ENCARTA®
CONCISE
ENGLISH
DICTIONARY

ENCARTA® CONCISE ENGLISH DICTIONARY

BLOOMSBURY

A BLOOMSBURY REFERENCE BOOK
Created from the Bloomsbury Database of World English

First published in 2001 by Bloomsbury Publishing Plc
38 Soho Square
London
W1D 3HB

This Dictionary includes words on the basis of their usage in the
English language today. Some words are identified as being
trademarks or service marks, but no attempt has been made to
identify all of the words in which proprietary rights might exist.
Neither the presence nor absence of any such identification in this
Dictionary is to be regarded as affecting in any way, or expressing
a judgment on, the validity or legal status of any trademark,
service mark, or other proprietary rights anywhere in the world.

www.bloomsburymagazine.com

British Library Cataloguing in Publication Data

ISBN 0 7475 4809 9

Typeset by Selwood Systems, Midsomer Norton, Bath, United Kingdom
Printed in the United States of America

Contents

Editor-in-Chief
Dr Kathy Rooney

Publisher
Nigel Newton

Dictionaries' Publisher
Faye Carney

Executive Editor
Susan Jellis

US General Editor
Anne H. Soukhanov

Database Manager
Edmund Wright

Senior Lexicographer
Lesley Brown

Project Manager
Katy McAdam

Chief Etymologist
John Ayto

Chief Phonetician
Dinah Jackson

Production Director
Penny Edwards

Production Editor
Nicky Thompson

Project Coordinators	**Corpus Resources**
Katherine Hill	Gloria George
James Randall	Ian Spackman

Marketing Manager
Gordon Kerr

INTERNATIONAL PUBLISHING PARTNERS

Bloomsbury Publishing Plc	**Microsoft Corporation**	**St. Martin's Press**	**Macmillan Australia**
Nigel Newton	Craig Bartholomew	Matthew Shear	Ross Gibb
Kathy Rooney	Richard Bready	Lisa Senz	James Fraser
	Robert Lindsey		

SPECIAL CONTRIBUTORS AND CONSULTANTS

ACADEMIC ADVISORY BOARD ON ENGLISH USAGE

UNITED KINGDOM

Dr Bethan Benwell
Department of English
Studies, University of Stirling

Tracy Donkersley
Head of English, Skegness
Grammar School, Skegness

Stephen Dundas, MA
Teacher of English, St Bede's
School, Redhill, Surrey

Dr Catherine Emmott
Senior Lecturer, Department
of English Language,
University of Glasgow

Dr Anthea Fraser Gupta
School of English,
University of Leeds

Sandra Poulton
Teacher of English language,
Weald of Kent Grammar
School, Tonbridge, Kent

Mary Scott
Former Head of English,
Hills Road Sixth Form
College, Cambridge

Dr Rebecca Stott
Director of the Speak-Write
Project, Department of
English, Anglia Polytechnic
University, Cambridge

Robert Veltman, MA
Lecturer in Applied
Linguistics, Department of
English Language and
Linguistics, University of
Kent at Canterbury, Kent

Dr Alison Wray
Senior Research Fellow,
Centre for Language and
Communication Research,
Cardiff University

AUSTRALIA

Dr Joy McEntee
Associate Lecturer,
Department of English,
Adelaide University,
Australia

Dr Frank Molloy
Senior Lecturer, Department
of English, School of
Humanities, Charles Sturt
University, New South
Wales, Australia

CANADA

Dr Terry K. Pratt
Professor Emeritus,
Department of English
Language and Literature,
University of Prince Edward
Island

Elizabeth (Betsy) Sargent
Writing Coordinator and
Associate Professor,
Department of English,
University of Alberta

Diane Tolomeo
Associate Professor,
Department of English,
University of Victoria,
British Columbia

Deborah Wills
Assistant Professor,
Department of English,
Mount Allison University,
New Brunswick

UNITED STATES

Michele Aina Barale
Associate Professor of
English and of Women's and
Gender Studies, Amherst
College, Massachusetts

LynDianne Beene
Professor, Department of
English, University of New
Mexico

Stephen C. Behrendt
George Holmes Distinguished
Professor of English,
University of Nebraska

Phillip D. Beidler
Professor of English,
University of Alabama

Erin Belieu
Assistant Professor,
Department of English, Ohio
State University

Joseph Donald Blount
Professor of English,
University of South Carolina
Aiken

Suzanne Bordelon
Assistant Professor of English/
Director of Composition,
University of Alaska Fairbanks

Robert H. Brinkmeyer, Jr.
Professor and Chair,
Department of English,
University of Arkansas

Teena A. M Carnegie
Assistant Professor,
Department of English,
University of Iowa

William Leon Coburn
Associate Professor,
Department of English,
University of Nevada, Las
Vegas

Paul B. Diehl
Associate Professor,
Department of English,
University of Iowa

Kenneth L. Donelson
Professor, Department of
English, Arizona State
University

Shirley Nelson Garner
Professor of English,
Associate Dean of the
Graduate School, University
of Minnesota

Eugene Green
Professor, Department of
English, Boston University

David Hoover
Associate Professor of
English, Department of
English, New York University

Kate Kiefer
Professor of English,
Colorado State University

Donald G. Marshall
Professor of English,
University of Illinois at
Chicago

Aya Matsuda
Assistant Professor,
Department of English,
University of New Hampshire

Ronald B. Newman
Associate Professor of
English, University of Miami

Thomas S. Oliver Jr.
Former Chair, Department
of English, University of the
District of Columbia

Verbie Lovorn Prevost,
Katharine Pryor Professor
of English, University of
Tennessee at Chattanooga

Gregory A. Waller
Professor and Chair,
Department of English,
University of Kentucky

Susan J. Wolfe
Professor, Department
of English, University of
South Dakota

Shawn H. Wong
Chairman and Professor,
Department of English,
University of Washington

Ben Yagoda
Associate Professor of
English, University of
Delaware

SPECIAL SUBJECT CONTRIBUTORS

Jane Dorner
Freelance writer, author of
*The Internet: A Writer's
Guide*

Dr Andrew Goldsbrough
molecular biologist,
Cambridge, UK
(Biotechnology)

WORLD ENGLISH AND LANGUAGE CONSULTANTS

Robert Allen
Editor and lexicographer

David Blair
Senior Lecturer, Department of Linguistics, Macquarie University (Australia)

Nikolas Coupland
Professor, Centre for Applied English Language Studies, University of Wales (English in Wales)

Tony Deverson
Senior Lecturer, Department of English, University of Canterbury, New Zealand (New Zealand)

Dr Scott Delancey
Department of Linguistics, University of Oregon (Native American English)

Margery Fee
Professor, Department of English, University of British Columbia; author, *Oxford Guide to Canadian Usage* (Canada)

Joshua Fishman
Professor, City University of New York (Yiddish)

Dr Eva Hertel
English Language and Linguistics, TU Chemnitz (East Africa)

Betty Kirkpatrick
Editor and lexicographer, editor *Roget's Thesaurus*

Jacqueline Lam
Senior Lecturer, Hong Kong University of Science and Technology (Hong Kong)

Naomi C. Losch
Assistant Professor in Hawaiian, Department of Hawaiian and Indo-Pacific Languages, University of Hawaii at Manoa (Hawaiian English)

Dr Catherine Macafee
University of Aberdeen (Scottish, Northern Irish)

Rajend Mesthrie
Senior Lecturer, Department of Linguistics, University of Capetown (South Africa)

Dr Mark Newbrook
Senior Lecturer, Department of Linguistics, Monash University (Malaysia and Singapore)

Dr Mark Sebba
Department of Linguistics, Lancaster University (US Black English)

Geneva Smitherman
University Distinguished Professor; Director, African American Language and Literacy Program; Director, "My Brother's Keeper" Program, Department of English, Michigan State University (African American English)

Kamal Keskar Sridhar
Associate Professor, Department of Linguistics, State University of New York, Stony Brook (South Asia)

Loreto Todd
Honorary Reader in International English, English Department, University of Leeds (Irish)

Don Winford
Professor, Department of Linguistics, Ohio State University (Caribbean)

SUBJECT CONSULTANTS

Clark Adams
Professor, Department of Wildlife and Fisheries Sciences, Texas A & M University (Hunting)

Michael Allaby
Writer and science consultant (Life Sciences)

Christopher Arnison
Professor, Royal Agricultural College (Agriculture)

Dr Tallis Barker
(Music)

Dr Alan Barnard
University of Edinburgh (Anthropology)

Joseph Bel Bruno
Professor, Dartmouth College, Hanover, New Hampshire (Chemistry)

David Bjorklund
Professor, Department of Psychology, Florida Atlantic University (Psychology)

Donald Black
Professor, College of Food and Natural Resources, University of Massachusetts (Agriculture)

Dr Sheila Blair
Editor for Islam and Central Asia, *The Dictionary of Art* (Arabic Words and Places)

Dr Clive Bloom
Middlesex University (Media)

Allan Brooks
Editor and writer; member, US Government technical committees (Engineering)

Charles Butcher
Specialist writer and editor (Chemical Engineering)

Colin Callander
Editor, *Golf Monthly* (Golf)

Col. John A. Calabro
Professor of English, US Military Academy, West Point (Military)

Paul A. Carling
Professor, University of Lancaster (Geography)

Dr Christopher Chippendale
Museum of Archaeology and Anthropology, University of Cambridge (Archaeology)

Timothy Collings
Motor racing correspondent, Reuters and *Daily Telegraph* (Motor Sports)

Helen Cowie
Professor, Roehampton Institute, London (Psychology)

Michael Crane
Director, British Isles Backgammon Association (Backgammon)

Dr Andrew Dalby
Honorary Librarian, Institute of Linguists, author, *Bloomsbury Dictionary of Languages* (Languages)

Robert Day
Chairman, Suffolk Advanced Motorcyclists Group (DIY, Motorcycles)

Col. Michael Dewar
Formerly Institute of Strategic Studies (Military)

Robert Ditton
Professor, Department of Wildlife and Fisheries Sciences, Texas A & M University (Ecology)

Bethany K. Dumas
Professor, Department of Linguistics, Language and Law, University of Tennessee (Law)

Dr Roy Evans
Formerly Faculty of Education, Roehampton Institute, London (Education)

Dr Alan Ewert
University of Northern British Columbia (Mountaineering/Climbing)

Nancy Flynn
Cornell University (Botany)

Tom Gallagher
Writer (Baseball)

Bruce Ganem
Professor, Department of Chemistry, Cornell University (Chemistry)

James Gramman
Professor, Department of Recreation, Park, and Tourism Sciences, Texas A & M University (Leisure)

Fayal Greene
Gardening writer and editor (Gardening)

Lynne Goldstein
Professor and Chair, Department of Anthropology, Michigan State University; editor, *American Antiquity* (Anthropology and Archaeology)

Jeremy Gray
Open University (Mathematics)

Steven Griffiths
UK civil servant (Transport/Environment)

Trevor Griffiths
Professor, Programme Director, School of Arts and Humanities, University of North London (Theater)

Andrew Howard
Middlesex University (Politics)

Alastair Hudson
Queen Mary and Westfield College, University of London (Law)

Philip Johansson
Naturalist and writer (Zoology)

Bridget Jones
Cookery editor and writer, member of the Guild of Food Writers (Food)

Darlene Juschka
Professor, University of Toronto (World Religions)

David Kemp
VP and Euro Director, London, ABN-AMRO Bank N.V. (Currencies)

Alison Kervin
Editor, *Rugby World* (Rugby)

Ira Konigsberg
Professor, University of Michigan, Ann Arbor; author, *Complete Film Dictionary* (Cinema)

Dr John Laurence
Boyce Thomson Institute, Cornell University (Botany)

Bryan Lawson
Professor, School of Architecture, University of Sheffield (Architecture)

Andrew Leclair
Professor, Newman Laboratory, Cornell University (Physics)

Dr Becky Lee
Centre for Religion, University of Toronto (Christianity and the Bible)

Franklin M. Loew
Professor, President, Becker College, Worcester, MA; formerly Dean of Veterinary Medicine, Tufts and Cornell Universities (Veterinary Science)

Alastair McIver
Editor, *Tennis World* (Tennis)

Jeffrey McQuain
Writer and researcher, *New York Times*; word columnist and researcher for William Safire; author, *Power Language* (Politics)

Carolyn Marcus
Gardening writer and editor (Gardening)

Anthony Middleton
Formerly editor, RAF in-house publications service; formerly, Technical Publications Editor, GEC-Marconi (Engineering)

Mark Miller
Editor (Literature)

Martyn Moore
Editor, *Practical Photography* (Photography)

Philip D. Morehead
Chicago Lyric Opera (Music)

David Morton
Professor, School of Biomedical Science and Ethics, University of Birmingham (Veterinary Science)

Bruce Murphy
Professor, Faculty of Veterinary Medicine, University of Montreal (Biology)

Adrian Napper
formerly Department of Architecture, Edinburgh College of Art (Building and Construction)

Susan North
Department of Textiles and Dress, Victoria and Albert Museum (Fashion)

Kathleen O'Grady
Trinity College, University of Cambridge (Religion and Mythology)

Alex Orenstein
Professor, City University of New York (Philosophy)

Anthony Pellegrini
Department of Educational Psychology, University of Minnesota (Education)

Michael Quinion
Lexicographer and editor (New Words)

John Ross
Writer and editor (Computing)

Dr Edward Ruddell
Department of Parks, Recreation, and Tourism, University of Utah (Martial Arts)

Richard Soffe
Seale-Hayne Faculty of Agriculture, Food and Land Use, University of Plymouth (Agriculture)

Tony Spybey
Professor, Department of Sociology, Staffordshire University (Sociology)

Peter N. Stearns
Professor, Dean, College of Humanities and Social Sciences, Carnegie Mellon University; author, *Encyclopedia of World History* (History)

James M. Steele
Professor, School of Architecture, University of Southern California; author, *Architecture Today* (Architecture and Building)

Robert Strong
Professor, Department of Economics, University of Maine (Finance)

Bruce Thom
Emeritus Professor, Visiting Professor, University of New South Wales (Geography)

Peter Timmer
University College London (Computing)

Dr Amos Turk
Professor Emeritus, Department of Chemistry, City College of New York (Chemical Engineering)

Dr Heather Valencia
University of Stirling (Judaism)

Michael J. Walsh
Librarian, Heythrop College, University of London (the Bible)

Rosemary Wilkinson
Freelance writer and editor (Crafts and Design)

Gillian Williams
Editor, *Ski and Board* magazine (Skiing)

John Williams
Sir Norman Chester Centre for Football Research, University of Leicester (Soccer)

Ellen Wohl
Associate Professor, Colorado State University (Geography)

Philip C. Wright
Professor, University of New Brunswick (Business and Management)

Dr Robert Youngson, MB, ChB
Author, *Royal Society of Medicine Encyclopedia of Family Health,* formerly consultant adviser on ophthalmology to British Army (Medicine and Pharmacology)

Introduction to the First Edition

Dr Kathy Rooney
Editor-in-Chief

WE, THE EDITORS of the *Encarta® Concise English Dictionary*, would like you to feel that your dictionary, this dictionary, is your best friend—or at least a very good one. Dictionaries can be regarded as dry and rather intimidating, only to be consulted in times of extreme need or as a last resort. The *Encarta Concise English Dictionary*, written especially for family and student use, will, we hope, provide you with an accessible and pleasurable route to the information you need.

Why should your dictionary be a good friend? As we continued to develop the Bloomsbury World English Dictionary database—from which the *Encarta Concise English Dictionary* is derived—we undertook research to find out what people like you actually **want** their dictionary to help them with, and what particular needs different types of dictionary users have. We tailored the *Encarta Concise English Dictionary* to meet these requirements.

People like you said they wanted answers to the following questions. Am I spelling this word correctly? What does this word mean? Am I using the word correctly? How do I pronounce this word? Where does the word come from? We also established that you set great store by the ease with which you can understand the information in the dictionary, the clarity with which it is presented, and the speed with which you can navigate through long entries.

In addition, we asked 41 professors of English from the UK, Australia, the United States, and Canada about the language problems their students faced. This survey revealed surprisingly similar findings across the globe. All expressed concern that students increasingly have difficulties with basic language skills—especially spelling and grammar. This is a shared international problem. When asked about the main problems students have with spelling, grammar, and punctuation, professors said that students need help with basic concepts like clause, noun, subjunctive, and also with punctuation: comma, colon, apostrophe, etc.

These are problems that the *Encarta Concise English Dictionary* helps you, its readers, solve. Two specific features help you with spelling. First, we list 700 incorrect spellings and refer you to the correct spelling. These are clearly indicated in the text, crossed through so that you cannot mistake them for the correct spelling, which is clearly shown. They look like this:

~~aquire~~ incorrect spelling of **acquire**

This feature also helps answer a perennial dictionary conundrum, 'How can I find a word in a dictionary if I don't know how to spell it?'

Another difficulty for many people is how to distinguish between words that sound alike but are spelt differently. This was another problem area highlighted by our Advisory Board of professors and teachers of English. We have therefore included 400 'Spellcheck' notes to point out potentially confusable words, for example: *your/you're, principle/principal, peel/peal, horde/ hoard, discreet/discrete*.

SPELLCHECK Do not confuse *discreet* with *discrete*, which has a similar sound. Beware: your spellchecker will not catch this error.

We also point out cases where, our Advisory Board has told us, students and others tend to make mistakes with grammar, syntax, and word choice. Over 600 Usage Notes give concrete guidance on language problems like these.

former[1] /fáwrmər/ *adj* **1 PREVIOUS** occurring at or existing in an earlier time or period ○ *met her on a former occasion* **2 HAVING BEEN** having had the name or status specified during an earlier period ○ *the former Soviet Union* **3 FIRST OF TWO** being the first of two things or people mentioned **4 PRECEDING** earlier or near the beginning of a text or list ○ *a conclusion inconsistent with the argument in the former part of the paper* ■ *n* **THE FIRST OF TWO** the first of two things or people mentioned ○ *Smith and Brown both work here, the former is an accountant and the latter is an engineer.* [12C. < Old English *forma* 'first' < Germanic + ER.]

USAGE former and **latter** The word *former* means the first of two, and *latter* means the second of two. To be clear, use these words in references to two and not more than two persons or things previously mentioned, as in *The symposium is for medical and nursing students, with the morning lectures directed to the former and the afternoon lectures directed to the latter.*

So what can you find in a dictionary? A dictionary entry is made up of many different elements, the main ones being the **headword**-the word you look up; the **pronunciation**-how to say it; the **part of speech**-is the word a noun, verb, or adjective etc; the **definition**-an explanation of what the word means; the **etymology**-where it comes from, its history, if known. Other elements include information on how to use the word (**usage**) and definitions of related phrases (**idioms** and **phrasal verbs**).

These are the types of information traditionally associated with any dictionary entry. The *Encarta Concise English Dictionary* offers many additional features to meet your unique needs. We include approximately 9,000 entries about people and places and 700 illustrations and tables. 'Quick Facts' on 70 key concepts amplify on the information in the definitions:

QUICK FACTS ON... **BAROQUE**

Key dates: late 16th-early 18th centuries
Key locations: W Europe, originating in Italy
Key elements: sense of movement and vitality, rich colours, strong contrasts in light and shade; illusionism; naturalism; integration of architecture, painting, and sculpture
Key figures: Carracci, Caravaggio, Pietro da Cortona, Velázquez, Rubens, Rembrandt, Vermeer (painting); Bernini (sculpture and architecture); Borromini, Churriguera (architecture)
Key works: Ceiling frescoes, Palazzo Farnese, Rome (Carracci) 1597-1600, *Allegory of Divine Providence and Barberini Power* (Pietro da Cortona) 1633-39, *The Ecstasy of Saint Theresa* (Bernini) 1645-52, Church of Santa Agnese, Rome (Borromini), 1653
Key developments: chiaroscuro, integrated design, rococo, classicism

---

Science and technology terms can be puzzling to the nonspecialist, so we have paid particular attention to creating definitions that are both clear and succinct. For example, at entries such as chemical compounds we put the formula in boldface letters first, after the part-of-speech label, followed by a clear and concise definition, in turn followed by other information titled 'Source' or 'Use'. That way, you can find what you need-fast, and without having to pore over line after line of small type.

calcium carbonate *n* $CaCO_3$ a white crystalline solid that is one of the most common natural substances. Source: chalk, limestone, marble, animal shells, bones. Use: antacids, paint, cement, toothpaste.

We have also included 'Quick Facts' in these specialist areas. Quick Facts spell out the development of theories, concepts, and discoveries that have resonated beyond the academic community, including cloning, psychoanalysis, and relativity. We also summarize recent influential trends in science such as quantum theory, string theory, chaos theory, and big bang theory. Technology Quick Facts put into perspective the development of the personal computer, microprocessors, the Internet, and artificial intelligence.

QUICK FACTS ON... **HUMAN GENOME PROJECT**

Key elements: sequencing and identifying genes of the human genome and recording their positions on the 46 individual chromosomes
Key dates: 1990 launch of publicly funded international reseach initiative; 1999 chromosome 22 fully mapped; 2000 chromosomes 5, 16, 19, and 21 mapped and draft genetic map completed; private company, Celera Genomics, also announces completion of a working draft; estimate of number of human genes is 30,000 to 40,000; 2003 expected completion date of project
Key technologies: bacterial artificial chromosomes; DNA sequencing, mapping; bioinformatics and computational biology; comparative and functional genomics
Key developments: medical benefits expected in: improved diagnosis of genetic and degenerative disease; earlier detection of genetic predisposition to disease; drug design and custom drugs; gene therapy. Nonmedical benefits expected in human evolutionary studies, anthropology, and forensic science
Key publications: *The DNA sequence of human chromosome 22* (Dunham et al.) 1999, Nature 402: 489- 495; *Your Genes, Your Choices? Exploring the issues raised by Genetic Research* (Catherine Baker) 1999; *Cracking the Genome* (Kevin Davies) 2001

The *Encarta Concise English Dictionary* also includes Literary Links, which reveal interesting, sometimes surprising, literary associations of selected words, as this one at the entry for *expectation*:

LITERARY LINK *Great Expectations*, a novel (1861) by Charles Dickens. It is the story of the orphan Pip, his early encounter with the convict Magwitch, and his love for the beautiful Estella, who lives with her eccentric guardian Miss Havisham. Pip subsequently receives a fortune from an unknown benefactor and moves to London, but is forced to return penniless to the humble blacksmith's home where he grew up.

Another important point highlighted by our research was that people often find it difficult to find their way through longer dictionary entries. The words in our language often have more than one meaning. A dictionary divides these meanings up and defines each one separately. These are called 'senses'. The word *take*, for example, has over 40 senses. To help you find just the right meaning fast, we have included 'Quick Definitions' in **boldface** capitalized type at the start of each sense of a word with more than three meanings. The Quick Definitions give the broad meanings. They are followed by the full definitions. This makes those longer entries easier for you to navigate.

bring /bring/ (brings, bringing, brought /brawt/, brought) v **1** vt ACCOMPANY OR CARRY to come from one place to another with somebody or something ○ *Please bring me a glass of water.* **2** vt ATTRACT to draw something to yourself or another person ○ *This charm is supposed to bring luck.* **3** vt MAKE SOMETHING HAPPEN to cause something to take place ○ *The heavy rain brought flooding.* **4** vt CAUSE TO BE IN A PARTICULAR STATE to force something or somebody to arrive at a particular situation or condition ○ *The chairperson brought the meeting to a close.* **5** vt CAUSE TO ENTER MIND to cause something to enter somebody's mind ○ *Seeing you brings memories of good times.* **6** vr MAKE YOURSELF DO to persuade or force yourself to do something (*usually with negatives or in questions*) ○ *She still can't bring herself to think about the tragedy.* **7** vt SELL FOR PARTICULAR PRICE to be sold for a particular price **8** vt BEGIN LEGAL ACTION to begin a legal action **9** vt PRESENT EVIDENCE to present evidence before a court **10** vt *Malaysia, Singapore, UK* TAKE SOMEWHERE to take somebody or something somewhere (*regional*) ○ *I brought my friend to the airport when she left.* [Old English *bringan* < Indo-European] - **bringer** n

account, unprotected, shopping experience, and *stickiness.* We have used a lightning bolt symbol [⚡] to indicate entries that include such terms.

⚡**backbone** /bák bōn/ n **1** = spinal column **2** SOMETHING SIMILAR TO SPINAL COLUMN something that is similar in shape or position to a spinal column ○ *the Pennines, the backbone of England* **3** CENTRAL SUPPORTING PART the part of an organization or system that is its strongest unifying factor and main support ○ *The middle classes are the backbone of this nation.* **4** FORTITUDE strength of character and determination ○ *He doesn't have the backbone to stand up to his critics.* **5** HIGH-SPEED RELAY a high-speed relay that feeds smaller channels in corporate networks and the Internet **6** CORE OF ELECTRONIC NETWORK the core of an electronic network, e.g. a physical cable connection or a routing protocol

Where did the *Encarta Concise English Dictionary*'s editors find the information on which to base their definitions? The Bloomsbury Corpus of World English, which now has over 150 million words, provided the main evidence. We amplified this with a tailored reading programme in science, technology, business, and other key areas in order to find evidence of word use in varied fields. Lastly we used the Internet as a research source.

Many of you also use the Internet, so we have included a specially commissioned essay on how to use the Web as a research tool, in particular for projects and assignments.

Language never stands still, and one result of English being used across the globe is that many new words and new senses are reaching a world audience faster than ever before. Pop culture, worldwide TV and film broadcasts, e-mail, and the Internet propel new words into national and international cultures. Some of the words appearing in this Dictionary for the first time include *blog, resistin, reality TV, cyberlaw, digital forensics, usability engineer, dotgov, microscooter, genetic discrimination, symbion,* and *rolling blackout.* As this list shows, terms associated with the widespread use of computers and the Internet constitute one of fastest-growing areas of the language.

The *Encarta Concise English Dictionary* contains many new words derived from high technology—more than any other Concise dictionary. The English language has taken in a host of new words, and new senses of existing words, as a result of the proliferation of personal computers and increased use of e-mail and the Internet. Now-familiar new meanings of old words include *mouse, virus, dot, Trojan horse, domain, browse, surf, cookie,* and *icon.* More recent examples are the high-tech senses of words like

As new and more informal forms of communication, such as e-mail and now text-messaging, emerge, dictionary editors have to monitor the extent to which, for example, the informality of the latest abbreviations used in e-mails and text messages may in time come to be regarded as acceptable usage. But beware: as our Advisory Board confirms, those abbreviations have not yet achieved that status. We have included a selection of them in the *Encarta Concise English Dictionary* because some of you may be unfamiliar with them when communicating with others online. For example:

⚡**L8R** abbr later (*in e-mails*)

The *Encarta Concise English Dictionary* defines the whole range of language, from formal through to slang. Slang words are clearly labelled *slang* and informal words are labelled *informal.* Offensive and taboo terms are labelled *offensive, taboo, insult,* or a combination thereof. Such labels are included to indicate that the terms may not only cause offence but are also a direct reflection on the user, not the target.

So why should your dictionary be a good friend in the 21st century? In an era of ever-faster communication, the *Encarta Concise English Dictionary* can help you to communicate clearly and accurately, understand words you don't know, improve your spelling and use of English, and succeed in coursework. It can also help you to enjoy and appreciate the huge richness of English, truly a language of the world.

Language is a powerful tool – use the new manual.

Kathy Rooney
Editor-in-Chief
April 2001   xiii

How to use the Dictionary

Faye Carney

INTRODUCTION

A dictionary is a complex amalgam of different elements that relate to what users want from a dictionary—spelling, pronunciation, meaning, examples of use, advice on grammar or usage, and the explanation of the origins of a word. This section outlines briefly the different elements in the text, so that you can find what you want in the *Encarta® Concise English Dictionary* quickly and easily.

Guide Words

Each page has two **guide words** that show, on the left, the first **boldface** dictionary entry on that page, and, on the right, the last, so that you can quickly find the word you are looking for.

Pronunciation Key

Each double-page spread shows the **pronunciation key** along the foot of the page for ease of reference. (For full details on the **Pronunciation System**, see pp.xxiv–xxv.)

Text Layout

The text is designed in three columns for maximum coverage and legibility. Important elements of the text appear in **boldface** type. Quick Definitions appear in **boldface SMALL CAPITALS**. Full definitions appear in roman type and examples and quotations in *italic* type.

Illustrations

Illustrations appear as close as possible to the entries to which they refer. Over 600 items are illustrated in this Dictionary, and over 30 tables and charts are integrated in the A–Z text at the relevant entry.

THE TEXT

The text of a dictionary combines many different elements, which are explained briefly here.

Headwords

The *Encarta Concise English Dictionary* contains over 90,000 **headwords** (the words you look up), including approximately 9,000 entries about people and places—the biographical and geographical entries.

Alphabetical order

Headwords are listed in strict letter order, ignoring punctuation and other characters:

box beam *n* CONSTR = **box girder**

box bed *n* an old-fashioned bed, enclosed on three sides and the top by a wooden structure resembling a box

boxboard /bóks bawrd/ *n* a tough cardboard made from wood and wastepaper pulp, used for making boxes

box calf *n* black calfskin leather that has been tanned with chromium salts [Early 20C. After Joseph *Box*, 19C London bootmaker.]

box camera *n* a camera shaped like a box, with a simple lens that has a fixed focus and a single shutter speed

box canyon *n* a canyon with steep walls that can be entered readily only from the downstream direction

boxcar /bóks kaar/ *n US* in North America, a fully enclosed railway wagon, usually with sliding doors, which is used to transport freight

box coat *n* a coat that hangs loosely from the shoulders

box elder *n* a fast-growing maple tree. Native to: North America. *Acer negundo*. [< BOX³]

Biographical and geographical entries are listed alphabetically. If one name appears in more than one entry, the entries appear in alphabetical order of the word following the comma:

Adams /áddəmz/, **Abigail** (1744–1818) US feminist
Adams, Ansel (1902–84) US photographer
Adams, Gerry (*b.* 1948) Northern Irish politician
Adams, John (1735–1826) US statesman and 2nd president of the United States (1797–1801)

Phrasal verbs are listed with their root verb. See p. xviii.

Words with the same spelling

Words with the same spelling but with different pronunciations or origins (**homographs**) are listed with superscript numbers to differentiate them. The order of these numbers broadly reflects usage and frequency.

bow[1] /bō/ n **1 LOOPED KNOT** a knot in which the loops remain visible, e.g. in tied shoelaces or in ribbons used for decorating gifts or hair. ◊ **bow tie 2 WEAPON FOR FIRING ARROWS** a weapon used to fire arrows, consisting of a curved flexible piece of wood and a taut string fastened to the two ends **3 ROD FOR PLAYING STRINGED INSTRUMENTS** a wooden rod with fibres tightly stretched between the two ends, used for playing stringed instruments **4 CURVED SHAPE OR PART** a rounded or semicircular shape, e.g. a part of a building or a loop in a river **5** ARCHERY, HIST = **bowman**[1] (literary) **6** METEOROL = **rainbow** n. 1 ■ v **1** vti **BEND SOMETHING INTO BOW SHAPE** to bend, or bend something, into a rounded or bow shape **2** vti **DRAW BOW ACROSS STRINGED INSTRUMENT** to draw a bow across the strings of a stringed instrument **3** vt **INDICATE BOWING FOR MUSIC** to mark a piece of music to indicate which notes are to be played with the bow moving in one direction across the strings and which are to be played with it moving in the opposite direction [Old English boga < Germanic, 'to bend']

bow[2] /bow/ v **1** vti **BEND HEAD OR BODY FORWARD** to bend the head forward, or to bend forward from the waist, as a signal of respect, greeting, consent, submission, or acknowledgment ○ bowing her head in shame **2** vti **BEND SOMETHING OR DROOP** to bend something over so that it droops, or to be bent in this way ○ branches bowed down with fruit. **3** vi **YIELD** to accept something and yield to it, often unwillingly ○ In the end they had to bow to the inevitable and sell up. ■ n **BENDING FORWARD OF UPPER BODY** a bending forward of the upper part of the body to show respect, acknowledgment, subservience, courtesy, or greeting [Old English būgan < Germanic, 'to bend'] ◊ **bow and scrape** to be excessively polite or attentive in an attempt to ingratiate yourself with somebody

bow[3] /bow/ n **1** the front section of a boat or other vessel **2** the rower closest to the front of a boat [Early 17C. < Low German booq or Middle Dutch boeq.]

Pronunciation

Our pronunciation system has been developed specifically for the *Encarta Concise English Dictionary*. It relies on familiar combinations of letters of the alphabet, so that you can use it without constant reference to a table of explanations and symbols. The system is explained in full on pp. xxiv–xxv.

Variant spellings

The Dictionary takes note whenever a word has more than one possible spelling **variant**. Such entries appear in **boldface type** following their headword. Variant spellings are cross-referred back to the entry where they are defined using an equals sign [=].

cagey /káyji/ (**-gier, -giest**), **cagy** (**-gier, -giest**) adj cautious and secretive rather than open, honest, or direct (informal) [Late 19C. < ?] - **cagily** adv - **caginess** n

cagy adj = **cagey**

Inflections

Inflections are forms of words that are different from the headword. These include the principal parts of verbs, the comparative and superlative forms of adjectives and adverbs, and plurals of nouns. These forms are shown where they are not predictable or regular, after the pronunciation when the inflection applies to the whole headword or at a specific sense or group of senses, as appropriate.

bully[1] /bŏolli/ n (plural **-lies**) an aggressive person who intimidates or mistreats weaker people ■ vt (**-lies, -lying, -lied**) to intimidate or mistreat a weaker person [Mid-16C. Probably < Middle Dutch boele 'lover'.] - **bullying** n ◊ **bully for you!** used to express approval (ironic)

adieu /ə dyŏŏ/ interj, n (plural **adieux** /ə dyŏŏz/ or **adieus** /ə dyŏŏz/) used to say goodbye ○ '…the more gentle adieus of her sisters were uttered without being heard' (Jane Austen, *Pride And Prejudice*; 1813) [14C. < French, '(I commend you) to God'.]

Important irregular inflections also appear as headwords in their own right:

fora plural of **forum**

laid past tense, past participle of **lay**[1]

Parts of Speech

Part-of-speech labels, in *italic* type, indicate the linguistic function of the headword. They are:

abbr	abbreviation
adj	adjective
adv	adverb
aux v	auxiliary verb
conj	conjunction
contr	contraction
det	determiner
interj	interjection
modal v	modal verb
n	noun
npl	plural noun
prefix	prefix
prep	preposition
pron	pronoun
symbol	symbol
suffix	suffix
tdmk	trademark
v	verb
vi	intransitive verb
vr	reflexive verb
vt	transitive verb
vti	transitive and intransitive verb

Abbreviations and Acronyms

Abbreviations and acronyms are grouped together according to their punctuation and their status as either an abbreviation or symbol. Our Corpus has shown that punctuation within abbreviations varies considerably. This Dictionary gives the most common form; important variants are also shown. Senses are ordered alphabetically.

⚡ca abbr Canada (in Internet addresses)

Ca symbol calcium

⚡CA abbr **1** California **2** Central America **3** Central American **4** chartered accountant **5** chief accountant **6** chronological age **7** consular agent **8** Consumers' Association **9** certificate authority (in e-mails)

ca. abbr circa (before dates)

c/a abbr current account

C/A abbr **1** capital account **2** credit account **3** current account

CAA abbr Civil Aviation Authority

⚡CAAT abbr certificate authority administration tool (in e-commerce)

When an abbreviation is more frequently used than its full form, we give the definition at the abbreviation:

DNA n a nucleic acid molecule in the form of a twisted double strand (**double helix**) that is the major component of chromosomes and carries genetic information. Full form **deoxyribonucleic acid**

Meanings

Many words have more than one meaning. The different meanings are indicated by definition numbers that appear in **boldface** type. Definitions are ordered according to usage and frequency; they are grouped according to part of speech (all noun definitions together, all verb definitions together, and so on).

The symbol [■] introduces a new part of speech within an entry.

> **baby** /báybi/ n (plural **-bies**) **1 VERY YOUNG CHILD** a very young child who is not yet able to walk or talk **2 UNBORN CHILD** a child that is still in the womb **3 CHILDISH PERSON** a childish or overly dependent person ○ told him not to be such a baby **4 YOUNGEST MEMBER** the youngest member of a family or group ○ the baby of the team **5 IMMATURE ANIMAL** a very young animal **6 TERM OF ENDEARMENT** an affectionate term of endearment, especially for a woman (slang; sometimes offensive) ■ adj **SMALLER AND YOUNGER** describes vegetables that are smaller and younger than usual ■ vt (**-bies, -bying, -bied**) **TREAT SOMEBODY WITH GREAT CARE** to show a great or inordinate amount of care to something or somebody [14C. Pet form of BABE.] - **babyhood** n ◇ **be left holding the baby** to be left in a situation of being solely responsible for something because other people have abdicated their own responsibility ◇ **throw out the baby with the bathwater** to reject something in its entirety without discriminating between good and bad parts

Undefined Terms (Runons)

At the end of many entries there are additional **boldface** entries that have no definitions. These are called **undefined runons**, and they consist of the headword plus a standard derivative suffix such as –ly or –ness, or the headword shown in another part of speech. They do not require definitions because they correlate predictably in meaning and usage with the main entry. Where appropriate, runons have been given pronunciations, for example where their stress pattern differs significantly from that of the headword.

> **changeable** /cháynjəb'l/ adj **1** capable of or liable to change **2** variable in colour according to viewpoint or lighting —**changeability** /cháynjə bíllati/ n —**changeableness** n —**changeably** adv

When we have had evidence from our Corpus that a potential runon in fact has a different pattern of linguistic behaviour, that term has been defined fully.

Subject Labels

Many definitions are for terms belonging to specific subject areas. **Subject area labels** indicate the subject area to which a meaning belongs. Where it is not possible to indicate the subject area in the definition, a label is provided:

> **aclinic line** /ay klínnik-/ n GEOG = **magnetic equator** [< Greek aklinēs 'not leaning' < klinein 'lean']

Quick Definitions

The **Quick Definitions**, like subject labels, are designed to guide you through longer entries. They appear in **boldface SMALL CAPITALS** and act as a brief summary of the full definition, so that you can easily find your way to the appropriate sense.

> **booth** /booth/ (plural **booths** /boothz/) n **1 SMALL PARTITIONED ENCLOSURE** a partitioned enclosure or small room shaped like a box that offers privacy, e.g. when telephoning, selling tickets, or voting **2 SMALL TENT OR STALL** a tent, stall, or other light structure at a fair or exhibition, offering some form of entertainment or goods for sale **3 RESTAURANT COMPARTMENT** a small, partly enclosed area in a restaurant with a table and high backed seats **4 SMALL ROOM USED IN BROADCASTING** a small soundproof room used for recording sound or for broadcasting [12C. < N Germanic.]

Definitions

The definitions in the *Encarta Concise English Dictionary* explain the meaning of a word clearly and comprehensibly and differentiate it from related terms and words meaning almost the same thing.

> **cadence** /káyd'nss/ n **1 RHYTHM** the beat or measure of something that follows a set rhythm, e.g. a dance or a march **2 FALLING TONE** a drop in the pitch of the voice, e.g. at the end of a sentence **3 INTONATION** the way in which the voice rises and falls in pitch when somebody is speaking **4 RHYTHM IN LANGUAGE** the way in which poetry or prose flows according to a rhythm **5 MUSICAL SEQUENCE** a short sequence of notes that marks the end of a piece or passage of music [14C. Via Old French, 'rhythm' < Italian cadenza 'falling away' < Latin cadere 'to fall'.] - **cadenced** adj

Specialist Terminology

The Dictionary includes as headwords the main specialized language you are likely to encounter in general publications and consumer magazines, and in particular the principal terminology likely to be encountered by college students. Entries containing high-technology meanings are preceded by a symbol [✦].

> ✦**clone** /klōn/ n **1 GENETICALLY IDENTICAL ORGANISM** a plant, animal, or other organism that is genetically identical to its parent, having developed by vegetative reproduction, e.g. from a bulb or a cutting, or experimentally from a single cell **2 GROUP OF GENETICALLY IDENTICAL PROGENY** a collection of organisms, cells, or molecular segments that are genetically identical direct descendants of a single parent by asexual reproduction, e.g. plant cuttings or grafts **3 NEAR COPY OF HARDWARE OR SOFTWARE** a hardware device, e.g. a PC, or a piece of software that is a functional copy of another, popular, more expensive product developed by another manufacturer ■ v (**clones, cloning, cloned**) **1** vti **PRODUCE GENETICALLY IDENTICAL ORGANISMS** to produce an organism that is genetically identical to its parent, by vegetative reproduction or a laboratory technique, or to be produced in this way **2** vt **MAKE COPY OF** to produce an exact or near copy of an object or product [Early 20C. < Greek klōn 'twig'.] - **clonal** adj - **clonally** adv - **cloner** n

Some information that occurs routinely in scientific and technical definitions, for example the sources of minerals or the uses to which chemicals are put, is shown in a formulaic way for greater accessibility:

> **agapanthus** /ággə pánthəss/ (plural **-thus** or **-thuses**) n a plant of the lily family. Flowers: bluish or white, funnel-shaped, in ball-shaped clusters. Native to: southern Africa. Genus: *Agapanthus*. US term **African lily** [Late 18C. < modern Latin, < Greek agapē 'love' + anthos 'flower'.]
>
> **calcium antagonist** n a drug that dilates the arteries and slows the heart. Use: treatment of angina.
>
> **calcium carbonate** n $CaCO_3$ a white crystalline solid that is one of the most common natural substances. Source: chalk, limestone, marble, animal shells, bones. Use: antacids, paint, cement, toothpaste.

Dated and Archaic Language

The Dictionary includes usages that are no longer current but that you may encounter in works of literature, such as prominent archaic or dated terms.

alack /ə láck/ *interj* used to express regret (*archaic or literary*) [15C. < LACK, after ALAS.]

Examples

The *Encarta Concise English Dictionary* has thousands of illustrative examples that clarify the definitions and place them in context. These are drawn from our Corpus of World English.

The symbol [○] introduces examples.

believe /bi leev/ (**-lieves, -lieving, -lieved**) *v* **1** *vt* ACCEPT AS TRUE to accept that something is true or real ○ *I don't know which story to believe.* **2** *vt* ACCEPT AS TRUTHFUL to accept that somebody is telling the truth ○ *Nobody will believe you!* **3** *vt* CREDIT WITH to accept that somebody or something has a particular quality or ability ○ *No one believed her capable of such a malicious remark.* **4** *vi* THINK THAT SOMETHING EXISTS to be of the opinion that something exists or is a reality, especially when there is no absolute proof of its existence or reality ○ *believe in reincarnation* **5** *vi* TRUST to be confident that somebody or something is worthwhile or effective ○ *We all believe in you.* **6** *vi* THINK SOMETHING IS GOOD to be of the opinion that something is right or beneficial, and, usually, to act in accordance with that belief ○ *believes strongly in freedom of expression* **7** *vi* HAVE RELIGIOUS FAITH to have a religious belief [Old English *belyfan*, alteration of *geléfan* < Germanic, 'to love, trust'] — **believer** *n* ◇ **make believe** to pretend

Citations

The Dictionary also includes many quotations taken from written sources (**citations**) such as fiction, nonfiction, and journalism. These citations are drawn from our Corpus of World English.

adage /áddij/ *n* a traditional saying that expresses something taken as a general truth ○ *'Oysters are said to be best in months containing the letter R, according to an old adage'.* (Barbara Sturm, *Living Page*; 1997) [Mid-16C. Via French < Latin *adagium* < *ad* 'to' + variant of *aio* 'I say'.]

Word Origins

The principal aim of the word origins (**etymologies**) in the Dictionary is to present the history of the entries with as much accuracy as present-day knowledge will permit, in a way that is accessible and interesting to the general reader. Etymologies have as far as possible been written in plain English, with few abbreviations or technical terms. Where possible, etymologies include the date when the headword was first recorded, an account of the word's origin, and other relevant information likely to be of interest to readers. The symbol [<], meaning 'from', indicates the various stages in a word's development. A question mark [?] is used when the ultimate origin of a word is not definitely known:

aardvark /aárd vaark/ *n* a burrowing mammal with a long snout, powerful claws, long tongue, and heavy tail. Native to: southern Africa. *Orycteropus afer.* [Late 18C. < Afrikaans, 'earth pig'.]

calypso /kə lípsō/ (*plural* **-sos**) *n* **1** a Caribbean, especially Trinidadian, ballad with a lively dance rhythm, that deals satirically with social and political topics **2** Caribbean dance music that has syncopated rhythms, is usually improvised, and is often played by a steel band [Early 20C. < ?]

Where space permits, we explain why a word is used with a particular meaning. This may be because of a development of meaning in English or in a source language, an association with a person or place, or some visual image or stereotype. We call these 'Why?' etymologies, since telling an interesting story is a key feature of the word histories in the Dictionary.

alstroemeria /álstrə meéri ə/ (*plural* **-as** *or* **-a**) *n* a tuberous plant of the amaryllis family. Flowers: long-lasting, variously coloured. Native to: South America. Genus: *Alstroemeria*. [Late 18C. < modern Latin, after Klas von *Alstroemer* (1736- 96), Swedish naturalist.]

camelopard /kə méllə paard, kámmilə-/ *n* **1** a giraffe (*archaic*) **2** ASTRON = **Camelopardalis** [14C. < Latin *camelopardus* < Greek *kamēlopardalis* < *kamēlos* 'camel' + *pardalis* 'pard' (because the animal has a head like a camel and spots like a leopard).]

Dandie Dinmont /dándi dínmont/, **Dandie Dinmont terrier** *n* a small terrier of a breed from the Scottish Borders with a long body, short legs, drooping ears, and a long wiry greyish or brownish coat [Early 19C. After the fictional owner of such dogs in *Guy Mannering* by Sir Walter Scott.]

Function Words

Function words are grammatical words such as the common prepositions, adverbs, conjunctions, and pronouns (*up, down, at, so, what, when, many, such, a, the,* and so on); the modal verbs and auxiliaries; and verbs such as *come, do, get,* and *give*.

Speakers of a language rarely look up common terms such as these. They tend to look up rare or archaic uses, such as the Shakespearean use of *and* to mean 'if'; technical and specialist uses, such as the nautical use of *after;* dialectal terms, or uses from other varieties of English, such as the regional use of *aye* to mean 'always'; uses that present a style or usage problem, such as *a* or *an* used before 'h'; least frequently of all, users might want to verify grammar points, for example whether *after* is an adverb or a preposition.

An introductory summary of the word's 'core', or central, meaning appears at the start of the entry. Remaining meanings appear in the usual way, except that parts of speech may be combined at one definition. Definitions are ordered by frequency.

below /bi ló/ CORE MEANING: a grammatical word indicating something situated or placed beneath something else or lower than something else ○ (prep) *a river below the town* ○ (adv) *on the shelf below*
1 *prep, adv* IN LOWER GRADE at or to a level, standard, or grade that is lower than that specified or understood ○ *animals ranked below humans* ○ *below average* ○ *30 degrees below* **2** *adv* FURTHER DOWN lower down or later on in a text, especially on the same page ○ *see below* ○ *on page 29 below* **3** *adv* LOWER THAN THE DECK on or to a level of a ship or boat that is lower than the deck [14C. < earlier form of BY + LOW[1].]

Foreign Words and Phrases

Based on information in our Corpus of World English, foreign words and phrases are included in the A–Z list as entries if they have established English pronunciations and are used without being explained in contemporary literature, journalism, general writing, or general conversation.

du jour /dyoo zhoŏr/ adj offered or served today ○ the soup du jour [< French, 'of the day']

Cross-References

The *Encarta Concise English Dictionary* contains two main types of cross-reference.

Direct cross-references

A direct cross-reference takes the place of a definition, and indicates that the information you need is given at another dictionary entry that has the same meaning.

Calif. abbr California

call-in n US BROADCAST = **phone-in**

The sign [=] refers from a variant spelling to its main form. *Plural of, past tense of,* and so on refer from an inflected form to its root word. *Abbr of, symbol for,* or *full form of* refer from an abbreviation or acronym or symbol to its full form, or vice versa.

The sign [♦] indicates that the information you need is given at another entry (not necessarily one with the same meaning).

Babel /báyb'l/ ♦ **Tower of Babel**

Indirect cross-references

The symbol [◊] indicates an indirect cross-reference to another entry where you will find additional relevant information:

carnivore /kaàrni vawr/ n **1 FLESH-EATING ANIMAL** an animal that eats other animals. ◊ **herbivore, omnivore** n. **1 2** a carnivorous plant **3 SOMEBODY WHO ENJOYS MEAT** a meat eater (*humorous*) [Mid-19C. Via French < Latin *carnivorus* (see CARNIVOROUS).]

Idioms and Phrases

Phrases and idioms are important lexical groups that deserve to be fully represented in dictionaries. The *Encarta Concise English Dictionary* gives particular attention to such items.

carpet /kaàrpit/ n **1 FLOOR COVERING** thick fabric for covering a floor **2 PIECE OF FLOOR COVERING** a piece of thick heavy fabric covering the floor of a room or area **3 LAYER OR COVERING** a layer or covering (*literary*) ○ a carpet of snow ■ vt **1 COVER FLOOR WITH CARPET** to cover a floor, or the floor of a room, with a carpet ○ We could carpet every room in the house with the money she spent on that rug. **2 COVER** to cover something in a layer (*literary*) ○ The valley was carpeted with flowers. **3 REPRIMAND** to reprimand somebody severely (*informal*) [14C. < Old French *carpite* or medieval Latin *carpita* < Latin *carpere* 'to pluck'.] ◇ **roll out the red carpet** to give a special welcome to a distinguished visitor ◇ **sweep something under the carpet** to conceal or ignore something that needs attention

Idioms and phrases are preceded by the symbol [◇].

Phrasal Verbs

The Dictionary gives a considerable amount of space to phrasal verbs. Phrasal verbs are verb-plus-particle combinations in which the total meanings are not literally the sum of the parts. They appear after the root form of the verb (**clear away**, **clear out**, and **clear up** come after **clear**, etc).

clear away vti to remove unwanted objects from a place and leave it tidy
clear off vi to go away (*informal; often a command*) ○ Clear off and don't come back!
clear out v **1** vi **LEAVE FAST** to leave a place quickly or urgently (*informal*) ○ We cleared out as fast as we could. **2** vt **REMOVE** to remove the contents of something, e.g. a room or cupboard, or to tidy something by removing some of its contents ○ clearing out the attic **3** vt **USE ALL OF SOMEBODY'S MONEY** to leave somebody without money or other resources (*slang*) ○ It will clear us out if we have to pay all the legal expenses.
clear up v **1** vi **BECOME BRIGHTER** to become brighter, e.g. after rain **2** vti **GET OR MAKE BETTER** to alleviate or cure something, or be alleviated or cured **3** vti **PUT SOMETHING IN ORDER** to tidy something by removing or arranging disorganized contents ○ Will you please clear up all this mess before you leave? **4** vt **SOLVE MYSTERY OR EXPLAIN MISUNDERSTANDING** to solve a mystery or explain a misunderstanding ○ Here is a big problem that has never been fully cleared up.

Illustrations and Tables

The *Encarta Concise English Dictionary* illustrates over 600 items. The main function of the illustrations is to help the reader by adding to and complementing the text, placing the definition in its context.

The Dictionary also contains over 30 tables of encyclopedic information that provide an invaluable supplement to the dictionary entries. A definition for an artistic movement, for example, can be better understood in the context of the development of art in general, so we have provided a table called **Key movements in Western painting**.

Style Level and Register

The Dictionary uses *italic* labels to indicate style, register, and currency:

Currency

archaic	not used since before 1945
dated	used at some stage between 1945 and 1990 but no longer part of the current idiom

Register

literary	used in literature and poetry and for special effect but not in everyday contexts
formal	used in formal situations and formal writing, but inappropriate in everyday contexts
technical	marks specialist terms that have an everyday equivalent
informal	used in relaxed conversation or writing but avoided in more formal contexts; often has an innocuous or euphemistic feel
humorous	pompous or formal or dated terms typically used self-consciously for humorous effect

disapproving	marks a derogatory attitude on the part of the speaker
slang	highly informal, completely inappropriate in formal contexts, and often with a crude edge
babytalk	used by adults when talking to young children and babies
nonstandard	not considered part of correct or educated usage, though current in spoken usage
regional	used in the dialect of a particular area

Offensiveness

insult	a pejorative term that would be likely to insult or upset somebody if said directly to the person
offensive	likely to be offensive to many people, for example because of being racist or sexual
taboo	for classic taboo words referring to race, sex, and bodily functions

Some lexical entries commonly regarded as offensive or taboo require inclusion in a dictionary of this size and scope. The editors have attempted to ensure that these and other offensive or potentially offensive lexical items and areas of reference are not used in the defining language and other elements of the text.

Words not universally regarded as offensive but likely to give offence in varying degrees are qualified accordingly: *often considered offensive*, *sometimes considered offensive*, and *offensive in some contexts*.

Offensive terms have been defined by a gloss rather than a substitutable definition.

World English and Regional Varieties of English

In the *Encarta Concise English Dictionary* we have attempted to give a world view of the English language that is relevant to the general or student user. We have included information on the two main spelling forms of English – American and British – as well as reflecting words and patterns of usage from a world perspective:

Aotearoa /aà ô tee ə rô ə/ *n NZ* the preferred Maori name for New Zealand (*often in combination*) ○ *Aotearoa-New Zealand*

chair class *n S Asia* a class of travel on Indian railway trains in which passengers are provided with reclinable seats similar to those in aircraft

The Dictionary uses the following *italic* labels to indicate the geographical area where a word is used:

ANZ	Australian and New Zealand English
Aus	Australian English
Can	Canadian English
Carib	Caribbean English
E Africa	East African English
Hawaii	Hawaiian English
Hong Kong	Hong Kong English
Ireland	Irish English
Malaysia	Malaysian English
Midwest	Midwestern United States
N England	Northern England
NZ	New Zealand English
New England	New England
Northeast US	Northeastern United States
Northwest US	Northwestern United States
Philippines	Philippines English
Quebec	Quebec
S Africa	South African English
S Asia	South Asian English
S Atlantic US	South Atlantic United States
S England	Southern England
Scotland	Scottish English
Singapore	Singapore
Southeast US	Southeastern United States
Southern US	Southern United States
Southwest US	Southwestern United States
UK	British English
US	American English
Wales	Welsh English
W Africa	West African English
Western US	Western United States

Restrictions on Usage

Restrictions on the usage of a word are shown by italic comments in brackets. They spell out useful syntactic information beyond the basic part of speech, for example *+ singular verb*; they give information on the typical users of a word or phrase, for example *used mainly by children*; and they give information on the speaker's attitude or tone of voice, for example *often ironic*.

Celsius /sélssi əss/ *adj* using or measured on an international metric temperature scale on which water freezes at 0° and boils at 100° under normal atmospheric conditions (*generally not in scientific contexts apart from meteorology*) ◊ **Fahrenheit** [Mid-19C. After Anders *Celsius* (1701- 44), Swedish astronomer.]

Trademarks, Trade Names, and Proprietary Terms

The Dictionary includes words on the basis of their usage in the English language today. Words that are known to have current trademark or proprietary registrations have been given the label *tdmk*.

Guidance on Spelling, Grammar, and Usage

This Dictionary is unique in reflecting the advice of an Academic Advisory Board of professors and teachers of English, whom we consulted in order to find out the particular difficulties today's students were experiencing with writing English. The main areas the Board was invited to comment on were spelling, grammar, syntax, and style.

As a result of this survey and our own research, we have included in the Dictionary a series of notes that address the problems identified, entered under the rubrics **Usage**, **Language Note**, **Punctuation**, and **Spellcheck**.

Incorrect Spellings

This Dictionary is unique in including in its A–Z text a list of frequent misspellings, entered at their own alphabetical places where users are most likely to look them up. This list has been compiled from the findings of our Academic Advisory Board and the evidence of our own Corpus of World English and research on the Internet. In order to avoid reinforcing an erroneous idea of the spelling of a word we have shown the incorrect form with a line through it:

> ~~Carribean~~ incorrect spelling of **Caribbean**

Spellcheck Notes

Another spelling-related problem identified by our Academic Advisory Board is confusion over homophones, or words with a similar sound but a different meaning or spelling such as *horde* and *hoard*. The Dictionary features pairs of common homophones that may be confused in written texts, often as a result of mistyping, under the rubric **Spellcheck**. These Spellcheck Notes are entered at the first word of the pair, regardless of relative frequency, with a cross-reference from the second homophone. Unlike incorrect spellings, Spellcheck terms are all valid forms.

> **broach** /brōch/ *v* **1** *vt* **BRING UP DIFFICULT SUBJECT** to introduce a subject for discussion, usually one that is awkward ○ *He finally broached the question of the loan.* **2** *vt* **OPEN CONTAINER** to open a container for the first time **3** *vt* **PIERCE CASK** to make a hole in a cask to draw off liquid **4** *vt* **BORE HOLE** to make or enlarge a hole in something **5** *vi* **COME THROUGH SURFACE OF WATER** to break the surface of water from below without completely emerging (*refers to a submarine*) **6** *vi* **TURN SIDEWAYS TO WIND** to be turned broadside to the wind, e.g. by heavy seas, with a risk of capsizing (*refers to a boat*) ■ *n* **1** **TOOL FOR ENLARGING HOLES** a tool for enlarging holes **2** **ROASTING SPIT** a roasting spit **3** **TOOL FOR PIERCING CASKS** a tool used for making holes in casks **4** = **brooch** [14C. < Old French *brocher* 'to stitch' < *broche* 'skewer, long needle'.] - **broacher** *n*
>
> **SPELLCHECK** Do not confuse **broach** with **brooch**, which has a similar sound. Beware: your spellchecker will not catch this error.

Some confusable pairs of words are also dealt with in Usage Notes (see below) because the confusion arises from underlying questions of meaning or usage that need to be explained in more detail.

Usage Notes

The Dictionary's Usage Notes again reflect the language difficulties identified by our Academic Advisory Board. The Notes address the thornier problems of grammar, style, and usage that recur in student and other forms of writing, and give clear and incisive guidance:

> **bored** /bawrd/ *adj* feeling irritable, either because of being exposed to something uninteresting or because of having nothing to do ○ *She grew bored with living in the country.*
>
> **SPELLCHECK** See *board*.
>
> **USAGE** The usual preposition to use after the adjective **bored** is *with*, as in *I grew bored with all their squabbling.* However nowadays the preposition *of* is sometimes seen, especially in speech or informal writing, perhaps by analogy with *tired of*. This usage is to be avoided in careful speech or writing.

Language and Punctuation Notes

The Language Notes and Punctuation Notes provide information on the nuts and bolts of language – information that students need to be able to write correctly constructed sentences. The notes give guidance on topics such as nouns, clauses, the passive, and the use of the apostrophe and the colon, written in clear, nontechnical language. Each Note appears at its relevant dictionary entry:

> **auxiliary verb** *n* a verb that is used with another verb to indicate person, number, mood, tense, or aspect. Some auxiliary verbs in English are 'be', 'have', and 'do'.
>
> **LANGUAGE NOTE Auxiliary verbs:** The auxiliary verbs in English are *be*, *do*, and *have*, which together with the so-called modal verbs (or modal auxiliaries) *can*, *could*, *may*, *might*, *must*, *ought to*, *shall*, *should*, *will*, and *would* (and in some classifications *dare*, *need*, and *used*), are all used with other verbs to form past and future tenses, negatives, questions, the passive voice, and other special functions. Most ordinary verbs cannot fulfil these functions by themselves; for example you have to use the auxiliary verb *do* to form negatives and questions (*They don't like it. Do you want to leave?*), the auxiliary verb *be* to form the progressive aspect (*I am going.*), the auxiliary verbs *be* and *have* to form past, progressive, and imperfect tenses (*We were leaving. They haven't decided.*), and the modal verbs *shall* and *will* to form future tenses (*He will drive you to the station. Shall we go now?*). Sometimes more than one auxiliary verb is used to form a tense, as in *We will be going* and *They have been paid*. The verb *be* is used to form the passive voice: *The letter was posted last night.*

Synonym Essays

The Synonym Essays bring together words that are close in meaning and help distinguish between them:

> **accomplish** /ə kúmplish, ə kóm-/ *vt* **1** to succeed in doing or achieving something **2** to arrive at the end of a period of time (*literary; usually passive*) [14C. < Old French *accompliss-*, a stem of *acomplir* 'complete to' < Latin *complere* (see COMPLETE).] - **accomplishable** *adj* - **accomplisher** *n*
>
> **SYNONYMS** *accomplish, achieve, attain, realize, carry out, pull off*
>
> CORE MEANING: to bring something to a successful conclusion **accomplish** to succeed in doing something; **achieve** to succeed in something, usually with effort; **attain** to reach a specific objective; **realize** to fulfil a specific vision or plan; **carry out** to perform or accomplish a task or activity; **pull off** (*informal*) to accomplish something, despite difficulties.

Literary Links

Literary Links are a unique feature in the Dictionary. They form a stepping-stone from a particular use of a word to its wider cultural context. They typically refer to titles of books or plays, especially those that have passed into the language.

> **comedy** /kómmədi/ (*plural* **-dies**) *n* **1** **FUNNY PLAY, FILM, OR BOOK** a play, film, or book depicting amusing events **2** **COMIC GENRE** comic works, especially plays, considered as a literary genre **3** **COMIC ENTERTAINMENT** entertainment that is amusing **4** **COMIC ELEMENT** the humorous elements of a situation or work of art [14C. Via French *comédie* < Greek *kōmōidia* < *kōmōidos* 'comic actor' < *kōmos* 'revel' + *aoidos* 'singer' < *aeidein* 'sing'.] - **comedic** /kə meédik/ *adj* - **comedically** *adv*

Quick Facts

Defining a complex encyclopedic term such as *chaos theory* in the limited space of a dictionary entry involves distilling a huge amount of possible information. People, places, and concepts associated with the term may be scattered throughout the text, but it is not generally the role of a language dictionary to link them explicitly. And yet for some more significant terms it can be enormously helpful to know the wider context. Recognizing this fact, the editors have chosen to highlight certain key artistic, scientific, and technical topics in a unique feature called **Quick Facts.**

Quick Facts give a brief synopsis of, say, an art movement, drawing together the people, concepts, and developments associated with it that are defined elsewhere in the Dictionary. Quick Facts also cover scientific or technical topics such as the personal computer or the Human Genome Project, giving an outline of the key theories and milestones in their development and attempting to sum up their overall significance.

QUICK FACTS ON... **CHAOS THEORY**

Key elements: mathematical techniques and theories describing highly complex systems, arising from the study of patterns in natural systems, e.g. the motion of the Sun and planets, the principles determining order in the shapes of clouds and crystals, the complexity of living organisms, and the interactions between synthetic chemicals and natural ecosystems

Key dates: 1963 use of three linked nonlinear differential equations to describe a weather system that exhibited sensitive dependence on initial conditions, 'the butterfly effect': the proposition that a butterfly flapping its wings in Hong Kong can effect the course of a tornado in Texas (Lorenz); 1975 first use of the term 'chaos' in a mathematical application (Li and Yorke)

Key technologies: artificial intelligence, computer modelling, fractal geometry, information theory, neural networks

Key developments: astrophysics, cognitive science, evolutionary and developmental biology, meteorology, particle physics, population dynamics

Subject Labels for Specialist Areas

ACCT	Accounting	CLOTHING	Clothing and costume	GENETICS	Genetics
ACOUSTICS	Acoustics	COINS	Coins and coin	GEOG	Geography
AEROSP	Aerospace		collecting	GEOL	Geology
AGRIC	Agriculture	COLLECTING	Collecting	GLASS	Glassware
AIR FORCE	Air force	COLOURS	Colours	GOLF	Golf
ALTERN MED	Alternative medicine	COMM	Commerce	GRAM	Grammar
AMERICAN FOOTBALL	American football	COMPASS	Compass points	GYM	Gym
AMPHIB	Amphibians	COMPUT	Computing	GYMNASTICS	Gymnastics
ANAT	Anatomy	CONSTR	Construction	HAIR	Hairdressing
ANTHROP	Anthropology	COOK	Cooking	HEALTH	Health
ANTIQUES	Antiques	COSMETICS	Cosmetics	HERALDRY	Heraldry
ARCHAEOL	Archaeology	COSMOL	Cosmology	HIKING	Hiking
ARCHERY	Archery	CRAFT	Crafts	HIST	History
ARCHIT	Architecture	CRICKET	Cricket	HOBBIES	Hobbies
ARMS	Arms and weapons	CRIME	Crime	HOCKEY	Hockey
ARMY	Armed forces	CRYSTALS	Crystals	HORSERACING	Horseracing
ART	Art	CUE GAMES	Cue games	HOUSEHOLD	Household items
ARTS	Arts	CYCLING	Cycling	HR	Human resources
ASTRON	Astronomy	DANCE	Dance	ICE HOCKEY	Ice hockey
ATHLETICS	Athletics	DARTS	Darts	ICE SKATING	Ice skating
AUTOMOT	Automotive	DENT	Dentistry	IMMUNOL	Immunology
AVIAT	Aviation	DESIGN	Design	INDUST	Industry
BABYWARE	Babyware	DIY	Home Maintenance	INFO SCI	Information science
BALLET	Ballet	DOMESTIC	Domestic and	INSECTS	Insects
BANKING	Banking		household items	INSUR	Insurance
BASEBALL	Baseball	DRUGS	Drugs	INTERNAT REL	International relations
BASKETBALL	Basketball	ECOL	Ecology	ISLAM	Islam
BEVERAGES	Beverages	E-COMMERCE	E-commerce	JEWELLERY	Jewellery
BIBLE	Biblical terms	ECON	Economics	JUDAISM	Judaism
BIOCHEM	Biochemistry	EDUC	Education	JUD-CHR	Judaeo-Christian
BIOL	Biology	ELEC	Electricity		religion
BIOTECH	Biotechnology	ELEC ENG	Electrical engineering	LACROSSE	Lacrosse
BIRDS	Birds	ELECTRONICS	Electronics	LANG	Language
BOARD GAMES	Board games	ENG	Engineering	LAW	Law
BOBSLEIGHING	Bobsleighing	ENVIRON	Environment	LEISURE	Leisure
BOWLS	Bowls	EQUESTRIAN	Equestrianism	LIBRARIES	Libraries
BOXING	Boxing	ETHICS	Ethics	LING	Linguistics
BROADCAST	Broadcasting	ETHNOL	Ethnology	LITERAT	Literature
BUDDHISM	Buddhism	FASHION	Fashion	LOGIC	Logic
BUILDING	Building	FENCING	Fencing	MAIL	Mail
BUSINESS	Business	FIELD SPORTS	Field sports, hunting, etc	MANAGEMT	Management
CALENDAR	Calendar terms	FIN	Finance	MANUF	Manufacturing
CAMPING	Camping	FISH	Fish	MAPS	Maps
CANOEING	Canoeing	FISHING	Fishing	MARINE BIOL	Marine biology
CARDS	Card games	FITNESS	Fitness	MARKETING	Marketing
CARS	Cars	FOOD	Food	MARTIAL ARTS	Martial arts
CERAMICS	Ceramics and pottery	FOOD TECH	Food technology	MATH	Mathematics
CHEM	Chemistry	FORESTRY	Forestry	MEASURE	Measurements
CHEM ELEM	Chemical elements	FREEMASONRY	Freemasonry	MECH ENG	Mechanical engineering
CHESS	Chess	FREIGHT	Freight	MED	Medicine
CHR	Christianity	FUNGI	Fungi	MEDIA	Media
CINEMA	Cinema	FURNITURE	Furniture	METALL	Metallurgy
CIV ENG	Civil engineering	GAMBLING	Gambling	METEOROL	Meteorology
CLIMBING	Climbing	GARDENING	Gardening	MICROBIOL	Microbiology

Abbreviations and Symbols

b.	born
C	century (in etymologies)
cgs	centimetre-gram-second
cl	centilitre(s)
d.	died
cm	centimetre(s)
cu.	cubic
e.g.	for example
fl.	flourished
fl.	fluid
ft	foot/feet
gal.	gallon(s)
in.	inch(es)
kg	kilogram(s)
km	kilometre(s)
kmph	kilometres per hour
l	litre(s)
lb.	pound(s)
m	metre(s)
mi.	mile(s)
ml	millilitre(s)
mm	millimetre(s)
mph	miles per hour
oz	ounce(s)
sq.	square
pt	pint(s)
yd	yard(s)

■ precedes new part of speech

○ precedes illustrative example

◇ precedes idiomatic phrase

= precedes cross-reference to word with same meaning

◊ precedes cross-reference to related entry

♦ precedes cross-reference to entry where meaning is given

⚡ precedes entry containing a high-tech usage

Pronunciation Guide

Pronunciations in the *Encarta® Concise English Dictionary* are given in a pronunciation system specially developed for the Dictionary. It relies on familiar combinations of letters of the alphabet so that it can be interpreted without constant reference to a table of explanations. The only symbol taken from outside the ordinary alphabet is the *schwa* /ə/, which stands for the sound represented by **a** in **approve** and **megabyte**. In the Dictionary the pronunciations follow the headword or sense number and appear between forward slashes / /.

Pronunciation Key

a	**at**
aa	**father**
aw	**all**
ay	**day**
air	**hair**
b, bb	**but**, **ribbon**
ch	**chin**
d, dd	**do**, la**dd**er
ə	**a**bout, **e**dible, **i**tem, c**o**mmon, circ**u**s
e	**egg**
ee	**eel**
f, ff	**fond**, di**ff**er
g, gg	**go**, gi**gg**le
h	**hot**
hw	**when**
i	**it**, happ**y**, med**i**um
ī	**ice**
j, jj	**juice**, pi**g**eon
k	**key**, thi**ck**
l, ll	**let**, si**ll**y
m, mm	**mother**, ha**mm**er
n, nn	**not**, fu**nn**y
ng	so**ng**
o	**odd**
ō	**open**
oŏ	**good**
oo	**school**
ow	**owl**
oy	**oil**
p, pp	**pen**, ha**pp**y
r, rr	**road**, ca**rr**y, ha**r**d
s, ss	**say**, le**ss**on
sh	**sheep**
th	**thin**
th	**this**
t, tt	**tell**, bu**tt**er
u	**up**
ur	**urge**
v, vv	**very**, sa**vv**y
w	**wet**
y	**yes**
z, zz	**zoo**, bli**zz**ard
zh	**vision**

ʹ over a vowel indicates the syllable with the strongest (primary) stress.

ʹ over a vowel indicates the syllable with medium (secondary) stress.

ʹ before /l/, /m/, or /n/ shows that the consonant is syllabic (takes the function of a vowel).

I. Consonants

The following are used to describe the sound they usually stand for in ordinary spelling: /b d f g h j k l m n p r s t v w y z/.

befriend	/bi frénd/
hug	/hug/
strap	/strap/
milk	/milk/
jazz	/jaz/
yes	/yess/

The following two-consonant combinations (**consonantal digraphs**) also denote the sound they stand for in ordinary spelling: /ch ng th/:

church	/church/
thing	/thing/
shop	/shop/

For the sound in '**the**' (**voiced dental fricative**) we have used th:

mother	/múthər/
that	/that/

For the central sound in '**vision**' (**voiced palatoalveolar fricative**) we use zh:

vision	/vízhʹn/
pleasure	/plézhər/

Doubling

This Dictionary uses double consonants to show many sounds in the middle of words because English spelling normally doubles letters in these positions. Consonants are doubled when they are preceded by the stressed vowels /á, é, í, ó, ú, oŏ/ and followed by either a vowel or a syllabic consonant, or by /l, r, y, or w/:

rubber	/rúbbər/
petrol	/péttrəl/
travel	/trávvʹl/
inward	/ínnwərd/
deputy	/déppyəti/
supposition	/súppə zíshʹn/
teakettle	/teé kettʹl/

In order to show clearly that /s/ is required, not /z/, we double the /s/ additionally at the end of a syllable and with voiced consonants:

face	/fayss/
miscue	/miss kyoŏ/
mincer	/mínssər/

But not with voiceless consonants:

wasp	/wosp/
first	/furst/
tax	/taks/

The consonant /k/ is not doubled:

flicker	/flíkər/
tackle	/tákʹl/

There is no doubling of the two-consonant combinations /ch, sh, th, ng, th, zh/:

touching	/túching/
passion	/páshʹn/
rhythm	/ríthʹm/
measure	/mézhər/
hanger	/hángər/

II. Vowels

The traditional short vowels /a, e, i, o, u/ denote the sounds they usually stand for in ordinary spelling:

cat	/kat/
head	/hed/
myth	/mith/
swan	/swon/
double	/dúbbʹl/

For the short vowel as in '**put**' we use /oŏ/:

good	/goŏd/
could	/koŏd/
full	/foŏl/

For the weak vowel as in the first syllable of '**along**' and the second syllable of '**butter**' we use the symbol /ə/ (schwa):

along	/ə lóng/
butter	/búttər/
flattering	/fláttəring/

For the vowel in '**goose**' and '**soup**' we use /oo/:

food	/food/
move	/moov/
rude	/rood/

When this is preceded by a y-sound (**palatal semivowel**) we use /yoo/:

music	/myoózik/
acute	/ə kyoŏt/
sinuous	/sínnyoo əss/

In words such as '**sure**' and '**pure**' we have used /oor/ and /yoor/ respectively:

poor	/poor, pawr/
cure	/kyoor/
during	/dyooring/

For the diphthongs in '**gray**', '**flee**', and '**boy**', the respellings /ay/, /ee/, and /oy/ are used:

great	/grayt/
niece	/neess/
voice	/voyss/

For the diphthongs in 'high', 'low', and 'cow' we use /ī/, /ō/, and /ow/ respectively:

write	/rīt/
goat	/gōt/
micro	/míkrō/
loud	/lowd/
frown	/frown/

For the vowel of 'nurse', we use /ur/:

turn	/turn/
stern	/sturn/
first	/furst/

For the stressed vowel of 'father' we use /aa/:

father	/fa͟ath̷ər/
bravado	/brə va͟adō/

For the vowel of 'start' in words where there is an 'r' in the spelling, we use /aar/:

farm	/faarm/
starry	/sta͟ari/

We have used /aw/ for the vowel of 'thought':

thought	/thawt/
tall	/tawl/

For the vowel of 'north' in words where there is an 'r' in the spelling, we have used /awr/:

short	/shawrt/
war	/wawr/
sport	/spawrt/
story	/stáwri/

For the vowels in 'near' and 'square' we have used /eer/ and /air/ respectively:

beer	/beer/
beard	/beerd/
weary	/wéeri/
declare	/di kláir/
scarce	/skairss/
vary	/váiri/

For the vowels in 'fire' and 'sour' we have used /īr/ and /owr/:

inspire	/in spír/
virus	/vírəss/
flour	/flowr/
dowry	/dówri/

Consonants that take the place of a vowel in a syllable (**syllabic consonants**) are preceded by /'/:

apple	/ápp'l/

garden	/ga͟ard'n/
station	/stáysh'n/
dental	/dént'l/
rhythm	/ríth̷'m/

In the vowel at the end of words such as 'happy', we have used /i/. The same applies to vowels such as the central one in 'various':

happy	/háppi/
coffee	/kóffi/
various	/váiri əss/
radiate	/ráydi ayt/

II. Stress

Single syllable words (**monosyllables**) have no stress marks. In words with more than one syllable (**polysyllables**) we have indicated the primary stress with an acute accent:

another	/ə núth̷ər/
collide	/kə líd/
cosmetic	/koz méttik/

We have also used the acute accent to show secondary stress **before** the main stress (**pretonic stresses**).

seventeen	/sévv'n te͟en/
academic	/ákə démmik/

IV. When are pronunciations given?

The *Encarta Concise English Dictionary* shows pronunciations at headwords except where the headword is made up of separate or hyphenated words that are given pronunciations elsewhere in the Dictionary. Thus we include pronunciations for all entries that are different headwords with the same spelling (**homographs**) such as *bank* or *bow*. Capitalized forms of common names are not given a pronunciation unless they are geographical or biographical entries. In geographical and biographical entries where the names are repeated, the first occurrence only is given a pronunciation. Important variants in pronunciation are covered in the Dictionary, as are significant changes in pronunciation or stress in undefined entries (**runons**) and pronunciations of plural or other forms where the pronunciation or stress changes from that of the headword.

V. Spacing

As it is easier to work out the pronunciation of a word if longer respellings are broken up into easily processed pieces, we have inserted spaces within the respelling of a word in the following cases:

(i) before a stressed syllable or other syllable containing a strong vowel (which means, for this purpose, any vowel other than / ə i ō oo yoo oͦo /):

allow	/ə lów/
detect	/di tékt/
unknown	/un nón/
celebrate	/séll ə brayt/
cucumber	/kyoͦo kumbər/

(ii) between the elements of a compound in which each element retains its usual pronunciation:

bedtime	/béd tīm/
getaway	/géttə way/

(iii) between any two successive vowel or diphthong symbols:

payee	/pay e͟e/
chaos	/káy oss/

(iv) between /ng/ and a following /g/:

anger	/áng gər/

VI. Foreign pronunciations

In occasional cases - particularly proper names - we have used the following to indicate non-English sounds:

/hl/	as in Welsh **Ll**ango**ll**en
/kh/	as in Scottish lo**ch**, German Ba**ch**, Spanish Gi**j**ón
/N/	to show nasalization of the preceding vowel as in the French pronunciation of **un bon vin** blanc /öN boN vaN blaaN/
/ö/	as in French b**oeu**f, German sch**ö**n
/ü/	as in French r**u**e, German gem**ü**tlich

Using the Internet for Research

Jane Dorner

Introduction

The Internet is inescapable – newspapers, the radio, and television refer readers and audiences to further information on designated websites. From the computer console, anyone can get background documents to explore a subject in greater depth, or 'chat online' to programme-makers and experts for a limited time after a show. Thus the conventional media, which tend to simplify their subject material, increasingly act as a conduit to electronic knowledge banks all over the world, so making available a full range of detail and opinion.

Some of the information is 'fixed' and hence reliable: it comes from published sources whose reputation depends on the public perception of that source. Some of the information is anecdotal: it comes from online forums, e-mail exchange, and a variety of interactive conversation venues that operate through text, voice, and video messaging. The reliability of anecdotal material is the same as in everyday life. Any serious researcher will always check and double-check everything.

Media reporters themselves think information provided by online sources is as valid as other reference, and indeed the Internet is as good a starting place as any. Better, as it is open at all times. So further personal research is at your own leisure – not when libraries or businesses are open – whether you want to know more about an illness and its cures, an unusual recipe, a date in history, weather forecasts, or train timetables.

Yet many people who are devoted to e-mail forget or ignore the power of this global network of interconnected information. It may be because it is not as intuitive as reaching for a book or the telephone. Effective search techniques need to be learnt and questions of reliability and currency of sources need to be explored. This article offers advice in the following areas:

- finding information online
- how to search
- evaluating material
- free and paid-for information
- copyright
- good online practice.

Finding information online

There are a number of different search strategies:
1. follow up sources suggested by the media
2. query a general search engine (software that searches the Web looking for specific words or subjects)
3. start at subject-based websites (or 'portals'), dictionaries, encyclopedias, and knowledge databases.

1. Sources suggested by the media

If you start searching, or 'surfing', from sites suggested by the media, you can be reasonably sure that a certain amount of sifting and sorting has been done for you. Source material will quickly snowball. Each site that you visit will lead on to a dozen or so others on the same topic. It then depends how thorough you wish to be. For most private purposes, it suffices to trawl through a number of links until you feel you are getting more or less the same information from each one. If it is important to be exhaustive, you will want to follow up every single lead and then perhaps use several different search engines to find material as well.

If the media route appeals, try:
Infogate – personalized news, continually updated, delivered to your computer by e-mail
<http://www.infogate.com>

2. General search engines

A search engine trawls the Web for requested content. There is always a search box (to enter the word or subject you are searching for) and an activating box (marked *Go, Fetch, Search,* or similar) that starts the engine hunting out words and phrases across hundreds of millions of pages of material over the entire connected world and comes back to the searcher with 'hits' – its best guesses at what you are looking for.

Every individual will find a favourite engine from the many hundreds that exist (see below for a selection). Trial and error is the only way of finding out which one is best for your own purposes, but some knowledge of how they work will help you select. Be warned that some of the well-known engines charge for prime positions in a listing, which means that those who pay most will be at the top of the list. No single search engine indexes more than one sixth of available Web pages – if that. It may also take six months before a new site makes its way into the indexes.

Searches all work on different principles, though all build up databases with powerful indexing and text-retrieval software. Some allow you to search the whole text of a book or article (full-text searching); others identify material categorized according to a specific theme or topic, for example literary works classified as 'romance' or 'adventure'. Common components are:

- the spiders, or software robots, with names like 'Web ferrets' or 'crawler' or 'search bots' that trawl the Web looking for new pages
- the machine that indexes specific search terms, or 'keywords' (and excludes common words such as prepositions, the definite and indefinite articles, parts of the verb 'to be', and so on)
- the retrieval software that searches the database when you submit a word or phrase.

The description (or abstract) of each 'hit' might come from the beginning of the first page of the site (something to bear in mind both when searching and when creating your own pages). The search engines may:

- index only the first 17 words of the page
- search on encoded keywords
- index every word
- index only sites that have registered with the engine (some free, others paid for)
- send out software spiders that collect up all new pages.

If you are looking for very specific or esoteric information, you may have to try several different engines and advanced techniques. After all, no one goes to just one library for research; they use several to discover which is the right one.

All-One-Search - 500 search engines, databases, indexes, and directories in a single site; worth looking at if only to find the engine that specializes in something esoteric
<http://www.allonesearch.com>
AltaVista - has an interesting foreign-language translation feature
<http://altavista.com>
Askjeeves - has only selected sites picked by real editors and searches across AltaVista, Excite, Infoseek, Webcrawler, and Yahoo!; a good starting point with a UK weighting
<http://www.askjeeves.co.uk>
Google - very useful, especially for the sciences
<http://www.google.com>
Infomine scholarly directory - librarian-selected with flexible search options
<http://www.infomine.ucr.edu/main.html>
Librarians' Index to the Internet - frequently updated
<http://www.lii.org>
Lycos - nice coverage of communities (like-minded people who 'meet' in virtual space)
<http://www.lycos.co.uk>
SearchIQ - tells users which search engine to try for their particular needs; also suggests a successful 3-phase strategy; a good starting point
<http://www.zdnet.com/searchiq>
WWW Virtual Library - search or browse subject-organized full-text documents, databases, and gateways
<http://www.vlib.org/overview.html>

---

3. Subject portals and knowledge databases

Just as most people go to an expert library for subject-related information, so they turn to subject portals on the Web. Portals are websites that list links to related websites on specific subjects. A good portal will have a directory structure with finer and finer subdivisions of the subject so that users can click along in a linear fashion to refine their search. The top-level departments – business, entertainment, music, sport, and so on – are called

channels. Some people prefer to look for information on a portal as it has a structure and some degree of vetting for content. Search engines tend to be more random, which is good for serendipity, but not always efficient.

Building such gateways to trusted sources of material is now a growing activity on the Web. Governments and corporations are putting a great deal of money into resourcing archives of factual and educational links.

Here are some examples:
About.com – popular/commercial subject guides
<http://www.home.about.com/index.htm>
AlphaSearch – points to gateways for a subject, discipline, or idea
<http://www.calvin.edu/library/searreso/internet/as/>
Argus Clearinghouse – librarian/academic subject guides
<http://www.clearinghouse.net/index/html>
UK Central Government – contains a database of virtually all government and related websites via its organization and topic indexes
<http://www.open.gov.uk>

How to search

Start with a few central words and be prepared to keep trying. Sophisticated searching is an art in itself and needs special training. Most of us will find the following tactics quite effective.

Start with a generalized but reasonably specific search term. Received wisdom is that you should not run one-word searches, but type in multiple words or a phrase in double quotes to increase your chances of finding useful results.

Guessing the relevant keyword or unique combination of several words is half the battle and it always pays to think of as many synonyms as possible and run the search several times in order to be sure of finding all material on a topic.

There is a halfway house somewhere in between making a search as wide as possible and refining down so you isolate a unique phrase. Thus 'gardens' is already more specific than 'garden'. Typing in '18th+century+gardens' might bring up Humphrey Repton, Capability Brown, Stowe, Stourhead, Burghley House, and others you had not thought of. If you just wanted Capability Brown, you would put his name in double quotes.

Search tips

All search engines have slightly different search rules, but a few general principles can be extrapolated.

Choose useful keywords

Typing one keyword usually returns too many results to be useful. Try to narrow your search by adding refining terms. Try two related words or a phrase in double quotes (called a string) to increase your chances of finding useful results, e.g. "french window".

Use lower case

When you use lower-case text, the search service finds both upper- and lower-case results. When you use upper-case text, the search service may only find upper case. So "oval" will find *Oval*, *oval*, and *OVAL*, but "Oval" might only launch results for *Oval*.

Use the asterisk as a wild card

Used at the end of a word, the asterisk (*) is like a wild card and can replace up to five characters. It allows you to broaden your search by including plurals, adjectives, adverbs, and conjugated words. So "sky*" will find pages with *sky, skylight, skywriting, skydiving*, etc.

Excluding and including

Boolean operators are connecting words or symbols that enable you to refine the context of your search term by including or excluding words associated with it. The most common Boolean operators are:

AND (you are looking for all terms)
OR (you are looking for at least one of the terms)
NOT (you are excluding a term)
NEAR (you are looking for terms within a specified number of words: note that this operator is not recognized by every engine).

Operators are shown in upper-case letters, although you may be able to use plus or minus signs (no spaces) to include or exclude words. Look at the instructions in the engine you are going to use regularly. They are all slightly different and the subject listings do not lend themselves to complex searching at all.

For example, try:
(sky AND blue) AND NOT cloud (alternatively "sky +blue –cloud") to find pages where 'sky' and 'blue' appear, but where there is no instance of the word 'cloud'.

Evaluating material

One of the reasons people instinctively distrust the Internet is because it is a free-for-all. Anyone may publish, and many do. Pages revealed by a search engine may be from reliable sources or from a private hobby page. There are no guarantees and every individual needs to be wary.

You can tell quite a lot from the Internet address, or URL (Uniform Resource Locator) itself – it is like reading any other address. It is unadventurous to be prejudiced and you can be wrong, but here are a few pointers.

Individuals or organizations that have invested resources in creating Web pages that excel will have registered short domain names descriptive of their organizations. This is, after all, publishing and a background in design, editing, and communications is an advantage. So short and snappy is good; long is a giveaway indicating that a site is a subdirectory branching off another site.

A URL with the squiggly sign '~' (called a tilde) is probably someone's personal page on a public or academic server. However, this does not mean that the information is necessarily of poor quality. The same applies to URLs with series of forward slashes, '/', and a name or number interspersed.

The extensions '.ac' (UK) or '.edu' (US) indicate that the site is an academic institution. Anything with a '.uk' in it is British, whereas '.com' (= commercial organization), '.org' (= non-commercial organization), or '.net' (= networking organization) can be anywhere in the world. The most recent set of top-level domain names, including '.museum' (= museums) '.info' (= general use), '.biz' (= business), and '.pro'(= professional practice), offer the promise of further quality guarantees.

Checklist of questions

You must be sure in your own mind about what you are looking for and why you have come to the site. Otherwise, there is a risk you will sink into unfocused channel-hopping. Once at a website, you can tell a lot by the look and feel of it. Poor spelling and grammar abounds on the Internet: it is usually the sign of a poorly thought-out site (though even the best have spelling errors here and there).

Look for these things:
- a statement of the aims and objectives of the site
- author and publisher details and an e-mail link to back up authenticity
- details of the origin of any data or information
- mention of any quality checks or referencing of the information
- creation and modification dates - age may or may not matter
- clearly marked archival information
- good design and awareness of readability - though many excellent academic papers have poor design and less legible typefaces
- an effective search box - vital on an information-rich site.

In judging the content, ask yourself:
- Does the resource appear to be honest and genuine?
- Is the resource available in another format? (e.g. a book or CD-ROM)
- Do any of the materials potentially infringe copyright?
- Is the information well researched?
- Is any bias made clear and of an acceptable level?
- Is the information durable in nature?
- Is there adequate maintenance of the information content?

For more on evaluation, visit:
Evaluating Information Found on the Internet
<http://milton.mse.jhu.edu/research/education/net.html>
Evaluating Web Resources
<http://www2.widener.edu/Wolfgram-Memorial-Library/webevaluation/webeval.htm>
Information overload
Reuters business report
<http://www.reuters.com/rbb/research/overloadframe.htm>

Free and paid-for information

The Internet has changed the nature of reference-book publication. Nowadays the printed volume very often has a set of links to expand its fixed content so that buyers feel they are getting the extra value of updates on the Web. The online versions (and most important reference works now are online) often link directly to other vetted sources. They are arguably better than the volume equivalents because of their search facilities.

There are two models:

1. the free reference works, e.g.:

Bibliomania - excellent online literature library with hundreds of searchable full-text classics; includes fiction and language reference works such as *Brewer's Dictionary of Phrase & Fable*
<http://www.bibliomania.com>
CIA World Factbook - statistical data about countries and other useful data
<http://www.cia.gov/cia/publications/factbook/index.html>
Encarta' Encyclopedia - over 19,000 entries, photographs, videos, animations, audio clips, and numerous web links. It is searchable by topic and carries updates, study features and teacher resources. It is available online at
<http://www.encarta.msn.co.uk/reference/>
For Australia and New Zealand
<http://www.encarta.ninemsn.com.au>
Encarta' World English Dictionary has over 90,000 entries and in available online at
<http://dictionary.msn.co.uk/>
Encyclopaedia Britannica - the online version of the encyclopedia searchable by topic; includes updates and free links.
<http://www.britannica.com>

2. the library subscription model, offering free online access via a password to those who have already bought the paper versions, e.g.:

KnowUK - vast compendium site on people, institutions, and organizations of the UK: *Debrett, Hansard, Who's Who, Who Was Who, Dictionary of Biography, Writers' & Artists' Yearbook*, and 30-40 licensed texts.
http://www.knowuk.co.uk
Oxford English Dictionary - fully searchable 20-volume edition
http://www.oed.com

Many scientific and medical journals also follow the subscription model. Some journals are available in paid-for versions online only - a trend that is expected to grow.

Generally speaking (and this is a simplification to which there are exceptions) the paid-for resources offer higher guarantees of quality assurance than the rest since they have been through time-honoured processes of publishing quality control.

Copyright

It is a myth that anything that is freely available is available free. Researchers may want free research and educational materials, but everyone has a responsibility to honour copyright online in the same way as they would on paper. Posting something on the Internet is publishing no matter how small the readership is. Remember that there is no redress in British law if you have taken anyone's materials for anything other than personal information. Be aware of the following:

You **may**:
- copy something from an Internet site for individual research only
- print one paper copy from a screen copy
- print a list of URLs to show others.

You **may not**:
- copy the original again for a friend or colleague
- copy it for use in a classroom or business venue
- post a copyrighted cartoon, photo, video clip, or anything else on a personal page
- cut and paste any material that you did not write into your own work unless it is a very short quotation.

Some people may well feel that copyright is not appropriate to the Internet and that if it is hard to protect then no one can enforce it. Yet anyone can use search tools to detect plagiarism by searching the Web for texts containing identifiable strings of words - even whole paragraphs. Some images and music carry digital watermarks that will show up unauthorized use of copyrighted work. Watermarked texts exist too, but are harder to standardize because of the many text formats that are digitally readable.

But enforcement is not the issue. At the moment, and for the time being, copyright is all we have to protect an individual's work. Copyright is a right whether the work appears on paper, on screen, on film, over radio waves, or is just spoken or performed across a room. So electronic words, music, and pictures are protected by copyright as soon as they are created, and at all stages of being copied onto disks, retrieved from disks, or transmitted from any kind of host computer to any receiving computer.

If you want to reproduce a substantial part of a copyrighted source, ask permission to use it. You may refer to the source, or paraphrase or summarize its contents, citing the source appropriately. But even hyperlinking is something of a minefield. To be safe, only link to another site's home page (not an inside page) and make sure it opens up in a separate browser window.

For more on copyright:
IP - Government-backed portal of UK Intellectual Property on the Internet
<http://www.intellectual-property.gov.uk>
Plagiarism detector - designed for academia, but with interesting future possibilities; robots search for exact phrase matching from thousands of databases
<http://www.plagiarism.org>

Good online practice
Quoting sources
The same rules of citation apply to research material found on the Internet as anywhere else. The format you use depends on the discipline of your own subject area and will match the bibliographical styles, e.g. Harvard, Chicago, MLA (Modern Language Association), APA (American Psychological Association), and many more. All are different in detail, but the following principles apply to quoting Web-originated materials:

- Give information so a reader can find the online source you are citing.
- The citation for a Web document often follows a format similar to that for print, with some information omitted and some added.
- If you cannot find some elements of information, cite what is available. E.g.:
    - instead of a title, there may only be a file name
    - the place of publication and the name of the publisher may be replaced online by the URL
    - if the work was originally for print, it may be necessary to give the date of the original print publication
    - online authors may only use login names or aliases.
- Always include the date that you accessed the source (equivalent to the edition).
- Cite the complete URL accurately (within angled brackets is a typical convention). Include the access mode (shown by the abbreviation *http, ftp, telnet*, etc). If you have to divide the URL between two lines, break only after a slash mark and do not insert a hyphen at the break.

URLs do, unfortunately, change. Researchers generally realize that they may have to step back to the core domain name in a URL that has a long series of elements separated by forward slashes.

Full information at:
University of London library notes on citation (5 August 1998)
<http://www.ucl.ac.uk/Library/citing.htm>
The International Standard (ISO 690-2) on citing electronic documents (14 August 2000)
<http://www.nlc-bnc.ca/iso/tc46sc9/standard/690-2e.htm>

E-mail and Chat Etiquette
E-mail and computer conferencing (including chat rooms and forums) are also useful for research. Several people can exchange ideas using the computer to provide virtual spaces to 'meet' online. Audio and video outlets are improving, but for most individuals, this form of simultaneous exchange is still text-based.

There is a level of informality in e-mail and online chat that has become acceptable discourse, but the same rules of social awareness apply. If you would avoid saying something face to face, do not do it by e-mail or online chat. It is very easy to feel detached from what you are keying onto a screen, partly because there is the multiple distancing of silence, inherent problems of decoding text, lack of communication cues, and uncertainty about what time lags mean.

Some good practice guidelines have developed:
- Describe the content of your message clearly in the 'Subject' line and keep that subject in replies to the same conversational thread. Change the subject line in replies that start a new topic. This helps people to prioritize and to find information again later.
- Send short messages that can be clearly understood on their own.
- Make the top of the message count. People will decide whether or not to read on.
- Make sure your message is written in a style that is friendly, appealing, and logical. 'Who, why, what, where' is a formula that works well.
- Read messages carefully before sending.
- Ask permission before forwarding or copying other people's messages - they are not yours.
- Avoid sexist or racist language.
- Avoid using all upper-case letters (it looks as if you are SHOUTING).
- Be aware that all written communication is open to misunderstanding. If the message is very important or controversial consider a face-to-face discussion instead.
- Select the right forum - private e-mail or conference. If your comment is only of interest to a limited number of people, send it to the private mailboxes.
- When joining an online group that has been in existence for some time, read through all the contributions to date (and the FAQs, or frequently asked questions) to avoid asking a question or making a point that has already been covered.
- Do not assume that all outrageous messages are intended to inflame opinion (they may be a clumsy attempt at humour, or lack of familiarity with the medium).
- Check that you are sending the message to the right person or people. Be especially careful when replying.
- We need also to remember not to rely on instant answers: technologies can go wrong. It is always wise to allow time if you have an important deadline.

Web searching, online conferencing, and e-mail interviewing are research tools that are changing our lives, and we need to become expert at using them to serve us well.

Usage Notes in the *Encarta*® *Concise English Dictionary*

'Reading *Wuthering Heights*, Heathcliff never fails to make an impression.'
'There's players all over the field.'
'He gave it to John and I.'
'Helen and me went to class.'
'Whereas I don't want to go at all.'
'If it was true, things would be different.'
'This poem is'nt rhymed.'
'The main character was put in prison for two years and her husband left her, which served her right.'
'Humans use of sound is in no way unique.'
'If your planning on joining the workforce immediately, its a good idea to attend a job fair.'
'If a personality conflict arises, both proffessor and student will loose a wonderful opportunity.'
'The villain use to be seen lurking on foggy streets late at night.'

You have just read some examples of university students' writing that were submitted to the editors of the *Encarta*® *Concise English Dictionary* by an Academic Advisory Board of English professors and sixth-form teachers. These and many more such examples indicate a degree of crisis in many students' use of the English language. How did this silent usage slippage come to our attention?

Bloomsbury has been asking people – parents, grandparents, students, and teachers – what they want from dictionaries. Help with the English language as a key requirement. So, for the first time in the history of dictionary publishing, the editors of a Concise-level dictionary decided to escape the somewhat artificial confines of commercial publishing and find out directly from English professors and teachers the kinds of problem they are encountering in their students' prose. Our aim was to collect, directly from those in contact with students, information on the areas in which the potential future users of a Concise dictionary might need help in making choices in English. And because the *Encarta Concise* is a dictionary of World English we assembled an Advisory Board of academics and teachers from around the world – from Britain, Australia, the United States, and Canada.

We sent our Advisory Board questionnaires eliciting their responses to broad questions like these: What is the most pervasive usage problem that you see in your students' writing? What types of syntactic, grammatical, and stylistic difficulties are your students experiencing? What types of spelling problem do you see in your students' writing? We then sent usage notes on numerous usage and spelling problems identified by the Board as a whole, and invited their comments. In all we consulted 41 professors or teachers of English, 12 of whom are affiliated with universities and colleges in Britain and Australia.

The results were stunning, as the examples cited show. The Board reported strikingly similar problems, regardless of whether their students were British, Australian, or North American. Our current generation of students has grown up, after all, in the global village, and has had an unprecedented degree of exposure to rapid communication in the form of computers, e-mail, and the Internet.

The Board reported, for example, that many students do not understand the basic rules of subject/verb agreement, the difference between *there/their/they're*, the components required to construct a full sentence, the difference between possessives and contractions, the ways to avoid dangling participles and misplaced modifiers, and the most rudimentary rules of spelling and meaning.

In terms of usage and meaning, they reported that many students do not understand the difference between, say, *pretext* and *pretence*, *climatic* and *climactic*, *difference* and *differentiation*, and *cf.* and *ff.*

In terms of spelling, the mishearing of words is a central, pervasive problem, leading to major spelling difficulties. Students mishear words such as *used/supposed* as 'use/suppose', *humanist* as 'huminist', and *whether* as 'weather'. They write *incidents* in contexts where *incidence* is required. They mishear *past* for 'passed' and vice versa.

Many students have trouble with words having

doubled letters, writing 'refered' for *referred* and 'personell' for *personnel*.

Here are some more examples of the invaluable comments of our Board on matters of current misusage:

'Students are often unsure about subject-verb agreement, not only in the case of "one is/are" but also when compound subjects are involved, as in: "My friend and her parents was going to France to live".'

'Students use *would of, should of,* and *could of* when *would have/would've, should have/should've*, and *could have/could've* are the correct forms.'

'Students habitually confuse *childish/childlike, simple/ simplistic*.'

'Students do not understand pronoun use, as in "Us friends decided to go on holiday together" or "Joe and me want to do this project together".'

'Students do not know when to use the subjunctive in contrary-to-fact situations and instead use the incorrect indicative, as in "If I was you . . . .".'

'Students often use *issue/issues* as a catch-all term for *problem, difficulty, point of disagreement,* etc, as in "He has some issues with this premise."'

'Students habitually use informal, vague words in formal writing, e.g. *kind of, sort of*.'

'Students are unclear about appropriate punctuation, especially the use of commas, apostrophes, and inverted commas.'

'Students regularly mix misspellings, redundancies, and formal/informal registers, as in "The reason that I should of created the table is because the data isn't clear otherwise."'

'Students regularly produce incomplete sentences or rambling, poorly connected sentences.'

'Students overuse empty intensifiers (*very, extremely, literally*) and dull, devalued words (*interesting, good*).'

'Students have problems with the plurals of words like *phenomenon* and *criterion*, producing bogus plurals like *phenomenas* and *criterias*.'

'Students confuse *affect* and *effect*.'

'Students do not understand defining and non-defining clauses, subject-verb agreement, gerunds and participles, and other major components of good syntax and grammar.'

All these problems and a host of others are dealt with in the Dictionary's 600 Usage Notes, its A-Z list of over 700 commonly misspelt words, and its 400 'Spellcheck' notes that distinguish between pairs of words pronounced similarly but spelt differently and having different meanings - for example *faze/phase* and *pray/prey*.

Our Notes focus especially on uses that would be regarded by many people as unsuitable, incorrect, or just unhelpful to clear expression. Current teaching guidelines stress the importance of being able to communicate effectively in different situations. This Dictionary's Notes provide the information needed to make appropriate choices of grammar and vocabulary in a given context.

A good many of the errors highlighted above are not addressed by current dictionaries in their usage comments. The problems are not addressed because, we suspect, dictionary editors are unaware of the severity of the problem. Further, it has become clear to us that usage notes in current dictionaries presuppose a level of grammatical and syntactic literacy on the undergraduate level that simply does not exist today. Thus, in our Notes, when we explain things like gerunds, participles, and defining/non-defining clauses, we briefly gloss these terms in brackets before going on to explain the usage problems and how to avoid them.

As we continue into the 21st century it is our hope that the Usage Notes and other language guidance in the *Encarta Concise English Dictionary* - grounded in the classroom and reviewed and edited by English teachers - will help all students make informed choices in their writing.

In an era in which the English language is fast becoming the global lingua franca, it is essential that speakers and writers of it learn to use it with grace, accuracy, and concision, for it is a precious communicative medium.

Entries with Notes

The *Encarta® Concise English Dictionary* includes the Usage, Punctuation, and Language Notes and the Synonym Essays listed below.

USAGE

a[5]	Arab	century	definite	ever	incidence	parameter
about	Arabian	ceremonial	definitive	every	incident	part
absolutely	Arabic	ceremonious	déjà vu	everyday	Indian	participle
accept	aren't	cf	delusion	except	infer	passed
access	arguably	chair	denigrate	excepting	inflict	past[1]
acronym	as[1]	chairman	denote	exceptionable	ingenious	people
actual	Asian	chairperson	deprecate	exceptional	ingenuous	per cent
actually	Asiatic	chairwoman	depreciate	expect	inquire	percentage
A.D.[1]	assert	challenged	derisive	explicit	insert	person
adapt	assertive	childish	derisory	extrovert	inside	persuade
adjacent	assure	childlike	desert[2]	fact	insidious	persuasion
adjoining	at[1]	chord[1]	dessert	fame	insure	phenomenon
adopt	aural	chronic	devolve	farther	Inuit	plus
adoptive	avenge	cite	dialogue	farthest	invidious	pore[1]
adversarial	averse	classic	dice	few	ironic	possessive
adverse	avoid	classical	die[1]	finished	irregardless	pour
advise	avoidance	climactic	difference	flagrant	irrespective	preposition
adviser	await	climatic	different	flaunt	issue	pretext
affect[1]	awake	cohort	differentiation	flout	its	principal
afflict	awful	collective noun	disassociation	foetus	kind[2]	principle
age	awhile	comparable	disinterested	follow	kindly	proactive
agenda	back	compare	disputably	foot	large	prophecy
agendum	backward	compatriot	dissociation	for	late	prophesy
aggravate	bad	complacent	do[1]	foregone	lead[1]	prove
aggressive	balance	complaisant	done	former[1]	leave[1]	quantity
ago	baleful	complement	doubt	fortuitous	led	queer
agreement	baneful	complementary	double negative	fortunate	let[1]	quest
ain't	Bantu	compliment	each	free	like[1]	question
alibi	barely	complimentary	each other	from	literally	rational
all	basically	condole	eager	fulsome	loan	rationale
alleged	basis	conflicted	early	further	look	rationalization
all right	bath	conscientious	eatable	furthest	loose	re[2]
allude	bathe	conscious	economic	gender	lose	reason
allusion	battle	consensus	economical	gerund	lot	rebound
already	because	console[1]	edible	gift	majority	rebuff
alright	behalf	continual	effect	girl	man	rebut
alternate	beside	continually	e.g.	good	may	recuperate
alternative	besides	continuous	egoism	government	media[1]	recur
although	best	controversy	egotism	graffiti	militate	redound
altogether	better[1]	contribute	either	group	millennium	refer
ambiguous	between	conviction	elder[1]	grow	minimal	refute
ambivalent	biannual	convince	eldest	half	minimize	regardless
amend	biennial	cord	electric	halting	mitigate	regretful
America	billion	corporal[1]	electrical	hardly	myself	regrettable
among	bimonthly	corporeal	else	have	Native American	reiterate
amount	biweekly	council	elude	healthful	nauseate	relate
an[1]	biyearly	counsel	emend	healthy	Negro	reluctant
analogous	black	couple	end	help	neither	repellent
and	blatant	credible	enormity	home	nigger	replace
and/or	blond	creditable	enormousness	hopefully	none	represent
antecedent	bored	credulous	enquire	house	nothing	repulsive
anticipate	born[1]	crescendo	ensure	however	notoriety	research
anxious	borne	criterion	envisage	I[1]	number	respectfully
any	both	crone	envision	idea	observance	respectively
anybody	breath	crucial	equally	ideal	observation	reticent
any more	breathe	dangling	escalate	i.e.	obviate	reverend
anyone	bring	participle	Eskimo	if	off	reverent
anyplace	but	data	estimate	ill	old	revolve
anytime	can[2]	decade	estimation	illusion	one	same
appraise	cannot	deceptively	et al.[1]	impact	only	sank
appreciate	censor	decimate	etc.	implicit	oral	savage
apprise	censure	defective	evade	imply	ought[1]	saving
	centre	deficient	evasion	in[1]	pair	scarcely

scenario
Scot
Scotsman
Scotswoman
Scottish
seeing
self
sensibility
sensible
sensitive
sensual
sensuous
sentence adverb
sequence of
  tenses
serendipity
series
sex
should
sick
sight
similar
simple
simplistic
since
sink
site
slow
sneak
so-called
sociable
social
someday
someplace
sort
southward
specially
stratum
substitute
such
sulphur
sunk
sunken
sure
suspect
take
than
thankfully
that
their
theme
themselves
there
therefore
they
they're
this
though
till[1]
together
ton
tonne
tortuous
torturous[1]
transformation
transmigration
transpire
trillion
try
turbid
turgid
type

un-[1]
unanticipated
unaware
unawares
underlay[1]
underlie
under way
unexceptionable
unexceptional
uninterested
unique
until
up
use[1]
utilize
venal
venial
vicious circle
wait
wake
waken
we
well[2]
were
westward
what
whatever
when
whence
whenever
where
wherever
which
while
whilst
who
whoever
whom
whomever
who's
whose
why
will[1]
-wise
with
within
woman
work
worthwhile
would
wreak
wrought
yet
you
your
you're
yourself

PUNCTUATION

apostrophe[1]
bracket
colon[1]
comma
dash
ellipsis
full stop
hyphen
inverted comma
possessive
question mark
semicolon

slash
square bracket

LANGUAGE NOTES

abbreviation
auxiliary verb
clause
euphemism
figurative
functional shift
function word
insult
majority
noun
passive
phrase
progressive
shall
split infinitive
subjunctive
thankfully
transitive

SYNONYM ESSAYS

abhorrence
ability
able
aboriginal
abrogate
abstruse
abuse
accomplish
accumulate
achieve
acquiesce
acquire
admiration
advise
advocate
affection
agree
alive
alloy
alter
amalgam
amass
amplify
angel
anger
angst
animate
animosity
annoyance
annul
answer
antipathy
anxiety
apathetic
ape
applicant
apprentice
aptitude
arcane
arduous
argue
arid
aroma
arrogant
aspirant

assemble
assent
assiduous
assistant
assume
attain
attempt
augment
autochthonous
averse
aversion
aware
backer
battle
beginner
bent[2]
bestow
blast
blemish
blend
block
blunder
bother
bountiful
bouquet
bravery
bright
broadcast
bug
burden[2]
candidate
capability
capacity
capitulate
care
careful
carp[1]
cast
castigate
category
caustic
cautious
censure
change
chary
chatty
chicken
child
chuck[1]
circumspect
city
clandestine
clash
class
clever
clone
coach
cogent
cognizant
collect[1]
combination
competence
complain
composed
compound[1]
conceited
conclude
concur
condemn
confer
conflict
conscientious

conscious
consent
contender
contestant
contradict
conurbation
convert
convincing
copy
courage
covert
covet
cowardly
crave
craven
criticize
crush
cryptic
custom
customary
dead
deadly
dearth
debilitated
deceased
decrepit
decriminalize
deduce
defame
defect
defend
deficiency
deficit
defunct
delicate
demur
denounce
departed
deplore
derivation
desiccated
desire
differ
difficult
diffuse[2]
dirty
disagree
disapprove
disgust
dislike
dispute
disseminate
distaste
distribute
disturb
donate
doubt
doubtful
drag
draw
drill[1]
dry
dubious
ductile
duplicate
educate
effective
effectual
efficacious
efficient
elastic
emaciated

embezzle
emolument
employ
empty
emulate
engagement
enigmatic
enlarge
entrant
epidemic
error
essential
esteem
expand
expostulate
extant
extend
extinct
fabrication
failing
faint-hearted
falsehood
falter
fatal
fault
faux pas
favour
fee
feeble
fib
fight
filch
filthy
finicky
flair
flaw[1]
fleeting
flimsy
flinch
fling
forget
fragile
fragrance
frail
frangible
fresh
friable
furtive
fury
fussy
gain[1]
gape
garrulous
gather
gawk
gawp
gaze
generous
genius
genre
get[1]
gift
gifted
give
goad
grant
greenhorn
grimy
gripe
grouse[2]
grubby
grumble

guarantor
guard
guarded
gut
gutless
habit
habitual
hamper[1]
hard
hate
hatred
haul
heave
hesitant
hesitate
hinder[1]
hoard
hollow
honorarium
hurl
idle
illegal
illicit
ill-treat
imitate
impassive
impede
imperfection
inaccuracy
incentive
increase
indigenous
indignation
indispensable
inducement
infatuation
infer
infirm
instruct
intelligent
intensify
intermittent
intractable
invalidate
ire
irk
kid[1]
kind[2]
knack
laborious
labour
lack
language
late
lean[2]
legal
lethal
libel
liberal
licit
lie[2]
lifeless
liking
living
loath
loathing
long[2]
long-winded
loquacious
love
magnanimous
malign

malleable
maltreat
matter
meticulous
metropolis
mettle
mimic
mindful
misappropriate
mistake
mistreat
misuse
mixture
modern
modify
moist
mortal
motive
moving
municipality
munificent
nag[1]
native
necessary
need
negate
neglect
nerve
new
newfangled
nick
nitpick
nonlegal
novel[2]
novice
nullify
object
obscure
obstreperous
obstruct
obtain
occasional
odour
ogle
omit
oral
origin
original
overlook
painstaking
parched
passion
pathetic
patron
pause
pay[1]
peaceful
perfume
periodic
phlegmatic
pilfer
pinch
placid
pliable
pliant
pluck
practice
present[1]
prevalent
procure
prolix
protect

protest
proud
provenance
prudent
pull
punctilious
purloin
pusillanimous
quail[2]
quick
quiet
rage
rambling
realize
reason
reasonable
recalcitrant
recoil
recommend
recondite
recondition
re-create
reek
regard
rejoinder
reluctant
remonstrate
remuneration
rend
renew
renovate
replicate
reply
reproduce
requisite
respect
response
restore
reticent
retort[1]
revamp
reverence
rife
right hand
rip[1]
riposte
root[1]
routine
rubberneck
runner
safeguard
salary
sarcastic
sardonic
satirical
scatter
scent
sceptical
school[1]
scraggy
scrawny
scrupulous
secret
secure
sensible
sere[1]
serene
shield
shift
shortage
shrink
shrivel

silent
skill
skinny
skirmish
slander
slender
slim
slip[1]
slit
smart
smell
soil[2]
sort
sound[2]
source
species
spineless
spoken
sponsor
sporadic
spur
squalid
stare
steal
stealthy
stench
still[1]
stink
stipend
stockpile
stoic
stolid
strenuous
stress
stumble
subject
subject matter
submit
succumb
suggest
surrender
surreptitious
taciturn
talent
talkative
teach
tear[1]
teenager
temporary
terminal
theme
thin
thorough
throw
tongue
topic
toss
tough
tow[1]
town
tradition
train
tranquil
transform[1]
transmute
trouble
try
tug
tutor
type
tyro
uncertain

unclean
uncommunicative
unfilled
universal
unlawful
unmoved
unoccupied
unruffled
unruly
unsure
untruth
unwilling
use[1]
usual
utilize
vacant
vacillate
vain
valid
vary
veneration
verbal
verbose
vigilant
vilify
vital
vocabulary
void
wage
want
war
wary
waver
wayward
weak
whine
white lie
widespread
wild
wilful
wince
wish
wont
wonted
wordy
worry
wrath
wrongful
yank
yearn
yellow
yield
youngster
youth

QUICK FACTS

abstract
  expressionism
aestheticism
artificial
  intelligence
art nouveau
Arts and Crafts
atomic structure
baroque
big bang
biotechnology
chaos theory
classicism
clone
computer
conceptual art

constructivism
cubism
Dada
deconstructionism
DNA
  fingerprinting
empiricism
existentialism
expressionism
fascism
fauvism
feminism
film noir
Freudianism
futurism
genetic
  modification
global warming
Gothic
heredity
Human Genome
  Project
imagism
impressionism
Internet
Keynesianism
magic realism
mannerism[2]
microprocessor
modernism
monetarism
neoclassicism
neoimpressionism
new wave
op art
performance art
personal
  computer
pop art
postimpressionism
postmodernism
post-structuralism
Pre-Raphaelite
programming
  language
psychoanalysis
quantum theory
Reformation
relativity
Renaissance
rococo
Romanesque
Romanticism
string theory
surrealism
symbolism
Theater of the
  Absurd
transcendentalism

LITERARY LINKS

ado
afraid
alchemist
ambassador
angel
anger
ark
bell[1]
beloved
birthday

bleak
brave new world
brigade
builder
cabin
career
carol
catch-22
children
cider
circle
comedy
courage
crime
crucible
cry
elegy
expectation
experience
fable
fairy tale
farm
father
fellow
fringe
fire
front
fury
gable
gaol
garden
ghost
grape
grass
great
handful
hard
heart
height
helix
hollow
human
hunchback
hunter
if
inferno
innocence
labour
lad
lighthouse
like[2]
lover
lucky
lunch
Madame
madding
magic
magus
mariner
master builder
mayor
measure
merchant
merry
metamorphosis
mice
midsummer
milk
mill
miserable
mockingbird
moonstone

morgue
mourning
musketeer
naked
nightingale
nobody
odyssey
orchard
origin
outsider
paradise
park
passage[1]
picture
Pied Piper
pilgrim
playboy
portrait
prelude
pride
prime
purple
rainbow
raven[1]
remembrance
rival
road
roof
rye[1]
saga
salesman
scandal
seagull
sense
sentimental
shrew
sister
slaughterhouse
snowy
solitude
son
stoop
tale
tempest
tender[1]
term
time
travel
treasure
tree
trial
tropic[1]
Twelfth Night
twist
urn
vanity
view
volcano
wait
wake[1]
war
wasteland
willow
woman
wonderland
woods

Tables and Charts

Below is a list of tables and charts in the *Encarta® Concise English Dictionary*, together with the dictionary entries at which they can be found:

TABLE OR CHART	ENTERED AT
Key dates in astronomy	astronomy
Divisions of the Earth's atmosphere	atmosphere
Beaufort wind scale	Beaufort scale
Constellations	constellation
Currencies	currency
World's largest deserts	desert
Common diacritic marks	diacritic
Internet domains	domain name
Measuring earthquakes using the Richter scale	earthquake
Emoticons	emoticon
Member states of the European Union	European Union
Figures of speech	figure of speech
Key dates in the history of film	film
Key dates in the history of flight	flight
Main divisions of geological time	geological time
Geometry: shapes and solids	geometry
World's largest lakes	lake
Mathematical symbols	mathematics
Measurements	measurement
World's highest mountains	mountain

TABLE OR CHART	ENTERED AT
Key dates in Western classical music	music
Numbers	number
World's largest oceans and seas	ocean
Key movements in Western painting	painting
Periodic table	periodic table
Key movements in modern Western philosophy	philosophy
Key dates in the physical sciences	physical science
Planets	planet
Presidents of the United States	president
Prime ministers of Australia, Canada, New Zealand, and the United Kingdom	prime minister
World's longest rivers	river
Roman numerals	Roman numeral
Shakespeare's plays	Shakespeare
SI units with special designations	SI unit
Key dates in space travel	space
Time zones	time zone
Major volcanoes of the world	volcano
World's highest waterfalls	waterfall

a¹ /ay/ (*plural* **a's**), **A** (*plural* **A's** *or* **As**) *n* the first letter of the English alphabet, representing a vowel sound

a² *symbol* acceleration

a³ /ay/ used to refer to the first vertical row of squares from the left on a chessboard

a⁴ *abbr* are²

a⁵ (*stressed*) /ay/; (*unstressed*) /ə/ CORE MEANING: a determiner, used before a singular countable noun to refer to one person or thing not previously known or specified, in contrast with 'the', referring to somebody or something known to the listener ○ *I need a new car.*

det **1 INDICATES A TYPE** used before a noun to indicate that somebody or something has some of the same qualities as the person or thing mentioned ○ *a Hercules* **2 ONE** used instead of 'one' with words of measurement ○ *a teaspoonful of salt* **3 PER** in each or in every ○ *twice a day* **4 INDICATES SOMEBODY NOT KNOWN PERSONALLY** used to indicate somebody not personally known, but known of ○ *There's a Mr. O'Flynn here to see you.* **5 ANY** used in negative structures to emphasize a complete absence of something ○ *He doesn't have a hope!* [Old English, shortening of *ān* (see ONE)]

USAGE a *or* **an**? *A* is the form of the indefinite article used before words that are pronounced with an initial consonant sound (even if the spelling does not begin with a consonant): *a banana; a hunk; a ewe. An* is used before words that begin with a vowel sound (even if an unpronounced consonant comes first): *an elephant; an heir.* The same rule regarding sound rather than spelling applies to abbreviations: *a CD* but *an LP.* The practice of using *an* before words beginning with *h* and an unstressed syllable (for example *an hotel*) is falling out of use, and it is much more usual now to hear *a hotel*, with the *h* sounded.

A¹ /ay/ (*plural* **A's** *or* **As**) *n* **1 'A'-SHAPED OBJECT** something shaped like a letter 'A' **2 6TH NOTE IN C MAJOR** the sixth note of a scale in C major. The A above middle C is often used to tune instruments and is standardized at a frequency of 440 hertz. **3 SOMETHING THAT PRODUCES AN A** a string, key, or pipe tuned to produce the note A **4 SCALE BEGINNING ON A** a scale or key that starts on the note A **5 WRITTEN SYMBOL OF A** a graphic representation of the tone of A **6 HIGHEST GRADE** the highest grade in a series, e.g. a top grade for academic work ○ *solid As in her exams.* ◊ **alpha** *n.* **4 7 HUMAN BLOOD TYPE** a human blood type of the ABO system, containing the A antigen **8 SENIOR MANAGER OR PROFESSIONAL** somebody in a senior management, professional, or administrative position, in the market research system that classifies people according to their occupation ◊ **from A to B** from one place to another ◊ **from A to Z 1** extremely thoroughly **2** all the way from the beginning to the end

A² *symbol* **1** activity **2** adenine **3** ampere **4** A, Å **5** a main road other than a motorway **6** mass number **7** 10 (*in hexadecimal notation*)

a-¹ *prefix* in a particular place, condition, or manner ○ *abed* ○ *adrift* ○ *aloud* [Old English, < *an*, alternative for *on* (see ON)]

a-² *prefix* without, not ○ *agnostic* ○ *amoral* [< Greek]

A1, **A-1, A-one** *adj* **1** in excellent or first-rate condition (*informal*) **2** describes a ship as being well equipped and in excellent condition [Mid-19C. < Lloyd's Register, an annual British shipping list; *A* indicated a hull in first-class condition, *1* that the ship was well provisioned and equipped.]

aa /aʾà aaʾ/ *n* solidified lava with a rough jagged surface and sharp angular features [Mid-19C. < Hawaiian *a-ʾa.*]

AA *abbr* **1** Alcoholics Anonymous **2** Automobile Association

AAA *abbr* **1** Amateur Athletic Association **2** *US* American Automobile Association

⚡ **AAA server** *n* a computer file server that provides authentication, authorization, and accounting security functions

a.a.e. *abbr* according to age and experience

aah /aa/ *interj* EXPRESSING EMOTION used to express surprise, pleasure, satisfaction, or sympathy (*informal*) ■ *vi* SAY 'AAH' to say 'aah' (*informal*) ◆ **ooh** *v.* ■ *n* UTTERANCE OF 'AAH' an exclamation of 'aah' (*informal*) [Lengthened form of AH]

Aalto /aʾàltō/, **Alvar** (1898–1976) Finnish architect

AAM *abbr* air-to-air missile

⚡ **AAMOF** *abbr* as a matter of fact (*in e-mails*)

⚡ **AAMOI** *abbr* as a matter of interest (*in e-mails*)

A & E *abbr* accident and emergency

A & M *abbr* (Hymns) Ancient and Modern

A & R *abbr* artists and repertoire

Aardvark

aardvark /aʾàrd vaark/ *n* a burrowing mammal with a long snout, powerful claws, long tongue, and heavy tail. Native to: southern Africa. *Orycteropus afer.* [Late 18C. < Afrikaans, 'earth pig'.]

aardwolf /aʾàrd wŏŏlf/ (*plural* **-wolves** /-vz/) *n* a striped nocturnal mammal related to the hyena that feeds mainly on termites. Native to: southern Africa. *Proteles cristatus.* [Mid-19C. < Afrikaans, 'earth wolf'.]

Aarhus = **Århus**

Aaron /áiran/ *n* in the Bible, the first Jewish high priest and elder brother of Moses

Aaron's beard *n* PLANTS = **rose of Sharon** *n.* **1** [After AARON, who had a long beard (Psalms 133:2), because of the flower's prominent hairy stamens]

Aaron's rod *n* a tall smooth-stemmed plant. Flowers: yellow. Native to: Asia, Europe, North America. [After the rod bearing the name AARON, said to have flowered (Numbers 17:8)]

A'asia *abbr* Australasia

AAVE *abbr* African American Vernacular English

Ab /ab/, **Av** /av/ *n* in the Jewish calendar, the 11th month of the civil year and the fifth month of the religious year, occurring about the same time as July to August [Late 18C. < Hebrew *āb.*]

AB¹ *abbr* **1** able-bodied seaman **2** Alberta

AB² *n* a human blood type of the ABO group, containing the A and B antigens

A.B. *abbr* **1** *US* Bachelor of Arts **2** able-bodied seaman

ab- *prefix* away from, off ○ *aboral* [< Latin, < Indo-European, 'off, away']

aba /áb baʾ/ *n* **1** a cloth made in Syria using hair from goats or camels **2** a loose sleeveless outer garment worn by boys and men in the Middle East [Early 19C. < Arabic *'abā'.*]

ABA *abbr* **1** Amateur Boxing Association **2** ABA, A.B.A. American Bar Association

abaca /ábbəkə/ *n* **1** INDUST = **Manila hemp 2** a large plant from whose leaves Manila hemp is produced. *Musa textilis.* [Mid-18C. Via Spanish < Tagalog *abaká.*]

abaci *plural of* **abacus**

aback /ə bák/ *adv* **1** with the wind blowing against the forward part of a sail or sails, so that a vessel cannot move ahead **2** backwards or towards the back (*archaic*) [Old English *on bæc* 'towards the back, backwards'] ◊ **take somebody aback** to surprise somebody and make him or her unsure how to react

abacus /ábbəkəss/ (*plural* **-cuses** *or* **-ci** /-sī/) *n* **1** a mechanical device for making calculations consisting of a frame mounted with rods along which beads or balls are moved **2** a flat slab at the top of an architectural column [14C. Via Latin < Greek *abakos* 'board strewn with dust on which to draw or write' (later 'slab, table').]

Abadan /ábbə daʾàn/, **Ābādān** city in SW Iran. Population: 40,000 (1996).

abaft /ə baʾàft/ *adv* towards the rear of a ship or boat ■ *prep* to the rear of an area on a ship or boat [14C. < Old English *an* + *be* (see BY¹) + *æften* 'behind'.]

Abakan /aʾàbə kaʾàn/ city and administrative centre of the autonomous republic of Khakassa in NE Russia. Population: 158,200 (1992 est.).

abalone /ábbə lŏ́ ní/ *n* an edible sea mollusc that breathes through holes in its ear-shaped shell. Genus: *Haliotis.* [Mid-19C. Via American Spanish *abulón* < Shoshonean *aulun.*]

abampere /ab ám peer/ *n* the centimetre-gram-second unit of electromagnetic current equal to ten amperes

abandon /ə bándən/ *v* **1** *vt* LEAVE SOMEBODY BEHIND to leave somebody or something behind for others to look after, especially somebody or something meant to be a personal responsibility ○ *pets abandoned by their owners* **2** *vt* LEAVE A PLACE BECAUSE OF DANGER to leave a place or vehicle, especially for reasons of safety and without intending to return soon ○ *Drivers caught in the snowstorm had to abandon their vehicles.* **3** *vt* RENOUNCE to renounce or reject something previously done or used ○ *The practice was abandoned long ago.* **4** *vt* GIVE UP CONTROL OF to surrender control of something completely to somebody else ○ *As troops closed in the town was abandoned to its fate.* **5** *vt* HALT SOMETHING IN PROGRESS to stop doing something before it is completed, usually because of difficulty or danger **6** *vt* GIVE UP TO INSURER to surrender part of an insured property to the insurer in order to make a claim for total loss **7** *vr* GIVE IN TO EMOTION to give yourself over to a powerful emotion ○ *He abandoned himself to his grief.*

■ *n* **LACK OF RESTRAINT** complete lack of inhibition or self-restraint [14C. < Old French *abandoner* < *a bandon* 'under control' < Latin *bannum* 'proclamation' Originally 'bring under control'.] —**abandonment** *n*

abandoned /ə bándənd/ *adj* **1 EMPTY** left empty because of not being used or lived in any more **2 ALONE** left alone without being cared for or supported **3 UNRESTRAINED** without restraint or self-control

abase /ə báyss/ (**abases, abasing, abased**) *vt* to make somebody feel belittled or degraded [14C. < Old French *abaissier* < *baissier* 'to lower' < Latin *bassus* 'short of stature'.] —**abasement** *n* ◇ **abase yourself** to behave in a way that lowers your sense of dignity

abash /ə básh/ *vt* to make somebody feel ashamed, embarrassed, or uncomfortable [14C. < Anglo-Norman *abaïss-* < Old French *baïr* 'astound'.] —**abashedly** /ə báshidli/ *adv* —**abashment** *n*

abate /ə báyt/ (**abates, abating, abated**) *v* **1** *vti* **BECOME LESS** to lessen or make something lessen gradually (*formal or literary*) **2** *vti* **END** to suppress or end a nuisance, act, or writ **3** *vt* **REDUCE** to lower the amount or rate of something such as a tax (*formal*) [13C. < Old French *abatre* 'beat down' < Latin *batt(u)ere* 'fight, beat'.] —**abatement** *n*

abatis /ábbətiss, -tee/ (*plural* **-tis** *or* **-tises**) *n* a rampart made of felled trees placed so that their bent or sharpened branches face out towards the enemy [Mid-18C. < French < Old French *abatre* 'beat down, fell' (see ABATE).]

abattoir /ábbə twaar/ *n* a place where animals are slaughtered for their meat and by-products [Early 19C. < French, < *abattre* 'fell' < Old French *abatre* (see ABATE).]

abaxial /ab áksee əl/ *adj* describes the underside of a leaf or other surface that faces away from the stem. ◊ **adaxial**

Abba /ábbə/ *n* **1** a name used to address God in the Bible **2** a title given to bishops and patriarchs in the Syrian Orthodox and Coptic Churches [14C. Via ecclesiastical Latin and New Testament Greek < Aramaic *'abbā* 'father'.]

abbacy /ábbəssi/ (*plural* **-cies**) *n* the rank, jurisdiction, or term of office of an abbot or abbess [15C. < ecclesiastical Latin *abbacia* < *abbat-* (see ABBOT).]

Abbado /ə baádō/, **Claudio** (*b.* 1933) Italian conductor

Abbas /ábbəss/ (566?–653) Arabian merchant

Abbas I (1571–1629) shah of Persia (1588–1629). Known as **Abbas the Great**

Abbasid /ə bássid, ábbə sid/ *n* a member of a dynasty that ruled an Islamic empire from Baghdad from 750 to 1258 —**Abbasid** *adj*

abbatial /ə báysh'l/ *adj* relating to an abbey, abbot, or abbess [Late 17C. < French, or < medieval Latin *abatialis*, both < ecclesiastical Latin *abbat-* (see ABBOT).]

~~**abbatoir**~~ incorrect spelling of **abattoir**

abbé /ábbay/ *n* an abbot or member of a religious order in a French-speaking area [Mid-16C. Via French < ecclesiastical Latin *abbat-* (see ABBOT).]

abbess /ábbess/ *n* the nun in charge of a convent [13C. < Old French *abbesse* < ecclesiastical Latin *abbat-* (see ABBOT).]

Abbevillean /ab vílli ən/ *adj* relating to or typical of early Lower Palaeolithic culture in Europe [Mid-20C. < French *Abbevillien*, after the town of *Abbeville* in N France, where artefacts from this period were discovered.]

abbey /ábbi/ (*plural* **-beys**) *n* **1** a building or buildings occupied by monks under an abbot, or nuns under an abbess, especially the church building **2** a church that is or was used by a community of monks or nuns [13C. < Old French *ab(b)eïe* < ecclesiastical Latin *abbat-* (see ABBOT).]

abbot /ábbət/ *n* the monk in charge of a monastery [Pre-12C. Via ecclesiastical Latin *abbat-*, stem of *abbas* < Aramaic *'abbā* 'father'.] —**abbotship** *n*

abbr., abbrev. *abbr* abbreviation

abbreviate /ə breé vi ayt/ (**-ates, -ating, -ated**) *vt* **1** to shorten a word by leaving out some of its letters or sounds **2** to shorten a piece of text by cutting sections or paraphrasing it [15C. < Latin *abbreviat-*, past participle of *abbreviare* 'shorten' < *brevis* 'short'.] —**abbreviator** *n*

abbreviation /ə breévi áysh'n/ *n* **1** a shortened form of a word or phrase **2** the shortening of a word or phrase to be used to represent the full form

LANGUAGE NOTE Types of **abbreviation**: There are four main kinds of abbreviation: shortenings, contractions, initialisms, and acronyms. **1 Shortenings** of words usually consist of the first few letters of the full form and are usually spelt with a final full stop when they are still regarded as abbreviations, for example *cont.* = continued, *etc.* = et cetera. They may consist of the stressed syllable, e.g. *bus* or *gym*. In the cases where they form words in their own right, the full stop is omitted, for example *hippo* = hippopotamus. Such shortenings are often but not always informal. Some become the standard forms, and the full forms are then regarded as formal or technical, for example *bus* = omnibus, *pub* = public house, *zoo* = zoological garden. **2 Contractions** are abbreviated forms in which letters from the middle of the full form have been omitted, for example *Dr* = doctor, *St* = saint or street. Practice varies with regard to adding a full stop, but in modern usage it is increasingly usual to omit it. Another kind of contraction is the type with an apostrophe marking the omission of letters: *can't* = cannot, *didn't* = did not, *you've* = you have. **3 Initialisms** are made up of the initial letters of words and are pronounced as separate letters: *CIA* (or *C.I.A.*), *pm* (or *p.m.*), *US* (or *U.S.*). Practice again varies with regard to full stops, with current usage increasingly in favour of omitting them, especially when the initialism consists entirely of capital letters. **4 Acronyms** are initialisms that have become words in their own right or words formed from parts of several words. They are pronounced as words rather than as a series of letters, for example *Aids*, *laser*, *scuba*, *UNESCO*, and do not have full stops. In many cases the acronym becomes the standard term and the full form is only used in explanatory contexts.

ABC[1] *n* **1** the alphabet, especially in referring to basic reading and writing. US term **ABCs** *npl.* 1 **2** the basic facts or essential elements of a subject ○ *the ABC of building your own home.* US term **ABCs** *npl.* 2 ◇ **as easy as ABC** extremely easy

ABC[2] *abbr* **1** Australian Broadcasting Corporation **2** American Broadcasting Company

abcoulomb /ab kóo lom/ *n* the centimetre-gram-second unit of electrical charge equal to ten coulombs

ABCs *npl US* 1 = **ABC**[1] *n.* 1 2 = **ABC**[1] *n.* 2

Abd al-Hamid /ab daal hámmid/ = **Abdul-Hamid II**

Abd Allah /ab daálə/ (1846–99) Sudanese nationalist resistance leader

abdicate /ábdi kayt/ (**-cates, -cating, -cated**) *v* **1** *vti* to give up a high office formally or officially, especially the throne **2** *vt* to fail to fulfil a duty or responsibility ○ *The company seems to have abdicated all responsibility in this matter.* [Mid-16C. < Latin *abdicat-*, past participle of *abdicare* 'renounce' < *dicare* 'proclaim'.] —**abdication** /ábdi káysh'n/ *n* —**abdicator** *n*

abdomen /ábdəmən/ *n* **1 BODY SECTION CONTAINING STOMACH** the part of the body of a vertebrate that contains the stomach, intestines, and other organs **2 BELLY** the surface of the body of a vertebrate around the stomach **3 REAR PART OF INSECT** the elongated portion of the body of an arthropod, located behind the thorax [Mid-16C. < Latin.] —**abdominal** /ab dómmin'l/ *adj* —**abdominally** *adv*

abducens nerve /ab dyóoss'nz-/, **abducent nerve** /ab dyóoss'nt-/ *n* a nerve conveying impulses from the brain to the muscle that moves the eye laterally in its socket [*Abducens* < modern Latin, 'leading out' < present participle of *abducere* (see ABDUCT)]

abduct /əb dúkt/ *vt* **1** to take somebody away by force or deception **2** to pull something, e.g. a muscle, away from the midpoint or midline of the body or of a limb. ◊ **adduct** *v.* [Early 17C. < Latin *abduct-*, past participle of *abducere* 'lead out' < *ducere* 'lead'.] —**abduction** /-dúksh'n/ *n*

abductor /ab dúktər/ *n* **1** somebody who takes somebody else away by force or deception **2** a muscle that pulls the body or a limb away from a midpoint or midline

Abdul-Hamid II /áb dŏol hámmid/, **Abd al-Hamid** (1842–1918) Ottoman sultan

Abdullah II /ab dúllə/ (*b.* 1962) king of Jordan (1999–)

Abdullah ibn Husein /ab dúllə ib'n hŏo sáyn/ (1882–1951) king of Jordan (1921–51)

Abdul Rahman /ab dŏol raámən/, **Tunku** (1903–90) Malayan politician

abeam /ə beém/ *adv* to or at the side of a ship, boat, or aircraft, especially at right angles to its length

abecedarian /áy bee see dáiri ən/ *n* somebody learning the basics of literacy or a subject [Early 17C. < medieval Latin *abecedarium* 'book containing the alphabet' < the names of the first four letters of the alphabet.]

abed /ə béd/ *adv* in or confined to bed (*archaic*)

Abednego /ə bédni gō/ *n* in the Bible, one of Daniel's companions thrown into Nebuchadnezzar's furnace (Daniel 3:12–20)

Abel /áyb'l/ *n* in the Bible, the second son of Adam and Eve, who was killed by his brother Cain (Genesis 4)

Abelard /ábbə laard/, **Peter** (1079–1142) French philosopher and theologian

Abeles /áyb'lz/, **Sir Peter** (1924–99) Hungarian-born Australian business executive

abelia /ə beéli ə/ *n* a widespread bush. Flowers: white, pink, purple, tubular. Native to: E Asia. Genus: *Abelia*. [Mid-19C. < modern Latin, after the English botanist Clarke *Abel* (1780–1826).]

Abelian group /ə beéli ən-/ *n* an algebraic group in which the result of the operation is independent of the sequence of the operands, e.g. ab = ba or a+b = b+a [Mid-19C. After the Norwegian mathematician Niels *Abel* (1802–29).]

Abenaki /ab naáki, -náki/ (*plural* **-ki** *or* **-kis**), **Abnaki** (*plural* **-ki** *or* **-kis**) *n* a member of a Native North American people who once lived throughout New England and SE Canada, but who now live in Maine and S Quebec [Early 18C. Via French *Abénaqui* < Montagnais *ouabanăkionek* 'people of the eastern country'.] —**Abenaki** *adj*

ϟ **ABEND** /áb end/ *n* **1 ABEND, abend** a sudden failure of a computer program. Full form **abnormal end** **2** used in the subject line of e-mails to warn correspondents of an imminent loss of Internet access. Full form **absent by enforced Net deprivation**

Abeokuta /áybi ō kóotə/ port in SW Nigeria. Population: 367,900 (1990 est.).

Aberdeen /ábbər deén/ **1** port and industrial centre in NE Scotland. Population: 227,430 (1996 estimate). **2** council area in NE Scotland. Population: 218,220 (1993). Area: 186 sq. km/72 sq. mi. **3** port in W Washington State. Population: 16,598 (1996). —**Aberdonian** /ábbər dṓni ən/ *n, adj*

Aberdeen Angus (*plural* **Aberdeen Angus** *or* **Aberdeen Anguses**) *n* a cow belonging to a short-haired, black, hornless breed of beef cattle. US term **Angus**[1] [Mid-19C. After ABERDEENSHIRE and ANGUS[2].]

Aberdeenshire /ábbər deénshər/ Scottish administrative county. Area: 5,103 sq. km/1,971 sq. mi.

Aberfan /ábbərván/ coalmining village in S Wales, where in 1966 a landslide killed 144 people

abernethy /ábbər néthi/ (*plural* **-ies**) *n* a crisp semisweet biscuit [Mid-19C. Probably after the English physician John *Abernethy* (1764–1831).]

aberrant /ə bérrənt/ *adj* deviating from what is normal or desirable [Mid-16C. < Latin *aberrant-*, present participle of *aberrare* (see ABERRATION).] —**aberrance** *n* —**aberrantly** *adv*

aberration /ábbə ráysh'n/ *n* **1 DEVIATION** a departure from what is normal or desirable **2 LAPSE** a temporary departure from somebody's normal mental state **3 OPTICAL DEFECT** a defect in a lens or mirror, causing a distorted image or one with coloured edges **4 APPARENT DISPLACEMENT IN STAR'S POSITION** a small periodic change in the apparent position of a star or other astronomical object, caused by the motion of the Earth around the Sun [Late 16C. < Latin *aberration-* < *aberrare* 'go astray' < *errare* 'wander, err'.] —**aberrational** *adj*

Aberystwyth /ábbər rístwith, -rústwith/ seaside resort in W Wales. Population: 11,154 (1991).

abet /ə bét/ (**abets, abetting, abetted**) *vt* to assist somebody to do something, especially something illegal [14C. < Old French *abeter* 'urge, stimulate' < *beter* 'hound or drive on'.] —**abettor** *n*

abeyance /ə báy ənss/ *n* **1** temporary inactivity or nonoperation ○ *a law that has been in abeyance for some time* **2** a condition in which legal ownership of an estate has not been established [Late 16C. < Old French *abeance* 'expectation, desire' < *abaer* 'desire' < *baer* 'gape' < medieval Latin *batare*.] —**abeyant** *adj*

abfarad /ab fárrad, -fárrəd/ *n* the centimetre-gram-second unit of electrical capacitance equal to 10^9 farads

abhenry /ab hénri/ (*plural* **-ries**) *n* the centimetre-gram-second unit of electrical conductance equal to 10^{-9} of a henry

abhor /əb háwr/ (**-hors, -horring, -horred**) *vt* to dislike or reject something very strongly (*formal*) [15C. < Latin *abhorrere* 'shrink back in horror' < *horrere* 'shudder, bristle'.] —**abhorrer** *n*

abhorrence /əb hórrənss/ *n* **1** a feeling of loathing for or intense disapproval of something **2** somebody or something that is loathed or detested ○ *The idea became an abhorrence to her.*

SYNONYMS See ***dislike***.

abhorrent /əb hórrənt/ *adj* **1** arousing strong feelings of repugnance or disapproval (*formal*) ○ *a practice abhorrent to all animal lovers* **2** incompatible or conflicting with something (*literary*) —**abhorrently** *adv*

Abib /a beéb/ *n* the first month of the ancient Hebrew calendar, corresponding to Nisan in the modern Jewish calendar [Mid-16C. < Hebrew *'ābīb* 'ear of corn'.]

abide /ə bíd/ (**abides, abiding, abode** *or* **abided**) *v* **1** *vt* **TOLERATE** to find somebody or something acceptable or bearable ○ *couldn't abide his superior attitude* **2** *vt* **AWAIT** to wait for somebody or something (*archaic*) **3** *vi* **DWELL** to live or reside in a place (*archaic*) **4** *vt* **WITHSTAND** to endure or withstand something (*archaic*) [Old English *ābīdan* 'wait for, expect' < *bīdan* 'wait' (see BIDE)] —**abidance** *n* —**abider** *n*

abide by *vt* to comply with or act in accordance with something such as a decision or rule ○ *Applicants must agree to abide by the rules of the competition.*

abiding /ə bíding/ *adj* permanent or long-lasting ○ *my abiding memory of her* —**abidingly** *adv*

Abidjan /ábbi jaán/ cultural and commercial capital of the Côte d'Ivoire, in the SE of the country. Population: 2,700,000 (1990 est.).

abietic acid /ábbi éttik-/ *n* $C_{20}H_{30}O_2$ a naturally occurring yellowish powder. Source: rosin. Use: varnishes, lacquers, soaps. [< Latin *abiet-* 'fir', from which rosin is obtained]

Abigail /ábbi gayl/ *n* in the Bible, a woman who averted an attack by David and his followers by taking provisions to them. (1 Samuel 25).

Abilene /ábbə leen/ **1** city in central Texas. Population: 108,257 (1998 estimate). **2** city in east-central Kansas. Population: 6,519 (1998 estimate).

ability /ə bílləti/ (*plural* **-ties**) *n* **1 BEING ABLE** the capacity to do something or perform successfully ○ *It has the ability to perform well on really rough terrain.* **2 EXCEPTIONAL SKILL OR INTELLIGENCE** a high degree of general skill or competence ○ *We need people of your ability.* **3 TALENT** a particular talent or acquired skill ○ *a student with great musical abilities* [14C. Via Old French *ablete* < Latin *habilitas* 'suitability, aptness' < *habilis* (see ABLE).]

SYNONYMS ***ability, skill, competence, aptitude, talent, capacity, capability***

CORE MEANING: the necessary skill, knowledge, or experience to do something

ability natural and acquired skills or knowledge; **skill** proficiency gained through training or experience; **competence** ability measured against a standard; **aptitude** a natural tendency to do something well; **talent** an unusual natural ability to do something well; **capacity** mental or physical ability for something or to do something; **capability** the ability of a person or machine to do something.

ab initio /áb i níshi ō/ *adv* **1** from the beginning (*formal*) **2** without any previous knowledge of a subject ○ *study Spanish ab initio* [Early 17C. < Latin.]

abiogenesis /áy bī ō jénnəssiss/ *n* the hypothesis that life can come into being from non-living materials [Late 19C. < Greek *abios* 'without life' < *bios* 'life' + GENESIS.] —**abiogenetic** /áy bī ō jə néttik/ *adj* —**abiogenetical** *adj* —**abiogenist** /áy bī ójjənist/ *n*

abiotic /áy bī óttik/ *adj* **1** describes the physical and chemical aspects of an organism's environment **2** not containing or supporting life —**abiosis** /-ōssiss/ *n* —**abiotically** *adv*

abject /áb jekt/ *adj* **1 MISERABLE** allowing no hope of improvement or relief **2 HUMBLE** extremely or excessively humble, e.g. in making an apology or request **3 DESPICABLE** utterly despicable or contemptible [15C. < Latin *abjectus*, past participle of *abjicere* 'throw away, reject' < *jacere* 'throw'.] —**abjection** /ab jéksh'n/ *n* —**abjectly** *adv* —**abjectness** *n*

abjure /əb jóor/ (**-jures, -juring, -jured**) *vt* **1** to give up a previously held belief, especially formally or solemnly **2** to abstain from, reject, or avoid something (*literary*) [15C. < Latin *abjurare* 'deny on oath' < *jurare* 'swear'.] —**abjuration** /áb joor ráysh'n/ *n* —**abjurer** *n*

Abkhaz /ab kaáz/ *n* **1** somebody who comes from between the eastern shores of the Black Sea and the Great Caucasus mountain range in Georgia **2** an Abkhaz-Adyghean language spoken in NW Georgia. Native speakers: 80,000–100,000. [Mid-19C. A territory in the Caucasus.] —**Abkhaz** *adj*

Abkhaz-Adyghean /-aadi gáy ən/ *n* a group of Caucasian languages spoken in Georgia and S Russia —**Abkhaz-Adyghean** *adj*

Abkhazia /ab kaázi ə/ autonomous republic in NW Georgia. Area: 8,600 sq. km/3,320 sq. mi. Population: 537,500 (1990 est.).

ablate /ə bláyt/ (**-lates, -lating, -lated**) *vt* **1** to remove diseased or unwanted tissue from the body by surgical or other means **2** to remove or reduce snow and ice from a glacier by melting and evaporation [15C. < Latin *ablat-*, past participle of *auferre* (see ABLATIVE).]

ablation /ə bláysh'n/ *n* **1 REMOVAL OF TISSUE** the removal of diseased or unwanted tissue from the body by surgical or other means **2 MELTING OF SPACECRAFT'S OUTER SURFACE** the melting or erosion of the protective outer surface of a spacecraft during re-entry through the earth's atmosphere **3 MELTING OF SNOW AND ICE** the removal of snow and ice by melting and sublimation from a glacier or iceberg

ablative /ább lətiv/ *n* **1** a grammatical form (**case**) that identifies the source, agent, or instrument of action of the verb in some inflected languages and that affects nouns, pronouns, and adjectives **2** a word or phrase in the ablative [15C. Directly or via French *ablatif* < Latin *ablativus* < *ablatus*, past participle of *auferre* 'carry away'.]

ablator /ə bláytər/ *n* a heat shield on a spacecraft

ablaut /áb lowt/ *n* in Indo-European languages, a regular change of vowels in a related series of words or forms, e.g. 'sing', 'sang', 'sung' [Mid-19C. < German < *ab* 'off' + *Laut* 'sound'.]

ablaze /ə bláyz/ *adj* **1 ON FIRE** burning strongly **2 BRIGHTLY LIT** very brightly lit **3 SHOWING STRONG EMOTION** displaying great emotion or excitement, especially on the face

able /áyb'l/ (**abler, ablest**) *adj* **1** physically or mentally equipped to do something, especially because of circumstances and timing ○ *Were you able to reach her before she left?* **2** having the necessary resources or talent to do something ○ *a very able administrator* [14C. Via Old French *(h)able* < Latin *habilis* 'easy to hold or handle' < *habere* 'have, hold'.]

SYNONYMS See ***intelligent***.

-able, -ible *suffix* **1** capable of or fit for ○ *readable* **2** tending to ○ *changeable* [< Latin *-abilis*] —**-ability** *suffix*

able-bodied /-bóddid/ *adj* healthy and physically strong

able-bodied seaman *n* a member of a ship's crew, especially the crew of a merchant ship, who possesses basic skills and qualifications

abled /áyb'ld/ having abilities as specified ■ *adj* having all physical or mental functions

ableism /áyb'lizəm/ *n* discrimination in favour of those who are not physically or mentally disabled —**ableist** *adj, n*

able seaman *n* a sailor in the Royal or Canadian navy of a rank above ordinary seaman

abloom /ə blóom/ *adj* blooming or flowering

ablution /ə blóosh'n/ *n* **RITUAL WASHING** the ritual cleansing of a priest's hands or body, or of sacred vessels, during a religious ceremony ■ **ablutions** *npl* **1 WASHING YOURSELF** the act of washing the hands or the whole of the body (*formal or humorous*) **2 WASHING FACILITIES** washing facilities in a military camp or base [14C. Directly or via French < Latin *ablution-* < *abluere* 'wash away, wash clean' < *luere* 'wash'.] —**ablutionary** *adj*

ably /áybli/ *adv* in a skilful or competent way

ABM *abbr* antiballistic missile

Abnaki *n, adj* PEOPLES = **Abenaki**

abnegate /ábni gayt/ (**-gates, -gating, -gated**) *vt* to give up or renounce something (*formal*) [Early 17C. < Latin *abnegat-*, past participle of *abnegare* 'refuse, reject' < *negare* 'deny'.] —**abnegation** /ábni gáysh'n/ *n* —**abnegator** *n*

abnormal /ab náwrm'l/ *adj* unusual or unexpected, especially in a way that causes alarm or anxiety ○ *X-rays of the lung showed nothing abnormal.* [Mid-19C. From French *anormal*, from Latin *abnormis* 'deviating from a rule'.] —**abnormally** *adv*

abnormality /áb nawr málləti/ (*plural* **-ties**) *n* **1** a variation from a normal structure or function of the mind or body ○ *The blood test detected no abnormalities.* **2** any condition that is not the usual or expected one

Abo /ábbō/ (*plural* **Abos**), **abo** (*plural* **abos**) *n Aus* a highly offensive term for an Aboriginal (*taboo*) [Early 20C. Shortening.]

aboard /ə báwrd/ *adv, prep* **1** on, onto, in, or into a ship, aeroplane, train, or other vehicle **2** in or into an organization or group (*informal*)

abode[1] /ə bód/ *n* (*literary*) **1** the house or other place where a particular person lives **2** a period of living somewhere [13C. < ABIDE.] ◇ **of no fixed abode** having no permanent place in which to live (*formal*)

abode[2] past participle, past tense of **abide**

abohm /ab ōm/ *n* the centimetre-gram-second unit of electrical resistance equal to 10^{-9} ohms

abolish /ə bóllish/ *vt* to put an end to something, e.g. a law ○ *'Critics of advertising usually forget that if it were eliminated or abolished, other methods would necessarily be substituted for it'.* (Daniel Starch, *Principles of Advertising*; 1923) [15C. Via French *aboliss-*, stem of *abolir* < Latin *abolere* 'destroy'.] —**abolishable** *adj* —**abolisher** *n* —**abolishment** *n*

abolition /ábbə lísh'n/ *n* **1** the act of officially ending a law, regulation, or practice **2 abolition, Abolition** the official ending of the practice of slavery [Early 16C. Directly or via French < Latin *abolition-* < *abolere* 'destroy' (see ABOLISH).] —**abolitionary** *adj*

abolitionist /ábə líshənist/ *n* **1 abolitionist, Abolitionist** an anti-slavery campaigner in the 18th and 19th centuries **2** a supporter of the abolition of something, e.g. capital punishment —**abolitionism** *n*

abomasum /ábbō máyssəm/ (*plural* **-sa** /-sə/) *n* the fourth and final chamber of the multi-stomach digestive system of cattle and other ruminants, where enzymatic or true digestion takes place

A-bomb *n* an atom bomb [Mid-20C. Contraction.]

abominable /ə bómminəb'l/ *adj* **1** extremely repugnant or offensive **2** of very bad quality, or very unpleasant to experience [14C. Via Old French < Latin *abominabilis* < *abominari* 'shun something as being a bad omen' < *omen* 'omen'.] —**abominably** *adv*

Abominable Snowman *n* = **yeti**

abominate /ə bómin ayt/ (**-nates, -nating, -nated**) *vt* to dislike and disapprove of somebody or something intensely (*formal*) [Mid-17C. < Latin *abominat-*, past participle of *abominari* (see ABOMINABLE).] —**abominator** *n*

abomination /ə bómmi náysh'n/ *n* **1 SOMETHING HORRIBLE** an object of intense disapproval or dislike **2 SOMETHING SHAMEFUL** something that is immoral, disgusting, or shameful **3 INTENSE DISLIKE** a feeling of intense dislike or disapproval towards somebody or something (*literary*)

aboral /ab áwrəl/ *adj* situated away from or opposite the mouth ○ *the aboral surface of a starfish* —**aborally** *adv*

aboriginal /ábbə ríjjinəl/ *adj* existing from the earliest known times ■ *n* a member of a people that has lived in an area from the earliest known times [Mid-17C. < Latin *aborigines* (see ABORIGINE).] —**aboriginality** /ábbə rijji nálləti/ *n* —**aboriginally** *adv*

SYNONYMS See ***native***.

Aboriginal *n* a member of any of the indigenous peoples that inhabited Australia before the arrival of European settlers —**Aboriginal** *adj*

aborigine /ábbə ríjjini/ *n* a person, animal, or plant that has lived in an area from the earliest known times [16C. Back-formation < Latin *aborigines*, the pre-Roman inhabitants of Latium < *ab origine* 'from the beginning'.]

Aborigine *n* a member of any of the indigenous peoples that inhabited Australia before the arrival of European settlers

aborning /ə báwrning/ *adv US* while being born, created, or realized

ϟ **abort** /ə báwrt/ *v* **1** *vti* **REMOVE FOETUS** to remove an embryo or foetus from the womb in order to end a pregnancy **2** *vi* **HAVE MISCARRIAGE** to give birth to an embryo or foetus before its independent survival is possible (*technical*) **3** *vti* **END PREMATURELY** to bring something to an end or come to an end at an early stage **4** *vti* **ABANDON MISSION** to end a space flight or similar mission before it is completed **5** *vti* **QUIT COMPUTER PROGRAM** to abandon a computer program, command, or operation before it has finished [Mid-16C. < Latin *abort-*, past participle of *aboriri* 'miscarry' < *oriri* 'come into being'.]

abortifacient /ə báwrti fáysh'nt/ *adj* describes a drug or device that causes abortion —**abortifacient** *n*

abortion /ə báwrsh'n/ *n* 1 **OPERATION TO END PREGNANCY** an operation or other intervention to end a pregnancy by removing an embryo or foetus from the womb 2 **MISCARRIAGE** a miscarriage (*technical*) 3 **CANCELLATION** the ending of a flight or mission before it is completed 4 **OFFENSIVE TERM** something so badly done or made that it is a complete failure

abortionist /ə báwrsh'nist/ *n* an offensive term for somebody who performs abortions, especially suggesting the illegality of the procedure

abortion pill *n* a drug that induces an abortion at a very early stage of pregnancy

abortion trauma syndrome *n* a set of symptoms associated with the period following an abortion including guilt, anxiety, depression, low self-esteem, eating and sleeping disorders, and suicidal thoughts

abortive /ə báwr tiv/ *adj* 1 failing to reach completion 2 describes an organ that has had its development terminated —**abortively** *adv*

ABO system *n* a system that classifies human blood by dividing it into the four groups A, B, AB, and O

Aboukir, Bay of /ábboo keer/ = **Abukir, Bay of**

abound /ə bównd/ *vi* 1 to be present in large numbers or quantities 2 to contain something in large numbers or amounts [14C. Via Old French *abunder* < Latin *abundare* 'overflow' < *undare* 'surge' < *unda* 'wave'.] —**abounding** *adj* —**aboundingly** *adv*

about /ə bówt/ CORE MEANING: a grammatical word that refers to different sides or aspects of something from some point of orientation ○ (prep) *a book about a dog* ○ (adv) *There's a lot of laziness about.*

1 *prep* **IN CONNECTION WITH** in connection with or relating to ○ *think about problems* 2 *prep* **APPROXIMATELY** close to in number, time, or degree ○ *inviting about 15 people* 3 *prep* **DOING OR ATTENDING TO** with or in an activity ○ *go about your business* 4 *prep* **CLOSE BY** placed, located, or happening close by or around ○ *frantic activity going on all about us* 5 *prep* **AROUND** around or on a place or person ○ *a red scarf about her neck* 6 *adv, prep* **IN VARIOUS PLACES** positioned here and there ○ *scattered about the house* 7 *adv, prep* **IN DIFFERENT DIRECTIONS** from place to place in different directions or in no particular direction ○ *children running about everywhere* 8 *adv* **IN CIRCULATION** available or in circulation ○ *there was never much money about* 9 *adv* **INTO A REVERSED POSITION** in or to the opposite direction ○ *the wrong way about* 10 *adv* **ALL AROUND** on every side of or all the way around ○ *'He proceeded to the banks of the Hudson, and looked about among the vessels'.* (Jules Verne, *Around the World in 80 Days*; 1873) 11 *adv* **USED AS INTENSIFIER** used to emphasize a statement, usually when expressing impatience or anger (*informal*) ○ *Well, it's about time you showed up!* 12 *adv* **TO OPPOSITE TACK** on or to the opposite tack [Old English *onbūtan* 'on or around the outside of' < *on* (see ON) + *būtan* (see BUT[1])] ◇ ⚠ **be about** to have something as an essential characteristic ○ *Being successful is all about energy, drive, and commitment.* ◇ **be about to** be on the point of doing something ○ *The game was about to start.* ◇ **be what something or somebody is (all) about** to be what something or somebody involves or has as a purpose (*informal*) ◇ ⚠ **not about to** used to emphasize that somebody is certainly not going to do something (*informal*) ○ *I'm not about to apologize!*

USAGE ***About***: If you use the preposition ***about*** meaning 'having as an essential characteristic' in formal contexts, you are likely to be criticized. Avoid usages like these: *The main character in the novel is about power. She's about winning and nothing more.* Here, the contested use of ***about*** is an attempt to establish equivalent relationships, however vague they may be, among pairs of entities (i.e., *main character, she*) and the things those entities supposedly illustrate or represent (i.e., *power, winning*). Say instead: *The central interest of the main character in the novel is power. She is obsessed with winning and nothing more.*
Another problematic use of ***about*** is that of an intensifier after a negative indicating an unwillingness to do something, as in *I'm not about to apologize.* Avoid this usage in formal writing, for many people object to it. Say instead: *I have no intention of apologizing.*

about-face *vi* (**about-faces, about-facing, about-faced**), *n* US = **about-turn**

about-ship (**about-ships, about-shipping, about-shipped**) *vi* to turn to a new tack in sailing

about-turn *vi* **TURN AROUND** to turn to face in the opposite direction (*usually a command*) ■ *n* 1 **REVERSAL** a sudden and complete reversal of a previous opinion or policy 2 **TURN** a turn to face in the opposite direction

above /ə búv/ CORE MEANING: a grammatical word indicating a position directly overhead, on top of, or higher than something ○ (prep) *The bird flew up above the trees.* ○ (adv) *gazing at the sky above*

1 *prep, adv* **MORE THAN** greater than an amount or level ○ *100 pounds above the ideal body weight* 2 *prep, adv* **SUPERIOR TO** higher in status or power ○ *You can rise above your station.* 3 *prep* **TOO GOOD FOR** too good or important to be affected by or involved in something ○ *They felt they were above small town gossip.* 4 *prep* **BEYOND** not subject to something negative such as criticism or reproach ○ *'He wanted her to know that here too his conduct should be above suspicion'.* (George Eliot, *Middlemarch*; 1872) 5 *prep* **IN POSITION OF HIGHER RESPECT THAN** in a position that is valued more or considered more important than other people or things ○ *We put the people above everything else.* 6 *prep* **TOO DIFFICULT FOR** outside or beyond somebody's understanding ○ *The lecture was completely above me.* 7 *prep* **LOUDER THAN** louder than or over another sound ○ *She couldn't hear him above the roar of the band.* 8 *prep* **NORTH OF** lying north of a place ○ *a small town just above London* 9 *prep* **UPSTREAM FROM** lying upstream from a place 10 *adv, adj* **IN A PREVIOUS PLACE IN WRITING** appearing previously in a piece of writing (*often in hyphenated compounds*) ○ *using the information from the table above* 11 *adv* **IN HEAVEN** to or in heaven (*literary*) ○ *pray to God above* [Old English, < *an* (see ON) + *bufan* 'above' < Indo-European] ◇ **above all** used to indicate the most important thing or the main point of a statement ◇ **get above yourself** to become conceited

aboveboard /ə búv báwrd/ *adj* honest, legal, and without deception ■ *adv* **aboveboard, above board** honestly, legally, and without deception [Late 16C. Originally a gambling term indicating that the player's hands were above the gaming table and nothing was being concealed.]

above-mentioned *adj* written or listed above, or referred to previously ■ *n* a person previously referred to in a text

above-the-title *adj* shown in film credits before the title is seen, and therefore in a starring role ○ *an above-the-title mention*

ab ovo /ab ṓvō/ *adv* from the very beginning [Late 16C. < Latin, 'from the egg'.]

abracadabra /ábbrəkə dábbrə/ *interj* **MAGIC WORD** a word spoken by magicians and conjurors supposedly to ensure the success of a trick ■ *n* 1 **MAGIC SPELL** a supposedly magical charm or spell 2 **GIBBERISH** deliberately nonsensical language [Mid-16C. Via Latin < Greek.]

abrade /ə bráyd/ (**abrades, abrading, abraded**) *vti* to wear something away or be worn away by friction [Late 17C. < Latin *abradere* < *radere* 'scrape'.]

Abraham /áybrə ham/, **Abram** /áybrəm/ *n* the first patriarch in the Bible, seen by Jewish people as the father of the Israelites through his son Isaac, and by Muslims as the father of Arab peoples through his son Ishmael

Abraham, Plains of /áybrə ham/ plateau in the city of Quebec, E Canada. It was the scene of a battle between British and French forces in 1759.

Abrahams /áybrə hamz/, **Harold** (1899–1978) British athlete

Abram *n* BIBLE = **Abraham**

abrasion /ə bráyzh'n/ *n* 1 **WEARING AWAY** the process of wearing away by friction 2 **SCRAPED AREA OF SKIN** an area on the skin, or some other surface of the body, that has been damaged by scraping or rubbing ○ *dental abrasion* 3 **WEARING AWAY OF ROCK** the erosion of bedrock by continuous friction caused by rock fragments in water, wind, or ice [Mid-17C. < Latin *abrasion-* < *abradere* (see ABRADE).]

abrasive /ə bráy siv/ *adj* 1 **USING FRICTION** using friction and roughness of texture to smooth or clean a surface ○ *an abrasive cleaner* 2 **HARSH IN MANNER** aggressively direct and insensitive ■ *n* **SMOOTHING SUBSTANCE** a substance used to smooth or polish a surface by grinding or scraping [Mid-19C. < Latin *abras-*, past participle of *abradere* (see ABRADE).]

abreact /ábbri ákt/ *vt* to release unconscious tension by talking about or reliving the events that caused it —**abreaction** *n*

abreast /ə brést/ *adv* side by side and facing the front ■ *adj* up to date with something

~~**abreviation**~~ incorrect spelling of **abbreviation**

abridge /ə bríj/ (**abridges, abridging, abridged**) *vt* 1 **SHORTEN** to shorten a text, e.g. by cutting or summarizing it ○ *abridged for television in three episodes* 2 **CUT SOMETHING SHORT** to reduce something in scope or extent ○ *They abridged the meeting as best they could.* 3 **RESTRICT** to deprive somebody of rights or privileges (*archaic*) [14C. Via Old French *abreg(i)er* < Latin *abbreviare* 'shorten' < *brevis* 'short'.] —**abridgable** *adj* —**abridged** *adj* —**abridger** *n* —**abridgment** *n*

abroad /ə bráwd/ *adv* 1 **AWAY FROM YOUR OWN COUNTRY** in or to another country or other countries 2 **IN CIRCULATION** in public or into general circulation 3 **EVERYWHERE** over a wide area 4 **OFF TARGET** wide of the mark (*literary*) 5 *Ireland* **NOT AT HOME** out of your house or home ■ *n* **OTHER COUNTRIES** countries other than a specified one (*informal*)

abrogate /ábbrə gayt/ (**-gates, -gating, -gated**) *vt* to repeal or abolish something formally and publicly (*formal*) [Early 16C. < Latin *abrogat-*, past participle of *abrogare* 'repeal a law' < *rogare* 'ask, propose a law'.] —**abrogation** /ábbrə gáysh'n/ *n*

SYNONYMS See ***nullify***.

abrupt /ə brúpt/ *adj* 1 **SUDDEN** sudden and unexpected 2 **BRUSQUE** brief and making no effort to be friendly 3 **STEEP** with a sudden steep slope 4 **DISCONNECTED** not passing smoothly from topic to topic [Late 16C. < Latin *abruptus* 'broken off, steep', past participle of *abrumpere* 'break off' < *rumpere* 'break'.] —**abruptly** *adv* —**abruptness** *n*

abruption /ə brúpsh'n/ *n* the sudden breaking off of a part from a larger mass (*formal*) [Early 17C. < Latin *abruption-* < *abrumpere* (see ABRUPT).]

abruptio placentae /ab rŏopti ō plə séntī/ *n* the sudden premature detachment of a placenta, often accompanied by shock and bleeding [Early 20C. < modern Latin, 'breaking of the placenta'.]

Abruzzi /ə brŏotsi/ agricultural region of central S Italy. Area: 10,794 sq. km/4,168 sq. mi. Population: 1,249,388 (1991).

abs /abz/ *npl* the abdominal muscles, or exercises done to firm them (*informal*) [Late 20C. Shortening.]

ABS[1] *n* a type of strong plastic (**copolymer**). Use: moulded casings, pipes, car parts. Full form **acrylonitrile-butachene-styrene**

ABS[2] *abbr* anti-lock braking system

Absalom /ábssələm/ *n* in the Bible, the third son of David, King of Israel. He rebelled against his father and was killed by Joab (2 Samuel 13–18).

abscess /áb sess/ *n* a pus-filled cavity resulting from inflammation and usually caused by bacterial infection ■ *vi* to form an abscess, or be the site where one develops [Mid-16C. < Latin *abscessus* < *abscedere* 'go away' (referring to bodily humours going away in the pus) < *cedere* 'go'.] —**abscessed** *adj*

abscisic acid /ab síssik-/ *n* a plant hormone that promotes leaf and fruit fall, and dormancy in seeds and buds

abscissa /ab síssə/ (*plural* **-sas** *or* **-sae** /-see/) *n* the horizontal coordinate or x-coordinate of a point in a two-dimensional system of Cartesian coordinates. ◊ **ordinate** [Late 17C. < modern Latin *abscissa linea* 'line cut off'.]

abscission /ab sísh'n/ *n* 1 the natural process by which leaves or other parts are shed from a plant 2 the act of suddenly cutting something off [Early 17C. < Latin *abscission-* < *abscindere* 'cut off' < *scindere* 'cut up, divide'.]

abscond /əb skónd, ab-/ *vi* 1 to run away secretly, especially in order to avoid arrest or prosecution 2 to escape from a place of detention [Mid-16C. < Latin *abscondere* 'hide or put away' < *condere* 'stow'.] —**absconder** *n*

abseil /áb sayl/ *vi* to descend a steep slope or vertical face using a rope that is secured at the top and passed around the body. US term **rappel** *v.* ■ *n* a descent of a steep slope or vertical face by abseiling. US term **rappel** *n.* [Mid-20C. < German *abseilen* < *ab* 'down' + *Seil* 'rope'.] —**abseiler** *n*

absence /ábs'nss/ *n* **1 NOT BEING PRESENT** the fact of somebody's not being in a particular place **2 TIME AWAY** a period during which somebody is away **3 NONEXISTENCE** the lack or nonexistence of a particular quality or feature ○ *in the absence of any fresh information* [14C. Via French < Latin *absentia* < *abesse* (see ABSENT[1]).]

~~absense~~ incorrect spelling of **absence**

absent[1] /ábs'nt/ *adj* **1** not attending a place or event, especially when expected to ○ *absent from school* **2** not paying attention [14C. < Latin *absent-*, present participle of *abesse* 'be away' < *esse* 'be'.]

absent[2] /ab sént/ *vr* to stay away from or leave something such as an event or occasion ○ *She absented herself from the gathering and went outside.* [14C. Directly or via French *absenter* < Latin *absentare* 'keep or be away' < *absent-* (see ABSENT[1]).]

absentee /ábs'n teé/ *n* somebody who is not present at an event

absentee ballot *n US* POL = **postal vote**

absenteeism /ábs'n teé izəm/ *n* persistent absence from work or some other place without good reason

absentee landlord *n* a landlord who lives away from the accommodation or land rented out, especially one who neglects the needs of tenants

absently /ábs'ntli/ *adv* in an inattentive or absent-minded way

absent-minded *adj* tending to be preoccupied or forgetful —**absent-mindedly** *adv* —**absent-mindedness** *n*

absent without leave *adj* absent from military duties without permission, but not assumed to have deserted

absinthe /ábssinth/, **absinth** *n* **1** a highly alcoholic liqueur tasting of aniseed and made from wormwood and herbs **2** PLANTS = **wormwood** *n.* 1 [Early 17C. Via French < Greek *apsinthion* 'wormwood'.]

absolute /ábssə loot/ *adj* **1 OUT-AND-OUT** used for emphasis ○ *an absolute fool* **2 UNBOUNDED** to the very greatest degree possible ○ *absolute confidence in her ability to win* **3 DESPOTIC** having total power and authority **4 TOTAL AND UNEQUIVOCAL** completely unequivocal and not capable of being viewed as partial or relative ○ *No absolute correlation has been established.* **5 INDEPENDENT AND UNMODIFIABLE** not depending on or qualified by anything else ○ *absolute truth* **6 GRAMMATICALLY INDEPENDENT** not syntactically dependent on the main clause of a sentence **7 WITHOUT DIRECT OBJECT** used without an explicit direct object **8 USED AS NOUN** used without an explicit noun **9 MEASURED RELATIVE TO VACUUM** involving or relating to measurements made relative to the vacuum state **10 ACCORDING TO STANDARDIZED MEASURES** relating to or using basic units of length, time, mass, and charge **11 MEASURED RELATIVE TO ABSOLUTE ZERO** measured on or relating to a scale that has as its lowest temperature absolute zero, the point at which all molecular motion ceases **12 FULL AND UNCONDITIONAL** complete and in no way conditional on any future evidence or behaviour **13 OWNED OUTRIGHT** having unconditional ownership of a title or property, unrestricted by trusts or entails (*often after nouns*) **14 ALWAYS TRUE ALGEBRAICALLY** true for all values of a variable in an algebraic expression **15 CONSTANT IN VALUE** not changing in value in varying mathematical expressions **16 WITHOUT VARIABLES** not containing an algebraic variable ■ *n* **1 UNQUESTIONABLE RULE** a principle or value that is held to be always true or valid **2 absolute, Absolute ULTIMATE REALITY** in some schools of philosophy, the one ultimate reality that does not depend on anything, and is not relative to anything else [14C. < Latin *absolutus*, past participle of *absolvere* 'set free' (see ABSOLVE).]

absolute ceiling *n* the maximum height above sea level at which an aircraft can maintain horizontal flight

absolutely /ábssə lootli, -lóotli/ *adv* **1** ⚠ **TOTALLY** used to give strong emphasis to what is being said. **2** ⚠ **THAT'S RIGHT** used in speech or dialogue as an emphatic way of agreeing with the other speaker ○ *Absolutely!* **3 NOT IN RELATIVE WAY** in a way that is independent of circumstances and never variable or modified **4 WITH NO GRAMMATICAL OBJECT** used syntactically with an implied direct object or noun head **5 UNCONDITIONALLY** with no conditions or restrictions, especially constitutional or legal ones

USAGE Some people dislike the use of ***absolutely*** to give strong emphasis (*That is absolutely disgraceful.*). Also controversial is its use to express agreement. It retains some meaning in uses such as *'Do you like it?' 'Yes, absolutely'*, but is simply an intensifier when used with answers that are factual rather than expressing an opinion: *'Have you been to Paris?' 'Yes, absolutely'.*

absolute magnitude *n* the brightness of a star as it would be seen at a distance of 10 parsecs (32.6 light-years)

absolute majority (*plural* **absolute majorities**) *n* the winning total of votes that amounts to more than half of the votes cast

absolute music *n* music whose meaning is derived solely from the music itself and which does not evoke another source, e.g. a visual scene. ◊ **programme music**

absolute pitch *n* **1** the ability to identify the pitch of a single note without reference to any other sound **2** the exact pitch a tone is expected to have, measured by its rate of vibrations per second

absolute temperature *n* temperature derived from the laws of thermodynamics rather than being primarily derived from properties of substances

absolute value *n* **1** the magnitude of a number, irrespective of whether it is positive or negative, symbolized by placing the number within vertical bars, thus $|7| = |-7| = 7$ **2** MATH = **modulus**

absolute zero *n* the temperature at which hypothetically all molecular motion ceases, equal to 0 degrees K and equivalent to -273.16°C or -459.69°F

absolution /ábssə lóosh'n/ *n* **1** forgiveness for somebody's sins, especially when formally given in a Christian church **2** a spoken blessing used in a Christian church to grant absolution to somebody [13C. Via French < Latin *absolution-* 'acquittal, perfection' < *absolvere* (see ABSOLVE).]

absolutism /ábssə lootizəm/ *n* **1 POLITICAL SYSTEM** a political system in which the power of a ruler is unchecked and absolute **2 SOMETHING ABSOLUTE** a standard, principle, or theory that is absolute **3 THEORY OF OBJECTIVE VALUES** a philosophical theory in which values such as truth or morality are absolute and not conditional upon human perception **4 PREDESTINATION** a strict form of the doctrine of predestination —**absolutist** *n, adj*

absolve /əb zólv/ (**-solves, -solving, -solved**) *vt* **1 PRONOUNCE SOMEBODY BLAMELESS** to state publicly or officially that somebody is not guilty and not to be held responsible **2 RELIEVE SOMEBODY OF OBLIGATION** to release somebody from an obligation or requirement **3 FORGIVE** to forgive somebody's sins, especially formally in a Christian church service or sacrament [15C. < Latin *absolvere* 'set free' < *solvere* 'loosen'.] —**absolvable** *adj* —**absolver** *n*

absorb /əb sáwrb, -záwrb/ *vt* **1 TAKE UP** to soak up a liquid or take in nutrients or chemicals gradually **2 NOT TRANSMIT** to take up light, noise, or energy and not transmit it at all **3 INCORPORATE INTO WHOLE** to incorporate something into a larger entity in such a way that it loses much of its own identity **4 ADAPT** to adapt to changing situations without being adversely affected **5 REQUIRE IN QUANTITY** to require something in considerable quantities, usually without the results being precisely itemizable ○ *absorbing a huge amount of money* **6 NOT PASS ON** to accept increased costs without passing them on to customers **7 TAKE IN MENTALLY** to see, read, or hear something and realize its implications mentally **8 ENGROSS** to hold somebody's attention or occupy somebody's time completely [15C. Via French *absorber* < Latin *absorbere* 'swallow' < *sorbere* 'suck in'.] —**absorbable** *adj* —**absorbed** *adj* —**absorbedly** *adv* —**absorber** *n*

absorbance /əb sáwrbənss, -záwrb-/ *n* (*symbol* α) the capacity of a substance to absorb radiation

absorbent /əb sáwrbənt, -záwrb-/ *adj* **1** capable of soaking up liquid **2** capable of absorbing light, noise, or energy instead of reflecting it (*often in combination*) [Early 18C. < Latin *absorbent-*, present participle of *absorbere* 'swallow' (see ABSORB).] —**absorbency** *n*

absorbent cotton *n US* = **cotton wool** *n.* 1

absorbing /əb sáwrbing, -záwrb-/ *adj* occupying the attention completely —**absorbingly** *adv*

~~absorbtion~~ incorrect spelling of **absorption**

absorptance /əb sáwrptənss, -záwrp-/ *n* (*symbol* α) a measure of the ability of an object or substance to absorb radiant energy, equal to the ratio of the absorbed energy to the total energy reaching the object or substance [Mid-20C. < Latin *absorptus* (see ABSORPTION).]

absorption /əb sáwrpsh'n, -záwrp-/ *n* **1 PREOCCUPATION** a state in which the whole attention is occupied **2 SOAKING UP** the uptake of liquid into the fibres of a substance **3 NONREFLECTION** the ability of a substance to absorb light, noise, or energy, or the fact that it does so **4 INCORPORATION** the incorporation of something into a larger group or entity **5 ASSIMILATION BY THE BODY** the passage of material through the lining of the intestine into the blood or through a cell membrane into a cell **6 REDUCTION IN RADIATED ENERGY** the reduction in intensity of radiated energy within a medium caused by converting some or all of the energy into another form **7 REMOVAL OF ANTIBODIES** the elimination of antibodies or antigens by the use of a chemical reagent [Late 16C. < Latin *absorption-* < *absorptus*, past participle of *absorbere* 'swallow' (see ABSORB).] —**absorptive** *adj* —**absorptivity** /əb sawrp tívvəti, -zawrp-/ *n*

absorption spectrum *n* the pattern of dark bands that is seen when electromagnetic radiation passes through an absorbing medium and is observed with a spectroscope

absquatulate /əb skwóttyoo layt/ (**-lates, -lating, -lated**) *vi US* to leave, especially in a hurry or under suspicious circumstances (*archaic or humorous*) [Mid-19C. < Latin *ab* 'away' + SQUAT + *-ulate* (as in CONGRATULATE).]

abstain /əb stáyn/ *vi* **1** to choose deliberately not to do something **2** not vote for or against a proposal when a vote is held [14C. Via Old French *abstenir* < Latin *abstinere* 'hold yourself away' < *tenere* 'hold'.] —**abstainer** *n*

abstemious /əb steémi əss/ *adj* not indulging in or involving excessive eating or drinking [Early 17C. < Latin *abstemius* < *abs-* 'away from' + *temetum* 'intoxicating liquor'.] —**abstemiously** *adv* —**abstemiousness** *n*

abstention /əb sténsh'n/ *n* **1** the deliberate choice not to do something **2** a vote or voting neither for nor against a proposal [Early 16C. < late Latin *abstention-* < Latin *abstentus*, past participle of *abstinere* (see ABSTAIN).]

abstinence /ábstinənss/ *n* restraint from indulging a desire for something pleasurable, e.g. alcohol or sexual relations [14C. Via Old French < Latin *abstinentia* < *abstinent-*, present participle of *abstinere* (see ABSTAIN).] —**abstinent** *adj* —**abstinently** *adv*

abstract *adj* /áb strakt/ **1 NOT CONCRETE** not relating to concrete objects but expressing something that can only be appreciated intellectually **2 THEORETICAL** based on general principles or theories rather than on specific instances ○ *abstract arguments* **3 NONREPRESENTATIONAL** not aiming to depict an object but composed with the focus on internal structure and form **4 CONCEPTUAL** describes music that is intended to have no programmatic or emotional content **5 WITH IRREGULAR PATTERN** decorated with irregular areas of colour that do not represent anything concrete **6 IMPERSONAL** emotionally detached or distanced from something ■ *n* /áb strakt/ **1 PRINTED SUMMARY** a summary of a longer text, especially of an academic article **2 INTELLECTUAL CONCEPT** a concept or term that does not refer to a concrete object but that denotes a quality, an emotion, or an idea **3 ABSTRACT ARTWORK** a work of art, especially a painting, in an abstract style ■ *vt* /əb strákt/ **1 CONCEPTUALIZE** to develop a line of thought from a concrete reality to a general principle or an intellectual idea **2 SUMMARIZE** to make a summary of the main points of an argument or some information **3 EXTRACT** to remove something from a place, usually with some difficulty **4 STEAL** to steal something by taking it unobtrusively (*used euphemistically*) **5 PUMP WATER** to remove water from a river or other source for industrial use [14C. < Latin *abstractus*, past participle of *abstrahere* 'drag away' < *trahere* 'drag'.] —**abstracted** *adj* —**abstractedly** *adv* —**abstractedness** *n* —**abstracter** /əb stráktər/ *n* —**abstractly** *adv* —**abstractness** *n*

abstract expressionism *n* a school of painting, originating in New York in the 1940s, that combined abstract forms with spontaneity of artistic expression

QUICK FACTS ON... **ABSTRACT EXPRESSIONISM**

Key dates: mid-1940s–early 1960s
Key locations: New York
Key elements: reliance on the subconscious, monumental scale, spontaneity, emphasis on expressive qualities of paint and flat surface of canvas
Key figures: Jackson Pollock, Mark Rothko, Clyfford Still, Barnett Newman, Willem de Kooning, Franz Kline
Key works: *Number 1 (1948)* (Jackson Pollock) 1948, *Covenant* (Barnett Newman) 1949, *Excavation* (Willem de Kooning) 1950, *Ochre and Red on Red* (Mark Rothko) 1954
Key developments: action painting, colour-field painting, minimalism, tachism

abstraction /əb stráksh'n/ n 1 PREOCCUPATION a state in which somebody is deep in thought and not concentrating on his or her surroundings 2 GENERALIZED CONCEPT a generalized idea or theory developed from specific concrete examples of events 3 GENERALIZING PROCESS the forming of general ideas or concepts from specific concrete examples 4 CONCEPTUALIZATION the philosophical process by which people develop concepts either from experience or from other concepts 5 ABSTRACT ART an abstract painting or sculpture 6 EXTRACTION the removal or theft of something, usually with some difficulty 7 PUMPING WATER FROM RIVER the pumping of water from a river or other source for industrial use

abstractionism /əb stráksh'nizəm/ n the principles and practice of abstract art —**abstractionist** n

abstract noun n a noun signifying a concept, quality, or other abstract idea

abstract of title n a summary of the details of the ownership of a piece of land

abstruse /əb strooss/ adj obscure and not easily understood [Late 16C. Directly or via French < Latin abstrusus, past participle of abstrudere 'thrust away' < trudere 'thrust'.] —**abstrusely** adv —**abstruseness** n

SYNONYMS See obscure.

absurd /əb súrd/ adj 1 LUDICROUS ridiculous because of being irrational, incongruous, or illogical ○ an absurd notion 2 MEANINGLESS lacking any meaning that would give purpose to life ■ n absurd, Absurd MEANINGLESSNESS the condition of living in a meaningless universe where life has no purpose, especially as a concept in certain 20th-century philosophical movements. ◊ Theatre of the Absurd [Mid-16C. Via French < Latin absurdus 'inharmonious', literally 'away from the (right) sound'.] —**absurdly** adv —**absurdness** n

absurdism /əb súrdizəm/, **Absurdism** n the idea that the universe is without meaning or rational order and that human beings, in attempting to find a sense of order, conflict with it —**absurdist** n adj

absurdity /əb súrdəti/ (plural -ties) n 1 ridiculousness or silliness 2 something that is irrational, incongruous, or illogical

ABTA /ábtə/ abbr Association of British Travel Agents

Abu Bakr /ə boò bákər/ (573–634) Arabian religious leader

Abu Dhabi /ábboo daábi/ capital of the United Arab Emirates, on an island in the Persian Gulf. Population: 605,000 (1990 estimate).

Abuja /ə boò jaa/ official capital of Nigeria, in central Nigeria. Population: 339,100 (1995 estimate).

Abukir, Bay of /ábboo keer/, **Aboukir, Abū Qīr** bay in the Nile Delta that was the site of Lord Nelson's defeat of the French fleet in 1798

abundance /ə búndənss/ n 1 LARGE AMOUNT a more than plentiful quantity of something ○ Florence, with its abundance of art treasures 2 AFFLUENCE a lifestyle with more than adequate material provisions 3 FULLNESS a fullness of spirit that overflows 4 RATE OF INCIDENCE the extent to which an element is present in the earth or in certain rocks 5 PROPORTION OF ISOTOPE ATOMS the proportion of one isotope of an element, expressed by number of atoms, to the total quantity of the element [14C. Via Old French < Latin abundantia < abundant- (see ABUNDANT).]

abundant /ə búndənt/ adj 1 PLENTIFUL present in great quantities 2 WELL-SUPPLIED providing a more than plentiful supply of something 3 FOUND IN QUANTITY existing in large quantities [14C. Latin abundant-, present participle of abundare 'overflow' (see ABOUND).] —**abundantly** adv

Abū Qīr, Bay of = Abukir, Bay of

abuse n /ə byooss/ 1 MALTREATMENT the physical or psychological maltreatment of a person or animal 2 IMPROPER USE the illegal, improper, or harmful use of something, or an illegal, improper, or harmful practice 3 INSULTS insulting or offensive language 4 DRUG USE the harmful use of drugs or alcohol ■ v /ə byooz/ (abuses, abusing, abused) 1 vt MALTREAT to maltreat a person or animal physically, sexually, or psychologically 2 vt MISUSE to use something in an improper, illegal, or damaging way 3 vt INSULT to speak insultingly or offensively to somebody 4 vr MASTURBATE to masturbate (disapproving) [15C. Via French abus < Latin abusus, past participle of abuti 'use up, misuse' < uti 'use'.] —**abuser** /ə byoòzər/ n

SYNONYMS See misuse.

Great Temple of Rameses II

Abu Simbel /ábboo símb'l/ n the site of two carved rock temples in S Egypt, built in the reign of Rameses II in the 13th century BC

abusive /ə byoòssiv/ adj 1 INSULTING meant to insult or offend somebody ○ abusive language 2 HARMFUL involving physical or psychological damage ○ an abusive relationship 3 WRONGFUL involving illegal, improper, or harmful activities ○ using abusive methods to secure power —**abusively** adv —**abusiveness** n

abut /ə bút/ (abuts, abutting, abutted) vti to touch or be adjacent to something along one side [15C. Partly < Anglo-Latin abuttare < butta 'ridge or strip of land'; partly < Old French aboter 'aim at' < boter 'strike' < Germanic.]

abutilon /ə byoòtilən/ n a tropical plant or shrub. Flowers: red, yellow, or white, bell-shaped. Genus: Abutilon. US term **flowering maple** [Late 16C. Via modern Latin < Arabic ubutilun.]

abutment /ə bútmənt/ n 1 abutment, abuttal ADJACENCY the immediate adjacency of two objects or pieces of land 2 abutment, abuttal MEETING POINT the point at which two things abut 3 MAKING THINGS ABUT the positioning of two things so that they abut 4 SUPPORT STRUCTURE a structure that supports or bears the thrust of something

abuttals /ə bútt'lz/ npl the boundaries of a piece of land in relation to an adjoining piece of land

abuzz /ə búz/ adj full of lively conversation or activity

abwatt /áb wot/ n the centimetre-gram-second unit of electrical power, equal to one ten millionth (10^{-7}) of a watt

abysmal /ə bízm'l/ adj 1 appallingly bad or extremely severe 2 similar to the great depth of an abyss [Mid-17C. < abysm, via Old French < medieval Latin abysmus, alteration of late Latin abyssus (see ABYSS).] —**abysmally** adv

abyss /ə bíss/ n 1 CHASM a chasm or gorge so deep or vast that its extent is not visible 2 ENDLESS SPACE something that is immeasurably deep or infinite 3 TERRIBLE SITUATION a situation of apparently unending awfulness 4 HELL hell thought of as a bottomless pit [14C. Via late Latin abyssus < Greek abussos 'bottomless' < bussos 'bottom'.]

abyssal /ə bíss'l/ adj found in the very deepest areas of the oceans or on the deep ocean floor

abyssal plain n a broad flat area of seafloor at the deepest part of an ocean basin

Abyssinia /ábbə sí nni ə/ n former name for **Ethiopia** — **Abyssinian** adj, n

Abyssinian cat n a domestic cat belonging to a breed with dark brown or black markings on its short-haired brown coat

abyssopelagic /ə bíssō pə lájik/ adj relating to or living in the water just above the deep ocean floor [< Greek abussos 'abyss' (see ABYSS) + pelagikos 'of the sea' (see PELAGIC)]

Abzug /áb tsoog/, **Bella** (1920–98) US feminist, lawyer, and politician. Born Bella Savitsky

⚡**ac** abbr (in Internet addresses) 1 Ascension Island 2 academic organization

Ac symbol actinium

AC abbr 1 alternating current. ◊ DC 2 2 Athletic Club (in club names) 3 ante Christum (before dates) 4 appellation contrôlée 5 air conditioning

ac- prefix = ad- (before c, k, and q)

-ac suffix person affected with a condition ○ amnesiac [Via modern Latin -acus < Greek -akos]

A/C abbr 1 A/C, a/c account 2 A/C, a/c account current 3 air conditioning

acacia /ə káyshə/ (plural -cias or -cia) n 1 a bush or tree that has narrow leaves and dark fruit pods. Flowers: small, yellow. Native to: tropics, subtropics. Genus: Acacia. 2 any tree or like acacia 3 = **gum arabic** [14C. Via Latin < Greek akakia.]

academe /ákə deem/ n 1 = **academia** 2 a place of learning, especially a college or university [Late 16C. Partly < Latin academia, partly < Greek Akademeia (see ACADEMY).]

academia /ákə deèmi ə/ n scholars and students of the academic world and their activities [Mid-20C. < Latin (see ACADEMY).]

academic /ákə démmik/ adj 1 EDUCATIONAL connected with the education system 2 SCHOLARLY scholarly and intellectual, as opposed to vocational or practical 3 IRRELEVANT IN PRACTICE theoretical and not of any practical relevance 4 NOT LIVELY dry and intellectual in approach, concentrating on structure, form, or historical conventions ■ n 1 UNIVERSITY TEACHER somebody teaching or conducting research at an institution of higher learning 2 SCHOLARLY PERSON somebody with a scholarly background or attitudes —**academical** adj —**academically** adv

academic dress n formal garments for students or university staff, usually including a gown and hood

academician /ə káddə mísh'n/ n a member of an academy or society concerned with the arts or sciences

academicism /ákə démməsizəm/ n artistry that relies on conventional techniques or emphasizes the formal aspects of an art form such as painting or poetry

academic year n the annual cycle of teaching and study at an educational institution

academism /ə káddəmizəm/ n = **academicism**

academy /ə káddəmi/ (plural -mies) n 1 SOCIETY a formal society whose purpose is to promote a particular aspect of knowledge or culture 2 SPECIALIZED SCHOOL an educational institution devoted to a particular subject 3 SCHOOL NAME a secondary school, often a private one (usually in school names) [Mid-16C. Via Latin academia < Greek Akademeia, the school of philosophy founded by Plato, after the park on the outskirts of Athens where he taught.]

Academy n the school Plato founded to teach his philosophy

Academy Award n an award, known as an Oscar, given annually by the Academy of Motion Picture Arts and Sciences in the United States for work in film-making or acting

Acadia /ə káydi ə/ n former French colony in North America that comprised present-day New Brunswick, Nova Scotia, Prince Edward Island, and parts of Quebec and New England —**Acadian** n, adj

Acadian orogeny n the stage of mountain formation that occurred in the Appalachian Mountains of the United States during the Devonian Period

acalculia /áy kal kyoòli ə/ n an inability, or the loss of the ability, to carry out basic arithmetic calculations [Early 20C. < A-2 + Latin calculare (see CALCULATE).]

acanthi plural of **acanthus**

acantho- prefix thorn ○ acanthopterygian [< Greek akanthos 'thorn plant' (see ACANTHUS)]

acanthocephalan /ə kánthō séffələn/ n ZOOL = **spiny-headed worm** [Mid-19C. < ACANTHO- + Greek kephalē 'head' (see CEPHALO-).] —**acanthocephalan** adj

acanthopterygian /ákən thoptə ríjji ən/ n a fish with spiny-rayed fins and toothed scales. Superorder: Acanthopterygii. [Mid-19C. < Greek akantha 'thorn' + pterugion 'fin', literally 'small wing' < pterux 'wing'.] —**acanthopterygian** adj

acanthus /ə kánthəss/ (plural -thuses or -thi /-ī/ or -thus) n 1 a spiny-leaved bush or perennial plant. Flowers: white, purple. Native to: the Mediterranean. Genus: Acanthus. 2 a design characteristic of the capital of a Corinthian column, representing acanthus leaves [Mid-16C. Via Latin < Greek akanthos < akantha 'thorn'.]

a cappella /aàkə péllə, ákə-/ adv, adj unaccompanied by musical instruments [Late 19C. < Italian, 'in chapel style', that is, 'in the style of church music'.]

Acapulco /ákə poòlkō/ seaport and resort on the Pacific coast in S Mexico. Population: 687,292 (1995).

acari plural of **acarus**

acariasis /ákə rī́ əssiss/ *n* infestation of the skin with mites

acarid /ákərid/ *n* a mite or tick. Order: Acarina.

acaroid resin /ákəroyd-/, **acaroid gum** *n* a red resin exuded by certain grass trees, used in making varnishes and coating paper

acarology /ákə róllәji/ *n* the branch of zoology devoted to the study of mites and ticks —**acarologist** *n*

acarophobia /ákərə fṓbi ə/ *n* irrational fear of mites or ticks

acarus /ákərəss/ (*plural* **-ri** /-rī/) *n* a mite or tick (*technical*) [Mid-17C. Via modern Latin < Greek *akari* 'mite', literally 'too short to cut, tiny' < *kar-* 'cut'.]

ACAS /áy kass/, **Acas** *n* an organization that mediates between employers and workers or trade unions in industrial disputes. Full form **Advisory, Conciliation, and Arbitration Service**

acatalectic /áy kattə léktik/ *adj* having the full number of syllables in the final foot of a line of verse ■ *n* a line of verse that has the full number of syllables in the final foot [Late 16C. Via late Latin *acatalecticus* < Greek *akatalektos* 'complete' < *katalektos* 'incomplete'.]

acc. *abbr* **1** accusative **2** account

accede /ək séed/ (**-cedes, -ceding, -ceded**) *vi* **1 ASSENT** to give consent or agreement to something **2 COME TO POWER** to attain an important and powerful position **3 SIGN TREATY** to become a party to an international agreement or treaty [15C. < Latin *accedere* 'come to' < *cedere* 'come'.] —**accedence** *n* —**acceder** *n*

SPELLCHECK Do not confuse ***accede*** with ***exceed***, which has a similar sound. Beware: your spellchecker will not catch this error.

accelerando /ak séllə rándō, ə chéllə-/ *adv, adj* with gradually increasing speed (*musical direction*) [Early 19C. < Italian, 'accelerating'.]

accelerant /ək séllərənt/ *n* **1** CHEM = **accelerator** *n.* 3 **2** a substance that is used to intensify a fire

accelerate /ək séllə rayt/ (**-ates, -ating, -ated**) *vti* **1 GO FASTER** to move increasingly quickly, or cause something to move faster **2 PROGRESS FASTER** to happen or develop faster, or cause something to happen or develop faster **3 INCREASE VELOCITY** to cause an increase in the velocity of something, or experience an increase in velocity [Early 16C. < Latin *acceleratus*, past participle of *accelerare* 'quicken' < *celer* 'quick'.] —**accelerated** *adj* —**accelerative** /-rətiv/ *adj*

⚡**accelerated graphics port** *n* a computer interface that allows the display of three-dimensional graphics

acceleration /ək séllə ráysh'n/ *n* **1 INCREASE IN VELOCITY** the rate at which something increases in velocity **2 INCREASE IN RATE OF PROGRESS** an increase in the rate at which something happens or develops **3 ACT OF ACCELERATING** something's accelerating, or the causing of something to accelerate **4 INCREASE IN VELOCITY** (*symbol a*) the rate of increase in the velocity of something

acceleration clause *n* a clause in the terms of a loan or mortgage stipulating that payments must be made earlier in particular circumstances

accelerator /ək séllə raytər/ *n* **1 SPEED-INCREASING CONTROL** a pedal or other control mechanism used to cause a vehicle to increase speed **2 DEVICE FOR GIVING PARTICLES HIGH VELOCITIES** a machine used to increase the velocity, and hence the kinetic energy, of subatomic particles or nuclei, usually in preparation for collision with a target **3 CHEMICAL THAT SPEEDS UP REACTION** a substance that speeds up chemical reactions

⚡**accelerator card, accelerator board** *n* a circuit board that adds a faster central processing unit to a computer

accelerometer /ək séllə rómmitər/ *n* an instrument or device for measuring acceleration

accent *n* /áks'nt/ **1 MANNER OF PRONUNCIATION** a way of pronouncing words that indicates the place of origin or social background of the speaker **2 INTONATION** a way of using intonation or inflection to convey the speaker's mood or character **3 STRESS ON SYLLABLE** the prominence given to a syllable within a word or to a word within a phrase **4 MARK ABOVE LETTER** a symbol used in print or writing to indicate stress or the pronunciation of a vowel **5 MAIN EMPHASIS** an aspect of a situation, issue, or state of affairs that is emphasized ○ *the accent is on safety* **6 CONTRASTING DETAIL** a contrasting decorative feature used to add interest ○ *a blue room with green accents in the furnishings* **7 STYLE** a distinctive style that is characteristic of a particular person, region, or artistic school **8 STRESS ON NOTES** stress placed on particular notes in a piece of music, or the symbol printed above the notes to indicate this stress **9 RHYTHM** the rhythm of a piece of music, represented as the stress on the first beat of each bar **10 MATHEMATICAL SYMBOL** a superscript symbol, ′ or ″, used to indicate a unit of measurement such as feet and inches respectively or minutes and seconds of an arc respectively ■ *vt* /ak sént/ **1 EMPHASIZE** to stress something, e.g. by pronouncing a word or syllable more prominently **2 MARK SOMETHING WITH AN ACCENT** to mark a letter, word, or something else with a written or printed accent [Early 16C. Via French < Latin *accentus* < *ad* 'to' + *cantus* 'singing', a literal translation of Greek *prosōidia* 'accompanied song'.]

accent lighting *n* lighting that highlights an area or feature of a room, e.g. a painting or an alcove

accentor /ək séntər, -tawr/ *n* a songbird with a thinner, more pointed bill than the house sparrow. Native to: Europe, Asia, Africa. Family: Prunellidae.

accentual /ək sénchoo əl/ *adj* **1** involving or associated with accent or stress **2** employing a structure based on the number of stresses in a poetic line rather than on the number of syllables. ◊ **syllabic** *adj.* 4 —**accentually** *adv*

accentuate /ək sénchoo ayt/ (**-ates, -ating, -ated**) *vt* **1** to make a feature of something more noticeable **2** to emphasize a syllable, word, or phrase when saying it [Mid-18C. < medieval Latin *accentuatus*, past participle of *accentuare* 'emphasize' < Latin *accentus* (see ACCENT).] —**accentuation** /ək sénchoo áysh'n/ *n*

accept /ək sépt/ *v* **1** *vt* **TAKE SOMETHING OFFERED** to take something that is offered, e.g. a gift or payment **2** *vti* **SAY YES TO INVITATION** to reply in the affirmative to an invitation **3** *vt* **AGREE TO TERMS** to indicate formal agreement to the terms and conditions in a contract **4** *vt* **ENDURE SITUATION** to tolerate something without protesting or attempting to change it **5** *vt* **BELIEVE** to acknowledge that something is true **6** *vt* **COME TO TERMS WITH** to acknowledge a fact or truth and come to terms with it **7** *vt* **ADMIT** to admit the blame or responsibility for something **8** *vti* **TAKE ON DUTY** to agree to take on a duty, responsibility, or position **9** *vt* **PROCESS** to be able to process something or be operated by something ○ *old machines that won't accept the new cards* **10** *vt* **ALLOW SOMEBODY TO JOIN** to allow somebody to join an organization or attend an institution **11** *vt* **BE WELCOMING TO** to treat somebody as a member of a group or social circle **12** *vt* **RECEIVE FOR REVIEW** to receive something such as a report for official action or review **13** *vt* **AGREE TO MARRY** to reply in the affirmative to a marriage proposal (*dated*) [14C. Via French *accepter* < Latin *acceptare* < *accipere* 'take to (yourself)' < *capere* 'take'.] —**accepted** *adj* —**accepting** *adj* —**acceptingly** *adv*

USAGE accept or **except**? Do not confuse these two, even though they have similar pronunciations. ***Accept*** is a verb only; it means variously 'to take something offered', 'to believe something', and 'to agree to something', as in *We cannot accept* [not *except*] *such a lame excuse.* ***Except*** can work as a preposition meaning 'to the exclusion of', 'excluding', as in *All students except* [not *accept*] *the first years are eligible.* It is also a conjunction meaning 'if it were not for the fact that' and 'otherwise than', as in *I would have finished the course except* [not *accept*] *that I became ill at the end of term. The demonstrators did not quieten down except* [not *accept*] *to regroup and create new slogans for use later.* Finally, it is a verb used most often in the passive voice in the meaning 'to leave out or exclude', as in *Only children were excepted* [not *accepted*] *from attendance.*

acceptable /ək séptəb'l/ *adj* **1 ADEQUATE** considered to be satisfactory **2 APPROVED OF** likely to gain somebody's approval **3 WELCOME** likely to please the person who receives it (*usually modified by an adverb such as 'most' or 'quite'*) —**acceptability** /ək séptə bílləti/ *n* —**acceptableness** *n* —**acceptably** *adv*

acceptable daily intake *n* the highest daily intake level of a chemical that, if continued over the whole life of a person, appears to pose no health risk

acceptance /ək séptənss/ *n* **1 SAYING YES** a written or verbal indication that somebody agrees to an invitation **2 TAKING OF A GIFT** the willing receipt of a gift or payment **3 WILLINGNESS TO BELIEVE** willingness to believe that something is true **4 COMING TO TERMS WITH** the realization of a fact or truth resulting in somebody's coming to terms with it **5 TOLERATION** the tolerating of something without protesting **6 SOCIAL TOLERANCE** willingness to treat somebody as a member of a group or social circle **7 POSITIVE RESPONSE TO APPLICATION** an offer to allow somebody to join an organization or attend an institution **8 AGREEMENT TO TERMS** formal agreement, in writing or verbally, showing that somebody assents to the terms and conditions in a contract **9 AGREEMENT TO PAY** a formal agreement by a debtor to pay a draft or bill of exchange when it becomes payable

acceptation /áksep táysh'n/ *n* **1** a generally favourable reception of something **2** the sense in which a word or phrase is generally understood

~~acceptence~~ incorrect spelling of **acceptance**

accepter /ək séptər/ *n* **1** COMM = **acceptor** *n.* 1 **2** ELEC ENG = **acceptor**

accepting house *n* a financial institution that guarantees bills of exchange

acceptor /ək séptər/ *n* **1** somebody who accepts liability for a bill of exchange **2** an atom or group of atoms that accepts electrons to form a coordinate bond. ◊ **donor** *n.* 4

⚡**access** /ák sess/ *n* **1 ENTRY OR APPROACH** the possibility or means of entering or approaching a place ○ *Thieves gained access via a side door.* **2 OPPORTUNITY FOR USE** the opportunity or right to experience or make use of something **3 RIGHT TO MEET** the right or opportunity to meet somebody **4 OUTBURST** a sudden strongly felt burst of emotion (*literary*) ○ *'With a sudden access of tenderness he flung his arm about me'.* (Rider Haggard, *She*; 1887) **5 RIGHT TO USE COMPUTER** the right or ability to log on to a computer system or use a computer program ○ *software that allows network access* ■ *adj* **FOR UNQUALIFIED STUDENTS** designed as a course of study for people without formal educational qualifications, in order to give them entry to higher education ■ *vt* **1 ENTER PLACE** to find a way or means of entering or approaching a place **2** ⚠ **GET INFORMATION** to have the opportunity or right to experience or make use of something **3 CALL UP** to retrieve data or a computer file ○ *The program can be accessed using the correct password.* [14C. Directly or via Old French *acces* < Latin *accessus*, past participle of *accedere* 'come near' (see ACCEDE).]

SPELLCHECK Do not confuse ***access*** with ***excess***, which has a similar sound. Beware: your spellchecker will not catch this error.

USAGE *access* as a verb: There is normally no problem with using ***access*** as a verb in computing contexts (although even this is objected to by some people), but there is more resistance to using it in general contexts such as accessing bank accounts or biographical information.

accessary *n* LAW = **accessory**

SPELLCHECK See ***accessory***.

⚡**access code** *n* a sequence of letters or numbers that have to be keyed in to allow somebody access to a restricted area, e.g. a building or a computerized network

accessible /ək séssəb'l/ *adj* **1 EASILY REACHED** easy to enter or reach physically **2 EASILY UNDERSTOOD** able to be appreciated or understood without specialist knowledge **3 EASILY AVAILABLE** able to be obtained, used, or experienced without difficulty **4 APPROACHABLE** not aloof and not difficult to talk to or meet **5 SUSCEPTIBLE** susceptible to or likely to be influenced by something (*literary*) **6 OBSERVABLE FROM ANOTHER WORLD** able to be referred to from another possible world, so that the truth value of statements about it can be given —**accessibility** /ək séssə bílləti/ *n* —**accessibly** *adv*

accession /ək sésh'n/ *n* **1 TAKING UP POSITION** the assumption of an important position, usually a position of power **2 ACCEPTANCE OF TREATY** the formal acceptance by a state of an international treaty or convention **3 ASSENT** agreement or consent, usually when given unwillingly **4 SUDDEN MOOD** a sudden and unexpected display of a particular mood or emotion (*literary*) **5 ADDITION TO COLLECTION** an item added to a collection **6 INCREASE TO PROPERTY** addition to property by natural growth or by improvement **7 RIGHT TO INCREASE IN PROPERTY** the right of an owner to add to a property by natural growth or improvement ■ *vt* **CATALOGUE ADDITIONS TO COLLECTION** to make a formal record of an addition to a collection —**accessional** *adj*

accessorize /ək séssə rīz/ (**-izes, -izing, -ized**), **accessorise** (**-ises, -ising, -ised**) *v* **1** *vt* to fit accessories to something **2** *vti* to wear or use items such as gloves, hats, and handbags to complete an outfit of clothing

accessory /ək séssəri/ *n* (*plural* **-ries**) **1 OPTIONAL PART** an optional part that may be fitted to something to perform an additional function or enhance performance **2 FASHION ARTICLE** an item of clothing that is worn or used for fashionable effect with an outfit ○ *'designers who create neckties as fashion accessories'* (*International Herald Tribune*; June 1997) **3 accessory, accessary CRIMINAL HELPER** somebody who aids somebody else to commit a crime or avoid arrest ■ *adj* **1 ADDITIONAL** supplementary or subsidiary to the main thing **2 accessory, accessary ASSISTING IN CRIME** aiding a criminal act although not participating in the crime itself —**accessorial** /ák se sáwri əl/ *adj* —**accessorily** *adv* —**accessoriness** *n*

SPELLCHECK Do not confuse ***accessory*** with ***accessary***, which has a similar sound. ***Accessary*** is an older spelling, and you will find it is still occasionally used, especially in some legal contexts. Beware: your spellchecker will not catch this error.

accessory after the fact *n* somebody who helps a criminal after a crime

accessory before the fact *n* somebody who incites or helps a criminal before a crime

accessory mineral *n* a mineral in igneous rock that occurs in small quantities

accessory nerve *n* the eleventh cranial nerve, associated with the pharynx and muscles in the throat, larynx, palate, neck, and back

accessory shoe *n* a bracket on a camera allowing an accessory to be mounted on it

ϟ**access profile** *n* the details identifying a computer user held, e.g., on a server, specifying the name and password and the areas of a computer system the user is authorized to access

ϟ**access time** *n* the time a computer takes to locate and retrieve data

acciaccatura /ə chákə tóorə/ (*plural* **-ras** *or* **-re** /-ray/) *n* a brief grace note sounded at the same time as or just before a principal note [Early 19C. < Italian, 'crushed'.]

accidence /áksidənss/ *n* the area of traditional grammar dealing with the inflections of words [15C. < late Latin *accidentia* (plural) 'things that happen' (taken as singular) < Latin *accident-* (see ACCIDENT).]

accident /áksidənt/ *n* **1 CHANCE** the way things happen without any planning, apparent cause, or deliberate intent **2 CRASH** a collision or similar incident involving a moving vehicle, often resulting in injury or death **3 CHANCE HAPPENING** an event that happens completely by chance, with no planning or deliberate intent **4 MISHAP** an unplanned and unfortunate event that results in damage, injury, or upset of some kind **5 FAILURE TO REACH TOILET** an incident when somebody, particularly a small child, is incontinent (*used euphemistically*) **6 UNPLANNED PREGNANCY** a child conceived in an unplanned way **7 NONESSENTIAL ATTRIBUTE** a nonessential attribute or characteristic of something [14C. Via French < Latin *accident-*, present participle of *accidere* 'happen' < *cadere* 'fall, die'.]

accidental /áksi dént'l/ *adj* **1 CHANCE** happening by chance and not planned **2 INCIDENTAL** not specifically intended and arising as a side effect **3 NOT IN KEY SIGNATURE** sharp, flat, or natural, in a way not indicated in the key signature ■ *n* **1 UNPLANNED EFFECT** something not specifically intended that arises as a side effect **2 NOTE NOT IN KEY SIGNATURE** a musical note, marked with a sharp, flat, or natural sign, whose pitch does not correspond to the key signature —**accidentally** *adv*

accident and emergency *n* MED = **casualty** *n.* **4**

accident insurance *n* insurance against injury or death caused by an accident

~~accidently~~ incorrect spelling of **accidentally**

accident-prone *adj* having more accidents than average

accipiter /ak síppitər/ *n* **1** a hawk, typically with short broad wings and a long tail, e.g. a sparrowhawk or goshawk. Genus: *Accipiter.* **2** any bird in the family that includes all hawks, eagles, and kites. Family: Accipitidae. [Early 19C. < Latin, < *accipere* 'take to (yourself)' (see ACCEPT).]

accipitrine /ak síppi trin, -trīn/ *adj* describes the family of predatory birds including hawks, eagles, and kites

acclaim /ə kláym/ *v* **1** *vt* **PRAISE SOMEBODY LAVISHLY** to praise somebody or something publicly with great enthusiasm **2** *vt* **PRONOUNCE SOMEBODY TO BE** to declare enthusiastically and publicly that somebody holds a high position **3** *vi* **SHOUT ENTHUSIASTICALLY** to demonstrate enthusiastic approval by shouting and cheering ■ *n* **ENTHUSIASTIC RECEPTION** enthusiastic approval given to somebody or something publicly [Early 16C. < Latin *acclamare* 'shout to' < *clamare* 'shout'.] —**acclaimer** *n*

acclamation /áklə máysh'n/ *n* a public and enthusiastic display of approval [Mid-16C. < Latin *acclamation-* < *acclamare* (see ACCLAIM).] —**acclamatory** /ə klámmətri/ *adj*

acclimate /ákli mayt/ (**-mates, -mating, -mated**) *v* **1** *vti* = **acclimatize 2** *vi* to adjust in response to a change in environment [Late 18C. < French *acclimater* < *a-* 'to' + *climat* 'climate' (see CLIMATE).] —**acclimation** /áklə máysh'n/ *n*

acclimatize /ə klīmə tīz/ (**-tizes, -tizing, -tized**) *vti* to become accustomed to a new climate or environment, or help somebody become accustomed to it —**acclimatization** /ə klīmə tī záysh'n/ *n*

acclivity /ə klívvəti/ (*plural* **-ties**) *n* an upward slope on a hill [Early 17C. < Latin *acclivitat-* 'ascent' < *acclivis* 'uphill' < *clivus* 'slope'.]

accolade /ákə layd, -laad/ *n* **1 SIGN OF PRAISE** a sign or expression of high praise and esteem for somebody **2 PUBLIC RECOGNITION** praise and public recognition of somebody's achievements **3 KNIGHTING** the ceremonial bestowal of a knighthood by touching somebody's shoulders with a sword **4 CURVED MOULDING** an ornamental moulding shaped like a brace [Early 17C. Via French < Provençal *acolada* 'embrace' < Latin *collum* 'neck'; because knighthood was formerly conferred with an embrace.]

accommodate /ə kómmə dayt/ (**-dates, -dating, -dated**) *v* **1** *vt* **PROVIDE LODGING FOR** to provide somebody with a place to stay **2** *vt* **HAVE ROOM FOR** to have sufficient space for somebody or something **3** *vt* **ALLOW FOR** to be adaptable enough to allow something without major change **4** *vt* **OBLIGE** to adjust actions in response to somebody's needs **5** *vt* **LEND SOMEBODY MONEY** to give somebody money in response to a request for a loan (*formal*) **6** *vti* **REACH AGREEMENT** to settle a difference of opinion in a way that is acceptable to all **7** *vi* **ADJUST** to adapt to a new situation **8** *vi* **ADJUST FOCUS** to adjust focus automatically to give clear vision (*refers to the eyes*) [Mid-16C. < Latin *accommodare* 'make fit' < *commodus* 'suitable' < *modus* 'measure'.] —**accommodative** *adj*

accommodating /ə kómmə dayting/ *adj* willing to adjust actions in response to the needs of others —**accommodatingly** *adv*

accommodation /ə kómmə dáysh'n/ *n* **1 LODGING** a room or building to live in **2 SEATING** seating in a vehicle or public facility **3 WORKSPACE** a room or space to work in **4 HELPFULNESS** willingness to adjust actions in response to the needs of others **5 HELPFUL GESTURE** a modification of actions in response to the needs of others **6 AGREEMENT** an agreement acceptable to all parties in a dispute **7 FLEXIBILITY** the ability to include something without major change **8 ADJUSTMENT** adaptation to a new situation **9 ADJUSTMENT OF EYE FOCUS** the automatic adjustment of the focus of an eye to give clear vision **10 LOAN OF MONEY** a loan of money, especially by a financial institution as a favour to somebody before a formal credit arrangement is made

accommodation address *n* a mailing address used by a person or organization unwilling or unable to use an identifiable individual address

accommodation bill *n* a bill of exchange cosigned by another party in order to give added security

accommodationist /ə kómmə dáysh'nist/ *n* somebody who prefers compromise to confrontation —**accommodationist** *adj*

accommodation ladder *n* a ladder or flight of stairs hung over a ship's side to allow boarding or disembarking

accommodation platform, accommodation rig *n* a platform or rig used as living quarters for offshore oil or gas workers

accommodations /ə kómmə dáysh'nz/ *npl* US **1 LODGING** a room or building to live in **2 SEATING** seating in a vehicle or public facility **3 WORKSPACE** a room or space to work in

~~accomodate~~ incorrect spelling of **accommodate**

~~accomodation~~ incorrect spelling of **accommodation**

accompaniment /ə kúmpənimənt, -pni-/ *n* **1 MUSICAL BACKING** instrumental or vocal parts in a musical composition that support the more important parts **2 SIMULTANEOUS OCCURRENCE** something that occurs at the same time and in the same place as something else **3 SUPPLEMENT** an item that is added or served because it goes well with something

accompanist /ə kúmpənist, -pnist/ *n* a musician playing the accompaniment for a soloist

accompany /ə kúmpəni, -pni/ (**-nies, -nying, -nied**) *v* **1** *vt* **ESCORT** to go with somebody **2** *vt* **BE PRESENT WITH** to be enclosed, attached, or present with something **3** *vt* **OCCUR WITH** to happen at the same time as something else **4** *vt* **SUPPLEMENT** to be present or served with something as a supplement **5** *vti* **PROVIDE MUSICAL BACKING** to play or sing a part that supports a more important part [15C. < Old French *acompaignier* 'be a companion to' < *compaing* 'companion' (see COMPANION[1]).]

accomplice /ə kúmpliss, ə kóm-/ *n* somebody who helps somebody to commit a crime or misdeed [Mid-16C.< Archaic *complice* (by misunderstanding of *a complice*), via French < Latin *complic-*, stem of *complex* 'associate' < *complicare* (see COMPLICATE).]

accomplish /ə kúmplish, ə kóm-/ *vt* **1** to succeed in doing or achieving something **2** to arrive at the end of a period of time (*literary; usually passive*) [14C. < Old French *accompliss-*, a stem of *acomplir* 'complete to' < Latin *complere* (see COMPLETE).] —**accomplishable** *adj* —**accomplisher** *n*

SYNONYMS ***accomplish, achieve, attain, realize, carry out, pull off***

CORE MEANING: to bring something to a successful conclusion

accomplish to succeed in doing something; **achieve** to succeed in something, usually with effort; **attain** to reach a specific objective; **realize** to fulfil a specific vision or plan; **carry out** to perform or accomplish a task or activity; **pull off** (*informal*) to accomplish something, despite difficulties.

accomplished /ə kúmplisht, ə kóm-/ *adj* **1 TALENTED** having considerable talent and skill **2 WITH SOCIAL GRACES** possessing social skills and talents **3 COMPLETE** fully established

accomplishment /ə kúmplishmənt, ə kóm-/ *n* **1 ACHIEVING OF** the completion or fulfilment of something **2 FEAT** a remarkable or successful achievement **3 TALENT** a skill or talent that has been developed

Acconci /ə kónsi/, **Vito** (*b.* 1940) US artist

accord /ə káwrd/ *v* **1** *vt* **RENDER** to give somebody or something a particular status or treatment **2** *vi* **AGREE** to be in agreement or come to an agreement **3** *vt* **GRANT** to bestow something such as a blessing on somebody ■ *n* **1 AGREEMENT** a treaty or settlement agreed by two or more parties **2 CONSENSUS** general agreement as to what is right **3 HARMONY** a state in which things are in harmony with each other [Pre-12C. < Old French *acorder* < Latin *ad* 'to' + *cord-*, stem of *cor* 'heart'.] ◇ **of your own accord** of your own free will ◇ **with one accord** together and with everyone agreeing (*formal*)

accordance /ə káwrd'nss/ *n* **1 CONSENSUS** consensus as to the right course of action **2 ADHERENCE TO CORRECT PROCESS** conformity with specified procedures or actions ○ *in accordance with official guidelines* **3 BESTOWAL** the bestowal of a particular status or treatment on somebody or something

according as /ə káwrding-/ *conj* depending on whether, or corresponding to the extent to which

accordingly /ə káwrdingli/ *adv* **1** in a way that is appropriate **2** in accordance with what has been said or with a principle or practice

according to *prep* **1 ON SOMEBODY'S OR SOMETHING'S AUTHORITY** as stated by somebody or indicated by something ○ *the gospel according to St Luke* **2 RELATED TO** depending on and corresponding in extent to something ○ *salary according to experience* **3 AS DETERMINED BY** on the basis of and in line with a particular method, approach, or principle ○ *arranged according to alphabetical order* **4 AS LAID DOWN BY** in the way that a particular plan or system stipulates ○ *done exactly according to the instructions*

accordion /ə káwrdi ən/ *n* a musical instrument with a keyboard or buttons on one side, buttons on the other, and a bellows in the middle that forces air through metal reeds [Mid-19C. < German *Akkordion* < *Akkord* 'chord' < Italian *accordare* 'tune (an instrument)'.]

accordion pleats *npl* sharp pleats in a garment or piece of fabric, like the folds in an accordion's bellows

accost /ə kóst/ *vt* to approach and stop somebody in order to speak, especially in an aggressive, insistent, or suggestive way [Late 16C. Via French < Latin *accostare* 'adjoin' < *costa* 'rib, side'.] —**accoster** *n*

ϟ **account** /ə kównt/ *n* **1 REPORT** a written or verbal report of something **2 EXPLANATION** an explanation of something that has happened, especially one given to somebody in authority **3 BANK ARRANGEMENT** an arrangement in which a customer keeps money in a bank or building society and is offered certain services in exchange **4 MONEY IN BANK** the money that a customer keeps in a bank **5 FINANCIAL ARRANGEMENT** an arrangement with a store, company, stockbroker, or other business, which provides certain financial services, e.g. credit **6 NETWORK ACCESS CONTROL** a contractual agreement between a user and an Internet or e-mail service provider establishing a directory and other system information and giving the user access to a network, e.g. the Internet, in return for a fee or other consideration **7 RECORD OF FINANCES** a regular printed statement of financial transactions conducted through an account **8 PERIOD OF TRANSACTION** the period during which transactions are made, usually lasting two weeks, and at the end of which settlements are made **9 CUSTOMER** a customer who has a regular business relationship with a company **10 BUSINESS ON SOMEBODY'S BEHALF** an area of business handled by a company on behalf of another, e.g. advertising, design, or publicity **11 IMPORTANCE** importance, relevance, or value (*usually in negative statements*) ■ **accounts** *npl* **LIST OF FINANCIAL INFORMATION** a detailed list of everything that a company or individual earns or spends, kept primarily for tax purposes ■ *vt* **CONSIDER** to consider something, somebody, or yourself to have a specified quality (*dated*) [14C. < Old French *aconte* 'a counting up' < *aconter* < Latin *computare* 'sum up'.] ◇ **by all accounts** according to what most people say ◇ **call somebody to account** to demand that somebody explains what he or she has done ◇ **give a good account of yourself** to do something well, especially something difficult ◇ **of no account** of no importance ◇ **on account** on credit ◇ **on account of** because of ◇ **on no account** for no reason, whatever the circumstances ◇ **on somebody's account** out of concern for somebody's well-being ◇ **take account of something, take something into account** to consider something when making a decision ◇ **turn something to good account** to use or deal with something in a way that puts it to good use

account for *vt* **1 EXPLAIN** to provide an explanation for something ○ *And how do you account for the hole in the wall?* **2 BE RESPONSIBLE FOR** to be responsible for something or be an important factor in something ○ *Export sales account for at least half of our total business.* **3 KILL OR DESTROY** to be responsible for killing, destroying, or neutralizing somebody or something

accountable /ə kówntəb'l/ *adj* **1** responsible to somebody else or to others, or responsible for something **2** capable of being explained (*formal*) —**accountability** /ə kówntə bílləti/ *n* —**accountableness** *n* —**accountably** *adv*

accountancy /ə kówntənssi/ *n* the work or profession of an accountant

accountant /ə kówntənt/ *n* somebody who maintains the business records of an individual or organization and prepares tax reports

account day *n* the day on which payments and deliveries that have been agreed on during the preceding two-week period are made

account executive *n* an employee, especially in an advertising or public relations company, who handles all of the business of an individual client

accounting /ə kównting/ *n* the activity, practice, or profession of maintaining and checking the business records of an individual or organization and preparing reports for tax or other financial purposes

accounting rate of return (*plural* **accounting rates of return**) *n* a calculation of the anticipated net profit from an investment in an asset or project, expressed as a percentage of the money invested

accounts payable *npl* a record that shows how much a firm owes suppliers for the purchase of supplies or services on credit

accounts receivable *npl* a record that shows how much is owed to a company by customers who have purchased supplies or services on credit

~~**accoustic**~~ incorrect spelling of **acoustic**

accouter *vt* US = **accoutre**

accouterment *n* US = **accoutrement**

accoutre /ə kóotər/ (**-tres, -tring, -tred**) *vt* to equip and clothe somebody, especially for military purposes [Mid-16C. Via French *accoutrer* 'equip with something, especially clothes' < assumed Latin *consutura* 'sewn together' < *sutura* 'sewn'.]

accoutrement /ə kóotrəmənt/ *n* **1** an accessory or piece of equipment associated with a particular object, task, or role **2** a piece of military equipment carried by soldiers in addition to their standard uniform and weapons

Accra /ə kráa/ capital of Ghana, on the S coast. Population: 953,500 (1990 estimate).

accredit /ə kréddit/ *vt* **1 GIVE OFFICIAL RECOGNITION TO** officially to recognize a person or organization as having met a standard or criterion (*usually passive*) **2 GIVE AUTHORITY** to give somebody the authority to perform a function (*usually passive*) **3 APPOINT AS ENVOY** to appoint somebody as an envoy or ambassador representing his or her government or country **4** *NZ* **PASS FOR UNIVERSITY ENTRANCE** to pass a student for entrance to university without having to sit an external examination [Early 17C. < French *accréditer* 'believe (firmly)' < *crédit* (see CREDIT).] —**accreditation** /ə kréddi táysh'n/ *n*

accrete /ə kreét/ (**-cretes, -creting, -creted**) *vti* to become bigger, or make something become bigger, especially by adding to what is there or by two or more things growing together [Late 18C. < Latin *accret-*, past participle of *accrescere* < *crescere* 'grow'.]

accretion /ə kreésh'n/ *n* **1 INCREASE** an increase in size or amount as a result of something accumulating or being added gradually, or something accumulated in this way **2 ADDITION** something added to something else, e.g. a fund or account, from an external source **3 ATTRACTION OF MATTER BY GRAVITY** a process in which matter revolving around an astronomical object is gradually pulled in and added to the body's mass **4 INCREASE IN LAND MASS** a process by which a body of rock or a land mass increases in size as a result of material accumulating on or around it **5 INCREASE IN SIZE OF CONTINENTS** a process by which the size of a continent increases as a result of the moving together and deforming of tectonic plates —**accretionary** *adj*

accretion disc *n* a band of matter revolving around and being pulled into an astronomical object with an intense gravitational field, e.g. a star or black hole

~~**accross**~~ incorrect spelling of **across**

accrual /ə kroó əl/ *n* **1** something that has accrued **2** the process of accruing or of being accrued

accrual method *n* a method of accounting that counts income or expenses at the time they are earned or incurred, irrespective of when money is received or paid out. ◊ **cash method**

accrue /ə kroó/ (**-crues, -cruing, -crued**) *v* **1** *vi* **COME INTO SOMEBODY'S POSSESSION** to come into somebody's possession, often over a period of time **2** *vi* **INCREASE** to increase in amount or value **3** *vt* **GATHER TOGETHER** to gather together an amount, especially over a period of time **4** *vi* **BECOME ENFORCEABLE** to become legally enforceable (*refers to claims or rights*) [15C. Via Anglo-Norman < Latin *accrescent-*, present participle of *accrescere* (see ACCRETE).] —**accruement** *n*

acct *abbr* account

acculturate /ə kúlchə rayt/ (**-ates, -ating, -ated**) *v* **1** *vi* to absorb and assimilate the culture of another group of people or another individual **2** *vt* to change somebody's cultural behaviour and thinking through contact with another culture [Mid-20C. Back-formation < ACCULTURATION.] —**acculturative** *adj*

acculturation /ə kúlchə ráysh'n/ *n* **1** a change in the cultural behaviour and thinking of an individual or group through contact with another culture **2** the process by which somebody absorbs the culture of a society from birth onwards [Late 19C. < AC- + CULTURE + -ATION.] —**acculturational** *adj*

accumulate /ə kyoómyoo layt/ (**-lates, -lating, -lated**) *vti* to gather something together or collect something, or gather together or collect, over a period of time [15C. < Latin *accumulat-*, past participle of *accumulare* 'heap up in addition' < *cumulus* 'heap'.] —**accumulable** /ə kyoómyoolәb'l/ *adj*

SYNONYMS See ***collect***.

accumulation /ə kyoómyoo láysh'n/ *n* **1 PROCESS OF GATHERING** the process of gathering together and increasing in amount over a period of time **2 COLLECTION OF THINGS** a number of things that have collected or been collected over a period of time **3 GROWTH THROUGH INTEREST** the growth of a sum by the addition of earned interest

accumulative /ə kyoómyoolətiv/ *adj* **1** tending to gather or collect things **2** growing by gradual additions —**accumulatively** *adv* —**accumulativeness** *n*

ϟ **accumulator** /ə kyoómyoo laytər/ *n* **1 BATTERY** a rechargeable battery consisting of one or more cells for producing electrical energy from stored chemical energy. US term **storage battery** **2 MEMORY FOR SHORT-TERM STORAGE** a section of short-term memory in a computer or calculator **3 BET ON SEVERAL RACES** a bet made on a chosen number of horse races, with the stake and any winnings from one race being automatically bet on the next

accuracy /ákyoorəssi/ *n* **1** the correctness or truthfulness of something **2** the ability to be precise and avoid errors

accurate /ákyoorət/ *adj* **1 CORRECT** giving a correct or truthful representation of something ○ *Their account of the incident was not entirely accurate.* **2 FREE FROM ERRORS** precise or free from errors ○ *an accurate typist* **3 PROVIDING INFORMATION TO ACCEPTED STANDARD** providing correct information in accordance with an accepted standard [Late 16C. Via Latin *accuratus* 'done with care' < *cura* 'care'.] —**accurately** *adv* —**accurateness** *n*

accursed /ə kúrssid, ə kúrst/, **accurst** /ə kúrst/ *adj* (*archaic or literary*) **1** enduring the effects of a curse **2** horrible or hateful [12C. < *a-* 'on' (from Old English *ar-*) + CURSE.] —**accursedly** /ə kúrssidli/ *adv* —**accursedness** /ə kúrssidnəss/ *n*

accusation /ákyoo záysh'n/ *n* **1** a claim that somebody has done something illegal, wrong, or undesirable **2** the accusing of somebody, or the state of having been accused of something

accusative /ə kyoózətiv/ *n* **1** a grammatical form (**case**) that identifies the direct object of a verb or certain other grammatical parts in some inflected languages and that affects nouns, pronouns, and adjectives **2** a word or phrase in the accusative [15C. < Latin *accusativus* < *accusare* (see ACCUSE).] —**accusative** *adj* —**accusatively** *adv*

accusatorial /ə kyoózə táwri əl/, **accusatory** /-təri, ákyoo záytəri/ *adj* **1** containing or suggesting a claim that somebody has done something wrong (*formal*) **2** describes a legal system in which the prosecution is required to provide proof beyond reasonable doubt against an accused person, with the evidence being assessed by an impartial judge and jury. ◊ **inquisitorial** *adj*. 2 —**accusatorially** *adv*

accuse /ə kyoóz/ (**-cuses, -cusing, -cused**) *v* **1** *vti* to confront somebody with a charge of having done something illegal, wrong, or undesirable **2** *vt* to charge somebody formally with having committed a crime (*often passive*) [14C. Via French < Latin *accusare* 'call somebody to account' < *ad causa* 'the (legal) case'.] —**accuser** *n*

accused /ə kyoózd/ *n* the person or people being charged in a criminal case

accusing /ə kyoózing/ *adj* containing or suggesting a claim that somebody has done something wrong —**accusingly** *adv*

accustom /ə kústəm/ *vt* to make yourself or somebody else become used to something through frequent or prolonged contact or use [15C. < Anglo-Norman *acustomer* < *custome* 'habit' (see CUSTOM).]

accustomed /ə kústəmd/ *adj* habitual or usual ◇ **accustomed to** used to or familiar with something or somebody ○ *I've grown accustomed to life in a small town.*

AC/DC *adj* **1** able to be powered by battery or by connection to the mains. Full form **alternating current/direct current** **2** an offensive term meaning bisexual (*slang*)

ace /ayss/ *n* **1 PLAYING CARD** a playing card that has a single mark on it, or the single mark itself **2 SINGLE-SPOTTED SIDE** a single-spotted side of a dice or domino, or the single spot itself **3 WINNING SERVE** in tennis, a serve that an opponent cannot reach **4 HOLE IN ONE** the hitting of a golf ball from the tee into a hole in one stroke, or a score resulting from such a stroke **5 FIGHTER PILOT** a top fighter pilot, especially one who has shot down a number of enemy aircraft **6 SOMEBODY WITH AN EXCEPTIONAL SKILL** somebody who is outstandingly good at something, e.g. a sport (*informal*) ■ *vt* (**aces, acing, aced**) **BEAT WITH SERVE** in tennis, to beat an opponent by serving an ace ■ *adj* **EXCELLENT** very good (*informal*) [14C. Via French *as* < Latin, 'unit, unity'.] ◇ **have an ace up your sleeve** to have a concealed advantage ◇ **hold all the aces** to have all the advantages (*informal*) ◇ **within an ace of** very close to

ACE[1] /ayss/ *n* an enzyme that increases blood pressure [Late 20C. Acronym < *angiotensin-converting enzyme*.]

ACE[2] *abbr* **1** Allied Command Europe **2** Advisory Centre for Education

-acean *suffix* = **-aceous**

acebutolol /ássi byóotə lol/ *n* an adrenergic blocking agent that reduces the heart rate and the force of heart muscle contraction. Use: treatment of high blood pressure and heart rhythms. [Mid-20C. < ACETYL + BUTYL.]

acedapsone /ássə dápsōn/ *n* a sulphur-containing drug. Use: treatment of malaria and leprosy [Mid-20C. Blend of *acetylated* + DAPSONE.]

ACE inhibitor *n* a drug that blocks an enzyme that raises blood pressure. Full form **angiotensin-converting enzyme inhibitor**

acellular /ay séllyoolər/ *adj* describes a tissue or organism that lacks distinct cells

acentric /ay séntrik/ *adj* **1** without a centre **2** describes a chromosome that lacks the structure at which the two arms of a chromosome join (**centromere**). ◊ **acrocentric, metacentric** *adj.* 2, **telocentric**

-aceous, -acean *suffix* resembling or related to ○ *herbaceous* [< Latin *-aceus*]

acephalous /ay séffələss/ *adj* describes an animal that has no head [Mid-18C. Via medieval Latin < Greek *akephalos* 'without a head' < *kephalē* 'head' (see CEPHAL-).]

acer /áyssər/ *n* a deciduous tree or shrub grown for its ornamental foliage. Native to: Europe, Asia, North America. Genus: *Acer.*

acerb *adj* US = **acerbic** [Early 17C. < Latin *acerbus* (see ACERBIC).]

acerbate /ássər bayt/ (**-bates, -bating, -bated**) *vt* (*formal*) **1** to annoy or irritate somebody **2** to make something taste bitter [Mid-18C. < Latin *acerbat-*, past participle of *acerbare* 'make harsh' < *acerbus* (see ACERBIC).]

acerbic /ə sérbik/ *adj* bitter or sharp in tone, taste, or manner [Mid-19C. < Latin *acerbus* 'harsh' < Indo-European.] —**acerbically** *adv* —**acerbity** *n*

acervulus /ə súrvyooləss/ (*plural* **-li** /-lī/) *n* an asexual fruiting body shaped like a saucer, found in some fungi [Early 19C. < modern Latin, 'little heap'.]

~~**acessory**~~ incorrect spelling of **accessory**

acet- *prefix* = **aceto-** (*before vowels*)

acetabulum /ássi tábbyooləm/ (*plural* **-la** /-lə/) *n* **1** the curved cavity on the side of the hipbone where the end of the thighbone fits **2** a round cup-shaped sucker found on flatworms, leeches, and molluscs such as the octopus [14C. < Latin, 'vinegar cup, cup-shaped cavity' < *acetum* 'vinegar'.] —**acetabular** *adj*

acetal /ássi tal/ *n* **1** $C_6H_{14}O_2$ a colourless volatile liquid. Use: solvent, perfumes. **2** $-CH(OR_1)OR_2$ any organic compound similar to acetal that contains the given chemical group

acetaldehyde /ássi táldi hīd/ *n* C_2H_4O a colourless volatile liquid with a pungent smell. Use: manufacture of acetic acid, acetic anhydride, and butanol.

acetamide /ə séttə mīd, ássi tá-/ *n* CH_3CONH_2 a white crystalline solid that absorbs water readily. Use: solvent, manufacture of organic chemicals.

acetaminophen /ə séetə mínnəfən, ássitə-/ (*plural* **-phen** *or* **-phens**) *n* US **1** = **paracetamol** *n.* 1 **2** = **paracetamol** *n.* 2

acetanilide /ássi tánni līd/ *n* a white crystalline compound. Use: pain and fever relief, manufacture of chemicals, dyes, and rubber. [Mid-19C. < ACETYL + ANILINE + -IDE.]

acetate /ássi tayt/ *n* **1** a salt or ester of acetic acid **2** CHEM = **cellulose acetate 3** a product made of or containing acetate

acetazolamide /ə séetə zóllə mīd, ássitō-/ *n* a drug that increases the output of urine. Use: treatment of oedema, glaucoma, and epilepsy. [Mid-20C. < ACETO- + AZO- + -L- + AMIDE.]

acetic /ə séetik/ *adj* containing, producing, or made from vinegar or acetic acid [Late 18C. < French *acétique* < Latin *acetum* 'vinegar'.]

acetic acid *n* CH_3COOH a colourless acid with a pungent odour that is the main component of vinegar. Use: manufacture of drugs, dyes, plastics, fibres. ◊ **glacial acetic acid**

acetic anhydride *n* a colourless liquid with a pungent odour. Use: manufacture of aspirin and plastics.

acetify /ə sétti fī/ (**-fies, -fying, -fied**) *vti* to turn into, or cause something to turn into, acetic acid or vinegar —**acetification** /ə séttifi káysh'n/ *n* —**acetifier** *n*

aceto-, acet- *prefix* acetic acid ○ *acetify* [< Latin *acetum* 'vinegar']

acetohexamide /ə séetō héksə mīd/ *n* a sulphur-containing drug. Use: treatment of diabetes. [< ACETO- + HEXA- + AMIDE]

acetone /ássitōn/ *n* C_3H_6O a colourless flammable liquid with a sweetish smell. Use: paint and nail polish solvent, manufacture of organic chemicals.

acetone body *n* BIOCHEM = **ketone body**

acetonitrile /ə séetō nī trīl/ *n* CH_3CN a colourless poisonous liquid. Use: solvent.

acetophenetidin /ə séetō fə néttidin, ássitō-/ *n* CHEM, PHARM = **phenacetin** *n.* 1

acetophenone /ə séetō fénnōn/ *n* a colourless liquid with a sweet pungent smell and taste. Use: in perfumes and chemical synthesis, solvent, flavouring. [Mid-19C. < ACETO- + PHENYL + -ONE.]

acetous /ássitəss, ə sée-/ *adj* like, containing, or producing acetic acid or vinegar [14C. < late Latin *acetosus* < Latin *acetum* 'vinegar'.]

acetyl /ássi tīl, ə sée-/ *adj* relating to or containing the chemical group CH_3CO-

acetylate /ə sétti layt/ (**-lates, -lating, -lated**) *vt* to introduce the acetyl group into a compound —**acetylation** /ə sétti láysh'n/ *n*

acetylcholine /ássi tīl kó leen/ *n* $C_7H_{17}NO_3$ a white crystalline compound released from the ends of nerve fibres and involved in the transmission of nerve impulses

acetylcholinesterase /ássi tīl kōlin éstə rayz/ *n* an enzyme, present in blood and some nerve endings, that aids the breakdown of acetylcholine and suppresses its stimulatory effect on nerves

acetyl coenzyme A, acetyl CoA *n* a coenzyme produced during metabolism of carbohydrates, fatty acids, and amino acids

acetylene /ə sétti leen/ *n* C_2H_2 a colourless gaseous flammable hydrocarbon. Use: welding, manufacture of organic chemicals. —**acetylenic** /ə sétti lénnik/ *adj*

acetylide /ə sétti līd/ *n* any acetylene-derived compound containing a metal atom, often very explosive

acetylsalicylic acid /ássi tīl sálli síllik-/ *n* the drug aspirin (*technical*)

acey-deucy /áyssi dyóossi/ *n* a version of backgammon in which a dice throw of one or two wins an additional turn [< ACE and DEUCE[1]]

ach /aakh/ *interj Scotland* used to express emotion, e.g. annoyance, surprise, or resignation, often as an introduction to saying something [15C. < Celtic.]

⚡**ACH** *n* a wholesale payment network for interbank clearing and payment settlement in e-commerce, accessible by point-of-sale or automated teller machine systems. Full form **automated clearing house**

Achaea /ə kée ə/, **Achaia** /ə kī ə, ə káy ə/ **1** administrative department in S Greece. Area: 3,209 sq. km/1,239 sq. mi. Population: 300,078 (1991). **2** province in ancient Greece

Achaean /ə kée ən, ə káy ən/, **Achaian** *n* **1** a member of an ancient Hellenic people thought to have founded the Mycenaean civilization on the Peloponnese **2** somebody who comes from the modern Greek department of Achaea —**Achaean** *adj*

achalasia /ákə láyzi ə/ *n* a failure of certain smooth muscle bands, e.g. in the gullet, to relax [Early 20C. < A-[2] + Greek *khalasis* 'relaxation' < *khalan* 'loosen'.]

acharya /ə cháari ə/ *n S Asia* a learned religious teacher and guide

ache /ayk/ *vi* (**aches, aching, ached**) **1 FEEL PAIN** to feel or be the site of a dull constant pain **2 YEARN** to yearn for the presence of somebody or something **3 WANT BADLY** to want something very much (*informal*) ○ *aching to tell her the news* ■ *n* **CONSTANT PAIN** a feeling of constant dull pain [Old English *æce* (noun), *acan* (verb) < ? The *ch* spelling arose from a mistaken association with Greek *akhos* 'pain'.] —**achingly** *adv*

Achebe /ə cháybi/, **Chinua** (*b.* 1930) Nigerian novelist

~~**acheive**~~ incorrect spelling of **achieve**

achene /ə kéen/, **akene** *n* a dry single-seeded fruit that does not open to release its seed [Mid-19C. < modern Latin *achaenium* 'not gaping' < Greek *khainein* 'gape'.]

Acheron /ákərōn/ *n* in Greek mythology, one of the rivers that ran through Hades

Acheson /áchəss'n/, **Dean** (1893–1971) US statesman

Acheulian /ə shóoli ən/ *n* a period of the Palaeolithic era during which people made symmetrical stone hand axes [Early 20C. After the French village of Saint-*Acheul* near Amiens, where distinctive tools were found in the 19C.] —**Acheulian** *adj*

à cheval /áshə vál/ *adv* describes a bet made on two adjacent numbers, e.g. in roulette or cards [< French, 'on horseback', used to mean 'with one foot on either side'. Because the risk is shared equally between two cards.]

achieve /ə chéev/ (**achieves, achieving, achieved**) *vt* to succeed in doing or gaining something, usually with effort [14C. < French *achever* 'bring to an end or head' < *a chief* 'to a head' (see CHIEF).] —**achievability** /ə chéevə bílləti/ *n* —**achievable** *adj* —**achievably** *adv*

SYNONYMS See ***accomplish***.

achieved /ə chéevd/ *adj* US showing great skill or accomplishment

achievement /ə chéevmənt/ *n* **1 SUCCESS** something that somebody has succeeded in doing, usually with effort **2 FINISHING WELL** the act or process of finishing something successfully **3 FULL COAT OF ARMS** a full coat of arms that includes standing figures such as lions or unicorns (**supporters**), the family symbol (**crest**), and the family motto

achievement age *n* the age at which a child should be able to perform a particular task successfully

achiever /ə chéevər/ *n* **1** a successful and motivated person **2** somebody who succeeds in a particular activity ○ *low achievers*

Achilles /ə kílleez/ *n* in Greek mythology, the principal hero of the Trojan War, made invulnerable by being dipped in the river Styx as a baby by his mother, except for the heel she held him by

Achilles heel *n* a weakness that seems small but makes somebody or something fatally vulnerable

Achilles tendon *n* the tendon that connects the heel bone to the calf muscles

achiral /ay kīrəl/ *adj* describes a molecule having neither left-handed nor right-handed configuration

achlorhydria /áy klaw hīdri ə/ *n* an absence of or reduction in hydrochloric acid in the gastric juice —**achlorhydric** *adj*

achondrite /ay kón drīt/ *n* a stony meteorite that does not contain rounded grains (**chondrules**) —**achondritic** /áy kon dríttik/ *adj*

achondroplasia /áy kondrō pláyzi ə/ *n* a genetic disorder in which cartilage fails to develop into bone at the early stages of development, resulting in dwarfism [Late 19C. < Greek *akhondros* 'without cartilage' + -PLASIA.] —**achondroplastic** /-plástik/ *adj*

achromat /ákrə mat/ *n* **1** PHYS = **achromatic lens 2** OPHTHALMOL = **monochromat** [Early 20C. Back-formation < ACHROMATIC.]

achromatic /áykrō máttik/ *adj* **1 WITHOUT COLOUR** without colour and therefore white, grey, or black in appearance **2 WITHOUT SPECTRUM COLOURS** able to reflect or refract light without spectral colour separation **3 NOT EASILY STAINED** describes cells not easily stained with standard dyes **4 WITHOUT SHARPS OR FLATS** using a musical scale with no sharps or flats —**achromatically** *adv* —**achromaticity** /áykrōmə tíssəti/ *n* —**achromatism** /ə krṓmətizəm/ *n*

achromatic colour *n* a colour with no hue or chromatic component

achromatic lens *n* a composite lens in which two or

more lenses with different properties are combined to prevent distortion (**chromatic aberration**)

achromatic prism *n* a composite prism in which two or more prisms deflect, but do not disperse, light

achromatopsia /áy krōmə tópsi ə/ *n* MED = **monochromatism** [Mid-19C. < Greek *akhrōmatos* 'without colour' < *a-* 'without, not' + khrômato- (see CHROMATO-) + *-opsia* (see -OPSY).]

achy /áyki/ (**-ier, -iest**) *adj* feeling or being the site of a constant dull pain —**achiness** *n*

acicula /ə síkyŏŏlə/ (*plural* **-lae** /-lee/) *n* a needle-shaped part, e.g. a spine, bristle, or crystal (*technical*) [Mid-19C. < late Latin, 'little needle'.] —**aciculate** /ə síkyŏŏ layt/ *adj* —**aciculated** *adj*

acid /ássid/ *n* **1 CORROSIVE SUBSTANCE** a sour-tasting compound that releases hydrogen ions to form a solution with a pH of less than 7, reacts with a base to form a salt, and turns blue litmus red. ◊ **alkali** *n.* 1 **2 COMPOUND FORMING COVALENT BOND WITH BASE** a compound that can donate a proton or accept a pair of electrons to form a covalent bond with a base **3 LSD** LSD (*slang*) **4 SHARPNESS** a sharp, bitter, or sarcastic quality in speech or writing ■ *adj* **1 RELATING TO AN ACID** with the properties of or containing an acid **2 SOUR-TASTING** having a sour or sharp taste **3 SHARP** sharp, bitter, or sarcastic **4 POLLUTED** describes rain or snow that contains dilute acid resulting from pollution **5 HIGH IN SILICA** describes igneous rocks that have a high silica content [Late 17C. Directly or via French < Latin *acidus* < *acere* 'be sour'.] —**acidly** *adv*

acid anhydride *n* CHEM = **anhydride**

acid chloride *n* CHEM = **acylchloride**

acid deposition *n* a deposit of water vapour, e.g. dew, rain, snow, hail, or fog, that is high in acid content because of atmospheric pollution

acid drop *n* a boiled sweet that has a sharp lemony taste

acid house *n* electronic dance music of the late 1980s, using pulsating rhythms and associated with the use of the drug ecstasy

acidic /ə síddik/ *adj* **1 SOUR-TASTING** sour or bitter in taste **2 SARCASTIC** sour, bitter, or sarcastic in manner or tone **3 FORMING ACID IN WATER** forming an acid in water

acidify /ə síddi fī/ (**-fies, -fying, -fied**) *vti* to turn something acid, or become acid —**acidifiable** *adj* —**acidification** /ə síddifi káysh'n/ *n* —**acidifier** *n*

acidimeter /ássi dímmitər/ *n* an instrument for measuring the amount of acid in a solution —**acidimetric** /ássidi méttrik/ *adj* —**acidimetry** *n*

acidity /ə síddəti/ (*plural* **-ties**) *n* **1** the concentration of acid in a substance, of which pH is a measure **2** MED = **hyperacidity 3** the quality or condition of being acid

acid jazz *n* a mixture of funk, jazz, and soul music that first appeared in the 1980s

acidophil /ássi dōfil, ə síddōfil/, **acidophile** /ássi dō fīl, ə síddōfīl/ *n* **1** a microorganism or plant that flourishes in an acid environment **2** a cell that stains readily with acidic dyes

acidophilic /ássidō fíllik/ *adj* **1** describes cells that are easily stained by an acid dye **2** describes microorganisms or plants that flourish in an acid environment

acidophilus /ássi dóffiləss/ (*plural* **acidophili** /-lī/) *n* a bacterium with slender rod-shaped cells, usually in chains, that thrives in acidic conditions. Use: yoghurt manufacture. *Lactobacillus acidophilus.* [Mid-19C. < modern Latin, 'acid-loving'.]

acidophilus milk *n* milk fermented using bacterial cultures, used to treat digestive disorders

acidosis /ássi dṓsiss/ *n* a failure of the mechanism that controls the acidity of the blood, common in untreated diabetes

acid protease *n* a protein-digesting enzyme activated in stomach acid

acid rain *n* rain that contains dilute acid derived from burning fossil fuels and that is potentially harmful to the environment

acid reflux *n* a painful burning sensation caused by the stomach contents being repeatedly returned to the oesophagus, a result of the inadequate functioning of, e.g. the lower oesophageal sphincter

acid rock *n* electric rock music popular in the late 1960s, with instrumental effects and lyrics suggesting or promoting psychedelic experiences

Acid rain: Detail of tree in Norway damaged by acid rain

acid test *n* a decisive test that establishes the worth or credibility of something ○ *'The treatment accorded Russia by her sister nations in the months to come will be the acid test of their good will'.* (Woodrow Wilson, *Speech on the Fourteen Points*; 1918) [< the use of nitric acid to test gold]

acidulate /ə síddyŏŏ layt/ (**-lates, -lating, -lated**) *vti* to make something slightly acid, or become slightly acid —**acidulation** /ə síddyŏŏ láysh'n/ *n*

acidulous /ə síddyŏŏləss/ *adj* **1** slightly sour in taste (*formal*) **2** cutting and sharp in speech or tone [Mid-18C. < Latin *acidulus* < *acidus* (see ACID).]

acierate /ássi ə rayt/ (**-ates, -ating, -ated**) *vt* to make iron into steel by combining it with carbon and other elements [Mid-19C. < French *aciérer* < *acier* 'steel'.]

ACII *abbr* Associate of the Chartered Insurance Institute

acinus /ássinəss/ (*plural* **-ni** /-nī/) *n* **1** a rounded sac, containing secretory cells, found at the ends of the ducts in an exocrine gland **2** ANAT = **alveolus** *n.* 1 **3** one of the small globes (**drupelets**) that make up an aggregate fruit such as a blackberry or raspberry [Mid-18C. < Latin, 'berry growing in a cluster, kernel'.] —**acinar** *adj* —**acinous** *adj*

ack-ack /ák ak/ *n* (*informal*) **1** an antiaircraft gun **2** antiaircraft fire [Representing *AA* 'antiaircraft' in a former system of spelling out messages]

ackee /ákee/ (*plural* **ackees** *or* **ackee**), **akee** (*plural* **-ees** *or* **-ee**) *n* **1** a red pear-shaped fruit only edible when ripe and with poisonous seeds **2** an evergreen tree cultivated in the Caribbean and Florida for ackees. Native to: tropical W Africa. *Blighia sapida.* [Late 18C. Perhaps < Kru.]

ack-emma /ák émmə/ *adv* in the morning (*dated informal*) [Representing A.M. in a former system of spelling out messages]

Ackerman steering /ákərmən-/ *n* the steering system used in most motor vehicles, in which the wheels swivel at each end of the axle

acknowledge /ək nóllij/ (**-edges, -edging, -edged**) *v* **1** *vti* **ADMIT** to admit or accept that something exists, is true, or is real **2** *vti* **SHOW AWARENESS OF** to respond to something such as a greeting or message to show it has been noticed or received **3** *vti* **SHOW APPRECIATION OF** to show appreciation or express thanks for something such as a letter or gift **4** *vt* **RECOGNIZE LEGALLY** to recognize or admit the existence, rights, or authority of somebody or something, especially in a legal context **5** *vt* **THANK OFFICIALLY** to give official or public recognition of the help somebody has given or the work somebody has done [15C. Probably < KNOWLEDGE after obsolete English *aknow* 'recognize, acknowledge' (< KNOW).] —**acknowledgable** *adj* —**acknowledged** *adj* —**acknowledger** *n*

acknowledgment /ək nóllijmənt/, **acknowledgement** *n* **1 ACT OF ACKNOWLEDGING** the act of acknowledging something, or the condition of being acknowledged **2 SIGN OF RECOGNITION** a sign showing that somebody has seen or heard somebody else's greeting or presence **3 INDICATION OF RECEIPT** a letter or other message sent to say that something has been received **4 THANKS** an expression of thanks or appreciation for something **5 OFFICIAL RECOGNITION** official or public recognition of the help somebody has given or the work somebody has done ■ **acknowledgments** *npl* **AUTHOR'S THANKS** a section at the beginning or end of a book or other piece of writing where an author thanks those who have helped

aclarubicin /áklə rŏŏbissin/ *n* a cytotoxic antibiotic. Use: treatment of leukaemia.

aclinic line /ay klínnik-/ *n* GEOG = **magnetic equator** [< Greek *aklinēs* 'not leaning' < *klinein* 'lean']

ACLU *abbr* American Civil Liberties Union

ACM *abbr* **1** air chief marshal **2** Association for Computing Machinery

acme /ákmi/ *n* the highest point of perfection or achievement [Late 16C. < Greek *akmē* 'highest point'.]

acne /ákni/ *n* a disease of the oil-secreting glands of the skin that often affects adolescents, producing eruptions on the face, neck, and shoulders that can leave pitted scars [Mid-19C. < Latin, misreading of Greek *akmē* (see ACME).] —**acned** *adj*

acne rosacea *n* MED = **rosacea**

acoelomate /ə seélə mayt/ *n* an organism with no cavity (**coelom**) between its digestive tract and outer wall, e.g. a flatworm or jellyfish

acolyte /ákə līt/ *n* **1** somebody, especially a young person, who assists a member of the clergy in the performance of rites **2** a follower or assistant ○ *the acolytes of this powerful leader* [14C. Directly or via Old French < ecclesiastical Latin *acolytus* < Greek *akolouthos* 'follower' < *a-* 'together' + *keleuthos* 'path'.]

~~**acompany**~~ incorrect spelling of **accompany**

Aconcagua /ákən kágwə/ highest mountain in the Andes and in the W hemisphere, located in W Argentina. Height: 6,960 m/22,834 ft.

aconite /ákə nīt/ *n* **1** a plant with poisonous roots. Flowers: purplish blue white, hooded. Native to: northern temperate regions. Genus: *Aconitum.* **2** PLANTS = **winter aconite 3** an extract of the dried poisonous root of some aconite plants. Use: homeopathic remedy. [Mid-16C. Directly or via French < Latin *aconitum* < Greek *akoniton.*]

~~**acording**~~ incorrect spelling of **according**

acorn /áy kawrn/ *n* the hard fruit of an oak tree, consisting of a smooth single-seeded nut that is set in a cup-shaped base and ripens from green to brown [Old English *æcern*, perhaps < *æcer* 'open land'; later interpreted as 'oak-corn']

acorn barnacle *n* a marine organism with a conical shell that attaches itself to rocks and catches food using tendrils. *Balanus balanoides.*

acorn squash *n* US an acorn-shaped winter squash with a ridged dark-green rind and yellow or orange flesh

acorn worm *n* a small burrowing sea animal resembling a worm that has an acorn-shaped snout that it uses to dig for food. Phylum: Chordata.

acouchi /ə kŏŏshi/ (*plural* **-chis** *or* **-chies**), **acouchy** (*plural* **-chies**) *n* an agile South American rodent similar to an agouti. Genus: *Myoprocta.* [Late 18C. Via French < Tupi.]

acoustic /ə kŏŏstik/, **acoustical** /-stik'l/ *adj* **1 RELATING TO SOUND** concerning sound, hearing, or the study of sound **2 DESIGNED FOR USE WITH SOUND** designed to control sound, absorb it, or carry it better **3 NOT AMPLIFIED** without electronic amplification in music or a musical instrument, e.g. a guitar ■ *n* MUSIC = **acoustics** *npl.* [Early 18C. < Greek *akoustikos* < *akouein* 'hear' < Indo-European.] —**acoustically** *adv*

acoustic nerve *n* MED = **auditory nerve**

acoustic neuroma *n* a benign tumour of the auditory canal of the ear that causes hearing loss, loss of balance, and headaches

acoustics /ə kŏŏstiks/ *n* the scientific study of sound (+ *singular verb*) ■ *npl* the characteristic way in which sound carries or can be heard within a particular enclosed space, e.g. an auditorium —**acoustician** /ákoo stísh'n/ *n*

acoustic tile *n* a ceiling or wall tile designed to stop or diminish the transmission of sound

acoustic trauma *n* physical damage or changes in the body caused by sound waves, e.g. hearing loss, disorientation, motion sickness, and dizziness

acoustoelectric /ə kŏŏstō i léktrik/ *adj* = **electroacoustic** —**acoustoelectrically** *adv*

acquaint /ə kwáynt/ *vt* to make somebody, or yourself, aware of or familiar with something [13C. Via French *acointier* 'make known' < Latin *accognoscere* 'know perfectly' < *cognoscere* 'know'.]

acquaintance /ə kwáyntənss/ *n* **1 SOMEBODY KNOWN** somebody who is known slightly **2 KNOWLEDGE** knowledge, usually slight, of somebody or something **3 PEOPLE SLIGHTLY KNOWN** people who are known slightly but not well ○ *a wide circle of acquaintance* —**acquaintanceship** *n* ◇ **have a nodding acquaintance with somebody** *or* **something** to know somebody or something slightly ◇ **make somebody's acquaintance** to meet somebody for the first time

acquainted /ə kwáyntid/ *adj* **1** having some, often not very much, knowledge of something **2** known to somebody or to each other from a previous introduction

acquiesce /àkwi éss/ (**-esces, -escing, -esced**) *vi* to agree to or comply with something passively rather than expressing approval or support [Early 17C. < Latin *acquiescere* 'remain resting', hence 'agree tacitly' < *quiescere* 'rest'.] —**acquiescence** *n* —**acquiescent** *adj* —**acquiescently** *adv*

SYNONYMS See ***agree***.

acquire /ə kwír/ (**-quires, -quiring, -quired**) *vt* **1 GET** to get or obtain possession of something **2 DEVELOP** to learn or develop something ○ *a habit I acquired in the army* **3 LOCATE BY RADAR** to locate an object such as an aircraft by the use of radar or another detector [15C. Via Old French *acquerre* < Latin *acquirere* 'get something extra' < *quaerere* 'try to get or obtain' (see QUERY).] —**acquirable** *adj* —**acquired** *adj* —**acquirer** *n*

SYNONYMS See ***get***.

acquired character, acquired characteristic *n* a characteristic that an organism develops in response to its environment and that cannot be passed on to the next generation

acquired immune deficiency syndrome, acquired immunodeficiency syndrome *n* full form of **Aids**

acquired taste *n* a liking that develops for something that seems unpleasant at first

acquirement /ə kwírmənt/ *n* **1** the act or process of acquiring something **2** something learned or attained, especially a skill

⚡**acquirer** /ak kwírər/ *n* a financial institution that processes transactions paid for by credit or debit card, supplying payment to the retailer and notifying the card issuer of the debt incurred by the purchaser

acquisition /àkwi zísh'n/ *n* **1 ACQUIRING** the act of acquiring something **2 NEW POSSESSION** something that has recently been bought or obtained **3 SKILL DEVELOPMENT** developing a new skill, practice, or way of doing things ○ *language acquisition* **4 LOCATING BY RADAR** the location of an object such as an aircraft by the use of radar or some other detector ■ **acquisitions** *npl* **COMPANY DEPARTMENT** the department in a company responsible for taking over other businesses (*takes a singular verb*) ○ *I work in acquisitions and mergers.* [14C. < Latin *acquisition-* < *acquisit-*, past participle of *acquirere* (see ACQUIRE).]

acquisitive /ə kwízzətiv/ *adj* eager to acquire things, especially possessions [Mid-17C. < Latin *acquisit-* (see ACQUISITION), after French *acquisitif*.] —**acquisitively** *adv* —**acquisitiveness** *n*

acquit /ə kwít/ (**-quits, -quitting, -quitted**) *v* **1** *vt* **DECLARE INNOCENT** to declare officially that somebody is not guilty of a charge or accusation **2** *vr* **BEHAVE** to conduct yourself in a particular way ○ *The band acquitted itself well at the performance.* **3** *vt* **FREE FROM OBLIGATION** to free somebody from a duty or obligation (*formal*) **4** *vt* **REPAY** to repay something such as a debt (*formal*) [13C. Via Old French *a(c)quiter* < assumed Latin *acquitare* 'bring to rest', hence 'set free' < *quies* 'quiet'.] —**acquitter** *n*

acquittal /ə kwítt'l/ *n* a judgment given by a court of law that somebody is not guilty of a charge or accusation

acquittance /ə kwítt'nss/ *n* release from a debt or obligation, or a written receipt or other record of this (*dated*)

acre /áykər/ *n* **UNIT OF AREA** a unit of area used in some countries, including the United States and the United Kingdom, equal to 4,046.86 sq. m./4,840 sq. yd ■ **acres** *npl* **1 LAND** land, especially a large amount of land **2 LARGE AMOUNT** a large amount or area of something (*informal*) [Old English *æcer*. Ultimately probably 'area over which ploughing oxen can be driven in a day' < Indo-European, 'drive'.]

Acre /áykər/ seaport in N Israel. Population: 45,035 (1998 estimate).

acreage /áykərij/ *n* land, or an area of land, measured in acres

acre-foot *n* the volume of water that would cover an area of one acre to a depth of one foot, equivalent to 1,233.5 cu m/43,560 cu ft

acre-inch *n* one-twelfth of an acre-foot, or the volume of water that would cover an area of one acre to a depth of one inch, equivalent to 102.8 cu m./3,630 cu ft

acrid /ákrid/ *adj* **1** unpleasantly strong and bitter in smell or taste **2** sharp or bitter in tone or character [Early 18C. < Latin *acri-* 'sharp, pungent', after ACID.] —**acridity** /ə kríddəti/ *n* —**acridly** *adv* —**acridness** /-nəss/ *n*

acridine /ákri deen/ *n* $C_{13}H_9N$ a colourless crystalline solid. Source: coal tar. Use: manufacture of dyes and pharmaceuticals. [Late 19C. < German *Acridin* < Latin *acri-* (see ACRID).]

acriflavine /ákri fláy veen/ *n* an orange-brown crystalline solid. Use: as an antiseptic in solution.

~~**acrilic**~~ incorrect spelling of **acrylic**

acrimonious /ákri móni əss/ *adj* full of or displaying anger and resentment —**acrimoniously** *adv* —**acrimoniousness** *n*

acrimony /ákriməni/ *n* bitterness and resentment, especially in speech, attitude, or tone [Mid-16C. Directly or via French < Latin *acrimonia* < *acri-* (see ACRID).]

acrivastine /ə krívvə steen/ *n* a drug that is a histamine antagonist. Use: treatment of rhinitis, urticaria, and eczema. [Late 20C. < ACRIDINE + *vastine*.]

acro- *prefix* top, tip, height ○ *acrocentric* ○ *acrophobia* [< Greek *akros* 'extreme, topmost' < Indo-European]

acrobat /ákrə bat/ *n* **1** a performer of gymnastic feats as entertainment **2** somebody whose opinions or positions change readily to suit the circumstances [Early 19C. Via French < Greek *akrobatos* 'walking on tiptoe' < *akros* (see ACRO-) + *bainein* 'walk'.]

acrobatic /ákrə báttik/ *adj* **1** relating to or involving acrobatics **2** showing or demanding agility and energy —**acrobatically** *adv*

acrobatics /ákrə báttiks/ *n* (*+ singular or plural verb*) **1 GYMNASTICS** the skill or performance routines of an acrobat **2 ACTIVITY REQUIRING AGILITY** an activity that requires great skill or agility **3 VIRTUOSO PERFORMANCE** performance of something that is marked by virtuosic skill ○ *verbal acrobatics in her summing-up*

acrocentric /ákrō séntrik/ *adj* describes a chromosome that has arms of unequal length because the structure at which the two arms join (**centromere**) is located towards one end. ◊ **acentric** *adj.* **2**, **metacentric** *adj.* **2**, **telocentric**

acrocephaly /ákrō séffəli/ *n* MED = **oxycephaly** —**acrocephalic** /ákrō sə fállik/ *adj* —**acrocephalous** *adj*

acrocyanosis /ákrō sī ə nṓssis/ *n* a condition characterized by cyanosis, sweating, and coldness of the toes and fingers

acrodont /ákrə dont/ *adj* describes the teeth of some reptiles that have no roots and are joined to the jawbone, or reptiles with teeth of this type

acrolect /ákrō lekt/ *n* the language variety among a group of related varieties that is closest to the standard form of the language

acrolein /ə krṓli in/ *n* CH_2CHCHO a colourless poisonous pungent aldehyde. Use: manufacture of chemicals and pharmaceuticals.

acrolith /ákrō lith/ *n* a statue, especially in ancient Greece, with a wooden body and hands, feet, and head of stone

acromegaly /ákrō méggəli/ *n* overproduction of growth hormones, resulting in enlarged bones in the hands, feet, jaw, nose, and ribs of adults —**acromegalic** /ákrō mi gállik/ *adj*

acromion /ə krṓmi ən/ (*plural* **-a** /-mi ə/) *n* a bony projection from the outer end of the spine of the shoulder blade, to which the collarbone is attached [Late 16C. < Greek *akrōmion* < *akros* (see ACRO-) + *ōmos* 'shoulder'.]

acronym /ákrənim/ *n* a word formed from the initials or other parts of several words [Mid-20C. <ACRO- + *-nym* < Greek *onuma* 'name', after SYNONYM etc.] —**acronymic** /ákrə nímmik/ *adj* —**acronymous** /ə krónniməss/ *adj*

USAGE See ***abbreviation***.

acropetal /ə króppit'l/ *adj* describes leaves or flowers that grow in order from the base of a plant or stem towards the apex. ◊ **basipetal** —**acropetally** *adv*

acrophobia /ákrə fṓbi ə/ *n* an irrational fear of being in high places —**acrophobic** *adj*

acropolis /ə króppəliss/ *n* the fortified citadel of a city in ancient Greece [Early 17C. < Greek *akropolis*.]

Acropolis /ə króppəliss/ *n* the ancient citadel of Athens in Greece that was the religious focus of the city

acrosome /ákrō sōm/ *n* a structure at the end of a sperm cell that releases enzymes to digest the cell membrane of an egg, enabling the sperm to penetrate

across /ə króss/ CORE MEANING: a grammatical word indicating that somebody or something is on the opposite side of something or moves or reaches from one side to the other ○ (prep) *I live across the street from you.* ○ (adv) *a bridge wide enough to walk across*

1 *prep* **ON OPPOSITE SIDE** at or on the opposite side of something ○ *across the road* **2** *prep* **FROM ONE SIDE TO OTHER** from one side of something to the opposite side ○ *ran across the road* ○ *a bridge across the river* **3** *prep* **IN SPITE OF BOUNDARIES** in such a way that boundaries or borders are transcended ○ *united across cultures* **4** *adj, adv* **SO AS TO CROSS** in such a way as to intersect or form a cross with something ○ *placed one board across the other* **5** *prep* **THROUGHOUT** all over something or somewhere ○ *all across America* **6** *adv* **AT OR TO OTHER SIDE** at, on, or to the other side of something ○ *Once we were across, we felt safe.* **7** *adv* **MEASURED IN WIDTH** as measured from one side of something to the other ○ *about an inch across* **8** *adv* **HORIZONTALLY ON CROSSWORD** in a horizontal position in a crossword ○ *couldn't find the solution to 3 across.* ◊ **down**[1] **18** [13C. Via Old French *à croix* or *en croix* 'transversely' < Latin *crux* (see CROSS).]

across-the-board *adj, adv* affecting everyone or everything equally or proportionally ■ *adj US* wagering an equal amount to win if a horse or other competitor finishes first, second, or third

acrostic /ə króstik/ *n* a number of lines of writing, especially a poem or word puzzle, in which particular letters, e.g. the first, in each line spell a word or phrase [Late 16C. Via French *acrostiche* < Greek *akrostikhis* < *akros* 'outermost' + *stikhos* 'line of verse' (< *steikhein* 'go').] —**acrostically** *adv*

acrylamide /ə kríllə mīd/ *n* **1** $C_{17}H_{10}O$ a poisonous colourless crystalline solid. Use: manufacture of polymers **2** a polymer made with acrylamide [Late 19C. < ACRYLIC + AMIDE.]

acrylate /ə kríllayt/ *n* a salt or ester of acrylic acid [Mid-19C. < ACRYLIC + -ATE.]

acrylate resin /ákri layt-/ *n* a resin derived from acrylic or other related acids. Use: paints, sizing, adhesives, plastics.

acrylic /ə kríllik/ *n* **1 SYNTHETIC FIBRE** a synthetic textile fibre produced from acrylonitrile **2 SOMETHING MADE WITH ACRYLIC ACID** something containing or made from acrylic acid **3 PAINT** a paint containing acrylate resin, used especially in painting pictures —**acrylic** *adj*

acrylic acid *n* $C_3H_4O_2$ a colourless corrosive acid. Use: manufacture of acrylate resins.

acrylic resin *n* CHEM = **acrylate resin**

acrylonitrile /ákrilō nī trīl/ *n* C_3H_3N a colourless toxic liquid. Use: manufacture of acrylic fibres and resins, rubbers, thermoplastics. [Late 19C. < ACRYLIC + NITRILE.]

act /akt/ *n* **1 SOMETHING DONE** something that somebody does **2 DOING** the action of carrying something out **3 PART OF PLAY** one of the main sections of a play or other dramatic performance **4 ONE OF SEVERAL PERFORMANCES** a short performance, especially one that is part of a varied programme or show ○ *The next act is a barbershop quartet.* **5 PERFORMER** the performer or performers who take part in an act **6 PERSONAL BEHAVIOUR** somebody's actions or behaviour considered as entertainment or used as an assessment of that person's worth (*informal*) ○ *a class act* **7 PRETENCE** behaviour that is intended to impress or deceive other people ○ *He's just putting on an act.* **8 STATEMENT OF INSTRUCTION REGARDING LAW** a record or statement of the decision made by a law-making or judicial body such as Parliament **9 FORMAL RECORD** a formal written record of the proceedings of a society, committee, or elected group **10 SOMETHING DONE INTENTIONALLY** something brought about by human will ■ *v* **1** *vi* **DO** to do something to change a situation, e.g. to solve a problem or prevent one arising **2** *vti* **BEHAVE IN CERTAIN WAY** to adopt a particular way of behaving ○ *You've been acting funny all morning.* ○ *Stop acting the fool.* ○ *'I even liked him when he was 'difficult' and official, because I thought I knew why he acted like that'.* (Paul Scott, *The Jewel in the Crown*; 1966) **3** *vi*

PRETEND to behave in a way intended to impress or deceive other people **4** *vi* **FUNCTION** to serve a particular purpose or perform a particular function ○ *The ozone layer acts as a barrier against harmful radiation.* **5** *vi* **REPLACE** to be a substitute for somebody or something else ○ *Since the director cannot attend, his deputy will act for him.* **6** *vi* **HAVE AN EFFECT** to create, produce, or bring about an effect or result ○ *Once the medicine acts, you'll feel better.* **7** *vti* **PLAY A ROLE** to play the part of a character in a dramatic performance ○ *a chance to act Othello* **8** *vi* **BE ACTOR** to pursue a career in films or drama **9** *vti* **PERFORM SOMETHING OR BE PERFORMED** to stage a dramatic performance, or be capable of being staged ○ *The company will act a different play tomorrow night.* [14C. Directly or via French *acte* < Latin *actus, actum* 'public transaction' < past participle of *agere* 'do'.] —**actable** *adj* ◇ **a hard** *or* **tough act to follow** somebody or something that sets a standard difficult to reach by others who come later ◇ **catch somebody in the act** to see or meet somebody just as he or she is doing something, especially something wrong ◇ **clean up your act** to improve your behaviour ◇ **get in on the act** to join in something in order to share in its success or profit (*informal*) ◇ **get your act together** to do something to become more organized (*informal*)

act on, act upon *vt* **1** to be guided by somebody's advice or suggestion **2** to have an effect on something

act out *vt* **1** to perform something or portray it in action **2** to express a negative feeling or impulse by behaving in a socially unacceptable way

act up *vi* to cause trouble or pain

ACT *abbr* **1** *Aus* Australian Capital Territory **2** advance corporation tax

Actaeon /ak tée ən/ *n* in Greek mythology, a hunter who was turned into a stag after inadvertently seeing the goddess Artemis bathing

ACTH *n* a pituitary hormone that stimulates the adrenal cortex to produce steroid hormones. Full form **adrenocorticotrophic hormone**

actin /áktin/ *n* a protein present in all cells and in muscle tissue where it plays a role in contraction [Mid-20C. < Latin *actus* (see ACT).]

actin- *prefix* = **actino-** (*before vowels*)

actinal /áktənəl/ *adj* **1** describes the side of a marine animal such as a jellyfish or sea anemone from which the arms or tentacles radiate **2** with rays or tentacles

acting /ákting/ *n* **PERFORMING IN PLAYS** the art, profession, or performance of an actor ■ *adj* **1 TEMPORARY** carrying out certain duties or doing somebody else's job temporarily ○ *the acting manager* **2 WITH DIRECTIONS FOR STAGING** including directions in a play's text to be used in staging a performance ○ *a copy of the acting edition of the play*

actinian /ak tínni ən/ *n* a sea anemone (*technical*) [Late 19C. < modern Latin *Actinia* < Greek *aktin-* 'ray'.]

actinic /ak tínnik/ *adj* relating to radiation such as ultraviolet radiation that produces a chemical effect —**actinically** *adv*

actinide /ákti nīd/ *n* any element in the series of radioactive elements beginning with actinium and ending with lawrencium [Mid-20C. < ACTINIUM, after LANTHANIDE.]

actinism /áktinizəm/ *n* the property of radiation that makes photochemical change possible

actinium /ak tínni əm/ *n* (*symbol* **Ac**) a radioactive silvery-white metallic element. Source: pitchblende. Use: source of alpha rays. [Early 20C. < Greek *aktin-* 'ray'.]

actino-, actin- *prefix* **1** radial ○ *actinomorphic* **2** radiation [< Greek *aktin-*, stem of *aktis* 'ray']

actinolite /ak tínnə līt/ *n* a green or greyish-green silicate mineral of the amphibole group, containing calcium, magnesium, and iron

actinometer /ákti nómmitər/ *n* a device for measuring the intensity of radiation, especially that from the sun —**actinometric** /áktinō méttrik/ *adj* —**actinometry** /ákti nómmətri/ *n*

actinomorphic /áktinō máwrfik/, **actinomorphous** /-máwrfəss/ *adj* spreading out symmetrically around a central point and so making identical halves when divided along any vertical axis —**actinomorphy** *n*

actinomycete /áktinō mī séet/ *n* a rod-shaped or filamentous bacterium belonging to a large group that includes some that cause diseases and some that are the sources of antibiotics. Order: Actinomycetales. [Early 20C. Back-formation < modern Latin *actinomycetes*, plural of *actinomyces* < ACTINO- + Greek *mukēs* 'fungus'.] —**actinomycetous** *adj*

actinomycin /áktinō míssin/ *n* an antibiotic. Use: treatment of childhood cancers.

actinouranium /áktinō yoo ráyni əm/ *n* the only naturally occurring, naturally fissile, radioactive isotope of uranium. Use: nuclear reactors, weapons.

action /áksh'n/ *n* **1 DOING SOMETHING TOWARD GOAL** the process of doing something in order to achieve a purpose **2 SOMETHING DONE** something that somebody or something does **3 MOVEMENT** the way somebody or something moves or works, or the movement itself ○ *the action of a piston* **4 VERVE** energetic activity ○ *a woman of action* **5 LEGAL PROCEEDINGS** legal proceedings in a court to obtain compensation for something or to enforce a right ○ *decided not to take action* **6 EVENTS** the important events in any form of narrative composition such as a novel or film **7 FUNCTION OR INFLUENCE** the way in which something functions, or the effect it produces ○ *the action of water on stone* **8 FIGHTING DURING WAR** a small battle, or the fighting that takes place during a war ○ *wounded in action* ○ *a campaign of brief actions* **9 EXCITING OR PROFITABLE ACTIVITY** involvement in something that brings excitement, profit, or pleasure (*informal*) ○ *a piece of the action* **10 OPERATING MECHANISM** the operating parts of a mechanism or instrument, e.g. a watch or piano **11 SPACE UNDER STRINGS** the space between the fingerboard and strings of a string instrument such as a violin or a guitar **12 FORCE** the force applied to a body **13 PROPERTY OF SYSTEM USED IN DYNAMICS** twice the average kinetic energy of a system in a given time multiplied by the time **14 VOLUNTARY BEHAVIOUR** voluntary or intended behaviour, as opposed to forced behaviour ■ *interj* **START PERFORMING** a command from a film director telling actors to begin acting as filming has begun ■ *vt* ⚠ **PUT INTO OPERATION** to take action on something such as a proposal or request.

USAGE The use of ***action*** as a verb, as in *Criticism was levelled at the way the operation was actioned*, has crept into ordinary usage from business jargon. It is disliked by people who maintain that simpler words such as *do*, *achieve*, and *complete* are just as effective. The use is particularly unwelcome in cases such as *to action dismissal*, as in *Dismissal will be actioned if any employee violates this rule*, when a simple verb is available (*Any employee who violates this rule will be dismissed*). It is always better to use the more straightforward word when this conveys the meaning just as well.

---

actionable /áksh'nəb'l/ *adj* giving a basis for somebody to take legal action

actioner /áksh'nər/ *n* a film that features a great deal of usually extreme action (*informal*) ○ *a made-for-TV actioner with a little-known cast*

action group *n* a group of people formed to achieve some purpose, e.g. to support or oppose a proposal

action-packed *adj* involving or containing a large number of exciting events

action painting *n* a technique used by artists of the Abstract Expressionism movement in which paintings are created by splashing, dripping, spattering, or smearing paint

action potential *n* a temporary change in electrical potential that occurs between the inside and the outside of a nerve or muscle fibre when a nerve impulse is transmitted

action replay *n* a reshowing of a brief part of a televised event, often in slow motion. US term **instant replay**

action stations *npl* **POST FOR COMBAT** the posts assigned to people in combat. US term **battle stations** *npl.* ■ *interj* **1 GO TO COMBAT POSTS** used as a command ordering people to take up the posts assigned to them during or in readiness for combat. US term **battle stations** *interj.* 1 **2 GET READY** used to warn people to get ready to carry out their assigned tasks (*informal*) US term **battle stations** *interj.* 2

activate /ákti vayt/ (**-vates, -vating, -vated**) *v* **1** *vt* **MAKE SOMETHING ACTIVE** to make something active **2** *vi* **BECOME ACTIVE** to become active or begin to operate **3** *vt* **MAKE SOMETHING RADIOACTIVE** to make something radioactive **4** *vt* **MAKE SOMETHING REACTIVE** to increase the rate of a chemical reaction **5** *vt* **INCREASE POWER OF ADSORPTION** to treat a substance such as charcoal so as to increase its capacity for adsorption **6** *vt* **PREPARE BY STIMULATION OR CONVERSION** to prepare an organ, body part, or body chemical for activity by stimulating it or converting an inactive form into one capable of action **7** *vt* **PURIFY WITH AIR** to purify sewage by aerating it —**activation** /ákti váysh'n/ *n* —**activator** *n*

activated alumina *n* a highly adsorbent form of aluminium oxide. Use: removing moisture from gases, filtering oil, catalyst.

activated carbon, activated charcoal *n* a highly adsorbent powdered or granular form of carbon. Use: liquid and gas purification, chemical extraction, solvent recovery, poison antidote.

activated sludge *n* aerated sewage containing microorganisms added to untreated sewage to purify it by accelerating its bacterial decomposition

activation energy *n* the energy needed to make molecules of a substance take part in a chemical reaction

active /áktiv/ *adj* **1 MOVING ABOUT** moving about, working, or doing something as opposed to resting or sleeping **2 BUSY** full of or involved in busy activity ○ *an active life* **3 DOING** carrying out some action or process, or able to do so ○ *an active ingredient* **4 SHOWING ENERGY AND INVOLVEMENT** marked by involvement, energy, or action ○ *played an active part* **5 NEEDING AND USING ENERGY** requiring a lot of energy and movement ○ *active pastimes* **6 NOT EXTINCT** describes a volcano that is not extinct and still erupts occasionally **7 RELATING TO ROLE OF VERB'S SUBJECT** describes a verb whose subject is the person or thing performing the action described by the verb. ◊ **passive** *adj.* 5 **8 SHOWING VARIABLE SURFACE FEATURES** describes the sun when it is displaying large numbers of dark patches (**sunspots**) and bright patches (**faculae**) and high variability in radio-wave emissions **9 USED TO PRODUCE PROFIT** producing or being used to produce profits or dividends **10 TRADING IN LARGE VOLUME** being bought and sold in large quantities **11 INVOLVING FREQUENT TRADING** describes a form of portfolio management in which the manager adds value to the portfolio by frequent trades **12 WITH POWER SOURCE** describes electronic networks and components that contain a power source and are capable of operating ■ *n* **VERB VOICE** the active voice of a verb —**actively** *adv* —**activeness** *n*

ϟ**active cell** *n* a spreadsheet cell in which values or formulas may be entered

active duty, active service *n US* full-time service in the armed forces with full pay and benefits

active immunity *n* immunity generated by the production of antibodies within a body when it is exposed to antigens

active list *n* a list of officers on or available for full duty

ϟ**active-matrix display** *n* a flat liquid-crystal display with high colour resolution that is particularly suited to use in laptop and notebook computers

ϟ**active server page** *n* a page in HyperText Markup Language with scripts that are processed on a server before being sent to a user

active service *n* **1** service with the armed forces in an operational area **2** *US* MIL = **active duty**

active site *n* the part of an enzyme molecule that binds the substance the enzyme acts on (**substrate**)

active transport *n* the movement of substances across cell membranes from low to high concentrations, requiring energy and carrier proteins

active vocabulary *n* the range of words that somebody normally uses in speech or writing

activism /áktivizəm/ *n* vigorous and sometimes aggressive action in pursuing a political or social end —**activist** *n, adj* —**activistic** /ákti vístik/ *adj*

activity /ak tívvəti/ (*plural* **-ties**) *n* **1 SOMETHING SOMEBODY DOES** something that somebody takes part in or does (*often plural*) **2 PHYSICAL EXERCISE** energetic physical movement or exercise **3 STATE OF DOING** work, movement, or whatever somebody or something is doing ○ *Activity in the newsroom has reached fever pitch.* **4 MEASURE OF POTENTIAL FOR CHEMICAL REACTION** the ability of a substance to undergo a chemical reaction **5 NATURAL PROCESS** a process or function that takes place naturally in a living organism ○ *activities such as eating or sleeping* **6 LEARNING EXPERIENCE** an educational exercise designed to provide direct experience of something ○ *an activity to accompany the geography lesson* **7 RADIOACTIVITY** (*symbol A*) radioactivity (*technical*)

act of contrition *n* a short prayer of penitence

act of faith *n* an action motivated by belief in something for which there is no concrete evidence

act of God n a sudden uncontrollable event produced by natural forces, e.g. an earthquake or a tornado

actomyosin /áktō mí əssin/ n a complex of actin and myosin formed in muscle cells during contraction

actor /áktər/ n 1 somebody who acts in plays, films, or television 2 somebody who pretends to be somebody else or to feel something

actress /áktrəss/ n 1 a woman or girl who acts in plays, films, or television 2 a woman who behaves in a way intended to deceive or impress others (*disapproving*)

Acts of the Apostles n a book of the Bible in which the early history of the Christian church is described (+ *singular verb*)

actual /ákchoo əl, ákchəl/ adj 1 REAL real and existing as fact ○ *Is that her actual title?* 2 △ USED FOR EMPHASIS used for emphasis, e.g. to stress that somebody or something being referred to is genuinely the person or thing involved ○ *This is the actual place where Wellington stood.* 3 EXISTING NOW existing or occurring at the moment ○ *actual as opposed to projected income*

USAGE **Actual** is often overused as a mere emphatic term, often without any real meaning: *He wanted to know if any (actual) damage had been done.* In this sentence **actual** could be removed without any significant change to the sense. In the sentence *The actual total was much higher than we had expected,* **actual** is legitimately used to mark a contrast with projected or estimated totals.

actualise vti = actualize

actuality /ákchoo álləti/ (plural **-ties**) n 1 something that is real, as opposed to what is expected, intended, or feared ○ *Let's deal with actualities.* 2 everything that does or could exist or happen in real life

actualize /ákchoo ə līz/ (-izes, -izing, -ized), **actualise** (-ises, -ising, -ised) vt 1 to make something real or actual ○ *expectations actualized by deeds* 2 to portray or represent something realistically —**actualization** /ákchoo ə lī záysh'n/ n

actually /ákchoo əli, ákchəli/ adv 1 △ used to emphasize that something really is so or really exists, e.g. when it may be hard to believe or contrasts with what has already been said ○ *He's actually over 35, although he looks much younger.* 2 used to express an opinion, often a contradictory one, or to change the subject ○ *Actually I'd prefer it if you left right now.* ○ *He's in India – he's always wanted to go there, actually*

USAGE **Actually**, like **actual**, is used most effectively when it contrasts with what is theoretical or only apparent: *It sounds difficult, but it's actually quite straightforward.* It is regarded as poor style to use it as a sentence filler with no real meaning, although this practice is common in informal conversation: *Actually, I prefer her to her cousin.*

actuarial /ákchoo áiri əl/ adj 1 relating to the statistical calculation of risk or life expectancy for insurance purposes 2 relating to actuaries and their work

actuarial science n the branch of statistics that deals with the calculation of risk, life expectancy, and insurance premiums

actuary /ákchoo əri/ (plural **-ies**) n a statistician who calculates insurance premiums, risks, dividends, and annuity rates

actuate /ákchoo ayt/ (-ates, -ating, -ated) vt 1 to make somebody act or behave in a certain way (*often passive*) ○ *actuated by self-interest* 2 to make a device move or start working (*formal*) [Late 16C. < medieval Latin *actuatus*, past participle of *actuare* 'cause something to be done' < Latin *actus* (see ACT).] —**actuation** /ákchoo áysh'n/ n —**actuator** n

ACT-UP /ákt up/ n an Aids activist organization in the United States and United Kingdom. Full form **Aids Coalition To Unleash Power**

acuity /ə kyoo əti/ n keenness of hearing, sight, or intellect [Mid-16C. Directly or via French *acuité* < medieval Latin *acuitas* < Latin *acuere* (see ACUTE).]

aculeate /ə kyoōli ət/ adj 1 describes an insect that has a sting 2 describes a plant or plant part that has prickles [Mid-17C. < Latin *aculeatus* < *aculeus* 'small needle' < *acus* (see ACUTE).]

acumen /ákyoōmən/ n the ability to make quick accurate judgments of people or situations ○ *political acumen* [Late 16C. < Latin, 'point, sharpness' < *acuere* (see ACUTE).]

acuminate adj /ə kyoóminət/ describes leaves that taper to a sharp point [Late 16C. < late Latin *acuminatus*, past participle of *acuminare* 'sharpen to a point' < Latin *acumen* (see ACUMEN).]

acupressure /ákyoō preshər/ n a form of alternative therapy similar to acupuncture that uses manual pressure rather than needles [Mid-19C. Acu- < ACUPUNCTURE.]

acupuncture /ákyoō pungkchər/ n the treatment of disorders by inserting needles into the skin at points where the flow of energy is thought to be blocked (**meridians**) [Late 17C. Acu- < Latin *acus* 'needle'.] —**acupuncturist** n

~~**accurate**~~ incorrect spelling of **accurate**

acute /ə kyoōt/ adj 1 VERY GREAT OR BAD extremely serious, severe, or painful ○ *an acute financial crisis* 2 PERCEPTIVE keenly perceptive and intelligent ○ *an acute grasp of foreign affairs* 3 SENSITIVE very powerful and sensitive to detail ○ *acute eyesight* 4 LESS THAN 90° describes an angle that is less than 90° 5 WITH ANGLES LESS THAN 90° describes a triangle that has three internal angles of less than 90° 6 SEVERE AND OF SHORT DURATION describes a disease that is brief, severe, and quickly comes to a crisis 7 POINTED describes leaves that end in a short narrow point ■ n **acute, acute accent** MARK ABOVE LETTER in some languages, a mark placed above a letter to show it is sounded in a particular way, as in á, ó [14C. < Latin *acutus*, past participle of *acuere* 'sharpen' < *acus* 'needle'.] —**acutely** adv —**acuteness** n

USAGE See **chronic**.

acute arch n ARCHIT = lancet arch

acute dose n a fatal amount of radiation received over a short period

acute lymphocytic leukaemia n a form of leukaemia affecting mainly children, characterized by anaemia, weight loss, bone pain, and fatigue

acute nonlymphocytic leukaemia n a form of leukaemia affecting mainly adults, characterized by anaemia, fatigue, and weight loss

ACW abbr aircraftwoman

acyclic /ay síklik, -síklik/ adj 1 having a molecular structure in which the atoms are arranged in a string whose ends do not meet (**open chain**) 2 describes flowers that have their parts arranged in a spiral rather than a whorl

acyclovir /ay síklə veer/ n an antiviral drug. Use: treatment of herpes and cold sores.

acyl /áy síl/ adj relating to or containing the chemical group derived from a carboxylic acid, e.g. the acetyl group

acylation /áy sī láysh'n/ n the introduction of an acyl group into a chemical compound

acyl chloride n a chemical group containing the compound -COCl

ad[1] /ad/ n an advertisement (*informal*) [Mid-19C. Shortening.]

⚡ad[2] abbr Andorra (*in Internet addresses*)

ad[3] abbr advantage

AD[1], **A.D.** adv used to indicate a date that is a specified number of years after the birth of Jesus Christ [< Latin *anno domini* 'in the year of our Lord']

USAGE **AD** before or after the date? Because of its literal Latin meaning, AD is traditionally put before the numeral to which it relates, so that it makes grammatical sense if understood in its expanded form: AD 1453. In practice, AD is often put after the numeral, and it is normally acceptable to put it after the identification of a century, as in *the fifth century* AD. Some writers prefer to use PE (Present Era) or CE (Common Era) as alternatives in order to avoid the association with Christianity.

AD[2] abbr Alzheimer's disease

ad-, ac-, af-, ag-, as-, ap- prefix 1 to, toward ○ *adsorb* ○ *advance* 2 near ○ *adrenal* [< Latin *ad* 'towards, near' < Indo-European]

-ad suffix to, toward ○ *cephalad* [< Latin *ad* (see AD-)]

⚡A/D abbr **A/D** analog to digital

⚡Ada /áydə/ n a high-level general-purpose programming language used for military and other complex applications [Late 20C. After the English mathematician Augusta *Ada* Byron, Countess of Lovelace (1815–52).]

ADA deficiency n a genetic disease resulting from the deficiency of a metabolic enzyme (**adenosine deaminase**) characterized by low numbers of certain lymphomas and increased susceptibility to lymphomas and chronic infections [*ADA* shortening of adenosine deaminase]

adage /áddij/ n a traditional saying that expresses something taken as a general truth ○ *'Oysters are said to be best in months containing the letter R, according to an old adage'.* (Barbara Sturm, *Living Page*; 1997) [Mid-16C. Via French < Latin *adagium* < *ad* 'to' + variant of *aio* 'I say'.]

adagio /ə daaji ō/ adv slowly, but faster than lento (*musical direction*) ■ n (*plural* **adagios**) a movement or piece of music played or marked adagio [Late 17C. < Italian, 'at ease'.] —**adagio** n

Adam /áddəm/ n in the Bible, the first man, created by God ○ **not know somebody from Adam** to have never met or seen somebody before ○ **the old Adam** a natural tendency in people to do wrong

Adam /áddəm/, **Adolphe Charles** (1803–56) French composer

Adam, Robert (1728–92) British architect and interior designer

Adama-Eastern /ə daamə-/ n a branch of the Niger-Congo family of languages, spoken in N Central Africa [After the Fula Muslim leader Modibbo *Adama* (died 1848)] —**Adama-Eastern** adj

adamant /áddəmənt/ adj very determined and not influenced by appeals to reconsider ○ *'They did their best to persuade her, but Mother was adamant'.* (Gerald Durrell, *Birds, Beasts and Relatives*; 1969) ■ n an extremely hard legendary stone, sometimes identified as diamond or lodestone (*archaic*) [Pre-12C. Via Old French *adamaunt* and Latin *adamant-* 'adamant, steel, diamond' < Greek *adamas* 'unbreakable' < *daman* 'break down'.] —**adamantly** adv

adamantine /áddə mán tīn/ adj (*literary*) 1 extremely hard or unyielding 2 like a diamond in hardness and brilliance

Adamawa-Eastern /áddə maàwə-/ n one of the major branches of the Niger-Congo family of African languages [Mid-20C. After the *Adamawa* Massif in Cameroon.] —**Adamawa-Eastern** adj

Adamite /áddə mīt/ n 1 a human being regarded as a descendant of Adam 2 a member of a Christian religious group in 2nd-century North Africa whose members preferred not to wear clothes

Adamov, Arthur (1908–70) Russian poet and dramatist

Adams /áddəmz/, **Abigail** (1744–1818) US feminist

Adams, Ansel (1902–84) US photographer

Adams, Gerry (b. 1948) Northern Irish politician

Adams, John (1735–1826) US statesman and 2nd president of the United States (1797–1801)

John Quincy Adams

Adams, John Quincy (1767–1848) US statesman and 6th president of the United States (1825–29)

Adams, Philip Andrew (b. 1939) Australian writer and film producer

Adam's apple n the hard lump at the front of the throat formed by the thyroid cartilage of the larynx [< the belief that it results from the forbidden apple being stuck in Adam's throat]

Adam-Smith /áddəm smíth/, **Patsy** (b. 1926) Australian writer and historian

Adam's needle *n* a yucca with spiny pointed leaves. Flowers: white, in spikes. Native to: North America. *Yucca filamentosa*. [In allusion to Adam and Eve sewing fig leaves together to cover themselves (Genesis 3:7)]

Adana /áddənə/ city in S Turkey and capital of Adana province. Population: 1,047,300 (1994 est.).

adapt /ə dápt/ *v* **1** *vti* CHANGE SOMETHING TO MEET REQUIREMENTS to change, or change something, to suit different conditions or a different purpose ○ *adapted the novel for radio* **2** *vti* ADJUST TO to make or become used to a new environment or different conditions **3** *vt* REWRITE BOOK OR PLAY to rewrite a book or a play so that it can be made into a film or a television programme [15C. Via French *adapter* and Latin *adaptare* 'fit to' < *aptus* 'attached'.]

USAGE adapt or **adopt**? ***Adapt*** means 'to change something to meet requirements', 'to adjust to something', or 'to rewrite something', as in *adapted* [not *adopted*] *the cottage to a year-round dwelling; flora and fauna that had adapted* [not *adopted*] *to an arid climate; adapted* [not *adopted*] *the novel for television.* ***Adopt*** means 'to raise legally another's child', 'to choose and decide to use something', and 'to assume a behaviour pattern', as in *adopted* [not *adapted*] *two boys; adopted* [not *adapted*] *a new ideology; adopted* [not *adapted*] *an attitude of superiority.*

adaptable /ə dáptəb'l/ *adj* **1** able to adjust easily to changes and new conditions **2** capable of being modified to suit different purposes or conditions ○ *adaptable for different voltages* —**adaptability** /ə dáptə bílləti/ *n* —**adaptableness** *n* —**adaptably** *adv*

adaptation /áddap táysh'n, -əp-/, **adaption** /ə dápsh'n/ *n* **1** ADAPTING the process or state of changing to fit new circumstances or conditions, or the resulting change **2** SOMETHING ADAPTED TO FIT NEED something that has been modified for a purpose ○ *a film adaptation of a novel* **3** CHANGE TO SUIT ENVIRONMENT the development of physical and behavioural characteristics that allow organisms to survive and reproduce in their habitats **4** DIMINISHING SENSORY RESPONSE the diminishing response of a sense organ to a sustained stimulus —**adaptational** *adj* —**adaptationally** *adv*

adapter /ə dáptər/, **adaptor** *n* **1** ELECTRIC CONNECTOR a device used to connect an electrical appliance to a power source with a different voltage or a different plug shape, or several appliances to one mains socket **2** DEVICE FOR CONNECTING UNLIKE PARTS a device for connecting two nonmatching parts **3** SOMEBODY OR SOMETHING THAT ADAPTS somebody who or something that changes something or is able to adjust

adaption *n* = **adaptation**

adaptive /ə dáptiv/ *adj* able to be adjusted for use in different conditions —**adaptively** *adv*

adaptive radiation *n* the evolutionary diversification of a group of organisms from an ancestral form into several different forms that adapt to different environments

adaptive reuse *n* a use of a building that is different from its original or previous use, often involving conversion work

adaptor *n* = **adapter**

Adar /ə daár/ *n* in the Jewish calendar, the sixth month of the civil year and the twelfth month of the religious year, renamed Adar Rishon in leap years [14C. < Hebrew *ădār*.]

Adar Rishon /-ríshon/ *n* in the Jewish calendar, the name given to the month of Adar during a leap year, when an additional month (**Adar Sheni**) follows it

Adar Sheni /-sháyni/ *n* a 13th month added to the Jewish calendar after Adar in leap years [*Sheni* < Hebrew *šēnî* 'second']

adaxial /ad áksi əl/ *adj* describes the upper side of a leaf or other surface that faces towards the stem. ◊ **abaxial**

⚡**ADC** *abbr* analogue-to-digital converter

Adcock /ád kok/, **Fleur** (*b.* 1934) New Zealand poet

⚡**A-D conversion** *n* an electronic process that converts an analogue signal to a multilevel digital signal

ad court *n* the left-hand side of a tennis court, from which alternate, odd points are played [< shortening of ADVANTAGE]

add /ad/ *v* **1** *vt* UNITE OR COMBINE THINGS to put something into or join something onto something else ○ *I'll add your name to the list.* **2** *vti* FIGURE TOTAL to calculate the total of two or more numbers or amounts **3** *vt* PUT IN INGREDIENT to mix in an ingredient that is part of a recipe ○ *Add six eggs to the flour.* **4** *vt* INTRODUCE to give something a particular quality or more of a particular quality ○ *The flowers add a touch of cheerfulness.* **5** *vi* INTENSIFY to increase the effect of something ○ *This adds to our problems.* **6** *vt* SUPPLEMENT SPEECH OR WRITING to say or write something else after you have written or said something ○ *'Don't forget your umbrella', she added.* [14C. < Latin *addere* < *dare* 'give'.] —**addable** *adj*

add up *v* **1** *vti* MAKE TOTAL to calculate the total of two or more numbers or amounts **2** *vi* MAKE SENSE to make a sensible or believable story or explanation ○ *His story just doesn't add up.* **3** *vi* FORM LARGE AMOUNT to make a large total or amount ○ *If everyone gives a little, it soon adds up.*

add up to *vt* to amount to or result in a particular sum or thing

ADD *abbr* attention deficit disorder

add. *abbr* **1** addendum **2** addition **3** address

addax /áddaks/ (*plural* **-daxes** *or* **-dax**) *n* an antelope that has long spiralling horns. Native to: desert regions of North Africa. *Addax nasomaculatus*. [Late 17C. < Latin, < an African word.]

addend /áddend, ə dénd/ *n* a number that is to be added [Late 17C. Shortening of ADDENDUM.]

addendum /ə déndəm/ (*plural* **-da** /-də/) *n* **1** something that is or has been added **2** a supplement to a book or magazine [Late 17C. < Latin, < *addere* (see ADD).]

adder[1] /áddər/ *n* somebody or something that adds, especially an electronic device that adds numbers

adder[2] /áddər/ *n* a small venomous snake that is dark grey with a black zigzag pattern on its back. Native to: Europe. *Vipera berus*. [Old English *nǣd(d)re* 'snake' < Germanic. The initial *n* was lost when 'a nadder' was misanalysed as 'an adder'.]

adder's tongue *n* **1** a fern with a spore-bearing stalk at the base of a pointed frond. Native to: N hemisphere. Genus: *Ophioglossum*. **2** PLANTS = **dogtooth violet**

addict /áddikt/ *n* **1** somebody who is dependent on a potentially damaging drug **2** a devotee of something ○ *soap opera addicts* [Mid-16C. < Latin *addictus*, past participle of *addicere* 'award, devote' < *dicere* 'say'.]

addicted /ə díktid/ *adj* **1** physiologically or mentally dependent on a harmful drug **2** very interested in something and devoting a lot of time to it ○ *addicted to football*

addiction /ə díksh'n/ *n* **1** a state of physiological or psychological dependence on a drug liable to have a damaging effect **2** great interest in something to which a lot of time is devoted

addictionology /ə díksh'n ólləji/ *n* the study and treatment of addictions —**addictionologist** *n*

addictive /ə díktiv/ *adj* making or likely to make somebody an addict —**addictively** *adv*

addictive personality *n* a personality predisposed towards becoming addicted to something

⚡**add-in** *n* COMPUT = **add-on**

Addington /áddingtən/, **Henry, 1st Viscount Sidmouth** (1757–1844) British statesman

Addis Ababa /áddiss ábbəbə/ capital of Ethiopia. Population: 1,047,300 (1994 estimate).

Addison /áddiss'n/, **Joseph** (1672–1719) English essayist and politician

Addison, Thomas (1793–1860) British physician

Addison's disease *n* a wasting disease caused by underactivity of the adrenal glands and characterized by bronzing of the skin, low blood pressure, and weakness [Mid-19C. After Thomas ADDISON.]

addition /ə dísh'n/ *n* **1** PUTTING IN OR ON the act of adding something onto or into something else **2** SOMETHING ADDED something that or somebody who is added **3** CALCULATION the process of calculating the sum of two or more numbers or amounts **4** CHEMICAL REACTION a chemical reaction in which two or more compounds combine to produce a new compound ○ *an addition-type reaction* [14C. Directly or via French < Latin *addition-* < *additus*, past participle of *addere* (see ADD).] ◇ **in addition 1** used to introduce an additional point or a relevant fact **2** also ◇ **in addition to** as well as

additional /ə dísh'nəl/ *adj* added on to something else

additionality /ə díshə nálləti/ *n* a principle of funding in the European Union by which funds for a project are only granted to a member state if the latter also contributes

additionally /ə dísh'nəli/ *adv* **1** FURTHER further to what has just been said ○ *Additionally, each machine is checked hourly.* **2** EVEN MORE to an even greater extent (*literary*) ○ *'The atmosphere of the place was heavy and mouldy, being rendered additionally oppressive by the closing of the door which led into the church'.* (Wilkie Collins, *The Woman in White*; 1860) **3** ALSO as well as

Additional Member System *n* a method of voting in which votes are cast separately for parties and candidates and parties may acquire extra seats according to their share of the total vote. ◊ **proportional representation**

additive /áddətiv/ *n* something added to something else to alter or improve it in some way, e.g. to change the colour or texture of food ■ *adj* involving or produced by addition or by the addition of something (*formal*) [Late 17C. < late Latin *additivus* < *additus* (see ADDITION).]

additive identity *n* a quantity that, when added to another, leaves it unchanged. For ordinary numbers this is zero.

additive inverse *n* a number or quantity that gives zero when added to another. For example, the additive inverse of 3 is –3.

additive printing *n* a process in printing in which colours are produced by adding proportionate amounts of three primary colours

addle /ádd'l/ (**-dles, -dling, -dled**) *vti* **1** to confuse or muddle somebody, or become confused or muddled **2** to make something rotten or spoiled [Old English *adela* 'filth, liquid manure' < Germanic]

⚡**add-on, add-in** *n* a piece of computer equipment added to another to expand its capabilities

⚡**address** /ə dréss/ *n* **1** PHYSICAL LOCATION the number, street name, and other information that describes where a building is or where somebody lives **2** WRITTEN FORM OF ADDRESS the address of a person or organization when written on a letter or an item of mail **3** FORMAL TALK a formal speech or report **4** NUMBER FOR LOCATION a number that specifies a location in a computer's memory **5** STATEMENT FROM PARLIAMENT a statement of opinions or desires sent to the sovereign by either or both of the Houses of Parliament ■ **addresses** *npl* COURTSHIP attention paid to somebody that is intended as courtship (*archaic*) ■ *v* **1** *vt* WRITE DIRECTIONS ON to write or print on an item of mail details of where it is to be delivered **2** *vt* SPEAK OR MAKE SPEECH TO to say something to somebody, or make a speech to an audience **3** *vr* BEGIN JOB to set about doing some task ○ *'Through this program of action we address ourselves to putting our own national house in order'* (Franklin D. Roosevelt, *First Inaugural Address*; 1933) **4** *vt* DEAL WITH to face up to and deal with a problem or issue ○ *failure to address the main issue* **5** *vt* FACE to move to face or stand facing a target in a sport or a partner in a dance ○ *address the target* **6** *vt* AIM GOLF CLUB to take up the correct stance before hitting a golf shot ○ *address the ball* [14C. Via Old French *adresser* and assumed Vulgar Latin *addrictiare* 'direct to' < Latin *directus* (see DIRECT).] —**addressability** *n* —**addressable** *adj*

addressee /áddre sée, ə dréss ée/ *n* a person or organization to whom an item of mail is to be delivered

⚡**address harvester** *n* a computer program that collects e-mail addresses from the Internet

adduce /ə dyóoss/ (**-duces, -ducing, -duced**) *vt* to offer something as evidence, reason, or proof (*formal*) [15C. < Latin *adducere* 'bring forward' < *ducere* 'lead'.] —**adduceable** *adj*

adduct /ə dúkt, a-/ *vt* to pull a leg or arm towards the central line of the body or a toe or finger towards the axis of a leg or arm. ◊ **abduct** *v.* 2 ■ *n* a chemical compound formed by an addition reaction between two or more different compounds or elements [Mid-19C. Back-formation < *adduction*, directly or via French < Latin *adduction-* < *adductus*, past participle of *adducere* (see ADDUCE).] —**adduction** *n* —**adductive** *adj*

adductor /ə dúktər/ *n* a muscle that pulls a leg or arm towards the central line of the body or a toe or finger towards the axis of a leg or arm [Early 17C. < modern Latin, < Latin *adductus* (see ADDUCT).]

Ade /ayd/, **George** (1866–1944) US writer

-ade *suffix* **1** a sweetened drink ○ *orangeade* **2** an action ○ *cannonade* [Via Old French < Latin *-ata*, feminine of *-atus* (see -ATE)]

Adelaide /ádd'l ayd/ city in SE Australia. Population: 978,100 (1996).

Aden /áyd'n/ n 1 former British protectorate that is now part of Yemen 2 port and second largest city of Yemen. Population: 400,783 (1993 estimate).

aden- prefix = adeno- (before vowels)

Adenauer /áddə now ər/, **Konrad** (1876–1967) German statesman

adenectomy /áddə néktəmi/ (plural -mies) n the surgical removal of a gland

adenine /áddə neen/ n (symbol A) a purine base found in DNA, RNA, and energy-carrying molecules such as ATP

adenitis /áddə nítiss/ n inflammation of a gland or a lymph node

adeno-, **aden-** prefix gland ○ adenovirus [< Greek adēn]

adenocarcinoma /áddinō kaàrssi nómə/ (plural -mas or -mata /-mətə/) n 1 a malignant tumour in glandular tissue 2 a malignant tumour with cells arranged in patterns similar to those of a gland —**adenocarcinomatous** adj

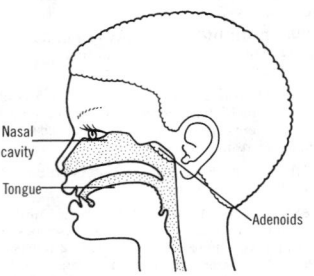

Nasal
cavity

Tongue

Adenoids

Adenoids

adenoid /áddə noyd/ adj 1 RELATING TO GLANDS relating to or similar to a gland 2 CONCERNING LYMPHOID TISSUE relating to lymphoid tissue 3 ANAT = adenoidal adj. 1 ■ adenoids npl THROAT TISSUE a mass of tissue at the back of the nose and throat that can restrict breathing if enlarged

adenoidal /áddi nóyd'l/ adj 1 displaying symptoms caused by enlarged adenoids, e.g. a nasal voice or breathing difficulties 2 relating to the adenoids

adenoidectomy /áddi noy déktəmi/ (plural -ies) n surgical removal of adenoids

adenoma /áddi nómə/ (plural -mas or -mata /-mətə/) n 1 a benign tumour in glandular tissue 2 a benign tumour with cells arranged in patterns similar to those found in a gland —**adenomatoid** adj

adenoma sebaceum /-sə báyshəm/ n a skin condition of the face characterized by raised, red, vascular bumps, usually begining in late childhood or early adolescence [< modern Latin, 'sebaceous adenoma']

adenopathy /áddi nóppəthi/ (plural -nopathies) n a diseased condition, e.g. inflammation or enlargement, in a gland or lymph node

adenosine /ə dénnō seen/ n a compound of adenine and a ribose found in nucleic acids and energy-carrying molecules such as ATP [Early 20C. Blend of ADENINE + RIBOSE.]

adenosine deaminase n an enzyme that catalyses the removal of an amino group from adenosine to form inosine during purine metabolism

adenosine diphosphate full form of ADP[1] n.

adenosine monophosphate /-monō fós fayt/ full form of AMP n.

adenosine triphosphatase /-trī fósfə tayz/ n an enzyme that catalyses the breakdown of ATP into ADP with energy release

adenosine triphosphate full form of ATP[1] n.

adenosis /áddi nóssiss/ n 1 the abnormal enlargement or development of a gland 2 any disease characterized by adenosis

adenovirus /áddinō vírəss/ n a virus that causes respiratory infections in humans [< its occurrence in adenoid tissue]

adenylate cyclase /ə dénnə layt-/, **adenyl cyclase** /áddənīl-/ n an enzyme involved in the formation of cyclic AMP from ATP

adept adj /ə dépt/ highly proficient or expert ■ n /ádd ept/ somebody who is highly proficient or expert at something [Mid-17C. < Latin adeptus, past participle of adipisci 'acquire' < apisci 'pursue'.] —**adeptly** adv —**adeptness** n

adequate /áddikwət/ adj 1 sufficient in quality or quantity to meet a need 2 just barely sufficient in quality or quantity to meet a need or qualify for something [Late 16C. < Latin adaequatus, past participle of adaequare 'make equal, match' < aequus 'even'.] —**adequacy** n —**adequately** adv —**adequateness** n

~~adequatly~~ incorrect spelling of **adequately**

Ader /a dáir/, **Clément** (1841–1926) French engineer

à deux /aa dő/ adv, adj involving only two people and therefore private [Late 19C. < French.]

ADH abbr antidiuretic hormone. ◊ **vasopressin**

ADHD abbr attention deficit hyperactivity disorder

adhere /əd heer/ (-heres, -hering, -hered) vi 1 OBEY to be devoted in supporting or following somebody or something 2 SUPPORT to hold firmly to a belief, idea, or opinion 3 STICK FIRMLY to stick firmly to a surface or an object [15C. Directly or via French adhérer < Latin adhaerere < haerere 'stick'.] —**adherence** n

adherent /əd heerənt/ n a supporter of a cause or leader ■ adj able to stick firmly to a surface or an object (formal)

adhesion /əd heezh'n/ n 1 STICKING POWER the ability to stick firmly to something 2 ABSENCE OF SLIPPINESS the ability to make firm contact with a surface without slipping 3 SUPPORT loyal support for a cause or a leader 4 INTERMOLECULAR ATTRACTION the intermolecular attraction between substances that are unlike and in surface contact, causing them to cling together 5 JOINING OF BODY PARTS the joining of normally unconnected body parts by bands of fibrous tissue [15C. Directly or via French < Latin adhaesion- < adhaes-, past participle of adhaerere (see ADHERE).]

adhesive /əd heessiv, -ziv/ n a substance used to stick things together ■ adj able to stick to something or to stick things together [Late 17C. < Latin adhaes- (see ADHESION).] —**adhesively** adv —**adhesiveness** n

ad hoc /ad hók/ adj done or set up solely in response to a particular situation or problem and without considering wider issues ○ ad hoc measures [Mid-17C. < Latin, 'to this'.] —**ad hoc** adv

ad hocism /ad hókizəm/ n taking decisions or implementing measures according to the nature and needs of each specific case individually rather than on the basis of a set, well-thought-out policy (disapproving)

adhocracy /ad hókrəssi/ (plural -cies) n an organization with a fluid command structure that can alter to suit changing circumstances [Late 20C. Blend of AD HOC + BUREAUCRACY.]

ad hominem /ad hómmi nem/ adj 1 appealing to people's emotions and prejudices rather than their ability to think (formal) 2 S Africa on the basis of personal merit ○ ad hominem promotion [Late 16C. < Latin, 'to the person'.] —**ad hominem** adv

adiabatic /áddi ə báttik/ adj describes a thermodynamic process that happens without loss or gain of heat [Late 19C. < Greek adiabatos 'impassable' < diabainein 'go through'.] —**adiabatically** adv

adiaphorism /áddi áffərizəm/ n especially in Protestant Christianity, the view that things not specifically forbidden by the Scriptures may be treated with indifference [Early 17C. < Greek adiaphoros 'indifferent' < a- 'not' + diaphoros 'different'.] —**adiaphoristic** /-áffə rístik/ adj

~~adict~~ incorrect spelling of **addict**

Adie's pupil /áydiz-/ n a condition of the eyes in which one pupil is much larger than the other and less responsive to light [Early 20C. After Australian-born British neurologist William John Adie (1886–1935).]

adieu /ə dyoo/ interj, n (plural **adieux** /ə dyooz/ or **adieus** /ə dyooz/) used to say goodbye ○ '...the more gentle adieus of her sisters were uttered without being heard' (Jane Austen, Pride And Prejudice; 1813) [14C. < French, '(I commend you) to God'.]

Adi Granth /aàdi grúnt/ n the principal Sikh scripture, which contains the teachings of the first five gurus and also poems and hymns [< Sanskrit ādigrantha 'first book' < grantha 'tying, work of literature']

ad infinitum /ádd infi nítəm/ adv endlessly [Early 17C. < Latin, 'to infinity'.]

ad interim /ád intərim/ adv for the meantime [< Latin, 'to the meanwhile'.] —**ad interim** adj

adios /áddi óss/ interj used to say goodbye (informal) [Mid-19C. < Spanish, 'to God' (see ADIEU).]

adipic acid /ə díppik-/ n $C_6H_{10}O_4$ a white crystalline solid. Use: making nylon, the production of chemicals. [< Latin adip- 'fat' (see ADIPO-), because the acid was originally made by oxidizing fats]

adipo- prefix fat, fatty ○ adipocyte [< Latin adip-, stem of adeps 'fat']

adipocyte /áddi pō sīt/ n a cell that synthesizes and stores fat [Mid-20C. < modern Latin adiposus (see ADIPOSE).]

adipose /áddi pōss/ adj containing fat ■ n fat under the skin and surrounding major organs, providing stored energy, insulation, and protection [Mid-18C. < modern Latin adiposus 'fatty' < Latin adip- (see ADIPO-).] —**adiposeness** n —**adiposity** /áddi póssəti/ n

adipose tissue n connective tissue in animal bodies that contains fat

adipsin /ay dípsin/ n a protein that is believed to control appetite. Use: obesity treatment. [Late 20C. < adipsia 'abstaining from liquids']

Adirondack Mountains /áddə rón dak-/, **Adirondacks** /áddə rón daks/ mountain chain in NE New York State. Highest peak: Mount Marcy 1,629 m/5,344 ft.

adit /áddit/ n a nearly horizontal shaft used for giving access to a mine or for drainage [Early 17C. < Latin aditus 'approach, entrance' < past participle of adire 'go towards' < ire 'go'.]

adj. abbr 1 adjective 2 adjoint 3 adjunct 4 adjustment 5 adj., Adj. adjutant

adjacent /ə jáyss'nt/ adj 1 situated near or close to something or each other, especially without touching 2 describes either a pair of vertices in a graph that have common edges, or a pair of edges in a graph that have a common vertex [15C. < Latin adjacent-, present participle of adjacere 'lie near' < jacere 'lie'.] —**adjacency** n

USAGE adjacent or adjoining? Two houses are said to be **adjoining** when they are next to each other with a common wall. **Adjoining** tables are next to each other end to end, forming one surface (they are, to use a more technical word, contiguous). In other words, **adjoining** items join. **Adjacent** houses, on the other hand, can have a space between them or even be on opposite sides of the road, as long as there is nothing significant between them (e.g. another house) and they are close enough for you to pass easily from one to the other. **Adjacent** tables are next to each other but not necessarily touching. Note also that **adjoining**, being a form of a verb, can govern an object (the house adjoining ours), whereas **adjacent** needs the addition of to (the house adjacent to ours).

adjacent angle n either of the two angles that are formed by the intersection of two straight lines and lie on the same side of one line

adjective /ájjiktiv/ n WORD QUALIFYING NOUN a word that qualifies or describes a noun or pronoun ■ adj 1 ACTING AS ADJECTIVE relating to, forming, or functioning as an adjective 2 PRACTISED IN COURT relating to court practice and procedure rather than the principles of law. ◊ **substantive** adj. 7 [14C. Via French adjectif < Latin adjectivus < adjicere 'throw to' < jacere 'throw'.] —**adjectival** /ájjik tīv'l/ adj —**adjectivally** adv —**adjectively** adv

adjoin /ə jóyn/ v 1 vti to be next to or share a common border with something, especially an area of land ○ The two properties adjoin. 2 vt to attach or add to something (archaic) [14C. Via Old French ajoin-, stem of ajoindre < Latin adjungere 'join to' < jungere 'join'.]

adjoining /ə jóyning/ adj situated next to or touching something or each other

USAGE See **adjacent**.

adjoint /ájjoynt/ n a matrix formed from a given square matrix, each element being derived from its cofactors, the determinants of the given matrix obtained by removing the row and column containing the element [Late 16C. < French, past participle of adjoindre (see ADJOIN).]

adjourn /ə júrn/ *v* **1** *vti* **POSTPONE PROCEEDINGS** to suspend the business of a court, legislature, or committee temporarily or indefinitely, or become suspended temporarily or indefinitely ○ *The court adjourned at one o'clock.* **2** *vti* **POSTPONE** to postpone a meeting to another time, or become postponed **3** *vt* **DEFER** to defer a matter or an action to another time **4** *vi* **MOVE AS GROUP** to move together from one place to another **5** *vi* **STOP WORKING** to stop working (*informal*) [14C. < Old French *ajourner* < *à jorn (nomé)* 'to an (appointed) day'.] —**adjournment** *n*

adjournment debate *n* in the House of Commons, a debate on the motion that Parliament be adjourned, used as a formal device for raising other topics

Adjt *abbr* adjutant

adjudge /ə júj/ (**-judges, -judging, -judged**) *vt* **1** **MAKE DECLARATION ABOUT** to judge somebody or something in a particular way ○ *She was adjudged to be an accomplished musician.* **2** **DETERMINE JUDICIALLY** to decide something in a judicial proceeding **3** **DECREE LEGALLY** to pronounce something by law **4** **GRANT MONEY IN JUDGMENT** to make somebody an award of damages or costs in a legal judgment [14C. Via Old French *ajuger* < Latin *adjudicare* (see ADJUDICATE).]

adjudicate /ə jóodi kayt/ (**-cates, -cating, -cated**) *vti* **1** to reach a judicial decision on something **2** to make an official decision about a problem or dispute [Early 18C. < Latin *adjudicat-*, past participle of *adjudicare* 'award in arbitration' < *judic-* 'judge'.] —**adjudication** /ə jóodi káysh'n/ *n* —**adjudicative** /ə jóodikətiv/ *adj* —**adjudicator** *n*

adjunct /ájjungkt/ *n* **1** **SOMETHING EXTRA ADDED ON** something inessential added to something else **2** **ASSISTANT** an assistant or subordinate **3** **INESSENTIAL PART OF SENTENCE** a part of a sentence that is not the subject or predicate [Early 16C. < Latin *adjunctus*, past participle of *adjungere* (see ADJOIN).] —**adjunction** /ə júngksh'n/ *n* —**adjunctive** *adj*

adjure /ə jóor/ (**-jures, -juring, -jured**) *vt* **1** to order somebody to do something, especially under oath **2** to make an earnest appeal to somebody [14C. < Latin *adjurare* 'swear by oath' < *jurare* 'swear' (see JURY).] —**adjuration** /ájjoo ráysh'n/ *n* —**adjuratory** *adj* —**adjurer** *n*

adjust /ə júst/ *v* **1** *vt* **CHANGE SLIGHTLY** to make slight changes in something to make it fit or function better **2** *vti* **ADAPT TO NEW CIRCUMSTANCES** to adapt to a new environment or condition **3** *vt* **REARRANGE** to put something back in order, especially clothing, so that it is tidy **4** *vt* **DECIDE AMOUNT OF MONEY OWED** to decide what sums are payable in the settlement of an insurance claim [Early 17C. Via obsolete French *adjuster* < assumed Vulgar Latin *adjuxtare* 'put close to' < Latin *juxta* 'close'.] —**adjustability** /ə jústə bílləti/ *n* —**adjustable** *adj* —**adjustably** *adv* —**adjustment** *n*

adjustable-rate mortgage *n US* FIN = **variable-rate mortgage**

adjuster /ə júster/ *n US* INSUR = **loss adjuster**

adjutant /ájjootənt/ *n* an officer who acts as an administrative assistant to a commanding officer [Early 17C. < Latin *adjutant-*, present participle of *adjutare* 'keep on helping' < *adjuvare* (see ADJUVANT).]

adjutant general (*plural* **adjutants general**) *n* **1** an army general responsible for administration and personnel **2** an executive officer of an army general

adjutant stork *n* a carrion-eating stork with a pink neck and white feathers on its underside. Native to: Southeast Asia. *Leptoptilos dubius* and *Leptoptilos javanicus*. [< the similarity of its walk to that of a military staff officer]

adjuvant /ájjoovənt/ *n* **1** **DRUG-ENHANCING AGENT** a drug or agent added to another drug or agent to enhance its medical effectiveness **2** **ANTIGEN-ENHANCING DRUG** a substance injected along with an antigen to enhance the immune response stimulated by the antigen **3** **HELPING AGENT** something that helps or assists ■ *adj* **SUPPLEMENTARY** helping by supplementing [Late 16C. Directly or via French < Latin *adjuvant-*, present participle of *adjuvare* 'give help to' < *juvare* 'help'.]

Adler /áddlər/, **Alfred** (1870–1937) Austrian psychiatrist

ad lib /ád líb/ *adj* = **ad libitum** ■ *adv* **1** = **ad libitum** **2** without any advance preparation [Early 19C. Shortening of AD LIBITUM.]

ad-lib /ád líb/ *vti* (**ad-libs, ad-libbing, ad-libbed**) **IMPROVISE SPEECH OR PERFORMANCE** to make up a speech or a musical or dramatic performance on the spot without a fixed text or score ■ *adj* **UNPLANNED** improvised or made up on the spot ■ *n* **IMPROVISED REMARK IN PERFORMANCE** something said by an actor or other performer that is not in the script —**ad-libber** *n*

ad libitum /ád líbbitəm/ *adj, adv* to be performed in the way the performer chooses [Early 17C. < Latin, 'at your pleasure'.]

ad litem /ád lítem/ *adj* appointed by a court to represent a minor [Mid-18C. < Latin, 'for the purpose of a lawsuit'.]

Adm. *abbr* **1** Admiral **2** Admiralty

adman /ád man/ (*plural* **-men** /-men/) *n* a worker in advertising (*informal*)

admass /ád mass/ *n* the part of society that can be influenced by advertising or publicity [Mid-20C. Coined by the English writer J. B. Priestley from AD- + MASS.]

admeasure /ad mézhər/ (**-ures, -uring, -ured**) *vt* to divide something up to be shared out [14C. Via Old French *amesurer* < medieval Latin *admensurare* 'apply a measure to'.]

admin /ád min/ *n* **1** the administrative work involved in running a business or organization (*informal*) **2** *US* an administrative assistant [Mid-20C. Shortening.]

administer /əd mínnistər/ *v* **1** *vti* **BE IN CHARGE OF** to manage the affairs of a business, organization, or institution **2** *vt* **DISPENSE** to preside over the dispensation of something ○ *He administered justice in the fairest possible manner.* **3** *vt* **GIVE AS MEDICATION** to give somebody a measured amount of a medication, often also physically introducing it into the body **4** *vt* **PERFORM AS MEDICAL PROCEDURE** to apply a medical technique or procedure to somebody **5** *vt* **PERFORM AS RITUAL** to carry out a set ritual or religious ceremony on behalf of an individual or group **6** *vi* **SUPERVISE OATH-TAKING** to oversee the taking of an oath by somebody **7** *vi* **LOOK AFTER** to look after and tend to the needs of somebody **8** *vt* **ORGANIZE HANDOVER OF PROPERTY** to manage the distribution of a deceased person's property in accordance with the law [14C. Via Old French *aministrer* < Latin *administrare* 'serve, manage' < *ministrare* 'serve'.] —**administrable** *adj*

administrate /əd mínni strayt/ (**-trates, -trating, -trated**) *vti* to oversee or organize the affairs of something, especially a business, organization, or institution [Mid-16C. < Latin *administrat-*, past participle of *administrare* (see ADMINISTER).]

administration /əd mínni stráysh'n/ *n* **1** **MANAGEMENT OF BUSINESS** the management of the affairs of a business or organization **2** **MANAGEMENT STAFF** the staff of a business or institution whose task is to manage its affairs **3** **MANAGEMENT OF GOVERNMENT** the management of public affairs or the affairs of a government **4** **STAFF OF GOVERNMENT** a government's staff whose task is to manage its affairs **5** **TERM OF OFFICE** the duration of a particular office, usually a political one **6** **GOVERNMENT** a government, especially its executive branch **7** **LEGAL DISPOSAL OF ESTATE** the disposal or management of a deceased person's estate or an estate held in trust **8** **ADMINISTERING SOMETHING TO** the act of administering something such as an oath, medicine, or sacrament **9** **SOMETHING ADMINISTERED** something that is administered to somebody, especially an oath, medicine, or sacrament

administration order *n* **1** a court order appointing somebody to run a company in financial trouble, in order to return it to successful trading or to oversee the sale of its assets **2** a court order appointing somebody to administer the estate of a debtor

administrative /əd mínnistrətiv/ *adj* relating to the administration of a business or organization —**administratively** *adv*

administrative area *n* a part of a country under the control of a particular local government administration

administrative assistant *n* an employee whose task is to assist a superior with the day-to-day affairs of running a business or department

administrative law *n* the area of law dealing with the affairs of agencies of the executive branch of a government, and with the judicial review of public bodies generally

administrative officer *n* an employee who carries out administrative tasks in an institution or government body, usually at a fairly junior level

administrator /əd mínni straytər/ *n* **1** somebody whose job is to manage the affairs of a business or organization **2** somebody appointed by a court to manage the estate of a deceased person, especially when there is no competent executor

admirable /ádmərəb'l/ *adj* deserving to be admired [15C. < Latin *admirabilis* < *admirari* (see ADMIRE).] —**admirableness** *n* —**admirably** *adv*

admiral /ádmərəl/ *n* **1** the officer in command of a navy or fleet, of a rank above vice admiral **2** a brightly coloured butterfly of temperate regions. Family: Nymphalidae. ◊ **red admiral, white admiral** [13C. Via French *amiral* < Arabic *amir-al* 'commander of' in such phrases as *amir-al-bahr* 'commander of the sea'.] —**admiralship** *n*

Admiral of the Fleet *n* the officer of the highest rank in the Royal Navy

admiralty /ádmərəlti/ *n* the office or jurisdiction of an admiral

Admiralty *n* a former UK government department that administered the affairs of the Navy

Admiralty Board *n* the department of the British Ministry of Defence responsible for the administration of the Royal Navy

Admiralty Islands /ádmərəlti-/ island group in the W Pacific Ocean, part of Papua New Guinea. Area: 2,072 sq. km/800 sq. mi.

admiration /ádmə ráysh'n/ *n* **1** a feeling of pleasure, approval, and, often, surprise **2** something or somebody regarded with a feeling of pleasure, approval, and, often, surprise

SYNONYMS See ***regard***.

admire /əd mír/ (**-mires, -miring, -mired**) *vt* **1** to regard somebody or something with a feeling of pleasure, approval, and, often, surprise **2** to have a high opinion of somebody or something, e.g. a quality or attribute [Late 16C. Directly or via French *admirer* < Latin *admirari* 'wonder at' < *mirari* 'wonder'.] —**admirer** *n*

admiring /əd míring/ *adj* full of admiration for somebody or something —**admiringly** *adv*

~~**admision**~~ incorrect spelling of **admission**

~~**admissable**~~ incorrect spelling of **admissible**

admissible /əd míssəb'l/ *adj* **1** **ALLOWABLE** allowed to be done **2** **ALLOWED TO COME IN** able or deserving to enter **3** **ALLOWED TO BE GIVEN IN COURT** accepted as evidence in court [Early 17C. Directly or via French < medieval Latin *admissibilis* < Latin *admiss-* (see ADMISSION).] —**admissibility** /əd míssə bílləti/ *n* —**admissibleness** *n* —**admissibly** *adv*

admission /əd mísh'n/ *n* **1** **ENTRY** the right, ability, or permission to enter **2** **FEE FOR ENTRY** a fee paid for entrance to a place or event **3** **CONFESSION** a confession to having committed a crime or having made a mistake **4** **DECLARATION** an acknowledgment that something is true [15C. < Latin *admission-* < *admiss-*, past participle of *admittere* (see ADMIT).]

admissive /əd míssiv/ *adj* granting or showing admission

admit /əd mít/ (**-mits, -mitting, -mitted**) *v* **1** *vti* **CONFESS** to confess to having committed a crime or having made a mistake **2** *vti* **ACKNOWLEDGE TRUTH** to acknowledge that something is true ○ *You must admit it is a tempting offer.* **3** *vt* **ALLOW TO ENTER** to allow somebody or something entrance or access ○ *'Admits one'* **4** *vti* **OFFER POSSIBILITY** to permit the possibility of something ○ *Their conduct admits of only one explanation.* [14C. < Latin *admittere* 'let go into' < *mittere* 'let go'.]

admittance /əd mítt'nss/ *n* **1** **PERMISSION TO GO IN** the permission or right to enter a place **2** **ENTRANCE TO PLACE** physical entry to a place **3** **MEASURE OF FLOW OF CURRENT** (*symbol* Y) the reciprocal of impedance, a measure of the ability of an electrical current to flow

admittedly /əd míttidli/ *adv* as must be acknowledged

admix /əd míks/ *vt* to mix something into something else [Early 16C. Probably a back-formation < ADMIXTURE.]

admixture /əd míkschər/ *n* **1** **PRODUCT OF MIXING** something produced by mixing something into something else **2** **INGREDIENT** something added to something else by mixing **3** **PROCESS OF MIXING INGREDIENTS** the mixing of something into something else [Early 17C. < MIXTURE.]

admonish /əd mónnish/ *vt* **1** **REBUKE** to rebuke somebody mildly but earnestly **2** **ADVISE** to advise somebody to do or, more often, not to do something **3** **REPRIMAND OFFICIALLY** in the UK police force, to reprimand an employee severely for misconduct [14C. Anglicization of Old French *amonester* < assumed Vulgar Latin *admonere* < Latin *monere* 'warn'.] —**admonisher** *n* —**admonishment** *n*

admonition /ádmə nísh'n/ *n* **1** a mild but earnest rebuke **2** advice for or against doing something —**admonitory** /əd mónnitəri/ *adj*

⚡**ADN** *abbr* any day now (*in e-mails*)

ad nauseam /ad náwzi am/ *adv* to an extreme or annoying extent [Mid-17C. < Latin, 'to sickness'.]

~~ad nauseum~~ incorrect spelling of **ad nauseam**

adnexa /ad néksə/ *npl* adjoining structural parts of the body [Late 19C. < Latin, < *adnectere* 'tie together' < *nectere* 'tie'.] —**adnexal** *adj*

adnominal /əd nómmin'l/ *n* a word that modifies a noun [Mid-19C. < Latin *adnomen*, alteration of *agnomen* (see AGNOMEN).] —**adnominal** *adj*

adnoun /ád nown/ *n* an adjective that is used as a noun, e.g. 'meek' in 'Blessed are the meek' [Mid-18C. < AD- + NOUN, after *adverb*.]

ado /ə dóo/ *n* excited activity or bother [14C. Contraction of N English dialect *at do* < Old Norse *at* 'to' + DO.] ◊ **without further** *or* **more ado** without wasting any time

> **LITERARY LINK** *Much Ado About Nothing*, a play (1598?) by William Shakespeare. A comedy set in the court of the Duke of Messina in Sicily, it tells of the love of a soldier, Claudio, for the Duke's daughter, Hero, and the eventually unsuccessful attempts of Claudio's enemy, Don John, to prevent their marriage.

adobe /ə dóbi/ *n* **1** EARTHEN BRICK brick made from earth and straw and dried by the sun **2** BUILDING MADE OF ADOBE a structure made with adobe bricks **3** EARTH THAT FORMS ADOBE earth used to make adobe bricks [Mid-18C. Via Spanish < Arabic *at-tūb* 'the bricks'.]

adobe flat *n* in the United States, a gently sloping plain of clay soil deposited by desert floods

adolescence /ádda léss'nss/ *n* **1** the period from puberty to adulthood in human beings **2** the stage in the development of something such as a civilization before it reaches maturity

adolescent /ádda léss'n't/ *n* SOMEBODY IN PERIOD PRECEDING ADULTHOOD somebody who has reached puberty but is not yet an adult ■ *adj* **1** EXPERIENCING ADOLESCENCE going through the period of adolescence ○ *adolescent males* **2** HAPPENING DURING ADOLESCENCE typically occurring during the period of adolescence **3** IMMATURE typical of somebody who is immature [15C. Via French < Latin *adolescent-*, present participle of *adolescere* 'be nourished, grow up' < *alere* 'nourish'.]

~~adolesent~~ incorrect spelling of **adolescent**

Adonai /áddo ní/ *n* a name used in Judaism instead of the unspeakable name of God [14C. < Hebrew *'ădōnay*.]

Adonic /ə dónnik/ *adj* **1** OF CLASSICAL VERSE STYLE describes a line in classical verse consisting of a dactyl followed by either a spondee or trochee **2** RELATING TO ADONIS like or typical of Adonis ■ *n* CLASSICAL LINE OR POEM an Adonic line or poem [Late 16C. Via French < medieval Latin *adonicus* < Greek *Adōnis* (see ADONIS).]

Adonis /ə dóniss/ *n* **1** In Greek mythology, a handsome youth loved by Aphrodite and Persephone **2 Adonis, adonis** an extremely handsome young man [Late 16C. < Greek *Adōnis* < Phoenician *ædōnī* 'my lord'.]

adopt /ə dópt/ *vt* **1** LEGALLY RAISE ANOTHER'S CHILD to raise a child of other biological parents as if it were your own, in accordance with formal legal procedures **2** CHOOSE AND DECIDE TO USE to take up something such as a plan, idea, cause, or practice and use or follow it **3** ASSUME WAY OF ACTING to assume a particular attitude or way of behaving **4** TAKE OVER to take over something such as an idea that originated elsewhere and use it as your own **5** CHOOSE AS CANDIDATE to choose somebody as a political candidate **6** START USING to take on and use a new name or title **7** VOTE IN FAVOUR OF to vote to accept something such as a committee's decision or a parliamentary bill [15C. Directly or via French < Latin *adoptare* 'choose for yourself' < *optare* 'choose'.] —**adoptable** *adj* —**adopted** *adj* —**adoptee** *n* —**adopter** *n*

> **USAGE adopted** or **adoptive**? Parents who adopt a child have an *adopted* child, and the child has *adoptive* parents. Any children related to the parents by birth have an *adopted* brother or sister; the *adopted* child has *adoptive* siblings.

> **USAGE** See *adapt*.

adoption /ə dópsh'n/ *n* **1** a formal legal process to adopt a child **2** an instance of adopting somebody or something such as an idea, name, or attitude

adoptive /ə dóptiv/ *adj* describes a parent who adopts a child or somebody related to another by adoption (*see usage note*)

> **USAGE** See *adopt*.

adorable /ə dáwrəb'l/ *adj* charming, lovable, and usually very attractive —**adorability** /ə dáwrə bílləti/ *n* —**adorableness** *n* —**adorably** *adv*

adore /ə dáwr/ (**adores, adoring, adored**) *vt* **1** LOVE DEEPLY to love somebody intensely **2** WORSHIP to worship God, a god, or a spirit **3** LIKE VERY MUCH to like something or somebody very much (*informal*) [14C. Via Old French < late Latin *adorare* 'pray to' < Latin *orare* 'pray'.] —**adoration** /áddə ráysh'n/ *n* —**adorer** *n*

adoring /ə dáwring/ *adj* showing love or admiration for somebody —**adoringly** *adv*

adorn /ə dáwrn/ *vt* **1** to add decoration or ornamentation to something **2** to add to the beauty or glory of something or somebody [14C. Via Old French < Latin *adornare* 'embellish with ornaments' < *ornare* 'embellish'.] —**adorner** *n* —**adornment** *n*

ADP[1] *n* a chemical compound (**nucleotide**) involved in energy transfer reactions in living cells See **ATP**. Full form **adenosine diphosphate**

⚡**ADP**[2] *abbr* automatic data processing

Adrastea /ə drásti ə/ *n* a small natural satellite of Jupiter, discovered in 1979

ad rem /ad rém/ *adv* to the point or purpose [Late 16C. < Latin, 'to the matter or business'.] —**ad rem** *adj*

adren- *prefix* = **adreno-** (*before vowels*)

adrenal /ə dreen'l/ *adj* **1** relating to or on the kidneys **2** describes parts or effects of the adrenal glands ■ *n* ANAT = **adrenal gland** [Late 19C. < AD- + RENAL.] —**adrenally** *adv*

adrenalectomy /ə dreenə léktəmi/ (*plural* **-mies**) *n* the surgical removal of one or both of the adrenal glands

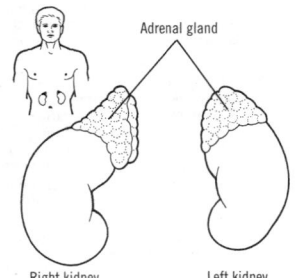

Adrenal glands

adrenal gland *n* an endocrine gland located above each kidney. The inner part (**medulla**) of each gland secretes adrenalin and the outer part (**cortex**) secretes steroids.

adrenalin /ə drénnəlin/, **adrenaline** *n* a hormone secreted by the adrenal glands and by some nerve endings, involved in the stress reaction (*often nontechnical*) ○ *get the adrenalin pumping* [Early 20C. < ADRENAL + -IN.]

> **USAGE adrenalin** or **adrenaline**? In British English, the usual spelling is *adrenalin*, but *adrenaline* is also used. In American usage, *adrenaline* is the more usual spelling, and *Adrenalin* (with a capital initial letter) is a trademark for a commercial drug. An alternative spelling, especially in American English, is *epinephrine*.

adrenergic /áddrə núrjik/ *adj* producing or activated by adrenalin or a similar substance —**adrenergically** *adv*

adreno-, adren- *prefix* pertaining to adrenaline or the adrenal glands ○ *adrenochrome* [< AD- + RENAL, because the adrenal glands are next to the kidneys]

adrenocortical /ə dreenō káwrtik'l/ *adj* involving, located in, or produced by the cortex of the adrenal glands

adrenocorticosteroid /ə dreenō káwrtikō steˈer oyd, -stérr oyd/ *n* **1** any steroid hormone released from the adrenal

cortex **2** a drug that mimics steroids produced by the adrenal cortex

adrenocorticotrophic /ə dreenō káwrtikō tróffik/, **adrenocorticotropic** /-tróppik/ *adj* describes hormones or drugs that stimulate the adrenal cortex to produce corticosteroids

adrenocorticotrophic hormone *n* full form of **ACTH**

adrenocorticotrophin /ə dreenō káwrtikō trófin/, **adrenocorticotropin** /-trópin/ *n* = **ACTH**

adrenocorticotropic *adj* = **adrenocorticotrophic**

adrenoleukodystrophy /ə dreenō loòka dístrəfi/ *n* a hereditary disorder of the nervous system in boys that affects the adrenal glands

adrenolytic /ə dreenō líttik/ *adj* blocking the action of the adrenergic nerves or inhibiting the response to adrenalin ■ *n* an adrenolytic drug or agent

adrenoreceptor /ə drénnō ri séptər/ *n* a nerve ending that is activated by adrenalin or related substances

~~adress~~ incorrect spelling of **address**

Adriatic Sea /áydri áttik-/ *arm* of the Mediterranean Sea, east of Italy. Area: about 155,000 sq. km/60,000 sq. mi.

adrift /ə dríft/ *adj, adv* **1** FLOATING WITHOUT DIRECTION floating freely without being steered in a particular direction **2** WITHOUT PURPOSE living life without a goal **3** OFF TARGET astray, off target, or amiss

adroit /ə dróyt/ *adj* **1** displaying physical or mental skill **2** able to react quickly in thought or actions [Mid-17C. < French *à droit* 'by right, properly'.] —**adroitly** *adv* —**adroitness** *n*

⚡**ADSL** *abbr* asymmetrical digital subscriber line

adsorb /ad sáwrb, -záwrb/ *vti* to undergo or cause something to undergo adsorption [Late 19C. Back-formation < ADSORPTION.] —**adsorbable** *adj*

adsorbate /ad sáwr bayt, -sáwrb-/ *n* a substance that is adsorbed

adsorbent /ad sáwrbənt, -záwrbənt/ *adj* able to adsorb ■ *n* a substance capable of adsorbing

adsorption /ad sáwrpsh'n, -záwrp-/ *n* the adhesion of a thin layer of molecules of some substance to the surface of a solid or liquid [Late 19C. Blend of AD- + ABSORPTION.] —**adsorptive** *adj*

adspend /ád spend/ *n* the amount of money spent on advertising for a particular product or campaign

ADT *abbr* US Atlantic Daylight Time

aduki bean *n* PLANTS, FOOD = **adzuki bean**

adularia /áddyoò láiri ə/ *n* a precious stone that is a white or transparent variety of the mineral orthoclase. Use: gems. [Late 18C. < French *adulaire* < *Adula*, mountains in the Swiss Alps where the mineral was first found.]

adulate /áddyoo layt/ (**-lates, -lating, -lated**) *vt* to admire or flatter somebody excessively [Mid-18C. Back-formation < ADULATION.] —**adulator** *n* —**adulatory** /áddyoò láytəri/ *adj*

adulation /áddyoò láysh'n/ *n* excessive flattery or admiration [14C. Directly or via French < Latin *adulation-* < *adulari* 'flatter'.]

adult /áddult, ə dúlt/ *adj* **1** COMPLETELY GROWN fully developed and mature **2** FOR SOMEBODY MATURE involving, typical of, or meant for mature people **3** UNSUITABLE FOR CHILDREN considered unsuitable for young people because of pornography, violence, or sexually explicit language ■ *n* **1** FULLY GROWN LIFE FORM a fully mature person, animal, plant, or other form of life **2** SOMEBODY LEGALLY AN ADULT somebody who has reached the age of legal majority [Mid-16C. < Latin *adultus*, past participle of *adolescere* (see ADOLESCENT).] —**adulthood** *n* —**adultness** *n*

adult education *n* = **continuing education** *n*. 1

adulterant /ə dúltərənt/ *n* something that makes something else less pure —**adulterant** *adj*

adulterate /ə dúltə rayt/ *vt* (**-ates, -ating, -ated**) MAKE IMPURE to make something less pure by adding inferior or unsuitable elements or substances to it ■ *adj* **1** IMPURE made less pure **2** ADULTEROUS adulterous (*literary*) [Mid-16C. < Latin *adulterat-*, past participle of *adulterare* 'change, corrupt, commit adultery' < *alterare* (see ALTER).] —**adulterative** /-rətiv/ *adj*

adulterine /ə dúltərin/ *adj* **1** IMPURE characterized by adulteration **2** BORN FROM ADULTERY born from an adulterous relationship (*literary*) **3** ILLEGAL not within the law

adulterous /ə dúltərəss/ *adj* relating to or involved in adultery [Early 17C. < earlier *adulter* 'adulterer' < Latin *adulterare* (see ADULTERATE).] —**adulterously** *adv*

adultery /ə dúltəri/ *n* voluntary sexual relations between a married person and somebody other than his or her spouse [15C. Directly and via Old French *avout(e)rie* < Latin *adulterare* (see ADULTERATE).] —**adulterer** *n*

adult-onset diabetes *n* a form of diabetes mellitus that develops slowly in some adults as the body becomes unable to use insulin effectively

adumbrate /áddum brayt/ (**-brates, -brating, -brated**) *vt* **1 SKETCHILY INDICATE** to give an incomplete or faint outline or indication of something **2 FORESHADOW** to give a vague indication or warning of something to come **3 CONCEAL** to overshadow and obscure something [Late 16C. < Latin *adumbrat-*, past participle of *adumbrare* 'overshadow' < *umbra* 'shade'.] —**adumbration** /áddum bráysh'n/ *n* —**adumbrative** /ə dúmbrətiv/ *adj* —**adumbratively** *adv*

adv. *abbr* **1** adverb **2** adverbial **3** advertisement **4** advisory

ad val. *abbr* ad valorem

ad valorem /ád və láw rem/ *adj, adv* in proportion to the value of something [Late 17C. < Latin.]

advance /əd vaánss/ *v* (**-vances, -vancing, -vanced**) **1** *vti* **MOVE AHEAD** to move, or move somebody or something, forward in position **2** *vt* **SUGGEST** to put something forward as a proposal **3** *vt* **GIVE BEFOREHAND** to supply something or part of something, especially money, before it is due **4** *vt* **LEND MONEY OR GOODS** to supply money or goods on credit **5** *vti* **RISE IN STATUS** to rise, or make or help somebody rise, in rank or position **6** *vt* **BRING FORWARD IN TIME** to make something happen earlier than originally expected **7** *vti* **PROGRESS** to further the progress or improvement of something, e.g. a cause, or undergo such progress or improvement **8** *vti* **RISE IN AMOUNT** to increase in price, rate, or amount, or increase the price, rate or amount of something ■ *n* **1 DEVELOPMENT** a progress or improvement **2 PAYMENT AHEAD OF TIME** a sum of money paid before it is due **3 MOVEMENT AHEAD** a forward movement in position **4 FRIENDLY APPROACH** an approach made to somebody in an attempt to form a relationship or come to an agreement (*often plural*) **5 PROVIDING SOMETHING BEFORE BEING PAID** the act of supplying money or goods before payment is received **6 SOMETHING RECEIVED BEFORE BEING PAID FOR** a quantity of money or goods supplied before payment is made or repayments begin **7 LOAN** a loan of money **8 PRICE RISE** an increase in price or rate ■ *adj* **1 AHEAD OF TIME** made, given, or sent ahead of time **2 GOING IN FRONT** going ahead of the main group [13C. Via Old French *avancer* < assumed Vulgar Latin *abantiare* < *abante* '(from) before' < Latin *ante* 'before'.] —**advancer** *n* ◇ **in advance** before a particular event takes place

advance copy (*plural* **advance copies**) *n* a copy of a book made available before the actual publication date

advance corporation tax *n* a tax paid by any company that pays a dividend, calculated by deducting the basic rate of income tax from the grossed-up value of the dividend

advanced /əd vaánst/ *adj* **1 MORE HIGHLY DEVELOPED** at a higher stage of development or progress than other similar people or things **2 FAR ALONG** at a point late in the progress or development of something **3 FUTURISTIC** considered to be radical or ahead of its time

advanced degree *n US* a university degree higher than a bachelor's

advance guard *n* a body of troops sent ahead of a main force to prepare an area for operations

advancement /əd vaánssmənt/ *n* **1 PROMOTION** a promotion in rank or position **2 ADVANCING** an act or instance of moving ahead **3 DEVELOPMENT** an improvement or progress in something **4 USE OF LEGACY BEFORE DUE** the use of money from a legacy by or on behalf of its beneficiary before the person is strictly entitled to it

advance party (*plural* **advance parties**) *n* **1** a group of soldiers or units sent ahead of a larger force to prepare an area for operations **2** a small group sent on ahead of any main party, e.g. on an expedition

advance poll *n* in Canada, an early vote held for voters who will be absent from their regular polling place on election day

advance woman *n US* a woman employed by a politician or other public figure to travel ahead on trips to organize timetables, publicity, security, and other arrangements

advantage /əd vaántij/ *n* **1 SUPERIOR POSITION** a superior or favourable position in relation to somebody or something **2 FACTOR FAVOURING** a circumstance or factor that places somebody in a favourable position in relation to others ○ *These children have the advantage of a stable home.* **3 PROFIT** a benefit or gain ○ *Their mistakes in the race worked to our advantage.* **4 POINT AFTER DEUCE** in tennis, the point scored after deuce ■ *vt* (**-tages, -taging, -taged**) **BENEFIT** to put somebody in a superior or favourable position in relation to other people [14C. Alteration of Old French *avantage* < *avant* 'before' < assumed Vulgar Latin *abante* (see ADVANCE).] ◇ **take advantage of somebody** to use somebody in a selfish way in order to achieve a personal benefit, usually by exploiting a weakness ◇ **take advantage of something** to make use of something that is available for personal benefit ◇ **to advantage** in a way that emphasizes the positive aspects of somebody or something

advantageous /ádvən táyjəss/ *adj* **1** giving an advantage **2** of use or benefit —**advantageously** *adv* —**advantageousness** *n*

advect /əd vékt/ *vt* to transfer something by advection [Mid-20C. Back-formation < ADVECTION.]

advection /əd véksh'n/ *n* the horizontal transfer of a property such as heat, caused by air movement [Early 20C. < Latin *advection-* < *advehere* 'carry to' < *vehere* 'carry'.]

advent /ád vent/ *n* the arrival of something important or awaited

Advent *n* the four-week period leading up to Christmas, beginning on the fourth Sunday before Christmas Day [Pre-12C. < Latin *adventus* 'arrival' < *advenire* 'come to' < *venire* 'come'.]

Advent calendar *n* a large decorated card with numbered doors on it, one of which is opened each day from 1 to 24 December, revealing a picture

Adventist /ádvəntist/ *n* a member of a Christian denomination, e.g. the Seventh-Day Adventists, that believes that the Second Coming of Jesus Christ is imminent —**Adventism** *n*

adventitia /ád ven tíshi ə/ *n* the outer covering of an organ or body part, especially that of a blood vessel [Late 19C. < medieval Latin, < neuter plural of *adventitius* (see ADVENTITIOUS).]

adventitious /ádvən tíshəss/ *adj* **1** added from an outside and often unexpected source rather than intrinsic **2** developing in an unusual position, as does, e.g., a root growing downward from a branch [Early 17C. < medieval Latin *adventitius* 'coming from outside', alteration of Latin *adventicius* < *adventus* (see ADVENT).] —**adventitiously** *adv* —**adventitiousness** *n*

adventive /əd véntiv/ *adj* describes a plant or animal found in an environment where it is not native and is not fully established ■ *n* an adventive plant or animal —**adventively** *adv*

Advent Sunday *n* the fourth Sunday before Christmas

adventure /əd vénchər/ *n* **1 EXCITING EXPERIENCE** an exciting or extraordinary event or series of events **2 BOLD UNDERTAKING** an undertaking involving uncertainty and risk **3 INVOLVEMENT IN BOLD UNDERTAKINGS** the participation or willingness to participate in things that involve uncertainty and risk ○ *Where's your sense of adventure?* **4 FINANCIAL SPECULATION** a risky or speculative financial undertaking ■ *v* (**-tures, -turing, -tured**) **1** *vt* **PUT AT RISK** to put something at risk **2** *vt* **RISK SAYING** to risk saying something that other people may disagree with or find offensive **3** *vi* **RISK DANGER** to dare to go somewhere new or engage in something dangerous [13C. Via French *aventure* < Latin *adventurus* 'about to arrive', future participle of *advenire* (see ADVENT).]

adventure playground *n* an outdoor play area for children with slides, climbing frames, ropes, and sometimes materials with which to build things

adventurer /əd vénchərər/ *n* **1 SOMEBODY IN SEARCH OF ADVENTURE** somebody who enjoys exciting or risky activities **2 SOMEBODY PURSUING MONEY OR POSITION** somebody who is unscrupulous in trying to gain wealth or status (*disapproving*) **3 SPECULATOR** a financial speculator

adventuresome /əd vénchərsəm/ *adj* willing or eager to participate in risky or exciting activities —**adventuresomely** *adv* —**adventuresomeness** *n*

adventuress /əd vénchərəss/ *n* a woman who uses unscrupulous means in order to gain wealth or social position (*dated disapproving*)

adventurism /əd vénchərizəm/ *n* **1** involvement in risky financial enterprises **2** reckless intervention by one government in the affairs of another —**adventurist** *n*

adventurous /əd vénchərəss/ *adj* **1** willing or eager to participate in risky or exciting activities **2** involving risk —**adventurously** *adv* —**adventurousness** *n*

adverb /ád vurb/ *n* a word that modifies a verb, an adjective, another adverb, or a sentence, e.g. 'happily', 'very', or 'frankly' [15C. Directly or via French < Latin *adverbium* (after Greek *epirrhēma* 'added word').]

adverbial /əd vúrbi əl/ *adj* relating to or functioning as an adverb ■ *n* an adverb, or a phrase or clause that functions as an adverb —**adverbially** *adv*

ad verbum /ad vúrbəm/ *adv* word for word [< Latin, 'in accordance with the word']

adversarial /ád vur sáiri əl/ *adj* **1** relating to conflict or adversaries **2** involving conflicting parties or interests, in relation to a legal proceeding. US term **adversary** *adj.*

adversary /ádvərsəri/ *n* (*plural* **-ies**) an opponent in a conflict, contest, or debate ■ *adj US* LAW = **adversarial** *adj.* **2** [14C. Via Old French < Latin *adversarius* 'enemy' < *adversus* (see ADVERSE).]

adversative /əd vúrssətiv/ *adj* expressing opposition or contrast ■ *n* a word, phrase, or clause that expresses opposition or contrast, e.g. 'but' or 'although' [Mid-16C. Directly or via French < late Latin *adversativus* 'opposed' < Latin *adversus* (see ADVERSE).] —**adversatively** *adv*

adverse /ád vurss, ad vúrss/ *adj* **1 HARMFUL** creating unfavourable or undesirable results **2 ANTAGONISTIC** acting with or characterized by opposition or antagonism **3 CONTRARY** creating momentum in a direction opposite from that desired **4 FACING THE STEM** describes a leaf or flower that faces the main stem [14C. Via Old French < Latin *adversus* 'turned against, hostile' < past participle of *advertere* (see ADVERT[1]).] —**adversely** *adv* —**adverseness** *n*

USAGE adverse or **averse**? Both words mean 'opposed' in different ways. ***Adverse*** describes something unfavourable or difficult and is normally used before an abstract noun: *adverse circumstances, adverse conditions.* ***Averse*** describes people who are disinclined to do something or have a strong dislike specified by the word that follows *to*: *Are you averse to publicity?* ***Averse*** is never used attributively (i.e. before a noun), as ***adverse*** normally is.

---

adverse possession *n* the possession or occupation of land or property without the owner's permission as a method of acquiring legal ownership

adversity /əd vúrssəti/ (*plural* **-ties**) *n* **1** hardship and suffering **2** an extremely unfavourable experience or event

advert[1] /əd vúrt/ *vi* to call attention or make reference to something [15C. Via Old French *advertir* 'notice' < Latin *advertere* 'turn towards' < *vertere* 'turn'.] —**advertence** *n*

advert[2] /ád vurt/ *n* an advertisement (*informal*) [Mid-19C. Shortening.]

advertise /ádvər tīz/ (**-tises, -tising, -tised**) *v* **1** *vti* **PRAISE COMMERCIAL PRODUCT** to publicize the qualities of a product, service, business, or event in order to encourage people to buy or use it **2** *vti* **PUBLICLY ANNOUNCE AVAILABILITY OR NEED** to publicize something such as a job vacancy or item for sale in a newspaper or on the radio, television, or Internet ○ *advertise for a new flatmate* **3** *vt* **TELL OTHERS ABOUT** to make something known to others [15C. < Old French *advertiss-*, stem of *advertir* (see ADVERT[1]).] —**advertiser** *n*

advertisement /əd vúrtissmənt/ *n* **1** the act of advertising something **2** a public announcement in a newspaper or on the radio, television, or Internet advertising something such as a product for sale or an event

advertising /ádvər tīzing/ *n* **1 PUBLIC PROMOTION OF** the public promotion of something such as a product, service, business, or event, in order to attract or increase interest in it **2 BUSINESS OF PRODUCING ADVERTISEMENTS** the business of producing advertisements **3 ADVERTISEMENTS** advertisements considered collectively

~~advertisment~~ incorrect spelling of **advertisement**

advertorial /ádvər táwri əl/ *n* an advertisement in a publication that looks like one of its normal articles [Mid-20C. Blend of ADVERTISEMENT + EDITORIAL.]

advice /əd vīss/ *n* **1** somebody's opinion about what another person should do ○ *I followed her advice and changed jobs.* **2** formal or official information about something, usually received from a distance (*often* *plural*) [13C. Via French *avis* 'opinion' < Latin *ad (meum) visum* 'in (my) view or opinion' (*visum*, past participle of *videre* 'see').]

advice note *n* a formal document from a supplier to a customer containing details of goods that have been sent

advisable /əd vīzəb'l/ *adj* being a sensible or desirable thing to do —**advisability** /əd vīzə bílləti/ *n* —**advisableness** *n* —**advisably** *adv*

advise /əd vīz/ (**-vises, -vising, -vised**) *v* **1** *vti* OFFER ADVICE to offer advice to somebody ○ *We were advised to leave.* **2** *vt* RECOMMEND to suggest or recommend a course of action to somebody ○ *'I have advised him to join a club or get a hobby but he is determined to feel sorry for himself'.* (Sue Townsend, *The Secret Diary of Adrian Mole Aged 13 ¾*, 1982) **3** △ *vt* INFORM to tell somebody about something. [14C. < Old French *aviser* < *avis* 'opinion' (see ADVICE).]

SYNONYMS See **recommend**.

USAGE The use of the verb **advise** to mean 'tell somebody about something' is often regarded as jargon and is best avoided in formal usage: *Please advise us of* [or *tell us*] *your new address. I will advise them* [or *inform them*] *of the new time of the meeting.*

advisedly /əd vīzidli/ *adv* after careful consideration

advisee /əd vī zee/ *n* somebody who receives advice

adviser /əd vīzər/, **advisor** *n* **1** GIVER OF ADVICE somebody who gives advice **2** SOMEBODY ADVISING STUDENTS somebody who advises students on academic matters **3** SUBJECT SPECIALIST a teacher who is a specialist in a particular subject and is appointed by an education authority to advise school heads and teachers on the teaching of that subject

USAGE **adviser** or **advisor**? Both spellings are used for 'somebody who gives advice'. **Adviser** is often regarded as more correct because *-er* is the more usual suffix for words formed directly from other English words; **advisor** is common in American English and is probably influenced by the form of the adjective **advisory** or the spelling of Latin *advisor*.

advisory /əd vīzəri/ *adj* **1** GIVING ADVICE providing or of the nature of advice **2** HAVING THE FUNCTION OF GIVING ADVICE having the function of giving advice, usually with the implication that the advice given need not be followed ■ *n* US WARNING OF SOMETHING TO COME an advance notice of something, e.g. a warning of impending severe weather ○ *traffic advisory*

advisory teacher *n* EDUC = adviser *n*. 3

advocaat /ádvō kaa, -kaat/ *n* an alcoholic beverage similar to eggnog, containing eggs, sugar, and brandy [Mid-20C. < Dutch, 'advocate', because it was supposed to help clear the throat.]

advocacy /ádvəkəssi/ (*plural* **-cies**) *n* **1** active verbal support for a cause or position **2** support for people who are thought likely to be disregarded or to have difficulty in gaining attention, so that their opinion is listened to [14C. Via Old French *advocacie* < Latin *advocatus* (see ADVOCATE).]

advocate *vt* /ádvə kayt/ (**-cates, -cating, -cated**) GIVE SUPPORT TO to support or speak in favour of something ■ *n* /ádvəkət, -kayt/ **1** SOMEBODY GIVING SUPPORT somebody who supports or speaks in favour of something ○ *a tireless advocate of social reform* **2** HELPER somebody who acts or intercedes on behalf of another **3** LEGAL REPRESENTATIVE somebody, e.g. a lawyer, who pleads another's case in a legal forum **4** SCOTTISH BARRISTER the equivalent of an English barrister in Scotland [14C. Via Old French *avocat* 'advocate' < Latin *advocare* 'call to' < *vocare* 'call'.] —**advocator** *n* —**advocatory** /ádvə káytəri, ádvəkətəri/ *adj*

SYNONYMS See **recommend**.

Advocate Depute (*plural* **Advocates Depute**) *n* a law officer in Scotland, appointed to prosecute cases on behalf of the Lord Advocate

advt *abbr* advertisement

Adyghe /aádi gay, -gáy/, **Adygei** *n* an Abkhaz-Adyghean language spoken in the NW region of the Georgian Republic. Native speakers: 100,000. —**Adyghe** *adj*

adynamic /ay dT námmik/ *adj* characterized by loss of normal function ○ *adynamic ileus*

adytum /áddɪtəm/ (*plural* **-ta** /-tə/) *n* the most sacred part in an ancient temple, restricted to priests [Early 17C. Via Latin < Greek *adutos* 'not to be entered' < *duein* 'enter'.]

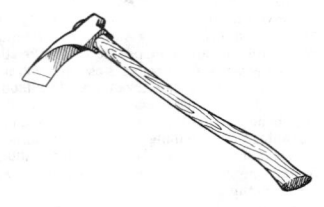

Adze

adze /adz/, **adz** *n* a tool similar to an axe, with an arched blade set at right angles to the handle. Use: trimming and shaping wood. [Old English *adesa, eadesa* < ?]

adzuki bean /ad zóoki-/, **aduki bean** /ə dóoki-/, **azuki bean** /ə zóoki-/ *n* **1** a small, slightly sweet, red-brown bean. Use: in vegetarian dishes in Europe and North America, in sweet dishes in Asian cooking. **2** a plant that produces adzuki beans. *Vigna angularis.* [< Japanese *azuki* 'red bean']

ae /ay/ *det* Scotland a single (*literary*) [Variant of A²]

AEA *abbr* Atomic Energy Authority

aecidiospore *n* FUNGI = aeciospore

aecidium *n* FUNGI = aecium

aeciospore /éessi ə spawr/, **aecidiospore** /-síddi ō-/ *n* a spore produced in the reproductive organ (**aecium**) of a rust fungus with two genetically distinct nuclei [Early 20C. < AECIUM + SPORE.]

aecium /éessi əm/ (*plural* **-a** /-ə/), **aecidium** /ee síddi əm/ (*plural* **-a** /-ə/) *n* a cup-shaped reproductive organ (**fruiting body**) produced by some rust fungi in the tissue of their host plant, in which spores (**aeciospores**) are formed [Early 20C. Via modern Latin < Greek *aikia* 'injury'; from the harm caused by the fungi.]

aedes /ay eé deez/ (*plural* **-des**) *n* a tropical and sub-tropical mosquito that can transmit serious diseases, e.g. yellow fever and dengue. *Aedes aegypti.* [Early 20C. < modern Latin, < Greek *aēdēs* 'unpleasant', because it carries diseases.]

aedile /eé dīl/ *n* a magistrate in ancient Rome responsible for public works and buildings, games, markets, and the grain and water supplies [Mid-16C. < Latin *aedilis* > *aedes* 'building'.]

AEEU *abbr* Amalgamated Engineering and Electrical Union

Aegean Sea /i jeé ən-/ arm of the Mediterranean Sea, between Greece and Turkey. Area: about 179,000 sq. km/69,000 sq. mi.

aegis /eéjiss/ *n* **1** in Greek mythology, the shield of Zeus or Athena [Early 17C. Via Latin < Greek *aigis* 'goatskin shield of Zeus'.] ○ **under the aegis of somebody** *or* **something** with the support or protection of somebody or something (*formal*)

aegrotat /īgrō tat, eégrō-, ee grō-/ *n* **1** a certificate granted to a university student crediting the student with passing an examination missed because of illness **2** a degree or other qualification granted to a university student by an aegrotat [Late 18C. < Latin, 'he or she is ill'.]

Aelfric /álfrik/ (955?–1020?) Anglo-Saxon monk and writer

-aemia, **-haemia**, **-emia**, **-hemia** *suffix* blood ○ *anaemia* [Via modern Latin < Greek *-aimia* < *haima* 'blood']

Aeneas /i neé əss/ *n* in Greek and Roman mythology, a Trojan hero who escaped after the fall of Troy and spent seven years travelling before settling near the site of Rome in Italy

Aeolia = Aeolis

aeolian /ee óli ən/ *adj* carried or produced by the wind ○ *aeolian deposits* [Early 20C. < AEOLUS.]

Aeolian /ee óli ən/, **Eolian** *n* LANG = Aeolic ■ *adj* **1** relating to Aeolis, or its people, language, or culture **2** relating to Aeolus

aeolian harp, **Aeolian harp** *n* a box-shaped musical instrument with strings of equal length that are tuned in unison and sounded when the wind blows over them

Aeolian Islands ♦ Lipari Islands

Aeolis /eé ə liss/, **Aeolia** /ee óli ə/ ancient region on the NW coast of Asia Minor

Aeolus /eé ə ləss/ *n* in Greek mythology, the god of wind

aeon /eé ən, ee on/, **eon** *n* **1** a length of time that is too long to measure (*informal*) **2** a division of geological time comprising two or more eras [Mid-17C. Via late Latin < Greek *aiōn* 'age, lifetime'.] —**aeonian** *adj*

aepyornis /eépi áwrniss/ (*plural* **-nises** *or* **-nis**) *n* a giant extinct flightless bird that lived in Madagascar. Genus: *Aepyornis.* Also called **elephant bird** [Mid-19C. < modern Latin < Greek *aipus* 'high' + *ornis* (see ORNITHO-).]

aer- *prefix* = aero- (before vowels)

aerate /áir rayt/ (**-ates, -ating, -ated**) *vt* **1** to allow circulating air to reach or penetrate something **2** to charge a liquid with a gas, especially when using carbon dioxide to make carbonated drinks **3** PHYSIOL = oxygenate *v.* [Late 18C. < Latin *aer* 'air' < Greek *aēr.*] —**aeration** /air ráysh'n/ *n* —**aerator** *n*

aerenchyma /ə réngkəmə/ *n* the spongy tissue in some aquatic plants that keeps them afloat and helps in the exchange of gases [Late 19C. < Greek *aēr* 'air' + *egkhuma* 'infusion'.]

aeri- *prefix* = aero-

aerial /áiri əl/ *adj* **1** RELATING TO AIR consisting of, typical of, or relating to the air **2** IN AIR living, happening, or moving in the air ○ *a plant with aerial roots* **3** LIGHT IN WEIGHT like the air in being light and insubstantial **4** IMAGINARY existing only in the imagination **5** INVOLVING AIRCRAFT done by or involving aircraft ○ *an aerial bombardment* ■ *n* **1** METAL ROD FOR RADIO WAVES a metallic rod or wire for sending and receiving radio waves or microwaves. US term **antenna** *n.* **3** **2** HIGH BALL IN HOCKEY in hockey, a ball passed by being raised off the ground [Early 17C. < Latin *aerius* < Greek *aerios* < *aēr* 'air'.]

aerialist /áiri əlist/ *n* an acrobat who performs on a tightrope or trapeze

aerial ladder *n* US = turntable ladder

aerial perspective *n* the use in painting of gradations in colour and definition to suggest distance

aerie *n* US = eyrie

aeriform /áiri fawrm/ *adj* **1** existing as air or gas **2** having no substance or material form

aero¹ /áirō/ *adj* used in aircraft or aeronautics

✦aero² *abbr* aviation industry (*in Internet addresses*)

aero-, **aeri-**, **aer-** *prefix* **1** air, atmosphere, gas ○ *aerodynamic* **2** aviation ○ *aerospace* [< Greek *aēr* 'air']

aeroballistics /áirō bə lístiks/ *n* the branch of ballistics that deals with projectiles fired or dropped from aircraft (+ *singular verb*) —**aeroballistic** *adj*

aerobatics /áirō báttiks/ *n* the flying of an aircraft in daring manoeuvres, often as an entertainment (+ *singular or plural verb*) [Early 20C. < AERO-, after ACROBATICS.] —**aerobatic** *adj*

aerobe /áirōb/ *n* a microorganism that requires oxygen for metabolism [Late 19C. < AERO- + Greek *bios* 'life'.]

aerobic¹ /air róbik/ *adj* **1** living or taking place only in the presence of oxygen **2** having or providing oxygen [Late 19C. < French *aérobie*, coined by Louis Pasteur < Greek *aēr* 'air' + *bios* 'life'.] —**aerobically** *adv*

aerobic² /air róbik/ *adj* **1** increasing respiration and heart rates ○ *aerobic exercise* **2** used in or relating to aerobics [Mid-20C. < AEROBICS.]

aerobic respiration *n* the breakdown of foodstuffs to create energy in the presence of oxygen. ◊ **anaerobic respiration**

aerobics /air róbiks/ *n* (+ *singular or plural verb*) **1** an active exercise programme done to music, often in a class **2** exercises, e.g. walking, jogging, bicycling, and swimming, that increase respiration and heart rates [Mid-20C. < AEROBIC¹, after GYMNASTICS.]

aerobiology /áirō bī óllaji/ *n* the study of airborne biological materials and organisms, e.g. airborne allergens and disease-causing microorganisms —**aerobiological** /áirō bī ə lójjik'l/ *adj* —**aerobiologically** *adv*

aerobiosis /áirō bī óssiss/ *n* life in the presence of oxygen [Early 20C. < modern Latin, < Greek *aēr* 'air' + *biōsis* (see -BIOSIS).]

aerodrome /áirō drōm/ *n* a small airfield with limited facilities [Early 20C. < AERO- + -DROME.]

aerodynamic /áirō dī námmik/ *adj* **1** involving or typical of aerodynamics **2** designed to reduce air resistance, especially to increase fuel efficiency or maximum speed —**aerodynamically** *adv*

aerodynamics /áirō dī námmiks/ *n* the study of moving gases, especially the study of the forces experienced by objects moving through air (+ *singular verb*) ■ *npl* the aerodynamic properties of an object (+ *plural verb*) —**aerodynamicist** /-námmissist/ *n*

aerodyne /áirō dīn/ *n* an aircraft such as an aeroplane or helicopter that is heavier than air and whose lift in flight results from forces caused by its motion through the air [Early 20C. Back-formation < AERODYNAMIC.]

aeroembolism /áirō émbəlizəm/ *n* MED = **air embolism**

aerofoil /áirō foyl/ *n* a part of an aircraft's or other vehicle's surface, e.g. an aileron, wing, or propeller, that acts on the air to provide lift or control

aerogram /áirə gram/, **aerogramme** *n* a single sheet of lightweight paper for airmail use that, once written on, can be folded and sealed to form an envelope [Late 19C. After TELEGRAM.]

aerography /air róggrəfi/ *n* the study of atmospheric conditions

aerolite /áirō līt/ *n* a meteorite with a high silicate content [Early 19C. < AERO- + -LITE.] —**aerolitic** /áirō líttik/ *adj*

aerology /air rólləji/ *n* the study of the lower layers of the Earth's atmosphere —**aerologic** /áirə lójjik/ *adj* —**aerological** *adj* —**aerologist** *n*

aeromechanics /áirō mi kánniks/ *n* the study of gases in motion and in equilibrium, including the study of the mechanical effects of gases upon objects (+ *singular verb*) —**aeromechanical** *adj* —**aeromechanically** *adv*

aeromedicine /áirō médss'n/ *n* MED = **aviation medicine** —**aeromedical** /-méddik'l/ *adj*

aerometeorograph /áirō meéti ərə graaf, -graf/ *n* an instrument on board an aircraft that records temperature, atmospheric pressure, and humidity

aerometer /air rómmitər/ *n* an instrument for measuring the mass or density of air or another gas [Late 18C. < French *aéromètre*.]

aeronaut /áirə nawt/ *n* somebody who flies in an airship or balloon [Late 18C. < French *aéronaute* < *aéro-* (< Greek *aēr* 'air') + Greek *nautēs* 'sailor'.]

aeronautical /áirə náwtik'l/, **aeronautic** /-náwtik/ *adj* relating to aircraft or their flight [Early 19C. < French *aéronautique* (see AERONAUT).] —**aeronautically** *adv*

aeronautics /áirə náwtiks/ *n* the science, art, theory, and practice of designing, building, and operating aircraft (+ *singular verb*)

aeroneurosis /áirō nyoō rōssiss/ *n* anxiety and fatigue in airline pilots brought on by prolonged periods of flying

aeronomy /air ónnəmi/ *n* the study of the upper atmosphere of the Earth or other planets —**aeronomer** *n* —**aeronomic** /áirə nómmik/ *adj* —**aeronomical** *adj* —**aeronomist** *n*

aeropause /áirə pawz/ *n* the part of the Earth's upper atmosphere above which air is too thin for aircraft to fly

aerophagy /air róffəji/, **aerophagia** /áirə fáyji ə, -fáyjə/ *n* the abnormal spasmodic swallowing of air, a common cause of flatulence and belching [Late 19C. After French *aérophagie*.]

aerophobia /áirə fōbi ə/ *n* an abnormal fear of draughts of air —**aerophobic** *adj*

aerophyte /áirə fīt/ *n* PLANTS = **epiphyte**

aeroplane /áirə playn/ *n* a vehicle with wings and a jet engine or propellers, that is heavier than air, and is able to fly [Late 19C. < French *aéroplane* < *aéro-* (< Greek *aēr* 'air') + *-plane*.]

aerosol /áirə sol/ *n* **1** CONTAINER WITH GAS UNDER PRESSURE a small container holding a substance that can be dispensed under pressure by a propellant as a spray **2** SUBSTANCE SPRAYED a substance held in a small container from which it can be dispensed under pressure by a propellant as a spray **3** SUSPENSION OF PARTICLES IN GAS a suspension of solid or liquid particles in a gaseous medium

aerosolize /áirəsə līz/, **aerosolise** *vt* to convert a substance into a fine spray or colloidal suspension

aerospace /áirō spayss/ *n* the Earth's atmosphere and outer space ■ *adj* relating to the design, manufacture, and flight of vehicles or missiles that fly in and beyond the Earth's atmosphere

aerostat /áirə stat/ *n* a hot-air or gas-filled aircraft such as an airship or balloon [Late 18C. < French *aérostat* < *aéro-* 'AERO-' + Greek *statos* 'standing'.] —**aerostatic** /áirə státtik/ *adj*

aerostatics /áirə státtiks/ *n* **1** the study of gases in equilibrium and objects in equilibrium in gases **2** the science of aircraft that are lighter than air, e.g. dirigibles and balloons

aerothermodynamics /áirō thúrmō dī námmiks/ *n* the study of the heat exchange between gases and solid objects, especially between air and aircraft flying at high velocity (+ *singular verb*) —**aerothermodynamic** *adj*

aery /áiri/ (**-ier, -iest**) *adj* insubstantial and unworldly [Late 16C. < Latin *aerius* (see AERIAL).]

Aeschylus /eéskələss/ (525?–426 BC) Greek dramatist

Aesculapian /eéskyoō láypi ən/ *adj* relating to medicine and the healing arts [Early 17C. < Latin *Aesculapius*, the Roman god of medicine.]

aesculapian snake *n* a long slender brown non-venomous snake. Native to: forests in Europe and W Asia. *Elaphe longissima*. [< the common depiction of Aesculapius (see AESCULAPIAN) in antiquity with such a snake]

Aesop /eéssop/ (*fl.* 6th century BC) Greek writer

AEST *abbr Aus* Australian Eastern Standard Time

aesthesia /eess theézi ə/ *n* the ability to feel or experience through the senses [Early 18C. Via modern Latin < Greek *aisthēsis* 'perceiving' < *aisthesthai* 'perceive'.]

aesthete /eés theet/ *n* somebody who has or affects a highly developed appreciation of beauty, especially in the arts [Late 19C. Back-formation < AESTHETIC, after ATHLETE.]

aesthetic /eess théttik, iss-/ *adj* **1** RELATING TO AESTHETICS relating to the philosophical principles of aesthetics **2** APPRECIATING BEAUTY sensitive to or appreciative of art or beauty **3** BEAUTIFUL pleasing in appearance ■ *n* SET OF PRINCIPLES a set of principles about art [Early 19C. < Greek *aisthētikos* 'perceptual' < *aisthesthai* 'perceive'.] —**aesthetically** *adv*

aestheticism /eess théttisizəm, iss-/ *n* **1** DERIVATION OF MORAL PRINCIPLES FROM BEAUTY the philosophical doctrine that all moral principles are derived from beauty **2** BELIEF IN IMPORTANCE OF AESTHETICS the belief that the principles of aesthetics are of the highest importance in the arts **3** LOVE OF BEAUTY appreciation of and devotion to beauty

QUICK FACTS ON... **AESTHETICISM**

Key dates: late 19th century, especially the 1890s
Key locations: W Europe, especially England
Key elements: rejection of social role of art, focus on aesthetics – 'art for art's sake' (Pater); belief in moral value of beauty; search for new sensations and experiences, refined sensibility
Key figures: John Ruskin, Victor Cousin, Walter Pater (philosophy); Oscar Wilde, Ernest Dowson (literature); Aubrey Beardsley, James Abbott McNeill Whistler (art)
Key works: *Studies in the History of the Renaissance* (Walter Pater) 1873, *Nocturne in Blue and Silver* (James Abbott McNeill Whistler) 1872–73, *The Picture of Dorian Gray* (Oscar Wilde) 1891, *The Yellow Book* (periodical) 1894–97
Key developments: Arts and Crafts movement, art nouveau, modernism, formalism, avant-gardism

aestheticize /eess théttı sīz, iss-/ (**-cizes, -cizing, -cized**) *vt* to show something in its best or most artistic light

aesthetics /eess théttiks, iss-/ *n* **1** STUDY OF BEAUTY the branch of philosophy dealing with the study of aesthetic values such as the beautiful and the sublime (+ *singular verb*) **2** STUDY OF ART the study of the rules and principles of art (+ *singular verb*) **3** IDEA OF BEAUTY a particular idea of what is beautiful or artistic (+ *singular or plural verb*) **4** HOW SOMETHING LOOKS how something looks, especially when considered in terms of how pleasing it is (+ *singular or plural verb*) [Early 19C. Via modern Latin *aesthetica* < Greek *aisthētikos* (see AESTHETIC), perhaps after ATHLETICS.] —**aesthetician** /eéssthə tísh'n, éss-/ *n*

aesthetic surgery *n* SURG = **cosmetic surgery**

aestival[1] *adj* = **estival**

aestival[2] /ee stív'l, éstiv'l/ *adj* relating to or happening during summer [14C. Via Old French < Latin *aestivalis* < *aestas* 'summer'.]

aestivate /eésti vayt, ésti-/ (**-vates, -vating, -vated**) *vi* **1** to spend the summer in a particular place or activity (*formal*) **2** to be dormant during the summer or during months of drought (*refers to animals, especially certain amphibians, reptiles, and insects*) [Early 17C. < Latin *aestivat-*, past participle of *aestivare* < *aestus* 'summer'.]

aestivation /eésti váysh'n, ésti-/ *n* **1** PARTICULAR SUMMER ACTIVITY spending summer in a particular place or activity **2** SUMMER DORMANCY dormancy in certain animals during the summer or months of drought **3** ARRANGEMENT OF FLOWER BUD PARTS the arrangement of the sepals and petals in a flower bud

aether *n* = **ether** *n*. 3, **ether** *n*. 4

aethereal *adj* ethereal (*literary archaic*)

aetiology /eéti óllәji/, **etiology** *n* **1** STUDY OF CAUSES the philosophical investigation of causes and origins **2** MEDICAL STUDY OF CAUSE OF DISEASE the study of the causes and origins of disease **3** CAUSE OF DISEASE the set of factors that contributes to the occurrence of a disease [Mid-16C. Via Latin *aetiologia* < Greek *aitiologiā* 'statement of the cause' < *aitiā* 'cause'.] —**aetiologic** /eéti ə lójjik/ *adj* —**aetiologically** *adv* —**aetiologist** *n*

ϟ **af** *abbr* Afghanistan (*in Internet addresses*)

AF *abbr* **1** air force **2** Anglo-French **3** audio frequency **4** autofocus

Af. *abbr* **1** Africa **2** African

af- *prefix* = **ad-** (*before f*)

ϟ **AFAIK** *abbr* as far as I know (*in e-mails*)

afar /ə faár/ *adv* at, to, or from a great distance (*literary*) ■ *n* a great distance away [14C. < A-[1] + FAR.]

AFC *abbr* **1** automatic flight control **2** automatic frequency control

afeard /ə feérd/, **afeared** *adj* afraid (*archaic regional*) [Old English, past participle of *afǣren* 'frighten' < *fǣren* 'to fear']

afebrile /a feéb rīl, ay-/ *adj* having no fever

affable /áffəb'l/ *adj* good-natured, friendly and easy to talk to [15C. Via French < Latin *affabilis* 'easy to speak to' < *(af)fari* 'speak (to)'.] —**affability** /àffə bílləti/ *n* —**affably** *adv*

affair /ə fáir/ *n* **1** BUSINESS MATTER a matter that has been attended to or that needs attention, especially business **2** OCCURRENCE an event or occurrence that has been referred to or is known about ○ *that odd affair at work last week* **3** SOCIAL EVENT a social event **4** SOMETHING OF A PARTICULAR KIND an object or item of a particular kind ○ *The house is a ramshackle affair.* **5** SEXUAL RELATIONSHIP a sexual relationship between two people not married to each other **6** SCANDALOUS INCIDENT an incident that attracts public attention or notoriety ○ *the Profumo affair* ■ **affairs** *npl* BUSINESS TO ATTEND TO professional, public, or personal business [12C. Via French, 'do' < Latin *facere*.]

affaire /ə fáir/ *n* a love affair [Early 20C. Shortening of AFFAIRE DE COEUR.]

affaire de coeur /a fáir də kúr/ (*plural* **affaires de coeur** /a fáir də kúr/) *n* a love affair or romantic attachment [Early 19C. < French, 'affair of the heart'.]

affect[1] /ə fékt/ *vt* **1** INFLUENCE to act upon or have an effect on somebody or something **2** MOVE EMOTIONALLY to move somebody emotionally **3** CAUSE DISEASE to infect or damage somebody or something with disease [14C. < Latin *affect-*, past participle of *afficere* 'act on' < *facere* 'do'.]

USAGE affect or **effect**? In general use, ***affect*** is only used as a verb, whereas ***effect*** is commonly used as a noun and only in formal contexts as a verb. What causes confusion is that they have the same pronunciations and closely related meanings. If one thing ***affects*** [acts upon] another, it has an ***effect*** on it [causes it to change]. Notice also that you can ***affect*** [cause a change in] people as well as things, but you can only ***effect*** [bring about] things: *The election has affected our entire society, for it has effected major changes in the government. The bad weather has a bad effect* [not *affect*] *on him.*

affect[2] /ə fékt/ *vt* **1** PRETEND TO BE to give the appearance or pretence of something **2** ADOPT to adopt a use, style, or manner as your own **3** ACT LIKE to imitate somebody else's style or character **4** COME TO BE OR HAVE to assume a particular form or state ○ *affect a liquid state* [15C. Directly or via French *affecter* < Latin *affectare* 'strive for' < *affect-* (see AFFECT[1]).] —**affecter** *n*

affect[3] /áffekt, ə fékt/ *n* an emotion or mood associated with an idea or action, or the external expression of such a feeling ○ *blunted affect* [Late 19C. < German *Affekt*.]

affectation /áffek táysh'n/ *n* **1** feigned or unnatural behaviour that is often meant to impress others **2** an appearance or manner assumed or put on as a show or pretence, often to impress others [Mid-16C. Directly or via French < Latin *affectation-* 'influence' < *affectare* (see AFFECT[1]).]

affected /ə féktid/ *adj* **1 INFLUENCED BY** acted upon or influenced by something or somebody **2 MOVED EMOTIONALLY** emotionally moved by something **3 INFECTED OR DAMAGED** infected or damaged by disease **4 TRYING TO IMPRESS** behaving in an unnatural way intended to impress others **5 INTENDED TO IMPRESS** done or assumed with the intention of impressing others —**affectedly** *adv* —**affectedness** *n*

affecting /ə fékting/ *adj* able to stir the emotions —**affectingly** *adv*

affection /ə féksh'n/ *n* fond or tender feeling towards somebody or something ■ **affections** *npl* feelings of fondness or tenderness, sometimes as opposed to reason [12C. Via Old French, 'emotion' < Latin *affection-* 'inclination' < *afficere* (see AFFECT[1]).] —**affectional** *adj* —**affectionally** *adv*

SYNONYMS See ***love***.

affectionate /ə féksh'nət/ *adj* having or showing affection [15C. Directly or via French < Latin *affectionatus* 'devoted' < *affection-* (see AFFECTION).] —**affectionately** *adv* —**affectionateness** *n*

affective /ə féktiv/ *adj* **1** relating to an external expression of emotion associated with an idea or action **2** = **affecting** [15C. Via French *affectif* < late Latin *affectivus* < Latin *affect-* (see AFFECT[1]).] —**affectively** *adv* —**affectivity** /áffek tívvəti/ *n*

affective disorder *n* a psychiatric disorder with a central emotional component, e.g. depression

affectless /ə féktləss/ *adj* feeling or showing no emotion —**affectlessness** *n*

affenpinscher /áffən pinshər/ *n* a European breed of small dog with wiry hair and tufted muzzle [Early 20C. < German, 'ape terrier'.]

afferent /áffərənt/ *adj* describes nerves that carry impulses from the body towards the brain or spinal cord, or blood vessels that carry blood to an organ. ◊ **efferent** [Mid-19C. < Latin *afferent-*, present participle of *afferre* 'bring towards'.] —**afferently** *adv*

affettuoso /ə féchoo óssō/ *adv, adj* played or sung musically with feeling (*musical direction*) [Early 18C. < Italian, < Latin *affect-* (see AFFECT[1]).]

affiance /ə fī́ ənss/ (**-ances, -ancing, -anced**) *vt* to promise yourself or somebody else in marriage to somebody (*literary; often passive*) [14C. Via Old French *afiancer* < *afiance* 'trust' < medieval Latin *affidare* 'to trust'.]

affidavit /áffi dáyvit/ *n* a written declaration made on oath before somebody authorized to administer oaths, usually setting out the statement of a witness for court proceedings [Late 16C. < medieval Latin, 'he or she has sworn', a form of *affidare* 'trust, affirm' < *fidus* 'faithful'.]

affiliate *vti* /ə fílli ayt/ (**-ates, -ating, -ated**) to come, or bring a person or group, into a close relationship with another, usually larger, group ■ *n* /ə fílli ət, -ayt/ a group that is closely connected with a larger group, or an individual who combines with others to form a group [Mid-18C. < Latin *affiliare* 'adopt as a son' < *filius* 'son'.] —**affiliated** *adj* —**affiliation** /ə fílli áysh'n/ *n*

affiliation order *n* a court order requiring a man adjudged to be the father of an illegitimate child to pay money towards its maintenance

affiliation proceedings *npl* legal proceedings usually initiated by a woman seeking to prove that a particular man is the father of her child, especially in order to claim monetary support from him

affine /áffīn/ *n* **1** a geometric transformation that maps points and parallel lines to points and parallel lines **2** a relative by marriage [Early 20C. < Latin *affinis* (see AFFINITY).] —**affinal** *adj*

affinity /ə fínnəti/ (*plural* **-ties**) *n* **1 FEELING OF IDENTIFICATION** a natural liking for or identification with somebody or something **2 SOMEBODY ATTRACTIVE** somebody to whom somebody else is attracted **3 CONNECTION** a similarity or likeness that connects persons or things **4 KINSHIP BY MARRIAGE** a relationship by marriage rather than blood **5 SIMILARITY IN STRUCTURE** a similarity in structure between groups that may suggest a common origin **6 LIKELIHOOD OF CHEMICAL REACTION** a measure of the likelihood of a chemical reaction taking place between two substances **7 ANTIGEN-ANTIBODY ATTRACTION** the attraction between an antigen and an antibody [14C. Via Old French *afinité* 'close relationship' < Latin *affinis* 'bordering on something' < *finis* 'border'.]

affinity card *n* a credit card that benefits a named charity or charities every time it is used

affirm /ə fúrm/ *v* **1** *vti* **DECLARE POSITIVELY** to declare positively that something is true ○ *They affirmed their continued support for the initiative* **2** *vt* **CONFIRM** to confirm something as binding or valid **3** *vi* **MAKE A FORMAL STATEMENT** to make a statement formally but not under oath [13C. Via Old French < Latin *affirmare* 'strengthen' < *firmus* 'firm'.] —**affirmable** *adj* —**affirmably** *adv* —**affirmant** *n* —**affirmer** *n*

affirmation /áffər máysh'n/ *n* **1 ASSERTION OF TRUTH** an assertion of truth **2 SOMETHING SAID TO BE TRUE** something asserted as being true **3 FORMAL LEGAL DECLARATION** a formal declaration acceptable in a court, usually made by somebody who has a conscientious objection to taking an oath **4 POSITIVE STATEMENT OF ACHIEVEMENT** a positive statement asserting that a goal the speaker or thinker wishes to achieve is already happening ○ *Start the day by repeating 20 times the affirmation 'I am a non-smoker'.* [15C. Directly or via French < Latin *affirmation-* < *affirmare* (see AFFIRM).]

affirmative /ə fúrmətiv/ *adj* **1 TRUE** confirming or asserting that something is true **2 INDICATING AGREEMENT** indicating agreement or giving assent **3 RELATING TO A TYPE OF PROPOSITION** relating to or being a categorical proposition in which the predicate's extension is contained partially or wholly within the subject, e.g. 'All humans are mammals' ■ *n* **1 POSITIVE ASSERTION** a positive assertion **2 WORD CONVEYING AGREEMENT** a word or statement conveying agreement or approval **3** *US* **SIDE FOR A PROPOSITION** the side in a debate that supports a proposition ■ *interj* **YES** a signal code word expressing agreement or compliance —**affirmatively** *adv*

affirmative action *n US* = **positive discrimination**

affix *vt* /ə fíks/ **1 FASTEN TO SOMETHING ELSE** to fasten something to something else **2 ADD ON TO** to add something at the end of something, e.g. a signature to a document **3 ATTRIBUTE TO** to ascribe something, e.g. responsibility or blame, to somebody ■ *n* /áffiks/ **1 PART ADDED TO A WORD** a form added to the beginning, middle, or end of another word that creates a derivative word or inflection **2 SOMETHING ATTACHED** something attached or added [Mid-16C. Directly or via French *affixer* < medieval Latin *affixare* 'keep on fastening to' < Latin *affigere* 'fasten to' < *figere* 'fasten'.] —**affixable** *adj* —**affixer** *n*

affixation /áffik sáysh'n/ *n* the addition of a prefix, suffix, or infix to a word in order to create a new word or an inflected form

afflatus /ə fláytəss/ *n* creative inspiration, usually thought of as divine (*formal*) [Mid-17C. < Latin, 'act of blowing on' < *flare* 'to blow'.]

afflict /ə flíkt/ *vt* to cause severe mental or physical distress to somebody [14C. < Latin *afflict-*, past participle of *affligere* 'strike down, cause to suffer' < *fligere* 'strike'.] —**afflicter** *n* —**afflictive** *adj* —**afflictively** *adv*

USAGE afflict or **inflict**? The chief difference is in the grammatical construction: you ***inflict*** something unpleasant *on* somebody, whereas you ***afflict*** somebody (or, more usually, somebody is ***afflicted***) *with* or *by* something unpleasant: *They promoted measures to avoid inflicting further harm on the environment. The population was afflicted by a series of natural disasters.*

affliction /ə flíksh'n/ *n* **1** a condition of great physical or mental distress **2** something that causes great physical or mental distress [14C. Via Old French < Latin *affliction-* < *affligere* (see AFFLICT).]

affluent /áffloo ənt/ *adj* having an abundance of material wealth ■ *n* a stream or river that flows into another [15C. Via Old French < Latin *affluent-*, present participle of *affluere* 'flow towards' < *fluere* 'flow'.] —**affluence** *n* —**affluently** *adv*

afflux /áffluks/ *n* an inward flow or flow towards a point, especially of blood in the body [Early 17C. < medieval Latin *affluxus* < *affluere* (see AFFLUENT).]

afford /ə fáwrd/ *vt* **1 BE ABLE TO BUY** to be able to meet the cost of something without unacceptable difficulty **2 BE ABLE TO DO** to be able to do or provide something without unacceptable or disadvantageous consequences **3 BE ABLE TO SPARE** to be able to spare something without unacceptable or disadvantageous consequences **4 PROVIDE** to supply or provide something (*formal*) [Old English *geforþian* 'accomplish' < *forþian* 'to further'] —**affordability** *n* —**affordable** *adj* —**affordably** *adv*

afforest /ə fórrist/ *vt* to convert land not previously forested into forest by planting trees [Early 16C. < medieval Latin *afforestare* < *foresta* 'forest'.] —**afforestation** /ə fórri stáysh'n/ *n*

affray /ə fráy/ *n* a fight or violent disturbance in a public place [14C. Via Anglo-Norman *afrayer* 'disturb' < assumed Vulgar Latin *exfridare* 'take out of peace'.]

affricate /áffrikət/, **affricative** /ə fríkətiv/ *n* a composite speech sound made up of a stop immediately followed by a fricative [Late 19C. < Latin *affricat-*, past participle of *affricare* 'rub against' < *fricare* 'rub'.] —**affricative** *adj*

affright /ə frī́t/ *vt* to overwhelm somebody with sudden fear (*archaic literary*) [Late 16C. < obsolete *fright* 'frighten' < Old English *fryhtan* < Germanic.] —**affright** *n* —**affrightment** *n*

affront /ə frúnt/ *n* an open insult or giving of offence to somebody ■ *vt* to insult or offend somebody openly [14C. Via Old French < Vulgar Latin *affrontare* 'strike in the face' < *ad frontem* 'to the face'.]

afghan /áf gan, áfgən/ *n* **1** a knitted or crocheted blanket or shawl, often with geometric designs **2** a large carpet woven in a geometric design [Early 18C. < Pashto *afghāni* 'of Afghanistan'.]

Afghan *n* **1** somebody who comes from Afghanistan **2** LANG = **Pashto** *n.* 1 **3** ZOOL = **Afghan hound** —**Afghan** *adj*

Afghan hound *n* a tall dog with a long silky coat

afghani /af gánni, -gaáni/ (*plural* **-is**) *n* see table at **currency** [Early 20C. < Pashto *afghānī*.]

Afghanistan

Afghanistan /af gánni staan, -stan/ republic in SW Asia. Capital: Kabul. Population: 23,738,085 (1997). Area: 652,225 sq. km/251,825 sq. mi.

aficionada /ə físhə naádə, ə físsi ə-/ *n* a woman who is enthusiastic and knowledgeable about something

aficionado /ə físhə naádō, ə físsi ə-/ (*plural* **-dos**) *n* **1** somebody who is enthusiastic and knowledgeable about something **2** a devotee of bullfighting [Mid-19C. Via Spanish, 'somebody who likes something' < Latin *affection-* (see AFFECTION).]

afield /ə feéld/ *adv, adj* **1** distant from home or your usual surroundings ○ *wandered far afield* **2** off the point or subject

afikomen /aáfi kṓmən/ *n* in Judaism, the unleavened bread that completes the festive meal (**Seder**) on the first night of Passover [Late 19C. Via Hebrew *aphīqōmān* < Greek, 'festival'.]

afire /ə fī́r/ *adj, adv* **1** on fire or blazing **2** passionately interested in something

AFL *abbr* Australian Football League

aflame /ə fláym/ *adj* **1** in flames or blazing **2** highly aroused or impassioned

aflatoxin /áfflə tóksin/ *n* a toxin produced by some moulds in crops, especially peanuts [Mid-20C. < modern Latin *Aspergillus flavus* + TOXIN.]

AFL-CIO *abbr* American Federation of Labor and Congress of Industrial Organizations

afloat /ə flṓt/ *adj, adv* **1 FLOATING ON WATER** floating on water **2 ON BOARD SHIP** on board a ship or at sea **3 FLOODED** covered with water **4 DRIFTING PURPOSELESSLY** without purpose or guidance **5 IN CIRCULATION** circulating among the public **6 FINANCIALLY SOLVENT** free of debt or financial problems

AFLP *abbr* amplified fragment length polymorphism

aflutter /ə flúttər/ *adj, adv* **1** in a state of agitation or excitement **2** flapping or waving, e.g. as a flag does in the breeze

AFNOR /áf nawr/ *n* the French industrial standards authority. Full form **Association française de normalisation**

afoot /ə fŏŏt/ *adj, adv* **1** in the process of happening **2** on foot or by walking [13C. Partly after Old Norse *á fótum* 'on foot'.]

afore /ə fáwr/ *adv, prep, conj* before (*regional*) [Old English *onforan* < *foran* 'in front, before']

aforementioned /ə fáwr mensh'nd/ *adj* previously mentioned (*formal*) ■ *n* the previously mentioned person or people (*formal*)

aforesaid /ə fáwr sed/ *adj* previously named (*formal*)

aforethought /ə fáwr thawt/ *adj* thought about or planned beforehand

a fortiori /ay fáwrti áwr ī, aa fáwrti áwree/ *adv* for an even stronger reason [Early 17C. < Latin, 'from the stronger (reason)' < *fortis* 'strong'.]

afoul /ə fówl/ *adj, adv* **1** in or into trouble or conflict with somebody or something **2** entangled or in collision with something

AFP *abbr* **1** alpha-foetoprotein **2** *Aus* Australian Federal Police

Afr. *abbr* **1** Africa **2** African

afraid /ə fráyd/ *adj* **1 FRIGHTENED** frightened or apprehensive about something **2 RELUCTANT** feeling hesitation or disinclination towards something **3 REGRETFUL** regretful that something is or is not the case [14C. Originally past participle of AFFRAY, after Anglo-Norman *affrayé*.]

LITERARY LINK ***Who's Afraid of Virginia Woolf?***, a play (1962) by US dramatist Edward Albee. It examines the sour relationship between a middle-aged, underachieving academic and his embittered wife. A dinner party with a younger, not dissimilar, couple forces them to confront the reality of their past and present.

A-frame *adj* built in the shape of a capital letter A ■ *n* a building shaped like a capital letter A, with a triangular front and back and a roof that slopes to the ground forming the sides of the building

afreet /áffreet, ə fréet/, **afrit** *n* an evil spirit or powerful monster in Arabian mythology [Late 18C. < Arabic *afrīt*.]

afresh /ə frésh/ *adv* once again, especially from the beginning

Africa /áffrikə/ second largest continent, lying south of Europe with the Atlantic Ocean to the west and the Indian Ocean to the east. Population: 728,000,000 (1995). Area: 30,330,000 sq. km/11,699,000 sq. mi.

African /áffrikən/ *adj* **OF AFRICA** relating to any part of the African continent, or its people, language, or culture ■ *n* **1 SOMEBODY FROM AFRICA** somebody who comes from Africa **2 SOMEBODY OF AFRICAN DESCENT** somebody descended from a people of Africa [Pre-12C. < Latin *Africanus* < *Afri* 'the ancient inhabitants of N Africa'.]

African American *n* an American of African descent —**African American** *adj*

African American Vernacular English *n* the variety of English spoken by many African Americans

African-Caribbean *n* somebody of African descent who lives in or comes from the Caribbean —**African-Caribbean** *adj*

Africander *n* ZOOL = **Afrikander**

Africanism /áffrikənizəm/ *n* a cultural feature associated with Africa or Africans, especially a linguistic feature found in a language that is not itself African

Africanist /áffrikənist/ *n* a specialist in African affairs, cultures, or languages

Africanized bee /áfrikə nīzd-/ *n* an aggressive honeybee that was accidentally hybridized in Brazil from African and European strains and has spread north into Mexico and S Texas

African lily *n* = **agapanthus**

African mahogany *n* **1** a hard wood similar in appearance to that of tropical American mahogany. Use: furniture-making. **2** a tree that produces African mahogany. Native to: Africa. Genera: *Khaya* and *Entandrophragma.*

African National Congress *n* full form of **ANC**

African sleeping sickness *n* MED = **sleeping sickness**

African violet *n* a tropical plant with fleshy leaves, grown as a houseplant. Flowers: violet, white, or pink. Native to: Africa. Genus: *Saintpaulia.*

Afrikaans /áffri kaánss/ *n* an official language of South Africa, also spoken in Namibia, that is descended from the Dutch spoken by 17th-century settlers. Native speakers: 10 million. ■ *adj* relating to the Afrikaner people, or their language or culture [Early 20C. < Dutch, 'African'.]

Afrikander /áffri kándər/, **Africander** *n* **1** a long-horned hump-backed animal with a reddish colour, belonging to a South African breed of beef cattle **2** a sheep belonging to an indigenous South African breed [Variant of AFRIKANER]

Afrikaner /áffri kaánər/ *n* a South African whose first language is Afrikaans, usually descended from 17th century settlers (**Boers**) [Early 19C. < Afrikaans, < *Afrikaan* 'African person', after *Hollander* 'Dutch person'.] —**Afrikaner** *adj*

afrit *n* = **afreet**

Afro /áffrō/ *n* (*plural* **-ros**) a hairstyle with rounded thick curls ■ *adj* of African origin or style [Mid-20C. < AFRO-AMERICAN or AFRO-.]

Afro- *prefix* Africa, African ○ *Afro-Cuban* [< Latin *Afr-*, stem of *Afer* 'an African']

Afro-American *n* an American of African descent —**Afro-American** *adj*

Afro-American English *n* LANG = **African American Vernacular English**

Afro-Asian *adj* relating to the continents of Africa and Asia or their peoples or shared cultural phenomena

Afro-Asiatic *n* a large family of languages spoken across North Africa and the Middle East. Native speakers: 250 million. —**Afro-Asiatic** *adj*

Afro-Caribbean *n* = **African-Caribbean** —**Afro-Caribbean** *adj*

Afro-Cuban *adj* relating to Cuban culture as influenced by Africa, especially a style of jazz based on Cuban interpretations of African rhythms

afrormosia /áffrawr mṓzi ə/ *n* a hard wood, similar to teak, from tropical African trees [Mid-20C. < modern Latin, < *Afro-* + *Ormosia*, genus name (from Greek *hormos* 'necklace', probably because the wood was used to make jewellery).]

aft /aaft/ *adv, adj* towards or at the rear of a ship, submarine, or aircraft [Early 17C. Shortening of ABAFT.]

after /áaftər/ *prep* **1 LATER THAN** later in time than **2 BEHIND** behind in order or place **3 IN PURSUIT OF** in pursuit of or looking for **4 REGARDING** about or regarding **5 FOLLOWING FROM** subsequent to and considering **6 LIKE** in imitation or in the manner of somebody or something **7 AGREEING WITH** in agreement with or in conformity to **8 WITH THE SAME NAME AS** with a name from that of a specified person or thing because of family relationships or respect **9** *US* **PAST THE HOUR OF** past the hour of ■ *adv* **1 LATER** later in time or place **2 FARTHER BACK** farther towards the rear of a ship, submarine, or aircraft ■ *conj* **FOLLOWING A TIME WHEN** following a time when, and sometimes as a result ■ *adj* **1 SUBSEQUENT** later in time **2 REAR** nearer to the rear of a ship, submarine, or aircraft [Old English *æfter*. Assumed to be a comparative form, 'farther away' < Indo-European, 'away, off'.] ◇ **after all 1** used to emphasize something that should be taken into consideration in spite of what has happened or been said **2** used to show that in the end something happened, was done, or was recognized in spite of expectations to the contrary or efforts to prevent it

afterbeat /áaftər beet/ *n* MUSIC = **backbeat**

afterbirth /áaftər burth/ *n* the placenta and foetal membranes expelled from the womb after a birth [Late 16C. Perhaps after German *Aftergeburt*.]

afterburner /áftər burnər/ *n* **1** a system for increasing the thrust of an aircraft jet engine by feeding fuel into the hot exhaust gases **2** a device in the exhaust system of an internal combustion engine for burning or catalytically destroying potentially harmful unburned or incompletely burned carbon compounds

aftercare /áaftər kair/ *n* **1 CARE AFTER LEAVING HOSPITAL** care or support somebody receives after leaving a hospital, prison, or other institution, often provided by a community nurse or social worker **2 CARE AFTER ILLNESS** care given in a hospital to a patient who is recovering from an illness or operation **3 UPKEEP OF PRODUCT PURCHASED** the maintenance in good condition of a product after purchase, or a service provided by a company to its customers to support this **4 POLLUTION PREVENTION** arrangements for preventing pollution from occurring after a potentially polluting activity such as landfill of waste has ended

afterdamp /áaftər damp/ *n* gaseous fumes remaining in a mine after an explosion of firedamp

afterdeck /áaftər dek/ *n* the part of the main open deck of a ship that extends from the bridge or midships to the stern

aftereffect /áaftər i fekt/ *n* **1 DELAYED RESULT** an effect, usually unpleasant, that follows its cause after an interval of time ○ *The stock markets are still showing the aftereffects of last month's rise in interest rates.* **2 SECONDARY REACTION** a secondary response that follows the primary response to a physiological stimulus **3 DELAYED REACTION** a delayed reaction to a psychological stimulus

afterglow /áaftər glō/ *n* **1** radiated light that remains visible after a source of light or energy has been removed, e.g. the glow sometimes seen in the sky after sunset **2** a feeling of pleasure or a favourable impression that remains after a positive experience ○ *In the afterglow of the victory, we forgot our leading scorer had been injured.*

after-hours *adj* taking place after the time a business or service closes for the day

afterimage /áaftər immij/ *n* a visual image that remains briefly after light stimulation has ended

afterlife /áaftər līf/ *n* **1** a form of existence believed to continue after death **2** the period of somebody's life that follows a particular event ○ *Is there an afterlife for retired football players?*

aftermarket /áaftər maarkit/ *n* subsequent sales opportunities resulting from an original sale, especially the demand for parts and services

aftermath /áaftə math, -maath/ *n* **1** ⚠ the consequences of an event, especially a disastrous one, or the period of time during which these consequences are felt ○ *in the aftermath of the war.* **2** a second crop or growth of grass in the same season, after the first harvest or mowing [15C. Literally 'grass that springs up after mowing' < *math* 'mowing' < Old English *mæþ*.]

USAGE aftermath = 'what comes after': Some people insist that an ***aftermath*** should be the same kind of thing as the thing it comes after, as it is in its older literal meaning, 'a second crop or growth of grass', but the word is now normally used as follows: *House prices fell in the aftermath of the recession.*

aftermost /áaftər mōst/, **aftmost** /áaft mōst/ *adj* nearest to the stern of a ship

afternoon /áaftər nóon/ *n* **1 DAYTIME BETWEEN MIDDAY AND EVENING** the period of the day between noon or lunchtime, and evening **2 LATTER PART** a latter part of something, especially of somebody's life (*literary*) ■ *interj* **GREETING** a greeting used to say 'good afternoon' (*informal*)

afternoons /áaftər nóonz/ *adv* in any or during every afternoon (*informal*)

afterpains /áaftər paynz/ *npl* pains experienced by some women just after giving birth, caused by contractions of the womb

afterpiece /áaftər peess/ *n* a short entertainment, usually comic, performed after a play

afters /áaftərz/ *n* the sweet or dessert course of a meal (*informal; + singular or plural verb*) ○ *What's for afters?*

aftersales /áaftə saylz/ *adj* occurring or provided after the sale of a product

aftersensation /áaftər sen sáysh'n/ *n* any sense impression, e.g. an aftertaste or afterimage, that remains after the immediate stimulus has been removed

aftershave /áaftər shayv/ *n* a liquid applied after shaving, to soothe and scent the skin of the face

aftershock /áaftər shok/ *n* **1** a small earthquake, usually one of several, that follows a larger one after a period of time **2** a delayed psychological or physical reaction to a serious event or trauma

aftertaste /áaftər tayst/ *n* **1** a taste left in the mouth by food or drink after swallowing **2** a feeling or sensation, especially an unpleasant one, left behind after an experience

afterthought /áaftər thawt/ *n* **1** something not thought of, said, or done originally, but added afterwards **2** a child born several years after other children in the same family (*humorous*)

afterward /áaftərwərd/ *adv* US = **afterwards**

afterwards /-wərdz/ *adv* at a later time or after an event that has been mentioned previously ○ *Let's have breakfast now and go skiing afterwards.*

afterword /áaftər wurd/ *n* a short concluding section added at the end of a literary work

afterworld /áaftər wurld/ *n* in some religions, a world that people are believed to go to and live in after death

aftmost *adj* = **aftermost**

AFV *abbr* armoured fighting vehicle

ϟ **ag** *abbr* Antigua and Barbuda (*in Internet addresses*)

Ag *symbol* silver [Shortening of Latin *argentum* 'silver']

AG *abbr* **1** Adjutant General **2** Attorney General

ag- *prefix* = **ad-** (*before g*)

aga /áagə/, **agha** *n* used as a title for a military commander or important official in Islamic countries, especially during the Ottoman Empire ○ *the Aga Khan* [Mid-16C. < Turkish *aghā* 'chief, master, lord'.]

Aga /áagə/ *tdmk* a trademark for a large iron stove used for both cooking and heating

Agadir /ággə déer/ port in Morocco. Population: 779,000 (1990).

again /ə gén, ə gáyn/ *adv* **1 AT ANOTHER TIME** at another time or on another occasion, repeating what has happened or been done before ○ *I hope to come here again some day.* **2 AS BEFORE** to the place, person, or state where somebody or something was earlier ○ *Will I ever be able to walk again?* **3 IN ADDITION** in addition to a previously mentioned quantity ○ *You'll need all that and half as much again.* **4 MOREOVER** similarly and in addition (*formal*) ○ *Again, that is something that the court must take into account.* [Old English *ongēan* 'in a direct line with, facing' or 'back to a starting point' < Germanic] ◇ **again and again** repeatedly

against /ə génst, ə gáynst/ CORE MEANING: a preposition indicating opposition to or conflict with somebody or something, either physically or intellectually ○ (prep) *a battle against cancer*

prep **1 IN COMPETITION WITH** with somebody or something as an opponent in a competitive situation, especially in sport ○ *It's Australia against Sweden in the finals.* **2 IN CONTACT WITH BY LEANING** in a position such that part or all of something touches another object or surface, by leaning or resting on the side of it rather than resting on top of it ○ *I leaned against a tree.* **3 INTO SUDDEN CONTACT OR COLLISION WITH** so as to briefly touch or suddenly collide with a usually stationary object while in movement ○ *banged his head against the beam* **4 IN THE OPPOSITE DIRECTION OF** in the opposite direction to the movement, angle, or position of something or somebody ○ *to swim against the current* **5 SEEN IN CONTRAST WITH** seen in contrast with something, e.g. a colour that is behind or surrounding something ○ *The dark green pines are lovely against the blue sky.* **6 IN RELATION TO EVENTS** in relation to, or contrasted with, a set of events or circumstances ○ *Government action makes sense against the background of rising tensions.* **7 AS PROTECTION FROM** in order to prevent or avoid something, or to be protected from something ○ *vaccinate against disease* **8 IN PAYMENT OF** in partial or total payment of, or as a charge on ○ *I'd like to put this money against the amount I owe you.* **9 AS A DISADVANTAGE TO** to the disadvantage of somebody or something ○ *Will you hold it against me if I don't come to your party?* **10 COMPARED WITH** in comparison with something ○ *weighed the cost of hiring someone against that of promoting existing staff* **11 CONTRARY TO** contrary to or not approved or allowed by something or somebody ○ *It's against the law.* [14C. < AGAIN + adverbial suffix *-es* + *-t*, after such words as AMIDST.]

Aga Khan III /áagə kaán/ (1877–1957) religious leader, born in Karachi, India, now Pakistan

Aga Khan IV (*b.* 1936) Swiss-born Muslim leader. Born **Karim al Hussaini Shah**

agama /ággəmə/ *n* **1** a small long-tailed, often colourful lizard. Native to: tropical Africa, Asia. Genus: *Agama.* **2** ZOOL = **agamid** [Late 18C. < modern Latin and Spanish, probably < Carib *mami* 'lizard'.]

Agamemnon /ággə mém non/ *n* the commander of the Greek army in the Trojan War

agamic /ə gámmik/, **agamous** /ə gámməss/ *adj* describes an organism that multiplies asexually [Mid-19C. < Greek *agamos* 'unmarried' < *gamos* 'marriage'.] —**agamically** *adv*

agamid /ággəmid/ *n* a small long-tailed insect-eating lizard. Native to: tropical Africa and Asia. Family: Agamidae. [Late 19C. < modern Latin *Agamidae* < *agama* (see AGAMA).]

agamogenesis /áy gamō jénnəsiss, ággəmō-/ *n* asexual reproduction, e.g. by cell division or budding [Mid-19C. < Greek *agamos* 'unmarried' + -GENESIS.]

agamospermy /ággəmō spurmi/ *n* the asexual formation of seeds without fertilization [Mid-20C. < Greek *agamos* 'unmarried' + SPERM[1] + -Y[1].]

agamous *adj* = **agamic**

agapanthus /ággə pánthəss/ (*plural* **-thus** *or* **-thuses**) *n* a plant of the lily family. Flowers: bluish or white, funnel-shaped, in ball-shaped clusters. Native to: southern Africa. Genus: *Agapanthus.* US term **African lily** [Late 18C. < modern Latin, < Greek *agapē* 'love' + *anthos* 'flower'.]

agape[1] /ə gáyp/ *adv, adj* (*literary*) **1** opened quite widely ○ *The door to the room was agape.* **2** with the mouth wide open, usually in surprise or wonder

agape[2] /ággəpi/ *n* **1 NON-SEXUAL LOVE** love that is wholly selfless and spiritual **2 CHRISTIAN LOVE** selfless love felt by Christians for their fellow human beings **3 CHRISTIAN COMMUNAL MEAL** a communal meal held by a Christian community, especially in early Christian times, in commemoration of the Last Supper [Mid-17C. < Greek *agapē* 'brotherly love'.]

agar /áygər, -gaar/, **agar-agar** *n* **1** a powdered seaweed extract. Use: setting agent, thickener. **2** a culture medium based on a seaweed extract. Use: for growing microorganisms in laboratories [Late 19C. < Malay *agar-agar* 'jelly'.]

agaric /ággərik, ə gárrik/ *n* a fungus with a large cap resembling an umbrella with numerous radiating gills on the underside. Family: Agaricaceae. [15C. Directly or via French < Latin *agaricum* < Greek *agarikon* 'tree fungus'.]

agarose /ággə rōss, -rōz/ *n* a complex carbohydrate (**polysaccharide**) obtained from agar. Use: as a medium in chromatography and electrophoresis.

Aga saga *n* a novel about middle-class people, especially those living in the shire counties of Britain [Because the AGA™ is thought to symbolize the lifestyle of the main characters]

Agassi /ággəssi/, **Andre** (*b.* 1970) US tennis player

agate /ággət/ *n* **1** a semi-precious stone that is a hard fine-grained form of chalcedony with variously coloured bands, markings, and areas of clouding. Use: gems. **2** a playing marble made of agate or of glass that looks like agate [Late 16C. Via French < Greek *akhatēs*, perhaps after *Achates*, river in Sicily.]

agateware /ággət wair/ *n* decorative pottery made using a cross-section of layers of clay of contrasting colours

agave /ə gáyvi, ə gáavi, ággayv/ (*plural* **-ves** *or* **-ve**) *n* a spiny-leaved plant with a single tall flower stalk. Use: fibre, alcoholic drinks, especially tequila. Native to: America. Genus: *Agave.* [Late 18C. Via Latin < Greek *Agauē*, mother of Pentheus in Greek mythology.]

AGC *abbr* automatic gain control

age /ayj/ *n* **1 HOW OLD SOMEBODY OR SOMETHING IS** the length of time that somebody or something has existed, usually expressed in years **2 STAGE OF LIFE** one of the stages or phases in the lifetime of somebody or something ○ *at an early age* **3 LEGAL ADULTHOOD** the age at which somebody is legally considered as an adult **4 STATE OF HAVING LIVED LONG** the condition of having lived many years ○ *the wisdom of age* **5 age, Age HISTORICAL ERA** a period in history, especially a long period or one associated with and named after a distinctive characteristic, achievement, or influential person ○ *the space age* **6 age, Age GEOLOGICAL ERA** a relatively short division of recent geological time, shorter than an epoch ○ *the Ice Age* **7 LEVEL OF DEVELOPMENT** a level of development equivalent to that of an average person of the stated age ○ *a reading age of 7* **8 GENERATION** a generation of people (*literary*) ○ *the greatest writer of her age* ■ **ages** *npl* **1 LONG TIME** a very long time (*informal*) **2 HISTORY** human history ○ *People have warred with one another throughout the ages.* ■ *v* (**ages, ageing** *or* **aging, aged**) **1** *vti* **GROW OR CAUSE TO GROW OLD** to become old, develop the characteristics of being old, or cause somebody or something to become or seem old ○ *Too much sun ages the skin.* **2** *vti* **IMPROVE OVER TIME** to cause a food or wine to mature, develop a desired flavour, or become more tender, or to become improved in this way over time ○ *The wine is aged in oak barrels.* **3** *vt* **STABILIZE THROUGH USE** to stabilize an electronic device by using it [13C. Via Old French *aage* < Latin *aetat-* 'period of life' < Indo-European.] ◇ **come of age** to reach the age when somebody is legally considered an adult ◇ **of a certain age** no longer young (*humorous*)

USAGE of age or **old**? It is more concise and less formal to write: *She is 40 years old* instead of *She is 40 years of age.*

-age *suffix* **1** action or result of an action ○ *breakage* ○ *coinage* **2** collection of things ○ *signage* **3** housing ○ *orphanage* **4** condition, office ○ *brigandage* ○ *peerage* **5** charge ○ *dockage* [Via French < assumed Vulgar Latin *-aticum* < Latin *-aticus*, suffix forming adjectives]

aged /áyjid/ *adj* **1 OLD** very advanced in years **2 OF PARTICULAR AGE** of the stated age ○ *a person aged 50* **3 IMPROVED WITH TIME** stored for a period of time in order to mature and produce the best flavour ○ *well-aged wine* **4 ERODED** showing evidence of advanced erosion ■ *npl* **OLD PEOPLE** people of advanced years, especially those whose physical or mental health has diminished (*formal*) [15C. Probably after French *âgé*.]

age discrimination *n* discrimination against people of particular ages, particularly in employment

Agee /áyji/, **James** (1909–55) US poet, novelist, screenwriter, and film critic

age-grade *n* a group of people in a society who are the same sex and approximately the same age

age group *n* a group of people whose ages are approximately the same or fall within a stated range

ageing /áyjing/, **aging** *n* **1 GROWING OLD** the process of growing old, especially of acquiring the physical and mental characteristics of old age **2 MATURING PROCESS** the natural or chemically assisted process of bringing foods to maturity or of making materials like wood appear older ■ *adj* **BECOMING OLD** growing old or elderly ○ *caring for an ageing parent* ■ present participle of **age**

ageism /áyjizəm/, **agism** *n* discrimination or prejudice against people of particular ages, especially in employment —**ageist** *adj*

ageless /áyjləss/ *adj* **1** never growing or seeming to grow older **2** not typical of or confined to a particular period of time ○ *the ageless search for the truth* —**agelessly** *adv* —**agelessness** *n*

agency /áyjənssi/ (*plural* **-cies**) *n* **1 COMPANY ACTING AS AGENT** an organization, especially a company, acting as the representative, agent, or subcontractor of a person or another company ○ *an employment agency* **2 GOVERNMENT ORGANIZATION** a division of a government or international organization that carries out administrative duties ○ *a United Nations agency* **3 SEPARATE PART OF UK CIVIL SERVICE** a part of the civil service in the United Kingdom that has some autonomy to deal with a particular aspect of administration such as issuing passports or benefits ○ *the Child Support Agency* **4 OFFICE OF AGENCY** the building or offices where an agency is located **5 ACTION OR OPERATION** the action, medium, or means by which something is accomplished [Mid-17C. < medieval Latin *agentia* < Latin *agent-* (see AGENT).]

agenda /ə jéndə/ *n* **1 LIST OF THINGS TO DO** a formal list of things to be done in a particular order, especially a list of things to be discussed at a meeting **2 MATTERS NEEDING ATTENTION** the various matters that somebody needs to deal with at a given time ○ *What's your agenda for today?* **3 SOMEBODY'S PARTICULAR MOTIVE** an underlying personal viewpoint or bias ○ *Of course she's in favour, but then she has her own agenda.* ■ plural of **agendum** [Early 17C. < Latin, plural of *agendum* 'thing to be done' < *agere* 'do' (see AGENT).] ◇ **set the agenda** to be the major influence or force affecting something ○ *It is the environmental lobby that is setting the agenda in this round of negotiations.*

USAGE Although ***agenda*** is strictly speaking a plural noun meaning 'things to be done', the singular form *agendum* is formal and no longer used; ***agenda*** is used in the singular as if it were 'a list of things to be done', with a plural form ***agendas***: *The agenda for tomorrow's meeting has been changed. This item has appeared on a number of previous agendas.* The use of ***agenda*** as a verb (*We will agenda that for the next meeting*) is criticized and is better avoided.

Agenda 21 *n* the global environmental programme and statement of principles agreed at the Earth Summit in Rio de Janeiro in 1992

agendum /ə jéndəm/ (*plural* **-dums** *or* **-da** /-ə/) *n* an item on an agenda (*formal*) [Early 17C. < Latin (see AGENDA).]

USAGE See ***agenda***.

agenesis /ay jénnəsiss/ *n* the incomplete development or total absence of a body part ○ *ovarian agenesis*

⚡**agent** /áyjənt/ *n* **1 SOMEBODY REPRESENTING ANOTHER** somebody who officially represents somebody else in business **2 CAUSATIVE SUBSTANCE** something, e.g. a chemical substance, organism, or natural force, that causes an effect ○ *a cleansing agent* **3 MEANS EFFECTING RESULT** the means by which an effect or result is produced ○ *As director you will be expected to be the main agent of change.* **4 COMPUTER PROGRAM** a program that works automatically on routine tasks, e.g. sorting e-mail or gathering information [15C. < Latin *agent-*, present participle of *agere* 'drive, lead, act, do'.] —**agential** /ay jénsh'l/ *adj*

agent-general (*plural* **agents-general**) *n* a representative of a Canadian province or Australian state in a foreign country

Agent Orange *n* a toxic herbicide sprayed by the US military during the Vietnam War to defoliate jungle areas and expose enemy forces [< the orange stripe on its storage drums]

agent provocateur /ázhoN prə vókə túr/ (*plural* **agents provocateurs** /ázhoN prə vókə túr/) *n* somebody employed to gain the trust of suspects and then tempt them to do something illegal so that they can be arrested and punished [< French, 'provocative agent']

Age of Aquarius *n* an astrological era in which increased spirituality and harmony is said to characterize people's lives

age of consent *n* the age at which somebody is legally old enough to consent to marriage or sexual intercourse

age-old *adj* dating from a very long time ago and still in existence

age pension *n Aus* a social security payment made to men over 65 and women over 60

ageratum /ájjə ráytəm/ (*plural* **-tum** *or* **-tums**) *n* a low-growing garden plant. Flowers: blue, white, or purplish, in thick clusters. Genus: *Ageratum.* [Mid-16C. Via modern Latin < Greek *agēratos* 'ageless, everlasting' < *gēras* 'old age'.]

age-related *adj* relating to or governed by the age that somebody has reached

Aggadah /əgə daá/ (*plural* **-doth** /-dáwt/) *n* **1** those sections of the Talmud and other rabbinic literature dealing with biblical narrative and stories and legends on biblical themes, rather than with religious law and regulations **2** = **Haggadah** *n.* **2, Haggadah** *n.* **3** [Mid-19C. < Rabbinic Hebrew *haggādāh* 'tale'.]

aggiornamento /ə jáwrnə méntō/ *n* the process of modernizing Roman Catholic Church ritual and policy [Mid-20C. < Italian, < *aggiornare* 'bring up to date'.]

agglomerate *vti* /ə glómmə rayt/ (**-ates, -ating, -ated**) **1 FORM A MASS** to collect together into a mass **2 COLLECT IN ROUND MASS** to gather or accumulate something in a roughly ball-shaped mass ■ *n* /ə glómmərət/ **1 JUMBLED COLLECTION** a jumbled mass or collection of something (*formal*) **2 VOLCANIC ROCK** rock produced by a volcanic eruption, consisting of fragments of different rock types, sizes, and shapes set in fine-grained solidified volcanic ash ■ *adj* /ə glómmərət/ **IN ROUND MASS** gathered into or forming a rounded mass [Mid-17C. < Latin *agglomerat-*, past participle of *agglomerare* 'heap up' < *glomer-* 'ball'.] —**agglomeration** /ə glómmə ráysh'n/ *n* —**agglomerative** /ə glómmərətiv, -raytiv/ *adj* —**agglomerator** *n*

agglutinate /ə glóoti nayt/ (**-nates, -nating, -nated**) *vti* **1 ADHERE OR CAUSE SOMETHING TO ADHERE** to be joined or glued together, or cause things to stick to each other **2 CLUMP OR CAUSE CELLS TO CLUMP** to cause cells such as red blood cells or bacteria to form clumps, or stick together in clumps **3 FORM COMPOUND WORD** to combine simple words together without changing their form to make a new word, or be combined in a new word in this way [Mid-16C. < Latin *agglutinat-*, past participle of *agglutinare* 'fasten with glue' < *gluten* 'glue'.] —**agglutinability** /ə glóotinə bílləti/ *n* —**agglutinable** *adj* —**agglutinant** *n, adj* —**agglutination** /ə glóoti náysh'n/ *n*

agglutinative /ə glóotinətiv/ *adj* **1** able or likely to agglutinate **2** forming words by combining simple words or word components without alteration ○ *an agglutinative language*

agglutinin /ə glóotinin/ *n* a substance that causes cells to clump together, e.g. an antibody or lectin

agglutinogen /ágglōō tínnəjən/ *n* an antigen responsible for the formation of a specific agglutinin

aggrade /ə gráyd/ (**-grades, -grading, -graded**) *vt* to build up a land surface or stream bed through the natural deposition of material. ◊ **degrade** *v.* **4** [Early 20C. Back-formation < *aggradation* < AG- + DEGRADATION.] —**aggradation** /ággrə dáysh'n/ *n* —**aggradational** *adj*

aggrandize /ə grán dīz, ággrən-/ (**-dizes, -dizing, -dized**), **aggrandise** (**-dises, -dising, -dised**) *vt* **1** to increase or improve the power, wealth, influence, or status of somebody or something, especially by deliberate plan **2** to make somebody or something seem bigger or better than is actually the case, especially through exaggerated praise (*formal*) ○ *aggrandizing the value of her accomplishments* [Mid-17C. < French *agrandiss-*, stem of *agrandir* < *grandir* 'increase' < Latin *grandis* 'great' (see GRAND).] —**aggrandizement** /ə grán dizmənt, -dīzmənt/ *n* —**aggrandizer** *n*

aggravate /ággrə vayt/ (**-vates, -vating, -vated**) *vt* **1** ⚠ to irritate or anger somebody, especially with a continuing or trivial annoyance (*informal*) **2** to make something that is already bad or serious worse or more severe [Mid-16C. Probably via Old French < Latin *aggravat-*, past participle of *aggravare* 'make heavier' < *gravis* 'heavy'.] —**aggravating** *adj* —**aggravatingly** *adv* —**aggravator** *n*

USAGE **aggravate** meaning 'annoy': Many people still dislike the use of ***aggravate*** to mean 'irritate' or 'anger' somebody, despite a history of usage dating back to the 17th century: *We were aggravated by the continuous loud noise from the street. Their bad behaviour has been very aggravating.* Except in informal conversation, it is usually better to use an alternative word such as *annoy, exasperate,* or *irritate.*

aggravated /ággrə vaytid/ *adj* having features that make something a worse criminal offence ○ *aggravated assault*

aggravation /ággrə váysh'n/ *n* **1 IRRITATION** a feeling of exasperation or irritation, especially when caused by a continuing problem **2 SOURCE OF IRRITATION** somebody or something that causes continuing exasperation, irritation, or trouble **3 WORSENING** the worsening of an already bad situation, or something that or somebody who makes a bad situation worse ○ *Exercising before you have fully recovered may lead to an aggravation of your condition.* **4 TROUBLE** annoyance or bother, often aggressive in nature (*informal*) ○ *I get a lot of aggravation from dissatisfied customers.*

aggregate *adj* /ággrigət, -gayt/ **1 FORMING A TOTAL** collected together from different sources and considered as a whole (*formal*) **2 RESEMBLING ROCK** describes a mixture of minerals or rock fragments that resembles rock ○ *an aggregate structure* ■ *n* /ággrigət, -gayt/ **1 SUM TOTAL** a total or whole made up of different parts from often disparate sources (*formal*) ○ *Her portfolio consisted of an aggregate of shares from different countries.* **2 INGREDIENTS OF CONCRETE** broken stone, gravel, and sand used in road construction and, when mixed with cement and water, for making concrete **3 MINERAL MIXTURE RESEMBLING ROCK** a mixture of minerals or rock fragments that resembles rock ■ *v* /ággri gayt/ (**-gates, -gating, -gated**) **1** *vti* **UNITE** to come together, or bring different things together, into a total, mass, or whole ○ *Aggregate the different totals to get the overall cost.* **2** *vt* **ADD UP TO A NUMBER** to amount or add up to a particular number ○ *The company's earnings aggregate £175,000.* [15C. < Latin *aggregat-*, past participle of *aggregare* 'add to' < *greg-* 'flock'.] —**aggregately** *adv* —**aggregation** /ággri gáysh'n/ *n* —**aggregative** *adj* —**aggregator** *n* ◇ **in the aggregate** considered or taken together as a whole

aggress /ə gréss/ *vi* to attack first, or begin a fight, argument, or war (*formal*) [Late 16C. Via obsolete French *aggresser* < Latin *aggress-*, past participle of *aggredi* 'approach, attack' < *gradi* 'walk'.]

aggression /ə grésh'n/ *n* **1** hostile action, especially a physical or military attack, directed against another person or country, often without provocation **2** threatening behaviour or actions [Early 17C. Directly or via French < Latin *aggression-* < *aggress-* (see AGGRESS).]

aggressive /ə gréssiv/ *adj* **1 LIKELY TO HARM** showing a readiness or having a tendency to attack or do harm to others **2 ATTACKING** attacking or taking action without provocation or without waiting for an enemy to make the first move **3** ⚠ **ASSERTIVE** characterized by or exhibiting determination, energy, and initiative ○ *an aggressive investment policy* **4 SPREADING QUICKLY** describes a disease process or pathological growth, e.g. a tumour, that is fast-growing or spreading to other parts of the body —**aggressively** *adv* —**aggressiveness** *n*

USAGE **Aggressive** or **assertive**? ***Aggressive*** normally implies hostility and even the threat of violence, and is best avoided when the meaning required is 'forceful' or 'assertive': *The sales team is encouraged to be assertive but not to use aggressive methods.*

aggressor /ə gréssər/ *n* a person or country that attacks or starts a war, fight, or argument, often without being provoked [Mid-17C. < late Latin, < *aggress-* (see AGGRESS).]

aggrieve /ə gréev/ (**-grieves, -grieving, -grieved**) *vt* **1** to cause somebody pain, trouble, or distress (*formal*) **2** to inflict an actionable injury on somebody [13C. Via Old French *agrever* 'make heavier' < Latin *aggravare* (see AGGRAVATE).] —**aggrieved** *adj* —**aggrievedly** /ə gréevidli/ *adv* —**aggrievedness** /-vidnəss/ *n*

aggro /ággrō/ *n* (*slang*) **1** threatening behaviour, especially trouble-making or fighting ○ *we don't want any aggro* **2** trouble or difficulty ○ *He's having a lot of aggro with the garage.* [Mid-20C. Shortening of AGGRAVATION or AGGRESSION.]

aggrupation /ággroo páysh'n/ *n Philippines* a group [< Spanish *agrupación* 'group']

agha *n* POL = **aga**

Agha Mohammad Khan /aágə mə hámməd kaán/ (1742–97) Iranian ruler

aghast /ə gaást/ *adj* overcome with shock and dismay [13C. < the past participle of obsolete *agast* 'frighten' < Old English *gǣst* 'spirit, ghost'.]

agile /ájjīl/ *adj* **1** able to move quickly and with suppleness, skill, and control **2** able to think quickly and intelligently [Late 16C. Via French < Latin *agilis* 'that can be moved easily, nimble, quick' < *agere* 'move, do'.] —**agilely** *adv* —**agileness** *n* —**agility** /ə jílləti/

aging *n, adj* = **ageing**

agio /ájji ō/ (*plural* **-os**) *n* **1** an amount charged as a premium or percentage for changing one country's currency into that of another **2** an allowance or discount given when paying in a foreign currency to compensate for the costs of exchanging the currency [Late 17C. Via Italian < medieval Greek *allagion* 'exchange' < *allagē* 'change' < *allos* 'other'.]

agiotage /ájjətij/ *n* **1** the business of exchanging currencies between countries **2** speculation in stocks, securities, or foreign currencies [Late 18C. < French, < Italian *agio* (see AGIO).]

agism *n* = **ageism**

agist *adj* = **ageist**

agitate /ájji tayt/ (**-tates, -tating, -tated**) *v* **1** *vt* **MAKE SOMEBODY ANXIOUS** to make somebody feel anxious, nervous, or disturbed **2** *vi* **AROUSE PUBLIC INTEREST** to attempt to arouse public feeling, interest, or support for or against something such as a cause **3** *vt* **MOVE SOMETHING VIOLENTLY** to cause something to move vigorously or violently, e.g. by shaking or blowing it ○ *Agitate the mixture until the sediment is thoroughly dispersed.* [Late 16C. < Latin *agitat-*, past participle of *agitare* 'move to and fro' < *agere* 'drive, move'.] —**agitated** /ájji taytid/ *adj* —**agitatedly** *adv* —**agitative** /ájjitətiv/ *adj*

agitation /ájji táysh'n/ *n* **1 ANXIETY** nervous anxiety **2 PUBLIC CAMPAIGNING** actions intended to arouse public feeling, interest, or support for or against something such as a cause **3 SHAKING** vigorous or violent shaking, stirring, or other disturbance of something, especially a liquid ○ *Observe the mixture after agitation.* —**agitational** *adj*

agitato /ájji taátō/ *adj, adv* in a restless, tense, or excited manner (*musical direction*) [Early 19C. Via Italian < Latin *agitat-* (see AGITATE).]

agitator /ájji taytər/ *n* **1** somebody who attempts to arouse feeling about something, especially a political cause **2** a machine or machine part that causes vigorous movement in a liquid or other substance

agitprop /ájjit prop/ *n* **1** political propaganda, especially when disseminated through literature, drama, music, or art **2** artistic work or works serving as a vehicle for political propaganda [Early 20C. < Russian, < *agitatsiya* 'agitation' + *propaganda* 'propaganda'.]

Aglaia /ə glí ə, ə gláy ə/ *n* in Greek mythology, one of the three Graces who lived on Mount Olympus and tended the goddess Aphrodite

agleam /ə gléem/ *adj* glowing, gleaming, or emitting a soft light (*literary*) ○ *She was laughing, her eyes agleam.*

aglet /ágglət/ *n* **1** a plain or ornamental metal or plastic sheath covering the end of a shoelace or ribbon **2** a metallic ornament such as a stud, cord, or badge worn on clothing [15C. < French *aiguillette* (see AIGUILLETTE).]

agley /ə gláy, ə glí, ə glée/ *adv, adj Scotland, N England* awry or askew ○ *'The best laid schemes o' mice and men/ Gang aft agley'* (Robert Burns, *To a mouse;* 1785) [Late 18C. < A-[1] + *gley* 'squint' < ?]

aglimmer /ə glímmər/ *adj* glimmering with light (*literary*)

aglitter /ə glíttər/ *adj* glittering or sparkling with light (*literary*)

aglow /ə glṓ/ *adj* radiating light, warmth, excitement, or happy emotion

AGM *abbr* annual general meeting

agma /ágmə/ *n* the symbol (ŋ) used to represent a velar nasal consonant, as in the final sound of 'long' [Mid-20C. < Greek, 'fragment'.]

agnail /ág nayl/ *n* = **hangnail** [Old English *angnægl* < *ang-* 'narrow, painful' + *nægl* 'nail']

agnate /ág nayt/ *n* **RELATIVE DESCENDED FROM SAME MAN** a relative who is descended from a man who is also the ancestor of other relatives, especially through the male line (*formal*) ■ *adj* (*formal*) **1 PATRILINEAL** patrilineal **2 RELATED** related or akin in any way [15C. < Latin *agnatus* 'born in addition' < Old Latin *gnatus*, past participle of *gnasci* 'be born'.] —**agnatic** /ag náttik/ *adj* —**agnatically** *adv* —**agnation** /ag náysh'n/ *n*

agnathan /ag náythən/ *n* a vertebrate aquatic animal that has no jaw, e.g. a lamprey or hagfish. Subphylum: Agnatha. [Mid-20C. < modern Latin *Agnatha* < Greek *a-* 'without, not' + *gnathos* 'jaw'.]

Agnes /ágnəss/, **St** (*d.* 304?) Roman Christian martyr and saint

Agnew /ág nyoo/, **Spiro T.** (1918–96) US politician

Agni /úgni/ *n* the Hindu god of fire [< Sanskrit, 'fire, the fire god']

agnolotti /ánnyə lótti/ *npl* small pieces of semicircular pasta stuffed with meat, cheese, or other filling and sealed at the edges [Late 20C. < Italian dialect, alteration of Italian *anellotto* 'little ring'.]

agnomen /ag nṓm en/ (*plural* **-nomina** /-minə/) *n* a nickname (*literary*) [Mid-17C. < Latin, 'additional name' < *(g)nomen* 'name'.]

agnosia /ag nṓzi ə/ *n* the total or partial loss of the ability to recognize familiar people or objects, usually caused by brain damage [Early 20C. < Greek, 'lack of knowledge' < *gnōsis* (see GNOSIS).]

agnostic /ag nóstik/ *n* **1** somebody who believes that it is impossible to know whether or not God exists **2** somebody who doubts that a question has one correct answer or that something can be completely understood ○ *I'm an agnostic concerning space aliens.* [Mid-19C. < A-[2] + GNOSTIC.] —**agnostic** *adj* —**agnostically** *adv*

agnosticism /ag nóstissizəm/ *n* the belief that it is impossible to know whether or not God exists

Agnus Dei /ágnooss dáy ee/ *n* **1 LAMB WITH CROSS** a lamb, usually depicted with a halo and holding a cross and banner, symbolizing Jesus Christ **2 CHRISTIAN PRAYER** a Christian prayer that begins in Latin with the words 'Agnus Dei', or 'Lamb of God', part of the liturgy of the Mass **3 MUSIC FOR AGNUS DEI PRAYER** a musical setting of the Christian prayer beginning 'Agnus Dei' [15C. < Latin, 'Lamb of God'.]

ago /ə gṓ/ *adv, adj* before the present time ○ *He only left about five minutes ago.* [14C. < the past participle of Old English *āgān* 'go away, pass by' < *gān* 'go'.]

USAGE ago and **since**: If ***ago*** is used it should be followed by *that* and not ***since*** in a following clause: *It was several weeks ago that I saw them.* If **ago** is left out, then ***since*** is used: *It is several weeks since I last saw them.* Note also that in sentences of this type, ***ago*** is preceded by a verb in the past tense (*was*) and ***since*** by a verb in the present tense (*is*).

agog /ə góg/ *adj* intensely interested, excited, or eager ○ *agog at the new twist to the scandal* [15C. Probably based on Old French *en gogues* 'enjoying yourself', literally 'in enjoyment'.]

-agog *suffix* = **-agogue**

à gogo /ə gṓ gō/ *adj* as much as anybody could want (*dated informal*) ○ *caviare à gogo* [Mid-20C. < French, 'joyfully' < *en gogues* (see AGOG) by repeating the *go-*.]

-agogue, -agog *suffix* substance promoting the flow of something ○ *galactagogue* [Via French < Greek *agōgos* 'a drawing off' < *agein* 'lead']

agonise *vti* = **agonize**

agonised *adj* = **agonized**

agonising *adj* = **agonizing**

agonist /ággənist/ *n* **1 MUSCLE ACTING AGAINST ANOTHER** a muscle whose action is balanced by that of another associated muscle **2 DRUG MIMICKING BODILY CHEMICAL** a hormone, neurotransmitter, or drug that triggers a response by binding to specific cell receptors **3 COMPETITOR** somebody involved in a struggle, contest, or competition with somebody else (*formal*) [Early 17C. < Greek *agōnistēs* 'contestant, actor' < *agōn* 'contest'.]

agonistic /ággə nístik/, **agonistical** /ággə nístik'l/ *adj* **1 TRYING FOR EFFECT** striving to achieve an effect but appearing contrived or exaggerated (*literary*) **2 ARGUMENTATIVE** tending to argue and eager to win an argument (*literary*) **3 AGGRESSIVE** characteristic of aggressive interaction between individuals, usually of the same species [Mid-17C. Via late Latin < Greek *agōnistikos* < *agōnistēs* (see AGONIST).] —**agonistically** *adv*

agonize /ággə nīz/ (**-nizes, -nizing, -nized**), **agonise** (**-nises, -nising, -nised**) *v* **1** *vi* **SPEND TIME WORRYING** to think about something intensely and anxiously before making a decision ○ *to agonize over the answer to every question* **2** *vti* **SUFFER OR CAUSE SOMEBODY PAIN** to suffer, or cause somebody to suffer, extreme pain or mental anguish **3** *vi* **STRUGGLE** to make a desperate or strenuous effort (*literary*) [Late 16C. Directly or via French < late Latin *agonizare*, after Greek *agōnizesthai* 'take part in a contest' < *agōn* 'contest'.]

agonized /ággə nīzd/, **agonised** *adj* expressing or characterized by severe pain or anxiety ○ *an agonized scream* ○ *an agonized search for the missing person*

agonizing /ággə nīzing/, **agonising** *adj* **1** extremely painful **2** causing much difficulty or unpleasantness ○ *an agonizing decision* —**agonizingly** *adv*

agony /ággəni/ (*plural* **-nies**) *n* **1 GREAT PAIN OR ANGUISH** intense physical pain or mental anguish **2 INTENSE EMOTION** a consuming emotion ○ *in an agony of indecision* **3 SUFFERING PRECEDING DEATH** a period of struggle or suffering immediately preceding death (*literary*) ○ *last agony* [14C. Directly or via French < Latin *agonia* < Greek *agōnia* '(mental) struggle, anguish' < *agōn* 'contest'.] —**agonal** *adj* ◇ **prolong the agony** to make a period of misfortune or anxiety last longer than necessary

agony aunt *n* a woman who gives personal advice to readers in a regular column in a newspaper or magazine or to callers on a radio or television programme

agony column *n* **1** a regular column in a newspaper or magazine in which a columnist gives advice to readers who have written in about their personal problems **2** a newspaper column of personal advertisements, usually inquiring about missing relatives or friends (*archaic*)

agony uncle *n* a man who gives personal advice to readers in a regular column in a newspaper or magazine or to callers on a radio or television programme

agora[1] /ággərə/ (*plural* **-rae** /ággərī/ *or* **-ras**) *n* an open space in a town where people gather, especially a marketplace in ancient Greece [Late 16C. < Greek, 'marketplace, place of assembly' < *ageirein* 'assemble'.]

agora[2] /ággə ráa/ (*plural* **-rot** /-rṓt/) *n* see table at **currency** [Mid-20C. < Hebrew *agōrāh* 'small coin'.]

agorae plural of **agora**[1]

agoraphobia /ággərə fṓbi ə/ *n* a condition characterized by an irrational fear of public or open spaces [Late 19C. < Greek *agora* 'open place' (see AGORA[1]) + -PHOBIA.] —**agoraphobic** *adj, n*

agorot plural of **agora**[2]

agouti /ə góoti/ (*plural* **-tis** *or* **-ties**) *n* **1** a rabbit-sized rodent with short ears and clawed feet. Native to: tropical Central and South America. Genus: *Dasyprocta.* **2** an irregularly striped pattern in the individual hairs of the fur of an agouti [Early 17C. Via French or Spanish < Tupi-Guarani *akutí.*]

AGP *abbr* accelerated graphics port

Agra /áagrə/, **Āgra** city in N India, famous as the site of the Taj Mahal. Population: 891,790 (1991).

agranulocytosis /ə grànnyòolō sī tṓsiss, ay-/ *n* a sometimes fatal acute illness characterized by a decrease in granular white blood cells, and lesions of the throat, gastrointestinal tract, and skin [Early 20C. < A-[2] + GRANULOCYTE.]

agrapha /ággrəfə/ *npl* sayings of Jesus Christ not recorded in the Bible but found in other early Christian writings [Late 19C. < plural of Greek *agraphon* 'unwritten'.]

agraphia /ə gráffi ə, ay-/ *n* loss of the ability to write, resulting from neurological damage such as a brain lesion [Mid-19C. < A-[2] + Greek *graphia* 'writing'.] —**agraphic** *adj*

agrarian /ə gráiri ən/ *adj* **1 OF LAND** relating to land, especially its ownership and cultivation **2 OF RURAL LIFE** dominated by or relating to farming or rural life **3 PRO-FARMER** promoting the interests of farmers, especially in seeking a more equitable basis of land ownership ○ *an agrarian political party* ■ *n* **LAND REFORMER** somebody, often a member of an agrarian political movement, who believes in the fair distribution of land, especially the redistribution of large amounts of land owned by the rich [Early 17C. < Latin *agrarius* < *agr-* 'field, land'.]

agrarianism /ə gráiri ənizəm/ *n* a political movement or philosophy that promotes the interests of the farmer, especially the redistribution of land owned by the rich or by government

agree /ə grée/ (**agrees, agreeing, agreed**) *v* **1** *vi* **BE IN ACCORD** to have the same opinion about something as somebody or each other ○ *Scientists don't agree about what causes these reactions.* **2** *vi* **CONSENT** to consent to or approve something ○ *They agreed to a postponement.* **3** *vi* **ADMIT AS TRUE** to admit that something is true ○ *I had to agree that the room looked better with a coat of paint.* **4** *vti* **DECIDE** to come to an understanding or reach a settlement regarding something ○ *Do you think we can agree on a plan?* **5** *vi* **BE CONSISTENT** to be consistent in content, meaning, or characteristics with something ○ *The witnesses' stories agree in most details with the accused's.* **6** *vi* **BE SUITABLE** to suit or be good for somebody ○ *The climate doesn't agree with me.* **7** *vt* **CAUSE TO CORRESPOND** to make something equal or consistent with something else ○ *to agree the incomings with the outgoings* **8** *vi* **MATCH GRAMMATICALLY** to have the same grammatical number, case, person, or gender, especially in the same sentence [14C. < French *agréer* 'please' < Latin *ad* 'to' + *gratus* 'pleasing'.]

SYNONYMS ***agree, consent, concur, acquiesce, assent***
CORE MEANING: to accept an idea, plan, or course of action that has been put forward
agree to be in agreement with somebody else about a course of action; **consent** to give formal permission for something to happen; **concur** to agree or reach agreement independently on a specified point; **acquiesce** to agree to or comply with something passively; **assent** to agree to something formally.

agreeable /ə grée əb'l/ *adj* **1 PLEASING** pleasing to the senses or to somebody's taste ○ *The climate here is very agreeable.* **2 FRIENDLY** pleasant, friendly, and ready to please others ○ *an agreeable companion* **3 WILLING TO COMPLY** willing to consent to or consider something ○ *If the committee is agreeable, you can start work straight away.* **4 CONSISTENT** consistent or in keeping with something —**agreeability** /ə grée ə bílləti/ *n* —**agreeableness** *n* —**agreeably** *adv*

agreed /ə gréed/ *adj* **1 DETERMINED BY CONSENSUS** previously decided and assented to by two or more people ○ *the agreed procedure* **2 SHARING OPINION** sharing the same view as somebody else or others ○ *Are we all agreed on the proposal?* ■ *interj* **YES** used to confirm agreement with somebody else

agreement /ə gréemənt/ *n* **1 FORMAL CONTRACT** a contract or arrangement, either written or verbal and sometimes enforceable by law **2 ACT OR STATE OF AGREEING** the reaching or sharing of the same opinion that somebody or others hold ○ *Do we have your agreement on this issue?* **3 CON-**

SENSUS OF OPINION a situation in which everyone accepts the same terms or has the same opinion ○ *everyone is in agreement* **4 CONSENT** an expression of consent ○ *my parents' agreement to the marriage* **5 GRAMMATICAL CORRESPONDENCE** correspondence of the number, case, gender, or person of one word with that of another word, especially in the same sentence

USAGE Person agreement Many centuries ago, English verbs had a fully fledged system of ***person agreement***: that is to say, the form of the verb showed whether the subject was the person speaking (*first person*), the person being spoken to (*second person*), or the person or thing being spoken about (*third person*). Today almost the only survivor of this is the third person present singular, which ends in an s (*it rains*), although the verb *to be* retains distinctive first and second person forms (*am, are*). Otherwise, English verbs have no distinctive person endings, a situation that makes for simplicity in matching subject with verb. Problems can arise, however, with multiple subjects joined by *or, neither...nor*, or *either...or*, especially where one subject is in the third person. Should it be *Neither I nor my friend intend to stay* or *Neither I nor my friend intends to stay*? In other words, should the verb agree with *I* (first person) or *my friend* (third person)? Probably the best way of avoiding the problem is to recast the sentence so that it does not arise; for example, *I do not intend to stay, and nor does my friend*. But if a multiple subject is unavoidable, it is preferable for the verb to agree with the noun or pronoun closest to it: *Neither I nor my friend intends to stay.*

~~agression~~ incorrect spelling of **aggression**

~~agressive~~ incorrect spelling of **aggressive**

agrestal /ə grést'l/ *adj* describes a plant that grows on cultivated land or among crops [Mid-19C. < Latin *agrestis* 'of fields' < *agr-* 'field, land'.]

agrestic /ə gréstik/ *adj* (*literary*) **1** associated with the rural or rustic life **2** lacking the qualities associated with sophistication [Early 17C. < Latin *agrestis* (see AGRESTAL).]

agri- *prefix* = **agro-**

agribusiness /ággri biznəss/ *n* the operations and businesses that are associated with large-scale farming

agrichemical *n* = **agrochemical**

Agricola /ə gríkələ/, **Gnaeus Julius** (37–93) Roman colonial administrator

agricultural /àggri kúlchərəl/ *adj* **1** involving or relating to agriculture ○ *agricultural equipment* ○ *agricultural college* **2** with farming as the dominant way of life ○ *one of the earliest agricultural communities* —**agriculturalist** /àggri kúlchərəlist/ *n* —**agriculturally** *adv*

agriculture /ággri kulchər/ *n* the occupation or business of cultivating the land, producing crops, and raising livestock [15C. Directly or via French < Latin *agricultura* < *agri* 'of the land' (< *agr-* 'field, land') + *cultura* 'cultivation'.] —**agriculturist** /àggri kúlchərist/ *n*

agrimony /àggriməni/ (*plural* **-ny** *or* **-nies**) *n* **1** a perennial plant with compound leaves and spiny fruits. Flowers: small, yellow, in spikes. Genus: *Agrimonia*. **2** PLANTS = **hemp agrimony** [Pre-12C. Via Old French < Latin *agrimonia*, misreading of *argemonia* < Greek *argemōnē* 'poppy'.]

Agrippa /ə gríppə/, **Marcus Vipsanius** (63–12 BC) Roman general.

Agrippina /àggrə peénə/ (13? BC–AD 33) Roman noblewoman. Known as **Agrippina the Elder**. **2** (15–AD 59) Roman noblewoman. Known as **Agrippina the Younger**

agro-, agri- *prefix* **1** soil ○ *agrology* **2** agriculture ○ *agroindustrial* [< Latin *agri* (form of *ager*) and Greek *agros* 'field' < Indo-European]

agrobiology /àggrō bī óllәji/ *n* the branch of biology concerned with agricultural production, especially crop growth —**agrobiological** /àggrō bī ə lójjik'l/ *adj* —**agrobiologically** *adv* —**agrobiologist** *n*

agrochemical /àggrō kémmik'l/, **agrichemical** /àggri-/ *n* a chemical used in farming, e.g. a fertilizer or pesticide

agroforestry /àggrō fórristri/ *n* **1** the method or practice of integrating the raising of trees into farming **2** forestry conducted purely to produce timber, without any regard for sporting or recreational pursuits

agroindustrial /àggrō in dústri əl/ *adj* **1** relating to the production or provision of materials needed by both agriculture and industry, e.g. water **2** used in, produced by, or involved in the industrial processing of agricultural products —**agroindustry** *n*

agronomic /àggrə nómmik/, **agronomical** /-nómmik'l/ *adj* **1** relating to the scientific study of soil management, land cultivation, and crop production **2** describes plant characteristics that are important during growth and development of a crop, e.g. height and stem strength

agronomics /àggrə nómmiks/ *n* the branch of economics that is concerned with the use and productivity of land (+ *singular verb*) [Mid-19C. < AGRO- + ECONOMICS.]

agronomy /ə grónnəmi/ *n* the science of soil management, land cultivation, and crop production [Early 19C. < French *agronomie* < Greek *agronomos* 'overseer of land' < *agros* 'land' + *-nomos* 'dispensing, administering'.] —**agronomist** *n*

aground /ə grównd/ *adj, adv* onto or on ground, especially a shore, a reef, rocks, or the bottom of shallow water

aguardiente /àg waardi énti/ *n* rough brandy distilled in Spain, Portugal, or Latin America, sometimes flavoured with anise [Early 19C. < Spanish, < *agua* 'water' + *ardiente* 'fiery'.]

Aguascalientes /àggwə skal yén tayz/ state in central Mexico. Capital: Aguascalientes. Population: 862,335 (1995). Area: 5,589 sq. km/2,158 sq. mi.

ague /áy gyoo/ *n* **1** a feverish condition involving alternating hot, cold, and sweating stages, especially as a symptom of malaria **2** a fever or shivering fit (*archaic*) [14C. Via French < medieval Latin *acuta*, short for *febris acuta* 'sharp fever'.] —**aguish** *adj* —**aguishly** *adv* —**aguishness** *n*

ah /aa/ *interj* **1 EXPRESSING EMOTION** used to express emotions ranging from blissful contentment to acute discomfort to disgust, depending on the speaker's tone of voice **2 EXPRESSING RECOGNITION** used to express surprise or recognition and understanding ○ *Ah, I see.* ■ *vi* **SAY 'AH'** to say 'ah' ■ *n* **UTTERANCE OF 'AH'** an exclamation of 'ah' expressing any of various emotions

AH *adv* used to indicate the number of years from the Hegira (AD 622), a key date in the Islamic calendar. Full form **anno Hegirae**

aha /aa haá/ *interj* used when discovering something, especially to express triumphant satisfaction or excitement ○ *Aha, I caught you in the act!* [14C. < AH + HA[1].]

AHA *abbr* alpha-hydroxy acid

ahead /ə héd/ *adv, adj* **1 IN FRONT** in front of somebody or something ○ *They are in the white car just ahead.* **2 FORWARDS** onwards or in a forward direction ○ *Keep walking straight ahead and it's on your left.* **3 TO THE FUTURE** in or into the future ○ *We expect more news in the weeks ahead.* **4 EARLIER** before or in advance of something or somebody ○ *You need to learn to plan ahead!* **5 IN BETTER SHAPE** in or into a more advanced or desirable state ○ *Our company is definitely ahead compared to competition.* **6 IN FIRST PLACE** in a winning position in a contest or competition ○ *They were ahead by 6 points to 4.* ◇ **ahead of 1** in front of **2** at an earlier time than **3** in a more advanced or advantageous position than

ahem /ə hém/ *interj* used in writing to indicate the sound of a quiet cough made to attract attention, express disapproval or doubt, or gain time [Mid-18C. An imitation of the sound.]

Ahern /ə húrn/, **Bertie** (*b.* 1951) Irish Taoiseach (prime minister) (1997–)

ahimsa /ə hím saa/ *n* the Hindu, Buddhist, and Jainist philosophy of revering all life and refraining from harm to any living thing [Late 19C. < Sanskrit, < A-[2] 'without' + *hiṁsā* 'injury'.]

ahistorical /áy hi stórrik'l/, **ahistoric** /áy hi stórrik/ *adj* not taking into account historical development

-aholic *suffix* dependent on or with an extreme fondness for ○ *workaholic* [< ALCOHOLIC]

A-horizon *n* the uppermost layer of soil containing humus, topsoil, and organic debris

ahoy /ə hóy/ *interj* **1** used by sailors to greet another ship or person or to attract attention ○ *Ahoy there!* **2** used by sailors to announce that something, usually another ship or land, is in sight [Mid-18C. Probably blend of AHA + *hoy* < Middle Dutch *hoei* 'barge, ship' < ?]

Ahriman /aárimən/ *n* the spirit of evil in Zoroastrianism, and the opponent of Ahura Mazda [Via Persian < Avestan *angrō mainiiuš* 'evil spirit']

Ahura Mazda /ə hoórə mázdə/ *n* the creator god in Zoroastrianism, and the opponent of Ahriman [< Avestan *ahurō mazdā* 'wise lord']

⚡ **ai** *abbr* Anguilla (*in Internet addresses*)

⚡ **AI** *abbr* **1** artificial insemination **2** artificial intelligence

aid /ayd/ *vti* **GIVE HELP TO** to provide somebody or something with help or with what is needed to achieve something ○ *Better sewage systems aid in the fight against cholera.* ■ *n* **1 MONEY OR SUPPLIES** financial or material assistance, e.g. that provided by a government or international organization, especially in times of crisis **2 ASSISTANCE** anything done or provided that assists somebody or something ○ *I wouldn't have made it without the aid of my friends.* **3 SOMEBODY OR SOMETHING HELPFUL** somebody or something, e.g. a device, resource, or material, that helps or assists with something ○ *visual aids such as maps* ○ *This book is an aid to using the Internet for research.* **4 ASSISTANT** an assistant or aide **5 DEVICE TO AID CLIMBING** any device that is used to help a climber ascend a cliff or mountain face **6 PAYMENT TO LORD** a monetary payment by a vassal to an English feudal lord **7 SUBSIDY FOR ENGLISH KING** a special subsidy formerly granted to the English king by parliament [15C. Via French < Latin *adjutare* 'to help'.] ◇ **aid and abet** to assist somebody in commission of a crime ◇ **in aid of** in order to help or for a particular reason or purpose (*informal*)

AID *abbr* **1** Agency for International Development **2** acute infectious disease **3** artificial insemination by donor (*dated*)

aida /ī eédə/ *n* a fabric that comes in different sizes of weave. Use: cross-stitch.

Aidan /áyd'n/, **St** (600?–651) Irish monk

aid climbing *n* climbing mountains or rocks with the assistance of artificial aids such as pitons

aide /ayd/ *n* **1** an assistant to somebody in public office or to somebody providing a professional service ○ *The letter was signed by one of the Prince's aides.* **2** MIL = **aide-de-camp** [Late 18C. Shortening of AIDE-DE-CAMP.]

aide-de-camp /àyd də kaáN/ (*plural* **aides-de-camp** /àyd də kaáN/), **aide** /ayd/ *n* a military officer acting as confidential assistant to a general or senior officer [Late 17C. < French, 'camp assistant'.]

aide-mémoire /àyd mem waár/ (*plural* **aide-mémoire** /àyd mem waár/ *or* **aide-mémoires** *or* **aides-mémoire**) *n* (*formal*) **1** a brief written summary or outline of the items on which agreement was reached in a meeting **2** something, e.g. a mnemonic device, book, or document, that is an aid to remembering something else [Mid-19C. < French, 'help-memory'.]

Aids /aydz/, **AIDS** *n* a disease of the immune system caused by infection with the retrovirus HIV, which destroys certain white blood cells and is transmitted through blood or bodily secretions such as semen [Late 20C. Acronym < *Acquired Immune Deficiency Syndrome.*]

AIDS dementia *n* a dementia caused by HIV infection of the brain and characterized by neurological and psychiatric symptoms, e.g. severe cognitive impairment and degeneration of motor nerves and the spinal cord

Aids-related complex *n* the set of symptoms associated with infection by HIV, including weight loss and fever

aid station *n US* a military medical installation for troops in the field

aigrette /áy gret, ay grét/ *n* **1** a tuft of long upright plumes, especially the tail feathers of an egret, worn on the head or on a hat for decoration **2** a piece of jewellery that resembles a plume of feathers, usually worn on the head or on a hat [Mid-17C. < French, 'egret, heron'.]

aiguille /ay gweél, àggweel/ *n* a mountain peak or large rock that is tall and sharply pointed [Early 19C. < French, 'needle'.]

aiguillette /àygwi lét/ *n* a decorative cord with hanging points worn on the shoulder of some military uniforms [Mid-16C. < French, 'little needle' < *aiguille* 'needle'.]

AIH *abbr* artificial insemination by husband

aikido /ī keédō, īki-/ *n* a martial art originating in Japan that is similar to judo but incorporates blows made with the hands and feet [Mid-20C. < Japanese, 'way of coordinated breathing'.]

ail /ayl/ *vt* to cause pain or discomfort to somebody or something (*archaic or literary*) ○ *'Oh what can ail thee, knight at arms/Alone and palely loitering'* (John Keats, *La Belle Dame Sans Merci*; 1820) [Old English *eglian* < Indo-European, 'be afraid or distressed']

SPELLCHECK Do not confuse ***ail*** with ***ale***, which has a similar sound. Beware: your spellchecker will not catch this error.

ailanthus /ay lánthəss, ī-/ *n* a tree or bush with long feathery leaves, winged fruit, and dense flower clusters. Native to: Asia. Genus: *Ailanthus.* [Early 19C. Via modern Latin < Amboinese *ai lanto* 'tree of heaven', influenced by plant names ending in *-anthus.*]

aileron /áylə ron/ *n* a hinged flap on the trailing edge of an aircraft wing, used to control banking or rolling movements [Early 20C. < French, 'small wing' < *aile* 'wing' < Latin *ala.*]

Ailey /áyli/, **Alvin** (1931–89) US dancer and choreographer

ailing /áyling/ *adj* **1** performing below an expected standard ○ *the nation's ailing steel industry* **2** suffering from or weakened by an illness (*dated*)

ailment /áylmənt/ *n* a mild illness or injury, especially a persistent one

Ailsa Craig /áylssə kráyg/ rocky islet in the Firth of Clyde, Scotland. Height: 340 m/1,114 ft.

ailurophile /ī lóorə fīl, ī lyóorə-/ *n* somebody who loves cats [Mid-20C. < Greek *ailuros* 'cat' + -PHILE.]

ailurophobe /ī lóorə fōb, ī lyóorə-/ *n* somebody who hates or fears cats [Early 20C. < Greek *ailuros* 'cat'.] —**ailurophobia** /ī lóorə fōbi ə, ī lyóorə-/ *n*

aim /aym/ *v* **1** *vi* **PLAN TO DO** to intend or plan to do something **2** *vt* **DIRECT A MESSAGE** to target words, a message, an action, or a product at a particular person or group **3** *vti* **POINT AN OBJECT** to point a weapon or object or direct a blow at somebody or something ■ *n* **1 INTENTION** a plan to do or achieve something **2 ACT OF AIMING** an act or manner of aiming ○ *Take aim and fire.* **3 SKILL IN AIMING** skill at hitting a target ○ *Her aim was perfect.* **4 DEGREE OF ACCURACY** the level of accuracy of a weapon ○ *A rifle has more precise aim than a shotgun.* [14C. < Old French *esmer* 'estimate', *aesmer* 'aim at' < Latin *aestimare* (see ESTIMATE).] —**aimer** *n*

aimless /áymləss/ *adj* without purpose or direction —**aimlessly** *adv* —**aimlessness** *n*

aina /aá eenə/ *n Hawaii* land or country [20C. < Hawaiian *'āina.*]

ain't /aynt/ *contr* a contraction of 'am not', 'is not', 'are not', 'have not', or 'has not' (*nonstandard*)

Ainu /ī noo/ (*plural* **-nu** *or* **-nus**) *n* **1** a member of a Japanese people who now live in the north of the Japanese island of Hokkaido, and on the Kurile Islands and the island of Sakhalin **2** a language spoken by the Ainu on Hokkaido, considered to be unrelated to any other language [Early 19C. < Ainu, 'person'.] —**Ainu** *adj*

aioli /ī ōli/ *n* mayonnaise flavoured with garlic [Early 20C. Via French < Provençal, < *ai* 'garlic' + *oli* 'oil'.]

air /air/ *n* **1 GASES FORMING ATMOSPHERE** the mixture of gases, mainly nitrogen and oxygen, that forms the Earth's atmosphere **2 ATMOSPHERE IN OPEN SPACE** the atmosphere of an open space as opposed to that of an enclosed space ○ *in the open air* **3 ATMOSPHERE WE BREATHE** the particular atmosphere in a place or enclosed space ○ *fresh air* ○ *He dived, then came up for air.* **4 SKY** the sky or the empty space above the Earth ○ *It flew through the air and landed at our feet.* **5 TRAVEL IN AIRCRAFT** travel in or transportation by aircraft (*often before nouns*) ○ *sending the package by air* ○ *an air terminal* **6 AURA** an aura or particular quality ○ *an air of sadness about him* **7 SOMEBODY'S DISTINCTIVE QUALITY** a distinctive quality in somebody's appearance or manner ○ *her air of superiority* **8 MELODY** a melody or tune, especially a light or cheerful one **9 LIGHT WIND** a very light wind ■ *adj* **OF ZODIAC SIGNS** relating to the Aquarius, Gemini, or Libra signs of the zodiac ■ *v* **1** *vti* **BROADCAST OR BE BROADCAST** to be broadcast or broadcast something on radio or television ○ *aired in the spring* **2** *vt* **MAKE KNOWN** to express something such as an opinion or complaint ○ *air your views* **3** *vti* **EXPOSE TO AIR** to be exposed to the air, or expose something to the air in order to dry it, remove damp from it, cool it, or ventilate it [13C. Partly via Old French and Latin < Greek *aēr* 'air, atmosphere', partly via French, 'nature, place of origin' < Latin *ager* 'field', *area* 'open space'.] ◇ **airs and graces** affected or pretentious behaviour ◇ **clear the air** to remove the tension, uncertainty, or misunderstanding from a situation ◇ **in the air** happening or about to happen ○ *The rumour is that a merger is in the air.* ◇ **off (the) air** not being broadcast on radio or television, e.g. because a person or programme has stopped or finished broadcasting ◇ **on (the) air** being broadcast on radio or television ◇ **punch the air** to make a gesture of triumph by raising and throwing out a clenched fist in the air ◇ **take the air** to go for a walk (*formal*) ◇ **up in the air** undecided or uncertain ◇ **vanish into thin air** to disappear completely ◇ **walk** *or* **tread on air** to be extremely happy

SPELLCHECK Do not confuse ***air*** with ***ere***, ***err***, or ***heir***, which sound similar. Beware: your spellchecker will not catch this error.

AIR *abbr S Asia* All India Radio

air bag *n* **1** a safety device in a car consisting of a bag that automatically inflates on impact to protect the occupant of the seat **2** a strong inflatable bag used to bring sunken items to the surface or by rescue workers to lift heavy machinery or debris under which somebody is trapped

air base *n* a place from which military aircraft operate

air bladder *n* **1** an air-filled sac above the alimentary canal in most fishes that regulates buoyancy and, in some, aids in respiration **2** an air-filled sac that aids buoyancy in certain types of seaweed

airboat /áir bōt/ *n* TRANSP = **swamp boat** [Because it is driven with a propellor and steered with a rudder like an aeroplane's]

airborne /áir bawrn/ *adj* **1 CARRIED BY AIR** carried along by movements of air **2 BY AIRCRAFT** carried out or transported by aircraft **3 IN FLIGHT** in flight or in the air

air brake *n* **1** a brake operated by compressed air, especially in a heavy motor vehicle **2** a flap or small parachute on an aircraft operated to increase drag and thus slow the aircraft

airbrick /áir brik/ *n* a brick with holes through it, incorporated in structures to increase ventilation

air bridge *n* an air transport link between two places, especially where travel by land is not possible

airbrush /áir brush/ *n* a device for spraying paint using compressed air ■ *vt* to paint something or alter or improve a picture using an airbrush ○ *The blemish had been airbrushed out.*

airburst /áir burst/ *n* an explosion of a bomb, shell, or missile in the air

air chamber *n* **1** an enclosed space with air in it **2** a chamber in a hydraulic system in which air expands and compresses to control the flow of a fluid

air chief marshal *n* an officer in the Royal Air Force of a rank above air marshal

air commodore *n* an officer in the Royal Air Force of a rank above group captain

air-condition *vt* to cool and control the humidity and purity of the air circulating in a building with an air conditioner —**air conditioned** *adj*

air conditioner *n* a device for cooling and controlling the humidity and purity of the air circulating in a building

air conditioning *n* a system for cooling and controlling the humidity and purity of the air circulating in a building

air-cool *vt* to cool something, especially an engine, by a flow of air rather than a water system —**air-cooled** *adj*

air cooler *n* a device, such as a portable air-conditioning unit, for cooling the air inside a building, room, or vehicle

Air Corps *n* the airborne division of the US Army that later became the US Air Force

air corridor *n* a specified route that aircraft should take through airspace in which flying is restricted

air cover *n* the provision of an airborne defence for ground forces against an enemy air attack, or the aircraft providing the defence

aircraft /áir kraaft/ (*plural* **-craft**) *n* any vehicle capable of flight

aircraft carrier *n* a warship with a long flat deck designed to allow aircraft to take off and land on it

aircraftman /áir kraaftmən/ (*plural* **-men** /-mən/) *n* a serviceman of the lowest rank in the Royal Air Force

aircraftwoman /áir kraaft wòomən/ (*plural* **-en** /-wimin/) *n* a servicewoman of the lowest rank in the Royal Air Force

aircrew /áir kroo/ *n* the pilot, navigator, and other crew members of an aircraft

air curtain *n* a stream of air directed across a doorway, especially to prevent draughts

air cushion *n* **1** the pocket of air that is forced down to support a hovercraft **2** a type of suspension that uses enclosed air to absorb shocks —**air-cushioned** *adj*

air cushion vehicle *n US* TRANSP = **hovercraft**

air dam *n* a device for reducing the air resistance of a vehicle, especially a strip of metal or plastic fitted across the width of a car below the front bumper

airdate /áir dayt/ *n* the date on which a radio or television programme is scheduled to be broadcast

air division *n* a unit of the US Air Force of a size between a wing and an air force

air door *n* a strong current of air directed upwards in an entrance to take the place of a door

airdrome /áir drōm/ *n* US = **aerodrome**

airdrop /áir drop/ *n* a landing of troops or supplies by parachute from an aircraft ■ *vt* (**-drops, -dropping, -dropped**) to land troops or supplies by parachute from an aircraft

air-dry *v* (**air-dries, air-drying, air-dried**) to dry something by exposing it to air ■ *adj* dry to the point where continued exposure to air will remove no further moisture

Airedale /áir dayl/, **Airedale terrier** *n* a large terrier belonging to a breed with rough tan-coloured hair and a black patch on the back [Late 19C. A district in W Yorkshire.]

air embolism *n* the presence of air in a blood vessel resulting from injury, from moving too rapidly from high to lower atmospheric pressure, or from using a heart-lung machine during cardiopulmonary bypass

air exchanger *n* a device that expels stale air from a room and brings in fresh air from outside, and may also heat or cool the incoming air

airfare /áir fair/ *n* the price of a journey in an aircraft

airfield /áir feeld/ *n* an area where aircraft can take off and land

airflow /áir flō/ *n* a flow of air, especially around a moving vehicle

airfoil /áir foyl/ *n* US = **aerofoil**

air force *n* a military organization that uses aircraft in war, especially a branch of a nation's armed forces

Air Force One *n* the official aeroplane of the President of the United States

airframe /áir fraym/ *n* the whole body of an aircraft, apart from its engines

airfreight /áir frayt/ *n* **1 TRANSPORTATION OF GOODS BY AIR** the transportation of freight by air **2 CHARGE FOR AIRFREIGHT** the charge made for transporting freight by air ■ *vt* **TRANSPORT GOODS BY AIR** to transport goods by air

air gas *n* CHEM = **producer gas**

airglow /áir glō/ *n* a faint light observed in the night sky from low latitudes, caused by photochemical reactions generated by solar radiation in the upper atmosphere

air guitar *n* an imaginary guitar held by somebody pretending to play a real instrument, especially when miming to rock music (*informal*)

air gun *n* a pistol or rifle that fires a projectile by releasing compressed air

airhead[1] /áir hed/ *n* somebody regarded as unintelligent and superficial (*slang insult*)

airhead[2] /áir hed/ *n* an area in enemy territory captured and held by airborne forces and used when flying troops and supplies in or out of the territory [Mid-20C. After BEACHHEAD.]

air hole *n* **1** an unfrozen area in the surface of a frozen body of water, especially one where aquatic mammals surface to breathe **2** METEOROL = **air pocket** *n.* 1

air hostess *n* a woman flight attendant on a large passenger aeroplane (*dated*)

airily /áirili/ *adv* **1** in a carefree or light-hearted way as if something was unimportant **2** in a delicate or light way

airing /áiring/ *n* **1 DRYING** exposure to air or heat, especially for drying, removal of dampness, or ventilation **2 WALK OR DRIVE** a walk or drive in the open air **3 MAKING SOMETHING KNOWN** the exposure to public attention of somebody's opinions or ideas

airing cupboard *n* a warm or heated cupboard where laundry can be aired or kept dry

air intake *n* an opening through which air enters a duct, a confined space, or a fuel-burning engine

air jacket *n* **1** an air-filled casing around a machine to insulate it against heat loss or gain **2** = **life jacket**

air-kiss *vt* greet somebody by making a kissing gesture near to, but not actually making contact with, his or her cheek (*informal*) ○ *The guests were welcomed in a flurry of air-kissing and delighted squeals.* —**air kiss** *n*

air lane *n* a regular route used in air travel

air layering *n* a plant propagation method in which a growing branch is cut or stripped of bark and the area wrapped in moist compost to encourage root formation

airless /áirləss/ *adj* **1 WITH STALE AIR** with stale rather than fresh air **2 WITHOUT AIR** completely lacking any air **3 STILL** without wind or movement of air —**airlessness** *n*

airlift /áir lift/ *n* the transport of people or things by air, especially when alternative means cannot be used ■ *vt* to transport people or things by air, especially when alternative means cannot be used

airline /áir līn/ *n* **1** a system of commercial scheduled flights transporting people and goods, or a company that operates such a system **2** a tube through which air is passed under pressure

airliner /áir līnər/ *n* a large commercial passenger-carrying aircraft

airlock /áir lok/ *n* **1** an obstruction to the flow of a liquid in a pipe, caused by a bubble of air **2** an airtight chamber between two areas of differing air pressure in which air pressure can be altered to match that of either area

airmail /áir mayl/ *n* **1 SENDING OF MAIL BY AIR** the system of transporting letters and parcels in aircraft **2 MAIL SENT BY AIR** mail transported in aircraft ■ *adj* **SENT BY AIR** sent by airmail ■ *vt* **SEND BY AIR** to send something, e.g. a letter or parcel, by airmail

airman /áirmən/ (*plural* **-men** /-mən/) *n* **1** a pilot, especially of a military aircraft **2** an enlisted person in the US Air Force

airman basic (*plural* **airmen basic**) *n* somebody of the lowest rank in the US Air Force

airman first class (*plural* **airmen first class**) *n* somebody in the US Air Force of a rank above airman

air marshal *n* an officer in the Royal Air Force of a rank above air vice-marshal

air mass *n* a large body of air with temperature, pressure, and moisture uniform throughout its mass but changed by the environment through which it passes

Air Medal *n* a decoration for meritorious conduct in the air awarded by the US Army, Navy, or Air Force

air mile *n* a unit of distance used in air travel, equal to one international nautical mile

Air Miles *tdmk* a trademark for points worth miles of free or discounted air travel, issued by retailers and other businesses

airmobile /áir mō bīl/ *adj* able to be transported into a combat zone by air, especially by helicopter

air officer *n* an officer in the Royal Air Force of any rank above group captain

airpack /áir pak/ *n* a device consisting of a portable supply of oxygen connected to a face mask that allows somebody to enter an area where the air is unsafe to breathe

air pistol *n* a pistol that fires a projectile by releasing compressed air or another gas

airplane /áir playn/ *n* US = **aeroplane**

air plant *n* a plant that obtains nutrients and moisture from the air and rain, especially one grown as a houseplant. ◊ **epiphyte**

airplay /áir play/ *n* the playing on radio of a piece of recorded music

air pocket *n* **1** a small area of lower air density or a downward air current that makes an aircraft abruptly lose height **2** an air bubble that impedes the flow of liquid or gas, e.g. in a pipe

airport /áir pawrt/ *n* an area where civil aircraft may take off and land

airpower /áir powər/ *n* military capability in terms of combat power delivered from the air

air pressure *n* METEOROL = **atmospheric pressure**

air pump *n* a device for compressing air or forcing it into or out of something

air quality index *n* a numerical scale that indicates how polluted the air is

air rage *n* disruptive or aggressive behaviour by passengers aboard an aircraft that is liable to endanger the safety of other passengers

air raid *n* an attack by aircraft on something on the ground, especially a nonmilitary target (*hyphenated when used before a noun*)

air rifle *n* a rifle that fires a projectile by releasing compressed air or another gas

air sac *n* **1** ZOOL = **alveolus** *n.* 1 **2** an air-filled cavity in a bird, formed as an extension of the respiratory system and growing into the bones, that aids respiration and decreases bone mass **3** a thin-walled bulge (**diverticulum**) that aids respiration, located in the tubes that transport air through the bodies of some insects

Air Scout *n* a member of the Scout movement who belongs to a troop that goes flying or gliding

airscrew /áir skroo/ *n* a propeller on an aircraft

air-sea rescue *n* a rescue at sea in which aircraft are used

airship /áir ship/ *n* an aircraft that is lighter than air, powered, and navigable

airshow /áir shō/ *n* a public exhibition at an airfield of aircraft in flight and on the ground

airsickness /áir siknəss/ *n* motion sickness caused by air travel —**airsick** *adj*

airside /áir sīd/ *n* the area of an airport where the aircraft take off and land, load, or unload

air sock *n* AIR = **windsock**

airspace /áir spayss/ *n* **1** the part of the atmosphere directly above an area of land or water, especially a part over which a state claims jurisdiction **2** the space in the air that a flying aircraft occupies or needs to manoeuvre

air speed *n* the speed of an aircraft in relation to the air through which it moves

air splint *n* a splint consisting of an inflatable cylinder that surrounds the injured limb

air spray *n* **1** = **aerosol** *n.* 1 **2** = **aerosol** *n.* 2

air station *n* a small airfield with facilities for maintenance of aircraft

airstream /áir streem/ *n* **1** a wind, especially one blowing at a high altitude **2** AEROSP = **airflow**

air strike *n* an attack by aircraft on something on the ground, especially an enemy position or formation —**airstrike** *vt*

airstrip /áir strip/ *n* a place for aircraft to take off and land that has no facilities and is often temporary

air stripping *n* a technique for removing pollutants from water by breaking the water into minute particles

airt /airt/ *n Scotland* a direction or quarter, especially one of the cardinal compass points [15C. Via Scottish Gaelic *aird* < Old Irish, 'point of the compass'.]

air taxi *n* a small commercial aircraft used for brief flights between places that do not have regularly scheduled flights

air terminal *n* a building in a city used by passengers being transported to or from an airport by train or bus

air terrorism *n* the use of terrorist acts involving aeroplanes in an attempt to achieve a political objective or get international publicity

airtight /áir tīt/ *adj* **1 IMPERMEABLE BY AIR** not allowing air in or out **2 FLAWLESS** without flaws or vulnerable points ■ *n W Africa* **METAL BOX** a metal box

airtime /áir tīm/ *n* **1** the amount of time given to a programme or subject in radio or television broadcasting **2** the time at which an item is scheduled to be broadcast

air-to-air *adj* moving or passing from one aircraft to another while in flight

air-to-surface *adj* moving or passing from a flying aircraft to a point on the ground

air traffic *n* the movement of aircraft in a particular area

air-traffic control *n* the system or organization responsible for directing the movement of aircraft over a particular area, operated by ground staff in radio contact with pilots —**air-traffic controller** *n*

air vice-marshal *n* an officer in the Royal Air Force and formerly in the Royal Canadian Air Force of a rank above air commodore

air walk *n US* a high-level passageway connecting two buildings, usually made from a transparent material

airwaves /áir wayvz/ *npl* radio waves as used in broadcasting

airway /áir way/ *n* **1 AIR ROUTE** an air route, especially one used by regular commercial flights (*often plural*) **2 Airways AIR TRANSPORT COMPANY** a company that operates a system of commercial flights (*in company names*) **3 BREATHING PASSAGE** a passage for air from the nose or mouth to the lungs **4 TUBE TO KEEP AIRWAY OPEN** a device for keeping an unconscious person's airway open, incorporating a tube inserted into the throat **5 VENTILATION PASSAGE** a passage for ventilation in a mine or tunnel

airworthy /áir wur*th*i/ *adj* in good enough condition to be safe to fly [Early 19C. After SEAWORTHY.] —**airworthiness** *n*

airy /áiri/ (**-ier, -iest**) *adj* **1 ROOMY** having plenty of space **2 VENTILATED** having plenty of fresh air **3 CAREFREE** carefree or lighthearted and unconcerned **4 ETHEREAL** ethereal or insubstantial **5 OF AIR** connected with, like, or taking place in the air **6 GRACEFUL** light and graceful in movement **7 HIGH IN THE AIR** at a great height in the sky —**airiness** *n*

airy-fairy *adj* fanciful or not grounded in reality (*informal*)

Aisha /aá ee shaá/, **Ayeshah** (614?–678) wife of the prophet Muhammad

aisle /īl/ *n* **1 PASSAGEWAY BETWEEN SEATS** a passageway between areas of seating, especially in a church, theatre, or passenger vehicle **2 PASSAGEWAY BETWEEN GOODS** a passageway between stacks or displays of goods, especially in a supermarket or warehouse **3 DIVISION IN CHURCH** an area of a church separated from the nave or central area by pillars, especially one forming a passage between seats [14C. Alteration of Old French *ele* 'wing' < Latin *ala*, under the influence of ISLE and, later, French *aile* 'wing'.] ◇ **rolling in the aisles** laughing very heartily

SPELLCHECK Do not confuse ***aisle*** with ***isle***, which has a similar sound. Beware: your spellchecker will not catch this error.

ait /ayt/ *n* a small island, especially in a river (*regional*) [Old English *īgeþ* 'small island' < *īeg* (see ISLAND)]

aitch /aych/ *n* the letter 'h', or its sound [Mid-16C. < French *hache*, via late Latin *ach* < Latin *ah*, alteration of *ha*.]

Aix-en-Provence /éks aaN pro vaáNss/ city in SE France. Population: 134,222 (1999).

Ajaccio /ə jáksi ō/ capital and main port of Corse-du-Sud Department, W Corsica, France. Population: 59,318 (1990).

ajar /ə jaár/ *adj, adv* neither shut nor wide open ○ *left the door ajar* [Late 17C. < later form of Old English *cierr* 'turn'.]

Ajax /áy jaks/ *n* in Greek mythology, a powerful warrior who fought in the Trojan War as leader of the Salamis forces

AK *abbr* Alaska

a.k.a., AKA *abbr* also known as

Akan /aá kaan/ (*plural* **Akan** *or* **Akans**) *n* **1** a member of a people who live in S Ghana, the SE Ivory Coast, and parts of Togo **2** a language spoken in Ghana and Ivory Coast, belonging to the Kwa group of Niger-Congo languages. Native speakers: 8 million. [Late 17C. < Twi *akan*.] —**Akan** *adj*

akaryote /áy kárri ōt/ *n* a cell that has no nucleus —**akaryotic** /ay kárri óttik/ *adj*

Akbar /ák baar/ (1542–1605) emperor of India (1556–1605). Known as **Akbar the Great**

akee *n* TREES = **ackee**

Akela /aa káylə/ *n UK, Can* the adult leader of a Cub Scout pack [Early 20C. A wolf in Kipling's *Jungle Book*.]

akene *n* PLANT SCI = **achene**

Akhenaton /aákə naát'n, aák-/, **Ikhnaton** /ik naátən/ (*fl.* 14th century BC) Egyptian pharaoh

Akhmatova /ákmə tōvə/, **Anna** (1889–1966) Russian poet. Pseudonym of **Anna Andreyevna Gorenko**

Akiba ben Joseph /ə keébə ben jṓzəf, -jṓssəf/ (AD50?–135?) Palestinian Jewish rabbi

Akihito /áki heé tō/ (*b.* 1933) emperor of Japan (1989–)

akimbo /ə kímbō/ *adj, adv* with the hands on the hips and the elbows turned outwards [14C. < ?]

akin /ə kín/ *adj* **1** SIMILAR similar or closely related to something **2** RELATED related by blood **3** WITH COMMON ORIGIN describes languages that share a common origin or ancient forms

akinesia /áy ki neéssi ə, -kī-, á-/ *n* the loss or reduction of the normal power of movement [Mid-19C. < Greek *akinēsia*, 'lack of movement' < *kinein* 'to move'.] —**akinetic** /áy ki néttik/ *adj*

Akira Yoshimura /a keèrə yóshi moòrə/ (*b.* 1927) Japanese writer

Akita /a keétə/ capital of Akita Prefecture, NW Honshu Island, Japan. Population: 311,723 (1999).

Akkad /á kad/ ancient region situated in central N Mesopotamia that corresponds approximately to biblical Babylonia

Akkadian /a káydi ən/ *n* **1** somebody who came from the ancient city or region of Akkad **2** the extinct Semitic language of Mesopotamia, written in cuneiform [Mid-19C. < *Akkad*, city in ancient Babylonia.] —**Akkadian** *adj*

Akmolinsk /ak móllinsk/ former name for **Astana** (1824–1960)

~~akknowledge~~ incorrect spelling of **acknowledge**

akrasia /ə kráyzi ə/ *n* weakness of will, especially a failure to act according to a sense of moral obligation [< Greek, variant of *akrateia* 'powerlessness' < *kratos* 'strength' (see -CRACY)] —**akratic** /ə kráttik/ *adj*

Akron /ákrən/ city in NE Ohio. Population: 215,712 (1998 estimate).

Akutagawa Ryunosuke /a·a koota gaàwa roònə soòki/, **Akutagawa Ryūnosuke** (1892–1927) Japanese author

akvavit *n* BEVERAGES = **aquavit**

⚡**al** *abbr* Albania (*in Internet addresses*)

Al *symbol* aluminium

AL *abbr* **1** Alabama **2** Albania (*international vehicle registration*)

al. *abbr* **1** alcohol **2** alcoholic

-al[1] *suffix* **al** relating to or characterized by ○ *delusional* [Via French < Latin *-alis*]

-al[2] *suffix* action, process ○ *disposal* [Via Old French *-aille* < Latin *-alia*, neuter plural of *-alis*]

-al[3] *suffix* aldehyde ○ *chloral* [< ALDEHYDE]

à la /a·a laa, állə/, **a la** *prep* in the style of somebody or something [Late 16C. < French, shortening of *à la mode de* 'in the fashion of'.]

Ala. *abbr* Alabama

Alabama /állə bámmə/ state of the SE United States. Capital: Montgomery. Population: 4,319,154 (1997). Area: 135,293 sq. km/52,237 sq. mi. —**Alabaman** *adj*, *n* —**Alabamian** *adj*, *n*

alabaster /állə baastər, -bastər/ *n* **1** TYPE OF GYPSUM a white or transparent form of gypsum. Use: decorative carving. **2** TYPE OF CALCITE a hard semitranslucent type of calcite, occasionally with banding ■ *adj* OF ALABASTER made of alabaster, or white and translucent like alabaster [14C. Via Old French < Greek *alabastros*.]

à la carte /a·a laa kaàrt, állə-/, **a la carte** *adj*, *adv* with each dish on a menu priced separately [Early 19C. < French, 'by the menu'.]

alack /ə lák/ *interj* used to express regret (*archaic or literary*) [15C. < LACK, after ALAS.]

alacrity /ə lákrəti/ *n* promptness or eager and speedy readiness [Early 16C. < Latin *alacritas* < *alacer* 'lively'.] —**alacritous** *adj*

Aladdin's cave /ə láddinz-/ *n* a suddenly discovered place containing great riches

al-Adha /ál aàda/ *n* CALENDAR = **Eid-ul-Adha**

à la grecque /a·a laa grék, állə-/, **a la grecque** *adj* cooked in a sauce made with olive oil, lemon, usually wine, and herbs and served cold [< French, 'in the Greek style']

Alain-Fournier /álla·N foòr nyay/ (1886–1914) French writer and journalist. Pseudonym of **Henri-Alban Fournier**

à la king /a·a laa kíng, álllə-/, **a la king** /ál aa kíng/ *adj* cooked in a cream sauce with peppers and mushrooms

Alamo /államō/ chapel in San Antonio, Texas, besieged by Mexican forces in 1836 when all 187 Texan defenders were killed

alamode /álləmōd/ *n US* a light silk. Use: shawls. [Mid-17C. < French (see À LA MODE).]

à la mode /a·a laa mōd, állə-/, **a la mode** *adj* in the latest fashion (*dated*) [Late 16C. < French, 'in the style'.]

Alamogordo /álləmə gáwrdō/ city in S New Mexico, northeast of White Sands Missile Range, the site of the first atom bomb explosion, on 16 July, 1945. Population: 28,312 (1998 estimate).

alanine /állə neen, -nīn/ *n* an amino acid found in protein foods and also synthesized by the body [Mid-19C. < German *Alanin* < *Aldehyd* 'aldehyde'.]

alannah /ə lánnə/ *interj* Ireland used to address a child affectionately [Mid-19C. < Irish *a leanbh* 'O child' < Old Irish *lenab* 'child'.]

alar /áylər/ *adj* describes a part of an animal or plant that is shaped like a wing or is associated with such a part [Mid-19C. < Latin *alaris* < *ala* 'wing'.]

alarm /ə laàrm/ *n* **1** FEAR fear caused by perception of imminent danger **2** WARNING DEVICE a device for giving a warning of danger **3** SECURITY DEVICE a security device fitted to property, especially a house or car, to make a warning sound if a break-in or theft is attempted **4** SOUND OF SECURITY OR WARNING DEVICE the sound made by a security or warning device **5** = **alarm clock 6** CHALLENGE MADE BY STAMPING a warning or challenge to a fencer made by stamping the leading foot ■ *vt* **1** FRIGHTEN to make somebody frightened or apprehensive **2** WARN to give somebody warning of danger **3** FIT WITH WARNING DEVICE to fit a building or vehicle with a security warning device [Early 16C. Via French < Italian *all' arme* 'to arms!'.] —**alarmed** *adj*

alarm clock, **alarm** *n* a clock that can be set to sound an alarm at a desired time, especially to wake somebody

alarming /ə laàrming/ *adj* frightening or disturbing —**alarmingly** *adv*

alarmist /ə laàrmist/ *n* **1** somebody who spreads unnecessary fear **2** somebody who becomes afraid easily —**alarmism** *n* —**alarmíst** *adj*

alarm reaction *n* the initial response of a person or animal to stress, including an increased heart rate and hormonal activity

alarum /ə lárrəm, ə laàrəm/ *n* an alarm (*archaic*) [Variant]

alas /ə láss/ *interj* used to express sorrow or pity ■ *adv* unfortunately or regrettably [13C. Via French *hélas* < Latin *lassus* 'weary'.]

Alas. *abbr* Alaska

Alaska

Alaska /ə láskə/ US state of NW North America. Capital: Juneau. Population: 609,311 (1997). Area: 1,593,438 sq. km/615,230 sq. mi. —**Alaskan** *adj*, *n*

Alaska Highway *n* a road built in 1942 from Dawson Creek, British Columbia, to Fairbanks, Alaska

Alaskan king crab *n US* MARINE BIOL = **king crab**

Alaska Range mountain range in S Alaska. Highest peak: Mount McKinley 6,194 m/20,320 ft.

Alaska Standard Time *n* the local standard time in the ninth zone west of the Greenwich meridian, calculated at 135° west and used throughout Alaska apart from the W Aleutian Islands

alastrim /ə lástrim/ *n* a mild form of smallpox, found especially in South America and West Africa [Early 20C. <lt, Portuguese, < *alastrar* 'spread'.]

alate /áy layt/, **alated** /-laytid/ *adj* describes insects with wings or seeds with parts resembling wings [Mid-17C. < Latin *alatus* < *ala* 'wing'.]

alb /alb/ *n* a long white robe with long sleeves worn by priests [Pre-12C. Via ecclesiastical Latin (*vestis*) *alba* 'white (garment)' < Latin *albus* 'white'.]

Alb. *abbr* **1** Albania **2** Albanian

albacore /álbə kawr/ (*plural* **-core** *or* **-cores**) *n* **1** a large tuna with a long pectoral fin. Native to: warm waters of the Atlantic and Pacific. *Thunnus alalunga*. **2** the flesh of an albacore used as food [Late 16C. < Portuguese *albacor*.]

Alban /áwlbən/, **St** (*fl.* 3rd century) Roman-born English martyr

Albania

Albania /al báyni ə/ republic in SE Europe, bordering the Adriatic Sea. Capital: Tirana. Population: 3,260,000 (1995). Area: 28,748 sq. km/11,100 sq. mi.

Albanian /al báyni ən/ *n* **1** the official language of Albania that is also spoken in parts of nearby countries, and is a branch of the Indo-European languages. Native speakers: 4 million. **2** somebody who comes from Albania —**Albanian** *adj*

Albany /áwlbəni/ coastal town in SW Western Australia. Population: 20,493 (1996).

albatross /álbə tross/ (*plural* **-trosses** *or* **-tross**) *n* **1** LARGE SEABIRD a large long-winged seabird that spends most of its life in flight. Native to: cool S oceans. Family: Diomedeidae. **2** OPPRESSIVE BURDEN an oppressive burden or hindrance **3** THREE BELOW PAR in golf, a score of three below par for a hole. US term **double eagle** *n*. **2** [Late 17C. Alteration (after Latin *albus* 'white') of Portuguese *alcatraz* < Arabic *al-ġaṭṭās* 'the diver'.] ◇ **an albatross round somebody's neck** a burden from which somebody cannot escape

albedo /al beédō/ (*plural* **-dos**) *n* the fraction of incident light that is reflected by an object, especially a planet reflecting the Sun's light [Mid-19C. < ecclesiastical Latin, 'whiteness' < Latin *albus* 'white'.]

Albee /álbi/, **Edward Franklin** (*b.* 1928) US playwright

albeit /áwl bee it/ *conj* used to add information that is different from what you have already said ○ *a difficult, albeit rewarding job* [14C. < ALL + BE + IT, 'all though it may be'.]

Alberich /álbərikh/ *n* in medieval German legend, king of the dwarves and guardian of the treasures of the Nibelung

Albers /álbərz, áwl-/, **Josef** (1888–1976) German painter and designer

albert /álbərt/ *n* a short chain used to attach a pocket watch to a waistcoat [Mid-19C. After Prince ALBERT, who wore such a chain.]

Albert /álbərt/, **Prince** (1819–61) German-born prince consort to Queen Victoria

Albert, Lake lake in east-central Africa, on the border between Uganda and Democratic Republic of the Congo. Area: 5,600 sq. km/2,160 sq. mi. Length: 160 m/100 mi.

Alberta /al búrtə/ province in W Canada. Capital: Edmonton. Population: 2,696,826 (1996). Area: 661,848 sq. km/255,541 sq. mi.

Albert Edward Nyanza /-ni ánzə/ former name for **Edward, Lake**

Alberti /al báirti/, **Leon Battista** (1404–72) Italian architect

albertite /álbər tīt/ *n* a solid black variety of bitumen found in oil-bearing rock strata [Mid-19C. After *Albert* County, New Brunswick, Canada, where it was originally found.]

Albertus Magnus /al búrtəss mágnəss/, **St** (1200?–80) German cleric and philosopher

albescent /al béss'nt/ *adj* becoming white or whitish [Early 18C. < Latin *albescent-* < *albus* 'white'.]

Albigenses /álbi jén seez/ *npl* a heretical Christian religious group in S France during the 12th and 13th centuries [Early 17C. < medieval Latin < *Albiga*, the city of Albi in S France, where the group originated.] —**Albigensian** *adj* —**Albigensianism** *n*

albinism /álbinizəm/ *n* congenital lack of normal pigmentation in the skin and hair of a person or animal or in the coloration of a plant —**albinistic** /álbi nístik/ *adj*

albino /al beénō/ (*plural* **-nos**) *n* **1** a person or animal whose skin and hair lack pigmentation and whose irises are pink because of a hereditary condition (**albinism**) **2** a plant that lacks normal coloration because of a hereditary condition (**albinism**) [Early 18C. < Portuguese, < Latin *albus* 'white'.] —**albinic** /al bínnik/ *adj* —**albinotic** /álbi nóttik/ *adj*

Albion /álbi ən/ ancient name for England or the island of Britain

albite /ál bīt/ *n* a usually white form of feldspar. Use: glass, ceramics. [Early 19C. < Latin *albus* 'white'.] —**albitic** /al bíttik/ *adj*

ALBM *abbr* air-launched ballistic missile

Albright /áwl brīt/, **Madeleine** (*b.* 1937) Czech-born US stateswoman

album /álbəm/ *n* **1 BLANK BOOK** a book or binder with blank pages or pockets in which valuable or fragile items like postage stamps, photographs, mementos, or autographs are kept **2 MUSIC RECORDING** a music recording, sometimes including more than one disk or cassette, issued as an individual item **3 RECORD HOLDER** a cardboard holder for gramophone records, similar to a book in shape [Early 17C. < Latin, 'blank tablet' < *albus* 'white'.]

albumblatt /álbəm blat/ (*plural* **-blatts** *or* **-blätter** /-blettər/) *n* a short light instrumental piece popular in the 19th century, usually bound together in a set with other similar pieces [< German, 'page from an album']

albumen /álbyoòmin, al byoòmin/ *n* **1** the clear water-soluble protein that surrounds the yolk of an egg and provides nutrition for the embryo (*technical*) **2** the protein component of egg white, which includes albumin [Late 16C. < Latin, < *albus* 'white'.]

albumin /álbyoòmin, al byoòmin/ *n* a common water-soluble protein coagulated by heat, found in egg white, blood plasma, and milk —**albuminous** /al byoòminəss/ *adj*

albuminoid /al byoòmi noyd/ *adj* resembling albumin ■ *n* BIOCHEM = **scleroprotein** —**albuminoidal** /al byoòmi nóyd'l/ *adj*

albuminuria /al byoòmi nyoòri ə, ál byoòmi-/ *n* the presence of albumin in urine, usually an indication of kidney disease

Albuquerque /álbəkərki/ largest city in New Mexico, United States, in the centre of the state. Population: 419,311 (1998 estimate).

Albury-Wodonga /áwlbəri wə dóng gə/ urban area in SE Australia. Population: 67,316 (1996).

alc. *abbr* US **1** alcohol **2** alcoholic

alcahest *n* = **alkahest**

Alcaic /al káy ik/ *adj* in poetry, written in the metrical form of a stanza of four lines, each containing four feet ■ *n* a poem or lines written in the Alcaic form (*often plural*) [Mid-17C. < late Latin *alcaicus* < Greek *Alkaios*, lyric poet credited with inventing the form.]

alcaide /al káyd, -kīdi/, **alcayde** *n* **1** a commander of a fortress in a Spanish-speaking area **2** a governor of a prison in a Spanish-speaking area [Early 16C. Via Spanish < Arabic *al-kā-'id* 'the commander'.]

alcalde /al káldi, -kaáldi/ *n* the mayor or chief magistrate of a town in a Spanish-speaking area [Mid-16C. Via Spanish < Arabic *al-kāḍī* 'the judge'.]

Alcan Highway /ál kan/ *n* former name for **Alaska Highway** [Contraction of *Alaska-Canada*]

Alcatraz /álkə traz/ island in San Francisco Bay, California, site of a federal prison from 1933 to 1963

alcayde *n* MIL = **alcaide**

alcazar /álkə zaàr/ *n* a fortress or palace in Spain, especially one built by the Moors [Early 17C. Via Spanish < Arabic *al-kaṣr* 'the castle' < Latin *castrum* 'camp'.]

Alcestis /al séstiss/ *n* in Greek mythology, daughter of Pelias and wife of Admetus, King of Phaerae

alchemise *vt* = **alchemize**

alchemist /álkəmist/ *n* somebody who practises alchemy —**alchemistic** /álkə místik/ *adj*

> **LITERARY LINK** *The Alchemist*, a play (1610) by Ben Jonson. Set in London, it tells the story of a servant, Face, and his friends Subtle and Doll Common. They pose as alchemists, convincing a series of gullible characters that they can help them attain wealth and happiness.

alchemy /álkəmi/ *n* **1** an early, unscientific form of chemistry that sought to change base metals into gold and discover a life-prolonging elixir, a universal cure for disease, and a universal solvent (**alkahest**) **2** a power supposedly like alchemy, especially of enchantment or transformation [14C. Via Old French *alquemie* and medieval Latin *alchimia* < Arabic *al-kīmiyā* 'the chemistry' < Greek *khēmeia*.] —**alchemic** /al kémmik/ *adj* —**alchemical** *adj* —**alchemize** *vt*

alclometazone *n* a synthetic steroid drug. Use: treatment of dermatosis.

ALCM *abbr* air-launched cruise missile

Alcmene /alk meéni/ *n* in Greek mythology, wife of Amphitryon and mother of Hercules and Iphicles

Alcock /áwl kok/, **Sir John William** (1892–1919) British aviator

alcohol /álkə hol/ *n* **1 LIQUID FOR DRINKS OR SOLVENTS** C_2H_5OH a colourless liquid, produced by the fermentation of sugar or starch, that is the intoxicating agent in fermented drinks **2 DRINKS WITH ALCOHOL** intoxicating drinks containing alcohol **3 ORGANIC COMPOUND** any organic compound containing one or more hydroxyl groups bound to carbon atoms [Mid-16C. Via medieval Latin, 'fine powder, distilled essence' < Arabic *al-kuḥl* 'the antimony powder'.]

alcoholic /álkə hóllik/ *adj* **1 CONTAINING ALCOHOL** containing alcohol or concerning alcohol **2 CAUSED BY ALCOHOL** caused by alcohol consumption ○ *alcoholic dehydration* **3 ADDICTED TO ALCOHOL** addicted to drinking beverages containing alcohol ■ *n* **ALCOHOL ADDICT** somebody who is addicted to alcohol

alcoholic cardiomyopathy *n* a disease (**cardiomyopathy**) of the heart muscle caused by prolonged exposure to the toxic effects of alcohol or its byproducts

alcoholic dementia *n* MED = **Wenicke-Korsakoff syndrome**

alcoholic hepatitis *n* inflammation (**hepatitis**) of the liver caused by prolonged exposure to the toxic effects of alcohol or its byproducts, often a precursor to cirrhosis

alcoholicity /álkə ho líssəti/ *n* the amount of alcohol contained in something

Alcoholics Anonymous *n* an organization for alcoholics that offers mutual support to members to help them overcome their dependency

alcoholism /álkə holizəm/ *n* **1** dependence on alcohol consumption to an extent that adversely affects behaviour and social or work function and produces withdrawal symptoms when intake is stopped or greatly reduced **2** a physical disorder caused by the toxic effects of excessive alcohol consumption

alcopop /álkō pòp/ *n* a drink made of a soft drink, e.g. lemonade, mixed with alcohol [Late 20C. < ALCOHOL + POP[1].]

Alcoran /ál kaw raàn/ *n* ISLAM = **Koran** —**Alcoranic** /-ránnik/ *adj*

Alcott /áwlkət/, **Amos Bronson** (1799–1888) US transcendentalist and writer

Alcott, Louisa May (1832–88) US novelist

alcove /álkōv/ *n* **1 INTERNAL RECESS** a recess in the wall of a room **2 EXTERNAL RECESS** a recess in an exterior wall, usually with a roof or some covering structure **3 SECLUDED PLACE** a shady or secluded place in a garden [Late 16C. Via French *alcôve* and Spanish *alcoba* < Arabic *al-kubba* 'the vault, the arch'.]

alcuronium /álkyoò rōni əm/ *n* a drug used as a muscle relaxant

Aldabra /al dábbrə/ group of four islands in the Seychelles in the Indian Ocean. Area: 154 sq. km/59 sq. mi.

Aldebaran /al débbərən/ *n* the brightest star in the constellation Taurus and one of the brightest stars in the sky

Louisa May Alcott

Aldeburgh /áwldbərə/ seaside town in E England. Population: 2,654 (1991).

aldehyde /áldi hīd/ *n* a reactive organic compound with a CHO group, produced by the oxidation of an alcohol [Mid-19C. Contraction of modern Latin *alcohol dehydrogenatum* 'dehydrogenated alcohol'.] —**aldehydic** /áldi híddik/ *adj*

Alden /áwldən/, **John** (1599?–1687) English-born American colonist

al dente /al dén tay, -dénti/ *adj* cooked just long enough to be firm rather than soft [< Italian, 'to the tooth']

alder /áwldər/ *n* **1** a deciduous tree or shrub with male catkins and cone-shaped fruits, common in wet places in northern temperate areas. Genus: *Alnus*. **2** the rot-resistant wood of the alder tree. Use: in underwater structures, carving, furniture making. [Old English *alor* < Indo-European, 'reddish-brown']

alderman /áwldərmən/ (*plural* **-men** /-mən/) *n* **1 SENIOR COUNCIL MEMBER** a senior member of an English or Welsh local council before the local government reorganization of 1974 **2 MEMBER OF US TOWN LEGISLATING BODY** a member of the legislating body of a town or city in the United States or Canada **3 LOCAL GOVERNMENT MEMBER IN AUSTRALIA** a member of local government elected by the constituents of a municipality in Australia **4** HIST = **ealdorman** [Old English *ealdorman* < *ealdor* 'an elder' + MAN] —**aldermancy** *n* —**aldermanic** /áwldər mánnik/ *adj*

Aldermaston /áwldər maastən/ village in Berkshire, S England, the site of the Atomic Weapons Research Establishment

Alderney[1] /áwldərni/ third largest and most northerly of the Channel Islands. Population: 2,297 (1991). Area: 1,795 hectares /1,962 acres.

Alderney[2] *n* a cow belonging to a breed of small dairy cattle originally from the Channel Islands

Aldershot /áwldər shot/ town and military centre in S England. Population: 51,356 (1991).

alderwoman /áwldər woòmman/ (*plural* **-en** /-wimmin/) *n* **1 WOMAN ALDERMAN** a woman alderman **2 SENIOR COUNCIL MEMBER** a woman who was a senior member of an English or Welsh local council before the local government reorganization of 1974 **3 MEMBER OF US TOWN LEGISLATING BODY** a woman who is a member of the legislating body of a town or city in the United States or Canada **4 LOCAL GOVERNMENT MEMBER IN AUSTRALIA** a woman who is a member of local government elected by the constituents of a municipality in Australia

aldesleukin /ál dez lookin/ *n* a genetically engineered drug. Use: treatment of cancer.

Aldington /áwl ding t'n/, **Richard** (1892–1962) British writer

Aldis lamp /áwldiss-/ *n* a signalling device in the form of a portable lamp used to flash messages in Morse code [Early 20C. After the British inventor A. C. W. *Aldis*.]

aldohexose /áldō héksōss, -héksōz/ *n* a six-carbon sugar that contains a CHO group [Early 20C. Contraction of ALDEHYDE + HEXOSE.]

aldol /ál dol/ *n* **1** a colourless or pale yellow oily liquid. Use: catalyst in the vulcanization of rubber, solvent, in perfumery. **2** a colourless liquid formed by the condensation of acetaldehyde. Use: organic syntheses, denaturing alcohol.

aldolase /áldə layss, -layz/ *n* an enzyme that aids the breakdown of fructose [Mid-20C. < German.]

aldose /áldōss, -dōz/ n a sugar (**monosaccharide**) that contains a CHO group

aldosterone /al dóstərōn/ n a steroid hormone, secreted by the adrenal cortex, that controls mineral and water balance

aldosteronism /al dóstərənizəm/ n a condition caused by excessive secretion of aldosterone by the adrenal cortex, characterized by weakness, high blood pressure, and large fluid intake and urinary output

Aldrich /áwldrich/, **Thomas Bailey** (1836–1907) US writer

Aldrin, **Buzz** (b. 1930) US astronaut. Full name **Edwin Eugene Aldrin, Jr.**

ale /ayl/ n 1 a type of beer, brewed from a cereal and originally distinguished from beer by the absence of hops 2 = **beer** n. 1 3 US an alcoholic drink made from rapidly fermented malt to which hops have been added [Old English ealu < Germanic, perhaps 'intoxicating drink']

SPELLCHECK See **ail**.

aleatory /áyli ətəri/ adj 1 depending on chance or contingency 2 **aleatory, aleatoric** having the sequence of given notes or passages in a piece of music chosen at random by the performer or left to chance [Late 17C. < Latin aleatorius < alea 'dice'.]

alec /álik/, **aleck** n Aus somebody regarded as unintelligent and thoughtless (slang insult) [Early 20C. Shortening of SMART ALEC.]

aleck /álik/ n Aus = **alec** (slang)

Alecto /ə léktō/ n in Greek mythology, one of the three Furies

alee /ə lee/ adv, adj on or to the leeward side

alef n = **aleph**

alehouse /áyl howss/ n a pub (dated)

alein incorrect spelling of **alien**

Alemannic /álla mánnik/ n a group of High German dialects spoken in Alsace, Switzerland, and SW Germany —**Alemannic** adj

Alembert /a lam bér, a laaN bér/, **Jean le Rond d'** (1717–83) French philosopher, mathematician, and encyclopedist

alembic /ə lémbik/ n an apparatus formerly used in distillation [14C. Via Old French and medieval Latin alembicus < Arabic al-'anbīq 'the still' < Greek ambix 'cup'.]

aleph /állef, aà lef/, **alef** n the first letter of the Hebrew alphabet [14C. From Hebrew and Phoenician āleph 'first letter of the alphabet, ox', perhaps because its form derived from a hieroglyph resembling an ox's head.]

Aleppo /ə léppō/ city in NW Syria. Population: 1,582,930 (1994).

Aleppo boil n a skin disease caused by infection with a protozoan and characterized by the formation of nodules and sores

alert /ə lúrt/ adj 1 WATCHFUL watchful and ready to deal with whatever happens 2 MENTALLY LIVELY clear-headed and responsive ■ n 1 WARNING OF DANGER an alarm or warning of danger 2 TIME OF DANGER a period of time during which an alert remains in force ■ v WARN to make somebody aware of possible dangers or difficulties ○ Police have alerted the public to the danger. [Late 16C. Via French alerte < Italian all'erta 'on the lookout'.] —**alertly** adv —**alertness** n ◇ **on red alert** prepared for any trouble or danger that may occur ◇ **on the alert** watchful and ready to deal with whatever happens

Alessandri Palma /álla sándri pálma/, **Arturo** (1868–1950) Chilean statesman

alethic /ə leéthik/ adj relating to the philosophical concepts of truth and possibility and especially to the branch of logic that formalizes them [Late 20C. < Greek alētheia 'truth' < alēthēs 'true'.]

aleurone /ə lyoorōn/, **aleuron** /-on/ n a protein occurring as granules in various plants, especially in seeds [Mid-19C. Alteration of Greek aleuron 'wheat flour'.] —**aleuronic** /állyoō rónnik/ adj

Aleut /álli oot, ə lyoót/ (plural **Aleut** or **Aleuts**) n 1 a member of an indigenous people who live in the Aleutian Islands and coastal SW Alaska 2 an Eskimo-Aleut language spoken in the Aleutian Islands and coastal parts of Alaska. Native speakers: 500. [Late 18C. < Russian.] —**Aleut** adj —**Aleutian** /ə loósh'n/ adj

Aleutian Islands chain of islands off SW Alaska, between the Pacific Ocean and the Bering Sea

A level n 1 the advanced level of any subject studied to gain a General Certificate of Education qualification in England, Wales, and Northern Ireland 2 a pass in an examination in a subject studied at A level [Shortening of Advanced level]

alevin /álləvin/ n a young salmon or trout with the yolk sac still attached [Mid-19C. Via French < assumed Vulgar Latin allevamen 'something that is raised' < Latin levare (see LEVER).]

alewife /áyl wīf/ (plural **-wives** /-wīvz/) n a herring that migrates up rivers to spawn. Alosa pseudoharengus. [14C. < ALE + WIFE 'woman'.]

alexander /állig zaándər/ n a cocktail made from crème de cacao, sweet cream, and gin or brandy [Early 20C. < the name Alexander.]

Alexander II /állig zándər/ (1818–81) tsar of Russia (1855–81)

Alexander III (1105?–81) pope (1159–81). Born **Rolando Bandinelli**

Alexander, William, Earl of Stirling (1567?–1640) Scots poet

Alexander technique n a method of improving the posture that involves developing awareness of it [Mid-20C. After the Australian physiotherapist Frederick Alexander (1869–1955), who developed it.]

Alexander the Great (356–323 BC) king of Macedonia (336–323 BC)

Alexandra /állig zaándra/ (1872–1918) empress of Russia

Alexandria /állig zaándri ə/ port in N Egypt, on the Nile delta. Founded by Alexander the Great in 332 BC, it was a major cultural centre of the ancient world. Population: 3,328,000 (1998 estimate). —**Alexandrian** adj

Alexandrina /állig zan dreéna/ coastal lagoon in SE South Australia. Area: 680 sq. km/260 sq. mi.

alexandrine /állig zán drīn, -zaàn-, -drin/ n 1 ENGLISH VERSE FORM in English poetry, a line of verse that has six iambic feet and usually a caesura after the third foot 2 FRENCH VERSE FORM in French poetry, a line of verse that has twelve syllables and usually a caesura after the sixth syllable ■ adj LIKE OR IN ALEXANDRINES typical of or written in alexandrines [Late 16C. < French, after the romance Alexandre about Alexander the Great, which was written in this metre.]

alexandrite /állig zán drīt, -zaàn-/ n a precious stone that is a green chrysoberyl. Use: gems. [Mid-19C. < German Alexandrit, after Alexander II (1818–81), tsar of Russia, because it was discovered on the day of his majority.]

alexia /ə léksi ə/ n a loss of the ability to read, caused by a disorder of the central nervous system [Late 19C. < A-² + Greek lexis 'speech'; meaning influenced by Latin legere 'read'.]

Alexis Mikhailovich /ə léksiss mi kī'lə vich/ (1629–76) tsar of Russia (1654–76)

alf /alf/ n Aus somebody, especially an Australian, regarded as unsophisticated (informal insult)

ALF abbr Animal Liberation Front

alfa n, adj = **alpha**

alfacalcidol /álfə kálssə dœl/ n a derivative of vitamin D used by the body in the regulation of calcium and phosphate, and as a drug in the treatment of vitamin D deficiency

alfalfa /al fálfə/ n a plant of the pea family. Use: hay, forage crop. Native to: Europe, Asia. Medicago sativa. [Mid-19C. Via Spanish < Arabic al-faṣfaṣa 'the best kind of fodder'.]

Al Fatah n = **Fatah, Al**

alfentanil hydrochloride /al fént'nil-/ n an opioid drug. Use: general anaesthesia.

Alfieri /álfi áiri/, **Vittorio, Count** (1749–1803) Italian poet and dramatist

al-Fitr /al fíttər/ n CALENDAR = **Eid-ul-Fitr**

Alfred (the Great) /álfrid/ (849–901) king of Wessex (871–901)

alfresco /al fréskō/ adv outdoors or in the open air ■ adj taking place or located outdoors [Mid-18C. < Italian, 'in the fresh air'.]

Alfven /al vén/, **Hannes Olof Gosta** (1908–95) Swedish theoretical physicist

Alg. abbr 1 Algeria 2 Algerian

alga /álgə/ (plural **-gae** /áljee, álgee/) n a mainly aquatic photosynthetic organism that differs from plants in not having true leaves, roots, or stems and includes the seaweeds [Mid-16C. < Latin, 'seaweed'.] —**algal** adj —**algoid** /ál goyd/ adj

algal bloom n an excessive growth of algae on or near the surface of water, occurring naturally or as a result of an oversupply of nutrients from organic pollution

Algarve /aal gaàrv/ region in S Portugal

algebra /áljibrə/ n 1 a branch of mathematics in which symbols, usually letters of the alphabet, represent unknown numbers 2 the study of structures in mathematics such as groups, rings, fields, and categories [Mid-16C. Via Italian and medieval Latin < Arabic al-jabr 'the reuniting', in the title of a treatise by the mathematician al-Khwarizmi.] —**algebraist** /álji bráyist/ n

algebraic /álji bráyik/, **algebraical** /-bráyik'l/ adj 1 involving or relating to algebra 2 relating to or using only finite numbers, expressions, and operations —**algebraically** adv

Algeciras /álja seérass/ port and resort in S Spain. Population: 101,972 (1998 estimate).

Alger /áljər/, **Horatio** (1832–99) US writer and clergyman

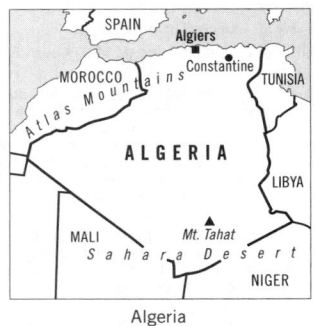

Algeria

Algeria /al jeérri ə/ country in NW Africa. Capital: Algiers. Population: 29,830,371 (1997). Area: 2,381,741 sq. km/919,595 sq. mi. —**Algerian** adj, n

algesia /al jeézi ə, -ssi ə/ n sensitivity to or perception of pain [< modern Latin, < Greek algesis]

-algia suffix pain ○ neuralgia [< Greek algos 'pain']

algicide /álji sīd/ n a substance that kills algae or prevents their growth —**algicidal** /álji sīd'l/ adj

algid /áljid/ adj describes an episode during a severe fever when the patient's body temperature suddenly drops to an abnormally low level [Early 17C. < Latin algidus < algere 'be cold'.] —**algidity** /al jíddəti/ n

Algiers /al jeérz/ capital, chief port, and largest city of Algeria. Population: 2,561,992 (1998).

algin /áljin/ n a viscous liquid, especially alginic acid or an alginate. Source: seaweed. Use: thickener or emulsifier in plastics or food. [Late 19C. < ALGA + -IN.]

alginate /álji nayt/ n a salt or ester of alginic acid. Use: thickener or emulsifier in plastics or food.

alginic acid /al jínnik-/ n ($C_6H_8O_6$)ₙ an insoluble powdery acid. Source: brown seaweed. Use: food, pharmaceuticals, cosmetics, textiles.

algo- prefix pain ○ algophobia [< Greek algos 'pain']

ALGOL /ál gol/, **Algol** n a high-level computer programming language that uses algebraic symbols in solving mathematical and scientific problems [Mid-20C. Contraction of algorithm-oriented language.]

algolagnia /álgō lágni ə/ n sexual pleasure experienced through inflicting or experiencing pain (technical) [Early 20C. < Greek algos 'pain' + lagneia 'lust'.] —**algolagnic** adj —**algolagnist** n

algology /al góllaji/ n the branch of botany concerned with the scientific study of algae —**algological** /álgə lójjik'l/ adj —**algologist** n

Algonkian n LANG, PEOPLES = **Algonquian**

Algonkin n LANG, PEOPLES = **Algonquin**¹

Algonquian /al góngki ən, -kwi-/ (plural **-an** or **-ans**), **Algonkian** /-ki-/ (plural **-an** or **-ans**) n 1 a group of Native North American languages that are, or were, spoken in central and E Canada, and parts of the central and E United States **2** a member of an Algonquian-speaking people [Late 19C. < ALGONQUIN[1].] —**Algonquian** *adj*

Algonquian-Wakashan *n* a family of over 40 Native American languages spoken throughout wide areas of Canada and in the central, E, and S United States —**Algonquian-Wakashan** *adj*

Algonquin[1] /al góngkin, -kwin/, **Algonkin** /-kin/ (*plural* **-kin** *or* **-kins**) *n* **1** a member of a group of Native North American peoples living along the Ottawa and St Lawrence Rivers in E Canada **2** a Native North American language spoken in Quebec and Ontario. Native speakers: 3,000. [Early 17C. Via Canadian French < Algonquian.] —**Algonquin** *adj*

Algonquin[2] /al góngkin, -kwin/ village in NE Illinois. Population: 20,093 (1998 estimate).

algophobia /álgə fóbi ə/ *n* an abnormally intense fear of pain

ϟ **algorithm** /álgə rithəm/ *n* **1** a logical step-by-step procedure for solving a mathematical problem in a finite number of steps, often involving repetition of the same basic operation **2** a logical sequence of steps for solving a problem, often written out as a flow chart, that can be translated into a computer program [Late 17C. Alteration of *algorism* after Greek *arithmos* 'number'.] —**algorithmic** /álgə ríthmik/ *adj*

Algren /áwlgrin/, **Nelson** (1909–81) US writer

Alhambra /al hámbrə/ citadel and palace in Granada, Spain, built for Moorish kings in the 12th and 13th centuries

Alhazen /ál hə zén/ (965–1040) Arab scientist

Muhammad Ali

Ali /aa lí/, **Muhammad** (*b.* 1942) US boxer. Born **Cassius Marcellus Clay**

Alia /áali ə/, **Ramiz** (*b.* 1925) Albanian statesman

ϟ **alias** /áyli əss/ *adv* **ALSO KNOWN AS** otherwise or also known as ■ *n* **1 NAME TAKEN** an assumed name **2 FILE OR DIRECTORY NAME** a name assigned to a computer file or directory, e.g. to make it more convenient to locate or manipulate [15C. < Latin, 'otherwise'.]

alibi /álli bī/ *n* (*plural* **-bis**) **1 ACCUSED'S CLAIM OF HAVING BEEN ELSEWHERE** a form of defence against an accusation in which the accused person claims to have been somewhere other than at the scene of the crime when the crime was committed **2 SOMEBODY USED TO ESTABLISH ALIBI** somebody or something used to prove that somebody else was elsewhere at the time that a crime was committed **3** ⚠ **EXCUSE** an explanation offered to justify something (*informal*) ■ *vt* (**-bis, -biing, -bied**) **PROVIDE ALIBI FOR** to provide an alibi or excuse for somebody [Late 17C. < Latin, 'elsewhere'.]

USAGE alibi meaning 'excuse': ***Alibi*** should only be used informally in the weakened meaning 'an explanation offered to justify something', because it has a precise legal meaning that is in danger of being compromised. Avoid overuse when *excuse* is the more natural word to use: *He used his illness as an excuse* [not *as an alibi*] *for leaving work early.*

Alicante /álli kánti/ port in SE Spain. Population: 272,432 (1998 estimate).

Alice band /álliss-/ *n* a band of velvet or ribbon worn across the top of the head to hold the hair back [Because Alice is shown wearing one in the original illustrations to *Through the Looking-Glass* by Lewis Carroll]

Alice-in-Wonderland /állis in wúndər land/ *adj* absurd, fantastic, or completely at odds with reality [Early 20C. < the well-known fantasy by Lewis Carroll (1832–98), *Alice's Adventures in Wonderland* (1865).]

Alice Springs /álliss-/ town in S Northern Territory, Australia. Population: 22,488 (1996).

alicyclic /álli síklik, -sík-/ *adj* describes organic compounds that have carbon atoms joined in a string (**open chain**) as well as in rings. ◊ **aliphatic** [Late 19C. Blend of ALIPHATIC + CYCLIC.]

alidade /álli dayd/ *n* an instrument consisting of a rule with sights at both ends, used in surveying for measuring angles and directions [14C. Via French and Spanish < Arabic *al-idada* 'the revolving radius'.]

alien /áyli ən/ *n* **1 EXTRATERRESTRIAL BEING** a being from another planet or another part of the universe, especially in works of science fiction **2 NONCITIZEN RESIDENT OF COUNTRY** a citizen of a country other than the one he or she is currently in **3 OUTSIDER** somebody who does not belong to or feels unaccepted by a group or society ■ *adj* **1 STRANGE** outside somebody's normal or previous experience and seeming strange and sometimes threatening **2 INCONSISTENT** not in keeping or totally incompatible with the nature of something or somebody ○ *The idea was alien to her nature.* **3 NOT OF A COUNTRY** not a citizen of, or not belonging to, the country in question **4 EXTRATERRESTRIAL** from another world or part of the universe, or relating to extraterrestrial beings ■ *vt* LAW = **alienate** *v.* **4** [14C. Directly or via Old French < Latin *alienus* < *alius* 'other'.]

alienable /áyli ənəb'l/ *adj* capable of being transferred by a legal process to another owner —**alienability** /áyli ənə bílləti/ *n*

alienate /áyli ə nayt/ (**-ates, -ating, -ated**) *vt* **1 MAKE UNFRIENDLY** to cause somebody to become unfriendly, unsympathetic, or hostile ○ *His selfishness succeeded in alienating all of his friends.* **2 MAKE FEEL DISAFFECTED** to make somebody feel that he or she does not belong to or share in something (*often passive*) ○ *The long-term unemployed often feel alienated from society.* **3 TURN SOMETHING AWAY** to cause something, especially somebody's affections, to be directed at somebody or something else **4 TRANSFER OWNERSHIP** to transfer the ownership of a property or right to somebody [15C. < Latin *alienat-*, past participle of *alienare* 'make somebody else's, alienate' < *alienus* (see ALIEN).] —**alienation** /áyli ə náysh'n/ *n* —**alienator** /áylyə naytər, áyli ə naytər/ *n*

alienee /áyli ə neé/ *n* somebody to whom property or a right is transferred by a legal process

alienist /áyli ənist/ *n* **1** *US* an expert witness, usually a psychiatrist, who is accepted by a court of law as qualified to assess the psychological state of people appearing in court **2** a psychiatrist (*archaic*) [Mid-19C. < French *aliéniste* < Latin *alienare* 'estrange, make irrational' (see ALIENATE).]

alienor /áyli ənər/ *n* somebody who transfers property or a right to somebody else by legal process

aliform /álli fawrm, áyli-/ *adj* shaped like a wing (*technical*) [Early 18C. < Latin *ala* 'wing'.]

Alighieri ♦ **Dante Alighieri**

alight[1] /ə lít/ (**alights, alighting, alighted** *or* **alit** /ə lít/, **alighted** *or* **alit**) *vi* **1 GET OUT OF VEHICLE** to step down or dismount from something onto the ground or a platform ○ *The VIPs alighted from their train.* **2 LAND** to land or settle after a flight ○ *A magpie alighted on a branch.* **3 FIND BY CHANCE** to happen to find, spot, or come to rest on something ○ *to alight on a suitable candidate* [Old English *alīhtan* < *a-* 'away, up, out' + *līhtan* 'make lighter in weight']

alight[2] /ə lít/ *adj* **1 ON FIRE** on fire or burning ○ *Try to keep the fire alight.* ○ *set the bonfire alight* **2 LIT UP** lit up or full of light ○ *The sky was alight with fireworks.* **3 FULL OF ENERGY** filled with or radiating energy, excitement, interest, or pleasure ○ *His face was alight with joy.* [Old English *aliht* 'illuminated', past participle of *alihtan* 'light up']

align /ə lín/, **aline** (**alines, alining, alined**) *v* **1** *vt* **BRING INTO LINE** to place something in a line, or in an orderly spatial relationship, e.g. parallel, with something else **2** *vti* **BRING INTO CORRECT POSITION** to bring something, e.g. different parts of a machine or structure, into the correct position with respect to each other or something else, or come into this position **3** *vti* **DECLARE SUPPORT FOR** to declare your support, or the support of somebody or something you represent, for a particular person, group, argument, or point of view ○ *The government aligned itself behind NATO.* ○ *The issue has aligned many citizens behind the candidate.* **4** *vi* **FORM LINE** to become arranged in a line [15C. < Old French *alignier* < Latin *linea* 'line'.] —**aligner** *n*

alignment /ə línmənt/, **alinement** *n* **1 LINEAR OR ORDERLY ARRANGEMENT** the arrangement of something in a straight line or in an orderly position relative to something else **2 POSITIONING OF SOMETHING FOR PROPER PERFORMANCE** the correct position or positioning of different components relative to one another, so that they perform properly ○ *the wheels are out of alignment* **3 SUPPORT OR ALLIANCE** support for, or a political alliance with, a particular person, group, or point of view ○ *shifting alignments within the legislature* **4 GROUND PLAN** a ground plan, especially one showing the course of a road or railway line **5 ORDERING OF TYPE** the ordering of lines of type relative to a margin or line ○ *Try changing the alignment from left to right.* ○ *The vertical alignment looks uneven.*

alike /ə lík/ *adj* similar in appearance or character ○ *They're so alike, it's difficult to tell them apart.* ■ *adv* in a similar or the same way ○ *The film will please young and old alike.* [Old English *gelīc* 'alike, similar' < Germanic, 'body, form'] —**alikeness** *n*

aliment /állimənt/ *n* something that feeds, sustains, or supports something else (*formal*) [15C. Via French < Latin *alimentum* < *alere* 'nourish'.] —**aliment** *vt* —**alimental** /álli mént'l/ *adj* —**alimentally** *adv*

alimentary /álli méntəri/ *adj* (*formal*) **1** relating to food or nutrition **2** providing nourishment, sustenance, support, or maintenance

alimentary canal *n* the tubular passage between the mouth and the anus, including the organs through which food passes for digestion and elimination as waste

alimentation /álli men táysh'n/ *n* (*formal*) **1** the providing of food or nourishment **2** the providing of maintenance or support —**alimentative** /álli méntətiv/ *adj*

alimony /álliməni/ *n* maintenance paid to a former spouse [Early 17C. < Latin *alimonia* 'subsistence' < *alere* (see ALIMENT).]

aliphatic /álli fáttik/ *adj* describes organic compounds that have carbon atoms linked in a string (**open chain**). ◊ **alicyclic** [Late 19C. < Greek *aleiphat-* 'fat', because originally applied to fatty acids.]

aliquant /állikwənt, -kwont/ *adj* describes a number or quantity that cannot divide another number or quantity without leaving a remainder. ◊ **aliquot** *adj.* [Late 17C. < Latin *aliquantum* 'somewhat'.]

aliquot /álli kwot/ *adj* describes a number or quantity that will divide another number or quantity without leaving a remainder. ◊ **aliquant** ■ *n* an aliquot part, including fractional parts, e.g. $\frac{1}{2}$, $\frac{1}{4}$, or $\frac{1}{8}$ [Late 16C. Via French < Latin, 'a certain number'.]

A list *n* the people most sought after or most in demand for any activity, e.g. as guests at social functions or for recruitment to a team or organization (*hyphenated before nouns*)

alit past tense and past participle of **alight**[1]

aliterate /ay líttərət/ *n* somebody who, though usually able to read, is completely uninterested in reading and literature —**aliteracy** *n* —**aliterate** *adj*

alive /ə lív/ *adj* **1 LIVING** living, especially still living, and not dead **2 OF ALL PEOPLE LIVING** of all people currently living (*usually with a superlative*) ○ *the luckiest person alive* **3 STILL IN EXISTENCE** still existing, continuing, or functioning ○ *The movement remained alive by going underground.* **4 STILL INTERESTING** still interesting, relevant, or vividly imaginable for people in the present day **5 FULL OF LIFE** full of energy and vigour, and with a zest for and interest in life **6 ANIMATED** active or animated, especially full of busy activity or a sense of excitement ○ *The place doesn't come alive till after midnight.* **7 SWARMING WITH** full of or swarming with people or animals ○ *The floor of the tent was alive with ants.* **8 AWARE OF** sensitive to or aware of things ○ *alive to the danger involved in the operation* [Old English *on life* 'in life'] —**aliveness** *n* ◇ **alive and kicking** still active, healthy, or functioning vigorously (*humorous*)

SYNONYMS See ***living***.

aliyah /álli yaá/ *n* **1** immigration into Israel by Jews **2** the honour of being nominated to give a reading from the Torah [Mid-20C. < Hebrew, 'ascent'.]

alizarin /ə lízzərin/ *n* $C_{14}H_8O_4$ an orange-red or brownish-yellow crystalline compound. Source: coal tar, formerly madder root. Use: dyes. [Mid-19C. < French *alizarine*, probably < Arabic *alizari* 'madder'.]

al-Kadr *n* ISLAM, CALENDAR = **Lailat-ul-Qadr**

alkahest /álkə hest/, **alcahest** *n* a hypothetical universal solvent sought by alchemists [Mid-17C. Coined by Paracelsus, in imitation of Arabic.] —**alkahestic** /álkə héstik/ *adj*

alkalescent /álkə léss'nt/ *adj* slightly alkaline or becoming alkaline —**alkalescence** *n*

alkali /álkə lī/ (*plural* **-lis** *or* **-li**) *n* **1** a water-soluble chemical that reacts with acids to form salts, has a pH above 7, and turns red litmus paper blue. ◊ **acid** *n.* 1 **2** a soluble mineral salt found in some arid soils and natural waters at levels harmful to agriculture [14C. Via medieval Latin < Arabic *al-ḳalī* 'the ashes of saltwort', from which it was first obtained.]

alkali metal *n* a soft, white, reactive metallic element belonging to group 1 of the periodic table, comprising lithium, sodium, potassium, rubidium, caesium, and francium

alkalimeter /álkə límmitər/ *n* an instrument used for measuring the concentration of alkalis in a solution —**alkalimetric** /álkəli méttrik/ *adj* —**alkalimetrically** *adv* —**alkalimetry** *n*

alkaline /álkə līn/ *adj* having the properties of an alkali, or containing an alkali or alkalis

alkaline-earth metal, alkaline earth *n* a metallic element belonging to group 2 of the periodic table, comprising beryllium, magnesium, calcium, strontium, barium, and radium

alkaline phosphatase *n* an enzyme that controls hydrolysis, used in the clinical diagnosis of many illnesses

alkalinity /álkə línnəti/ *n* the concentration of alkali in a solution, measured in terms of pH

alkalise /álkə līz/ *vti* = **alkalize**

alkalize /álkə līz/ (**-lizes, -lizing, -lized**), **alkalise** (**-lises, -lising, -lised**) *vti* to make something alkaline, or become alkaline

alkaloid /álkə loyd/ *n* a group of nitrogen-containing compounds that are physiologically active as poisons or drugs [Early 19C. < ALKALI, because their chemical properties are similar to it.] —**alkaloidal** /álkə lóyd'l/ *adj*

alkalosis /álkə lṓssiss/ *n* an abnormally high level of alkalinity in the blood, other body fluids, or body tissues, causing a high blood pH —**alkalotic** /álkə lóttik/ *adj*

alkane /ál kayn/ *n* C_nH_{2n+2} an open-chain hydrocarbon containing only carbon-to-carbon or carbon-to-hydrogen single bonds and belonging to a series whose members all have the same general chemical formula

alkanet /álkə net/ (*plural* **-nets** *or* **-net**) *n* **1** RED DYE a red dye obtained from the roots of a European plant **2** EUROPEAN DYE PLANT a plant related to borage with red roots that produce alkanet. Flowers: small, blue. Native to: Europe. *Alkanna tinctoria.* **3** PLANT RELATED TO ALKANET a bristly plant related to alkanet. Flowers: blue. Native to: Europe, Asia, Africa. Genus: *Anchusa.* [14C. Probably via Old Spanish *alcaneta* < Arabic *al-ḥinnā'* (see HENNA).]

alkaptonuria /al káptə nyŏori ə/ *n* a rare genetic disease characterized by arthritis and the destruction of connective tissue and bone [Late 19C. < German *Alkapton*, an acid + -URIA.]

alkene /ál keen/ *n* C_nH_{2n} an open-chain hydrocarbon containing one carbon-to-carbon double bond and belonging to a series whose members all have the same general chemical formula

alkoxide /al kóksīd/ *n* a salt formed by replacing the hydroxyl ion of an alcohol with a metal [Late 19C. < ALKALI + OXY- + -IDE.]

alky /álki/ (*plural* **-kies**), **alkie** *n* an offensive term for somebody who is an alcoholic or who drinks to excess (*slang*) [Mid-20C. Shortening.]

alkyd /ál kid/, **alkyd resin** *n* a sticky resin that is prepared from phthalic acid and glycerol and becomes liquid or plastic when heated. Use: paints, lacquer. [Early 20C. < ALKYL + ACID.]

alkyl /ál kil/ *adj* describes a hydrocarbon group derived from an alkane, e.g. the ethyl group [Late 19C. < German < *Alkohol* 'alcohol' + -YL.]

alkylation /álki láysh'n/ *n* the addition of an alkyl group to a chemical compound through the replacement of a hydrogen atom

alkyne /ál kīn/ *n* C_nH_{2n-2} an open-chain hydrocarbon containing one carbon-to-carbon triple bond and belonging to a series whose members all have the same general chemical formula

all /awl/ CORE MEANING: a grammatical word used to indicate that the whole of a particular thing, amount, group, or area is involved or affected ○ (det) *all men and all women* ○ (pron) *All of the computers are down.* ○ (pron) *All that glitters is not gold.*
1 *det* THE WHOLE OF used to indicate that the whole of a particular amount, area, quantity, or thing is involved or affected ○ *All Europe was cold this winter.* **2** *det* EVERY every one of ○ *all men over 30* **3** *det* ANY any whatever (*after a negative word such as 'refuse' or 'deny'*) ○ *Deny all connection with the plot.* **4** *det* MOST the greatest possible ○ *with all speed* **5** *det* CHARACTERIZED BY dominated in mood or character by something (*informal*) ○ *He was all smiles.* **6** *adv* VERY very, completely, or totally (*informal*) ○ *I got all confused.* **7** *pron* EVERY ONE OR THE WHOLE the whole number or amount (+ *plural verb*) ○ *All of us are going to the game.* **8** *pron* EVERYTHING OR EVERYONE the whole quantity or group ○ *All that glitters is not gold.* **9** *n* SOMEBODY'S BEST EFFORT the greatest amount of somebody's ability or effort ○ *He gave his all in the performance.* [Old English *eall* < Germanic] ◇ **all along** from the start, or for the whole time that something else was taking place ◇ **all but** almost ○ *I was all but asleep when the phone rang.* ◇ **(all) in all** when everything has been taken into account ◇ **all of** no less than (*informal*) ○ *It took us all of three hours to get here.* ◇ **all or nothing** used to indicate that only complete success or obtaining everything counts and anything less than that has no value ◇ **all that** very, particularly, or to that extent (*informal; usually in negative statements or questions*) ○ *I'm not all that worried about it.* ◇ **all the same 1** nevertheless **2** used to indicate that it is unimportant to the speaker which of two or more things is done or chosen ◇ **all there** fully alert, aware of what is going on, and able to deal with it (*informal*) ◇ **all very well** used to indicate that there is some kind of objection or drawback, despite the fact that somebody else is apparently satisfied with the situation ○ *That's all very well, but it's still my responsibility.* ◇ **be all over somebody** to be extremely or excessively friendly or effusive towards somebody (*informal*) ◇ **in all** in total ○ *That makes 52 votes in all for our candidate.*

SPELLCHECK Do not confuse ***all*** with ***awl***, which has a similar sound. Beware: your spellchecker will not catch this error.

USAGE all or **all of**? You have a choice between ***all*** and ***all of*** when the following noun is qualified by *the, this, that, these, those*, or a possessive determiner such as *my* and *your*: *All my life I've wanted to be a singer. All of my life I've wanted to be a singer. All these things worried them. All of these things worried them.*

alla breve /állə bráyvi/ *n* a time signature in music, represented by a C with a slash through it, specifying a beat of two or four minims to the bar. US term **cut time** ■ *adv* at twice the normal speed (*musical direction*) [< Italian, 'according to the breve'] —**alla breve** *adj*

Allah /állə/ *n* in Islam, the name of God [Late 16C. < Arabic *'allāh.*]

all-American *adj* **1** OF OR ABOUT THE UNITED STATES of or about the United States, its people, or their way of life, or representing them at their best **2** BEST IN THE UNITED STATES selected and honoured as the best amateur player or athlete in the United States in a particular position or event ○ *an all-American linebacker* **3** MADE OF US COMPONENTS made up entirely of people from the United States, or of materials or components from the United States **4** OF ALL THE AMERICAS including all the countries of North and South America or representatives from them ○ *an all-American agreement* ■ *n* **1** BEST US ATHLETE a player or athlete chosen as being the best in a position or event in the United States **2** TEAM OF BEST US PLAYERS a team made up of US players or athletes selected for their excellence in a particular position or event

allantois /állən tṓ iss/ (*plural* **-ides** /-ideez/) *n* a membranous sac that grows from the lower gut in mammal, bird, and reptile embryos [Mid-17C. Via modern Latin < Greek *allantoeidēs* 'sausage-like', because of its shape.] —**allantoic** *adj*

allargando /állaar gándō/ *adv* at a gradually slower tempo, with a broadening stately sound (*musical direction*) [Late 19C. < Italian, 'broadening'.] —**allargando** *adj*

all-around *adj* US = **all-round**

allay /ə láy/ *vt* **1** to calm a strong emotion, e.g. anger, or diminish and set at rest somebody's fears or suspicions **2** to relieve or reduce the severity of pain or a painful emotion [Old English *ālecgan* 'lay aside' (see LAY[1]). The meaning was influenced by Old French *alleger* 'lighten' and *aleier* 'moderate'.] —**allayer** *n* —**allayment** *n*

all-choice *adj US* describes a school system that allows people to choose a particular school to attend

all clear *n* **1** a signal that a period of danger is over, especially one sounded on a siren after an air raid **2** a signal or notification that something may proceed ○ *We've got the all clear to start building.*

all-consuming *adj* absorbing somebody's attention, time, or energy to the exclusion of everything else

~~**alledged**~~ incorrect spelling of **alleged**

allegation /álli gáysh'n/ *n* **1** an assertion, especially relating to wrongdoing or misconduct on somebody's part, that has yet to be proved or supported by evidence **2** the alleging of something, especially wrongdoing

allege /ə léj/ (**-leges, -leging, -leged**) *vti* **1** to state or assert something, especially to accuse somebody of wrongdoing, without offering proof of it or with a view to proving it later ○ *The prosecutor alleged that Simmons knew about the planned hold-up.* **2** to put something forward as a reason or excuse for your actions or conduct (*formal*) ○ *He declined the invitation, alleging a prior appointment.* [14C. Via Anglo-Norman, 'declare before a legal tribunal' < assumed Vulgar Latin *exlitigare* 'clear of charges' (see LITIGATE).] —**allegeable** *adj* —**alleger** *n*

alleged /ə léjd/ *adj* claimed but not yet proven to have taken place, have been committed, or be as described —**allegedly** /ə léjjidli/ *adv*

USAGE alleged and **allegedly** ***Alleged*** is often used to describe a crime or other wrongdoing; it denotes uncertainty about whether the incident happened at all or whether a particular person was responsible for it and may be used in media reports as a protection against legal action: *The alleged fraud took place over a number of months.* It is also used to describe somebody associated with a crime, not necessarily the culprit: *The alleged victims all live in the suburbs.* The adverb form ***allegedly*** has the same force: *The accused had allegedly been filing false expenses claims.*

Alleghenies /állə gáyniz/ ➧ **Allegheny Mountains**

Allegheny /állə gayni/ river in Pennsylvania and New York. Length: 523 km/325 mi.

Allegheny Mountains, Alleghenies range of the Appalachian Mountains in Pennsylvania, Maryland, West Virginia, and Virginia. Highest peak: Spruce Knob 1,482 m/4,861ft.

allegiance /ə leéjənss/ *n* **1** LOYALTY TO RULER OR STATE a subject's or citizen's loyalty to a ruler or state **2** DEVOTED SUPPORT loyalty to or support for a particular person, cause, or group ○ *The match was a treat for all fans, whatever their allegiance.* **3** FEUDAL OBLIGATION the feudal obligation of vassals to their liege lord [14C. Via Anglo-Norman < Old French *ligeance* < *lige* 'liege' (see LIEGE).] —**allegiant** *adj*

~~**allegience**~~ incorrect spelling of **allegiance**

allegorical /álli górrik'l/, **allegoric** /-górrik/ *adj* **1** expressing something through an allegory **2** used in or relating to allegory —**allegorically** *adv*

allegorize /álligə rīz/ (**-rizes, -rizing, -rized**), **allegorise** (**-rises, -rising, -rised**) *v* **1** *vti* to express something in the form of an allegory **2** *vt* to interpret or treat something as an allegory —**allegorization** /álligə rī záysh'n/ *n* —**allegorizer** *n*

allegory /álligəri/ (*plural* **-ries**) *n* **1** SYMBOLIC WORK a work in which the characters and events are to be understood as representing other things and symbolically expressing a deeper, often spiritual, moral, or political meaning **2** SYMBOLIC EXPRESSION OF MEANING IN STORY the symbolic expression of a deeper meaning through a story or scene acted out by human, animal, or mythical characters **3** GENRE allegories considered as a literary or artistic genre **4** SYMBOLIC REPRESENTATION a symbolic representation of something [14C. < Latin *allegoria* < Greek *allegorein* 'say otherwise' < *allos* 'other' + *agoreuein* 'speak in public'.] —**allegorist** *n*

allegretto /álli gréttō/ *adv* at a fairly quick tempo (*musical direction*) ■ *n* (*plural* **-tos**) a piece of music, or a section of a piece, played allegretto [Mid-18C. < Italian, 'less than allegro'.] —**allegretto** *adj*

allegro /ə láygrō, ə léggrō/ *adv* at a quick and lively tempo (*musical direction*) ■ *n* (*plural* **-gros**) a piece of music, or a section of a piece, played allegro [Late 17C. < Italian, 'lively'.] —**allegro** *adj*

allele /ə léel/ *n* one of two or more alternative forms of a gene, occupying the same position (**locus**) on paired chromosomes and controlling the same inherited characteristic [Mid-20C. < German *Allel*, shortening of *Allelomorph* 'allelomorph'.] —**allelic** *adj* —**allelism** *n*

allelo- *prefix* one another ○ *allelopathy* [< Greek *allēlon* < *allos* 'other' (see ALLO-)]

allelochemical /ə léelə kémmik'l/ *n* a chemical produced by one plant that is toxic to another

allelomorph /ə léelə mawrf, ə léllə-/ *n* GENETICS = **allele** —**allelomorphic** /ə léelə máwrfik, ə léllə-/ *adj* —**allelomorphism** *n*

allelopathy /álli lóppəthi/ *n* the release into the environment by one plant of a substance that inhibits the germination or growth of other potential competitor plants of the same or another species —**allelopathic** /ə léelə páthik, -léllə-/ *adj*

allelotoxin /ə léelə tóksin/ *n* PLANT SCI = **allelochemical**

alleluia *interj, n* = **hallelujah**

allemande /álli mand/ *n* **1** MUSICAL MOVEMENT FORMING PART OF SUITE a stately piece of music in moderate tempo and four-four time, often used as the opening movement of a baroque or classical suite **2** DANCE POPULAR IN 18C a stately dance of German origin popular in France in the 18th century **3** DANCE MOVEMENT a movement used in country dancing that involves partners changing positions, often by interlinking arms [Late 17C. < French, 'German'.]

all-embracing *adj* including all or everything without discrimination

Allen /állən/, **Paul** (*b.* 1953) US business executive

Allen, Peter (1944–92) Australian singer and songwriter. Born **Peter Woolnough**

Allen, Woody (*b.* 1935) US film director, actor, screenwriter, playwright, and humorous essayist. Born **Allen Stewart Konigsberg**

Allenby /állənbi/, **Edmund Henry Hynman, 1st Viscount** (1861–1936) British soldier

all-encompassing *adj* including or affecting everyone or everything

Allende /ə yén day/, **Isabel** (*b.* 1942) Chilean author

Allende Gossens /aa yén day gáw sens/, **Salvador** (1908–73) Chilean statesman

allene /álleen/ *n* a colourless unstable gas. Use: manufacture of chemicals. [Late 19C. Contraction of *allylene*, a gaseous hydrocarbon.]

Allen key *n* a tool in the form of an L-shaped rod, hexagonal in cross section, made in different sizes to turn corresponding sizes of Allen screws. US term **Allen wrench** [See ALLEN SCREW]

Allen screw *n* a screw with a hexagonal recess in its head that allows it to be turned using an Allen key [Mid-20C. After the *Allen* Manufacturing Company of Hartford, Connecticut, US.]

Allen wrench *n US* = **Allen key** [See ALLEN SCREW]

allergen /állər jen, állərjən/ *n* any substance that causes an allergic reaction —**allergenic** /állər jénnik/ *adj*

allergic /ə lúrjik/ *adj* **1** HAVING ALLERGY having an allergy to a substance ○ *allergic to dust mites* **2** CAUSED BY ALLERGY typical of or caused by an allergy ○ *an allergic reaction* **3** HAVING A DISLIKE having a strong dislike for or aversion to something or somebody (*informal*) ○ *allergic to loud music*

allergic purpura *n* a form of purpura caused by inflammation of blood vessels, found most often in children

allergist /állərjist/ *n* a doctor who specializes in allergies and their treatment

allergy /állərji/ (*plural* **-gies**) *n* **1** unusual sensitivity to a normally harmless substance that provokes a strong reaction from a person's body **2** a strong dislike for or aversion to something (*informal*) ○ *an allergy to washing* [Early 20C. < German *Allergie* < Greek *allos* 'other' (see ALLO-), after *Energie* 'energy'.]

allethrin /ə léthrin/ *n* $C_{19}H_{26}O_3$ a clear or amber-coloured viscous liquid. Use: insecticide. [Mid-20C. Blend of ALLYL + PYRETHRIN.]

alleviate /ə léevi ayt/ (**-ates, -ating, -ated**) *vt* to make something, e.g. pain or hardship, more bearable or less severe ○ *Nothing could alleviate her despair.* [Early 16C. < late Latin *alleviat-*, past participle of *alleviare* 'lighten' < Latin *levis* 'light (in weight)'.] —**alleviation** /ə léevi áysh'n/ *n* —**alleviative** *adj* —**alleviator** *n* —**alleviatory** /ə léevi áytəri/ *adj*

alley[1] /álli/ (*plural* **-leys**) *n* **1** SMALL STREET a short or narrow street **2** NARROW PASSAGE a narrow passageway or lane, especially one running between or behind buildings **3** PATH IN GARDEN OR PARK a path or walk in a garden or park, especially one between trees or shrubs **4** SPORTS = **bowling alley** *n.* 2 **5** *US* PART OF TENNIS COURT either of the two spaces, one on each side of a court, between the singles and doubles sidelines [14C. < Old French *alee* 'a walk' < Latin *ambulare* (see AMBULATE).] ◇ **right up** *or* **down somebody's alley** *US* completely suited to somebody's interest, expertise, or line of work

alley[2] /álli/ *n* a large playing marble [Early 18C. Shortening of ALABASTER, from which they were originally made.]

Alley /álli/, **Rewi** (1897–1987) New Zealand poet and translator

alley cat *n US* **1** a homeless or stray cat, usually in bad condition or half wild, that lives on the streets **2** somebody thought to resemble an alley cat, especially in being disreputable or fierce-tempered, or having loose morals (*disapproving*)

alley-oop /álli óop/ *interj* ENCOURAGEMENT ON GETTING UP used as a word of encouragement when somebody is getting up or being helped up, or something is being lifted (*dated*) ■ *n* **1** TYPE OF MOVE IN BASKETBALL a play in basketball in which a player jumps up to receive a pass over the basket and immediately puts the ball into the net from above **2** TYPE OF PASS IN BASKETBALL a pass in basketball aimed to allow a player to jump up to receive it over the basket [Early 20C. < French *allez* 'come on!' + *houp* 'upsadaisy!'.]

alleyway /álli way/ *n* an alley or narrow passageway

all-fired *adv US* in an excessive or inordinate way (*informal*) ○ *Don't act so all-fired high and mighty.* [Early 19C. Alteration of *hell-fired*.]

All Fools' Day *n* CALENDAR = **April Fools' Day**

all fours *n* CARDS = **seven-up** ◇ **on all fours** crawling along or crouched down on the hands and knees

Allhallows /awl hállōz/ (*plural* **-lows**), **Allhallowmas** /-hállōməss/ *n* All Saints' Day (*archaic; + singular verb*) [Old English *ealra hālgena* 'of all saints' < *hālga* 'saint' < *hālig* 'holy' (see HOLY)]

Allhallows' Eve *n* Hallowe'en (*archaic*)

allheal /áwl heel/ (*plural* **-heals** *or* **-heal**) *n* a plant traditionally believed to have healing powers, e.g. valerian or selfheal

alliance /ə lí ənss/ *n* **1** ASSOCIATION OF GROUPS WITH COMMON AIM an association of two or more groups, individuals, or nations who agree to cooperate with one another to achieve a common goal **2** FORMING OF ALLIANCE the establishment of or participation in an alliance with somebody **3** MEMBERS OF ALLIANCE the nations, individuals, or groups that make up an alliance ○ *the enemy alliance* **4** CLOSE RELATIONSHIP a close relationship, based on the possession of similar aims or characteristics, between two or more people or things [13C. < Old French *aliance* < *alier* 'ally' (see ALLY).]

allied /állīd, ə líd/ *adj* **1** JOINED WITH OTHERS IN ALLIANCE joined in an alliance with other nations, groups, or individuals by agreement or treaty **2** ASSOCIATED having a close relationship or connection with each other ○ *allied banks* **3** OF SIMILAR TYPE of a similar or related type ○ *sociology and allied studies*

alligator /álli gaytər/ *n* **1** (*plural* **-tors** *or* **-tor**) LARGE REPTILE a large reptile that lives near water, has thick scaly skin, powerful jaws, a long tail, and a shorter and broader snout than a crocodile. Native to: S United States, China. Genus: *Alligator*. **2** LEATHER FROM ALLIGATOR SKIN leather made from alligator skin **3** TOOL OR MACHINE WITH MOVABLE JAW a tool or machine with a strong, movable, often toothed jaw for gripping or crushing [Mid-16C. Alteration of Spanish *el lagarto* 'the lizard' < Latin *lacertus*.]

alligator clip *n US* ELEC ENG = **crocodile clip** [Because it resembles an alligator's jaws]

alligator pear *n US* FOOD = **avocado** *n.* 1 [Mid-18C. Alteration of American Spanish *aguacate* 'avocado', perhaps because of the rough dark skin of some varieties.]

alligator snapping turtle, alligator snapper *n* a large freshwater snapping turtle. Native to: Gulf States of the United States. *Macroclemys temmincki.*

all-important *adj* extremely or vitally important or necessary

all in *adj* **1** including everything, especially all costs (*hyphenated before nouns*) ○ *Is that the all-in price?* **2** extremely tired ○ *We were all in by the time we got back to the hotel.*

all-inclusive *adj* including or encompassing everything that is expected or appropriate —**all-inclusiveness** *n*

Allingham /állingəm/, **Margery** (1904–66) British writer

all-in-one *adj* **1** performing two or more functions or made up of two or more elements that are often separate **2** describes a garment made in a single piece —**all-in-one** *n*

all-in wrestling *n* a style of professional wrestling with relatively few restrictions on the permissible types of holds, blows, or throws ○ *an all-in wrestling tournament*

alliterate /ə lítti rayt/ (**-ates, -ating, -ated**) *v* **1** *vi* to begin words that are consecutive or close to each other with the same or a similar consonant, or to contain alliteration **2** *vti* to use alliteration in speaking or writing [Late 18C. Back-formation < ALLITERATION.] —**alliterative** /ə líttirətiv/ *adj* —**alliteratively** *adv*

alliteration /ə lítti ráysh'n/ *n* a poetic or literary effect achieved by using several words that begin with the same or similar consonants. ◊ **assonance** [Early 17C. < medieval Latin *alliteration-* < Latin *littera* 'letter of the alphabet'.]

~~**allmost**~~ incorrect spelling of **almost**

all-night *adj* lasting, open, or available throughout the night, or throughout a particular night ○ *an all-night rave*

allo- *prefix* other, different, alternate ○ *allosteric* ○ *allophone* [< Greek *allos* 'other' < Indo-European, 'other of more than two']

Alloa /állō ə/ seaport on the River Forth in Scotland. Population: 18,842 (1991).

allocate /állə kayt/ (**-cates, -cating, -cated**) *vt* **1** to give something to a particular person, or set something aside for a particular purpose, when dividing something between different people or projects ○ *Each team member has been allocated a specific task.* **2** to share out or divide up something between a number of different people or projects ○ *Much depends on how we allocate the time available for discussion.* [Mid-17C. < medieval Latin *allocat-*, past participle of *allocare* 'put in place' < Latin *locus* 'place'.] —**allocable** /álləkəb'l/ *adj* —**allocatable** /állə káytəb'l/ *adj* —**allocator** *n*

allocation /állə káysh'n/ *n* **1** ACT OF ALLOCATING the assignment or earmarking of something ○ *allocation of duties* **2** SOMETHING ALLOCATED a thing, amount, or share of something allocated to somebody or something ○ *The department has already used its entire allocation.* **3** SYSTEM OF DIVIDING INCOME AMONG DEPARTMENTS the system or practice of dividing a company's income and overheads among its various departments

allochthonous /ə lókthənəss/ *adj* **1** describes features of the landscape or elements of its geological structure that have been moved to their current position through tectonic forces. ◊ **autochthonous** *adj.* 1 **2** describes flora, fauna, or inhabitants that have moved to the region in which they are found from elsewhere. ◊ **autochthonous** *adj.* 2 [Early 20C. < Greek *allochthon* < ALLO- + *khthōn* 'soil'.]

allocution /állə kyóosh'n/ *n* a formal speech or address, especially one that contains an authoritative statement on a subject or an exhortation to somebody [Early 17C. < Latin *allocution-* < *alloqui* 'speak to' < *loqui* 'speak'.]

allogamy /ə lóggəmi/ *n* the process of cross-fertilization in flowering plants —**allogamous** *adj*

allogeneic /állō jə née ik/, **allogenic** /-jénnik/ *adj* describes tissues that are genetically different and therefore incompatible when transplanted [Mid-20C. < ALLO- + Greek *genea* 'race, generation'.] —**allogeneically** *adv*

allograft /állō graaft/ *n* a graft of tissue from one member of a species to a genetically different member of the same species. ◊ **homograft**

allograph /állə graaf, -graf/ *n* **1** something, especially a signature, written by one person on another's behalf **2** a letter or combination of letters that is one of a set that can be used to represent the same speech sound (**phoneme**), as, e.g., 's', 'ss', and 'c' in English

allomerism /ə lómmərizəm/ *n* similarity in the crystal structure of substances that are chemically different —**allomerous** *adj*

allometry /ə lómmətri/ *n* measurement of the rate of growth of a part or parts of an organism relative to the growth of the whole organism —**allometric** /állə méttrik/ *adj*

allomone /állə mōn/ *n* a chemical substance produced by a plant in response to attack by other organisms [Late 20C. < ALLO- + PLANT HORMONE.]

allomorph /állə mawrf/ *n* **1** a letter or combination of letters that is part of a set used to represent the same basic grammatical element (**morpheme**) of a language, as, e.g., '-ed' and '-t' both form the English past tense **2** a different crystal form of the same mineral, chemical compound, or element [Mid-20C. < ALLO- + MORPHEME.] —**allomorphic** /állə máwrfik/ *adj* —**allomorphism** /-fizəm/ *n*

allopathy /ə lóppəthi/ *n* the treatment of a disease by using remedies whose effects differ from those produced by that disease —**allopath** /állə path/ *n* —**allopathic** /állə páthik/ *adj* —**allopathically** *adv*

allopatric /állə páttrik/ *adj* describes species or populations that do not interbreed because they are geographically isolated from one another [Mid-20C. < ALLO- + Greek *patra* 'homeland' < *patēr* 'father'.] —**allopatrically** *adv* —**allopatry** /ə lóppətri/ *n*

allophane /állə fayn/ *n* an amorphous, variously coloured, hydrated aluminosilicate mineral [Early 19C. < Greek *allophanēs* 'appearing otherwise' (because it changes colour when heated) < *allos* 'other' + *phainesthai* 'appear'.]

allophone /állə fōn/ *n* one of the slightly differing forms that the same single speech sound (**phoneme**) can take [Mid-20C. < ALLO- + PHONEME.] —**allophonic** /állə fónnik/ *adj* —**allophonically** *adv*

allopurinol /állō pyóori nol/ *n* a drug that blocks production of uric acid. Use: gout treatment. [Mid-20C. < ALLO- + PURINE.]

All-Ordinaries Index *n* an index of the daily change in share prices on the Australian Stock Market, based on the average price change in the shares of a selection of top Australian companies

All-Ords *n Aus* the All-Ordinaries Index (*informal*)

all-or-none *adj US* functioning or taking effect either completely or not at all

all-or-nothing *adj* **1** bound to result either in complete success or total failure, with no possibility of anything in between **2** unwilling to accept anything less than all ○ *an all-or-nothing approach to negotiating*

allosaurus /állə sawrəss/ *n* a very large carnivorous theropod dinosaur of the late Upper Jurassic period. Native to: North America. Genus: *Allosaurus*. [Late 19C. < modern Latin, < Greek *allos* 'other' + *saurus* 'lizard'.]

allosteric /állō stéerik/ *adj* describes a binding site on an enzyme at which interaction induces altered activity at another site —**allosterically** *adv* —**allostery** /ə lóstəri/ *n*

allot /ə lót/ (**-lots, -lotting, -lotted**) *vt* **1** to give something to somebody as his or her share of what is available or what has to be done ○ *I was allotted the task of sweeping up.* **2** to earmark or reserve something for a particular purpose ○ *alloting ten shelves to books* [15C. < Old French *aloter* < *lot* 'portion' < Germanic.] —**allottee** /ə lot ée/ *n* —**allotter** *n*

allotment /ə lótmənt/ *n* **1 PLOT OF LAND** a small plot of publicly owned land rented to a person for growing vegetables or flowers **2 ALLOTTING OF** the assignment or earmarking of something ○ *the allotment of shares* **3 SOMETHING ALLOTTED** a thing, amount, or share allotted to somebody or something

allotransplant *vt* /állō transs plaánt, -traanss-/ to transplant an organ or body tissue from one member of a species to a genetically different member of the same species ■ *n* /állō tránss plaant, -traánss-/ an organ or piece of body tissue transplanted from one member of a species to a genetically different member of the same species

allotrope /állə trōp/ *n* one of many forms in which a chemical element occurs, each differing in physical properties, e.g. diamonds and coal as forms of carbon —**allotropic** /állə tróppik/ *adj* —**allotropically** *adv*

allotropy /ə lóttrəpi/, **allotropism** /-izəm/ *n* the existence of a chemical element in more than one form (**allotrope**), each having different physical but the same chemical properties

all'ottava /állə taávə/ *adv* to be played an octave higher or lower than written (*musical direction*) [Early 19C. < Italian, 'on the octave'.] —**all'ottava** *adj*

all out *adv* with maximum effort, at full power, or at top speed

all-out *adj* **1** involving the maximum possible effort or every available resource ○ *an all-out attempt to break the record* **2** describes a strike involving the whole workforce

all over *adv* (*informal*) **1** everywhere **2** used to stress that a particular description or action is utterly typical of the person or type of person stated ○ *That's Jackie all over: late again!*

all-over *adj* covering the whole surface area of something ○ *an all-over tan*

allow /ə lów/ *v* **1** *vt* **LET SOMEBODY DO** to give permission for something to happen or somebody to do something, or take no action or make no rule to prevent it ○ *I can't allow you to throw this chance away.* **2** *vt* **LET SOMEBODY ENTER OR BE PRESENT** to let somebody or something enter or be present in a place ○ *Children are not allowed after nine o'clock.* **3** *vt* **LET SOMEBODY HAVE** to let somebody or yourself have something, often a benefit or pleasure of some kind ○ *Allow yourself a few minutes to catch your breath.* **4** *vt* **CREDIT SOMEBODY MONEY FOR** to give or credit somebody with an amount of money as a discount or in exchange for something ○ *How much will you allow on our old machine?* **5** *vt* **ADMIT** to admit something or accept it to be true or valid (*dated*) ○ *You must allow that it was rather harsh.* **6** *vi* **PRESENT AS POSSIBLE** to present something as possible or reasonable (*formal*) ○ *The events allow of only one interpretation.* **7** *vi Southern US* **SAY OR THINK** to state or suppose ○ *He allowed it was time to go.* [14C. Via Old French *allouer* < Latin *allaudare* 'praise' and medieval Latin *allocare* 'assign' (see ALLOCATE).] —**allowable** *adj* —**allowably** *adv* —**allowed** *adj*

allow for *vti* to set aside or make available something such as a period of time or amount of material for a particular purpose ○ *Allow extra for shrinkage.*

allowance /ə lówənss/ *n* **1 BUDGETED AMOUNT** an amount of something, especially money, given out at regular intervals or for a specific purpose ○ *a mileage allowance as well as expenses* **2** *US* = **pocket money** *n.* 1 **3 DISCOUNT** money deducted from the selling price of something by the seller as a discount or in exchange for something **4 INCOME NOT TAXABLE** an amount of a person's income that is exempt from taxation and is deducted from the total to be taxed ○ *the married person's allowance* **5 SALARY SUPPLEMENT GIVEN TO TEACHER** a salary supplement paid to a teacher for taking on extra duties or responsibilities **6 TOLERATION** the allowing of something to happen **7 AMOUNT OF VARIATION ALLOWED** a small amount of variation permitted in the dimensions of closely fitting machine parts **8** *US* **HANDICAP** a handicap or advantage in certain sports ■ *vt* (**-ances, -ancing, -anced**) *US* **GIVE SOMEBODY ALLOWANCE** to restrict somebody to a fixed regular amount of something ○ *Members of the sales staff are allowanced for monthly expenses.* ◇ **make allowance** *or* **allowances (for somebody** *or* **something) 1** to take a charitable view of somebody or something and take mitigating circumstances into account **2** to take something into consideration when making a plan, decision, or judgment

allowedly /ə lówidli/ *adv* admittedly or by general agreement ○ *Allowedly, the salary is modest.*

alloy *n* /álloy/ **1 MIXTURE OF METALS** a substance that is a mixture of two or more metals, or of a metal with a nonmetallic material **2 DEBASING ADDITION** something that detracts from the value or quality of the thing it is added to or mixed with ○ *The film is weakened by the alloy of sentimentality.* **3 BLEND** any mixture, amalgam, or compound of different materials ■ *vt* /ə lóy/ **1 MIX METALS** to mix one metal with another, or mix a metal with a nonmetallic material **2 DEBASE** to detract from the quality, purity, or value of something by being added to or by adding an inferior material to it ○ *principles alloyed with cynicism* **3 COMBINE** to mix or combine different things [Mid-17C. Via Old French dialect *allai* (noun), *allayer* (verb) < Latin *alligare* 'bind to' < *ligare* 'bind'.]

SYNONYMS See ***mixture***.

all-pervading *adj* spread or present throughout everything ○ *a sense of all pervading gloom*

all-points bulletin *n US* a message broadcast to all police in a particular area, usually containing urgent information or a warning

all-powerful *adj* possessing unlimited authority or power —**all-powerfulness** *n*

all-purpose *adj* suitable for a wide variety of uses

~~**allready**~~ incorrect spelling of **already**

all right *adj* **1 SATISFACTORY** generally good, satisfactory, or pleasing (*hyphenated before nouns*) ○ *Everything's going to be all right.* **2 JUST ADEQUATE** just about acceptable or adequate, but not very good ○ *The new job's all right, I guess.* **3 UNINJURED** not injured or unwell **4 IN GOOD CONDITION** in good condition or order, and not defective or damaged ■ *interj* **1 YES** used to express agreement or approval ○ *'Will you come along?' 'All right'.* **2 GREETING** used as a greeting and friendly inquiry, meaning hello and how are you (*informal*) ■ *adv* **1 SATISFACTORILY** in a generally good, satisfactory, or pleasing way ○ *My old drill still works all right.* **2 CERTAINLY** without any doubt ○ *He's his father's son all right.* ◇ **it's all right for some** some people are more privileged or have more advantages than others (*humorous*)

USAGE All right or **alright**? Some people think the one-word spelling is justified by the analogy of *already* and *altogether*, and that it is sometimes useful to be able to distinguish between ***all right*** and ***alright*** (as with *altogether* and *all together*): *The answers were alright* (= satisfactory). *The answers were all right* (= all correct). But ***alright*** has never been accepted as good usage.

all round *adv* **1** in every respect or taking everything into consideration ○ *I think, all round, it was a pretty successful effort, don't you?* **2** for, from, or involving everyone ○ *There was a sigh of relief all round when he made the announcement.*

all-round *adj* **1 WITH MANY ABILITIES** able to do many things well, or useful in a number of different ways, not specialized ○ *the best all-round player for both attack and defence* **2 ALL-INCLUSIVE** broad or comprehensive in scope ○ *for all-round news coverage* **3 IN ALL DIRECTIONS** in all directions

all-rounder *n* somebody who is good at many things, especially in sports

All Saints' Day, All Saints *n* the day in the Christian calendar set aside to celebrate the lives of saints. Date: 1 November

all-season *adj* usable in every season of the year, regardless of weather conditions

all-seater *adj* providing seats for all spectators and no standing room ○ *an all-seater stadium*

all-seeing *adj* seeing or appearing to see everything

all-singing-all-dancing *adj* extraordinarily versatile or impressive (*informal humorous*)

All Souls' Day, All Souls *n* the day set aside in the Roman Catholic Church calendar for prayer for the souls of those who have died and are believed to be in purgatory. Date: 2 November.

allspice /áwl spīss/ *n* **1** the ground dried berries of a tropical evergreen tree, used as a spice **2** (*plural* **-spices** *or* **-spice**) an evergreen tree whose aromatic berries make allspice. Native to: tropical America. *Pimenta dioica*. [Because it is thought to combine the flavours of cinnamon, cloves, and nutmeg]

all-star *adj* made up mainly or completely of very famous and talented performers or players ■ *n US* a member of an all-star team

Allston /áwlstən/, **Washington** (1779–1843) US artist and writer

all-suite *adj* describes a hotel room that has a sitting-room and kitchenette as well as the standard features of hotel accommodation

all-terrain bike *n* a bicycle or motorcycle designed for use in open country as well as on roads

all-terrain vehicle *n* a motor vehicle designed for use on rough, sandy, or marshy ground, as well as on roads

~~**allthough**~~ incorrect spelling of **although**

all-ticket *adj* describes an event to which people are only admitted if they have bought a ticket in advance

all-time *adj* having never yet been bettered, or the best, greatest, or most popular ever ○ *an all-time record for this distance*

all told *adv* when everything or everyone is counted, included, or taken into account ○ *A dozen people made it, all told.*

allude /ə lo͞od/ (**-ludes, -luding, -luded**) *vi* to mention something or somebody indirectly, without giving a precise name or explicit identification ○ *I presume you are alluding to the alleged financial discrepancy.* [Mid-16C. < Latin *alludere* 'play to' < *ludere* < *ludus* 'play'.]

SPELLCHECK Do not confuse ***allude*** with ***elude***, which has a similar sound. Beware: your spellchecker will not catch this error.

USAGE allude or **refer**? The sentence *She alluded to her husband by name* is a self-contradiction, because ***allude*** means 'to mention indirectly'. When the reference is direct, the word to use is ***refer***. So if she mentioned 'the man at home looking after the children', she was ***alluding*** to her husband, whereas if she mentioned 'George' or 'my husband' directly, she was ***referring*** to him: *She referred to her husband frequently.*

allure /ə lyo͝or, ə lo͝or/ *n* an attractive or tempting quality possessed by somebody or something, often a glamorous and sometimes risky one ○ *They couldn't resist the allure of the big city.* ■ *vti* (**-lures, -luring, -lured**) to exert a very powerful and often dangerous attraction on somebody [15C. < Anglo-Norman *alurer*, Old French *aloirrier, aleurier* 'bring to the bait' < *leure* 'bait' (see LURE).] —**allurement** *n*

alluring /ə lyo͝oring, ə lo͝oring/ *adj* extremely attractive, tempting, or glamorous, and able to arouse strong desire in people —**alluringly** *adv*

allusion /ə lo͞ozh'n/ *n* **1** a reference that is made indirectly, subtly suggested, or implied ○ *a poem typical of its period in its use of classical allusions* **2** the act of making an indirect reference to somebody or something [Early 17C. Directly or via French < late Latin *allusion-* < Latin *allus-*, past participle of *alludere* (see ALLUDE).]

USAGE allusion, delusion, or **illusion**? ***Allusion*** and ***illusion*** are the closest in sound but the furthest apart in meaning: an ***allusion*** is an indirect reference to a person, thing, or event: *The story contained an allusion to her childhood in Africa.* An ***illusion*** is something that deceives the senses or mind: *The shimmering effect on a hot road is an optical illusion. By shutting himself in his room for hours he kept up an illusion of studying hard.* ***Illusion*** and ***delusion*** are similar in meaning, but ***delusion*** denotes a false or mistaken belief or idea, rather than a wrong impression received: *Visitors often suffer under the delusion that the weather is always hot here.*

allusive /ə lo͞ossiv/ *adj* **1** that makes or contains an indirect reference to something or somebody **2** characterized by the use of indirect references or subtle suggestion —**allusively** *adv* —**allusiveness** *n*

alluvia plural of **alluvium**

alluvial /ə lo͞ovi əl/ *adj* describes the environment, action, and sedimentary deposits of rivers or streams

alluvial fan *n* a fan-shaped deposit of sediment formed at the point where a stream enters a valley or plain or another, larger stream

alluvion /ə lo͞ovi ən/ *n* the expansion of a land area through the build-up of alluvial deposits or the receding of a body of water [Mid-16C. Via French < Latin *alluvion-* < *alluvius* (see ALLUVIUM).]

alluvium /ə lo͞ovi əm/ (*plural* **-ums** *or* **-a** /-vi ə/) *n* sediment deposited by running water, especially soil formed in river valleys and deltas from material washed down by the river [Mid-17C. < Latin, form of *alluvius* 'washed against' < *lavare* 'wash'.]

~~**allways**~~ incorrect spelling of **always**

all-weather *adj* usable in or able to stand up to all types of weather

ally /ə lī, állī/ *v* (**-lies, -lying, -lied**) **1** *vti* **JOIN IN MUTUALLY SUPPORTIVE ASSOCIATION** to join, or enlist somebody, in an association with others for mutual help and support or the achievement of a common purpose **2** *vt* **AFFILIATE** to connect something with something else through similarity or common features (*usually passive*) ○ *These plants are allied to lilies.* **3** *vti* **CONNECT THROUGH MARRIAGE** to connect individuals or families, or form a connection with another individual or family, through marriage or a similar tie ■ *n* (*plural* **-lies**) **1 MEMBER OF ALLIANCE** a person, group, or state that is joined in an association with another or others for mutual help and support or the achievement of a common purpose **2 RELATED ORGANISM** an organism that is closely related to another [14C. Via Old French *al(e)ier* < Latin *alligare* 'bind to' (see ALLOY).]

allyl /állīl, állil/ *adj* describes a compound containing the chemical group C_3H_5– [Mid-19C. < Latin *allium* 'garlic' (because first obtained from garlic).]

allyl alcohol *n* a colourless, strong-smelling liquid. Use: manufacture of resins, plasticizers.

Alma-Ata former name for **Almaty**

Almagest /álmə jest/ *n* **1** a text on astronomy written by Ptolemy in the second century AD setting out his view of the universe with the Earth at its centre surrounded by spheres **2 Almagest, almagest** an important medieval treatise on a subject, especially on astronomy, astrology, or alchemy [14C. Via Old French < Arabic *al-mijistī* 'the greatest' < Greek *megistē* 'greatest', superlative of *megas* 'great' (see MEGA-).]

alma mater /álmə maatər, -máytər/, **Alma Mater** *n* the school, college, or university that somebody formerly attended [< Latin, 'bounteous mother', title given by the Romans to several goddesses]

almanac /áwlmə nak, álmə-/ *n* **1** an annual publication that includes a calendar for the year as well as astronomical information and details of anniversaries and events **2** an annually published book of information relating to a particular subject or activity ○ *a sports almanac* [14C. < medieval Latin *almanac(h)*.]

almandine /álməndin, -dīn/ *n* a precious stone that is a form of garnet coloured deep red by iron. Use: gems. [15C. Via French < Latin *alabandina (gemma)* '(gem) of Alabanda' (city in Asia Minor where the gem was originally cut and polished).]

Alma-Tadema /álmə táddimə/, **Sir Lawrence** (1836–1912) Dutch-born British painter

Almaty /al maáti/ former capital of Kazakhstan, in the SE of the country. Population: 1,180,000 (1993).

almighty /awl mīti/ *adj* **1 ALL-POWERFUL** having supreme unquestionable power over everything **2 EXTREME** extreme or excessive of its kind (*informal*) ○ *an almighty quarrel* ■ *adv* **EXTREMELY** to an extreme or excessive degree (*informal*) ○ *almighty proud* [Old English *ælmeahtig* < *æl* 'completely' (see ALL) + *meahtig* (see MIGHTY)] —**almightiness** *n*

Almighty *n* God ○ *pray to the Almighty*

almirah /al mīrə/ *n S Asia* a wardrobe, cabinet, or cupboard

Almodóvar /álmə dṓvər/, **Pedro** (*b.* 1951) Spanish film director

almond /aámənd, aálmənd/ *n* **1 NUT** an edible, oval-shaped, brown-skinned nut that is widely used ground or flaked in cooking **2 SMALL TREE PRODUCING ALMONDS** a tree that bears almonds. Native to: W Asia. *Prunus dulcis.* **3 ALMOND-SHAPED OBJECT** something oval and pointed in shape like an almond ■ *adj* **SHAPED LIKE AN ALMOND** oval and pointed in shape like an almond [14C. Via Old French *alemande, a(l)mande* < Greek *amugdalē*.]

almoner /aámənər/ *n* **1** formerly, somebody attached to a hospital as a social worker for its patients **2** in former times, somebody who distributed alms to the needy, especially on behalf of a church, monastery, or wealthy family [15C. Alteration of obsolete *aumener*, via Old French *aumoner* < ecclesiastical Latin *eleemosynarius* 'connected with alms' < *eleemosyna* (see ALMS).]

almost /áwlmōst, awl mṓst/ *adv* not exactly, not yet, or not in fact, but very close to being or happening as described ○ *I almost wrecked the car.*

alms /aamz/ *npl* in former times, money or other assistance given to people in need as charity [Pre-12C. Via assumed Vulgar Latin *alimosina* < ecclesiastical Latin *eleemosyna* < Greek *eleēmosynē* 'compassionateness' < *eleos* 'compassion, mercy'.]

almshouse /aámz howss/ (*plural* **-houses** /-howziz/) *n* **1** a house built and maintained by private charitable funds and intended as accommodation for a poor family or an old person or couple **2** = **poorhouse**

alnico /álnikō/ (*plural* **-coes**) *n* an alloy of iron, aluminium, and nickel together with one or more of cobalt, copper, and titanium. Use: strong permanent magnets. [Mid-20C. < ALUMINIUM + NICKEL + COBALT.]

Aloe

aloe /állō/ *n* **1** a plant with fleshy toothed leaves. Flowers: red, yellow. Native to: southern Africa. Genus: *Aloe.* **2** = **aloe vera** *n.* **2** [14C. Via Latin < Greek *aloē*, probably of Asian origin.]

aloes /állōz/ *n* (+ *singular verb*) **1** a bitter-tasting aloe leaf extract. Use: laxative. **2 aloes, aloes wood** the fragrant wood of the eaglewood tree from which a resin is obtained. Use: making perfumes

aloe vera /-veérə/ *n* **1** a Mediterranean species of aloe. *Aloe barbadensis.* **2** a soothing, moisturizing extract made from the leaves of the aloe vera plant. Use: drugs, cosmetics. [< modern Latin, 'true aloe']

aloft /ə lóft/ *adv* **1** upwards, high up, or in a higher position **2** in or into the rigging of a sailing ship [13C. < Old Norse *á lopt(i)* 'in the air' < *lopt* 'air, sky' (see LOFT).]

alogical /ay lójjik'l/ *adj* that cannot be dealt with by, or has nothing to do with, logic —**alogically** *adv* —**alogicalness** *n*

aloha /ə lṓ ə, aa lṓ haa/ *interj Hawaii* used as a greeting or farewell [Early 19C. < Hawaiian, 'love, affection'.]

Aloha State *n US* the state of Hawaii (*informal*)

aloin /állō in/ *n* a bitter-tasting aloe derivative. Use: manufacture of laxatives. [Mid-19C. < ALOE + -INE.]

alone /ə lṓn/ CORE MEANING: a grammatical word meaning without any other person or thing nearby ○ (adj) *I like to be alone sometimes.* ○ (adv) *wandering alone in the wilderness*

1 *adv* **WITHOUT HELP FROM OTHERS** without help or support from anybody or anything else ○ *I can't do this job alone.* **2** *adj* **UNIQUE IN SOME RESPECT** describes the only one of a group to do, achieve, or think something ○ *Am I alone in thinking this?* **3** *adj* **DONE WITHOUT OTHERS** carried out by somebody or assigned to somebody without the assistance or company of others **4** *adv, adj* **WITHOUT COMPANY** without any other person or thing nearby or in attendance, for company, or to give assistance ○ *She left with the others but returned alone.* [13C. < *all one* 'completely by yourself'.] —**aloneness** *n*

along /ə lóng/ CORE MEANING: a preposition indicating that something is situated or moves over all or part of the length of something ○ *came racing along the path*

1 *prep* **PARALLEL WITH** following a course or line parallel with or beside ○ *freighters sailing along the coastline* **2** *prep* **SIMILAR TO** in accordance with or similar to **3** *adv* **FORWARDS** forwards, onwards, or in a particular direction ○ *Move along there!* **4** *adv* **WITH** with you, with somebody, or with the rest of the group when going somewhere ○ *I asked if I could come along.* ○ *Next time you come, bring your guitar along.* **5** *adv* **AT OR TO A PLACE** arriving at or coming or going to a particular place ○ *There'll be a bus along in a minute.* [14C. < Old English *andlang* 'against the long' < *lang* 'long'.] ◇ **along with** together with, or as well as

alongshore /ə lóng sháwr/ *adv* near to, beside, or along a shore ○ *The water was too shallow to bring the ship alongshore.* ■ *adj* located on or near a shore or moving along a shore

alongside /ə lóng sīd, ə lóng sīd/ *prep* **alongside, alongside of** close up against, near, or parallel to the side of ○ *pulled the boat alongside the pier* ■ *adv* in or into a position along or by the side of something

Alonso /ə lónzō/, **Alicia** (*b.* 1921) Cuban ballerina, choreographer, and dance teacher

aloof /ə lo͞of/ *adj* **1** uninvolved or unwilling to become involved with other people or events, often out of a sense of lofty superiority to them **2** physically distant or apart from somebody or something [Mid-16C. Probably < *a luff* 'in a windward direction', hence 'away from the shore', after Dutch *te loef*.] —**aloofly** *adv* —**aloofness** *n*

alopecia /állə péeshi ə, -péeshə/ *n* loss or the absence of hair, especially from the human head [14C. Via Latin < Greek *alōpekia* 'baldness, fox mange' < *alōpek-* 'fox'.] —**alopecic** *adj*

alopecia areata /-ari áttə/ *n* a reversible patchy hair loss of the scalp and beard caused by inflammation [< modern Latin, 'alopecia with patches']

aloud /ə lówd/ *adv* **1** using an audible speaking voice ○ *reading aloud* **2** in a loud voice ○ *cried aloud for mercy*

aloxiprin /ə lóksə prīn/ *n* a compound of aluminium hydroxide and aspirin. Use: analgesic. [Blend of AL-IMINIUM + OXY- + ASPIRIN]

alp /alp/ *n* **1** a high mountain. ◊ **Alps 2** a high mountain pasture in Switzerland [15C. Via French *Alpes* 'Alps' < Latin < Greek *Alpeis*.]

ALP *abbr Aus* Australian Labor Party

alpaca /al pákə/ *n* **1** (*plural* **-as** *or* **-a**) **S AMERICAN MAMMAL** a domesticated, long-haired South American mammal of the camel family, related to the llama and similar in appearance. *Lama pacos.* **2 WOOL FROM ALPACA** wool or cloth made from the long shaggy hair of the alpaca **3 GLOSSY CLOTH** a thin glossy cotton, wool, or rayon fabric made to simulate alpaca cloth [Late 18C. Via Spanish < Aymara *alpako* < *pako* 'reddish-brown', from the colour of its hair.]

alpenglow /álpən glō/ *n* a reddish glow on snow-covered mountain peaks at sunset or sunrise, caused by reflected weak sunlight [Late 19C. Partial translation of German *Alpenglühen* 'glowing of the Alps'.]

alpenhorn /álpən hawrn/, **alphorn** /álp-/ *n* a traditional wooden wind instrument with a long tube that rests on the ground and curves up at the end [Late 19C. < German, 'horn of the Alps'.]

alpenstock /álpən stok/ *n* a long staff with an iron spike at one end, formerly used by mountain climbers [Early 19C. < German, 'staff of the Alps'.]

alpestrine /al péstrin/ *adj* describes a plant that grows at high altitudes [Late 19C. < Latin *alpestris* 'alpine' < *Alpes* (see ALP).]

alpha /álfə/, **alfa** *n* **1 1ST LETTER OF GREEK ALPHABET** the first letter of the Greek alphabet **2 CODE WORD FOR LETTER 'A'** the NATO phonetic alphabet code word for the letter 'A', used in international radio communications **3 alpha, Alpha BRIGHTEST STAR** the brightest or main star in a constellation (*followed by Latin genitive*) ○ *Alpha Centauri* **4 HIGHEST MARK** the highest mark in a system that uses Greek letters to grade examinations or pieces of academic work ■ *adj* **1 MOST IMPORTANT** first or most important ○ *the alpha male in a group of chimpanzees* **2 RELATING TO THE NEAREST ATOM** describes the atom nearest to a designated atom or group of atoms in an organic molecule **3 RELATING TO THE MAJOR FORM OF ELEMENT** describes the major form of a chemical element with more than one physical form (**allotrope**) [13C. Via Latin < Greek, related to Hebrew and Phoenician *āleph* (see ALEPH).]

alpha and omega *n* **1** the beginning and end of something **2** the most important aspect of something [< their being the first and last letters of the Greek alphabet]

alphabet /álfə bet/ *n* **1 LETTERS USED TO REPRESENT LANGUAGE** a set of letters, usually listed in a fixed order, used in writing a language and representing its basic speech sounds ○ *the Cyrillic alphabet* **2 SYMBOLS FOR COMMUNICATING** a set of symbols representing units used in communication, especially speech sounds or words ○ *the alphabet in Braille* **3 BASIC PRINCIPLES** the basic principles of something (*formal*) **4** *Malaysia, Singapore* **LETTER OF ALPHABET** a single letter of an alphabet [Early 16C. Via late Latin *alphabetum* < Greek *alphabētos* < Greek *alpha* and *bēta*, the first and second letters of the alphabet.]

alphabetical /álfə béttik'l/, **alphabetic** /álfə béttik/ *adj* **1** ordered like the letters of the alphabet **2** based on, typical of, or relating to an alphabet —**alphabetically** *adv*

alphabetize /álfə bet īz/ (**-izes, -izing, -ized**), **alphabetise** (**-tises, -tising, -tised**) *vt* **1** to arrange words or items in alphabetical order **2** to provide a language with an alphabet —**alphabetization** /álfə bet ī záysh'n/ *n* —**alphabetizer** *n*

alphabet soup *n* **1** soup containing small pieces of pasta formed as letters of the alphabet **2** a confusing mass of letters, especially with unintelligible abbreviations

alpha-blocker *n* a drug that prevents vasoconstriction. Use: treatment of high blood pressure.

Alpha Centauri /álfə sen táwri, -táwrī/ *n* the brightest star in the constellation Centaurus and the nearest bright star to Earth

alpha-chymotrypsin /álfə kīmō trípsin/ *n* a hydrolytic enzyme (**chymotrypsin**), synthesized in the pancreas, that has an unusually reactive serine residue in the active site

alpha decay *n* a radioactive decay process in which an alpha particle is emitted from a nucleus

alpha emission *n* the emission of alpha particles from an atomic nucleus —**alpha emitter** *n*

alpha-foetoprotein *n* **1** a protein in the liver of a human foetus, the presence of which in very high or low quantities in the amniotic fluid may indicate spina bifida or Down's syndrome **2** a blood protein produced in the liver, yolk sac, and gastrointestinal tract of a foetus and used as an indicator of cancer and other diseases in adults

alpha-hydroxy acid *n* an organic acid in which a hydroxyl acid is bonded to a carbon atom. Use: skin care products.

alphanumeric /álfənyoo mérrik/, **alphanumerical** /-mérrik'l/, **alphameric** /álfə mérrik/ *adj* using both letters and numbers ○ *an alphanumeric code* [Mid-20C. Blend of ALPHABET + *numeric*.] —**alphanumerically** *adv*

alpha particle *n* a particle consisting of two neutrons and two protons that is identical to the helium nucleus and is emitted during certain radioactive transformations

alpha ray *n* a stream of alpha particles

alpha-receptor *n* a protein molecule in the cell membrane that specifically binds adrenaline or noradrenaline, triggering a response in the cell

alpha rhythm *n* the pattern of electrical activity in the brain of somebody awake but relaxed or drowsy, registering on an electroencephalograph at a reading between 8 and 13 hertz

alpha source *n* a radioactive atom that emits alpha particles, e.g. polonium

alpha stock *n* any of the 100–200 most profitable securities on the Stock Exchange

ϟ **alpha test** *n* a first test by the manufacturer of new or upgraded software or hardware [< the idea of being first in a series] —**alpha-test** *vt*

alphatocopherol /álfə to kóffə rol/ *n* ♦ **vitamin E**

Alphege /álfij/, **St, Archbishop of Canterbury** (954–1012) English martyr

alphorn *n* MUSIC = **alpenhorn**

alpine /álp īn/ *adj* **1 TYPICAL OF HIGH MOUNTAINS** relating to, typical of, or found in high mountains ○ *an alpine climate* **2 SITUATED OR GROWING ABOVE TREE LINE** describes the zone of vegetation on high mountains between the tree line and snow line and any plant that grows in or originates from that zone **3 USED IN MOUNTAINEERING** used in or involving mountain climbing ■ *n* **MOUNTAIN PLANT** a plant that originates from or can grow in the alpine zone on mountains, above the tree line [15C. < Latin *alpinus* < *Alpes* (see ALP).]

Alpine *adj* **1** relating to the Alps and those who live in them **2 Alpine, alpine** describes competitive skiing on steep downhill courses, especially downhill and slalom events

alpine-style *adj* describes a type of mountaineering in which the climbers carry all the necessary equipment with them on a single ascent to a mountain summit —**alpine-style** *adv*

alpinist /álpinist/ *n* a mountain climber, especially one who climbs in the Alps or mountains of similar height [Late 19C. < French *alpiniste* < Latin *alpinus* (see ALPINE).] —**alpinism** *n*

Alport's syndrome /ál pawrts-/, **Alport syndrome** *n* a genetic disease characterized by kidney disease and hearing and sight loss

alprostadil /al próstə dil/ *n* a vasodilator drug. Use: impotence, prevention of coagulation, treatment of neonates.

Alps /alps/ mountain range in S Europe, stretching from SE France to Austria. Highest peak: Mont Blanc 4,807 m/15,771 ft.

al-Quds /al ko͝odz/ *n* the Islamic name for Jerusalem, the third most important of the sacred sites of Islam

already /awl réddi, áwl redi/ CORE MEANING: an adverb indicating that something has happened before now, happened in the past before a particular time, or will have happened by or before a particular time in the future ○ *I already know what you're going to say.* ○ *She had already left when I arrived.*

adv **1** by or at an earlier time than expected ○ *Have you finished already?* **2** *US* used after a command, exclamation, or other statement to give it emphasis or express exasperation (*informal*) ○ *Enough already!* [14C. < *all ready* 'completely ready'.]

USAGE already or **all ready**? These words do not mean the same thing, and so they are not interchangeable. ***Already***, an adverb, means 'by or at an earlier time than expected', as in *Have they already* [not *all ready*] *left?* ***All ready*** means 'all or totally prepared', as in *Is everything all ready* [not *already*] *for tomorrow?*

alright /awl rít, áwl rīt/ *adv* ⚠ in a generally good, satisfactory, or pleasing way (*informal*) ■ *adj* generally good, satisfactory, or pleasant (*informal*)

USAGE See ***all right***.

ALS *abbr* amyotrophic lateral sclerosis

Alsace /al sáss/ region in E France. Capital: Strasbourg. Population: 1,642,000 (1990). Area: 8,280 sq. km/3,197 sq. mi.

Alsace-Lorraine /-lə ráyn/ area of France on the German border, now divided into two administrative regions, Alsace and Lorraine

Alsatian /al sáysh'n/ *n* **1 LARGE DOG** a large powerful dog belonging to a short-haired breed with erect ears, a face rather like a wolf's, and a brown and black coat. US term **German shepherd 2 SOMEBODY FROM ALSACE** somebody who comes from Alsace ■ *adj* **FROM ALSACE** relating to Alsace, or its people, language, or culture [Late 19C. < medieval Latin *Alsatia* 'Alsace'.]

alsike clover /ál sīk-, álsik-/ *n* a perennial clover widely grown for forage. Flowers: white or pink. Native to: Europe. *Trifolium hybridum.* [Mid-19C. After *Alsike*, town in Sweden.]

also /áwlsō/ *adv* **1 IN ADDITION** used to indicate that something is true or is the case in addition ○ *got his picture in the paper and also won a prize* **2 LIKEWISE OR SIMILARLY** like or in the same way as somebody or something else ○ *Her niece was also called Jean.* ○ *When they withdraw their forces, we shall also withdraw ours.* **3 MOREOVER** and in addition to that (*modifies a whole sentence or clause*) ○ *Also, you must complete the task in one hour.* [Old English *ealswā, allswā* (see ALL, SO)]

Alsop /áwlsəp, ólsəp/, **Joseph, Jr** (1910–89) US journalist

also-ran *n* **1 LOSING RUNNER** a horse or other entrant in a race that does not finish in any of the winning places **2 LOSING COMPETITOR** a losing entrant in any contest **3 SOMEBODY UNIMPORTANT** somebody of little or no consequence or significance [Because newspaper racing results formerly listed horses that finished fourth or lower under the heading 'Also Ran']

alstroemeria /álstrə méeri ə/ (*plural* **-as** *or* **-a**) *n* a tuberous plant of the amaryllis family. Flowers: long-lasting, variously coloured. Native to: South America. Genus: *Alstroemeria.* [Late 18C. < modern Latin, after Klas von *Alstroemer* (1736–96), Swedish naturalist.]

alt *abbr* **1** alteration **2** alternate **3** altitude **4** alto

Alt *abbr* Alt key

alt- *prefix* = **alto-** (*before vowels*)

Alta *abbr* Alberta

Altaic /al táy ik/ *n* a family of languages that consists of Turkic, Mongolic, and Tungusic, sometimes considered as part of the Ural-Altaic family [Mid-19C. After the ALTAI MOUNTAINS.] —**Altaic** *adj*

Altai Mountains /al tī-/ mountain range in central Asia, on the Kazakhstan-Mongolia border. Highest peak: Mount Belukha 4,620 m/m/15,157 ft.

altar /áwltər/ *n* **1** a raised structure, typically a flat-topped rock or a table of wood or stone, or raised area where religious ceremonies are performed **2** the table or other raised structure in a Christian church on which the bread and wine of Communion are prepared [Pre-12C.

< Latin *altare* < *altaria* 'burnt offerings', probably < *adolere* 'burn up'.] ◇ **lead somebody to the altar** to marry somebody (*dated informal*)

SPELLCHECK Do not confuse ***altar*** with ***alter***, which has a similar sound. Beware: your spellchecker will not catch this error.

altarpiece /áwltər peess/ *n* a work of art, usually a painting, placed above and behind an altar

altazimuth /al tázzimәth/ *n* **1** an instrument, incorporating a telescope that can move vertically and horizontally, used to measure the altitude and azimuth of a celestial body **2** an instrument similar to a theodolite used in surveying to measure horizontal and vertical angles [Mid-19C. Blend of ALTITUDE + AZIMUTH.]

alteplase /áltə playz, -playss/ *n* a tissue plasminogen activator produced by recombinant DNA technology. Use: treatment of heart failure.

alter /áwltər/ *v* **1** *vti* **CHANGE** to make changes to something or somebody, or be changed or become different ○ *We'll have to alter our plans.* **2** *vt* **ADJUST GARMENT FOR BETTER FIT** to make adjustments to a piece of clothing so that it fits better ○ *The trousers are fine, but the jacket will have to be altered.* **3** *vt US, Aus* **CASTRATE** to castrate or spay an animal (*informal*) [14C. Via French < late Latin *alterare* < Latin *alter* 'other'.] —**alterability** /áwltərə bíllәti/ *n* —**alterable** *adj*

SPELLCHECK See ***altar***.

SYNONYMS See ***change***.

alteration /àwltə ráysh'n/ *n* **1 CHANGE** a change, modification, or adjustment made to something **2 DIFFERENCE** a difference in something resulting from change ○ *I don't see any alteration in the patient's condition.* **3 PROCESS OF CHANGING** the process of changing something or of being changed ○ *undergoing alteration*

altercation /àwltər káysh'n/ *n* a heated argument, quarrel, or confrontation [14C. Via Old French < Latin *altercation-* < *altercari* 'to dispute' < *alter* 'other'.] —**altercate** /áwltər kayt/ *vi*

alter ego /áwltər éegō/ (*plural* **alter egos**) *n* **1** a second side to an individual's personality, different from the one that most people know **2** a very close and trusted friend [< Latin, 'other self']

alternant /awl túrnənt/ *adj* alternating (*formal*)

alternate *vi* /áwltər nayt/ (**-nates, -nating, -nated**) **1 FOLLOW IN INTERCHANGING PATTERN** to follow each other and take each other's place in a regular pattern of events ○ *as night alternates with day* **2 FLUCTUATE** to shift back and forth, especially regularly or constantly, between one state and another ○ *Her mood alternates between elation and despair.* **3 BE AN UNDERSTUDY** to act as an understudy for another performer ■ *adj* /awl túrnət/ **1 ARRANGED IN ALTERNATING PATTERN** arranged or happening in a regular pattern in which the one thing alternates with the other ○ *alternate spells of sun and showers* **2 EVERY OTHER** every other or second of a series ○ *They babysit for each other on alternate weekends.* **3** *US* = **alternative** *adj.* 1 **4 NOT ALIGNED** describes flowers, buds, or leaves that are arranged singly and at different levels on either side of the stem of a plant, as opposed to being in pairs or groups ■ *n* /awl túrnət/ *US* **SOMEBODY WHO FILLS IN** somebody who substitutes for somebody else [Early 16C. < Latin *alternat-*, past participle of *alternare* 'do things one after another' < *alternus* 'one after another' < *alter* 'other'.] —**alternateness** /awl túrnətnəss/ *n*

USAGE alternate or **alternative**?: The adjective ***alternate*** is often used, especially in US English, instead of ***alternative*** to mean 'different from or able to serve as a substitute', as in *The band decided to go with the song's alternate title.* However ***alternate*** has a quite distinct meaning, namely 'every other', as in *We meet on alternate Sundays* (=every other Sunday).

alternate angle *n* one of a pair of angles on opposite sides and at opposite ends of a line that cuts two other lines

alternately /awl túrnətli/ *adv* **1** by following one immediately after the other in a regular repeated pattern or sequence **2** = **alternatively**

alternating current *n* an electric current that regularly reverses direction

alternation /àwltər náysh'n/ *n* **1** a process of change in which one thing follows, or is made to follow, another in a regular repeated pattern **2** a proposition of the form 'p or q', that is, either sentence 'p' is true or sentence 'q' is true

alternation of generations *n* the existence in the life cycle of an organism of two or more alternating forms or reproductive modes, e.g. sexual and asexual cycles

alternative /awl túrnətiv/ *n* **1 OTHER POSSIBILITY** something different from, and able to serve as a substitute for, something else ○ *You could take the bus as an alternative to driving.* **2 POSSIBILITY OF CHOOSING** the possibility of choosing between two different things or courses of action ○ *We gave you the alternative; you decided to stay.* **3 OPTION** either one of two, or one of several, things or courses of action to choose between ○ *I can't decide which of the two alternatives is worse.* ■ *adj* **1 SERVING AS A BACKUP** different and serving, or able to serve, as a substitute for something else ○ *There are alternative courses we can take.* US term **alternate** *adj.* 3 **2 MUTUALLY EXCLUSIVE** of which only one can be true, or only one can be used or chosen, or take place at any one time ○ *There are two alternative theories as to why this phenomenon occurs.* **3 UNCONVENTIONALLY NONTRADITIONAL** outside the establishment or mainstream, and often presented as being less institutionalized or conventional, or more natural or economical with resources ○ *alternative methods of painting* **4** LOGIC = **disjunctive** *adj.* 3

USAGE See ***alternate***.

USAGE alternative = two or more? Some people maintain that the noun sense of ***alternative***, 'either of two or more options', cannot in fact apply to more than two choices. However this distinction is largely dying out.

alternative comedy *n* any form of comedy characterized by subject matter and a style of presentation deliberately made different from mainstream comedy —**alternative comedian** *n*

alternative curriculum *n* in England and Wales, any available course of study that is not included in the National Curriculum

alternative energy *n* any form of energy obtained from the sun, wind, waves, or other natural renewable source, in contrast to energy generated from fossil fuels

alternatively /awl túrnətivli/ *adv* or instead of that ○ *Alternatively, you could drive there.*

alternative medicine *n* the treatment of illness using remedies not considered part of mainstream medicine, e.g. homoeopathy or naturopathy

alternative vote *n* a system of voting in which electors vote for several candidates in order of preference, their votes being transferred to the second choice if the first choice fails to receive a majority

alternator /áwltər naytər/ *n* a device that generates alternating current

altho /awl thṓ/ *conj US* although (*informal*)

althorn /ált hawrn/ *n* an alto brass wind instrument of either the saxhorn or the flügelhorn family, used mainly in brass or military bands [Mid-19C. < German, < *Alt* 'alto' + *Horn* 'horn'.]

although /awl thṓ/ *conj* granting or in spite of the fact that ○ *Although the children were sleepy, they kept watching the movie.* [14C. < ALL in the sense 'even' + THOUGH.]

USAGE although or **though**? In many uses ***although*** and ***though*** are interchangeable, but ***though*** is a generally more versatile word, capable of occupying different positions in a sentence and having more grammatical flexibility. It is the only choice in the phrases *as though* and *even though*, and in the following types of use: *I don't like them, though. It is true, though, that they have been kind to us. The chair, though damaged, could still be used. We enjoyed the day out, cold though it was.*

USAGE although or **however**? Do not use the conjunction ***although*** as a substitute for the adverb ***however***. ***However*** is used to add contrasting and surprising information, and, unlike ***although***, is followed by a comma. Compare *We were from different backgrounds. However, we got along really well* and *We got along very well, although we were from different backgrounds.*

alti- *prefix* = **alto-**

altimeter /al tímmitər, álti meetər/ *n* an instrument that shows height above sea level, especially one mounted in an aircraft and incorporating an aneroid barometer that senses differences in pressure caused by changes in altitude —**altimetric** /àlti méttrik/ *adj* —**altimetry** /al tímmətri/ *n*

altiplano /àlti plaánō/ (*plural* **-nos**) *n* a high plateau, especially in Mexico or the Andes of South America [Early 20C. < American Spanish, 'high plain'.]

Altiplano /àlti plaá nō/ region of the Andes Mountains from SW Bolivia to S Peru. Height: about 3,650 m/12,000 ft.

altitude /álti tyood/ *n* **1 HEIGHT ABOVE SEA LEVEL** the height of something above a particular specified level, especially above sea level or the Earth's surface **2 HIGH PLACE** a place or region situated high above sea level (*often plural*) **3 DISTANCE** in a geometrical figure, the perpendicular distance from the vertex to the base **4 ANGLE CELESTIAL BODY IS ABOVE HORIZON** the angle of a celestial body above an observer's horizon, measured from the horizon along the circle passing through the object and the point above the observer **5 HIGH RANK OR POSITION** a high rank or high position in a society or group [14C. < Latin *altitudo* < *altus* 'high'.] —**altitudinal** /àlti tyóodin'l/ *adj*

altitude sickness *n* a condition caused by low levels of oxygen in the air at high altitudes, resulting in nausea and breathlessness

ϟ**Alt key** /áwlt-/ *n* a computer key that is pressed together with another key to change its function

Altman /áwltmən/, **Robert** (*b.* 1925) US film director and screenwriter

alto /áltō/ (*plural* **-tos**) *n* **1** = **contralto** *n.* 1 **2 HIGHEST MAN'S VOICE** the highest singing voice for a man, achieved by using falsetto **3 ALTO SINGER** a singer with an alto or contralto voice **4 INSTRUMENT BETWEEN SOPRANO AND TENOR** in a family of instruments, the instrument whose size and pitch fall between the soprano and tenor instruments [Late 16C. Via Italian, 'high' < Latin *altus*.]

alto-, alti-, alt- *prefix* high, altitude ○ *altocumulus, altimeter* [< Latin *altus* 'high, deep' < Indo-European, 'grow']

alto clef *n* the C clef indicating that middle C is on the third line of the stave

altocumulus /àltō kyóomyooləss/ (*plural* **-li** /-lī/) *n* white or grey patchy cloud with a rounded outline

altogether /àwltə géthər, -geth-/ *adv* **1 WITH EVERYTHING INCLUDED** when everything is included or taken into account ○ *Altogether, your bill comes to £75.99.* **2 TOTALLY** entirely or utterly ○ *I'm not altogether satisfied.* **3 ON THE WHOLE** considered as a whole ○ *Altogether, it's been a highly successful day.* [12C. < ALL 'the whole group' + TOGETHER.] ◇ **in the altogether** naked (*informal*)

USAGE altogether or **all together**? These words mean different things. ***Altogether*** means 'with everything included', 'totally', or 'on the whole' and is an adverb. ***All together*** means 'everyone together', 'all at the same place or time', and functions as an adjectival phrase. Usually the word *all* can be removed without affecting the grammar or the sense: *They arrived (all) together at nine. The plates are (all) together on a separate shelf.*

altoist /áltō ist/ *n* a musician who plays an alto saxophone

alto-relievo /àltō ri léevō/ (*plural* **alto-relievos**), **alto-rilievo** /-rillee áy vō/ (*plural* **alto-rilievos**) *n* SCULPTURE = **high relief** [Mid-17C. < Italian *alto-rilievo* 'high relief'.]

altostratus /àltō straátəss, -stráytəss/ (*plural* **-ti** /-stráy tī/) *n* greyish cloud in thin sheets or layers of uniform appearance, through which the Sun can be seen

altricial /al trísh'l/ *adj* describes birds or mammals that are helpless when young and dependent on their parents for food ■ *n* a bird or mammal that produces young that are unable to move or feed themselves without help [Late 19C. < modern Latin *Altrices* (former division of birds), plural of Latin *altrix* 'female nourisher' < *alere* 'nourish'.]

alt rock /áwlt-/ *n* rock music played by lesser known performers and considered as alternative to the music promoted by large record companies [< shortening of ALTERNATIVE]

altruism /áltroo izəm/ *n* **1** an attitude or way of behaving marked by unselfish concern for the welfare of others **2** the belief that acting for the benefit of others is right and good [Mid-19C. < French *altruisme* < Italian *altrui* 'that which belongs to other people' < Latin *alter* 'other'.] —**altruist** /áltroo ist/ *n* —**altruistic** /àltroo ístik/ *adj* —**altruistically** *adv*

⚡**ALU** *abbr* arithmetic logic unit

alula /ályoŏlə/ (*plural* **-lae** /-lee/) *n* a bastard wing (*technical*) [Late 18C. < modern Latin, 'little wing' < Latin *ala* 'wing'.] —**alular** *adj*

alum /álləm/ *n* **1** $KAl(SO_4)_2.12H_2O$ a colourless crystalline solid that turns white in air. Use: astringents, pigments, dyes, water purification, leather dressing. **2** an inorganic chemical having a structure like alum [14C. Via Old French < Latin *alumen* (see ALUMINIUM).]

alumina /ə lóomìnə/ *n* Al_2O_3 white or colourless aluminium oxide. Source: corundum, bauxite. Use: catalysts, abrasives, manufacture of artificial rubies and sapphires. [Late 18C. < Latin *alumin-* (see ALUMINIUM), after words such as SODA and MAGNESIA.]

aluminate /ə lóomi nayt/ *n* any salt of aluminium and a metallic oxide

aluminiferous /ə lóomi nífərəss/ *adj* that contains or is a source of alumina or aluminium

aluminise *vt* = **aluminize**

aluminium /állə mínni əm/ *n* (*symbol* **Al**) a silvery-white, light metallic element that is ductile, malleable, and resistant to corrosion. Source: bauxite. Use: lightweight construction, corrosion-resistant materials. [Early 19C. < Latin *alumin-*, stem of *alumen* 'alum'.]

aluminium chloride *n* $AlCl_3$ **or** Al_2Cl_6 a white or yellowish crystalline powder. Use: in medicines, cosmetics, pigments, and antiperspirants.

aluminium hydroxide *n* $Al(OH)_3$ **or** $Al_2O_3.3H_2O$ a white solid. Use: antacid, catalyst, drying agent, glass and ceramics manufacturing.

aluminium oxide *n* CHEM = **alumina**

aluminium sulphate *n* $Al_2(SO_4)_3$ a white crystalline solid. Use: paper, textiles, water purification.

aluminize /ə lóomi nīz/ (**-nizes, -nizing, -nized**), **aluminise** (**-minises, -minising, -minised**) *vt* to treat or coat something with aluminium

aluminosilicate /ə lóominō sílli kayt/ *n* an inorganic compound whose negatively charged ion (**anion**) consists of aluminium, silicon, and oxygen

aluminothermy /ə lóominō thúrmi/ *n* a process for extracting a metal from its oxide that involves burning the oxide together with aluminium powder

aluminous /ə lóominəss/ *adj* **1** resembling aluminium or alum **2** CHEM = **aluminiferous** [15C. < Latin *aluminosus* < *alumin-* (see ALUMINIUM).]

aluminum /ə lóominəm/ *n* US = **aluminium**

alumna /ə lúmnə/ (*plural* **-nae** /-nī, -nee/) *n* a female graduate or former student of a school, college, or university [Late 19C. < Latin, feminine form of ALUMNUS.]

alumnus /ə lúmnəss/ (*plural* **-ni** /-nī, -nee/) *n* a male graduate or former student of a school, college, or university [Mid-17C. < Latin, 'pupil, foster child' < *alere* 'nourish'.]

alunite /állyoŏ nīt/ *n* a white, grey, or reddish mineral composed of hydrated potassium aluminium sulphate. Source: altered volcanic rocks. Use: fertilizers. [Mid-19C. < French, < *alun* 'alum' < Latin *alumen* (see ALUMINIUM).]

Alvarez /álvərrez/, **Luis W.** (1911–88) US physicist. Full name **Luis Walter Alvarez**

alveolar /álvi ólər, al vée ələr/ *adj* **1 RELATING TO AIR SAC IN LUNG** relating to the air sacs in the lungs (**alveoli**) **2 RELATING TO THE JAWBONE** relating to the part of the upper or lower jaw that contains the roots of the teeth **3 WITH TONGUE NEAR UPPER TEETH RIDGE** describes a consonant that is sounded with the tongue touching or close to the ridge behind the teeth of the upper jaw ■ *n* **ALVEOLAR CONSONANT** an alveolar consonant, e.g. 't', 'd', or 's' in English —**alveolarly** *adv*

alveolar ridge *n* a hard ridge in the mouth immediately behind the roots of the teeth

alveolectomy /álvi ə léktəmi/ *n* surgical excision of a portion of the tooth socket or ridge

alveolitis /álvi ə lítiss/ *n* inflammation of the air sacs of the lungs

alveolus /álvi óləss, al vée ələss/ (*plural* **-li** /-lee, -lī/) *n* **1** a tiny thin-walled air sac found in large numbers in each lung, through which oxygen enters and carbon dioxide leaves the blood **2** a socket in the jaw bone in which a tooth is rooted [Late 17C. < Latin, 'little cavity' < *alveus* 'cavity' < *alvus* 'belly'.]

always /áwl wayz, -wiz/ *adv* **1 EVERY TIME OR CONTINUOUSLY** used to indicate that something happens or is done at all times, either continuously, repetitively, or on every occasion ○ *She's always very polite.* **2 THROUGH ALL PAST OR FUTURE TIME** throughout all past time or all future time ○ *I will always love you.* **3 IF NECESSARY** if necessary ○ *I could always stay an extra day if you need help.* [14C. < Old English *ealne weg* 'all the way'.] ◇ **for always** for all time

⚡**always-on** *adj* **1** describes a home or business with several computers and mobile phones, in which Internet access is not restricted to particular times **2** describes a modem that is continuously switched on

Alwyn /áwlwin/, **William** (1905–85) British composer

alyssum /állissəm/ *n* **1** = **sweet alyssum 2** a perennial plant with oval, hairy, grey-green leaves. Flowers: bright yellow. Native to: Europe. *Aurinia saxatilis.* US term **basket-of-gold** [Mid-16C. Via modern Latin < Greek *alysson* 'madwort' (believed to cure rabies) < A-[2] 'without' + *lyssa* 'rabies'.]

Alzheimer's disease /álts hīmərz-/, **Alzheimer's** *n* a degenerative disorder that affects the brain and causes dementia, especially late in life [Early 20C. After Alois *Alzheimer* (1864–1915), German neurologist.]

am[1], **AM** *abbr* amplitude modulation

am[2] (*stressed*) /am/; (*unstressed*) /əm/ 1st person present singular of **be** [Old English *eom* < Indo-European]

⚡**am**[3] *abbr* Armenia (*in Internet addresses*)

Am *abbr* **1** Amos **2** americium

AM *abbr* **1** anno mundi **2** ante meridiem **3** Artium Magister **4** associate member **5** Albert Medal

Am. *abbr* American

a.m., A.M. *adj, adv* in the period between midnight and noon. Full form **ante meridiem**

AMA *abbr* American Medical Association

Amadeus, Lake /ə maádi əss/ large salt lake in S Northern Territory, Australia. Area: 2,400 sq. km/927 sq. mi.

Amado /ə maádō, ə maá doo/, **Jorge** (*b.* 1912) Brazilian novelist and Communist politician

amah /aámə/ *n* in East and South Asia, a woman employed as a children's nurse, domestic servant, office cleaner, or attendant [Mid-19C. Via Portuguese *ama* 'nurse' < medieval Latin *amma* 'mother'.]

amalgam /ə málgəm/ *n* **1 MIXTURE** a blend of two or more elements or characteristics **2 FILLING MATERIAL FOR TEETH** a substance used as filling for tooth cavities, consisting of a paste of powdered mercury, silver, and tin that quickly hardens. ◊ **cement** *n.* 5 **3 MERCURY ALLOY** an alloy of mercury and another metal [15C. Directly or via French < medieval Latin *amalgama*.]

SYNONYMS See ***mixture***.

amalgamate /ə málgə mayt/ (**-mates, -mating, -mated**) *vti* **1** to combine two or more organizations or things into one unified whole, or take the form of one unified whole **2** to alloy a metal with mercury, or be alloyed with mercury —**amalgamative** /ə málgəmətiv/ *adj* —**amalgamator** *n*

amalgamation /ə málgə máysh'n/ *n* **1 COMBINING THINGS** the process of amalgamating things into a unified whole **2 RESULT OF COMBINING THINGS** something that is a combination of different things or results from their amalgamation **3 BUSINESS MERGER** a combination of two or more business concerns so as to form one **4 METAL EXTRACTION FROM ORE** a method of extracting a precious metal from an ore by using mercury to form an amalgam with the metal

Amalthea /ámmal thée ə/ *n* a natural satellite of Jupiter, discovered in 1892

amantadine /ə mántə deen/ *n* an anti-viral drug that also treats Parkinson's disease. Use: influenza treatment. [Mid-20C. Blend of AMINE + ADAMANTANE.]

amanuensis /ə mánnyoo énssiss/ (*plural* **-ses** /-seez/) *n* **1** somebody employed by an individual to write from his or her dictation or to copy manuscripts **2** a writer's assistant with research and secretarial duties [Early 17C. < Latin < *a manu*, 'by hand' (in *servus a manu* 'enslaved servant with secretarial duties').]

amaranth /ámmə ranth/ (*plural* **-ranths** *or* **-ranth**) *n* **1 FLOWERING PLANT WITH DROOPING FLOWER HEADS** a plant sometimes grown as a grain crop or as a leafy vegetable. Flowers: long drooping heads of green, red, or purple. Genus: *Amaranthus.* **2 LEGENDARY FLOWER** a flower that, according to legend, never fades **3 FOOD DYE** a synthetic red food dye [Mid-16C. Via either French *amarante* or modern Latin *amaranthus* < Latin *amarantus* < Greek *amarantos* 'not corruptible, not fading'.]

amaranthine /ámmə rán thīn, -thin/ *adj* **1** undying or unfading, like the legendary amaranth (*literary*) **2** of a dark reddish-purple colour

amaretti /ámmə rétti/ *npl* small crisp Italian biscuits flavoured with almonds [See AMARETTO]

amaretto /ámmə réttō/ (*plural* **-tos**) *n* an Italian almond-flavoured liqueur [Mid-20C. < Italian, 'little bitter (one)' < *amaro* 'bitter' < Latin *amarus*.]

Amarillo /ámmə ríllō/ city in NW Texas. Population: 171,207 (1998 estimate).

amaryllis /ámmə rílliss/ (*plural* **-lises** *or* **-lis**) *n* **1** a plant grown from a bulb. Flowers: large, red, pink, or white, trumpet-shaped, facing in opposite directions at the head of a single stalk. Native to: southern Africa. *Amaryllis belladonna.* **2** a tropical American plant related to the southern African amaryllis. Genus: *Hippeastrum.* [Late 18C. Via modern Latin < Greek *Amarullis*, shepherdess in pastorals.]

amass /ə máss/ *vti* to gather a large quantity of things together over time, or accumulate in this way ○ *amassed a fortune in the 1950s* [15C. < French *amasser* < *masser* 'gather into a mass' < Latin *massa* (see MASS).] —**amassable** *adj* —**amasser** *n* —**amassment** *n*

SYNONYMS See ***collect***.

amateur /ámmətər, -choor/ *n* **1 SOMEBODY DOING SOMETHING FOR PLEASURE** somebody who does something for pleasure rather than payment ○ *a talented amateur golfer* **2 UNSKILLED PERSON** somebody with limited skill in, or knowledge of, an activity ○ *Whoever handled your rewiring must have been an amateur.* **3 ENJOYER** somebody who loves or is greatly interested in something (*literary*) ○ *She is an amateur of classical sculpture.* ■ *adj* **1 BY AMATEURS** for, by, or consisting of amateurs **2 NOT DONE WITH SKILL** unskilful or unprofessional [Late 18C. Via French < Latin *amator* 'lover' < *amare* 'to love'.]

amateurish /ámmətərish, -choor-/ *adj* lacking the skill of a professional —**amateurishly** *adv* —**amateurishness** *n*

amateurism /ámmətərizəm, -choor-/ *n* amateur status, participation by amateurs, or the principle that something should be reserved for amateurs ○ *one of the last bastions of true amateurism in sport*

amatol /ámmə tol/ *n* an explosive made from ammonium nitrate and TNT and used in bombs [Early 20C. < AMMONIUM + TOLUENE.]

amatory /ámmətəri/, **amatorial** /ámmə táwri əl/ *adj* relating to, involving, expressing, or typical of physical love ○ *amatory adventures* [Late 16C. < Latin *amatorius* < *amator* (see AMATEUR).]

~~**amatuer**~~ incorrect spelling of **amateur**

amaurosis /ámmaw rṓssiss/ *n* partial or complete vision impairment, especially when there is no obvious damage to the eye [Mid-17C. < Greek *amaurōsis* < *amauroun* 'darken' < *amauros* 'dark'.] —**amaurotic** /ámmaw róttik/ *adj*

amaurosis fugax /-fyóo gaks/ *n* a brief episode of partial blindness occurring when there is no obvious damage to the eye [*Fugax* < Latin < *fugere* 'flee']

amaze /ə máyz/ (**amazes, amazing, amazed**) *vt* to fill somebody with wonder, astonishment, or extreme surprise ○ *We were amazed at the news.* [Old English *āmasian* 'stupefy, stun' < ?] —**amazed** *adj* —**amazedly** /ə máyzidli/ *adv* —**amazedness** *n*

amazement /ə máyzmənt/ *n* a strong feeling of wonder or surprise at the extraordinariness of something

amazing /ə máyzing/ *adj* **1** so extraordinary or wonderful as to be barely believable or to cause extreme surprise ○ *an amazing escape* **2** outstandingly good, skilful, or admirable (*informal*) ○ *an amazing concert* —**amazingly** *adv* —**amazingness** *n*

amazon /ámməz'n/ *n* a parrot that typically has green plumage. Native to: tropical America. Genus: *Amazona.* [Late 19C. After the AMAZON[2].]

Amazon[1] /ámməz'n/ *n* **1** in Greek mythology, a member of a group of women warriors who lived in Scythia, an area of present-day Ukraine, or elsewhere at the northern limits of the world **2 Amazon, amazon** a notably tall, physically strong, or strong-willed woman —**Amazonian** /ámmə zṓni ən/ *adj*

Amazon

Amazon^2 /ámməz'n/ world's second longest river. It flows east from N Peru, through N South America and into the Atlantic Ocean in Brazil. Length: about 6,400 km/4,000 mi. —**Amazonian** *adj*

Amazonas /ámmə zṓnəss/ state in NW Brazil. Capital: Manaus. Population: 2,390,102 (1996). Area: 1,577,820 sq. km/609,039 sq. mi.

amazonite /ámməzə nīt/ *n* a precious stone that is a green or bluish-green form of microcline. Use: gems. [After the AMAZON^2, where similar green stones were formerly found]

ambassador /am bássədər/ *n* **1 DIPLOMATIC REPRESENTATIVE** a diplomatic official of the highest rank sent by one country as its long-term representative to another **2 OFFICIAL REPRESENTATIVE** an official representative of something, e.g. a movement ○ *visiting this country as an ambassador for an organization dedicated to saving endangered species* **3 UNOFFICIAL REPRESENTATIVE** somebody or something regarded as an unofficial representative or a symbol of something ○ *The swallow is an ambassador of spring.* [14C. Via French *ambassadeur* < Italian *ambasciator* < Latin *ambactus* 'vassal' < Gaulish, 'servant'.] —**ambassadorial** /am bássə dáwri əl/ *adj* —**ambassadorship** *n*

LITERARY LINK ***The Ambassadors***, a novel (1903) by US writer Henry James. It tells the story of Lambert Strether, a middle-aged editor sent by his wealthy New England patron and fiancée to Paris to persuade her expatriate son Chad to return home.

ambassador at large (*plural* **ambassadors at large**) *n US* an ambassador not assigned to one particular country

amber /ámbər/ *n* **1 YELLOW FOSSIL RESIN** a hard translucent fossil resin varying in colour from yellow to light brown. Use: jewellery, ornaments. **2 BROWNISH-YELLOW COLOUR** a yellow to brown colour **3 SIGNAL FOR CAUTION** in a system of traffic signals, the yellow-coloured light that advises caution [14C. Via French *ambre* < Arabic *anbar* 'ambergris', from a perceived similarity between the two.] —**amber** *adj*

amber fluid, amber nectar *n Aus* beer (*informal*)

amber gambler *n* a driver who takes risks by not stopping at traffic lights when they are at amber (*informal*)

ambergris /ámbər greess, -griss/ *n* a grey waxy substance, consisting mainly of cholesterol, secreted from the intestines of the sperm whale [15C. < French *ambre gris* 'grey amber'.]

amberjack /ámbər jak/ (*plural* **-jacks** *or* **-jack**) *n* **1** a large sea fish that has golden markings. Native to: warm Atlantic waters. Genus: *Seriola.* **2** a fish found in waters off the east and west coasts of Australia with a black-blue, yellow-banded body and a mouth that is a brilliant orange colour inside. *Seriola purpurascens.*

amber nectar *n Aus* = **amber fluid** (*informal*)

amberoid /ámbə royd/ *n* a synthetic form of amber made by heating and compressing valueless small pieces of amber with other resins

ambi- *prefix* both ○ *ambiversion* [< Latin *ambi* 'around, on both sides' < Indo-European]

ambiance *n* = **ambience**

ambidextrous /ámbi dékstrəss/ *adj* **1** able to use either the right or the left hand with equal skill **2** very skilful and versatile [Mid-17C. < late Latin *ambidexter* 'right-handed on both sides' < Latin *dexter* 'right-handed' (see DEXTEROUS).] —**ambidexterity** /ámbi dek stérrəti/ *n* —**ambidextrously** *adv*

ambience /ámbi ənss, ámbi onss/, **ambiance** *n* the typical atmosphere or mood of a place ○ *a restaurant with a welcoming ambience* [Mid-20C. < French *ambiance* < *ambiant* < Latin *ambient-* (see AMBIENT).]

ambient /ámbi ənt/ *adj* in the immediately surrounding area ○ *ambient temperature* ■ *n* **ambient, ambient music** music that is usually instrumental and repetitive and often contains soothing electronic sounds, used to create an atmosphere of calm or relaxation [Late 16C. Directly or via French < Latin *ambient-*, present participle of *ambire* 'go round' (see AMBITION).]

ambiguity /ámbi gyoó əti/ (*plural* **-ties**) *n* **1** a situation in which something can be understood in more than one way and it is not clear which meaning is intended **2** an expression or statement that has more than one meaning

ambiguous /am bíggyoo əss/ *adj* **1** having more than one possible meaning or interpretation ○ *an ambiguous response* **2** causing uncertainty or confusion ○ *an ambiguous result* [Early 16C. < Latin *ambiguus* 'undecided' < *ambigere* 'wander about' < *agere* 'lead'.] —**ambiguously** *adv* —**ambiguousness** *n*

USAGE ambiguous or **ambivalent**? Both words describe uncertainty in understanding what is meant. The principal difference is that ***ambivalent*** is used of people and their attitudes, whereas ***ambiguous*** refers to information or context. If people are ***ambivalent*** about disarmament, they are unsure about the advantages and disadvantages and cannot easily decide between the various arguments, whereas if a political leader makes an ***ambiguous*** statement about disarmament, then the statement has more than one possible interpretation.

ambiguous genitalia *n* a congenital condition in which the outer genitals do not have the typical appearance of either sex

ambisexual /ámbi sékshoo əl/ *adj* **1** describes secondary sexual characteristics that are common to both sexes **2** sexually responsive or attracted to both sexes —**ambisexuality** /ámbi sékshoo állәti/ *n*

ambisonics /ámbi sónniks/ *n* a recording and reproduction system that uses separate channels and speakers to create the effect of being surrounded by sound (+ *singular verb*) —**ambisonic** *adj*

ambit /ámbit/ *n* the scope, extent, or limits of something ○ *within the ambit of the court's jurisdiction* [Late 16C. < Latin *ambitus* 'circuit' < *ambire* (see AMBITION).]

ambit claim *n Aus* a claim made to an arbitration authority by workers who expect to negotiate and therefore make extravagant initial demands

ambition /am bísh'n/ *n* **1** a strong feeling of wanting to be successful in life and achieve great things **2** an aim or objective that somebody is trying to achieve [14C. Via French < Latin *ambition-* < *ambire* 'canvass for votes, go round' < *ire* 'go'.]

ambitious /am bíshəss/ *adj* **1 HAVING STRONG DESIRE FOR SUCCESS** having a strong desire to be successful in life **2 NEEDING GREAT EFFORT TO SUCCEED** sounding impressive but difficult to achieve because very high standards have been set or a great deal of work is required ○ *an ambitious plan to increase market share* **3 STRONGLY DESIROUS** with a strong desire to have or do something ○ *ambitious to be the youngest person ever to win the championship* —**ambitiously** *adv* —**ambitiousness** *n*

ambivalence /am bívvələnss/ *n* **1** the presence of two opposing ideas, attitudes, or emotions at the same time **2** a feeling of uncertainty about something due to a mental conflict [Early 20C. < German *Ambivalenz*, after *Äquivalenz* 'equivalence'.]

ambivalent /am bívvələnt/ *adj* having mixed, uncertain, or conflicting feelings about something

USAGE See ***ambiguous***.

ambiversion /ámbi vúrsh'n/ *n* a personality pattern that has characteristics of both introversion and extroversion —**ambivert** /ámbi vurt/ *n*

amble /ámb'l/ *vi* (**-bles, -bling, -bled**) to walk slowly in a relaxed way ○ *'I took off shoes and socks and ambled along carrying them, enjoying the evening sun'.* (Dick Francis, *The Danger*; 1983) ■ *n* a slow and relaxed walk or style of walking [14C. Via French *ambler* < Latin *ambulare* 'walk'.] —**ambler** *n*

amblygonite /am blíggə nīt/ *n* a white or greyish-green mineral consisting of lithium aluminium fluophosphate. Use: source of lithium. [Early 19C. < Greek *amblugōnios* 'obtuse-angled'.]

amblyopia /ámbli ṓpi ə/ *n* an impairment of the vision in one eye that does not have a physical cause [Early 18C. Via modern Latin < Greek *ambluōpia* 'dim-sightedness'.] —**amblyopic** /ámbli óppik/ *adj*

ambo /ámbō/ (*plural* **-bos** *or* **-bones** /am bṓ neez/) *n* a lectern or pulpit in early Christian churches [Mid-17C. Via medieval Latin < Greek *ambōn* 'raised edge (of a dish)'.]

ambones plural of **ambo**

Ambonese /ámbə neéz/ (*plural* **-nese**), **Amboinese** /ámboy neéz/ (*plural* **-nese**) *n* **1** somebody who was born or brought up on the island of Ambon in E Indonesia **2** the form of Malay spoken on the island of Ambon [Mid-19C. < *Ambon.*] —**Ambonese** *adj*

Ambrose /ámbrōz/, **St** (340?–397) Roman priest and theologian

ambrosia /am brṓzi ə/ *n* **1 FOOD OF THE DEITIES** in classical mythology, the food of the deities, which was supposed to make those who ate it immortal **2 SOMETHING DELICIOUS** a substance that tastes or smells delicious (*literary*) **3** = **beebread 4 FRUIT AND COCONUT DISH** a dessert or salad made from oranges, bananas, and coconut [Mid-16C. Via Latin < Greek, < *ambrotos* 'immortal'.] —**ambrosial** *adj* —**ambrosially** *adv*

ambry /ámbri/ (*plural* **-bries**), **aumbry** /áwmbri/ (*plural* **-bries**) *n* a small recess near the altar in a church, where sacred vessels are kept [14C. Via French *armarie* < Latin *armarium* (see ARMOIRE).]

ambulacrum /ámbyoō láykrəm/ (*plural* **-ra** /-rə/) *n* any one of the five radial areas on the underside of a starfish, sea urchin, or similar animal, along which the blood vessels and nerves run and through which the feet extend [Early 19C. < Latin, 'avenue' < *ambulare* 'walk'.] —**ambulacral** *adj*

ambulance /ámbyoōlənss/ *n* a vehicle designed and equipped for carrying people to and from hospital [Mid-19C. < French < *hôpital ambulant* 'field hospital', literally 'walking hospital' < Latin *ambulare* 'walk'.]

ambulance chaser *n* a lawyer who, in order to earn large fees, seeks out accident victims and encourages them to claim heavy damages (*slang disapproving*)

ambulant /ámbyoōlənt/ *adj* **1** moving around from place to place **2** MED = **ambulatory** *adj.* **3** [Early 17C. < French, < Latin *ambulare* 'walk'.]

ambulate /ámbyoō layt/ (**-lates, -lating, -lated**) *vi* to walk or move from one place to another (*formal*) [Early 17C. < Latin *ambulat-*, past participle of *ambulare* 'walk'.]

ambulatory /ámbyoō láytəri/ *adj* **1 RELATING TO WALKING** relating to or equipped for walking (*formal*) **2 WALKING OR MOVING** walking or moving around, or done while walking or moving (*formal*) ○ *ambulatory activities* **3 MOBILE** describes a patient who is able to walk and does not have to be kept in bed **4 REVOCABLE** able to be revoked ○ *an ambulatory will* ■ *n* (*plural* **-ries**) **WALKWAY IN CHURCH OR CLOISTER** an aisle at the end of a choir or chancel in a church, or a covered walkway of a cloister —**ambulatorily** *adv*

ambuscade /ámbə skáyd/ *n* an ambush set for somebody (*literary*) ■ *vt* (**-cades, -cading, -caded**) to ambush somebody (*literary*) [Late 16C. Via French *embuscade* and Italian *imboscata* < assumed Vulgar Latin *imboscare* (see AMBUSH).]

ambush /ámboŏsh/ *n* **1 SURPRISE ATTACK** an unexpected attack from a concealed position **2 CONCEALMENT BEFORE ATTACK** a concealment before a surprise attack ○ *They lay in ambush and waited for their victims.* **3 SOMEBODY WAITING IN AMBUSH** one or more people concealed in order to make a surprise attack ■ *vt* **ATTACK** to attack somebody or something suddenly from a concealed position [14C. Via Old French *embusche* < assumed Vulgar Latin *imboscare* 'hide in a bush' < assumed *boscus* 'bush'.] —**ambusher** *n*

am dram /ám dram/ *n* amateur dramatics (*informal*) [Shortening]

ameba *n* BIOL = **amoeba**

amebiasis *n* US = **amoebiasis**

ameliorate /ə meéli ə rayt/ (**-rates, -rating, -rated**) *vti* to improve something or make it better (*formal*) [Mid-18C. Alteration of MELIORATE (after French *améliorer*).] —**ameliorable** /ə meéli ərəb'l/ *adj* —**amelioration** /ə meéli ə ráysh'n/ *n* —**ameliorative** /-rətiv/ *adj* —**ameliorator** *n*

amen /aá mén, áy-/ *interj* **1** said or sung at the end of a prayer or hymn to affirm its content **2** used to express strong agreement ○ *amen to that* [Pre-12C. Via late Latin and Greek < Hebrew *'āmēn* 'truly' < *'āman* 'confirm'.]

amenable /ə meènəb'l/ *adj* **1** WILLING TO COOPERATE responsive to suggestion and likely to cooperate **2** ACCOUNTABLE required to account for your behaviour to an authority **3** LIABLE TO BE JUDGED likely or available to be tested or judged [Late 16C. < Anglo-Norman, < Old French *amener* 'bring to' < Latin *minari* 'threaten' < *minae* 'threats'.] —**amenability** /ə meènə bílləti/ *n* —**amenableness** *n* —**amenably** *adv*

amend /ə ménd/ *vt* **1** to make changes to something, especially a piece of text, in order to improve or correct it **2** to revise or alter formally a motion, bill, or constitution [13C. Via French *amender* < Latin *emendare* 'to correct' < *menda* 'error'.] —**amendable** *adj* —**amendatory** *adj*

USAGE **amend** or **emend**? The word to use in general contexts involving change for the better or legislative alterations is **amend**. **Emend** is normally restricted to the correction of errors in a printed or written text: *The ambiguous wording at the beginning of the document needs amending* (= changing to something clearer). *By emending two words* (= suggesting alternatives for them because they may have been copied wrongly) *it is possible to make the sentence intelligible.*

amendment /ə méndmənt/ *n* **1** ALTERATION TO a change, correction, or improvement to something **2** CHANGE TO LEGAL INSTRUMENT an addition or alteration to a motion, bill, or constitution **3** PROCESS OF CHANGING OR IMPROVING the process of changing, correcting, or improving something ○ *The bill was passed without amendment.*

amends /ə méndz/ *n* something done or given as compensation for a wrong (+ *singular or plural verb*) ○ *a desire to make amends after the misunderstanding* ○ *No amends were forthcoming even after we proved that they were in the wrong.* [14C. < Old French *amendes*, plural of *amende* 'reparation' < *amender* (see AMEND).]

amenity /ə meènəti/ (*plural* **-ties**) *n* a useful or attractive feature or service, e.g. leisure facilities (*often plural*) [14C. Directly or via French *aménité* < Latin *amoenitas* < *amoenus* 'pleasant'.]

amenorrhoea /áy menə reè ə/, **amenorrhea** *n* the abnormal absence or suppression of menstruation —**amenorrhoeic** *adj*

ament /ə mént/, **amentum** (*plural* **-ta**) *n* a catkin (*technical*) [Mid-18C. < Latin *amentum* 'strap'.]

Amer. *abbr* American

Amerasian /ámmə ráyzh'n/ *n* somebody of mixed American and Asian parentage ■ *adj* having mixed American and Asian parentage [Mid-20C. Blend of AMERICAN + ASIAN.]

America /ə mérrikə/ **1** △ United States **2** a landmass comprising North America, South America, and Central America **3** North America (*informal*) [Early 16C. < *Americus*, Latinized form of *Amerigo* Vespucci (1454–1512), Italian navigator.]

USAGE The use of **America** to mean the United States may cause offence to people from Canada and Central and South America, and should be avoided. The term North America may be used to refer to the United States and Canada together.

American /ə mérrikən/ *n* SOMEBODY FROM UNITED STATES somebody who comes from the United States ■ *adj* **1** OF THE UNITED STATES relating to the United States, or its people, language, or culture **2** OF THE AMERICAN CONTINENTS relating to North, South, or Central America [Mid-16C. < modern Latin *Americanus* < AMERICA.] —**Americanness** *n*

Americana /ə mérri kaànə/ *n* things from or about the United States, especially items that are valued by collectors (+ *singular or plural verb*)

American aloe *n* PLANTS = **century plant**

American chameleon *n* ZOOL = **anole**

American dream, **American Dream** *n* the idea that everyone in the United States has the chance to achieve success and prosperity

American eagle *n* BIRDS = **bald eagle**

American football *n* a game played in the United States by two teams of 11 players who advance an oval ball by carrying or throwing it. Points are scored by carrying the ball across the opposing team's goal line or by kicking it through open-topped goal posts. US term **football** *n*. **2**

American Gothic (1930) by Grant Wood

American gothic, **American Gothic** *adj* depicting or representing hard work, frugality, and conservative social attitudes associated with rural and small-town United States [After a 1930 painting by the Iowan painter Grant Wood (1892–1942), which depicts a dour farm couple and their surroundings]

American Indian *n* a Native American —**American Indian** *adj*

Americanise *vti* = **Americanize**

Americanism /ə mérrikənizəm/ *n* **1** a word, phrase, or custom that originated in, or is regarded as characteristic of, the United States **2** strong affection for or support for the United States

Americanist /ə mérrikənist/ *n* **1** an expert on the life, history, language, or culture of the United States **2** a student of or specialist in the languages and cultures of Native Americans

Americanize /ə mérrika nīz/ (**-izes, -izing, -ized**), **Americanise** (**-ises, -ising, -ised**) *vti* to give something the form, style, or qualities associated with or used in the United States, or take on such qualities —**Americanization** /ə mérrika nī záysh'n/ *n*

American kestrel *n* BIRDS = **sparrowhawk** *n*. **2**

American Legion *n* an organization of veterans of the US armed services, founded in 1919

American plan *n* US = **full board**

American Revolution *n* US = **American War of Independence**

American saddle horse *n* a high-stepping saddle horse, originally bred in Kentucky and trained to walk, trot, canter, gallop, and pace

American Samoa US territory, consisting of a group of islands in the South Pacific. Population: 59,566 (1996). Area: 200 sq. km/77 sq. mi.

American shorthair *n* a domestic cat belonging to a US breed with a broad head and short thick coat

American Sign Language *n* a system of communication used by people with impaired hearing that uses motions or gestures of the hands

⚡ **American Standard Code for Information Interchange** *n* full form of **ASCII**

American War of Independence *n* the war in which the American colonies won independence from Great Britain (1775–83). US term **American Revolution**

Americas /ə mérrikəss/ = **America 2**

americium /ámmə ríssi əm/ *n* (*symbol* **Am**) a white radioactive metallic element. Source: beta decay of plutonium. Use: alpha particle source for research. [Mid-20C. After AMERICA, where it was first produced.]

Amerindian /ámmə ríndi ən/ *n*, *adj* a member of an indigenous people of North, South, or Central America (*sometimes offensive*) [Late 19C. Blend of AMERICAN + INDIAN.] —**Amerindic** *adj*

Ameslan /ámmə slan/ *n* = **American Sign Language** [Late 20C. Acronym.]

Ames test /áymz-/ *n* a test used to determine the cancer-causing potential of a chemical or other agent by meas-

uring its effect on bacteria [Late 20C. After the US biochemist Bruce Ames (born 1928).]

amethocaine /ə méthō kayn/ *n* MED = **tetracaine** [Mid-20C. < ?]

amethyst /ámməthist/ *n* **1** VIOLET QUARTZ a precious stone that is a translucent violet variety of quartz. Use: gems. **2** PURPLE SAPPHIRE a purple variety of sapphire. Use: gems. **3** BLUISH-PURPLE a bluish-purple colour [13C. Via Old French and Latin < Greek *amethustos* 'not intoxicating' < *methu* 'wine'.] —**amethyst** *adj* —**amethystine** /ámmə thís tīn/ *adj*

Amex /ámmeks/, **AMEX** *abbr* American Stock Exchange

Amharic /am hárrik/ *n* the official language of Ethiopia, belonging to the Semitic branch of Afro-Asiatic languages and written in Ethiopic script. Native speakers: 15 million. [Early 19C. < *Amhara*, province in NW Ethiopia.] —**Amharic** *adj*

Amherst /ám hurst/ **1** town in W Massachusetts. Population: 35,468 (1996 estimate). **2** town in N Ohio. Population: 11,311 (1996).

amiable /áymi əb'l/ *adj* **1** friendly and pleasant to be with **2** characterized by friendly feelings [14C. Via French < late Latin *amicabilis* (see AMICABLE), influenced in meaning by French *aimable* 'lovable'.] —**amiability** /áymi ə bílləti/ *n* —**amiableness** *n* —**amiably** *adv*

amianthus /ámmi ánthəss/ *n* a type of asbestos with thin silky fibres [Early 17C. Via Latin < Greek *amiantos* 'undefiled' < *miainein* 'defile'.]

amicable /ámmikəb'l/ *adj* characterized by or done in friendliness, without anger or bad feelings ○ *an amicable divorce* [15C. < late Latin *amicabilis* < Latin *amicus* 'friend' < *amare* 'to love'.] —**amicability** /ámmika bílləti/ *n* —**amicableness** /ámmikəb'lnəss/ *n* —**amicably** *adv*

amice /ámmiss/ *n* a length of white fabric worn by a Christian priest around the neck [13C. Probably via Old French *amit* < Latin *amictus* 'cloak' < *amicire* 'to cover' < *iacere* 'throw'.]

amicus curiae /ə míkəss kyoòri ee/ (*plural* **amici curiae** /ə míssee-/), **amicus** (*plural* **-ci**) *n* somebody whose counsel provides information to a court on legal issues involved in a case [Early 17C. < modern Latin, 'friend of the court'.]

amid /ə míd/, **amidst** /ə mídst/ *prep* **1** surrounded by things or people ○ *a small lake amid the hills* **2** used to indicate the circumstances or events around or accompanying something ○ *I sat down amid roars of laughter.* [12C. < an earlier form of MIDDLE.]

amide /ámmīd/ *n* **1** any organic compound derived from ammonia, formed by the replacement of one or more hydrogen atoms with acyl groups **2** any inorganic compound derived from ammonia and containing the NH_2 ion [Mid-19C. < AMMONIA.] —**amidic** /ə míddik/ *adj*

amidol /ámmi dol/ *n* $C_6H_3(NH_2)_2OH·HC$ a colourless, water-soluble, crystalline compound. Use: photographic developer. [Late 19C. < German, a trademark.]

amidships /ə mídships/ *adv*, *adj* near or in the middle of a boat or ship

amidst *prep* = **amid**

amigo /ə meègō/ (*plural* **-gos**) *n* a friend (*in Spanish-speaking regions*) [Mid-19C. Via Spanish < Latin *amicus* 'friend'.]

Amin /aa meèn/, **Idi** (*b.* 1925) Ugandan head of state (1971–79)

amine /ámmeen/ *n* any organic derivative of ammonia formed by the replacement of hydrogen with one or more alkyl groups [Mid-19C. < AMMONIA.]

-amine *suffix* amine ○ *tryptamine* [< AMINE]

amino /ə meènō/ *adj* describes a chemical compound containing the NH_2 group

amino- *prefix* containing an NH_2 group combined with a nonacid radical ○ *aminophenol* [< AMINE]

amino acid *n* a compound belonging to a class that contains an amino group and makes up proteins

aminobenzoic acid /ə meènō ben zō ik-/ *n* $C_7H_7NO_2$ any of three crystalline solids derived from benzoic acid, especially PABA. Use: sunscreen lotions.

amino caproic acid *n* a type of amino acid. Use: treatment of excessive bleeding.

aminoglutethimide /ə meènō gloo téthə mīd/ *n* a drug that acts on the adrenal cortex, affecting the production of steroids. Use: treatment of breast cancer.

aminoglycoside /ə meènð glīkð sīd/ *n* any of a group of soluble basic antibiotics. Use: treatment of aerobic bacterial infections.

aminopeptidase /ə meènð pépti dayz, -dayss/ *n* an enzyme that breaks down dietary peptides into amino acids

aminophenol /ə meènð feè nol/ *n* C_6H_7NO any of three white soluble organic compounds. Use: dyes, photographic developers.

aminophylline /ámmi nóffi leen, -nóffilin/ *n* a white crystalline drug. Use: bronchodilator, treatment of asthma, in veterinary medicine. [Mid-20C. < AMINO- + THEOPHYLLINE.]

aminoquinolone /ə meènð kwinnə lōn/ *n* an oral antibiotic. Use: prevention of malaria.

aminotransferase /ə meènð tránsfə rayz, -rayss/ *n* BIOCHEM = **transaminase**

amiodarone /ámmi óddərōn/ *a* drug that acts as a potassium channel blocker. Use: treatment of heart arryhthmia.

amir *n* = **emir**

Amish /aámish/ *npl* members of a Protestant group who migrated from Europe to North America in the 18th century [Late 19C. Probably < German *amisch*.] —**Amish** *adj*

amiss /ə míss/ *adj* incorrect, inappropriate, or not as it should be ○ *We knew immediately from the disorder in the house that something was amiss.* ■ *adv* incorrectly or inappropriately ○ *Things began to go amiss after she left.* [13C. < Old Norse *á mis* 'so as to miss'.] ◇ **not go or come amiss** to be welcome or useful ◇ **take something amiss** to be upset or offended by something, even though no offence was intended

amitosis /ámmi tôssiss/ *n* cell division by simple division of the nucleus and cytoplasm, without the appearance of chromosomes [Late 19C. < MITOSIS.] —**amitotic** /ámmi tóttik/ *adj*

amitriptyline /ámmi tríptə leen/ *n* a sedative drug. Use: treatment of depression and chronic pain

amity /ámmati/ *n* friendliness and peaceful relations (*formal*) [15C. Via French *amitié* < medieval Latin *amicitas* < Latin *amicus* 'friend' (see AMICABLE).]

amlodipine /am lóddi peen/ *n* a drug that acts as a calcium channel blocker. Use: treatment of hypertension and angina.

Amman /ə maàn/ capital of the Hashemite Kingdom of Jordan. Population: 1,187,000 (1995 estimate).

ammeter /ámmeetər/ *n* an instrument used for measuring electric current in amperes [Late 19C. < AMPERE + -METER.]

ammine /ámmeen/ *n* a compound containing one or more ammonia molecules attached to a salt or similar compound through coordinate bonds [Late 19C. < AMMONIA.]

ammo /ámmð/ *n* ammunition (*informal*) [Early 20C. Shortening.]

ammocoete /ámmə seet/ *n* the filter-feeding larva of the lamprey [Mid-19C. < modern Latin *Ammocoetes* < Greek *ammos* 'sand' + *koitē* 'bed'.]

ammonate /ámmə nayt/ *n* CHEM = **ammine**

ammonia /ə mőni ə/ *n* 1 NH_3 a colourless, pungent gas that is highly soluble in water. Use: refrigerant, manufacture of fertilizers, explosives, plastics. 2 a solution of ammonia in water. Use: household cleaner, manufacture of fertilizers and textiles. [Late 18C. < modern Latin, < Latin *sal ammoniacus* 'salt of Ammon' < Greek *Ammōn* 'Ammon', Egyptian god near whose temple ammonia and ammoniac were said to be obtained.]

ammoniac /ə mőni ak/ *n* a strong-smelling brownish-yellow gum resin. Source: Asian plant of the carrot family. Use: medicine, porcelain, cement. ■ *adj* = **ammoniacal** [14C. Via French < Latin *ammoniacus* (see AMMONIA).]

ammoniacal /ámmə nĭ ək'l/, **ammoniac** /ə mőni ak/ *adj* containing or resembling ammonia

ammoniate /ə mőni ayt/ (**-ates, -ating, -ated**) *vt* to treat or combine something with ammonia or an ammonia compound —**ammoniation** /ə mőni áysh'n/ *n*

ammonia water *n* CHEM = **ammonia** *n.* 2

ammonification /ə mónnifi káysh'n/ *n* 1 treatment with ammonia or an ammonium compound 2 the formation of ammonia or ammonium compounds through the bacterial decomposition of organic matter

ammonify /ə mónni fī/ (**-fies, -fying, -fied**) *vti* to treat something with ammonia or to undergo ammonification —**ammonifier** *n*

ammonite /ámmə nīt/ *n* 1 an extinct marine mollusc with a flat partitioned spiral shell, belonging to the ammonoids 2 the fossilized shell of an ammonite [Mid-18C. < modern Latin *ammonites* < medieval Latin *cornu Ammonis* 'horn of Ammon'.] —**ammonitic** /ámmə níttik/ *adj*

Ammonite /ámmə nīt/ *n* a member of an ancient Semitic people in the Bible who lived between the Syrian desert and the River Jordan from the 13th to the 6th centuries BC [Mid-16C. < late Latin, < Hebrew *'Ammōn* 'Ammon (son of Lot)'.]

ammonium /ə mőni əm/ *adj* relating to or containing the NH_4+ ion derived from ammonia [Early 19C. < AMMONIA.]

ammonium bicarbonate *n* NH_4HCO_3 a white crystalline solid. Use: baking powder.

ammonium carbonate *n* $(NH_4)_2CO_3$ a white crystalline solid. Use: smelling salts, baking powder.

ammonium chloride *n* NH_4Cl a white crystalline solid. Use: expectorant, soldering flux, dry cell electrolyte.

ammonium hydroxide *n* a solution of ammonia in water

ammonium nitrate *n* NH_4NO_3 a colourless crystalline solid. Use: fertilizers, herbicides, insecticides, explosives.

ammonium sulphate *n* $(NH_4)_2SO_4$ a colourless crystalline solid. Use: fertilizer, water purification.

ammonoid /ámmə noyd/ *n* an extinct cephalopod mollusc with a partitioned shell [Mid-19C. < modern Latin *Ammonoidea* < *ammonites* (see AMMONITE).]

ammunition /ámmyoö nísh'n/ *n* 1 BULLETS AND MISSILES bullets, shells, missiles, and other projectiles used as weapons 2 EXPLOSIVE MATERIAL bombs, grenades, and other explosive devices or substances used as weapons 3 SUPPORTING FACTS facts and information that can be used to support a point of view in an argument [Late 16C. < French, alteration (due to mistaking *la munition* for *l'amunition*) of *munition* (see MUNITION).]

amnesia /am neèzi ə/ *n* loss of memory as a result of shock, injury, psychological disturbance, or medical disorder [Late 18C. < Greek *amnēsia*, alteration of *amnēstia* 'forgetfulness' < *amnēstos* 'not remembered' < *mnasthai* 'remember'.] —**amnesiac** /am neèzi ak/ *n, adj* —**amnestic** /-néstik/ *adj*

amnesty /ámnəsti/ *n* (*plural* **-ties**) 1 PARDON a general pardon, especially for those who have committed political crimes 2 PROSECUTION-FREE PERIOD a period during which crimes can be admitted or illegal weapons handed in without prosecution ■ *vt* (**-ties, -tying, -tied**) PARDON to grant amnesty to somebody [Late 16C. Via French < Greek *amnēstia* (see AMNESIA).]

Amnesty International *n* an international human rights organization concerned with prisoners of conscience under any type of political regime

amnia plural of **amnion**

amnio /ámni ð/ *n* (*plural* **-os**) *n* an amniocentesis (*informal*) [Late 20C. Shortening.]

amniocentesis /ámni ð sen teèssiss/ (*plural* **-ses** /-seez/) *n* a test performed to determine the health, sex, or genetic constitution of a foetus by taking a sample of amniotic fluid through a needle inserted into the womb of the mother [Mid-20C. < AMNION + Greek *kentēsis* 'pricking' (from *kentein* 'prick').]

amniography /ámni ógrəfi/ *n* an X-ray of the womb [Mid-20C. < AMNION + -GRAPHY.]

amnion /ámni ən/ (*plural* **-ons** or **-a** /-ə/) *n* 1 the inner of the two membranes enclosing the embryo of a bird, reptile, or mammal and its surrounding fluid. ◊ **chorion** 2 the fluid-filled sac within which the embryo of a bird, reptile, or mammal develops [Mid-17C. < Greek, 'caul' < *amnos* 'lamb'.] —**amniotic** /ámni óttik/ *adj*

amniote /ámni ōt/ *n* any vertebrate that develops from an embryo within an amnion, e.g. a bird, reptile, or mammal [Early 20C. < modern Latin *Amniota* < AMNION.]

amniotic fluid /ámni óttik-/ *n* the fluid that surrounds a foetus while it is developing

amniotic sac *n* ANAT, MED = **amnion** *n.* 2

amodiaquine /ámmð dī ə kween/ *n* a bitter yellow crystalline solid. Use: prevention of malaria.

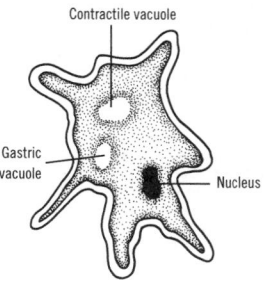

Amoeba

amoeba /ə meèbə/ (*plural* **-bae** /-bee/ or **-bas**), **ameba** (*plural* **-bas** or **-bae**) *n* a single-celled organism found in water and in damp soil on land, and as a parasite of other organisms. Genus: *Amoeba*. [Mid-19C. Via modern Latin < Greek *amoibē* 'change' < *ameibein* 'to change'.] —**amoebic** *adj* —**amoeboid** /ə meè boyd/ *adj*

amoebiasis /ámmi bĭ əssiss/ *n* an infection or disease affecting the bowel, caused by an amoeba *Entamoeba histolytica*

amoebic dysentery *n* an inflammation of the colon causing diarrhoea of varying degrees of severity that results from infection by an amoeba *Entamoeba histolytica*

amoebicide /ə meèbə sīd/ *n* a chemical agent used to kill amoebas

amoebocyte /ə meèbə sīt/ *n* a cell that moves like an amoeba, e.g. a blood cell that can engulf particles

amok /ə mók/, **amuck** /ə múk/ *adj* frenzied and out of control [Early 16C. Directly or via Portuguese *am(o)uco* < Malay *amuk* 'fighting frenziedly'.] ◇ **run amok** to be or become out of control, especially in a frenzied way

among /ə múng/, **amongst** /-múngst/ CORE MEANING: a preposition indicating that something or somebody is surrounded by people, things, ideas, or circumstances ○ *You're among friends here.*
prep 1 OF A GROUP of the stated group or class ○ *Her carvings are among the world's finest.* 2 IN A GROUP in a group or by the particular group stated ○ *a widely-held notion among physicists* 3 BETWEEN GROUP MEMBERS by, between, or to each person or thing in a group ○ *divided among six of us* 4 IN ADDITION TO in addition to other things or people ○ *The photos showed, among other things, a birthday party.* [Old English *on (ge)mong* < *on* 'in' + *(ge)mong* 'crowd'. Ultimately < Indo-European.]

USAGE See **between**.

amontillado /ámmonti laàdð/ (*plural* **-dos**) *n* a pale medium-dry sherry from Spain [Early 19C. < Spanish.]

amoral /ay mórrəl/ *adj* 1 not concerned with or amenable to moral judgments 2 not caring about good behaviour or morals (*disapproving*) —**amoralism** *n* —**amorality** /áymo rálləti/ *n* —**amorally** *adv*

amoretto /ámmə réttð/ (*plural* **-ti** /-rétti/) *n* an artistic representation of a small naked boy or winged cherub as a symbol of love [Early 17C. < Italian, 'small cupid' < *amore* 'love' < Latin *amor*.]

amorist /ámmərist/ *n* somebody who writes about love or is in love (*literary*) [Late 16C. < French *amour* 'love' or Latin *amor*.]

Amorite /ámmə rīt/ *n* a member of an ancient Semitic people who lived in Mesopotamia, Syria, and Palestine between about 2600 and 1200 BC [Mid-16C. < Hebrew *'ĕmōrī* < Akkadian *Amurru(m)*, the land inhabited by the Amorites.]

amoroso[1] /ámmə rôssð/ *adv, adj* to be played or sung in a gentle loving way (*musical direction*) [Late 18C. Via Italian < medieval Latin *amorosus* (see AMOROUS).]

amoroso[2] /ámmə rôssð/ (*plural* **amorosos**) *n* a sweet dark sherry [Late 19C. Via Spanish < medieval Latin *amorosus* (see AMOROUS).]

amorous /ámmərəss/ *adj* showing or feeling romantic love or sexual attraction [14C. Via Old French < medieval Latin *amorosus* < Latin *amor* 'love'.] —**amorously** *adv* —**amorousness** *n*

amorphous /ə máwrfəss/ *adj* **1 WITHOUT SHAPE** without any clear shape, form, or structure **2 NOT CLASSIFIABLE** not obviously belonging to any particular category or type **3 WITHOUT CRYSTALLINE STRUCTURE** without a crystalline structure [Mid-18C. Via modern Latin < Greek *amorphos* 'without shape' < *morphē* 'shape'.] —**amorphously** *adv* —**amorphousness** *n*

amortise *vt* FIN = **amortize**

amortize /ə máwr tīz/ (**-tizes, -tizing, -tized**), **amortise** (**-tises, -tising, -tised**) *vt* **1 REDUCE DEBT BY INSTALMENTS** to reduce a debt by making payments against the principal balance in instalments or regular transfers **2 WRITE OFF COST OF ASSET** to write off the cost of an asset over a period of time in a statement of accounts **3 TRANSFER PROPERTY** to transfer land or other assets to an ecclesiastical body (*archaic*) [14C. Via French *amortiss-* 'alienate in mortmain' < assumed Vulgar Latin *admortire* 'deaden' < Latin *mort-* 'death'.] —**amortizable** *adj* —**amortization** /ə máwr tī záysh'n/ *n*

Amos /áymoss/ a Hebrew prophet in the Bible who lived in the 8th century BC ■ *n* a book of the Bible that contains the prophecies of Amos

amotivational syndrome /áy mōti váysh'nəl-/ *n* a psychological condition characterized by a loss of the motivation to carry out socially accepted behaviours and tasks, usually associated with the use of marijuana

amount /ə mównt/ *n* a quantity or degree of something, considered as a unit or total [14C. < Old French *amonter* 'rise' < *amont* 'upwards' < Latin *ad montem* 'to the mountain'.]

USAGE amount or **number**? ***Amount*** is normally used with singular words or words that have no plural, that is so-called uncountable or mass nouns such as *cheese, happiness*, and *warfare*: *a large amount of cheese; any amount of happiness*. In contrast, ***number*** is used with plural nouns such as *books, questions, ships*, and *cheeses* (= *types of cheese*): *a large number of books; an excessive number of questions; a good number of cheeses*. In everyday speech, ***amount*** is sometimes used when ***number*** is strictly called for: *a large amount of books*. This should be avoided in more formal speaking and writing.

amount to *vt* **1** to come to a particular total when added up **2** to be equivalent to something ○ *Their statement amounts to nothing more than a slick evasion.*

amour /ə mŏŏr/ *n* a love affair, especially one that is clandestine (*dated*) [14C. Via French < Latin *amor* 'love'.]

amour-propre /ámmoor própprə/ *n* self-respect or estimation of your true worth (*formal*) [Late 18C. < French, 'self-love'.]

amoxapine /ə móksə peen/ *n* a depressant drug taken orally. Use: treatment of neurotic and psychotic depressive disorders.

amoxycillin /ə móksi síllin/ *n* a broad-spectrum, synthetic penicillin taken orally [Late 20C. < AMINO- + OXY- + PENICILLIN.]

Amoy /ə móy/ *n* the dialect of Chinese spoken on the island of Xiamen and in neighbouring areas in SE China [Mid-19C. After *Amoy* (XIAMEN).]

amp /amp/ *n* **1** an ampere **2** an amplifier (*informal*) [Late 19C. Shortening.]

AMP *n* a compound (**nucleotide**) involved in energy transfer reactions in living cells. Full form **adenosine monophosphate**. ◊ **cyclic AMP**

amperage /ámpərij/ *n* the number of amperes measured in an electric current

ampere /ám pair/ *n* (*symbol* **A**) the basic unit of electric current in the SI system, equal to a current that produces a force of 2x10^{-7} newtons per metre between two parallel conductors in a vacuum [Late 19C. After the French physicist André-Marie *Ampère* (1775–1836).]

ampere-hour *n* a measure of quantity of electricity equal to the amount of electricity that passes in one hour through a conductor with a current of one ampere

ampersand /ámpər sand/ *n* the symbol '&', meaning 'and' [Mid-19C. < *and per se and* '(the character) '&' by itself (means) and'.]

amphetamine /am féttə meen/ *n* a drug or any of its derivatives. Use: formerly, to treat depression and as an appetite suppressant. [Mid-20C. Contraction of *alpha-methyl-phenethylamine*.]

amphi- *prefix* both ○ *amphibious* [Via Latin < Greek *amphi* 'on both sides' < Indo-European]

amphibian /am fíbbi ən/ *n* **1** a cold-blooded vertebrate that spends some time on land but must breed and develop into an adult in water. Class: Amphibia. **2** an aircraft or vehicle designed to operate on land or water ■ *adj* = **amphibious** *adj*. 1 [Mid-19C. < modern Latin *Amphibia* < Greek *amphibion* 'amphibious being' < *amphibios* (see AMPHIBIOUS).]

amphibious /am fíbbi əss/ *adj* **1 LIVING ON LAND AND IN WATER** describes an animal that lives in water during early development and on land as an adult **2 ON LAND AND IN WATER** taking place or operating both on land and in water ○ *made an amphibious assault on the island* ○ *amphibious vehicles* **3 OF MIXED TYPE** with two different qualities or features resulting in a mixed type [Mid-17C. < Greek *amphibios* 'living on both (land and water)' < *bios* 'life'.] —**amphibiously** *adv* —**amphibiousness** *n*

amphibole /ámfi bōl/ *n* a hydrous silicate mineral containing varying amounts of aluminium, calcium, iron, magnesium, and sodium [Early 19C. < French, < Greek *amphibolos* 'ambiguous' < *ballein* 'throw'; because the mineral is able to appear in a variety of forms.] —**amphibolic** /ámfi bóllik/ *adj*

amphibolite /am fíbbə līt/ *n* a metamorphic rock consisting mainly of amphibole with some plagioclase

amphibology /ámfi bólləji/ (*plural* **-gies**), **amphiboly** /am fíbbəli/ (*plural* **-lies**) *n* a phrase or sentence that can be interpreted in two ways, usually because of the grammatical construction rather than the meanings of the words themselves [Late 16C. < late Latin *amphibologia* 'ambiguity' < Latin *amphibolia* + Greek *-logia* 'speech'.] —**amphibological** /am fíbbə lójjik'l/ *adj* —**amphibologically** *adv* —**amphibolous** /am fíbbələss/ *adj*

amphibrach /ámfi brak/ *n* a metrical foot of three syllables with the stress on the second syllable, or of one long syllable between two short syllables [Late 16C. Via Latin *amphibrachys* < Greek *amphibrakhus* 'short on both sides' < *brakhus* 'short'.] —**amphibrachic** /ámfi brákik/ *adj*

amphictyony /am fíkti əni/ (*plural* **-nies**) *n* a group of neighbouring states or communities in ancient Greece that shared responsibility for shrines and temples — **amphictyonic** /am fíkti ónnik/ *adj*

amphigenetic /ámfijə néttik/ *adj* produced by or involving both sexes, as in reproduction

amphigory /ám figgəri/ (*plural* **-ries**), **amphigouri** /ámfi goori/ (*plural* **-ris**) *n* a nonsensical piece of writing, usually in verse [Early 19C. < French *amphigouri*.]

amphimacer /am fímməssər/ *n* a metrical foot of three syllables with the stress on the first and third syllables, or of one short syllable between two long syllables [Late 16C. Via Latin < Greek *amphimakros* 'long on both sides' < *makros* 'long'.]

amphimixis /ámfi míksiss/ *n* sexual reproduction involving the fusion of reproductive cells (**gametes**) from two organisms [Late 19C. < modern Latin < Greek *amphi-* 'on both sides' + *mixis* 'mingling' < *mignunai* 'mix'.] — **amphimictic** *adj*

amphioxus /ámfi óksəss/ (*plural* **-i** /-sī/ *or* **-uses**) *n* = **lancelet** [Mid-19C. < modern Latin, 'sharp at both sides' < Greek *amphi-* 'at both sides' + *oxus* 'sharp'.]

amphipod /ámfi pod/ *n* a small freshwater or marine crustacean with a thin body and without a carapace. Order: Amphipoda. [Mid-19C. < modern Latin *Amphipoda* < Greek *amphi-* 'both' + *pod-* stem of *pous* 'foot', because there are two types of feet in this order.] —**amphipodous** /am físpədəss/ *adj*

amphiprostyle /ámfi prṓ stīl/ *n* a classical temple or other building with a set of columns at each end but not at the sides [Early 18C. Via French and Latin < Greek *amphiprostulos* 'with pillars at both ends' < *prostulos* 'having pillars' (see PROSTYLE).]

amphiprotic /ámfi prṓtik/ *adj* producing and reacting with protons as a solvent and therefore having properties of both an acid and an alkali [Mid-20C. < AMPHI- + PROTON + *-ic*.]

amphisbaena /ámfiss béenə/ (*plural* **-nae** /-nee/ *or* **-nas**) *n* **1** a legless lizard with a rounded tail resembling a second head. Native to: tropical America. Family: Amphisbaenidae. **2** in classical mythology, a poisonous snake that has a head at each end of its body, allowing it to move in either direction [14C. Via Latin < Greek *amphisbaina* 'going both ways' < *amphis* 'both ways' + *bainein* 'go'.] —**amphisbaenic** *adj*

amphistylar /ámfi stīlər/ *adj* describes a building, especially a classical temple, that has a set of columns on both ends or sides [19C. < AMPHI- + Greek *stulos* 'column'.]

amphitheatre /ámfi theertər/ *n* **1 CIRCULAR BUILDING** a round or oval building without a roof that has a central open space surrounded by tiers of seats, especially one used by the ancient Romans for public entertainments **2 PLACE FOR SPORTS** a large enclosure where sporting activities or public entertainments take place **3 SEATING FOR SPECTATORS** a gallery of seats arranged in semicircular tiers for the audience in a theatre or lecture room **4 LECTURE ROOM** a lecture hall or operating room where seating is arranged in semicircular tiers [Mid-14C. Via Latin < Greek *amphitheatron*, 'theatre on both sides' (because the typical classical Greek theatre had seating on one side only) < *theatron* (see THEATRE).] —**amphitheatric** /ámfithi áttrik/ *adj* —**amphitheatrically** *adv*

amphora /ámfərə/ (*plural* **-rae** /-ree/ *or* **-ras**) *n* a jar, usually made of clay, with a narrow neck and two handles, used by ancient Greeks and Romans for holding oil or wine [15C. Via Latin < Greek *amphiphoreus* < *amphi-* 'on both sides' + *phoreus* 'bearer' < *pherein* 'bear'; from its two handles.] —**amphoral** *adj*

amphoteric /ámfə térrik/ *adj* able to react chemically as either an acid or a base [Mid-19C. < Greek *amphoteroi* 'both of two', comparative form of *amphō* 'both'.]

amphotericin /ámfə térrissin/ *n* either of two antibiotic drugs used intravenously. Use: treatment of fungal infections.

ampicillin /ámpi síllin/ *n* a semisynthetic form of penicillin. Use: treatment of respiratory infections. [Mid-20C. Blend of AMINO- + PENICILLIN.]

ample /ámp'l/ (**-pler, -plest**) *adj* **1** as much or as many as required, usually with some left over **2** large, especially in physical size (*often used euphemistically*) [15C. Via French < Latin *amplus* 'large, plentiful'.] —**ampleness** *n*

amplexus /am pléksəss/ *n* the mating posture of a pair of frogs or toads, in which the male clasps the female from behind during egg release and fertilization [Mid-20C. < Latin, < past participle of *amplecti* 'embrace'.]

amplicon /ámpli kón/ *n* a nucleic acid fragment that is the product of the artificial large-scale reproduction of genetic material

amplidyne /ámpli dīn/ *n* a specialized direct-current generator in which small changes in power input produce large changes in output [Mid-20C. Blend of AMPLIFIER + Greek *dynamis* 'power' (see DYNAMIC).]

amplification /ámpli fi káysh'n/ *n* **1 ENLARGEMENT OF** the act or process of making something larger, greater, or stronger **2 PROCESS OF MAKING LOUDER** the act or process of making something louder **3 ADDITION OF DETAIL** the act or process of making a spoken or written account fuller or clearer **4 DETAIL ADDED** a detail, explanation, or illustration added to a spoken or written account to make it fuller or clearer **5 INCREASE IN SIGNAL MAGNITUDE** the increase in the magnitude of a signal produced by an amplifier **6 GENE REPRODUCTION** the artificial large-scale reproduction of genes or DNA sequences

amplified fragment length polymorphism *n* a rapid method for detecting variations in DNA sequences between individuals, using the polymerase chain reaction technique

amplifier /ámpli fī ər/ *n* **1** a device that makes sounds louder, especially one increasing the sound level of musical instruments **2** an electronic device that increases the magnitude of a signal, voltage, or current

amplify /ámpli fī/ (**-fies, -fying, -fied**) *vti* **1 INCREASE** to become, or cause something to become, larger, greater, or stronger **2 MAKE LOUDER** to become louder, or make a sound become louder, by electronic or other means **3 ADD DETAIL** to make a spoken or written account fuller, clearer, or more detailed **4 INCREASE SIGNAL** to increase the magnitude of a signal using an amplifier, or undergo such an increase [15C. Via French *amplifier* < Latin *amplificare* 'enlarge' < *amplus* 'large' + *fic-*, a stem of *facere* 'make'.] —**amplifiable** *adj*

SYNONYMS See ***increase***.

amplitude /ámpli tyood/ *n* **1 LARGENESS** a largeness in size, volume, or extent **2 BREADTH** a breadth of range **3 ABUNDANCE** an amount that is more than required **4 DISTANCE FROM MEAN POINT** the farthest distance that a vibrating or oscillating system such as a pendulum travels from a mean or zero point **5 SIGNAL'S MAXIMUM VALUE** the maximum value of an alternating signal **6 ANGLE OF VECTOR REPRESENTING COMPLEX NUMBER** the angle between a vector representing a complex number and the positive real axis [Mid-16C. Via French < Latin *amplitudo* 'size, greatness, grandeur' < *amplus* 'large'.]

amplitude modulation *n* the modulation of the amplitude of a radio wave in such a way as to encode the wave with audio or visual information

amply /ámpli/ *adv* to a more than adequate degree

ampoule /ám pool, -pyool/, **ampule** *n* a small sealed glass container that holds a measured amount of a medicinal substance to be injected [Early 20C. Via French < Latin *ampulla* (see AMPULLA).]

ampulla /am pŏŏllə/ (*plural* **-lae** /-lee/) *n* **1** a small container for a consecrated substance, especially oil, water, or the wine used in the Christian Communion **2** a round two-handled bottle used by the ancient Romans to hold wine, oil, or perfume [Late 14C. < Latin, 'little amphora' < *ampora*, variant of *amphora* (see AMPHORA).]

amputate /ámpyŏŏ tayt/ (**-tates, -tating, -tated**) *vti* to cut off a limb or other appendage of the body, especially in a surgical operation [Mid-16C. < Latin *amputat-*, past participle of *amputare* 'cut around' < *ambi-* 'around' + *putare* 'cut'.] —**amputation** /ámpyŏŏ táysh'n/ *n* —**amputator** *n*

amputee /ámpyŏŏ tée/ *n* somebody who has had a limb or part of a limb cut off

amrita /am réetə/, **amreeta** *n* **1** in Hindu mythology, a substance prepared by the deities that makes those who drink it immortal **2** immortality gained by drinking amrita [Late 18C. < Sanskrit *amṛta* 'without death' < *mṛta* 'death'.]

Amritsar /əm rítsər/ city in Punjab state in NW India. Population: 708,835 (1991).

Amsterdam /ámstər dam/ capital and commercial centre in the Netherlands. Population: 731,200 (2000).

amu *abbr* atomic mass unit

amuck *adj, adv* = **amok**

Amu Darya /àa moo daaryə/ longest river in central Asia, flowing from the Pamir plateau to the Aral Sea. Length: 1,415 km/879 mi.

amulet /ámmyŏŏlət/ *n* **1** a piece of jewellery worn to provide protection against evil, injury, disease, or bad luck **2** an ordinary object that is supposed to provide protection against bad luck or negative forces [Late 16C. < Latin *amuletum*.]

Amun /aamən/ *n* a supreme god of ancient Egypt

Amundsen /ámmənds'n/, **Roald** (1872–1928) Norwegian explorer

Amur /ə múr/ river in east-central Asia. Length: 4,345 km/2,700 mi. (total river system)

amuse /ə myóoz/ (**amuses, amusing, amused**) *v* **1** *vti* to make somebody smile or laugh or think that something is funny **2** *vt* to keep somebody occupied or entertained by providing entertainment or an interesting task [15C. < French *amuser* 'cause to stare stupidly' < *muser* 'stare stupidly'.] —**amused** *adj*

amusement /ə myóozmənt/ *n* **1 FEELING SOMETHING IS FUNNY** the feeling that something is funny or entertaining **2 RECREATIONAL ACTIVITY** an enjoyable activity such as a game, a hobby, or a form of entertainment **3 RIDE OR GAME** a ride, game, or other attraction found in an amusement park or arcade **4 KEEPING HAPPILY OCCUPIED** the act of keeping somebody or a group of people occupied or entertained

amusement arcade *n* an indoor or covered area containing a variety of coin-operated machines for playing games. US term **penny arcade**

amusement park *n* an outdoor area with a variety of mechanical rides, games, and other attractions that people pay to use

amusing /ə myóozing/ *adj* causing somebody to smile or laugh or be amused, often in a subdued way — **amusingly** *adv* —**amusingness** *n*

amygdala /ə mígdələ/ (*plural* **-lae** /-lee/) *n* an almond-shaped mass of grey matter, one in each hemisphere of the brain, associated with feelings of fear and aggression and important for visual learning and memory [Pre-12C. Via Latin < Greek *amugdalē* 'almond'.]

amygdalin /ə mígdəlin/, **amygdaline** /-lin, -leen/ *n* a white crystalline bitter-tasting sugar derivative (**glycoside**). Source: almond, apricot, and peach seeds. Use: expectorant. [Mid-19C. < Latin *amygdala* 'almond' (see AMYGDALA).]

amyl /ámmil, áy mīl/ *adj* relating to or containing any of eight possible forms of a chemical group with the same basic formula C_5H_{11}– [Mid-19C. < Latin *amylum* < Greek *amulon* 'finely ground meal' < *mulē* 'mill'.]

amyl- *prefix* = **amylo-** (*before vowels*)

amylaceous /ámmi láyshəss/ *adj* having or resembling starch (*technical*)

amyl acetate *n* $CH_3CO_2C_5H_{11}$ a colourless volatile liquid that smells like pears. Use: flavouring agent, solvent.

amyl alcohol *n* $C_5H_{12}O$ a colourless alcohol or mixture of any of the eight related amyl alcohols. Use: solvent, manufacture of organic chemicals and drugs.

amylase /ámmi layz, -layss/ *n* an enzyme, in saliva and pancreatic juice, that breaks down starch into simple sugars

amyl nitrite *n* $C_5H_{11}NO_2$ a pale yellow fragrant liquid. Use: inhalant to dilate blood vessels.

amylo-, **amyl-** *prefix* starch ○ *amylopectin* [< Latin *amylum* (see AMYL)]

amyloid /ámmi loyd/ *n* **1 WAXY PROTEIN** a waxy translucent substance composed of complex protein fibres and polysaccharides that is formed in body tissues in some degenerative diseases, e.g. Alzheimer's disease **2 STARCHY SUBSTANCE** a substance that resembles starch ■ *adj* **STARCHY** resembling a starch (*technical*)

amyloidosis /ámmi loy dṓssiss/ *n* a condition marked by the accumulation of a protein-based substance (**amyloid**) in the body's organs and tissues

amylopectin /ámmilō péktin/ *n* a branched polysaccharide that is an insoluble component of starch. ◊ **amylose**

amyloplast /ámmilō plaast, -plast/ *n* a microscopic sac, bound by a double membrane, that is found inside plant cells and contains starch granules

amylose /ámmi lōz, -lōss/ *n* an unbranched polysaccharide that is a soluble component of starch. ◊ **amylopectin**

amyotonia /áy mī ə tṓni ə/ *n* a medically significant lack of muscle tension

amyotrophic lateral sclerosis /ə mī ə trṓfik-, -tróffik-/ *n* a fatal degenerative disease of the nervous system marked by progressive muscle weakness and atrophy

amyotrophy /ámmi óttrəfi/ *n* a degeneration of the muscles caused by nerve disease [Late 19C. < A-[2] + MYO- + -TROPHY.]

an[1] (*stressed*) /an/; (*unstressed*) /ən/ *det* used instead of 'a', the indefinite article, in front of words with an initial vowel sound [Old English, stressless form of *ān* 'one']

USAGE See ***a***.

an[2] *abbr* Netherlands Antilles (*in Internet addresses*)

an[3] /an, ən/, **an'** *conj* if (*archaic*) [12C. Reduced form of AND 'if'.]

an- *prefix* = **a-**[2] *prefix.* (*before vowels*)

-an[1] *suffix* an unsaturated carbon compound ○ *benzofuran* [Alteration of -ANE]

-an[2] *suffix* **1** of or relating to ○ *Minoan* ○ *agrarian* **2** a person of or resembling a certain kind ○ *librarian* [Via Old French < Latin *-anus*]

ana[1] /aanə/ (*plural* **-a** *or* **-as**) *n* **1** a collection of things connected with a famous person, place, or period, especially spoken or written information, anecdotes, or sayings **2** an item in an ana

ana[2] /ánnə/ *adv* of each of the ingredients specified in a medical prescription in equal amounts [< Greek *ana-* 'up, back, again']

ana- *prefix* **1** up, upward ○ *anamorphic* **2** back, backward, away ○ *anaphase* **3** again ○ *anaplastic* [< Greek *ana.* Ultimately < Indo-European 'on', which is also the ancestor of English *on*.]

-ana *suffix* a collection of objects or information about a topic, person, or place ○ *Shakespeareana* [Via modern Latin < Latin, neuter plural of *-anus* 'relating to']

anabaptism /ánnə báptizəm/ *n* the advocacy of adult baptism on the grounds that only as adults can people responsibly accept and declare their faith [See ANABAPTISM]

Anabaptism *n* the doctrines or beliefs of the Anabaptists [Mid-16C. Via ecclesiastical Latin *anabaptismus* < Greek *anabaptismos* 'second baptism' < *baptismos* 'baptism'.]

Anabaptist /ánnə báptist/ *n* a member of a 16th-century Protestant movement promoting the doctrine of adult baptism on the grounds that only adults can accept and declare their faith on their own behalf [Mid-16C. < ecclesiastical Latin *anabaptista* < Greek *ana-* 'again, afresh' + *baptistēs* 'baptizer' (see BAPTIZE).] —**Anabaptist** *adj*

anabatic /ánnə báttik/ *adj* describes winds that move or blow upwards during the daytime as warm air rises up mountain slopes. ◊ **katabatic** [Mid-20C. < Greek *anabatikos* 'relating to mounting' < *anabainein* 'go up, mount' < *bainein* 'go'.]

anabolic /ánnə bóllik/ *adj* promoting tissue growth [Late 19C. Blend of ANA- + METABOLIC.]

anabolic steroid *n* **1** a synthetic steroid hormone. Use: to increase muscle mass and strength. **2** a naturally occurring hormone that promotes tissue growth

anabolism /ə nábbəlizəm/ *n* a metabolic process in which energy is used to make compounds and tissues from simple molecules [Late 19C. Blend of ANA- + METABOLISM.]

anabolite /ə nábbə līt/ *n* a substance resulting from anabolism

anabranch /ánnə braanch/ *n* a stream that separates from a river and follows its own course before re-entering the same river farther downstream [Mid-19C. Blend of *anastomosing* (< ANASTOMOSE) + BRANCH.]

anachronism /ə nákrənizəm/ *n* **1 CHRONOLOGICAL MISTAKE** something from a different period of time, e.g. a modern idea or invention wrongly placed in a historical setting in fiction or drama **2 SOMETHING OUT OF TIME** a person, thing, idea, or custom that seems to belong to a different time in history **3 MAKING OF CHRONOLOGICAL MISTAKE** the representation of somebody or something out of chronological order or in the wrong historical setting [Mid-17C. Via French *anachronisme* < late Greek *anakhronizesthai* 'be timed backwards' < *khronos* 'time'.] —**anachronous** *adj* —**anachronously** *adv*

anachronistic /ə nákrə nístik/ *adj* **1** belonging to a time other than the one being represented, especially in fiction or drama **2** out-of-date or inappropriate at the time in question —**anachronistically** *adv*

anaclitic /ánnə klíttik/ *adj* characterized by strong emotional dependence on a mother or other nurturing person, especially to the extent of exhibiting or causing serious developmental and psychological disturbances [Early 20C. < Greek *anaklitos* 'for reclining' < *anaklinein* 'lean upon' < *klinein* 'lean'.] —**anaclisis** /ánnə klīssiss/ *n*

anacoluthon /ánnəkə lóo thon, -lóoth'n/ (*plural* **-tha** /-lóothə/) *n* an instance of abandoning a grammatical construction in speech or writing before it is complete and continuing with another. The sentence 'The subject of the lecture was – I didn't really understand it' contains an anacoluthon. [Early 18C. Via late Latin < Greek *anakolouthon* 'illogicality, inconsistency' < *anakolouthos* 'not following' < *akolouthos* 'following'.] —**anacoluthic** *adj*

anaconda /ánnə kóndə/ *n* a nonvenomous snake, the largest in the boa family, that lives in or near water and in trees. Native to: South America. *Eunectes murinus.* [Mid-18C. < ?]

Anacreon /ə nákri on/ (570?–478 BC) Greek lyric poet

Anacreontic /ə nákri óntik/, **anacreontic** *adj* written in the style or treating the subjects of the Greek poet Anacreon [Early 17C. < Latin *Anacreonticus* < Greek *Anakreont-*, stem of *Anakreōn* 'Anacreon'.] —**Anacreontic** *n*

anacrusis /ánnə kroossiss/ (*plural* **-ses** /-seez/) *n* **1** one or more unstressed syllables at the beginning of a line of verse that are not considered part of the metrical pattern of the line **2** one or more unaccented notes immediately before the first downbeat of a bar of music [Mid-19C. < modern Latin, < Greek *anakrouein* 'strike up (a tune)' < *krouein* 'strike'.] —**anacrustic** /ánnə krústik/ *adj*

anadiplosis /ánnə di plṓssiss/ (*plural* **-ses** /-seez/) *n* the rhetorical repetition of the last word or words of one phrase or sentence at the beginning of the next [Late 16C. < Latin, < Greek *anadiploein* 'double back' < *diploein* 'double'.]

anadromous /ə náddrəməss/ *adj* describes fish such as salmon and shad that return from the sea to the rivers where they were born in order to breed. ◊ **catadromous** [Mid-18C. < Greek *anadromos* 'running up (a river from the sea)' < *dromos* 'a running'.]

anaemia /ə néemi ə/, **anemia** *n* **1** a blood condition in which there are too few red blood cells or the red blood cells are deficient in haemoglobin, resulting in poor health **2** lack of vitality or courage [Early 19C. Via modern Latin < Greek *anaimia* 'being without blood' < *haima* 'blood'.]

anaemic /ə néemik/, **anemic** *adj* **1 HAVING ANAEMIA** having some form of anaemia **2 SICK-LOOKING** pale and not looking well **3 WEAK** lacking vitality, strength, or courage —**anaemically** *adv*

anaerobe /ánnə rōb/ *n* a microorganism that does not require oxygen for metabolism [Late 19C. Back-formation < French *anaérobie* 'living without air' < Greek *an-* 'not' + French *aéro-* 'air' + Greek *bios* 'life'.]

anaerobic /ánnə rṓbik, án air-/ *adj* **1** living or taking place in the absence of oxygen, especially not requiring oxygen for metabolism **2** having or providing no oxygen —**anaerobically** *adv*

anaerobic process *n* a chemical or biological process such as decay or decomposition that does not require oxygen

anaerobic respiration *n* the production of energy without the presence of oxygen. ◊ **aerobic respiration**

anaerobiosis /ánnərō bī ṓssiss, án airō-/ *n* life in the absence of free or atmospheric oxygen [Late 19C. < ANAEROBIC + -BIOSIS.] —**anaerobiotic** /ánnərō bī óttik, án airō-/ *adj*

anaesthesia /ánnəss théezi ə/, **anesthesia** *n* **1 MEDICALLY INDUCED INSENSITIVITY TO PAIN** induced loss of sensitivity to pain in all or a part of the body for medical reasons **2 LOSS OF SENSATION** the loss of sensation caused by damage to a nerve **3 APATHY** a state of apathy or mindlessness [Early 18C. Via modern Latin < Greek *anaisthēsia* 'lack of sensation' < *aisthēsis* 'feeling, sensation' (see AESTHETIC).]

anaesthesiologist *n* US = **anaesthetist** *n.* 1

anaesthesiology *n* US= **anaesthetics**

anaesthetic /ánnəss théttik/, **anesthetic** *n* a substance that reduces sensitivity to pain and may cause unconsciousness, especially a drug used in medicine [Mid-19C. < Greek *anaisthētos* 'without feeling' < *aisthētos* 'capable of feeling' < *aisthesthai* (see AESTHESIA).] —**anaesthetic** *adj* —**anaesthetically** *adv*

anaesthetics /ánnəss théttiks/ *n* the medical study and application of anaesthetic substances. US term **anesthesiology**

anaesthetise *vt* SURG = **anaesthetize**

anaesthetist /ə néesthətist/, **anesthetist** *n* **1** a senior doctor who specializes in administering anaesthetics. US term **anesthesiologist** **2** *US* somebody qualified to administer anaesthetics, especially a nurse or technician

anaesthetize /ə néesthə tīz/ (**-tizes, -tizing, -tized**), **anesthetize** (**-tizes, -tizing, -tized**), **anaesthetise** /ə néesthətīz/ (**-tises, -tising, -tised**) *vt* to administer an anaesthetic to somebody —**anaesthetization** *n*

anaglyph /ánnə glif/ *n* **1** a decoration carved in low relief, so that the shape of the design projects only slightly from the background **2** a three-dimensional visual effect created by dyeing each of two images a different colour, usually red and green, and then viewing them through complementary-coloured filters, one over each eye [Late 16C. < Greek *anagluphē* 'low-relief sculpture' < *gluphein* 'carve'.] —**anaglyphic** /ánnə glíffik/ *adj* —**anaglyptic** /-glíptik/ *adj*

anagoge /ánnə gōji/, **anagogy** /ánnə gōji, -gogi/ (*plural* **-gies**) *n* **1** a spiritual or mystical interpretation of a word or passage, especially in a sacred text, in contrast to a literal or moral interpretation **2** an allegorical interpretation of a passage in the Bible as an allusion to or foreshadowing of people or events in the New Testament [18C. Via Latin < Greek *anagōgē* 'reference' < *anagein* 'take back' < *agein* 'take'.] —**anagogic** /ánnə gójjik/ *adj* —**anagogical** *adj* —**anagogically** *adv*

anagram /ánnə gram/ *n* a word or phrase that contains all the letters of another word or phrase in a different order [Late 16C. Directly or via French *anagramme* < modern Latin *anagramma*, probably < Greek *anagrammatismos* 'transposition of letters' < *anagrammatizein* (see ANAGRAMMATIZE).] —**anagrammatic** /ánnəgrə máttik/ *adj* —**anagrammatically** /ánnəgrə máttikli/ *adv*

anagrammatize /ánnə grámmə tīz/ (**-tizes, -tizing, -tized**), **anagrammatise** (**-tises, -tising, -tised**) *vt* to rearrange the letters of a word or phrase to form a different word or phrase [Late 16C. Perhaps < Greek *anagrammatizein* 'rearrange the letters of a word' < *gramma* 'letter'.]

Anaheim /ánnə hīm/ city in SW California, site of Disneyland. Population: 295,153 (1998 estimate).

anal /áyn'l/ *adj* **1 RELATING TO ANUS** relating to or situated near the anus **2 RELATING TO CHILDHOOD INTEREST IN DEFECATION** in Freudian theory, relating to a stage of childhood psychosexual development during which the focus is on the anal region and functions **3 OBSESSIVELY SELF-CONTROLLED** in Freudian theory, relating to adult personality traits, e.g. obsessive neatness, stubbornness, and meanness, that are considered to have originated during or be characteristic of the anal stage of development [Mid-18C. < modern Latin *analis* < *anus* (see ANUS).] —**anally** *adv*

anal. *abbr* **1** analogous **2** analogy **3** analysis **4** analytic

analcime /ə nál seem/, **analcite** /-sīt/ *n* a white or light-coloured form of the mineral zeolite composed of hydrated sodium aluminium silicate. Source: igneous rocks. [Early 19C. < French, < Greek *analkimos* 'not strong' (in reference to the mineral's weak electric current) < *alkimos* 'strong' < *alkē* 'strength'.] —**analcimic** /ánn'l símmik/ *adj*

analects /ánnə lekts/, **analecta** /ánnə léktə/ *npl* passages selected from one or more literary or philosophical works, especially when published as a collection [Early 17C. Via Latin < Greek *analekta* 'collected, or selected, things' < *analegein* 'gather up' < *legein* 'gather'.] —**analectic** /ánnə léktik/ *adj*

analemma /ánnə lémmə/ (*plural* **-mas** *or* **-mata** /-lémmətə/) *n* a scale, found on some sundials and globes, that is shaped like a figure eight and marked to indicate the declination of the sun and to allow the calculation of apparent solar time [Mid-17C. Via Latin, 'sundial, pedestal of a sundial' < Greek *analēmma* 'pedestal, support' < *analambanein* 'take up, support' < *lambanein* 'take'.]

analeptic /ánnə léptik/ *adj* restorative or invigorating, especially after an illness ■ *n* a drug that stimulates the central nervous system [Mid-17C. Via Latin < Greek *analēptikos* 'restorative' < *analambanein* (see ANALEMMA).]

analgesia /ánn'l jéezi ə/ *n* **1** the lack of sensibility to pain while somebody is conscious **2** treatment to control pain [Early 18C. Via modern Latin < Greek *analgēsia* 'lack of feeling, insensibility' < *algeein* 'feel pain' < *algos* 'pain'.] —**analgetic** /ánn'l jéttik/ *adj*

analgesic /ánn'l jéezik/ *adj* describes a type of medication that alleviates pain without loss of consciousness —**analgesic** *n*

anal intercourse *n* a form of sexual intercourse in which a man puts his penis into the anus of a man or woman

⚡**analog** /ánnə log/ *n* US CHEM = **analogue** *n.* 3 ■ *adj* US COMPUT = **analogue** *adj.* [Mid-20C. Variant.]

analogical /ánnə lójjik'l/ *adj* relating to or working by means of analogy [Late 16C. Directly or via French *analogique* < Latin *analogicus* < Greek *analogikos* < *analogos* (see ANALOGOUS).] —**analogically** *adv*

analogise *vti* = **analogize**

analogize /ə nállə jīz/ (**-gizes, -gizing, -gized**), **analogise** (**-gises, -gising, -gised**) *v* **1** *vt* to compare two things that are similar in some respects, especially in order to explain something or to support an argument **2** *vi* to make use of an analogy

analogous /ə nállagəss/ *adj* **1** similar in some respects, allowing an analogy to be drawn **2** describes body parts and organs that have equivalent functions but that appear to be independent of one another in different plants or animals. The wings of birds, bats, and insects are analogous. [Mid-17C. Via French *analogue* or Latin *analogus* < Greek *analogos* < *analogon* 'in due ratio' < *ana* 'according to' + *logos* 'ratio'.] —**analogously** *adv* —**analogousness** *n*

USAGE ***Analogous***, correctly used, should include a notion of *analogy*, that is of similarity in some particular respects: *The Commission has set up guidelines for broadcasters that are analogous to those for journalists.* It is better to avoid ***analogous*** when the comparison is only general and when more straightforward words such as *similar, equivalent, comparable*, or *corresponding* serve just as well, as in *The new system is comparable* [not *analogous*] *to that used in the electronics industry.*

⚡**analogue** /ánnə log/ *n* **1 CORRESPONDING THING** a thing, idea, or institution that is similar to or has the same function as another ○ *'They had no exact analogue for our word "home", any more than they had for our Roman-based "family".'* (Charlotte Perkins Gilman, *Herland*; 1915) **2 EQUIVALENT BUT INDEPENDENT ORGAN** a body part or organ that has an equivalent function to one in a different plant or animal but that appeared independently **3 SIMILAR CHEMICAL** a chemical with a similar structure to another but differing slightly in composition. US term **analog** *n.* **4 FOOD SUBSTITUTE** a food or dish made to resemble another by the substitution of inferior ingredients ■ *adj* **USING PHYSICAL REPRESENTATION** relating to a system or device that represents data variation by a measurable physical entity. US term **analog** *adj.* ◊ **digital** *adj.* 1 [Early 19C. Via French < Greek *analogon* (see ANALOGOUS).]

analogue clock *n* a clock that shows the time by means of hands on a dial

⚡**analogue computer** *n* a computer that uses a variable physical quantity such as voltage to represent data

analogue watch *n* a watch that shows the time by means of hands on a dial

analogy /ə nálləji/ (*plural* **-gies**) *n* **1 COMPARISON** a comparison between two things that are similar in some specific respects, often used to help explain something or make it easier to understand **2 SIMILARITY** a similarity in some respects **3 EQUIVALENCE BETWEEN INDEPENDENT PARTS** equivalence in biological function between body parts or organs that have appeared independently in different plants and animals **4 FORM OF REASONING** a form of logical inference, reasoning that if two things are taken to be alike in a particular way, they are alike in certain other ways **5 STANDARDIZATION OF LINGUISTIC FORMS** the development or production of linguistic forms and patterns that resemble those already predominating in a language [15C. Via French *analogie* or Latin *analogia* < Greek *analogia* 'proportion' < *analogos* (see ANALOGOUS).]

analphabetic /án alfə béttik, an álfə-/ *adj* **1 NOT ALPHABETICAL** not in alphabetical order (*formal*) **2 ILLITERATE** not knowing how to read or write (*formal*) **3 NOT OF ALPHABET** not belonging to or concerning an alphabet ■ *n* **1 PRINTING CHARACTER** a typographical character used with the alphabet but not part of its order, e.g. a punctuation mark **2 ILLITERATE PERSON** somebody who cannot read or write (*formal*) [Late 19C. < Greek *analphabētos* 'not knowing the alphabet' < *alphabētos* 'alphabet'.]

anal-retentive *adj* = **anal** *adj.* 3 —**anal retention** *n* —**anal-retentive** *n* —**anal-retentiveness** *n*

anal sex *n* = **anal intercourse**

analysand /ə nálli sand/ *n* somebody who is undergoing psychoanalysis [Mid-20C. < ANALYSE, after *operand*.]

analyse /ánnə līz/ (**-lyses, -lysing, -lysed**), **analyze** (**-lyzes, -lyzing, -lyzed**) *vt* **1 BREAK DOWN INTO COMPONENTS** to find out what something is made up of by identifying its constituent parts **2 EXAMINE STRUCTURE** to study or examine the structure of something or how its constituent parts are put together **3 STUDY CLOSELY** to examine something in great detail in order to understand it better or discover more about it **4 EXPRESS BY USING FUNCTION WORDS** to express grammatical relationships by using function words or word order rather than inflectional endings **5** = **psychoanalyse** [Early 17C. Perhaps back-formation < ANALYSIS, or < French *analyse* 'analysis' used as a verb; reinforced by French *analyser* 'analyse'.] —**analysable** *adj* —**analysation** /ánnə lī záysh'n/ *n* —**analyser** *n*

analysis /ə nállississ/ (*plural* **-ses** /-seez/) *n* **1 SEPARATION INTO COMPONENTS** the separation of something into its constituents in order to find out what it contains, to examine individual parts, or to study the structure of the whole **2 LIST OF PARTS** a statement giving details of all the constituent elements of something and how they relate to each other **3 CLOSE EXAMINATION** the examination of something in detail in order to understand it better or draw conclusions from it **4 ASSESSMENT** an assessment, description, or explanation of something, usually based on careful consideration or investigation **5 BRANCH OF MATHEMATICS** the branch of mathematics dealing with differential calculus, functions, and limits **6 WAY OF EXPRESSING GRAMMATICAL RELATIONSHIPS** the use of function words or word order, rather than inflectional forms, to express grammatical relationships in a language **7** = **psychoanalysis** *n.* 2 [Late 16C. Via medieval Latin < Greek *analusis* 'a breaking up into elements' < *analuein* 'unloose, dissolve into elements' < *luein* 'loosen'.] ◇ **in the final** *or* **last analysis** used to introduce or indicate a summary conclusion to a complex subject

analysis of variance *n* the analysis of the difference in outcomes of an experiment to determine the factors contributing to the variations

analyst /ánnəlist/ *n* **1** somebody with specialist knowledge or skill who studies or examines something and gives an assessment **2** a person who practises psychoanalysis [Mid-17C. < French *analyste* < *analyse* 'analysis' (see ANALYSE).]

analytic /ánnə líttik/, **analytical** /-líttik'l/ *adj* **1 OF ANALYSIS** connected with or involving analysis **2 USING ANALYSIS** able or inclined to separate things into their constituent elements in order to study or examine them, draw conclusions, or solve problems **3 TRUE BY MEANING ALONE** true by definition or by virtue of the meaning of the words used **4 DIFFERENTIABLE AT ALL POINTS IN DOMAIN** describes a function of a complex variable that is differentiable at all points in its domain **5 USING FUNCTION WORDS** expressing grammatical relationships by means of function words or word order rather than inflections [Late 16C. Via late Latin < Greek *analutikos* < *analuein* (see ANALYSIS).] —**analytically** *adv*

analytical balance *n* an accurate scale used in laboratories for weighing minute objects or quantities

⚡**analytical engine** *n* a programmable calculating machine, the forerunner of the modern computer, invented by Charles Babbage in 1833

analytical geometry, analytic geometry *n* a branch of mathematics dealing with geometric properties using algebraic operations and notation to locate points within a coordinate system

analytical philosophy, analytic philosophy *n* a 20th-century philosophy primarily concerned with resolving philosophical problems through the analysis and clarification of language

analytical psychology, analytic psychology *n* a system of psychoanalysis based on the psychological theories of Carl Jung

analytical reagent *n* a chemical virtually free of impurities

analytic geometry *n* = **analytical geometry**

analytic philosophy *n* = **analytical philosophy**

analytic psychology *n* = **analytical psychology**

analytics /ánnə líttiks/ *n* the branch of logic involved with the analysis of propositions (+ *singular or plural verb*)

analyze *vt* = **analyse**

anamnesis /án am néessiss/ (*plural* **-ses** /-seez/) *n* the medical history of a patient, especially in the patient's own words [Late 16C. < Greek, 'remembrance' < *anamimnēskein* 'call back to mind' < *mimnēskein* 'call to mind'.]

anamnestic /án am néstik/ *adj* showing a secondary immunological response to an antigen at some time after initial immunization [Early 18C. < Greek *anamnēstikos* < *anamimnēskein* (see ANAMNESIS).] —**anamnestically** *adv*

anamorphic /ánnə máwrfik/ *adj* relating to or producing image distortion caused by unequal magnification along different perpendicular axes

anamorphosis /ánnə mawr fóssiss, -máwrfəssiss/ (*plural* **-ses** /-seez/) *n* **1** a distorted image or drawing of a distorted image that appears normal when viewed with or reflected from a special device **2** the process of making distorted images by means of special mirrors or other devices [Mid-18C. < Greek, 'transformation' < *anamorphoein* 'change shape again' < *morphoein* 'change shape' < *morphē* 'shape'.]

Ananke /ə nángki/ *n* a small natural satellite of Jupiter, discovered in 1951

anapaest /ánnə peest, -pest/, **anapest** *n* a metrical foot of three syllables with the stress on the third syllable, or of two short syllables followed by a long syllable [Late 16C. Via Latin < Greek *anapaistos* 'struck backwards' (from its being a reversed dactyl), past participle of *anapaiein* < *paiein* 'strike'.] —**anapaestic** /ánnə péestik, -pést-/ *adj*

anaphase /ánnə fayz/ *n* a late stage of cell division during which chromosomes move to the poles of the spindle. ◊ **prophase, metaphase, telophase**

anaphora /ə náffərə/ *n* **1 REFERRING BACK** reference to a word or phrase used earlier, especially to avoid repeating the word or phrase by replacing it with something else such as a pronoun. In the sentence 'I told Paul to close the door and he did so', the clause 'he did so' makes use of anaphora. **2 REPETITION FOR EFFECT** the use of the same word or phrase at the beginning of several successive clauses, sentences, lines, or verses, usually for emphasis or rhetorical effect. 'She didn't speak. She didn't stand. She didn't even look up when we came in' is an example of anaphora. (*formal*) **3 PART OF COMMUNION** the offering of the bread and wine in Communion [Late 16C. Via Latin < Greek, 'reference, repetition' < *anapherein* 'carry back' < *pherein* 'carry'.] —**anaphoric** /ánnə fórrik/ *adj* —**anaphorically** *adv*

anaphoresis /ánnə fə réessiss/ *n* the movement towards the anode of suspended particles in solution

anaphrodisia /án affrə dízzi ə/ *n* absence or reduction of sexual desire [20C. < Greek, 'inability to inspire love' < *aphrodisia* (see APHRODISIAC).]

anaphrodisiac /án affrə dízzi ak/ *adj* tending to reduce sexual desire [Early 19C. < Greek *an-* 'not' + *aphrodisiakos* (see APHRODISIAC).] —**anaphrodisiac** *n*

anaphylactic /ánnəfi láktik/ *adj* relating to or caused or characterized by extreme sensitivity to a substance (**anaphylaxis**) —**anaphylactically** *adv*

anaphylactic shock *n* a sudden severe and potentially fatal allergic reaction in somebody sensitive to a particular substance, marked by a drop in blood pressure, difficulty in breathing, itching, and swelling

anaphylaxis /ánnəfi láksiss/ *n* **1** extreme sensitivity to a particular substance such as a specific protein or drug **2** MED = **anaphylactic shock** [Early 20C. < modern Latin < Greek *ana-* 'again' (because a substance is reintroduced) + *-phylaxis* 'guarding, watching'.] —**anaphylactoid** *adj*

anaplasia /ánnə pláyzi ə/ *n* the reversion of cells, usually within a tumour, to a simpler or less differentiated form

anaplastic /ánnə plástik/ *adj* relating to or characterized by the loss of distinctive cell features (**anaplasia**)

anaptyxis /ánnap tíksiss/ *n* the insertion of a weak vowel sound between two consonants in order to make a word or phrase easier to pronounce [Late 19C. Via modern Latin < Greek *anaptuxis* 'an unfolding' < *anaptussein* 'unfold' < *ptussein* 'fold'.]

anarchic /an áarkik, ən-/, **anarchical** /-kik'l/ *adj* **1 LAWLESS** showing no respect for established laws, rules, institutions, or authority **2 CHAOTIC** characterized by a lack of organization or control **3 ENCOURAGING ANARCHY** likely to cause the overthrow of a formal system of government or a breakdown of law and order —**anarchically** *adv*

anarchism /ánnər kizəm/ *n* **1 DOCTRINE REJECTING GOVERNMENT** an ideology that rejects the need for a system of government in society and proposes its abolition **2 ACTIONS OF ANARCHISTS** behaviour intended to overthrow or weaken a society's formal system of government **3 RESISTANCE TO CONTROL** resistance to all forms of authority or control

anarchist /ánnərkist/ *n* **1** somebody who believes that governments should be abolished as unnecessary **2** somebody who tries to overthrow a government or behaves in a lawless way (*disapproving*) —**anarchistic** /ánnər kístik/ *adj*

anarchy /ánnərki/ *n* **1** the absence of any formal system of government in a society **2** a situation in which there is a total lack of organization or control [Mid-16C. Via medieval Latin < Greek *anarkhia* < *anarkhos* 'without a ruler' < *arkhos* 'ruler'.]

anarthria /an áarthri ə/ *n* the loss of the ability to articulate words [Late 19C. Via modern Latin < Greek < *anarthros* 'inarticulate, disjointed' < *arthron* 'joint'.] —**anarthric** *adj*

anarthrous /an áarthrəss/ *adj* used or occurring without a definite or indefinite article [Early 19C. < Greek *anarthros* 'not articulated' < *arthron* 'article, joint'.]

anasarca /ánnə sáarkə/ *n* the accumulation of watery fluid in connective tissue and cavities, resulting in swelling (**oedema**) [14C. Via medieval Latin < Greek *anasarx*, describing oedema, < *ana sarka* 'throughout the flesh'.] —**anasarcous** *adj*

Anastasia /ánnə stáyzi ə, -staázi ə/, **Grand Duchess** (1901–18). daughter of Tsar Nicholas II.

anastigmat /an ástig mat, ánnə stíg mat/ *n* a lens or combination of lenses free from astigmatism [Late 19C. < German, back-formation < *anastigmatisch* 'anastigmatic' < Greek *stigmat-* 'point'.]

anastigmatic /ánnə stig máttik/ *adj* describes a lens that is corrected for or free from astigmatism

anastomose /ə nástə mōz, -stə mōss/ (**-moses, -mosing, -mosed**) *vt* to join blood vessels or other tubular parts in a surgical operation (**anastomosis**) [Late 17C. Probably back-formation < ANASTOMOSIS.]

anastomosis /ə nástə mṓssiss/ (*plural* **-ses** /-seez/) *n* **1 NATURAL JOINT** the connection or place of connection of two or more parts of a natural branching system, e.g. of blood vessels, leaf veins, stems of woody plants, or rivers **2 SURGICAL UNION OF TUBULAR PARTS** the surgical union of two hollow organs, e.g. blood vessels or parts of the intestine, to ensure continuity of the passageway **3 NETWORK OF FUNGAL FILAMENTS** a fusion between fungal filaments (**hyphae**) to form a network [Early 17C. Via modern Latin < Greek, 'outlet, opening, interconnection of openings' < *anastomoein* 'supply with a mouth or opening' < *stoma* 'mouth'.] —**anastomotic** /ə nástə móttik/ *adj*

anastrophe /ə nástrəfi/ *n* an alteration of the normal order of words or phrases in a grammatical construction, usually for rhetorical effect. Coleridge's 'The helmsman steered; the ship moved on; yet never a breeze up blew' ends with an anastrophe. [Mid-16C. < Greek, 'a turning back, inversion' < *stroph-*, stem of *strephein* 'turn'.]

anat. *abbr* **1** anatomical **2** anatomy

anatase /ánnə tayz/ *n* a blue or yellowish-brown mineral consisting of titanium dioxide. Source: igneous rocks. [Early 19C. Via French < Greek *anatasis* 'extension' (from the elongated crystals) < *teinein* 'stretch'.]

anathema /ə náthəmə/ *n* **1 OBJECT OF LOATHING** somebody or something that is greatly disliked or detested and is therefore shunned **2 ECCLESIASTICAL CURSE** a curse from a religious authority that denounces something or excommunicates somebody **3 GENERAL CURSE** any forceful curse or denunciation **4 SOMEBODY OR SOMETHING FORMALLY DENOUNCED** somebody or something cursed, denounced, or excommunicated by a religious authority [Early 16C. Via ecclesiastical Latin < Greek, 'something devoted to evil' < *anatithenai* 'set up'.]

anathematize /ə náthəmə tīz/ (**-tizes, -tizing, -tized**), **anathematise** (**-tises, -tising, -tised**) *vti* to formally curse, denounce, or excommunicate somebody or something [Mid-16C. Via ecclesiastical Latin *anathematizare* 'ban, curse' < Greek *anathematizein* 'dedicate to evil' < *anathemat-*, stem of *anathema* (see ANATHEMA).] —**anathematization** /ə náthəmə tī záysh'n/ *n*

Anatolia /ánnə tṓli ə/ *n* the Asian part of Turkey —**Anatolian** *n, adj*

Anatolian Plateau mountainous region extending across much of Turkey. Highest peak: Mount Erciyes 3,916 m/12,848 ft.

anatomical /ánnə tómmik'l/, **anatomic** /-tómmik/ *adj* relating to or showing the physical structure of animals or plants —**anatomically** *adv*

anatomically correct *adj* having an accurate representation of the genitals and other bodily details

anatomical position *n* the standard position of the body in the study of anatomy from which all directions and positions are derived and in which the body is assumed to be standing, the feet together, the arms to the side, and the head, eyes, and palms facing forward

anatomise *vt* = **anatomize**

anatomize /ə náttə mīz/ (**-mizes, -mizing, -mized**), **anatomise** (**-mises, -mising, -mised**) *vt* **1** = **dissect** *v.* **1** **2** to analyse or examine something in great detail, thus revealing features that are not obvious —**anatomization** /ə náttə mī záysh'n/ *n*

anatomy /ə náttəmi/ (*plural* **-mies**) *n* **1 STUDY OF STRUCTURE OF BODY** the branch of science that studies the physical structure of animals, plants, and other organisms **2 PHYSICAL STRUCTURE OF ORGANISM** the physical structure, especially the internal structure, of an animal, plant, or other organism, or of any of its parts **3 BOOK ABOUT ANATOMY** a book or other written work about the physical structure of animals, plants, or other organisms **4 BODY** the human body (*informal*) **5 ANALYSIS** a detailed analysis of something [14C. Via French *anatomie* and late Latin *anatomia* < Greek *anatomē* 'cutting up' < *temnein* 'cut'.] —**anatomist** *n*

anatropous /ə náttrəpəss/ *adj* describes a plant ovule that has bent during development so that its tip faces its point of attachment to the ovary wall

Anaxagoras /á nak sággərəss/ (500?–428 BC) Greek philosopher

Anaximander /ə náksi mándər/ (611?–547? BC) Greek philosopher

Anaximenes /á nak símmə neez/ (570?–500? BC) Greek philosopher

ANC *n* a South African political party founded in 1912 that fought against apartheid and formed South Africa's first multiracial, democratically elected government in 1994. Full form **African National Congress**

ancestor /án sestər, ánsəstər/ *n* **1 DISTANT RELATION SOMEBODY IS DESCENDED FROM** somebody from whom somebody else is directly descended, especially somebody more distant than a grandparent **2 FORERUNNER** a predecessor of somebody, e.g. in the development of a certain art form **3 EARLIER SPECIES** an animal or plant from which a species has evolved **4 EARLIER MODEL** a device that was an earlier form of a modern invention or was used as a basis for developing it [14C. Via Old French *ancestre* < Latin *antecessor* 'somebody who goes before' < *cess-*, past participle of *cedere* 'give way'.]

ancestral /an séstrəl/ *adj* relating to something belonging to former generations of somebody's family [15C. < Old French *ancestrel* < *ancestre* (see ANCESTOR).] —**ancestrally** *adv*

ancestry /án sestri, ánsəs-/ *n* somebody's ancestors regarded as a line linking the modern generation to its past [14C. Alteration of Old French *ancesserie* < *ancessour* < Latin *antecessor* (see ANCESTOR).]

Anchises /an kī́ seez/ *n* in Greek and Roman mythology, a Trojan prince and the father of Aeneas by the goddess Aphrodite

anchor /ángkər/ *n* **1 DEVICE TO HOLD SHIP IN PLACE** a heavy, traditionally double-hooked, device for keeping a ship or floating object in place **2 DEVICE KEEPING OBJECT IN PLACE** any device that keeps an object in place **3 SOMETHING DEPENDABLE** somebody who or something that provides stability ○ *She was my anchor during the crisis.* **4 PRESENTER OF NEWS PROGRAMME** a presenter on a news programme, providing links between the studio and reporters based outside. ◊ **anchorman, anchorwoman 5 SOMEBODY POSITIONED LAST** the team member who is responsible for the last leg in a relay race or who is at the back in a tug of war **6 SOMETHING CLIMBER IS TIED TO** a rock feature, piton, or other feature to which a climber is tied ■ *adj* **ATTACHING** used for securing or connecting something ■ *v* **1** *vt* **HOLD SOMETHING IN PLACE** to hold something securely in place **2** *vti* **PUT DOWN ANCHOR** to moor a ship by lowering its anchor so that it remains stationary in a particular place ○ *The vessel was anchored off the Nigerian coast.* **3** *vt* **BE NEWS PROGRAMME'S PRESENTER** to be the presenter on a news programme [Pre-12C. Via Latin *ancora* < Greek *agkura*.] ◇ **at anchor** held on the water by an anchor

anchorage /ángkərij/ *n* **1 PLACE TO HOLD BOATS SECURE** a place in or near a harbour where boats are moored **2 CHARGE FOR ANCHORING BOAT** a charge for anchoring a boat in a harbour **3 SOMETHING HOLDING OBJECT IN PLACE** any device used to hold an object in place **4 ANCHORING** the securing of a ship with an anchor **5 SECURITY** a source of stability, or a stable condition

Anchorage /ánkərij/ port in S Alaska. Population: 253,649 (1994).

anchorite /ángkə rīt/ *n* somebody who lives a reclusive life of prayer [15C. Via medieval Latin *anc(h)orita* < ecclesiastical Greek *anakhōrētēs* < Greek *anakhōrein* 'withdraw' < *ana-* 'away' + *khōrein* 'move'.]

anchorman /ángkər man/ (*plural* **-men** /-men/) *n* **1** a man or boy who is the anchor in a relay race or for a tug-of-war team **2** a man who is an anchor for a news programme

anchorperson /ángkər purss'n/ (*plural* **-persons** *or* **-people**) *n* BROADCAST = **anchor** *n.* 4

anchorwoman /ángkər wòomən/ (*plural* **-en** /-wimmin/) *n* **1** a woman or girl who is the anchor in a relay race or for a tug-of-war team **2** a woman who is an anchor for a news programme

anchovy /ánchəvi, an chṓvi/ (*plural* **-vies** *or* **-vy**) *n* **1** a small silvery sea fish that travels in large schools. Family: Engraulidae. **2** the flesh of an anchovy as food, often sold salted and canned in oil [Late 16C. < Spanish *anchova*.]

ancien régime /aàN syaN ray zheém/ (*plural* **anciens régimes** /aàN syaN ray zheém/) *n* **1** the political and social system of France before the revolution of 1789 **2** an outmoded system, method, or way of life [Late 18C. < French, 'old regime'.]

ancient /áynshənt/ *adj* **1 OF DISTANT PAST** belonging to the distant past, especially to the time before the collapse of the Western Roman Empire in AD 476 **2 OLD** very old ■ *n* **1 SOMEBODY FROM PAST CIVILIZATION** a member of a civilization of the distant past **2 SOMEBODY OF ADVANCED YEARS** a very mature or venerable person ■ **ancients** *npl* **1 PEOPLE OF ANCIENT WESTERN CIVILIZATIONS** the people who lived in one of the ancient civilizations, especially Greece and Rome **2 ANCIENT GREEK AND ROMAN AUTHORS** the authors of ancient Greece and Rome, whose writings form the basis of the classics as a subject of study [14C. Via French *ancien* < assumed Vulgar Latin *anteanus* < Latin *ante* 'before'.] —**anciently** *adv* —**ancientness** *n*

Ancient Greek *n* the forms of the Greek language spoken from about 1500 BC to about AD 500

ancient history *n* **1** the study of the cultures of the distant past, especially those of Greece and Rome **2** things that happened a long time ago (*informal*)

ancient lights *n* the legal right to receive daylight through windows (+ *singular verb*)

Ancient Mariner *n* somebody who tends to talk at length (*informal humorous*) ◊ **mariner** [From the title of the poem by Samuel Taylor Coleridge]

ancient monument *n* a building or part of a building, usually dating from at least medieval times, that is preserved and protected by law

Ancient of Days *n* a name for God, used in the King James Bible (Daniel 7:9) [Translation of Latin *antiquus dierum*]

ancillary /an síllәri/ *adj* **1 PROVIDING SUPPORT** providing support for somebody or something, e.g. nontechnical assistance to people who work in an industry or profession **2 SUBORDINATE** in a position of lesser importance ■ *n* (*plural* **-ies**) **1 SUBORDINATE PART** a subordinate part or element, e.g. a branch of an organization **2 NONTECHNICAL SUPPORT EMPLOYEE** a worker who provides nontechnical assistance or support to the core workers in an industry or profession [Mid-17C. < Latin *ancillaris* < *ancilla* 'handmaid', feminine of *anculus* 'manservant'.]

ancylostomiasis /ángki lōstə mī́ əssiss, ánssi-/, **ankylostomiasis** /ángki-/ *n* a tropical disease caused by infestation of the small intestine by hookworms, with symptoms of anaemia and tiredness [Late 19C. < modern Latin *Ancyclostoma*, genus of hookworms < Greek *agkulos* 'hooked' + *stoma* 'mouth'.]

and (*stressed*) /and/; (*unstressed*) /ənd, ən/ CORE MEANING: a conjunction used to indicate an additional thing, situation, or fact. 'And' in this case links words and phrases of the same grammatical value. ○ *a sister and two brothers* ○ *We need to clean the house and pack our suitcases.* ○ *switching back and forth between different systems*
conj **1 THEN** used to link two verbs or statements about events to indicate that the second follows the first ○ *Just add water and stir.* **2 AS A RESULT** used to introduce a situation or event that is a consequence of something just mentioned ○ *Their work was excellent and won several awards.* **3 USED TO STRESS REPETITION OR CONTINUITY** used to link identical words or phrases in order to emphasize repetition or continuity ○ *It gets better and better.* **4 PLUS** used to link two numbers or quantities to indicate that they are to be added together ○ *One and one are two.* **5 BUT** used to introduce a contrasting statement ○ *My dentist says to eat fruit and avoid refined sugar.* **6 MOREOVER** used to introduce a statement that continues or adds weight to a statement just made ○ *Kim needed clothes, and I hadn't been paid in weeks.* **7 USED TO CONNECT IDEAS** used to connect clauses or sentences, especially in spoken conversation ○ *I like Pierre, the head waiter, but the work's hard. And the hours are very long.* **8 INDICATES AN INFINITIVE VERB** used instead of 'to' before an infinitive verb, usually with verbs such as 'try', 'go', and 'come' (*informal*) ○ *I usually try and visit her once a week.* **9 IF** used to introduce a conditional clause (*archaic*) ○ *and it please you* [Old English *and, ond* < Germanic] ◇ **and (all) that** and everything else that is similar or included (*informal*) ○ *I've painted the doors and window frames and all that.* ◇ **and how** used to show strong agreement with or to emphasize something that has just been said (*informal*)

USAGE The notion that ***and*** should not be used at the beginning of a sentence arose from too literal an understanding of the 'joining' function of conjunctions. The same objection is also raised with regard to *but*. If initial ***and*** is overdone, the effect is of poor style, but it is not a matter of grammatical correctness. Using ***and*** at the beginning of a sentence can often be an effective way of drawing attention to what follows: *'You can't get away with this', he threatened. And we knew he meant it.*

ϟ **AND** /and/ *n* **1** a binary operator in Boolean algebra whose result is true if both its operands are true and false otherwise **2 AND, AND circuit** a logic circuit, used especially in computers, that gives a high-voltage output if its input carries a low voltage and a low-voltage output otherwise [Mid-20C. < AND.]

Andalusia /ándə lòozi ə/ autonomous region of S Spain bordered by the Mediterranean Sea and the Atlantic Ocean. Population: 6,940,522 (1991). Area: 87,268 sq. km/33,694 sq. mi. Spanish **Andalucía** —**Andalusian** *adj, n*

andalusite /ándə lòo sīt/ *n* a precious stone in various colours composed of aluminium silicate. Use: gems. [Early 19C. After ANDALUSIA.]

Andaman Islands /ándəmən-/ northern part of the Indian union territory of the Andaman and Nicobar Islands, between the Bay of Bengal and the Andaman Sea. Population: 240,089 (1991). Area: 6,500 sq. km/2,500 sq. mi.

andante /an dánti, -tay/ *adj, adv* at a moderate musical tempo but slower than moderato (*musical direction*) ■ *n* a title given to certain musical pieces or movements that are to be played andante [Early 18C. < Italian, 'walking', present participle of *andare* 'go, walk'.]

andantino /án dan teé nō/ *adj, adv* at a moderate musical tempo slightly faster than andante (*musical direction*) ■ *n* (*plural* **-nos**) a title given to certain musical pieces or movements that are to be played andantino [Early 19C. < Italian, 'little andante'.]

Andean-Equatorial *n* a family of Native South American languages, one of whose main branches is Tupi-Guarani —**Andean-Equatorial** *adj*

Andean margin *n* an area of tectonic plate convergence along the Andes Mountain Range, characterized by thicker than normal crust and high mountains

Andersen /ándərs'n/**, Hans Christian** (1805–75) Danish writer

Anderson /ándərss'n/**, Elizabeth Garrett** (1836–1917) British physician

Anderson, John (1893–1962) Scottish-born Australian philosopher

Anderson, Laurie (*b.* 1947) US composer and performance artist

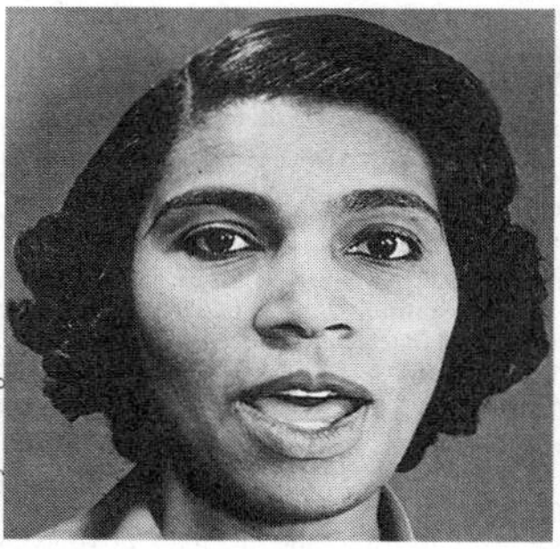

Library of Congress

Marian Anderson

Anderson, Marian (1897–1993) US contralto

Anderson, Philip W. (*b.* 1923) US physicist. Full name **Philip Warren Anderson**

Anderson shelter *n* a small arch of corrugated metal designed to act as a shelter during air raids in World War II [Mid-20C. After its designer, David A. *Anderson*, but popularly associated with British Home Secretary Sir John Anderson.]

Andersson /ándərss'n/**, Adolf** (1818–79) Prussian chess master

Andes /án deez/ South American mountain system extending along the west coast from Panama to Tierra del Fuego. Highest peak: Aconcagua 6,960 m/22,835 ft. —**Andean** /ándi ən/ *adj, n*

andesine /ándi zeen, -zin/ *n* a hard colourless mineral of the feldspar group. Source: andesite. [Because found in the ANDES]

andesite /ándi zīt/ *n* a fine-grained greyish volcanic rock characterized by feldspar minerals [Because found in the ANDES] —**andesitic** /ándi zíttik/ *adj*

Andhra Pradesh /ándrəprə désh/ state in SE India. Capital: Hyderabad. Population: 71,800,000 (1994). Area: 275,045 sq. km/106,195 sq. mi.

Andes

andiron /ánd ī ərn/ n either of a pair of metal stands used to hold logs in a fireplace [14C. Alteration (influenced by IRON) of Old French *andier* < Celtic.]

andolan /áan dōlən/ n S Asia an angry protest or other act of opposition by a group of people

and/or /ánd áwr/ conj a short way of saying that either or both of two options may be valid ○ *Bring mosquito netting and/or insect repellent.*

USAGE When to use **and/or**. *And/or* is a useful device to express three possibilities in a concise form: *A and/or B* gives the three possibilities A only, B only, or both A and B. On the other hand, since it is not a particularly elegant expression, it is usually more appropriate to legal and business contexts. An alternative that is often preferable in general contexts is *A or B or both*.

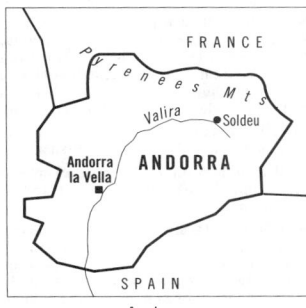

Andorra

Andorra /an dáwrə/ principality between France and Spain. Capital: Andorra la Vella. Population: 64,000 (1997). Area: 468 sq. km / 181 sq. mi. —**Andorran** *adj, n*

Andorra la Vella /-lə véllə/ capital of Andorra. Population: 21,985 (1996 estimate).

andouille /on doō i, aaN dwée/ n a black-skinned French sausage (**chitterlings**) [Early 17C. < French.]

andr- *prefix* = **andro-** (before vowels)

andradite /ándrə dīt/ n a variously coloured precious stone that is a type of garnet consisting of calcium iron silicate. Use: gems. [Mid-19C. After José Bonifácio de Andrada e Silva.]

Andre /áan dray/, **Carl** (b. 1935) US sculptor

Andreessen /an dráyss'n/, **Marc** (b. 1970) US computer scientist

Andreotti /án dray ótti/, **Giulio** (b. 1919) Italian statesman and seven-time Italian prime minister

Andrew /án drooʹ/, **Prince, Duke of York** (b. 1960). second son of Queen Elizabeth II and Prince Philip, Duke of Edinburgh.

Andrew, St (d. AD 60) apostle and saint

Andrewes /án drooz/, **Lancelot** (1555–1626) English Anglican bishop and writer

Andrews /án drooz/, **Julie** (b. 1935) British-born US actor and singer. Born **Julia Elizabeth Wells**

andro-, andr- *prefix* male, masculine ○ *androgen* [< Greek, < *andr-*, stem of *anēr* 'man']

Androcles /ándrə kleez/ n a legendary Roman slave who was forced to fight a lion, which spared his life after recognizing Androcles as the man who had once removed a thorn from its paw

androecium /an drèessi əm/ (*plural* **-a** /-ə/) n the set of stamens in a single flower [Mid-19C. < modern Latin < Greek *andro-* 'man, male' + *oikion* 'house'.] —**androecial** *adj*

androgen /ándrəjən/ n a natural or artificial male sex hormone responsible for the development of male sexual characteristics —**androgenic** /ándrə jénnik/ *adj*

androgenize /an drójjə nīz/ (**-nizes, -nizing, -nized**), **androgenise** (**-nises, -nising, -nised**) *vt* to cause a female to acquire some male sexual characteristics —**androgenization** /an drójjə nī záysh'n/ n

androgyne /ándrə jīn/ n 1 somebody who seems to have both male and female sexual characteristics 2 BIOL = **hermaphrodite** n. 1 [Mid-16C. Via French and Latin < Greek *androgunos* < *andro-* 'man' + *gunē* 'woman']

androgynous /an drójjənəss/ *adj* 1 neither male nor female in appearance but having both conventional masculine and feminine traits and giving an impression of ambiguous sexual identity 2 describes a plant species in which both male and female flowers occur in the same flower head 3 PHYSIOL = **hermaphrodite** *adj.* [Early 17C. < Latin *androgynus* 'hermaphrodite' (see ANDROGYNE).] —**androgynously** *adv* —**androgyny** n

android /án droyd/ n in science fiction, a robot that looks and behaves like a human being [Early 18C. < modern Latin *androides* < Greek *andro-* 'man'.]

Andromache /an drómmaki/ n in Greek mythology, a princess of Troy and the wife of Hector, who led the Trojan women throughout the Trojan War

andromeda /an drómmidə/ (*plural* **-da** *or* **-das**) n an evergreen bush of the heath family. Flowers: pink, drooping in clusters. Genera: *Andromeda* and *Pieris*. [Mid-18C. < modern Latin.]

Andromeda /an drómmidə/ n 1 in Greek mythology, the daughter of Cassiopeia, who was saved from a sea monster by her future husband, Perseus 2 a constellation of the northern hemisphere containing a spiral galaxy (**Andromeda Galaxy**) that can be seen with the naked eye. See illustration at **constellation**

Andropov /an dróppov/, **Yuri** (1914–84) Soviet statesman and president of the Soviet Union (1983–84)

androsterone /an dróstə rōn/ n a weak male sex hormone produced by males and females [Mid-20C. < ANDRO- + STEROL + -ONE.]

-andry *suffix* 1 the condition of having a particular number of males or husbands ○ *polyandry* 2 the condition of having a particular number of stamens ○ *monandry* [< Greek *-andria* < *andr-*, stem of *anēr* 'man'] —**-androus** *suffix*

-ane *suffix* a saturated hydrocarbon ○ *methane* [After -ENE, -ONE]

anecdotal /ánnik dót'l/, **anecdotic** /ánnik dótik/ *adj* 1 consisting of or based on second-hand accounts rather than firsthand knowledge or experience or scientific investigation ○ *anecdotal evidence* 2 relating to anecdotes or in the form of anecdotes —**anecdotally** *adv*

anecdote /ánnik dōt/ n a short personal account of an incident or event [Early 18C. Directly or via French < modern Latin *anecdota* < Greek *anekdota* 'things unpublished' < *an-* 'not' + *ekdidonai* 'publish'.]

anecdotic *adj* = anecdotal

anechoic /ánni kō ik/ *adj* producing or characterized by few or no echoes

Aneirin /a nírin/ (*fl.* AD early 6th century) Scottish-born Welsh court poet

anemia n = anaemia

anemic *adj* = anaemic

anemo- *prefix* wind ○ *anemography* [< Greek *anemos* 'wind' < Indo-European, 'breathe']

anemography /ánni móggrəfi/ n the process of measuring wind speed

anemometry /ánni mómmətri/ n the process of measuring the force and direction of the wind —**anemometer** n —**anemometrical** /ánnimə méttrik'l/ *adj*

anemone /ə némməni/ (*plural* **-nes** *or* **-ne**) n 1 a perennial flowering plant of the buttercup family with wild and cultivated types. Genus: *Anemone*. 2 ♦ **sea anemone** [Mid-16C. Via Latin < Greek *anemōnē*.]

anemone fish n a small colourful damselfish with stinging cells, found on tropical coral reefs in close association with sea anemones. Genus: *Amphiprion*.

anemophilous /ánni móffələss/ *adj* describes a plant species that is pollinated by the wind —**anemophily** n

anencephaly /án en séffəli/ n the absence of all or a part of the brain and part of the skull at birth —**anencephalic** /án ensə fállik/ *adj*

~~anenome~~ incorrect spelling of **anemone**

anergy /ánnərji/ n decreased immunity or lack of immunity to an antigen [Late 19C. < modern Latin *anergia* < Greek *an-* 'without' + *ergon* 'work'.] —**anergic** /a núrjik/ *adj*

aneroid /ánnə royd/ *adj* not containing or using liquid [Mid-19C. < French *anéroïde* < Greek *a-* 'without' + *nēron* 'water, liquid'.]

aneroid barometer n an instrument for indicating atmospheric pressure on a circular dial

anesthesia n = anaesthesia

anesthesiologist /ánnəss theezi ólləjist/, **anaesthesiologist** n US = anaesthetist n. 1

anesthesiology /ánnəss theezi ólləji/, **anaesthesiology** n US = anaesthetics

anesthetic n, *adj* = anaesthetic

anesthetist n = anaesthetist

anesthetize *vt* = anaesthetize

aneuploid /ánnyöö employ/ *adj* describes a cell or organism with fewer or more chromosomes than usual —**aneuploid** n —**aneuploidy** n

aneurysm /ánnyöörizm/, **aneurism** n a fluid-filled sac in the wall of an artery that can weaken the wall [< Greek *aneurusma* 'dilation, swelling' < *aneurunein* 'widen out' < *ana-* 'through' + *eurus* 'wide'] —**aneurysmal** /ánnyöö rízm'l/ *adj*

anew /ə nyóó/ *adv* 1 again or once more 2 in a new way or form that is unlike the previous one [14C. < *a-* (reduced form of *of*) + NEW; probably after Old French *de neuf, de nouveau*.]

anfractuosity /án frakchoo óssəti/ (*plural* **-ties**) n (*literary*) 1 a twist or turn, e.g. in a road or in the plot of a novel 2 the twisting, turning nature of something [Late 16C. < French *anfractuosité* < late Latin *anfractuosus* < Latin *anfractus* 'bending'.] —**anfractuous** /an frákchoo ass/ *adj*

Angas /áng gass/, **George Fife** (1789–1879) British-born Australian philanthropist

angel /áynjəl/ n 1 HEAVENLY BEING a divine being who acts as a messenger of God 2 PICTURE OF HEAVENLY BEING a picture of an angel as a human figure with wings 3 KIND PERSON somebody who is kind or beautiful (*informal*) 4 MEMBER OF LOWEST ANGELIC ORDER a member of the lowest order of angels in the medieval Christian celestial hierarchy, ranked below archangels 5 GUARDIAN AND GUIDE a spirit that protects and offers guidance 6 FINANCIAL BACKER a financial backer, especially for a theatrical production (*informal*) 7 OLD ENGLISH COIN a gold coin that was a unit of currency in England from the 15th to the early 17th centuries [13C. Via Old French < Greek *aggelos* 'messenger'.]

LITERARY LINK *An Angel at My Table*, the second volume of a three-part autobiography by New Zealand writer Janet Frame. It describes the author's commitment to a mental institution where she was erroneously diagnosed as schizophrenic.

SYNONYMS See *backer*.

angel cake n a whitish light-textured cake made with egg whites but without yolks

angel dust n the illegal hallucinogenic drug phencyclidine (*slang*)

Angeleno /anjə leenō/ (*plural* **-nos**) n US somebody who comes from Los Angeles, California [Late 19C. < American Spanish *angeleño*.]

Angel Falls /áyngəl fáwlz/ world's highest waterfall, located in SE Venezuela. Height: 979 m / 3,212 ft.

angelfish /áynjəl fish/ (*plural* **-fish** *or* **-fishes**) n 1 a freshwater fish with a broad striped body and large fins that is often kept in aquariums. Native to: the tropical rivers of South America. *Pterophyllum scalare*. 2 a brightly coloured tropical fish that has a broad flat body. Native to: tropics. Family: Chaetodontidae and Pomacanthidae. 3 ZOOL = angel shark

angel food cake *n* US = **angel cake**

angel hair *n* pasta in the form of long, very fine strands

angelic /an jéllik/, **angelical** /-jéllik'l/ *adj* **1** very kind or beautiful **2** relating to angels —**angelically** *adv* —**angelicalness** *n*

angelica /an jéllikə/ (*plural* **-cas** *or* **-ca**) *n* **1** bright green, candied plant stems. Use: decorating cakes and biscuits. **2** a tall hollow-stemmed plant of the carrot family. Native to: Europe, Asia. Genus: *Angelica*. [Early 16C. < medieval Latin, short for *herba angelica* 'angelic plant'.]

angelical *adj* = **angelic**

Angelico /an jélli kō/, **Fra** (1400?–55) Italian religious painter. Born **Guido di Pietro**

angel of mercy *n* somebody who brings welcome assistance

Angel of the North *n* a large metal sculpture by Antony Gormley of an angel, erected on a hill outside Gateshead, NE England, in 1997

Angelou /ánjə loo/, **Maya** (*b.* 1928) US writer

angel shark *n* a small shark with a flat body, broad head, and enlarged pectoral fins, giving it the appearance of a ray. Genus: *Squatina*. [< its wing-like pectoral fins]

Angelus /ánjiləss/, **angelus** *n* **1** in the Roman Catholic Church, a set of prayers to commemorate the Annunciation and the Incarnation **2** a bell rung to announce the time for the Angelus [Mid-17C. < Latin *Angelus domini* 'the angel of the Lord', the first words of the prayer.]

anger /áng gər/ *n* a feeling of extreme annoyance ■ *vti* to become or make somebody extremely annoyed [13C. < Old Norse *angr* 'trouble, sorrow'.]

LITERARY LINK ***Look Back in Anger***, a play (1956) by John Osborne. Seen at the time of its first performances as a landmark play that reflected the disaffection of many young people, this domestic drama focusses on Jimmy Porter, a working-class graduate who feels trapped by social conventions.

SYNONYMS ***anger, annoyance, irritation, resentment, indignation, fury, rage, ire, wrath***

CORE MEANING: a feeling of strong displeasure in response to an assumed injury

anger a strong feeling of grievance; **annoyance** mild anger and impatience; **irritation** impatience and exasperation; **resentment** aggrieved feelings caused by a sense of unfair treatment; **indignation** anger because something seems unfair or unreasonable; **fury** violent anger; **rage** sudden and extreme anger; **ire** (*literary*) strong anger; **wrath** strong anger, often with a desire for revenge.

Angers /aáN zhay/ capital of Maine-et-Loire Department, W France. Population: 146,163 (1990).

Angevin /ánjəvin/ *n* **SOMEBODY FROM ANJOU** somebody who comes from the Anjou region in SW France ■ *adj* **1 OF ANJOU** relating to the Anjou region in France **2 OF ANJOU AND PLANTAGENET DYNASTIES** relating to the House of Anjou, especially the branch that includes the Plantagenet kings of England [Mid-17C. Via French < medieval Latin *Andegavinus* < *Andegavia* 'Anjou'.]

angina /an jínə/, **angina pectoris** /-péktəriss/ *n* a medical condition in which lack of blood to the heart causes severe chest pains [Mid-16C. < Latin, 'quinsy', alteration (after *angere* 'to squeeze') of Greek *agkhonē* 'strangling' < *agkhein* 'to squeeze, strangle'.]

angio- *prefix* **1** blood or lymph vessel ○ *angiogram* **2** pericarp ○ *angiosperm* [< modern Latin < Greek *aggeion* 'blood vessel' < *aggos* 'vessel']

angiocardiography /ánji ō kaardi óggrəfi/ *n* X-ray examination of the heart and related blood vessels —**angiocardiographic** /ánji ō kaardi ə gráffik/ *adj*

angiogenesis /ánji ō jénnississ/ *n* the formation of new blood vessels, e.g. in an embryo or as a result of a tumour

angiogram /ánji ō gram/ *n* an X-ray photograph of a blood vessel

angiography /ánji óggrəfi/ *n* X-ray examination of blood vessels —**angiographic** /ánji ə gráffik/ *adj*

angiology /ánji ólləji/ *n* the branch of medicine that deals with blood vessels and the lymphatic system

angioma /ánji ṓmə/ (*plural* **-mas** *or* **-mata** /-mətə/) *n* a benign tumour made up of blood or lymph vessels —**angiomatous** *adj*

angiopathy /ánji óppəthi/ (*plural* **-thies**) *n* a disease of the blood vessels or lymph vessels

angioplasty /ánji ō plasti/ (*plural* **-ties**) *n* a surgical operation to clear a narrowed or blocked artery

angiosarcoma /ánji ō saar kṓmə/ *n* a malignant tumour consisting of vascular cells, often in the liver

angioscope /ánji ə skōp/ *n* a long fine surgical viewing instrument threaded into a patient's blood vessels to allow surgeons to observe and perform operations without large incisions —**angioscopy** /ánji óskəpi/ *n*

angiospasm /ánji ō spazəm/ *n* a spasmodic contraction of a blood vessel

angiosperm /ánji ō spurm/ *n* a plant in which the sex organs are within flowers and the seeds are in a fruit. ◊ **gymnosperm** [Early 19C. < ANGIO- + Greek *sperma* 'seed'.]

angiotensin /ánji ō ténssin/ *n* a hormone that causes blood pressure to rise [Mid-20C. < ANGIO- + HYPERTENSION + -IN.]

angiotensin-converting enzyme inhibitor *n* full form of **ACE inhibitor**

Angkor /áng kawr/, **Ângkôr** ancient capital of the early Khmer civilization in NW Cambodia, noted for its temples and monuments

angle[1] /áng g'l/ *n* **1 SPACE BETWEEN DIVERGING LINES** the space between two diverging lines or planes, or a measure of the space **2 FIGURE FORMED BY DIVERGING LINES** a figure formed by two lines diverging from a common point or two planes diverging from a common line **3** MATH = **solid angle 4 PART THAT STICKS OUT** a projecting part of something **5 POSITION FOR VIEWING** a position from which somebody can look at something ○ *a sculpture seen from three angles* **6 WAY OF CONSIDERING** a way of looking at a situation ○ *Consider the matter from this angle.* ■ *v* (**-gles, -gling, -gled**) **1** *vti* **DIRECT OR PLACE OBLIQUELY** to direct or place something obliquely, or move or be placed obliquely **2** *vt* **PRESENT SOMETHING WITH BIAS** to present something with a particular audience in mind or in order to express a particular point of view **3** *vi* **CHANGE DIRECTION SHARPLY** to turn in a sharply different direction [14C. Directly or via French < Latin *angulus* 'corner'.]

angle[2] /áng g'l/ (**-gles, -gling, -gled**) *vi* **1** to fish with a hook, line, and rod **2** to attempt to obtain a compliment or an advantage (*informal*) [Old English *angul* 'fishhook' < Indo-European, 'to bend, hook']

Angle /áng g'l/ *n* a member of a Germanic people who invaded and settled E and N England in the 5th and 6th centuries AD [Pre-12C. < Latin *Angli* 'people from Angul' (in N Germany).] —**Anglian** /áng gli ən/ *adj, n*

angle bar *n* BUILDING = **angle iron**

angle bracket *n* one of a pair of marks (< or >) used to enclose text

angle iron *n* an iron or steel bar that is L-shaped in cross section

angle of attack *n* the acute angle between the direction of airflow and the line linking the leading and trailing edges of an aircraft wing

angle of incidence *n* the angle between an incoming ray of light and the line perpendicular to the surface at the point of arrival

angle of reflection *n* the angle between a reflected ray of light and the line perpendicular to the surface at the point of reflection

angle of refraction *n* the angle between a refracted ray of light and the line perpendicular to the surface at the point of refraction

angle of repose *n* the maximum slope or angle at which unconsolidated material such as sand can be made into a mound before it begins to slide

angle plate *n* an L-shaped metal plate used to support a framework

angler /áng glər/ *n* **1** somebody who fishes with a hook, line, and rod **2** ZOOL = **anglerfish**

anglerfish /áng glər fish/ (*plural* **-fish** *or* **-fishes**) *n* a marine fish that uses a long dorsal fin extending over its mouth to attract prey. Order: Lophiiformes.

Anglesey /áng g'lssi/ island off the coast of NW Wales. Population: 67,200 (1995). Area: 620 sq. km/276 sq. mi.

anglesite /áng g'l sīt/ *n* a colourless, white, or lightly tinted lead sulphate mineral

Anglican /áng glikən/ *adj* relating to the Anglican Church ■ *n* a member of an Anglican Church [Early 17C. < medieval Latin *Anglicanus* 'English' < Latin *Angli* 'the Angles'; from its originally denoting the Church of England.]

Anglican Church, Anglican Communion *n* a group of Christian churches including the Churches of England, Ireland, and Wales, and the Episcopal Church of Scotland

Anglicanism /áng glikənizəm/ *n* the doctrines of the Church of England and other Anglican churches

anglicise *vti* = **anglicize**

Anglicism /áng gli sizəm/, **anglicism** *n* **1** a term that is peculiar to British English as opposed to other varieties of English **2** an English word or phrase used in a foreign language [Mid-17C. < medieval Latin *Anglicus* 'English' < Latin *Angli* 'the Angles'.]

anglicize /áng gli sīz/, **Anglicize** (**-cizes, -cizing, -cized**), **anglicise** (**-cises, -cising, -cised**), **Anglicise** (**-cises, -cising, -cised**) *vti* to become or make somebody or something more English [Early 18C. < medieval Latin *Anglicus* (see ANGLICISM).] —**anglicization** /áng gli sī záysh'n/ *n*

angling /áng gling/ *n* the sport of catching fish with a hook, line, and rod

Anglo /áng glō/ (*plural* **-glos**), **anglo** (*plural* **-glos**) *n* **1** *Aus* **AUSTRALIAN OF BRITISH ORIGIN** an Australian citizen of British, Irish, or American origin (*insult*) **2** *US* **NON-HISPANIC WHITE PERSON** an English-speaking white person in the United States who is not of Hispanic origin (*informal*) **3** *Can* **NON-FRENCH-SPEAKING CANADIAN** an English-speaking person in Canada, especially in Quebec (*informal*) [Early 19C. < ANGLO-.]

Anglo- *prefix* England, the English ○ *Anglophile* [< Latin *Angli* 'the Angles']

Anglo-French *adj* relating to the links that exist between France and the United Kingdom

Anglo-Indian *adj* **FROM INDIAN LANGUAGE** introduced into English from an Indian language ■ *n* **1 SOMEBODY WITH BRITISH AND INDIAN ANCESTRY** somebody of both British and Indian descent **2 BRITISH PERSON RESIDENT IN INDIA** a British person who has lived a long time in India, especially during the time when India was a British colony

Anglo-Irish *npl* people of English descent who were born or who live in Ireland —**Anglo-Irish** *adj*

Anglo-Latin *n* a form of Latin used in medieval England, having some English loanwords and forms —**Anglo-Latin** *adj*

Anglo-Norman *adj* **ENGLISH AND NORMAN** connected with the 11th-century Norman conquerors of England ■ *n* **1 NORMAN IN ENGLAND** a Norman inhabitant of England after 1066 **2 FRENCH SPOKEN IN MEDIEVAL ENGLAND** the form of Norman French spoken in medieval England

Anglophile /áng glō fīl/ *n* an admirer of England or the English —**Anglophilia** /áng glō fílli ə/ *n* —**Anglophilic** *adj*

Anglophobe /áng glō fōb/ *n* somebody who hates England or the English —**Anglophobia** /áng glō fṓbi ə/ *n* —**Anglophobic** /-fṓbik/ *adj*

anglophone /áng glə fōn/ *n* somebody who speaks English ■ *adj* where English is spoken by most people as their first language

Anglo-Saxon *n* **1 MEMBER OF GERMANIC PEOPLE** a member of a West Germanic people who settled in Britain from the 5th century AD and were dominant until 1066 **2** LANG = **Old English** *n*. 1 **3 WHITE ENGLISH NATIVE SPEAKER** a white speaker of English as a first language ■ *adj* **1 FROM OLD ENGLISH** describes a word in Modern English that comes from Old English **2 OF ENGLISH SPEAKERS** relating to white English speakers

Angola /ang gṓlə/ republic in west-central Africa. Capital: Luanda. Population: 10,548,000 (1997). Area: 1,246,700 sq. km/481,530 sq. mi. —**Angolan** *adj, n*

angora /ang gáwrə/ *n* **1** a rabbit, goat, or cat belonging to a breed with long silky fur **2** wool made from the hair of an angora goat or rabbit (*often before nouns*) [Early 19C. < ANGORA.]

Angora /ang gáwrə/ former name for **Ankara** (until 1930)

angostura /áng gə styóorə/, **angostura bark** *n* the bitter aromatic bark of either of two South American citrus trees. Use: flavouring in bitters and formerly to relieve fever. [After *Angostura*, Venezuela]

Angostura bitters /áng gə styóorə bíttərz/ *tdmk* a trade-

Angola

mark for a bitter-tasting flavouring for alcoholic drinks, made from herbs and spices

Angoulême /aàN goo lem/, **Charles, Duc d'** (1573–1650) French soldier

angrily /áng grəli/ adv **1** in a way that conveys extreme annoyance or displeasure **2** in a stormy threatening way

angry /áng gri/ (**-grier, -griest**) adj **1 FEELING VERY ANNOYED** feeling extremely annoyed, often about an insult or a wrong **2 EXPRESSING ANNOYANCE** expressing extreme annoyance ○ *'Low growls and angry snarls assailed our ears on every side…'* (Edgar Rice Burroughs, *The Gods of Mars*; 1913) **3 STORMY** stormy-looking **4 INFLAMED** inflamed and painful-looking [14C. < ANGER.]

angry young man n **1 angry young man, Angry Young Man** a member of a group of British men writing in the 1950s who were hostile to authority. The setting for their works is typically working-class, and the central character typically a lone man. (*often plural*) **2** a young man who is hostile to authority

angst /angst/ n **1** in existentialist philosophy, a feeling of dread arising from an awareness of free choice **2** any feeling of dread or anxiety [Early 20C. < German.]

SYNONYMS See *worry*.

angst-ridden adj dominated by a feeling of dread or anxiety

angstrom /ángstrəm, -strom/ n **1 angstrom, angstrom unit** (*symbol* Å) a unit of length equal to one ten-billionth of a metre (10^{-10} m), used to measure the wavelengths of electromagnetic radiations **2** a mark (°) placed over the letter 'a' in some Scandinavian languages to indicate a change in pronunciation from 'a' to 'aw' [Late 19C. After Anders Jonas *Ångström*.]

angsty /ángsti/ (**-stier, -stiest**) adj feeling nervous, anxious, and afraid, or causing anxiety or nervousness (*slang*)

Anguilla /ang gwíllə/ one of the Leeward Islands, in the West Indies. Area: 91 sq. km/35 sq. mi.

anguish /áng gwish/ n extreme anxiety or emotional torment ■ vti to feel or cause somebody to feel anguish [12C. < Old French *anguis* < Latin *angustus* 'narrow, tight'.]

anguished /áng gwisht/ adj **1** feeling or showing extreme anxiety or torment **2** producing extreme anxiety or other torment

angular /áng gyōōlər/ adj **1 THIN** thin and bony **2 AWKWARD AND UNGAINLY** stiff, awkward, and ungainly **3 SHARPLY DEFINED** describes an object with a lot of angles **4 MEASURED BY ANGLES** measured by an angle or rate of change of an angle [14C. < Latin *angularis* < *angulus* 'corner'.] —**angularly** adv

angular acceleration n (*symbol* α) the rate at which the rotation of a rotating body changes

angular displacement n the angle through which something has been rotated about an axis, usually measured in radians

angular frequency n (*symbol* ω) the frequency of a repeating rotation expressed in radians per second and multiplied by 2π

angularity /áng gyōō lárrəti/ (*plural* **-ties**) n **1** the thin and bony appearance of somebody's body **2** a sharp corner or angle (*often plural*)

angular momentum n (*symbol* L) the momentum that a body has due to its rotation about an axis, calculated as the product of its mass and its angular velocity

angular stomatitis n a condition of the lips, mouth, and cheeks characterized by cracks and fissures and caused by a bacterial infection

angular velocity n (*symbol* ω) the rate of rotation of a body around an axis

Angus[1] /áng gəss/ (*plural* **-gus** *or* **-guses**) n AGRIC = **Aberdeen Angus**

Angus[2] /áng gəss/ historic Scottish county

anhidrotic /ánhi dróttik/ n a medication or other agent that reduces sweating

anhinga /an híng gə/ (*plural* **-gas** *or* **-ga**) n US ZOOL = **darter** n. **2** [Mid-18C. Via Portuguese < Tupi *áyinga*.]

Anhui /án hwáy/, **Anhwei** province in east-central China. Capital: Hefei. Population: 59,550,000 (1994). Area: 139,899 sq. km/54,015 sq. mi.

anhydride /an hí drīd, -drid/ n a compound formed from another by the removal of water [Mid-19C. < ANHYDROUS.]

anhydrite /an hí drīt/ n a colourless or lightly tinted anhydrous calcium sulphate mineral. Use: cement, fertilizers. [Early 19C. < ANHYDROUS.]

anhydrous /an hídrəss/ adj describes compounds that contain no water [Early 19C. < Greek *anudros* 'waterless' < *hudōr* 'water'.]

ani /aáni/ (*plural* **anis** *or* **ani**) n a black long-tailed bird that has a heavy arched bill and lays eggs in a communal nest. Native to: tropical America. Genus: *Crotophaga*. [Early 19C. Via Spanish or Portuguese < Tupi *anū*.]

anicca /ánnikə/ n in Buddhism, the cycle of birth, life, and death [Via Pali < Sanskrit *anitya-* 'not eternal' < *nitya-* 'constant, perpetual']

aniconic /án T kónnik/ adj describes images of deities that are not human or animal in form

~~anihilation~~ incorrect spelling of **annihilation**

anil /ánnil/ (*plural* **-ils** *or* **-il**) n a bush that is the source of indigo dye. Native to: West Indies. *Indigofera suffruticosa*. [Late 16C. Via French, Portuguese, Arabic, and Persian < Sanskrit *nīla-* 'dark blue'.]

anile /ánnīl, áy-/ adj resembling a woman of advanced years [Mid-17C. < Latin *anilis* < *anus* 'venerable woman'.]

aniline /ánnilin, -leen/ n $C_6H_5NH_2$ a colourless poisonous oily liquid. Use: manufacture of dyes, inks, pharmaceuticals, explosives. [Mid-19C. < ANIL, because first obtained by distilling indigo with alkali.]

aniline dye n a synthetic dye derived from aniline

anilingus /áyni líng gəss/ n the act of sexually stimulating the anus with the tongue or mouth [Mid-20C. < modern Latin < Latin *anus* 'anus', after CUNNILINGUS.]

anima /ánnimə/ n **1** in Jungian psychology, the true inner self as opposed to the outer persona **2** in Jungian psychology, the feminine aspect of a man's personality [Early 20C. < Latin, 'breath, soul, spirit'.]

animadversion /ánni mad vúrsh'n/ n a critical comment or comments, especially those reproaching somebody

animadvert /ánni mad vúrt, -məd-/ vi to comment critically or unfavourably [Mid-17C. < Latin *animadvertere* 'turn the mind towards' < *animus* 'mind' + *advertere* (see ADVERT[1]).]

animal /ánnim'l/ n **1 LIVING ORGANISM WITH INDEPENDENT MOVEMENT** a living organism that is distinguished from plants by independent movement and responsive sense organs **2 MAMMAL** a land mammal other than a human being **3 BRUTISH PERSON** a vulgar or brutish person (*informal*) **4 INSTINCT-DRIVEN INNER SELF** the instinctive inner self as opposed to the one subject to self-restraint **5 PERSON OR THING** any particular person or thing (*informal*) ■ adj **1 FROM ANIMALS** derived from animals **2 INSTINCTIVE** belonging to the realm of instincts and urges [14C. < Latin *animal(e)* < *animalis* 'living, breathing' < *anima* 'breath, life, soul'.]

animalcule /ánni mál kyool/, **animalculum** /ánni málkyōōləm/ (*plural* **-la** /-kyōōlə/) n a microscopic organism, e.g. an amoeba, that moves about, eats other microbes, or resembles an animal in some other way (*archaic*) [Late 16C. < modern Latin *animalculum* 'little animal' < Latin *animal(e)* (see ANIMAL).] —**animalcular** adj

animal husbandry n the branch of agriculture concerned with breeding and rearing farm animals

animalise vt = **animalize**

animalism /ánniməlizəm/ n **1 THEORY OF HUMANS' NON-SPIRITUAL NATURE** the theory that human beings are driven by physical appetites rather than spiritual needs **2 PREOCCUPATION WITH PHYSICAL SIDE OF LIFE** preoccupation with physical rather than spiritual needs **3 TYPICAL ANIMAL BEHAVIOUR** behaviour that is typical of animals —**animalistic** /ánnimə lístik/ adj

animalist /ánnim'list/ n **1 SOMEBODY PREOCCUPIED WITH PHYSICAL NEEDS** somebody who is preoccupied with physical rather than spiritual needs **2 SOMEBODY DENYING HUMANS' SPIRITUAL NATURE** somebody who holds that humans are driven by physical rather than spiritual needs **3 ANIMAL RIGHTS SUPPORTER** a supporter of animal rights, especially a militant one (*informal*)

animality /ánni málləti/ n **1** the characteristics of animals, as opposed to plants **2** = **animalism** n. **2**

animalize /ánnimə līz/ (**-izes, -izing, -ized**), **animalise** (**-ises, -ising, -ised**) vt to bring out somebody's brutal or instinctive nature —**animalization** /ánnimə īT záysh'n/ n

animal liberation n the movement to free animals from what is held to be human exploitation (*often before nouns*)

animal magnetism n somebody's strong physical attractiveness (*informal humorous*)

animal rights npl basic rights for animals, e.g. the right to live free from suffering inflicted by human beings ○ *an animal rights activist*

animal spirits npl natural energy and high spirits

animal welfarist n a supporter of animal rights

animate vt /ánni mayt/ (**-mates, -mating, -mated**) **1 MAKE LIVELY** to make somebody or something lively **2 INSPIRE** to rouse or inspire somebody to take action or to have strong feelings **3 PRESENT USING ANIMATION TECHNIQUES** to present or record something in the form of a sequence of moving still images **4 MAKE ACTIVE** to arouse somebody or something into activity **5 CAUSE TO LIVE** to bring somebody or something to life ■ adj /ánnimat/ **1 PHYSICALLY ALIVE** in a physically live state, as opposed to being dead or inert **2 FULL OF LIVELINESS** full of liveliness or energy [14C. < Latin *animat-*, past participle of *animare* 'give life to' < *anima* 'breath, soul, spirit'.] —**animated** adj —**animatedly** adv

SYNONYMS See *living*.

animation /ánni máysh'n/ n **1 LIVELINESS** liveliness in the way somebody speaks or behaves **2 PRODUCTION OF ANIMATED FILMS** the making of films by photographing a sequence of slightly varying drawings or models so that they appear to move and change when the sequence is shown **3 ANIMATED FILM OR FILMS** a film or films consisting of a series of drawn, painted, or modelled scenes

animato /ánni maàtō/ adj, adv to be played in a lively animated manner (*musical direction*) [Early 18C. < Italian, < Latin *animare* (see ANIMATE).]

animator /ánnimaytər/ n **1** a maker of animated films **2** somebody or something that makes things lively, exciting, or interesting

animatronics /ánnimə trónniks/ n the use of computer technology and a form of radio control to animate puppets or other models (+ *singular verb*) [Late 20C. Blend of ANIMATE + ELECTRONICS.] —**animatronic** adj

animé /ánni may/ n resin obtained from various tropical American trees. Use: varnishes, perfumes. [Late 16C. Via French < Tupi *wana'ni*.]

animism /ánnimizəm/ n **1 BELIEF THAT NATURE HAS A SOUL** the belief that things in nature, e.g. trees, mountains, and the sky, have souls or consciousness **2 BELIEF IN ORGANIZING FORCE IN UNIVERSE** the belief that a supernatural force animates and organizes the universe **3 BELIEF IN EXISTENCE OF SEPARATE SPIRIT** the belief that people have spirits that do or can exist separately from their bodies [Mid-19C. < Latin *anima* 'soul'.] —**animist** adj, n —**animistic** /ánni místik/ adj

animosity /ánni móssəti/ (*plural* **-ties**) n a feeling or spirit of hostility and resentment [15C. Directly or via French *animosité* < late Latin *animositas* 'spiritedness' < *animosus* 'spirited' < *animus* 'mind, spirit'.]

SYNONYMS See *dislike*.

animus /ánniməss/ n **1 HOSTILITY** a feeling or display of animosity **2 DISPOSITION** an attitude or feeling that motivates somebody's actions **3 WOMAN'S MASCULINE SIDE** in Jungian psychology, the masculine aspect of a woman's personality [Early 19C. < Latin, 'mind, spirit'.]

anion /án ī ən/ *n* a negatively charged ion, especially one that is attracted to an anode [Mid-19C. Blend of ANODE + ION.] —**anionic** /án ī ónnik/ *adj* —**anionically** *adv*

anion-exchange resin *n* a solid resin in which the functional group is positive and thus attracts negative ions. Use: chemical and radioactive waste cleanup, chemical separation.

anise /ánniss/ *n* **1** an aromatic plant with liquorice-flavoured seeds (**aniseed**). Use: medicines, flavouring for food and drink. Native to: Mediterranean. *Pimpinella anisum.* **2** FOOD = **aniseed** [13C. Via French *anis* and Latin *anisum* < Greek *anison.*]

aniseed /ánnis seed/ *n* the liquorice-flavoured seeds of anise, used whole or in ground spice mixtures as a flavouring in foods and drinks

aniseikonia /án ī sī kṓni ə/ *n* a defect in the lens of one eye that results in its seeing an image that differs in size and shape from the image seen by the other eye [Mid-20C. < ANISO- + Greek *eikōn* 'image'.]

anisette /ánni zét, -sét/ *n* a sweet liqueur flavoured with aniseed [Mid-19C. < French, 'a little anise' < *anis* 'ANISE'.]

aniso- *prefix* differing, not equal ○ *anisogamy* [< Greek *anisos* < *an-* 'not' + *isos* 'equal']

anisogamete /án ī sō gámmeet, -gə meét/ *n* BIOL = **heterogamete** *n.* 1

anisogamy /án ī sóggəmi/ *n* BIOL = **heterogamy** *n.* 1 —**anisogamic** /án īssə gámmik/ *adj* —**anisogamous** /án ī sóggəməss/ *adj*

anisole /ánni sōl/ *n* $C_6H_5OCH_3$ a colourless liquid with a pleasant smell. Use: solvent, perfume, flavouring. [Mid-19C. < ANISE + -OLE.]

anisomeric /án īssō mérrik/ *adj* describes a compound that does not form structurally different molecules (**isomers**)

anisometric /á n īssō méttrik/ *adj* **1** not isometric or symmetrical ○ *an anisometric particle* **2** describes a crystal that does not have three perpendicular axes of equal length and is therefore not regular

anisometropia /án īssōmə trṓpi ə/ *n* lack of balance between each eye's ability to refract light [Late 19C. < ANISO- + Greek *metron* 'measure' + -OPIA.] —**anisometropic** /án īssōmə tróppik/ *adj*

anisotropic /án īssō tróppik/ *adj* describes something with physical properties that are different in different directions, e.g. crystals that measure differently along each of two or more axes —**anisotropically** *adv* —**anisotropism** /án ī sóttrəpizəm/ *n* —**anisotropy** /án ī sóttrəpi/ *n*

anistreplase /a nístrə playz, -playss/ *n* a drug that is effective in dissolving blood clots

Anjou[1] /aán zhoō, óN-/, **Anjou pear** *n* a variety of pear with green skin and firm flesh [After ANJOU[2]]

Anjou[2] /aán zhoō, óN-/ former province in W France

Ankara /ángkərə/ capital of Turkey, in the north-central part of the country. Population: 2,782,200 (1994).

ankerite /ángkə rīt/ *n* a white, grey, brown, or reddish carbonate mineral containing calcium, magnesium, iron, and sometimes manganese [Mid-19C. < German *Ankerit.*]

ankh /angk/ *n* a symbol consisting of a cross with a loop for the top extension and a short crossbar, used in ancient Egypt to signify life [Late 19C. < Egyptian, 'life'.]

ankle /ángk'l/ *n* **1** the joint that connects the leg bones with the highest bone in the foot **2** the slender part of the leg immediately above the ankle [14C. < assumed Old Norse *ankula*, which replaced related Old English *anclēow*, < Indo-European.]

anklebone /ángk'l bōn/ *n* ANAT = **talus**[2] *n.*

ankle boot *n* a boot that extends up to the ankle but not much beyond

ankle sock *n* a sock that extends up to the ankle but not much past it. US term **anklet** *n.* 2

anklet /ángklət/ *n* **1** a piece of jewellery or some other ornament worn round the ankle **2** *US* = **ankle sock**

anklewarmer /ángk'l wawrmər/ *n* a knitted tube that covers the ankles and sometimes also the calves and top of the foot

ankylosaur /ángkələ sawr/ *n* a plant-eating dinosaur with short legs, a heavy thickset body, and bony dorsal plates [Late 20C. < modern Latin *Ankylosaurus* < Greek *agkulōsis* (see ANKYLOSIS) + *sauros* 'lizard'.]

ankylose /ángkilōz, -lōss/ (**-loses, -losing, -losed**) *vti* to fuse together and become stiff, or cause bones to fuse together and a joint to become stiff, as a result of injury or disease [Late 18C. Back-formation < ANKYLOSIS.]

ankylosing spondylitis /ángkilōssing-, -lōzing-/ *n* a disease of the spine that causes the vertebrae to form a solid inflexible column

ankylosis /ángki lṓssiss/ (*plural* **-loses** /-lṓ seez/) *n* **1** the fusion of the bones of a joint, often as a result of disease or injury, or intentionally through surgery **2** stiffness or immobility in a joint caused by bones fusing together as a result of disease or injury or arising from surgery to join one bone or part to another [Early 18C. Via modern Latin < Greek *agkulōsis* 'stiffening of the joints' < *agkuloun* 'bend' < *agkulos* 'bent'.] —**ankylotic** /ángki lóttik/ *adj*

ankylostomiasis *n* MED = **ancylostomiasis**

anlage /án laagə/ (*plural* **-lagen** /-gən/ *or* **-lages**) *n* **1** a part or organ in its earliest stage of development **2** something, often a principle, on which something else is based or founded (*literary*) [Late 19C. < German, 'layout'.]

ANLL *abbr* acute non-lymphocytic leukaemia

ann. *abbr* **1** annals **2** annual **3** annuity

Anna Ivanovna /ánnə i vaánəvnə/ (1693–1740) empress of Russia (1730–40)

annalist /ánn'list/ *n* somebody who compiles annals

annals /ánn'lz/ *npl* **1 ANNUAL RECORDS** a record of events arranged chronologically by year **2 RECORDED HISTORY** history in general, as it is recorded in books and other documents ○ *Her achievements have secured her place in the annals of our nation.* **3 LEARNED JOURNAL** a periodical that records events and reports in a specific field of research [Mid-16C. Directly or via French < Latin *annales* < *annalis* (see ANNUAL).]

Annam /a nám/ region in Vietnam forming a narrow strip along the South China Sea —**Annamese** /ánnə meéz/ *adj, n*

Annan /a nán, ánnən/, **Kofi** (*b.* 1938) Ghanaian statesman, Secretary General of the United Nations (1997-)

Annapolis /ə náppəliss/ capital of Maryland, in the central part of the state. Population: 33,234 (1996).

Annapurna /ánnə púrnə/ mountain in the Himalayas in north-central Nepal. Height: 8,078 m/26,504 ft.

Ann Arbor /an aárbər/ city in SE Michigan. Population: 109,967 (1998 estimate).

annatto /ə náttō/ (*plural* **-tos**) *n* **1** a yellowish-red dye made from the pulp around the seeds of a tropical tree. Use: food colouring, fabric dye. **2** the tree from whose seeds annatto dye is made. Native to: tropical America. *Bixa orellana.* [Early 17C. < Carib.]

Anne /an/ (1665–1714) queen of Great Britain and Ireland (1702–14)

Anne, the Princess Royal (*b.* 1950) daughter of Queen Elizabeth II and Prince Philip, Duke of Edinburgh.

Anne (of Austria) (1601–66) queen regent of France (1643–51)

Anne (of Cleves) /-kleévz/ (1515–57) queen consort of Henry VIII of England (1540)

Anne (of Denmark) (1574–1619) queen consort of James I of England (1603–19)

anneal /ə neél/ *v* **1** *vti* **MAKE SOMETHING STRONGER THROUGH HEATING** to subject an alloy, metal, or glass to a process of heating and slow cooling to make it tougher and less brittle **2** *vti* **SEPARATE STRANDS OF NUCLEIC ACID** to subject nucleic acid to a process of heating and cooling in order to separate its strands **3** *vt* **MAKE SOMETHING MORE RESOLUTE** to make something, especially an opinion, a feeling, or an intention, stronger, firmer, or more resolute (*literary*) [Old English *onǣlan* < *ǣlan* 'burn' < Germanic]

annelid /ánnəlid/ *n* an invertebrate organism with a flat body that is divided into segments. Earthworms and leeches are annelids. Phylum: Anelida. [Mid-19C. < modern Latin *Annelida* < French *annelés* 'ringed' < Latin *an(n)ulus* (see ANNULUS).]

annex /ə néks/ *vt* **1 ADD SOMETHING TO** to attach something subsidiary to a larger thing (*usually passive*) ○ *The new pool will be annexed to the gymnasium.* **2 TAKE OVER TERRITORY** to take over territory and incorporate it into another political entity, e.g. a country or state **3 ATTACH A QUALITY TO** to add something such as a consequence, quality, or condition (*usually passive*) ○ *Annexed to his feeling of guilt was a sense of having let everybody down.* **4 STEAL** to take something without permission (*informal*) ○ *He returned to find that his assistant had annexed his chair.* ■ *n* **1** = **annexe** *n.* 1 **2** = **annexe** *n.* 2 [14C. Via French *annexer* < Latin *annectere* 'tie together' < *nectere* 'to tie'.] —**annexation** /ánnek sáysh'n/ *n* —**annexationism** *n* —**annexationist** *n*

annexe /ánneks/ *n* **1** a building added onto another building or serving as an auxiliary building to a larger one. US term **annex** *n.* 1 **2** an appendix, epilogue, or other additional material attached to a larger document. US term **annex** *n.* 2

Annigoni /ánni gṓni/, **Pietro** (1910–88) Italian painter

annihilate /ə nī́ ə layt/ (**-lates, -lating, -lated**) *v* **1** *vt* **DESTROY** to destroy something completely, especially so that it ceases to exist **2** *vt* **DEFEAT** to defeat somebody easily and convincingly (*informal*) **3** *vi* **BE DESTROYED IN PARTICLE COLLISION** to be mutually destroyed when a particle collides with a corresponding antiparticle [Early 16C. < late Latin *annihilat-*, past participle of *annihilare* 'reduce to nothing' < Latin *nihil* 'nothing'.] —**annihilable** /ə nī́ələb'l/ *adj* —**annihilator** *n*

annihilation /ə nī́ ə láysh'n/ *n* **1 DESTRUCTION** the complete destruction of something **2 DEFEAT OF OPPONENT** the complete and convincing defeat of an opponent (*informal*) **3 DESTRUCTIVE COLLISION OF PARTICLE AND ANTIPARTICLE** the process in which a particle combines with its antiparticle, destroying both and releasing their energy in the form of radiation or other particles ○ *annihilation radiation*

anniversary /ánni vúrssəri/ (*plural* **-ries**) *n* **1** a date that is observed on an annual basis because it is the same date as a remarkable event in a past year **2** a celebration or other commemorative ritual marking the date of a noteworthy event, often a wedding [13C. Directly or via French *anniversaire* < medieval Latin *anniversarium* < Latin *anniversarius* 'returning yearly' < *annus* 'year' + *versus*, past participle of *vertere* 'turn'.]

anno Domini /ánnō dómminī/ *adv* full form of **AD** [Mid-16C. < Latin, 'in the year of the Lord'.]

anno Hegirae /ánnō hə jī́ri/ *adv* full form of **AH** [Late 19C. < Latin, 'in the year of the Hegira'.]

~~**annonymous**~~ incorrect spelling of **anonymous**

annotate /ánnə tayt/ (**-tates, -tating, -tated**) *vt* to add critical or explanatory notes to a text (*usually passive*) [Mid-18C. < Latin *annotat-*, past participle of *annotare* 'note down' < *nota* 'mark'.] —**annotative** *adj* —**annotator** *n*

annotation /ánnə táysh'n/ *n* **1** the adding of explanatory or critical notes to a text **2** an explanatory or critical comment that has been added to a text

announce /ə nównss/ (**-nounces, -nouncing, -nounced**) *v* **1** *vt* **TELL PUBLICLY** to declare or report something publicly **2** *vt* **SAY** to say something in a formal, forceful, or aggressive way **3** *vt* **DECLARE ARRIVAL OF** to tell others formally that somebody or something has arrived **4** *vt* **SIGNIFY OR FORETELL** to be a sign that something has arrived or is imminent **5** *vti US* **SERVE AS PRESENTER OF** to act as a presenter of something, e.g. a television or radio show [15C. Directly or via French *annoncer* < Latin *annuntiare* < *nuntius* 'messenger'.]

announcement /ə nównssmənt/ *n* **1** a public statement giving people information or news, or the making of the statement **2** a formal written notice, often a card or newspaper item, giving the news of a birth, wedding, or other event

announcer /ə nównssər/ *n* **1** somebody who makes announcements, e.g. on a public address system at an airport **2** a television or radio commentator who gives news bulletins or programme information

annoy /ə nóy/ *v* **1** *vt* **IRRITATE** to make somebody feel impatient or angry **2** *vt* **HARASS** to harass or bother somebody repeatedly **3** *vi* **BE IRRITATING** to be a source of irritation ○ *Barking dogs are bound to annoy.* [13C. Via Old French *anoier* < late Latin *inodiare* 'make loathsome' < Latin *in odio* 'in hatred'.]

annoyance /ə nóy ənss/ *n* **1** feelings of mild anger and impatience **2** something that causes somebody to be mildly angry or impatient ○ *Living in this neighbourhood is not without its annoyances.*

SYNONYMS See ***anger.***

annoying /ə nóy ing/ *adj* causing mild anger or impatience —**annoyingly** *adv*

annual /ánnyoo əl/ *adj* **1 ONCE A YEAR** happening once a year **2 FOR PERIOD OF ONE YEAR** based on or accumulating over one year **3 DYING AFTER ONE SEASON** describes a plant that flowers, produces seed, and dies in one growing season ■ *n* **1 PLANT THAT DIES AFTER ONE SEASON** a plant that flowers, produces seed, and dies in one growing season **2 YEARLY BOOK OR MAGAZINE** a book or magazine published once a year, especially one for children [14C. Directly or via French *annuel* < late Latin *annualis*, blend of Latin *annuus* + *annalis* 'yearly' < *annus* 'year'.]

annual general meeting *n* a yearly gathering of members of an organization, at which officers are elected and the year's activities, including financial dealings, are discussed

annualise *vt* = **annualize**

annualize /ánnyoo ə līz/ (**-izes, -izing, -ized**), **annualise** (**-alises, -alising, -alised**) *vt* **1** to calculate or adjust figures so that they reflect a period of a year **2** to put something on, or change something to, a once-a-year schedule ○ *Let's annualize the newsletter.*

annually /ánnyoo əli/ *adv* every year or once a year

annual report *n* a document that outlines and analyses the activities, especially the financial dealings, of a company or other organization over the past year

Annual ring: Cross-section through pine log

annual ring *n* TREES = **growth ring**

annuitant /ə nyoó itənt/ *n* somebody who receives an annuity

annuity /ə nyoó əti/ (*plural* **-ties**) *n* **1 MONEY PAID AT REGULAR INTERVALS** an amount of money paid to somebody yearly or at some other regular interval **2 INVESTMENT PAYING ANNUAL SUM** an investment that earns the investor a fixed amount of money each year for a number of years, often the investor's lifetime **3 CONTRACT FOR ANNUAL PAYMENT** the right to receive or the obligation to pay an annuity [15C. Via French *annuité* < medieval Latin *annuitas* < Latin *annuus* (see ANNUAL).]

annul /ə núl/ (**-nuls, -nulling, -nulled**) *vt* **1 MAKE SOMETHING INVALID** to render a legal document or agreement invalid **2 DECLARE MARRIAGE INVALID** to declare that a marriage was never a proper marriage in the eyes of a church, e.g. because one of the parties was not completely committed to it **3 DESTROY** to wipe out or destroy the effect or existence of something ○ *not able to annul my fears* [14C. Via Old French *anuller* < late Latin *annullare* 'make into nothing' < Latin *nullus* 'nothing'.] —**annulment** *n*

SYNONYMS See ***nullify***.

annular /ánnyŏŏlər/ *adj* shaped like or forming a ring [Late 16C. Directly or via French *annulaire* < Latin *an(n)ularis* < *an(n)ulus* (see ANNULUS).]

annular eclipse *n* a solar eclipse in which all but the outermost rim of the sun is blocked by the moon, leaving a ring of sunlight visible round the moon

annular ligament *n* a ring-shaped ligament that surrounds an ankle joint or a wrist joint and holds other ligaments in place

annulate /ányŏŏ layt/, **annulated** /ányoolaytid/ *adj* with ring-shaped parts [Early 19C. < Latin *an(n)ulatus* < *an(n)ulus* (see ANNULUS).]

annulation /ánnyŏŏ láysh'n/ *n* **1** the formation of rings or ring-shaped parts **2** any part that is shaped like a ring

annulet /ánnyŏŏlət/ *n* **1** a ring-shaped moulding round a column **2** a ring-shaped object on a heraldic shield [Late 16C. < Latin *an(n)ulus* (see ANNULUS).]

annuli plural of **annulus**

annulus /ánnyŏŏləss/ (*plural* **-li** /-lī/ *or* **-luses**) *n* **1** a ring-shaped part or arrangement of parts in a plant or animal, e.g. a growth ring on fish scales **2** the area bounded by two concentric circles [Mid-16C. < Latin *an(n)ulus* 'small ring' < *anus* 'ring'.]

annunciation /ə núnssi áysh'n/ *n* the announcing of something, or an announcement (*archaic*) [14C. Via Old French < late Latin *annuntiation-* < Latin *annuntiare* (see ANNOUNCE).]

Annunciation *n* **1** in the Bible, the archangel Gabriel's visit to the Virgin Mary to announce that she had been chosen to be the mother of Jesus Christ (Luke 1:26–38) **2** the Christian festival known as the feast of the Annunciation. Date: 25 March.

annunciator /ə núnssi aytər/ *n* an electronic signalling device, e.g. a switchboard device that indicates the source of incoming telephone calls

annus horribilis /ánnəss hə ríbbiliss/ (*plural* **anni horribiles** /ánnī hə ríbbi layz/) *n* a year of great unhappiness or misfortune [Late 20C. < Latin, 'horrible year'.]

annus mirabilis /ánnəss mi ráabiliss/ (*plural* **anni mirabiles** /ánnī mi ráabi layz/) *n* a year that is remarkable for its great events [Mid-17C. < Latin, 'wonderful year'.]

anode /ánnōd/ *n* **1** the negative terminal of a battery **2** the positive electrode in an electrolytic cell [Mid-19C. < Greek *anodos* 'way up' < *hodos* 'way'.]

anodise *vt* = **anodize**

anodize /ánnō dīz/ (**-dizes, -dizing, -dized**), **anodise** (**-dises, -dising, -dised**) *vt* to coat a metal, e.g. aluminium, with a protective or decorative oxide by making the metal the anode of an electrolytic cell —**anodization** /ánnō dī záysh'n/ *n*

anodontia /ánnə dónshə, -dónshi ə/ *n* the absence of some or all teeth because the teeth have never developed

anodyne /ánnō dīn/ *adj* **1 PAINKILLING** bringing relief from pain or discomfort **2 SOOTHING** serving to soothe, relax, or comfort (*literary*) ○ *the anodyne effects of a weekend in the mountains after a hard working week* **3 BLAND** harmless, inoffensive, or uncontroversial to the point of being dull (*literary*) ○ *a rather anodyne speech, given the nature of the crisis* ■ *n* **1 PAINKILLER** a drug such as aspirin or codeine that relieves pain **2 COMFORTING THING** something that soothes, comforts, or relaxes (*literary*) [Mid-16C. Via Latin < Greek *anōdunos* 'without pain' < *odunē* 'pain'.]

anoestrous /an éestrəss/ *adj* **1** describes a female mammal that is sexually inactive between breeding periods **2** describes the period of sexual inactivity between breeding periods in certain female mammals

anoestrus /an éestrəss/ *n* the period of sexual inactivity between the breeding periods of certain female mammals

anoint /ə nóynt/ *vt* **1** to rub oil or ointment on a part of somebody's body, usually the head or feet, as part of a religious ceremony **2** to install somebody officially or ceremonially in a position or office [14C. < Old French *enoint*, past participle of *enoindre* < Latin *inungere* < *ungere* 'to smear'.] —**anointment** *n*

anointing of the sick *n* in the Roman Catholic Church, the sacrament of anointing people who are very ill, praying for their recovery, and offering confession and absolution of sins

anole /ə nṓ li/ *n* a tree-climbing lizard that can change colour. Genus: *Anolis*. [Early 18C. Via modern Latin *Anolis* < Carib *anoli*.]

anomalistic month /ə nómmə lístik-/ *n* the average time taken by the Moon to orbit the Earth once, starting from the point in its orbit at which it is nearest the Earth, measured as 27.554 days

anomalistic year *n* the time taken by the Earth to orbit the Sun once, starting from the point in its orbit at which the Earth is nearest the Sun, measured as 365.26 days

anomalous /ə nómmələss/ *adj* **1** deviating from the norm or from what people expect ○ *We're getting anomalous readings on the heart monitor.* **2** strange and difficult to identify or classify ○ *'Individuals would occasionally give rise to new species having anomalous habits'.* (Charles Darwin, *On the Origin of Species*; 1859) [Mid-17C. < late Latin *anomalus* < Greek *anōmalos* 'uneven' < *homalos* 'even'.]

anomaly /ə nómməli/ (*plural* **-lies**) *n* **1 IRREGULARITY** something that deviates from the norm or from expectations ○ *looking for anomalies in the patient's blood tests* **2 PECULIARITY** something strange and difficult to identify or classify ○ *The space probe has encountered an anomaly.* **3 ANGLE IN PLANET'S ORBIT** the angle between a planet's position, the Sun, and the point in the planet's orbit when it is closest to the Sun

anomic /ə nómmik/ *adj* **1 UNSTABLE BECAUSE OF MORAL BREAKDOWN** unstable because moral and social codes have been eroded or abandoned ○ *an anomic society* **2 AFFECTED BY ALIENATION** feeling alienated from society and disorientated by the perceived absence of a social or moral framework ■ *n* **SOMEBODY AFFECTED BY ALIENATION** somebody who feels alienated and disorientated because of the lack of a social and moral framework

anomie /ánnōmi/, **anomy** *n* **1** instability in society caused by the erosion or abandonment of moral and social codes **2** a feeling of disorientation and alienation from society caused by the perceived absence of a supporting social or moral framework [Late 16C. Via French < Greek *anomia* 'lawlessness' < *anomos* 'lawless' < *nomos* 'law'.]

anon /ə nón/ *adv* (*archaic or literary*) **1** at an unspecified future time ○ *I'll see you anon.* **2** in a short while ○ *more of these grotesque escapades anon* [Old English *on ān* 'in one']

anon. *abbr* anonymous

anonym /ánnənim/ *n* **1 UNNAMED AUTHOR** an author whose name is not known or not given **2 PSEUDONYM** a name used by somebody to hide his or her identity **3 PUBLICATION WITH UNNAMED AUTHOR** a publication whose author is unnamed or unknown [Early 19C. < French *anonyme* < Greek *anōnumos* (see ANONYMOUS).]

anonymity /ánnə nímməti/ (*plural* **-ties**) *n* **1 FREEDOM FROM IDENTIFICATION** the state of not being known or identified by name, e.g. as the author or donor of something **2 LACK OF DISTINCTIVENESS** a lack of distinctive features that makes things seem bland or interchangeable ○ *detested the anonymity of the city-centre hotels* **3 UNNAMED PERSON** an unnamed or unacknowledged person **4 STATE OF BEING UNNOTICED** the state of blending into a crowd and going unnoticed ○ *I always preferred the anonymity of the big city.*

anonymous /ə nónniməss/ *adj* **1 UNNAMED** whose name is not known or not given **2 WITH NAME WITHHELD** with the performer's, maker's, or creator's identity withheld **3 INDISTINCTIVE** lacking individuality or distinctiveness ○ *a quirkiness unsuited to an anonymous shopping mall* [Early 17C. < late Latin *anonymus* < Greek *anōnumos* 'unnamed' < *onuma* 'name'.] —**anonymousness** *n*

anonymous FTP *n* a method of connecting to a computer on the Internet without a password

anonymously /ə nónniməssli/ *adv* without being named or acknowledged

anorak /ánnə rak/ *n* **1** a warm thick waterproof hip-length jacket with a hood **2** a boring, unfashionable, or studious person, especially somebody who is excessively devoted to a particular hobby or interest (*humorous*) ○ *You can be into something without becoming a total anorak about it.* [Early 20C. < (Greenlandic) Inuit *annoraaq*.]

anorectic /ánnə réktik/ *adj* relating to pathological loss of appetite ■ *n* medication that suppresses the appetite [Late 19C. < Greek *anorektos* 'without appetite' < *orexein* 'to desire'.]

anorexia /ánnə réksi ə/ *n* **1** MED = **anorexia nervosa** **2** persistent loss of appetite [Late 16C. Via modern Latin, < Greek, 'lack of appetite' < *orexis* 'appetite' < *orexein* 'to desire'.]

anorexia nervosa /-nur vṓssə/ *n* an eating disorder, marked by an extreme fear of becoming overweight, that leads to excessive dieting to the point of serious ill-health and sometimes death [< modern Latin, 'nervous anorexia']

anorexic /ánnə réksik/ *adj* **1 OF ANOREXIA NERVOSA** relating to or affected by anorexia nervosa **2 VERY THIN** extremely thin, especially unhealthily or unattractively so (*informal*) ■ *n* **SOMEBODY WITH ANOREXIA NERVOSA** somebody who is affected by anorexia nervosa

anorthite /a náwr thīt/ *n* a rare white, grey, or reddish-grey feldspar mineral. Source: mainly in igneous rocks. Use: glass, ceramics. —**anorthitic** /ánnawr thíttik/ *adj*

anorthosite /ə náwrthə sīt/ *n* a coarse-grained igneous rock comprising at least 90% feldspar [Mid-19C. < French *anorthose* 'type of feldspar' < Greek *anorthos* 'not straight'.] —**anorthositic** /ə náwrthə síttik/ *adj*

anosmia /ə nózmi ə/ *n* absence or loss of the sense of smell [Early 19C. < AN- + Greek *osmē* 'smell'.] —**anosmic** *adj*

another /ə núthər/ *det, pron* 1 ONE MORE an additional ○ *need another person to help* ○ *May I have another?* 1 ONE THAT IS DIFFERENT somebody who or something that is separate or different ○ *We need another accountant because ours is moving.* ○ *This one is too dark; I would prefer another.* SOME OTHER some other one ◇ **another place** used by the House of Lords to refer to the House of Commons, and vice versa

A N Other /áy en úthər/ *n* an as-yet-unnamed person, e.g. in an incomplete list of participants or contestants

Anouilh /ánnoo ee/, **Jean** (1910–87) French dramatist

anovulant /ə nóvvyōōlant/ *n* a drug that prevents ovulation, e.g. a birth-control pill [Mid-20C. < AN- + OVULATE.] —**anovulant** *adj* —**anovulatory** /án ovvyōō láytəri/ *adj, n*

anovulation /án ovvyōō láysh'n/ *n* the state of not ovulating because of a medical condition, suppression by drugs, or menopause

anoxaemia /ánnok seémi ə/ *n* a deficiency of oxygen in the blood flowing through the arteries —**anoxaemic** *adj*

anoxemia *n* US = anoxaemia

anoxia /ə nóksi ə/ *n* MED = hypoxia *n.* —**anoxic** *adj*

ansate /án sayt/ *adj* with a handle or a part shaped like a handle [Late 19C. < Latin *ansatus < ansa* 'handle'.]

ansate cross *n* = ankh

Anselm /ánselm/, **St** (1033–1109) Italian theologian and philosopher

Ansermet /aánssər may/, **Ernest** (1883–1969) Swiss conductor

Ansett /ánssət/, **Sir Reginald Myles** (1909–81) Australian aviator and business executive

ANSI /ánssi/ *abbr* American National Standards Institute

answer /aánssər/ *n* 1 RESPONSE TO QUESTION the information requested by a question 2 WAY OF SOLVING PROBLEM the solution to a problem ○ *trying to find an answer to our ecological problems* 3 RESPONSE TO ACTION a response to something that somebody says or does ○ *She had no answer to her opponent's lethal backhand.* 4 CORRESPONDING THING something designed to match or correspond to something else 5 PLEA IN COURT a defendant's plea in response to a charge, lawsuit, or summons ■ *v* 1 *vti* REPLY to reply to something written or spoken 2 *vti* RESPOND TO CALL to respond to a summons, e.g. a ringing telephone, a doorbell, or somebody calling your name 3 *vti* CORRESPOND to match something or correspond to it ○ *We haven't found anyone who answers to that description.* 4 *vt* MEET A NEED to fulfil a need or wish 5 *vi* SERVE A PURPOSE to be adequate in meeting a requirement or serving a purpose (*formal*) ○ *an upturned box that answers for a seat* 6 *vt* RESPOND TO CHARGE IN COURT to offer a plea in response to a charge, lawsuit, or summons ○ *The defendant will now answer the charges.* [Old English *andswaru* < Germanic, 'swear against'] ◇ **be the answer to a maiden's prayer** to be exactly what is desired or sought after ◇ **know** *or* **have all the answers** to be admirably knowledgeable about a subject, or be irritatingly eager to demonstrate or claim superior knowledge

---

SYNONYMS *answer, reply, response, rejoinder, retort, riposte*

CORE MEANING: something said, written, or done in acknowledgment of a question or remark, or in reaction to a situation

answer an acknowledgment of a question, letter, or situation; **reply** a spoken or written answer, or a reaction to a situation; **response** a spoken or written answer, or a reaction to a situation; **rejoinder** a sharp, critical, angry, or clever reply, usually spoken; **retort** a sharp spoken reply, often to criticism; **riposte** a quick or witty spoken reply.

---

answer back *vti* to reply to somebody boldly or with impudence when silence is expected

answer for *vt* 1 to give an excuse or explanation for a wrong that has been committed ○ *You'll have to answer for this broken window.* 2 to give an assurance about somebody's good character ○ *She can be trusted, but I can't answer for the rest of the team.*

answer to *vt* to be accountable to somebody for something

answerable /aánssərəb'l/ *adj* 1 responsible for something ○ *You're answerable to your boss for any losses you incur.* 2 having a possible solution or a correct response —**answerability** /aánssərə bílləti/ *n* —**answerably** *adv*

answerback /aánssər bak/ *n* a response in a two-way radio transmission

answering machine *n* a recording device that is connected to a telephone and can be activated to play a message to callers and record messages from them

answering service *n* a business that receives telephone calls on behalf of other individuals and organizations and takes messages for them

ant /ant/ *n* an insect that lives in complex well-organized colonies and is noted for its ability to carry objects heavier than itself. Male ants have wings, as do fertile females (**queens**) after mating. Family: Formicidae. [Old English *æmette* < Germanic, 'cut off'] ◇ **have ants in your pants** to be excited or impatient about something (*informal*)

ant. *abbr* 1 antiquarian 2 antiquity 3 antonym

Ant. *abbr* Antarctica

ant- *prefix* = anti- (*before vowels*)

-ant *suffix* 1 performing a particular action ○ *desiccant* 2 being in a particular condition ○ *hesitant* [< Latin *-ant-,* stem of *-ans,* a present participle ending] —**-ance** *suffix* —**-ancy** *suffix*

anta /ántə/ (*plural* **-tae** /ántí/) *n* a thicker end of the side wall of a Greek temple that forms one side of a porch [Mid-18C. Back-formation < Latin *antae* 'square pilasters'.]

antacid /an tássid/ *adj* preventing, counteracting, or neutralizing acidity, especially in the stomach ■ *n* a drug that reduces or neutralizes stomach acid

antae *plural of* anta

antagonise *vt* = antagonize

antagonism /an tággənizəm/ *n* 1 HOSTILITY hostility or hatred causing opposition and ill will 2 OPPOSITION opposition between forces or principles ○ *the antagonism between good and evil* 3 NEUTRALIZING INTERACTION the interaction between two or more chemical substances in the body that diminishes the effect each of them has individually 4 MUSCLE OPPOSITION the opposing force that usually exists between pairs of muscles

antagonist /an tággənist/ *n* 1 OPPONENT somebody or something opposing or in conflict with another ○ *several antagonists locked in a power struggle* 2 CHARACTER IN CONFLICT WITH HERO a major character in a book, play, or film whose values or behaviour are in conflict with those of the protagonist or hero 3 NEUTRALIZING AGENT a drug that neutralizes the effect of a substance on the body 4 OPPOSING MUSCLE a muscle that acts with and limits the action of another muscle

antagonistic /an tággə nístik/ *adj* showing or expressing hostility —**antagonistically** *adv*

antagonize /an tággənīz/ (*-nizes, -nizing, -nized*), **antagonise** (*-nises, -nising, -nised*) *vt* to cause a person or animal to be hostile [Mid-17C. < Greek *antagōnizesthai* 'struggle against' < *agōnizesthai* 'struggle' < *agōn* 'contest'.]

Antakya /an taákyə/ city in S Turkey. Population: 123,871 (1990).

Antalya /an taályə/ city in SW Turkey. Population: 378,208 (1990).

Antananarivo /ántə nánnə reè vō/ capital of Madagascar. Population: 1,052,835 (1993).

Antarctic /an taárktik/ *n* the region lying south of the Antarctic Circle. ◇ **Arctic** —**Antarctic** *adj*

Antarctica /an taárktikə/ uninhabited continent surrounding the South Pole, consisting of an ice-covered plateau and high mountain peaks. Area: 14,245,000 sq. km/5,500,000 sq. mi.

Antarctic Circle the parallel of latitude at 66°30'S, encircling Antarctica and its surrounding seas

Antarctic Current ocean current circling Antarctica, circulating water eastwards through the Southern Ocean. Length: 21,000km/13,050mi.

Antarctic Ocean the waters of the S Atlantic, Indian, and Pacific oceans that surround Antarctica. Depths exceed 6,000 m/20,000 ft.

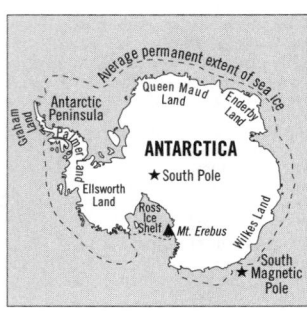

Antarctica

Antartic incorrect spelling of **Antarctic**

antazoline /an tázzə leen/ *n* a white odourless compound. Use: antihistamine.

ant bear *n* ZOOL = aardvark

ante /ánti/ *n* an amount a card player puts into the gambling pot before cards are dealt [Early 19C. < Latin (see ANTE-).] —**ante** *vti* ◇ **up the ante** 1 to increase the amount of money required to do or get something (*informal*) 2 to demand more in a situation, especially in an extortionate way (*informal*)

ante up *vti* US to pay money that is due to be paid (*informal*) ○ *We know you've got the cash, so ante up now!*

ante- *prefix* before, in front ○ *antechamber* [< Latin *ante* 'before' < Indo-European, 'front']

Anteater

anteater /ánt eetər/ *n* 1 a long-snouted toothless mammal that has long claws and a sticky tongue for catching prey, usually ants and termites. Native to: Central and South America. Family: Myrmecophagidae. 2 ZOOL = pangolin 3 ZOOL = aardvark

antebellum /ánti bélləm/ *adj* preceding a war [Mid-19C. < Latin *ante bellum* 'before the war'.]

antecede /ánti seéd/ (*-cedes, -ceding, -ceded*) *vt* to precede something in time or order (*formal*) ○ *Economic depressions often antecede wars.* [Early 17C. < Latin *antecedere* 'go before' < *cedere* 'give way'.]

antecedent /ánti seéd'nt/ *n* 1 THING COMING BEFORE something that happened or existed before something else ○ *The book deals with the historical antecedents of the revolution.* 2 WORD THAT SUBSEQUENT WORD REFERS TO a word or phrase that a subsequent word refers back to. 'Mary' is the antecedent of 'her' in the sentence 'I'll give this to Mary if I see her'. 3 CLAUSE EXPRESSING CONDITION the first part of a conditional proposition, which states the condition and is the p component in a proposition phrased 'if p then q' ■ **antecedents** *npl* 1 ANCESTORS somebody's ancestors 2 SOMEBODY'S HISTORY the events or circumstances in somebody's past ○ *He's done pretty well for himself, considering what we know of his antecedents.* ■ *adj* OCCURRING EARLIER IN TIME happening or existing before something else (*formal*) ○ *A high fever is usually an antecedent condition to other effects of the disease.* [14C. Directly or via French < Latin *antecedent-,* present participle of *antecedere* (see ANTECEDE).] —**antecedence** *n* —**antecedently** *adv*

USAGE Antecedents *Relative clauses* need something, such as *nouns*, to refer to, and the relationship ought to be clear. In formal writing, avoid constructions like these where the antecedents (words or phrases that subsequent material refers to) are either absent or unclear: *I'd sign up for advanced calculus if I were smart, which I'm not.* The clause *which I'm not* has no antecedent; also, *if I were smart* already tells the reader that I am not smart. Don't try to make an entire clause an antecedent for a *relative clause*; recast the sentence. Instead of *I need to purchase an entirely new computer system, which upsets me* use *I am upset that I need to purchase an entirely new computer system.* Similarly, avoid *relative clause* constructions with vague antecedents: *She crashed the ultralight aircraft into the freeway, which was her own fault.* Since the freeway was definitely not her own fault but the crash indeed was, reword the sentence: *Crashing the ultralight aircraft into the freeway was her own fault* or *She crashed the ultralight aircraft into the freeway in an accident that was her own fault.*

antechamber /ánti chaymbər/ *n* a small room leading into a larger main room and often used as a waiting area [Mid-17C. < French *antichambre*, translation of Italian *anticamera* 'room in front'.]

antechoir /ánti kwīr/ *n* an area at the entrance to the choir in a church, reserved for clergy and choir members

antedate /ánti dáyt/ *vt* (**-dates, -dating, -dated**) **1 OCCUR EARLIER THAN** to exist or happen at an earlier date than something else ○ *These tapestries antedate the development of synthetic dyes.* **2 PUT EARLIER DATE ON** to assign something a date that is earlier than its true or original date ○ *This vase was mistakenly antedated to the Ming dynasty.* ■ *n* **EARLIER DATE** a date assigned to something that is earlier than its true or original date

antediluvian /ánti di lóovi ən/ *adj* **1** in or from the time before the biblical Flood **2** extremely old-fashioned or out-of-date (*informal*) [Mid-17C. < ANTE- + Latin *diluvium* 'flood'.]

antefix /ánti fiks/ (*plural* **-fixes** *or* **-fixa** /-fiksə/) *n* an ornamental edging on the eaves of ancient buildings with tiled roofs that hides the joints of the roof tiles [Mid-19C. < Latin *antefixum* < *antefigere* 'fasten before' < *figere* 'fasten'.] —**antefixal** /ánti fíks'l/ *adj*

antegrade amnesia /ántə grayd-/ *n* a form of amnesia in which the memory loss relates to events occurring after a traumatic event

antelope /ántəlōp/ (*plural* **-lopes** *or* **-lope**) *n* a cud-chewing mammal with smooth brown or grey hair, two-toed hooves, and unbranched horns. Native to: Africa, SW Asia. Family: Bovidae. [15C. Via Old French *antelop*, < medieval Greek *antholops*.]

antemeridian /ánti mə ríddi ən/ *adj* relating to or taking place in the morning

ante meridiem /-mə ríddi əm/ *adj, adv* full form of **a.m.** [Mid-16C. < Latin, 'before noon'.]

antemortem /ánti máwrtəm/ *adj* existing or happening before death (*formal*) [Late 19C. < Latin *ante mortem* 'before death'.] —**ante mortem** *adv*

antenatal /ánti náyt'l/ *adj* existing or happening during pregnancy but before childbirth. US term **prenatal** —**antenatally** *adv*

antenna /an ténnə/ (*plural* **-nae** /-nee/ *or* **-nas**) *n* **1** a thin movable sensory organ found in pairs on the heads of some organisms, including insects and crustaceans **2** somebody's inquisitive or inquiring sense (*informal; often plural*) **3** *US* BROADCAST = **aerial** *n.* 1 [Mid-17C. < Latin, 'pole supporting a sail'.] —**antennal** *adj*

antenna head *n US* a person, especially a child, who spends a great deal of time watching television (*slang*)

antenuptial contract /ánti nûpsh'l-/ *n S Africa* LAW = **prenuptial agreement**

antepartum /ánti paártəm/ *adj* relating to the period before birth, especially the period of labour before a baby is delivered [Late 19C. < ANTE- + Latin *partus* 'birth'.]

antependium /ánti péndi əm/ (*plural* **-a** /-di ə/) *n* a decorative cloth that hangs on the front of an altar or lectern [Late 16C. < medieval Latin < Latin *pendere* 'hang'.]

antepenult /ánti pi núlt/ *n* the third from last syllable in a word ○ *The antepenult is stressed in the word 'superfluous'.*

antepenultimate /ánti pi núltimət/ *adj* third from last in a series ○ *the antepenultimate word in the paragraph* ■ *n* = **antepenult**

ante-post *adj* describes odds offered, or bets placed, before the starting places of the competitors are known, especially in horseracing

anterior /an teéri ər/ *adj* **1 IN FRONT** at or near the front of something (*formal*) ○ *an anterior view of the building* **2 EARLIER** existing or happening before something else (*formal*) **3 NEAR FRONT OF BODY** situated at or near the front of the body or of a body part **4 AWAY FROM STEM** describes a leaf or flower part that is situated furthest away or facing away from the stem of a plant [Mid-16C. Directly or via French < Latin, 'earlier' < *ante* 'before'.] —**anteriority** /an teéri órrəti/ *n*

anteroom /ánti room, -rŏŏm/ *n* a subsidiary room that opens into a larger main room, often used as a waiting area

antetype /ánti tīp/ *n* an earlier form of something

anteversion /ánti vúrsh'n/ *n* an unusual tilting forward of an organ, especially the uterus, without bending

anthelion /an theéli ən/ (*plural* **-a** /-i ə/) *n* a luminous spot appearing occasionally in the sky opposite the Sun [Late 17C. < Greek, 'opposite the sun' < *hēlios* 'sun'.]

anthelix /ant heéliks, an theé-/ (*plural* **-lixes** /-heéliksiz/ *or* **-lices** /-li seez/), **antihelix** /ánti heéliks/ (*plural* **-lixes** *or* **-lices** /-li seez/) *n* a ridge of cartilage located behind the folded edge (**helix**) of the outer ear and running more or less parallel to it

anthelmintic /ánthəl mínthik, ánthəl-/, **anthelminthic** /ant hel mínthik/ *adj* describes a drug that destroys or expels intestinal parasitic worms [Late 17C. < Greek *anti-* (see ANTI-) + *helmint-* 'worm'.] —**anthelmintic** *n*

anthem /ánthəm/ *n* **1** a stirring, often commercially popular song that has become associated with a particular group, period, or cause and celebrates a sense of solidarity with it ○ *The aria became the anthem of World Cup fans around the world.* **2 SONG OF ALLEGIANCE** a song praising and declaring loyalty to something, e.g. a country, cause or organization ○ *a national anthem* **3 SHORT HYMN FOR CHOIR** a short hymn with words from the Bible, sung by a choir as part of a church service **4 RELIGIOUS SONG WITH PARTS** a religious song with parts for different singers or groups, especially a church hymn with parts sung by different members of the congregation, e.g. a responsal psalm [Pre-12C. Via late Latin *antiphona* 'antiphon' < Greek *antiphōnos* 'responsive' < *phonē* 'sound'.]

anthemion /an theémi ən/ (*plural* **-a** /-ə/) *n* a motif of radiating leaves found in classical Greek art and design [Mid-19C. < Greek, 'small flower' < *anthos* 'flower'.]

anther /ánthər/ *n* a male flower part, the top part of a stamen, that bears the pollen in pollen sacs. ◊ **filament** *n.* 3 [Early 18C. Via Latin, 'medicine made from (the pollen-bearing part of) flowers' < Greek *anthēra* 'flowery' < *anthos* 'flower'.]

antheridium /ánthə ríddi əm/ (*plural* **-a** /-di ə/) *n* the male reproductive organ in algae, ferns, fungi, and mosses

anthesis /an theéssiss/ *n* **1** the opening of a flower bud **2** the period of time between the opening of a flower and the formation of the fruit [Mid-19C. Via modern Latin, < Greek *anthēsis* 'bloom' < *anthein* 'to flower' < *anthos* 'flower'.]

anthill /ánt hil/ *n* a mound of earth formed by ants during the construction of their nest

antho- *prefix* flower ○ *anthozoan* [< Greek *anthos*]

anthocyanin /ánthō sī ənin/ *n* a water-soluble pigment that produces blue, violet, and red colours in plants [Mid-19C. < ANTHO- + CYANINE.]

anthologise *vti* = **anthologize**

anthologize /an thóllə jīz/ (**-gizes, -gizing, -gized**), **anthologise** (**-gises, -gising, -gised**) *v* **1** *vt* to gather works from different writers or other artists, e.g. songwriters or painters, into a collection, or include somebody's work in a collection **2** *vi* to compile or publish an anthology

anthology /an thólləji/ (*plural* **-gies**) *n* **1** a book that consists of essays, stories, or poems by different writers **2** anything that brings together various things or ideas [Mid-17C. Via medieval Latin < medieval Greek *anthologiā* 'collection of flowers' < Greek *anthos* 'flower'.] —**anthologist** *n*

Anthony (of Padua) /ántəni/, **St** (1195–1231) Italian friar

Anthony, Susan B. (1820–1906) US social reformer. Full name **Susan Brownell Anthony**

anthophilous /an thóffiləss/ *adj* describes an insect that feeds on or lives among flowers

anthozoan /ánthə zṓ ən/ *n* a marine invertebrate animal with a roundish hollow body, e.g. a coral or sea anemone. Class: Anthozoa. [Late 19C. < modern Latin *Anthozoa* < ANTHO- + Greek *zōia* 'animals'.] —**anthozoic** *adj*

anthracene /ánthrə seen/ *n* $C_{14}H_{10}$ an aromatic crystalline solid with a faint blue glow. Source: coal tar. Use: manufacture of dyes, organic chemicals. [Mid-19C. < Greek *anthrax* 'coal'.]

anthraces plural of **anthrax**

anthracite /ánthrə sīt/ *n* a hard shiny black type of coal that is clean-burning, high in carbon content, and low in volatile matter [Early 19C. Via Latin < Greek *anthrakitēs* < *anthrax* 'coal'.] —**anthracitic** /ánthrə síttik/ *adj*

anthracnose /an thrákn ōss/ *n* a fungal disease of beans and vines that produces dark sunken spots on fruit, stems, and leaves [Late 19C. < French < Greek *anthrax* 'coal' + *nosos* 'disease'.]

anthracosis /ánthrə kṓssiss/ *n* pneumoconiosis caused by long-term inhalation of coal dust [Mid-19C. < Greek *anthrax* 'coal'.]

anthraquinone /ánthrə kwínnōn/ *n* $C_{14}H_8O_2$ a yellow crystalline chemical. Use: manufacture of dyes. [Late 19C. Blend of ANTHRACENE + QUINONE.]

anthrax /ánthraks/ (*plural* **-thraces** /-thrə seez/) *n* **1** a highly infectious fatal bacterial disease of mammals, especially cattle and sheep, that is transmittable to humans **2** an open sore on the skin that results from infection with anthrax [14C. < Greek, 'coal'.]

anthrobotics /ánthrō bóttiks/ *n* the study and development of robots that are intended to behave like or resemble human beings (+ *singular verb*) [Late 20C. Blend of ANTHROPO- + ROBOTICS.]

anthrop. *abbr* **1** anthropology **2** anthropological

anthropo- *prefix* human being ○ *anthropocentric* [< Greek *anthrōpos*]

anthropocentric /ánthrəpō séntrik/ *adj* **1** regarding humans as the universe's most important entity **2** seeing things in human terms, especially judging things according to human perceptions, values, and experiences ○ *anthropocentric responses to the condition of animals* —**anthropocentrically** *adv* —**anthropocentrism** *n*

anthropogenesis /ánthrəpō jénnəsiss/, **anthropogeny** /ánthrō pójjəni/ *n* the scientific study of the origin of humankind and how it has developed

anthropogenic /ánthrəpō jénnik/, **anthropogenetic** /ánthrəpōjə néttik/ *adj* **1** relating to or resulting from the influence humans have on the natural world **2** relating to the origin and development of human beings —**anthropogeny** *n*

anthropoid /ánthrə poyd/ *adj* **1 RELATING TO APES** describes monkeys and apes **2 LIKE HUMANS** physically resembling human beings or human parts **3 RESEMBLING A STEREOTYPED APE** rough-mannered, clumsy, ugly, or unintelligent, as apes are sometimes characterized (*informal*) ■ *n* **1 PRIMATE** an animal belonging to the group that includes monkeys, gibbons, great apes, and humans. Suborder: Anthropoidea. **2** ZOOL = **anthropoid ape** —**anthropoidal** /ánthrə póyd'l/ *adj*

anthropoid ape *n* a tailless animal with long arms and a highly developed brain that belongs to the family that includes the gorillas, chimpanzees, orangutans, and gibbons

anthropological /ánthrəpə lójjik'l/ *adj* relating to the study of humankind, especially the study of cultures —**anthropologically** *adv*

anthropological linguistics *n* a branch of linguistic research that investigates the relationship between language and culture (+ *singular verb*)

anthropology /ánthrə pólləji/ *n* **1** the study of humankind in all its aspects, especially human culture or human development **2** the parts of Christian doctrine that are concerned with the nature, origin, and destiny of humankind —**anthropologist** *n*

anthropometry /ánthrə pómmətri/ *n* the study of human body measurements —**anthropometric** /ánthrəpə méttrik/ *adj* —**anthropometrically** *adv* —**anthropometrist** *n*

anthropomorphise *vt* = **anthropomorphize**

anthropomorphism /ánthrōpō máwrfizəm/ *n* the attribution of a human form, human characteristics, or human behaviour to nonhuman things such as deities in mythology and animals in children's stories —**anthropomorphic** *adj* —**anthropomorphically** *adv*

anthropomorphize /ánthrəpə máwr fīz/ (**-phizes, -phizing, -phized**), **anthropomorphise** (**-phises, -phising, -phised**) *vt* to give a nonhuman thing a human form or human characteristics ○ *Mythology and children's stories anthropomorphize animals and inanimate objects.* —**anthropomorphization** /ánthrəpə máwr fī záysh'n/ *n*

anthropomorphous /ánthrəpə máwrfəss/ *adj* with the shape of the human body or a human body part

anthropopathism /ánthrə póppəthizəm/, **anthropopathy** /ánthrə póppəthi/ *n* the attribution of human emotions to a nonhuman thing, e.g. a deity or an object of worship [Mid-19C. < ANTHROPO- + -PATHY + -ISM.]

anthropophagus /ánthrə póffəgəss/ (*plural* **-gi** /-póffəjī/) *n* somebody who eats human flesh (*technical*) [Mid-16C. Via Latin, < Greek *anthrōpophagos* 'man-eating' < *anthrōpos* (see ANTHROPO-).] —**anthropophagic** /ánthrəpə fájjik/ *adj* —**anthropophagous** *adj* —**anthropophagy** /-póffəji/ *n*

anthroposophy /ánthrə póssəfi/ *n* a religious philosophy developed by Rudolf Steiner from theosophy, holding that spiritual development should be humanity's foremost concern —**anthroposophical** /ánthrəpə sóffik'l/ *adj* —**anthroposophist** *n*

anthurium /an thyoóri əm/ *n* a tropical evergreen plant with showy foliage. Flowers: glossy, heart-shaped, red or white, enclosing a spike of yellow florets. Native to: America. Genus: *Anthurium*. [Mid-19C. < modern Latin, < Greek *anthos* 'flower' (see ANTHO-) + *oura* 'tail'.]

anti /ánti/ *adj* expressing or holding an opposing view, particularly regarding a political issue or moral principle (*informal*) ○ *When it comes to smoking, she's very anti.* ■ *n* (*plural* **-tis**) somebody with an opposing view, particularly on a political issue (*informal*) ○ *Are you a pro or an anti?* [Late 18C. < ANTI-.]

anti-, **ant-** *prefix* against, opposite ○ *anticonvulsive* [Via Latin < Greek *anti* 'opposite, against']

antiabortion /ánti ə báwrsh'n/ *adj* opposed to the practice of abortion —**antiabortionist** *n*

antiadrenergic /ánti áddrə núrjik/ *adj* neutralizing the physiological effects of adrenaline ■ *n* a drug that counteracts the effects of adrenaline

antiageing /ánti áyjing/ *adj* intended to reduce or combat the effects of ageing, especially on the skin or personal appearance

antiaircraft /ánti áir kraaft/ *adj* designed and used to destroy enemy aircraft

antiaircraft gun *n* a piece of artillery designed and used to destroy enemy aircraft

⚡ **antialiasing** /ánti áyli əssing/ *n* smoothing the jagged edges of diagonal lines in computer graphics by varying the colour at the edges

antiangina /ánti an jínə/ *adj* relating to or preventing the symptoms of angina

antiarrhythmic /ánti ay ríthmik/ *adj* counteracting irregular heart action ■ *n* a drug that regulates the action of the heart

anti-art *n* the rebellion against easel painting and conventional art launched by the Dada movement during World War I ■ *adj* rejecting established artistic conventions

antiatom /ánti áttəm/ *n* an atom made up of antiparticles

antibacterial /ánti bak téeri əl/ *adj* preventing, killing, or reducing the growth of bacteria ■ *n* an agent that prevents, kills, or reduces the growth of bacteria

antiballistic missile /ánti bə lístik-/ *n* a missile used to prevent a ballistic missile from reaching its target by destroying it in flight

Antibes /on téeb/ port in SE France. Population: 72,412 (1999).

antibiosis /ánti bī óssiss/ *n* a relationship between organisms that is harmful to one of them, e.g. the production by one microorganism of chemicals that harm another [Late 19C. < ANTI-, after *symbiosis*.]

antibiotic /ánti bī óttik/ *n* a substance that kills or inactivates bacteria —**antibiotic** *adj* —**antibiotically** *adv*

antibody /ánti bodi/ (*plural* **-ies**) *n* a protein produced by B cells in the body in response to the presence of an antigen, e.g. a bacterium or virus [Early 20C. Translation of German *Antikörper*, contraction of *anti-toxischer Körper* 'antitoxic body' or a similar phrase.]

antic /ántik/ *npl* **antics** amusing, frivolous, or eccentric behaviour ■ *adj* ludicrously or amusingly strange and eccentric (*archaic*) [Early 16C. Via Italian *antico* 'old, old-fashioned' < Latin *anticus, antiquus*.] —**antically** *adv*

anticancer /ánti kánssər/ *adj* preventing or arresting the development of cancer

anticatalyst /ánti káttəlist/ *n* **1** CHEM = **inhibitor** *n*. 1 **2** a substance that inhibits or prevents the action of a catalyst

anticathode /ánti káthōd/ *n* the anode in a vacuum tube, e.g. an X-ray tube, towards which electrons flow

anti-choice *adj* against the principle or practice of legal abortion

anticholinergic /ántikōli núrjik/ *adj* blocking nerve impulses that are part of the stress response ■ *n* an anticholinergic agent

anticholinesterase /ántikōl néstə rayz, -rayss/ *n* a substance that blocks the activity of the enzyme cholinesterase, increasing the concentration of acetylcholine in the body

Antichrist /ánti krīst/ *n* **1** an antagonist of Jesus Christ, expected by the early Christians to spread evil throughout the world, but then to be overcome by the second coming of Christ **2 Antichrist, antichrist** any person or power opposed to Jesus Christ [Pre-12C. Via ecclesiastical Latin < Greek *antikhristos*.]

anticipate /an tíssi payt/ (**-pates, -pating, -pated**) *vt* **1 ACT BEFOREHAND TO ADDRESS SOMETHING IMMINENT** to imagine or consider something before it happens and make any necessary preparations or changes **2 EXPECT** to think or be fairly sure that a certain thing will happen or come. **3 LOOK FORWARD TO** to feel excited, hopeful, or eager about something that is going to happen **4 PREVENT** to imagine or consider something that might happen and take action to prevent it **5 START SOMETHING AHEAD OF TIME** to say or do something before it becomes fashionable or comes into widespread use (*formal*) **6 USE SOMETHING NOT YET RECEIVED** to make use of something before it has actually been received (*formal*) [Mid-16C. < Latin *anticipat-*, past participle of *anticipare* 'catch beforehand' < *capere* 'seize, take'.] —**anticipatable** *adj* —**anticipative** /-tíssipətiv/ *adj* —**anticipatively** *adv* —**anticipator** *n*

USAGE Anticipating trouble: If you ***anticipate*** trouble, it often just means that you are expecting or foreseeing trouble; the word's more traditional meaning is that you are taking steps to prevent trouble, that is forestalling rather than expecting it.

anticipation /an tíssi páysh'n/ *n* **1 EXPECTANT WAITING** the feeling of looking forward, usually excitedly or eagerly, to something that is going to happen **2 PREMATURE USE OF FUNDS** the seizure or use of funds before they are legally available, especially from a trust fund **3 NOTE PLAYED BEFORE CHORD** a note related to a chord that is played just before the chord itself

anticipatory /an tíssipətəri/ *adj* experienced or done in the expectation of a future event

anticlerical /ánti klérrik'l/ *adj* opposed to the involvement by the church or clergy in politics and public affairs —**anticlericalism** *n*

anticlimax /ánti klī maks/ *n* **1** an ordinary or unsatisfying event that follows an increasingly exciting, dramatic, or unusual series of events or a period of increasing anticipation and excitement **2** an unexpected change in tone or subject matter from the high-minded, serious, or compelling to the trivial, comic, or dull —**anticlimactic** /ánti klī máktik/ *adj* —**anticlimactically** *adv*

anticline /ánti klīn/ *n* an arch-shaped formation of layers of sedimentary rock folded upwards by movements in the earth's crust [Mid-19C < ANTI- + Greek *klinein* 'to lean', after INCLINE] —**anticlinal** /ánti klīn'l/ *adj*

anticlockwise /ánti klók wīz/ *adj, adv* in the opposite direction to the way the hands of a clock move. US term **counterclockwise**

anticoagulant /ánti kō ággyoolənt/ *adj* preventing normal blood clotting ■ *n* a natural or synthetic agent that prevents blood clots from forming

anticodon /ánti kō don/ *n* a set of three nucleotides in transfer RNA involved in the formation of a specific protein

anticoincidence /ánti kō ínssidənss/ *adj* describes an electronic circuit that produces an output pulse if one, but not both, of its input terminals receives a pulse within a specified time frame

anticompetitive /ántikəm péttətiv/ *adj* likely or certain to discourage competition

anticonvulsant /ántikən vúlssənt/ *adj* preventing or reducing seizures ■ *n* a drug that prevents or reduces seizures. Use: epilepsy control. —**anticonvulsive** *n, adj*

anticorrosive /ánti kə róssiv/ *adj* likely or certain to prevent corrosion

Anticosti Island /ánti kówsti-/ island in the Gulf of St. Lawrence, Canada. Area: 7,941 sq. km/3,066 sq. mi.

anticrime /ánti krīm/ *adj* designed to prevent or reduce the incidence of crime

anticyclone /ánti sīklōn/ *n* a large system of atmospheric high pressure marked by circulating winds moving clockwise from the centre in the northern hemisphere and anticlockwise in the southern hemisphere, bringing generally settled weather —**anticyclonic** /ánti sī klónnik/ *adj*

antidemocratic /ánti demmə kráttik/ *adj* opposed to or working in a way that undermines democratic procedures or policies, especially the political institution of representative government

antidepressant /ánti di préss'nt/ *n* a drug used to prevent or reduce depression ■ *adj* acting to prevent or reduce depression —**antidepressive** *adj*

antidiabetic /ánti dī ə béttik/ *adj* reducing the effects of diabetes

antidiarrhoeal /ánti dī ə rée əl/, **antidiarrheal** *adj* preventing or reducing diarrhoea ■ *n* a drug for preventing or reducing diarrhoea

antidiuretic /ánti dīyoo réttik/ *adj* preventing the excessive output of urine ■ *n* a drug for preventing or reducing the excessive output of urine

antidiuretic hormone *n* BIOCHEM = **vasopressin**

antidote /ántidōt/ *n* **1** a substance that counteracts the effects of a toxin **2** something that will take away or reduce the bad effects of something experienced earlier [15C. Via Latin, < Greek *antidoton* < *antididonai* 'give against' < *didonai* 'give'.] —**antidotal** /ánti dṓt'l/ *adj* —**antidotally** *adv*

antiemetic /ánti i méttik/ *adj* preventing vomiting ■ *n* a drug that prevents vomiting

Antietam /an téetəm/ creek near Sharpsburg, Maryland, the site of one of the bloodiest battles of the US Civil War in September 1862

antifebrile /ánti féeb rīl/ *adj, n* MED = **antipyretic**

antifederalist /ánti féddərəlist/ *n* an opponent of the division of power between a central government and regional governments —**antifederalism** *n* —**antifederalist** *adj*

antiferromagnetic /ánti férrō mag néttik/ *adj* describes substances that behave like paramagnetic substances with respect to their permeability but behave like ferromagnetic substances when their temperature is changed —**antiferromagnet** /ánti férrō mágnit/ *n* —**antiferromagnetism** /-mágnitizəm/ *n*

antifouling paint /ánti fówling-/ *n* a poisonous paint used to prevent barnacles and other organisms from growing on the bottoms of boats or ships

antifreeze /ánti freez/ *n* a substance added to a liquid to lower its freezing point

antifungal /ánti fúng g'l/ *adj* preventing or reducing the growth of fungi

antigen /ántijən/ *n* a substance, usually a protein, on the surface of a cell or bacterium that stimulates the production of an antibody [Early 20C. Via German, < French *antigène* < ANTI- + Greek *-genēs* (see -GEN).] —**antigenic** /ánti jénnik/ *adj* —**antigenically** *adv* —**antigenicity** /ántijə níssəti/ *n*

antigen feeding *n* the oral administration of a specific protein antigen to encourage immune-system tolerance to it

antigenic drift *n* changes of a minor nature in the antigenic structure of a virus strain

Antigone /an tíggəni/ *n* in Greek mythology, the daughter of Oedipus and his mother and wife Jocasta. She committed suicide.

Antigonus I /an tíggənəss/ (382?–301 BC) Greek general

antigravity /ánti grávvəti/ *n* a hypothetical force that would cancel the force of gravity ■ *adj* counteracting the effects of gravity or of high acceleration

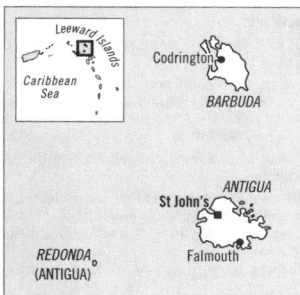

Antigua and Barbuda

Antigua and Barbuda /an teegə ənd baar boòdə/ island nation in the Leeward Islands in the Caribbean Sea. Capital: Saint John's. Population: 63,739 (1997). Area: 440 sq. km/170 sq. mi. —**Antiguan** *adj, n*

antihelix *n* ANAT = **anthelix**

antihero /ánti heerō/ (*plural* **-roes**) *n* a central character in a story who is not a traditionally brave or good hero —**antiheroic** /ánti hə rō ik/ *adj* —**antiheroism** /ánti hérrō izəm/ *n*

antihistamine /ánti hístə meen/ *n* a drug that blocks the action of histamine. Use: to control allergies. —**antihistaminic** /ánti hístə mínnik/ *adj*

antihypertensive /ánti hīpər ténssiv/ *adj* controlling high blood pressure ■ *n* an agent or means to control high blood pressure

anti-inflammatory (*plural* **anti-inflammatories**) *n* a drug that reduces inflammation, such as aspirin —**anti-inflammatory** *adj*

antiknock /ánti nók/ *n* a substance added to petrol to reduce or stop faulty fuel combustion associated with a knocking sound

Anti-Lebanon Mountains /ánti lébbənən-/ mountain range in SW Syria and E Lebanon. Highest peak: Mount Hermon 2,814 m/9,232 ft.

antilepton /ánti lépton/ *n* the antiparticle of a lepton

antilife /ánti līf/ *adj* preventing or opposed to living life to the full or fully in tune with the natural world (*informal*)

antilock brake /ánti lók-/ *n* an electronically controlled brake or braking system designed so that the vehicle's wheels do not lock if the driver brakes very suddenly

antilogarithm /ánti lóggərithəm/, **antilog** /ánti log/ *n* a number for which the logarithm is a given number, so for logarithm$_b$c = c, then antilogarithm$_b$c = b

antilogy /an tílləji/ (*plural* **-ogies**) *n* a phrase that contradicts itself or negates what it says < Greek *antilogia* 'speaking against' < *-logia* (see -LOGY).]

antimacassar /ánti mə kássər/ *n* a piece of fabric placed over the back of an armchair to keep it clean (*dated*) [Mid-19C. < ANTI- + *Macassar*, brand of hair oil.]

antimagnetic /ánti mag néttik/ *adj* describes a material that does not become permanently magnetized in a magnetic field

antimalarial /ánti mə láiri əl/ *adj* preventing or curing malaria ■ *n* a drug that prevents or cures malaria

antimasque /ánti maask/, **antimask** *n* an interlude in or prelude to a 17th-century masque that contrasts with the main performance and often involves grotesque costume and dancing

antimatter /ánti mattər/ *n* a hypothetical form of matter composed of subatomic particles (**antiparticles**) that correspond to and can annihilate other elementary particles

antimetabolite /ánti mə tábbə līt/ *n* a substance that disrupts cell growth by replacing normal cell nutrients. Use: some cancer treatments.

antimicrobial /ánti mī krōbi əl/ *adj* **1** CONTROLLING MICRO-ORGANISMS neutralizing microorganisms **2** CAPABLE OF KILLING MICROBES capable of killing or inhibiting the growth of microorganisms, especially bacteria, fungi, or viruses ■ *n* **1** AGENT THAT CONTROLS MICROORGANISMS an agent that neutralizes microorganisms **2** CHEMICAL THAT KILLS MICROBES a chemical that kills or inhibits the growth of microorganisms, especially bacteria, fungi, or viruses

antimissile missile /ánti míssīl-/ *n* a missile used to prevent another missile from reaching its target by destroying it in flight

antimitotic /ánti mī tóttik/ *adj* preventing cell division (**mitosis**) —**antimitotic** *n*

antimonial /ánti mōni əl/ *adj* describes drugs that contain antimony ■ *n* a drug or other substance containing antimony

antimony /ántiməni, an tímməni/ *n* (*symbol* Sb) a toxic crystalline element that occurs in metallic and non-metallic forms. Source: ores, e.g. stibnite. Use: alloys, electronics. [15C. < medieval Latin *antimonium*.]

antimycotic /ánti mī kóttik/ *adj* preventing, killing, or reducing the growth of fungi [< ANTI- + Greek *mukhētes* 'fungi']

antineoplastic /ánti nee ō plástik/ *adj* preventing or inhibiting the growth of cancers —**antineoplastic** *n*

antineutrino /ánti nyoo treenō/ (*plural* **-nos**) *n* the antiparticle of a neutrino

antineutron /ánti nyoò tron/ *n* the antiparticle of a neutron

antinode /ántinōd/ *n* a point of maximum amplitude of a wave characteristic in a system in which the wave form is stationary in time

antinomian /ánti nōmi ən/ *n* CHRISTIAN BELIEVING SALVATION DEPENDS ON FAITH a Christian who believes that faith and divine grace bring about salvation and that established laws are not binding ■ *adj* **1** OPPOSING FIXED MORAL LAWS disagreeing with the philosophy that the same fixed rules of morality and other laws should apply to everybody **2** HOLDING ANTINOMIAN BELIEFS accepting antinomianism in Christian belief [Mid-17C. < medieval Latin *Antinomi* 'antinomians' < Latin *antinomia* (see ANTINOMY).]

antinomianism /ánti nōmi ənizəm/ *n* **1** a belief that Christians are not bound by established laws, especially moral laws, but should rely on faith and divine grace for salvation **2** the belief that it is impossible to apply a universal moral code because it will have a different meaning for different people

antinomy /an tínnəmi/ (*plural* **-mies**) *n* **1** a contradictory and illogical conclusion produced by two apparently correct and reasonable statements or facts **2** a contradiction between two laws, principles, or authorities [Late 16C. Via Latin < Greek *antinomia* 'against law' < *nomos* 'law, rule'.] —**antinomic** /ánti nómmik/ *adj*

antinovel /ánti nov'l/ *n* a work of fiction that lacks the elements traditionally used in a novel, especially one with no coherent plot and characters, or in which the writer's perspective is deliberately inconsistent —**antinovelist** *n*

antinuclear /ánti nyoòkli ər/ *adj* **1** opposed to nuclear weapons or power **2** reactive with or destructive to cell nuclei

antinucleon /ánti nyoòkli on/ *n* an antiproton or antineutron

Antioch /ánti ok/ former name for **Antakya**

anti-oncogene *n* a recessive gene that is thought to suppress cancers by limiting cell multiplication

antioxidant /ánti óksidənt/ *n* any substance that inhibits the destructive effects of oxidation, e.g. in the body or in foodstuffs and plastics

antiparallel /ánti párrə lel/ *adj* parallel but opposite in linear or rotational direction

antiparticle /ánti paartik'l/ *n* an elementary particle with the same mass as its corresponding particle but having opposite values for other properties such as charge. When an antiparticle and its particle interact mutual annihilation occurs.

antipasto /ánti pastō/ (*plural* **-ti** /-pasti/ *or* **-tos**) *n* food served at the beginning of an Italian meal or as a snack [Early 17C. < Italian, 'before food'.]

antipathetic /ántipə théttik/ *adj* **1** feeling or expressing anger, hostility, strong opposition, or disgust, especially towards a particular person or thing **2** stirring up or causing strongly negative feelings such as anger, hostility, or disgust [Early 17C. < ANTIPATHY, after PATHETIC.] —**antipathetically** *adv*

antipathy /an típpəthi/ (*plural* **-thies**) *n* **1** anger, hostility, fixed opposition, or disgust directed towards a particular person or thing **2** a source of somebody's anger, hostility, fixed opposition, or disgust [Late 16C. Via French *antipathie* < Greek *antipathēs* 'feeling the opposite' < *pathos* 'feeling'.]

SYNONYMS See *dislike*.

antiperiodic /ánti peeri óddik/ *adj* preventing the periodic recurrence of symptoms or of a disease such as malaria —**antiperiodic** *n*

antiperistalsis /ánti perri stálsiss/ (*plural* **-ses** /-seez/) *n* contractions of the intestine in the reverse direction to what is usual, tending to cause vomiting —**antiperistaltic** *adj*

antipersonnel /ánti purssə nél/ *adj* intended to injure and kill enemy personnel rather than to blow up buildings, structures, arsenals, or missiles

antiperspirant /ánti púrspərənt/ *n* an astringent preparation applied especially under the arms to help prevent perspiration ■ *adj* used to reduce or prevent perspiration

antiphase /ánti fáyz/ *adj* relating to a boundary, e.g. in an alloy, where an ordered pattern of atoms meets a random pattern

antiphon /ántifən/ *n* **1** MUSIC SUNG IN ALTERNATING PARTS a hymn or psalm performed by two groups of singers chanting alternate sections **2** SECTION OF FORMAL CHURCH SERVICE a short piece of biblical or devotional text that is chanted or sung before or after a psalm verse in a Roman Catholic or Anglican church service **3** RESPONSE a response or reply (*literary*) [15C. Via ecclesiastical Latin *antiphona* < Greek *antiphōnos* 'sounding in response' < *phōnē* 'sound'.]

antiphonary /an tíffənə ri/ (*plural* **-ies**) *n* a book, often large and richly decorated, containing antiphons or anthems to be sung or chanted responsively

antiphony /an tíffəni/ (*plural* **-nies**) *n* **1** CHR = **antiphon** *n*. **1 2** responsive chanting, recitation, or singing, e.g. of liturgical antiphons **3** a musical response or answering phrase —**antiphonal** *adj* —**antiphonally** *adv*

antiphrasis /an tíffrəsiss/ *n* the use of a word or phrase to mean the opposite of its usual or literal sense, e.g. saying on a rainy day, 'What a lovely day for a picnic!' [Mid-16C. < late Latin, < Greek *antiphrazein* 'express opposity' < *phrazein* 'declare'.]

antipode /ántipōd/ *n* an exact or diametrical opposite [Early 17C. Back-formation < ANTIPODES.]

antipodean /ánti típpə deè ən/, **Antipodean** *adj* coming from or relating to Australia or New Zealand

antipodes /an típpə deez/ *npl* **1** places at opposite sides of the world **2** two points, places, or things that are diametrically opposite each other [14C. Via French or late Latin < Greek *antipodes* 'those who have their feet opposite' < *pod-*, stem of *pous* 'foot'.] —**antipodal** *adj*

Antipodes /an típpə deez/ *n* Australia and New Zealand, from the perspective of the United Kingdom or Europe (*informal*)

antipollution /ánti pə loòsh'n/ *adj* designed to stop or reduce pollution of the environment

antipope /ántipōp/ *n* an alternative pope elected in opposition to a standing pope [15C. Via French *antipape* < medieval Latin *antipapa* < *papa* 'pope', after *antichristus* 'Antichrist'.]

antiprostaglandin /ánti próstə glándin/ *n* a drug or agent used to limit the release of prostaglandins

antiproton /ántiprō ton/ *n* the antiparticle of a proton

antipruritic /ánti proor ríttik/ *adj* controlling itching ■ *n* a drug or other agent that controls itching

antipsoriasis /ánti sə rí əssiss/ *adj* alleviating the symptoms of psoriasis —**antipsoriatic** /ánti sáwri áttik/ *adj*

antipsychiatry /ántī sī kí ətri/ *n* a way of treating people with psychiatric disorders that is derived from psychoanalysis and is opposed to conventional medication

antipsychotic /ánti sī kóttik/ *adj* relieving the symptoms of psychosis ■ *n* a drug that relieves the symptoms of a psychiatric disorder

antipyretic /ánti pī réttik/ *adj* reducing fever ■ *n* a drug or other agent that reduces fever —**antipyresis** /ánti pī reéssiss/ *n*

antiq. *abbr* **1** antiquarian **2** antiquity

antiquarian /ánti kwáiri ən/ *adj* dealing with or relating to antiques or antiquities, especially rare and old books ■ *n* = **antiquary** —**antiquarianism** *n*

antiquark /ánti kwaark/ *n* the antiparticle of a quark

antiquary /ántikwəri/ (*plural* **-ies**) *n* a collector, scholar, or seller of antiques or antiquities [Mid-16C. < Latin *antiquarius* < *antiquus* 'old'.]

antiquate /ánti kwayt/ (**-quates, -quating, -quated**) *vt* **1** to cause something to become out of date or old by replacing it with something newer **2** CRAFT = **antique** *v.* [Late 16C. Via ecclesiastical Latin *antiquare* 'make old' < Latin *antiquus* (see ANTIQUE).]

antiquated /ánti kwaytid/ *adj* quaint, extremely out of date, or badly in need of updating or replacing —**antiquatedness** *n*

antique /an téek/ *n* (*plural* **-tiques**) **1 OLD ITEM** a collectable decorative or household object, often a piece of furniture, which is valued because of its age **2 CLASSICAL ART** the style, traditions, and qualities of ancient times, usually specifically the art and sculpture of ancient Greece and Rome ■ *adj* **1 MADE LONG AGO** old and often valuable, of interest to collectors, and characteristic of a particular period and style of manufacture **2 FROM CLASSICAL TIMES** derived from a period of ancient history, especially ancient Greece or Rome, or stylistically typical of such a period (*formal*) **3 ANCIENT** very old or old-fashioned (*informal*) ■ *vt* (**-tiquing, -tiqued**) **MAKE SOMETHING APPEAR OLD** to treat something, especially a new object, so that it looks antique or worn with time [15C. Via French < Latin *antiquus* 'old'.] —**antiquely** *adv* —**antiqueness** *n*

antiquity /an tíkwəti/ (*plural* **-ties**) *n* **1 ANCIENT HISTORY** ancient history, especially the period of time during which the ancient Greek or Roman civilizations flourished **2 OLDNESS** the state of being very old or ancient ○ *a sculpture of great antiquity* **3 OLD OBJECT** an object, especially something collectable, decorative, valuable, or interesting, that dates from a previous era **4 PEOPLE OF ANCIENT TIME** the people of ancient civilizations, especially those of ancient Greece or Rome

antiracism /ánti ráyssizəm/ *n* policies, views, or actions that oppose racial prejudice and discrimination and promote racial equality —**antiracist** *adj, n*

antirejection /ánti ri jéksh'n/ *adj* designed to prevent the immune system from rejecting a newly grafted organ or tissue

antiretroviral /ánti réttrō vírəl/ *adj* effective against retroviruses

antirheumatoid /ánti róomə toyd/ *adj* preventing or relieving the symptoms of rheumatism

anti-roll bar *n* a cross-mounted metal bar incorporated in the suspension system of a motor vehicle, designed to prevent the vehicle from swinging dangerously or overturning

antirrhinum /ánti rínəm/ *n* PLANTS = **snapdragon** [Mid-16C. Via Latin < Greek *antirrhinon* 'counterfeiting a nose' < *rhin-* 'nose'; from the flower's shape.]

antisatellite /ánti sátt'l īt/ *adj* designed to destroy or incapacitate satellites

anti-Semitic /ánti sə míttik/ *adj* hating or discriminating against Jewish people (*disapproving*)

anti-Semitism *n* policies, views, or actions that harm or discriminate against Jewish people (*disapproving*) —**anti-Semite** /ánti séemīt, ánti sémmīt/ *n*

antisense /ánti sénss/ *adj* relating to or having a strand of DNA complementary to other genetic material, enabling the expression of a trait to be regulated

antisepsis /ánti sépsiss/ *n* **1** eliminating or reducing the spread of microorganisms causing disease or decay, especially with chemicals **2** the condition of being free from microorganisms

antiseptic /ánti séptik/ *adj* **1 CONTROLLING INFECTION** reducing or preventing infection, especially by the elimination or reduction of the growth of microorganisms **2 DULL** unexciting and unimaginative ■ *n* **AGENT FOR CONTROLLING INFECTION** an agent that prevents or reduces infection, especially by eliminating or reducing the growth of microorganisms —**antiseptically** *adv*

antiserum /ánti seerəm/ (*plural* **-rums** *or* **-ra** /-rə/) *n* an animal or human blood serum containing one or more specific ready-made antibodies. Use: to provide immunity against a disease, to counteract venom.

antisexist /ánti séksist/ *adj* opposed to discrimination on the basis of sex, particularly discrimination against women —**antisexism** *n*

antislavery /ánti sláyvəri/ *adj* in favour of abolishing slavery or preventing people from enslaving others

antismog /ánti smóg/ *adj* designed to stop or reduce smog

antismoking /ánti smṓking/ *adj* established or designed to stop people smoking tobacco

antisocial /ánti sṓsh'l/ *adj* **1** annoying, inconsiderate, or indifferent to the comfort or needs of neighbours, or to society as a whole **2** preferring not to spend time with other people —**antisociality** /ánti sṓshi állәti/ *n* —**antisocially** *adv*

antispasmodic /ánti spaz móddik/ *adj* controlling spasms ■ *n* a drug or other agent that controls muscle spasms

antistatic /ánti státtik/, **antistat** /ánti stat/ *adj* preventing or controlling the effects of static electricity

Antisthenes /an tísthə neez/ (444?–365? BC) Greek philosopher

antistrophe /an tístrəfi/ *n* **1** the second of two movements made by the chorus in a classical Greek drama, or the section of an ode sung during this movement **2** the second type of metrical form in a poem that alternates two contrasting metrical forms. ◊ **strophe** *n.* 1 [Mid-16C. Via late Latin < Greek *antistrophē* < *antistrephein* 'turn back' < *strophē* (see STROPHE).] —**antistrophic** /ánti strόffik/ *adj* —**antistrophically** *adv*

antisubmarine /ánti súbmə reen/ *adj* designed to destroy or incapacitate submarines

antitank /ánti tánk/ *adj* designed to destroy or incapacitate military tanks

antitheft /ánti théft/ *adj* designed to prevent something, e.g. a motor vehicle, from being stolen

antithesis /an títhəssiss/ (*plural* **-ses** /-seez/) *n* **1 DIRECT OPPOSITE** the complete or exact opposite of something **2 FIGURE OF SPEECH** a use of words or phrases that contrast with each other to create a balanced effect **3 CONTRASTING PROPOSITION** a proposition that is the opposite of another already proposed [Early 16C. < late Latin, < Greek *antitithenai* 'set against' < *tithenai* 'set'.]

antithetical /ánti théttik'l/, **antithetic** /ánti théttik/ *adj* **1** expressing or constituting the complete or exact opposite (*formal*) ○ *policies that are antithetical to the prevailing mood of the country* **2** amounting or relating to a proposition that is the opposite of another already proposed [Late 16C. < Greek *antithetikos* < *antitithenai* (see ANTITHESIS).] —**antithetically** *adv*

antithyroid /ánti thī́ royd/ *adj* counteracting thyroid overactivity, especially in its production of thyroid hormone

antitoxic /ánti tóksik/ *adj* acting to counteract toxins

antitoxin /ánti tóksin/ *n* **1** an antibody produced in response to a particular toxin **2** MED = **antiserum**

antitrade /ánti trayd/ *n* a wind in the planetary wind system that is above the trade winds and blows in the opposite direction from them

antitragus /an títtrəgəss/ (*plural* **-gi** /-jī/) *n* a bump of cartilage just below the opening of the external ear

antitrust /ánti trúst/ *adj US* intended to oppose trusts and cartels, e.g. from using monopolistic business practices to make unfair profits

antituberculosis /ánti tyoo búrkyoo lṓssiss/ *adj* effective against tuberculosis

antitussive /ánti tússiv/ *adj* controlling coughing ■ *n* a drug that controls coughing

antitype /ánti tīp/ *n* **1** somebody or something seen as being foreshadowed by or having striking similarities to an earlier person or thing (**type**) in the Bible **2** an opposite or contrasting type [Early 17C. Via late Latin < Greek *antitupos* 'corresponding as an impression (to the die in which it was cast)' < *tupos* (see TYPE).] —**antitypical** /ánti típpik'l/ *adj*

antivenin /ánti vénnin/, **antivenom** /-vénnəm/ *n* **1** an antitoxin to a particular venom **2** an antiserum containing antibodies to venom [Early 20C. < ANTI- + VENOM + -IN.]

antiviral /ánti vī́rəl/ *adj* used to eliminate or inactivate a virus

⚡**antivirus** /ánti vī́rəss/ *adj* **1** describes a utility program that identifies and removes viruses in a computer's memory or on disks before damage occurs to the computer system

antivitamin /ánti víttəmin/ *n* a substance that neutralizes a vitamin

antivivisectionist /ánti vivvi séksh'nist/ *n* an opponent of scientific experiments on live animals (**vivisection**) —**antivivisectionism** *n* —**antivivisectionist** *adj*

antiwar /ánti wáwr/ *adj* wanting to prevent a war or bring a war to an end

antler /ántlər/ *n* a solid bony branched horn found in pairs on the head of animals, especially males, of the deer family [14C. < Anglo-Norman variant of Old French *antoillier.*] —**antlered** *adj*

Antlia /ántli ə/ *n* a faint constellation of the southern hemisphere

ant lion *n* a nocturnal insect that resembles a damselfly when adult. Family: Myrmeleontidae. [Translation of Greek *murmēko-leōn*; from its usual prey and its fierce-looking jaws]

Antofagasta /ántōfə gástə/ city in N Chile. Population: 251,429 (1998).

Antonello da Messina /ántə néllō daa mə séenə/ (1430?–79) Italian painter

Antonescu /ántə nés kyoo, -nés koo/, **Ion** (1882–1946) Romanian general and politician

Antoninus Pius /ántə nī́nəss pī́ əss/ (AD 86–161) Roman emperor (AD 138–161)

Antonioni /án tōni ṓni/, **Michelangelo** (*b.* 1912) Italian filmmaker

antonomasia /ántənə máyzi ə/ *n* **1** the use of a title or formal description such as 'Your Highness' or 'His Excellency' in place of somebody's proper name **2** the use of a proper name as a common noun to refer to somebody or something with associated characteristics, e.g. when a strong young man is called 'a Hercules' [Mid-16C. < Latin, < Greek *antonomazein* 'name instead' < *anti-* 'against, instead' + *onuma* 'name'.]

Antony /ántəni/, **Mark** (83?–30 BC) Roman politician and general

antonym /ántənim/ *n* a word that means the opposite of another word. For example 'hot' is the antonym of 'cold'. [Mid-19C. < French *antonyme* < Greek *anti-* 'against, opposite' + *onuma* 'name'.] —**antonymic** /ántə nímmik/ *adj* —**antonymous** /an tónnəməss/ *adj* —**antonymy** /-mi/ *n*

antra /ántrə/ plural of **antrum**

Antrim /ántrim/ **1** town in NE Northern Ireland. Population: 20,878 (1991). **2** former county in NE Northern Ireland

Antrim Coast and Glens /-glénz/ Area of Outstanding Natural Beauty in Northern Ireland. Area: 706 sq. km/273 sq. mi.

antrostomy /an tróstəmi/ *n* the surgical creation of an opening into an antrum, usually for drainage purposes [< ANTRUM]

antrum /ántrəm/ (*plural* **-tra** /ántrə/) *n* a cavity within a bone, especially a sinus cavity [Early 19C. Via Latin, 'cave' < Greek *antron.*]

antsy /ántsi/ (**-sier, -siest**) *adj US* (*informal*) **1** tensely nervous or apprehensive **2** moving or squirming about in a restless, bored, or impatient way [Mid-20C. Probably < *have ants in your pants.*]

Antwerp /án twurp/ city in Belgium, on the Schelde River estuary. Population: 449,745 (1998 estimate).

ANU *abbr Aus* Australian National University

Anubis /ə nyóobiss/ *n* in Egyptian mythology, a god represented with the head of a jackal, who leads the dead to judgment

anuran /ə nyóorən/ *n* an amphibian such as a frog or toad that does not have a tail as an adult and has long powerful hind legs. Order: Anura. [Late 19C. < modern Latin *Anura* < Greek *an-* 'without' + *oura* 'tail'.]

anuria /a nyóori ə, ə-/ *n* inability of the kidneys to form urine, leading to a build-up of toxic waste in the blood —**anuric** *adj*

anus /áynəss/ *n* the opening at the lower end of the alimentary canal through which faeces are released [15C. < Latin, 'ring'.]

Anuszkiewicz /a núskəvich/, **Richard** (*b.* 1930) US artist

anvil /ánvil/ *n* **1** a sturdy piece of iron onto which heated metal is placed to be beaten into the required shape **2** ANAT = **incus** [Old English *anfilte*, *anfealt* < Indo-European, 'to beat']

anvil technique *n* a prehistoric method of making chipped stone tools that involves striking a stone repeatedly against a static boulder used as an anvil

anxiety /ang zī əti/ (*plural* **-ties**) *n* **1 FEELING OF WORRY** nervousness or agitation, often about something that is going to happen **2 SOMETHING THAT WORRIES** a subject or concern that causes worry **3 STRONG WISH** the strong wish to do a particular thing, especially if the wish is unnecessarily or unhealthily strong **4 EXTREME APPREHENSION** a medical condition marked by abnormal and intense apprehension or fear of real or imagined danger [Early 16C. < French *anxiété* < Latin *anxius* (see ANXIOUS).]

SYNONYMS See *worry*.

anxiety disorder *n* a psychiatric disorder causing feelings of persistent anxiety, e.g. panic disorder or post-traumatic stress disorder

anxiety neurosis *n* a persistent panic disorder characterized by emotional distress, constant worry, and a strong tendency to avoid specific situations

anxiolytic /ángzi ə líttik/ *adj* relieving anxiety ■ *n* a drug that relieves anxiety [Mid-20C. < ANXIETY + *-lytic*.]

anxious /ánkshəss/ *adj* **1 FEELING NERVOUS** worried or afraid, especially about something that is going to happen or might happen **2** ⚠ **EAGER** wanting to do or receive something very much, or in a tense or uneasy way. **3 PRODUCING ANXIETY** producing feelings of fear, uncertainty, or nervousness [Early 17C. < Latin *anxius* < *anx-*, past participle of *angere* 'torment', literally 'strangle'.] —**anxiously** *adv* —**anxiousness** *n*

USAGE anxious or **eager**? In formal writing avoid using ***anxious*** to mean ***eager***, as in *She was anxious to attend the concert.* Say instead: *She was eager to attend the concert.*

any /énni/ CORE MEANING: a grammatical word used to indicate one, some, or several, when the quality, type, or number is not important ○ (det) *Do you have any books on gardening?* ○ (pron) *for any who wish to enter*

1 *det, pron* **EVEN ONE OR A LITTLE** even one or even the least amount (*in negatives*) ○ *I don't want any dessert.* ○ *I didn't see any.* ○ *This isn't any of your business.* **2** *det, pron* **EVERY** every person or thing stated, no matter who or what ○ *Any financial advisor would agree.* **3** *det* **WITHOUT LIMIT** an unlimited or indefinite amount or number of ○ *any number of foods including soups, stews, and salads* **4** *adv* **IN SOME DEGREE** to even the smallest extent or degree (*before adjectives and adverbs*) ○ *Is it getting any louder?* **5** ⚠ *adv US* **AT ALL** used after a verb to add emphasis (*informal*) ○ *I still don't like him any.* [Old English *ǣnig* < Indo-European, 'one of a kind']

USAGE Singular or plural? ***Any*** used as a pronoun is followed by a singular or plural verb depending on the intended meaning: *Any of these suggestions is acceptable. Are any of the children* [i.e. more than one of several children] *coming?* (*Is any of the children coming?* implies that one is expected, with uncertainty as to which).

USAGE American **any**. The use of ***any*** as an adverb meaning 'at all' is a distinctly American idiom that is not yet used in British English: *Her manners haven't improved any.*

anybody /énni bodi, -bədi/ *pron* = **anyone**

USAGE See *anyone*.

ϟ **anycast** /énni kaast/ *n* an act of sending data across a computer network from a single user to the nearest receiver —**anycasting** *n*

anyhow /énni how/ CORE MEANING: an adverb meaning no matter what the situation is or no matter what may be true ○ *What does it matter, anyhow?* ○ *and anyhow I have to go*

adv **1 IN ANY CASE** no matter what the situation is or no matter what may be true ○ *What does it matter, anyhow?* **2 IN A CARELESS WAY** in a haphazard, careless, or untidy way ○ *ideas produced anyhow* **3 NEVERTHELESS** in spite of something ○ *I asked him to wait, but he left anyhow.*

any more /énni máwr/ *adv* (*in negative statements or questions*) **1** at present and continuing from a point in the past ○ *They don't make them like this any more!* **2** from the present and ongoing ○ *I'm not tolerating this any more.*

USAGE anymore or **any more**? In British English, ***any more*** used as an adverbial phrase after a negative or a question is normally written as two words: *She doesn't live here any more.* In American English and in some other varieties (for example Australian and South African English) it is also, though not exclusively, written as one word, ***anymore***, and there are signs that this is occurring in British contexts too, although this is not yet standard.

anyone /énni wun/ CORE MEANING: an indefinite pronoun used to mean one or more people, when exactly which person or which people is not known or not important ○ *Can I get anyone more coffee?* ○ *Did anyone show up?* ○ *There isn't anyone home.*

pron **1 EVERY PERSON** any or every particular person who could be named or thought of ○ *more qualified than anyone in the business* **2 EVEN ONE PERSON** used to emphasize the unlikelihood of finding even one person to match the stated description or criteria ○ *Why would anyone want to hurt me?* **3 UNIMPORTANT PERSON** an unimportant and unknown person ○ *It's not just anyone, it's your sister!*

USAGE anyone or **any one**? ***Anyone*** is rather more common than *anybody* (which has the same meaning), and is used only of people after a negative or a question: *Has anyone seen my pen?* The words *any* and *one* are written separately when they mean any one particular person or thing: *Any one of them could have started the fire. The tables are all free, so you can sit at any one you like.*

anyplace /énni playss/ *adv US, Can* at, in, or to any place (*informal*)

USAGE American **anyplace** and **anytime**: In British English, **any place** and **any time** are not yet regarded as a unit and are usually spelt as two words in each case, whereas in US English they are more often spelt as single words and are entered that way in dictionaries: *I don't recall seeing him anyplace. You can come anytime you like.*

anyroad /énni rōd/ *adv N England* anyway

anyroads /énni rōdz/ *adv N England* in any case or no matter what (*informal*) ○ *Anyroads, that's what I heard.*

anything /énni thing/ *pron* any object, event, action, situation, or fact ○ *Is there anything I need to know?* ■ *adv* in any way (*in negative statements or questions*) ○ *He isn't anything like his brother.* ◇ **anything but** used as an emphatic way of contradicting or negating a statement

anytime /énni tīm/ *adv US, Can* at some undecided time, whenever you like, or whenever seems appropriate (*informal*)

USAGE See *anyplace*.

anyway /énni way/ CORE MEANING: an adverb meaning no matter what the situation is ○ *Anyway, we have to pay whether it was accidental or not.* ○ *Recycling, according to some anyway, is the best way of teaching respect for the environment.*

adv **1 IN ANY CASE** no matter what **2 REGARDLESS OF** in spite of the situation already stated ○ *I knew it would be a sad movie but I went anyway.* **3 IN A CARELESS WAY** in a careless, haphazard, or lazy way ○ *According to my mother, packing is a skilled operation, not throwing your clothes into a case just anyway.* **4 anyway, any way BY ANY MEANS** in any manner or way (*informal*) ○ *We have to teach our children moral values anyway we can.*

anyways /énni wayz/ *adv regional or nonstandard US* anyway

anywear /énni wair/ *n* clothing that can be worn for both casual and more formal occasions (*informal*)

anywhere /énni wair/ CORE MEANING: an indefinite pronoun and adverb referring to one or many places unknown or unspecified ○ (pron-indef) *Is there anywhere you prefer?* ○ (pron-indef) *Anywhere we live now will seem warm.* ○ (adv) *She can sleep anywhere.*

1 *pron* **SOME UNIDENTIFIED PLACE** one or many places unknown or unspecified **2** *adv* **TO ANY PLACE** to one or many places unknown or unspecified ○ *I'll follow you anywhere!* **3** *adv* **AT OR IN ANY PLACE** in, at, or to any place ○ *We couldn't find her anywhere.* ○ *will live anywhere with a beach* ◇ **anywhere from...to...** used to state an approximate measurement of something by stating the smallest and largest possible measurements ○ *weighing anywhere from six to ten pounds*

anywise /énni wīz/ *adv US* in any way or in any case (*archaic regional; usually in negative statements*)

Anzac /án zak/ *n* **1** *ANZ* **WORLD WAR I SOLDIER** a soldier who served in the Australian and New Zealand Army Corps in World War I **2** *Aus* **AUSTRALIAN SOLDIER** an Australian soldier **3** *Aus* **TYPICAL AUSTRALIAN MAN** a typical Australian man seen as having the courage and spirit shown by the Anzacs at Gallipoli in World War I

Anzac Day *n* in Australia and New Zealand, a public holiday marking the anniversary of the landing of the Australian and New Zealand Army Corps at Gallipoli in 1915 and commemorating all those who have fought in recent times. Date: 25 April.

Anzio /ánzi ō/ port in W Italy, the site of heavy fighting during World War II. Population: 33,497 (1996).

ϟ **ao** *abbr* Angola (*in Internet addresses*)

AO *abbr Aus* Officer of the Order of Australia

a/o, A/O *abbr* account of

AOAI *abbr UK* Area of Archaeological Importance

AOB *abbr* any other business

AOC *abbr* appellation d'origine contrôlée (*describes appellation contrôlée wines*)

ao dai /ów dī/ *n* a long tunic worn over trousers by Vietnamese women that has a high neck and is slit at both sides below the waist [Mid-20C. < Vietnamese *áo dài* 'long blouse'.]

A-OK, A-okay *adj* in excellent condition or working order (*informal*) [Mid-20C. < *all (systems) OK*.]

AONB *n* an area of countryside officially designated for the purposes of town and country planning as being special and deserving of protection. Full form **Area of Outstanding Natural Beauty**

AOR *abbr* adult-oriented rock

aorist /áy ərist, áirist/ *n* a verb tense used to express a past action in an unqualified way, without specifying whether that action was repeated, continuing, or completed or how long it lasted, found especially in classical Greek [Late 16C. < Greek *aoristos* 'indefinite' < *a-* 'not' + *horistos* 'delimited' < *horizein* 'delimit' (see HORIZON).] —**aoristic** /áy ə rístik, air-/ *adj* —**aoristically** *adv*

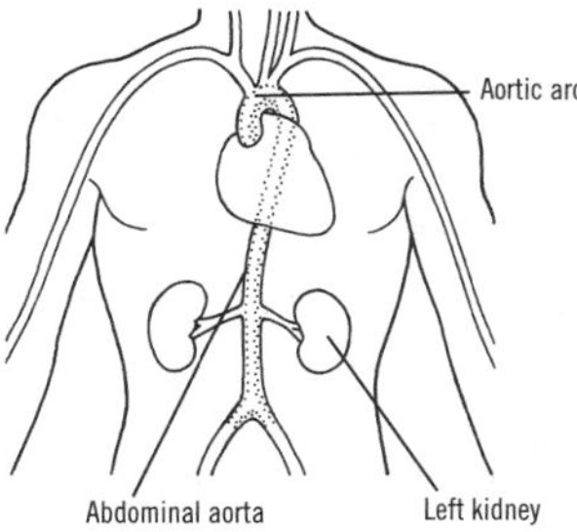

Aorta

aorta /ay áwrtə/ (*plural* **-tas** *or* **-tae** /-tee/) *n* the main artery in mammals that carries blood from the left ventricle of the heart to all the branch arteries in the body except those in the lungs [Mid-16C. Via modern Latin < Greek *aortē* < *aeirein* 'raise'; perhaps from the notion that the heart was held up by the aorta.] —**aortal** *adj* —**aortic** *adj*

aortic arch *n* **1** the section of the largest artery (**aorta**) in the body that forms the curve between the ascending and descending parts **2** a set of paired curved arteries, one of several in the vertebrate embryo that begin in the aorta, rise through the pharynx, and join with the dorsal arterial system

aortic valve *n* the valve in the largest artery (**aorta**) in the body at the point where it leaves the heart

aortography /áy awr tóggrəfi/ *n* X-ray examination of the largest artery (**aorta**) in the body —**aortographic** /áy awrtə gráffik/ *adj*

Aotearoa /áa ō tee ə rṓ ə/ *n NZ* the preferred Maori name for New Zealand (*often in combination*) ○ *Aotearoa-New Zealand*

aoudad /ów dad, áa oo dad/ *n* a wild sheep that has long curved horns and a long fringe of hair on the neck and forelegs. Native to: North Africa. *Ammotragus lervia*. [Early 19C. Via French < Berber *udād*.]

Aouita /ow éetə/, **Said** (*b.* 1960) Moroccan runner

AP *abbr* **1** Associated Press **2** Air Police **3** American plan **4** antipersonnel

a.p. *abbr* **1** additional premium **2** before a meal (*in prescriptions*) **3** author's proof

ap-[1] *prefix* = **ad-** (*before p*)

ap-[2] *prefix* = **apo-** (*before vowels and h*)

apace /ə páyss/ *adv* **1** at a good or fast pace **2** *US* at a sufficient rate to keep up with or be alongside somebody or something [14C. < Old French *a pas* 'on step'.]

Apache /ə páchi/ (*plural* **-e** *or* **-es**) *n* **1** a member of a Native North American people who once lived throughout the present-day SW United States and N Mexico, but now live in Arizona, New Mexico, and Oklahoma **2** an Athabaskan language spoken in parts of Arizona, New Mexico, and Oklahoma. Native speakers: 50,000. [Mid-18C. < American Spanish.] —**Apache** *adj* —**Apachean** *adj*

~~**apalling**~~ incorrect spelling of **appalling**

apanage *n* HIST = **appanage**

~~**aparatus**~~ incorrect spelling of **apparatus**

~~**aparent**~~ incorrect spelling of **apparent**

~~**aparently**~~ incorrect spelling of **apparently**

apart /ə pa͡art/ CORE MEANING: a grammatical word meaning separated in space or time ○ (adv) *scheduled appointments a month apart* ○ (adv) *living apart* ○ (adj) *hard to be apart* ○ (adj) *sitting with legs apart*

1 *adv* **NOT TOGETHER** separated in space or time ○ *She placed the chairs some distance apart.* **2** *adv* **INTO PIECES** into separate parts or sections ○ *take the machine apart* ○ *pulled the two scuffling children apart* **3** *adv* **MOVING AWAY AFTER BEING TOGETHER** away from somebody or something after previously being together ○ *We've drifted apart over the years.* **4** *adv* **REMOVED FROM CONSIDERATION** set aside or excluded from consideration ○ *The orange flowered tie apart, it was a rather smart outfit.* **5** *adv* **INTO DIFFICULTY** into a bad or difficult condition **6** *adv* **OF A SEPARATE KIND** different and consequently separate from others ○ *a world apart* **7** *adj* **SEPARATED** away from each other in position or location ○ *think of her all the time we're apart* [14C. < Old French *a part* 'to the side'.] —**apartness** *n* ◇ **apart from 1** with the exception of somebody or something **2** in addition to something

apartheid /ə pa͡art hayt, -hīt/ *n* a political system in South Africa from 1948 to the early 1990s that separated the different peoples living there and gave particular privileges to those of European origin [Mid-20C. < Afrikaans, 'separateness' < Dutch *apart* 'separate' < French.]

apartment /ə pa͡artmənt/ *n* **1** *US* = **flat**[2] *n.* 1 **2** a single room in a residential building (*formal*) ■ **apartments** *npl* a suite of adjoining rooms used for a particular purpose, e.g. as an office, entertainment suite, or place to live (*formal*) [Mid-17C. < French *appartement* < Italian *a parte* 'apart', literally 'to the side'.]

apartment building, apartment block *n* a block of flats

apathetic /àppə théttik/ *adj* not taking any interest in anything [Mid-18C. < APATHY, after *pathetic*.] —**apathetically** *adv*

SYNONYMS See ***impassive***.

apathy /áppəthi/ *n* **1** lack of interest in anything **2** inability to feel normal or passionate human feelings or to respond emotionally [Early 17C. < French *apathie* < Greek *apathēs* 'without feeling' < *pathos* 'feeling'.]

apatite /áppə tīt/ *n* a glassy, variously coloured calcium phosphate mineral. Use: fertilizers, source of phosphorus. [Early 19C. < Greek *apatē* 'deceit'; from its diversity of form and colour.]

apatosaurus /ə páttə sáwrəss/, **apatosaur** /ə páttə sawr/ *n* a large plant-eating dinosaur that lived in North America during the Jurassic period and had a small head, short front legs, and a long neck and tail. Genus: *Apatosaurus*. [Late 19C. < modern Latin, < Greek *apatē* 'deceit' + *sauros* 'lizard'.]

APB *abbr* all-points bulletin

APD *abbr* adult polycyclic disease

ape /ayp/ *n* **1 TAILLESS PRIMATE** any tailless primate such as a chimpanzee, gorilla, or orangutan. Family: Pongidae. **2 PRIMATE** any primate (*informal*) **3 IMITATOR** an imitator or mimic of somebody or something **4** *US* **CLUMSY PERSON** a clumsy or unintelligent person (*informal insult*) ■ *vt* (**apes, aping, aped**) **IMITATE** to copy somebody or something in an absurd or mindless way [Old English *apa* < Germanic] ◇ **go ape** to lose self-control, because of either anger or excitement (*slang*)

SYNONYMS See ***imitate***.

apeak /ə pe͡ek/ *adj, adv* in a vertical position or direction [Late 16C. < French *à pic* 'at the peak'.]

~~**apear**~~ incorrect spelling of **appear**

APEC /áy pek/ *abbr* Asia-Pacific Economic Co-operation

apeman /áyp man/ (*plural* **-men** /-men/) *n* a nontechnical name for any of various extinct primates believed to be ancestors of modern humans

Apennines /áppə nīnz/ mountain range that forms the backbone of peninsular Italy. Highest peak: Monte Corno 2,912 m/9,554 ft.

aperçu /àppər syóo/ *n* (*formal*) **1** a revealing glimpse or insight **2** a concise outline or summary [Early 19C. < French, 'something perceived'.]

aperient /ə pe͡eri ənt/ *n* a mild laxative [Early 17C. < Latin *aperient-*, present participle of *aperire* 'open'.] —**aperient** *adj*

aperiodic /áy peeri óddik/ *adj* **1** happening at irregular intervals ○ *aperiodic floods* **2** describes a mechanical or electrical system that does not exhibit resonance when a periodic disturbance is applied —**aperiodically** *adv*—**aperiodicity** /áy peeri ə díssəti/ *n*

aperitif /ə pérrə te͡ef/ *n* an alcoholic beverage to be drunk before a meal [Late 19C. < French *apéritif* < Latin *apertus*, past participle of *aperire* 'open'.]

aperture /áppər tyoor/ *n* **1 NARROW OPENING** a small narrow opening **2 OPENING THROUGH LENS OR MIRROR** a fixed or adjustable opening in a device, e.g. a camera or microscope, that lets light pass through a lens or mirror **3 DIAMETER OF APERTURE** the diameter of an aperture, e.g. in a camera [Mid-17C. < Latin *apert-*, past participle of *aperire* 'open'.] —**apertural** *adj*

aperture card *n* a card for mounting microfilmed pages

aperture priority *n* the system in a semi-automatic camera in which the user sets the lens aperture and the camera then selects the appropriate shutter speed automatically

aperture stop *n* PHOTOG = **f-stop**

apeshit /áyp shit/ *adj* an offensive term meaning unreasonably angry or excited (*taboo slang*)

~~**apetite**~~ incorrect spelling of **appetite**

apex /áy peks/ (*plural* **apexes** *or* **apices** /áypi seez, áp-/) *n* **1 HIGHEST POINT** the highest point of something **2 HIGHEST POINT OF SOMEBODY'S CAREER** the most successful part of something, especially somebody's career or life **3 TIP OF** the tip or top of something, especially something that is pointed, e.g. a triangle [Early 17C. < Latin.]

Apex, APEX *n* a system whereby air or rail tickets are available at a reduced price when bought a certain period of time in advance [Acronym < *advance-purchase excursion*]

Apgar score /áp gaar-/ *n* a score that is given after assessing the condition of a newborn baby in the five areas of heart rate, breathing, skin colour, muscle tone, and reflex response [After Virginia *Apgar* (1909–74)]

aphaeresis /ə fe͡erəssiss, ə-/, **apheresis** *n* the loss of a syllable from the beginning of a word, e.g. in 'coon' for 'raccoon' [Mid-16C. Via late Latin < Greek *aphairesis* < *aphairein* 'take away' < *hairein* 'take'.] —**aphaeretic** /àffə réttik/ *adj*

aphagia /ə fáyji ə/ *n* the inability or refusal to swallow

aphakia /ə fáyki ə/ *n* a medical condition in which the internal crystalline lens of the eye is absent [Mid-19C. < A-[2] + Greek *phakos* 'lentil', because of the lens's shape.]

aphanite /áffə nīt/ *n* an igneous rock with mineral components that are too fine to be seen by the naked eye [Early 19C. < Greek *aphanēs* 'unseen' < *phan-*, stem of *phainein* (see PHENOMENON).] —**aphanitic** /àffə níttik/ *adj*

aphasia /ə fáyzi ə, -zhə/ *n* the partial or total inability to produce and understand speech as a result of brain damage caused by injury or disease [Mid-19C. < Greek, < *aphatos* 'speechless' < *phanai* 'speak'.] —**aphasic** /ə fáyzik/ *adj*

aphelandra /àffə lándrə/ *n* an evergreen shrub with shiny leaves and brightly coloured flowers, often grown as a house plant. Native to: tropical America. Genus: *Aphelandra*.

aphelion /ə fe͡eli ən, ap he͡eli ən/ (*plural* **-a** /-li ə/) *n* the point in the orbit of a planet, comet, or other celestial body that is farthest from the Sun [Mid-17C. < modern Latin *aphelium* < Greek *apo-* 'away' + *hēlios* 'sun'.] —**aphelian** *adj*

apheresis /àffə re͡essiss/ *n* **1** the retransfusion of a donor's or patient's own blood from which certain constituents have been removed **2** LING = **aphaeresis**

aphesis /áffississ/ *n* the loss of an unstressed vowel at the beginning of a word, e.g. in 'round' for 'around' [Late 19C. < Greek, 'letting go' < *aphienai* 'send away' < *hienai* 'send'.] —**aphetic** /ə féttik/ *adj* —**aphetically** *adv*

aphid /áy fid/ *n* an insect that has specially adapted mouthparts for piercing and sucking the sap from plants. Family: Aphididae. [Late 19C. < modern Latin *aphid-*, stem of *Aphis*, genus name.] —**aphidian** /ə fíddi ən/ *adj* —**aphidious** *adj*

aphonia /áy fṓni ə/ *n* the loss of the voice as a result of injury or disease of the larynx or mouth or of various psychological conditions [Late 17C. < Greek, < *aphōnos* 'having no voice' < *phōnē* 'sound'.] —**aphonic** /áy fónnik/ *adj*

aphorise *vi* = **aphorize**

aphorism /áffərizəm/ *n* a succinct statement expressing an opinion or a general truth [Early 16C. < French *aphorisme* < Greek *aphorizein* 'define' < *horizein* 'delimit' (see HORIZON).] —**aphorist** *n* —**aphoristic** /àffə rístik/ *adj* —**aphoristically** /-rístikli/ *adv*

aphorize /áffə rīz/ (**-rizes, -rizing, -rized**), **aphorise** (**-rises, -rising, -rised**) *vi* to speak or write using aphorisms

aphotic /ə fóttik/ *adj* describes those parts of the ocean that are not reached by sunlight, or plants that grow there without photosynthesizing

aphrodisiac /àffrə dízzi ak/ *n* something that arouses or intensifies sexual desire [Early 18C. < Greek *aphrodisiakos* 'arousing sexual desire' < *aphrodisia* 'sexual pleasures' < *Aphroditē* 'Aphrodite'.] —**aphrodisiac** *adj* —**aphrodisiacal** /àffrədi zī ək'l/ *adj*

Aphrodite /àffrə dīti/ *n* in Greek mythology, the goddess of love and beauty. Roman equivalent **Venus**

aphtha /áfthə/ (*plural* **-thae** /-thee/) *n* a small white ulcer that appears in groups in the mouth and on the tongue as a result of the fungal condition thrush (*technical; usually plural*) [Mid-17C. Via Latin < Greek.] —**aphthous** *adj*

Apia /ə pe͡e ə/ capital of Samoa, on Upolu Island. Population: 34,126 (1991).

apian /áypi ən/ *adj* relating to or resembling bees [Early 19C. < Latin *apianus* < *apis* 'bee'.]

apiarist /áypi ərist/ *n* somebody who keeps bees

apiary /áypi əri/ (*plural* **-ies**) *n* a place where beehives are kept and bees are raised for their honey [Mid-17C. < Latin *apiarium* 'beehive' < *apis* 'bee'.]

apical /áppik'l, áy-/ *adj* **1** describes the top of something **2** used to classify a consonant that is pronounced with the tip of the tongue, e.g. 't' or 'd' [Early 19C. < Latin *apic-*, stem of *apex* 'apex'.] —**apically** *adv*

apices plural of **apex**

apiculture /áypi kulchər/ *n* the keeping of bees, especially for commercial purposes [Mid-19C. < Latin *apis* 'bee' + CULTURE.] —**apicultural** /áypi kúlchərəl/ *adj* —**apiculturist** /-kúlchərist/ *n*

apiece /ə pe͡ess/ *adv* to or for each one ○ *gold watches, from £150 to £550 apiece* [Mid-16C. < A[5] + PIECE.]

apish /áypish/ *adj* **1** silly, ridiculous, or boorish **2** imitating somebody else or somebody's style —**apishly** *adv* —**apishness** *n*

aplacental /áyplə sént'l/ *adj* describes mammals such as marsupials that do not develop a placenta

aplanatic /àpplə náttik/ *adj* describes a lens that does not have, or is corrected for, spherical aberration and so produces a clear undistorted image [Late 18C. < Greek *aplanētos* 'without error' < *planasthai* 'wander'.]

aplasia /ə pláyzi ə/ *n* the absence or partial development of an organ, part of an organ, or tissue

aplastic /ay plástik/ *adj* unable to develop new cells or tissue

aplastic anaemia *n* severe anaemia in which the capacity of bone marrow cells to generate red blood cells is diminished

aplenty /ə plénti/ *adj* in large or excessive amounts ○ *There are apples aplenty for all of you.*

aplite /áp plīt/ *n* a light-coloured, fine-grained igneous rock [Late 19C. < German *Aplit* < Greek *haplous* 'single', because of its chemical composition.] —**aplitic** /a plíttik/ *adj*

aplomb /ə plóm/ *n* confidence, skill, and poise, especially in difficult or challenging circumstances [Early 19C. < French *à plomb* 'perpendiculars'.]

apnea *n* US = **apnoea**

apneusis /ap nyóossiss/ *n* a form of breathing caused by brain damage, in which each full inhalation is held for a prolonged period —**apneustic** *adj*

apnoea /ápni ə, apní ə/ *n* a temporary suspension or absence of breathing [Early 18C. Via modern Latin < Greek *apnoia* 'not breathing' < *pnein* 'breathe'.]

apo-, ap- *prefix* away from, detached ○ *apolune* ○ *apocarp* [< Greek *apo* 'off, away' < Indo-European]

Apoc. *abbr* **1** Apocalypse **2** Apocrypha

apocalypse /ə póka lips/ *n* **1** the destruction or devastation of something, or an instance of this **2** a revelation made concerning the future [13C. Via late Latin < Greek *apokalupsis* 'revelation' < *apokaluptein* 'uncover' < *kaluptein* 'cover'.]

Apocalypse *n* BIBLE = **Revelation**

apocalyptic /ə póka líptik/ *adj* **1 PREDICTING DISASTER** warning about or predicting a disastrous future or outcome ○ *an apocalyptic scenario of global warming* **2 RELATING TO THE APOCALYPSE** relating to the events in the Book of Revelation in the Bible **3 INVOLVING DESTRUCTION** involving widespread destruction and devastation —**apocalyptically** *adv*

apocarpous /áppə kaárpəss/ *adj* describes a flower that has separate carpels [Mid-19C. < APO- + Greek *karpos* 'fruit'.] —**apocarpy** /áppə kaarpi/ *n*

apochromat /áppə krṓmat/ *n* a lens that is corrected for chromatic aberration by incorporating different types of glass

apochromatic /áppəkrō máttik/ *adj* describes a lens that has been corrected for chromatic aberration —**apochromatism** /áppə krṓmətizəm/ *n*

apocope /ə pókəpi/ *n* the loss or omission of one or more sounds from the end of a word, e.g. the shortening of 'margarine' to 'marge' [Mid-16C. Via late Latin < Greek *apokopē* 'cutting off' < *koptein* 'to cut'.] —**apocopate** *vt*

apocrine /áppə krīn, -krin/ *adj* describes glands that secrete part of their secreting cells with the secretory products [Early 20C. < APO- + Greek *krinein* 'to separate'.]

Apocrypha /ə pókrifə/ *n* **1** books of the Bible that are included in the Vulgate and Septuagint versions of the Christian Bible, but not in the Protestant Bible or the Hebrew canon (+ *singular or plural verb*) **2** a group of Christian writings dating from the early centuries AD that are not included in the Bible [14C. Via ecclesiastical Latin, < Greek *apokruphos* 'hidden away' < *kruptein* 'to hide'.]

apocryphal /ə pókrif'l/ *adj* **1** probably not true, but widely believed to be true **2** relating to the Apocrypha —**apocryphally** *adv*

apodal /áppəd'l/, **apodous** /áppədəss/ *adj* without limbs, feet, or pelvic fins [Mid-18C. < Greek *apod-* 'footless' < *pous* 'foot'.]

apodictic /áppə díktik/, **apodeictic** /-dík-/ *adj* demonstrably or indisputably true [Mid-17C. < Latin *apodicticus* < Greek *apodeiknunai* 'demonstrate' < *deiknunai* 'show' (see DEICTIC).]

apodosis /ə póddəssiss/ (*plural* **-ses** /-seez/) *n* the main clause explaining the consequence in a conditional statement, e.g. 'we can watch the film' in 'If you come early, we can watch the film' [Early 17C. < late Latin, < Greek *apodidonai* 'give back' < *didonai* (see DOSE).]

apodous *adj* = **apodal**

apoenzyme /áppō én zīm/ *n* the inactive protein component of an enzyme that has no physiological effect without attachment of a specific molecule (**coenzyme**)

apogamy /ə póggəmi/ *n* the development of an embryo without prior fertilization —**apogamic** /áppə gámmik/ *adj*

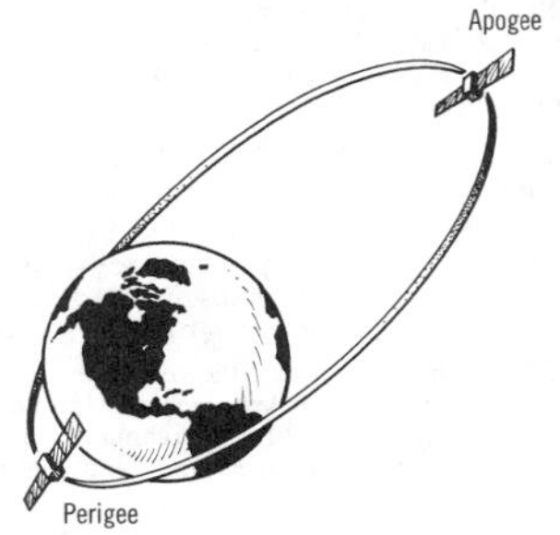

Apogee

apogee /áppə jee/ *n* **1** the best or greatest point **2** the point when the Moon, or a satellite or other object orbiting around the Earth, is farthest from the centre of the Earth [Late 16C. < French, < Greek *apogaios* 'away from the Earth' < *gaia* 'Earth'.] —**apogean** /áppə jée ən/ *adj*

apolipoprotein /áppō lipō prṓ teen/ a protein that combines with a lipid to form a constituent of lipoproteins

apolitical /áypə líttik'l/ *adj* having no interest in politics —**apolitically** *adv*

Apollinaire /ə pólli náir/, **Guillaume** (1880–1918) Italian-born French poet

Apollo /ə póllō/ *n* **1** in Greek mythology, the god of prophecy, sunlight, music, and healing, also worshipped by the Romans **2 Apollo** (*plural* **-los**), **apollo** (*plural* **-los**) a very handsome young man (*literary*) [Via Latin < Greek *Apollōn*] —**Apollonian** /áppə lṓni ən/ *adj*

apologetic /ə póllə jéttik/ *adj* **1** expressing apology or contrition for something **2** defending something in speech or writing [Mid-17C. Via French and Latin, < Greek *apologētikos* < *apologeisthai* 'speak in your own defence' < *apologia* (see APOLOGY).] —**apologetically** *adv*

apologetics /ə póllə jéttiks/ *n* a branch of theology that is concerned with proving the truth of Christianity (+ *singular verb*)

apologia /áppə lṓji ə/ *n* a formal, usually written, defence or justification of a belief, theory, or policy (*formal*) [Late 18C. < Latin (see APOLOGY).]

apologise *vi* = **apologize**

apologist /ə pólləjist/ *n* somebody who defends or justifies a doctrine or ideology

apologize /ə póllə jīz/ (**-gizes, -gizing, -gized**), **apologise** (**-gises, -gising, -gised**) *vi* **1 EXPRESS REMORSE FOR** to say you are sorry for something that has upset or inconvenienced somebody else **2 ACKNOWLEDGE THAT SOMETHING IS NOT IDEAL** to acknowledge that something is not as it should be, especially when you feel embarrassed or guilty about it **3 DEFEND FORMALLY** to defend something formally in writing or speech [Late 16C. < Greek *apologizesthai* < *apologia* (see APOLOGY).] —**apologizer** *n*

apologue /áppə log/ *n* a fable that is intended to teach a moral lesson, especially one that has animals as characters [Mid-16C. Via French or late Latin, < Greek *apologos* 'story' < *logos* 'speech' (see LOGOS).]

apology /ə pólləji/ (*plural* **-gies**) *n* **1 STATEMENT EXPRESSING REMORSE** a written or spoken statement expressing remorse for something **2 NOTIFICATION OF NONATTENDANCE AT MEETING** a notification that somebody cannot attend a meeting (*formal*) **3 INFERIOR EXAMPLE** an inferior or bad example of something (*humorous*) ○ *I can't work in this apology for an office!* **4 FORMAL JUSTIFICATION** a formal defence or justification of something [Mid-16C. Via French *apologie* and Latin *apologia* < Greek, 'speech in defence' < *logos* 'speech' (see LOGOS).]

apolune /áppə loon/ *n* the point in the orbit of a spacecraft circling the Moon when it is farthest from the Moon's centre [Mid-20C. < APO- + Latin *luna* 'moon' (see LUNAR), after English *apogee*.]

apomictic /áppə míktik/ *adj* describes an organism that reproduces asexually —**apomict** /áppə mikt/ *n* —**apomictically** *adv*

apomixis /áppə míksiss/ *n* asexual reproduction in organisms that are also able to reproduce sexually, in which embryos are formed without fertilization or the creation of specialized reproductive cells [Early 20C. < APO- + Greek *mixis* 'mingling' (see AMPHIMIXIS).]

aponeurosis /áppō nyoo rṓssiss/ (*plural* **-ses** /-seez/) *n* a broad sheet of fibrous tissue or expanded tendon that joins muscles together or connects muscle to bone [Late 17C. < modern Latin, < Greek *aponeurousthai* 'become like a tendon' < *neuron* 'sinew'.] —**aponeurotic** /áppō nyoo róttik/ *adj*

apophthegm /áppə them/, **apothegm** *n* a terse saying that embodies an important truth, e.g. 'Haste makes waste' [Mid-16C. < Greek *apophthegma* < *apophtheggesthai* 'speak plainly' < *phtheggesthai* 'speak'.] —**apophthegmatic** /áppə theg máttik/ *adj* —**apophthegmatically** *adv*

apophyge /ə póffəji/ *n* the outward curve at the top of an architectural column where it joins the capital, or at the bottom where it joins the base [Mid-16C. < Greek *apophugē* 'fleeing away' < *pheugein* 'flee'.]

apophyllite /áppə fíllīt, ə póffi līt/ *n* a white, pale pink, or pale green hydrated silicate mineral containing potassium, calcium, and fluorine [Early 19C. < APO- + Greek *phullon* 'leaf', because it peels when heated.]

apophysis /ə póffəssiss/ (*plural* **-ses** /-seez/) *n* **1** a natural swelling or outgrowth on an animal or plant, e.g. a bony protuberance on a vertebra **2** a small offshoot or network of veins from a large igneous mass of rock such as granite [Late 16C. Via modern Latin, < Greek, < *apophuein* 'grow out' < *phuein* 'grow'.] —**apophysate** *adj* —**apophysial** /ə póffə sée əl/ *adj*

apoplectic /áppə pléktik/ *adj* **1** overcome with anger **2** having the symptoms of a stroke (*archaic*) [Early 17C. Via French or late Latin < Greek *apoplēktikos* < *apoplēxia* (see APOPLEXY).] —**apoplectically** *adv*

apoplexy /áppə pleksi/ *n* **1** a fit of anger **2** a cerebral stroke, usually caused by a haemorrhage in the brain (*archaic*) [14C. Via French and Latin, < Greek *apoplēxia* < *apoplēssein* 'strike completely' < *plēssein* 'to strike'.]

apoptosis /áppəp tṓsiss, áppə tṓsiss/ *n* a form of cell death necessary to make way for new cells and to remove cells whose DNA has been damaged to the point at which cancerous change is liable to occur [Late 20C. < Greek, 'falling off' (see APO-, PTOSIS).]

aporia /ə páwri ə/ *n* a confusion in establishing the truth of a proposition [Mid-16C. Via late Latin, < Greek, < *aporos* 'without passage' < *poros* 'passage' (see PORE[1]).] —**aporetic** /áppə réttik/ *adj*

aport /ə páwrt/ *adv, adj* on or towards the port or left-hand side of a ship as you face forward

aposematic /áppə se máttik/ *adj* describes natural colours and bright markings on an animal that warn predators that it is poisonous ○ *aposematic coloration*

aposiopesis /áppə sī ə péessiss/ (*plural* **-ses** /-seez/) *n* a sudden break in speaking, giving the impression that the speaker does not want to or cannot continue, e.g. in the sentence 'On Tuesday morning I came in just as I always do, and I saw—I can't go on' [Late 16C. Via Latin, < Greek *aposiōpēsis* < *aposiopan* 'stop speaking' < *siopē* 'silence'.] —**aposiopetic** /áppə sī ə péttik/ *adj*

apospory /áppə spawri, ə póspəri/ *n* the process of asexual reproduction in certain ferns and mosses without the occurrence of cell division (**meiosis**) or spore formation [Late 19C. < APO- + SPORE + -Y[2].]

apostasy /ə póstəssi/ *n* the renunciation of a religious or political belief or allegiance [14C. Via French, < Greek *apostasis* 'standing away' < *histasthai* 'stand'.]

apostate /ə pó stayt/ *n* somebody who renounces a belief or allegiance [14C. Via French and Latin, < Greek *apostatēs* 'somebody caused to stand away' < *stat-*, related to *histanai* 'cause to stand'.]

apostatize /ə póstə tīz/ (**-tizes, -tizing, -tized**), **apostatise** (**-tises, -tising, -tised**) *vi* to renounce a religious faith, a political party, a set of principles, or a moral allegiance (*formal*)

a posteriori /áy pos térri áw rī, aá-, -teeri-/ *adj, adv* reasoning from observed facts or events back to their causes [< Latin, 'from what comes later']

apostle /ə póss'l/ *n* **1 STRONG BELIEVER** somebody who tries to persuade others to share an idea or cause ○ *an apostle of free trade* **2 PROMINENT CHRISTIAN MISSIONARY** a prominent Christian missionary, especially one who is responsible for first converting a people **3 MORMON OFFICIAL** a member of the 12-person administrative council of the Church of Jesus Christ of Latter-Day Saints [Pre-12C. Via ecclesiastical Latin *apostolus* < Greek *apostolos* 'somebody sent out' < *stellein* 'send'.] —**apostleship** *n*

Apostle *n* one of the 12 followers of Jesus Christ chosen by him to preach the news about Christianity

apostlebird /ə póss'l burd/ *n* a medium-sized grey bird, usually found in small flocks. Native to: Australia. *Struthidea cinerea.* [Because they congregate in flocks]

Apostles' Creed *n* a statement of Christian belief ascribed to the Apostles and dating from around AD 500. It is frequently used in services in Eastern Orthodox, Anglican, and Lutheran churches.

apostle spoon *n* a silver spoon with the figure of an Apostle on the handle

apostolate /ə póstə layt/ *n* **1** the duties or mission of an apostle **2** a group involved in converting new followers to a religion or doctrine [Mid-17C. < Ecclesiastical Latin *apostolatus* < *apostolus* 'apostle' (see APOSTLE).]

apostolic /áppə stóllik/ *adj* **1** relating to, given by, or on behalf of the pope **2** relating to the Apostles or their teachings [Mid-16C. Via French and ecclesiastical Latin < Greek *apostolos* 'apostle' (see APOSTLE).] —**apostolical** *adj* —**apostolically** *adv*

apostolic delegate *n* a representative of the pope who is sent to a country that has no formal diplomatic relations with the Vatican

Apostolic Father *n* a Christian church leader of the first or second century AD

Apostolic See *n* the area of jurisdiction (**see**) of the pope

apostolic succession *n* the doctrine of some Christian denominations that the ordination of bishops follows in an unbroken line of succession from the Apostles, providing the basis of their spiritual authority

apostrophe[1] /ə póstrəfi/ *n* the punctuation mark (') used to show where letters are omitted from a word, to mark the possessive, and sometimes to form the plural of numbers, letters, and symbols [Mid-16C. Via French, < Greek *apostrophos* 'turned away' < *apostrephein* 'turn away' < *strephein* 'to turn'.]

PUNCTUATION Use of ***apostrophe***: The ***apostrophe*** is used in contractions (e.g. *we've, it's, hadn't, 'em*) and some literary words (e.g. *e'en, ne'er*) to show that a letter or letters have been omitted. Do not confuse the contraction *it's*, meaning *it is* or *it has*, with the possessive *its*, which does not have an apostrophe: *It's [= it has] lost all its hair.* When used to mark the possessive form of nouns, the apostrophe is followed by *s* unless the noun is plural and already ends in *s*: *the cat's tail; London's theatres; my children's computer; the companies' accounts; the boys' behaviour.* For singular nouns ending in *s* it is often acceptable to use either *'* or *'s*: *Dickens' best-loved novel* or *Dickens's best-loved novel.* Note that the possessives *its, hers, yours,* and *theirs* do not have an apostrophe. An apostrophe may also be used to indicate relationships of description (*a summer's day*) or measurement (*ten days' absence*). The use of an apostrophe in forming the plural of numbers and letters is optional: *the word has two Ts/T's; in the 1990s/1990's.* However, *'s* is preferable where confusion may arise, especially in showing plural forms of lower-case letters: *dot the i's and cross the t's.*

---

apostrophe[2] /ə póstrəfi/ *n* a rhetorical passage in which an absent or imaginary person or an abstract or inanimate entity is addressed directly [Mid-16C. Via Latin, < Greek *apostrophē* < *apostrephein* (see APOSTROPHE[1]).] —**apostrophic** /áppə stróffik/ *adj*

apostrophize /ə póstrə fīz/ (**-phizes, -phizing, -phized**), **apostrophise** (**-phises, -phising, -phised**) *vti* to address an absent or imaginary person or a personified abstraction

apothecaries' measure *n* a system of liquid measures formerly used in pharmacy

apothecaries' weight *n* a system of weights formerly used in pharmacy

apothegm *n* = **apophthegm**

apotheosis /ə póthi óssiss/ (*plural* **-ses** /-seez/) *n* **1 HIGHEST LEVEL OF GLORY OR POWER** the highest point of glory, power, or importance **2 BEST EXAMPLE** the best or most glorious example of something ○ *the apotheosis of romantic music* **3 TRANSFORMATION INTO DEITY** the transformation of a human being into a deity [Late 16C. Via late Latin, < Greek *apotheōsis* < *apotheoun* 'make into a god completely' < *theos* 'god'.]

apotheosize /ə póthi ə sīz/ (**-sizes, -sizing, -sized**), **apotheosise** (**-sises, -sising, -sised**) *vt* **1** to elevate somebody to the status of a deity **2** to glorify or exalt somebody or something

apotropaic /áppətrə páy ik/ *adj* intended to ward off evil or bad luck [Late 19C. < Greek *apotropaios* < *apotrepein* 'turn away' < *trepein* 'to turn'.] —**apotropaically** *adv* —**apotropaism** *n*

⚡**app** /ap/ *n* computer application (*informal*)

app. *abbr* **1** apparatus **2** appendix **3** applied **4** appointed **5** apprentice **6** approved **7** approximate

appal /ə páwl/ (**-pals, -palling, -palled**) *vt* to make somebody feel shock, horror, or disgust [Mid-16C. < Old French *apallir* 'grow pale or faint' < *pale* (see PALE[1]).]

Appalachia /áppə láychi ə/ *n* the region in the United States that includes the S Appalachian Mountains, extending roughly from SW Pennsylvania through West Virginia and parts of Kentucky and Tennessee to NW Georgia

Appalachian /áppə láychi ən/ *adj* **1 OF APPALACHIAN MOUNTAINS** relating to the Appalachian Mountains **2 OF APPALACHIA** relating to Appalachia, or its people or culture ■ *n* **SOMEBODY FROM APPALACHIA** somebody who comes from Appalachia in the United States [Late 17C. < *Apalachee*, Native North American people.]

Appalachian Mountains, Appalachians North American mountain system, stretching from SE Canada to central Alabama. Highest peak: Mount Mitchell 2,037 m/6,684 ft.

Appalachian Trail *n* a mountain trail in the E United States, extending about 3,298 km/2,050 mi. from central Maine to N Georgia

appall *vt* US = **appal**

appalled /ə páwld/ *adj* feeling or appearing to be shocked by something dreadful or awful ○ *an appalled look*

appalling /ə páwling/ *adj* **1** causing shock or horror **2** causing dismay —**appallingly** *adv*

Appaloosa /áppə lóossə/, **appaloosa** *n* a saddle horse with white hair and dark patches, first bred in NW North America and formerly much used by Native Americans [Mid-19C. < ?]

appanage /áppənij/, **apanage** *n* **1** a source of revenue e.g. land given by a sovereign for the maintenance of a member of the royal family, especially a younger son **2** a thing that naturally or usually accompanies something else [Early 17C. < French, < medieval Latin *appanare* 'provide with subsistence' < *panis* 'bread'.]

~~**apparantly**~~ incorrect spelling of **apparently**

apparat /áppə raát/ *n* the administrative organization or staff of the Communist Party in the former Soviet Union and other Communist states [Mid-20C. Via Russian < German, 'apparatus'.]

apparatchik /áppə rátchik, -raát-/ *n* **1** a subordinate who is unquestioningly loyal to a powerful political leader or organization **2** a member of the administrative organization or staff (**apparat**) of the Communist Party in the former Soviet Union and other Communist states [Mid-20C. < Russian.]

apparatus /áppə ráytəss, -raá-, -ráttəss/ (*plural* **-tuses** *or* **-tus**) *n* **1 EQUIPMENT** a piece of machinery, a tool, or a device used for a particular purpose **2 SYSTEM ALLOWING SOMETHING TO FUNCTION** the system or structure in which a process occurs or an organization functions ○ *a complex bureaucratic apparatus* **3 SYSTEM OF ORGANS** a group or system of organs that work together to perform a particular function [Early 17C. < Latin, past participle of *apparare* 'prepare' < *parare* 'prepare'.]

apparel /ə párrəl/ *n* **1 CLOTHING** clothing or garments, especially outer or decorative clothing (*formal*) ○ *Olympics-related sports apparel* **2 SHIP'S EQUIPMENT** a ship's gear and equipment ■ *vt* (**-els, -elling, -elled**) **CLOTHE** to dress somebody, especially in formal clothes (*archaic*) [13C. < Old French *apareil* 'preparation' < Latin *apparare* (see APPARATUS).]

apparent /ə párrənt/ *adj* **1 CLEAR** clearly seen or understood **2 SEEMING** appearing to show particular qualities, feelings, or attributes that may not be genuine ○ *her apparent indifference* **3 DIRECTLY OBSERVED BUT NEGLECTING MODIFYING FACTORS** directly observed or measured but not taking into account factors or effects that should be allowed for, e.g. distortion caused by the measuring instruments themselves [14C. < Old French *aparant*, present participle of *aparoir* (see APPEAR).] —**apparentness** *n*

apparent horizon *n* GEOG = **horizon** *n.* **1**

apparently /ə párrəntli/ *adv* according to what seems to be the case but may not actually be so

apparent magnitude *n* ASTRON = **magnitude** *n.* **6**

apparent wind /-wínd/ *n* a combination of the actual wind and the wind created by a ship's motion

apparition /áppə rísh'n/ *n* **1** an appearance of a supposed ghost or something ghostly **2** an appearance of something or somebody unexpected or strange (*humorous*) [15C. Directly or via French, < Latin, < *apparere* (see APPEAR).] —**apparitional** *adj*

~~**appartment**~~ incorrect spelling of **apartment**

appassionato /ə pássyə naá tō/ *adj, adv* to be performed in an impassioned way (*musical direction*) [< Italian, 'impassioned']

appeal /ə peél/ *n* **1 EARNEST OR URGENT REQUEST** an earnest or urgent request to somebody for something ○ *an emotional appeal for forgiveness* **2 CAMPAIGN TO RAISE MONEY** a request or campaign to raise money or resources ○ *The hospital has launched an appeal for funds.* **3 ATTRACTION** the quality that makes somebody or something pleasant or desirable ○ *The film's appeal lies in its humour and charm.* **4 FORMAL REQUEST** a formal request to a higher authority requesting a change in or confirmation of a decision ○ *An appeal to the boss might solve the matter.* **5 HEARING OF CASE BEFORE SUPERIOR COURT** the hearing of part or the whole of a previously tried case by a superior court, a request for a hearing, or the right to have such a hearing **6 REQUEST FOR UMPIRE TO DISMISS BATSMAN** a verbal request to the umpire to declare a batsman out ■ *v* **1** *vi* **REQUEST MONEY** to ask for or campaign to raise money or resources ○ *The charity is appealing for books and toys.* **2** *vi* **EARNESTLY REQUEST** to make an earnest and urgent request for something ○ *We are appealing to the public to let us know if they see anything suspicious.* **3** *vi* **MAKE A FORMAL REQUEST TO SUPERIOR** to make a formal request to a higher authority requesting a change in or confirmation of a decision ○ *You will have to appeal to a senior officer.* **4** *vi* **ATTRACT OR FASCINATE** to be interesting or desirable ○ *Starting up my own business really appeals to me.* **5** *vti* **APPLY TO SUPERIOR COURT FOR HEARING** to apply to a superior court for a hearing of the whole or part of a case previously tried in a lower court **6** *vi* **ASK UMPIRE TO DISMISS BATSMAN** to make a verbal request to the umpire to declare a batsman out **7** *vi* **CHALLENGE UMPIRE'S DECISION** to challenge the decision of an umpire or referee [14C. Via Old French *apeler* < Latin *appellare* 'address, entreat', related to *pellere* 'push'.] —**appealable** *adj* —**appealer** *n* ◇ **on appeal** at the stage of a court case that involves reconsideration of the decision made at the original trial

Appeal Court *n* LAW = **Court of Appeal**

appealing /ə peéling/ *adj* **1** pleasing and interesting or desirable **2** appearing to request help or sympathy ○ *a timid, appealing glance* —**appealingly** *adv*

appear /ə peér/ *v* **1** *vi* **COME INTO VIEW** to come into view ○ *The main menu will appear whenever you turn on the computer.* **2** *vi* **BEGIN TO EXIST** to come into existence ○ *When did this rash appear?* **3** *vi* **BECOME AVAILABLE FOR SALE** to become available, especially as a product for sale ○ *Cheaper and better printers have appeared on the market.* **4** *vti* **SEEM LIKELY** to seem likely or true ○ *The three men appear to have left the city.* **5** *vi* **BE SEEN IN PUBLIC** to come before the public, especially to perform a duty or to act ○ *His dream was to appear on Broadway.* **6** *vi* **BE IN LAW COURT OFFICIALLY** to be present in a court of law as a defendant, plaintiff, witness, or legal adviser ○ *due to appear in court next week* **7** *vi* **FORMALLY PRESENT YOURSELF TO** to present yourself formally to somebody after receiving an official request ○ *He was ordered to appear in the district superintendent's office.* [13C. Via Old French *aparoir* < Latin *apparere* 'show, become visible to' < *parere* 'show'.]

appearance /ə peéranss/ *n* **1 COMING INTO EXISTENCE** the act of emerging, arriving, or coming into existence ○ *the appearance of the first daffodils* **2 WAY SOMEBODY OR SOMETHING LOOKS** the way somebody or something looks or seems to other people ○ *a youthful appearance* **3 OUTWARD ASPECT** an outward aspect of somebody or something that creates a particular impression (*often plural*) ○ *The place gives the appearance of prosperity.* ○ *I know the dog looks friendly, but don't be fooled by appearances.* **4 PERFORMANCE OR EXHIBITION IN PUBLIC** a performance or exhibition before a public audience ○ *It was the band's first British appearance.* **5 ATTENDANCE IN COURT** attendance in court as a defendant, plaintiff, witness, or legal adviser ○ *The prospect of an appearance in court was daunting.* ◇ **keep up appearances** to maintain an appearance of well-being despite difficulties ◇ **put in an appearance (at something)** to attend something, often only for a short time or to fulfil an obligation

~~appearence~~ incorrect spelling of **appearance**

appease /ə peéz/ (**-peases, -peasing, -peased**) *vt* **1** to pacify somebody, especially by acceding to demands **2** to satisfy or relieve something, especially a physical appetite [14C. < Old French *apaisier* < *pais* 'peace'.] —**appeasable** *adj* —**appeasably** *adv* —**appeaser** *n*

appeasement /ə peézmənt/ *n* **1** the political strategy of pacifying a potentially hostile nation in the hope of avoiding war, often by granting concessions **2** an attempt to stop complaints or reduce difficulties by making concessions

appel /ə pél/ *n* **1** a stamp of the foot that signals a fencer's intention to start attacking **2** in fencing, a sharp blow with the blade made to procure an opening [< French, 'call']

appellant /ə péllənt/ *n* the person or group of people in a legal action who bring an appeal [Late 16C. < Old French *apelant*, present participle of *apeler* (see APPEAL).]

appellate /ə péllət/ *adj* having the jurisdiction to hear appeals and review the decisions of lower courts [Mid-18C. < Latin *appellatus*, past participle of *appellare* (see APPEAL).]

appellate court *n* a court with the power to review and reverse the decisions of lower courts

appellate jurisdiction *n* the power vested in an appellate court authorizing it to review the decisions of lower courts

appellation /áppə láysh'n/ *n* the name or title by which something or somebody is known (*formal*) [15C. Via French, 'naming' < Latin, < *appellare* (see APPEAL).]

appellation contrôlée /áppe lássyoN koN trő lay/ (*plural* **appellations contrôlées** /áppe lássyoN koN trő lay/) *n* a certification for French wine that guarantees its origin and verifies that it meets production regulations [< French, 'controlled name']

appellative /ə péllətiv/ *n* **1** = **appellation** (*formal*) **2** GRAM = **common noun** ■ *adj* **1** connected with a name or title **2** used as a common noun to describe a class of things —**appellatively** *adv*

append /ə pénd/ *vt* **1 ADD EXTRA INFORMATION** to add extra information to something, especially to attach extra information to a document **2 ADD AUTHORIZED SIGNATURE** to add an authorized signature to a bill or an official agreement as a final part of the ratification or agreement process (*formal*) ○ *All principals to the sale must append their signatures.* **3 ATTACH** to attach something or fasten it to something else [Mid-17C. < Latin *appendere* 'hang upon' < *pendere* 'hang'.]

appendage /ə péndij/ *n* **1** something fastened to something else as a small or secondary attachment ○ *feeling like an appendage of a large company* **2** a body part or organ e.g. a tail, wing, or fin that projects from the main part of the body

appendant /ə péndənt/ *n* **1 ATTACHMENT** something that is attached or added to something larger or more important **2 SOMETHING ADDED TO LEGAL DOCUMENT** a secondary document that is attached to the main body of a legal document, e.g. a codicil altering the terms of a will ■ *adj* **ATTACHED** attached or added to something larger or more important [Early 16C. < Old French *apendant*, present participle of *apendre* < Latin *appendere* (see APPEND).]

appendicectomy /àppəndə séktəmi/ (*plural* **-mies** /-miz/), **appendectomy** /àppən déktəmi/ (*plural* **-mies** /-miz/) *n* a surgical operation to remove the appendix [Late 19C. < Latin of *appendix* 'APPENDIX' + -ECTOMY.]

appendices plural of **appendix**

appendicitis /ə péndi sítiss/ *n* inflammation of the appendix, causing severe pain

appendicular /àppən díkyoolər/ *adj* **1** describes body parts that are associated with the limbs ○ *appendicular muscles* **2** describes the appendix [Mid-17C. < Latin *appendicula* 'small appendix'.]

appendix /ə péndiks/ (*plural* **-dixes** *or* **-dices** /-di seez/) *n* **1 SMALL OUTGROWTH FROM LARGE INTESTINE** a blind-ended tube leading from the large intestine (**caecum**), near its junction with the small intestine **2 ADDITIONAL INFORMATION** a collection of separate material at the end of a book or document **3 PROJECTING PART** a part that projects from something larger [Mid-16C. < Latin, < *appendere* (see APPEND).]

apperceive /àppər seév/ (**-ceives, -ceiving, -ceived**) *vt* to comprehend or assimilate something, e.g. a new idea, in terms of previous experiences or perceptions [Late 19C. < APPERCEPTION.]

apperception /àppər sépsh'n/ *n* the comprehension or assimilation of something, e.g. a new idea, in terms of previous experiences or perceptions [Mid-18C. < modern Latin stem *apperception-* < Latin *perception-* 'perception' (see PERCEPTION).] —**apperceptive** *adj*

appertain /àppər táyn/ *vi* to belong or relate to something (*formal*) ○ *another issue that appertains to the policy under discussion* [14C. Via Old French *apartenir* < late Latin *appertinere* 'belong completely to' < *pertinere* 'belong to' (see PERTAIN).]

appestat /áppə stat/ *n* the region of the brain that controls appetite and eating [< APPETITE + -STAT]

appetence /áppətənss/, **appetency** /-tənssi/ (*plural* **-cies**) *n* a desire or longing for something [Early 17C. Via French < Latin *appetentia* < *appetent-*, present participle of *appetere* (see APPETITE).]

appetiser *n* = **appetizer**

appetising *adj* = **appetizing**

appetite /áppi tīt/ *n* **1** a natural desire for food **2** a strong desire or craving for something [14C. Via French < Latin *appetitus* 'desire' < *appetere* 'seek after' < *petere* 'seek' (see PETITION).] —**appetitive** /ə péttitiv/ *adj*

appetizer /áppi tīzər/, **appetiser** *n* **1** a small dish of food served at the beginning of a meal to stimulate the appetite **2** a sample of something that is meant to stimulate an interest [Mid-19C. Back-formation < APPETIZING.]

appetizing /áppi tīzing/, **appetising** *adj* appealing to or stimulating the appetite [Mid-17C. Anglicization of French *appétissant* < *appétit* (see APPETITE).] —**appetizingly** *adv*

applanation tonometry /àpple náysh'n tə nómmetri/ *n* a technique for measuring the force per unit area required to flatten the cornea, used in diagnosing glaucoma [< modern Latin *applanare* 'flatten, level' < Latin *planus* 'flat']

applaud /ə pláwd/ *v* **1** *vti* to clap hands as a sign of welcome, appreciation, or approval **2** *vt* to praise somebody or something ○ *applauded the students' achievement* [15C. Directly and via French < Latin *applaudere* 'clap at' < *plaudere* 'clap'.] —**applaudable** *adj* —**applauder** *n* —**applaudingly** *adv*

applause /ə pláwz/ *n* the clapping of hands to express welcome, enjoyment, appreciation, or approval [Late 16C. < Latin *applausus* < *applaus-*, past participle of *applaudere* (see APPLAUD).]

apple /ápp'l/ *n* **1** a firm round fruit with a central core, red or green skin, and white flesh **2** a tree that bears apples. *Malus pumila.* [Old English *æppel* < Indo-European] ◇ **the apple of somebody's eye** somebody or something very much loved and favoured by another person

apple butter *n* a smooth spread made of stewed apples flavoured with spices

applecart /ápp'l kaart/ ◇ **upset the applecart** to spoil a plan or arrangement

apple green *n* a bright yellowish-green colour —**apple-green** *adj*

Apple Isle /ápp'l-/ *n Aus* Tasmania (*informal*)

applejack /ápp'l jak/ *n* **1** a brandy distilled from cider **2** an alcoholic beverage made from the liquid remaining after cider has been frozen

apple pie *n* a dessert made by cooking sliced apples in a pastry case

apple-pie *adj US* characteristic of or embodying the virtues that Americans believe to be typical of US culture, e.g. neighbourliness, civic pride, and honesty (*informal*) ○ *apple-pie honesty* ◇ **in apple-pie order** neat and tidy

apple-pie bed *n* a way of making a bed with the sheet folded up on itself so that it is impossible to lie full length in the bed [Probably alteration of French *nappe pliée* 'folded sheet']

apples and pears *npl Cockney* stairs (*informal*) [Rhyming slang]

apple sauce /ápp'l sawss/ *n* a sauce of sweetened stewed apples

ϟ **applet** /ápplit/ *n* **1** a simple computer program that performs a single task, run from within a larger application **2** a small piece of computer code, often embedded in a web page, that is transferred over the Internet and executed by the recipient's computer [Late 20C. < APPLICATION + -LET.]

Appleton /ápp'ltən/, **Edward Victor** (1892–1965) British physicist

Appleton layer *n* METEOROL = **F region** [After Edward V. APPLETON.]

appliance /ə plī́ ənss/ *n* **1** an electrical device or machine such as a vacuum cleaner that is used for a particular purpose in the home **2** = **fire engine** **3** the act of putting something into effect

applicable /ə plíkəb'l, ápplikəb'l/ *adj* affecting, connected with, or relevant to a particular person, group of people, or situation [Mid-16C. < French, < Latin *applicare* (see APPLY).] —**applicability** /àpplikə bíllәti/ *n* —**applicably** /ápplikəbli/ *adv*

applicant /ápplikənt/ *n* somebody who formally applies for something [Early 19C. < Latin *applicant-*, present participle of *applicare* (see APPLY).]

SYNONYMS See ***candidate***.

ϟ **application** /àppli káysh'n/ *n* **1 FORMAL REQUEST** a formal and usually written request for something, e.g. a job, a grant of money, or a place at a university **2 USE** the use something is put to or the process of putting it to use **3 RELEVANCE** the relevance or value that something has, especially when it is applied to a certain field or area ○ *the industrial applications of biochemical research* **4 SPREADING LIQUID ON SURFACE** the act of spreading a liquid such as paint or medicine on a surface **5 HARD WORK** concentration and hard work **6 COMPUTER SOFTWARE** a computer program or piece of software designed to perform a specific task [15C. Via French, < Latin, < *applicare* (see APPLY).]

ϟ **application service provider** *n* a company that provides one or more program functions, e.g. accounting, on behalf of an enterprise, freeing it to concentrate on its primary business

applicative /ə plíkətiv/ *adj* capable of being applied [Mid-17C. < Latin *applicat-* (see APPLICATOR).] —**applicatively** *adv*

applicator /áppli kaytər/ *n* a device used to apply a liquid or powder to a surface [Mid-17C. < Latin *applicat-*, past participle of *applicare* (see APPLY).]

applicatory /ə plíkətəri/ *adj* easily or suitably applied [Mid-17C. < Latin *applicat-* (see APPLICATOR).]

applied /ə plī́d/ *adj* able to be put to practical use, especially as a branch of a subject that has both practical and theoretical aspects. ◊ **pure**

appliqué /ə pleé kay/ *n* shaped pieces of fabric sewn on a foundation fabric to form a design [Mid-18C. < French, 'applied'.] —**appliqué** *vt*

apply /ə plī́/ (**-plies, -plying, -plied**) *v* **1** *vi* **MAKE A FORMAL REQUEST FOR** to make a formal, usually written, request for something ○ *How do I apply for the job?* **2** *vt* **USE** to make use of something to achieve a result ○ *He applied his first-aid skills to help the accident victims.* **3** *vi* **BE RELEVANT** to be relevant to somebody or something ○ *The requirement applies only if you are over 65.* **4** *vt* **SPREAD** to spread a liquid or other material over a surface ○ *Apply a thin layer of cream to the face and neck.* **5** *vt* **WORK HARD** to work hard or spend a significant amount of time on something ○ *I could have done better if I'd applied myself a bit more.* [14C. Via Old French *aplier* < Latin *applicare* 'fold towards' < *plicare* 'fold' (see PLY²).] —**applier** *n*

appoggiatura /ə pójjə toórə/ (*plural* **-ras** *or* **-re** /-ray/) *n* in music, an ornamental dissonant note resolving, usually downwards by a step, into a principal note [Mid-18C. < Italian, 'something supported by another'.]

appoint /ə póynt/ *vt* **1 SELECT SOMEBODY FOR POSITION OR JOB** to select a person or a group of people for an official position or to do a particular job ○ *She's been appointed director.* **2 AGREE UPON A TIME OR PLACE** to fix or agree upon a particular time or place for something to happen (*formal*) **3 EMPOWER TRUSTEE** to authorize a trustee to transfer trust property to particular beneficiaries [14C. < Old French *apointier* 'arrange, settle' < *a point* 'to a point'.] —**appointee** *n*

appointed /ə póyntid/ *adj* decorated, furnished, or equipped (*usually in combination*) ○ *a well-appointed flat*

appointive /ə póyntiv/ *adj* **1** *US* being or relating to a position to which somebody is appointed **2** relating to trust property that is managed by a trustee with the power to transfer it to beneficiaries

appointment /ə póyntmənt/ *n* **1 ARRANGEMENT TO MEET** an arrangement to have a meeting or to be somewhere at a particular time **2 CHOICE OF SOMEBODY FOR JOB** the selection of somebody for a position, office, or job **3 POSITION OR JOB** a position, office, or job to which somebody is appointed **4 SOMEBODY APPOINTED TO JOB** somebody who has been appointed to an office or job **5 SELECTION OF TRUSTEE** the selection of a trustee to whom power is given to transfer trust property to beneficiaries ■ **appointments** *npl* **FURNITURE AND FITTINGS** the furniture, fittings, and equipment belonging to a particular place

appointment book *n US* = **diary** *n.* 3

appointor /ə póyntər/ *n* somebody responsible for selecting a trustee to supervise and transfer trust property

~~**appologize**~~ incorrect spelling of **apologize**

~~**appology**~~ incorrect spelling of **apology**

Appomattox /àppə máttəks/ town in central Virginia, site of the 1865 Confederate surrender to the Union Army that ended the US Civil War. Population: 1,838 (1996).

apport /ə páwrt/ *n* **1** the production of objects at a spiritualist's seance, supposedly by paranormal means **2** an object produced at a spiritualist's seance, supposedly by paranormal means [15C. < French *aport* 'bringing to' < *aporter* 'carry to' < *porter* 'carry'.]

apportion /ə páwrsh'n/ *vt* to divide and allocate something among different people or groups [Late 16C. Via French, < Latin *portion-* (see PORTION).]

apportionment /ə páwrsh'nmənt/ *n* **1** the division and allocation of something among people or groups **2** *US* the distribution of seats in the US House of Representatives or a state legislature, based proportionally on the population of states or electoral districts

appose /ə pṓz/ (**-poses, -posing, -posed**) *vt* to be placed near something, or place or move something next to something else [Late 16C. < Latin *apponere*, after English *compose* and *expose*.]

apposite /áppəzit/ *adj* especially well suited to the circumstances [Early 17C. < Latin *appositus*, past participle of *apponere* 'add to, put near' < *ponere* 'put' (see POSITION).] —**appositely** *adv* —**appositeness** *n*

apposition /àppə zísh'n/ *n* **1 JUXTAPOSITION** the relative position of two things that are next to each other **2 RELATIONSHIP BETWEEN NOUN PHRASES** the relationship between two usually consecutive nouns or noun phrases that refer to the same person or thing and have the same relationship to other sentence elements. In the sentence 'My son, an actor, lives with me', the phrase 'My son, an actor' is an example of apposition. **3 CELL GROWTH IN LAYERS** cell growth in which layers of material are deposited on already existing ones —**appositional** *adj* —**appositionally** *adv*

appositive /ə pózzətiv/ *adj* describes words or phrases that refer to the same person or thing and have the same relationship to other sentence elements —**appositive** *n* —**appositively** *adv*

appraisal /ə práyz'l/ *n* **1** a judgment or opinion on something or somebody, especially one that assesses how effective or useful something or somebody is **2** an estimate of the value of something

appraise /ə práyz/ (**-praises, -praising, -praised**) *vt* **1 VALUE** to give an estimate of how much money something is worth **2 ASSESS MERITS OR QUALITY** to give an opinion of somebody's merits or something's quality **3 ASSESS FORMALLY** to make a formal assessment of an employee's performance following an agreed set of criteria [15C. Alteration of APPRIZE, after PRAISE.] —**appraisable** *adj* —**appraisement** *n* —**appraiser** *n*

USAGE appraise or **apprise**? ***Appraise***, meaning 'evaluate', is used with reference to people or (more usually) the things they do or achieve: *She appraised their work at the end of each week.* ***Apprise***, meaning 'inform', is a more formal word, and is used with reference to people: *He apprised them of the decisions.*

appreciable /ə préeshəb'l/ *adj* large or important enough to be noticed ○ *There is no appreciable difference between them.* —**appreciably** *adv*

appreciate /ə préeshi ayt/ (**-ates, -ating, -ated**) *v* **1** *vt* **FEEL GRATITUDE** to feel grateful for something ○ *I'd appreciate it if you didn't repeat this to anyone.* **2** *vt* **VALUE SOMEBODY OR SOMETHING HIGHLY** to recognize and like the qualities in somebody or something ○ *I don't feel appreciated.* **3** *vt* **UNDERSTAND** to understand fully the meaning or significance of a particular situation ○ *I hadn't appreciated how upset he felt.* **4** ⚠ **ACKNOWLEDGE** to accept something as valid ○ *I don't appreciate being called a time-waster.* **5** *vi* **GAIN IN VALUE** to increase in value, especially over time [Mid-17C. < late Latin *appretiare* 'value, estimate, rate, appraise' < *pretium* 'money spent, worth, value'.]

USAGE Opinions on ***appreciate*** vary widely. Some people, explaining that the word's history has to do with accurate valuation, consider that it should be used only in neutral contexts (*I appreciate your position*). Others, pointing out that ***appreciation*** is admiration or gratitude, say it should be used only in favourable contexts (*I appreciate your frankness*). Still others argue that the object of this verb should always be a noun (*I appreciate your annoyance*), not a clause (*I appreciate how angry you must feel*). Certainly it is worth remembering the verb's continuing ties to the ideas of valuation and gratitude, and worth remembering, too, that no one objects to *recognize*, *realize*, or *understand* in negative contexts or before clauses.

appreciation /ə prèeshi áysh'n/ *n* **1 GRATEFULNESS** a feeling or expression of gratitude ○ *a token of my appreciation* **2 POSITIVE OPINION** a favourable opinion of something **3 VALUING SOMETHING HIGHLY** recognition and liking of something's qualities **4 FULL UNDERSTANDING** a full understanding of the meaning and importance of something **5 GROWTH IN VALUE** an increase in value, especially over time

appreciative /ə préeshi ətiv, -shətiv/ *adj* expressing or feeling gratitude or approval —**appreciatively** *adv* —**appreciativeness** *n*

apprehend /àppri hénd/ *vt* **1 ARREST** to put somebody suspected of wrongdoing into legal custody **2 UNDERSTAND** to grasp the importance or meaning of something **3 BECOME AWARE OF** to become aware of something by use of the senses (*formal*) **4 BE FEARFUL OF** to await an impending disaster or other calamity with fear or dread (*formal*) [14C. Directly or via Old French, < Latin *apprehendere* 'take hold of' < *prehendere* 'seize'.]

apprehensible /àppri hénssəb'l/ *adj* capable of being understood

apprehension /àppri hénsh'n/ *n* **1 DREAD** a feeling of anxiety or fear that something bad or unpleasant will happen **2 IDEA** an idea formed by observation or experience **3 ARREST** the taking of a criminal suspect into custody (*formal*) **4 ABILITY TO UNDERSTAND** the power or ability to grasp the importance, significance, or meaning of something (*formal*) [14C. Directly or via Old French < late Latin *apprehension-* < *apprehens-*, past participle of Latin *apprehendere* (see APPREHEND).]

apprehensive /àppri hénssiv/ *adj* **1** worried that something bad will happen **2** aware or cognizant of something nonphysical, e.g. implications or results (*formal*) —**apprehensively** *adv* —**apprehensiveness** *n*

apprentice /ə préntiss/ *n* **1 TRAINEE** somebody being trained by a skilled professional in an art, craft, or trade **2 INEXPERIENCED PERSON** a novice or amateur ■ *vt* (**-tices, -ticing, -ticed**) **MAKE SOMEBODY APPRENTICE** to give somebody work as an apprentice to a skilled professional ○ *He was apprenticed to a master sailmaker for five years.* [14C. < Old French *aprentis* < *aprendre* 'learn' < Latin *apprehendere* (see APPREHEND).] —**apprenticeship** *n*

SYNONYMS See ***beginner***.

appressed /ə prést/ *adj* describes a part of a plant that is pressed closely against another part without being joined to it ○ *appressed leaves* [Late 18C. < Latin *appressus*, past participle of *apprimere* 'press to' < *premere* 'press'.]

apprise /ə príz/ (**-prises, -prising, -prised**) *vt* to inform or give notice to somebody about something (*formal*) [Late 17C. < French *appris*, past participle of *apprendre* 'make learn, teach' (see APPRENTICE).]

USAGE See ***appraise***.

apprize /ə príz/ (**-prizes, -prizing, -prized**) *vt* to value something very highly, e.g. because of its monetary worth (*archaic*) [15C. Via Old French *aprisier* < Latin *appretiare* (see APPRECIATE).]

approach /ə prṓch/ *v* **1** *vti* **MOVE CLOSER** to move closer to somebody or something ○ *He motioned to us to approach.* **2** *vt* **ASK** to speak to somebody with a view to asking for something **3** *vt* **TREAT IN PARTICULAR WAY** to deal with something in a particular way ○ *Try approaching the article from a fresh angle.* **4** *vt* **COME CLOSE TO BEING** to be almost at a particular level or state **5** *vti* **COME CLOSER IN TIME** to come nearer in time to something ○ *As spring approaches I notice people smiling more.* **6** *vi* **HIT BALL FROM FAIRWAY TO GREEN** to make a golf shot from the fairway towards a green ■ *n* **1 COMING** a coming nearer in space or time **2 METHOD** a way of doing or solving something **3 CONTACT** an informal request, offer, suggestion, or proposal made to somebody (*often plural*) **4 SIMILAR THING** one thing that is very similar in its nature or qualities to another **5 ACCESS** a way of reaching or gaining access to a building or place **6 AIRCRAFT'S COURSE** the path that an aircraft follows as it prepares to land **7 BOWLING MOVEMENT** the steps a bowler takes before releasing the ball, or the part of the bowling lane used for doing this **8 GOLF SHOT** a golf shot made from the fairway towards the green [14C. Via Old French *aproch(i)er* < late Latin *appropiare* 'go nearer to' < *prope* 'near'.]

approachable /ə prṓchəb'l/ *adj* **1 INVITINGLY FRIENDLY** friendly and easy to talk to **2 EASILY ACCESSIBLE** able to be reached with ease, especially in terms of transportation **3 USER-FRIENDLY** easy for nonspecialists to understand —**approachability** /ə prṓchə bílləti/ *n* —**approachableness** *n* —**approachably** *adv*

approaching /ə prṓching/ *adj* coming near in space or time

approach shot *n* **1** a tennis shot hit deep into the opponent's court, designed to give the player time to approach the net for the next shot **2** GOLF = **approach** *n.* 8

approbation /àpprə báysh'n/ *n* **1** approval, consent, or appreciation **2** the official approving, authorizing, or sanctioning of something —**approbative** /áppra baytiv/ *adj* —**approbatory** *adj*

~~**approch**~~ incorrect spelling of **approach**

appropriate *adj* /ə prṓpri ət/ **FITTING** suitable for the occasion or circumstances ■ *vt* /ə prṓpri ayt/ (**-ates, -ating, -ated**) **1 TAKE SOMETHING FOR OWN USE** to take or use something forcefully or without permission ○ *They should act before rival parties appropriate the moral high ground.* **2 USE MONEY FOR PARTICULAR PURPOSE** to set aside an amount of money for a particular use [15C. < late Latin *appropriatus*, past participle of Latin *appropriare* 'make your own' < *propius* 'own'.] —**appropriable** *adj* —**appropriately** *adv* —**appropriateness** *n* —**appropriative** *adj* —**appropriator** *n*

appropriation /əprṓpri áysh'n/ *n* **1** the taking or using of something forcefully or without permission **2** a sum of money that has been set aside from a budget, especially a government budget, for a particular purpose (*often plural*)

approval /ə pro͞ov'l/ *n* **1** a favourable opinion or feeling about something **2** formal or official agreement or permission ◇ **on approval** with the opportunity to try something before deciding whether you really want to buy it

approve /ə pro͞ov/ (**-proves, -proving, -proved**) *v* **1** *vi* to have a favourable opinion of somebody or something **2** *vt* to formally confirm that something is satisfactory [14C. Via Old French < Latin *approbare* 'assent to as good' < *probus* 'good'.] —**approvable** *adj* —**approved** *adj* —**approving** *adj* —**approvingly** *adv*

approved school *n* a reform school or detention centre for young offenders (*dated*)

approx. *abbr* **1** approximate **2** approximately

approximal /ə próksim'l/ *adj* describes, or relating to, teeth that are side by side or set close together

approximate *adj* /ə próksimət/ **1 NEARLY EXACT** not quite exact, but only slightly more or less in number or quantity **2 SIMILAR** similar in nature, appearance, or characteristics to something else ■ *v* /ə próksi mayt/ (**-mates, -mating, -mated**) **1** *vti* **BE SIMILAR** to be or become similar to something in nature, size, or extent ○ *There was nothing in the terms of the treaty that even approximated to the negotiators' original thinking.* **2** *vt* **ESTIMATE** to make or provide an estimate, usually a rough estimate, of something **3** *vti* **COME OR BRING CLOSE** to come or bring something close to something else [15C. < late Latin *approximatus*, past participle of *approximare* 'draw near to' < Latin *proximus* 'near'.] —**approximateness** *n* —**approximation** /ə próksi máysh'n/ *n* —**approximative** *adj*

approximately /ə próksimətli/ *adv* not exactly, but nearly or roughly

~~**approximatly**~~ incorrect spelling of **approximately**

appt *abbr* appointment

appulse /ə púlss/ *n* a near approach of two celestial bodies that does not result in a partial concealment or an eclipse [Early 17C. < Latin *appulsus*, past participle of *appellere* 'drive to, force towards' < *pellere* 'drive'.]

appurtenance /ə púrtinənsz/ *n* **1 ACCESSORY** an accompanying part or feature of something (*formal; often* *plural*) ○ *an athletic club with all the usual appurtenances* **2 PROPERTY RIGHT** a legal right or privilege attached to a property and inherited with it ■ **appurtenances** *npl* **EQUIPMENT** the equipment needed for a particular activity (*formal*) [14C. < Anglo-Norman, < late Latin *appertinere* (see APPERTAIN).] —**appurtenant** *adj*

APR *abbr* **1** annual percentage rate **2** annual purchase rate (*used to show repayment rates in hire-purchase schemes*)

Apr. *abbr* April

apraxia /ay práksi ə, ə-/ *n* the inability to perform complex movements, often as a result of brain damage, e.g. following a stroke [Late 19C. Via German < Greek, 'in-action'.] —**apraxic** *adj*

~~**apreciate**~~ incorrect spelling of **appreciate**

après /ápray/ *prep* after an activity [Mid-20C. < French, 'after'.]

après-ski /ápray skee/ *n* social activities taking place after skiing ■ *adj* taking place during or appropriate to the period of time after skiing [Mid-20C. < French, 'after skiing'.]

apricot /áypri kot/ *n* **1 FRUIT** a small round fruit with a soft furry yellowish-orange skin and a single stone **2 FRUIT TREE** a tree that bears apricots. *Prunus armeniaca*. **3 YELLOWISH-ORANGE COLOUR** a pale yellowish-orange colour [Mid-16C. Via obsolete Catalan *abrecoc* < Arabic *al-barqūq* 'the apricot'.] —**apricot** *adj*

April /áypral/ *n* in the Gregorian calendar, the fourth month of the year, made up of 30 days [14C. < Latin *Aprilis* < Etruscan *apru* < Greek *Aphrō*, shortening of *Aphroditē* 'Aphrodite'.]

April fool *n* **1 TARGET OF JOKE** the target of a practical joke on April Fools' Day **2 JOKE** a practical joke played on somebody on April Fools' Day ■ *interj* **ANNOUNCING THAT JOKE HAS BEEN PLAYED** used to tell somebody that he or she has been the target of an April Fools' Day joke

April Fools' Day *n* 1 April, traditionally a day on which practical jokes are played on other people

a priori /áy prī áwrī, aá pri áwri/ *adj* **1 BASED ON SOMETHING KNOWN** working from something that is already known or self-evident to arrive at a conclusion **2 ASSUMED** known or assumed without reference to experience **3 MADE BEFOREHAND** conceived or formulated before investigation or experience [Mid-17C. < Latin, 'from the previous (one, cause, hypothesis)'.] —**a priori** *adv*—**apriority** /áyprī órrəti/ *n*

apron /áyprən/ *n* **1 PROTECTIVE GARMENT TIED OVER CLOTHES** a garment worn over the front of clothes to keep them clean during working, especially cooking **2 PROTECTIVE PART** a shield or plate fitted to a machine that protects the user from flying debris **3 PROJECTING EDGE** the projecting edge of a platform, e.g. a theatre stage, dock, or loading bay **4 PARKING AREA FOR PLANES** the hard-surfaced area immediately in front of airport buildings, on which aircraft are loaded and unloaded **5 BORDER AROUND GREEN** the outer edge of a green on a golf course **6 AREA OUTSIDE BOXING RING** the part of the floor of a boxing ring that is outside the ropes **7 LOW-ANGLED SURFACE** a gently sloping surface of sand, gravel, or bare rock, usually in front of a mountain range **8 CURVING CONVEYOR BELT** a conveyor belt made of slats loosely attached to each other in a way that allows the belt to go around curves **9** ENG = **skirt** *n.* 4 [14C. < Old French *naperon* 'small cloth' < *nape* 'tablecloth' < Latin *mappa* 'napkin'; by interpreting 'a napron' as 'an apron'.]

apron stage *n* a stage that juts out into the auditorium

apropos /áppra pó/ *prep* **IN REGARD TO** on the subject of (*formal*) ○ *We've had further correspondence from them apropos our application for funds.* ■ *adj* **JUST RIGHT** appropriate in a particular situation (*formal*) ■ *adv* **INCIDENTALLY** by the way (*formal*) ○ *Apropos, do you think we should delay the announcement?* [Mid-17C. < French *à propos* 'to the purpose'.]

aprotic /ay prótik/ *adj* describes a solvent that is unable to donate protons [Mid-20C. < A-[2] + PROTON + -IC.]

aprotinin /ay prótinin/ *n* a polypeptide obtained from animal organs. Use: treatment of pancreatitis.

~~**aproximately**~~ incorrect spelling of **approximately**

apse /aps/ *n* **1** a semicircular projecting part of a building, especially the east end of a church that contains the altar **2** ASTRON = **apsis** *n.* 1 [Early 19C. < Latin *apsis* (see APSIS).] —**apsidal** /ap sīd'l, ápsid'l/ *adj*

apsis /ápsiss/ (*plural* **-sides** /-deez/) *n* **1** either of the two points in an orbit that are nearest to and farthest from the centre of gravitational attraction **2** ARCHIT = **apse** *n.* 1 [Late 16C. Via Latin < Greek *(h)apsis* 'rim of a wheel, wheel, arch, vault', perhaps < *haptein* 'fasten'.] —**apsidal** /ápsid'l, ápsīd'l/ *adj*

apt /apt/ *adj* **1 VERY APPROPRIATE** especially suited to the circumstances **2 LIKELY** often doing something and likely to do it again ○ *He is apt to get angry when people question him.* **3 QUICK TO LEARN** enthusiastic and quick to learn new things [14C. Directly or via Old French < Latin *aptus*, past participle of *apere* 'fit, fasten, join'.] —**aptly** *adv*—**aptness** *n*

APT *abbr* advanced passenger train

apt. *abbr* apartment

apteral /áptərəl/ *adj* **1** describes a classical temple that has no columns along its sides **2** describes a church that has no aisles [Mid-19C. < Greek *apteros* 'wingless' < *pteron* 'wing, feather'.]

apterous /áptərəss/ *adj* describes an insect that has no wings [Late 18C. < Greek *apteros* (see APTERAL).]

apteryx /áptəriks/ *n* BIRDS = **kiwi** *n.* 1 [Early 19C. < modern Latin, < Greek *a-* 'without' + *pterux* 'wing'.]

aptitude /ápti tyood/ *n* **1** a natural talent or ability for something, especially one that is not yet fully developed ○ *pupils of varying aptitudes* **2** quickness and ease in learning

SYNONYMS See ***ability***. See ***talent***.

aptitude test *n* a test to determine how readily somebody is likely to be able to develop certain skills, especially in order to do a particular kind of work

Apuleius /ápyoō leé əss/, **Lucius** (125?–200?) Numidian-born Roman philosopher and writer

Apus /áypəss/ *n* a faint constellation near the south celestial pole. See illustration at **constellation**

apyrase /áppə rayz, -rays/ *n* an enzyme that aids the breakdown of ATP, producing energy [Mid-20C. Contraction of *adenypyrophosphatase*.]

apyrexia /áypī réksi ə, áppī-/ *n* absence of fever, or a period during which a patient experiences no fever [Mid-17C. Via modern Latin, < Greek, < *purexis* (see PYREXIA).] —**apyretic** *adj* —**apyrexial** *adj*

ϟ **aq** *abbr* Antarctica (*in Internet addresses*)

AQ *abbr* achievement quotient

aq. *abbr* **1** aqua **2** aqueous

Aqaba, Gulf of /ákəbə/ northeastern arm of the Red Sea, bordered by Egypt, Israel, Jordan, and Saudi Arabia. Length: 160 km/100 mi.

Aqmola /aak móllə/ former name for **Astana** (1991–98)

aqua /ákwə/ (*plural* **-uae** /-wee, -wī/ *or* **-uas**) *n* **1** water, especially when used as a solvent (*technical*) **2** COLOURS = **aquamarine** *n.* 2 [14C. < Latin, 'water'.] —**aqua** *adj*

aqua- *prefix* water ○ *aquanaut* [< Latin *aqua* (see AQUA)]

aquaculture /ákwə kulchər/, **aquiculture** /ákwi-/ *n* **1** the farming of marine and freshwater plants and animals for human consumption **2** PLANT SCI = **hydroponics** [Mid-19C. After AGRICULTURE.] —**aquacultural** /ákwə kúlchərəl/ *adj* —**aquaculturist** *n*

~~**aquaduct**~~ incorrect spelling of **aqueduct**

aquadynamic /ákwə dī námmik/ *adj* having a smooth or streamlined surface in order to reduce drag when passing through water [Late 20C. After AERODYNAMIC.]

aquae plural of **aqua**

aquaerobics *n* = **aquarobics**

~~**aquaint**~~ incorrect spelling of **acquaint**

~~**aquaintance**~~ incorrect spelling of **acquaintance**

aqualung /ákwə lung/ *n* an underwater breathing apparatus used by divers

aquamarine /ákwə mə reén/ *n* **1** a greenish-blue variety of beryl. Use: gems. **2** a greenish-blue colour [Late 16C. < Latin *aqua marina* 'sea water'.] —**aquamarine** *adj*

aquanaut /ákwə nawt/ *n* somebody with training and equipment to spend long periods working or swimming underwater [Late 19C. < AQUA- + Greek *nautēs* 'sailor', after ARGONAUT.]

aquaphobia /ákwə fóbi ə/ *n* an irrational fear of water

aquaplane /ákwə playn/ *n* **WATER-SKIING BOARD** a water-skiing board on which somebody stands while being towed by a motorboat ■ *vi* (**-planes, -planing, -planed**) **1 RIDE ON AN AQUAPLANE** to ride on an aquaplane **2 LOSE CONTROL IN WET CONDITIONS** to skid out of control at high speed on a surface that is so wet that it causes the vehicle's tyres to lose contact with the road. US term **hydroplane** *v.* 2

aqua regia /-reéji ə/ *n* a fuming, highly corrosive mixture of nitric and hydrochloric acid. Use: dissolving metals, including gold. [Early 17C. < Latin, 'royal water'; because it can dissolve 'noble' metals.]

aquarelle /ákwə rél/ *n* **1** a painting technique that uses transparent washes of watercolour **2** a painting produced using the aquarelle technique [Mid-19C. Via French < obsolete Italian *acquarella* 'watercolour' < *acqua* 'water'.] —**aquarellist** *n*

aquaria plural of **aquarium**

aquarist /ákwərist/ *n* somebody who looks after an aquarium

aquarium /ə kwáiri əm/ (*plural* **-ums** *or* **-a** /-ri ə/) *n* **1** a water-filled transparent container, often box-shaped, in which fish and other aquatic animals and plants are kept **2** a building in which fish and other aquatic animals are kept and shown to the public [Mid-19C. < Latin *aquarius* (see AQUARIUS) after VIVARIUM.]

Aquarius /ə kwáiri əss/ *n* **1 CONSTELLATION IN SOUTHERN HEMISPHERE** a constellation of the southern hemisphere. See illustration at **constellation** **2 11TH SIGN OF ZODIAC** the 11th sign of the zodiac, represented by a man pouring water, and lasting from approximately 20 January to 18 February **3 SOMEBODY BORN UNDER AQUARIUS** somebody whose birthday falls between 20 January and 18 February [14C. < Latin, 'water carrier' < *aquarius* 'of water' < *aqua* 'water'.] —**Aquarian** *n* —**Aquarius** *adj*

aquarobics /ákwə róbiks/, **aquaerobics** *n* aerobic exercises done to music in a swimming pool (+ *singular or plural verb*) [Late 20C. Blend of AQUA- + AEROBICS.]

aquatic /ə kwáttik/ *adj* **1 OF WATER** connected with, consisting of, or dependent upon water **2 LIVING IN WATER** living or growing in water **3 DONE IN WATER** played or performed in or on water ■ *n* **WATER PLANT OR ANIMAL** a plant or animal that lives or grows in water —**aquatically** *adv*

aquatics /ə kwáttiks/ *n* sports played in or on water (+ *singular or plural verb*)

aquatint /ákwə tint/ *n* **1** a method of etching a copper plate in which the prints produced from it show areas similar to watercolours **2** an etching produced by the aquatint process [Late 18C. Via French *aquatinte* < Italian *acquatinta* 'tinted water'.] —**aquatinter** *n* —**aquatintist** *n*

aquavit /ákwəvit/ *n* a potato- or grain-based spirit flavoured with caraway seeds, produced in Scandinavia [Late 19C. Via Danish, Norwegian, Swedish *aquavit* < Latin *aqua vitae* (see AQUA VITAE).]

aqua vitae /ákwə vī tee, -veé tī/ *n* a strong spirit, especially brandy [14C. < Latin, 'water of life'.]

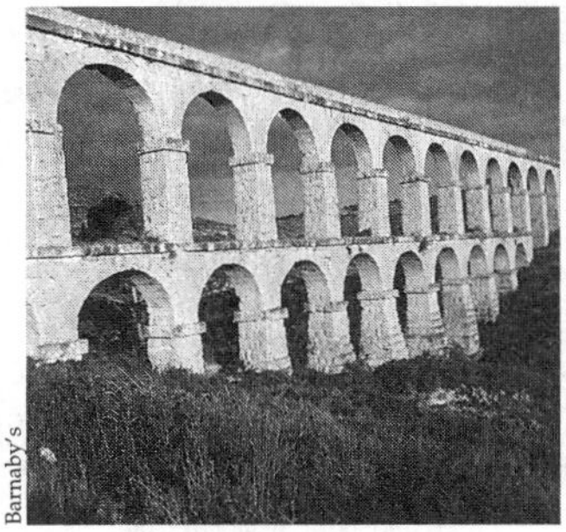

Barnaby's

Aqueduct: Ancient Roman aqueduct in Tarragona, Spain

aqueduct /ákwi dukt/ *n* **1 STRUCTURE CARRYING CANAL** a structure in the form of a bridge that carries a canal across a valley or river **2 CHANNEL FOR WATER** a pipe or channel for moving water to a lower level, often across a great distance **3 CHANNEL CARRYING FLUID IN BODY** a channel in an organ or body part through which fluid passes [Mid-16C. Via medieval Latin *aqueductus* < Latin *aquae ductus* 'water conveyance'.]

aqueous /áykwi əss, ákwi-/ *adj* containing, dissolved in, or consisting mostly of water [Mid-17C. < medieval Latin *aqueus* < Latin *aqua* 'water'.]

aqueous humour *n* the transparent fluid that circulates in the eye chamber between the back of the cornea and the front of the iris and pupil

aqui- *prefix* water ○ *aquifer* [< Latin *aqua* 'water']

aquiculture *n* AGRIC = **aquaculture**

aquifer /ákwifər/ *n* a layer of permeable rock, sand, or gravel through which ground water flows, containing enough water to supply wells and springs

Aquila /ákwilə, ə kwíllə/ *n* a constellation near the celestial equator containing the bright star Altair. See illustration at **constellation**

aquilegia /ákwi leéji ə/ (*plural* **-as** *or* **-a**) *n* a perennial plant with leaves that have five rounded lobes. Flowers: drooping, purple, pink, blue, or red, on tall stalks. Genus: *Aquilegia*. US term **columbine**[1] [Late 16C. < medieval Latin.]

aquiline /ákwi līn/ *adj* **1** thin, curved, and pointed like an eagle's beak **2** resembling or connected with eagles [Mid-17C. < Latin *aquilinus* < *aquila* 'eagle'.] — **aquilinity** /ákwi línnəti/ *n*

Aquinas /ə kwínəss/**, Thomas, St** (1225–74) Italian philosopher and theologian

Aquino /ə keénō/**, Corazón** (*b.* 1933) Filipino government leader and president of the Philippines (1986–92)

~~aquire~~ incorrect spelling of **acquire**

~~aquit~~ incorrect spelling of **acquit**

Aquitaine /ákwi tayn/ region of SW France. Population: 2,795,800 (1990). Area: 41,309 sq. km/15,949 sq. mi.

aquiver /ə kwívvər/ *adj* quivering, especially from excitement or agitation

Ar *symbol* argon

AR *abbr* **1 A/R** account receivable **2** Arkansas

ar. *abbr* **1** arrival **2** arrive

Ar. *abbr* **1** Arabia **2** Arabian **3** Arabic

-ar *suffix* of, relating to, or resembling ○ *nebular* [Via Old French *-ar* < Latin *-aris*, alternative for *-alis*]

Ara /áərə/ *n* a faint constellation of the southern hemisphere. See illustration at **constellation**

ARA *abbr* Associate of the Royal Academy

ara-A /árrə áy/ *n* an antiviral drug. Use: treatment of herpes, chickenpox, shingles, hepatitis B. Full name **adenine arabinoside** [Late 20C. < contraction of *arabinoside* (< ARABINOSE) + A[2] 2.]

Arab /árrəb/ *n* a member of a Semitic Arabic-speaking people who live throughout North Africa and the Middle East ■ *adj* PEOPLES = **Arabian** *adj*. [14C. Via Old French and Latin, < Greek *Arab-* < Arabic *arab*.]

> **USAGE Arab, Arabic,** or **Arabian**? *Arab* denotes a person, and is also used attributively (i.e. before a noun) as a kind of adjective (*the Arab world*; *Arab customs*). *Arabian* is an adjective referring to *Arabia* in geographical terms (*the Arabian Peninsula*; *an Arabian stallion*); and *Arabic* is a noun and an adjective meaning the language of the *Arab* people (*She speaks Arabic and knows Arabic literature*). *Arabic* is written with a capital initial letter in *Arabic numerals* (1, 2, 3, etc.), and with a small initial letter in the term *gum arabic*, a substance obtained from African acacia trees.

Arab. *abbr* **1** Arabia **2** Arabian **3** Arabic

arabesque /árrə bésk/ *n* **1** ORNATE DESIGN an intricate and often symmetrical design, or style of design, incorporating curves, geometric patterns, leaves, flowers, and animal shapes **2** BALLET POSTURE a ballet position in which the dancer stands on one leg with the other extended back and both arms stretched out, usually one forward and the other backward **3** MUSIC WITH ORNATE MELODY a piece of classical music characterized by decorative melodies [Early 17C. Via French, < Italian *arabesco* 'in the Arabian style'.]

Arabia /ə ráybi ə/ peninsula of SW Asia, bordering the Persian Gulf, the Arabian Sea, and the Red Sea. Area: 3,000,000 sq. km/1,158,306 sq. mi.

Arabian /ə ráybi ən/ *adj* relating to Arabia, or its peoples or cultures ■ *n* **1** somebody who comes from a country of the Arabian Peninsula **2** ZOOL = **Arabian horse**

> **USAGE See Arab.**

Arabian camel *n* = **dromedary**

Arabian horse *n* a horse of a breed known for its intelligence, graceful build, and speed. Native to: Arabia.

Arabian Peninsula ♦ **Arabia**

Arabian Sea arm of the Indian Ocean between the Arabian Peninsula and the Indian subcontinent

Arabic /árrəbik/ *n* SEMITIC LANGUAGE a Semitic language that is the official language of several countries of North Africa and the Middle East. Native speakers: 150 million. Other speakers: 175 million. ■ *adj* **1** OF ARABIA relating to Arabia, or its people, language, or culture **2** OF ARABIC relating or belonging to the Arabic language

> **USAGE See Arab.**

arabica /ə rábbikə/ *n* **1** a widely grown species of coffee bush producing high-quality coffee. *Coffea arabica*. **2** coffee made with arabica coffee beans [Early 20C. < modern Latin, 'Arabic'.]

Arabicize /ə rábbi sīz/ (**-cizes, -cizing, -cized**), **Arabicise** (**-cises, -cising, -cised**) *v* **1** *vt* to adapt a word or other language feature for use in Arabic **2** *vti* = **Arabize** — **Arabicization** /ə rábbi sī záysh'n/ *n*

Arabic numeral *n* any of the symbols 0, 1, 2, 3, 4, 5, 6, 7, 8, and 9 that are used to represent numbers

arabinose /ə rábbinōz, -noss/ *n* a sugar (**aldose**) derived from various plant gums and used in culturing [Late 19C. < GUM ARABIC + -IN + -OSE[2].]

Arabise *vti* = **Arabize**

Arabist /árrəbist/ *n* a student of or expert on the Arabs, their language, or their culture **2** somebody who favours Arab causes or political positions

Arabize /árrə bīz/ (**-izes, -izing, -ized**), **Arabise** (**-ises, -ising, -ised**) *vti* to conform, or make something conform, to Arab customs or culture — **Arabization** /árrə bī záysh'n/ *n*

arable /árrəb'l/ *adj* **1** SUITABLE FOR GROWING CROPS capable of being cultivated for growing crops **2** RELATING TO LARGE-SCALE CULTIVATION relating to, involving, or produced by the large-scale cultivation of field crops such as cereals and potatoes ■ *n* LAND SUITABLE FOR CULTIVATION land that is fit for planting crops [15C. Via Old French, < Latin *arabilis* < *arare* 'to plough'.] — **arability** /árrə bílləti/ *n*

Arab League *n* a political and economic association of Arab states, formed in 1945

arachidonic acid /árrəkə dónnik-/ *n* an essential fatty acid found in most animal fats that is a precursor to prostaglandins [*arachidonic* < modern Latin *arachid-* 'peanut' (< Greek *arakhos* 'type of leguminous plant') + -ONE]

arachis oil /árrəkiss-/ *n* FOOD = **peanut oil**

arachnid /ə ráknid/ *n* an animal with four pairs of legs and a body with two segments, belonging to a large class that includes spiders, scorpions, and mites. Class: Arachnida. [Mid-19C. < modern Latin *Arachnida* < Greek *arakhnē* 'spider, spider's web'.] — **arachnidan** *adj*

arachnodactyly /ə ráknō dáktəli/ *n* a condition characterized by unusually long fingers and toes

arachnoid /ə rák noyd/ *n* **1** middle of the three membranes that envelop the brain and spinal cord **2** ZOOL = **arachnid** [Mid-18C. Via modern Latin < Greek *arakhnoeidēs* 'like a spider's web' < *arakhnē* 'spider's web'.] — **arachnoid** *adj*

arachnology /árrak nólləji/ *n* the branch of zoology concerned with the study of spiders and other arachnids [Mid-19C. < Greek *arakhnē* 'spider' + -LOGY.] — **arachnologist** *n*

arachnophobia /ə ráknə fóbi ə/ *n* an abnormally strong fear of spiders [Early 20C. < Greek *arakhnē* 'spider' + -PHOBIA.] — **arachnophobe** /ə ráknəfōb/ *n* — **arachnophobic** *adj*

Arafat /árrə fat/**, Yasir** (*b.* 1929) Palestinian statesman

Arafura Sea /árrə foörə-/ arm of the Pacific Ocean between N Australia and E Indonesia

Aragon /árrə gon/**, Louis** (1897–1982) French writer

aragonite /árrə rággə nīt/ *n* a colourless, blue to violet, or yellow mineral consisting of calcium carbonate [Late 18C. After *Aragon*.]

aralia /ə ráyli ə/ (*plural* **-as** *or* **-a**) *n* a plant widely grown as a houseplant for its ornamental leaves. Genera: *Aralia* and *Polyscias*. [Mid-18C. < modern Latin.]

Aral Sea /árrəl-/ inland sea in SW Kazakhstan and NW Uzbekistan. Area: 31,220 sq. km/12,050 sq. mi.

Aram /áirəm/**, Eugene** (1704–59) English scholar

Aramaic /árrə máy ik/ *n* a Semitic language of the ancient Near East, dating from about 300 BC and still spoken in the region. Native speakers: 50,000–100,000. [Mid-19C. < Greek *Aramaios* 'of Aram' (ancient Syria).] — **Aramaic** *adj*

Aran /árrən/ *adj* describes a traditional style of heavy knitted garments made from thick unbleached wool with complex cable patterns [Mid-20C. After the ARAN ISLANDS.]

Aranda /árrəndə, ə rándə/ (*plural* **-da** *or* **-das**) *n* **1** a Pama-Nyungan language spoken in parts of Australia's Northern Territory. Native speakers: 2,000. **2** a member of an Aboriginal people who live in S central Australia [Late 19C. < Aranda.] — **Aranda** *adj*

Aran Islands /árrən-/ group of three islands, Inishmoor, Inishmaan, and Inisheer, situated at the mouth of Galway Bay in W Ireland. Population: 803 (1981). Area: 47 sq. km/18 sq. mi.

Arapaho /ə ráppəhō/ (*plural* **-ho** *or* **-hos**) *n* **1** a member of a Native North American people who formerly lived on the Great Plains, and now live in Colorado, Wyoming, and Montana **2** an Algonquian language of W North America. Native speakers: 1,500. [Early 19C. < Crow *alappahó* 'many tattoo marks'.] — **Arapaho** *adj*

Ararat, Mount /árrə rat/ mountain in E Turkey, the landing place of Noah's Ark according to the Bible. Height: 5,137 m/16,854 ft.

Araucanian /árraw káyni ən/ *n* **1** a member of a Native South American people who live in central Chile and W Argentina **2** a South American language spoken in parts of Chile and W Argentina. Native speakers: 300,000. [Early 19C. < Spanish *Araucanía*, region of Chile.] — **Araucanian** *adj*

araucaria /árraw káiri ə/ (*plural* **-as** *or* **-a**) *n* an evergreen coniferous tree with stiff sharp leaves. Native to: S hemisphere. Genus: *Araucaria*. [Mid-19C. < modern Latin, < *Arauco*, province in Chile.]

Arawak /árrə wak/ (*plural* **-wak** *or* **-waks**) *n* **1** a member of a native South American people who live in Guyana, Suriname, and French Guiana **2** a South American language of the Arawakan family, spoken in Guyana and neighbouring countries [Mid-18C. < Carib *aruac*.]

Arawakan /árrə wákən/ *n* a family of Native South American languages, spoken by widely scattered peoples in Central and South America. Native speakers: 300,000. — **Arawakan** *adj*

arbalest /áarbalist/**, arbalist** *n* a large medieval crossbow used to propel stones, arrows, and other missiles [Pre-12C. Via Old French *arbaleste* < late Latin *arcuballista* < *arcus* 'bow' + *ballista* (see BALLISTA).] — **arbalester** *n*

arbiter /áarbitər/ *n* **1** SOMEBODY MAKING JUDGMENT somebody who can settle a dispute or decide an issue **2** INFLUENTIAL PERSON OR THING somebody or something with great influence over what people say, think, or do **3** SCOTTISH JUDGE OF DISPUTE in the Scottish legal system, somebody designated to hear both sides of a dispute and make a judgment [14C. Directly or via Old French *arbitre* < Latin *arbiter* 'judge, umpire'.] — **arbitral** /áarbitrəl/ *adj*

arbitrage /áarbitrij, -traazh/ *n* the simultaneous buying and selling of the same negotiables or commodities in different markets in order to make an immediate risk-less profit ■ *vi* (**-trages, -traging, -traged**) to participate in arbitrage [Mid-19C. < French, < *arbitrer* 'to judge' < Latin *arbitrari* (see ARBITRATE).]

Yasir Arafat

arbitrageur /a̋arbi traa zhúr/ *n* somebody who engages in arbitrage [Mid-19C. < French, < *arbitrage* (see ARBITRAGE).]

arbitrary /a̋arbitrəri/ *adj* 1 BASED ON WHIM based solely on personal wishes, feelings, or perceptions, rather than on objective facts, reasons, or principles 2 RANDOMLY CHOSEN chosen or determined at random 3 NOT ACCORDING TO RULE based on the decision of a particular judge or court rather than in accordance with any rule or law 4 AUTHORITARIAN with unlimited power 5 ASSIGNED NO SPECIFIC VALUE describes a mathematical constant that is not assigned a specific value [15C. < Latin *arbitrarius* 'uncertain, depending on the judgment of an arbiter' < *arbiter* 'judge'.] —**arbitrarily** /a̋arbitrərəli, a̋arbi tráirəli/ *adv* —**arbitrariness** *n*

arbitrate /a̋arbi trayt/ (-**trates**, -**trating**, -**trated**) *v* 1 *vti* to act as a judge in a dispute between others 2 *vt* to submit a dispute to be decided by a third party [Late 16C. < Latin *arbitrat-*, past participle of *arbitrari* 'judge, decide' < *arbiter* 'judge'.] —**arbitrable** *adj*

arbitration /a̋arbi tráysh'n/ *n* the process of resolving disputes between people or groups by referring them to a third party, either agreed by them or provided by law, who makes a judgment —**arbitrational** *adj*

arbitrator /a̋arbi traytər/ *n* somebody designated to hear both sides of a dispute and make a judgment

arbor[1] *n* US = **arbour**

arbor[2] /a̋arbər/ *n* 1 AXLE ON MACHINE OR POWER TOOL a shaft, axle, or spindle on a machine or a power tool, e.g. a lathe 2 SUPPORTING PIECE a machine part that holds an object being worked on, or the tools being used to work on the object 3 REINFORCING PART OF MOULD a part that reinforces the core of a mould used to cast metal [Mid-17C. Via Old French *arbre* < Latin *arbor* 'tree, mast, lever, shaft'.]

Arbor Day *n* in the United States, a day set aside for the planting and appreciation of trees. Date: typically the last Friday in April, but varying from state to state.

arboreal /aar báwri əl/ *adj* 1 relating to, resembling, or consisting of trees 2 describes a species that lives in trees —**arboreally** *adv*

arboreous /aar báwri əss/ *adj* covered with trees

arborescent /a̋arbə réss'nt/ *adj* resembling a tree, especially in developing branches or similar parts [Mid-17C. < Latin *arborescent-*, present participle of *arborescere* 'grow into a tree' < *arbor* 'tree'.] —**arborescence** *n*

arboretum /a̋arbə reétəm/ (*plural* -**tums** *or* -**ta** /-tə/) *n* an area planted with many types of trees for study, display, and preservation [Mid-19C. < Latin, 'place grown with trees, plantation of trees' < *arbor* 'tree'.]

arboriculture /a̋arbəri kulchər, aar báwri-/ *n* the cultivation of trees and shrubs for study, ornamentation, or profit [Mid-19C. Blend of Latin *arbor* 'tree' + AGRICULTURE.] —**arboricultural** *adj* —**arboriculturist** *n*

arborise *vi* = **arborize**

arborist /a̋arbərist/ *n* an expert in the cultivation and care of trees

arborize /a̋arbə rīz/ (-**rizes**, -**rizing**, -**rized**), **arborise** (-**rises**, -**rising**, -**rised**) *vi* to develop many branching parts or formations —**arborization** /a̋arbə rī záysh'n/ *n*

arbor vitae /a̋arbər vītee, -veétī/ (*plural* **arbor vitaes**), **arborvitae** (*plural* -**taes**) *n* an ornamental coniferous tree with flat closely-fitted leaves resembling scales. Native to: Asia, North America. Genus: *Thuja*. [Mid-17C. < Latin, 'tree of life'.]

arbour /a̋arbər/ *n* 1 a shaded place formed by the leaves and branches of trees and plants that interweave naturally or are trained to grow around a trellis 2 a trellis or other structure used to support plants that form an arbour [14C. Via Old French *(h)erb(i)er* < late Latin *herbarium* (see HERBARIUM).]

arbovirus /a̋arbə vīrəss/ *n* a virus transmitted by blood-sucking arthropods such as ticks and fleas [Mid-20C. Contraction of *arthropod-borne virus*.] —**arboviral** /a̋arbə vīrəl/ *adj*

Arbus /a̋arbəss/, **Diane** (1923–71) US photographer

arbutus /aar byóotəss/ (*plural* -**tuses** *or* -**tus**) *n* 1 a bush or tree that bears reddish fruits. Flowers: white, pink. Native to: S Europe. Genus: *Arbutus*. 2 PLANTS = **trailing arbutus** [Mid-16C. < Latin, 'wild strawberry', from the shape of the leaves.]

arc /aark/ *n* 1 CURVE a curved or semicircular line, direction of movement, or arrangement of items ○ *The ball curved in a high arc.* 2 SECTION OF CIRCLE a section of a circle, ellipse, or other curved figure 3 VISIBLE PART OF CELESTIAL BODY'S PATH a section of the path that a planet or other celestial body appears to follow, especially that between rising above the horizon and disappearing below it 4 ELECTRIC DISCHARGE a luminous discharge caused by an electric current flowing across a gap in an electrical circuit 5 GEOL = **island arc** ■ *vi* (**arcs**, **arcing** *or* **arcking**, **arced** *or* **arcked**) 1 FORM OR MOVE IN ARC to form a curve or move along a curved path 2 SPARK ACROSS GAP to produce a luminous discharge across a gap in an electrical circuit [14C. Via Old French < Latin *arcus* 'bow, curve'.]

ARC *abbr* Aids-related complex

arcade /aar káyd/ *n* 1 SERIES OF ARCHES a series of arches and the columns supporting them 2 PASSAGEWAY WITH ARCHES a passageway or building with a series of arches and supporting columns 3 AVENUE OF SHOPS a covered passage with shops on both sides 4 ENCLOSED AREA WITH GAMES MACHINES an enclosed area where people can play on coin-operated games machines such as pinball machines or video games [Mid-18C. Via French < Italian *arcata* < Latin *arcus* 'bow, curve, arch'.] —**arcaded** *adj*

arcade game *n* a coin-operated game played in amusement arcades, e.g. one-armed bandits, pinball machines, or video games

Arcadia[1] /aar káydi ə/, **arcadia** *n* a place in which people are imagined or believed to enjoy a perfect life of rustic simplicity [Late 19C. Via Latin, < Greek *Arkadia*, mountainous district in the Peloponnese.] —**Arcadian** *adj*

Arcadia[2] /aar káydi ə/ mountainous region of the central Peloponnese, SW Greece —**Arcadian** *adj, n*

arcana /aar káynə/ *n* either of two divisions of a pack of tarot cards ■ plural of **arcanum**

arcane /aa káyn/ *adj* 1 requiring secret knowledge to be understood 2 difficult or impossible to understand [Early 16C. < Latin *arcanus* 'closed, secret' < *arca* 'box'.] —**arcanely** *adv* —**arcaneness** *n*

SYNONYMS See ***obscure***.

arcanum /aar káynəm/ (*plural* -**na** /-nə/) *n* (*usually plural*) 1 a secret known only to the members of a small select group 2 a secret of nature, of the kind that was sought by alchemists [Late 16C. < Latin, form of *arcanus* (see ARCANE).]

arc cosine *n* the inverse of the cosine function

Arc de Triomphe /a̋ark də treé ómf/ *n* a triumphal arch at the end of the Avenue des Champs Elysées in Paris, completed in 1835

arc furnace *n* a furnace in which an electric arc supplies the heat

arch[1] /aarch/ *n* 1 CURVED STRUCTURE a curved structure that forms the upper edge of an open space, e.g. a window, a doorway, or the space between a bridge's supports 2 PASSAGE UNDER ARCH an entrance or passageway under an arch 3 ARCH SHAPE the shape of an arch, resembling an inverted U, or an object with such a shape ○ *the arch of his eyebrows* 4 CURVED BODY PART a body part with the shape of an arch, especially the bony structure in the foot 5 CURVED ROCK FORMATION a naturally occurring arch-shaped span of rock found in arid, especially desert, regions ■ *v* 1 *vt* FORM CURVED SHAPE to form something into the shape of an arch 2 *vi* MOVE IN CURVING LINE to follow a trajectory in the shape of an arch 3 *vt* CROSS to extend across something 4 *vt* BUILD ARCH to build something in the shape of an arch or with arch-shaped supports [13C. Via Old French *arche* < Latin *arcus* 'bow, curve, arch'.] —**arched** *adj*

arch[2] /aarch/ *adj* 1 greatest, especially most hostile 2 expressing playfulness, mischief, or shared humour in a knowing way [Mid-16C. < ARCH-.] —**archly** *adv* —**archness** *n*

arch. *abbr* 1 archaic 2 archaism 3 archery 4 archipelago 5 architect 6 architecture

arch- *prefix* 1 chief, most important ○ *archrival* 2 extreme ○ *archconservative* [Via Latin and Old French *arche* < Greek *arkhi-* 'first, chief' (see ARCHI-)]

-arch *suffix* leader, ruler ○ *matriarch* [Via Old French and late Latin, < Greek *arkhos* < *arkhein* 'to rule'] —**-archic** *suffix* —**-archy** *suffix*

archaea /a̋arkeé ə/ *npl* members of one of two distinct groups of the most primitive living single-celled organisms, similar in size to bacteria but different in molecular organization [Late 20C. Shortening of ARCHAEBACTERIA.]

Archaean /aar keé ən/, **Archean** *adj* 1 OF OLDEST ROCK describes the oldest known kinds of rock 2 OF EARLIEST GEOLOGICAL PERIOD describes the earliest geological period of time, dating from about four billion years ago ■ *n* ARCHAEAN ERA the Archaean era [Late 19C. < Greek *arkhaios* 'old, ancient' + AN[3].]

archaebacteria /a̋arki bak teéri ə/ *npl* MICROBIOL = **archaea** [Late 20C. Because believed to be of ancient origin.] —**archaebacterial** *adj*

archaeo-, **archae-**, **archeo-** *prefix* ancient ○ *archaeoastronomy* [Via modern Latin < Greek *arkhaios*]

archaeoastronomy /a̋arki ō ə strónnəmi/, **archeoastronomy** *n* the study of the astronomical beliefs, practices, and discoveries of prehistoric and ancient cultures —**archaeoastronomer** *n* —**archaeoastronomical** /a̋arki ō astrə nómmik'l/ *adj*

archaeobotany /a̋arki ō bóttəni/, **archeobotany** *n* the scientific study of excavated plant remains from ancient times —**archaeobotanist** *n*

archaeological dating *n* the use of the decay rates of biological specimens to determine the age of an archaeological site, effective to about 50,000 years back

archaeology /a̋arki óllәji/, **archeology** *n* the scientific study of ancient cultures through the examination of their material remains —**archaeological** /a̋arki ə lójjik'l/ *adj* —**archaeologically** *adv* —**archaeologist** *n*

archaeomagnetism /a̋arki ō mágnətizəm/, **archeomagnetism** *n* a method of dating excavated artefacts by measuring the degree of their magnetization

archaeometry /a̋arki ómmətri/, **archeometry** *n* the systematic dating of archaeological objects —**archaeometrical** /a̋arki ə méttrik'l/ *adj* —**archaeometrically** *adv* —**archaeometrist** *n*

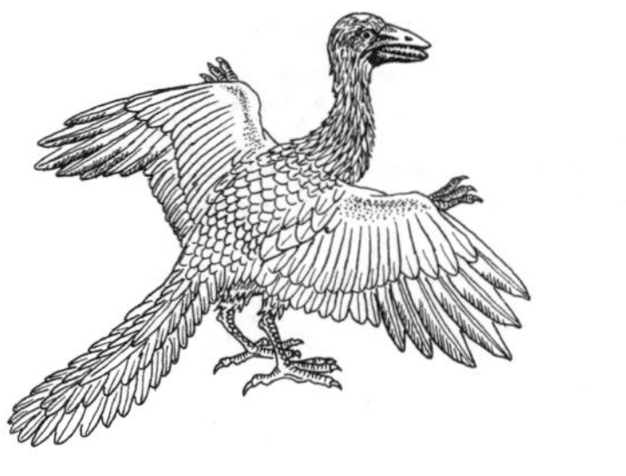

Archaeopteryx

archaeopteryx /a̋arki óptəriks/ *n* an extinct bird of the Jurassic period that had the feathers of modern birds but the jaw and sharp teeth of reptiles. *Archaeopteryx lithographica*. [Mid-19C. < ARCHAEO- + Greek *pterux* 'wing'.]

archaic /aar káyik/ *adj* 1 ANCIENT belonging or relating to a much earlier period 2 NO LONGER IN ORDINARY LANGUAGE describes a word or phrase that is no longer in general use but is still encountered in older literature and still sometimes used for special effect 3 OUTMODED no longer useful or efficient [Mid-19C. Via French < Greek *arkhaikos* < *arkhaios* 'old, ancient' < *arkhē* 'beginning'.] —**archaically** *adv*

archaise *vt* = **archaize**

archaism /a̋ar kay izəm, -ki-/ *n* 1 a word, expression, practice, or method from an earlier time that is no longer used 2 the use of expressions, techniques, and fashions from an earlier period [Mid-17C. Via modern Latin < Greek *arkhaismos* < *arkhaizein* 'copy the ancients, give an archaic air to' < *arkhaios* (see ARCHAIC).] —**archaist** *n* —**archaistic** /a̋ar kay ístik, -ki-/ *adj*

archaize /a̋ark ay īz/ (-**izes**, -**izing**, -**ized**), **archaise** (-**ises**, -**ising**, -**ised**) *vt* to cause something to seem much older than it is by using old forms or styles —**archaizer** *n*

archangel /a̋ark aynjəl/ *n* 1 a chief or principal angel 2 a member of the second-lowest rank in the medieval order of celestial beings, ranking above angels and below principalities 3 PLANTS = **angelica** *n.* 2 [Pre-12C. Via Anglo-Norman, < ecclesiastical Greek *arkhaggelos* < Greek *arkhi-* 'chief' (see ARCHI-) + *aggelos* 'messenger'.] —**archangelic** *adj*

archbishop /aarch bíshəp/ n a bishop of the highest rank, who heads an archdiocese or an ecclesiastical province

archbishopric /aarch bíshəprik/ n 1 the area of an archbishop's jurisdiction 2 the status or term of office of an archbishop [Pre-12C. < ARCHBISHOP + Old English rice 'realm'.]

arch bridge n a bridge whose span curves in the shape of an arch

archd. abbr 1 archdeacon 2 archduke

archdeacon /aarch deékən/ n a member of the clergy who ranks just below a bishop and assists the bishop with ceremonial and administrative duties —**archdeaconate** n —**archdeaconship** /-ship/ n

archdeaconry /aarch deékənri/ (plural -ries) n 1 the status or term of office of an archdeacon 2 the residence of an archdeacon

archdiocese /aarch dí əssiss/ n the area for which an archbishop has ecclesiastical responsibility —**archdiocesan** /aarch dī óssass'n/ adj

archducal /aarch dyoók'l/ adj relating or belonging to archdukes, archduchesses, or archduchies

archduchess /aarch dúchiss/ n 1 an archduke's wife or widow 2 a princess of the former Austrian imperial family

archduchy /aarch dúchi/ (plural -ies) n the land ruled by an archduke or archduchess

archduke /aarch dyoók/ n a senior duke in some countries, especially Austria [Early 16C. Via Old French archeduc < late Latin archidux < archi- 'chief, first' + dux 'leader'.]

Archean adj, n = Archaean

archegonia plural of archegonium

archegoniate /aarki góni ət/ adj bearing archegonia ▪ n a plant that bears archegonia

archegonium /aarki góni əm/ (plural -a /-ə/) n the female reproductive organ of mosses, ferns, liverworts, and most gymnosperms [Mid-19C. < modern Latin, < Greek arkhegonos < arkhe- 'chief, first' + gonos 'people'.] —**archegonial** adj

archenemy /aarch énnəmi/ (plural -mies) n 1 somebody's main or worst enemy 2 **archenemy, Archenemy** the Devil

archenteron /aar kéntə ron, -tərən/ n a digestive cavity in animal embryos that develops into the gut [Late 19C. < Greek arkhē 'beginning'+ enteron 'intestine'.] —**archenteric** adj

archeo- prefix = archaeo-

archeoastronomy n = archaeoastronomy

archeobotany n = archaeobotany

archeological, archeologic adj = archaeological

archeology n = archaeology

archeomagnetism n ARCHAEOL = archaeomagnetism

archeometry n ARCHAEOL = archaeometry

archer /aarchər/ n somebody who uses a bow and arrow [13C. Via Anglo-Norman and Old French, < Latin arcus 'bow, curve'.]

Archer n ZODIAC = Sagittarius n. 2

Archer /aarchər/, **Frederick Scott** (1813–57) British photographer

Archer, Jeffrey, Baron Archer of Weston-super-Mare (b. 1940) British politician and writer

Archer, Robyn (b. 1948) Australian singer and actor

Archer, William (1856–1924) British drama critic

archerfish /aarchər fish/ (plural -fish or -fishes) n a freshwater fish of Australia and Southeast Asia that hunts insects by spitting water at them. Family: Toxotidae.

archery /aarchəri/ n 1 SHOOTING WITH BOW AND ARROW the activity of shooting with a bow and arrow 2 TROOP OF ARCHERS a troop of soldiers armed with bows and arrows 3 ARCHERS' WEAPONS the bows and arrows used by archers

archesporium /aarki spáwri əm/ (plural -a /-ə/), **archespore** /aarki spawr/ n the tissue that gives rise to spore-producing cells in a sporangium in fungi [Late 19C. < arche-, alteration of ARCHI- + SPORE + -IUM.]

archetype /aarki tīp/ n 1 ORIGINAL MODEL something that served as the model or pattern for other things of the same type ○ The film was one of the archetypes of the American Western. 2 TYPICAL SPECIMEN a typical, ideal, or classic example of something ○ It was described as an archetype of the interior design of the period. 3 IMAGE FROM COLLECTIVE UNCONSCIOUS in Jungian psychology, an inherited memory represented in the mind by a universal symbol and observed in dreams and myths 4 RECURRING SYMBOL an image or symbol that is used repeatedly in art or literature [Mid-16C. Via Latin archetypum < Greek arkhetupon 'first moulded as a model' < arkhe- 'first, chief' + tupon 'mould, model'.] —**archetypal** /aarki típ'l, -tīp'l/ adj —**archetypally** adv —**archetypic** /aarki típpik/ adj —**archetypical** adj —**archetypically** adv

archi- prefix 1 chief, most important ○ archimage 2 primitive, primary ○ archenteron [Via French archi- < Greek arkhi- < arkhein 'be first, rule']

Archibald /aarchi bawld/, **Jules François** (1856–1919) Australian journalist

Archibald Prize n an annual prize awarded for portrait painting in Australia

archidiaconal /aarki dī ákənəl/ adj relating to the work or position of an archdeacon [15C. < Latin archidiaconus < diaconus (see DEACON).]

archidiaconate /aarki dī ákənət/ n an archdeacon's position, area of jurisdiction, or term of office [Mid-18C. < Latin archidiaconus (see ARCHIDIACONAL).]

⚡**Archie** /aarchi/ n an Internet database used to search for files and programs that can be downloaded using File Transfer Protocol [Late 20C. < ARCHIVE + -IE, after the name Archie.]

archiepiscopal /aarki ə pískəp'l/ adj relating to archbishops or archdioceses [Early 17C. < ecclesiastical Latin archiepiscopus 'archbishop' < ecclesiastical Greek arkhiepiskopos.] —**archiepiscopality** /aarki ə pískə pálləti/ n —**archiepiscopally** adv —**archiepiscopate** n

archimandrite /aarki mán drīt/ n in the Eastern Orthodox Church, a senior priest who heads a monastery or group of monasteries [Mid-17C. Directly or via French < ecclesiastical Latin archimandrita < ecclesiastical Greek arkhimandritēs < arkhi- 'first, chief' + mandra 'enclosure, monastery'.]

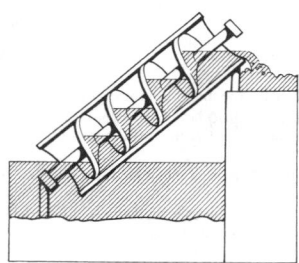

Archimedean screw

Archimedean screw /aarkə meé dee ən-/ n an ancient method of raising water using either a large screw inside a sloping tube or a spiral tube curling around a sloping axis [After ARCHIMEDES]

Archimedes /aarkə meé deez/ (287–212 BC) Greek mathematician

Archimedes' principle n the principle stating that an object immersed in a liquid experiences an upward thrust equal to the weight of liquid it displaces, thus light objects float and heavy objects sink

Archimedes' screw n = Archimedean screw

archipelago /aarki péllə gō/ (plural -gos or -goes) n 1 a group or chain of islands (often in placenames) 2 an area of sea with many islands [Early 16C. < Italian arcipelago < Greek arkhi- 'chief, main' + pelagos 'sea'.] —**archipelagic** /aarkipə lájjik/ adj

archit. abbr architecture

architect /aarki tekt/ n 1 somebody whose job is to design buildings and advise on their construction 2 the person who created or invented something ○ the architect of her own fortune [Mid-16C. Directly or via French and Italian < Latin architectus < Greek arkhitektōn 'chief builder' < tektōn 'builder'.]

architectonic /aarki tek tónnik/ adj 1 relating to architecture or the qualities, e.g. design and structure, that architecture requires 2 relating to the classification of knowledge used in metaphysics [Mid-17C. Via Latin < Greek arkhitektonikos < arkhitektōn (see ARCHITECT).] —**architectonically** adv

architectonics /aarki tek tónniks/ n (+ singular verb) 1 SCIENCE OF ARCHITECTURE the science of architecture 2 STRUCTURAL DESIGN OF COMPLEX THING the way in which the parts of a complex object or system fit together ○ the architectonics of a good novel 3 CLASSIFICATION OF KNOWLEDGE in metaphysics, the classification of knowledge

⚡**architecture** /aarki tekchər/ n 1 BUILDING DESIGN the art and science of designing and constructing buildings 2 BUILDING STYLE a particular style or fashion of building, especially one that is typical of a period of history or of a particular place 3 STRUCTURE OF COMPUTER SYSTEM the design, structure, and behaviour of a computer system, microprocessor, or system program, including the characteristics of individual components and how they interact ○ network architecture —**architectural** /aarki tékchərəl/ adj —**architecturally** adv

architrave /aarki trayv/ n 1 in classical architecture, the lowest section of an entablature, which comes into contact with the top of the columns 2 a decorative strip of wood or plaster forming a frame around a door or window [Mid-16C. Via French < Italian, 'main beam' < trave 'beam' < Latin trab-.]

⚡**archive** /aar kīv/ n 1 COLLECTION OF DOCUMENTS a collection of documents such as letters, official papers, photographs, or recorded material, kept for their historical interest (often plural) ○ archive material ○ We'll have to check the archives. 2 PLACE WHERE ARCHIVES ARE HELD the building or room that houses archives 3 BACKUP COMPUTER FILE a copy of computer files stored, often in compressed form, on tape or disk 4 COMPUTER FILE OF COMPRESSED FILES a computer file containing other compressed files 5 INTERNET DIRECTORY a directory of files that Internet users can access using anonymous File Transfer Protocol ▪ vt (-chiving, -chived, -chives, -chived) 1 PUT DOCUMENT IN ARCHIVE to store a document in an archive 2 STORE DATA EXTERNALLY to transfer data from a computer's hard disk to a tape or disk for storage 3 COMBINE COMPUTER FILES to store compressed copies of computer files in a single file [Early 17C. Via French, < Latin archiva, archia < Greek arkheia 'things kept at the public office', plural of arkheion 'ruler's house, public office' < arkhē 'beginning, government'.] —**archival** /aar kīv'l/ adj

archivist /aarkivist/ n somebody employed to collect, catalogue, and look after the items in an archive

archivolt /aarki vōlt/ n 1 a decorative moulding or band on the face of an arch 2 the underside of an arch [Mid-17C. Directly or via French archivolte < Italian archivolto < Latin arcus 'arch' + volta 'vault'.]

archon /aarkən, -kon/ n one of the nine chief magistrates in ancient Athens [Late 16C. < Greek arkhōn < arkhein 'to rule'.] —**archonship** n

archosaur /aarkə sawr/, **archosaurian** /aarkə sáwri ən/ n a relatively advanced and active reptile that became predominant on land during the Mesozoic era. Superorder: Archosauria. [Mid-20C. < modern Latin Archosauria < Greek arkhos 'chief' + sauros 'lizard'.]

archpriest /aarch preést/ n 1 HIGH-RANKING EASTERN ORTHODOX PRIEST in the Eastern Orthodox Church, a married priest of the highest rank 2 SPECIAL ROMAN CATHOLIC TITLE in the Roman Catholic Church, a title given to a priest who has a specific important duty or function 3 BISHOP'S SENIOR ASSISTANT formerly, a title given to the senior Roman Catholic priest in a cathedral chapter, who acted as the bishop's principal assistant [14C. Via Old French archeprestre < late Latin archipresbyter 'chief priest'.]

archway /aarch way/ n an entrance or passage under one or more arches, or an arch that forms an entrance

Archytas /aar kítəss/ (fl. early 4thC BC) Greek mathematician

Arcimboldo /aarchim bóldō/, **Giuseppe** (1530?–93) Italian painter and designer

arc lamp, arc light n an intensely bright electric lamp with numerous uses, e.g. in floodlights

arco /aarkō/ adv played using the bow of a stringed instrument, usually after a passage played by plucking the strings (**pizzicato**) (musical direction) [Mid-18C. < Italian, 'bow'.] —**arco** adj

arc sine n the inverse of the sine function

arc tangent n the inverse of the tangent function

arctic /aarktik/ adj extremely cold (informal) ▪ n US a high waterproof overshoe with a warm lining [14C. Via

Old French *artique* < Greek *arktikos* < *arktos* 'bear', also 'the constellation Ursa Major (the Great Bear)'.]

Arctic /aárktik/ *n* the region that lies around the North Pole, inside the Arctic Circle. ◊ **Antarctic** —**Arctic** *adj*

Arctic Circle

Arctic Circle *n* the line of latitude at 66°30′N that marks the boundary of the Arctic

arctic fox *n* a small fox with thick fur that is brownish-grey in summer and white or blue in winter. Native to: Arctic. *Alopex lagopus.*

arctic hare *n* 1 a large hare with white fur that in southern regions turns brown in the summer. Native to: Arctic North America, Greenland. *Lepus arcticus.* 2 ZOOL = **mountain hare**

Arctic Ocean world's smallest ocean, mostly ice-covered, situated north of the Arctic Circle. Area: 14,055,930 sq. km/5,427,000 sq.mi. Depth: 5,500 m/17,880 ft.

arctic tern *n* a black-headed seabird that breeds in Arctic regions and migrates to southern Africa, South America, and the Antarctic. *Sterna paradisaea.*

arctophile /aárktō fīl/ *n* a collector of teddy bears [Late 20C. < Greek *arktos* 'bear' + -PHILE.]

Arcturus /aark tyoórass/ *n* the brightest star in the constellation Boötes and the fourth brightest star in the sky

arcuate /aárkyoo at/ *adj* in the shape of an arc or a bow [15C. < Latin *arcuatus* < *arcus* 'bow, arch'.] —**arcuately** *adv*

arcus senilis /aárkōoss se neéliss/ *n* an opaque circle around the cornea of the eye that can develop late in life [Latin, 'bow of advanced age']

arc welding *n* the joining of metal components by fusing them with heat from an electric arc struck between two electrodes

ARD *abbr* acute respiratory disease

-ard, -art *suffix* somebody characterized by a given quality ◊ *dullard* [< Old French, < Germanic]

Arden /aárd'n/, **John** (*b.* 1930) British playwright

Ardennes /aar dén/ forested plateau in SE Belgium, Luxembourg, and NE France

ardent /aárd'nt/ *adj* 1 PASSIONATE felt passionately 2 ENTHUSIASTIC feeling or showing great enthusiasm or eagerness ◊ *one of his most ardent supporters* 3 GLOWING shining or glowing brightly, with a fiery quality (*literary*) ◊ *her ardent gaze* [14C. Via Old French *ardant* < Latin *ardent-*, present participle of *ardere* 'burn'.] —**ardently** *adv*

ardent spirits *npl* distilled alcoholic beverages, e.g. whisky and rum

ardor *n* US = **ardour**

ardour /aárdər/ *n* fierce intensity of feelings ◊ *repeated attempts to dampen their revolutionary ardour* [14C. Via Old French < Latin *ardor* < *ardere* 'to burn'.]

Ards /aardz/ local government region in E Northern Ireland. Population: 64,764 (1991). Area: 381 sq. km/147 sq. mi.

arduous /aárdyoo ass/ *adj* 1 requiring hard work or continuous strenuous effort 2 very difficult to traverse, endure, or overcome [Mid-16C. < Latin *arduus* 'steep, difficult'.] —**arduously** *adv* —**arduousness** *n*

SYNONYMS See **hard**.

are[1] (*stressed*) /aar/; (*unstressed*) /ər/ the plural and second

person singular present tense of the verb 'be' [Old English *earon* < Germanic]

are[2] /aar/ *n* a metric unit of area, equal to 100 sq. m [Late 18C. Via French < Latin *area* (see AREA).]

area /áiri ə/ *n* 1 MEASUREMENT OF SURFACE the extent of part of a surface enclosed within a boundary, or the extent of the surface of all or part of a solid 2 PART OF SURFACE a distinct part of the surface of something, especially a piece of land ◊ *The storms resulted in flooding over a large area.* 3 SPACE OR PART FOR SPECIFIC FUNCTION a space, part, or surface of something, especially when intended for a specific use ◊ *an area of the brain used for memory* 4 REGION OR DISTRICT a region or district, either a distinct political or administrative division or a place that has particular qualities or features 5 SUBJECT a particular subject, field of knowledge, or sphere of activity ◊ *in the area of genetic research* 6 SOCCER = **penalty area** [Mid-16C. < Latin, 'flat piece of unoccupied land'.]

area code *n* digits indicating a particular area of a country that are dialled before the local number in calls from outside that area

Area of Archaeological Importance *n* an area of land, usually an urban one, designated and protected by law because there are known to be concentrations of archaeological remains

Area of Outstanding Natural Beauty *n* full form of **AONB**

areca /ə reékə, árri-/ *n* a tall palm tree with white flowers. Native to: Southeast Asia. Genus: *Areca*. [Late 16C. Via Portuguese, < Malayalam *atekka*.]

areg plural of **erg**[2]

ARELS /árrəlz/ *abbr* Association of Recognized English Language Schools

arena /ə reé nə/ *n* 1 STADIUM an indoor or outdoor area, surrounded by seating for spectators, where shows or sports events take place 2 SCENE OF ACTIVITY a place or situation where there is conflict or intense activity ◊ *A new contestant has entered the political arena.* 3 CENTRE OF ROMAN AMPHITHEATRE the open area inside a Roman amphitheatre, in which gladiatorial contests and other entertainments were staged [Early 17C. < Latin, 'sand, sand-strewn place'.]

arenaceous /árri náyshəss/ *adj* 1 describes rocks or deposits that are composed of sand grains or have a sandy texture 2 describes plants that grow best in sandy soil [Mid-17C. < Latin *arenaceus* 'of sand' < *arena* 'sand'.]

arena theatre *n* THEATRE = **theatre-in-the-round** *n.* 1

arenavirus /ə reénə vírəss/ *n* a virus of the family that causes diseases such as Lassa fever. Family: Arenaviridae. [Late 20C. < Latin *arena* 'sand' + VIRUS, because when the viruses are viewed under an electron microscope they appear to have sandy granules in them.]

Arendt /aárənt/, **Hannah** (1906–75) German-born US philosopher and political theorist

arene /árreen/ *n* an aromatic hydrocarbon [Mid-20C. <lt. AROMATIC.]

arenicolous /árri níkələss/ *adj* living, burrowing, or thriving in sand [Mid-18C. < Latin *arena* 'sand' + *-cola* 'inhabiting'.]

aren't /aarnt/ *contr* (*informal*) 1 short form of 'are not' ◊ *They aren't coming.* 2 short form of 'am not', which can only be used in questions ◊ *I'm allowed to go too, aren't I?*

USAGE Use of **aren't**: English does not have a convenient contracted form of *am I not?* (The logically expected form *amn't I* is used in some parts of Scotland and Ireland but has never been part of standard English.) The usual form used is *aren't I*, borrowing *are* from other parts of the verb *be*, whereas in American English *ain't I* is used, though only informally. There is no contraction for *I am not* that corresponds to *I don't* and *I haven't* (as distinct from *I'm not*, which places greater emphasis on the *not*), and this is why the nonstandard form *ain't* tends to be used for want of anything better, although it is extremely informal.

areola /ə reé ələ/ (*plural* **-lae** /-lee/ *or* **-las**) *n* 1 the small circular dark area around the nipple in humans 2 a small circular area, e.g. an inflamed ring around a spot [Mid-17C. < Latin, 'little area'.] —**areolar** *adj* —**areolate** /ə reé ələt/ —**areolation** /-láysh'n/ *n*

areole /árri ōl/ *n* 1 a small clearly defined space, e.g. that between veins on a leaf 2 a depression on the surface of a cactus that the spines, hairs, or flowers grow from [Mid-19C. Via French < Latin *areola* 'little area'.]

Arequipa /árri keépa/ city in S Peru. Population: 620,471 (1993).

Ares /aá reez/ *n* in Greek mythology, the god of war and the son of Zeus and Hera. Roman equivalent **Mars**

arête /ə ráyt, -rét/ *n* a narrow ridge of bare rock situated between two or more deep smooth-sided semicircular areas (**cirques**) [Early 19C. Via French, < Latin *arista* 'ear of grain, fish bone, spine', from its shape.]

Aretino /árra teénō/, **Pietro** (1492–1556) Italian poet

argal *n* CHEM = **argol**

argali /aárgəli/ (*plural* **-li**) *n* a large wild mountain sheep. Native to: central and N Asia. *Ovis ammon.* [Late 18C. < Mongolian.]

argent /aárjənt/ *n* 1 the metal or the colour silver (*archaic or literary*) 2 the colour white or silver on a coat of arms [14C. Via French < Latin *argentum* 'silver'.] —**argent** *adj*

argentic /aar jéntik/ *adj* containing silver with a valency of 2

argentiferous /aárjən tíffərəss/ *adj* describes rocks or deposits containing silver

Argentina

Argentina /aárjən teénə/ republic in S South America. Capital: Buenos Aires. Population: 35,797,981 (1997). Area: 2,780,400 sq. km/1,073,518 sq. mi. —**Argentinian** /aárjən tínni ən/ *adj*, *n*

argentine /aárjən tīn/ *adj* silvery in colour (*archaic or literary*) ■ *n* the metal silver, or any material that looks like silver

Argentine /aárjən teen, -tīn/ *n* = **Argentina**

argentite /aárjən tīt/ *n* a grey to black silver sulphide mineral, forming cubic crystals [Mid-19C. < Latin *argentum* 'silver'.]

argie-bargie *n* = **argy-bargy**

argil /aárjil/ *n* clay, especially potter's clay [14C. Via Old French *argille* < Greek *argillos* 'clay'.]

argillaceous /aárji láyshəss/ *adj* describes sedimentary rock that is made up of fine silt or clay particles

argillite /aárji līt/ *n* rock that is made up of clay or silt particles, especially a hardened mudstone

arginase /aárji nayz, -nayss/ *n* a liver enzyme involved in the production of urea

arginine /aárji neen, -nīn/ *n* an essential amino acid, one of the constituents of protein [Late 19C. < German, perhaps < Greek *arginoeis* 'bright-shining, white'.]

Argive /aár gīv, -jīv/ *adj* GREEK relating to ancient Greece, especially the city of Argos ■ *n* 1 ANCIENT GREEK somebody from ancient Greece (*literary*) 2 CITIZEN OF ARGOS somebody from the city of Argos [Mid-16C. < Latin *Argivus* 'of Argos'.]

Argo /aárgō/ *n* a large constellation in the southern hemisphere

argol /aár gol/, **argal** /aárg'l/ *n* potassium hydrogen tartrate, formed in wine casks [14C. < Anglo-Norman *argoile*.]

argon /aár gon/ *n* (*symbol* **Ar**) an inert, gaseous element that makes up about one per cent of the Earth's atmosphere. Use: electric lights, gas shield in welding. [Late 19C. < Greek, < *argos* 'inactive, idle' < *a-* 'without' + *ergon* 'work'.]

argonaut /aárgə nawt/ *n* ZOOL = **paper nautilus** [Mid-19C. < modern Latin *Argonauta*, (see ARGONAUT).]

Argonaut *n* 1 one of the heroes in Greek mythology who sailed with Jason to find the Golden Fleece 2 **Argonaut,**

argonaut an adventurer, especially somebody who took part in the Californian gold rush of 1849 [Late 16C. Via Latin *argonauta* < Greek *argonautēs* 'sailor in the ship Argo'.]

Argonne /aar gón, áar gon/ wooded highland region in NE France

argosy /áargəssi/ (*plural* **-sies**) *n* a large richly laden merchant ship, or a fleet of such ships (*literary*) [Late 16C. Probably < Italian *Ragusea* '(ship from the port of) Ragusa'.]

argot /áargō, -gət/ *n* jargon used by a particular group [Mid-19C. < French, originally 'criminals' jargon'.] —**argotic** /aar góttik/ *adj*

arguable /áargyoo əb'l/ *adj* **1** able to be supported or proved with evidence or arguments ○ *an arguable case for global warming* **2** not obviously true or accurate, and therefore likely to be questioned or argued about ○ *It's arguable whether he really is the world's best guitarist.*

arguably /áargyoo əbli/ *adv* used to mean that a statement is open to dispute but could be defended in an argument ○ *They are arguably the best team to come out of Europe this decade.*

USAGE arguably, debatably, or **disputably**? ***Arguably***, the most common of the three words, suggests that the speaker assumes widespread agreement with what is being said: *arguably the most influential legislator in the county.* ***Disputably***, the least common word, tends to emphasize the potential for disagreement: *The cause was disputably his work habits, although some say it was his temper that got him into trouble.* ***Debatably*** is the most nearly neutral of the three: *It was a debatably rude thing to do.*

argue /áargyoo/ (**-gues, -guing, -gued**) *v* **1** *vi* **EXPRESS DISAGREEMENT** to express disagreement with somebody, especially continuously or angrily **2** *vti* **GIVE REASONS FOR** to give reasons for an opinion in order to support it ○ *You could argue that this calls for greater freedom, not less.* **3** *vt* **PERSUADE** to persuade somebody to do something by giving reasons ○ *argued her out of leaving* **4** *vti* **PROVIDE EVIDENCE FOR** to be evidence or a sign of something ○ *The increase in crime argued for tougher jail sentences, said some.* [14C. Via French *arguer* < Latin *argutari* 'assert repeatedly' < *arguere* 'make clear, assert'.] —**arguer** *n*

SYNONYMS See ***disagree***.

~~**argueing**~~ incorrect spelling of **arguing**

~~**arguement**~~ incorrect spelling of **argument**

argufy /áargyoo fī/ (**-fies, -fying, -fied**) *vi* to argue about something that is unimportant (*informal*)

ϟ **argument** /áargyoomənt/ *n* **1 QUARREL** a disagreement in which different views are expressed, often angrily **2 REASON** a reason put forward in support of a point of view ○ *the arguments for and against the planned development* **3 STATED POINT OF VIEW** the main point of view expressed in a book, report, or speech **4 DISCUSSION** debate or discussion about whether something is correct **5 NOUN ELEMENT IN CLAUSE** any noun element in a clause that relates directly to the verb, e.g. the subject or object **6 VARIABLE ELEMENT** an independent variable whose value determines the value of a mathematical expression **7 FEATURE CONTROLLING COMPUTER PROGRAM** a value that modifies how a command or function operates in a computer program

argumenta plural of **argumentum**

argumentation /áargyoomən táysh'n/ *n* **1** a process of debating or discussing something **2** reasoning that proceeds methodically from a statement to a conclusion

argumentative /áargyoo méntətiv/ *adj* **1** tending to disagree and argue **2** characterized by disagreement or argument —**argumentatively** *adv* —**argumentativeness** *n*

Argus /áargəss/ *n* **1** in Greek mythology, a giant with a hundred eyes **2** an alert watchful person (*literary*)

argus pheasant *n* a large pheasant, the male of which has a tail like a peacock's. Native to: Southeast Asia, Indonesia. *Argusianus argus.* [From its tail-spots, reminiscent of Argus's eyes]

argy-bargy /áarji báarji/ (*plural* **argy-bargies**), **argie-bargie** *n* an animated or heated quarrel (*informal*) [Late 19C. Playful development of ARGUMENT.]

argyle /aar gī́l/ *adj* knitted with a pattern of coloured diamonds ■ *n* a sock or sweater made in an argyle design [Mid-20C. From being based on the tartan of Campbells from Argyll in Scotland.]

Argyle, Lake /áar gīl/ large reservoir in NW Australia. Area: 2,400 sq. km/927 sq. mi.

Argyll and Bute /aar gī́l-/ administrative area in W Scotland

arhat /áarhət/ *n* a Buddhist who has reached the highest state of peace and enlightenment [Late 19C. Via Pali < Sanskrit, 'deserving, meritorious'.] —**arhatship** *n*

Århus /áwr hooss, áar-/, **Aarhus** port in E Jutland, Denmark. Population: 213,826 (1996).

aria /áari ə/ *n* a melody sung solo or as a duet in an opera, oratorio, or cantata [Early 18C. Via Italian < Latin *aer* 'air' (see AIR).]

Ariadne /árri ádni/ *n* in Greek mythology, the daughter of King Minos of Crete

Arian[1] /áiri ən/ *n* ZODIAC = **Aries** *n.* 2 —**Arian** *adj*

Arian[2] /áiri ən/ *n* a follower of the ancient Greek Christian theologian Arius, who argued that Jesus Christ was the highest created being, but was not divine —**Arianism** *n*

Arias Sanchez /áari aass sán chez/, **Oscar** (*b.* 1941) Costa Rican statesman and president (1986–90)

ariboflavinosis /ay rī́bō fláyvi nóssiss/ *n* a condition caused by a dietary deficiency of vitamin B_2 (**riboflavin**) [Mid-20C. < A-[2] + RIBOFLAVIN.]

arid /árrid/ *adj* **1** describes a region in which annual rainfall is less than 25 cm/10 in **2** completely lacking in interest or excitement [Mid-17C. Directly or via French, < Latin *aridus* < *arere* 'be dry'.] —**aridity** /ə ríddəti/ *n* —**aridly** /árridli/ *adv* —**aridness** *n*

SYNONYMS See ***dry***.

arid zone *n* either of two zones of latitude that are between 15° and 30° north and south of the equator, consisting mostly of desert or semidesert

Ariel /áiri əl/ *n* a natural satellite of Uranus having a radius of 580 km, discovered in 1851

Aries /áireez/ *n* **1 FIRST SIGN OF THE ZODIAC** the first sign of the zodiac, represented by a ram and lasting from approximately 21 March to 19 April **2 SOMEBODY BORN UNDER ARIES** somebody whose birthday falls between 21 March and 19 April **3 CONSTELLATION** a zodiacal constellation of the northern hemisphere. See illustration at **constellation** [Pre-12C. < Latin *aries* 'ram'.] —**Aries** *adj*

arietta /árri éttə/ *n* a short simple aria in an opera, oratorio, or cantata [Early 18C. < Italian, 'little aria'.]

aright /ə rī́t/ *adv* in the correct or proper way (*archaic*)

aril /árril/ *n* a fleshy, often brightly coloured seed covering in some plants [Mid-18C. Via modern Latin *arillus* < medieval Latin *arilli* 'dried grape pips'.] —**ariled** *adj* —**arillate** /árri layt/ *adj*

arioso /áari ṓzō, árri óssō/ *adj, adv* with intense lyricism or feeling (*musical direction*) ■ *n* (*plural* **-sos**) a short lyrical aria or instrumental work [Early 18C. < Italian, 'like an aria'.]

Ariosto /árri óstō/, **Ludovico** (1474–1533) Italian poet

arise /ə rī́z/ (**arises, arising, arose** /ə rṓz/, **arisen** /ə rízz'n/) *vi* **1 OCCUR** to appear or come into existence ○ *When did the problem arise?* **2 BE CAUSED** to happen or exist as a result of something **3 BECOME ACTIVE OR VOCAL** to rise from a quiet, inactive, or subjugated state to become active, vocal, or rebellious (*literary*) **4 STAND UP** to stand up from a sitting, lying, or kneeling position (*archaic or literary*) [Old English *arisan* 'rise up' < Germanic]

arista /ə rístə/ (*plural* **-tae** /-tay, -tee/) *n* **1** PLANT SCI = **awn** **2** a bristly part of the antennae of some flies [Late 17C. < Latin, 'ear of grain'.]

Aristarchus of Samos /árri stáarkəss-/ (310?–250? BC) Greek astronomer

Aristide /árri stéed/, **Jean-Bertrand** (*b.* 1953) Haitian political leader and president of Haiti (1991–96)

Aristides the Just /árri stī́ deez-/ (530–468 BC) Greek soldier-statesman

Aristippus /árri stíppəss/ (435?–360? BC) Greek philosopher

aristo /ə rístō/ (*plural* **-tos**) *n* an aristocrat (*informal*) [Mid-19C. < French, abbreviation of *aristocrate* 'aristocrat'.]

aristocracy /árris tókrəssi/ (*plural* **-cies**) *n* **1 PEOPLE OF HIGHEST CLASS** people of noble families or the highest social class **2 SUPERIOR GROUP** a group acknowledged to be superior to all others of the same kind **3 GOVERNMENT BY ELITE** government of a country by a small group of people, especially a hereditary nobility **4 STATE GOVERNED BY ARISTOCRACY** a state governed by an aristocracy [15C. Via French *aristocratie* < Greek *aristokratia* 'rule by the best' < *aristos* 'best' + *kratos* 'power, rule' (see -CRACY).]

aristocrat /árristə krat/ *n* **1 MEMBER OF NOBILITY** a member of the highest social class in a country **2 SUPPORTER OF ARISTOCRATIC RULE** a member of a governing aristocracy, or somebody who supports government by aristocracy **3 SUPERIOR PERSON** a person, thing, or group believed to be superior to all others of the same kind

aristocratic /árristə kráttik/ *adj* **1** belonging or relating to the highest social class, especially the nobility **2** of or about people belonging to noble families, e.g. in having a grand lifestyle or elegant manners —**aristocratically** *adv*

Aristophanes /árri stóffə neez/ (448?–385 BC) Greek dramatist

Aristotelian /árristə téeli ən/ *adj* expressing or based on the ideas of the Greek philosopher Aristotle ■ *n* a follower of Aristotle's philosophy

Aristotelian logic *n* the system of logic developed by Aristotle, based on the kind of reasoning (**syllogism**) that reaches a conclusion from two independent statements with a common factor

Aristotle /árri stótt'l/ (384–322 BC) Greek philosopher and scientist

arithmetic *n* /ə ríthmə tik/ **1 BASIC MATHS** the branch of mathematics that deals with addition, subtraction, multiplication, and division **2 CALCULATION** one or more calculations using basic mathematics **3 USE OF NUMBERS** the use of numbers in calculation, or educational exercises involving this **4 ABILITY TO DO ARITHMETIC** somebody's ability to add, subtract, multiply, and divide (*informal*) ■ *adj* /árrith méttik/ **RELATING TO ARITHMETIC** using, involving, or based on arithmetic [13C. Via Old French *arismetique* < Greek *arithmētikē (tekhnē)* 'counting (art)' < *arithmein* 'reckon' < *arithmos* 'number'.] —**arithmetical** /árrith méttik'l/ *adj* —**arithmetically** *adv* —**arithmetician** /ə ríthmə tísh'n/ *n*

ϟ **arithmetic logic unit** *n* the circuit in a computer's central processing unit that makes decisions based on the results of calculations

arithmetic mean *n* the average of a set of numbers, calculated by adding them together and then dividing their sum by the number of terms

arithmetic progression *n* a sequence of numbers in which a constant figure (**common difference**) is added to each term to give the next. For example, 3, 8, 13, 18 is an arithmetic progression in which the common difference is 5.

-arium *suffix* a place or device connected with something ○ *herbarium* [< Latin]

Ariz. *abbr* Arizona

Arizona /árri zṓnə/ state in the SW United States. Capital: Phoenix. Population: 4,554,966 (1997). Area: 295,274 sq. km/114,006 sq. mi. —**Arizonan** *adj, n* —**Arizonian** *adj, n*

Arjuna /áarjoonə/ *n* a major character in the *Mahabharata*. Serving as his charioteer, Krishna explains Hindu doctrine to him.

ark /aark/ *n* **1 NOAH'S SHIP** the ship that, according to biblical accounts, Noah was instructed to build by God to save his family and the animals from the Flood **2 SANCTUARY** a place providing refuge **3 ark, Ark** JUD-CHR = **Ark of the Covenant** **4 ark, Ark CABINET CONTAINING TORAH SCROLLS** a cupboard in a synagogue in which the scrolls of the Torah are kept [Old English *ærc*, via Germanic < Latin *arca* 'chest, box'] ◇ **out of the ark** extremely old or old-fashioned (*informal*)

Ark. *abbr* Arkansas

Arkansas /áarkən saw/ **1** state of the south-central United States. Capital: Little Rock. Population: 2,522,819 (1996). Area: 137,741 sq. km/53,182 sq. mi. **2** river of the central United States. Length: 2,350 km/1,460 mi. —**Arkansan** /aar kánz'n/ *n, adj*

Ark of the Covenant, Ark of the Testimony *n* the chest in which, according to biblical accounts, Moses placed the two stone tablets containing the Ten Commandments

arkose /áarkōss, -ōz/ *n* a coarse-grained sedimentary rock rich in feldspar and quartz [Mid-19C. < French, probably < Greek *arkhaios* 'ancient'.]

Arkwright /áark rīt/, **Sir Richard** (1732–92) British inventor and manufacturer

Arles /aarl/ city in S France. Population: 50,513 (1999).

Arlington /aárlingtən/ 1 city in NE Virginia. Population: 174,603 (1994). 2 city in NE Texas. Population: 306,497 (1998 estimate).

arm[1] /aarm/ n 1 **UPPER HUMAN LIMB** a limb attached to the shoulder of the human body 2 **PART OF GARMENT** the part of a piece of clothing that covers the arm 3 **PART OF CHAIR** a side piece of a seat designed to support the arms 4 **ANIMAL'S LIMB** a part of an animal's body that is similar to the human arm 5 **PROJECTING PART** a part of something that is similar to a human arm in function or appearance ○ *an arm of the sea* 6 **DIVISION OF LARGER GROUP** a branch of an organization, especially a section of the armed forces [Old English *arm, earm* < Indo-European, 'fit, join'] — **armful** n ◇ **an arm and a leg** a lot of money (*informal*) ○ *It would cost an arm and a leg to repair.* ◇ **arm in arm** holding each other affectionately by linking arms ◇ **at arm's length** in a position or situation that avoids involvement or familiarity ◇ **chance your arm** to attempt something despite unfavourable odds (*informal*) ◇ **put the arm on somebody** 1 *US* to try to force somebody to do something (*informal*) 2 *US* to borrow money from somebody (*informal*) ◇ **the long arm of the law** the far-reaching power of the police (*humorous*) ◇ **twist somebody's arm** to try to persuade somebody to do something against his or her will ◇ **with open arms** in a friendly and welcoming way ◇ **would give your right arm for something** would be willing to do or give almost anything to get something that you want (*informal*)

arm[2] /aarm/ v 1 *vti* **EQUIP WITH WEAPONS** to equip a person or a country with weapons 2 *vt* **ACTIVATE** to prepare a weapon so that it is ready to use 3 *vt* **PROVIDE WITH TOOLS** to provide somebody with the information or equipment needed to do something ○ *armed myself with statistics before the meeting* ■ n **WEAPON** a weapon, especially one used in warfare (*often plural*) ■ **arms** npl 1 **WARFARE** fighting and military activity 2 **COAT OF ARMS** a coat of arms [12C. Via Old French *armer* < Latin *armare* < *arma* (plural) 'weapons'.] ◇ **be up in arms** to protest or complain angrily ◇ **lay down your arms** to stop fighting ◇ **take up arms** to enter, or prepare to enter, a battle

armada /aar maáda/ n a large fleet of ships [Mid-16C. Via Spanish < medieval Latin *armata* (see ARMY).]

armadillo /aarmə díllō/ (*plural* **-los** *or* **-lo**) n a burrowing mammal with a hard-plated body, related to the anteater and sloth. Native to: temperate and tropical Americas. Family: Dasypodidae. [Late 16C. < Spanish, 'little armed man' < Latin *armare* (see ARM[2]).]

Armageddon /aarmə géddʾn/ n 1 in the Bible, the battle between the forces of good and evil that is predicted to mark the end of the world and precede the Day of Judgment. (Revelation 16:16). 2 any final and decisive war or conflict, e.g. a worldwide nuclear war [Early 19C. Via late Latin < Hebrew *har megiddōn* 'hill of Megiddo'.]

Armagh /aar maá/ 1 town in S Northern Ireland. Population: 14,640 (1991). 2 former county in S Northern Ireland

armament /aármamant/ n 1 the guns and other weapons on a military aircraft, vehicle, or ship (*often plural*) 2 the provision of weapons and equipment in preparation for war [Late 17C. < Latin *armamentum* < *armare* (see ARM[2]).]

armamentarium /aarmə men táiri am/ (*plural* **-ums** *or* **-a** /-ri ə/) n the complete range of equipment, medications, and techniques that a medical practitioner has at his or her disposal [Late 19C. < Latin, 'arsenal, armoury' < *armare* (see ARM[2]).]

Armani /aar maáni/, **Giorgio** (*b.* 1934) Italian fashion designer

armature /aármachar/ n 1 **MOVING PART IN ELECTROMAGNETIC DEVICE** the moving part in an electromagnetic device, wound with coils that carry a current 2 **KEEPER FOR MAGNET** a bar of soft iron or steel placed across the poles of a magnet to maintain its strength 3 **PROTECTIVE PART** a protective outer covering or structure, e.g. quills on a porcupine or spines on a plant 4 **FRAMEWORK FOR A SCULPTURE** a framework that supports a sculpture while it is being modelled [15C. Via French < Latin *armatura* < *armat-*, past participle of *armare* (see ARM[2]).]

armband /aarm band/ n a band of fabric worn around the upper arm

arm candy n *US* a good-looking woman who accompanies a man to a social event by prior arrangement, often for a fee (*slang humorous*)

armchair /aárm chair/ n a chair with arms, especially a comfortable upholstered chair ■ adj with no direct experience, only theoretical knowledge ○ *an armchair tourist*

armed /aarmd/ adj 1 **EQUIPPED WITH WEAPONS** equipped with one or more weapons ○ *armed robbers* 2 **USING WEAPONS** involving the use of weapons ○ *armed conflict* 3 **WITH EXPLODING MECHANISM ACTIVE** prepared and ready for use as a weapon, especially with a fuse or detonator activated 4 **PROVIDED WITH NECESSARY THINGS** equipped with the information or tools needed to achieve something ○ *armed with the latest statistics*

armed forces npl the combined bodies of troops of a country who fight on land, at sea, or in the air

Armenia

Armenia /aar meéni ə/ republic in W Asia, between the Black and Caspian seas. Capital: Yerevan. Population: 3,433,629 (1997). Area: 29,800 sq. km/11,500 sq. mi. — **Armenian** n, adj

armhole /aarm hōl/ n either of the holes at the top of a garment for the wearer's arms to go through

Armidale /aarmi dayl/ town in E New South Wales, Australia. Population: 21,330 (1996).

armiger /aármijar/ n somebody entitled to have a coat of arms (*archaic*) [Mid-16C. < Latin, 'bearing weapons' < *arma* 'weapons'.]

armillary sphere /aar mílləri-, aármiləri-/ n a spherical model of the universe in which the relative positions of the Earth and other celestial bodies are represented by intersecting metal rings [< modern Latin *armillaris* < Latin *armilla* 'arm bracelet' < *armus* 'shoulder'.]

Arminian /aar mínni ən/ adj relating to or following the Protestant theologian Arminius or his doctrines, which rejected the Calvinist view of absolute predestination ■ n a follower of Arminius or his doctrines [Early 17C. < *Arminius*, Latinized surname of Jakob Hermandszoon (1560–1609).] —**Arminianism** n

armistice /aármistiss/ n a truce in a war to discuss terms for peace [Early 18C. Directly or via French < modern Latin *armistitium* 'stoppage of weapons' < Latin *arma* 'weapons'.]

Armistice Day n the former annual celebration of the armistice that ended World War I on 11 November, 1918, now incorporated into the observance of Remembrance Sunday

armlet /aarmlət/ n 1 a band worn on the upper arm 2 a short narrow arm of a lake or the sea

armlock /aarm lok/ n a tight immobilizing grip around one or both of somebody's upper arms, e.g. in wrestling or judo

armoire /aar mwaár/ n a tall cupboard or wardrobe, often ornately decorated [Late 16C. Via French, < Latin *armarium* 'chest' < *arma* 'weapons'.]

armor n *US* = **armour**

armorial /aar máwri əl/ adj relating to coats of arms or decorated with a coat of arms ○ *armorial bearings* [Late 16C. < obsolete *armory* 'heraldry' < Old French *armoi(e)rie* < *armoier* 'to blazon' < *armes* 'weapons' < Latin *arma*.]

armour /aármar/ n 1 **PROTECTION FOR SOLDIERS** protective clothing of metal or leather worn in battle by soldiers in former times 2 **PROTECTION FOR MILITARY VEHICLES** the protective layer of metal covering military vehicles, ships, and aircraft 3 **COVERING ON PLANTS OR ANIMALS** a protective layer covering an animal or plant 4 **PROTECTION** anything that gives protection or acts as a safeguard 5 **GRAVEL ON RIVER BED** a surface layer of gravel in a river bed preventing erosion of the material below 6 **COATS OF**

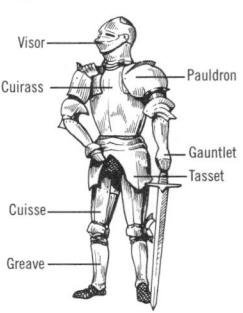

Armour

ARMS coats of arms or the symbols and designs used on them [13C. < French *armure* < Latin *armatura* (see ARMATURE).]

armoured /aármard/ adj 1 **WITH PROTECTIVE METAL COVERING** with a protective metal covering to protect from bullets or missiles 2 **WITH ARMOURED VEHICLES** using armoured vehicles 3 **WITH PROTECTIVE COVERING** with a natural protective covering, e.g. a shell

armoured car n 1 a lightly armoured military vehicle used mainly for reconnaissance 2 any vehicle, e.g. a security van, with an extra layer of thick metal to protect the occupants from bullets or other weapons

armourer /aármarar/ n 1 somebody who makes armour and weapons 2 a soldier who repairs and maintains small arms

armour plate n strong metal sheets used for protecting military vehicles, aircraft, and ships —**armour-plated** adj

armoury /aármari/ (*plural* **-ies**) n 1 **STORE FOR WEAPONS** a building in which weapons are stored 2 **COLLECTION OF WEAPONS** a store or collection of weapons 3 **BUILDING FOR MILITARY TRAINING** a building used for drilling and training militia 4 **RESOURCES OF ANY KIND** a range of equipment and skills available to somebody, used especially in dealing with opponents [14C. < Old French *armoi(e)rie* 'weaponry' (see ARMORIAL).]

armpit /aarm pit/ n 1 the hollow area under the arm where it joins the body 2 a place that is the worst of its kind (*slang*)

armrest /aarm rest/ n a projecting part, e.g. on a chair, designed to support the arm of somebody sitting down

arm's-length adj without close contact or an intimate relationship ○ *the companies' arm's-length trading arrangement*

arms race n the competition between countries for superiority in the number and power of weapons held

Armstrong /aárm strong/, **Gillian** (*b.* 1950) Australian filmmaker

Armstrong, Louis (1900–71) US jazz musician. Known as **Satchmo**

Neil Armstrong

Armstrong, Neil (*b.* 1930) US astronaut

Armstrong, William (1810–1900) British engineer and industrialist

arm-twisting *n* heavy-handed or unfair pressure on somebody to do something

arm wrestling *n* a contest of strength between two people in which they sit opposite each other with one elbow each on a table, clasp hands, and try to force the opponent's hand onto the table

army /aármi/ (*plural* **-mies**) *n* **1 BRANCH OF ARMED FORCES** the branch of a country's armed forces trained to fight on land **2 LARGE ARMED GROUP** any trained or armed fighting force **3 LARGE ORGANIZED GROUP** a large group that has been organized to do a particular task ○ *an army of volunteers* **4 LARGE NUMBER OF THINGS** a very large number of things [14C. Via French *armée* < medieval Latin *armata* < past participle of Latin *armare* (see ARM[2]).]

army ant *n* any nomadic tropical ant that forages in large groups

army brat *n* a person who is born into, or grows up in, the family of a member of the army (*disapproving*) ○ *As an army brat, she's lived all over the world.*

Army List *n* an official list of all serving commissioned officers and reserve officers in the army

armyworm /aármi wurm/ *n* the larva of any insect that travels in large migratory groups destroying vegetation and crops

Arne /aarn/, **Thomas** (1710–78) British composer

Arnhem /aárnəm/ city in the E Netherlands. Population: 138,020 (2000).

Arnhem Land region in N Australia, site of one of Australia's largest Aboriginal reserves

arnica /aárnikə/ (*plural* **-cas** *or* **-ca**) *n* **1** a liquid preparation made from the dried flower heads of a perennial herb. Use: treating bruises and sprains in alternative medicine. **2** a perennial plant from which arnica is prepared. Flowers: yellow, daisy-like. Native to: N Europe. Genus: *Arnica*. [Mid-18C. < modern Latin.]

Arno /aárnō/ river in Tuscany, central Italy. Length: 240 km/150 mi.

Arnold /aárn'ld/, **Benedict** (1741–1801) American Revolutionary general and traitor

Arnold, Sir Malcolm (*b.* 1921) British composer

Arnold, Matthew (1822–88) British poet and critic

Arnold, Thomas (1795–1842) British educator

Arnside and Silverdale /aárn sīd ənd sílvər dayl/ Area of Outstanding Natural Beauty in NW England. Area: 75 sq. km/29 sq. mi.

A-road *n* a primary route other than a motorway, having the prefix 'A' in the national road numbering and classification system

aroha /aárōhə/ *n NZ* love and compassion for others [< Maori]

aroid /árroyd/ *adj* belonging to the arum family of perennial plants [Late 19C. < ARUM + -OID.]

aroma /ə rṓmə/ *n* **1** a smell, especially a pleasant smell **2** a subtle impression or quality [12C. Via Latin, < Greek *arōma* 'spice'.]

SYNONYMS See ***smell***.

---

aromatherapy /ə rṓmə thérrəpi/ *n* the use of oils extracted from plants to alleviate physical and psychological disorders, usually through massage or inhalation [Mid-20C. < French *aromathérapie*.] —**aromatherapist** *n*

aromatic /árrə máttik/ *adj* **1 WITH PLEASANT SMELL** with a distinctive and pleasant smell **2 OF CLASS OF COMPOUNDS** describes organic compounds that contain one or more rings of carbon atoms and undergo chemical reactions that are characteristic of benzene. ◊ **aliphatic** ■ *n* **FRAGRANT SUBSTANCE OR PLANT** an aromatic substance or plant [14C. Via French, < Greek *arōmatikos* < *arōma* 'spice'.] —**aromatically** *adv*

aromatize /ə rṓmə tīz/ (**-tizes, -tizing, -tized**), **aromatise** (**-tises, -tising, -tised**) *vt* **1** to make something fragrant, or release the fragrance of something **2** to convert a nonaromatic (**aliphatic**) chemical compound to an aromatic compound —**aromatization** /ə rōmə tī záysh'n/ *n*

arose past tense of **arise**

around /ə równd/ CORE MEANING: a grammatical word used to indicate that something surrounds a place or object or is situated on or moves around all sides of it ○ (prep) *She came in and looked at the mess all around her.* ○ (prep) *A crumbling wall still stood around the old town.* ○ (adv) *From this spot you could see the countryside for miles around.*

1 *prep* **TO THE OTHER SIDE OF** moving or looking to the other side of ○ *around the corner* **2** *adv* **IN OPPOSITE DIRECTION** in the opposite direction ○ *turned around and walked away* **3** *adv* **PRESENT** present or existing ○ *since computers have been around* **4** *adv, prep* **FROM PLACE TO PLACE** from place to place, in every or most parts ○ *rushing around* **5** *adv, prep* **IN THE VICINITY** in the vicinity, especially with no particular purpose or intent ○ *hanging around* **6** *adv, prep* **HERE AND THERE** in various unspecified parts of a place or area ○ *travelled around the country* **7** *adv, prep* **APPROXIMATELY** approximately ○ *around £600 a month* [13C. < A-[1] 'on' + ROUND[1], probably after Old French *a la reond* 'in the round, roundabout'.] ◇ **have been around** to have had enough experience of life and the ways of the world not to be easily deceived (*informal*)

around-the-clock *adj* happening constantly with no breaks, for 24 hours a day

arouse /ə rówz/ (**arouses, arousing, aroused**) *v* **1** *vt* **STIMULATE** to evoke a feeling, response, or desire **2** *vt* **STIMULATE SEXUAL DESIRE IN** to cause feelings of sexual desire in somebody **3** *vt* **ANGER** to make somebody angry **4** *vti* **WAKE UP** to wake up, or wake somebody up from sleep or unconsciousness (*formal*) [Late 16C. < ROUSE.] —**arousal** *n*

Arp /aarp/, **Jean** (1887–1966) French sculptor

ϟ **ARPANET** /aárpə net/ *n* a wide area network of the late 1960s linking government, academic, business, and military sites

arpeggio /aar péjji ō/ (*plural* **-os**) *n* a sounding of the notes of a chord one after the other in rapid succession, rather than simultaneously [Early 18C. < Italian, < *arpeggiare* 'play on the harp' < *arpa* 'harp'.]

arquebus *n* ARMS = **harquebus**

arr. *abbr* **1** arranged **2** arrival **3** arrived **4** arrives

Arrabal /árrə bál/, **Fernando** (*b.* 1932) Moroccan-born Spanish dramatist and novelist

arraign /ə ráyn/ *vt* **1** to bring somebody to court to answer a charge (*usually passive*) **2** to call somebody to account for a fault or mistake [14C. Via Anglo-Norman *arainer* < assumed Vulgar Latin *adrationare* 'call to account' < Latin *ratio* 'reason'.] —**arraigner** *n* —**arraignment** *n*

Arran /árrən/ island in the Firth of Clyde in W Scotland. Area: 433 sq. km/167 sq. mi.

arrange /ə ráynj/ (**-ranges, -ranging, -ranged**) *v* **1** *vt* **PREPARE FOR** to do what is necessary to make something happen in the future ○ *arrange a meeting* **2** *vt* **MAKE AGREEMENT FOR** to make an agreement so that something can happen or somebody can have something **3** *vt* **PUT IN ORDER** to put people or things in a position or order **4** *vti* **ADAPT MUSIC** to adapt a piece of music for playing or singing in a different manner (*often passive*) [Mid-18C. < Old French *arangier* 'put in a line to' < *rangier* (see RANGE).] —**arrangeable** *adj* —**arranged** *adj* —**arranger** *n*

arrangee /aa ráynjee/ *n W Africa* somebody who deals illegally in foreign currency

arrangement /ə ráynjmənt/ *n* **1 PREPARATION** something that has to be done so that something else can happen in the future, or the making of such preparations (*often plural*) **2 AGREEMENT** an agreement made with somebody to do something, or the making of such an agreement **3 PLEASING DISPLAY** a group of things organized in a way that is meant to be pleasing to look at, or the arranging of such a group **4 ORGANIZATION** the way in which something is organized **5 MUSICAL ADAPTATION** a version of a piece of music adapted for playing or singing in a different manner, or the scoring of such a version

arrant /árrənt/ *adj* used to emphasize that somebody or something is an extreme example of something disapproved of [Mid-16C. Alteration of ERRANT 'wandering'.] —**arrantly** *adv*

arras /árrəss/ *n* a tapestry used as a wall-hanging or hanging screen [15C. < Anglo-Norman *draps d'Arras* 'cloth of Arras' (French town famous for its woollens and tapestry).]

ϟ **array** /ə ráy/ *n* **1 COLLECTION** a large number or wide range of people or things ○ *a dazzling array of talent* **2 STRIKING ARRANGEMENT** a group of things arranged in an impressive or structured way ○ *an array of Greek sculptures* **3 FINE CLOTHES** fine, expensive, or impressive clothes (*literary*) **4 ORDERED SET OF NUMBERS** a set of numbers or symbols, e.g. experimental data, usually arranged in a particular order **5 GROUP OF AERIALS** a group of aerials arranged to increase their effectiveness **6 JURORS** a panel of jurors, or the group of people from whom a jury is selected **7 DATA STRUCTURE** an arrangement of items of computerized data in tabular form for easy reference ■ *vt* **1 ARRANGE** to arrange something for display or in readiness for use (*formal; usually passive*) **2 DEPLOY TROOPS** to arrange troops for battle (*literary; usually passive*) **3 DRESS** to dress somebody in particular clothes (*literary; often passive*) [14C. Via Anglo-Norman, < Old French *arei* < *areer* 'to array' < assumed Vulgar Latin *arredare* 'arrange' < Latin *ad* 'to' + a Germanic word, 'prepare'.]

arrearage /ə reérij/ *n* **1** the debt that remains after part of an overdue debt has been paid **2** the state of being overdue in the payment of a debt

arrears /ə reérz/ *npl* unpaid debts, especially debts accumulating as a result of the debtor's failure to make regular payments [15C. < obsolete *arrear* 'to the rear, overdue' via Old French, < medieval Latin *adretro* < Latin *ad* 'to' + *retro* 'backward, behind'.] ◇ **in arrears 1** behind in making regular payments of money owed **2** paid only after some work has been done or a period of time has elapsed

arrest /ə rést/ *vt* **1 TAKE INTO CUSTODY** to take somebody into custody on suspicion of having committed a crime **2 STOP OR SLOW** to stop or slow a process (*formal*) ○ *a mechanism that arrests the motion of the flywheel* **3 TAKE HOLD OF** to capture suddenly and hold something, especially somebody's attention (*formal*) **4 SEIZE LEGALLY** to seize something by legal authority (*formal*) ■ *n* **1 TAKING OF SOMEBODY INTO CUSTODY** the taking of somebody into custody on suspicion of having committed a crime ○ *a case of wrongful arrest* **2 CUSTODY** the state of being held in custody on suspicion of having committed a crime ○ *You're under arrest!* **3 SUDDEN STOP** a sudden stopping of the movement or operation of something **4 LEGAL SEIZURE** the legal seizure or detention of something (*formal*) [14C. Via Old French, < assumed Vulgar Latin *arrestare* 'cause to stop' < Latin *restare* 'stay behind' (see REST[2]).] —**arrestee** /ə rés teé/ *n* —**arrestment** *n*

arrester /ə réstər/, **arrestor** /ə réstər, -awr/ *n* **1** one of a set of cables on an aircraft carrier used to slow and stop landing aircraft **2** somebody who takes a suspect into legal custody

arresting /ə résting/ *adj* so good-looking or so unusual that people's attention is immediately caught —**arrestingly** *adv*

arresting cable *n* one of a set of cables strung across the deck of an aircraft carrier to catch the tail hook of a landing aircraft and bring it to a halt (*usually plural*)

arrest of judgment *n* a delay in acting on the verdict of a court on the grounds of possible error

arrestor *n* = **arrester**

Arrhenius /ə reé nee əs/, **Svante August** (1859–1927) Swedish chemist

Arrhenius equation *n* an equation in physical chemistry that relates the increase in the rate of a chemical reaction to a rise in temperature

arrhythmia /ə rít͟hmi ə, ay-/ *n* an irregularity in the normal rhythm or force of a rhythmical action such as heartbeat or breathing [Late 19C. < Greek, < *arruthmos* 'without measure' < *rhuthmos* (see RHYTHM).]

arrhythmic /ə rít͟hmik, ay-/ *adj* **1** describes a rhythmical action such as heartbeart or breathing that is irregular **2** without a regular or recognizable rhythm —**arrhythmically** *adv*

arrière-pensée /árri air póN say/ *n* (*formal*) **1** a mental reservation **2** an unspoken intention [Early 19C. < French, literally 'behind-thought'.]

arris /árriss/ (*plural* **-ris** *or* **-rises**) *n* a sharp edge or ridge made by the meeting of two surfaces on an architectural column or moulding [Late 17C. Via French *areste* 'sharp edge' < Latin *arista* (see ARÊTE).]

arrival /ə rív'l/ *n* **1 ARRIVING** the reaching of a place after coming from another place ○ *Her arrival caused a buzz of comment.* **2 NEWCOMER** somebody or something recently arriving at a place or joining a group ○ *a late arrival* **3 PASSENGER VEHICLE ARRIVING SOMEWHERE** an aircraft, train, or bus arriving at an airport or station **4 TIME OF ARRIVING** the time when somebody or something reaches a place after coming from another place ○ *date of arrival* **5 BEGINNING** the moment when something begins or becomes important ○ *The arrival of television changed the world.* **6 BIRTH** the birth of a baby **7 REACHING OF** the achieving or reaching of something after much work or effort ○ *Their arrival at a decision seems unlikely.*

arrive /ə rív/ (**-rives, -riving, -rived**) *vi* **1 GET TO PLACE** to reach a place after coming from another place **2 BE DELIVERED** to be delivered or brought to somebody or something **3 BECOME AVAILABLE OR COMMON** to become available or common **4 BEGIN** to begin or happen after a period of time or waiting **5 BE BORN** to be born **6 WORK OUT SOLUTION** to reach a decision after thinking about or discussing a problem ○ *How did you arrive at the idea of using strings?* **7 SUCCEED** to become successful or famous (*informal*) ○ *You haven't arrived until you've eaten in this restaurant.* [12C. Via Old French < assumed Vulgar Latin *arripare* 'come to shore' < Latin *ripa* 'shore'.] —**arriver** *n*

arrivederci /ə reévə dúrchi/ *interj* goodbye for now [Late 20C. < Italian *a rivederci* 'until we see each other again' < *rivedere* 'see again'.]

arriviste /árri veést/ *n* somebody who has recently become influential or socially prominent, especially when seen as disreputable (*disapproving*) [Early 20C. < French, 'somebody who arrives'.]

arrogant /árrəgənt/ *adj* feeling or showing proud self-importance and contempt for others [14C. Via French, < Latin *arrogant-*, present participle of *arrogare* 'claim for yourself' < *rogare* 'ask'.] —**arrogance** *n* —**arrogantly** *adv*

SYNONYMS See ***proud.***

arrogate /árrə gayt/ (**-gates, -gating, -gated**) *vt* (*formal*) **1** to take or claim something for yourself without the right to do so **2** to assign or attribute something to another in a way that is not warranted [Mid-16C. < Latin *arrogat-*, past participle of *arrogare* (see ARROGANT).] —**arrogation** /árrə gáysh'n/ *n* —**arrogator** *n*

arrondissement /a róN deess móN/ (*plural* **-ments** /-móN/) *n* **1** an administrative area in France that is the largest subdivision of a department **2** an administrative area in some large cities in France, including Paris [Early 19C. < French, < *arrondiss-*, stem of *arrondir* 'make round'.]

arrow /árrō/ *n* **1 MISSILE SHOT FROM BOW** a long thin missile pointed at one end and usually with feathers at the other, fired from a bow **2 DIRECTION SIGN** a direction sign consisting of a horizontal stroke finishing in the middle of a V shape ■ *v* **1** *vi* **DART** to move quickly like an arrow shot from a bow **2** *vt Malaysia* **SELECT FOR UNPLEASANT TASK** to choose somebody to do something unpleasant (*informal*) ○ *The teacher arrowed me because I was dreaming in class.* [Old English *arwe* < Old Norse *ǫrv-* < Indo-European]

arrowhead /árrō hed/ *n* **1** a sharp pointed tip fixed to an arrow **2** an aquatic plant with arrow-shaped leaves. Flowers: white, in clusters. Native to: Asia, North America. Genus: *Sagittaria.*

⚡**arrow key** *n* one of four computer keys marked with an up, down, left, or right arrow, used to move the cursor

arrow-poison frog *n* a brightly coloured frog whose skin glands produce poison that is used by local peoples for their arrow tips. Native to: South America. Family: Dendrobatidae.

arrowroot /árrō root/ (*plural* **-root** *or* **-roots**) *n* **1** edible starch obtained from the rhizomes of a West Indian plant. Use: thickener for clear sauces. **2** a plant with rhizomes that yield arrowroot. Native to: W Indies. *Maranta arundinacea.* [Late 17C. By folk etymology, < Arawak *aru-aru* 'meal of meals', from its use to absorb poison from arrow wounds.]

arrow worm *n* a marine invertebrate animal that has an arrow-shaped body and spines on its head for catching prey. Phylum: Chaetognatha. [From the head with its curved bristles on each side]

arroyo /ə róy ō/ (*plural* **-os**) *n Southwest US* **1** a steep-sided dry gully in a desert area that is wet only after heavy rain **2** a small stream of running water [Mid-19C. Via Spanish, < Latin *arrugia* 'mineshaft'.]

arse /aarss/ *n* (*taboo*) **1** a highly offensive term for a person's buttocks or anus. US term **ass**[2] *n.* 1 **2** a highly offensive term for an unintelligent or contemptible person [Old English *ærs, ears* < Indo-European] ◇ **move** *or* **shift your arse** a highly offensive phrase meaning to hurry up (*taboo*) ◇ **not know your arse from your elbow** a highly offensive phrase meaning to know very little (*taboo*)
arse about, arse around *vi* a highly offensive term meaning to waste time behaving in a silly irritating way (*taboo*)

arsehole /áars hōl/ *n* **1** a highly offensive term for a contemptible person (*taboo insult*) **2** a highly offensive term for the anus (*taboo*)

arse licker *n* a highly offensive term for somebody who flatters or obediently carries out the orders of a superior in order to gain favour (*taboo*)

arsenal /áarss'nəl/ *n* **1 ARMAMENTS** a stockpile of weapons and military equipment **2 STORE FOR WEAPONS** a building where weapons and military equipment are stored **3 RESOURCES** a supply of methods or resources [Early 16C. Directly or via French < Italian *arzanale* < Venetian Italian *arzanà* < Arabic *dār-(aṣ-)ṣināʻa* 'workshop, factory'.]

arsenate /áarssə nayt, -nit/ *n* any salt of arsenic acid [Early 19C. < ARSENIC + -ATE.]

arsenic /áarssnik/ *n* **1** (*symbol* **As**) a steel-grey poisonous solid element that is a brittle crystalline metalloid. Source: realgar, arsenopyrite. Use: alloys. **2** CHEM = **arsenic trioxide** ■ *adj* relating to or containing arsenic, especially with a valency of 5 [14C. Via French, < Greek *arsenikon* 'yellow orpiment' < Arabic *az-zarnīk* 'the orpiment' < Persian *zar* 'gold'.]

arsenic acid /aar sénnik-/ *n* H_3AsO_4 a white poisonous crystalline solid containing arsenic. Use: manufacture of arsenates and insecticides.

arsenical /aar sénnik'l/ *adj* relating to or containing arsenic ■ *n* a substance, e.g. a drug or insecticide, that contains arsenic

arsenic trioxide /áarssnik trī óksīd, aar sénnik trī óksīd/ *n* As_2O_3 a white poisonous solid that contains arsenic. Use: insecticide, rodenticide, herbicide, manufacture of glass and pigments.

arsenide /áarssə nīd/ *n* a chemical compound of arsenic and a metal [Mid-19C. < ARSENIC + -IDE.]

arsenious /aar seéni əss/ *adj* relating to or containing arsenic, especially with a valency of 3 [Early 19C. < ARSENIC.]

arsenopyrite /áarssinō pīr īt, aar sénnə-/ *n* a grey to white metallic mineral consisting of a sulphide of iron and arsenic [Mid-19C. < ARSENIC + PYRITE.]

arsenotherapy /áarsənō thérrəpi/ the treatment of disease with arsenic or one of its derivatives or preparations [< ARSENIC]

arses plural of **arsis**

arsine /áar seen/ *n* AsH_3 a colourless, very poisonous gas with an odour like garlic. Use: manufacture of organic chemicals, transistors, chemical weapons. [Late 19C. < ARSENIC + -INE.]

arsis /áarssiss/ (*plural* **-ses** /-seez/) *n* **1** in classical Greek and Roman verse, the short syllable or syllables in a metrical foot. ◊ **thesis** *n.* 6 **2** in modern verse, the accented syllable in a metrical foot. ◊ **thesis** *n.* 7 [14C. Via late Latin, 'raising of the voice to greater force, accented part of the metrical foot' < Greek, 'raising (of the foot in beating time)'.]

ars nova /áarz nṓvə/ *n* a late medieval style of music characterized by variety and complexity of rhythm and melody and the use of such forms as the motet and madrigal (+ *singular verb*) [Late 20C. < medieval Latin, 'new art'.]

arson /áarss'n/ *n* the burning of a building or other property for a criminal or malicious reason [Late 17C. Via legal Anglo-Norman *arsoun* < Latin *arsus*, past participle of *ardere* 'burn'.] —**arsonist** *n*

arsy-versy /áarssi vúrssi/ *adv* backwards or upside down (*dated informal; sometimes offensive*) [Mid-16C. < ARSE + Latin *versus* 'turned', perhaps after VICE VERSA.]

art[1] /aart/ *n* **1 CREATION OF BEAUTIFUL THINGS** the creation of beautiful or thought-provoking works, e.g. in painting, music, or writing **2 BEAUTIFUL OBJECTS** beautiful or thought-provoking works produced through creative activity **3 BRANCH OF ART** a branch or category of art, especially one of the visual arts **4 ARTISTIC SKILL** the skill and technique involved in producing visual representations **5 STUDY OF ART** the study of a branch of the visual arts **6 CREATION BY HUMANS** creation by human endeavour rather than by nature **7 TECHNIQUES OR CRAFT** the techniques used by somebody in a particular field, or the use of those techniques ○ *the art of the typographer* **8 ABILITY** the skill or ability to do something well **9 CUNNING** the ability to achieve things by deceitful or cunning methods (*literary*) ■ **arts** *npl* **1 FORMS OF CREATIVE BEAUTY** activities enjoyed for the beauty they create or the way they present ideas, e.g. painting, music, and literature **2 NONSCIENTIFIC SUBJECTS** nonscientific and nontechnical subjects at school or university [13C. Via French, < Latin *art-* 'skill'.] ◇ **have something down to a fine art** to be able to do something very skilfully

art[2] /aart/ 2nd person present singular of **be** (*archaic or literary*)

art. *abbr* **1** article **2** artificial **3** artillery **4** artist

-art *suffix* = **-ard**

artal plural of **rotl**

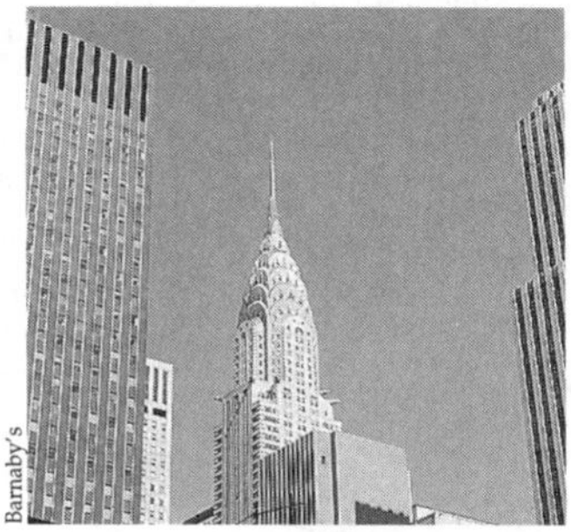

Art deco: Chrysler Building, New York City (1930), designed by William van Alen

art deco /-dékō/, **Art Deco** *n* a style of architecture, interior design, and jewellery most popular in the 1930s that used geometrical designs and bold colours and outlines [Mid-20C. < French, shortening of *arts décoratifs* 'decorative arts'.]

art director *n* the person in charge of the sets and costumes when something is being filmed or photographed

artefact /áarti fakt/, **artifact** *n* **1** an object made by a human being, especially one that has archaeological or cultural interest **2** something in a biological specimen that is not present naturally but has been introduced or produced during some procedure [Early 19C. < Latin *arte* 'skill' + *factum* 'thing made' (see FACT).]

artel /aar tél/ *n* a workers' or producers' cooperative in pre-Revolutionary Russia or the Soviet Union [Late 19C. < Russian.]

Artemis /áartəmiss/ *n* in Greek mythology, the goddess of hunting and the moon, and of childbirth. Roman equivalent **Diana**

artemisia /áarti meézi ə, -mízzi ə/ (*plural* **-as** *or* **-a**) *n* an aromatic plant with greyish-green leaves. Flowers: profuse, small. Native to: N hemisphere. Genus: *Artemisia.* [14C. Via Latin < Greek, 'wormwood' < *Artemis* 'Artemis', to whom it was sacred.]

Arte Povere /áartay póvərə/ *n* an Italian art movement of the 1960s that used happenings, sculptures, performance art, and banal everyday materials to question the conventional role of the artist [Late 20C. Italian, 'impoverished art'; coined by art critic Germano Celant in 1967.]

arterial /aar teéri əl/ *adj* **1 OF ARTERIES** relating to, affecting, or used in arteries **2 OXYGENATED** describes the bright red blood in the arteries that has absorbed oxygen **3 MAIN** constituting a main route in a road, rail, or river system —**arterially** *adv*

arterialize /aar teéri ə līz/ (**-izes, -izing, -ized**), **arterialise** (**-ises, -ising, -ised**) *vt* to convert venous blood into arterial blood by replenishing its oxygen —**arterialization** /aar teéri ə lī záysh'n/ *n*

arterio- *prefix* artery, arterial ○ *arteriovenous* [< Greek *artēria* 'artery']

arteriogram /aar teéri ə gram/ *n* an X-ray of the arteries

arteriography /aar teéri óggrəfi/ *n* X-ray examination of the arteries —**arteriographic** /aar teéri ə gráffik/ *adj*

arteriole /aar teéri ōl/ *n* a blood vessel that branches off from an artery [Mid-19C. < French *artériole* 'little artery' < *artère* 'artery' < Latin *arteria* (see ARTERY).] —**arteriolar** /aar teéri ṓlər/ *adj*

arteriosclerosis /aar teéri ō sklə rṓssiss/ *n* the arterial disease atherosclerosis —**arteriosclerotic** /-sklə róttik/ *adj*

arteriovenous /aar teéri ō veénəss/ *adj* involving both a vein and an artery

arteritis /áartə rītiss/ *n* inflammation of the walls of an artery

artery /áartəri/ (*plural* **-ies**) *n* **1** a blood vessel that is part of the system carrying blood under pressure from the heart to the rest of the body **2** a main route in a road, rail, or river system [14C. Via Latin < Greek *artēria*.]

artesian aquifer /aar teézi ən-/ *n* an aquifer that has an impermeable bed both above and below it and is under enough pressure for water to be forced upward

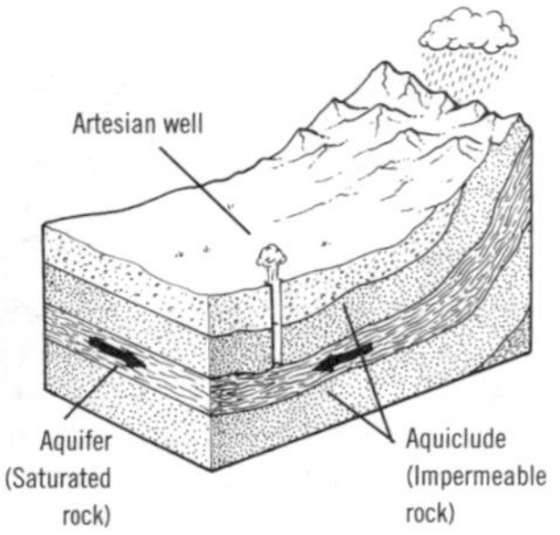

Artesian well

artesian well *n* a well drilled through impermeable rocks into strata where water is under enough pressure to force it to the surface without pumping [Mid-19C. < French *artésien* 'of Artois' (*Arteis* in Old French), region in NE France where such wells were first drilled.]

art film *n* a film that is made as a work of art rather than for mass entertainment

art form *n* **1** a creative activity or type of artistic expression that is intended to be beautiful or thought-provoking **2** something that is done in such a sophisticated or skilful way that it can be seen as artistic

artful /aártf'l/ *adj* **1 CUNNING** using subtle and clever means to achieve things **2 PERFORMED WITH CLEVERNESS** performed with cleverness and subtlety **3 SKILFUL** done skilfully or with taste —**artfully** *adv* —**artfulness** *n*

art gallery *n* **1** a building where works of art are displayed **2** an establishment that displays and sells works of art

art house *n* a cinema where art films are shown

arthr- *prefix* = **arthro-** (*before vowels*)

arthralgia /aar thráljə/ *n* pain in a joint —**arthralgic** *adj*

arthrectomy /aar thréktəmi/ (*plural* **-mies**) *n* the surgical removal of a joint

arthritis /aar thrítiss/ *n* a medical condition affecting a joint or joints, causing pain, swelling, and stiffness [Mid-16C. Via Latin, < Greek, 'joint disease' < *arthron* 'joint' (see ARTHRO-).] —**arthritic** /aar thríttik/ *adj, n* —**arthritically** *adv*

arthro-, arthr- *prefix* joint ○ *arthroscopic* [< Greek *arthron* < Indo-European, 'fit together']

arthrogram /aárthrə gram/ *n* an X-ray of the inside of a damaged joint

arthrography /aar thróggrəfi/ *n* X-ray examination of the inside of a damaged joint

arthropathy /aar thróppəthi/ *n* a disease or medically noteworthy condition of a joint

arthroplasty /aárthrə plasti/ (*plural* **-ties**) *n* surgical repair of a joint or replacement of a joint or part of one by metal or plastic parts

arthropod /aárthrə pod/ *n* an invertebrate animal that has jointed limbs, a segmented body, and an exoskeleton made of chitin, e.g. an insect, arachnid, centipede, or crustacean. Phylum: Arthropoda. [Late 19C. < modern Latin *Arthropoda* < Greek *arthron* 'joint' (see ARTHRO-) + *pod-* 'foot' (see -POD).] —**arthropod** *adj* —**arthropodal** /aar thróppəd'l/ *adj* —**arthropodous** /-əss/ *adj*

arthroscopy /aar thróskəpi/ (*plural* **-pies**) *n* inspection of the inside of a joint of the body using an endoscope —**arthroscope** /aárthrəskōp/ *n* —**arthroscopic** /aárthrə skóppik/ *adj* —**arthroscopically** *adv*

arthrosis /aar thróssiss/ (*plural* **-ses** /-seez/) *n* **1** a joint between two bones (*technical*) **2** a degenerative disease of a joint [Mid-17C. Via Latin, < Greek *arthrōsis* < *arthroun* 'to articulate' < *arthron* 'joint' (see ARTHRO-).]

arthrotomy /aar thróttəmi/ (*plural* **-mies**) *n* a surgical operation that involves cutting into a joint of the body

Arthur /aárthər/**, Chester A.** (1829–86) US statesman and 21st president of the United States (1881–85)

Arthur I *n* in medieval legend, a king of the Britons whose court was based at Camelot —**Arthurian** /aar thyóori ən/ *adj*

Arthurs Pass National Park national park in the South Island of New Zealand. Area: 980 sq. km/380 sq. mi.

artic[1] /aar tík/ *n* an articulated lorry (*informal*) [Mid-20C. Shortening.]

~~**artic**~~[2] incorrect spelling of **arctic**

artichoke /aártichōk/ (*plural* **-chokes** *or* **-choke**) *n* **1** a large flower bud with parts that can be eaten after cooking **2** a plant that produces artichokes. Native to: Europe, Asia. *Cynara scolymus*. **3 FOOD** = **Jerusalem artichoke** *n*. 1 [Mid-16C. < N Italian *articiocco, arciciocco* < Italian *arcicioffo* < Spanish *alcarchofa* < Arabic *al-karšūf(a)* 'artichoke'.]

article /aártik'l/ *n* **1 NEWSPAPER OR REFERENCE PIECE** a piece of nonfiction writing in a newspaper, magazine, or reference book ○ *an article on ecology* **2 ITEM** an object or item, especially one that is part of a group ○ *articles of clothing* **3 LEGAL PARAGRAPH** a section of a legal document that deals with a particular point **4 WORD BEFORE NOUN** a word used with a noun that specifies whether the noun is definite or indefinite, e.g. the indefinite articles 'a' and 'an' and the definite article 'the' in English ■ *vt* (**-cles, -cling, -cled**) **BIND SOMEBODY BY CONTRACT** to bind somebody by the articles of a contract, especially somebody training in the legal profession [12C. Via French, < Latin *articulus* 'joint, section' < *artus* 'joint, limb'.]

articled clerk *n* in the United Kingdom, a former title of a person being trained as a solicitor while working in a solicitor's office

article of faith *n* **1** any one of the items that must be believed as part of a creed or statement of faith **2** something that somebody believes completely

articles of association *npl* the regulations and constitution that a registered company is legally required to have by the British Companies Acts

articular /aar tíkyóolər/ *adj* relating to or involving a joint of the body [15C. < Latin *articularis* < *articulus* 'joint' (see ARTICLE).] —**articularly** *adv*

articulate *adj* /aar tíkyóolət/ **1 ELOQUENT** able to express thoughts, ideas, and feelings coherently **2 COHERENT** spoken or expressed clearly **3 ABLE TO SPEAK** possessing the power of speech **4 JOINTED** with joints or jointed segments, as in the bodies of higher vertebrates and arthropods (*technical*) ■ *v* /aar tíkyoo layt/ (**-lates, -lating, -lated**) **1** *vt* **COMMUNICATE** to express thoughts, ideas, or feelings coherently ○ *unable to articulate his grief* **2** *vti* **SPEAK DISTINCTLY** to pronounce something or speak clearly **3** *vti* **JOIN TO ALLOW MOVEMENT** to form the kind of joint that allows movement **4** *vi* **SPEAK INTELLIGIBLY** to utter intelligible speech [Mid-16C. < Latin *articulatus*, past participle of *articulare* 'divide into joints, speak distinctly' < *articulus* 'joint' (see ARTICLE).] —**articulable** *adj* —**articulacy** *n* —**articulately** *adv* —**articulateness** *n*

articulated /aar tíkyoo laytid/ *adj* made up of two or more sections connected by a joint that can pivot

articulated lorry *n* a lorry made up of two parts, tractor and trailer, connected by a joint that can pivot

articulation /aar tíkyoo láysh'n/ *n* **1 SPEECH** the pronouncing of words, or the manner in which they are pronounced **2 COMMUNICATION** the coherent expression of thoughts, ideas, or feelings **3 JOINTING** the connection of the different parts of something by joints, or the way the parts fit together **4 ANIMAL'S JOINT** a joint in an animal (*technical*) **5 PLANT NODE** a node of a plant, or the space on a stem between two nodes (*technical*) —**articulative** /aar tíkyóolətiv/ *adj* —**articulatory** /-lətəri, -tíkyoo láytəri/ *adj*

articulator /aar tíkyoo laytər/ *n* **1** somebody who communicates clearly **2** a part of the vocal organs that helps form speech sounds

artifact /aárti fakt/ *n* = **artefact**

artifice /aártifiss/ *n* (*formal*) **1 CLEVER TRICK** a clever trick or stratagem **2 CLEVERNESS** the use of clever stratagems or tricks **3 INSINCERE BEHAVIOUR** the deceiving of people in a clever or subtle way [Early 17C. Via French, < Latin *artificium* 'craft, art, cunning' < *artific-* 'artisan, contriver' < *art-* 'skill' + *facere* 'make'.]

artificer /aar tíffissər/ *n* (*dated*) **1** somebody whose work requires manual skill **2** an inventor [14C. < Anglo-Norman, probably < Old French *artificien* < Latin *artificium* 'craft, cunning'.]

artificial /aárti físh'l/ *adj* **1 MADE BY HUMANS** made by human beings rather than occurring naturally **2 SYNTHETIC** made in imitation of something natural **3 INSINCERE** without sincerity or spontaneity ○ *an artificial smile* **4 CREATED BY CULTURE** produced as a result of political or cultural forces ○ *artificial barriers to promotion* [14C. Directly or via Old French, < Latin *artificialis* < *artificium* 'craft, cunning' (see ARTIFICE).] —**artificiality** /aártifishi álləti/ *n* —**artificially** *adv*

artificial climbing *n* climbing on indoor or other human-made environments such as special walls designed and built for this

artificial feeding *n* the feeding of somebody by means that do not occur naturally, such as feeding a patient on life support intravenously or bottle-feeding a baby

artificial horizon *n* an instrument that displays, usually pictorially, the amount of pitch or bank of an aircraft relative to the horizon

artificial insemination *n* a method of inducing pregnancy in a female mammal by injecting sperm into the womb

⚡**artificial intelligence** *n* **1** a branch of computer science that develops programs to allow machines to perform functions normally requiring human intelligence **2** the ability of computers to perform functions that normally require human intelligence

QUICK FACTS ON... **ARTIFICIAL INTELLIGENCE**

Key elements: simulation of the behavioural aspects of human learning and reasoning through the use of computers (advances in artificial intelligence research have been linked to advances in computer science, particularly speed and memory size, and branches of mathematics); development of computers able to perform highly complicated albeit very specialized tasks; through popularization by the media progress in chess-playing programs has become symbolic of advances in artificial intelligence research

Key dates: 1847 Boole develops a mathematical symbolic logic; 1879 Frege invents predicate logic, making it possible to prove general theories from rules; 1921 Čapek, in his play *RUR*, coins the term 'robot' to describe intelligent machines; 1928 von Neumann introduces the minimax theorem, which is still the foundation for game-playing programs; 1943 Pitts and McCulloch show that neural networks can compute using feedback loops; 1948 Wiener publishes *Cybernetics*, a landmark book on control systems; 1962 first industrial robots are marketed; 1970 first ACM-sponsored computer chess tournament is held; 1988 Hitech, a chess-playing program developed at Carnegie-Mellon University, is the first computer to defeat a grandmaster; 1990 Mephisto-Portrose, a German computer program, becomes the first computer to defeat a former world champion, Anatoly Karpov; 1996 Deep Blue, a program developed by the IBM Corporation, is the first computer to defeat a reigning world champion, Garry Kasparov

Key publications: *Brainmakers: How Scientists are Moving Beyond Computers to Create a Rival to the Human Brain* (David H. Freedman) 1995; *The Muse in the Machine: Computerizing the Poetry of Human Thought* (David Hillel Gelernter) 1994

artificialize /aárti físhə līz/ (**-izes, -izing, -ized**), **artificialise** (**-ises, -ising, -ised**) *vt* to give something an artificial appearance or quality —**artificialization** /aárti físhə lī záysh'n/ *n*

artificial language *n* a language that has been invented for international communication or for use with computers

artificial respiration *n* any method of forcing air into the lungs of somebody who has stopped breathing, especially the method that involves blowing air into the mouth

artificial selection *n* selection by humans of animals and plants with desirable characteristics for use in breeding over several generations. ◊ **natural selection**

artificial sweetener *n* a synthetic sugar substitute used in low-calorie drinks or food or added to hot drinks by slimmers or people with diabetes

artillery /aar tílləri/ *n* **1** heavy-calibre firearms, e.g. cannons, howitzers, missile-launchers, and mortars **2** soldiers who specialize in operating large powerful firearms, regarded as a group or unit [14C. < French *artillerie* < *artiller*, variant of *atillier* 'equip, arm', influenced by *art* 'skill'.]

artilleryman /aar tíllərimən/ (*plural* **-men** /-mən/) *n* a soldier in an artillery unit

artillery plant *n* a plant with fleshy leaves and stamens that discharge their pollen by exploding. Native to: tropical America. *Pilea microphylla.*

artiodactyl /àarti ō dáktil/ *n* any herbivorous, hooved mammal with an even number of toes on each foot, e.g. cows and deer. Order: Artiodactyla. [Mid-19C. < modern Latin *artiodactyla* < Greek *artios* 'even, fitting' + *dactylos* 'finger, toe'.] —**artiodactyl** *adj* —**artiodactylous** *adj*

artisan /àarti zan, -zán/ *n* somebody who is skilled at a craft [Mid-16C. Via French < Italian *artigiano* < Latin *artit-*, past participle of *artire* 'instruct in the arts' < *art-* 'skill'.] —**artisanship** /àartiz'n ship/ *n*

artist /àartist/ *n* **1 CREATOR OF ART** somebody who creates art, especially paintings or sculptures **2 PERFORMER** a professional entertainer **3 SKILLED PERSON** somebody who does something skilfully and creatively **4 PERSON GOOD AT SOMETHING** somebody who is very good at something (*slang*) ○ *a ripoff artist* [Late 16C. Via French *artiste* < Italian *artista* < *arte* 'art'.]

artiste /aar tèest/ *n* **1** a professional entertainer, especially a singer or dancer **2** somebody who aspires to being artistic (*humorous*) [Early 19C. < French, 'artist' (see ARTIST).]

artistic /aar tístik/ *adj* **1 GOOD AT ART** good at a form of creative expression **2 OF ART** involving or typical of art or artists **3 TASTEFUL** showing taste, skill, and imagination **4 APPRECIATIVE OF ART** able to appreciate the beauty and worth of art —**artistically** *adv*

artistic director *n* somebody responsible for the artistic content of an enterprise in one of the arts

artistry /àartistri/ *n* **1** the creative ability and skill of an artist, or the expression of this **2** great ability and skill in doing something

artless /àartləss/ *adj* **1 WITHOUT DECEPTION** without guile or deception **2 TOTALLY NATURAL** completely natural and unforced **3 INELEGANT** lacking skill, knowledge, or elegance —**artlessly** *adv* —**artlessness** *n*

art nouveau /àart noo vó, àar-/, **Art Nouveau** *n* a style of art, architecture, and decoration popular in the 1890s that used stylized natural forms and flowing lines [Early 20C. < French, 'new art'.]

QUICK FACTS ON... **ART NOUVEAU**

Key dates: 1890–1910
Key locations: Europe, United States
Key elements: designs incorporating sinuous lines and organic forms; integration of architecture, art, and applied arts; use of modern materials, preference for handcrafting; rejection of established styles
Key figures: Henry van de Velde, Victor Horta, Hector Guimard, Charles Rennie Mackintosh, Antoni Gaudí (architecture); Louis Comfort Tiffany (applied arts); Aubrey Beardsley, Gustav Klimt, Henri de Toulouse-Lautrec (painting)
Key works: Hotel Tassel, Brussels (Victor Horta), 1892–93, Glasgow School of Art (Charles Rennie Mackintosh), 1897–1909, Casa Milà, Barcelona (Antoni Gaudí), 1905–07, *The Kiss* (Gustav Klimt), 1907–08
Key developments: Jugendstil, Vienna Secession, Liberty Style, modernism, integrated design

art paper *n* a high-quality paper coated with china clay or something similar to give it a smooth shiny surface

arts and crafts *n* the art of decorative design applied to everyday objects (*+ singular or plural verb*)

Arts and Crafts *n* a movement in the late 19th and early 20th centuries in Britain and the United States that stressed the value of artisanship

QUICK FACTS ON... **ARTS AND CRAFTS**

Key dates: late 19th–early 20th centuries
Key locations: Europe, especially England, and United States
Key elements: opposition to industrial mass production; concern with artisanship; aestheticism; integration of architecture, arts, and applied arts; medievalism
Key figures: William Morris, Edward Burne-Jones, Walter Crane (design); Philip Webb, C.F.A. Voysey, Arthur Mackmurdo, Charles Rennie Mackintosh (architecture)
Key events: founding of Morris, Marshall & Faulkner 1860; founding of the Arts and Crafts Exhibition Society 1888; founding of Kelmscott Press 1891
Key works: The Red House, Bexleyheath (Philip Webb), 1859–60, stained-glass windows, Salisbury Cathedral (Edward Burne-Jones and William Morris), 1879, *Marigold* wallpaper design (William Morris), 1875
Key developments: aestheticism, art nouveau, , Vienna Workshop; integrated design, continuation of craft traditions

artsy /àartsi/ *adj* US = **arty**[1]

artsy-craftsy *adj* US = **arty-crafty** (*informal disapproving*)

artsy-fartsy /àartsi fàartsi/ *adj* US = **arty-farty**

artwork /àart wurk/ *n* **1** a work or works of art **2** the illustrations that are to be printed in a publication

arty[1] /àarti/ (**-ier, -iest**) *adj* self-consciously and pretentiously artistic (*informal*)

arty[2] *abbr* artillery

arty-crafty *adj* **1** relating to handicrafts or objects decorated by hand (*informal*) **2** decorated in a pretentiously artistic or cute way (*informal disapproving*) [Early 20C. < ARTS AND CRAFTS.]

arty-farty /àarti fàarti/ *adj* representing an elitist or self-indulgent side of the arts (*informal*)

Aruba /ə ròobə/ island off the Venezuelan coast, a self-governing part of the Netherlands. Population: 67,794 (1996). Area: 193 sq. km/75 sq. mi.

arugula /ə ròogyòolə/ (*plural* **-las** *or* **-la**) *n US* PLANTS, FOOD = **rocket**[2] *n.* 1 [Mid-20C. Probably related to dialectal Italian (Lombard) *arigola* and Venetian Italian *rucola*.]

arum /áirəm/ (*plural* **-ums** *or* **-um**) *n* a perennial plant that grows from tubers and has arrow-shaped leaves. Native to: Europe. Genus: *Arum.* [14C. Via Latin, < Greek *aron*.]

arum lily *n* an ornamental lily with a white funnel-shaped cone around a long yellow spike bearing the actual flowers. Native to: S Africa. *Zantedeschia aethiopica.* US term **calla lily** *n.*

Arunachal Pradesh /àarə nàak'l prə désh/, **Arunāchal Pradesh** union state of India. Situated in NE India, it has borders with China and Myanmar. A portion of this state's territory is claimed by China. Capital: Itanagar. Population: 965,000 (1994). Area: 83,743 sq. km/32,333 sq. mi.

Arup /áwrəp/, **Sir Ove** (1895–1988) Danish-born British civil engineer

aruspex *n* HIST = **haruspex**

arvo /àarvō/ (*plural* **-vos**) *n Aus* an afternoon (*informal*) [Mid-20C. < *arv-* (representing an Australian pronunciation of the first syllable of *afternoon*) + -o.]

-ary *suffix* of or relating to ○ *functionary* [Via Old French *-arie* < Latin *-arius*]

Aryan /áiri ən, árri-/ *n* **1 INDO-EUROPEAN LANGUAGE** the hypothetical parent language of the Indo-European languages (*dated*) **2 INDO-EUROPEAN ANCESTOR** somebody who spoke the hypothetical parent language of Indo-European languages (*dated*) **3 NAZI IDEAL** in Nazi ideology, a person of non-Semitic descent regarded as racially superior [Mid-19C. < Sanskrit *ārya* 'noble, of good family'.] —**Aryan** *adj*

aryl /árril/ *adj* describes a chemical group derived from an aromatic hydrocarbon

arytenoid /àrri tèen oyd/ *adj* **arytenoid, arytenoidal** **1 RELATING TO LARYNX CARTILAGE** describes either of the two small cartilages of the larynx to which the vocal cords are attached **2 RELATING TO LARYNX MUSCLE** describes any of the small muscles of the larynx ■ *n* **ARYTENOID CARTILAGE OR MUSCLE** an arytenoid cartilage or muscle [Early 18C. Via modern Latin < Greek *arutainoeidēs* 'ladle-shaped' < *arutaina* 'ladle, funnel' < *aruein* 'draw water'.]

as[1] (*stressed*) /az/; (*unstressed*) /əz/ CORE MEANING: a grammatical word indicating simultaneity, causality, comparison, or the identity or function of somebody or something ○ (conj) *Once again, as I started my interview, the telephone rang.* ○ (conj) *I'll drop the book off, as I'll be passing your house anyway.* ○ (conj) *Here, take this pencil as it's sharper than yours.* ○ (prep) *Data is stored on the disk as magnetic patterns, much as music is stored on an audio tape or cassette.*

1 *conj* **AT THE TIME THAT** used to indicate that something happens at the same time as something else ○ *A woman stands near the water's edge as two large golden retrievers frolic in the river.* **2** *conj* **WHAT** that which ○ *Do as you like!* **3** *conj* **BECAUSE** seeing that ○ *I'm not sure where we are in mathematics, as I've been absent for the last week.* **4** *conj* **USED FOR COMPARISON** used to compare things, people, or situations ○ (conj-coord) *He is almost as tall as she.* ○ (conj-subord) *I'm working as hard as before but getting less done.* **5** *conj* **EMPHASIZES AMOUNTS** used to indicate that an amount is small or large **6** *conj* **INTRODUCES CLAUSE** used to introduce a short clause referring to a previous or subsequent statement ○ *As you know, I have been in this job for a long time.* **7** *conj* **IN THE WAY THAT** used to indicate the way that something happens or exists ○ *Did everything go as planned?* **8** *conj* **IN THE SAME WAY THAT** used to indicate that something happens or exists in the same way as something else ○ *Her attitude to life was very practical, as her mother's had been.* **9** *conj* **DESPITE** in spite of ○ *Hard-working as she is, she can't compete with the others.* **10** *prep* **AT THE TIME WHEN** used to indicate a stage in somebody's life ○ *As a teenager I was quite shy.* **11** ⚠ *prep* **IN THE CAPACITY OF** used to indicate the capacity in which somebody or something exists or acts ○ *uses it as a short cut.* [12C. Contraction of earlier form of ALSO.] ◇ **as against** used to indicate comparison or contrast between two facts or amounts ◇ **as ever** used to indicate that a situation is the same as usual ◇ **as far as** to the extent to which a situation holds or is relevant ◇ **as for, as to** used to introduce a topic related to what has been mentioned before ◇ **as from, as of** on and after a given date or time (*formal*) ◇ **as how** used to mean 'that' in the phrases 'seeing as how' and 'allowed as how' (*informal*) ○ *Seeing as how they were almost finished, I waited.* ○ *She allowed as how I had helped her more than anybody.* ◇ **as if, as though 1** in a way that suggests something ○ *He looked as though he'd been crying.* **2** used to indicate that the speaker is saying something ridiculous ○ *As if I'd say a thing like that!* ◇ **as is** in the present condition, with whatever faults there may be ◇ **as it were** used to indicate qualification, uncertainty, or lack of definiteness in a statement (*formal*) ◇ **as long as 1** provided that ○ *You can go, as long as you're home by midnight.* **2** because or seeing that ○ *As long as we're here we may as well look round.* ◇ **as much again** twice as much ◇ **as per** in accordance with ◇ **as such 1** used to indicate that a word or phrase does not apply exactly to a situation (*often used with a negative*) ○ *I have no qualifications as such, but I feel I could do the job.* **2** used to indicate that something is being considered separately ○ *After the earthquake, the village as such virtually ceased to exist.* ◇ **as to** with reference to ◇ **as yet** used to indicate that a situation has lasted up to the present time ○ *She has never once mentioned the terrible accusation nor has she, as yet, said that she is sorry for all the pain it inflicted.* ◇ **as you were** a military command to return to the same position as before

USAGE As meaning 'in the capacity of': In this use, the preposition ***as*** is used to show the capacity in which somebody or something exists or acts: *She has a job as a copywriter. As a doctor I understand these problems.* Avoid false links with the ***as*** clause when they result in ambiguity or apparent absurdity: *As a journalist, you know I do not like being asked such questions.* (Which one is the journalist?).

USAGE See ***because***.

⚡ **as**[2] *abbr* American Samoa (*in Internet addresses*)

As *symbol* arsenic

AS *abbr* **1** after sight **2 AS, A.S.** Anglo-Saxon **3** antisubmarine

As. *abbr* **1** Asia **2** Asian

ASA[1] *adj* used to indicate the speed of photographic film

ASA[2] *abbr* Advertising Standards Authority

Asadha /àasədə/ *n* in the Hindu calendar, the fourth month of the year, with 29 or 30 days and occurring about the same time as June to July. It is followed in certain leap years by an extra month (**Dvitiya Asadha**).

asafoetida /àssə féttidə, -fèe-/, **asafetida** *n* **1** a bitter, brownish, acrid-smelling plant extract. Use: Indian cooking. **2** a plant of the parsley family that produces asafoetida. *Ferula assafoetida.*

asana /àassənə/ *n* a posture used in yoga [Mid-20C. < Sanskrit *āsana* 'manner of sitting' < *āste* 'he sits'.]

a.s.a.p. *abbr* as soon as possible

ASAT, Asat *abbr* antisatellite

asbestos /ass béss toss, əz béstəss/ *n* a fibrous carcinogenic silicate mineral. Use: formerly, heat-resistant materials. [Early 17C. < Greek, 'unslaked lime' < *sbestos* 'extinguished' < *sbennunai* 'extinguish'.] —**asbestine** /ass béss teen, -béstin/ *adj*

asbestosis /àss bess tőssiss, ász-/ *n* inflammation of the lungs caused by prolonged inhalation of asbestos fibres [Early 20C. < ASBESTOS + -OSIS.]

ASCAP *abbr* American Society of Composers, Authors, and Publishers

ascariasis /áskə rī́ əssiss/ *n* infestation of the intestines by common roundworms or related nematode worms (**ascarids**) [Late 19C. < ASCARID + -IASIS.]

ascarid /áskərid/ *n* a parasitic nematode worm such as the common roundworm. Family: Ascaridae. [Late 17C. Back-formation < modern Latin *ascarides*, plural of *ascaris* < Greek *askaris* 'intestinal worm' < *askarizein* 'to jump'.]

ascend /ə sénd/ *v* **1** *vi* **MOVE UPWARDS** to go upwards, usually vertically or into the air **2** *vti* **CLIMB** to climb up something, e.g. a hill or staircase **3** *vi* **LEAD UPWARDS** to rise or lead to a higher level **4** *vt* **TAKE UP POSITION** to succeed to an important position, especially as a monarch (*formal*) **5** *vti* **RISE THROUGH IN CAREER** to rise through the ranks to a higher status [14C. < Latin *ascendere* 'climb to' < *scandere* 'to climb'.] —**ascendable** *adj*

ascendance /ə séndənss/, **ascendence** *n* **1** succeeding or rising to a powerful position **2** = **ascendancy**

ascendancy /ə séndənssi/, **ascendency** *n* a position of power or domination over others

ascendant /ə séndənt/, **ascendent** *adj* **1** **MOVING UPWARDS** moving upwards (*literary*) **2** **DOMINANT** having a position of power or domination over others (*formal*) **3** PLANT SCI = **ascending** *adj.* 2 ■ *n* **POINT ON ECLIPTIC** in astrology, the point on the ecliptic or the sign of the zodiac that is rising in the east at a particular time

ascendence *n* = **ascendance**

ascendency *n* = **ascendancy**

ascendent *adj, n* = **ascendant**

ascender /ə séndər/ *n* **1** **SOMEBODY OR SOMETHING THAT ASCENDS** somebody or something that ascends something **2** **LETTER PART EXTENDING UPWARDS** the part of a lowercase letter, e.g. h, d, or b, that projects above the body of the letter **3** **LETTER WITH ASCENDER** a letter with an ascender

ascendeur /ássoN dúr/ *n* a metal grip on a rope that can be loosened, moved up, and tightened to help a climber ascend the rope [Late 20C. < French, 'ascender'.]

ascending /ə sénding/ *adj* **1** moving upwards, especially on a scale **2** **ascending, ascendant** describes a plant part that grows upwards

ascension /ə sénsh'n/ *n* an act of ascending something (*formal*) [14C. Via French < Latin *ascension-* < *ascens-*, present participle of *ascendere* (see ASCEND).] —**ascensional** *adj*

Ascension *n* according to Christianity, the rising of Jesus Christ from earth to heaven after the Resurrection

Ascension Day *n* the day when Christians celebrate the rising of Jesus Christ from earth to heaven after the Resurrection. Date: Thursday, forty days after Easter Day.

Ascension Island island in the S Atlantic Ocean, a British dependency. Population: 1,007 (1988). Area: 88 sq. km/34 sq. mi.

ascent /ə sént/ *n* **1** **CLIMB** an act of climbing a mountain or hill ○ *the ascent of Everest* **2** **UPWARD MOVEMENT** an upward vertical movement **3** **UPWARD SLOPE** an upward slope **4** **WAY UP MOUNTAIN** a climbers' route up a mountain or hill **5** **RISE TO IMPORTANCE** the process by which somebody becomes more important, successful, or powerful [Late 16C. < ASCEND, after DESCEND, DESCENT.]

SPELLCHECK See ***assent***.

ascertain /ássər táyn/ *vti* to find out something with certainty (*formal*) [Late 16C. < Old French *acertain-*, stem of *acertener* < *certain* (see CERTAIN).] —**ascertainable** *adj* —**ascertainably** *adv* —**ascertainment** *n*

ascetic /ə séttik/ *adj* choosing or reflecting austerity and self-denial as personal or religious discipline ■ *n* somebody who is self-denying and lives with minimal material comforts [Mid-17C. Directly or via medieval Latin, < Greek *askētikos* < *askētēs* 'monk, hermit' < *askein* 'to exercise'.] —**ascetically** *adv*

asceticism /ə séttisizəm/ *n* austerity and self-denial, especially as a principled way of life

Ascham /áskəm/, **Roger** (1515–68) English humanist and scholar

aschelminth /a skélminth/ *n* a tiny animal belonging to a group that resembles worms and has a cavity filled with fluid between the body wall and the gut [< Latin *ascus* 'sac' + HELMINTH]

asci plural of **ascus**

ascidia plural of **ascidium**

ascidian /ə síddi ən/ (*plural* **-ans** *or* **-an**) *n* any marine invertebrate animal that has a body with openings through which water passes, e.g. a sea squirt. Class: Ascidiacea. [Mid-19C. < modern Latin *Ascidia* < Greek *askidion* 'little wineskin' < *askos* 'wineskin, leather bag'.]

ascidium /ə síddi əm/ (*plural* **-a** /-ə/) *n* a part of a plant or fungus shaped like a pitcher [Mid-18C. Via modern Latin < Greek *askidion* (see ASCIDIAN).]

ASCII /áski/ *n* a standard identifying letters, numbers, and symbols by code numbers for exchanging data between different computer systems. Full form **American Standard Code for Information Interchange**

ASCII art *n* illustrations using only ASCII characters, often used in e-mails

ASCII file *n* a computer file that contains only ASCII characters. ◊ **binary file**

ascites /ə sī́t eez/ *n* an accumulation of fluid (**serous fluid**) in the peritoneal cavity, causing abdominal swelling [14C. Via late Latin, < Greek *askitēs* 'oedema' < *askos* 'wineskin, leather bag'.] —**ascitic** /ə síttik/ *adj*

asco- *prefix* ascus ○ *ascocarp* [Via modern Latin, < Greek *askos* 'wineskin, leather bag']

ascocarp /áskə kaarp/ *n* a fleshy structure in certain fungi (**ascomycetes**) containing sexually produced spores (**ascospores**) in a membranous spore case (**ascus**)

ascogonium /áskə gṓni əm/ (*plural* **-a** /-ni ə/) *n* a female reproductive part in certain fungi (**ascomycetes**)

ascoma /a skṓmə/ (*plural* **-mata** /-mətə/) *n* FUNGI = **ascocarp**

ascomycete /áskə mī seet/ *n* a fungus that produces spores sexually inside a membranous spore case (**ascus**), e.g. a yeast or truffle. Class: Ascomycetes. —**ascomycetous** *adj*

ascorbate /ə skáwr bayt, -bət/ *n* any salt of ascorbic acid

ascorbic acid /ə skáwrbik-/ *n* = **vitamin C** [< A-[2] + SCORBUTIC]

ascospore /áskə spawr/ *n* a fungal spore produced sexually inside a membranous spore case (**ascus**) —**ascosporic** /áskə spáwrik/ *adj* —**ascosporous** /-spáwrəss/ *adj*

ascot /áskət/ *n* a broad cravat with square ends, often held in place with an ornamental stud [Early 20C. After ASCOT.]

Ascot /áskət/ town in S England where horse races are held. Population: 13,500.

ascribe /ə skrī́b/ (**-cribes, -cribing, -cribed**) *vt* (*formal*) **1** **GIVE AS CAUSE** to believe or say that something was caused by something else that is named ○ *His rivals could only ascribe his success to sheer good luck.* **2** **GIVE AS AUTHOR** to believe or say that something was originally written or said by somebody who is named ○ *The researcher was confident enough to ascribe the newly discovered poems to Burns.* **3** **GIVE AS CHARACTERISTIC** to believe that something that is named belongs to or is typical of a person or group ○ *to ascribe contentment to the unambitious* [15C. < Latin *ascribere* 'add to in writing' < *scribere* 'write'.] —**ascribable** *adj*

ascribed status *n* the status that an individual possesses by reason of age, sex, ethnic background, family background, or another factor outside the control of the individual

ascription /ə skrípsh'n/ *n* **1** **ATTRIBUTION** the attributing of a relationship between something and somebody or something else (*formal*) **2** **STATEMENT OF ATTRIBUTION** a statement that assigns or attributes something to somebody or something else (*formal*) **3** **SOCIAL STATUS BY BIRTH** the social status derived from the circumstances into which somebody is born [Late 16C. < Latin *ascription-* < *ascript-*, past participle of *ascribere* (see ASCRIBE).]

ascus /áskəss/ (*plural* **-ci** /-sī, -s kī/) *n* a membranous spore case formed by certain fungi (**ascomycetes**) that contains eight sexually produced spores (**ascospores**) [Mid-19C. Via modern Latin, < Greek *askos* 'wineskin, leather bag'.]

asdic /ázdik/ *n* an early version of sonar [Early 20C. Acronym < *Anti-Submarine Detection Investigation Committee.*]

-ase *suffix* enzyme ○ *polymerase* [< DIASTASE]

ASEAN /ássi an/ *abbr* Association of Southeast Asian Nations

aseismic /ay sī́zmik/ *adj* **1** not subject to earthquakes **2** built to withstand earthquakes

aseismic creep *n* movement of tectonic plates below the Earth's crust that is not caused by earthquakes or other seismic disturbance

aseismic ridge *n* a long linear mountainous ridge in an ocean basin, usually the result of volcanic activity generated as an ocean plate travels over a hot spot in the Earth's mantle

asepsis /ay sépsiss, ə-/ *n* **1** a condition in which no living disease-causing microorganisms are present **2** the process or methods of bringing about a condition in which no disease-causing microorganisms are present

aseptic /ay séptik, ə-/ *adj* **1** free of disease-causing microorganisms **2** designed to prevent infection from pathogenic microorganisms —**aseptically** *adv* —**asepticism** *n*

asexual /ay sékshoo əl/ *adj* **1** **WITHOUT SEX-LINKED FEATURES** lacking any apparent sex or sex organs **2** **WITHOUT SEXUAL FUSION** describes reproduction in which there is no fusion of male and female sex cells (**gametes**), e.g. vegetative reproduction or budding **3** **SEXUALLY INACTIVE** without sexual desire or activity —**asexuality** /áy sekshoo álləti/ *n* —**asexually** *adv*

Asgard /áss gaard/ *n* in Norse mythology, the home of the deities and of heroes killed in battle

ash[1] /ash/ *n* **1** **REMAINS OF FIRE** the powdery substance that is left when something has been burnt (*often plural*) **2** **VOLCANIC DUST** fine-grained lava that erupts or flows from a volcano before settling on the ground ■ **ashes** *npl* **BURNT REMAINS OF BODY** the remains of somebody's body after it has been cremated ■ *adj* **SILVERY GREY** of a silvery grey colour [Old English *æsce* < Indo-European, 'burn, be dry'] ◇ **rise (like a phoenix) from the ashes** to come into existence or popularity again, seemingly from a state of ruin or destruction

ash[2] /ash/ (*plural* **ashes** *or* **ash**) *n* **1** **DECIDUOUS TREE** a deciduous tree that has compound leaves with paired leaflets and winged fruits. Native to: temperate regions. Genus: *Fraxinus*. **2** **HARD WOOD OF ASH** the hard durable wood of the ash tree. Use: furniture, tool handles. **3** **SYMBOL FOR VOWEL SOUND** the character 'æ', representing the vowel sound of the modern English word 'pad', used in Old English and the International Phonetic Alphabet [Old English *æsc* < Germanic]

ashamed /ə sháymd/ *adj* **1** feeling full of shame **2** embarrassed or regretful ○ *I'm ashamed to say I didn't acknowledge their invitation.* [Old English *āscamod* < *sceamu* 'shame'] —**ashamedly** /-mədli/ *adv*

Ashanti[1] /ə shánti/ (*plural* **-ti** *or* **-tis**), **Ashante** (*plural* **-te** *or* **-tes**) *n* **1** somebody who comes from Ashanti **2** a language spoken in central Ghana, often regarded as a form of Akan [Early 18C. < Twi *Asante*.] —**Ashanti** *adj*

Ashanti[2] /ə shánti/ administrative area and former kingdom in central Ghana

A share *n* a share in a company that does not entitle the holder to voting rights and that may carry other restrictions

ash blonde, ash blond *adj* light or whitish blonde in colour (*hyphenated when used before a noun*) ■ *n* somebody with ash blonde hair

Ashburton /ásh burt'n/ **1** river in Western Australia. Length: 650 km/404 mi. **2** reservoir in NW Australia

ashcan /ásh kan/ *n* US **1** = **dustbin** **2** a depth charge (*slang*)

Ashcroft /ásh kroft/, **Dame Peggy** (1907–91) British actor. Born **Edith Margaret Emily Ashcroft**

Ashdown /ásh down/, **Paddy** (*b.* 1941) British politician

Ashe /ash/, **Arthur** (1943–93) US tennis player

ashen[1] /ásh'n/ *adj* **1** extremely pale in appearance **2** resembling or consisting of ashes

ashen[2] /ásh'n/ *adj* relating to the ash tree or its wood (*archaic*)

Ashes /áshiz/ *n* in cricket, the trophy awarded to the winner of a series of test matches between England and Australia [Late 19C. < a mock obituary for English cricket after a defeat, and the subsequent presentation to the English of an urn containing ashes, which became the trophy.]

ashet /áshit/ *n* Scotland, N England, NZ a large plate or shallow dish, usually oval in shape, used for serving food [Mid-19C. < French *assiette* 'place at table, plate' < *asseoir* 'to seat' (see ASSIZE).]

ash flow *n* **1** an avalanche of hot volcanic ash and debris down the sides of a volcano **2** a deposit of volcanic ash and debris resulting from an ash flow

Ashgabat /áshgə bat/ capital of Turkmenistan. Population: 517,200 (1993 estimate).

Ashkenazi /áshkə naázi/ (*plural* **-im** /-im/) *n* a member of a Jewish people originating in Germany and N Europe [Mid-19C. < modern Hebrew, < medieval Hebrew *Ashkenaz* 'Germany' < Hebrew *Ashkĕnāz*, a grandson of Noah.] —**Ashkenazi** *adj* —**Ashkenazic** *adj*

Ashkhabad /áshkə bad/ former name for **Ashgabat**

ashlar /áshlər/, **ashler** *n* **1** a thin slab of squared stone, used for facing walls or building **2** masonry using thin slabs of squared stone as facing material [14C. Via Old French *aisselier* 'plank' < medieval Latin *axicellus* < Latin *axis* 'plank, axletree'.]

ashlaring /áshləring/ *n* the construction of a building using ashlars

ashler *n* BUILDING = **ashlar**

Ashley /áshli/, **Laura** (1925–85) British fashion designer. Born **Laura Mountney**

Ashmore and Cartier Islands /ásh mawr ənd kaárti ay-/ island group in the Indian Ocean, NW of Australia, a territory of Australia. Area: 5 sq. km/2 sq. mi.

Ashora /ə sháwrə/, **Ashura** /ə shoórə/ *n* an Islamic festival associated by Sunni Muslims with the death of Muhammad's grandson Husain. Date: tenth day of Muharram. [Mid-19C. < Arabic *'āšūrā*, 'tenth'.]

ashore /ə sháwr/ *adv* to the land from the water, or on land as opposed to on a ship or boat ○ *All but the captain went ashore.*

~~**ashphalt**~~ incorrect spelling of **asphalt**

ashram /áshrəm, aásh-/ *n* **1** a retreat for the practice of yoga or other Hindu disciplines **2** a commune or communal house whose members share spiritual goals and practices [Early 20C. < Sanskrit *āśramaḥ* 'hermitage'.]

Ashton /áshtən/, **Sir Frederick** (1904–88) British dancer and choreographer

Ashton-under-Lyne /-līn/ town in NW England. Population: 43,906 (1991).

Ashton-Warner /-wáwrnər/, **Sylvia** (1905–84) New Zealand novelist and teacher

Ashtoreth /áshtə reth/ *n* ♦ **Ishtar**

ashtray /ásh tray/ *n* an open receptacle for the ash from a cigarette, cigar, or pipe and for cigarette ends

Ashura *n* ISLAM, CALENDAR = **Ashora**

Ashurbanipal /áshoor bánni pal/ king of Assyria

Ash Wednesday *n* a Christian holy day marking the first day of Lent [Because of the Roman Catholic custom of marking the heads of penitents with ashes on this day]

ashy /áshi/ (**-ier, -iest**) *adj* **1** extremely pale or greyish in appearance (*literary*) **2** resembling or covered in ash

Asia /áyshə, áyzhə/ world's largest continent, bordered by the Ural and Caucasus mountains and the Arctic, Pacific, and Indian oceans. Population: estimated 3.46 billion (1995). Area: 44,936,000 sq. km/17,350,000 sq. mi.

Asiadollar /áyshə dollər, áyzhə-/ *n* a US dollar used in Asian banks and currency markets

Asia Minor peninsula in W Asia, roughly corresponding to Asian Turkey

Asian /áysh'n, áyzh'n/ *adj* OF ASIA relating to Asia, or its peoples, languages, or cultures ■ *n* **1** SOMEBODY FROM ASIA somebody who comes from Asia, or is of Asian descent **2** SOMEBODY FROM THE INDIAN SUBCONTINENT somebody who comes from, or is descended from those who came from, the Indian subcontinent [15C. Via Latin < Greek *Asianos* < *Asia* 'Asia'.]

USAGE ***Asian*** has largely replaced *Asiatic*, both as a noun and as an adjective. When the reference is to people, *Asiatic* is now regarded as derogatory and should be strictly avoided. In British English, ***Asian*** is also used to refer to people from South Asia (the Indian subcontinent), or their descendants, now living in Britain. In US English, ***Asian*** usually refers to people of East Asian origin or ancestry, for example from China, Japan, or Korea.

Asian-American *n* an American of Asian descent — **Asian-American** *adj*

Asian flu, Asian influenza *n* influenza that occurs in sporadic worldwide epidemics, caused by a virus strain thought to have originated in China in the mid-1950s, and related strains

Asian pear *n* **1** a fruit resembling a brownish-yellow apple with crisp juicy flesh **2** a tree that bears Asian pears. Genus: *Pyrus*.

Asia-Pacific *n* a commercial region encompassing the countries of Asia and the Pacific Rim

Asiatic /áyshi áttik, áyzi-/ *adj* describes things Asian, e.g. flora, fauna, or climatic conditions ○ *Asiatic plants and animals* ○ *parts of the Asiatic steppes* [Early 17C. Via Latin < Greek *Asiatikos* < *Asia* 'Asia'.]

USAGE See ***Asian***.

Asiatic cholera *n* MED = **cholera**

aside /ə síd/ *adv* **1** AWAY OR TO ONE SIDE to one side of somebody or something ○ *Stand aside and let the people through.* **2** OUT OF THE WAY out of the way ○ *brush aside all criticism* **3** IGNORED ignored for the sake of argument ○ *Budget constraints aside, is the deadline feasible?* **4** FOR FUTURE USE for special or future use ○ *put aside some money each week* ■ *n* **1** ACTOR'S COMMENT a remark made by an actor, usually to the audience, that the other characters on stage supposedly cannot hear **2** CONFIDENTIAL COMMENT IN UNDERTONE a spoken remark not directed to all listeners and usually made in a quiet voice **3** DIGRESSION a digression from a main point

A-side *n* the side of a pop, rock, or jazz single that contains the more important recording, usually the title track (*dated*)

aside from *prep US* **1** in addition to or besides somebody or something ○ *Aside from his medical practice he is also a lawyer.* **2** except for or not considering the stated thing ○ *Aside from the cold weather, I love it here.*

Asimov /ázzi mof/, **Isaac** (1920–92) Russian-born US scientist and writer

asinine /ássi nīn/ *adj* **1** utterly ridiculous or lacking sense **2** relating to or resembling an ass [15C. < Latin *asininus* < *asinus* 'ass'.] —**asininely** *adv* —**asininity** /ássi nínnəti/ *n*

as is *adj* used to imply that goods may not be in perfect condition ○ *all merchandise sold as is*

ask /aask/ *v* **1** *vti* QUESTION to put a question to somebody ○ *Ask them how long it will take.* **2** *vti* MAKE REQUEST to make a request for something ○ *They asked me for my opinion.* **3** *vt* INVITE to invite somebody to a social event ○ *Only close friends were asked to dine.* **4** *vt* REQUIRE to require somebody to give or contribute something ○ *The job asks a lot more of me than I expected.* **5** *vt* NAME AS PRICE to name an amount as an acceptable price ○ *They're asking £100,000 for the house.* [Old English *āscian* < Indo-European, 'to wish'] —**asker** *n* ◇ **for the asking** available at no cost

ask after *vt* to inquire about somebody's welfare ○ *She asks after the children whenever we meet.*

ask for *v* **1** *vti* REQUEST to request that something be provided ○ *I asked for a cup of coffee.* **2** *vt* REQUEST SOMEBODY'S APPEARANCE to request somebody's appearance, especially to speak to **3** *vt* REQUEST TELEPHONE CONVERSATION WITH to request that somebody be called to the telephone ○ *A man on the phone is asking for the manager.* **4** *vt* INVITE SOMETHING UNPLEASANT to behave in a way that deserves something unpleasant ○ *You're asking for a lot of problems if you do that.*

ask out *vt* to invite somebody to go on a date

askance /ə skánss, ə skaánss/ *adv* with doubt or suspicion ○ *'They surveyed each other askance, feeling that they were rivals, and mentally calculating each other's chances'.* (Horatio Alger, Jr., *Ragged Dick*; 1868) [15C. < ?]

askari /a skaári/, **askar** /áss kaar/ *n* a soldier or police officer in various Islamic countries of E Africa [Late 19C. < Arabic *askarī* 'soldier'.]

askew /ə skyoó/ *adj, adv* at an angle ○ *with his hat askew*

asking price *n* the price set by a seller before any negotiation

ϟ **ASL** *abbr* **1** *US* American Sign Language **2** age, sex, location (*in e-mails*)

aslant /ə slaánt/ *adv* sloping or at an angle ○ *books all aslant on the shelves*

asleep /ə sleép/ *adj* **1** NOT AWAKE in or into a state of sleep ○ *After tossing and turning for some hours I eventually fell asleep.* **2** NOT ALERT not alert enough to function or operate properly ○ *asleep on the job* **3** NUMB numb for lack of proper blood circulation

ASLEF /ázz lef/, **Aslef** *abbr* Associated Society of Locomotive Engineers and Firemen

A/S level *n* in England and Wales, a school examination taken at an advanced level in a particular subject but involving less coursework than an A level (*hyphenated before nouns*) ○ *A/S-level biology*. Full form **Advanced Supplementary level**

aslope /ə slṓp/ *adj, adv* at a sloping angle

ASM *abbr* air-to-surface missile

Asmara /ass maárə/ capital of Eritrea, in the W of the country. Population: 359,000 (1990 estimate).

asocial /ay sṓsh'l/ *adj* **1** UNWILLING TO MIX SOCIALLY disinclined or averse to human social interaction **2** NOT INTERACTING SOCIALLY lacking a need or capacity for social interaction **3** UNSUITED TO SOCIETY not conforming to normal social standards, or showing a lack of consideration for others

~~**asociation**~~ incorrect spelling of **association**

Asoka /ə sṓkə/ (291?–232 BC) king of Maghada (273?–232 BC)

asp /asp/ *n* **1** a small poisonous snake that caused the death of Cleopatra, thought to have been a member of the cobra family. Native to: Africa, Asia, Europe. *Naja haje.* **2** a snake of the viper family, resembling a small adder. Native to: S Europe. **3** ZOOL = **horned viper** [14C. Directly or via Old French *aspe* < Latin *aspis* < Greek.]

ϟ **ASP** *abbr* **1** active server page **2** application service provider

asparaginase /ə spárrəji nayz, -nayss/ *n* an enzyme that catalyzes the breakdown of asparagine

asparagine /ə spárrə jeen, -jin/ *n* an amino acid found in many plant seeds that can also be produced by humans and animals [Early 19C. < ASPARAGUS, from which it was first obtained.]

asparagus /ə spárrəgəss/ (*plural* **-gus**) *n* **1** spear-shaped young plant shoots, eaten cooked as a vegetable **2** a perennial plant that produces asparagus. *Asparagus officinalis.* [Pre-12C. Via Latin, < Greek *asparagos.*]

asparagus fern *n* a plant with feathery leaves and purplish-black berries grown as a houseplant. Flowers: small, white. Use: foliage for bouquets. Native to: South Africa. *Asparagus setaceus.*

aspartame /ə spaár taym/ *n* a protein produced from aspartic acid. Use: synthetic sweetener. [Late 20C. < ASPARTIC ACID.]

aspartate /ə spaár tayt/ *n* a salt or ester of aspartic acid

aspartic acid /ə spaártik-/ *n* an amino acid occurring in many plant proteins that can also be produced by humans and animals [Mid-19C. < French *aspartique* < Latin *asparagus* (see ASPARAGUS).]

aspect /áspekt/ *n* **1** ONE SIDE OR PART a facet, phase, or part of a whole ○ *consider the various aspects of the problem* **2** APPEARANCE the appearance of something to the mind or eye ○ *The stone has a greenish aspect in this light.* **3** VIEWPOINT a particular view or point of view ○ *seeing life from a new aspect* ○ *the aspect of the mountain from the river* **4** EXPOSURE exposure to a particular direction, weather, or other influence ○ *This plant requires a sunny aspect.* **5** ANGLE BETWEEN CELESTIAL BODIES the apparent angular separation of two celestial bodies, especially as observed from the Earth **6** POSITIONS OF PLANETS in astrology, the relative positions of the stars and planets, believed to influence human affairs **7** GRAMMATICAL CATEGORY a grammatical category of verbs that considers qualities of action independent of tense, e.g. the progressive or continuous and perfect aspects in English [14C. < Latin *aspectus*, past participle of *aspicere* < *specere* 'look at'.]

aspect ratio *n* **1** in television and the cinema, the ratio of the width of the picture on the screen to its height **2** the ratio of the length of an aircraft's wing to the mean distance between the front and back edge of the wing

aspectual /a spéktyoo əl/ *adj* relating to the aspects of a verb

aspen /áspən/ (*plural* **-pens** *or* **-pen**) *n* a poplar with leaves that rustle and flutter in the breeze. Native to: Europe, N United States. *Populus tremens* and *Populus tremuloides.* [14C. <.]

Aspen /áspən/ city in west-central Colorado, a fashionable ski resort. Population: 5,245 (1996).

asper /áspər/ *n* a minor unit of currency in Turkey, 120 of which are worth a piastre [15C. Via French *aspre* < medieval Greek *aspros* 'newly minted' < Latin *asper* 'rough'.]

Asperger's syndrome /áspurjərz-/, **Asperger syndrome** /áspurjər-/ *n* a severe developmental disorder, akin to autism, characterized by difficulties with social relations, strange behaviour patterns, concentration on details of objects, and often a heightened ability to memorize [After Hans *Asperger* (1906–80), Austrian paediatrician]

asperges /ə spúr jeez/ *n* a religious ceremony of the Roman Catholic Church in which holy water is sprinkled over the altar, clergy, and congregation before High Mass [Late 16C. < Latin, 'you will sprinkle', the first word of the rite.]

aspergill *n* RELIG = **aspergillum**

aspergillosis /ə spúrji lóssiss/ *n* a disease affecting mucous membranes, lungs, and sometimes bones that is caused by infection with the fungus *Aspergillus*

aspergillum /áspər jíləm/ (*plural* **-la** /-ə/ *or* **-lums**), **aspergill** /áspər jíl/ (*plural* **-gilla** *or* **-gills**) *n* a brush or perforated container for sprinkling holy water [Mid-17C. < modern Latin, 'little sprinkler' < Latin *aspergere* 'sprinkle'.]

asperity /a spérrəti/ (*plural* **-ties**) *n* **1 HARSHNESS OR SEVERITY** harshness or severity of manner or tone (*formal*) **2 ROUGHNESS** the roughness of a surface (*literary*) **3 HARDSHIP** something that is hard to bear because of its harshness or severity **4 AREA WHERE SURFACES TOUCH** a region of contact between two load-bearing flat surfaces [13C. Via French *asperité* < Latin *asperitas* < *asper* 'rough'.]

aspermia /ə spúrmi ə/ *n* a medical condition in which no spermatozoa are present in the seminal fluid [Mid-19C. < A-[2] + Greek *sperma* 'seed'.] —**aspermic** *adj*

aspersion /ə spúrsh'n/ *n* **1** a statement that attacks somebody's character or reputation (*often plural*) **2** the making of defamatory remarks

aspersorium /áspər sáwri əm/ (*plural* **-ria** /-ri ə/) *n* RELIG = **aspergillum** [Mid-19C. < medieval Latin, < Latin *aspers-*, the past participle stem of *aspergere* 'to spatter on'.]

asphalt /áss falt, -fawlt/ *n* **1 SEMISOLID BITUMINOUS SUBSTANCE** a brownish-black solid or semisolid substance. Source: oil-bearing rocks, by-product of petroleum distillation. Use: surfacing roads and paths, waterproofing, fungicides. **2 MATERIAL USED FOR SURFACING ROADS** surfacing material composed mainly of asphalt and gravel or crushed rock that hardens on cooling and is used for making roads and paths ■ *vt* **COVER SOMETHING WITH ASPHALT** to surface a roadway, pavement, or other area with asphalt [14C. Via late Latin, < Greek *asphaltos*.] —**asphaltic** /ass fáltik/ *adj*

asphalt jungle *n* a big city or urban area with little natural landscape

aspheric /ay sférrik/, **aspherical** /ay sférrik'l/ *adj* not perfectly spherical

asphodel /ásfə del/ (*plural* **-dels** *or* **-del**) *n* **1 FLOWERING PLANT** a perennial plant of the lily family. Flowers: white, pink, yellow, in clusters. Native to: S Europe. Genera: *Asphodelus* and *Asphodeline*. **2 PLANT RESEMBLING TRUE ASPHODEL** a plant similar to asphodel proper, e.g. bog asphodel **3 FLOWER OF HADES** in Greek mythology, the flower of Hades that was sacred to Persephone [15C. Via Latin *asphodilus* < Greek *asphodelos*.]

asphyxia /ass fíksi ə, əss-/ *n* suffocation as a result of physical blockage of the airway or inhalation of toxic gases, causing a lack of oxygen and unconsciousness [Early 18C. Via modern Latin, < Greek *asphuxia* 'lack of pulse' < *sphuxis* 'heartbeat' < *sphuzein* 'to throb'.] —**asphyxiant** *adj*, *n*

asphyxiate /ass fíksi ayt, əss-/ (**-ates, -ating, -ated**) *vti* to deprive a person or animal of oxygen, or be deprived of oxygen, usually leading to unconsciousness or death —**asphyxiation** /ass fíksi áysh'n, əss-/ *n* —**asphyxiator** *n*

aspic /áspik/ *n* a cold jelly often used as a mould for fish, meat, eggs, or vegetables [Late 18C. < French, 'asp', alteration of Old French *aspe* (see ASP).]

aspidistra /áspi dístrə/ *n* a common houseplant of the lily family with large glossy leaves. Flowers: small, brownish. Native to: Asia. Genus: *Aspidistra*. [Early 19C. < modern Latin, < Greek *aspid-*, stem of *aspis* 'shield', because of the shape of the leaves.]

aspirant /áspirənt, ə spírənt/ *n* somebody who seeks or hopes to attain something ○ *an aspirant to the presidency* ■ *adj* seeking or hoping to attain something

SYNONYMS See ***candidate***.

aspirate *vt* /áspi rayt/ (**-rates, -rating, -rated**) **1 PRONOUNCE WHILE BREATHING OUT** to pronounce a sound or word while breathing out, e.g. the letter h at the beginning of such words as 'house' and 'hat' in standard English **2 REMOVE LIQUID** to remove liquid or gas by suction, especially from a body cavity **3 INHALE** to inhale something, especially a liquid, into the lungs ■ *n* /áspərət/ **BREATHY LETTER** a sound pronounced while breathing out, e.g. the sound of the letter h at the beginning of many English words ■ *adj* /áspərət/ **BREATHY SOUNDING** pronounced while breathing out [Late 17C. < Latin *aspirat-*, past participle of *aspirare* 'breathe towards' < *spirare* 'breathe'.]

aspiration /áspi ráysh'n/ *n* **1 AMBITION** a desire or ambition to achieve something **2 BREATHY PRONUNCIATION** pronunciation accompanied by breathing out **3 SUCTION** the withdrawal by suction of fluids or gases from the body or a body cavity **4 INHALATION** drawing matter into the lungs along with the breath —**aspirational** *adj* —**aspiratory** /ə spírətəri, áspirətəri/ *adj*

aspiration pneumonia *n* pneumonia caused by foreign matter such as food entering the lungs

aspirator /áspi raytər/ *n* an apparatus for drawing out fluids or gases by suction

aspire /ə spír/ (**-pires, -piring, -pired**) *vi* **1** to seek to attain a particular goal ○ *aspire to public office* **2** to soar to a great height (*literary*) [14C. < Latin *aspirare* 'breathe towards' (see ASPIRATE).] —**aspirer** *n* —**aspiring** *adj*

aspirin /ásprin/ (*plural* **-rins** *or* **-rin**) *n* **1** a drug that relieves pain and inflammation, lowers fever, and reduces blood clotting **2** a tablet containing aspirin [Late 19C. < German, < contraction of *acetylierte Spirsäure* 'acetylated spiraeic acid' (former name of salicylic acid).]

Aspiring, Mount /ə spíring/ mountain in SW South Island. Height: 3,035 m/9,957 ft.

~~**asprin**~~ incorrect spelling of **aspirin**

asquint /ə skwínt/ *adv* from the corner of the eye, as if suspiciously

Asquith /áskwith/, **Herbert Henry, 1st Earl of Oxford and Asquith** (1852–1928) British statesman and prime minister (1908–16)

ass[1] /ass/ *n* **1** an animal resembling a small horse with long ears, sometimes used as a beast of burden. Genus: *Equus*. **2** an offensive term for somebody regarded as unintelligent, thoughtless, or ridiculous (*slang insult*) [Old English *assa*, via Celtic, < Latin *asinus*]

ass[2] /ass/ *n* US **1** = **arse** *n*. 1 (*taboo offensive*) **2** a highly offensive term for sexual intercourse (*taboo*) [Mid-19C. Euphemistic alteration of ARSE.] ◇ **cover your ass** *US* a highly offensive phrase meaning to behave in a way that ensures you will not be blamed for something later (*taboo*) ◇ **haul ass** *US* a highly offensive phrase meaning to move or start to move quickly (*taboo*) ◇ **have somebody's ass in a sling** *or* **bind** *US* a highly offensive phrase meaning to get somebody into trouble (*taboo*) ◇ **kick (some) ass** *US* a highly offensive phrase meaning to behave aggressively or ruthlessly in order to achieve a goal (*taboo*) ◇ **kiss ass** *US* a highly offensive phrase meaning to be very polite or obsequious to somebody in authority (*taboo*)

Assad /a sád/, **Hafez al-** (1928–2000) Syrian statesman and president (1971–2000)

assagai *n* ARMS = **assegai**

assail /ə sáyl/ *vt* **1** to attack somebody vigorously with words or actions ○ *assailed by furious criticism* **2** to overwhelm the mind or senses of somebody ○ *'Low growls and angry snarls assailed our ears on every side'*. (Edgar Rice Burroughs, *The Gods of Mars*; 1913) [13C. Via Old French *asaill-*, stem of *asalir* < assumed Vulgar Latin *assalire* 'leap at' < Latin *salire* 'leap'.] —**assailable** *adj* —**assailer** *n* —**assailment** *n*

assailant /ə sáylənt/ *n* somebody who violently attacks somebody else

Assam /a sám/ union state of NE India. Capital: Dispur. Population: 24,200,000 (1994). Area: 78,438 sq. km/30,285 sq. mi.

Assamese /ássə meéz/ (*plural* **-ese**) *n* **1** somebody who comes from Assam, India **2** an Indic language spoken in the state of Assam in NE India and in Bangladesh, written in Bengali script. Native speakers: 11 million. —**Assamese** *adj*

~~**assasin**~~ incorrect spelling of **assassin**

assassin /ə sássin/ *n* a killer, especially of a political leader or other public figure [Mid-16C. Via French, < Arabic *ḥašāšīn* 'hashish users'.]

assassinate /ə sássi nayt/ (**-nates, -nating, -nated**) *vt* **1** to kill somebody, especially a political leader or other public figure, by a sudden violent attack **2** to harm or destroy something such as somebody's reputation maliciously or treacherously —**assassinator** *n*

assassination /ə sássi náysh'n/ *n* **1** the killing of a political leader or other public figure by a sudden violent attack ○ *an unsuccessful assassination attempt* **2** the destruction of something such as somebody's reputation by malicious or treacherous means

assassin bug *n* a large long-legged insect with powerful mouthparts that kills and sucks the blood of other animals. Family: Reduviidae.

assassin fly (*plural* **assassin flies**) *n* INSECTS = **robber fly**

assault /ə sáwlt/ *n* **1 PHYSICAL OR VERBAL ATTACK** a violent physical or verbal attack **2 THREAT OF BODILY HARM** an unlawful threat or attempt to do violence or harm to somebody else **3** LAW = **sexual assault 4 ATTEMPT TO DESTROY** a campaign or series of actions that aims to challenge or destroy something ○ *The proposals are under assault by various special interest groups.* ■ *vt* **1 ATTACK** to attack somebody physically or verbally in a violent way **2 MAKE MILITARY ATTACK** to attack a place with a military force [13C. Via Old French *assaut* < assumed Vulgar Latin *assaltus*, past participle of *assalire* (see ASSAIL).] —**assaulter** *n*

assault and battery *n* the crime of doing bodily harm to somebody

assault course *n* an area of land on which there are various obstacles to be climbed over, crawled under, and run through, used by soldiers for training and keeping fit. US term **obstacle course** *n*. 1

assaultive /ə sáwltiv/ *adj* extremely aggressive or disposed to attack

assault weapon *n* a weapon designed for use in warfare, especially when used in noncombat situations such as terrorism

assay /ə sáy, ássay/ *n* **1 EXAMINATION** an examination and analysis of something **2 CHEMICAL ANALYSIS OF SUBSTANCE** chemical testing carried out to determine the composition of a substance or the concentration of its components **3 SAMPLE OF MATERIAL** a sample of material for analysis ■ *vt* **1 EXAMINE** to examine or test something with a view to evaluating it **2 ANALYSE** to analyse a substance such as an ore in order to discover its components and their concentration **3 ATTEMPT TO DO** to attempt to do something (*literary*) [14C. < Old French *assai* 'test' and its source *assaier* 'to test', variant of *essaier* (see ESSAY).] —**assayable** /ə sáy əb'l/ *adj* —**assayer** /ə sáyər/ *n*

assegai /ássə gī/, **assagai** *n* a slender hardwood spear with an iron tip, used especially by the Zulu peoples of southern Africa [Early 17C. Via obsolete French *azagaie* < Berber *zaḡāya* 'spear'.]

assemblage /ə sémblij/ *n* **1 GATHERING TOGETHER** a gathering of things or people at one point ○ *an assemblage of world-famous actors and directors at the awards ceremony* **2 COLLECTION** a collection of people or things ○ *an assemblage of ideas* **3 ARTISTIC ARRANGEMENT OF MISCELLANEOUS ITEMS** a work of art made from a collection of different objects

assemble /ə sémb'l/ (**-bles, -bling, -bled**) *v* **1** *vti* to bring people or things together or gather together in one place ○ *A crowd began to assemble.* **2** *vt* to fit the parts of something together to make a finished whole ○ *assembled a model* [13C. Via French *assembler* < assumed Vulgar Latin *assimulare* 'put together' < Latin *simul* 'together'.] —**assembled** *adj*

SYNONYMS See ***collect***.

assembler /ə sémblər/ *n* **1** a person, machine, or company that puts together the parts of a machine or piece of equipment when it is being built **2** a computer program that converts assembly language into machine language **3** COMPUT = **assembly language**

assembly /ə sémbli/ (*plural* **-blies**) *n* **1 GATHERING** the coming together of people for a common purpose ○ *freedom of assembly* **2 SCHOOL MEETING** a regular formal gathering of all the students in a school **3 assembly,**

Assembly **LEGISLATIVE MEETING** a group of people meeting as a deliberative or law-making body **4 FITTING COMPONENTS TOGETHER** the putting together of parts to make a finished product **5 COMPONENTS** a set of components before they are put together to make a finished product **6 MILITARY GATHERING** the gathering together of a military unit prior to an event or operation **7 MILITARY SIGNAL** a signal for soldiers or other personnel to gather **8 TRANSLATION OF COMPUTER LANGUAGE** the translation of assembly language into machine language [14C. < French *assemblée*, feminine past participle of *assembler* (see ASSEMBLE).]

assembly language *n* a low-level computer language consisting of mnemonic codes and symbolic addresses corresponding to machine-language instructions

assembly line *n* a series of work stations at which individual steps in the assembly of a product are carried out by workers or machines as the product is moved along

assemblyman /ə sémblimən/ (*plural* **-men** /-mən/) *n* a member of a legislative assembly

assembly point *n* a designated place for people to gather, especially in the event of an evacuation of a building

assemblywoman /ə sémbli wŏŏmən/ (*plural* **-en** /-wimmin/) *n* a woman member of a legislative assembly

assent /ə sént/ *vi* to agree to something or express agreement ○ *She will never assent to their marriage.* ■ *n* an expression of agreement or acceptance [13C. Via Old French *assenter* < Latin *assentire* 'feel towards' < *sentire* 'feel'.] —**assenter** *n* —**assentingly** *adv*

SPELLCHECK Do not confuse ***assent*** with ***ascent***, which has a similar sound. Beware: your spellchecker will not catch this error.

SYNONYMS See ***agree***.

assentient /ə sénshi ənt/ *adj* agreeing or accepting (*formal*) ■ *n* a person or party that agrees (*formal*) [Mid-19C. < Latin *assentient-*, present participle of *assentire* (see ASSENT).]

assert /ə súrt/ *v* **1** *vt* **CLAIM** to state something as being true ○ *She asserted that she had never seen the man before.* **2** *vt* **INSIST ON RIGHTS** to insist on or exercise your rights ○ *He asserted his right to remain silent and refused to testify.* **3** *vr* **BEHAVE FORCEFULLY** to exercise and reveal your power, influence, and prerogatives ○ *The new management quickly began to assert itself after the takeover.* **4** *vr* **BECOME KNOWN OR EFFECTIVE** to start to have an effect or become noticeable ○ *The relationship went well until their age difference began to assert itself.* [Early 17C. < Latin *assert-*, past participle of *asserere* 'join to' < *serere* 'join, connect'.] —**assertable** *adj* —**asserter** *n*

USAGE assert or **insert**? If you ***assert*** something, you claim it or insist on it, as in *She asserted her innocence. He asserted that his debating opponent's position was flawed. The prosecutor asserted* [not *inserted*] *her opinion that the bail had been set too low.* If you ***insert*** something, you put it into something else or you add material to a larger unit of printed material, as in *We inserted [not asserted] the key into the lock. I inserted* [not *asserted*] *an editorial on page 12.*

assertion /ə súrsh'n/ *n* **1** a strong statement that something is true **2** the act of stating emphatically that something is true ○ *the assertion of their rights*

assertive /ə súrtiv/ *adj* confident in stating your position or claim ○ *Modern education encourages the assertive student.* —**assertively** *adv* —**assertiveness** *n*

USAGE See ***aggressive***.

assertiveness training *n* teaching people how to overcome shyness and assert themselves

assess /ə séss/ *vt* **1 JUDGE** to examine something in order to judge or evaluate it ○ *not enough information to assess whether the event occurred* **2 DETERMINE AMOUNT** to calculate a value based on various factors ○ *Loss adjustors are assessing the damage.* **3 CALCULATE VALUE FOR TAX** to calculate the value of something in order to establish how much tax must be paid ○ *property assessed at £300,000* [15C. < Old French *assesser* < Latin *assess-*, past participle of *assidere* 'sit beside' < *sedere* 'sit'.] —**assessable** *adj*

assessment /ə séssmənt/ *n* **1 EVALUATION** a judgment about something based on an understanding of the situation ○ *a fair assessment of the project* **2 PROPERTY VALUATION** a calculation of the value of something in order to know how much tax must be paid **3 AMOUNT CALCULATED** an amount assessed, e.g. on a property **4 EDUCATIONAL EVALUATION** a method of evaluating student performance and attainment

assessor /ə séssər/ *n* **1 SOMEBODY WHO CALCULATES** somebody who calculates amounts to be paid or assessed for tax or insurance purposes **2 SOMEBODY WHO EVALUATES** somebody who evaluates the work of somebody else **3 JUDGE'S ADVISOR** a specialist in a particular subject who advises a judge or committee of inquiry

asset /ásset/ *n* **1 SOMEBODY OR SOMETHING USEFUL** somebody or something that is useful and contributes to the success of something **2 VALUABLE THING** a property to which a value can be assigned ■ **assets** *npl* **1 OWNED ITEMS** the property that is owned by a particular person or organization **2 SEIZABLE PROPERTY** the property of a person that can be taken by law for the settlement of debts or that forms part of a dead person's estate **3 BALANCE SHEET ITEMS** the items on a balance sheet that constitute the total value of an organization [Mid-16C. Via Anglo-Norman *assetz* 'sufficient goods' (to settle an estate) < Latin *ad satis* 'sufficiency'.]

asset demand *n* the desire of an individual or organization to acquire money, property, or other assets

asset-stripping *n* the practice of buying a company cheaply and making a profit by selling all its assets individually —**asset-stripper** *n*

asseverate /ə sévvə rayt/ (**-ates, -ating, -ated**) *vt* to state something earnestly or solemnly (*formal*) [Mid-16C. < Latin *asseverat-*, past participle of *asseverare* < *severus* 'serious'.] —**asseveration** /ə sévvə ráysh'n/ *n*

asshole /áss hōl/ *n* US = **arsehole** (*taboo offensive*)

assibilate /ə síbbi layt/ (**-lates, -lating, -lated**) *v* **1** *vt* to utter something with a hissing sound like that of the letter s or z **2** *vi* to be transformed into a hissing sound (**sibilant**) [Mid-19C. < Latin *assibilat-*, past participle of *assibilare* 'hiss at' < *sibilare* (see SIBILANT).] —**assibilation** /ə síbbi láysh'n/ *n*

assiduity /ássi dyŏŏ əti/ *n* great care and attention in doing something ■ **assiduities** *npl* constant attentiveness shown towards somebody

assiduous /ə síddyoo əss/ *adj* undeviating in effort and care [Mid-16C. < Latin *assiduus* < *assidere* (see ASSESS), in a late sense 'apply yourself'.] —**assiduously** *adv* —**assiduousness** *n*

SYNONYMS See ***careful***.

assign /ə sín/ *vt* **1 GIVE SOMEBODY TASK OR DUTY** to give somebody a particular job to do ○ *assign extra duties to the latecomers* **2 SEND SOMEBODY TO DO SOMETHING** to send somebody to work in a particular place or with a particular group of people ○ *I assigned him to the post room.* **3 ORDER A SOLDIER** to put a soldier or military unit under a particular command **4 TRANSFER PROPERTY** to transfer property or rights to another person by an official act **5 SET SOMETHING ASIDE FOR** to designate something for a particular use ○ *The new radio station has been assigned a frequency by the authorities.* **6 PLACE A VALUE** to designate a value for a computer memory location corresponding to a named variable ■ *n* LAW = **assignee** *n.* 1 [14C. Via French *assigner* < Latin *assignare* < *signare* 'mark out, designate' < *signum* 'mark'.] —**assignability** /ə sínə bílləti/ *n* —**assignable** *adj* —**assignably** *adv* —**assigner** *n* —**assignor** *n*

assignation /ássig náysh'n/ *n* **1** an appointment to meet a lover, especially secretly **2** the act of giving somebody a particular job or designating something for a particular use **3** LAW = **assignment** *n.* 4 [14C. Via French, < Latin *assignation-* < *assignare* (see ASSIGN).]

assignee /ássī née/ *n* **1** somebody to whom a right over property is given or transferred **2** a person appointed to act for another

assignment /ə sínmənt/ *n* **1 TASK** a specific task assigned or undertaken ○ *All team members have received their assignments.* **2 APPOINTMENT** a position, duty, or job for which somebody is chosen ○ *an assignment in Japan* **3 LEGAL TRANSFER DOCUMENT** a document, e.g. a deed, that effects a legal transfer of rights **4 LEGAL TRANSFER** the transfer of a right in or over property to another **5** *Aus* **CONVICT LABOUR** the system by which convicts were assigned to work for free settlers as fulfilment of their sentences in colonial Australia

assimilate /ə símmi layt/ (**-lates, -lating, -lated**) *v* **1** *vti* **INTEGRATE** to integrate somebody into a larger group, so that differences are minimized or eliminated, or to become integrated in this way **2** *vt* **ABSORB INFORMATION** to integrate knowledge or information with what is already known **3** *vt* **ABSORB NUTRIENTS** to incorporate digested food materials into the cells and tissues of the body ○ *assimilate protein* **4** *vti* **SOUND LIKE ADJACENT SOUND** to make a speech sound similar to an adjacent sound or to become similar to an adjacent sound [15C. < Latin *assimilat-*, past participle of *assimilare* 'make the same' < *similis* 'like'.] —**assimilability** /ə símmilə bílləti/ *n* —**assimilable** *adj* —**assimilator** *n* —**assimilatory** /ə símmilətəri, -láytəri/ *adj*

assimilation /ə símmi láysh'n/ *n* **1 ACT OF BECOMING PART OF** the process of becoming part of or more like something greater **2 INTEGRATION INTO GROUP** the process in which one group takes on the cultural and other traits of a larger group **3 LEARNING PROCESS** the integration of new knowledge or information with what is already known **4 NUTRIENT CONVERSION** incorporation of nutrients into the cells and tissues of plants and animals involving digestion, photosynthesis, and root absorption **5 SPEECH SOUND CHANGE** the changing of a speech sound under the influence of an adjacent sound

assimilationism /ə símmi láysh'nizəm/ *n* a policy of assimilating differing ethnic or cultural groups —**assimilationist** *n, adj*

Assiniboin /ə sínnə boyn/ (*plural* **-boin** *or* **-boins**), **Assiniboine** (*plural* **-boine** *or* **-boines**) *n* **1** a member of a Native North American people who once lived in the N Great Plains, and who now live mainly in Saskatchewan, Alberta, and Montana **2** a Siouan language spoken in S and W Canada and in Montana by the Assiniboin [Late 17C. Via Canadian French, < Ojibwa *assini:-pwa:n* 'stone Sioux'.] —**Assiniboin** *adj*

Assisi /ə sée si/ town in central Italy. Population: 24,626 (1996).

Assisi embroidery *n* embroidery in which designs are outlined, some design areas are left open, and the background is filled in with cross stitch

assist /ə síst/ *vti* **HELP** to help somebody to do or accomplish something ■ *n* **1 HELP BY TEAM PLAYER** an act by a player in a sport that enables another member of the team to score or achieve a successful defensive move **2** *US* **ACT OF HELPING** an act or series of actions helping another person [15C. Via French *assister* < Latin *assistere* 'stand beside' < *sistere* < *stare* 'to stand'.] —**assister** *n*

assistance /ə sístənss/ *n* help given or made available to another ○ *technical assistance*

assistant /ə sístənt/ *n* **1 HELPER** somebody, especially a subordinate, who helps somebody else to do something **2 SHOP EMPLOYEE** somebody who serves in a shop ■ *adj* **1 HELPING** subordinate to or helping another person ○ *an assistant teacher* **2 HELPFUL** serving to help or be useful

SYNONYMS ***assistant, helper, deputy, aide***

CORE MEANING: somebody who helps another person in carrying out a task

assistant somebody who works to somebody else's instructions, often in a paid capacity; **helper** somebody who takes on an informal, often voluntary, role; **deputy** an officially designated chief assistant authorized to act on a superior's behalf; **aide** an assistant in military, political, or commercial contexts.

assistant professor *n* *US* a member of a college or university faculty ranking typically above an instructor and below an associate professor

assistantship /ə sístəntship/ *n* *US* an academic position that provides financial support in exchange for teaching or research services, typically for a postgraduate student

assisted conception *n* MED = **assisted reproduction**

assisted place *n* a place at a fee-paying school or university for which funding is granted by an official body

assisted reproduction, assisted conception *n* the use of a technique, e.g. in vitro fertilization, to aid human reproduction in cases where this is problematic

assisted suicide *n* the suicide of a patient, usually somebody who is terminally ill, that is aided by a carer or especially a doctor, by the express wish and consent of the patient

assize /ə sīz/ *n US* a judicial inquest, or the verdict of the jurors involved ■ **assizes** *npl* periodic judicial proceedings held until 1971 in the counties of England and Wales and presided over by itinerant judges [14C. < Old French *assise*, past participle of *asseoir* 'settle' < Latin *assidere* (see ASSESS).]

associate *v* /ə sṓshi ayt, ə sṓssi-/ (**-ates, -ating, -ated**) **1** *vt* **CONNECT THINGS IN MIND** to connect one thing with another in the mind **2** *vi* **SPEND TIME** to spend time together with somebody ○ *Before the race she associated only with other skiers.* **3** *vr* **JOIN AS PARTNER** to join other people in a professional or social relationship **4** *vi* **FORM AN ASSOCIATION** to form an association ■ *n* /ə sṓshi ət, -ayt, ə sṓssi ət, -ayt/ **1 PARTNER** a partner in a business or other undertaking ○ *my associates in the firm* **2 CONNECTED PERSON** somebody who is known to spend time with another person ○ *I couldn't identify any of his associates.* **3 MEMBER** a member of an organization such as a club or a law firm, especially a newly licensed attorney, who does not have full status, rights, or privileges ■ *adj* /ə sṓshi ət, -ayt, ə sṓssi ət, -ayt/ **1 ALLIED** joined with others in purpose on an equal or nearly equal basis **2 SECONDARY** with subordinate status or less than full membership in an organization ○ *an associate member* [14C. < Latin *associat-*, past participle of *associare* < *socius* 'ally, companion'.] —**associability** /ə sṓshi ə bílləti, ə sṓshə-, ə sṓssi-/ *n* —**associable** /ə sṓshi əb'l, ə sṓshəb'l, ə sṓssi-/ *adj* —**associateship** /ə sṓshi ət ship, ə sṓssi-/ *n* —**associator** *n*

associate degree *n* in the United States, a degree earned on completion of a two-year course at a institution of higher education

associated statehood *n* the status of several former British colonies, mostly in the Caribbean, after dissolution of direct rule from Britain but before full independence

associate professor *n US* a member of a college or university faculty ranking typically above an assistant professor and below a professor

association /ə sṓssi áysh'n, ə sṓshi-/ *n* **1 GROUP** a group of people or organizations joined together for a purpose ○ *form an association to represent dairy farmers* **2 CONNECTION** a linking or joining of people or things ○ *She hasn't profited from her association with him.* **3 COMING TOGETHER** coming together and social interaction between people ○ *freedom of association* **4 PSYCHOLOGICAL CONNECTION** a connection of ideas, memories, or feelings with each other, or with events. ◊ **free association** *n.* **2 5 LINKED IDEA** a thought, idea, or feeling that is linked with an event **6 GROUPING OF MOLECULES** the formation of groups of loosely bound molecules **7 GROUPING OF ORGANISMS** a major ecological community dominated by one or more species, e.g. oak in a deciduous forest —**associational** *adj*

association football *n* football played according to the rules of the Football Association (*formal*)

associationism /ə sṓssi áysh'nizəm, ə sṓshi-/ *n* a psychological theory that explains complex thought and feelings in terms of associations with simpler elements —**associationist** *n* —**associationistic** /ə sṓssi áyshə nístik, ə sṓshi-/ *adj*

associative /ə sṓshi ətiv, ə sṓssi-/ *adj* **1** relating to the association of ideas, events, or experiences **2** giving the same result irrespective of the order taken, thus since a + (b + c) = (a + b) + c, addition is associative —**associatively** *adv*

associative learning *n* a learning process in which separate ideas and beliefs are linked in order to increase learning effectiveness

ϟ**associative memory** *n* computer memory organization in which stored information is accessed by content rather than memory address

assonance /ássənənss/ *n* the similarity of two or more vowel sounds or the repetition of two or more consonant sounds, especially in words that are close together in a poem. ◊ **alliteration** [Early 18C. < French, < Latin *assonare* 'respond to' < *sonare* 'to sound'.] —**assonant** *adj*

assort /ə sáwrt/ *v* **1** *vt* to sort things by type or category **2** *vi* to fit into a particular group [15C. < Old French *assorter* < *sorte* 'a sort' (see SORT).] —**assorter** *n*

assorted /ə sáwrtid/ *adj* **1** consisting of various kinds ○ *arrived with assorted excuses* **2** arranged in groups

assortment /ə sáwrtmənt/ *n* a collection of various kinds ○ *an assortment of drawings*

asst *abbr* assistant

asstd *abbr* **1** assisted **2** assorted

assuage /ə swáyj/ (**-suages, -suaging, -suaged**) *vt* to provide relief from something distressing or painful ○ *Constant reassurance could not assuage their fears.* [13C. Via Old French *assuagier* < assumed Vulgar Latin *assuaviare* 'sweeten' < Latin *suavis* 'sweet'.] —**assuagement** *n* —**assuager** *n* —**assuasive** /ə swáyssiv, -ziv/ *adj*

assume /ə syo͞om/ (**-sumes, -suming, -sumed**) *vt* **1 SUPPOSE** to think that something is true even though you have no evidence for it ○ *Don't assume that all has been revealed.* **2 TAKE RESPONSIBILITY FOR** to start being responsible for something ○ *She assumed all of her brother's debts when he died.* **3 ADOPT** to adopt or take on a particular quality ○ *The task facing them assumed Herculean proportions.* **4 UNDERTAKE ROLE** to undertake a particular role or function ○ *assume a new role as sales director* **5 PRETEND** to put on a pretence of something, usually in order to hide your true feelings ○ *He assumed an air of indifference.* [15C. < Latin *assumere* 'take up' < *sumere* (see SUMPTUARY).] —**assumable** *adj* —**assumably** *adv* —**assumed** *adj* —**assumedly** *adv* —**assumer** *n*

SYNONYMS See ***deduce***.

assuming /ə syo͞oming/ *adj* expecting too much of other people ■ *conj* if it is assumed that —**assumingly** *adv*

assumpsit /ə súmpsit/ *n* **1** an oral or written agreement, contract, or promise that exists without being on the record or under seal **2** an attempt to recover damages from a breached assumpsit [Late 16C. < Latin, 'he or she has undertaken'.]

assumption /ə súmpsh'n/ *n* **1 SOMETHING TAKEN FOR GRANTED** something that is believed to be true without proof ○ *Make no assumptions before looking at the evidence.* ○ *'Cruelty will be slyly advocated by the assumption that its only opposite is sentimentality'.* (C. S. Lewis, *Reflections on the Psalms*; 1961) **2 TAKING SOMETHING FOR GRANTED** believing something to be true without proof **3 UNDERTAKING** taking something upon yourself ○ *With the assumption of power comes responsibility.* **4 TAKING RESPONSIBILITY** taking over responsibility for something **5 INCLINATION TO HIGH EXPECTATIONS** the tendency to expect too much **6 UNPROVED STARTING POINT** something taken as a starting point of a logical proof rather than given as a premise [13C. < Latin *assumption-* < *assumpt-*, past participle of *assumere* (see ASSUME).]

Assumption, Assumption of the Virgin Mary *n* **1** the ascent of the Virgin Mary to heaven at her death, as believed by some Christians **2** a Christian feast that celebrates the Assumption. Date: 15 August.

assumptive /ə súmptiv/ *adj* predicated on an assumption or a set of assumptions

assurance /ə sháwrənss, ə sho͝orənss/ *n* **1 PLEDGE OR PROMISE** a declaration that inspires or is intended to inspire confidence ○ *They gave us every assurance it would arrive on time.* **2 CONFIDENCE** confidence in your ability or status ○ *He steered the ungainly machine with smooth assurance.* **3 CERTAINTY** freedom from uncertainty ○ *took heart in the assurance that the problem was solved* **4 MAKING SOMETHING CERTAIN** making something certain or overcoming doubt **5 INSURANCE AGAINST CERTAINTY** insurance against something that is certain to happen, e.g. death, rather than something that might happen, e.g. loss of or damage to property ○ *life assurance*

assure /ə sháwr, ə sho͝or/ (**-sures, -suring, -sured**) *vt* **1 MAKE SOMEBODY CONFIDENT** to overcome somebody's doubt or disbelief about something ○ *I can assure you that every word is true.* **2 CONVINCE** to convince somebody of something ○ *assured us of her sincerity* **3 MAKE SOMETHING CERTAIN** to make something certain ○ *Proper planning assures that the job will be done right.* **4 INSURE AGAINST CERTAINTY** to insure somebody against something that is certain to happen, e.g. death, rather than something that might happen, e.g. loss of or damage to property [14C. Via French *assurer* < assumed Vulgar Latin *assecurare* 'make secure' < Latin *securus* (see SECURE).] —**assurable** *adj* —**assurer** *n*

USAGE assure, ensure, or **insure**? You use ***assure*** when you are referring to somebody being made sure about something, and ***ensure*** when you are referring to something that you want to be sure of: *I assure you it doesn't hurt. She wanted to ensure that it wouldn't hurt.* ***Insure*** is used generally in connection with insurance (i.e. financial protection), and is also a variant spelling of ***ensure*** in US English.

assured /ə sháwrd, ə sho͝ord/ *adj* **1 GUARANTEED** certain to happen ○ *an assured victory* **2 SELF-CONFIDENT** confident about your abilities or other qualities ○ *the most assured conductor the orchestra had ever seen* **3 WITH LIFE ASSURANCE** covered by a life assurance policy ■ *n* **1** (*plural* **assured**) **PERSON WITH LIFE ASSURANCE** the person whose life is covered by assurance **2 SOMEBODY RECEIVING ASSURANCE MONEY** the person named as the beneficiary in a life assurance policy —**assuredly** /ə sháwridli, ə sho͝or-/ *adv* —**assuredness** /ə sháwridnəss, ə sho͝or-/ *n*

Assyria /ə sírri ə/ ancient kingdom in present-day N Iraq

Assyrian /ə sírri ən/ *n* **1** the Akkadian language, especially as recorded in cuneiform tablets from Assyria **2** somebody who lived in Assyria —**Assyrian** *adj*

AST /ast/ *abbr* Atlantic Standard Time

astable /ay stáyb'l/ *adj* **1** lacking stability **2** oscillating between two unstable states

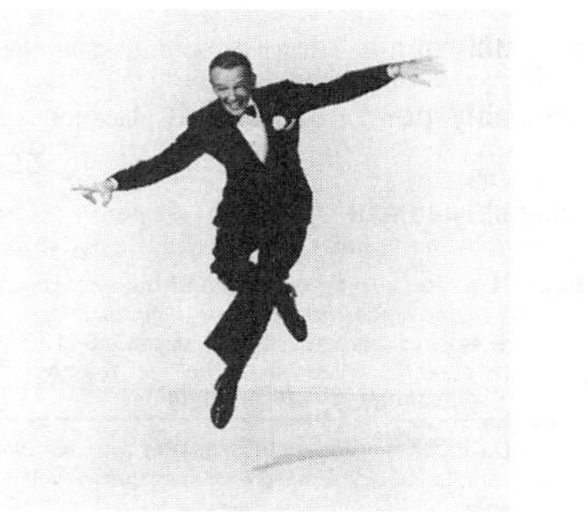

Fred Astaire

Astaire /ə stáir/, **Fred** (1899–1987) US dancer and actor. Born **Fred Austerlitz**

Astana /ə staána/ capital of Kazakhstan, in the north-central part of the country. Population: 287,000 (1993 estimate).

Astarte /ə staárti/ *n* ◊ **Ishtar**

astatic /ay státtik/ *adj* unsteady because of poor muscle coordination [Early 19C. < Greek *astatos* 'unstable' < *statos* 'standing'.] —**astatically** *adv* —**astaticism** /ay státtissizəm/ *n*

astatic galvanometer *n* an instrument for measuring electric current (**galvanometer**) that is not significantly affected by the Earth's magnetic field

astatine /ásstə teen/ *n* (*symbol* **At**) an unstable radioactive element, the heaviest in the halogen series. Source: bombardment of bismuth with alpha particles. Use: in medicine as a tracer. [Mid-20C. < Greek *astatos* (see ASTATIC).]

aster /ástər/ *n* **1** an annual plant of the daisy family. Flowers: white, pink, violet. **2** a star-shaped structure seen during cell division (**mitosis**) [Early 18C. Via Latin, < Greek *astēr* 'star'.]

-aster *suffix* one that is inferior ○ *criticaster* [< Latin]

asteriated /a steéri aytid/ *adj* describes a crystal that reflects light in a star shape [Early 19C. < Greek *asterios* 'starry' < *astēr* 'star'.]

asterisk /ástərisk/ *n* **1 STAR-SHAPED SYMBOL** a star-shaped symbol (*) used in printing **2 ASTERISK AS LINGUISTIC SYMBOL** in linguistics, an asterisk used to mark a sound, form, or structure that is believed to have existed but is unrecorded, or that is wrong or ungrammatical ■ *vt* **MARK SOMETHING WITH ASTERISK** to mark a printed or written item with an asterisk, especially to draw attention to it [14C. Via late Latin, < Greek *asteriskos* 'little star' < *astēr* 'star'.]

asterism /ástərizzm/ *n* **1 PRINTER'S MARK OF THREE ASTERISKS** a triangle formed of three asterisks that calls the reader's attention to a following passage **2 STAR CLUSTER** a cluster of stars smaller than a constellation **3 REFLECTION IN CRYSTALS** an optical effect appearing as a star in the light reflected from certain crystals [Late 16C. < Greek *asterismos* 'constellation' < *astēr* 'star'.]

astern /ə stúrn/ *adv* **1 IN OR TO THE STERN** in, on, to, or towards the stern of a ship or boat ○ *The deckhand walked astern.* **2 WITH STERN FOREMOST** into a position with the stern pointing in the direction of motion ○ *Bring the captain's gig astern.* ■ *adj* **BEHIND BOAT** positioned behind a boat ○ *The astern line has been cut.*

asteroid /ástə royd/ *n* **1** an irregularly shaped rock that orbits the Sun, mostly occurring in a band between the orbits of Mars and Jupiter **2** a starfish (*technical*) [Early 19C. < Greek *asteroeidēs* 'starlike' < *astēr* 'star'.] —**asteroidal** /ástə róyd'l/ *adj*

asteroid belt *n* a region of space where the density of asteroids is high, located between the orbits of Mars and Jupiter

asthenia /ass théeni ə/ *n* a condition marked by loss of strength in the body [Late 18C. < modern Latin, < Greek *asthenēs* (see ASTHENIC).]

asthenic /ass thénnik/ *adj* **1** showing marked physical weakness **2** having a slender and lightly muscled build [Late 18C. < Greek *asthenikos* < *asthenēs* 'without strength' < *sthenos* 'strength'.]

asthenosphere /ass thénnə sfeer/ *n* a weak zone in the upper part of the Earth's mantle where rock can be deformed in response to stress, resulting in movement of the overlying crust [Early 20C. < Greek *asthenēs* (see ASTHENIC) + SPHERE.]

asthma /ásmə/ *n* a disease of the respiratory system, sometimes caused by allergies, with symptoms including coughing, sudden difficulty in breathing, and a tight feeling in the chest [14C. Via medieval Latin, < Greek, < *azein* 'breathe hard'.]

asthmatic /ass máttik/ *adj* **1 WITH ASTHMA** affected with or prone to attacks of asthma **2 OF ASTHMA** relating to the respiratory difficulties associated with asthma ■ *n* **SOMEBODY WITH ASTHMA** somebody who is affected by asthma [Early 16C. Via Latin, < Greek *asthmatikos* < *asthma* (see ASTHMA).] —**asthmatically** *adv*

astigmatism /ə stígmətizəm/ *n* **1** a visual defect caused by the unequal curving of one or more of the refractive surfaces of the eye, usually the cornea **2** a defect in a lens or mirror that prevents light rays from meeting at a single point, producing an imperfect image [Mid-19C. < A-[2] + Greek *stigmat-* 'point'.] —**astigmatic** /ástig máttik/ *adj* —**astigmatically** *adv*

astilbe /ə stílbi/ (*plural* **-bes** *or* **-be**) *n* a perennial plant widely cultivated in shady damp gardens. Flowers: plume-shaped. Native to: E Asia. Genus: *Astilbe*. [Mid-19C. < modern Latin, 'not glittering' < Greek *a-* 'not' + *stilbos* 'glittering'.]

astir /ə stúr/ *adj* **1** awake and moving around, especially out of bed ○ *The children were astir early as usual.* **2** moving around ○ *leaves astir in the breeze*

Asti spumante /ásti spyoo mánti/ *n* sparkling white wine from Asti in NW Italy

Astley /ástli/, **Thea** (*b.* 1925) Australian novelist

astonish /ə stónnish/ *vt* to amaze somebody to a great degree [Early 16C. < *astone* (see ASTOUND).] —**astonishing** *adj* —**astonishingly** *adv*

astonishment /ə stónnishmənt/ *n* great amazement, often eliciting shock ○ *He was on time, to my astonishment.*

Astor /ástər/, **John Jacob** (1763–1848) German-born US fur trader and property millionaire

Astor, Nancy, Viscountess (1879–1964) US-born British politician. Born **Nancy Langhorne**

Astoria /ə stáwri ə/ city in NW Oregon. Population: 9,676 (1998 estimate).

astound /ə stównd/ *vt* to overwhelm and stun somebody with sudden surprise ○ *astounded by the viciousness of the attacks* [14C. Alteration of *astoned*, past participle of *astone* 'stun', via Old French *estoner* < assumed Vulgar Latin *extonare* 'thunder out'.] —**astounding** *adj* —**astoundingly** *adv*

astr- *prefix* = **astro-** (*before vowels*)

astraddle /ə strádd'l/ *prep, adv* with one leg or part on either side of something

astragal /ástrəg'l/ *n* **1** a narrow convex moulding, often taking the form of beads **2** *Scotland* any of the bars framing the individual panes that make up a window [Mid-17C. Via French, < Latin *astragalus* (see ASTRAGALUS).]

astragalus /ə strággələss/ (*plural* **-li** /-lee/) *n* ANAT = **talus**[2] *n*. [Mid-16C. Via Latin < Greek *astragalos*.]

astrakhan /ástrə kán, -kaán/ *n* fur fabric made from the curly dark fleece of lambs from Astrakhan, S Russia, or an acrylic imitation. Use: hats, trims on coats.

astral /ástrəl/ *adj* **1 ABOVE MATERIAL WORLD** in theosophical belief, belonging to the ethereal region that is believed to exist throughout and at a higher level than the material world **2 EXALTED** likened to stars, e.g. in height or distance from ordinary places or people ○ *the astral position of king or president* **3 RELATING TO STARS** relating to, characteristic of, or consisting of stars [Early 17C. < late Latin *astralis* < Greek *astron* (see ASTRO-).] —**astrally** *adv*

astral body *n* in theosophical belief, a second body, not directly perceivable by the human senses, believed to coexist with and survive the death of the physical body

astral plane *n* in theosophical belief, a level of existence where the spirit goes between death and entry into the spirit world

astral projection *n* in theosophical belief, the ability to send the astral body outside of the physical body, while both remain connected

astray /ə stráy/ *adv* **1 OFF RIGHT PATH** away from the right path **2 INTO ERROR OR SIN** in or into an evil or undesirable course of life ○ *led astray by unsuitable companions* ■ *adj Ireland* **UPSET** deeply upset and disturbed [13C. < Old French *estraie*, past participle of *estraier* 'stray'.] ◇ **go astray** to be mislaid or missing

astride /ə stríd/ *prep* **1 WITH LEGS AROUND** on top of and with a leg on each side of something ○ *astride a horse* **2 EXTENDING ACROSS** extending across in terms of influence or power ○ *a military colossus astride the world* ■ *adv* **WITH LEGS APART** with legs spread wide apart ○ *He stood with arms folded and legs astride*

astringent /ə strínjənt/ *n* a substance that draws tissue together ■ *adj* speaking or writing in a manner that is critical and hurtful in tone and content [Mid-16C. < Latin *astringent-*, present participle of *astringere* 'bind to' < *stringere* 'bind'.] —**astringency** *n* —**astringently** *adv*

astro-, astr- *prefix* **1** star, the stars, outer space ○ *astrobiology* **2** aster of a cell ○ *astrocyte* [< Greek < *astron* 'star' < *astēr* (see ASTER)]

astrobleme /ástrə bleem/ *n* a depression, usually circular, on the surface of the Earth that is caused by the impact of a meteorite [Mid-20C. < ASTRO- + Greek *blēma* 'wound from a missile'.]

astrochemistry /ástrō kémmistri/ *n* the chemistry of celestial bodies and interstellar space —**astrochemist** *n*

astrocompass /ástrō kumpəss/ *n* a nonmagnetic navigational instrument used to determine the position of true north relative to a celestial body

astrocyte /ástrə sīt/ *n* a star-shaped cell in the central nervous system's supportive tissue (**glia**)

astrocytoma /ástrə sī tṓmə/ (*plural* **-mas** *or* **-mata** /-mətə/) *n* a commonly occurring malignant brain tumour made up of star-shaped cells (**astrocytes**)

astrodome /ástrədōm/ *n* a transparent dome on an aircraft or spacecraft through which celestial observations are made in order to navigate

astrodynamics /ástrō dī námmiks/ *n* the study of the effects of gravitational and other forces on the motion of natural and artificial bodies in outer space (+ *singular verb*) —**astrodynamic** *adj*

astrogeology /ástrō ji óllәji/ *n* the study of the origin, history, and structure of cosmic bodies other than the Earth —**astrogeologist** *n*

astrol. *abbr* **1** astrologer **2** astrological **3** astrology

astrolabe /ástrə layb/ *n* an early instrument used to observe the position and determine the altitude of the Sun or other celestial body [14C. Via Old French and medieval Latin < Greek *astrolabon* 'take a star'.]

astrology /ə strólləji/ *n* the study of the positions of the Moon, Sun, and other planets in the belief that their motions affect human beings [14C. Via French, < Greek *astrologia* 'account of the stars' < *astron* (see ASTRO-) + *-logia* (see -LOGY).] —**astrologer** *n* —**astrological** /ástrə lójjik'l/ *adj* —**astrologically** *adv* —**astrologist** *n*

astrometry /ə strómmətri/ *n* the measurement of the real and apparent motions and the positions of celestial bodies —**astrometrical** /ástrə méttrik'l/ *adj*

astron. *abbr* **1** astronomer **2** astronomical **3** astronomy

astronaut /ástrə nawt/ *n* somebody trained to travel and perform tasks in space [Early 20C. < ASTRO-, after *aeronaut*.]

astronautics /ástrə náwtiks/ *n* **1** the science and technology of designing and building spacecraft (+ *singular verb*) **2** the skills and activities associated with the operation of a spacecraft (+ *plural verb*) [Early 20C. < ASTRO-, after *aeronautics*.] —**astronautic** *adj* —**astronautically** *adv*

astronavigation /ástrō navi gáysh'n/ *n* **1** = **celestial navigation** **2** the navigation of a spacecraft among celestial bodies, especially stars —**astronavigator** /ástrō návvi gaytər/ *n*

astronomical /ástrə nómmik'l/, **astronomic** *adj* **1** immeasurably numerous, high, or great (*informal*) ○ *reached astronomical proportions* **2** relating to astronomy —**astronomically** *adv*

astronomical clock *n* a clock that shows astronomical information such as the phases of the Moon

astronomical telescope *n* a telescope used to view celestial objects

astronomical twilight *n* the period of time during which the Sun is at 18° below the horizon

astronomical unit *n* a unit of astronomical distances, especially within the solar system, equal to the mean distance between the Earth and the Sun, about 150 million km/93 million mi

astronomical year *n* ASTRON = **solar year**

astronomy /ə strónnəmi/ *n* the scientific study of the universe, especially of the motions, positions, sizes, composition, and behaviour of celestial objects [13C. Via Old French and Latin, < Greek *astronomia* 'star-arranging' < *astron* (see ASTRO-) + *-nomia* (see -NOMY).] See illustration overleaf. —**astronomer** *n*

astrophotography /ástrō fə tóggrəfi/ *n* the art of photographing celestial objects and events for astronomical studies

astrophysics /ástrō fízziks/ *n* the study of the physical properties, origin, and development of celestial objects and events (+ *singular verb*) —**astrophysical** *adj* —**astrophysically** *adv* —**astrophysicist** *n*

AstroTurf /ástrō turf/ *tdmk* a trademark for synthetic turf resembling grass

Asturias /ə stóori əss/, **Miguel Angel** (1899–1974) Guatemalan writer

astute /ə styóot/ *adj* shrewd and discerning, especially where personal benefit is to be derived ○ *an astute investor* [Early 17C. < Latin *astutus* < *astus* 'cleverness, skill'.] —**astutely** *adv* —**astuteness** *n*

astylar /ay stílər/ *adj* describes a classical building that has no columns [Mid-19C. < Greek *astulos* 'without pillars' < *stulos* 'pillar'.]

Asuncion /ə soónssi ón/ capital of Paraguay, in the SW of the country. Population: 502,400 (1992).

asunder /ə súndər/ *adv* into separate parts, pieces, or places (*literary*) [Old English *onsundran* 'into parts' < *on* 'into' + *sundran* 'parts' < Germanic]

asura /ússoorə/ *n* in Hindu mythology, a member of a class of nonhuman beings who are enemies of heavenly beings [< Sanskrit, 'demon']

Asvina /áshvinə/ *n* in the Hindu calendar, the seventh month of the year, occurring approximately the same time as September to October

Aswan /a swaán/ city in S Egypt, on the River Nile, near the Aswan High Dam. Population: 220,000 (1992 estimate).

aswarm /ə swáwrm/ *adj* full of moving living beings

aswirl /ə swúrl/ *adj* moving with a swirling or twirling motion

aswoon /ə swoón/ *adj* experiencing a swoon or faint (*literary*)

ASX *abbr Aus* Australian Stock Exchange

asyllabic /áy si lábbik/ *adj* describes a speech sound that does not constitute a syllable

asylum /ə sílәm/ *n* **1 SHELTER AND PROTECTION** protection or safety from danger or imminent harm provided by a sheltered place ○ *They sought asylum in a neutral country.* **2 PROTECTION FROM EXTRADITION** protection and immunity from extradition **3 OFFENSIVE TERM** an offensive term for an institution for people with psychiatric disorders (*dated*) **4 PLACE OF SANCTUARY** a place that once offered shelter to criminals and debtors, especially a church [15C. Via Latin < Greek *asulon* 'refuge' < *asulos* 'without right of seizure' < *sulon* 'right of seizure'.]

asylum seeker *n* somebody who applies for asylum

asymmetric /ássi méttrik, áy si-/, **asymmetrical** /-méttrik'l/ *adj* **1 NOT SYMMETRIC** not arranged in a symmetrical way ○ *an asymmetric flower arrangement* **2 WITH PARTICULAR ATOMIC ARRANGEMENT** describes a carbon atom bonded to four different atoms or radicals whose arrangement in space may occur in two different configurations

KEY DATES IN ASTRONOMY

about 6500 BC	Earliest-known calendar marked on bone in Congo	1796–98	French astronomer Pierre-Simon Laplace theorizes that solar system formed by condensing gas, also postulates black holes
about 2770 BC	Egyptians develop first calendar with 365-day year		
about 2000 BC	Stonehenge built as astronomical observatory	1877	'Canals' first observed on Mars
6th century BC	Greek philosopher and mathematician Pythagoras proposes that Earth is spherical	1916	German-born US physicist Albert Einstein proposes that universe is curved owing to effects of gravitation
AD 1260	Observatory built in Beijing, China	1927	Belgian astrophysicist Georges-Henri Lemâitre publishes 'big bang' theory that universe began with explosion
1543	Polish astronomer Nicolaus Copernicus proposes idea that planets move around Sun	1929	US astronomer Edwin Hubble develops law of uniform expansion of universe
1609–19	German astronomer Johannes Kepler publishes three laws of planetary motion	1931	US engineer Karl Jansky discovers radio waves emitted in Milky Way, beginning of radio astronomy
1609	Italian scientist Galileo Galilei builds telescope and discovers phases of Venus, Saturn's rings, mountains on Moon	1970	First black hole located
		1986	Astronomers witness the birth of a star 500 light-years away
1668	English physicist Isaac Newton invents reflecting telescope, enabling greater magnification	1994	Hubble Space Telescope locates supermassive black hole at centre of M87 galaxy
1705	English astronomer Edmond Halley proves that comets orbit Sun	1998	Observations of supernovae in distant galaxies suggest that expansion of universe is actually accelerating
1755	German philosopher Immanuel Kant proposes that solar system is part of one of many larger systems, later called galaxies	1999	First multiple-planet system discovered outside solar system

(stereoisomerism) 3 WITH VARYING CONDUCTIVITY describes a substance or a device that exhibits varying or different conductivities for currents flowing through it in different directions **4 WITH UNEQUAL THRUST** unbalanced because of unequal thrust from two or more sources, e.g. when one engine of a pair is not functioning properly **5 NOT INTERCHANGEABLE** describes a relation between two things where the first has a relation to the second, but the second cannot have the same relation to the first —**asymmetrically** adv

⚡**asymmetrical digital subscriber line** n a high-speed telephone line that can transmit voice and video data over copper lines

asymmetry /a símmətri, ay-/ n **1** the condition of being asymmetric in arrangement ○ some asymmetry in the design **2** a relation between two things where the first has a relation to the second, but the second cannot have the same relation to the first. Asymmetry is illustrated in the statement 'A is the father of B', since B cannot be the father of A.

asymptomatic /áyssimptə máttik/ adj not showing or producing indications of a disease or other medical condition ○ The operation was successful, and she has remained asymptomatic ever since. —**asymptomatically** adv

asymptote /ássimptōt/ n a line that draws increasingly nearer to a curve without ever meeting it [Mid-17C. Via modern Latin, < Greek asumptōtos 'not adapted to fall together' < sun- 'together' + ptōtos 'adapted to fall'.] —**asymptotic** /ássimp tóttik/ adj —**asymptotically** adv

asynapsis /áy si nápsiss/ n the failure of chromosomes that are alike (**homologous**) to pair during cell division (**meiosis**)

⚡**asynchronism** /ay síngkrənizəm/, **asynchrony** /ay sínkrəni/ n in computing and electronics, the occurrence of two or more processes at different times —**asynchronous** adj —**asynchronously** adv

⚡**asynchronous communication** /ay síngkrənəss-/ n an electronic communication method that sends data in one direction, one character at a time

asyndeton /a síndítən, ə-/ (plural **-ta** /-tə/) n the leaving out of conjunctions in sentence constructions in which they would usually be used. ◊ **parataxis** [Mid-16C. Via late Latin, < Greek asundeton 'not bound together' < sundein 'bind together'.] —**asyndetic** /ássin déttik/ adj —**asyndetically** adv

asynergy /ay sínnərji/, **asynergia** /áy si núrji ə/ n a failure of coordination between different muscle groups so that delicate, skilled, or rapid movements become impossible [Mid-19C. < A-² + Greek sunergia (see SYNERGY).] —**asynergic** /áy si núrjik/ adj

asystole /ay sístəli/ n the absence of any heartbeat —**asystolic** /áy si stóllik/ adj

at[1] (stressed) /at/; (unstressed) /ət/ **CORE MEANING:** a preposition used to indicate general position or location. In order to be more precise about exact physical location, other prepositions such as 'on', 'over', 'under', and 'by' are used instead. ○ a conference at the school ○ Someone's at the door. ○ I work at home.

prep 1 ATTENDING attending regularly ○ not at school yet **2 FROM AN INTERVAL OF** describes the position of something by indicating its distance or angle ○ She followed them at a distance. **3 INDICATES WHEN SOMETHING HAPPENS** used to indicate the time or age when something happens ○ Lunch is at noon. **4 DURING AN EVENT** while present during an event ○ had a good time at the carnival **5 INDICATES RATE OR FREQUENCY** used to indicate the rate, frequency, level, or price of something ○ driving at 65 miles per hour **6 TOWARDS** towards or in the direction of somebody or something ○ He glanced over at her. **7 AS A REACTION TO** used to indicate what somebody is reacting to ○ amazed at what had happened **8 IN THE STATED ACTIVITY** used to indicate an activity or subject that a judgment about somebody relates to ○ an expert at windsurfing **9 IN A STATE OF** indicating the state or condition that somebody or some-thing is in ○ at risk of infection **10 DOING** engaged or occupied in ○ hard at work **11 IN THE MANNER OF** used to indicate how something is done ○ set off at a run **12 INDICATES REPEATED ACTIONS** used to indicate the object of a repeated action ○ She just picks at her food. **13 ACCORDING TO SOMEBODY'S WISHES** in response to or based on some-body's wish or decision ○ Spend this money at your discretion. [Old English æt < Indo-European] ◊ **at all 1** in any way, to any extent, or under any conditions ○ don't like it at all **2** in any way ◊ **at that 1** in addition ○ It was a coincidence, and a happy one at that. **2** nevertheless, or in spite of something else ○ It just might work at that. **3** at a specific point or place ○ I think we'll leave it at that for today. ◊ **where it's** or **something is at** where all the action and excitement is happening (informal)

PUNCTUATION use of **@**: The symbol **@** means at, and until the 1990s it was mainly used in commercial or technical contexts: 25 kg @ £3.50 per kg; 150 miles @ 30 mph. Its most familiar use today, however, is in e-mail addresses, where it usually comes between the user's personal screen name and the domain name of his or her organization or Internet service provider: rtjackson@scotrack.com.

⚡**at**[2] abbr Austria (in Internet addresses)

At symbol astatine

AT abbr **1** antitank **2** attainment target **3** Atlantic Time

at. abbr **1** atomic **2** atmosphere

at-[1] = **ad-** [< Latin ad-]

at-[2] prefix = **ad-** (before t-)

Atacama Desert /áttə kaámə-/ dry plateau in N Chile. Area: 363,000 sq. km/140,000 sq. mi.

ataghan n ARMS = **yataghan**

at-a-glance adj presenting information in a clear and simple form so that it can be understood very quickly

Atahualpa /áttə waálpə/ (1500?–33) Inca king (1532–33)

ataman /áttəmən, -man/ n a Cossack chieftain [Mid-19C. Via Russian < Turkic, 'great father'.]

Atanasoff /ə tánnə sof/, **John V.** (1903–95) US math-ematical physicist

ataractic /áttə ráktik/, **ataraxic** /-ráksik/ adj describes a drug or other agent that tranquillizes ■ n a tranquillizer (technical) [Mid-20C. < Greek ataraktos 'not disturbed' < tarassein 'disturb'.]

ataraxia /áttə ráksi ə/ n freedom from worry or any other preoccupation [Mid-19C. < Greek, < ataraktos (see ATARACTIC).]

ataraxic adj, n MED = **ataractic**

AKG London

Mustafa Kemal Atatürk

Atatürk /áttə turk/, **Kemal** (1881–1938) Turkish statesman. Born **Mustafa Kemal Pasha**

atavism /áttəvizəm/ n **1** the recurrence of a genetically controlled feature in an organism after it has been absent for several generations, usually because of an accidental recombination of genes **2** atavism, atavist an individual showing atavism [Mid-19C. < French ata-visme < Latin atavus 'beyond a grandfather' < avus 'grand-father'.]

atavistic /áttə vístik/ adj **1** relating to or displaying the recurrence of a genetic feature that has been absent for several generations **2** relating to or displaying the kind of behaviour that seems to be a product of impulses long since suppressed by society's rules —**atavistically** adv

ataxia /ə táksi ə/, **ataxy** /ə táksi/ n the inability to co-ordinate the movements of muscles [Late 19C. Via modern Latin < Greek, 'without order' < *taxis* (see TAXIS).] —**ataxic** adj

ATB abbr all-terrain bike

ATC abbr 1 air-traffic control 2 Air Training Corps

ate past tense of **eat**

-ate suffix 1 having, characterized by ○ *lobate* 2 office, rank ○ *archdeaconate* 3 to act on in a particular way ○ *fluoridate* 4 a chemical compound derived from a particular element or compound ○ *borate* [< Latin *-atus*, past participle ending of verbs in *-are*]

A-team n a group of people who are the very best of their type

atelectasis /áttə léktəssiss/ n 1 a partial or total collapse of a lung 2 a condition in which the lungs fail to expand completely at birth [Mid-19C. < Greek *atelēs* 'incomplete' + *ektasis* 'extension'.]

atelier /ə télli ay/ n a studio or workshop where an artist works [Late 17C. < French, 'carpenter's workshop' < late Latin *astella* 'board'.]

a tempo /aa témpō/ adv, adj in or back into a previous musical tempo (*musical direction*) [< Italian, 'in time']

atemporal /ay témpərəl/ adj independent of or unaffected by time

~~atempt~~ incorrect spelling of **attempt**

atenolol /ə ténnə lol/ n a drug. Use: blood pressure control and angina management.

Athabasca /áthə báskə/ river in Alberta, Canada. Length: 1,231 km/765 mi.

Athabasca, Lake lake in N Alberta and N Saskatchewan, Canada. Area: 7,936 sq. km/3,064 sq. mi.

Athabaskan /áthə báskən/, **Athapaskan** /-páskən/ n 1 a group of Na-Dene languages spoken in NW Canada and parts of Alaska, Oregon, and California. Native speakers: 180,000. 2 a member of an Athabaskan-speaking people [Mid-19C. After Lake ATHABASCA.] —**Athabaskan** adj

Athanasian Creed /áthə náyzh'n-, -náysh'n-/ n a 5th-century Christian statement of belief of unknown authorship, formerly attributed to St Athanasius, Greek patriarch of Alexandria

Athanasius /áthə náyshəss/, **St** (293?–373?) Greek theologian and prelate

Athapaskan n, adj LANG = **Athabaskan**

atheism /áythi izəm/ n disbelief in the existence of God or deities [Late 16C. < French *athéisme* < Greek *atheos* 'godless' < *theos* 'god'.]

atheist /áythi ist/ n somebody who does not believe in God or deities

atheistic /áythi ístik/, **atheistical** /-ístik'l/ adj relating to or characteristic of atheists or atheism —**atheistically** adv

~~athelete~~ incorrect spelling of **athlete**

atheling /áthəling/ n an Anglo-Saxon nobleman or prince, usually the heir to a throne [Old English *æpeling* < Germanic, 'noble']

Athelstan /áthəlstən/ (895?–939) king of Wessex and Mercia (926?–939)

athematic /áthi máttik, áy thee-/ adj describes music that is not based on themes or tunes

Athena /ə theenə/, **Athene** /ə theeni/ n in Greek mythology, the goddess of wisdom and warfare, and the patron goddess of Athens. Roman equivalent **Minerva**

athenaeum /áthi nee əm/ n 1 an institution that encourages learning, e.g. an academy of science 2 any institution where reading materials are made available to the public, e.g. a library [Mid-18C. Via Latin < *Athēnaion*, the temple of Athena in Athens, used for teaching.]

Athenagoras I /ə theenə gáwrəss/ (1886–1972) Greek religious leader

Athene n MYTHOL = **Athena**

atheneum n US = **athenaeum**

Athens /áthənz/ capital of Greece, in the SE of the country. Population: 772,072 (1991). —**Athenian** /ə theeni ən/ adj, n

atheoretical /áytheər réttik'l/ adj without a theoretical basis

atherogenesis /áthərō jénnəssiss/ n the origination and formation of fatty deposits (**atheromas**) in arteries [Mid-20C. < ATHEROMA + -GENESIS.] —**atherogenic** adj —**atherogenicity** /áthərōjə níssəti/ n

atheroma /áthə rōmə/ n (*plural* **-mas** or **-mata** /-mətə/) n an accumulation in the inner lining of an artery of a plaque of cholesterol and other constituents (**atheromatous plaque**) [Late 16C. Via Latin, < Greek *athērōma < athērē* 'porridge', from its texture.] —**atheromatosis** /áthərōmə tōssiss/ n —**atheromatous** /áthə rómmətəss, -rōmətəss/ adj

atherosclerosis /áthərōsklə róssiss/ n a common arterial disease in which raised areas of degeneration and cholesterol deposits (**plaques**) form on the inner surfaces of the arteries obstructing blood flow [Early 20C. < ATHEROMA + SCLEROSIS.] —**atherosclerotic** /-sklə róttik/ adj —**atherosclerotically** adv

Atherton /áthərtən/, **Mike** (b. 1968) British cricketer. Full name **Michael Andrew Atherton**

athetosis /áthə tōssiss/ n a condition characterized by involuntary slow movements of the fingers, toes, hands, and feet and usually caused by a brain lesion [Late 19C. < Greek *athetos* 'without a place' < *tithenai* 'to place'.]

~~athiest~~ incorrect spelling of **atheist**

athirst /ə thúrst/ adj 1 eager or longing for something (*literary*) 2 thirsty (*archaic*) [Old English *ofpyrst < past participle of *ofpyrstan* 'thirst greatly' < *þurst* (see THIRST)]

athlete /áth leet/ n 1 somebody with the abilities to participate in physical exercise, especially in competitive games and races 2 a competitor in track or field events [15C. Via Latin, < Greek *athlētēs < athlein* 'contend for a prize'.]

athlete's foot n a contagious fungal infection affecting the feet

athletic /ath léttik/ adj 1 relating to athletes, athletics, or other sports activities ○ *athletic uniforms* 2 possessing a large skeletal structure and having strong muscles ○ *an athletic build* [Early 17C. Via French and Latin < Greek *athlētikos < athlētēs* (see ATHLETE).] —**athletically** adv —**athleticism** n

athletics /ath léttiks/ n 1 TRACK-AND-FIELD EVENTS sports activities carried out on a field, e.g. discus, high jump, and long jump, or on a track, e.g. running (+ *singular or plural verb*) US term **track and field** 2 US SPORTS ACTIVITIES activities such as sports and exercises that require physical skill and strength (+ *singular or plural verb*) 3 METHODS OF ATHLETIC TRAINING the methods, systems, or principles of training and practice for activities involving athletics (+ *plural verb*)

athletic support n SPORTS, CLOTHING = **jockstrap**

athodyd /áthədid/ n a simple tubular jet engine [Mid-20C. Contraction of *aero-thermodynamic duct*.]

at-home n an informal social gathering in somebody's own home

athwart /ə thwáwrt/ prep 1 so as to be across or positioned crosswise over something 2 so as to oppose or obstruct something

athwartships /ə thwáwrtships/ adv from one side of a ship to the other

atilt /ə tílt/ adv, adj in or into a slanting position ○ *Her hat was atilt on her head.*

atingle /ə ting g'l/ adj feeling a tingling sensation, often associated with excitement ○ *atingle with anticipation*

-ation suffix an action or process, or the result of it ○ *alienation* [Via French < Latin *-ation-*, forming nouns from verbs in *-are*]

~~atitude~~ incorrect spelling of **attitude**

-ative suffix having a particular characteristic ○ *argumentative* [Via French < Latin *-ativus < -atus* (see -ATE)]

Atkinson /átkins'n/, **Sir Harry** (1831–92) British-born New Zealand statesman

Atlanta /at lántə/ capital of Georgia, United States. Population: 403,819 (1998 estimate).

atlantes /at lán teez/ plural of **atlas** n. 3

Atlantic /ət lántik/ adj relating to or situated in or near the Atlantic Ocean ■ n 1 = **Atlantic Ocean** 2 a group of West African languages, often considered to be related and to belong to the Niger-Congo language family [15C. Via Latin, < Greek *Atlantikos < Atlas* (see ATLAS).]

Atlantic City city in SE New Jersey. Population: 38,063 (1998 estimate).

Atlantic Intracoastal Waterway /-intrə cṓst'l-/ system of protected inland waterways along the US Atlantic coast

Atlanticism /ət lántissizəm/ n a doctrine assuming that both W Europe and the United States can benefit politically and economically from cooperation, especially in military matters —**Atlanticist** n

Atlantic Ocean, Atlantic world's second largest ocean, separating Europe and Africa from North and South America. Area: 82,362,000 sq. km/31,800,000 sq. mi.

Atlantic Provinces Canadian provinces of New Brunswick, Nova Scotia, Prince Edward Island, and Newfoundland

Atlantic Rim n those regions that have shores on the Atlantic Ocean, especially the north Atlantic

Atlantic salmon n the flesh of an Atlantic salmon as food

Atlantic Standard Time, Atlantic Time n the standard time in the fourth time zone west of Greenwich, reckoned at 60° West. It is used e.g. in Puerto Rico and the Canadian Maritime Provinces.

Atlantis /at lántiss, ət-/ n in ancient mythology, an idyllic island that sank in an earthquake

atlas /átlass/ n 1 MAP BOOK a book containing maps and vital statistics relating to geographical regions 2 TOP BONE IN THE NECK the vertebra that is at the top of the spinal column and supports the skull 3 (*plural* **-lantes**) FIGURE OF MAN USED AS SUPPORT a figure of a man, either standing or kneeling, used as a support for the upper part of a classical building [Late 16C. < Greek.]

Atlas[1] /átlass/ n in Greek mythology, a Titan who was forced by Zeus to support the heavens on his shoulders as a punishment

Atlas[2] /átlass/ n a small natural satellite of Saturn, discovered in 1980

atlas moth n a large moth with a wingspan of 25 cm/10 in or more and strongly hooked and boldly patterned wings. Native to: tropical Asia and Australia. *Attacus atlas*.

Atlas Mountains /átləss-/ system of mountain ranges in Morocco, Algeria, and Tunisia. Highest peak: Jebel Toubkal 4,165 m/13,665 ft.

atlatl /át latt'l/ n a spear-throwing device, usually a stick fitted with a thong or socket, used to steady the butt of the spear during the throwing motion [Late 19C. < Nahuatl *ahtlatl*.]

ATM n BANKING = **cashpoint** [Acronym for *automated teller machine*]

atm. abbr 1 atmosphere 2 atmospheric

atman /aatmən/ n in Hinduism, the essence of an individual [Late 18C. < Sanskrit *ātman* 'breath, spirit'.]

Atman /aatmən/ n in Hinduism, Brahman regarded as the Universal Soul

atmo- prefix gas, vapour [< Greek *atmos* 'breath, vapour' < Indo-European, 'to blow']

atmosphere /átməss feer/ n 1 GAS AROUND CELESTIAL BODY the mixture of gases that surrounds a celestial body such as the Earth. See illustration overleaf. 2 AIR OR CLIMATE the air or climate in a given place 3 MOOD OR TONE a prevailing emotional tone or attitude, especially one associated with a specific place or time ○ '*The atmosphere of the place was heavy and mouldy, being rendered additionally oppressive by the closing of the door which led into the church*'. (Wilkie Collins, *The Woman in White*; 1860) 4 MOOD OR TONE OF ARTWORK the prevailing tone or mood of a work of art 5 INTERESTING MOOD OF PLACE an interesting or exciting mood existing in a particular place ○ *a jazz club with lots of atmosphere* 6 UNIT OF PRESSURE a unit of pressure defined as the pressure that will support a 760 mm column of mercury at 0°C at sea level, equal to 1.01325 x 10⁵ newtons per square metre [Mid-17C. < modern Latin *atmosphaera* 'sphere of vapour' < Greek *atmos* (see ATMO-) + Latin *sphaera* (see SPHERE).]

atmospheric /átmoss férrik/, **atmospherical** /-férrik'l/ adj 1 relating to the atmosphere of a celestial body or of a particular place ○ *atmospheric pollution* 2 evoking or producing an emotional tone or aesthetic quality ○ *a mural with a misty atmospheric effect* —**atmospherically** adv

atmospheric pressure n the downward pressure exerted by the weight of the overlying atmosphere

atmospherics /átməss férriks/ n STUDY OF ATMOSPHERIC INTERFERENCE the study of electromagnetic radiation em-

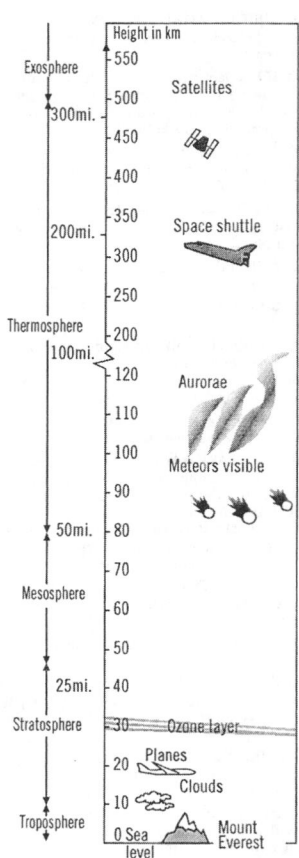

Height in km

550	Exosphere	Satellites
300mi. 500		
450		
400		
200mi. 350	Space shuttle	
300		
250		
Thermosphere 200		
100mi. 120	Aurorae	
110		
100	Meteors visible	
90		
50mi. 80		
70		
Mesosphere 60		
50		
25mi. 40		
Stratosphere 30	Ozone layer	
20	Planes	
10	Clouds	
Troposphere 0 Sea level		Mount Everest

Atmosphere: Divisions of the
Earth's atmosphere

anating from natural sources in the atmosphere (+ *singular verb*) ∎ *npl* (+ *plural verb*) **1 ATMOSPHERIC INTERFERENCE WITH ELECTRONIC SIGNALS** static on a radio or flickering white spots (**snow**) on a television screen caused by electromagnetic radiation from natural sources in the atmosphere **2 PREVAILING MOOD** the mood or atmosphere suffusing a situation, group, or place

at. no. *abbr* atomic number

ATOL *abbr* Air Travel Organizers' Licence

atoll /áttol, ə tól/ *n* a ring-shaped coral reef and small island, enclosing a lagoon and surrounded by open sea (*often in placenames*) ○ *Bikini Atoll* [Early 17C. < Maldivian *atolu*.]

atom /áttəm/ *n* **1 SMALLEST PART OF ELEMENT** the smallest portion into which an element can be divided and still retain its properties, made up of a dense, positively charged nucleus surrounded by a system of electrons **2 VERY SMALL AMOUNT** a very small part or amount ○ *not an atom of truth* **3 PARTICLE OF MATTER IN GREEK PHILOSOPHY** the basic particle of matter, indestructible and indivisible, first proposed by ancient Greek philosophers as the fundamental component of the universe [16C. Via Latin *atomus* < Greek *atomos* 'unable to be cut' < *temnein* 'to cut'.]

atom bomb *n* an explosive device whose great destructive power is due to the uncontrollable release of energy from the fission of heavy nuclei, such as uranium-235 or plutonium-239, by neutrons sustaining a rapid chain reaction. US term **atomic bomb**

atomic /ə tómmik/ *adj* **1 BASED ON NUCLEAR ENERGY** based on or using nuclear energy **2 RELATING TO ATOM** relating to an atom or atoms ○ *atomic theory* **3 TINY** extremely small **4 UNANALYSABLE** describes a proposition, sentence, or

formula that cannot be analysed into a coherent structure —**atomically** *adv*

atomic bomb *n* PHYS = **atom bomb**

atomic clock *n* an extremely accurate timekeeping device regulated by the natural regular oscillations of an atom or molecule

atomic cocktail *n* a radioactive substance in liquid form, used to diagnose or treat cancer (*informal*)

atomic energy *n* PHYS = **nuclear energy**

atomic heat *n* a value obtained by multiplying the specific heat of an element by its relative atomic mass

atomicity /áttə míssəti/ *n* **1** the number of atoms in a molecule of a chemical element **2** the state of being composed of atoms **3** CHEM = **valency** *n*. **1**

atomic mass *n* PHYS = **relative atomic mass**

atomic mass unit *n* (*symbol* **u**) a unit used to express the masses of atoms and molecules, equal to one-twelfth of the mass of a carbon-12 atom or about 1.660 x 10^{-27} kg

atomic number *n* (*symbol* **Z**) the number of protons in the nucleus of an atom of an element and its isotopes, used to determine that element's position in the periodic table ○ *The atomic number of carbon is 6.*

atomic particle *n* any of the particles making up an atom, namely the proton, electron, or neutrons

atomic physics *n* the physics of elementary particles and their interactions and processes

atomic radius *n* a length equal to half the distance between the nuclei of two covalently bonded atoms

atomic structure *n* the composition of the atom, consisting of a small, dense, positively-charged nucleus surrounded by a cloud of electrons in defined orbits

QUICK FACTS ON... **ATOMIC STRUCTURE**

Key elements: the atom (the smallest unit of an element having the properties of that element) consists of a nucleus that contains protons and neutrons and together with its system of electrons in various orbits has a diameter of approximately 10^{-8} cm. Atoms usually do not divide in chemical reactions except for the transfer or exchange of electrons. Electrons in the outermost orbits determine the atom's chemical and electrical properties

Key dates: 5th century BC Greek philosophers Leucippus and Democritus propose the particle theory of matter; 1808 Dalton concludes that all atoms of an element have exactly the same size and relative atomic mass; 1897 Thomson discovers the electron; 1911 Rutherford proposes an atom with a positively charged nucleus surrounded by negatively charged electrons in orbit; 1913 Bohr incorporates quantum theory; 1923 de Broglie proposes that all matter and radiations have both particle- and wave-like characteristics; 1938 Hahn and Strassman discover nuclear fission; 1945 US scientists produce the first atom bomb

atomic theory *n* any theory proposing that matter is composed of atoms

atomic weight *n* relative atomic mass

atomise *vti* = **atomize**

atomism /áttəmizəm/ *n* **1** the theory that all matter in the universe is made up of small, individual, finite, and indivisible particles **2** a theory of psychological states that attempts to reduce them to simple elements —**atomist** *n* —**atomistic** /áttə místik/ *adj* —**atomistically** *adv*

atomize /áttə mīz/ (**-izes**, **-izing**, **-ized**), **atomise** (**-ises**, **-ising**, **-ised**) *v* **1** *vt* **SEPARATE SOMETHING INTO ATOMS** to reduce something to atoms or separate something into free atoms **2** *vti* **MAKE INTO SPRAY** to convert a liquid into fine particles or to spray particles converted in this way **3** *vt* **DESTROY** to destroy something with atomic weapons —**atomization** /áttə mī záysh'n/ *n*

atomizer /áttə mīzər/, **atomiser** *n* a device that converts a liquid into a fine spray

atom smasher *n* a device that speeds up subatomic particles (*informal*)

atonal /ay tón'l/ *adj* describes music in which the notes are not related by any mode or key. ◊ **tonal** *adj*. **2** —**atonally** *adv*

atonalism /ay tón'lizəm/ *n* the process of composing music in an atonal style or using atonality —**atonalist** *n, adj*

atonality /áy tō nálləti/ *n* in music, the fact of consisting of notes that are not related by any mode or key. ◊ **tonality** *n*. **2**

atone /ə tốn/ (**atones**, **atoning**, **atoned**) *vi* to make reparation for a sin or a mistake (*formal*) ○ *< at one* 'in agreement', as in *(set) at one* 'reconcile'.] —**atonable** *adj* —**atoner** *n*

atonement /ə tốnmənt/ *n* **1** the making of reparation for a sin or a mistake **2 atonement, Atonement** in Christian belief, the reconciliation between God and people brought about by the death of Jesus Christ

atonic /ay tónnik/ *adj* **1** describes a syllable or sound that is not accented or stressed **2** connected with, caused by, or showing a lack of muscle tone [Mid-18C. < TONIC and ATONY.] —**atonicity** /áytə níssəti/ *n*

atony /átt'ni/ *n* **1** lack of stress or accent **2** lack of normal muscle tone [Late 17C. Via French or late Latin *atonia* 'weakness' < Greek < *atonos* 'lacking tone' < *tonos* (see TONE).]

atop /ə tóp/ *prep, adv* on or at the top of something

atopic /ay tóppik, ə-/ *adj* describes a condition that is caused by a hereditary tendency to react to certain allergens, as in hay fever, some skin irritations, and asthma [Early 20C. < Greek *atopia* 'unusualness' < *atopos* 'out of place' < *topos* 'place'.] —**atopy** /áttəpi/ *n*

-ator *suffix* something or somebody that acts in a given way ○ *demonstrator* —**-atory** *suffix*

ATP[1] *n* a chemical compound (**nucleotide**) in living organisms that releases energy for cellular reactions when it converts to ADP. Full form **adenosine triphosphate**

ATP[2] *abbr* Association of Tennis Professionals

ATPase /áy tee pèe ayz, -ayss/ *abbr* adenosine triphosphatase

atrabilious /áttrə bílli əss/ *adj* (*literary*) **1** tending to feel very sad **2** inclined to peevishness and irritability [Mid-17C. < Latin *atra bilis* 'black bile' (translation of Greek *melankholia*), the bodily fluid thought to cause sadness and irritability.] —**atrabiliousness** *n*

atracurium besylate /áttrə kyoori əm bə síllat/ *n* a drug administered intravenously that acts as a neuromuscular blocking agent. Use: anesthesia.

atrazine /áttrə zeen/ *n* $C_8H_{14}N_5Cl$ a white compound. Use: agricultural herbicide. [Mid-20C. < Latin *atr-* 'black' (because it prevents photosynthesis) + TRIAZINE.]

atremble /ə trémb'l/ *adj* shaking or trembling from a strong emotion such as fear or excitement (*literary*)

atresia /ə treézi ə, -zhə/ *n* the often hereditary absence of a usual body opening such as the anus or ear canal [Early 19C. < A-[2] + Greek *trēsis* 'perforation'.]

Atreus /áytri əss/ *n* in Greek mythology, king of Mycenae and father of Agamemnon and Menelaus

atria plural of **atrium**

atrial fibrillation /áytri əl-/ *n* an irregularity in heartbeat (**arrhythmia**) caused by involuntary contractions of small areas of heart-wall muscle

atrioventricular /áytri ō ven tríkyōölər/ *adj* relating to the atria and ventricles of the heart or to their interconnection [Mid-19C. < ATRIUM + VENTRICULAR.]

atrip /ə tríp/ *adj* describes an anchor that has just been raised clear of the sea bottom

at-risk *adj* exposed to danger or harm of some kind

atrium /áytri əm/ (*plural* **-ums** *or* **-a** /-ə/) *n* **1 CENTRAL HALL WITH SKYLIGHT** a central hall usually with a glass roof or skylight and extending the full height or several storeys of a building **2 ROMAN COURTYARD** the open central courtyard of an ancient Roman house **3 BODY CHAMBER OR CAVITY** a cavity or chamber of the body, especially one of the upper chambers of the heart that takes blood from the veins and pumps it into a ventricle [Late 16C. < Latin.]

atrocious /ə trốshəss/ *adj* **1** appallingly bad ○ *atrocious manners* **2** extremely evil or cruel ○ *atrocious crimes* [Mid-17C. < Latin *atroc-* < *atrox* 'dark' < *ater* 'dark'.] —**atrociously** *adv* —**atrociousness** *n*

atrocity /ə tróssəti/ (*plural* **-ties**) *n* **1 SHOCKINGLY CRUEL ACT** a shockingly cruel act, especially an act of wanton violence against an enemy in wartime ○ *to deplore the atrocities of war* **2 EXTREME CRUELTY** extreme evil or cruelty ○ *an act of atrocity* **3 SOMETHING VERY BAD** something repellent or extremely bad of its kind [Mid-16C. Directly or via French < Latin *atrocitas* < *atrox* (see ATROCIOUS).]

atrophic vaginitis *n* inflammation of the vagina (**vaginitis**) caused by oestrogen deficiency and characterized by thinning and shrinking of the tissues of the vagina

atrophy /áttrəfi/ *n* 1 WASTING AWAY the shrinking in size of some part or organ of the body, usually caused by injury, disease, or lack of use 2 LESSENING OF ABILITY weakening or lessening of some ability ■ *vi* (-phies, -phying, -phied) WEAKEN to weaken or waste away through disuse or the effects of disease [Early 17C. Via late Latin *atrophia* < Greek, 'lack of food' < *trophē* 'food'.] —**atrophic** /a tróffik/ *adj*

atropine /áttrə peen, -pin/, **atropin** /-pin/ *n* a poisonous alkaloid obtained from the belladonna plant. Use: muscle relaxant. [Mid-19C. < modern Latin *Atropa*, genus name of belladonna.]

Atropos /áttrə poss/ *n* in Greek mythology, one of the Fates, who were three goddesses who influenced human destiny. Atropos was known as the Inexorable, and carried the shears that cut the thread of life. ◊ **Clotho, Lachesis**

ATS *abbr* Applications Technology Satellite

ϟ **ATST** *abbr* at the same time (*in e-mails*)

att. *abbr* 1 attached 2 attention 3 attorney

attaboy /áttə boy/ *interj US* used to express enthusiastic encouragement or approval to a man or boy (*slang*) [Early 20C. Alteration of *That's the boy!*]

attach /ə tách/ *v* 1 *vt* SECURE SOMETHING TO SOMETHING ELSE to secure one thing to another ○ *attached the door to the frame* 2 *vt* ADD SOMETHING TO SOMETHING ELSE to append one thing to another as a separate piece, the two being held together ○ *attached copies of the contracts* 3 *vt* ASCRIBE to assign a certain character or quality to something under consideration ○ *I attach no importance whatsoever to their claims.* 4 *vi* BE ASSOCIATED WITH to have a close inherent relationship to something ○ *little prestige attached to this post* 5 *vr* JOIN IN WITH to join and go along with somebody or something, often without an invitation 6 *vt* PLACE SOMEBODY ON TEMPORARY DUTY to assign military personnel to a military group on a temporary basis 7 *vt* SEIZE SOMETHING LEGALLY to seize people or property by legal writ ○ *They've attached her salary for nonpayment of taxes.* 8 *vt* BIND EMOTIONALLY to bind somebody emotionally to somebody else or to something (*usually passive*) [14C. < Old French *atachier*, alteration of *estachier* 'fasten with a stake' < Germanic.] —**attachable** *adj* —**attacher** *n*

attaché /ə tásh ay/ *n* somebody on the staff of a diplomatic mission who has responsibilities in a specific area [Early 19C. < French, past participle of *attacher* 'attach'.]

attaché case *n* a hard flat rectangular briefcase used for carrying business documents

attached /ə tácht/ *adj* 1 ENCLOSED fastened to or enclosed with something else ○ *Please see the attached documents and call if you have any questions.* 2 DEVOTED devoted to or fond of somebody or something 3 COMMITTED EMOTIONALLY TO committed to an emotional relationship with somebody else (*informal*) 4 TOUCHING ANOTHER STRUCTURE sharing a wall with another building, and thus not standing alone 5 *Malaysia, Singapore* EMPLOYED having a permanent job with a person or organization ○ *My brother is attached to the Ministry.*

ϟ **attachment** /ə táchmənt/ *n* 1 PART ATTACHED an accessory attached or to be attached to a machine 2 MEANS OF ATTACHING a means by which something is attached to something else 3 EMOTIONAL BOND an emotional bond or tie to somebody or something 4 ATTACHED TEXT a document or file attached to another or to an e-mail message 5 ACT OF ATTACHING the action of attaching one thing to another 6 LEGAL SEIZURE the legal seizure of people or property, especially to acquire jurisdiction over them or it

attachment of earnings *n* a court order directing a third party, usually an employer, to withhold somebody's wages in order to satisfy unpaid debts or to pay maintenance to the person's former spouse

attack /ə ták/ *v* 1 *vti* HARM to try to harm somebody by using violence or try to defeat an enemy or capture an enemy position 2 *vt* CRITICIZE to subject somebody or something to strong or vehement criticism ○ *The press has repeatedly attacked his plan.* 3 *vti* INFECT SOMEBODY OR DAMAGE to cause an infection, illness, or damage in somebody or something ○ *The disease can attack at any age.* 4 *vt* MAKE A VIGOROUS START ON to begin something such as work with enthusiasm or determination and deal vigorously with it 5 *vti* TRY TO WIN to attempt to defeat, or score against, an opponent or an opposing team in a competitive game or team sport ○ *The chess game began sluggishly, with both sides slow to attack.* ■ *n* 1 ACTION OF ATTACKING the process or an instance of attacking ○ *The proposals have come under attack.* 2 BOUT OF ILLNESS an occurrence of something such as a medical disorder that is temporarily debilitating ○ *an attack of asthma* 3 ATTACKING MEMBERS OF TEAM the attacking members of a team, especially the forwards in a football team (+ *singular or plural verb*) 4 ENERGETIC WAY OF PLAYING the decisive or energetic way in which a musician begins to play a piece or passage [Early 17C. Via French *attaquer* < Italian *attacare battaglia* 'join battle'.] —**attacker** *n*

attack dog *n* 1 a powerful dog of a breed that is naturally fierce and aggressive, or is trained to be so 2 an aggressive proponent, mouthpiece, or supporter of a politician or political party (*slang*)

attain /ə táyn/ *vt* 1 to achieve a goal or desired state, usually with effort 2 to reach a specified age, speed, or size [13C. Via Old French *ataindre* < Latin *attingere* 'reach to' < *tangere* 'to touch'.] —**attainability** /ə táynə bíllәti/ *n* —**attainable** *adj* —**attainableness** *n*

SYNONYMS See ***accomplish***.

attainder /ə táyndər/ *n* formerly, the removal of the rights or the confiscation of the property of somebody outlawed or sentenced to death for a serious crime, often treason [15C. < Anglo-Norman, variant of Old French *ataindre* 'affect, dishonour' (see ATTAIN).]

attainment /ə táynmənt/ *n* 1 the achievement of the goals that somebody has set 2 a skill, accomplishment, or distinction, especially one achieved through effort (*often plural*)

attainment target *n* the required level of ability that schoolchildren should demonstrate in any subject at certain key stages in the National Curriculum

attaint /ə táynt/ *vt* formerly, to take away the civil rights of somebody outlawed or sentenced to death for committing a serious crime, often treason (*archaic; often passive*) [14C. < Old French *atainte*, feminine past participle of *ataindre* 'affect, dishonour' (see ATTAIN).]

attapulgite /áttə púlgīt/ *n* a hydrated silicate of aluminium and magnesium. Use: in filters, an absorbent in medicine.

attar /áttər, á taar/, **atar** *n* essential oil extracted from flowers, especially rose petals ○ *attar of roses* [Mid-17C. < Arabic dialect *aṭar*.]

attempt /ə témpt/ *vti* TRY TO DO to try to do something, especially without much expectation of success ■ *n* 1 EFFORT TO DO an act of trying to do something ○ *a successful attempt at cooking* 2 ATTACK an attack or assault ○ *an attempt on his life* [14C. Via Old French, < Latin *attemptare* 'try for' < *temptare* 'to try, test'.] —**attemptable** *adj* —**attempter** *n*

SYNONYMS See ***try***.

Attenborough /átt'nbərə/, **Sir David** (*b.* 1926) British naturalist and broadcaster

Attenborough, Sir Richard, Baron Attenborough of Richmond-upon-Thames (*b.* 1923) British actor and director

attend /ə ténd/ *v* 1 *vti* GO TO EVENT to go to or be present at an event ○ *Hundreds attended the wedding.* 2 *vti* REGULARLY GO TO SPECIFIC ESTABLISHMENT to go regularly to an institution such as a school, church, or hospital for instruction, worship, or treatment 3 *vi* LISTEN OR WATCH CAREFULLY to listen or pay close attention to somebody or something 4 *vt* OCCUR WITH SOMETHING ELSE to accompany something or be associated with it (*usually passive*) 5 *vt* BE SOMEBODY'S ATTENDANT to escort somebody or act as an attendant to somebody (*usually passive*) 6 *vi* RESULT to be the consequence of something (*literary*) [14C. Via Old French *atendre* < Latin *attendere* 'reach towards' < *tendere* 'to stretch'.] —**attender** *n*

attend to *vti* to deal with or look after somebody or something ○ *patients to attend to* ○ *attend to business*

attendance /ə téndənss/ *n* 1 an instance of being at an event or regularly going to a school, church, or other institution 2 the number of people who are present at an event or institution ◇ **dance attendance on somebody** to be ready to carry out all somebody's wishes

attendance allowance *n* a tax-free state benefit paid to disabled people to cover the cost of constant care or supervision

attendance centre *n* a centre to which young offenders are required to report regularly by the court, as an alternative to a custodial sentence

attendant /ə téndənt/ *n* 1 SOMEBODY SERVING IN A PUBLIC PLACE somebody employed to serve or help members of the public in a public institution or place ○ *a museum attendant* 2 ESCORT somebody who escorts or serves another person ■ *adj* OCCURRING WITH SOMETHING ELSE associated with something, or resulting or following from it ○ *parenthood and its attendant anxieties*

attendee /ə tén dée, á ten-/ *n* a person attending something, especially a conference, course, or seminar

attention /ə ténsh'n/ *n* 1 CONCENTRATION mental focus, serious consideration, or concentration 2 INTEREST notice or interest ○ *media attention* ○ *A letter for the attention of Mr Brown.* 3 APPROPRIATE TREATMENT care, tending, or appropriate treatment 4 AFFECTIONATE ACT a polite, considerate, or affectionate act (*formal; often plural*) 5 FORMAL MILITARY POSTURE a formal standing attitude assumed by members of the armed forces in drill and often when receiving orders, with feet together, eyes forward, and arms at the sides ■ *interj* MILITARY ORDER a shouted military order to assume posture of attention [14C. < Latin *attention-* < stem of *attendere* (see ATTEND).]

attention deficit disorder, attention deficit hyperactivity disorder *n* a condition, occurring mainly in children, characterized by hyperactivity, inability to concentrate, and impulsive or inappropriate behaviour

ϟ **attention economy** *n* a view of the economy in late 20th century that suggests that people's attention to websites is a valuable and tradable commodity

attention-grabbing *adj* attracting notice or interest, especially by being sensational or lurid ○ *attention-grabbing headlines*

attention line *n* a line in a formally addressed letter indicating for whom, especially for which employee or member of staff, the letter is intended

attention-seeker *n* somebody who tries to attract attention, especially from somebody whose notice is craved —**attention-seeking** *n*

attention span *n* the length of time that somebody can concentrate effectively on a particular task or activity

attentive /ə téntiv/ *adj* 1 behaving towards somebody in a way that shows special regard or affection 2 listening or watching carefully and with concentration [14C. < French *attentif* < *atendre* (see ATTEND).] —**attentively** *adv* —**attentiveness** *n*

attenuate /ə ténnyoo ayt/ (-ates, -ating, -ated) *v* 1 *vti* to reduce the size, strength, or density of something, or to become thinner, weaker, or less dense 2 *vt* to reduce the virulence of a bacterium or virus, e.g. by exposing it to heat or producing a culture of it in a special medium [Mid-16C. < Latin *attenuat-*, past participle of *attenuare* 'make thin' < *tenuis* 'thin'.] —**attenuation** /ə ténnyoo áysh'n/ *n*

attenuated /ə ténnyoo aytid/ *adj* long, narrow, and sometimes tapering

attenuator /ə ténnyoo aytər/ *n* a device for reducing the strength of a wave, especially an electrical signal

attest /ə tést/ *vti* 1 to show that something exists or is true or valid 2 to state that something is true, especially in a formal written statement [15C. Via French, < Latin *attestari* 'to witness to' < *testis* 'witness'.] —**attestant** *n* —**attestation** /á te stáysh'n/ *n* —**attestor** *n*

Att. Gen. *abbr* Attorney General

attic /áttik/ *n* a room or the area that occupies the space under a pitched roof [Late 17C. Via French *attique* 'Attic' < Latin *Atticus* (see ATTIC).]

Attic /áttik/ *adj* 1 OF ATTICA relating to the ancient Greek territory of Attica or to the modern Greek department of Attica 2 ELEGANTLY WITTY elegantly succinct or drily witty ■ *n* EXTINCT GREEK DIALECT a dialect of ancient Greek that was spoken in Attica [Late 16C. Via Latin, < Greek *Attikos* < *Attikē* 'Attica'.]

Attica /áttikə/ region of ancient Greece around Athens

Atticism /áttisizəm/ *n* a witty or elegantly simple and concise turn of phrase [Late 16C. < Greek *Attikismos* < *Attikos* (see ATTIC.]

Attila /ə tíllə/ (406?–453?) Hunnish warrior king

attire /ə tír/ *n* clothing, especially a garment or combination of garments, worn on a particular occasion (*formal*) ■ *vt* (-tires, -tiring, -tired) to dress yourself or somebody else, especially in clothes of a particular type (*formal*) [13C. < Old French *atirier* 'to array' < *tire* 'order' (see TIER).]

attitude /átti tyood/ *n* **1** PERSONAL VIEW an opinion or general feeling about something ○ *a positive attitude to change* **2** BODILY POSTURE a physical posture, either conscious or unconscious, especially while interacting with others **3** CHALLENGING MANNER an arrogant or assertive manner or stance assumed as a challenge or for effect (*informal*) ○ *a streetwise teenager with attitude* **4** ORIENTATION OF AIRCRAFT'S AXES the angle of an aircraft in relation to the direction of the airflow or to the horizontal plane **5** ORIENTATION OF SPACECRAFT the angle of a spacecraft in relation to its direction of movement [Late 17C. Via French < late Latin *aptitudo* 'disposition' < Latin *aptus* (see APT).]

attitudinal /átti tyóodinəl/ *adj* US insisting strongly on your rights

attitudinize /átti tyoodi nīz/ (**-nizes, -nizing, -nized**), **attitudinise** (**-dinises, -dinising, -dinised**) *vi* to strike exaggerated or unspontaneous poses, or adopt extreme opinions, for effect

Attlee /átlli/, **Clement, 1st Earl Attlee** (1883–1967) British statesman and prime minister (1945–51)

attn *abbr* attention

atto- *prefix* one quintillionth (10^{-18}) [< Danish or Norwegian *atten* 'eighteen']

attorney /ə túrni/ (*plural* **-neys**) *n* **1** somebody legally empowered by a document (**power of attorney**) to make decisions and act on behalf of somebody else **2** US a qualified lawyer, especially one who represents clients in court proceedings [14C. < Old French *atorne*, past participle of *atorner* 'appoint' < *torner* < Latin *tornare* (see TURN).] —**attorneyship** *n*

attorney general (*plural* **attorney generals** *or* **attorneys general**) *n* **1** COUNTRY'S CHIEF LEGAL OFFICER a country's chief legal officer, and its government's chief legal adviser **2** US CHIEF LEGAL OFFICER OF US STATE in the United States, the chief law officer of a state, and its government's chief legal adviser **3** CHIEF LAW OFFICER OF AUSTRALIA the chief law officer of the Australian Commonwealth or one of its states or territories

~~**attornies**~~ incorrect spelling of **attorneys**

attract /ə trákt/ *v* **1** *vt* DRAW CLOSER to draw objects nearer, e.g. as a magnet draws iron objects towards it **2** *vt* ENTICE to be appealing enough to make people visit a place or spend their money **3** *vt* GET A RESPONSE to win or elicit a response from people, especially support or encouragement **4** *vt* DRAW SOMEBODY'S ATTENTION to draw or secure somebody's attention, or become the focus of somebody's attention ○ *'It takes a big idea to attract the attention of consumers and get them to buy your product'.* (David Ogilvy, *Ogilvy on Advertising*; 1985) **5** *vt* HAVE APPEAL to appeal to people or awaken a response in them **6** *vti* BE THE OBJECT OF SEXUAL FEELINGS to be the focus or object of sexual interest [15C. < Latin *attract-*, past participle of *attrahere* 'draw towards' < *trahere* 'to draw, pull'.] —**attractable** *adj* —**attracter** *n*

attraction /ə tráksh'n/ *n* **1** POWER OF ATTRACTING the power of attracting or the feeling of being attracted ○ *'Our mutual attraction was immediate, and we enjoyed one another's company'.* (Peter Ustinov, *Dear Me*; 1977) **2** APPEALING QUALITY OR FEATURE a quality or feature that attracts somebody ○ *The idea has its attractions.* **3** THING OR PLACE THAT DRAWS TOURISTS something, e.g. a historical site or building, that people, especially tourists, like to see or visit

attractive /ə tráktiv/ *adj* **1** AGREEABLE pleasing in appearance or manner **2** GOOD-LOOKING good-looking or sexually desirable **3** INTERESTING interesting or appealing because of the probable advantages ○ *an attractive proposition* —**attractiveness** *n*

attractively /ə tráktivli/ *adv* in a pleasing, appealing, or sexually interesting way ○ *attractively priced furnishings* ○ *attractively situated a few minutes from the beach*

attractor /ə tráktər/ *n* a fixed point or state of equilibrium that the behaviour of a system is attracted to and tends to imitate

attrib. *abbr* attributive

attribute *vt* /ə tríbbyoot/ (**-utes, -uting, -uted**) **1** ASCRIBE A FEATURE to think of something as caused by a particular circumstance ○ *To what do you attribute your success?* **2** GIVE CREDIT to give credit for a certain thing, such as a work of art or literature, or a saying, to a particular person, often wrongly ○ *It's a bon mot that is often wrongly attributed to Saki.* **3** ASSIGN QUALITIES to regard somebody or something as having particular qualities ○ *the wisdom that she attributes to her favourite writers* ■ *n* /áttri byoot/ QUALITY OR PROPERTY a quality, property, or characteristic of somebody or something [14C. Directly or via French < Latin *attribut-*, past participle of *attribuere* 'allot to' < *tribuere* (see TRIBUTE).] —**attributable** *adj* —**attributer** *n*

attribution /áttri byóosh'n/ *n* the ascribing of something to somebody or something, e.g. a work of art to a certain artist or circumstances to a particular cause

attributive /ə tríbbyootiv/ *adj* forming part of a noun phrase and typically preceding the noun —**attributively** *adv* —**attributiveness** *n*

attrit /ə trít/ (**-trits, -tritting, -tritted**) *vt* US to wear something down little by little, especially enemy forces by constant attacks (*informal*) [Mid-20C. Back-formation < ATTRITION.]

attrition /ə trísh'n/ *n* **1** WEARING AWAY OF SURFACE the wearing away of a surface, typically by friction or abrasion **2** WEAKENING BY PERSISTENT ATTACK the gradual wearing away of morale and the powers of resistance by persistent attacks **3** LOSS OF STAFF the gradual reduction of the size of a workforce by not replacing staff lost through retirement or resignation **4** SORROW FOR SIN remorse for sin engendered by the fear of damnation [15C. Via French, < Latin *attrit-*, past participle of *atterere* 'rub away' < *terere* 'rub'.]

attune /ə tyóon/ (**-tunes, -tuning, -tuned**) *vt* to adjust or accustom something to become receptive or responsive to something else

Atty. Gen. *abbr* attorney general

ATV *abbr* all-terrain vehicle

Atwood /át wòod/, **Margaret** (*b.* 1939) Canadian writer

at. wt. *abbr* atomic weight

atypical /ay típpik'l/ *adj* not conforming to the usual type or expected pattern

ϟ **au** *abbr* Australia (*in Internet addresses*)

Au *symbol* gold [< Latin *aurum*]

AU, a.u. *abbr* **1** angstrom unit **2** astronomical unit

aubade /ō baád/ *n* a song, poem, or piece of instrumental music celebrating or greeting the dawn [Late 17C. Via French, < Provençal *albada* < *alba* 'dawn' < Latin *albus* 'white'.]

aubergine /óbər zheen/ *n* **1** VEGETABLE a large fruit with shiny purple skin, eaten cooked as a vegetable. ◊ **eggplant** *n.* 2 **2** AUBERGINE PLANT a bushy perennial plant of the potato family that bears aubergines. *Solanum melongena.* ◊ **eggplant** *n.* 1 ■ *adj* DARK PURPLE a dark reddish-purple colour. ◊ **eggplant** *n.* 3 [Late 18C. Via French, Catalan, and Arabic, < Persian *bādingān*.]

Aubrey /áwbri/, **John** (1626–97) English antiquary

auburn /áwbən, áw burn/ *adj* dark coppery red or reddish-brown ○ *auburn hair* [15C. < Old French (influenced in sense by the similarity of the variant spelling *abrun* to *brun* 'brown') < medieval Latin *alburnus* 'whitish' < Latin *albus* 'white'.] —**auburn** *n*

AUC *abbr* **1** ab urbe condita (*used by Roman classical writers to specify the dates of events in terms of the number of years since Rome's foundation in 753 BC*) **2** Australian Universities Commission

Auckland /áwklənd/ **1** administrative region of New Zealand, in NW North Island. Population: 1,077,205 (1996). Area: 16,282 sq. km/6,287 sq. mi. **2** largest city and port in New Zealand, in NW North Island. Population: 997,940 (1996).

Auckland Islands group of uninhabited islands in the S Pacific Ocean, part of New Zealand. Area: 606 sq. km/234 sq. mi.

au contraire /ō kon tráir/ *adv* indeed, the opposite is really the case [< French, 'to the contrary']

au courant /ō kóo raáN/ *adj* abreast of the latest developments [< French, 'in the current']

auction /áwksh'n/ *n* **1** SALE BY BIDDING a sale of goods or property at which intending buyers bid against one another for individual items ○ *an Internet auction* **2** BIDDING IN GAME OF BRIDGE the bidding phase in a game of bridge, during which players contract to win a certain number of tricks if a certain suit is trumps ■ *vti* SELL AT AUCTION to sell goods by auction [Late 16C. < Latin *auction-* 'increase' < *augere* 'to increase'.] —**auctionable** *adj*

auction bridge *n* a form of bridge in which all tricks won count towards the score

auctioneer /áwkshə néer/ *n* somebody who is in charge of an auction —**auctioneering** *n*

AUD *abbr* Australian dollar

aud. *abbr* **1** audit **2** auditor

audacious /aw dáyshəss/ *adj* bold, daring, or fearless, especially in challenging assumptions or conventions [Mid-16C. < Latin *audac-*, stem of *audax* 'bold' < *audere* 'to dare' < *avidus* (see AVIDITY).] —**audaciously** *adv* —**audaciousness** *n*

audacity /aw dássəti/ *n* **1** daring or willingness to challenge assumptions or conventions or tackle something difficult or dangerous **2** lack of respect in somebody's behaviour towards another

Auden /áwd'n/, **W. H.** (1907–73) British-born US poet and dramatist. Full name **Wystan Hugh Auden**

audi- *prefix* = **audio-**

audial /áwdi əl/ *adj* relating to hearing or sounds [Mid-20C. < AUDIO.]

~~**audiance**~~ incorrect spelling of **audience**

audible /áwdəb'l/ *adj* loud or clear enough to be heard ○ *an audible gasp from the crowd* [15C. < late Latin *audibilis* < Latin *audire* 'hear'.] —**audibility** /áwdə bíllәti/ *n* —**audibleness** *n* —**audibly** *adv*

audience /áwdi ənss/ *n* **1** PEOPLE WATCHING LIVE PERFORMANCE a group of people who are watching and listening to a show, concert, or other live performance **2** PEOPLE WATCHING OR LISTENING TO BROADCAST the viewers of a film or a television programme, or the listeners to a radio programme, **3** AUTHOR'S READERSHIP the people who read a particular writer's books **4** FORMAL INTERVIEW a formal, usually prearranged, interview with somebody important [14C. Via French, < Latin *audientia* 'a hearing' < *audire* 'hear'.]

audile /áw dīl/ *adj* PHYSIOL = **auditory** [Late 19C. < Latin *audire* 'hear'.]

audio /áwdi ō/ *n* the recording and reproduction of sound [Early 20C. < AUDIO-.]

audio-, audi- *prefix* sound, hearing ○ *audiogram* [< Latin *audire* 'hear']

audio book *n* a commercial recording, usually on a cassette tape, of somebody reading the text of a well-known book

audiocassette /áwdi ō kə sét/ *n* a cassette containing an audiotape, for use in a tape recorder

audio clip *n* an extract from a longer sound recording, e.g. from a film soundtrack, that can be listened to on a personal computer

audio console *n* a cabinet for vertically stacked pieces of audio equipment

audio frequency *n* a frequency that is audible to the human ear, between 20 and 20,000 hertz in people with normal hearing

audiogram /áwdi ō gram/ *n* a tracing produced by an audiometer, recording the sharpness of somebody's hearing

audiology /áwdi óllәji/ *n* the scientific study of hearing, especially for diagnosing and treating hearing defects —**audiological** /áwdi ə lójjik'l/ *adj* —**audiologist** *n*

audiometer /áwdi ómmitər/ *n* an instrument for testing the ability of a human ear to detect sounds over a range of frequencies and intensities —**audiometric** /áwdi ō méttrik/ *adj* —**audiometry** *n*

audiophile /áwdi ō fīl/ *n* an enthusiast for sound reproduction, especially high-fidelity music recordings

audiotape /áwdi ō tayp/ *n* **1** magnetic tape for recording sound, or a length of this, typically in a cassette **2** a sound recording on magnetic tape, especially an audiocassette for use in a tape recorder

audiotyping /áwdi ō tīping/ *n* the skill or activity of typing up recorded dictation as you are listening to it —**audiotypist** *n*

audiovisual /áwdi ō vízhoo əl/ *adj* **1** relating to sound and vision, especially when combined, e.g. in a presentation using both film and sound recordings **2** relating to the faculties of hearing and seeing ■ *n* US = **audiovisual aid**

audiovisual aid *n* any aid to teaching or lecturing that combines sound and vision. US term **audiovisual** *n.*

audit /áwdit/ *n* **1** CHECK OF ACCOUNTS a formal examination, correction, and official endorsing of financial accounts, especially those of a business, undertaken annually by an accountant **2** EFFICIENCY CHECK a systematic check or assessment, especially of the efficiency or effectiveness of an organization or department, typically carried out by an independent assessor ■ *vt* **1 CARRY OUT AUDIT** to carry out an audit of the financial accounts of a firm, department, or organization to establish accuracy or efficiency **2** *US* **SIT IN ON CLASS** to attend a class without asking for or receiving graduation credit for it, usually attending all the sessions but not doing the assignments [15C. < Latin *auditus* 'hearing' < *audit-*, past participle of *audire* 'hear'.] —**auditable** *adj*

auditee /áwdi teé/ *n* a person or organization that is being audited

audition /aw dísh'n/ *n* **1 TEST PERFORMANCE BY CANDIDATE** a test in the form of a short performance, e.g. by an actor applying for a role in a film or play **2 HEARING** the sense, faculty, or process of hearing ■ *vti* **DO OR GIVE AN AUDITION** to do an audition or give somebody an audition for a role [Late 16C. < Latin *audition-* 'hearing' < *audire* 'hear'.]

auditive /áwditiv/ *adj* = **auditory** [Early 17C. Via French, < Latin *audire* 'hear'.]

auditor /áwditər/ *n* **1 SOMEBODY CHECKING ACCOUNTS OR SYSTEMS** somebody who checks accounts or conducts an audit of an organization **2** *US* **STUDENT SITTING IN ON CLASS** a student who attends a class without asking for or receiving graduation credit **3 HEARER** a hearer or listener, e.g. a member of an audience or somebody listening to somebody who is talking (*formal*) [14C. Via Anglo-Norman, < Latin *auditor* 'hearer' < *audire* 'hear'.]

auditor-general (*plural* **auditor-generals** *or* **auditors-general**) *n* an officer of the Australian government who monitors government expenditure and ensures that it is authorized by Act or regulation

auditorium /áwdi táwri əm/ (*plural* **-ums** *or* **-a** /-ri ə/) *n* **1** the area of a theatre or concert hall where the audience sits **2** a lecture theatre or a hall that is used for lectures, concerts, and other events [Early 17C. < Latin, 'place for hearing' < *audire* 'hear'.]

auditory /áwditəri/ *adj* relating to the hearing organs, or the process of hearing [Late 16C. < late Latin *auditorius* < Latin *audire* 'hear'.]

auditory nerve *n* a nerve that conveys impulses relating to hearing and balance from the inner ear to the brain

audit trail *n* a record kept, e.g. by a computer, of a sequence of events or transactions

Audubon /áwdəbən/, **John James** (1785–1851) Haitian-born US ornithologist, naturalist, and artist

Auerbach /ówər bak/, **Frank** (*b.* 1931) German-born British painter

au fait /ō fáy/ *adj* familiar with the latest developments in or facts about something [< French, 'to the fact']

Aufbau principle *n* a principle in chemistry holding that each successive element in a sequence can be created by adding a proton to the nucleus and an electron to an orbital of the preceding element

Aug. *abbr* August

Augean /aw jeé ən/ *adj* **1** disgustingly dirty, like the Augean stables **2** extremely difficult and unpleasant

Augean stables *n* in Greek mythology, the stables owned by King Augeas that had not been cleaned in 30 years. One of Hercules' tasks was to clean them in one day, which he achieved by diverting two rivers through them. ◇ **cleanse the Augean stables** to put something that is extremely untidy and disorganized into a state of order and tidiness

auger /áwgər/ *n* a hand tool with a corkscrew-shaped bit for boring holes, or a larger tool, using the same principle, for boring holes in the ground [Old English *nafogār* < NAVE² *gār* 'spear' (see GORE¹); *n* lost in the 16C by false division of *a nauger* as *an auger*]

SPELLCHECK Do not confuse *auger* with *augur*, which has a similar sound. Beware: your spellchecker will not catch this error.

Auger effect /ō zhay-/, **Auger process** *n* the emission of an electron from an excited positive ion resulting in a doubly charged ion [Mid-20C. After the French physicist Pierre *Auger* (1899–1993).]

aught /awt/ *pron* anything whatever (*archaic literary*) [Old English *āwiht* 'ever a thing' < Germanic]

augite /áw gīt/ *n* a dark green mineral of the pyroxene group, containing aluminium, calcium, iron, and magnesium. Source: igneous rocks. [Early 19C. Via Latin

augites, a precious stone (possibly turquoise) < Greek *augitēs* < *augē* 'lustre'.]

augment /awg mént/ *v* **1** *vti* **INCREASE** to grow, or to increase something in number, amount, size, strength, or intensity (*formal*) **2** *vt* **ENLARGE MUSICAL INTERVAL** in music, to enlarge a perfect or major interval by a semitone ■ *n* **PREFIXED VOWEL** in Greek or Sanskrit grammar, a vowel prefixed to a verb, or added to its initial vowel so as to lengthen it into a diphthong, to form a past tense [14C. < French *augmenter* < Latin *augere* 'to increase' < Indo-European.] —**augmented** *adj* —**augmenter** *n*

SYNONYMS See *increase*.

augmentation /áwg men táysh'n, -mən-/ *n* **1** the increasing, or growth, of something in number, amount, size, strength, or intensity, or the amount by which something grows or is added to ◇ *augmentation in costs* **2** in music, the technique of varying a theme by increasing its note values proportionally

augmentation mammoplasty *n* surgical enlargement of the breasts

augmentative /awg méntativ/ *adj* **1 CAUSING AN INCREASE** tending to add to or increase something or to enable something to grow or increase (*formal*) **2 DENOTING GREAT SIZE OR IMPORTANCE** describes an affix, such as Spanish '-ote' or Italian '-one', that signifies great size or importance, or a word to which an affix of this kind has been added ■ *n* **AUGMENTATIVE AFFIX OR WORD** an affix signifying great size or importance, or a word to which an affix of this kind has been added

au gratin /ō gráttaN/ *adj* sprinkled with breadcrumbs, sometimes mixed with grated cheese, and browned before serving [< French, 'with a gratin crust']

Augsburg /ówgz burg/ city in S Germany. Population: 262,110 (1997).

augur /áwgər/ *n* **1 INTERPRETER OF MESSAGES FROM ROMAN DEITIES** a religious official in ancient Rome who interpreted natural phenomena, such as the flight of birds, as signs that the deities favoured or disapproved of actions proposed by the city **2 SOOTHSAYER OR PROPHET** any soothsayer, prophet, or diviner ■ *vt* **INDICATE WHAT WILL HAPPEN** to suggest or indicate what will happen in the future [14C. < Latin.] —**augural** /áwgyōōrəl/ *adj*

SPELLCHECK See *auger*.

augury /áwgyōōri/ (*plural* **-ries**) *n* **1** the art, activity, prophecies, or pronouncements of an augur, soothsayer, or diviner **2** an indication of what will happen in the future

august /aw gúst/ *adj* full of solemn splendour and dignity (*formal*) [Mid-17C. Directly or via French, < Latin *augustus*.] —**augustly** *adv*

August /áwgəst/ *n* the eighth month of the year in the Gregorian calendar. It has 31 days. [Pre-12C. < Latin *augustus*, after the Roman emperor AUGUSTUS.]

Augusta /ə gústə/ **1** city in east-central Georgia, United States. Population: 187,689 (1998 estimate). **2** capital of Maine, in the SW of the state. Population: 19,978 (1998 estimate).

Augustan /aw gústən/ *adj* **1 OF AUGUSTUS OR HIS TIME** relating to the Roman emperor Augustus, to his reign, or to the classical writers, including Virgil, Ovid, and Horace, who flourished during this period **2 CHARACTERIZED BY CLASSICAL WRITING** relating to any period or the writers or works of a period during which writing in the classical style flourished, especially in 17th-century France and 18th-century England ■ *n* **AUGUSTAN WRITER OR STUDENT** a writer from an Augustan period, or somebody who studies Augustan literature

Augustine /aw gústin/, **St** (354–430) Roman priest and theologian

Augustine, St (*d.* 604) Roman priest and Archbishop of Canterbury (597–604)

Augustinian /áwgə stínni ən/ *adj* relating to St Augustine of Hippo, or to his teachings, or to any of the Christian religious orders living according to his rule or system of monastic life ■ *n* a follower of St Augustine, especially a member of one of the religious orders living according to his rule

Augustus /aw gústəss/ (63 BC–AD 14) Roman emperor (27 BC–14 AD)

auk /awk/ *n* a small black-and-white heavy-bodied seabird of the puffin family. Native to: cool northern

seas. Family: Alcidae. [Late 17C. Via Norwegian *alk* < Old Norse *álka*.]

auklet /áwklət/ *n* a small auk that nests in burrows or rock slides. Native to: N Pacific. Family: Alcidae.

auld lang syne /áwld lang zīn/ *n Scotland* old times or times long gone (*archaic*) [Literally 'old long since', 'old long ago']

aum *n* RELIG, BUDDHISM = **Om**

aumbry *n* RELIG = **ambry**

au naturel /ō náttyōō rél/ *adv, adj* **1** served simply and plainly, e.g. uncooked or without seasoning or salt **2** wearing no clothes (*humorous*) [< French, 'in the natural state']

Aung San /áwng sán/, **U** (1916?–47) Burmese national leader

Aung San Suu Kyi

Popperfoto

Aung San Suu Kyi /áwng san soo keé/, **Daw** (*b.* 1945) Burmese human rights activist

aunt /aant/ *n* the sister of somebody's mother or father, or the wife of somebody's uncle (*before a first name as a title or form of address, now rather formal*) [13C. Via Anglo-Norman < Latin *amita* 'father's sister'.] —**aunthood** *n*

auntie /áanti/, **aunty** (*plural* **-ies**) *n* an aunt or close woman friend of a child's parents (*informal*)

Auntie, Aunty *n* (*informal*) **1** *BBC* a nickname for the British Broadcasting Corporation, or BBC, in reference to its image as a kindly and well-intentioned, if old-fashioned, guardian of standards **2** *Aus* **AUSTRALIAN BROADCASTING CORPORATION** a nickname for the Australian Broadcasting Corporation **3** *S Asia, Malaysia, Singapore* **FORM OF ADDRESS TO WOMAN** used as a form of address to a woman of middle age or beyond, e.g. one who is not a relative of the speaker and whose name is not known ◇ *Hey, Auntie, do you want to buy some?*

Aunt Sally /-sálli/ (*plural* **Aunt Sallies**) *n* **1 FAIRGROUND TARGET** a traditional target used in throwing-games in fairgrounds, shaped like the head of a woman of advanced years, typically with a clay pipe in her mouth, that throwers try to break **2 BUTT OF CRITICISM** a person or organization that is the constant target of criticism and abusive comment **3 ARGUMENT TO BE DEMOLISHED** in formal discussion, an argument put forward so that it can be demolished and dismissed

aunty *n* = **auntie**

Aunty *n* = **Auntie**

au pair /ō paír/ *n* a young person from abroad living with a family to learn the language, and helping with childcare and domestic work in return for board and accommodation [< French, 'on equal terms']

aura /áwrə/ (*plural* **-ras** *or* **-rae** /-reé/) *n* **1 DISTINCTIVE QUALITY** a characteristic or distinctive impression created by somebody or something ◇ *an aura of mystery* **2 EMANATING FORCE** a force that is said to surround all people and objects, discernible often as a bright glow, only to people of unusual psychic sensitivity **3 WARNING SENSATION BEFORE EPILEPTIC EPISODE** a distinctive sensation or visual disturbance that may signal the beginning of an epileptic episode or a migraine [Mid-18C. Via Latin, 'gentle breeze' < Greek.]

aural /áwrəl/ *adj* relating to the ear, hearing, or to receptiveness and response to speech or other sounds ◇ *the extent to which our visual and aural perceptions of painting and music depend on our prior knowledge of the pieces* [Mid-19C. < Latin *auris* 'ear'.] —**aurally** *adv*

USAGE aural or **oral**? These two words are often confused because they are pronounced in a similar way and have meanings that are close. Essentially **aural** is to do with hearing whereas **oral** is to do with speaking or the mouth. An *aural test* is an examination testing comprehension by listening, whereas in an *oral test* the answers are spoken rather than written.

auranofin /aw ránnəfin/ *n* a gold-containing compound taken orally. Use: treatment of arthritis.

aurar plural of **eyrir**

aureate /áwri ayt, -ət/ *adj* **1** gold, gilded, golden, or gold-coloured **2** expressed or written in a highly or excessively ornamented, florid, or elaborate style [15C. < Latin *aureatus* < *aureus* 'golden' < *aurum* 'gold'.]

aurei plural of **aureus**

Aurelian /aw reéli ən/ (215?–275) Roman soldier and emperor (270–275)

aureole /aw ri ōl/, **aureola** /aw reè ələ, áw ri ólə/ *n* **1** a painted or carved representation of a circle of light around the head of a divine being or a saint **2** METEOROL = **corona** *n.* **2** [Mid-19C. Via French < late Latin *corona aureola* 'golden crown'.]

aureus /áwri əss/ (*plural* **-i** /-ī/) *n* a gold coin that was a unit of currency in the Roman Empire between 30 BC and AD 310 [Early 17C. < Latin, noun use of *aureus* 'golden' (see AUREATE).]

au revoir /ō rə vwaár/ *interj* goodbye till we see each other again [< French, 'until seeing again']

auri-[1] *prefix* ear, hearing ○ *auriform* [< Latin *auris* 'ear']

auri-[2] *prefix* gold ○ *auriferous* [< Latin *aurum*]

auric /áwrik/ *adj* containing gold with a valency of three ○ *auric oxide* [Early 19C. < Latin *aurum* 'gold'.]

Auric /aw reék/, **Georges** (1899–1983) French composer

auricle /áwrik'l/ *n* **1** VISIBLE PART OF EAR the part of the external ear that projects outwards from the head **2** PART OF HEART CHAMBER an ear-shaped muscular part that sticks out from the surface of each upper chamber (**atrium**) of the heart **3** ATRIUM an atrium of the heart (*dated*) [Mid-17C. < Latin *auricula* 'little ear' < *auris* 'ear'.] —**auricled** *adj*

auricula /aw ríkyōōlə/ (*plural* **-las** *or* **-lae** /-lee/) *n* an alpine primrose with leaves shaped like a bear's ear. Flowers: yellow. *Primula auricula.* [Mid-17C. < Latin (see AURICLE).]

auricular /aw ríkyōōlər/ *adj* **1** EAR-SHAPED shaped like an ear **2** RELATING TO HEARING ORGANS relating to the ear or to the sense of hearing **3** RELATING TO HEART CHAMBERS relating to the ear-shaped muscular part (**auricle**) on the surface of each upper chamber (**atrium**) of the heart

auriculate /aw ríkyōō layt/ *adj* **1** describes leaves that have an attachment at the base that is shaped like an ear **2** relating to an animal that has ears, auricles, or extensions that resemble earlobes

auriferous /aw ríffərəss/ *adj* describes rock or minerals that contain gold

Auriga /aw rígə/ *n* a prominent constellation of the northern hemisphere containing the bright star Capella. See illustration at **constellation**

Aurignacian /áwrig náysh'n/ *adj* belonging to a prehistoric culture associated with Cro-Magnon people in Europe around the period 30,000 to 22,000 BC [Early 20C. After *Aurignac*, France.]

Auriol /áwri ol/, **Vincent** (1884–1966) French statesman

aurochs /áwroks/ (*plural* **-rochs**) *n* a long-horned wild ox, now extinct but thought to be an ancestor of modern domestic cattle. Native to: North Africa, Europe, Southwest Asia. [Late 18C. < German, variant of *Auerochs* 'original ox'.]

aurora /ə ráwrə/ (*plural* **-ras** *or* **-rae** /-ree/) *n* **1** a phenomenon occurring in the night sky around the polar regions, caused by atmospheric gases interacting with solar particles to create streamers, folds, or arches of coloured light **2 aurora, Aurora** the dawn, usually personified or regarded, as in classical literature, as a goddess [15C. < Latin, 'dawn'.] —**auroral** *adj*

aurora australis /-o stráyliss/ *n* the coloured lights seen in the skies around the South Pole [< modern Latin, 'southern aurora']

aurora borealis /-bawri áyliss/ *n* the coloured lights seen in the skies around the North Pole [< modern Latin, 'northern aurora']

AUS *abbr* **1** Australia (*international vehicle registration*) **2** Australian Union of Students

Aus. *abbr* **1** Australia **2** Australian **3** Austria **4** Austrian

Auschwitz /ów shvits/ site in S Poland of the largest Nazi concentration camp

Auschwitz Lie *n* denial that the attempted extermination of the Jews by the Nazis ever took place

auscultation /áwsk'l táysh'n/ *n* listening to the sounds made by a patient's internal organs, especially the heart, lungs, and abdominal organs, usually with a stethoscope, in order to make a diagnosis [Mid-17C. < Latin *auscultation-* < *auscultare* 'listen to'.] —**auscultate** /áwsk'l tayt/ *vt* —**auscultative** /aw skúltətiv/ *adj* —**auscultatory** *adj*

auslese /ówss layzə/ *n* a middle grade of high-quality German table wine, made from selected late-picked grapes and typically medium sweet to sweet [Mid-19C. < German, 'selection'.]

auspice /áwspiss/ (*plural* **-pices** /-iz/) *n* a sign or token for the future, especially a happy or promising one [Mid-17C. Via French, < Latin *auspicium* 'taking omens' < *auspex* 'soothsayer', originally 'somebody who foretells the future by studying the flight pattern of birds' < *avis* 'bird' + *specere* 'to look'.] ◇ **under the auspices of** with the help or support of a person or organization

auspicious /aw spíshəss/ *adj* marked by lucky signs or good omens, and therefore by the promise of success or happiness —**auspiciously** *adv* —**auspiciousness** *n*

Aussie /ózzi/ *n* an Australian (*informal*) [Early 20C. Shortening.] —**Aussie** *adj*

Aust. *abbr* **1** Australia **2** Australian **3** Austria **4** Austrian

Jane Austen

Austen /óstin/, **Jane** (1775–1817) British novelist

austenite /áwstə nīt, óstə-/ *n* a solid solution of carbon in iron that occurs as a component of steel at a certain stage of manufacture [Early 20C. After Sir William Roberts-Austen.] —**austenitic** /áwstə níttik, óstə-/ *adj*

austere /aw steér, o-/ *adj* **1** SUGGESTING PHYSICAL HARDSHIP imposing or suggesting physical hardship **2** UNSMILING grimly unsmiling, humourless, or suggesting strict self-denial **3** PLAIN AND WITHOUT LUXURY plain and simple, without luxury or self-indulgence **4** PLAIN IN STYLE OR DESIGN severely plain in design or lines, without distractions or decoration [14C. Via French and Latin < Greek *austēros*.] —**austerely** *adv* —**austereness** *n*

austerity /aw stérrəti, o-/ (*plural* **-ties**) *n* **1** SEVERITY OR PLAINNESS severity of discipline, regime, expression, or design **2** ECONOMY MEASURE a saving, economy, or act of self-denial, especially in respect of something regarded as a luxury **3** ENFORCED THRIFT thrift imposed as government policy, with restricted access to or availability of consumer goods

Austerlitz /áwsterlits, ówsterlits/ site of a major battle in 1805 in present-day E Czech Republic, when Napoleon defeated Russian and Austrian forces

Austin /áwstin/ capital of Texas, in the S of the state. Population: 541,278 (1996).

austral /áwstrəl/ *adj* relating to, belonging to, or coming from the south [15C. < Latin *australis* < *auster* 'south'.]

Austral. *abbr* **1** Australasia **2** Australia **3** Australian

Australasia /áwstra láyzhə/ Australia, New Zealand, New Guinea, and neighbouring islands of the S Pacific Ocean —**Australasian** *adj, n*

Australia /o stráyli ə/ country comprising the continent of Australia, southeast of Asia, and the island of Tasmania. Capital: Canberra. Population: 18,311,000 (1996). Area: 7,682,300 sq. km/2,966,200 sq. mi.

Australia Day *n* an Australian public holiday marking the landing of the British First Fleet at Port Jackson, now Sydney Harbour, in 1788. Date: first Monday after 26 January.

Australian /o stráyli ən/ *adj* **1** OF AUSTRALIA relating to Australia, or its people, language, or culture **2** OF ABORIGINAL LANGUAGES OF AUSTRALIA relating to the family of languages spoken in Australia before European settlement ■ *n* **1** SOMEBODY FROM AUSTRALIA somebody who comes from Australia **2** AUSTRALIAN ENGLISH the form of English that is spoken in Australia

Australian Alps mountain range in SE Australia. Highest peak: Mount Kosciuszko 2,228 m./7,310 ft.

Australian Antarctic Territory region of E Antarctica formally claimed by Australia. Area: 6,119,818 sq. km/2,362,862 sq. mi.

Australian ballot *n US* POL = **secret ballot**

Australian Capital Territory federal district in SE Australia incorporating Canberra, the national capital. Population: 308,000 (1996). Area: 2,400 sq. km/930 sq. mi.

Australian English *n* the form of English spoken in Australia as distinct from other forms of English such as American English or British English

Australianism /o stráyli ənizəm/ *n* a word or expression that originated in, or is used mainly in, Australia

Australian Museum *n* a museum in Sydney that contains the Australian national collections of natural history and anthropology

Australian Rules *n* an Australian game resembling rugby, played on an oval pitch with 18 to a team and a large oval ball that can be punched, kicked, or carried (+ *singular verb*)

Australoid /óstrə loyd/ *adj* relating to the Australian Aborigines and certain other S Asian and Pacific peoples — **Australoid** *n*

australopithecine /óstralō píthə seen/ *adj* relating to a prehistoric primate whose fossilized remains resemble those of humans. Native to: S and E Africa. [Mid-20C. < modern Latin *Australopithecus* < Latin *australis* 'southern' + Greek *pithēkos* 'ape'.] —**australopithecine** *n*

Austrasia /aw stráyzhə/ eastern part of an ancient Frankish kingdom, in present-day NE France, Germany, and the Netherlands

Austria

Austria /óstri ə/ republic in central Europe. Capital: Vienna. Population: 8,054,000 (1995). Area: 83,858 sq. km/32,378 sq. mi. —**Austrian** *adj, n*

Austrian blind *n* a fabric window blind with panels that can be gathered up vertically into loose folds

Austro- *prefix* southern ○ *Austroasiatic* [< Latin *auster*]

Austro-Asiatic /óstrō-, -ayzi-/ *n* a large family of languages spoken in Southeast Asia and central India. Native speakers: 70 million.

Austronesia /óstrō neézhə, -neéshə/ region consisting of Indonesia, Melanesia, Micronesia, Polynesia, and neighbouring islands in the Pacific Ocean

Austronesian /óstrō neézh'n, -neésh'n/ *adj* relating to Austronesia, or its peoples, languages, or cultures ■ *n* a family of languages spoken in Taiwan, Southeast Asia, the Philippines, the Malay Archipelago, the

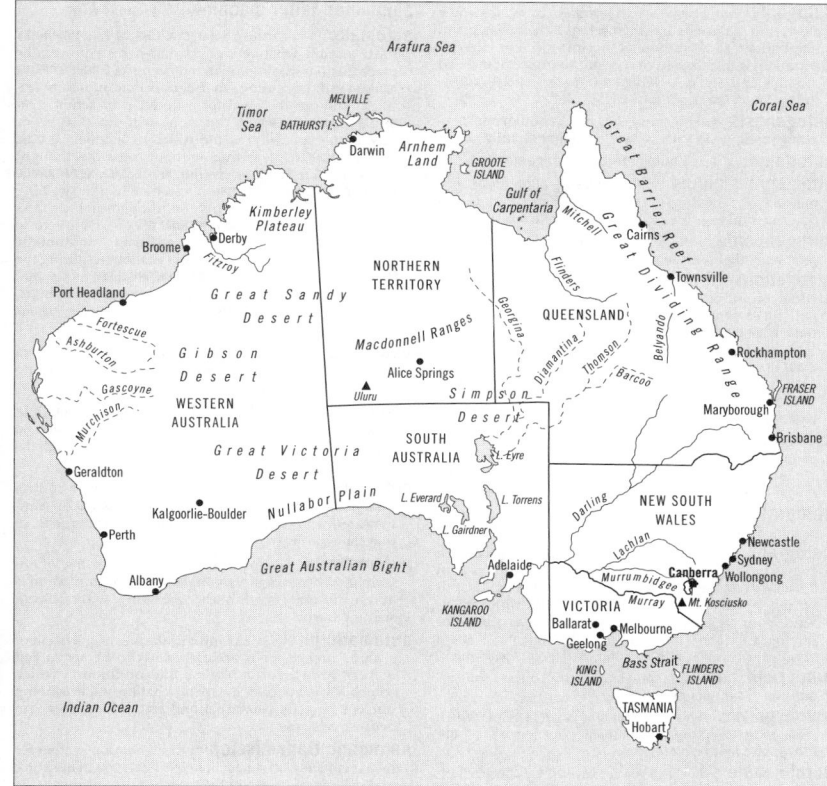

Australia

Pacific Islands, New Zealand, and Madagascar. Native speakers: 250 million.

AUT *abbr* Association of University Teachers

aut- *prefix* = **auto** (*before vowels*)

autarchy /áw taarki/ (*plural* **-chies**) *n* **1 UNLIMITED POLITICAL POWER** absolute power, especially such power wielded by a despotic ruler **2 SELF-GOVERNMENT** self-government of a country by representatives drawn from among its own citizens **3 COUNTRY WITH DESPOTIC RULER** a country governed by a ruler who has absolute power **4 SELF-GOVERNING COUNTRY** an independent country with its own government, as distinct from a colony or dependency [Mid-17C. < Greek *autarkhos* 'self-governing' < *arkhein* 'rule'.] —**autarchic** /aw taárkik/ *adj* —**autarchical** *adj* —**autarchist** *n*

autarky /áw taarki/ (*plural* **-kies**) *n* **1** an economic policy or situation in which a nation is independent of international trade and not reliant upon imported goods **2** a nation that is economically self-sufficient [Early 17C. < Greek *autarkeia* 'self-sufficiency' < *autarkēs* 'self-sufficient' < *arkein* 'be sufficient'.] —**autarkic** /aw taárkik/ *adj* —**autarkical** *adj*

autecology /áwti kólləji/ *n* the study of individuals or populations of a single species and their relationship to their environment —**autecological** /áwtikə lójjik'l/ *adj*

auteur /aw túr/ *n* a film director whose films are so distinctive that he or she is perceived as a film's creator [Mid-20C. < French, 'author'.]

auteurism /aw túriz əm/ *n CINEMA* = **auteur theory** —**auteurist** *adj*

auteur theory /aw túr theeri/ *n* film criticism that considers the director of a film to be its primary creator

auth. *abbr* **1** authentic **2** author **3** authority **4** authorized

authentic /aw théntik/ *adj* **1 NOT FALSE OR COPIED** genuine and original, as opposed to something that is a fake or reproduction **2 TRUSTWORTHY** shown to be true and trustworthy **3 VALID** legally valid because all necessary procedures have been followed correctly **4 IN STYLE OF ORIGINAL PERIOD** performed in the style current at the time of composition, and on instruments similar to those of the time **5 WITH UPWARD RANGE FROM MAIN NOTE** describes church music, such as Gregorian chant, that has an upward range from the keynote of the scale [14C. Via Old French < Greek *authentikos* 'genuine' < *authentes* 'master, doer' < *autos* 'self'.] —**authentically** *adv*

authenticate /aw thénti kayt/ (**-cates**, **-cating**, **-cated**) *vt* **1** to establish that something is genuine or that an account is true **2** to establish something such as a deed or document as legally valid —**authenticator** *n*

authentication /aw thénti káysh'n/ *n* **1** the act of proving something to be genuine or valid, or the evidence used in so doing **2** a security measure using data encryption that identifies the user and verifies that the message was not tampered with (*in e-commerce*)

authenticity /áw then tíssəti, áwthən-/ *n* **1** the genuineness or truth of something **2** the legal validity or correctness of a legal document

author /áwthər/ *n* **1 WRITER** somebody who writes a book or other text **2 PROFESSIONAL WRITER** a professional book writer **3 CREATOR OR SOURCE** the creator or cause of something ■ *vt* **1 WRITE** to write or be responsible for the final form of a book, report, or other text **2 CAUSE** to be the cause, creator, or originator of something [14C. Via Old French, < Latin *auctor* 'creator, originator' < *augere* 'originate, increase'.] —**authorial** /aw tháwri əl/ *adj* —**authorship** *n*

authoring /áwthəring/ *n* the creation of computer applications such as multimedia documents using special software for non-programmers

authoring language *n* a software development system that lets users develop applications without using formal programming language

authorisation *n* = authorization

authorise *vt* = authorize

authoritarian /aw thórri táiri ən/ *adj* **1** favouring strict rules and established authority **2** belonging to or believing in a political system in which obedience to the ruling person or group is strongly enforced —**authoritarian** *n* —**authoritarianism** *n*

authoritative /aw thórritətiv/ *adj* **1 RELIABLE** convincing, reliable, backed by evidence, and showing deep knowledge **2 BACKED BY AUTHORITY** backed by an established and accepted authority **3 SHOWING AUTHORITY** showing that the person is used to being obeyed or expects to be obeyed —**authoritatively** *adv* —**authoritativeness** *n*

authority /aw thórriti/ (*plural* **-ties**) *n* **1 RIGHT TO COMMAND** the right or power to enforce rules or give orders **2 HOLDER OF POWER** somebody or something with official power **3 POWER GIVEN TO SOMEBODY** power to act on behalf of somebody else or official permission to do something **4 SOURCE OF RELIABLE INFORMATION** a source of reliable information on a subject **5 ADMINISTRATIVE BODY** an official body that is set up by a government to administer an area of activity (*often plural*) **6 JUSTIFICATION** a statement that makes somebody believe something is true **7 QUALITY THAT IS RESPECTED** the ability to gain the respect of other people and to influence or control what they do **8 OBVIOUS KNOWLEDGE AND EXPERIENCE** knowledge, skill, or experience worthy of respect **9 SOURCE OF PRECEDENT OR PRINCIPLE** a law or legal decision that is cited as establishing a precedent or a principle **10 LEGITIMATE POWER** a form of rule that is seen as legitimate [13C. Via French, < Latin *auctoritas* < *auctor* (see AUTHOR).]

authority figure *n* somebody who is, or appears to be, strong and powerful

⚡ **authorization** /áwthə rī záysh'n/, **authorisation** *n* **1 PERMISSION** official power or permission to do something **2 DOCUMENT GIVING PERMISSION** a letter or document that confirms that somebody has permission to do something or be somewhere **3 TRANSACTION RISK ASSESSMENT** the process of assessing the degree of risk involved in an e-commerce transaction in terms of a customer's debt limits and available credit (*in e-commerce*)

authorize /áwthə rīz/ (**-izes**, **-izing**, **-ized**), **authorise** (**-rises**, **-rising**, **-rised**) *vt* to give somebody or something power or permission to do something or be somewhere [14C. Via French < medieval Latin *auctorizare* < Latin *auctor* (see AUTHOR).] —**authorized** *adj* —**authorizer** *n*

Authorized Version, **Authorised Version** *n* a version of the Bible published in England in 1611 and authorized by James I for use in the Church of England. US term **King James Bible**

autism /áwtizəm/ *n* a disturbance in psychological development in which use of language, reaction to stimuli, interpretation of the world, and the formation of relationships are not fully established and follow unusual patterns [Early 20C. < Greek *autos* 'self' + -ISM.]

autistic /aw tístik/ *adj* showing evidence of autism, e.g. failure to use language and perceive surroundings normally —**autistically** *adv*

auto /áwtō/ (*plural* **-tos**) *n US* a motor car (*informal*) [Late 19C. Shortening of AUTOMOBILE.]

auto. *abbr* **1** automatic **2** automotive

auto-, **aut-** *prefix* **1** self ○ *autograft* **2** automatic ○ *autorotation* [< Greek *autos* 'self']

autoantibody /áwtō ánti bodi/ (*plural* **-ies**) *n* an antibody that reacts against normal substances present in the organism producing it and is present in certain diseases (**autoimmune diseases**)

autobahn /áwtō baan, ówtō-/ *n* a motorway in a German-speaking country or region [Mid-20C. < German, 'automobile track'.]

autobiography /áwtō bī óggrəfi/ (*plural* **-phies**) *n* an account of somebody's life written by that person —**autobiographer** *n* —**autobiographical** /-bī ə gráffik'l/ *adj* —**autobiographically** *adv*

autobus /áwtō buss/ *n US* a bus or motor coach

autocatalysis /áwtō kə tálləsiss/ *n* the speeding up of a chemical reaction by a catalyst that is a product of the reaction —**autocatalytic** /áwtō kátta líttik/ *adj* —**autocatalytically** *adv*

autocephalous /áwtō séffələss/, **autocephalic** /áwtō si fállik/ *adj* describes an Eastern Orthodox church that is governed by its own elected bishop or patriarch [Mid-19C. < AUTO- + Greek *kephalē* 'head'.]

autochthon /aw tókthən, -thon/ (*plural* **-thons** *or* **-thones** /-thə neez/) *n* **1 NATIVE PLANT OR ANIMAL** a plant or animal that originated in the country where it is found **2 ABORIGINAL**

PERSON a descendant of the earliest inhabitants of a region **3 GEOLOGICAL DEPOSIT ORIGINATING WHERE FOUND** a rock formation, mineral deposit, or geological feature that was formed in the area where it is now found [Early 19C. < Greek *autokhthōn* 'indigenous' < *khthōn* 'earth, soil'.]

autochthonous /aw tókthənəss/ *adj* **1 FORMED WHERE FOUND** describes a rock, mineral deposit, or geological feature that was formed in the area where it is found **2 PRESENT FROM EARLIEST TIMES** descended from the original flora, fauna, or inhabitants of the region in which it is found. ◊ **allochthonous** *adj.* 2 **3 PRODUCED WHERE SITUATED** produced or originating as a physical function or disorder in the place where it is found —**autochthonism** *n* —**autochthonously** *adv* —**autochthony** *n*

SYNONYMS See ***native***.

autocidal /áwtō sīd'l/ *adj* describes a method of pest control in which sterile or genetically altered insects are released to reduce the breeding success of the local insect population

autoclave /áwtō klayv, áwtə-/ *n* **1 STERILIZATION EQUIPMENT** a strong steel vessel. Use: steam sterilization, pressurized reaction of chemicals at high temperature. **2 STEAMER FOR CONCRETE** an apparatus with which newly cast concrete is cured by steam under pressure ■ *vt* (**-claves, -claving, -claved**) **USE AUTOCLAVE** to use an autoclave to steam something [Late 19C. < French, < Greek *autos* 'self' + Latin *clavus* 'nail' or *clavis* 'key'; because it is self-fastening.]

autocorrelation /áwtō kórri láysh'n/ *n* a property displayed by some sequences of adjacent items not being independent of each other

autocracy /aw tókrəssi/ (*plural* **-cies**) *n* **1 RULE BY ONE PERSON** a government in which somebody holds unlimited power **2 RULER'S ABSOLUTE POWER** the unlimited political power of a single ruler **3 PLACE RULED BY ONE PERSON** a country governed by a single ruler who has unlimited power [Mid-17C. < Greek *autokrateia* < *autokratēs* (see AUTOCRAT).]

autocrat /áwtə krat/ *n* **1** a ruler who holds unlimited power and is answerable to no other person **2** somebody who dominates others [Early 19C. Via French *autocrate* < Greek *autokratēs* 'independent authority' < *kratos* 'power'.] —**autocratic** /áwtə kráttik/ *adj* —**autocratically** *adv*

autocross /áwtō kross/ *n* timed motor racing across rough ground [Mid-20C. Contraction of AUTOMOBILE + CROSS-COUNTRY.]

Autocue /áwtō kyoo/ *tdmk* a trademark for a device that displays an enlarged line-by-line text on a television screen to a speaker while remaining unseen to the audience

auto-da-fé /áwtō də fáy/ (*plural* **autos-da-fé** /áwtō də fáy/) *n* a sentence of death pronounced on a heretic by a court of the Spanish Inquisition and carried out by the civil authorities [Early 18C. < Portuguese, 'act of the faith'.]

autodeconstruction /áwtō deekən strúksh'n/ *n* critical analysis of artistic works that is done by the artists themselves rather than critics

autodestruct /áwtō di strúkt/ *vi* to undergo self-destruction (*technical*) ○ *The missile auto-destructed after a failed launch.* ■ *adj* allowing or causing something to destroy itself

autodial /áwtō dī əl/ *n* a device that automatically dials a prerecorded number in response to an input signal, e.g. pressing a button [Late 20C. Contraction.] —**autodialler** *n*

autodidact /áwtō dī dakt/ *n* somebody whose knowledge is self-taught [Mid-18C. < Greek *autodidaktos* < *didaskein* 'teach'.] —**autodidactic** /áwtō dī dáktik, -di-/ *adj*

autodyne /áwtō dīn/ *n* an electronic circuit containing an element such as a transistor that acts simultaneously as a detector and oscillator ■ *adj* describes a radio device containing an element, such as a transistor, that acts simultaneously as a detector and oscillator [Early 20C. < AUTO- + Greek *dunamis* 'force, power'.]

autoecious /aw teeshəss/ *adj* living as a pest or parasite on a single host species [Late 19C. < AUTO- + Greek *oikia* 'house'.] —**autoecism** *n*

autoeroticism /áwtō i róttisizəm/, **autoerotism** /áwtō érrətizəm/ *n* sexual arousal and gratification from self-stimulation —**autoerotic** *adj*

autofocus /áwtō fōkəss/ *n* a device that automatically adjusts the focus of a camera

autogamy /aw tóggəmi/ *n* **1** the process by which some flowering plants fertilize themselves **2** the division and subsequent reunification of a single cell in the reproductive processes of certain simple one-celled animals and algae —**autogamic** /áwtə gámmik/ *adj* —**autogamous** /aw tóggəməss/ *adj*

autogenesis /áwtō jénnississ/ *n* BIOL = **abiogenesis** —**autogenetic** /áwtō ji néttik/ *adj* —**autogenetically** *adv*

autogenic *adj* BIOL = **autogenous** —**autogenically** *adv*

autogenic training /áwtō jénniks/, **autogenics** *n* a method of relieving stress by using meditation and other mental exercises to produce physical relaxation

autogenocide /áwtō jénnə sīd/ *n* the extermination of people by their fellow citizens [Late 20C]

autogenous /aw tójjənəss/, **autogenic** *adj* **1 PRODUCED INSIDE** produced or created within something itself, without external help or influence **2 PRODUCED FROM SOMETHING FROM RECIPIENT'S BODY** produced in, or with tissue from, the body of the person to whom it will be given **3 NOT NEEDING BLOOD** describes insects that do not require a meal of blood in order to produce viable eggs [Mid-19C. < Greek *autogenēs* < *gignesthai* 'be born'.] —**autogenously** *adv*

autogiro /áwtō jīrō/ (*plural* **-ros**) *n* an aircraft that uses a propeller for forward motion and an unpowered horizontal rotor for lift and stability. ◊ **gyroplane** [Early 20C. < Spanish, 'self-turning' < *giro* 'gyration'.]

autograft /áwtə graaft/ *n* a graft of skin or other tissue obtained from the patient's own body

autograph /áwtə graaf, -graf/ *n* **1 SOMEBODY'S SIGNATURE** a signature, especially the signature of a famous person **2 HANDWRITTEN TEXT** a copy of a document or text handwritten by its creator (*technical*) ■ *vt* **SIGN WITH NAME** to write your signature on something such as a book or photograph [Early 17C. Via French or late Latin, < Greek *autographon* 'written with your own hand' < *graphein* 'write'.]

autograph hunter *n* somebody who collects the signatures of famous people (*informal*)

autohypnosis /áwtō hip nṓssiss/ *n* a process by which somebody hypnotizes himself or herself —**autohypnotic** /áwtō hip nóttik/ *adj*

autoimmune /áwtō i myoón/ *adj* caused by the reaction of an antibody to substances that occur naturally in the body —**autoimmunity** *n* —**autoimmunization** /áwtō ímmyoo nī záysh'n/ *n*

autoimmune disease *n* a disease caused by the reaction of antibodies to substances occurring naturally in the body

autoimmune haemolytic anaemia *n* a form of anaemia involving autoantibodies of red cell antigens

autoinfection /áwtō in féksh'n/ *n* infection caused by an organism already present in another part of the body or by the larval reproduction of a parasite already present in the body

autoinoculation /áwtō i nókyoo láysh'n/ *n* a disease that occurs when an infection spreads from one part of the body to another —**autoinoculable** /áwtō i nókyooləb'l/ *adj*

autointoxication /áwtō in tóksi káysh'n/ *n* poisoning by a substance that has been produced within the body of the person who is poisoned

autojumble /áwtō jumb'l/ *n* components and spares for obsolete vehicles, often found on sale at classic car and commercial vehicle rallies, country shows, or car boot sales (*informal*)

autoload /áwtō lōd/ *adj US* ARMS = **semiautomatic** *adj.* 1 —**autoloader** *n*

autologous /aw tólləgəss/ *adj* derived from the patient's own body [Early 20C. < AUTO- + *-logous* < -LOGY.]

autolysate /aw tóllə sayt, -zayt/ *n* a product of the process (**autolysis**) by which cells are broken down by enzymes produced in the cells themselves

autolysin /aw tóllissin, áwtə līssin/ *n* an enzyme that causes autolysis

autolysis /aw tóllississ/ *n* the digestion of cells by their own enzymes —**autolytic** /áwtə líttik/ *adj*

automata plural of **automaton**

automate /áwtə mayt/ (**-mates, -mating, -mated**) *vti* to convert a process or workplace to automation [Mid-20C. Back-formation < AUTOMATION.]

automated external defibrillator *n* a small portable device used on a person who has suffered a heart attack to restore a regular heartbeat

automated teller machine *n* full form of **ATM**

automatic /áwtə máttik/ *adj* **1 STARTING OR FUNCTIONING BY ITSELF** started, operated, or regulated by a process or mechanism without human intervention **2 DONE BY PRIOR ARRANGEMENT** beginning when certain conditions are fulfilled, without the need for a decision or action **3 INDEPENDENT OF SOMEBODY'S WILL** done without thought or intention, especially as the result of a reflex **4 DONE WITHOUT THOUGHT** performed without conscious thought as the result of habit or custom ■ *n* **1 MACHINE OPERATING WITHOUT HUMAN INTERVENTION** a machine, e.g. a washing machine, that controls its own operating process **2 MOTOR VEHICLE NOT REQUIRING MANUAL GEAR** a motor vehicle that has a built-in mechanism (**automatic transmission**) for changing gears without requiring the driver to do it **3 GUN THAT FIRES CONTINUOUSLY** a gun that continues to fire for as long as the trigger is pressed, automatically ejecting used cartridges [18C. < Greek *automatos* (see AUTOMATON).] —**automatically** *adv*

automatic exposure *n* a control system in a camera that sets the lens aperture and shutter speed according to the amount of light that is present

automatic frequency control *n* a control system in a radio or television receiver that keeps it tuned to a signal in spite of minor variations in the signal's frequency

automatic gain control *n* a radio receiver control system by which the amplifier is adjusted to compensate for variations in the volume of the signal, so that the volume of the output is constant

automaticity /áwtəmə tíssiti/ *n* the processing of information by an organism in response to stimuli that is automatic and involuntary, occurring without conscious control

automatic pilot *n* **1** a control in the steering system of a ship, aircraft, or spacecraft that can be set to put or keep it on a steady course **2** a condition in which somebody is not fully aware of what he or she is doing but is acting in a habitual and unthinking way, e.g. because of stress

automatic transmission *n* a transmission system for motor vehicles in which changes of gear are made automatically in response to the speed of the vehicle

automatic writing *n* the production of writing while in a trance or similar state as an attempt to make contact with the writer's unconscious or a supposed spirit

automation /áwtə máysh'n/ *n* the conversion of a workplace to one that replaces or minimizes human labour with mechanical or electronic equipment [Mid-20C. < AUTOMATIC.]

automatise *vt* = **automatize**

automatism /aw tómmətizəm/ *n* **1 INVOLUNTARY ORGANIC FUNCTION** a physical reflex or involuntary activity of the body **2 THEORY THAT ACTIONS ARE PERFORMED AUTOMATICALLY** the philosophical theory that all bodily actions have involuntary physical or physiological causes, or the legal defence that an action had such a cause **3 ACTIVITY NOT CONSCIOUSLY CAUSED** behaviour that is not consciously motivated, e.g. sleepwalking or involuntary repetitive actions **4 ARTISTIC METHOD** an artistic approach, associated with the surrealists, in which the painter or writer empties the mind and allows the unconscious to direct the work —**automatist** *n*

automatize /aw tómmə tīz/ (**-tizes, -tizing, -tized**), **automatise** (**-tises, -tising, -tised**) *vt* to make a process or workplace operate automatically using electronic or mechanical devices —**automatization** /aw tómmə tī záysh'n/ *n*

automaton /aw tómmətən, -ton/ (*plural* **-tons** *or* **-ta** /-mətə/) *n* **1** a machine that contains its own power source and can perform a complicated series of actions, including responses to external stimuli, without human intervention **2** somebody who behaves like a machine in emotionlessly obeying instructions and performing repetitive actions [Early 17C. Via Latin, < Greek, neuter of *automatos* 'acting by itself'.] —**automatous** *adj*

automobile /áwtə mə beel/ *n* a road vehicle, usually with four wheels and powered by an internal-combustion engine, designed to carry a small number of passengers [Late 19C. < French, 'self-mobile'.]

automobilia /áwtə mə beéli ə/ *npl* things to do with cars or motoring that appeal to collectors and enthusiasts [Late 20C. < AUTOMOBILE, after MEMORABILIA.]

automotive /áwtə mṓtiv/ *adj* **1** relating to or involving motor vehicles **2** propelled by its own motor or engine

autonomic /áwtə nómmik/ *adj* **1 CONTROLLED BY AUTOMATIC RESPONSES** describes functions of the nervous system not under the voluntary control of the individual, e.g. the regulation of heartbeat or gland secretions **2 WITHOUT THOUGHT** describes an action or response that occurs without conscious control **3 FROM INTERNAL STIMULI** produced or caused by internal stimuli —**autonomically** *adv*

autonomic nervous system *n* the part of the nervous system in humans and other vertebrates that controls involuntary activity, e.g. the action of the heart and glands, breathing, digestive processes, and reflex actions. ◊ **somatic nervous system**

autonomous /aw tónnəməss/ *adj* **1 SELF-GOVERNING** politically independent and self-governing **2 ABLE TO CHOOSE** able to make decisions and act on them as a free and independent moral agent **3 SELF-SUFFICIENT** existing, reacting, or developing as an independent, self-regulating organism —**autonomously** *adv*

autonomy /aw tónnəmi/ *n* **1 SELF-GOVERNMENT** political independence and self-government **2 EXISTENCE AS INDEPENDENT MORAL AGENT** personal independence and the capacity to make moral decisions and act on them **3 INDEPENDENCE OF A TEXT** the status of a text as an aesthetic object not to be judged or commented on in the light of external knowledge, e.g. of the biography of the author [Early 17C. < Greek *autonomia* < *autonomos* 'having its own laws' < *nomos* 'law'.] —**autonomist** *n*

autopilot /áwtō pīlət/ *n* AEROSP, NAUT = **automatic pilot** *n.* 1 ◇ **on autopilot** without guidance, control, or proper attention (*informal*) ○ *The business has been on autopilot since the manager resigned.*

autopista /áwtō pe͞estə/ *n* a motorway in a Spanish-speaking country or region [Mid-20C. < Spanish, 'automobile track'.]

autoplasty /áwtə plasti/ (*plural* **-ties**) *n* the repair of a patient's body using tissue, e.g. skin, taken from another part of the patient's body —**autoplastic** /áwtə plástik/ *adj* —**autoplastically** *adv*

autopsy /áwt opsi/ *n* (*plural* **-sies**) **1 EXAMINATION TO FIND CAUSE OF DEATH** the medical examination of a dead body in order to establish the cause and circumstances of death **2 EXHAUSTIVE EXAMINATION** an exhaustive critical examination of something ■ *vt* (**-sies, -sying, -sied**) **PERFORM AUTOPSY ON** to perform an autopsy on a person or organ [Mid-17C. Via French or modern Latin < Greek *autopsia* 'seeing with your own eyes' < *autoptēs* 'eyewitness'.]

auto racing *n US* MOTOR SPORTS = **motor racing**

autoradiograph /áwtō ráydi ə graaf, -graf/, **autoradiogram** /-gram/ *n* a photograph that reveals how radioactivity is distributed in a specimen or sample, made by exposing a photographic plate to the radiation —**autoradiographic** /áwtō ráydi ə gráffik/ *adj* —**autoradiography** /-ráydi óggrəfi/ *n*

autorickshaw /áwtō rík shaw/ *n* a vehicle with three wheels, like a covered motor scooter with a back seat for passengers, that is used as a taxi in South Asia

autorotation /áwtō rō táysh'n/ *n* the continuous rotation of an object, e.g. a propeller, caused by aerodynamic forces only

autoroute /áwtō root/ *n* a motorway in a French-speaking country or region [Mid-20C. < French, 'automobile route'.]

⚡**autosave** /áwtō sayv/ *n* a computer program feature in which data is saved automatically at predetermined intervals

autosome /áwtə sōm/ *n* a chromosome other than one that determines sex —**autosomal** /áwtə sṓm'l/ *adj* —**autosomally** *adv*

autostrada /áwtō straadə/ *n* a motorway in an Italian-speaking country or region [Early 20C. < Italian, 'automobile road'.]

autosuggestion /áwtō sə jéschən/ *n* the process by which somebody's perceptions, behaviour, or physical condition may be altered by means of his or her power of suggestion —**autosuggest** *vt* —**autosuggestibility** /áwtō sə jéstə bílləti/ *n* —**autosuggestible** *adj* —**autosuggestive** *adj*

autotelic /áwtō téllik, -te͞elik/ *adj* **1** concerning an entity or event that has within itself the purpose of its existence or occurrence **2** done for its own sake rather than to gain a material reward or avoid a punishment [Early 20C. < Greek *autotelēs* < *autos* 'self' + *telos* 'end'.] —**autotelism** *n*

autotimer /áwtō tīmər/ *n* an automatic timing device, e.g. on a cooker

autotomy /aw tóttəmi/ *n* the casting off of part of the body by an animal such as a lizard, snake, worm, or crustacean when it is caught or attacked by a predator —**autotomic** /áwtə tómmik/ *adj*

autotoxaemia /áwtō tok se͞emi ə/ *n* MED = **autointoxication**

autotoxin /áwtə tóksin/ *n* a substance that poisons the system within which it is formed

autotransformer /áwtō transs fáwrmər/ *n* a transformer in which the primary and secondary coils share all or some windings

autotransfusion /áwtō transs fyo͞ozh'n/ *n* a blood transfusion using the patient's own blood

autotrophic /áwtə tróffik/ *adj* describes organisms, especially green plants, that are capable of making nutrients from inorganic materials —**autotroph** /áwtə trōf/ *n* —**autrotrophically** /-tróffikli/ *adv* —**autotrophy** /aw tóttrəfi/ *n*

autowinder /áwtō wīndər/ *n* a device that automatically winds the film in a camera forward after a photograph is taken

autoxidation /aw tóksi dáysh'n/ *n* **1** oxidation of certain substances at normal temperatures due to contact with air **2** oxidation that occurs only in the presence of another substance undergoing oxidation

~~**autum**~~ incorrect spelling of **autumn**

autumn /áwtəm/ *n* **1** the season occurring between summer and winter. Autumn traditionally lasts from 22 September to 21 December in the northern hemisphere, and from 21 March to 21 June in the southern hemisphere. US term **fall** *n.* 6 **2** a time in the development of something that follows its most vigorous and successful phase, before its decline ○ *in the autumn of his career as a cellist* [14C. < Latin *autumnus*.] —**autumnal** /aw túmn'l/ *adj*

autumnal equinox *n* **1** the first day of autumn, when the sun crosses the plane of the Earth's equator and makes day and night approximately of equal length **2** the position of the sun during the autumnal equinox

autumn crocus *n* an autumn-flowering plant. Flowers: crocus-shaped, purple or pink, growing directly from the ground after the leaves have died down. *Colchicum autumnale.*

autunite /áwtə nīt/ *n* a yellow radioactive fluorescent mineral consisting of hydrated calcium uranium phosphate [Mid-19C. After *Autun*, France.]

aux. *abbr* auxiliary

auxesis /awg ze͞essiss, -se͞essiss/ *n* growth in animals or plants caused by an increase in the size of cells, not by cellular division [Mid-19C. Via late Latin, < Greek.] —**auxetic** /awk séttik/ *adj* —**auxetically** *adv*

auxiliary /awg zíllyəri, -zílləri/ *adj* **1 GIVING SUPPORT** acting to support or supplement a group of people **2 HELD IN RESERVE** available as backup for a system, process, or piece of equipment **3 SECONDARY** secondary to something larger **4 WITH MOTOR AND SAILS** describes a boat with an engine to supplement or replace the sails ■ *n* (*plural* **-ries**) **1 SUPPORTING PERSON OR THING** somebody who or something that has a supporting or supplementary role **2** GRAM = **auxiliary verb 3 SAILING SHIP WITH ENGINE** a sailing ship equipped with an engine **4 NAVAL SUPPORT VESSEL** a naval vessel, e.g. a tug or transport ship, that does not engage in combat **5 MEMBER OF SUPPORTING TROOPS** a member of a separate troop, often from another country, that fights with an army as allies or mercenaries and has its own command structure (*often plural*) [Early 17C. < Latin *auxiliarius* < *auxilium* 'help, assistance'.]

⚡**auxiliary device** *n* a peripheral piece of computer hardware, e.g. a printer or scanner

auxiliary note *n* in music, a note that falls between two adjacent notes of the same pitch and is not an overtone

auxiliary rotor *n* the tail rotor of a helicopter

auxiliary verb *n* a verb that is used with another verb to indicate person, number, mood, tense, or aspect. Some auxiliary verbs in English are 'be', 'have', and 'do'.

LANGUAGE NOTE Auxiliary verbs: The auxiliary verbs in English are *be, do,* and *have,* which together with the so-called modal verbs (or modal auxiliaries) *can, could, may, might, must, ought to, shall, should, will,* and *would* (and in some classifications *dare, need,* and *used*), are all used with other verbs to form past and future tenses, negatives, questions, the passive voice, and other special functions. Most ordinary verbs cannot fulfil these functions by themselves; for example you have to use the auxiliary verb *do* to form negatives and questions (*They don't like it. Do you want to leave?*), the auxiliary verb *be* to form the progressive aspect (*I am going.*), the auxiliary verbs *be* and *have* to form past, progressive, and imperfect tenses (*We were leaving. They haven't decided.*), and the modal verbs *shall* and *will* to form future tenses (*He will drive you to the station. Shall we go now?*). Sometimes more than one auxiliary verb is used to form a tense, as in *We will be going* and *They have been paid.* The verb *be* is used to form the passive voice: *The letter was posted last night.*

~~**auxillary**~~ incorrect spelling of **auxiliary**

auxin /áwksin/ *n* a natural plant hormone or synthetic substance that affects the growth and development of all plant parts [Mid-20C. < Greek *auxein* 'to increase'.] —**auxinic** /awk sínnik/ *adj* —**auxinically** *adv*

auxotonic /áwksə tónnik/ *adj* occurring against increasing force as part of a muscle contraction [< Greek *auxein* 'to increase' + TONIC]

auxotroph /áwksə trōf/ *n* a mutant strain of an organism, e.g. a bacterium, that has lost the ability to synthesize a particular nutrient (**growth factor**) and must obtain it from its environment to survive. ◊ **prototroph** [Mid-20C. Back-formation < *auxotrophic* < Greek *auxein* 'to increase'.] —**auxotrophic** *adj*

Av *n* CALENDAR, JUDAISM = **Ab**

AV *abbr* **1** audiovisual **2** Authorized Version

av. *abbr* **1 av., Av.** avenue **2** average **3** avoirdupois

A/V, a/v, a.v. *abbr* ad valorem

avadavat /ávvədə vát/ *n* an Asian waxbill often kept as a cagebird. Genus: *Estrilda.* [Late 17C. Alteration of *Ahmadabad*, city in W India where these birds were sold.]

avail /ə váyl/ *v* **1** *vr* **USE** to make use of something useful or helpful while you have the opportunity **2** *vti* **HELP** to be helpful or useful to somebody or to help somebody succeed ■ *n* **HELP OR ADVANTAGE** help, advantage, or success in achieving something (*in negatives*) ○ *His defence was to no avail, a conviction was secured.* [14C. < Old French *vail-*, stem of *valoir* 'be worth' < Latin *valere* 'be strong'.]

available /ə váyləb'l/ *adj* **1 ABLE TO BE GOT** able to be used, obtained, or relied on **2** *US* **ELIGIBLE FOR OFFICE** eligible and willing to undertake a public office or stand for election **3 UNATTACHED** not currently involved in a romantic or sexual relationship but ready to engage in one (*informal*) —**availability** /ə váylə bílləti/ *n* —**availably** *adv*

~~**availible**~~ incorrect spelling of **available**

avalanche /ávvə laanch/ *n* **1 DOWNHILL FALL OF SNOW** a rapid downhill flow of a large mass of something dislodged from a mountainside or the top of a precipice, especially snow or ice **2 OVERWHELMING QUANTITY** a sudden overwhelming quantity of something **3 INCREASE IN NUMBER OF IONS** an increase in the number of ions or electrons, usually within a medium exposed to an applied electromagnetic field, caused by collisions of the ions or electrons with the medium ■ *vti* (**-lanches, -lanching, -lanched**) **FLOW DOWN IN LARGE QUANTITY** to descend in a large mass on something or somebody [Late 18C. Via French, < Romansh *avalantze* < assumed Vulgar Latin *labanca.*]

Avalon /ávvə lon/ *n* in Celtic mythology, an island paradise in the West

avant-garde /ávong gaárd/ *n* **ARTISTS WITH NEW IDEAS AND METHODS** writers, artists, filmmakers, or musicians whose work is innovative, experimental, or unconventional (*takes a singular or plural verb*) ■ *adj* **1 ARTISTICALLY NEW** artistically new, experimental, or unconventional **2 OF THE AVANT-GARDE** belonging to the artistically innovative [Early 20C. < French, 'before the guard'.] —**avant-gardism** *n* —**avant-gardist** *n*

Avar /aá vaar, áv-/ *n* a Caucasian language spoken in Dagestan —**Avar** *adj*

avarice /ávvəriss/ *n* an unreasonably strong desire to obtain and keep money [13C. Via French, < Latin *avaritia* < *avarus* 'greedy' < *avere* 'to desire'.]

avaricious /ávvə ríshəss/ *adj* showing an unreasonably strong desire for money —**avariciously** *adv* —**avariciousness** *n*

avascular /ə váskyŏŏlər/ *adj* lacking blood vessels in body tissue —**avascularity** /ə váskyŏŏ lárrəti/ *n*

avascular necrosis *n* the death of cells in tissue or organs as a result of deficient blood supply

avast /ə vaást/ *interj* used by sailors as a command to stop doing something or to ignore a previous order [Early 17C. Alteration of Dutch *hou'vast*, shortening of *houd vast* 'hold fast'.]

ϟ **avatar** /ávvə taar/ *n* **1 INCARNATION OF HINDU DEITY** an incarnation of a Hindu deity in human or animal form, especially one of the incarnations of Vishnu such as Rama and Krishna **2 EMBODIMENT OF** somebody who embodies an idea or concept **3 IMAGE OF PERSON IN VIRTUAL REALITY** a movable three-dimensional image used to represent somebody in cyberspace [Late 18C. < Sanskrit *avatāra* 'descent' (of a god to earth).]

AVC *abbr* additional voluntary contribution

avdp. *abbr* avoirdupois

ave /aá vay, aávi/, **Ave** *n* **1** RELIG = **Hail Mary** *n.* **2** the time when the Hail Mary is to be said, marked by the ringing of a bell **3** a small bead on a rosary, used for keeping track of how many times the Hail Mary has been said [13C. < Latin, imperative of *avere* 'be or fare well'.]

Ave., ave. *abbr* avenue

Avebury /áyvbəri/ village in SW England, site of the largest ancient stone circle in the country

Avedon /ávvə don/, **Richard** (*b.* 1923) US photographer

Ave Maria, ave, Ave *n* RELIG = **Hail Mary** *n.* [13C. < Latin.]

avenge /ə vénj/ (**avenges, avenging, avenged**) *vt* to inflict punishment on somebody for a wrong done [14C. < Old French *avengier* < *vengier* < Latin *vindicare* (see VINDICATE).] —**avenger** *n* —**avenging** *adj* —**avengingly** *adv*

USAGE avenge or **revenge**? Both words are about repaying a wrong. The differences between them have to do with grammar and shades of meaning, though there is considerable overlap in meaning, dictated by usage over time. Grammatically speaking, ***avenge*** is a verb only; ***revenge*** is a verb and more usually a noun. ***Avenge*** traditionally relates not only to repaying a wrong but to getting justice on somebody else's behalf as a remedy for that wrong (*They sought to avenge their sister's murder* [or *their murdered sister*] *by pursuing her killer through the courts*). ***Revenge***, often connoting malice, traditionally relates to getting even with an adversary by inflicting punishment or harm (*In an act of revenge for the bombing of the ship, the navy shelled the terrorists' training camps*). Though both ***avenge*** and ***revenge*** can be used as transitive verbs with reflexive pronouns, ***revenge*** is the one most commonly used: *The dictatorship revenged itself on the partisans' radio station by burning it to the ground.*

avens /ávvinz, áyvənz/ (*plural* **-ens**) *n* PLANTS = **mountain avens** [12C. < Old French *avence*.]

aventurine /ə véntyŏŏrin, -reen/, **aventurin** /-rin/ *n* **1** dark brown or green glass that contains sparkling mineral particles **2** a variety of quartz or feldspar containing minute particles of mica or haematite. Use: gems. [Early 18C. Via French, < Italian *avventurino* 'chance' (because discovered accidentally).]

avenue /ávvə nyoo/ *n* **1 WIDE STREET** a wide street or road in a town **2 MEANS OF APPROACH** a course of action to be taken in order to approach, attain, or gain access to somebody or something ○ *need to explore all avenues* **3 TREE-LINED ROAD** a road lined with trees, especially a tree-lined path leading through grounds to a country residence [Early 17C. < French, 'approach', feminine past participle of *avenir* 'arrive' < Latin *advenire* (see ADVENT).]

aver /ə vúr/ (**avers, averring, averred**) *vt* **1** to assert or allege something confidently (*formal*) **2** to state or allege that something is true [14C. < French *avérer* < Latin *verus* 'true'.] —**averment** *n* —**averrable** *adj*

average /ávvərij/ *n* **1 TYPICAL AMOUNT** the level, amount, or degree of something that is typical of a group or class of people or things **2 NUMBER CONSIDERED TYPICAL OF NUMBER GROUP** a number that can be regarded as typical of a group of numbers, calculated by adding the numbers together, then dividing the total by the number of numbers **3 MEASURE OF PLAYING PERFORMANCE** a measure of a player's or team's achievement, reached by dividing the number of opportunities for successful performances by how many times a successful performance was achieved **4 LOSS AT SEA** in maritime law, the loss or damage of a ship and its cargo, or the division of the costs of this loss or damage among the owner or partners involved **5 INTERMEDIATE PRICE** a measure of stock exchange performance, based on the total of prices for a group or class of securities, divided by the number of securities ■ *adj* **1 TYPICAL** without any extraordinary, untypical, or exceptional characteristic ○ *just an average guy* **2 CALCULATED AS TOTAL DIVIDED BY MEMBERS** obtained by adding the numerical value for each member or part of a group or class and dividing the total by the number of members **3 NOT VERY GOOD** not terrible but not very good either ○ *The performance was no better than average.* ■ *vt* (**-ages, -aging, -aged**) **1 CALCULATE NUMERICAL AVERAGE** to calculate a numerical average of something, by finding the total amount and dividing it by the number of members in the group **2 HAVE AS AVERAGE** to have or show as an average **3 ACHIEVE OR GET AS AVERAGE** to do, produce, or receive a particular amount of something as an average ○ *She averages one trip to Asia each year.* [15C. Alteration, after DAMAGE, of French *avarie* < Arabic *'awār* 'damage to goods'.] —**averagely** *adv* —**averageness** *n*

average down *vi* to purchase more shares of a security when its price is falling, in the hope of reducing costs and increasing profits

average out *v* **1** *vi* to have or show as an average **2** *vt* to calculate the numerical average of something

average up *vi* to purchase more shares of a security when its price is rising, in the hope of increasing profits

average deviation *n* STATS = **mean deviation**

averse /ə vúrss/ *adj* **1** strongly opposed to or disliking something (*formal; see usage note*) **2** describes a leaf or flower that is turned away from the main stem or axis [Late 16C. < Latin *aversus* 'turned away', past participle of *avertere* (see AVERT).] —**aversely** *adv* —**averseness** *n*

SYNONYMS See ***unwilling***.

USAGE See ***adverse***.

aversion /ə vúrsh'n/ *n* **1** a strong feeling of dislike or hatred of somebody or something **2** somebody or something strongly disliked

SYNONYMS See ***dislike***.

aversion therapy *n* **1** a method of therapy that attempts to eliminate undesired behaviour by associating it repeatedly with painful or unpleasant effects **2** therapy aimed at eliminating an irrational fear or dislike by making somebody experience the thing feared or disliked in remote or indirect ways that gradually become closer and more direct

aversive /ə vúrssiv/ *adj* inducing dislike or loathing of something —**aversively** *adv* —**aversiveness** *n*

avert /ə vúrt/ *vt* **1** to prevent something from occurring, especially something harmful **2** to turn your eyes away from something [14C. Via Old French, < Latin *avertere* 'to turn away' < *vertere* 'turn'.] —**avertible** *adj*

Avery /áyvəri/, **Oswald** (1877–1955) US bacteriologist and geneticist

Avesta /ə véstə/ *n* the sacred book of the Zoroastrian religion [Early 16C. < Middle Persian *Avastāk* 'original text'.]

Avestan /ə véstən/, **Avestic** /ə véstik/ *n* an ancient Iranian language once spoken in various parts of the Middle East —**Avestan** *adj*

avg. *abbr* average

avian /áyvi ən/ *adj* belonging to, relating to, or characteristic of birds [Late 19C. < Latin *avis* 'bird'.]

aviary /áyvi əri/ (*plural* **-ies**) *n* an enclosure or large cage for birds [Late 16C. < Latin *aviarium* < *avis* 'bird'.]

aviate /áyvi ayt/ (**-ates, -ating, -ated**) *vi* to pilot or fly in an aircraft (*formal*) [Late 19C. Back-formation < AVIATION.]

aviation /áyvi áysh'n/ *n* the design, manufacture, use, or operation of aircraft [Mid-19C. < French, < Latin *avis* 'bird'.]

aviator /áyvi aytər/ *n* the pilot of an aircraft

aviator glasses *npl US* spectacles with oval tinted lenses and a metal frame

aviculture /áyvi kulchər, ávvi-/ *n* the care and rearing of birds in cages, aviaries, or enclosures [Late 19C. < Latin *avis* 'bird' + CULTURE.] —**aviculturist** *n*

avid /ávvid/ *adj* eager for, dedicated to, or enthusiastic about something [Mid-18C. Back-formation < AVIDITY.] —**avidly** *adv* —**avidness** *n*

avidin /ávvidin/ *n* an egg white protein that inactivates the vitamin biotin [Mid-20C. < AVID, because of its 'avidity' for BIOTIN.]

avidity /ə víddəti/ *n* **1** great eagerness or greed for something **2** CHEM = **affinity** *n.* **6 3** a measure of the strength with which an antibody binds to an antigen [15C. Directly or via French, < Latin *aviditas* < *avidus* < *avere* 'to desire'.]

Aviemore /ávvi mawr/ ski resort in NE Scotland. Population: 2,214 (1991).

avifauna /áyvi fáwnə, ávvi-/ (*plural* **-nas** *or* **-nae** /-fáwnee/) *n* all the birds present in a region [Late 19C. < Latin *avis* 'bird' + FAUNA.] —**avifaunal** *adj*

Avignon /ávvee nyoN/ city in SE France. Population: 85,935 (1999).

avionics /áyvi ónniks/ *n* the development and use of electric and electronic equipment for aircraft and spacecraft (+ *singular verb*) ■ *npl* the electrical and electronic equipment of an aircraft or spacecraft (+ *plural verb*) [Mid-20C. Blend of AVIATION + ELECTRONICS.] —**avionic** *adj*

avirulent /ay vírrŏŏlənt, -ryŏŏ-/ *adj* describes microorganisms that are not likely to cause disease in another organism —**avirulence** *n*

avitaminosis /áy víttəmin ṓssiss/ (*plural* **-ses** /-seez/) *n* a disease caused by deficiency of a particular vitamin —**avitaminotic** /-óttik/ *adj*

Aviv /ə veév/ *n* JUDAISM = **Nisan**

AVM *abbr Can, UK* Air Vice-Marshal

avo /ávvoo/ (*plural* **avos**) *n* a subunit of currency in Macau [Early 20C. < Portuguese, shortened < *oitavo* 'eighth' < Latin *octavus* < *octo* 'eight'.]

avocado /ávvə kaádō/ (*plural* **-dos**) *n* **1 avocado, avocado pear GREEN-FLESHED EDIBLE FRUIT** a fruit with a leathery dark green or blackish skin, soft smooth-tasting pale green flesh, and a large stony seed, eaten raw in salads or dips **2 TREE ON WHICH AVOCADOS GROW** a tropical tree that bears avocados. *Persea americana.* **3 CREAMY GREEN** a dull creamy green colour [Mid-17C. < Spanish, alteration of *aguacate* < Nahuatl *ahuacatl* 'testicle' (because of the shape of the fruit).] —**avocado** *adj*

avocation /ávvə káysh'n/ *n* (*formal*) **1** a calling or occupation **2** a hobby or pastime [Early 17C. < Latin *avocation-*, 'distraction' < *vocare* 'to call'.] —**avocational** *adj* —**avocationally** *adv*

avocet /ávvə set/ *n* a shore bird with black and white plumage and a long slender upward-curving beak. Genus: *Recurvirostra.* [Late 17C. Via French *avocette* < Italian *avosetta*.]

Avogadro /ávvə gaá drō/, **Amedeo, Conte di Quaregna e Ceretto** (1776–1856) Italian physicist and chemist

Avogadro's constant *n* PHYS, CHEM = **Avogadro's number**

Avogadro's law *n* a principle in physics stating that equal volumes of different gases at the same temperature and pressure contain the same number of molecules [Late 19C. After Amedeo AVOGADRO.]

Avogadro's number, Avogadro's constant *n* (*symbol* N_A) the number of atoms or molecules, approximately 6.022×10^{23}, contained in one mole of a substance [Late 19C. After Amedeo AVOGADRO.]

avoid /ə vóyd/ *v* **1** *vt* **NOT GO NEAR** to keep away from somebody or something ○ *a place to be avoided* **2** *vti* **NOT DO OR PREVENT** to manage not to do something or to stop something happening ○ *I narrowly avoided colliding with it.* **3** *vt* **STATE SOMETHING IS NOT VALID** to say that something is void or invalid [14C. < Anglo-Norman, < Old French *vuide, voide* 'empty' (see VOID).] —**avoidable** *adj* —**avoidably** *adv* —**avoider** *n*

USAGE avoid, evade, or **elude**? All three words involve keeping away from somebody or something or keeping somebody or something away from you. The main difference between ***avoid*** and ***evade*** is that ***avoid*** is neutral in tone whereas ***evade*** implies dishonesty or deception, or at least some sort of ulterior motive. If you ***avoid*** a responsibility, you take measures to prevent it from being necessary, whereas if you ***evade*** a responsibility you get out of it in an underhand or deceitful way. ***Avoid*** can be followed by a verbal noun in *-ing*, whereas ***evade*** must be followed by an ordinary noun: *We avoided having to pay. We evaded payment.* ***Elude*** implies clever or ingenious avoidance. It also has the extended meaning 'be beyond understanding or recall', as in *Her name eludes me.*

avoidance /ə vóydənss/ *n* **1 ACT OF KEEPING AWAY** the act of staying away from somebody or something **2 ACT OF NOT DOING** the act of refraining from doing something or preventing something from happening or applying **3 ACT OF MAKING SOMETHING INVALID** the act of making something void or invalid

USAGE avoidance or **evasion**? The difference between these two nouns corresponds to the difference between *avoid* and *evade*. In particular, *tax avoidance* means a legal method of reducing a liability to pay tax, whereas *tax evasion* means an illegal method.

avoirdupois /ávv waar dyoo pwaá, ávvərdə poyz/ *n* **1** MEASURE = **avoirdupois weight 2** the amount that somebody weighs (*humorous*) [14C. < Old French *aveir de peis* 'goods of weight'.]

avoirdupois weight, avoirdupois *n* a system for measuring weights based on the pound

Avon /áyvən/ **1** former county in W England **2** river in central England. Length: 154 km/96 mi. **3** river in SW England. Length: 120 km/75 mi. **4** river in S England. Length: 96 km/60 mi.

avow /ə vów/ *vt* to state or affirm that something is a fact (*formal*) [13C. Via Old French *avouer* 'acknowledge' < Latin *advocare* 'summon' (see ADVOCATE).] —**avowable** *adj* —**avowably** *adv* —**avowedly** /ə vówidli/ *adv*

avowal /ə vów əl/ *n* a frank statement or admission (*formal*)

avulsion /ə vúlsh'n/ *n* **1** the tearing away or separation of part of the body, resulting from an accident or performed during surgery **2** the removal of soil from one person's land to another's, especially by a flood [Early 17C. Directly or via French < Latin *avulsion-* < *vellere* 'pull'.]

avuncular /ə vúngkyŏŏlər/ *adj* **1** resembling an uncle, especially one who is friendly, helpful, or good-humoured **2** relating to or deriving from an uncle (*formal or humorous*) [Mid-19C. < Latin *avunculus* 'maternal uncle'.] —**avuncularity** /ə vúngkyŏŏ lárrəti/ *n* —**avuncularly** *adv*

avunculate /ə vúngkyŏŏlət/ *n* in some patrilineal societies, a special relationship similar to that of father and son that exists between a man and his sister's sons —**avunculate** *adj*

aw /aw/ *interj US, Scotland* used to express surprise, disappointment, or pity (*informal*) [Mid-19C. Natural exclamation.]

AWACS /áy waks/ *n* a radar and computer system carried in an aircraft to track large numbers of low-flying aircraft [Acronym < *airborne warning and control system*]

await /ə wáyt/ *v* **1** *vti* to expect or be looking for somebody or something **2** *vt* to be going to happen or be given to somebody ○ *'Where we find a difficulty we may always expect that a discovery awaits us'.* (C. S. Lewis, *Reflections on the Psalms*; 1961) [13C. Via Anglo-Norman *awaitier* < Old French *guaitier* < Germanic.]

USAGE await, await for, wait, or **wait for**? You ***await*** or ***wait for*** test results or the arrival of a professor, and you travel to exotic lands where great adventures ***wait*** or ***await***. You do not *await for* anybody: *Let's take a break as we wait for [not await for] the judge to arrive in the courtroom* or *...while we await the judge's arrival.*

Awakabal /ə wákə bal/ (*plural* **-bal** *or* **-bals**) *n* **1** a member of an Australian Aboriginal people of New South Wales **2** the language of the Awakabal people, now extinct [Early 19C. < an Aboriginal language.] —**Awakabal** *adj*

awake /ə wáyk/ *adj* **1 NOT ASLEEP** fully conscious and not asleep **2 ALERT** alert and vigilant about what is going on all around you ○ *'The colour had come back to his face, and his eyes were clear, and fully awake and aware'.* (J. R. R. Tolkien, *The Fellowship of the Ring*; 1954) **3 AWARE** fully aware of something or alert to it ■ *vti* (**awakes, awaking, awoke** /ə wṓk/ *or* **awaked, awoken** /ə wṓkən/ *or* **awaked**) **1 EMERGE FROM SLEEP** to rouse somebody or be roused from sleep **2 BECOME OR MAKE SOMEBODY AWARE** to become or make somebody become alert to something **3 AROUSE SOMEBODY** to arouse yourself or somebody else from a dazed or dreamlike state **4 AROUSE FEELINGS** to arouse feelings or memories [Old English *āwæcnan* < *wacian* 'be awake' and assumed *wacen* 'wake up' < Germanic]

USAGE awake, awaken, wake, or **waken**? Although all four verbs are interchangeable in both the transitive (with an object) and the intransitive (without an object) uses, in practice ***awake*** and ***awaken*** are preferred in figurative meanings: *At last we awoke to the dangers that faced us.* When used in literal meanings ***awake*** and ***awaken*** are normally used intransitively or in the passive: *He awoke at four in the morning. I was awoken by shouts in the street. Will you wake us at four?* ***Wake*** is the only one of these verbs that can be followed by *up*.

awaken /ə wáykən/ *vti* to wake up from a state of sleep or a state likened to sleep [Old English *āwæcnian* < *wæcnan* 'waken' < Germanic] —**awakener** *n*

awakening /ə wáykəning/ *adj* **JUST BEGINNING** just beginning or growing ■ *n* **1 AROUSAL FROM SLEEP** the act or process of waking from sleep **2 RENEWED ATTENTION TO** a revival or renewal of interest in something, especially religion **3 SUDDEN AWARENESS** a sudden recognition or realization of something

award /ə wáwrd/ *n* **1 SOMETHING GIVEN FOR ACHIEVEMENT** something, e.g. a prize, that is given in recognition of somebody's merit or an achievement **2 SOMETHING GRANTED BY LAW COURT** something bestowed, granted, or assigned to somebody by a court of law or by arbitration ■ *vt* **1 GIVE SOMETHING FOR MERIT** to give somebody something in recognition of merit **2 BESTOW AS RESULT OF COURT'S DECISION** to bestow or grant something by a judicial decision or by arbitration [14C. Via Anglo-Norman, 'decide a legal case' < Old French *warder* 'to judge' < Germanic.] —**awardable** *adj* —**awardee** /ə wáwr deé/ *n* —**awarder** *n*

award wage, award rate *n ANZ* a statutory minimum wage set by an industrial court for a specified type of work

aware /ə wáir/ *adj* **1 KNOWING** having knowledge of something because you have observed it or somebody has told you about it ○ *We are already aware of the problem, and we are dealing with it.* **2 NOTICING OR REALIZING** mindful that something exists because you notice it or realize that it is happening ○ *He became aware of a pain in his left side.* **3 KNOWLEDGEABLE** well-informed about what is going on in the world or about the latest developments in a particular sphere of activity ○ *More financially aware investors were starting to sell their stock.* [Old English *gewær* 'very watchful' < *wær* 'watchful' < Indo-European, 'perceive, watch out for'] —**awareness** *n*

SYNONYMS ***aware, conscious, mindful, cognizant, sensible***

CORE MEANING: having knowledge of the existence of something

aware knowing something either intellectually or intuitively; **conscious** keenly aware of something and regarding it as important; **mindful** actively attentive, or deliberately keeping something in mind; **cognizant** (*formal*) having special knowledge about something; **sensible** (*formal*) keenly aware of something.

awash /ə wósh/ *adj* **1 COVERED IN WATER** covered in water or some other liquid **2 OVERSUPPLIED** having more of something than is desirable or manageable ○ *an office awash with letters of complaint* **3 WITH WATER RUNNING OVER THE SIDES** sunk so low that water is able to come in over the sides of the vessel

away /ə wáy/ CORE MEANING: an adverb used to indicate that something or somebody moves so as to leave a particular place ○ *I really need to go away for a while.* ○ *The truck drove away leaving us stranded.* ○ *The cat has run away.*

1 *adv* **UNINVOLVED** separated or far from somebody or something ○ *I try to stay away from trouble.* **2** *adv* **IN A DIFFERENT DIRECTION** in a different direction from the one somebody was originally facing or looking in ○ *He turned his face away.* **3** *adv* **INTO THE DISTANCE** towards the distance ○ *olive groves stretching away towards the sea* **4** *adv* **IN THE FUTURE** at a particular time in the future (*follows a span of time*) ○ *Christmas is only a week away.* **5** *adv* **INTO STORAGE OR SAFEKEEPING** into the place where something is normally stored or kept safe ○ *We put the cutlery away.* **6** *adv* **OFF** so as to remove or separate something, or so as to be removed or separated (*follows a verb*) ○ *a tool to chip away the old paint* **7** *adv* **TO OR FROM** into or out of the possession of somebody or something (*follows the verb or object of the verb*) ○ *decided to give the old car away* **8** *adv* **UNTIL SOMETHING IS USED UP** so as to make something disappear or be expended (*follows a verb and precedes the object*) **9** *adv* **GRADUALLY** gradually until it ceases or is no longer noticed ○ *The music gradually died away.* **10** *adv* **SO AS TO SHOW A CHANGE** so that a perceptible change from one thing to another occurs ○ *a shift away from heavier taxation* **11** *adv* **WITHOUT STOPPING** continuously and usually energetically over a period of time ○ *hammering away in the garage* **12** *adv* **SO AS TO SET OUT** so as to be on a journey ○ *hope to get away after breakfast* **13** *adv, adj* **IN ANOTHER PLACE** not in the particular place or the place where somebody usually is, especially at home or at work ○ *I'll be away until Thursday.* ○ *She works away from the office.* **14** *adv, adj* **IN DISTANCE OR TIME** as measured in distance or time from here (*follows a measure or indication of distance or time*) ○ *The mountains are not far away.* **15** *adv, adj* **ON OPPOSING TEAM'S GROUND** played on an opponent's ground ○ *Their next three games will be played away.* ○ *Their away record has been very bad this season.* **16** *adj* **FURTHEST FROM THE HOLE** placed furthest from the hole in a game of golf [Old English *aweg* < *on weg* 'on (your) way']

awe /aw/ *n* **1 MIXTURE OF WONDER AND DREAD** a feeling of amazement and respect mixed with fear that is often coupled with a feeling of personal insignificance or powerlessness ○ *Filled with awe, they gazed at the ruins of the massive temple.* ○ *I was completely in awe of her.* **2 ABILITY TO INSPIRE DREAD** the ability to inspire dread or reverence (*archaic*) ■ *vt* (**awes, awing, awed**) **CAUSE AWE IN** to make somebody feel awe (*usually passive*) ○ *The visiting ambassadors were awed by this display of military might.* [13C. < Old Norse *agi*.]

aweary /ə weéri/ *adj* feeling very tired (*archaic or literary*) ○ *'By my troth, Nerissa, my little body is aweary of this great world!'* (Shakespeare *The Merchant of Venice*; 1596)

aweather /ə wéthər/ *adv* towards the windward side

~~**aweful**~~ incorrect spelling of **awful**

aweigh /ə wáy/ *adj* hanging clear of the bottom of a body of water ○ *Anchors aweigh!*

awe-inspiring *adj* so impressive as to make a person feel humble or slightly afraid

awesome /áwsəm/ *adj* **1** so impressive or overwhelming as to inspire a strong feeling of admiration or fear ○ *the awesome destructive power of a tornado* **2** used as a general term of enthusiastic approval (*slang*) ○ *The second track on this CD is totally awesome.* —**awesomely** *adv* —**awesomeness** *n*

awestruck /áw struk/, **awestricken** /-strikən/ *adj* filled with a feeling of awe

awful /áwf'l/ *adj* **1 EXTREMELY BAD** very bad or unpleasant ○ *an awful smell* **2 CAUSING SHOCK OR SADNESS** extremely shocking, saddening, or unpleasant ○ *an awful accident* **3 NOT VERY WELL** in very poor health ○ *I feel awful this morning.* **4 VERY GREAT** enormous in size, amount, number, or extent (*informal*) ○ *We spent an awful lot of money on furniture.* **5 AWE-INSPIRING** so impressive as to inspire awe (*literary*) ■ *adv* **EXTREMELY** to an extreme degree or extent (*informal*) ○ *It's awful hot this morning.* [13C. < AWE.] —**awfulness** *n*

USAGE The most common use of ***awful*** in current English has nothing to do with inspiring awe but has the generalized meaning 'very bad or unpleasant', as in the example *The weather has been awful*, and in certain common phrases, for example *an awful shame* and *an awful cheat*, in which ***awful*** intensifies the meaning of the word it accompanies (here, *shame* and *cheat*). This use of ***awful*** is deep-rooted in idiomatic English and is normally unexceptionable, but it is often better to avoid it in more formal contexts.

awfully /áwfli, -fəli/ *adv* **1** to an extremely great degree ○ *I'm awfully grateful to you for helping me out.* **2** in a very bad or unpleasant way ○ *treated them awfully*

awhile /ə wíl/ *adv* for a short time

USAGE awhile or **a while**? Both expressions are derived from the word *while*, but they have a different role in the sentence. ***Awhile*** is an adverb *Let us wait awhile* [not *for awhile*]. ***A while*** – written as two words – is a noun phrase and is normally preceded by *for*: *I'm going to be away for a while.* Sometimes, however, the word *for* is left out, making ***a while*** look more like an adverbial phrase, although it is still strictly a noun phrase: *We had to wait quite a while.* This use is fairly easy to identify because *while* is qualified in some way, for example *quite a while* or *a long while*.

awhirl /ə wúrl/ *adj* **1** in a dizzy state of excitement or confusion ○ *Her mind was awhirl with new ideas.* **2** moving round and round (*literary*) ○ *red and golden leaves awhirl in the autumn breeze*

awkward /áwkwərd/ *adj* **1 EMBARRASSING** embarrassing and requiring great tact or skill to resolve ○ *I find myself in an awkward situation.* **2 DIFFICULT OR UNCOMFORTABLE TO USE** difficult to use because you have to move your body into an uncomfortable position **3 PERFORMED GRACELESSLY** performed in a way that lacks grace and looks uncomfortable **4 WITHOUT GRACEFUL COORDINATION** lacking physical coordination and grace ○ *an awkward, gangling adolescent* **5 SHYLY UNCOMFORTABLE** shy, uncomfortable, and embarrassed ○ *He was always awkward around kids.* **6 UNCOOPERATIVE** showing no willingness to cooperate or be reasonable ○ *I think she's being deliberately awkward.* [Mid-16C. < obsolete *awke* 'turned the wrong way' (< Old Norse *afugr* 'turned backwards') + -WARD.] —**awkwardly** *adv* —**awkwardness** *n*

awl /awl/ *n* a tool consisting of a handle and a slim metal shaft with a sharp point, used for boring small holes in leather or wood [Old English *æl* < ?]

SPELLCHECK See *all*.

awn /awn/ *n* a stiff bristle projecting from the tip of a plant organ, e.g. from the sheath surrounding a cereal or grass seed [12C. < Old Norse *agn-* 'chaff'.] —**awned** *adj* —**awnless** *adj*

awning /áwning/ *n* a plastic, canvas, or metal roof supported by a frame and often foldable, that is placed over a shop front, doorway, window, or side of a caravan [Early 17C. < ?]

awoke past tense of **awake**

awoken past participle of **awake**

AWOL /áy wol/ *adj* absent from a post, especially a military post, without official permission [< *a(bsent) w(ith)o(ut) l(eave)*]

Awolowo /ə wólləwə/, **Obafemi** (1909–87) Nigerian Yoruba chief and political leader

awry /ə rī/ *adj* **1** not in the proper position but turned or twisted to one side ○ *The cushions were awry and there was mud on the carpet.* **2** not in keeping with plans or expectations ○ *Our plans have gone awry.* [14C. <*on wry* 'in a twist'.]

ax *n, vt* US = **axe**

axe /aks/ *n* **1 TOOL FOR CUTTING** a tool consisting of a flat heavy metal head with a sharpened edge attached to a long handle, used to chop wood or fell trees **2 JOB LOSS** dismissal from a job (*slang*) ○ *Her secretary got the axe yesterday.* **3 IMMEDIATE CLOSURE** the immediate closure of an institution or the sudden discontinuation of a project or funding (*slang*) ○ *schemes facing the axe* **4 MUSICAL INSTRUMENT** a rock guitar or a jazz saxophone (*slang*) ■ *vt* (**axes, axing, axed**) **1 TERMINATE** to end something, e.g. a job, a service, or a television programme, usually without prior warning or discussion (*informal; usually passive*) ○ *The show was axed after only five episodes.* **2 FIRE** to dismiss somebody from a job, especially abruptly (*informal*) **3 REDUCE SOMETHING DRASTICALLY** to cut something, e.g. expenditures or services, drastically ○ *Most of the welfare provisions were axed from the budget.* [Old English *æcs* < Indo-European] ◇ **have an axe to grind** to be motivated by some personal consideration, usually a negative one ○ *It was clear from their hostile questioning that certain reporters had an axe to grind on this issue.*

axel /áks'l/ *n* a figure-skating jump in which the skater takes off from the forward outside edge of one skate, turns in midair, and lands on the rear outside edge of the other skate [Mid-20C. After *Axel* Rudolph Paulser (1885–1938), Norwegian skater.]

axeman /áksmən, -man/ (*plural* **-men** /-mən, -men/) *n* **1** a man who carries or uses an axe as either a tool or a weapon **2** a rock guitarist or a jazz saxophone player (*slang*)

axenic /ay zéenik/ *adj* describes a culture of an organism that is free from contamination by other living organisms [Mid-20C. < Greek *a-* 'not' + *xenikos* 'alien, strange'.]

axes plural of **axis**[1]

axial /áksi əl/ *adj* **1 OF AXIS** relating to or forming an axis **2 LOCATED ALONG PLANE OF AXIS** located on or in the plane of an axis of a crystal **3 OF AXIS OF ORGANISM** located in or relating to the axis of an organism —**axially** *adv*

axial plane *n* a plane that intersects the crest or trough of a geological fold in such a way that the sides of the fold are symmetrical about the plane

axial skeleton *n* the bones that make up the vertebral column and skull

axil /áksil/ *n* the space between a leaf or branch and the stem to which it is attached [Late 18C. < Latin *axilla* (see AXILLA).]

axilla /ak sílla/ (*plural* **-lae** /-síllee/) *n* **1** a person's armpit (*technical*) **2** the hollow underneath the wing of a bird [Early 17C. < Latin, 'little wing' < *ala* 'wing, upper arm'.]

axillary /ak síllәri/ *adj* **1** relating to or near the armpit **2** relating to or growing in the space (**axil**) between a leaf or branch and the stem ■ *n* (*plural* **-ies**) ZOOL = **axillar**

axinite /áksi nīt/ *n* a brilliant brown borosilicate mineral containing calcium and aluminium, occurring in wedge-shaped crystals [Early 19C. < Greek *axinē* 'axe'.]

axiology /áksi óllәji/ *n* the study of the nature, types, and governing criteria of values and value judgments [Early 20C. < French *axiologie* < Greek *axia* 'value'.] —**axiological** /áksi ə lójjik'l/ *adj* —**axiologically** *adv* —**axiologist** *n*

axiom /áksi əm/ *n* **1** a statement or idea that people accept as self-evidently true **2** a basic proposition of a system that, although unproven, is used to prove the other propositions in the system [15C. Directly or via French < Latin *axioma* < Greek *axiōma* 'something worthy' < *axios* 'weighty, worthy'.]

axiomatic /áksi ə máttik/ *adj* **1** self-evidently true **2** consisting of or based on axioms [Late 18C. < Greek *axiōmatikos* < stem of *axiōma* (see AXIOM).] —**axiomatically** *adv*

axion /áksi on/ *n* a hypothetical subatomic particle that has small mass, zero spin, and no electrical charge [Late 20C. < AXIAL + -ON.]

axis[1] /áksiss/ (*plural* **-es** /ák seez/) *n* **1 LINE AROUND WHICH OBJECT ROTATES** an imaginary straight line around which an object, such as the earth, rotates **2 LINE AROUND WHICH SHAPE IS SYMMETRICAL** a straight line around which a geometric figure or three-dimensional object is symmetrical **3 LINE FOR MEASURING COORDINATES** one of two or more lines on which coordinates are measured **4 ALLIANCE** an alliance or association between two or more people, organizations, or countries that is thought of as forming a centre of power or influence ○ *the Paris-Bonn axis* **5 LINE DEFINING DIRECTION OF AIRCRAFT** any one of the three mutually perpendicular lines in an aircraft that define its orientation **6 SECOND VERTEBRA IN NECK** the second vertebra in the neck, which acts as the pivot on which the head and first vertebra turn **7 CENTRAL PART OF PLANT** the main part of a plant, usually the stem and the root, from which all subsidiary parts develop **8 LINE PERPENDICULAR TO LENS OR MIRROR** the axis of symmetry of an optical system, especially a line perpendicular to the surface of a lens or mirror **9 LINE AT MAXIMUM CURVATURE** an imaginary line along the crest of an anticline or the trough of a syncline at the point of maximum curvature **10 LINE PASSING THROUGH CRYSTAL** an imaginary line, one of three or four that pass through the centre of a crystal and are used to define its symmetry and the arrangement of its atoms [14C. < Latin, 'axle, pivot'.]

axis[2] *n* ZOOL = **axis deer** [Early 17C. < Latin, an unidentified wild animal in India.]

Axis *n* the military and political alliance of Germany, Italy, and, later, Japan that fought the Allies in World War II [Mid-20C. < Mussolini's idea of 'an axis round which nations could assemble'.]

axis deer, axis *n* a deer with a reddish-brown, white-spotted coat that lives in India and central Asia. *Axis axis.*

axisymmetric /áksi si méttrik/, **axisymmetrical** /-méttrik'l/ *adj* symmetrical with respect to an axis —**axisymmetrically** *adv*

axle /áks'l/ *n* **1** a shaft on which a wheel or set of wheels revolves, especially a shaft under the body of a vehicle that connects a pair of wheels **2** the spindle on which one or more wheels revolve [Late 16C. Shortening of AXLETREE.]

axletree /áks'l tree/ *n* a shaft that runs underneath the body of a vehicle such as a cart or carriage and connects a pair of wheels [13C. < Old Norse *öxultré* < *öxull* 'axle' + *tré* 'tree, beam'.]

Axminster /áksminstər/ *n* a high-quality carpet with a cut pile that is usually woven into a colourful pattern [Early 19C. After *Axminster*, SW England.]

axolemma /áksə lémmə/ *n* the membranous sheath that encloses the long thin extension of a nerve cell (**axon**) [Late 19C. < Greek *axōn* 'axis' + *lemma* 'skin, husk'.]

Axolotl

axolotl /áksə lott'l/ (*plural* **-lotls** *or* **-lotl**) *n* an aquatic salamander that often retains its external gills as an adult. Native to: Mexico, W United States. Genus: *Ambystoma.* [Late 18C. < Nahuatl < *atl* 'water' + *xolotl* 'servant'.]

axon /ák son/, **axone** /áksōn/ *n* an extension of a nerve cell, similar in shape to a thread, that transmits impulses outwards from the cell body [Late 19C. < Greek *axōn* 'axis'.]

axoneme /áksə neem/ *n* a bundle of fibrils that form the central core of a cilium or flagellum [Early 20C. < Greek *axōn* 'axis' + *nēma* 'thread'.]

axonometric /áksənō méttrik/ *adj* describes a method of drawing a three-dimensional object so that the vertical and horizontal axes are drawn to scale but the curves and diagonals appear distorted

axoplasm /áksə plazəm/ *n* the cytoplasm of a nerve cell extension (**axon**) —**axoplasmic** /áksə plázmik/ *adj*

ay[1] *interj, n* = **aye**[1]

ay[2] *adv* = **aye**[2]

Ayacucho /ī ə kóochō/ city in S Peru. Population: 118,960 (1998 estimate).

ayah /ī yə/ *n S Asia* a maid whose duties include the care of children [Late 18C. Via Portuguese *aia* 'woman tutor' < Latin *avia* 'grandmother'.]

ayatollah /ī ə tóllə/ *n* a Shiite religious leader in Iran, often one who takes an important political as well as religious role [Mid-20C. Via Persian < Arabic *'āyatu-llāh* 'miraculous sign of God' < *'āya* 'sign, miracle' + *allāh* 'God'.]

Ayckbourn /áyk bawrn/, **Alan** (*b.* 1939) British dramatist

aye[1] /ī/, **ay** /ay/ *interj* used to say yes ■ *n* (*plural* **ayes**) a vote in favour of a motion, or somebody who casts a vote in favour [Late 16C. < ?]

aye[2] /ī/, **ay** *adv* always or forever (*archaic or regional*) [13C. < Old Norse *ei, ey.*]

aye-aye /ī ī/ *n* a small nocturnal primate that lives in trees and has a long bushy tail, long bony fingers, and teeth resembling those of a rodent. Native to: Madagascar. *Daubentonia madagascariensis.* [Late 18C. Via French, < Malagasy *aiay*; probably an imitation of its cry.]

Ayer /air/, **A. J.** (1910–89) British philosopher

Ayers Rock /áirz-/ former name for **Uluru**

Ayeshah = **Aisha**

ayin /áa yin/ *n* the 16th letter of the Hebrew alphabet [Early 19C. < Hebrew *'ayin* 'eye'.]

Aylesbury /áylzbəri/ town in S England. Population: 58,058 (1991).

Aylesbury Vale local government district in S England

Aymara /īmə ráa/ (*plural* **-ra** *or* **-ras**) *n* **1** a member of a Native South American people who live around Lake Titicaca in Bolivia and Peru **2** a language of Bolivia and Peru, related to Quechua. Native speakers: 2 million. [Mid-19C. < Bolivian Spanish.] —**Aymaran** *adj*

Aymé /e máy/, **Marcel** (1902–67) French writer

Ayr /air/ city in SW Scotland. Population: 47,962 (1991).

Ayrshire[1] /áirshər/ former county of SW Scotland

Ayrshire[2] *n* a cow of a largely white breed of dairy cattle

Ayub Khan /īyoob kaán/, **Muhammad** (1907–74) Pakistani soldier and head of state

Ayurveda /aà yoor vayda, -veeda/ *n* ALTERN MED = **Ayurvedic medicine** [Early 20C. < Sanskrit *āyur-veda* 'medicine' < *āyur-* 'life, vital power' + *veda* 'knowledge'.] —**Ayurvedic** *adj*

Ayurvedic medicine /aà yoor váydik-, -veédik-/ *n* an ancient Indian system of healing that assesses an individual's constitution and lifestyle, and recommends treatment based on herbal preparations, diet, yoga, and purification

⚡**az** *abbr* Azerbaijan (*in Internet addresses*)

AZ *abbr* Arizona

az. *abbr* **1** azimuth **2** azure

azalea /ə záyli ə/ (*plural* **-eas** *or* **-ea**) *n* a flowering shrub widely grown for its large pink, purple, white, or yellow flowers. Genus: *Rhododendron.* [Mid-18C. Via modern Latin, < Greek, < *azaleos* 'dry'.]

azan /aa zaàn/ *n* the Islamic call to prayer that a muezzin repeats five times a day from the minaret of a mosque [Mid-19C. < Arabic *aḏān* 'announcement'.]

Azania /ə záyni ə/ *n* S *African* a name for South Africa used by resistance movements in the apartheid era

Azapo /ə záppō/ *n* a Socialist political movement in South Africa [Late 20C. Acronym < *Azanian People's Organization.*]

azapropazone /ázzə próppə zōn/ *n* a ketone derivative of pyrazole with analgesic and anti-inflammatory properties. Use: treatment of rheumatoid arthritis.

azatadine /ə záttə deen, ay-/ *n* an antihistamine taken orally. Use: treatment of allergic rhinitis, urticaria.

azathioprine /ázzə thī̆ ō preen/ *n* a drug that suppresses the immune response. Use: after transplant surgery to prevent rejection. [Mid-20C. < *aza-* + THI-² + PURINE.]

azelaic acid /ázzə láy ik-/ *n* a dicarboxylic acid that is a yellowish to white powder. Use: treatment of skin cancer and other skin disorders. [< AZO- + Greek *elaion* 'oil']

azelastine /ázzə lásteen/ *n* an antihistamine taken nasally

azeotrope /ə zeè ə trōp/ *n* a mixture of liquids that has a different boiling point from any of its components and that retains its composition as a vapour [Early 20C. A-² + Greek *zeo-*, form of *zein* 'to boil' + *-tropos* 'turning, changing'.] —**azeotropic** /áyzi ə tróppik/ *adj* —**azeotropy** /áyzi óttrəpi/ *n*

Azerbaijan /ázzər bī̆ jaàn/ republic in W Asia, bordered to the east by the Caspian Sea. Capital: Baku. Population: 7,797,476 (1997). Area: 86,600 sq. km/33,400 sq. mi. — **Azerbaijani** *n, adj*

Azeri /ə záiri/ *n, adj* the Turkic official language of the country of Azerbaijan, also spoken in the province of Azerbaijan in NW Iran, belonging to the Altaic family of languages. Native speakers: 14 million.

azerty /ə zúrti/, **AZERTY** *adj* describes a computer or typewriter keyboard layout in continental Europe, where the top row of letters, beginning from the left, runs A, Z, E, R, T, Y. ◊ **qwerty**

azide /áy zīd/ *n* **N₃** any chemical compound containing a group of three adjacent nitrogen atoms [Early 20C. < AZO- + -IDE.]

azidothymidine /ə zíddō thī̆mə deen/ *n* full form of **AZT**

Azerbaijan

Azikiwe /aà zee keè way/, **Nnamdi** (1904–96) Nigerian statesman and president of Nigeria (1963–66)

Azilian /ə zílli ən/ *n* a prehistoric culture that existed in Spain and SW France from around 10,000 to 8,000 BC [Late 19C. After Mas d' *Azil* in the French Pyrenees, where a cave containing bone and flint implements was found.]

azimuth /ázziməth/ *n* **1** the angle measured from north, eastwards along the horizon to the point where a vertical circle through a celestial object intersects the horizon **2** the angular distance along the horizon between a point of reference, usually the observer's bearing, and another object [Early 17C. Via French *azimut* < Arabic *as-samūt*, plural of *as-samt* 'the way' < *samt* 'way, direction'.] —**azimuthal** /ázzi múth'l/ *adj* —**azimuthally** *adv*

azimuthal equidistant projection *n* a method of map projection in which a straight line from the centre to any given point represents the shortest distance to that point and can be measured to scale

azine /áyzin/ *n* an organic chemical compound with a six-sided ring structure containing one or more atoms of nitrogen [Late 19C. < AZO- + -INE.]

azithromycin /ázzithrō mī̆ssin/ *n* an antibiotic taken in combination with other drugs. Use: treatment of toxoplasmosis, heart disease.

azlocillin /ázzlō síllin/ *n* a form of penicillin used to treat a broad range of infections

azo /áyzō, ázzō/ *adj* **-N=N-** relating to or containing two adjacent nitrogen atoms. ◊ **diazo** *adj*. [Late 19C. < AZO-.]

azo- *prefix* containing a nitrogen group ○ *azole* [< French *azote* 'nitrogen' < Greek *a-* 'not' + *zōē* 'life'; because living creatures cannot breathe it]

azobenzene /áyzō bén zeen/ *n* $C_6H_5N=NC_6H_5$ a yellow or orange crystalline solid. Use: making dyes.

azo compound *n* any compound containing two adjacent nitrogen atoms attached to aromatic groups

azo dye *n* an artificial dye, usually orange, yellow, or brown, containing an azo group. Source: amines.

azoic /ə zố ik/ *adj* **1** belonging to a geological period before the appearance of living organisms on Earth **2** without any trace of life or organic remains [Mid-19C. < Greek *azōos* 'without life' < *zōē* 'life'.]

azole /áyzōl, ə zốl/ *n* an organic chemical compound with a ring structure comprising five linked atoms, of which at least one is nitrogen [Late 19C. < AZO- + -OLE.]

azonal /ay zốn'l/ *adj* **1** not divided into zones **2** not restricted to a specific zone or geographical area

azonic /ay zốnik/ *adj* GEOG = **azonal** *adj*. **2**

azoospermia /ay zố ə spúrmi ə/ *n* MED = **aspermia**

Azores /ə záwrz/ archipelago in the N Atlantic Ocean, west of Portugal, an autonomous region of that country. Population: 239,900 (1992). Area: 2,247 sq. km/868 sq. mi.

Azorín /ázzə reèn/ (1873–1967) Spanish writer. Born **José Martínez Ruiz**

azotaemia /ázzə teèmi ə/ *n* MED = **uraemia** [Early 20C. < obsolete *azote* 'nitrogen' (see AZO-) + -EMIA.] —**azotaemic** *adj*

azothioprine /ázzə thī̆ ə prin/ *n* an immunosuppressive drug. Use: transplant therapy, treatment of rheumatoid arthritis, psoriasis, lupus, and other inflammatory diseases.

azotic /ay zóttik/ *adj* relating to or containing nitrogen [Late 18C. < obsolete *azote* < French (see AZO-).]

azotobacter /ə zốtō baktər/ *n* a rod-shaped or spherical bacterium found in soil and water that fixes atmospheric nitrogen. Family: Azotobacter. [Early 20C. < modern Latin, < French *azote* 'nitrogen' (see AZO-) + *bacterium.*]

Azov, Sea of /ázzov, áy zov/ shallow inland sea in SW Russia. Area: 37,555 sq. km/14,500 sq. mi.

AZT *n* an antiviral drug. Use: Aids treatment. Full form **azidothymidine**

Aztec /áz tek/ *n* **1** a member of a Native Middle American people whose empire dominated central Mexico during the 14th and 15th centuries **2** LANG = **Nahuatl** *n*. **2** ■ *adj* **Aztec, Aztecan** relating to the Aztecs or their people, language, or culture [Late 18C. Via French *Aztèque* or Spanish *Azteca* < Nahuatl *aztecatl* 'somebody from Aztlan'.]

Aztec-Tanoan *n* a family of Native North and Central American languages, one of whose main branches is Uto-Aztecan. —**Aztec-Tanoan** *adj*

aztreonam /az treè ə nam/ *n* an antibiotic administered intravenously, effective against a broad range of infections

azuki bean *n* = **adzuki bean**

azure /ázhər, áy-/ *adj* **1** DEEP BLUE deep blue, like the colour of a clear sky on a warm day (*literary*) ○ *the azure depths of the ocean* **2** BLUE coloured blue on a coat of arms ■ *n* (*literary*) **1** BLUE SKY a clear blue sky **2** DEEP BLUE HUE a deep blue colour ○ *the azure of her eyes* [13C. Via Old French *azur* < medieval Latin *azzurum* < Arabic *al-lāzaward* 'the lapis lazuli' < Persian *lāžward* 'lapis lazuli'.]

azurite /ázhōō rīt/ *n* a deep blue semiprecious stone composed of hydrated copper carbonate. Use: source of copper, gems.

azygous /ázzigəss/ *adj* occurring as a single muscle or vein rather than as a pair [Mid-17C. < Greek *azugos* 'without yoke' < *zugon* 'yoke'.]

b[1] /bee/ (*plural* **b's**), **B** (*plural* **B's** *or* **Bs**) *n* the second letter of the English alphabet, representing a consonant sound

b[2] refers to the second vertical row of squares from the left on a chessboard

b[3] *abbr* **1** barn **2** bass[1] **3** basso **4 b, B** bel **5** billion **6** book **7** born **8** bowled **9** breadth **10** bye[1]

B[1] (*plural* **B's** *or* **Bs**) *n* **1 'B'-SHAPED OBJECT** something shaped like a letter 'B' **2 7TH NOTE IN C MAJOR** the seventh note of a scale in C major **3 SOMETHING THAT PRODUCES A B** a string, key, or pipe tuned to produce the note B **4 SCALE BEGINNING ON B** a scale or key that starts on the note B **5 WRITTEN SYMBOL OF B** a graphic representation of the tone of B **6 2ND HIGHEST GRADE** the second highest grade in a series, e.g. an above-average grade for academic work **7 HUMAN BLOOD TYPE** a human blood type of the ABO system **8 MIDDLE MANAGER OR INTERMEDIATE PROFESSIONAL** somebody in a middle-management or intermediate professional or administrative position, in the market research system that classifies people according to their occupation

B[2] *symbol* **1** black (*used on pencils to indicate that the lead is soft*) **2** boron **3** eleven (*in hexadecimal notation*) **4** magnetic flux density **5** a secondary road

⚡**B**[3] *abbr* **1** bachelor (*in degree titles*) **2** back (*in e-mails*) **3** bass[1] **4** basso **5** Baumé scale **6** Bay (*on maps*) **7** Bible **8** billion **9** bishop **10** book **11** breadth

⚡**B2B** *abbr* business-to-business

⚡**B2C** *abbr* business-to-consumer

⚡**B4** *abbr* before (*in e-mails*)

⚡**B4N** *abbr* bye for now (*in e-mails*)

Ba *symbol* barium

BA *abbr* **1** Bachelor of Arts **2** British Academy **3** British Airways **4** British Association (for the Advancement of Science)

baa /baa/ *vi* (**baas, baaing, baaed**) **BLEAT LIKE SHEEP** to make the long wavering cry characteristic of a sheep or lamb ■ *n* (*plural* **baas**) **1 CRY OF SHEEP** the long wavering cry characteristic of a sheep or lamb **2** *N England, Ireland* **CHILD** a child, especially a youngest child (*informal*) ○ *Where's the baa? Is he sleeping?* [Early 16C. An imitation of the sound.]

BAA, **B.A.A.** *abbr* Bachelor of Applied Arts

Baal /baal, báyal/ (*plural* **-alim** /baàlim, báyalim/ *or* **-als**) *n* **1** any of the fertility or nature gods worshipped by the Canaanites and the Phoenicians, and considered false idols by the ancient Hebrews **2 Baal, baal** an idol or false god

Baalbek /baàl bek/ town in E Lebanon, site of the ancient ruins of Heliopolis. Population: 50,000 (1981 estimate).

baal teshuvah (*plural* **baalei teshuvah**), **baal tshuva** (*plural* **baalei tshuva**) *n* somebody who returns to Orthodox Jewish practice after abandoning it [< Hebrew, 'master of return']

baas /baass/ *n S Africa* a form of address used mainly during apartheid by non-whites to show respect when addressing a white man or boy, especially an employer [Late 18C. Via Afrikaans < Dutch, 'master'.]

Baath /baath/, **Ba'ath** /baa aáth/ *n* a Socialist party in several Arab countries, including Iraq and Syria, founded in 1943 [Mid-20C. < Arabic *ba't* 'resurrection'.]

Bab /baab/ *n* title of a Persian religious leader, Mirza Ali Muhammad (1819–50), who founded Babism [Mid-19C. Via Persian < Arabic *bāb* 'gate, intermediary'.]

baba /baá baa, -bə/ (*plural* **-bas**) *n* a dessert made of leavened dough soaked in a rum-flavoured syrup and baked in a tin [Early 19C. Via French < Polish, 'married (peasant) woman'.]

Babangida /bə báng geeda/, **Ibrahim** (*b.* 1941) Nigerian soldier, politician, and president (1985–93)

Babbage /bábbij/, **Charles** (1792–1871) British mathematician and inventor

babbitt /bábbit/ *n* a bearing made of babbitt metal ■ *vt* to cover or line a surface with babbitt metal or a similar alloy [Late 19C. See BABBITT METAL.]

Babbitt /bábbit/ *n US* a self-satisfied narrow-minded man who cannot see beyond his own business and social interests [Early 20C. After the main character in the novel *Babbitt* (1922) by Sinclair Lewis.] —**Babbittry** *n*

Babbitt /bábbit/, **Milton** (*b.* 1916) US composer

babbitt metal *n* a soft alloy used especially in the manufacture of antifriction bearings [Late 19C. After Isaac Babbitt (1799–1862).]

babble /bább'l/ *v* (**-bles, -bling, -bled**) **1** *vti* **SPEAK INCOHERENTLY** to say something rapidly and incoherently without pausing, usually because of excitement or fear ○ *He babbled something about leaving a deposit and then dashed out.* **2** *vi* **SPEAK IRRELEVANTLY** to talk rapidly or at length in a way people find irrelevant or foolish ○ *He babbled on about the importance of some new gadget.* **3** *vi* **MURMUR** to make a continuous low murmuring or bubbling sound ○ *a brook babbling through the pasture* **4** *vti* **BLURT OUT** to reveal something thoughtlessly or impulsively that is supposed to be secret or confidential ○ *immediately babbled the whole story to the neighbours* ■ *n* **BACKGROUND INTERFERENCE ON PHONE LINES** background noise on a telephone line caused by interference from other conversations [13C. Probably < Middle Low German or Middle Dutch *babbelen*, an imitation of the sound, or a similar formation in English.] —**babble** *n* —**babblement** *n*

babbler /bábblər/ *n* **1** somebody who babbles, especially giving away secrets **2** a small bird of the family that includes the laughing thrush, a popular cage bird. Native to: forests and bush of Europe, Asia, and Africa. Family: Timaliidae.

babe /bayb/ *n* **1 LOVER** used as an affectionate term of address to a lover or somebody you love (*slang*) **2 YOUNG WOMAN CONSIDERED GOOD-LOOKING** a young woman who is considered good-looking (*slang; sometimes offensive*) **3 BABY** a baby or small child (*literary or archaic*) **4** *US* **HANDSOME YOUTH** an attractive young man (*slang*) [14C. Probably < obsolete *baban* 'baby', an imitation of childish utterances.] ◇ **a babe in arms** an innocent inexperienced person ◇ **a babe in the woods** a naive excessively trusting person

babel /báyb'l/ *n* (*literary*) **1** a confused noise, especially the noise of loud unintelligible voices all talking at once **2** a scene or place of noisy confusion [Early 16C. < the TOWER OF BABEL.]

Babel /báyb'l/ ♦ **Tower of Babel**

babesiosis /ba beèzi ṓssiss/, **babesiasis** /baàbi zí əssiss/ *n* a disease of humans and animals caused by protozoan infection of red blood cells and transmitted by a tick bite [Early 20C. < modern Latin *Babesia*, after Victor Babès (1854–1926), Romanian bacteriologist.]

Babi /baá abi/ (*plural* **-bis**) *n* a follower of the Bab or of Babism [Mid-19C. Via Persian < Arabic < *bāb* (see BAB).]

Babington /bábbingtən/, **Antony** (1561–86) English conspirator

Babinski reflex /bə bínski reè fleks/, **Babinski's reflex** /bə bínskiz-/ *n* a curling upwards of the big toe when the sole of the foot is stroked, an indicator of disease of the brain or spinal cord in older people [Early 20C. After J. F. F. Babinski (1857–1932), French neurologist.]

babirusa /baàbi roóssa/ (*plural* **-sas** *or* **-sa**), **babirussa** (*plural* **-sas** *or* **-sa**), **babirousa** (*plural* **-sas** *or* **-sa**) *n* a wild pig that has almost hairless skin and very large curved tusks. Native to: Indonesia, Malaysia. *Babyrousa babyrussa*. [Late 17C. < Malay, < *babi* 'pig' + *rusa* 'deer'.]

Babism /baàbizəm/ *n* a religion founded by the Bab as a reform of Shiite Islam in Persia in the 19th century

baboon /ba boòn/ *n* **1** a large ground-dwelling monkey with a prominent snout resembling a dog's muzzle, large teeth, and bare pink patches on the buttocks. Native to: Africa, Asia. Genus: *Papio*. **2** somebody considered to be rude or oafishly clumsy (*insult*) [15C. < French *babuin* 'gaping figure, baboon' or medieval Latin *babewynus*.]

babu /baá boo/, **baboo** *n* **1** a courtesy title or form of address in Hindi equivalent to 'Mr' **2** an offensive term, in the former colonial period of the 19th and 20th centuries, for an Indian, especially a clerk or official, with limited knowledge of the English language and culture [Late 18C. < Hindi *bābū* 'father'.]

babul /baa boól, baà bool/ (*plural* **-buls** *or* **-bul**) *n* a tree that produces gum arabic, tannin, and hardwood. Native to: North Africa, India. *Acacia nilotica.* [Early 19C. Via Hindi *babūl*, Bengali *bābul* < Sanskrit *babbūla*.]

babushka /bə boòshka/ *n* **1** a headscarf folded and tied under the chin in the style of Russian peasant women **2** a traditional Russian grandmother figure [Mid-20C. < Russian, 'grandmother'.]

baby /báybi/ *n* (*plural* **-bies**) **1 VERY YOUNG CHILD** a very young child who is not yet able to walk or talk **2 UNBORN CHILD** a child that is still in the womb **3 CHILDISH PERSON** a childish or overly dependent person ○ *told him not to be such a baby* **4 YOUNGEST MEMBER** the youngest member of a family or group ○ *the baby of the team* **5 IMMATURE ANIMAL** a very young animal **6 TERM OF ENDEARMENT** an affectionate term of endearment, especially for a woman (*slang; sometimes offensive*) ■ *adj* **SMALLER AND YOUNGER** describes vegetables that are smaller and younger than usual ■ *vt* (**-bies, -bying, -bied**) **TREAT SOMEBODY WITH GREAT CARE** to show a great or inordinate amount of care to something or somebody [14C. Pet form of BABE.] —**babyhood** *n* ◇ **be left holding the baby** to be left in a situation of being solely responsible for something because other people have abdicated their own responsibility ◇ **throw out the baby with the bathwater** to reject something in its entirety without discriminating between good and bad parts

baby blue *n* a pale blue colour —**baby-blue** *adj*

baby blues *n* post-natal depression (*informal; + singular or plural verb*)

baby bond *n US* a bond issued for an amount lower than $1,000, usually between $25 and $500

baby bonus *n* = child tax benefit

baby boom *n* a sudden large increase in the birthrate

over a particular period, especially the 15 years after World War II

baby boomer *n* somebody born during a baby boom, especially the one following the end of World War II

baby bouncer *n* a harness with elastic straps that allows a baby to be seated within it and suspended from a doorway, letting the infant bounce up and down

baby buggy *n* a pushchair

baby carriage *n US* = **pram**[1] *n.*

Baby Doc ➧ **Jean-Claude Duvalier**

baby-dolls *npl* women's nightwear consisting of a short loose top and loose shorts [Because worn in the film *Baby Doll* (1956)]

baby face *n* **1** a smooth round face that gives somebody a childlike innocent look **2** somebody with a baby face

baby grand *n* a small grand piano about 1.5 m/5 ft long

Babygro /báybigrō/ *tdmk* a trademark for a baby's all-in-one suit made from stretch fabric

babyish /báybi ish/ *adj* **1** like a baby in appearance, sound or behaviour ○ *She has a really babyish voice* **2** suitable for a baby or for a younger child ○ *Clothes like these are too babyish for a child his age.* —**babyishly** *adv* —**babyishness** *n*

Babylon[1] /bábbilən, -lon/ capital of ancient Babylonia

Babylon[2] /bábbilən, -lon/ *n* **1** a place of great luxury or immorality (*disapproving*) **2** a place of exile or captivity

Babylonia /bábbi lṓni ə/ ancient empire in Mesopotamia, in present-day Iraq

Babylonian /bábbi lṓni ən/ *n* **1** somebody who lived in ancient Babylon or Babylonia **2** the Akkadian language, particularly as recorded in cuneiform texts from Babylonia —**Babylonian** *adj*

Babylonian captivity *n* the period of time that the Jews spent in exile in Babylonia in the 6th century BC

baby minder *n* somebody whose job is to look after other people's babies or very young children, especially while their parents are at work

baby's breath (*plural* **baby's breath** *or* **baby's breaths**) *n* **1** a plant with a mass of delicate branched stems, often used in bouquets and floral arrangements. Flowers: small, fragrant white or pink. *Gypsophila paniculata.* **2** a perennial plant with a mass of tiny flowers, especially a bedstraw [< its delicate scent]

babysit /báybisit/ (**-sits, -sitting, -sat**) *v* **1** *vti* to look after a child or children in the child's home while the parents are out **2** *vt* to look after somebody or something unable to be left unsupervised or needing constant attention (*informal*) ○ *Would you babysit my plants next week?* —**babysitter** *n*

baby snatcher *n* **1** somebody who steals a baby (*slang*) **2** = **cradle snatcher** (*informal humorous*)

baby talk, babytalk *n* the simplified or specially modified language and exaggerated intonation that adults use when talking to very small children

baby tooth *n* = **milk tooth**

baby walker *n* a frame mounted on wheels that helps keep babies upright when they are learning to walk. US term **walker** *n.* **2**

babywear /báybi wair/ *n* clothing designed to be worn by babies

ϟ**BAC** *abbr* **1** bacterial artificial chromosome **2** by any chance (*in e-mails*)

Bacall /bə káwl/, **Lauren** (*b.* 1924) US actor. Born **Betty Joan Perske**

Bacău /bə ków/ city in E Romania. Population: 209,689 (1997 estimate).

baccalaureate /bákə láwri ət/ *n* **1** an examination taken at the conclusion of a student's secondary school studies, especially in France, that enables successful candidates to enter university **2** a bachelor's degree (*formal*) [Mid-17C. Directly or via French < medieval Latin *baccalaureatus* < *baccalaureus* 'bachelor'.]

baccarat /bákə raa, -raá/ *n* a gambling card game, in which the winning hand is the one that totals nine points or is closest to nine points without exceeding it [Mid-19C. < French *baccara.*]

baccate /bák ayt/ *adj* resembling a berry in shape [Early 19C. < Latin *baccatus* < *bacca* 'berry'.]

Bacchae /bákee/ *npl* in Greek and Roman mythology, the priestesses and women who participated in the orgiastic rites of Bacchus [Early 20C. Via Latin < Greek *Bakkhai*, plural of *Bakkhē* 'priest of Bacchus' < *Bakkhos* 'Bacchus'.]

bacchanal /bákə nál/ *n* **1 PARTICIPANT IN ORGIASTIC RITES** a participant in the orgiastic rites of Bacchus **2 LOUD DRUNK** a riotous drunken reveller (*literary*) **3 DRUNKEN PARTY** a noisy drunken celebration or spree (*literary*) ■ *adj* **RELATING TO BACCHUS** relating to Bacchus or the worship of Bacchus [Mid-16C. < Latin *bacchanalis* 'of Bacchus'.]

bacchanalia /bákə náyli ə/ *npl* riotous drunken revels [Late 16C. < Latin *bacchanalia*, plural of *bacchanalis* (see BACCHANAL).] —**bacchanalian** *adj*

Bacchanalia /bákə náyli ə/ *n* ancient Roman festivities in honour of Bacchus that involved orgiastic rites (+ *singular or plural verb*) —**Bacchanalian** *adj*

bacchant /bákənt/ *n* a priest, priestess, or other devotee of Bacchus [Late 16C. Via French *bacchante* < Latin *bacchant-*, present participle of *bacchari* 'celebrate the feast of Bacchus' < *Bacchus* 'Bacchus'.]

bacchante /bə kánti/ *n* a priestess or woman devotee of Bacchus [Late 18C. < French *bacchante* (see BACCHANT).]

bacchantic /bə kántik/ *adj* relating to the worship of Bacchus and the orgiastic rites associated with it

bacchic /bákik/ *adj* characterized by riotous drunkenness

Bacchic /bákik/ *adj* relating to Bacchus

bacchius /ba kī́ əss/ (*plural* **-i** /ba kī́ ī/) *n* a metrical foot consisting of one short syllable followed by two long ones [Late 16C. Via Latin < Greek *bakkheios (pous)* 'Bacchic (foot)' < *Bakkhos* 'Bacchus'.]

Bacchus /bákəss/ *n* in classical mythology, the god of wine, identified with the Greek god Dionysus and the Roman god Liber [Via Latin < Greek *Bakkhos*]

Bacchus Marsh /bákəss-/ town in Victoria, SE Australia. Population: 9,689 (1991).

baccy /báki/ *n* tobacco (*informal regional*) [Early 19C. Shortening and alteration.]

bach[1] /bach/, **batch** *vi US, ANZ* to live alone as a single man and keep house for yourself (*informal*) ■ *n ANZ* a cottage or holiday home (*informal*) [Mid-19C. Shortening of BACHELOR.]

bach[2] /baakh, baak/ *n Wales* used as an affectionate form of address to a man or boy, alone or after somebody's name ○ *Alan bach, how are you?* [Late 19C. < Welsh, 'little'.]

Bach /baak, baakh/, **C. P. E.** (1714–88) German composer. Full name **Carl Philipp Emanuel Bach**

Bach, J. C. (1735–82) German composer. Full name **Johann Christian Bach**

AKG London

Johann Sebastian Bach

Bach, Johann Sebastian (1685–1750) German composer and organist

Bach, W. F. (1710–84) German composer. Full name **Wilhelm Friedemann Bach**

bachelor /báchələr/ *n* **1 UNMARRIED MAN** a man who is not or has never been married **2 YOUNG KNIGHT** a young knight in feudal times who served under the banner of another knight or a great lord **3 UNMATED YOUNG MALE SEAL** a young male seal, especially a fur seal, that older male seals keep from having access to breeding grounds [13C. Via Old French *bacheler* 'young man aspiring to knighthood' < assumed Vulgar Latin *baccalaris.*] —**bachelordom** *n* —**bachelorhood** *n* —**bachelorship** *n*

bachelorette /báchələ rét/ *n US* a young unmarried woman

bachelorette party *n US* = **hen party**

bachelor girl *n* a young unmarried woman, usually one who is self-supporting (*dated*)

Bachelor of Arts *n* a college or university degree awarded to somebody who has successfully completed an undergraduate course in an aspect of the arts or humanities

Bachelor of Science *n* a college or university degree awarded to somebody who has successfully completed an undergraduate course in an aspect of the sciences or technology

bachelor party *n US* = **stag party**

bachelor's degree *n* a degree awarded on the successful completion of an undergraduate course at a college or university and, at some universities, on completion of a usually short postgraduate course

Bach flower remedy /bách-/ *n* a healing method using extracts of 38 flowers, each treating a different emotional disorder, to promote physical health [Late 20C. After Edward *Bach* (1886–1936), British physician.]

Bach trumpet /baák-, baákh-/ *n* a modern valve trumpet, smaller than an ordinary trumpet, specially designed for playing the high-pitched trumpet parts in baroque music [After J. S. BACH.]

bacillary /bə sílləri/ *adj* **1** relating to or caused by rod-shaped bacteria (**bacilli**) **2** shaped like a small rod, or consisting of small rod-shaped parts

bacillus /bə sílləss/ (*plural* **-li** /-seé lī/) *n* **1** an aerobic, rod-shaped, spore-producing bacterium. Genus: *Bacillus.* **2** a rod-shaped bacterium [Late 19C. < late Latin, 'little rod' < *baculus* 'rod, stick'.]

bacitracin /bássi tráyssin/ *n* an antibiotic. Use: treatment of skin infections. [Mid-20C. < BACILLUS + Margaret *Tracy*, in whom the substance was discovered in a wound.]

back /bak/ *n* **1 REAR PART OF BODY** the rear part of the human body between the neck and the pelvis ○ *carrying a baby on her back* ○ *back pain* **2 SPINE** the spinal column **3 BACK OF AN ANIMAL** the area of a vertebrate animal's body on either side of the backbone **4 PART OF GARMENT** the part of a garment designed to cover the wearer's back **5 PART AT THE REAR** the part that is at the rear of something or is furthest from the front ○ *Someone at the back of the crowd called out.* **6 SIDE NOT USUALLY SEEN** the side of something such as a sheet of paper or a photograph that carries less information or is away from the viewer **7 PART OF PIECE OF FURNITURE** the part of a seat designed to support somebody's spine **8 DEFENSIVE PLAYER** a player in sports such as soccer or hockey whose role is mainly to prevent the other team scoring **9 PART OF BOOK OR PERIODICAL** the part of a book, magazine, or newspaper that is located towards the last page ○ *the index at the back of the book* **10 PART TO WHICH PAGES ARE FIXED** the part of the book where the pages are glued or stitched to the binding ■ *adv* **1 IN A REVERSE DIRECTION** in the opposite direction to the one in which somebody or something was previously facing or travelling ○ *He looked back at us over his shoulder.* **2 AT A DISTANCE** at a distance from where something is situated or taking place ○ *Stay back, the dog might bite.* **3 IN RESERVE** as a reserve or supply kept for future use ○ *I kept back part of the proceeds.* **4 SO AS TO UNCOVER** away from something so as to leave something else uncovered or revealed ○ *roll back the carpet* **5 SO AS TO RECLINE** in or into a reclining position ○ *Sit back and relax.* **6 IN OR INTO THE PAST** indicates a time in the past ○ *Back then, people grew their own food.* ○ *It happened about three weeks back.* **7 TO A MORE DISTANT TIME** indicates movement in time away from the present ○ *will put the clocks back* ○ *postponed the wedding and moved it back to next year* **8 TO THE ORIGINAL OWNER** to or into the keeping of the original or former owner or possessor ○ *You can have it back now, because I've finished with it.* **9 IN RETURN** as a reaction or response to something ○ *She called me while I was out, so I called her back.* **10 INDICATES DIRECTION AND DISTANCE** in the distance behind something, especially somebody's present position ○ *We passed it about two miles back.* **11 RETURNED TO CONDITION OR TOPIC** used to indicate a return to a state, situation, or subject of discussion ○ *to get back to your point* **12 POPULAR AGAIN** into fashion or popularity again ○ *The 70s are back.* ○ *Do you think Depression glass will ever come back?* ■ *adj* **1 LOCATED AT THE REAR** located at the rear of something or at the part furthest from the front ○ *Use the back entrance.* **2 ISSUED EARLIER** published or issued at an earlier date ○ *a back issue* **3 DUE EARLIER** due at or owed from an earlier date ○ *paid the back taxes in full* **4 LOCATED AWAY FROM MAIN ROADS** located away from the main roads or the centre of a town ○ *a quiet back* *street* 5 **REMOTE** situated away from the main centres of population or activity ○ *explored the back areas of the canyon* 6 **REVERSE** moving in an opposite direction to the usual one 7 **FORMED AT REAR OF MOUTH** formed at or towards the rear of the mouth, as the vowel in 'ball' is ○ *a back vowel* ■ *v* 1 *vti* **MOVE BACKWARDS** to move backwards, or make somebody or something move backwards ○ *The vehicle in front backed into me.* 2 *vt* **SUPPORT PERSON OR CAUSE** to give a person or cause financial, political, or moral support 3 *vt* **BET ON OUTCOME OF RACE** to bet money on the person, team, or animal thought likely to win a race or competition 4 *vt* **PROVIDE PROOF TO SUPPORT** to provide evidence or proof in support of a statement ○ *But can they back their allegations?* 5 *vt* **REINFORCE** to reinforce something by adding a support or backing ○ *coloured paper backed with cardboard* 6 *vt* **BE BEHIND** to be situated behind something (*usually passive*) ○ *a lake backed by a range of mountains* 7 *vt* **PROVIDE MUSICAL ACCOMPANIMENT FOR** to provide an instrumental or vocal accompaniment for the main performer of a piece of popular music or jazz 8 *vi* **CHANGE DIRECTION** to change direction, moving in an anticlockwise direction (*refers to wind*) [Old English *bæc* < Germanic] ◇ **back and fill** 1 to dither or vacillate in actions or decision-making 2 to adjust the sails of a vessel in order to allow the wind to move in and out of them in an alternating manner as the boat is manoeuvred in a narrow channel ◇ **back of** *US, Can* at the back of or behind something ◇ **behind somebody's back** when somebody is not present ◇ **be** *or* **get on somebody's back** to criticize or pressurize somebody (*slang*) ◇ **get off somebody's back** 1 to stop criticizing or pressurizing somebody (*slang*) 2 to make somebody feel annoyed or defensive ◇ **have your back to the wall** to be in a very difficult situation, with little chance of getting out of it ◇ **in back (of something)** *US, Can* at the back of or behind something (*informal*) ◇ **put somebody's back up** to annoy or antagonize somebody (*informal*) ◇ **put your back into something** to put effort, especially physical strength, into doing something ◇ **the back of beyond** a remote inaccessible place that has few amenities ○ *They bought a small cottage in the back of beyond, just to get away from it all.* ◇ **turn your back on somebody** *or* **something** to ignore or reject somebody or something ◇ **you scratch my back, I'll scratch yours** if you help me, I will help you in return (*often refers to unofficial or dishonest business dealings*)

USAGE back of and **in back of**: The phrase ***back of*** is standard in American English and ***in back of*** is its informal variant. They would not be normally used elsewhere except as consciously adopted Americanisms. Both mean 'behind', and ***in back of*** is formed on the direct analogy of *in front of*, which is standard in both American and British varieties of English: *There was a swimming pool (in) back of the house.*

USAGE Movement in time: ***Back*** as it applies to the past refers to a change to an earlier time. *They have moved its estimated date of origin back a hundred years* would mean a change from, say, AD 1000 to AD 900. As the word applies to the future, however, it usually signifies a change to a later time: *The forecast is for rain, so let's move the picnic back a week.* What the two uses have in common is movement in time away from the present. *Forward* in future contexts is used less consistently than ***back***; it is best avoided. All these words become particularly confusing when the subject is, for example, a decision, now in the past, about what was at the time the future: *Last month she told me she wanted to move my appointment back.* In a context like this, *make earlier* or *make later* is clearer.

back away *vi* 1 to walk backwards away from somebody or something, usually because of fear 2 to withdraw from a situation or previous position ○ *We think they'll back away from any direct confrontation over sanctions.*

back down *vi* to abandon a claim, opinion, or commitment because of the degree of opposition it arouses

back off *vi* 1 to move away backwards 2 to stop putting pressure on somebody to do something

back out *v* 1 *vi* to withdraw from a previous commitment ○ *The buyer backed out before the papers were signed.* 2 *vti* to move out backwards, or cause something to move out backwards

⚡**back up** *v* 1 *vt* **TO SUPPORT** to provide support for a person or idea ○ *I'm sure you'll back me up on this.* 2 *vt* **COPY COMPUTER FILES** to make a copy of computer data to keep in case anything goes wrong with the original 3 *vti* **GO BACKWARDS** to go or move something backwards 4 *vt* **PRINT OTHER SIDE OF SHEET** to print the other side of a sheet that has already been printed on one side 5 *vti* **ACCUMULATE** to build up, or cause something to build up, especially because normal flow is obstructed ○ *Traffic was backed up three miles from the accident.* 6 *vi* **START TO RUN EARLY** to begin moving down the wicket towards the receiving batsman in anticipation of a run before the ball is bowled 7 *vt* **PROVE STATEMENT** to supply proof that a statement is true ○ *Evidence of growth is backed up by recent economic statistics.*

backache /bák ayk/ *n* an ache or pain affecting the back, most commonly the lower back

back-and-forth *n* the repeated exchange of ideas, opinions, or information

back bacon *n* a cut of bacon from the back of the pig that provides very lean rashers

backbeat /bák beet/ *n* a loud rhythmic beat occurring on the off beats of the bar, used especially in rock music

backbench /bák bénch/ *n UK, Can, ANZ* a bench in a legislative assembly reserved for Members of Parliament who do not hold office or are not official spokespersons for the Opposition (*usually plural*) ○ *on the back benches* ■ *adj* relating to Members of Parliament who are not members of the government or official spokespersons for the Opposition

backbencher /bák benchər/ *n* 1 *UK, Can, ANZ* a member of the lower house of a legislative assembly who is not a government minister or an official Opposition spokesperson 2 *US* a member of Congress who has low seniority

backbend /bák bend/ *n* an exercise in gymnastics in which somebody bends over backwards from a standing position until the hands touch the floor

backbite /bák bīt/ (**-bites, -biting, -bit** /-bitt/, **-bitten** /-bitt'n/ *or* **-bit**) *vti* to make spiteful or slanderous comments about somebody who is not present —**backbiter** *n*

backboard /bák bawrd/ *n* 1 a board that forms the back of something, e.g. a cart or boat 2 in basketball, the vertical board situated behind the basket that serves to rebound the ball into the basket or onto the court

back boiler *n* a water tank or set of pipes placed behind a fireplace so that a domestic fire will also heat water

⚡**backbone** /bák bōn/ *n* 1 = **spinal column** 2 **SOMETHING SIMILAR TO SPINAL COLUMN** something that is similar in shape or position to a spinal column ○ *the Pennines, the backbone of England* 3 **CENTRAL SUPPORTING PART** the part of an organization or system that is its strongest unifying factor and main support ○ *The middle classes are the backbone of this nation.* 4 **FORTITUDE** strength of character and determination ○ *He doesn't have the backbone to stand up to his critics.* 5 **HIGH-SPEED RELAY** a high-speed relay that feeds smaller channels in corporate networks and the Internet 6 **CORE OF ELECTRONIC NETWORK** the core of an electronic network, e.g. a physical cable connection or a routing protocol

back boundary line *n* either of two lines parallel to the net that mark the rear limit of the playing area on a badminton court

backbreaker /bák braykər/ *n* 1 a wrestling hold in which somebody's back is bent backwards over the opponent's knee or shoulder 2 an exhausting or greatly demanding taxing task (*informal*)

backbreaking /bák brayking/ *adj* involving enormous physical effort

back burner ◇ **put something on the back burner** to assign something a lower priority or give something less prominence ○ *The project has been put on the back burner.*

back channel *n* a covert way of exchanging sensitive information in politics or diplomacy that circumvents the usual procedures

backchat /bák chat/ *n* rude or impertinent answers or comments ○ *I don't want any backchat if he asks you whether you like school.* US term **back talk**

backcheck /bák chek/ *vti* to skate back towards your own goal in ice hockey while trying to block an opponent with your body or stick —**backchecker** *n*

backcloth /bák kloth/ (*plural* **-cloths**) *n* THEATRE = **backdrop** *n.* 1

backcomb /bák kōm/ *vt* to comb hair with quick short movements towards the roots so that it stands up away from the head and can be brushed into a bouffant hairstyle. US term **tease** *v.* 8

back country *n US, Can, ANZ* a remote, sparsely populated rural area, often used for various forms of outdoor recreation, including backpacking and camping ○ *backpacking in rugged back country*

backcourt /bák kawrt/ *n* 1 **REAR OF COURT** the area between the baseline and the service line on a tennis court or the area of the court nearest the back boundary line or back wall in similar games 2 **DEFENDED HALF OF BASKETBALL COURT** the half of a basketball court where the basket being defended is located 3 **DEFENSIVE PLAYERS** the basketball players who defend the backcourt

back crawl *n* SWIMMING = **backstroke** *n.* 1

backcross /bák kross/ *vt* **CROSS HYBRID WITH PARENT** to cross an organism, especially a hybrid, with one of its parents or an individual genetically identical to that parent ■ *n* 1 **HYBRID OBTAINED BY BACKCROSSING** a hybrid obtained by backcrossing 2 **ACT OF BACKCROSSING** the act or the process of backcrossing organisms

backdate /bák dayt/ (**-dates, -dating, -dated**) *vt* 1 to put a date on a document that is earlier than the actual date of its writing or signing 2 to make an agreement or document valid from an earlier date than the present date

back dive *n* a dive made when the diver's back is facing the water

⚡**back door** *n* 1 **REAR DOOR** a door or entrance at the rear of a building 2 **back door, backdoor DISHONEST ADVANTAGE** underhand or indirect access that gives somebody an unfair advantage 3 **DELIBERATE GAP IN SECURITY SYSTEM** an opening deliberately left in a security system to allow access for technicians

backdoor /bák dawr/ *adj* carried out in secrecy or in a surreptitious way ○ *There's been a lot of backdoor pressure on her to step down.* ■ *n* = **back door** *n.* 2

backdown /bák down/ *n* the abandonment of a course of action or an opinion in the face of opposition from other people

backdrop /bák drop/ *n* 1 a large painted cloth hung at the back of the stage that usually depicts the setting in which the action of a scene takes place 2 a setting or context ○ *The ski-jumping took place against the backdrop of jagged mountain peaks.*

back EMF /-émf/ *n* an electromagnetic force that opposes any change of current in an inductive circuit

back emission *n* the production of electrons from the anode of a vacuum tube

⚡**back end** *n* 1 a main processing computer, often with a smaller interactive computer 2 a software program that controls operations not specified by the user

back end load *n* a unit trust sales charge paid when shares are sold

backer /bákər/ *n* 1 somebody who gives moral or financial support 2 somebody who bets

SYNONYMS ***backer, angel, guarantor, patron, sponsor***
CORE MEANING: somebody who provides financial support
backer a person who gives moral or financial support; **angel** a person who provides financial support for an enterprise, e.g. a theatrical venture; **guarantor** a person who gives a legal undertaking to be responsible for somebody else's debts or obligations; **patron** a person who gives financial or moral support to a person, institution, or charity, especially in the arts; **sponsor** a person or organization that contributes money to help fund an event, usually in return for publicity, or gives money to a person taking part in a fundraising activity.

backfield /bák feeld/ *n* 1 **AREA OF FIELD** in American football, the area of the playing field behind the line of scrimmage 2 **PLAYERS** the players who line up behind the line of scrimmage 3 **POSITIONS** the positions of the players who line up behind the line of scrimmage

backfile /bák fīl/ *n* an archive consisting of previous issues of a newspaper or magazine

backfill /bákfil/ *vt* to refill a trench or other excavation with the soil dug out of it ■ *n* the soil used to refill a trench

backfire /bák fīr/ *vi* (**-fires, -firing, -fired**) 1 **HAVE OPPOSITE EFFECT** to have an effect opposite to the one intended ○ *The policy of mandatory testing may well backfire and do more harm than good.* 2 **MAKE EXPLOSION IN EXHAUST PIPE** to produce an explosion of prematurely ignited fuel in an internal-combustion engine or of unburnt exhaust gases in the exhaust pipe 3 **START FIRE TO CREATE FIREBREAK** to start a fire in the path of an advancing wildfire in order to halt its advance ■ *n* 1 **EXPLOSION IN CAR EXHAUST** an explosion of prematurely ignited fuel in an internal-combustion engine or of unburnt exhaust gases in the exhaust pipe **2 FIRE STARTED TO CREATE FIREBREAK** a fire deliberately started in order to clear the ground in front of an advancing wildfire so as to halt it

backflow /bák flō/ *n* the flowing back of something towards the source

back-formation *n* **1** a process of word formation in which a new word is coined by removing a real or imagined affix from an existing word **2** a word formed by back-formation, e.g. 'greed' from 'greedy', or 'televise' from 'television'

back four *n* a defensive formation in football that consists of two wing backs and two centre backs deployed in a straight line across the field

backgammon /bák gamən/ *n* **1** a board game for two players who move pieces according to throws of a pair of dice, the object being to remove all your counters from the board **2** the most complete form of victory in backgammon [Mid-17C. < BACK + *gamen*, early form of GAME[1]; probably from the pieces sometimes being put 'back' on the table.]

ϟ **background** /bák grownd/ *n* **1 PERSONAL CIRCUMSTANCES AND EXPERIENCES** the personal circumstances and experiences that shape somebody's life, e.g. ethnic and social origins, upbringing, education, and work experience ○ *a group of people from very different backgrounds* **2 CAUSES OF AN EVENT** the circumstances leading up to an event that explain its cause ○ *The meeting takes place against a background of rising tension.* **3 SCENERY BEHIND** the setting for a scene ○ *A silvery lake shone against a background of tall dark firs.* **4 PART OF PICTURE** the part of a picture or pattern that appears to be in the distance or behind the most important part **5 INFORMATION** information that helps to explain what somebody or something is like or why something is happening **6 INCONSPICUOUS POSITION** a position of relative inconspicuousness or unimportance ○ *working tirelessly in the background* **7** PHYS = **background radiation** **8 SIGNAL CAUSING DISTORTION OR INTERFERENCE** an extraneous signal, often in the form of electronic or acoustic noise, that can cause distortion or affect an instrument reading (*often before nouns*) ○ *background interference* **9 LOW-PRIORITY ENVIRONMENT IN COMPUTERS** the low-priority environment in computers that can perform multiple tasks ■ *adj* **1 AS PART OF THE BACKGROUND** situated or depicted in, or forming part of, the background to something **2 ACCOMPANYING** functioning or suitable as an accompaniment to something else

background music *n* music used as an accompaniment to action or dialogue in a film, or to create a pleasant atmosphere for an activity or in a public place

ϟ **background processing** *n* execution of computer tasks that continues while the user is working on something else

background radiation *n* low-level radiation occurring naturally as a result of radioactivity present in the air, soil, and buildings and other structures

backhand /bák hand/ *n* **1 BACKHANDED STROKE** in tennis and similar games, a stroke made with the back of the hand turned towards the ball as the arm moves outwards from a position across the body **2 BACKHAND SIDE** the side of a tennis court, or of the body, on which a player would naturally play a backhand stroke **3 HANDWRITING SLOPING LEFTWARDS** a style of handwriting in which the letters slope to the left ■ *adj* **WITH BACK OF HAND TOWARDS BALL** carried out with the back of the hand facing in the direction in which the stroke, movement, or blow is made ■ *adv* **BACKHANDEDLY** with a backhand stroke ■ *vt* **1 CONTACT BALL WITH BACKHAND** to strike a ball with a backhand stroke ○ *She backhanded the ball just over the net.* **2 HIT SOMEBODY WITH BACK OF HAND** to hit somebody or something with the back of the hand ○ *accidentally backhanded an opponent*

backhanded /bák hándid/ *adj* **1 PLAYED BACKHAND** carried out with the back of the hand facing in the direction in which the stroke, movement, or blow is made ○ *a backhanded return* **2 WITH DOUBLE MEANING** with a doubtful or double meaning, especially one that can be understood equally as a compliment or as an insult ○ *a backhanded compliment* **3 WRITTEN WITH LETTERS SLOPING LEFTWARDS** written in a style of handwriting in which the letters slope to the left —**backhandedly** *adv* —**backhandedness** *n*

backhander /bák handər/ *n* **1 BACKHANDED BLOW** a blow struck with the back of the hand ○ *caught the opposing team member with a terrific backhander across the face during hard play* **2 BACKHAND STROKE** a backhand stroke in tennis and similar games **3 BRIBE** an illicit payment made as a bribe (*informal*) **4 BACKHANDED COMPLIMENT** a backhanded compliment or veiled verbal attack on somebody (*informal*)

backhoe /bák hō/ *n* a digging machine or attachment consisting of a hinged scoop attached to a jointed mechanical arm that drags the scoop back towards the tractor from which it is operated

backing /báking/ *n* **1 SUPPORT OR HELP** active approval, support, or help, often in financial form, given to an individual, organization, or cause **2 SUPPORTERS** the people or organizations giving support to a person or cause **3 REAR SURFACE** material forming or covering the back of something, especially to strengthen, stiffen, or protect it **4 MUSICAL ACCOMPANIMENT** the music or singing that accompanies the playing or singing of the main performer of a piece of popular music or jazz

backing track *n* a recorded musical accompaniment for use by a solo performer

back issue *n* PUBL = **back number** *n.* 1

back kitchen *n* a pantry or other small room off a kitchen (*informal*)

backlash /bák lash/ *n* **1 STRONG REACTION** a strong adverse reaction among a group of people to an event, development, or trend, especially one that benefits another group **2 VIOLENT BACKWARD MOVEMENT** a sudden violent backward jerking movement, e.g. when a cable breaks under strain **3 RECOIL BETWEEN MACHINE PARTS** a jarring recoil that sometimes occurs when worn or badly fitting parts of a mechanism come together **4 PLAY BETWEEN MACHINE PARTS** excessive play between adjacent parts in a mechanism such as a set of gears, usually as a result of the parts being worn or badly fitted **5 FISHING LINE TANGLE** a tangle in a fishing line wound on the reel

backless /bákləss/ *adj* with the back cut very low ○ *a backless dress*

backlight /bák līt/ *n* light that illuminates the subject of a photograph or painting from behind ■ *vt* (**-lights, -lighting, -lighted** *or* **-lit** /-lit/, **-lighted** *or* **-lit**) to illuminate a subject from behind —**backlighting** *n*

backlist /bák list/ *n* the range of books already published by a publisher that are still in print ○ *The departing editor had built up a highly respectable backlist.*

backlit past tense, past participle of **backlight**

backlog /bák log/ *n* **1** a quantity of unfinished business or work that has built up over a period of time and must be dealt with before progress can be made ○ *She faced a backlog of work when she came back.* **2** a large log placed at the back of an open fire

back matter *n* the parts of a book that appear after the main text, e.g. the index or an appendix

backmost /bák mōst/ *adj* furthest back from a given point ○ *Spectators in the backmost seats couldn't hear a thing.*

back mutation *n* the reversion of a mutated gene to its original form

back number *n* **1** a previous issue of a magazine or newspaper. US term **back issue** **2** a person or thing considered to be out of date (*informal*)

ϟ **back office** *n* **1 BUSINESS OPERATIONS OTHER THAN POLICYMAKING** the business operations performed by people who do not make policy, or the place where they work **2 SECURE AREA OF SOFTWARE** a secure area of e-commerce software where details of store properties, tax tables, and products are held (*in e-commerce*) ■ *adj* **RELATING TO INTERNAL MATTERS** relating to or concerned with the administration and internal workings of a business organization rather than its contacts with the public

backpack /bák pak/ *n* **1 RUCKSACK** a large canvas bag, often on a metal frame, worn on the back and used by walkers **2 EQUIPMENT CARRIED ON THE BACK** a pack or carrier for a piece of equipment, such as an astronaut's personal life-support system, that is designed to be strapped on the user's back ■ *v* **1** *vi* **HIKE WITH BACKPACK** to travel, especially hike, carrying belongings or supplies in a backpack ○ *She spent a month backpacking in the Rockies.* **2** *vt* **CARRY SOMETHING ON THE BACK** to transport something, usually equipment or supplies, in a pack on the back ○ *astronauts backpacking oxygen during a spacewalk* —**backpacker** *n*

back pass *n* in football, a pass from an outfield player back to the goalkeeper

back passage *n* the anal canal (*informal*)

back pay *n* pay that is owed to an employee for work done before the current payment period and is either overdue or results from a backdated pay increase

backpedal /bák pedd'l/ (**-als, -alling, -alled**) *v* **1** *vti* **PEDAL BACKWARDS** to turn the pedals of a bicycle backwards, e.g. in order to operate a brake **2** *vi* **MOVE BACKWARDS** to move quickly backwards, e.g. in order to get away from an opponent or to catch a ball **3** *vi* **RETREAT** to try to escape the consequences of a statement or action by retracting it, modifying it, or toning it down

backplate /bák playt/ *n* a piece of armour protecting the back

back pressure *n* **1 RESISTANT PRESSURE** resistant pressure exerted by any solid, liquid, or gas to the forward motion of a system, especially the pressure opposing the exhaust stroke of a piston in an internal-combustion engine **2 OIL OR GAS PRESSURE** the pressure exerted by fluids in the bore of an oil well on the oil and gas in the reservoir **3 PRESSURE DUE TO OBSTRUCTION** pressure within a blood vessel or the urinary system that builds up when there is an obstruction to the flow of fluid

back projection *n* the cinematic technique of projecting a film onto a translucent screen from behind, usually to provide a moving background against which other action can be filmed

backrest /bák rest/ *n* a part of a seat designed to support the user's back

backroom /bák room, -ròòm/, **back room** *n* a place away from the centre of activities where important and usually secret research or planning is supposed to be carried out ■ *adj* **backroom, back-room** taking place unobtrusively, but usually important or influential nonetheless

back row *n* the players forming the third row of a rugby union scrum, traditionally the two wing forwards and the number eight

backsaw /bák saw/ *n* a small saw stiffened and strengthened by a strip of metal on its noncutting edge

backscatter /bák skatər/ *n* **1** the deflection of radiation or particles through angles of greater than 90 degrees measured with respect to the original direction of travel through a medium **2** radiation or particles deflected more than 90 degrees while passing through a medium

back seat *n* **1** a seat at the back of a vehicle **2** a less important or active role ◇ **take a back seat (to somebody)** to allow somebody else to direct or control something while taking on a relatively less important role yourself

back-seat driver *n* (*informal*) **1** a passenger in a vehicle who continually pesters the driver with unwanted advice or criticism **2** somebody who gives unwanted advice or criticism while somebody else does something

backset /bák set/ *n* an eddy or a current flowing against the direction of the main current in a body of water

back shift *n* **1** a period of work beginning in the afternoon and ending at night overlapping with the day shift and the night shift. US term **swing shift** *n.* 1 **2** a group of employees working on a back shift. US term **swing shift** *n.* 2

backshore /bák shawr/ *n* the area of the shore that is above the high-water mark except in very severe weather

backside /bák sīd, bák sīd/ *n* **1** a person's buttocks (*informal*) **2** *Malaysia* the rear part of a vehicle or building

backsight /bák sīt/ *n* **1** a sight on the part of a firearm nearest to the aimer's eye **2** a sight or reading taken by a surveyor back towards a position from which a previous sight has been made

back slang *n* slang in which words are disguised by being pronounced as if spelt backwards

backslap /bák slap/ (**-slaps, -slapping, -slapped**) *vti* to treat somebody, or treat each other, in a hearty, jovial, and enthusiastically complimentary way, with or without physical slaps on the back ○ *a political candidate who backslapped his way around the country* —**backslapper** *n*

ϟ **backslash** /bák slash/ (*plural* **-slashes**) *n* a keyboard character (\) with various uses in computing and programming

backslide /bák slīd/ (**-slides, -sliding, -slid** /-slid/, **-slid**

or **-slidden** /-slidd'n/) *vi* to fall back into wrongdoing after attempting to live morally —**backslider** *n*

backspin /bák spin/ *n* spin that makes a ball rotate in the opposite direction to its line of movement so that when it lands or strikes something its forward momentum will be reduced

backstab /bák stab/ (**-stabs, -stabbing, -stabbed**) *vt* to do or say something harmful to somebody after pretending to be a friend [Early 20C. < *stab somebody in the back.*] —**backstabber** *n* —**backstabbing** *n*

backstage /bák stáyj/ *adv* **1** behind the area of a theatre stage that is visible to an audience ○ *Journalists were allowed backstage to interview the star.* **2** in private or out of the view of the general public —**backstage** *adj*

backstairs /bák stairz/ *npl* a set of stairs in a private part of a house, often originally for the use of servants ■ *adj* carried on secretly or furtively

backstay /bák stay/ *n* **1** a rope leading backwards from the top of a mast to the side or stern and giving support to the mast **2** a thing that supports or strengthens the back of something else, e.g. a piece of leather covering the back seam of a shoe

backstitch /bák stich/ *n* a method of stitching in which each new stitch starts from the middle of the previous stitch —**backstitch** *vti*

backstop /bák stop/ *n* **1** SCREEN TO STOP A BALL a screen or barrier to stop the ball travelling out of the playing area **2** BASEBALL = **catcher** *n.* **2** **3** CATCH STOPPING BACKWARD MOVEMENT a catch on a mechanism designed to prevent it from moving back too far **4** ADDITIONAL SUPPORT somebody or something providing additional support or protection

back-story (*plural* **back-stories**) *n* **1** the events that are supposed to have taken place before the action of a film, television programme, or novel begins (*informal*) **2** CINEMA, MEDIA = **prequel**

back straight *n* the straight section of a racing circuit opposite the home straight. US term **back stretch**

backstreet /bák street/ *n* **backstreet, back street** MINOR STREET a small street off the main roads in a city or town ■ *adj* **1** **backstreet, back-street** IN A BACKSTREET situated or taking place in a backstreet **2** **backstreet, back-street** ILLICIT carried out furtively or illicitly in a place where it is unlikely to attract public attention

back stretch *n US* SPORTS = **back straight**

backstroke /bák strōk/ *n* **1** SWIMMING ON THE BACK a method of swimming on the back in which the swimmer makes circular backward movements with each arm alternately while kicking the legs rhythmically up and down **2** RETURN STROKE a stroke or movement in the opposite direction to that of the original or forward one **3** *US* BACKHAND STROKE a backhand stroke in tennis and similar games —**backstroke** *vi* —**backstroker** *n*

backswept /bák swept/ *adj* angled, slanting, or brushed backwards ○ *a backswept hairstyle*

backswing /bák swing/ *n* the backward movement of a player's club, bat, or racket away from the eventual point of contact with the ball in preparation for playing the actual stroke

backsword /bák sawrd/ *n* **1** a sword with a cutting edge on one side of the blade only **2** a stick with a basket-shaped hilt used in fencing practice

back talk *n US* = **backchat**

back-to-back *adj* **1** WITH BACKS TO EACH OTHER standing or sitting with backs turned to, and sometimes touching, one another **2** BUILT CLOSE TOGETHER describes houses that are built so that their backs join or are only narrowly separated ○ *street after street of back-to-back houses* **3** CONSECUTIVE following immediately one after the other ○ *We had back-to-back meetings prior to the new-product launch.* ■ *n* HOUSE BUILT BACK TO BACK a house built with its back touching the back of another house or only narrowly separated from it —**back to back** *adv*

back to front *adv* with the back part at the front ○ *I hadn't noticed I'd put my sweater on back to front.*

backtrack /bák trak/ *vi* **1** to go back in the direction from which you have come **2** to change, or distance yourself from, a previous action, opinion, statement, or policy, especially as a result of other people's opposition to it ○ *After a lot of public outrage, the government backtracked on its proposed ban.*

⚡**backup** /bák up/ *n* **1** SUPPORT support or assistance from other people, e.g. from the supplier of a product **2** REINFORCEMENTS reinforcements to help personnel already committed, especially police officers ○ *The officers at the scene are calling for backup from another force.* **3** SUBSTITUTE OR RESERVE a substitute or reserve that can be used if the thing normally used fails **4** SECURITY COPY a copy of computer data that is stored, e.g. on a floppy disk **5** COPYING the procedure for copying computer data with which somebody is working ○ *The backup is done automatically every morning.* **6** OVERFLOW an overflow from a pipe caused by a blockage ○ *a backup of water* **7** an excess quantity of something that builds up when normal flow is obstructed —**backup** *adj*

backward /bákwərd/ *adj* **1** TO THE REAR in the opposite direction to the one in which somebody or something is facing **2** REVERSED positioned the opposite way round, arranged in the opposite order, or proceeding in the opposite direction to the normal one **3** NOT ACHIEVING USUAL OR EXPECTED STANDARD lagging behind the progress and development of others of comparable status (*offensive in some contexts*) ○ *a backward economy* **4** RETROGRADE causing or representing a return to a previous or less advanced, and usually less satisfactory, state ○ *a backward step developmentally* **5** TOWARDS THE PAST directed towards the past ○ *a backward look over the city's progress during the last century* **6** SHY shy or lacking in self-confidence ■ *adv* **1** = **backwards** *adv.* **1** **2** = **backwards** *adv.* **2** **3** in the reverse order or direction from the usual. = **backwards** *adv.* **3** **4** = **backwards** *adv.* **4** **5** = **backwards** *adv.* **5** —**backwardness** *n* ◇ **not be backward in coming forward** to be quick and eager to present yourself for something, especially to claim something that could benefit you (*informal*)

USAGE backward or **backwards**? ***Backward*** is the only form available for the adjective: *a backward glance*. In British, Canadian, Australian, and New Zealand English, ***backwards*** is used more often than ***backward*** for the adverb, but in American English ***backward*** is more common for the adverb: *The vehicle moved slowly backwards/backward.*

backwardation /bákwər dáysh'n/ *n* **1** the amount by which the price of goods for immediate delivery differs from the price of goods for delivery at a future time **2** on the London Stock Exchange, the right to delay delivery of securities purchased by somebody until the next settlement period, or the percentage paid by the seller for this right (*dated*)

backward-looking *adj* more concerned with or relevant to a past state of affairs than the present

backwards, backward *adv* **1** BACK FIRST with your back or the back of an object facing in the direction in which you move or it moves ○ *She walked backwards out of the room.* US term **backward** *adv.* **1** **2** TOWARDS THE REAR behind you or in a direction away from the front of something **3** WRONG WAY ROUND the opposite way round, or in the reverse order or direction to the usual ○ *The kids are trying to say the alphabet backwards.* **4** TOWARDS THE PAST towards or into the past ○ *Critics accused the report of going backwards in time* **5** INTO A WORSE CONDITION into a state that is worse or less advanced than the previous or original one ○ *Everything's gone backwards since the new committee took over.* ◇ **bend** *or* **lean over backwards** to make an exceptional effort to do something, especially to help somebody ◇ **know something backwards** know something very well

backwash /bák wosh/ *n* **1** RETREATING WAVE the movement of water back down a beach after a wave has broken **2** WATER PUSHED BACKWARDS a backward movement or flow in water produced by a ship's propeller or by oars **3** AIR PUSHED BACKWARDS a backward rush of air produced by an aircraft propeller or jet engine **4** CONSEQUENCES the consequential effects of an event or action, especially unpleasant or unsettling ones

backwater /bák wawtər/ *n* **1** SMALL STAGNANT BRANCH OF RIVER a still body of water connected to a river but not affected by its current **2** STILL WATER a still body of water held back by a dam, obstruction, or prevailing countercurrent **3** DULL PLACE a place or situation regarded as cut off from the mainstream of activity and consequently seen as quiet or unimportant

backwoods /bák wŏŏdz/ *npl* **1** a sparsely inhabited forested area distant from the main centres of population **2** an area regarded as remote, rustic, and culturally unsophisticated —**backwoods** *adj*

backwoodsman /bák wŏŏdzmən/ (*plural* **-men** /-mən/) *n* **1** somebody who lives in the backwoods **2** a member of the House of Lords who does not often attend (*informal*)

back yard *n* **1** YARD BEHIND A HOUSE a yard behind a house **2** *US, Can* GARDEN a back garden **3** SOMEBODY'S NEIGHBOURHOOD somebody's immediate neighbourhood, or the area considered as somebody's home ground ○ *The gangs know better than to cause trouble in each other's back yards.* —**backyard** *adj*

bacon /báykən/ *n* meat from the back and sides of a pig that has been salted, dried, and often smoked [14C. Via Old French < Germanic, 'back meat'.] ◇ **bring home the bacon** to earn the money on which a family lives (*informal*) ◇ **save somebody's bacon** to save somebody from serious trouble, punishment, injury, or danger (*informal*)

Bacon /báykən/, **Sir Francis, 1st Baron Verulam and Viscount St Albans** (1561–1626) English philosopher, lawyer, and statesman

Bacon, Francis (1909–92) Irish-born British painter

Bacon, Roger (1214?–94) English philosopher and scientist. Known as **Doctor Mirabilis ('Wonderful Doctor')**

bacon-and-eggs *n* PLANTS = **bird's-foot trefoil** [< its yellow flowers streaked with red]

baconer /báykənər/ *n* a pig reared to produce bacon

Baconian /bay kṓni ən/ *adj* OF WORKS OF SIR FRANCIS BACON typical of or similar to the philosophy of Sir Francis Bacon, particularly his method of inductive reasoning in which the emphasis is placed on collecting instances rather than testing theories ■ *n* **1** FOLLOWER OF SIR FRANCIS BACON a student or follower of the philosophy of Sir Francis Bacon **2** BELIEVER IN BACON AS AUTHOR OF SHAKESPEARE'S PLAYS somebody who believes that Shakespeare's plays were actually written by Sir Francis Bacon

bact. *abbr* **1** bacteria **2** bacteriology

bacteraemia /báktə reémi ə/ *n* the presence of bacteria in the blood —**bacteraemic** *adj* —**bacteraemically** *adv*

bacteremia *n* US = **bacteraemia**

bacteri- *prefix* = **bacterio-**

bacteria plural of **bacterium**

bacterial /bak teéri əl/ *adj* consisting of, caused by, or connected with bacteria —**bacterially** *adv*

bacterial artificial chromosome *n* a sequence of DNA taken from another organism and inserted in a bacterium to reveal its function

bactericide /bak teéri sīd/ *n* a substance or agent that destroys bacteria —**bactericidal** *adj*

bacterio- *prefix* bacteria, bacterial ○ *bacteriostat* [< BACTERIUM]

bacteriol. *abbr* bacteriology

bacteriology /bak teéri óllәji/ *n* the scientific study of bacteria, especially in relation to medicine and agriculture —**bacteriological** /bak teéri ə lójjik'l/ *adj* —**bacteriologically** *adv* —**bacteriologist** *n*

bacteriolysis /bak teéri óllississ/ (*plural* **-ses** /-seez/) *n* the dissolution or destruction of a bacterial cell —**bacteriolytic** /bak teéri ə líttik/ *adj*

bacteriophage /bak teéri ə fayj/ *n* a virus that infects bacteria and may integrate into the genetic material of its host cell. Bacteriophages are used as vectors in gene cloning and have other biotechnological uses. —**bacteriophagic** /bak teéri ə fájjik/ *adj* —**bacteriophagous** /-óffəgəss/ *adj* —**bacteriophagy** /-óffəji/ *n*

bacteriostasis /bak teéri ō stáyssiss/ *n* inhibition of bacterial growth and multiplication by a chemical agent

bacteriostat /bak teéri ə stat/ *n* a substance that restricts the growth and activity of bacteria without killing them —**bacteriostatic** /bak teéri ə státtik/ *adj* —**bacteriostatically** *adv*

bacterium /bak teéri əm/ (*plural* **-a** /-ri ə/) *n* a single-celled, often parasitic microorganism without distinct nuclei or organized cell structures. Various species are responsible for decay, fermentation, nitrogen fixation, and many plant and animal diseases. Kingdom: *Eubacteria.* [Mid-19C. < Greek *baktērion* 'little rod' (because the first ones discovered were rod-shaped) < *baktron* 'rod'.] —**bacteroid** /báktə royd/ *adj*

bacteriuria /bak teéri yŏŏri ə/ *n* the presence of bacteria in urine

Bactrian camel /báktri ən-/ *n* a two-humped camel. Native to: Gobi Desert. *Camelus bactrianus.* [Early 17C. < Latin *Bactrianus* < *Bactria*, ancient country in central Asia.]

baculiform /bə kyóoli fawrm/ *adj* shaped like a rod [< Latin *baculum* 'rod']

bad /bad/ *adj* (**worse** /wurss/, **worst** /wurst/) **1 OF POOR QUALITY** below an acceptable standard in quality or performance ○ *bad driving* **2 UNSKILFUL** lacking the skill or competence to perform a task adequately ○ *I've always been bad at remembering dates.* **3 NOT FUNCTIONING PROPERLY** not functioning properly because of a fault ○ *bad TV reception* **4 INCORRECT** incorrect according to the normal rules, especially those governing the use of language ○ *used bad grammar in the essay* **5 WICKED** morally evil, blameworthy, or unacceptable ○ *It's how you tell the good guys from the bad guys.* **6 MISBEHAVING AND DISOBEDIENT** troublesome or annoying, usually through rudeness, disobedience, or mischievousness ○ *Bad dog!* **7 ANGRY AND UNPLEASANT TOWARDS OTHERS** characterized by anger and unpleasantness towards other people ○ *in a bad mood* **8 OFFENSIVE** likely to cause offence to other people because it deals with a taboo subject or expresses violent feelings ○ *swearing and other bad language* **9 HARMFUL** liable to damage health or cause injury ○ *Reading in a dim light is bad for the eyes.* **10 ROTTEN** rotted or deteriorated in quality to the point of being unfit to eat or drink ○ *This milk is bad.* **11 INJURED OR DISEASED** affected by an injury or disease, or not functioning properly, and often causing pain ○ *She's got a bad tooth.* **12 UNWELL** unwell or in pain ○ *I've been feeling bad for a couple of days.* **13 UNEASY** uneasy or regretful about something, or causing somebody to feel this way ○ *I feel really bad about having had to reprimand you.* **14 MORE UNPLEASANT THAN USUAL** possessing an unpleasant, painful, or troublesome quality to a higher degree than usual ○ *Was the pain very bad?* **15 DISTRESSING** likely to cause unhappiness or disappointment ○ *I'm afraid the news is bad.* **16 UNFAVOURABLE** containing or indicating an unfavourable assessment of somebody's performance, work, or character ○ *received a bad job evaluation* **17** (*comparative* **badder**, *superlative* **baddest**) **VERY GOOD** extremely good (*slang*) ○ *the baddest outfit at the party* ■ *n* **1 EVIL** wrong or immoral behaviour ○ *You're old enough to know good from bad.* **2 UNSATISFACTORY OR UNPLEASANT THINGS** things or events that are unsatisfactory or unpleasant ○ *You've got to take the good with the bad.* ■ *adv* (*informal*) **1 BADLY** in an unsatisfactory manner ○ *We didn't do too bad.* **2 VERY MUCH** to an intense or extreme degree ○ *He's got it bad!* [13C. Perhaps < Old English *bæddel* 'effeminate man'.] —**baddish** *adj* —**badness** *n* ◇ **go bad** to become rotten or unfit to eat ◇ **go from bad to worse** to become even more unpleasant, unsatisfactory, or morally unacceptable than before ◇ **go to the bad** to adopt or fall into a way of life that other people consider morally or socially debased and unacceptable (*dated*) ◇ **not bad** fairly good or of a standard that is admitted to be satisfactory, sometimes grudgingly or cautiously, but often in a positive or definitely approving way ○ *That's not bad for a first attempt.*

bad apple *n* somebody thought to be a bad influence on others (*informal*) [< the idea that one bad apple can spoil a whole batch]

badass /bád ass/ *n US* a highly offensive term for somebody who is regarded as bad-tempered or aggressive (*taboo insult*) ■ *adj US* a highly offensive term meaning tough, intimidating, or powerful (*slang*)

bad blood *n* an intense and usually long-lasting feeling of hatred, anger, or resentment

bad breath *n* unpleasant-smelling breath

bad cheque *n* a cheque that is invalid because there are insufficient funds in the account to cover it

bad debt *n* a sum of money owed that is unlikely to be repaid

baddie /báddi/, **baddy** (*plural* **-dies**) *n* somebody, especially a character in a film or a novel, who does evil or criminal things (*informal*)

bade past tense of **bid**

Baden-Baden /baád'n baád'n/ spa town in SW Germany. Population: 52,570 (1997).

Baden-Powell /báyd'n pṓ əl, -pówəl/, **Agnes** (1858–1945) British founder of the Girl Guides Association

Baden-Powell, Robert, 1st Baron Baden-Powell of Gilwell (1857–1941) British soldier and founder of the Scout Movement

Baden-Württemberg /baád'n vúrtəm burg/ state in SW Germany. Capital: Stuttgart. Population: 10,272,000 (1994). Area: 35,752 sq. km/13,804 sq. mi.

Bader /baádər/, **Sir Douglas** (1910–82) British fighter pilot

bad faith *n* insincerity, especially as evidenced by actions that do not accord with somebody's stated intentions

bad feeling *n* = **ill feeling**

badge /baj/ *n* **1 EMBLEM** a small distinctive piece of fabric, metal, or plastic worn on clothing to show rank, membership, or personal enthusiasm and support for something **2 IDENTIFYING FEATURE** a characteristic or identifying mark of a particular brand, quality, or type of person ■ *vt* (**badges, badging, badged**) **1 PUT IDENTIFYING MARK ON** to put a badge or a distinctive identifying mark on something **2 SELL WITH BADGE ON** to market a product under different badges or brand names [14C. < Old French *bage.*]

badger /bájjər/ *n* a medium-sized burrowing animal that is related to the weasel and has short legs, strong claws, and a thick coat. It usually has black and white stripes on the sides of its head. Subfamily: Melinae. ■ *vt* to pester or annoy somebody continually ○ *kept badgering me to go shopping* [Early 16C. Perhaps < BADGE, because of the markings on its head.]

bad hair day *n* a day during which somebody experiences a series of difficulties or annoyances (*slang*)

badinage /báddi naazh, -naaj, báddi naázh/ *n* the exchange of playful or joking remarks between people in conversation [Mid-17C. < French, < *badin* 'fool, joker' < assumed Vulgar Latin *badare* 'yawn, gape'.]

badlands /bád landz/ *npl* a barren area of gullies and bare mountain peaks or mesas formed by erosion

bad lot *n* somebody whose character and behaviour is strongly disapproved of and who is considered to be immoral or pernicious (*dated insult*)

bad luck *n* an unpleasant experience, disappointment, or failure that seems to happen to somebody by chance or undeservedly ■ *interj* used to show sympathy for somebody when something has gone wrong and to suggest that what happened was probably beyond his or her control

badly /báddli/ *adv* (**worse, worst**) **1 POORLY** in an unsatisfactory, incompetent, or incorrect way ○ *The paintwork had been badly finished.* **2 UNHAPPILY** in such a way as to cause suffering, sorrow, or disappointment to the people involved ○ *felt badly about the mistake* **3 SEVERELY** to a degree that causes serious concern for the person or thing involved ○ *Two of the survivors were very badly burned.* **4 VERY MUCH** to a great extent ○ *We're badly in need of new ideas.* **5 WICKEDLY** in a way that is immoral, or that causes trouble, offence, or annoyance to other people ○ *had been behaving badly* **6 REMORSEFUL** full of remorse or regret ○ *feel badly about it* ■ *adj N England* **ILL** unwell or ill ○ *She's still badly after that accident.*

badly off (**worse off, worst off**) *adj* **1** short of money or having a lower than average income (*hyphenated before nouns*) ○ *badly-off families* **2** poorly or inadequately supplied with something ○ *We're badly off for good singers at the moment.*

badminton /bádmintən/ *n* **1** a game similar to tennis, played usually on an indoor court, using rackets to strike a shuttlecock back and forth across a high net **2** a long drink based on claret, with sugar and soda water added [Mid-19C. After BADMINTON.]

Badminton /bádmintən/ village in SW England where horse trials are held annually

badmouth /bád mowth, -mowth/ *vt* to make disparaging remarks about somebody (*slang*)

bad news *n* somebody or something that is likely to cause trouble and should be avoided (*slang*) ○ *Something tells me this guy's bad news.*

bad-tempered *adj* characterized by anger and unpleasantness towards other people —**bad-temperedly** *adv* —**bad-temperedness** *n*

Baeda /beédə/ = **Bede**

Baedeker /báydikər/, **baedeker** *n* a guidebook for travellers [Mid-19C. < Karl BAEDEKER.]

Baedeker /báydikər/, **Karl** (1801–59) German publisher

Baekeland /báykələnd/, **Leo** (1863–1944) Belgian-born US chemist

bael /báy əl/ *n* a pear-shaped thick-shelled fruit similar to a quince. Use: in India, food, medicine for dysentery. [Early 17C. Via Hindi *bel* < Tamil *vilavu.*]

Baeyer /bī́ ər/, **Johann** (1835–1917) German chemist

Baez /bī́ ez, bī éz, bīz/, **Joan** (*b.* 1941) US folk singer and activist

Baffin /báffin/, **William** (1584–1622) English navigator

Baffin Bay /báffin-/ large bay separating Greenland and Canada

Baffin Island large island in Nunavut Territory, NE Canada. Area: 507,451 sq. km/195,928 sq. mi.

baffle /báff'l/ *vt* (**-fles, -fling, -fled**) **1 PUZZLE** to prove too difficult or complicated for somebody to understand, solve, or deal with, causing a feeling of confusion or helplessness **2 FRUSTRATE** to hinder or thwart an action or intention (*formal*) **3 CONTROL** to impede or control the movement of a fluid or gas or the emission of sound or light waves ■ *n* **1 RESTRAINING DEVICE** a device used to control or impede the flow or emission of something and reduce its force **2 PARTITION IN LOUDSPEAKER** a partition in a loudspeaker or microphone intended to prevent sound waves of different frequencies from interfering with one another [Mid-16C. Perhaps blend of French *bafouer* 'ridicule' + Scots *bauchle* 'revile'.] —**bafflement** *n*

bafflegab /báff'l gab/ *n US, Can* pretentious and obscure talk full of technical terminology or circumlocutions (*slang*)

baffling /báffling/ *adj* impossible for the mind to understand, and causing a feeling of confusion or helplessness —**bafflingly** *adv*

Bafta /báftə/ *n* an award given for films and television programmes in Britain ○ *The film won two Baftas.*

BAFTA /báftə/ *abbr* British Academy of Film and Television Arts

bag /bag/ *n* **1 FLEXIBLE CONTAINER** a flexible container that opens at one end and is used for carrying things **2 AMOUNT IN FLEXIBLE CONTAINER** the amount that can be contained in a bag, often used as a measure ○ *eating a bag of crisps* **3 PORTABLE CONTAINER FOR EQUIPMENT OR BELONGINGS** a portable container made of strong flexible material for carrying somebody's belongings or equipment ○ *I threw everything into a bag and rushed out.* **4 ITEM OF BAGGAGE** an item of traveller's baggage, e.g. a suitcase, that can be carried by hand (*often plural*) ○ *Our bags went missing at the airport.* **5 HANDBAG** a handbag **6 NUMBER OF ANIMALS SHOT** the number of animals shot or captured by an individual hunter or party **7 OFFENSIVE TERM** an offensive term deliberately insulting a woman's age and appearance (*slang offensive insult*) **8 SOMEBODY'S SPECIALITY** something that somebody is particularly interested in or good at (*slang dated*) **9** BASEBALL = **base**[1] *n.* 20 **10 SMALL QUANTITY OF ILLEGAL DRUG** a small quantity of an illegal drug in a piece of folded paper, a plastic bag, or a similar container (*slang*) ■ *v* (**bags, bagging, bagged**) **1** *vt* **CLAIM SOMETHING FOR YOURSELF** to claim or get possession of something for yourself before anyone else can claim it (*informal*) ○ *She quickly bagged the window seat.* **2** *vt* **PUT INTO BAG** to put something into a bag **3** *vti* **BULGE** to bulge or become baggy, or cause something to do this **4** *vt* **SHOOT OR CAPTURE ANIMAL** to shoot or capture a game animal or bird ○ *He bagged a six-point buck.* **5** *vt* **OBTAIN** to take, catch, seize, or steal something, usually in an opportunistic way (*informal*) ○ *They've got hold of our address list and are using it to try and bag some of our customers.* **6** *vt* **SPOT** to do, acquire, or see something that is of particular interest or value to you and counts as an achievement in terms of one of your regular hobbies or pursuits (*informal*) **7** *vt Aus* **CRITICIZE** to make disapproving comments about something (*slang*) ■ *interj* **bags I WANT** used to indicate that the speaker wants to claim the right to have or do something, or demands that a particular thing should happen (*informal; usually by children*) ○ *Bags I go first!* [13C. < Old Norse *baggi.*] —**bagful** *n* —**bagger** *n* ◇ **bag and baggage** with all your belongings ◇ **bag of tricks 1** everything, especially all the equipment necessary to do something (*informal*) ○ *They picked up the whole bag of tricks and slung it onto the back of a truck.* **2** a magician's collection of equipment and props ◇ **bags of** a huge amount or number of something (*informal*) ◇ **in the bag** certain to be achieved or obtained (*informal*)

bagasse /bə gáss/ *n* **1** the pulp or dry refuse left after the juice has been extracted from sugar cane. Use: fuel, cattle feed, making paper. **2** paper made from bagasse [Early 19C. Via French < Spanish *bagazo* 'dregs' < Latin *baca* 'berry'.]

bagatelle /bággə tél/ *n* **1 SOMETHING UNIMPORTANT** a thing of little importance (*formal*) ○ *a mere bagatelle* **2 BOARD GAME** a game played on a board or table, in which balls have to be propelled by a cue or spring-loaded launcher past obstacles and into numbered holes **3 SHORT PLAYFUL PIECE OF MUSIC** a short piece of classical music, usually for piano, written in a playful style [Mid-17C. Via French < Italian *bagatella*.]

Bagdad ♦ Baghdad

Bagehot /bájjət/, **Walter** (1826–77) British economist and journalist

bagel /báyg'l/ *n* a glazed ring-shaped bread roll with a slightly chewy texture [Early 20C. < Yiddish *beygl* < Old High German *boug* 'ring'.]

baggage /bággij/ *n* **1 PACKED SUITCASES AND BAGS** suitcases and other containers holding the belongings of people who are travelling **2 PORTABLE EQUIPMENT** the equipment and supplies that a military force carries with it on campaign **3 PRECONCEIVED IDEAS** ideas, beliefs, or practices retained from somebody's previous life experiences, especially insofar as they affect a new situation where they may be no longer relevant or appropriate (*informal*) ○ *emotional baggage* **4 IMPUDENT GIRL OR WOMAN** a girl or woman who is thought of as impudent or obstinate (*often considered offensive*) [15C. < French *bagage* < Old French *bague* 'bundle'.]

baggage handler *n* somebody whose job it is to load and unload baggage onto and off aeroplanes

baggies /bággiz/ *npl US* clothing that is cut extra large for the size of the wearer and hangs loosely on the body (*informal*)

bagging /bágging/ *n* coarse material used for making bags

baggy /bággi/ (**-gier**, **-giest**) *adj* hanging loosely —**baggily** *adv* —**bagginess** *n*

bagh /baag/ *n S Asia* a garden [Via Hindi < Persian *bāg*]

Baghdad /bág dád/, **Bagdad, Baghdād** capital of Iraq, in the E of the country. Population: 3,841,268 (1987).

bag lady *n* a homeless woman who carries her possessions in shopping bags (*informal*)

bagnio /bánnyō, bá-an-/ (*plural* **-gnios**) *n* **1** a house of prostitution (*literary*) **2** a prison, especially a prison in Asia (*archaic*) [Late 16C. Via Italian *bagno* 'bath' < Latin *balneus*.]

Bagnold /bág nōld/, **Enid** (1889–1981) British author and playwright

bag person *n* a homeless person who carries his or her possessions in shopping bags (*informal*)

bagpipes /bág pīps/ *npl* a wind instrument consisting of an inflatable bag with an inlet pipe and one or more outlet pipes that each produce either one fixed note or several notes (*sometimes singular*) —**bagpiper** *n*

bags /bagz/ *npl* **1** prominent folds of skin beneath the eyes, often caused by fatigue **2** a pair of trousers (*dated informal*)

bag-snatcher *n* a thief who specializes in taking women's handbags from them in public places and running away (*informal*) —**bag-snatch** *n* —**bag-snatching** *n*

baguette /ba gét/ *n* **1 STICK-SHAPED LOAF** a long thin loaf of French bread **2 RECTANGULAR GEM** a gem cut into a long rectangular shape **3 SHAPE OF BAGUETTE GEM** the shape of a baguette gem **4 CONVEX MOULDING** a small narrow rounded convex moulding on a wall or column [Early 18C. < French, < Latin *baculum* 'rod'.]

Baguio /bággi ō/ *city* on Luzon Island, the Philippines. It is the country's summer capital. Population: 268,772 (1999 estimate).

bagwash /bág wosh/ (*plural* **-washes**) *n* the process or business of washing clothes but not drying or pressing them, or an amount of washing to be dealt with in this way (*archaic*) [Because finished when the clothes are in the bag]

bagworm /bág wurm/ *n* a moth larva that constructs a case of sand grains, bark, or similar material attached to a leaf or twig. Family: Psychidae.

bah /baa/ *interj* expresses scornful irritation, disgust, or contempt

bahadur /baàhə dòor, bə haàdər/ *n S Asia* a title of respect used before an Indian surname in British India, originally applied to officers [Late 18C. Via Urdu and Persian *bahādur* < Mongolian.]

Baha'i /bə hī́, baa-, bə haà i, -hī́ i/ (*plural* **-ha'is**) *n* **1** a religion founded in Iran in 1863 that maintains that the teachings of all religions are of value and humankind

is spiritually one, and advocates world peace **2** a follower of the teachings of Baha'i [Late 19C. Via Persian *bahā'ī*T < Arabic *bahā'* 'splendour'.] —**Baha'i** *adj* —**Baha'ism** *n* —**Baha'ist** *n*

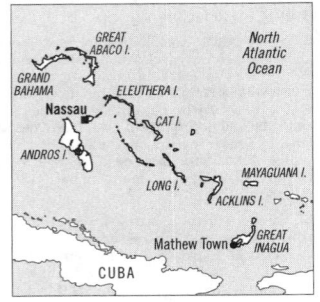
Bahamas

Bahamas /bə haàməz/ *nation* consisting of hundreds of islands in the Atlantic Ocean southeast of Florida. Capital: Nassau. Population: 259,367 (1996). Area: 13,940 sq. km/5,380 sq. mi. —**Bahamian** /bə háymi ən/ *n, adj*

Bahasa Indonesia /baa haàssə-/ *n* the form of Malay that is the official language of Indonesia [< Malay, 'language of Indonesia']

Bahasa Malaysia /ba haàssə-/ *n* the form of Malay that is the official language of Malaysia [< Malay, 'language of Malaysia']

Bahawalpur /bə haàwəl poor, báhə wólpər/ *city* in E Pakistan. Population: 180,263 (1981).

Bahia /bə hee ə, -eè ə/ **1** *state* in E Brazil. Capital: Salvador. Population: 12,531,895 (1996). Area: 566,970 sq. km/218,850 sq. mi. **2** former name for **Salvador**

Bahía Blanca /bə hee ə blángkə, baa eè ə-/ *port* in E Argentina. Population: 260,096 (1991).

Bahia grass /bə hee ə-/ *n* a perennial tropical American grass, grown in the S United States. Use: lawns, forage. *Paspalum notatum.*

bahookie /bə hoòki/ *n Scotland* the buttocks (*humorous*)

Bahrain

Bahrain /baa rayn/, **Bahrein** *island state* on the Persian Gulf off the coast of Saudi Arabia. Capital: Manama. Population: 603,318 (1997). Area: 707 sq. km/273 sq. mi. —**Bahraini** *n, adj*

baht /baat/ (*plural* **bahts** *or* **baht**) *n* see table at **currency** [Early 20C. < Thai *bāt*.]

bahuvrihi /baà hoo vreè hee/ (*plural* **-his**) *n* a compound word in which the first part describes the second or governs it grammatically, and the second element cannot be substituted for the whole, e.g. 'yellowhammer' or 'afternoon' [Mid-19C. < Sanskrit *bahuvrīhi* 'possessing much rice', a typical example of this class.]

Baikal, Lake /bī kaàl/ *world's deepest lake, in S Siberia, Russia. Area: 31,500 sq. km/12,200 sq. mi. Depth: 1,637 m/5,371 ft.

bail[1] /bayl/ *n* **1 SECURITY FOR APPEARANCE IN COURT** a sum of money deposited to secure an accused person's temporary release from custody and to guarantee that person's appearance in court at a later date **2 SOMEBODY**

WHO PAYS BAIL somebody who pays bail **3 RELEASE UNDER SECURITY** temporary release from custody after bail has been paid ○ *Her brother was out on bail.* ■ *vt* **FREE SOMEBODY BY PAYING BAIL** to release an accused person from custody after bail has been paid (*usually passive*) ○ *He has been bailed to appear before the magistrates again on 11th October.* [14C. < Old French, 'temporary custody' < *baillier* 'take charge of' < Latin *bajulus* 'somebody who carries (responsibility)'.] —**bailable** *adj* ◇ **jump** *or* **skip bail** to fail to appear in court as promised at the end of a bail period (*informal*)

bail out *vt* to secure somebody's release from legal custody by paying bail or posting bond

bail[2] /bayl/, **bale** (**bales, baling, baled**) *vti* to empty water out of a boat, using a bucket or similar container ○ *We bailed the sinking boat for an hour.* [Early 17C. < *baille* 'bucket', via Old French < assumed Vulgar Latin *bajula* 'water carrier'.] —**bailer** *n*

bail out, bale out *v* **1** *vti* **EMPTY WATER OUT OF BOAT** to empty water out of a boat, using a bucket or similar container ○ *bailing water out as the boat slowly sank* **2** *vi* **PARACHUTE FROM PLANE** to escape from a plane that is in danger of crashing by making a parachute jump **3** *vi* **ESCAPE FROM DIFFICULT SITUATION** to abandon hurriedly and unceremoniously a situation that is dangerous or difficult ○ *When the company hit the skids, she was the first to bail out.* **4** *vt* **HELP SOMEBODY OUT OF TROUBLE** to help somebody out of a difficult situation

bail[3] /bayl/ *n* **1** in cricket, either of the two short pieces of wood laid on top of the stumps to make the wicket **2** a pole or framework used to separate horses in a barn or stable [Mid-18C. Probably via Old French < Latin *baculum* 'rod'.]

bail up *vt Aus* to stop a person in order to speak to him or her, often in a situation where that person does not want to be stopped or spoken to (*informal*) ○ *I was hoping I wouldn't have to speak to him, but he bailed me up as I was leaving.* [< BAIL[3]]

bail[4] /bayl/, **bale** *n* **1 HINGED BAR** a hinged bar on a typewriter or printer that holds the paper against the platen **2 SEMICIRCULAR HANDLE** a semicircular handle, e.g. on a bucket **3 SEMICIRCULAR SUPPORT** a semicircular support, e.g. to hold up the canopy on a covered wagon [15C. Probably < Old Norse.]

Bail /bayl/, **Murray** (*b.* 1941) Australian writer

bail bar *n* = **bail**[4] *n.* 1

bail bond *n* a document in which the prisoner released on bail and the person who pays the bail money promise that the prisoner will appear in court at a set time

bail bondsman *n US* somebody engaged in the business of providing bail money, or acting as surety, for an accused person

bailee /báy leè/ *n* somebody to whom goods are temporarily entrusted by bailment

bailey /báyli/ (*plural* **-leys**) *n* **1** the outermost wall surrounding a castle **2** a courtyard inside the walls, especially the outermost walls, of a castle [13C. Probably alteration of BAIL[3], influenced by medieval Latin *ballium*.]

Bailey /báyli/, **David** (*b.* 1938) British photographer

Bailey bridge *n* a temporary steel bridge made of prefabricated parts and designed for quick construction [Mid-20C. After Sir D. Coleman *Bailey* (1901–85), British engineer.]

bailie /báyli/ *n Scotland* an honorary title sometimes given to senior members of a local council in Scotland. Formerly, the title was reserved for municipal magistrates. [13C. Variant of BAILIFF.]

bailiff /báylif/ *n* **1 STEWARD** a steward or agent of a landowner or landlord **2 SHERIFF'S OFFICER** a legal officer who serves under a sheriff and is empowered to take possession of a debtor's property, forcibly if necessary, to serve writs, or to make arrests **3 SENIOR OFFICIAL** a senior officer with judicial powers representing the sovereign in a district, e.g. a mayor or sheriff, especially the chief officer of a hundred [13C. Via Old French *baillif*- 'overseer' < assumed medieval Latin *bajulivus* < Latin *bajulus* (see BAIL[1]).]

bailiwick /báyliwik/ *n* an area of activity in which somebody has specific responsibility, knowledge, or ability ○ *Export permits are her bailiwick.* [15C. < BAILIFF + *wik* 'town' (via Old English *wīc* < Latin *vicus* 'village, homestead').]

Baillie /báyli/, **Dame Isobel** (1895–1983) British soprano

bailment /báylmənt/ *n* **1** the temporary entrustment, subject to a contract, of goods to somebody for a particular purpose **2** the granting of bail to somebody in custody

bailor /báy láwr, báylər/ *n* somebody who entrusts goods to another by bailment

bailout /báyl owt/ *n* an intervention by a person or company to help another person or company out of financial difficulties

bailsman /báylzmən/ (*plural* **-men** /-mən/) *n US* LAW = **bail bondsman**

Baily's beads /báyliz-/ *npl* bright points of sunlight that briefly appear around the Moon immediately before and after a total eclipse of the Sun [Mid-19C. After Francis *Baily* (1774–1844), British astronomer.]

báinín /baá neen/, **bawneen** /báw-/ *n Ireland* **1** a collarless jacket for men, made of white wool **2** white wool prepared with some of the natural oil retained. Use: jackets, skirts. [Early 20C. < Irish *bán* 'white'.]

bain-marie /báN mə reé/ (*plural* **bain-maries**) *n* a cooking utensil containing heated water into which another container is placed to be kept warm or cooked gently [Early 19C. < French, via medieval Latin translation < Greek *kaminos Marias* 'alchemist's apparatus', literally 'furnace of Maria' (alchemist and sister of Moses).]

Bairam /bī raám/ *n* either of two Islamic festivals, the Lesser Bairam marking the end of Ramadan or the Greater Bairam seventy days later, marking the end of the Islamic year [Late 16C. Via Turkish *bayram* < Persian *bazrām*.]

Baird /baird/, **John Logie** (1888–1946) British inventor

Bairiki /bī reéki/ administrative centre of Kiribati. Population: 25,000 (1990 estimate).

bairn /bairn/ *n* a young child (*regional*) [Old English *bearn* < Indo-European, 'carry, bear children']

Bairnsdale /báirnz dayl/ town in SE Victoria, Australia. Population: 10,770 (1991).

Baisakhi /bī sáki/ *n* a Sikh festival commemorating the founding of the Khalsa order by Gobind Singh in 1699 and marking the New Year. Date: 13 April.

bait[1] /bayt/ *n* **1 FOOD FOR ATTRACTING ANIMALS** a piece of food used as a lure in fishing or trapping ○ *fishing with live bait* **2 ENTICEMENT** something used to attract or tempt somebody or something else into being caught ■ *vt* **1 PUT FOOD ON HOOK** to put a food attractant on a hook or in a trap ○ *This line's baited with a minnow.* **2 HARASS** to persecute, tease, or harass somebody ○ *Stop baiting the dog, please.* **3 ATTACK ANIMAL WITH DOGS** to set dogs onto a tethered animal, usually a bear or bull, for sport [13C. < Old Norse *beit* 'food', *beita* 'hunt with dogs'.] —**baiter** *n* ◇ **rise to the bait** to react to something, especially to temptation or provocation, in precisely the way that somebody wants you to, e.g. by getting angry when somebody teases you

bait[2] /bayt/ *vi* = **bate**[1]

bait advertising *n* the advertising of cheap products that may or may not be available in order to lure customers into a shop so that they will then buy more expensive products

bait and switch *n* = **bait advertising** (*slang*)

baiza /bízə/ (*plural* **-zas** *or* **-za**) *n* see table at **currency** [Late 20C. Via Arabic < Hindi *paisā*.]

baize /bayz/ *n* a green woollen cloth, similar to felt. Use: tops of billiard, snooker, and card tables. [Late 16C. < French *baies*, plural of *bai* 'bay-coloured' (see BAY[4]), probably because of its original colour.]

Baja California /baá haa-/ peninsula in NW Mexico. Length: 1,220 km/760 mi.

bajada /bə haádə/ *n* a broad plain formed at the base of a mountain or mountain range as a result of the coalescing of sedimentary deposits from a number of streams [Mid-19C. < Spanish, 'slope, descent'.]

Bajazet ♦ **Bayazid I**

bajee *n* FOOD = **bhaji**

bake /bayk/ *v* (**bakes, baking, baked**) **1** *vti* **COOK FOOD IN OVEN** to cook food in an oven by dry heat, or be cooked in this way **2** *vti* **HARDEN BY HEAT** to become hardened, or harden something, by exposing it to dry heat **3** *vi* **BE VERY HOT** to be or feel very hot (*informal*) ○ *You must be baking in that heavy coat.* ■ *n* **1 AMOUNT BAKED** a number of things baked at the same time **2** *Scotland* **TYPE OF BISCUIT** a type of biscuit **3 OVEN-COOKED DISH** a dish of food that is cooked in the oven ○ *a cheese and vegetable bake* [Old English *bacan* < Indo-European, 'to warm']

baked Alaska *n* a dessert of cake that is topped with ice cream, covered with meringue, and then quickly browned in a very hot oven

baked beans *npl* baked haricot beans in a tomato sauce, usually bought in tins

bakehouse /báyk howss/ *n* COMM = **bakery** *n*. 1

Bakelite /báykə līt/ *tdmk* a trademark for any of various synthetic resins used in many manufacturing applications

baker /báykər/ *n* **1** somebody who makes baked foods, especially bread and cakes **2** a portable oven

Baker /báykər/, **Dame Janet** (*b.* 1933) British mezzo-soprano

AKG London

Josephine Baker

Baker, Josephine (1906–75) US-born French dancer and entertainer. Born **Freda Josephine McDonald**

Baker, Sir Samuel (1821–93) British explorer

baker's dozen *n* a set of thirteen items [Because retailers of bread formerly received an extra loaf with each dozen from the baker, which they were entitled to keep as profit]

bakery /báykəri/ (*plural* **-ies**) *n* **1** a building or part of a building where items of food, especially bread and cakes, are baked **2** a shop or part of a store where items of baked food, especially bread and cakes, are sold

Bakewell /báyk wel/, **Robert** (1725–95) British agriculturalist

Bakewell tart *n* a tart with a pastry base covered with jam and topped with almond-flavoured sponge [After the town of *Bakewell* in Derbyshire]

Bakhtaran /báktə raán/, **Bākhtarān** capital of Bakhtaran Province, W Iran. Population: 692,986 (1996).

baking /báyking/ *n* **1 COOKING OF BREAD AND CAKES** the cooking of bread, cakes, and other foods by dry heat in an oven ○ *did the baking early in the morning* **2 AMOUNT BAKED AT ONE TIME** a quantity of items baked at one time ○ *a baking of 46 rolls* ■ *adj* **VERY HOT** very hot and dry ○ *a baking sun*

baking powder *n* a mixture containing sodium bicarbonate, starch, and acids. Use: leavening agent, especially for cakes.

baking sheet *n* US = **baking tray**

baking soda *n* = **bicarbonate of soda** *n.*

baking tray *n* a flat metal tray used for cooking, especially baking, food in an oven

bakkie /báki/ *n S Africa* **1** a pick-up truck with an open back **2** a bowl or basin

baklava /baáklə vaa, bákləvə/ *n* a dessert of filo pastry layered with nuts, with syrup or honey poured over it after baking [Mid-17C. < Turkish.]

baksheesh /bák sheésh, bák sheesh/ *n* in the Middle East, money given as a tip or bribe, or as charity [Mid-18C. < Persian *bakšīš*.]

Baku /baa koó/ capital of Azerbaijan, on the Caspian Sea. Population: 1,853,000 (1995 estimate).

Bakunin /bə koónin/, **Mikhail** (1814–76) Russian-born anarchist

BAL *n* MED = **dimercaprol** [Acronym < *British anti-lewisite*]

Bala, Lake /bállə/ lake in N Wales. Area: 10 sq. km/ 4 sq. mi.

Balaam /báyləm, báy lam/ *n* in the Bible, a Mesopotamian seer who, when called on to curse the Israelites, instead praised them after being reproached by his ass (Numbers 22–24)

balaclava /bállə klaávə/, **balaclava helmet** *n* a close-fitting knitted covering for the head and neck that leaves only the face, or parts of it, exposed [Late 19C. After the village of *Balaklava* in the Crimea, probably because the cap was worn by infantry involved in the campaign there.]

balalaika /bállə líkə/ *n* a Russian musical instrument with a triangular soundbox and three strings that are plucked or strummed [Late 18C. Via Russian < Turkic.]

balance /bállənss/ *n* **1 STEADY STATE ON A NARROW BASE** a state in which a body or object remains reasonably steady in a particular position while resting on a base that is narrow or small relative to its other dimensions ○ *He lost his balance and fell from the beam.* **2 OPPOSITION OF EQUAL FORCES** a state in which two opposing forces or factors are of equal strength or importance so that they effectively cancel each other out and stability is maintained **3 HARMONY** a state in which various elements form a satisfying and harmonious whole and nothing is out of proportion or unduly emphasized at the expense of the rest **4 EMOTIONAL STABILITY** a state of emotional and mental stability in which somebody is calm and able to make rational decisions and judgments **5 WEIGHING MACHINE** a simple mechanical device for weighing objects or samples, often consisting of a pivoted horizontal beam with a pan suspended from each end **6 COUNTERWEIGHT** something that offsets or counters the weight or influence of another element ○ *a system of checks and balances* **7 GREATER PART** the greater, more significant, or more influential part of something, such as evidence or opinion that is likely to sway a decision **8 REMAINDER** a remaining or outstanding amount, e.g. the amount remaining in a bank account after a withdrawal or the amount still to be paid to settle a bill **9 EQUAL DEBIT AND CREDIT** a position where the amounts on the debit and credit sides of an account are equal and cancel each other out **10 DIFFERENCE BETWEEN DEBIT AND CREDIT** the amount by which the debit and credit sides of an account differ **11 EQUALITY OF ELEMENTS IN AN EQUATION** a state of a chemical equation where the number of atoms of each element are equal on both sides of the equation ■ *v* (**-ances, -ancing, -anced**) **1** *vti* **REMAIN IN OR GIVE SOMETHING EQUILIBRIUM** to achieve or maintain, or cause somebody or something to achieve or maintain, a position of steadiness while resting on a narrow base ○ *balanced precariously on a branch* **2** *vti* **PLACE IN PRECARIOUS POSITION** to place an object in a position where it is or seems to be in imminent danger of falling over or of falling off something (*often passive*) **3** *vt* **ASSESS** to assess and compare the relative importance of different factors or alternatives before making a choice or decision ○ *balanced the pros and cons of the plan before moving ahead with it* **4** *vt* **WEIGH IN BALANCE** to weigh something in a balance or by an action or method that resembles the working of a balance **5** *vti* **EQUAL OR CANCEL OUT** to be equal to something in force, weight, or importance, or cancel it out **6** *vt* **BRING ELEMENTS INTO HARMONY** to arrange the different elements of something so that they form a harmonious and well-proportioned whole **7** *vt* **BRING EQUATION INTO EQUALITY** to bring the elements of a chemical or mathematical equation into a state of equality **8** *vt* **ASSESS ACCOUNT** to assess the relative positions of the debit and credit sides of an account **9** *vt* **EQUALIZE ACCOUNT** to make the debit and credit sides of an account equal [13C. Via Old French < Latin *(libra) bilanx* '(scales) with two pans' < *lanx* 'plate, pan'.] —**balanceable** *adj* ◇ **balance the books** to ensure that the debit and credit or income and expenditure sides of an account show the same total, usually by making additional entries ◇ **hang in the balance** to be in a dramatic and tense situation where two diametrically opposed outcomes are possible and the possibility of an unfavourable one is real and greatly feared ◇ **hold the balance 1** to have the power to decide in which way a situation will develop or which of two opposing sides will prevail **2** to control the key to maintaining an existing state of equilibrium between two opposing forces ◇ **on balance** having taken all the relevant factors into consideration and assessed their relative significance ○ *The situation, on balance, is relatively hopeful.* ◇ **redress the balance** to make the situation more fair or equal, usually by giving something to or assisting somebody who was previously at a disadvantage ◇ **strike a balance** to reach a compromise between two extremes ◇ **throw somebody off balance** to surprise or confuse somebody

balance out *v* **1** *vti* to act as an equal and opposing weight, force, or value to something and either neutralize or complement its effect ○ *This gain balances out last month's losses.* **2** *vi* to arrive at a state of equality or harmony, usually through one thing offsetting the other over a period of time ○ *These things tend to balance out in the end.*

Balance *n* ZODIAC = **Libra** *n*. 2

balance beam *n* GYMNASTICS = **beam** *n*. 13

balanced /bállənst/ *adj* **1** EVEN-HANDED taking account of all sides on their merits without prejudice or favouritism ○ *a balanced assessment* **2** HEALTHY containing different elements in suitable quantities or suitably arranged to produce a satisfying and effective whole ○ *a balanced diet* **3** MENTALLY STABLE in a state of mental and emotional stability and able to make rational judgments

balance of payments *n* the difference between the amount paid by a national government to other countries and the amount it receives from them

balance of power *n* **1** the distribution of power among two or more states, where the pattern of force and dominance among them is balanced in such a way that no single state has dominance over the others **2** the power of a single country, group, or individual to affect a situation decisively by supporting either of two opposing sides whose powers are equally balanced

balance of trade *n* the difference between the value of the total imports and total exports of a country as assessed over a fixed period

balance sheet *n* a statement showing the assets and liabilities of a company or institution at a particular time

balance weight *n* a weight used to counterbalance a moving part in a machine

balance wheel *n* a wheel in a machine, especially in a clock, that regulates the rate of movement of the main mechanism

Balanchine /bállən cheen, bállən cheen/, **George** (1904–83) Russian-born US dancer and choreographer. Born **Georgy Melitonovich Balanchivadze**

balancing act *n* **1** a skilful or precarious attempt to deal with or survive a situation where you have to conciliate opposing groups, reconcile opposing views, or perform a large variety of tasks (*informal*) **2** an entertainment in which the performer keeps objects balanced in precarious positions, or balances himself or herself on an unstable object, such as an upended chair

balanitis /bállə nítiss/ *n* inflammation of the head of the penis, usually caused by an infection [Mid-19C. < Greek *balanos* 'acorn, glans penis'.]

balas /bálləss, báyləss/, **balas ruby** *n* a ruby that is a red spinel. Use: gems. [15C. Via Old French *balais*, Spanish *balax* < Arabic *balakš* < Persian *Badakšān*, region of Afghanistan.]

balata /bállətə/ *n* **1** a gum made from tree sap and resembling rubber. Use: gaskets, chewing gum, gutta percha substitute. **2** a tropical tree that yields the sap from which balata is made. *Manilkara bidentata*. US term **bully tree** [Early 17C. < Carib *balatá*.]

Balaton, Lake /bállə ton/ lake in west-central Hungary. Area: 601 sq. km/232 sq. mi.

balboa /bal bố ə/ *n* see table at **currency** [Early 20C. After Vasco Núñez de BALBOA.]

Balboa /bal bố ə/, **Vasco Núñez de** (1475?–1519) Spanish explorer

balbriggan /bal bríggən/ *n* a knitted unbleached cotton fabric. Use: making underwear. [Late 19C. After the town of *Balbriggan*, Ireland.]

Balcon /báwlkən/, **Sir Michael** (1896–1977) British film producer

balcony /bálkəni/ (*plural* **-nies**) *n* **1** a platform projecting from the interior or exterior of a building, usually enclosed by a rail or parapet **2** one of the separate areas of seating raised entirely above the floor level in a theatre, cinema, or concert hall [Early 17C. Via Italian *balcone* < Old Italian, 'scaffold' < Germanic.] —**balconied** *adj*

bald /bawld/ *adj* **1** WITH HAIRLESS HEAD having little or no hair on the head **2** WITHOUT NATURAL COVERING with little or no hair, fur, grass, or other natural covering, and with the bare skin or surface showing ○ *a bald patch on the grass* **3** WORN having a very worn-down tread ○ *Bald tyres are dangerous.* **4** PLAIN plain and direct, with no attempt to elaborate or explain ○ *a bald statement of the facts* **5** UNORNAMENTED plain, bare, and without ornamentation, often to the point of seeming dull or prosaic **6** WITH WHITE MARKINGS describes birds and mammals that have white markings on the face or head [14C. Perhaps < obsolete *bal* 'white spot or streak, especially on a horse's face'.] —**baldness** *n*

baldachin /báwldəkin/ *n* **1** CANOPY a canopy made of cloth or stone erected over an altar, shrine, or throne in a Christian church **2** PORTABLE CANOPY a canopy carried above a priest or venerated object during a religious procession **3** BROCADE a rich silk and gold brocade [Late 16C. < Italian *baldacchino* < *Baldacco* 'Baghdad'.]

bald cypress *n* a deciduous coniferous tree, often found in swamps or near water, that yields hard timber. Native to: United States. *Taxodium distichum*. [Bald because it sheds its needles, unlike most members of its family]

bald eagle *n* a large eagle, the adult of which has a white head and tail. Native to: lakes and rivers of North America. *Haliaeetus leucocephalus*.

Balder /báwldər/ *n* in Norse mythology, one of Odin's sons, who was god of the summer sun. He was vulnerable only to mistletoe, by which he was killed.

balderdash /báwldər dash/ *n* senseless or pointless talk or writing [Late 16C. < ?]

bald-faced *adj* US = **barefaced** *adj*. 1 —**bald-facedly** *adv* —**bald-facedness** *n*

baldheaded /báwld héddid/ *adj* with a bald head ■ *adv* impetuously or without restraint (*informal*) —**bald-headedness** *n*

baldie *n* = **baldy**

balding /báwlding/ *adj* in the process of losing the hair on the head

baldly /báwldli/ *adv* in a simple and blunt way ○ *To put it baldly, she did a lousy job.*

baldpate /báwld payt/ *n* BIRDS = **wigeon** *n*.

baldric /báwldrik/ *n* a sash or belt worn from one shoulder to the opposite hip, used to support a sword [13C. Directly and via Old French *baudre* < Middle High German *balderich*.]

Baldwin /báwldwin/, **James** (1924–87) US writer

Baldwin, **Stanley, 1st Earl Baldwin of Bewdley** (1867–1947) British statesman

baldy /báwldi/ (*plural* **baldies**), **baldie** *n* an offensive term for somebody who is bald or balding (*informal insult*)

bale[1] /bayl/ *n* a large bundle or package of hay or a raw material such as cotton, tightly bound with string or wire ■ *vti* (**bales**, **baling**, **baled**) to gather and fasten material or goods into bales ○ *baling hay* [14C. < Old French, < Germanic.] —**baler** *n*

bale out *v* **1** *vti* = **bail out** 2 *vi* to escape from a plane that is in danger of crashing by making a parachute jump. US term **bail out** *v*. 2 **3** *vi* to abandon hurriedly and unceremoniously a situation that is dangerous or difficult for you ○ *When the company hit the skids she was the first to bale out.* US term **bail out** *v*. 3

bale[2] /bayl/ *n* evil or suffering (*archaic or literary*) [Old English *bealu* < Germanic]

bale[3] /bayl/ *vti* = **bail**[2]

Balearic /bálli árrik/ *adj* belonging to the Balearic Islands

Balearic Islands island group in the W Mediterranean including Majorca, Menorca, and Ibiza. It is an autonomous region of Spain. Population: 736,865 (1991). Area: 5,014 sq. km/1,936 sq. mi.

baleen /bə leen/ *n* a horny substance that grows as fringed plates from the upper jaws of certain whales, acting to strain food, especially small crustaceans, from the water [14C. Via Old French *balaine* < Latin *balaena* 'whale' < Greek *phalaina*.]

baleen whale *n* a large whale that has two blowholes and a set of horny fringed plates instead of teeth

Balearic Islands

baleful /báylf'l/ *adj* threatening, or seeming to threaten, harm or misfortune ○ *a baleful stare* —**balefully** *adv* —**balefulness** *n*

~~balence~~ incorrect spelling of **balance**

Balfour /bálfər, -fawr/, **Arthur James, 1st Earl of Balfour** (1848–1930) British statesman

Bali /baáli/ island east of Java, S Indonesia. Population: 2,895,600 (1995). Area: 5,623 sq. km/2,171 sq. mi.

balibuntal /bálli búnt'l/ *n* **1** fine straw woven into material. Use: hat making. **2** a hat made from balibuntal [Early 20C. < *Baliuag* in the Philippines, + Tagalog *buntal* 'straw from the talipot palm tree'.]

Balikpapan /baálik paá paan/ port in E Borneo, Indonesia. Population: 433,494 (1997 estimate).

Balinese /baáli neéz/ (*plural* **-nese**) *n* **1** somebody who comes from Bali **2** an Austronesian language spoken on Bali. Native speakers: 2–3 million. [Early 19C. < Dutch *Balinees* < *Bali* 'Bali'.] —**Balinese** *adj*

balisier /ba líz yay/ *n* a small bushy shrub. Flowers: yellow to bright red, the symbol of the People's National Movement of Trinidad. Family: Heliconia.

balk *v*, *n* = **baulk**

Balkanization /báwlkə nī záysh'n, bólkə-/, **balkanization**, **Balkanisation** *n* division of an area, region, or group into smaller and often mutually hostile units [Early 20C. < the political fragmentation of the Balkan States between the Treaty of Berlin (1878) and the Balkan Wars (1912–13).] —**Balkanize** *vt*

Balkan Mountains /báwlkən-/ mountain range in Yugoslavia and Bulgaria. Highest peak: Botev Peak 2,376 m/7,795 ft.

Balkan Peninsula peninsula in SE Europe between the Adriatic and Ionian seas in the west and the Aegean and Black seas in the east

Balkans = **Balkan States**

Balkan States, **Balkans** /báwlkənz/ the countries in the Balkan Peninsula

balky /báwki, báwlki/ (**balkier, balkiest**), **baulky** (**baulkier, baulkiest**) *adj* US difficult and uncooperative ○ *a balky mule that stopped dead in its tracks* —**balkily** *adv* —**balkiness** *n*

ball[1] /bawl/ *n* **1** ROUND OBJECT PLAYED WITH an object, usually round in shape and often hollow and flexible, used in many games and sports in which it is thrown, struck, or kicked **2** ROUNDED THING something spherical or almost spherical, especially a spherical mass or arrangement of material ○ *a ball of wool* **3** GAME WITH A BALL a game, especially one played by children, in which a ball is used and, e.g., is thrown from one player to another ○ *Who's coming out to play ball?* **4** BALL PLAYED IN A PARTICULAR WAY a particular use, movement, or way of transferring the ball to another player in the course of a game ○ *a long ball into the penalty area* **5** DELIVERY BY BOWLER a single instance of a bowler bowling the ball to a batsman in cricket ○ *The last ball of the over.* **6** PITCH THAT IS NOT A STRIKE in baseball, any pitch that does not pass through the strike zone and at which the batter does not swing **7** POSSESSION AFTER SET PIECE useful possession, usually with an opportunity to develop an attacking movement, arising from skilful delivery of the ball by another player **8 SOLID PROJECTILE** a solid nonexplosive and usually round projectile shot from an old-fashioned pistol, musket, or cannon **9 SOLID PROJECTILES COLLECTIVELY** a collective term for the solid projectiles fired from old-fashioned guns ○ *The gunners were ordered to change from ball to case-shot.* **10 ROUNDED BODY PART** a rounded part of the body, e.g. at the base of the thumb or just behind the toes ○ *the ball of the foot* **11 TABOO TERM** a highly offensive term for a testicle (*taboo*) ■ *vti* **1 MAKE INTO OR FORM BALL** to mould, gather, or wind something into a ball, or become a ball-shaped mass ○ *She balled her fists.* **2 TABOO TERM** a highly offensive term meaning to have sexual intercourse (*taboo*) [13C. < Old Norse *böllr* or assumed Old English *beall* < Germanic.] ◇ **get** *or* **set** *or* **start the ball rolling** to start something off, especially a conversation or project ◇ **keep the ball rolling** to ensure that an activity continues ◇ **on the ball** aware of what is going on and quick to respond and take action (*informal*) ◇ **play ball (with somebody)** to cooperate together or with somebody (*informal*) ◇ **the ball is in somebody's court** used to say that it is somebody's turn to take action (*informal*)

balls up *vt* a highly offensive term meaning to make a complete mess of something by mistake or through lack of skill (*taboo*) US term **ball up**

ball up *vt US* = **balls up** (*slang offensive*)

ball[2] /bawl/ *n* a large-scale formal social event at which the main activity is dancing [Early 17C. Via French *bal* < late Latin *ballare* 'to dance' < Greek *ballizein*.] ◇ **have a ball** to enjoy yourself very much (*informal*) ○ *It was a great party; we really had a ball!*

Ball /bawl/, **Hugo** (1886–1927) German poet and musician

Ball, John (1338?–81) English rebel

Ball, Lucille (1911–89) US actor

Ball, Murray Hone (*b.* 1939) New Zealand cartoonist

Balla /bállə/, **Giacomo** (1871–1958) Italian painter

ballad /bálləd/ *n* **1** a song or poem, especially a traditional one or one in a traditional style, telling a story in a number of short regular stanzas, often with a refrain ○ *The Ballad of Bonnie and Clyde* **2** a slow romantic popular song ○ *two up-tempo numbers followed by a ballad* [Late 15C. < French *ballade* < late Latin *ballare* (see BALL).] —**balladic** /bə láddik/ *adj* —**balladist** /bálləddist/ *n* —**balladry** *n*

ballade /ba laád, bə-/ *n* **1** a poem consisting of three stanzas of eight or ten lines and a short concluding explanatory stanza (**envoy**), all of which end with the same refrain **2** an instrumental piece, usually for piano, intended to suggest the telling of a story as in a ballad [14C. Variant of BALLAD.]

balladeer /bállə déer/ *n* a ballad singer

ballad opera *n* a form of opera with spoken dialogue and popular tunes made into songs

Ballance /bálləns/, **John** (1839–93) British-born New Zealand statesman

ball and chain *n* something considered to be a great hindrance or restraint ○ *Censorship can be a ball and chain fettering artistic freedom of expression.*

ball-and-claw *adj* having a foot or another part modelled in the shape of an animal's claw holding a ball ○ *a ball-and-claw bathtub*

ball and socket joint, ball joint *n* **1** a joint such as the hip joint in which a bone with a rounded end fits into a concave area of the adjoining bone, allowing a wide range of movement **2** a junction between two moving parts of a mechanism in which the rounded end of one part fits into a cup-shaped socket on the other

Ballarat /bállə rat/ city in S Victoria, Australia. Population: 64,831 (1996).

ballast /bálləst/ *n* **1 STABILIZING HEAVY WEIGHTS** heavy material carried in the hold of a ship, especially one that has no cargo, or in the gondola of a balloon, to give the craft increased stability **2 SOMETHING THAT GIVES BULK OR STABILITY** anything that serves no particular purpose except to give bulk or weight to something or that provides additional stability **3 FOUNDATION MATERIAL** stones or gravel used as a foundation for a road or a railway track **4 GRAVEL USED IN MAKING CONCRETE** gravel used in making concrete and in earthworks ■ *vt* **1 LOAD SOMETHING WITH BALLAST** to load ballast onto something **2 STABILIZE** to give stability to something [Mid-16C. Probably < Old Danish, 'mere weight' < *bar* 'bare, mere' + *last* 'load'.]

ball bearing *n* **1** a metal ball used to reduce friction between moving parts **2** a bearing containing a number of metal balls that rotate freely to reduce friction between moving parts

ball boy *n* **1** a boy who retrieves balls that go out of play during a tennis match and delivers them to the server when required **2** a boy who takes care of the balls that are out of play during a baseball game or practice

ballbreaker /báwl braykər/ *n US* a highly offensive term that deliberately insults a woman who is regarded as aggressive towards men (*taboo*)

ballbuster /báwl bustər/ *n US* **1** an offensive term for a difficult and unpleasant job (*taboo*) **2** = **ballbreaker** (*taboo offensive*)

ball clay *n* a sedimentary clay containing kaolin, mica, other minerals, and organic matter. Use: ceramics. [< an obsolete mining process in which clay was handled as rounded cubes ('balls')]

ballcock *n* a floating ball on the end of an arm that is connected to a valve controlling the water level in a cistern or tank

ballerina /bállə réenə/ *n* **1** a woman ballet dancer **2** *US* a woman dancer in a ballet company who is regularly given principal parts [Late 18C. < Italian, 'woman dancing teacher' < *ballare* 'to dance' < Greek *ballizein*.]

Ballesteros /bállə stéer oss/, **Severiano** (*b.* 1957) Spanish golfer

ballet /bállay/ *n* **1 FORM OF DANCE** a form of dance characterized by conventional steps, poses, and graceful movements including leaps and spins **2 STORY PERFORMED BY DANCERS** a choreographed presentation of a story or theme performed to music by ballet dancers, or the musical score written for this **3 GROUP OF DANCERS** a company of ballet dancers who perform together [Mid-17C. Via French < Italian *balletto* < *ballo* 'ball (with dancing)'.]

balletic /ba léttik/ *adj* with the grace of somebody dancing in a ballet

balletomane /bállətō mayn/ *n* a lover of ballet —**balletomania** /-máyni ə/ *n*

ball game *n* **1** any game played with a ball **2** *US, Can* a game of baseball ◇ **a whole new ball game** a completely new or different set of circumstances (*informal*)

ball girl *n* a girl who retrieves balls that go out of play during a tennis match and delivers them to the server when required

ballgown /báwl gown/ *n* a full-length formal dress suitable for wearing to a ball

Ballina /bállinə/ coastal town in NE New South Wales, Australia. Population: 16,056 (1996).

Balliol /báyli əl/, **John** (1250?–1314) king of Scots (1292–96)

ballista /bə lístə/ (*plural* **-tae** /-tee/) *n* a piece of military equipment that was used in ancient times to hurl stones and other missiles over a distance [Early 16C. < Latin, < Greek *ballein* 'throw'.]

ballistic /bə lístik/ *adj* relating to the movements of objects propelled through the air [Mid-18C. < BALLISTA.] —**ballistically** *adv* ◇ **go ballistic** to become extremely angry (*informal*)

ballistic missile *n* a missile that maintains a course determined by its initial orientation and engine thrust, rather than one calculated by guidance systems during flight

ballistics /bə lístiks/ *n* **1 STUDY OF PROJECTILES** the study of the movements and forces involved in the propulsion of objects through the air (+ *singular verb*) **2 STUDY OF FIREARMS** the study of firearms and ammunition (+ *singular verb*) **3 FIRING CHARACTERISTICS OF WEAPON** the characteristics of a firearm that affect the way missiles are fired (+ *singular or plural verb*)

ball joint *n* MECH ENG = **ball and socket joint** *n.* 2

ball lightning *n* a rare form of lightning that takes the shape of a moving glowing ball, typically disappearing without explosion

ballocks /bólləks/ *npl, interj, vt* = **bollocks** (*taboo offensive*) [Old English *beallucc* < Germanic, 'little (round) ball']

ball of fire *n* an extremely energetic and dynamic person (*informal*)

ballon d'essai /ba láwn de sáy/ (*plural* **ballons d'essai**) *n* = **trial balloon** [< French]

balloon /bə lóon/ *n* **1 GAS-FILLED BAG USED AS TOY** a small coloured bag made of thin rubber or plastic that is inflated with air or helium and used as a toy or decoration **2 GAS-FILLED BAG USED IN AIR TRANSPORT** an extremely large bag filled with a lighter-than-air gas and used as a form of air transport, carrying passengers or equipment in a suspended basket or gondola **3 SPEECH CIRCLE IN CARTOON** a rounded outline with a point directed towards a character in a cartoon that encloses the text of the character's speech or thought **4 BRANDY GLASS** a glass with a large rounded bowl, used for drinking brandy ■ *vi* **1 SWELL** to form a large round swollen shape **2 INCREASE IN AMOUNT** to increase in amount suddenly and rapidly [Late 16C. < French *ballon* or Italian *ballone* 'large (round) ball'.] ◇ **go over** *or* **down like a lead balloon** to be completely unsuccessful (*informal*) ◇ **if** *or* **when the balloon goes up** if *or* when the expected or likely trouble or excitement starts (*informal*)

balloon angioplasty *n* the use of a balloon catheter to widen a narrowed artery

balloon catheter *n* a tube that can be inserted into a blood vessel or other body part and inflated while inside, e.g. to widen a narrowed artery

ballooning /bə lóoning/ *n* the sport of riding in or piloting a balloon

balloonist /bə lóonist/ *n* the pilot of a balloon

balloon loan *n* a loan that is repaid with a series of regular payments and one much larger payment at the end

balloon mortgage *n* a mortgage that is paid back in a series of regular payments with one much larger payment at the end

balloon tyre *n* a pneumatic tyre with a wide tread inflated to a low pressure, used to drive on soft surfaces such as deep sand

balloon whisk *n* a hand-held whisk made of stiff wires that form a loop at one end and are gathered into a covered handle at the other

ballot /bállət/ *n* **1 VOTING SYSTEM** a system in which eligible people vote, usually in secret, to determine the outcome of an election or make some other collective decision **2 SECRET VOTE** a secret vote held to determine the outcome of an election or some other decision **3** = **ballot paper** **4 TOTAL VOTES** the total number of votes that have been cast in an election ■ *v* **1** *vt* **ASK PEOPLE TO VOTE** to carry out a ballot on members of an organization or an electorate **2** *vi* **VOTE** to vote in a ballot [Mid-16C. < Italian *ballotta* 'little ball' < *balla* '(round) ball'.] —**balloter** *n*

ballot box *n* **1** a box in which voters put their ballot papers after marking them **2** the system in which leaders are elected or decisions are made using a ballot ○ *The people will decide at the ballot box.*

ballot paper *n* a piece of paper or card on which somebody can record a vote

ballot rigging *n* the use of dishonest or illegal methods of voting to ensure victory for a particular candidate or party in an election

ballpark /báwl paark/ *n US, Can* **1 PARK FOR PLAYING BALL GAMES** a stadium or area of land for playing ball games, especially baseball **2 TOUCHDOWN AREA FOR SPACECRAFT** the approximate area within which a spacecraft is intended to touch down ■ *adj US* **APPROXIMATE** rough or approximate (*informal*) ○ *a ballpark figure* ◇ **in the right ballpark** within the right general range or scope (*slang*)

ballpoint /báwl poynt/, **ballpoint pen** *n* a pen with a small rotating ball at its tip that transfers the ink from an inner tube onto the writing surface

ballroom /báwl room, -rŏŏm/ *n* a very large room with a smooth floor and a high ceiling, used for formal dances

ballroom dancing *n* formal dancing with a partner in dances that use a set pattern of steps, e.g. the foxtrot, quickstep, and waltz

balls-up *n* a highly offensive term for a complete mistake or totally unsuccessful attempt at something (*taboo*)

ballsy /báwlzi/ (**-ier, -iest**) *adj US* a highly offensive term meaning unusually tough, courageous, or determined (*slang taboo*) [Mid-20C. < BALL[1].]

ball valve *n* a nonreturn valve in which a ball moves in and out of an aperture in response to changes in fluid or mechanical pressure

bally /bálli/ *adj, adv* used to express anger, frustration, or additional emphasis (*dated informal*) [Late 19C. Alteration of BLOODY, perhaps influenced by the written form *bl-y*.]

ballyhoo /bálli hoō/ *n* (*plural* **-hoos**) **1** UPROAR a noisy argument or disturbance **2** SENSATIONAL ADVERTISING sensational, loud, or sustained advertising ■ *vt* (**-hoos, -hooing, -hooed**) ADVERTISE SOMETHING LOUDLY to advertise or publicize something loudly and insistently [Mid-19C. < ?]

Ballymena /bálli meēnə/ town in NE Northern Ireland. Population: 28,717 (1991).

Ballymoney /bálli múnni/ district in NE Northern Ireland. Area: 417 sq. km/161 sq. mi.

ballyrag *vt* = **bullyrag**

balm /baam/ *n* **1** SOOTHING OIL a fragrant oily substance obtained as a resin from various trees. Use: soothing ointments. **2** PLEASANT SCENT a pleasant scent (*literary*) **3** SOMETHING THAT SOOTHES something that has the effect of calming, soothing, or comforting ○ *balm to his wounded ego* **4** PLANTS = **lemon balm** [13C. Via French *bame* < Latin *balsamum* (see BALSAM).]

Balmain /bál maN/, **Pierre** (1914–86) French couturier

Balmer series /bálmər-/ *n* a series of lines in the visible part of the atomic spectrum of hydrogen [Early 20C. After J. J. *Balmer* (1825–98) Swiss physicist.]

balm of Gilead /-gílli ad/ *n* **1** TREES = **balsam fir 2** a hybrid poplar tree that has heart-shaped leaves and resinous buds. Genus: *Populus.* **3** a fragrant resin produced by various trees

Balmoral /bal mórrəl/, **balmoral** *n* **1** a strong walking shoe that is fastened with laces **2** a traditional Scottish flat woollen cap [Mid-19C. After the royal estate of *Balmoral* in Scotland.]

balmy /baámi/ (**-ier, -iest**) *adj* **1** describes weather that is pleasantly mild ○ *a balmy summer's evening* **2** = **barmy** (*informal*) —**balmily** *adv* —**balminess** *n*

balneology /bálni óllәji/ *n* a branch of medicine concerned with therapeutic bathing, especially in natural mineral spring water [Mid-19C. < Latin *balneum* 'bath'.] —**balneological** /-ə lójjik'l/ *adj* —**balneologist** *n*

balneotherapy /bálni ə thérrəpi/ *n* the medical practice of treatment by immersion in baths, especially those in spas containing water with a high mineral content [Late 19C. < Latin *balneum* 'bath'.]

baloney /bə lṓni/ *n* (*informal*) **1** *US* FOOD = **bologna** *n.* **2** any silly or stupid talk ○ *Don't talk baloney.* [Early 20C. < ?]

~~baloon~~ incorrect spelling of **balloon**

Balqash, Lake /bal kásh/ shallow lake in SE Kazakhstan. Area: 18,200 sq. km/7,030 sq. mi.

balsa /báwlssə/ (*plural* **-sas** *or* **-sa**) *n* **1** a tree that yields lightweight timber. Native to: South America. Genus: *Ochroma.* **2 balsa, balsa wood** a lightweight softwood. Use: rafts, toy models, insulation. [Early 17C. < Spanish, 'raft'.]

balsam /báwlssəm/ *n* **1** OILY RESINOUS PLANT SUBSTANCE an oily resinous substance (**oleoresin**) obtained from plants, especially one containing benzoic acid or cinnamic acid. Use: perfumes, medicines. **2** PREPARATION CONTAINING BALSAM a preparation containing or resembling balsam **3** FLOWERING PLANT a plant of the family that includes Busy Lizzie. Family: Balsaminaceae. [Pre-12C. Via Latin < Greek *balsamon.*] —**balsamic** /bawl sámmik/ *adj*

balsam fir *n* a pyramid-shaped tree that is the source of Canada balsam. Native to: North America. *Abies balsamea.*

balsamic vinegar *n* Italian vinegar made from the juice of white grapes matured in wood for 10 to 50 years

balsam of Peru *n* **1** a tree that produces high-quality timber and is also the source of a balsam. Native to: South America. *Myroxylon balsamum var. pareirae.* **2** an aromatic resin. Source: balsam of Peru tree. Use: perfumes, skin lotions.

Balt /bawlt/ *n* **1** somebody who comes from Lithuania, Latvia, or Estonia **2** somebody whose native language is Lithuanian, Latvian, or Estonian [Late 19C. < late Latin *balthae.*] —**Balt** *adj*

Balthazar[1] /bal thάzzə, bálthə zaar/ *n* a bottle that contains 12 litres of wine, the equivalent of 16 bottles [Mid-20C. After *Balshazzar,* King of Babylon, who, according to the book of Daniel in the Bible, 'made a great feast . . . and drank wine before the thousand'.]

Balthazar[2], **Balthasar** *n* one of the three wise men who, according to the Bible, brought gifts to Bethlehem to honour the birth of Jesus Christ (Matthew 2:1–12)

balti /báwlti, bál-/ *n* a spicy dish originally from Pakistan that is traditionally served in the bowl-shaped pan it is cooked in

Balti /báwlti, bál-/ *n* a Tibetan language spoken in N Kashmir [Early 20C. < Ladakhi dialect.] —**Balti** *adj*

Baltic[1] /báwltik/ *n* a group of Indo-European languages in NE Europe, closely related to the Slavonic group. Native speakers: 5 million. [Late 16C. < late Latin *Balticus.*]

Baltic[2] /báwltik/ **1** = **Baltic Sea 2** = **Baltic States**

Baltic Exchange *n* a commodity market in the City of London that deals in international trade, especially international bulk shipping

Baltic Sea sea in N Europe between Sweden, Finland, Russia, Estonia, Latvia, Lithuania, Poland, Germany, and Denmark. Area: 422,000 sq. km/163,000 sq. mi.

Baltic States Estonia, Latvia, and Lithuania, considered as a group

Baltimore /báwltəmōr/ port and largest city in Maryland. Population: 645,593 (1998 estimate).

Baltimore oriole *n* a bird, the male of which has a black head and upper body with orange underside and tail. Native to: North America. *Icterus galbula.* [Late 17C. After George Calvert, Lord *Baltimore* (1580?-1632), English proprietor of Maryland.]

Balto-Slavonic /báwl tō-/, **Balto-Slavic** *n* the Baltic and Slavonic branches of the Indo-European language family, sometimes considered to form a unified grouping —**Balto-Slavonic** *adj*

Baluchi /bə loōchi/ (*plural* **-chis** *or* **-chi**), **Balochi** /-lṓchi/ (*plural* **-chis** *or* **-chi**) *n* **1** somebody who comes from Baluchistan **2** an Eastern Iranian language spoken in Baluchistan. Native speakers: 5 million. [Early 17C. < Persian *Balučī.*] —**Baluchi** *adj*

Baluchistan /bə loōchi staán/ mountainous arid region in SW Pakistan and SE Iran

balun /bállən/ *n* a transformer used to couple balanced and unbalanced transmission lines [Contraction of BALANCED + UNBALANCED]

baluster /bálləstər/ *n* **1** an upright post supporting a handrail, e.g. in the banister of a staircase **2** a support, e.g. a chair leg or the stem of a glass, that is shaped like a long narrow vase [Early 17C. Via French *balustre* < Italian *balaustro* < Greek *balaustion* 'blossom of the wild pomegranate', because early balusters resembled its shape.]

balustrade /bállə stráyd/ *n* a decorative railing together with its supporting balusters, often used at the front of a parapet or gallery [Mid-17C. Via French < Spanish *balastrada* or Italian *balaustrata* < *balaustro* (see BALUSTER).]

Balzac /bál zak/, **Honoré de** (1799–1850) French novelist —**Balzacian** /bal záki ən/ *adj*

bam /bam/ *vti* (**bams, bamming, bammed**) *US* MAKE LOUD NOISE to make a loud hammering or thudding noise ○ *The police bammed on the door with a battering ram.* ■ *n* LOUD NOISE a loud thudding or hammering noise ○ *The dictionary fell to the floor with a bam.* ■ *interj* USED TO INDICATE SUDDEN IMPACT used to indicate sudden impact, the result of such impact, or the sudden occurrence of an event of great significance (*informal*) ○ *All of a sudden, bam! I was 30!* [Early 20C. An imitation of the sound.]

Bamako /bámməkō/ capital of Mali, in the SW of the country. Population: 880,000 (1993 estimate).

Bambara /bám baárə, baám-/ (*plural* **-ra** *or* **-ras**) *n* **1** a member of an African people living mainly in Mali **2** a Niger-Congo language spoken in Mali, Senegal, Burkina Faso, and Côte d'Ivoire. Native speakers: 1–2 million. [Late 19C. < Bambara.] —**Bambara** *adj*

Bamberg /baám burg/ river port in S Germany. Population: 70,216 (1997).

bambino /bam beénō/ (*plural* **-nos** *or* **-ni** /-ni/) *n* **1** a baby or young child (*informal*) **2** a representation of Jesus Christ as a baby [Early 18C. < Italian, 'baby' < *bambo* 'silly'.]

bamboo /bam boō/ (*plural* **-boos**) *n* **1** a plant with long woody, often hollow, stems that grows in dense clumps. Native to: tropical and semitropical areas. Family: Bambusaceae. **2** the strong hollow stems of bamboo plants. Use: building, furniture, canes, fishing rods. [Late 16C. Via Dutch *bamboes,* modern Latin *bambusa* < Malay *mambu.*]

bamboo curtain *n* the political, military, and ideological barrier that effectively isolated China from Western countries from the Communist revolution of 1949 until China's relaxation of trade barriers in 1979 [After IRON CURTAIN]

bamboozle /bam boōz'l/ (**-zles, -zling, -zled**) *vt* (*informal*) **1** to trick or deceive somebody through misleading statements or falsehoods **2** to make somebody confused [Early 18C. < ?] —**bamboozler** *n*

ban[1] /ban/ *vt* (**bans, banning, banned**) **1** FORBID to forbid something officially or legally **2** STOP SOMEBODY DOING SOMETHING to forbid somebody to do something or go somewhere **3** RESTRICT RIGHTS IN SOUTH AFRICA during the apartheid era in South Africa, to punish somebody suspected of breaking the apartheid laws by preventing the person from moving around freely and having contact with other people ■ *n* **1** ORDER FORBIDDING SOMETHING an order officially or legally forbidding something so that it cannot be done, used, seen, or read **2** PUBLIC REVILEMENT public condemnation (*archaic*) **3** CURSE a powerful curse (*archaic*) [Old English *bannan* 'summon, proclaim' < Germanic; noun via Old French *ban* 'summons for military duty, proclamation' < same Germanic word]

ban[2] /ban/ (*plural* **bani** /baánni/) *n* see table at **currency** [Late 19C. Via Romanian < Serbo-Croat *bān* 'lord' < Turkic *bayan* 'very rich person' < *bay* 'rich gentleman'.]

Banaba /bə naábə/ island of Kiribati in the W Pacific Ocean. Population: 284 (1990). Area: 5.7 sq. km/2.2 sq. mi.

banal /bə naál/ *adj* boringly ordinary and lacking in originality [Mid-19C. < French, < *ban* (see BAN[1]), which developed in French < 'compulsory military service' via '(something) common to all' to 'commonplace'.] —**banally** *adv*

banality /bə nálləti/ (*plural* **-ties**) *n* **1** conventional or dull ordinariness **2** an ordinary remark or feature that lacks originality

banana /bə naánə/ (*plural* **-as** *or* **-a**) *n* **1** a long and slightly curved fruit with creamy coloured soft flesh and a skin that turns from green to yellow when ripe **2** a large-leaved tropical plant that bears bananas. Genus: *Musa.* [Late 16C. Via Spanish and Portuguese < Mande.] ◇ **go bananas** to become uncontrollably or unreasonably angry or excited (*informal*)

banana plug *n* a single conductor plug with a spring metal tip shaped like a banana

bananaquit /bə naánə kwit/ *n* a bird that resembles a warbler with a downturned bill. Native to: Central and S America. *Coereba flaveola.*

banana republic *n* a small country with an unstable government and an economy dependent on the export of a single product or on outside financial help (*disapproving*)

banana split *n* a dessert of peeled banana cut in half lengthways, filled with ice cream, sweet sauce, whipped cream, and chopped nuts

banausic /bə náwzik/ *adj* **1** with no art, creativity, or imagination **2** practical or materialistic rather than uplifting or inspiring [Mid-19C. < Greek *banausikos* 'of or for artisans'.]

Banbridge /bán brij/ district council in SE Northern Ireland

banco /bángkō/ *interj* used in baccarat and chemin de fer to declare that a player wishes to place a bet equivalent to the total worth of the bank ■ *n* in baccarat and chemin de fer, a bet placed equivalent to to the total worth of the bank [Late 18C. Via French < Italian, variant of *banca* (see BANK[1]).]

~~bancrupcy~~ incorrect spelling of **bankruptcy**

band[1] /band/ *n* **1** MUSICIANS PLAYING TOGETHER a group of musicians who play together, particularly a group playing popular or rock music **2** GROUP WITH SAME BELIEFS OR PURPOSE a group of people who have the same ideas or beliefs or who are pursuing the same activity together ○ *a growing band of supporters* **3** SMALL SIMPLY-STRUCTURED GROUP a small group of people with a relatively simple social structure [15C. < French *bande.*] ◇ **to beat the band** to a very great extent or degree (*dated*)

band together *vi* to form a group in order to achieve a goal

band[2] /band/ *n* **1** STRIP OR LOOP OF MATERIAL a strip of fabric, metal, or elastic placed around something to strengthen it or around several things to hold them together **2** CONTRASTING STRIPE a long narrow area that is different in material, colour, or texture from the adjacent parts **3** STRIP OR CIRCLE OF MATERIAL a strip or circle of fabric or elastic used for decoration, identification, or absorbing sweat on the forehead or hands **4 RING** a plain ring worn on a finger ○ *a wedding band* **5 MOVING BELT** a moving belt in a piece of machinery **6 RANGE OF VALUES WITHIN LARGER RANGE** a range of values relating to people, e.g. age or amount of tax paid, within the overall range of all people ○ *the highest tax band* **7 RANGE OF RADIO FREQUENCIES** a range of frequencies or wavelengths assigned to a radio station or radio broadcaster **8 GROUP OF PUPILS TAUGHT TOGETHER** a group of pupils from the same school year, taught together because they are at a similar level of ability **9 RANGE OF ENERGIES** the range of energies possessed by electrons in a solid **10 ORE OR MINERAL LAYER** a layer of rock with a different composition or texture from the adjacent layers ■ *vt* **1 PUT BAND ON OR ROUND** to put a strip on or round something to decorate or identify it or to hold a number of things together **2 CATEGORIZE THINGS** to divide things into ranges of value **3 DIVIDE PUPILS INTO GROUPS** to divide pupils from one school year into groups to be taught together because they are at a similar ability level [13C. < Old Norse < Germanic, reinforced by French *bande* < the same Germanic word.]

Banda /bándə/, **Hastings** (1906?–97) Malawi statesman

bandage /bándij/ *n* a long strip of thin or elasticated fabric that is wrapped around a wound or injured part of the body to protect or support it [Late 16C. < French < *bande* (see BAND²).] —**bandage** *vt* —**bandager** *n*

bandanna /ban dánnə/, **bandana** *n* a large square of brightly coloured cotton or silk cloth worn over the hair or around the neck [Mid-18C. Probably via Portuguese < Hindi *bāndhnū*, method of tie-dyeing < *bāndhnā* 'to tie'.]

Bandaranaike /bándərə nī əkə/, **Chandrika** (*b.* 1945) Sri Lankan stateswoman

Bandaranaike, Sirimavo (1916–2000) Sri Lankan stateswoman

Bandaranaike, S.W.R.D. (1899–1959) Sri Lankan statesman. Full name **Solomon West Ridgeway Dias Bandaranaike**

Bandar Seri Begawan /bán daar sérri bə gaáwən/ capital of Brunei. Population: 50,000 (1995 estimate).

Banda Sea /bándə-/ sea in the Pacific Ocean in E Indonesia, north of Timor and southeast of Sulawesi. Area: 738,150 sq. km/285,000 sq. mi.

B & B *abbr* bed and breakfast (*informal*)

bandbox /bánd boks/ *n* a round lightweight box for carrying accessories such as hats [Mid-17C. Because originally used to carry neckbands.]

bandeau /bándō/ (*plural* **-deaux** /-dōz/) *n* **1** *US* a ribbon or band of material worn around the head to keep the hair in place **2** a piece of material worn round the chest to cover the breasts [Early 18C. < French, < Old French *bandel* 'little band' < *bande* (see BAND²).]

banded /bándid/ *adj* marked with bands of different or contrasting colours ○ *banded agate*

banded-iron formation *n* a thin, extremely old, iron-rich layer of sedimentary material of unknown origin, deposited on all continents and containing haematite, magnetite, goethite, and limonite

banderilla /bándə reé ə, -reéyə/ *n* in a bullfight, a long decorated barbed dart that is thrust into the neck or shoulder of a bull by a bullfighter's assistant [Late 18C. < Spanish, 'little banner' < *bandera* 'banner'.]

banderillero /bándə ree áirrō, -lyáirō/ (*plural* **-ros**) *n* a bullfighter's assistant who sticks a banderilla into the bull during a bullfight [Late 18C. < Spanish, < *banderilla* (see BANDERILLA).]

banderole /bándə rōl/, **banderol, bannerol** /bánnə-/ *n* **1 FLAG ON MASTHEAD** a long narrow flag with a divided end that is flown on a ship's masthead **2 FLAG AT FUNERAL** a flag that is carried at a funeral or used to cover a tomb **3 INSCRIBED BAND** a sculpted scroll or band bearing an inscription **4 RIBBON ON KNIGHT'S LANCE** a ribbon or streamer hanging from a knight's lance [Mid-16C. Via French < Italian *banderuola* 'small banner' < *bandiera* 'banner'.]

bandh /bund/, **bundh** *n S Asia* a short general strike called in a city or district [< Hindi, 'a tying up']

bandicoot /bándi koot/ *n* a marsupial that has a long nose, strong hind legs, and a long tail and eats mainly insects and plants. Native to: Australia, Tasmania, New Guinea. Family: Peramelidae. [Late 18C. < Telugu *pandikokku* 'pig-rat'.]

bandicoot rat *n* a large rodent that is a serious pest to farmers. Native to: South Asia. *Bandicota indica.*

banding /bánding/ *n* the grouping of pupils from the same school year into bands, usually of a similar ability level, to be taught together

bandit /bándit/ (*plural* **-dits** *or* **-ditti** /-dítti/) *n* **1 ARMED ROBBER** an armed robber who steals from travellers and other people, usually at gunpoint **2 GANGSTER** a member of a gang of violent criminals **3** *US* **EXPLOITATIVE PERSON** a swindler or cheat **4 ENEMY AIRCRAFT** an enemy aircraft sighted by a crew while flying (*informal*) ○ *Bandits at twelve o'clock high!* [Late 16C. < Italian *bandito* < *bandire* 'to ban'.] ◇ **make out like a bandit** *or* **bandits** *US* to be extremely successful, especially by making a lot of money in a short period of time (*informal*)

banditry /bánditri/ *n* the occurrence or prevalence of armed robbery and violent crime

banditti plural of **bandit**

Bandjarmasin ♦ **Banjarmasin**

bandleader /bánd leedər/ *n* the conductor of a band, especially of a dance band

Bandler /bándlər/, **Faith** (*b.* 1918) Australian writer and activist

bandmaster /bánd maastər/ *n* the conductor of a band, especially of a brass band or a military band

bandog /bán dog/ *n* an aggressive dog produced by crossbreeding a pit bull terrier with a mastiff, Rottweiler, or Rhodesian ridgeback [15C. Blend of BAND² + DOG; originally a dog that was chained up or bound.]

bandoleer /bándə leér/, **bandolier** *n* a soldier's belt with loops or small pockets for storing cartridges, worn over the shoulder and across the chest [Late 16C. < French, perhaps < Spanish *bandolera* < *banda* 'sash', or < Catalan *bandolera* < *bandoler* 'bandit'.]

bandoneon /ban dṓni ən/ *n* a square concertina, used especially in Argentina [Early 20C. Via Spanish *bandoneón* < German *Bandonion*, after its German inventor Heinrich *Band* (1821–60).] —**bandoneonist** *n*

bandore /ban dáwr, bán dawr/ *n* a musical instrument of the 16th and 17th centuries, similar to a large guitar or lute [Mid-16C. < ?]

band-pass filter *n* **1** an electronic filter that passes only those frequencies within a specified range **2** a device transmitting electromagnetic radiation, especially visible light, within a restricted wavelength range

band saw *n* a stationary power saw with a continuous vertically mounted blade

B and S Ball *n* a social event held in the Australian outback for young people, typically comprising a weekend of music, dancing, and drinking [Shortening of *Bachelor and Spinsters Ball*]

band shell *n* a bandstand with a curved wall at the back that is designed to reflect the sound towards the audience

bandsman /bándzmən/ (*plural* **-men** /-mən/) *n* a player in a brass band or military band

bandspreading /bánd spreding/ *n* a function of some radios that allows the user to select a narrow band of frequencies and space them further apart, to make tuning into a specific frequency easier

bandstand /bánd stand/ *n* a platform for a band or small orchestra to perform on, especially outdoors

band theory *n* a theory that explains the electrical conductivity of solids in terms of energy bands containing electrons

Bandung /bán dŏŏng/ city in W Java, Indonesia. Population: 2,056,915 (1990).

B & W, b & w *abbr* black-and-white

bandwagon /bánd wagən/ *n* **1** a cause or movement that is gaining popularity and support **2** *US* an ornately decorated wagon that musicians perform on during a parade ◇ **jump** *or* **climb on the bandwagon** to join in something only because it is fashionable or likely to be profitable

ϟ **bandwidth** /bánd width/ *n* **1** a range of radio frequencies used in radio or telecommunications transmission and reception **2** the capacity of a communication channel, e.g. a connection to the Internet, often measured in bits per second

bandy /bándi/ *vt* (**-dies, -dying, -died**) to toss words back and forth casually, often without caring whether they are true or what effect they may have ○ *I've heard the name being bandied about.* ■ *adj* (**-dier, -diest**) describes legs that curve outward so that the knees cannot meet [Late 16C. Perhaps < French *bander* 'take sides at tennis'.] ◇ **bandy words (with somebody)** to have an argument or discussion with somebody, often one that is unnecessary or a waste of time

bandy-bandy (*plural* **bandy-bandies**) *n ANZ* a small, mildly venomous Australian snake marked with black-and-white bands. *Vermicella annulata.* [Early 20C. < an Aboriginal language.]

bandy-legged *adj* having legs that curve outward, so that the knees do not touch

bane /bayn/ *n* **1 SOMETHING THAT CAUSES MISERY** something that continually causes problems or misery ○ *It's the bane of my life.* **2 SOMETHING THAT CAUSES RUIN** something that causes death, destruction, or ruin (*literary or archaic*) **3 DEADLY POISON** a fatal poison (*often in combination in the names of poisonous plants*) [Old English *bana* < Germanic] ◇ **the bane of somebody's life** somebody or something that is a constant source of trouble or annoyance

baneberry /báyn berri/ (*plural* **-ries**) *n* **1** a poisonous fleshy red or white berry **2** a plant that bears baneberries. Native to: North America, Europe, Asia. Genus: *Rubus fruticosus.*

baneful /báynf'l/ *adj* causing ruin or destruction (*literary*) —**banefully** *adv* —**banefulness** *n*

USAGE See ***baleful***.

Banff /bamf/ port in NE Scotland. Population: 4,110 (1991).

Banff National Park national park in SW Alberta, Canada. Area: 6,641 sq. km/2,564 sq. mi.

Banffshire /bámfshər/ former county in NE Scotland

bang¹ /bang/ *n* **1 SUDDEN LOUD NOISE** a sudden loud noise, e.g. the sound of a gun firing or a door slamming shut **2 SHARP HIT** a sharp blow or hit ○ *a nasty bang on the head* **3 ENERGY BURST** a burst of energy or activity (*informal*) ○ *The party started with a bang.* **4 OFFENSIVE TERM** an offensive term for the act of having sexual intercourse (*slang*) **5 INJECTION OF DRUG** an injection of an illegal drug such as heroin (*slang*) **6** *US* **CHARACTER IN TYPESETTING** the character ! in typesetting ■ **bangs** *npl US* **FRINGE OF HAIR ACROSS FOREHEAD** the hair falling over the forehead when it is cut square above the eyes ■ *v* **1** *vti* **HIT** to hit something hard, or slam something against a surface ○ *He banged his fist on the table.* **2** *vti* **HIT ACCIDENTALLY** to hit something unintentionally ○ *She banged her knee.* ○ *I pulled up sharply and banged into the car in front.* **3** *vti* **CLOSE HARD AND NOISILY** to close suddenly and loudly, or make something close with a sudden loud noise ○ *The door banged shut.* **4** *vi* **MAKE LOUD NOISE** to make a sudden loud noise ○ *children banging on pots and pans* **5** *vi* **MOVE AROUND NOISILY** to move around making a lot of noise ○ *I could hear her banging about in the kitchen.* **6** *vti* **OFFENSIVE TERM** an offensive term meaning to have sexual intercourse with somebody (*slang*) **7** *vt* **MAKE SHARE PRICES FALL** to cause share prices to fall **8** *vi* **INJECT A DRUG** to inject an illegal drug such as heroin (*slang*) ■ *adv* **1** exactly or precisely ○ *Our hotel is bang in the centre of the town.* **2 SUDDENLY** suddenly and unexpectedly ○ *I turned round and bang, there he was!* ■ *interj* **IMITATING EXPLOSIVE SOUND** used especially by children to imitate the sound of a gun firing (*informal*) ○ *Bang! You're dead!* [Mid-16C. An imitation of the sound.] ◇ **bang for your buck** *US* value for money spent or effort expended (*slang*) ◇ **bang goes something!** used as a rueful acknowledgment that something is no longer available or likely to happen (*informal*) ◇ **bang on** *UK, Can* exactly right (*informal*) ◇ **go out with a bang** to end or finish something in a dramatic way (*informal*) ◇ **go (off) with a bang** to be very successful

bang away *vi* to keep doing something persistently and determinedly

bang on to keep on talking about the same topic (*informal*)

bang out *vt* (*informal*) **1** to produce something speedily ○ *bang out an essay overnight* **2** to play a tune on a musical instrument, especially a piano, loudly and coarsely

bang up to lock a prisoner in a cell (*informal*)

bang² /bang/ *n* = **bhang**

Bangalore /bángg ə láwr/ capital of Karnataka State in south-central India. Population: 2,660,088 (1991).

bangalore torpedo *n* an explosive device in a metal tube, used to blow holes in barbed-wire fences or to detonate land mines [Early 20C. After BANGALORE.]

bangalow /báng gəlō/ *n* an Australian palm tree. Native to: New South Wales, Queensland. *Archontophoenix cunninghamiana*. [Early 19C. < an Aboriginal name.]

banger /bángər/ *n* **1 SAUSAGE** a fried or grilled sausage (*informal*) **2 OLD CAR** an old car that is not in very good condition (*informal*) **3 LOUD FIREWORK** a firework that explodes very noisily

Banghāzī ♦ **Benghazi**

Bangka /bángkə/, **Banka** island in W Indonesia. Area: 11,940 sq. km/4,609 sq. mi.

Bangkok /báng kók, báng kok/ capital and main port of Thailand. Population: 5,882,000 (1990).

Bangla /báng glə/ *n* LANG = **Bengali** *n.* 2 [< Bengali *bāṅglā*] —**Bangla** *adj*

Bangladesh

Bangladesh /bán glə désh/ republic in South Asia, on the Bay of Bengal, east of India. Capital: Dhaka. Population: 125,340,261 (1997). Area: 147,570 sq. km/56,977 sq. mi. —**Bangladeshi** *n, adj*

bangle /báng g'l/ *n* **1** a stiff metal, plastic, or wooden bracelet that is worn around the arm, wrist, or ankle **2** a decorative disc, charm, or other ornament that hangs from a bracelet [Late 18C. < Hindi *baṅglī* 'coloured glass bracelet'.]

Bangor /báng gər/ coastal town in E Northern Ireland. Population: 52,437 (1991). ■ city on the Menai Strait, N Wales. Population: 12,330 (1991).

Bang's disease /bángz-/ *n* brucellosis in animals, especially in cattle [Early 20C. After Bernhard L. F. Bang, Danish veterinary surgeon (d. 1932).]

bangtail /báng tayl/ *n US* an envelope with a detachable section that can be used as an order form or to provide marketing information

Bangui /baang gée/ capital of the Central African Republic, on the River Ubangi. Population: 451,690 (1988).

bani plural of **ban**[2]

banish /bánnish/ *vt* **1** to exile somebody from a place **2** to put something out of your mind ○ *Let us banish from our minds all dark thoughts.* [14C. < French *baniss-*, stem of *banir* 'proclaim' < assumed Vulgar Latin *bannire* < Germanic.] —**banisher** *n* —**banishment** *n*

banister /bánnistər/, **bannister** *n* **1** a handrail supported by posts running up the outside edge of a staircase (*often used in the plural*) **2** any one of the posts supporting a handrail on a staircase [Mid-17C. Alteration of BALUSTER.]

Banja Luka /bánnyə lóokə/ city in N Bosnia-Herzegovina. Population: 142,644 (1991).

Banjarmasin /bánjə maá sin/, **Bandjarmasin** city in SE Borneo, Indonesia. Population: 480,737 (1990).

banjax /bán jaks/ *vt Ireland* to damage or ruin something (*informal*) [Mid-20C. < ?]

banjo /bánjō/ (*plural* **-jos** *or* **-joes**) *n* a musical instrument that has a round sound box covered with parchment, a long neck, and five strings that are plucked or strummed [Mid-18C. Related to Jamaican English *banja* 'fiddle' and probably to Kimbundu *mbanza* 'stringed musical instrument'.]

Banjul /ban jóol/ capital of the Gambia, at the mouth of the River Gambia. Population: 44,200 (1994).

bank[1] /bangk/ *n* **1 BUSINESS OFFERING FINANCIAL SERVICES** a business that keeps money for individuals or companies, exchanges currencies, makes loans, and offers other financial services **2 BANK'S LOCAL OFFICE** a local office of a bank **3 FUND OF MONEY OR TOKENS** the fund of money, tokens, chips, or other pieces that players can draw out in certain games, or the player who holds the fund **4 SOMETHING STORED** a supply of something stored, ready for immediate use, e.g. data, food, or blood ■ *v* **1** *vt* **DEPOSIT MONEY IN BANK** to pay money into a bank ○ *banked the cheque immediately* **2** *vi* **HAVE ACCOUNT WITH FINANCIAL INSTITUTION** to have an account with or use a particular bank [15C. Directly or via French *banque* < Italian *banca* 'bank, bench, table' < Germanic.] ◇ **break the bank 1** *US* to win more money than is available **2** to leave somebody very short of or without money (*informal*)

bank on *vt* to count on something happening ○ *We're banking on your support.*

bank[2] /bangk/ *n* **1 SIDE OF WATERWAY** the steep side of a river, stream, lake, or canal **2 RAISED AREA OF LAND BELOW WATER** a ridge of sand or other sedimentary deposit in a river or coastal sea that decreases the depth of the water above it and may become visible at low tide **3 EARTH OR SNOW WITH SLOPING SIDE** a pile of earth, snow, or sand, or a raised area of ground with a sloping side **4 MASS OF CLOUD** a large dense area of cloud or fog **5 LONG TRACK GRADIENT** a long gradient or slope on a railway **6 SLOPE AT BEND IN RACETRACK** an upward slope at a bend in a road or racetrack, designed to reduce the likelihood of drivers going off the road or track when travelling around the bend at speed **7 TURNING ANGLE OF AIRCRAFT** the angle made by an aeroplane as it turns **8 CUSHION OF BILLIARD TABLE** the cushion of a billiard or pool table **9 MOUTH OF MINE SHAFT** the area around the mouth of a mine shaft ■ *v* **1** *vti* **FORM INTO PILE** to make something into a pile or a large heap or form a pile or heap ○ *snow banked against the fence* **2** *vt* **MAKE RAISED SLOPE** to make a raised slope as an edge or border to something ○ *bank earth along the river* **3** *vt* **COVER FIRE** to cover a fire with ashes or fuel so that it will continue to burn slowly for a long time **4** *vti* **TILT WHILE TURNING PLANE** to tilt an aeroplane with one wing higher than the other while turning **5** *vti* **TILT WHILE DRIVING** to tilt a vehicle, especially a motorcycle, while travelling around a bend at speed, or travel around a bend like this **6** *vt* **BUILD SLOPE INTO ROAD OR RACETRACK** to build a slope into a road or racetrack at a bend **7** *vt* **HIT BALL INTO CUSHION** to hit a billiard or pool ball into the cushion [12C. < assumed Old Norse *banki* 'ridge, bank' < Germanic.]

bank[3] /bangk/ *n* **1 ROW OF SIMILAR THINGS** a row or several rows of things of one type ○ *a bank of switches* **2 GALLEY ROWERS' BENCH** a bench for rowers in a galley **3 GALLEY OARS** a row of oars in a galley ■ *vt* **PUT THINGS INTO ROWS** to arrange things in rows or tiers [13C. < French *banc* 'bench' < Germanic.]

Banka = **Bangka**

bankable /bángkəb'l/ *adj* **1** likely to become financially profitable ○ *a bankable movie star* **2** readily and legally acceptable to a bank —**bankability** /bángkə bílləti/ *n*

bank account *n* an arrangement according to which a bank accepts deposits of money and keeps that money available for withdrawal by the named account holder or holders

bank annuities *npl* FIN = **consols**

bank balance *n* the amount of money in a bank account at any given time

bank bill *n* FIN = **bank draft**

bankbook /bángk bòòk/ *n* BANKING = **passbook** *n.* 1

bank card *n UK* BANKING = **cheque card**

bank discount *n* the interest on a loan that is deducted from the amount borrowed at the time the loan is taken out

bank draft *n* a bill of exchange drawn by one bank on another

banker /bángkər/ *n* **1** an owner or senior employee of a bank **2** the player in charge of the bank in a gambling game [Mid-16C. < BANK[1].] —**bankerly** *adj*

banker's draft *n* an order for the payment of money from one bank to another bank's own funds

banker's order *n* BANKING = **standing order** *n.* 1

banket /bángkit/ *n* rock containing gold, found in South Africa [Late 19C. < Afrikaans, 'almond toffee'.]

Bankhead /bángk hed/, **Tallulah** (1902–68) US actor. Born **Tallulah Brockman**

bank holiday *n* a weekday public holiday on which banks, government offices, shops, and many businesses are closed

banking /bángking/ *n* the work carried out by banks or bankers

⚡**bank Internet payment system** *n US* a number that uniquely identifies a financial institution for the purposes of Internet transactions

bank manager *n* somebody in charge of a branch of a bank

banknote /bángk nōt/ *n* a piece of paper money issued by a bank that may be freely exchanged for goods or services

Bank of Canada *n* the federal central bank of Canada

Bank of England *n* the central bank of England and Wales

bank rate *n* = **base rate** *n.*

bankroll /bángk rōl/ *n* **1 FUND OF MONEY** a fund of money used to finance a project **2** *US* **ROLL OF PAPER MONEY** a roll of banknotes ■ *vt* **FINANCE** to provide the money needed to finance a project on a continuing basis (*informal*) —**bankroller** *n*

bankrupt /bángk rupt/ *adj* **1 UNABLE TO PAY DEBTS** judged legally to be unable to pay off personal debts **2 WITHOUT RESOURCES** completely lacking in a particular quality, especially in good or ethical qualities ○ *morally bankrupt* ■ *n* **1 SOMEBODY WHO CANNOT PAY DEBTS** somebody who is unable to pay his or her debts **2 SOMEBODY WITHOUT RESOURCES** somebody who completely lacks a particular quality ■ *vt* **DEPLETE SOMEBODY'S FUNDS** to cost so much that a person or business will have hardly any money left or will be declared bankrupt [Mid-16C. < Italian *banca rotta* 'broken table' < *banca* (see BANK[1]) + *rotto* < Latin *ruptus* 'broken'.]

bankruptcy /bángk ruptsi/ (*plural* **-cies**) *n* **1** the state of having been legally declared bankrupt **2** the complete lack of a particular quality, especially good or ethical qualities ○ *moral bankruptcy*

Banks /bangks/, **Sir Joseph** (1743–1820) British naturalist

banksia /bángksi ə/ (*plural* **-as** *or* **-a**) *n* a small evergreen tree or shrub with leathery narrow leaves and cylindrical flowers. Native to: Australia. Family: Proteaceae. [Early 19C. < modern Latin, after Sir Joseph BANKS.]

Banks Island /bángks-/ island in the Arctic Ocean, Northwest Territories, Canada. Area: 70,028 sq. km/27,038 sq. mi.

Banks Peninsula peninsula on the E coast of the South Island, New Zealand. Length: 48 km/30 mi.

bank statement *n* a document showing all the transactions in a bank account over a specific period of time

⚡**banner** /bánnər/ *n* **1 CLOTH SUSPENDED BETWEEN TWO POLES** a long piece of cloth, often bearing a symbol or slogan, and attached at each end to a pole or hanging from the top of a pole **2 GUIDING PRINCIPLE** a guiding principle, cause, or philosophy ○ *under the banner of the trade union movement* **3 NATION'S OR ARMY'S FLAG** the flag of a country or army **4 FLAG OF KING, EMPEROR, OR KNIGHT** a flag used by a king, emperor, or knight when going into battle **5** MEDIA = **banner headline 6 WEBSITE ADVERT** a rectangular graphic across a web page, used as an advertisement, heading, or link [13C. < Anglo-Norman *banere*, Old French *banière* < medieval Latin *bandum* 'standard'.]

banneret /bánnərət, -ret/ *n* **1** a knight of high rank who was entitled to lead his own men into battle **2** formerly, a title given by a king or queen for bravery in battle [13C. < Old French *baneret* 'bannered' < *banière* (see BANNER).]

banner headline *n* a headline in large letters that runs across an entire page of a newspaper

bannerol *n* = **banderole**

bannister *n* = **banister**

Bannister /bánnistər/, **Sir Roger** (*b.* 1929) British athlete

bannock /bánnək/ *n* a traditional Scottish bread in the shape of a round flat savoury cake cooked on a griddle [Old English *bannuc* < Celtic]

Bannockburn /bánnək burn/ town in central Scotland where the Scots defeated English forces in 1314. Population: 2,675 (1991).

banns /banz/ *npl* an announcement of a forthcoming marriage, proclaimed in the parish churches of the engaged couple on three successive Sundays [14C. < BAN[1].]

banoffee /bə nóffi/, **banoffi** *n* a creamy filling made from bananas and soft toffee, eaten in a pastry or biscuit base ○ *banoffee pie* [Late 20C. Blend of BANANA + TOFFEE.]

banquet /bángkwit/ *n* **1** an elaborate formal meal attended by many guests, often held in honour of a particular person or occasion and followed by speeches **2** an elaborate or lavish meal of many courses [15C. < French, 'little bank' < *banc* (see BANK[3]).] —**banquet** *vi* —**banqueter** *n*

banqueting hall *n* a room large enough to accommodate a banquet, usually in a palace, castle, or stately home

banqueting room *n* a room large enough to accommodate a banquet in a hotel or restaurant

banquette /bang két/ *n* 1 an upholstered bench along a wall, especially in a restaurant 2 a raised step in a trench or behind a parapet on which a soldier may stand to fire or a gun may be mounted [Early 17C. Via French < Italian *banchetta* 'little bench' < *banca* (see BANK¹).]

bansela *n* = **bonsela** *n*. 2

banshee /bán shee/ *n* 1 in Gaelic folklore, a spirit of a woman who appears, wailing, to signal that somebody in the household is going to die 2 *Ireland* a female fairy [Late 17C. < Irish *bean sidhe* < Old Irish *ben* 'woman' + *side* 'of the fairy world'.]

Banstead /bán sted/ town in south-central England. Population: 56,706 (1991).

bantam /bántəm/ *n* 1 a bird belonging to a breed of small domestic fowl 2 BOXING = **bantamweight** *n*. 1 ■ *adj US* overconfident and slightly aggressive [Mid-18C. After the town of *Bantam* in Java.]

bantamweight /bántəm wayt/ *n* 1 a professional boxer weighing 51–53.5 kg/112–118 lb, or an amateur weighing 51–54 kg/112–119 lb 2 a wrestler weighing 52–57 kg/115–126 lb

banter /bántər/ *n* lighthearted teasing or amusing remarks that are exchanged between people ■ *vi* to exchange lighthearted teasing remarks [Late 17C. < ?] —**banterer** *n*

Banting /bánting/, **Sir Frederick Grant** (1891–1941) Canadian physician

Bantu /bán tòò/ (*plural* **-tu** *or* **-tus**) *n* (*offensive in some contexts*) 1 a large group of languages, spoken in central, eastern, and southern Africa, belonging to the Benue-Congo subfamily of Niger-Congo languages. Native speakers: 150 million. 2 ⚠ a member of a large group of peoples living in equatorial and southern Africa. [Mid-19C. In some Bantu languages the plural of *-ntu* 'person'.] —**Bantu** *adj*

> **USAGE** In South Africa after the apartheid era, *Bantu* is considered highly offensive when used with reference to Black people, especially in the singular to refer to one person, and *Black* or *African* are the normally accepted terms. In technical contexts outside South Africa, for example academic discussions of anthropology and language, *Bantu* continues in use.

bantustan /bán tòò staan, bán tòò staàn/, **Bantustan** *n* an area in South Africa where Black people lived with limited self-government during the apartheid era from the 1950s until 1994 (*sometimes offensive*) [Mid-20C. < BANTU, after such names as HINDUSTAN.]

Banville /baàn veel/, **Théodore de** (1823–91) French poet and playwright

Banyan

banyan /bánnyən, -yan/ *n* 1 a tree with roots that grow down from the branches into the ground to form new secondary trunks. Native to: South Asia. *Ficus benghalensis*. 2 a loose jacket, shirt, or gown, worn by men in parts of South Asia [Late 16C. Via Portuguese < Gujarati *vāṇiyo* 'man of the trading class' < Sanskrit *nāṇija* 'merchant'.]

banzai /ban zí, baan-/ *interj* a patriotic Japanese battle cry or shout ■ *adj* reckless and utterly ferocious in a

military attack [Late 19C. < Japanese, '(may you live) ten thousand years'.]

baobab /báy ō bab/ *n* a tree with a thick short trunk and edible fruit. Native to: S Africa and NW Australia. *Adansonia digitata*. [Mid-17C. < ?]

Bao Dai /bów dí/ (*b.* 1913) emperor of Annam (1926–45) and Vietnamese national leader (1949–55). Born **Nguyen Vinh Duy**

Baotou /bów tǒ/ city on the Huang He, Inner Mongolia, N China. Population: 1,574,291 (1991).

bap /bap/ *n* a large soft flattish bread roll [Late 16C. < ?]

baptise *vt* = **baptize**

baptism /báptizəm/ *n* 1 a religious ceremony in which somebody is sprinkled with or immersed in water to symbolize purification. In Christian baptisms, the person is often named and accepted into the Christian faith. 2 a ceremony that serves as an initiation or naming ritual —**baptismal** /bap tízm'l/ *adj* —**baptismally** *adv*

baptism of fire *n* 1 a difficult or dangerous first experience in a new situation 2 a soldier's first experience of battle

Baptist /báptist/ *n* a member of a Protestant denomination that baptizes people by total immersion when they are old enough to understand and declare their faith —**Baptist** *adj*

baptistery /báptistri/ (*plural* **-ies**), **baptistry** (*plural* **-tries**) *n* 1 a part of a Christian church used for baptisms 2 a tank or pool in a Baptist church used for baptisms by total immersion

baptize /báp tíz/ (**-tizes, -tizing, -tized**), **baptise** (**-tises, -tising, -tised**) *v* 1 *vti* to sprinkle somebody with or immerse somebody in water as a sign that the person has been accepted into the Christian faith 2 *vt* to give a personal name to somebody during the Christian ceremony of baptism [13C. Via French *baptiser* and ecclesiastical Latin *baptisare* < Greek *baptizein* 'baptize' < *baptein* 'dip'.] —**baptizer** *n*

bar¹ /baar/ *n* 1 LENGTH OF SOLID MATERIAL a length of metal, wood, or other solid material used as a barrier, or as part of a structure 2 SMALL BLOCK a small, solid, usually rectangular, block of some substance ○ *a bar of soap* 3 BARRIER something that blocks or hinders progress ○ *Aloofness is a bar to making friends easily.* 4 PLACE FOR DRINKING a place where alcoholic drinks can be bought and drunk 5 DRINKS COUNTER a counter where alcoholic drinks are served 6 PLACE PROVIDING PRODUCT OR SERVICE a commercial establishment, or a counter inside one, where a product or service is provided ○ *a juice bar* 7 NARROW BAND a narrow stripe or band of colour or light 8 SOMETHING USED AS A STANDARD something referred to as an authority or standard ○ *We need to raise the bar of academic courses for all our students.* 9 PART OF LAW COURT the railing in a law court that separates the judge, jury, and Queen's Counsel from solicitors, junior barristers, and the public 10 PLACE FOR DEFENDANT IN COURT the place in a law court where somebody on trial stands or sits 11 TRIBUNAL a tribunal or court of law 12 DEFEAT OF LEGAL ACTION the defeat, prevention, or nullification of an action or claim, or the process by which this is achieved 13 PLACE IN BRITISH PARLIAMENT the place in the House of Commons or House of Lords where nonmembers must stand to address either House 14 UNIT OF TIME IN MUSIC a fundamental unit of time into which all music is divided, according to the number of beats 15 VERTICAL LINE SEPARATING MUSICAL UNITS any one of the vertical lines on a sheet of music that separates each unit of musical time 16 INSIGNIA an insignia added to a decoration to show that an award has been won twice 17 SPORTS = **crossbar** *n*. 1 GYMNASTICS = **horizontal bar** *n*. 1 BALLET = **barre** 18 LINE ACROSS SHIELD a horizontal line on a shield, usually one of two or three parallel lines 21 RIDGE OF SAND a low ridge of sand or shingle in the shallow part of the bed of a body of water 22 RIVER'S CRESCENT-SHAPED SAND DEPOSIT a crescent-shaped area of alluvium deposited on the convex bend of a river bed 23 STRIP IN BACKGAMMON BOARD the central dividing strip on a backgammon board ■ *vt* (**bars, barring, barred**) 1 FASTEN WITH BAR to fasten something with a bar ○ *barred the door* 2 BLOCK to block something by means of bars or barriers 3 NOT ALLOW SOMEBODY ENTRY to refuse somebody entry to a place ○ *He was barred from the club.* 4 MARK SOMETHING WITH BARS to mark something with stripes or bands of colour (*usually passive*) 5 HALT COURT CASE to prevent a court case from going ahead by making a legal objection to it ■ *prep* EXCLUDING except for ○ *The*

fight was all over, bar the shouting. [12C. Via Old French *barre* < Vulgar Latin *barra*.] ◇ **behind bars** in prison ○ *a convicted felon who spent 20 years behind bars*

bar² /baar/ *n* a cgs unit of pressure that can be used in combination with SI units and prefixes, equal to 10⁵ newtons per square metre [Early 20C. < Greek *baros* 'weight'.]

Bar *n* 1 barristers considered collectively 2 in the United States, lawyers considered collectively ○ *the federal and state Bars*

bar. *abbr* 1 barometer 2 barrel

Bar. *abbr* 1 barrister 2 Baruch

Bara /bárrə/, **Theda** (1890?–1955) US actor. Born **Theodosia Goodman.** Known as **the Vamp**

Barabbas /bə rábbəss/ *n* in the Bible, a condemned thief who was freed by Pilate at Passover instead of Jesus Christ (Matthew 27)

Barak /baa rák/, **Ehud** (*b.* 1942) Israeli soldier, politician, and prime minister (1999–2001)

Baranof Island /bárrənəf-/ island off SE Alaska. Population: 9,000. Area: 4,162 sq. km/1,607 sq. mi.

Barassi /bə rássi/, **Ron** (*b.* 1936) Australian footballer and coach

barathea /bárrə thee ə/ *n* a fabric made from a combination of silk, cotton, wool, or synthetic material. Use: coats. [Mid-19C. < ?]

baraza /bə raázə/ *n* a public meeting or a place where meetings are held in East Africa [Late 19C. < Kiswahili.]

barb¹ /baarb/ *n* 1 REVERSE POINT OF ARROW a sharp point facing away from the head of an arrow, fishhook, or harpoon, designed to make it difficult to remove 2 WOUNDING REMARK a pointed or wounding remark 3 (*plural* **barbs** *or* **barb**) AQUARIUM FISH a small fish often kept in aquariums. Genera: *Barbus* and *Puntius*. 4 MEDIEVAL HEADDRESS a white cloth headdress covering the chin and throat, worn by women in the Middle Ages 5 PART OF FEATHER a stiff filament that forms the framework of a feather. The barbs stick out on each side of the main shaft. 6 WHISKER ON ANIMAL'S HEAD a growth on an animal's head like a beard or whisker 7 BRISTLE OF A PLANT a hooked projection on some plants and fruits ■ *vt* FIT WITH BARB to provide something with a barb or barbs [14C. Via Old French *barbe* 'beard, appendage like a beard' < Latin *barba* 'beard'.]

barb² /baarb/ (*plural* **barbs** *or* **barb**) *n* a horse noted for speed and stamina belonging to a breed originally from North Africa [Mid-17C. Via French *barbe* < Italian *barbero* 'of Barbary'.]

barb³ /baarb/ *n* a barbiturate (*slang*) [Mid-20C. Shortening.]

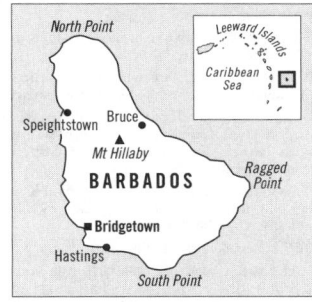

Barbados

Barbados /baar báy doss/ island nation in the Caribbean off NE South America. Capital: Bridgetown. Population: 258,756 (1997). Area: 430 sq. km/166 sq. mi. —**Barbadian** *n, adj*

barbarian /baar báiri ən/ *n* 1 UNCIVILIZED PERSON especially in ancient times, a member of a people whose culture and behaviour was considered uncivilized (*offensive in some contexts*) 2 UNCULTURED PERSON somebody with no interest in culture 3 AGGRESSIVE PERSON an extremely aggressive or violent person [14C. < Old French *barbarien* or Latin *barbarianus* < *barbarus* (see BARBAROUS).] —**barbarianism** *n*

barbaric /baar bárrik/ *adj* 1 cruel or extremely brutal 2 uncivilized or unsophisticated when compared to highly developed civilizations (*offensive in some* *contexts*) [14C. Directly or via Old French *barbarique* < Latin *barbaricus* < Greek *barbarikos* < *barbaros* (see BARBAROUS).] —**barbarically** *adv*

barbarise *vti* = **barbarize**

barbarism /báarbərizəm/ *n* **1 CRUEL ACT** a cruel or brutal act **2 UNCIVILIZED QUALITY** the uncivilized nature of a culture or civilization (*offensive in some contexts*) **3 UNGRAMMATICAL WORD** a word or expression considered to be grammatically incorrect **4 UNCONVENTIONAL OR UNACCEPTABLE THING** something that breaks rules of convention or good taste [15C. Via French *barbarisme* < Latin *barbarismus* < Greek *barbarismos* < *barbarizein* (see BARBARIZE).]

barbarity /baar bárrəti/ (*plural* **-ties**) *n* **1** a cruel act **2** an uncivilized condition [Mid-16C. < Latin *barbarus* (see BARBAROUS).]

barbarize /báarbə rīz/ (**-rizes, -rizing, -rized**), **barbarise** (**-rises, -rising, -rised**) *vti* **1** to become, or make somebody, cruel or brutal **2** to become less civilized, or less cultured, or reduce something to this state [15C. < Greek *barbarizein* 'act or speak like a foreigner, speak gibberish' < *barbaros* (see BARBAROUS).] —**barbarization** /báarbə rī záysh'n/ *n*

Barbarossa /báarbə róssə/ (1483?–1546) Greek-born Ottoman admiral and pirate. Born **Khair ad-Din**

barbarous /báarbərəss/ *adj* **1 EXTREMELY CRUEL** showing extreme cruelty **2 UNCIVILIZED** characterized by an uncivilized culture (*offensive in some contexts*) **3 NOT SOPHISTICATED** lacking sophistication or refinement **4 UNGRAMMATICAL** using ungrammatical language [15C. Via Latin *barbarus* < Greek *barbaros* 'non-Greek, foreign, ignorant, uncivilized'.] —**barbarously** *adv* —**barbarousness** *n*

Barbary /báarbəri/ former region of North Africa stretching from the Atlantic coast to W Egypt

Barbary ape *n* a tailless monkey with greenish-brown hair. Native to: NW Africa, introduced to Gibraltar. *Macaca sylvana*.

Barbary Coast formerly, the Mediterranean coast of North Africa

Barbary sheep *n* ZOOL = **aoudad**

barbastelle /báarbə stél/ *n* an insect-eating bat with large ears and a wrinkly face. Native to: Europe, Asia. *Barbastella barbastellus*. [Late 18C. Via French < Italian *barbastello* < Latin *vespertilio* 'bat'.]

barbecue /báarbi kyoo/, **barbeque** *n* **1** an apparatus, including a grill and fuel, used for cooking food outdoors **2** an outdoor party where people eat food cooked on a barbecue [Mid-17C. < American Spanish *barbacoa*, probably < Arawak *barbakoa* 'frame of sticks'.] —**barbecue** *vt*

barbecue sauce *n* a sweet-sour and spicy sauce, sometimes with chilli, used to marinate meat or served as an accompaniment to meat

barbed /baarbd/ *adj* **1** with one or more backward-facing points **2** critical or biting ○ *a barbed comment*

barbed wire *n* strong wire with pointed projections along its length, used to make fences and barriers

barbel /báarb'l/ *n* **1** a slender feeler resembling a whisker on the lips or jaws of some fishes **2** a toothless European fish with barbels that resembles the carp. Genus: *Barbus*. [14C. < Latin *barba* 'beard'.]

barbell /báar bel/ *n* a metal bar with removable weights at either end, used in weightlifting [Late 19C. Blend of BAR[1] + DUMBBELL.] —**barbeller** *n*

barbeque *n* LEISURE, FOOD = **barbecue**

barber /báarbər/ *n* **SOMEBODY WHO CUTS HAIR** somebody whose profession it is to cut men's hair and shave their beards ■ *v* **1** *vt* **CUT SOMEBODY'S HAIR** to cut or shave somebody's hair, especially a man's **2** *vi* **WORK AS BARBER** to work as a barber [13C. < Anglo-Norman *barbour* < French *barbe* (see BARB[1]).]

Barber /báarbər/, **Samuel** (1910–81) US composer

barberry /báarbəri/ (*plural* **-ries**) *n* a thorny flowering shrub widely grown as a garden or hedge plant, especially a yellow-flowered variety that has orange or red berries. Native to: Asia. Genus: *Berberis*. [14C. < Old French *berberis* < medieval Latin *barbaris*, influenced by BERRY.]

barbershop /báarbər shop/ *n* a style of popular music for unaccompanied single-sex voices in close harmony, originally for four male voices

barber's itch *n* any rash or skin eruption on the face and neck, especially around the beard, caused by a fungal infection

barber's pole *n* a short pole with red and white stripes found outside a barber's shop

barber's rash *n* MED = **barber's itch**

barbet /báarbit/ *n* a small brightly coloured bird related to the toucan. Native to: tropics. Family: Capitonidae. [Late 16C. < French, 'small beard' < *barbe* (see BARB[1]).]

barbette /baar bét/ *n* **1** a metal cylinder giving armoured protection to a gun turret on a warship **2** a mound of earth inside a fortress used as a platform for cannons [Late 18C. < French, 'small beard' (perhaps from the idea of cannon sticking over the parapet like a line of bristles) < *barbe* (see BARB[1]).]

barbican /báarbikən/ *n* a strong defensive tower at the entrance to a town or fortress [13C. Via Old French *barbacane* < Persian *barbarkhana* 'guard house'.]

Barbican /báarbikən/ *n* a major arts centre in the City of London, completed in 1982

barbicel /báarbi sel/ *n* a tiny projection linking the filaments (**barbules**) of feathers [Mid-19C. < Italian or modern Latin *barbicella* 'small beard' < Latin *barba* 'beard'.]

barbie /báarbi/ *n Aus* a barbecue (*informal*) [Late 20C. Shortening.]

Barbie /báarbi/, **Klaus** (1913–91) German SS officer. Known as **The Butcher of Lyons**

bar billiards *n* a billiards-style game, once popular in British pubs, played on a small table with holes instead of pockets and peg-shaped obstacles

Barbirolli /báarbə rólli/, **Sir John** (1899–1970) British conductor. Born **Giovanni Battista Barbirolli**

barbiturate /baar bíchŏŏrət/ *n* a derivative of barbituric acid with sedative and hypnotic properties [Late 19C. < BARBITURIC ACID.]

barbituric acid /báarbi tyŏŏrik-/ *n* $C_4H_4N_2O$ a white crystalline solid. Use: manufacture of barbiturates. [< French *acide barbiturique*, translating German *Barbitursäure* < the name *Barbara*]

Barbizon School /báarbizon-/ *n* a group of mid-19th-century French painters, which included Corot, Millet, Daubigny, and Rousseau, noted for their realistic depictions of landscapes [Late 19C. After the village of *Barbizon* in France, where the artists met.]

Barbour /báarbər/ *tdmk* a trademark for a waxed waterproof jacket

Barbuda /baar bóodə/ island of the state of Antigua and Barbuda in the E Caribbean Sea. Population: 1,280 (1995). Area: 417 sq. km/161 sq. mi. ◆ **Antigua and Barbuda** —**Barbudan** *n, adj*

barbule /báarbyool/ *n* a slender filament attached to the thicker spines (**barbs**) on a feather's central shaft that interlocks with others [Mid-19C. < Latin *barbula* 'little beard' < *barba* 'beard'.]

barbwire /báarb wīr/ *n US* = **barbed wire**

barcarole /báarkə rōl/, **barcarolle** *n* **1** a song traditionally sung by Venetian gondoliers **2** a piece of instrumental music that imitates a barcarole [Early 17C. Via French < Venetian Italian *barcaruola* < *barcarolo* 'gondolier' < late Latin *barca* 'barque'.]

Barcelona /báarssə lṓnə/ city and port in NE Spain. Population: 1,505,581 (1998 estimate).

BArch *abbr* Bachelor of Architecture

barchan /báar kaan/ *n* a crescent-shaped sand dune in which the tips of the crescent point in the direction of dune movement [Late 19C. < Turkic *barkhan*.]

bar chart *n* STATS = **bar graph**

⚡**bar code** *n* a sequence of numbers and vertical lines identifying an item and often its price when interpreted by an optical scanner

Barcoo /baar kóo/ river in central Queensland, Australia. Length: 480 km/298 mi.

bard[1] /baard/ *n* **1 ANCIENT CELTIC POET** in ancient Celtic culture, a poet who composed and recited epic poems describing important events **2 POET WINNING EISTEDDFOD PRIZE** a poet who has won a prize at a modern Welsh eisteddfod **3 POET** a poet, especially one of national importance (*literary or humorous*) [15C. Via Gaelic *bàrd* < Celtic.] —**bardic** *adj*

bard[2] /baard/ *n* **ARMOUR FOR HORSE** a piece of armour for a horse ■ *vt* **1 DECORATE HORSE WITH BARD** to put a bard on a horse **2 COVER MEAT WITH FAT** to cover meat with fat before roasting it to prevent it from drying out [15C. Via French *barde* < Arabic *barda'a* 'saddle cloth, padded saddle'.]

Bard, Bard of Avon *n* an informal name for William Shakespeare

Bardeen /baar déen/, **John** (1908–91) US physicist

bar diagram *n* = **bar graph**

bardolatry /baar dóllətri/ *n* the idolizing of a poet, especially Shakespeare (*disapproving*)

Bardot /baar dṓ/, **Brigitte** (*b.* 1934) French actor and activist. Born **Camille Javal**

bare /bair/ *adj* (**barer, barest**) **1 NOT COVERED** not covered by clothing ○ *bare legs* **2 WITHOUT DECORATION** without the usual furnishings or decorations ○ *The room was bare except for an iron bedstead.* **3 WITHOUT PLANTS** without vegetation ○ *a bare hillside* **4 BASIC** simple or essential ○ *the bare facts* **5 EMPHASIZING SMALLNESS** used to emphasize how small something is ○ *the bare minimum of supplies* **6 MINIMUM** only just sufficient ○ *the bare essentials* ■ *vt* (**bares, baring, bared**) **EXPOSE** to reveal or expose something ○ *The dog bared its teeth.* ○ *an investigative report that bared the details of the conspiracy* ■ *adv* very (*slang*) [Old English *bær* < Germanic] —**bareness** *n* ◇ **lay something bare** to expose something that has been concealed or hidden ○ *finally laid bare the whole sorry tale of mismanagement*

SPELLCHECK Do not confuse ***bare*** with ***bear***, which has a similar sound. Beware: your spellchecker will not catch this error.

bareback /báir bak/, **barebacked** /-bakt/ *adv, adj* on the bare back of a horse that is usually saddled

bare bones *npl* the essential elements or structure of something, without any elaboration (*informal*)—**barebones** *adj*

barefaced /báir fáyst/ *adj* **1** shamelessly undisguised ○ *a barefaced lie.* US term **bald-faced 2** with an uncovered or clean-shaven face —**barefacedly** /báir fáystli, -fáysidli/ *adv* —**barefacedness** /-fáystnəss, -fáysidnəss/ *n*

barefoot /báir fŏŏt/, **barefooted** /-fŏŏtid/ *adj, adv* wearing nothing on the feet

barefoot doctor *n* an auxiliary healthcare worker, especially in rural areas of China

barefooted *adj, adv* = **barefoot**

barehanded /báir hándid/ *adj, adv* without weapons, or with hands not protected by gloves —**barehandedness** *n*

bareheaded /báir héddid/ *adj, adv* wearing nothing on the head —**bareheadedness** *n*

Bareilly /bə ráyli/ city in north-central India. Population: 587,211 (1991).

bareknuckle /báir nuk'l/, **bareknuckled** /-nuk'ld/ *adv* **WITHOUT BOXING GLOVES** not wearing boxing gloves ■ *adj* **1 USING BARE HANDS** using hands not protected by gloves ○ *He was a great bareknuckle champion in his time.* **2 AGGRESSIVE AND COMPETITIVE** characterized by open aggression or competitiveness ○ *a bareknuckle exchange in the House*

barelegged /báir légd, -léggid/ *adj, adv* with nothing covering the legs —**bareleggedness** /-léggidnəss/ *n*

barely /báirli/ *adv* **1** scarcely or almost not ○ *They had barely enough money to pay the rent.* ○ *She had barely sat down when the phone rang.* **2** sparsely or simply, with no adornments ○ *a barely furnished office*

USAGE See ***hardly***.

Barenboim /bárrən boym/, **Daniel** (*b.* 1942) Argentinian-born Israeli pianist and conductor

Barents /bárrənts/, **Barentz, Willem** (1550?–97) Dutch explorer

Barents Sea /bárrənts-/ part of the Arctic Ocean, north of Norway, Finland, and Russia and south of Franz Josef Land. Area: 1,370,350 sq. km/529,096 sq. mi.

Barentz = **Barents**

barf /baarf/ *vti US* to vomit (*informal*) ■ *n US* vomited food (*informal*) [Mid-20C. Probably an imitation of the sound.] —**barfy** *adj*

barfly /báar flī/ (*plural* **-flies**) *n US* a frequent drinker in bars (*slang*) [Early 20C. Because regarded as a pest.]

bargain /báargin/ *n* **1 CHEAP PURCHASE** something offered or bought at less than the normal price **2 MUTUAL PACT** an agreement between two people or parties in which each side promises to carry out an obligation **3 PRICE AGREEMENT** a commercial agreement between two parties that fixes the price of something **4 THINGS RECEIVED BY AGREEMENT** goods or services obtained by a commercial agreement ■ *v* **1** *vi* **NEGOTIATE** to negotiate the terms of an agreement with somebody **2** *vt* **EXCHANGE** to exchange one thing for another [14C. < Old French *bargaignier* 'trade, negotiate, dispute', probably < Germanic.] —**bargainer** *n* ◇ **into the bargain** as well ○ *hard-working and very intelligent into the bargain*

bargain away *vt* to lose something by giving it away as part of an agreement that is ultimately disadvantageous

bargain for *vt* to expect or believe something to be of a certain nature, and prepare for it ○ *The bill was a lot more than we'd bargained for.*

bargain on *vt* expect or believe something will happen, and prepare for it ○ *We hadn't bargained on the train arriving early.*

bargain basement *n* an area of a shop, often in the basement, selling goods cheaply ■ *adj* **bargain-basement** lower than normal ○ *at bargain-basement prices*

bargain hunter *n* somebody who enjoys finding bargains —**bargain hunting** *n*

bargaining chip, bargaining counter *n* something that can be used as leverage in negotiations

barge /baarj/ *n* **1 FREIGHT BOAT** a long narrow flat-bottomed boat used for transporting freight on rivers or canals **2 OPEN BOAT USED CEREMONIALLY** a large open boat used during ceremonies **3 SMALL NAVAL BOAT** a motor launch used by a high-ranking naval officer for ceremonial occasions ■ *v* (**barges, barging, barged**) **1** *vti* **MOVE ROUGHLY** to move roughly, colliding with other people **2** *vti* **PUSH** to push somebody or something roughly ○ *people barging into you with bags* **3** *vt* **TRANSPORT BY BARGE** to transport freight by barge [13C. < Old French *barge* or medieval Latin *bargia.*]

barge in *vt* to enter or intrude suddenly or rudely ○ *Don't just barge in without knocking.*

barge in on *vt* to interrupt somebody in a clumsy or rude manner ○ *Don't barge in on them; they are having a private meeting.*

bargeboard /baárj bawrd/ *n* an ornamental board along the gable end of a roof [Mid-19C. < medieval Latin *bargus*, a kind of gallows.]

bargee /baar jeé/ *n* a crew member or captain of a barge. US term **bargeman**

bargello /baar jéllō/ (*plural* **-los**) *n* a straight needlepoint stitch that is worked in zigzags to create chevron or scallop patterns [Mid-20C. After the *Bargello* Palace in Florence.]

bargeman /baárjmən/ (*plural* **-men** /-mən/) *n US* = **bargee**

bargepole /baárj pōl/ *n* a long pole used to propel barges ◇ **not touch somebody** *or* **something with a bargepole** to be unwilling to have any involvement with somebody or something

~~bargin~~ incorrect spelling of **bargain**

bar graph *n* a graph consisting of a series of vertical or horizontal bars representing statistical data. Also called **bar diagram**

Bari /baári/ port in SE Italy. Population: 1,569,133 (1997 estimate).

bariatrics /bárri áttriks/ *n* the branch of medicine concerned with the treatment of obesity (+ *singular verb*) [Mid-20C. < BARO- + -IATRICS.] —**bariatric** *adj*

baric /báirik/ *adj* **1** relating to or containing barium **2** relating to barometric pressure

barilla /bə rílla/ *n* **1** a sodium carbonate and sodium sulphate alkali ash. Source: derived from various plants. Use: formerly, manufacture of soap, glass. **2** a plant belonging to various species formerly burned to produce an alkali ash. Native to: Mediterranean, some now naturalized in North America and Australia. *Salsola spp.* and *Suaeda spp.* and *Halogeton sativus.* [Early 17C. < Spanish, 'small bar' < *barra* 'bar'.]

barista /ba rístə/ *n* **1** a maker and server of coffee in a coffee bar **2** a connoisseur of coffee or coffee drinking [Late 20C. < Italian, 'worker in or owner of a bar'.]

barite /báir īt/ *n US* MINERALS = **barytes** [Mid-19C. < BARIUM.]

baritone /bárritōn/, **barytone** *n* **1** a man's singing voice with a range lower than a tenor and higher than a bass, or a singer with this voice **2** a wind instrument with the second lowest range in its family [Early 17C. Via Italian *baritono* < Greek *barutonos* 'deep-sounding, baritone'.]

barium /báiri əm/ *n* (*symbol* **Ba**) a soft silver-white toxic chemical element used in alloys [Early 19C. < BARYTA + -IUM.]

barium enema *n* the introduction of a barium salt suspension into the rectum and colon before an X-ray is taken

barium meal *n* a barium salt suspension, given by mouth before X-raying the oesophagus, stomach, and upper intestine

barium sulphate *n* $BaSO_4$ a white or yellowish odourless powder. Use: pigment, contrast medium for X-ray photography.

bark[1] /baark/ *n* **1 DOG'S NOISE** the natural loud abrupt sound made by a dog or fox **2 SHORT REPEATED SOUND** a loud, abrupt, repeated sound ○ *the bark of guns in the distance* ■ *v* **1 MAKE DOG'S SOUND** to make the loud abrupt sound of a dog or fox **2** *vi* **MAKE ABRUPT, HARSH SOUND** to make a short, abrupt, harsh sound **3** *vti* **SPEAK AGGRESSIVELY** to say something in a loud or aggressive manner ○ *He barked out an order.* [Old English *(ge)beorc* (noun), *beorcan* (verb) < Germanic]

bark[2] /baark/ *n* **OUTER LAYER OF TREE** the rough outer covering of the woody stems of trees or bushes ■ *vt* **1 GRAZE SKIN** to have the skin rubbed off a part of the body through abrasive contact with another object ○ *I barked my shins climbing the fence.* **2 STRIP BARK FROM TREE** to remove the bark from a tree or log **3 TAN LEATHER USING BARK** to tan leather using tannins derived from bark [13C. < Old Norse *börkr.*] —**barky** *adj*

bark[3] *n* SAILING = **barque** [15C. < Old French, via provençal < Latin *barca* 'ship's boat'.]

bark beetle *n* a beetle that burrows under the bark of trees. Family: Scolytidae.

barkeeper /baár keepər/ *n US* **1** somebody who runs a bar **2** = **bartender**

barker[1] /baárkər/ *n* **1** somebody who stands outside a fair or carnival and shouts out its attractions **2** a dog that barks

barker[2] /baárkər/ *n* a person or machine that strips bark off trees and logs or prepares bark for tanning

barking /baárking/ *adj* extremely irrational (*informal insult*)

barking deer *n* ZOOL = **muntjac**

Barkly Tableland /baárkli táyb'l land/ plateau region in NE Northern Territory and NW Queensland, Australia. Area: 130,000 sq. km/50,200 sq. mi.

Barlee, Lake /baárli/ lake in SW Western Australia. Area: 1944 sq. km/750 sq. mi.

barley /baárli/ *n* **1** a cereal plant with a long head of whiskered grains. Use: food, malt production, livestock feed. *Hordeum vulgare.* **2** the grain from a barley plant [Old English *bærlic* 'barley-like' < *bære, bere* 'barley' < Indo-European]

barleycorn /baárli kawrn/ *n* barley grain, especially used for malt

barley sugar *n* a clear hard orange-yellow sweet made from boiled-down sugar

barley water *n* a sweet cordial made from water, barley extract, and sugar

barley wine *n* very strong, slightly sweet beer

bar line *n* MUSIC = **bar**[1] *n.* 15

Barlow knife /baárlō-/ *n* a penknife with one blade for cutting and another for poking or gouging [Late 18C. After a family of cutlers in Sheffield.]

barm /baarm/ *n* the foam that rises to the surface during the fermentation of malt liquor [Old English *beorma* < Germanic]

barmaid /baár mayd/ *n* a woman who serves in a pub or bar

barman /baármən/ (*plural* **-men** /-mən/) *n* a man who serves in a pub or a bar

barmbrack /baárm brak/, **barnbrack** /baárn brak/ *n Ireland* rich sweet bread with currants in it [Mid-19C. < Irish *bairin breac* 'speckled cake'.]

Barmecidal /baármi sīd'l/, **Barmecide** /-sīd/ *adj* abundant or lavish only in appearance and not in reality (*literary*) [Mid-18C. < *Barmecide*, prince in *The Arabian Nights' Entertainments* who served a series of empty dishes to a hungry beggar to test his sense of humour.]

bar mitzvah /baar mítsvə/ *n* **1** the ritual ceremony that marks the 13th birthday of a Jewish boy, after which he takes full responsibility for his moral and spiritual conduct **2** a Jewish boy who has reached the age of 13, the age of religious responsibility [Early 19C. < Hebrew *bar miṣwāh* 'son of the commandment'.]

barmy /baármi/ (**-ier, -iest**) *adj* (*informal*) **1** unconventional or slightly irrational in behaviour **2** completely lacking in good sense or reason ○ *That's a barmy idea and you know it.*

barn /baarn/ *n* **1** a large outbuilding on a farm used to store grain or shelter livestock **2** any large building, especially one that is plain and functional [Old English *ber(e)n* 'barley house' < *bere* 'barley' + *ærn* 'house, place']

Barnabas /baárnəbəss/, **St** (*fl.* 1st century AD) Cypriot missionary

barnacle /baárnək'l/ *n* **1** a small marine organism that clings to rocks and ships and draws food by using slender hairs (**cirri**). Subclass: Cirripedia. **2** ZOOL = **barnacle goose** **3** a clinging or dependent person or thing [12C. < medieval Latin *berneca.*]

barnacle goose *n* a wild goose with grey wings and a black-and-white head and body. Native to: N Europe, Greenland. *Branta leucopsis.*

Barnard /baár naard/, **Christiaan** (1922–2000) South African surgeon

Barnardo /bər naárdō/, **Thomas** (1845–1905) Irish-born British physician and philanthropist

Barnard's star /baárnərdz-, baár naardz-/ *n* a red dwarf star in the constellation Ophiuchus [Early 20C. After Edward Emerson *Barnard* (1857–1923), US astronomer.]

Barnaul /baárnə oól/ capital of Attay Territory, SW Siberia, Russia. Population: 616,299 (1995).

barnbrack *n* FOOD = **barmbrack**

barn dance *n* **1** a party, originally held in a barn, with country dancing **2** a country dance

barn door *n* **1** either of the huge doors that close the entrance to a traditional wooden barn **2** any of the four rectangular adjustable flaps on the front of a large industrial light used, e.g., on film sets and in the theatre

barney /baárni/ (*plural* **-neys**) *n* a noisy argument (*informal*) [Mid-19C. < ?]

barn owl *n* an owl with white and pale brown feathers that often nests in barns

Barnsley /baárnzli/ industrial town in N England. Population: 217,300 (1991).

barnstorm /baárn stawrm/ *v* **1** *vti* to travel from place to place giving performances **2** *vi* to perform exhibitions of aerial acrobatics at shows and fairs —**barnstormer** *n* —**barnstorming** *adj*

Barnum /baárnəm/, **P. T.** (1810–91) US showman. Full name **Phineas Taylor Barnum**

barnyard /baárn yaard/ *n* the area around a barn ■ *adj* crude or vulgar (*informal*) ○ *barnyard humour*

barnyard grass *n* a coarse weedy grass with spiky clusters of flowers, sometimes grown as forage. *Echinochloa crusgalli.*

baro- pressure, weight ○ *barometer* [< Greek *baros* 'weight']

baroceptor /bárrə septər/ PHYSIOL = **baroreceptor**

Baroda /bə rṓdə/ former name for **Vadodara**

barogram /bárrə gram/ *n* a record of atmospheric pressure produced by a barograph or other meteorological instrument

barograph /bárrə graaf, -graf/ *n* a barometer that gives a continuous printed record of variations in atmospheric pressure —**barographic** /bárrə gráffik/ *adj*

Barolo /bə róllō/ *n* a full-bodied red wine made in the area around Barolo in NW Italy

barometer /bə rómmitər/ *n* **1** an instrument measuring changes in atmospheric pressure, used in weather forecasting **2** something that indicates an atmosphere or mood ○ *the barometer of public opinion* —**barometric** /bárrə méttrik/ *adj* —**barometrical** *adj* —**barometrically** *adv* —**barometry** *n*

barometric pressure *n* atmospheric pressure as recorded by a barometer

baron /bárrən/ *n* **1 NOBLEMAN** a nobleman of the lowest rank of British or Japanese nobility, or various ranks in some European countries **2 POWERFUL PERSON** somebody with power or influence ○ *an oil baron* **3 MEDIEVAL NOBLEMAN** in the Middle Ages, a nobleman who was given land in return for loyal service [12C. Via Anglo-Norman *barun*, Old French *baron* < medieval Latin *baron-* 'man'.]

SPELLCHECK Do not confuse ***baron*** with ***barren***, which has a similar sound. Beware: your spellchecker will not catch this error.

baronage /bárrənij/ *n* **1** barons considered collectively **2** a baron's rank or position

baroness /bárrənəss/ *n* **1** a noblewoman who belongs to the lowest rank of British or Japanese nobility, or to various ranks in some European countries **2** a baron's wife or widow

baronet /bárrənət/ *n* a British nobleman who holds the lowest hereditary rank

baronetage /bárrənitəj/ *n* **1** baronets collectively **2** = **baronetcy**

baronetcy /bárrənətsi/ *n* a baronet's rank or position

barong /ba róng/ *n* a large knife with a broad blade, used by the Moro people of the Philippines [Late 19C. < Austronesian.]

baronial /bə rṓni əl/ *adj* **1** RELATING TO BARONS relating to or associated with barons **2** LARGE AND IMPRESSIVE large, imposing, or sumptuous ○ *a baronial fireplace* **3** *Scot* LARGE AND WITH TURRETS describes a large solid-looking country house with turrets

baron of beef *n* a cut of beef consisting of a double sirloin, joined at the backbone

barony /bárrəni/ (*plural* **-nies**) *n* **1** a baron's rank or position, or the land held by a baron **2** a powerful businessperson's area of influence ○ *a newspaper tycoon zealously guarding his barony*

barophilic /bárrə fíllik/ *adj* describes an organism that can tolerate high atmospheric pressure —**barophile** /bárrə fīl/ *n*

baroque /bə rók/, **Baroque** *n* FLAMBOYANT STYLE OF ARCHITECTURE AND ART a highly ornamental style of European architecture and art that lasted from the mid-16th to the early 18th centuries, or this period in European history ■ *adj* IN 17C STYLE in the baroque style of art, architecture, or music ■ *n* 17C CLASSICAL MUSIC classical music of the 17th century, the period of such composers as Purcell, Vivaldi, and Telemann ■ *adj* IN VERY ORNAMENTAL STYLE bizarre or highly exaggerated in style [Mid-18C. Via French, applied to ornate architecture < Italian *barocco*, Portuguese *barroco* 'irregularly shaped pearl'.] —**baroquely** *adv*

QUICK FACTS ON... **BAROQUE**

Key dates: late 16th–early 18th centuries
Key locations: W Europe, originating in Italy
Key elements: sense of movement and vitality, rich colours, strong contrasts in light and shade; illusionism; naturalism; integration of architecture, painting, and sculpture
Key figures: Carracci, Caravaggio, Pietro da Cortona, Velázquez, Rubens, Rembrandt, Vermeer (painting); Bernini (sculpture and architecture); Borromini, Churriguera (architecture)
Key works: Ceiling frescoes, Palazzo Farnese, Rome (Carracci) 1597–1600, *Allegory of Divine Providence and Barberini Power* (Pietro da Cortona) 1633–39, *The Ecstasy of Saint Theresa* (Bernini) 1645–52, Church of Santa Agnese, Rome (Borromini), 1653
Key developments: chiaroscuro, integrated design, rococo, classicism

baroreceptor /bárrō ri septər/ *n* a nerve ending that is sensitive to blood pressure changes

Barossa Valley /bə róssə-/ grape-growing region in South Australia

barothermograph /bárrə thúrmə graaf, -graf/ *n* an instrument that records atmospheric pressure and temperature simultaneously

barotitis *n* pain in the ear caused by pressure differences, e.g. during air travel (*informal*)

barotrauma /bárrō trawmə/ *n* pain in and possible damage to an organ occurring as a result of changes in atmospheric pressure

barouche /bə róosh/ *n* a four-wheeled horse-drawn carriage, with two facing double seats, a retractable hood, and a box seat at the front for the driver [Early 19C. Via German dialect *Barutsche* < Italian *baroccio* 'two-wheeled' < Latin *birotus* < *rota* 'wheel'.]

barperson /baár purss'n/ (*plural* **-people** /-peep'l/) *n* somebody who serves in a pub or bar

bar point *n* the seventh point on a large backgammon board, near the bar

barque /baark/, **bark** *n* **1** a small sailing ship with masts whose sails are fixed breadthways (**square**) except for the last mast, which has its sail running lengthwise (**fore-and-aft**) **2** any small sailing ship or boat [15C. Via French *barque* < late Latin *barca*.]

Barquisimeto /baár kissi méttō/ capital of Lara State, NW Venezuela. Population: 602,662 (1991).

Barra /bárrə/ island in the S Outer Hebrides, W Scotland. Population: 1,200. Area: 90 sq. km/35 sq. mi.

barrack[1] /bárrək/ *n* MIL = **barracks** *n.* 1 ■ *vt* **1** to house soldiers in a barracks **2** to house people in any kind of temporary accommodation (*often passive*) [Late 17C. < BARRACKS.]

barrack[2] /bárrək/ *vti* (*informal*) **1** to shout at somebody in criticism or protest **2** *Aus* to shout support for somebody, especially a player or team [Late 19C. Probably < N Irish dialect *barrack* 'brag'.] —**barracker** *n*

barrack-room lawyer *n* somebody who gives unwanted advice or opinions (*disapproving*)

barracks /bárrəks/ *n* (+ *singular or plural verb*) **1** a building used to accommodate military personnel **2** any temporary accommodation [Late 17C. Via French *baraque* < Italian *baracca* or Spanish *barraca* 'soldier's tent, barracks'.]

barracoon /bárrə kóon/ *n* formerly, a large building used to confine convicts or enslaved people temporarily [Mid-19C. < Spanish *barracón* 'large barracks' < *barraca* 'barracks'.]

barracouta /bárrə kóotə/ (*plural* **-tas** *or* **-ta**) *n* **1** a large predatory sea fish with strong teeth and a projecting lower jaw. Native to: Pacific Ocean. Family: Gempylidae. **2** *NZ* a long bread loaf [Late 17C. Alteration of BARRACUDA.]

barracuda /bárrə kyóodə/ (*plural* **-das** *or* **-da**) *n* a predatory sea fish with a long body and protruding jaws and teeth. Native to: tropical seas. Genus: *Sphyraena*. [Late 17C. Via American Spanish < Spanish dialect *barraco* 'overlapping tooth'.]

barrage /bárraazh, -j/ *n* **1** MILITARY BOMBARDMENT a long continuous burst of gunfire **2** ATTACKING FLOW a rapid attacking outpouring of something ○ *a barrage of criticism* **3** RIVER BARRIER an artificial barrier built across a river or canal to provide water or prevent flooding ■ *vt* (**-rages, -raging, -raged**) **1** FIRE CONTINUOUSLY ON ENEMY to attack an enemy with rapid and continuous gunfire **2** ATTACK SOMEBODY CONTINUOUSLY to subject somebody to a relentless onslaught ○ *Those two have been barraging me with questions all morning.* [Mid-19C. < French, 'barrier' < *barrer* 'to block' < *barre* (see BAR[1]).]

barrage balloon *n* a large balloon anchored to the ground in wartime to deter enemy aircraft

barramundi /bárrə múndi/ (*plural* **-dis** *or* **-dies** *or* **-di**), **barramunda** /-múndə/ (*plural* **-das** *or* **-da**) *n* **1** an edible fish of the perch family. Native to: Australia. *Lates calcarifer*. **2** a tropical freshwater fish with a long robust body and a single dorsal fin near the rounded tail fin. Family: Osteoglossidae. [Late 19C. Probably < a Queensland Aboriginal word.]

Barranquilla /bárran keé yə/ capital of Atlántico Department, N Colombia. Population: 1,157,826 (1997 estimate).

barratry /bárrətri/, **barretry** *n* **1** BRINGING OF UNREASONABLE LAWSUITS the illegal action of persistently bringing lawsuits for little or no reason **2** ILLEGAL SHIPPING PRACTICE any unlawful practice committed by a ship's master or crew that harms its owner or charterer **3** BUYING OF CHURCH OR GOVERNMENT POSITION the sale or purchase of a position in government or the church [15C. < French *baraterie* 'combat, deceit' < *barater* 'fight, cheat' < Greek *prattein* 'do'.] —**barrator** *n* —**barratrous** *adj* —**barratrously** *adv*

Barrault /ba rṓ/, **Jean-Louis** (1910–94) French actor and producer

Barr body /baár-/ *n* an inactive X chromosome present in the cells of females, used in a test to determine sex [Mid-20C. After Murray L. *Barr* (b. 1908), Canadian anatomist.]

barre /baar/ *n* a rail fixed to a wall, at about hip height, used by ballet dancers when exercising [Mid-20C. < French (see BAR[1]).]

barré /bárray/ *n* **1** the placing of the index finger over all the strings of a guitar or similar string instrument to raise the pitch of each string simultaneously **2** a chord played on a guitar or similar string instrument in a barré fashion [Late 19C. < French, past participle of *barrer* (see BARRAGE).]

barred /baard/ *adj* **1** having strips of colour **2** fitted with or made of bars

barred owl *n* a large owl with dark eyes, broad brownish stripes across its breast, and streaked underparts. Native to: North America. *Strix varia*.

barred spiral galaxy *n* a galaxy in which the stars form a spiral with a bright bar across the centre

barrel /bárrəl/ *n* **1** LARGE CASK a cylindrical container with a flat top and bottom, used to store liquids **2** AMOUNT HELD BY BARREL the amount held by a barrel **3** UNIT OF VOLUME IN OIL INDUSTRY a unit of liquid volume used in the oil industry, usually taken to be 35 imperial gallons or 42 US gallons (approximately 159 litres) **4** UNIT OF VOLUME IN BREWING INDUSTRY a unit of liquid volume used in the brewing industry, equal to 36 imperial gallons or 43 US gallons (approximately 164 litres) **5** TUBE-SHAPED PART OF A GUN the tube-shaped part of gun through which bullets are fired **6** CYLINDRICAL PART a hollow cylindrical device that forms part of a mechanism, e.g. in clocks ■ *vti* (**-rels, -relling, -relled**) *US* TRAVEL FAST to move somewhere at high speed (*informal*) [13C. Via Old French *barril* < medieval Latin *barriclus* 'small cask'.] —**barrelful** *n* ◇ **have somebody over a barrel** to place somebody in a situation in which he or she is unable to act freely ◇ **scrape the bottom of the barrel** to use somebody or something of very poor quality because nothing or no one else is available ◇ **not be a barrel of laughs** to be far from being interesting or amusing

barrel chair *n US* an upholstered chair with a high, curved, solid back

barrel-chested *adj* with a large rounded chest

barrelhead /bárrəl hed/ *n* the flat circular top of a barrel

barrelhouse /bárrəl howss/ (*plural* **-houses** /-howziz/) *n* **1** *US* a cheap disreputable bar, especially one where there is music and dancing (*dated*) **2** a loud rough style of jazz characterized by a heavy two-beat rhythm [Late 19C. < the barrels of liquor along the walls.]

barrel organ *n* a mechanical musical instrument consisting of a cylinder turned by a handle that allows air to pass through a set of pipes

barrel roll *n* a flight manoeuvre in which an aircraft makes one complete sideways revolution ■ *vi* to carry out a barrel roll

barrel vault *n* a ceiling in the shape of a half cylinder

barren /bárrən/ *adj* **1** BARE OF VEGETATION with no trees or other plants growing **2** NOT FRUITING producing no fruit or seed **3** UNABLE TO HAVE CHILDREN not able to bear children (*archaic or literary*) **4** WITH NO USEFUL RESULT not producing valuable results or interesting effects ○ *It was a barren period in his career.* **5** LACKING lacking in a particular thing (*literary*) ○ *Our writers seem somewhat barren of new ideas.* [12C. < Old French *baraigne*.] —**barrenly** *adv* —**barrenness** *n*

SPELLCHECK See ***baron***.

barretry *n* LAW = **barratry**

barricade /bárri káyd, -kayd/ *n* a barrier that protects defenders or blocks a route ■ *vt* (**-cades, -cading, -caded**) to obstruct or protect something, or protect yourself, using barricades [Late 16C. < French, < *barrique* 'barrel'.]

Barrie /bárri/, **Sir J. M.** (1860–1937) British playwright and author. Full name **Sir James Matthew Barrie**

barrier /bárri ər/ *n* **1** STRUCTURE BLOCKING ACCESS a structure, e.g. a fence, intended to stop access or keep one place separate from another **2** THING THAT OBSTRUCTS something that obstructs or separates, often by emphasizing differences **3** LIMIT OR STANDARD something considered as a limit, standard, or boundary **4** ICE SHELF the part of the Antarctic ice shelf that extends over the sea and partly rests on the ocean floor [14C. Via Old French *barriere* < Vulgar Latin *barra* 'bar'.]

barrier cream *n* any cream that protects the skin against dirt, harmful moisture, or infection

barrier island *n* a long sandy island that runs parallel to a coastline and serves to protect the shore from erosion

barrier method *n* a method of contraception in which the access of sperm to the womb is blocked, e.g. by use of a condom or diaphragm

barrier nursing *n* the nursing of patients with infectious diseases in isolation, to prevent the spread of infection —**barrier-nurse** *vt*

barrier reef *n* a narrow ridge of coral lying parallel and close to a coastline and separated from it by a wide deep lagoon

barring /baáring/ *prep* excepting or except for something ○ *Barring delays, we'll arrive this afternoon.*

Barrington /bárringtən/, **Jonah** (*b.* 1940) British squash player

barrio /bárri ō/ (*plural* **-os**) *n* **1** an area of a town in a Spanish-speaking country **2** *US* a Spanish-speaking quarter in a city or town in the United States [Mid-19C. Via Spanish < Arabic *barr* 'open area'.]

barrister /báristər/ *n* **1** a lawyer who is qualified to represent clients in the higher law courts in England and Wales **2** *Can* a lawyer who represents clients in any law court in Canada [15C. < BAR[1], probably after words such as *minister, chorister.*]

barrow[1] /bárrō/ *n* **1** a two-wheeled cart used by street vendors to sell their wares. US term **pushcart 2** = **wheelbarrow** *n.* [Old English *bearwe* 'stretcher, bier' < Germanic, 'to bear']

barrow[2] /bárrō/ *n* a large mound of earth above a prehistoric tomb [Old English *beorg* 'hill, tumulus' < Germanic, 'hide, protect']

barrow[3] /bárrō/ *n* a pig that has been castrated before sexual maturity [Old English *b(e)arg* < Germanic]

Barrow /bárrō/ village in NW Alaska near Point Barrow, the northernmost point of the United States. Population: 4,047 (1998 estimate).

Barrow, Clyde (1909–34) US outlaw

barrow boy *n* a man who sells wares from a barrow

Barrow-in-Furness /-fúrniss/ industrial town in NW England. Population: 48,947 (1991).

Barrow Island island off the NW coast of Western Australia. Population: 100. Area: 200 sq. km/78 sq. mi.

Barry /bárri/ port on the Bristol Channel, Wales. Population: 49,887 (1991).

Barry, Sir Charles (1795–1860) British architect

Barrymore /bárri mawr/, **Ethel** (1879–1959) US actor

Barrymore, John (1882–1942) US actor

Barrymore, Lionel (1878–1954) US actor

Barsac /baár sak/ *n* a sweet white Bordeaux wine from the area around the town of Barsac, France

bar sinister (*plural* **bars sinister**) *n* **1** HERALDRY = **bend sinister 2** evidence suggesting that somebody is of illegitimate birth

Bart. *abbr* baronet

bar tack *n* a straight stitch that crosses a piece of cloth at a right angle to a slit, e.g. at the end of a buttonhole

bartender /baár tendər/ *n* somebody who serves in a pub or bar

barter /baártər/ *v* **1** *vti* **EXCHANGE GOODS OR SERVICES** to exchange goods or services in return for other goods or services **2** *vi* **NEGOTIATE TERMS OF AGREEMENT** to negotiate or argue over the terms of a transaction ■ *n* **1 BARTERING** the practice or system of bartering **2 THINGS BARTERED** goods or services that are bartered [15C. Probably < Old French *barater* (see BARRATRY).] —**barterer** *n*

Barth /baarth/, **John** (*b.* 1930) US writer and educator

Barth /baarth, baart/, **Karl** (1886–1968) Swiss theologian

Barthes /baart/, **Roland** (1915–80) French philosopher and writer

Bartholin's gland /baárthəlinz-/ *n* either of two small glands on either side of the lower vagina that secrete a lubricating mucus during sexual stimulation. ◊ **Cowper's gland** [Early 20C. After Kaspar *Bartholin* (1655–1738), Danish anatomist.]

bartizan /baártiz'n, baárti zán/ *n* a small turret that projects from a tower or wall of a fortress or castle, used as a lookout or a defensive position [Mid-16C. Scots variant of *bratticing* 'timberwork' < BRATTICE.] —**bartizaned** *adj*

Bartle Frere /baárt'l freer/ highest mountain in Queensland, Australia, in the north of the state. Height: 1,612 m/5,287 ft.

Bartlett /baártlət/, **Bartlett pear** *n* *US* FOOD = **Williams** *n.* [Mid-19C. After Enoch *Bartlett* (1779–1860), US merchant.]

Bartók /baár tok/, **Béla** (1881–1945) Hungarian composer

Barton, Sir Edmund (1849–1920) Australian statesman

Baruch /bə roók/ *n* a book in the Roman Catholic Bible and the Protestant Apocrypha traditionally ascribed to Baruch, a disciple of the prophet Jeremiah

Barwick /bárrik/, **Sir Garfield** (1903–97) Australian judge and politician

barycentre /bárri sentər/ *n* the centre of the mass of a system, especially a system of celestial bodies [Late 19C. < Greek *barus* 'heavy'.] —**barycentric** /bárri séntrik/ *adj*

baryon /bárri on/ *n* a subatomic particle belonging to a group that undergo strong interactions, have a mass greater than or equal to that of the proton, and consist of three quarks [Mid-20C. < Greek *barus* 'heavy' + -ON[1].] —**baryonic** /bárri ónnik/ *adj*

Baryshnikov /bə ríshnikof/, **Mikhail** (*b.* 1948) Russian-born US dancer and choreographer

baryta /bə rītə/ *n* barium oxide or hydroxide [Early 19C. < BARYTES, after SODA.] —**barytic** /bə ríttik/ *adj*

barytes /bə rī teez/ *n* a yellow, white, or colourless mineral consisting of barium sulphate. Use: source of barium. US term **barite** [Late 18C. < Greek *barutēs* 'weight'.]

basal /báyss'l/ *adj* **1** at or forming the bottom of something **2** basic or fundamental —**basally** *adv*

basal body *n* a structure found near the base of cells that have projecting threads (**cilia**)

basal cell *n* a cell forming the deepest layer of the skin

basal cell carcinoma *n* a slow-growing malignant tumour that typically affects the facial skin of older persons. It rarely spreads to other parts, and is generally curable by surgery or radiotherapy.

basal ganglion *n* a mass of grey matter that lies in the white matter near the base of each cerebral hemisphere of the brain

basal metabolic rate *n* the rate at which an organism consumes oxygen while awake but at rest, measured in kilocalories per square metre of body surface per hour

basal metabolism *n* the amount of energy consumed by a resting organism simply in maintaining its basic functions

basalt /bássawlt/ *n* **1** a hard black, often glassy, volcanic rock. It was produced by the partial melting of the Earth's mantle. **2** a hard black unglazed pottery [Early 17C. Via Latin *basaltes*, variant of *basanites* < Greek *basanitēs* 'very hard stone, touchstone' < Egyptian *bakhan* 'slate'.] —**basaltic** /bə sáwltik/ *adj*

basalt plateau *n* an extensive continental deposit of basaltic volcanic rock

basaltware /bássawlt wair/ *n* a hard black stoneware pottery made in England and parts of continental Europe in the 18th century

basanite /bássə nīt/ *n* volcanic basaltic rock containing olivine and additional alkaline minerals [Mid-18C. < Latin *basanites* (see BASALT).]

bascule /báss kyool/ *n* **1** a counterbalanced device that pivots on a central axis so that the unweighted end rises as the weighted end is allowed to fall **2 bascule, bascule bridge** a bridge with a roadway that can be raised to allow tall boats and ships to pass through [Late 17C. < French, 'seesaw' < *battre* 'to batter' + *cul* 'buttocks'.]

base[1] /bayss/ *n* **1 LOWEST PART** the lowest, bottom, or supporting part or layer of something **2 LOWER PART OF BUILT STRUCTURE** the lower part of a built structure, e.g. a wall, pillar, or column, regarded as a separate feature **3 MAIN SUPPORTING ELEMENT** the main source of an important component in an economy or sphere of influence ○ *improve our customer base* **4 FUNDAMENTAL PRINCIPLE** the main principle or starting point of a system or theory **5 CENTRE FROM WHICH ACTIVITIES START** a centre from which activities start or are coordinated **6 MILITARY CENTRE** a coordinating or supply centre for military operations **7 MAIN INGREDIENT** a main ingredient to which others are added **8 SOLVENT** a medium in which ingredients or constituents may be dissolved or carried **9 ATTACHING PART OF ORGAN** the part of an organ or body part by which it is attached to a more central structure **10 LOWER PART OF HERALDIC SHIELD** the lower part of a heraldic shield **11 REFERENCE NUMBER** the number that is the basis for a system of calculation, represented by the total countable digits in the system. The base 10 system contains the ten digits 0–9. **12 LOGARITHM REFERENCE** a number raised to a power denoted by a superscript **13 LOWER SIDE OF FIGURE** the lower side or face of a geometric figure **14** MEASURE = **baseline** *n.* **1** **15 LOWEST STOCK PRICE** the lowest recorded price level of a tradable commodity or security **16 CHEMICAL COMPOUND** a compound that releases hydroxyl ions to form a solution with a pH greater than 7, reacts with acids to form salts, and turns red litmus paper blue **17 CHEMICAL COMPOUND FORMING COVALENT BOND** a compound that can accept a proton or donate a pair of electrons to form a covalent bond with an acid **18 FILM FOUNDATION** an inert medium supporting the photographic emulsion of films **19 MIDDLE REGION OF TRANSISTOR** the middle region of a transistor between the emitter and the collector **20 FIELD MARKER** in baseball, any one of the four corners of the diamond-shaped infield that a batter must touch in order to score a run ■ *vt* (**bases, basing, based**) **1 MAKE A BASE** to create or provide a base for something **2 ASSIGN SOMEBODY TO BASE** to station, post, or assign somebody to a base **3 USE SOMETHING AS A BASIS** to use something as a base or basis for something else [14C. Directly or via Old French < Latin *basis* < Greek *basis* (see BASIS).] ◇ **off base** *US* wrong or inexact ○ *Your calculations are all off base.*

SPELLCHECK Do not confuse ***base*** with ***bass***, which can have a similar sound. Beware: your spellchecker will not catch this error.

base[2] /bayss/ (*comparative* **baser**) *adj* **1 LACKING MORALS** lacking proper social values or moral principles **2 OF POOR QUALITY** inferior in value or quality **3 COUNTERFEIT** containing a higher proportion of base metals than usual **4 ILLEGITIMATE** of humble or illegitimate birth (*archaic*) **5 RELATING TO PEASANTS** relating to a peasant (**villein**) renting land from a feudal lord (*archaic*) [14C. Via French *bas* < medieval Latin *bassus* 'short, low'.] —**basely** *adv* —**baseness** *n*

baseball /báyss bawl/ *n* **1** a game played with a bat and ball by two teams of nine players, on a field that has four bases arranged in a diamond pattern to mark the course a batter must take to score a run **2** a hard leather-covered ball, about 23 cm/9 in in circumference, used in the game of baseball

baseball cap *n* a close-fitting cap with a long peak, originally worn by baseball players

baseband /báyss band/ *n* the frequency band of a transmitted message

baseboard /báyss bawrd/ *n* **1** a board that serves as the base of something **2** *US* CONSTR = **skirting board**

baseborn /báyss bawrn/ *adj* (*archaic*) **1 OF HUMBLE BIRTH** born of poor or disgraced parents **2 ILLEGITIMATE** born of unmarried parents **3 IGNOBLE** dishonourable or unworthy

base coin *n* a counterfeit coin made of cheap metal

base currency *n* a currency in which a business maintains its accounts and that it uses for buying and selling

Basedow's disease /bázzidōz-/ *n* = **Graves' disease** [Late 19C. After Karl Adolph von *Basedow* (1799–1854), German physician.]

base hit *n* in baseball, a hit that enables the batter to reach a base safely without causing an error, a force play, or a fielder's choice

base hospital *n* *Aus* a central hospital that serves an extensive rural area

Basel /baáz'l/, **Basle** /baal/ city in NW Switzerland. Population: 168,735 (1998).

baseless /báyssləss/ *adj* **1** without grounds or a factual basis **2** lacking a base or foundation —**baselessly** *adv* —**baselessness** *n*

base level *n* the lowest level to which moving water can erode a land surface, e.g. the bed of a stream, lake, or sea

baseline /báysslīn/ *n* **1 MEASURING LINE** a line used as a basis for measurement, calculation, or location, e.g. in surveying or navigation **2 STANDARD OF VALUE** a standard of value to which other similar things are compared **3 REFERENCE DATA** the data used as a reference with which to compare future observations or results **4 BOUNDARY LINE AT END OF COURT** a boundary line at each end of a court that marks the limit of play in tennis, badminton, or basketball

baseliner /báysslīnər/ *n* a tennis player who prefers to play on or near the baseline, and who only occasionally moves to the net

base load *n* the average demand placed on an electrical power supply system

baseman /báyssmən/ (*plural* **-men** /-mən/) *n* in baseball, a fielder positioned near first, second, or third base

basement /báyssmənt/ *n* **1 UNDERGROUND STOREY OF BUILDING** a storey of a building that is wholly or partly below ground level **2 LOWEST PART OF WALL OR BUILDING** the foundation, substructure, or lowest part of a wall or building **3 PART OF EARTH'S CRUST** the highly folded igneous or metamorphic layer of rocks that lies beneath more recent, softer sedimentary rocks [Mid-18C. Probably via Dutch < Italian *basamento* 'base of a column' < *basare* 'to base'.]

base metal *n* any common inexpensive metal

basenji /bə sénji/ *n* a dog belonging to a small curly-tailed African breed that rarely barks and has a short smooth coat varying from black to chestnut [Mid-20C. < Bantu.]

base on balls *n* in baseball, an advance to first base awarded to a batter who receives four pitches outside the strike zone at which the batter does not swing

base pair *n* a chemical unit linking complementary strands of DNA or RNA

base pairing *n* the hydrogen bonding between complementary bases that holds together the two strands of the double helix of DNA and RNA

base rate *n* the rate of interest used by UK clearing banks as a basis for calculating their lending rates

base runner *n* in baseball, a player on the team batting who is on a base or is trying to get to one safely

bases plural of **basis**

base unit *n* a fundamental unit within a system of measurement from which other units in the system are derived

bash /bash/ *v* **1** *vt* **STRIKE WITH HEAVY BLOW** to strike something or somebody with a heavy blow (*informal*) **2** *vt* **SMASH** to smash or strike something violently or damagingly (*informal*) **3** *vt* **MAKE DENT** to make a dent in something (*informal*) **4** *vi* **COLLIDE WITH** to crash into or collide with something (*informal*) **5** *vt* **CRITICIZE** to criticize somebody or something harshly (*informal*) **6** *vt* **BATTER** to beat somebody severely (*dated informal*) ■ *n* **1 HEAVY BLOW** a forceful blow (*informal*) **2 DENT** a dent (*informal*) **3 CELEBRATION** a party or celebration [Mid-17C. Probably an imitation of the sound of hitting.] ◇ **have a bash (at something)** to make an attempt to do something (*informal*)

bash out *vt* to produce something quickly or in large quantities, but without much care or attention (*informal*)

bash up *vt* to attack and injure somebody (*informal*)

bashful /báshf'l/ *adj* shy, self-conscious, or modest [15C. < shortened form of ABASH.] —**bashfully** *adv* —**bashfulness** *n*

bashing /báshing/ *n* (*slang; usually in combination*) **1 PHYSICAL ASSAULT** mugging or violence, especially when directed at a particular group of people **2 CRITICISM** hostile comment directed at a particular individual or group ○ *male-bashing* **3** *UK, ANZ, Can* **EXCESSIVE USE** the exposure of something to repetitive or prolonged use ○ *spud-bashing* ○ *an ear-bashing*

Bashkir /bash kéer/ (*plural* **-kirs** *or* **-kir**) *n* **1** somebody from east-central Russia who is a member of a Turkic-speaking Muslim people **2** a Turkic language spoken in an area west of the Ural Mountains in central Russia. Native speakers: 1 million. [Early 19C. Via Russian < Turkic *Başkurt*.] —**Bashkir** *adj*

Bashkortostan /bash káwrtə staan/ autonomous republic in central Russia, west of the Ural Mountains, bordering the republic of Tatarstan to the northwest and the republic of Udmurtia to the north. Capital: Ufa. Population: 4,055,300 (1994). Area: 143,600 sq. km/55,444 sq. mi.

basho /báshō/ (*plural* **-os**) *n* a sumo wrestling tournament [Late 20C. < Japanese.]

Basho /báshō/, **Bashō** (1644–94) Japanese poet. Pseudonym of **Matsuo Munefusa**

basi- *prefix* = **baso-**

basic /báyssik/ *adj* **1 MOST IMPORTANT** most important or essential ○ *a few basic guidelines* **2 ELEMENTARY** serving as a starting point or minimum **3 WITHOUT EXTRA** without anything extra ○ *a basic salary* **4 PLAIN** plain and utilitarian rather than luxurious or fancy (*informal*) **5 RELATING TO CHEMICAL BASE** containing, relating to, or being a chemical base **6 ALKALINE** having an alkaline reaction **7 CONTAINING HYDROXIDE OR OXIDE GROUPS** describes a salt that contains hydroxide or oxide anions **8 LOW IN SILICA** describes rock that contains 45–53 percent total silica by weight, e.g. basalt **9 USING A BASE IN MAKING STEEL** describes a process of making steel in which the furnace is lined with a base that combines with acidic impurities in the ore to produce basic slag ■ **basics** *npl* **MOST IMPORTANT THINGS** the most important or fundamental elements of something —**basicity** /bay síssiti/ *n*

⚡**BASIC** /báyssik/, **Basic** *n* a high-level computer programming language that uses common English terms and algebra [Acronym < *Beginners All-purpose Symbolic Instruction Code*]

basically /báyssikli/ *adv* **1** ⚠ **ESSENTIALLY** used to emphasize the most important aspect of something ○ *Basically, I'm not interested.* **2** ⚠ **IN GENERAL** generally or in most respects ○ *He's basically not a bad player.* **3 SIMPLY** in a simple way, using only essentials

USAGE Basically as a sentence adverb: This use, in which ***basically*** is reduced to adding emphasis (*Basically it's a waste of time.*) is common in informal conversation but should be avoided otherwise. So too should the meaning 'generally', as in *It is basically the case that fats can cause heart disease.*

Basic Curriculum *n* in schools in England and Wales, the National Curriculum plus religious education

Basic English *n* a simplified form of English intended as an introductory version of the language for non-native speakers and for use as an auxiliary international language

~~**basicly**~~ incorrect spelling of **basically**

basic rate *n* **1** the standard cost or rate of pay excluding any discounts or additions **2** the standard rate of income tax

basic slag *n* the phosphate-rich slag from making steel using a basic process. Use: fertilizer.

basic training *n* the initial training of a military recruit

basidiomycete /bə síddi ō mī séet/ *n* a fungus that produces spores in a specialized structure (**basidium**). Class: Basidiomycetes. [Late 19C. < modern Latin *Basidiomycetes* < *basidium* (see BASIDIUM) + Greek *mukētes* 'fungi'.] —**basidiomycetous** *adj*

basidiomycote /bə síddi ō mī́kōt/ *n* a fungus such as a mushroom, puffball, smut, or rust that produces its spores in a characteristic club-shaped cell (**basidium**). Phylum: Basidiomycota. —**basidiomycote** *adj*

basidiospore /bə síddi ō spawr/ *n* a spore produced by a basidiomycote fungus such as a mushroom, puffball, smut, or rust —**basidiosporous** /bə síddi ō spáwrəss/ *adj*

basidium /bə síddi əm/ (*plural* **-a** /-ə/) *n* a cell or organ found in certain fungi from which external sexual spores are produced [Mid-19C. < modern Latin, 'small base' < Greek *basis* 'step, base'.] —**basidial** *adj*

Basie /báyzi/, **Count** (1904–84) US composer and bandleader. Born **William Basie**

basify /báyssifī/ (**-fies, -fying, -fied**) *vt* **1** to change a chemical into a base **2** to make something alkaline —**basification** /báyssifi káysh'n/ *n*

basil /bázz'l/ *n* a herb with aromatic leaves, especially sweet basil. Use: seasoning. *Ocimum basilicum*. [15C. Via Old French *basile* < Latin *basilicum* < Greek *basilikon (phuton)* 'royal (herb)'.]

Basil /bázz'l/, **St** (329?–379 AD) Greek prelate and scholar. Known as **Basil the Great**

basilar /bássilər/ *adj* relating to or situated at the base of something, e.g. the skull [Mid-16C. < modern Latin *basilaris* < Latin *basis* (see BASIS).]

Basildon /bázz'ldən/ town in SE England. Population: 100,924 (1991).

basilica /bə zíllikə, -síllikə/ *n* **1 PRIVILEGED ROMAN CATHOLIC CHURCH** a Roman Catholic church or cathedral given ceremonial privileges by the Pope **2 ANCIENT ROMAN BUILDING** an ancient Roman building with a central nave, a columned aisle on each side, and typically a terminal semicircular apse **3 LARGE CHRISTIAN CHURCH** a Christian church building formed out of a Roman basilica or built to a similar design [Mid-16C. Via Latin, 'royal palace' < Greek *basilikē* < *basilikos* 'royal' < *basileus* 'king'.] —**basilican** *adj*

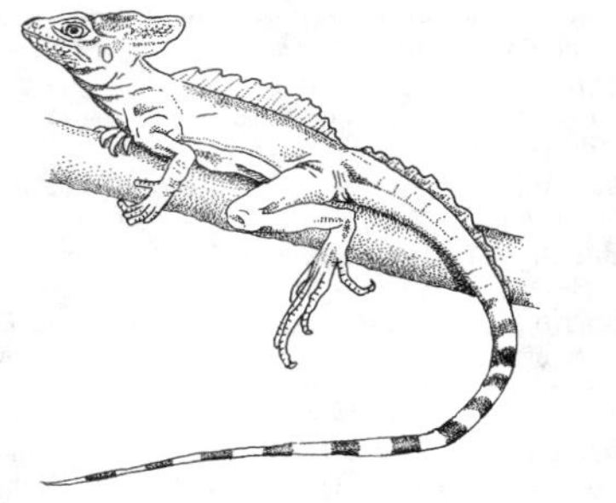

Basilisk

basilisk /bázzə lisk/ *n* **1** a legendary reptile whose look or breath was supposed to be fatal **2** a lizard, related to the iguana, that is able to run upright on its long hind legs. Native to: Central and South America. Genus: *Basiliscus*. [14C. Via Latin < Greek *basiliskos* 'minor king, kind of serpent' < *basileus* 'king'.]

basin /báyss'n/ *n* **1 OPEN CONTAINER FOR WASHING** an open metal, ceramic, or plastic container with sloping sides, typically used for holding water or washing **2 BOWL FOR PREPARING FOOD** a deep bowl, especially a round one, used for storing, mixing, or cooking food **3 BASIN CONTENTS** the contents of or amount contained in a basin **4 DOCK NEAR SEA** a dock built in a harbour or river that opens to the sea **5 DEPRESSION IN LAND FILLED WITH WATER** any depression in the Earth's surface that contains water **6 LAND DRAINING INTO RIVER OR LAKE** a broad area of land drained by a single river and its tributaries **7 BOWL-SHAPED DEPRESSION** a bowl-shaped depression on land or on the ocean floor into which sediments may be deposited **8 CIRCULAR FORMATION OF SLOPING ROCK STRATA** a large circular outcrop of rock in which strata dip inwards towards the centre [13C. Via Old French < medieval Latin *ba(s)cinus* < *bacca* 'water container'.] —**basinful** *n*

basinet /bássinət/ *n* a lightweight steel helmet, sometimes with a visor, worn in medieval times [14C. < Old French *bacinet* 'little basin', from its shape.]

Basingstoke /báyzing stōk/ town in south-central England. Population: 77,837 (1991).

Basingstoke and Deane /-déen/ local government district in south-central England. Population: 147,400 (1991).

basipetal /bay síppit'l/ *adj* developing from the top of a stem towards the base so that the oldest leaves or flowers are at the top —**basipetally** *adv*

basis /báyssiss/ (*plural* **-ses** /-seez/) *n* **1 FOUNDATION** something that acts as a support or foundation, especially of an idea or argument **2 STARTING POINT** the point from which something, e.g. a discussion, starts or is developed **3 WAY OF PROCEEDING** the basic method or system according to which something is done or organized ○ *work on a part-time basis* **4 MAIN COMPONENT** the main component or ingredient of something **5 SET OF VECTORS** in a vector space, the minimal set of vectors necessary to define all other vectors in the space [Late 16C. Via Latin < Greek, 'step, base' < *bainen* 'go'.]

USAGE *Basis* does a number of jobs that other words can do better or that need not be done at all. Expressions such as *on a continuing basis, on a daily basis,* and *on a regular basis* are sometimes only wordier ways of saying *continually, daily,* and *regularly.* By the same token, *providing expert resources on a global basis* means providing them everywhere. *We can help develop your basis for facilities design* means, essentially, *We can help you plan.* Careful writers should avoid the unnecessary use of ***basis***.

bask /baask/ *vi* **1** to lie in or expose yourself to enjoyable warmth, especially from the sun **2** to derive great satisfaction or pleasure from something [14C. Probably < Old Norse *bathask* 'bathe yourself' < Germanic.]

Baskerville /báskər vil/ *n* a typeface characterized by serifs [Early 19C. After John BASKERVILLE.]

Baskerville /báskər vil/, **John** (1706–75) British printer

basket /baáskit/ *n* **1 WOVEN CONTAINER** a container made of woven strips of material, often with a handle or handles **2 BASKET CONTENTS** the contents of or amount contained in a basket **3 CONTAINER** a container resembling a basket, e.g. the open gondola attached to a hot-air balloon **4 BASKETBALL NET** a mounted horizontal metal hoop with a hanging open net, through which a basketball player must throw the ball in order to score **5 GOAL** a goal scored in basketball **6 GROUP OF RELATED ITEMS** a group or collection of similar or related things or ideas **7 EUPHEMISTIC USE** used as a euphemism for 'bastard' (*informal insult*) [14C. < ?] —**basketful** *n*

basketball /baáskit bawl/ *n* **1** a game played by two teams of five players, who score points by throwing a ball through a basket mounted at the opponent's end of a rectangular court **2** a ball of the type used in the game of basketball

basket case *n* **1** an offensive term for somebody who is suffering from severe nervous strain (*insult*) **2** somebody who is completely incapacitated (*informal*)

basket chair *n* a deep chair made of wickerwork or cane

basket hilt *n* a sword hilt with a guard made of interwoven strips —**basket-hilted** *adj*

basket of currencies *n* a group of currencies of which the average value is used as a basis for comparison with another currency

basketry /baáskitri/ *n* **1** the art or craft of making baskets **2** baskets collectively

basket weave *n* a textile weave like the chequered pattern of a woven basket

basketwork /baáskit wurk/ *n* CRAFT = **basketry** *n.* 1

basking shark *n* a large plankton-eating shark measuring up to 13 m/43 ft that often floats on the surface of the sea. Native to: temperate waters. genus: *cetorhinus.*

Basle = **Basel**

basmati /baz maáti/ *n* a long-grained aromatic rice originally grown in N India and Pakistan [Mid-19C. < Hindi *bāsamatī* 'fragrant'.]

bas mitzvah /baass mítsvə/ *n* JUDAISM = **bat mitzvah**

baso- *prefix* **1** bottom, base ○ *basipetal* **2** chemical base ○ *basophil* [< Latin *basis* (see BASIS)]

basophil /báyssə fil/, **basophile** /-fīl/ *n* a white blood cell with granules that are readily stained by basic dyes, occurring in some blood diseases

basophilia /báyssə fílli ə/, **basiphilia** *n* **1** the property of microorganisms and white blood cells of being stained with basic dyes **2** an increase in the blood of the type of cells that stain with basic dyes, occurring in a variety of blood diseases

basophilic /báyssə fíllik/, **basophilous** /bə sóffələss/ *adj* describes cells or cell components that are readily stained by basic dyes

Basotho /bə sóo too/ *npl* a Sotho people who live in Lesotho in southern Africa [Mid-19C. < Sesotho.]

basque /bask, baask/ *n* **1** a woman's tight-fitting corset that covers the area from the breasts to the top of the thighs **2** a part of the bodice of a woman's jacket that extends below the waist [Mid-19C. < ?]

Basque /bask, baask/ *n* **1** a member of a people of unknown origin living in the W Pyrenees, in NW Spain and SW France **2** the language spoken by the Basques, having no known relationship with another language. Native speakers: 700,000. [Early 19C. Via French < Latin *Vasco*.] —**Basque** *adj*

Basque Country autonomous region of N Spain. Population: 2,130,783 (1995). Area: 7,261 sq. km/2,803 sq. mi. Spanish **País Vasco**. Basque **Euskadi**

Basra /bázzrə/ port in SE Iraq. Population: 406,296 (1987).

bas-relief /baá-/ *n* **1** a sculpture in which the design projects slightly from a flat background, but without any part being totally detached from the background. ◊ **high relief** **2** an example or piece of bas-relief sculpture [Early 17C. < BASSO-RELIEVO, altered after French.]

bass[1] /bayss/ *n* **1 LOWEST SINGING VOICE** a voice of the lowest range **2 LOWEST PITCHES** the lower half of all the pitches produced by a voice or a musical instrument **3 LOWEST MUSICAL PART** the lowest part in instrumental or vocal part music **4 LOWEST INSTRUMENT IN FAMILY** the instrument with the lowest range in a family of musical instruments **5 LOW FREQUENCY IN AUDIO REPRODUCTION** the low-frequency sound output from an electric amplifier **6 BASS CONTROL** a knob on a piece of audio equipment that controls low-frequency sound output ■ *adj* **1 DEEP IN TONE** deep or grave in tone **2 LOW IN PITCH** low in pitch **3 RELATING TO BASS** relating to a bass [15C. Via French *bas* < medieval Latin *bassus*, influenced by Italian *basso* (see BASSO).]

SPELLCHECK See ***base***.

---

bass[2] /bass/ (*plural* **bass** *or* **basses**) *n* a spiny-finned fish found in rivers, lakes, and seas that is caught for food. Families: Centrarchidae and Percichthyidae and Serranidae. [15C. Alteration of Old English *bærs, bears* < Germanic.]

bass[3] /bass/ *n* INDUST = **bast** *n.* 2 [Late 17C. Alteration of BAST.]

bass-baritone *n* a singing voice between baritone and bass, or somebody with that voice

bass clef *n* a symbol on a musical staff indicating that a note on the fourth line from the bottom represents the F a fifth below middle C

bass drum *n* a large drum that has a cylindrical body, two drumheads, and a low indefinite pitch

Bassein /ba sáyn/ city in S Myanmar. Population: 144,092 (1983).

basset *n* = **basset hound**

Basseterre /bass táir/ capital of St Kitts and Nevis, on the SW coast of St Kitts island. Population: 12,600 (1994).

basset horn /bássit-/ *n* an alto clarinet in F, used in classical music [Mid-19C. < German, translating French *cor de basset* < Italian *corno di bassetto*, literally 'cello-horn'.]

basset hound *n* a dog of a breed with short legs, long ears, and a short-haired, white, black, and tan coat, originally bred for hunting [Early 17C. < French, < *bas* 'low', from its short legs.]

bass guitar *n* a four-string guitar, usually electric, that has the same pitch and tuning as a double bass

bassinet /bássi nét/ *n* a baby's bed or pram in the shape of a basket, often with a hood over one end and commonly made of wood or wickerwork [Mid-19C. < French, 'little basin'.]

bassist /báyssist/ *n* a player of a bass guitar or a double bass

basso /bássō/ (*plural* **-sos** *or* **-si** /-see/) *n* a bass singer, especially of opera [Early 18C. Via Italian < medieval Latin *bassus* 'low'.]

basso continuo *n* = **continuo**

bassoon /bə sóon/ *n* a low-pitched double-reed instrument of the oboe family. Its wooden body is a long U-shaped tube, attached to the mouthpiece by means of a thin metal pipe. [Early 18C. Via French < Italian *bassone* 'large bass' < *basso* (see BASSO).] —**bassoonist** *n*

basso profundo /-prō fúndō/ (*plural* **basso profundos**) *n* a bass singer with an exceptionally low range [Mid-19C. < Italian, 'deep bass'.]

basso-relievo /bássō ri léevō/ (*plural* **basso-relievos**), **basso-rilievo** /-rillee áy vō/ (*plural* **basso-rilievos**) *n* SCULPTURE = **bas-relief** *n.* 1 [Mid-17C. < Italian *basso-rilievo* 'low relief'.]

Bass Rock /báss-/ islet in the Firth of Forth, Scotland

Bass Strait /báss-/ channel between mainland Australia and Tasmania, approximately 225 km/140 mi. wide

bass viol *n* **1** = **viola da gamba** **2** *US* = **double bass**

bast /bast/ *n* **1** PLANT SCI = **phloem** *n.* **2** a strong woody fibrous material obtained chiefly from the phloem of plants such as flax, hemp, and jute. Use: ropes, mats, textiles. US term **bast fiber** [Old English *bæst* < ?]

bastard /baástərd/ *n* **1 OFFENSIVE TERM** an offensive term for a disagreeable or obnoxious person (*slang*) **2 OFFENSIVE TERM** an offensive term for somebody born to unmarried parents **3 OFFENSIVE TERM** an offensive term for something that is extremely difficult, trying, or unpleasant (*slang*) **4 ABNORMAL THING** something that is abnormal, inferior, or of questionable or mixed origin (*sometimes offensive*) **5 PERSON** used to refer to somebody, especially a man, sometimes affectionately or humorously (*informal; sometimes offensive*) ■ *adj* **1 NOT GENUINE** not the real thing **2 OF INFERIOR OR MIXED ORIGIN** of an inferior, ill-conceived, or mixed origin **3 SIMILAR** describes plants and animals that are similar but not identical to, and usually slightly inferior to, a particular kind or species **4 UNUSUAL** unusual or irregular in shape, size, or appearance (*sometimes offensive*) [14C. Via Old French *bastart* < medieval Latin *bastardus*, probably < *bastum* 'pack saddle', the idea probably being of a child produced from a relationship with a traveller.] —**bastardly** *adj*

bastardise *vt* = **bastardize**

bastardize /baástər dīz/ (**-izes, -izing, -ized**), **bastardise** (**-ises, -ising, -ised**) *vt* **1** to lower the value or quality of something **2** to prove or declare somebody to be illegitimate (*archaic*) —**bastardization** /baástər dī záysh'n/ *n*

bastard title *n* PUBL = **half title**

bastard wing *n* the part of a bird's wing that corresponds to a thumb and contains a few short feathers

bastardy /baástərdi/ *n* the state of being a child with unmarried parents (*archaic; sometimes offensive*)

baste[1] /bayst/ (**bastes, basting, basted**) *vt* to moisten meat or fish at intervals during cooking with a liquid such as melted fat or cooking juices [14C. Via Old French *bastir* < Germanic, 'join together with bast'.]

baste[2] /bayst/ (**bastes, basting, basted**) *vt* to beat somebody severely [15C. < ?]

baste[3] /bayst/ (**bastes, basting, basted**) *vt* **1** to sew fabric with long loose stitches in order to hold pieces of material together temporarily **2** to sew fabric with rows of long diagonal stitches [Mid-16C. < ?]

bast fiber *n US* INDUST = **bast** *n.* 2

basti /bústi/ *n S Asia* a slum [Late 19C. < Hindi *bastī*.]

Bastia /ba stée ə/ capital of Haute-Corse Department, NE Corsica, France. Population: 37,884 (1999).

Bastille /ba stéel/ *n* a prison in Paris that was stormed and destroyed by a mob at the beginning of the French Revolution on 14 July, 1789

bastinado /básti náydō/ *n* (*plural* **-does**) **1 PUNISHMENT BY BEATING FEET** a punishment or torture in which the soles of the victim's feet are beaten with a stick **2 THRASHING** a beating or a blow with a club **3 CLUB** a stick or club ■ *vt* (**-does, -doing, -doed**) **BEAT WITH STICK** to beat somebody with a stick, especially on the soles of the feet [Late 16C. < Spanish *bastonada* < *bastón* 'cudgel'.]

basting /báysting/ *n* loose or temporary stitches

bastion /básti ən/ *n* **1 PROJECTING PART** a projecting part of a wall, rampart, or other fortification **2 FORTIFICATION** a fortified place **3 STRONG SUPPORTER** somebody or something regarded as providing strong defence or support, especially for a belief or cause [Mid-16C. Via French < Italian *bastione* < *bastire* 'build'.]

bastnaesite /bástnə sīt/, **bastnasite** *n* a rare yellow to reddish-brown fluorocarbonate mineral containing lanthanum and cerium. Use: source of rare-earth elements. [Late 19C. After *Bastnäs* in Sweden.]

bat[1] /bat/ *n* **1 CLUB USED IN SPORTS** a club used to strike the ball in sports such as cricket, table tennis, and baseball, usually wooden but sometimes made of metal or plastic **2 DEVICE FOR GUIDING AIRCRAFT** either of a pair of hand-held devices that look like table-tennis bats and are used by somebody on the ground to guide taxiing or landing aircraft **3 HEAVY STICK OR CLUB** a heavy stick or wooden club **4 BLOW FROM STICK** a blow from a stout stick or club **5 CRICKET BATSMAN** a batsman or batswoman in cricket **6 PACE** rate, pace, or speed (*informal*) ■ *v* (**bats, batting, batted**) **1** *vt* **STRIKE WITH BAT** to strike somebody or something with a bat **2** *vi* **HAVE TURN AT BATTING** to take a turn at batting in sports such as cricket or baseball [Old English *batt* < ?] ◇ **off your own bat** on your own initiative and without instructions or help from anyone (*informal*)

bat[2] /bat/ *n* a small nocturnal flying mammal with leathery wings stretching from the forelimbs to the rear legs and tail. Order: Chiroptera. [Late 16C. Alteration of *backe* < N Germanic.] ◇ **have bats in the belfry** to be slightly but harmlessly eccentric (*informal*)

bat[3] /bat/ (**bats, batting, batted**) *vt* to wink or flutter something, especially the eyes or eyelids [Early 19C. Variant of BATE[1].]

ϟ **bat.** *abbr* **1** batch[1] **2** battalion

Bataan /bə tán, -taán/ peninsula of Luzon Island in the Philippines. Area: 1,400 sq. km/530 sq. mi.

Batak /báttək/ *n* a group of Austronesian languages spoken in Sumatra, Indonesia. Native speakers: 3 million. [Early 19C. < Batak.] —**Batak** *adj*

~~**batallion**~~ incorrect spelling of **battalion**

Batangas /bə táng gass/ port on Luzon Island in the Philippines. Population: 185,000 (1990).

Batavia /bə táyvi ə/ former name for **Jakarta**

ϟ **batch**[1] /bach/ *n* **1 QUANTITY REGARDED AS GROUP** a quantity of people or things treated or regarded as a group, especially when subdivided from a larger group **2 AMOUNT BAKED** the amount of something baked at one time or produced at one baking **3 AMOUNT FOR ONE OPERATION** the amount of material prepared or needed for, or produced in, one operation **4 PROGRAMS PROCESSED TOGETHER** a set of programs or jobs processed on a computer at one time ■ *vt* **PROCESS ITEMS AS BATCH** to process or assemble items as a batch or in batches [15C. < assumed Old English *bæcce* 'something baked' < *bacan* (see BAKE).]

batch[2] *vi US, ANZ* = **bach**[1] *v.*

bat chayil /baat khaáyil/, **bat hayill** *n* JUDAISM = **bat mitzvah** *n.* 2 [Late 20C. < Hebrew, 'daughter of valour'.]

~~**batchelor**~~ incorrect spelling of **bachelor**

ϟ**batch file** *n* a computer file containing a series of commands to be processed by a computer, as if they were entered from the keyboard consecutively

ϟ**batch processing** *n* a mode of computer operation in which programs are executed without the user being able to influence processing while it is in progress

bate[1] /bayt/ (**bates, bating, bated**), **bait** (**baits, baiting, baited**) *vi* to beat the wings wildly or impatiently in an attempt to fly off something, e.g. a perch or a falconer's fist, when still attached by a leash (*refers to a falcon or other hunting bird*) [13C. < Old French *batre* (see BATTER[1]).]

bate[2] /bayt/ *n* a fit of anger (*dated informal*)

bat-eared fox *n* a yellowish-grey fox with large ears. Native to: eastern and southern Africa. *Otocyon megalotis.*

bated past participle of **bate**

Batei Din *n* plural of **Beth Din**

bateleur /bátta lur/, **bateleur eagle** *n* a crested eagle that has a short tail and long broad wings and feeds mainly on carrion. Native to: Africa. *Terathopius ecaudatus.* [Mid-19C. < French, 'juggler, rogue'.]

Bates /bayts/, **Daisy May** (1863–1951) Irish-born Australian journalist and anthropologist. Born **Daisy May O'Dwyer**

Bates, H.W. (1825–92) British naturalist. Full name **Henry Walter Bates**

Batesian mimicry /báytsi ən-/ *n* mimicry in which a harmless species is protected from predators by its resemblance to a species that is harmful or unpalatable to them [Late 19C. After H. W. BATES.]

batfish /bátfish/ (*plural* **-fish** *or* **-fishes**) *n* a marine angler fish that has a flattened head and body and waddles on the sea bottom using pectoral and pelvic fins. Family: Ogcocephalidae.

bath /baath/ *n* (*plural* **baths** /baathz/) **1 LARGE CONTAINER FOR WASHING BODY IN** a large container, usually oblong in shape and made of plastic or enamelled metal, that you sit in to wash your body. US term **bathtub 2 IMMERSION OF BODY** the act of immersing all or part of the body in a bath in order to wash it **3 BODY TREATMENT** the act of immersing all or part of the body in an enveloping substance, e.g. mud, usually for therapeutic reasons **4 WATER IN BATH** water used for bathing **5 LIQUID** a liquid, or a liquid and its container, in which something is immersed ■ **baths** *npl* **1 BATHHOUSE** a building with facilities for people to have baths **2 SWIMMING POOL** a swimming pool for public use ■ *vi* **WASH IN BATH** to wash yourself or somebody else in a bath. US term **bathe** *v.* 6 [Old English *bæþ* < Germanic] ◇ **take a bath** to suffer a severe financial setback (*slang*)

USAGE bath or **bathe**? In US English, ***bath*** is normally used only as a noun (*The bath was deep.*) and ***bathe*** is used only as a verb (*She bathed daily.*). However in many other varieties of English, both words can be used as noun or verb, with ***bath*** referring to washing and ***bathe*** to swimming. In most varieties of English, ***bathe*** is also used of immersing things in water to clean or moisten them: *The nurse bathed the wound.*

Bath /baath/ city in SW England, a spa since Roman times. Population: 84,100 (1994 estimate).

bat hayill *n* JUDAISM = **bat chayil**

Bath bun *n* a sweet sticky spiced bun containing dried fruit

bath chair *n* an old-fashioned type of wheelchair, often with a hood [< After BATH]

bath cube *n* a cube of soluble material used to perfume and soften bathwater

bathe /bayth/ *v* (**bathes, bathing, bathed**) **1** *vi* **SWIM OR PADDLE IN OPEN WATER** to swim or paddle, especially for pleasure, in an area of open water such as the sea or a river **2** *vt* **CLEANSE WOUND** to apply water or another liquid to a wound or part of the body in order to cleanse, heal, or soothe it **3** *vt* **DIP SOMETHING IN LIQUID** to immerse something in liquid **4** *vt* **COVER** to cover or surround something with light, colour, or a substance ○ *bathed in a golden glow* **5** *vt* **FLOW ALONG EDGE OF** to flow along the edge of something **6** *vti US* HOUSEHOLD = **bath** *v.* ■ *n* **ACT OF SWIMMING OR BATHING** an act of swimming or bathing, especially in an area of open water (*dated*) [Old English *baþian* < Germanic]

USAGE See ***bath.***

bather /báythər/ *n* somebody who is swimming

bathers /báytharz/ *npl Aus* a swimming costume (*informal*)

bathetic /bə théttik/ *adj* **1** showing or characterized by bathos **2** trite, commonplace, or absurdly sentimental [Late 18C. < BATHOS, after *pathos, pathetic.*] —**bathetically** *adv*

bathhouse /baáth howss/ (*plural* **-houses** /-howziz/) *n* a building equipped with baths, especially for public use

bathing costume *n* a swimming costume (*dated*)

bathing machine *n* in the 18th and 19th centuries, a small hut on wheels that bathers changed in

bathing suit *n US* CLOTHES = **swimsuit**

bathing waters *npl* bodies of seawater or fresh water that are used for public bathing and to which particular water quality standards apply under EU and UK law

bath mitzvah *n* JUDAISM = **bat mitzvah**

batho- deep, depth ○ *bathometer* [< Greek *bathos* 'depth']

bathochromic /báthə krṓmik/ *adj* describes a shift towards the red end in a compound's absorption spectrum

batholith /báthəlith/, **batholite** /-līt/ *n* a large mass of igneous rock, composed of granite or gabbro, formed deep in the Earth's crust and intruded in a molten state —**batholithic** /báthə líthik/ *adj*

Bath Oliver *n* a thin dry unsweetened biscuit, usually eaten with cheese [After its creator, Dr William *Oliver* (1695–1764) of BATH]

bathometer /bə thómmitər/ *n* an instrument for measuring the depth of a body of water —**bathometric** /báthə méttrik/ *adj* —**bathometry** *n*

bathophilous /bə thóffiləss/ *adj* describes organisms that are adapted to living in very deep water

bathos /báy thoss/ *n* **1** in writing or speech, a sudden descent in style or manner from the elevated or sublime to the commonplace, producing a ludicrous effect **2** insincere and excessively sentimental pathos [Early 18C. < Greek, 'depth' < *bathus* 'deep'.]

bathrobe /baáth rōb/ *n* **1** a loose-fitting garment with a belt usually made of towelling, worn before or after bathing **2** *US* = **dressing gown**

bathroom /baáth room, -ro͝om/ *n* **1** a room containing a bath or shower and, usually, a washbasin and a toilet **2** a room with a toilet

bathroom scales *npl* a step-on device for people to weigh themselves on at home, usually kept in a bathroom

bath salts *npl* soluble mineral salts used to perfume and soften bathwater

Bathsheba /bath sheébə, báthshibə/ in the Bible, the wife of Uriah and later of David, by whom she became the mother of Solomon (II Samuel 11–12)

Bath stone *n* a white limestone used for building, quarried near Bath

bathtub /baáth tub/ *n* HOUSEHOLD = **bath** *n.* 1

Bathurst[1] /báth urst/ *n* former name for **Banjul**

Bathurst[2] /báth urst/ **1** resort city in NE New Brunswick, Canada. Population: 13,815 (1996). **2** city in central New South Wales, Australia. Population: 26,029 (1996).

Bathurst Island island off the coast of N Northern Territory, Australia. Population: 1,000 (1996). Area: 2,600 sq. km/1,000 sq. mi.

bathwater /baáth wawtər/ *n* the water used for a bath

bathy- deep, depth ○ *bathysphere* [< Greek *bathus* 'deep']

bathyal /báthi əl/ *adj* relating to or living in ocean depths between 200 and 2,000 m/650 and 6,550 ft

bathymetry /bə thímmətri/ *n* **1** the measurement of the depth of large bodies of water, e.g. lakes, oceans, and seas **2** the data obtained by the use of bathymetry —**bathymetric** /báthi méttrik/ *adj* —**bathymetrically** *adv*

bathypelagic /báthipə lájjik/ *adj* relating to or living in the depths of the ocean, especially between 600 and 3,600 m/2,000 and 12,000 ft

bathyscaphe /báthi skayf/, **bathyscaph** *n* a deep-sea research vessel that has a large flotation hull and an observation cabin attached to its underside, and can dive to depths over 10,000 m/6.2 mi [Mid-20C. < BATHY- + Greek *skaphos* 'ship'.]

bathysphere /báthi sfeer/ *n* a strong steel diving sphere that can be lowered by cable to depths of 900 m/3,000 ft

batik /báttik, bə teék/, **battik** /báttik/ *n* **1** a method of hand-printing a fabric by covering with removable wax the parts that will not be dyed **2** fabric that has been hand-dyed by the batik method [Late 19C. < Javanese, 'painted'.]

Batista y Zaldívar /ba teéstə ee zal deé vaar/, **Fulgencio** (1901–73) Cuban soldier and head of state (1940–44, 1952–59)

batiste /ba teést/ *n* a fine soft plain-woven cotton or linen fabric. Use: clothing. [Early 19C. < French.]

Batley /báttli/ town in N England. Population: 48,030 (1991).

Batlle y Ordóñez /bátyay ee awr thón yess/, **José** (1856–1929) Uruguayan statesman

batman /bátmən/ (*plural* **-men** /-mən/) *n* a British military officer's personal servant [Mid-18C. Via Old French < medieval Latin *bastum* 'pack saddle'.]

Batman /bát man/, **John** (1801–39) Australian pioneer

bat mitzvah /baat mítsvə/, **bath mitzvah, bas mitzvah** /baass-/ *n* **1** the ritual that marks the 13th birthday of a Jewish girl, after which she takes full responsibility for her moral and spiritual conduct **2** a Jewish girl who has reached the age of 13, the age of religious responsibility [< Hebrew *bat miṣwāh* 'daughter of commandment']

BATNEEC /bát neek/ *n* a principle applied to the control of emissions into the air, land, and water from polluting processes, minimizing pollution without requiring technology or methods that are not yet available or unreasonably expensive. Full form **best available technology not entailing excessive cost**

baton /bátton, bátt'n/ *n* **1 CONDUCTING STICK** a short thin stick used by a conductor to direct musical performers **2 POLICE STICK** a short thick stick used as a weapon, especially by police ○ *a side-handled baton* **3 RELAY TEAM STICK** a short stick or hollow cylinder passed by each runner in a relay team to the next runner **4 OFFICIAL STAFF** a staff carried by an official, e.g. a field marshal, as a symbol of office **5 DRUM MAJOR'S STICK** a long stick with a knob at one or both ends, carried and twirled by a drum major or majorette **6 DIAGONAL LINE ON COAT OF ARMS** a shortened narrow diagonal line on a coat of arms, especially one signifying bastardy [Early 16C. Via French < late Latin *bastum* 'stick'.]

baton charge *n* a charge made by people armed with batons, especially police officers

Baton Rouge /bátt'n ro͞ozh/ capital of Louisiana, in the SE of the state. Population: 211,551 (1998 estimate).

baton round *n* a plastic or rubber bullet used in riot control

batrachian /bə tráyki ən/ *n* a tailless amphibian, e.g. a frog or toad [Mid-19C. < modern Latin *Batrachia*, < Greek *batrakhos* 'frog'.] —**batrachian** *adj*

bats /bats/ *adj* harmlessly eccentric (*informal*) [Early 20C. < *have bats in the belfry.*]

batsman /bátsmən/ (*plural* **-men** /-mən/) *n* **1 PLAYER WHO BATS OR IS BATTING** a cricket or baseball player who bats or is batting **2 PLAYER WHO SPECIALIZES IN BATTING** a cricket player who specializes in batting, rather than bowling or fielding **3 GROUND OFFICIAL WHO GUIDES AIRCRAFT** a ground official who uses a pair of bats to guide landing and taxiing aircraft

batswoman /báts wo͝omən/ (*plural* **-en** /-wimin/) *n* a woman cricketer who bats or is batting

batt /bat/ *n* TEXTILES = **batting**[2] [Late 19C. Shortening.]

battalion /bə tályən/ *n* **1 LARGE BODY OF SOLDIERS** a large body of soldiers organized to act together **2 MILITARY UNIT** a military unit typically consisting of a headquarters and three or more companies, batteries, or other subunits of similar size **3 LARGE NUMBER** a large group or number (*often plural*) [Late 16C. Via French < Italian *bataglione* 'great battle' < late Latin *bat(t)uere* 'to beat'.]

~~battallion~~ incorrect spelling of **battalion**

battels /bátt'lz/ *npl* at Oxford University, the bill or account of a member of a college for accommodation, food, and other expenses [Late 16C. < ?]

battement /bát maaN/ *n* a ballet movement in which one leg is extended, either once or repeatedly, to the front, side, or back, and then beaten against the supporting foot [Mid-19C. < French, 'beating'.]

batten /bátt'n/ *n* **1 BUILDING SUPPORT** a thin strip of wood used in building, e.g. to seal or reinforce a joint or to support laths, slates, or tiles **2 NARROW PIECE OF WOOD** a long narrow piece of wood used especially for flooring **3 STRIP FOR KEEPING SAILS IN SHAPE** a thin flexible strip of wood or plastic inserted in pockets at the edge of a sail to keep it taut and flat **4 SLAT FOR FASTENING DOWN TARPAULIN** a narrow metal or wooden slat used to fasten down the edges of a tarpaulin covering a ship's raised hatch in poor weather **5 LIGHTS IN THEATRE** a row of lights in a theatre, or the strip or bar that holds it ■ *vt* **PROVIDE WITH BATTENS** to provide, strengthen, or secure something with battens [Late 16C. < Old Norse *batna* 'improve, get better' < Germanic.]

Batten /bátt'n/, **Jean** (1909–82) New Zealand aviator

Battenberg /bátt'n burg/ *n* an oblong cake coated with marzipan and made of squares of yellow and pink sponge, so that a slice of it has two yellow and two pink squares [Early 20C. After Prince Louis of *Battenberg* (1820–93).]

batter[1] /báttər/ *vt* **1 HIT REPEATEDLY** to hit or beat something repeatedly using heavy blows in order to break, bruise, or damage it **2 SUBJECT TO ATTACK** to subject somebody to persistent attack or violence **3 DAMAGE BY HEAVY BLOWS OR WEAR** to damage or injure something by hard blows or heavy wear (*often passive*) ■ *n* **1 DAMAGED TYPE** a damaged or worn printing type or plate **2 FAULTY IMPRESSION** a defective impression produced by a faulty printing plate [14C. Via Old French *batre* < late Latin *bat(t)uere* 'to beat'.] —**battered** *adj* —**batterer** *n*

batter[2] /báttər/ *n* a liquid mixture of flour, milk, and eggs used in making cakes and pancakes, and for coating foods before frying ■ *vt* to cover food with batter before frying [14C. < Old French *bateüre* 'act of beating' < *batre* (see BATTER[1]); from the idea of beating the mixture.]

batter[3] /báttər/ *vt* to build something, e.g. a wall or similar structure, in a way that forms an upwardly receding slope ■ *n* a receding upwards slope of the outer face of a wall, hedge, or similar structure [Mid-16C. < ?]

batter[4] /báttər/ *n* a player who bats, especially in baseball

batterie /báttəri, ba trée/ *n* a ballet movement in which the dancer beats the feet or calves together during a leap [Early 18C. < French, 'battery'.]

battering ram *n* **1** a large heavy beam used in ancient times to break down the walls and doors of a fortification under siege **2** a heavy metal bar used by police officers and firefighters to break down doors

battery /báttəri/ (*plural* **-ies**) *n* **1 POWER SOURCE** a number of connected electric cells that produce a direct current through the conversion of chemical energy into electrical energy **2 ACT OF BATTERING** the act of battering, beating, or pounding something **3 UNLAWFUL USE OF FORCE** the unlawful use of any physical force on another person, including beating or offensive touching without the person's consent **4 GROUPING OF ARTILLERY** a grouping of similar artillery pieces, e.g. guns or missile launchers, that function as a single tactical unit **5 ARMY ARTILLERY UNIT** an army artillery unit corresponding to a company in an infantry regiment **6 GUN EMPLACEMENT** a prepared position for artillery **7 SYSTEM OF CAGES FOR REARING ANIMALS** a series of cages used for the intensive rearing of livestock, especially poultry **8 GROUPING OF SIMILAR THINGS USED TOGETHER** an array or grouping of similar things intended to be used together **9 SIMILAR THINGS TOGETHER** a cluster of similar things or ideas taken, used, or considered together **10 PERCUSSION SECTION** the percussion section of an orchestra [Mid-16C. < Old French *baterie* < *batre* (see BATTER[1]).]

battery charger *n* a device for restoring power to electrical batteries

battik *n* CRAFT, TEXTILES = **batik**

batting[1] /bátting/ *n* the action or ability of a player or team that hits with a bat, especially in cricket or baseball

batting[2] /bátting/ *n* bulky material made from fabric or other fibres. Use: padding, stuffing. [Early 19C. < BAT[1], from the beating out of impurities from cotton.]

batting average *n* **1** *US* a measure of a baseball batter's performance, calculated by dividing the total of base hits gained in a given period by the number of times at bat **2** a measure of a cricket batsman's performance, calculated by dividing the total number of runs scored in a given period by the number of innings or matches played

batting crease *n* CRICKET = **popping crease**

battle /bátt'l/ *n* **1 ARMED FIGHT** a large-scale fight between armed forces involving combat between armies, warships, or aircraft **2 STRUGGLE** a drawn-out conflict between adversaries ○ *the battle against malaria* ■ *v* (**-tles, -tling, -tled**) **1** *vi* **FIGHT** to fight in a battle **2** *vi US, Can* **STRIVE** to strive or contend in order to overcome or achieve something **3** *vt* **STRUGGLE AGAINST SOMEBODY OR SOMETHING** to struggle against or contend with somebody or something, in or as if in a battle [13C. Via French *bataille* < late Latin *battualia* 'military or gladiatorial exercises' < *bat(t)uere* 'to beat'.] ◇ **be half the battle** to be an important first part of a difficult task ○ *Shipping the books on time is only half the battle; we have to sell them too.* ◇ **do battle (with somebody** *or* **something)** to fight or struggle against somebody or something ◇ **fight a losing battle** to try hard with no prospect of success

SYNONYMS See *fight*.

USAGE The transitive use of ***battle*** (with a direct object, instead of *battle against* or *battle with*, as in *The people of South Carolina have been battling a hurricane*) is a feature of US usage that has begun to enter other varieties of English also. This is partly a revival of an older use that died out in the 19th century.

Battle /bátt'l/ town in SE England, the site of the Battle of Hastings in 1066. Population: 5,235 (1991).

Battle, Kathleen (*b.* 1948) US soprano

battleaxe /bátt'l aks/ *n* **1** a large heavy broad-headed axe used as a weapon **2** an offensive term for a woman who is considered domineering and fearsome (*insult*)

battle cruiser *n* a heavily armed warship but with lighter armour, fewer guns, greater manoeuvrability, and a faster speed than a battleship

battle cry *n* **1** a rallying or encouraging shout that soldiers make when going into battle **2** a slogan used by supporters of a cause to rally fellow supporters

battledore /bátt'l dawr/ *n* **1 EARLY RACKET GAME** an early racket game played by two people with flat wooden rackets and a shuttlecock **2 LIGHT RACKET USED IN BATTLEDORE** a light racket, smaller than a tennis racket, used for hitting the shuttlecock in battledore **3 WOODEN BAT** a wooden bat formerly used to beat clothes when washing them [15C. Probably < Provençal *batedor* 'beater' < *battre* 'to beat' < late Latin *bat(t)uere*.]

battledress /bátt'l dress/ *n* the ordinary uniform worn by a soldier

battle fatigue *n* MIL, MED = **combat fatigue**

battlefield /bátt'l feeld/ *n* **1** the place where a battle is fought **2** an area of conflict or contention

battlefront /bátt'l frunt/ *n* an area or sector in which combat between armed forces takes place

battleground *n* MIL = **battlefield** *n.* 1

battle line *n* a position along which a battle takes place

battlement /bátt'l mənt/ *n* a defensive or decorative parapet with indentations [14C. < French *bateiller* 'fortify'.]

battlements /bátt'l mənts/ *npl* a series of indentations forming a defensive or decorative parapet

Battle of Britain *n* an aerial battle fought in World War II in 1940 between the German Luftwaffe, which carried out extensive bombing in Britain, and the Royal Air Force, which offered successful resistance

battle plan *n* **1** a strategy for fighting a battle **2** a strategy for any operation or contest

battler /bátt'lər/ *n* a courageous or indomitable fighter

battle royal (*plural* **battles royal** *or* **battle royals**) *n* **1** a battle involving many combatants, especially a fight to the finish **2** a passionate conflict, especially one that unfolds in public

battleship /bátt'l ship/ *n* the largest type of warship that carries the heaviest armour

battleship grey *adj* of a medium grey colour tinged with blue —**battleship grey** *n*

battle stations *npl US* MIL = **action stations** *npl.* ■ *interj US* **1** MIL = **action stations** *interj.* 1 **2** = **action stations** *interj.* 2 (*informal*)

battue /ba tóo/ *n* **1 DRIVING OF GAME IN HUNT** the beating of woodland or cover in order to drive game towards hunters **2 HUNT USING BATTUE** a hunt in which battue is used **3 SLAUGHTER** a wholesale massacre or indiscriminate slaughter [Early 19C. < French, past participle of *battre* (see BATTER[1]).]

batty /bátti/ (**-tier, -tiest**) *adj* slightly eccentric (*informal*) [Early 20C. < *have bats in the belfry*.] —**battiness** *n*

Batumi /baa tóomi/, **Batum** /-tóom/ port in SW Georgia on the Black Sea. Population: 137,000 (1990 estimate).

batwing sleeve /bátwing-/ *n* a sleeve that is wide at the armhole and tight at the wrist

bauble /báwb'l/ *n* something that is small and decorative but of little real value [14C. < Old French, 'plaything'.]

baud /bawd/ *n* a unit of data transmission speed, equal to one unit element per second [Mid-20C. After J. M. E. *Baudot* (1845–1903), French engineer.]

Baudelaire /bṓd lair/, **Charles** (1821–67) French poet and critic

Baudouin I /bṓ dwaN/ (1930–93) king of the Belgians (1951–93)

Bauhaus /bów howss/ *n* an influential German school of architecture and design, founded in 1919 by Walter Gropius [Early 20C. < German, < *Bau* 'building' + *Haus* 'house'.]

baulk /bawk, bawlk/, **balk** *v* **1** *vi* **STOP SHORT** to stop suddenly and refuse to go on, especially when faced with an obstacle ○ *The horse baulked and refused the jump.* **2** *vi* **TURN AWAY** to hesitate or be unwilling to do something, usually because of a natural revulsion or moral scruples ○ *I baulked at getting down on my hands and knees to wipe the floor.* **3** *vti* **REFUSE TO TACKLE** to refuse to tackle something that presents a difficulty **4** *vt* **FOIL** to prevent somebody from carrying out a plan or intention (*often passive*) ○ *acted like a lion baulked of its prey* **5** *vi* **MAKE ILLEGAL PITCHING MOTION** to make an illegal motion in baseball, by pretending to pitch but not actually pitching ■ *n* **1 LARGE PIECE OF WOOD** a large squared wooden beam **2 WOODEN BEAM IN HOUSE ROOF** a wooden tie beam in the roof of a house **3 UNPLOUGHED RIDGE** a ridge of land left unploughed to serve as a boundary or to counter erosion **4 OBSTACLE** something that hinders or frustrates ○ *a baulk to further progress in the peace negotiations* **5 ILLEGAL PITCHING MOVE** an illegal motion in baseball in which the pitcher pretends to throw the ball towards the plate or to a base but does not release it **6** *US* **AREA BEHIND BAULK LINE** the area between the baulk line and the bottom cushion on a billiard table, or in baulk-line billiards between any baulk line and the cushion **7 BILLIARDS SHOT** a shot from behind the baulk line on a billiards table [< Old English *balca* 'ridge' and Old Norse *bálkr* 'beam, bar' < Indo-European, 'beam'] —**balker** *n*

baulk line, baukline, baukline billiards *n* **1 LINE ON BILLIARD TABLE** a straight line parallel to the end of a billiard table, from behind which opening shots with the cue ball are made **2 DIVIDING LINE ON BILLIARD TABLE** one of four lines parallel to the edges of a billiard table that divide it into the central area and eight smaller compartments that are used in a particular variety of billiards **3 VARIETY OF BILLIARDS** the variety of billiards in which baulk lines are used —**baulk-line** *adj*

baulky /báwki, báwlki/ *adj* = **balky**

Baumé scale /bō máy-, bṓ may-/ *n* a scale for calibrating hydrometers that are used to ascertain the relative density of liquids [Mid-19C. After Antoine *Baumé* (1728–1804), French chemist.]

Baur /bów ər/, **Ferdinand Christian** (1792–1860) German theologian

Bausch /bowsh/, **Pina** (*b.* 1940) German dancer and choreographer

bauxite /báwk sīt/ *n* a rock containing aluminium hydroxides that is the principal ore of aluminium [Mid-19C. After the S French village of Les *Baux*.]

Bavaria /bə váiri ə/ state in SE Germany. Capital: Munich. Population: 11,922,000 (1994). Area: 70,548 sq. km/27,239 sq. mi.

bavarois /bávvər waá/ (*plural* **-rois**) *n* a dessert of flavoured rich set custard, eaten cold [Mid-19C. < French, 'Bavarian'.]

bawbee /baw beé, báw bee/ *n Scotland* a former Scottish silver coin ■ **bawbees** *npl Scotland* money, especially scarce or hard-earned money (*informal*) [Mid-16C. < *Sillebawby*, an estate whose owner, Alexander Orok, was Scottish mintmaster.]

bawd /bawd/ *n* a woman who runs a brothel [14C. Probably < Old French *baude* 'bold, lively' < Germanic.]

bawdy /báwdi/ (**-ier, -iest**) *adj* ribald in a frank, humorous, and often crude way —**bawdily** *adv* —**bawdiness** *n*

bawdyhouse /báwdi howss/ (*plural* **-houses** /-howziz/) *n* a house of prostitution (*archaic*)

bawl /báwl/ *vti* **1 SHOUT** to shout something in a loud and usually aggressive voice **2 CRY NOISILY** to cry very loudly and energetically (*informal*) ■ *n* **LOUD SHOUT** a loud cry or shout [15C. < ?] —**bawler** *n*

bawl out *vt* to tell somebody off loudly and angrily (*informal*)

bawneen *n Ireland* = **báinín**

Baxter /bákstər/, **James K.** (1926–72) New Zealand poet

bay[1] /bay/ *n* **1** an area of sea enclosed by a wide inward-curving stretch of coastline **2** a lowland area with curving hills partly surrounding it [14C. Via French *baie* < Spanish *bahía*.]

bay[2] /bay/ *n* **1 SPECIAL AREA OR COMPARTMENT** an area, e.g. in a building, bus station, or aircraft, that is divided off and used for a particular purpose **2 SPACE BETWEEN TWO PILLARS** a section of a wall or building between two vertical structures such as pillars or buttresses **3 RECESS** a recess or alcove in a wall **4** ARCHIT = **bay window** *n.* [14C. < French *baie* 'opening' < *bayer* 'gape, stand open' < assumed Vulgar Latin *batare* 'yawn, gape'.]

bay[3] /bay/ *n* **1** a small evergreen Mediterranean tree of the laurel family with stiff dark green aromatic leaves. Use: dried as a seasoning. *Laurus nobilis.* **2** PLANTS = **laurel** *n.* **2** ■ **bays** *npl* a wreath woven out of laurel leaves, classically presented to poets and victors, or the honour conferred by this (*literary*) [14C. Via Old French *baie* < Latin *baca* 'berry'.]

bay[4] /bay/ *n* **1** an animal with a reddish-brown coat, especially a horse **2** a reddish-brown colour [14C. Via Old French *bai* < Latin *badius* 'chestnut-coloured'.] —**bay** *adj*

bay[5] /bay/ *v* **1** *vi* **HOWL** to make the howling sound of a hunting dog on the trail of an animal **2** *vi* **MAKE LOUD OUTCRY FOR** to call noisily and aggressively for something bad to happen to somebody ○ *an outraged public baying for blood* **3** *vt* **CORNER HUNTED ANIMAL** to corner or exhaust a hunted animal so that it must turn and face its hunters ■ *n* **POSITION OF NO ESCAPE** the position in which a hunted animal or a person being pursued has to face the hunters or pursuers [13C. Via Old French *(a)baier* < assumed Vulgar Latin *abbaiare*; an imitation of the sound.] ◇ **keep somebody** *or* **something at bay** to keep somebody or something unpleasant at a distance to avoid difficulty or harm

bayadere /bī ə deér/ *n* fabric with horizontal stripes of bold contrasting colours [Mid-19C. Via French < Portuguese *bailladeira* 'woman dancer' < *bailar* 'to dance'.]

Bayamón /bī́ ə món/ city in NE Puerto Rico. Population: 220,262 (1990).

Bayazid I /bī́ əzid/, **Bayezit I, Bajazet** (1360?–1403?) sultan of the Ottoman Empire (1389–1402). Known as **Yilderim ('Lightning')**

Bayazid II (1448–1512) sultan of the Ottoman Empire (1481–1512)

Baybars I /bī baárss/ (1233?–77) sultan of Egypt and Syria (1260–77)

bayberry /báybəri/ (*plural* **-ries**) *n* **1** a fruit covered with a waxy substance, borne by a North American shrub. Use: making candles. **2** the shrub that bears bayberries. Native to: coast of E North America. Genus: *Myrica.* **3** = **bay rum tree**

Bayes' theorem /báyz-/ *n* a theorem of conditional probability that allows estimates of probability to be continually revised based on observations of occurrences of events [Mid-19C. After Thomas *Bayes* (1702–61), British mathematician.]

Bayeux /bī yúr/ town in N France. Population: 14,961 (1999).

Bayeux tapestry *n* a linen embroidery from the 11th century that hangs in Bayeux, France, and depicts the Norman conquest of England

Bayezit I ♦ **Bayazid I**

bay laurel *n* TREES = **bay**[3] *n.* **1**

Bayle /bayl, bel/, **Pierre** (1647–1706) French philosopher

bay leaf *n* the aromatic leaf of the Mediterranean bay tree, used for flavouring in cooking

Bay of Pigs bay on the SW coast of Cuba, site of an abortive attempt by US-backed Cuban exiles to overthrow the government of Fidel Castro in 1961

bayonet /báyənit/ *n* **1 BLADE FITTED TO RIFLE** a blade that can be attached to the end of a rifle and used for stabbing **2 FITTING WITH PROJECTING PINS** a fitting with projecting pins that are pushed into a socket and then twisted into slots, used, e.g., on electric light bulbs ■ *vt* **STAB WITH BAYONET** to stab or kill somebody with a bayonet [Early 17C. < French *baïonnette*, after BAYONNE.]

Bayonne /bī ón/ city in SW France. Population: 61,051 (1998 estimate).

bayou /bī́ yoo/ (*plural* **-ous**) *n* in the S United States, an area of slow-moving water, often overgrown with reeds, leading from a river or lake [Mid-18C. Via Louisiana French < Choctaw *bayuk* 'small river forming part of a delta'.]

bay platform *n* a railway platform at which a line ends in a station where other lines continue, often where a branch line ends in a mainline station

Bayreuth /bī róyt/ city in S Germany, site of an annual Wagner opera festival. Population: 72,840 (1997).

bay rum *n* a liquid made by dissolving the oil of the leaves of the bay rum tree and other fragrant oils in alcohol and water. Use: men's cosmetics. [Because originally made by distilling oil with rum]

bay rum tree *n* a tree whose leaves produce oil used for making bay rum. Native to: Central and South America *Pimenta racemosa.*

Bay Street *n* the controlling financial interests of Toronto, Canada

bay window *n* a rounded or three-sided window that sticks out from an outside wall and forms a recess on the inside

baywood /báy wòòd/ *n* a light variety of mahogany from S Mexico [After the *Bay* of Campeche, Mexico]

bazaar /bə zaár/ *n* **1 CHARITABLE SALE** a sale of goods to raise money for charity **2 SHOP SELLING MISCELLANEOUS ITEMS** a retail store that sells a wide variety of items (*dated*) **3 MIDDLE EASTERN MARKET** a street market in Middle Eastern countries [Late 16C. Via Italian and Turkish < Persian *bāzār* 'market'.]

~~**bazar**~~ incorrect spelling of **bazaar**

bazillion /bə zíllyən/, **bizillion** *n US* a very large indefinite number (*slang*) [*Ba-* expressing emphasis]

bazooka /bə zóòkə/ *n* a tube-shaped weapon, fired from the shoulder, that launches a missile that can disable a tank [Mid-20C. < ?]

⚡**bb** *abbr* Barbados (*in Internet addresses*)

BB[1] *n US* a pellet fired from a shotgun or airgun [Late 19C. < the official designation of shot that is 0.18 in.]

BB[2] *abbr* **1** Boys' Brigade ■ *symbol* **2** double black (*describes pencils with very soft leads*)

BBA *abbr* Bachelor of Business Administration

BBC *abbr* British Broadcasting Corporation

BBFC *abbr* British Board of Film Classification

⚡**BBFN** *abbr* bye-bye for now (*in e-mails*)

bbl, bbl. *abbr* barrel

⚡**BBL** *abbr* be back later (*in e-mails*)

⚡**BBN** *abbr* bye-bye now (*in e-mails*)

BBQ *abbr* barbecue

⚡**BBS** *abbr* bulletin board system

BC, B.C. *adv* used to indicate a date that is a specified number of years before the birth of Jesus Christ (*after a date*) Full form **before Christ**

B.C. *abbr* British Columbia

bcc, b.c.c. *abbr* blind carbon copy

BCC *abbr* British Coal Corporation

⚡**BCD** *abbr* binary coded decimal

BCE[1] *abbr US* **1** Bachelor of Chemical Engineering **2** Bachelor of Civil Engineering

BCE[2], BCE *adv* used after a date as the non-Christian equivalent of BC. Full form **Before the Common Era**

B-cell *n* a white blood cell (**lymphocyte**), formed in bone marrow in mammals and present in blood and lymph, that creates antibodies in response to a specific antigen

BCG *n* an anti-tuberculosis vaccine made from a weakened strain of the tubercle bacillus. Full form **bacillus Calmette-Guérin (vaccine)**

BCh *abbr* Bachelor of Surgery [< Latin *Baccalaureus Chirurgiae*]

BCL *abbr* Bachelor of Civil Law

⚡**BCNU** *abbr* be seeing you (*in e-mails*)

BCNZ *abbr NZ* Broadcasting Corporation of New Zealand

B complex *n* BIOCHEM = **vitamin B complex**

BC soil *n* soil made up of two distinct layers

⚡**bd** *abbr* **1** Bangladesh (*in Internet addresses*) **2** board **3** bond **4** bound **5** bundle

BD *abbr US* Bachelor of Divinity

B/D, b/d *abbr* **1** bank draft **2** bills discounted **3** brought down

BDA *abbr* British Dental Association

bdellium /délli əm/ *n* **1** a transparent yellowish resin, valued for its perfume **2** a tree that produces bdellium resin. Native to: Africa, W Asia. Genus: *Commiphora.* [14C. Via Latin and Greek < Semitic.]

bd ft *abbr* board foot

Bdr *abbr* Bombardier

bds *abbr* **1** bound in boards **2** bundles

BDS *abbr* Bachelor of Dental Surgery

be[1] (*stressed*) /bee/; (*unstressed*) /bi/ (*1st person present singular* **am** (*stressed*) /am/; (*unstressed*) /əm/, *2nd person present singular* **are** (*stressed*) /aar/; (*unstressed*) /ər/, *3rd person present singular* **is** /iz/, *1st person present plural* **are,** *2nd person present plural* **are,** *present subjunctive* **be,** *1st person singular past indicative* **was** (*stressed*) /woz/; (*unstressed*) /wəz/, *2nd person singular past indicative* **were,** *3rd person singular past indicative* **was,** *1st person plural past indicative* **were,** *2nd person plural past indicative* **were,** *3rd person plural past indicative* **were,** *past subjunctive* **were,** *past participle* **been** (*stressed*) /been/; (*unstressed*) /bin/) CORE MEANING: a verb used most commonly to link the subject of a clause to a complement in order to give more information about the subject, e.g. its identity, nature, attributes, position, or value ○ *This is my colleague.* ○ *He's a very sweet person.* ○ *Her new car is blue.* ○ *The supermarket is on the left.* ○ *The clock was worth £3000*

vi **1 GIVING A DESCRIPTION** used after 'it' as the subject of the clause, to give a description or judgment of something ○ *It was a good thing they didn't go after all.* ○ *It is up to you to make a success of the business.* **2 EXIST OR BE TRUE** used after 'there' to indicate that something exists or is true ○ *There was nothing in the news today about the resignation.* ○ *There are too many people in here.* **3 EXIST** to exist, have presence, or live ○ *I think, therefore I am.* ○ *Our cat has ceased to be.* **4 HAPPEN** to happen or take place ○ *The meeting will be at 2 o'clock in the conference room.* **5 STAY** to stay or visit ○ *He wanted nothing but to be with the family.* ○ *Have you ever been to Italy?* **6 HAVE PARTICULAR QUALITY** to have a particular quality or attribute ○ *To be really precise, you must state the exact time at which the accident happened.* **7 REMAIN** used to indicate that a certain situation remains ○ *The fact of the matter is, I just don't want to stay here any more.* **8 EXPRESSING CONTINUATION** used with the present participle of verbs to express continuation ○ *The firm will be instituting more training programmes next year.* **9 FORMING THE PASSIVE** used with the past participle of transitive verbs to form the passive voice ○ *She was sent on the mission.* **10 FORMING PERFECT TENSE** used with the past participle of some intransitive verbs to form a perfect tense (*archaic*) ○ *She is gone.* **11 EXPRESSING THE FUTURE** used to indicate that something is planned, expected, intended, or supposed to happen in the future (*with infinitives*) ○ *The meeting is to take place tomorrow.* ○ *What am I to do?* **12 EXPRESSING UNPLANNED ACTION IN THE PAST** used when reporting past events to indicate that something happened later than the time reported and was unplanned or uncertain at the time (*with infinitives*) ○ *He kissed her goodbye; it was to be the last time he ever saw her.* [Old English *bēon*, via Germanic, 'exist, dwell' < Indo-European, 'exist, grow'] ◇ **been there, done that (bought the T-shirt)** used to indicate somebody's blasé attitude (*informal humorous*) ◇ **be off** go away ○ *It's already seven o'clock; I'm off.*

ϟ **be**[2] *abbr* Belgium (*in Internet addresses*)

Be *symbol* beryllium

BE *abbr* **1** *US* Bachelor of Education **2** *US* Bachelor of Engineering **3** bill of exchange

be- *prefix* **1** thoroughly, excessively ○ *bedazzle* ○ *bespatter* **2** on, over, about ○ *bewail* **3** to surround or cover with ○ *befog* ○ *bedew* **4** to furnish with ○ *befriend* **5** to make ○ *belittle* [Old English *be-*, *bi-* < Indo-European, 'around']

beach /beech/ *n* a strip of sand or pebbles at the point where land meets the sea or a lake ■ *vti* to pull or run a boat onto a beach, or be pulled onto a beach [Mid-16C. < ?]

SPELLCHECK Do not confuse ***beach*** with ***beech***, which has a similar sound. Beware: your spellchecker will not catch this error.

beach buggy *n* a motorized beach vehicle, usually without a top and with oversized tyres to prevent it from getting stuck in sand. US term **dune buggy**

beach bum *n* a person with no regular occupation who spends time idly on beaches (*informal*)

beachcomber /beéch kōmər/ *n* **1** somebody who looks for useful or valuable things on beaches **2** a long high wave that crashes onto a beach. US term **comber** *n.* 2

beach drift *n* the unconsolidated material and debris transported by the drifting movement of a beach

beached /beecht/ *adj* stranded on a beach or out of the water

beach flea *n* MARINE BIOL = **sand hopper** *n.*

beachhead /beéch hed/ *n* a part of an enemy shoreline that troops have captured and are using as a base for launching an attack [After BRIDGEHEAD]

Beach-la-Mar /beéch lə maár/ *n* a pidgin based on English that developed in Vanuatu, Fiji, and other nearby islands as a trading lingua franca [Early 19C. < Portuguese *bicho do mar* 'sea cucumber', by association with BEACH.] —**Beach-la-Mar** *adj*

beach plum *n* **1** a dark purple edible plum **2** a small shrubby plum tree with large white flowers that bears beach plums. Native to: coast of NE North America. *Prunus maritima.*

beachwear /beéch wair/ *n* casual clothing designed to be worn on a beach

Beachy Head /beéchi-/ chalk headland on the English Channel, SE England. Height: 171 m/570 ft.

beacon /beékən/ *n* **1 FLASHING LIGHT FOR SHIPS** a lighthouse or signalling buoy that produces a flashing light to warn or guide ships **2 RADIO TRANSMITTER PRODUCING NAVIGATION SIGNAL** a radio transmitter that continuously broadcasts a signal that aircraft use for guidance **3 SIGNALLING FIRE ON HILL** a fire lit on a hilltop or tower in former times as a signal, e.g. to warn of invasion **4 HILL SUITABLE FOR SIGNALLING FIRES** a prominent hill on which fires were formerly lit as a signal (*often in placenames*) **5** TRANSP = **Belisha beacon 6 SOURCE OF INSPIRATION** somebody or something that inspires or guides others (*literary*) [Old English *bēacen* 'signal, sign' < Germanic]

bead /beed/ *n* **1 BALL FOR A NECKLACE** a small gemstone or glass, plastic, or wooden ball, pierced for stringing on a necklace or sewing onto fabric **2 DROP OF MOISTURE** a drop of moisture, especially of sweat **3 BUILDING OR FURNITURE TRIM** an edge or rim that sticks out on a building or a piece of furniture, traditionally with a pattern of rounded knobs **4 GUN SIGHT** a knob sticking up on the end of the barrel of a gun, forming the front part of the gun's sight **5 SEAL ON A TYRE** a projecting lip on the tyre of a motor vehicle that seals to the wheel rim **6 DEPOSIT OF METAL** a deposit of metal used in welding ■ **beads** *npl* **1 ROSARY** a rosary **2 NECKLACE** a necklace made of beads ■ *v* **1** *vt* **DECORATE WITH BEADS** to trim or ornament something with beads **2** *vi* **FORM INTO BEADS** to form drops of moisture [Old English *gebed* 'prayer' < Germanic] —**beaded** *adj* ◇ **draw a bead on somebody** *or* **something** to take careful aim at somebody or something ◇ **tell** *or* **say** *or* **count your beads** to say prayers recited in sequence and counted using a rosary

beading /beéding/ *n* an edge or rim that sticks out on a building or a piece of furniture, traditionally with a pattern of rounded knobs

beadle /beéd'l/ *n* **1** a minor parish official once employed in the Church of England to usher and keep order **2** an official who acts as caretaker of a synagogue and oversees the running of the service [13C. < Old French *bedel* 'proclaimer, messenger' < Germanic.]

beadwork /beéd wurk/ *n* decoration using beads to form a design, e.g. on furniture or knitwear

beady /beédi/ (**-ier, -iest**) *adj* **1 LIKE BEADS** small, round, and shiny like glass beads **2 COVERED WITH BEADS** covered or ornamented with beads **3 WATCHFUL** carefully attentive (*informal*) ○ *a beady eye* —**beadily** *adv* —**beadiness** *n* ◇ **keep a** *or* **your beady eye on somebody** *or* **something** to watch somebody or something very carefully (*informal*)

beagle /beég'l/ *n* a small smooth-haired dog belonging to a breed with a white, tan, and black coat and long drooping ears, often used for hunting [15C. < ?]

Beagle Channel /beég'l-/ strait in the Tierra del Fuego archipelago at the southern tip of South America. Length: 240 km/150 mi.

beagling /beégling/ *n* hunting, especially for rabbits or hares, using beagles —**beagler** *n*

beak /beek/ *n* **1 BIRD'S MOUTH** the strong horny outer parts of a bird's mouth that stick out from its head **2 PROTRUDING PART OF ANIMAL'S MOUTH** a projecting part of the mouth or jaw of animals other than birds, e.g. the sucking mouthpart of an insect or the bony jaw projection of a fish **3 PART OF MOLLUSC'S SHELL** the oldest part of the shell of a mollusc with a hinged shell, found nearest the hinge **4 SOMEBODY'S NOSE** somebody's nose, especially when it is long or hooked (*slang*) **5 PROJECTING PART** a part that sticks out, e.g. the lip of a container **6 CURVED CORNICE OR MOULDING** a cornice or moulding with a downward-curving edge **7 MAGISTRATE** a court judge or a magistrate (*dated slang*) **8 TEACHER** a headmaster or schoolmaster (*dated slang*) [13C. Via Old French *bec* < Latin *beccus.*] —**beaked** *adj* —**beakless** *adj* —**beaklike** *adj*

beaked whale *n* a widely found, medium-sized, toothed whale with a long snout. Family: Ziphiidae.

beaker /beékər/ *n* **1** a wide-mouthed cup, especially a plastic one without a handle **2** a flat-bottomed glass container used in laboratories [14C. Via Old Norse *bikarr* < assumed Vulgar Latin *bicarium*, perhaps < Greek *bikos* 'wine jar, earthen vessel'.]

Beaker folk /beékər-/ *npl* a prehistoric people who lived throughout central Europe during the period 2000 to 1000 BC

beaky /beéki/ (**-ier, -iest**) *adj* with a large, long, or hooked nose (*informal insult*)

Beale /beel/, **Dorothea** (1831–1906) British educator and suffragette

be-all ◇ **the be-all and end-all** the thing that is most important

beam /beem/ *n* **1 HORIZONTAL STRUCTURAL SUPPORT** a horizontal structural member that carries the load by bending, e.g. a long piece of timber, metal, or concrete spanning a room and supporting the storey or roof above **2 LINE OF LIGHT** a narrow line of light, e.g. from a flashlight **3 STRUCTURAL CROSSPIECE IN SHIP** a structural member of a ship or boat that joins the sides and supports the deck **4 SHIP'S BREADTH** the full breadth of a ship **5 SIDE OF SHIP** either of the sides of a ship **6 FLOW OF RADIATION** a narrow stream of radiation or particles flowing in one direction **7 GUIDING SIGNAL** a radio or radar signal intended to guide a ship or aircraft, or the direction indicated by this **8 BROAD SMILE** a broad smile of happiness or satisfaction **9 HORIZONTAL PART OF BALANCE** the pivoted horizontal bar of a balance on which the two scales hang **10 MAIN SUPPORTING SHAFT** a main bar or shaft, e.g. either of the main stems of a deer's antlers or the central shaft of a plough **11 CONNECTING LEVER IN ENGINE** a lever connecting the piston rod and crankshaft in an engine **12 ROLLER IN LOOM** a cylinder in a loom on which either the warp or the cloth is wound **13 GYMNASTS' BALANCING BAR** a narrow horizontal wooden bar on legs that women gymnasts stand on to perform balancing exercises, or the event involving this. US term **balance beam** ■ *v* **1** *vti* **SMILE BROADLY** to smile broadly with happiness or satisfaction **2** *vt* **SEND AS RADIO OR TV SIGNAL** to send or transmit a programme to a distant place in the form of a radio or television signal **3** *vti* **SHINE** to shine in a particular direction **4** *vti* **CHANGE CIRCUMSTANCES SUDDENLY** to move between completely different places or situations in a sudden and disorienting way (*slang; with 'up' or 'down'*) [Old English *bēam* 'tree, piece of timber, column, ray' < Germanic] ◇ **broad** *or* **wide in the beam** having wide hips (*informal; sometimes offensive*) ◇ **off beam** missing the point or relevancy ◇ **on the beam 1** using a beam for guidance **2** on track or working effectively (*informal*)

beam aerial *n* a radio or television aerial designed to transmit or receive signals in or from a particular direction. US term **beam antenna**

beam bridge *n* a bridge, usually with a short span, supported on beams whose ends rest on piers or abutments

beam compass *n* a tool for drawing very large circles or arcs, consisting of a horizontal bar with sliding legs

beam-ends *npl* the ends of the beams supporting the deck of a vessel ◇ **on her** *or* **its beam-ends** describes a ship leaning so far to one side that its deck is vertical ◇ **on your beam-ends** having very little money to live on (*informal*)

beam engine *n* an early type of steam engine with a piston that pushes a pivoted horizontal beam up and down in a see-saw motion

Beamer /beémər/ *n* a BMW™ motor car (*informal*) [Late 20C. Alteration.]

Beamon /beémən/, **Bob** (*b.* 1946) US athlete. Full name **Robert Beamon**

beam splitter *n* a device used in holography to divide a laser light into two beams by means of a prism and mirror to produce a three-dimensional image

beamy /beémi/ (**-ier, -iest**) *adj* **1** sending out beams of light (*literary*) **2** describes a ship with a broad beam

bean /been/ *n* **1 EDIBLE GREEN POD** a long thin usually green seed pod eaten cooked whole as a vegetable **2 SMALL ROUND VEGETABLE** a small round or kidney-shaped seed of various colours that is eaten as a vegetable and can be dried to preserve it **3 PLANT WITH EDIBLE PODS AND SEEDS** a tall climbing or small bushy plant that produces beans. Genus: *Phaseolus*. **4 SEED USED IN FOOD OR DRINK** a coffee, cocoa, or carob seed that is processed and used in food or drink ■ **beans** *npl US* **NOTHING** nothing at all (*informal*) ■ *vt Can, US* **HIT ON HEAD** to hit somebody on the head (*slang*) [Old English *bēan* < Germanic] ◇ **full of beans** bright and energetic (*informal*) ◇ **not have a bean** to have no money (*informal*) ◇ **not know beans about something** *US* to have no knowledge or understanding of something (*informal*) ◇ **spill the beans** to reveal secret information (*informal*)

Bean /been/, **Charles Edwin Woodrow** (1879–1968) Australian writer

beanbag /beén bag/ *n* **1** a small cloth bag filled with dried beans or something similar, thrown or otherwise used in children's games **2** an oversized cushion filled with tiny polystyrene balls, laid on the floor and used as a chair

bean beetle *n* ZOOL = **Mexican bean beetle**

bean curd *n* tofu, especially as used in Chinese cookery

beanery /beénəri/ (*plural* **-ies**) *n US* a cheap restaurant (*informal*)

beanfeast /beén feest/ *n* (*dated informal*) **1** a party or social gathering **2** an annual dinner given to employees

beanie /beéni/ *n US* a round tight-fitting hat like a skullcap

beano /beénō/ *n* a noisy or enjoyable party or celebration (*dated informal*)

beanpole /beén pōl/ *n* **1** a stick or pole for supporting a climbing bean plant **2** a tall thin person (*informal*)

bean sprouts *npl* long pale shoots of sprouted bean seeds, particularly of mung bean, harvested while crisp and used raw or very lightly cooked

bear[1] /bair/ *n* **1 LARGE FURRY ANIMAL** a large strong omnivorous four-legged mammal that has thick shaggy fur and sharp claws and walks on the flat of its paws. Family: Ursidae. **2 MEDIUM-SIZED FURRY ANIMAL** an animal that resembles but is unrelated to the true bear, e.g. the koala **3** = **teddy bear 4 BAD-TEMPERED PERSON** an ill-tempered person (*informal*) **5 SOMEBODY WHO ANTICIPATES FALLING PRICES** somebody who sells stocks or commodities in anticipation of falling prices. ◊ **bull**[1] *n.* 4 [Old English *bera* < Germanic, 'the brown one']

SPELLCHECK See ***bare***.

bear[2] /bair/ (**bears, bearing, bore** /bawr/, **borne** /bawrn/) *v* **1** *vti* **TOLERATE** to be able to endure something without great distress or annoyance (*in negatives*) ○ *couldn't bear to see them unhappy* **2** *vt* **SUPPORT** to hold or support a weight or something heavy **3** *vti* **BE FIT FOR** to withstand being subjected to a particular action ○ *Will her theories bear scrutiny?* **4** *vt* **MERIT** to be worthy of an action ○ *These allegations bear further investigation.* **5** *vt* **ACCEPT AS RESPONSIBILITY** to accept something as a duty or responsibility **6** *vt* **BE CHARACTERIZED BY** to have something as a quality, characteristic, or permanent attribute ○ *The description bore no relation to reality.* **7** *vt* **BE MARKED BY** to show physical signs of something **8** *vt* **CARRY** to hold or support and transport somebody or something **9** *vt* **PRODUCE** to yield something by a natural process, or produce something desirable or valuable ○ *the tree that bore fruit* **10** *vt* **GIVE BIRTH** to give birth to a child or young **11** *vt* **THINK** to hold a particular thought, feeling, or idea in the mind ○ *I bore him no ill will.* **12** *vt* **TRANSMIT** to hold something in mind and communicate it to others (*formal*) **13** *vi* **HEAD IN A CERTAIN DIRECTION** to move or turn in a particular direction ○ *Bear right when the road divides.* **14** *vt* **BEHAVE IN A CERTAIN WAY** to conduct or carry yourself in a particular way [Old English *beran* < Indo-European] ◇ **bring something to bear (on something)** to use something to force a desired outcome

bear down *vi* to push with the vaginal muscles during childbirth

bear down on *vt* **1** to move quickly and menacingly towards somebody or something **2** to exert downward pressure on something

bear on, bear upon *vt* **1** to relate to or affect something **2** to be a problem for, or a burden to, somebody or something

bear out *vt* to prove something or somebody to be true or justified ○ *This bears out my theory.*

bear up *vi* **1** to remain cheerful and determined in spite of problems **2** to remain true or undamaged after being examined or criticized

bear upon *vt* = **bear on**

bear with *vt* to be patient with somebody trying to do something

bearable /báirəb'l/ *adj* not too unpleasant to put up with or accept —**bearably** *adv*

bearbaiting /báir bayting/ *n* the setting of fierce dogs onto a chained bear, once a popular form of public entertainment

bearberry /báirbəri/ (*plural* **-ries**) *n* a trailing evergreen shrub with red berries. Native to: Europe, Asia, North America. *Arctostaphylos uva-ursi.* [Early 17C. < BEAR[1].]

bearcat /báir kat/ *n* ZOOL = **red panda**

beard /beerd/ *n* **1** **HAIR GROWING ON MAN'S CHIN** the hair on a man's chin and, often, his neck and cheeks **2** **TUFTS GROWING ON PLANTS AND ANIMALS** a growth of longer hair on an animal, e.g. on a goat's chin, or a long slender growth on plants, e.g. on barley and wheat heads ■ *vt* **STAND UP TO SOMEBODY OPENLY** to oppose or confront something or somebody confidently or disrespectfully [Old English, < Indo-European] —**bearded** *adj* —**beardedness** *n* —**beardless** *adj*

bearded dragon, bearded lizard *n* a large lizard with a pouch under its chin, that inflates to ward off attackers. Native to: Australia. *Amphibolus barbatus.*

bearded iris *n* an iris that has large flowers, with numerous hairs, often coloured, along the centre of each drooping lower petal

bearded lizard *n* ZOOL = **bearded dragon**

bearded tit *n* BIRDS = **reedling**

bearded vulture *n* BIRDS = **lammergeier**

Beardsley /beérdzli/, **Aubrey** (1872–98) British artist and illustrator

bearer /báirər/ *n* **1** **BRINGER** somebody who brings or carries something **2** **HOLDER OF REDEEMABLE NOTE** somebody possessing a document redeemable for payment **3** = **pallbearer** **4** **PORTER** a local person employed to carry equipment on an expedition

bearer bond *n* a bond payable only to the person who presents it

bear garden *n* **1** a noisy or unruly place or occasion **2** in former times, a place where live bears were on public display and where bearbaiting took place

bear hug *n* **1** **TIGHT EMBRACE** an enthusiastic or energetic embrace **2** **SQUEEZING HOLD IN WRESTLING** in wrestling, a tight, squeezing hold around an opponent's chest and arms **3** **WARNING OF INTENDED TAKEOVER** one company's warning to another of its intention to assume control

bearing /báiring/ *n* **1** **RELEVANCE** a relation to something ○ *This has no bearing on the matter under discussion.* **2** **WAY OF MOVING OR STANDING** somebody's way of moving, standing, or behaving generally ○ *her dignified bearing* **3** **CALCULATION OF DIRECTION OR GEOGRAPHIC POSITION** somebody's location or direction of movement calculated using a map or compass **4** **HOUSING FOR A MOVING PART** the part of a machine that supports a sliding or rotating part **5** **SUPPORT FOR BEAM** a support for a beam or girder **6** **HERALDIC DEVICE** a heraldic device or charge ◇ **find** *or* **get your bearings** **1** to learn exactly where you are and in which direction you should proceed **2** to become familiar with a new environment ◇ **lose your bearings** **1** to become uncertain about where you are and in which direction you should proceed **2** to become unable to react in a normal manner

bearing rein *n* a short rein joining a horse's bit to a hook on the saddle, used to keep the horse's head up. US term **checkrein** *n.* 1

bearish /báirish/ *adj* **1** **BAD-TEMPERED** surly or ill-tempered towards people **2** **CLUMSY** moving or behaving roughly or clumsily **3** **ANTICIPATING FALLING PRICES** conducive to or characterized by selling rather than buying stocks or commodities in anticipation of falling prices

bear market *n* a situation in a stock or commodity market in which shareholders are selling in anticipation of falling prices

béarnaise sauce /báyər nayz-/ *n* a savoury sauce thickened with egg yolk and flavoured with tarragon [Late 19C. < French, < *Béarn*, district in SW France.]

bear raid *n* an attempt to lower a stock or commodity price by selling large numbers of shares, usually in order to buy them back at a lowered price

bear's breech *n* a large garden plant with spiky leaves. Flowers: whitish, purple-streaked. *Acanthus mollis.*

bearskin /báir skin/ *n* **1** **BEAR'S PELT** a bear's skin with the fur still attached, stripped from the animal **2** **SHAGGY WOOLLEN CLOTH** coarse woollen fabric. Use: overcoats. **3** **SOLDIER'S TALL FUR HAT** a tall fur hat worn as part of the ceremonial uniform of soldiers in the Guards regiments

beast /beest/ *n* **1** **LARGE ANIMAL** an animal, especially a large four-footed mammal **2** **IRRATIONAL SIDE OF SOMEBODY'S PERSONALITY** the instinctive, irrational, or aggressive part of somebody's personality **3** **BRUTAL PERSON** a cruel or aggressive person **4** **SOMETHING UNPLEASANT** a thing or situation that is difficult or unpleasant (*informal*) ○ *This is truly a beast of a job!* [12C. Via Old French *beste* < Latin *bestia*.] —**beastlike** *adj*

beastie /beésti/ *n US, Scotland* a small animal, especially an insect or small crawling creature (*informal*)

beastly /beéstli/ *adj* thoroughly unpleasant or objectionable (*dated informal*) ■ *adv* exceedingly (*dated informal*) —**beastliness** *n*

beast of burden *n* an animal, e.g. a donkey or an ox, used to carry or pull things or do other heavy work

beast of prey *n* a mammal that hunts other animals for food

beat /beet/ *v* (**beats, beating, beat, beaten** /beét'n/) **1** *vt* **DEFEAT** to defeat somebody in a contest ○ *She was beaten in the semifinal.* **2** *vt* **HIT REPEATEDLY** to hit somebody or something with repeated heavy blows ○ *beaten nearly to death.* **3** *vi* **KNOCK AGAINST REPEATEDLY** to knock or strike against something repeatedly ○ *waves beating against the rocks* **4** *vt* **FLOG** to inflict physical punishment or injury on somebody using an instrument such as a whip, stick, or belt **5** *vi* **PULSATE** to make natural short rhythmical movements (*refers to the heart or pulse*) **6** *vti* **HIT DRUM** to hit a drum repeatedly to produce a musical rhythm or a signal **7** *vt* **SET MUSICAL RHYTHM** to show or establish a musical rhythm, e.g. with a conductor's baton or by clapping hands **8** *vt* **STIR VIGOROUSLY** to mix moist ingredients vigorously to combine them, make them smooth, or incorporate air into them ○ *Now, beat the eggs.* **9** *vt* **OVERCOME OBSTACLES IN** to overcome the difficulties or obstacles created by something ○ *You can't beat the system.* **10** *vt* **ARRIVE AHEAD OF** to arrive or finish something sooner than somebody else or than a time limit ○ *She beat me to the office.* **11** *vt* **AVOID LATER DELAYS** to take early action to avoid being prevented or delayed by something ○ *Order now and beat the rush!* **12** *vt* **SURPASS** to surpass a previous best performance ○ *beat the long jump record* **13** *vti* **BE BETTER** to be or do better than a particular thing, activity, or quality (*informal*) ○ *Sitting by the pool certainly beats working.* **14** *vt* **MAKE BY BLOWS** to shape or make something by pounding or trampling ○ *beat silver into jewellery* **15** *vti* **FLAP WINGS** to move the wings up and down in flight or an attempt at flight, or be moved in this way **16** *vt* **FORCE TO WITHDRAW** to force somebody to retreat or accept a weaker position ○ *They beat back the enemy.* **17** *vti* **DRIVE GAME FROM BRUSH** to move through or disturb cover in order to frighten animals and birds for hunting **18** *vi* **SAIL INTO WIND** to sail a boat or ship as nearly as possible in the direction from which the wind is blowing ■ *n* **1** **STEADY THROBBING** a rhythmical sound or movement made by something throbbing or pulsating (*often in combination*) ○ *a fast heartbeat* **2** **STROKE** an act of striking one thing against another, or the sound of one thing striking against another, especially repeatedly and rhythmically ○ *a drum beat* **3** **SET RHYTHM** a single element of measured time in a musical piece or poem **4** **CONDUCTOR'S SIGNAL** a movement made by a conductor's baton or hand to indicate a musical rhythm **5** **DOMINANT RHYTHM** the dominant rhythm in a piece of music, especially a strong rhythm in rock music **6** **USUAL ROUTE** a regular route followed or area covered while working, e.g. by a police officer ○ *the local police officer on the beat* **7** **AREA SOMEBODY USUALLY GOES TO** the places somebody usually frequents, especially somebody's usual hunting or fishing area ■ *adj* **1** **TIRED OUT** completely exhausted (*informal*) **2** **PUZZLED** unable to understand or think how to proceed (*informal*) ○ *It has me beat.* **3** **beat, Beat OF THE BEAT GENERATION** typical of or produced by members of the Beat Generation [Old English *bēatan*, via Germanic < Indo-European, 'to strike'] ◇ **beat it!** used to tell somebody to go away (*informal*) ◇ **beat somebody to something** to succeed in doing something before somebody else can do it (*informal*) ◇ **it beats me** used to indicate you have no answer (*informal*) ◇ **not miss a beat** to show no sign of surprise or upset ◇ **take some beating** to be difficult to improve on because of its excellence ○ *Her speech will take some beating.*

SPELLCHECK Do not confuse ***beat*** with ***beet***, which has a similar sound. Beware: your spellchecker will not catch this error.

beat down *v* **1** *vi* to shine intensely or fall heavily from the sky (*refers to sun or rain*) **2** *vt* to persuade somebody to charge less than the intended selling price (*informal*)

beat off *v* **1** *vt* to stop an attack or challenge by vigorous action **2** *vi US* a highly offensive term meaning to masturbate (*slang taboo*)

beat up *vt* to injure somebody badly by repeated punches or kicks (*informal*)

beat upon *v US* = **beat up**

beatbox /beét bòks/ *n US* an electronic drum used mainly in hip-hop and rap music to provide accompanying rhythm and sounds (*informal*)

ϟ **beat-'em-up** *n* a video or computer game involving a large amount of simulated fighting

beaten past participle of **beat**

beater /beétər/ *n* **1** **TOOL FOR BEATING** a tool for beating something, e.g. a shaped stick for beating the dust out of carpets, or an electric food mixer attachment for beating eggs (*often in combination*) **2** **HUNTER'S ASSISTANT FOR DRIVING BIRDS OUT** somebody who flushes out game for hunters to shoot, usually by hitting bushes **3** **SOMEBODY WHO BEATS METAL** somebody who hammers metal

Beat Generation *n* **1** young people in the 1950s who rejected the traditional values, customs, and dress of Western society and experimented with Eastern philosophies, communal living, and illegal drugs **2** a group of writers associated with the attitudes of the Beat Generation, including Jack Kerouac, Allen Ginsberg, and Laurence Ferlinghetti

beatific /beé ə tíffik/ *adj* (*literary*) **1** expressing or radiating great happiness and serenity **2** bringing or expressing the perfect happiness and inner peace supposed to be enjoyed by the soul in heaven [Mid-17C. Directly or via French *béatifique* < Latin *beatificus* < *beatus* 'blessed'.] —**beatifically** *adv*

~~**beatiful**~~ incorrect spelling of **beautiful**

beatify /bi átti fī/ (**-fies, -fying, -fied**) *vt* **1** in the Roman Catholic Church, to state officially that a dead person lived a holy life, usually as the first step towards sainthood **2** to make somebody extremely happy (*literary*) [Mid-16C. Directly or via French *béatifier* < ecclesiastical Latin *beatificare* < Latin *beatificus* (see BEATIFIC).] —**beatification** /bi áttifi káysh'n/ *n*

beating /beeting/ n 1 an attack or punishment in which somebody is repeatedly hit 2 a severe defeat or setback, e.g. in a competition or in business

beating reed n a reed in woodwind instruments that vibrates as air passes over it

beatitude /bi átti tyood/ n (literary) 1 the perfect happiness and inner peace supposed to be enjoyed by the soul in heaven 2 extreme happiness and serenity [15C. Directly or via French < Latin beatitud- < beatus 'blessed'.]

Beatitude n 1 each of the sayings of Jesus Christ in the Sermon on the Mount about the eight groups of people who will receive blessing in heaven (Matthew 5:3–11) 2 a title given to a senior bishop in non-Orthodox churches of the E Mediterranean

The Beatles

Beatles /beet'lz/ (1959–70) British pop music group

beatnik /beetnik/ n a member of the Beat Generation of the 1950s

Beaton /beet'n/, **Sir Cecil** (1904–80) British photographer and designer

Beatrix /bee ətriks/ (b. 1938) queen of the Netherlands (1980–)

Beatty /beeti/, **David, 1st Earl** (1871–1936) British admiral

beat-up adj in bad condition because of overuse (informal)

beau /bō/ (plural **beaus** or **beaux** /bō, bōz/) n 1 a boyfriend or male admirer (dated) 2 a man who is always smartly dressed in the most fashionable clothes (archaic) [Late 17C. < French, < beau 'beautiful' < Latin bellus (see BEAUTY).]

Beaufort /bōfərt/, **Henry, Cardinal** (1377–1447) English prelate and statesman

Beaufort scale /bōfərt-/ n an international scale of wind speeds indicated by numbers ranging from 0 for calm to 12 for hurricane [Mid-19C. After Sir Francis Beaufort (1774–1857), Irish admiral and hydrographer.]

Beaufort Sea section of the Arctic Ocean northwest of Canada and north of Alaska. Area: 450,000 sq. km/170,000 sq. mi. Depth: 4,682 m/15,360 ft.

beau geste /bō zhést/ (plural **beaux gestes** /bō zhést/) n a kind or magnanimous act [Early 20C. < French, 'fine gesture'.]

Beauharnais /bō aar náy/, **Alexandre, vicomte de** (1760–94) French soldier and politician

beau ideal /bō ee day aàl/ n somebody's idea of perfection or beauty, or a perfect example of something [Early 19C. < French, 'ideal beauty' (but usually taken as meaning 'beautiful ideal').]

Beaujolais /bōzhə lay/ (plural **-lais** /-lay/) n a fruity fairly light red or white wine produced in the Beaujolais district of the Burgundy region in central France

Beaujolais nouveau /-noo vō/ n Beaujolais sold from November in the year of its production

Beaulieu /byōoli/ village in S England, site of the Montagu Motor Museum and the ruins of Beaulieu Abbey. Population: 1,200.

Beaumarchais /bō maar shay/, **Pierre Augustin Caron de** (1732–99) French dramatist. Born **Pierre Augustin Caron**

Beaumes-de-Venise /bōm də və neéz/ n a sweet fortified white wine made from the muscat grape in the area around Beaumes-de-Venise in the S Rhône valley, France

beau monde /bō mónd/ n the part of society made up of the richest and most fashionable people [Late 17C. < French, 'beautiful world'.]

Beaumont /bō mont/, **Francis** (1584–1616) English dramatist

Beaumont, William (1785–1853) US physician

beaut /byoot/ n ANZ, US a fine or impressive thing (informal) ■ adj, interj ANZ outstanding or first-rate (informal) [Mid-19C. Shortening of BEAUTY or BEAUTIFUL.]

beauteous /byóoti əss/ adj beautiful to look at (literary) —**beauteously** adv —**beauteousness** n

beautician /byoo tish'n/ n US somebody trained to give beauty treatments, e.g. application of makeup and facial treatments

beautiful /byóotəf'l/ adj 1 very pleasing and impressive to listen to, touch, or especially to look at 2 very good or enjoyable —**beautifully** adv —**beautifulness** n

beautiful people npl 1 HIGH SOCIETY rich fashionable people 2 PEOPLE PARADING THEIR GOOD LOOKS people who like to show off their good looks 3 HIPPIES in the 1960s, hippies collectively

beautify /byóoti fī/ (**-fies, -fying, -fied**) vt to make something pleasing and impressive to look at —**beautification** /byóotifi káysh'n/ n —**beautifier** n

beauty /byóoti/ (plural **-ties**) n 1 PLEASING AND IMPRESSIVE QUALITIES the combination of qualities that make something pleasing and impressive to listen to or touch, or especially to look at 2 PLEASING PERSONAL APPEARANCE personal physical attractiveness, especially with regard to the use of cosmetics and other methods of enhancing it 3 BEAUTIFUL WOMAN a beautiful woman or girl ○ her reputation as a great beauty 4 FINE EXAMPLE something very good, attractive, or impressive of its kind 5 EXCELLENT ASPECT an attractive, useful, or satisfying feature ○ Great fuel economy is one of the beauties of this vehicle. [13C. Via Old French bealte < Vulgar Latin bellitat- < Latin bellus 'handsome, fine' < bonus 'good'.]

beautybush /byóoti boosh/ n a shrub grown for its pink flowers and fruit with hairy knobbly skin. Native to: China. Kolkwitzia amabilis.

beauty mark n US = beauty spot n. 2

beauty parlour n = beauty salon

beauty quark n QUANTUM PHYS = bottom quark

beauty queen n a woman judged to be the most beautiful of all the candidates in a competition

beauty salon, beauty shop n a business establishment where beauty treatments are provided, e.g. hair styling, facials, and manicures. US term **beauty parlor**

beauty sleep n deep restful sleep, especially before midnight, supposed to preserve youthful good looks (informal)

beauty spot n 1 POPULAR SCENIC PLACE a place that people often visit because of its pleasing scenery 2 SMALL NATURAL MARK ON FACE a mole or other small round blemish on somebody's face 3 DOT WORN ON THE FACE a small black or brown dot of silk or makeup on somebody's face used to emphasize the skin's paleness or hide a blemish

Beauvoir /bō vwaar/, **Simone de** (1908–86) French writer

beaux plural of beau

beaver[1] /beevar/ n 1 (plural **-vers** or **-ver**) FURRY FLAT-TAILED WATER ANIMAL a semiaquatic rodent that has a broad flat tail and webbed hind feet. Native to: North America, Europe, Asia. Genus: Castor. 2 FUR FROM BEAVER the valuable fur of the beaver 3 MAN'S FUR HAT a man's hat made of beaver fur, felt, or a fabric imitating beaver fur 4 THICK FABRIC thick woollen or cotton fabric 5 TABOO TERM a highly offensive term for a woman's outer sex organs and pubic hair (taboo) ■ vi WORK HARD AND CONTINUOUSLY to work hard with unflagging energy and attention (informal) [Old English beofor < Indo-European, 'brown animal']

beaver[2] /beevar/ n the guard for the lower part of the face on a medieval helmet [15C. < French baviere, originally 'child's bib' < baver 'to slaver'.]

BEAUFORT SCALE

The Beaufort Scale was devised in 1805 by Sir Francis Beaufort, a captain (later admiral) in the British Royal Navy, to measure the observable effects of wind force at sea. It was later adapted to include effects on land, and wind speed equivalents were officially incorporated in 1926.

Sailors and forecasters use the Beaufort Scale as a standardized way to rate wind speed. Warnings of potentially dangerous conditions for people in small boats are usually issued at ratings of six on the scale. The Beaufort number is also referred to as a 'Force' number, for example, 'Force 10 Gale.'

Beaufort Scale	Wind speed km/h	Wind speed mph	Description
0	below 1	below 1	Calm
1	1 – 6	1 – 3	Light air
2	7 – 12	4 – 7	Light breeze
3	13 – 19	8 – 12	Gentle breeze
4	20 – 30	13 – 18	Moderate breeze
5	31 – 39	19 – 24	Fresh breeze
6	40 – 50	25 – 31	Strong breeze
7	51 – 62	32 – 38	Moderate gale
8	63 – 74	39 – 46	Fresh gale
9	75 – 87	47 – 54	Strong gale
10	88 – 102	55 – 63	Whole gale
11	103 – 117	64 – 72	Storm
12	above 118	above 73	Hurricane

Beaver /beévar/, **Beaver Scout** *n* a member of the most junior branch of the Scout Association, for boys and girls aged between six and eight

beaverboard /beévar bawrd/ *n* a thick board made of compressed wood fibres. Use: ceilings, inner walls.

Beaverbrook /beévar bro͝ok/, **Max Aitken, 1st Baron** (1879–1964) Canadian-born British newspaper owner and politician

Beazley /beézli/, **Kim** (*b.* 1948) Australian politician

Bebel /báyb'l/, **August** (1840–1913) German politician

bebop /beé bop/ *n* fast jazz music with complex harmonies and melodies [Mid-20C. An imitation of either the two-beat phrase of such music or the nonsense syllables of scat singing.] —**bebopper** *n*

becalm /bi kaám/ *vt* **1** to cause a sailing boat or sailing ship to stop moving because of lack of wind (*usually passive*) **2** to bring peace and quiet to somebody

became past tense of **become**

because /bi kóz, -kaz/ *conj* **1** for the reason that follows **2** on the basis of or taking into account what follows [14C. < *by cause* 'for the reason (that)', after Old French *par chance*.] ◇ **because of** indicating the reason or cause of something

USAGE because, as, for, or **since**? The conjunctions ***since***, ***because***, and ***as*** may be at the beginning of a sentence, especially when the reason is already well known or when the reason is considered not as important as the main statement: *As you're only staying a little while, we'd better eat now.* ***Because*** puts a greater emphasis on the cause: *He liked her because she was witty and lively.* ***Because*** and ***for*** are both used to introduce reasons that justify a statement as distinct from giving a reason for it, though ***for*** is more formal: *You must have forgotten to invite them, because/for they didn't turn up.* ***For*** as a conjunction is never used at the beginning of a sentence. ***As*** can also be understood to mean 'at the time that' as well as 'because': *As Luisa went back to work, Tony stayed behind to look after the baby.* In this case, it is better to avoid ambiguity and use either ***because*** or *while* as appropriate. Avoid using ***being as*** in place of ***because*** in formal writing: *They left for the game late, because* [not *being as*] *the car would not start.*

USAGE See ***reason***.

béchamel sauce /báysha mel-/ *n* a sauce made from milk thickened and made rich with butter and flour and served hot [Late 18C. After Louis, Marquis de *Béchamel* (1630–1703), steward to Louis XIV of France.]

bêche-de-mer /bésh da máir/ (*plural* **bêches-de-mer** /bésh da máir/ *or* **bêche-de-mer**) *n* ZOOL = **trepang** [Early 19C. < pseudo-French form of Portuguese *bicho do mar* 'sea cucumber'.]

Bechuanaland /béchoo aána land/ former name for **Botswana**

beck[1] /bek/ *n N England* a stream, especially a mountain stream [13C. < Old Norse *bekkr* < Germanic.]

beck[2] /bek/ *n* a nod, wave, or similar gesture to attract attention (*literary*) [14C. Shortening of BECKON.] ◇ **at somebody's beck and call** always available and ready to carry out somebody's wishes

Beckenbauer /békan bowar/, **Franz** (*b.* 1945) German footballer

Becker /békar/, **Boris** (*b.* 1967) German tennis player

becket /békit/ *n* a rope with a knot at one end and a small loop or hook at the other, used for tying down loose equipment on a ship or boat [Mid-18C. < ?]

Becket /békit/, **Thomas à, St** (1118?–70) English saint and martyr

Beckett /békit/, **Samuel** (1906–89) Irish writer

Beckford /békfard/, **William** (1760–1844) British writer and art collector

Beckmann /békman/, **Max** (1884–1950) German painter

beckon /békan/ *vti* **1** to signal to somebody to approach with a movement of the hand or head **2** to be an attraction or temptation to somebody (*literary*) [Old English *bēcnan* < Germanic] —**beckoner** *n* —**beckoningly** *adv*

becloud /bi klówd/ *vt* (*literary*) **1** to cover or conceal something with cloud or mist **2** to make something confused or difficult to understand

become /bi kúm/ (**-comes, -coming, -came** /-káym/, **-come**) *v* **1** *vi* COME TO BE to change or develop into something ○ *The caterpillar will soon become a moth.* **2** *vt* SUIT to suit the appearance or personality of somebody ○ *That colour really becomes you.* **3** *vt* BE APPROPRIATE to be an appropriate or socially acceptable thing for somebody to do or say (*formal*) [Old English *becuman* < Germanic]

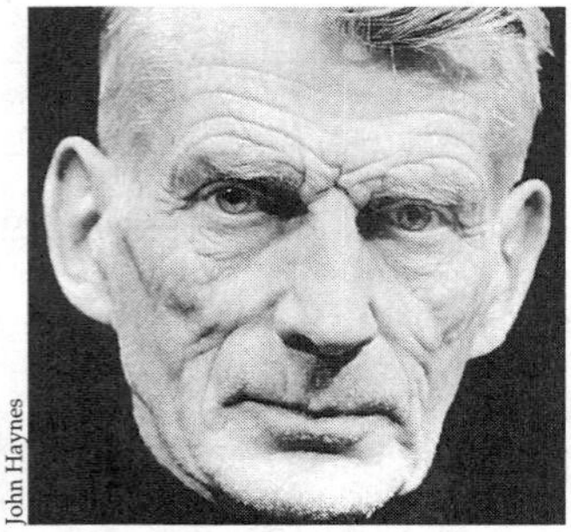

Samuel Beckett

become of *vt* to happen to somebody or something

becoming /bi kúmming/ *adj* **1** attractively suitable for somebody's appearance **2** appropriate or fitting for somebody —**becomingly** *adv* —**becomingness** *n*

becquerel /béka rel/ *n* (*symbol* **Bq**) the SI unit for measuring radioactivity, equal to the activity resulting from the decay of one nucleus of radioactive matter in one second [Late 19C. After Antoine Henri *Becquerel* (1852–1908), French physicist.]

BECTU /bék too/ *abbr* Broadcasting, Entertainment, and Cinematograph Technicians Union

bed /bed/ *n* **1** FURNITURE ON WHICH TO SLEEP a piece of furniture on which to sleep, usually consisting of a rectangular frame with a mattress on top **2** MATTRESS a mattress, especially with its coverings **3** SLEEP sleep or rest in bed, or the time for this **4** PLACE FOR SLEEPING a place in which to sleep, or an object on which to sleep ○ *looking for a bed for the night* **5** ACCOMMODATION FOR GUEST OR PATIENT a place for one person to stay or sleep as a guest in a hotel or a patient in a hospital **6** PATCH OF SOIL an area of soil prepared for plants, especially flowers, or an area where particular plants are growing ○ *a rose bed* **7** GROUND UNDER WATER the ground at the bottom of the sea, a river, or a lake **8** STATE OF INTIMACY the state of sexual intimacy associated with being in bed with somebody ○ *the marriage bed* **9** SURFACE ON WHICH TO BUILD a prepared surface on which something is built or laid, e.g. the foundation of a road or a railway **10** LAYER OF FOOD a layer of food on which another item of food is placed for serving **11** AREA OF WATER WITH SHELLFISH an area of the sea, a river, or a lake, where a particular kind of shellfish is found or cultivated ○ *oyster beds* **12** LAYER OF ROCK a layer of rock, normally sedimentary, that is generally homogeneous and was deposited more or less continuously without erosion ■ *v* (**beds, bedding, bedded**) **1** *vt* FIX INTO SURROUNDING SURFACE to embed something firmly in a surrounding mass of a substance such as rock or concrete **2** *vt* HAVE SEXUAL INTERCOURSE WITH to have sexual intercourse with somebody (*informal*) **3** *vti* FORM LAYER to arrange something, or be arranged, in a layer or stratum [Old English *bedd* < Germanic, 'dig'] ◇ **a bed of nails** an extremely difficult situation or existence ◇ **get out of bed on the wrong side** to be in an irritable or angry mood right from the start of the day ◇ **go to bed with somebody** to have sexual intercourse with somebody ◇ **put something to bed** to finish work on a newspaper or magazine so it is ready to go to press

bed down *v* **1** *vi* GO TO BED to settle down somewhere, not usually in a proper bed, ready for sleep **2** *vt* PUT TO BED to put a person to bed or an animal in a place with bedding for the night **3** *vi* SETTLE INTO POSITION to sink and settle into position or become flatter and denser

bed in *vti* to fit something firmly into place, or fit firmly into place

bed out *vt* to put young plants raised indoors into their final growing position outside

BEd /beé ed/ *abbr* Bachelor of Education

bed and board *n* accommodation and meals provided for somebody

bed and breakfast *n* **1** ROOM AND BREAKFAST overnight accommodation and breakfast provided for paying guests **2** GUESTHOUSE a small hotel or, more often, a private home that offers overnight accommodation and breakfast for paying guests ■ *adj* INVOLVING SELLING THEN QUICK REACQUISITION describes transactions involving selling shares late one day and buying them back for less the next morning, to create an apparent financial loss for tax purposes (*informal*)

bedaub /bi dáwb/ *vt* to smear a surface thickly or carelessly with something that spoils it or makes it dirty (*literary*)

bedazzle /bi dázz'l/ (**-zles, -zling, -zled**) *vt* (*literary*) **1** to astonish somebody by being immediately impressive (*usually passive*) **2** to make somebody temporarily unable to see by shining a bright light

bed bath *n* an all-over wash for somebody confined to bed. US term **sponge bath**

bedbug /béd bug/ *n* a small wingless bloodsucking insect that infests the bedding and furnishings of houses and the nests of mammals. Family: Cimicidae.

bedchamber /béd chaymbar/ *n* a bedroom (*archaic*)

bedclothes /béd klōthz, -klōz/ *npl* the sheets, blankets, duvet, and any other similar coverings on a bed

bedcover /béd kuvar/ *n* any of the coverings, e.g. sheets and blankets, for a bed

beddable /béddab'l/ *adj* considered desirable enough to make a good sexual partner (*informal*)

bedder /béddar/ *n* **1** somebody who cleans students' rooms in Cambridge University **2** GARDENING = **bedding plant**

bedding /bédding/ *n* **1** BED COVERINGS the coverings, e.g. sheets, quilts, and blankets, and the mattress and pillows used to prepare a bed **2** SOMETHING USED AS BED something used to make a bed **3** BED FOR ANIMALS material such as straw put down for animals to lie on **4** UNDER LAYER a layer of material put down under something else, especially to serve as a foundation **5** ARRANGEMENT OF ROCK STRATA the arrangement of a group of rock strata, or beds, in a particular area or outcrop

bedding plant *n* a plant suitable for planting in a flower bed for one season's display

Bede /beed/, **Baeda** /beéda/, **St** (673?–735) English theologian and historian. Known as **the Venerable Bede**

bedeck /bi dék/ *vt* to make something look pretty or festive, especially by decorating it with colourful flags, ribbons, or streamers

bedevil /bi dévv'l/ (**-ils, -illing, -illed**) *vt* to be a continual source of problems or irritation to something or somebody —**bedevilment** *n*

bedew /bi dyoó/ *vt* to wet or cover something with dew or drops of liquid (*literary*)

bedfellow /béd felō/ *n* **1** somebody or something paired or allied with somebody or something else **2** somebody who shares a bed with somebody else (*archaic*)

Bedford /bédfard/ town in south-central England. Population: 137,451 (1996 estimate).

Bedford cord *n* a heavy ribbed fabric like corduroy

Bedfordshire /bédfardshar/ county in central England. Population: 543,100 (1994). Area: 1,235 sq. km/477 sq. mi.

bedhead /béd hed/ *n* the upper end of a bed, often with a headboard or rail

bed-hopping *n* casual sex with successive partners (*informal*)

bedim /bi dím/ (**-dims, -dimming, -dimmed**) *vt* (*literary*) **1** to make the eyes or mind less able to perceive things clearly **2** to make something appear less bright or distinct

bedizen /bi díz'n, -dízz'n/ *vt* to dress or decorate somebody or something in a way that seems exaggeratedly or vulgarly showy (*literary*) [Mid-17C. < *dizen* 'put flax onto a rod'.] —**bedizenment** *n*

bed jacket *n* a woman's short light jacket worn over a nightdress when sitting up in bed

bedlam /bédlam/ *n* **1** a place or situation full of noise, frenzied activity, and confusion **2** a psychiatric hospital (*archaic; offensive in some contexts*) [15C. Alteration of BETHLEHEM.]

bed linen *n* the sheets, pillowcases, and other fabric coverings that go on a bed

Bedlington terrier /bédlingtan-/, **Bedlington** *n* a dog belonging to a breed of English terriers that have a tapering head and fleecy coat that makes them look similar to lambs [Mid-19C. After the N English town of Bedlington.]

bed load *n* the loose sand and gravel carried by a stream at or above its bed

Bedloe's Island /bédlōz-/ former name for **Liberty Island**

bed moulding *n* in classical architecture, the lowest section of a cornice, protruding less than the topmost part

Bedouin /béddoo in/ (*plural* **-ins** *or* **-in**), **Beduin** (*plural* **-ins** *or* **-in**) *n* a nomadic Arab of the desert regions of Arabia and North Africa [15C. Via Old French *beduin* < Arabic *badw* 'desert, nomadic desert people'.] —**Bedouin** *adj*

bedpan /béd pan/ *n* a shallow container into which a sick or frail person can urinate or defecate while lying in bed

bedplate /béd playt/ *n* a heavy metal base or platform to which the frame of an engine or machine is attached

bedpost /béd pōst/ *n* one of the posts at the corners of a bed, especially a four-poster bed

bedraggled /bi drágg'ld/ *adj* wet, dirty, and unkempt, or with hair or clothes in this state

bedrail /béd rayl/ *n* a rail at the head, foot, or side of a bed

bed rest *n* staying in bed to rest and recover when not well

bedridden /béd rid'n/ *adj* forced to remain in bed because of illness, weakness, or injury [14C. < Old English *bedrida* 'bed-rider'.]

bedrock /béd rok/ *n* **1** the solid rock beneath a layer of soil, rock fragments, or gravel **2** the facts or principles on which something is based

bedroll /béd rōl/ *n* a roll of bedding carried by somebody who is hiking or camping

bedroom /béd room, -rŏom/ *n* a room that has a bed in it and is used mainly for sleeping ■ *adj* involving, depicting, or suggesting sexual activity ○ *a bedroom comedy*

beds *abbr* bedrooms (*in advertisements*)

Beds. *abbr* Bedfordshire

bedside /béd sīd/ *n* the side of a bed, or the space next to it —**bedside** *adj*

bedside manner *n* a doctor's way of talking to and dealing with patients

bedsit /béd sit, béd sít/ *n* = **bedsitter** (*informal*) [Mid-20C. Shortening.]

bedsitter /béd sitar, -síttar/, **bedsit** /béd sit/ *n* a combined bedroom and living room, especially one that is rented and serves as somebody's residence [*sitter* < SITTING ROOM]

bedsock /béd sok/ *n* either of a pair of socks that are worn to keep the feet warm in bed

bedsore /béd sawr/ *n* an ulcer on the skin caused by pressure and friction from bedding when somebody is confined to bed for a long time

bedspread /béd spred/ *n* a decorative covering placed on top of bedclothes

bedstead /béd sted/ *n* the structural framework of a bed, excluding the mattress and coverings [Originally the place where a bed stood]

bedstraw /béd straw/ *n* a plant of the madder family with small pointed leaves and hairy stems. Flowers: small, white or yellow. Use: formerly, as stuffing for mattresses. Genus: *Galium*.

bedtime /béd tīm/ *n* the time when somebody normally goes to bed, or should go to bed

Beduin *n*, *adj* PEOPLES = **Bedouin**

bedwarmer /béd wawrmar/ *n* a covered metal container for hot coals, formerly used to warm a bed

bed-wetting *n* urination in bed during sleep, especially by a child —**bedwetter** *n*

bee /bee/ *n* **1** a flying insect with a furry body that makes a buzzing sound as it flies. Superfamily: Apoidea. ◊ **bumblebee, honeybee 2** *US* a gathering at which people combine working together at a particular activity or having a friendly competition while socializing ○ *a sewing bee* ○ *a quilting bee* [Old English *bēo* < Germanic]

Beeb /beeb/ *n* the BBC (*informal humorous*) [Mid-20C. Shortening of the pronunciation of BBC.]

beebread /bee bred/ *n* a yellow-brown pollen stored by bees and mixed with honey as food for their larvae

beech /beech/ *n* **1** a tall tree with smooth grey bark and glossy deciduous leaves. Native to: temperate regions. Genus: *Fagus*. **2** the wood of the beech tree. Use: furniture. [Old English *bēce* < Germanic]

SPELLCHECK See *beach*.

Beecham /beechəm/, **Sir Thomas** (1879–1961) British conductor and impresario

beech mast *n* the hard fruit of a beech tree enclosed in a prickly case

beechnut /beech nut/ *n* the small triangular hard edible fruit of a beech tree

beeda /beedə/ *n* a combination of betel leaf and areca nuts, eaten in India after a meal to aid digestion [Mid-20C. < Hindi.]

bee-eater *n* a small brightly coloured bird that preys on insects. Native to: Europe and Asia. Family: Meropidae.

beef /beef/ *n* **1** MEAT FROM CATTLE meat from a cow, heifer, bull, or bullock **2** (*plural* **beeves**) ANIMAL GIVING BEEF a cow, heifer, bull, or bullock being reared for meat **3** STRENGTH muscular strength or effort (*informal*) **4** COMPLAINT a complaint about something (*slang*) ■ *vi* COMPLAIN to complain about something (*slang*) [12C. Via Anglo-Norman *boef* < stem of Latin *bos* 'ox'.]

beef up *vt* to make something stronger or more effective (*informal*) —**beefed-up** *adj*

beefalo /beefə lō/ (*plural* **-lo** *or* **-loes**) *n* a cross between the North American bison and domestic cattle that is raised for its resistance to disease and its lean meat [Late 20C. Blend of BEEF + BUFFALO.]

beefburger /beef burgar/ *n* COOK = **hamburger** *n*. 1, **hamburger** *n*. 2

beefcake /beef kayk/ *n* muscular men or pictures of them, considered from the point of view of their physical appearance (*informal*) [After CHEESECAKE]

beefeater /beef eetar/ *n* one of the Yeomen of the Guard, a group who act as warders of the Tower of London wearing a uniform of Tudor dress

bee fly *n* a fly that resembles a bee, eats pollen and nectar, and whose larvae develop as parasites on insect larvae. Family: Bombyliidae.

beefsteak /beef stayk/ *n* a slice of lean, tender beef that can be grilled or fried

beefsteak fungus /beef stayk-/, **beefsteak mushroom** *n* an edible bracket fungus with a large reddish cap that grows especially on oak and ash trees. *Fistulina hepatica*.

beefsteak tomato *n* US PLANTS = **beef tomato**

beef tea *n* a drink made by boiling beef to extract the juices, formerly given to invalids

beef tomato *n* a large firm-fleshed tomato. US term **beefsteak tomato**

beef Wellington *n* a dish consisting of a fillet of beef, covered in pâté de foie gras, wrapped in pastry, and baked

beefwood /beef wŏod/ *n* **1** the hard red wood of an Australian tree. Use: construction, cabinet-making. **2** an evergreen hardwood tree that is the source of beefwood. Native to: Australia. Genus: *Casuarina*.

beefy /beefi/ (**-ier, -iest**) *adj* **1** MUSCULAR strong and muscular **2** POWERFUL having strength, power, or substance (*informal*) ○ *a novel with a really beefy plot* **3** LIKE BEEF containing, produced by, or resembling beef —**beefily** *adv* —**beefiness** *n*

beehive /bee hīv/ *n* **1** HIVE FOR BEES a structure housing a colony of bees **2** TALL HAIRSTYLE a hairstyle for women, popular around 1960, in which the hair is arranged in a high rounded shape on top of the head ■ *adj* BEEHIVE-SHAPED shaped like a beehive, with a round base rising in a cone to a domed top

beehive house *n* a round prehistoric house with a domed roof

beekeeper /bee keepar/ *n* somebody who keeps bees for honey or to pollinate crops —**beekeeping** *n*

beeline /bee līn/ *n* a very direct line, path, or other course from one point to another ○ *The kids made a beeline for the swimming pool as soon as we reached the motel.* [< the belief that bees return to their hives in a straight line]

Beelzebub /bi élzi bub/ *n* the Devil, or one of the chief devils in hell [Pre-12C. Via Latin < Hebrew *ba'al zĕbūb* 'Lord of Flies', a Philistine god.]

been past participle of **be**

Beenleigh /beénli/ *n* town in SE Queensland, Australia. Population: 16,387 (1991).

bee orchid *n* a European orchid. Flowers: resembling bees. *Ophrys apiphera*.

beep /beep/ *n* SHORT HIGH NOISE a short high-pitched noise emitted as a signal by a piece of electronic equipment or the horn of a vehicle ■ *v* **1** *vti* MAKE BEEP to make a beep **2** *vt* SIGNAL WITH CAR HORN to signal to somebody by using the horn of a vehicle [Early 20C. An imitation of the sound.]

beeper /beepar/ *n* COMMUNICATION = **pager** (*informal*)

bee plant *n* any plant that is particularly attractive to bees

beer /beer/ *n* **1** DRINK BREWED FROM MALT a typically bitter-tasting alcoholic drink brewed by fermenting malt with sugar and yeast and flavouring it with hops **2** DRINK OF BEER a drink or glass of beer **3** HERBAL DRINK a fizzy or slightly fermented drink made from, or flavoured with, the roots, leaves, or seeds of a plant [Old English *bēor* < late Latin *biber* 'drink' < *bibere* 'to drink']

SPELLCHECK Do not confuse *beer* with *bier*, which has a similar sound. Beware: your spellchecker will not catch this error.

beer and skittles *n* pleasure and amusement (*informal*)

beer belly *n* an extended stomach often associated with having drunk too much beer (*slang*)

Beerbohm /beer bōm/, **Sir Max** (1872–1956) British writer and caricaturist. Known as **the Incomparable Max**

beer garden *n* an open space or garden, often attached to a pub or similar establishment, where beer and other alcoholic drinks can be purchased and drunk in the open air

beer gut *n* = **beer belly** (*slang*)

Beersheba /beer sheebə/ *n* city in south-central Israel. In biblical times it was in the extreme south of Palestine. Population: 160,364 (1998 estimate).

beery /beeri/ (**-ier, -iest**) *adj* **1** typical of somebody who is slightly inebriated from having drunk too much beer **2** smelling or tasting of beer —**beerily** *adv* —**beeriness** *n*

beestings /beestingz/ *n* the first milk secreted by a mammal, especially a cow or goat, after it has given birth [Old English *bȳsting* < Germanic]

bee-stung *adj* full and rounded, as if stung by a bee ○ *bee-stung lips*

beeswax /beez waks/ *n* **1** WAX MADE BY BEES the dark yellow substance secreted by honeybees and used for building honeycombs **2** COMMERCIALLY PROCESSED BEESWAX wax produced by bees that has been commercially processed for use in furniture polishes, candles, and crayons ■ *vt* POLISH WITH BEESWAX to polish something with beeswax

beeswing /beez wing/ *n* a thin shiny sediment that forms in port and some other wines when they are kept for a long time after bottling

beet /beet/ *n* **1** a plant with a large swollen root. Use: some types as vegetable, some for animal feed, one for sugar. Genus: *Beta*. **2** *US* PLANTS = **beetroot** *n*. 1 **3** *US* FOOD = **beetroot** *n*. 2 [Old English *bēte* < Latin *beta*]

SPELLCHECK See *beat*.

Beethoven /báyt hōvən/, **Ludwig van** (1770–1827) German composer

beetle[1] /beet'l/ *n* **1** HARD-BACKED INSECT an insect belonging to a large order characterized by a modified outer pair of wings that form a hard covering for the inner pair. Order: Coleoptera. **2** DICE GAME a game in which players attempt to draw or assemble a complete beetle-shape by throwing a dice and drawing in or collecting the part corresponding to the number thrown ■ *vi* (**-tles, -tling, -tled**) GO QUICKLY to go somewhere quickly (*informal*) [Old English *bitula, bitela* < *bītan* 'to bite']

beetle[2] /beet'l/ *n* **1** LARGE MALLET a large tool with a long handle and a heavy wooden head. Use: driving in stakes, ramming, pounding. **2** TEXTILE-FINISHING MACHINE a machine that beats cloth to give it a smooth finish ■ *vt* (**-tles, -tling, -tled**) FINISH CLOTH to give a finishing treatment to cloth with a beetle [Old English *bētel, bīetel* < Germanic]

beetle[3] /beét'l/ *vi* (**-tles, -tling, -tled**) to overhang or jut out (*literary*) ■ *adj* jutting out and shaggy (*literary*) ○ *beetle brows* [14C. < ?] —**beetling** *adj*

beetle-browed *adj* having eyebrows that are thick, bushy, or jutting

beetle-crushers *npl* heavy, thick-soled boots or shoes (*informal*)

beetle drive *n* a social gathering to play the game of beetle

Beeton /beét'n/, **Isabella Mary** (1836–65) British cookery writer. Known as **Mrs Beeton**

beetroot /beét root/ *n* **1** the dark red root of a beet plant, cooked and usually eaten cold as a salad vegetable or pickled. US term **beet** *n*. 3 **2** a beet plant that produces beetroots. *Beta vulgaris.* US term **beet** *n*. 2

beet sugar *n* sugar that has been extracted from sugar beet

beeves plural of **beef** *n*. 2

BEF *n* the British Army that served overseas during World War I and World War II. Full form **British Expeditionary Force**

befall /bi fáwl/ (**-falls, -falling, -fell** /-fél/, **-fallen** /-fáwlən/) *vti* to happen, or happen to somebody, especially through the unexpected workings of chance or fate (*archaic or literary*)

befit /bi fít/ (**-fits, -fitting, -fitted**) *vt* to be suitable or appropriate for somebody or something —**befitting** *adj* —**befittingly** *adv*

befog /bi fóg/ (**-fogs, -fogging, -fogged**) *vt* (*literary*) **1** to make somebody or something vague or confused **2** to make something difficult to see or see through because it is covered in fog

before /bi fáwr/ CORE MEANING: a grammatical word indicating that a point in time, event, or situation precedes another in a sequence ○ (prep) *We try all of the products before deciding to stock them.* ○ (conj) *We lost a lot of manufacturing jobs in the 12 years before I became president.* ○ (conj) *She died at the hospital before her parents could reach her side.* ○ (adv) *He has had this nightmare before.*

1 *prep* **IN THE PRESENCE OF** in the presence of a person or body of people ○ *spoke before a huge crowd* **2** *prep* **WITH MORE IMPORTANCE THAN** indicating that one thing is preferable to or more important than another ○ *Their needs come before yours.* **3** *prep* **INDICATES LOCATION** located close to something but just ahead of it **4** *prep* **AHEAD OF** stretching ahead of somebody **5** *prep, conj, adv* **EARLIER** earlier than a particular date, time, or event **6** *prep, conj* **INDICATES SEQUENCE** used to indicate a sequence of actions, one preceding the other and closely connected with it **7** *adv* **PREVIOUSLY** on a previous occasion **8** *conj* **RATHER THAN** used to indicate that somebody would prefer to do one thing rather than what they consider to be a worse thing ○ *I'll quit before I report to him.* [Old English *beforan* < Germanic]

beforehand /bi fáwr hand/ *adv* used to indicate that a situation, action, or event happens ahead of time or in advance of something

befoul /bi fówl/ *vt* to make something dirty or impure (*archaic or literary*) —**befoulment** *n*

befriend /bi frénd/ *vt* to be friendly to somebody, especially to somebody who has no friends and needs help —**befriender** *n*

befuddle /bi fúdd'l/ (**-dles, -dling, -dled**) *vt* to make somebody confused or perplexed —**befuddled** *adj* —**befuddlement** *n*

beg /beg/ (**begs, begging, begged**) *v* **1** *vti* **ASK WITH EMOTION** to ask somebody for something in a very intense, humble, or even humiliating way **2** *vti* **ASK FOR CHARITY** to ask people for gifts of money or food, especially in the street **3** *vi* **SIT UP AND ASK FOR FOOD** to ask for food by performing an action that has been previously taught, especially, for a dog, by sitting up and holding out the front legs **4** *vt* **EVADE** to avoid answering or dealing with a point, especially by assuming that it has already been dealt with ○ *beg the question* [Probably < Old English *bedecian* < Germanic]

beg off *vi* to ask to be excused from doing something

begad /bi gád/ *interj* used to add emphasis to something that is said (*archaic*) [Late 16C. Alteration of *by God*.]

began past tense of **begin**

beget /bi gét/ (**-gets, -getting, -got** /-gót/ *or* **-gat** /-gát/, **-gotten** /-gótt'n/ *or* **-got**) *vt* **1** to be the father of a child (*archaic*) **2** to be the cause of something [Old English *begietan* 'get' < Germanic] —**begetter** *n*

beggar /béggər/ *n* **1** **SOMEBODY WHO BEGS** somebody who begs for money or food **2** **VERY POOR PERSON** a very poor person **3** **PERSON** a person (*informal*) ○ *You lucky beggar!* ■ *vt* **1** **MAKE POOR** to make somebody poor (*literary*) **2** **BE BEYOND SCOPE OF** to be so extraordinary as to make description or belief impossible

beggarly /béggərli/ *adj* insufficient and showing meanness —**beggarliness** *n*

beggar-my-neighbour *n* a simple card game for two players in which cards are won and lost until one person holds them all ■ *adj* involving a ruthless attitude towards another person, organization, or country, especially as regards taking over resources

beggar's lice (*plural* **beggar's lice**), **beggar ticks** (*plural* **beggar ticks**) *n* **1** PLANTS = **bur marigold** **2** the burs of a beggar's lice plant

beggary /béggəri/ *n* a state of extreme poverty

~~**begger**~~ incorrect spelling of **beggar**

begging bowl *n* a bowl carried by somebody who begs to collect gifts of food or money

begging letter *n* a letter asking for money or help

begin /bi gín/ (**-gins, -ginning, -gan** /-gán/, **-gun** /-gún/) *v* **1** *vti* **START** to do something that was not being done before ○ *People began to leave.* **2** *vti* **HAVE AS ITS STARTING POINT** to have as its starting point, first action, or first part, or be the starting point or first part of something ○ *The story begins with a birthday party.* **3** *vti* **COME OR BRING INTO BEING** to come into existence, or cause something to come into existence or take place ○ *The business began as a two-person operation.* **4** *vt* **UNDERTAKE FOR FIRST TIME** to undertake, use, or give attention to something for the first time **5** *vti* **START TO SPEAK** to start to say something **6** *vt* **BE CAPABLE OF** to be able to succeed in accomplishing a particular task (*in negatives*) ○ *The salary doesn't even begin to meet her expectations* ○ *I couldn't begin to explain how awful it was* [Old English *beginnan* < Germanic]

Begin /báygin/, **Menachem** (1913–92) Russian-born Israeli statesman

~~**begining**~~ incorrect spelling of **beginning**

beginner /bi gínnər/ *n* somebody who has just started to do something

SYNONYMS ***beginner, apprentice, greenhorn, novice, tyro***

CORE MEANING: a person who has not acquired the necessary experience or skills to do something

beginner somebody who has just started to learn or do something; **apprentice** somebody who is being taught the skills of a trade over an agreed period of time by somebody fully trained; **greenhorn** somebody who lacks experience and may be naïve or gullible; **novice** somebody with no previous experience or skill in the activity undertaken; **tyro** somebody who is raw and inexperienced.

beginner's luck *n* early success that seems inconsistent with somebody's lack of experience

beginning /bi gínning/ *n* **1** **FIRST PART** the first part or early stages of something **2** **START** the point in time or space at which something starts, comes into existence, or is first encountered ■ **beginnings** *npl* **EARLY CONDITIONS** the conditions in which something or somebody starts

begone /bi gón/ *interj* used to tell somebody to go away (*archaic*)

begonia /bi góni ə/ *n* a widely grown houseplant and garden plant with ragged-edged leaves. Flowers: round or drooping, brightly coloured. Genus: *Begonia.* [Mid-18C. < modern Latin, after Michel *Bégon*, (1638–1710), governor of French Canada.]

begorra /bi górrə/ *interj Ireland* used as an exclamation or a mild oath (*archaic*) [Mid-19C. Alteration of *by God*.]

begot past tense, past participle of **beget**

begotten past participle of **beget**

begrime /bi grím/ (**-grimes, -griming, -grimed**) *vt* to cover something with grime

begrudge /bi grúj/ (**-grudges, -grudging, -grudged**) *vt* **1** to resent the fact that somebody has something ○ *begrudged me my success* **2** to be unwilling to give or pay something

begrudging /bi grújjing/ *adj* showing unwillingness to give somebody something or to let somebody be admired or praised —**begrudgingly** *adv*

beguile /bi gíl/ (**-guiles, -guiling, -guiled**) *vt* **1** **CHARM** to win and hold somebody's attention, interest, or devotion **2** **DECEIVE** to mislead or deceive somebody (*literary*) **3** **CHEAT** to rob somebody of something (*literary*) **4** **PASS** to pass time in a pleasant way (*literary*) —**beguilement** *n* —**beguiler** *n*

beguiling /bi gíling/ *adj* having the power to gain people's interest or devotion —**beguilingly** *adv*

beguine /bi geén/ *n* a ballroom dance similar to the rumba, originating in the West Indies [Early 20C. < French *béguine* < *béguin* 'flirtation'.]

begum /báygəm, beé-/ *n* **1** a title of respect for a woman in some Muslim communities **2** a woman of high rank in some Muslim communities [Mid-17C. Via Urdu < East Turkic, 'my mistress'.]

begun past participle of **begin**

behalf /bi haáf/ [14C. Blend of *on his half* + *by half him*, both meaning 'on his side'.] ◇ **in somebody's behalf** *US* on somebody's behalf ◇ **on somebody's behalf** **1** as somebody's representative ○ *We chose James to speak on our behalf.* **2** for somebody's benefit or support, or in somebody's best interests

USAGE on somebody's behalf: It is important to distinguish ***on somebody's behalf*** from *on somebody's part* (= as far as somebody is concerned): *This is a serious error on the part of [not: on behalf of] the Minister.* In the United States, *in somebody's behalf* is also used but this variant has virtually died out in British English.

Behan /beé ən/, **Brendan** (1923–64) Irish playwright and author

behave /bi háyv/ (**-haves, -having, -haved**) *vi* **1** **ACT** to act in a particular way that expresses general character, state of mind, or response to a situation or other people ○ *He's been behaving oddly.* **2** **BEHAVE WELL** to act in an acceptable way, especially by being polite, good-tempered, and self-controlled **3** **PERFORM** to perform in or react to particular conditions or circumstances [15C. < HAVE in the obsolete sense 'conduct yourself'.]

behavior *n* US = **behaviour**

behaviour /bi háyvyər/ *n* **1** **THE WAY SOMEBODY BEHAVES** the way in which somebody behaves **2** **RESPONSE** the way in which a person, organism, or group responds to a certain set of conditions **3** **WHAT SOMETHING DOES** the way that a machine operates or a substance reacts under a certain set of conditions [15C. < BEHAVE, after *haviour* 'possession' < Old French *aveir* 'have'.] —**behavioural** *adj* —**behaviourally** *adv*

behavioural contagion *n* the spread of a type of behaviour first exhibited by a few people in a group to the group as a whole

behavioural psychology *n* a branch of psychology based on the observation and modification of the way that people behave

behavioural science *n* **1** a science such as sociology, psychology, or anthropology that is concerned with the ways in which people or animals behave **2** the use of scientific methods to study the behaviour of living creatures —**behavioural scientist** *n*

behavioural therapy *n* PSYCHIAT = **behaviour medicine**

behaviourism /bi háyvyərizəm/ *n* **1** an approach to the study of psychology that concentrates exclusively on observing, measuring, and modifying behaviour. ◊ **introspectionism** **2** the theory that statements about the mind and mental states are really about actual or potential behaviour —**behaviourist** *adj, n* —**behaviouristic** /-rístik/ *adj*

behaviour modification *n* psychological treatment that attempts to change somebody's behaviour by rewarding new and desirable responses and making accustomed undesirable ones less attractive

behaviour therapy *n* a form of psychotherapy, the goal of which is observable changes in problem behaviours rather than changes in mental state. US term **behavioral medicine**

behead /bi héd/ *vt* to cut the head off somebody or something, especially as a form of execution

beheld past tense, past participle of **behold**

behemoth /bi heé moth, -m əth/ *n* **1** **behemoth, Behemoth** a huge beast referred to in the Bible, usually thought to be a hippopotamus (Job 40:15) **2** something that is enormously big or powerful [14C. < Hebrew *bəhēmōṯ* < *bəhēmāh* 'beast'.]

behest /bi hést/ n an order or request (literary) ○ arrived at the conference only at her behest [Alteration of Old English behǽs < Germanic, 'to bid, call']

behind /bi hínd/ CORE MEANING: a grammatical word indicating that somebody or something is in or is going towards a position at the back or rear of something ○ (prep) From behind the door we heard country music. ○ (prep) She was behind the wheel, and I was in the back. ○ (adv) Their car was hit from behind. ○ (adv) She had to go back because she'd left her money behind.
1 prep, adv AT THE BACK OF in or towards a position farther back or at the rear of something **2** prep, adv FOLLOWING following somebody or something **3** adv IN DEBT in debt or in arrears on a payment ○ months behind on the payments **4** adv REMAINING used to indicate that somebody or something is left after another's departure **5** prep IN THE PAST indicates that an achievement or experience happened in the past ○ My best days are behind me. **6** prep LATE indicates that something is not as far advanced as it should be ○ seven weeks behind schedule **7** prep CAUSING causing or being responsible for something ○ the reason behind it **8** prep SUPPORTING backing or supporting somebody ○ I'm behind you all the way on this issue. **9** prep UNDERNEATH underneath the external appearance of somebody or something ○ Behind his calm exterior, he was very confused. **10** n BUTTOCKS somebody's buttocks (informal) [Old English behindan < hindan 'from behind' < Germanic] ◇ **put something behind you** to ensure that something unpleasant can no longer affect you detrimentally

behindhand /bi hínd hand/ adj **1** BEHIND SCHEDULE behind schedule **2** LAGGING BEHIND behind in development or achievement **3** IN ARREARS in arrears for payment of a debt [Mid-16C. After BEFOREHAND.]

behind-the-scenes adj carried out privately or secretly ○ a lot of frantic behind-the-scenes negotiation

Behn /ben/, **Aphra** (1640–89) English writer

behold /bi hóld/ (-holds, -holding, -held /-héld/, -held) vt to see or observe something or somebody (archaic or literary; often in commands) ○ 'Behold her, single in the field, / Yon solitary Highland lass!' (William Wordsworth, The Solitary Reaper) [Old English bihaldan < Germanic, 'watch, guard'] —**beholder** n

beholden /bi hóld'n/ adj under an obligation to somebody because of something helpful that person has done [14C. Originally past participle of BEHOLD, in the obsolete sense 'hold under obligation'.]

behove /bi hóov/ (-hoves, -hoving, -hoved) vt to be right and proper or appropriate for somebody (formal) ○ It ill behoves him to complain. [Old English behófian 'to need']

Behrens /báirənz/, **Peter** (1868–1940) German architect and designer

Behring /báiring/, **Emil von** (1854–1917) German bacteriologist

Beiderbecke /bídər bek/, **Bix** (1903–31) US musician. Born **Leon Bismarke Beiderbecke**

beige /bayzh/ adj VERY PALE BROWN of a very pale brown colour with a tinge of yellow or pink ■ n **1** BEIGE COLOUR a beige colour **2** UNDYED WOOLLEN CLOTH cloth made of undyed or unbleached wool [Mid-19C. < French, perhaps < late Latin bombax 'cotton'.]

Beijing /bay jíng/ capital of China, in the NE of the country. Population: 7,746,519 (1991).

being /bée ing/ present participle of **be** ■ n **1** EXISTENCE the state of existing ○ the turbulent years during which the new nation came into being **2** ESSENTIAL NATURE somebody's essential nature or character **3** LIVING THING a living thing, especially one conceived of as supernatural or not living on earth **4** PERSON a human individual

Beira /bíra/ capital of Sofala Province, E Mozambique. Population: 299,300 (1990).

Beirut /bay róot/ capital of Lebanon, and a major port on the Mediterranean Sea. Population: 1,500,000 (1998 estimate).

bejabers /bi jáybərz/ interj, n Ireland = **bejasus** [Early 19C. Alteration of by Jesus.]

Béjart /báy zhaar/, **Maurice** (b. 1928) French dancer and choreographer. Born **Maurice Jean de Berger**

bejasus /bi jáyzəss/, **bejesus** /-jéezəss, -jáyzəss/ n Ireland used to emphasize a statement or question ■ interj Ireland used as an exclamation or a mild oath [Early 20C. Alteration of by Jesus.]

bejewel /bi jóō əl/ (-els, -elling, -elled) vt to decorate something lavishly with jewels or colourful decorative objects —**bejewelled** adj

Bekaa Valley /bi kaáa/, **Bekáa Valley** valley in Lebanon, running down the centre of the country. Length: 120 km/75 mi.

bel /bel/ n a logarithmic unit for comparing the loudness or strength of signals, equal to an intensity ratio of 10 to 1 [Early 20C. After Alexander Graham BELL.]

belabor vt US = **belabour**

belabour /bi láybər/ vt **1** HARP ON to repeat or discuss something unnecessarily or at too great a length **2** CRITICIZE to subject somebody to a sustained verbal or literary attack (literary) **3** BEAT to hit somebody hard and repeatedly with something (literary or humorous)

Belarus

Belarus /béllə róoss, byéllə-/ republic in E Europe, formerly part of the USSR. Capital: Minsk. Population: 10,412,219 (1997). Area: 207,595 sq. km/80,153 sq. mi.

Belarusian /béllə rúsh'n/ n **1** somebody who comes from Belarus **2** the official language of the Republic of Belarus, belonging to the East Slavonic group of Indo-European languages. Native speakers: 11 million. —**Belarusian** adj

belated /bi láytid/ adj occurring after the appropriate or expected time, especially too late to be effective or useful [Early 17C. < belate 'make late, delay'.] —**belatedly** adv —**belatedness** n

Belau ♦ **Palau**

belay /bi láy/ vti **1** FASTEN LINE ON SHIP to fasten a rope or line to a securing point on a ship or boat **2** SECURE ROPE to fasten or control the rope to which a climber is attached by wrapping it round a metal device or another person ■ n **1** SECURING OF CLIMBER'S ROPE the fastening or controlling of a climber's rope by wrapping it around a metal device or another person, or the method by which this is done **2** FASTENING POINT the point to which a climber's rope is fastened [Old English belecgan 'surround' < Germanic]

belaying pin n a large wooden or metal pin that fits into a hole in a rail on a ship or boat and to which a rope can be fastened

bel canto /bel kántō/ n **1** a style of operatic singing that concentrates on producing a pure and even tone **2** a style of expressive melodic instrumental playing that uses the principles of bel canto singing [Late 19C. < Italian, 'fine song'.]

belch /belch/ vti **1** to let gas from the stomach out through the mouth, making a loud noise in the throat **2** to send out large amounts of steam, smoke, or gas, or come out of something in a thick cloud [Old English bealcettan, bælcan, perhaps < Germanic] —**belch** n

beleaguer /bi léegər/ vt (usually passive) **1** to make somebody feel harassed, hemmed in, or under severe pressure **2** to surround somebody or something with an army [Late 16C. < Dutch belegeren 'camp around, besiege'.] —**beleaguerment** n

~~beleif~~ incorrect spelling of **belief**

~~beleive~~ incorrect spelling of **believe**

Belém /bə lém/ port and capital of Pará State, N Brazil. Population: 1,144,312 (1996 estimate).

belemnite /bélləm nīt/ n a fossilized cylinder-shaped internal shell of an extinct order of cephalopods common in the Mesozoic era [Early 17C. < modern Latin, < Greek belemnon 'a dart', from its shape.]

bel esprit /bél ess prée/ (plural **beaux esprits** /bōz es prée/) n a witty, intelligent, and cultured person [Mid-17C. < French, 'fine mind'.]

Belfast /bél faast, bel faást/ capital of Northern Ireland, located at the head of Belfast Lough on the Lagan River. Population: 297,300 (1996 estimate).

Belfast roof n a wooden bow-string girder that is made of short lengths of timber but is able to span a length of up to 30 m/100 ft

belfry /bélfri/ (plural **-fries**) n **1** the part of a church steeple or tower in which bells are hung **2** a tower on a building, in which a bell or bells are hung [13C. < Old French berfrei 'movable siege tower', by association with BELL[1].] —**belfried** adj

Belgae /bél zhi, bél gī/ n an ancient Celtic people who lived in N Gaul and parts of S England

Belgaum /bel gówm/ city in SW India. Population: 401,619 (1991).

Belgian /béljən/ n SOMEBODY FROM BELGIUM somebody who comes from Belgium ■ adj **1** OF BELGIUM relating to Belgium, or its people, language, or culture **2** OF FLEMISH OR WALLOON relating to the Flemish or Walloon languages

Belgian Congo former name for **Democratic Republic of the Congo**

Belgian hare n a domestic rabbit belonging to a breed with slender reddish-brown fur and long legs and ears

Belgium

Belgium /béljəm/ kingdom in NW Europe, bordering the North Sea. Capital: Brussels. Population: 10,165,059 (1997). Area: 30,528 sq. km/11,787 sq. mi.

Belgrade /bél grayd/ capital of the Federal Republic of Yugoslavia, in north-central Serbia. Population: 1,136,786 (1991).

Belgrano /bel graánō/, **Manuel** (1770–1820) Argentine general and statesman

Belial /béeli əl/ n a personification of wickedness or worthlessness, mentioned in the Bible and often thought of as a devil or demon [13C. < Hebrew bĕliyya'al 'worthlessness'.]

belie /bi lí/ (-lies, -lying, -lied) vt **1** to disguise the true nature of something **2** to show that something is not true or real ○ The evidence belies the testimony of the witness. [Old English beléogan < Germanic]

belief /bi léef/ n **1** ACCEPTANCE OF TRUTH OF acceptance by the mind that something is true or real, often underpinned by an emotional or spiritual sense of certainty ○ belief in an afterlife **2** TRUST confidence that somebody or something is good or will be effective ○ belief in democracy **3** SOMETHING THAT SOMEBODY BELIEVES IN a statement, principle, or doctrine that a person or group accepts as true **4** OPINION an opinion, especially a firm and considered one **5** RELIGIOUS FAITH religious faith [12C. Alteration of Old English geléafa after BELIEVE.]

belief system n **1** a set of beliefs, e.g. in religion or politics, that form a unified system **2** a collection and organization of beliefs prevalent in a community or society

believable /bi léevəb'l/ adj seeming to be true or authentic, and capable of being believed or believed in —**believability** /bi léevə bíllətee/ n —**believably** adv

believe /bi léev/ (-lieves, -lieving, -lieved) v **1** ACCEPT AS TRUE to accept that something is true or real ○ I don't know which story to believe. **2** vt ACCEPT AS TRUTHFUL to accept that somebody is telling the truth ○ Nobody will *believe you!* **3** *vt* **CREDIT WITH** to accept that somebody or something has a particular quality or ability ○ *No one believed her capable of such a malicious remark.* **4** *vi* **THINK THAT SOMETHING EXISTS** to be of the opinion that something exists or is a reality, especially when there is no absolute proof of its existence or reality ○ *believe in reincarnation* **5** *vi* **TRUST** to be confident that somebody or something is worthwhile or effective ○ *We all believe in you.* **6** *vi* **THINK SOMETHING IS GOOD** to be of the opinion that something is right or beneficial, and, usually, to act in accordance with that belief ○ *believe strongly in freedom of expression* **7** *vi* **HAVE RELIGIOUS FAITH** to have a religious belief [Old English *belyfan*, alteration of *gelēfan* < Germanic, 'to love, trust'] —**believer** *n* ◇ **make believe** to pretend

~~**beligerent**~~ incorrect spelling of **belligerent**

Belinda /bə líndə/ *n* a small natural satellite of Uranus, discovered in 1986 by the Voyager 2 planetary probe

Belisha beacon /bə leésha-/ *n* a sign at each end of a zebra crossing consisting of an amber ball with a flashing light inside it on top of a black-and-white-striped pole [Mid-20C. After Leslie Hore-*Belisha* (1895–1957), British Minister of Transport who introduced it.]

belittle /bi lítt'l/ (**-tles, -tling, -tled**) *vt* to make something seem less good or important than it is —**belittlement** *n* —**belittler** *n* —**belittlingly** *adv*

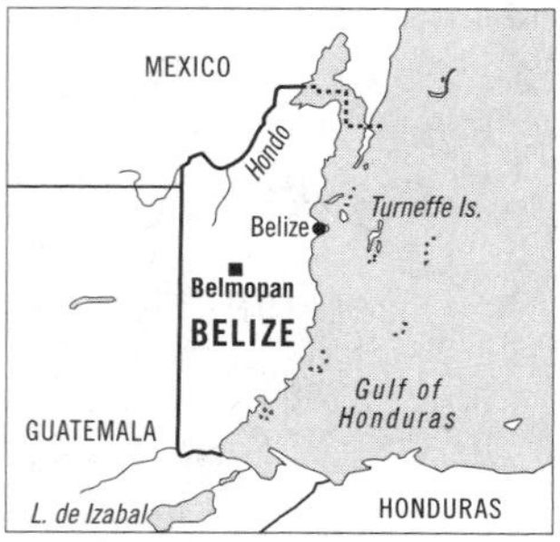

Belize

Belize /be leéz, bə-/ country in Central America on the Caribbean Sea. Capital: Belmopan. Population: 224,663 (1997). Area: 22,965 sq. km/8,867 sq. mi. —**Belizean** /be leézh'n, bə-/ *n, adj*

Belize City main port of Belize on the Caribbean Sea. Population: 50,000 (1990).

bell[1] /bel/ *n* **1** **OBJECT WITH RINGING SOUND** a hollow open-ended metal instrument with a rounded top that produces a ringing sound when struck **2** **ELECTRICAL DEVICE PRODUCING SOUND** a device activated by electricity that produces a ringing or buzzing signal **3** **SOMETHING BELL-SHAPED** something with the curved and open-ended shape of a bell, especially a flower **4** **FLARED END OF WIND INSTRUMENT** the flared end of a wind instrument, from which the sound emerges **5** **DURATION OF SHIP'S WATCH** the time during a watch on a ship, indicated by rings on a bell, one ring for each half hour that has passed ■ **bells** *npl* **PERCUSSION INSTRUMENT** a percussion instrument consisting of metal tubes or bars hung from a frame that give out a ringing sound when struck ■ *vti* **BECOME OR MAKE WIDER** to open out, or open something out, into a curved or flared shape similar to that of a bell [Old English *belle* < Germanic] ◇ **give somebody a bell** to telephone somebody (*informal*) ◇ **ring a bell** to evoke a vague memory of something or somebody (*informal*) ○ *Her name doesn't ring a bell*

LITERARY LINK ***For Whom the Bell Tolls***, a novel (1940) by US writer Ernest Hemingway. Set during the Spanish Civil War, it tells the story of Robert Jordan, a US volunteer fighting for the Republicans, who falls in love with a fellow volunteer called Maria.

LITERARY LINK ***Five Bells***, a long poem (1939) by Australian poet Kenneth Slessor. This meditation on time and the fragility of human existence is cast as an elegy for Joe Lynch, a friend of the author who drowned in Sydney Harbour.

bell[2] /bel/ *n* a bellowing sound made by a rutting stag or by a hunting dog during the chase ■ *vi* to make a bellowing sound [Old English *bellan* < Germanic]

Bell /bel/, **Alexander Graham** (1847–1922) Scottish-born US inventor and educator

Bell, Sir Francis Henry Dillon (1851–1936) New Zealand statesman

Bell, Gertrude (1868–1926) British archaeologist and traveller

Bell, Vanessa (1879–1961) British painter and designer. Born **Vanessa Stephen**

belladonna /béllə dónnə/ *n* **1** PLANTS = **deadly nightshade** **2** a drug, e.g. atropine, made from belladonna [Mid-18C. Via Modern Latin < Italian, 'beautiful lady', from the use of belladonna to dilate the pupils.]

belladonna lily *n* PLANTS = **amaryllis** *n.* 1

bellarmine /béll aar meen/ *n* a large earthenware or stoneware jug decorated with a bearded face [Mid-17C. After St Robert *Bellarmin* (1542–1621), Jesuit cardinal.]

Bell Bay bay on the N coast of Tasmania, Australia

bellbird /bél burd/ *n* a bird with a call that sounds like a bell. Native to: tropical America, Australasia.

bellboy /bél boy/ *n* a man working in a hotel as a porter or page. US term **bellhop**

bell buoy *n* a floating buoy with a bell on top that is rung by the movement of the waves and gives a warning or positional signal to shipping

bell crank *n* a lever with two arms that share a fulcrum at the point where they join

belle /bel/ *n* **1** a beautiful woman **2** a woman considered to be the most conspicuously good-looking of all those living in a particular place or attending a particular social event [Early 17C. < French, 'beautiful'.]

Belleek ware /bə leék-/, **Belleek** *n* very thin, typically cream-coloured porcelain with a lustrous glaze [Mid-19C. After a town in N Ireland.]

belle époque /bél ay pók/ *n* an era of cultural refinement, social elegance, and general prosperity and security, especially the last decades of the 19th century and the early years of the 20th prior to World War I [Mid-20C. French, 'fine period'.]

Bellerophon /bə lérrəfən/ *n* in Greek mythology, a hero who tamed the winged horse Pegasus and slew the fire-breathing monster Chimera

belles-lettres /bél léttrə/ *n* writings that are valued for their elegance and aesthetic qualities rather than for any human interest or moral or instructive content (+ *singular or plural verb*) [Mid-17C. French, 'fine letters'.] —**belletrism** /bél léttrizəm/ *n* —**belletrist** *n*

bellflower /bél flowər/ *n* PLANTS = **campanula**

bellfoundry /bél fowndri/ (*plural* **-ries**) *n* a foundry that specializes in making bells

bell glass *n* CHEM = **bell jar** *n.* 2

bell heather *n* a type of heather. Flowers: deep reddish-purple. Native to: Europe. *Erica cineria.*

bellhop /bél hop/ *n US, Can* OCCUPATIONS = **bellboy**

bellicose /béllikōss/ *adj* ready or inclined to quarrel, fight, or go to war [15C. < Latin *bellicosus* < *bellum* 'war'.] —**bellicosely** *adv* —**bellicoseness** *n* —**bellicosity** /bélli kóssəti/ *n*

belligerence /bə líjjərənss/ *n* the quality of being hostile, ready to start a fight, or ready to go to war

belligerency /bə líjjərənssi/ *n* **1** = **belligerence** **2** the state of being at war

belligerent /bə líjjərənt/ *adj* **1** **HOSTILE OR AGGRESSIVE** hostile, ready to start a fight, or ready to go to war **2** **ENGAGED IN WAR** taking part in warfare, especially in a war recognized by the law of nations **3** **RELATING TO BELLIGERENT NATION** relating to or characteristic of a participant in war or a fight ■ *n* **PARTICIPANT IN WAR** a participant in a war or fight, especially a nation engaged in a war recognized by the law of nations [Late 16C. < Latin *belligerare* 'wage war' < *belliger* 'carrying on war' < *bellum* 'war' + *gerere* 'carry on'.] —**belligerently** *adv*

Bellingshausen /béllingz howz'n/, **Fabian Gottlieb von** (1778–1852) Russian explorer

Bellingshausen Sea /béllingz howz'n-/ part of the S Pacific Ocean off the coast of W Antarctica

Bellini /be leéni/, **Giovanni** (1430?–1516) Italian painter

Bellini, Jacopo (1400?–70?) Italian painter

bell jar *n* **1** a glass cover, shaped like a bell, used to protect and display delicate items **2** a bell-shaped glass cover used to enclose equipment in experiments and prevent gases from escaping or entering

bell magpie *n* BIRDS = **currawong** [< its call]

bellman /bélmən/ (*plural* **-men** /-mən, -men/) *n* a man who rings a bell, especially a town crier

bell metal *n* an alloy of copper with 20 to 25 percent tin, used to cast bells and plain bearings

Belloc /béllok/, **Hilaire** (1870–1953) French-born British writer

bellow /béllō/ *v* **1** *vi* to give a bull's loud deep roar or a roar like that of a bull **2** *vti* to shout something in a loud deep voice [14C. < ?] —**bellow** *n* —**bellower** *n*

Bellow /béllō/, **Saul** (*b.* 1915) Canadian-born US writer

bellows /béllōz/ (*plural* **-lows**) *n* (+ *singular or plural verb*) **1** a device or piece of equipment with a chamber with flexible sides that can be expanded to draw air in and compressed to force the air out **2** something constructed of a pleated material and able to be expanded and contracted, e.g. the part enclosing the lenses on some cameras or photographic enlargers [12C. Probably < Old English *belga*, shortening of *blæstbelig* 'blowing bag'.]

bell pull *n* a handle or cord that when pulled makes a bell ring

bell push *n* a button that when pressed causes an electric bell to ring

bell-ringer *n* **1** somebody who rings church bells **2** a musician who plays handbells —**bell-ringing** *n*

bells and whistles *npl* special features that are not necessary but are incorporated in a product to make it appear more desirable or useful (*informal*)

bells of Ireland *n* an annual garden plant. Flowers: small, surrounded by green cup-shaped sepals. *Moluccella laevis.*

Bell's palsy /bélz-/ *n* the inability to move the muscles on one side of the face, causing a distorted facial expression [Mid-19C. After Sir Charles *Bell* (1774–1842), Scottish anatomist.]

bell tent *n* a tent shaped like a bell or a cone, held up by a central pole

bellwether /bél weṯhər/ *n* **1** **SHEEP LEADING FLOCK** a sheep that leads the rest of the flock, usually wearing a bell around its neck **2** **LEADER** somebody who leads others **3** **INDICATOR OF FUTURE DEVELOPMENTS** an indicator of future developments or trends

belly /bélli/ *n* (*plural* **-lies**) **1** **MIDDLE PART OF BODY** the part of the body of a vertebrate that contains the stomach, intestines, and other organs **2** **FRONT OF BODY AROUND STOMACH** the surface of the body of a vertebrate around the stomach **3** **STOMACH** the stomach (*informal*) **4** **APPETITE** the desire or need for food and drink **5** **DESIRE OR PERSISTENCE** the courage or desire to have or do something ○ *They have no belly for a fight.* **6** **BULGING PART** a part of something that bulges out, e.g. a sail **7** **INTERIOR CAVITY** the interior cavity of a structure, especially a ship **8** **UPPER SURFACE OF STRINGED INSTRUMENT** the top or front surface of the body of a stringed instrument, over which the strings are stretched ■ *vti* (**-lies, -lying, -lied**) **BULGE** to bulge or make something bulge ○ *The wind bellied out the sail.* [Old English *belig* 'bag' < Indo-European, 'to swell'] ◇ **go** *or* **turn belly up** to go bankrupt, fail, or fall through

bellyache /bélli ayk/ *n* a painful or upset stomach (*informal*) ■ *vi* (**-aches, -aching, -ached**) to complain in a whining manner (*informal*) —**bellyacher** *n*

bellyband /bélli band/ *n* a strap passed around the belly of a draught animal and attached to the shafts of the vehicle it is pulling

bellybutton /bélli butt'n/ *n* the human navel (*informal*)

belly chain *n* a chain designed to be worn around the waist or waist area, especially as an ornament

belly dance *n* a dance of Middle Eastern origin for women, in which the hips and abdomen are moved rapidly —**belly dancer** *n* —**belly dancing** *n*

belly flop *n* **1** a shallow dive where the front of the diver's body hits the water first **2** AIR = **belly landing** —**belly-flop** *vi*

bellyful /bélli fòòl/ *n* (*informal*) **1** all the food that somebody wants or is able to eat **2** an undesirable or excessive amount of something

belly landing *n* an emergency landing of an aircraft with the wheels not extended —**belly-land** *vti*

belly laugh *n* a deep and unrestrained laugh

belly pork *n* a streaky cut of pork from a pig's belly

Belmondo /bel móndō/, **Jean-Paul** (*b.* 1933) French actor

Belmopan /bélmə pán/ capital of Belize, in the centre of the country. Population: 6,785 (1997 estimate).

Belo Horizonte /béllō horri zóntay/ capital of Minas Gerais State in E Brazil. Population: 2,091,770 (1996).

belong /bi lóng/ *vi* **1 BE SOMEBODY'S PROPERTY** to be the property of a person or organization ○ *Who does this coat belong to?* **2 BE PERSONALLY LINKED** to be linked to a particular place or person by a relationship such as birth, affection, or membership **3 BE CLASSIFIED** to be part of a class or group ○ *Tulips belong to the lily family.* **4 BE PART OF** to be a part or component of something else **5 BE IN RIGHT PLACE** to be in an appropriate or usual place ○ *He belongs in jail.* **6 BE ACCEPTED** to be accepted or made welcome in a place or group ○ *feeling that I didn't belong* [14C. < obsolete *long* 'relate to'.]

belonging /bi lónging/ *n* the state of being comfortable and accepted in a place or community ■ **belongings** *npl* the things somebody owns or has with him or her

Belorussia /béllō rúshə/ ◊ **Belarus**

beloved /bi lúvvid/; *(predicatively)* /-lúvd/ *adj* very much loved ■ *n* somebody who is very much loved

LITERARY LINK ***Beloved***, a novel (1987) by US writer Toni Morrison. It explores the emotional legacy of slavery among Black people in the United States. Set in the years before, during, and after the Civil War, it centres on three generations of Black women, Baby Suggs, a woman freed from slavery, her daughter-in-law Sethe, who escapes to the North from vicious slave owners in Kentucky, and Sethe's daughter Denver, raised in freedom but scarred by her inheritance. They are haunted by the ghost of Beloved, another daughter whom Sethe murdered to save her from being raised in slavery. The novel weaves their memories as they come to terms with their personal and collective past.

below /bi lṓ/ CORE MEANING: a grammatical word indicating something situated or placed beneath something else or lower than something else ○ (prep) *a river below the town* ○ (adv) *on the shelf below*

1 *prep, adv* **IN LOWER GRADE** at or to a level, standard, or grade that is lower than that specified or understood ○ *animals ranked below humans* ○ *below average* ○ *30 degrees below* **2** *adv* **FURTHER DOWN** lower down or later on in a text, especially on the same page ○ *see below* ○ *on page 29 below* **3** *adv* **LOWER THAN THE DECK** on or to a level of a ship or boat that is lower than the deck [14C. < earlier form of BY + LOW[1].]

belowground /bi lṓ grownd, -grównd/ *adj* situated under the ground ■ *adv* into or under the ground

Belsen /bélss'n/ village in NW Germany, site of the Bergen-Belsen Nazi concentration camp (1943–45)

Belshazzar /bel sházzər/ *n* a king of Babylon in the sixth century BC. The Bible tells of the foretelling of his death in an inscription that mysteriously appears on the wall of his palace during a feast (Daniel 5).

belt /belt/ *n* **1 STRIP OF MATERIAL ROUND WAIST** a strip of material worn round the waist, used to hold up clothing for the lower body, as decoration, or to carry tools or weapons **2 STRIP OF SOMETHING DIFFERENT** a band or stripe of a different colour, texture, or substance from what it encircles or crosses **3 SPECIFIC AREA** an area or region where a particular item or quality is characteristic ○ *a wheat belt* ○ *the stockbroker belt* **4 BELT GIVEN FOR ACHIEVEMENT** a belt awarded to a sports competitor, especially in boxing or the martial arts, as a trophy or a sign of having attained a particular grade **5 SOMEBODY HOLDING BELT FOR ACHIEVEMENT** somebody awarded a particular belt for an achievement, usually in boxing or one of the martial arts **6 BELT AS SIGN OF RANK** a belt worn as a sign of a particular rank, e.g. by a knight or an earl **7** TRANSP = **seat belt 8 BAND AS PART OF MACHINE** a band of strong flexible material used in machinery to transmit motion or power or to move articles **9 BLOW** a hard blow *(informal)* **10** *US* **DRINK** a drink of spirits *(slang)* **11 STRAP USED TO PUNISH** a leather strap, usually split into several thongs at one end, formerly used in schools for corporal punishment ■ *v* **1** *vt* **FASTEN WITH BELT** to fasten or attach something with a belt **2** *vt* **HIT WITH BELT** to strike somebody with a belt **3** *vt* **HIT HARD** to strike somebody or something with a hard blow *(informal)* **4** *vi* **MOVE FAST** to move or travel very quickly *(informal)* [Old English, < Latin *balteus* 'girdle'] ◇ **below the belt** unfair and often hurtful ◇ **have something under your belt** to have done or acquired something that will be of benefit to you in the future ○ *She has 12 computer science courses under her belt.* ◇ **tighten your belt** to reduce your expenditure

belt out *vt* to sing or play something loudly and enthusiastically *(informal)*

belt up *v* **1** *vi* to be quiet or stop talking *(slang; usually a command)* **2** *vti* to fasten a safety belt, or secure somebody with a safety belt

Beltane /bél tayn/ *n* an ancient Celtic festival marked by the lighting of bonfires. Date: beginning of May. [15C. Via Gaelic *bealltainn* < Old Irish.]

belt drive *n* a system for transmitting power from one shaft to another by means of an endless flexible belt looped over pulleys mounted on the shafts

belted Galloway *n* a breed of hornless beef cattle with a white belt round a black body, originating in Galloway

belter /béltər/ *n (informal)* **1** somebody or something considered remarkable or outstanding **2** a popular song that lends itself to a loud and rousing performance

belting /bélting/ *n* **1** material used for making belts **2** belts considered collectively

belt sander *n* a sander that uses a continuous belt coated with an abrasive

belt-tightening *n* a reduction in spending that results in the loss of something previously enjoyed

beltway /bélt way/ *n US* TRANSP = **ring road** ◇ **inside** *or* **outside the Beltway** *US* inside *or* outside the ring road that surrounds the community of Washington DC, often viewed as politically and socially insular

beluga /bə lóogə/ (*plural* **-gas** *or* **-ga**) *n* **1** a large white sturgeon. Native to: Black Sea, Caspian Sea. *Huso huso* and *Acipenser huso.* **2 beluga, beluga caviar** caviar made from the eggs of the beluga sturgeon **3** ZOOL = **white whale** [Late 16C. < Russian, 'large white' < *belyĭ* 'white'.]

belvedere /bélvə deer/ *n* a building or part of a building positioned to offer a fine view of the surrounding area [Late 16C. < Italian, 'beautiful to see'.]

bema /beémə/ *n* **1 bema, bima, bimah** in a synagogue, the raised platform where the scriptures are read **2** in an Orthodox church, the raised area where the altar is located [Late 17C. < Greek *bēma* 'step, platform'.]

Bemba /bémbə/ (*plural* **-ba** *or* **-bas**) *n* **1** a member of an African people chiefly in Zambia **2** a Bantu language spoken in east-central Africa and belonging to the Benue-Congo group of languages. Native speakers: 2 million. [Mid-20C. < Bantu.] —**Bemba** *adj*

bemire /bi mī́ r/ (**-mires, -miring, -mired**) *vt* to soil something or somebody with mud or dirt *(archaic)*

bemoan /bi mṓn/ *vt* to express grief or disappointment about something

bemuse /bi myóoz/ (**-muses, -musing, -mused**) *vt* to cause somebody to be confused or puzzled —**bemusement** *n*

bemused /bi myóozd/ *adj* confused, puzzled, and unable to understand or think clearly —**bemusedly** /-zidli/ *adv*

ben[1] /ben/ *n Scotland, Ireland* a mountain *(often in placenames)* ○ *Ben Nevis* [Late 18C. < Scottish Gaelic and Irish *beann*.]

ben[2] /ben/ *n Scotland* the inner room of a house, especially of an old-fashioned rural cottage with two rooms. ◊ **but and ben** [14C. < Old English *binnan* 'within'.]

Ben Ali /ben aáli/, **Zine al-Abidine** (*b.* 1936) Tunisian statesman

Benares /bi naáriz/ former name for **Varanasi**

Benaud /bénnō/, **Richie** (*b.* 1930) Australian cricketer and broadcaster. Full name **Richard Benaud**

Ben Bella /bén béllə/, **Ahmed** (*b.* 1919) Algerian political leader

Benbow /bénbō/, **John** (1653–1702) English naval commander

bench /bench/ *n* **1 LONG BACKLESS SEAT** a long seat for two or more people, usually made without a back or arms **2 SEAT IN BOAT** a seat for a rower in a boat **3 WORK TABLE** a long strong work table **4 JUDGE'S SEAT** the seat where a judge sits in a court **5 JUDGE** a judge or magistrate presiding over a court **6 JUDGES** the judges of a court system **7 JUDGESHIP** the office or position of a judge **8 SEAT FOR NONPLAYING ATHLETES** in team sports, the seat for officials and for players not on the field or court during play **9 PEOPLE WHO OCCUPY BENCH** the people who sit on the bench in a team sports event **10 LEDGE OF LAND** a narrow flat ledge of land, often the remnant of a former shoreline **11 LEDGE IN MINE** a ledge formed by excavation in a mine **12 PLATFORM FOR SHOWING ANIMALS** a platform used for displaying dogs, cats, or other animals at a show ■ *vt* **1 PROVIDE WITH BENCHES** to provide something with benches **2 DISPLAY ANIMAL AT SHOW** to display a dog, cat, or other animal at a show on a bench **3 PUT ON NONPLAYERS' BENCH** to exclude or remove a member of a sports team from play [Old English *benc* < Germanic]

bencher /bénchər/ *n* a member of the governing body of an Inn of Court

ϟ**benchmark** /bénch maark/ *n* **1 STANDARD** a standard against which something can be measured or assessed **2 TEST OF COMPUTER PERFORMANCE** a standard test to measure the performance of computer hardware or software ■ *adj* **USED AS STANDARD** used as a standard for measuring or assessing something ■ *vt* **1 PROVIDE STANDARD** to provide a standard against which something can be measured or assessed **2 TEST COMPUTER PERFORMANCE** to test the performance of computer hardware or software for comparison with similar products

bench mark *n* a mark made by a surveyor on a permanent object that shows an established position and elevation and is used as a reference point

bench press *n* in weightlifting, a lift where somebody lies on a bench with the feet on the floor and raises a weight from chest level to arm's length —**bench-press** *vti*

bench seat *n* in a motor vehicle, a seat that extends across the full width of the vehicle

bench test *n* a trial of a machine or part in the laboratory or workshop to confirm that it works properly before it is installed —**bench-test** *vti*

bend[1] /bend/ *v* (**bends, bending, bent** /bent/) **1** *vti* **BECOME OR MAKE CURVED** to take on or cause something to take on a curved or angled shape ○ *The wooden struts bent under pressure.* **2** *vti* **STOOP** to make or cause somebody to make a stooping or inclined movement ○ *I bent to pick up the ball.* **3** *vti* **YIELD OR FORCE TO YIELD** to yield in response to a strong will or force, or force somebody or something to yield **4** *vti* **CHANGE OR CAUSE TO CHANGE DIRECTION** to change or cause something to change direction or course ○ *The path bends to the right.* **5** *vti* **CONCENTRATE ON DOING** to concentrate the mind on an activity ○ *bent her mind to the task in hand* **6** *vt* **DISTORT FOR SOMEBODY'S BENEFIT** to adapt or interpret something in a way that was not originally intended, especially for personal benefit or to help somebody else ○ *bend the rules* **7** *vt* **ATTACH** to attach or fasten something, especially a pair of lines or ropes ■ *n* **1 CURVE** a curved part of something, especially a sharp curve in a road **2 ACT OF BENDING** an act of bending **3 KNOT JOINING TWO ROPES** a knot that joins one line to another [Old English *bendan* 'tie, curve' < Germanic] —**bendability** /béndə bílləti/ *n* —**bendable** *adj* —**bendily** *adv* —**bendiness** *n* —**bendy** *adj* ◇ **round the bend** wild or distracted *(informal)*

bend[2] /bend/ *n* a band that crosses a heraldic shield diagonally from top right to bottom left [Old English, < Germanic; later < Old French *bende*]

benday /bén dáy/, **Ben Day** *adj* describes a printing process of adding tone to an image by overlaying a transparent sheet patterned with dots before the image is reproduced to make a plate [Early 20C. After *Benjamin Day* Jr (1838–1916), US printer.]

bended /béndid/ *adj* in a position so as to be curved or bent *(literary)* ○ *on bended knee*

bender /béndər/ *n* **1 DRINKING SPREE** a prolonged bout of drinking *(slang)* **2 OFFENSIVE TERM** an offensive term for a homosexual man *(slang offensive insult)* **3 TEMPORARY SHELTER** a usually dome-shaped temporary shelter made by bending and interweaving branches and covering them with plastic sheeting or tarpaulin *(informal)*

Bendigo /béndigō/ town in central Victoria, Australia. Population: 59,936 (1996).

bendrofluazide /béndrō flóo ə zīd/ *n* a diuretic drug that promotes excretion of salt and water by the kidneys. Use: treatment of oedema and hypertension. US term **bendroflumethiazide**

bendroflumethiazide /béndrō flóo methī́ ə zīd/ *n US* PHARM = **bendrofluazide**

bends /bendz/ *n* decompression sickness, especially in divers *(informal; + singular or plural verb)*

bend sinister (*plural* **bends sinister**) *n* a band that crosses a heraldic shield diagonally from top left to bottom right, used to indicate a line of descent from a birth outside marriage

beneath /bi neéth/ CORE MEANING: a grammatical word indicating a position underneath or lower than something

1 *prep, adv* **UNDERNEATH** in, at, or to a lower position or less superficial level than that specified or understood (*formal*) ○ *kept in a box beneath the bed* ○ *a door giving access to the cellar beneath* ○ *Beneath his veneer of politeness lay hostility.* 2 *prep, adv* **LOWER** in, at, or to a lower level, grade, or standard than that specified or understood (*formal*) ○ *She always supported those beneath her.* 3 *prep* **TOO LOW FOR** too low in status or character for ○ *beneath contempt* ○ *Telling tales should be beneath you.* [Old English *binithan, bineothan* 'by or from below' < Germanic]

benedicite /bénnə dĭssəti/ *n* a blessing or grace used in some Christian religious communities [13C. < Latin, 'may you bless'.]

Benedicite *n* a Latin hymn beginning 'Benedicite omnia opera Domini Domino', traditionally translated as 'O all ye works of the Lord, bless ye the Lord'

Benedict XV /bénnədikt/ (1854–1922) pope (1914–22). Born **Giacomo della Chiesa**

Benedictine /bénnі díktin/ *n* a monk or nun belonging to a religious order founded by St Benedict or following his rule ■ *adj* relating to or characteristic of St Benedict, his rule, or the monastic order that he founded

benediction /bénni díksh'n/ *n* 1 **EXPRESSION OF APPROVAL** an expression of approval or good wishes 2 **PRAYER ASKING FOR GOD'S BLESSING** a prayer asking for God's blessing, usually at the end of a Christian service 3 **Benediction, benediction CATHOLIC DEVOTIONAL SERVICE** in the Roman Catholic Church, a devotional service during which the congregation is blessed with the Host 4 **BLESSEDNESS** the state of being blessed [15C. Directly or via French *bénédiction* < Latin *benediction-* < *benedicere* 'say well to' < *bene* 'well' + *dicere* 'say'.] —**benedictive** *adj* —**benedictory** *adj*

Benedict's solution /bénnidikts-/, **Benedict's reagent** *n* a chemical solution that turns red in the presence of sugars like glucose that are reducing agents. Use: urine tests for diabetes. [Early 20C. After Stanley Rossiter *Benedict* (1884–1936), US chemist.]

Benedictus /bénni díktəss/ *n* 1 a Latin hymn, beginning 'Benedictus qui venit in nomine Domini' ('Blessed is he that cometh in the name of the Lord' Luke 1: 68–79) 2 a Latin hymn, beginning 'Benedictus Dominus Deus Israel' ('Blessed be the Lord God of Israel') [Mid-16C. < Latin, past participle of *benedicere* (see BENEDICTION).]

benefaction /bénni fáksh'n/ *n* 1 **DOING GOOD** an act of doing good 2 **GOOD DEED** a good deed, especially an act of charity 3 **DONATION** a donation given to a charity [Mid-17C. < late Latin *benefaction-* < Latin *bene* 'well' + *fact-*, past participle of *facere* 'do'.]

benefactor /bénni faktər/ *n* a financial supporter of a cause, institution, or individual

benefactress /bénni faktrəss/ *n* a woman who aids a cause, institution, or individual, especially with a gift of money

benefice /bénnifiss/ *n* 1 **ENDOWED CHURCH LIVING** a church office that provides a living for its holder through an endowment attached to it 2 **REVENUE FOR CHURCH LIVING** the revenue or property that provides the living of the holder of a church benefice 3 **FORM OF FEUDAL TENURE** a form of feudal tenure in which a vassal held land from a superior, especially in return for military service ■ *vt* (**-fices, -ficing, -ficed**) **PROVIDE WITH BENEFICE** to provide a member of the clergy with a church office that will yield a living [14C. Via Old French < Latin *beneficium* 'doing well' < *bene* 'well' + *fic-*, variant of stem of *facere* 'do'.]

beneficent /bə néffissənt/ *adj* 1 doing good or charitable acts 2 producing benefits or advantages [Early 17C. < Latin *beneficent-*, stem of *beneficentior* 'more beneficent' < *beneficus*.] —**beneficence** *n* —**beneficently** *adv*

beneficial /bénni físh'l/ *adj* 1 producing a good or advantageous effect ○ *The exercise should prove beneficial to his health.* 2 entitling somebody to or entitled to profits or property [15C. Directly or via French *bénéficial* < late Latin *beneficialis* < Latin *beneficium* (see BENEFICE).] —**beneficially** *adv* —**beneficialness** *n*

beneficiary /bénni físhəri/ *n* (*plural* **-ies**) 1 **SOMEBODY BENEFITING** somebody who receives a benefit 2 **LEGAL RECIPIENT OF MONEY** somebody entitled to money or property under a will, trust, or insurance policy 3 **HOLDER OF BENEFICE** a member of the clergy who holds an office that provides a living (**benefice**) 4 *NZ* **SOMEBODY RECEIVING GOVERNMENT ASSISTANCE** somebody who receives a state welfare benefit ■ *adj* **RELATING TO BENEFICE** relating to a church office that provides a living (**benefice**) or the member of the clergy who holds it [Early 17C. < Latin *beneficiarius* < *beneficium* (see BENEFICE).]

beneficiary bank *n* a bank that receives money, especially from another bank

benefit /bénnifit/ *n* 1 **ADVANTAGE** something that has a good effect or promotes wellbeing ○ *They eventually reaped the benefits of all their hard work.* 2 **GOVERNMENT PAYMENT TO SOMEBODY NEEDING ASSISTANCE** a regular payment made by the government under the national insurance scheme or social security to somebody qualified to receive it or in need of financial assistance (*often plural*) 3 **MONEY PAID TO CLAIMANT** a payment made to a claimant or entitled person by an employer, insurance company, or other institution 4 **PERFORMANCE FOR CHARITY** a performance by entertainers, athletes, or others to raise money for somebody or something, especially a charity ■ *vti* (**-fits, -fiting** *or* **-fitting, -fited** *or* **-fitted**) **GIVE OR RECEIVE BENEFIT** to give or receive help, an advantage, or another benefit ○ *The research would benefit from an injection of new ideas.* [14C. Via Anglo-Norman *benfet*, Old French *bienfait* < Latin *benefactum* 'good deed' < *bene* 'well' + *facere* 'do'.] ◇ **give somebody the benefit of the doubt** to assume that somebody is telling the truth about something or is innocent of something because there is not enough evidence that the person is lying or guilty

benefit of clergy *n* 1 the official approval or ministration of the church ○ *married without benefit of clergy* 2 the privilege held by the clergy in the Middle Ages that entitled them to trial by an ecclesiastical court and exemption from trial by secular authorities

Benelux /bénni luks/ *n* the countries of Belgium, the Netherlands, and Luxembourg as a group [Mid-20C. Acronym < *Belgium, Netherlands, Luxembourg*.]

Beneš /bénnesh/, **Eduard** (1884–1948) Czech statesman

Benét /bə náy/, **Stephen Vincent** (1898–1943) US author and poet

Benét, William Rose (1886–1950) US poet, critic, and editor

benevolent /bə névvələnt/ *adj* 1 showing kindness or goodwill 2 performing good or charitable acts and not seeking to make a profit [15C. Via French < Latin *benevolent-*, present participle of *bene velle* 'wish well'.] —**benevolence** *n* —**benevolently** *adv*

Bengal /ben gáwl, beng-/ former province of NE India, now divided into the Indian state of West Bengal and Bangladesh —**Bengalese** *n*

Bengal, Bay of northeastern arm of the Indian Ocean between India, Myanmar, and the Malay peninsula. Area: 2,172,000 sq. km/839,000 sq. mi.

Bengali /ben gáwli, beng gáwli/ *n* 1 somebody who comes from Bangladesh or the state of West Bengal in India 2 the Indic national language of Bangladesh and state language of West Bengal, India, also spoken in other parts of the world. Native speakers: 170 million. [Late 18C. < Hindi *baṅgālī*.] —**Bengali** *adj*

bengaline /béngəlin, -ə leén/ *n* a heavyweight corded cotton and silk or wool fabric [Late 19C. < French, because of its similarity to cloth made in Bengal.]

Bengasi ♦ **Benghazi**

Benghazi /ben gaázi, beng-/, **Bengasi, Banghāzī** port in NE Libya. Population: 800,000 (1994 estimate).

Benguela /ben gwéllə/ capital of Benguela District, W Angola. Population: 155,000 (1983 estimate).

Ben-Gurion /ben gŏori ən/, **David** (1886–1973) Polish-born Israeli statesman. Born **David Gruen**

~~**benificial**~~ incorrect spelling of **beneficial**

~~**benifit**~~ incorrect spelling of **benefit**

benighted /bi nítid/ *adj* 1 unenlightened intellectually, socially, or morally 2 overtaken by night or the dark —**benightedly** *adv* —**benightedness** *n*

benign /bi nín/ *adj* 1 **KINDLY** having a kind and gentle disposition or appearance 2 **FAVOURABLE** mild or favourable in effect ○ *a benign climate* 3 **HARMLESS** neutral or harmless in its effect or influence 4 **NOT LIFE-THREATENING** not a threat to life or long-term health, especially by being noncancerous [14C. Via French < Latin *benignus*.] —**benignly** *adv*

benignant /bə nígnənt/ *adj* kind and gracious in behaviour or appearance —**benignancy** *n*

benignity /bə nígnəti/ (*plural* **-ties**) *n* 1 kindness and gentleness of disposition or appearance 2 a kind or gracious act

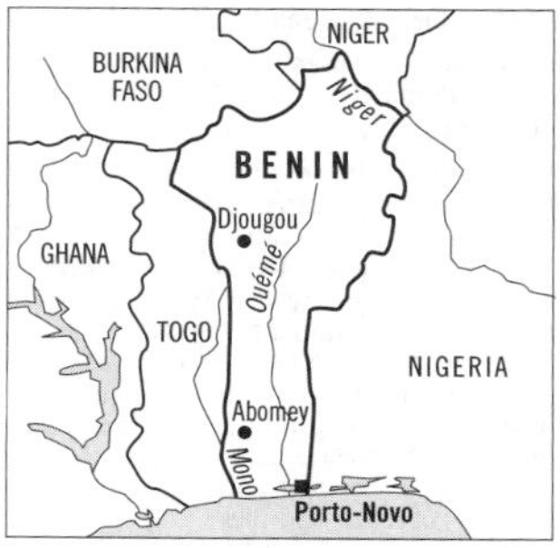

Benin

Benin /bə neén/ republic in W Africa between Togo and Nigeria. Capital: Porto-Novo. Population: 5,902,178 (1997). Area: 112,622 sq. km/43,484 sq. mi. —**Beninese** /bénni neéz/ *adj, n*

Benin, Bight of bay on the SW coast of Nigeria and the W coast of Benin. Length: approximately 720 km/450 mi.

Benin City capital of Edo State in S Nigeria. Population: 223,900 (1995 estimate).

Benioff zone /bénni əf-/ *n* a steeply-angled region along the edge of a continental plate where many earthquakes originate and the ocean floor is thought to descend [Mid-20C. After V. Hugo *Benioff* (1899–1968), US seismologist.]

benison /bénnizən, -ssən/ *n* a blessing or benediction (*literary*) [12C. Via Old French *benisson* < Latin *benediction-* (see BENEDICTION).]

benjamin /bénjəmin/ *n* CHEM = **benzoin** [Mid-16C. Alteration of earlier form of BENZOIN after the name *Benjamin*.]

Benjamin /bénjəmin/ *n* in the Bible, the youngest son of Jacob and Rachel and father of the smallest tribe of Israel

Benjamin /bénjəmin/, **Walter** (1892–1940) German literary critic

Ben Lomond /ben lṓmənd/ mountain in W Scotland. Height: 973 m/3,192 ft.

Benn /ben/, **Tony** (*b.* 1925) British politician. Full name **Anthony Neil Wedgwood Benn**

benne /bénni/ *n* FOOD = **sesame** *n.* 2 [Mid-18C. < Malay *bene*.]

Bennett /bénnit/, **Alan** (*b.* 1934) British playwright and actor

Bennett, Arnold (1867–1931) British novelist

Bennett, James Gordon (1841–1918) US newspaper owner and editor

Bennett, Richard Bedford, 1st Viscount (1870–1947) Canadian statesman and business executive. Known as **Iron Heel Bennett**

Bennett, Richard Rodney (*b.* 1936) British composer

Ben Nevis /ben névviss/ highest mountain in the British Isles, in W Scotland. Height: 1,343 m/4,406 ft.

benni /bénni/ *n* FOOD = **sesame** *n.* 2 [Mid-18thC. < Malay *bene*.]

benny /bénni/ (*plural* **-nies**) *n* an amphetamine tablet, especially Benzedrine™ (*slang*) [Mid-20C. Shortening of BENZEDRINE.]

Benny /bénni/, **Jack** (1894–1974) US comedian. Born **Benjamin Kubelsky**

Benoni /bi nṓni/ city in NE South Africa. Population: 103,501 (1991).

bensh /bench/, **bentsh** *vi* to say a Jewish benediction after eating a meal [Via Yiddish *bentshen* < Latin *benedicere* 'bless']

bent[1] past tense, past participle of **bend**[1]

bent[2] /bent/ *adj* 1 **CURVED** having a curved, twisted, or angled shape 2 **DETERMINED** having a fixed desire to do or accomplish something ○ *bent on making a name for herself* 3 **OFFENSIVE TERM** an offensive term for homosexual (*slang offensive insult*) 4 **CORRUPT** dishonest or corrupt in behaviour (*slang*) ○ *a bent cop* 5 **STOLEN** dishonestly acquired or made (*slang*) 6 **SUFFERING FROM THE BENDS** suffering from decompression sickness (*informal*) ■ *n* 1 **NATURAL INCLINATION** a strong natural inclination or talent for something **2 CROSSWISE SUPPORT** a crosswise framework or member used to strengthen a structure

SYNONYMS See ***talent***.

bent[3] /bent/ *n* **1 GRASS OF TEMPERATE REGIONS** a perennial grass of temperate regions. Use: hay, lawns, putting greens. Genus: *Agrostis*. **2 REEDY GRASS** a stiff reedy grass (*archaic*) **3 GRASS STALK** a flower stalk of a stiff grass (*archaic*) **4 HEATH** an area of open moor or grassland (*archaic*) [Old English *beonet* < Germanic]

Bentham /bénthəm/, **Jeremy** (1748–1832) British philosopher, jurist, and social reformer

Benthamism /bénthəmizəm/ *n* the utilitarian philosophy of Jeremy Bentham, which argues that the highest good is the happiness of the greatest number —**Benthamite** *n, adj*

benthic /bénthik/, **benthonic** /ben thónnik/ *adj* relating to or characteristic of the bottom of a sea, lake, or deep river, or the animals and plants that live there [< BENTHOS]

benthos /bénthoss/ *n* the animals and plants that live on or in the sediment at the bottom of a sea, lake, or deep river [Late 19C. < Greek, 'depth of the sea'.]

Bentley /béntli/, **E. C.** (1875–1956) British writer. Full name **Edmund Clerihew Bentley**

bento /béntō/ *n* FOOD = **obento** [Late 20C. < Japanese.]

bentonite /béntə nīt/ *n* a light-coloured clay that expands in water. Use: oil drilling, paper, pharmaceutical industries. [Late 19C. After Fort *Benton*, Montana, USA.] —**bentonitic** /béntə níttik/ *adj*

bentsh *vi* JUDAISM = **bensh**

bentwood /bént wŏŏd/ *n* wood that has been bent into a curved shape by being steamed and then put into a mould. Use: furniture.

Benue /bénnoo ay/ river in Cameroon and Nigeria, main tributary of the River Niger. Length: 1,400 km/870 mi.

Benue-Congo *n* a large group of Niger-Congo languages spoken across central and southern Africa, of which Bantu languages form the largest subgroup —**Benue-Congo** *adj*

benumb /bi núm/ *vt* **1** to remove the sense of feeling from a faculty or part of the body, especially by exposure to extreme cold **2** to make somebody incapable of activity or thought (*usually passive*) —**benumbment** *n*

Benz /benz/, **Karl** (1844–1929) German engineer and automobile manufacturer

benz- /benz, bents/ *prefix* = **benzo-** (*before vowels*)

benzaldehyde /ben záldi hīd/ *n* C_6H_5CHO a colourless volatile liquid found naturally in and smelling of almonds. Use: manufacture of dyes, flavourings, and perfumes.

benzene /bén zeen/ *n* C_6H_6 a colourless volatile toxic liquid with a distinctive odour. Source: petroleum. Use: manufacture of dyes, polymers, and industrial chemicals. [Mid-19C. < *benzoic*.]

benzene ring *n* a molecular structure common to benzene and its derivatives in which six carbon atoms are bonded in a hexagon by alternating single and double bonds

benzine /bén zeen/, **benzin** /-zin/ *n* a mixture of liquid hydrocarbons having a carefully selected boiling point range. Source: crude oil. Use: industrial solvent. [Mid-19C. < *benzoic*.]

benzo- *prefix* benzene, benzoic acid ○ *benzopyrene* [< BENZOIN]

benzodiazepine /bénzō dī áyzə peen/ *n* a minor tranquillizer. Use: short-term treatment for sleeping difficulties.

benzoic acid /ben zṓik-/ *n* C_6H_5COOH a colourless crystalline solid found in some natural resins. Use: food preservative, manufacture of pharmaceuticals and cosmetics.

benzoin /bénzō in/ *n* $C_{14}H_{12}O_2$ a toxic white crystalline solid occurring in natural resins or manufactured synthetically. Use: medications, perfumes, incense. [Mid-16C. Via French *benjoin* < Arabic *lubānjāwī* 'incense from Sumatra'.]

benzol /bén zol/, **benzole** *n* CHEM = **benzene** [Mid-19C. < *benzoic*.]

benzonitrile /bénzō nītrəl, -trīl/ *n* a colourless almond-scented oil with a pungent taste. Use: synthesis of chemicals and resins, solvent.

benzophenone /bénzō feénōn/ *n* $(C_6H_5)_2CO$ a sweet-smelling colourless, crystalline solid. Use: manufacture of perfumes, organic compounds. [Late 19C. < BENZO- + PHENO- + -ONE.]

benzopyrene /bénzō pīrin/ *n* $C_{20}H_{12}$ a yellow crystalline solid that is highly carcinogenic. Source: tobacco smoke, coal tar.

benzoquinone /bénzō kweénōn/ *n* $C_6H_4O_2$ a yellow crystalline solid with an unpleasant odour. Use: photographic developer, dyes, antioxidants.

benzoyl /bénzōil/ *adj* relating to or containing the group $C_6H_5CO–$ [Mid-19C. < German, < *Benzoësäure* 'benzoic acid' + Greek *hylē* 'wood, matter'.]

benzpyrene *n* CHEM = **benzopyrene**

Ben-Zvi /ben zveé/, **Itzhak** (1884–1963) Polish-born Israeli statesman

benzyl /bénzil/ *adj* relating to or containing the group $C_6H_5CH_2–$

benzyl alcohol *n* a colourless alcohol with a sharp, burning taste. Use: synthesis of chemicals, in perfumes and flavourings, solvent.

benzylamine /bénzil áymeen/ *n* an amber, toxic, strongly alkaline liquid. Use: synthesis of chemicals and drugs.

Beowulf /báyō wŏŏlf/ *n* an anonymous Old English epic poem of the eighth century AD describing the exploits of the hero Beowulf, in particular his slaying of the monster Grendel and Grendel's mother

bequeath /bi kweéth, -kweéth/ *vt* **1** to leave personal or other property to somebody after death by means of a will **2** to hand something, e.g. knowledge or a practice, down to future generations [Old English *becweðan* 'speak about' < *cweðan* 'speak'] —**bequeathal** /bi kweéth'l/ *n* —**bequeather** *n* —**bequeathment** *n*

bequest /bi kwést/ *n* **1 ACT OF BEQUEATHING** an act of bequeathing something **2 SOMETHING LEFT IN WILL** something disposed of in a will **3 SOMETHING HANDED DOWN TO POSTERITY** something passed down to future generations [14C. < BEQUEATH.]

Béranger /báy raaN zhay/, **Pierre Jean de** (1780–1857) French poet

berate /bi ráyt/ (**-rates, -rating, -rated**) *vt* to scold somebody vigorously and lengthily [Mid-16C. < *rate* 'berate' < ?]

Berber /búrbər/ (*plural* **-bers** *or* **-ber**) *n* **1** a member of a people living in North Africa **2** a group of Afro-Asiatic languages spoken across North Africa, especially in Algeria and Morocco, sometimes regarded as a single language with divergent dialects. Native speakers: 12 million. [Mid-18C. < Arabic *barbar*.] —**Berber** *adj*

Berbera /búrbərə/ port in NW Somalia. Population: 65,000 (1987).

berberis /búrbəriss/ *n* TREES = **barberry** [Late 16C. Via modern Latin or Old French < medieval Latin *barbaris*.]

berceuse /bair súrz/ *n* **1** a lullaby or cradlesong **2** an instrumental piece of music, usually in $\frac{6}{8}$ time, meant to sound like a lullaby [Late 19C. < French, < *bercer* 'to rock'.]

Berchtesgaden /báirktəss gaad'n, báirkhtəss-/ town in SE Bavaria, Germany, near the site of the Berghof, Adolf Hitler's fortified retreat. Population: 7,979 (1991).

bereave /bi reév/ (**-reaves, -reaving, -reaved**) *vt* to deprive somebody of a beloved person or a treasured thing, especially through death (*often passive*) [Old English *bereafian* 'deprive, rob' < Germanic] —**bereavement** *n* —**bereaver** *n*

bereaved /bi reévd/ *adj* having lost a loved one through death ■ *n* (*plural* **-reaved**) somebody who has suffered the death of a loved one

bereft /bi réft/ *adj* **1 DEPRIVED** deprived of somebody or something loved or valued **2 LACKING** lacking in something desirable or necessary ○ *'Lively as the Tabloid Decade (the 1990s) has been, it wouldn't be the worst thing if it uncharacteristically just dribbled out, bereft of new material'* (David Kamp *Vanity Fair*; February 1999) **3 FEELING SENSE OF LOSS** filled with a sense of loss [Late 16C. Old past participle of BEREAVE.]

Berenice's Hair /bérrə nīssiz-/ *n* ASTRON = **Coma Berenices**

Berenson /bérrənss'n/, **Bernard** (1865–1959) Lithuanian-born US art critic and collector. Born **Bernard Valvrojenski**

Beresford /bérrisfərd/, **Bruce** (*b.* 1940) Australian film director

beret /bérray/ *n* a flat round soft hat, usually woollen, with a tight-fitting headband [Early 19C. Via French < late Latin *birrus* 'hooded cloak'.]

berg[1] /burg/ *n* an iceberg [Early 19C. Shortening.]

berg[2] /burg/ *n S Africa* a mountain [Early 19C. Via Afrikaans < Dutch *bergh* 'mountain'.]

Berg /burg/, **Alban** (1885–1935) Austrian composer

Berg, Paul (*b.* 1926) US molecular biologist

bergamot /búrgə mot/ (*plural* **-mots** *or* **-mot**) *n* **1 bergamot, bergamot oil OIL FROM FRUIT OF BERGAMOT TREE** a fragrant yellow-green essential oil. Source: bergamot fruit rinds. Use: perfumes, flavouring in Earl Grey tea. **2 bergamot, bergamot orange SPINY ASIAN CITRUS TREE** a spiny citrus tree with sour pear-shaped fruit. Native to: Asia. *Citrus bergamia*. **3 MEDITERRANEAN MINT PLANT** a plant producing a fragrant oil similar to bergamot oil. Native to: Mediterranean. *Mentha citrata*. **4 N AMERICAN MINT PLANT** a wild or garden plant. Flowers: scarlet in the wild, white to purple in garden varieties. Native to: North America. *Monarda didyma*. US term **bee balm 5** PLANTS = **wild bergamot** [Late 17C. After *Bergamo* in N Italy.]

Bergen /búrgən/ capital of Hordaland County and port in SW Norway. Population: 225,439 (1998).

Bergen-Belsen ♦ **Belsen**

bergenia /bə geéni ə/ (*plural* **-ias** *or* **-ia**) *n* a low-growing perennial plant with large leathery leaves. Flowers: early, usually red, purple, or pink on long stalks. Genus: *Bergenia*. [Mid-19C. After Karl August von *Bergen* (1704–60), German botanist and physician.]

bergère /bər zháir/ (*plural* **-gères**) *n* a chair or sofa with sides and back made of woven cane [Mid-18C. < French, 'shepherdess'.]

Bergman /búrgmən/, **Ingmar** (*b.* 1918) Swedish film director

Bergman, Ingrid (1915–82) Swedish-born US film actor

bergschrund /búrk shrŏŏnt/ (*plural* **-schrunds** *or* **-schrunde** /-shrŏŏndə/) *n* a crevasse formed at the head of a glacier [Mid-19C. < German, 'mountain cleft'.]

Bergson /búrgss'n/, **Henri** (1859–1941) French philosopher —**Bergsonian** *n, adj*

Bergsonism /búrgss'nizəm/ *n* the philosophy of Henri Bergson, which posits the existence of a universal life-giving force (**élan vital**)

berg wind *n S Africa* a hot dry wind blowing from the South African interior to the coast [< BERG[2], because it comes from the mountains]

beriberi /bérri bérri/ *n* a degenerative disease of the nerves caused by a deficiency of the vitamin thiamine and marked by pain, inability to move, and swelling [Early 18C. < Sinhalese, 'weakness'.]

Bering /báiring/, **Vitus** (1681–1741) Danish-born Russian explorer

Bering land bridge *n* a link between Alaska and Siberia that was above sea level during the Ice Age between 13,000 and 10,000 years ago and provided a route for prehistoric people and animals into the Americas

Bering Sea arm of the North Pacific Ocean between the Aleutian Islands, Siberia, and Alaska. Area: 2,261,000 sq. km/873,000 sq. mi. Depth: 4,773 m/15,659 ft.

Bering Strait narrow stretch of sea between Russia and Alaska. At its narrowest point it is 82 km/51 mi. wide.

Berio /bérri ō/, **Luciano** (*b.* 1925) Italian composer

Berisha /bə reéshə/, **Sali** (*b.* 1944) Albanian statesman

berk /burk/, **burk** *n* somebody stupid or foolish (*slang insult*) [Mid-20C. < Rhyming slang *Berkeley Hunt* 'cunt'.]

Berkeleianism /baárkli ə nizzəm/ *n* the philosophy of George Berkeley, particularly his view that the material world is an idea in God's mind and that an object's existence consists in its being perceived [Early 19C. After Bishop BERKELEY.] —**Berkeleian** *adj, n*

Berkeley /búrkli/ city in W California on San Francisco Bay. Population: 108,101 (1998 estimate).

Berkeley /baárkli/, **Busby** (1895–1976) US film director and choreographer. Born **William Berkeley Enos**

Berkeley, George (1685–1753) Irish Anglican bishop and philosopher

Berkeley, Sir William (1606–77) English-born colonial governor

berkelium /bur keéli əm/ *n* (*symbol* **Bk**) a synthetic radioactive element. Source: bombardment of americium-241 with helium ions. [Mid-20C. After BERKELEY, California.]

Berkoff /búrk of/, **Steven** (*b.* 1937) British actor, director, and dramatist

Berks. /baarks/ *abbr* Berkshire

Berkshire /baàrkshər/ former county in south-central England

berlin /bur lín/, **berline** *n* a large and luxurious car with a glass partition between the driver and the passengers [Late 17C. After the city of BERLIN.]

Berlin /bur lín/ capital of Germany, in the northeast of the country. Population: 3,472,000 (1997). —**Berliner** *n*

Berlin, Irving (1888–1989) Russian-born US songwriter. Born **Israel Baline**

Berlin, Sir Isaiah (1909–97) Latvian-born British philosopher and historian

Berlin Wall fortified wall surrounding West Berlin, between 1961 and 1989

Berlin wool *n* a fine wool yarn. Use: clothes, tapestry.

Berlin woolwork *n* needlepoint embroidery stitched with Berlin wools from handpainted coloured charts, popular especially in the second half of the 19th century

Berlioz /báirli ōz/, **Hector** (1803–69) French composer

berm /burm/, **berme** *n* **1** NARROW PATH a ledge or narrow path along the top or bottom of a slope, at the edge of a road, or along a canal **2** RIDGE ABOVE HIGH TIDE MARK a natural ridge or flat platform formed at the rear of a beach, above the high tide mark **3** RIDGE OF SAND FOR ANTITANK DEFENCE a ridge of sand or soil erected as a defence against tanks, which in crossing it expose their vulnerable undersides to attack **4** LEDGE BETWEEN MOAT AND RAMPART a ledge or narrow path between a moat or ditch and a rampart **5** ROADWAY IN OPEN-CAST MINE a narrow roadway cut in the slope of an open-cast mine [Early 18C. Via French < Dutch.]

Bermuda /bər myoódə/ group of islands in the W North Atlantic Ocean, a self-governing British dependency. Capital: Hamilton. Population: 61,600 (1995). Area: 53 sq. km/20 sq. mi. —**Bermudan** *n*, *adj*

Bermuda grass *n* a creeping grass with wiry roots. Use: lawns, pastures, stabilizing sand dunes. Native to: S Europe. *Cynodon dactylon.*

Bermuda rig *n* a fore-and-aft arrangement of a boat's mast and sails that has a tall pointed mainsail on a sharply raked mast

Bermuda shorts, Bermudas *npl* tailored shorts whose legs extend almost to the knee

Bermuda Triangle *n* an area in the W Atlantic Ocean, between Bermuda, Florida, and Puerto Rico, where many ships and aircraft are believed to have disappeared in mysterious circumstances

Bern /burn/, **Berne** capital of Switzerland, in the northwestern part of the country. Population: 123,254 (1998).

Bernadette of Lourdes /búrnə dét əv loórd, -loórdz/, **St** (1844–79) French nun and visionary. Born **Marie Bernarde Soubirous**

Bernadotte /búrnə dot/, **Folke, Count** (1895–1948) Swedish diplomat

Bernanos /báirnə noss/, **Georges** (1888–1948) French novelist

Bernard /bair naàr, búrnərd/, **Claude** (1813–78) French physiologist

Bernardine /búrnədin/ *n* **1** CISTERCIAN MONK a monk belonging to a stricter branch of the Cistercian order **2** NUN a nun belonging to a non-Cistercian order that follows a rule based on the original Cistercian rule ■ *adj* **1** OF THE BERNARDINES relating to or characteristic of a Bernardine **2** OF ST BERNARD relating to or characteristic of St Bernard of Clairvaux or his monastic reforms

Bernard of Clairvaux /búrnərd əv klair vố/, **St** (1090–1153) French theologian

Berne ♦ **Bern**

Berners-Lee /búrnərz leè/, **Tim** (*b.* 1955) British computer scientist and Internet pioneer

Bernese Alps /búr neez-/ mountain range in SW Switzerland. Highest peak: Finsteraarhorn, 4,274 m/14,022 ft.

Sarah Bernhardt

Bernhardt /búrn haart/, **Sarah** (1844–1923) French actor. Born **Henriette Rosine Bernard**

Bernini /bur neéni/, **Gianlorenzo** (1598–1680) Italian sculptor and architect

Bernoulli /bur noóli/, **Daniel** (1700–82) Dutch-born Swiss mathematician and physicist

Bernoulli, Jacques (1654–1705) Swiss mathematician

Bernoulli, Johann *or* **Jean** (1667–1748) Swiss mathematician

Bernoulli distribution *n* STATS = **binomial distribution**

Bernoulli equation *n* US PHYS = **Bernoulli's theorem** *n.* 1

Bernoulli's principle *n* PHYS = **Bernoulli's theorem** *n.* 1 [After Jacques BERNOULLI]

Bernoulli's theorem, Bernoulli's law *n* **1** a law in physics whereby the sum of the pressure and the product of one half of the density times the velocity squared is constant along a streamline for steady flow in an incompressible nonviscous fluid at constant height **2** STATS = **law of large numbers**

Leonard Bernstein

Bernstein /búrn stīn/, **Leonard** (1918–90) US conductor, composer, and pianist

Berri /bérri/ town in SE South Australia. Population: 3,731 (1991).

berry /bérri/ *n* (*plural* **-ries**) **1** SMALL JUICY FRUIT any small juicy or fleshy fruit **2** FLESHY SEED-CONTAINING FRUIT a soft fleshy fruit that contains many seeds. Tomato, grape, and banana fruits are berries. (*technical*) **3** KERNEL a seed or kernel, e.g. a coffee bean **4** LOBSTER EGG an egg of a lobster or other egg-carrying crustacean ■ *vi* (**-ries, -rying, -ried**) **1** BEAR BERRIES to produce berries (*refers to bushes*) **2** SEARCH FOR EDIBLE BERRIES to gather or hunt for berries to eat [Old English *beri(g)e* < Germanic] —**berried** *adj*

SPELLCHECK Do not confuse *berry* with *bury*, which has a similar sound. Beware: your spellchecker will not catch this error.

Berryman /bérrimən/, **John** (1914–72) US poet, writer, and critic

berseem /bər seèm/ *n* a clover grown especially in the S United States and the Nile Valley. Use: forage, to improve soil quality. Native to: Mediterranean. *Trifolium alexandrinum.* [Early 20C. Via Arabic *birsīm* < Coptic *bersīm.*]

berserk /bə zúrk/ *adj* extremely aggressive or angry ○ *go berserk* ■ *n* **1** a violent or reckless person **2** ARMY = **berserker** [Early 19C. < Old Norse *berserk* 'wild warrior', probably < the stem of *bjorn* 'bear' + *serkr* 'shirt'.] —**berserkly** *adv*

berserker /bər zúrkər/ *n* a member of a group of Norse warriors who fought with wild unrestrained aggression

berth /burth/ *n* **1** BED ON SHIP OR TRAIN a bed, usually built-in, on a ship or a train **2** DOCK FOR SHIP a place, usually alongside a quay or dock, where a ship ties up or anchors **3** ROOM TO MANOEUVRE AT SEA sufficient room between a ship and the shore or between a ship and another vessel or object to allow the ship to manoeuvre safely **4** PARKING PLACE a place for a motor vehicle to park or be loaded or unloaded **5** JOB ON SHIP a post as part of a ship's crew **6** JOB a job or position of employment (*informal*) ■ *v* **1** *vti* DOCK A SHIP to dock or moor a vessel, or be docked or moored **2** *vt* ASSIGN MOORING TO VESSEL to assign a vessel a place to dock or moor **3** *vt* ASSIGN BERTH TO to assign somebody a berth on a ship or train [Early 17C. < BEAR² 'carry'.] ◇ **give somebody or something a wide berth** to keep well away from somebody or something

bertha /búrthə/ *n* a wide long collar around the shoulders of a woman's low-necked dress [Mid-19C. < French *berthe*, after the Carolingian Queen *Bertha* (d. AD 783).]

Bertillon system /búrtilən-/ *n* a former method of identifying people, especially criminals, on the basis of detailed records of their physical measurements and characteristics [Late 19C. After Alphonse *Bertillon* (1853–1914), French criminologist.]

Berwickshire /bérrikshər/ former county in SE Scotland

Berwick-upon-Tweed /bérrik ə pon tweéd/ town in NE England. Population: 13,544 (1991).

beryl /bérrəl/ *n* a hard, crystalline mineral, consisting of beryllium aluminium silicate, that occurs in white, yellow, pink, green, or blue forms. Use: gems. [12C. Via French and Latin *beryllus* < Greek *bērullos.*] —**berylline** *adj*

beryllium /bə rílli əm/ *n* (*symbol* **Be**) a grey-white metallic element that is light, hard, brittle, and resists corrosion. Source: beryl. Use: alloys, lightweight construction material, windows in X-ray tubes.

Berzelius /bər zeèli ass/, **Jöns Jakob, Baron** (1779–1848) Swedish chemist

Besançon /bə zóN soN/ capital of Doubs Department, E France. Population: 119,194 (1990).

Besant /bézz'nt/, **Annie** (1847–1933) British theosophist and politician. Born **Annie Wood**

Besant /bə zánt/, **Sir Walter** (1836–1901) British social reformer and novelist

beseech /bi seéch/ (**-seeches, -seeching, -sought** /-sáwt/ *or* **-seeched**) *vt* (*literary*) **1** to ask earnestly or beg somebody to do something **2** to ask urgently for something [12C. < SEEK.] —**beseecher** *n* —**beseeching** *adj* —**beseechingly** *adv*

beset /bi sét/ (**-sets, -setting, -set**) *vt* (*usually passive*) **1** HARASS to harass or trouble somebody or something continually (*formal*) **2** SURROUND to attack somebody or something on all sides (*formal*) **3** SET WITH JEWELS to surround or set something with jewels or other ornaments (*literary*) —**besetment** *n* —**besetter** *n*

besetting /bi sétting/ *adj* harassing or troubling somebody continually

beside /bi síd/ *prep* **1** AT THE SIDE OF in a position next to or alongside ○ *Sit beside me.* ○ *beside the seaside* **2** COMPARED WITH in comparison with ○ *handsome beside his brother* **3** AS WELL AS in addition to ○ *in another dictionary beside this one* [Old English *be sīdan* 'by the side of'] ◇ **beside yourself** in a very excited or agitated state

USAGE beside or **besides**? *Beside* is a preposition referring to physical position: *Come and sit beside me.* It is also used to mean 'in addition to', although this can lead to confusion with the meaning 'at the side of'. *Besides* is an adverb meaning 'moreover': *It's late and besides, the weather's too cold.* It is also a preposition meaning 'in addition to': *They've already paid a lot for the house besides what they'll need for improvements.* Note that *besides* is inclusive, whereas *except* is exclusive, so that *Besides Larry, we'll invite John, Jake, and Renée.* means that Larry is also invited, whereas *They are all invited except Larry* means that Larry is not invited.

besides /bi sídz/ *prep, adv* in addition to something or somebody specified or understood ○ *Besides fruit, we will also need cheese, and crackers.* ■ *adv* what is more ○ *He's my cousin. Besides, he's good company.*

USAGE See ***beside***.

besiege /bi seéj/ (**-sieges, -sieging, -sieged**) *vt* **1 SURROUND WITH ARMY** to surround a city or strongpoint with armed forces in order to bring about its surrender or capture **2 CROWD AROUND** to crowd around somebody in an oppressive way (*usually passive*) ○ *the newlyweds were besieged by reporters outside their hotel* **3 HARASS** to harass a person or organization with insistent demands or complaints (*usually passive*) ○ *The box office was besieged by fans wanting tickets.* [13C. < *assiege*, via Old French *asegier* < Latin *sedere* 'sit'.] —**besiegement** *n* —**besieger** *n*

besmear /bi smeér/ *vt* **1** to smear somebody or something with mud, dirt, or some greasy or sticky substance **2** to bring shame or disgrace on somebody or something

besmirch /bi smúrch/ *vt* **1** to bring shame or disgrace on somebody's reputation **2** to make something dirty (*literary*) —**besmircher** *n* —**besmirchment** *n*

besom /beézəm/ *n* **1 BROOM MADE FROM TWIGS** a broom, especially one made with a bundle of twigs **2 CURLING BROOM** in curling, a broom used to sweep the ice in front of a moving stone in order to help it slide **3 WOMAN OR GIRL** used as a mildly derogatory term for a woman or girl (*insult regional*) [Old English *bes(e)ma* < Germanic] —**besom** *vt*

besotted /bi sóttid/ *adj* **1** made confused through affection for or attraction to somebody **2** in a confused mental state, especially through having drunk too much alcohol (*archaic*) [Late 16C. < earlier *sot* 'stupefy' < Old French, 'fool'.]

besought past tense, past participle of **beseech**

bespangle /bi spáng g'l/ (**-gles, -gling, -gled**) *vt* to ornament something with something bright, especially spangles

bespatter /bi spáttər/ *vt* to splash something with mud, paint, or some other substance

bespeak /bi speék/ (**-speaks, -speaking, -spoke** /-spók/, **-spoken** /-spókən/) *vt* **1 SIGNIFY** to be a sign or indication of something **2 ORDER IN ADVANCE** to reserve or order something in advance **3 ASK FOR POLITELY** to ask politely for something, e.g. a favour (*formal*) **4 ADDRESS** to speak to somebody (*literary*)

bespectacled /bi spéktək'ld/ *adj* wearing spectacles

bespoke past tense of **bespeak** ■ *adj* **1** made to a customer's specifications **2** making clothes or shoes to customers' specifications ○ *a bespoke tailor*

bespoken past participle of **bespeak**

besprinkle /bi spríngk'l/ (**-kles, -kling, -kled**) *vt* to sprinkle small quantities of liquid or something light over the surface of something (*often passive*)

Bessarabia /béssə ráybi ə/ historic region in SE Europe, corresponding to present-day Moldova and part of Ukraine

Bessel /béss'l/, **Friedrich Wilhelm** (1784–1846) German mathematician and astronomer

Bessemer /béssəmər/, **Sir Henry** (1813–98) British metallurgist

Bessemer process *n* a largely obsolete method for making steel from impure iron by forcing air through the molten metal in a specialized furnace (**Bessemer converter**) [Late 19C. After Sir Henry BESSEMER.]

best /best/ CORE MEANING: better than anybody or anything else

1 *adj* **BETTER THAN ALL OTHERS** of the highest quality or standard or the most excellent type ○ *the best days of your life* ○ *wearing her best dress* ○ *the best sprinter this decade* **2** *adj* **MOST LIKELY TO SUCCEED** most likely to have or come near to the desired outcome ○ *the best thing to do in the circumstances* **3** *adj* **MOST INTIMATE** liked, trusted, and confided in more than anybody else ○ *my best friends* **4** *adv* **MORE THAN ALL OTHERS** in the highest degree or to the greatest extent ○ *likes me best* **5** *adv* **MOST SUCCESSFULLY** in a way that is most likely to have or come near to the desired outcome ○ *It works best if you warm it up first.* **6** *adv* **TO THE HIGHEST STANDARD** to a higher standard than anybody or anything else ○ *the best trained horse in the competition* **7** *n* **WHAT IS BEST** the best possible things or circumstances ○ *want the best for their family* ○ *will only buy the best* **8** *n* **SOMEBODY OR SOMETHING BETTER THAN OTHERS** somebody or something of the highest quality or standard ○ *is the best at hockey* **9** *n* **TOP QUALITY** the highest quality or standard that somebody or something is capable of ○ *do your best* ○ *past its best* **10** *n* **TOP ACHIEVEMENT** the best time or score that somebody has achieved in a sport or game ○ *trying to beat her personal best in the marathon* **11** *n* **ENDORSEMENT** used as an enthusiastic endorsement of something (*slang*) ○ *How is your hotel? – It's the best!* [Old English *betest*, superlative of GOOD and WELL[2], < Germanic] ◇ **at best** according to the most favourable interpretation ◇ **at the best of times** even when circumstances are at their most favourable ◇ **at somebody's** *or* **its best** performing at the peak of ability or effectiveness ◇ **make the best of something** to extract what benefit you can from an unsatisfactory or disadvantageous situation

USAGE ***best*** or ***better***? When you compare two persons or things, use *better* not *best* if you wish to avoid possible criticism. Thus, it is safer to write *Of the two properties, this one is the* ***better*** [not ***best***] *buy.* This advice also holds with other adjectives in dual comparisons: *We nursed the weaker* [not *weakest*] *of the two tiny pups; She's the older* [not *oldest*] *of the two sisters.* ***Best***, however, is the word used in set idiomatic expressions like *Put your best foot forward* and *May the best man win.*

Best /best/, **Charles H.** (1899–1978) US-born Canadian physiologist

Best, Elsdon (1856–1931) New Zealand ethnologist

Best, George (*b.* 1946) Northern Irish footballer

best-ball *adj* using a scoring method in which a golfer competes against a team of two or three other golfers, with the team recording only the best individual score for each hole

best boy *n* the chief assistant to the electrician in charge of lighting on a film or television set

best end *n* meat cut from the end of the neck nearest to the shoulder of a butchered animal

bestial /bésti əl/ *adj* **1 INHUMAN** lacking normal human feelings of pity or remorse ○ *bestial cruelty* **2 SEXUALLY DEPRAVED** sexual in a depraved or purely physical manner **3 BRUTISH** lacking intellect, reason, or culture **4 RELATING TO BEASTS** relating to or characteristic of a beast [14C. Via French < late Latin *bestialis* < Latin *bestia* 'beast'.] —**bestially** *adv*

bestialise *vt* = **bestialize**

bestiality /bésti állәti/ *n* **1** sexual activity between a human being and an animal **2** an act, behaviour, or condition more appropriate for an animal than a human being

bestialize /bésti ə līz/ (**-izes, -izing, -ized**), **bestialise** (**-ises, -ising, -ised**) *vt* **1** to make somebody behave or live like an animal **2** to make somebody inhuman or savage

bestiary /bésti əri/ (*plural* **-ies**) *n* a medieval book containing pictures and moralizing stories about real and imaginary animals [Mid-19C. < medieval Latin *bestiarium* < Latin *bestia* 'beast'.]

bestir /bi stúr/ (**-stirs, -stirring, -stirred**) *vr* to begin to do something after a period of inactivity (*formal*) ○ *After a long afternoon nap, they finally bestirred themselves to start the supper preparations.*

best maid *n Scotland* the chief bridesmaid at a wedding, the counterpart of the best man

best man *n* a man attending a bridegroom and carrying out important duties during the wedding celebrations

bestow /bi stów/ *vt* to present something to somebody (*formal*) —**bestowal** *n* —**bestowment** *n*

SYNONYMS See ***give***.

bestrew /bi stróo/ (**-strews, -strewing, -strewed, -strewn** /bi stróon/ *or* **-strewed**) *vt* (*literary*) **1** to scatter things over something ○ *a church aisle bestrewn with flowers* **2** to be scattered over something ○ *the confetti that bestrewed the church steps after the wedding*

bestride /bi stríd/ (**-strides, -striding, -strode** /-stród/ *or* **-strid, -stridden** /-strídd'n/ *or* **-strid** *archaic* /-stríd/) *vt* to sit or stand with one foot on or towards each side of something ○ *He bestrode the hearthrug, holding forth on the merits of the case.*

bestseller /bést séllər/ *n* **1** something, especially a book, that is commercially very successful **2** an author who writes bestsellers

bestselling /bést sélling/ *adj* far more popular and successful than other products on sale at the same time ○ *his bestselling account of life in Provence*

bet /bet/ *vti* (**bets, betting, bet** *or* **betted**) **1 RISK SOMETHING OF VALUE** to agree with somebody that something specified, usually money, will be forfeited by the person who incorrectly predicts the outcome of a future event to the other or fails in some other prearranged challenge **2 THINK SOMETHING IS TRUE** to express certainty that something will happen, has happened, or is true (*informal*) ○ *I bet he's forgotten to bring the keys.* ■ *n* **1 ACT OF BETTING** an agreement that the person who incorrectly predicts the outcome of a future event will forfeit something, usually money, to another **2 AMOUNT WAGERED** the amount of money that somebody agrees to pay as a bet ○ *She lost her £10 bet.* **3 WHAT SOMEBODY EXPECTS OR THINKS** what somebody expects to happen or thinks is true ○ *My bet is they'll decide to overlook the whole thing.* **4 SOMEBODY OR SOMETHING LIKELY TO WIN** somebody or something likely to be successful ○ *She's a good bet for a vice-presidency.* [Late 16C. < ?] ◇ **you bet!** used to show emphatic agreement (*informal*) ◇ **your best** *or* **safest bet** the course of action most likely to be productive

beta /beétə/ *n* **1 2ND LETTER OF GREEK ALPHABET** the second letter of the Greek alphabet **2 ACADEMIC GRADE** a letter such as 'B' used as a grade for good, but not excellent, academic work **3 MEASURE OF PRICE SENSITIVITY** a measure of how volatile the price of a security is, compared to the overall market ■ *adj* **1 RELATING TO ELECTRONS PRODUCED BY RADIOACTIVITY** describes electrons, especially those formed by the splitting of a neutron into a proton and an electron **2 SECOND NEAREST TO DESIGNATED ATOM** describes the second nearest atom to a designated atom or group of atoms in an organic molecule **3 DESCRIBING MINOR FORM OF ELEMENT** describes a minor form of a chemical element with more than one form (**allotrope**) **4 DESCRIBING ONE FORM OF A COMPOUND** describes a structural form of a chemical compound having more than one form (**isomer**) [14C. Via Latin and Greek < Canaanite *bet* 'house'.]

Beta /beétə/ *n* the second brightest star in a constellation (*followed by Latin genitive*) ○ *Beta Centauri*

beta-blocker *n* a drug that regulates the activity of the heart. Use: treatment of high blood pressure.

beta-carotene *n* BIOCHEM = **carotene**

beta decay *n* the radioactive transformation of an atomic nucleus during which an electron or positron is produced, although the mass number remains unchanged

beta emission *n* the emission of an electron by a radionuclide —**beta emitter** *n*

betaine /beétə een, -in, bi táy-/ *n* $C_5H_{11}NO_2$ a sweet-tasting organic compound. Source: sugar beet. Use: treatment of muscular degeneration. [Mid-19C. < Latin *beta* 'beet'.]

betake /bi táyk/ (**-takes, -taking, -took** /-tóok/, **-taken** /-táykən/) *vr* to go somewhere (*archaic or literary*)

Betancourt /béttən koor/, **Rómulo** (1908–81) Venezuelan statesman

beta-oxidation *n* the breakdown of fatty acids during cellular metabolism to produce acetyl coenzyme A

beta particle *n* a high-speed electron emitted from the nucleus of an atom during radioactive decay and created by the splitting of a neutron into a proton and an electron

beta process *n* PHYS = **beta decay**

beta ray *n* a stream of beta particles

beta-receptor *n* a site on cells in the autonomic nervous system that responds to hormones such as adrenalin and operates to control blood pressure, regulate the heartbeat, and contract muscles

beta rhythm *n* a pattern of electrical waves in the brain of somebody who is awake and active, registering on an electroencephalograph at a reading between 18 and 30 hertz. ◊ **beta wave**

ϟ **beta test** *n* **1** a test of a product, especially computer software, by giving it to a few customers to try out, before the final version is put on sale **2** a beta test (*informal*) —**beta-test** *vt*

beta transformation *n* PHYS = **beta decay**

betatron /beétə tron/ *n* a device that accelerates electrons in a circular orbit by means of a rapidly alternating magnetic field ϟ **betaware** /béetə wair/ *n* a version of computer software that is to be tested by giving it to customers before the final version is put on sale

beta wave *n* a high-frequency electrical wave produced in the human brain and associated with normal wakefulness. ◊ **beta rhythm**

betcha /béchə/ *contr* a form of 'bet you' used mainly in conversation (*nonstandard*) ○ *Betcha he asks me out before the weekend.*

betel /béet'l/ (*plural* **-tels** *or* **-tel**) *n* an evergreen climbing plant with broad leaves. Use: chewed as a mild stimulant and digestive aid. Native to: Asia. *Piper betle.* [Mid-16C. Via Portuguese < Malayalam *verrila* < Tamil *vrrilai.*]

Betelgeuse /béet'l júrz, béet'l jurz, béet'l jooz/ *n* a bright red variable supergiant star that is the second brightest star in the constellation Orion

betel nut *n* a dark red seed. Source: betel palm. Use: wrapped in betel leaves with lime and chewed by people in Asia as a mild stimulant.

betel palm *n* a palm tree that has orange fruit and dark red seeds. Native to: Asia. *Areca catechu.*

bete noire /bét nwaár/ (*plural* **betes noires** /bét nwaár/) *n* somebody or something you particularly dislike [Mid-19C. < French, 'black beast'.]

beth /beth/ *n* the second letter of the Hebrew alphabet [Early 19C. < Hebrew, < *bēṯ* 'house'.]

Bethany /béthəni/ village near Jerusalem in ancient Palestine. According to the Bible, Lazarus arose from the dead there.

Beth Din /bét dín, béth-/ (*plural* **Batei Din** /baá tay dín/) *n* a Jewish religious court regulating matters of Jewish law such as dietary laws, divorce, and conversion [Late 18C. < Hebrew *bēṯ dīn* 'house of judgment'.]

Bethe /báytə/, **Hans** (*b.* 1906) German-born US physicist

Bethesda /bə thézdə/ town in W Maryland. Population: 62,936 (1996 estimate).

bethink /bi thíngk/ (**-thinks, -thinking, -thought** /-tháwt/, **-thought**) *vr* to think of or remember something (*archaic*)

Bethlehem /béthli hem/ town in the West Bank near Jerusalem. Part of Israel since 1967, it has been administered by the Palestinian Authority since 1995. Thought to be the birthplace of King David and Jesus Christ. Population: 28,132 (1990).

bethought past tense, past participle of **bethink**

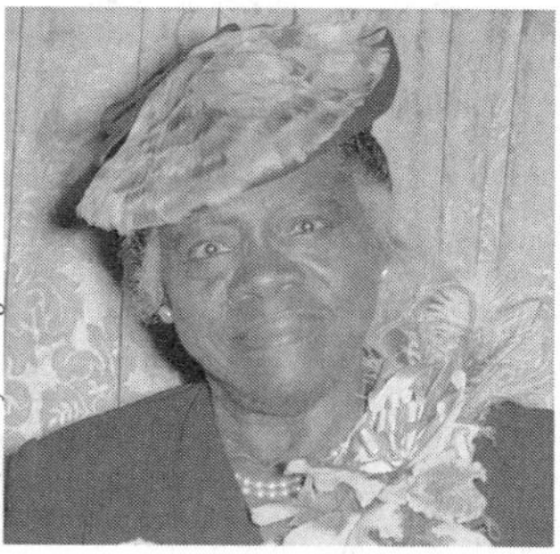

Corbis/Library of Congress

Mary McLeod Bethune

Bethune /be thyoón/, **Mary McLeod** (1875–1955) US educator and activist

betide /bi tíd/ *vti* to happen, or happen to somebody (*literary*) ○ *Whether good or ill betide you, trust in yourself.*

betimes /bi tímz/ *adv* early or in good time (*archaic*) [13C. *be-* a form of BY[1].]

Betjeman /béchəmən/, **Sir John** (1906–84) British poet

betoken /bi tókən/ *vt* to be a sign that something exists or will happen (*literary*)

betony /béttəni/ (*plural* **-nies**) *n* **1** a plant of the mint family. Flowers: purplish. Use: formerly, in medicine. Native to: Europe, Asia. *Stachys officinalis.* **2** any plant resembling true betony [14C. < Latin *betonica.*]

betook past tense of **betake**

betray /bi tráy/ *vt* **1** HELP AN ENEMY to harm or be disloyal to your own country or another person by helping or giving information to an enemy **2** SURRENDER SOMEBODY OR SOMETHING TREACHEROUSLY to deliver somebody or something to an enemy ○ *He betrayed his own brother to the secret police.* **3** GO AGAINST A PROMISE to act in a way that is contrary to a promise made ○ *'If an intelligent person is betrayed repeatedly, and humiliated publicly, yet chooses to remain in that situation, one must ask: what are the rewards?'* (Gail Sheehy, *Vanity Fair;* February 1999) **4** REVEAL to show something, often unintentionally ○ *She said nothing, but her bright eyes betrayed her excitement.* [13C. < BE- + Old French *trair* < Latin *tradere* 'hand over'.] —**betrayal** *n* —**betrayer** *n*

betroth /bi tróth/ *vt* to promise to marry somebody, or promise that somebody will marry somebody (*archaic*) [14C. < BE- + TRUTH.]

betrothal /bi tróthəl/ *n* the act of becoming engaged to marry somebody, or the state of being engaged to somebody (*formal*)

betrothed /bi tróthd/ (*plural* **-trotheds** *or* **-trothed**) *n* the person to whom somebody is engaged to be married (*formal*) —**betrothed** *adj*

Bettelheim /bétt'l hīm/, **Bruno** (1903–90) Austrian-born US psychologist

better[1] /béttər/ CORE MEANING: indicating that a thing or an action is superior in some way to something else or is an improvement upon a situation ○ (adj) *Concentrated laundry detergent is better because it requires a smaller box or bottle.* ○ (adj) *She is gradually getting better, albeit slowly.* ○ (adj) *That's hardly going to make things any better.* ○ (adv) *Treatment programmes may get the job done better.*

1 *adj* MORE ACCEPTABLE more pleasing or acceptable than something else ○ *That hairstyle is far better than the one you had before.* **2** *adj* OF GREATER QUALITY of greater quality, usefulness, or suitability than something else ○ *Economic security helps ensure a better future for our children.* ○ *It is better to light a candle than to curse the darkness.* **3** *adj* IMPROVED IN HEALTH in an improved state of health, after not being well ○ *I'm feeling much better today, thank you.* **4** *adv* MORE OR TO A HIGHER STANDARD in a more acceptable, appropriate or effective way ○ *He plays tennis much better than I do.* ○ *I liked her much better after I got to know her.* **5** *adv* PREFERABLY in a way that is preferable or more advantageous ○ *Such things are better left unsaid.* **6** *vt* SURPASS to improve on something ○ *She hopes to better the record that she set at the Commonwealth Games.* ○ *He summed the whole thing up in a way that I couldn't possibly better.* **7** *vt* IMPROVE SELF OR THING to improve yourself or something (*formal*) ○ *They tried to better themselves by attaining a good education.* ○ *attempts to better the lot of the refugees* **8** *n* SUPERIOR PERSON a person who is superior to another in some way (*often plural*) ○ *They think themselves our betters.* [Old English *bettra* < comparative of Germanic, 'advantageous'] ◇ **for better or worse** whatever the outcome may be ◇ **get the better of somebody 1** to defeat somebody in some way **2** to be too strong for somebody to control ◇ **go one better** to do something that has been done before but in a superior or preferable way ◇ **had better do something** ought to or must do something ○ *You'd better tell them soon.*

USAGE See ***best.***

better[2] /béttər/ *n* somebody who bets. US term **bettor**

better half *n* somebody's wife or husband (*informal*)

betterment /béttərmənt/ *n* **1** a change that improves something, especially somebody's financial or social condition (*formal*) **2** improvement of a building or land that increases its value

Betti /bétti/, **Ugo** (1892–1953) Italian dramatist and poet

betting /bétting/ *n* the activity of placing bets

bettong /be tóng/ *n* a small nocturnal member of the kangaroo family of Australia, with small rounded ears and a bushy tail. Genus: *Bettongia.* [Early 19C. < an Aboriginal language.]

bettor /béttər/ *n* GAMBLING = **better**[2]

between /bi twéen/ CORE MEANING: a grammatical word indicating an intermediate point between two places or times ○ (prep) *I was standing between two other women.* ○ (prep) *I intend to pay off my mortgage between now and 2010.* ○ (adv) *He worked two shifts, with an hour off between.*

prep **1** TO AND FROM from one place to another ○ *She travels between Oxford and Birmingham most days.* **2** TOGETHER together or in combination with ○ *Between us we should have enough money to pay for the trip.* **3** INDICATES COMPARISON indicates a comparison, discussion, or relationship involving two or more people or groups ○ *Reconciliation was hampered by personality conflicts between company executives.* **4** INDICATES CHOICES indicates two or more possible courses of action ○ *The court offers them a choice between a fine or community service.* [Old English *betwēonum* 'by two each' < *twēonum* 'two each' < Germanic] ◇ **(just) between you and me, (just) between ourselves, (just) between you, me, and the gatepost** *or* **bedpost** used to indicate that you are about to reveal something confidential

USAGE between or **among**? Although some people insist on using ***among*** and not ***between*** when more than two items are involved, it is established usage to use ***between*** in this meaning as well, especially when ***among*** might sound too formal: *They shared out the money equally between their five children.* ***Among*** is never used when only two items are involved.

betweenbrain /bi twéen brayn/ *n* ANAT = **diencephalon**

betweentimes /bi twéen tīmz/ *adv* in the intervals between doing other things

betwixt /bi twíkst/ *adv, prep* between (*literary*) [Old English *betwēohs* < *tweohs* 'for two' < Germanic] ◇ **betwixt and between** between two groups or categories, without belonging to one or the other

~~**beutiful**~~ incorrect spelling of **beautiful**

Beuys /boyz, boyss/, **Joseph** (1921–86) German artist

Bevan /bévv'n/, **Nye** (1897–1960) British politician. Full name **Aneurin Bevan**

bevel /bévv'l/ *n* **1** SLANTING EDGE a surface that joins another surface at an angle that is not a right angle **2** ANGLE the angle at which one surface joins another, when this is not a right angle **3** TOOL a tool with two legs that can be adjusted to make various angles, and used to measure or mark an angle on something ■ *vt* (**-els, -elling, -elled**) MAKE SLANTING EDGE to shape the edge of something so that it forms an angle other than a right angle with the main surface ○ *a mirror with bevelled edges* [Late 17C. < assumed Old French.]

bevel gear *n* either of a pair of gear wheels, one conical and the other flat or conical, connecting and transmitting power between shafts that are not parallel

bevel square *n* CONSTR = **bevel** *n.* **3**

beverage /bévvərij/ *n* a drink other than water (*used in commerce*) [14C. < Old French *bevrage* < *bevre,* variant of *boire* < Latin *bibere* 'to drink'.]

Beveridge /bévvərij/, **William, 1st Baron Beveridge of Tuggal** (1879–1963) Indian-born British economist

Beverley /bévvərli/ town in NE England. Population: 23,632 (1991).

Beverly Hills city in SW California. Population: 32,400 (1998 estimate).

Bevin /bévvin/, **Ernest** (1881–1951) British trade union leader and politician

bevvy /bévvi/ *n* (*plural* **-vies**) an alcoholic drink (*slang*) ○ *We went out for a few bevvies.* ■ *vi* (**-vies, -vying, -vied**) to drink alcohol (*slang*) [Late 19C. Shortening of BEVERAGE.] ◇ **on the bevvy** spending time drinking alcohol (*slang*)

bevy /bévvi/ (*plural* **-ies**) *n* **1** a group of people **2** a group of animals or birds, especially quail, larks, or roe deer [15C. < ?]

bewail /bi wáyl/ *vt* to express great sadness about something (*formal*)

beware /bi wáir/ *vti* to be on guard against somebody or something (*as a command and in the infinitive*) [13C. < *be ware* 'be careful' < Old English *wær* 'watchful' < Germanic.]

bewhiskered /bi wískərd/ *adj* having whiskers or a beard ○ *bewhiskered gentlemen in old photographs*

Bewick /byoó ik/, **Thomas** (1753–1828) British wood engraver

Bewick's swan *n* a small swan. Native to: marshy and swampy Arctic regions of Europe and Asia. *Cygnus bewickii.* [After Thomas *Bewick* (1753–1828), British illustrator of natural history books]

bewigged /bi wígd/ *adj* wearing a wig

bewilder /bi wíldər/ *vt* to confuse or puzzle somebody completely [Late 17C. < BE- + archaic *wilder* < ?] —**bewildered** *adj* —**bewilderedly** *adv* —**bewilderedness** *n* —**bewilderment** *n*

bewildering /bi wíldəring/ *adj* extremely confusing —**bewilderingly** *adv*

bewitch /bi wích/ *vt* **1** to fascinate or be very desirable to somebody (*often passive*) **2** to affect somebody or something using a supposed magic spell [13C. < BE- +

witch 'enchant' < WITCH.] —**bewitcher** *n* —**bewitchment** *n*

bewitching /bi wíching/ *adj* fascinating, charming, or very desirable —**bewitchingly** *adv*

bey /bay/ (*plural* **beys**) *n* **1** a title used for various high-ranking officials in the Ottoman Empire, especially governors of a province **2** a respectful form of address for men used in Turkey and Egypt [Late 16C. Via Turkish < Old Turkish *beg* 'prince'.]

beyond /bi yónd/ CORE MEANING: a grammatical word indicating that something is on the other side of something else, either physically or in the abstract ○ (prep) *They are expanding environmental protection programmes beyond the border area.* ○ (prep) *The gift of laughter is beyond price.*

1 *prep, adv* AFTER A STATED TIME indicates that something continues after a particular time ○ *will remain the world's leading economy in the next decade and beyond* **2** *prep* PAST past a particular stage or situation ○ *Don't attempt to live beyond your income.* **3** *prep* FURTHER THAN further than a particular state of mind or emotion ○ *The site has proved to be popular beyond anyone's wildest dreams.* **4** *prep* EXCEPT indicates an exception ○ *He was incapable of any emotion beyond a certain rueful irony.* **5** *prep* IMPOSSIBLE FOR indicates that something is impossible for somebody to do ○ *I find it quite beyond me to describe what this woman was to me.* **6** *n* THE HEREAFTER the form of existence that some people believe the spirit reaches after death ○ *He feels that his late parents watch over him from the beyond.* **7** *n* WHAT IS OUT THERE an area that lies outside what is known ○ *Humanity stands at the edge of the solar system, contemplating the beyond.* [Old English *begeondan* < *be* form of BY + *geondan* (see YOND).]

bezel /bézz'l/ *n* **1** the face of a cutting tool, especially a chisel, that slopes towards the cutting edge **2** the groove that holds the glass of a watch, light, or instrument dial in position [Late 16C. < Old French.]

Béziers /bézzi ay/ city in SW France. Population: 69,153 (1999).

bezique /bi zéek/ *n* **1** a card game like whist, played with the highest 64 cards from two packs **2** the combination of the queen of spades and the jack of diamonds, which gains a high score in the game of bezique [Mid-19C. < French *besigue*.]

bezoar /bée zawr/ *n* a hard mass of material such as fruit or hair found in the intestines of a ruminant animal, formerly believed to be an antidote to poison [15C. Via French *bezourd* < Arabic *badhizahr* < Persian *padzahr* < *pad* 'protection (against)' + *zahr* 'poison'.]

bf, **b.f.**, **B/F**, **b/f** *abbr* **1** bloody fool (*dated informal*) **2** boldface **3** brought forward

BF *abbr* Belgian franc

BFI *abbr* British Film Institute

BFPO *abbr* British Forces Post Office

⚡bg *abbr* Bulgaria (*in Internet addresses*)

BG *abbr* brigadier general

B-girl *n* a young woman who is a devotee of hip-hop and rap music culture (*slang*) [Abbreviation of *break* (see BREAKDANCING)]

⚡bh *abbr* Bahrain (*in Internet addresses*)

Bhadrapada /báàdra paada/ *n* in the Hindu calendar, the sixth month of the year, made up of 29 or 30 days and occurring about the same time as August to September

Bhagavadgita /búggavad geéta/, **Bhagavad-Gita** *n* a Hindu religious text in which the god Krishna teaches the importance of detachment from personal aims, the fulfilment of religious duties, and devotion to God [Late 18C. < Sanskrit *Bhagavadgītā* 'song of the blessed one' (Krishna) < *bhagavant-* 'blessed' + *gītā* 'song'.]

Bhagwan /bug waàn/ *n S Asia* **1** God **2** a teacher, especially somebody who is revered [Via Hindi *bhagwān* < Sanskrit *bhagavān* < *bhaj* 'adore']

bhai /bī/ *n S Asia* **1** a brother **2** used as a friendly form of address for a man [< Hindi *bhāi* related to Sanskrit *bhrātr* 'brother']

Bhai /bī/ *n* a title of respect that is used after a Sikh man's name to indicate distinction [< Hindi *bhāi* < Sanskrit *bhrātr* 'brother']

bhajan /búȷȷan/ *n S Asia* a Sikh or Hindu hymn [Early 20C. < Sanskrit *bhajana*]

bhaji /baáji/ (*plural* **-jis**), **bhajee**, **bajee** *n* a vegetable fritter, or a dish of vegetable fritters [< Hindi *bhāji* 'fried vegetables']

bhakti /baákti/ *n* in Hinduism, the practice of loving devotion to God as the means of salvation [Mid-19C. < Sanskrit, 'devotion'.]

bhang /bang/, **bang** *n* a drug made from the Indian hemp or cannabis plant [Late 16C. Via Portuguese *bangue* < Persian and Urdu *bang*, Hindi *bhan* < Sanskrit *bhanga*.]

bhangra /báng gra/ *n* a style of popular music that originated in the South Asian community in Britain and mixes Punjabi folk music with western pop music [Mid-20C. < Punjabi.]

bharal /búrral/ *n* a wild sheep from the Himalayas with a bluish-grey coat and curved-back horns. *Pseudois nayaur.* [Mid-19C. < Hindi.]

Bharat /búrrat/ *n S Asia* the Hindi name for India — **Bharatiya** /búrra tee ya/ *adj*

Bharat Natyam /búrrat naátyam/ *n* a classical dance from S India, usually performed by one dancer, with symbolic hand and arm movements

Bhatpara /baat paára/, **Bhātpāra** city in NE India. Population: 304,952 (1991).

bhavan /búv'n/ *n* a large important house or official building in South Asia (*often part of a building's name*) ○ *Rashtrapati Bhavan* [< Hindi]

Bhavnagar /baàvnagar/, **Bhāvnagar** port in W India. Population: 402,338 (1991).

bhindi /bíndi/ *n S Asia* FOOD = **okra** *n.* **2**

Bhindranwale /bíndran waali/, **Sant Jarnail Singh** (1947–84) Indian Sikh leader

Bhopal /bō paál/, **Bhōpal** capital of Madhya Pradesh State, central India. Population: 1,062,771 (1991).

B horizon *n* an intermediate layer of soil beneath the A horizon, containing some organic matter and clay

bhp *abbr* brake horsepower

BHT *abbr* butylated hydroxytoluene

Bhumibol Adulyadej /póòmi pōn aa dòòn la dayt/ (*b.* 1927) king of Thailand (1946-). Known as **Rama XI**

bhuna /bóòna/ *n* a type of curry from S India with a thick spicy sauce

Bhutan

Bhutan /boo taàn/ kingdom in the E Himalayas between India and the Tibet region of China. Capital: Thimphu. Population: 842,000 (1996). Area: 47,000 sq. km/18,100 sq. mi. —**Bhutanese** *n, adj*

Bhutto /bóòtō/, **Benazir** (*b.* 1953) Pakistani stateswoman

bi¹ /bī/ *adj* bisexual (*slang*) ■ *n* (*plural* **bi's**) a bisexual person (*slang*) [Mid-20C. Shortening.]

SPELLCHECK See **buy**.

⚡bi² *abbr* Burundi (*in Internet addresses*)

Bi *symbol* bismuth

bi- *prefix* two, twice, both ○ *biaxial* ○ *bimonthly* [< Latin *bi-*, stem of *bis* 'twice', *bini* 'two by two' < Indo-European, 'two']

Biafra /bi áffra/ region of E Nigeria that was declared a secessionist state between 1967 and 1970 —**Biafran** *n, adj*

Białystok /bi áwi stok/, **Bialystok** /bi álli stok/ capital of Białystok Province, NE Poland. Population: 282,500 (1997 estimate).

Bianca /bi ángka/ *n* a small natural satellite of Uranus, discovered in 1986 by the Voyager 2 planetary probe

biannual /bī ánnyoo al/ *adj* happening twice in a year

USAGE **biannual** or **biennial**? **Biannual** means 'twice a year' whereas **biennial** means 'every two years'. Because many people are unsure about which is which, it is often advisable to use the more straightforward expressions *twice-yearly* and *two-yearly*: *Interest is paid twice-yearly* (or, less formally, *Interest is paid twice a year*). *They met at a series of two-yearly conferences on the environment.*

USAGE See **biweekly**.

Biarritz /beer ríts/ resort town on the Bay of Biscay in SW France. Population: 30,055 (1999).

bias /bí ass/ *n* (*plural* **-ases** *or* **-asses**) **1** PREFERENCE an unfair preference for or dislike of something ○ *a bias in favour of internal candidates* **2** DIAGONAL LINE a line that runs diagonally across the weave of a fabric ○ *a dress cut on the bias* **3** VOLTAGE APPLIED the voltage applied across an electronic device, especially a transistor or valve, to determine the conditions under which it operates **4** UNBALANCED WEIGHT IN BOWLING a bulge or internal weight in one side of a bowl that makes it run in a curved path **5** CURVED PATH IN BOWLING the curved path in which a bowl containing a bulge or internal weight runs **6** DISTORTION OF RESULTS the distortion of a set of statistical results by a variable not considered in the calculation, or the variable itself ■ *vt* (*-ases or -asses, -asing or -assing, -ased or -assed*) INFLUENCE to influence somebody or something unfairly or in a biased way ■ *adj* DIAGONAL running diagonally across the weave of a fabric ○ *a bias seam* ■ *adv* DIAGONALLY diagonally across the weave of a fabric ○ *The sleeves are cut bias.* [Mid-16C. Via French < Old Provençal *biais* 'slant' < Greek *epikarsios* 'oblique'.] —**biased** *adj*

bias binding *n* a long narrow strip of material cut on the bias and used to form the edge of a hem or to bind the edges of a garment. US term **bias tape**

bias-ply *adj US* AUTOMOT = **cross-ply**

bias voltage *n* ELEC ENG = **bias** *n.* **3**

biathlon /bī áth lón/ *n* a competition that combines cross-country skiing with rifle shooting at targets along the course [Mid-20C. < BI- + Greek *athlon* 'prize from a contest'.] —**biathlete** *n*

biaxial /bī áksi al/ *adj* having two axes —**biaxially** *adv*

bib /bib/ *n* **1** PROTECTIVE CLOTHING a small piece of material fastened under a child's chin to protect the clothing while eating **2** PART OF GARMENT the front part of a pinafore, apron, or pair of dungarees that covers the chest **3** FISH OF COD FAMILY a sea fish of the cod family. Native to: European coastal waters. *Trisopterus luscus.* [Late 16C. Probably < *bib* 'drink frequently' < Latin *bibere* 'to drink'.] ◇ **somebody's best bib and tucker** somebody's finest clothes (*informal*)

Bib. *abbr* **1** Bible **2** biblical

bibb /bib/ *n* a part attached to the mast of a sailing ship to support the trestletrees [Late 18C. Variant of BIB.]

bibber /bibbar/ *n* a regular alcohol drinker (*archaic*) [Mid-16C. < *bib* 'drink frequently' (see BIB).]

bibcock /bíb kok/ *n* a tap with a nozzle that is bent downwards [Late 18C. < BIB.]

bibelot /bíbblō/ *n* a small and attractive ornament or piece of jewellery [Late 19C. < French, doubling of *bel* 'beautiful'.]

bibl. *abbr* bibliography

Bible /bíb'l/ *n* **1** CHRISTIAN HOLY BOOK the sacred book of the Christian religion **2** JEWISH HOLY BOOK the Hebrew scriptures, the sacred book of the Jewish religion **3** **Bible, bible** RELIGION'S HOLY BOOK the holy book of any religion **4** **Bible, bible** COPY OF BIBLE a copy or edition of the Bible **5** **Bible, bible** ESSENTIAL BOOK a book that is considered an authority on a particular subject ○ *a bible for amateur renovators* [14C. < Latin *biblia* (*sacra*) '(sacred) books' < Greek, plural of *biblion* 'book' < *biblos* (see BIBLIO-).]

Bible-basher *n* an offensive term for a committed Christian whose outspoken evangelizing is regarded by some as extreme (*slang; sometimes considered offensive*) US term **Bible-thumper** —**Bible-bashing** *n*

Bible belt *n* those areas of the southern and midwestern United States that are characterized by strong Protestant beliefs and strict interpretation of the Bible

Bible-thumper *n US* = **Bible-basher** (*slang*) —**Bible-thumping** *n*

biblical /bíbblik'l/, **Biblical** *adj* 1 relating to the Bible 2 like the Bible, especially in style of language —**biblically** *adv*

Biblicist /bíbblissist/, **biblicist** *n* 1 a scholar who studies the Bible 2 somebody who interprets the Bible strictly or literally —**Biblicism** *n*

biblio- *prefix* book ○ *bibliomania* [< Greek *biblion* 'small book' < *biblos* 'papyrus, scroll' < *Bublos*, Phoenician city from which papyrus was imported]

bibliography /bíbbli óggrəfi/ (*plural* **-phies**) *n* 1 BOOK SOURCES a list of books and articles consulted, appearing at the end of a book or other text 2 BOOKS ON SUBJECT a list of books and articles on a particular subject 3 LIST OF PUBLICATIONS a list of the books and articles written by a particular author or issued by a particular publisher 4 BOOK HISTORY the history of books and other publications, and the work of classifying and describing them [Late 17C. Directly or via French < modern Latin *bibliographia* < Greek *biblion* (see BIBLIO-) + Latin *graphia* (see -GRAPHY).] —**bibliographer** *n* —**bibliographic** /bíbbli ə gráffik/ *adj* —**bibliographical** *adj* —**bibliographically** *adv*

bibliomancy /bíbbli ə manssi/ *n* an attempt to foretell the future or answer a question by picking a passage at random from a book, especially the Bible

bibliomania /bíbbli ə máyni ə/ *n* an extreme fondness for books, especially the collecting of them —**bibliomaniac** *n*

bibliophile /bíbbli ə fīl/ *n* a collector of books

bib necklace *n* a necklace with decorative attachments hanging from it that form a V-shape

bibulous /bíbbyŏŏləss/ *adj* tending to drink too much alcohol (*formal*) [Late 17C. < Latin *bibulus* < *bibere* 'to drink'.] —**bibulously** *adv* —**bibulousness** *n*

bicameral /bī kámmərəl/ *adj* having two separate and distinct law-making assemblies, e.g. the House of Commons and House of Lords in Britain [Mid-19C. < BI- + Latin *camera* 'chamber, vault' (see CAMERA).] —**bicameralism** *n* —**bicameralist** *n*

bicarb /bī kaárb/ *n* sodium bicarbonate (*informal*) [Early 20C. Shortening.]

bicarbonate /bī kaárbənət, -nayt/ *n* CHEM = **hydrogen carbonate**

bicarbonate of soda *n* sodium bicarbonate. Use: raising agent, antacid. US term **baking soda**

bice /bīss/ *n* a dull blue colour or pigment [14C. < French *bis* 'dark grey'.]

bice blue *n* a deep sky-blue colour

bice green *n* a bright leaf-green colour

bicentenary /bī́ sen teénəri, -ténn-/ *n* (*plural* **-ries**) an anniversary on which something is 200 years old. US term **bicentennial** *n.* ■ *adj* marking or celebrating a 200th anniversary ○ *bicentenary celebrations.* US term **bicentennial** *adj.*

bicentennial /bī́ sen ténni əl/ *n US* = **bicentenary** *n.* ■ *adj US* = **bicentenary** *adj.* —**bicentennially** *adv*

bicephalous /bī séffələss/ *adj* having two heads [Early 19C. < BI- + Greek *kephalē* 'head'.]

biceps /bī́ seps/ (*plural* **-ceps**) *n* 1 a large muscle in the upper arm that contracts to bend the elbow 2 a muscle that has two points of attachment at one end, especially one (**biceps brachii**) in the upper arm and one (**biceps femoris**) in the back of the thigh [Mid-17C. Via French < Latin, 'two-headed' < *caput* 'head'.] —**bicipital** /bī síppit'l/ *adj*

bicker /bíkər/ *vi* to argue in a bad-tempered way about something unimportant [13C. < Middle Dutch *bicken* 'stab, attack' + English *-er* 'repeatedly'.]

bicolour /bī kúllər/, **bicoloured** /bī kúllərd/ *adj* having two colours

biconcave /bī kóng kayv/ *adj* describes a lens with two faces that are concave

biconditional /bī́ kən dísh'nəl/ *n* a proposition in logic involving two statements, one of which is true if, and only if, the other is true

biconvex /bī kón veks/ *adj* describes a lens with two faces that are convex

bicultural /bī kúlchərəl/ *adj* relating to or containing two cultures ○ *a bicultural society* —**biculturalism** *n*

bicurious /bī kyŏŏri əss/ *adj* heterosexual, but wishing to experiment with bisexuality

bicuspid /bī kúspid/ *adj* with two cusps or points ○ *a bicuspid tooth* ■ *n* a tooth with two points, especially one of the eight teeth (**premolars**) that come between the canines and the molars in adult humans [Mid-19C. < BI- + Latin *cuspid-*, stem of *cuspis* 'point, spear'.]

bicuspid valve *n* ANAT = **mitral valve**

bicycle /bī́ sik'l/ *n* a vehicle with two wheels and a seat that is moved by pushing pedals with the feet, and steered by handlebars at the front wheel ■ *vi* (**-cles, -cling, -cled**) to travel by bicycle —**bicycler** *n*

bicycle clip *n* one of a pair of circular clips used to prevent the ends of a cyclist's trousers getting in the way of the bicycle chain

bicycle motocross *n* full form of **BMX**

bicyclic /bī sīklik, -sík-/ *adj* 1 consisting of or arranged in two circles, rings, or cycles 2 describes a molecule containing atoms arranged in two rings

bid /bid/ *v* (**bids, bidding, bad** *archaic* /bad/ *or* **bade** /bad, bayd/ *or* **bid, bidden** /bídd'n/ *or* **bid**) 1 (*past and past participle* **bid**) *vti* OFFER MONEY AT AUCTION to offer a particular amount of money for something at an auction 2 (*past and past participle* **bid**) *vi* OFFER PRICE FOR WORK to offer to do a piece of work for a particular price 3 (*past and past participle* **bid**) *vti* STATE NUMBER OF TRICKS to declare the number of card tricks to be taken 4 *vt* ORDER to tell somebody to do something (*archaic*) ○ *We were bidden to sit quietly, and so we did.* 5 *vt* INVITE to invite somebody somewhere (*archaic*) 6 (*past and past participle* **bid**) *vi* TRY TO ACHIEVE to make an attempt to achieve a particular goal ○ *He hasn't decided whether or not he'll bid for the Presidency.* ■ *n* 1 OFFER MADE TO PAY an offer of money for something at an auction 2 OFFER an offer to do a piece of work for a particular price ○ *bids were invited for the contract* 3 ATTEMPT an attempt to do something or get something ○ *in a desperate bid to save the situation* 4 STATEMENT OF TRICKS a statement of the number of tricks that a player will take in a card game [Old English *biddan* 'request', *beodan* 'offer', both < Germanic] —**bidder** *n*

bid in *vt* to bid at an auction for something already owned, in order to increase its final selling price

bid up *vt* to make bids that are intended to increase the price of something, not to obtain it

b.i.d. *adv* twice a day (*in prescriptions*) [Abbreviation of Latin *bis in die*]

Bidault /bee dṓ/, **Georges** (1899–1983) French statesman

biddable /bíddəb'l/ *adj* likely to do as asked or ordered —**biddability** /bíddə bílləti/ *n* —**biddableness** *n* —**biddably** *adv*

bidden past participle of **bid**

bidding /bídding/ *n* 1 the making of bids at an auction or in a card game 2 somebody's orders or instructions ○ *lots of paperwork to do at the boss's bidding*

Biddle /bídd'l/, **Nicholas** (1786–1844) US financier

biddy /bíddi/ (*plural* **-dies**) *n* an offensive term deliberately insulting a woman's behaviour as fussing or interfering (*slang offensive insult*) [Early 17C. < ?]

biddy-biddy /bíddi bíddi/ (*plural* **biddy-biddies**), **bidi-bidi** (*plural* **bidi-bidis**) *n* a low-growing plant with a clinging seed case. Native to: New Zealand. *Acaena novae-zelandiae.* [Mid-19C. Alteration of Maori *piripiri.*]

bide /bīd/ (**bides, biding, bided** *or* **bode** *archaic* /bōd/, **bided**) *vi* 1 to stay, remain, or wait (*archaic*) ○ *Bide here with us a while.* 2 *Scotland* to remain, stay, or reside in a place or situation [Old English *bīdan* < Indo-European]

bidet /beé day/ *n* a low bathroom plumbing fixture resembling a toilet and equipped with a spray or jet of water, used for washing the genital and anal areas [Mid-17C. < French, 'pony' < *bider* 'to trot'.]

bidi /beédi/, **beedi, biri** /beéri/ *n S Asia* a cheap cigarette made with coarse tobacco [< Hindi *bīḍī* 'betel plug, cigar']

bid price *n* the price that a dealer on the stock exchange will pay for a security

Biedermeier /beédər mī ər/ *adj* belonging to or typical of a highly conventional neoclassical style of home decoration and furnishing that was popular among the middle class in 19th-century Germany [Early 20C. < the surname of a fictional poet created by Ludwig *Eichrodt* (1827–92).]

Bielefeld /beélə felt/ city NW Germany. Population: 324,067 (1997).

Bien Hoa /byén hṓ ə/ city in S Vietnam. Population: 273,953 (1989).

biennial /bī énni əl/ *adj* 1 happening every two years 2 describes a plant that lives for two years and produces flowers and fruit in the second year [Early 17C. < Latin *biennis* 'two-yearly' or *biennium* 'two year period'.] —**biennial** *n* —**biennially** *adv*

USAGE See ***biannual***.

bier /beer/ *n* 1 a table on which a coffin or a corpse is placed 2 a wooden frame on which a corpse or a coffin is carried to where it will be buried (*literary*) [Old English *bǣr* < Germanic]

SPELLCHECK See ***beer***.

Bierce /beerss/, **Ambrose** (1842–1914?) US writer

biethnic /bī éthnik/ *adj* belonging or relating to two different ethnic groups

bifacial /bī fáysh'l/ *adj* 1 describes leaves with upper and lower surfaces that are different from each other 2 having two sides or surfaces

biff /bif/ *vt* to hit somebody with the fist (*informal*) [Mid-19C. An imitation of the sound caused.] —**biff** *n*

bifid /bī́fid/ *adj* divided at one end into two equal parts [Mid-17C. < Latin *bifidus* 'twice divided' < *findere* 'to divide'.] —**bifidity** /bī fíddəti/ *n* —**bifidly** *adv*

bifilar /bī fīlər/ *adj* describes a part suspended on two parallel wires or threads, especially the moving part of an electrical measuring instrument [Mid-19C. < BI- + Latin *filum* 'thread'.]

biflagellate /bī flájjilət, -layt/ *adj* describes a cell that has two slender appendages (**flagella**)

bifocal /bī fṓk'l/ *adj* describes lenses with sections that have different focal lengths, especially in glasses for near and distant vision ■ **bifocals** *npl* a pair of glasses with bifocal lenses

bifurcate *vti* /bī́ fur kayt/ (**-cates, -cating, -cated**) to be split or branched off into two parts, or split something into two parts ■ *adj* /-kayt, -kət/ separating or branching off into two parts [Early 17C. < Latin *bifurcare* 'fork twice' < *furca* 'fork' (see FORK).] —**bifurcation** /bī́ fur káysh'n/ *n*

big /big/ *adj* (**bigger, biggest**) 1 OF GREAT SIZE of great size, number, or amount ○ *a big crowd* 2 OF GREAT POWER of great power or volume ○ *A big cheer went up.* 3 SIGNIFICANT significant or important to somebody ○ *your big moment* 4 SIGNIFICANTLY GREAT significantly or surprisingly great ○ *You're making a big mistake.* 5 OLDER older or grown-up (*usually by or to children*) ○ *When I'm big, I'll be rich and famous.* 6 IMPORTANT important and powerful ○ *one of the big fashion houses* 7 ENTHUSIASTIC enthusiastic about something or somebody (*informal*) ○ *I'm a big baseball fan.* 8 GREAT used to make a word convey greater dislike or disapproval (*informal*) ○ *It's all a big con, really.* 9 MAGNANIMOUS generous or noble ○ *She's a woman with a big heart.* 10 AMBITIOUS full of boastful or unrealistic ambition ○ *She's not likely to fall for his big talk.* 11 FILLED filled with or swollen by something (*literary*) ○ *eyes big with tears* 12 PREGNANT in an obvious state of pregnancy (*archaic*) ○ *She was big with child.* 13 FULL-BODIED full-bodied and full of flavour ○ *The best accompaniment to this dish would be a big Chianti.* ■ *adv* 1 AMBITIOUSLY in a way that is ambitious, and often boastful or unrealistic ○ *You have to think big if you want to get anywhere.* 2 SUCCESSFULLY in a highly successful way (*informal*) ○ *This approach should go over big at the convention.* [14C. < ?] —**bigness** *n* ◇ **big on** enthusiastic about something or recognizing its importance (*informal*) ◇ **make it big** to be extremely successful (*informal*)

bigamous /bíggəməss/ *adj* involved in or constituting an illegal marriage made when an existing marriage is still valid [Late 19C. < Latin *bigamus* (see BIGAMY).] —**bigamously** *adv*

bigamy /bíggəmi/ *n* the crime of marrying somebody while being legally married to somebody else [13C. < Latin *bigamus* 'marriage twice' < Greek *gamos* 'marriage'.] —**bigamist** *n*

Big Apple *n* an informal name for New York City [< use of *apple* by jazz musicians to mean 'job, engagement']

big band *n* a large jazz or dance band, especially one that was popular in the 1930s and 1940s ○ *the big band sound of Tommy Dorsey*

big bang *n* the explosion of a single extremely dense mass of matter that started the universe according to the big bang theory

QUICK FACTS ON... **BIG BANG THEORY**

Key elements: a popular theory of the origin of the universe, slowly replacing the steady-state theory, holds that the universe originated billions of years ago with a 'primordial fireball', an explosion at a single point of infinite density, followed by expansion. Through the effects of gravitational attraction, the initial uniform density at the time of the big bang gave way to clumping and the resulting evolution of galaxies, clusters, and superclusters as well as a constant low-level, nearly uniform, cosmic background radiation. One theory holds that, if there is enough mass in the universe, the current expansion will eventually slow and reverse, ending ultimately in an enormous implosion or 'big crunch'.

Key dates: 1920 steady-state theory; 1923 postulation of red shift; 1929 formulation of Hubble's law; 1948 Gamow proposed that the universe was created in a gigantic explosion; 1965 discovery of uniform cosmic microwave background radiation by Penzias and Wilson; 1989 precise measurements by the Cosmic Background Explorer (COBE) satellite showed the radiation had a uniform temperature of 2.735 kelvin

Big Ben *n* **1** the large clock above the Houses of Parliament in London, or the tower in which it stands **2** the large bell that chimes the hours in the clock tower of the Houses of Parliament in London [After Sir *Benjamin* Hall, Chief Commissioner of Works]

Big Board *n US* the New York Stock Exchange (*informal*)

Big Brother *n* a person or group who exerts dictatorial control and maintains a constant watch over others, often while presenting a caring image [Used in George Orwell's novel *Nineteen Eighty-Four* (1949)] —**Big Brotherism** *n*

big bucks *npl* a large amount of money (*slang*)

big business *n* the activity of large commercial organizations, or these organizations considered as a group

big cheese *n* an important person (*slang*)

big city *n* the largest city in an area ○ *the lure of the big city*

big-city *adj* typical of life in a large metropolitan area ○ *the fast-paced big-city lifestyle*

big crunch *n* the cosmic implosion that, according to one theory of the universe, will ultimately result if there is enough mass in the universe for gravity to slow, halt, and eventually reverse the current expansion

big daddy *n* (*slang*) **1** somebody who or something that is respected, powerful, or well known ○ *the big daddy of the blues guitar* **2** the head of an organization, especially one who exerts paternalistic control

big deal *interj* used to counter that something is less impressive or important than somebody thinks it is (*informal*) ○ *So he's head of department. Big deal.* ■ *n* something that is very important (*informal*) ○ *Let's not make a big deal out of a minor misunderstanding.*

big dipper *n* = **roller coaster** *n.* 1

Big Dipper *n US* = **Plough**

Big Easy *n* an informal name for New Orleans, Louisiana ○ *a night on the town in the Big Easy* [< *The Big Easy* (1970), novel by James Conaway]

big end *n* the larger end of the connecting rod in an internal-combustion engine

bigeneric /bī jə nérrik/ *adj* describes a hybrid produced from two different genera

~~**biger**~~ incorrect spelling of **bigger**

bigeye /bíg ī/ (*plural* **-eyes** *or* **-eye**) *n* a small tropical or subtropical sea fish with rough reddish or silvery scales and very large eyes. Family: Priacanthidae.

Bigfoot /bíg fòot/, **bigfoot** *n* a large hairy humanoid creature supposed to live in the wilderness areas of NW North America, and described as standing 2–3 m/7–10 ft tall [Mid-20C. < the size of the footprints it is said to leave.]

big game *n* large wild animals hunted for sport, especially the larger African mammals

biggie /bíggi/ *n* (*informal*) **1** something that is big **2** somebody or something that is very significant, important, powerful, or successful ◇ **no biggie** not particularly important or serious (*informal*)

big girl's blouse *n* a man who is thought to behave in ways traditionally attributed to women (*slang insult*)

biggish /bíggish/ *adj* fairly large, although not extremely large ○ *The house is quite nice, and it's got a biggish garden.*

big government *n* government perceived as being excessively high-spending and attempting to control too many aspects of people's lives

Biggs /bigz/, **Ronnie** (*b.* 1929) British train robber. Born **Ronald Biggs**

big gun *n* a powerful or influential person (*informal*)

big hair *n* hair that is rather long with a lot of body, often backcombed or sprayed so that it stands away from the head (*informal*)

bighead /bíg hed/ *n* somebody who is too proud of himself or herself (*informal*) —**bigheaded** /bíg héddid/ *adj*

big-hearted *adj* showing kindness and willingness to help and support others —**big-heartedly** *adv* —**big-heartedness** *n*

bighorn /bíg hawrn/ (*plural* **-horns** *or* **-horn**) *n* a large wild mountain sheep that has a long coarse brown coat and very large curving horns. Native to: W North America, NE Asia. Genus: *Ovis.* ◊ **mountain sheep**

big house *n* **1** the biggest house in a locality, especially that owned by a family of high social rank **2** a large prison (*slang*)

bight /bīt/ *n* **1** a wide curving indent in a shoreline, forming a bay **2** a loop or slack curve in a rope [Old English *byht* < Indo-European, 'to bend']

big league *n* the highest level of achievement in any field, or the people who occupy the top positions in it (*informal*)

big-league *adj* **1** among the most successful or influential in a particular field **2** of a wholehearted and unrestrained kind (*slang*) ○ *They're into big-league partying*

Big Man *n* in some cultures, a male leader whose leadership is based on influence, not official or formally recognized authority

bigmouth /bígg mowth/ (*plural* **-mouths**) *n* (*informal*) **1** somebody who cannot keep a secret **2** a noisy, vulgar, or boastful person

bigmouthed /bíg mowthd/ *adj* **1** unable to keep a secret (*informal*) **2** loud and boastful

big name *n* a well-known and successful person, organization, or product —**big-name** *adj*

bignonia /big nṓni ə/ *n* an evergreen woody climbing shrub. Flowers: trumpet-shaped, red, orange, or yellow. Native to: tropical America. Genus: *Bignonia.* [Late 18C. < modern Latin, after Abbé J. P. *Bignon* (1662–1743), French librarian.]

bigot /bíggət/ *n* somebody with strong opinions, especially on politics, religion, or ethnicity, who refuses to accept different views [Late 16C. < French.] —**bigoted** *adj* —**bigotedly** *adv* —**bigotedness** *n* —**bigotry** *n*

big science *n* any area of scientific research that needs major capital investment

big screen *n* the cinema and films made for the cinema, as opposed to television or video

big shot *n* a person with or claiming to possess much power or influence (*informal*)

Big Smoke *n* a nickname for a large city, especially a capital city (*informal*)

big stick *n* a threat of force or severe penalties

Big Sur /big súr/ coastal region of W California

big-ticket *adj Can, US* costing a lot of money (*informal*)

big time *n* the highest level of achievement and success in a profession or other activity (*slang*) ■ *adv* on a grand scale or to a significant degree (*slang*) ○ *He had messed up his life big time.* —**big timer** *n*

big toe *n* the largest and innermost digit of the foot

big top *n* **1** a large round tent, especially the main tent, used for circus performances **2** a circus

big wheel *n* = **Ferris wheel**

bigwig /bíg wig/ *n* an important person with considerable power or influence (*informal*) [Early 18C. Because important people once wore full-length wigs, whereas ordinary people wore short ones.]

Bihar /bi haár/, **Bihār** state in NE India. Capital: Patna. Population: 93,080,000 (1994). Area: 173,876 sq. km/ 67,134 sq. mi.

Bihari /bi haári/ (*plural* **-ri** *or* **-ris**) *n* **1** a member of a people who live mostly in the Indian state of Bihar, and also in Bangladesh and Pakistan **2** an Indic language of the state of Bihar in India, closely related to Hindi [Late 19C. < Hindi *bihārī*.] —**Bihari** *adj*

Bijapur /bi jaá poor/, **Bijāpur** city in SW India. Population: 186,939 (1991).

bijection /bī jéksh'n/ *n* a mathematical mapping between two spaces in which every element in each space corresponds to only one element of the other space for mapping in either direction [Mid-20C. < BI- + INJECTION.] —**bijective** *adj*

bijou /beé zhoo, beé zhóo/ *adj* small but fashionable and elegant (*humorous*) ○ *a bijou apartment* ■ *n* (*plural* **-jous** /-zhooz/ *or* **-joux** /-zhoo/) a small delicate jewel or ornamental object [Mid-17C. Via French, 'trinket' < Breton *bizoù* 'jewelled ring' < *biz* 'finger'.]

Bikaner /beékə neer/, **Bīkāner** city in NW India. Population: 416,289 (1991).

bike[1] /bīk/ *n* **1 BICYCLE OR MOTORCYCLE** a bicycle or a motorcycle (*informal*) **2 OFFENSIVE TERM** an offensive term for a woman who has many sexual relationships (*insult*) ■ *vi* (**bikes, biking, biked**) **GO BY BIKE** to ride somewhere on a bicycle or motorcycle (*informal*) [Late 19C. Shortening of BICYCLE.] ◇ **on your bike** used as a mildly rude way of telling somebody to go away or of dismissing somebody's suggestion (*informal*)

bike[2] /bīk/, **byke** *n Scotland* a nest of wasps or wild bees ■ *vi* (**bikes, biking, biked; bykes, byking, byked**) *Scotland* to swarm (*refers to bees and wasps*) [13C. < ?]

biker /bīkər/ *n* somebody who rides a motorcycle

bikeway /bīk way/ *n US* = **cycle path**

bikie /bīki/ *n ANZ* somebody who rides a motorcycle (*informal*)

Bikila /bi keélə/, **Abebe** (1932–73) Ethiopian athlete

bikini /bi keéni/ *n* **1** a woman's or girl's two-piece swimming costume consisting of a bra-style top and panties-style bottoms **2 bikini, bikinis** very scanty briefs for women [Mid-20C. After BIKINI ATOLL.] —**bikinied** *adj*

Bikini /bi keéni/ atoll consisting of 36 islets in the Marshall Islands, W Pacific Ocean, used as a nuclear testing site by the United States between 1946 and 1958. Area: 5 sq. km/2 sq. mi.

bikini line *n* the area where the top of a woman's thighs meets the lower edge of her bikini or underwear

Biko /beékō/, **Steve** (1946–77) South African political activist. Full name **Stephen Bantu Biko**

bilabial /bī láybi əl/ *adj* describes a consonant pronounced by closing or rounding both lips ■ *n* a consonant pronounced by bringing both lips into contact with each other or by rounding them —**bilabially** *adv*

bilateral /bī láttərəl/ *adj* **1** involving or carried out by two groups, especially the political representatives of two countries ○ *bilateral talks* **2** relating to or affecting both of two sides ○ *bilateral kidney failure* —**bilateralism** *n* —**bilaterally** *adv*

bilateral symmetry *n* symmetry in which an imaginary plane divides an object into right and left halves, each side being a mirror image of the other

bilayer /bī layər/ *n* a membrane that consists of two layers of molecules

Bilbao /bil baá ō/ port in N Spain. Population: 358,467 (1998 estimate).

bilberry /bílbəri/ (*plural* **-ries**) *n* **1** an edible blue-black berry **2** a wild shrub that produces bilberries. Native to: N Europe. Genus: *Vaccinium.* [Late 16C. < ?]

bilby /bílbi/ (*plural* **-bies**) *n* an Australasian marsupial resembling a rat with large ears, a pointed nose, and a long tail. Genus: *Macrotis.* [Late 19C. < Yuwaalaraay *bilbi.*]

bildungsroman /bíll dòongz rō maan/ *n* a novel about the early years of somebody's life, exploring the development of his or her character and personality [Early 20C. < German, 'education-novel'.]

bile /bīl/ *n* **1 DIGESTIVE FLUID** a yellowish-green fluid produced in the liver, stored in the gallbladder, and passed through ducts to the small intestine, where it plays an essential role in emulsifying fats **2 BITTERNESS** feelings of bitterness and irritability (*literary*) **3 BODILY HUMOUR** according to medieval medicine, one of the four basic fluids of the body (**humours**), an excess of which was thought to make somebody prone to anger [Mid-16C. Via French < Latin *bilis.*]

bilection /bīléksh'n/ *n* ARCHIT = **bolection**

bile duct *n* a tube that carries bile from the liver or gallbladder to the small intestine. The (**hepatic**) and (**cystic**) ducts merge to form the common bile duct.

bi-level *adj* 1 **TWO-LEVEL** with two levels for cargo or passengers 2 *Can, US* **HAVING TWO GROUND-FLOOR LEVELS** having two ground-floor levels divided by a vertical partition ■ *n Can, US* a bi-level house

bilge /bilj/ *n* 1 **LOWER HULL OF BOAT** the part of a boat below the water where the sides curve inwards to the keel 2 **LOWER HULL'S INSIDES** the area inside the bottom of a boat, beneath the lowest floorboards 3 **DIRTY WATER IN BOAT BOTTOM** dirty water that collects inside the bottom of a boat 4 **BARREL'S WIDEST PART** the widest part of a barrel or cask 5 **NONSENSE** ridiculous silly talk or ideas (*informal*) ○ *a load of bilge* ■ *vti* (**bilges, bilging, bilged**) **SPRING A LEAK** to be, or cause a boat to be, damaged in the lower part of the hull and start leaking [15C. Probably alteration of BULGE.]

bilge keel *n* either of two fin-shaped underwater projections on either side of a boat's hull, designed to control rolling

bilge water *n* NAUT = **bilge** *n.* 3

bilharzia /bil haár zi ə/ *n* 1 ZOOL = **schistosome** 2 MED = **schistosomiasis** [Mid-19C. < modern Latin, after Theodor *Bilharz* (1825–62), German physician.]

bilharziasis /bíl haar zí əssiss/ *n* = **schistosomiasis**

biliary /bíllyəri/ *adj* 1 relating to bile or the transporting of bile 2 affecting a bile duct or the system of ducts in the liver ○ *biliary cirrhosis* [Mid-18C. < Latin *bilis* 'bile'.]

bilinear /bī línni ər/ *adj* relating to or representing a mathematical expression with two variables, such as x + y, neither of which is squared, cubed, or raised to another power or exponent

bilingual /bī líng gwəl/ *adj* 1 **SPEAKING TWO LANGUAGES** able to speak two languages easily and naturally 2 **IN TWO LANGUAGES** written, expressed, or conducted in two languages ○ *a bilingual dictionary* ■ *n* **BILINGUAL SPEAKER** somebody who speaks two languages easily and naturally [Mid-19C. < Latin *bilinguis* < *bi-* 'two' + *lingua* 'tongue, speech'.] —**bilingually** *adv*

bilingualism /bī líng gwə lizəm/ *n* 1 the ability to speak two languages easily and naturally 2 the regular use of two languages in everyday communication

bilious /bílli əss/ *adj* 1 **FEELING NAUSEATED** feeling as if about to vomit 2 **NAUSEATINGLY UNPLEASANT** extremely unpleasant to look at ○ *The walls were painted bilious green.* 3 **SHOWING BAD MOOD** bad-tempered and irritable ○ *a bilious stare* [Mid-16C. < Latin *biliosus* < *bilis* 'bile'.] —**biliously** *adv* —**biliousness** *n*

bilirubin /bílli roóbin, bíli-/ *n* a reddish-yellow bile pigment [Late 19C. < German, < Latin *bilis* 'bile' + *ruber* 'red'.]

biliverdin /bílli vúrdin/ *n* a greenish bile pigment [Mid-19C. < German, < Latin *bilis* 'bile' + French *vert* 'green'.]

bilk /bilk/ *vt* 1 **CHEAT** to cheat somebody, especially by swindling him or her out of money (*informal*) 2 **AVOID PAYING** to avoid paying a debt or the person to whom money is owed (*informal*) 3 **AVOID OR EVADE** to escape from or elude somebody [Mid-17C. < ?] —**bilker** *n*

bill[1] /bil/ *n* 1 **STATEMENT OF MONEY OWED** a written statement of how much money has to be paid for items that have been bought or for services provided ○ *I'll send you the bill.* 2 **AMOUNT OWED** the amount of money owed for items or services provided, as shown on a statement ○ *The bill for the meal came to £550!* 3 **AMOUNT PAID** the amount that a person, company, or organization has to pay in taxes, salaries, or other charges 4 **LAW PROPOSAL** a written proposal for a new law, discussed and voted upon by the members of a legislative assembly 5 **ADVERTISING NOTICE** a notice, poster, or leaflet advertising something 6 **LIST OF ITEMS** a list, especially of entertainment features or acts in a show, or the programme of entertainment itself ○ *We've got a brilliant new comedian on the bill tonight.* 7 *US, Can* BANKING, FIN = **note** *n.* 7 ■ *vt* 1 **SEND REQUEST FOR PAYMENT** to send somebody a statement of how much money is owed for items bought or services provided ○ *Bill me for the cost of dry-cleaning.* 2 **ADVERTISE** to advertise an event or performance, especially using posters ○ *It's billed as the biggest ice show in Britain.* 3 **DESCRIBE** to describe an emerging or forthcoming thing in a particular way ○ *billed as the technological advance of the decade* [14C. Via Anglo-Norman *bille* < medieval Latin *bulla* 'seal on a document'.] —**biller** *n* ◇ **fill** *or* **fit the bill** to be suitable for a particular purpose

bill[2] /bil/ *n* 1 **BIRD'S BEAK** the beak of a bird, consisting of two pointed jaws protected by a horny covering 2 **MOUTHPART OF ANIMAL** the mouthparts of a platypus 3 **NARROW STRIP OF LAND** a narrow strip of land that juts out into the sea (*often in placenames*) 4 **POINT OF AN ANCHOR** the point at the very end of one of the arms of an anchor [Old English *bile* < ?] ◇ **bill and coo** to kiss and whisper intimately, as young lovers do, in a way thought to be reminiscent of the affectionate behaviour of doves

bill[3], **Bill** *n* the police (*informal; + plural verb*) ○ *Are the bill still after him for that jewellery job?* [Mid-20C. Probably shortening of Old Bill.]

billabong /bíllə bong/ *n Aus* a pool or water hole formed by a side-channel of a river during the wet season [Mid-19C. < Wiradhuri, < *bila* 'river' + *bang* 'watercourse that only runs after rain'.]

billboard[1] /bíll bawrd/ *n* a very large board erected by the roadside or attached to a building, used for displaying advertisements

billboard[2] *n* a ledge on the front of a boat or ship to which the anchor is secured

billet[1] /bíllət/ *n* 1 **ACCOMMODATION FOR SERVICE PEOPLE** a private home or a guest house providing temporary accommodation for people in the armed forces 2 **ORDER TO PROVIDE ACCOMMODATION** an official order stating that a householder has to provide temporary accommodation for a member of the armed forces 3 **EMPLOYMENT POSITION** a position of employment together with its tasks (*informal*) ■ *v* 1 *vti* **ASSIGN SOLDIER TO TEMPORARY ACCOMMODATION** to arrange for a member of the armed forces to have temporary accommodation in a particular house, or to have such temporary accommodation somewhere 2 *vt* **PROVIDE TEMPORARY ACCOMMODATION FOR SOLDIER** to provide temporary accommodation in your home for a member of the armed forces [15C. < Anglo-Norman *billette* 'written orders' < variant of Old French *bulle* (see BULL[2]).]

billet[2] /bíllət/ *n* 1 **CHUNK OF WOOD** a short thick piece of wood, especially firewood 2 **METAL BAR IN SEMI-FINISHED STATE** a metal bar or block with a simple shape that requires further working 3 **DECORATIVE MOULDING** any one of a series of short, evenly spaced blocks or cylinders forming part of a decorative moulding [15C. < Old French *billette* 'small log' < *bille* 'log'.]

billet-doux /bílli doó/ (*plural* **billets-doux** /bílli doóz/) *n* a letter expressing affectionate and romantic thoughts [Late 17C. < French, 'sweet note'.]

billfish /bíll fish/ (*plural* **-fish** *or* **-fishes**) *n* a large fish with jaws resembling spears that lives near the surface of tropical and semitropical waters and is hunted for sport. Marlin, sailfish, and swordfish are billfish. Family: Xiphiidae. [< BILL[2]]

billfold /bíll fōld/ *n Can, US* a pocket-sized folding container for paper money, credit cards, stamps, and photographs, sometimes with a compartment for loose change [< BILL[1]]

billhook /bíll hoŏk/ *n* a woodcutting tool with a wooden handle and a large broad curved blade. Use: especially to lop branches off trees. [< obsolete *bill* 'bladed or pointed weapon']

billiard /bíllyərd/ *adj* relating to or used in the cue game billiards ○ *a billiard table*

billiards /bíllyərdz/ *n* an indoor game in which a felt-tipped stick (**cue**) is used to hit three balls across a cloth-covered table into pockets (*+ singular verb*) [Late 16C. < French *billard* < *bille* 'log'.]

billing /bílling/ *n* 1 **POSITION IN TERMS OF ADVERTISING** the particular importance or prominence given to a performer or event in advertisements ○ *an exciting young band currently getting top billing* 2 **SENDING OUT CUSTOMERS' BILLS** the preparing and sending out of bills to customers 3 *US* **ADVERTISING** the advertising or promoting of a performance, event, or product [< BILL[1]]

Billingsgate /bíllingz gayt/ wholesale fish market in London

billion /bíllyən/ (*plural* **-lions** *or* **-lion**) *n* 1 **ONE THOUSAND MILLION** one thousand million, written as 1 followed by nine zeros. See table at **number** 2 **ONE MILLION MILLION** one million million, written as 1 followed by 12 zeros (*dated*) See table at **number** 3 **LARGE NUMBER** an extremely large but unspecified number of people or things (*informal; often plural*) [Late 17C. < French, 'million million' < *bis* 'twice' + *million* (see MILLION).] —**billionth** *n, adj*

USAGE A thousand million or a million million? In current use, a ***billion*** means a thousand million. In earlier use it often meant a million million, but a number as large as this is needed far less often. In its colloquial (singular or plural) use, ***billions*** (like *hundreds, thousands*, etc.) has no precise numerical meaning: *I've called his office billions of times.* The word now used to mean a million million is *trillion*.

billionaire /bíllyə náir/ *n* a very rich person, literally somebody who has money and property worth more than a billion pounds [Late 19C. After MILLIONAIRE.]

bill of entry *n* a list of goods to be imported or exported, presented to officials at a customs house

bill of exchange *n* a document setting out an instruction to pay a named person a fixed sum of money on a specified date or when the person requests payment

bill of fare *n* 1 a menu of food available in a restaurant or served at a special function 2 a list of items of any kind, especially events in a programme of entertainment (*informal*)

bill of health *n* a certificate stating that the crew of a ship are healthy and are not affected by infectious diseases ◇ **a clean bill of health** a good report on somebody's health, or a good report about the state of something, e.g. an organization's efficiency or profitability

bill of indictment *n* a document setting out the criminal charges against somebody, formerly presented to a grand jury

bill of lading *n* a list of goods being transported, especially by ship, together with the conditions that apply to their transportation

bill of rights *n* a list of basic human rights as guaranteed by the laws of a country

Bill of Rights *n* 1 an English act of law, passed in 1689, guaranteeing people, especially landowners and parliamentarians, freedom and basic rights 2 the first ten amendments to the US Constitution, which protect people's basic human rights

bill of sale *n* a document stating that something has been sold or transferred to the ownership of another party

billon /bíllən/ *n* 1 an alloy consisting of a small amount of silver or gold mixed with a base metal such as copper, used especially for making coins 2 an alloy of silver with copper in high proportion, used especially for making medals [Early 18C. < French, 'ingot, bronze money' < *bille* 'log'.]

billow /bíllō/ *v* 1 *vt* **SWELL WITH AIR** to fill with air, or cause something made of fabric to fill with air, and swell outwards ○ *the wind billowing their dresses* 2 *vi* **FLOW IN CURLING MASS** to flow upwards or along in a curling mass ■ *n* **FLOWING CURLING MASS** a curling or rolling mass of something, e.g. waves or clouds of smoke [Mid-16C. < Old Norse *bylgja* 'wave' < Indo-European, 'to swell'.] —**billowy** *adj*

billposter /bíll pōstər/, **billsticker** /bíl stikər/ *n* somebody who puts up advertising notices in public places ○ *Billposters will be prosecuted.* [< BILL[1]] —**billposting** *n*

billy goat *n* a male goat [< *Billy* pet form of *William*]

Billy the Kid /bílli-/ (1859–81) US outlaw. Born **Henry McCarty**. Known as **William H. Bonney**

bilobate /bī lō bayt/, **bilobed** /bī lōbd/ *adj* having or in the form of two lobes ○ *a bilobate leaf*

biltong /bíll tong/ *n S Africa* strips of lean meat dried in the sun [Early 19C. < Afrikaans, < Dutch *bil* 'buttock, rump' + *tong* 'tongue'.]

BIM *abbr* British Institute of Management

bima, bimah *n* JUDAISM = **bema** *n.* 1

bimanual /bī mánn yoo əl/ *adj* done with or needing the use of two hands —**bimanually** *adv*

Bimberi Peak /bímbəri-/ mountain in the Australian Capital Territory. Height: 1,912 m./6,273 ft.

bimbo /bímbō/ (*plural* **-bos** *or* **-boes**) *n* (*slang*) 1 an offensive term that deliberately insults a woman's intelligence while implying that she is good-looking 2 *US* an offensive term for a man or woman who is regarded as being unintelligent or superficial [Early 20C. Probably < Italian, 'baby, small child'.]

bimetallic /bī me tállik/ *adj* containing or consisting of two metals

bimetallic strip *n* a strip composed of two metals with different coefficients of expansion fixed together that bend at different rates when heated

bimillenary /bī mi lénnəri/ *adj* relating to or celebrating a 2,000th anniversary ■ *n* (*plural* **-ies**) the 2,000th anniversary of something

bimodal /bī mṓd'l/ *adj* relating to or consisting of a set of observations with two peaks, representing two values that occur with equal frequency and more often than any other value ○ *bimodal distribution* —**bimodality** /bīmō dálləti/ *n*

bimolecular /bī mə lékyōōlər/ *adj* relating to, consisting of, or formed from two molecules

bimonthly /bī múnthli/ *adj* **OCCURRING EVERY TWO MONTHS** produced or held every two months ■ *adj, adv* **OCCURRING TWICE A MONTH** produced or held twice a month ■ *n* (*plural* **-lies**) **PUBLICATION ISSUED BIMONTHLY** a publication, e.g. a magazine or journal, that appears every two months or twice a month

USAGE See ***biweekly***.

bimorphemic /bī mawr feémik/ *adj* consisting of two of the smallest units of meaning in language (**morphemes**). The word 'fallen' is bimorphemic, comprising the free morpheme 'fall' and the bound past participle morpheme '-en'.

bin /bin/ *n* **1 RUBBISH CONTAINER** a container for rubbish or waste paper (*often in combination*) **2 LARGE STORAGE CONTAINER** a large storage container, e.g. an industrial container for grain or coal or an open container holding goods in a shop **3 STORAGE SHELVES FOR WINE** a set of shelves with compartments for storing bottles of wine in a cellar ■ *vt* (**bins, binning, binned**) **1 DISPOSE OF** to throw something away ○ *I bin all the junk mail without even looking at it.* **2 STORE IN BIN** to put something in a storage bin [Old English *binn* < Celtic]

binary /bīnəri/ *adj* **1 IN TWO PARTS** consisting of two parts or two separate elements **2 RELATING TO NUMBER SYSTEM BASED ON TWO** describes a number system, or a number belonging to it, that has 2 rather than 10 as its base **3 HAVING ONLY TWO CHEMICAL ELEMENTS** consisting of two different chemical elements only **4 HAVING TWO CHEMICALS MIXING TOXICALLY** consisting of or using two harmless components that combine to form an extremely toxic product **5** MUSIC = **duple** ■ *n* (*plural* **-ries**) **1 BINARY NUMBER SYSTEM** the binary number system ○ *written in binary* **2 BINARY DIGIT** a binary number or digit **3** ASTRON = **binary star** **4** ARMS = **binary weapon** [15C. < late Latin *binarius* < Latin *bini* 'two by two'.]

binary code *n* a computer code that uses the binary number system. Numbers and letters are translated into signals that a computer reads as sequences of ones and zeros called binary digits (**bits**).

binary coded decimal *n* a numbering system in which each digit of a decimal is converted into a binary number

binary digit *n* either of the digits 0 and 1, used in the binary system

binary file *n* a computer file that contains data in a raw or nontext state made up of characters that only a computer can read. ◊ **ASCII file**

binary fission *n* the reproduction of a cell or a one-celled organism by division into two nearly equal parts

binary form *n* a musical form that has two complementary parts, both usually repeated

binary notation *n* = **binary system**

binary star *n* a pair of stars that revolve around their common centre of mass under mutual gravitational attraction

binary system *n* a number system with 2 as its base, numbers being expressed as sequences of the digits 0 and 1

binary weapon *n* a chemical weapon, e.g. a bomb or artillery shell, containing two chemicals that are harmless in isolation but combine to form a toxic compound before reaching the target

binational /bī násh'nəl/ *adj* relating to two nations

binaural /bī náwrəl, bi-/ *adj* **1** relating to both ears **2** recorded onto two separate channels using two microphones, so as to sound realistic when heard through headphones [Mid-19C. < Latin *bini* 'two together'.]

bind /bīnd/ *v* (**binds, binding, bound** /bownd/, **bound**) **1** *vt* **TIE FIRMLY** to tie something firmly to something else by winding a cord tightly round and round both things **2** *vt* **WRAP RIBBON OR BANDAGE ROUND** to wind a cord, tape, or bandage firmly round something to protect it or hold it together ○ *You have to bind the wound firmly.* **3** *vt* **TIE SOMEBODY'S HANDS OR FEET TOGETHER** to tie somebody's hands or feet together to make it difficult to escape (*often passive*) ○ *bound hand and foot* **4** *vt* **PROTECT EDGE OF FABRIC** to protect or decorate the edge of a piece of material by stitching over it or fixing a strip of fabric to it **5** *vti* **CAUSE FEELINGS OF LOYALTY OR CLOSENESS** to form a link or relationship based on loyalty, affection, or a shared experience ○ *the instinct that binds mother and child* **6** *vt* **FORCE TO DO** to oblige or compel somebody to do something, e.g. by invoking a law or a promise that has been made (*often passive*) ○ *bound by her oath of office* **7** *vt* **PUT BOOK TOGETHER** to fix pages together and put them in a cover to form a book, leaflet, or other publication **8** *vti* **STICK TOGETHER** to stick together, or cause elements or ingredients to stick together, so as to form a solid mass ○ *The water, sand, and cement bind to form workable mortar.* **9** *vti* **FORM CHEMICAL BOND** to form a chemical bond with a substance **10** *vt* **MAKE FAECES FIRMER** to make the faeces firmer and more solid, especially to curb diarrhoea ○ *White rice is said to bind you.* **11** *vi* **BECOME STIFF OR STUCK** to become stiff, stuck, or unable to move freely (*refers to mechanical parts*) ○ *The brakes are binding.* **12** *vt* **EMPLOY AS APPRENTICE** in former times, to employ somebody as an apprentice under the terms of an agreement that obliged the apprentice to work for a fixed period, often several years ■ *n* **1 NUISANCE** something that is annoying or causes inconvenience ○ *I have to go to the hospital every two weeks: it's a real bind.* **2 FENCING MOVEMENT** a fencing movement that pushes an opponent's blade out of line **3 DOMINANT POSITION IN CHESS** in chess, a position of dominance in the centre of the board that restricts an opponent's moves **4** MUSIC = **tie** *n.* 8 [Old English *bindan* < Indo-European] ◇ **in a bind** in a difficult or unpleasant situation, especially a situation in which every option leads to difficulties ◇ **bound up with somebody** *or* **something** closely involved with or connected to somebody or something

bind off *vti US* HANDICRAFT = **cast off** *v.* 3

bind over *vt* to place a legal order on somebody, stating that he or she must or must not behave in a particular way for a specified period of time (*often passive*) ○ *He was fined £200 and bound over to keep the peace for twelve months.*

binder /bīndər/ *n* **1 HARD COVER FOR PAPERS** a stiff cover with clips inside for holding loose sheets of paper or magazines **2 MACHINE FOR BINDING BOOKS OR PAPERS** a machine for fixing sheets of paper together to form a book or booklet **3 BOOKBINDER** somebody whose job is to make books by assembling the pages and putting on the cover **4 CORD OR TIE** a length of cord, string, or tape that is used to tie things together **5 SOMETHING THAT STICKS THINGS** a substance added to form dry ingredients into a solid mass or to maintain an even consistency throughout a liquid or semi-liquid substance **6 MACHINE FOR MAKING SHEAVES** an attachment on a reaping machine for bundling cut grain into sheaves, or a reaping machine with this attachment

bindery /bīndəri/ (*plural* **-ies**) *n* a place where the pages and covers of books are put together

bindi-eye /bíndi-/ (*plural* **bindi-eyes** *or* **bindi-eye**) *n* a small Australian plant of the daisy family with fruits that are covered in small hooks or prickles. Genus: *Calotis*. [Early 20C. Alteration of Kamilaroi, Yuwaalaraay *bindayaa*.]

binding /bīnding/ *n* **1 CORD USED FOR TYING** something that is used to tie or protect things, especially a cord or tape that is wound round and round something **2 BOOK COVERING** the cover of a book, or the material used to cover books **3 SOMETHING HOLDING BOOK'S PAGES TOGETHER** the glue, strip of plastic, or other material that holds the pages of a book or booklet together **4 FABRIC EDGING** a strip of fabric or tape attached to the edge of a piece of material to prevent it from fraying **5 SKI FASTENING** one of the fastenings on a ski or snowboard that hold the ski to the boot ■ *adj* **OBLIGING SOMEBODY TO DO** creating a legal or moral obligation to do something, with no possibility of withdrawal or avoidance

binding energy *n* **1** the energy required to remove a particle from a system, e.g. an electron from an atom **2** the energy required to separate a system into its individual particles or components

bindweed /bīnd weed/ *n* a plant with long twining stems, especially a wild plant with large white funnel-shaped flowers, generally regarded as a weed. Genera: *Convolvulus* and *Calystegia*.

bin end *n* one of the last bottles remaining from a single quantity of wine, often sold at a reduced price

bing /bing/ *n Scotland* a heap or pile of something, especially a slag heap [Early 16C. < Old Norse *bingr* 'heap, bolster'.]

binge /binj/ *n* **1 HEAVY DRINKING OR EATING SESSION** a short period when somebody drinks or eats far too much, especially a period of uncontrolled drinking or eating caused by a disorder such as alcoholism or bulimia **2 SPREE** a short period of time when something is done in an unrestrained way ○ *a shopping binge* ■ *vi* (**binges, bingeing** *or* **binging, binged**) **1 EAT TOO MUCH** to eat far too much food very quickly, sometimes as a symptom of an eating disorder such as bulimia **2 BE SELF-INDULGENT WITH** to do or consume something in an unrestrained self-indulgent way ○ *stay in all day and binge on old movies* [Early 19C. < ?] —**binger** *n*

bingo /bíng gō/ *n* **LOTTERY GAME WITH NUMBERED CARDS** a game played communally with numbered cards in which numbers are selected at random and the first person to cover all or specified numbered slots on his or her card wins ■ *interj* **1 CALL IN BINGO** a shout of success, called by a player who has won a game of bingo **2 EXCLAMATION OF SUCCESS** used to express satisfaction at sudden success or achievement [Early 20C. < ?]

Bini /bi neé/ (*plural* **-ni** *or* **-nis**) *n* LANG, PEOPLES = **Edo** [Mid-20C. < ?]

binman /bín man/ (*plural* **-men** /-men/) *n* a dustman (*informal*)

binnacle /bínnək'l/ *n* a support or mounting for a ship's compass [15C. Alteration of Spanish *bitácula* < Latin *habitaculum* 'housing' < *habitare* 'inhabit'.]

binocular /bī nókyōōlər, bi-/ *adj* involving or using both eyes [Mid-18C. < Latin *bini* 'two together' + *oculus* 'eye'.] —**binocularity** /bī nókyōō lárrəti, bi-/ *n*

binoculars /bī nók yōōlərz, bi-/ *npl* a device for looking at distant objects that magnifies what is seen using a lens for each eye

binomial /bī nṓmi əl/ *n* **1 EXPRESSION WITH TWO TERMS** a mathematical expression made up of two terms and a plus or minus sign **2 ORGANISM'S TWO-PART NAME** a pair of Latin or Latinized words forming a scientific name in the classification of plants, animals, and micro-organisms. The first word represents the genus and the second the species. ■ *adj* **HAVING TWO NAMES OR TERMS** relating to or consisting of two names, especially the two elements of a scientific name, or two terms, e.g. the terms of a mathematical expression [Mid-16C. < modern Latin *binomius* < Latin *bi-* 'two' + Greek *nomos* 'part'.] —**binomially** *adv*

binomial coefficient *n* a number that multiplies the variables in a two-part mathematical expression, e.g. the numbers 3 and 4 in the expression 3x-4y

binomial distribution *n* a formula that indicates the probability of achieving a given number of successful outcomes in a predetermined number of statistical trials when the probability of success is the same for each trial

binomial nomenclature *n* the system of assigning two-part Latin or Latinized scientific names to plants, animals, and microorganisms, with the first word denoting the genus and the second the species

binomial theorem *n* a mathematical formula used to calculate the value of a two-part mathematical expression that is squared, cubed, or raised to another power or exponent, e.g. $(x+y)^n$, without explicitly multiplying the parts themselves

bint /bint/ *n* an offensive term for a girl or woman (*slang*) [Mid-19C. < Arabic, 'girl, daughter'.]

binturong /bíntyōō rong, bin tyóor ong/ *n* a Southeast Asian mammal resembling a cat, with a thick black coat, a long tail, and tufts on its ears. *Arctictus binturong*. [Early 19C. < Malay.]

binucleate /bī nyóokli ət/, **binucleated** /-kli aytid/, **binuclear** /-kli ər/ *adj* having two distinct cell nuclei

Binyon /bínnyən/, **Laurence** (1869–1943) British poet. Born **Robert Laurence Binyon**

bio /bī ō/ (*plural* **-os**) *n Can, US* a biographical work (*informal*) ○ *mostly fiction and celebrity bios* [Mid-20th C. Shortening of BIOGRAPHY.]

bio- *prefix* life, biology ○ *bioengineering* [< Greek *bios* 'life, way of living' < Indo-European, 'to live']

bioaccumulation /bī ō ə kyoōmyoō láysh'n/ *n* the accumulation of a harmful substance such as a radioactive element, a heavy metal, or an organochlorine in a biological organism, especially one that forms part of the food chain —**bioaccumulative** /bī ō ə kyoōmyoōlətiv/ *adj*

bioactive /bī ō áktiv/ *adj* producing an effect in living tissue

bioactivity /bī ō ak tívvəti/ *n* the effect that a substance or agent has on living tissue or an organism

bioassay /bī ō ə sáy, -ássay/ *n* a technique for determining the concentration or potency of a substance such as a drug by measuring its effect on a living organism —**bioassay** *vt*

bioastronomy /bī ō ə strónnəmi/ *n* the study of the possibility of life in the universe other than on Earth

bioavailability /bī ō ə váylə bílləti/ *n* the degree to which a drug affects its target

bio-break *n US* a short break, e.g. during a meeting, when people go to the toilet and generally refresh themselves

biocenosis *n* ECOL = **biocoenosis**

biochemical /bī ō kémmik'l/ *adj* relating to the chemical substances present in living organisms —**biochemically** *adv*

biochemical oxygen demand *n* a measure of the pollution present in water, obtained by measuring the amount of oxygen absorbed from the water by the microorganisms present in it

biochemistry /bī ō kémmistri/ *n* **1** the scientific study of the chemical substances, processes, and reactions that occur in living organisms **2** the chemistry or composition of a particular organism or system —**biochemist** *n*

biocide /bī ō sīd/ *n* BIOCHEM = **pesticide** —**biocidal** /bī ō sīd'l/ *adj*

bioclastic rock /bī ō klastik-/ *n* rock formed from organic remains

bioclimatic /bī ō klī máttik/ *adj* relating to the relationship between climate and living organisms

biocoenosis /bī ō sə nóssiss/ (*plural* **-ses** /-seez/), **biocenosis** (*plural* **-cenoses**) *n* a diverse group of species or organisms with its own distinct habitat, interacting to form an ecological community [Late 19C. < modern Latin, < Greek *bios* 'life' + *koinōsis* 'sharing' < *koinos* 'common'.]

biocompatibility /bī ō kəm pátta bílləti/ *n* the compatibility of a donated organ or artificial limb with the living tissue into which it is implanted or with which it is brought into contact —**biocompatible** /bī ō kəm páttəb'l/ *adj*

⚡**biocomputer** /bī ō kəm pyoōtər/ *n* a very fast computer whose calculations are performed using biological processes instead of semiconductor technology

biocontrol /bī ō kən trṓl/ *n* = **biological control**

bioconversion /bī ō kən vúrsh'n/ *n* the conversion of one organic substance into another or into energy by biological processes or organisms

biodata /bī ō daytə, -daatə/ *n S Asia* somebody's curriculum vitae (+ *singular or plural noun*)

biodegradable /bī ō di gráydəb'l/ *adj* made of substances that will decay relatively quickly as a result of the action of bacteria and break down into elements such as carbon that are recycled naturally —**biodegradability** /bī ō di gráydə bílləti/ *n*

biodegrade /bī ō di gráyd/ (**-grades, -grading, -graded**) *vi* to decay naturally as the result of the action of bacteria —**biodegradation** /bī ō déggrə dáysh'n/ *n*

biodiesel /bī ō deez'l/ *n* a substitute for diesel fuel made wholly or partly from organic products, especially processed vegetable oils such as soya bean oil and groundnut oil

biodiversity /bī ō dī vúrssəti/ *n* the range of organisms present in a given ecological community or system

biodynamics /bī ō dī námmiks/ *n* the study of how energy, motion, and other forces affect living things (+ *singular verb*) —**biodynamic** *adj*

bioelectricity /bī ō ilek tríssəti/ *n* electric current generated by living tissue —**bioelectric** *adj*

bioenergetics /bī ō énnər jéttiks/ *n* (+ *singular verb*) **1** the study of the conversion of energy in organisms and biological systems, e.g. in photosynthesis **2** a therapy, devised by Wilhelm Reich in the 1940s, that uses an analysis of somebody's physical posture and movements to enhance emotional wellbeing —**bioenergetic** *adj*

bioengineering /bī ō énji neéring/ *n* the use of engineering principles and techniques to solve medical problems, e.g. in the design of artificial limbs or in organ replacement —**bioengineer** *n*

bioethics /bī ō éthiks/ *n* the study of the moral and ethical choices faced in medical research and in the treatment of patients, especially when the application of advanced technology is involved (+ *singular verb*) —**bioethical** *adj* —**bioethicist** *n*

biofeedback /bī ō feéd bak/ *n* the use of monitoring devices that display information about the operation of a bodily function, e.g. heart rate or blood pressure, that is not normally consciously controlled

bioflavonoid /bī ō fláyvə noyd/ *n* a biologically active compound found in citrus and other fruits

biofuel /bī ō fyoo əl/ *n* a renewable fuel, e.g. biodiesel, biogas, and methane, that is derived from biological matter

biog. *abbr* **1** biographer **2** biographical **3** biography

biogas /bī ō gass/ *n* a mixture of carbon dioxide and methane. Source: fermentation of organic waste. Use: fuel.

biogenesis /bī ō jénnəssiss/ *n* **1** the generation of living things from other pre-existing life forms **2** the theory that living things can arise only from other living things and cannot be spontaneously created **3** BIOL = **recapitulation** *n.* 2 —**biogenetic** /bī ō jə néttik/ *adj*

biogenic /bī ō jénnik/ *adj* resulting from biological activity or from living things ○ *a biogenic amine*

biogeochemistry /bī ō jee ō kémmistri/ *n* the study of the distribution of elements between organisms and their surroundings —**biogeochemical** *adj*

biogeography /bī ō ji óggrəfi/ *n* the study of the geographical distribution of plants and animals —**biogeographer** *n* —**biogeographic** /bī ō jee ə gráffik/ *adj* —**biogeographical** *adj*

biography /bī óggrəfi/ (*plural* **-phies**) *n* **1** an account of somebody's life, e.g. in the form of a book, film, or television programme, written or produced by another person **2** books about people's lives, considered as a whole or as a type of literature [Late 17C. Via French and Latin < medieval Greek *biographia* 'writing about lives' < Greek *bios* 'life' + *graphein* 'write'.] —**biographer** *n* —**biographical** /bī ə gráffik'l/ *adj* —**biographically** *adv*

biohazard /bī ō hazərd/ *n* a risk to human beings or their environment, especially one presented by a toxic or infectious agent —**biohazardous** /bī ō házzərdəss/ *adj*

bioinformatics /bī ō infər máttiks/ *n* the use of computers to extract and analyse biological data, especially in studying the nucleotide sequences of DNA and other nucleic acids (+ *singular verb*)

bioinstrumentation /bī ō instroōmən táysh'n/ *n* instruments used to record and display information about the body's functions

Bioko /bi ṓkō/ island in the Gulf of Guinea, part of Equatorial Guinea. Population: 57,190 (1983). Area: 2,020 sq. km/779 sq. mi.

biol. *abbr* **1** biological **2** biology

biological /bī ə lójik'l/ *adj* **1 CONCERNING LIVING THINGS** relating to living organisms ○ *biological diversity* **2 RELATING TO BIOLOGY** relating to the science of biology **3 CONTAINING ENZYMES** containing enzymes that are intended to digest stains caused by natural substances ○ *biological detergent* **4 GENETICALLY RELATED** related by birth rather than by adoption ○ *my biological mother* ■ *n* **MEDICATION OR VACCINE FROM LIVING ORGANISMS** a drug or other compound produced by living organisms —**biologically** *adv*

biological clock *n* the set of mechanisms within living organisms that link physiological processes with daily, monthly, or seasonal cycles or with stages of development and ageing

biological control *n* a method of reducing or eliminating plant pests by introducing predators or microorganisms that attack the targeted pests but spare other species in the area

biological oxygen demand *n* ENVIRON = **biochemical oxygen demand**

biological shield *n* a massive structure, usually made of concrete and steel, built around the core of a nuclear reactor to protect operating staff from radiation

biological warfare *n* the use of microorganisms to cause disease or death to humans, animals, and plants

biological weapon *n* a missile, bomb, or other device that delivers harmful biological agents

biology /bī óllәji/ *n* **1 SCIENCE OF LIFE** the science that deals with all forms of life, including their classification, physiology, chemistry, and interactions **2 LIFE IN ONE PLACE** the forms of life in a particular environment and their behaviour, development, and history ○ *the biology of desert regions* **3 PLANT'S OR ANIMAL'S MAKEUP** the physical makeup and functioning of a particular plant or animal ○ *the biology of the fruit fly* [Early 19C. Via French *biologie* < German, < Greek *bios* 'life'.] —**biologist** *n*

bioluminescence /bī ō loomi néss'nss/ *n* the generation and emission of light by living organisms such as fireflies, some bacteria and fungi, and many marine animals —**bioluminescent** *adj*

biomagnetics /bī ō mag néttiks/ *n* the use of magnets and magnetic fields in the treatment of medical conditions, or the study of this subject (+ *singular verb*)

biomagnification /bī ō mágnifi káysh'n/ *n* BIOL = **bioaccumulation**

biomass /bī ō mass/ *n* **1 MASS OF ORGANISMS IN ECOSYSTEM** the mass of living organisms within a given environment, measured in terms of weight per unit of area **2 PLANT AND ANIMAL WASTE AS FUEL** plant and animal material, e.g. agricultural waste products, used as a source of fuel **3 ORGANISM'S DRY WEIGHT** the mass of material in a living organism, or in a community of organisms, usually measured in terms of dry weight

biomaterial /bī ō mə teeri əl/ *n* material that can safely be implanted into the human body and left there without causing an adverse reaction

biomathematics /bī ō mathə máttiks/ *n* the application of mathematical methods and formulas to medical or biological phenomena (+ *singular verb*) —**biomathematical** *adj* —**biomathematician** /bī ō mathəmə tísh'n/ *n*

biome /bī ōm/ *n* a division of the world's vegetation that corresponds to a particular climate and is characterized by certain types of plants and animals, e.g. tropical rain forest or desert

biomechanics /bī ō mi kánniks/ *n* the study of body movements and of the forces acting on the musculoskeletal system (+ *singular verb*) ■ *npl* the mechanical forces at work in a particular body or organ (+ *plural verb*) —**biomechanical** *adj* —**biomechanically** *adv*

biomedical engineering *n* = **bioengineering**

biomedicine /bī ō médss'n/ *n* **1** the employing of the principles of biology, biochemistry, physiology, and other basic sciences to solve problems in clinical medicine **2** the study of the body's ability to withstand the stresses of unusual environments, e.g. outer space —**biomedical** *adj*

biometry /bī ómmətri/ *n* the application of statistical techniques to biological studies —**biometrist** *n*

biomimetic /bī ō mi méttik/ *n* a complex biochemical molecule such as a peptide protein that is synthesized to resemble a substance occurring naturally in the body

biomolecule /bī ō mólli kyool/ *n* **1** one of the molecules from which living organisms are made **2** a molecule of a compound produced by or important to a biological organism —**biomolecular** /bī ō mə lékyoōlər/ *adj*

bionic /bī ónnik/ *adj* **1 HAVING ELECTRONICALLY POWERED ORGANS** having many or most ordinary human organs or functions replaced or enhanced by electronically powered parts that give superhuman capabilities, in the realm of science fiction **2 HAVING SUPERHUMAN QUALITIES** having superhuman strength, speed, or intensity (*informal*) ○ *a bionic appetite* **3 INVOLVING BIONICS** involving or relating to bionics [Early 20C. < BIO- + ELECTRONIC.]

bionics /bī ónniks/ *n* (+ *singular verb*) **1** the study of biological function and mechanics, and the application of them to machine design **2** the use of electronic devices to replace damaged limbs and organs

bionomics /bī ō nómmiks/ *n* a theory suggesting that economics can usefully be thought of as similar to an evolving ecosystem (+ *singular verb*) [Late 19C. < BIO-, after ECONOMICS.]

-biont *suffix* an organism that lives under particular conditions ○ *halobiont* [< SYMBIONT]

bioorganic /bī ō awr gánnik/ *adj* describes a carbon-based (**organic**) compound produced by a living organism or of biological importance

biopharmaceutical /bī ō faarmə syoótik'l/ *n* a drug produced by biotechnological methods

biophysics /bī ō fízziks/ *n* the science that applies the laws and methods of physics to the study of biological processes (+ *singular verb*) —**biophysical** *adj* —**biophysically** *adv* —**biophysicist** *n*

biopic /bī ō pik/ *n* a film about the life of a well-known or interesting person (*informal*) [Mid-20C. Contraction of *biographical picture*.]

biopolymer /bī ō póllimər/ *n* a polymer produced in living organisms

bioprocess /bī ō prō sess/ *n* any method for producing commercially useful biological material

biopsy /bī opsi/ (*plural* **-sies**) *n* the removal of a sample of tissue from a living person for laboratory examination [Late 19C. < BIO- + Greek *opsis* 'a viewing' < *ōps* 'eye'.] —**biopsic** /bī ópsik/ *adj* —**bioptic** *adj*

biopsychology /bī ō sī kólləji/ *n* = **psychobiology**

bioreactor /bī ō ri áktər/ *n* **1** a microorganism that, through its biochemical reactions, can produce medically or commercially useful materials, e.g. beer from fermentation of yeast or insulin from genetically altered bacteria **2** a large tank for growing microorganisms used in industrial production

bioremediation /bī ō ri meédi áysh'n/ *n* the use of biological means to restore or clean up contaminated land, e.g. by adding bacteria and other organisms that consume or neutralize contaminants in the soil

biorhythm /bī ō ri*th*əm/ *n* a cyclical change, e.g. sleeping, waking, or the reproductive cycle, that takes place within living organisms (*often plural*) —**biorhythmic** /bī ō rí*th*mik/ *adj* —**biorhythmically** *adv*

biorhythmics /bī ō rí*th*miks/ *n* a branch of science dealing with biorhythms (+ *singular verb*)

⚡**BIOS** /bī oss/ *abbr* Basic Input-Output System

biosatellite /bī ō satt'l īt/ *n* a satellite designed for living beings, including humans, to live in

bioscience /bī ō sī ənss/ *n* a science, e.g. biology, ecology, physiology, or molecular biology that studies structures, functions, interactions, or other aspects of living organisms

bioscientist /bī ō sī əntist/ *n* a specialist in any of the life sciences, e.g. biology, ecology, physiology, or molecular biology

biosensor /bī ō senssər/ *n* an apparatus for detecting chemical or physical signals that provide information about specific biological activities such as blood pressure or heart monitors that use live organisms

-biosis *suffix* a particular mode of life ○ *necrobiosis* [< Greek *biōsis* 'way of living' < *bioun* 'to live' < *bios* 'life'] —**-biotic** *suffix*

biosphere /bī ə sfeer/ *n* the whole area of the Earth's surface, atmosphere, and sea that is inhabited by living things —**biospheric** /bī ə sférrik/ *adj*

biosphere reserve *n* a nationally or internationally protected area managed primarily to preserve natural ecological processes

biospheric cycles *npl* the natural recycling processes essential to life on Earth, involving the principal elements that make up the biosphere

biostatics /bī ō státtiks/ *n* a branch of science dealing with the relationship between the structure and the function of an organism (+ *singular verb*) —**biostatic** *adj* —**biostatically** *adv*

biostatistics /bī ō stə tístiks/ *n* the application of statistics to biological systems and organisms (+ *singular verb*) —**biostatistical** *adj*

biostratigraphy /bī ō strə tíggrəfi/ *n* the branch of science that uses animal and plant fossils to date and correlate sequences of sedimentary rocks

biostrome /bī ə strōm/ *n* a thin layer in a rock formation that consists of organic material such as fossils, deposited at the site where they lived [Early 20C. < modern Latin *biostroma* < Greek *bios* 'life' + *strōma* 'bed, covering'.]

biosurgery /bī ō surjəri/ *n* the use of living organisms in surgery and post-surgical treatment, especially the use of maggots or leeches to clean wounds

biosynthesis /bī ō sínthəssiss/ *n* the synthesis of chemical substances as the result of biological activity —**biosynthetic** /bī ō sin théttik/ *adj* —**biosynthetically** *adv*

biosystematics /bī ō sistə máttiks/ *n* the study of the relationships among groups of species using criteria such as morphology, biochemistry, and DNA comparisons, especially to determine the history of a species (+ *singular verb*) —**biosystematic** *adj*

biota /bī ṓtə/ *n* the total complement of animals and plants in a particular area ○ *The biotas of tropical forests are the richest of all.* [Early 20C. Via modern Latin < Greek *biotē* 'life' < *bios* 'life'.]

biotech /bī ō tek/ *n* biotechnology (*informal*) [Late 20C. Shortening.]

biotechnical /bī ō téknik'l/ *adj* relating to or involving biotechnology

biotechnology /bī ō tek nólləji/ *n* **1** the use of biological processes in industrial production **2** = **molecular biology** —**biotechnological** /bī ō teknə lójjik'l/ *adj* —**biotechnologically** *adv* —**biotechnologist** *n*

QUICK FACTS ON... **BIOTECHNOLOGY**

Key elements: the use of cellular and molecular processes in energy production and bioremediation, and to make products of benefit to medicine, agriculture, and the food industry
Key dates: 1972 first recombinant DNA produced (Berg); 1973 first recombinant organism produced (Cohen, Chang, and Boyer); 1975 monoclonal antibodies produced (Kohler and Milstein), with uses in blood group identification and vaccine production; 1982 human insulin produced in recombinant bacteria by Genentech approved for sale; first genetically modified (GM) crop approved for field trials (USA); 1994 first GM crop, Calgene's Flavr Savr tomato, approved by FDA (in United States); 1996 Dolly the sheep cloned (Wilmut and Campbell, Roslin Institute, Scotland); 1997 Polly, genetically modified cloned sheep
Key technologies: cell culture, genetic modification, antisense technology, protein engineering, cloning, polymerase chain reaction
Key developments: biosensors, monoclonal antibodies, gene therapy, modified plant varieties, pharmaceuticals

biotelemetry /bī ō tə lémmətri/ *n* the remote monitoring of vital processes, e.g. by attaching a signalling device to an animal

biotherapy /bī ō thérrəpi/ (*plural* **-pies**) *n* the treatment of disease with substances produced through the activity of living organisms such as sera, vaccines, or antibiotics

biotic /bī óttik/ *adj* describes the features of a natural system that are living [Early 17C. Via late Latin < Greek *biōtikos* 'of life, lively' < *bios* 'life'.]

biotic potential *n* the optimal ability of an organism or a species to survive and reproduce successfully

biotin /bī ətin/ *n* a B complex vitamin found in egg yolk and liver, used in fat metabolism [Mid-20C. < Greek *biōtos* 'life, sustenance' < *bios* 'life'.]

biotite /bī ə tīt/ *n* a black, dark brown, or green silicate mineral of the mica group. Source: igneous and metamorphic rocks. [Mid-19C. J.-B. *Biot* (1774–1862), After French physicist.]

biotope /bī ətōp/ *n* a small area with a distinct set of environmental conditions that supports a particular ecological community of plants and animals [Early 20C. < German *Biotop* < Greek *topos* 'place'.]

biotron /bī ə tron/ *n* a place in a laboratory in which temperature and other environmental conditions can be controlled

biotroph /bī ətrōf/ *n* a parasite that feeds on the living tissue of its host

biotype /bī ə tīp/ *n* a naturally occurring group of individuals with the same genetic make-up (**genotype**) —**biotypic** /bī ə típpik/ *adj*

biparental /bī pə rént'l/ *adj* descended from two parents, male and female, as opposed to being the product of asexual reproduction

biparietal /bī pə rī ət'l/ *adj* relating to or involving both parietal bones of the skull, particularly with respect to the measurement of the distance between their rounded projections

biparous /bíppərəss/ *adj* giving birth to two offspring at one time

bipartisan /bī paarti zán, bī paárti zan/ *adj* relating to, undertaken by, or including two political parties ○ *bipartisan support* —**bipartisanism** *n* —**bipartisanship** *n*

bipartite /bī paár tīt/ *adj* **1** made or shared by two groups of people ○ *a bipartite agreement* **2** describes leaves that are almost completely divided into two parts —**bipartitely** *adv* —**bipartition** /bī paar tísh'n/ *n*

biped /bī ped/ *n* an animal, e.g. a human, with only two legs for locomotion [Mid-17C. Directly or via French *bipède* < Latin *biped-* 'two-footed' < *ped-* 'foot'.]

bipedal /bī peéd'l, -pédd'l/ *adj* describes an animal that has two legs or feet [15C. < Latin *bipedalis* < *biped-* (see BIPED).]

bipedalism /bī peéd'l izəm, -pédd'l-/ *n* walking upright on two feet as opposed to moving on all four limbs

biphasic /bī fáyzik/ *adj* having two phases

biphenyl /bī fénn'l, -feén'l/ *n* $C_{12}H_{10}$ a white crystalline substance. Use: fungicide, heat transfer agent, synthesis of organic compounds.

bipinnate /bī pínnayt/ *adj* describes leaves divided into leaflets that are themselves subdivided —**bipinnately** *adv*

biplane /bī playn/ *n* an aeroplane with two sets of wings, one above the other

bipod /bī pod/ *n* a stand or support that has two legs

bipolar /bī pṓlər/ *adj* **1 TWO-POLED** with two poles **2 HAVING TWO DIFFERENT IDEAS** having two quite different opinions, attitudes, or natures **3 RELATING TO N AND S POLES** involving, found at, or relating to both the North and South Poles **4 HAVING MANIC AND DEPRESSED PERIODS** characterized by shifts between episodes of mania and depression **5 USING NEGATIVE AND POSITIVE CHARGE CARRIERS** describes electronic devices, especially transistors, in which both negative and positive charge carriers are utilized —**bipolarity** /bī pō lárrəti/ *n*

bipolar disorder *n* a psychiatric disorder characterized by extreme mood swings, ranging between episodes of acute euphoria (**mania**) and severe depression

bipotentiality /bīpə ténshi álləti/ *n* the potential early in embryological development for a cell or organ to differentiate in one of two ways, especially for a gonad to become either an ovary or a testis

biprism /bī prizəm/ *n* a glass prism that produces a double image of a single object

bipropellant /bī prə péllənt/ *n* a substance made up of two elements, usually a fuel and an oxidizer, that is used to propel a rocket

⚡**BIPS** /bips/ *abbr* bank Internet payment system (*in e-commerce*)

biquadratic /bī kwo dráttik/ *adj* relating to the fourth power of a number ○ *a biquadratic equation* ■ *n* an equation that involves the fourth power of a number

biracial /bī ráysh'l/ *adj* relating to, made up of, or involving people of two different races —**biracialism** *n* —**biracially** *adv*

biradial /bī ráydi əl/ *adj* with both bilateral and radial symmetry, as found in some primitive marine animals

biramous /bírrəməss, bī ráy-/ *adj* divided into or forming two branches ○ *a biramous appendage*

birch /burch/ *n* **1 TALL TREE WITH PEELING BARK** a tall slender tree with papery, peeling bark. Native to: N hemisphere. Genus: *Betula*. **2 WOOD OF A BIRCH** the pale wood of the birch tree **3 ROD FOR FLOGGING** a birch rod or bundle of twigs, formerly used to beat people as a punishment **4 PUNISHMENT BY BEATING** the action of beating somebody with a birch rod as a punishment ■ *vt* **PUNISH BY BEATING** to beat somebody with a birch rod as a punishment [Old English *birce* < Indo-European]

Bircher /búrchər/ *n* a member of the John Birch Society, a right-wing political organization in the United States with the prime mission of fighting Communism [Mid-20C. After John *Birch*, US Baptist missionary.]

bird /burd/ *n* **1 TWO-LEGGED WINGED ANIMAL** a two-legged, warm-blooded, egg-laying animal with wings, a hard beak, and a body covered with feathers. Class: Aves. **2 FOWL EATEN AS FOOD** a fowl, e.g. a turkey, chicken, duck, or goose, cooked and eaten as food **3 KIND OF PERSON** somebody of a particular type (*informal*) ○ *He's a wise old bird.* **4 OFFENSIVE TERM** an offensive term for a girl or woman (*dated informal*) **5** *US* **AEROPLANE OR SPACECRAFT** an aircraft, satellite, or rocket (*slang*) **6 PRISON** prison, or a period in prison (*slang*) **7** SPORTS = **clay pigeon** *n*. 1 [Old English *brid* 'young bird' < ?] ◇ **get the bird** to be received badly, often with booing (*informal*) ◇ **kill two birds with one stone** to achieve two aims with one action ◇ **(strictly) for the birds** worthless or unacceptable (*informal*) ◇ **the birds and the bees** the facts about sexual reproduction in humans (*informal humorous*)

birdbath /búrd baath/ (*plural* **-baths** /-baathz/) *n* a small shallow basin containing water that is placed outside a house for birds to bathe in

birdbrain /búrd brayn/ *n* a silly or mildly unintelligent person (*informal insult*) —**birdbrained** *adj*

birdcage /búrd kayj/ *n* a cage with wire or bamboo bars used to keep birds in captivity

birdcall /búrd kawl/ *n* **1** the sound or cry of a bird, especially a warning cry **2** a device that imitates a bird's call, used especially in trying to hunt or catch birds

bird colonel *n US* a full colonel in the United States Army, Air Force, or Marine Corps, as opposed to a lieutenant colonel (*informal*) [< the insignia of an eagle worn by a US colonel]

bird dog *n US, Can* a dog used to bring back game birds after they have been shot

bird-dog (**bird-dogs, bird-dogging, bird-dogged, bird-dogged**) *vti US* to watch somebody or something carefully and persistently (*informal*)

birder /búrdər/ *n US* = **birdwatcher**

birdhouse /búrd howss/ (*plural* **-houses** /-howziz/) *n* **1** *US* a small box or shelter built for birds to nest in **2** a large cage in which birds are kept in captivity

birdie /búrdi/ *n* **1 GOLF SCORE** a score in golf in which the ball is hit into the hole using one stroke fewer than the accepted standard number of strokes (**par**) for that hole **2 BIRD** a bird (*babytalk*) ■ *vt* (**-ies, -ieing, -ied**) **PLAY HOLE ONE STROKE UNDER PAR** to score a birdie in playing a hole in golf

birdlife /búrd līf/ *n* all the birds that live in a particular area or region

birdlime /búrd līm/ *n* a sticky substance made from plants that is spread on trees to catch birds ■ *vt* (**-limes, -liming, -limed**) to spread a sticky substance on trees in order to catch birds

bird louse *n* a wingless insect with a flattened body that is not truly parasitic but lives on the feathers and skin debris of birds, often causing skin irritation. Suborder: Mallophaga.

bird of paradise *n* **1** a bird, the male of which has bright feathers used in spectacular mating displays. Native to: New Guinea, Australia. Family: Paradisaeidae. **2** an ornamental plant. Flowers: orange-and-blue petals resembling a bird's head and crest. Native to: southern Africa, South America. Genus: *Strelitzia*.

bird of passage *n* **1** a bird that migrates from one region or country to another according to the season **2** somebody who rarely stays in the same place for long

bird of peace *n* a white dove as a symbol of peace

bird of prey *n* a bird, e.g. an owl, eagle, or hawk, that kills other birds and animals for food and has excellent eyesight, sharp talons, and a sharp curved beak

bird pepper *n* **1** a small pod-shaped hot-tasting fruit eaten cooked or raw as a vegetable **2** a tropical plant that produces bird peppers. *Capsicum frutescens*.

birdseed /búrd seed/ *n* seed or a mixture of seeds, usually used for feeding caged or wild birds

Birdseye /búrdz ī/, **Clarence** (1886–1956) US inventor and business executive

bird's-eye *n* **1** a pattern for fabric composed of diamond shapes with a dot in the middle of each **2** fabric with a bird's-eye pattern

bird's-eye maple *n* wood from the sugar maple that has a curled pattern in the grain reminiscent of a bird's eye

bird's-eye view *n* **1** a view that is seen from somewhere very high up **2** an overall impression or summary of something without details

bird's-foot trefoil *n* a creeping wild plant with seed pods in the shape of a bird's foot. Flowers: yellow with red tips. *Lotus corniculatus*.

birdshot /búrd shot/ *n* small lead shot designed to be fired from a shotgun

bird's nest *n* a food delicacy, usually used in soups, obtained from high cliffs in SE Asia, that is believed to be a swift's nest built with the bird's saliva (*hyphenated before nouns*) ○ *bird's-nest soup*

bird's-nest fern *n* a fern with long green fronds shaped like a bird's nest that grows on the ground or on trees in parts of Australia, India, and the South Pacific islands. *Asplenium nidus*.

birdsong /búrd song/ *n* the sounds made by a bird to attract a mate or defend territory

bird spider *n* a large hairy spider from tropical America that eats birds. Family: Aviculariidae.

bird strike *n* a collision between a bird and an aircraft in flight

Birdsville /búrdz vil/ town in SW Queensland, Australia. Population: 102 (1996).

bird table *n* a small table or platform in a garden on which food is laid out for birds to eat

birdwatcher /búrd wochər/ *n* somebody who as a hobby observes birds in their natural habitats —**birdwatching** *n*

birefringence /bī ri frínjənss/ *n* OPTICS = **double refraction** —**birefringent** *adj*

bireme /bī reem/ *n* an ancient warship that had two ranks of oars on each side [Late 16C. < Latin *biremis* 'two-oared' < *remus* 'oar'.]

Birendra Bir Bikram Shah Dev /bi réndrə beer bík ram shaa dév/ (*b.* 1945) king of Nepal (1972–)

biretta /bə réttə/, **beretta** *n* a stiff hat worn by Roman Catholic clerics that has three upright sections meeting at the centre on top [Late 16C. < Italian *berretta* or Spanish *birreta* < late Latin *birrus, birrum* 'hooded cape or cloak'.]

biri *n* = **bidi**

biriani *n* FOOD = **biryani**

Birinus /bi rīnəss/, **St** (*d.* 650?) Roman-born English missionary

Birkenhead /búrkən hed/ port in Merseyside, NW England. Population: 93,087 (1991).

Birkenhead, Frederick Edwin Smith, 1st Earl of (1872–1930) British lawyer and politician

Birkenstock /búrkən stok/ *tdmk* a trademark for a brand of footwear that includes sandals and clogs

birl /burl/ *v* **1** *vi Scotland* to spin round **2** *vt US, Can* to cause a floating log to spin round in water [Early 18C. Probably an imitation of the sound of something rotating rapidly.] —**birler** *n*

Birmingham /búrmingəm/ city and industrial centre in central England. Population: 1,020,589 (1996 estimate).

Biro /bīrō/ *tdmk* a trademark for a pen with a small metal ball at the tip that transfers the ink contained in the pen to the paper

Biro /bīrō/, **Lazio José** (1899–1985) Hungarian inventor [After Joseph BIRO]

birr[1] /bur/ *vti US, Scotland* **MAKE WHIR** to make a whirring sound, or cause something to make a whirring sound ■ *n* **1** *US, Scotland* **WHIR** a whirring sound **2** *Scotland, US* **FORCE** a forward-moving driving force [14C. < Old Norse *byrr* 'favourable wind'.]

birr[2] /bur/ *n* see table at **currency** [Late 20C. < Amharic.]

birth /burth/ *n* **1 EVENT OF BEING BORN** the emergence of the young of a human or animal from the mother's womb into the outside world ○ *The father was present at the birth.* ○ *articles give birth and death dates* **2 PROCESS OF BEING BORN** the process of bringing forth young from a mother's womb ○ *the growing number of home births* **3 TIME OR PLACE OF BIRTH** the time or place of birth **4 SOMEBODY'S HERITAGE** somebody's social or national origins ○ *a man of noble birth* ○ *Italian by birth* **5 ORIGIN** the origin, beginning, or formation of something ○ *the birth of jazz* ■ *adj* **BIOLOGICALLY RELATED AS A PARENT** biologically related to somebody, especially as a parent, rather than related by adoption [13C. < Old Norse *byrð* < Indo-European.] ◇ **give birth 1** to produce a child or young from the womb **2** to originate or be responsible for creating something ○ *a revolution that gave birth to a free nation*

birth canal *n* the passageway including the cervix and vagina through which a foetus emerges from the womb into the outside world

birth certificate *n* an official document that states when and where somebody was born and the parents' names

birth control *n* the deliberate limiting, usually by contraceptive means, of the number of children born

birthday /búrth day, -di/ *n* **1** the day in each year that is the anniversary of the day somebody was born (*often before nouns*) **2** the day on which somebody is born

LITERARY LINK ***The Birthday Party***, a play (1958) by Harold Pinter. It tells of a young man called Stanley whose comfortable life in a seaside boarding house is disrupted by the arrival of two mysterious and intimidating strangers, Goldberg and McCann.

Birthday Honours *npl* honorary titles given by the British sovereign on his or her official birthday to people who have in some way distinguished themselves

birthday suit *n* a state of nakedness (*slang humorous*)

birth father *n* a person's biological father, especially in the case of an adopted child

birthing /búrthing/ *n* the process of giving birth, especially when using natural childbirth methods ■ *adj* designed to facilitate childbirth ○ *a birthing pool*

birthing chair *n* a chair designed to support a woman and ease the process of childbirth by enabling gravity to act on the foetus as it moves through the birth canal

birthing room *n* an area with nonclinical-looking surroundings in a hospital or other building set up for childbirth

birthmark /búrth maark/ *n* a reddish or brown marking seen on the skin of some newborn babies that typically remains visible for life

birth mother *n* a person's biological mother, especially in the case of an adopted child

birth pangs *npl* a difficult or troubled period at the start of something ○ *the birth pangs of a new nation-state*

birth parent *n* somebody's biological mother or father, especially in the case of an adopted child

birthplace /búrth playss/ *n* a place where somebody was born or where something first started ○ *Shakespeare's birthplace* ○ *the birthplace of classical philosophy*

birthrate /búrth rayt/ *n* the number of live births per 1,000 members of the population in a year ○ *a declining birthrate*

birthright /búrth rīt/ *n* **1** a basic right that somebody has or is thought to be entitled to from birth ○ *Freedom of speech is our birthright.* **2** property or money that somebody feels entitled to because it belongs in the family, particularly if the person is the eldest son of the family

birthstone /búrth stōn/ *n* a precious or semi-precious stone such as an amethyst or garnet that is popularly associated with the month in which somebody was born

birthwort /búrth wurt/ *n* a European climbing plant. *Aristolochia clematitis*. [Because formerly used to help ease pain during childbirth]

Birtwistle /búrt wiss'l/, **Sir Harrison** (*b.* 1934) British composer

biryani /bírri aani/, **biriani** *n* an Indian dish containing spicy coloured rice mixed with meat, fish, or vegetables ○ *chicken biryani* [Mid-20C. Via Hindi < Persian *biriyān* 'fried, grilled'.]

bis /biss/ *adv* to be played or sung again (*musical direction*) ■ *interj* used by members of an audience to call for an encore [Early 17C. Via French and Italian < Latin, 'twice' < Indo-European, 'two'.]

Biscay, Bay of /bís kay/ arm of the North Atlantic Ocean between W France and N Spain. Area: 223,000 sq. km/86,000 sq. mi.

biscotto /bi skóttō/ (*plural* **-ti** /-ti/) *n* a hard oblong biscuit, often containing nuts [< Italian, 'biscuit']

biscuit /bískit/ *n* **1 SMALL FLAT CAKE** a small flat dry cake that is usually sweet and crisp and can additionally contain fruit, nuts, or chocolate. US term **cookie** *n.* 1 **2** *US* **SMALL ROUND PIECE OF BREAD** a small round plain piece of bread that rises with baking powder or soda and is then baked in an oven **3 LIGHT BROWN** a light brown colour **4 UNGLAZED POTTERY** pottery that has been fired but not glazed [14C. < Old French *bescuit* 'twice-cooked' < Latin *bis* 'twice' + *coctus*, past participle of *coquere* 'cook'.] —**biscuit** *adj* ◇ **take the biscuit** to be the worst in a series of bad or annoying things that have already happened (*informal*)

biscuit firing *n* the first firing of something made of clay, at a relatively low temperature

biscuit ware *n* pots or pottery that have been through a first firing at a relatively low temperature

bise /beez/ *n* a sharp dry northerly wind that blows in Switzerland and neighbouring parts of Italy and France [14C. < French.]

bisect /bī sékt/ *vt* **1** to split something into two parts ○ *The river bisects the town.* **2** to divide something into two exactly equal parts [Mid-17C. < BI- + Latin *sect-*, past participle of *secare* 'cut'.] —**bisection** *n* —**bisectional** *adj* —**bisectionally** *adv*

bisector /bī séktər/ *n* a straight line or plane that divides an angle or another line into two exactly equal parts

bisexual /bī sékshoo əl/ *adj* **1 ATTRACTED TO BOTH SEXES** sexually attracted to both men and women **2 BOTH MALE AND FEMALE IN CHARACTERISTICS** having both male and female characteristics **3 WITH MALE AND FEMALE REPRODUCTIVE ORGANS** describes something such as a flower that has both male and female reproductive organs —**bisexual** *n* —**bisexuality** /bī sékshoo állәti/ *n* —**bisexually** *adv*

Bishkek /bish kék/ capital of Kyrgyzstan, in the N of the country. Population: 585,800 (1996 estimate).

bishop /bíshəp/ *n* **1** a senior Christian cleric, especially in the Roman Catholic, Anglican, and Orthodox churches, who is in charge of the spiritual life and administration of a particular region (**diocese**) **2** a chess piece that can be moved diagonally across the board over any number of squares of the same colour [Pre-12C. Via Latin *episcopus* 'bishop, overseer' < Greek *episkopos* 'overseer' < *skopos* 'watcher'.]

Bishop /bíshəp/, **Elizabeth** (1911–79) US poet

bishopbird /bíshəp burd/ *n* a weaverbird, the males of which have black feathers with red or yellow markings. Native to: Africa. Genus: *Euplectes*.

bishopric /bíshəp rik/ *n* **1 BISHOP'S DIOCESE** an area that a bishop is in charge of **2 BISHOP'S SEE** a place where a bishop's cathedral is situated **3 RANK OF BISHOP** the rank or office of a bishop [Pre-12C. < BISHOP + Old English *rīce* 'realm, power'.]

bishop sleeve *n* a wide sleeve that is gathered at the wrist

Biskra /biss kraá/ oasis on the edge of the Sahara Desert in NE Algeria. Population: 128,280 (1987).

Bislama /bíshlə maá/ *n* the national language of Vanuatu in the Pacific, a modern form of Beach-la-Mar. Native speakers: 128,000. [Late 20C. Representing the local pronunciation of BEACH-LA-MAR.]

Bismarck /bíz maark/ capital of North Dakota, in the south-central part of the state. Population: 54,040 (1998 estimate).

Bismarck, Otto Edward Leopold von, Prince (1815–98) German statesman. Known as **the Iron Chancellor**

Bismarck Archipelago group of over 200 islands in the W Pacific Ocean, part of Papua New Guinea. Area: 49,658 sq. km/19,173 sq. mi.

bismuth /bízməth/ *n* (*symbol* **Bi**) a heavy, brittle, reddish-white, crystalline metallic element. Source: ores of lead, silver, copper, and gold. Use: alloys, medicines. [Mid-17C. < obsolete German *Bismut*, modern Latin *bisemutum* < Middle High German *wise* 'meadow' + *muth* 'claim to a mine'.]

bison /bíss'n/ (*plural* **-son**) *n* a large hairy animal resembling an ox, but with massive head and shoulders and a humped back. Native to: North America, Europe. Genus: *Bison*. [Early 17C. Directly or via French < Latin, < Germanic.]

bisque[1] /bisk/ *n* a rich soup made from shellfish ○ *lobster bisque* [Mid-17C. < French.]

bisque[2] /bisk/ *n* **1** CERAMICS = **biscuit** *n.* **4 2** a pinkish-brown colour [Mid-17C. Alteration of BISCUIT, perhaps after French.] —**bisque** *adj*

bisque[3] /bisk/ *n* an extra turn, stroke, or point that is given as an advantage to a weaker player in a game of tennis, golf, or croquet [Mid-17C. < French.]

Bissau /bi sów/ capital and main port of Guinea-Bissau. Population: 200,000 (1994 estimate).

bissextile /bi séks tīl/ *adj* having the extra day in a year that makes it a leap year ○ *bissextile month* ■ *n* a leap year [Late 16C. < late Latin *bis(s)extilus* < Latin *bi(s)sextus (dies)* 'twice-sixth (day)', 24 February, the sixth day before 1 March, counted twice in a leap year in the ancient Roman calendar.]

bistable /bī stáyb'l/ *adj* describes an electronic device or circuit that has two stable states at any given time so that it is possible to switch between them

bistort /bís tawrt/ *n* a plant with an S-shaped underground stem (**rhizome**). Use: formerly, in medicine. Native to: Europe, Asia. *Polygonum bistorta*. [Early 16C. Directly or via French < assumed medieval Latin *bistorta* < Latin *bis* 'twice' + *torta*, feminine past participle of *torquere* 'twist'.]

bistoury /bístəri/ (*plural* **-ries**) *n* a thin surgical knife designed to cut from the inside outwards, formerly used to cut open abscesses or enlarge fistulas [Mid-18C. < French.]

bistro /beéstrō/ (*plural* **-tros**) *n* a small restaurant or bar [Early 20C. < French.]

bisulphate /bī súl fayt/ *n* CHEM = **hydrogen sulphate**

bisulphide /bī súl fīd/ *n* CHEM = **disulphide**

bisulphite /bī súl fīt/ *n* CHEM = **hydrogen sulphite**

bit[1] /bit/ *n* **1 PIECE** a small piece of something ○ *There were bits of paper everywhere.* **2 SMALL AMOUNT** a small part or amount of something ○ *a bit of housework* **3 SHORT AMOUNT OF TIME** a very short period of time or distance ○ *I'll do it in a bit.* **4 SMALL COIN** a small coin of a particular value (*informal dated*) ○ *a threepenny bit* **5 SHORT PERFORMANCE** a short routine, joke, or skit in a performance **6 SMALL ACTING PART** a small part in a film or play (*often before nouns*) **7 EVERYTHING ABOUT A ROLE** all the aspects of a particular role in life (*informal*) ○ *did the whole two-career marriage bit* [Old English *bita* < *bītan* 'to bite' (see BITE)] ◇ **a bit** somewhat (*informal*) ◇ **a bit much** excessive or unacceptable (*informal*) ◇ **a bit of all right** very good-looking (*informal; offensive in some contexts*) ◇ **a bit of fluff** an offensive term for a young woman who is regarded as very good-looking but unintelligent, often somebody's girlfriend or lover (*informal*) ◇ **a bit of rough** an offensive term for a person, usually a man, whose physicality and lack of refinement are found sexually attractive by somebody from a higher social class (*informal*) ◇ **a bit of stuff** an offensive term for a woman or girl considered from the point of view of her sexual attractiveness (*dated informal*) ◇ **bit by bit** gradually ◇ **bits and pieces, bits and bobs 1** personal belongings (*informal*) **2** miscellaneous small objects (*informal*) ○ *I collected up my bits and pieces and left.* ◇ **do your bit** to contribute your share to work that needs to be done ◇ **every bit** in every way ○ *She is every bit as skilled as he is.* ◇ **fall to bits 1** to become broken into small pieces **2** to become unable to cope ◇ **to bits** very much or to the greatest degree possible (*informal*) ○ *I just love the kids to bits!*

bit[2] /bit/ *n* **1 MOUTHPIECE OF BRIDLE** a part of a bridle, consisting of a metal mouthpiece held in a horse's mouth by the reins and used to control the horse **2 DETACHABLE PART OF DRILL** a small metal tool that is inserted into a drill or brace and used for boring or drilling **3 TOOL BLADE** the part of a plane that is used for cutting **4 PART OF PINCERS** the gripping part of a pair of pincers **5 TIP OF SOLDERING IRON** the tip of a soldering iron that is made from copper ■ *vt* (**bits, bitting, bitted**) **1 INSERT BRIDLE BIT** to put a bit into the mouth of a horse **2 RESTRAIN** to restrain or hold somebody back [Old English *bite* < Indo-European] ◇ **champ** *or* **chafe at the bit** to be impatient for something to happen or because no action is possible ◇ **get** *or* **take** *or* **have the bit between your teeth** to start something and refuse stubbornly to stop

⚡**bit**[3] /bit/ *n* **1** in binary notation, either of the digits 0 or 1 used to represent one of only two outcomes, e.g. on or off **2** the smallest unit of information storable in a computer or a peripheral device, expressed as 0 or 1. Eight bits make a byte, the common measure of memory or storage capacity. [Mid-20C. Blend of BINARY + DIGIT.]

bit[4] /bit/ past tense, past participle of **bite**

bitch /bich/ *n* **1 FEMALE DOG** a female dog, or the female of another related animal, e.g. the fox, or another carnivore, e.g. the ferret **2 OFFENSIVE TERM** an offensive term that deliberately insults a woman's temperament (*slang*) **3 SPITEFUL CONVERSATION** a conversation that involves complaining or saying unpleasant things about somebody who is not present (*informal*) **4** *US* **COMPLAINT** a querulous nagging complaint (*slang; often considered offensive*) **5 SOMETHING DIFFICULT** a difficult thing or situation (*slang; often considered offensive*) ■ *vi* (*often considered offensive*) **1 BE NASTY** to talk about somebody who is not present in an unpleasant or malicious way (*slang*) **2** *US* **COMPLAIN CONTINUALLY** to complain or grumble about something continually [Old English *bicce*, perhaps < Old Norse]

bitch slap *n US* a physical slap as given by a dominant person to a subservient person who cannot hit back (*slang; offensive in some contexts*) —**bitch-slap** *vt*

bitchy /bíchi/ (**-ier, -iest**) *adj* malicious or unpleasant in speaking to, talking about, or behaving toward somebody (*slang; often considered offensive*) —**bitchily** *adv* —**bitchiness** *n*

bite /bīt/ *v* (**bites, biting, bit** /bit/, **bitten** /bítt'n/) **1** *vti* **GRIP WITH THE TEETH** to hold something tightly, tear something off, or cut through something using the teeth ○ *I bit into the fruit.* **2** *vt* **STING** to puncture or tear the skin of a person or animal using fangs, teeth, or mouthparts ○ *got bitten by a spider* **3** *vti* **GRIP SOMETHING FIRMLY** to make firm or secure contact with something ○ *The wheel's not biting.* **4** *vi* **CORRODE** to eat into something with a corrosive action ○ *The acid had bitten into the metal surface.* **5** *vi* **CAUSE DISCOMFORT** to penetrate somebody or something sharply, as if with a honed blade ○ *The icy wind bit into him.* **6** *vi* **TAKE BAIT** to attempt to take the bait that has been placed on the end of a fishing line (*refers to fish*) **7** *vi* **RISE TO SOMEBODY ELSE'S BAIT** to respond when somebody else tries to get you involved in a scheme or an argument (*informal*) ○ *Even though baited by the Opposition, she refused to bite.* **8** *vt* **ANNOY OR UPSET** to annoy or preoccupy somebody, or put somebody in a bad mood ○ *What's biting you today?* **9** *vi* **BE EFFECTIVE** to have an effect or influence ○ *The trade sanctions are at last beginning to bite.* ■ *n* **1 SEIZURE OF SOMETHING WITH TEETH** the action of taking something between the teeth and tearing it off **2 MOUTHFUL** a piece of food torn off with the teeth **3 INJURY FROM TEETH OR INSECT** an injury that has been caused by an animal or insect puncturing or tearing the skin with teeth, fangs, or mouthparts ○ *a mosquito bite* **4 ATTEMPT BY FISH TO TAKE BAIT** an attempt by a fish to eat the bait that has been put on the end of a fishing line **5 PIQUANCY** a pleasantly sharp taste **6 WIT AND INTELLIGENCE** a penetrating and intelligent quality **7 COLDNESS** a cold sharp sensation that is quite painful ○ *There's a bit of a bite in the air today.* **8 DEPTH OF MACHINE TOOL'S BLADE** the depth to which a machine tool can cut **9 GRIP** the grip that something such as a tool has on something else **10 FIT OF TEETH** the way the upper and lower teeth meet and fit together when the jaw is closed **11 CORROSIVE EFFECT** the corrosive effect of acid on a surface **12 PERIOD WHEN FISH EAT** a time when fish usually feed ○ *The catfish bite is usually the heaviest and best in the evening.* [Old English *bītan* < Indo-European] —**bitable** *adj* —**biter** *n* ◇ **bite off more than you can chew** to take on more than you can deal with (*informal*) ◇ **have two bites at the cherry** to have more than one attempt at doing something (*informal*)

bite back *v* **1** *vt* to hold back from saying something or openly crying ○ *I bit back my tears.* **2** *vti* to make a sharp retort

biteplate /bīt playt/ *n* a removable acrylic dental device that sticks to the roof of the mouth and is worn to encourage the back teeth to come through or to correct an overbite

bite-sized, bite-size *adj* small enough to be eaten as a single mouthful ○ *cut the meat into bite-sized pieces*

⚡**bit flip** *n* **1** the switching of a digital bit from 0 to 1 or from 1 to 0 **2** *US* a complete change in personality or attitude (*slang*)

Bithynia /bi thínni ə/ ancient country of NW Asia Minor, on the Black Sea in present-day Turkey

biting /bīting/ *adj* **1** cold enough to cause discomfort or pain ○ *a biting north wind* **2** sarcastic and clever

⚡**bit map** *n* a representation of a graphics image in computer memory consisting of rows and columns of dots, each corresponding to a pixel ■ *vt* (**bit-maps, bit-mapping, bit-mapped**) to represent a graphics image in computer memory as a matrix of dots or to recreate the image on a computer screen from such a bit map [< BIT[3]]

⚡**bitmapped font** /bít mapt-/ *n* a screen or printer font with characters formed as a pattern of pixels or dots

⚡**BITNET** /bít net/ *abbr* Because It's Time Network

bitok /bíttok/ *n* fried mince patties served with a sour cream sauce [Via Russian < French *bifteck (haché)* '(minced) beef' < English *beefsteak*]

⚡**bit stream** *n* a simple unstructured sequence of bits transmitting data in the form of binary digits

bitt /bit/ *n* either of a pair of posts on a ship's deck for fastening cables (*often plural*) ■ *vt* to fasten something round a bitt [15C. < ?]

bitten past participle of **bite**

bitter /bíttər/ *adj* 1 **STRONG AND SHARP IN TASTE** having a sharp strong unpleasant taste, e.g. like that of orange peel 2 **RESENTFUL** angry and resentful ○ *a bitter smile* 3 **DIFFICULT TO ACCEPT** painful or very hard to accept ○ *a bitter blow* 4 **HOSTILE** expressing intense hostility ○ *bitter fighting.* 5 **VERY COLD** penetratingly and unpleasantly cold ○ *a bitter wind* ■ *n UK* **BEER** beer that is made with a lot of hops and has a slightly sharp taste ○ *a pint of bitter* [Old English *biter* < Indo-European] —**bitterly** *adv* —**bitterness** *n*

bitter almond *n* an almond tree that bears nuts containing hydrogen cyanide. Use: food flavouring.

bitter aloes *n* = **aloes** *n.* 1

bitter cress *n* a plant belonging to the mustard family that often grows in damp places. Flowers: white, in clusters. Genus: *Cardamine.*

bitter end *n* the very end of something, however unpleasant it is ○ *They held out to the bitter end.* [Originally 'end of a cable or mooring rope secured on board ship', *bitter* perhaps < BITT, but now interpreted as 'painful']

bitter-ender *n US, S Africa* a highly obstinate, inflexible recalcitrant person who takes a stand, refusing to budge until he or she is forced by adverse circumstances to do so

bitter lemon *n* a fizzy nonalcoholic drink that is flavoured with lemon and is a greyish-green colour

bitterling /bíttərling/ *n* a small brightly-coloured freshwater fish from central Europe that is often kept in aquariums. *Rhodeus sericeus.* [Late 19C. < German, 'small bitter (fish)'.]

bittern[1] /bíttərn/ *n* a wading bird with mottled brownish plumage, and a booming call. Family: Ardeidae. [Early 16C. Alteration of *bitore*, probably < Anglo-Latin *butorius* or Old French *butor*, < Latin *butio* 'bittern' + *taurus* 'bull'.]

bittern[2] /bíttərn/ *n* the bitter liquid that is left after common salt has crystallized from sea water. Use: source of bromides, magnesium. [Late 17C. < BITTER + *-n* < ?]

bitternut /bíttər nut/ *n* 1 a thin-shelled nut with a bitter kernel 2 a tree that bears bitternuts. Native to: E North America. *Carya cordiformis.*

bitter orange *n* FOOD = **Seville orange**

bitter pill *n* something unpleasant that nonetheless must be accepted ○ *Not getting the job was a bitter pill for him to swallow.*

bitters /bíttərz/ *n* a slightly alcoholic liquid flavoured with plant extracts and used as a mixer with certain cocktails (+ *singular verb*) ■ *npl* a bitter-tasting liquid used as a digestive tonic

bittersweet /bíttər sweet/ *adj* 1 **BOTH BITTER AND SWEET** smelling or tasting both bitter and sweet at the same time 2 **BOTH HAPPY AND SAD** causing feelings of happiness and sadness at the same time ■ *n* 1 **PLANT WITH BRIGHT CAPSULES AND SEEDS** a poisonous climbing plant that has orange capsules containing bright red seeds. Native to: N America. Genus: *Celastus.* 2 = **woody nightshade**

bitty /bítti/ (**-tier, -tiest**) *adj* made up of lots of different parts that do not seem to fit together ○ *a very bitty film* —**bittiness** *n*

bitumen /bíttyoomən/ *n* 1 a sticky mixture of hydrocarbons found in substances such as asphalt and tar. Source: petroleum. 2 *Aus* a tarred road or sealed road or system of roads, as opposed to a dirt road [15C. < Latin, 'asphalt'.] —**bituminous** /bi tyóominəss/ *adj*

bituminize /bi tyóomi nīz/ (**-nizes, -nizing, -nized**), **bituminise** (**-nises, -nising, -nised**) *vt* to cover or treat something with bitumen, or convert something into bitumen —**bituminization** /bi tyóomi nī záysh'n/ *n*

bituminous coal *n* soft coal that burns with a smoky flame

bivalence /bī váylənss/, **bivalency** /-lənssi/ *n* the property that a proposition has in classical systems of logic of being either true or false

bivalent /bī váylənt/ *adj* 1 CHEM = **divalent** 2 describes structurally identical (**homologous**) chromosomes that come together during cell division (**meiosis**) ■ *n* a pair of structurally identical (**homologous**) chromosomes that come together during cell division (**meiosis**)

bivalve /bī valv/ *n* a marine or freshwater mollusc that has its body contained within two shells joined by a hinge. Oysters, mussels, and cockles are bivalves. —**bivalved** *adj* —**bivalvular** /bī válvyoolər/ *adj*

bivariate /bī váiri ət, -ayt/ *adj* relating to or involving two variables

bivouac /bívvoo ak/ *n* 1 **MILITARY OR MOUNTAINEERING CAMP** a very simple temporary camp that is set up and used by soldiers or mountaineers 2 **BRIEF OVERNIGHT STAY** a short stay, usually overnight, often with minimum equipment ■ *vi* (**-acs, -acking, -acked**) **MAKE CAMP** to set up and stay in a very simple temporary camp [Early 18C. < French, probably < Low German *bīwake* < *bi-* 'by' + *wake* 'watch, vigil'.]

bivvy /bívvi/ (*plural* **-vies**) *n* a very simple shelter or tent (*slang*) [Early 20C. < BIVOUAC.]

biweekly /bī weékli/ *adj* 1 **COMING OUT EVERY TWO WEEKS** produced or appearing every two weeks 2 **COMING OUT TWICE A WEEK** produced or appearing twice a week ■ *adv* 1 **ONCE EVERY TWO WEEKS** at two-week intervals 2 **TWICE A WEEK** twice during a one-week period ■ *n* (*plural* **-lies**) **TWICE-WEEKLY PUBLICATION** a publication that appears every two weeks

---

USAGE How many times is **biweekly**? Confusion is caused by the fact that ***biweekly***, *bimonthly*, and *biyearly* can mean either 'once every two weeks or months or years' or 'twice a week or month or year'. If you want to avoid doubt, it is better to reword the sentence: *The talks are held twice a week at the local school. The talks are held every two weeks at the local school.*

---

biyearly /bī yeérli/ *adj* 1 **COMING OUT EVERY TWO YEARS** produced or appearing every two years 2 **COMING OUT TWICE A YEAR** produced or appearing twice a year ■ *adv* 1 **ONCE EVERY TWO YEARS** at two-year intervals 2 **TWICE A YEAR** twice during a one-year period

---

USAGE See ***biweekly***.

---

biz[1] /biz/ *n* (*slang*) 1 something that is really excellent 2 a business of a particular type, typically involving fashion, entertainment, or the media [Mid-19C. Shortened < BUSINESS.]

⚡**biz**[2] *abbr* business (*in Internet addresses*)

~~**bizare**~~ incorrect spelling of **bizarre**

bizarre /bi zaár/ *adj* amusingly or grotesquely strange or unusual [Mid-17C. Via French, 'odd', formerly 'brave, handsome' < Spanish *bizarro* 'brave' < Italian *bizzarro* 'angry'.] —**bizarrely** *adv* —**bizarreness** *n*

bizarrerie /bi zaárəri/ *n* amusing or grotesque strangeness or oddity [Mid-18C. < French.]

Bizet /beé zay/, **Georges** (1838–75) French composer

bizillion *n US* = **bazillion** (*slang*)

bizonal /bī zṓn'l/ *adj* made up of two zones

Bjelke-Petersen /byélki peétərss'n/, **Sir Johannes** (*b.* 1911) New Zealand-born Australian politician

Bjørnson /byúrnss'n/, **Bjørnstjerne** (1832–1910) Norwegian writer and politician

bk *abbr* 1 bank[1] 2 book

Bk *symbol* berkelium

bks *abbr* 1 barracks 2 books

BL *abbr* 1 Bachelor of Law 2 Bachelor of Letters 3 *US* Barrister-at-Law 4 British Library 5 bill of lading

bl. *abbr* 1 black 2 blue 3 bale[1]

B/L *abbr* bill of lading

blab /blab/ *vi* (**blabs, blabbing, blabbed**) (*informal*) 1 to talk indiscreetly about something that is supposed to be secret 2 to chatter in a mildly incoherent way ■ *n* = **blabbermouth** [13C. Probably < Germanic, imitating the sound of vacuous talking.]

blabber /blábbər/ *vi* to chatter in a mildly incoherent way ■ *n* 1 = **blabbermouth** 2 the sound made by people talking loudly and incoherently [14C. Probably < BLAB.]

blabbermouth /blábbər mowth/ (*plural* **-mouths** /-mowthz/) *n* somebody who talks too much and reveals secrets (*informal*)

black /blak/ *adj* 1 **OF THE DARKEST COLOUR** being the colour of coal or carbon 2 **DEVOID OF LIGHT** completely dark, with no light 3 ⚠ **black, Black DARK-SKINNED** belonging to an African people or to another ethnic group with dark skin, e.g. Australian Aboriginals. 4 **WITHOUT MILK** served without adding milk or cream 5 **FUNNY AND MACABRE** dealing with very serious things in a humorous and often macabre way 6 **CLANDESTINE** carried out in the utmost secrecy 7 **FULL OF ANGER** filled with anger or hostility 8 **HOPELESS** so depressing as to end all hope 9 **DIRTY** covered with mud, soil, or any other dark substance 10 **BOYCOTTED** boycotted by trade unions, especially in support of industrial action that is being taken by other unions 11 **SERIOUSLY BAD OR UNFORTUNATE** causing or associated with severely bad conditions or misfortune 12 **DISHONOURABLE** extremely dishonourable and deserving the most serious criticism 13 **EVIL** relating to evil ■ *n* 1 **DARKEST COLOUR** a colour value that has no hue as a result of the absorption of nearly all light 2 **COAL-COLOURED DYE OR PIGMENT** a pigment or dye that is the colour of carbon or coal 3 ⚠ **black, Black MEMBER OF DARK-SKINNED PEOPLE** a member of an African ethnic group or another ethnic group with dark skin, e.g. Australian Aboriginals. 4 **BLACK MATERIAL OR CLOTHES** fabric or clothing that is black in colour 5 **TOTAL DARKNESS** complete darkness 6 **BLACK PIECE** a black piece in a game such as chess or draughts 7 **PLAYER WITH BLACK PIECES** a player in games such as chess or draughts who is playing with the black pieces 8 **BLACK BALL** a black ball in snooker, which is the last ball to be potted 9 **BLACK RING ON ARCHERY TARGET** a black ring on a target in archery, which gives a player a score of three 10 **BLACK COLOUR BETS ARE PLACED ON** one of the colours on which players can lay their bets when gambling at such games as roulette ■ *vt* 1 **MAKE BLACK** to make something black or cover something in black 2 **USE BLACK POLISH** to cover something, e.g. shoes or boots, with black polish 3 **BRUISE THE EYE** to hit somebody's eye so that it becomes very bruised and turns a purplish-black colour 4 **BOYCOTT** to organize a boycott of goods or some action, especially in support of industrial action being carried out by other trade unions [Old English *blæc* < ?] —**blackish** *adj* —**blackness** *n* ◇ **in the black** 1 not in debt or overdrawn 2 having or making money or a profit

---

USAGE Terms considered appropriate for different ethnic groups change from place to place and from time to time. The word ***Black*** is standard in current usage for a dark-skinned person of African or African-Caribbean origin or descent. It is the term that African-Caribbean people in the UK prefer and is also used by Australian Aborigines. However, many Americans of African descent prefer the more formal term *African American*, used both as noun and adjective. The term ***Black*** is sometimes extended to include other peoples who are not white, but this use is generally regarded as unacceptable, the preferable use being specific names such as *Indian* or *Malay*.

---

black out *v* 1 *vi* **LOSE CONSCIOUSNESS** to lose consciousness, sight, or memory temporarily 2 *vt* **TO EXTINGUISH OR HIDE LIGHTS** to ensure that all lights in an inhabited area are turned off or covered up at night to prevent it being seen from enemy aircraft 3 *vt* **REMOVE ELECTRICITY SUPPLY FROM** to cause a place to undergo a failure of its electricity supply 4 *vt* **MAKE SOMETHING UNREADABLE** to cover a piece of writing with black colour so that it cannot be read 5 *vt* **ERASE FROM MEMORY** to refuse to remember an upsetting fact, event, or experience 6 *vt* **WITHDRAW FROM BROADCASTING** to refuse to broadcast radio or television programmes, usually because of a strike 7 *vt* **WITHHOLD INFORMATION** to withhold news or information about a subject 8 *vi* **LOSE RADIO COMMUNICATION** to lose radio communication between an aircraft or ship and headquarters

Black /blak/, **Hugo** (1886–1971) US Supreme Court justice

Black, Sir James Whyte (*b.* 1924) British pharmacologist

Black, Shirley Temple (*b.* 1928) US actor and former ambassador

blackamoor /blákə moor, -mawr/ *n* an offensive term for a Black person or somebody with very dark skin (*archaic*) [Early 16C. Alteration of *black Moor.*]

black-and-blue *adj* covered with bruises, or feeling very bruised (*not hyphenated after verbs*)

Black and Tan *n* a member of the armed force that was sent by the British to Ireland in 1920–21 to fight Sinn Fein

black-and-tan *n* a drink consisting of ale mixed with stout or porter

black and white *n* 1 material either handwritten or printed 2 a visual medium without colours, and in hues of black, white, and shades of grey

black-and-white *adj* 1 **NOT IN COLOUR** representing an image in which colours have been converted to black, white, and shades of grey ○ *a black-and-white photograph* **2 REPRODUCING IMAGES NOT IN COLOUR** reproducing images in which colours have been converted to black, white, and shades of grey ○ *a black-and-white television* **3 CLEAR-CUT** clear-cut and straightforward, allowing no room for compromise or doubt (*not hyphenated after verbs*) ○ *Everything is black and white as far as she's concerned.*

black arts *npl* magic attempted for evil purposes, calling upon the help of the Devil

black-backed gull *n* a common gull with a black back and wings and white underparts. Native to: N Atlantic coastal waters. *Larus marinus* and *Larus fuscus*.

blackball /blák bawl/ *vt* **1 PREVENT FROM JOINING** to prevent somebody from becoming a member of a club by voting against the person **2 EXCLUDE FROM GROUP** to exclude somebody from a group or profession ■ *n* **1 NEGATIVE VOTE** a vote against somebody, especially somebody wanting to join a group **2 VOTING TOKEN** a black ball used to show a negative vote (*archaic*)

black bass *n* a large freshwater bass that is popular as a game fish. Native to: North America. Genus: *Micropterus*.

black bean *n* **1 DRIED BEAN** a small black seed dried and used in cooking **2 BEAN PLANT** any bean plant that produces black beans **3 TREE** a tree with smooth bark and dark green leaves. Use: furniture. Native to: rainforests of E Australia. *Castanospermum australe*. **4 FERMENTED SOYA BEAN** a soya bean used fermented in oriental cookery ○ *black bean sauce*

black bear *n* **1** a bear that lives in forests and ranges from brownish yellow to black in colour. Native to: North America. *Euarctos americanus*. **2** a bear that has a black coat with a whitish V-shaped mark on its chest. Native to: Central and E Asia. *Selenarctos thibetanus*.

black belt *n* **1 BELT SHOWING SKILL IN MARTIAL ARTS** a belt worn by somebody who has reached the highest level of skill in a martial art such as judo or karate **2 SOMEBODY WITH BLACK BELT** somebody at the highest level of skill in a martial art, entitled to wear a belt that is black **3 black belt, Black Belt FERTILE AGRICULTURAL REGION** a region in the S United States, stretching from Georgia across Alabama and Mississippi, with extremely fertile dark soil

blackberry /blákbəri/ (*plural* **-ries**) *n* **1** a small sweet purple fruit, composed of tight clusters of small round fruitlets **2** a large bush with arching, often thorny, stems that bears blackberries. Native to: Europe. *Rubus fruticosus*.

black bile *n* one of the four humours that were once believed to be the base of somebody's character, associated with a melancholy temperament

blackbird /blák burd/ *n* **1** a common bird, the male of which has black feathers and a yellow beak and the female, brown feathers. Native to: Europe. *Turdus merula*. **2** a bird with black feathers showing a metallic sheen or bold patterns of yellow, orange, or red. Native to: N and S America. Family: Icteridae.

blackboard /blák bawrd/ *n* a board of either a dark colour or white that is written on with contrasting chalk or erasable markers, used especially in classrooms

black body (*plural* **black bodies**) *n* an ideal object that would absorb all of the radiation incident on it without reflecting any

black-body radiation *n* the thermal radiation that would be emitted by a black body. The distribution of energy in such radiation depends solely on the temperature of the source.

black book *n* **1** a book in which the names of people who are to be punished or blacklisted are kept **2** a book in which somebody keeps the names and telephone numbers of private friends, especially boyfriends or girlfriends (*informal*)

⚡**black box** *n* **1** AIR = **flight recorder 2** an electronic component whose constituents or circuitry are unknown or irrelevant, but whose function is understood

black bread *n* a very dark rye bread that is particularly popular in Germany and Slavic countries

blackbuck /blák buk/ (*plural* **-bucks** *or* **-buck**) *n* a rare, small antelope, the male of which has a black back, white underbelly, and spiral horns. Native to: India. *Antilope cervicapra*.

black bun *n Scotland* a dark rich fruit cake in a pastry case, traditionally eaten at Hogmanay

Blackburn /blák burn/ town in NW England. Population: 132,800 (1991).

blackbutt /blák but/ *n Aus* a eucalyptus tree with sickle-shaped leaves and a tall straight trunk. Use: timber. Native to: E Australia. *Eucalyptus pilularis*.

blackcap /blák kap/ *n* **1 SMALL SONGBIRD** a small brown-grey warbler, the male of which has a black-topped head. Native to: Europe, Asia, Africa. *Sylvia atricapilla*. **2 BIRD WITH BLACK CROWN** any bird similar to the blackcap warbler with a black-topped head, e.g. a chickadee **3 JUDGE'S CAP** a black cap formerly worn by a judge when passing a death sentence

black cherry *n* a large wild cherry tree that has dark bark and white flowers and bears black cherries. Native to: North America. *Prunus serotina*.

blackcock /blák kok/ (*plural* **-cocks** *or* **-cock**) *n* **1** the male of the black grouse **2** a grouse that is smaller and duller than the black grouse. Native to: Caucasus mountains. *Lyrurus mlokosiewiczi*.

black comedy *n* comedy containing bitter jokes about unpleasant aspects of life

Black Country /blák kuntri/ region of the West Midlands, England

blackcurrant /blák kúrrənt/ *n* **1** a small black berry that grows in bunches **2** a fruit bush that bears blackcurrants. *Ribes nigrum*.

blackdamp /blák damp/ *n* atmospheric conditions in a mine that prevent normal breathing because insufficient oxygen remains after an explosion

Black Death *n* the bubonic plague epidemic that killed over 50 million people throughout Asia and Europe in the 14th century [Probably < the colour of the buboes]

black diamond *n* **1** MINERALS = **carbonado** *n*. **2** the black variety of haematite. Use: source of iron. ■ **black diamonds** *npl* coal (*informal*)

Blackdown Hills /blák down-/ Area of Outstanding Natural Beauty in SW England

black duck *n* a brownish duck. Native to: NE North America. *Anas rubripes*.

black dwarf *n* a very small star that cannot generate thermonuclear energy and emits little or no radiation

black economy *n* the part of an economy that consists of unofficial or illegal, and therefore untaxed, earnings

blacken /blákən/ *v* **1** *vti* to become, or cause something to become, darker or black **2** *vt* to harm or damage somebody's reputation

Black English *n* a variety of English that has developed in a Black community ■ = **African American Vernacular English**

Blacket /blákit/, **Edmund Thomas** (1817–83) British-born Australian architect

Blackett /blákit/, **Patrick M. S., Baron** (1897–1974) British physicist. Full name **Patrick Maynard Stuart**

black eye *n* an area of bruising round somebody's eye

black-eyed bean *n* **1** a small beige bean with a black spot. US term **black-eyed pea** *n*. 2 **2** a legume widely cultivated in the S United States for forage and for black-eyed beans. *Vigna unguiculata*. US term **black-eyed pea** *n*. 1

black-eyed pea *n US* **1** PLANTS = **black-eyed bean** *n*. 1 **2** FOOD = **black-eyed bean** *n*. 2

black-eyed Susan *n* **1** a type of rudbeckia. Flowers: yellowish-orange with a dark conical centre. Native to: North America. Genus: *Rudbeckia*. **2** a climbing plant. Flowers: yellow with purple centres. Native to: tropical Africa. *Thunbergia alata*.

blackfish /blák fish/ (*plural* **-fish** *or* **-fishes**) *n* **1** a small freshwater fish that is very abundant in Arctic North America and Siberia. *Dallia pectoralis*. **2** a female salmon that has spawned **3** = **pilot whale**

black flag *n* = **Jolly Roger** ■ *vt* (**black-flags, black-flagging, black-flagged**) to signal to a racing driver to pull into the pits by waving a black flag

black fly (*plural* **black flies** *or* **black fly**) *n* a small dark biting gnat that causes painful itchy welts in people and animals. Family: Simuliidae.

blackfly /blák flī/ (*plural* **-flies** *or* **-fly**) *n* a black aphid that infests many types of plant. Genus: *Aphis*.

Blackfoot /blák fòot/ (*plural* **-feet** /-feet/ *or* **-foot**) *n* **1** a member of a group of Native North American peoples living in Alberta, Saskatchewan, and Montana **2** an Algonquian language spoken in Alberta, Canada, and in Montana, the United States. Native speakers: 8,000. [Late 18C. Translation of Blackfoot *Siksika*, perhaps from walking across burnt prairies.] —**Blackfoot** *adj*

black-footed albatross *n* a dark albatross that spends most of its time at sea. Native to: Pacific. *Diomedea nigripes*.

Black Forest wooded highland region in SW Germany. Area: 5,180 sq. km/2,000 sq. mi.

Black Forest gateau *n* a rich chocolate cake that is topped and filled with cherries and whipped cream. US term **Black Forest cake**

Black Friar *n* a member of the Dominican order of friars

black grouse *n* a large grouse with a lyre-shaped tail, the male of which is black with white patches on its wings. Native to: Europe, W Asia. *Lyrurus tetrix*.

blackguard /blággərd, blágg aard/ *n* somebody despised for being dishonest or having few, if any, principles (*dated*) ■ *vt* to attack or criticize somebody using abusive language (*archaic*) —**blackguardism** *n* —**blackguardly** *adj*

black guillemot *n* a small seabird of the auk family that has black plumage with white wing patches in summer. Native to: NE North America. *Cepphus grylle*.

⚡**black hat hacker** *n* a hacker who makes malicious attempts to break into a computer system belonging to somebody else. ◊ **white hat hacker**

blackhead /blák hed/ *n* **1 DARK BLOCKED PORE** a small plug of dark fatty matter blocking a follicle on the skin, especially on the face **2 FOWL DISEASE** an infectious disease of turkeys and related fowl resulting in darkened head skin **3 BIRD WITH BLACK HEAD** a bird with a dark-coloured head, especially a duck or gull

Blackheath /blak heéth/ village and area of open ground in SE London

Black Hills mountainous region in W South Dakota and NE Wyoming, including Mount Rushmore National Memorial. Highest peak: Harney Peak 2,207 m/7,242 ft.

black hole *n* **1** an area in space with such a strong gravitational pull that no matter or energy can escape from it **2** a place or thing into which objects disappear and are not expected to be seen again (*humorous*)

Black Hole of Calcutta *n* **1** a dungeon in Calcutta in which, in 1756, 123 out of 146 prisoners were said to have died of suffocation **2** an uncomfortably overcrowded place (*informal*)

black ice *n* a thin, almost invisible, layer of ice formed when rain falls on a surface that is below freezing

blacking /bláking/ *n* polish formerly used to make shoes and stoves black

Black Isle peninsula in NE Scotland

blackjack /blák jak/ *n* **1** CARDS = **pontoon**[2] *n*. 1 **2** CARDS = **pontoon**[2] *n*. 2 **3 BLACK MINERAL** a black variety of the mineral sphalerite or zinc blende **4** *US* **SHORT CLUB** a weapon in the form of a short leather-covered club **5** *S Africa* **S AFRICAN WEED** a weed of South Africa with barbed seeds that cling to clothing and animals. *Bidens pilosa*. ■ *interj* **INDICATING A WIN AT BLACKJACK** used to indicate to other players that a blackjack has been dealt ■ *vt US* **1 HIT WITH CLUB** to hit somebody with a short club **2 FORCE** to force somebody to do something [Early 20C. < JACK[1] 'playing card'.]

black knight *n* a company that makes an unwelcome attempt to take over another

black lead *n* a commercial form of graphite

blackleg /blák leg/ *n* **1 DISEASE OF FARM ANIMALS** an infectious bacterial disease of farm animals that causes swellings on the legs **2 SOMEBODY WHO WORKS DURING STRIKE** a worker who is criticized and despised by striking colleagues for working during a strike (*slang*) **3 POTATO DISEASE** a disease of potato plants caused by the bacterium *Erwinia carotovora* that makes the lower stems rot **4 GAMBLER WHO CHEATS** a cheat at cards or horseracing (*informal*) ■ *vi* (**-legs, -legging, -legged**) **WORK DURING STRIKE** to continue to work while colleagues are on strike (*informal*)

black letter *n* PRINTING = **gothic** *n*. 3

black light *n* **1** any invisible electromagnetic radiation, e.g. ultraviolet or infrared light **2** a bulb, tube, or other device that emits black light when stimulated with electrical current

blacklist /blák list/ *n* a list of people or groups who are under suspicion or excluded from something ○ *a credit blacklist* ■ *vt* to add somebody's name to a blacklist

black lung *n* MED = **anthracosis**

blackly /blákli/ *adv* **1** in an angry or threatening way **2** showing or making use of the colour black

black magic *n* magic attempted for evil purposes, calling upon evil spirits or the Devil

blackmail /blák mayl/ *n* **1** the act of forcing somebody to pay money or do something by threatening to reveal shameful or incriminating facts about him or her **2** unfair threatening or incriminating of somebody, as a way of achieving a result [Mid-16C. < obsolete *mail* 'tribute, tax' < Old Norse *mál* 'speech, agreement'.] —**blackmail** *vt* —**blackmailer** *n*

Blackman /blákmən/, **Charles Raymond** (*b.* 1928) Australian painter

black mark *n* a record of something that somebody has done that gives people a bad opinion of him or her ○ *Avoiding the family reunion counted as a black mark against me.*

black market *n* a system of buying and selling officially controlled goods illegally —**black marketeer** *n* —**black marketeering** *n* —**black marketer** *n*

black mass *n* an imitation of a Christian Mass said to be conducted by worshippers of the Devil

black money *n* money earned unofficially or illegally

Black Monk *n* a member of the Benedictine order of monks, who wear black cloaks over their white habits

Blackmore /blák mawr/, **R. D.** (1825–1900) British writer. Full name **Richard Doddridge Blackmore**

Black Mountain mountain range in S Wales. Highest peak: Carmarthen Van 1,802 m/2,630 ft.

Black Mountains mountain range in SE Wales and W England. Highest peak: Waunfach, 811 m/2,660 ft.

Black Muslim *n* a member of the Nation of Islam, an almost exclusively African American Islamic denomination based in the United States

Black nationalist *n* a member of any political organization that promotes separate self-governing communities or states for Black people —**Black nationalism** *n*

black nightshade *n* a plant of the nightshade family that has poisonous leaves and black berries. Flowers: white, star-shaped. *Solanum nigrum.*

blackout /blák owt/ *n* **1** LOSS OF CONSCIOUSNESS a temporary loss of consciousness, sight, or memory **2** WITHDRAWAL OF BROADCASTING a refusal to broadcast radio or television programmes, usually because of a strike, **3** LOSS OF ELECTRIC LIGHT a failure of an electricity supply **4** WITHHOLDING OF INFORMATION the withholding of news or information about a subject, especially by official sources **5** LOSS OF RADIO COMMUNICATION a loss of radio communication between an aircraft or ship and headquarters **6** PERIOD OF EXTINGUISHING OR HIDING LIGHTS a period during wartime in which all lights are to be turned off or covered up at night to prevent towns being seen from enemy aircraft

Black Panther *n* a member of a militant African American political organization opposed to white domination that was active in the United States especially in the late 1960s and early 1970s [*Panther* from the emblem used by certain Black Power electoral candidates in Alabama in the mid-1960s]

black pepper *n* dark brown seasoning made by grinding pepper seeds that have not had their black outer covering removed

black pine *n* TREES = **matai**

blackpoll /blák pōl/, **blackpoll warbler** *n* a small bird with streaky plumage found in conifer forests. Native to: North America. *Dendroica striata.*

Blackpool /blák pool/ seaside resort in NW England, famous for its tower. Population: 153,600 (1995).

Black Power *n* a movement formed by Black people to engender social equality and emphasize pride in their racial identity via Black cultural and political institutions and organizations

black pudding *n UK, Southern US* a dark kind of sausage made from pig's blood and pork fat. US term **blood sausage**

black rat *n* a common dark-brown rat that is a household pest and a carrier of plague. It was originally from Asia but was imported to coastal cities throughout the world. *Rattus rattus.*

black rot *n* any plant disease that causes blackening as well as decay

Black Sash *n* an organization of white women in South Africa who campaigned against apartheid and now provide social services

Black Sea inland sea between SE Europe and Asia. Area: 436,400 sq. km/168,500 sq. mi.

black shale *n* a mudstone that contains organic carbon, e.g. an oil-bearing shale

black sheep *n* somebody regarded by the other members of a family or group as not living up to their standards and expectations [Because black wool is less valuable than white]

Blackshirt /blák shurt/ *n* a member of any European fascist movement active before and during World War II, especially a member of the Italian Fascist Party [< the party's uniform]

blacksmith /blák smith/ *n* somebody whose job is making and repairing iron and metal objects, including horseshoes [*black* applied to iron]

blacksnake /blák snayk/ *n* a dark-coloured poisonous snake that inhabits forests in E Australia. *Pseudechis porphyriacus.*

black spot *n* **1** a place where something bad exists or happens ○ *an unemployment black spot* **2** a plant disease that causes black patches to form on leaves, particularly on roses

Blackstone /blák stōn, -stən/, **Sir William** (1723–80) British jurist

Black Stone *n* the sacred stone in the Kaaba in the great mosque in Mecca, believed to have been given by God. It is reddish-black in colour.

Black Studies *n* an academic subject or curriculum taught mainly in the United States that deals with the history, culture, and literature of Black communities worldwide, often with an emphasis on African American culture (*+ singular verb*)

black swan *n* a large swan with black plumage and a red beak. Native to: Australia, New Zealand. *Cygnus atratus.*

black-tailed deer *n* a mule deer with a tail that is black on top. Native to: W North America. *Odocoileus hemionus columbianus.*

black tea *n* **1** dark-coloured tea leaves that have been fermented before being dried. ◊ **green tea 2** tea served without milk

blackthorn /blák thawrn/ *n* **1** a thorny black-stemmed bush with small blue-black berries (**sloes**). Native to: Europe, Asia. *Prunus spinosa.* **2** a walking stick made from the hard wood of the blackthorn

black tie *n* **1** a black bow tie worn on formal occasions **2** a formal style in men's dress that includes a black bow tie and a dinner jacket —**black-tie** *adj*

blacktop /blák top/ *n US, Can* **1** ROAD-SURFACING MATERIAL a road-surfacing material bound together with a tarry substance such as asphalt **2** ROAD MADE WITH BLACKTOP a road or other area with a blacktop surface ■ *vti* (**-tops, -topping, -topped**) *US, Can* COAT SURFACE WITH BLACKTOP to cover a road or other surface with blacktop

black treacle *n* FOOD = **treacle** *n.* 1

black velvet *n* an alcoholic drink consisting of stout and champagne

Black Vernacular English *n* LANG = **African American Vernacular English**

black vulture *n* **1** a large dark vulture. Native to: S Europe, W Asia. *Aegypius monachus.* **2** a common vulture with black plumage and a bald black head. Native to: North and South America. *Coragyps atratus.*

black walnut *n* **1** N AMERICAN WALNUT WOOD the hard dark wood of a North American walnut tree. Use: veneers, cabinets. **2** EDIBLE NUT the hard-shelled nut of the a North American walnut tree **3** N AMERICAN WALNUT TREE a walnut tree that yields black walnut wood and bears black walnuts. Native to: North America. *Juglans nigra.*

Black Watch *n* the Royal Highland Regiment in the British Army [Because of its dark tartan]

blackwater fever /blák wawtər-/ *n* a serious condition, developing from malaria, that causes a rapid and massive loss of red blood cells and turns the urine dark red or blackish

black widow *n* a highly poisonous spider, the female of which has a black body with an hourglass-shaped red marking on the abdomen. Native to: temperate North America and East Asia. *Latrodectus mactans.* [< the female's habit of eating her mate]

bladder /bláddər/ *n* **1** BODILY SAC FOR LIQUID OR GAS an organ or other body part for storing a liquid or gas, especially the sac that stores urine (**urinary bladder**) or the sac that stores bile (**gallbladder**) **2** INFLATABLE INNER BAG an inflatable part of something, especially a football, that resembles a bag **3** SAC IN PLANT a sac found in some plants, e.g. in bladder wrack to store air allowing the plant to float, or in bladderwort to trap insects **4** FLUID-FILLED BLISTER a blister or small sac filled with fluid [Old English *blǣdre, blæddre* < Indo-European] —**bladdery** *adj*

bladder campion *n* a wild plant with a swollen calyx. Flowers: white. Native to: Europe. *Silene vulgaris.*

bladdered /bláddərd/ *adj* extremely drunk (*slang*)

bladder fern *n* a small delicate fern that grows in rocks and walls and has a bulbous seed pod. *Cystoperis fragilis.*

bladder kelp *n* any brown alga with inflated bladders from which leaflike streamers are suspended

bladdernut /bláddər nut/ *n* **1** a small tree or shrub with clusters of small white flowers and bulbous seed pods. Genus: *Staphylea.* **2** the seed pod of a bladdernut tree

bladder worm *n* the larva of a tapeworm, shaped like a sac and armed with six hooks. Class: Cestoda.

bladderwort /bláddər wurt/ *n* an aquatic plant with floating leaves bearing small bladders that are used to trap insects. Genus: *Utricularia.*

bladder wrack *n* a brown seaweed that has bulbous air bladders on its fronds, allowing them to float. It grows between the high and low water line. *Fucus vesiculosus.*

blade /blayd/ *n* **1** CUTTING PART the flat sharp-edged cutting part of a tool or weapon **2** LONG THIN FLAT PART a long thin flat part of some tools or machines, e.g. a propeller **3** THIN LEAF a long thin leaf, especially of grass **4** FLAT STRIKING PART the flat striking part of something such as an oar or a golf club **5** RAZOR BLADE a razor blade **6** PART OF ICE SKATE the metal part of an ice skate that glides on the ice **7** PART OF TONGUE the flat upper part of the tongue just behind the tip **8** STONE FRAGMENT a parallel-sided stone flake that is at least twice as long as it is wide **9** SWORD a sword (*literary*) ○ *'And then dreams he of cutting foreign throats/ Of breaches, ambuscadoes, Spanish blades'* (William Shakespeare, *Romeo and Juliet*) **10** DASHING MAN an energetic fun-loving man (*dated informal*) ■ **blades** *npl* **1** *ANZ* SHEEP SHEARS hand-operated shears for shearing sheep **2** *US* in-line roller skates (*informal*) ■ *vi US, Can* to skate on in-line roller skates (*informal*) [Old English *blæd* < Germanic]

blag /blag/ *vt* (**blags, blagging, blagged**) (*slang*) **1** STEAL SOMETHING FROM SOMEWHERE to steal something, or rob a place, especially using an element of violence, speed, or surprise **2** to obtain something by deceit, scrounging, or cajoling ○ *He blagged his way into the party.* ■ *n* ROBBERY a theft or robbery, especially one using an element of violence, speed, or surprise (*slang*) ○ *He's done some big bank blags.* [Late 19C. < ?] —**blagger** *n* —**blagging** *n*

blah /blaa/ *n* NONSENSE talk or writing that is inane or pretentious (*informal*) ■ **blahs** *npl US* MALAISE a condition of feeling bored, restless, and listless ○ *She's got the blahs today.* ■ *vi* TALK NONSENSE to talk or write pretentious nonsense (*informal; often repeated for emphasis*) [Early 20C. An imitation of vacuous talk.]

Blair /blair/, **Tony** (*b.* 1953) British statesman and prime minister (1997–). Full name **Anthony Charles Lynton Blair**

Blairism /bláir izəm/ *n* the political policies and style of government of Tony Blair, typified by moderate and gradual social reform, financial prudence, and tight control over policy presentation

Blake /blayk/, **Peter** (*b.* 1932) British painter

Blake, Robert (1599–1657) English admiral

Blake, William (1757–1827) British poet, painter, and engraver —**Blakeian** *adj*

Blakey /bláyki/, **Art** (1919–90) US jazz musician. Full name **Arthur Blakey**

blame /blaym/ *vt* (**blames, blaming, blamed**) **1** CONSIDER SOMEBODY RESPONSIBLE to consider somebody to be responsible for something wrong or unfortunate that has happened **2** CRITICIZE to find fault with somebody (*in negative statements and questions*) ○ *I don't blame you* *for wanting to know what happened.* ■ *n* **RESPONSIBILITY** responsibility for something wrong or unfortunate that has happened ○ *It's still not clear where the blame lies.* ○ *I'm not taking the blame for your mistakes.* [12C. Via Old French *bla(s)mer* < Latin *blastemare*, alteration of *blasphemare* 'revile' (see BLASPHEME).] —**blamable** *adj* —**blameful** *adj* —**blameworthiness** —**blameworthy** *adj* ◇ **be to blame** to be responsible for something wrong or unfortunate that has happened ○ *Who's to blame for the mix-up?*

blameless /bláymləss/ *adj* **1** not responsible for something wrong or unfortunate that has happened ○ *No one involved is entirely blameless.* **2** doing nothing bad or wrong ○ *a blameless life* —**blamelessly** *adv* —**blamelessness** *n*

Blamey /bláymi/, **Sir Thomas Albert** (1884–1951) Australian soldier

blanch /blaanch/, **blench** /blench/ *v* **1** *vt* **PUT FOOD BRIEFLY IN BOILING WATER** to put food in boiling water for a few seconds in order to loosen the skin or to kill enzymes **2** *vi* **TURN PALE** to become pale suddenly **3** *vt* **WHITEN VEGETABLES BY GROWING IN DARK** to grow vegetables, especially celery and chicory, in dark conditions in order to whiten the stems and improve their flavour **4** *vti* **REMOVE OR LOSE COLOUR** to lose colour, or cause something to lose colour [14C. < French *blanchir* 'whiten' < *blanche*, feminine of *blanc* 'white'.] —**blancher** *n*

blancmange /blə maánj, -maánzh/ *n* a dessert similar to jelly made with milk, sugar, flavourings, and cornflour and eaten cold [14C. < Old French *blanc mangier* < *blanc* 'white' + *mangier* 'food' < *mangier* 'eat' (see MANGER).]

bland /bland/ *adj* **1 INSIPID** lacking flavour, character, or interest ○ *a bland diet* **2 FREE OF STRESS** free from anything annoying or upsetting **3 UNEMOTIONAL** without emotion [Mid-17C. < Latin *blandus* 'smooth, flattering'.] —**blandly** *adv* —**blandness** *n*

blandishment /blándishmənt/ *n* **1** a piece of flattery intended to persuade somebody to do something (*formal; often plural*) ○ *impervious to all blandishments* **2** the use of flattery and enticements to persuade somebody to do something [Late 16C. < archaic *blandish* < Old French *blandiss-*, stem of *blandir* < Latin *blandus* 'smooth, flattering'.]

blank /blangk/ *adj* **1 NOT MARKED** not written on, drawn on, or printed on ○ *a blank page* **2 UNBROKEN** plain and unvaried ○ *a blank wall* **3 LACKING INTEREST** having or showing no interest or awareness ○ *a blank expression* **4 UNEVENTFUL OR UNPRODUCTIVE** characterized by lack of useful action or result ○ *It was one of those blank periods when nothing particular was happening.* **5 DOWNRIGHT** complete or absolute ○ *She stared at me in blank amazement.* ■ *n* **1 SPACE IN WHICH TO WRITE** a space left blank in which to write, in a form or document ○ *Fill in the blanks.* **2 MARK INDICATING MISSING WORD** a mark (–) in writing or print indicating that a word or letter is missing ○ *a word meaning solitary, spelt a l – – e* **3 EMPTINESS OF MIND** a complete absence of awareness or memory ○ *I remember hearing a loud noise; the rest is a blank.* **4 VOID** a period about which nothing is known ○ *There are a lot of blanks in her account of the event.* **5** ARMS = **blank cartridge** **6 DOCUMENT WITH BLANK SPACES** a form or document with spaces for writing in **7 PIECE FROM WHICH ARTICLE IS MADE** a piece of metal or other material that will be shaped to produce a finished article **8 BULL'S EYE** the bull's eye of a target ■ *v* **1** *vt* **OBLITERATE** to delete or black something out ○ *The names had been blanked.* **2** *vi* **FORGET TEMPORARILY** to forget something suddenly and temporarily ○ *I tried to recall their names, but I just blanked.* **3** *vt US, Can* **PREVENT SCORING** to prevent an opponent from scoring **4** *vt* **IGNORE** to ignore or pretend not to see somebody (*informal*) [13C. < French *blanc* 'white'.] —**blankly** *adv* —**blankness** *n* ◇ **draw a blank** to be unsuccessful in a search or inquiry ◇ **fire** *or* **shoot blanks** to be unable to impregnate a woman because of a low sperm count (*slang; sometimes offensive*) ◇ **go (a) blank** to be unable to think of or remember something ○ *I tried to remember her name but my mind went blank.*

blank out *v* **1** *vt* **COVER** to cover something completely so that it cannot be seen or read **2** *vt* **ERASE FROM MIND** to refuse to remember or acknowledge a fact, event, or memory **3** *vi* **LOSE AWARENESS** to become dazed or unconscious **4** *vi* **FADE AWAY** to diminish in intensity or loudness

blank cartridge *n* a gun cartridge that contains explosive but no bullet

blank cheque *n* **1** a signed cheque that has not yet had the amount payable filled in **2** complete freedom to act or decide (*informal*) ○ *They gave us a blank cheque in our negotiations.*

blank endorsement *n* an endorsement on a bill of exchange that does not name a payee and so may benefit the bearer

blanket /blángkit/ *n* **1 LARGE PIECE OF THICK CLOTH** a piece of thick cloth used as a cover for a bed **2 COVERING LAYER** a layer of something, covering an area completely **3 LAYER AROUND CORE OF NUCLEAR REACTOR** in a nuclear reactor, a layer of material surrounding the radioactive core used to reflect neutrons or to create more fissile material ■ *adj* **APPLYING GENERALLY** applying to all areas or situations ○ *We have blanket approval for our proposals.* ■ *vt* **1 COVER WITH LAYER** to cover something with a thick layer ○ *The streets were blanketed with snow.* **2 COVER TO SUPPRESS** to cover something, especially a fire, in order to stop it or put it out ○ *Foam from the fire extinguisher quickly blanketed the flames.* **3 SUPPRESS** to prevent something from being heard or seen ○ *Background interference keeps blanketing out the recording.* **4 PREVENT WIND REACHING SAILS** to take the wind from the sails of another yacht or ship by sailing to windward of it [14C. < Old Northern French *blanquet*, Old French *blanchet* < *blanc* 'white'.]

blanket bath *n* MED = **bed bath**

blanket bog *n* a peat bog covering a wide area

blanket finish *n* a situation in which the runners in a race finish very close to one another

blanket stitch *n* looped stitching with wide gaps between stitches, used to reinforce the edge of a piece of fabric

blank verse *n* unrhymed poetry that has a regular rhythm and line length, especially iambic pentameter

blanquette /blong két, blaaN-/ *n* a dish consisting of white meat, e.g. veal, cooked in a white sauce ○ *blanquette of veal* [Mid-18C. < French, < Old N French *blanquet* (see BLANKET).]

Blantyre-Limbe /blán tīr lím bay/ largest city in Malawi, in the south of the country. Population: 446,800 (1994).

blare /blair/ (**blares, blaring, blared**) *v* **1** *vti* to make a loud harsh noise ○ *speakers blaring out rock music* **2** *vt* to proclaim something loudly ○ *'Heiress disappears', the headlines blared.* [14C. Probably an imitation of the sound.] —**blare** *n*

blarney /blaárni/ *n* unintelligent or insincere talk (*informal*) ■ *vti* (**-neys, -neying, -neyed**) to persuade somebody with flattery (*informal*) [Late 18C. After the BLARNEY STONE.]

Blarney /blaárni/ village in S Republic of Ireland. Population: 2,043 (1991).

Blarney Stone *n* a stone in Blarney Castle, near Cork in Ireland, that is said to give the power of persuasive talk to people who kiss it

blasé /blaá zay/ *adj* not impressed or worried by something, usually because of having experienced it before [Early 19C. < French, 'satiated'.]

blaspheme /blass feém, blaass-/ (**-phemes, -pheming, -phemed**) *v* **1** to swear in a way that insults religion **2** *vt* to treat God or sacred things disrespectfully through words or action [14C. Via Old French *blasfemer* < ecclesiastical Latin *blasphemare* 'revile' < Greek *blasphēmein* < *blasphēmos* 'evil-speaking'.] —**blasphemer** *n*

blasphemous /blássfəməss/ *adj* expressing or involving disrespect for God or sacred things —**blasphemously** *adv* —**blasphemousness** *n*

blasphemy /blássfəmi/ (*plural* **-mies**) *n* **1** disrespect for God or sacred things **2** something done or said that shows disrespect for God or sacred things

blast /blaast/ *n* **1 AIR OR GAS CURRENT** a sudden strong current of air or wind **2 EXPLOSION** an explosion, or a sudden rush of air caused by an explosion ○ *Several homes were destroyed by the blast.* **3 LOUD EXPLOSIVE SOUND** the sound made by an explosion ○ *We were almost deafened by the blasts.* **4 INSTRUMENT'S LOUD SOUND** a short loud sound made on an instrument, whistle, or car horn **5 OUTBURST** a loud or angry outburst ○ *a blast of criticism* ■ *v* **1** *vti* **BLOW UP WITH EXPLOSIVES** to destroy or break open something using explosives ○ *Rescuers blasted a hole in the rock.* ○ *Road crews had to blast a way through the mountains.* **2** *vti* **MAKE A LOUD NOISE** to come out with great force or volume, or make something do this (*informal*) **3** *vt* **HIT HARD** to strike something with great force (*informal*) ○ *She blasted the ball into the net* **4** *vt* **CRITICIZE** to subject somebody or something to severe criticism (*informal*) **5** *vt* **BLIGHT** to affect a plant with a withering disease (*often passive*) ■ *interj* **EXPRESSING ANNOYANCE** used to express mild annoyance (*informal*) [Old English *blǣst* < Indo-European] —**blaster** *n* ◇ **(at) full blast** at maximum volume or speed

SYNONYMS See ***criticize***.

blast away *vi* to fire a gun repeatedly (*informal*)

blast off *vti* to launch a rocket, spacecraft, or astronaut into space, or be launched into space

-blast *suffix* embryonic cell ○ *melanoblast* [< Greek *blastos* 'bud, germ, sprout'] —**-blastic** *suffix*

blasted /blaástid/ *adj, adv* used to express mild irritation (*informal*) ○ *Then the blasted handle broke.*

blastema /blas teémə/ (*plural* **-mas** *or* **-mata** /-mətə/) *n* a group of unspecialized animal cells from which an organ or new tissue develops [Mid-19C. < Greek *blastēma* 'sprout'.] —**blastemal** *adj* —**blastematic** /blástə máttik/ *adj* —**blastemic** *adj*

blast furnace *n* a vertical shaft furnace for smelting metals

blast injection *n* a method of fuel injection that uses air pressure to atomize the fuel as it enters the cylinder of an internal-combustion engine

blasto- *prefix* bud, germ ○ *blastomycete* [< Greek *blastos* 'bud, germ, sprout']

blastocoel /blástə seel/, **blastocoele** *n* the cavity that forms within the mass of cells (**blastula**) in a developing embryo and that fills with fluid [Late 19C. < BLASTO- + Greek *koilos* 'hollow'.] —**blastocoelic** /blástə seélik/ *adj*

blastocyst /blástəsist/ *n* a mammalian embryo at the stage where it is implanted in the wall of the womb —**blastocystic** /blástə sístik/ *adj*

blastoderm /blástə durm/ *n* a layer of cells arising from the repeated division of a fertilized mammalian egg that develops into an embryo [Mid-19C. < BLASTO- + Greek *derma* 'skin'.] —**blastodermatic** /blástə dur máttik/ *adj* —**blastodermic** /blástə dúrmik/ *adj*

blastodisc /blástō disk/, **blastodisk** *n* the disc-like part on the upper surface of the yolk of a fertilized egg where the embryo begins to form, as in reptiles and birds

blastoff /blaást of/ *n* a launch of a rocket, spacecraft, or missile

blastogenesis /blástə jénnəssiss/ *n* asexual reproduction by budding —**blastogenetic** /blástə jə néttik/ *adj* —**blastogenic** *adj*

blastomere /blástō meer/ *n* any one of the cells of the early animal embryo (**blastula**), formed by division of the fertilized egg cell

blastomycosis /blástō mī kṓssiss/ *n* a fungal infection causing lesions on the lungs, skin, or mucous membranes

blastopore /blástə pawr/ *n* an opening in a young embryo that develops into the anus in some mammals —**blastoporal** /blástə páwrəl/ *adj* —**blastoporic** *adj*

blastosphere /blástə sfeer/ *n* BIOL = **blastula**

blastospore /blástə spawr/ *n* a fungal spore produced by budding

blastula /blástyōōlə/ (*plural* **-las** *or* **-lae** /-lee/) *n* an embryo at an early stage of development, consisting of a hollow ball of cells [Late 19C. < modern Latin, < Greek *blastos* 'bud, germ, sprout'.] —**blastular** *adj* —**blastulation** /blástyōō láysh'n/ *n*

blat[1] /blat/ (**blats, blatting, blatted**) *vi* to make a bleating sound [Mid-19C. An imitation of the sound.]

blat[2] /blat/, **blatt** *n US* a tabloid newspaper (*slang*) [Mid-20C. < German *Blatt* 'leaf, sheet (of paper)'.]

blatant /bláyt'nt/ *adj* **1** offensively, often intentionally, obtrusive, and conspicuous ○ *blatant falsehoods* **2** excessively or offensively noisy (*literary*) [Late 16C. Perhaps alteration of Scottish *blatand* 'bleating', or < Latin *blatire* 'to babble'.] —**blatancy** *n* —**blatantly** *adv*

USAGE blatant or **flagrant**? Both words describe openly offensive behaviour, but there is a difference. ***Blatant*** emphasizes the brazen conspicuousness of the offence, as in *a blatant breach of good faith in the negotiations*, whereas ***flagrant*** emphasizes the shocking seriousness or gravity that the offence has: *flagrant racism*. A ***blatant*** lie is one so barefaced that no one can miss it, whereas ***flagrant*** disregard for human life is unforgivably shameless or outrageous. Avoid using ***blatant*** to mean merely 'obvious': *There seems to be* *a blatant contradiction.*... In sentences like this, substitute *obvious, clear,* or *glaring* for ***blatant***.

blate /blayt/ *adj Scotland* lacking in self-confidence [15C. < ?]

blather /bláthər/, **blither** /blíthər/ *vi* to talk in an unintelligent or inane manner, especially at length (*informal*) [15C. < Old Norse *blaðra* 'to chatter, babble'.] —**blather** *n* —**blatherer** *n*

blatt *n* = **blat**[2]

Blaxland /bláksland/, **Gregory** (1778–1853) British-born Australian explorer

blaxploitation /blák sploy táysh'n/ *n* depiction of Black people in films or other media in a way that appeals to people's popular and often inaccurate or negative notions of their experiences and qualities (*informal*) [Late 20C. Blend of *Blacks* + EXPLOITATION.]

blaze[1] /blayz/ *vi* (**blazes, blazing, blazed**) **1 BURN BRIGHTLY** to burn brightly and fiercely **2 SHINE** to shine or appear to shine brightly **3 EXPERIENCE STRONG EMOTION** to be affected by a strong emotion (*informal*) ○ *blazing with indignation* **4 FIRE GUN** to fire a gun repeatedly ■ *n* **1 BRIGHT FIRE** a bright flame or fire **2 CONSPICUOUS DISPLAY** a display that attracts attention ○ *a blaze of glory* [Old English *blæse* 'torch, bright flame' < Germanic]

blaze[2] /blayz/ *n* **1 WHITE MARK ON ANIMAL'S FACE** a white streak on the face of a horse or other animal **2 MARK SHOWING THE WAY** a mark indicating a path, originally a cut made in a tree trunk ■ *vt* (**blazes, blazing, blazed**) **1 MARK PATH** to indicate a new path by making marks **2 DO SOMETHING NEW** to lead the way in doing something new ○ *He blazed the way to the understanding of DNA's structure.* [Mid-17C. Perhaps < Old Norse *blesi*, Middle High German *blasse*, or Middle Low German *bles* 'white mark'.]

blaze[3] /blayz/ (**blazes, blazing, blazed**) *vt* to spread news or information loudly and clearly [14C. < Middle Dutch *blāzen* 'swell' < Indo-European.]

blazer /bláyzər/ *n* a jacket, often in the colours of, or with the badge of, a school or club [Mid-17C. < the typically bright colour.]

blazes /bláyziz/ *npl* used to add emphasis (*informal; used euphemistically*) ○ *What the blazes did you do that for?* ○ *run like blazes*

blazing /bláyzing/ *adj* **1 INTENSE** intense and impassioned ○ *a blazing row* **2 HOT** very hot ○ *sitting in the blazing sun* ■ *adv* **EXTREMELY** extremely or intensely ○ *blazing hot* —**blazingly** *adv*

blazing star *n* **1 WHITE-FLOWERED PLANT** a plant of the lily family. Flowers: white in long heads. Native to: North America. *Chamaelirium luteum.* **2 WHITE- OR PURPLE-FLOWERED PLANT** a flower of the daisy family. Flowers: white or purplish in long heads. Native to: North America. Genus: *Liatris.* **3 RED- OR PURPLE-FLOWERED PLANT** a plant with rough leaves. Flowers: red or purple. Native to: North America. Genus: *Laevicaulis.*

blazon /bláyz'n/ *vt* **1 PROCLAIM WIDELY** to announce something widely or ostentatiously **2 DEPICT COAT OF ARMS** to create or describe a coat of arms using the traditional symbols ■ *n* **COAT OF ARMS** a coat of arms, or a technical description of one [13C. < French *blason* 'shield'.] —**blazoner** *n* —**blazonment** *n*

blazonry /bláyzənri/ *n* **1 MAKING OR EXPLAINING COATS OF ARMS** the art of creating or explaining coats of arms **2 COATS OF ARMS** coats of arms individually or collectively **3 BRILLIANT DISPLAY** a bright or showy display (*literary*)

bldg *abbr* building

bleach /bleech/ *n* **1 COLOUR-REMOVING SUBSTANCE** a chemical that removes or whitens colour or staining and also cleans and disinfects **2 APPLICATION OF BLEACH** an act of using bleach on something ■ *v* **1** *vt* **USE BLEACH ON** to clean or whiten something using bleach **2** *vti* **LIGHTEN IN COLOUR** to make something whiter or lighter, or become lighter or whiter [Old English *blǣcan* 'make white' < *blǣc* 'pale, shining' < Germanic] —**bleacher** *n*

bleachers /bleéchərz/ *npl US* (*sometimes singular*) **1** seats in an uncovered area of a sports stadium **2** retractable tiered benches for spectators in a gymnasium, at a swimming pool, or in some other indoor sports arena [Late 19C. < the sun's bleaching of the exposed benches.]

bleaching powder *n* CaCl(OCl) a white powder obtained from calcium hydroxide and chlorine. Use: disinfectant, bleaching agent.

bleak /bleek/ *adj* **1 DISCOURAGING** without hope or expectation of success or improvement ○ *The company's future looks bleak.* **2 UNWELCOMING** providing little comfort or shelter ○ *a cabin on a bleak hilltop* **3 COLD AND CLOUDY** unpleasantly cold, dull, and windy ○ *bleak winter days* [14C. < Old Norse *bleikr* 'pale, white, shining' < Germanic.] —**bleakly** *adv* —**bleakness** *n*

LITERARY LINK ***Bleak House***, a novel (1852–53) by Charles Dickens. Among the strands of the complex plot are the interminable court case of Jarndyce and Jarndyce; the guilty secret of Lady Dedlock and the tragic consequences of her discovery that her illegitimate daughter, Esther Summerson, is still alive; and Esther's relationship with her kindly and devoted guardian John Jarndyce.

blear /bleer/ *vt* to make eyes misty or eyesight dim, e.g. with tears (*usually passive*) [14C. < ?]

bleary /bleéri/ (**-ier, -iest**) *adj* **1** not seeing clearly owing to mistiness or blurring, especially that associated with sleepiness ○ *a bleary gaze* **2** obscured and not easy to see —**blearily** *adv* —**bleariness** *n*

bleary-eyed *adj* seeing unclearly, especially because of sleepiness or drunkenness

Bleasdale /bleéz dayl/, **Alan** (*b.* 1946) British dramatist

bleat /bleet/ *v* **1** *vi* to make the wavering cry of a sheep, goat, or calf **2** *vti* to complain about something in an irritating way (*informal*) [Old English *blǣtan* < Germanic, an imitation of the sound] —**bleat** *n* —**bleater** *n*

bleb /bleb/ *n* **1** a small blister on the skin **2** a small bubble, e.g. in glass [Early 17C. Alteration of BLOB.] —**blebby** *adj*

bleed /bleed/ *v* (**bleeds, bleeding, bled** /bled/, **bled**) **1** *vi* **LOSE BLOOD** to lose blood from the body, through a wound or because of illness ○ *The wound was bleeding heavily.* **2** *vt* **TAKE BLOOD FROM** to take blood from a person or animal, especially in order to treat a disease **3** *vi* **FEEL SORROW** to feel sadness or pity ○ *My heart bleeds for her in her loss.* **4** *vi* **EXUDE SAP** to exude sap from a plant's wound **5** *vt* **TAKE MONEY OR RESOURCES FROM** to use up large amounts of money or resources from an individual or organization, especially dishonestly (*informal*) ○ *bleeding public funds* **6** *vt* **DRAW OFF LIQUID OR GAS** to draw liquid or gas out of a container or pressurized system ○ *bleed a radiator* **7** *vi* **RELEASE COLOUR** to release colour when wet or being washed (*refers to fabrics*) **8** *vti* **OVERRUN PAGE** to print something, or be printed, so that part of something is cut off by the edge of the page **9** *vti* **MAKE COLOURS OF ILLUSTRATION RUN** to print something, or be printed, so that colours run into other colours or over the edge of an illustration ■ *n* **1 SOMETHING THAT OVERRUNS PRINTED PAGE** an illustration or piece of text printed in such a way that part of it is cut off the page **2 INSTANCE OF BLEEDING** an instance of losing blood [Old English *blēdan* < Germanic]

bleeder /bleédər/ *n* **1** an offensive term for somebody who is disliked (*slang*) **2** a blood vessel that is bleeding during surgery and requires clamping or other measures to stop it

bleeder resistor *n* a resistor connected across the terminals of a power supply to regulate its output voltage or to discharge capacitors

bleeding /bleéding/ *adj, adv* used for emphasis, as a milder form of 'bloody' (*slang*)

bleeding heart *n* **1** a garden plant with arching stems. Flowers: pink, red, white, heart-shaped. Genus: *Dicentra.* **2** somebody regarded as naively kind or sympathetic, especially towards left-wing or liberal causes (*disapproving*)

bleed valve *n* a valve that can be opened to let liquid or gas out of a tank or pressurized system

bleep /bleep/ *n* **1 ELECTRONIC SOUND** a short high-pitched electronic noise, intended as a signal and repeated intermittently **2** = **pager** ■ *v* **1** *vi* **MAKE ELECTRONIC SOUND** to make a short high-pitched electronic noise **2** *vt* **CALL ON BLEEPER** to call somebody by sending a signal to a portable electronic receiver **3 bleep** *vt US* BROADCAST = **bleep out** [Mid-20C. An imitation of the sound.]

bleep out *vt* to remove an offensive word from a broadcast, and replace it with a short high-pitched electronic sound. US term **bleep** *v.* **3**

bleeper /bleépər/ *n* TELECOM = **pager**

blemish /blémmish/ *n* **1 SPOILING MARK OR FLAW** a mark or imperfection that spoils the appearance of something ○ *a cream that hides skin blemishes* **2 SPOILING FAULT** something that spoils a person's reputation or good record ■ *vt* **MAR** to spoil the appearance or reputation of something [14C. < Old French *ble(s)miss-* 'make pale, injure'.] —**blemisher** *n*

SYNONYMS See ***flaw***.

blench[1] /blench/ *vi* to move back or away in fear [Old English *blencan* 'deceive, cheat' < ?] —**blencher** *n*

blench[2] *vi* = **blanch**

blend /blend/ *v* **1** *vti* **MIX INGREDIENTS** to mix different substances together so that they do not readily separate ○ *blend the butter and sugar together* **2** *vt* **CREATE PRODUCT BY MIXING INGREDIENTS** to create food or drinks by mixing different types of ingredients (*often passive*) **3** *vti* **INTERMINGLE** to mix with other people or things without being conspicuous, or mix something in this way ○ *blend fact and fiction* **4** *vti* **MAKE PLEASING COMBINATION** to combine things or qualities to create a pleasing effect, or be combined in this way ○ *instruments blending harmoniously* **5** *vi* **SHADE IMPERCEPTIBLY INTO EACH OTHER** to shade from one colour to another without obvious transitions and boundaries ■ *n* **1 MIXTURE** a mixture or combination ○ *an interesting blend of traditional styles and modern materials* **2 FOOD OR DRINK MIXTURE** a food or type of drink created by mixing different types of ingredient ○ *an expensive coffee blend* **3 WORD MADE BY JOINING TWO WORDS** a new word made by joining parts of other words [14C. Probably < Old Norse *blend-* 'to mix'.]

SYNONYMS See ***mixture***.

blend in *vi* **1** to have personal qualities that suit a situation well ○ *He's a likable boy who blends in well.* **2** to be difficult to see or distinguish from similar things around

blende /blend/ *n* **1** MINERALS = **sphalerite** **2** a metallic sulphide ore [Late 17C. < German *blenden* 'deceive'.]

blender /bléndər/ *n* **1** an electrical kitchen appliance used to liquidize and blend foods **2** somebody or something that blends things, especially a person or company that blends foods or drinks

Blenheim[1] /blénnim/ *n* a dog belonging to a breed of spaniel with reddish markings [< *Blenheim* Palace in Oxfordshire]

Blenheim[2] /blénnim/ **1** wine-producing borough in the Wairau Valley in the South Island of New Zealand. Population: 26,500 (1998 estimate). **2** site of the Battle of Blenheim in 1704, where a British army defeated French and Bavarian troops in the War of the Spanish Succession. It is near the present-day village of Blindheim, SW Germany.

blenny /blénni/ (*plural* **-nies** *or* **-ny**) *n* a small scaleless long-bodied fish found in rocky coastal areas and coral reefs. Family: Blenniidae. [Mid-18C. < Latin *blennius* < Greek *blennos* 'slime', from the fish's covering of mucus.]

blephar- *prefix* = **blepharo-**

blepharitis /bléffə rítiss/ *n* inflammation of one or both eyelids [Mid-19C. < Greek *blepharon* 'eyelid'.]

blepharo- *prefix* **1** eyelid ○ *blepharospasm* **2** cilium, flagella ○ *blepharoplast* [< Greek *blepharon* 'eyelid']

Blériot /blérri ō/, **Louis** (1872–1936) French aviator

blesbok /bléss bok/ (*plural* **-boks** *or* **-bok**) *n* a reddish-brown antelope that has a white streak on its nose. Native to: southern Africa. *Damaliscus dorcas.* [Early 19C. < Afrikaans, < Dutch *bles* 'white facial streak' + *bok* 'buck'.]

bless /bless/ (**blesses, blessing, blessed, blest** /blest/) *vt* **1 MAKE HOLY** to bestow holiness on somebody or something in a religious ceremony ○ *The bishop blessed the new chapel.* **2 PROTECT** to watch over somebody or something protectively ○ *We prayed for God to bless our marriage.* **3 WISH WELL** to declare approval and support for somebody or something ○ *The governor has blessed the new scheme.* **4 CONFER PERSONAL BENEFIT ON** to give somebody a desirable quality or talent (*usually passive*) ○ *blessed with brains as well as good looks* **5 THANK** to express heart-felt thanks to somebody (*often expressing a wish*) ○ *Bless you for speaking up for my child!* [Old English *blētsian* < Germanic] —**blesser** *n*

blessed /bléssid/ *adj* **1 HOLY** made holy **2 BEATIFIED** declared holy by the pope, usually as the first stage towards being declared a saint **3 BESTOWING JOY** bringing happiness or good luck ○ *The rain has brought farmers blessed relief from the long drought.* ■ *adj, adv* **USED FOR EMPHASIS** used to add emphasis in an expression of annoyance (*informal*) ○ *She wouldn't say a blessed thing about it.* —**blessedly** *adv* —**blessedness** *n*

Blessed Sacrament *n* in various Christian churches, the bread and wine that has been blessed for use in Holy Communion

blessing /bléssing/ *n* **1** GOD'S HELP help from God or another deity **2** RELIGIOUS ACT a ceremony in which an ordained person invokes or bestows divine help **3** PRAYER BEFORE MEAL a prayer of thanks before a meal **4** EXPRESSION OF APPROVAL approval or good wishes **5** SOMETHING FORTUNATE something to be glad or relieved about ○ *It's a blessing that we had time to fix all the mistakes in the original version.*

blest past participle of **bless**

blether /bléthər/ *vi, n UK* = **blather** ■ *n Scotland* somebody who talks nonsense

blew **1** past tense of **blow**[1] **2** past tense of **blow**[3]

blewits /blóo its/ (*plural* **-wits**) *n* an edible fungus with a brown cap and a bluish stem. Genus: *Lepista*. (*takes a singular verb*) [Early 19C. Probably < *blue*, from the colour of its stem.]

blight /blīt/ *n* **1** DESTRUCTIVE FORCE something that spoils or damages things severely **2** RUINED STATE a severely spoiled or ruined state, especially of an urban area ○ *urban blight* **3** PLANT DISEASE a plant disease, caused by bacteria, fungi, or viruses, in which symptoms range from brownish blotches on the foliage to withering of the entire plant without rotting **4** PLANT SCI = **potato blight** **5** CAUSE OF BLIGHT IN PLANTS a bacterium, fungus, or virus that causes blight in plants ■ *vt* **1** RUIN to spoil or damage something severely ○ *a football career blighted by injury* **2** AFFECT PLANT WITH BLIGHT to cause a plant to wither without rotting [Mid-16C. < ?]

blighter /blītər/ *n* **1** somebody or something considered a source of annoyance (*dated informal insult*) **2** somebody who is envied or sympathized with (*dated informal*) ○ *poor little blighter* ○ *lucky blighter*

Blighty /blīti/, **blighty** *n UK* England or Britain (*dated humorous slang*) [Early 20C. < Hindi *bilāyatī* 'foreign, European', originally used by British soldiers in India for 'home'.]

blimey /blīmi/ *interj* used to express amazement or shock (*informal*) ○ *Blimey, that's expensive!* [Late 19C. Alteration of *blind me!* or *blame me!*]

blimp[1] /blimp/ *n* a nonrigid airship especially one used as a barrage balloon or for observation during World War II [Early 20C. < ?]

blimp[2] /blimp/, **Colonel Blimp** *n* a person, typically a middle-aged military officer, who is pompous and very conservative (*humorous*) [Mid-20C. After a cartoon character invented by David Low (1891–1963).]

blin /blin/ plural of **blini** [Late 19C. < Russian.]

blind /blīnd/ *adj* **1** UNABLE TO SEE unable to see, permanently or temporarily **2** UNABLE TO RECOGNIZE unwilling or unable to understand something ○ *blind to the consequences* **3** UNCONTROLLABLE so extreme and uncontrollable as to make somebody behave irrationally ○ *blind rage* ○ *blind fear* **4** UNQUESTIONING not based on fact and usually total and unquestioning ○ *blind prejudice* **5** UNAWARE lacking awareness ○ *a blind stupor* **6** NOT GIVING A CLEAR VIEW not giving a clear view and possibly dangerous ○ *a blind corner* **7** MADE ON UNDERSIDE OF FABRIC hidden from sight on the underside of a fabric **8** WITHOUT DOORS OR WINDOWS without doors, windows, or openings **9** CLOSED AT ONE END closed off at one end ○ *a blind unused tunnel* **10** DONE WITHOUT LOOKING done without looking or while unable to see ○ *blind taste tests* **11** DONE UNPREPARED done without preparation or the relevant information ○ *a blind presentation* **12** WITH INFORMATION CONCEALED FOR UNPREJUDICED RESULT describes scientific experiments or similar evaluations in which information is withheld in order to obtain an unprejudiced result **13** WITHOUT A GROWING POINT describes a plant in which growth stops because the growing point is damaged ■ *adv* **1** WITHOUT PRIOR EXAMINATION OR PREPARATION without previously thinking about or preparing for something ○ *You shouldn't buy livestock blind.* **2** USING INSTRUMENTS using information from aircraft instruments, without being able to see **3** TOTALLY totally or utterly (*informal*) ○ *an unscrupulous lawyer who robbed his clients blind* ■ *vt* **1** MAKE PERMANENTLY BLIND to make somebody permanently unable to see **2** MAKE TEMPORARILY BLIND to make somebody temporarily unable to see ○ *blinded by the lights* **3** MAKE UNABLE TO JUDGE PROPERLY to make somebody unable to judge or act rationally ○ *blinded by rage* **4** CONFUSE to make it difficult for somebody to understand something ○ *Stop trying to blind us with statistics.* ■ *n* **1** WINDOW COVERING a device that is pulled down to shut out the light from a window **2** COVER OR SUBTERFUGE something that is intended to conceal the true nature of somebody's activities **3** *US* FIELD SPORTS = **hide**[1] *n.* [Old English, < Indo-European, 'confusion, obscurity'] —**blindly** *adv* —**blindness** *n*

blind alley *n* **1** a narrow alley or passage that is closed off at one end **2** something that produces no worthwhile results

blind date *n* **1** a date arranged between people who have not seen or met each other before **2** somebody whom you meet on a blind date

blinder /blīndər/ *n* **1** something outstanding, especially a performance in a sport (*informal*) **2** a bout of excessive drinking (*slang*) ■ **blinders** *npl US, Can* HORSERACING = **blinker** *npl.* 1

blindfold /blīnd fōld/ *n* BANDAGE TIED OVER EYES a piece of cloth tied over the eyes to prevent the wearer from seeing ■ *vt* **1** PUT BANDAGE ON EYES to prevent somebody from seeing by putting a bandage or other material over the person's eyes **2** PREVENT FROM UNDERSTANDING to prevent somebody from understanding clearly ■ *adj* WEARING A BLINDFOLD wearing a blindfold ■ *adv* **1** WHILE BLINDFOLDED wearing a blindfold or being unable to see for some other reason **2** UNPREPARED without consideration or relevant information ○ *had to field their queries blindfold* [Early 16C. By folk etymology (from FOLD[1]) < past tense of obsolete *blindfell* 'make unable to see'.]

Blind Freddie /-fréddi/ *n Aus* an offensive term for a hypothetical person who represents incompetence and lack of intelligence

blind gut *n* ANAT = **caecum**

blinding /blīnding/ *adj* **1** IMPAIRING VISION causing inability to see, especially temporarily, by being bright ○ *a blinding flash of light* **2** OUTSTANDING outstanding or extraordinary (*informal*) ■ *n* BASE LAYER OF CONCRETE a thin layer of concrete used to seal a surface before more concrete is added —**blindingly** *adv*

blind man's buff *n* a children's game in which one player is blindfolded and has to catch and identify other players by touch [*Buff* shortening of BUFFET[2] 'stroke with the hand']

blind side *n* **1** the area that is out of your field of vision ○ *The cyclist came up on my blind side.* **2** in rugby, the side of a scrum opposite the main line of the backs belonging to the opposing team. ◊ **open side**

blind-side, blindside /blīnd sīd/ *vt US* **1** to attack somebody suddenly and physically by hitting the person on a side where his or her peripheral vision is obstructed **2** to take somebody unawares suddenly, with detrimental results

blind snake *n* a small tropical nonvenomous snake with scales over its eyes, adapted for burrowing and eating small soil invertebrates. Families: Typhlopidae and Anomalepididae.

blind spot *n* **1** ANAT = **optic disc** **2** AREA OF IGNORANCE a subject that somebody is ignorant about ○ *have a blind spot for maths* **3** DIRECTION IN WHICH VISION IS OBSCURED an area or direction, especially on a road, in which somebody's vision is obscured **4** ACOUSTICALLY UNSATISFACTORY AREA an area in an auditorium where things cannot be clearly heard **5** PLACE WITH POOR RADIO RECEPTION an area within the normal range of a radio transmitter where reception is poor

blind stamping *n* PUBL = **book tooling**

blindworm /blīnd wurm/ *n* ZOOL = **slowworm** [15C. < the animal's small eyes.]

blini /blínni, bléeni/ (*plural* **blinis** *or* **blin** *or* **blini**) *n* a small pancake made with yeast and buckwheat flour, traditional in Russia and other parts of Eastern Europe [Late 20C. < Russian *bliný*, plural of *blin*.]

blink /blingk/ *v* **1** *vti* CLOSE AND REOPEN EYES to close and reopen both eyes rapidly **2** *vti* LOOK WHILE BLINKING to look at somebody or something while blinking **3** *vt* HIDE OR REMOVE BY BLINKING to open and shut the eyes rapidly to remove something from them ○ *He blinked away his tears.* **4** *vti* FLASH to flash on and off, especially as a signal **5** *vi US* WAVER to waver or lose your nerve ○ *After a ten-week strike, it was the management that finally blinked.* ■ *n* **1** ACT OF BLINKING EYES a rapid closing and reopening of both eyes **2** *Scotland* QUICK LOOK a quick look or glance **3** METEOROL = **iceblink, snowblink** [13C. Partly variant of BLENCH[1], partly < Middle Dutch *blinken* 'glitter'.] ◇ **on the blink** not working properly (*informal*) ○ *The television's on the blink.*

blinker /blíngkər/ *n* FLASHING LIGHT a light that flashes in order to give a message or warning, especially on a motor vehicle ■ **blinkers** *npl* **1** EYE COVERS FOR HORSE a pair of flaps attached to a horse's bridle, one beside each eye, to keep the horse from looking anywhere but straight ahead. US term **blinder** *npl.* **2** OBSTRUCTION TO JUDGMENT a mental attitude that prevents somebody from considering a situation rationally ■ *vt* **1** FIT HORSE WITH BLINKERS to put blinkers on a horse **2** HINDER SOMEBODY'S JUDGMENT to prevent somebody from considering a situation rationally —**blinkered** *adj* —**blinkeredness** *n*

blinking /blíngking/ *adj* used to add force to an insult or an expression of annoyance (*slang*) ○ *I don't want the blinking thing!* —**blinking** *adv*

blip /blip/ *n* **1** SPOT ON DISPLAY SCREEN a spot of light, often accompanied by a high-pitched sound, indicating the position of something on a screen ○ *The submarine shows up as a series of faint blips on the screen.* **2** = **bleep** *n.* 1 **3** SUDDEN DEVIATION a sudden temporary problem in the normal progress of something ■ *vi* (**blips, blipping, blipped**) MAKE A BLIP to produce a blip [Late 19C. An imitation of the sound.]

bliss /bliss/ *n* **1** perfect untroubled happiness ○ *It was bliss to have a day at home.* **2** a state of spiritual joy [Old English, alteration of *blīps* < Germanic, 'gentle, kind']

Bliss /bliss/, **Sir Arthur** (1891–1975) British composer

blissful /blíssf'l/ *adj* **1** characterized by perfect happiness ○ *a look of blissful contentment* **2** serenely happy because of being unaware of something ○ *blissful ignorance* —**blissfully** *adv* —**blissfulness** *n*

blister /blístər/ *n* **1** PAINFUL SWELLING a painful swelling on the skin containing fluid (**serum**) **2** PLANT DISEASE a swelling in a leaf or other plant part indicating disease **3** BUBBLE ON PAINT a bubble containing liquid or air on paintwork or rubber **4** AIRCRAFT DOME a rounded, usually transparent dome on the fuselage of an aircraft, used for observation **5** *NZ* SHARP REBUKE a sharp and stinging rebuke (*slang*) ■ *vti* FORM BLISTERS to be raised in a blister or blisters, or to cause blisters to form [14C. < ?] —**blistery** *adj*

blister beetle *n* a soft-bodied beetle that secretes for its own defence a substance that raises burning blisters on the skin of vertebrates. Family: Meloidae.

blistering /blístəring/ *adj* **1** extremely hot **2** extremely scornful or critical ○ *a blistering attack on the government's failures* —**blisteringly** *adv*

blister pack *n* a packet in which small items are contained in raised domes of plastic

BLit /bée lít/ *n, abbr* Bachelor of Literature [Latin *Baccalaureus Litterarum*]

blithe /blīth/ *adj* **1** happy, cheerful, and carefree (*literary*) **2** casually indifferent ○ *with a blithe disregard for anyone's feelings* [Old English *blīþe* < Germanic, 'gentle, kind'] —**blithely** *adv* —**blitheness** *n*

blither *vi* = **blather** (*informal*)

blithering /blíthəring/ *adj* used to express annoyance and contempt for somebody or something (*informal*)

blithe spirit *n* somebody whose characteristic mood is one of carefree happiness

BLitt /bée lít/ *n, abbr* Bachelor of Literature [Latin *Baccalaureus Litterarum*]

blitz /blits/ *n* **1** SUSTAINED AERIAL ATTACK a heavy air raid intended to obliterate a target **2** MIL = **blitzkrieg** **3** CONCERTED EFFORT a concentrated effort to get something done (*informal*) **4** CHARGE ON PASSER in American football, a direct attack on the passer, by one or more players who usually stay behind the line of scrimmage, to try to prevent a pass ■ *v* **1** *vt* DESTROY BY AERIAL BOMBING to attack or destroy something by bombardment from the air **2** *vt* DEAL WITH ENERGETICALLY to concentrate a lot of effort on something to get it done (*informal*) **3** *vt* TRY TO OVERWHELM to subject somebody to an overwhelming amount of something, often in order to force him or her into agreement or submission (*informal*) ○ *blitzed with a stream of facts* **4** *vti* CHARGE PASSER in American football, to charge the passer in order to prevent a pass [Mid-20C. Shortening of BLITZKRIEG.]

Blitz /blits/ *n* the intensive bombing of British cities by the German Air Force between 1940 and 1941

blitzkrieg /blíts kreeg/ *n* a swift military offensive using ground and air forces [Mid-20C. < German, 'lightning war'.]

Blixen /blíks'n/, **Karen, Baroness** (1885–1962) Danish writer. Born **Karen Christence Dinesen**. Pseudonym **Isak Dinesen**

~~blizard~~ incorrect spelling of **blizzard**

blizzard /blízzərd/ *n* a severe snowstorm with strong winds and poor visibility [Early 19C. < ?]

blk *abbr* **1** block **2** bulk

BLL *abbr* Bachelor of Laws [Latin *Baccalaureus Legum*]

bloat /blōt/ *vti* **1 SWELL** to become swollen or inflated, or to make something do this **2 EXCESSIVELY EXPAND** to increase excessively or to make something do this ■ *n* **1** *US* **EXCESSIVE INCREASE** an excessive amount or excessive increase in something ○ *corporate bloat* **2 CATTLE DISEASE** a disease affecting cattle and sheep, characterized by excessive gas in the main stomach compartment (**rumen**) [Early 17C. Probably < Old Norse *blautr* 'soft, wet'.]

bloated /blṓtid/ *adj* **1 SWOLLEN** swollen with liquid, air, or gas **2 OVERFULL AFTER OVEREATING** overfull after eating too much **3 TOO LARGE** excessively large (*disapproving*) ○ *a bloated expense account* —**bloatedness** *n*

bloater /blṓtər/ *n* **1** a large herring that has been soaked in brine and smoked **2** a common freshwater whitefish native to the Great Lakes of North America. *Coregonus hoyi*. [Mid-19C. < obsolete *bloat herring* < ?]

⚡**bloatware** /blṓt wair/ *n* a computer program with many, often superfluous features that take up so much memory that the computer's performance is impaired (*informal*) [Late 20C. After SOFTWARE.]

blob /blob/ *n* **1 SOFT MASS** a soft lump or drop of something such as paint or glue **2 SMALL SPOT OF COLOUR** a small rounded spot of colour **3 INDISTINCT FORM** an indistinct or shapeless form or object ■ *vt* (**blobs, blobbing, blobbed**) **PUT BLOBS ON** to apply blobs of colour or a soft substance to something [15C. < ?]

bloc /blok/ *n* a group of countries with a shared aim ○ *former Eastern bloc countries* [Early 20C. < French (see BLOCK).]

SPELLCHECK See ***block***.

Bloch /blok/, **Ernest** (1880–1959) Swiss-born US composer

⚡**block** /blok/ *n* **1 SOLID LUMP** a large solid piece of a hard substance, usually with flat sides **2 BUILDING UNIT** a large flat-sided piece of hard material such as stone or wood, used in building **3** GAMES = **building block** *n*. **2** **4 CHOPPING BASE** a large piece of wood used for chopping things on **5 PLACE FOR BEHEADING PEOPLE** a large piece of wood or stone on which people were beheaded in former times **6 AUCTIONEER'S PLATFORM** a stand on which articles in an auction are displayed **7 PRINTING DEVICE** a piece of wood, metal, or stone with a design engraved on it used for printing **8** SPORTS = **starting block** **9 PAD OF PAPER** a pad of writing or drawing paper **10 LARGE BUILDING** a building divided into offices or flats **11 SPECIAL-PURPOSE BUILDING** a building or part of a building designed for a particular purpose ○ *the new science block* **12 GROUP OF BUILDINGS** a group of buildings in a town or city bounded on each side by a street ○ *I'm just taking the dog for a walk round the block.* **13** *US* **DISTANCE** the distance between two parallel streets ○ *They live only three blocks from here.* **14** *US* **STREET SECTION** the section of a street between two parallel streets ○ *The post office is in the middle of the next block.* **15 LAND AREA** an area of land marked for division or development **16** *ANZ* **LARGE AREA OF SETTLED LAND** an extensive area of land used for a particular purpose, e.g. housing or farming **17** *NZ* **AREA OF BUSH RESERVED BY HUNTER** an area of bushland reserved for an individual trapper or hunter **18 UNBROKEN EXPANSE OR AREA** a uniform expanse of something such as colour **19 SET OF SIMILAR ITEMS** a set of similar items sold as a unit ○ *a block of tickets* **20 GROUP OF POSTAGE STAMPS** a group of four or more postage stamps forming a rectangle **21 LENGTH OF TRACK** a length of railway track on which only one train is permitted at a time **22 UNIT OF DATA** in computing, a set of contiguous data that performs some action as a unit ○ *a block of text* **23** POL = **bloc** **24 OBSTRUCTION** something that obstructs or prevents progress **25 OBSTRUCTION OF PLAY** an act of deliberately preventing a ball or another player from moving forward **26 DEFENSIVE STROKE** in cricket, a defensive stroke made by a batsman, intended only to stop the ball **27 OBSTRUCTION OF PHYSIOLOGICAL FUNCTION** an interruption of the normal functioning of an organ of the body **28 DISRUPTION OF PSYCHOLOGICAL PROCESSES** an inability to begin or continue a psychological process, often attributed to emotional stress **29** MECH ENG = **cylinder block** **30 BATSMAN'S MARK ON CREASE** in cricket, a mark made by a batsman near the popping crease to indicate the position of his bat in relation to the wicket ■ *v* **1** *vt* **OBSTRUCT** to prevent or hinder movement through, into, or out of something ○ *The drains are blocked with leaves.* ○ *He stood in front of me, blocking my way.* **2** *vt* **HINDER SOMEBODY'S OR SOMETHING'S MOVEMENT OR PROGRESS** to prevent something from moving or developing ○ *Her appointment was blocked by the managing director* **3** *vt* **OBSTRUCT SIGHT OF** to obstruct somebody's line of sight **4** *vti* **OBSTRUCT PLAYER OR BALL** to prevent a ball or another player from moving forward **5** *vti* **OBSTRUCT PLAYER** in American football, to prevent a defensive player from interfering with movement towards the goal **6** *vti* **PREVENT NORMAL FUNCTIONING** to prevent the normal functioning of a physiological process ○ *a blocked tear duct* **7** *vti* **FAIL TO REMEMBER** to fail to remember something or to have a psychological block ○ *block a memory* **8** *vt* **MAKE INTO BLOCK** to shape something into a block **9** *vt* **SUPPORT WITH BLOCK** to support or strengthen something using a block **10** *vt* **SHAPE ON BLOCK** to mould something with or on a block **11** *vt* **STAMP USING BLOCK** to stamp a surface with a title or using an engraved block **12** *vti* **REHEARSE BASIC MOVEMENTS FOR SCENE** to plan and rehearse the basic movements and positions for the actors in a scene [14C. Via Old French *bloc* < Middle Dutch *blok* 'tree trunk'.] ◇ **knock somebody's block off** to punch somebody in the head (*slang*) ◇ **on the block** *US* for sale at an auction

SPELLCHECK Do not confuse ***block*** with ***bloc***, which has a similar sound. Beware: your spellchecker will not catch this error.

SYNONYMS See ***hinder***.

block in *vt* **1** to prevent somebody or something moving from a place by being, or placing something, in the way **2** to fill in the blank spaces on an outline design with colour

block off *vt* **1** to put up or form a barrier in order to prevent anybody or anything entering ○ *Police blocked off the street.* **2** to put up or form a barrier that prevents something from being seen

block out *vt* **1 PUT OUT OF MIND** to prevent a disturbing thought from entering the mind **2 DESCRIBE WITHOUT DETAIL** to describe something in a general fashion, without great detail ○ *block out a proposal* **3 COVER PART OF NEGATIVE** to cover part of a negative or stencil when printing from it to prevent that part appearing

block up *vti* to prevent movement through something by filling all the space in, or to become completely obstructed

blockade /blo káyd/ *n* **1 PREVENTION OF ACCESS** an organized action to prevent people or goods entering or leaving a place **2 FORCES FORMING BLOCKADE** the ships or forces used to maintain a blockade **3 OBSTACLE OR OBSTRUCTION** something that prevents access to a place ■ *vt* (**-ades, -ading, -aded**) **1 SUBJECT PLACE TO BLOCKADE** to impose a blockade on a place **2 BLOCK ACCESS TO PLACE** to obstruct access to a place [Late 17C. Perhaps after AMBUSCADE.] —**blockader** *n*

blockage /blókij/ *n* **1** something that obstructs movement through a pipe or channel ○ *a blockage in an artery* **2** the act of blocking something

block and tackle (*plural* **blocks and tackles**) *n* a system of two pulley blocks, each with at least one pulley with rope or cable threaded through them, used for hoisting or hauling

blockboard /blók bawrd/ *n* a plywood composed of soft wood squares or strips between outer layers of veneer

block booking *n* a booking of a large number of tickets for the same event or show

blockbuster /blók bustər/ *n* (*informal*) **1** something such as a book, play, or film that is either very large or achieves enormous commercial success **2** *US* somebody who persuades people to sell their houses by instilling fear of declining property values

blockbusting /blók busting/ *n* *US* the practice of persuading homeowners to sell low for fear of declining property values (*informal*) ■ *adj* sensational and enormously successful commercially ○ *a blockbusting novel*

block capital *n* a plain capital letter that is not joined to other letters ○ *Fill in the form in block capitals.*

block diagram *n* a diagram in which the essential parts of a system or process are represented by labelled rectangles

blocker /blókər/ *n* **1** a drug that prevents a physiological function **2** in American football, an offensive player who tries to keep the defence from reaching the ball, kicker, or passer

block grant *n* money from the government granted to local authorities to spend on local services

blockhead /blók hed/ *n* a person regarded as very unintelligent (*insult*)

blockhouse /blók howss/ *n* **1** a small military building with apertures to fire through, used as part of a defensive system or an observation post **2** a fort of former times in America constructed from heavy wooden beams

block letter *n* **1** = **block capital** **2** a compressed sans serif typeface or individual letter

block party (*plural* **block parties**) *n* *US* a party for all the people who live on the same block or street

block plane *n* a small carpenter's plane with the blade at a low pitch, used to cut across the grain of the wood

block printing *n* printing from hand-carved or engraved blocks

block vote *n* a single vote by a representative, typically of a trade union, on behalf of the members of his or her organization, weighted according to the number of members

blocky /blóki/ (**-ier, -iest**) *adj* three-dimensional, boxy in shape, and seemingly solid

Bloemfontein /blo͝om fon tayn/ capital of Free State Province, central South Africa. Population: 126,867 (1991).

⚡**blog** /blog/ *n* a weblog (*slang*) ■ *vi* (**blogs, blogging, blogged**) to create or run a weblog (*slang*) [Contraction]

⚡**blogger** /bloggər/ *n* somebody who creates or runs a weblog

Blois /blwaa/ capital of Loir-et-Cher Department, north-central France. Population: 49,171 (1999).

bloke /blōk/ *n* a man (*informal*) [Mid-19C. < Shelta.]

blokeish /blṓkish/, **blokish** *adj* relating to the stereotypical character, behaviour, or interests of men, especially when they are in all-male company (*informal*) —**blokeishness** *n*

blond /blond/, **blonde** *adj* **1 FAIR** yellowish or golden in colour **2 FAIR-HAIRED AND LIGHT-SKINNED** with fair hair and a light-coloured skin **3 LIGHT COLOURED** light-coloured, ranging from yellowish brown to greyish yellow ○ *blond wood* ■ *n* **FAIR-HAIRED PERSON** a person with blond hair [15C. Via French < medieval Latin *blundus* 'yellow'.] —**blondness** *n*

USAGE blond or **blonde**? When describing the colour of somebody's hair, ***blond*** is normally used of a person of either sex: *Jane has blond hair.* When used as a noun or adjective to describe somebody directly, ***blond*** is often used of a man or boy and ***blonde*** of a woman or girl: *He is blond. Jane is blonde/is a blonde.*

Blondin /bloN dáN/, **Charles** (1824–97) French acrobat

blood /blud/ *n* **1 RED FLUID CIRCULATING IN BODY** the red fluid that is pumped from the heart and circulates around the bodies of humans and other vertebrates **2 BODY FLUID OF INVERTEBRATES** a liquid found in invertebrates, with functions similar to those of vertebrate blood **3 BLOODSHED** bloodshed or killing **4 VITAL LIFE FORCE** blood considered as a vital life force **5 FAMILY OR KINSHIP** family background or descent from a particular ancestor, especially when viewed as determining a person's character or appearance **6 PURE BREEDING** pure breeding in animals, especially horses **7 MEMBERS OF GROUP** people considered for their potential to strengthen and improve an organization (*informal*) **8 YOUNG MAN** a fashionable and wealthy young man, especially in the 18th and 19th centuries (*informal humorous*) ■ *vt* **1 INITIATE TROOPS IN BATTLE** to subject troops to their first experience of battle **2 LET DOG TASTE BLOOD** to give a dog its first taste of the blood of a freshly killed animal in order to make it keen to hunt **3 SMEAR FACE WITH BLOOD** to smear somebody's face with the blood of a hunted animal as an initiation into hunting [Old English *blōd* < Germanic] ◇ **be out for** *or* **after somebody's blood** to be intending to punish somebody ◇ **blood is thicker than water** family ties and loyalties take precedence over other relationships ◇ **have blood on your hands** to be responsible for somebody's death ◇ **in cold blood** deliberately, and in a way that shows a complete lack of emotion ○ *was murdered in cold blood* ◇ **make somebody's blood boil** to make somebody extremely angry ◇ **make somebody's blood run cold** to frighten or horrify somebody ◇ **spill blood** to wound or kill people ◇ **sweat blood** to make a great effort

blood-and-thunder *adj* full of melodramatic adventure and action (*informal*)

blood bank *n* **1** a place where blood or blood plasma is stored for transfusion **2** the blood or blood plasma stored in a blood bank

bloodbath /blúd baath/ (*plural* **-baths** /-baathz/) *n* a battle or fight characterized by mass killing

blood brother *n* either one of two men or boys who have sworn mutual loyalty and friendship

blood clot *n* a thick mass of coagulated blood

blood count *n* **1** a counting of the number of red and white blood cells and platelets in a given volume of blood **2** the actual number of cells and platelets found in a blood count

bloodcurdling /blúd kurd'ling/, **blood-curdling** *adj* arousing extreme fear ○ *bloodcurdling screams*

blood donor *n* somebody who gives blood for use in transfusions

blood doping *n* the practice of reinjecting an athlete with his or her own red blood cells shortly before a competition in order to enhance performance. The practice is illegal in most organized competitions.

blooded /blúddid/ *adj* belonging to a superior breed ○ *blooded mares*

blood feud *n* a long-lasting feud between families or clans involving murder

bloodfin /blúd fin/ *n* a small red-finned freshwater fish often kept in aquariums. Native to: Argentina. *Aphyocharax rubripinnis.*

blood fluke *n* a parasitic flatworm found in human blood that relies on two hosts, humans and some types of snails, to complete its life cycle. Native to: tropical Asia and Africa. Genus: *Schistosoma.*

blood group *n* any class into which human blood is divided for transfusion purposes according to the presence or absence of genetically determined antigens that determine its immunological compatibility

bloodhound /blúd hownd/ *n* **1** a large powerful dog with drooping ears, sagging jowls, and a keen sense of smell, formerly used for tracking **2** a detective who is relentless in pursuing people or things (*informal*)

bloodless /blúdləss/ *adj* **1 WITHOUT KILLING OR VIOLENCE** conducted without killing or great violence ○ *a bloodless coup* **2 PALE AND ANAEMIC** pale and anaemic-looking **3 LACKING LIVELINESS** dull and lacking liveliness ○ *a bloodless performance* **4 LACKING EMOTION** cold and lacking in human emotion ○ *bloodless statistics* **5 LACKING BLOOD** lacking blood or the expected amount of blood — **bloodlessly** *adv* —**bloodlessness** *n*

Bloodless Revolution *n* = **Glorious Revolution**

bloodletting /blúd leting/ *n* **1 REMOVAL OF BLOOD FROM BODY** the removal of blood, usually by making an incision in a vein, for therapeutic purposes. ◊ **phlebotomy 2 BITTER QUARRELLING** bitter violent fighting between rival groups **3** *US* **EJECTION OF PEOPLE** the large-scale ejection, or laying off, of human resources in a corporation (*formal*) ○ *corporate bloodletting in which a number of senior managers were let go* —**bloodletter** *n*

bloodline /blúd līn/ *n* a direct line of descent from a particular human or animal ancestor, especially with respect to the common characteristics shared by that ancestor's descendants

blood lust *n* a strong desire for killing or violence

blood money *n* **1 COMPENSATION PAID FOR KILLING** in some cultures, compensation paid to the relatives of somebody who has been killed or murdered **2 FEE FOR HIRED KILLER** the fee paid to a hired killer or to somebody who reveals where the victim of a murder is to be found **3 REWARD FOR FINDING KILLER** the reward paid to somebody for giving information about a criminal, especially a murderer

blood orange *n* an orange that has deep red flesh

blood plasma *n* ANAT = **plasma** *n.* **1**, **plasma** *n.* **2**

blood poisoning *n* infection of the blood, generally caused either by the presence in the blood of microorganisms (**septicaemia**) or of toxins produced by body cells (**toxaemia**)

blood pressure *n* the pressure exerted by the blood against the walls of blood vessels

blood red *n* a deep vivid red colour —**blood red** *adj*

blood relation, blood relative *n* a person who is related to another person by birth rather than marriage

bloodroot /blúd root/ (*plural* **-roots** *or* **-root**) *n* a plant that has poisonous, deep red sap in its roots. Native to: E North America. *Sanguinaria canadensis.*

blood sausage *n* *US, Can* = **black pudding**

blood serum *n* MED = **serum** *n.* **1**

bloodshed /blúd shed/ *n* activity resulting in killings or injuries

bloodshot /blúd shot/ *adj* inflamed and red as a result of the widening of small blood vessels in the white of the eye ○ *bloodshot eyes*

blood sport *n* a sport in which animals are killed. Hunting and bullfighting are blood sports.

bloodstain /blúd stayn/ *n* a dark stain left by dried blood —**bloodstained** *adj*

bloodstock /blúd stok/ *n* thoroughbred horses, especially when bred and sold for horseracing

bloodstone /blúd stōn/ *n* a deep green variety of chalcedony with small red spots or streaks of red jasper. Use: gems.

bloodstream /blúd streem/ *n* the flow of blood circulating through the blood vessels of a person or animal

bloodsucker /blúd sukər/ *n* **1** a parasite that sucks blood from its host, e.g. a leech or mosquito **2** somebody who exploits somebody else, especially by extortion (*informal disapproving*) —**bloodsucking** *n, adj*

blood sugar *n* the concentration of glucose in the blood

blood test *n* a scientific analysis of a sample of blood

bloodthirsty /blúd thursti/ (**bloodthirstier, bloodthirstiest**) *adj* **1** eager to take part in or witness violence and bloodshed **2** full of intentional violence or killing —**bloodthirstily** *adv* —**bloodthirstiness** *n*

blood type *n* MED = **blood group**

blood vessel *n* any of the arteries, veins, or capillaries through which blood flows

bloody /blúddi/ *adj* (**-ier, -iest**) **1 BLOODSTAINED** covered or smeared with blood ○ *Her hands were bloody and shaking.* **2 RELATING TO BLOOD** resembling or containing blood **3 INVOLVING MUCH BLOODSHED** involving a great deal of killing and bloodshed **4 SWEARWORD** used as a swearword or to add emphasis (*slang; sometimes offensive*) **5 UNFAIR AND INCONSIDERATE** very unfair and inconsiderate (*dated informal*) ■ *adv* **SWEARWORD** used as a swearword or to add emphasis (*slang; sometimes offensive*) ■ *vt* (**-ies, -ying, -ied**) **STAIN WITH BLOOD** to stain or smear something with blood —**bloodily** *adv* —**bloodiness** *n* ◇ **bloody well** used to show anger or irritation when contradicting something (*slang*)

bloody mary (*plural* **bloody marys**), **Bloody Mary** *n* a cocktail consisting of vodka, tomato juice, and other spices

bloody-minded *adj* intentionally uncooperative and obstructive (*informal*) —**bloody-mindedly** *adv* —**bloody-mindedness** *n*

bloom[1] /bloom/ *n* **1 FLOWER** a flower, especially on a plant cultivated chiefly for its flowers **2 MASS OF FLOWERS** the mass of flowers on a single plant **3 FLOWERING** the state of being in flower ○ *roses in full bloom* **4 PRIME** the condition of greatest freshness or health (*literary*) ○ *in the bloom of youth* **5 HEALTHY APPEARANCE OR COMPLEXION** a fresh, youthful, healthy complexion **6 WHITE COATING ON LEAVES OR FRUIT** a thin white coating on the leaves of some plants and on fruits **7 WHITE POWDER ON COINS** a fine white powder sometimes found on newly minted coins **8 COATING ON CHOCOLATE** a mottled white coating on chocolate, usually caused by incorrect temperature during storage **9** ECOL = **algal bloom** ■ *vi* **1 COME INTO FLOWER** to open into flower ○ *The roses bloomed early this year.* **2 PRODUCE PLANTS** to produce abundant plant life, especially unexpectedly ○ *make the desert bloom* **3 PROSPER OR FLOURISH** to reach the fullest stage of development or maturity (*literary*) **4 APPEAR HEALTHY** to appear healthy and vigorous (*literary*) **5** *US* **APPEAR SUDDENLY** to appear suddenly, usually in a cloud ○ *A cloud of smoke bloomed under the rocket.* **6 BECOME COVERED WITH ALGAE** to become discoloured on the surface because of an excessive growth of algae or phytoplankton (*refers to bodies of water*) [13C. < Old Norse *blóm* < Indo-European.] —**bloomy** *adj*

bloom[2] /bloom/ *n* a bar of steel or wrought iron hammered or rolled from an ingot ■ *vt* to convert an ingot of iron or steel into a bloom [Old English *blóma* < ?]

bloomer /blóomər/ *n* **1** a flowering plant, especially considered with respect to the time of its flowering ○ *an early bloomer* **2** a mildly embarrassing mistake (*informal humorous*) [Mid-18C. 'Mistake' shortening and alteration of *blooming error.*]

Bloomer /blóomər/, **Amelia** (1818–94) US feminist and reformer

bloomers /blóomərz/ *npl* (*dated*) **1** baggy knickers for women or girls, especially garments that reach down to just above the knee **2** long loose trousers gathered at the ankle and formerly worn by women and girls under a shorter skirt [Mid-19C. After Amelia BLOOMER.]

blooming /blóoming/ *adj* flourishing and in exceptionally good health or condition ■ *adj, adv* used as a euphemistic alternative for 'bloody' (*dated informal*) ○ *a blooming nuisance* ○ *not blooming likely*

Bloomsbury Group /blóomzbəri-/ *n* a group of artists and writers who congregated in Bloomsbury in London after World War I

bloop /bloop/ *vt* to hit a baseball just over the infield ■ *n* BASEBALL = **blooper** *n.* **2** [Early 20C. An imitation of the sound.]

blooper /blóopər/ *n* **1** *US, Can* **EMBARRASSING MISTAKE** a mildly embarrassing mistake (*informal humorous*) **2 HIT** a hit just beyond the infield in baseball **3 BASEBALL PITCH** a lobbed underhand pitch in baseball

blossom /blóssəm/ *n* **1 MASS OF FLOWERS ON TREE** a mass of flowers appearing on a tree or bush **2 SINGLE FLOWER** a single flower **3 FLOWERING** the state of flowering ○ *cherry trees in blossom* ■ *vi* **1 COME INTO FLOWER** to open into flower **2 DEVELOP WELL** to develop in a pleasing or promising way **3 blossom, blossom out STOP BEING SHY** to stop being shy and reserved [Old English *blōstm* < Indo-European] — **blossomy** *adj*

blot[1] /blot/ *n* **1 STAIN** a stain or spot caused by a drop of liquid **2 EYESORE** something ugly that spoils the appearance of something ○ *a blot on the landscape* **3 BLEMISH** something that spoils somebody or something's good name or reputation ■ *v* (**blots, blotting, blotted**) **1** *vti* **CREATE BLOT** to make a blot on paper **2** *vt* **BRING DISREPUTE** to bring dishonour on somebody's reputation **3** *vt* **DRY WITH ABSORBENT MATERIAL** to soak up liquid from the surface of something using absorbent material [14C. Probably < N Germanic.]

blot out *vt* **1** to cover something so that it can no longer be seen **2** to remove something painful from the mind

blot[2] /blot/ *n* in backgammon, a piece placed alone on a point and therefore exposed to capture by the opposing player [Late 16C. Probably < Dutch *bloot* 'exposed, naked'.]

blotch /bloch/ *n* **1 SPOT OR MARK** an irregularly shaped spot or mark **2 BLEMISH ON SKIN** a reddish patch on the skin ■ *vti* **MARK WITH BLOTCHES** to mark or become marked with blotches [Early 17C. Blend of BLOT[1] + BOTCH.] —**blotchily** *adv* —**blotchiness** *n* —**blotchy** *adj*

blotter /blóttər/ *n* **1** a sheet of blotting paper that absorbs ink or water **2** *US* a book used for recording daily events and transactions ○ *a police blotter*

blotter acid *n* blotting paper soaked with LSD, designed to be an easy way of taking single doses

blotting paper *n* soft paper used for soaking up ink from paper

blotto /blóttō/ *adj* extremely inebriated (*slang*) [Early 20C. < BLOT[1].]

blouse /blowz/ (*plural* **blouses**) *n* **1 WOMAN'S SHIRT** a woman's loose-fitting shirt **2 ETHNIC SMOCK** a loose-fitting shirt or smock, often part of traditional costume **3 CADET'S OR SOLDIER'S TUNIC** a tunic, sometimes loose and sometimes very snug, that is a part of some military uniforms [Early 19C. < French.]

blouson /blóo zon/ *n* **1** a woman's garment resembling a shirt that is gathered at the waist **2** a short jacket that fits closely at the waist and becomes looser over the upper body [Early 20C. < French.]

blow[1] /blō/ *v* (**blows, blowing, blew** /bloo/, **blown** /blōn/) **1** *vi* **BE MOVING AS AIR** be in motion as an air current ○ *It blew all night.* **2** *vti* **MOVE WITH AIR CURRENT** to move something with an air current, especially air exhaled through the mouth ○ *I blew the dust off the shelf.* **3** *vti* **EXHALE** to expel a stream of air from the mouth ○ *She blew on her soup* **4** *vt* **MAKE BY BLOWING** to make bubbles or smoke rings by expelling a stream of air from the mouth **5** *vt* **CLEAR NOSE** to clear the nose by forcing air through it **6** *vt* **SHAPE HOT GLASS** to give shape to molten glass by forcing air into it **7** *vti* **SOUND BY BLOWING** to make a sound from a musical instrument by blowing air into it **8** *vt* **SEND A KISS** to send somebody a symbolic kiss by kissing your hand and then blowing across it **9** *vi* **EXPEL MOIST AIR** to expel moist air from the lungs up through the blowhole (*refers to whales, dolphins, and other cetaceans*) **10** *vi* **BREATHE HARD** to breathe hard or pant through exertion **11** *vt* **EXHAUST HORSE** to cause a horse to breathe hard through overexertion **12** *vti* **DESTROY OR MOVE BY EXPLOSION** to destroy or displace something or somebody violently ○ *The blast blew the roof off.* **13** *vt* **OPEN BY FORCE** to break open something that is firmly shut using explosives **14** *vti* **PUNCTURE** to cause or experience a puncture (*informal*) **15** *vti* **CAUSE FUSE TO BURN OUT** to burn out and break an electrical circuit ○ *The toaster blew when I plugged it in.* **16** *vti* **BREAK BECAUSE OF PRESSURE** to be ruptured or cause something to rupture under excess pressure **17** *vt* **MISS AN OPPORTUNITY** to fail to take advantage of an opportunity (*slang*) **18** *vt* **WASTE MONEY** to spend money wastefully (*slang*) ○ *blew a bundle of dough on fast cars* **19** *vt US* **ENTERTAIN LAVISHLY** to treat or entertain somebody lavishly (*informal*) ○ *The company blew us to a massive dinner.* **20** *vt* **EXPOSE** to expose something secret (*slang*) ○ *blew his cover* **21** *vt* **DISREGARD** to disregard something as trivial (*dated informal; usually a command*) ○ *Blow the expense!* **22** *vti US* **LEAVE SUDDENLY** to leave a place suddenly (*slang*) ○ *When the cops arrived, the thieves blew.* **23** *vti* **PLAY MUSIC INFORMALLY** to play music, especially informally or with other musicians (*slang*) **24** *vt US* **INHALE DRUG** to inhale a drug (*slang*) **25** *vt* **OFFENSIVE TERM** an offensive term meaning to fellate (*slang*) **26** *vt* **CAPTURE PIECE IN DRAUGHTS** to capture a piece in draughts ■ *interj* **blow, blow it EXPRESSING ANNOYANCE** used to express annoyance (*informal*) ■ *n* **1 ACT OF BLOWING** an act of blowing **2 STRONG WIND** a strong wind (*informal*) **3 SHORT WALK** a short walk in order to get some fresh air (*informal*) ○ *We went for a blow along the cliffs.* **4 JAM SESSION** a jam session (*slang*) **5** *US, ANZ* **BOAST** an act of boasting (*informal*) **6 CANNABIS** cannabis (*slang*) **7** *US* **COCAINE** the drug cocaine (*slang*) **8** *ANZ* **SHEAR STROKE** a stroke of the shears in sheep-shearing [Old English *blāwan* < Indo-European] ◇ **blow it** to spoil your chances of success (*slang*)

blow away *vt* (*slang*) **1 KILL** to shoot somebody dead **2** *US* **DEFEAT DECISIVELY** to subject somebody to an overwhelming defeat **3** *US* **OVERWHELM** to affect somebody emotionally ○ *an epic movie that just blew me away*

blow in *vi* **1** to arrive or enter a place in a casual way (*slang*) ○ *blew in at midnight from Toronto* **2** to start producing oil (*refers to oil wells*)

blow off *v* **1** *vti* **RELEASE GAS** to release a gas or liquid under pressure. ◊ **blow out 2** *vi* **FART** to noisily release stomach gases through the anus (*slang*) **3** *vt US* **FAIL TO MEET** to disregard an obligation to meet somebody (*slang*) ○ *Lee blew me off, so I'm free for lunch.*

blow out *v* **1** *vti* **EXTINGUISH** to extinguish a flame with a blast of air or wind **2** *vr* **DIE DOWN** to return to a state of calm after a storm (*refers to storms and winds*) **3** *vi* **PUNCTURE** to puncture suddenly and at speed (*refers to tyres*) **4** *vi* **EMIT UNCONTROLLABLY** to release oil or gas explosively (*refers to gas or oil wells*) **5** *vi* **OVERINDULGE** to overindulge in food or drink (*informal*) **6** *vt* **CANCEL MEETING** to cancel a meeting or a performance (*slang*)

blow over *vi* **1** to become less violent (*refers to storms*) **2** to no longer excite strong feelings (*informal*) ○ *It was quite a scandal but it all blew over.*

blow up *v* **1** *vti* **DESTROY BY EXPLOSION** to destroy something or kill somebody by causing an explosion, or to be destroyed in this way **2** *vti* **INFLATE** to blow air into something so that it becomes swollen, or to swell as a result of being filled with air **3** *vt* **ENLARGE IMAGE** to enlarge a photograph **4** *vi* **BECOME ANGRY** to lose your temper suddenly (*informal*) **5** *vi* **BEGIN TO BLOW** to begin to develop or gather force (*refers to winds or storms*) **6** *vi* **ARISE OR COME ABOUT** to develop, often unexpectedly, into something more serious **7** *vt* **EXAGGERATE** exaggerate the value or importance of something (*informal*) ○ *This affair has been blown up out of all proportion.*

blow[2] /blō/ *n* **1 HARD HIT** a hard hit with a fist or weapon ○ *a nasty blow on the head* **2 ACTION HELPING CAUSE** an important action that helps a cause or belief ○ *They struck an important blow for civil rights.* **3 SETBACK** a sudden setback ○ *a blow to his confidence* [15C. < ?]

blow[3] /blō/ (**blows, blowing, blew** /bloo/, **blown** /blōn/) *vti* to blossom, or cause something to blossom [Old English *blōwan* < Germanic]

Blow /blō/, **John** (1649–1708) English composer

blowback /blṓ bak/ *n* **1 REARWARD FLOW OF GASES** the reverse flow of gases in a system, e.g., through the carburettor of an internal-combustion engine during the compression cycle **2 FIREARM POWER RESIDUE** the powdery residue that is released or ejected upon firing bullets or shells from a weapon **3 REACTION** a reaction or effect resulting from an action or cause, usually a negative reaction (*informal*) ○ *The blowback from the press revelations was terrific.*

blow-by-blow *adj* describing something in great detail ○ *a blow-by-blow account*

blow-dry *vt* to dry and style hair using a hairdryer ■ *n* a hairstyle produced by blow-drying

blower /blṓ ər/ *n* **1 BLOWING MACHINE** a machine that produces a current of air or gas ○ *a leaf blower* **2 LOW-PRESSURE COMPRESSOR** an air compressor that produces air at low pressure **3 THE TELEPHONE** the telephone (*dated informal*)

blowfish /blṓ fish/ (*plural* **-fish** *or* **-fishes**) *n* FISH = **puffer** *n.* 2

blowfly /blṓ flī/ (*plural* **-flies**) *n* a large fly such as a bluebottle that lays its eggs in rotting meat, in dung, or in open wounds. Family: Calliphoridae. [Early 19C. < BLOW[1] 'deposit eggs'.]

blowgun /blṓ gun/ *n US* ARMS = **blowpipe** *n.* 1

blowhard /blṓ haard/ *n US* somebody who boasts but is considered ineffectual

blowhole /blṓ hōl/ *n* **1 NOSTRIL OF WHALE OR SIMILAR MAMMAL** a nostril in the top of the head of a whale, dolphin, or similar sea mammal **2 BREATHING HOLE IN ICE** a hole in ice where aquatic mammals come to the surface to breathe **3 AIR VENT** a vent to permit the escape of air or gas from a tunnel or passage **4** *NZ* **VOLCANIC VENT** a vent or hole in the ground in a volcanic or thermal area through which gas or steam is forced out

blowie /blṓ i/ *n Aus* a blowfly (*informal*) [Mid-20C. Shortening.]

blow-in *n ANZ* somebody who has just arrived, especially a stranger (*informal*)

blow job *n* an offensive term for the act of fellatio (*slang*)

blowlamp *n* CONSTR = **blowtorch**

blown past participle of **blow**[1]

blowoff /blṓ of/, **blow-off** *n* **1** a discharge of surplus gas or fluid under pressure **2** a device through which surplus gas or liquid under pressure is released

blowout /blṓ owt/ *n* **1 TYRE PUNCTURE** a sudden puncture of a tyre **2 FAILURE OF FUSE** a sudden burning of a fuse, caused by an electrical overload **3 GUSH OF OIL OR GAS** a sudden rush of oil or gas from an oil well to the surface **4** = **flameout 5 BIG PARTY** a big party with ample food and drink (*slang*)

blowpipe /blṓ pīp/ *n* **1 TUBE FOR SHOOTING DARTS** a long narrow tube through which darts or pellets are shot by blowing. US term **blowgun 2 TUBE FOR CONCENTRATING HEAT** a small tube that leads a jet of air into a flame to increase its heat **3 GLASSBLOWER'S TUBE** a long narrow iron tube used in glassblowing to shape molten glass

blowsy *adj* = **blowzy**

blowtorch /blṓ tawrch/, **blowlamp** /blṓ lamp/ *n* a small, usually portable, gas burner that intensifies the heat of its flame by a blast of air or oxygen. = **blowlamp**

blowup /blṓ up/, **blow-up** *n* **1 PHOTOGRAPHIC ENLARGEMENT** an enlargement of a photograph or picture **2 OUTBURST OF TEMPER** a sudden outburst of temper (*informal*) **3 EXPLOSION** an explosion caused by a bomb or similar device

blowy /blṓ i/ (**-ier, -iest**) *adj* windy or breezy (*informal*)

blowzy /blówzi/ (**-zier, -ziest**), **blowsy** (**-sier, -siest**) *adj* **1** with a reddish face and coarse complexion (*disapproving*) **2** slovenly and careless in appearance [Early 17C. < obsolete *blowze* 'wench'.] —**blowzily** *adv* —**blowziness** *n*

BLT (*plural* **BLTs** *or* **BLT's**) *n* a sandwich with a filling of bacon, lettuce, and tomato

blubber /blúbbər/ *v* (*informal*) **1** *vi* **SOB LOUDLY** to sob in a loud and unattractive manner **2** *vt* **SAY WHILE SOBBING** to say something while sobbing ■ *n* **1 FAT OF MARINE MAMMALS** the insulating fat of whales and other large sea mammals, used as a source of oil and food **2 UNSIGHTLY FAT** unsightly body fat (*informal; sometimes offensive*) [14C. < ?] —**blubberer** *n* —**blubbery** *adj*

bludge /bluj/ *v* (**bludges, bludging, bludged**) *ANZ* (*informal*) **1** *vi* **LIVE OFF OTHERS** to live off somebody else's earnings or on state benefits **2** *vi* **AVOID WORK** to avoid work and shirk responsibilities **3** *vti* **BEG** to beg something from somebody ■ *n ANZ* **EASY TASK** an easy task (*informal*) [Early 20C. Back-formation < *bludger*, contraction of *bludgeoner*.] —**bludger** *n*

bludgeon /blújjən/ *n* **SHORT CLUB** a short stout club used as a weapon ■ *vt* **1 HIT WITH HEAVY OBJECT** to hit somebody repeatedly with a heavy object ○ *bludgeoned to death* **2 COERCE OR BULLY** to coerce or bully somebody into doing something [Mid-18C. < ?] —**bludgeoner** *n*

blue /bloo/ *adj* (**bluer, bluest**) **1 OF THE COLOUR OF THE SKY** having or resembling the colour of the sky on a cloudless day **2 SLIGHTLY PURPLE IN SKIN COLOUR** with the skin appearing slightly purple because of cold, bruising, or exertion **3 BLUEISH** describes animals and plants that are blueish or blue-grey in colour ○ *a blue whale* ○ *a blue spruce* **4 GLOOMY** gloomy or melancholy (*informal*) ○ *feeling blue* ○ *a blue day* **5 EXPLICIT** depicting or referring to sex in an explicit or offensive way (*informal*) **6 CONSERVATIVE** holding or supporting right-wing views ■ *n* **1 COLOUR OF THE SKY** the colour of the sky on a cloudless day. Blue is one of the three primary colours of light and pigment. **2 BLUE PIGMENT** a blue dye or pigment **3 THE DISTANCE** the far distance (*informal*) ○ *disappeared off into the blue* **4 blue, Blue OXBRIDGE ATHLETE** an athlete who has represented Oxford or Cambridge University in a match between the two universities, winning the right to wear the university's blue colours **5 BLUE RING ON TARGET** the blue ring on the target in archery **6 BLUE BALL IN SNOOKER** the blue ball in snooker and similar games **7 blue, Blue** *US* **MEMBER OF UNION ARMY** a member of the Union Army in the American Civil War **8** *ANZ* **FIGHT** a fight or quarrel (*slang*) **9** *ANZ* **MISTAKE** a mistake or error (*informal*) **10 blue, Blue** *ANZ* **RED-HAIRED PERSON** somebody with red hair (*informal*) **11 BLUE BUTTERFLY** a common blue small-winged butterfly. Subfamily: Plebeiinae. ■ *v* (**blues, blueing** *or* **bluing, blued**) **1** *vti* **MAKE OR BECOME BLUE** to make something blue, or become blue **2** *vt* **TREAT WITH BLUING** to treat something with bluing **3** *vt* **SQUANDER MONEY** to spend money wastefully (*dated informal disapproving*) [13C. < Old French *bleu* < Indo-European.] —**blueness** *n* ◇ **out of the blue** unexpectedly ○ *The offer came out of the blue.*

blue baby *n* a baby born with a bluish skin colour (**cyanosis**) as a result of a congenital heart defect that causes the mixing of venous and arterial blood

bluebeard /bloō beerd/, **Bluebeard** *n* a man who marries and then kills successive wives [Early 19C. After *Blue Beard*, translation of French *Barbe Bleue*, character in a story by Charles Perrault (1628–1703).]

bluebell /bloō bel/ *n* **1** a woodland plant of the lily family with long thin leaves. Flowers: small, blue, bell-shaped. Native to: Europe. Genus: *Endymion*. **2** PLANTS = **harebell 3** *US* a plant of the borage family. Flowers: blue. Native to: E North America. Genus: *Mertenia*.

blueberry /bloōbəri/ (*plural* **-ries**) *n* **1** a blueish-black edible berry **2** a cultivated fruit bush that bears blueberries. Native to: North America. Genus: *Vaccinium*.

bluebill /bloō bil/ *n* **1** *US* BIRDS = **scaup 2** any African waxbill with a heavy metallic-blue bill. Genus: *Spermophaga*.

bluebird /bloō burd/ *n* **1** a thrush that has bright blue plumage with a bluish or reddish-brown breast. Native to: North America. Genus: *Sialia*. **2** any bird with blue feathers

blue-black *adj* black tinged with blue or with a blue sheen —**blue-black** *n*

blue blood, blueblood /bloō blud/ *n* **1** the quality of being royal or aristocratic by birth **2** an aristocrat, or a noble, or a person born into a respectable and very wealthy family —**blue-blooded** *adj*

bluebonnet /bloō bonit/ *n* **1** a wide round flat cap of blue wool, formerly worn in Scotland **2** a low-growing lupin. Flowers: light blue, in spikes. Native to: Texas. *Lupinus texensis* and *Lupinus subcarnosus*.

blue book *n* **1** a real or imaginary book listing names and details of socially prominent people (*informal*) **2** an official government report bound in a blue cover, especially one published by the British or Canadian government

bluebottle /bloō bott'l/ *n* **1 LARGE BUZZING FLY** a large buzzing blowfly with an iridescent blue body that lays its eggs in decaying plant and animal material. Genus: *Calliphora*. **2 BLUE-FLOWERED PLANT** a blue-flowered plant, especially a cornflower or grape hyacinth **3** *ANZ* **PORTUGUESE MAN-OF-WAR** a Portuguese man-of-war (*informal*)

blue cheese *n* any whitish cheese with veins of blue mould

blue chip *n* **1 VALUABLE STOCK IN RELIABLE COMPANY** a stock selling for a high price because it belongs to a company that is considered to be well-established, highly successful, and reliable **2 VALUABLE ASSET OR COMPANY** an extremely valuable asset, especially a well-established, reliable, and successful company **3 POKER CHIP** a blue-coloured gambling chip of high value —**blue-chip** *adj*

blue-chipper *n US* a blue-chip company

blue cod *n* **1** a sea fish related to perches that is a popular food in New Zealand. *Parapercis colias.* **2** the flesh of a blue cod used as food

blue-collar *adj* relating to or belonging to workers who do manual or industrial work, and who often require work clothes or protective clothing —**blue-collar** *n*

blue devil *n US* a capsule containing the barbiturate amylobarbitone (*slang*)

blue duck *n* a grey-blue mountain duck. Native to: New Zealand. *Hymenolaimus malacorhynchos.*

Blue Ensign *n* a blue flag with a Union Jack at the top inner corner, flown by auxiliary vessels of the Royal Navy and by some yacht clubs

blue-eyed boy *n* somebody who is the favourite of another person or group (*informal*) US term **fair-haired boy**

bluefin /blóo fin/, **bluefin tuna** *n* a large tuna found in temperate seas that is caught for sport and food. *Thunnus thynnus.*

bluefish /blóo fish/ (*plural* **-fish** *or* **-fishes**) *n* **1** a bluish fish with a silver underside, caught for sport and food in temperate and tropical regions of the Atlantic and Indian oceans. *Pomatomus saltatrix.* **2** any fish with bluish colouring

blue fox *n* **1** an Arctic fox with a tawny-brown coat that turns pale blue-grey in winter. *Alopex lagopus.* **2** the fur of a blue fox

bluegill /blóo gil/ (*plural* **-gills** *or* **-gill**) *n* a freshwater sunfish common in eastern and central North America. *Lepomis macrochirus.*

bluegrass /blóo graass/ *n* **1** a style of country music from the S United States, usually played on fiddle, banjo, guitar, and mandolin and featuring close harmony and instrumental solos (*often before nouns*) **2** a blue-green grass. Native to: North America, Europe. Use: fodder, lawns. Genus: *Poa.*

blue-green algae *npl* BIOL = **cyanobacteria**

blue ground *n* unweathered kimberlite rock lying beneath an oxidized yellow surface layer

blue gum *n* a tall eucalyptus tree with aromatic leaves and smooth blue-grey bark. Use: medicinal oil, timber. Native to: Australia. *Eucalyptus globulus.*

blue heeler *n Aus* **1** a dog with a blue-speckled coat, belonging to an Australian breed used for controlling cattle (*informal*) **2** a police officer (*slang*) [< the dog's practice of urging cattle on by biting their heels]

blueing *n* = **bluing**

blueish *adj* = **bluish**

blue jay *n* a bird with blue plumage, a crested head, and a white underside. Native to: North America. *Cyanocitta cristata.*

blue jeans *npl US* a pair of jeans made of blue denim

blue john *n* a blue or purple form of the mineral fluorspar found only in Derbyshire

blue law *n* **1** in the United States, a law regulating moral conduct, e.g. a law prohibiting the sale of alcohol on Sundays **2** a law intended to govern moral conduct in colonial New England [*Blue* in the US sense of 'puritanical']

blue line *n* either of two blue lines that divide an ice hockey rink into the defensive, neutral, and offensive zones

Blue Mantle *n* one of the four lowest-ranked heraldic officers of the British College of Arms

blue moon *n* **1** a long period of time (*informal*) ○ *once in a blue moon* **2** a second full moon in a calendar month

Blue Mountains plateau region in E New South Wales, Australia, part of the Great Dividing Range. Highest peak: Bird Rock, 1,134 m/3,871 ft.

blue murder *n* a noisy protest (*informal*) ○ *screaming blue murder*

Blue Nile river in Ethiopia and Sudan that joins the White Nile to form the Nile at Khartoum. Length: 1,370 km/850 mi.

bluenose /blóo nōz/ *n* **1** *US* somebody excessively concerned with morals (*dated informal*) **2** *Can* somebody from Nova Scotia (*informal*)

blue note *n* a musical note played or sung slightly lower than usual, especially in blues and jazz

blue pages *npl* in the United States and Canada, the section of the telephone book that contains listings of government agencies and departments [Because usually printed on blue paper]

blue-pencil (**blue-pencils, blue-pencilling, blue-pencilled**) *vt* to edit a piece of writing by marking it, in order to shorten, censor, or delete it [< the use of a blue pencil in the editing process]

Blue Peter *n* a blue flag with a white square in the middle, used by ships to signal that they are ready to sail [because the pattern on the flag represents P in the International Code of Symbols]

blue-plate *adj US* describes a main course offered by a restaurant at a lower price than usual ○ *We had the blue-plate special.*

blueprint /blóo print/ *n* **1 PRINT OF PLAN** a photographic print of a technical drawing with white lines printed on a blue background, usually used as a reference before and during the building process **2 PLAN OR GUIDE** a plan of action or guide to doing something ○ *His administration's policies became a blueprint for those that followed.* ■ *vt* **1 MAKE BLUEPRINT OF** to make a blueprint of something, especially a technical drawing **2 MAKE PLAN FOR** to make or be a plan for something

blue racer *n* a blue-green subspecies of the blacksnake. Native to: central United States. *Coluber constrictor flaviventris.*

blue riband *n* the highest distinction or first prize in a particular field. US term **blue ribbon** *n.* 2 —**blue-riband** *adj*

blue ribbon *n* **1** an emblem or badge made of blue ribbon and awarded for first prize in a competition **2** *US* = **blue riband 3** a badge made of blue ribbon, worn by members of the Order of the Garter —**blue-ribbon** *adj*

Blue Ridge, Blue Ridge Mountains mountain range in N Georgia, W North Carolina, and W Virginia, the easternmost range of the Appalachian Mountains. Highest peak: Mount Mitchell 2,037 m/6,684 ft.

blues /blooz/ *n* (*plural* **blues**) a song or instrumental piece of music in the style of a type of popular music that developed from African American folk songs in the early 20th century, consisting mainly of slow sad songs often performed over a repeating harmonic pattern (+ *singular or plural verb*) ■ *npl* a feeling of unhappiness or low spirits (*informal*) [Mid-18C. < BLUE DEVILS.]

Blues /blooz/ *npl* the Royal Horse Guards

blue shark *n* a shark that has a dark blue back and white underside and lives in tropical and temperate seas. *Prionace glauca.*

blueshift /blóo shift/ *n* a displacement in the wavelengths of spectral lines towards the blue end of the visible spectrum, indicating that the radiation source and observer are approaching each other. ◊ **Doppler effect, red shift**

blue-sky *adj* (*informal*) **1** purely theoretical and having no concrete goal **2** idealistic or visionary and not practical —**blue-sky** *vi*

bluesman /blóozmən/ (*plural* **-men** /-mən/) *n* somebody who plays or sings the blues

bluestocking /blóo stoking/ *n* an offensive term for a woman who is considered highly educated or has scholarly or literary interests

bluestone /blóo stōn/ *n* **1** a blue-grey sandstone. Use: building, paving. **2** the blue mineral form of copper sulphate

blue streak *n* a fast-moving person or thing (*informal humorous*) ◇ **talk a blue streak** *US* to talk very quickly and without pausing (*informal*)

bluesy /blóozi/ (**bluesier, bluesiest**) *adj* composed or performed in or like the style of the blues (*informal*) ○ *a bluesy ballad*

bluet /blóo it/ *n* a plant of the madder family. Flowers: small, pale blue to white, four-petalled, with yellow centres. Native to: North America. Genus: *Hedyotis.* [Early 18C. < French *bl(e)uet* 'small blue' < *bleu* 'blue'.]

bluetit /blóo tit/ (*plural* **-tits** *or* **-tit**) *n* a small bird of the tit family that has a blue cap, blue in its wings and tail, and a yellow breast. Native to: Europe. *Parus caeruleus.*

bluetongue /blóo tung/ (*plural* **-tongues** *or* **-tongue**), **blue-tongued lizard** *n* a Australian lizard that displays its bright blue tongue when threatened. Genus: *Tiliqua.*

blue vitriol *n* copper sulphate (*archaic*)

blue water *n* the ocean far away from the shore

blue whale *n* a slate-blue whale, the world's largest living animal, that migrates between polar and equatorial seas. *Balaenoptera musculus.*

bluff[1] /bluf/ *v* **1** *vti* **PRETEND TO BE CONFIDENT** to pretend to have strength, confidence, or the intention of doing something, in order to deceive somebody **2** *vti* **DECEIVE PLAYERS ABOUT CARDS** to try to deceive other players in a card game about the true value of your hand **3** *vt Malaysia, Singapore* **DECEIVE SOMEBODY IN MINOR WAY** to try to mislead somebody about something relatively unimportant (*informal*) [Late 17C. < Dutch *bluffen* 'brag' or *bluf* 'bragging'.] —**bluff** *n* —**bluffable** *adj* —**bluffer** *n*

bluff[2] /bluf/ *n* **CLIFF WITH BROAD FACE** a high steep bank, cliff, or headland, especially one with a broad face ■ *adj* **1 STEEP AND BROAD** having a broad, flattened, or rounded steep front **2 BLUNT BUT KIND IN MANNER** cheerful and friendly but outspoken and often insensitive to others' feelings [Early 17C. < Dutch *blaf* 'flat'.] —**bluffly** *adv* —**bluffness** *n*

bluing /blóo ing/, **blueing** *n* a substance used in laundering to prevent white materials turning yellow

bluish /blóo ish/, **blueish** *adj* of a colour that is near to blue or contains some blue

Blum /bloom/, **Léon** (1872–1950) French statesman

Blume /bloom/, **Judy** (*b.* 1938) US writer

blunder /blúndər/ *n* **STUPID MISTAKE** a serious or embarrassing mistake, usually the result of carelessness or ignorance ■ *v* **1** *vi* **MAKE A SERIOUS MISTAKE** to make a serious or embarrassing mistake as a result of carelessness or ignorance **2** *vi* **MOVE CLUMSILY** to stumble or move clumsily **3** *vti* **ACT IN CONFUSED WAY** to act or speak in a manner that is clumsy, ignorant, or thoughtless [14C. Via a N Germanic language < Indo-European.] —**blunderer** *n* —**blunderingly** *adv*

SYNONYMS See ***mistake.***

blunderbuss /blúndər buss/ *n* **1** a short, wide-muzzled firearm of the 17th century, used to fire shot with a scattering effect at close range **2** a clumsy person (*informal*) [Mid-17C. Alteration of Dutch *donderbus* < *donder* 'thunder' + *bus* 'gun'.]

blunge /blunj/ (**blunges, blunging, blunged**) *vt* to mix clay with water and chemicals to create the material for making pottery commercially [Early 19C. Blend of PLUNGE + other *bl-* words such as BLOW[1] and BLEND.] —**blunger** *n*

blunt /blunt/ *adj* **1 NOT SHARP** having a cutting edge or point that is not sharp **2 FRANK OR HONEST WITHOUT SENSITIVITY** very frank or straightforward and showing no delicacy or consideration ■ *v* **1** *vti* **MAKE SOMETHING LESS SHARP** to make the point or cutting edge of something dull rather than sharp **2** *vt* **LESSEN OR WEAKEN** to make something such as a sense or an emotion less effective or less intense [13C. Perhaps < Old Norse *blundr* 'dozing'.] —**bluntly** *adv* —**bluntness** *n*

Blunt /blunt/, **Anthony** (1907–83) British art historian and Soviet spy

blur /blur/ *n* **1 FUZZY OR INDISTINCT IMAGE** something that cannot be seen clearly, e.g. because it moves too quickly or because it is not distinctly remembered **2 SMEAR OR SMEARED AREA** a mark on something that makes it unclear, or an area of something that is unclear ■ *vti* (**blurs, blurring, blurred**) **1 MAKE OR BECOME VAGUE** to become less clear or distinct, or make something such as an idea less clear or distinct **2 MAKE OR BECOME FUZZY** to become fuzzy or unclear, or make something fuzzy or unclear ■ *adj Malaysia, Singapore* **CONFUSED** confused or uncertain about something (*informal*) ○ *I am very blur about linguistics.* [Mid-16C. Probably variant of BLEAR.] —**blurredness** *n* —**blurrily** *adv* —**blurriness** *n* —**blurry** *adj*

blurb /blurb/ *n* a short piece of writing that praises and promotes something, especially a paragraph on the cover of a book (*slang*) [Early 20C. Coined by Gelett Burgess (1866–1951), US humorist.] —**blurb** *vt*

blurt /blurt/ *vti* to say something suddenly or impulsively, as if by accident ○ *blurted out an apology* [Late 16C. Probably an imitation of the sound.]

blush /blush/ *vi* **1 BECOME RED IN FACE** to turn red in the face because of emotion, especially embarrassment, shame, modesty, or pleasure **2 BECOME EMBARRASSED** to feel embarrassed or ashamed (*formal*) **3 TURN RED OR PINK** to become red or pink (*literary*) ■ *n* **1 REDDENING OF FACE** a reddening of the face caused by emotion, especially embarrassment, shame, modesty, or pleasure **2 RED OR PINK** a red colour or rosy glow **3** *US* COSMETICS = **blusher 4** WINE = **blush wine** [Old English *blyscan* < Indo-European] —**blushful** *adj* —**blushing** *adj* —**blushingly** *adv*

blusher /blúshər/ *n* a pink or reddish powder or cream applied to the face, especially to accentuate the cheekbones. US term **blush** *n.* 3

blush wine *n* wine with a slight pink tinge

bluster /blústər/ *v* **1** *vti* **SPEAK OR UTTER LOUDLY OR ARROGANTLY** to speak loudly, boisterously, or arrogantly, or to say something in this way **2** *vti* **BEHAVE IN BULLYING WAY** to behave or do something in a bullying or threatening way **3** *vi* **BLOW LOUDLY IN GUSTS** to blow in loud gusts (*refers to wind*) ■ *n* **1 LOUD BULLYING OR BRAGGING SPEECH** loud arrogant or threatening speech or behaviour **2 SUDDEN LOUD GUST OF WIND** a loud gust of wind **3 LOUD FUSS** a loud or angry commotion [Early 15C. < Middle Low German *blustern* 'blow violently'.] —**blusterer** *n* —**blusteringly** *adv* —**blustery** *adj*

Blu-tack /bloo tak/ *tdmk* a trademark for a soft malleable substance that is used to stick paper temporarily to walls and other surfaces

Blvd *abbr* Boulevard

B-lymphocyte *n* IMMUNOL = **B cell**

Blyth /blīth/ industrial port in N England. Population: 35,327 (1991).

Blyth, Chay (*b.* 1940) British yachtsman. Born **Charles Blyth**

Blyton /blít'n/, **Enid** (1897–1968) British writer

bm *abbr* **1** board measure **2** bowel movement

BM *abbr* **1** bench mark **2** British Museum

BMA *abbr* British Medical Association

BMJ *abbr* British Medical Journal

B movie *n* a low-budget film that was formerly shown in addition to the main feature —**B-movie** *adj*

⚡**bmp, BMP** *suffix* used after the dot in a DOS-based computer file to show that the file is an image stored as a series of pixels

BMus /bee múz/ *abbr* Bachelor of Music

BMX *n* the riding of bicycles over rough terrain and open country or a racing course. Full form **bicycle motocross**

bn[1] *abbr* **1 Bn** battalion **2** billion

⚡**bn**[2] *abbr* Brunei (*in Internet addresses*)

Bn *abbr* **1** baron **2** battalion

B'nai B'rith /bə náy bə reeth, bə náy bríth/ *n* an international Jewish social service organization founded in New York in 1843 [< Hebrew, 'Sons of the Covenant']

⚡**bo** *abbr* Bolivia (*in Internet addresses*)

BO *n* an unpleasant smell that comes from a person because of sweat, lack of hygiene, or a physical disorder (*informal*) Full form **body odour** ■ *abbr* box office

b.o. *abbr* **1** branch office **2** broker's order **3** buyer's option

B/O *abbr* brought over

boa /bó ə/ *n* **1** a nonvenomous, often large snake that kills by winding its body around its prey and suffocating it. Native to: tropical America, Africa, Asia. Family: Boidae. **2** a long fluffy scarf of feathers or fur worn by women around the neck [14C. < Latin, 'large water snake'.]

boa constrictor *n* a large snake of the boa family that kills by winding its body around its prey and crushing it. Native to: tropical America, West Indies. *Boa constrictor.*

Boadicea = **Boudicca**

boar /bawr/ (*plural* **boars** *or* **boar**) *n* **1 UNCASTRATED PIG** a male pig that has not been castrated **2 MALE MAMMAL** a male mammal, e.g. a male badger, beaver, or raccoon **3 WILD BOAR** a wild boar [Old English *bār* < W Germanic]

SPELLCHECK Do not confuse ***boar*** with ***bore***, which has a similar sound. Beware: your spellchecker will not catch this error.

board /bawrd/ *n* **1 FLAT PIECE OF WOOD** a piece of wood cut into a flat rectangular shape, especially a long and narrow piece used for building **2 FLAT SURFACE FOR PARTICULAR PURPOSE** a flat piece of wood, plastic, or other rigid material, used for a particular purpose, e.g. chopping food **3 FLAT SURFACE FOR GAME** a flat surface on which a game is played, especially a piece of wood or cardboard marked with coloured areas for a particular game such as chess **4 COMPOSITE MATERIAL PRESSED INTO A SHEET** a rigid sheet material made by compressing layers of other materials, e.g. plywood **5 CONTROL PANEL** a panel on which the controls of a piece of electrical equipment are mounted **6** EDUC = **blackboard 7 NOTICEBOARD** a noticeboard **8 SHIP'S SIDE** the side of a ship **9 CIRCUIT BOARD** a printed circuit board **10 DIVING BOARD** a diving board **11 SURFBOARD** a surfboard **12 SCOREBOARD** a scoreboard **13 SNOWBOARD** a snowboard **14** BASKETBALL = **backboard** *n.* 2 **15 BOOK COVER** either of the pair of pieces of stiff cardboard that together form the front and back covers of a book **16 GROUP CHOSEN TO MAKE DECISIONS** a group of people chosen to make executive or managerial decisions for an organization (*takes a singular or plural verb*) **17 DAILY MEALS** daily meals provided at the place where somebody lives, usually for money or in return for work **18 TABLE WITH FOOD** a table used for meals, especially one spread with food (*archaic*) **19 DISTANCE SAILED INTO WIND** the distance covered by a sailing vessel in one period of sailing as near as possible into the wind **20** *ANZ* **SHEEP-SHEARING FLOOR** the area, sometimes raised like a platform or stage, where sheep are sheared inside a shearing shed ■ **boards** *npl* **ICE HOCKEY RINK ENCLOSURE** the wooden wall that surrounds an ice hockey rink ■ *v* **1** *vti* **GET ONTO VEHICLE AS PASSENGER** to get onto a vehicle, especially a ship, train, or aircraft, as a passenger **2** *vti* **TAKE PASSENGERS ON FOR JOURNEY** to take passengers onto a ship, plane, or other vehicle ○ *This flight is now boarding.* **3** *vt* **ATTACK OR INSPECT SHIP** to come alongside a ship in order for people to go from one ship to another for the purposes of attack or inspection **4** *vti* **COVER SOMETHING WITH BOARDS** to fix boards onto something, especially to cover any openings ○ *The house had been boarded up for the winter.* ○ *The windows were boarded over.* **5** *vti* **BE PROVIDED WITH ROOM AND MEALS** to be provided with accommodation and meals, e.g. in a school or guesthouse, in return for money or work, or to arrange for this to happen [Old English *bord* < Germanic, 'board, plank' and 'border, ship's side'] ◇ **go by the board** to be neglected, no longer used, cast aside, or destroyed ◇ **on board 1** into or on a vehicle, especially a train, boat, or aircraft **2** into an existing group or project (*informal*) ○ *As soon as we bring this new analyst on board, the workload should return to normal.* ◇ **take something on board 1** to understand or realize something fully **2** to accept or include something, e.g. a suggestion or new idea

SPELLCHECK Do not confuse ***board*** with ***bored***, which has a similar sound. Beware: your spellchecker will not catch this error.

board bridge *n* BOARD GAMES = **duplicate bridge**

boarder /báwrdər/ *n* **1 SOMEBODY PAYING FOR FOOD AND BED** somebody who pays to sleep and eat in a private home or boarding house **2 PUPIL LIVING AT SCHOOL** a school pupil who lives at the school during term time **3 SOMEBODY TRYING TO CAPTURE SHIP** somebody who tries to get onto a ship to capture it

board foot *n* a unit of volume for measuring timber, equal to the volume of a board that is one foot square and one inch thick

board game *n* a game that involves moving pieces around on a board marked with coloured areas for a particular game, e.g. chess or backgammon

boarding card *n* TRANSP = **boarding pass**

boarding house *n* a private home that provides a room and meals to paying guests who are usually long-term residents. ◊ **bed and breakfast**

boarding pass *n* an additional ticket, or part of a ticket, that somebody must have in order to be allowed onto an aircraft or ship as a passenger

boarding school *n* a school that provides some or all pupils with accommodation and daily meals

Boardman /báwrdmən/, **Chris** (*b.* 1968) British cyclist. Full name **Christopher Miles Boardman**

board measure *n* a system for measuring timber volume based on the board foot

Board of Deputies *n* a representative body that concerns itself with the collective legal and political interests of British Jews

board of trade *n US* an organization of business and banks that has the goal of promoting commercial interest in a state, city, or other area

Board of Trade *n* a British government department that regulates commerce and promotes exports

boardroom /báwrd room, -rŏom/ *n* a room where the members of a board meet

boardsailing /báwrd sayling/ *n* = **windsurfing** —**boardsailor** *n*

boardwalk /báwrd wawk/ *n* a raised walkway made of boards, built across marshy ground or sand

Boas /bó az/, **Franz** (1858–1942) German-born US anthropologist

boast[1] /bōst/ *v* **1** *vti* **SPEAK PROUDLY ABOUT POSSESSIONS OR ACCOMPLISHMENTS** to praise yourself or brag about something you possess or have achieved **2** *vt* **POSSESS SOMETHING DESIRABLE** to possess something, especially something very desirable ○ *Our town boasts the world's biggest roller coaster.* ■ *n* **1 EXCESSIVELY PROUD STATEMENT** something you say or write that praises yourself or brags about your possessions or achievements **2 DESIRABLE POSSESSION** something possessed that is very desirable [13C. < Anglo-Norman *bost* 'boasting' < N Germanic.] —**boaster** *n* —**boastful** *adj* —**boastfully** *adv* —**boastfulness** *n*

boast[2] /bōst/ *vt* to shape stone roughly using a chisel [Early 19C. < ?]

boat /bōt/ *n* **1 SMALL VESSEL FOR TRAVELLING ON WATER** a small, often open vessel for travelling on water **2 SHIP OR SUBMARINE** any watercraft, e.g. a ship or submarine **3 SOMETHING SHAPED LIKE A BOAT** an open container shaped like a boat, e.g. one for holding gravy or incense ■ *v* **1** *vi* **TRAVEL BY BOAT** to travel by boat or ride in a boat for pleasure **2** *vt* **CARRY BY BOAT** to move or transport something by boat **3** *vt* **PULL FISH TO BOAT** to bring a caught fish to a boat [Old English *bāt* < Germanic] ◇ **in the same boat** in the same situation or having the same problems as somebody else (*informal*) ◇ **miss the boat** to fail to take advantage of an opportunity (*informal*) ◇ **push the boat out** to spend a lot of money when celebrating something or entertaining somebody (*informal*) ◇ **rock the boat** to cause trouble, especially by questioning an accepted situation (*informal*)

boatbill /bót bil/ *n* a heron with a large, dark, heavy bill. Native to: tropical America. *Cochlearius cochlearius.*

boat deck *n* a deck on a ship where the lifeboats are carried

boatel /bō tél/, **botel** *n* **1** a waterside hotel where people travelling in boats can stay and moor their boats **2** a ship that functions as a hotel [Mid-20C. Blend of BOAT + HOTEL.]

boater /bótər/ *n* **1** a straw hat with a flat brim, a flat crown, and a hatband **2** somebody who rides in a boat

boathook /bót hook/ *n* a long pole with a hook on one end, used for pulling or pushing boats, rafts, or logs

boathouse /bót howss/ (*plural* **-houses** /-howziz/) *n* a small building beside water, in which boats are kept

boating /bóting/ *n* riding in a boat for pleasure

boatload /bót lōd/ *n* **1** an amount of something or a number of people that fills a boat **2** a large amount of something or a large number of people (*informal*)

boatman /bótmən/ (*plural* **-men** /-mən/) *n* somebody who operates or works on a boat —**boatmanship** *n*

boat neck *n* a wide shallow neckline that runs from shoulder to shoulder and is equally deep at the front and back, similar to the neckline of a traditional sailor's blouse

boat people *npl* refugees who leave their country by boat

Boat Race *n* **1** an annual rowing race on the Thames between Oxford and Cambridge Universities, each represented by one boat with a crew of eight **2 Boat Race, boat race** *Cockney* a face (*rhyming slang*)

boatswain /bóss'n/, **bo's'n, bosun** *n* a noncommissioned officer or a warrant officer on a ship in charge of the maintenance of the vessel, its boats, and other equipment [Old English *bātswegen* < BOAT + Old Norse *sveinn* 'boy' (see SWAIN)]

boatswain's chair *n* a board supported by ropes, slung over the side of a ship or up in the rigging so that somebody can sit on it while working

boat train *n* a train that takes people between a dockside and a town, usually timed to coincide with the arrival or departure of a ferry or liner

boatyard /bṓt yaard/ *n* an area where boats are built and maintained

bob[1] /bob/ *vi* (**bobs, bobbing, bobbed**) **1 BOUNCE** to bounce up and down quickly and repeatedly, especially in and out of the water while floating **2 MAKE CURTSY, BOW, OR NOD** to make a quick movement, especially a curtsy, bow, or nod ■ *n* **1 SMALL HANGING OR BOUNCING OBJECT** a small hanging or bouncing object, e.g. a weight on a plumb line or a fishing bobber **2 CURTSY, BOW, OR NOD** a quick movement such as a curtsy, bow, or nod [14C. Probably an imitation of the sound.]

bob[2] /bob/ *n* **1 WOMAN'S SHORT HAIRCUT** a woman's short haircut, especially a straight cut at chin length **2 SOMETHING CUT SHORT** something that has been cut short, e.g. a horse's tail when docked, a dog's ears when clipped, or a short line of poetry at the end of a stanza **3 BOBSLEIGH** a bobsleigh (*informal*) ■ *vt* (**bobs, bobbing, bobbed**) **CUT HAIR SHORT** to cut a person's hair or a horse's tail short so that it is all one length [14C. < ?]

bob[3] /bob/ (*plural* **bob**) *n* a shilling in the former currency system (*informal*) [Late 18C. < ?]

bob[4] /bob/ *n* a small polishing wheel of felt or leather ■ *vt* (**bobs, bobbing, bobbed**) to polish something with a small polishing wheel of felt or leather [Probably < BOB[2]]

Bob /bob/ ◇ **Bob's your uncle** used after an explanation of how to do something to say that it will be easy or simple to do (*informal*)

bobber /bóbbər/ *n* a light object attached to a fishing line that floats on the surface of the water to keep the bait at the proper depth

bobbin /bóbbin/ *n* **1** a cylinder wound with thread, yarn, or wire used for sewing, spinning, weaving, knitting, or making lace **2** a narrow cotton cord, often braided, formerly used for trimming and binding [Mid-16C. < French *bobine* 'sewing instrument' < Old French *balbiner*, probably alteration of *balbier* 'to stutter' < Latin *balbus* 'stuttering'.]

bobbinet /bóbbi nét/ *n* a machine-made net fabric with a hexagonal mesh

bobbin lace *n* a lace made by winding thread on bobbins around pins stuck into a pillow

bobble /bóbb'l/ *n* **1 WOOLLEN BALL** a woollen ball used as decoration on clothing, especially on a woollen hat **2 UP-AND-DOWN MOVEMENT** a fast repeated up-and-down movement ■ *vti* (**-bles, -bling, -bled**) **MOVE UP AND DOWN** to move, or to cause something to move, quickly and repeatedly up and down [Early 19C. Probably < BOB[1].]

bobble hat *n* a woollen hat with a woollen ball on its crown as decoration

bobby /bóbbi/ (*plural* **-bies**) *n* a policeman (*dated informal*) [Mid-19C. < Pet form of *Robert*, after Sir Robert PEEL, who introduced the 1828 Police Act.]

bobby calf *n* a male calf of a dairy cow that is slaughtered before weaning and used for veal [*Bobby* probably < BOB[2]]

bobby-dazzler *n* an excellent thing or person, especially a good-looking woman (*dated informal*) [*Bobby* < ?]

bobby pin *n US, Can, ANZ* a hair clip made of a tightly folded piece of wire that slides into the hair and holds it in place [Probably < BOB[2] 'short haircut']

bobby socks, bobby sox *npl US* ankle socks that fold over at the top, popular among teenage girls in the 1940s and 1950s [*Bobby* probably < BOB[2]]

bobbysoxer /bóbbi soksər/ *n US* a teenage girl of the 1940s and 1950s (*informal*)

bobcat /bób kat/ *n* a medium-sized wildcat that is related to the lynx and has reddish-brown fur with black markings, tufted ears, and a short tail. Native to: North America. *Lynx rufus*. [Late 19C. < BOB[2], from its short tail.]

bobol /bó bol/, **bobbol** *n Carib* corrupt behaviour, usually involving misappropriation of money, the acceptance of bribes, and other fraudulent practices (*slang*)

bobolink /bóbbə lingk/ (*plural* **-links** *or* **-link**) *n* a bird with a distinctive bubbly song. Native to: North America, migrating to South America. *Dolichonyx oryzivorus*. [Late 18C. An imitation of the bird's call.]

bob skate *n US, Can* an ice skate that has two parallel blades, usually used by children [< BOB[2], from its shortness]

bobsled /bób sled/ *vi* (**-sleds, -sledding, -sledded**) *US* = **bobsleigh** *v.* ■ *n US* **1** = **bobsleigh** *n.* 1 **2** = **bobsleigh** *n.* 2

bobsleigh /bób slay/ *n* **1 RACING SLEDGE** a long racing sledge with steering, brakes, a seat for two or more, and two pairs of runners, one in front and one at the back. US term **bobsled** *n.* 1 **2 SLEDGE MADE OF TWO SHORT SLEDGES** a long sledge made up of two short sledges attached one behind the other, used for recreation or for carrying things over snow. US term **bobsled** *n.* 2 ■ *vi* **RIDE IN BOBSLEIGH** to ride or race in a bobsleigh. US term **bobsled** *v.*

bobstay /bób stay/ *n* a rope used to hold down a ship's bowsprit [*Bob* < ?]

bobtail /bób tayl/ *n* **1** an animal's tail that is naturally short or has been cut short **2** an animal, especially a horse or dog, that has a short or shortened tail [Mid-16C. < BOB[2], from its shortness.] —**bobtailed** *adj*

bobwhite /bób wīt/ (*plural* **-whites** *or* **-white**) *n* a small brown mottled quail with white markings on its head that has been introduced into Europe. Native to: central and E North America. *Colinus virginianus*. [Early 19C. An imitation of the bird's call.]

Boccaccio /bo káchi ō/, **Giovanni** (1313–75) Italian writer and humanist

bocce /bó chee/, **bocci** *n* an Italian game similar to bowling, usually played on a long earth-floored court [Early 20C. Via Italian *bocce*, plural of *boccia* '(round) ball' < Vulgar Latin *bottia* 'boss'.]

Boccherini /bókə réeni/, **Luigi** (1743–1805) Italian composer and cellist

Boccioni /bo chṓni/, **Umberto** (1882–1916) Italian painter and sculptor

Boche /bosh/ (*plural* **Boches** *or* **Boche**), **boche** (*plural* **boches** *or* **boche**) *n* an offensive term for Germans considered collectively, especially German soldiers of World War I (*dated*) [Early 20C. Shortening of French *alboche*, blend of *allemand* 'German' + *caboche* 'cabbage, blockhead'.]

Bochum /bókəm, bókhəm/ city in west-central Germany. Population: 401,129 (1997).

bod /bod/ *n* (*slang*) **1** somebody's body or figure **2** a person [Late 18C. Shortening.]

BOD *abbr* biochemical oxygen demand

bodacious /bō dáyshəss/, **bowdacious** *adj US* (*informal humorous regional*) **1 IMPRESSIVE** remarkable or excellent ○ *That's one bodacious boat!* **2 BOLD** outrageously arrogant or uninhibited ○ *a bodacious lie* ■ *adv US* **VERY** extremely (*informal humorous regional*) ○ *I'm bodacious hungry.* [Mid-19C. Perhaps alteration of dialect blend of BOLD + AUDACIOUS.] —**bodaciously** *adv*

bode[1] /bōd/ (**bodes, boding, boded**) *vti* to be an indication of something particular that is about to happen ○ *This does not bode well for the future of the organization.* [Old English *bodian* 'announce, foretell' < *boda* 'messenger' < Germanic]

bode[2] *v* past tense of **bide**

bodega /bō dáygə/ *n* a wine shop or warehouse for the storage of wine in a Spanish-speaking country [Mid-19C. Via Spanish < Latin *apotheca* 'storehouse'.]

bodge /boj/ *vti* (**bodges, bodging, bodged**) to make or repair something badly (*informal*) ■ *n* a clumsy piece of work or a badly done repair (*informal*) [Mid-16C. Alteration of BOTCH.]

bodgie /bójji/ *adj Aus* false or fake (*slang*)

Bodhidharma /bóddi daármə/ (*fl.* 6th century) Indian Buddhist monk

bodhisattva /bóddi sátvə/ *n* in Buddhism, a deity or being who has attained enlightenment worthy of nirvana but who remains in the human world to help others [Early 19C. < Sanskrit *bodhi* 'perfect knowledge' + *sattva* 'being, reality'.]

bodhrán /bów raan/ *n* a shallow drum used in Irish and sometimes Scottish folk music, covered on one side with goat skin, held in one hand, and played with the other using a stick [Late 20C. < Irish.]

bodice /bóddiss/ *n* **1** the part of a woman's dress or undergarment that covers the upper body **2** a close-fitting, often laced-up top worn over a blouse in the past or as part of some national costumes [Mid-16C. < Plural of BODY.]

bodiless /bóddiləss/ *adj* having no body or physical substance

bodily /bóddili/ *adj* **PHYSICAL** relating to, involving, or typical of the body ■ *adv* **1 PHYSICALLY** physically or in the flesh **2 USING PHYSICAL FORCE** by taking hold of something with the hands and using physical strength ○ *bodily removed him from the building*

bodkin /bódkin/ *n* **1 LARGE BLUNT NEEDLE** a long thick blunt needle with a large eye **2 HOLE-PUNCHING TOOL** a small slender sharply pointed tool used for making holes in cloth or leather **3 TYPESETTING TOOL** a long sharp typesetting tool [14C. Probably < Celtic, 'small dagger'.]

Bodleian /bóddli ən/ *n* the library of Oxford University [Mid-17C. After Sir Thomas *Bodley*, English diplomat who refounded the library in 1603.]

Bodmin /bódmin/ town in SW England, near Bodmin Moor, an Area of Outstanding Natural Beauty. Population: 12,553 (1991).

Bodoni /bə dṓni/ *n* a font or style of typeface [Late 19C. After Giambattista *Bodoni* (1740–1813), Italian printer.]

body /bóddi/ *n* (*plural* **-ies**) **1 PHYSICAL FORM OF HUMAN OR ANIMAL** the complete material structure or physical form of a human being or an animal **2 DEAD HUMAN OR ANIMAL REMAINS** the physical remains of a dead person or animal **3 TORSO** the main part of the physical structure of a human being or animal, not including the head, arms, legs, or wings **4 SOMEBODY'S FIGURE** somebody's figure or build, especially with regard to shape and muscle tone ○ *a great body* **5 GROUP** an organized group of individuals, e.g. lawmakers, students, or soldiers ○ *a legislative body* **6 COLLECTION** a collection or amount of something, seen as a whole ○ *a body of evidence* **7 MASS** an individual mass of something, especially water or land ○ *a large body of water* **8 MAIN PART** the main or central part of something, e.g. the majority of a quantity **9 NAVE** the nave or central part of a church **10 MAIN PART OF VEHICLE** the main part of a vehicle, e.g. the fuselage of an aircraft or the outer shell of a motor car **11 MAIN PART OF MUSICAL INSTRUMENT** the largest part of a musical instrument, especially the soundbox of a stringed instrument **12 MAIN PART OF SOMETHING WRITTEN** the main part of a piece of writing ○ *in the body of the text* **13 FULLNESS OF FLAVOUR IN WINE** the extent to which a wine seems full when tasted ○ *a French red with plenty of body* **14 THICKNESS OF LIQUID** the thickness or opacity of a liquid such as paint or soup **15 FULLNESS OF TEXTURE** a fullness and bounciness in texture or appearance ○ *designed to give hair more body* **16 FIRMNESS OF FABRIC** the firmness of a type of cloth **17 GARMENT FOR TORSO** a tight one-piece garment that covers the torso and is fastened at the crotch. US term **body suit** **18 UPPER PART OF GARMENT** the part of a garment that covers the torso **19 PERSON** used to refer to a person or yourself in an impersonal way (*informal*) ○ *This treatment could make a body feel unwelcome!* **20 MATERIAL FOR MAKING CERAMICS** the blend of clay and other raw materials used in a ceramic piece **21 PHYSICAL OBJECT** a distinguishable physical object **22 OBJECT REPRESENTED MATHEMATICALLY** a physical object represented mathematically ■ *vt* (**-ies, -ying, -ied**) **GIVE SHAPE** to give shape or substance to something (*literary*) [Old English *bodig* < ?]

body armour *n* a protective covering for the upper part of the torso

body bag *n* a bag designed to hold a dead body, usually made of plastic and fitted with a zip

body blow *n* **1** something that causes great physical, financial, or emotional damage to somebody or something **2** a punch that lands between the neck and the waist

body board *n* a short polystyrene surfboard on which a surfer lies rather than stands

body building *n* the practice of developing the muscles of the body through weightlifting and diet (*hyphenated before a noun*) —**body builder** *n*

body cavity *n* **1** ZOOL = **coelom** **2** an opening into the body, e.g. the mouth, oesophagus, vagina, rectum, or ear

body-centred *adj* describes crystals that have an atom in the middle of each unit cell as well as at the corners. ◊ **face-centred**

bodycheck /bóddi chek/ *n* an illegal act of using the body to obstruct an opposing player in a game, especially ice hockey or soccer ■ *vt* to use your body illegally to obstruct an opposing player in a game, especially ice hockey or soccer

body clock *n* BIOL = **biological clock**

body corporate (*plural* **bodies corporate**) *n* **1** a group of people legally recognized as being able to act as one body **2** *Aus* a committee that manages the common property of an apartment building, e.g. the gardens or foyer

body count *n* a count of the number of dead bodies, especially of soldiers killed after combat

body double *n* somebody whose body is filmed instead of that of an actor, especially in a scene involving nudity

body fluid *n* **1** a liquid produced by the body, including blood, saliva, semen, vaginal secretions, milk, urine, sweat, and tears **2** the water content of the body

bodyguard /bóddi gaard/ *n* a person or group of people paid to protect somebody from physical attack

body image *n* a person's own impression of how his or her body looks

body language *n* bodily mannerisms, postures, and facial expressions that can be interpreted as unconsciously communicating a person's feelings or psychological state

bodyline bowling *n* in cricket, fast bowling in which the bowler deliberately aims the ball at the batsman's body

body odour *n* a rank, unpleasant smell associated with an unclean human being. Full form of **BO**

body packer *n* somebody who swallows illegal narcotics in order to smuggle them (*slang*)

body politic *n* the people of a nation or any politically organized state, considered as a group

body popping *n* dancing, popular especially in the 1980s, involving convulsive, sinuous, or robotic movements (*slang*) —**body popper** *n*

body search *n* a detailed physical examination of somebody suspected of hiding something such as weapons or narcotics on his or her person

bodyshaper /bóddi shaypər/ *n* a woman's elasticated undergarment reaching from bust to hips, intended to produce a more streamlined body shape

body shop *n* a workshop where car bodies are repaired (*informal*)

body snatcher *n* somebody who stole corpses from graves in the past, usually to sell for medical study —**body snatching** *n*

body stocking *n* a close-fitting, usually sheer, one-piece garment that covers the body and sometimes the arms and legs

bodysuit *n* CLOTHING = **body** *n*. 17

bodysurf /bóddi surf/ *vi* to surf without a board by lying on a wave and using the body as a surfboard —**bodysurfer** *n* —**bodysurfing** *n*

body wall *n* the part of an animal's body that forms its external surface, encloses the body cavity, and consists of layers of skin and muscle

bodywork /bóddi wurk/ *n* **1** CAR BODY the outer frame of a car or other motor vehicle **2** REPAIR OF MOTOR VEHICLE BODY the work of repairing the outer frame of a car or other motor vehicle **3** MASSAGE OR PHYSICAL MANIPULATION OF BODY physical manipulation of the human body, including all types of massage, to improve general health or posture or to treat injuries

boehmite /búr mīt/ *n* a light grey to dark red-brown mineral consisting of hydrous aluminium oxide. Source: bauxite. [Early 20C. After Johann *Böhm* (1895–1952), German chemist.]

Boeotia /bi ôshə/ *n* region of ancient Greece —**Boeotian** *n, adj*

Boer /boor, bawr/ *n* **1** somebody of Dutch descent who lives in South Africa **2** *S Africa* a police officer (*slang*) [Mid-19C. < Dutch *boer* 'farmer'.] —**Boer** *adj*

boeremusiek /bóorə myoozik/ *n S Africa* country dance music popular among Afrikaners, usually played by a small band [Mid-20 C. < Afrikaans, < *boere* 'Afrikaner' + *musiek* 'music'.]

boerewors /bóorə vawrss/ *n S Africa* a large spicy homemade sausage, traditionally eaten by Afrikaners [Mid-20 C. < Afrikaans, < *boere* 'Afrikaner' + *wors* 'sausage'.]

Boer War *n* a war fought in South Africa from 1899 to 1902 between the British and the descendants of the Dutch, ending eventually in a British victory

Boethius /bō éethi əss/, **Anicius Manlius Severinus** (480?–524) Roman statesman and philosopher

⚡**BOF** *abbr* beginning of file

boff /bof/ *n US* **1** FUNNY JOKE a joke that gets a big laugh (*informal dated*) **2** BIG LAUGH a big hearty laugh (*informal dated*) **3** SUCCESS something that is a conspicuous success, especially a hit show (*informal dated*) **4** PUNCH OR SLAP a blow with the fist or open hand (*informal*) **5** OFFENSIVE TERM an offensive term for sexual intercourse (*slang*) ■ *v US* **1** *vt* PUNCH OR SLAP to hit somebody with the fist or open hand (*informal*) **2** *vti* OFFENSIVE TERM an offensive term meaning to have sexual intercourse with somebody (*slang*) [Mid-20C. Probably contraction of BOX OFFICE, indicating a box-office success.]

boffin /bóffin/ *n* a scientific expert, especially one involved in research and who appears unconventional or absentminded (*informal*) [Mid-20C. < ?]

boffo /bóffō/ *adj* excellent or extremely successful (*informal dated*)

Bofors gun /bófərz-/ *n* a 40 mm anti-aircraft gun with one or two barrels [After a munitions site in Sweden]

bog /bog/ *n* **1** an area of wet marshy ground, largely consisting of accumulated decomposing plant material **2** *UK* a toilet (*slang*) [14C. < Gaelic *boghan* 'marsh' < *bog* 'soft'.] —**boggy** *adj*

bog down *vt* to slow somebody's general progress (*informal*) ○ *got bogged down in unimportant details*

bog off *vi* to go away (*slang; usually a command*)

Humphrey Bogart

Bogart /bō gaart/, **Humphrey** (1899–1957) US film actor

bog asphodel *n* a plant of the lily family with grassy leaves that is common in boggy areas. Flowers: small, yellow, in clusters. Native to: Europe. *Narthecium ossifragum*.

bogey /bógi/ *n* **1** CAUSE OF TROUBLE something that troubles, annoys, or frightens somebody **2** ONE OVER PAR a golf score of one over par for a particular hole **3** PIECE OF NASAL MUCUS a lump of mucus in or from somebody's nose (*slang*) US term **booger** *n*. **4** UNIDENTIFIED FLYING AIRCRAFT an aircraft in flight that cannot be identified, especially one assumed to be hostile (*slang*) **5** = **bogeyman** *n*. **6** POLICE OFFICER a police officer or detective (*slang dated*) ■ *vt* (**-geying, -geys, -geyed**) SCORE ONE OVER PAR FOR HOLE to score one over par for a particular hole in golf [Mid-19C. Alteration of BOGLE.]

bogeyman /bógi man/ (*plural* **-men** /-men/), **bogyman** (*plural* **-men**) *n* **1** a real or imaginary person or monster that causes fear or is invoked to cause fear, especially in children **2** somebody considered to be especially hateful, evil, or frightening ○ *The press treated him as a bogeyman.*

boggle /bógg'l/ (**-gles, -gling, -gled**) *v* **1** *vti* BAFFLE OR BECOME BAFFLED to astonish or confuse somebody, or to become astonished or confused (*informal*) **2** *vi* HESITATE WITH SECOND THOUGHTS to hesitate before doing something, usually because of being overwhelmed, afraid, or concerned **3** *vti US* MAKE A TRIVIAL MISTAKE to make a trivial mistake or mismanage something (*informal*) [Late 16C. Probably related to BOGLE.] —**boggler** *n*

bogie /bógi/ *n* **1** FRAMEWORK WITH WHEELS a framework mounted on a set of wheels on the undercarriage of a vehicle **2** **bogie, bogy** (*plural* **-gies**) SMALL RAILWAY TRUCK a small railway truck used for carrying heavy loads

3 *S Asia* TRAIN COMPARTMENT a railway compartment [Mid-19C. < ?]

bogle /bóg'l/ *n* a bogeyman (*archaic or regional*) [Early 16C. < ?]

Bognor Regis /bógnər réejiss/ coastal town in S England. Population: 56,744 (1991).

bogong /bó gong/, **bogong moth, bugong** /boó gong/, **bugong moth** *n* a large Australian nocturnal moth that is eaten by Aboriginals. *Agrotis infusa*. [Mid-19C. < an Aboriginal language.]

Bogong, Mount /bó gong/ highest peak in Victoria, Australia, in the NE of the state. Height: 1,986 m./6,516 ft.

Bogor /bó gawr/ city in Indonesia, on W Java. Population: 271,711 (1990).

Bogotá /bógga taá/ capital of Colombia, in the centre of the country. Population: 6,004,782 (1997 estimate).

bog rosemary *n* a evergreen shrub of the heath family. Flowers: pink or white, urn-shaped. *Andromeda polifolia*.

bog spavin *n* a chronic puffy inflammation of the soft tissue of the hock joint of horses

bog-standard *adj* basic, ordinary, or lacking any special features (*informal*) ○ *For that price you get your bog-standard production model, without accessories.*

bogtrotter /bóg trottər/ *n* a highly offensive term for an Irish person (*slang*)

bogus /bốgəss/ *adj* **1** false, dishonest, or fraudulently imitating something **2** *US* not good, pleasant, or acceptable (*slang*) [Early 19C. < *Bogus*, a machine for producing counterfeit money < ?] —**bogusly** *adv* —**bogusness** *n*

bogy *n* RAIL = **bogie** *n*. 2

bogyman *n* = **bogeyman**

bohea /bō heé/ *n* a low-quality black Chinese tea [Early 18C. < Chinese dialect *Bu-yi*, variant of *Wu-yi*, after the Wu-Yi hills in SE China.]

bohemia /bō heémi ə/ *n* **1** a community of artists and other people who live unconventional lives **2** the unconventional lifestyle characteristic of bohemians

Bohemia /bō heémi ə/ *n* historic region in present-day W Czech Republic —**Bohemian** *adj, n*

bohemian /bō heémi ən/ *n* somebody, often a writer or an artist, who does not live according to the conventions of society —**bohemian** *adj* —**bohemianism** *n*

Böhm /burm/, **Karl** (1894–1981) Austrian conductor

boho /bốhō/ *n* (*plural* **-hos**) a bohemian (*slang*) ■ *adj* bohemian (*slang*) ○ *a flat furnished in boho style*

Bohr /bawr/, **Niels** (1885–1962) Danish physicist

Bohr effect *n* the effect of carbon dioxide on the binding of oxygen to haemoglobin [Mid-20C. After Christian *Bohr* (1855–1911), Danish physiologist.]

Bohr theory *n* a theory of atomic structure postulating that electrons move around a nucleus in distinct orbits and a jump between orbits is accompanied by the absorption or emission of a photon [Mid-20C. After Niels BOHR.]

bohunk /bó hungk/ *n US, Can* an offensive term for a person from central or SE Europe (*slang*) [Early 20C. Blend of *Bohemian* + *hunk*, shortening of HUNGARIAN.]

boil[1] /boyl/ *v* **1** *vti* REACH BOILING POINT to heat a liquid until it forms bubbles and turns to gas, or to reach this state **2** *vti* CONTAIN OR CAUSE TO CONTAIN BOILING LIQUID to contain liquid that has reached boiling point, or to cause the liquid in a container to boil **3** *vti* COOK IN BOILING LIQUID to cook something by submerging it in boiling liquid for a certain amount of time, or to be cooked in this way **4** *vti* PLACE IN BOILING WATER to put something such as clothing in boiling water, e.g. to clean or sterilize it, or to be put in boiling water for these purposes **5** *vi* GET VERY HOT to be or become extremely hot (*informal*) ○ *It's boiling in there!* **6** *vi* BUBBLE ON SURFACE to be stirred up and have bubbles breaking on the surface **7** *vi* GET VERY ANGRY to be or become very angry ○ *boiling with rage* ■ *n* **1** STATE OF BUBBLING AT HIGH TEMPERATURE the point at which a liquid bubbles because of having reached the temperature at which it turns to gas, or the state of bubbling at this temperature **2** *Southern US* OUTDOOR PICNIC an outdoor picnic at which shellfish are boiled and eaten (*informal*) ○ *a Low Country crab boil* [13C. Via Old French *boillir* < Latin *bullire* 'to bubble' < *bulla* 'a bubble'.]

boil away *vti* to turn completely into steam, or turn all of a quantity of liquid into steam by boiling it

boil down *v* **1** *vti* to make a liquid mixture thicker and reduce its volume by heating it rapidly until much of the liquid turns to steam, or to be made thicker in this way **2** *vt* to condense or summarize something such as information or text (*informal*)
boil down to *vt* to mean or amount to something in essence (*informal*) ○ *It all boils down to the single question: Is he telling the truth?*
boil off *vti* to remove something from a mixture by heating the mixture rapidly until it turns to steam, or to be removed in this way
boil over *v* **1** *vti* to reach or to cause a liquid to reach boiling point and be so full of bubbles that some of it spills from the container **2** *vi* to become too intense or out of control ○ *her anger boiled over*

boil[2] /boyl/ *n* a painful pus-filled abscess on the skin caused by bacterial infection of a hair follicle [Old English *byl* 'inflammation' < W Germanic]

Boileau /bwaálō/, **Nicolas** (1636–1711) French writer

boiled sweet *n* a hard sweet made by boiling water, sugar, and flavouring

boiler /bóylər/ *n* **1** a large tank in which water is heated and stored, either as hot water or as steam, and used for heating or generating power **2** an old chicken with flesh that is so tough that it must be boiled to make it palatable

boilermaker /bóylər maykər/ *n* **1** an industrial worker who makes large metal objects, especially boilers **2** *US* a drink of whisky followed by a beer

ϟ **boilerplate** /bóylər playt/ *n* **1 PLATE USED FOR MAKING BOILERS** steel plate used for making boilers **2** *US, Can* **CLICHÉD WRITING** writing that says nothing new, informative, or interesting **3** *US, Can* **FORMULAIC LANGUAGE** stock or formulaic language such as that used in legal forms and documents like powers of attorney and authors' contracts **4 REUSABLE UNIT OF CODE** a unit of IT code writing that can be reused

boiler room *n* an area or room that houses one or more boilers

boiler-room *adj US* relating to or being political campaign workers who perform administrative support tasks and make polling phone calls for the candidate

boiler suit *n* a one-piece long-sleeved garment worn over other clothes to protect them while doing manual labour or dirty jobs

boiling /bóyling/ *adj* **1** extremely hot **2** extremely angry ■ *n Scotland* = **boiled sweet**

boiling point *n* **1** the temperature at which a heated liquid turns to gas, e.g. 100°C or 212°F for water at sea level **2** the point at which people lose their tempers or a situation becomes critical

boing /boyng/ *n* the sound made by something that bounces [Mid-20C. An imitation of the sound.]

Boise /bóyssi, bóyzi/ **1** capital city of Idaho, in the SW of the state. Population: 157,452 (1998 estimate). **2** river in SW Idaho. Length: 150 km/95 mi.

boisterous /bóystərəss/ *adj* **1** full of noisy enthusiasm and energy, and often roughness or wildness **2** wild, rough, or stormy [13C. Alteration of *boistous*, via Old French *boistos* 'clumsy, rough' < Latin *buxus* 'made from box-tree wood'.] —**boisterously** *adv* —**boisterousness** *n*

Boito /bō éetō/, **Arrigo** (1842–1918) Italian composer and librettist. Original name **Enrico Giuseppe Giovanni Boito**

Bokassa /bə kássə/, **Jean Bédel** (1921–96) Central African national leader and president (1966–77) and emperor (1977–79) of the Central African Republic

bok choy /bók chóy/ *n US* FOOD = **pak choi** [Mid-20C. < Chinese Guangdang dialect *baahk-choi* 'white vegetable'.]

boke /bōk/ *vti* (**bokes, boking, boked**) *Scotland* **RETCH** to retch or vomit (*informal*) ■ *n Scotland* (*informal*) **1 ACT OF RETCHING OR VOMITING** an act or instance of retching or vomiting **2 SOMETHING VOMITED** something that has been vomited [Mid-16C. Variant of POKE[1].]

Bol. *abbr* **1** Bolivia **2** Bolivian

bola /bṓlə/, **bolas** /-ləss/ *n* a strong cord with weights attached to the ends, used for catching cows by South American cowhands (**gauchos**) who throw it to entangle the cows' legs [Early 19C. Via Spanish, 'ball' < Latin *bulla* 'bubble'.]

bold /bōld/ *adj* **1 FEARLESS AND ADVENTUROUS** willing and eager to face danger or adventure with a sense of confidence and fearlessness **2 REQUIRING OR SHOWING A DARING PERSONALITY** requiring or showing fearlessness, daring, and often originality **3 IMPUDENT OR PRESUMPTUOUS** lacking in modesty or impolitely assertive **4 CLEAR AND CONSPICUOUS** standing out and therefore easily noticed ○ *bold colours* **5 STEEP** rising abruptly and steeply from the surroundings ○ *a bold cliff* **6 DARKER THAN STANDARD** having darker thicker lines than standard type, fonts, or lettering ■ *n* **TYPE DARKER THAN STANDARD** type, fonts, or lettering with darker thicker lines than is standard ■ *vt* **SET BOLDFACE TYPE** to set, print, or display text in boldface type [Old English *bald* < Indo-European] —**boldly** *adv* —**boldness** *n*

boldface /bṓld fayss/ *adj* PRINTING = **bold** *adj.* **6** ■ *vt* to make letters darker and thicker for emphasis

bold-faced /bṓld fáyst/, **boldfaced** *adj* **1** showing impudence or lack of shame or modesty **2** PRINTING = **bold** *adj.* **6**

bole[1] /bōl/ *n* the trunk of a tree [14C. < Old Norse *bolr*.]

SPELLCHECK Do not confuse ***bole*** with ***bowl***, which has a similar sound. Beware: your spellchecker will not catch this error.

bole[2] /bōl/ *n* a reddish-brown clay used as a pigment [14C. < late Latin *bolus* 'clod of earth' (see BOLUS).]

bolection /bō léksh'n/ *n* a moulding covering an architectural joint and projecting beyond it, usually S-shaped in cross section [Mid-17C. < ?]

bolero /bə láirō/ (*plural* **-ros**) *n* **1 SPANISH DANCE** a Spanish dance in triple time that involves much foot-stamping and dramatic posing **2 SPANISH DANCE MUSIC** the music for a bolero **3 SHORT OPEN JACKET** a short jacket, with or without sleeves, worn open over a blouse or shirt [Late 18C. < Spanish, < *bola* 'ball' (see BOLA).]

boletus /bō léetəss/ (*plural* **-tuses** *or* **-ti** /-tī/) *n* a fungus that has a rounded cap with pores rather than gills on the underside. Genus: *Boletus*. [Early 16C. < Latin.]

Boleyn /bōō lín/, **Anne** (1507?–36) queen consort of Henry VIII (1533–36)

Bolger /bóljər/, **Jim** (*b.* 1935) New Zealand statesman. Full name **James Brendan Bolger**

bolide /bṓ līd/ *n* a bright meteor that explodes [Early 19C. < French, < Greek *bolis* 'missile'.]

bolivar /bólli vaar/ *n* see table at **currency** [Late 19C. After Simón BOLÍVAR.]

Bolívar /bólli vaar/, **Simón** (1783–1830) South American revolutionary. Known as **the Liberator**

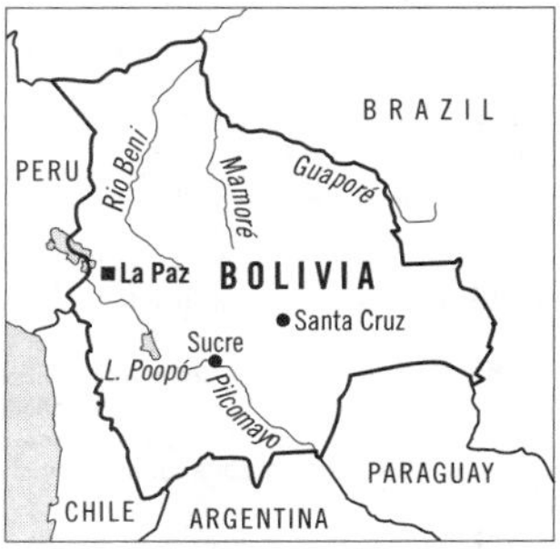

Bolivia

Bolivia /bə lívvi ə/ landlocked republic in west-central South America. Capital: Sucre.La Paz Population: 7,669,868 (1997). Area: 1,098,581 sq. km/424,164 sq. mi. —**Bolivian** *n, adj*

boliviano /bə lívvi aánō/ (*plural* **-nos**) *n* see table at **currency** [Late 19C. < Spanish, 'Bolivian'.]

boll /bōl/ *n* a rounded seed pod or capsule, especially of cotton [15C. < Middle Dutch *bolle* 'round object'.]

Böll /böl/, **Heinrich** (1917–85) German novelist

bollard /bóll aard/ *n* **1 POST FOR MOORING SHIPS** a strong post on a quay or wharf, or on the deck of a ship, used for securing ropes **2 POST FOR GUIDING TRAFFIC** a small post marking the edge of an area traffic must keep off **3 ROCK SUITABLE FOR SECURING ROPE** a spike of rock or a pillar of ice round which a rope can be secured [Mid-19C. Probably < BOLE[1].]

bollocking /bólləking/ *n* a highly offensive term for a severe telling-off (*taboo*) [Mid-20C. < BOLLOCKS.]

bollocks /bólləks/ *npl* a highly offensive term for the testicles (*taboo*) ■ *n* a highly offensive term meaning nonsense (*taboo*) ■ *interj* a highly offensive term indicating strong disbelief or disagreement (*taboo*) ■ *vt* a highly offensive term meaning to make a mess or muddle of something (*taboo*) [Mid-18C. Variant of BALLOCKS.]

boll weevil *n* a weevil whose larvae infest and destroy cotton bolls. Native to: S United States, Mexico. *Anthonomus grandis.*

bollworm /bṓl wurm/ *n* a moth caterpillar, especially the corn earworm or pink bollworm, that feeds on and destroys cotton and other crops

Bollywood /bólli wŏŏd/ *n* a nickname given to the Indian film industry [Mid-20C. Blend of BOMBAY + HOLLYWOOD.]

bolo /bṓlō/ (*plural* **-los**) *n* a machete from the Philippines with a single-edged blade [Early 20C. < Philippine Spanish.]

bologna /bə lṓnyə/ *n US* a large smoked sausage made with a variety of finely minced seasoned meats, usually including beef and pork [Mid-19C. After BOLOGNA, Italy.]

Bologna /bə lṓnyə, -lón-/ capital of Emilia-Romagna Region, N Italy. Population: 384,015 (1997 estimate).

bolognese /bóllə náyz/, **Bolognese** *adj* describes an Italian sauce for pasta, made with minced meat and tomato [Early 19C. < Italian, '(in the style) of Bologna'.]

bolometer /bō lómmitər/ *n* an instrument for measuring radiant energy by determining the changes of resistance in an electrical conductor [Late 19C. < Greek *bolē* 'ray'.] —**bolometric** /bṓlə méttrik/ *adj* —**bolometry** *n*

bolo tie, **bola tie** *n US* a thin tie of cord fastened in front by a clasp [Alteration of BOLA]

Bolshevik /bólshəvik/ *n* **1 RUSSIAN COMMUNIST** a member of the radical group within the Russian Social Democratic Labour Party that became the Communist Party in 1918 **2 Bolshevik, bolshevik COMMUNIST OR COMMUNIST SYMPATHIZER** a Communist or Communist sympathizer **3 Bolshevik, bolshevik POLITICAL RADICAL** a revolutionary or radical socialist (*disapproving*) [Early 20C. < Russian *bol'shevik* < *bol'she* 'more'; because the radicals were in the majority.]

Bolshevism /bólshəvizəm/, **bolshevism** *n* **1** the ideology and policies of the Bolsheviks, especially advocacy of the forcible overthrow of capitalism **2** Communism or revolutionary socialism (*dated*) —**Bolshevist** *n* —**Bolshevistic** /bólshə vístik/ *adj*

bolshie /bólshi/, **bolshy** *n* (*plural* **-shies**) **BOLSHEVIK** a Bolshevik (*informal dated*) ■ *adj UK, Can* (*informal*) **1 UNCOOPERATIVE** tending to be argumentative or uncooperative **2 POLITICALLY RADICAL** politically radical or subversive [Early 20C. < BOLSHEVIK.] —**bolshily** *adv* —**bolshiness** *n*

bolster[1] /bṓlstər/ *n* **1 LONG CYLINDRICAL PILLOW** a long firm cylindrical pillow placed under other pillows to support them **2 PAD PREVENTING FRICTION** a pad or cushion fitted to machinery to prevent friction or give support **3 HORIZONTAL SUPPORTING TIMBER** a short horizontal timber positioned between the top of a post and the beam it supports, to spread the load of the post ■ *vt* **1 ENCOURAGE THROUGH SUPPORT** to strengthen something through support or encouragement **2 KEEP RAISED** to prop something up [Old English, 'cushion' < Indo-European, 'to swell'] —**bolsterer** *n*

bolster[2] /bṓlstə/ *n* a chisel with a wide cutting edge. Use: cutting stone. [Early 20C. Alteration of *boaster* < *boast* 'cut with a chisel' < ?]

bolt[1] /bōlt/ *n* **1 BAR FOR FASTENING DOOR** a sliding bar that fits into a socket and secures a door or gate **2 SHORT SCREW** a short cylindrical metal bar with a screw thread, used with a nut **3 ARROW FOR CROSSBOW** a short arrow for use with a crossbow **4 PART OF GUN** in a breech-loading firearm, a sliding rod, bar, or plate that ejects a used cartridge and closes the breech **5 LIGHTNING FLASH** a flash of lightning **6 ROLL OF FABRIC** a rolled length of fabric or wallpaper **7 METAL PIN** a nail-like metal shaft used to provide an anchor in rock faces ■ *v* **1** *vt* **LOCK WITH BOLT** to fasten a door or gate by sliding a bolt into a socket **2** *vi* **RUSH AWAY** to move suddenly and quickly, especially out of fright **3** *vt* **EXPEL FROM HIDING-PLACE** to flush out a wild animal that is hidden or concealed **4** *vt* **DEVOUR HURRIEDLY** to swallow food hurriedly without chewing **5** *vi* **PREMATURELY PRODUCE SEEDS** to flower and produce seeds earlier than expected or wanted **6** *vt* **ROLL INTO BOLT** to roll fabric or wallpaper into a bolt [Old English, 'crossbow bolt' < ?] —**bolter** *n* ◇ **like a bolt from the blue**

very suddenly and unexpectedly ◇ **make a bolt for something** to make a sudden rush towards something ◇ **shoot your bolt** to use all your resources

bolt[2] /bōlt/, **boult** *vt* to filter a substance through a cloth or sieve, especially flour [12C. < Old French *buleter* < Germanic.]

Bolt /bōlt/, **Robert** (1924–95) British playwright

bolt-action *adj* describes a gun with a sliding bolt that replaces the used cartridge and closes the breech

bolthole /bṓlt hōl/ *n* a place of escape, especially for an animal fleeing from danger ○ *The rabbit ran down a bolthole.*

Bolton /bṓltən/ town in NW England. Population: 253,300 (1991).

bolt-on *adj* **1 ATTACHABLE WITH A BOLT** attachable by means of a bolt **2 ATTACHABLE AS AN EXTRA** attachable as an extra without affecting or requiring change to the rest ■ *n* **ADDITIONAL PART** something that can be added to a larger structure (*informal*)

boltrope /bṓlt rōp/ *n* a rope sewn along the lower edge or leading edge of a sail to strengthen it

Boltzmann constant /bóltsmən-/ *n* (*symbol k*) the ratio of the universal gas constant to Avogadro's number [After Ludwig *Boltzmann* (1844–1906), Austrian physicist]

bolus /bṓləss/ *n* **1 INTRAVENOUS INJECTION OF DRUG** a rapidly absorbed, intravenous injection of a drug **2 LARGE PILL** a very large pill **3 ROUND MASS** a soft rounded ball, especially of chewed food [Mid-16C. Via late Latin < Greek *bōlos* 'clod of earth'.]

boma /bṓmə/ *n* in central and eastern Africa, a police post or magistrate's office [Late 19C. < Kiswahili.]

⚡**bomb** /bom/ *n* **1 EXPLOSIVE PROJECTILE** a missile containing explosive or other destructive material **2 SPECIALIZED EXPLOSIVE DEVICE** a device that contains explosive material, especially one designed to explode after some time **3 bomb, Bomb ATOM BOMB** the atom bomb considered as the absolute weapon of mass destruction ○ *lived in dread of the Bomb during the Cold War* **4 LOT OF MONEY** a great deal of money (*informal*) ○ *It cost a bomb.* **5 DEVICE FOR DIRECTING RADIATION** a device that contains radioactive material and is used to beam therapeutic radiation at a patient **6 SOLIDIFIED LAVA** a solidified rounded or teardrop-shaped mass of lava from a volcano **7** *US, Can, ANZ* **ARTISTIC FAILURE** a performance that is a commercial or artistic failure (*informal*) **8** *ANZ* **DILAPIDATED VEHICLE** a battered or dilapidated vehicle (*informal*) **9** *US* **SOMETHING OR SOMEBODY GOOD** something or somebody extremely good or exciting (*slang*) ○ *Their lead singer is the bomb.* ■ *v* **1** *vti* **ATTACK PEOPLE AND PLACES WITH BOMBS** to drop bombs on people or places, or attack or destroy them with bombs ○ *bombing enemy territory* **2** *vt* **DAMAGE BUILDING WITH EXPLOSION** to destroy or damage a building by placing an explosive device there (*often with 'out'*) ○ *the wreckage of bombed-out homes* **3** *vi* **MOVE VERY FAST** to move exceptionally fast, especially in a vehicle (*informal*) **4** *vi* **FAIL MISERABLY** to fail badly as a performance (*informal*) **5** *vi* **CRASH** of a computer, to fail suddenly (*informal*) [Late 17C. Via French, Italian, and Latin, < Greek *bombos* 'booming sound'.]

bomb out *vt* (*usually passive*) **1** to destroy a home or workplace completely by bombing it **2** to drive somebody out of a home or workplace by bombing

bombard /bom baád/ *vt* **1 ATTACK WITH MISSILES** to attack an enemy or enemy territory intensively with sustained artillery fire or bombs **2 HIT REPEATEDLY** to attack somebody persistently and vigorously **3 OVERWHELM** to overwhelm somebody, e.g. with questions **4 HIT WITH HIGH-ENERGY PARTICLES** to direct high-energy particles against atoms or nuclei ■ *n* **MEDIEVAL CANNON** a cannon used in medieval times to throw large stones [15C. < French *bombarder* < *bombarde* 'cannon' < Latin *bombus* < Greek *bombos* 'booming sound'.] —**bombarder** *n* —**bombardment** *n*

bombardier /bómbə deér/ *n* **1** a member of a military aircraft crew who releases bombs **2** a noncommissioned officer in the Royal Artillery of a rank below sergeant [Mid-16C. < French, < *bombarde* 'cannon' (see BOMBARD).]

bombardier beetle *n* a beetle that squirts volatile acrid liquid when attacked. *Brachinus crepitans.*

bombardon /bómbərdən/ *n* **1** a brass wind instrument of the tuba family **2** a bass reed stop on an organ [Mid-19C. Via Italian *bombardone* < medieval Latin *bombarda* 'bombard' (see BOMBARD).]

bombasine *n* TEXTILES = **bombazine**

bombast /bóm bast/ *n* language that is full of long or pretentious words, used to impress others [Late 16C. Alteration of Old French *bombace* 'cotton stuffing', via medieval Latin *bombax* 'cotton' < Greek *bombux* 'silk, silkworm'.] —**bombastic** /bom bástik/ *adj* —**bombastically** *adv*

Bombay /bom báy/ former name for **Mumbai**

Bombay duck *n* **1** a fish, especially the bummalo, dried, salted, grilled, and served as a pungent accompaniment to Indian foods **2** = **bummalo** [Mid-19C. < Marathi *bombīla* 'bummalo', by association with BOMBAY, from where the fish were exported.]

bombay mix *n* a spiced mixture of fried lentils and other Asian dried foods, eaten as a snack or appetizer [After BOMBAY]

bombazine /bómbə zeén, bómbə zeen/, **bombasine** *n* a twilled silk or cotton and worsted material, usually dyed black. Use: formerly, mourning clothes. [Late 16C. Via French *bombasin* < medieval Latin *bombycinus* 'silken' < Latin *bombyx* 'silk, silkworm' < Greek *bombux*.]

bomb bay *n* the compartment on board a bomber aircraft in which the bombs are carried

bomb calorimeter *n* a device for measuring calorific values in which substances are burned inside a sealed vessel

bomb disposal *n* the task or process of rendering bombs harmless by defusing, removing, or detonating them in a controlled explosion (*hyphenated before nouns*) ○ *a bomb-disposal expert*

bombé /bom báy/ *adj* describes furniture with a bulging convex shape, typical of French rococo furniture of the 18th century [Early 20C. < French, 'swollen'.]

bombed /bomd/ *adj* **1** severely damaged or destroyed by bombing **2** intoxicated by alcohol or a drug (*slang*)

bomber /bómmər/ *n* **1** an aircraft designed for carrying and dropping bombs **2** somebody who plants bombs

bomber jacket *n* a short jacket, usually leather, with an elasticated waist and usually a zip at the front [< the wearing of such jackets by the crew of US bomber aircraft]

bombinate /bómbi nayt/ (**-nates, -nating, -nated**), **bombilate** /-layt/ (**-lates, -lating, -lated**) *vi* to make a humming or buzzing noise [Late 19C. < medieval Latin *bombinat-*, past participle of *bombinare* 'to buzz' < Latin *bombus* < Greek *bombos* 'booming sound'.] —**bombination** /bómbi náysh'n/ *n*

bombing /bómming/ *n* the act or process of dropping bombs from aircraft

bomblet /bómmlət/ *n* a small bomb or explosive device packed into a larger bomb

bombora /bom báwrə/ *n Aus* **1** a reef lying just below sea level **2** a dangerous patch of sea where waves break over a reef [Mid-20C. < an Aboriginal language.]

bombproof /bóm proof/ *adj* constructed to withstand the impact of bombs

bombshell /bóm shel/ *n* **1 SURPRISING NEWS** an unexpected and shocking piece of news (*informal*) **2 STUNNING WOMAN** a very good-looking and glamorous woman (*dated informal*) **3 ARTILLERY SHELL OR BOMB** an artillery shell or a bomb

bombsight /bóm sīt/ *n* a device in an aircraft for aiming bombs

bomb site *n* an area devastated by bombs

Bon, Cape /bon/ peninsula in NE Tunisia

Bona, Mount /bṓnə/ highest peak in the Wrangell Mountains, S Alaska. Height: 5,032 m/16,500 ft.

bona fide /bṓnə fídi/ *adj* **1** authentic and genuine in nature ○ *a bona fide offer* **2** without any intention to deceive [< Latin, 'with good faith']

bona fides /-fídeez/ *npl* a sincere statement or evidence of good intentions

bonanza /bə nánzə/ *n* **1** a source that yields great riches or success **2** an extremely valuable mineral deposit [Early 19C. Via Spanish < medieval Latin *bonacia* 'calm seas', alteration of *malacia* 'calm seas' after Latin *bonus* 'good'.]

Bonaparte /bṓnə paárt/ ♦ **Napoleon I**

Bonapartism /bṓnə paartizəm/ *n* **1** government by or on the pattern of Napoleon I **2** support for Napoleon I or Napoleon III or their dynasty —**Bonapartist** *n, adj*

bona vacantia /bṓnə və kánti ə/ *n* in law, property that is unclaimed or that has no known owner (+ *singular or plural verb*) [< Latin, 'ownerless goods']

Bonaventure /bonə vénchər/, **Bonaventura** /bónnə ven tyóorə/, **St** (1221?–74) Italian friar and theologian

bonbon /bón bon/ *n* **1** a sweet confection **2** something that is sweet and unsubstantial [Late 18C. < French, 'good-good' < Latin *bonus* 'good'.]

bonbonnière /bónbə neér, -nyáir/ *n* an ornamental bowl or box for sweets [Early 19C. < French, < *bonbon* (see BONBON).]

bonce /bonss/ *n* somebody's head (*informal*) [Mid-19C. < ?]

bond /bond/ *n* **1 SOMETHING THAT BINDS** an object such as a rope, band, or chain that binds somebody or something **2 SOLEMN PROMISE** a solemn agreement promising to do something **3 PROMISE TO PAY** a document that legally obliges one party to pay money to another **4 CERTIFICATE PROMISING DEPT REPAYMENT** a certificate issued by the government or a company promising to pay back borrowed money at a fixed rate of interest on a specified date **5 ADHESION** the way in which one surface sticks to another **6 ADHESIVE SUBSTANCE** a substance that makes objects adhere **7 ATTRACTIVE FORCE** a fundamental attractive force that binds atoms and ions in a molecule **8 TECHNIQUE FOR OVERLAPPING BRICKS** an overlapping pattern in which bricks or tiles can be laid **9 LINK BETWEEN PEOPLE** a link that binds people together in a relationship **10 RESTRAINT** a situation that limits somebody socially, psychologically, or emotionally **11 SECURE STORAGE** secure storage of goods before payment of duty **12** INDUST = **bond paper 13** *Aus* **SURETY** a deposit, especially on rented accommodation ■ *v* **1** *vti* **ADHERE OR MAKE SURFACES ADHERE** to stick together, or make two surfaces stick together **2** *vti* **LINK EMOTIONALLY** to link together, or cause people to be linked together, emotionally or psychologically **3** *vt* **STORE SECURELY** to store goods securely until duty is paid **4** *vti* **CONVERT INTO DEBT UNDER BOND** to convert something, or be converted, into a debt with a bond as security **5** *vt* **LINK WITH CHEMICAL BOND** to link atoms or ions with a chemical bond **6** *vt* **OVERLAP** to lay bricks or tiles so that they overlap in a pattern **7** *vt* **FUSE TOGETHER** to fuse two fabrics together **8** *vt Aus* **GIVE MONEY DEPOSIT** to provide a bond against unforeseen losses [13C. Variant of BAND[2].] —**bondable** *adj*

Bond /bond/, **Alan** (*b.* 1938) British-born Australian business executive

Bond, Edward (*b.* 1934) British playwright and director

bondage /bóndij/ *n* **1 SLAVERY** the condition of being enslaved or a serf **2 RESTRICTION** the condition of being controlled by something that limits freedom **3 PHYSICAL RESTRAINT** the practice of being tied up or restrained physically during sexual intercourse **4** HIST = **villeinage** *n.* 1 [14C. < Anglo-Norman, < Old Norse *bóndi* 'husbandman' < present participle of *búa* 'dwell'.]

bonded /bóndid/ *adj* **1** stored securely until duty or tax is paid **2** chemically attached or fused together in layers

bonded warehouse *n* a warehouse that holds goods awaiting duty or tax to be paid on them

bond energy *n* the energy required to dissociate the bonds of a specific type within a molecule

bonder /bóndər/ *n* **1** somebody who or something that bonds **2** CONSTR = **bondstone**

bondholder /bónd hōldər/ *n* an owner of government or company bonds

Bondi Beach /bóndī-/ coastal suburb of Sydney, Australia, a popular surfing centre

bonding /bónding/ *n* **1 FORMATION OF EMOTIONAL BONDS** the formation of a close emotional tie between people, e.g. between a mother and her newly born infant **2 COATING A TOOTH** the process of coating a tooth with a durable resinous substance **3 PROCESS OF BONDING** the process by which something is bonded

bondman /bóndmən/ (*plural* **-men** /-mən/) *n US* HIST = **bondsman** *n.* 2

bond paper *n* a strong, white, high-quality paper

bondsman /bóndzmən/ (*plural* **-men** /-mən/) *n* **1** somebody responsible for a legal bond **2** an enslaved man or serf. US term **bondman** [13C. < *bond* 'bound in servitude'.]

bondstone /bónd stōn/ *n* a stone that extends into the interior of a wall in order to strengthen it

bone /bōn/ *n* **1 SECTION OF THE SKELETON** any one of the hard parts forming the skeleton in vertebrate animals **2 MATERIAL MAKING UP BONES** the main material that makes up a vertebrate skeleton, formed principally from collagen fibres and calcium phosphate **3 SUBSTANCE RESEMBLING BONE** something hard that resembles the bone of the vertebrate skeleton, e.g. whalebone or ivory **4 IVORY COLOUR** the ivory or off-white colour of bone **5 STRIP USED AS STIFFENING** a flat strip of hard material, e.g. whalebone or plastic, used to stiffen a garment ■ **bones** *npl* **1 LIVING BODY** somebody's living body (*humorous*) ○ *I must rest my weary bones.* **2 DEAD BODY** the skeleton or corpse of a dead person or animal **3 PAIR OF RHYTHMICALLY CLACKING BARS** a pair of bars or strips of wood, metal, or bone, that are struck together sharply to make musical rhythms **4 STRUCTURE** the structure or framework of something **5 DICE** a pair of dice (*informal*) ■ *vt* (**bones, boning, boned**) **1 REMOVE BONES FROM** to remove the bones from fish, meat, or poultry when preparing it for cooking or eating **2 STIFFEN** to add flat strips to stiffen a garment **3** *US* **OFFENSIVE TERM** an offensive term meaning to have sexual intercourse with somebody (*slang*) ■ *adv* **VERY** extremely or totally ○ *He's bone idle!* [Old English *bān* < Germanic, 'long bone'] ◇ **feel** *or* **know it in your bones** to be sure that something is true without having any proof or being able to explain why ◇ **have a bone to pick with somebody** to have cause for disagreement with somebody ◇ **make no bones about something** to say something openly and frankly

bone up *vi* to review or study something intensely (*informal*)

bone ash *n* the residue, composed mostly of calcium phosphate, that remains when bones of animals are burnt to a powder. Use: fertilizer, bone china manufacture.

bone china *n* **1** a fine white porcelain made from a mixture of clay and bone ash **2** articles made of bone china

bone dry *adj* containing no moisture at all

bonefire /bṓn fīr/ *n Ireland* a bonfire [Variant of BONFIRE]

bonefish /bṓn fish/ (*plural* **-fish** *or* **-fishes**) *n* a large game fish found in warm shallow waters. *Albula vulpes.*

bonehead /bṓn hed/ *n* an offensive term that deliberately insults somebody's intelligence (*insult*) —**boneheaded** /bṓn héddid/ *adj* —**boneheadedness** *n*

boneless /bṓnləss/ *adj* having the bones removed in preparation for cooking or eating

bone marrow *n* a soft reddish substance inside some bones that is involved in the production of blood cells. New white and red blood cells are formed only in the marrow of the flat bones such as the ribs, breastbone, or pelvis in adults.

bone meal *n* ground animal bones, used as a fertilizer or in animal feed [< MEAL[2]]

bone of contention *n* a subject of constant argument or disagreement between people [< dogs fighting over a bone]

boner /bṓnər/ *n* **1 EMBARRASSING MISTAKE** an embarrassing mistake (*informal*) **2** *US* **ERECTION** an erect penis (*slang*) **3 DEVICE THAT BONES** something that is designed for boning something, or somebody who bones something ○ *a fish boner*

boneset /bṓn set/ (*plural* **-set** *or* **-sets**) *n* a plant of the daisy family believed to have healing properties. Native to: North America. Genus: *Eupatorium.*

bonesetter /bṓn setər/ *n* somebody who sets broken or dislocated bones

boneshaker /bṓn shaykər/ *n* **1** a decrepit or uncomfortable vehicle (*informal*) **2** an early type of bicycle with solid tyres and no springs

bone spavin *n* an inflammation of the bones in a horse's hock, resulting in swelling and lameness

boneyard /bṓn yaard/ *n* a cemetery (*informal*)

bonfire /bón fīr/ *n* a large fire built outside for burning rubbish or garden refuse, as part of a celebration, or as a signal [14C. < BONE.]

Bonfire Night *n* the anniversary of the day on which Guy Fawkes' plot to blow up Parliament (**the Gunpowder Plot**) was discovered in 1605, marked with fireworks and bonfires in the United Kingdom and other Commonwealth countries. Date: 5 November.

bong[1] /bong/ *n, interj* a deep resonant sound, especially from a bell ■ *vi* to make a deep resonant sound [Mid-19C. An imitation of the sound.]

bong[2] /bong/ *n* **1** a water pipe for smoking hashish or other drugs (*slang*) **2** a large metal device resembling a tube, used in providing protection for climbers [Late 20C. Probably < Thai *baung.*]

Bongaree /bóng gə rée/ resort on Bribie Island, off the coast of SE Queensland, Australia. Population: 11,166 (1996).

bongo /bóng gō/ (*plural* **-gos** *or* **-goes** *or* **-go**) *n* a forest-dwelling antelope with a reddish coat and vertical white stripes and spiralling horns. Native to: central Africa. *Boocercus euryceros.* [Mid-19C. < Kikongo.]

bongo drums, bongos *npl* a set of two small deep-bodied drums that are held between the knees and beaten with the fingers [< American Spanish *bongó*]

Bonhoeffer /bón h-fər/, **Dietrich** (1906–45) German pastor and theologian

bonhomie /bónnə mee/ *n* easy good-humoured friendliness [Late 18C. < French *bonhomme* 'good man'.] —**bonhomous** /bónnəməss/ *adj*

Boniface /bónni fayss/, **St** (675?–754?) Saxon missionary. Born **Wynfrith**. Known as **the Apostle of Germany**

Boniface VIII (1234?–1303) pope (1294–1303). Born **Benedetto Caetani**

Bonington /bónningtən/, **Sir Chris** (*b.* 1934) British mountaineer. Full name **Sir Christian John Storey Bonington**

Bonin Islands /bṓnin-/ Japanese island group in the W Pacific Ocean. Population: 2,303 (1985). Area: 104 sq. km/40 sq. mi.

bonito /bə néetō/ (*plural* **-tos** *or* **-to**) *n* **1 FISH OF MACKEREL FAMILY** a striped fish. Native to: Atlantic and Pacific waters. Genus: *Sarda.* **2 BONITO AS FOOD** the flesh of a bonito used as food **3 FISH RESEMBLING TRUE BONITO** a fish such as the skipjack that resembles or is related to the bonito [Late 16C. Probably < Spanish, 'pretty' < Latin *bonus* 'good'.]

bonk /bongk/ *v* **1** *vt* **BANG** to bang or hit something or somebody (*informal*) **2** *vti* **OFFENSIVE TERM** to have sexual intercourse (*slang offensive*) ■ *n* **1 SHARP BLOW** a sharp blow, typically on the head **2 OFFENSIVE TERM** an offensive term for sexual intercourse (*slang*) [Early 20C. An imitation of the sound.]

bonkers /bóngkərz/ *adj* an offensive term meaning irrational (*informal*) [Mid-20C. < ?]

bon mot /bóN mṓ/ (*plural* **bons mots** /bóN mṓ/) *n* a witty comment [< French, 'good word']

Bonn /bon/ city in west-central Germany. Population: 293,072 (1997).

Bonnard /bónnaar, bo náar/, **Pierre** (1867–1947) French painter

bonne /bon/ *n* a French woman servant (*dated*) [Late 18C. < French, 'good girl'.]

bonne bouche /bón bóosh/ (*plural* **bonnes bouches** /bón bóosh/) *n* a small piece of tasty food [< French, 'good mouth']

Bonner /bónnər/, **Neville Thomas** (*b.* 1922) Australian politician

bonnet /bónnit/ *n* **1 WOMAN'S HAT** a hat framing the face and usually tied under the chin, worn by a woman or girl **2 COVER OF CAR ENGINE** the hinged cover over the engine of a car or other vehicle, usually at the front. US term **hood**[1] *n.* 3 **3** *Scotland* **SOFT FLAT CAP** a soft flat cap, worn by men or boys **4 NATIVE NORTH AMERICAN HEADDRESS** a ceremonial feathered headdress traditionally worn by some Native North Americans **5 CHIMNEY COWL** a wire cover fitted over a chimney pot **6 PROTECTIVE COVER** a protective cap or cover fitting over a machine part **7 EXTRA PIECE OF SAIL** an extra strip of canvas laced to the base of a foresail, used to extend it when the wind is light [14C. < Old French *bonet* < medieval Latin *abonnis* 'headgear'.] —**bonneted** *adj*

bonnethead /bónnət hed/ (*plural* **-heads** *or* **-head**), **bonnethead shark** *n* ZOOL = **shovelhead**

Bonneville Salt Flats /bónnəvil-/ barren salt plain in NW Utah, used for setting world land speed records. Area: 260 sq. km/100 sq. mi.

Bonnie Prince Charlie /bónni prinss cháarli/ ➧ **Charles Edward Stuart**

bonny /bónni/ (**-nier, -niest**), **bonnie** (**-nier, -niest**) *adj Scotland, N England* **1 ATTRACTIVE** pleasing to look at **2 SUBSTANTIAL** fairly large **3 EXCELLENT** extremely good **4 PLUMP AND HEALTHY** plump and healthy [15C. < ?] —**bonnily** *adv* —**bonniness** *n*

bonsai /bón sī/ (*plural* **-sai** *or* **-sais**) *n* **1** the art of growing miniaturized forms of trees and shrubs by rigorous pruning of roots and branches **2** a tree or shrub miniaturized using bonsai techniques [Early 20C. < Japanese, 'tray planting'.]

bonsela /bon séllə/, **bonsella** *n S Africa* **1** a tip or gratuity **2** a small reward, usually of sweets, given to a good customer by a trader [< ?]

bonspiel /bón speel/ *n* a curling match or tournament [Mid-16C. Probably < Dutch or Low German.]

bontebok /bónti buk/ (*plural* **-boks** *or* **-bok**) *n* a S African antelope with a reddish coat, white markings on the face and rump, and white legs. *Damaliscus pygargus.* [Late 18C. < Afrikaans, 'pied buck'.]

bon ton /bóN tóN/ *n* (*literary*) **1** good taste, style, or manners ○ *People thought it bon ton to be seen attending such an occasion.* **2** fashionable society [< French, 'good tone']

bonus /bṓnəss/ *n* **1 UNEXPECTED EXTRA** an extra unexpected advantage **2 EXTRA MONEY** an amount of money given in addition to normal pay, especially as a reward **3 PREMIUM PAID TO** an extra dividend or premium paid to the purchaser, holder, promoter, or vendor of a stock or insurance policy [Late 18C. < Latin, 'good'.]

bonus issue *n* an issue of free shares, distributed pro rata by a company to existing shareholders

bon vivant /bóN vee vóN/ (*plural* **bons vivants** /bóN vee vóN/), **bon viveur** /-vee vúr/ (*plural* **bons viveurs** /bóN vee vúr/) *n* somebody who enjoys the luxuries in life [*Bon vivant* < French, 'somebody who lives well'; *bon viveur* formed in English after *bon vivant* and French *viveur* 'living person']

bon voyage /bóN vwaa yáazh, bón voy áazh/ *interj* used to wish somebody an enjoyable and safe journey [< French, 'good journey']

bony /bṓni/ (**-ier, -iest**) *adj* **1 HAVING PROMINENT BONES** extremely thin and with prominent bones **2 CONTAINING MANY BONES** containing a lot of bones, and often difficult to eat **3 OF OR LIKE BONE** consisting of or like bone **4 WITH A BACKBONE** describes fish that have a skeleton of bone, as distinct from cartilaginous fish such as sharks. Class: Osteichthyes. —**boniness** *n*

bonze /bonz/ *n* a Buddhist monk in Southeast Asia, China, or Japan [Late 16C. Via French < Japanese *bonsō.*]

bonzer /bónzər/ *adj ANZ* with the best or most pleasing qualities (*dated informal*) [Early 20C. < ?]

boo /boo/ *interj* **1 EXPRESSING DISAPPROVAL** used to express dissatisfaction or contempt, especially at a speaker or performer **2 USED TO STARTLE** used to surprise or startle somebody ■ *n* **SOUND 'BOO!'** an utterance of 'boo!' ■ *vti* **EXPRESS DISAPPROVAL** to shout 'boo!' in order to express disapproval or contempt of somebody, especially a speaker or performer [Early 19C. Originally an imitation of a cow's lowing.] ◇ **would not say boo to a goose** to be extremely timid and shy (*informal*)

booai *n NZ* = **boohai**

booay *n NZ* = **boohai**

boob[1] /boob/, **booby** /bóobi/ (*plural* **-bies**) *n* a woman's breast (*slang; often considered offensive; usually plural*) [Mid-20C. < *bubby* < ?]

boob[2] /boob/ *n* **1 UNFORTUNATE MISTAKE** an unfortunate and embarrassing mistake (*informal*) **2 UNINTELLIGENT PERSON** somebody who is considered unintelligent ■ *vi UK, Can* **MAKE AN UNFORTUNATE MISTAKE** to make an unfortunate and embarrassing mistake (*informal*) [Early 20C. Shortening of BOOBY[1].]

boo-boo *n* a mistake or tactless remark (*informal*) [Mid-20C. Probably < BOOB[2].]

boobook /bóobòók/ (*plural* **-books** *or* **-book**) *n* a small owl with greyish-brown to dark-brown plumage and greenish-yellow eyes set in a large facial mask. Native to: Australia, New Zealand. *Ninox novaeseelandiae.* [Early 19C. < an Aboriginal language; an imitation of the bird's call.]

boob tube[1] *n* a short strapless stretchy top for women (*slang*)

boob tube[2] *n US, Can* television (*informal*)

booby[1] /bóobi/ (*plural* **-bies**) *n* **1** somebody considered silly or unintelligent (*dated informal*) **2** a large seabird of the gannet family, with brown, black, or white plumage, often with a brightly coloured bill and feet. Native to: tropical regions. Family: Sulidae. [Early 17C. Probably alteration of Spanish *bobo* < Latin *balbus* 'stammering'.]

booby[2] *n* ANAT = **boob**[1]

booby hatch *n* a cover for a small hatchway on a sailing ship [< BOOBY[1], because a favourite haunt for these birds]

booby prize *n* a prize given as a joke to the person or team coming last in a competition

booby trap *n* **1** a trap set as a practical joke **2** a bomb that is hidden or disguised and is designed to explode when touched or moved

booby-trap (**booby-traps, booby-trapping, booby-trapped**) *vt* to place a booby trap in a place or attach one to something (*often passive*)

boodle /bŏŏd'l/ *n* a large amount of money that has been acquired or used in a corrupt way (*slang*) [Early 17C. < Dutch *boedel* 'estate, possessions'.]

boofhead /bŏŏf hed/ *n Aus* somebody who is considered unintelligent or thoughtless (*informal insult*) [Mid-20C. Perhaps < BUFFLEHEAD in the obsolete sense 'simpleton'.]

booger /bŏŏggər/ *n US* = **bogey** *n.* 3 (*slang*) [Mid-19C. Probably alteration of BUGGER[1].]

boogie /bŏŏgi/ *vi* (**-ies, -ieing, -ied**) to dance to fast rock music (*informal*) ■ *n* MUSIC = **boogie-woogie** [Mid-20C. < ?]

boogie on down *vi* to go off somewhere (*slang*)

boogie-woogie /bŏŏgi wŏŏgi/ *n* a jazz piano style derived from the blues

boohai /bŏŏ hī/, **booai** /bŏŏ ī/, **booay** *n NZ* a remote rural area (*informal*) [Mid-20C. < ?]

boohoo /boo hŏŏ/ *n, interj* used to represent the sound of noisy weeping ■ *vi* (**-hoos, -hooing, -hooed**) to cry noisily [Mid-19C. An imitation of the sound.]

book /bŏŏk/ *n* **1 BOUND COLLECTION OF PAGES** a collection of printed or manuscript pages sewn or glued together along one side and bound between rigid boards or flexible covers **2 PUBLISHED WORK** a published work of literature, science, or reference, or one intended for publication **3 BOUND SET OF BLANK SHEETS** a bound set of blank sheets of paper, e.g. for writing in **4 SET OF THINGS BOUND TOGETHER** a set of objects, e.g. matches or fabric samples, that are bound together **5 DIVISION OF LITERARY WORK** each of several major divisions of a literary work or of the Bible **6 SCRIPT OR LIBRETTO** the script of a play or the libretto of an opera **7 BOOKMAKER'S RECORD** a record kept by a bookmaker of the bets made and of the money paid out **8 TELEPHONE DIRECTORY** a telephone directory (*informal*) **9 NUMBER OF TRICKS NEEDED IN SCORING** in cards, the number of tricks that need to be won by a player or side in order to be scored **10 MAGAZINE** a magazine for reading or looking at (*informal*) **11 SET OF RULES** the body of rules or procedures relevant to a situation ○ *likes to do things by the book* **12 IMAGINARY RECORD** an imaginary record, archive, or repository of knowledge **13** THEATRE = **promptbook 14 book, Book** BIBLE the Christian Bible or Hebrew scripture ■ **books** *npl* **1 FINANCIAL ACCOUNTS** the financial records and accounts of an organization **2 LEARNING** academic study ■ *v* **1** *vti* **MAKE RESERVATION** to arrange for somebody to keep a place available at a specified time, e.g. at the theatre or in a restaurant **2** *vt* **RESERVE A PLACE FOR** to reserve a place for somebody somewhere, especially on some form of transport **3** *vt* **ENGAGE SOMEONE** to engage somebody in advance to do something or be somewhere, especially as a performer (*often passive*) **4** *vt* **CHARGE WITH CRIMINAL OFFENCE** to charge somebody with a criminal offence, pending legal proceedings (*often passive*) **5** *vt* **TAKE NAME OF OFFENDING PLAYER** in sports, officially to take the name of a player who has committed an offence (*often passive*) **6** *vi US* **LEAVE A PLACE** to leave a place (*slang*) ○ *Yo man, let's book!* [Old English *bōc* 'written document' < Indo-European, 'beech'] —**booker** *n* ◇ **a closed book** a person or thing about which little, if anything, is known or understood ◇ **an open book** a person or thing that is fully understood ◇ **bring somebody to book** to admonish somebody ◇ **cook the books** to alter records, especially financial accounts, to conceal irregularities or wrongdoing (*slang*) ◇ **in somebody's book** in somebody's opinion ◇ **in somebody's good** *or* **bad books** in *or* out of favour with somebody ◇ **throw the book at somebody** to charge somebody with all the offences he or she may be guilty of, or punish somebody with the maximum penalty

book in *v* **1** *vti* to reserve accommodation at a hotel or other lodgings **2** *vi* to sign in at a hotel or other lodgings

book out *vti* to register that you have or somebody else has completed a stay at a hotel or other accommodation

book up *vi* to reserve accommodation or buy a ticket for something in advance

bookable /bŏŏkəb'l/ *adj* **1** able to be applied for in advance and reserved **2** serious enough for the referee to give a warning and record it officially

bookbinder /bŏŏk bīndər/ *n* somebody who binds books —**bookbindery** *n* —**bookbinding** *n*

bookcase /bŏŏk kayss/ *n* a set of shelves, either fixed to a wall or free-standing, used for holding books

book club *n* an organization that offers its members books at reduced prices

~~**bookeeping**~~ incorrect spelling of **bookkeeping**

bookend /bŏŏk end/ *n* either of a pair of supports placed at each end of a row of books ■ *vt* to occur on both sides or at the beginning and end of something (*informal*) ○ *bookend a speech with anecdotes*

Booker Prize /bŏŏkər-/ *n* a cash prize awarded annually by the company Booker McConnell for a recently published work of fiction by a UK, Irish, or Commonwealth writer —**Booker Prizewinner** *n*

bookie /bŏŏki/ *n* a bookmaker (*informal*) [Late 19C. < BOOKMAKER.]

booking /bŏŏking/ *n* **1** an arrangement by which something such as a theatre seat or hotel room is kept for somebody's use at a specified time **2** a contract or arrangement for an entertainer to perform somewhere

bookish /bŏŏkish/ *adj* devoted to reading, especially to the exclusion of other things —**bookishly** *adv* —**bookishness** *n*

bookkeeping /bŏŏk keeping/, **book-keeping** *n* the activity or profession of recording the money received and spent by an individual, business, or organization —**bookkeeper** *n*

book learning *n* knowledge obtained from books rather than from experience

booklet /bŏŏklət/ *n* a small book with a paper cover and few pages, usually containing information about a particular subject

booklore /bŏŏk lawr/ *n* **1** = **book learning 2** information about books, especially their authors and circumstances of publication

booklouse /bŏŏk lowss/ (*plural* **-lice** /-līss/) *n* a small wingless insect that destroys books by feeding on the paste used in the binding. Order: Psocoptera.

book lung *n* the breathing organ in spiders and other arachnids, with membranous tissue arranged in folds that resemble the leaves of a book

bookmaker /bŏŏk maykər/ *n* **1** somebody who takes bets and pays winners **2** a book designer, printer, or binder —**bookmaking** *n*

bookman /bŏŏkmən/ (*plural* **-men** /-mən/) *n* a book enthusiast or collector

ϟ**bookmark** /bŏŏk maark/ *n* **1 MARKER IN BOOK** a strip of leather or other material inserted between the pages of a book to mark a place in it **2 MARKER IN ELECTRONIC TEXT** an electronic marker in a word-processed document, identifying it for reference or retrieval **3 ADDRESS OF INTERNET SITE** the address of a favourite Internet site electronically listed ■ *vt* **LIST AN INTERNET ADDRESS** to list the address of an Internet site

bookmobile /bŏŏk mō beel/ *n US, Can* a large motor vehicle equipped as a small lending library, used for taking books to people, especially in rural areas

Book of Changes *n* PHILOSOPHY = **I Ching** *n.* 2

Book of Common Prayer *n* the official book giving the order and content of services in the Anglican Church

book of hours *n* a medieval service book, used especially in monasteries, containing the offices, prayers, and services prescribed for the various canonical hours

Book of Kells /-kéllz/ *n* an illuminated manuscript of the Christian Gospels, produced at Kells in Ireland in the 8th century and now kept in Trinity College, Dublin

Book of Life *n* **1** a comprehensive personal identity document carried by South Africans. ◊ **dompas 2** the Bible

Book of Mormon *n* a book believed by members of the Church of Jesus Christ of Latter-Day Saints to have been revealed by the prophet Mormon to Joseph Smith. It contains the history of an ancient American people to whom Jesus Christ is believed to have appeared.

bookplate /bŏŏk playt/ *n* a label for sticking into the front of a book, bearing the name of the owner and sometimes a coat of arms or personal design

bookrest /bŏŏk rest/ *n* a support, often angled, for an open book

bookseller /bŏŏk selər/ *n* somebody who deals in books

bookshelf /bŏŏk shelf/ (*plural* **-shelves** /-shelvz/) *n* a shelf designed for holding books

bookshop /bŏŏk shop/ *n* a shop that specializes in selling books

bookstall /bŏŏk stawl/ *n* **1** a stand in the street or at a railway or bus station where newspapers, magazines, and books are sold **2** a stall where books are sold

bookstand /bŏŏk stand/ *n* **1** = **bookstall 2** a support for an open book, often adjustable and made of wood, metal, or plastic

bookstore /bŏŏk stawr/ *n US* a shop that sells books

book token *n* a voucher for a specified value that can be exchanged for books and is often given as a present

book value *n* **1** the value of a commodity or asset according to the accounting records of the firm owning it **2** the net value of a business after liabilities have been deducted from assets

bookworm /bŏŏk wurm/ *n* **1** any insect whose larvae eat the paper or binding paste in books **2** somebody who loves reading (*informal*)

Boole /bool/, **George** (1815–64) British mathematician and logician

ϟ**Boolean** /bŏŏli ən/ *adj* using a system of symbolic logic that uses combinations of such logical operators as 'AND', 'OR', and 'NOT' to determine relationships between entities [Mid-19C. After George BOOLE.]

ϟ**Boolean algebra** *n* a form of algebra concerned with the logical functions of variables that are restricted to two values, true or false

boom[1] /boom/ *v* **1** *vi* **MAKE A LOUD DEEP SOUND** to make a loud deep reverberating sound **2** *vt* **UTTER WITH DEEP SOUND** to utter something, e.g. a warning, in a loud deep voice ■ *n* **1 LOUD DEEP SOUND** a loud deep reverberating sound **2 SIGNIFICANT INCREASE IN BUSINESS** a significant expansion of business and investment, either across an economy or in a specific market **3 SIGNIFICANT INCREASE IN AMOUNT** a significant increase in the amount of something, e.g. a population level **4 DEEP LOUD BIRD OR ANIMAL NOISE** a deep loud cry made by some birds and animals, e.g. bitterns or grouse [15C. Perhaps < Dutch *bommen* 'to hum, buzz'; an imitation of the sound.] —**boomy** *adj*

boom[2] /boom/ *n* **1 BEAM HOLDING SAIL AT ANGLE** a beam to which the bottom edge of a sail is attached in order to hold the sail at an advantageous angle to the wind **2 EXTENDABLE OVERHEAD POLE** an extendable pole carrying overhead equipment, such as a camera, for positioning over a television or film set **3 FLOATING BARRIER** a floating barrier used to confine or restrict something, e.g. a barrier to protect a harbour from attack or to confine an oil spill **4 POLE USED TO MOVE CARGO** a long pole extending from the mast of a derrick to lift or lower cargo **5 CONNECTING SPAR FOR AIRCRAFT** a spar that connects the tail and the fuselage in some aircraft [Mid-16C. < Dutch, 'beam, pole'.]

boom and bust, boom or bust *n* the alternation in an economy or market between immoderate growth and collapse and recession

boom box *n* a large radio and cassette or CD player with a built-in speaker at each end, carried by a handle at the top

boomer /bŏŏmər/ *n* **1** *US* **BABY BOOMER** a baby boomer (*informal*) **2** *Aus* **LARGE KANGAROO** a very large male kangaroo (*informal*) **3 SUBMARINE** a nuclear-powered submarine armed with ballistic missiles (*slang*)

boomerang /bŏŏmə rang/ *n* **1 CURVED MISSILE** a flat curved piece of wood used as a weapon by Australian Aborigines that is designed to return to the person who throws it **2 SOMETHING HARMFUL TO INITIATOR** something that does inadvertent harm to its initiator ■ *vi* **BACKFIRE ON INITIATOR** to backfire on an initiator of an action, causing harm [Late 18C. < an Aboriginal language.]

boomlet /bŏŏmlət/ *n* a short period of sudden and intense economic growth

boomslang /bŏŏm slang/ (*plural* **-slangs** *or* **-slang**) *n* a large greenish tree-dwelling poisonous snake. Native to: Southern Africa. *Dispholidus typus.* [Late 18C. < Afrikaans, 'tree snake'.]

boom town *n* a town that significantly increases in size and wealth, often as the result of new and profitable industry

boon /boon/ *n* something that functions as a blessing or benefit to somebody [12C. < Old Norse *bón* 'prayer, petition' < Indo-European, 'speak'.]

boon companion *n* an intimate and inseparable friend [Via French *bon* < Latin *bonus* 'good']

boondocks /bo͝on doks/ *npl US, Can* anywhere far from civilization, used as an archetype of a provincial way of life and lack of sophistication (*informal*)

boondoggle /bo͝on dog'l/ *n US, Can* an activity or project that is unnecessary and wasteful of time or money, especially one undertaken for personal or political gain (*informal*) [Mid-20C. An invented word: originally a plaited leather cord made by Scouts.] —**boondoggle** *vi* —**boondoggler** *n* —**boondoggling** *n*

Boone /boon/, **Daniel** (1734–1820) American pioneer

boongary /bo͝ong gari/ (*plural* **-ries** *or* **-ry**) *n* a kangaroo that lives in trees. Native to: N Australia. *Dendrolagus lumholtzi.* [Late 19C. < an Aboriginal language.]

boonies /bo͝oniz/ *npl US, Can* = **boondocks**

boor /boor/ *n* a crass, insensitive, or ill-mannered person [Mid-16C. < Dutch *boer* 'peasant'.] —**boorish** *adj* —**boorishly** *adv* —**boorishness** *n*

Boorman /báwrmən/, **John** (*b.* 1933) British film director

boost /boost/ *vt* **1 IMPROVE** to improve or strengthen something **2 INCREASE** to cause something to increase ○ *measures to boost productivity* **3 VIGOROUSLY PROMOTE** to promote something widely and intensively so that people will buy it **4 RAISE VOLTAGE IN** to increase the voltage in an electrical circuit **5 ASSIST BY PUSHING OR LIFTING** to assist somebody or something to get up or over something by giving a push or lift from below ■ *n* **1 ENCOURAGEMENT** something that helps to encourage or improve somebody or something in some way ○ *gave his career a much-needed boost* **2 INCREASE IN** an increase in something ○ *a boost in income* **3 ADVERTISING CAMPAIGN** a campaign advertising or promoting something **4 PUSH OR LIFT FROM BELOW** a push from below to help somebody up or over something [Early 19C. < ?]

booster /bo͝ostər/ *n* **1 RADIO-FREQUENCY AMPLIFIER** a radio-frequency amplifier that amplifies weak television or radio signals and retransmits them so that they can be received by viewers or listeners **2** AEROSP = **booster rocket 3 SOMEBODY OR SOMETHING THAT IMPROVES CONFIDENCE** somebody or something that encourages or improves something such as confidence (*usually in combination*) ○ *a morale-booster* **4 DEVICE THAT ASSISTS** a device used to increase the effectiveness of some piece of equipment **5 SUPPLEMENTARY DOSE OF VACCINE** a repeat dose of a vaccine given some time after the initial course to maintain the level of immunity provided by the previous dose

booster rocket *n* an engine in a space vehicle that is used to give thrust during the launch and extra thrust during another stage of the flight

booster seat *n* a seat that can be placed over another seat in a motor vehicle or at a table to raise a child into a higher position

boot[1] /boot/ *n* **1 STRONG SHOE EXTENDING UP LOWER LEG** a strong item of footwear that covers part of the lower leg (*often in combination*) ○ *an ankle boot* **2 LUGGAGE COMPARTMENT IN A CAR** the luggage compartment of a car. US term **trunk** *n.* 6 **3 HARD KICK** the act of kicking something hard **4 DISMISSAL FROM JOB** dismissal from employment or from a personal relationship (*informal*) **5 COVERING FOR HORSE'S LEG** a protective covering for the lower part of a horse's leg **6 INSTRUMENT OF TORTURE** an instrument of torture that was used in the past to enclose and crush the victim's foot **7 OFFENSIVE TERM** an offensive term that deliberately insults a person's age and appearance (*insult*) **8 PROTECTIVE COVERING** a protective covering, e.g. a rubber sheath for protecting a coupling between two shafts **9** *US* AUTOMOT = **wheel clamp** ■ *vt* **1 KICK SOMEBODY OR SOMETHING HARD** to kick somebody or something hard **2** *US* CARS = **clamp** *v.* 3 [14C. < Old French *bote.*] ◇ **get too big for your boots** to become overconfident (*informal*) ◇ **lick somebody's boots** to be extremely obsequious to somebody ◇ **put the boot in** to attack somebody, often somebody who is vulnerable or already hurt (*informal*)

boot out *vt* to force somebody to leave a place, group of people, or job (*informal*)

⚡**boot**[2] /boot/ *n* the process of starting or restarting a computer and loading the operating system ■ *vi* to start or restart a computer and load the operating system, or be started up in this way [Late 20C. Shortening of BOOTSTRAP in *bootstrap loader*, a simple program that enables a computer to start up and load its full operating system.]

boot up *vt* to start or restart a computer

boot[3] /boot/ [Old English *bōt* 'remedy' < Indo-European, 'good'] ◇ **to boot** in addition

Boot /boot/, **Sir Jesse, Baron Trent** (1850–1931) British pharmaceutical manufacturer

boot and saddle *n* MIL = **boots and saddles**

bootblack /bo͝ot blak/ *n US* = **shoeblack**

boot camp *n* (*informal*) **1** *US* a training camp for military recruits **2** a prison with military-style discipline to which juvenile offenders are sent [< BOOT[1] 'naval or marine corps recruit']

bootee /bo͝o tee/, **bootie** *n* **1** a soft woollen boot for a baby **2** an ankle boot for a woman or child

Boötes /bō ṓ teez/ *n* a constellation of the northern hemisphere, dominated by the bright star Arcturus. See illustration at **constellation**

booth /booth/ (*plural* **booths** /boothz/) *n* **1 SMALL PARTITIONED ENCLOSURE** a partitioned enclosure or small room shaped like a box that offers privacy, e.g. when telephoning, selling tickets, or voting **2 SMALL TENT OR STALL** a tent, stall, or other light structure at a fair or exhibition, offering some form of entertainment or goods for sale **3 RESTAURANT COMPARTMENT** a small, partly enclosed area in a restaurant with a table and high backed seats **4 SMALL ROOM USED IN BROADCASTING** a small soundproof room used for recording sound or for broadcasting [12C. < N Germanic.]

Booth /booth/, **John Wilkes** (1838–65) US actor and assassin of Abraham Lincoln

Booth /booth/, **William** (1829–1912) British religious leader

Boothia Peninsula /bo͝othi ə-/ northernmost tip of mainland North America, in Northwest Territories, Canada. Area: 32,300 sq. km/12,500 sq. mi.

Boothroyd /bo͝oth royd/, **Betty** (*b.* 1929) British politician

bootie *n* CLOTHING = **bootee**

bootjack /bo͝ot jak/ *n* a device similar to a yoke, used for gripping the back of a boot when removing it

bootlace /bo͝ot layss/ *n* a long shoelace, traditionally a narrow cord or a leather thong, for lacing up boots

bootleg /bo͝ot leg/ *vti* (**-legs, -legging, -legged**) **DEAL IN ILLEGAL GOODS** to make, transport, or sell illegal goods, especially illegally copied or recorded material ■ *n* **1 SOMETHING ILLEGALLY MADE** an illegally made product, especially an illegal recording **2 ILLEGAL ALCOHOL** alcohol or an alcoholic beverage that has been smuggled or illegally distilled [Early 20C. Back-formation < *bootlegger* (late 19C), from liquor smugglers carrying bottles in their boots.] —**bootlegger** *n*

bootless /bo͝otləss/ *adj* having little or no success [< BOOT[3]] —**bootlessly** *adv* —**bootlessness** *n*

bootlick /bo͝ot lik/ *vti* to flatter somebody in a position of authority in order to gain an advantage (*informal disapproving*) —**bootlicker** *n* —**bootlicking** *n, adj*

boots /boots/ (*plural* **boots**) *n* somebody who polishes boots and shoes (*dated*)

boot sale *n* = **car boot sale**

bootstrap /bo͝ot strap/ *n* a leather or fabric loop on the back or side of a boot to help pull it on ◇ **pull yourself up by your (own) bootstraps** to improve your situation in life by your own efforts

boot tree *n* **1** a wooden or metal device shaped like a foot and lower leg, placed inside a boot to preserve its shape **2** a foot-shaped support for making or repairing boots

booty /bo͝oti/ *n* money or valuables seized or stolen, especially by soldiers in war [15C. Directly or via Old French *butin* < Middle Low German *būte* 'exchange'.]

booze /booz/ *vi* (**boozes, boozing, boozed**) **OVERINDULGE IN ALCOHOL** to drink alcoholic beverages, especially to excess (*slang*) ■ *n* (*slang*) **1 ALCOHOL** alcoholic drink **2 SESSION OF HEAVY DRINKING** a period of time spent overindulging in alcohol [13C. < Middle Dutch *būsen* 'drink to excess'.]

boozer /bo͝ozər/ *n* (*slang*) **1** a public house or bar **2** a heavy drinker of alcohol

booze-up *n* an occasion when alcohol is drunk to excess (*slang*)

boozy /bo͝ozi/ (**-ier, -iest**) *adj* (*slang*) **1 WITH EXCESSIVE DRINKING** featuring the drinking of alcohol to excess **2 CONTAINING ALCOHOL** containing or flavoured with alcohol **3 DRINKING EXCESSIVELY** tending to drink alcohol excessively **4 SHOWING EFFECTS OF EXCESSIVE DRINKING** showing the effects of prolonged excessive drinking —**boozily** *adv*

bop[1] /bop/ *vi* (**bops, bopping, bopped**) **DANCE** to dance to pop music, especially in a disco (*informal*) ■ *n* **1 A SPELL OF DANCING** a session of dancing to pop music (*informal*) ○ *We had one quick bop and left.* **2 DANCE** a social event organized for the purpose of dancing to pop music (*informal*) **3** MUSIC = **bebop** [Mid-20C. Shortening of BEBOP.]

bop[2] /bop/ *vt* (**bops, bopping, bopped**) to hit somebody, especially to punch somebody in the face (*informal*) ■ *n* a blow, especially a punch in the face (*informal*) [Late 19C. An imitation of the sound.]

bopper /bóppər/ *n* a jazz musician who plays bebop

~~**boquet**~~ incorrect spelling of **bouquet**

bora /báwrə/, **Bora** *n* a cold, dry, strong northeasterly wind that blows down the mountains of central Europe and along the shores of the Adriatic [Mid-19C. < dialect variant of Italian *borea* < Latin *boreas* 'north wind'.]

Bora-Bora /báwrə báwrə/ one of the Leeward Islands of French Polynesia. Population: 4,225 (1988). Area: 39 sq. km/15 sq. mi.

boracic /bə rássik/ *adj* **1** CHEM = **boric 2** *Cockney* having no money (*slang*) [Late 18C. < medieval Latin *borac-*, stem of *borax* (see BORAX).]

borage /bórrij/ *n* a hairy plant that has thick leaves that taste of cucumber and produces oil with pharmaceutical uses. Flowers: blue, star-shaped. Native to: Mediterranean. *Borago officinalis.* [13C. Via French *bourrache* < Latin *bor(r)ago.*]

borane /báw rayn/ *n* any compound containing only boron and hydrogen. Use: rocket and jet engine fuels. [Early 20C. < BORON.]

borate /báw rayt/ *n* a boric acid salt or ester [Late 18C. < BORAX.]

borax /báw raks/ *n* $Na_2B_4O_7.10H_2O$ a white crystalline solid. Source: alkaline soils, salt deposits. Use: boron ore, cleaning agent, water softener, preservative. [14C. Via medieval Latin and colloquial Arabic, < Pahlavi *būrak.*]

borborygmus /báwrbə rígməss/ *n* the rumbling sounds made by the movement of gases in the stomach and intestine (*technical*) [Early 18C. < Greek *borborugmos* < *borboruzein* 'have a rumbling in the bowels'.] —**borborygmic** *adj*

Bordeaux[1] /bawr dṓ/ capital of Gironde Department, SW France. Population: 215,363 (1999).

Bordeaux[2] /bawr dṓ/ (*plural* **-deaux**) *n* red or white wine produced in the region around Bordeaux, France

Bordeaux mixture *n* a solution of copper sulphate and calcium hydroxide in water that is used as a plant fungicide

bordello /bawr déllō/ (*plural* **-los**) *n* a house of prostitution [Late 16C. Via Italian < French *bordel* 'cabin, small hut'.]

Borden /báwrd'n/, **Sir Robert** (1854–1937) Canadian statesman

border /báwrdər/ *n* **1 LINE DIVIDING TWO AREAS** the line that officially separates two countries or regions, or the land on either side of it (*often before nouns*) ○ *across the border* ○ *border country* **2 STRIP AROUND EDGE** a band that runs along the edge of something, e.g. a printed page or a length of fabric, often decorated or itself added for decoration ○ *a handkerchief with a patterned border* **3 LAND AT EDGE** the edge of an area of land, or the ground near the edge ○ *a shy animal that rarely comes nearer than the border of the field* **4 NARROW FLOWERBED** a narrow flowerbed along a wall or at the edge of a lawn or path ■ *vti* **1 FORM FRONTIER WITH PLACE** to form the frontier with another country or the boundary between two regions ○ *Italy borders Austria in the Alps.* **2 BE NEXT TO** to form a line along the edge of something ○ *a field bordered by willow trees* [14C. < Old French *bordeüre* < Germanic.]

border on *vt* to be almost the same as something ○ *an admissions policy bordering on the ridiculous*

Border /báwrdər/, **Allan** (*b.* 1955) Australian cricketer

Border collie *n* a dog with a long silky black-and-white coat, belonging to a breed often kept as sheepdogs [Because originally bred in the border region between England and Scotland]

borderer /báwrdərər/ n somebody who lives in a border area between countries or regions

borderland /báwrdər land/ n **1** the area near the edge of a country or region, especially a remote area **2** the indeterminate area between two conditions, categories, or activities that is hard to define because it contains features or qualities of both

borderline /báwrdər līn/ n **SEPARATING LINE** the notional line that separates one state or quality from another very similar one ○ *the borderline between frankness and rudeness* ■ adj **1 AT CATEGORY'S EDGE** not clearly belonging to one or other of two categories ○ *Borderline candidates will take a further oral exam.* **2 PSYCHOLOGICALLY UNSTABLE** describes a psychological condition characterized by emotional instability and marked by self-destructive, manipulative, and erratic behaviour **3 ALMOST DEVELOPED** describes a medical condition that a patient is likely to develop unless preventive steps are taken ○ *borderline hypertension*

Border terrier n a small short dog belonging to a breed of terriers with rough coats that are kept as pets [Because originally bred in the border region between England and Scotland]

Bordet /báwr day/, **Jules** (1870–1961) Belgian physiologist and bacteriologist

Borduas /báwrdoo aa/, **Paul Émile** (1905–60) Canadian painter

bordure /báwr dyoor/ n the decorated edge running round the edge of the shield on a coat of arms, signifying that the bearer is not the chief of the family [14C. Variant of BORDER.]

bore[1] /báwr/ vt (**bores, boring, bored**) to make somebody lose interest and so feel tired and annoyed ○ *He bored us stiff with a detailed explanation of his holiday itinerary.* ■ n somebody or something regarded as wholly uninteresting or tiresome ○ *Peeling potatoes is a bore!* [Mid-18C. < ?]

SPELLCHECK See **boar**.

bore[2] /báwr/ vti (**bores, boring, bored**) **1 MAKE DEEP HOLE IN** to make a deep hole in something, such as one made by a drill, a bullet, or a boring insect **2 PENETRATE** to penetrate into the inner or hidden parts of somebody or something ○ *questioning that bores deep into their private affairs* ■ n **SIZE OF PIPE** the internal diameter of a pipe, gun barrel, or other hollow cylindrical part [Old English *borian* < Indo-European]

bore[3] /báwr/ n a large powerful wave that the tide causes to move up a river or narrow estuary [Early 17C. < ?]

bore[4] /báwr/ v past participle of **bear**[2]

boreal /báwri əl/ adj describes a region that has a northern temperate climate, with cold winters and warm summers [15C. Directly or via French < late Latin *borealis* < Latin *Boreas* (see BOREAS).]

Boreas /báwri ass/ n **1** in Greek mythology, the god who personifies the north wind. ◊ **Zephyrus 2 Boreas, boreas** a wind blowing from the north (*literary*) [14C. Via Latin < Greek.]

bored /bawrd/ adj feeling irritable, either because of being exposed to something uninteresting or because of having nothing to do ○ *She grew bored with living in the country.*

SPELLCHECK See **board**.

USAGE The usual preposition to use after the adjective **bored** is *with*, as in *I grew bored with all their squabbling.* However nowadays the preposition of is sometimes seen, especially in speech or informal writing, perhaps by analogy with *tired of.* This usage is to be avoided in careful speech or writing.

boredom /báwrdəm/ n the feeling of being bored ○ *I nearly died of boredom.*

borehole /báwr hōl/ n a deep hole drilled into the ground to obtain samples for geological study or to release or extract water or oil

~~boreing~~ incorrect spelling of **boring**

borer /báwrər/ n **1** a machine or hand tool used for boring holes **2** an organism, especially an insect or a mollusc, that bores into a plant or into wood or rock

Borg /bawrg/, **Björn** (b. 1956) Swedish tennis player

Borges /báwr hess/, **Jorge Luis** (1899–1986) Argentinian writer

Borgia /báwrjə/, **Cesare, Duke of the Romagna** (1476?–1507) Italian soldier

Borgia, Lucrezia (1480–1519) Italian art patron

boric /báwrik/ adj containing or relating to boron [Mid-19C. < BORON.]

boric acid n H_3BO_3 a weak acidic white crystalline solid. Use: fire retardant, antiseptic, manufacture of heat-resistant glass and ceramics.

boring[1] /báwring/ adj stimulating no interest or enthusiasm —**boringly** adv —**boringness** n

boring[2] /báwring/ adj describes animals or tools that make holes in things

Bormann /báwrmən, -man/, **Martin** (1900–45?) German Nazi official

born /bawrn/ adj **1 BROUGHT INTO LIFE** brought into existence as a baby or as young from a mother's womb ○ *a child born in Birmingham* **2 BEGUN** developed from a particular source or root cause ○ *a realization born of long experience* **3 NATURALLY PREDISPOSED** having a particular natural talent or innate character trait ○ *describes the young Napoleon as a born leader* **4 WITH SPECIFIED ORIGINAL STATUS** given a particular status or condition by or at birth (*often in combination*) ○ *the Canadian-born singer-songwriter* [Old English *boren*, past participle of BEAR[2]] ◊ **born and bred** coming from a particular place or background and usually having the qualities or character regarded as typical of it

USAGE See **borne**.

Born /bawrn/, **Max** (1882–1970) German-born British physicist

born-again adj with all the enthusiasm of somebody who has been recently converted to a cause or an idea

born-again Christian n somebody with a new and passionately felt and expressed Christian faith [< John 3:3 'Except a man be born again, he cannot see the kingdom of God' (referring to a spiritual rebirth)]

borne past participle of **bear**[2]

USAGE **borne** or **born**? *Borne* is the primary past participle of the verb *to bear*: *The following points should be borne in mind. His account is simply not borne out by the facts.* In meanings relating to birth, *borne* is used when the mother is the subject of the verb, or when the verb is passive followed by the preposition 'by': *Maria had already borne six children. The twins were borne by an Italian mother.* But when the subject is the child, *born* is used as an adjective: *I was born on a Tuesday. A child was born to Helga that evening.*

Borneo /báwrni ō/ island of the Malay Archipelago in the W Pacific Ocean. Population: 12,500,000 (1991). Area: 751,100 sq. km/290,000 sq. mi. —**Bornean** n, adj

Born-Haber cycle /báwrn háybər-/ n a cycle of chemical reactions used for calculating either the energy required to break down a crystalline solid into its constituent ions (**lattice energy**) or the bond energy of noncrystalline solids [Mid-20C. After Max BORN and Fritz HABER (1868–1934), German chemist.]

Bornholm /báwrn hōlm/ island of SE Denmark, in the Baltic Sea. Population: 45,067 (1994). Area: 588 sq. km/227 sq. mi.

Bornholm disease n an acute epidemic viral infection whose symptoms include fever and chest pain [Because first identified on BORNHOLM]

bornite /báwr nīt/ n a brown metallic mineral. Use: source of copper. [Early 19C. After Ignatius von Born (1742–91), Austrian mineralogist.]

boro- prefix boron ○ *borosilicate* [< BORON]

Borodin /bórrədin/, **Aleksander Porfiryevich** (1833–87) Russian composer and chemist

Borodino /bórrə deènō/ village in W Russia, site in 1812 of an important victory by Napoleon

boron /báw ron/ n (*symbol* **B**) a yellow-brown element that is hard and brittle, with properties intermediate between a metal and nonmetal. Source: borax, kernite. Use: alloys, glass, ceramics, in nuclear reactors to absorb radiation. [Early 19C. < BORAX, after CARBON.]

boronia /bə rōni ə/ n an aromatic evergreen shrub. Flowers: bowl-shaped, crimson, yellow, or purplish-brown. Native to: Australia. Genus: *Boronia*. [Late 18C. < modern Latin, after Francesco Borone (1769–94), Italian botanist.]

borosilicate /báwrō síllikət, -kayt/ n a salt of boric and silicic acids. Use: manufacture of heat- and chemical-resistant glass.

borough /búrrə/ n **1** an administrative division of a large city, responsible for running local services such as housing and education **2** in England, a town that once had special privileges granted to it by royal charter [Old English *burg* 'fortress, fortified town' < Germanic, 'protect']

Borromini /bórrə meèni/, **Francesco** (1599–1667) Italian architect. Born **Francesco Castelli**

borrow /bórrō/ v **1** vt **USE SOMEBODY ELSE'S PROPERTY** to get temporary possession or use of something belonging to somebody else, usually after asking permission ○ *Dad, can I borrow the car?* **2** vti **RECEIVE MONEY AS LOAN** to arrange to be given money by somebody or by a bank or other financial institution for a fixed period of time ○ *We've already borrowed heavily this year.* **3** vt **TAKE FROM LIBRARY** to take out a book or other item from a library **4** vt **COPY FROM SOMEBODY'S WORK** to copy something from somebody else's work, especially a work of art of some kind ○ *some shots clearly borrowed from Hitchcock* **5** vt **TAKE FROM ANOTHER LANGUAGE** to adopt a word from another language **6** vi **PUTT ALLOWING FOR SLOPE** in golf, to putt to the left or right of a straight line on a green to allow for the effect of the slope **7** vt **LEND** to lend something to somebody (*nonstandard*) ■ n **EXTENT OF VEERING** the degree to which a golf ball veers to the left or right as a result of the slope of a green [Old English *borgian* 'borrow against security' < Germanic, 'protect'] —**borrower** n

Borrow /bórrō/, **George** (1803–81) British writer and traveller

borrowing /bórrō ing/ n **1 ACT OF BORROWING** an act of borrowing something **2 PROCESS OF BORROWING** the process of agreeing to accept money from a bank and pay it back later ○ *an increase in government borrowing* **3 AMOUNT BORROWED** an amount of money borrowed ○ *substantial borrowings in the region of half a million pounds* **4 ADOPTED WORD** a word that has been adopted from another language **5 COPIED IDEA** an idea copied from somebody else's work, especially a work of art of some kind

borrow pit n a hole left where stones or other materials have been dug up for use in construction work elsewhere

borscht /bawrsht/ n a Russian or Polish soup whose main ingredient is beetroot [Early 19C. < Russian *borshch*.]

borstal /báwrst'l/ n before 1953, an institution for young offenders that combined features of prison and school (*often before nouns*) ○ *a multimillionaire and former borstal boy* [Early 20C. After the village of *Borstal* in S England.]

bort /bawrt/ n a diamond of inferior quality that is used industrially on grinding wheels and other abrasive devices [Early 17C. < ?]

borzoi /báwr zoy/ (*plural* -**zois**) n a tall graceful domestic dog with a long silky coat, belonging to a breed formerly used in Russia to hunt wolves [Late 19C. < Russian, < *borzyȳ* 'swift'.]

boscage /bóskij/ n densely growing trees and bushes [14C. < Old French, < Germanic.]

AKG London

Hieronymus Bosch

Bosch /bosh/, **Hieronymus** (1450?–1516) Dutch painter. Born **Jerome van Aken**

Bose /bōss/, **Sir Jagadis Chandra** (1858–1937) Indian physicist and botanist

bosh /bosh/ interj used to dismiss as nonsense what has just been said (*dated informal*) [Mid-19C. < Turkish *boş* 'empty, worthless'.]

bosie /bṓzi/, **bosey** (*plural* **-seys**) *n Aus* a googly [Early 20C. After the English cricketer B. T. *Bosanquet* (1877–1936), who used it.]

bosky /bóski/ (**-ier, -iest**) *adj* densely covered with small trees or bushes (*literary*) [Late 16C. < variant of BUSH¹.]

Bosman Ruling /bózmən-/ *n* the European Court ruling that made it possible for football players to leave their club at the end of a contract with no transfer fee payable [After Jean-Marc *Bosman*, player who brought the test case to the European Court]

bo's'n *n* = **boatswain**

Bosnia /bózni ə/ *n* the northern region of Bosnia and Herzegovina —**Bosnian** *adj, n*

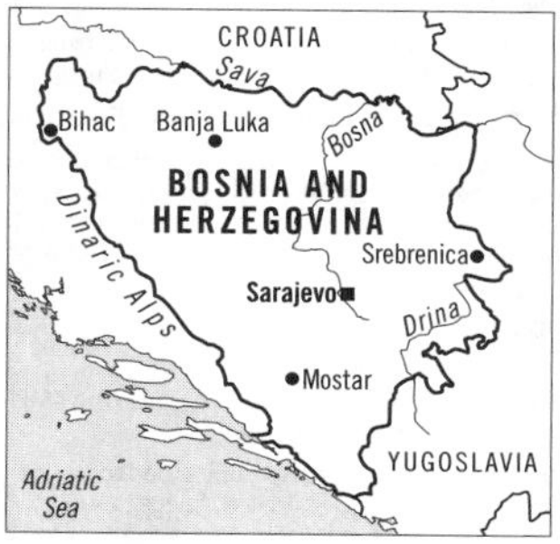

Bosnia and Herzegovina

Bosnia and Herzegovina /bózni ə and húrtsə gō véenə/ republic in SE Europe, between Croatia and the Federal Republic of Yugoslavia. Capital: Sarajevo. Population: 3,222,584 (1997). Area: 51,129 sq. km/19,745 sq. mi.

bosom /bo͝ozzəm/ *n* **1 WOMAN'S BREASTS** a woman's breasts or chest **2 CLOTHES COVERING BREASTS** a part of a garment, e.g. a dress, that covers the chest **3 PROTECTIVE PLACE** a familiar source of protection, security, or affection (*literary*) ○ *back in the bosom of her family* **4 SEAT OF EMOTION** the place where emotions are felt (*literary*) ■ *adj* **CLOSE IN FRIENDSHIP** describes a friend to whom somebody is very close (*informal*) ○ *a bosom buddy* [Old English *bōsm* < ?]

bosomy /bo͝ozzəmi/ (**-ier, -iest**) *adj* with large breasts

boson /bṓ zon/ *n* an elementary particle that has zero or integral spin and obeys statistical rules that place no restriction on the number of identical particles that may be in the same state [Mid-20C. After Satyendra Nuath *Bose* (1894–1974), Indian physicist.]

Bosporus /bóspərəss/, **Bosphorus** /bósfərəss/ strait linking the Black Sea and the Sea of Marmara that separates European and Asian Turkey. Length: 31 km/19 mi.

boss¹ /boss/ *n* **1 SOMEBODY IN CHARGE** somebody who is in charge of others ○ *asked the boss for some time off* **2 DOMINANT PERSON** the person who is the dominant partner in a relationship or the dominant member of a group, who tends to make decisions and give instructions (*informal; often ironic*) **3** *US* **POWERFUL POLITICIAN** a politician who exerts a controlling influence, e.g. by applying pressure on others to vote in a particular way (*informal*) ■ *vt* **GIVE ORDERS** to give others orders in a way that seeks to demonstrate or establish authority and is often resisted or resented ○ *You find the big kids trying to boss the little kids about.* ■ *adj* **EXCELLENT** so good as to dominate in a group (*slang*) ○ *a boss drummer* [Early 19C. < Dutch *baas* 'master'.] ◇ **be your own boss 1** to work under your own authority, e.g. with freelance or self-employed status **2** to make decisions relating to your own life, rather than have them dictated by others

boss² /boss/ *n* **1 KNOB** a round raised part that sticks out from a surface, e.g. a stud at the centre of a shield **2 CEILING DECORATION** a decorative knob on a vaulted ceiling at points where the ribs meet **3 SWELLING** a round swelling on a plant or the horn of an animal **4 SHAFT PART** a thicker part of a shaft at a point where another part is attached to it **5 VOLCANIC ROCK MASS** a mass of volcanic rock with a roughly circular cross section and vertical sides [14C. < Old French *boce*.]

BOSS /boss/ *n* a South African intelligence organization. Full form **Bureau of State Security**

bossa nova /bóssə nṓvə/ *n* **1** a lively ballroom dance of Brazilian origin similar to the samba **2** the music for a bossa nova [Mid-20C. < Portuguese, 'new trend'.]

boss cocky *n Aus* a boss who likes giving orders (*informal*) [COCKY]

bosset /bóssit/ *n* a rudimentary antler that grows on each side of a young deer's head [Mid-19C. < French, 'little boss knob'.]

boss-eyed *adj* with one or both eyes out of alignment (*informal*) [< ?]

bossy /bóssi/ (**-ier, -iest**) *adj* fond of giving people orders ○ *The other children don't like it when you're bossy.* —**bossily** *adv* —**bossiness** *n*

boston /bóstən/ *n* a version of whist in which two packs of cards are used and players bid for the right to name trumps [Early 19C. < French, probably after BOSTON, Massachusetts.]

Boston /bóstən/ **1** port in E England. Population: 34,606 (1991). **2** capital city of Massachusetts, in the E part of the state. Population: 555,447 (1998 estimate). —**Bostonian** /bo stṓni ən/ *n, adj*

Boston crab *n* a wrestling hold in which a wrestler is grabbed by the legs, turned face down, and sat on [After BOSTON, Massachusetts]

Boston ivy *n* a climbing plant with leaves having three black lobes that turn red in autumn. *Parthenocissus tricuspidata*. [After BOSTON, Massachusetts]

Boston Tea Party *n* a protest against British taxes made by the citizens of Boston in 1773, leading to the American Revolution. The protesters boarded three British ships and threw their cargoes of tea overboard.

Boston terrier *n* a stocky dog with a smooth, brindled, or black coat and white markings, belonging to a breed originating in Boston, Massachusetts that is a cross between a bulldog and a terrier

bosun /bṓss'n/ *n* ♦ **boatswain** [Mid-17C. Representing a pronunciation of BOATSWAIN.]

Boswell /bóz wel, -wəl/, **James** (1740–95) Scottish lawyer and biographer

Bosworth Field /bózwərth-/ site in central England of a decisive battle in 1485 when Henry Tudor defeated Richard III

bot¹ /bot/ *n* a parasitic larva of the botfly [Early 16C. Probably < Low Dutch.]

⚡**bot²** /bot/ *n* a computer program performing routine or time-consuming tasks, e.g. searching websites, automatically or semi-independently (*usually in combination*) [Late 20C. Shortening of ROBOT.]

⚡**BOT** *abbr* **1 BOT, BoT** Board of Trade **2** beginning of tape

bot. *abbr* **1** botanical **2** botany

botanical /bə tánnik'l/, **botanic** /bə tánnik/ *adj* relating to plants, especially to the scientific study of plants ■ *n* a drug or product made from plants (*often plural*) [Mid-17C. Directly or via French *botanique* < late Latin *botanicus* < Greek *botanikos* < *botanē* 'plant'.] —**botanically** *adv*

botanical garden, botanic garden *n* an area, often open to the public, in which exotic, rare, or scientifically interesting plants are grown and studied

botanise *vti* = **botanize**

botanist /bótə nist/ *n* somebody with an expert scientific knowledge of, or a strong interest in, plants [Mid-17C. < French *botaniste* < *botanique* (see BOTANICAL).]

botanize /bótə nīz/ (**-nizes, -nizing, -nized**), **botanise** (**botanises, botanising, botanised, botanised**) *vti* to collect or study plants (*informal*) [Mid-18C. Via modern Latin *botanizare* < Greek *botanizein* 'gather plants' < *botanē* 'plant'.] —**botanizer** *n*

botany /bótəni/ (*plural* **-nies**) *n* **1 STUDY OF PLANTS** the scientific study of plants **2 PLANT LIFE OF SPECIFIC AREA** the plant life that exists within a particular area **3 BIOLOGICAL CHARACTERISTICS OF PLANT** the biological description of a single plant or group of plants [Late 17C. < BOTANICAL.]

Botany Bay /bóttəni-/ bay in New South Wales, Australia, site of Captain Cook's first landing in 1770

Botany wool *n* a fine merino wool. Use: yarns, fabrics. [After BOTANY BAY]

botch /boch/ *vt* to do something very badly out of clumsiness or lack of care ○ *managed to botch a simple repair job* ■ *n* **botch, botch-up** a job or task that has been done very badly (*informal*) ○ *made a complete botch of translating the songs* [14C. < ?] —**botcher** *n* —**botchily** *adv* —**botchiness** *n* —**botchy** *adj*

botel *n* SAILING = **boatel**

botfly /bót flī/ (*plural* **-flies**) *n* a two-winged hairy parasitic fly that lays its eggs under the skin or in the digestive tract, sometimes causing serious illness. Families: Oestridae and Gasterophilidae.

both /bōth/ *det* relating to or being two people or things considered together ○ *For the first time I find that I like both candidates.* ○ *There are only two banks in the town, and both are shut on Saturdays.* ■ *conj* used with two facts or alternatives joined by 'and' to indicate that not just one but also the other one is included ○ *Truancy is now treated as both a policing and an educational issue.* [13C. < Old Norse *báðir*.]

USAGE ***Both*** has many roles, as a pronoun (*I like both*), adjective or determiner (*I like both boys*), and adverb or conjunction (*They are both pleasant and cheerful*). Its mobility in a sentence is so great that its meaning can become ambiguous. In the last example, it is not immediately clear whether ***both*** belongs with 'they' or with the complement of the sentence, 'pleasant and cheerful'; in speech, intonation will normally clarify the intention. However, when writing, you need to ensure that you are not leaving the reader in doubt. The principal restriction that applies to ***both*** is that it should refer to two people or things and no more; if three or more are meant it is necessary to use *each*, which behaves grammatically in ways quite similar to ***both***. (However, *each* is regarded as singular while ***both*** is plural, and ***both*** alone allows the construction *I saw them both*.) When pairing ***both*** with *and*, it is important to retain a balance between the two parts of the construction, with regard to the position of ***both*** and the types of words linked: *She is both charming and intellectual* [not *She is both charming and an intellectual*] or *He both sings well and likes to paint* [not *He is both a fine singer and likes to paint*]. In terms of possession, *of* + ***both*** is clearer, as in *the parents of both, the responsibility of both*, as opposed to *both their parents* and *both their responsibility* or *both their responsibilities*.

Botha /bo͝ortə, bṓ-/, **P. W.** (*b.* 1916) South African statesman and prime minister (1978–84), and president (1984–89). Full name **Pieter Willem Botha**

Botham /bṓthəm/, **Ian** (*b.* 1955) British cricketer

bother /bóthər/ *v* **1** *vi* **MAKE EFFORT** to take the time or trouble to do something (*often in negatives*) ○ *He didn't even bother to get out of the car.* ○ *I shouldn't bother about a raincoat. It's clearing up.* **2** *vti* **WORRY** to make somebody feel worried, anxious, or upset ○ *I never bother about what the neighbours think.* ○ *It bothers me to think of you all on your own.* **3** *vt* **DISTURB** to annoy or disturb somebody, e.g. by interrupting or by making unwelcome advances ○ *Is the music bothering you?* **4** *vt* **GIVE PAIN** to make somebody feel physical discomfort or pain ○ *My back is bothering me again.* ■ *n* **1 EFFORT** trouble or effort to do something ○ *Don't go to all that bother for me.* **2 SOURCE OF ANNOYANCE** somebody or something that causes annoyance, e.g. by making noise ○ *I'm sorry to be a bother, but could I use your phone?* ■ *interj* **EXPRESSING MILD ANNOYANCE** used as an expression of mild annoyance ○ *Bother! I've left my glasses in the car.* [Late 17C. < ?]

SYNONYMS ***bother, annoy, bug, disturb, irk, trouble, worry***

CORE MEANING: to interfere with somebody's composure

bother to make somebody feel worried, anxious, or upset, or to disturb or interrupt somebody; **annoy** to irritate or harass somebody; **bug** (*informal*) to cause persistent trouble and annoyance; **disturb** to interrupt or distract somebody in the process of doing something, or to upset somebody's peace of mind; **irk** to annoy somebody slightly, especially by being tedious; **trouble** to cause distress or inconvenience; **worry** to cause anxiety in somebody.

botheration /bóthə ráysh'n/ *interj* used as an expression of mild annoyance (*dated informal*)

bothersome /bóthərsəm/ *adj* causing annoyance and inconvenience

Bothnia, Gulf of /bóthni ə/ northern arm of the Baltic Sea, between Finland and Sweden. Area: 117,000 sq. km/45,200 sq. mi.

bothy /bóthi/ (*plural* **-ies**) *n Scotland* a simple house or hut, originally a farmer's or crofter's cottage, now usually a hut providing shelter for hillwalkers or climbers [Late 18C. Probably < variant of BOOTH.]

bo tree /bṓ tree/ *n* a tree of the fig family that is regarded as sacred by Buddhists. Native to: India. *Ficus religiosa*. [Mid-19C. Partial translation of Sinhalese *bōgaha* < *bō* (< Pali, Sanskrit *bodhi* 'perfect knowledge') + *gaha* 'tree'.]

botryoidal /bóttri óyd'l/ *adj* describes minerals and plant parts shaped like a bunch of grapes [Late 18C. < Greek *botruoeidēs* < *botrus* 'bunch of grapes'.]

bots /bots/ *n* an intestinal disease of horses, sheep, and cattle, caused by infection with botfly larvae (+ *singular or plural verb*)

Botswana

Botswana /bot swaána/ *n* republic in central-southern Africa. Capital: Gaborone. Population: 1,431,981 (1997). Area: 581,730 sq. km/224,607 sq. mi. —**Botswanan** *n*, *adj*

botte /bot/ *n* a thrust or hit in fencing [14C. < Old French *bot(te)* 'blow, hit'.]

Sandro Botticelli: *The Birth of Venus* (after 1482)

Botticelli /bótti chélli/, **Sandro** (1445–1510) Italian painter. Born **Alessandro di Mariano Filipepi**

bottle /bótt'l/ *n* 1 CONTAINER FOR LIQUIDS a container for liquids, usually made of glass or plastic, with a narrow neck and no handle 2 AMOUNT IN BOTTLE the amount of liquid contained in a bottle 3 CONTAINER FOR BABY'S MILK a plastic or glass container with a rubber teat used for feeding a baby, or a feed of milk given by using one of these ○ *Has he had his bottle yet?* 4 ALCOHOL alcoholic beverages, or the habit of drinking it to excess (*informal*) ○ *fond of the bottle* 5 COURAGE boldness or nerve (*informal*) ○ *didn't have the bottle to say it to her face* ■ *vt* (**-tles, -tling, -tled**) 1 PUT IN BOTTLE to put a liquid, e.g. wine, beer, or milk, in a bottle for storage or sale 2 PRESERVE IN JARS to store fruit or vegetables in a preserving liquid in a glass container [14C. Via Old French *boteille* < medieval Latin *butticula* 'little cask' < late Latin *buttis* 'cask, barrel'.] **bottle out** to lose courage at a crucial moment (*informal*) ○ *He was going to tell her, then he bottled out.* **bottle up** *vt* 1 to contain, hold, or entrap something or somebody, especially a group of people 2 to conceal or repress strong feelings ○ *all the resentment she's been bottling up for years*

bottle bank *n* a large container or group of containers in which members of the public can deposit used glass bottles and jars for recycling

bottlebrush /bótt'l brush/ *n* a bush or small tree that has a mass of spiky flowers with large stamens. Native to: Australia. Genus: *Callistemon* and *Melaleuca*. [< the plant's resemblance to a cylindrical brush for cleaning bottles]

bottled /bótt'ld/ *adj* 1 stored or sold in bottles 2 completely inebriated (*slang*)

bottle-feed *vt* to feed a baby or a young animal formula milk from a bottle, as distinct from breast-feeding or suckling it

bottle gourd *n* a climbing plant that produces bottle-shaped fruits. Use: containers for liquids, when dried. Native to: Europe. *Lagenaria siceraria.*

bottle-green *adj* of a dark green colour, like certain wine bottles —**bottle green** *n*

bottleneck /bótt'l nek/ *n* 1 a junction or a narrow section of a road that slows traffic or causes traffic jams 2 a delay caused when one part of a process or activity is slower than the others and so hinders overall progress

bottle-nosed dolphin, bottlenose dolphin /bótt'l nōz-/ *n* a dolphin with a long snout. Native to: warm waters. *Tursiops truncatus.*

bottle party *n* a party to which guests bring alcoholic drink

bottler /bótt'lər/ *n* a company that bottles beverages as part of a manufacturing process

bottle store, bottle shop *n* ANZ, S Africa = **off-licence**

bottle tree *n* a tree with a swollen bottle-shaped trunk and an unpleasant smell. Native to: Australia. Genus: *Brachychiton.*

bottom /bóttəm/ *n* 1 LOWEST PART the lowest or deepest part of something ○ *From the bottom of the hill it seems a long way up.* 2 UNDERSIDE the underneath side or surface of something ○ *rust on the bottom of the boat* 3 FARTHEST POINT the part of something that is farthest away ○ *ponies grazing at the bottom of the field* 4 LAND UNDER WATER the ground underneath a sea, lake, or river ○ *Can you dive down and touch the bottom?* 5 END OF LIST the end of a list or series, especially the lowest level of excellence or achievement ○ *teams at the bottom of the league* 6 ROOT CAUSE the fundamental, often hidden, cause or origin of something ○ *get to the bottom of the problem* 7 LOWEST RANK the lowest level in a hierarchy ○ *worked her way up from the bottom* 8 BUTTOCKS somebody's buttocks, or, particularly when speaking to children, any body part in this general area 9 PART COVERING LOWER BODY the part of a two-piece garment, e.g. a tracksuit or bikini, that covers the lower body (*often plural*) 10 VALLEY a dry valley or hollow (*often in placenames*) ○ *Six Mile Bottom* ■ *adj* 1 LOWEST in the lower or lowest position ○ *Look on the bottom shelf.* 2 LEAST SUCCESSFUL in the position of least excellence or achievement ○ *determined not to come bottom of the class again* ○ *the bottom five teams* ■ *v* 1 *vi* HIT SEA FLOOR to scrape the underside against the floor of the sea or a river, because the water is too shallow (*refers to ships*) 2 *vt* OVERLOAD TRANSISTOR to overload a transistor to the point where additional input produces no additional output [Old English *botm* < Indo-European] ◇ **at bottom** in reality, when external appearances are stripped away ◇ **bottoms up** used as a drinking toast ◇ **from the bottom of your heart** with the utmost sincerity ◇ **hit rock bottom** to reach the lowest point in your personal, professional, or emotional life **bottom out** *vi* after a decline, to stop falling any lower and stabilize at a low level ○ *After plummeting 200 points, the stock market finally bottomed out.*

bottom drawer *n* a collection of household items, e.g. linens, that a young woman traditionally accumulates in anticipation of marriage. US term **hope chest** *n*. [Traditionally kept in the lowest drawer of a chest of drawers]

bottom feeder *n* 1 a fresh- or saltwater animal, especially a fish that feeds on material drifting to the bottom of a body of water 2 *US* a person regarded as contemptible and unworthy (*slang insult*)

bottomless /bóttəmləss/ *adj* 1 VERY DEEP so deep that what is specified appears to have no bottom 2 PLENTIFUL with unlimited or seemingly unlimited resources, especially of money ○ *a bottomless fund* 3 UNFATHOMABLE too well hidden to be discovered or too mysterious to be understood —**bottomlessness** *n*

bottom line *n* 1 UNAVOIDABLE FACTOR the most important factor that must be accepted, however reluctantly ○ *The bottom line is that the sponsors want a French driver on the team.* 2 PROFIT OR LOSS the final profit or loss that a company makes at the end of a given period of time 3 LOWEST ACCEPTABLE AMOUNT the least amount of money regarded as acceptable, e.g. in a business deal

bottommost /bóttəm mōst/ *adj* at the very lowest level ○ *the bottommost rung of the ladder*

bottom quark *n* a quark with an electric charge $-\frac{1}{3}$ that of the electron, zero charm, zero isotopic spin, and zero strangeness

bottomset bed /bóttəmset-/ *n* a layer of sediment deposited by a river at the base of an accumulating delta

botulin /bóttyŏolin/ *n* a toxin produced by the bacterium *Clostridium botulinum* that causes botulism [Early 20C. < modern Latin *botulinus* (see BOTULINUM).]

botulinum /bóttyŏo línəm/, **botulinus** /-línəss/ *n* an anaerobic bacterium that causes botulism when it is present in food. *Clostridium botulinum.* [Early 20C. < modern Latin, neuter of *botulinus* < Latin *botulus* 'sausage'.] —**botulinal** *adj*

botulism /bóttyŏolizəm/ *n* a serious form of food poisoning caused by eating preserved food that has been contaminated with botulinum organisms [Late 19C. < German *Botulismus* 'sausage-poisoning' < Latin *botulus* 'sausage'.]

Bouaké /bwaá kay/ capital of Bouaké Department, central Côte d'Ivoire. Population: 329,850 (1988).

Boucher /boo shay/, **François** (1703–70) French painter

bouclé /boo klay/ *n* a yarn with loops or bumps along its length that give a knobbly effect when knitted or woven (*often before nouns*) [Late 19C. < French, past participle of *boucler* 'curl' < Latin *buccula* 'cheek strap of a helmet' < *bucca* 'cheek'.]

Boudicca /boódika/, **Boadicea** /bó ədi seé ə/ (d. AD 62) English tribal queen

boudin /boo daN/ *n* a French black pudding [Mid-19C. < French, < Latin *botulus* 'sausage'.]

boudoir /boo dwaar/ *n* a woman's bedroom or private sitting room [Late 18C. < French, 'place to sulk in' < *bouder* 'to pout, sulk'.]

bouffant /boo foN/ *adj* describes a woman's hairstyle in which hair is backcombed or teased to give fullness and height [Early 19C. < French, present participle of *bouffer* 'swell or puff up'.] —**bouffant** *n*

bougainvillaea *n* PLANTS = **bougainvillea**

Bougainville /boóganvil/ largest island of the Solomon Island group in E Papua New Guinea, in the SW Pacific Ocean. Area: 8,730 sq. km/3,492 sq. mi.

Bougainville /boóganvil, boo gaN veél/, **Louis Antoine de** (1729–1811) French navigator

bougainvillea /boógan vílli ə/, **bougainvillaea** *n* a climbing woody ornamental plant with attractive red, purple, or pink leaves (**bracts**) around insignificant flowers. Native to: South America. Genus: *Bougainvillea.* [Mid-19C. < modern Latin, after Louis Antoine de BOUGAINVILLE.]

bough /bow/ *n* a large main branch of a tree, from which smaller branches grow [Old English *bōg* 'bough, shoulder' < Indo-European, 'arm']

SPELLCHECK Do not confuse **bough** with **bow**[2] or **bow**[3], which sound similar. Beware: your spellchecker will not catch this error.

bought[1] /bawt/ past tense, past participle of **buy**

bought[2] /bawt/ *adj* commercially made rather than home-made

bougie /boo zhee, boo zheé/ *n* a medical instrument in the form of a flexible tube, inserted into a body passage such as the rectum to open it to allow medicines or instruments to be introduced [Mid-18C. < French, after the town of *Bougie* (Arabic *Bijāya*) in Algeria, which traded in wax.]

bouillabaisse /boóya béss, -báyss/ *n* a rich soup made with fish and originating from the south of France [Mid-19C. Via French < modern Provençal *bouiabaisso*.]

bouillon /boo yoN/ *n* a clear liquid that is traditionally made by boiling meat, bones, and vegetables together [Mid-17C. < French, < *bouillir* (see BOIL[1]).]

Boulanger /boo loN zhay/, **Nadia** (1887–1979) French composer and music teacher

boulder /bōldər/ *n* 1 a large round rock 2 a large fragment of rock greater than 200 mm/8 in in diameter [15C. Shortening of *boulderstone*, partial translation of a N Germanic word.]

Boulder /bōldər/ city in N Colorado. Population: 90,928 (1996).

boulder clay *n* GEOL = **till**[4] *n*.

bouldering /bōldəring/ *n* rock climbing that involves climbing short and extremely difficult slopes —**boulderer** *n*

boule /bool/ *n* a pear-shaped imitation gemstone made in a furnace from synthetic aluminium oxide (**corundum**) [Early 20C. < French (see BOWL²).]

boules /bool/ *n* an outdoor game of French origin, similar to bowls (+ *singular verb*) [Early 20C. < French, plural of *boule* (see BOWL²).]

boulevard /bóol vaar, bóolə vaard/ *n* a wide street, especially one lined with trees (*often in placenames*) [Mid-18C. Via French, '(promenade on the site of) a rampart' < Middle Low German, Middle Dutch *bolwerk* (see BULWARK).]

boulevardier /bool vaárdi ay, boolə vaárdi ay/ *n* a fashionable, sophisticated man who treats life with light-hearted cynicism (*dated*) [Late 19C. < French, < *boulevard* (see BOULEVARD).]

Boulez /bóo lez/, **Pierre** (*b.* 1925) French composer and conductor

boulle /bool/ *n* elaborate inlay work on furniture, using tortoiseshell, ivory, or brass in scroll shapes (*often before nouns*) [Early 19C. < French, after André Charles *Boulle* (1642–1732), French cabinetmaker.]

Boulogne-sur-Mer /boo lóyn syoor máir/, **Boulogne** port in NW France. Population: 44,859 (1999).

boult *vt* = **bolt**²

Boumédienne /boo máydi én/, **Houari** (1932–78) Algerian nationalist and president of Algeria (1965–78). Born **Muhammad Brahim Boukharouba**

bounce /bownss/ *v* (**bounces, bouncing, bounced**) **1** *vti* **SPRING AWAY FROM SURFACE** to move away quickly after hitting a surface, or throw something so that it hits a surface and moves away ○ *bouncing a tennis ball against a wall* ○ *Onlookers saw the car bounce off a tree.* **2** *vi* **JUMP UP AND DOWN** to jump up and down repeatedly on a soft surface ○ *children bouncing on trampolines* **3** *vt* **LIFT CHILD ON KNEE** to lift a baby or child up and down on your knee for fun **4** *vti* **REFLECT FROM SURFACE** to strike a surface, or cause something to strike a surface, and be reflected back ○ *the use of a fixed orbiting satellite to bounce the transmission signal back to earth* **5** *vi* **MOVE SWINGINGLY** to move in an up-and-down or swinging way ○ *with her long blonde hair bouncing as she walked* **6** *vi* **GO ENERGETICALLY** to walk quickly and energetically ○ *She bounced up to the guests and breezily said hello.* **7** *vti* **REFUSE TO PAY** to refuse payment of a cheque, or be refused by a bank, because there is insufficient money in the account on which it is drawn **8** *vt* **WRITE BAD CHEQUE** to write a cheque that the bank will not honour **9** *vt* **SOLICIT OPINIONS** to put something, especially an idea or suggestion, to somebody in order to get reactions or opinions (*slang*) ○ *She bounced a couple of theories off the students.* **10** *vt* **COERCE INTO DOING** to force somebody into doing something by restricting the alternatives (*informal*) ○ *I don't want to get bounced into making unwise investments.* **11** *vt* **THROW OUT** to eject somebody from a place or expel somebody from a club or other organization (*slang*) ○ *managed to get themselves bounced out of the restaurant* **12** *vi* **COME BACK** to be returned undelivered to a sender of an e-mail message ○ *My last e-mail to you bounced.* ■ *n* **1 ACT OF REBOUNDING** a springing away from a surface after hitting it ○ *hit the ball before the second bounce* **2 SPRINGINESS** the capacity of a ball or other object to bounce, or of a surface to cause objects hitting it to bounce ○ *not so much bounce in the pitch* **3 BOBBING MOVEMENT** swinging or bobbing movement, or the capacity to swing or bob up and down ○ *a conditioner guaranteed to give your hair added bounce* **4 ENERGY** lively energy [13C. < ?]
bounce back *vi* to recover quickly and completely after a bad experience

bouncer /bównssər/ *n* **1 GUARD AT NIGHTCLUB** a security guard who usually stands at the door of a nightclub or other place of entertainment and is responsible for preventing undesirable people from entering and for ejecting troublemakers **2 BALL BOUNCING HEAD HIGH** in cricket, a ball that is pitched short and bounces at chest or head height to intimidate the batsman **3 STRUCK BALL THAT BOUNCES** a ball that bounces along the ground after being hit

bouncing /bównssing/ *adj* describes a healthy active baby ○ *the proud parents of a beautiful bouncing boy*

bouncing Bet *n* PLANTS = **soapwort** [Pet form of *Elizabeth*]

bouncy /bównssi/ (**-ier, -iest**) *adj* **1 LIVELY** lively and energetic **2 BOUNCING WELL** tending to bounce or capable of bouncing well ○ *bouncy material used in making tennis balls* **3 SPRINGY** tending to bounce objects hitting it or resting on it —**bouncily** *adv* —**bounciness** *n*

bouncy castle *n* a large inflatable object in the shape of a castle which children can bounce on for fun

bound¹ /bownd/ *v* past participle, past tense of **bind**

bound² /bownd/ *adj* **1 CERTAIN TO DO** certain to happen or do something because custom, experience, or common sense dictates it ○ *If you play music late at night, people are bound to complain.* **2 OBLIGED** obliged to do something or behave in a certain way, e.g. for legal or moral reasons **3 WITH PERMANENT COVER** describes a book or other written document that has a permanent, usually hard, cover **4** *US* **DETERMINED** firmly resolved ○ *She was bound to become the best in the business.* [14C. Shortening of BOUNDEN.]

bound³ /bownd/ *vi* to move quickly and energetically, with large strides or jumps ○ *A puppy came bounding across the lawn.* [Early 16C. Via French *bondir* 'resound, rebound' < Latin *bombire* 'to buzz' < *bombus* < Greek *bombos* 'booming sound'.] —**bound** *n*

bound⁴ /bownd/ *adj* **1** travelling towards a particular place (*often in combination*) ○ *a Spanish trawler bound for the Irish Sea* ○ *homeward bound* **2** certain to reach or achieve something ○ *young performers bound for international stardom* [Late 16C. Originally *boun* < Old Norse *búinn*, past participle of *búa* 'prepare'; probably influenced by BOUND¹.]

bound⁵ /bownd/ *vt* **1 SURROUND** to form the boundary to an area or site ○ *grounds bounded on three sides by the river* **2 RESTRICT** to impose limits on something ○ *political views not bounded by moral convictions* ■ *n* **LIMITING NUMBER** a number that represents the upper or lower end of a range of possible values ■ *adj* **1 NOT ABLE TO BE USED ALONE** describes a unit of meaning (**morpheme**) that cannot be used on its own as a word. ◊ **free** *adj.* 20 **2 NOT ABLE TO BE USED ALONE** describes a grammatical element such as a clause that can only be used with another element [14C. < Anglo-Norman *bounde*, Old French *bodne* < medieval Latin *butina*; originally 'boundary marker'.]

boundary /bówndəri/ (*plural* **-ries**) *n* **1 BORDER** the official line that divides one area of land from another ○ *Multinational companies operate across national boundaries.* **2 LIMIT** the point at which something ends or beyond which it becomes something else ○ *pushing back the boundaries of human knowledge* **3 EDGE OF CRICKET PITCH** the outer limit of the playing area of a cricket pitch **4 SHOT CROSSING BOUNDARY** in cricket, a shot that crosses the boundary, scoring either four or six runs [Early 17C. Alteration of *bounder* < BOUND⁴.]

Boundary Commission *n* a public body that monitors the boundaries of parliamentary constituencies between elections and recommends changes to them based on shifts in the population

boundary condition *n* the set of requirements that must be met in order for the solution to a set of differential equations to be found

boundary layer *n* the region of a viscous fluid, e.g. air or water, closest to the surface of a solid that is in motion relative to the fluid

boundary rider *n Aus* an employee on a sheep or cattle station whose job is to check that boundary fences are in good repair

bounded /bówndid/ *adj* describes a mathematical set that has an upper and lower limiting number (**bound**⁵)

bounden /bówndən/ *v* past participle of **bind** (*literary*)

bounder /bówndər/ *n* somebody, especially a man, who behaves in a dishonourable or morally unacceptable way (*dated; insult*) [Late 19C. < BOUND³.]

boundless /bówndləss/ *adj* seeming to have no end or limit —**boundlessly** *adv* —**boundlessness** *n*

~~**boundry**~~ incorrect spelling of **boundary**

bounds /bowndz/ *npl* limits, especially restrictions on what can happen or what can be done ○ *a joke that goes beyond the bounds of good taste* ◇ **know no bounds** to be very great, strong, or intense ○ *an ego that knows no bounds* ◇ **out of bounds 1** outside the area where somebody is allowed to go ○ *a basketball that is out of bounds* **2** not open or available ○ *Discussion of the candidate's private life is out of bounds.*

bounteous /bównti əss/ *adj* (*literary*) **1** giving generously **2** given in generous measure [14C. Alteration (after PLENTEOUS) of Old French *bontif* < *bonté* (see BOUNTY).] —**bounteously** *adv* —**bounteousness** *n*

bountiful /bówntif'l/ *adj* (*literary*) **1** giving generously **2** in plentiful supply —**bountifully** *adv* —**bountifulness** *n*

SYNONYMS See ***generous***.

bounty /bównti/ (*plural* **-ties**) *n* **1 REWARD** a reward of money offered for finding a criminal or other wanted person, or for killing a person or a predator **2 GENEROSITY** generosity in giving (*literary*) ○ *'a trifling additional claim upon your bounty and good nature'* (Sir Walter Scott, *Waverley*; 1814) **3 ABUNDANT SUPPLY** a plentiful or generous supply (*literary*) ○ *'As a grand mansion, 'The Broadway Estate' is home to a bounty of rooms, each with a distinct personality'.* (Patti Martinhome, *Living Page*, (*Asbury Park Press*; 1997) [14C. Via French *bonté* < Latin *bonitas* 'goodness' < *bonus* 'good'.]

Bounty /bównti/ *n* the British naval ship commanded by Captain William Bligh on a scientific voyage to Tahiti in 1789. Bligh's cruelty provoked a mutiny led by Fletcher Christian.

bounty hunter *n* **1** somebody who captures criminals for reward money **2** somebody who hunts animals for reward money

Bounty Islands /bownti-/ uninhabited island group in the SW Pacific Ocean, part of New Zealand. Area: 1.4 sq. km/0.54 sq. mi.

bouquet /boo káy, bō-/ *n* **1 BUNCH OF FLOWERS** a bunch of cut flowers that have been specially chosen or arranged **2 SCENT OF WINE** a wine's characteristic scent **3 PRAISE** an expression of congratulation or praise (*literary*) [Early 18C. < French, 'thicket' < Old French *bois* 'forest' < Germanic.]

SYNONYMS See ***smell***.

bouquet garni /bóo kay gaárni/ (*plural* **bouquets garnis** /bóo kay gaárni/) *n* a bunch of mixed herbs, or an equivalent dried herb mixture in a sachet, that is used to add flavour to stews, soups, sauces, and other dishes [Mid-19C. < French, 'garnished bouquet'.]

bourbon¹ /búrbən/ *n* a type of whisky distilled mainly in the United States from a fermented mixture of hot water and grain (**mash**) containing at least 51% maize [Mid-19C. After *Bourbon* County, Kentucky.]

bourbon² /bóorbən/, **Bourbon** *n* a rectangular chocolate-flavoured biscuit that has two layers sandwiched together with a chocolate cream filling [Mid-18C. After the *Bourbon* dynasty of France.]

Bourbon /bóorbən/ *adj* relating to a branch of the French royal family who reigned from 1589 to 1793 and again after the French Revolution until the revolution of 1830. The Spanish royal family also belongs to this branch. [Mid-18C. < French, after the town of *Bourbon l'Archambault* in central France.]

bourdon /bóord'n/ *n* **1** the bass pipe on a set of bagpipes, or the bass note it produces **2** the bass stop on an organ, especially on a 16-foot pipe [Mid-19C. < French, 'drone'.]

Bourdon gauge /bóord'n-/ *n* a pressure gauge with a flattened curved tube that straightens under pressure, allowing the force to be measured [After Eugène *Bourdon*, French hydraulic engineer]

bourgeois /boor zhwaá, bóor zhwaa/ *adj* **1** associated with affluent middle-class people, who are often characterized as conventional, conservative, or materialistic in outlook **2** according to Marxist theory, relating to the social class that owns the means of producing wealth and is regarded as exploiting the working class [Mid-16C. < French, 'citizen of a city or borough' < Latin *burgus* 'castle, borough'.] —**bourgeois** *n*

Bourgeois /bóor zhwaa/, **Léon Victor** (1851–1925) French statesman

bourgeoisie /bóor zhwaa zée/ *n* **1** the social class that, according to Marxist theory, owns the means of producing wealth and is regarded as exploiting the working class **2** affluent middle-class people characterized as conventional, conservative, or materialistic in outlook [Early 18C. < French, < *bourgeois* (see BOURGEOIS).]

bourgeoisify /boor zhwaázi fī/ (**-fies, -fying, -fied**) *vt* to impose bourgeois values on somebody or something, or make somebody or something bourgeois in character —**bourgeoisification** /boor zhwaázifi káysh'n/ *n*

Bourguiba /boor géebə/, **Habib** (1903–2000) Tunisian statesman and prime minister (1956–57) and president (1957–87) of Tunisia

bourguignonne /bóor geen yón/ *adj* cooked in a red wine sauce with mushrooms and small whole onions, in a style that originated in the Burgundy region of France [Early 20C. < French, < *Bourgogne* 'Burgundy'.]

Bourke /burk/ town in N New South Wales, Australia. Population: 2,976 (1991).

Bourke-White /búrk wīt/, **Margaret** (1906–71) US photographer and writer

bourn[1] /bawrn, boorn/ *n* (*archaic*) **1** a boundary between one place or one thing and another ○ *'I'll set a bourn how far to be beloved'*. (William Shakespeare, *Antony & Cleopatra*; 1606) **2** something that is aimed for or aspired to [Early 16C. Via French *borne* < Old French *bodne* (see BOUND[5]).]

bourn[2] /bawrn, boorn/, **bourne** *n* a small stream that flows only in the winter months [14C. S English variant of BURN[2].]

Bournemouth /báwrnməth/ coastal town in SW England. Population: 160,900 (1995).

bourse /boorss/, **Bourse** *n* a European stock exchange, especially the one in Paris [Late 16C. Via French < medieval Latin *bursa* 'bag, purse' < Greek *bursa* 'leather'.]

boustrophedon /boóstrə feéd'n, bówstrə-/ *n* an ancient method of inscribing and writing in which lines are written alternately from right to left and from left to right [Early 17C. < Greek, 'as the ox turns in ploughing' < *bous* 'ox' + *-strophos* 'turning' < *strephein* 'to turn'.] —**boustrophedonic** /boóstrə fee dónnik, bówstrə-/ *adj*

bout /bowt/ *n* **1 ATTACK OF ILLNESS** a temporary or short-lived attack of illness, usually a common and not very serious illness ○ *a recent bout of flu* **2 SHORT PERIOD OF ACTIVITY** a short time spent doing something, often something considered distasteful **3 FIGHT** a boxing or wrestling match [Mid-16C. < ?]

boutique /boo teék/ *n* **1** a small shop that sells fashionable clothes **2** a small shop selling specialist goods or services of any kind, e.g. imported foods and wines [Mid-18C. Via French < Greek *apothēkē* 'storehouse'.]

boutique brewery *n US* = **microbrewery**

boutique hotel *n* an upmarket, often stylish hotel with an individual character and decor

bouton /boó toN/ *n* the knob or swelling on a nerve-cell extension (**axon**) at the point where it forms a junction (**synapse**) with a neuron [Mid-19C. < French (see BUTTON).]

boutonniere /boó ton yáir, -tonni áir/, **boutonnière** *n* = **buttonhole** *n*. 2 [Late 19C. < French, < *bouton* (see BUTTON).]

Boutros-Ghali /boó tross gaáli/, **Boutros** (*b.* 1922) Egyptian diplomat and secretary general of the UN (1992–96)

bouvier /boóvi ay/ *n* a large powerful dog with a rough fawn or black coat, originally bred in Belgium to herd cattle [Early 20C. < French, shortened < *bouvier des Flandres* 'cowherd of Flanders'.]

~~**bouy**~~ incorrect spelling of **buoy**

~~**bouyant**~~ incorrect spelling of **buoyant**

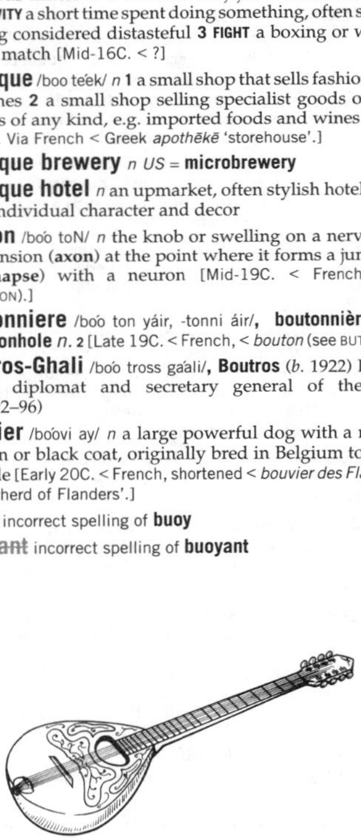

Bouzouki

bouzouki /boo zoóki/ (*plural* **-kis**) *n* a long-necked stringed musical instrument of Greek origin, resembling a mandolin [Mid-20C. < modern Greek *mpouzouki*.]

bovid /bṓvid/ *adj* relating or belonging to the family of hollow-horned, hoofed, ruminant animals that includes cattle, sheep, and antelopes. Family: Bovidae. [Late 19C. < Latin *bov-* (see BOVINE).] —**bovid** *n*

bovine /bṓ vīn/ *adj* **1 OF CATTLE GENUS** relating or belonging to the genus of ruminant animals that includes cattle, oxen, and buffalo. Genus: *Bos*. **2 SLOW** displaying the slowness regarded as typical of cattle and related animals (*literary*) ■ *n* **BOVINE ANIMAL** an animal belonging to the same genus as cattle [Early 19C. < late Latin *bovinus* < Latin *bov-*, stem of *bos* 'ox'.]

bovine somatotrophin, bovine growth hormone *n* a hormone in cattle that regulates growth and milk production

bovine spongiform encephalopathy *n* full form of **BSE**

bovver /bóvvər/ (*plural* **-ver**) *n* aggressive behaviour (*slang*) [Mid-20C. Representing a Cockney pronunciation of BOTHER.]

bovver boot *n UK* a heavy-duty boot, often one with a steel toecap, worn by members of gangs as a fighting weapon and a symbol of toughness (*dated informal*)

bow[1] /bō/ *n* **1 LOOPED KNOT** a knot in which the loops remain visible, e.g. in tied shoelaces or in ribbons used for decorating gifts or hair. ◊ **bow tie 2 WEAPON FOR FIRING ARROWS** a weapon used to fire arrows, consisting of a curved flexible piece of wood and a taut string fastened to the two ends **3 ROD FOR PLAYING STRINGED INSTRUMENTS** a wooden rod with fibres tightly stretched between the two ends, used for playing stringed instruments **4 CURVED SHAPE OR PART** a rounded or semicircular shape, e.g. a part of a building or a loop in a river **5** ARCHERY, HIST = **bowman**[1] (*literary*) **6** METEOROL = **rainbow** *n*. 1 ■ *v* **1** *vti* **BEND SOMETHING INTO BOW SHAPE** to bend, or bend something, into a rounded or bow shape **2** *vti* **DRAW BOW ACROSS STRINGED INSTRUMENT** to draw a bow across the strings of a stringed instrument **3** *vt* **INDICATE BOWING FOR MUSIC** to mark a piece of music to indicate which notes are to be played with the bow moving in one direction across the strings and which are to be played with it moving in the opposite direction [Old English *boga* < Germanic, 'to bend']

bow[2] /bow/ *v* **1** *vti* **BEND HEAD OR BODY FORWARD** to bend the head forward, or to bend forward from the waist, as a signal of respect, greeting, consent, submission, or acknowledgment ○ *bowing her head in shame* **2** *vti* **BEND SOMETHING OR DROOP** to bend something over so that it droops, or to be bent in this way ○ *branches bowed down with fruit*. **3** *vi* **YIELD** to accept something and yield to it, often unwillingly ○ *In the end they had to bow to the inevitable and sell up*. ■ *n* **BENDING FORWARD OF UPPER BODY** a bending forward of the upper part of the body to show respect, acknowledgment, subservience, courtesy, or greeting [Old English *būgan* < Germanic, 'to bend'] ◇ **bow and scrape** to be excessively polite or attentive in an attempt to ingratiate yourself with somebody

bow[3] /bow/ *n* **1** the front section of a boat or other vessel **2** the rower closest to the front of a boat [Early 17C. < Low German *boog* or Middle Dutch *boeg*.]

SPELLCHECK See ***bough***.

Bow /bō/, **Clara** (1905–65) US actor. Known as **the It Girl**

bowdlerise *vti* = **bowdlerize**

bowdlerize /bówdlə rīz/ (**-izes, -izing, -ized**), **bowdlerise** (**-lerises, -lerising, -lerised**) *vti* to remove parts of a work of literature that are considered indecent [Mid-19C. < Thomas *Bowdler* (1754–1825), who published an edition of Shakespeare omitting scenes that he considered unsuitable.] —**bowdlerism** *n* —**bowdlerization** /bówdlə rī záysh'n/ *n* —**bowdlerizer** *n*

bowel /bówəl/ *n* **1 INTESTINE** the intestine **2 PART OF THE INTESTINE** a section or part of the intestines, especially the part of the intestine that connects to the anus ○ *empty your bowels* ■ **bowels** *npl* **DEPTHS OF** the deepest or innermost part of something ○ *the bowels of the ship* [13C. Via Anglo-Norman *buel*, Old French *boël* < Latin *botellus* 'small sausage' < *botulus* 'sausage'.]

bowel movement *n* **1** the passing of faeces out of the body through the anus **2** faeces passed through the anus

Bowen /bṓ in/, **Elizabeth** (1899–1973) Irish writer

Bowen therapy /bṓ in-/ *n* a therapeutic technique that initiates healing and encourages emotional stability using manipulation of muscles and connective tissues [Mid-20C. After its Australian originator Tom *Bowen* (1916–82).]

bower[1] /bówər/ *n* **1 SHADY SHELTER** a shady leafy shelter or recess, especially in a garden or wood **2 WOMAN'S BEDROOM OR APARTMENTS** a woman's bedroom or private apartments, especially in a medieval castle **3 PICTURESQUE COTTAGE** a picturesque country cottage, especially one that is used as a retreat (*literary*) [Old English *būr* 'dwelling' < Indo-European, 'be, live'] —**bowery** *adj*

bower[2] /bówər/ *n* the anchor at a ship's bow

bower[3] /bówər/ *n* the jack in euchre and other similar card games [Late 19C. < German *Bauer* 'peasant'.]

bowerbird /bówər burd/ *n* a bird that is noted for the elaborate structures that the male builds for courtship. Native to: New Guinea, Australia. Family: Ptilonorynchidae.

bowfin /bṓ fin/ (*plural* **-fins** *or* **-fin**) *n* a freshwater fish with a mottled greenish-brown body and a long dorsal fin. Native to: E North America. *Amia calva*.

bowfront /bṓ frunt/ *adj* describes a piece of furniture with a front that curves outwards ○ *a bowfront desk*

bowhead /bṓ hed/ (*plural* **-heads** *or* **-head**) *n* a baleen whale that lives in the Arctic seas and has an arched upper jaw. *Balaena mysticetus*.

Bowie /bṓwi/, **David** (*b.* 1947) British pop singer and actor. Born **David Robert Jones**

Bowie /bṓ i/, **Jim** (1796?–1836) US pioneer. Full name **James Bowie**

bowie knife /bṓ i nīf/ *n* a single-edged hunting knife, about 38 cm / 15 in long and curved near the point, with a short hilt and a guard for the hand [Mid-19C. Named after Jim BOWIE, who popularized it.]

bowknot /bṓ not/ *n* a decorative knot in the form of a bow

bowl[1] /bōl/ *n* **1 ROUND CONTAINER** an open container, usually round in shape and wider than it is deep, and typically used for holding food and liquids **2 AMOUNT IN BOWL** the amount a bowl can hold **3 PART LIKE BOWL** a bowl-shaped part of something ○ *a toilet bowl* **4 DEPRESSION IN GROUND** a round depression in the surface of the land. ◊ **dust bowl 5 MILDLY ALCOHOLIC DRINK** a mildly alcoholic beverage, or the type of cup used for drinking it (*literary*) [Old English *bolla* < Indo-European, 'swell, be round'] —**bowlful** *n*

SPELLCHECK See ***bole***.

bowl[2] /bōl/ *v* **1** *vti* **ROLL SMOOTHLY ALONG** to roll smoothly, or to make something such as a ball, roll smoothly along the ground or some other flat surface ○ *Bowl the ball more gently this time*. **2** *vti* **SEND BALL TO PERSON BATTING** in cricket, to send a ball, usually overarm, to a batsman or batswoman **3** *vt* **DISMISS BATSMAN OR BATSWOMAN** to get a batsman or batswoman out by bowling ○ *He's been bowled!* **4** *vi* **GO BOWLING** to take part in a game of bowls or bowling **5** *vt* **SCORE POINTS IN BOWLING** to score a given number of points in bowling ○ *He bowled 250 last night*. **6** *vi* **MOVE QUICKLY** to move smoothly and quickly ○ *bowling along down the country lanes* ■ *n* **1 WOODEN BALL USED IN BOWLS** a wooden ball used in the game of bowls, which has slightly flattened sides in order to make it roll in a curve **2 BOWLING BALL** a bowling ball **3 ROLL OF THE BALL** one roll of the ball in bowling [15C. Via French *boule* < Latin *bulla* 'bubble'.]

bowl out *vt* = **bowl**[2] *v*. 3

bowl over *vt* **1** to amaze or delight somebody (*often passive*) ○ *I was completely bowled over by their generous offer*. **2** to knock something or somebody down, especially accidentally during a headlong rush ○ *The dog bowled three chairs over in its excitement*.

bowlegged /bō léggid, bō légd/ *adj* having legs that curve outwards around or below the knee area [Mid-16C. < BOW[1].]

bow legs *n* a condition in which the legs curve outwards around the knee area (+ *singular verb*) —**bowleg** *n*

bowler /bṓlər/ *n* **1** the player who bowls the ball in cricket **2** somebody who plays in bowling ■ ACCESSORIES = **bowler hat**

bowler hat, bowler *n* a hard felt hat with a round crown and narrow upturned brim. US term **derby** *n*. 3 [Mid-19C. After its designer William *Bowler*, British hatter.]

Bowles /bōlz/, **Paul** (1910–99) US writer and composer

bowline /bṓ lin/ *n* **1 KNOT FORMING TIGHT LOOP** a knot used to form a loop that will not slip at the end of a piece of rope **2 LINE FOR CONTROLLING SAIL** a line for controlling one of the vertical edges of a square sail **3 KNOT IN END OF CLIMBING ROPE** a fixed knot in the end of a climbing rope [14C. < Middle Low German *bōlīne* or Middle Dutch *boechline* 'line from the ship's bow'.]

bowling /bṓling/ *n* **1 GAME CONSISTING OF ROLLING BALL** a game played by rolling a ball so that it either hits pins, as in tenpin bowling, or moves close to another ball, as in bowls **2** **PLAYING OF BOWLING** the playing of any form of bowling **3** **THROWING BALL TO PERSON BATTING** in cricket, the throwing of the ball, usually overarm, to the person who is batting

bowling alley *n* **1** a building for tenpin bowling **2** the long, narrow, smooth expanse of floor down which a ball is rolled in tenpin bowling or skittles

bowling ball *n* the heavy ball used in the game of bowling, especially tenpin bowling, that has holes in it for the bowler's thumb and two fingers

bowling crease *n* in cricket, a line that a bowler must not cross before the ball has been bowled

bowling green *n* a piece of natural grass outdoors or a piece of artificial grass indoors for playing the game of bowls

bowls /bōlz/ *n* a game in which heavy wooden balls are rolled on a flat surface with the object of coming close to a smaller target ball (+ *singular verb*) US term **lawn bowling**

bowman[1] /bṓmən/ (*plural* **-men** /-mən/) *n* somebody who uses a bow and arrows —**bowmanship** *n*

bowman[2] /bówmən/ (*plural* **-men** /-mən/) *n* a man or boy who rows at the bow of a boat

Bowman's capsule /bṓmənz káp syool/ *n* a cup-shaped part of the kidney that extracts waste and water from the blood and produces urine [Late 19C. Sir William *Bowman* (1816–92), British surgeon.]

Bowral /bówrəl/ town in east-central New South Wales, Australia. Population: 7,919 (1991).

bow saw /bṓ saw/ *n* a saw with a thin blade held in a bow-shaped frame with a narrow handle at each end, used for cutting curves

bowshot /bṓ shot/ *n* the distance that an arrow travels when it has been shot from a bow

bowsprit /bṓ sprit/ *n* a spar that projects forward from the stem of a ship, to which the stays of the foremast are fastened [14C. < Low German *bōgsprēt* or Middle Dutch *boechspriet* 'pole at the ship's bow'.]

Bow Street Runner /bṓ-/ *n* one of the officers at Bow Street magistrates' court, London, from 1749 to 1829, whose duty was to pursue and arrest criminals

bowstring /bṓ string/ *n* the taut string on an archer's bow, usually made of strands of hemp

bowstring hemp *n* **1** fibre from the leaves of a tropical perennial plant. Use: bowstrings, mats, nets. **2** a tropical plant with thick leaves grouped in rosettes, from which bowstring hemp is obtained. Native to: Africa, Asia. Genus: *Sansevieria*.

bow tie /bṓ tī/ *n* a short tie, knotted in a bow at the neck

bow weight /bṓ-/ *n* the amount of force needed to pull a bowstring back to its fullest extent

bow window /bṓ-/ *n* a bay window that is curved

bow-wow /bów wów, bów wow/ *interj* **IMITATION OF BARKING** used to imitate the bark of a dog ■ *n* **DOG** a dog (*babytalk*) ■ *vi* **BARK OR IMITATE BARKING** to bark, or imitate the sound of barking [Late 16C. An imitation of the sound.]

bowyangs /bṓ yangz/ *npl ANZ* a pair of strings or straps secured round each trouser leg below the knee, worn in Australia and New Zealand by agricultural workers [Mid-19C. < ?]

bowyer /bṓyər/ *n* somebody who makes bows for archery [13C. < BOW[1] + -IER.]

box[1] /boks/ *n* **1** **CONTAINER** a container for objects or dry goods, often with a removable or hinged lid, and usually square or rectangular **2** **AMOUNT BOX HOLDS** the amount of something a box holds or could hold **3** **RECTANGULAR SHAPE** a square or rectangular shape printed on paper, or on a computer screen, usually containing information or requiring information to be entered in it ○ *Tick the boxes if the following items apply to you.* **4** **AREA OR STRUCTURE WITH BEST SEATS** an enclosed area in a public building or at a sports venue, especially a theatre, football stadium, or racetrack, that contains the best and most luxurious seats **5** **ENCLOSED AREA IN COURTROOM** the enclosed area in a courtroom that is reserved for certain participants in a court case ○ *in the witness box* **6** **SMALL BUILDING PROVIDING SHELTER** a small building that is used as a shelter, especially by military personnel (*usually in combination*) **7** **SMALL BUILDING THAT HOUSES EQUIPMENT** a small building that houses equipment and provides shelter for those who use this equipment (*always in combination*) ○ *a police box* **8** **EQUIPMENT CONTAINER** a container, usually affixed to a wall or on a stand, that houses equipment such as a fire extinguisher, emergency telephone, or first-aid materials **9** **ANONYMOUS ADDRESS FOR MAIL** an anonymous address for mail to be sent to, used either for administrative purposes or to protect the privacy of the addressee **10** **PART OF PLAYING AREA** a marked-off part of the playing area in certain sports, e.g. baseball and football, used for a specific purpose, or subject to special rules **11** **PENALTY AREA** the penalty area in front of a football goal (*informal*) **12** **PROTECTIVE COVERING FOR SPORTSMAN'S GENITALS** a protective plastic covering for a sportsman's genitals, worn especially in cricket **13** FIELD SPORTS = **shooting box** **14** **DRIVER'S SEAT IN HORSE-DRAWN COACH** a raised seat for the driver in a horse-drawn coach **15** **COMPARTMENT FOR LIVESTOCK** a compartment for horses or other farm animals, either in a building or in a vehicle **16** **TELEVISION** the television set (*slang*) ○ *What's on the box tonight, then?* **17** **COFFIN** a casket for a corpse (*informal*) ○ *The next time he leaves that house it'll be in a box.* **18** *NZ* **WHEELED CONTAINER FOR COAL** a wheeled container used for transporting coal in a mine **19** *Aus, US* **OFFENSIVE TERM** an offensive term for a woman's vulva and vagina (*taboo slang*) **20** **HOLE IN TREE TO COLLECT SAP** a hole or hollow cut into the base of a tree in order to collect sap ■ *vt* **1** **PACK IN BOXES** to pack individual items into boxes ○ *There are 300 pieces waiting to be boxed before shipping.* **2** **OUTLINE SOMETHING WITH BOX** to enclose something on a page or on a computer screen in a box ○ *Box the title to make it stand out more.* **3** **CUT HOLE IN TREE FOR SAP** to cut a box in the base of a tree to collect the sap **4** *ANZ* **MIX FLOCKS OR HERDS** to mix flocks or herds of animals either accidentally or on purpose [Pre-12C. Via late Latin *buxis* < Greek *puxis* 'wooden container' < *puxos* 'boxwood, box tree'.] —**boxful** *n*

box in *vt* to surround somebody, or a vehicle, by or with something, especially other people or cars, so that it is impossible to move

box up *vt* = **box**[1] *v.* 1

box[2] /boks/ *vti* to fight using the techniques of boxing, or fight somebody in a boxing match ○ *He boxed in exhibition bouts to entertain the crowds.* [14C. < ?] ◇ **box clever** to act in a clever and wily manner so as to defeat an opponent

box on *vi* to continue with a boxing match

box[3] /boks/ (*plural* **box** *or* **boxes**) *n* **1** a dense evergreen tree or shrub with shiny dark green oval leaves. Use: hedges. Genus: *Buxus*. **2** INDUST = **boxwood** *n.* 2 [Pre-12C. Via Latin *buxus* < Greek *puxos*.]

box[4] /boks/ *vti* SAILING = **boxhaul** [Mid-18C. < ?]

Box and Cox /bóks ən kóks/ *npl* an arrangement whereby two people can share the use of something in strict rotation (especially accommodation) because they need it at different times [< a farce by J. M. Morton (1811–91).]

box beam *n* CONSTR = **box girder**

box bed *n* an old-fashioned bed, enclosed on three sides and the top by a wooden structure resembling a box

boxboard /bóks bawrd/ *n* a tough cardboard made from wood and wastepaper pulp, used for making boxes

box calf *n* black calfskin leather that has been tanned with chromium salts [Early 20C. After Joseph *Box*, 19C London bootmaker.]

box camera *n* a camera shaped like a box, with a simple lens that has a fixed focus and a single shutter speed

box canyon *n* a canyon with steep walls that can be entered readily only from the downstream direction

boxcar /bóks kaar/ *n US* in North America, a fully enclosed railway wagon, usually with sliding doors, which is used to transport freight

box coat *n* a coat that hangs loosely from the shoulders

box elder *n* a fast-growing maple tree. Native to: North America. *Acer negundo*. [< BOX[3]]

boxer[1] /bóksər/ *n* a fighter in boxing matches

boxer[2] /bóksər/ *n* a medium-sized smooth-haired dog belonging to a breed developed in Germany [Early 20C. Via German, < English *boxer*; because of its wide flattened nose.]

boxer[3] /bóksər/ *n* a person or machine whose task it is to pack things into boxes

Boxer /bóksər/ *n* a member of a secret society in China that launched the Boxer Rebellion [Early 20C. Translation of Mandarin Chinese *yì hé quán* 'righteous harmonious fists'.]

Boxer Rebellion *n* an unsuccessful rebellion in China in 1900, the aim of which was to drive out all foreigners, remove all foreign influence, and compel Chinese Christians to give up their religion

boxer shorts *npl* underpants with a gathered waistband and loose-fitting short legs [Because they resemble trunks worn by boxers]

boxfish /bóks fish/ (*plural* **-fish** *or* **-fishes**) *n* = **trunkfish**

box girder *n* a hollow girder or beam that is square or rectangular in section

boxhaul /bóks hawl/ *vti* to turn a square-rigged ship onto a new tack by backwinding the foresails and steering hard round [Mid-18C. < BOX[4].]

boxing /bóksing/ *n* the sport of fighting with the fists, with the aim of knocking out the opposing boxer, or inflicting enough punishment to cause the other boxer to retire or be judged defeated

Boxing Day *n* a public holiday in England, Wales, and some Commonwealth countries. Date: 26 December. [Because traditionally the day on which Christmas boxes were given to service workers]

boxing glove *n* a thick padded glove tied at the wrist, worn by boxers for fighting

boxing ring *n* the square raised platform with roped-in sides, used as the fighting arena in boxing matches

box junction *n* a road junction with yellow crossed lines painted on the road surface, marking an area that traffic is not permitted to block

box kite *n* a square kite without a tail, consisting of two open-ended boxes joined by thin sticks

box lunch *n US* = **packed lunch**

box lyre *n* a plucked stringed instrument, formed from a hollow wooden box with strings running across the soundboard, which are attached to arms jutting out to form a crossbar

box number *n* the number assigned to an anonymous address for mail, either at a post office or as a reference for a reply to a newspaper advertisement

box office *n* **1** **PLACE WHERE TICKETS ARE BOUGHT** the place where tickets are bought for entertainments such as films, plays, or concerts (*often before nouns*) ○ *box office takings* **2** **MONEY FROM TICKET SALES** ticket sales for a theatrical or cinematic entertainment, or the income from these sales (*informal; often before nouns*) **3** **AUDIENCE POPULARITY** drawing power to attract an audience to a theatre (*informal*) ○ *The show makes great box office.* [Originally where a box in the theatre could be reserved]

box-on *n Australian* a fight

box pleat *n* a pleat in which fabric is folded under and back again on both sides, and pressed flat

boxroom /bóks room, -ro͝om/ *n* a small room used for storage of household items not in regular use or sometimes as a bedroom [Early 20C. Because used to store boxes and trunks.]

box score *n US* a printed summary of a game, especially a baseball game, in table form, listing the players and their positions and performance in the game

box seat *n* **1** a seat in a box in a theatre or a sports stadium **2** the box on a horse-drawn carriage on which the driver sits

box set *n* **1** a stage set with a ceiling and three walls **2** **box set, boxed set** a set of similar items, e.g. recordings of music, that are packaged together in a box and sold as a single unit ○ *a four-CD box set*

box spanner *n* a spanner in the form of a steel cylinder with a hexagonal end that slips over a nut. US term **box wrench**

box spring *n* a base for a mattress consisting of a set of coiled springs in a frame, covered with fabric

box stall *n US* RIDING = **loosebox**

box step *n* the basic step in ballroom dancing, in which the feet are moved in a square-shaped pattern

boxthorn /bóks thawrn/ (*plural* **-thorns** *or* **-thorns**) *n* = **matrimony vine** [< BOX[3]]

box turtle *n* a land turtle with a hinged shell on the underside of its body that can close up over its head and forelimbs for protection. Native to: North America. Genus: *Terrapene*.

boxwood /bóks wo͝od/ (*plural* **-wood** *or* **-woods**) *n* **1** TREES = **box**[3] *n.* 1 **2** the hard close-grained yellow wood of the evergreen box shrub

box wrench *n US* = **box spanner**

boxy /bóksi/ (**-ier, -iest**) *adj* shaped like a cube or rectangular box —**boxiness** *n*

boy /boy/ *n* 1 **YOUNG MALE** a young male person ○ *I've had this hobby since I was a boy.* 2 **SON** somebody's male child ○ *I'm very proud of that boy of mine.* 3 **YOUNG MAN WITH A SPECIFIC JOB** a male child or teenager described in terms of his job ○ *a newspaper boy* 4 **MALE FROM CERTAIN AREA** a youth or man who comes from or was brought up in a particular area or has a particular background ○ *He's a local boy.* 5 **WAY OF ADDRESSING MALE ANIMAL** a way of addressing a male animal, especially a dog or a horse ○ *Get down, boy!* 6 **SUITABLE TOOL** a tool that will do a particular job (*informal regional*) ○ *That's just the boy I need to tighten this nut.* ■ **boys** *npl* **A GROUP OF MALE FRIENDS** a group of men of any age who often socialize together ○ *I'm off out with the boys.* ■ *interj* **EXCLAMATION OF SURPRISE** used to express surprise, pleasure, or disgust ○ *Oh boy! Would you just take a look at that!* [13C. < ?] —**boyhood** *n* ◇ **boys and their toys** a way of saying that men are fascinated by machines or gadgets, especially in a way that women find hard to understand

SPELLCHECK See ***buoy***.

boyar /bō yaar, bóyər/ *n* from the 12th century to the early 18th century, a member of a class of the higher Russian nobility ranking below a prince [Late 16C. < Russian *boyarin* 'grandee'.]

boy band *n* a pop group made up of personable young men who sing and dance to synthesized music but do not play instruments

boycott /bóy kot/ *vt* to cease or refuse to deal with something such as an organization, a company, or a process, as a protest against it or an effort to force it to become more acceptable ○ *Some called for the elections to be boycotted, insisting they were flawed.* [Late 19C. After Captain Charles *Boycott* (1832–97), estate manager in Ireland.] —**boycott** *n* —**boycotter** *n*

Boycott /bóy kot/, **Geoff** (*b.* 1940) British cricketer. Full name **Geoffrey Boycott**

Boyd /boyd/, **Arthur Merric** (1862–1940) New Zealand-born Australian painter

Boyd, Arthur Merric Bloomfield (1920–99) Australian artist

Boyd, Benjamin (1803?–51) British-born Australian pioneer and entrepreneur

Boyd, Martin Beckett (1893–1972) Australian writer

Boyd, Merric (1888–1959) Australian potter

Boyer /bóy ay/, **Charles** (1897–1978) French actor

Boyer /bóy ər/, **Herbert W.** (*b.* 1936) US biochemist

boyfriend /bóy frend/ *n* a man with whom somebody has a romantic or sexual relationship

boyish /bóyish/ *adj* resembling a very young man's fresh looks or youthful behaviour in a way that is pleasing or attractive —**boyishly** *adv* —**boyishness** *n*

Boyle's law /bóylz-/ *n* the principle that the volume of a confined gas at constant temperature varies inversely with its pressure [After Robert *Boyle* (1627–91), Irish-born scientist]

boy-meets-girl *adj* based on a developing romance between a young man and a young woman, and treated in a predictable or hackneyed way in film or print ○ *It's a typical boy-meets-girl story where they live happily ever afterwards.*

Boyne /boyn/ river in E Ireland, site of the Battle of the Boyne, in which forces led by William III of England defeated the army of James II in 1690

boyo /bóy ō/ *n* used as a form of address for a boy or man, or a way of referring, sometimes disparagingly, to a boy or a man, particularly one who is Welsh (*informal; sometimes disapproving*) ○ *Relax, boyo.*

boy racer *n* a young man with a tendency to drive very fast to impress people (*informal disapproving*)

Boys' Brigade *n* a Christian organization for boys founded in Britain in 1883 by William Alexander Smith to promote obedience, reverence, discipline, and self-respect

Boy Scout *n* 1 in the United States, a member of the Boy Scouts of America, an organization whose objectives are to develop character, physical fitness, and citizenship, often through community and outdoor activities 2 **boy scout, Boy Scout** a man who is considered to be naive or overzealous (*insult*)

boysenberry /bóyz'nbəri/ (*plural* **-ries**) *n* 1 a large purplish-black fruit with a taste similar to a loganberry 2 a plant that bears boysenberries, a hybrid of the loganberry, blackberry, and raspberry. Genus: *Rubus*. [Mid-20C. After Rudolph *Boysen* (1895–1950), US botanist.]

boys in blue *npl* the police (*informal*)

boy toy *n US, Can* a young woman who appears deliberately to try to attract and please men (*informal insult; sometimes offensive*)

boy wonder *n* a talented and bright young man

bozo /bṓzō/ *n* somebody who says or does something unwise (*informal insult*) [Early 20C. < ?]

bozon /bṓ zon/ *n US* a supposed unit measuring somebody's degree of stupidity (*slang*) [< BOZO + -ON[1]]

bp *abbr* 1 baptized 2 base pair 3 bills payable 4 birthplace 5 bishop 6 **bp, b.p.** boiling point

BP *abbr* 1 **BP, B/P** bills payable 2 blood pressure 3 before the present

BPC *abbr* British Pharmaceutical Codex

BPharm /beé faárm/ *abbr* Bachelor of Pharmacy

BPhil /beé fíl/ *abbr* Bachelor of Philosophy

ϟ **bps** *n* a measurement of data transfer speed, e.g. in modems. Full form **bits per second**

Bq *symbol* becquerel

b quark *n* PHYS = **bottom quark**

br[1] *abbr* bills receivable

ϟ **br**[2] *abbr* Brazil (*in Internet addresses*)

Br *symbol* bromine

ϟ **BR** *abbr* 1 bedroom 2 British Rail 3 bathroom (*in e-mails*)

br. *abbr* 1 branch 2 brass 3 brief 4 bronze 5 brother 6 brown 7 bills receivable

Br. *abbr* 1 Britain 2 British 3 Brother

bra /braa/ *n* an undergarment designed to support and shape a woman's breasts [Mid-20C. Shortening of BRASSIERE.]

braai /brī/ *n S Africa* 1 a barbecue 2 = **braaivleis** ■ *vti S Africa* to grill or roast meat over an open fire, usually outdoors [Mid-20C. Shortening of BRAAIVLEIS.]

braaivleis /brī flayss/ (*plural* **-vleis**) *n S African* in South Africa, a meal eaten outdoors where meat is grilled [Mid-20C. < Afrikaans, 'grilled meat'.]

Brabant /brə bánt/ former duchy in W Europe, now divided between the Netherlands and Belgium

Brabham /brábbəm/, **Sir Jack** (*b.* 1926) Australian racing driver. Full name **Sir John Arthur Brabham**

brace[1] /brayss/ *n* 1 **SUPPORT FOR PART OF BODY** an orthopaedic appliance that holds or supports part of the body 2 **CLAMP** a device that keeps something steady or holds two things together 3 **SUPPORT FOR SOMETHING CONSTRUCTED** a device used in the building trade to hold a structure or part steady or upright, e.g. a beam or wooden framework 4 **brace** (*plural* **brace**) **PAIR** a pair of similar things, e.g. wild game, hunting dogs, or pistols ○ *two brace of pheasant* 5 **TOOL FOR HOLDING DRILL BIT** a tool with an adjustable socket at one end for holding a drill bit, and a handle like a crank at the other for turning the bit. ◊ **brace and bit** 6 **EITHER OF THE SYMBOLS** either of a pair of symbols, , used in printing or writing 7 **ADJUSTER FOR DRUM TENSION** a sliding loop on the cords of a drum, used to change its tension 8 **BRACKET CONNECTING LINES OF MUSIC** a thick line or bracket connecting a group of the staves in a piece of music, e.g. all the choral parts, or the accompaniment 9 **SYMBOL OF MATHEMATICAL GROUPING** either of a pair of symbols, , for additional grouping of mathematical quantities after parentheses and square brackets have been used 10 ARCHERY, FENCING = **bracer**[2] *n.* ■ **braces** *npl* 1 **APPLIANCE FIXED TO TEETH** a dental appliance that is fixed to the teeth, and that can be tightened in order to straighten them (*sometimes singular*) 2 **STRAPS FOR HOLDING UP TROUSERS** a pair of elasticated shoulder straps attached to the front and back waist of trousers ■ *v* (**braces, bracing, braced**) 1 *vt* **SUPPORT OR STRENGTHEN** to support or strengthen something, especially part of a building, with a brace ○ *Anchor bolts cannot be used to brace these shelves.* 2 *vr* **PREPARE YOURSELF** to prepare yourself for something dangerous or unknown that is about to happen ○ *The financial markets braced themselves for a rise in interest rates.* [14C. Via Old French, 'two outstretched arms' < Latin *bracchia*, plural of *brachium* 'arm' (see BRACHIUM).]

brace up *vi* to be strong and resolute in facing difficulty ○ *Brace up and face the facts.*

brace[2] /brayss/ *n* on a square-rigged ship, a rope used to control the spar that extends a sail [Early 17C. Perhaps alteration of French *bras de vergue* 'yard arm', after BRACE[1].]

brace and bit *n* a hand tool for boring holes, consisting of a crank handle at one end and a drill bit at the other. ◊ **brace**[1] *n.* 5

bracelet /bráysslət/ *n* 1 **JEWELLERY WORN AROUND WRIST OR ARM** a piece of jewellery, e.g. a chain or a bangle, that is worn around the wrist or arm 2 **METAL BAND FOR WRISTWATCH** a metal band for a wristwatch ■ **bracelets** *npl* **HANDCUFFS** a pair of handcuffs (*slang*) [15C. < French, < Latin *bracchiale* 'armlet' < *brachium* 'arm' (see BRACHIUM).]

brace position *n* a protective position that somebody adopts before impact in a crash, protecting the head with the arms and bringing the legs up underneath the chest

bracer[1] /bráyssər/ *n* 1 somebody or something that braces 2 an invigorating often alcoholic drink [Mid-16C. < BRACE[1].]

bracer[2] /bráyssər/, **brace** /brayss/ *n* a leather guard worn by fencers and archers to protect the arm [14C. < Old French *bracière* < *bras* 'arm' < Latin *brachium* (see BRACHIUM).]

brace root *n* PLANT = **prop root**

brachia plural of **brachium**

brachial /bráyki əl/ *adj* relating to or situated in the arm, foreleg, or wing [Late 16C. < Latin *brachialis* < *brachium* (see BRACHIUM).]

brachiate /bráyki ayt/ (**-ates, -ating, -ated**) *vi* to move along by swinging from one hold to the next with the arms (*refers to tree-dwelling animals*) [Mid-18C. < Latin *brachiatus* < *brachium* (see BRACHIUM).] —**brachiation** /bráyki áysh'n/ *n*

brachio- *prefix* arm ○ *brachiocephalic* [< Latin *brachium* (see BRACHIUM)]

brachiocephalic /bráki ō sə fállik, bráyki ō-/ *adj* relating to or supplying the arms and the head

brachiocephalic artery *n* ANAT = **innominate artery**

brachiopod /bráki ə pod, bráyki-/ *n* a marine invertebrate animal with hinged shells enclosing tentacles. Phylum: Brachiopoda. [Mid-19C. < modern Latin *Brachiopoda* < Latin *brachium* (see BRACHIUM) + Greek *-pod* (see -POD).] —**brachiopod** *adj*

brachiosaurus /bráki ə sáwrəss, bráyki-/ (*plural* **-ruses** *or* **-ri** /-rī/), **brachiosaur** /bráki ə sawr/ *n* a dinosaur with a massive sloping body up to 30 m/100 ft long. Genus: *Brachiosaurus*. [Early 20C. < modern Latin, < Latin *brachium* (see BRACHIUM) (from the unusual length of the animal's humerus bones) + Greek *sauros* 'lizard'.]

brachium /bráyki əm/ (*plural* **-a** /-ki ə/) *n* 1 an arm, especially the upper arm (*technical*) 2 a structure, e.g. a wing, that corresponds to an arm [Mid-18C. Via Latin, < Greek *brakhiōn* 'upper arm', literally 'shorter' < *brakhus* (see BRACHY-).]

brachy- *prefix* short ○ *brachyodont* [< Greek *brakhus* < Indo-European, 'short']

brachycephalic /bráki sə fállik/, **brachycephalous** /-séffələss/ *adj* with a short, broad, and almost spherical head —**brachycephalism** /-séffəlizəm/ *n* —**brachycephaly** /-séffəli/ *n*

brachydactylic /bráki dak tíllik/, **brachydactylous** /-dáktiləss/ *adj* with abnormally short fingers or toes —**brachydactylia** *n* —**brachydactyly** /-dáktili/ *n*

brachylogy /bra kílləji/ *n* 1 brevity in speech or writing, or an instance of such brevity 2 a shortened form of an expression, used in informal speech [Mid-16C. Via late Latin < Greek *brakhulogia* 'shortness of speech'.] —**brachylogous** *adj*

brachypterous /bra kíptərəss/ *adj* describes insects and some species of diving birds with short or not fully developed wings —**brachypterism** *n*

bracing /bráyssing/ *adj* refreshing or invigorating ○ *a bracing cold shower* ■ *n* a system of braces that are used to support or strengthen a structure —**bracingly** *adv*

bracken /brákən/ (*plural* **-en** *or* **-ens**) *n* a large fern, common in most temperate and tropical regions, with extensive underground stems and large triangular fronds. *Pteridium aquilinum*. [14C. < assumed Old Norse *brakni*.]

bracket /brákit/ *n* 1 **UPRIGHT CURVED MARK IN PUNCTUATION** one of a pair of shallow, curved signs, (), used to enclose an explanatory word or comment and distinguish it from the sentence in which it occurs (*often plural*) US term

parenthesis n. 1 2 US PRINTING = **square bracket** 3 L-SHAPED STRUCTURE ON WALL an L-shaped structure that is fixed to a wall to hold up something, e.g. a shelf or speaker 4 TYPE OF SHELF a shelf that usually has an integral part that fixes to the wall as its support and can sometimes be swivelled ○ *This TV bracket is too low.* 5 GROUP WITHIN CERTAIN LIMITS a section of the population that falls within specific defined limits ○ *taxpayers in the £50,000 to £70,000 bracket* ■ vt 1 PUT SOMETHING INSIDE BRACKETS to put something, especially text or a mathematical equation, inside brackets 2 SUPPORT SOMETHING WITH BRACKETS to fix brackets to something, especially a wall, or support something with brackets 3 GROUP THINGS OR PEOPLE TOGETHER to group or class things or people together, usually because they are similar in some way ○ *Rail and bus travel can be bracketed together under public transport.* [Late 16C. Perhaps < French *braguette* 'codpiece' (because of the shape) < Latin *bracae* 'breeches'.] —**bracketing** n

PUNCTUATION *Brackets* are used around text that adds extra information to what has gone before: *She was suffering from rubella (German measles). The noun 'dessert' (with a double 's') is pronounced the same as the verb 'desert'. He read an article on GM (genetically modified) crops.* The information within the **brackets** can usually be omitted without affecting the structure of the sentence. Note that there should be no punctuation directly before the opening **bracket** in such cases. Brackets are also used around optional or alternative material: *Please write your forename(s) in full*, or to separate something, e.g. a number or symbol, from the surrounding text: *I disagree with the proposal, (a) because it is too expensive and (b) because it is unlikely to be effective in the long term.* See also **square bracket**.

bracket clock n a clock that is designed to stand on a shelf or a wall bracket

bracket fungus n a fungus that forms growths that stick out like shelves

brackish /brákish/ adj rather salty, especially from being a mixture of fresh and salt water [Mid-16C. < Dutch *brak* 'salty water'.] —**brackishness** n

Bracknell /brákn'l/ town in S England. Population: 60,895 (1991).

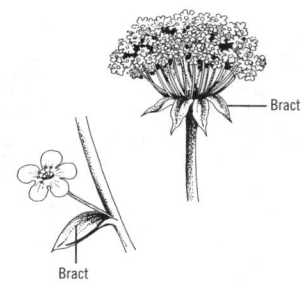

Bract

Bract

Bract

bract /brakt/ n a modified leaf that arises from the stem at the point where the flower or flower cluster develops [Late 18C. < Latin *bractea* 'thin metal plate, gold leaf'.] —**bracteal** /brákti əl/ adj

bracteate /brákti ət/ adj describes a plant that has bracts ■ n a decorated dish or plate made of precious metal [Early 19C. < Latin *bracteatus* < *bractea* 'thin metal plate, gold leaf'.]

bracteole /brákti ōl/ n an organ resembling a leaf or scale that arises from a branch of a flower cluster where the flowers develop, and where the entire cluster itself develops above a bract [Early 19C. < Latin *bracteola* 'small bract' < *bractea* 'thin metal plate, gold leaf'.] —**bracteolate** /brákti əlat, -layt/ adj

brad /brad/ n a thin tapered nail with a small head that is either symmetrical or formed on one side only [13C. < Old Norse *broddr* 'spike'.]

bradawl /brád awl/ n a hand tool with a pointed tip, used for making holes in wood, leather, and other materials, to allow screws and nails to be inserted

Bradbury /brádbəri/, **Malcolm Stanley** (1932–2000) British novelist, critic, and scholar

Bradfield /brád feeld/, **John Job Crew** (1867–1943) Australian civil engineer

Bradford /brádfərd/ city in north-central England. Population: 289,376 (1992).

Bradlaugh /brád law/, **Charles** (1833–91) British social reformer and freethinker

Bradley /brádli/, **A.C.** (1851–1935) British literary critic. Full name **Andrew Cecil Bradley**

Bradley, **Francis Herbert** (1846–1924) British philosopher

Bradley, **James** (1693–1762) British astronomer

Sir Don Bradman

Bradman /brádmən/, **Sir Don** (1908–2001) Australian cricketer. Full name **Sir Donald George Bradman**

Bradstreet /brád street/, **Ann** (1612?–72) English-born American New England poet. Born **Ann Dudley**

Brady, **James** US presidential aide

brady- prefix slow ○ *bradycardia* [< Greek *bradus*]

bradycardia /bráddi ka'ardi ə/ n slowness of the heart rate, usually measured as fewer than 60 beats per minute in an adult human [Late 19C. < BRADY- + Greek *kardia* 'heart'.] —**bradycardiac** adj —**bradycardic** adj

bradykinin /bráddi kínin/ n a chemical (**peptide**) produced in the blood when tissues are injured, and playing a role in inflammation [Mid-20C. < BRADY- + Greek *kinein* 'to move'.]

brae /bray/ n Scotland a hill or slope (often in place-names) [14C. < Old Norse *brá* 'eyelash'.]

brag /brag/ vi (**brags, bragging, bragged**) TALK WITH TOO MUCH PRIDE to talk shamelessly or with excessive pride about achievements or possessions ○ *The police arrested him after he bragged about the bank robbery to his friends.* ■ n 1 BOASTFUL REMARK a boastful statement or display of arrogant behaviour 2 CARD GAME a card game similar to poker [14C. < ?] —**bragger** n —**bragging** n, adj —**braggingly** adv

Braga /bráàgə/ town in NW Portugal. Population: 90,535 (1991).

Brage n MYTHOL = **Bragi**

Bragg, Sir William Henry (1862–1942) British physicist

Bragg, Sir William Lawrence (1890–1971) Australian-born British physicist

braggadocio /brággə dóchi ō/ (plural **-os**) n 1 empty boasting and swaggering self-aggrandisement 2 somebody who boasts [Late 16C. Alteration of *Braggadocchio*, personification of boastfulness in Spenser's *Faerie Queene*.]

braggart /brággərt/ n somebody who talks immodestly or with excessive pride about himself or herself [Late 16C. < French *bragard* < *braguer* 'brag'.]

Bragg's law /brágz-/ n a law stating the directions in which X-rays reflected from a crystal are most intense [Early 20C. After Sir William Henry BRAGG and Sir Lawrence BRAGG (1890–1971).]

Bragi /bráàgi/, **Brage** /-gə/ n in Nordic mythology, the god of poetry, eloquence, and music

Brahe /braa, braà ə, braàhi/, **Tycho** (1546–1601) Danish astronomer

Brahma[1] /braàmə/ n 1 a Hindu god, the source of knowledge and understanding, regarded as the protector of the world and in later tradition called the creator 2 RELIG = **Brahman** n. 1 [< Sanskrit *brahmana-* < *brahman-* 'priest']

Brahma[2] /braàmə/ n a large domestic fowl with heavily feathered legs and feet and a small tail and wings [Mid-19C. Shortening of *Brahmaputra fowl*; because first imported from a town on the Brahmaputra river in India.]

Brahman /braàmən/ n 1 in Hinduism, the ultimate impersonal reality underlying everything in the universe, from which everything comes to and comes to which it returns 2 RELIG = **Brahma** n. 1 3 RELIG = **Brahmin** n. 1, **Brahmin** n. 2 [Late 18C. < Sanskrit *brahman-* 'priest'.] —**Brahmanic** /braa mánnik/ adj —**Brahmanical** adj

Brahmana /braàmənə/ n a sacred Hindu text, belonging to a group of commentaries on the Vedas [< Sanskrit *brāhmaṇam* < *brāhmaṇa-* (see BRAHMIN)]

Brahmani /braàməni/, **brahmani** n a woman of the Brahmin caste [Late 18C. < Sanskrit *brāhmaṇī*, feminine of *brāhmaṇa-* (see BRAHMIN).]

Brahmanism, **brahmanism** n = **Brahminism** —**Brahmanist** n

Brahmaputra /braàmə poo'tra/ river in Tibet and NE India, emptying into the Ganges delta in Bangladesh. Length: 2,900 km/1,800 mi.

Brahmin

Brahmin /braàmin/ (plural **-mins** or **-min**), **brahmin** (plural **-mins** or **-min**) n 1 the first of the four Hindu castes, the members of which are priests and scholars of Vedic literature 2 a member of the Brahmin caste [15C. < Sanskrit *brāhmaṇa-* < *brahman-* 'priest'.] —**Brahminic** /braa mínnik/ adj —**Brahminical** adj

Brahminism /braàminizəm/, **brahminism, Brahmanism, brahmanism** n the traditional social and religious system of Vedic Hinduism —**Brahminist** n

Brahms /braamz/, **Johannes** (1833–97) German composer

Brahui /braa hoò i/ (plural **-is** or **-i**) n 1 a Dravidian language spoken in SW Pakistan. Native speakers: 2 million. 2 a member of a Brahui-speaking people who live in SW Pakistan [Early 19C. < Brahui.] —**Brahui** adj

braid /brayd/ n 1 DECORATIVE SILKY CORD decorative and often silky cord or interwoven thread, used especially to trim and bind, in decorating uniforms, and as edging for soft furnishings 2 SOMETHING INTERWOVEN something that is made of three or more interwoven strands ■ vt 1 INTERWEAVE STRANDS to interweave three or more strands of something, especially hair 2 MAKE SOMETHING BY BRAIDING to make something by interweaving strands, strips, or other elements 3 DECORATE SOMETHING WITH BRAID to decorate uniforms or edge furnishings with braid [Old English *bregdan* 'weave, lay hold of' < Germanic]

braided /bráydid/ adj 1 INTERWOVEN interwoven from three or more strands 2 EDGED WITH CORD decorated or edged with silky, especially gold, cord 3 CONSISTING OF INTERCONNECTED TRACKS OR CHANNELS composed of several interconnected tracks or channels that divide and reunite ○ *a braided river*

braiding /bráyding/ n 1 decorative silky thread or cord, used especially to trim uniforms and furnishings 2 embroidery worked in decorative silky thread

Brăila /brə eèlə/ city in SE Romania. Population: 235,763 (1994).

Braille /brayl/ n a writing system for visually impaired or sightless people, consisting of patterns of raised dots that are read by touch [Mid-19C. After Louis BRAILLE.]

Braille /brayl/, **Louis** (1809–52) French educationist

Brailler /bráylər/, **Braillewriter** /brayl rītər/ n a machine similar to a typewriter that prints Braille

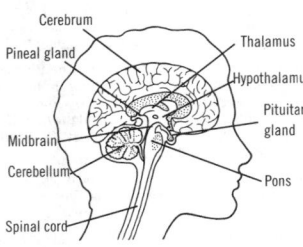

Brain: Cross-section of human brain

brain /brayn/ n **1 ORGAN OF THOUGHT AND FEELING** the controlling centre of the nervous system in vertebrates, connected to the spinal cord and enclosed in the cranium **2 CENTRE OF INVERTEBRATE NERVOUS SYSTEM** a nervous-system centre in some invertebrates that is functionally similar to the brain in vertebrates **3 INTELLECT** somebody's intellectual abilities or intellectual centre ○ *His heart was beating violently and his brain was in a turmoil.* **4 BRAINY PERSON** a very intelligent person, especially the most intelligent person in a certain group (*informal*) ○ *Lee's the brain of the family.* ■ *vt* **HIT SOMEBODY ON HEAD** to hit somebody violently on the head (*slang*) [Old English *brægen* < W Germanic] ◇ **have something on the brain** to be unable to stop thinking about something ◇ **pick somebody's brains** to ask questions of somebody, in order to learn what he or she knows about something ◇ **rack your brains** to try to solve a problem by thinking very hard about it

brainbox /brayn boks/ n a very clever person (*informal; often used by children*)

brain bucket n a protective helmet worn when engaging in sports such as climbing or motorcycling (*slang*)

braincase /brayn kayss/ n the part of the skull enclosing the brain

brainchild /brayn chīld/ (*plural* **-children**) n an original plan or idea attributed to a single person or to a group of people

brain coral n coral that forms rounded colonies resembling the convex folds of the human brain. Genus: *Meandrina.*

brain damage n injury to the brain tissue that can impair normal functioning —**brain-damaged** *adj*

brain dead *adj* **1** lacking functions of the brain and central nervous system as measured by brain wave activity on an electroencephalogram over a set period of time **2** an offensive term meaning of extremely low intellectual ability (*slang*)

brain death n the end of all functions of the brain and central nervous system as measured by brain wave activity on an electroencephalogram over a set period of time

brain drain n the movement of highly skilled people to a country offering better opportunities

brain fever n a term for inflammation of the brain or its covering membranes (*archaic*)

brainless /braynləss/ *adj* lacking intelligence —**brainlessly** *adv* —**brainlessness** n

brainpan /brayn pan/ n = braincase

brainpower /brayn powər/ n somebody's intellectual capability

brain stem n the part of the brain between the spinal column and the cerebral hemispheres

brainstorm /brayn stawrm/ n **1** US = **brain wave** n. 2 (*informal*) **2** a momentary psychological disturbance ■ *vti* to have an intensive group discussion without allowing time for reflection, in order to generate creative ideas and usually to stimulate problem-solving —**brainstormer** n —**brainstorming** n

brains trust n **1** a group of experts who informally discuss issues of public interest, especially on television or radio **2** a group of high-level advisors, usually un-

official, to a government or administration. US term **brain trust** n. 1

brainteaser /brayn teezər/ n a difficult or complex problem that requires careful thought in order to solve it, often done for amusement

brain trust n US POL = **brains trust** n. 2 **2 brain trust, Brain Trust** a group of high-level academics who helped President Franklin Delano Roosevelt to formulate the New Deal, especially prior to his taking office

brainwash /brayn wosh/ *vt* **1** to impose a set of usually political or religious beliefs on somebody by the use of various coercive methods of indoctrination, including destruction of the victim's prior beliefs **2** to induce somebody to believe or do something, e.g. to buy a new product, especially by constant repetition or advertising

brain wave n **1** one of the rhythmic waves of voltage arising from electrical activity within brain tissue **2** a sudden exciting idea (*informal*) US term **brainstorm** n. 1

brainy /brayni/ (**-ier, -iest**) *adj* extremely intelligent (*informal*) —**brainily** *adv* —**braininess** n

braise /brayz/ (**braises, braising, braised**) *vt* to cook food, especially meat or vegetables, by browning briefly in hot fat, adding a little liquid, and cooking at a low temperature in a covered pot [Mid-18C. < French *braiser* < *braise* 'live coals'.]

SPELLCHECK Do not confuse **braise** with **braze**, which has a similar sound. Beware: your spellchecker will not catch this error.

brake[1] /brayk/ n **1 DEVICE THAT SLOWS OR STOPS MACHINE** the part of a machine or vehicle that slows it down or stops it (*often plural*) **2 RESTRAINT** a slowing down or stopping of something such as expenditure or development, or something that causes this ○ *The brake on investment is largely a result of political factors.* **3 = brake van** ■ *v* (**brakes, braking, braked**) **1** *vti* **SLOW OR STOP MACHINE** to slow down or stop, or to make something such as a vehicle or a machine go more slowly or stop ○ *The driver braked hard.* **2** *vt* **SLOW OR HALT DEVELOPMENT** to slow down or halt the progress of something or an increase in something [Late 18C. Perhaps < BRAKE[4].]

SPELLCHECK See **break**.

brake[2] /brayk/ (*plural* **brake** *or* **brakes**) n = **bracken** [14C. Perhaps back-formation < BRACKEN.]

brake[3] /brayk/ n an area of dense undergrowth, shrubs, and brushwood [Old English *bracu* < ?]

brake[4] /brayk/ n **1** a tool or machine for crushing and separating flax or hemp fibres **2** a machine, frequently hydraulically powered, for precision bending and folding of sheet metal [15C. < Middle Low German or Middle Dutch.]

brake[5] /brayk/ n a lever or handle on a pump or other machine [Early 17C. < ?]

brake[6] /brayk/, **break** n an open four-wheeled horse-drawn carriage [Mid-19C. < ?]

brake block n a small rectangular block of rubber that is pressed against the rim of a bicycle wheel when the brake is applied

brake chute n = **brake parachute**

brake drum n the metal cylinder attached to the wheel of a vehicle that slows the rotation of the wheel when pressure is applied

brake-fade n a decrease in braking efficiency of a motor vehicle, caused by the brakes overheating

brake fluid n the oily liquid used in hydraulic brakes and clutches to transmit pressure

brake horsepower n a measure of the work produced by an engine, calibrated in horsepower and determined by the force exerted on a friction brake

brake light n a rear light on a motor vehicle that lights up when the driver brakes. US term **stoplight** n. 2

brake lining n the renewable thin strip of material attached to a brake shoe

brakeman /braykmən/ (*plural* **-men** /-mən/) n a member of a train crew or other railway employee who operates, inspects, or repairs brakes

brake pad n a renewable block of material that presses against the surface of a disc brake

brake parachute, brake chute n a parachute that is attached to the back of a vehicle and acts as a brake

brake shoe n a curved block that presses against a wheel or brake drum to slow it down

brakesman /brayksmən/ (*plural* **-men** /-mən/) n the person who operates the winch at a pithead

brake van n formerly, a railway vehicle attached to a goods train from which the guard applied the brakes

braking distance n the distance a vehicle needs to come to a complete stop when the brakes have been applied

braless /braaləss/ *adj, adv* not wearing a bra

Bramante /brə mán tay/, **Donato** (1444–1514) Italian architect and painter. Born **Donato di Pascuccio d'Antonio**

bramble /brámb'l/ n **1 BLACKBERRY BUSH** a prickly shrub that produces blackberries, especially when growing wild (*often plural*) **2 PRICKLY SHRUB** a prickly shrub or bush similar to, or related to, the blackberry, e.g. a dog rose **3 BLACKBERRY** a blackberry ■ *vi* (**-bles, -bling, -bled**) **COLLECT BERRIES FROM BRAMBLES** to collect berries from brambles in hedgerows [Old English *bræmbel* < Germanic, 'thorny bush']

brambling /brámbling/ n a bird related to the chaffinch, with a speckled head and back and rusty-brown breast. Native to: N Europe, Asia. *Fringilla montifringilla.* [Mid-16C. Perhaps < BRAMBLE + -LING.]

brambly /brámbli/ (**-blier, -bliest**) *adj* covered in or containing prickly shrubs, especially blackberries or wild roses ○ *a brambly garden*

bran /bran/ n the husks of cereal grain that are removed during milling. Use: supplementary source of dietary fibre. [13C. < French.]

Bran n in Celtic mythology, a giant god who ruled Britain and installed his son, Gwern, as king of Ireland

Branagh /bránnə/, **Kenneth** (b. 1960) British actor and director

⚡**branch** /braanch/ n **1 PART OF TREE GROWING FROM TRUNK** a woody limb of a tree that grows out from a larger limb or from the trunk **2 PART OF PLANT STEM OR ROOT** a subdivision of the stem, root, or flower cluster of a plant **3 SOMETHING LIKE TREE BRANCH** something that resembles a branch of a tree in structure **4 LOCAL UNIT IN ORGANIZATION** a shop, a bank, or another organization that is part of a larger group and is located in a different part of a geographical area from the parent organization ○ *The account is held at the bank's Oxford branch.* **5 DISTINCT PART OF LARGE ORGANIZATION** a subdivision of a large organization, usually with a specialized mission **6 PART OF SUBJECT AREA** one part of a large area of study or subject ○ *Ethics is a branch of philosophy.* **7 FAMILY LINE** one line of a family that is descended from a common ancestor ○ *the Peruvian branch of the family* **8 PART OF CURVE** a distinctive part of a curve that is separated from the rest of the curve, e.g. by discontinuities or extreme points **9 TRIBUTARY STREAM** a river or stream flowing into another river ○ *a branch of the Colorado River* **10 ALTERNATIVE SEQUENCE OF COMPUTER INSTRUCTIONS** one of several alternative sequences of computer program instructions that may be activated according to certain specific conditions, e.g. the value of a variable ■ *v* **1** *vti* **DIVIDE INTO SMALLER PARTS** to divide or cause something to divide into lesser parts ○ *Part of the track branches off towards the river.* **2** *vi* **HAVE BRANCHES** to grow branches **3** *vi* **EXPAND ACTIVITIES OR INTERESTS** to become involved in something new, especially as a way of extending or expanding personal interests or business activities ○ *The company has branched into multimedia upgrade kits.* [13C. Via French *branche* < late Latin *branca* 'paw'.]

branch out *vi* to do something different, especially if it involves an element of risk

-branch *suffix* gills ○ *opisthobranch* [< Latin *branchia* (see BRANCHIA)]

branchia /brángki ə/ (*plural* **-ae** /-ki ee/) n a gill in aquatic animals or a similar structure found in the embryos of higher animals, including humans [Late 17C. Via Latin < Greek *bragkhia* 'gills'.] —**branchial** *adj* —**branchiate** *adj*

branchial cleft, branchial groove n a gill slit (*technical*)

branchiopod /brángki ə pod/ n a small, usually freshwater, crustacean with a segmented body and flat gill-bearing appendages. Subclass: Branchiopoda. [Early 19C. < modern Latin *Branchiopoda* < Latin *branchia* 'gills' + Greek *-pod* (see -POD).] —**branchiopod** *adj* —**branchiopodous** /brángki óppədəss/ *adj*

Labels on diagram:
Cerebrum, Pineal gland, Thalamus, Hypothalamus, Pituitary gland, Midbrain, Pons, Cerebellum, Spinal cord

branch line *n* part of a railway system that is routed to smaller towns and villages that are not served by a main line. ◊ **main line**

branch officer *n* a warrant officer in the Royal Navy

Brancusi /bran kóozi/, **Constantin** (1876–1957) Romanian sculptor

brand /brand/ *n* **1 PRODUCT OR MANUFACTURER** a name, usually a trademark, of a manufacturer or product, or the product identified by this name ○ *What brand of cosmetics does she use?* **2 PARTICULAR TYPE** a distinctive type or kind of something ○ *Hollywood makes a certain brand of movies.* **3 MARK BURNED ON ANIMAL** a mark burned into the hide of an animal to identify it as the property of a particular farm or owner ○ *The Triple S is the brand on all our steers.* **4 MARK ON CRIMINAL OR ENSLAVED PERSON** formerly, a mark made on the skin of a criminal or an enslaved person, especially to identify the owner **5 SIGN OR MARK OF DISGRACE** a sign or mark of disgrace, infamy, or notoriety ○ *He bore the brand of disloyalty.* **6 BURNT OR BURNING PIECE OF WOOD** a piece of wood that is burnt or smouldering (*archaic*) **7 SWORD** a sword (*literary*) **8 FUNGAL DISEASE OF PLANTS** a fungal disease that affects garden plants by causing brown spots to appear on leaves ■ *vt* **1 MARK SKIN OR HIDE** to mark an animal's skin or hide with a hot iron, especially as a means of identification ○ *All the cattle have been branded.* **2 DESCRIBE SOMEBODY OR SOMETHING AS BAD** to class somebody or something as bad, illegal, or undesirable, often arbitrarily ○ *branded a cheat* **3 MAKE INDELIBLE MARK ON** to make an indelible mark or impression on somebody or something (*literary*) ○ *The traditions of this sport have been branded into my heart.* [Old English, 'burning stick' < Indo-European, 'be hot'] —**brander** *n*

branded /brándid/ *adj* bearing a company name or trademark, usually considered a mark of prestige or quality

Brandeis /brán dīss/, **Louis** (1856–1941) US supreme court justice

Brandenburg Gate /brándən burg-/ *n* a large neoclassical stone gateway in Berlin, a symbol of the city and a focal point for public gatherings

brandied /brándid/ *adj* cooked or preserved in brandy

branding iron *n* an iron tool that is heated and pressed onto a surface, especially an animal's hide, in order to leave a permanent identifying mark. ◊ **brand** *n*. 3

brandish /brándish/ *vt* to wave something about, especially a weapon, in a menacing, theatrical, or triumphant way [14C. < French *brandiss-*, stem of *brandir* < *brand* 'sword'.] —**brandisher** *n*

brand leader *n* the best-selling product in a particular category

brandling /brándling/ *n* a small, reddish-brown earthworm that is often used as bait by anglers. *Eisenia foetida*. [Mid-17C. Because of its colouring, like a burning brand.]

brand loyalty *n* the tendency to buy a particular brand of a product

brand name *n* a trade name for a product or service produced by a particular company ○ *A computer with a brand name can cost 10 per cent more.* —**brand-named** *adj*

brand-new *adj* completely new and unused [As if newly made in a furnace]

Brando /brándō/, **Marlon** (*b.* 1924) US actor

Brandt /brant/, **Bill** (1904–83) German-born British photographer. Full name **William Brandt**

Brandt, Willy (1913–92) German statesman and Chancellor of west Germany (1969–74). Born **Herbert Ernst Karl Frahm**

brandy /brándi/ (*plural* **-dies**) *n* a spirit that is distilled from the fermented juice of grapes or other fruit [Early 17C. Shortening of *brandy-wine* < Dutch *brandewijn* 'burnt (i.e. distilled) wine'.]

brandy Alexander *n* a cocktail with a base of brandy

brandy butter *n* a creamed mixture of butter, sugar, and brandy, traditionally served with Christmas pudding. US term **hard sauce**

brandy snap *n* a sweet crisp biscuit with a thin lacy texture that is rolled into a cylinder and often filled with cream

branks /brangks/ *npl* a device consisting of a metal frame for the head and a bit to restrain the tongue, formerly used to restrain and punish women thought to be quarrelsome or nagging [Mid-16C. < ?]

Branson /bránss'n/, **Richard** (*b.* 1950) British entrepreneur

brant /brant/ (*plural* **brants** *or* **brant**) *n US* = **brent goose** [14C. Variant of BRENT GOOSE.]

Brantôme /braaN tōm/, **Pierre de Bourdeille, seigneur de** (1540–1614) French writer and courtier

bran tub *n* a tub or barrel containing bran in which small wrapped gifts are hidden at parties or fairs, to be pulled out by people in a game of lucky dip

Braque /braak, brak/, **Georges** (1882–1963) French painter

brash[1] /brash/ *adj* self-assertive in an aggressive or rude way [Early 19C. < ?] —**brashly** *adv* —**brashness** *n*

brash[2] /brash/ *adj* easily cracked or broken [Mid-16C. < ?]

brash[3] /brash/ *n* = **heartburn** [Early 19C. < ?]

brash[4] /brash/ *n* a pile of loose rubbish, e.g. broken rock or garden refuse [Late 18C. < ?]

brashy /bráshi/ (**-ier, -iest**) *adj* **1** loosely broken or fragmented ○ *soft, brashy ice* **2** easily cracked or broken

Brasília /brə zíllyə/ capital of Brazil, in the east-central part of the country. Population: 1,821,946 (1996 estimate).

Braşov /brásh ov/ city in central Romania. Population: 319,908 (1997 estimate).

brass /braass/ *n* **1 YELLOW ALLOY** a hard yellow shiny metal that is an alloy of zinc and copper, frequently with the addition of other metallic elements ○ *candlesticks made of brass* **2 ITEMS MADE OF BRASS** a collection of ornaments or items made of brass **3 ITEM MADE OF BRASS** an individual ornament or item made of brass (*usually plural*) **4 ENGRAVED BRASS PLAQUE OR TABLET** an engraved plaque or tablet made of brass, especially one set into the floor or wall of a church **5 BRASS MUSICAL INSTRUMENTS** the musical instruments made of brass, e.g. the trumpet and trombone **6 PLAYERS OF BRASS INSTRUMENTS** the players of brass instruments, especially when considered as one of the four main sections of an orchestra **7 HIGH-RANKING OFFICERS** high-ranking officers, especially in the military (*informal*) **8** *N England* **MONEY** money or cash (*informal*) ○ *Where there's muck, there's brass.* **9 RENEWABLE BRASS LINER FOR BEARING** a renewable brass or bronze liner for a bearing **10 EXCESSIVE SELF-ASSURANCE** extreme, and usually excessive, self-confidence (*informal*) ○ *He had the brass to lie about every aspect of his background.* [Old English *bræs* < ?]

Brassaï /bra sī/ (1899–1984) Hungarian-born French photographer. Pseudonym of **Gyula Halasz**

brass band *n* a band consisting of brass wind instruments and sometimes percussion instruments

brassbound /bráass bownd/ *adj* **1** trimmed or banded with brass or similar metal **2** unreasonably inflexible in manner or character

brassed off /bráast-/ *adj* feeling irritated and disappointed (*informal dated*)

brasserie /brássəri/ *n* a restaurant serving a wide range of food and drinks [Mid-19C. < French, 'brewery' < Old French *bracier* 'brew' < Latin *brace* 'malt' < Celtic.]

brassica /brássikə/ *n* a plant of the mustard family, e.g. cabbage, kale, broccoli, cauliflower, or mustard. Genus: *Brassica*. [Early 19C. Via modern Latin, genus name < Latin, 'cabbage'.]

brassie /brássi, bráassi/ *n* a golf club (a number 2 wood) with a brass-plated sole (*informal*)

brassiere /brássi ər, brázzi ər/ *n* CLOTHES = **bra** [Early 20C. < French, 'bodice' < *bras* 'arm' < Latin *brachium* (see BRACHIUM).]

brass knuckles *npl* = **knuckle-duster**

brass-monkey weather, brass monkeys *n* extremely cold weather (*informal*) [< *cold enough to freeze the balls off a brass monkey*]

brass neck *n* impudence and a lack of respect (*informal*)

brass rubbing *n* **1** a copy of an engraved plaque or tablet made by putting a piece of paper over the engraving and rubbing it with something soft such as chalk or graphite **2** the process of making a brass rubbing

brass tacks *npl* the most basic or fundamental parts of a situation or issue ○ *Let's get down to brass tacks.*

brassware /bráass wair/ *n* items such as plates and ornaments made from brass

brassy /bráassi/ (**-ier, -iest**) *adj* **1 FLASHY AND VULGAR** brightly dressed in a cheap and showy way, and behaving too confidently or noisily (*insult*) **2 SOUNDING LIKE BRASS INSTRUMENTS** dominated by or resembling the sounds of brass musical instruments ○ *a brassy mixture of reggae, funk, calypso, and jazz* **3 BRAZENLY OVERBEARING** brazen or strident in style **4 OF BRASS** made of or containing brass **5 OF GOLDEN-YELLOW COLOUR** golden-yellow in colour or hue —**brassily** *adv* —**brassiness** *n*

brat /brat/ *n* somebody, either a child or an adult, who is regarded as tiresomely demanding and selfish [Mid-16C. < ?] —**brattiness** *n* —**brattish** *adj* —**bratty** *adj*

Bratby /brátbi/, **John** (1928–92) British painter

Bratislava /brátti slaávə/ capital of Slovakia, in the SW of the country. Population: 451,395 (1998 estimate).

brat pack *n* a group of successful or affluent young people, especially actors [After RAT PACK]

Bratsk /braatsk/ town in Siberia, E Russia. Population: 301,742 (1995).

Brattain /brátt'n/, **Walter H.** (1902–87) Chinese-born US physicist. Full name **Walter Houser Brattain**

brattice /bráttiss/ *n* **1** a partition used to assist ventilation in a mine **2** in medieval times, a temporary wooden parapet or gallery erected on the battlements of a fortress and used during a siege [13C. Via Anglo-Norman, Old French *bretesche* < medieval Latin *bretescha (turris)* 'British (tower)'.]

bratwurst /brát wurst/ *n* a highly seasoned fresh German sausage made of pork or of pork and veal [Early 20C. < German, 'frying-sausage'.]

brava /braá vaa/ *interj, n* a shout of approval for a woman or girl performer [Early 19C. < Italian, 'excellent'.]

bravado /brə vaádō/ *n* a real or pretended display of courage or boldness ○ *a breathtaking act of bravado* [Late 16C. Alteration of Spanish *bravada* < *bravo* (see BRAVE).]

brave /brayv/ *adj* (**braver, bravest**) **HAVING OR SHOWING COURAGE** having or showing courage, especially when facing danger, difficulty, or pain ■ *n* **1 BRAVE PEOPLE** those people who are courageous **2 NATIVE NORTH AMERICAN WARRIOR** a Native North American warrior ■ *vt* (**braves, braving, braved**) **1 FACE ONSLAUGHT OF** to face the onslaught of something unpleasant with courage and resolution **2 CHALLENGE** to defy something despite there being only a small chance of being victorious [15C. Via French < Italian *bravo* 'bold' or Spanish *bravo* 'brave, savage', < Latin *barbarus* (see BARBAROUS).] —**bravely** *adv* —**braveness** *n*
brave out *vt* to live through something that is difficult or unpleasant

brave new world *n* the world of the future, usually either a technology-based utopia or a sinister totalitarian world devoid of human values (*often ironical*) [Mid-20C. < *Brave New World* (1932), novel by Aldous HUXLEY.]

LITERARY LINK ***Brave New World***, a novel (1932) by Aldous Huxley. Written partly as a response to more utopian writers of the day, it depicts a bleak and sterile future civilization in which feelings are stimulated by drugs, and babies are bred in factories.

bravery /bráyvəri/ *n* extreme courage in the face of danger or difficulty, or an example of this [Mid-16C. < French *braverie* or Italian *braveria*, both < Italian *bravo* 'bold'.]

SYNONYMS See ***courage***.

bravissimo /braa víssimō/ *interj* used as a cry of great and enthusiastic approval by members of a theatre audience (*formal*) [Mid-18C. < Italian, 'most excellent'.]

bravo /braávō, braa vō/ *interj* **AUDIENCE'S SHOUT OF APPROVAL** used as a cry of approval by members of a theatre audience ■ *n* (*plural* **-vos**) **1 CRY OF 'BRAVO'** a shout of 'bravo' to express admiration **2 HIRED ASSASSIN** a hired assassin (*archaic*) [Mid-18C. < Italian, 'excellent'.]

Bravo /braávō/ *n* the code word for the letter 'b', used in international radio communications

bravura /brə vyóorə/ *n* **1** great skill that is shown when something artistic is done in an exciting or innovative way (*often used before a noun*) ○ *a bravura performance* **2** showy style or behaviour [Mid-18C. < Italian, 'courage, spirit' < *bravo* 'bold'.]

braw /braw/ *adj Scotland* attractive or pleasant [Late 16C. Variant of BRAVE.]

brawl /brawl/ *n* **1 NOISY FIGHT** a rough and noisy fight, usually in a public place and between large numbers of people **2 LOUD NOISE** a loud deep noise, especially the noise of rushing water **3** *US, Can* **LOUD PARTY** a noisy boisterous party (*slang*) ■ *vi* 1 FIGHT NOISILY to fight or wrestle noisily, especially in a public place 2 MAKE DEEP LOUD SOUND to make a deep loud roaring sound, especially the sound of rushing water [14C. < ?] —**brawler** *n* —**brawling** *n*

brawn /brawn/ *n* 1 STRONG MUSCLES very strong muscles, especially on the arms and legs 2 BODILY STRENGTH physical strength, especially as opposed to intellectual power 3 COOKED MEAT FROM ANIMALS' HEADS boiled and jellied meat from the head and feet of pigs or calves. US term **headcheese** [14C. < Anglo-Norman *braun* 'fleshy part of the leg' < Germanic.]

brawny /bráwni/ (**-ier, -iest**) *adj* muscular and strong-looking —**brawnily** *adv* —**brawniness** *n*

bray[1] /bray/ *v* 1 *vi* to make the sound a donkey makes 2 *vti* to speak, laugh, or say something in a harsh high-pitched rasping voice [13C. < Old French *braire* 'to cry'.] —**bray** *n* —**brayer** *n*

bray[2] /bray/ *vt* 1 to crush something to a fine powder or consistency 2 to spread ink in a thin layer on a surface [14C. < Anglo-Norman *braier*, Old French *breier* < Germanic.]

Braz. *abbr* 1 Brazil 2 Brazilian

braze[1] /brayz/ (**brazes, brazing, brazed**) *vt* 1 to make something out of brass or decorate something with brass 2 to give something a hardness like that of brass [Old English *brasian* < BRASS] —**brazer** *n*

SPELLCHECK See ***braise***.

braze[2] /brayz/ (**brazes, brazing, brazed**) *vt* to join two pieces of metal together with a solder that has a high melting point [Mid-16C. < Old French *braser* 'to burn'.] —**brazer** *n*

brazen /bráyz'n/ *adj* 1 BOLD AND UNASHAMED showing or expressing boldness and complete lack of shame 2 HARSH-SOUNDING with an unpleasantly loud and resonant sound 3 OF OR LIKE BRASS made of brass or resembling it, especially in colour or hardness (*literary*) [Old English *bræsen* 'made of brass' < BRASS] —**brazenly** *adv* —**brazenness** *n*

brazen out *vt* to face a difficult situation confidently, without showing shame or embarrassment

brazier[1] /bráyzi ər/ *n* somebody who works on brass articles [14C. Probably < BRASS, after GLAZIER.]

brazier[2] /bráyzi ər/ *n* a metal drum with holes in it, used outdoors as a container for burning coal or charcoal, either for cooking or to keep people warm [Late 17C. < French *brasier* < *braise* 'hot coals'.]

brazil /brə zíl/ *n* 1 INDUST = **brazilwood** 2 FOOD = **Brazil nut** *n.* 1 [14C. < medieval Latin *brasilium*.]

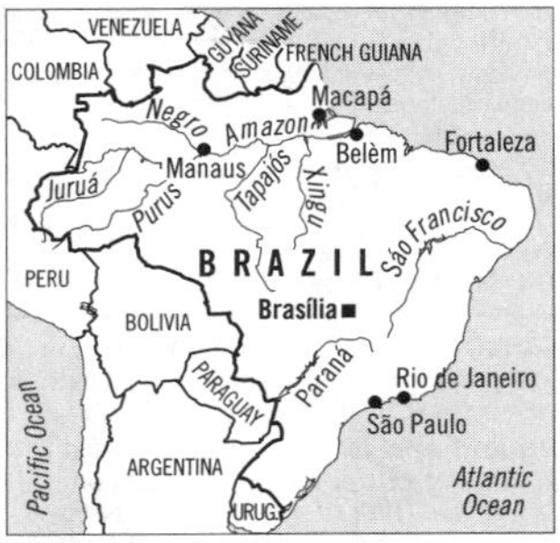

Brazil

Brazil /brə zíl/ republic in E South America, the largest country in the continent. Capital: Brasília. Population: 167,660,687 (1997). Area: 8,547,404 sq. km/3,300,171 sq. mi. —**Brazilian** *n, adj*

Brazil Basin basin of the Atlantic Ocean on the American side of the Mid-Atlantic Ridge. Depth: 5,000 m/16,400 ft.

Brazil nut *n* 1 a long thick edible seed with a hard shell that is nearly triangular in cross-section, borne in clusters inside large round capsules 2 an evergreen tree that bears Brazil nuts. Native to: tropical S America. *Bertholletia excelsa*.

brazilwood /brə zíl wŏŏd/, **brazil** *n* red wood from various tropical and North American trees, especially one native to Brazil. Use: manufacture of red dyes, violin bows.

Brazzaville /brázzə vil/ capital of the Republic of the Congo, in the SE of the country. Population: 1,009,000 (1995 estimate).

BRB *abbr* be right back (*in e-mails*)

BRCS *abbr* British Red Cross Society

BRE *abbr* 1 Bachelor of Religious Education 2 Building Research Establishment

breach /breech/ *v* 1 *vt* MAKE OPENING THROUGH to break down an obstruction to allow something to pass through it 2 *vt* SURPASS LIMIT to go beyond a target or limit 3 *vt* BREAK LAW OR PROMISE to fail to obey, or preserve something, for such as a law or trust 4 *vi* LEAP OUT to leap above the surface of the water (*refers to whales*) ■ *n* 1 HOLE a hole in something that is caused by something else forcing its way through 2 GAP a gap that results when something or somebody leaves 3 FAILURE a failure to obey, keep, or preserve something, e.g. a law, a trust, or a promise ○ *a breach of confidentiality* 4 ESTRANGEMENT a breakdown in friendly relations 5 WHALE'S LEAP a leap out of the water by a whale [13C. < Old French *breche* < Germanic.]

SPELLCHECK Do not confuse ***breach*** with ***breech***, which has a similar sound. Beware: your spellchecker will not catch this error.

breach of promise *n* failure in fulfilling a promise, especially in former times the breaking of a promise to marry somebody

breach of the peace *n* the criminal offence of behaving in a noisy and violent way in public

bread /bred/ *n* 1 FOOD MADE FROM FLOUR AND WATER a food typically made by mixing flour, water, and yeast and allowing it to swell before baking it 2 MEANS OF SURVIVAL food, sustenance, or a means of survival or support 3 MONEY money to live on (*dated slang*) [Old English *brēad* < ?] ◇ **cast your bread upon the waters** to spend time and effort, especially to help others, without expecting any immediate advantage for yourself (*formal*) ◇ **know which side your bread is buttered (on)** to know what is to your advantage (*informal*)

SPELLCHECK Do not confuse ***bread*** with ***bred***, which has a similar sound. Beware: your spellchecker will not catch this error.

bread and butter *n* 1 a dependable source of income 2 something that is the essential or sustaining part of something else

bread-and-butter *adj* 1 concerned with basic but important things 2 providing the main source of somebody's income or livelihood ○ *a bread-and-butter job*

bread-and-butter letter *n* a letter or note expressing thanks for somebody's hospitality

bread-and-butter pudding *n* a baked pudding that is made from bread and butter layered in a dish with dried fruit and covered in a mixture of egg, sugar, milk, and spices. US term **bread pudding**

bread and circuses *npl* something done or given to keep people happy, especially something provided or encouraged by governments to win popular appeal or avert public unrest [Translation of Latin *panis et circenses*]

breadbasket /bréd baaskit/ *n* 1 a region that is an important grower of cereal crops 2 the stomach or abdomen (*slang dated*)

bread bin *n* a container for storing bread. US term **breadbox**

breadboard /bréd bawrd/ *n* a preliminary version of an electrical or electronic circuit put together for test purposes ■ *vt* to make a preliminary version of an electrical or electronic circuit for test purposes —**breadboarding** *n*

breadbox /bréd boks/ *n US* = **bread bin**

breadcrumb /bréd krum/ *n* a tiny piece of bread, either soft or hard (*often plural*)

breadfruit /bréd froot/ (*plural* **-fruit** *or* **-fruits**) *n* 1 a large round seedless tropical fruit 2 an evergreen tree that bears breadfruit. Native to: Pacific Islands. *Artocarpus altilis*.

breadline /bréd līn/ *n* 1 a very low standard of living, with only just enough food and money to survive 2 *US* a queue of people waiting for handouts of free food [Originally 'queue of people for unsold bread']

bread mould *n* a fungus that grows on decaying bread and other foods, forming a dense cottony growth. *Rhizopus nigricans*.

breadnut /bréd nut/ *n* 1 the large edible seed of a yellow fruit 2 a large tree with yellow fruits containing breadnuts. Native to: Central America, Mexico, West Indies. *Brosimum alicastrum*.

breadroot /bréd root/ *n* 1 a starchy tuber, formerly used as food by many Native American people 2 a perennial plant of the pea family that produces breadroot. Native to: North America. *Psoralea esculenta*.

bread sauce *n* a milk-based sauce thickened with breadcrumbs and flavoured with onion, traditionally served with poultry

breadth /bredth, bretth/ *n* 1 DISTANCE FROM SIDE TO SIDE the distance or measurement of something from one side to the other 2 PIECE OF FABRIC IN STANDARD WIDTH a standardized width that a product, especially fabric, is manufactured in, or a piece of fabric in a standardized width 3 GREAT EXTENT the extent of something, especially when it is impressively great 4 BROAD-MINDEDNESS an open and tolerant view of life and the world [Early 16C. < obsolete *brede* 'breadth' < Germanic, after LENGTH.]

breadwinner /bréd winnər/ *n* somebody whose earnings are a family's main income

break /brayk/ *v* (**breaks, breaking, broke** /brōk/, **broken** /brōkən/) 1 *vti* SEPARATE SOMETHING INTO PIECES to become damaged or damage something so that it separates into pieces ○ *It broke in two.* 2 *vt* DAMAGE BODY to damage a body part, e.g. a bone ○ *She broke her leg.* 3 *vti* DAMAGE PART OF MACHINE to damage a part of a tool or machine so that it stops functioning properly, or become damaged and stop functioning properly ○ *The washing machine is broken.* 4 *vti* TEAR SURFACE to become torn, or make a tear or hole in a surface or seal, allowing the possibility of a leak or spill ○ *Store in the fridge after breaking open the seal on the bottle.* 5 *vt* DISOBEY RULE to disobey a rule or law 6 *vt* GO BACK ON WORD to renege on a promise or agreement 7 *vt* END BAD SITUATION to end, change, or rectify a difficult or disadvantageous situation ○ *break the deadlock between rival factions* 8 *vt* END SILENCE to end a period of silence 9 *vti* FINISH RELATIONSHIP to end an involvement with an individual or group ○ *Divorce broke my links with his friends.* 10 *vt* END to finish something, bring it to an end, or stop somebody doing it ○ *break the coffee-drinking habit* 11 *vt* INTERRUPT to interrupt something temporarily ○ *The distraction broke her train of thought.* 12 *vt* RUIN SOMEBODY'S LIFE to destroy somebody's career, resolve, courage, or hope of success ○ *The media can make or break her.* 13 *vti* ESCAPE to escape from a restraint ○ *break free* 14 *vi* TAKE PERIOD FOR REST to take a period of leisure ○ *break for lunch* 15 *vt* STAND IN THE WAY OF to stand in the way of or weaken the effect of something, e.g. a fall or blow ○ *He tried to break her fall.* 16 *vt* BEAT RECORD to beat a previous record 17 *vt* EXCEED LIMIT to exceed a limit or constraint ○ *break the speed limit* 18 *vti* REVEAL OR BE REVEALED to reveal something personally, or be revealed, particularly by the media ○ *She broke it to me gently.* ○ *Panic ensued when the news broke.* 19 *vi* BECOME DEEPER to settle into an adult man's register (*refers to a boy's voice*) 20 *vi* STOP SPEAKING FROM EMOTION to stop speaking and hesitate when overcome with emotion ○ *Her voice broke and tears slid down her face.* 21 *vi* CHANGE TONE WITH REGISTER to change in tone or quality when changing register (*refers to a voice or musical instrument*) 22 *vi* BECOME DAYLIGHT to become light at sunrise 23 *vi* CHANGE WEATHER PATTERN to change after a settled period 24 *vi* SUDDENLY START to suddenly begin to rain, snow, or hail ○ *The storm broke.* 25 *vi* TURN TO SURF to start collapsing into surf when close to shore or hitting rocks or similar objects (*refers to a wave*) 26 *vt* INTERPRET A CODE to understand a code and be able to translate it accurately 27 *vt* PROVE UNTRUE to prove that something is untrue or wrong 28 *vt* INVALIDATE WILL to use legal means to declare a will invalid 29 *vt* BLOW OPEN SAFE to open a safe using explosives 30 *vt* TRAIN HORSE TO ACCEPT HARNESS to train a horse to become accustomed to a saddle, bit, and rider 31 *vt* SWAP NOTE FOR CHANGE to exchange a note of money for smaller units of money, either coins or smaller notes and coins ○ *break a £20 note* 32 *vi* FLOW OUT IN CHILDBIRTH to flow out when the amniotic sac around an unborn baby breaks during the first stage of labour (*refers to amniotic fluid*) ○ *Her waters have broken.* 33 *vi US* TURN OUT to happen or turn out in a particular way ○ *Things are breaking well.* 34 *vt* REDUCE TO POVERTY to cause somebody to be extremely poor or bankrupt **35** *vti* **EMERGE OUT OF WATER** to emerge or erupt above the surface of a body of water **36** *vt* **DEMOTE** to demote somebody to a lower rank **37** *vt* **INTERRUPT FLOW OF ELECTRIC CURRENT** to interrupt the flow of electricity in an electrical circuit **38** *vi* **FALL SHARPLY** to fall in price (*refers to stock exchange quotations*) **39** *vti* **WIN GAME OFF OPPONENT'S SERVICE** to win a game in tennis in which the other player is serving **40** *vi* **SEPARATE FROM CLINCH** to separate after being in a boxing or wrestling clinch **41** *vi* **SPEED UP IN RACE** to increase speed suddenly in a race **42** *vi* **CHANGE DIRECTION IN AIR** to change direction while moving through the air (*refers to a baseball*) **43** *vi* **CHANGE DIRECTION ON BOUNCING** to change direction after bouncing (*refers to a cricket ball*) **44** *vt* **KNOCK OVER WICKET** to hit and knock over a bail from the wicket when playing cricket **45** *vi* **START OFF IN HORSE RACE** to start off at the start of a race in horseracing **46** *vi* **TAKE THE FIRST SHOT** to take the first shot in a game or frame in billiards or snooker **47** *vi* **BECOME DIPHTHONG** to change in pronunciation, becoming a diphthong (*refers to a vowel*) ■ *n* **1 PERIOD OFF FROM ACTIVITY** a period taken away from an activity for a rest, change, or meal ○ *a lunch break* ○ *Let's take a break now.* **2 BRIEF HOLIDAY** a short holiday away from home ○ *a weekend break* ○ *We needed to get away for a short break.* **3 PERIOD OFF BEFORE CONTINUING** a period away from something before continuing it again ○ *a career break* **4 TIME OFF IN SCHOOL DAY** time off from classes during the school day when pupils can play or rest. US term **recess** *n.* 4 **5 END TO RELATIONSHIP** the severance of links with a person or group or an end to a relationship ○ *He wanted to make the break with his partner.* **6 END** an end to something ○ *a break with tradition* **7** BROADCAST = **commercial break** **8 INTERVAL IN MATCH** an interval in a sports match **9 PAUSE IN SPEECH** a pause when speaking ○ *a break in the conversation* **10 FRACTURE** a fracture in a bone **11 CRACK** a crack in something **12 CHANGE IN WEATHER** a change in the weather **13 LUCKY OPPORTUNITY FOR SUCCESS** an unexpected opportunity that allows somebody to achieve something or become successful (*informal*) ○ *He got his first break when he was spotted playing for his college.* **14 PIECE OF LUCK** a piece of good luck or bad luck ○ *a lucky break* **15 ADVANTAGEOUS FINANCIAL SITUATION** an advantageous financial situation in which somebody is repaid or makes a reduced payment ○ *a tax break* **16 ESCAPE ATTEMPT** a sudden attempt to escape ○ *make a break for it* **17 DISCONTINUITY** a discontinuity in something, by which it changes in quality or level **18 SUNRISE** the time when the sun first rises (*literary*) ○ *at the break of day* **19 WINNING OF GAME OFF OPPONENT'S SERVICE** the winning of a game in tennis in which the other player is serving **20 START OF HORSE RACE** the start of a horse race **21 INTERRUPTION IN FLOW OF ELECTRICITY** an interruption in the flow of electricity in an electrical circuit **22 INSTRUMENTAL PART IN SONG** an instrumental part in a piece of pop music **23 IMPROVISED JAZZ SOLO** an improvised solo part in a piece of jazz music **24 CHANGE IN REGISTER** a change in register in a voice or musical instrument **25** LITERAT = **caesura** *n.* 1, **caesura** *n.* 2 **26 FALL IN PRICES** a sudden fall in prices, particularly in a stock market **27 SERIES OF SUCCESSFUL SHOTS** a sequence of successful shots in one player's turn in billiards or snooker, or the points scored from them **28 FIRST SHOT THAT SCATTERS BALLS** an opening shot in billiards or snooker, which in snooker often scatters the balls **29 FAILURE TO KNOCK DOWN ALL PINS** a failure to knock down all the pins in ten pin bowling after the second throw **30 ACCESS TO CB RADIO CHANNEL** access for a CB radio operator to a radio channel **31** TRANSP = **brake**[6] *n.* ■ *interj* **USED TO SEPARATE FIGHTERS** used to command boxers or wrestlers to separate from a clinch [Old English *brecan* < Indo-European] ◇ **break even** to make neither a profit nor a loss from a venture ◇ **give somebody a break** to stop nagging or criticizing somebody or to start treating somebody fairly (*informal*)

SPELLCHECK Do not confuse ***break*** with ***brake***, which has a similar sound. Beware: your spellchecker will not catch this error.

break away *vi* **1 LEAVE OR GET AWAY** to sever relations with or detach from a person or group **2 DEPART FROM CUSTOM** to change or depart from established customs or procedures **3 PULL AWAY QUICKLY** to depart or pull away from somebody or something, usually at high speed

break down *v* **1** *vi* **FAIL TO FUNCTION PROPERLY** to stop working, or to stop working properly, effectively, or usefully **2** *vt* **TEAR DOWN** to destroy something or cause something to fall or collapse **3** *vti* **BECOME OR MAKE EMOTIONAL** to become upset emotionally, or to cause somebody to become upset emotionally **4** *vti* **EXPERIENCE OR CAUSE HEALTH COLLAPSE** to experience, or cause somebody to experience, a physical or psychological collapse **5** *vti* **STOP RESISTING** to yield or end any resistance, or to cause somebody to yield or somebody's resistance to end **6** *vti* **WEAKEN** to become or cause somebody or something to become weak and ineffective **7** *vt* **ANALYSE BY DIVIDING INTO PARTS** to analyse or examine something by reducing it to its simplest terms or component parts **8** *vi* **BE DIVISIBLE INTO ELEMENTS** to divide into or be reducible to separate parts when analysed **9** *vti* **DECOMPOSE CHEMICALLY** to decompose chemically, or to cause something to undergo chemical decomposition **10** *vi* **EXPERIENCE ELECTRICAL INSULATION FAILURE** to experience a sudden failure of an insulating material to halt the current flow

break in *v* **1** *vi* **ENTER FORCIBLY** to enter a place or building forcibly and usually illegally **2** *vt* **BEGIN USING SOMEBODY OR SOMETHING NEW** to begin to employ somebody new or use something new, supplying the training or modifications needed for good performance **3** *vi* **START TALKING** to interrupt a conversation or discussion

break into *vt* **1 ENTER BUILDING FORCIBLY AND ILLEGALLY** to enter a building forcibly and usually illegally **2 BEGIN SPEAKING** to interrupt something that is being said or discussed **3 DO SOMETHING SUDDENLY** to begin doing something suddenly, e.g. running or singing **4 START WORK IN NEW FIELD** to begin working in a profession or field, often after having tried to do so for some time without success

break off *v* **1** *vt* **TAKE OFF PIECE OF** to separate a piece from a solid mass or the main part of something **2** *vti* **END BEING OR DOING SOMETHING TOGETHER** to discontinue a relationship or interaction with somebody or a group **3** *vi* **STOP SPEAKING** to stop talking, usually abruptly

break out *v* **1** *vi* **HAVE SKIN RASH** to develop skin blemishes or a rash, especially suddenly **2** *vi* **BEGIN ABRUPTLY** to happen or begin suddenly and strongly (*refers to wars and violence*) **3** *vi* **BECOME FREE FROM** to escape or emerge from something that confines, restrains, or traps, such as a prison cell **4** *vt* **PREPARE SOMETHING FOR USE** to open something or get something ready for use or action **5** *vt* **CLASSIFY DATA ITEMS** to classify, summarize, outline, or separate data items in order to analyse, explain, or identify something

break through *vti* to burst or advance quickly and suddenly through an obstruction or opposition, e.g. from an enemy

break up *v* **1** *vt* **DIVIDE OR INTERRUPT** to divide or separate something into pieces or to interrupt its continuity **2** *vi* **DISPERSE** to separate, or have members separate, and go in different directions **3** *vti* **END** to cause a relationship, interaction, or gathering to end, or to come to an end **4** *vti* **CAUSE EMOTIONAL RESPONSE** to cause somebody to burst into tears or laughter **5** *vi* **LOSE PHONE COMMUNICATION** to start to lose clear communication when using a mobile phone ○ *You're breaking up.*

break with *vt* to separate from somebody or from a tradition, rule, or trend

breakable /bráykəb'l/ *adj* likely to be broken if not handled carefully ■ *n* something that is easily broken if not handled carefully (*usually plural*) —**breakability** /bráykə bílləti/ *n* —**breakableness** *n*

breakage /bráykij/ *n* **1** something that has been broken, usually accidentally (*usually plural*) ○ *All breakages must be paid for.* **2** the breaking of something

breakaway /bráykə way/ *n* **1 SOMETHING BREAKING OFF** somebody or something that breaks or has broken away **2 SOMETHING MADE TO BREAK OFF** something that is designed to break away or break apart from the whole **3 BREAKING AWAY** the breaking away of somebody or something ■ *adj* **1 MADE TO BREAK OFF** designed to break away or apart, either as a safety mechanism or to create an illusion, e.g. a theatre prop **2 HAVING SEVERED TIES WITH** having broken ties or connections to somebody or a group

breakbeat /bráyk beet/ *n* a drum pattern with a syncopated beat that is electronically looped, used mostly in jungle, drum and bass, and hard-core music

breakbone fever /bráyk bōn-/ *n* MED = **dengue**

breakdancing /bráyk daanssing/ *n* an acrobatic style of solo dancing to rap music, typically involving spinning of the body on the ground [Perhaps related to BREAKDOWN 'fast dance'] —**breakdance** *n, vi* —**breakdancer** *n*

breakdown /bráyk down/ *n* **1 FAILURE TO OPERATE** a failure to operate or an interruption of the operation of a machine or vehicle **2 DISRUPTION IN COMMUNICATIONS** a disruption of the understanding and interaction between people or groups ○ *breakdown in the talks* **3 PERSONAL HEALTH CRISIS** a sudden physical or psychological collapse **4 DATA SUMMARY OR EXPLANATION** a summary, explanation or analysis of data items collected **5 CAR OR MACHINERY FAILURE** a time when a car or piece of machinery stops working **6 DECOMPOSITION INTO PARTS** a breaking down of something into its essential components, parts, or elements **7 SUDDEN PASSAGE OF CURRENT THROUGH INSULATOR** the sudden passage of electrical current through an insulator **8 COUNTRY DANCE** a fast US country dance

breakdown lorry, breakdown truck *n* a lorry that tows a vehicle that has broken down to a garage where it can be repaired. US term **wrecker**

breakdown voltage *n* the voltage at which a sudden and large increase in current through an insulator or semiconductor happens

breaker[1] /bráykər/ *n* **1** ELEC ENG = **circuit breaker** **2 LARGE WHITE-CAPPED WAVE** a large, usually white-capped, wave that is cresting or breaking, especially onto the shore **3 BREAKDANCER** a breakdancer (*slang*) **4 BREAKING MACHINE** something that is used to crush or break up rocks, fibres, or other substances **5 HORSE TRAINER** somebody who trains horses to be ridden ■ *interj* **OPENING MESSAGE** used by CB radio operators to announce that they are beginning to transmit on a channel

breaker[2] /bráykər/ *n* a small cask for water, used especially on lifeboats [Mid-19C. < Spanish *barrica* 'cask'.]

breakeven /bráyk éev'n/, **breakeven point** *n* the point or level of financial activity at which expenditure equals income or the value of an investment equals its cost, and the result is neither a profit nor loss

breakfast /brékfəst/ *n* the first meal of the day, usually eaten in the morning (*often before nouns*) [15C. < FAST[2].] —**breakfast** *vi* —**breakfaster** *n*

breakfast television *n* informal, magazine-style television programmes broadcast in the morning

breakfront /bráyk frunt/ *adj* describes a piece of furniture, e.g. a cabinet or bookcase, with a central section that juts forward slightly —**breakfront** *n*

break-in *n* an illegal forced entry into a building or place

breaking[1] /bráyking/ *n* the changing of a simple vowel into a diphthong when certain other speech sounds come before or after it. For example the vowel in 'feet' becomes a diphthong in 'feel'.

breaking[2] /bráyking/ *n* breakdancing (*slang*)

breaking and entering *n* the crime of forcibly entering property, usually in order to steal from it

breaking point *n* **1** the point at which somebody loses the ability to deal physically, psychologically, or emotionally with a stressful situation **2** the point at which a condition or situation reaches a crisis

breakneck /bráyk nek/ *adj* so fast or quick as to be hazardous or reckless ○ *at breakneck speed*

break of day *n* the time when the sun rises in the morning

breakoff /bráyk of/ *n* a discontinuation of something, especially when this is abrupt ○ *the breakoff of negotiations*

breakout /bráyk owt/ *n* a forceful escape or emergence from being confined, restrained, or trapped

⚡**breakpoint** /bráyk poynt/ *n* **1** a pause inserted into a computer program so that the registers and memory locations can be examined to correct a programming logic error **2** a point where something stops, pauses, changes, or breaks apart

break point *n* a point in tennis which, if won, results in the player who is not serving winning the game

breakthrough /bráyk throo/ *n* **1 IMPORTANT DISCOVERY** an important new discovery, especially in science, medicine, or technology, that has a dramatic and far-reaching effect **2 REMOVAL OF BARRIER TO PROGRESS** an event that causes or marks the breaking down of a barrier to progress, e.g. in negotiations **3 PENETRATION OF ENEMY LINE** an attacking army's breaking through and beyond an enemy's line of defence ■ *adj* **BRINGING PUBLIC RECOGNITION** bringing public attention and fame to a performing artist

breakthrough bleeding *n* bleeding from the womb that occurs between menstrual periods

breakup /bráyk up/ *n* **1 BREAKING APART OR UP** a breaking into separate pieces or sections that are not connected or continuous **2 END OF RELATIONSHIP** the breaking off or discontinuation of a personal relationship **3 SPRING THAW OF LODGED ICE** the melting or breaking apart of lodged ice in rivers and harbours in the spring **4 EMOTIONAL BREAKDOWN** a loss of control over the emotions

breakwater /bráyk wawtər/ *n* an offshore barrier that protects a harbour or other coastal area from the full force of the sea

bream[1] /breem/ (*plural* **bream** *or* **breams**) *n* **1 EURASIAN FRESHWATER FISH** a freshwater fish that has a deep thin body and is yellowish in colour. Native to: Europe, Asia. *Abramis brama.* **2 FRESHWATER FISH LIKE BREAM** a freshwater fish that resembles the bream, introduced into Europe and Asia. Native to: North America. Genus: *Lepomis.* **3** ZOOL = **sea bream** *n.* 1 **4** the flesh of a bream as food [14C. < Old French *bre(s)me* < Germanic.]

bream[2] /breem/ *vt* to scrape the shells, seaweed, and mud off the bottom of a ship (*archaic*) [Early 17C. Probably < Middle Dutch *bremme* 'broom, furze'.]

Bream /breem/, **Julian** (*b.* 1933) British guitarist and lutenist

breast /brest/ *n* **1 ORGAN ON CHEST** soft rounded organs on each side of the chest in women and men. In women the organs are more prominent and produce milk after childbirth. **2 ANIMAL'S MILK GLAND** a gland in mammals corresponding to the human breast **3 SOMEBODY'S CHEST** the front of the human chest **4 GARMENT SECTION** the part or section of clothing covering the front of the chest **5 SEAT OF EMOTIONS** the chest regarded as the place where human emotions reside (*literary*) ○ *with pride filling my breast* **6 ANIMAL'S CHEST** the chest of an animal, especially a mammal or bird **7 MEAT FROM ANIMAL'S CHEST** meat from the chest of an animal, especially from a chicken or other poultry **8 FONT OF NOURISHMENT** a source of sustenance or protection (*literary*) **9 PART STICKING OUT OR UP** a part that is rounded, projects, or in some way resembles a breast ■ *vt* **1 PUSH SOMETHING WITH CHEST** to touch or push against something with the chest ○ *managed to breast the tape ahead of her rival* **2 REACH HILLTOP** to reach the summit of a hill **3 FACE SOMETHING BOLDLY** to confront a difficulty squarely and boldly and deal with it in a determined way [Old English *brēost* < Germanic, perhaps < Indo-European, 'swelling'] ◇ **make a clean breast of something** to confess or admit to something, especially something previously denied or withheld

breastbone /brést bōn/ *n* a long bone running down the front of the chest, flat in many animals but ridged in most birds. In humans, the top seven pairs of ribs are connected to it.

breast-feed *vti* to feed a baby with milk from the breast

breastplate /brést playt/ *n* **1** a piece of armour that covers the chest **2** a garment worn over the breast by Jewish high priests in ancient times, set with twelve precious stones representing the twelve tribes of Israel

breaststroke /brést strōk/ *n* a swimming stroke in which the arms are extended and pulled back together in a circular motion while the legs are thrust out and pulled together —**breaststroke** *vi* —**breaststroker** *n*

breastwork /brést wurk/ *n* in former times, an earth wall built at chest height as a temporary barrier for defence

breath /breth/ *n* **1 AIR BREATHED IN AND OUT** the air that a person or animal inhales and exhales **2 AIR EXHALED** the air that somebody exhales, especially with reference to how it feels or smells to somebody nearby **3 BREATHING OF AIR** an inhaling or exhaling of air ○ *take a deep breath* **4 HINT** a faint hint of something ○ *a breath of scandal* **5 LIFE** the vital force or spirit of a living person or animal **6 SHORT PAUSE** a momentary pause or respite **7 WAFT** a fleeting or slight fragrance or movement of air ○ *not a breath of wind* **8 SOFT SOUND** a sound or whispering that is soft and almost inaudible [Old English *bræþ* 'odour, especially of something burning or cooking' < Indo-European, 'heat'] ◇ **a breath of fresh air** somebody or something that is refreshingly new and exciting ◇ **catch your breath 1** to stop breathing for an instant, e.g. from shock or physical pain **2** to regain a normal breathing rhythm after exertion ◇ **don't hold your breath!** used to indicate that it is extremely unlikely that something will happen (*informal*) ◇ **in the same breath** at the same time or shortly afterwards ◇ **out of breath** breathing heavily because of physical exertion ◇ **take somebody's breath away** to astonish or greatly impress somebody ◇ **under your breath** in a whispering or muttering voice ◇ **with bated breath** full of anxious anticipation

USAGE breath or **breathe**? The noun is ***breath*** (*not a breath of air moving*), and the verb is ***breathe*** (*hard to breathe in the sultry air*). Only the verb has the *-e* at the end.

breathable /brée*th*əb'l/ *adj* **1** suitable or possible for people to breathe **2** allowing air in and body moisture out in order to keep the wearer cool and dry (*refers to fabric*) —**breathability** /brée*th*ə bíllәti/ *n*

breathalyse /bré*th*ə līz/ (**-lyses, -lysing, -lysed**) *vt* to test somebody, especially a driver, for drunkenness by making him or her breathe into a Breathalyser™ [Mid-20C. Back-formation < BREATHALYZER.]

Breathalyzer /bré*th*ə līzər/ *tdmk* a trademark for an apparatus that measures a subject's blood alcohol concentration

breathe /bree*th*/ (**breathes, breathing, breathed**) *v* **1** *vti* **TAKE IN AIR** to repeatedly and alternately take in and blow out air in order to stay alive ○ *breathe in deeply* **2** *vti* **EXPEL SUBSTANCE WITH BREATH** to expel a substance, e.g. cigarette smoke, from the mouth or nose along with the breath, or to be exhaled in this way **3** *vt* **SMELL** to take in the aroma of something **4** *vti* **TAKE IN AIR** to take in air, e.g. for combustion or in order to equalize internal and external pressure (*refers to machines*) **5** *vi* **ALLOW AIR THROUGH** to allow air and moisture to pass through fabric or clothing **6** *vt* **SAY SOMETHING SECRETIVELY** to say something in a soft voice or secretively **7** *vt* **GIVE SOMEBODY OR SOMETHING A QUALITY** to instil a particular quality in somebody or something ○ *breathed new life into the group* **8** *vti* **EXUDE QUALITY** to suggest a particular quality in abundance, or to be suggested or displayed noticeably **9** *vi* **LIVE** to be alive **10** *vi* **DEVELOP FLAVOUR THROUGH EXPOSURE TO AIR** to be exposed to air in order to develop flavour (*refers to wine*) **11** *vti* **PAUSE TO REST** to allow a person or animal, e.g. a horse, to pause to rest or catch a breath **12** *vi* **WAFT** to blow softly or move gently [13C. < BREATH.] ◇ **breathe easy** *or* **easily** to relax and stop worrying about something or things in general

USAGE See ***breath***.

breathed /bretht, bree*th*d/ *adj* **1** pronounced without vibrating the vocal cords **2** with a particular type of breathing (*usually in combination*)

breather /brée*th*ər/ *n* **1 PAUSE TO REST** a short rest while in the middle of doing something (*informal*) ○ *In extreme heat you have to make sure you take a breather every hour or so.* **2 BREATHING PERSON** somebody who breathes in a particular way (*in combination*) ○ *a heavy breather* **3 VENT** a vent in an area or enclosure that is otherwise sealed

breathing /brée*th*ing/ *n* **1** the process of taking air into the lungs and pushing it out again **2** in ancient Greek, the pronouncing of an initial vowel with an 'h' sound before it (**rough breathing**), or without an 'h'sound (**smooth breathing**), or either of the symbols indicating these pronunciations

breathing space, breathing room *n* the opportunity to relax or sort out problems without pressures, constraints, interruptions, or interference ○ *Going away should give you some breathing space to sort out any relationship problems.*

breathing spell *n US* = **breathing space**

breathless /bréthləss/ *adj* **1 UNABLE TO BREATHE PROPERLY** experiencing difficulty in breathing, or breathing faster than normal, because of physical exertion or illness **2 WITH SHALLOW BREATHING** breathing very shallowly because of intense emotion, e.g. fear or excitement **3 EXCITING OR INTENSE** capable of causing difficulties in breathing because of intense excitement, emotion, or speed **4 HOT AND WITHOUT BREEZE** lacking any air movement or breeze **5 NOT ALIVE** dead and no longer breathing (*literary*) —**breathlessly** *adv* —**breathlessness** *n*

breathtaking /bréth tayking/ *adj* evoking strong emotions, especially excitement, awe, or shock —**breathtakingly** *adv*

breath test *n* a test using a device that a person breathes into to determine the level of alcohol in the breath, especially one conducted by police on the driver of a road vehicle

breathy /bréthi/ (**-ier, -iest**) *adj* **1** with a discernible sound of breathing accompanying spoken words **2** without proper control of the breath, which creates an uneven or weak vocal or instrumental sound —**breathily** *adv* —**breathiness** *n*

Brébeuf /bráy bŏŏf/, **Jean de, St** (1593–1649) French-born Canadian missionary

breccia /bréchi ə/ *n* coarse-grained sedimentary rock made of sharp fragments of rock and stone cemented together by finer material [Late 18C. < Italian, 'gravel'.] —**breccial** *adj* —**brecciate** /-ayt/ *vti* —**brecciation** /bréchi áysh'n/ *n*

Brecht /brekht/, **Bertolt** (1898–1956) German playwright and director

Brecon Beacons National Park /brékən beekənz-/ national park in SE Wales

bred[1] /bred/ past tense, past participle of **breed**

SPELLCHECK See ***bread***.

bred[2] /bred/ *adj* raised in a particular manner (*in combination*) ○ *city-bred*

Breda /brédə/ city in S Netherlands. Population: 160,398 (2000).

bred-in-the-bone *adj* **1** deeply instilled or firmly established **2** describes a habit, especially a bad habit, that has become deeply ingrained over time

breech /breech/ *n* **1 BACK OF GUN BARREL** the rear part of the barrel of a rifle or shotgun, near the stock **2 PART OF PULLEY** the lower part of a pulley block, to which the rope, cable, or chain is fixed **3 BUTTOCKS** the back lower portion of the trunk of the body [Old English *brēc*, plural of *brōc* 'garment covering the thighs and lower trunk' < Germanic]

SPELLCHECK See ***breach***.

breech birth *n* the delivery of a baby with its buttocks or feet, rather than its head, emerging first

breechblock /breech blok/ *n* the part of a breechloading gun that is detached from the barrel to allow cartridges to be loaded into the back of the barrel

breech delivery *n* = **breech birth**

breeches /bríchiz/, **britches** *npl* **1** trousers with legs that come down to the knee **2** trousers of any kind (*informal*) [13C. Plural of BREECH.]

breeches buoy *n* a piece of equipment used for transferring people between moving ships, consisting of a canvas harness suspended from a pulley and line that links the ships

breeching /bríching, bree-/ *n* **1 STRAP ON HORSE'S HARNESS** the strap of a harness that passes behind the hindquarters of a horse or donkey **2 ROPE SECURING SHIP'S GUN** in former times, ropes used to secure guns to the side of a ship to control the recoil **3 GUN'S BREECH PARTS** parts of a gun that form or make up the breech

breechloader /breech lōdər/ *n* a gun that is loaded by inserting cartridges through the back of the barrel —**breechloading** *adj*

breed /breed/ *n* **1 DISTINCT ANIMAL OR PLANT** a strain of an animal or plant with identifiable characteristics that distinguish it from other members of its species, especially one whose characteristics are preserved by controlled mating or propagation **2 SOMEBODY OR SOMETHING OF PARTICULAR TYPE** a particular type of thing or person, especially one that can be easily distinguished from other similar things or people ○ *a new breed of managers* ■ *v* (**breeds, breeding, bred** /bred/, **bred**) **1** *vti* **MATE AND PRODUCE YOUNG** to mate and give birth to offspring **2** *vt* **RAISE ANIMALS OR PLANTS** to reproduce and raise animals or plants, especially for commercial purposes or for shows and competitions **3** *vt* **SELECT ANIMALS OR PLANTS** to select animals or plants as part of a process of improving or preserving their special characteristics **4** *vti* **PRODUCE** to produce or create something, or be produced or created ○ *Experience breeds confidence.* **5** *vt* **MAKE NUCLEAR FUEL** to make fissionable substances using a breeder reactor [Old English *brēdan* < Indo-European,'heat']

breeder /breedər/ *n* **1 SOMEBODY WHO BREEDS ANIMALS OR PLANTS** somebody who breeds animals or propagates plants **2 ANIMAL OR PLANT USED FOR BREEDING** an animal or plant kept to produce offspring **3 CAUSAL FACTOR** a cause or a source of something **4** INDUST = **breeder reactor**

breeder reactor *n* a nuclear reactor that produces more fuel than it consumes

breeding /breeding/ *n* **1 ANCESTRY** somebody's family or ancestry **2 REPRODUCTION** the mating and producing of young (*often before nouns*) ○ *prime breeding stock* **3 DEVELOPMENT OF IMPROVED ANIMALS AND PLANTS** the development of new types of plants or animals with improved characteristics **4 UPBRINGING** somebody's upbringing, education, and training in manners and other social skills, especially an upbringing that produces the polished manners and self-assurance thought typical of the upper classes **5 REACTOR'S FUEL PRODUCTION EXCEEDING CONSUMPTION** production of fissionable material in a breeder reactor in quantities in excess of the fuel it consumes

breeding ground *n* **1** an area where animals mate and produce young **2** an environment or situation that is likely to produce or encourage a particular phenomenon ○ *The festival is a breeding ground for new comedy talent.*

breeks /breeks/ *npl Scotland, N England* trousers or breeches (*informal*) [14C. Variant of BREECHES.]

breeze /breez/ *n* **1 LIGHT TO MODERATE WIND** a wind ranging in strength from light to moderate, with a speed of 6 to 50 kph/4 to 31 mph **2 SOMETHING EASY** a task or object that is easily achieved (*informal*) ■ *vi* (**breezes, breezing, breezed**) **GO SOMEWHERE BRISKLY** to move quickly and confidently or cheerfully [Mid-16C. Probably < Spanish *brisa*, Portuguese *briza* 'northeast wind'.]

breeze through *vti* to do something quickly and easily

breeze block *n* a light rectangular block made from a mixture of cement and the ashes of coal and coke. Use: lightweight walls, e.g. interior walls. US term **cinder block** [< French *braise* 'hot coals']

breezeway /bréez way/ *n US* a roofed passageway with open sides that connects two buildings, e.g. a house and garage

breezily /bréezili/ *adv* in a lively, cheerful, and relaxed way

breezy /bréezi/ (**-ier, -iest**) *adj* **1** with a light to moderate wind **2** lively, cheerful, and relaxed —**breeziness** *n*

bregma /brégmə/ (*plural* **-mata** /-mətə/) *n* the place on the skull at the top of the forehead where the frontal bone and the two parietal bones meet, used as a reference point when measuring skulls [Late 16C. < Greek, 'front of the head'.] —**bregmatic** /breg máttik/ *adj*

brei /brī/ (**breis, breiing, breid**) *vi S Africa* to make the sound of 'r' deep in the back of the throat when speaking Afrikaans (*informal*) [Mid-20C. Via Afrikaans *bry* < Dutch *brijen* < *brouwen* 'speak thickly'.]

brekky /bréki/ (*plural* **-kies**) *n* breakfast (*informal*) [Early 20C. Shortening and alteration.]

Brel /brel/, **Jacques** (1929–78) Belgian-born French singer and songwriter

Bremen /bráymən/ port in NW Germany. Population: 551,000 (1994).

Bremerhaven /bráymər haavən/ port in NW Germany, on the River Weser estuary. Population: 130,847 (1997).

bremsstrahlung /brémz shtraaloong/ *n* the electromagnetic radiation that is produced by an electrically charged subatomic particle such as an electron when it is suddenly slowed down by the electric field of an atomic nucleus [Mid-20C. < German, < *bremsen* 'brake' + *Strahlung* 'radiation'.]

Brendan /bréndən/, **St.** (484–577) Irish saint and traveller. Known as **the Navigator**

Bren gun /brén-/ *n* a light machine gun, used by British and Commonwealth forces in World War II, that is air-cooled and gas-operated and takes .303 calibre ammunition. [Mid-20C. Blend of BRNO, where originally made + *Enfield*, town in S England where later made under licence.]

Brennan /brénnən/, **Christopher** (1870–1932) Australian poet

Brennan, William J., Jr (1906–97) US associate justice of the US Supreme Court

Brenner /brénnər/, **Sydney** (*b.* 1927) South African molecular biologist

Brenner Pass /brénnər-/ mountain pass between SW Austria and NE Italy

Brentano /bren taanō/, **Clemens Maria von** (1778–1842) German writer

brent goose /brént-/, **brent** *n* a small dark-coloured goose with a white band around its neck. Native to: Pacific coasts of Europe, Asia, and North America. *Branta bernicula.* US term **brant**

Brenton /bréntən/, **Howard** (*b.* 1942) British dramatist

Brentwood /brént wood/ town in SE England. Population: 49,463 (1991).

Brescia /bréshə/ capital of Brescia Province, N Italy. Population: 190,089 (1997 estimate).

Bresson /brésson/, **Robert** (*b.* 1907) French film director

Brest /brést/ port in NW France. Population: 149,634 (1999).

brethren /bréthrən/ plural of **brother** (*archaic*) ■ *npl* **1** members of the same family, group, class, or community (*literary or humorous*) ○ *the weaker brethren among us* **2** the members, especially men, of a particular church or other religious group, especially a Protestant Christian denomination (*archaic or literary*) [12C. Old plural of BROTHER.]

Breton /brétton, brétt'n/ *n* **1** somebody who comes from Brittany **2** a Celtic language, related to Cornish, that is spoken in mostly rural areas of Brittany. Native speakers: 500,000. —**Breton** *adj*

Breton /bréttoN/, **André** (1896–1966) French poet and essayist

Bretton Woods /brétt'n-/ resort in N New Hampshire, site of the 1944 conference where the International Monetary Fund and the International Bank for Reconstruction and Development were set up

Breuer /bróy ər/, **Josef** (1842–1925) Austrian physician

Breuer, Marcel (1902–81) Hungarian-born US architect

Breughel ◆ **Brueghel**

breve /breev/ *n* **1 MARK OVER SHORT VOWEL** a mark, ˘, placed over a vowel to show that it has a short sound **2 MARK OVER UNSTRESSED POETIC SYLLABLE** a mark, ˘, that is used to show a short or unstressed syllable in poetry **3 LONG MUSICAL NOTE** a musical note that is equal in length to two semibreves [14C. Variant of BRIEF.]

brevet /brévit/ *n* (*plural* **-vets**) a temporary promotion of a military officer without an increase in pay ■ *vt* (**-vets, -vetting** *or* **-veting, -vetted** *or* **-veted, -veted** *or* **-vetted**) to promote a military officer by brevet [14C. < French, 'little letter' < Old French *brief* 'letter'.] —**brevetcy** *n*

breviary /breévi əri/ (*plural* **-ies**) *n* in the Roman Catholic Church, a book that contains the hymns, psalms, and prayers prescribed for each day [15C. < Latin *breviarium* 'summary, abridgment' < *breviare* 'shorten'.]

brevity /brévvəti/ *n* **1** shortness in time **2** the economical use of words in speech or writing [15C. Via Old French *brievete* < Latin *brevitat-* < *brevis* 'short'.]

brew /broo/ *vti* **1 MAKE BEER** to make beer or similar alcoholic drinks by a process of steeping, boiling, and fermenting grain with hops, sugar, and other ingredients **2 MAKE TEA OR COFFEE** to prepare tea or coffee for drinking by infusing it to develop its flavour **3 DEVELOP THREATENINGLY** to form, concoct, or develop ominously or threateningly ○ *a scandal was brewing* ■ *n* **1 KIND OF BEER** a type of beer, e.g. a lager or ale **2 BREWED BEVERAGE** a drink such as coffee or tea, or a serving of such a drink (*informal*) **3 MIXTURE** a combination of ingredients or elements of any kind [Old English *breowan* < Germanic] —**brewer** *n* —**brewing** *n*

brew up *vi* to make tea (*informal or regional*)

brewer's yeast *n* the yeast that is used in brewing beer, also used as a dietary source of vitamins, especially vitamin B. *Saccharomyces cerevisiae.*

brewery /broó əri/ (*plural* **-ies**) *n* a building where beer or a similar drink is brewed or a company that brews beer

brewpub /broó pub/ *n US, Can* a restaurant or bar where the beer is made on the premises

Brewster /broóstər/, **Sir David** (1781–1868) British physicist

Brewster's law *n* a law relating a material's index of refraction to the tangent of the material's angle of polarization [After Sir David BREWSTER]

brewup /broó up/ *n* a cup or pot of tea (*informal or regional*)

Brezhnev /brézh nef/, **Leonid Ilyich** (1906–82) Soviet statesman and leader of the Communist Party of the Soviet Union(1964–82)

Brian Bórú /brī ən bə roó/ (926?–1014) king of Ireland (1002–14)

Briand /bree aaN/, **Aristide** (1862–1932) French statesman and prime minister of France on eleven occasions

briar[1] /brī ər/ (*plural* **-ars** *or* **-ar**), **brier** (*plural* **-ers** *or* **-er**) *n* **1** a shrub of the heather family with hard woody roots. Native to: S Europe. *Erica arborea.* **2** a tobacco pipe made from the wood of the roots of the briar [Mid-19C. < French *bruyère* 'wild heather'.]

briar[2] /brī ər/, **brier** *n* a thorny wild plant, especially a trailing rose [Old English *brēr* < ?] —**briery** *adj*

Briareus /brī áiri əss/ *n* in Greek mythology, a giant with fifty heads who fought alongside Zeus against the Titans

briarroot /brīər root/ *n* the root of the European briar, a source of wood for making tobacco pipes [Mid-19C. < BRIAR[1].]

briarwood /brī ər wood/ *n* wood from the root of the European briar, used for making tobacco pipes

bribe /brīb/ *vti* (**bribes, bribing, bribed**) to give somebody money or some other incentive to do something, especially something illegal or dishonest ■ *n* money or some other incentive that is given to persuade somebody to do something, especially something illegal or dishonest [14C. < Old French *briber, brimber* 'beg' < *bribe* 'morsel of food given to a beggar'.] —**bribable** *adj* —**briber** *n*

bribery /brībəri/ (*plural* **-ies**) *n* the offering of money or other incentives to persuade somebody to do something, especially something dishonest or illegal

bric-a-brac /bríkə brak/ *n* small ornamental objects that are of interest or sentimental value but of little monetary value [Mid-19C. < French, < obsolete *à bric et à brac* 'at random'.]

brick /brik/ *n* **1 HARD BLOCK USED FOR CONSTRUCTION WORK** a rectangular block of clay or a similar material that is baked until it is hard and is used for building houses, walls, and other large permanent structures **2 BRICKS OR THEIR MATERIAL** bricks collectively, or the material they are made of **3 CHILD'S BUILDING BLOCK** a child's wooden or plastic block used with others to make shapes or structures **4 BLOCK** a rectangular block of something, e.g. ice cream **5 RELIABLE SUPPORTIVE PERSON** a helpful or supportive person (*informal dated*) ■ *vt* **1 MAKE SOMETHING WITH BRICKS** to use bricks to build something or as a liner or paving material **2 CLOSE UP WITH BRICKS** to close something up or wall something off with bricks and mortar ○ *the window had been bricked up* [15C. < Middle Dutch *bricke*, later reinforced by French *brique*.]

ϟ **brick-and-mortar** *adj* E-COMMERCE = **bricks-and-mortar**

brickbat /brík bat/ *n* **1** a harshly unfavourable criticism **2** a broken fragment of something hard that is used as a missile [Mid-16C. < BAT[1] 'piece, lump'.]

brickie /bríki/ *n* a bricklayer (*informal*)

bricklayer /brík layər/ *n* somebody trained to construct houses, walls, and other large permanent structures by cementing bricks together with mortar —**bricklaying** *n*

brick-red *adj* of a warm brownish-red colour similar to that of bricks —**brick red** *n*

ϟ **bricks-and-mortar, brick-and-mortar** *adj* having and using actual business or retail premises, as opposed to operating solely or mainly via the Internet. ◊ **clicks-and-mortar**

brick veneer *n Aus* an external wall that consists of a timber frame with a decorative facing of bricks (*hyphenated before nouns*)

brickwork /brík wurk/ *n* **1** something, e.g. a wall, building, or walk that is made up of bricks **2** the technique or skill of laying bricks

brickyard /brík yaard/ *n* a place where bricks are made, stored, or sold

bricolage /bree kō laazh, bríkō-/ *n* something that is made or put together with whatever materials happen to be available [Mid-20C. < French, < *bricoler* 'do odd jobs' < *bricole* (see BRICOLE).]

bricole /brík'l, bri kōl/ *n* **1 TYPE OF BILLIARDS SHOT** in billiards, a shot where the cue ball touches the cushion after hitting the target ball and before hitting another ball **2 ANCIENT MILITARY CATAPULT** a catapult that ancient and medieval soldiers used to launch stones **3 SOLDIER'S HARNESS FOR HAULING GUNS** a harness worn by soldiers in the past for hauling guns [Early 16C. Via French < Provençal *bricola* or Italian *briccola*.]

bridal /brīd'l/ *adj* for or associated with brides or weddings [Old English *bryd-ealu* 'wedding with much ale' < BRIDE + ALE, altered after -AL[1]]

SPELLCHECK Do not confuse ***bridal*** with ***bridle***, which has a similar sound. Beware: your spellchecker will not catch this error.

bridal wreath *n* a shrub with arching branches. Flowers: small, white. Genus: *Spiraea.*

bride /brīd/ *n* a woman who is about to marry or has just married [Old English *bryd* < Germanic]

bridegroom /bríd groom, -gro͝om/ *n* a man who is about to marry or has just married [Old English *brȳdguma* < BRIDE + *guma* 'man', altered after GROOM]

bride price *n* in some societies, a payment in the form of money or property made by the groom to the bride or her family

bridesmaid /brídz mayd/ *n* a girl or woman who helps the bride on her wedding day

⚡**bridge**[1] /brij/ *n* **1 STRUCTURE ALLOWING PASSAGE ACROSS OBSTACLE** a structure that is built above and across a river, road, or other obstacle to allow people or vehicles to cross it **2 LINK OR MEANS OF APPROACH** something that provides a link, connection, or means of coming together **3 SHIP'S CONTROL ROOM OR PLATFORM** the platform or room on a ship or other vessel from which the captain controls its course **4 PARTIAL FALSE TEETH** a set of one or more false teeth that act as a replacement for missing natural teeth **5 TOP OF NOSE** the top part of the nose between the eyes **6 PART OF GLASSES** the part of a pair of glasses that connects the two lenses together at the front and rests on the nose **7 PART OF STRINGED INSTRUMENT** the part of a stringed instrument that keeps the strings away from the body **8 MUSICAL PASSAGE** a transitional or connecting section in a musical work **9 CUE REST WITH HIGH END** a long-handled support for a player's cue in snooker and billiards, with a high arching end **10 HAND USED AS REST** the player's hand used as a rest for the cue in billiards and snooker **11 PART OF ELECTRICAL CIRCUIT** a part of an electrical circuit fitted with a device that measures electrical resistance or capacitance **12 TELECOMMUNICATIONS CONNECTION** a telecommunications connection between two local area networks ■ *vt* (**bridges, bridging, bridged**) **1 BUILD BRIDGE ACROSS OBSTACLE** to build a bridge across an obstacle to allow people or vehicles to get across it **2 CREATE UNDERSTANDING BETWEEN PEOPLE** to create a means of communication or understanding between people or a means of reconciling their differences [Old English *brycg* < Germanic] —**bridgeable** *adj* ◇ **build bridges** to try to make friends with somebody who has previously been an enemy ◇ **burn your bridges** to do something that makes it difficult or impossible to return to your former position ◇ **cross that bridge when you come to it** to think about or worry about something only when it becomes a reality or a priority

bridge[2] /brij/ *n* a card game derived from whist and played with one deck of cards divided among four players, who play in two pairs [Late 19C. < ?]

bridgehead /bríj hed/ *n* **1 END OF BRIDGE** the area immediately surrounding the end of a bridge **2 DEFENSIVE MILITARY POSITION** a fortified position from which troops defend the end of a bridge that is nearest to the enemy **3 ARMY'S POSITION SEIZED IN ENEMY TERRITORY** a forward position seized by advancing troops in enemy territory and serving as a basis for further advances **4 PIONEERING FOOTHOLD** any position from which further advancement can be attained

bridge loan *n US* = **bridging loan**

Bridgend /bri jénd/ county in S Wales. Area: 264 sq. km/102 sq. mi.

Bridge of Sighs *n* a 16th century canal bridge in Venice, Italy, believed to be named after the sighs of prisoners crossing the bridge to be tried or executed

bridge roll *n* a small torpedo-shaped soft bread roll [Perhaps because eaten at afternoon bridge parties]

Bridges /bríjjiz/, **Robert** (1844–1930) British poet

Bridget /bríjjit/, **St** (453?–524?) Irish abbess

Bridgetown /bríj town/ capital of Barbados, in the SW of the island. Population: 7,500 (1994).

bridgework /bríj wurk/ *n* **1** provision of false teeth to replace missing or removed natural teeth **2** DENT = **bridge**[1] *n*. 4

bridging loan *n* money borrowed temporarily until a specific event occurs, especially a loan to finance the purchase of a property while another is being sold. US term **bridge loan**

Bridgman /bríjmən/, **P.W.** (1882–1961) US physicist. Full name **Percy Williams Bridgman**

Bridgwater /bríj wawtər/ town in SW England. Population: 34,610 (1991).

bridie /brídi/ *n Scotland* a meat pie made with a circle of puff pasty folded over a meat filling

Bridie /brídi/, **James** (1888–1951) British dramatist. Born **Henry Mavor Osborne**

bridle /bríd'l/ *n* **1 HARNESS FOR HORSE'S HEAD** a set of leather straps fitted to a horse's head and incorporating the bit and the reins **2 RESTRAINING THING** something that acts as a control or restraint ■ *v* (**-dles, -dling, -dled**) **1** *vt* **PUT BRIDLE ON HORSE** to provide a horse with a bridle **2** *vi* **SHOW ANGER OR INDIGNATION** to react with slight anger or indignation **3** *vt* **EXERCISE CONTROL OR RESTRAINT** to show restraint in expressing a feeling or control or in curbing something [Old English *brīdel* < Germanic]

SPELLCHECK See ***bridal***.

bridle path, bridleway /bríd'l way/ *n* a path or trail for horse riding

Brie /bree/ *n* soft cow's-milk cheese with a whitish rind, originally made in Brie in NE France

brief /breef/ *adj* **1 NOT LENGTHY** lasting for only a short time ○ *a brief conversation* **2 CONCISE** containing only the necessary information without any extra details **3 SCANTY** leaving much of the wearer's body exposed **4 CURT** curt or abrupt speech or conversation ■ *n* **1 SYNOPSIS OF DOCUMENTS** a digest or synopsis of a larger document or group of documents **2 BRIEFING** a briefing, or the information conveyed during one **3 ASSIGNED DUTIES** the details of what somebody's job or duties involve **4 SUMMARY OF LEGAL CASE FOR BARRISTER** a summary of a client's case prepared for the barrister who will deal with it in court **5 LEGAL REPRESENTATIVE** a legal representative, especially a barrister (*informal*) **6 PAPAL LETTER** a letter from the Pope, less formal than a papal bull ■ **briefs** *npl* **SNUG UNDERWEAR FOR LOWER BODY** men's or women's close-fitting underwear, as distinct from boxer shorts or camiknickers ■ *vt* **1 GIVE INFORMATION TO PREPARE** to give somebody all the necessary information about something in preparation for a discussion or decision **2 SUMMARIZE** to make a summary of something, especially a written summary [13C. Via Old French < Latin *brevis* 'short'.] —**briefer** *n* —**briefly** *adv* —**briefness** *n* ◇ **in brief** used to introduce a summary ○ *In brief, then, you think he should resign.*

briefcase /bréef kayss/ *n* a small rectangular case with a handle, used for carrying books and papers

briefing /bréefing/ *n* **1** a meeting held to provide information about the main facts of an issue or a situation **2** the information conveyed at a briefing

brier /brī ər/ *n* = **briar**[1]

brig[1] /brig/ *n* **1 SAILING SHIP** a two-masted sailing ship with square-rigged sails on both masts **2** *US* **SHIP'S PRISON** a secure area in a ship of the US Navy, which can be used as a prison while the ship is at sea **3** *US* **MILITARY PRISON** a building or part of a building that is used as a prison in a US military installation [Early 18C. Shortening of BRIGANTINE.]

brig[2] /brig/ *n N England, Scotland* a bridge [13C. Form of BRIDGE[1], influenced by Old Norse *bryggja*.]

Brig. *abbr* **1** brigadier **2** brigade

brigade /bri gáyd/ *n* **1 MILITARY UNIT** a military unit consisting of two or more combat battalions or regiments and associated support units **2 GROUP WITH COMMON GOAL OR CHARACTERISTIC** a group of people organized to achieve a particular goal, or characterized by a common trait such as attitude, background, appearance, or activities ■ *vt* (**-gades, -gading, -gaded**) **ORGANIZE INTO A TASK FORCE** to organize a group of people in order to achieve a particular goal [Mid-17C. Via French, < Italian *brigata* 'military company' < *brigare* 'contend, brawl' < *briga* 'strife'.]

LITERARY LINK ***The Charge of the Light Brigade***, a poem (1845) by Alfred, Lord Tennyson. Based on a contemporary newspaper report, it describes a suicidal but heroic attack by the British Light Brigade on the Russian army at Balaclava in the Crimea, on October 25, 1854.

brigade major *n* the chief staff officer of a brigade, not necessarily holding the rank of major

brigadier /briggə déer/ *n* an officer in the British Army or Royal Marines of a rank above colonel [Late 17C. < French, < *brigade* (see BRIGADE).]

brigadier general (*plural* **brigadiers general**), **brigadier** *n* an officer in the US or Royal Canadian Army, Air force or Marines of a rank above colonel

brigalow /bríggə lō/ (*plural* **-lows** *or* **-low**) *n* an acacia tree found in semi-arid regions. Native to: Australia. *Acacia harpophylla*. [Mid-19C. < ?]

brigand /bríggənd/ *n* a bandit operating in wild or isolated terrain, usually as a member of a roving band (*literary*) [14C. Via Old French < Italian *brigante* < present participle of *brigare* (see BRIGADE).] —**brigandage** *n* —**brigandism** *n* —**brigandry** *n*

brigandine /bríggən deen/ *n* a coat chain-mail body armour, worn in medieval times [15C. Directly or via Old French < Italian *brigantina* < *brigante* (see BRIGAND).]

brigantine /bríggən teen, -tīn/ *n* a two-masted sailing ship with square-rigged sails on the foremast and fore-and-aft sails on the mainmast [Early 16C. Directly or via Old French *brigandine* < Italian *brigantino* 'fighting ship' < *brigante* (see BRIGAND).]

Brig. Gen. *abbr* brigadier general

Briggs /brigz/, **Henry** (1561–1630) English mathematician

bright /brīt/ *adj* **1 SHOWING LIGHT** reflecting or giving off strong light ○ *It was a bright moonlit night.* **2 ILLUMINATED** illuminated with strong natural or artificial light **3 INTENSELY COLOURED** intense in colour ○ *bright blue* **4 INTELLIGENT** showing an ability to think, learn, or respond quickly ○ *She was brighter than other children of her age.* **5 CHEERFUL** cheerful and lively ○ *He seems much brighter this morning.* **6 PROMISING SUCCESS** promising a successful outcome **7 ADMIRABLE** deserving admiration and glory ○ *one of the brightest stars of the theatre* **8 CLEAR-SOUNDING** describes sounds with a clear crisp quality and little harmonic resonance **9 BEAUTIFUL** remarkably beautiful or handsome (*archaic*) ■ *adv* **WITH LIGHT** with a great deal of light ■ **brights** *npl US* **HEADLIGHTS** the headlights on a motor vehicle when set to full beam [Old English *beorht* < Indo-European, 'shine'] —**brightish** *adj* —**brightly** *adv*

SYNONYMS See ***intelligent***.

Bright /brīt/, **John** (1811–89) British politician

brighten /brīt'n/ *v* **1** *vi* **LOOK HAPPY** to become enthusiastic, lively, or happy ○ *She brightened visibly at the suggestion.* **2** *vt* **ADD INTEREST** to add colour or interest to something ○ *Their visit brightened the day for us.* **3** *vi* **BECOME CLEARER** to become less overcast or rainy ○ *It's supposed to brighten this afternoon.* **4** *vti* **ILLUMINATE OR GET LIGHTER** to increase the amount of light emitted or reflected, or be filled with an increasing amount of light **5** *vti* **MAKE OR BECOME MORE PROMISING** to make something seem more promising, or appear more likely to be successful

brighten up *vti* to make somebody or something that is dark, colourless, or gloomy become brighter, or to become lighter, more colourful, or livelier

brightener /brīt'nər/, **brightening agent** /brīt'ning-/ *n* a compound added to some washing powders and liquids to make white fabrics look brighter

bright lights *npl* the entertainment and activities of a big city (*informal*)

bright nebula *n* a cloud of material in space that appears bright because it is illuminated by the stars around it

brightness /brītnəss/ *n* **1 STRONG LIGHT** the intensity of light reflected or given off by something **2 CLEVERNESS** the ability to think, learn, or respond quickly **3 CHEERFULNESS** a happy or animated attitude or manner **4 PROMISE OF SUCCESS** the promise of a successful outcome **5 CLARITY OF SOUND** a clear crisp sound quality **6 LIGHT EMITTED IN PARTICULAR DIRECTION** the intensity of light (**luminosity**) emitted by an object in a particular direction, used by an observer to compare the luminosity of other visible objects

Brighton /brīt'n/ coastal city in S England. Population: 133,400 (1991).

Bright's disease /brīts-/ *n* an inflammatory disease of the kidneys, such as glomerulonephritis [Mid-19C. After Richard *Bright* (1789–1858), English physician.]

bright spark *n* a clever or ingenious person (*informal; often ironic*) ○ *Some bright spark had the idea of hiding my glasses.*

brightwork /brīt wurk/ *n* fittings or trimmings of polished metal or varnished wood, e.g. on a vehicle or boat

bright young thing *n* **1** a young clever person thought likely to succeed **2** a member of a young and fashionable social set in Great Britain in the 1920s and 1930s who regarded themselves as setting new fashions in dress, music, behaviour, and style

~~**briliant**~~ incorrect spelling of **brilliant**

brill[1] /bril/ (*plural* **brill** *or* **brills**) *n* an edible European flatfish that is closely related to the turbot. *Scophthalmus rhombus*. [15C. < ?]

brill[2] /bril/ *adj, interj* used to express satisfaction with somebody or something (*informal*) [Late 20C. Shortening of BRILLIANT.]

Brillat-Savarin /breè yaa sávvə raN/, **Anthelme** (1755–1826) French politician and writer

brilliance /brillyənss/, **brilliancy** /-yənssi/ *n* 1 BRIGHTNESS dazzling brightness 2 GREAT ABILITY OR SKILL exceptional ability, skill, or success ○ *the technical brilliance of the pianist's performance* 3 SPLENDOUR imposing splendour

brilliant /brillyənt/ *adj* 1 EXTREMELY BRIGHT OR RADIANT extremely bright or radiant ○ *brilliant sunshine* 2 VIVID vividly coloured ○ *a brilliant shade of green* 3 INTELLIGENT OR TALENTED showing exceptional intelligence, skill, or talent ○ *a brilliant mathematician* 4 EXCELLENT distinguished by excellence 5 MAGNIFICENT imposing in splendour and magnificence ■ *adj, interj* GREAT used to express great satisfaction with somebody or something (*informal*) [Late 17C. < French *brillant*, present participle of *briller* 'shine' < Italian *brillare*.] —**brilliantly** *adv* —**brilliantness** *n*

brilliant-cut *adj* describes a gemstone that is cut into a multifaceted shape to maximize brilliance

brilliantine /brillyən teen/ *n* 1 an oily hair cream, used by men to keep hair in place and make it look glossy 2 a shiny lightweight fabric, often made from cotton woven with mohair or worsted [Late 19C. < French *brillantine* < *brillant* (see BRILLIANT).]

brim /brim/ *n* 1 HAT EDGE the rim around the edge of a hat, shaped to stand out from the head 2 TOP EDGE the top edge of a container such as a cup or bowl ■ *v* (**brims, brimming, brimmed**) 1 *vti* BE FULL TO THE TOP to fill something or to be full to the top edge ○ *The cup was brimming with hot coffee.* 2 *vi* BURST to have an unusually plentiful supply of something ○ *She was brimming with ideas.* 3 *vi* OVERFLOW to be so full as to be overflowing ○ *eyes brimming with tears* [13C. < ?] —**brimless** *adj*

brimful /brímfo͝ol/ *adj* 1 full to the top edge of something 2 with an unusually plentiful supply of something ○ *brimful of energy*

brimstone /brím stōn/ *n* 1 sulphur (*archaic*) 2 **brimstone, brimstone butterfly** a medium-sized butterfly the male of which is bright yellow and the female greenish-white. Native to: gardens and woodlands in Europe and Asia. *Gonepteryx rhamni.* [12C. < Old English *byrne* 'burning' < *birnan* (see BURN[1]).]

Brindisi /brin deèzi/ port in SE Italy. Population: 94,540 (1997 estimate).

brindle /brínd'l/ *adj* = **brindled** ■ *n* brindled colouring [Late 17C. Back-formation < BRINDLED.]

brindled /brínd'ld/ *adj* tawny brown or grey marked with darker streaks or patches [Late 17C. Alteration of *brinded* (influenced by GRIZZLED or SPECKLED) < ?]

Brindley /bríndli/, **James** (1716–72) British engineer

brine /brīn/ *n* 1 SALT WATER FOR PRESERVING water containing a significant amount of salt, used for curing, preserving, and developing flavour in food 2 SEA WATER the salt water of the sea (*literary*) 3 STRONG SALT SOLUTION a strong salt solution ■ *vt* (**brines, brining, brined**) TREAT SOMETHING WITH SALT WATER to preserve, can, pickle, or soak something in salt water [Old English *brīne* < ?] —**brinish** *adj*

Brinell hardness /bri nél-/ *n* the hardness of a metal or alloy, determined by pressing a steel ball into its surface under standard pressure and measuring the surface area of the resulting indentation [Early 20C. After Johan *Brinell* (1849–1925), Swedish engineer.]

Brinell hardness number, Brinell number *n* a number expressing the hardness of a metal or alloy

brine shrimp *n* a small crustacean that lives in salt lakes and brine pools and is used as food for aquarium fish. Genus: *Artemia.*

bring /bring/ (**brings, bringing, brought** /brawt/, **brought**) *v* 1 *vt* ACCOMPANY OR CARRY to come from one place to another with somebody or something ○ *Please bring me a glass of water.* 2 *vt* ATTRACT to draw something to yourself or another person ○ *This charm is supposed to bring luck.* 3 *vt* MAKE SOMETHING HAPPEN to cause something to take place ○ *The heavy rain brought flooding.* 4 *vt* CAUSE TO BE IN A PARTICULAR STATE to force something or somebody to arrive at a particular situation or condition ○ *The chairperson brought the meeting to a close.* 5 *vt* CAUSE TO ENTER MIND to cause something to enter somebody's mind ○ *Seeing you brings memories of good times.* 6 *vr* MAKE YOURSELF DO to persuade or force yourself to do something (*usually with negatives or in questions*) ○ *She still can't bring herself to think about the tragedy.* 7 *vt* SELL FOR PARTICULAR PRICE to be sold for a particular price 8 *vt* BEGIN LEGAL ACTION to begin a legal action 9 *vt* PRESENT EVIDENCE to present evidence before a court 10 *vt Malaysia, Singapore, UK* TAKE SOMEWHERE to take somebody or something somewhere (*regional*) ○ *I brought my friend to the airport when she left.* [Old English *bringan* < Indo-European] —**bringer** *n*

USAGE ***Bring*** or ***take***? The terms ***bring*** and ***take*** relate to the location of speaker or writer, hearer, and event. It can sometimes be difficult to decide which one to use. Generally, use ***bring*** to indicate movement *towards* the speaker or writer: *Please bring the papers over here.* Use *bring* to indicate movement *towards* the location from which the speaker seems to be observing the movement: *The visiting team is bringing a coachload of supporters.* Use ***take*** to indicate movement *away* from the speaker: *Please take the papers downstairs. Our team is taking a coachload of supporters to the away match.* Avoid the nonstandard verb form *brung*; the only correct form in the past is *brought*: *They brought* [not *brung*] *in the groceries.*

bring about *vt* to make something happen

bring back *vt* 1 to evoke memories of something forgotten 2 to restore something that has been discontinued ○ *widespread support for bringing back on-the-spot fines*

bring down *vt* 1 TOPPLE to cause the downfall of an authority or institution 2 KILL OR WOUND to make a person or animal fall by wounding or killing it 3 *Can, ANZ* PRESENT A BILL to present a bill or other piece of legislation in a parliament

bring forth *vt* 1 to bear young 2 to produce fruit or flowers

bring forward *vt* 1 BRING CLOSER IN TIME to move something, e.g. an appointment, to an earlier date or time 2 SUGGEST FOR DISCUSSION OR CONSIDERATION to offer something for discussion or consideration 3 CARRY AMOUNT TO NEXT PAGE to carry a sum from one column or page to the next

bring in *vt* 1 INTRODUCE to introduce something, e.g. a new policy or law 2 EARN OR ACQUIRE to acquire money as profits, pay, or interest ○ *She barely brings in enough to live on.* 3 PRESENT SOMETHING IN COURT to present something in a court of law

bring off *vt* 1 to succeed in doing something difficult 2 an offensive term meaning to cause somebody to have an orgasm (*slang*)

bring on *vt* 1 to be the cause of something happening or appearing ○ *exhaustion brought on by overwork* 2 to further the development of a quality, or of the person having it

bring out *vt* 1 MAKE KNOWN to make something known 2 CALL ATTENTION TO to emphasize a quality in somebody or something ○ *That outfit brings out the red in your hair.* 3 INTRODUCE FOR SALE to produce or issue something for sale to the public ○ *The company has just brought out a new version.* 4 INTRODUCE TO SOCIETY to introduce a debutante to society

bring round, bring around *vt* 1 to sway somebody's opinion or thinking ○ *We'll bring them round eventually.* 2 to revive a person who has lost consciousness

bring to *vt* 1 to restore somebody to consciousness 2 to head a boat or ship into the wind in order to slow it down or stop it

bring up *vt* 1 RAISE SUBJECT to raise a subject for discussion 2 REAR A CHILD to provide care, training, and education for a child until maturity 3 VOMIT to cough something up or to expel it from the stomach through the mouth 4 MAKE SOMETHING STOP SUDDENLY to cause somebody or something to come to a standstill

bring-and-buy sale *n* a sale, usually organized to raise funds for a school, church, or charity, in which people bring things to sell and buy things others have brought

brinjal /brínjəl/ *n S Asia* an aubergine [Early 17C. < Portuguese *berinjela* < Arabic *al-bāḏinjān*.]

brink /bringk/ *n* 1 the crucial point in a situation when something disastrous or momentous is about to happen ○ *teetering on the brink of bankruptcy* 2 the very edge of something, e.g. a steep drop or a river bank [13C. < Old Norse *brekka* 'slope'.]

brinkmanship /bríngkmən ship/ *n* the practice, especially in international relations, of taking a dispute to the verge of conflict in the hope of forcing the opposition to make concessions

briny /brīni/ *adj* (**-ier, -iest**) relating to, containing, or tasting like sea water ■ *n* the sea (*literary*) —**brininess** *n*

brio /breè ō/ *n* energy or vigour [Mid-18C. < Italian.]

brioche /bri ósh/ *n* a sweet French bread roll made from a dough enriched with eggs and butter [Early 19C. < French, < Old French *brier* 'knead'.]

briolette /breè ō lét/ *n* a gem cut in the shape of a teardrop or oval [Mid-19C. < French.]

briquette /bri két/, **briquet** *n* a small block of compressed material, e.g. charcoal, sawdust, or coal dust, use as fuel for cooking or heating ■ *vt* (**-quettes, -quetting, -quetted; -quets, -quetting, -quetted**) to form a material into rectangular blocks [Late 19C. < French, 'little brick' < *brique* 'brick'.]

bris /briss/, **brith** /brit/ *n* the religious circumcision ceremony for Jewish boys [Early 20C. < Hebrew *bərīṯ (mīlāh)* 'covenant (of circumcision)'.]

Brisbane /brízbən/ capital and main port of Queensland, Australia, in the SE of the state. Population: 1,291,117 (1996).

brisk /brisk/ *adj* 1 QUICK done quickly and energetically ○ *a brisk walk* 2 HURRIED speaking or behaving in an abrupt way ○ *a brisk reply* 3 BUSY showing or experiencing much activity ○ *business was brisk* 4 INVIGORATING refreshingly cool ○ *brisk autumn days* ■ *vti* BECOME LIVELY to become more active or lively or to liven something up ○ *Business brisks up in summer.* [Late 16C. Probably < French *brusque* (see BRUSQUE).] —**briskly** *adv* —**briskness** *n*

brisken /brískən/ *vti* to become faster or livelier or to make something faster or livelier ○ *She briskened her pace.*

brisket /brískit/ *n* 1 a cut of meat, especially of beef, taken from an animal's breast 2 the breast of a four-legged animal [14C. < ?]

brisling /bríssling, brízz-/ (*plural* **-ling** *or* **-lings**) *n* 1 a small fish of the herring family. *Clupea sprattus.* 2 the flesh of a brisling used as food [Early 20C. < Norwegian or Danish.]

bristle /bríss'l/ *n* 1 STIFF HAIR a short stiff hair on an animal or plant or a mass of short stiff hairs growing, e.g. on a pig's back or a man's face 2 HAIR ON BRUSH the short stiff natural or synthetic hair on a brush ■ *v* (**-tles, -tling, -tled**) 1 *vti* HAVE OR SET HAIR ON END to make the hair or fur stand upright in response to fear or anger, or to show such a response 2 *vi* BECOME OFFENDED BY to react somewhat angrily or indignantly to something or somebody ○ *He bristled at the suggestion.* 3 *vi* HAVE LARGE AMOUNT to have an abundance of something ○ *a mighty battleship bristling with guns* 4 *vt* GIVE SOMETHING BRISTLES to provide or cover something with bristles [13C. < Old English *byrst* 'bristle'.]

bristlebird /bríss'l burd/ *n* a small brown endangered bird. Native to: coastal scrub in E Australia. *Dasyornis brachypterus.* [Early 19C. < the bristles on its face.]

bristlecone pine /bríss'l kōn-/ *n* a small pine tree with bristly cones, the longest-living tree in the world. Native to: California. Genus: *Pinus.*

bristletail /bríss'l tayl/ (*plural* **-tails** *or* **-tail**) *n* a wingless insect that has a long segmented abdomen with two or three long bristles at the end. Order: Thysanura.

bristle worm *n* ZOOL = **polychaete**

bristling /bríssling/ *adj* 1 thick with stiff hairs 2 reacting with anger and indignation

bristly /bríss'li/ (**-tlier, -tliest**) *adj* 1 prickly and rough with bristles 2 quick to anger or take offence —**bristliness** *n*

Bristol /bríst'l/ port in SW England. Population: 399,633 (1996 estimate).

Bristol board *n* fine smooth lightweight cardboard, used in design and drawing [Early 19C. After BRISTOL.]

Bristol Channel arm of the Atlantic Ocean between S Wales and SW England. Length: 140 km/85 mi.

bristols /bríst'lz/ *npl* an offensive term for a woman's breasts (*slang*) [Mid-20C. Shortening of *Bristol Cities*, rhyming slang for 'titties'.]

brit /brit/ (*plural* **brits** *or* **brit**) *n* 1 the young form of some fish including the herring and the sprat 2 a mass of tiny marine organisms, especially crustaceans, that is a source of food for whalebone whales and some fish [Early 17C. < ?]

Brit /brit/ *n* a British person (*informal*) [Early 20C. Shortening.]

Brit. *abbr* 1 Britain 2 British

Britain /brítt'n/ ➧ **Great Britain**

Britannia[1] /bri tánnyə/ *n* 1 the personification and symbol of Britain, shown as a seated woman wearing a helmet and holding a trident 2 **Britannia, britannia** = **Britannia metal** [Pre-12C. < Latin *Brit(t)annia*.]

Britannia[2] /bri tánnyə/ Roman name for the southern part of Britain

Britannia coin, Britannia *n* a British gold coin worth £10, £25, £50, or £100 [< the figure depicted on the coin]

Britannia metal, britannia metal *n* an alloy of tin, antimony, and copper that is similar to pewter and is used for decorative items and for bearings

Britannic /bri tánnik/ *adj* belonging to Britain (*dated formal*) ○ *Her Britannic Majesty*

~~**Britanny**~~ incorrect spelling of **Brittany**

britches /bríchiz/ *npl* = **breeches** ◇ **too big for your britches** behaving in a self-important manner

brith /brit/ *n* JUDAISM = **bris**

Briticism /brítti sizəm/ *n* something, e.g. a word or custom, that is characteristic of the British or of Britain [Mid-19C. < BRITISH, after SCOTTICISM or GALLICISM.]

British /bríttish/ *n* 1 the people of the United Kingdom of Great Britain and Northern Ireland 2 LANG = **British English** 3 the language spoken by the ancient Celtic people who lived in S Britain [Old English *Brettisc, Brittisc* < *Bret* 'ancient Briton', directly or via Latin *Britto* < Celtic] — **British** *adj*

British Columbia westernmost province of Canada, on the Pacific coast. Capital: Victoria. Population: 3,724,500 (1996). Area: 944,735 sq. km/364,764 sq. mi.

British Commonwealth of Nations *n* = **Commonwealth of Nations**

British Council *n* a London-based organization founded by the Royal Charter in 1942 to promote the English language and British culture around the world

British Empire *n* a group of colonies, protectorates, and other territories brought under British rule after the late 16th century, and by the 19th century comprising more than one-quarter of the world's population. Most of Britain's former colonies became independent after World War II, and as sovereign states, many joined the Commonwealth.

Britisher /bríttishər/ *n* US a British subject or a person from Britain (*informal*)

British Guiana former name for **Guyana**

British Honduras former name for **Belize**

British India *n* the part of the Indian subcontinent under British administration from 1765 to 1947, when the independent states of India and Pakistan were created

British Indian Ocean Territory British overseas territory in the central Indian Ocean, comprising an island group including Diego Garcia, site of a communications and defence installation. Area: 60 sq. km/23 sq. mi.

British Isles group of islands in the Atlantic Ocean off the NW coast of Europe, comprising Britain, Ireland, and many smaller islands

British Legion *n* a charitable organization in the UK that provides help for former members of the armed forces

British Somaliland former British protectorate in present-day N Somalia

British Standards Institution *n* an organization that issues standards for manufacturing practice and quality control, as well as for measurements and technical terms used in the United Kingdom

British Standard Time *n* the time that was used from 1968 to 1971 in the United Kingdom, one hour ahead of Greenwich Mean Time

British Summer Time *n* the time, one hour ahead of Greenwich Mean Time, used in the United Kingdom from the beginning of April to the end of October

British thermal unit *n* the amount of heat needed to raise the temperature of one pound of water by one degree Fahrenheit, equal to approximately 1055 joules

British Union of Fascists *n* a fascist organization founded by Sir Oswald Mosley in the 1930s

British West Indies the islands of the Caribbean that were formerly administered by Great Britain, including Anguilla, the British Virgin Islands, the Cayman Islands, Montserrat, and the Turks and Caicos

Briton /brítt'n/ *n* 1 somebody who comes from Great Britain 2 a member of an ancient Celtic people who once lived in S Britain [13C. Via French *Breton* < Latin *Britton-* < Celtic.]

britska *n* = **britzka**

Brittain /brítt'n/, **Vera** (1893–1970) British writer

Brittany /brítt'ni/ peninsular region in NW France. Population: 2,795,600 (1990). Area: 27,209 sq. km/10,505 sq. mi.

Britten /brítt'n/, **Benjamin, Lord Britten of Aldeburgh** (1913–76) British composer

brittle /brítt'l/ *adj* 1 **HARD AND BREAKABLE** hard and likely to break or crack ○ *plastic that has become brittle with age.* 2 **SHARP-SOUNDING** having a sharp, unnerving quality or tone 3 **NOT LASTING** lacking durability or permanence 4 **NOT FRIENDLY** lacking personal warmth ○ *a brittle quality to her that I didn't like* 5 **IRRITABLE** easily irritated or annoyed ■ *n* **TOFFEE-NUT SWEET** a crunchy sweet made from caramel and nuts [14C. < Old English *gebryttan* 'shatter'.] —**brittlely** *adv* —**brittleness** *n*

brittle-bone disease *n* 1 = **osteoporosis** 2 = **osteogenesis imperfecta**

brittle star *n* a marine animal similar to a starfish but with thinner, longer, and more flexible arms. Class: Ophiuroidea.

Brittonic *adj, n* LANG, PEOPLES = **Brythonic**

britzka /brítskə/, **britska** *n* a horse-drawn carriage with a rear-facing front seat and a folding top over the back seat [Early 19C. < Polish *bryczka*.]

Brix scale /bríks-/ *n* a hydrometer scale used for measuring the sugar content of a solution at a particular temperature [Late 19C. After Adolf *Brix* (1798–1890), German scientist.]

Brno /búrnō/ city in SE Czech Republic. Population: 385,866 (1998 estimate).

bro /brō/ *n* a brother (*informal*)

bro., Bro. *abbr* brother

broach /brōch/ *v* 1 *vt* **BRING UP DIFFICULT SUBJECT** to introduce a subject for discussion, usually one that is awkward ○ *He finally broached the question of the loan.* 2 *vt* **OPEN CONTAINER** to open a container for the first time 3 *vt* **PIERCE CASK** to make a hole in a cask to draw off liquid 4 *vt* **BORE HOLE** to make or enlarge a hole in something 5 *vi* **COME THROUGH SURFACE OF WATER** to break the surface of water from below without completely emerging (*refers to a submarine*) 6 *vi* **TURN SIDEWAYS TO WIND** to be turned broadside to the wind, e.g. by heavy seas, with a risk of capsizing (*refers to a boat*) ■ *n* 1 **TOOL FOR ENLARGING HOLES** a tool for enlarging holes 2 **ROASTING SPIT** a roasting spit 3 **TOOL FOR PIERCING CASKS** a tool used for making holes in casks 4 = **brooch** [14C. < Old French *brocher* 'to stitch' < *broche* 'skewer, long needle'.] —**broacher** *n*

SPELLCHECK Do not confuse ***broach*** with ***brooch***, which has a similar sound. Beware: your spellchecker will not catch this error.

broad /brawd/ *adj* 1 **VERY WIDE** large from one side to the other ○ *a broad forehead* 2 **LARGE AND SPACIOUS** extending a great distance in all directions ○ *the broad steppes* 3 **MEASURED ACROSS** measured from side to side ○ *as broad as it is long* 4 **FULL AND CLEAR** full and clear to see ○ *a broad grin* ○ *broad daylight* 5 **COVERING A WIDE RANGE** comprehensive in content, knowledge, experience, ability, or application ○ *She has very broad interests.* 6 **NOT DETAILED** general, rather than detailed ○ *I'll give you a broad outline of the project.* 7 **WIDESPREAD OR GENERALIZED** widespread or generalized throughout a large and diverse group of people ○ *a broad feeling of disillusionment in the party* 8 **OBVIOUS** meant to be easily understood ○ *dropping broad hints about their plans* 9 **UNOBSTRUCTED** with nothing blocking the way 10 **TOLERANT** tending to tolerate or accept rather than to condemn the ideas and conduct of other people ○ *I think I have fairly broad views on the whole.* 11 **POTENTIALLY OFFENSIVE** potentially offensive to accepted standards of propriety 12 **STRONGLY REGIONAL** describes a regional accent that is very strong or pronounced 13 **SHOWING ONLY MAIN DIFFERENCES** describes a phonetic transcription that gives only major differences 14 **PRONOUNCED WITH THE TONGUE DOWN** describes a vowel pronounced with the tongue low and flat and the mouth open wide ■ *n* 1 **WIDE PART** the wide part of something ○ *He slapped Jack across the broad of his back.* 2 **RIVER COVERING LAND** a river that expands to cover low-lying land 3 US **OFFENSIVE TERM** an offensive term for a woman (*slang*) ■ *adv* **COMPLETELY** to the fullest extent [Old English *brād* < Germanic] —**broadness** *n*

B-road *n* a road given the prefix 'B' in the national road numbering and classification system because it is less important than an A-road

broad arrow *n* 1 a mark in the shape of a wide arrowhead that identifies government property and was used formerly on prison clothing 2 an arrow with a wide barbed head

Broad Australian *n* Australian English spoken with a strong Australian accent. ◊ **Cultivated Australian**

broadaxe /bráwd aks/ *n* a heavy battleaxe with a wide blade

⚡**broadband** /bráwd band/ *adj* 1 using a wide range of electromagnetic frequencies 2 able to transfer large amounts of data at high speed

broad bean *n* 1 a large flat green seed. Use: cooked as a vegetable. 2 a plant of the pea family with long pods that produces broad beans. Native to: Europe. *Vicia faba.*

broadbill /bráwd bil/ (*plural* **-bills** *or* **-bill**) *n* a bird with brightly coloured feathers and a short broad bill. Native to: tropical Africa and Asia. Family: Eurylaemidae.

broad-brush *adj* attempting to cover all conditions and instances ○ *a broad-brush approach*

broadcast /bráwd kaast/ *v* (**-casts, -casting, -cast** *or* **-casted**) 1 *vti* **TRANSMIT RADIO SIGNALS** to transmit a programme or information on television or radio 2 *vi* **PERFORM ON TELEVISION OR RADIO** to take part in a radio or television programme 3 *vt* **MAKE SOMETHING WIDELY KNOWN** to make something widely known ○ *They broadcast the rumours all over town.* 4 *vt* **SCATTER SEED** to sow seed by scattering it ■ *n* 1 **PROGRAMME** a television or radio programme 2 **TRANSMISSION** a transmission of radio or television signals 3 **SCATTERING SEED** a sowing of seed by scattering it ■ *adv* **WIDELY** over a wide area —**broadcast** *adj* —**broadcaster** *n*

SYNONYMS See ***scatter***.

broadcasting /bráwd kaasting/ *n* the making and transmission of television and radio programmes

broad church *n* a group, institution, or political party that has liberal and inclusive attitudes

Broad Church *n* a group within the Church of England that favours a liberal interpretation of doctrine

broadcloth /bráwd kloth/ *n* 1 a shiny, closely woven woollen, cotton, or silk cloth. Use: clothing. 2 a smooth woollen fabric with a plain weave and dense texture region

broaden /bráwd'n/ *vti* 1 to make something wider or to become wider 2 to enlarge the range or magnitude of something, or to become more wide-ranging

broad gauge *n* a railway track that has a distance between the tracks greater than the standard 123.2 cm/48.5 in

broad-gauge *adj* 1 relating to or designed for a railway using broad gauge 2 wide in application or range

broad-leaved /bráwd leevd/ *adj* describes deciduous or evergreen trees that have wide leaves rather than leaves that are like pine needles

broadloom /bráwd loom/ *adj* describes carpet that is woven on a wide loom ■ *n* a carpet woven on a wide loom that can be laid with few or no seams

broadly /bráwdli/ *adv* 1 **GENERALLY** in general terms, not allowing for exceptions ○ *Broadly speaking, there are two types of tourist.* 2 **MOSTLY** for the most part ○ *It is broadly based on the German prototype.* 3 **WITH AN ENTHUSIASTIC SMILE** with a smile that shows great enthusiasm or friendliness ○ *smiling broadly*

broadly-based *adj* involving or covering a wide range of people or things

broad-minded *adj* willing to tolerate a wide range of ideas and behaviour —**broad-mindedly** *adv* —**broad-mindedness** *n*

broad money *n* ECON = **M2**

Broads /brawdz/ area of shallow freshwater lakes and lagoons in E England

broadsheet /bráwd sheet/ *n* **1** a newspaper that is printed in a large format and is associated with serious journalism as opposed to the smaller-format tabloids **2** a large sheet of paper printed on one side. US term **broadside** *n.* 5

broadside /bráwd sīd/ *n* **1 SHIP'S SIDE** the side of a ship above the water line from bow to quarter **2 SHIP'S GUNS AND GUNFIRE** all the guns on one side of a ship or the simultaneous firing of them **3 STRONG VERBAL OR WRITTEN ATTACK** a strong verbal or written attack on somebody ○ *a vicious broadside on the Prime Minister* **4 LARGE FLAT SURFACE** a large flat and usually vertical surface ○ *the broadside of the barn* **5** PRINTING = **broadsheet** *n.* 2 ■ *adv* **1 FROM THE SIDE** with the side facing towards something ○ *The ship hit the rocks broadside on.* **2 WITH NO APPARENT OBJECTIVE** with no apparent objective ○ *Her proposals were attacked broadside.* ■ *vt* (**-sides, -siding, -sided**) *US* **HIT SIDE OF** to collide with something sideways on ○ *The car was broadsided by the train.*

broad-spectrum *adj* describes antibiotics and other chemicals that destroy a wide range of organisms, e.g. bacteria and agricultural pests

broadsword /bráwd sawrd/ *n* a sword with a wide flat blade designed for cutting rather than for thrusting

broadtail /bráwd tayl/ *n* **1** the black wavy fur of a prematurely born karakul lamb **2** ZOOL = **karakul** *n.* 1

Broadway /bráwd way/ *n* **1** a long avenue in Manhattan, New York City, part of which is the main thoroughfare of the city's theatre district **2** used to refer to the commercial theatre business in the United States ○ *This is not Broadway material.*

broad-winged hawk *n* a common woodland hawk with broad wings that are white on the underside, and a broadly banded tail. Native to: E North America. *Buteo platypterus.*

Broadwood /bráwd wŏŏd/, **John** (1732–1812) British piano manufacturer

Brobdingnagian /bróbding nággi ən/ *adj* extraordinarily large (*literary*) [Early 18C. < *Brobdingnag*, fictitious land of giants in Jonathan Swift's *Gulliver's Travels* (1726).]

brocade /brō káyd, brə-/ *n* a heavy silk, cotton, or woollen fabric with a raised design, often in metallic threads ■ *vt* (**-cades, -cading, -caded**) to weave fabric with a raised design [Late 16C. Via Spanish or Portuguese *brocado* < Italian *broccato* < *brocco* 'twisted thread, shoot' < Latin *brocchus*.] —**brocaded** *adj*

broccoli /brókəli/ *n* **1** heads of tight green, purple, or white flower buds, eaten cooked as a vegetable **2** a plant of the cabbage family that produces broccoli. *Brassica oleracea italica.* [Mid-17C. < Italian, plural of *broccolo* 'cabbage sprout' < *brocco* 'shoot' < Latin *brocchus*.]

broch /brok, brokh/ *n* a prehistoric fortified dwelling in the shape of a circular stone tower, found especially on the islands and northern mainland of Scotland [Mid-17C. Dialect form of BURGH.]

brochette /bro shét/ *n* **1** a small skewer on which chunks of food are grilled or roasted **2** food, e.g. meat or fish, that has been cooked on a brochette [15C. < French, 'little skewer' < *broche* 'skewer, long needle'.]

brochure /brṓshər, bro shŏŏr/ *n* a booklet or pamphlet that contains descriptive information or advertising [Mid-18C. < French, 'something stitched together' < *brocher* (see BROACH).]

ϟ**brochure site** *n* a simple, often one-page website giving details of how to contact a company and advertising its products

brock /brok/ (*plural* **brocks** *or* **brock**) *n* ZOOL = **badger** [Pre-12C. < Celtic.]

Brocken /brókən/ highest point in the Harz Mountains, central Germany. Height: 1,141 m/3,743 ft.

~~**brocoli**~~ incorrect spelling of **broccoli**

broderie anglaise /brṓdəri ong gláyz/ *n* **1** white cotton or synthetic fabric decorated with an ornamental pattern of small holes with stitched edges (**eyelet embroidery**). Use: decorative trimming. **2** embroidery in the form of an ornamental pattern of small holes with stitched edges [Mid-19C. < French, 'English embroidery'.]

broderie perse /-púrss/ *n* an appliqué technique in which designs are cut from patterned fabric and sewn onto plain fabric [< French, 'chintz embroidery']

Brodsky /bródski/, **Joseph** (1940–96) Soviet-born US poet and essayist

Broederbond /brŏŏdər bont/ *n S Africa* a secret society of Afrikaner nationalists in South Africa, committed to gaining control of vital areas of government [Mid-20C. Via Afrikaans < Dutch, 'league of brothers'.]

brog /brog/ *n Scotland* a bradawl [15C. < ?]

brogan /brṓgən/ *n* a heavy ankle-high work boot [Mid-19C. < Irish or Scots Gaelic *brōgan* 'little shoe' < *brōg* (see BROGUE[2]).]

Broglie /broy/, **Louis Victor, Prince de** (1892–1987) French physicist

brogue[1] /brōg/ *n* a regional accent, especially the accent of Irish people speaking English [Early 18C. < ?]

brogue[2] /brōg/ *n* **1** a rugged shoe, usually with a decorative pattern of small holes in the leather across the toe and along the sides. US term **wing tip** *n.* 2 **2** a simple heavy untanned shoe formerly worn in Ireland and Scotland [Late 16C. Via Irish and Scots Gaelic *brōg* < Old Norse *brók* 'leg covering'.]

broil /broyl/ *v* **1** *vti* to make somebody or something extremely hot, or be extremely hot ○ *We had been broiling in the sun all morning.* **2** *vt US, Can* COOK = **grill**[1] *v.* 1 **3** *vi US* to be extremely angry [14C. < Old French *bruler*.]

broiler /bróylər/ *n* **1** a young chicken for roasting **2** *US* COOK = **grill**[1] *n.* 1

broiler house *n* a building where broiler chickens are reared

broke[1] past tense of **break**

broke[2] /brōk/ *adj* (*informal*) **1** without any money to spend **2** totally bankrupt [Early 18C. Alteration of BROKEN[2].] ◇ **go for broke** to risk everything to achieve a goal (*informal*)

broke[3] /brōk/ *vt* to broker a deal, sale, or contract [Early 20C. Back-formation < BROKER.] —**broking** *n*

broken[1] past participle of **break**

broken[2] /brṓkən/ *adj* **1 NO LONGER WHOLE** in two or more pieces, e.g. after having been dropped or struck with something hard **2 OUT OF ORDER** no longer in working condition ○ *The CD player is broken.* **3 NOT KEPT** not honoured or fulfilled ○ *a broken promise* **4 NOT CONTINUOUS** lacking continuity **5 UNEVEN** having an uneven surface ○ *We travelled over broken terrain.* **6 WEAKENED** physically weakened ○ *His health was broken.* **7 DESTROYED BY ADVERSITY** destroyed or badly hurt by grief or misfortune **8 SPLIT APART** split apart by divorce, separation, or desertion **9 INCOMPLETE** lacking parts necessary to be complete **10 DISORGANIZED** lacking order or harmony ○ *escaping in broken ranks* **11 IMPERFECTLY SPOKEN** spoken in an imperfect or halting manner [Old English *brocen*, past participle of BREAK] —**brokenly** *adv* —**brokenness** *n*

Broken Bay /brṓkən-/ bay on the coast of New South Wales, Australia

broken chord *n* a chord played as a quick succession of notes (**arpeggio**) rather than simultaneously

broken consort *n* a musical ensemble made up of instruments of different types, used especially in music of the Renaissance

broken-down *adj* **1** damaged or not working ○ *a broken-down old machine* **2** in very poor condition

broken-field *adj* in American football, making quick changes in direction while carrying the ball downfield in order to avoid widely scattered opposing players ○ *broken-field running*

brokenhearted /brṓkən haártid/ *adj* extremely sad, e.g. after bereavement, great disappointment, or the end of a love affair —**brokenheartedly** *adv* —**brokenheartedness** *n*

Broken Hill city in W New South Wales, Australia. Population: 20,963 (1996).

broker /brṓkər/ *n* **1** a person who is paid to act as an agent for others, e.g. in negotiating contracts or buying and selling goods and services **2** FIN = **stockbroker 3** POL = **power broker** ■ *vt* to act as an agent in arranging a deal, sale, or contract [14C. < Anglo-Norman *brocour* 'small trader'.]

brokerage /brṓkərij/ *n* **1 PAYMENT TO A BROKER** a fee paid to somebody who acts as a financial agent for somebody else **2 BROKER'S BUSINESS** the business of being a broker **3 STOCKBROKER'S BUSINESS** a company whose business is buying and selling stocks, shares, and bonds for its clients

brokered CD *n* a certificate of deposit issued by a bank and sold in bulk to a brokerage for selling on to its customers

brolga /brólgə/ (*plural* **-gas** *or* **-ga**) *n* a large grey crane with a red band round its neck, known for its elaborate courtship dance. Native to: N Australia. *Grus rubicunda.* [Late 19C. < Kamilaroi *buralga*.]

brolly /brólli/ (*plural* **-lies**) *n* an umbrella (*informal*) [Late 19C. Alteration of UMBRELLA.]

brom- *prefix* bromine, bromic ○ *bromate* [< BROMINE, BROMIDE]

bromate /brṓ mayt/ *n* a salt, ester, or ion of bromic acid ■ *vt* (**-mates, -mating, -mated**) CHEM = **brominate**

bromegrass /brṓm graass/, **brome** /brōm/ *n* a tall grass with small drooping flower spikes that grows in temperate regions. Some types of bromegrass are cultivated for hay, while others are weeds. Genus: *Bromus.* [Mid-18C. Via modern Latin *Bromus* < Greek *bromos*, *brōmos* 'oats'.]

bromeliad /brō méeli ad/ *n* a tropical plant with fleshy leaves forming a funnel that holds water, that often grows on another plant for physical support. Native to: America. Family: Bromeliaceae. [Mid-19C. After Olaf *Bromel* (1639–1705), Swedish botanist.]

bromic /brṓmik/ *adj* relating to or containing bromine with a valency of five

bromic acid *n* $HBrO_3$ an unstable colourless acid that is a strong oxidizing agent. Use: manufacture of pharmaceuticals and dyes.

bromide /brṓ mīd/ *n* **1 BROMINE COMPOUND** a compound containing bromine and another element or group, e.g. silver bromide **2 POTASSIUM BROMIDE** potassium bromide, especially when used as a sedative **3 UNORIGINAL SAYING** a saying that lacks originality or significance (*dated*)

bromide paper *n* a light-sensitive photographic paper that is coated with silver bromide emulsion

bromidic /brō míddik/ *adj* without originality or interest

brominate /brṓmi nayt/ (**-nates, -nating, -nated**) *vt* to treat or combine a substance with bromine or a bromine compound —**bromination** /brṓmi náysh'n/ *n*

bromine /brṓ meen, -min/ *n* (*symbol* **Br**) a pungent, dark red, volatile liquid nonmetallic element of the halogen series. Use: sedatives, photographic materials. [Early 19C. < French *brome* < Greek *brōmos* 'stench'.]

Bromley /brómli/ borough of London. Population: 293,400 (1995).

bromobenzene /brṓmō bén zeen/ *n* a heavy colourless liquid with a pungent odour. Use: synthesis of chemicals, solvent.

Bromsgrove /brómz grōv/ town in west-central England. Population: 26,366 (1991).

bronch- *prefix* = **broncho-**

bronchi plural of **bronchus**

bronchial /bróngki əl/ *adj* relating to or affecting the tubes (**bronchi**) that carry air from the windpipe into the lungs ○ *a bronchial infection* —**bronchially** *adv*

bronchial pneumonia *n* MED = **bronchopneumonia**

bronchial tube *n* a tubular passage forming part of a network of airways to and within the lungs

bronchiectasis /bróngki éktəssiss/ *n* chronic dilation of the airways to and within the lungs, causing coughing and excessive mucus production [Late 19C. < late Latin *bronchia* (see BRONCHIOLE) + Greek *ektasis* 'dilation'.]

bronchiole /bróngki ōl/ *n* a narrow tube inside the lungs that branches off the main air passages (**bronchi**) [Mid-19C. < modern Latin *bronchiolus* 'little bronchium' < late Latin *bronchia* < Greek *brogkhos* (see BRONCHUS).] —**bronchiolar** /bróngki ṓlər/ *adj*

bronchitis /brong kī́tiss/ *n* inflammation of the mucous membrane in the airways (**bronchial tubes**) of the lungs, resulting from infection or irritation and causing breathing problems and severe coughing —**bronchitic** /brong kíttik/ *adj*

broncho *n* = **bronco**

broncho- *prefix* bronchus, bronchial ○ *bronchoscope* [Via late Latin < Greek *brogkhos* (see BRONCHUS)]

bronchodilator /bróngkō dī láytər/ *n* a drug that relaxes the bronchi and eases breathing. Use: asthma treatment.

bronchopneumonia /bróngkō nyoo mṓni ə/ *n* inflammation of the lungs caused by an infection in the air passages (**bronchioles**)

bronchoscope /bróngkə skōp/ *n* a thin instrument with a light on the end, used for looking inside the air passages (**bronchi**) leading to the lungs —**bronchoscopic**

/bróngkə skóppik/ *adj* —**bronchoscopically** *adv* —**bronchoscopist** /brong kóskəpist/ *n* —**bronchoscopy** /-kóskəpi/ *n*

bronchus /bróngkəss/ (*plural* **-chi** /-kī, -kee/) *n* a tube leading from the windpipe to a lung, which provides for the passage of air [Late 17C. Via modern Latin < Greek *brogkhos* 'windpipe' < Indo-European.]

bronco /bróng kō/, **broncho** *n* a wild or partly broken horse of the W United States, used in rodeos [Mid-19C. < Spanish, 'rough, wild'.]

broncobuster /bróngkō bustər/ *n US* a person who breaks in wild horses (*informal*)

Brontë /brónti/, **Anne** (1820–49) British novelist and poet

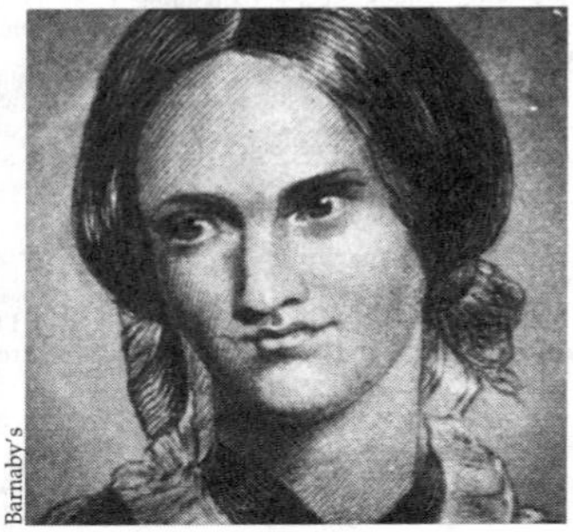

Charlotte Brontë

Brontë, Charlotte (1816–55) British novelist

Brontë, Emily (1818–48) British novelist and poet

brontosaurus /bróntə sáwrəss/, **brontosaur** /bróntə sawr/ *n* PALAEONT = **apatosaurus** [Late 19C. < modern Latin *Brontosaurus* < Greek *brontē* 'thunder' + *sauros* 'lizard'.]

Bronx /bronks/ borough of New York City, on the mainland north of Manhattan. Population: 1,203,789 (1990).

Bronx cheer *n US* = **raspberry** *n.* 3 (*informal*)

bronze /bronz/ *n* 1 **COPPER AND TIN ALLOY** a hard yellowish-brown alloy of copper and tin, sometimes containing small amounts of other metals 2 **COPPER-BASED ALLOY** an alloy of copper with a substance other than tin, e.g. aluminium or silicon 3 **BRONZE WORK OF ART** an object that is made from bronze, especially a statue or other piece of cast sculpture 4 **BRONZE MEDAL** a bronze medal (*informal*) 5 **DEEP YELLOWISH-BROWN COLOUR** a deep yellowish-brown colour ■ *v* (**bronzes, bronzing, bronzed**) 1 *vt* **MAKE SOMETHING LOOK LIKE BRONZE** to give something the yellowish-brown sheen or weathered patina of bronze 2 *vti* **TAN SKIN** to make somebody's skin suntanned, or become suntanned (*informal*) [Early 18C. Via French, < Italian *bronzo*.] —**bronze** *adj* —**bronzed** *adj* —**bronzer** *n* —**bronzy** *adj*

Bronze Age *n* a period of cultural history, approximately between 3500 and 1500 BC, that succeeded the Stone Age and was characterized by the use of tools made of bronze

bronze medal *n* a medal that is awarded to a person who is placed third in a competition, especially a sporting event —**bronze medallist** *n*

Bronzino /bron dzeénō/, **il** (1503–72) Italian painter. Born **Agnoli Tori di Cosimo di Mariano**

bronzite /brón zīt/ *n* an iron-containing form of orthopyroxene with a metallic sheen

brooch /brōch/ *n* a piece of jewellery that is fastened to a garment by a hinged pin and catch [13C. < Old French *broche* 'skewer, long needle'.]

SPELLCHECK See ***broach***.

brood /brood/ *n* 1 **YOUNG OF BIRDS OR ANIMALS** the young of an animal, especially young birds, that are born and reared together 2 **FAMILY'S CHILDREN** the children of one family (*informal humorous*) 3 **GROUP OF SIMILAR PEOPLE** a group whose members share a common origin or background ○ *the latest brood of avant-garde artists* ■ *adj* **KEPT FOR BREEDING** describes a female farm animal that is kept for the purpose of producing young ■ *v* 1 *vi* **WORRY** to be preoccupied with a troublesome or unwelcome thought 2 *vi* **THINK UNPLEASANT THOUGHTS** to think resentful, dark, or miserable thoughts 3 *vti* **HATCH EGGS** to sit on or hatch eggs, or cover nestlings for warmth 4 *vi* **BE HEAVY OR OMINOUS** to loom or hang heavily and ominously (*literary*) ○ *the dark clouds brooding overhead* [Old English *brōd* < Indo-European, 'heat']

brooder /broódər/ *n* 1 **HEATED PLACE FOR YOUNG ANIMAL** a heated area or enclosure for rearing young animals, especially young fowl, with or without the presence of their mother 2 **HEN THAT BROODS EGGS** a hen that sits on eggs to keep them warm before they hatch 3 **PERSON WHO WORRIES** a person who worries persistently over things

brooding /broóding/ *adj* seeming to contain some silent threat or danger (*literary*) ■ *n* somebody's private thoughts about a situation that is a source of anxiety ○ *Her broodings were disturbed by Colette's arrival.* —**broodingly** *adv*

brood mare *n* a mare that is kept specially for breeding

broody /broódi/ (**-ier, -iest**) *adj* 1 **READY TO INCUBATE EGGS** describes a hen that is ready to sit on eggs to keep them warm before they hatch, especially a hen that is no longer able to lay eggs 2 **THOUGHTFUL OR SULLEN** showing deep thought, anxiety, or resentment ○ *His long broody silences were hard to bear.* 3 **WANTING A BABY** eager or anxious to have a baby (*informal*) —**broodily** *adv* —**broodiness** *n*

brook[1] /brŏŏk/ *n* a small freshwater stream [Old English *brōc* < Germanic]

brook[2] /brŏŏk/ *vt* to put up with something (*literary; in negatives*) ○ *I will brook no interference in this matter.* [Old English *brūcan* < Indo-European]

Brook /brŏŏk/, **Peter** (*b.* 1925) British-born director

Brooke /brŏŏk/, **Rupert** (1887–1915) British poet

Brookeborough /brŏŏkbərə/, **Basil Stanlake Brooke, 1st Viscount** (1883–1973) British statesman

Brook Farm *n* an experimental cooperative community established by a group of writers and scholars on a farm at West Roxbury, Massachusetts

brookite /brŏŏk īt/ *n* a translucent or reddish-brown to black crystalline mineral composed of titanium dioxide [Early 19C. After Henry *Brook* (1771–1857), English mineralogist.]

Brooklyn /brŏŏklin/ borough of New York City, on the W tip of Long Island. Population: 2,300,664 (1990).

Brookner /brŏŏknər/, **Anita** (*b.* 1928) British writer

Brooks /brŏŏks/, **Mel** (*b.* 1926) US film actor and director. Born **Melvin Kaminsky**

brook trout *n* 1 a freshwater fish of the salmon family that is a popular game fish throughout N America and in Europe. Native to: E North America. *Salvelinus fontinalis.* 2 the flesh of a brook trout as food

broom /broom, brŏŏm/ *n* 1 **BRUSH FOR SWEEPING** a brush with a head of twigs or bristles attached to a long thin handle, used for sweeping indoors or outdoors 2 **PLANT WITH BRIGHT YELLOW FLOWERS** a widely cultivated leguminous shrub. Flowers: bright yellow. Native to: Europe, Asia. *Cytisus scoparius.* 3 **PLANT RESEMBLING BROOM** a shrub resembling broom. Native to: Europe, Asia. Genera: *Genista* and *Spartium.* ■ *vt* **SWEEP** to sweep something with a broom or brush [Old English *brōm* < Germanic]

Broome /broom/ coastal town in NW Western Australia. Population: 11,368 (1996).

broomrape /broóm rayp, brŏŏm-/ *n* a plant that lives on the roots of other plants, including crops. Flowers: tubular on a leafless stem. Genus: *Orobanche.* [Late 16C. < medieval Latin *rapum* 'tuber'.]

broomstick /broóm stik, brŏŏm-/ *n* the long handle of a broom

Broonzy /broónzi/, **Big Bill** (1893–1953) US musician. Born **William Lee Conley**

bros., Bros. *abbr* brothers

broth /broth/ *n* 1 a thin nourishing soup of poultry, meat, or vegetables 2 a liquid made by cooking vegetables, meat, seafood, or poultry in water for a long time, used as a base for soups and sauces [Old English *broþ* < Indo-European, 'heat, boil']

brothel /bróth'l/ *n* a place where people pay to have sexual intercourse with prostitutes [14C. < Old English *broþen* 'ruined'. Originally 'worthless person, prostitute'; current use a shortening of *brothel-house*.]

brothel creepers *npl* men's suede shoes with thick crepe soles, popular in the 1950s and 1960s

brother /brú*th*ər/ *n* 1 **MALE SIBLING** a boy or man who has the same father and mother as another person 2 (*plural* **brothers** *or* **brethren**) **FELLOW MEMBER** a man who belongs to the same ethnic group, religion, profession, trade, or organization as another man 3 (*plural* **brothers** *or* **brethren**) **LAY MEMBER** a member of a religious order for men 4 (*plural* **brothers** *or* **brethren**) **DEVOTED RELIGIOUS WORKER** a man who devotes himself to the work of a men's religious order without having been professed ■ *interj* **EXPRESSING SURPRISE OR ANNOYANCE** used to express surprise, annoyance, or disappointment (*informal*) ○ *Oh, brother! What happened here today?* [Old English *brōþor* < Indo-European]

brotherhood /brú*th*ər hŏŏd/ *n* 1 **HAVING SAME PARENTS** the relationship of brothers 2 **GROUP OF MEN** an organization of men, e.g. a trade union, that is united for a common purpose 3 **ALL THE MEMBERS** all the members of a particular profession or trade 4 **GOODWILL** a feeling of fellowship and sympathy for other people

brother-in-law (*plural* **brothers-in-law**) *n* 1 **SISTER'S HUSBAND** the husband of somebody's sister 2 **SPOUSE'S BROTHER** the brother of somebody's husband or wife 3 **SPOUSE'S SISTER'S HUSBAND** the husband of the sister of somebody's husband or wife

brotherly /brú*th*ərli/ *adj* showing feelings that a brother might be expected to have towards his sister or brother —**brotherliness** *n*

brougham /broom, broó əm/ *n* a one-horse carriage with an open seat at the front for the driver and a closed compartment at the back for passengers, used in the 19th century [Mid-19C. After Lord *Brougham* (1778–1868).]

brought *v* past tense, past participle of **bring**

brouhaha /broó haa haa/ *n* a noisy commotion or uproar [Late 19C. < French.]

brow /brow/ *n* 1 **FOREHEAD** the area on somebody's face above the eyes and below the hairline 2 ANAT = **eyebrow** *n.* 1 3 **TOP OF HILL** the top edge of a hill 4 **TOP OF MINE** the top of a mineshaft [Old English *brū* < Indo-European]

browallia /brə wáali ə/ (*plural* **-a** *or* **-as**) *n* an ornamental plant of the nightshade family. Flowers: blue, white, violet. Native to: America. Genus: *Browallia.* [Late 18C. < modern Latin, after Johann *Browall* (1707–55), Swedish botanist.]

browband /brów band/ *n* a strap that is part of a horse's bridle and goes across its forehead

browbeat /brów beet/ (**-beats, -beating, -beat, -beaten** /-beet'n/) *vt* to bully or intimidate somebody sternly ○ *His friends tried to browbeat him, but he made his own decision.* —**browbeater** *n*

brown /brown/ *n* 1 **COLOUR BETWEEN RED AND YELLOW** a colour that varies between red and yellow, e.g. the colour of wood or soil 2 **BROWN CLOTHING** fabric or clothing that is brown in colour ○ *We had to wear brown for school.* 3 **BROWN PIGMENT OR DYE** a pigment or dye that is formed from a combination of red, yellow, and black, and has or is near to the colour of wood or soil 4 **BROWN OBJECT** a brown object ○ *She decided to take the brown.* ■ *adj* 1 **BROWN IN COLOUR** of the colour brown ○ *the fruit was brown and rotten* 2 **SUNTANNED** deeply suntanned or sunburnt 3 **UNPROCESSED** describes foodstuffs that are partially or wholly unprocessed so that their natural brown colour remains ■ *vti* **MAKE OR BECOME BROWN** to make something brown or become brown, e.g. in cooking or sunbathing [Old English *brūn* < Indo-European, 'bright, brown'] —**brownish** *adj* —**brownness** *n*

Brown /brown/, **Sir Arthur Whitten** (1886–1948) British aviator

Brown, Capability (1715–83) British landscape gardener. Born **Lancelot Brown**

Brown, Ford Madox (1821–93) French-born British painter

Brown, George Mackay (1921–96) British poet and novelist

Brown, John (1800–59) US abolitionist

brown adipose tissue *n* PHYSIOL = **brown fat**

brown alga *n* a marine alga that has chlorophyll masked by brown pigment, including kelps and wracks. Division: *Phaeophyta.*

brown bear *n* a bear that is mainly brown in colour, e.g. the Kodiak and grizzly bears. Native to: W North America, N Europe, N Asia. *Ursus arctos.*

brown bread *n* bread made using wholemeal flour

brown coal *n* a soft, brown-black fossil fuel with visible plant remains and a high moisture content

brown dwarf *n* a star that is smaller than a planet and has a mass equivalent to less than one-tenth of the Sun's mass

brown earth *n* soil formed in temperate humid regions under deciduous forests and characterized by a dark brown layer rich in organic material

browned-off *adj* (*dated informal*) **1** in a state of boredom or low spirits **2** feeling discouraged or disheartened

brownette /brow nét/ *n US* a woman with light brown hair —**brownette** *adj*

brown fat *n* a dark-coloured fatty tissue in many mammals, especially hibernating animals and human babies, that produces heat in order to control body temperature

brownfield /brówn feeld/ *n US* ENVIRON = **brownfield site**

brownfield site /brówn feeld-/ *n* an urban development site that has been previously built on but is currently unused. US term **brownfield** [After GREENFIELD]

brown goods *npl* electrical consumer goods such as televisions and audio equipment that are mainly used for home entertainment, as opposed to conventionally 'white' kitchen appliances such as refrigerators and washing machines

Brownian movement /brówni ən-/, **Brownian motion** *n* the random movement of microscopic particles suspended in a liquid or gas that occurs as a result of collisions with molecules of the surrounding medium [After Robert *Brown* (1773–1858), British botanist]

brownie /brówni/ *n* **1** a piece of flat rich chocolate cake baked in a square or rectangular tin and sometimes containing chopped nuts **2** in folklore, a small supernatural being believed to do helpful work at night

Brownie /brówni/, **Brownie Guide** *n* in the UK, a member of the junior section of the Guides, aged between seven and ten years [Because of the brown uniform]

Brownie Guider *n* an adult leader of a pack of Brownie Guides, formerly known as 'Brown Owl'

brownie point, Brownie point *n* a credit earned for doing something helpful, especially in order to please (*informal*) [< the idea that Brownies use points for advancement]

browning /brówning/ *n* a substance, e.g. caramelized sugar, used to give a brown colour to soup or gravy

Browning /brówning/, **Elizabeth Barrett** (1806–61) British poet. Born **Elizabeth Barrett**

Browning, Robert (1812–89) British poet

Browning automatic rifle *n* an air-cooled, gas-operated, magazine-fed rifle with a .30 in calibre barrel [After John M. *Browning* (1855–1926), US arms designer.]

Browning machine gun *n* an air- or water-cooled, belt-fed, automatic machine gun with either a .30 or .50 calibre barrel [See BROWNING AUTOMATIC RIFLE]

brown lacewing *n* an insect with brownish wings that often feeds on agricultural pests. Family: Hemerobiidae.

brownlands /brówn landz/ *npl* land for development that has been previously developed but is currently unused. ◊ **brownfield site**

brown lung disease, brown lung *n* MED = **byssinosis**

brown mustard *n* **1** the ground dark reddish-brown oil-rich seeds of the mustard plant. Use: cooking spice. **2** *US* an annual plant of the mustard family with irregularly lobed leaves that produces brown mustardseeds. Flowers: pale yellow. *Brassica juncea*.

brownnose /brówn nōz/ (**-noses, -nosing, -nosed**) *vti* to be unnaturally subservient or obsequious to somebody in authority (*slang; sometimes offensive*) [Implying willingness to undertake stigmatized intimacy] —**brownnose** *n* —**brownnoser** *n*

brownout /brówn owt/ *n* **1** *US* **DIMMING OF LIGHTS** a dimming of lights or reduction in the use of electrical appliances in a city or region, especially as an economy measure **2** *US* **POWER REDUCTION** a temporary reduction in electrical power caused by high consumer demand or by technical malfunction **3** **LAPSE OF CONCENTRATION** a temporary lapse of concentration or focus [Mid-20C. After BLACKOUT.]

brown owl *n* BIRDS = **tawny owl**

Brown Owl *n* formerly, the adult leader of a pack of Brownies. Now called **Brownie Guider**

brown paper *n* thick strong brown-coloured paper used for wrapping parcels

brown patch *n* a soil-borne fungal disease of grass that produces round dead patches

brown rat *n* an extremely destructive rat, now found worldwide in populated areas. Native to: originally Europe, Asia. *Rattus norvegicus*.

brown recluse spider *n* a pale brown poisonous spider with a violin-shaped mark on the head area. Native to: United States, South America. *Loxosceles reclusa*.

brown rice *n* unpolished rice in which the yellowish-brown outer layer containing the bran remains intact, thus making it more nutritious than white rice. ◊ **white rice**

brown rot *n* a disease of ripe tree fruits such as apples and peaches, caused by fungi. Genus: *Rhizoctonia*.

brown sauce *n* **1** a sauce made from a dark meat stock, thickened with flour that has been browned in fat **2** a dark-brown savoury sauce made from fruit, vinegar, sugar, and spices

brown seaweed *n* MARINE BIOL = **brown alga**

Brownshirt /brówn shurt/ *n* **1** a member of a Nazi uniformed paramilitary organization that originally formed Adolf Hitler's personal bodyguard and was later used as a militia **2** *US* an offensive term for somebody who is viewed as being a violent racist (*insult*) [Translation of German *Braunhemd*, from the brown uniform shirts of the Nazi storm troopers]

brown snake *n Aus* a poisonous brown-coloured snake. Native to: Australia. Genus: *Pseudonaja*.

brownstone /brówn stōn/ *n US* **1** a reddish-brown sandstone used as a building material **2** a house or building made from or faced with reddish-brown sandstone, especially houses in New York City

brown study *n* a state of deep thought or serious absorption (*dated*) [Probably < BROWN 'gloomy']

brown sugar *n* **1** **REFINED SUGAR WITH TREACLE** a soft light or dark brown sugar made from refined white sugar combined with mild refined treacle and used in cooking **2** **UNREFINED SUGAR** unrefined or partially refined sugar **3** **HEROIN** the drug heroin (*slang*)

brown trout *n* **1** a common brownish freshwater fish. Native to: Europe, N America. *Salmo trutta*. **2** the flesh of a brown trout as food

ϟ **browse** /browz/ *v* (**browses, browsing, browsed**) **1** *vti* **READ CASUALLY** to read through something quickly or superficially **2** *vi* **LOOK THROUGH OR OVER CASUALLY** to look through or over something, especially goods in a shop, in a leisurely manner with the hope of finding something of interest **3** *vti* **FEED ON VEGETATION** to feed or graze on tender vegetation such as the shoots, leaves, or twigs of shrubs or trees **4** *vti* **SCAN COMPUTER FILES** to scan and view files in a computer database or on the Internet, especially on the World Wide Web ■ *n* **1** **SESSION OF BROWSING** a superficial read through something, e.g. a newspaper, or a leisurely look over something, e.g. the goods in a shop **2** **FEEDING PERIOD** a session of feeding on tender shoots or twigs of shrubs and trees **3** **TENDER VEGETATION USED AS FOOD** the tender shoots, leaves, or twigs of shrubs and trees used as food by animals such as deer and cattle [Early 16C. Via obsolete French *broust* < Old French *brost* < Germanic.]

ϟ **browser** /brówzər/ *n* **1** a piece of computer software used to search for information on the World Wide Web **2** somebody who looks at something, e.g. a book or goods for sale, in a leisurely or superficial manner

Broxbourne /bróks bawrn/ town in SE England. Population: 82,200 (1995).

ϟ **BRS** *n* refers to personal computer on-off switch when used to power down in the case of a sudden failure of a program. Full form **big red switch**

Brubeck /broō bek/, **Dave** (*b.* 1920) US jazz pianist and composer. Full name **David William Brubeck**

Bruce /brooss/, **Christopher** (*b.* 1945) British dancer and choreographer

Bruce, James (1730–94) British explorer

Bruce, Stanley Melbourne, 1st Viscount Bruce of Melbourne (1883–1967) Australian statesman and prime minister of Australia (1923–29)

brucellosis /broōssə lṓssiss/ *n* a chronic infectious disease of some domestic animals that can be transmitted to human beings through contaminated milk. ◊ **Bang's disease** [Mid-20C. < modern Latin *Brucella*, genus name of causative bacteria afer Sir David *Bruce* (1855–1931), Scottish physician.]

Bruch /broōkh/, **Max** (1838–1920) German composer

brucine /broō seen/ *n* $C_{23}H_{26}N_2O_4$ a poisonous white crystalline alkaloid. Source: nux vomica seeds. Use: denaturation of alcohol. *Strychnos nux-vomica*. [Early 19C. < modern Latin *Brucea*, genus name of a tree formerly thought to bear the bark that the substance is derived from.]

brucite /broōss īt/ *n* a magnesium hydroxide mineral. Source: hydrothermal deposits, metamorphosed limestone. [Early 19C. After Archibald *Bruce* (1777–1818), US mineralogist.]

Bruckner /broōknər/, **Anton** (1824–96) Austrian composer

Brueghel /bróyg'l/, **Breughel, Jan** (1568–1625) Flemish painter

Brueghel, Breughel, Pieter (1520–69) Flemish painter. Known as **Pieter Brueghel the Elder**

Bruges /broozh/ capital of West Flanders Province, W Belgium. Population: 115,573 (1998 estimate).

bruin /broō in/, **Bruin** *n* used as a name for a bear in folklore, fables, and children's stories [15C. < Middle Dutch, 'brown'.]

bruise /brooz/ *n* (*plural* **bruises**) **1** **SKIN DISCOLORATION CAUSED BY INJURY** a tender area of skin discoloration caused by blood leaking from blood vessels damaged by pressure or impact **2** **DAMAGE TO PLANT TISSUE** damage to underlying plant or fruit tissue, visible as a soft discoloured area on the unbroken surface and caused by pressure or impact **3** **EMOTIONAL INJURY** an injury that is not physical, e.g. hurt feelings or damaged self-esteem ■ *v* (**bruises, bruising, bruised**) **1** *vti* **INJURE CAUSING SKIN DISCOLORATION** to injure, or sustain an injury to, a part of the body resulting in discoloration caused by blood leaking from damaged blood vessels **2** *vti* **DAMAGE PLANT TISSUE** to damage plant tissue or to sustain damage by pressure or impact, leaving a softened and discoloured surface area **3** *vt* **CRUSH FOOD** to crush or pound food, especially to extract juice from it or bring out its flavour **4** *vt* **UPSET** to injure somebody's feelings or harm somebody's self-esteem ○ *I was bruised by the criticism* [Partly < Old English *brȳsan* 'crush', and partly < Anglo-Norman *bruser* 'break' < Germanic]

bruiser /broōzər/ *n* a large strong man or youth, e.g. a boxer, bodyguard, or club bouncer (*informal*)

bruising /broōzing/ *n* bruises or the dark patches left on the surface of bruised skin ■ *adj* causing emotional, psychological, or physical pain

bruit /broot/ *n* **1** **SIGNIFICANT SOUND INSIDE BODY** a medically significant sound heard inside the body, usually with the aid of a stethoscope, and caused by turbulent blood flow **2** **RUMOUR OR REPORT** a story, true or untrue, that is passed about among people (*archaic*) ■ *vt* **SPREAD STORY** to circulate stories, whether true or untrue [15C. < Old French, < past participle of *bruire* 'roar'.]

Brum /brum/ *n* = **Brummagem** [Mid-19C. Shortening.]

brumby /brúmbi/ (*plural* **-bies**) *n ANZ* a wild unbroken horse [Late 19C. < ?]

brume /broom/ *n* a weather condition in which fog or mist is present, or the fog or mist itself (*literary*) [Early 18C. Via French, 'fog' < Latin *bruma* 'winter'.] —**brumous** *adj*

brummagem /brúmməjəm/, **Brummagem** *n* something, especially imitation jewellery, that is cheap and gaudy [Mid-17C. < BRUMMAGEM, originally referring to counterfeit coins made there.] —**brummagem** *adj*

Brummagem /brúmməjəm/ *n* a nickname for Birmingham (*informal*) [Mid-17C. Dialectal form of BIRMINGHAM.]

Brummell /brúmm'l/, **Beau** (1778–1840) British dandy. Born **George Bryan Brummell**

Brummie /brúmmi/, **Brummy** (*plural* **-mies**) *n* somebody who comes from Birmingham in the United Kingdom (*informal*) —**Brummie** *adj*

brunch /brunch/ (*plural* **brunches**) *n* a meal that combines breakfast and lunch, eaten late in the morning [Late 19C. Blend of BREAKFAST + LUNCH.]

Brunei

Brunei /broo ní/ sultanate in NW Borneo. Capital: Bandar Seri Begawan. Population: 307,612 (1997). Area: 5,765 sq. km/2,226 sq. mi.

Brunel /broo nél/, **Isambard Kingdom** (1806–59) British engineer

Brunelleschi /broòna léski/, **Filippo** (1377–1446) Italian architect and sculptor. Born **Filippo di Ser Brunellesco**

brunette /broo nét/ n a girl or woman with dark brown hair [Early 17C. < French, feminine form of *brunet* (see BRUNET).] —**brunette** adj

Brunhild /broòn híld/, **Brünnhilde** /-híldə/ n in medieval Germanic mythology, the queen of Iceland who promises to marry whoever can defeat her in battle

Bruno /broònō/, **St** (1030?–1101) German monk. Known as **Bruno the Carthusian**

brunt /brunt/ n 1 the main force or effect of something, e.g. a blow or an attack ○ *We always had to bear the brunt of her anger.* 2 the greater part or the main burden [14C. < ?]

bruschetta /broò skéttə, -shéttə/ n Italian bread toasted and drizzled with olive oil, usually served with added garlic and chopped tomatoes [< Italian, < *bruscare* 'roast over coals']

brush[1] /brush/ n 1 TOOL WITH BRISTLES ATTACHED TO HANDLE an implement consisting of bristles, hair, or wire set into a handle, used for grooming the hair, painting, polishing, scrubbing, sweeping 2 USE OF BRUSH the use of a brush, e.g. to groom the hair or to sweep a surface 3 LIGHT CONTACT a light stroke or momentary contact 4 SHORT UNPLEASANT ENCOUNTER a brief unpleasant encounter ○ *a brush with evil* 5 BUSHY TAIL OF FOX a bushy tail, especially the tail of a fox as a hunting trophy 6 ELECTRICAL CONDUCTOR an electrical conductor that makes sliding contact between a stationary and a moving part of a generator or motor while completing a circuit and conveying a current 7 ELEC = **brush discharge** ■ v 1 vti USE BRUSH to use a brush to clean, groom, paint, polish, or scrub something 2 vt APPLY WITH BRUSH to apply something such as paint or varnish to a surface using a brush 3 vt REMOVE WITH BRUSH to remove with a brush or a sweeping motion 4 vt REJECT to dismiss, ignore, or rebuff something or somebody in an abrupt or curt manner ○ *They brushed aside the suggestion.* 5 vti GRAZE AGAINST to touch something lightly and briefly in passing [14C. < Old French *broisse*, probably variant of *broce* (see BRUSH[2]).] —**brusher** n —**brushy** adj ◇ **tar somebody with the same brush** to attribute unfairly the faults and deficits of somebody to another person
  brush off vt to dismiss or disregard somebody or something in an abrupt manner
  brush up vt to refresh or renew knowledge of or skill in something

brush[2] /brush/ n 1 THICK UNDERGROWTH a dense undergrowth of small trees and bushes 2 LAND COVERED WITH THICK UNDERGROWTH land covered with a dense undergrowth of small trees and bushes 3 = **brushwood** n. 1 4 BACKWOODS wild and sparsely populated woodland [14C. < Anglo-Norman *brousse*, variant of Old French *broce* 'broken branches'.]

brush border n a dense layer of tiny protuberances that lines certain absorbing cells, e.g. in the intestine and kidney

brush discharge n a luminous electric discharge between two conductors, consisting of a flow of ionized particles with less intensity than a spark [< its appearance]

brushed /brusht/ adj 1 describes a knitted or woven fabric that has a nap produced by brushing it during manufacture 2 describes a metallic surface with a non-reflective sheen

brush fire n 1 FIRE IN DRY BRUSH a fire in dry brush and scrub that usually spreads quickly 2 A SMALL WAR a localized but often intensely fought war ■ adj INVOLVING LOCAL MILITARY involving only small-scale and local military mobilization

brushmark /brush maark/ n a mark or line left by the bristles of a brush on a painted or varnished surface

brushoff /brush of/ n an abrupt dismissal, rejection, or snub (*informal*)

brushstroke /brush strōk/ n a movement of a paintbrush that produces a particular look or mark on a painted surface, or the mark itself

brush turkey n a heavy-bodied bird resembling a turkey, with a bare head, black plumage, and red and yellow wattles. Native to: forests of NE Australia. *Alectura lathami*. [Because of the appearance of its wattles]

brushwood /brush wŏod/ n 1 cut or broken branches and twigs 2 = **brush**[2] n. 1 3 = **brush**[2] n. 2

brushwork /brush wurk/ n 1 the characteristic manner in which an artist applies paint with a brush 2 the product of an artist's use of a brush in painting

brusque /broosk/ adj abrupt, blunt, or curt in manner or speech [Early 17C. Via French < late Latin *bruscum* 'coarse, rough'.] —**brusquely** adv —**brusqueness** n —**brusquerie** /broòskəri, broòs-/ n

Brussels /brúss'lz/ capital of Belgium, in the centre of the country. Population: 953,175 (1998 estimate).

Brussels carpet n a carpet with a heavy patterned pile of small woollen loops attached to a linen base

Brussels lace n 1 a fine lace with a floral design, made with bobbins or with needle and thread, that originated in or near Brussels 2 a machine-made net lace with an appliqué design

Brussels sprout n 1 a small green swollen bud like a tiny cabbage cooked as a vegetable 2 a plant related to cabbage that has a thick stalk lined with Brussels sprouts. *Brassica oleracea.* [Because first grown near Brussels]

brut /broot/ adj describes wine, especially sparkling white wine, that is extremely dry in taste [Late 19C. < French.]

brutal /broot'l/ adj 1 RUTHLESS AND CRUEL extremely ruthless or cruel 2 HARSH AND SEVERE unrelentingly harsh and severe ○ *a brutal regimen* 3 DIRECT IN MANNER direct or insensitive in manner or speech ○ *with brutal frankness* [15C. Directly or via French, < medieval Latin *brutalis* < Latin *brutus* (see BRUTE).] —**brutalness** n —**brutally** adv

brutalise vt = **brutalize**

brutalism /broot'lizəm/ n a style of modern architecture characterized by massiveness, a lack of exterior decoration, harsh lines, and the exposure of structural materials —**brutalist** n, adj

brutality /broo táləti/ (*plural* **-ties**) n 1 cruel, harsh, or ruthless behaviour or treatment 2 a cruel, harsh, or ruthless act

brutalize /broot' īz/ (**-izes**, **-izing**, **-ized**), **brutalise** (**-talises**, **-talising**, **-talised**) vt 1 to make somebody brutal or unfeeling 2 to treat somebody brutally, cruelly, or harshly —**brutalization** /broot' ī záysh'n/ n

brute /broot/ n 1 SOMEBODY BRUTAL a cruel, ruthless, or insensitive person 2 ANIMAL an animal other than a human being (*literary*) ■ adj 1 PURELY PHYSICAL purely physical or instinctive, rather than intellectual or reasoned 2 CRUEL OR SAVAGE displaying extreme cruelty and savagery 3 STARK unremittingly harsh or severe 4 CRUDE OR BARBARIC describes behaviour, actions, or instincts that are considered crude, especially those prompted by physical desire and hunger 5 OF BEASTS relating or belonging to lower animals, as opposed to human beings [15C. Via French *brut* < Latin *brutus* 'stupid, like an animal' < Indo-European, 'heavy'.] —**brutism** n

brutish /broòtish/ adj 1 RELATING TO BEASTS relating to or characteristic of lower animals 2 CRUEL cruel, ruthless, or insensitive 3 COARSELY UNINTELLIGENT coarse, crude, unintelligent, or lacking sensitivity —**brutishly** adv —**brutishness** n

Bruton /broòt'n/, **John** (b. 1947) Irish statesman

Brutus /broòtass/, **Lucius Junius** (fl. late 6th century BC) Roman statesman

Brutus, Marcus Junius (85?–42 BC) Roman general and statesman

bruxism /broòksizəm/ n the unconscious habit of grinding or gritting the teeth that occurs during sleep or in stressful situations and can lead to excessive wear of the teeth [Mid-20C. < Greek *brukein* 'gnash the teeth'.]

Brynhild /brínhild/ n in Norse mythology, a Valkyrie who is woken from an enchanted sleep by Sigurd and later tricked into marrying his brother-in-law, Gunnar

bryo- prefix moss ○ *bryophyte* [< Greek *bruon*]

bryology /brī óllэji/ n the branch of botany concerned with the study of hornworts, mosses, and liverworts —**bryological** /brī ə lójjik'l/ adj —**bryologist** n

bryony /brī əni/ n (*plural* **-nies**) a climbing plant with large leaves, tendrils, and red or black berries. Native to: Europe, North Africa. Genus: *Bryonia.* [Pre-12C. Via medieval < Greek *bruonia* < *bruein* 'teem'.]

bryophyte /brī ə fīt/ n a nonflowering plant, often growing in damp places, that has separate gamete-bearing and spore-bearing forms, e.g. moss. Division: *Bryophyta.* —**bryophytic** /brī ə fíttik/ adj

bryozoan /brī ə zō ən/ n an aquatic invertebrate animal that reproduces by budding. Phylum: Bryozoa. [Late 19C. < modern Latin *Bryozoa* < Greek *bruon* 'moss' + *zoion* 'animal'.] —**bryozoan** adj

Brythonic /bri thónnik/, **Brittonic** /-tónnik/ n a group of languages that belongs to the Celtic branch of Indo-European and includes Breton, Cornish, and Welsh. Native speakers: 1 million. ■ adj relating to the Brythons, or their language or culture [Late 19C. < Welsh *Brython* 'Briton'.]

⚡**bs** abbr Bahamas (*in Internet addresses*)

BS abbr 1 British Standard (*as part of the number of a British Standards Institution publication*) 2 US Bachelor of Surgery 3 bill of sale

b.s. abbr 1 balance sheet 2 **b.s., B/S, b/s** bill of sale

B.S. abbr US bullshit (*slang taboo*)

BSB abbr British Standard brass (*identifies a type of screw thread*)

BSc abbr Bachelor of Science

BSE n a disease that affects the nervous system of cattle, believed to be caused by an abnormal transmissible protein (**prion**) and related to Creutzfeldt-Jakob disease in humans. Full form **bovine spongiform encephalopathy**

BSF abbr British Standard fine (*identifies a type of screw thread*)

bsh. abbr bushel

BSI abbr British Standards Institution

B-side n the side of a pop-music or jazz single that does not contain the title track and is considered less important

BSL abbr British Sign Language

Bs/L abbr bills of lading

BSN abbr Bachelor of Science in Nursing

BSP abbr British Standard pipe (*identifies a type of screw thread*)

BST abbr 1 bovine somatotrophin 2 British Summer Time

BSW abbr British Standard Whitworth (*identifies a type of screw thread*)

⚡**bt** abbr Bhutan (*in Internet addresses*)

Bt abbr baronet

BT abbr British Telecom

⚡**BTA** abbr but then again (*in e-mails*)

⚡**BTAIM** abbr be that as it may (*in e-mails*)

⚡**BTDT** abbr been there, done that (*in e-mails*)

BTEC /beè tek/ abbr Business and Technology Education Council

BThU abbr British thermal unit

⚡**b-to-b** adj relating to Internet transactions between business organizations [Abbreviation of *business-to-business*]

⚡**b-to-c** adj relating to Internet transactions between a business and consumers [Abbreviation of *business-to-consumer*]

btry abbr battery

btu, Btu abbr British thermal unit

BTU n a unit for measuring electrical energy, equal to 1 kilowatt-hour. Full form **Board of Trade Unit**

⚡**BTW, btw** *abbr* by the way (*in e-mails*)

bty *abbr* battery

bu. *abbr* bushel

bub /bub/ *n US* used as a term of address to an unnamed male person, especially one encountered and spoken to casually (*slang*) [Mid-19C. Shortening and alteration of BROTHER.]

bubble /búbb'l/ *n* **1 THIN GLOBE-SHAPED FILM** a thin film of something, usually spherical or dome-shaped and filled with air or a gas **2 SOMETHING LIKE A BUBBLE** something spherical or dome-shaped like a bubble **3 GLOBULE WITHIN LIQUID OR SOLID** a globule of air or a gas within a liquid or a solid, e.g. in a fizzy drink or in glass **4 GURGLING SOUND** a gurgling sound made by a boiling or effervescent liquid **5 SOUND OF MANY BUBBLES BURSTING** a sound produced by bubbles forming and bursting **6** = **balloon** *n.* 3 **7 DOME** a dome, usually made of transparent glass or plastic **8 PROTECTED AREA** a protected, isolated, or exempted area **9 FALSE CONFIDENCE** a false feeling of confidence or security ○ *The rocketing housing market is a bubble that will surely burst.* **10 RISKY SCHEME** a risky or unreliable business enterprise or speculative scheme, especially one proving to be fraudulent or unsuccessful ■ *v* (**-bles, -bling, -bled**) **1** *vi* **EFFERVESCE OR BOIL UP** to form or produce spherical or dome-shaped pockets of air or gas in a liquid **2** *vi* **GURGLE** to move or flow with a gurgling sound **3** *vi* **EMERGE OR APPEAR** to emerge or rise to the surface **4** *vi* **BE ESPECIALLY LIVELY WITH EMOTION** to be animated with or display an emotion such as excitement, happiness, or anger ○ *bubbling with mirth* **5** *vt* **EXPRESS SOMETHING ENTHUSIASTICALLY** to say something with great animation and friendly enthusiasm **6** *vi Scotland* **SOB** to blubber or snivel **7** *vt* **MAKE SOMETHING BUBBLE** to cause something to form bubbles or to move in bubbles through a liquid [14C. Probably an imitation of the sound of bubbling water.]

bubble and squeak *n* **1** a dish consisting of leftover cooked potatoes and cabbage chopped up and fried together **2** *Cockney* an offensive term for a Greek person (*rhyming slang offensive*) [Because of the sounds during cooking]

bubble bath *n* **1** a usually perfumed and coloured preparation in liquid or crystal form that is added to bath water in order to make it foam **2** a bath to which a preparation has been added to make the bath water foam

bubble car *n* a small two-seater car, usually three-wheeled, with a transparent, bubble-shaped dome or a single door in place of a bonnet

bubble chamber *n* a chamber containing a liquid, usually liquid hydrogen just above its boiling point, in which the trail of a particle can be observed as a line of bubbles created by the particle

bubble cut *n* a woman's hairstyle of short full curls

bubblegum /búbb'l gum/ *n* **1 CHEWING GUM THAT FORMS BUBBLES** chewing gum that can be blown from the mouth into large bubbles **2 POP MUSIC FOR TEENAGERS** commercial pop music aimed at the younger teenage market and usually considered to be lacking originality (*informal*) ■ *adj US* (*informal*) **1 APPEALING TO ADOLESCENTS** appealing to or characteristic of the style, taste, or behaviour of adolescents, especially when considered immature **2 BLAND, INSIPID, OR VAPID** lacking originality, careful mature thought, or seriousness

⚡**bubble-jet printer** *n* a printer in which heated ink forms bubbles that burst onto the paper

⚡**bubble memory** *n* computer memory in which data is stored as binary digits represented by the presence or absence of minute areas of magnetization in a semiconductor

bubble pack *n* = **blister pack**

bubble point *n* the temperature at which bubbles first appear when a liquid mixture is heated

bubbler /búbblər/ *n* **1** a device for bubbling gas through a liquid **2** something that emits bubbles, e.g. a mountain spring

bubble top *n* a transparent glass or plastic dome used in building, e.g. one forming a roof over a swimming pool

bubblewrap /búbb'l rap/ *n* a sheet of plastic material covered with air-filled bubbles, used for wrapping fragile objects in order to protect them in transit

bubbly /búbb'li/ *adj* (**-blier, -bliest**) **1 FOAMY OR EFFERVESCENT** full of or producing bubbles **2 LIKE BUBBLES** resembling a bubble or bubbles **3 CHEERFULLY EXCITED** feeling and exhibiting cheerful excitement ■ *n* **CHAMPAGNE** sparkling wine, especially champagne (*informal*) —**bubbliness** *n*

Buber /bóobər/, **Martin** (1878–1965) Austrian-born Israeli theologian and philosopher

bubo /byóobō/ (*plural* **-boes**) *n* swelling and inflammation of a lymph node, especially in the area of the armpit or groin [14C. Via Latin < Greek *boubōn* 'swelling in the groin'.]

bubonic /byoo bónnik/ *adj* describes a swelling (**bubo**) of the lymph nodes

bubonic plague *n* an infectious fatal epidemic disease caused by a bacterium *Yersinia pestis* transmitted by fleas that have bitten an infected host, and characterized by fever, chills, and the formation of swellings (**buboes**) [< Latin *bubon-*, stem of *bubo* (see BUBO)]

bubonocele /byoo bónnə seel/ *n* an incomplete hernia of the groin accompanied by swelling [Early 17C. Via modern Latin < Greek *boubōnokēlē* 'groin rupture'.]

buccal /búk'l/ *adj* **1** relating to or forming part of the cheek ○ *the buccal surface of a tooth* **2** relating to the mouth [Early 19C. < Latin *bucca* 'cheek'.]

buccaneer /búkə néer/ *n* **1 PIRATE** a pirate, especially one who preyed on Spanish colonies and shipping in the West Indies in the 17th century **2 UNSCRUPULOUS ADVENTURER OR BUSINESSPERSON** a ruthless or unscrupulous adventurer, businessperson, or politician ■ *vi* **ACT LIKE BUCCANEER** to be or behave like a buccaneer [Mid-17C. < French *boucanier* < *boucaner* 'cook over an open fire'.] —**buccaneering** *adj, n*

buccinator /búksi naytər/ *n* a flat thin muscle that compresses the cheek and is used in blowing and chewing [Late 17C. < Latin < *buccinare* 'blow the trumpet' < *buccina*, a kind of trumpet.]

Bucephalus /byoo séffələss/ *n* the favourite war horse of Alexander the Great, which he tamed when still a boy

Buchan /búkən/, **John, 1st Baron Tweedsmuir** (1875–1940) British writer and statesman

Buchanan /byoo kánnən/, **George** (1506–82) Scottish scholar and humanist

Buchanan, James (1791–1868) US statesman and 15th president of the United States (1857–61)

Bucharest /bóokə rést/ capital of Romania, in the SE of the country. Population: 2,037,000 (1997 estimate).

Buchenwald /bóokhən vald/ village in central Germany, site of a World War II Nazi concentration camp

Buchner /búknər, bóokhnər/, **Eduard** (1860–1917) German chemist

Büchner /byóokhnər/, **Georg** (1813–37) German dramatist

Buchner funnel /búknər-/, **Büchner funnel** *n* a cylindrical filter funnel with a flat perforated base through which liquids are drawn under reduced pressure [After Eduard BÜCHNER]

buchu /bóo koo/ (*plural* **-chus** *or* **-chu**), **bucku** (*plural* **-ckus** *or* **-cku**) *n* a southern African shrub with leaves that have medicinal properties. Use: mild diuretic, urinary antiseptic. Genus: *Agathosma.* [Mid-18C. Via Afrikaans < Nama.]

Buchwald /búk wawld/, **Art** (*b.* 1925) US journalist. Full name **Arthur Buchwald**

buck[1] /buk/ *n* **1 MALE ANIMAL** a male animal of some species, including antelope, deer, goat, kangaroo, and rabbit **2** (*plural* **buck** *or* **bucks**) *S Africa* **ANTELOPE OR DEER** an antelope or deer of either sex **3 VIRILE YOUNG MAN** a man, especially a strong, virile, impetuous, or spirited young man (*informal dated*) **4 DANDY OR FOP** a young man who takes elaborate care to be neat and stylish (*archaic*) [Old English *buc* 'male deer', *bucca* 'male goat' < Germanic]

buck up *v* **1** *vti* **MAKE OR BECOME MORE CHEERFUL** to raise the morale or spirits of somebody or to become more cheerful, confident, or encouraged (*informal*) **2** *vt* **IMPROVE** to make something better or smarter (*informal*) **3** *vi* **HURRY UP** to hurry or act more quickly (*informal dated*)

buck[2] /buk/ *v* **1** *vi* **JUMP UPWARDS** to jump or rear upwards with the back arched and the legs stiff **2** *vt* **THROW RIDER** to throw a rider by rearing or jumping upwards on the hind legs or forelegs **3** *vi US, Can* **MAKE JOLTING MOTION** to move in a jerky or erratic manner **4** *vti* **STAND IN OPPOSITION** to oppose or resist something obstinately (*informal*) **5** *vt* **GAMBLE AGAINST** to take a risk against something ○ *buck the odds* **6** *vt* **ENCOURAGE** to raise somebody's spirits or hopes (*usually passive*) **7** *vti US, Can* **BUTT WITH LOWERED HEAD** to charge against somebody or something with the head lowered ■ *n* **ACT OF BUCKING** the movement or action of bucking [Mid-19C. < BUCK[1].]

buck[3] /buk/ *n US, Can, ANZ* (*informal*) **1** a United States, Canadian, Australian, or New Zealand dollar **2** a specified or unspecified amount of money [Mid-19C. Shortening of BUCKSKIN, used as a unit of exchange on the American frontier.] ◇ **make a fast** *or* **quick buck** *US* to make a profit on a quick and often dishonest transaction

buck[4] /buk/ *n* **1** a covered block used as a vaulting horse **2** *US, Can* CONSTR = **sawhorse** [Early 19C. < BUCK[1].]

buck[5] /buk/ *n* a counter or marker formerly used in poker and passed from one player to another to indicate some obligation, especially somebody's turn to deal [Mid-19C. < ?] ◇ **pass the buck** to shift responsibility to somebody else (*informal*)

Buck /buk/, **Pearl S.** (1892–1973) US writer. Born **Pearl Sydenstricker**

Buck, Sir Peter (1879–1951) New Zealand anthropologist and politician. Born **Te Rangi Hiroa**

buckaroo /búkə róo/ (*plural* **-roos**), **buckeroo** (*plural* **-oos**) *n US* a cowhand in the SW United States (*informal*) [Early 19C. Alteration of Spanish *vaquero* 'cowboy', after BUCK[2].]

buckbean /búk been/ *n* a marsh plant of the gentian family. Flowers: white, pink, purplish. Native to: N hemisphere. *Menyanthes trifoliata.* [Late 16C. Translation of Flemish *boks boonen* 'goat's beans'.]

buckboard /búk bawrd/ *n US, Can* an open four-wheeled horse-drawn carriage with the seat or seats mounted on a flexible board between the front and rear axles [Late 17C. < obsolete *buck* 'belly, body (of a wagon)'.]

bucket /búkit/ *n* **1 CYLINDRICAL CONTAINER** a container, usually cylindrical in shape with an open top and a semicircular handle, used for catching or holding liquids or solids **2 BUCKETFUL** the contents of a bucket, or the amount that a bucket will hold **3 LARGE QUANTITY** a very large quantity or amount of something (*informal; often plural*) **4 SOMETHING LIKE A BUCKET** something resembling or suggesting a bucket in shape or function, e.g. a compartment on the outer edge of a water wheel **5 MACHINE PART** a machine part that resembles a bucket, e.g. the scoop on a mechanical shovel **6 FOOD CONTAINER** a large plastic or paper container for food, e.g. fried chicken or ice cream **7** TRANSP = **bucket seat** **8** BASKETBALL = **basket** *n.* 4 ■ *v* **1** *vt* **CARRY OR PUT SOMETHING IN BUCKET** to carry, hold, lift, or put something in a bucket **2** *vi* **POUR WITH RAIN** to rain very heavily (*informal*) **3** *vi* **MOVE FAST** to move or drive fast, jerkily, haphazardly, or recklessly (*informal*) ○ *We went bucketing down the motorway.* **4** *vt* **RIDE HORSE HARD** to ride a horse hard without consideration for the animal **5** *vt Aus* **ATTACK SOMEBODY VERBALLY** to criticize somebody severely, or denigrate somebody (*informal*) [13C. < Anglo-Norman *buket* < Germanic.] ◇ **kick the bucket** to die (*slang*)

bucket down *vi* to rain very heavily (*informal*)

bucket chain *n* a line of people formed to pass buckets of water from hand to hand in order to put out a fire

bucketful /búkitfòol/ *n* **1** the contents of a bucket or the amount that a bucket will hold **2** a very large quantity or amount of something (*usually plural*)

bucket ladder *n* a continuous chain of buckets used for excavating land or dredging riverbeds (*hyphenated before nouns*) ○ *bucket-ladder dredger*

bucket seat *n* an individual seat with a rounded back in a vehicle or aircraft

bucket shop *n* **1** a dishonest unregistered stockbroking firm that speculates on stocks and commodities using its clients' capital **2** any small business that cannot be relied on by customers, especially an unlicensed travel agency that buys airline tickets in bulk and sells them cheaply [Originally a saloon selling liquor from buckets]

buckeye /búk ī/ *n* **1** (*plural* **-eyes** *or* **-eye**) a tree or shrub of the horse chestnut family. Native to: North America. Genus: *Aesculus.* **2** a prickly or smooth fruit of a buckeye tree, or the large shiny brown poisonous seed it contains [Mid-18C. Because of the seed's resemblance to a deer's eye.]

buck fever *n* (*informal*) **1** nervous excitement felt by an inexperienced hunter at the sight of game **2** nervous excitement felt by somebody faced with a new situation, experience, or responsibility

buckhorn /búk hawrn/ *n* **1 MATERIAL FROM A BUCK'S HORN** the material from the horn of a male deer or antelope. Use: handles for knives and tools. **2 HORN OF BUCK** the horn of a male deer or antelope 3 (*plural* **-horns** *or* **-horn**) **PLANT WITH LEAVES RESEMBLING ANIMAL'S HORN** a plant with leaves shaped like the horn of a deer or antelope. Native to: Europe, Asia. *Plantago coronopus*.

buckie /búki/ *n Scotland* 1 **SHELLFISH OR SHELL** a shellfish with a spiral shell, or the shell itself 2 **OBSTINATE PERSON** an obstinate person 3 **LIVELY PERSON** a lively person [Early 16C. Probably alteration of Latin *buccinum* 'whelk'.]

Buckingham /búkingəm/, **George Villiers, 2nd Duke of** (1628–87) English courtier

Buckingham Palace *n* the official London residence of the British monarch, built in 1703

Buckinghamshire /búkingəmshər/ county in S England. Population: 473,000 (1995). Area: 727sq. km/1,883 sq. mi.

Buckland /búklənd/, **William** (1784–1856) British geologist and cleric

buckle /búk'l/ *n* 1 **METAL FASTENER** a clasp, typically consisting of a metal frame with a hinged prong, for fastening two loose ends, especially of a belt, shoe, or strap 2 **ORNAMENT RESEMBLING BUCKLE** an ornament that resembles a buckle, e.g. on a shoe or a hat 3 **BULGING OR BENDING PART** a bend or kink in something such as a rope, or a bulge in something such as a piece of wood ■ *v* (**-les, -ling, -led**) 1 *vti* **FASTEN SOMETHING WITH BUCKLE** to fasten something, e.g. a shoe or seat belt, with a buckle, or be fastened with such a device 2 *vti* **BEND OR CAUSE SOMETHING TO BEND** to bend out of shape, warp, or crumple, usually because of heat or pressure, or distort something in this way 3 *vi* **COLLAPSE** to collapse or lose strength completely, sometimes as a result of a structural defect or weakness 4 *vi* **GIVE IN** to succumb or yield to pressure, especially emotional strain or fear [14C. Via Anglo-Norman *bucle*, Old French *bocle* < Latin *buccula* 'cheek strap of a helmet' < *bucca* 'cheek'.]
buckle down *vi* to set out to accomplish something with vigour or determination (*informal*)
buckle to *vi* to make a determined or special effort
buckle under *vi* to give in under pressure or stress
buckle up *vti* to fasten the buckle on a seat belt, e.g. in a motor vehicle or an aircraft

buckler /búklər/ *n* a small round shield either worn on the forearm or held by a short handle at arm's length [13C. < Old French *bocler* < *bocle* 'boss of a shield' (see BUCKLE).]

buckler fern *n* a perennial deciduous or semi-evergreen fern that grows to about 1 m/3 ft in height. Native to: Europe. Genus: *Dryopteris*. [Because of the flap of tissue covering the receptacle in which its spores are formed]

Buckley /búkli/, **William F. Jr** (*b.* 1925) US writer and editor. Full name **William Frank Buckley, Jr**

Buckley's chance /búkliz-/, **Buckley's hope** *n ANZ* no chance whatsoever of doing or accomplishing something (*informal*) [Late 19C. < ?]

buckminsterfullerene /búkminstər fóòlə reen/ *n* a stable form (**allotrope**) of carbon containing 60 atoms [Late 20C. < the molecule's resemblance to the geodesic dome structure invented by R. Buckminster FULLER.]

bucko /búkō/ (*plural* **-os**) *n* 1 a swaggering bully or bossy person (*slang*) 2 *Ireland, US* a boy or man (*informal*) [Late 19C. < BUCK[1].]

buck-passing *n* the shifting of blame or responsibility to somebody else (*informal*) [< BUCK[5]] —**buck-passer** *n*

buckram /búkrəm/ *n* **STIFF FABRIC** a coarse cotton or linen fabric that has been stiffened with starch, gum, or latex. Use: bookbinding, clothes stiffener. ■ *adj* **LIKE BUCKRAM** resembling buckram in rigidity ■ *vt* **STIFFEN SOMETHING WITH BUCKRAM** to stiffen or strengthen something with buckram [14C. < Old French *boquerant* 'cloth from Bukhara'.]

buck rarebit *n* Welsh rarebit topped with a poached egg

Bucks. *abbr* Buckinghamshire

bucksaw /búk saw/ *n* a woodcutting saw in which the blade is set in an H-shaped frame [Mid-19C. < BUCK[4].]

buck's fizz, Buck's fizz *n* a cocktail made of champagne mixed with orange juice [Mid-20C. After *Buck's Club* in London.]

buckshee /búk shée/ *adj* (*informal*) 1 **FREE** given or obtained without charge 2 **NOT ASKED FOR** given without being asked for ■ *adv* **WITHOUT CHARGING** free of charge (*informal*) [Early 17C. Alteration of BAKSHEESH.]

buckshot /búk shot/ *n* a large size of lead shot used in shotgun shells, especially for hunting game

buckskin /búk skin/ *n* 1 **DEERSKIN** the skin of a male deer 2 **SOFT LEATHER** a soft pliable greyish-yellow leather, usually with a suede finish, originally made from deerskin and now usually from sheepskin ■ **buckskins** *npl US* **BUCKSKIN GARMENTS** clothing made from buckskin leather, especially jackets, chaps, hats, and moccasins ■ *adj* **GREYISH-YELLOW** greyish-yellow in colour

buckthorn /búk thawrn/ (*plural* **-thorns** *or* **-thorn**) *n* a thorny shrub or small tree with black berries. Genus: *Rhamnus*. [Late 16C. Translation of modern Latin *cervi spina* 'stag's thorn'.]

bucktooth /búk tòoth/ (*plural* **-teeth** /búk tèeth/) *n* a protruding upper front tooth (*informal*) —**bucktoothed** *adj*

bucku *n* TREES = **buchu**

buckwheat /búk weet/ *n* 1 a triangular seed 2 a plant that produces buckwheat that is ground into flour. Native to: Asia. *Fagopyrum esculentum*. [Mid-16C. Anglicization of Middle Dutch *boecweite* 'beech wheat'; because its grains resemble beech nuts.]

buckyball /búki bawl/ *n* a stable ball-shaped molecule of carbon (**fullerene**), especially the molecule containing 60 atoms (**buckminsterfullerene**) (*informal*) [Late 20C. < *Bucky*, nickname of R. Buckminster FULLER.]

bucolic /byoo kóllik/ *adj* 1 **OF COUNTRYSIDE** relating to or characteristic of the countryside or country life ○ *a writer of bucolic poems* 2 **OF SHEPHERDS** relating to or characteristic of shepherds, herdsmen, or flocks ■ *n* 1 **PASTORAL POEM** a poem about the countryside or country life 2 **COUNTRY PERSON** a farmer, shepherd, or other person from the country [Early 16C. Via Latin, < Greek *boukolikos* < *boukolos* 'cowherd'.] —**bucolically** *adv*

bud[1] /bud/ *n* 1 **OUTGROWTH ON PLANT STEM** an outgrowth on a stem or branch consisting of a shortened stem and immature leaves or flowers, often enclosed by protective scales 2 **UNOPENED FLOWER** a flower that has not yet opened 3 **REPRODUCTIVE OUTGROWTH OF SIMPLE ORGANISM** an asexually produced outgrowth of a simple organism, e.g. an invertebrate or a yeast, that breaks away from the parent and develops into a new individual 4 **SOMETHING RESEMBLING PLANT BUD** something shaped like a plant bud 5 **SOMEBODY OR SOMETHING IMMATURE** somebody or something that is small, immature, or not yet fully developed ■ *v* (**buds, budding, budded**) 1 *vi* **PRODUCE PLANT BUDS** to produce outgrowths that develop into flowers or leaves 2 *vi* **START TO GROW** to start to develop or grow from a plant bud 3 *vi* **BEGIN TO DEVELOP** to begin to develop or grow from something small into another, usually larger, thing ○ *Seeds of dissent are budding in the heartland.* 4 *vi* **REPRODUCE ASEXUALLY** to reproduce asexually by producing an outgrowth that eventually separates to form a new individual, as occurs in invertebrates and yeasts 5 *vt* **GRAFT BUD INTO ANOTHER PLANT** to insert a bud from one plant into the bark of another, usually one of a different variety, in order to propagate a plant from the bud [14C. < ?] —**budder** *n* —**budless** *adj* ◇ **nip something in the bud** to put an end to a plan or idea before it can be developed (*informal*) ◇ **in bud** having new buds that have not yet opened

bud[2] /bud/ *n US* = **buddy** *n.* 2 (*informal*) [Mid-19C. Shortening.]

Budapest /bóòdə pést/ capital of Hungary, in the N of the country. Population: 1,861,383 (1998 estimate).

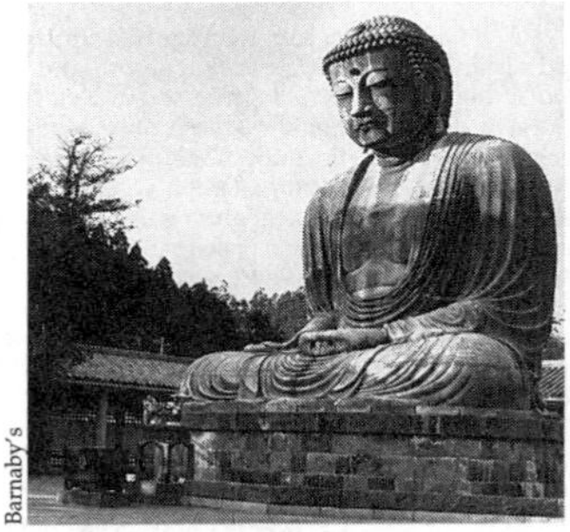

Barnaby's

Buddha: Daibutsu (Great Buddha), Kamakura, Japan

buddha /bóòddə/, **Buddha** *n* 1 in Buddhism, somebody who has attained perfect enlightenment 2 a statue, picture, or other representation of the Buddha [Late 17C. < Sanskrit, past participle of *budh-* 'wake up, be enlightened'.]

Buddha /bóòddə/ (563?–483? BC) Nepalese-born Indian philosopher. Born **Siddharta Gautama**

Buddhahood /bóòddəhòod/ *n* the state of spiritual enlightenment attained by the Buddha

Buddhism /bóòddizəm/ *n* a world religion or philosophy based on the teaching of the Buddha and holding that a state of enlightenment can be attained by suppressing worldly desires

Buddhist /bóòddist/ *n* somebody who professes Buddhism —**Buddhist** *adj* —**Buddhistic** /boo dístik/ *adj*

budding /búdding/ *adj* **PROMISING** beginning to show a particular talent ○ *a budding actor* ■ *n* 1 **DEVELOPMENT OF BUDS** the formation and growth of buds on a plant stem 2 **GRAFTING A BUD** artificial propagation, especially of woody plants, by grafting a bud from one variety onto the stem of another 3 **ASEXUAL REPRODUCTION** a form of asexual reproduction in which an outgrowth of the parent becomes constricted and eventually separates to form a new individual, as occurs in invertebrates and yeasts

buddle /búdd'l/ *n* a sloping trough in which crushed ore is separated from waste by washing with water [Mid-16C. < ?]

buddleia /búdli ə/ (*plural* **-ias** *or* **-ia**) *n* a deciduous ornamental shrub or small tree with flowers that attract butterflies. Flowers: small, scented, purple, in tapering heads. Native to: South America. *Buddleja davidii*. [Late 18C. < modern Latin, after Adam *Buddle*.]

buddy /búddi/ *n* (*plural* **-dies**) 1 *US, Can* **FRIEND** a good friend, colleague, companion, or partner (*informal*) 2 *US, Can* **TERM OF ADDRESS** a form of address to a man or boy (*informal*) ○ *Hey, buddy!* 3 **HELPER TO AIDS PATIENT** a volunteer who gives help and support to somebody who has Aids ■ *vi* (**-dies, -dying, -died**) **ACT AS AIDS HELPER** to act as a helper to somebody with Aids [Mid-19C. Perhaps alteration of BROTHER.]

buddy-buddy *adj US* appearing to enjoy a close friendship (*informal*)

buddy movie, buddy film *n* a style of film focusing on the adventures and friendship of two central characters of the same gender

buddy system *n US* an arrangement by which individuals are paired for mutual safety, e.g. in mountain climbing

Buderim /búddərəm/ coastal town in S Queensland, Australia. Population: 12,458 (1996).

budge[1] /buj/ (**budges, budging, budged**) *vti* 1 to move, or to alter the position of something by movement (*usually with negatives*) ○ *I tried moving the machine, but it wouldn't budge.* 2 to change or make somebody change an attitude, decision, or opinion ○ *Once she's made up her mind, no amount of persuasion will budge her.* [Late 16C. Via French *bouger* < assumed Vulgar Latin *bullicare* 'keep bubbling up' < Latin *bullire* (see BOIL[1]).]

budge[2] /buj/ *n* a type of fur, usually lambskin, worn with the wool outwards ■ *adj* made from, trimmed with, or lined with budge [14C. < ?]

Budge /buj/, **Don** (1915–2000) US tennis player. Full name **John Donald Budge**

budgerigar /bújjəri gaar/ *n* a small bright green parrot with a yellow head that is a popular cagebird. Native to: central Australia. *Melopsittacus undulatus*. [Mid-19C. < Yuwaalaraay *gijirigaa*.]

budget /bújjit/ *n* 1 **SUMMARY OF INCOME AND SPENDING** an often itemized estimate of income and spending, e.g. of a country or company, during a specified period 2 **PLAN FOR ALLOCATING RESOURCES** a plan specifying how resources, especially time or money, will be spent or allocated during a particular period 3 **MONEY FOR SPECIFIC PURPOSE** the total amount of money allocated or needed for a specific purpose or period of time 4 **QUANTITY OR SUPPLY** a specified quantity, stock, or supply ■ *adj* **CHEAP OR ECONOMICAL** suitable for people with a limited amount of money to spend ■ *v* 1 *vti* **PLAN SPENDING** to plan the allocation, expenditure, or use of resources, especially money or time 2 *vt* **ENTER IN BUDGET** to make provision for something, or enter something in a budget 3 *vi* **LIVE WITHIN SPENDING LIMITS** to live within a budget ○ *Having budgeted well all their lives, they can afford to retire early.* [15C. < Old French *bougette* 'leather pouch, purse' < *bouge* (see BULGE).] —**budgetary** *adj*

Budget /bújjit/ *n* a statement of the financial position of the United Kingdom for the financial year, with proposals for spending and taxation, presented in a speech by the Chancellor of the Exchequer

budget account *n* an account with a department store or other large organization that enables a customer to pay in regular or monthly instalments for goods or services obtained on credit

budget deficit *n* the amount of government expenditure that exceeds revenue

budgie /bújji/ *n* a budgerigar, especially one kept as a domestic pet (*informal*) [Early 20C. Shortening.]

bud scale *n* any of the scaly leaves that form a protective sheath around a plant bud and are sometimes hairy or resinous

budworm /búd wurm/ *n* a moth larva that feeds on conifer buds and is one of the most destructive pests in North America. *Harmolga fumiferana.*

Buenaventura /bwáynə ven tóorə, -tyóorə/ major port on the Pacific Coast of W Colombia. Population: 266,988 (1985).

Bueno /bwáynō/, **Maria** (*b.* 1940) Brazilian tennis player

Buenos Aires /bwáy noss íriz/ capital of Argentina, in the E of the country. Population: 2,965,403 (1991).

buff[1] /buf/ *n* **1 PALE YELLOWISH-BROWN** a dull yellowish-beige colour **2 SOFT LEATHER** a soft thick undyed leather that is made chiefly from the skins of buffalo, elk, or oxen and has a light yellow colour **3 POLISHING CLOTH** a cloth of soft material such as leather or velvet, often mounted on a block and used for polishing **4 POLISHING DISC** a revolving disc consisting of layers of cloth impregnated with abrasive powders. Use: polishing metal or other hard bright surfaces. **5 LEATHER GARMENT** a garment made of buff leather, e.g. a military uniform coat ■ *adj* **1 PALE YELLOWISH-BROWN** of a buff colour **2 OF BUFF LEATHER** made of buff leather ■ *vt* **1 POLISH** to clean or polish something with a piece of soft material **2 MAKE SURFACE SOFT** to make the surface of something, especially of leather, soft and velvety like buff by raising a nap [Late 16C. Alteration of French *buffle* 'buffalo' < late Latin *bufalus* (see BUFFALO).]
◇ **in the buff** naked (*informal*)

buff up *vi US* to become or make yourself physically fit and strong through exercise and diet (*informal*)

buff[2] /buf/ *n* somebody who is enthusiastic and knowledgeable about something ○ *a movie buff* ○ *an opera buff* [Early 19C. < the buff-leather overcoats formerly worn by volunteer firefighters ('fire buffs') in New York City.]

buff[3] /buf/ *vt* to deaden or reduce the force of something [15C. < Old French *bufe* (see BUFFET[2]).]

buff[4] /buf/ *adj US* physically fit and strong, especially through exercise and a controlled diet (*Informal*) [Late 20C. Probably < BUFF[1].]

buffalo /búffəlō/ *n* (*plural* **-loes** *or* **-los** *or* **-lo**) **1 TYPE OF HORNED CATTLE** a type of horned cattle belonging to various species, including the African buffalo and domesticated breeds of the Asian water buffalo. Family: Bovidae. **2** *US* **N AMERICAN BISON** the North American bison **3** ZOOL = **buffalo fish** ■ *vt* (**-loes, -loing, -loed**) (*informal*) **1** *US, Can* **BAFFLE** to throw somebody into a state of confusion and puzzled bewilderment **2** *Can* **INTIMIDATE** to coerce or inhibit somebody aggressively [Mid-16C. Via Portuguese or Italian < late Latin *bufalus* < Greek *boubalos* 'gazelle'.]

Buffalo /búffəlō/ port in W New York State. Population: 300,717 (1998 estimate).

Buffalo, Mount mountain in N Victoria, Australia. Height: 1,723 m/5,653 ft.

Buffalo Bill /búffəlō bíl/ (1846–1917) US scout and statesman. Born **William Frederick Cody**

buffalo fish *n* a large freshwater fish of the sucker family that resembles the carp and has a humped back. Native to: Mississippi Valley. Genus: *Ictiobus.*

buffalo grass *n* a short grey-green grass of the plains of central North America that is used as forage and for lawns. *Buchloë dactyloides.*

Buffalo wings *npl US, Can* fried chicken wings, typically served in barbecue sauce [Because supposedly first served in a restaurant in or named after BUFFALO]

ϟ **buffer**[1] /búffər/ *n* **1 PROTECTOR AGAINST IMPACT** somebody or something that reduces shock or impact or protects against other harm, usually by interception **2 DEVICE ON TRAIN OR TRACK** a spring-loaded or hydraulic pad attached to the end of rolling stock or at the end of a railway track that stops the train running off the end of the track **3 SUBSTANCE MAINTAINING PH** a substance that minimizes a change in pH of a solution by neutralizing added acids and bases, or a solution containing such a substance **4 MEMORY AREA** a temporary storage area for data being transmitted between two devices that function at different speeds ■ *vt* **1 CUSHION SOMETHING AGAINST SHOCK** to protect something against impact, or reduce the shock of an impact **2 ADD BUFFER TO SOLUTION** to add to a solution a substance that will keep its pH constant [Mid-19C. < obsolete *buff* 'hit something softly', perhaps < French *bufe* (see BUFFET[2]).]

buffer[2] /búffər/ *n* **1** somebody who polishes something with a buffer **2** INDUST = **buff**[1] *n.* **2** **3** TEXTILES = **buff**[1] *n.* **3** **4** ENG = **buff**[1] *n.* **4** [Mid-19C. < BUFF[1].]

buffer[3] /búffər/ *n* a bumbling or indecisive person, especially a man (*informal insult*) [Mid-18C. < obsolete *buff* 'stammer', probably an imitation of the sound.]

buffer state *n* a small neutral state that lies between two potentially hostile powers and reduces the risk of conflict between them

buffer stock *n* a stock of a basic commodity accumulated by a government, e.g. when supplies are plentiful and prices low, and held for use when supplies are short to stabilize the price

buffer zone *n* **1** a neutral area that lies between hostile forces and reduces the risk of conflict between them **2** any area designed to form a barrier that prevents potential conflict or harmful contact

buffet[1] /bóo fay/ *n* **1 SELF-SERVICE MEAL** a meal at which people serve themselves from various dishes set out on a table, sideboard, or counter **2 TABLE WITH REFRESHMENTS** a serving counter or table on which meals or refreshments are displayed **3** RAIL = **buffet car** **4 DINING-ROOM SERVING TABLE** a piece of dining-room furniture with drawers for storing tableware [Early 18C. < French, 'footstool, sideboard'.]

buffet[2] /búffit/ *n* **1 BLOW WITH HAND** a blow struck with the fist or hand **2 REPEATED BLOW** a heavy or repeated blow or stroke **3** AIR = **buffeting** ■ *v* **1** *vt* **BATTER** to knock or strike against something forcefully or repeatedly **2** *vt* **HIT SOMETHING SHARPLY** to hit something sharply, especially with the hand **3** *vi* **STRUGGLE TO PROGRESS** to proceed under difficult conditions [Pre-12C. < Old French, 'small blow' < *bufe* 'blow', originally an imitation of the sound.] —**buffeter** *n*

buffet car *n* a railway carriage where light refreshments and beverages are served

buffeting /búffiting/ *n* an irregular shaking of a part or the whole of an aircraft during flight, typically caused by strong winds

buffi plural of **buffo**

buffing wheel *n* a wheel covered with a soft material such as lamb's wool, leather, or velvet and used to shine or polish something, especially metal

bufflehead /búff'l hed/ (*plural* **-heads** *or* **-head**) *n* a small diving duck, the male of which has black and white plumage and a large fluffy head, while the female is dark brown. Native to: North America. *Bucephala albeola.* [Mid-17C. < obsolete *buffle* 'buffalo' < French (see BUFF[1]); because of its large head.]

buffo /bóoffō/ (*plural* **-fi** /-fee/ *or* **-fos**) *n* a male singer of comic roles in opera [Mid-18C. < Italian, < *buffare* (see BUFFOON).] —**buffo** *adj*

buffoon /bə fóon/ *n* **1** somebody who amuses others by clowning or joking **2** somebody behaving in a mildly inappropriate way [Mid-16C. Via French < Italian *buffone* < *buffare* 'puff, act the clown', an imitation of the sound.]

buffoonery /bə fóonəri/ *n* silly behaviour

buff-tip moth *n* a large European moth that resembles a twig when it wraps its cream-tipped wings around its body. *Phalera bucephala.*

buff wheel *n* = **buffing wheel**

ϟ **bug** /bug/ *n* **1 TYPE OF INSECT** an insect with thickened forewings and mouthparts adapted for piercing and sucking. Order: Hemiptera. **2** *US, Can* **ANY INSECT** any insect or similar organism, especially one considered to be a pest, e.g. an aphid, bedbug, or cockroach **3 GERM** any unspecified germ or microorganism that causes mild illness (*informal*) **4 AILMENT CAUSED BY GERM** any mild ailment that is caused by an unspecified microorganism (*informal*) **5 CRAZE OR OBSESSION** a strong and often widespread enthusiasm for or obsession with something (*informal*) **6 DEVOTEE** a fan or devotee of something (*informal dated*) **7 DEFECT** a defect or flaw in a design, machine, or system (*informal*) **8 PROGRAMMING ERROR** an error in a computer program (*informal*) **9 HIDDEN LISTENING DEVICE** a concealed electronic device, usually a small microphone, that is used for listening to or recording private conversations (*informal*) ■ *vt* (**bugs, bugging, bugged**) **1 PESTER** to cause somebody persistent trouble and annoyance (*informal*) ○ *Go away and stop bugging me!* **2 HIDE LISTENING DEVICE IN** to conceal an electronic listening device in something ○ *She suspected her phone had been bugged.* **3 LISTEN TO SOMETHING SECRETLY** to listen to or eavesdrop on a conversation using an electronic surveillance device ○ *He thinks someone is bugging his phone conversations.* [14C. < ?]

SYNONYMS See ***bother***.

bugaboo /búggə boo/ (*plural* **-boos**) *n* something that causes fear, annoyance, or trouble, especially an imagined threat or problem [Mid-18C. < ?]

Buganda /bóo gándə/ former kingdom in S Uganda

Bugatti /boo gátti/, **Ettore** (1882–1947) Italian automobile designer and manufacturer

bugbane /búg bayn/ *n* a perennial plant that has large compound leaves. Flowers: small, white, in spike-shaped clusters. Native to: Europe. *Cimicifuga foetida.* [Because its flowers are reputed to repel insects]

bugbear /búg bair/ *n* **1 SOURCE OF FEAR** a source of obsessive or groundless fear **2 CONTINUING PROBLEM** a continuing source of annoyance or difficulty **3 GOBLIN** a goblin invented to frighten children, traditionally in the form of a bear that eats those who misbehave [Late 16C. < obsolete *bug* 'hobgoblin' + BEAR[1] *n.* 1.]

bug-eyed *adj* (*informal*) **1** having protruding eyes **2** wide-eyed with amazement or fear

bugger[1] /búggər/ *n* **1 TABOO TERM** a highly offensive term for somebody who practises anal intercourse (*taboo*) **2 OFFENSIVE TERM** an offensive term for a person or thing regarded as unpleasant, difficult, or contemptible (*slang*) **3 PERSON OF A PARTICULAR TYPE** used to refer to somebody with a particular characteristic or in a particular situation (*slang; often considered offensive*) ■ *v* **1** *vti* **TABOO TERM** a highly offensive term meaning to practise anal intercourse with somebody (*taboo*) **2** *vt* **OFFENSIVE TERM** an offensive term meaning to damage, ruin, or spoil something (*slang*) **3** *vt* **OFFENSIVE TERM** an offensive term meaning to make somebody thoroughly exhausted (*slang*) **4** *vt* **OFFENSIVE TERM** an offensive term used as a swearword to express annoyance or frustration (*slang; can be in the passive, especially to express an absolute refusal*) ■ *interj* **OFFENSIVE TERM** an offensive term used as swearword to express annoyance or frustration (*slang*) [Mid-16C. Via French *bougre* 'heretic' < medieval Latin *Bulgarus* 'Bulgarian (belonging to the Orthodox Church)'; from a Western Christian association of heresy with anal intercourse.]

bugger off *vi* a highly offensive term meaning to go away or get out, usually inopportunely (*taboo*)

bugger up *vt* a highly offensive term meaning to spoil or ruin something (*taboo*)

bugger[2] /búggər/ *n* somebody who plants listening devices in something

buggery /búggəri/ *n* **1** a highly offensive term for anal intercourse (*taboo*) **2** an offensive term used as an intensifier (*slang*)

buggy[1] /búggi/ (*plural* **-gies**) *n* **1 HORSE-DRAWN VEHICLE** a lightweight horse-drawn carriage **2 BATTERY-POWERED VEHICLE** a small battery-powered vehicle used for a special purpose ○ *a golf buggy* **3** *US* **PRAM** a light pram **4 PUSHCHAIR** a lightweight pushchair for young children [Mid-18C. < ?]

buggy[2] /búggi/ (**-gier, -giest**) *adj* infested with insects [Early 18C. < BUG.] —**bugginess** *n*

bugle[1] /byóog'l/ *n* a brass instrument like a short trumpet without valves, used for military signals [14C. Via Old French < Latin *buculus*, diminutive of *bos* 'ox'.] —**bugle** *vi* —**bugler** *n*

bugle[2] /byóog'l/ *n* a creeping plant related to mint. Flowers: blue, pink, white. Native to: Europe, Asia. Genus: *Ajuga*. US term **bugleweed** *n.* [13C. Directly or via Old French, < late Latin *bugula*.]

bugle bead, bugle *n* a tube-shaped bead made of glass or plastic used in embroidery or bead trimmings [Late 16C. < ?]

bugleweed /byóog'l weed/ *n US* = **bugle**[2]

bugloss /byoo gloss/ n a hairy plant related to borage. Flowers: blue, drooping in clusters. Genus: *Lycopsis*. [14C. < Latin *buglossus* < Greek *buglõssus* 'oxtongued' (from the shape and roughness of the leaves).]

bugong, bugong moth n = **bogong**

buhl /bool/ n FURNITURE = **boulle** [Early 19C. Via German < French *boulle* (SEE BOULLE).]

buhrstone /búr stòn/, **burstone, burrstone** n 1 rough hard quartz rock. Use: formerly, millstones, grindstones. 2 a millstone or grindstone made from buhrstone [Mid-17C. < variant of BURR[1] (because of the stone's roughness).]

⫯build /bild/ v (**builds, building, built** /bilt/, **built**) 1 vt MAKE SOMETHING BY JOINING PARTS to make a structure by fitting the parts of it together ○ *to build a wall* 2 vt HAVE SOMETHING BUILT to have a building or other structure made ○ *The emperor built a number of these pavilions.* 3 vti FORM OR DEVELOP to form or develop an enterprise or relationship ○ *building a solid business reputation* 4 vt COLLECT A SET OF PLAYING CARDS in card games, to form a set by gathering related cards 5 vi INCREASE to increase or mount steadily ○ *Tension is starting to build.* ■ n 1 BODY STRUCTURE the physical structure, shape, and size of a person ○ *the wrestler's heavy build* 2 STAGE OF SOFTWARE DEVELOPMENT a stage in the development of computer software in which two or more independently developed software components are linked so that they can be tested in conjunction with one another ○ *testing the first build of the software* 3 STANDARD OF CONSTRUCTION the standard of construction of something, e.g. a vehicle [Old English *byldan* 'construct a house' < *bold* 'dwelling' < Germanic, 'dwell'.]

build in vt 1 to construct a piece of furniture so that it becomes part of the structure of a room or to add an object so that it becomes part of something else 2 to create or add something to a system or organization ○ *They built in the shelves.*

build into vt to create or add something as a permanent feature ○ *These safeguards will be built into the system.*

build on v 1 vt to use something as a basis for further development or improvement ○ *hoping to build on the success of their first CD* 2 vi to add something as an extra part joined to an existing building ○ *The porch was built on about ten years later.*

build up v 1 vti DEVELOP to increase or develop gradually ○ *Traffic is building up on the motorway.* 2 vt PRAISE EXCESSIVELY to emphasize or exaggerate the good qualities of somebody or something ○ *I expected someone more impressive after the way she built him up.* 3 vt MAKE SOMEBODY STRONGER AND HEALTHIER to make somebody stronger and healthier, especially by feeding

build up to vt to develop towards a point or climax

builder /bíldər/ n 1 a person or company engaged in building or repairing houses or other large structures 2 a detergent additive that improves cleaning properties

LITERARY LINK *The Master Builder*, a play (1845) by Norwegian dramatist Henrik Ibsen. It is the story of a successful architect, Halvard Solness, who is disturbed by his continued good fortune. His search for redemption eventually leads to his own death.

building /bílding/ n 1 a structure with walls and a roof, e.g. a house or factory 2 the business or task of constructing houses, factories, bridges, and other large structures (often before nouns) ○ *building materials*

building block n 1 BRICK-SHAPED CONSTRUCTION BLOCK a large block of concrete or similar hard material, used for building houses and other large structures 2 CHILD'S TOY BLOCK one of a set of children's wooden or plastic bricks 3 COMPONENT an element or component regarded as contributing to the growth of an organization, plan, or system ○ *He acquired companies as building blocks for his financial empire.*

building line n a line on a property beyond which no building is allowed

building paper n a damp-proofing and insulating material consisting of a bitumen and fibre mix sandwiched between heavy-duty paper

building society n a financial organization that pays interest on savings accounts, lends money for buying and improving houses, and provides other banking services

buildup /bíld up/ n 1 a large amount of something or a number of things gradually accumulated or developed ○ *prevents the buildup of plaque* 2 a description that em-

phasizes or exaggerates the good qualities of somebody or something

built past tense and past participle of **build**

built environment n the part of the environment that consists of buildings and structures, as opposed to the countryside or the natural world

built heritage n the part of a country's heritage that consists of buildings and structures, as opposed to natural or aesthetic assets

built-in adj 1 designed or fitted as a fixed or permanent part 2 forming a natural feature or characteristic

built-in obsolescence n MANUF = **planned obsolescence**

built-up adj 1 describes an area that has many buildings 2 having several layers or added thickness ○ *built-up heels*

Bujumbura /boojəm boorə/ capital of Burundi, in the W of the country. Population: 634,479 (1991 estimate).

Bukavu /boo kaa voo/ city in E Democratic Republic of the Congo. Population: 418,000 (1985).

Bukhara /boo khaarə/ city in S Uzbekistan. Population: 236,000 (1994).

Bukhari /boo khaari/ (810–870) Arabian scholar. Full name **Muhammad Ibn-Ismail al- Bukhari**

Bukharin /boo kaarin, -khaarin/, **Nicolay Ivanovich** (1888–1938) Russian revolutionary and political theorist

Bulawayo /boolla wáyó/ city in SW Zimbabwe. Population: 620,936 (1992).

bulb /bulb/ n 1 UNDERGROUND PLANT PART any underground plant storage organ, e.g. a corm, tuber, or rhizome, from which a new plant grows every year 2 PLANT GROWING FROM BULB a plant that develops from a bulb or other underground storage organ, e.g. a tulip or crocus 3 ROUNDED PART a rounded part of something, e.g. the mercury reservoir of a thermometer or the squeezable rubber ball on a dropper 4 = **light bulb** 5 ROUNDED PART OF BODY ORGAN a rounded or enlarged section of a cylindrical body part [Mid-16C. Via Latin *bulbus* < Greek *bolbos* 'bulbous root, onion'.]

bulbil /búl bil/, **bulbel** /búlb'l/ n a new bulb growing like a bud on a plant or leaf stem [Mid-19C. < modern Latin *bulbillus*, diminutive of Latin *bulbus* (SEE BULB).]

bulbourethral gland /búlbō yoo reéthral-/ n ANAT = **Cowper's gland** [Mid-18C. < Latin *bulbus* (SEE BULB)]

bulbous /búlbəss/ adj 1 rounded and swollen-looking 2 growing from a plant bulb —**bulbously** adv —**bulbousness** n

bulbul /bool bool/ n 1 a greyish or brownish songbird. Native to: tropical Africa and Asia. Family: Pycnonotidae. 2 a songbird frequently mentioned in Persian poetry, taken to be the nightingale [Mid-17C. < Persian, an imitation of its song.]

Bulgakov /bool gaa kof/, **Mikhail** (1891–1940) Ukrainian writer

bulgar n = **bulgur**

Bulgar /búl gaar/ n a member of an ancient Slavic people who settled in areas of present-day Bulgaria around the 7th century AD [Mid-18C. < medieval Latin *Bulgarus* < Old Church Slavonic *Blugary* (plural) 'Bulgars'.]

Bulgaria

Bulgaria /bul gáiri ə/ republic in SE Europe, on the Black Sea. Capital: Sofia. Population: 8,290,988 (1997). Area: 110,994 sq. km/42,855 sq. mi.

Bulgarian /bul gáiri ən/ n 1 somebody who comes from Bulgaria 2 the official language of Bulgaria, belonging to the South Slavonic group of Indo-European languages. Native speakers: 9 million. —**Bulgarian** adj

bulge /bulj/ vi (**bulges, bulging, bulged**) 1 SWELL to expand or swell 2 BE OVERFILLED to contain so much that the sides expand outwards (*informal*) ■ n 1 PART THAT EXPANDS OUTWARDS an area or part that curves or has expanded outwards 2 INCREASE a sudden temporary increase ○ *a bulge in the population figures* 3 BABY BOOM a baby boom (*informal*) [12C. Via Old French *boulge* 'leather sack, bag' < Latin *bulga* < Gaulish.] —**bulginess** n —**bulging** adj —**bulgingly** adv —**bulgy** adj

bulgur /búlgər/, **bulghur, bulgar, bulgur wheat** n wheat that has been parboiled, dried, and cracked into small pieces, and is a common ingredient in Middle Eastern and vegetarian cooking [Mid-20C. Via Turkish < Persian *bulgūr* 'bruised grain'.]

bulimia /byoo límmi ə/ n a condition in which bouts of overeating are followed by undereating, use of laxatives, or self-induced vomiting [14C. Via modern Latin < Greek *boulimia* 'hunger of an ox' < *bous* 'ox' + *limos* 'hunger'.] —**bulimic** adj, n

bulk /bulk/ n 1 LARGE SIZE large size or mass 2 THE GREATER PART the greater part of something 3 LARGE BODY a large or overweight person's body 4 CARGO a ship's cargo 5 PART OF SHIP the part of a ship where cargo is stored 6 FIBRE IN FOOD the indigestible fibre that is a constituent of some food ■ adj IN LARGE QUANTITY in or of a large quantity [15C. Partly < Old Norse *búlki* 'heap' (< Indo-European, 'swell'); partly < Old English *búc* 'belly' (< Germanic).] ◇ **bulk large** to play an important part

bulk up vti to increase in size or volume (*informal*) ○ *We're hoping student numbers will bulk up this year.*

bulk buy n a large amount or number of something bought at one time, usually at a reduced rate —**bulk buying** n

bulk carrier n a ship that carries loose unpackaged cargo, e.g. coal or grain

bulkhead /búlk hed/ n a partition inside a ship, aircraft, or large vehicle [15C. < Old Norse *bálkr* 'partition'.]

bulking /búlking/ n the increase in the volume of sand, cement, and other building materials when they become damp

bulky /búlki/ (**-ier, -iest**) adj 1 large and awkward to carry or move 2 heavily built, broad, or muscular —**bulkily** adv —**bulkiness** n

bull[1] /bool/ n 1 MALE OF CATTLE an uncastrated adult male of any breed of domestic cattle or other bovine animal 2 MALE MAMMAL a sexually mature male of any of various large mammals, including whales, seals, moose, and elephants 3 BIG MAN a hefty or aggressive man 4 BUYER OF RISING SECURITIES an investor who buys securities in anticipation of rising prices, intending to resell them for profit. ◇ **bear[1]** n 5. 5 BULL'S EYE the bull's eye of a target, or a shot that hits this 5 ■ vt RAISE PRICES WITH SPECULATIVE BUYING to attempt to raise prices in a particular commodity or market by buying large quantities and thus reducing availability and increasing demand [Old English *bula* < Old Norse *boli*] ◇ **shoot the bull** US to chatter idly (*slang*) ◇ **take the bull by the horns** to deal with a difficult situation forcefully and decisively

bull[2] /bool/ n a written statement formally issued by the pope and bearing an official seal [13C. Via French < Latin *bulla* 'bubble, seal, sealed document'.]

bull[3] /bool/ n Ireland a glaring mistake in speech, especially a self-contradictory statement [Early 17C. < ?]

bull[4] /bool/ n an offensive term for talk or writing dismissed as foolish or inaccurate (*slang*) [Early 17C. < ? Now often taken as an abbreviation of BULLSHIT.]

Bull /bool/ n ASTRON, ZODIAC = **Taurus** n. 2 [Early 16C. Translation of Latin *Taurus*.]

Bull /bool/, **John** (1563?–1628) English organist and composer

bulla /boollə/ (*plural* **-lae** /-lee/) n 1 BLISTER a blister (*technical*) 2 BONY PART any rounded, bony, and protruding part of the body 3 POPE'S SEAL the pope's official seal [14C. < Latin, 'bubble, seal, sealed document'.]

bullbaiting /bool bayting/ n the former entertainment of setting fierce dogs to attack a bull, popular in medieval times

bull bars npl a metal framework mounted on the front of a vehicle to protect it against impact

bulldog /bŏŏl dog/ *n* **1** a smooth-haired muscular dog belonging to a breed developed in England for bull-baiting **2** an assistant to a proctor at Oxford and Cambridge universities (*informal*)

bulldoze /bŏŏl dōz/ (**-dozes, -dozing, -dozed**) *v* **1** *vt* **DEMOLISH WITH BULLDOZERS** to demolish a building or clear debris using bulldozers **2** *vti* **FORCE A WAY** to force way past or through an obstruction (*informal*) **3** *vt* **FORCE ACTION** to force somebody to do something or to insist on a course of action stubbornly or ruthlessly (*informal*) [Late 19C. < ?]

bulldozer /bŏŏl dōzər/ *n* a construction vehicle with tracks or large wheels and a wide blade used for moving earth or debris

bull dyke *n* an offensive term for a lesbian who chooses masculine dress and manners (*slang*)

Bullen /bŏŏllən/, **Keith** (1906–76) New Zealand geophysicist and mathematician

Buller /bŏŏllər/ river in the NW of the South Island, New Zealand. Length: 177 km/110 mi.

bullet /bŏŏllit/ *n* **1 AMMUNITION USED IN FIREARM** a projectile fire from a handgun, rifle, or other small firearm, usually pointed and cylindrical and made of metal **2 bullet, bullet point DOT** a large printed dot used to highlight items in a printed list **3 REPAYMENT OF LOAN** the repayment of a loan, representing the initial sum borrowed excluding interest [Early 16C. < French *boulet* 'small ball' < *boule* (see BOWL[2]).] ◇ **bite the bullet** to deal with a situation that is unpleasant but unavoidable ◇ **get** *or* **be given the bullet** to be dismissed from a job (*informal*)

bulletin /bŏŏllətin/ *n* **1 NEWS BROADCAST** a short broadcast containing a single item of news **2 OFFICIAL NEWS** an official announcement of public news **3 NEWSLETTER** a newsletter issued by an organization or institution [Mid-18C. < Italian *bulletino* 'small papal bull' < *bulla* < Latin (see BULL[2]).]

ϟ**bulletin board** *n* **1** *US, Can* = **noticeboard 2 bulletin board, bulletin board system** an online forum used to exchange e-mails, chat, and access software

bullet loan *n* a loan that is repaid in full in a single payment on a set date

bullet point *n* PRINTING = **bullet** *n*. 2

bulletproof /bŏŏllit proof/ *adj* **1** able to resist the penetration of bullets ○ *bulletproof glass* **2** invulnerable to attack or criticism (*informal*) ○ *Nobody's bulletproof in this company.*

~~**bullettin**~~ incorrect spelling of **bulletin**

bullet train *n* a high-speed passenger train in Japan

bulletwood /bŏŏllit wŏŏd/ *n* **1** the tough durable wood of a tropical American tree **2** a tropical American tree grown for bulletwood. *Manilkara bidentata.*

bull fiddle *n US* a double bass (*informal*)

bullfight /bŏŏl fīt/ *n* a traditional public entertainment, especially in Spain and Mexico, in which a bull is baited and killed —**bullfighter** *n* —**bullfighting** *n*

bullfinch /bŏŏl finch/ *n* a small bird with a short thick beak, a black head, and a pink to red breast. Native to: Europe, Asia. *Pyrrhula pyrrhula.*

bullfrog /bŏŏl frog/ *n* a large frog with a deep croak. Native to: E North America. Genus: *Rana.* [Mid-18C. < its strong croak.]

bullhead /bŏŏl hed/ *n* **1** a large-headed fish such as the freshwater sculpin. Genus: *Cottus.* **2** a common catfish of rivers and lakes. Native to: North America. Genus: *Ictalurus.*

bullheaded /bŏŏl héddid/ *adj* stubborn and uncooperative (*informal*) —**bullheadedly** *adv* —**bullheadedness** *n*

bullhead rail *n* a railway rail with a narrow base and a bulbous top when viewed in cross-section

bullhorn /bŏŏl hawrn/ *n US, Can* = **loudhailer**

bullion /bŏŏlli ən/ *n* **1 BARS OF GOLD OR SILVER** gold or silver in the form of bars or ingots **2 MASS OF METAL** any metal in the form of an unshaped mass **3 GOLD OR SILVER BRAID** gold or silver ornamental braid [15C. < Anglo-Norman, 'mint' < Latin *bullire* 'boil' < *bulla* 'bubble'.]

bullish /bŏŏllish/ *adj* **1 BRAWNY** broad and strong **2 EXPECTING GOOD STOCK MARKET FIGURES** expecting or producing good results, especially rising stock market prices **3 OPTIMISTIC** confident and optimistic (*informal*) —**bullishly** *adv* —**bullishness** *n*

bull market *n* a stock market in which prices are rising and are expected to continue rising. ◊ **bear market**

bullnecked /bŏŏl nékt/ *adj* having a short thick neck

bullnose /bŏŏl nōz/ *n* **1** a brick with a rounded end **2** a disease of pigs that causes the snout to swell

bullnosed /bŏŏl nōzd/ *adj* having a rounded protruding front part

bullock /bŏŏllək/ *n* **1** a young domestic bull **2** a castrated domestic bull [Old English *bulluc* < *bula* 'bull']

bullock's heart *n* FOOD = **custard apple** *n*. 1

bullocky /bŏŏlləki/ (*plural* **-ies**) *n Aus* somebody who drives a team of bullocks (*informal*)

bullpen /bŏŏl pen/ *n* **1** the part of a baseball field where the relief pitchers warm up **2** *US* a cell for prisoners waiting to be brought into court (*informal*)

bullring /bŏŏl ring/ *n* an arena where bullfights are held

bull session *n US* an informal discussion

bull's eye *n* **1 MIDDLE OF TARGET** the centre of a target, which usually carries the highest score ○ *She hit the the bull's eye perfectly.* **2 TOP-SCORING SHOT** a shot that hits the centre of a target **3 ROUND WINDOW** a small round window, especially a disc of thick glass in a ship's deck for letting in light below deck **4 HARD SWEET** a hard round peppermint boiled sweet, usually striped **5 THICK LENS** a small thick lens for intensifying light **6 TYPE OF LAMP** a lamp fitted with a bull's-eye lens **7 PRECISE ACHIEVEMENT** a precise or highly effective achievement (*informal*) ■ *interj* **RECOGNIZING PRECISE ACHIEVEMENT** used to acknowledge and commend a precise or highly effective achievement (*informal*)

bullshit /bŏŏl shit/ *n* an offensive term for talk or writing dismissed as foolish or inaccurate (*slang*) ■ *vti* (**-shits, -shitting, -shitted**) (*slang*) **1** an offensive term meaning to say things that are completely untrue or very foolish **2** an offensive term meaning to try to intimidate, deceive, or persuade somebody with deceitful or foolish talk —**bullshitter** *n*

bull snake *n* a large, burrowing, nonpoisonous snake with yellow and brown markings that feeds mainly on rodents. Native to: North America. Genus: *Pituophis.*

bull terrier *n* a smooth-haired muscular dog belonging to a breed developed in England by crossing the bulldog with a breed of terrier

bullwhip /bŏŏl wip/ *n* a long heavy whip made of plaited strips of hide, knotted at the end ■ *vt* (**-whips, -whipping, -whipped**) to beat somebody with a bullwhip

bully[1] /bŏŏlli/ *n* (*plural* **-lies**) an aggressive person who intimidates or mistreats weaker people ■ *vt* (**-lies, -lying, -lied**) to intimidate or mistreat a weaker person [Mid-16C. Probably < Middle Dutch *boele* 'lover'.] —**bullying** *n* ◇ **bully for you!** used to express approval (*ironic*)

bully[2] /bŏŏlli/ (*plural* **-lies**) *n* a small New Zealand river fish. Genera: *Gobiomorphus* and *Phylinodon.* [Mid-19C. Probably shortened < BULLHEAD.]

bully beef *n* tinned corned or pickled beef (*dated*) [Mid-18C. Anglicization of *bouilli* 'boiled beef' < French, past participle of *bouillir* 'boil' < Latin *bullire.*]

bullyboy /bŏŏlli boy/ *n* an aggressive bully or thug

bully-off *n* formerly, a way of starting a hockey match, in which two opposing players hit sticks over the ball before each tries to hit it first. ◆ **pushback** [Late 19C. < ?]

bully pulpit *n US* a position of prominent authority, e.g. political office, that gives the holder a wide audience

bullyrag /bŏŏlli rag/ (**-rags, -ragging, -ragged**), **ballyrag** /bálli-/ (**-rags, -ragging, -ragged**) *vt US* to persecute somebody with insults or cruel practical jokes (*informal*) [Late 18C. < ?]

bully tree *n US* = **balata** *n*. 2

bulrush /bŏŏl rush/ *n* **1 TALL MARSH PLANT** a tall marsh plant. Flowers: brown, in furry spikes. Genus: *Typha.* **2 WATERSIDE PLANT** a plant that grows in wet conditions, with leaves like grass. Flowers: brown, in drooping clusters. Genus: *Scirpus.* **3 PAPYRUS** in the Bible, a papyrus plant [15C. Probably blend of BULL[1] + RUSH[2].]

bulwark /bŏŏlwərk/ *n* **1 DEFENSIVE WALL** a wall-like structure built to keep out attackers **2 HARBOUR WALL** a wall built in the sea to shelter a harbour **3 PROTECTION** a person or thing that gives protection or support ■ **bulwarks** *npl* **SHIP'S SIDES** the sides of a ship projecting above the deck ■ *vt* **1 PROTECT WITH WALLS** to fortify or protect a place by building walls round it **2 SAFEGUARD** to defend or support somebody or something strongly [15C. < Middle Dutch, Middle Low German *bolwerk* 'rampart made of tree trunks' < *bole* 'tree trunk' + *werk* 'work'.]

bum[1] /bum/ *n* (*informal*) **1 GOOD-FOR-NOTHING** somebody considered to be irresponsible or worthless **2** *US* **VAGRANT** a homeless person living on the street (*sometimes offensive*) **3 DEVOTEE** a person excessively devoted to a particular activity or place ○ *a ski bum* ■ *vt* (**bums, bumming, bummed**) **CADGE** to get something by asking or begging (*informal*) ■ *adj* **USELESS** useless, worthless, or of poor quality (*informal*) ○ *gave me some pretty bum advice* [Mid-19C. Shortening of BUMMER.] ◇ **give somebody the bum's rush** *US* to order or force somebody abruptly to leave a place (*slang*)

bum[2] /bum/ *n* the buttocks (*informal*) [14C. < ?]

bum bag *n* a pouch for valuables, worn on a belt. US term **fanny pack**

bumble[1] /búmb'l/ (**-bles, -bling, -bled**) *v* **1** *vti* to speak in a hesitant or muddled way **2** *vt* to move or proceed clumsily [Mid-16C. < ?] —**bumbler** *n*

bumble[2] /búmb'l/ (**-bles, -bling, -bled**) *vi* to make a humming sound [14C. An imitation of the sound.]

bumblebee /búmb'l bee/ *n* a large hairy bee that nests in burrows and makes a loud droning noise in flight. Native to: North America, Europe, Asia. Genus: *Bombus.*

bumble-puppy *n* **1** a game that involves hitting a ball attached to a string on a post, so that the string winds round the post. US term **tetherball 2** bridge or whist played badly (*informal*) [Early 19C. < ?]

bumbling /búmbling/ *adj* speaking or behaving in a clumsy or confused way (*informal*)

bumboat /búm bōt/ *n* a small boat that is used for selling goods to ships at anchor [Late 17C. < BUM[1].]

bumf /bumf/, **bumph** *n* unwanted or uninteresting printed material, especially official forms and documents (*informal*) [Late 19C. Shortening of *bum fodder* 'toilet paper'.]

bumfreezer /búm freezər/ *n* a short jacket for men, especially one that finishes above the waist (*informal*)

bummalo /búmməlō/ (*plural* **-lo**) *n* a small blunt-nosed edible fish found in brackish Indian waters. *Harpadon nehereus.* [Late 17C. Probably alteration of Marathi *bombīl.*]

bummed /bumd/ *adj US* unhappy as a result of an unpleasant experience (*slang*)

bummer /búmmər/ *n* (*slang*) **1** something annoying or unpleasant **2** a bad reaction to a hallucinogenic drug [Mid-19C. Probably < German *Bummler* 'idler, layabout' < *bummeln* 'stroll or loaf around'.]

bump /bump/ *v* **1** *vti* **KNOCK** to hit or knock something **2** *vti* **MOVE UNSTEADILY** to move in a jolting or bouncing way ○ *We bumped along the dirt track.* **3** *vt* **TURN AWAY A PASSENGER** to turn away an airline passenger with a reserved seat because the flight has been overbooked (*informal*) ■ *n* **1 ACCIDENTAL KNOCK** a light blow or impact ○ *that bump dented the bodywork* **2 SWELLING ON BODY** a swelling on the body caused by an impact ○ *a bump on the elbow* **3 LUMP ON SURFACE** a raised area on a flat surface ○ *a bump in the road* **4 SOUND OF IMPACT** the dull sound of one thing hitting another **5 RAISED AREA ON SKULL** any of numerous raised areas on the skull, formerly thought to indicate intelligence or personality type [Mid-16C. An imitation of the sound.] ◇ **bump and grind** *US* to dance erotically, thrusting and rotating the pelvis (*slang*)

bump into *vt* **1** to knock against or hit somebody or something accidentally **2** to meet somebody by chance

bump off *vt* to murder somebody (*slang*)

bump up *vt* to increase prices suddenly and sharply (*informal*)

bump up against *vt* **1** to come into contact with something, usually with a sound **2** to come into conflict with somebody

bumper /búmpər/ *n* **1 PROTECTING BAR ON VEHICLE** a projecting rim or bar on the front or back of a vehicle, designed to protect it from damage **2** *US* **DEVICE SEPARATING SECTIONS OF PROGRAMME** a device, e.g. a piece of music, that separates the content of a radio or television programme from a commercial break (*slang*) ■ *adj* **LARGE** unusually large ○ *a bumper crop*

bumper car *n* a small electric car used as part of a fairground entertainment

bumper sticker *n* a small adhesive sign, typically mounted on a car bumper or window

bumper-to-bumper *adj, adv* forming a line of close slow-moving vehicles ○ *bumper-to-bumper traffic* ○ *drive bumper-to-bumper*

bumph *n* = **bumf**

bumpkin[1] /búmpkin/ *n* a country person regarded as unsophisticated (*informal*) [Late 16C. < ?]

bumpkin[2] /búmpkin/, **bumkin** /búm-/ *n* a pole at the back of a ship or boat to which a sail is attached by a rope [Mid-17C. < Dutch *boomken* < *boom* 'tree'.]

bump-start *vt* = **push-start** *v.* ■ *n* = **push-start** *n.*

bumptious /búmpshəss/ *adj* stating opinions aggressively or self-importantly [Early 19C. Blend of BUMP + FRACTIOUS.] —**bumptiously** *adv* —**bumptiousness** *n*

bumpy /búmpi/ (**-ier, -iest**) *adj* **1** having a rough or uneven surface ○ *a bumpy road* **2** uncomfortably bouncy or rough ○ *a bumpy ride* —**bumpily** *adv* —**bumpiness** *n*

bum rap *n US* a false or fraudulent accusation or appraisal (*slang*)

bum steer *n US* a piece of misleading information or bad advice (*slang*)

bun /bun/ *n* **1 ROUND BREAD ROLL** a small round bread roll, sometimes sweetened and with added fruit or spice **2 SMALL CAKE** a small round sweet cake **3 HAIR COILED AT BACK OF HEAD** hair gathered in a tight round coil on the back or top of the head ■ **buns** *npl US* **BUTTOCKS** the buttocks (*slang*) [14C. < ?] ◇ **have a bun in the oven** to be pregnant (*informal; sometimes offensive*)

Bunbury /búnbəri/ coastal town in SW Western Australia. Population: 24,021 (1991).

bunch /bunch/ *n* **1 COLLECTION OF THINGS** a number of things grouped or joined together **2 CLUSTER OF FRUITS** a cluster of fruits growing on a stem **3 GROUP OF PEOPLE** a group of people, especially friends or associates (*informal*) ■ **bunches** *npl* **HAIR TIED IN TWO CLUMPS** hair gathered and tied in two clumps, one at each side of the head ■ *vti* **GATHER** to gather things or people into a cluster or close group [14C. < ?] —**bunchiness** *n* —**bunchy** *adj*

Buncho Tani /búnchō taáni/ (1763–1840) Japanese artist

bunco /búngkō/ (*plural* **-coes**), **bunko** (*plural* **-koes**) *n US* a trick or scheme that deceives people into parting with money (*slang*) [Late 19C. < ?] —**bunco** *vt*

bund[1] /bund/ *n S Asia* an embankment or dyke surrounding rice fields or acting as a breakwater to prevent flooding [Early 19C. Via Urdu *band* < Persian.]

bund[2] /bŏŏnd/, **Bund** *n* a political organization, especially a socialist Jewish labour movement in Tsarist Russia or a German-American group of Nazi sympathizers in the United States in the 1930s and 1940s [Late 19C. < German, 'association'.]

Bundaberg /búndə burg/ port on the Pacific coast of S Queensland, Australia. Population: 41,025 (1996).

bundh *n S Asia* POL = **bandh**

ϟ**bundle** /búnd'l/ *n* **1 COLLECTION OF THINGS HELD TOGETHER** a number of things tied, wrapped, or held together **2 A LOT OF MONEY** a large sum of money (*slang*) **3 BAND OF PARALLEL TISSUES** a band of tissue, e.g. muscle or nerve fibres, or vascular tissue in plants **4 SET OF COMPUTER EQUIPMENT** a package of computer hardware and software supplied at an inclusive price ■ *vt* (**-dles, -dling, -dled**) **1 TIE TOGETHER** to tie or wrap a number of things together **2 SHOVE** to push somebody or something roughly and hurriedly (*informal*) **3 SUPPLY COMPUTER EQUIPMENT** to package computer hardware and software together at an inclusive price [14C. < Dutch *bundel*.] —**bundler** *n* ◇ **drop your bundle** *ANZ* to lose your nerve and run away (*informal*) ◇ **go a bundle on something** to be very fond of or enthusiastic about something (*informal*)

bundle off *vt* to send somebody away hurriedly (*informal*) ○ *We bundled the children off to school.*

bundle up *v* **1** *vt* to gather things into a bundle **2** *vti* to dress in warm clothes, or dress somebody in warm clothes (*informal*) ○ *Bundle up, it's cold outside.*

bundle sheath cell *n* a specialized photosynthetic cell in some vascular plants where the initial products of photosynthesis are imported and decarboxylated

bundu /bŏŏn doo/ *n S Africa* any remote uninhabited area (*slang*) [Mid-20C. Probably < Shona *bundo* 'grasslands'.]

bundwall /búnd wawl/ *n* a casing of concrete or earth around an oil storage tank

bundy /búndi/ (**-dies, -dying, -died**) *vi ANZ* to clock on or off for work [Mid-20C. < Trade name of a time clock.]

bun fight *n* **1** a party or large gathering, especially an official dinner (*humorous*) **2** a heated argument (*slang*)

bung /bung/ *n* **1 STOPPER** a stopper or plug, especially one made of cork or rubber **2 PAYOFF** an illicit fee paid to a football player, manager, or agent to facilitate a player transfer (*slang*) ■ *vt* **1 PLUG** to plug or seal a hole with a bung **2 PLACE CARELESSLY** to put something somewhere roughly or hurriedly (*informal*) ○ *Bung it in the bin when you're finished.* [15C. < Middle Dutch *bonghe*, probably < late Latin *puncta* 'puncture' < Latin *pungere* 'to prick'.]

bung up *vt* to block or obstruct a hole or passage (*informal*)

bungalow /búng gəlō/ *n* **1 SINGLE-STOREY HOUSE** a single-storey house **2 LIGHTWEIGHT TROPICAL HOUSE** in Southeast Asia and the South Pacific, a simply built one-storey house with a veranda and a wide, gently sloping roof **3** *Malaysia, Singapore* **DETACHED HOUSE** a detached house, usually of two or more storeys [Late 17C. < Hindi *banglā* 'of Bengal'.]

bungee /búnji/ *n* a cord or rope made from elastic material [Early 20C. < ?]

bungee jump *n* a dive from a high place using an elastic cord tied to the ankles as a restraint —**bungee jumping** *n*

bunghole /búng hōl/ *n* a hole in a barrel or vat, used for drawing off the contents and closed with a bung

bungle /búng g'l/ *vt* (**-gles, -gling, -gled**) to cause something to fail through carelessness or incompetence (*informal*) ■ *n* a careless or clumsy action or mistake (*informal*) [Mid-16C. Thought to suggest the action.] —**bungler** *n* —**bungling** *adj* —**bunglingly** *adv*

bunion /búnyən/ *n* inflammation of the sac (**bursa**) around the first joint of the big toe, accompanied by swelling and sideways displacement of the joint [Early 18C. Directly or via English dialect *bunny* 'lump, swelling' < Old French *buigne* 'bump on the head'.]

bunk[1] /bungk/ *n* **1 SIMPLE BED** a simple narrow bed built on a shelf or in a recess **2** = **bunk bed 3 SLEEPING PLACE** any bed or place to sleep (*informal*) ■ *vi* **SLEEP** to sleep in a place away from home (*informal*) ○ *'You may as well bunk at the YMCA and get in on their recreation programs'.* (Garrison Keillor, *We Are Still Married*; 1989) [Mid-18C. < ?]

bunk off *vt* to sneak away or be absent from somewhere without permission, especially from school (*informal*)

bunk[2] /bungk/ *n* talk or writing dismissed as nonsensical or inaccurate (*slang*) [Early 20C. Shortened < BUNKUM.]

bunk[3] /bungk/ *vi* to disappear or depart hurriedly [Late 19C. < ?] ◇ **do a bunk** to leave unexpectedly and hurriedly (*informal*)

bunk bed *n* either of a pair of single beds fitted one on top of the other

bunker /búngkə/ *n* **1 LARGE OUTDOOR CONTAINER** a large outdoor bin or chest **2 FUEL STORAGE CONTAINER** a fuel-storage container on a ship **3 UNDERGROUND SHELTER** an underground shelter, especially one built for troops, with a fortified gun position above ground **4 SAND HAZARD** a sand-filled hollow on a golf course, built as a hazard ■ *vt* **1 PUT SOMETHING IN OUTDOOR BIN** to put or store something in a large outdoor bin or chest **2 SEND GOLF BALL INTO BUNKER** to hit a golf ball into a bunker [Mid-16C. < ?]

Bunker Hill /búngkər-/ hill in Boston, Massachusetts, near the site of the first battle of the American Revolution in 1775. Height: 34 m/110 ft.

bunkhouse /búngk howss/ (*plural* **-houses** /-howziz/) *n US* a building providing simple sleeping facilities

bunkum /búngkəm/ *n* talk or writing dismissed as nonsensical or inaccurate (*informal*) [Mid-19C. Alteration of *Buncombe* County, N Carolina, United States, whose congressman defended a dull and irrelevant speech by saying he made it to impress the people of Buncombe.]

bunny /búnni/ (*plural* **-nies**) *n* **1** a child's word for a rabbit **2** *Aus* a gullible person or scapegoat (*informal*) [Early 17C. < English dialect *bun* 'rabbit's tail, rabbit' < Gaelic *bun* 'stump, bottom'.]

bunny hug *n* a lively ballroom dance popular in the United States in the early 20th century

bunny slopes *npl US* SKIING = **nursery slopes**

bunodont /byŏŏnə dont/ *adj* having molars with separate rounded ridges (**cusps**), typical of omnivores [Late 19C. < Greek *bounos* 'mound'.]

Bunraku /bŏŏn raá koo/ *n* traditional Japanese puppetry using large wooden puppets, each worked by several puppeteers who are visible to the audience and with a separate narrator offstage [Early 20C. < Japanese, after the *Bunraku-za* theatre.]

Bunsen /búnss'n/, **Robert Wilhelm** (1811–99) German chemist and physicist

Bunsen burner *n* a portable tube-shaped gas burner with an adjustable hole to control air intake and flame type, used in laboratories [Late 19C. After R. W. BUNSEN.]

bunt[1] /bunt/ *vt* **1** = **butt**[1] *v.* 1 **2** in baseball, to hit a pitched ball very gently, holding the bat horizontally with both hands [Mid-18C. An imitation of the sound.] —**bunter** *n*

bunt[2] /bunt/ *n* the baggy middle part of a sail [Late 16C. < ?]

buntal /búnt'l/ *n* straw from the large leaves of the talipot palm tree of Southeast Asia [Early 20C. < Tagalog.]

bunting[1] /búnting/ *n* a small seed-eating songbird related to the finch, with a short stout bill and usually brown or grey feathers. Family: Emberizidae. [13C. < ?]

bunting[2] /búnting/ *n* strings of cloth or paper decorations for hanging outdoors [Early 18C. < ?]

buntline /búnt līn/ *n* a rope attached to the bottom of a square sail, used to roll up the sail

Buñuel /boon wél/, **Luis** (1900–83) Spanish film director

bunya /búnnyə/, **bunya-bunya, bunya pine** *n* a tall tree with cones containing edible seeds. Native to: Australia. *Araucaria bidwillii.* [Mid-19C. < Yagara *bunya-bunya.*]

Bunyan /búnnyən/, **John** (1628–88) English preacher and writer

bunyip /búnnyip/ *n Aus* in Aboriginal legend, a monster said to inhabit swamps and water holes of the Australian interior [Mid-19C. < Wemba-Wemba *banib.*]

Buonarroti /bwónnə rótti/, **Michelangelo** ➧ **Michelangelo**

buoy[1] /boy/ *n* **1** a large anchored float, often equipped with lights or bells, that serves as a guide or warning to ships **2** EMERGENCIES = **life buoy** ■ *vt* to use a buoy to mark the location of something in water, e.g. a hazard or channel [13C. < ?]

SPELLCHECK Do not confuse ***buoy*** with ***boy***, which has a similar sound. Beware: your spellchecker will not catch this error.

buoy[2] /boy/ *vt* to keep something from falling or sinking ○ *steps to buoy the country's currency* [Late 16C. < Spanish *boyar* 'to float' < *boya* 'buoy'.]

buoy up *vt* **1** to give support or encouragement to somebody ○ *Buoyed up by a few wise investments, the company went on to prosper the following year.* **2** to keep somebody cheerful or optimistic in spite of difficulties ○ *The arrival of the children has buoyed us all up.*

buoyancy /bóyənssi/, **buoyance** /-ənss/ *n* **1 FORCE CAUSING FLOATING** the tendency of a liquid or gas to cause less dense objects to float or rise to the surface **2 TENDENCY TO FLOAT** the tendency of an object to float **3 POWER TO RECOVER EMOTIONALLY** the ability to recover quickly from a disappointment or failure **4 CHEERFULNESS** cheerfulness or optimism

buoyant /bóyənt/ *adj* **1 PUSHING UPWARDS** causing immersed objects to float or rise to the surface of a liquid or upwards in a gas **2 ABLE TO FLOAT** tending to float or rise to the surface of a liquid or upwards in a gas **3 QUICK TO RECOVER EMOTIONALLY** tending to recover quickly from a disappointment or failure **4 CHEERFUL** cheerful or optimistic [Late 16C. Directly or via Old French < Spanish *boyante*, present participle of *boyar* (see BUOY[2]).] —**buoyantly** *adv*

bupivacaine /byoo pívvə kayn/ *n* a powerful local anaesthetic. Use: epidural anaesthesia.

buprestid /byoo préstid/ *n* a metallic-coloured tropical beetle found worldwide that bores into wood during the larval stage. Family: Buprestidae. [Mid-19C. < modern Latin *Buprestidae* (plural) < Greek *bouprēstis* 'ox-sweller' < *bous* 'ox'.]

bur *n* ENG = **burr**[1] *n.* 2 ■ **1** = **burr**[1] *n.* 3 **2** = **burr**[1] *n.* 4 **3** = **burr**[1] *n.* 5

Bur. *abbr* Burma

Burakumin /bŏŏ rákō min/ *npl* members of the lowest Japanese sector of society [Mid-20C. < Japanese, 'hamlet people'.]

buran /boo raán/ *n* a strong wind in central Asia, bringing dust storms in summer and blizzards in winter [Mid-19C. Via Russian < Turkic *boran.*]

Buraydah /boo rídə/ city in central Saudi Arabia. Population: 69,940.

burb /burb/ n US a suburb (slang) [Shortening]

burble /búrb'l/ v 1 (-bles, -bling, -bled) 1 vi MAKE BUBBLING SOUND to make a gentle bubbling sound, like the sound of running water 2 vti SPEAK EXCITEDLY to speak or say something in a fast excited way (informal) 3 vi BECOME TURBULENT to become turbulent (refers to the airflow around an aircraft's wing) ■ n 1 GENTLE SOUND a gentle bubbling or gurgling sound 2 STREAM OF TALK a flow of fast excited talking (informal) 3 BREAK IN AIRFLOW a break in the flow of air around an aircraft's wing, which causes turbulence [14C. An imitation of the sound.] —**burbler** n —**burbly** adv

burbot /búrbət/ (plural **-bot** or **-bots**) n a freshwater fish of the cod family. Native to: North America, N Europe, Asia. Lota lota. [14C. < Old French borbette.]

Burckhardt /búrk haart/, **Jakob** (1818–97) Swiss art historian

Burdekin /búrdəkən/ river in Queensland, Australia. Length: 720 km/447 mi.

burden¹ /búrd'n/ n 1 SOMETHING CARRIED a load being carried ○ carrying a heavy burden on his back 2 WORRYING RESPONSIBILITY a difficult or worrying responsibility or duty ○ the burdens of parenthood 3 SHIP'S CAPACITY the maximum weight of cargo that a ship can carry ■ vt 1 GIVE RESPONSIBILITY to give somebody a task that is difficult to deal with or something worrying to think about 2 IMPOSE BURDEN ON to cause somebody or something to carry a burden [Old English byrthen < Indo-European, 'to bear']

burden² /búrd'n/ n 1 a chorus in a song 2 a main or recurring theme in music or literature (literary) [14C. < French bourdon 'bass, drone', influenced by BURDEN¹.]

SYNONYMS See **subject**.

burden of proof n the responsibility of proving a case or argument, especially in a court of law

burdensome /búrd'nsəm/ adj difficult or worrying to bear or deal with

burdock /búr dok/ n a tall biennial plant with a long taproot. Flowers: small, prickly, purple. Native to: temperate areas. Genus: Arctium. [Late 16C. < BURR¹ + DOCK¹.]

bureau /byoor ō/ (plural **-reaus** or **-reaux** /-rōz/) n 1 ORGANIZATION an organization or one of its branches 2 GOVERNMENT DEPARTMENT a government department or one of its branches 3 WRITING DESK a narrow desk with a writing surface and drawers 4 US CHEST OF DRAWERS a chest of drawers, especially a low one [Late 17C. < French, literally 'baize' (used for desks).]

bureaucracy /byoor rókrəssi/ (plural **-cies**) n 1 ADMINISTRATIVE SYSTEM an administrative system, especially in a government, that divides work into specific categories carried out by special departments of nonelected officials 2 OFFICIALS COLLECTIVELY the nonelected officials of an organization or department 3 FRUSTRATING RULES complex rules and regulations applied rigidly 4 STATE OR ORGANIZATION a state or organization operated by a hierarchy of paid officials [Early 19C. < French bureaucratie < bureau 'office' + -cratie 'rule'.]

bureaucrat /byoor ə krat/ n 1 an administrative or government official 2 an official who applies rules rigidly —**bureaucratism** /byoo rókrətizəm/ n

bureaucratic /byoor rə kráttik/ adj 1 relating to the way administrative systems are organized ○ the bureaucratic structure 2 describes an administrative system or official that applies rules rigidly —**bureaucratically** adv

bureaucratise vt = **bureaucratize**

bureaucratize /byoo rókrə tīz/ (-**tizes**, -**tizing**, -**tized**), **bureaucratise** (-**tises**, -**tising**, -**tised**) vt 1 to change a system into a bureaucracy 2 to make a system or procedure rigid or complex —**bureaucratization** /byoo rókrə tī záysh'n/ n

bureau de change /byoor rō də shónZh/ (plural **bureaus de change** /byoor rō-/ or **bureaux de change** /byoor rō-/) n an office or part of a bank where foreign currency is exchanged [< French, 'office of exchange']

Buren /búrrən/, **Daniel** (b. 1938) French artist

burette /byoo rét/ n a glass tube with measurements marked on the side and a stopcock at the bottom, used in laboratories to release an accurately measured quantity of liquid [Mid-19C. < French, < buire 'jug'.]

burg /burg/ n 1 an ancient fortress or walled town 2 US a city or town (informal) [Mid-18C. 'Fortress' < late Latin burgus, 'town' < German Burg < Germanic.]

Burgas /boor gáss/ capital of Burgas Province, E Bulgaria. Population: 199,869 (1995).

burgee /búr jee/ n a light identification flag flown from the top of a mast [Mid-18C. < ?]

burgeon /búrjən/ vi (literary) 1 to produce new buds and leaves or to swell and develop into leaves and flowers 2 to flourish or develop rapidly [14C. < French bourgeonner < bourgeon 'a shoot or bud' < late Latin burra 'wool'.]

burgeoning /búrjəning/ adj growing or expanding rapidly ○ burgeoning wealth

burger /búrgər/ n 1 FOOD = **hamburger** n. 2 2 a round flat cake made of chicken, fish, vegetables, or nuts, usually served in a bun [Mid-20C. Shortened < HAMBURGER.]

-burger suffix resembling minced beef or a hamburger ○ veggieburger

Burgess /búrjiss/, **Anthony** (1917–93) British writer and critic. Born **John Anthony Burgess Wilson**

Burgess, **Guy** (1911–63) British Soviet spy. Full name **Guy Francis de Moncy Burgess**

burgh /búrrə/ n 1 Scotland a town, especially one incorporated by royal charter 2 a borough (archaic) [variant of BOROUGH]

Burgh /burg/, **Hubert de, Earl of Kent** (1197–1243?) English statesman

burgher /búrgər/ n 1 a merchant in a medieval European town 2 a citizen, especially a prosperous or conservative member of the middle class (humorous) [Late 16C. Partly < BURGH, partly < German or Dutch burger < burg (SEE BURG).]

Burghley /búrli/, **Sir William Cecil, 1st Baron** (1520–98) English statesman

burglar /búrglər/ n somebody who enters a building illegally [Mid-16C. < obsolete legal French burgier.]

burglar alarm n an electronic device designed to make a loud noise when somebody enters a building illegally

burglarize /búrglə rīz/ (-**izes**, -**izing**, -**ized**) vt US, Can = **burgle** (often passive)

burglarproof /búrglər proof/ adj secured with locks, alarms, or other devices so as to discourage or prevent unauthorized entry

burglary /búrgləri/ (plural **-ries**) n the crime of entering a building illegally, or an instance of such a crime — **burglarious** /bur gláiri əss/ adj —**burglariously** adv

burgle /búrg'l/ (-**gles**, -**gling**, -**gled**) vt to enter a building illegally, usually in order to steal something (often passive) US term **burglarize** [Late 19C. Back-formation < BURGLAR.]

~~burgler~~ incorrect spelling of **burglar**

burgomaster /búrgə maastər/ n the mayor or chief magistrate in some N European towns [Late 16C. < Dutch burgomeester 'town master'.]

Burgos /búr goss/ capital of Burgos Province, N Spain. Population: 166,732 (1997).

Burgoyne /bur góyn/, **John** (1722–92) British army general

Burgundian /bər gúndi ən/ n 1 somebody who comes from the Burgundy region of central France 2 member of a 15th-century group of European composers noted for their chansons and masses [Early 17C. < Burgundy, region of central France.]

burgundy /búrgəndi/ (plural **-dies**), **Burgundy** n 1 red or white wine produced in the Burgundy region of central France 2 a deep red colour —**burgundy** adj

burial /bérri əl/ n the act or ceremony of putting a dead body into the ground or into the sea (often before nouns) ○ a burial place [Old English byrgels < byrgan (see BURY)]

burial chamber n a small room or enclosed space where somebody has been buried

burial ground n an area of land where dead bodies are buried, especially an ancient site

Buridan's ass /byoor rid'nz-/ n a situation used to demonstrate the impracticality of making choices according to a formal system of reasoning [After Jean Buridan (1300–58), French philosopher]

burin /byoor rin/ n 1 an engraver's chisel for making grooves 2 a prehistoric chisel-like flint tool, used for cutting and engraving during the Upper Palaeolithic period [Mid-17C. < French.]

burk /burk/ n = **berk** (slang)

burka /búrkə/ n an all-over garment with veiled eyeholes, worn by some Muslim women [Mid-19C. Via Urdu or Persian burka' < Arabic burku'.]

burke /burk/ (**burkes**, **burking**, **burked**) vt 1 KEEP SOMETHING QUIET to prevent information from becoming known 2 KEEP SOMEBODY QUIET to prevent somebody from revealing information 3 EVADE to evade an issue or question 4 MURDER DISCREETLY to murder somebody silently and without leaving marks or wounds, especially by suffocation [Early 19C. After William BURKE.]

Burke /burk/, **Edmund** (1729–97) Irish-born British political philosopher and statesman

Burke, **Robert O'Hara** (1820–61) Irish-born Australian explorer

Burke, **William** (1792–1829) Irish murderer and grave robber

Burkina Faso

Burkina Faso /burk ee̱nə fássō/ landlocked republic in W Africa. Capital: Ouagadougou. Population: 10,963,300 (1997). Area: 274,200 sq. km/105,900 sq. mi.

Burkitt's lymphoma /búrkits-/ n a rare malignant tumour attacking white blood cells, associated with a virus spread by insects [Mid-20C. After Denis Burkitt (1911–93), British surgeon.]

burl¹ /burl/ n 1 KNOT ON TREE a knotty growth on a tree trunk 2 KNOTTY WOOD knotty wood or a decorative veneer made from it 3 KNOT IN CLOTH a knot in thread or cloth 4 Ireland, UK ACT OF SWINGING an act of swinging (informal regional) ○ How would you like a burl? ■ vt 1 REMOVE KNOTS FROM CLOTH to pick knots off newly woven cloth 2 Ireland, UK MAKE SOMEBODY SWING to cause someone to swing (informal regional) ○ He swung me off my feet and burled me through the air. [15C. Via Old French bourle 'tuft of wool' < late Latin burra 'wool'.] —**burler** n

burl² /burl/ n ANZ an attempt (informal) [Early 20C. < Variant of BIRL.]

burlap /búr lap/ n coarse cloth woven from jute, hemp, or a similar rough thread [Late 17C. < ?]

burlesque /bur lésk/ n 1 MOCKERY BY LUDICROUS IMITATION the mocking of a serious matter or style by imitating it in an incongruous way 2 WORK USING BURLESQUE a literary or dramatic work that uses burlesque 3 LUDICROUS IMITATION an incongruous imitation of something 4 US VARIETY SHOW a variety show of a type that often includes striptease ■ vt (**burlesques**, **burlesquing**, **burlesqued**) MOCK BY LUDICROUS IMITATION to mock something serious by imitating it in an incongruous way [Mid-17C. Via French < Italian burlesco < burla 'mockery, fun'.] —**burlesquer** n

burly /búrli/ (-**lier**, -**liest**) adj strong and with a broad sturdy frame ○ flanked by two burly bodyguards [14C. Probably < assumed Old English borlic 'excellent' < Indo-European, 'carry'.] —**burliness** n

Burma /búrmə/ former name for **Myanmar**

bur marigold n a wild plant that produces barbs that stick to hair, fur, and clothing. Flowers: yellow. Genus: Bidens. US term **beggar's lice** n. 1

Burmese /búr meéz/ (plural **-mese**) n 1 a person who comes from Myanmar, formerly Burma 2 the official language of Myanmar, one of the Tibeto-Burman group of Sino-Tibetan languages. Native speakers: 20–27 million. —**Burmese** adj

Burmese cat n a domestic cat with a chocolate-coloured or silvery-brown coat and yellow eyes, similar in build to the Siamese cat

burn[1] /burn/ *v* (**burns, burning, burnt** /burnt/ *or* **burned, burnt** *or* **burned**) **1** *vti* BE OR SET ON FIRE to be on fire, or cause something to be on fire **2** *vti* DESTROY SOMETHING BY FIRE to destroy something or be destroyed by fire ○ *The house was burnt to the ground.* **3** *vt* DAMAGE SOMETHING BY FIRE to injure, damage, or affect somebody or something with fire or extreme heat ○ *I burnt my hand on the iron.* **4** *vt* OVERCOOK to spoil food or a cooking pan by subjecting it to extreme heat **5** *vi* BE OVERCOOKED to be spoiled because of being subjected to too intense a heat or being cooked for too long **6** *vt* USE SOMETHING UP to use up or consume something ○ *You won't burn many calories watching TV.* **7** *vt* USE SOMETHING AS FUEL to use something as fuel ○ *burn gas* **8** *vti* KILL OR DIE BY FIRE to kill somebody with fire or die by fire, usually as a form of execution **9** *vi* SUFFER PAIN to suffer pain through fire **10** *vi* FEEL FEVERISH to feel or look extremely hot or feverish because of illness or embarrassment ○ *Her cheeks were burning.* **11** *vti* CAUSE OR FEEL STINGING to feel an intense stinging or smarting sensation, or cause such a sensation in a part of the body ○ *That hot coffee will burn your throat.* **12** *vi* IMPRESS DEEPLY to create a deep and lasting impression on somebody or something ○ *His words were burning in my brain.* **13** *vt* MAKE MARK to cause a mark, hole, or other sign of damage to appear in something because of intense heat or fire ○ *I burnt a hole in my shirt with the iron.* **14** *vti* SUNBURN to become sunburnt, or cause a person or part of the body to become sunburnt ○ *My skin burns easily.* **15** *vi* EMIT HEAT OR LIGHT to emit heat or light ○ *A light was burning in the front room.* **16** *vi* CONTAIN A FIRE to contain a fire, or operate by means of fire ○ *a fireplace burning brightly* **17** *vti US* ELECTROCUTE to electrocute somebody, or be electrocuted (*informal*) **18** *vt US* CHEAT to cheat or swindle somebody (*informal; usually passive*) ○ *We really got burnt on that deal.* **19** *vi* FEEL STRONG EMOTION to feel an emotion very intensely ○ *burning with shame* **20** *vi* YEARN to yearn to do or acquire something ○ *burning to succeed* **21** *vti* COMBUST to undergo combustion, or cause something to undergo combustion **22** *vti* DISCARD to exchange or discard unwanted playing cards in the course of a game (*informal*) **23** *vi* DRIVE FAST to drive a motor vehicle at high speed (*informal*) ■ *n* **1** HEAT INJURY an injury caused by fire, heat, radiation, chemical action, electricity, or friction, resulting in redness and blistering of the skin and often causing damage to underlying tissues **2** FIRE OR HEAT MARK a mark or hole left on or in something such as fabric, wood, or plastic as a result of burning **3** ROCKET ADJUSTMENT a controlled firing of a rocket's engine for adjusting course and position **4** STINGING a stinging sensation or feeling of intense heat ○ *the burn of the iodine on my skin* **5** SKIN BURN sunburn or windburn **6** SENSATION OF BURNING a sensation of burning that occurs during strenuous exercise, and the positive psychological sensation associated with it ○ *You can feel the burn after an hour of aerobics.* [Old English *birnan* 'be on fire', *bærnan* 'cause something to burn' < Germanic] —**burnable** *adj*

burn down *vti* to catch fire and burn until virtually nothing remains, or to burn something such as a building in order to destroy it

⚡**burn in** *vt* **1** to expose a specific part of an image on photographic paper while masking other areas so that they are not exposed any further **2** to operate a semiconductor-based device or piece of software continuously to test for defects

burn off *v* **1** *vt* GET RID OF EXCESS FAT to use up energy or get rid of unwanted fat by exercising ○ *burn off a few extra calories* **2** *vt* REMOVE VEGETATION to remove vegetation by fire or with chemicals, either to clear the land or in preparation for harvesting a root crop **3** *vt* GET RID OF EXCESS GAS to get rid of unwanted gas, e.g. at an oil-well head, by burning it **4** *vti* DISSIPATE to dissipate fog or clouds by the heat of the sun, or to be dissipated in this way

burn out *v* **1** *vi* FINISH BURNING to stop burning when reduced to nothing **2** *vti* WEAR OUT THROUGH HEAT to stop working or to cause something to stop working because of too much heat or friction ○ *The car's clutch has burned out* **3** *vti* BECOME EXHAUSTED to become or make somebody exhausted or unwell through too much hard work, stress, or reckless living (*informal*) ○ *You'll burn yourself out if you don't slow down.*

burn up *v* **1** *vti* DESTROY BY FIRE to destroy something or be destroyed by intense heat or fire **2** *vt* USE FUEL to use up fuel by burning **3** *vi* BE VERY HOT to be very hot or overheated ○ *burning up with fever* **4** *vt* DRIVE AT HIGH SPEED to drive at high speed on a road or track (*informal*) **5** *vt* DRIVE FASTER THAN to drive faster than somebody else (*informal*) ○ *some idiot tried to burn me up on the motorway*

burn[2] /burn/ *n Scotland, N England* a stream or brook [Old English *burna* < Indo-European, 'to boil']

burned-out *adj* = **burnt-out**

Burne-Jones /búrn-/, **Sir Edward** (1833–98) British painter and designer. Born **Edward Coley Jones**

burner /búrnər/ *n* **1** PART OF STOVE OR LAMP the part of a fuel-burning stove, lamp, or heater that produces a flame when lit **2** RING ON COOKER one of the circular rings or plates on a gas or electric cooker that produces heat or a flame **3** FURNACE an incinerator or furnace that burns fuel, waste products, or rubbish

burnet /búrnit/ (*plural* **-nets** *or* **-net**) *n* a perennial herb of the rose family. Genus: *Sanguisorba.* [14C. < Old French *brunet, brunete* < *brun* 'brown' < Germanic.]

Burnet /bər nét, búrnit/, **Sir Macfarlane** (1899–1985) Australian biologist

Burnett /bər nét/, **Frances Hodgson** (1849–1924) British-born US writer. Born **Frances Eliza Hodgson**

Burney /búrni/, **Fanny** (1752–1840) British novelist and diarist. Born **Frances Burney**

Burnie-Somerset /búrni-/ port in N Tasmania, Australia. Population: 19,134 (1996).

⚡**burn-in** *n* a final test for semiconductor-based devices or software in which they are operated for a prescribed period to find defects

burning /búrning/ *adj* **1** ON FIRE producing flames or on fire **2** VERY HOT extremely hot **3** ARDENT emotionally intense or strong ○ *He spoke with a burning passion.* **4** IMPORTANT of immediate or urgent importance ○ *one of the burning issues of the day* ■ *adv* EXTREMELY extremely ○ *a burning hot day*

burning bush *n* **1** a bushy annual plant with narrow light green leaves that turn red in autumn **2** PLANTS = **gas plant 3** *US* a shrub with bright red berries or foliage. Genus: *Euonymus.* [Alluding to Exodus 3]

burnish /búrnish/ *vt* **1** POLISH to polish metal until it shines **2** MAKE SOMETHING SHINY to make something such as pottery or fabric shine by rubbing it with a smooth instrument ■ *n* SHINY SURFACE a smooth shiny finish ○ *a bowl with a bright burnish* [14C. < Old French *burniss-*, stem of variant of *brunir* 'make bright or brown' < *brun* (see BURNET).] —**burnisher** *n*

burnished *adj* **1** polished until shiny **2** brown and lustrous or smooth (*literary*) ○ *the burnished coat of the chestnut mare*

Burnley /búrnli/ town in NW England. Population: 74,661 (1991).

burnoose /bur nóoss/, **burnous, burnouse** *n* a long hooded cloak worn by some Arabs, or a garment resembling this [Late 16C. Via French *burnous* < Arabic *burnus* < Greek *birros* 'hooded cloak'.]

burnout /búrn owt/ *n* **1** EXHAUSTION psychological exhaustion and diminished efficiency resulting from overwork or prolonged exposure to stress ○ *reported a high rate of burnout among nurses* **2** EXTREMELY EXHAUSTED PERSON somebody affected by psychological exhaustion (*informal*) **3** MACHINE FAILURE THROUGH HEAT failure of a machine or part of a machine to work because of overuse or excessive heat or friction **4** ROCKET FAILURE failure of a rocket or jet engine to work because the fuel supply has been exhausted or cut off

Burns /burnz/, **George** (1896–1996) US comedian and actor

Burns, Robert (1759–96) Scottish poet

burnsides /búrn sīdz/ *npl US* heavy side whiskers and a moustache worn with a clean-shaven chin [Late 19C. After Ambrose *Burnside* (1824–81), US general.]

Burns Night *n Scotland* the anniversary of the birth of (**Robert Burns**), which is traditionally celebrated with a Burns Supper. Date: 25 January.

Burns Supper *n Scotland* a celebration marking the birthday of (**Robert Burns**). Date: 25 January.

burnt[1] /burnt/ past tense, past participle of **burn**[1]

burnt[2] /burnt/ *adj* **1** affected or spoiled by burning, especially by overcooking **2** describes a pigment or dye that has been darkened through a heating process ○ *burnt umber*

burnt almond *n* sweet with an almond in the centre and a coating of burnt sugar

burnt offering *n* **1** an animal or other offering that is burnt on an altar as a sacrifice in some religions **2** burnt or overcooked food that is nevertheless served up (*humorous*)

burnt-out, burned-out *adj* **1** exhausted physically or emotionally through too much hard work, stress, or reckless living **2** destroyed on the inside by fire

burnt sienna *n* **1** a reddish-brown pigment or dye originally obtained by roasting raw sienna **2** a dark reddish-brown colour

burnt umber *n* **1** a dark brown pigment or dye originally obtained by roasting raw umber **2** a deep brown colour

Burnum /búrnəm/, **Burnum** (1936–97) Australian political activist and writer

burn-up *n* a high-speed drive in a motor vehicle (*slang*)

buroo /bə róo/ *n Ireland, Scotland* **1** an office where unemployed people go to seek work and sign on for state benefit (*dated slang*) **2** a state allowance paid to unemployed people seeking work (*dated informal*) [Mid-20C. Alteration of BUREAU.]

burp /burp/ *n* NOISE MADE THROUGH MOUTH a noise made through the mouth when air is suddenly forced up through the oesophagus from the stomach ■ *v* **1** *vi* BELCH to make a noise through the mouth when air is suddenly forced up through the oesophagus from the stomach **2** *vt* MAKE BABY BRING UP WIND to make a baby expel air from its stomach through its oesophagus after feeding by rubbing or patting its back [Mid-20C. An imitation of the sound.]

burp gun *n US* a lightweight submachine gun (*informal*)

burr[1] /bur/ *n* **1** PRICKLY SEED HUSK a prickly husk covering the seeds of plants such as burdock **2 burr, bur** ROUGH EDGE a rough edge on material such as metal after it has been cut or drilled **3 burr, bur** TOOL FOR REMOVING BURRS a tool used for removing the rough edges from metal that has been cut or drilled **4 burr, bur** DRILL FOR BONE an instrument for drilling holes in bone, especially into the skull **5 burr, bur** TREE GROWTH a lumpy outgrowth of wood on a tree ■ *vt* **1** CREATE ROUGH EDGE to create a rough edge on a piece of metal or other piece of work by cutting or drilling **2** REMOVE ROUGH EDGE to remove a rough edge from a piece of metal or other piece of work [Early 17C. Probably < a N Germanic language.]

burr[2] /bur/ *n* **1** a whirring or buzzing sound ○ *the steady burr of the machines downstairs* **2** a way of speaking the letter 'r' in some regional accents of English, in which the sound is rolled or trilled [Mid-18C. < ?] —**burr** *vti*

burr[3] /bur/ *n* a washer that fits around the end of a rivet [14C. Shortening of Old English *burg* (see BOROUGH); originally 'circle'.]

Burr /bur/, **Aaron** (1756–1836) US statesman and vice president of the United States (1801–05)

Burra /búrrə/, **Edward** (1905–76) British painter

Burrell Collection /búrrəl-/ *n* an art collection in Glasgow that contains paintings, textiles, glass, ceramics, and many other artefacts that once belonged to the 19th-century Scottish shipping magnate, Sir William Burrell (1861–1958)

burrito /bə réetō/ (*plural* **-tos**) *n* in Mexican cooking, a flour tortilla wrapped round a filling of meat, beans, or cheese [Mid-20C. < American Spanish, 'small burro' < Spanish *burro* (see BURRO).]

burro /b-rrō/ (*plural* **-ros**) *n US* a small donkey, especially one that is used as a pack animal [Early 19C. < Spanish, back-formation < *borrico* 'donkey' < late Latin *burricus* 'small horse'.]

Burroughs /búrrōz/, **Edgar Rice** (1875–1950) US writer

Burroughs, William S. (1914–97) US writer. Full name **William Seward Burroughs**

burrow /búrrō/ *n* **1** RABBIT'S HOME a hole or tunnel dug as a living space by a small animal such as a rabbit **2** SNUG PLACE a small snug place created by digging or hollowing ■ *v* **1** *vti* DIG HOLE OR TUNNEL to make a hole or tunnel by digging **2** *vi* PENETRATE BY DIGGING to move through something solid by digging or by creating a space ○ *He burrowed through the undergrowth.* **3** *vi* HIDE OR LIVE IN BURROW to hide or live in a burrow **4** *vi* LOOK INTO THOROUGHLY to research or investigate something very thoroughly ○ *had spent years burrowing into the history of the era* [13C. Variant of BOROUGH.] —**burrower** *n*

burrstone *n* GEOL, INDUST = **buhrstone**

burry[1] /búri/ (**-rier, -riest**) *adj* **1** covered in burrs **2** resembling a burr or burrs

burry[2] /búri/ (**-rier, -riest**) *adj* characterized by or spoken with a burr

bursa /búrssə/ (*plural* **-sas** *or* **-sae** /-see/) *n* a fluid-filled body sac that reduces friction around joints or between other parts that rub against one another [Early 19C. Via modern Latin < medieval Latin, 'bag, purse' < Greek, 'wineskin'.] —**bursal** *adj*

Bursa /búrssə/ city in NW Turkey. Population: 1,057,016 (1996 estimate).

bursa of Fabricius /-fə bríshəss/ *n* an organ in immature birds that produces B lymphocytes [After Girolamo *Fabrici* (1533–1619), Italian anatomist (Latinized)]

bursar /búrssər/ *n* **1** an official who has charge of funds, particularly in a university, college, school, or monastery **2** a student who holds a bursary [13C. Directly or via French *boursier* < medieval Latin *bursarius* < *bursa* (see BURSA).] —**bursarship** *n*

bursary /búrssəri/ (*plural* **-ries**) *n* **1** a grant or scholarship offered to a student at a school, college, or university in some countries, e.g. Scotland and Canada **2** the office or room where a bursar works [Late 17C. < medieval Latin *bursaria* 'bursar's office' < *bursa* (see BURSA).] —**bursarial** /bur sáiri əl/ *adj*

burse /burss/ *n* in the Roman Catholic Church, a flat case that is used for carrying a special linen cloth (**corporal**) when celebrating Mass [13C. Directly or via French *bourse* < medieval Latin *bursa* (see BURSA).]

bursitis /bur sítiss/ *n* inflammation of a fluid-filled sac (**bursa**) of the body, particularly at the elbow, knee, or shoulder joint

ϟ **burst** /burst/ *v* (**bursts, bursting, burst**) **1** *vi* **SPLIT OR BREAK** to split or break apart suddenly and violently because of excess internal pressure ○ *The suitcase had burst open.* **2** *vt* **MAKE SOMETHING SPLIT** to cause something to split open suddenly and disgorge its contents, e.g. by piercing it or applying external pressure **3** *vi* **BE VERY FULL** to be so full as to appear close to splitting open or overflowing ○ *Every hotel in town was bursting with tourists.* **4** *vt* **RUPTURE** to rupture an internal organ or blood vessel **5** *vt* **FLOW OVER** to overflow the normal limit of containment ○ *The river burst its banks.* **6** *vi* **MOVE SUDDENLY** to go, come, or move suddenly and with great energy and speed ○ *Angry protestors burst in on the meeting.* **7** *vi* **BE OVERWHELMED** to feel an emotion so intensely that it is almost overwhelming ○ *I thought I would burst with excitement.* **8** *vi* **BECOME SUDDENLY NOTICED** to appear suddenly and become noticed and prominent at a particular time and in a particular situation ○ *an exciting new product about to burst onto the market* **9** *vt* **DIVIDE PAPER** to separate continuous stationery, e.g. computer printout, into individual sheets ■ *n* **1 EXPLOSION OR RUPTURE** a sudden and often noisy splitting or breaking open of something ○ *There's a burst in the mains.* **2 SHORT INTENSE PERIOD** a short, sudden, and intense period of some activity or phenomenon ○ *a burst of publicity* **3 SUSTAINED ACTIVITY** a period of sustained activity ○ *I read it in two bursts.* **4 GUNFIRE** a short, sudden, and noisy volley of gunfire **5 SINGLE AMOUNT OF DATA** an amount of data sent or received in one operation [Old English *berstan* < Germanic] —**burster** *n*

burst into *vt* **1** to start to happen or appear suddenly and often dramatically ○ *The truck crashed and burst into flames.* ○ *Spring saw the landscape burst into life.* **2** to give sudden and full expression to a strong emotion such as laughter or tears

burst out *v* **1** *vi* to start expressing something suddenly and fully ○ *burst out laughing* **2** *vt* to say something suddenly, as if a suppressed emotion or opinion had been welling up inside

bursting /búrsting/ *adj* **1 ABSOLUTELY FULL** full to the point of overflowing **2 OVERFLOWING** so full of an emotion or quality that it is almost impossible to contain it **3 EAGER** wanting to do something very much (*informal*) ○ *I was bursting to tell her the news.* **4 WITH FULL BLADDER** needing desperately to urinate (*informal*)

bursting disc *n* a process vessel safety device consisting of a thin metal disc that is designed to rupture when subjected to abnormal pressure

burstone *n* GEOL, INDUST = **buhrstone**

ϟ **bursty** /búrsti/ *adj* moving, transferred, or transmitted in short uneven spurts, as is stellar radiation from a pulsar, traffic at a toll booth, or data in a computer network —**burstiness** *n*

burthen /búrthən/ *n* a burden (*archaic*) ■ *vt* to burden somebody (*archaic*) [Variant of BURDEN[1]]

burton /búrt'n/ *n* a type of light tackle with double or single blocks used for hoisting [Early 18C. Alteration of obsolete *Breton (tackle)* < ?] ◇ **go for a burton** to be destroyed, ruined, or dead (*informal; usually past progressive*)

Burton /búrt'n/, **Richard** (1925–84) Welsh-born British actor

Burton-upon-Trent /búrt'n ə pon trént/ town in central England. Population: 60,000 (1991).

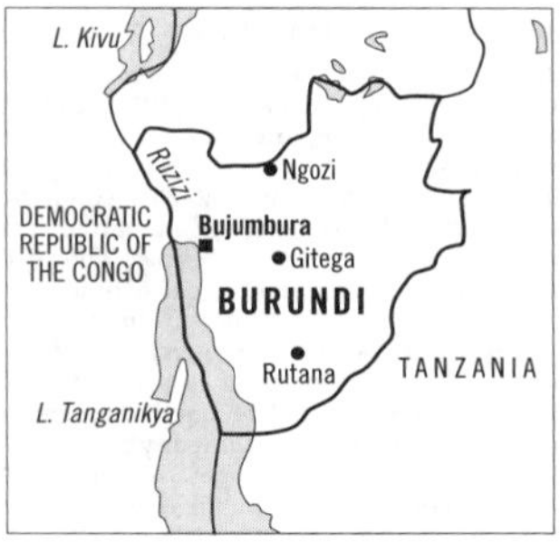

Burundi

Burundi /boo róondi/ republic in east-central Africa, northwest of Tanzania. Capital: Bujumbura. Population: 5,397,107 (1997). Area: 27,834 sq. km/10,747 sq. mi. —**Burundian** *n, adj*

bury /bérri/ (**-ies, -ying, -ied**) *v* **1** *vt* **PUT SOMETHING IN HOLE** to dig a hole, put something in it, and replace the soil or other material removed ○ *a dog burying its bone* **2** *vt* **INTER DEAD BODY** to put a dead body in a grave dug in the ground, or sometimes under water, usually as part of a religious ritual ○ *He asked to be buried at sea.* **3** *vt* **LOSE SOMEBODY THROUGH DEATH** to lose somebody, especially a spouse or a close relative, through death ○ *She has buried four husbands.* **4** *vt* **HIDE SOMETHING BY COVERING** to hide something by covering it with a lot of things so it cannot be seen ○ *He buried the letter under a pile of books.* **5** *vt* **COVER SOMETHING UP** to cover something or somebody completely with something ○ *buried alive under the rubble* **6** *vt* **OBSCURE** to make something difficult to find or distinguish ○ *The announcement was buried at the end of the programme.* **7** *vt* **SINK SOMETHING DEEPLY** to sink deeply into something so that it is difficult to see or retrieve ○ *The splinter had buried itself under his nail.* **8** *vt* **HIDE SOMETHING FROM SIGHT** to put the face or head somewhere, usually on or under a soft and yielding surface ○ *She buried her face in her hands.* **9** *vr* **CONCENTRATE INTENSELY** to concentrate exclusively and intensely on something ○ *She tended to bury herself in her work.* **10** *vt* **SUPPRESS OR FORGET** to suppress or forget something unpleasant or undesirable ○ *their efforts to bury the past* [Old English *byrgan* < Germanic, 'protection, shelter']

SPELLCHECK See ***berry***.

Bury /bérri/ town in NW England. Population: 62,633 (1991).

Buryat /bóori aát/, **Buriat** *n* **1** a member of a people living in SE Russia **2** an Altaic language spoken by the Buryats, considered to be a dialect of Mongolian. Native speakers: 300,000. [Mid-19C. < Mongolian *Buriyad*.] —**Buryat** *adj*

Bury St Edmunds /bérri s'nt édməndz/ town in E England. Population: 31,237 (1991).

ϟ **bus** /buss/ *n* (*plural* **buses** *or* **busses**) **1 LARGE PASSENGER VEHICLE** a long motor vehicle with many seats, usually divided by a central aisle and often on two decks **2 CAR OR PLANE** a vehicle, especially a car or plane (*informal*) ○ *I can't get this old bus to start!* **3 DATA CHANNEL** a channel or path for transferring computer data, particularly between the central processing unit and a peripheral device **4 ROCKET WARHEAD** the final stage of a multistage rocket, containing the warhead **5 SPACECRAFT COMPONENT** the part of a space exploration vehicle that contains the atmospheric re-entry probes ■ *v* (**buses** *or* **busses, busing** *or* **bussing, bused** *or* **bussed**) **1** *vti* **TRAVEL OR CARRY PASSENGERS BY BUS** to travel or transport passengers to a particular destination by bus **2** *vi* *US* **TRANSPORT SCHOOLCHILDREN** to transport schoolchildren by bus to another school distant from their homes, especially in an effort to achieve ethnic balance in the school population [Early 19C. Shortening of OMNIBUS.] ◇ **miss the bus** to fail to take advantage of an opportunity (*informal*)

bus. *abbr* business

busboy /búss boy/ *n* *US* somebody employed in a restaurant or café to clear away dishes, set tables, and assist the servers

busby /búzbi/ (*plural* **-bies**) *n* a tall fur helmet worn by some soldiers, including some British guards regiments [Mid-18C. < ?]

Busby /búzbi/, **James** (1800–71) British government official

Busby, Sir Matt (1909–94) British footballer and manager. Full name **Sir Matthew Busby**

bush[1] /bo͝osh/ *n* **1 WOODY BRANCHED PLANT** a woody plant that is smaller than a tree and has many branches growing up from the lower part of the main stem **2 THICKET** a thick clump of bushes **3 UNCULTIVATED AND UNSETTLED LAND** wild, uncultivated, and sparsely populated areas of land covered with natural vegetation, especially in Africa and Australia ○ *living in the bush* **4 DENSE MASS** a dense large mass of something, especially hair or beard ○ *a great bush of black hair* **5** *NZ* **NEW ZEALAND FOREST** the forest of New Zealand **6 BUSHY TAIL** a bushy tail, especially of a fox ■ *vi* **BRANCH OUT** to branch out, spread, or grow thick like a bush ○ *hair bushing out round her head* [< assumed Old English *bysc* and Old Norse *buski* < Germanic] ◇ **beat about the bush** to discuss a subject without coming to the point

bush[2] /bo͝osh/ *n* a cylindrical metal sleeve used to prevent abrasion, functioning as a bearing or as a guide for certain tool parts such as valve rods. US term **bushing** *n*. 3 [Mid-16C. < Middle Dutch *busse*, via Germanic < Latin *pyxis* 'box, cap' < late Greek *puxis* 'box'.]

Bush /bo͝osh/, **Barbara** (*b.* 1925) US first lady (1989–93)

Bush, George (*b.* 1924) US statesman and 41st president of the United States (1989–93)

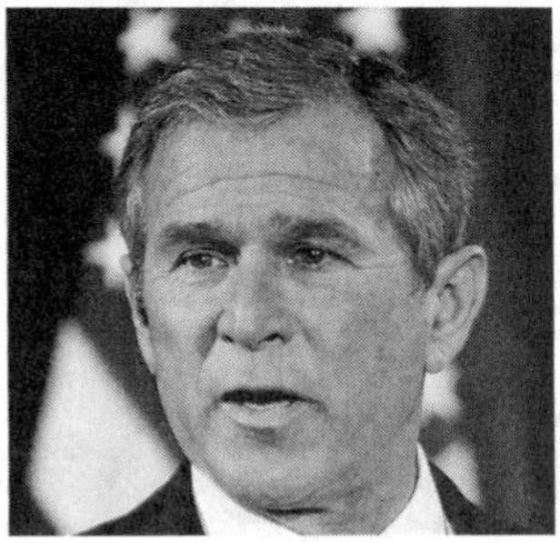
George W. Bush

Bush, George W. (*b.* 1946) US statesman and 43rd president of the United States (2001–). Full name **George Walker Bush**. Known as **Dubya**

bushbaby /bo͝osh baybi/ *n* a small nocturnal primate that lives in trees and has big round eyes, large ears, and a long tail. Native to: Africa. Family: Galagidae.

bushbuck /bo͝osh buk/ (*plural* **-bucks** *or* **-buck**) *n* a small antelope that has a reddish-brown coat, usually with white stripes, and twisted horns. Native to: sub-Saharan Africa. *Tragelaphus scriptus*. [Mid-19C. Translation of Afrikaans *bosbok* < Dutch *bosch* 'bush' + *bok* 'buck'.]

bush clover *n* a plant with three-leaved compound leaves. Genus: *Lespedeza*.

bushcraft /bo͝osh kraaft/ *n* *ANZ* the skills and knowledge that enable somebody to live and function successfully in the bush

bush dog *n* a wild dog that lives in dense undergrowth, usually near rivers and is sometimes kept as a pet. Native to: South America. *Speothos venaticus*.

bushed /bo͝osht/ *adj* (*informal*) **1** exhausted from overwork or lack of sleep **2** *ANZ* perplexed and confused [Late 19C. The state typical of somebody wandering in the bush.]

Bushehr /boo sheér/, **Bushire** /boo shír/ port in SW Iran. Population: 132,824 (1991).

bushel /bo͝osh'l/ *n* **1 FORMER UK UNIT OF VOLUME** a unit of dry or liquid measure in the British Imperial system, equal to 8 imperial gallons (36.37 litres), formerly used for measuring items such as wheat, fruit, and liquids **2 US UNIT OF VOLUME** a unit of measure in the US Customary system used for measuring dry goods, equal to 64 US pints (35.24 litres) 3 **CONTAINER** a container that has a capacity of one bushel [15C. < Old French *boisell*.]

bushfire /bo͝osh fīr/ *n* a fire in the bush or in a forest area that spreads quickly and easily goes out of control

bushfly /bo͝osh flī/ (*plural* **-flies** *or* **-fly**) *n* an Australian fly that lays its eggs in animal dung. *Musca vetustissima.*

bush grass *n* grass with leaves that grow tall like reeds in damp clay soils. Native to: Europe, Asia. *Calamagrostis epigejos.*

bushhammer /bo͝osh hamər/ *n* a powered hammer with small pyramidal points cut into the working surface, used to form a rough surface on stonework [Late 19C. Probably translation of German *Boszhammer* < *boszen* 'to beat'.]

Bushido /boo shéedō/ *n* the code of honour and behaviour of the Japanese warrior class (**samurai**), emphasizing self-discipline, courage, and loyalty [Late 19C. < Japanese.]

bushing /bo͝oshing/ *n* 1 a layer of electrical insulation that allows a live conductor to pass through an earthed wall 2 an adaptor or screw-piece for connecting two different sizes of pipe 3 ENG = **bush**² [Mid-19C. < BUSH².]

Bushire /byoo shīr/ = **Bushehr**

bush jacket *n* a lightweight cotton jacket resembling a shirt, with patch pockets and a belt

bush lawyer *n ANZ* 1 any Australian prickly, trailing plant 2 somebody who offers legal advice without being qualified (*informal disapproving*)

bush league *n US* 1 a minor league in baseball 2 a sphere of activity for those who cannot compete with the best ○ *a lawyer in the bush leagues* —**bush-league** *adj* —**bush-leaguer** *n*

bush line *n NZ* the height on a mountain or other elevation above which the native forest does not grow

bushman /bo͝oshmən/ (*plural* **-men** /-mən/) *n ANZ* somebody with experience of living or travelling in remote areas

Bushman /bo͝oshmən/ (*plural* **-men** /-mən/) *n* an offensive term for a member of the San people

bushmaster /bo͝osh maastər/ *n* a large venomous snake with greyish-brown markings, growing up to 3.6 m/12 ft in length. Native to: Central and South America. *Lachesis mutus.*

bush pig *n* a black or brown wild pig that has small tusks and long tufts of hair on the face and ears. Native to: southern Africa. *Potamochoerus porcus.*

bush pilot *n* a pilot who flies a small plane into and out of areas that are difficult to reach with other means of transportation

bushranger /bo͝osh raynjər/ *n* 1 *US* somebody who lives in the wilderness 2 *ANZ* formerly, a criminal or escaped convict living on the run in the bush

bush telegraph *n* 1 a method of communicating over distances, e.g. with drumbeats 2 a method of communicating information or rumours swiftly and unofficially by word of mouth or other means (*informal*)

bushtit /bo͝osh tit/ *n* a small grey bird known for building hanging nests. Native to: North America. Genus: *Psaltriparus.*

bush tucker *n Aus* (*informal*) 1 simple food that can be cooked over a campfire in the bush 2 food consisting of items collected in the bush, e.g. native plants and fruits

bushwalk /bo͝osh wawk/ *n ANZ* a hike through the bush —**bushwalker** *n* —**bushwalking** *n*

bushwhack /bo͝osh wak/ *v* 1 *vi US, Can, Aus* **TRAVEL THROUGH WOODS** to travel through woods, forest, or the bush 2 *vi US, Can, Aus* **CUT THROUGH WOODS** to cut a way through thick woods or forest 3 *vt US, Can* **AMBUSH** to ambush somebody (*informal*) 4 *vi US, Can* **FIGHT AS GUERRILLA** to fight as a guerrilla 5 *vi NZ* **FELL TIMBER** to fell timber in the native forest of New Zealand for a living

bushwhacker /bo͝osh wakər/ *n* 1 *US, Can, Aus* **SOMEBODY WHO LIVES IN THE BUSH** somebody who travels or lives in wooded isolated regions 2 **CLEARER OF BUSH** somebody who clears away bush 3 **CONFEDERATE GUERRILLA IN AMERICAN CIVIL WAR** a Confederate guerrilla in the American Civil War 4 *US* **RURAL GUERRILLA** a guerrilla who fights in remote or rural areas 5 *NZ* **NEW ZEALAND LUMBERJACK** somebody who fells timber in the bush 6 *ANZ* **UNSOPHISTICATED RUSTIC** an unsophisticated person from the country (*slang*) 7 **CLEARING TOOL** a tool for clearing or cutting a way through bush, trees, or undergrowth

bushy /bo͝oshi/ (**-ier, -iest**) *adj* 1 **THICK AND FULL** very thick and full 2 **DENSE AND WOODY** with many branches growing up together, producing a rounded shape like a bush 3 **COVERED WITH BUSHES** covered or overgrown with bushes —**bushily** *adv* —**bushiness** *n*

busily /bízzili/ *adv* in an active, energetic, and concentrated way ○ *busily cleaning the house*

~~**busines**~~ incorrect spelling of **business**

business /bíznəss/ *n* 1 **LINE OF WORK** a particular trade or profession ○ *the retail business* 2 **COMMERCIAL ORGANIZATION** a company or other organization that buys and sells goods, makes products, or provides services ○ *take over an ailing business* 3 **COMMERCIAL ACTIVITY** commercial activity involving the exchange of money for goods or services ○ *a good person to do business with* 4 **LEVEL OF COMMERCE** the amount of commercial activity or custom that exists at a particular time ○ *Business is poor right now.* 5 **COMMERCIAL PRACTICE** commercial practice or procedure ○ *It's bad business to neglect smaller clients.* 6 **CUSTOM** the commercial dealings that a person or organization has with another company or individual ○ *If this goes on, I shall take my business elsewhere!* 7 **IMPORTANT MATTERS** tasks or important things that a person has to do or deal with ○ *We have important business to discuss.* 8 **PRIVATE MATTERS** personal responsibilities and concerns ○ *What business is it of yours?* 9 **AFFAIR** a situation or event that is characterized by difficulty, fuss, or unpleasantness ○ *that business about the tickets* 10 **UNSPECIFIED ACTIVITIES** activities or things that are not clearly described or defined ○ *designing, measuring, and all that kind of business* 11 **COMPLICATED TASK** an overcomplicated or irritating task or activity ○ *It's such a business even getting served in here!* 12 **ACTOR'S SMALL ACTIONS** an action or series of actions performed by an actor for dramatic or comic effect or to fill in a pause when little is happening on stage 13 **SOMETHING EXCELLENT** something very impressive or excellent (*informal*) ○ *He thinks his new car is really the business.* ■ *adj* **OF COMMERCE** relating to, belonging to, or involving commerce and the world of professional workers ○ *good business practice* [Old English *bisignis* 'anxiety, distress' < *bisig* 'anxious, busy'] ◇ **do your business** to defecate (*informal; euphemistic*) ◇ **get down to business** to deal with important matters, leaving extraneous ones behind ◇ **have no business doing something** to have no right to do something ◇ **like nobody's business** very hard or strongly ◇ **mean business** to have sincere and forthright intentions ◇ **mind your own business** to attend to your own affairs and not interfere in other people's concerns ◇ **not be in the business of doing something** to consider something inappropriate or outside the usual area of responsibility ◇ **out of business** not or no longer trading or operating as a business ○ *restaurants that go out of business within a few months of opening*

business administration *n* a course of study at a university, college, or other institute of higher education that teaches the basic principles of business and business practices

business card *n* a small card printed with a person's name, job title, business address, and contact numbers

business class *n* a superior level of service in air travel that is less expensive than first class and caters for business travellers (*hyphenated before nouns*) —**business class** *adv*

business college *n* a college of higher education where students learn basic business skills such as accounting, and management

business cycle *n* ECON = **trade cycle**

business end *n* the part of a tool or device that does the work, as opposed to the body or handle (*informal*) ○ *the business end of a gun*

business hours *npl* 1 the hours during which business is conducted 2 the normal hours that most offices and shops are open, usually between about 9 AM and 5:30 PM

businesslike /bíznəss līk/ *adj* 1 showing qualities or attributes that are useful and desirable in a business context, e.g. efficiency, practicality, and methodicalness ○ *a very businesslike operation* 2 practical and unemotional

businessman /bíznəss man/ (*plural* **-men** /-mən, -men/) *n* a man who works in business, especially at a senior level

business park *n* an area designed to accommodate businesses and light industry, with large numbers of companies all grouped together, usually on the outskirts of a town or city

businessperson /bíznəss purss'n/ (*plural* **-people** /-peep'l/) *n* a person who works in business, especially at a senior level

business plan *n* a plan that sets out the future strategy and financial development of a business, usually covering a period of several years

business school *n US* a postgraduate educational establishment that offers MBAs and related courses of study

business suit *n* a suit consisting of a jacket and trousers, or a jacket and skirt, made from the same cloth that is worn during the day, especially in the office

businesswoman /bíznəss wo͝omən/ (*plural* **-en** /-wimmin/) *n* a woman who works in business, especially at a senior level

busing /bússing/, **bussing** *n US* the transporting of children by bus to school distant from their homes in an effort to achieve ethnic balance in school populations

busk /busk/ *vi* to entertain in the street or another public place in the hope of receiving money from passers-by [Mid-17C. Via obsolete French *busquer* 'seek, hunt for' < Italian *buscare* or Spanish *buscar* < Germanic.] —**busker** *n*

buskin /búskin/ *n* 1 a thick-soled laced boot worn by tragic actors in ancient Greece to give them extra height 2 a calf-length laced boot worn in the Middle Ages [Early 16C. Probably via Old French *bousequin*, variant of *brousequin* < Middle Dutch *broseken*.]

bus lane *n* a lane on a road in some cities or towns that during certain hours of the day can only be used by buses

busman's holiday *n* a holiday or leisure activity that is similar to the work somebody normally engages in (*informal*) [Probably < drivers of horse-drawn buses being driven around on their own bus]

ϟ **bus mouse** *n* a mouse attached to a computer bus using a special card or port

ϟ **bus network** *n* a computer network in which all nodes are connected to a single bus

Buson /bo͞o son/ (1716–84) Japanese poet and artist. Full name **Yosa Buson**

bus pass *n* a ticket that entitles the holder to multiple rides on buses over a set period of time, either free or at a reduced rate

Buss /buss/, **Frances Mary** (1827–94) British pioneer of women's education

Busselton /búss'ltən/ coastal city in S Western Australia. Population: 13,528 (1991).

bussing *n US* = **busing**

bus stop *n* a designated place along a specific route where a bus stops to pick up or set down passengers

bust¹ /bust/ *n* 1 a woman's upper torso 2 a sculpture of the head and shoulders of a person [Mid-17C. Via French *buste* < Italian *busto*.]

bust up *vt* (*informal*) 1 to disrupt or stop something such as a meeting or gathering 2 *US* to cause damage to something

bust² /bust/ *v* (**busts, busting, busted** *or* **bust**) 1 *vti* **MAKE OR BECOME USELESS** to break something mechanical or electrical, or to cease operating properly (*informal*) ○ *Your brother just busted our telly!* 2 *vti* **BREAK OR GET BROKEN** to break or damage something by hitting it or by subjecting it to a powerful impact, or be broken in this way (*informal*) ○ *I busted my leg skiing.* 3 *vti* **BURST** to burst something, or undergo bursting 4 *vt* **RAID PLACE OR ARREST PERSON** to mount a police raid, especially in connection with illegal drugs (*slang*) 5 *vti* **MAKE OR BECOME BANKRUPT** to make somebody bankrupt, or become bankrupt (*informal*) 6 *vt US, Can* **DEMOTE** to demote a member of the armed forces (*informal*) 7 *vt US* **BREAK IN HORSE** to break in a horse (*informal*) 8 *vt US* **BREAK UP ORGANIZATION** to break up an organization when it has become too powerful (*informal*) 9 *vt US* **HIT** to hit or punch somebody (*informal*) ○ *He busted the villain over the head.* 10 *vi* **GO OVER LIMIT** in pontoon, to have cards totalling more than 21 points 11 *vi* **FAIL TO COMPLETE HAND** in poker, to fail to complete a flush or straight ■ *n* 1 *US* **FAILURE** somebody or something that fails completely (*informal*) ○ *The plan seemed perfect in theory, but it was a bust in reality.* 2 *US* **BANKRUPTCY** bankruptcy or financial failure (*informal*) ○ *periods of boom and bust* 3 *US* **PUNCH** a punch or blow (*informal*) 4 **PARTY** a disorganized party or celebration (*informal*) 5 **POLICE RAID** a police raid or arrest, especially in connection with illegal drugs (*slang*) ■ *adj* (*informal*) 1 **DAMAGED** broken or no longer working 2 **BANKRUPT** bankrupt [Mid-18C. Alteration of BURST.]

Bustamante /bústə mánti/, **Sir Alexander** (1884–1977) Jamaican statesman. Born **William Alexander Clarke**

bustard /bústərd/ (*plural* **-tards** *or* **-tard**) *n* a bird with long legs, a rotund body, and a long neck. Native to: open grassy land in S Europe, Asia, Africa, and Australia. Family: Otididae. [15C. Probably < assumed Anglo-Norman *bustarde*, blend of *bistarde* + *oustarde*, both < Latin *avis tarda* 'slow bird'.]

buster /bústər/ *n* 1 *US, Can* used as a jocular or mildly threatening term of address, usually for a man or boy (*informal*) 2 *US, Can* RIDING = **broncobuster** 3 somebody or something that breaks up or destroys something (*informal; usually in combination*) [Mid-19C. < BUST[1], or alteration of *burster*.]

bustier /bústi ay/ *n* a close-fitting sleeveless and usually strapless bodice worn by women as lingerie or evening wear [Late 20C. < French, < *buste* (see BUST[1]).]

bustle[1] /búss'l/ *vi* (**-tles, -tling, -tled**) to work or do something in an ostentatiously hurried and energetic way ○ *He bustled about in preparation for their arrival.* ■ *n* energetic, busy, and noisy activity ○ *a great bustle surrounding the arriving guests* [14C. < ?] —**bustler** *n*

bustle[2] /búss'l/ *n* a pad or frame worn in the 19th century under the top of a woman's long skirt to fill it out at the back [Late 18C. < ?]

bustling /búss'ling/ *adj* full of or characterized by energetic and noisy activity —**bustlingly** *adv*

bust-up *n* (*informal*) 1 a breaking up of something such as a relationship or an organization 2 a fight or brawl ○ *There was a big bust-up in the bar last night.*

busty /bústi/ (**-ier, -iest**) *adj* having large breasts (*informal*)

busulphan /byoo súlfən/ *n* a drug used in the treatment of certain chronic leukaemias [Mid-20C. Blend of BUTANE + SULPHONYL.]

busy /bízzi/ *adj* (**-ier, -iest**) 1 **OCCUPIED** fully occupied in a particular activity, especially work ○ *She seemed too busy even to talk to me.* ○ *He was busy writing letters all morning.* 2 **FULL OF BUSTLE** full of activity, with a large number of people moving around ○ *the busy city streets* 3 **NOT FREE** committed to something that has previously been planned or arranged and so unable to undertake another activity ○ *I'm sorry but I'm busy tomorrow night.* 4 **ACTIVE** engaged in or characterized by constant, and usually purposeful, activity ○ *busy people who lead busy lives* 5 **ELABORATE** characterized by overcomplex detail, colours, or patterns ○ *a very busy painting* 6 TELECOM = **engaged** *adj.* 5 ■ *v* (**-ies, -ying, -ied**) 1 *vr* **OCCUPY YOURSELF** to start doing something that will keep you occupied and working for a period of time 2 *vt* **OCCUPY** to occupy somebody ○ *The work busied him all afternoon.* [Old English *bisig* 'busy, anxious'] —**busyness** *n*

busybody /bízzi bodi/ (*plural* **-ies**) *n* somebody who meddles in other people's business (*informal*)

Busy Lizzie /bízzi lízzi/ (*plural* **Busy Lizzie** *or* **Busy Lizzies**) *n* a low-growing cultivated species of the balsam family. Use: house and garden plant. Flowers: numerous, colourful. *Impatiens walleriana.* US term **impatiens**

busy signal *n US* TELECOM = **engaged tone**

busywork /bízzi wurk/ *n US* activities assigned or undertaken that take up time but do not necessarily yield productive results

but[1] *stressed* /but/; *unstressed* /bət/ CORE MEANING: a grammatical word used in the middle of or at the beginning of a sentence to introduce something that is true in spite of either being or seeming contrary to what has just been said ○ *I thought it was late, but it was only 9 o'clock.* ○ *Not one, but two offers were received.* ○ *Yes, but not now.* ○ *It's true her name is Spanish, but she's actually Greek.* ○ *I'm a blonde, but both my mother and father have dark hair.*

1 *conj* **INTRODUCING AN OPPOSING PROPOSITION** used to introduce a statement that disagrees with something just said, or that expresses an emotion such as surprise or disbelief at what was just said ○ *'I don't think you're suitable for the job'.'But I have all the right qualifications!'* 2 *conj* **INTRODUCING FURTHER INFORMATION** used to introduce a clause or a new sentence that adds information such as background or reasoning ○ *Jeff isn't coming with us. But he doesn't like horror movies anyway.* 3 *conj* **EXCEPT THAT** used to introduce a dependent clause, e.g. a reason for doing or not doing something ○ *I would have called, but I couldn't find a phone.* 4 *conj* **WITHOUT SOMETHING HAPPENING** used to indicate that something does not happen without something else happening or being the case (*formal; usually after a negative*) ○ *She never leaves home but she forgets her keys.* 5 *conj* **THAT** used to introduce a subordinate clause ○ *It's not so difficult but I can't understand it.* 6 *conj* **WHEN** than or when (*informal*) ○ *I'd no sooner put the phone down but it rang again.* 7 *conj, prep* **EXCEPT** used to indicate the exception to a statement just made ○ *He could do nothing but stand and watch her leave.* ○ *There was nothing but a lump of mouldy bread in the cupboard.* 8 *adv* **ONLY, JUST, OR MERELY** used to indicate that something happens or is true just to the extent mentioned and not more ○ *This is but one of the bread-making techniques used.* ○ *He arrived but a minute ago.* ○ *We can but try.* 9 *adv Aus* **THOUGH** however 10 *adv US* **FOR EMPHASIS** used to emphasize a statement (*slang*) ○ *Man, but he's fast!* 11 *npl* **buts OBJECTIONS** objections to something (*informal*) ○ *Allow time to consider all the ifs and buts from the children.* [Old English *būtan* 'outside, without, except, but' < Germanic] ◇ **but for** if not for, or if it had not been for

USAGE Can **but** begin a sentence? Some people object to the use of ***but***, like *and*, at the beginning of a sentence, regarding it as a joining word that has to have words on either side of it. However, this is a mistaken notion that has no foundation in English structure and usage. It is, however, advisable to reserve this use for occasions when the special effect that initial position affords is needed; otherwise it can become an awkward affectation.
But is not usually followed by a comma. A comma may precede ***but*** when an independent clause follows, thus: *I wanted to leave early, but the rest of the group did not*, not *I wanted to leave early, but* [,] *the rest of the group did not.* Avoid unnecessary redundancy in using ***but*** and other terms such as *however* together. Write *However,* [or *But*] *the Foreign Office have lodged a formal protest*, not *But the Foreign Office have, however, lodged a formal protest.*
When ***but*** is used to indicate an exception, as in *No one but me has* (or *No one but I have*) *seen the document*, either wording can be used, according to your interpretation of the function of ***but***: is it a preposition, as in the first variation, or is it a conjunction, as in the second, parenthetic, variation? Though strong cases have been made for both wordings, the prepositional wording does carry slightly more weight. You can recast the sentence to *No one has seen the document but me*, where its prepositional function is quite clear.

USAGE See ***help***.

but[2] /but/ *n Scotland* the outer room of a two-roomed cottage in Scotland, usually the living or cooking area. ◊ **but and ben** ■ *adv Scotland* in or towards the outer part of a house, cottage, or other dwelling [Early 18C. < BUT[1].]

but- *prefix* containing a group of four carbon atoms ○ *butene* [< BUTYRIC]

butadiene /byoótə dī́ een/ *n* $CH_2=CHCH=CH_2$ a colourless flammable gas. Source: petroleum. Use: manufacture of synthetic rubber, nylon, latex paints. [Early 20C. < BUTANE.]

butanal /byoótənal/ *n* CHEM = **butyraldehyde** [Late 20C. < BUTANOL.]

but and ben *n Scotland* in parts of Scotland, a two-roomed cottage that consists of a living room and a bedroom. ◊ **ben**[2]

butane /byoó tayn/ *n* C_4H_{10} a colourless, highly flammable gas that has two different molecular structures (**isomers**). Source: natural gas. Use: lighter fluid, fuel. [Late 19C. < BUTYL.]

butanoic acid /byoótənō ik-/ *n* C_3H_7COOH a thick colourless liquid that causes the smell of rancid butter. Use: in flavourings, scents. [< BUTANE]

butanol /byoótə nol/ *n* C_4H_9OH a colourless toxic liquid with four different molecular structures (**isomers**). Use: solvents, manufacture of organic compounds.

butanone /byoótə nōn/ *n* a colourless flammable liquid with an odour similar to acetone. Use: solvent, paint stripper, in resins. [Early 20C. < BUTANE.]

butch /booch/ *adj* 1 **MASCULINE AND STRONG** describes a man who is extremely masculine and strong 2 **OFFENSIVE TERM** an offensive term insulting a woman's appearance and sexuality (*slang*) ■ *n* 1 **OFFENSIVE TERM** an offensive term for a woman whose appearance and sexuality is considered unfeminine (*slang*) 2 *US* HAIR = **crew cut** [Mid-20C. Probably < the nickname *Butch*.]

butcher /boóchər/ *n* 1 **MEAT SELLER** somebody who sells meat 2 **SLAUGHTERER** somebody who slaughters animals for their meat 3 **butcher, butcher's PREMISES OF BUTCHER** a shop that sells prepared raw meat and meat products 4 **BRUTAL KILLER** somebody who kills many people in a brutal manner 5 **BOTCHER** somebody who does something badly ○ *a butcher of the sonnet form* ■ *vt* 1 **KILL ANIMAL FOR FOOD** to slaughter and prepare the meat of an animal for food 2 **KILL PEOPLE BRUTALLY** to kill people in a brutal way 3 **BOTCH** to do, perform, or make something very incompetently (*informal*) ○ *The original script had been butchered.* [13C. < Anglo-Norman form of Old French *bo(u)chier* 'slaughterer of he-goats' < *boc* 'he-goat'.] —**butcherer** *n*

butcherbird /boóchər burd/ *n* 1 a bird of the shrike family that impales its prey on thorns and barbed wire. Genus: *Lanius.* 2 a songbird of the magpie family, usually with black or black-and-white plumage, that impales insects and other prey on thorns. Native to: Australasia. Genus: *Cracticus.*

butcher's /boóchərz/ *n Cockney* a look (*informal*) ○ *Let's have a quick butcher's at that.* [Mid-20C. < Rhyming slang *butcher's hook* 'a look'.]

butcher's broom *n* an evergreen shrub with stiff stems. Use: formerly, making brooms. Native to: Mediterranean. *Ruscus aculeatus.*

butchery /boóchəri/ (*plural* **-ies**) *n* 1 **MASS KILLING** brutal, senseless, and cruel slaughter of people, usually in large numbers ○ *an act of appalling butchery* 2 **USE OF KNIVES ON CARCASS** the use of knives or other tools to remove meat from an animal's carcass ○ *'The tools are often found in association with broken animal bones, which sometimes show signs of butchery'.* (*'Ape at the Brink', Discover Magazine*; 1994) 3 **BUTCHER'S WORK** the work or trade of a butcher 4 **BOTCHING** a terrible botching of a job, performance, or activity (*informal*) ○ *the singer's butchery of the melody* 5 *S Africa* **BUTCHER'S SHOP** a butcher's shop [14C. < French *boucherie* < Old French *bo(u)chier* (see BUTCHER).]

butch haircut *n US* HAIR = **crew cut**

Bute /byoot/ island off the coast of SW Scotland. Area: 119 sq. km/46 sq. mi.

butene /byoó teen/ *n* C_4H_8 a colourless, flammable, easily liquefiable gas with three different molecular structures (**isomers**). Use: manufacture of polymers. [Late 19C. < BUTYL.]

buteo /byoóti ō/ (*plural* **-os**) *n US* BIRDS = **buzzard** *n.* 1 [Mid-20C. Via modern Latin (genus name) < Latin, '(kind of) hawk or falcon'.]

Buteshire /byoótshər/ former county in SW Scotland, now part of Argyll and Bute council area

Buthelezi /boótə láyzi/, **Mangosuthu Gatsha** (*b.* 1928) South African politician. Known as **Chief Buthelezi**

butler /búttlər/ *n* the male head servant in a large or important household [13C. < Anglo-Norman *buteler*, Old French *boteillier* 'cup-bearer' < *boteille* (see BOTTLE).]

Butler /búttlər/, **Rab** (1902–82) British politician. Full name **Richard Austen Butler**

Butler, Reg (1913–81) British sculptor. Full name **Reginald Cotterell Butler**

Butler, Samuel (1612–80) English satirist

butler's pantry, butlery /bútləri/ *n* a room situated between a kitchen and dining room, used for serving food and for storage

Butlin /búttlin/, **Sir Billy** (1899–1980) British holiday camp organizer. Full name **Sir William Edmund Butlin**

Butskellism /bútskillizəm/ *n* the perceived consensus politics of the Labour and Conservative parties in the United Kingdom in the 1950s, when R. A. Butler and Hugh Gaitskell were the chancellors of the two parties when in power. [Mid-20C. Blend of *Butler* + *Gaitskell*.]

butt[1] /but/ *v* 1 *vt* **RAM** to hit or push against somebody or something with the head or horns 2 *vi* **STICK OUT** to project or jut out ■ *n* **A PUSH** a push with the head or horns [15C. Via Anglo-Norman *buter*, Old French *bo(u)ter* < Germanic.] —**butter** *n*

butt in *vi* to interrupt and attempt to join in a conversation or activity without being invited ○ *He's always trying to butt in on our conversations.*

butt out *vi US, ANZ* to keep out of other people's business or conversation (*slang*)

butt[2] /but/ *n* 1 **OBJECT OF RIDICULE OR CONTEMPT** somebody or something that is an object of ridicule or contempt ○ *He became the butt of their satire.* 2 **HINGE** a butt hinge, or either of its two parts 3 BUILDING = **butt joint** ■ **butts** *npl*

1 MOUND BEHIND TARGET in archery and rifle shooting, a mound of earth behind the target, designed to stop any stray bullets or arrows **2 TARGET RANGE** a target range **3 TARGET** a target at a shooting or archery range ■ *vti* **ABUT** to lie with one flat end against the flat end of something else, or place something in such a position ○ *The beam butts against the wall.* [14C. < French *but* 'goal'.]

butt[3] /but/ *n* **1 THICK END** the thicker or larger end of something, such as the part of a rifle held against the shoulder **2 CIGARETTE END** the part of a cigarette that remains after the rest has been smoked **3** *US* **BUTTOCKS** a person's or animal's buttocks (*informal; sometimes offensive*) [15C. < ?]

butt[4] *n NZ* = **butty**[2]

butt[5] /but/ *n* a large cask for holding wine or ale [15C. Via Anglo-Norman *but*, Old French *bot* < late Latin *buttis*.]

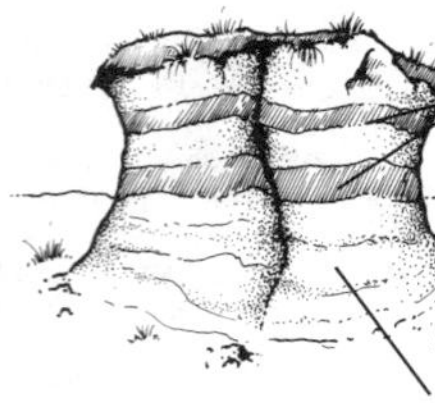
Strata of hard rock
Softer layer of rock
Butte

butte /byoot/ *n* in the W United States and Canada, a hill that rises abruptly from a flat area of land, with steep sides and a flat top. ◊ **mesa** [Mid-19C. < French, 'mound, hillock'.]

butter /búttər/ *n* **1 SOFT CREAMY SPREAD** a soft, pale yellow, fatty food made by churning cream. Use: cooking, spreading on food. ○ *bread and butter* **2 SUBSTANCE RESEMBLING BUTTER** any substance that is similar to butter in consistency or appearance ○ *apple butter* ■ *vt* **PUT BUTTER ON** to spread butter on something, or add butter to something [Old English *butere*, via Germanic < Latin *butyrum* < Greek *bouturon*] ◇ **look as if butter wouldn't melt in your mouth** to look more innocent than you really are

butter up *vt* to flatter somebody in the hope of winning favour or cooperation (*informal*)

butter-and-eggs (*plural* **butter-and-eggs**) *n* = **toadflax** *n.* 1 (+ *singular or plural verb*)

butterball /búttər bawl/ *n US* **1** a chubby person (*informal insult; sometimes offensive*) **2** BIRDS = **bufflehead**

butter bean *n* **1** a large flat cream-coloured bean, dried before cooking **2** *US* a wax bean (*regional*)

butterbur /búttər bur/ (*plural* **-burs** *or* **-bur**) *n* a waterside plant with large soft leaves. Flowers: purple. Native to: Europe, Aisa. Genus: *Petasites*. [Because butter was formerly wrapped in its leaves]

buttercup /búttər kup/ *n* a plant that grows in grassland. Flowers: yellow, cup-shaped. Native to: cold or temperate regions. Genus: *Ranunculus*.

butterfat /búttər fat/ *n* the natural fats found in dairy products

Butterfield /búttər feeld/, **William** (1814–1900) British architect

butterfingers /búttər fingərz/ (*plural* **-gers**) *n* somebody who tends to drop things accidentally (*informal*) —**butterfingered** *adj*

butterfish /búttər fish/ (*plural* **-fish** *or* **-fishes**) *n* **1** a small inshore fish, found worldwide. Family: Stromateidae. **2** the flesh of a butterfish as food [Late 17C. < its slippery mucous coating.]

butterflies /búttər flīz/ *npl* a fluttering feeling in the stomach caused by nervousness (*informal*)

butterfly /búttər flī/ *n* (*plural* **-flies**) **1 INSECT WITH BIG COLOURFUL WINGS** an insect with two pairs of often brightly coloured wings and knobbed antennae. Order: Lepidoptera. **2 PERSON LACKING CONCENTRATION** somebody who is unable to concentrate for long **3 butterfly, butterfly stroke SWIMMING STROKE** a swimming stroke in which both arms are lifted simultaneously above and over the head while both feet are kicked up and down **4 SWIMMING COMPETITION** a race in which swimmers do the butterfly stroke **5 PIECE OF METAL FOR FASTENING EARRING** a small piece of metal worn on the underside of the lobe of a pierced ear, into which the pin of an earring is fastened **6 TYPE OF DEAL ON STOCK MARKET** the buying and selling of options on the stock market on the same day but at different prices or with different expiry dates ■ *vt* (**-flies, -flying, -flied**) **SPLIT FOOD** to split a piece of food, e.g. meat or fish, along its length, separating it into halves [Old English *buttorflēoge*; reference to 'butter' unexplained]

butterfly ballot *n US* a ballot paper with the candidates' names printed on either or both sides of a central spine, in which the voter has to punch holes with a stylus to register a vote [< its resemblance to the outspread wings of a butterfly]

butterfly bush *n* PLANTS = **buddleia** [Because its flowers attract butterflies]

butterfly chair *n* a chair made from a continuous folded metal rod with four upward-pointing corners on which a fitted canvas seat rests

butterfly diagram *n* a graphic representation of the appearance of sunspots over an 11-year cycle [< its shape]

butterfly effect *n* the supposed influence exerted on a dynamic system by a small change in initial conditions. ◊ **chaos theory** [After a 1979 scientific paper 'Does the flap of a butterfly's wings in Brazil set off a tornado in Texas?' by Edward N. Lorenz.]

butterfly fish *n* a small boldly patterned fish with a flattish body and a tapered snout. Native to: tropics. Family: Chaetodontidae.

butterfly nut *n* DIY, CONSTR = **wing nut**

butterfly stroke *n* SWIMMING = **butterfly** *n.* **3**

butterfly valve *n* **1** a valve consisting of a disc that turns inside a pipe, especially one used as a throttle valve in a carburettor **2** a valve consisting of two semicircular plates that are hinged around a central spindle, used to allow flow in one direction only [< its shape]

butterfly weed *n* a wild plant whose roots have medicinal properties. Flowers: bright orange, in clusters. Native to: North America. *Asclepias tuberosa*. [Because it attracts butterflies]

butterie /búttəri/ *n Scotland* a rich breakfast roll, eaten in the northeast of Scotland

butter knife *n* a small knife with a broad blunt blade used for spreading butter

Buttermere /búttər meer/ lake in the Lake District, NW England. Area: 1.6 sq. km/0.63 sq. mi.

buttermilk /búttər milk/ *n* **1** a sour-tasting drink that is made by adding certain microorganisms to milk **2** the sour-tasting liquid that is left over after milk or cream has been churned to make butter. Use: in baking.

butter muslin *n* a thin, loosely woven cotton fabric. Use: originally, to wrap butter.

butternut /búttər nut/ *n* **1 NUT** an oily nut, similar in appearance to a walnut and with a sweetish taste **2 WOOD** a hard light-brown walnut wood. Use: furniture. **3 TREE** a walnut tree that produces butternuts and yiekds butternut wood. Native to: North America. *Juglans cinerea*.

butternut squash *n* a beige-coloured winter squash shaped like a club with a bulbous end and firm yellow-orange flesh. *Cucurbita moschata*.

butterscotch /búttər skoch/ *n* **1 BRITTLE SUGAR SWEET** a brittle brown-coloured sweet made from butter and brown sugar **2 BUTTERSCOTCH FLAVOURING** a flavouring made from the ingredients used in butterscotch **3 LIGHT BROWN** a light brown colour [Mid-19C. Probably because first made in Scotland.] —**butterscotch** *adj*

butterweed /búttər weed/ *n* a wild plant with yellow flowers. Family: Compositae.

butterwort /búttər wurt/ (*plural* **-worts** *or* **-wort**) *n* a carnivorous bog plant with a rosette of sticky fleshy leaves that trap and digest insects. Native to: Europe, Asia, North America. Genus: *Pinguicula*.

buttery[1] /búttəri/ (**-ier, -iest**) *adj* resembling, tasting like, or containing butter ○ *a smooth, buttery taste* —**butteriness** *n*

buttery[2] /búttəri/ (*plural* **-ies**) *n* **1** a room in which food or drinks are stored **2** a bar or room in certain universities where students can buy food and drinks to consume on the premises [14C. < Anglo-Norman *boterie*.]

butt hinge *n* a hinge consisting of two parts, one of which is attached to a door jamb, the other to the door itself, allowing the door to swing open and shut [< BUTT[2]]

butt joint *n* a joint consisting of two parts of wood or other material that are placed squarely together rather than overlapping or interlocking [< BUTT[2]]

buttock /búttək/ *n* **1** in humans, either of the two fleshy mounds above the legs and below the hollow of the back (*often plural*) **2** the rump of an animal [Old English *buttuc* 'end ridge of land' < assumed *butt* 'ridge']

ϟ**button** /bútt'n/ *n* **1 DISC FOR HOLDING CLOTHES TOGETHER** a flat and usually round piece of plastic or other material on a piece of clothing that fits into a slit or loop on another part and holds the two parts together **2 ELECTRICAL SWITCH** a small disc fitted in an electrical appliance or attached to a surface that activates an electrical connection when pressed **3 SMALL ROUND OBJECT** a small round object that resembles a button **4** *US, Aus* **SMALL SIGN WORN ON CLOTHES** a small round flat metal or plastic object with an image or words printed on it, worn attached to clothes **5 ROUNDED PART** a rounded knob-shaped part or organ, e.g. the head of an unripe mushroom **6 SMALL ACTIVATING ICON ON COMPUTER SCREEN** a small oblong image in a dialogue box of a computer-screen display, activated to perform a task by clicking with the mouse or pressing the 'Enter' key **7 ACTIVATING PART OF COMPUTER MOUSE** the part of a computer mouse that when pressed or clicked performs a function, e.g. inserting the cursor at a specific point **8 PROTECTIVE COVERING ON FOIL** a small rounded plastic or rubber covering placed on the tip of a fencing foil to protect participants from injury **9 END OF RATTLESNAKE'S TAIL** the terminal section of a rattlesnake's tail ■ *v* **1** *vt* **FASTEN WITH BUTTONS** to fasten something with a button or buttons **2** *vi* to have buttons that can be fastened on a particular side of a garment opening or in a particular place on the garment ○ *The dress buttons at the back.* **3** *vt* **PUT BUTTON IN HOLE** to put a button through a slit or loop designed to receive it ○ *I never button the top button of my shirt.* **4** *vt* **SHUT MOUTH** to close the mouth or lips and be quiet (*informal*) ○ *Just button your mouth.* [14C. < French *bouton* 'bud, knob' < Germanic.] —**buttoner** *n* ◇ **on the button 1** exactly right (*informal*) **2** precisely (*informal*) ○ *She was able to guess the price on the button.* ◇ **press** *or* **push all the right buttons** to do all the right or appropriate things ◇ **push somebody's buttons** to provoke a reaction in somebody deliberately

button up *v* **1** *vt* **DO UP BUTTONS** to fasten something with buttons **2** *vi* **STOP TALKING** to stop talking or refuse to talk (*informal*) **3** *vt* **CLOSE SOMETHING TIGHTLY** to close or seal something tightly

button-down *adj* **1** describes a collar that has a buttonhole at the end of each flap to fasten it to the front of a shirt **2** *US* = **buttoned-down** (*informal*)

buttoned-down *adj US* conservative and traditional (*informal*)

buttoned-up *adj* unwilling or unable to express feelings (*informal*)

buttonhole /búttən hōl/ *n* **1 HOLE FOR BUTTON** a slit in a garment through which a button is passed to fasten two pieces of material together **2 FLOWER WORN ON LAPEL** a flower or a small spray of flowers worn in or pinned over the buttonhole of a jacket or coat lapel. US term **boutonniere** ■ *vt* (**-holes, -holing, -holed**) **1 ACCOST** to compel somebody to listen, allowing no avenue of escape (*informal*) ○ *He buttonholed me outside my office.* **2 GIVE SOMETHING BUTTONHOLES** to make buttonholes in something **3 SEW WITH BUTTONHOLE STITCH** to sew something with buttonhole stitch —**buttonholer** *n*

buttonhole stitch *n* a tightly worked looped stitch used for reinforcing buttonholes

buttonhook /bútt'n hŏŏk/ *n* a small hook formerly used for pulling small buttons through buttonholes on tight boots or gloves

button mushroom *n* an immature unopened mushroom [< its shape]

button quail *n* a small terrestrial bird that has no hind toes and resembles a quail. Native to: S Europe, Asia, Africa, Australia. Family: Turnicidae.

buttons /bútt'nz/ *n* a pageboy who wears a livery with rows of buttons up the jacket (*archaic informal;* + *singular verb*)

button-through *adj* fastened by a row of buttons from the top to the bottom hem

button tow *n* a ski lift in which the occupant straddles a disc attached to a metal pole suspended from a moving cable

buttonwood /bútt'n wŏŏd/ *n* a mangrove tree that yields button wood. Native to: American and African tropics. *Conocarpus erectus.*

buttress /búttrəss/ *n* 1 SUPPORT FOR WALL a solid structure, usually made of brick or stone, that is built against a wall to support it 2 SOMEBODY OR SOMETHING THAT GIVES SUPPORT somebody or something that acts as a source of support, help, or reinforcement ○ *The constitution is a buttress of our civil rights.* 3 PROJECTING ROCK a large projecting rock mass that appears to support the rock above it 4 HOOF PART the pointed horny rear part of a horse's hoof ■ *vt* 1 SUPPORT WALL to support a wall with a buttress 2 SUPPORT OR REINFORCE to support or reinforce something, especially an argument, piece of analysis, or point of view ○ *He buttressed his views with lengthy quotations from the scriptures.* [14C. < Old French *(ars) bouterez* 'thrusting (arch)' < *bouter* (see BUTT[1]).]

butt shaft *n* a blunt-headed arrow used for archery practice [< BUTT[3]]

butt-weld *vt* to weld a joint in which the two pieces are placed end to end rather than overlapped —**butt weld** *n*

butty[1] /bútti, bŏŏtti/ (*plural* **-ties**) *n N England* a sandwich (*informal*) [Mid-19C. < BUTTER.]

butty[2] /bútti/ (*plural* **-ties**) *n* a friend, companion, or workmate, especially in a coal mine (*regional*) [Late 18C. Probably < archaic *play booty* 'unite against another player (and share winnings)'.]

butut /bŏŏt oot/ *n* see table at **currency** [Late 20C. < Wolof.]

butyl /byŏŏ tīl/ *n* C_4H_9- a hydrocarbon group having four molecular structures (**isomers**) [Mid-19C. < BUTYRIC.]

butyl acetate *n* CHEM = **butyl ethanoate**

butyl alcohol *n* CHEM = **butanol**

butylate /byŏŏti layt/ (**-ates, -ating, -ated**) *vt* to introduce a butyl group or groups into a chemical compound —**butylation** /byŏŏti láysh'n/ *n*

butylated hydroxytoluene /byŏŏti laytəd hī dróksi tóllyoo een/ *n* $[(CH_3)_3C]_2C_6H_2OH(CH_3)$ a crystalline solid. Use: antioxidant for fats and oils.

butylene /byŏŏti leen/ *n* = **butene**

butyl ethanoate /-i thánnō ayt/ *n* $CH_3COOC_4H_9$ a colourless flammable toxic liquid with a fruity odour and having three molecular structures (**isomers**). Use: lacquer solvent.

butyl rubber *n* a synthetic rubber that is extremely resistant to abrasion, tearing, sunlight, and chemical attack. Use: inner tubes, hosepipes, insulation, seals for food jars.

butyraceous /byŏŏtə ráyshəss/ *adj* containing, resembling, or producing butter (*technical*) [Mid-17C. < BUTYRIC.]

butyraldehyde /byŏŏtə ráldə hīd/ *n* C_4H_8O a colourless flammable liquid. Use: manufacture of solvents, resins, and plasticizers.

butyrate /byŏŏtə rayt/ *n* a salt or ester of butyric acid [Mid-19C. < BUTYRIC.]

butyric /byoo tírrik/ *adj* 1 relating to or containing butanoic acid 2 relating to or containing butter (*technical*) [Early 19C. < Latin *butyrum* (see BUTTER).]

butyric acid *n* CHEM = **butanoic acid**

butyrin /byŏŏtərin/ *n* a colourless liquid ester or oil having three molecular structures (**isomers**). Source: formed from butanoic acid and glycerol and found in butter. [Early 19C. Blend of BUTYRIC + GLYCERIN.]

butyrophenone /byŏŏtirō feénōn/ *n* a drug similar to the phenothiazines. Use: treatment of severe psychiatric disorders. [Early 20C. < BUTYRIC.]

buxom /búksəm/ *adj* describes a woman having a full figure (*humorous*) [Assumed Old English *(ge)būhsum* 'pliable' < *(ge)būgan* 'to bend' < Germanic] —**buxomly** *adv* —**buxomness** *n*

Buxtehude /bŏŏkstə hoódə/, **Dietrich** (1637?–1707) Danish-born German organist and composer

Buxton /búkstən/ spa town in the Peak District, central England. Population: 19,854 (1991).

buy /bī/ *v* (**buys, buying, bought** /bawt/, **bought**) 1 *vti* ACQUIRE SOMETHING BY PAYMENT to pay money for something in order to obtain it ○ *They bought me a bike for my birthday.* ○ *Money won't buy you happiness.* 2 *vt* BRIBE to obtain information, help, or loyalty from somebody in exchange for money 3 *vt* OBTAIN TIME to obtain more time to reach a desired end by taking strategic action ○ *a manoeuvre that should buy us another week* 4 *vt* OBTAIN SOMETHING BY SACRIFICE to obtain something by sacrificing a thing of equivalent value ○ *buy peace with land* 5 *vi* BE BUYER FOR COMPANY OR INDIVIDUAL to purchase goods on behalf of a company or another individual ○ *She buys for Harrods.* 6 *vt* BELIEVE to accept or believe something proposed as true (*informal*) ○ *I don't buy the part about an international conspiracy.* ■ *n* 1 SOMETHING BOUGHT something that you pay money for, considered relative to its worth ○ *a good buy* 2 EXCHANGE OF MONEY FOR GOODS an exchange of money for goods or services [Old English *bycgan* < Germanic] —**buyable** *adj*

SPELLCHECK Do not confuse ***buy*** with ***bi***, ***by***, or ***bye***, which sound similar. Beware: your spellchecker will not catch this error.

buy back *vt Malaysia* to buy something and take it home ○ *We bought back pizzas for supper.*

buy in *v* 1 *vt* WITHDRAW ITEM FROM AUCTION to withdraw an item from sale at an auction because it has failed to reach its reserve price 2 *vi* BUY SHARES IN COMPANY to buy shares in a company as the controlling interest 3 *vi* PAY TO TAKE PART IN to pay in order to take part in or have a share of something 4 *vti* BUY SOMETHING IN QUANTITY to buy something in large quantities, usually in preparation for an expected period of hardship

buy into *vt* 1 BUY SHARES IN COMPANY to buy shares in a company 2 PAY TO PARTICIPATE IN to pay money in order to take part in something ○ *buy into a timeshare* 3 *US* ACCEPT to accept or believe in a proposition or idea (*informal*) ○ *I don't buy into that 'greed is good' attitude.*

buy off *vt* to bribe somebody in order to prevent something happening or ensure cooperation ○ *They tried to buy off the entire jury.*

buy out *vt* 1 PURCHASE ENTIRE SHARES OF COMPANY to purchase the entire shares of or controlling financial interest in a company or business 2 RELEASE SOMEBODY FROM MILITARY SERVICE to pay money to release somebody from military service ○ *He bought himself out of the army and set up a business in London.* 3 PAY SOMEBODY TO RELINQUISH INTEREST to pay somebody to relinquish interest in a property or other enterprise ○ *She was bought out by her partners.*

buy up *vt* 1 to buy all, or all that is available, of a commodity ○ *They've been buying up property in the area.* 2 to buy something in great quantity without regard to expense ○ *buying up modern paintings*

buy-back *n* the repurchase by a company or an individual of something, e.g. shares or goods, according to a previously made contractual agreement

buyer /bī ər/ *n* 1 somebody who buys or intends to buy something 2 a person whose job is to choose and buy goods or merchandise for a company, factory, or store

buyer's market *n* a situation in which supply exceeds demand, prices are relatively low, and buyers therefore have an advantage. ◊ **seller's market**

buyout /bī owt/ *n* 1 the purchase of a controlling interest in a company ○ *a management buyout* 2 the purchase of an entire amount or quantity of something

buzz /buz/ *n* 1 STEADY HUMMING SOUND a steady low humming sound like that of a bee ○ *the low buzz of insects flitting over the flowers* 2 HUM OF TALK a low murmur of conversation made by a group of people, especially when they are excited or interested in something ○ *a buzz of voices emerging from the living room* 3 SOUND the sound made by a buzzer 4 TELEPHONE CALL a telephone call (*informal*) 5 FEELING OF EXCITEMENT a feeling of excitement or satisfaction often linked with a sense of achievement (*informal*) ○ *It gives me a tremendous buzz to hear someone saying the lines that I've written.* 6 INTOXICATION a feeling of intoxication (*slang*) 7 LATEST GOSSIP the latest gossip or information within a particular industry or locale (*informal*) ○ *The buzz at the festival was that he'd pick up an award for best director.* 8 FAD a short-lived interest or enthusiasm (*informal*) 9 PUBLICITY publicity, or interest generated by publicity (*informal*) ■ *v* 1 *vi* MAKE STEADY HUMMING SOUND to make a steady low humming sound like that of a bee 2 *vi* BE ANIMATED to be animated by the talk or activity of people ○ *The room was buzzing with excitement.* 3 *vi* MOVE SPEEDILY to move around speedily and busily ○ *buzzing about in small cars that dodged through traffic* 4 *vti* WORK BUZZER to activate a buzzer 5 *vt* LET SOMEBODY INTO BUILDING ELECTRONICALLY to admit somebody to a building by activating an electronic system that controls a door ○ *waiting for them to buzz me in* 6 *vi* MAKING ELECTRONIC HUMMING SOUND to make an electronic humming noise when activated ○ *When the timer buzzes, turn the oven down.* 7 *vi* BE EXCITED to be filled with anxious or excited thoughts ○ *My head was buzzing with all the things I'd heard that night.* 8 *vi* BE RINGING to be filled with a continuous ringing sound, e.g. after being exposed to loud noise ○ *My ears were buzzing after the concert.* 9 *vt* TELEPHONE to call somebody on the telephone (*informal*) 10 *vt* FLY LOW OVER PEOPLE OR PLACE to fly an aircraft low over people or buildings, or across the path of other aircraft (*informal*) [14C. An imitation of the sound.]

buzz off *vi* to go away (*informal*)

buzzard /búzzərd/ (*plural* **-zards** *or* **-zard**) *n* 1 a large hawk with broad wings and a broad tail. Native to: Europe, Asia. Genus: *Buteo.* US term **buteo** 2 *US* any North American vulture, e.g. the turkey vulture [14C. < Old French *busard.*]

buzz bomb *n* MIL = **V-1**

buzz cut *n US* a hairstyle in which the hair is cut very close to the skull with a razor

buzzer /búzzər/ *n* an electronic device that makes a humming or buzzing sound when activated

buzz saw *n US, Can* INDUST = **circular saw**

buzzword /búz wurd/ *n* a fashionable word or concept, often associated with a particular group of people and not understood by outsiders (*informal*) ○ *the latest media buzzword*

b.v. *abbr* book value

B vitamin *n* one of a group of water-soluble vitamins that are involved in many chemical reactions in the body

BVM *abbr* Blessed Virgin Mary [Latin *Beata Virgo Maria*]

⚡**bw** *abbr* Botswana (*in Internet addresses*)

BW *abbr* 1 bacteriological warfare 2 biological warfare 3 **BW, B/W, b/w** black-and-white

bwana /bwáanə/ *n* used as a respectful term of address for a man in East Africa [Late 19C. < Kiswahili.]

BWG *n* a numerical system for specifying the diameter of metal rods. Full form **Birmingham Wire Gauge**

BWI *abbr* 1 Baltimore-Washington International Airport 2 British West Indies

BWR *abbr* boiling-water reactor

BWV *abbr* Bach Werke-Verzeichnis (*before a number identifying the works by J. S. Bach*)

by[1] /bī/ CORE MEANING: a grammatical word expressing a spatial relationship ○ (prep) *standing by the window* ○ (adv) *A large crowd of shoppers stood by watching.*

1 *prep, adv* PAST SOMEBODY OR SOMETHING IN SPACE indicates movement past somebody or something, sometimes including a brief stop (*after a verb of movement*) ○ *He drove by his apartment building.* ○ *The waiter came by, pouring us some more coffee.* 2 *prep, adv* AT THAT PLACE at the place specified or understood, usually for a short visit ○ *We stopped by Jan's place.* ○ *Drop by any time.* 3 *prep* THROUGH passing through something ○ *entering by the back door* 4 *prep* BEFORE THAT TIME happening or required at or before the time stated ○ *reservations required by Sunday* 5 *prep* DURING happening during a particular time period ○ *By day he worked in a canning factory.* 6 *prep* IN MEASURES OF at a rate based on a particular measure such as time, weight, or volume ○ *These vegetables are sold by weight.* 7 *prep* INDICATES FACTOR OR DIVISOR used in multiplication and division to indicate any number or quantity being multiplied, or to indicate the number or quantity that divides another ○ *What is 144 divided by 12?* 8 *prep* INDICATES DIMENSIONS used between the measurements of the dimensions of an object, expressing area or volume 9 *prep* DIFFERING IN THE AMOUNT OF used to indicate an amount, extent, or rate at which something increases, decreases, or differs ○ *Tax rates are to be cut by 0.25%.* 10 *prep* INDICATES DIRECTION used to indicate a direction ○ *north by northwest* 11 *prep* IN AMOUNTS OF PARTICULAR SIZE in groups or amounts of a particular size ○ *Visitors arrived by the truckload.* 12 *prep* GRADUALLY used to link two identical words to indicate a progression or sequence ○ *One by one we told our stories.* ○ *You can see an improvement day by day.* 13 *prep* INDICATES CAUSE used to indicate the person or thing performing an action, or causing a situation or reaction (*after a passive verb*) ○ *He was hit by a ball.* 14 *prep* INDICATES CREATOR, AUTHOR, OR ARTIST used to indicate the person who wrote or created something such as a written piece or work of art ○ *written by A. A. Milne* 15 *prep* USING A METHOD OR MEDIUM used to indicate the particular mode, method, or action through which something occurs or is done ○ *travelling*

by ocean liner ○ *She earns a living by playing the harp.* **16** *prep* **INDICATES MEANS** indicating the action used to achieve something (*followed by a gerund*) ○ *The key to attracting banks back to inner cities is attracting business.* **17** *prep* **IN A PARTICULAR MANNER** with, in, or through a particular manner of doing something ○ *used by permission of the author* **18** *prep* **ACCORDING TO AN UNCHANGING QUALITY** in terms of a particular attribute or function ○ *a teacher by profession and a learner by nature* **19** *prep* **IN COMPLIANCE WITH** in order to comply with something, especially the law ○ *By law, patients must have access to their records.* **20** *prep* **AT A PARTICULAR PART** at a particular part of something, e.g. a hand or corner ○ *held the dancer by the waist* **21** *adv* **IN THE NAME OF SOMETHING SACRED** used to indicate something considered holy when making a solemn oath or promise ○ *By all that is sacred, I ask you to stop.* **22** *adv* **PAST IN TIME** indicates the passage of the stated amount of time (*following a verb expressing movement*) ○ *as time goes by* **23** *adv* Scotland **PAST** over and done with **24** *adv* **AWAY OR ASIDE** into a place for safekeeping for use later ○ *I spent some of the money and put some by for hard times.* [Old English *bī* < Germanic] ◇ **by and by** after a while (*literary*) ◇ **by the by, by the bye** used to introduce a question or piece of information that is not connected with the subject being discussed

SPELLCHECK See *buy*.

⚡**by**[2] *abbr* Belarus (*in Internet addresses*) ·

by- *prefix* **1** secondary ○ *byroad* ○ *by-product* **2** past ○ *bygone* [< BY[1]]

⚡**BYAM** *abbr* between you and me (*in e-mails*)

Byatt /bī ət/, **A. S.** (*b.* 1936) British novelist and academic. Born **Antonia Susan Drabble**

by-bidder *n* somebody who bids at an auction to raise the price —**by-bidding** *n*

Byblos /bíbbləss/ ancient Phoenician city, near modern-day Beirut, Lebanon

by-blow *n* an illegitimate child (*dated*)

by-catch *n* fish that are caught unintentionally in addition to the required species. ◊ **rough fish**

~~byciele~~ incorrect spelling of **bicycle**

bye[1] /bī/ *n* **1** **AUTOMATIC ADVANCE TO NEXT ROUND** the right to proceed to the next round of a competition without contesting the present round, often through non-appearance of an opponent **2** **INFORMAL MATCH** in golf, an informal match contested over remaining holes, once the main competition is over **3** **EXTRA RUN WITHOUT HITTING BALL** in cricket, a run scored off a ball that has not been hit by a batsman, awarded to the team as a whole rather than to an individual batsman [Mid-16C. < BY.]

SPELLCHECK See *buy*.

bye[2] /bī/ *interj* used to say goodbye (*informal*) [Early 18C. Shortening of GOODBYE.]

bye- *prefix* = by-

bye-bye[1] *interj* used to say goodbye (*informal*) [Child's variation of GOODBYE]

bye-bye[2] *n US* = **bye-byes**

bye-byes *n* bed or sleep (*babytalk*) US term **bye-bye**[2] *n.* [< a refrain used in lullabies]

by-election, bye-election *n* an election held between official general or local elections to fill a vacant seat, e.g. to replace a member of parliament or local councillor who has died or resigned

Byelorussia /byéllō rúshə/ *n* former name for **Belarus** — **Byelorussian** *n, adj*

bygone /bī gon/ *adj* existing or having happened a long time ago ○ *reminders of a bygone age* ■ *n* something that happened, existed, or was manufactured a long time ago (*often plural*) ◇ **let bygones be bygones** to forgive past offences or resentments

~~by in large~~ incorrect spelling of **by and large**

⚡**BYKT** *abbr* but you know/knew that (*in e-mails*)

bylaw /bī law/ *n* **1** **LOCAL LAW** a law made by a local authority that applies only in the area that the authority governs **2** **INTERNAL RULE** a law or regulation that governs the internal affairs of a company or other organization **3** **SECONDARY LAW** a secondary law [13C. Probably < Old Norse *bȳlagu* 'town law' < *bȳr* 'town' + *lagu* 'law'.]

byline /bī līn/ *n* **1** the name of the author of an article in a newspaper or magazine, printed at the head of the article **2** SOCCER = **goal line** ■ *vt* (**-lines, -lining, -lined**) to write an article that will include a byline

byname /bī naym/ *n* somebody's nickname

BYOB *abbr* bring your own bottle (*on party invitations*)

bypass /bī paass/ *n* **1** **ROAD ROUND TOWN** a road built round a town or city to keep through traffic away from the centre **2** **OPERATION TO REROUTE BLOOD** a surgical operation to redirect the blood, usually via a grafted blood vessel, carried out when the existing blood vessel has become blocked ○ *a heart bypass* **3** **NEW ROUTE FOR BLOOD** a new route for the blood, created by a bypass operation **4** ELEC ENG = **shunt** *n.* **4 5** **EMERGENCY CHANNEL** a channel, e.g. a pipe carrying gas or water, brought into use when the main channel is blocked ■ *vt* **1** **GO ROUND A PLACE** to avoid a place by travelling round it **2** **BUILD BYPASS** to build a bypass round a place **3** **AVOID** to avoid an obstacle, obstruction, or problem by using an alternative route or method **4** **AVOID STANDARD PROCEDURE** to ignore or avoid a standard procedure for doing something or ignore somebody who is usually consulted

bypath /bī paath/ *n* a rarely used path, especially in the country

by-play *n* matters of subsidiary importance or interest that take place while the main action is going on, e.g. in a stage play

byproduct /bī produkt/ *n* **1** something produced as a secondary result of the manufacture or production of something else, often something useful or commercially valuable **2** something that happens as an incidental result of something else

Byrd /burd/, **William** (1543–1623) English composer

byre /bīr/ *n* a cowshed (*regional*) [Old English *byre.* < ?]

byroad /bī rōd/ *n* a side road carrying a small volume of traffic

Byron, Cape /bírən/ cape in NE New South Wales, Australia, the most easterly point on the Australian mainland

Byron, George Gordon Noel, 6th Baron Byron (1788–1824) British poet. Known as **Lord Byron**

Byron Bay resort town in NE New South Wales, Australia. Population: 5,007 (1991).

Byronic /bī rónnik/ *adj* **1** relating to or characteristic of Lord Byron or his poetry **2** describes a brooding and solitary man who seems capable of great passion and suffering

byssi plural of **byssus**

byssinosis /bíssi nṓssiss/ *n* a respiratory disease caused by prolonged inhalation of dust from textile fibres [Late 19C. < Latin *byssinus* 'of fine linen' < *byssus* (see BYSSUS).]

byssus /bíssəss/ (*plural* **-suses** *or* **-si** /-sī/) *n* **1** a mass of strong silky threads that molluscs such as mussels use to attach themselves to rocks and other hard surfaces **2** fine linen used by the ancient Egyptians to wrap mummies [14C. Via Latin, 'fine linen' < Greek *bussos* < Semitic.]

bystander /bī standər/ *n* somebody who observes but is not involved in something

bystander effect *n* the reluctance of members of a crowd to intervene in an incident they are witnessing

⚡**byte** /bīt/ *n* **1** a group of eight bits of computer information, representing a unit of data such as a number or letter **2** a unit of computer memory equal to that needed to store a single character [Mid-20C. Probably alteration of BIT[3] after BITE 'morsel', or acronym < *binary digit eight*.]

byway /bī way/ *n* **1** a small side road not regularly used by people or traffic **2** the less important aspects of a particular pursuit or field of knowledge ○ *the byways of numismatics*

byword /bī wurd/ *n* **1** **WELL-KNOWN EXAMPLE** somebody or something that is well known for a particular quality ○ *The magazine became a byword for cutting-edge style.* **2** **CATCH PHRASE** a word or phrase that is in common use at a particular time **3** **PROVERB** a proverb common to a particular place, group, or time [Old English *bīwyrde* 'proverb', translation of Latin *proverbium*]

Byzantine /bī zán tīn, -teen, bízz'n tīn, -teen/ *adj* **1 OF BYZANTIUM** relating to the ancient city of Byzantium, or its people or culture **2 OF BYZANTINE EMPIRE** relating to the Byzantine Empire **3 OF BYZANTINE ART OR ARCHITECTURE** relating to or typical of the colourful religious art or the ornate architecture developed under the Byzantine Empire **4 OF EASTERN ORTHODOX CHURCH** relating to the Eastern Orthodox Church and its traditions **5 Byzantine, byzantine** VERY COMPLEX extremely complex or intricate **6 Byzantine, byzantine** DEVIOUS marked by deviousness or scheming ■ *n* **SOMEBODY FROM BYZANTIUM** somebody who came from the ancient city of Byzantium or the Byzantine Empire [Late 16C. < Latin *Byzantinus* < *Byzantium* < Greek *Buzantion*.]

Byzantine Church *n* CHR = **Orthodox Church**

Byzantine Empire *n* the eastern part of the late Roman Empire, from AD 330 to 1453, when its capital Constantinople fell to the Ottoman Turks

Byzantium /bī zánti əm, bi-, bī zánshi əm, bi-/ ancient Greek city on the site of modern Istanbul

⚡**bz** *abbr* Belize (*in Internet addresses*)

C[1] /see/ (*plural* **c's**), **C** (*plural* **C's** *or* **Cs**) *n* **1** the third letter of the English alphabet, representing a consonant sound **2** the Roman numeral for 100

C[2] *symbol* concentration

C[3] **1** used to refer to the speed of light in a vacuum **2** used to refer to the third vertical row of squares from the left on a chessboard

C[4] *abbr* **1** cancelled **2** canine **3** carat **4** carbon (paper) **5** carton **6** case **7** catcher **8** caught by **9** cedi **10** cent **11** centavo **12** centi- **13** centime **14** centimetre **15** centre **16** centum **17** century **18** chapter **19** charm **20** church **21** circa **22** circuit **23** circumference **24** clockwise **25** cloudy **26** codex **27** coefficient **28** cold **29** colon **30** colour **31** colt **32** constant **33** consul **34** contralto **35** copy **36** copyright **37** corps **38** cost **39** cubic **40** curie

♪**C++** /see pluss plúss/ *n* a superset of the C language that incorporates the benefits of object-oriented programming

♪**C**[1] (*plural* **C's** *or* **Cs**) *n* **1** **'C'-SHAPED OBJECT** something shaped like a letter 'C' **2** **1ST NOTE IN C MAJOR** the first note of a scale in C major **3** **SOMETHING THAT PRODUCES A C** a string, key, or pipe tuned to produce the note C **4** **SCALE BEGINNING ON C** a scale or key that starts on the note C **5** **WRITTEN SYMBOL OF C** a graphic representation of the tone of C **6** **3RD HIGHEST GRADE** the third highest grade in a series, e.g. an average grade for academic work **7** **PROGRAMMING LANGUAGE** a high-level computer programming language **8** **COCAINE** cocaine (*slang*) ◇ **the big C** cancer (*informal*)

C[2] *symbol* **1** capacitance **2** carbon **3** cytosine **4** heat capacity

♪**C**[3] *abbr* **1** cape **2** castle **3** Catholic **4** Celsius **5** Centigrade **6** Chancellor **7** charm **8** chief **9** city **10** College **11** Companion **12** Congress **13** Conservative **14** corps **15** coulomb **16** court **17** see (*in e-mails*)

C1 (*plural* **C1s**) *n* somebody in a clerical or junior management position, in the market research system that classifies people according to their occupation

C2 (*plural* **C2s**) *n* somebody in a skilled manual job, in the market research system that classifies people according to their occupation

♪**C2C** /see tə seé/ *abbr* consumer-to-consumer

♪**ca** *abbr* Canada (*in Internet addresses*)

Ca *symbol* calcium

♪**CA** *abbr* **1** California **2** Central America **3** Central American **4** chartered accountant **5** chief accountant **6** chronological age **7** consular agent **8** Consumers' Association **9** certificate authority (*in e-mails*)

ca. *abbr* circa (*before dates*)

c/a *abbr* current account

C/A *abbr* **1** capital account **2** credit account **3** current account

CAA *abbr* Civil Aviation Authority

♪**CAAT** *abbr* certificate authority administration tool (*in e-commerce*)

cab /kab/ *n* **1** TRANSP = **taxi** *n*. **2** the part of a large vehicle, e.g. a lorry, a locomotive, or a large crane, where the driver or operator sits **3** a lightweight horse-drawn carriage formerly used for public hire [Early 19C. Shortening of CABRIOLET.]

CAB *abbr* **1** Civil Aeronautics Board **2** Citizens' Advice Bureau

cabal /kə bál/ *n* **1** **GROUP OF PLOTTERS** a group of conspirators or plotters, particularly one formed for political purposes **2** **SECRET PLOT** a secret plot or conspiracy, especially a political one **3** **CLIQUE** an exclusive group of people ■ *vi* (**-bals, -balling, -balled**) **CONSPIRE AS GROUP** to form a group and plot together against somebody or something [Early 17C. Via French *cabale* < medieval Latin *cab(b)ala* 'secret teaching' (SEE CABALA).]

Cabal /kə bál/ *n* a group of ministers in the court of the English king Charles II, who governed the country between 1667 and 1673. Their surnames were Clifford, Arlington, Buckingham, Ashley, and Lauderdale. [Mid-17C. Acronym < the initials of their names, after CABAL.]

cabala *n* = **kabbalah**

cabaletta /kábbə léttə/ *n* **1** a short simple aria in 19th-century Italian opera, usually found in conjunction with a preceding cavatina **2** the final section of an aria or duet, typically with a lively rhythm [Mid-19C. < Italian, 'little stanza' < Latin *copula* 'link'.]

cabalistic /kábbə lístik/, **cabbalistic, kabalistic, kabbalistic** *adj* **1** relating to the teachings of the cabala **2** mysterious or esoteric ○ *the cabalistic teachings of the alchemists*

Caballé /kə bál yay, káb ə yáy/, **Montserrat** (*b.* 1933) Spanish soprano

caballero /kábbə láirō, kább'l yáirō/ (*plural* **-ros**) *n* **1** a Spanish knight, cavalier, or gentleman **2** *Southwest US* a horseman, especially of Spanish-speaking regions [Mid-19C. Via Spanish < late Latin *caballarius* < Latin *caballus* 'horse'.]

cabaret /kábbə ray/ *n* **1** a floor show consisting of singing, dancing, and comic acts performed in a restaurant, club, or bar **2** a restaurant, club, or bar offering a cabaret [Mid-17C. Via French < Old French dialect *camberet* 'little room' < Latin *camera* 'room' (SEE CAMERA).]

cabbage /kábbij/ *n* **1** **LEAVES AS FOOD** a roundish head of closely layered green, white, or red leaves, eaten raw or cooked as a vegetable **2** **PLANT WITH CLOSELY LAYERED LEAVES** a short-stemmed plant that produces cabbage. *Brassica oleracea* var. *capitata*. **3** **PLANT RELATED TO CABBAGE** a plant related to cabbage, e.g. Chinese cabbage **4** **EDIBLE PALM BUD** the bud of a number of species of palm, eaten as a vegetable **5** **OFFENSIVE TERM** a highly offensive term for somebody who has no mental awareness or mental activity, usually as a result of brain injury, and who is completely dependent on other people **6** **BORING PERSON** a physically and mentally inactive person (*informal insult*) [15C. < Old French *caboche*, variant of *caboce* 'head'.] —**cabbagy** *adj*

cabbage lettuce *n* a variety of lettuce that has a rounded head like a cabbage

cabbage palm *n* **1** a palm tree whose leaf buds resemble cabbages and are eaten as a vegetable. *Roystonea oleracea*. **2** any palm or similar plant resembling a cabbage

cabbage palmetto *n* a palm tree with edible leaf buds and fan-shaped leaves that are used in Christian celebrations on Palm Sunday. Native to: SE United States, Bahamas. *Sabal palmetto*.

cabbage root fly (*plural* **cabbage root flies**) *n* a fly whose larvae feed on cabbages and other plants of the cabbage family such as broccoli, cauliflowers, and brussels sprouts. *Delia radicum*.

cabbage rose *n* a hybrid bush rose grown in gardens. Flowers: fragrant, double-petalled. *Rosa centifolia*.

cabbage tree *n* **1** a small tree with a top that resembles that of a palm tree. Native to: New Zealand. *Cordyline australis*. **2** a large palm tree. Native to: coast of E Australia. *Livistona australis*.

cabbage white *n* a light-coloured butterfly whose larvae feed on the leaves of cabbages and related plants. Family: Pieridae. US term **cabbage butterfly**

cabbageworm /kábbij wurm/ *n* a larva that feeds on cabbages and related plants, especially the larva of the cabbage white butterfly

cabbala *n* = **kabbalah**

cabby /kábbi/ (*plural* **-bies**), **cabbie** *n* a taxi driver (*informal*)

caber /káybər/ *n* a long thick wooden pole used in Scottish Highland Games in an event known as 'tossing the caber', in which contestants have to throw a caber end over end [Early 16C. < Gaelic *cabar* 'pole'.]

cabernet sauvignon /kábbər nay sóvin yon/ *n* **1** a variety of black grape. **2** dry red wine made from the cabernet sauvignon grape [< French]

cabezon /kábbi zon/ (*plural* **-zons** *or* **-zon**) *n* a spiny striped and mottled fish found in N Pacific waters, popular as a food fish. *Scorpaenichthys marmoratus*.

cabin /kábbin/ *n* **1** **WOODEN HUT** a small simple house, especially one made of wood in forest or mountain areas **2** **SMALL ROOM ON SHIP** a small room on a boat or ship, where people live or sleep **3** **SHELTER ON SMALL BOAT** a covered compartment that houses the wheel on a small boat, used for shelter in bad weather and often as a living space **4** TRANSP = **cab** *n*. **2 5** **AEROPLANE INTERIOR** the part of a passenger aeroplane where the passengers sit, or the part of a cargo aeroplane where the cargo is carried **6** **CREW QUARTERS ON SPACECRAFT** the part of a spacecraft where the crew work, live, or sleep **7** **ROOM ON SHIP** the commanding officer's room on a warship **8** RAIL = **signal box** ■ *vti* **KEEP SOMEBODY CONFINED** to confine somebody, or live confined, in a small enclosed space (*literary; usually passive*) [14C. Via Old French *cabane* < late Latin *capanna* 'hut'.]

LITERARY LINK *Uncle Tom's Cabin*, a novel (1852) by US writer and abolitionist Harriet Beecher Stowe. Set in the American South, it is the story of an enslaved Black person, Uncle Tom, who is sold by his kindly owners and eventually dies at the hands of a vicious Yankee master.

---

cabin boy *n* a boy who acted as a servant on board a sailing ship, waiting on officers and passengers

cabin class *n* a class of accommodation on some passenger ships that is lower than first class and higher than tourist class ■ *adj, adv* in cabin class on a passenger ship

cabin crew *n* the staff on a passenger aircraft whose job is to attend to passengers

cabin cruiser *n* a large, powerful, and luxurious motor boat with generous living space

Cabinda /kə beéndə/ Angolan exclave on the Atlantic coast of central Africa, between the Republic of Congo and the Democratic Republic of Congo. Capital: Cabinda. Population: 152,100 (1992). Area: 7,270 sq. km/2,807 sq. mi.

cabinet /kábbinət/ *n* **1 cabinet, Cabinet GROUP OF SENIOR MINISTERS** a group of senior government ministers chosen by a prime minister to act as the executive decision-making body of the country (*+ singular or plural verb*) **2 PIECE OF FURNITURE** an upright piece of furniture usually made of wood and consisting of drawers, shelves, and compartments for storing or displaying objects **3 TV OR RADIO COVERING** the outer casing of a television or hi-fi system, especially the wooden casing of an old-fashioned model **4 PRIVATE ROOM** a small private room (*archaic*) ■ *adj* **1 FOR SMALL ROOM** describes furniture and other items intended for a small room or a room in a private home **2 FOR DISPLAY IN CABINET** small or decorative enough to be displayed in a cabinet [Mid-16C. < French, 'small room' < Old Picard *cabine* 'room for gambling'.]

cabinetmaker /kábbinət maykər/ *n* a skilled woodworker who specializes in making furniture —**cabinetmaking** *n*

cabinet minister *n* a senior government minister who is in the Cabinet

cabinetry *n* = **cabinetwork**

cabinetwork /kábbinət wurk/, **cabinetry** /kábbinətri/ *n* wooden furniture made to a high standard by a cabinetmaker

cabin fever *n* an emotional condition, marked by irritability, distress, or depression, caused by prolonged isolation or confined living quarters

cable /káyb'l/ *n* **1 STRONG ROPE OR WIRE** a strong thick rope or steel wire, used for lifting, pulling, towing, or securing things **2 BUNDLE OF ELECTRICAL WIRES** a group of wires for transmitting electrical signals that are bound together and usually have shared or common insulation. ◊ **coaxial cable 3 MOORING ROPE OR CHAIN** a rope or chain attached to an anchor or used for mooring a ship **4 OVERSEAS TELEGRAM** a telegram, originally sent by undersea cable, now usually by telephone, radio, or satellite **5** MEDIA = **cable television 6** HANDICRAFT = **cable stitch** ■ *v* (**-bles, -bling, -bled**) **1** *vti* **SEND TELEGRAM** to send somebody a telegram **2** *vt* **SEND SOMETHING VIA TELEGRAM** to send something, e.g. money or information, to somebody in a distant place by sending a telegram **3** *vt* **FASTEN OR FIT SOMETHING WITH CABLES** to fasten something with cables, or fit cables to something **4** *vt* **SUPPLY PLACE WITH CABLE TV** to connect a building or area to a cable television network [Pre-12C. Via Old French dialect < late Latin *capulum* 'halter' < Latin *capere* 'seize'.] —**cabler** *n* —**cabling** *n*

cable-access *adj US* showing programmes that are made locally, often of local interest only, as opposed to commercially produced material ○ *cable-access television*

cable car *n* **1** a compartment or cabin suspended from an overhead cable, used to transport passengers up and down steep hills or across valleys **2** a car on a cable railway

cablecast /káyb'l kaast/ *n* a broadcast over a cable television network [Late 20C. < CABLE + '-cast' < BROADCAST.] —**cablecaster** *n* —**cablecasting** *n*

cablegram /káyb'l gram/ *n* TELECOM = **cable** *n.* 4

cable-laid *adj* describes thick ropes made of three thinner ropes, each with three strands, twisted together anticlockwise

ϟ**cable modem** *n* a high-speed modem connecting a computer with a cable television network

cable railway *n* a hillside railway consisting of a track along which cars are pulled by a moving cable that is operated by a stationary engine

cable release *n* a cable fitted with a control button and attached to a camera in order to take photographs without shaking the camera, e.g. on long exposures

cable-stayed bridge *n* a suspension bridge with the cables that support the deck connected directly to the bridge's piers rather than to suspenders

cable stitch *n* a knitting stitch that produces a pattern resembling twisted rope

cablet /káyblət/ *n* a cable-laid rope that has a circumference of less than 25 cm/10 in

cable television /káyb'l télevizh'n/, **cablevision** /káyb'l vizh'n/, **cable TV** *n* a television system in which signals are sent to a central antenna and then transmitted by cable to subscribers

cableway /káyb'l way/ *n* any transportation system consisting of an overhead cable used for transporting suspended cars or containers

cabochon /kábbə shon/ *n* **1** a highly polished rounded unfaceted gem **2** the gem-cutting style that results in a cabochon [Mid-16C. < French, 'little head' < Old French *caboche* 'head'.] —**cabochon** *adj, adv*

caboodle /kə boód'l/ *n* a lot of things or people (*informal*) ○ *the whole kit and caboodle* [Late 19C. Probably an alteration of BOODLE < Dutch *boedel* 'goods'.]

Caboolture /kə boólchər/ town in SE Queensland, Australia. Population: 17,571 (1996).

caboose /kə boóss/ *n* the galley of a ship (*archaic*) [Mid-18C. < Dutch *cabuyse*.]

Cabot /kábbət/, **John** (1450?–99?) Italian explorer. Born **Giovanni Caboto**

Cabot, Sebastian (1476?–1557) Italian-born English navigator and cartographer

cabotage /kábbə taazh, -tij/ *n* **1** trade, shipping, or navigation that takes place in coastal waters within the boundaries of a single country **2** the right of a country to operate internal traffic, especially air traffic, using its own carriers and not those of other countries [Mid-19C. < French < *caboter* 'coast along' < Spanish *cabo* 'cape, headland' < Latin *caput* 'head'.]

Cabral /kə braál/, **Pedro Álvares** (1460?–1526?) Portuguese explorer

cabriole /kábbri ōl/ *n* **1** a curving furniture leg tapering into a decorative foot, popular in the early 18th century and used in Chippendale furniture **2** a ballet movement in which the dancer leaps into the air with one leg outstretched sideways and the other beating against it [Late 18C. < French, 'leap' < *cabrioler*, variant of *caprioler* 'to caper'.]

cabriolet /kábbri ə láy/ *n* **1** a two-door convertible car **2** a two-wheeled, two-seater, horse-drawn carriage with a folding roof [Mid-18C. < French, < *cabrioler* 'to caper'; from the bouncing motion of a horse-drawn vehicle.]

cac- *prefix* = **caco-** (*before vowels*)

cacao /kə ków, kə káy ō, kə kaá ō/ (*plural* **-os** *or* **-o**) *n* **1** a dried fatty seed from which cocoa, chocolate, and other foods and products are derived **2** a tropical American evergreen tree with fleshy pods containing cacao seeds. *Theobroma cacao*. **3 cacao, cacao butter** = **cocoa butter** [Mid-16C. Via Spanish < Nahuatl *cacauatl* < *uatl* 'tree'.]

cacao bean *n* = **cocoa bean**

cacciatore /káchə táwri/ *adj* cooked with mushrooms, tomatoes, and herbs (*usually after a noun*) ○ *chicken cacciatore* [Mid-20C. < Italian, 'hunter'; from its original use as a sauce for game.]

cachaca /kə shaássə/ *n* a Brazilian rum made from sugar cane

cachalot /káshə lot/ *n* = **sperm whale** [Mid-18C. Via French < Spanish or Portuguese *cachalote*.]

ϟ**cache** /kash/ *n* **1 HIDDEN SUPPLY** a hidden store of things, especially weapons or valuables **2 SECRET PLACE FOR HIDING THINGS** a secret place where a store of things is kept hidden **3 MEMORY FOR COMPUTER DATA** an area of high-speed computer memory used for temporary storage of frequently used data ■ *vt* (**caches, caching, cached**) **1 HIDE SUPPLY OF THINGS** to store a hidden supply of things, especially weapons or valuables, in a secret place **2 HOLD DATA IN CACHE** to store data in a cache [Late 18C. < French, < *cacher* (see CACHET).]

SPELLCHECK Do not confuse ***cache*** with ***cash***, which has a similar sound. Beware: your spellchecker will not catch this error.

---

cachectic /kə kéktik, ka-/ *adj* affected by or relating to cachexia [Early 17C. < Greek *kakhektikos*, related to *kakhexia* (see CACHEXIA).]

ϟ**cache memory** *n* = **cache** *n.* 3

cachepot /kásh pō, -pot/ *n* a decorative container for a flowerpot [Late 19C. < French, 'hide pot'.]

cachet /káshay/ *n* **1 QUALITY THAT ATTRACTS ADMIRATION** a quality of distinction and style that people admire and approve of **2 OFFICIAL MARK** an official seal or stamp on a letter or other document **3 COMMEMORATIVE POSTMARK** a commemorative mark stamped on mail to mark a particular event **4 EDIBLE MEDICINE SACHET** an edible capsule formerly used for containing unpleasant-tasting medicine [Early 17C. < French, 'stamp' < Old French *cacher* 'press'.]

cachexia /kə kéksi ə, ka-/ *n* a condition marked by loss of appetite, weight loss, muscle wastage, and general mental and physical debilitation, caused by chronic disease [Mid-16C. Via French *cachexie* or late Latin *cachexia* < Greek *kakhexia* < *kakos* 'bad' + *hexis* 'habit'.]

cachinnate /káki nayt/ (**-nates, -nating, -nated**) *vi* to laugh convulsively and loudly (*literary*) [Early 19C. < Latin *cachinnat-*, past participle of *cachinnare*, an imitation of the sound.] —**cachinnation** *n* —**cachinnator** *n*

cachou /ka shoó, káshoo/ *n* **1** a perfumed pastille that sweetens the breath **2** = **catechu** [Late 16C. Via French < Malayalam *kaccu*.]

cachucha /kə choóchə/ *n* **1** a lively Andalusian dance in 3/4 time for a solo dancer with castanets **2** the music for a cachucha [Mid-19C. < Spanish.]

cacique /kə seék/ *n* **1 NATIVE AMERICAN CHIEF** a Native American chief in Latin America during colonial times **2 POLITICAL LEADER** a local political boss, especially in Latin America or Spain **3 TROPICAL AMERICAN SONGBIRD** a boldly coloured blackbird that feeds on fruit and insects, and nests in colonies. Native to: tropical Central and South America. Genus: *Cacicus*. [Mid-16C. Via Spanish or French < Taino.]

cack-handed /kák hándid/ *adj* **1** clumsy (*informal*) **2** an offensive term meaning naturally left-handed (*regional*) [Mid-19C. < ?] —**cack-handedness** *n*

cackle /kák'l/ *v* (**-les, -ling, -led**) **1** *vi* **LAUGH HARSHLY AND SHRILLY** to laugh a harsh high-pitched malicious laugh, often suggesting pleasure at others' misfortune **2** *vt* **SAY SOMETHING WITH HARSH SHRILL LAUGH** to say something with a malicious high-pitched laugh **3** *vi* **MAKE SQUAWKING NOISE** to squawk shrilly, especially after laying an egg (*refers to hens*) ■ *n* **MALICIOUS LAUGH** a high-pitched malicious laugh or tone of voice [12C. < Middle Low German or Middle Dutch *kākel(e)n*, of imitative origin.] —**cackler** *n*

caco- *prefix* bad ○ *cacology* [< Greek *kakos*]

cacodemon /kákə deémən/, **cacodaemon** *n* an evil spirit [Late 16C. < Greek *kakodaimōn*.]

cacodyl /kákədil, kákədīl/ *n* $C_4H_{12}As_2$ a poisonous oily flammable liquid that contains arsenic and has an unpleasant garlicky smell [Mid-19C. < Greek *kakōdēs* 'bad-smelling'.] —**cacodylic** /kákə díllik/ *adj*

cacography /kə kóggrəfi, ka-/ *n* (*formal*) **1** poor handwriting **2** incorrect spelling —**cacographic** /kákə gráffik/ *adj* —**cacographical** *adj*

cacomistle /kákə miss'l/, **cacomixle** /-miks'l/ *n* a carnivorous mammal resembling a cat with brown fur and a long black-banded tail. Native to: SW United States and Mexico. *Bassariscus astutus*. [Mid-19C. Via American Spanish *cacomixtle* < Nahuatl *tlacomiztli* 'half mountain lion'.]

cacophony /kə kóffəni/ (*plural* **-nies**) *n* **1** an unpleasant combination of loud, often jarring, sounds **2** the use of harsh unpleasant sounds in language, e.g. for literary effect [Mid-17C. Via French < Greek *kakophōnia* < *kakophōnos* 'bad-sounding'.] —**cacophonous** *adj* —**cacophonously** *adv*

cactus /káktəs/ *n* (*plural* **-ti** /-tī/ *or* **-tuses** *or* **-tus**) **SPIKY DESERT PLANT** a plant belonging to a large family of spiny leafless plants with fleshy stems and branches. Native to: dry desert regions of the Americas. Family: Cactaceae. ■ *adj* (*slang*) **1 BROKEN DOWN** broken down **2** *ANZ* **DRUNK** drunk [Mid-18C. Via Latin, 'cardoon' < Greek *kaktos*.] —**cactaceous** /kak táyshəss/ *adj*

cacuminal /kə kyoómin'l, ka-/ *adj* PHON = **retroflex** *adj.* 2 [Mid-19C. < Latin *cacuminare* 'make pointed' < *cacumen* 'point'.]

cad /kad/ *n* **1** a man who does not behave as a gentleman should, especially towards a woman (*dated*) **2** the smallest or weakest piglet in a litter (*regional*) [Mid-19C. Shortening of CADDIE 'errand-boy'.] —**caddish** *adj* —**caddishly** *adv* —**caddishness** *n*

ϟ**CAD** /kad/ *abbr* computer-aided design

cadaster /kə dástər/, **cadastre** *n* an official register containing information on the value, extent, and ownership of land for the purposes of taxation [Late 18C. Via French < Italian *catastico* < Greek *katastikhon* 'list' < *kata stikhon* 'line by line'.] —**cadastral** *adj*

cadaver /kə dávvər, -dáy-, -daá-/ *n* a dead body, especially one that is to be dissected [14C. < Latin, < *cadere* 'to fall'.] —**cadaveric** *adj*

cadaverine /kə dávvə reen/ *n* a thick toxic colourless liquid with an extremely unpleasant smell, produced when flesh rots.

cadaverous /kə dávvərəss/ *adj* **1 EXTREMELY THIN** thin to the point of resembling a skeleton or corpse **2 PALE** deathly pale (*literary*) **3 OF CORPSES** suggesting death or corpses (*formal or literary*) —**cadaverously** *adv* —**cadaverousness** *n*

CADCAM /kád kam/ *abbr* computer-aided design and manufacturing

caddice *n* TEXTILES = **caddis**

caddice fly *n* = **caddis fly**

caddice worm *n* = **caddis worm**

caddie /káddi/, **caddy** *n* (*plural* **-dies**) a golfer's assistant who carries a bag of clubs and performs other duties ■ *vi* (**-dies, -dying, -died**) to act as a caddie for a golfer [Late 18C. Originally a Scots form of CADET.]

caddis /káddiss/, **caddice** *n* a coarse woollen fabric, braid, or yarn [Mid-16C. Via Old French < Provençal.]

caddis fly (*plural* **caddis fly**), **caddice fly** (*plural* **caddice fly**) *n* an insect with four membranous wings, multi-jointed antennae, and larvae (**caddis worms**) that live in water. Order: Trichoptera. [Perhaps < CADDIS, because the larva makes a protective case from coarse silken material]

caddis worm, caddice worm *n* a larva of a caddis fly [See CADDIS FLY]

Caddo /káddō/ (*plural* **-do** *or* **-dos**) *n* a member of a confederacy of Native Americans in central Oklahoma who formerly lived in the Red River area of Arkansas, Louisiana, and east Texas [Via American French from Caddo *kaduhdā-ču?*] —**Caddo** *adj*

Caddoan /káddō ən/ *n* a family of Native North American languages spoken by members of the Caddo confederacy, including Pawnee —**Caddoan** *adj*

caddy[1] /káddi/ (*plural* **-dies**) *n* **1** a small box or tin used for storing something, especially tea **2** a plastic or metal case for a CD-ROM [Late 18C. Alteration of *catty* < Malay *kati*, a standard measure for tea.]

caddy[2] *n, vi* = **caddie**

cade[1] /kayd/ *n* a juniper tree whose wood yields a medicinal oil (**cade oil**). Use: treating skin conditions. Native to: S Europe. *Juniperus oxycedrus*. [Late 16C. Via French < medieval Latin *catanus*.]

cade[2] /kayd/ *adj* describes animals that have been abandoned by their mother and reared by humans [14C. < ?]

Cade /kayd/**, Jack** (?–1450) Irish-born English rebel leader

-cade *suffix* procession ○ *motorcade* [< CAVALCADE]

cadelle /kə dél/ *n* a small black beetle that feeds on grain and other stored foods, found throughout the world. *Tenebroides mauritanicus*. [Mid-19C. Via French < Latin *cadellus* 'little dog'.]

cadence /káyd'nss/ *n* **1 RHYTHM** the beat or measure of something that follows a set rhythm, e.g. a dance or a march **2 FALLING TONE** a drop in the pitch of the voice, e.g. at the end of a sentence **3 INTONATION** the way in which the voice rises and falls in pitch when somebody is speaking **4 RHYTHM IN LANGUAGE** the way in which poetry or prose flows according to a rhythm **5 MUSICAL SEQUENCE** a short sequence of notes that marks the end of a piece or passage of music [14C. Via Old French, 'rhythm' < Italian *cadenza* 'falling away' < Latin *cadere* 'to fall'.] —**cadenced** *adj*

cadency /káyd'nssi/ (*plural* **-cies**) *n* a genealogical line that descends from a younger member of a family

cadential /kə dénsh'l/ *adj* **1** relating to rhythm or a rhythmical cadence **2** relating to cadenzas or a musical cadence

cadenza /kə dénzə/ *n* an elaborate solo passage of virtuoso singing or playing near the end of a section or piece of music, sometimes improvised by the soloist [Mid-18C. < Italian (see CADENCE).]

cade oil /káyd-/ *n* CHEM, PHARM = **juniper tar**

cadet /kə dét/ *n* **1 MILITARY TRAINEE** a young man or woman who is training to become a full member of the armed forces or the police force, especially as an officer **2 YOUNG PERSON IN UNIFORMED ORGANIZATION** somebody of school age who is a member of a uniformed organization offering military training **3 YOUNGER SON** a younger son or brother (*dated*) **4 ENGLISH GENTLEMAN TRAINEE** in England in former times, a gentleman, often a younger son, who entered the army without a commission, intending to work his way up to officer rank [Early 17C. < French, originally Gascon dialect *capdet* 'younger son' (because noble Gascon families traditionally sent these into the army), < Latin *caput* 'head'.] —**cadetship** *n*

cadge /kaj/ (**cadges, cadging, cadged**) *vti* to scrounge or beg something from somebody (*informal*) [Early 17C. Back-formation < CADGER.]

cadger /kájjər/ *n* an habitual borrower or requester of favours (*informal*) [15C. < ?]

cadi /kaádi, káydi/, **qadi** *n* a minor judge in a Muslim community where Islamic law is followed [Late 16C. < Arabic *ḳāḍi*.]

Cádiz /kə diz/ capital of Cádiz Province, SW Spain. Population: 143,129 (1998 estimate).

cadmium /kádmi əm/ *n* (*symbol* **Cd**) a soft malleable toxic bluish-white metallic element. Source: ores of copper and lead. Use: alloys, electroplating, nuclear reactors, dental amalgams, pigments, electronics. [Early 19C. < Latin *cadmia* 'zinc ore' < Greek *kadm(e)ia gē* 'earth of Cadmus', because the substance came originally from Thebes.]

cadmium sulphide *n* **CdS** an orange or yellowish-brown poisonous salt. Use: in paints as a pigment, in medicine, in electronic parts.

cadmium yellow *n* a bright yellow pigment that contains cadmium sulphide, or paint prepared with this pigment

Cadmus /kádməss/ *n* in Greek mythology, a prince who slew a dragon and planted its teeth in the ground, from which armed men sprouted and fought each other. With the five survivors Cadmus founded Thebes.

cadre /kaádər, káy-/ *n* **1 MILITARY UNIT** a group of experienced professionals at the core of a military organization who are able to train new recruits and expand the operations of the unit **2 CORE OF ACTIVISTS** a core group of political activists or revolutionaries **3 CORE GROUP** a controlling or representative group at the centre of an organization **4 SMALL GROUP OF TEAM-SPIRITED PEOPLE** a tightly knit, highly trained group of people **5 MEMBER OF CADRE** a member of a cadre [Mid-19C. Via French, 'frame' < Italian *quadro* 'framework' < Latin *quadrum* 'square'.]

caduceus /kə dyoóssi əss, -dyoóshi-/ (*plural* **-i** /-ī/) *n* **1** in classical mythology, a winged staff entwined with two serpents, the symbol of Hermes or Mercury and associated with the Greek god of healing, Asclepius **2** a symbol of various medical organizations that is modelled on Hermes' caduceus. ◊ **staff of Aesculapius** [Late 16C. Via Latin < Doric Greek *karuk(e)ion* < *kērux* 'herald'.] —**caducean** *adj*

caducity /kə dyoóssəti/ *n* (*literary*) **1** the frailty or senility that sometimes characterizes old age **2** the quality of being perishable or impermanent [Mid-18C. < French *caducité* < *caduc* 'transitory' < Latin *caducus* (see CADUCOUS).]

caducous /kə dyoókəss/ *adj* describes a plant or animal part that drops off or is shed in the early stages of development [Late 18C. < Latin *caducus* 'liable to fall'.]

CAE *abbr* computer-aided engineering

caeca plural of **caecum**

caecilian /see sílli ən/ *n* a limbless tropical amphibian that looks like an earthworm, has small or no eyes, and burrows in the soil. Order: Gymnophiona. [Late 19C. < modern Latin *Caecilia* < Latin *caecilia* 'slow-worm'.]

caecum /seékəm/ (*plural* **-ca** /seékə/) *n* the pouch in which the large intestine begins, which is open at one end [Early 18C. < Latin *(intestinum) caecum* 'blind (gut)' < *caecus* 'blind'.] —**caecal** *adj* —**caecally** *adv*

Caedmon /kádmən/ (650?–680?) English monk and poet

Caelum /seéləm/ *n* a constellation of the southern hemisphere [< Latin, 'chisel'; from its shape]

Caen /koN/ capital of Calvados Department, NW France. Population: 113,987 (1999).

caenogenesis, cainogenesis, cenogenesis *n* the development by an embryo, foetus, or larva of organs or body parts that are lost in adult life

Caenozoic *adj, n* = **Cenozoic**

Caerleon /kaar leé ən/ town in SE Wales. Population: 8,931 (1991).

Caernarvon /kər naárv'n/ town in NW Wales. Population: 9,695 (1991). Welsh **Caernarfon**

Caernarvonshire /kər naárv'nshər/ former county in NW Wales

caerphilly /kər fílli, kair-/ *n* a pale crumbly cheese made in Wales [Early 20C. After CAERPHILLY.]

Caerphilly /kər fílli, kair-/ town in SE Wales. Population: 42,736 (1986).

caeruloplasmin *n* = **ceruloplasmin**

Caesar /seézər/ *n* **1** the title given to a Roman emperor, especially from the reign of Augustus to that of Hadrian **2 Caesar, caesar** somebody, such as a ruler or leader, who acts like a dictator [Old English *casere* < Latin *Caesar*, family name of Julius CAESAR]

Caesar /seézər/**, Gaius Julius** (100–44 BC) Roman general and statesman

Caesarea /seézə reé ə/ ancient port and Roman capital of Palestine, in present-day NW Israel

Caesarean /si záiri ən/, **Caesarian** *adj* **1 OF OR LIKE CAESAR OR CAESARS** referring to or resembling Julius Caesar or the Caesars in general **2 OF CAESAREAN** relating to or involving a Caesarean operation ■ *n* **Caesarean, caesarean, Caesarian, caesarian SURGICAL DELIVERY OF BABY** an operation to deliver a baby by cutting through the mother's abdominal wall and womb. US term **cesarean** [In the medical sense, from the belief that Julius CAESAR was born this way]

Caesarean section *n* = **Caesarean** *n*.

caesar salad *n* a salad made with lettuce, croutons, parmesan cheese, and anchovies, with an egg-based dressing [After *Caesar* Gardini, restaurant proprietor]

caesium /seézi əm/ *n* (*symbol* **Cs**) a rare ductile silver-white element of the alkali metals group that is the most reactive of the elements. Use: photoelectric cells. [Mid-19C. < modern Latin < Latin *caesius* 'bluish-grey'; < its blue spectral lines.]

caesium clock *n* a clock in which caesium atoms are stimulated by an alternating magnetic field

caespitose /sésspi tōss/ *adj* describes a plant that grows in tufts or clumps [Late 18C. < Latin *caespit-* 'turf'.]

caesura /si zyoórə/ (*plural* **-ras** *or* **-rae** /-ree/), **cesura** (*plural* **-ras** *or* **-rae**) *n* **1 PAUSE IN LINE OF VERSE** a pause in a line of poetry, especially to allow its sense to be made clear or to follow the rhythms of natural speech, often near the middle of the line **2 BREAK IN LINE OF VERSE** in classical poetry, especially Greek, a break between two words that are part of the same unit of rhythm (**foot**), usually near the middle of the line **3 PAUSE** a pause or break in speech or conversation (*formal*) **4 MUSICAL INTERRUPTION** a brief interruption in a musical phrase [Mid-16C. < Latin, 'cut' < *caedere* 'cut'.] —**caesural** *adj* —**caesuric** *adj*

CAF *abbr* cost and freight

café /káffay/ *n* a small informal restaurant serving drinks, snacks, and often light meals [Early 19C. Via French, 'coffee(-house)' < Turkish *kahveh* 'coffee' or Arabic *qahwah* 'coffee, wine'.]

café au lait /káffay ō láy/ (*plural* **café au laits** /káffay ō láy/ *or* **cafés au lait**) *n* **1** strong coffee with hot milk **2** a pale brown colour, like that of milky coffee [Mid-18C. < French, 'coffee with milk'.] —**café au lait** *adj*

café latte /káffay láttay/ (*plural* **café lattes** *or* **cafés latte**) *n* = **latte**

café noir /káffay nwaár/ (*plural* **cafés noirs** /káffay nwaár/) *n* coffee without milk or cream [< French, 'black coffee']

café society *n* celebrities and media people who attend fashionable events and visit fashionable restaurants, clubs, and resorts

cafeteria /káffə teéri ə/ *n* a self-service restaurant or coffee bar, especially one in a workplace or department store [Mid-19C. < American Spanish < *café* 'coffee'.]

cafetière /káffə tyáir, -teér/ *n* a coffee pot fitted with a plunger that is used to push the floating coffee grounds to the bottom of the pot when the coffee is ready to drink. US term **French press pot** [Mid-19C. < French, < *café* (see CAFÉ).]

caff /kaf/ *n* a café, especially an old-fashioned British one serving tea and fried breakfasts in unstylish surroundings (*informal*) [Mid-20C. Anglicization of French *café* (see CAFÉ).]

caffeinated /káffi naytid/ *adj* containing caffeine

caffeine /káffeen, káffi een/, **caffein** *n* a stimulant found in coffee, tea, and cola nuts. Use: in soft drinks, cocoa, medicine, and painkillers. [Mid-19C. < French, < *café* 'coffee'.]

caffeinism /káffee nizəm, káffi een-/ *n* a condition caused by an excessive amount of caffeine in the body, resulting in symptoms of high blood pressure, diarrhoea, palpitations, accelerated breathing, and insomnia

caffè latte /káffay láttay/ *n* BEVERAGES = **latte**

~~**caffiene**~~ incorrect spelling of **caffeine**

caftan *n* CLOTHING = **kaftan**

cag /kag/ *n* a cagoule (*informal*) [Late 20C. Shortening.]

cage /kayj/ *n* **1** **ANIMAL ENCLOSURE** an enclosure, usually made from bars or wire, in which to keep animals or birds **2** **ENCLOSING OR PROTECTING WIRE-MESH STRUCTURE** a wire-mesh structure used to protect or enclose something **3** **LIFT PLATFORM** the part of a lift that people stand in, particularly one in a lift that goes down a mine shaft **4** **SCREEN TO STOP BALLS** in baseball, a screen behind home plate that stops thrown or fouled balls **5** **BASKET** the basket in the game of basketball (*informal*) **6** **HOCKEY GOAL** the goal in ice hockey (*informal*) **7** *US* **TEMPORARY PRISON CELL** a barred room or strong mesh enclosure for confining prisoners temporarily, e.g. in a police station ■ *vt* (**cages, caging, caged**) **PUT PERSON OR ANIMAL IN CAGE** to place or keep a person or animal in a cage [12C. Via Old French < Latin *cavea* 'enclosure, dungeon'.] —**caged** *adj* ◇ **rattle somebody's cage** to annoy or upset somebody deliberately ○ *'We kept after him and kept after him and finally rattled his cage a little bit, he said'.* (*Cincinnati Post*; 1997)

Cage /kayj/, **John** (1912–92) US composer

Cage, Nicholas (*b.* 1964) US actor

cagey /káyji/ (**-gier, -giest**), **cagy** (**-gier, -giest**) *adj* cautious and secretive rather than open, honest, or direct (*informal*) [Late 19C. < ?] —**cagily** *adv* —**caginess** *n*

Cagney /kágni/, **James** (1904–86) US film actor

cagoule /kə góol, ka-/ *n* a lightweight hooded waterproof top that often folds up small and can be carried easily [Mid-20C. Via French, 'cowl' < Latin *cucullus* 'cap, hood'.]

cagy *adj* = **cagey**

cahier /kaá yay/ *n* **1** a notebook **2** a written report of a meeting, e.g. of a parliamentary group [Late 18C. Via French < Latin *quaternis* 'set of four', because it was originally used for a pamphlet made from four folded sheets of paper < *quattuor* 'four'.]

Cahokia Mounds /kə hóki ə-/ group of prehistoric Native North American mounds in SW Illinois

cahoots /kə hóots/ [Early 19C. < ?] ◇ **be in cahoots (with somebody)** to have a secret agreement with somebody, especially to do something dishonest or illegal (*informal*)

Cahuilla /kə weé ə/ (*plural* **-la** *or* **-las**) *n* **1** a member of a Native North American people who live in the Sonoran and Mojave desert regions of S California **2** the language of the Cahuilla, belonging to the Shoshone group of Uto-Aztecan languages, now spoken by very few people [Mid-19C. < Cahuilla, 'masters'.] —**Cahuilla** *adj*

ϟ**CAI** *abbr* computer-aided instruction

Caiaphas /kí ə fass/ (*fl.* AD 18–37) Jewish high priest

Caicos Islands /káykəss-/ ➧ **Turks and Caicos Islands**

caiman /káymən/ (*plural* **-mans** *or* **-man**), **cayman** (*plural* **-mans** *or* **-man**) *n* a tropical American reptile smaller and slimmer than the related alligator, with a proportionally longer tail. Genus: *Caiman*. [Late 16C. Via Spanish *caimán* < Carib *caymán*.]

Cain /kayn/ *n* in the Bible, the elder son of Adam and Eve, who killed his brother Abel (Genesis 4) ◇ **raise Cain** to cause a noisy disturbance (*informal*)

Caine /kayn/, **Sir Michael** (*b.* 1933) British actor. Born **Maurice Joseph Micklewhite**

-caine *suffix* a synthetic alkaloid anaesthetic ○ *phenacaine* [< COCAINE]

cainogenesis *n* BIOL = **caenogenesis**

Cainozoic *adj, n* = **Cenozoic**

caïque /kī eék, kaa-/ *n* **1** a long narrow rowing boat used in the waters around Turkey **2** any small rowing, sailing, or motor boat used in the Greek Islands and the E Mediterranean [Early 17C. Via French < Turkish *kayık*.]

cairn /kairn/ *n* **1** a pile of stones set on a hill or mountain to mark a spot for walkers and climbers, or as a memorial to somebody who died there **2** = **Cairn terrier** [Mid-16C. < Gaelic *carn* 'heap of stones'.] —**cairned** *adj*

cairngorm /káirn gawrm/, **cairngorm stone** *n* a smoky yellow, grey, or brown form of quartz, found in Scotland. Use: jewellery. [Late 18C. After the CAIRNGORM MOUNTAINS.]

Cairngorm Mountains /káirn gawrm-/, **Cairngorms** range of the Grampian Mountains in NE Scotland. Highest peak: Ben Macdhui, 1,309 m/4,296 ft.

Cairns /kairnz/ coastal city in NE Queensland, Australia. Population: 92,273 (1996).

Cairn terrier *n* a small terrier with a shaggy coat of rough hair

Cairo /kí rō/ capital of Egypt and Africa's largest city, situated on the River Nile in N Egypt. Population: 6,789,000 (1998 estimate).

caisson /káyss'n, kə sóon/ *n* **1** **UNDERWATER WORK CHAMBER** a bottomless watertight chamber filled with compressed air, used as a base from which construction work is carried out underwater **2** **FLOAT TO RAISE SHIPS** a hollow structure attached to a sunken object, e.g. a wrecked ship, then pumped full of air until it acts as a float, raising the object to the surface **3** **WATER BLOCK** a floating watertight structure used to keep water from entering a dry dock, canal lock, or basin **4** **AMMUNITION BOX** a large container for ammunition **5** **HORSE-DRAWN VEHICLE** a two-wheeled horse-drawn vehicle, formerly used to carry ammunition but now often used to carry coffins at state or military funerals **6** **BOX OF EXPLOSIVES USED AS MINE** a box of explosives, formerly used as a land mine **7** ARCHIT = **coffer** *n.* **2** [Late 17C. Via French < Italian *cassone* 'large box' < *cassa* 'box' < Latin *capsa*.]

caisson disease *n* MED = **decompression sickness**

Caithness /káyth ness, kayth néss/ former county of NE Scotland

caitiff /káytif/ *n* a coward (*archaic*) [13C. Via Old French *caitif* 'captive, wretched person' < Latin *captivus* < *capere* 'take'.]

Caitra /káy trə/ *n* in the Hindu calendar, the first month of the year, made up of 29 or 30 days and falling approximately March to April

cajeput /kájjəpòot/ *n* a pungent medicinal oil [Late 18C. < Malay *kayuputih* 'white tree'.]

cajole /kə jṓl/ (**-joles, -joling, -joled**) *vti* to persuade somebody to do something by flattery or gentle but persistent argument [Mid-17C. < French *cajoler*.] —**cajolement** *n* —**cajoler** *n* —**cajolery** *n* —**cajolingly** *adv*

Cajun /káyjən/ *n* **1** **LOUISIANAN OF FRENCH DESCENT** somebody from Louisiana who is descended from French colonists exiled in the 18th century from Acadia in present-day Canada **2** **FRENCH DIALECT** a dialect of French spoken in Louisiana **3** **MUSIC MIXING BLUES AND FOLK** the musical style, consisting of a mixture of blues and folk music, that originated among the Cajuns **4** **SOMEBODY OF MIXED ANCESTRY** a native of S Alabama or SE Mississippi who is of mixed European, African American, and Native American ancestry [Mid-19C. Alteration of *Acadian* '(inhabitant) of Acadia'.] —**Cajun** *adj*

cake /kayk/ *n* **1** **BAKED SWEET FLOUR-BASED FOOD** a baked sweet food usually made from flour, fat, sugar, eggs, and other ingredients **2** **SHAPED PORTION OF SAVOURY FOOD** an individual portion of ground or chopped savoury food, shaped into a flat round piece and cooked, often by frying or grilling ○ *potato cakes* **3** **BLOCK OF** a solid block of something, e.g. soap, ice, or chocolate **4** **THICK LAYER** a thick layer of something that has collected over a period of time **5** **THING DIVIDED UP** something, e.g. a fund of money, that is to be shared or divided up ○ *Everyone wants a slice of the cake.* ■ *v* (**cakes, caking, caked**) **1** *vti* **FORM CRUST ON** to form, or cover an object with, a thick layer of something, especially dirt, grease, or grime ○ *My boots were caked with mud after I walked through the field.* **2** *vi* **FORM INTO A CAKE** to form into a solid mass [12C. < Old Norse *kaka* 'flat round loaf'.] —**cakey** *adj* ◇ **have your cake and eat it (too)** to try to enjoy the advantages of two things, each of which tends to make the other impossible

cakehole /káyk hōl/ *n* somebody's mouth (*slang*)

cakewalk /káyk wawk/ *n* **1** **COMPETITION BASED ON WALKING** an informal contest to music, with a cake as a prize for executing the most elaborate or amusing walking steps, popular among African Americans in the 19th century **2** **STRUTTING DANCE** any popular dance with elaborate or strutting steps **3** **MUSIC FOR CAKEWALK** the music for a cakewalk **4** **SOMETHING VERY EASY** something that is very easy to do or to achieve (*informal*) —**cakewalker** *n*

Cal *abbr* large calorie

CAL[1] *abbr* **1** calendar **2** calibre

ϟ**CAL**[2] *abbr* computer-assisted learning

Cal. *abbr* California

Calabar bean /kállə baar-/ *n* the dark-brown poisonous seed of a tropical climbing plant. Use: source of drug physostigmine. Native to: Africa. *Physostigma venenosum*. [After *Calabar*, Nigeria]

calabash /kállə bash/ *n* **1** **FRUIT OR GOURD** a large ball-shaped fruit of a tropical American tree, or of the bottle gourd or some other gourd **2** **CONTAINER** the hollowed-out dried shell of a calabash, a bottle gourd, or other gourd **3** **TROPICAL AMERICAN EVERGREEN TREE** a tropical evergreen tree that bears calabashes. Flowers: bell-shaped. Native to: America. *Crescentia cujete*. **4** = **bottle gourd** [Mid-17C. Via French *calabasse* < Persian *karbuz* 'melon'.]

Calabash /kállə bash/ *n* a way of preparing food in the SE United States that involves deep-frying seafood and piling it up on serving plates [After *Calabash*, town in North Carolina]

calabrese /kállə bráyzi, -breez/ *n* a variety of green broccoli [Mid-20C. < Italian, 'of Calabria', where it was developed.]

Calabria /kə lábbri ə/ region in S Italy forming the 'toe' of the Italian peninsula. Population: 2,076,128 (1995). Area: 15,080 sq. km/5,822 sq. mi.

caladium /kə láydi əm/ *n* a tropical plant with white, green, red, or pink variegated leaves, widely grown as a houseplant. Native to: America. Genus: *Caladium*. [Mid-19C. < modern Latin, < Malay *keladi*.]

Calais /kállay/ port in N France, on the English Channel. Population: 77,333 (1999).

calamanco /kállə máng kō/ *n* a glossy woollen fabric with a checked pattern on one side [Late 16C. < ?]

calamander /kállə mandər/ *n* the hard black-and-brown striped wood of a number of Asian trees. Use: furniture-making. [Early 19C. < Sinhalese *kalumādirriya*.]

calamari /kállə maári/ *npl* squid served as food, especially in Mediterranean cuisine [Late 20C. < Italian, plural of *calamaro* 'squid' < medieval Latin *calamarium* 'pen-case' (from the shape of the squid's internal shell) < Latin *calamus* (see CALAMUS).]

calami plural of **calamus**

calamine /kállə mīn/ *n* a pink zinc oxide and ferric oxide powder. Use: in lotions and creams to soothe irritated skin. [Late 16C. Via Old French < medieval Latin *calamina*, alteration of Latin *cadmia* 'zinc ore' (see CADMIUM).]

calamint /kálləmint/ (*plural* **-mints** *or* **-mint**) *n* a plant of the mint family. Flowers: drooping, white, pink, or purple. Genera: *Satureja* and *Calamintha*. [14C. Via Old French *calament* < Greek *kalaminthē*.]

calamite /kállə mīt/ *n* a plant that grew in the Palaeozoic era, related to the horsetail. Genus: *Calamites*. [Mid-19C. < modern Latin *calamites* < Latin *calamus* (see CALAMUS).]

calamitous /kə lámmitəss/ *adj* causing great trouble, tragedy, or disaster [Mid-16C. Directly or via French *calamiteux* < Latin *calamitosus* < *calamitas* 'disaster'.] —**calamitously** *adv* —**calamitousness** *n*

calamity /kə lámməti/ (*plural* **-ties**) *n* a disastrous situation or event (*often ironic*) [14C. Via Old French *calamité* < Latin *calamitas* 'disaster'.]

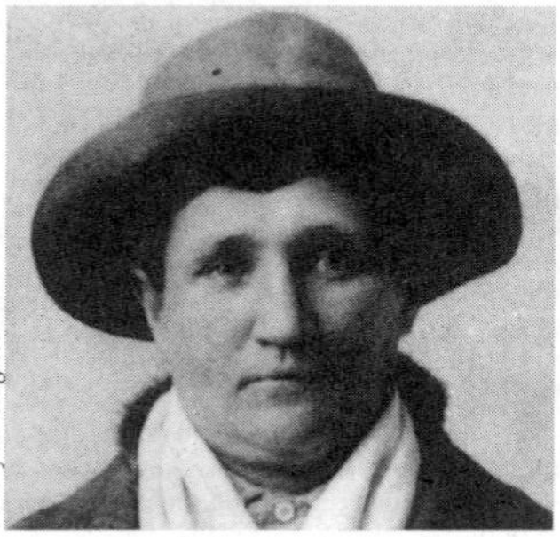

Library of Congress

Calamity Jane

Calamity Jane /kə lámməti jáyn/ (1852?–1903) US frontierswoman. Born **Martha Jane Canary**

calamondin /kállə mundin/ *n* **1** a small sour orange-yellow citrus fruit **2** a hybrid citrus tree that bears calamondins. Native to: Philippines. *Citrofortunella mitis*. [Early 20C. < Tagalog *kalamunding*.]

calamus /kálləməss/ (*plural* **-mi** /-mī/) *n* **1 ASIAN PALM** a tropical Asian palm tree. Use: rattan. Genus: *Calamus*. **2** PLANTS = **sweet flag 3 ROOT OF SWEET FLAG** the aromatic root of the sweet flag plant. Use: source of an oil used in perfumery. **4 FEATHER SHAFT** the hollow shaft of a feather [14C. Via Latin < Greek *kalamos* 'reed, pen'.]

calando /kə lándō/ *adv, adj* played with gradually decreasing volume and slowing tempo (*musical direction*) [Early 19C. < Italian, 'slackening'.]

calandria /kə lándri ə/ *n* the cylindrical core of a nuclear reactor with vertical holes [Early 20C. < Spanish, < Greek *kylindros* 'cylinder'.]

calathea /kállə theé ə/ *n* a tropical evergreen plant with showy variegated leaves, widely grown as a greenhouse plant and houseplant. Native to: South America. Genus: *Calathea*. [< modern Latin, < Greek *kalathos* 'basket']

calaverite /kə lávvə rīt, kállə váir īt/ *n* a silvery-white or yellowish mineral that contains gold [Mid-19C. After *Calaveras* County, California.]

calc- *prefix* = **calci-**

calcaneus /kal káyni əss/ (*plural* **-i** /-ī/) *n* the heel bone (*technical*) [Mid-18C. < late Latin, 'heel' < Latin *calc-*.] —**calcaneal** *adj*

calcar[1] /kál kaar/ (*plural* **-caria** /-káiri ə/) *n* a spur on a plant or animal part, e.g. on a bird's leg or at the base of a petal [Early 19C. < Latin, 'spur' < *calc-* 'heel'.]

calcar[2] /kál kaar/ *n* a furnace formerly used in glass-making for burning materials to make frit, the viscous substance from which glass is subsequently made [Mid-17C. < Italian *calcara*.]

calcareous /kal káiri əss/ *adj* **1** containing or characteristic of calcium carbonate **2** growing on limestone or in earth containing limestone ○ *calcareous algae* [Late 17C. < Latin *calcarius* 'of lime' < *calc-* 'lime'.] —**calcareously** *adv*

calcaria plural of **calcar**[1]

calcariferous /kálkə ríffərəss/ *adj* describes a plant or animal part that has a spur on it [Mid-19C. < Latin *calcar* (see CALCAR[1]) + -IFEROUS.]

calceolaria /kálssi ə láiri ə/ *n* a tropical American plant. Flowers: speckled, slipper-shaped. Genus: *Calceolaria*. [Late 18C. < modern Latin, < Latin *calceolus* 'little shoe'.]

Calchas /kál kass/ *n* in Greek mythology, a soothsayer who accompanied the Greeks during the Trojan War, advising them, amongst other things, to build the Trojan Horse

calci- *prefix* calcium, calcium salt, lime ○ *calcific* [< Latin *calc-*, stem of *calx* (see CALX)]

calcic /kálssik/ *adj* containing, derived from, or relating to calcium or lime

calciferol /kal síffə rol/ *n* = **vitamin D_2** [Mid-20C. < CALCIFEROUS + -OL.]

calciferous /kal síffərəss/ *adj* producing or containing calcium carbonate or other calcium salts

calcific /kal síffik/ *adj* producing lime salts, or involved in their production

calcifuge /kálssi fyooj/ *n* a plant that is best suited for growth in an acid soil —**calcifugal** /kal síffyoog'l, kálssi fyoóg'l/ *adj* —**calcifugous** /kal síffyoogəss, kálssi fyoógəss/ *adj*

calcify /kálssi fī/ (**-fies, -fying, -fied**) *vti* **1 TURN INTO LIME** to convert a substance into lime, or be converted into lime **2 TURN HARD WITH CALCIUM** to become, or cause a body part to become, abnormally hard or stiff as a result of the deposit of calcium salts **3 BECOME RIGID AND UNCHANGING** to become, or cause something to become, rigid and unchanging (*formal*) —**calcification** /kálssifi káysh'n/ *n*

calcimine /kálssi mīn, -min/ *n* a mixture of zinc oxide, water, and glue, sometimes with a colouring added, brushed onto interior walls as a decorative and sealing finish ■ *vt* (**-mines, -mining, -mined**) to cover a wall with calcimine [Mid-19C. Alteration of KALSOMINE, influenced by *calci-*.]

calcine /kál sīn, -sin/ (**-cines, -cining, -cined**) *vti* to heat a solid to a high temperature, converting it to a powdery residue by drying, decomposing, or oxidizing it, or to undergo this process [14C. < medieval Latin *calcinare* 'burn until like lime' < Latin *calc-* (see CALCIUM).] —**calcination** /kálssi náysh'n/ *n*

calcinosis /kálssi nóssiss/ *n* a medical condition in which nodules of calcium are deposited in soft body tissues

calcite /kál sīt/ *n* $CaCO_3$ a colourless or white crystalline mineral that is a form of calcium carbonate. Source: limestone, marble, chalk. Use: cement, plaster, glass, paints. —**calcitic** /kal síttik/ *adj*

calcitonin /kálssi tónin/ *n* a hormone, produced by the thyroid and parathyroid glands, that increases the deposition of calcium in bones

calcitriol /kal síttri ol/ *n* a form of Vitamin D. Use: to control or reverse bone loss. [Late 20C. Probably < CALCIUM + TRIOL.]

calcium /kálssi əm/ *n* (*symbol* **Ca**) a soft silvery-white element that is an alkaline earth metal constituting about three per cent of the earth's crust [Early 19C. < Latin *calc-*, stem of *calx* (see CALX).]

calcium acetylide *n* CHEM = **calcium carbide**

calcium antagonist *n* a drug that dilates the arteries and slows the heart. Use: treatment of angina.

calcium carbide *n* CaC_2 a colourless or greyish-black powdery compound. Use: generation of acetylene gas.

calcium carbonate *n* $CaCO_3$ a white crystalline solid that is one of the most common natural substances. Source: chalk, limestone, marble, animal shells, bones. Use: antacids, paint, cement, toothpaste.

calcium chloride *n* $CaCl_2$ a white salt that absorbs moisture easily and quickly. Use: drying gases, de-icing roads, in pulp and paper treatment.

calcium cyanamide *n* $CaCN_2$ a white or greyish-black crystalline compound that releases ammonia slowly in the presence of water. Use: fertilizers.

calcium cyanide *n* $Ca(CN)_2$ a white or greyish-black powder that decomposes in humid conditions to produce hydrogen cyanide. Use: formerly, insecticide, rodent poison, in fumigation.

calcium cyclamate *n* $Ca(C_6H_{11}NHSO_3)_2.2H_2O$ a sweet-tasting salt of cyclamic acid. Use: formerly, sugar substitute.

calcium fluoride *n* CaF_2 a colourless or white substance. Source: fluorspar.

calcium gluconate *n* $CaC_{12}H_{22}O_{14}$ a calcium salt. Use: mineral supplement, treatment of calcium deficiency and osteoporosis.

calcium hydroxide *n* $Ca(OH)_2$ a white alkaline powder. Source: action of water on calcium oxide. Use: treatment of acid soil, manufacture of cement, plaster, and glass.

calcium hypochlorite *n* $Ca(OCl)_2$ a white crystalline solid, soluble in water, that is a stable chlorine carrier. Use: bleaching agent, disinfectant, bactericide.

calcium nitrate *n* $Ca(NO_3)_2.4H_2O$ a white solid that absorbs moisture very quickly and is a strong oxidizer. Use: fertilizer, explosives.

calcium oxide *n* CaO a white crystalline powder. Use: manufacture of steel and glass, refining of aluminium, copper, and zinc, treatment of sewage.

calcium phosphate *n* any of several phosphates of calcium. Source: rocks, animal bones. Use: as fertilizer in the form of bone ash.

calcium sulphate *n* a white odourless crystal or powder. Source: anhydrite, gypsum. Use: drying agent, building material.

calcrete /kál kreet/ *n* an accumulation in the soil of a layer of calcium carbonate and other alkaline minerals just below the surface [Early 20C. < CALC- + (*con*)*crete*.]

calcspar /kálk spaar/ *n* MINERALS = **calcite** [Early 19C. < Latin *calc-* (see CALCIUM) + SPAR[3].]

calc-tufa /kálk-/ *n* MINERALS = **tufa** [Early 19C. < Latin *calc-* (see CALCIUM).]

calculable /kálkyoōləb'l/ *adj* **1** able to be worked out or estimated, using mathematics **2** likely to behave in the way that is expected —**calculability** /kálkyoōlə bílləti/ *n*

calculate /kálkyoō layt/ (**-lates, -lating, -lated**) *v* **1** *vti* **WORK OUT MATHEMATICALLY** to figure out or estimate a figure using mathematics **2** *vti* **DECIDE** to consider a situation carefully and decide what is likely to happen **3** *vt* **INTEND SOMETHING TO HAVE PARTICULAR EFFECT** to intend or design something to have a particular effect or result (*usually passive*) ○ *The attack was calculated to cause maximum loss of life.* **4** *vi US* **INTEND** to be planning or intending to do a particular thing (*regional*) ○ *We were calculating on going home around midnight.* [Late 16C. < late Latin *calculat-*, past participle of *calculare* < Latin *calculus* 'pebble' (see CALCULUS).] —**calculated** *adj* —**calculatedly** *adv* —**calculatedness** *n*

calculating /kálkyoō layting/ *adj* **1** determined to gain the greatest personal advantage **2** indicative of somebody's scheming nature —**calculatingly** *adv*

calculation /kálkyoō láysh'n/ *n* **1 PROCESS OF CALCULATING** the process, or a step in the process, of working out the answer to a mathematical problem **2 ESTIMATE** an estimate or answer obtained by calculating **3 DELIBERATENESS** consideration of something, especially when thinking of personal advantage —**calculational** *adj* —**calculative** /kálkyoōlətiv, -laytiv/ *adj*

calculator /kálkyoō laytər/ *n* a device used to carry out arithmetical operations, especially a small hand-held electronic device

calculous /kálkyoōləss/ *adj* relating to abnormal hard formations of minerals (**calculi**) in the body

calculus /kálkyoōləss/ (*plural* **-li** /-lī/ *or* **-luses**) *n* **1 BRANCH OF MATHEMATICS** a branch of mathematics dealing with the way that relations between certain sets (**functions**) are affected by very small changes in one of their variables (**independent variables**) as they approach zero. ◊ **differential calculus, integral calculus 2 METHOD OF CALCULATION** a method or system of calculation using symbols or symbolic logic **3 STONE** a stone or concretion, especially one in the kidney, gall bladder, or urinary bladder (*technical*) **4** DENT = **tartar** *n.* 1 [Mid-17C. < Latin, 'pebble', diminutive of *calx* (see CALX).]

Calcutta /kal kúttə/ capital of West Bengal State and port in NE India. Population: 4,309,819 (1991).

caldarium /kal dáiri əm/ (*plural* **-a** /-ri ə/) *n* the hot room in an ancient Roman bathhouse [Mid-18C. < Latin, < *calere* 'be warm'.]

Calder /káwldər, kóld-/, **Alexander Young** (1898–1976) US painter and sculptor

caldera /kal dáirə, káwldərə/ (*plural* **-ras**) *n* a large crater in a volcano, caused by a major eruption followed by the collapse of the volcanic pipe walls that form the volcano's cone [Late 17C. Via Spanish < late Latin *caldaria* 'cooking pot' < Latin *caldus* 'warm'.]

Calderdale /káwldər dayl/ local government unitary authority in N England, established 1997. Population: 193,200 (1995).

Calderón de la Barca /káldə rón də la baárkə/, **Pedro** (1600–81) Spanish dramatist and poet

Caldey Island /káwldi-/ small island off the coast of SW Wales. Population: 50. Area: 2.6 sq. km/1 sq. mi. Welsh **Ynys Pyr**

caldron *n* = **cauldron**

Caldwell /káwld wel/ city in SW Idaho. Population: 21,089 (1996).

Caldwell, Erskine (1903–87) US writer

Caledonia /kállə dóni ə/ **1** Roman name for the northern part of Britain **2** poetic name for Scotland

Caledonian /kálli dóni ən/ *adj* **1 OF SCOTLAND** relating to Scotland or its people, language, or culture (*literary*) **2 OF PALAEOZOIC EUROPE** relating to the Palaeozoic era in NW Europe, when many mountains were formed ■ *n* **SCOT** a Scottish person (*literary*)

Caledonian Canal major waterway in N Scotland linking east and west, comprising canals and lochs. Length: 60 km/97 mi.

calendar /kállindər/ *n* **1 SYSTEM OF CALCULATING YEAR** a system of calculating the days and months of the year and when the year begins and ends **2 CHART OF YEAR** a chart showing the days and months of the year, especially a particular year **3 TIMETABLE** a timetable of events, usually covering a period of a year **4 LIST** an official list of things to be done or considered ■ *vt* **SCHEDULE** to enter something in a calendar or diary [12C. Via Anglo-Norman *calender* < Latin *calendarium* 'money-lender's account-book' < *calendae* 'first day of the month'.]

calendar day *n* the period of 24 hours from midnight to midnight

calendar month *n* **1** = **month** *n.* 1 **2** = **month** *n.* 3

calendar year *n* the period of 365 or 366 days from 1 January to 31 December

calender /kállindər/ *n* a machine with rollers, used to form thin sheets from paper, plastic, or other material, or to impart a desired surface finish [Early 16C. < French *calendre* < Latin *cylindrus* 'roller' (influenced by Latin *columna* 'column').] —**calender** *vt* —**calenderer** *n*

calends /kállendz/, **kalends** *npl* the first day of the month in the ancient Roman calendar [14C. Via French *calendes* < Latin *calendae* 'first day of the month'.]

calendula /kə léndyoolə/ (*plural* **-las** *or* **-la**) *n US* PLANTS = **pot marigold** [Late 16C. < modern Latin, < Latin *calendae* (see CALENDS).]

calenture /kállən tyoor, -choor/ *n* a fever occurring in tropical regions, formerly believed to be caused by heat [Late 16C. Via French < Spanish *calentura* < Latin *calere* 'be warm'.]

calf[1] /kaaf/ (*plural* **calves** /kaavz/) *n* **1 YOUNG COW OR BULL** a very young cow or bull of domestic cattle **2 YOUNG ANIMAL** the young of some other animals besides the cow, e.g. the elephant, whale, giraffe, and buffalo **3** = **calfskin** *n.* 1 **4 PIECE OF ICEBERG** a large piece of ice that has broken away from an iceberg [Old English *cælf* < Germanic]

calf[2] /kaaf/ (*plural* **calves** /kaavz/) *n* the fleshy part at the back of the leg below the knee [14C. < Old Norse *kálfi*.]

calf love *n* = **puppy love** (*literary*)

calfskin /kaáf skin/ *n* **1** fine leather made from the skin of calves **2** the skin of a calf

Calgary /kálgəri/ city in S Alberta, Canada. Population: 768,082 (1996).

Cali /kaáli/ capital of Valle de Cauca Department, W Colombia. Population: 1,985,906 (1997 estimate).

caliber *n US* = **calibre**

calibrate /kálli brayt/ (**-brates, -brating, -brated**) *vt* **1 MARK SCALE ON** to establish and mark the units shown on a measuring instrument **2 ENSURE ACCURACY OF** to test and adjust the accuracy of a measuring instrument or process **3 MEASURE BORE OF** to measure the internal diameter of a gun or cylinder —**calibrator** *n*

calibration /kálli bráysh'n/ *n* **1** the checking of a measuring instrument against an accurate standard to determine any deviation and correct for errors **2** a mark showing one of the units of measurement on a measuring instrument

calibre /kállibər/ *n* **1 ABILITY** a person's ability, intelligence, or character ○ *We don't often get candidates of her calibre.* **2 BORE OF FIREARM** the inner diameter of a pipe or cylinder, especially the barrel of a firearm **3 SIZE OF BULLET** the external diameter of a projectile, e.g. a bullet or a shell [Mid-16C. Via French < Arabic *kālib* 'mould' < Greek *kalapous* 'shoemaker's last'.]

calices plural of **calix**

caliche /ka leéchi/ *n* **1** a layer of clay or sand containing minerals, e.g. sodium nitrate and sodium chloride, found in dry regions of South America **2** GEOL = **calcrete** [Mid-19C. < American Spanish.]

calico /kállikō/ (*plural* **-coes**) *n* **1 WHITE COTTON CLOTH** a white or unbleached cotton cloth **2** *US* **BRIGHT COTTON CLOTH** a coarse cotton cloth with a bright printed pattern **3** *US* **ANIMAL WITH BLOTCHED COAT** an animal with a blotched coat, usually white with black and reddish patches [Mid-16C. Alteration of *Calicut* (now Kozhikode), India, from which such cloth was exported.]

calif *n* = **caliph**

Calif. *abbr* California

califate *n* = **caliphate**

California /kálli fáwrnyə/ state in the W United States, on the Pacific Ocean. Capital: Sacramento. Population: 32,268,301 (1997). Area: 411,469 sq. km/158,869 sq. mi. —**Californian** *n, adj*

California, Gulf of arm of the Pacific Ocean between mainland Mexico and Baja California. Area: 152,810 sq. km/59,000 sq. mi.

California condor *n* a large dark grey or brown vulture with a wingspan of about 3 m/10 ft and a naked head and neck. Native to: SE United States. *Gymnogyps californianus.*

California Current Pacific Ocean current flowing southwards along the western coast of North America before turning west

California poppy, Californian poppy *n* an annual plant with bluish divided leaves. Flowers: bright red to yellow. *Eschscholzia californica.*

californium /kálli fáwrni əm/ *n* (*symbol* **Cf**) a synthetic radioactive metallic element. Source: bombardment of curium or americium with neutrons. Use: neutron source. [Mid-20C. Because first synthesized at the University of California.]

Caligula /kə líggyoolə/ (AD 12–41) Roman emperor (AD 37–41)

caliper *n US* = **calliper**

caliph /káylif, kállif/, **calif, kalif, khalif** *n* a title taken by Islamic rulers, e.g. the Turkish sultans, that asserts religious authority to rule derived from that of Muhammad [14C. Via French *caliphe* < Arabic *ḵalīfa* 'successor, deputy' < *ḵalafa* 'succeed'.]

caliphate /kálli fayt, káyli-, -fit/, **califate, kalifate, khalifate** *n* the territory over which a caliph's rule extends, or the time for which it lasts

calix /káyliks, káll-/ (*plural* **-lices** /-li seez/) *n* **1** a chalice or cup **2** ANAT = **calyx** *n.* 2 [Early 18C. < Latin (see CHALICE).]

calk[1] /kawk/ *n* a metal spike on a horseshoe to prevent slipping [Late 16C. < ?]

calk[2] *vt* = **caulk**

call /kawl/ *v* **1** *vt* **GIVE A NAME TO** to give somebody or something a name ○ *What are you going to call the baby?* **2** *vt* **REFER TO** to use a particular term to address or refer to somebody ○ *He always called his father 'Sir'.* **3** *vt* **DESCRIBE AS** to describe or think of somebody or something in a particular way ○ *I'd call him a fool.* **4** *vti* **SAY LOUDLY** to say something in a loud voice ○ *'Supper's ready', he called from the kitchen.* **5** *vt* **SUMMON** to summon or alert somebody or something by means of a formal request ○ *I'll call a taxi.* **6** *vti* **TELEPHONE** to contact somebody by telephone or radio **7** *vi* **VISIT** to visit somebody, or the place where somebody lives or works ○ *I called to see her yesterday.* **8** *vi* **STOP SOMEWHERE** to stop at a particular place on a regular bus, coach, or train route ○ *Do you call at George Square?* **9** *vti* **REQUEST SOMETHING TO HAPPEN** to make an official order or request for something, e.g. a meeting ○ *A council meeting has been called for July 15th.* **10** *vt* **READ OUT** to read names or numbers from a list **11** *vti* **DECLARE CHOICE IN GAME** to make a declaration in a game, e.g. to choose heads or tails, or choose trumps in a card game ○ *I'll toss, you call.* **12** *vi* **CRY** to give a cry (*refers to birds or animals*) **13** *vt US* **PREDICT** to predict what is going to happen, especially in politics ○ *It's a very hard result to call.* **14** *vt* **OFFICIALLY DECIDE IN GAME** to make an official decision in a sporting event or a game ○ *called a foul* **15** *vti* **INSTRUCT DANCERS** to direct people who are dancing, e.g. in a square dance **16** *vt* **DEMAND REPAYMENT OF** to demand repayment of a loan or bond issue **17** *vt Aus, NZ* **ACT AS SPORTS COMMENTATOR FOR** to commentate on radio or television on a sporting event, particularly a horse race ■ *n* **1 SHOUT** a shout or cry **2 BIRD OR ANIMAL CRY** the sound made by a bird or animal **3 SIGNAL** a signal given by a sound, e.g. on a horn or whistle **4 TELEPHONE COMMUNICATION** a telephone conversation, or an attempt to get in touch with somebody by telephone **5 VISIT** a short visit to somebody at his or her house or place of work ○ *made a few calls on the way home.* **6 REQUEST TO COME** a request for somebody to come ○ *The emergency services answer thousands of calls a year.* **7 EXPRESSED WISH** a demand or request for something to be done ○ *There have been calls for him to resign.* **8 STRONG APPEAL OF PLACE OR LIFESTYLE** the feeling of strong attraction exerted by a particular place or way of life ○ *the call of the wild* **9 FEELING OF DUTY** a feeling that a particular job or way of life is a personal duty **10 DEMAND OR OBLIGATION** a demand or obligation that somebody has to fulfil ○ *I'd like to help, but I have a great many calls on my time.* **11 REMINDER** a reminder, given electronically, by telephone, or in person, that somebody should wake up or that something is about to happen **12 DECLARATION IN GAME** a declaration made during a game, e.g. the choice of heads or tails when a coin is tossed ○ *It's your call.* **13 REFEREE'S DECISION** a decision made by a referee **14** *US* **PREDICTION** a prediction of what is about to happen, especially in politics **15 HUNTER'S DEVICE TO ATTRACT GAME** a device that imitates the cry of a bird or other animal, used as a lure in hunting [12C. < Old Norse *kalla*.] ◇ **be on call** to be on duty away from the workplace, available to be summoned

call back *v* **1** *vti* **TELEPHONE SOMEBODY AGAIN** to contact somebody by telephone again **2** *vi* **VISIT SOMEBODY AGAIN** to visit somebody again **3** *vt* **ASK TO RETURN** to recall somebody, e.g. for a second audition or to return to a job **4** *vt* **ASK WORKERS BACK TO WORK** to contact previously laid-off workers to ask them to return to a job site

call down *vt* **1** to pray or appeal for good or bad things to happen to somebody **2** *US* to rebuke somebody who has done something wrong ○ *The judge called the lawyers down for their unseemly courtroom antics.*

call for *vt* **1 REQUEST FOR SOMETHING TO HAPPEN** to make a demand or request for some action to take place **2 NEED** to need or require a particular thing or quality **3 COLLECT** to collect somebody

call forth *vt* to inspire an emotion, energy, or courage

call in *v* **1** *vt* **ASK HELP FROM** to ask somebody to come and give advice or help **2** *vi* **PAY QUICK VISIT** to make a brief visit to somebody **3** *vi* **TELEPHONE PLACE OF WORK** to telephone a place of work in order to collect or leave a message **4** *vt* **ASK FOR SOMETHING TO BE REPAID** to ask for a debt or loan to be repaid **5** *vt* **ARRANGE RETURN OF** to arrange for or request that something to be returned, e.g. outdated currency or defective goods

call off *vt* **1** to cancel or stop an event **2** to order a dog or a person to stop attacking somebody

call on *vt* **1** to ask or tell somebody to do something **2** to visit somebody, often in a formal manner

call out *vt* **1 SUMMON PEOPLE TO HELP** to summon somebody or an organization to come and help **2 ORDER TO STRIKE** to tell workers to stop work and go on strike **3 CHALLENGE TO A FIGHT** to challenge somebody to a duel or fight

⚡**call up** *vt* **1 RECRUIT TO FIGHT** to order somebody to join the armed services in time of war. US term **draught** **2 SUMMON** to summon somebody who or something that is available in reserve **3 TELEPHONE** to telephone somebody (*informal*) **4 DISPLAY ON COMPUTER SCREEN** to instruct a computer to find and display a particular piece of information ○ *call up last month's sales figures* **5 EVOKE** to bring back memories of something

call upon *vt* **1** to ask somebody in a formal way to do something **2** to make demands on somebody or on somebody's abilities

calla /kállə/ *n* PLANTS = **arum lily**

callable /káwləb'l/ *adj* **1** describes a loan that is repayable on demand **2** describes a share or bond that is convertible before reaching maturity

Callaghan /kállə hən, -han/, **James, Baron Callaghan of Cardiff** (*b.* 1912) British statesman

call alarm *n* a personal alarm used for summoning help in an emergency

calla lily *n* PLANTS = **arum lily**

callaloo /kállə loó/ (*plural* **-loos**) *n Carib* **1** a thick soup made of the leaves of the dasheen plant (**callaloo bush**) with okra, green peppers, coconut milk, onions, herbs, and crab **2** a complex mixture or confusion [Mid-18C. < American Spanish *calalu*.]

Callao /kə yów/ chief port of Peru, in the west of the country. Population: 424,294 (1998 estimate).

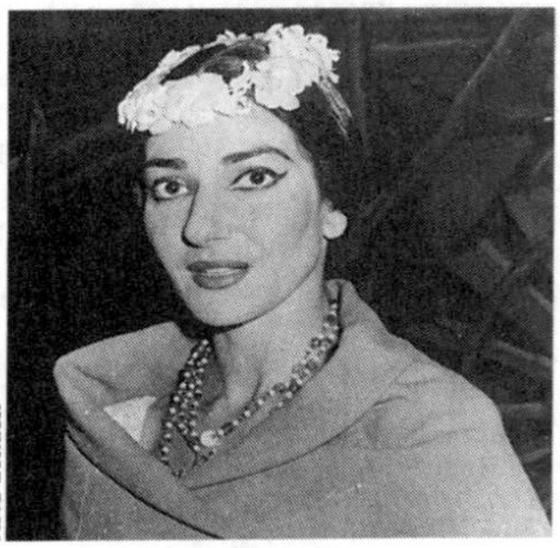

Maria Callas

Callas /kálləss, kál ass/, **Maria** (1923–77) US-born opera soprano. Born **Maria Anna Sofia Cecilia Kalogeropoulos**

callback /káwl bak/ *n* **1 RETURN CALL** a telephone call made to somebody who has recently phoned **2** *US* **RECALLING OF** an act of asking somebody to return **3** *US* **PRODUCT RECALL** the recalling of a faulty product by a manufacturer

call bird *n* a cheap article displayed to attract customers

callboard /káwl bawrd/ *n* a board backstage in a theatre, giving information to actors and other people involved in a production

call box *n UK* a telephone box

callboy /káwl boy/ *n* somebody in a theatre who tells the actors when the time for them to go on stage is approaching

call centre *n* a place that handles high-volume incoming telephone calls on behalf of a large organization

caller /káwlər/ *n* **1 SOMEBODY PHONING OR VISITING** a maker of telephone calls, or a visitor **2 ANNOUNCER** an announcer, e.g. of moves in a square dance or of numbers in a game of bingo **3** *Aus* **SPORTS COMMENTATOR** a broadcast commentator for a sporting event, especially a horse race

caller ID *n* an electronic device attached to a telephone that, on a small screen, shows the name and telephone number of somebody who is calling or has called

call girl *n* a prostitute who makes appointments with clients by telephone

calli- *prefix* beautiful ○ *callipygian* [< Greek *kallos* 'beauty']

calligraphy /kə líggrəfi/ *n* **1** the art or skill of producing beautiful handwriting **2** beautiful or artistic handwriting [Early 17C. < Greek *kalligraphia* 'beautiful writing' < *kallos* 'beauty' + *graphein* 'write'.] —**calligrapher** *n* —**calligraphic** /kálli gráffik/ *adj* —**calligraphically** *adv* —**calligraphist** *n*

Callil /kə líl/, **Carmen** (*b.* 1938) Australian publisher

call-in *n US* BROADCAST = **phone-in**

calling /káwling/ *n* **1** a strong urge to follow a particular career or do a particular type of work **2** a job or profession

calling card *n US, Can* = **visiting card**

calliope /kə lī́ əpi/ *n US, Can* MUSIC = **steam organ** [Mid-19C. < Latin *Calliope* 'CALLIOPE'.]

Calliope /kə lī́ əpi/ *n* the Muse of epic poetry, one of the nine Muses believed to inspire and nurture the arts in Greek mythology. ◊ **Muse** [Via Latin < Greek *Kalliopē* 'beautiful-voiced']

calliper /kállipər/ *n* **1 MEASURING INSTRUMENT** an instrument used to measure the internal or external dimensions of objects and consisting of two curved hinged legs joined at one end **2 LEG BRACE** a leg splint consisting of metal rods and straps, that enables the hip bone, rather than the foot, to support weight when walking ■ *vt* **MEASURE WITH CALLIPERS** to measure something using a calliper [Late 16C. < ?]

calliper rule *n* a graduated scale with jaws, one fixed and one sliding, set at right angles to it, used to measure the thickness of boards or the diameters of pipes or shafts

callipers /kállipəz/ *npl* a measuring instrument with two hinged legs and an attached scale that measures the distance between the tips of the legs, used particularly for measuring diameters

callipygian /kálli píjji ən/, **callipygous** /kálli pīgəss/ *adj* having well-shaped buttocks (*literary*) [Late 18C. < Greek *kallipūgos* 'beautiful buttocks' (applied to a statue of Aphrodite) < *kallos* 'beauty' + *pūgē* 'buttocks'.]

callisthenics /kálliss thénniks/ *npl* vigorous physical exercises for improving fitness and muscle tone (+ *plural verb*) ■ *n* the practice of performing callisthenics (+ *singular verb*) [Early 19C. < Greek *kalli-* 'beauty' + *sthenos* 'strength'.] —**callisthenic** *adj*

Callisto /kə lístō/ *n* **1** in Greek mythology, a nymph who was changed into a bear by Hera and later became the constellation Ursa Major **2** a large satellite of Jupiter [Via Latin, < Greek *Kallistō* < *kalos* 'beautiful']

call letters *npl US, Can* MEDIA = **call sign**

call loan *n* a loan that must be repaid on demand

call mark *n* LIBRARIES = **shelf mark**

call money *n* money that has been borrowed and that is repayable on demand

call number *n* LIBRARIES = **shelf mark**

call of nature *n* a need to urinate or defecate (*humorous*)

callose /kállōz/ *n* a polysaccharide found in plant cell walls and formed in flowering plants in response to injury [Mid-19C. < Latin *callosus* (see CALLOUS).]

callosity /kə lóssəti/ (*plural* **-ties**) *n* a local thickening of the outer layer of the skin caused by repeated friction or pressure

Callot /kə lót/, **Jacques** (1592–1635) French artist

callous /kálləss/ *adj* showing no concern if other people are hurt or upset [14C. Directly or via French *calleux* < Latin *callosus* < *callus* 'hard skin'.] —**callously** *adv* —**callousness** *n*

SPELLCHECK Do not confuse ***callous*** with ***callus***, which has a similar sound. Beware: your spellchecker will not catch this error.

calloused /kálləst/ *adj* having an area of hard thickened skin

callow /kállō/ *adj* young or immature, and lacking the experience of life that comes with adulthood [Old English *calu* < Germanic] —**callowness** *n*

Calloway /kállə way/, **Cab** (1907–94) US jazz musician. Full name **Cabel Calloway**

call sign *n* a signal, usually a group of letters and numbers, used for identification by a radio transmitting station or a unit or operator in radio communication with others. US term **call letters**

call slip *n* a form for requesting a library book that is not kept on the shelves used by the public

call-up *n* the order to join the armed services in time of war. US term **draught**

callus /kálləss/ *n* **1 PATCH OF THICKENED SKIN** a hard thickened area of skin, especially on the palm of the hand or the sole of the foot, caused by repeated pressure or friction **2 MASS FORMED IN HEALING BONE** a mass of fibrous tissue, calcium, cartilage, and bone that forms progressively during the healing of a bone fracture **3 PLANT TISSUE** plant tissue that forms at the site of a wound, or that develops during tissue culture of plant parts, giving rise to new plantlets [Mid-16C. < Latin.]

SPELLCHECK See ***callous***.

calm /kaam/ *adj* **1 NOT ANXIOUS** without anxiety or strong emotion **2 NOT WINDY** without wind or storms **3 AT LOWEST POINT OF BEAUFORT SCALE** relating to or having a wind speed of not more than 1.6 km/1 mi. per hour **4 NOT STORMY** smooth and without any large waves ○ *smooth sailing on calm seas* ■ *n* **1 PEACE AND QUIET** a situation of complete peace and quiet, with no noise, trouble, or anxiety **2 ABSENCE OF WIND** still weather, without wind or waves caused by wind ■ *vt* **MAKE LESS TENSE** to make somebody less anxious or upset [14C. Probably via French *calme* or directly < late Latin *cauma* < Greek *kauma* 'heat of the day'.] —**calmly** *adv* —**calmness** *n*

calm down *vti* to become or make somebody become less excited, anxious, or upset

calmative /kaámətiv/ *adj* having a calming or quietening effect ■ *n* a drug or treatment that has a calming or quietening effect

calmodulin /kal móddyōōlin/ *n* a calcium-binding protein found in the cells of most living organisms that controls many enzyme processes [Late 20C. Contraction of CALCIUM + MODULATE + -IN.]

calomel /kállə mel, -məl/ *n* a mercury compound. Use: fungicide, insecticide, formerly, as a purgative. [Late 17C. < modern Latin.]

Calor Gas /kállər-/ *tdmk* a trademark for liquid butane gas sold in cylinders for domestic use

caloric /kə lórrik, kállərik/ *adj* relating to calories or heat transfer —**calorically** /kə lórrikli/ *adv*

calorie /kálləri/ *n* **1 UNIT OF ENERGY** a unit of energy equal to 4.1855 joules, originally defined as the quantity of heat required to raise the temperature of 1 g of pure water by 1° C. It has now been superseded by the joule in scientific usage. **2 LARGER UNIT OF ENERGY** a unit of energy equal to the heat required to raise the temperature of 1 kg of pure water by 1° C **3 UNIT OF FOOD ENERGY** a unit of energy-producing potential in food, equal to one large calorie [Mid-19C. < French, < Latin *calor* 'heat' < *calere* 'be warm'.]

calorific /kállə ríffik/ *adj* relating to or generating heat or calories

calorific value *n* the amount of heat released by the combustion of a specified mass of fuel, typically measured in joules per kilogram

calorimeter /kállə rímmitər/ *n* an apparatus for measuring the amount of heat given out or taken in during a process such as combustion or change of state —**calorimetric** /kálləri méttrik/ *adj* —**calorimetrically** *adv* —**calorimetry** *n*

calorize /kállə rīz/ (**-rizes, -rizing, -rized**), **calorise** (**-rises, -rising, -rised**) *v* to treat the surface of steel or iron with aluminium powder and heat to 800–1,000° C to prevent or reduce rusting [Mid-20C. < Latin *calor* 'heat'.]

calotype /kállō tīp/ *n* **1** a 19th-century photographic process producing a negative on a plate wetted with silver iodide **2** a photograph produced by the calotype process [Mid-19C. < Greek *kalos* 'beautiful'.]

Caloundra /kə lówndrə/ city in SE Queensland, Australia. Population: 22,057 (1991).

calque /kalk/ *n* LANGUAGE = **loan translation** [Mid-20C. < French, 'copy' < Latin *calcare* (see CAULK).]

caltrop /káltrəp/ *n* **1** (*plural* **-trops** *or* **-trop**) a spiny plant harmful to livestock. Native to: Europe, naturalized in California. *Tribulus terrestris.* **2** a military device with four spikes arranged so that one will always point upwards, scattered on the ground to lame horses or puncture tyres **3** PLANTS = **water chestnut** *n.* 1 **4** PLANTS = **star thistle** [Pre-12C. Variant of obsolete *calcatrippe* 'thistle' < medieval Latin *calcatrippa*.]

calumet /kállyōō met/ *n* a long-stemmed ceremonial pipe used by some Native American peoples [Late 17C. < French, 'pipe', dialect variant of *chalumeau* < Latin *calamus* 'reed'.]

calumniate /kə lúmni ayt/ (**-ates, -ating, -ated**) *vt* to accuse somebody falsely, or slander somebody (*formal*) [Mid-16C. < Latin *calumniat-* < *calumnia* (see CALUMNY).] —**calumniable** *adj* —**calumniation** /kə lúmni áysh'n/ *n* —**calumniator** *n*

calumny /kálləmni/ (*plural* **-nies**) *n* (*formal*) **1** the making of false statements about somebody with malicious intent **2** a slanderous statement or false accusation [15C. < Latin *calumnia* 'false accusation' < *calvi* 'deceive'.] —**calumnious** /kə lúmni əss/ *adj* —**calumniously** *adv*

calvados /kálvə doss/ *n* apple brandy distilled from cider, made in the Normandy region of France [Early 20C. After *Calvados*, Normandy.]

calvarium /kal váiri əm/ (*plural* **-a** /-ə/) *n* the upper domed portion of the skull (*technical*) [Late 19C. Alteration of Latin *calvaria* 'skull' < *calvus* 'bald'.]

calvary /kálvəri/ (*plural* **-ries**) *n* a sculpture representing Jesus Christ's crucifixion

Calvary /kálvəri/ hill outside ancient Jerusalem where the Crucifixion of Jesus Christ took place, according to the Bible

Calvary cross *n* a Christian cross mounted on three symmetrical steps

calve /kaav/ (**calves, calving, calved**) *vti* **1** to give birth to a calf **2** to release a mass of ice that breaks away (*used of a glacier or iceberg*) [Old English *calfian* < *cælf* 'calf']

Calvert /kálvərt, káwl-/, **Cecilius, 2nd Baron Baltimore** (1605–75) English-born American colonial administrator

Calvert, Charles, 3rd Baron Baltimore (1637–1715) English-born American colonial administrator

Calvert, George, 1st Baron Baltimore (1580?–1632) English-born American absentee colonial administrator

calves plural of **calf**[1], **calf**[2]

Calvin /kálvin/, **John** (1509–64) French-born Swiss Protestant theologian and reformer

Calvin cycle *n* a series of reactions that take place in photosynthesis by which carbon dioxide is converted to glucose [After Melvin *Calvin* (1911–97), US chemist]

Calvinism /kálvinizəm/ *n* the religious doctrine of John Calvin, which emphasizes that salvation comes through faith in God, and also that God has already chosen those who will believe and be saved —**Calvinist** *n, adj* —**Calvinistic** /kálvi nístik/ *adj* —**Calvinistically** *adv*

Calvino /kal véenō/, **Italo** (1923–85) Cuban-born Italian novelist

calvities /kal víshi eez/ *n* baldness (*technical*) [Early 17C. < Latin < *calvus* 'bald'.]

calx /kalks/ (*plural* **calxes** *or* **calces** /kál seez/) *n* **1** the powdery oxide of a metal that is formed when an ore or a mineral is roasted **2** the rounded part at the back of the heel [15C. < Latin, 'lime, limestone' < Greek *khalix* 'pebble'.]

calyces plural of **calyx**

calypso /kə lípsō/ (*plural* **-sos**) *n* **1** a Caribbean, especially Trinidadian, ballad with a lively dance rhythm, that deals satirically with social and political topics **2** Caribbean dance music that has syncopated rhythms, is usually improvised, and is often played by a steel band [Early 20C. < ?]

Calypso[1] /kə lípsō/ *n* in Greek mythology, a nymph who kept Odysseus on her island for seven years

Calypso[2] /kə lípsō/ *n* a small irregularly-shaped natural satellite of Saturn, discovered in 1980

calyx /káyliks, kálliks/ *(plural* **calyxes** *or* **calyces** /-li seez/*)* *n* **1** the group of sepals, usually green, around the outside of a flower that encloses and protects the flower bud **2** one of the funnel-shaped hollows in the pelvis of the kidney, through which urine passes to the ureter [Late 17C. Via Latin < Greek *kalux* 'husk, shell' < *kaluptein* 'conceal'.]

calzone /kal zŏ nay, -ni/ *(plural* **-nes** /-nis/ *or* **-ni** /-ni/*)* *n* a semi-circular Italian turnover made from pizza dough with a savoury filling [Late 20C. < Italian, 'trouser leg' < Latin *calceus* 'shoe' < *calx* 'heel'.]

cam /kam/ *n* an irregularly-shaped projection on a rotating shaft that changes rotary motion into a reciprocating up and down motion in another machine part (**cam follower**) that touches it [Late 18C. < Dutch *kam* 'comb'.]

✦ **CAM** /kam/ *abbr* computer-aided manufacturing

Camagüey Archipelago /kámmə gwáy-/ group of coral islands off east-central Cuba

camaraderie /kámmə ráàdəri, -ráádəri/ *n* a feeling of close friendship and trust among a particular group of people [Mid-19C. < French, < *camarade* (see COMRADE).]

Camargue /ka maàrg/ delta region of marshes, lagoons, and farmland in S France

camarilla /kámmə rílla/ *n* a group of advisers, especially a secretive group advising an important person [Mid-19C. < Spanish, 'small room' < *camara* 'room'.]

camas /kámmass/ *(plural* **camasses** *or* **camas**), **camass** *(plural* **camasses** *or* **camass**) *n* **1** a plant with grassy leaves and an edible bulb. Flowers: blue and white, in clusters. Native to: North America. *Camassia quamash.* **2** PLANTS = **death camas** [Early 19C. < Chinook Jargon *qamaš*.]

Camb. *abbr* Cambridge

camber /kámbər/ *n* **1** CONVEX CURVE IN ROAD a slight convex curve in a structure, especially the curve in the surface of a road **2** SLANT OF VEHICLE'S WHEELS a slant in the steerable wheels on a vehicle that makes them slightly closer together at the bottom than at the top ▪ *vti* MAKE CURVED SHAPE to form something or be formed with a camber [Early 17C. Via French *cambre* 'arched' < Latin *camur* 'curved inwards'.] —**cambered** *adj*

Camberley /kámbərli/ town in SE England. Population: 46,120 (1991).

Camberwell beauty /kámbər wel-/ *(plural* **Camberwell beauties** *or* **Camberwell beauty**) *n* a European and North American butterfly with purplish-brown wings that are spotted and rimmed with bright yellow. *Nymphalis antiopa.* US term **mourning cloak** [Mid-18C. After *Camberwell*, district of SE London.]

cambist /kámbist/ *n* a dealer in foreign exchange [Early 19C. Via French < Italian *cambista* < medieval Latin *cambium* (see CAMBIUM).]

cambium /kámbi əm/ *(plural* **-biums** *or* **-bia** /-bi ə/*)* *n* a cylindrical layer of cells in plant roots and stems that produces the new tissue responsible for increased girth, particularly sap-conducting tissues, xylem and phloem, and bark [Late 17C. < medieval Latin *cambium* 'exchange' < Latin *cambire* 'exchange'.] —**cambial** *adj*

Cambodia

Cambodia /kam bŏdi ə/ republic in SE Asia. Capital: Phnom Penh. Population: 11,163,861 (1997). Area: 181,035 sq. km/69,898 sq. mi. —**Cambodian** *n, adj*

Camborne-Redruth /kám bawrn réd rooth/ district in SW England. Population: 35,915 (1991).

Cambrai /kám bray, kaàN-/ town in NE France. Population: 33,738 (1999).

Cambrian /kámbri ən/ *adj* **1** relating to the earliest part of the Palaeozoic era, in which invertebrate animal life, including trilobites, appeared, and marine algae developed **2** relating to or from Wales [Mid-17C. < medieval Latin *Cambria* 'Wales' < Welsh *Cymry*.]

Cambrian Mountains Welsh mountain system running from N to S Wales. Highest peak: Aran Fawddwy 905 m/2,970 ft.

cambric /kámbrik/ *n* a thin white linen or cotton fabric [14C. After *Kamerijk* 'Cambrai', where the fabric was originally made.]

Cambridge /káym brij/ **1** city in E England. Population: 116,701 (1996 estimate). **2** city in E Massachusetts. Population: 93,352 (1998 estimate)

Cambridge blue ▪ *n* LIGHT BLUE a light bright blue. ◊ **Oxford blue** ▪ *n* ◊ **Oxford blue 1** LIGHT BLUE COLOUR a light blue colour **2** CAMBRIDGE ATHLETE a representative of Cambridge University in a sports event who has been awarded a blue

Cambridgeshire /káym brijshər/ county of E England. Area: 3,409 sq. km/1,316 sq. mi.

Cambs. *abbr* Cambridgeshire

Cambyses I /kam bī seez/ *(fl.* 6th century BC) Persian king (600–559 BC)

Cambyses II *(d.* 523? BC) Persian king (529–522 BC)

camcorder /kám kawrdər/ *n* a portable video camera and recorder [Late 20C. Blend of CAMERA + RECORDER.]

Camden /kámdən/ **1** borough in N London. Population: 184,900 (1995). **2** port in SW New Jersey. Population: 84,844 (1996).

Camden, William (1551–1623) English antiquary and historian

came past tense of **come**

camel /kámm'l/ *n* **1** *(plural* **-els** *or* **-el**) a ruminant animal of S Eurasia that has either one or two humps on its back and is adapted to a dry climate. Genus: *Camelus.* ◊ **Arabian camel, Bactrian camel** ◊ NAUT = **caisson** *n.* **2 3** a light sandy brown colour [Pre-12C. Via Latin < Greek *kamēlos* < Semitic.] —**camel** *adj*

cameleer /kámmə leèr/ *n* a rider or controller of a camel

camel hair, camel's hair *n* **1** HAIR OF CAMEL hair from the camel. Use: clothing, rugs. **2** FABRIC soft fabric containing camel hair or a similar fibre. Use: coats. **3** PAINTBRUSH an artist's paintbrush, normally made of squirrel hair and used primarily for watercolours

camelia incorrect spelling of **camellia**

camelid /kámm'lid/ *n* a member of the family that includes camels, llamas, and their relatives, all of which have feet with two toes and thick leathery soles. Family: Camelidae.

camellia /kə meèli ə/ *(plural* **-lias** *or* **-lia**) *n* **1** an ornamental bush of the tea family with glossy evergreen leaves and rose-shaped flowers. *Camellia japonica.* **2** any tree or bush of the tea family that resembles a camellia. Genus: *Camellia.* [Mid-18C. < modern Latin, < *Camellus*, Latinized name of Joseph *Kamel* (1661–1706), Moravian Jesuit missionary and botanist.]

camelopard /kə méllə paard, kámmilə-/ *n* **1** a giraffe *(archaic)* **2** ASTRON = **Camelopardalis** [14C. < Latin *camelopardus* < Greek *kamēlopardalis* < *kamēlos* 'camel' + *pardalis* 'pard' (because the animal has a head like a camel and spots like a leopard).]

Camelopardalis /kə méllə paàrd'liss/, **Camelopardus** /-dəss/ *n* a large faint constellation of the northern hemisphere. See illustration at **constellation** [via Latin, < Greek *kamēlopardalis* (see CAMELOPARD)]

Camelot /kámmə lot/ *n* the legendary city of King Arthur

camel's hair *n* = camel hair

Camembert /kámməm bair/ *n* a small round soft French cheese with an edible white rind [Late 19C. After *Camembert*, France.]

cameo /kámmi ŏ/ *n* **1** a semiprecious stone carved to give a raised design in one colour against a background of another, especially a pale head against a darker background **2** a single brief appearance by a distinguished actor in a film or play [15C. < Italian.]

camera /kámmərə/ *n* **1** a device for taking photographs by letting light from an image fall briefly onto sensitized film, usually by means of a lens-and-shutter mechanism. ◊ **cine camera 2** a device that converts images into electrical signals for television transmission, video recording, or digital storage [Early 18C. Via Latin, 'vault' < Greek *kamara*.]

cameraderie incorrect spelling of **camaraderie**

camera lucida /-loòssidə/ *(plural* **camera lucidas**) *n* a box or chamber that allows images to be projected onto a surface so they can be traced [Early 18C. < Latin, 'bright chamber'.]

cameraman /kámmrə man, -mən/ *(plural* **-men** /-men/*)* *n* a male operator of a film or television camera

camera obscura /-ob skyoòrə/ *n* a box or small darkened room into which an image of what is outside is projected using a small hole, and sometimes a simple lens, in one of the sides of the box or room [Early 18C. < Latin, 'dark chamber', because the room is darkened.]

cameraperson /kámmrə purss'n/ *n* an operator of a film or television camera

camera-ready *adj* describes or relating to material in its final publishable format, ready to be photographed or electronically scanned for the purpose of preparing printing plates

camera-shy *adj* with a dislike of being photographed or filmed

camerawoman /kámmrə woòmən/ *(plural* **-men** /-wimin/*)* *n* a woman who operates a film or television camera

camerawork /kámmrə wurk/ *n* the ways in which cameras are used in films and television, especially their positioning and movement

camerlingo /kámmər líng gŏ/ *(plural* **-gos**), **camerlengo** /-léng gŏ/ *(plural* **-gos**) *n* in the Roman Catholic Church, a cardinal who deals with the Pope's financial and other secular affairs [Early 17C. Via Italian, < Frankish.]

Cameron /kámmərən/, **Julia Margaret** (1815–79) British photographer

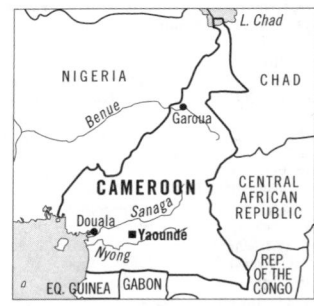

Cameroon

Cameroon[1] /kámmə roòn/ republic in west-central Africa. Capital: Yaoundé. Population: 14,611,357 (1997). Area: 475,442 sq. km/183,569 sq. mi.

Cameroon[2] active volcano in SW Cameroon, highest mountain in West Africa. Height: 4,095 m/13,435 ft.

camisado /kámmi saàdŏ/ *(plural* **-dos**) *n* a surprise attack at night [Mid-16C. < Spanish *camisada* 'attack in your shirt' (because attackers wore shirts over their armour in order to recognize each other) < *camisa* 'shirt'.]

camisole /kámmi sŏl/ *n* **1** a woman's sleeveless undergarment covering the upper torso **2** a woman's sleeveless top with thin shoulder straps and a straight neckline ◊ *a camisole top* [Early 19C. Via French < late Latin *camisia* 'linen shirt, nightgown'.]

Camlan /kámlən/ *n* in Arthurian legend, the battlefield in the southwest of England where King Arthur was mortally wounded by his traitorous nephew Modred before being carried away to Avalon

camo /kámmŏ/ *n* camouflage clothes or material used by military personnel *(slang)* [Shortening of CAMOUFLAGE.]

camoflage incorrect spelling of **camouflage**

camogie /kə mŏgi/ *n* an Irish stick and ball game that is a form of hurling played by women [Early 20C. < Irish Gaelic *camógaíocht* < *camóg* 'crooked stick'.]

camomile /kámmə mīl/, **chamomile** *n* **1** the leaves and flowers of an aromatic plant. Use: medicine, herbal teas. **2** an aromatic perennial plant with delicate leaves. Flowers: yellow and white, similar to daisies. Native to: Europe, Asia. Genera: *Anthemis* and *Matricaria.* [14C.

Via Old French *camomille* < medieval Latin *chamomilla* < Greek *khamaimēlon* 'earth-apple'; because the flowers smell like apples.]

camoodi /kə mo͞odi/ (*plural* **-dis**) *n* ZOOL = **anaconda** [Early 19C. < Arawak *kamudu*.]

Camorra /kə mórrə/ *n* a secret society formed in Italy in the early 1800s that was involved in criminal and terrorist activities [Mid-19C. < Italian.]

camouflage /kámmə flaazh, -flaaj/ *n* **1 CONCEALMENT OF THINGS** concealment of things, especially troops and military equipment, by disguising them to look like their surroundings, e.g. by covering them with branches or leaf-clad netting **2 CONCEALING DEVICES** devices designed to conceal by imitating the colours of the surrounding environment ○ *a camouflage jacket* **3 PROTECTIVE COLOURATION IN ANIMALS** the devices that animals use to blend into their environment in order to avoid being seen by predators or prey, especially colouration **4 DISGUISE** something that is intended to hide, disguise, or mislead ■ *vt* (**-flages, -flaging, -flaged**) **DISGUISE** to disguise something in order to mislead somebody, often somebody perceived as a threat [Early 20C. < French, < *camoufler* 'to disguise' < Italian *camuffare*.] —**camouflager** *n*

camp[1] /kamp/ *n* **1 PLACE WITH REMOVABLE ACCOMMODATION** a place where short-term accommodation has been temporarily erected or sited **2 PLACE FOR TEMPORARY STAY** a set of buildings where people are housed temporarily, e.g. as prisoners, refugees, or troops **3 GROUP** a group of people who share the same ideas, beliefs, or aims, or who form one of the sides in a debate ○ *the President's camp* ○ *members of the environmentalist camp* ■ *vi* **1 STAY TEMPORARILY** to stay in temporary accommodation, especially in a tent ○ *We camped by a stream.* **2 TAKE TEMPORARY POSITION** to take up a temporary position somewhere, e.g. as a protester or in alternative accommodation ○ *We'll camp on his doorstep until we get some action.* [Early 16C. Via French < Latin *campus* 'field, site for military exercises'.]

camp out *vi* **1** to live or sleep outdoors, with or without a tent ○ *We would be camping out under the stars for the next three nights.* **2** to take up a temporary position somewhere, e.g. as a protester or in alternative accommodation ○ *Hordes of journalists camped out in the palace grounds.*

camp[2] /kamp/ *adj* **1** exaggeratedly or affectedly feminine, especially in a man **2** deliberately and exaggeratedly brash or vulgar in an amusing, often self-parodying way [Early 20C. < ?] —**camp** *n* —**campily** *adv* —**campiness** *n* —**campy** *adj* ◇ **camp it up 1** to behave in a deliberately outrageous way for humorous effect (*informal*) **2** to behave in an exaggeratedly or affectedly feminine way, especially as a flaunting of male homosexuality (*informal*)

campaign /kam páyn/ *n* **1 PLANNED ACTIONS** a planned and organized series of actions intended to achieve a specific goal ○ *a national TV advertising campaign* **2 VOTE-SEEKING ACTIVITIES** a series of events, such as rallies and speeches, that are intended to persuade voters to vote for a particular politician or party ○ *kept her campaign promises* ○ *ran an expensive nationwide campaign* **3 MILITARY OPERATIONS** a series of military or terrorist operations taking place in one area over a particular period, intended to achieve a specific objective ○ *the Falklands campaign* ■ *vi* **1 PARTICIPATE IN CAMPAIGN** to take part in a campaign to achieve a specific goal ○ *parents campaigning to get the school re-opened* **2 PARTICIPATE IN POLITICAL CAMPAIGN** to take part in a political campaign ○ *We campaigned particularly strongly in the south.* [Early 17C. < French *campagne* 'open country' < Latin *campus* 'field'.] —**campaigner** *n*

~~campain~~ incorrect spelling of **campaign**

Campanella /kámpə néllə/, **Tommaso** (1568–1639) Italian philosopher. Born **Giovanni Domenico Campanella**

campanile /kámpə néeli/ (*plural* **-les** *or* **-li** /-li/) *n* a bell tower, especially a freestanding bell tower of the kind found in Italy [Mid-17C. < Italian *campanile* < *campana* 'bell' < late Latin *campana* (see CAMPANOLOGY).]

campanology /kámpə nólləji/ *n* the study or practice of bell-ringing [Mid-19C. < modern Latin *campanologia* < late Latin *campana* 'bell' < Latin *campanus* 'of Campania' (S Italy), a former source of bronze for making bells.] —**campanologist** *n*

campanula /kam pánnyo͝olə/ *n* an annual or perennial plant, widely grown as a garden plant. Flowers: bell-shaped, blue, white, or pink. Native to: northern temperate regions. Genus: *Campanula*. [Early 17C. < modern Latin, 'little bell' < late Latin *campana* (see CAMPANOLOGY).]

camp bed *n* a small narrow bed for occasional use that folds for easy storage and carriage, especially one consisting of a canvas sling supported on a sectional framework of metal tubing. US term **cot**[1] *n.* **2**

Campbell /kámb'l/, **Donald** (1921–67) British motor-racing driver

Campbell, Keith British microbiologist

Campbell, Kim (*b.* 1947) Canadian political leader. Born **Avril Phaedra Campbell**

Campbell, Sir Malcolm (1885–1948) British motor-racing driver

Campbell, Mrs Patrick (1865–1940) British actor. Born **Beatrice Stella Tanner**

Campbell, Roy (1901–57) South African-born British poet, translator, and journalist

Campbell, Thomas (1777–1844) British poet

Campbell-Bannerman /-bánnərmən/, **Sir Henry** (1836–1908) British statesman

Campbell Island /kámb'l-/ uninhabited island in the SW Pacific Ocean, south of New Zealand. Area: 166 sq. km/64 sq. mi.

Camp David /kámp dáyvid/ presidential retreat in Catoctin Mountain Park, central Maryland

Campeche /kam péechi, -péchay/ capital of Campeche State, SE Mexico. Population: 172,200 (1990).

camper /kámpər/ *n* **1 SOMEBODY WHO CAMPS** somebody who goes camping ○ *accessories for campers and hikers* **2 RECREATIONAL VEHICLE** a motor vehicle equipped as a self-contained travelling home, smaller than a motor caravan. It has basic facilities for cooking, washing, and sleeping. **3** *US* **TRAILER FOR LIVING IN** a trailer equipped as a self-contained travelling home, pulled by a car

camper van *n* TRANSP = **camper** *n.* **2**

Campese /kam péezi/, **David Ian** (*b.* 1962) Australian rugby player

campfire /kámp fī ər/ *n* a wood fire built outside by campers, for cooking on or for warmth

camp follower *n* **1** a civilian who follows a military unit from place to place in order to earn money by supplying products or services, e.g. services as a prostitute **2** a supporter of a group or an organization who does not belong to it

campground /kámp grownd/ *n* *US* LEISURE = **campsite** *n.* 1

camphor /kámfər/ *n* a strong-smelling compound. Use: in medicinal creams, manufacture of celluloid, plastics, and explosives. [14C. Directly or via Old French < medieval Latin *camphora*, via Arabic and Malay < Sanskrit *karpūra*.] —**camphoric** /kam fórrik/ *adj*

camphorate /kámfə rayt/ (**-ates, -ating, -ated**) *vt* to treat or impregnate something with camphor

camphor ice *n* an ointment used to relieve minor skin ailments, made of camphor mixed with white wax and castor oil

camphor oil *n* the oil that is distilled from the steamed bark and wood of the camphor tree

camphor tree *n* an evergreen tree, sometimes cultivated as an ornamental, with aromatic wood and bark that are a source of camphor. Native to: E Asia. *Cinnamomum camphora*.

campimetry /kam pímmətri/ *n* the measuring of the field of vision or the sensitivity of the retina to colour and space [Early 20C. < Latin *campus* 'field' + -METRY.]

Campinas /kam péenəss/ city in SE Brazil. Population: 908,906 (1996 estimate).

camping /kámping/ *n* living outdoors in a tent while on holiday or as a recreational activity ○ *a camping holiday*

campion /kámpi ən/ *n* a flowering plant of the pink family. Flowers: pink, red, white. Native to: N hemisphere. Genera: *Lychnis* and *Silene*. [Mid-16C. < ?]

Campion /kámpi ən/, **Jane** (*b.* 1954) New Zealand film director

Campion, St Edmund (1540–81) English Jesuit

Campion, Thomas (1567–1620) English poet

campo /kámpō/ (*plural* **-pos**) *n* a large grassy plain in South America, with scattered bushes and small stunted trees [Mid-19C. Via American Spanish or Portuguese, 'field' < Latin *campus*.]

Campo Grande /kámpō grándi/ capital of Mato Grosso do Sul State, SW Brazil. Population: 565,943 (1993).

Campos /kám poss/ city in SE Brazil. Population: 389,547 (1996 estimate).

campsite /kámp sīt/ *n* **1** an outdoor area designed for camping, usually providing campers with some facilities, e.g. showers, toilets, and a shop. US term **campground 2** *US* a single unit of land within a campground, for a camper to pitch a tent on or park a trailer or camper on

campus /kámpəss/ *n* **1** an area of land that contains the main buildings and grounds of a university or college ○ *accommodation on campus* **2** a site on which the buildings of an organization or institution are located ○ *a dormitory for nursing students on the hospital campus* [Late 18C. < Latin, 'field'.]

campus novel *n* a novel that satirizes university life. The genre appeared in Britain in the late 1970s and early 1980s.

campus university *n* a university whose teaching, administration, and accommodation buildings are located on one main site, usually a rural site, as opposed to being spread around different sites throughout a town

campylobacter /kámpilō báktər/ *n* a rod- or spiral-shaped bacterium that is a common cause of food poisoning in humans and of spontaneous abortion in farm animals [Late 20C. < modern Latin, < Greek *kampulos* 'bent' + BACTERIUM.]

CAMRA /kámrə/ *abbr* Campaign for Real Ale

camshaft /kám shaaft/ *n* a shaft that has one or more cams attached, especially one that operates the valves in a vehicle's internal combustion engine

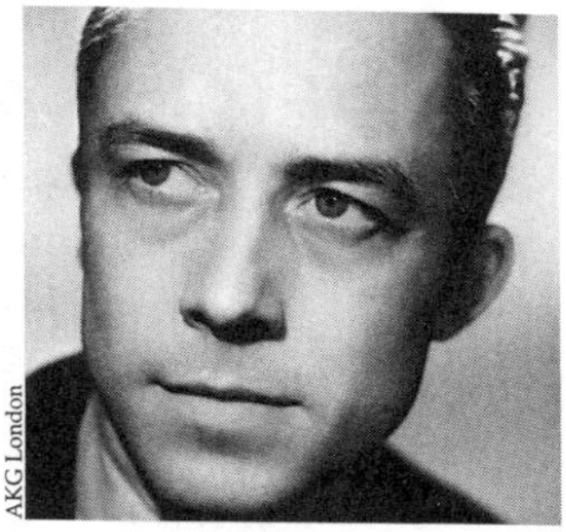
AKG London

Albert Camus

Camus /ka mo͞o/, **Albert** (1913–60) Algerian-born French novelist, essayist, and dramatist

cam wheel *n* a wheel that functions as a cam

camwood /kám wo͝od/ *n* **1** the hard red wood of a West African tree. Use: formerly, cabinet making, red dye. **2** a West African tree that produces camwood. *Baphia nitida*. [Late 17C. Probably < Temne *k'am*.]

can[1] /kan/ *n* **1** FOOD TECH = **tin 2 METAL CONTAINER** a metal container with a removable lid or cap, especially one for storing or packaging liquids, such as chemicals or paint **3 CONTENTS OF CAN** the contents of a metal container ○ *I drank two cans of beer.* ○ *We used up three cans of paint.* **4 PRESSURIZED CONTAINER** a metal container that holds liquid under pressure so that it can be released as a spray ○ *a can of hairspray* **5 PRISON** prison (*slang*) ○ *in the can* **6** *US, Can* **TOILET** a toilet (*slang*) **7 SHIP** a ship (*slang*) **8** *US* SHIPPING = **can buoy** ■ *vt* (**cans, canning, canned**) **1** FOOD TECH = **tin** *v.* 1 **2** *US* **STOP** to stop something regarded as inappropriate under the circumstances, e.g. laughter, tears, or jokes (*slang*) ○ *Just can the giggling.* [Old English *canne* < Germanic or late Latin *canna*] —**canful** *n* —**canner** *n* ◇ **carry the can** *UK, Can* to take the blame or responsibility (*informal*) ○ *An unsuspecting junior was left to carry the can.* ◇ **in the can 1** in the final edited form ready for broadcasting or distribution (*informal*) ○ *There's a lot more to do before the film's in the can.* **2** having been successfully completed or negotiated (*informal*) ○ *At last, after three weeks of tough negotiations, the contract was in the can.*

can[2] (*stressed*) /kan/; (*unstressed*) /kən/ CORE MEANING: a modal verb used to indicate that it is possible for some-

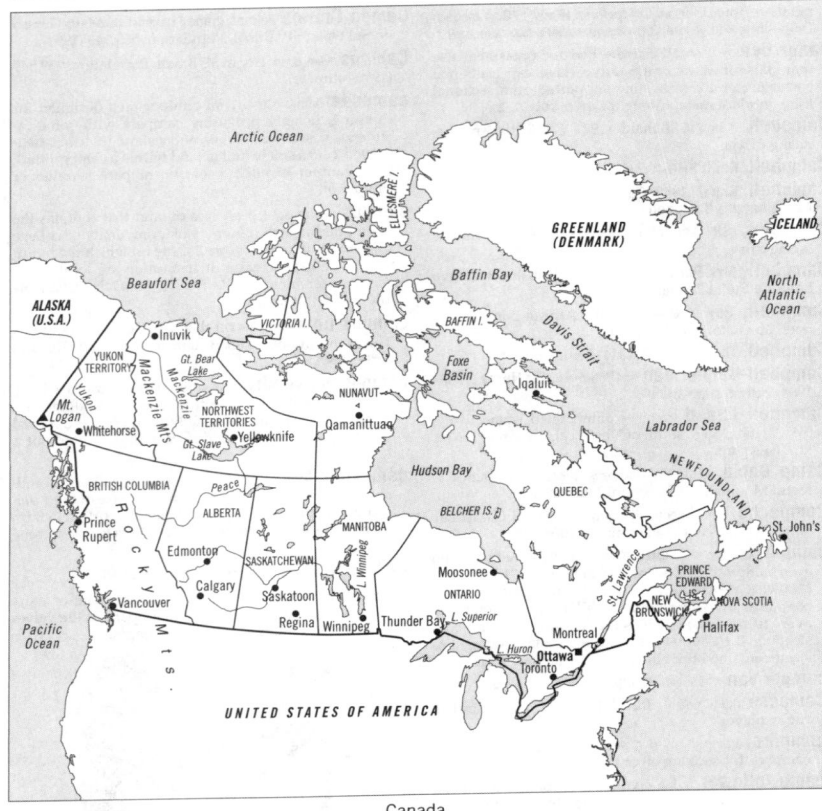

Canada

thing to be done or made use of in the way mentioned ○ *Loans can be made over the phone.*

vi **1 BE ABLE TO** to have the ability, knowledge, or opportunity to do something ○ *If you can keep a secret, so can I.* **2 BE LIKELY** to be likely to be true or to be the case ○ *Truancy can also signal more severe problems.* **3 BE ALLOWED TO** to be allowed to do something, either by legal or moral right or by permission ○ *In Britain, you can get married at 16.* **4 BE ACCEPTABLE** used to make polite requests, suggestions, or offers ○ *Can I get anybody any more coffee?* **5 BE POSSIBLE** used in questions to emphasize strong feelings about something ○ *How can you say that?* ○ *What on earth can be the matter?* [Old English *cunnan* < Indo-European]

USAGE can or **may**? Many people draw a distinction between **can**, meaning 'be able to', and **may**, meaning 'be allowed to', but the distinction is hard to maintain in practice and the meanings often overlap. In everyday conversation, *Can I go?* is as likely to be used as *May I go?*, and the context, together with intonation, usually makes it clear what is meant. In more formal situations it is wise to maintain the distinction, if only because many people expect it. Note that **may** has ambiguities of its own. *He may go* can mean either 'he is allowed to go' or 'it is possible that he will go'; again, intonation and context clarify the matter. The negative contraction **mayn't** is awkward, and **can't** is usually used instead: *Can't we come too?*

can³ *abbr* **1** cancelled **2** cancellation **3** cannon **4** canon¹ *n.* 6. **5** canto

Can. *abbr* Canada

Canaanite /káynə nīt/ *n* **1** a member of a Semitic people who lived in Canaan from around 3000 BC until 1000 BC **2** an extinct Semitic language once spoken in the region between the River Jordan and the Mediterranean Sea — **Canaanite** *adj*

Canada /kánnədə/ federation occupying the northern half of North America and the second largest country

in the world. Capital: Ottawa. Population: 31,000,000 (1997). Area: 9,970,610 sq. km/3,849,674 sq. mi. — **Canadian** /kə náydi ən/ *adj, n*

Canada balsam *n* a thick resin secreted from the bark of the balsam fir

Canada goose *n* a large goose with a brownish body, a black head and neck, and a white patch on its throat. Native to: North America, introduced into Europe. *Branta canadensis.*

Canada jay *n* BIRDS = **grey jay**

Canada lily *n* a lily with small orange funnel-shaped flowers. Native to: North America. *Lilium canadense.*

Canada thistle *n US, Can* PLANTS = **creeping thistle**

Canadian /kə náydi ən/ river in Colorado, New Mexico, Texas, and Oklahoma. Length: 1,460 km/906 mi.

Canadian football *n* a form of football that is similar to American football but takes place on a larger field, has 12 players on each team, and uses three rather than four plays to advance at least ten yards or score

Canadianism /kə náydi ə nizəm/ *n* a word or other expression originating in or restricted in use to Canada

Canadianize /kə náydi ə nīz/ (**-izes, -izing, -ized**), **Canadianise** (**-ises, -ising, -ised**) *vti* to make something Canadian in form, content, or status, or become Canadian — **Canadianization** /kə náydi ə nī záysh'n/ *n*

Canadian jay *n* BIRDS = **grey jay**

Canadian Shield plateau region of E Canada extending southwards and eastwards from Hudson Bay. Area: 4,600,000 sq. km/1,776,070 sq. mi.

canaille /kə nî/ *n* the lowest class of people (*disapproving*) ○ *'But to think of her partaking of hospitality; all alone, too; with the canaille of Wynford!'* (L. T. Meade, *A Very Naughty Girl*; 1907) [Late 16C. Via French < Italian *canaglia* 'pack of dogs' < Latin *canis* 'dog'.]

canal /kə nál/ *n* **1 WATERWAY** an artificial waterway constructed for use by shipping, for irrigation, or for recreational use **2 TUBE IN BODY** a tube-shaped passage in the body, carrying air, liquids, or semi-solid material **3 FEATURE ON MARS** an apparent surface marking on Mars, formerly thought to be part of a system of water channels [15C. < French, alteration (based on Italian *canale* < Latin *canalis*) of *chanel* < Latin *canalis* 'pipe, canal' < *canna* (see CANE).]

canal boat *n* a long boat used on canals to carry freight or for recreational boating

Canaletto /kánnə léttő/, **Antonio** (1697–1768) Italian artist

canaliculus /kánnə líkyōōlass/ (*plural* **-li** /-lī/) *n* a minute canal or duct in the body, especially one of the four narrow tubes that carry tears from behind the eyelids to the lacrimal sac [Mid-16C. < Latin, 'little pipe' < *canalis* (see CANAL).] — **canalicular** *adj* — **canaliculate** /kánnə líkyōōlət, -layt/ *adj*

canalise *vti* = **canalize**

canalize /kánn'l īz/ (**-lizes, -lizing, -lized**), **canalise** (**-lises, -lising, -lised**) *v* **1 BUILD CANALS** to provide an area with canals, or convert existing waterways into canals **2** *vt* **DIRECT** to direct or focus something, e.g. energy or enthusiasm, in a particular direction (*formal*) **3** *vi* **FLOW INTO CHANNEL** to flow into or form a new channel **4** *vt* **PUSH ENEMY FORCES** to drive enemy forces into a narrow space, either by firing on them or by erecting obstacles in their way — **canalization** /kánn'l ī záysh'n/ *n*

canapé /kánnə pay/ *n* a bite-sized base of bread, cracker, or pastry with a topping, usually highly garnished, and served as an appetizer or to accompany drinks [Late 19C. Via French, 'sofa' < medieval Latin *canopeum* (see CANOPY).]

canard /kánnaard, ka naárd/ *n* **1 HOAX** a deliberately false report or rumour, especially something silly intended as a joke (*literary*) **2 AIRCRAFT PART LIKE WING** a small projection like a wing near the nose of an aircraft, fitted to create extra horizontal stability **3 AIRCRAFT** an aircraft fitted with a canard [Mid-19C. < French, literally 'duck', an imitation of the sound.]

Canaries /kə náiriz/ = **Canary Islands**

Canaries Current /kə náiriz-/ cold North Atlantic current flowing south from the Canary Islands down the coast of W North Africa

canary /kə náiri/ (*plural* **-ies**) *n* **1 YELLOW FINCH** a small yellow finch. Native to: Canaries and adjacent islands. *Serinus canarius.* **2 WINE** a sweet wine from the Canary Islands, similar to Madeira **3** COLOURS = **canary yellow 4 DANCE** a lively court dance popular in the 16th century [Late 16C. < French *Canarie*, chief island of the Canary Islands < Latin *Canaria Insula* 'Isle of Dogs', from the large dogs that inhabited it in Roman times.]

canary creeper *n* a climbing plant. Flowers: small, yellow. Native to: Peru. *Tropaeolum peregrinum.*

canary grass *n* an annual grass plant cultivated for its seeds that are sold as birdseed. Native to: NW Africa, Canary Islands. *Phalaris canariensis.*

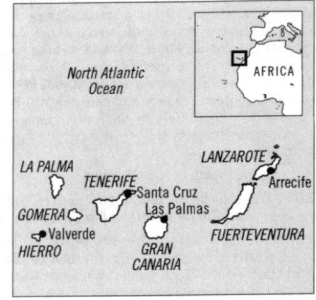

Canary Islands

Canary Islands /kə náiri-/, **Canaries** island group in the Atlantic Ocean, off the coast of NW Africa, an autonomous region of Spain. Population: 1,631,498 (1995). Area: 7,273 sq. km/2,808 sq. mi. Spanish **Islas Canarias**

canary yellow *adj* of a bright yellow colour, like the plumage of certain canaries — **canary yellow** *n*

canasta /kə nástə/ *n* **1** a variant of the card game rummy played with two 52-card packs. Players are dealt 15 cards, the aim being to collect groups of seven similar cards. **2** a point-scoring set of cards in canasta [Mid-20C. Via Spanish, 'basket' < Latin *canistrum*, because two packs of cards (a 'basketful') are used.]

Canaveral, Cape /kə návvərəl/ cape in east-central Florida, the launching site of US crewed space flights

Canberra /kánbərə/ capital of Australia, in Australian Capital Territory, SE Australia. Population: 322,723 (1996).

can buoy *n* an unlighted marker buoy for shipping, cylindrical or cone-shaped above the water

canc. *abbr* **1** cancelled **2** cancellation

cancan /kán kan/ *n* a dance of French origin in which a chorus line of women perform high kicks to reveal their underwear [Mid-19C. < French.]

cancel /kánss'l/ *v* (**-cels, -celling, -celled**) **1** *vti* **STOP SOMETHING HAPPENING** to stop a previously arranged event from happening ○ *We had to cancel five classes because nobody showed up.* ○ *The guest speaker is ill and has had to cancel.* **2** *vti* **END CONTRACT** to withdraw officially or legally from a contract ○ *Members are free to cancel at any time.* **3** *vt* **REVERSE INSTRUCTION** to reverse an instruction to a machine, especially a computer, or bring a machine's operation to an end ○ *Cancel the download from the Internet.* **4** *vt* **MARK AS USED** to invalidate a legal or official document to show that it has been used and cannot be reused ○ *machines that cancel postage stamps* **5** *vt* **DELETE** to mark something for deletion, usually by drawing a line through it **6** *vti* **REMOVE COMMON FACTOR** to remove a common factor from the numerator and denominator of a fraction or the common terms from the two sides of an equation ○ *The twelves cancel and you end up with 8 by 6 again.* ■ *n* **1 INSERTED PAGE** a new page or section of a book inserted to replace a missing original or an original that contained errors **2 PAGE TO BE REPLACED** a faulty page or section of a book replaced by another **3** = **cancellation** *n.* 3 [14C. Via French *canceller* < Latin *cancellare* 'cross out' < *cancelli* 'lattice' < *cancer* 'grating, lattice'.] —**cancellable** *adj* —**canceller** *n*
cancel out *vt* to combine two opposite or equally powerful things with the result that their strengths, qualities, or effects are neutralized

cancelation[1] *n US* = **cancellation**

~~**cancelation**~~[2] incorrect spelling of **cancellation**

⚡ **cancelbot** /kánss'l bot/ *n* a computer program that cancels unwanted articles sent to an Internet newsgroup by a specific user [Late 20C. Blend of CANCEL + ROBOT.]

cancellate /kánssə layt/, **cancellated** /-laytid/ *adj* **1** ANAT = **cancellous 2** forming a mesh or network

cancellation /kánssə láysh'n/ *n* **1 CANCELLING** the cancelling of something, e.g. an appointment or order ○ *We had one cancellation for two o'clock, so we can fit you in then.* ○ *There is a cancellation charge if you withdraw your order at the last minute.* **2 THING MADE AVAILABLE** something, e.g. a seat in a theatre, that has become available because the person who reserved it has cancelled **3 CANCELLING MARK** a mark that officially or legally invalidates something, especially a postage stamp [Mid-16C. < Latin *cancellat-*, past participle of *cancellare* (see CANCEL).]

cancellous /kánssələss/ *adj* describes bone that has a mesh of hollows on the inside, as opposed to being compact or dense [Mid-19C. < Latin *cancelli* (see CANCEL).]

cancer /kánssər/ *n* **1 MALIGNANT TUMOUR** a malignant tumour or growth caused when cells multiply uncontrollably, destroying healthy tissue **2 ILLNESS CAUSED BY TUMOUR** the illness or condition that is caused by the presence of a malignant tumour **3 FAST-SPREADING BAD PHENOMENON** something, usually something negative, that develops or spreads quickly and usually destructively [Pre-12C. < Latin, 'crab', translation of Greek *karkinos*.] —**cancerous** *adj*

Cancer /kánssər/ *n* **1 CONSTELLATION BETWEEN GEMINI AND LEO** a constellation of the northern hemisphere. See illustration at **constellation 2 4TH SIGN OF ZODIAC** the fourth sign of the zodiac, represented by a crab and lasting from approximately 21 June to 22 July **3 SOMEBODY BORN UNDER CANCER SIGN** somebody whose birthday falls between 21 June and 22 July [Pre-12C. < Latin (see CANCER); from the constellation's sideways movement across the sky.] —**Cancerian** /kan seéri ən, -sáiri ən/ *n, adj*

cancerophobia /kánsərō fṓbi ə/ *n* an obsessive fear of developing cancer

cancer stick *n* a cigarette (*slang*)

cancroid /káng kroyd/ *adj* like a crab in shape, structure, or movement ■ *n* = **squamous cell carcinoma** [Early 19C. < Latin *cancr-*, stem of *cancer* (see CANCER).]

Cancún /kàn kóon/ island on the NE Yucatán peninsula, SE Mexico. Population: 27,500 (1980).

candela /kan deélə, -déllə/ *n* (*symbol* **cd**) the basic SI unit of luminous intensity [Mid-20C. < Latin (see CANDLE).]

candelabrum /kándə laábrəm/ (*plural* **-bra** /-laábrə/ *or* **-brums**) *n* a large decorative candle holder with several arms or branches, or a similarly shaped electric light fitting [Early 19C. < Latin, < *candela* (see CANDLE).]

C and F *abbr* cost and freight

C and G *abbr* City and Guilds

c & i *abbr* cost and insurance

candid /kándid/ *adj* **1 HONEST** honest or direct in a way that people find either refreshing or distasteful ○ *a surprisingly candid admission* **2 PHOTOGRAPHED INFORMALLY** photographed or filmed without the subject knowing or having the opportunity to prepare or pose ○ *a candid documentary* ■ *n US* **UNPOSED PHOTOGRAPH** a photograph that is taken, unposed and informally, of a person or group [Mid-17C. Directly or via French *candide* 'guileless' < Latin *candidus* 'white, shining' < *candere* 'be white'.] —**candidly** *adv* —**candidness** *n*

candida /kándidə/ *n* a fungus that can cause yeast infection, especially in the mouth and vagina. *Candida albicans.* [Mid-20C. < Latin, feminine of *candidus* 'white' (see CANDID); from its colour.]

candidate /kándi dayt, -dət/ *n* **1 APPLICANT FOR OFFICE** a seeker of a political office or an official position ○ *names of candidates for the leadership of the party* **2 APPLICANT FOR JOB** an applicant or suitable person for a job ○ *The successful candidate will have had experience with market research.* **3 PERSON SUSCEPTIBLE TO DISEASE OR TREATMENT** a patient who seems suitable for a specific treatment, or is likely to be affected by a specific disease ○ *Men in this group are prime candidates for a heart attack.* **4 EXAM TAKER** somebody sitting an examination **5 COMPETITOR** somebody competing with others for a prize or award ○ *Candidates for Oscars include two Canadians and two Americans.* [Early 17C. Directly or via French *candidat* < Latin *candidatus* 'clothed in white'; from the white togas worn by candidates for election in ancient Rome.] —**candidacy** *n*

SYNONYMS ***candidate, contender, contestant, aspirant, applicant, entrant***
CORE MEANING: somebody who is seeking to be chosen for something or to win something
candidate somebody who is being considered for a job, grant, or prize, standing for election, or taking part in an examination; **contender** a competitor, especially somebody who has a good chance of winning; **contestant** somebody who takes part in a contest or competitive event; **aspirant** somebody aspiring to distinction or advancement; **applicant** somebody who has formally applied to be a candidate for something; **entrant** somebody who enters a competition or examination.

candid camera *n* the use of hidden cameras to film subjects unawares, often in stage-managed situations intended to elicit amusing responses (*hyphenated before nouns*)

candidiasis /kándi dī́ əssiss/ (*plural* **-ases** /-seez/) *n* yeast infection (*technical*) [Mid-20C. < CANDIDA + -IASIS.]

candle /kánd'l/ *n* a moulded piece of wax, tallow, or other fatty substance, usually cylindrical in shape, with a wick running through it ■ *vt* (**-dles, -dling, -dled**) to test an egg for freshness by looking at it against a bright light [Pre-12C. < Latin *candella*, earlier *candela* < *candere* 'be white, glisten'.] ◇ **burn the candle at both ends** to get up very early and go to bed very late, allowing for very little rest ◇ **not hold a candle to somebody** to be not nearly as good at something as somebody ○ *As a writer, he does not hold a candle to his mother.*

candleberry /kánd'lbəri/ (*plural* **-ries**) *n* any bush or tree that has berries that can be used for making candles

candlefish /kánd'l fish/ (*plural* **-fishes** *or* **-fish**) *n* an oily saltwater fish found in the N Pacific Ocean. *Thaleichthys pacificus.* [< the former use of the dried fish as a lamp by pushing a piece of bark through it as a wick]

candleholder /kánd'l hōldər/ *n* a holder for a candle, often a decorative one

candlelight /kánd'l līt/ *n* **1** the light that a burning candle provides ○ *reading by candlelight* **2** twilight, the time when candles are lit (*literary*)

candlelit /kánd'l lit/ *adj* lit by candles, or done by candlelight ○ *a silent, candlelit march through the streets*

Candlemas /kánd'l mass, -məss/ *n* **1** a Christian feast marking the purification of the Virgin Mary and the presentation of the infant Jesus Christ in the Temple. Date: 2 February. **2** in Scotland, one of the four days marking the traditional three-month divisions of the year (**quarter days**). Date: 2 February [Pre-12C. *-mas* < ecclesiastical Latin *missa* 'the mass'.]

candlenut /kánd'l nut/ *n* **1** a seed of a tropical tree. Use: source of oil in paints and varnishes, threaded with a wick as a candle in Asia and Polynesia. **2** a tropical tree of the spurge family that bears candlenuts. Native to: Asia, Polynesia. *Aleurites moluccana.*

candlepin /kánd'l pin/ *n* a slim pin used in the bowling game candlepins [< its shape]

candlepins /kánd'l pinz/ *n* a bowling game using slender pins and a ball smaller than that used in tenpins (+ *singular verb*)

candlepower /kánd'l powər/ *n* luminous intensity measured in candelas

candlesnuffer /kánd'l snufər/ *n* a device, usually made of metal, consisting of a small cone on the end of a long thin handle, placed over the flame of a candle to put it out

candlestick /kánd'l stik/ *n* a tall thin holder for a candle

candlewick /kánd'l wik/ *n* **1 COTTON FABRIC** tufted cotton fabric. Use: bedcovers, dressing gowns. **2 EMBROIDERY YARN** soft cotton yarn used for embroidery **3 THICK STRING** thick string used for candle wicks

candlewood /kánd'l wŏŏd/ *n* **1** the resinous wood of various trees or bushes, burnt for light and fuel **2** any tree or bush that produces candlewood

C and M *abbr* care and maintenance

can-do *adj* keen to take on a job or challenge and confident of success (*informal*) ○ *We're only looking at can-do executives with proven track records.*

Candolle /kan dṓl/, **Augustin Pyrame de** (1778–1841) Swiss botanist

candor *n* US = **candour**

candour /kándər/ *n* honesty or directness, whether refreshing or distasteful ○ *He spoke of their conspicuous candour and bravery.* [14C. < Latin *candor* 'glossy whiteness' < *cand-*, base of *candidus* (see CANDID).]

CANDU reactor /kán doo-/ *n* a form of nuclear reactor designed and built in Canada that uses replaceable fuel bundles and heavy water to moderate fission and cool the reactor core [Acronym < CANADA + DEUTERIUM + URANIUM]

C and W *abbr* country and western

candy /kándi/ *n* (*plural* **-dies**) **1** *US, Can* **SMALL CONFECTION** small sweet food items such as chocolate bars, mints, and toffee, usually eaten for pleasure and not as part of a meal **2** *US, Can* FOOD = **sweet** *n.* 1 **3 HARD DRUGS** heroin, cocaine, or any other hard drug (*slang*) ■ *v* (**-dies, -dying, -died**) **1** *vti* **TURN SUGAR SOLUTION INTO CRYSTALS** to turn a sugar solution into crystals, especially by boiling it, or be converted into sugar crystals **2** *vt* **STEEP IN SUGAR** to dress a food by impregnating it with sugar, in order either to preserve it or to make it more pleasant to eat **3** *vt* **COAT WITH SUGAR SYRUP** to coat food with sugar or sugar syrup, or be coated with sugar or sugar syrup [13C. Via Old French *candi* < Arabic *qandī* 'crystallized into sugar' < *qand* 'cane sugar'.]

candy apple *n US* FOOD = **toffee apple**

candyfloss /kándi floss/ *n* cooked sugar syrup, coloured and spun from a machine onto a stick in fine strands, eaten traditionally at fairgrounds. US term **cotton candy**

candy man *n US* **1** a drug trafficker (*slang*) **2** formerly, an itinerant seller of sweets

candy store *n US* = **sweet shop**

candy-striped *adj* with a pattern of narrow stripes in a single colour on a white background

candytuft /kándi tuft/ *n* a flowering plant with thin leaves. Flowers: white, red, or purple, in clusters. Native to: Europe, the Mediterranean. Genus: *Iberis.* [Early 17C. < *Candy*, an obsolete form of *Candia* 'Crete'.]

cane /kayn/ *n* 1 **WALKING STICK** a stick that people use to help them walk 2 **STICK FOR PUNISHMENT BEATINGS** a long flexible stick for administering beatings, especially one formerly used to punish schoolchildren 3 **BAMBOO STEM** a hollow lightweight stem of a tropical plant, especially bamboo 4 **WOVEN STEMS** the stems of various palms and grass plants, e.g. rattan, woven together to make furniture, baskets, and other household items 5 **STEM OF FRUIT PLANT** the long woody stem of various fruit-bearing plants, such as the raspberry or blackberry 6 **LONG-STEMMED PLANT** a coarse grass or reed with long stiff stems, e.g. sugar cane or sorghum ■ *vt* (**canes, caning, caned**) 1 **BEAT** to beat somebody, especially, formerly, a schoolchild, with a cane 2 **DEFEAT** to subject somebody to a crushing defeat (*slang*) [14C. Via Old French *cane* < Latin *canna* 'reed' < Greek *kanna* < Semitic.]

cane beetle *n* a large beetle that lays its eggs in sugar cane. Native to: Australia. *Demolepida albohirtum.*

canebrake /káyn brayk/ *n US* an area of land planted or overgrown with cane

cane grass *n* a tall stiff-stemmed grass found in inland wetland areas of Australia. *Eragrostis australasica.*

canelle knife /kə nél nīf/ *n* a small kitchen implement, similar to a vegetable peeler or zester, with a slot and a V-shaped blade for cutting strips from the skins of citrus fruits [< French *canneler* 'to groove, flute', from *cane* (see CANE)]

cane piece *n* in the Caribbean, a field of sugar cane, especially one that is isolated and belongs to a small farmer

caner /káynər/ *n US* a maker or repairer of furniture and other items made of cane

cane rat *n* a large rat measuring up to 60 cm/2 ft without the tail, and eaten locally as a delicacy. Native to: sub-Saharan Africa. Genus: *Thryonomys.* [Because it eats sugar cane]

canescent /kə néss'nt/ *adj* 1 describes plant parts that have a white or whitish-grey covering of fine hairs 2 becoming white or greyish [Mid-19C. < the present participle of Latin *canescere* 'grow white' < *canus* 'white, hoary'.] —**canescence** *n*

cane sugar *n* sucrose obtained from sugar cane or sugar beet

Canes Venatici /káy neez və nátti sī/ *n* a constellation of the northern hemisphere. See illustration at **constellation** [< Latin, 'hunting dogs']

cane toad *n* a large toad introduced into Australia to control pests in sugar cane but now a pest in its own right. Native to: South America. *Bufo marinus.*

Canetti /ka nétti/, **Elias** (1905–94) Bulgarian-born British writer

canfield /kán feeld/ *n* a gambling game developed from the card game patience [Early 20C. After Richard Albert *Canfield* (1855–1914), US gambler.]

Canicula /kə níkyŏŏlə/ *n* = **Sirius** [12C. < Latin (see CANICULAR).]

canicular /kə níkyŏŏlər/ *adj* relating to the star Sirius [14C. < late Latin *canicularis* < *canicula* 'little dog' < *canis* 'dog'.]

canid /kánnid, káy-/ *n* any carnivorous mammal of the dog family, which includes the foxes, wolves, jackals, dingos, coyotes, and domestic breeds [Late 19C. < modern Latin *Canidae* < Latin *canis* 'dog'.]

canine /káynīn, kánn-/ *adj* **OF DOGS** relating to dogs ○ *a canine trainer* ○ *members of the canine family* ■ *n* 1 **POINTED TOOTH** a pointed tooth between the incisors and the first bicuspids 2 **DOG** a dog (*often humorous*) [15C. Directly or via French, < Latin *caninus* < *canis* 'dog'.]

canine distemper *n* a viral disease of dogs that causes high fever and is often fatal. ◊ **distemper**[1]

canine tooth *n* DENT = **canine** *n.* 1

caning /káyning/ *n* 1 a punishment beating with a cane, especially the beatings formerly administered to schoolchildren 2 a resounding defeat (*informal*)

Canis Major /káyniss-/ *n* a constellation of the southern hemisphere containing the star Sirius. ◊ **Canis Minor**. See illustration at **constellation** [< Latin, 'greater dog']

Canis Minor /káyniss-/ *n* a constellation near the celestial equator containing the star Procyon. ◊ **Canis Major**. See illustration at **constellation** [< Latin, 'lesser dog']

canister /kánnistər/ *n* 1 **PRESSURIZED CONTAINER** a pressurized metal container holding a substance released as a spray 2 **SEALED CONTAINER** a strong sealed metal container for hazardous chemicals 3 **FOOD CONTAINER** a metal container with a lid, for storing tea, coffee, or other dry foods 4 **EXPLOSIVE** a weapon used in former times consisting of a metal shell filled with gas and shot or shrapnel, designed to explode when thrown or fired from a cannon [Late 15C. Via Latin *canistrum* < Greek *kanastron* 'wicker basket' < *kanna* 'reed'.]

canker /kángkər/ *n* 1 **PLANT DISEASE** a disease that creates open wounds on the trunks and branches of woody plants 2 **ANIMAL DISEASE** any of several diseases of animals, e.g. a disease of horses that makes their hooves spongy, a disease that can cause ulcers in the outer ears of some animals, or a throat infection of some birds 3 **EVIL** an evil or corrupting influence that spreads and is difficult to wipe out ○ *'This canker that eats up Love's tender spring'* (William Shakespeare, *Venus and Adonis*; 1593) ■ *vti* 1 **DEVELOP CANKER** to develop canker, or cause the trunks and branches of woody plants to develop canker 2 **MAKE OR BECOME CORRUPT** to become a source of spreading corruption or evil, or cause something to decay as a result of spreading corruption or evil [14C. Via Old N French *cancre* < Latin *cancr-* 'crab'.] —**cankerous** *adj*

canker sore *n US* an ulcer on the lips or inside the mouth

canna /kánnə/ *n* a perennial tropical plant with luxuriant foliage. Flowers: red or yellow, in clusters. Native to: Caribbean, Central America. Genus: *Canna.* [Mid-18C. Via modern Latin *Canna* < Latin *canna* (see CANE).]

cannabidiol /kánnəbə dī ol, kə nábbə-/ *n* $C_{21}H_{28}(OH)_2$ one of the chemical constituents of cannabis [Mid-20C. < CANNABIS + DI-[1] + -OL.]

cannabis /kánnəbiss/ *n* 1 a drug produced in various forms from the dried leaves and flowers of the hemp plant, smoked or chewed. Its recreational use is illegal in most countries. 2 the hemp plant, especially when grown as a source of cannabis. *Cannabis sativa.* [Early 18C. Via Latin < Greek *kannabis.*]

cannabis resin *n* the drug cannabis in the form of a greenish-black resin

Cannae /kánnee/ battlefield in SE Italy, site of Hannibal's major defeat of the Roman army during the Second Punic War in 216 BC

canned /kand/ *adj* 1 FOOD TECH = **tinned** 2 **PRE-RECORDED** pre-recorded in a standardized form for general use, rather than recorded for a specific broadcast or performance ○ *The actors learn to leave pauses where the canned laughter is to be inserted.* 3 **UNVARYING** used repeatedly with little or no variation, and therefore lacking freshness or originality ○ *the familiar canned claim to know about the problem already* 4 **DRUNK** extremely drunk (*slang*)

cannel /kánn'l/, **cannel coal** *n* a bituminous coal that burns brightly and creates a lot of smoke [Mid-16C. < English dialect *cannel* 'candle'; from its bright flame.]

cannelloni /kánnə lṓni/ *n* wide tubes or rolls of pasta that are stuffed with a filling, topped with sauce, then baked [Mid-20C. < Italian, plural of *cannellone* 'tubular noodle' < Latin *canna* (see CANE).]

cannelure /kánnəlyoor/ *n* a groove around the cylindrical part of a bullet [Mid-18C. < French, < *canneler* 'make a groove in' < *canne* 'reed' < Old French *cane* (see CANE).]

cannery /kánnəri/ (*plural* **-ies**) *n* a factory where food is packaged into tins

Cannes /kan/ city in SE France, on the Mediterranean Sea. Population: 67,304 (1999).

cannibal /kánnib'l/ *n* 1 an eater of human flesh 2 an animal that eats the flesh of other animals of the same species [Mid-16C. < Spanish *Canibales*, variant of *Caribes* < Arawak *carib*, the Carib people.]

cannibalise *vt* = **cannibalize**

cannibalism /kánnibə lizəm/ *n* 1 the eating of human flesh by other human beings, whether for food or as a religious ritual 2 the eating of animal flesh by animals of the same species

cannibalistic /kánnibə lístik/ *adj* relating to, involving, or practising cannibalism —**cannibalistically** *adv*

cannibalize /kánnibə līz/ (**-izes, -izing, -ized**), **cannibalise** (**-ises, -ising, -ised**) *vt* 1 to take parts from something, especially a machine, in order to use them elsewhere ○ *The troops, hard-pressed for spare parts, cannibalized the tracks from a wrecked tank to repair their own damaged vehicle.* 2 to eat the flesh of another human being or of an animal of the same species —**cannibalization** /kánnibə lī záysh'n/ *n*

cannikin /kánnikin/ *n* a small can, especially one used for drinking from [Late 16C. < Dutch *kanneken* 'little can' < Middle Dutch *canne* 'can'.]

Canning /kánning/, **Charles John, 1st Earl Canning** (1812–62) British colonial administrator

Canning, George (1770–1827) British statesman

Canning Basin /kánning-/ dry lowland region in the Great Sandy Desert, Western Australia

Cannizzaro reaction /kánni tsaárō-/ *n* a chemical process in which certain aldehydes are broken down into alcohols and acid salts in the presence of a strong alkali [After Stanislao *Cannizzaro* (1826–1910), Italian chemist]

Cannock /kánnək/ town in central England. Population: 60,106 (1991).

Cannock Chase Area of Outstanding Natural Beauty in central England. Area: 6,720 hectares/16,800 acres.

cannon /kánnən/ *n* 1 (*plural* **-nons** or **-non**) **HISTORICAL WEAPON** a weapon used in former times that fired heavy iron balls or other projectiles through a simple iron tube 2 **MODERN WEAPON** a modern heavy artillery weapon large enough to need to be mounted for firing, e.g. one mounted on a warship or on a tracked vehicle 3 **AIRCRAFT GUN** a rapid-firing gun mounted on an aircraft 4 **BILLIARDS SHOT** in cue games, a shot in which the cue ball hits one ball that then hits another ball. US term **carom** *n.* 1 5 **BELL LOOP** the loop at the top of a bell from which it is suspended ■ *v* 1 *vt* MIL = **cannonade** *v.* 1 2 *vi* **COLLIDE** to collide with something or bounce off it at great speed and with a lot of force ○ *a 35-yard shot that cannoned back off the post* ○ *The car, out of control on the icy road, cannoned into the bridge abutment and burst into flames.* 3 *vi* **MAKE A CANNON SHOT** in cue games, to make a cannon shot. US term **carom** *v.* 1 [14C. Via French *canon* < Italian *cannone* 'large tube' < Latin *canna* (see CANE).]

SPELLCHECK Do not confuse ***cannon*** with ***canon***, which has a similar sound. Beware: your spellchecker will not catch this error.

cannonade /kánnə náyd/ *n* 1 **BOMBARDMENT** a sustained bombardment with heavy artillery 2 **SOMETHING LIKE A BOMBARDMENT** something that sounds or feels like an artillery bombardment ○ *'The deep cannonade of roaring thunder belched forth its fearsome challenge'.* (Edgar Rice Burroughs, *Tarzan of the Apes*; 1914) ■ *v* (**-ades, -ading, -aded**) 1 *vti* **BOMBARD** to subject an enemy to, or be subjected to, a cannonade 2 *vt* **ATTACK** to subject somebody to a sustained attack, e.g. with words of criticism or reproach [Mid-16C. Via French < Italian *cannonata* < *cannone* (see CANNON).]

cannonball /kánnən bawl/ *n* 1 **BALL FIRED FROM CANNON** a heavy metal or stone ball fired from an old-fashioned cannon 2 **JUMP INTO WATER** a jump into water with the body tucked into a ball, usually with head down and knees drawn up to the chest ■ *vi* **TRAVEL QUICKLY** to travel at great speed (*informal*) ○ *The train cannonballed through the dark tunnel.*

cannon bone *n* a bone in the lower limbs of some hoofed animals, evolved from the fusing of the metatarsals or metacarpals [< its tubular shape]

cannoneer /kánnə néer/ *n* formerly, a soldier who fired a cannon [Mid-16C. Via French *canonnier* < Italian *cannoniere* < *cannone* (see CANNON).]

cannon fodder *n* (*informal*) 1 members of the lowest ranks of the military, regarded as an expendable resource in wartime 2 any person or group regarded as a resource to be exploited or sacrificed ○ *Our team ended up as cannon fodder for the opponents in the first championship game.*

cannot /kánnot, -ət, kə nót/ *contr* an alternative way of writing 'can not'

USAGE See ***help***.

cannula /kánnyŏŏlə/ (*plural* **-las** or **-lae** /-lī/), **canula** (*plural* **-las** or **-lae**) *n* a flexible tube with a sharp-pointed part at one end that is inserted into a duct, vein, or cavity in order to drain away fluid or to administer drugs [Late 17C. < Latin, 'little tube' < *canna* (see CANE).]

cannulate /kánnyŏŏ layt/, **canulate** *vt* (**-lates, -lating, -lated**) to insert a tube (**cannula**) into a vein or cavity in order to drain away fluid or to administer drugs ■ *adj* tubular in shape (*technical*) —**cannulation** /kánnyŏŏ láysh'n/ *n*

canny /kánni/ *adj* (**-nier, -niest**) **1 SHREWDLY KNOWING** shrewd enough not to be easily deceived ○ *a canny negotiator* **2** *N England* **GOOD** good, pleasant, or excellent (*informal*) **3** *Scotland* **MILD-TEMPERED** docile and obedient **4** *Scotland* **PRUDENT** careful and shrewd in money matters ■ *adv* **EXCEEDINGLY** used to emphasize the degree or extent of something (*regional*) ○ *We walked a canny long way.* [Late 16C. < CAN[2] 'know'.] —**cannily** *adv* —**canniness** *n*

canoe /kə nóo/ *n* a lightweight boat identically pointed at each end ■ *vi* (**-noes, -noeing, -noed**) to travel or paddle in a canoe, often as a sport or hobby [Mid-16C. Alteration of Spanish *canoa* < Carib *canaoua*.] —**canoeable** *adj* ◇ **paddle your own canoe** to take control of and responsibility for your own life and affairs (*informal*)

canoeing /kə nóo ing/ *n* the sport, hobby, or activity of paddling a canoe

canoeist /kə nóo ist/ *n* somebody who canoes

can of worms *n* a complicated situation that results from unforeseen problems, especially an issue that seems likely to create conflicts (*informal*)

canola /kə nṓlə/ *n* = **canola oil** [Late 20C. < CANADA.]

canola oil *n* a rapeseed oil that has a high level of monounsaturated fatty acids. Use: cooking oil.

canon[1] /kánnən/ *n* **1 GENERAL RULE** a general rule, principle, or standard ○ *one of the fundamental canons of free-market economics* **2 RELIGIOUS DECREE** a decree issued by a religious authority, especially one ruling on religious practices **3 BODY OF RELIGIOUS WRITINGS** a set of religious writings regarded as authentic and definitive and forming a religion's body of scripture **4 SET OF ARTISTIC WORKS** a set of artistic works established as genuine and complete, e.g. the works of a particular writer, painter, or filmmaker ○ *It's not one of the best-known pictures in the Welles canon.* **5 PART OF MASS** in the Roman Catholic Mass, the prayer during which the bread and wine are consecrated **6 STAGGERED SINGING OR PLAYING** a musical technique in which different instruments or voices enter one after the other, each playing or singing exactly the same sequence of notes, resulting in often complex counterpoint [Pre-12C. Via Latin < Greek *kanōn* 'rule'.]

SPELLCHECK See ***cannon***.

canon[2] /kánnən/ *n* **1** a member of the Christian clergy who is on the permanent staff of a cathedral and has specific duties in relation to the running of it **2** = **canon regular** [12C. Via Old French *canonie* < ecclesiastical Latin *canonicus* 'according to a rule' < Latin *canon* (see CANON[1]).]

cañon *n* = **canyon**

canoness /kánnə néss/ *n* in the Roman Catholic Church, a woman who belongs to one of several religious orders in which members live under a rule, not a vow

canonical /kə nónnik'l/, **canonic** /kə nónnik/ *adj* **1 OF A CANON OF WORKS** relating or belonging to the biblical canon or a canon of artistic works established as genuine and complete **2 FOLLOWING CANON LAW** conforming to or authorized by canon law **3 CONFORMING TO GENERAL PRINCIPLES** conforming to accepted principles or standard practice **4 OF CATHEDRAL OR REGULAR CANONS** relating to members of the clergy who are canons **5 OF MUSICAL CANON** relating to musical canons [15C. < medieval Latin *canonicalis* < Greek *kanōn* 'rule'.] —**canonically** *adv*

canonical hour *n* **1** in the Roman Catholic Church, any of the daily prayer times when specific prayers are said **2** in the Church of England, any time between 8 am and 6 pm when marriages can be officially celebrated

canonicals /kə nónnik'lz/ *npl* ceremonial robes worn by members of the clergy during a religious ceremony

canonicity /kánnə níssəti/ *n* inclusion in a religious or secular canon, or status as an included item

canonise *vt* = **canonize**

canonize /kánnə nīz/ (**-izes, -izing, -ized**), **canonise** (**-ises, -ising, -ised**) *vt* **1 DECLARE AS SAINT** in the Roman Catholic Church, to declare a deceased person to be a saint **2 GIVE RELIGIOUS APPROVAL TO** to declare something to be acceptable or valid according to canon law **3 GLORIFY** to idolize somebody or glorify something ○ *'And fame in time to come canonize us'* (William Shakespeare, *Troilus and Cressida*; 1601) [14C. < medieval Latin *canonizare* < Greek *kanōn* 'rule'.] —**canonization** /kánnən ī záysh'n/ *n* —**canonizer** *n*

canon law *n* the body of laws that governs the affairs of the Christian church or a particular branch of it

canon regular (*plural* **canons regular**) *n* a member of any of several Roman Catholic orders of monks living in communities that follow Augustinian rules

canonry /kánnənri/ (*plural* **-ries**) *n* the status or position of a religious canon

canoodle /kə nóod'l/ (**-noodles, -noodling, -noodled**) *vti* to kiss and cuddle somebody in a mildly romantic or sexual way (*informal*) ○ *couples canoodling on the back row of the dark theatre* [Mid-19C. < ?]

can opener *n* = **tin-opener**

Canopic jar

canopic jar /kə nṓpik-/, **Canopic jar** *n* a jar used in ancient Egypt to hold the embalmed entrails of a mummy [Late 19C. < Latin *Canopicus* < *Canopus*, port in ancient Egypt.]

Canopus /kə nṓpəss/ *n* the second brightest star in the sky after Sirius, in the constellation Argo

canopy /kánnəpi/ (*plural* **-pies**) *n* **1 COVERING FOR SHELTER** a covering fixed above something to provide shelter or for decoration, especially a fabric covering that can be removed or folded away **2 TREETOPS** the uppermost layer of vegetation in a forest, consisting of the tops of trees forming a kind of ceiling **3 SKY** the sky as a covering or ceiling (*literary*) ○ *the vast canopy of stars* **4 ROOFED STRUCTURE** a roofed structure that covers an area, especially one that shelters a passageway between two buildings **5 PART OF PARACHUTE** the part of a parachute that opens and fills with air **6 COCKPIT COVER** the transparent cover of an aircraft's cockpit [14C. Via medieval Latin *canopeum* 'canopy above an altar' < Greek *kōnōpeion* 'bed with a mosquito net' < *kōnōps* 'mosquito'.] —**canopied** *adj*

Canova /ka nṓvə/, **Antonio, Marquis of Ischia** (1757–1822) Italian sculptor

Canso /kánssō/ town in E Nova Scotia, Canada. Population: 1,228 (1991).

canst *stressed form* /kanst/; *unstressed form* /kənst/ *v* an archaic form of the verb 'can' used with 'thou'

cant[1] /kant/ *n* **1 CLICHÉD TALK** boring talk filled with clichés and platitudes **2 HYPOCRITICAL TALK** insincere talk, especially where morals and religion are concerned **3 JARGON** the special language or vocabulary of a particular group, especially a group whom some people look down on [Mid-16C. Probably < Latin *cantare* 'sing'.] —**cant** *vi* —**canter** *n* —**canting** *adj* —**cantingly** *adv*

cant[2] /kant/ *n* **1 SLOPE** slope, degree of slope, or a sloping surface **2 JOLT** a jolt that knocks something out of its straight or level position ■ *vt* **JOLT** to knock something out of its straight or level position [14C. Via Middle Low German *kante* or Middle Dutch *cant* 'edge' < Latin *cantus* 'tyre'.]

can't /kaant/ *contr* cannot

Cant. *abbr* **1** Canticle of Canticles **2** Canterbury

Cantab /kán tab/ *adj* of the University of Cambridge (*after titles of academic awards*) ◊ **Oxon.** [Shortening of Latin *Cantabrigiensis*]

cantabile /kan taá bi lay/ *adv* in a smooth, flowing, and melodious style (*musical direction*) ■ *n* a cantabile passage or piece of music [Early 18C. < Italian, 'that can be sung'.] —**cantabile** *adj*

Cantabrian Mountains /kan táybri ən-/ mountain range in N Spain. Highest peak: Torre Cerredo 2,648 m/8,688 ft.

Cantabrigian /kántə bríji ən/ *n* **1** a student or graduate of the University of Cambridge, England **2** somebody who comes from Cambridge, England, or Cambridge, Massachusetts [Mid-16C. < Latin *Cantabrigia* 'Cambridge (England)'.] —**Cantabrigian** *adj*

cantaloupe /kántə loop/, **cantaloup** *n* **1** a small round melon with a ridged scaly rind and aromatic orange flesh. *Cucumis melo cantalupensis.* **2** any orange-fleshed melon [Late 18C. Via French < Italian *Cantaluppi*, papal villa near Rome where the melon was introduced from Armenia.]

cantankerous /kan tángkərəss/ *adj* easily angered and difficult to get on with [Mid-18C. Probably blend of RANCOROUS + an unknown element.] —**cantankerously** *adv* —**cantankerousness** *n*

cantata /kan taátə/ *n* a musical composition for voices and instruments, usually on a religious theme, containing arias, choruses, and recitatives [Early 18C. Via Italian < Latin, feminine past participle of *cantare* 'sing' < *canere*.]

cant dog *n* FORESTRY = **cant hook** [< CANT[2] + DOG 'mechanical device']

canteen /kan téen/ *n* **1 CAFETERIA** a place where food is served, especially in a school or workplace **2 SOLDIERS' SHOP** a shop selling food, toiletries, and other items on a military base **3 CUTLERY BOX** a box or chest with compartments for storing cutlery **4 TEMPORARY FOOD STAND** a mobile or temporary food stand **5 PORTABLE DRINKING FLASK** a small container used by campers or soldiers for carrying liquids such as drinking water [Mid-18C. Via French *cantine* < Italian *cantina* 'cellar'.]

~~canteloupe~~ incorrect spelling of **cantaloupe**

canter /kántər/ *n* **1 HORSE'S MEDIUM PACE** a smooth easy gait of a horse or donkey, slower than a gallop but faster than a trot **2 HORSE RIDE AT CANTER** a horse ride at a canter ■ *v* **1** *vi* **MOVE AT CANTER** to move or ride at a canter **2** *vt* **MAKE HORSE CANTER** to make a horse go at a canter [Early 18C. Shortening of *Canterbury gallop*; from the pace of medieval pilgrims who rode to the shrine of St Thomas à Becket in Canterbury.]

canterbury /kántərbəri/ (*plural* **-ies**) *n* **1** a stand with partitions for holding sheet music or magazines **2** a stand with partitions for holding cutlery and plates [Early 19C. Probably after Charles Manners-Sutton, first Viscount *Canterbury*.]

Canterbury /kántərbəri/ **1** city in SE England. Population: 136,481 (1996 estimate). **2** administrative region of New Zealand, in E South Island. Population: 478,912 (1996). Area: 56,612 sq. km/21,858 sq. mi.

Canterbury bells *n* an ornamental garden plant. Flowers: blue, bell-shaped. Native to: Europe. *Campanula medium.* [< ?]

Canterbury Bight wide bay on the coast of E South Island, New Zealand

Canterbury Plains fertile lowland area in E South Island, New Zealand

cantharis /kánthəriss/ (*plural* **-tharides** /-thárri deez/) *n* INSECTS = **Spanish fly** *n.* 1 [14C. Via Latin < Greek *kantharis*.]

canthi plural of **canthus**

cant hook *n* a wooden pole with a pivoting metal hook at one end, used in forestry for handling logs [< CANT[2]]

canthus /kánthəss/ (*plural* **-thi** /-thī/) *n* the corner or angle at either side of the eye [Mid-17C. Via Latin < Greek *kanthos*.]

canticle /kántik'l/ *n* a song or chant, especially a hymn containing words derived from the Bible, used in the Christian liturgy [13C. < Latin *canticulum* 'little song' < *canticum* 'song' < *cantus* (see CANTO).]

Canticle of Canticles /kántik'l əv kántik'lz/ *n* = **Song of Solomon**

cantilena /kánti láynə/ *n* a smooth-flowing melodious line in vocal or instrumental music [Mid-18C. Directly or via Italian < Latin, 'song' < *cantus* (see CANTO).]

cantilever /kánti leevər/ *n* **1 PROJECTION SUPPORTED AT ONE END** a projecting structure that is attached or supported at only one end **2 SUPPORTING BRACKET** a bracket that supports a balcony or a cornice **3 WING WITH NO EXTERNAL BRACE** an aircraft wing constructed without external braces ■ *v* **1** *vt* **ATTACH SOMETHING AT ONE END** to construct something in such a way that it is attached or supported at only one end **2** *vi* **EXTEND LIKE CANTILEVER** to project outwards like a cantilever [Mid-17C. < ?]

cantilever bridge *n* a bridge consisting of arms projecting outwards from supporting piers and meeting in the middle of each span

cantillate /kánti layt/ (**-lates, -lating, -lated**) *vti* to chant or intone something, especially passages of the Hebrew scriptures [Mid-19C. < Latin *cantillat-*, past participle of *cantillare* 'sing low' < *cantare* (see CANTATA).] —**cantillation** /kánti láysh'n/ *n*

cantina /kan téenə/ *n* a bar or wine shop, especially in a Spanish-speaking country [Late 19C. Via Spanish, 'bar, wine cellar' < Italian (see CANTEEN).]

canting arms /kánting aarmz/ *npl* a coat of arms that makes a visual reference to the bearer's name [< CANT[1] (verb)]

cantle /kánt'l/ *n* the raised back part of a saddle for a horse [14C. Via Anglo-Norman *cantel* < medieval Latin *cantellus* 'small corner' < Latin *cant(h)us* (see CANT[2]).]

canto /kánt ō/ (*plural* **-tos**) *n* **1** any of the main divisions of a long poem **2** MUSIC = **cantus** *n.* 2 [Late 16C. Via Italian < Latin *cantus* 'song' < *cantare* (see CANTATA).]

canton /kán ton, kan tón/ *n* **1** PART OF COUNTRY a division of a country, especially one of the states into which Switzerland is divided **2** PART OF FRENCH ARRONDISSEMENT a division of a French arrondissement **3** PART OF FLAG a rectangular division in the top corner of a flag, next to the staff **4** PART OF SHIELD a small square or oblong division of a shield, usually in the top left corner [Early 16C. Via French < Provençal, < Latin *cant(h)us* (see CANT[2]).] —**cantonal** /kántən'l/ *adj*

Canton /kan tón/ = **Guangzhou**

Cantonese /kántə néez/ (*plural* **-ese**) *n* **1** the Chinese language of Guangzhou (Canton) and the province of Guangdong, China, also widely spoken elsewhere in the world. Native speakers: 70 million. **2** somebody who comes from Guangzhou or the surrounding province of Guangdong —**Cantonese** *adj*

cantonment /kan tóonmənt/ *n* **1** MILITARY TRAINING CAMP a large military training camp, especially in former times **2** TEMPORARY TROOP ACCOMMODATION temporary accommodation for troops, especially the winter quarters of an army **3** ASSIGNMENT TO QUARTERS the assignment of troops to temporary quarters **4** MILITARY CAMP IN BRITISH INDIA a permanent military station in India during the time of British imperial rule [Mid-18C. < French *cantonnement* < *cantonner* 'quarter, billet' < *canton* (see CANTON).]

Canton ware *n* Chinese porcelain and other ceramic ware of types exported during the 18th and 19th centuries [Early 20C. Because exported from China by way of CANTON (Guangzhou).]

cantor /kán tawr, kántər/ *n* **1** a Jewish religious official who is the chief singer of the liturgy in a synagogue **2** a leader of the singing in a synagogue or congregation [Mid-16C. < Latin, 'singer' < *cantare* (see CANTATA).]

cantorial /kan táwri əl/ *adj* **1** relating to the chief singer of a synagogue or church **2** describes the part of the choir on the north side of a cathedral or church **3** CHR, MUSIC = **cantoris**

cantoris /kan táwriss/ *adj* sung by the part of the choir on the north side of a cathedral or church. ◊ **decani** [Mid-17C. < Latin *cantoris* 'of the singer', form of *cantor* (see CANTOR).]

cantrip /kántrip/ *n Scotland* **1** WITCH'S SPELL a witch's trick or spell **2** PRANK a mischievous trick or prank (*often plural*) ■ *adj Scotland* DONE BY MAGIC supposedly carried out by means of magic [Late 16C. < ?]

cantus /kántəss/ (*plural* **-tus**) *n* **1** MUSIC = **cantus firmus** **2** the highest vocal part of a harmony in a piece of choral music **3** a melody or style of singing used in the medieval Christian church [Late 16C. < Latin (see CANTO).]

cantus firmus /-fúrməss/ (*plural* **cantus firmi** /-fúrmī/) *n* a melody, often derived from chant, that forms the basis of a composition to which other melodic lines are added [< Latin, 'firm song']

canty /kánti/ (**-tier, -tiest**) *adj N England, Scotland* cheerful, lively, or sprightly [Early 18C. < Scots and English dialect *cant* 'bold'.] —**cantily** *adv* —**cantiness** *n*

Canuck /kə núk/ *n US, Can* (*slang*) **1** somebody from Canada **2** an offensive term for a French-Canadian person [Mid-19C. Probably < (a Native American pronunciation of) CANADA.]

canula *n* = **cannula**

canvas /kánvəss/ *n* **1** HEAVY FABRIC a strong heavy cotton, hemp, or jute fabric. Use: sails, tents, furnishings. **2** FABRIC FOR PAINTING ON a piece of canvas on which a painting is done, especially in oils **3** PAINTING a painting that has been done on a canvas **4** BACKGROUND the background against which events happen **5** CLOTH FOR NEEDLEWORK a fabric with a coarse loose weave. Use: embroidery, tapestry. **6** SAIL a vessel's sail or sails **7** FLOOR OF ATHLETIC RING the floor of a boxing or wrestling ring when covered with canvas **8** END OF BOAT the covered section at either end of a racing boat, sometimes used as a unit of length ■ *vt* (**-vases** *or* **-vasses, -vasing** *or* **-vassing, -vased** *or* **-vassed**) COVER SOMETHING WITH CANVAS to cover or line something with canvas [14C. Via Old French *canevas* < Latin *cannabis* 'hemp' (from which the cloth was made).] ◇ **under canvas** living in a tent

SPELLCHECK Do not confuse ***canvas*** with ***canvass***, which has a similar sound. Beware: your spellchecker will not catch this error.

canvasback /kánvəss bak/ *n* a wild duck, the male of which has a white back and a reddish-brown head and neck. Native to: North America. *Aythya valisineria*.

canvass /kánvəss/ *v* **1** *vti* VISIT FOR SUPPORT OR CUSTOM to travel around an area asking people for something, e.g. sale orders, opinions, or votes **2** *vt* DEBATE to debate or discuss something thoroughly **3** *vt* LOOK AT CAREFULLY to examine something in detail ■ *n* (*plural* **-vasses** *or* **-vases**) **1** OPINION POLL a survey of public opinion, especially before an election **2** SALE OFFER TO MEMBERS OF GROUP an offer of something, especially something for sale, to people in a particular area or group **3** CAREFUL INSPECTION a close inspection or examination [Early 16C. < CANVAS.] —**canvasser** *n*

SPELLCHECK See ***canvas***.

canyon /kányən/, **cañon** /kányən/ *n* a deep narrow valley with steep sides, often with a stream running through it [Mid-19C. Via Mexican Spanish *cañón* < Spanish, 'large tube' < *caña* 'pipe' < Latin *canna* (see CANE).]

canzona /kan zṓnə/ *n* **1** a song resembling a madrigal but simpler and less serious in form and content **2** an instrumental piece in the style of a canzona **3** LITERAT = **canzone** *n.* 1 [Late 19C. < Italian, < *canzone* 'song' (see CANZONE).]

canzone /kan zṓ nay/ (*plural* **-ni** /-ni/) *n* **1** a love poem written by the troubadours of medieval Italy and Provence **2** MUSIC = **canzona** *n.* 1, **canzona** *n.* 2 [Late 16C. Via Italian < Latin *cant-*, past participle of *canere* 'sing'.]

canzonet /kánzə nét/, **canzonetta** /-néttə/ *n* **1** a short light English song of the 17th or 18th centuries, originally intended for a group of singers or for a soloist with accompaniment **2** a Renaissance song with different parts for different singers, similar to the madrigal [Late 16C. < Italian *canzonetta* 'small canzone' < *canzone* (see CANZONE).]

canzoni plural of **canzone**

cap /kap/ *n* **1** HAT a covering for the head, usually soft and close-fitting and often with a peak and no brim **2** UNIFORM HAT a head covering, usually part of a uniform, worn to identify the wearer's occupation or rank **3** PROTECTIVE COVERING FOR HAIR a head covering worn to protect the hair, usually close-fitting or elasticated around the edge **4** HAT AWARDED TO PLAYER a hat or beret awarded to a player selected for a special team **5** PLAYER AWARDED HAT a player who has been selected for a special team, e.g. a national cricket, football, or rugby team **6** HAT WORN AT GRADUATION an academic mortarboard, worn with a gown on a ceremonial occasion **7** COVER a removable cover or lid that closes the end of something when it is not in use ○ *a lens cap* **8** COVERING AT TIP something that covers the top or tip of something, especially as protection **9** TOP PART the top part of something, e.g. a hill or mountain **10** UPPER LIMIT an upper limit on something, e.g. the amount that may be spent on an item **11** ARMS = **percussion cap** **12** EXPLOSIVE FOR TOY GUN a small quantity of explosive enclosed in paper for use in a toy gun **13** COVERING FOR TOOTH a covering to preserve or replace the crown of a tooth **14** CONTRACEPTIVE DEVICE a contraceptive device that fits over the cervix, e.g. a Dutch cap or a diaphragm (*informal*) **15** TOP OF COLUMN the upper part of a column or pedestal **16** WINDMILL ROOF the roof of a windmill (*technical*) **17** TOP OF MUSHROOM the dome-shaped upper part of certain fungi, e.g. mushrooms **18** SPORE-CAPSULE COVERING the hood that covers the spore-bearing capsule of mosses and liverworts **19** PATCH ON BIRD'S HEAD a patch of feathers of a different colour on the top of a bird's head **20** MOLECULE CLUSTER an aggregation of molecules at one end of something such as a cell or virus **21** SET INTERSECTION SYMBOL a mathematical symbol (∩) representing the intersection of two sets **22** COLLECTION AT HUNT a collection of money taken at a fox hunt **23** GEOL = **cap rock** ■ *v* (**caps, capping, capped**) **1** *vt* COVER SOMETHING WITH CAP to put a cap over something **2** *vt* LIE ON TOP OF to cover the top or tip of something **3** *vt* SURPASS to improve on something that has already happened or been done **4** *vt* COMPLETE to add the finishing touch to something, e.g. an effort or a process **5** *vt* IMPOSE LIMIT ON to put an upper limit on something, e.g. the amount of money to be charged or spent **6** *vt* AWARD PLAYER CAP to select a player for a special team, e.g. a national side, for which a cap is awarded **7** *vt NZ, Scotland* GIVE SOMEBODY DEGREE to award an academic degree to somebody **8** *vt* ASK FOR MONEY AT HUNT to take a collection of money at a fox hunt from participants who are not members of the hunt **9** *vti* FORM CLUSTER OF MOLECULES to form a cluster of molecules on something [Pre-12C. < late Latin *cappa* 'hood, hooded cloak'.] —**capful** *n* ◇ **cap in hand** with a humble or apologetic attitude ◇ **if the cap fits (wear it)** if you think that a remark could apply to you, then you should take note of it ◇ **set your cap for** *or* **at somebody** to try to attract somebody, especially with a view to marriage (*dated*) ◇ **to cap it all** used to say that something has made a bad situation as bad as it can get

⚡**CAP** *abbr* **1** Common Agricultural Policy **2** computer-aided production **3** computer-aided publishing

cap. *abbr* **1** capacity **2** capital **3** capitalize **4** capital letter **5** caput

Capa /káppə/, **Robert** (1913–54) Hungarian-born US photographer

capability /káypə bíllәti/ (*plural* **-ties**) *n* **1** COMPETENCE the ability necessary to do something **2** TALENT THAT COULD BE DEVELOPED an ability or characteristic that has potential for development ○ *a man of immense capabilities* **3** POTENTIAL FOR USE the potential to be used for a particular purpose or treated in a particular manner

SYNONYMS See ***ability***.

capable /káypəb'l/ *adj* **1** DOING SOMETHING WELL good at a particular task or job or at a number of different things **2** ABLE TO DO PARTICULAR THING possessing the qualities needed to do a particular thing **3** LIABLE TO permitting or susceptible to something ○ *an action capable of being misinterpreted* **4** LEGALLY COMPETENT the ability or the legal power to do something [Mid-16C. Via French < late Latin *capabilis* < Latin *capere* 'take'.] —**capableness** *n*

capably /káypəbli/ *adv* in a competent or efficient way

capacious /kə páyshəss/ *adj* big enough to contain a large quantity [Early 17C. < Latin *capac-* 'able to hold' < *capere* 'take'.] —**capaciously** *adv* —**capaciousness** *n*

capacitance /kə pássitənss/ *n* **1** ABILITY TO STORE ELECTRICAL CHARGE the ability of a substance to store an electric charge **2** ABILITY OF COMPONENT TO STORE CHARGE the ability of an electronic component to store an electric charge **3** MEASURE OF ELECTRIC CHARGE STORAGE (*symbol C*) a measure of the capacitance of a substance, equal to the surface charge divided by the electric potential **4** PART OF ELECTRICAL CIRCUIT the part of an electrical circuit that has capacitance

capacitate /kə pássi tayt/ (**-tates, -tating, -tated**) *vt* **1** MAKE SOMEBODY CAPABLE to make somebody able, fit, or qualified to do something (*formal*) **2** GIVE SOMEBODY LEGAL POWER to make somebody legally able to do something **3** CAUSE CHANGE IN SPERM COATING to cause the coatings on a sperm to be able to interact with proteins on the ovum —**capacitation** /kə pássi táysh'n/ *n*

capacitive /kə pássətiv/ *adj* relating to electrical capacitance —**capacitively** *adv*

capacitor /kə pássitər/ *n* an electrical component, used to store a charge temporarily

⚡**capacity** /kə pássəti/ (*plural* **-ties**) *n* **1** MENTAL OR PHYSICAL ABILITY the ability to do or experience something **2** VOLUME a measure of the amount that can be held or contained **3** MAXIMUM VOLUME the maximum amount that can be held or taken in **4** MAXIMUM PRODUCTIVITY the maximum amount of output or productivity **5** OFFICIAL ROLE an official function or position that somebody has **6** MEASURE OF ELECTRICAL OUTPUT a measure of the electric output of a battery, generator, or motor **7** COMPUTER STORAGE SPACE the amount of data that can be stored by a specific computer device **8** LEGAL COMPETENCE the legal ability or qualification to do something, e.g. make an arrest or a will [15C. Via French *capacité* < Latin *capac-* (see CAPACIOUS).]

SYNONYMS See ***ability***.

caparison /kə párriss'n/ n 1 FANCY COVERING FOR HORSE an ornamental covering for a horse, especially for a war-horse in former times 2 HARNESS OR SADDLE DECORATIONS a decorative harness for a horse or decorations for its saddle or other fittings 3 ELABORATE CLOTHING OR ORNAMENTS elaborate or rich clothing and ornaments [Early 16C. < obsolete French caparasson.] —**caparison** vt

cape[1] /kayp/ n 1 LOOSE OUTER GARMENT a sleeveless outer garment, shorter than a cloak, that is fastened at the neck and hangs loosely from the shoulders 2 COAT PART LIKE CAPE a piece of material like a cape that forms part of a coat or other garment 3 FEATHERS ON BIRD'S SHOULDER a covering of short feathers on the shoulders of certain birds, especially fowl [Mid-16C. Via French < late Latin cappa (see CAP).]

cape[2] /kayp/ n a point of land that juts out into water, especially a headland significant for navigation [14C. Via French cap < Latin caput 'head'.]

Cape Breton Island island in NE Nova Scotia, Canada. Area: 10,311 sq. km/3,981 sq. mi.

Cape Coast capital of Central Region, Ghana, situated on the Gulf of Guinea. Population: 57,224 (1984).

Cape Coloured n in South Africa, somebody of mixed ethnic descent in the Western Cape Province, speaking Afrikaans or English [After the Cape of GOOD HOPE.]

Cape Dutch n 1 18C ARCHITECTURAL STYLE an 18th-century style of architecture characterized by whitewashed houses with high gables 2 18C FURNITURE STYLE a heavy style of furniture that developed in the Cape of Good Hope, South Africa, in the 18th century 3 DUTCH FORE-RUNNER OF AFRIKAANS the form of Dutch that developed into Afrikaans [Cape after the Cape of GOOD HOPE; Dutch refers to the early settlers or the language] —**Cape Dutch** adj

Cape gooseberry n PLANTS = physalis [< its cultivation in the Cape of GOOD HOPE]

Cape jasmine n PLANTS = gardenia

Čapek /cháp ek/, **Karel** (1890–1938) Czech writer

capelin /káyp'lin/, **caplin** /káplin/ n a small edible sea fish of the smelt family. Native to: northern and Arctic seas. Mallotus villosus. [Early 17C. Via French < medieval Latin cappellanus 'custodian of St Martin's cloak' < late Latin cappa (see CAP).]

Capella /kə péllə/ n a double star that is the brightest star in the constellation Auriga

Cape Peninsula peninsula south of Cape Town, South Africa, ending in the Cape of Good Hope

Cape pigeon n a seabird with dappled black and white plumage. Native to: S Atlantic and Antarctic seas. Daption capense. [After the Cape of GOOD HOPE.]

Cape primrose n PLANT SCI = streptocarpus [Probably after the Cape of GOOD HOPE or CAPE PROVINCE]

Cape Province former province of South Africa

caper[1] /káypər/ n 1 PLAYFUL JUMP a playful leap or dancing step 2 PLAYFUL ACT OR TRICK a light-hearted adventurous act or prank 3 QUESTIONABLE ACTIVITY a dangerous or illegal activity, especially one involving robbery (informal) ■ vi PRANCE HAPPILY to leap or dance about in a happy playful manner [Late 16C. Shortening of CAPRIOLE.]

caper[2] /káypər/ n 1 PICKLED FLOWER BUD a flower bud of a bush, eaten pickled or salted as a flavouring (often plural) 2 PLANT WITH EDIBLE BUDS a bush with spiny trailing stems, cultivated for its capers. Native to: the Mediterranean. Capparis spinosa. 3 PLANT RELATED TO THE CAPER any plant in the same family as caper. Family: Capparidaceae. [14C. Back-formation from caperis (taken as plural), directly or via French câpres < Latin capparis < Greek kapparis.]

capercaillie /káppər káyli/, **capercailzie** /-káyli, -káylzi/ n a large woodland bird of the grouse family, with dark grey plumage. Native to: Europe, Asia. Tetrao urogallus. [16C. Gaelic capull coille 'horse of the wood'.]

Capernaum /kə púrni əm/ city of ancient Palestine, on the northwestern shore of the Sea of Galilee

caper spurge n a plant of the spurge family that produces a milky fluid (latex). Native to: Europe. Euphorbia lathyris. [< CAPER[2]]

capeskin /kayp skin/ n a soft light leather made from South African sheepskin [After the Cape of GOOD HOPE]

Cape sparrow n a common sparrow. Native to: South Africa. Passer melanurus.

Capetian /kə peesh'n/ n a member of the royal dynasty founded by Hugh Capet that ruled France from AD 987 to 1328 ■ adj relating to the Capetians or the period of their rule

Cape Town legislative capital of South Africa and capital of Western Cape Province. Population: 854,616 (1991). Afrikaans **Kaapstad**

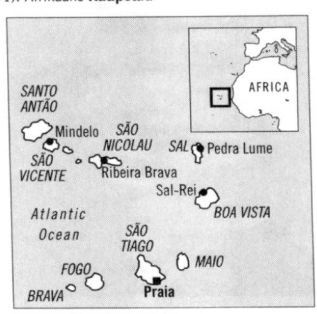

Cape Verde

Cape Verde /-vúrd/ 1 island republic in the Atlantic Ocean, west of Senegal. Capital: Praia. Population: 393,843 (1997). Area: 4,033 sq. km/1,557 sq. mi. 2 = **Cape Vert**

Cape Vert /kap váir/, **Cape Verde** peninsula in W Senegal forming the westernmost point of the African mainland. Length: 32 km/20 mi.

capework /káyp wurk/ n the skill of a bullfighter in using a cape to control the movements of a bull

Cape York Peninsula peninsula in N Queensland, Australia, the most northerly point on the Australian mainland. Area: 127,200 sq. km/49,100 sq. mi.

cap gun n a toy gun that can be loaded with a small quantity of explosive enclosed in paper (**cap**)

capias /káypi as, káppi as/ n a warrant authorizing an officer of the law to arrest a named person [< Latin, 'you are to seize' < capere 'take'.]

capillaceous /káppi láyshass/ adj 1 resembling a hair 2 having many filaments that resemble a hair or thread [Early 18C. < Latin capillaceus < capillus 'hair'.]

capillarity /káppi lárrəti/ n 1 PHYS = capillary action 2 the state of being capillary [Mid-19C. < French capillarité < Latin capillus 'hair'.]

capillary /kə pílləri/ n (plural -ies) 1 THIN BLOOD VESSEL an extremely narrow thin-walled blood vessel that connects small arteries (arterioles) with small veins (venules) to form a network throughout the body 2 SCI = capillary tube ■ adj 1 RELATING TO CAPILLARY ACTION involving or relating to capillary action 2 OF BLOOD CAPILLARIES relating to the capillaries of the blood system 3 RESEMBLING HAIR as fine and slender as a hair 4 SMALL IN DIAMETER with a very small internal diameter [Mid-17C. < Latin capillaris < capillus 'hair'.]

capillary action n a phenomenon in which a liquid's surface rises, falls, or becomes distorted in shape where it is in contact with a solid

capillary bed n the collective mass of capillaries of the body or in any particular site

capillary tube n a tube with a very small internal diameter, especially a glass tube with a fine bore and thick walls used in thermometers and similar pieces of equipment

capita /káppitə/ 1 plural of caput 2 ◊ per capita

capital[1] /káppit'l/ n 1 SEAT OF GOVERNMENT a city that is the seat of government of a country, state, or province 2 CENTRE OF ACTIVITY a city that is the centre of a specified activity 3 MATERIAL WEALTH material wealth in the form of money or property 4 CASH FOR INVESTMENT money that can be used to produce further wealth 5 ADVANTAGE advantage derived from or useful in a particular situation ◊ make political capital out of the dispute 6 ECONOMIC RESOURCE any resource or resources that can be used to generate economic wealth ◊ a waste of human capital 7 WEALTHY PEOPLE the capitalist class considered as a group ◊ capital's influence on government policy 8 NET WORTH the assets of a business that remain after its debts and other liabilities are paid or deducted 9 LING = capital letter (often plural) ■ adj 1 RELATING TO DEATH PENALTY

---

relating to or incurring punishment by death 2 GRAVE having extremely serious consequences ◊ a capital blunder that sealed their fate 3 PRINCIPAL constituting the highest category, or among those in the highest category 4 UPPER CASE describes the form of letters used at the beginning of sentences and names, e.g. A, B, and C as distinct from a, b, and c 5 GOVERNMENT functioning as or relating to a seat of government 6 OF FINANCIAL CAPITAL involving or relating to financial capital 7 EXCELLENT used to indicate that somebody thinks something is excellent (dated) [12C. Via French < Latin capitalis 'of the head' < caput 'head'.]

SPELLCHECK Do not confuse **capital** with **capitol**, which has a similar sound. Beware: your spellchecker will not catch this error.

capital[2] /káppit'l/ n the upper part of an architectural pillar or column, on top of the shaft and supporting the entablature [Via Old French capitel < late Latin capitellum (see CAPITELLUM)]

capital account n a statement of the value of a company's capital at a given time

capital allowance n money spent by a company on fixed assets and deducted from its profits before taxes are calculated

capital asset n = fixed asset

capital expenditure n an expenditure on long-term business assets (fixed assets) such as buildings

capital gain n a profit made from the sale of a financial asset such as shares or a house (often plural)

capital gains tax n a tax on profit above a fixed level made from the sale of financial assets

capital goods npl goods that are used in the production of other goods rather than being sold to consumers. ◊ consumer goods

capital-intensive adj using or requiring a proportionately large financial expenditure relative to the amount of labour involved

capitalise vt = capitalize

capitalism /káppitalizəm/ n an economic system based on the private ownership of the means of production and distribution of goods, characterized by a free competitive market and motivation by profit

capitalist /káppitalist/ n 1 INVESTOR an investor of money in business for profit 2 BELIEVER IN CAPITALISM a supporter of capitalism or a participant in a capitalist economy 3 RICH PERSON a wealthy person, especially somebody made rich by capitalism and considered to be greedy (informal) ■ adj 1 OF CAPITALISM involving or relating to capitalism or capitalists 2 capitalist, capitalistic FAVOURING CAPITALISM practising or supporting capitalism —**capitalistically** adv

capitalize /káppita líz/ (-izes, -izing, -ized), **capitalise** (-ises, -ising, -ised) v 1 USE CAPITAL LETTERS to write or print something with capital letters or an initial capital letter 2 vi BENEFIT FROM to profit by or take advantage of something ◊ to capitalize on an opponent's mistake 3 vt USE SOMETHING AS CAPITAL to use debt or budgeted expenditure as capital for development 4 vt AUTHORIZE ISSUE OF CAPITAL STOCK to authorize a business enterprise to issue a specified amount of capital stock 5 vt FINANCE to supply capital for a business enterprise 6 vt EXCHANGE DEBT FOR STOCK to convert a corporation's debt into shares of stock 7 vt TREAT EXPENSES AS ASSETS to treat an expenditure as an asset in a business account instead of as an expense 8 vt VALUE FUTURE INCOME to determine the current value of a future cash flow, earnings, or other income —**capitalizable** adj —**capitalization** /káppita lí zǎysh'n/ n

capital letter n an alphabetical letter in the larger form used to begin sentences and names, e.g. A, B, and C as distinct from a, b, and c

capital levy n a tax on fixed assets or property

capital market n a financial market involving institutions that deal with securities with a life of more than one year

capital punishment n the punishment of death for committing a crime

capital ship n a ship that belongs to the largest and most heavily armed class of warships

capital stock n 1 FIN = stock n. 4 2 the face value of the share capital that a company issues

capital transfer tax *n* in the United Kingdom, a tax levied until 1986 on the total value of gifts and bequests somebody made

capitate /káppi tayt/ *adj* **1** describes a flower head composed of small flowers arranged in a dense cluster **2** describes a body part that is enlarged and rounded [Mid-17C. < Latin *capitatus* 'having a head' < *caput* 'head'.]

capitated /káppi taytid/ *adj* numbered or assessed by or for each individual person ○ *capitated payments* [Late 20C. < CAPITATION.]

capitation /káppi táysh'n/ *n* **1 FIXED TAX PER PERSON** a form of taxation in which each person pays the same fixed amount **2 FIXED FEE PER PERSON** a payment or fee charged at an equal amount per person **3 COUNTING HEADS** a method of assessing the number of individuals by counting heads (*formal*) [Early 17C. Directly or via French < late Latin *capitation-* 'poll tax' < Latin *capit-* 'head'.] —**capitative** /káppitətiv/ *adj*

capitellum /káppi télləm/ (*plural* **-la** /-lə/) *n* a rounded enlarged part at the end of a bone, especially that of the upper arm bone (**humerus**) that forms the elbow joint with one of the lower bones (**radius**) [Early 18C. < Latin, 'little head' < *caput* 'head'.]

capitol /káppit'l/ *n* in the United States, a building or group of buildings in which a state legislature meets and where other state government offices may be housed [14C. < Old French *capitolie* < Latin *Capitolium*, temple of Jupiter in Rome < *caput* 'head'.]

SPELLCHECK See ***capital***.

Capitol /káppit'l/ *n* the white marble domed building in Washington, D.C. where the United States Congress meets

Capitol Hill *n* the United States Congress (*informal*)

capitula plural of **capitulum**

capitular /kə píttyŏŏlər/ *adj* **1 OF AN ECCLESIASTICAL CHAPTER** belonging or relating to a cathedral or other ecclesiastical chapter **2 DENSELY CLUSTERED** describes a flower head (**capitulum**) consisting of many small flowers **3 ROUNDED** describes the rounded end (**capitulum**) of a bone [Early 16C. < late Latin *capitularis* < *capitulum* (see CAPITULUM).] —**capitularly** *adv*

capitulary /kə píttyŏŏləri/ (*plural* **-ies**) *n* **1** a member of an ecclesiastical chapter **2** a civil or ecclesiastical decree or set of decrees [Mid-17C. < late Latin *capitularius* < Latin *capitulum* (see CAPITULUM).]

capitulate /kə píttyŏŏ layt/ (**-lates, -lating, -lated**) *vi* **1** to surrender, especially under specified conditions **2** to give in to an argument, request, pressure, or something unavoidable [Late 17C. Directly and via French *capituler* 'come to terms' < Latin *capitulare* 'draw up under distinct heads' < *capitulum* (see CAPITULUM).] —**capitulant** *n* — **capitulator** *n* —**capitulatory** /kə píttyŏŏlətəri/ *adj*

SYNONYMS See ***yield***.

capitulation /kə píttyŏŏ láysh'n/ *n* (*formal*) **1 GIVING UP** surrender or a giving up of resistance **2 TERMS OF SURRENDER** a document that sets out the agreed terms of surrender **3 SUMMARY** an outline or summary in document form

capitulum /kə píttyŏŏləm/ (*plural* **-la** /-lə/) *n* **1** a flower head that looks like a large single flower but consists of numerous tiny flowers clustered together on a disc **2** a rounded enlarged body part, e.g. at the end of a bone or at the tips of an insect's antennae [Early 18C. < Latin, 'little head' < *caput* 'head'.]

capiz /káppiz/ *n* **1** a small mollusc with a hinged shell. Native to: Philippines. *Placuna placenta*. **2 capiz, capiz shell** the shell of the capiz. Use: jewellery, lampshades, ornaments. [< a language in the Philippines]

caplet /káplət/ *n* a small oval tablet of medicine taken orally

caplin *n* = **capelin**

capo[1] /káp ō, káy pō/ (*plural* **-pos**) *n* a small movable bar fitted across all the strings of a guitar or similar instrument to raise the pitch [Mid-20C. Shortening of *capo tasto* < Italian, 'head stop'.]

capo[2] /káp ō, káyp ō/ (*plural* **-pos**) *n* the title of a leader in the Mafia or a similar criminal organization [Mid-20C. Via Italian < Latin *caput* 'head'.]

capoeira /kápoo áyrə/ *n* a martial art and dance form, originally from Brazil, that is used to promote physical fitness and grace of movement [Late 20C. < Portuguese.]

capon /káypən, -pon/ *n* a male chicken castrated to improve its growth and the quality of its flesh for eating [Pre-12C. Via Anglo-Norman < Latin.]

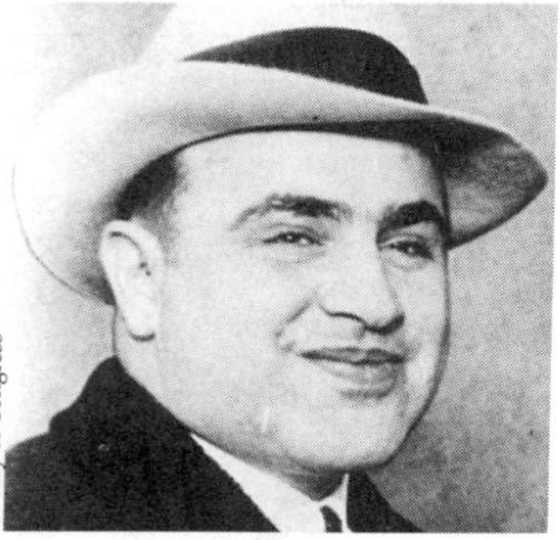

Library of Congress

Al Capone

Capone /kə pṓn/, **Al** (1899–1947) Italian-born US gangster and racketeer. Full name **Alphonse Capone**. Known as **Scarface**

caporal /káppə ráal/ *n* a strong dark coarse tobacco [Mid-19C. < French *tabac du caporal* 'corporal's tobacco' (being superior to *tabac du soldat* 'soldier's tobacco').]

capot /kə pót/ *n* the winning of all the tricks by one player in a game of piquet ■ *vt* to win all the tricks from an opponent in the game of piquet [Mid-17C. < French.]

Capote /kə pṓti/, **Truman** (1924–84) US writer

Capp /kap/, **Al** (1909–79) US cartoonist. Full name **Alfred Gerald Chaplin**

cappelletti /káppi létti/ *n* small pieces of pasta shaped like pointed hats, filled with a savoury mixture of cheese or meat (+ *singular or plural verb*) [Mid-20C. < Italian, 'little hats' < *capella* 'hat' < medieval Latin *capellus* 'little hat' < late Latin *cappa* (see CAP).]

capper /káppər/ *n* something good or bad that is the last in a string of such events (*informal*)

cap pistol *n* = **cap gun**

cappuccino /káppŏŏ chéen ō/ (*plural* **-nos**) *n* a drink made with espresso coffee and frothed hot milk, sometimes topped with powdered chocolate or cinnamon [Mid-20C. < Italian, 'Capuchin (friar)' < *cappuccio* 'hood' < late Latin *cappa* (see CAP); from the colour of the habit.]

~~cappucino~~ incorrect spelling of **cappuccino**

Capri /kə prée, kápri/ island in the Bay of Naples, S Italy. Population: 7,400 (1990). Area: 10 sq. km/4.02 sq. mi.

capric acid /káprik-/ *n* $C_{10}H_{20}O_2$ a white crystalline acid. Source: animal fats, oils. Use: manufacture of artificial fruit flavours, perfumes, plasticizers, and resins. [< Latin *capr-* 'goat'; from its smell]

capriccio /kə préechi ō, -prích-/ (*plural* **-cios** *or* **-ci** /-chi/) *n* **1 LIVELY INSTRUMENTAL WORK** a piece of instrumental music with a free form, an improvisatory style, and usually a lively tempo **2 PRANK** a lighthearted act or prank **3 WHIM** a sudden idea, impulsive decision, or change of mind [Early 17C. < Italian (see CAPRICE).]

capriccioso /kə préechi ósső, -prích-/ *adv* in a lively and fanciful manner (*musical direction*) [Mid-18C. < Italian, < *capriccio* (see CAPRICE).] —**capriccioso** *adj*

caprice /kə préess/ *n* **1 WHIM** a sudden idea, impulsive decision, or change of mind **2 SUDDEN CHANGE OR ACTION** a sudden unexpected action or change of mind **3 IMPULSIVE TENDENCY** a tendency to sudden impulsive decisions or changes of mind **4** MUSIC = **capriccio** *n.* 1 [Mid-17C. Via French < Italian *capriccio* 'head with hair standing on end' < *capo* 'head' (< Latin *caput*) + *riccio* 'hedgehog' (< Latin *(h)ericius*).]

capricious /kə príshəss/ *adj* tending to make sudden and unpredictable changes —**capriciously** *adv* —**capriciousness** *n*

Capricorn /káppri kawrn/ *n* **1** the tenth sign of the zodiac, represented by a goat with a fish's tail and extending from 22 December to 19 January **2 Capricorn, Capricornian, Capricornean** somebody whose birthday falls between 22 December and 19 January **3** ASTRON = **Capricornus** **4** GEOG = **tropic of Capricorn** [Pre-12C. < Latin *capricornus* 'goat's horn' < *caper* 'goat' + *cornu* 'horn'.] —**Capricorn** *adj*

Capricornia /káppri káwrni ə/ district in central Queensland, Australia

Capricornus /káppri káwrnəss/ *n* a faint zodiacal constellation of the equatorial southern hemisphere. See illustration at **constellation**

caprifig /káppri fig/ *n* **1** a fig borne by a wild fig tree **2** a wild fig tree that bears caprifigs. Use: pollination of some edible figs. Native to: S Europe, Asia Minor. *Ficus carica sylvestris*. [15C. Partial translation of Latin *caprificus*.]

caprine /ká prīn/ *adj* relating to or resembling a goat [15C. < Latin *caprinus* < *caper* 'goat'.]

capriole /kápri ōl/ *n* **1** in dressage, a vertical leap in which all four of the horse's feet leave the ground and then its hind legs are kicked out **2** a playful leap or jump performed in ballet [Late 16C. Via French < Latin *capreolus* 'little goat' < *caper* 'goat'.] —**capriole** *vi*

capri pants /kə prée-/, **Capri pants, capris** /kə préez/, **Capris** *npl* close-fitting women's trousers that end just below the knee [Mid-20C. After the island of *Capri*.]

Caprivi Strip /kə préevi-/ narrow extension of NE Namibia, between Angola, Zambia, and Botswana

cap rock *n* **1** a layer of rock that lies above a salt dome and consists of anhydrite, gypsum, or limestone **2** an impermeable layer of rock that lies above a deposit of gas or oil and prevents it from percolating upwards

caproic acid /kə prṓ ik-/ *n* $C_6H_{12}O_2$ a liquid fatty acid. Source: fats, oils, made synthetically. Use: flavourings, in medicine. [< Latin *capr-* 'goat'; from its smell]

caprylic acid /kə príllik-/ *n* $C_8H_{16}O_2$ an oily fatty acid with an unpleasant taste and smell. Source: animal fats. Use: in dyes and perfumes. [< Latin *capr-* 'goat'; from its smell]

caps. *abbr* **1** capsule **2** capital letters

capsaicin /kap sáy issin/ *n* $C_{18}H_{27}NO_3$ a colourless compound. Source: hot peppers. Use: medicine, flavouring. [Late 19C. Alteration of *capsicine* < CAPSICUM.]

cap screw *n* a long-threaded bolt with a head that may be square, hexagonal, slotted, or socketed

Capsian /kápsi ən/ *adj* belonging to a late Palaeolithic culture of N Africa and S Europe [Early 20C. < French *capsien* < Latin *Capsa* 'Gafsa', town in Tunisia.]

capsicum /kápsikəm/ *n* **1** a hot red pepper fruit, eaten raw or cooked as a vegetable, and often dried **2** FOOD = **pepper** *n.* 4. ◊ **chilli** [Late 16C. < modern Latin.]

capsid /kápsid/ *n* the outer coat of protein that surrounds a virus particle [Mid-20C. < Latin *capsa* 'box'.]

capsize /kap sīz/ (**-sizes, -sizing, -sized**) *vti* to overturn on the surface of the water, or cause a boat to overturn [Late 18C. < ?]

cap sleeve *n* a very short sleeve that hangs over the shoulder but does not extend beyond the armhole on the underside

caps lock *n* a key on a computer keyboard or typewriter that, if pressed once, causes all subsequent letters to be typed as capital letters

capsomere /kápsə meer/ *n* one of the individual protein units that make up the outer coat (**capsid**) of a virus [Mid-20C. < CAPSID.]

capstan /kápstən/ *n* **1** a device consisting of a vertical rotatable drum around which a cable is wound. Use: moving heavy weights, hauling in ropes on a ship. **2** a rotating shaft in a tape recorder that pulls the magnetic tape past the head [14C. Via Provençal *cabestan* < Latin *capistrum* 'halter' < *capere* 'seize'.]

capstan bar *n* a long lever used to turn a capstan by hand

capstan lathe *n* a lathe with a head holding several tools that can be rotated so that the tool needed for each operation can be brought in turn into the exact position required. US term **turret lathe**

capstone /káp stōn/ *n* **1** a stone used at the top of a wall or another structure **2** something considered the highest achievement or most important action in a series of actions

capsular /kápsyŏŏlər/ *adj* **1** relating to or resembling a capsule **2** enclosed in or in the form of a capsule

capsule /káp syool/ *n* **1 PILL OR CASING** a small cylindrical soluble container enclosing a dose of medicine, or the container itself **2 SEED CASE** a fruit containing seeds that it releases by splitting open when it is dry and mature **3 SPORE SAC** a sac containing the spores of a moss or a liverwort **4 GELATINOUS COVERING OF MICROORGANISM** a gelatinous covering that surrounds certain microorganisms **5 MEMBRANE SURROUNDING BODY PART** a membrane or sac enclosing an organ or body part **6 WHITE MATTER IN BRAIN** a layer of white fibres in the forebrain **7** AEROSP = **space capsule 8 EJECTABLE COCKPIT** a sealed cockpit in an aircraft that can be ejected in an emergency **9 SEAL ON CONTAINER** a protective seal such as the metal, plastic, or wax covering that protects the cork of a wine bottle **10 SHORT SUMMARY** a very brief summary ■ *adj* **1 VERY BRIEF** expressed in an extremely brief or highly condensed way **2 COMPACT** very small or compact ■ *vt US* = **capsulize** [Mid-17C. Via French < Latin *capsula* 'little box' < *capsa* 'box' < *capere* 'take'.] — **capsulate** /kápsyoo layt/ *adj* —**capsulation** /kápsyoo láysh'n/ *n*

capsulize /káp syoo līz/ (**-izes, -izing, -ized**), **capsulise** (**-ises, -ising, -ised**) *vt* to put something into a capsule or into the form of a capsule

capsulotomy /kápsyoo lóttəmi/ (*plural* **-mies**) *n* a surgical procedure involving cutting into the capsule surrounding a body part, e.g. that of the lens of the eye in the removal of a cataract

Capt. *abbr* Captain

captain /káptin/ *n* **1 SAILOR IN COMMAND** the commander of a ship **2 PILOT IN COMMAND** the person in command of a civil aircraft **3 NAVY OFFICER** a naval officer of a rank above commander **4 OFFICER IN CANADIAN FORCES** an officer in the Royal Canadian Army or Air force of a rank above lieutenant **5 OFFICER IN BRITISH FORCES** an officer in the British Army or Royal Marines of a rank above lieutenant **6 TEAM LEADER** a leader of a team in a sport or game **7 IMPORTANT PERSON** an influential leader in a field or organization **8 HEAD BOY OR GIRL** a senior pupil chosen to represent a school and sometimes given certain supervisory or disciplinary responsibilities **9 SUPERVISOR** a title sometimes given to somebody who supervises others ■ *vt* **COMMAND** to be the captain of something [14C. Via late Old French *capitain* < late Latin *capitaneus* 'chief' < Latin *caput* 'head'.] —**captaincy** *n*

Captain Cooker *n NZ* a wild pig (*informal*) [Late 19C. After Captain James COOK, whose crew released pigs into the wild in New Zealand.]

captain's chair *n* a wooden chair with a saddle seat and a low curved back and arms supported on vertical spindles

captain's mast *n* a disciplinary hearing at which a captain or commanding officer of a navy ship or force hears and acts on cases against enlisted personnel

captan /káp tan/ *n* $C_9H_8Cl_3NO_2S$ an agricultural fungicide in the form of a white powder, used on fruits, flowers, and vegetables [Mid-20C. Shortening of MERCAPTAN.]

caption /kápsh'n/ *n* **1 DESCRIPTION OF ILLUSTRATION** a short description or title accompanying an illustration in a printed text **2 FILM OR TELEVISION SUBTITLE** a printed explanation in a film or on television, especially a translation of dialogue accompanying a scene or an explanation preceding a scene **3 HEADING OR SUBHEADING** a heading or subheading in a document or article **4 HEADING OF LEGAL DOCUMENT** an attachment to or heading of a legal document that identifies the circumstances of its production and the sources of its authority [14C. < Latin *caption-* 'act of taking' < *capt-*, past participle of *capere* 'take'.] —**caption** *vt* —**captionless** *adj*

captious /kápshəss/ *adj* **1** tending to find fault and make trivial and excessive criticisms **2** intended to confuse or entrap an opponent in an argument [Directly or via French *captieux* < Latin *captiosus* < *caption-* (see CAPTION)] —**captiously** *adv* —**captiousness** *n*

captivate /kápti vayt/ (**-vates, -vating, -vated**) *vt* to attract and hold somebody's attention by charm or other pleasing or irresistible features [Early 16C. < late Latin *captivat-*, past participle of *captivare* 'capture' < Latin *captivus* (see CAPTIVE).] —**captivation** /kápti váysh'n/ *n* —**captivator** *n*

captivating /kápti vayting/ *adj* attracting and holding somebody's attention by charm or other pleasing or irresistible features —**captivatingly** *adv*

captive /káptiv/ *n* **1 PRISONER** a person or animal that is forcibly confined or restrained, especially somebody held prisoner **2 SOMEBODY DOMINATED BY EMOTION** a person gripped by a strong emotion such as love or anger ■ *adj* **1 UNABLE TO ESCAPE** prevented from escaping **2 FORCED TO USE OR ACCEPT** forced by circumstances to buy, accept, or pay attention to something, usually because there is no other option or no means of escape **3 VERY ATTRACTED** irresistibly attracted to somebody or something [15C. < Latin *captivus* < *capt-*, past participle of *capere* 'take'.]

captivity /kap tívvəti/ *n* the state of being a prisoner or a period of time that somebody is held prisoner

captopril /káptəpril/ *n* a drug that blocks the action of a vasoconstrictor (**angiotensin**). Use: control of high blood pressure. [Late 20C. < MERCAPTAN + -O- + PROLINE + *-il* (alteration of -YL).]

captor /káptər/ *n* a person who or animal that takes or holds another person or animal prisoner [Mid-16C. < Latin, < *capt-* (see CAPTIVE).]

⚡**capture** /kápchər/ *vt* (**-tures, -turing, -tured**) **1 TAKE SOMEBODY PRISONER** to catch and then forcibly lock up or restrain a person or animal **2 SEIZE PLACE** to seize or gain control over a place **3 TAKE SOMETHING IN GAME** to win control or gain possession of something in a game or contest **4 DOMINATE SOMEBODY'S THOUGHTS** to enchant or dominate somebody's mind, especially somebody's imagination, or to hold somebody's attention ○ *The stories about travel captured their imaginations most.* **5 REPRESENT SOMETHING ACCURATELY** to describe or represent something, especially something fleeting or intangible, in a lasting medium such as painting, writing, filmmaking, or sculpture **6 GAIN PARTICLE** to gain an additional elementary particle **7 RECORD DATA ON COMPUTER** to record and store data in the memory of a computer or as a computer file ■ *n* **1 BEING TAKEN OR TAKING PRISONER** the act of being captured or of capturing somebody or something **2 SOMEBODY OR SOMETHING CAPTURED** somebody or something that has been captured and held in captivity **3 GAIN OF PARTICLE** a process in which an atom, ion, molecule, or nucleus gains an additional elementary particle, often followed by an emission of radiation **4 RECORDING OF DATA** the recording and storage of data in the memory of a computer or as a computer file **5 DIVERSION OF RIVER OVER TIME** the diversion of the headwaters of one river into the channel of another, brought about by erosion over a long period of time [Mid-16C. Via French < Latin *captura* 'seizure' < *capt-* (see CAPTIVE).] — **capturer** *n*

Capua /káppyoo ə/ town in S Italy. Population: 18,845 (1996).

~~**capuccino**~~ incorrect spelling of **cappuccino**

capuche /kə poósh, -poóch/ *n* a large hood on a cloak, especially the cowl worn by a Capuchin monk [Late 16C. Via obsolete French, < Italian *cappuccio* (see CAPPUCCINO).]

capuchin /kápyoochin, -shin/ *n* **1 capuchin, capuchin monkey** an agile and intelligent long-tailed monkey with a tuft of hair on its head that resembles a monk's cowl. Native to: forests of Central and South America. *Cebus capucinus.* **2** a hooded cloak formerly worn by women [Mid-18C. < CAPUCHIN.]

Capuchin /kápyoochin, -shin/ *n* a member of an independent order of Franciscan friars founded in 1525 in Italy [Late 16C. Via French < Italian *cappuccino* (see CAPPUCCINO).]

capuchin monkey *n* ZOOL = **capuchin** *n.* 1

caput /káypət, káppət/ (*plural* **-pita** /káppitə/) *n* **1** the head (*technical*) **2** the most prominent part of something such as a bodily organ [< Latin]

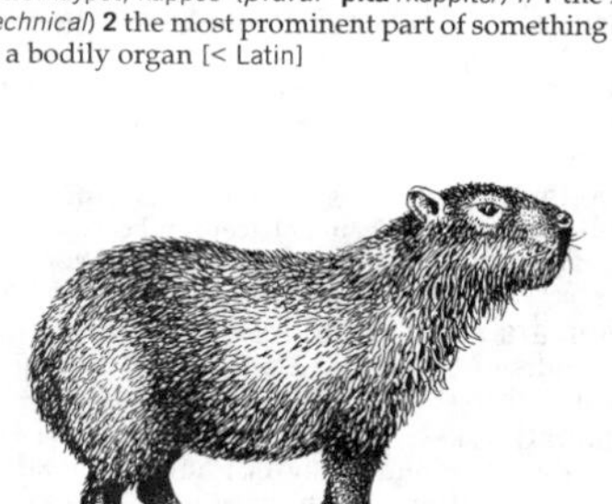

Capybara

capybara /káppi baárə/ (*plural* **-ras** *or* **-ra**) *n* the largest living rodent, resembling a large guinea pig, which can grow to a length of more than 1.2 m/4 ft. Native to: Central and South America. *Hydrochoerus hydrochaeris.* [Early 17C. Via Spanish *capibara* or Portuguese *capivara* < Tupi *capiuára* < *capī* 'grass' + *uára* 'eater'.]

car /kaar/ *n* **1 PASSENGER-CARRYING ROAD VEHICLE** a road vehicle, usually with four wheels and powered by an internal-combustion engine, designed to carry a small number of passengers **2 RAILWAY PASSENGER VEHICLE** a railway vehicle for carrying passengers rather than freight **3 TRAVELLING COMPARTMENT FOR PEOPLE OR THINGS** the part of an airship, balloon, or cable car for carrying passengers and cargo **4** *US* **VEHICLE ON RAILS** a vehicle designed to run on rails, e.g. a tram or a railway carriage or wagon [14C. Via Anglo-Norman, Old French *carre* < Latin *carrum*, *carrus* < Celtic.] —**carful** *n*

car. *abbr* carat

carabid /kárrəbid/ *n* a beetle that lives in the soil. Family: Carabidae. [Late 19C. < modern Latin *Carabidae* < Latin *carabus* 'sea crab' < Greek *karabos* 'horned beetle'.]

carabineer /kárribi neér/, **carabinier** *n* a soldier armed with a lightweight short-barrelled rifle (**carbine**) [Mid-17C. < French *carabinier* < *carabine* (see CARBINE).]

carabiner *n* CLIMBING = **karabiner**

carabinero /kárrəbi nái rō/ (*plural* **-bineros**) *n* **1** a member of the national police force of Spain **2** a customs, coast guard, or revenue officer in the Philippines [Mid-19C. < Spanish, < *carabina* 'carbine' < French *carabine* (see CARBINE).]

carabinier *n* = **carabineer**

carabiniere /kárrə binni áiri/ (*plural* **-ri** /-ri/) *n* a member of the national police force of Italy [Mid-19C. Via Italian < French *carabinier* (see CARABINEER).]

caracal /kárrə kal/ (*plural* **-cals** *or* **-cal**) *n* **1** a medium-sized wildcat with long legs, a smooth reddish-brown coat, a short tail, and long tufted ears. Native to: dry savannas of Africa and S Asia. *Lynx caracal.* **2** the fur of the caracal [Mid-18C. Via French or Spanish < Turkish *karakulak* < *kara* 'black' + *kulak* 'ear'.]

caracara /kárrə kaárə/ *n* a large long-legged carrion-eating or predatory bird of the falcon family. Native to: Central and South America. Genus: *Polyborus.* [Mid-19C. Via Spanish or Portuguese *caracará* < Tupi-Guarani, an imitation of its cry.]

Caracas /kə rákəss/ capital of Venezuela, near the Caribbean coast. Population: 1,964,846 (1992).

carack *n* = **carrack**

caracole /kárrəkōl/, **caracol** *n* in dressage, a half turn to the left or right performed by a horse and rider ■ *vti* (**-coles, -coling, -coled**) to perform or cause a horse to perform a caracole [Early 17C. < French *caracoler* < *caracol(e)* 'snail's shell, spiral'.]

Caractacus /kə ráktəkəss/ (*fl.* AD 50) British tribal ruler

caracul *n* = **karakul**

carafe /kə ráf, kə raáf/ *n* **1** a container with a wide cylindrical base, a narrow neck, and a flared open top, usually made of glass and used to serve liquids, especially wine or water at table **2** the contents or capacity of a carafe [Late 18C. Via French < Italian *caraffa.*]

caramba /kə rámbə/ *interj* used to express surprise, amazement, or dismay (*slang*) [Spanish]

carambola /kárrəm bṓlə/ *n* **1** a smooth, thin-skinned, crisp yellow fruit with lengthways ridges that give it a star-shaped cross section **2** a tropical evergreen tree that bears carambolas. *Averrhoa carambolas.* [Late 16C. < Portuguese, probably < Marathi *karambal.*]

caramel /kárrəmel, -m'l/ *n* **1 BURNT SUGAR** sugar melted or dissolved in a small amount of water and heated until it turns golden or dark brown. It is usually used as a syrup for ice cream and other desserts. **2 CHEWY SWEET** a chewy sweet that can be soft or firm, made with butter, milk, and sugar **3 YELLOWISH-BROWN COLOUR** a yellowish-brown colour ■ *adj* **OF YELLOWISH-BROWN COLOUR** yellowish-brown in colour [Early 18C. Via French < Spanish *caramelo*, alteration of Provençal *canamel* 'sugar cane' < Latin *canna* 'cane' + *mel* 'honey'.]

caramelize /kárrəmə līz/ (**-izes, -izing, -ized**), **caramelise** (**-ises, -ising, -ised**) *vti* to heat sugar or boil dissolved sugar until it turns dark brown, or to undergo this process [Mid-19C. < French *caraméliser* < *caramel* (see CARAMEL).] —**caramelization** /kárrəmə lī záysh'n/ *n*

carangid /kə ránjid, kə ráng gid/ *n* a spiny-finned sea fish of the family that includes the jack and pompano.

Family: Carangidae. [Late 19C. < modern Latin *Carangidae* < *Caranx* < Spanish *caranga* 'shad, horse mackerel'.]

carapace /kárrəpayss/ *n* **1** a thick hard case or shell made of bone or chitin that covers part of the body, especially the back, of an animal such as a crab or turtle **2** self-protection or a disguise that shelters somebody as a shell does a turtle, e.g. shy or arrogant behaviour [Mid-19C. Via French < Spanish *carapacho*.]

carat /kárrət/ *n* **1** a standard unit of mass used for precious stones, especially diamonds, equal to 200 milligrams **2** a unit for expressing the proportion of gold in an alloy on a scale from 1 to 24. US term **karat** [15C. Via French < Greek *keration* 'fruit of the carob' < *keras* 'horn'; because carob beans were used as standard weights for small quantities.]

SPELLCHECK Do not confuse ***carat*** with ***carrot***, which has a similar sound. Beware: your spellchecker will not catch this error.

Caravaggio /kárrə vájji ō/, **Michelangelo Merisi da** (1573–1610) Italian painter

caravan /kárrə van/ *n* **1 UNPOWERED VEHICLE FOR LIVING IN** a large vehicle equipped for living in, and designed to be towed by another vehicle. US term **trailer 2 VEHICLE FOR LIVING IN** a large covered vehicle or van used as a travelling home, particularly by Roma people or circus performers **3 GROUP OF DESERT MERCHANTS WITH CAMELS** a group of traders, especially in N Africa and Asia, crossing the desert together for safety, usually with a train of camels **4 GROUP OF TRAVELLERS** a group of people, vehicles, or supervised animals that are travelling together for security ■ *vi* (**-vans, -vanning, -vanned**) **SPEND TIME IN CARAVAN** to holiday or travel about in a caravan [Late 16C. Via French *caravane* < Persian *kārvān* 'group of desert travellers'.] —**caravanner** *n*

caravanning /kárrə vanning/ *n* travelling or staying in a caravan for pleasure or a holiday

caravanserai /kárrə vánssərī/ (*plural* **-rais**), **caravansary** (*plural* **-ries**) *n* **1** a large inn with a central courtyard, found in some eastern countries and used by caravans crossing the desert **2** = **caravan** *n.* **3**, **caravan** *n.* **4** [Late 16C. < Persian *kārwānsarāī* < *kārwān* (see CARAVAN) + *sarāī* 'inn' (see SERAI).]

caravel /kárrə vel/, **carvel** /kaárv'l/ *n* a light sailing ship with two or three masts, used in the Mediterranean from the 14th to the 17th centuries [Early 16C. < French *caravelle*.]

caraway /kárrə way/ *n* **1** a plant with finely divided leaves that bears caraway seeds. Flowers: small, white or pinkish, in clusters. Native to: Europe, Asia. *Carum carvi*. **2** FOOD = **caraway seed** *n.* [13C. Directly or via Old French *carvi* < medieval Latin *carui*.]

caraway seed *n* the aromatic dried ripe fruit of the caraway plant, used as a spice for flavouring a variety of sweet and savoury foods

carb[1] /kaarb/ *n* a carburettor (*informal*) [Mid-20C. Shortening.]

carb[2] /kaarb/ *n* a carbohydrate or a high-carbohydrate food (*slang*) [Mid-20C. Shortening of CARBOHYDRATE.]

carb- *prefix* CHEM = **carbo-** (*before vowels*)

carbamate /kaárbə mayt/ *n* any salt or ester of carbamic acid. Use: pesticides. [Mid-19C. < CARBO- + AMIDE.]

carbamazepine /kaárbə mázzə peen/ *n* an analgesic, anticonvulsant drug. Use: treatment of epilepsy, pain, manic-depressive psychosis. [Rearrangement of *dibenzazepinecarboxamide*]

carbamic acid /kaar bámmik-/ *n* NH_2COOH an acid that exists only in the form of its salt or ester [< CARBO- + AMIDE]

carbamide /kaárbə mīd/ *n* CHEM = **urea** [Mid-19C. < CARBO- + AMIDE.]

carbanion /kaár bánn ī ən/ *n* an organic ion that has a carbon atom with a negative charge [Mid-20C. < CARB- + ANION.]

carbaryl /kaárbə ril/ *n* an insecticide used as a substitute for DDT in a broad range of applications [Mid-20C. Blend of CARBAMATE + ARYL.]

carbene /kaár been/ *n* a highly reactive, short-lived molecule containing a carbon atom with only three bonds

carbenicillin /kaár bénni síllin/ *n* an antibiotic derived from penicillin [Contraction of *carb(boxy)ben(zylpen)icillin*]

carbide /kaár bīd/ *n* **1** a compound containing carbon and one other element, especially a metal **2** CHEM = **calcium carbide** [Mid-19C. < CARBON.]

carbimazole /kaar bímmə zōl/ *n* a drug that inhibits the formation of thyroid hormones. Use: management of hyperthyroidism.

carbine /kaár bīn/ *n* a lightweight rifle with a short barrel [Early 17C. < French *carabine* < *carabin* 'mounted musketeer'.]

carbineer /kaárbi neér/ *n* = **carabineer**

carbinol /kaárbi nol/ *n* CHEM = **methanol** [Mid-19C. < CARBON + -INE + -OL.]

carbo /kaábō/ (*plural* **-bos**) *n* carbohydrate (*slang*) ○ *pasta is a good source of carbo* [Shortening]

carbo- *prefix* carbon, carbonic ○ *carbocyclic* [< French < *carbone* (see CARBON)]

carbocyclic /kaárbō síklik/ *adj* describes a chemical compound containing a closed ring of carbon atoms

carbohydrase /kaárbō hī drayz/ *n* any enzyme that aids the breakdown of a carbohydrate [Early 20C. < CARBOHYDRATE.]

carbohydrate /kaárbō hī drayt/ *n* **1** a biological compound containing carbon, hydrogen, and oxygen that is an important source of food and energy **2** food containing carbohydrates

carbohydrate loading *n* a controversial practice of first starving the body of carbohydrates, then following a high-carbohydrate diet just before an athletic event in an attempt to increase performance

carbolic /kaar bóllik/ *n* carbolic acid [Mid-19C. < CARBO- + -OL + -IC.]

carbolic acid *n* CHEM = **phenol** *n.* **1**

carbo-loading /kaárbō-/ *n* carbohydrate loading (*slang*)

car bomb *n* an explosive device concealed inside or under a vehicle and detonated by remote control or when the engine is started

car-bomb *vt* to place a car bomb in or under a vehicle, or use such an explosive-laden vehicle against a target

carbon /kaárbən/ *n* **1 NONMETALLIC CHEMICAL ELEMENT** (*symbol* **C**) a nonmetallic element that exists in two main forms, diamond and graphite, and has the ability to form large numbers of organic compounds. Source: coal, petroleum. **2 CARBON COPY** a carbon copy of a document (*informal*) **3 CARBON PAPER** carbon paper (*informal*) **4 ELECTRICAL COMPONENT MADE OF CARBON** something made of carbon, especially an electrode or a lamp filament [Late 18C. Via French *carbone* < Latin *carbon-* 'coal'.] —**carbonous** *adj*

carbon 12 *n* an isotope of carbon with relative atomic mass of 12. Use: as a baseline in determining atomic mass.

carbon 14 *n* a naturally radioactive isotope of carbon with atomic mass of 14 and a half-life of 5780 years. Use: tracer, carbon dating.

carbon-14 dating, carbon-14 method *n* ARCHAEOL = **carbon dating**

carbonaceous /kaárbə náyshəss/ *adj* relating to, containing, or resembling carbon

carbonade /kaárbə náyd, -naád/, **carbonnade** *n* a stew made with beef and onions cooked in beer [Mid-17C. < French < *carbone* (see CARBON).]

carbonado /kaárbə náydō, -naádō/ (*plural* **-dos** *or* **-does**) *n* a dark diamond or cluster of diamonds. Use: drilling, polishing. [Mid-19C. < Portuguese.]

carbonara /kaárbə naárə/ *n* a hot pasta dish prepared with eggs, chopped ham or bacon, and cheese ○ *spaghetti carbonara* [Mid-20C. < Italian (*alla*) *carbonara* 'on the charcoal grill' < *carbone* 'charcoal' < Latin *carbon-* 'coal'.]

carbon arc *n* an electric discharge between two carbon electrodes or between an electrode and a metal to be welded, characterized by bright light and intense heat

Carbonari /kaárbə naári/ *npl* members of a secret society in early 19th-century Italy that aimed to establish a unified liberal republican government [Early 19C. < Italian, plural of *carbonaro* 'charcoal burner' < Latin *carbon-* 'coal'; from their use of symbols from the charcoal-burning trade.]

carbonate *n* /kaárbə nayt, -nət/ **1 SALT OR ESTER OF CARBONIC ACID** salt or ester of carbonic acid **2 MINERAL COMPOSED OF CARBONATES** a mineral composed of carbonates ■ *vt* /kaárbə nayt/ (**-ates, -ating, -ated**) **1 CONVERT TO CARBONATE** to convert a chemical compound into a carbonate **2 MAKE LIQUID FIZZY** to make a liquid fizzy by introducing carbon dioxide into it **3** CHEM = **carbonize** *v.* **1** —**carbonation** /kaárbə náysh'n/ *n* —**carbonator** *n*

carbonate platform *n* a broad extensive belt-like deposit of carbonate materials created in shallow warm oceanic waters during the Cambrian period

carbonatite /kaar bónnə tīt/ *n* an unusual alkaline igneous rock high in carbonate materials, found in E Africa and thought to derive from the Earth's mantle [Early 20C. < CARBONATE.]

carbon bisulphide *n* CHEM = **carbon disulphide**

carbon black *n* a form of finely divided carbon. Source: partial combustion of petroleum or natural gas. Use: manufacture of pigment, ink, rubber.

carbon brush *n* a block of carbon in an engine or generator that conveys current between the moving and the stationary parts

carbon copy *n* **1** a duplicate of written or drawn material that is made by using carbon paper **2** somebody or something that is identical to or very like somebody or something else (*informal*) ○ *This situation is a carbon copy of last year's crisis.*

carbon cycle *n* **1** the exchange of carbon between living organisms and the environment **2** a chain reaction believed to generate significant energy in some stars, in which carbon is used as a catalyst to fuse four hydrogen nuclei into one helium nucleus

carbon dating *n* a method of dating organic remains based on their content of carbon 14

carbon dioxide *n* CO_2 a heavy colourless odourless atmospheric gas. Source: respiration, combustion. Use: during photosynthesis, in refrigeration, carbonated drinks, fire extinguishers.

carbon disulphide *n* CS_2 a colourless poisonous flammable liquid containing impurities that give it a rotten-egg smell. Use: solvents, fumigants, manufacture of Cellophane and rayon.

carbon fibre *n* a very strong light carbonized acrylic thread. Use: reinforcing resins, metals, and ceramics, and making turbine blades.

carbon fixation *n* the process by which plants synthesize carbon dioxide into organic compounds

carbonic /kaar bónnik/ *adj* containing carbon

carbonic acid *n* H_2CO_3 a weak acid. Source: dissolving of carbon dioxide in water.

carbonic anhydrase /-an hīdrayz, -drayss/ *n* an enzyme in living tissue, e.g. blood cells, that contains zinc and aids the transfer of carbon dioxide from the tissues to the lungs

carboniferous /kaárbə níffərəss/ *adj* containing or yielding coal or carbon

Carboniferous *n* the period of geological time when true reptiles first appeared and when much of the Earth's surface was covered by forests, 362.5 million to 290 million years ago [Because numerous coal deposits were formed] —**Carboniferous** *adj*

carbonisation *n* = **carbonization**

carbonise *vti* = **carbonize**

carbonium ion /kaar bōni əm-/ *n* an organic ion that has a carbon atom bearing a positive charge [Early 20C. < CARBO-, after AMMONIUM.]

carbonization /kaárbən ī záysh'n/, **carbonisation** *n* **1** the burning, fossilization, or chemical treatment of something that turns it into carbon **2** the process of covering or coating something with carbon **3** CHEM = **destructive distillation**

carbonize /kaárbə nīz/ (**-izes, -izing, -ized**), **carbonise** (**-ises, -ising, -ised**) *v* **1** *vti* to turn into carbon, or turn something into carbon, by partial burning, by fossilization, or through chemical treatment **2** *vt* to cover or coat the surface of something with carbon —**carbonizer** *n*

carbon microphone *n* a microphone containing carbon granules that change resistance according to the vibrating pressure of sound waves, thereby modulating the frequency of the sound waves

carbon monoxide *n* CO a colourless odourless toxic gas. Source: the burning of carbon-containing compounds or fuels with insufficient air.

carbonnade *n* = **carbonade**

carbon-nitrogen cycle *n* CHEM = **carbon cycle** *n.* 2

carbon paper *n* paper used for making copies, coated on one side with a waxy pigment that often contains carbon

carbon process, carbon printing *n* a printing process that uses sensitized carbon tissue to produce positive prints

carbon sink *n* a forest or other area of vegetation that absorbs large quantities of carbon dioxide from the atmosphere, especially one planted specifically for this purpose

carbon star *n* a star that has a lower temperature and proportionately more carbon in relation to nitrogen than other stars

carbon steel *n* steel containing carbon with properties that vary according to the carbon content

carbon tetrachloride *n* CCl_4 a colourless nonflammable toxic liquid. Use: as a solvent, refrigerant, drycleaning agent, in fire extinguishers.

carbon value *n* a measurement of the extent to which a lubricant forms carbon when in use

carbonyl /kaárbə nil, -nīl/ *adj* relating to or containing the group of atoms =C=O found in certain organic and inorganic compounds ■ *n* a compound that has a metal bound to a carbonyl group —**carbonylic** /kaárbə níllik/ *adj*

carbonyl chloride *n* = **phosgene**

car boot sale *n* a sale of second-hand and new goods from the boots of people's cars, usually taking place on an open-air site hired for the purpose

carborundum /kaárbə rúndəm/ *n* an abrasive composed of silicon carbide

carboxy- *prefix* carboxyl ○ *carboxypeptidase* [< CARBOXYL]

carboxyhaemoglobin /kaar bóksi heémə glṓbin/ *n* a compound formed when inhaled carbon monoxide binds to haemoglobin

carboxylase /kaar bóksi layz, -layss/ *n* an enzyme that aids the transfer of carbon dioxide

carboxylate *n* /kaar bóksi layt, -lət/ any salt or ester of a carboxylic acid ■ *vt* /kaar bóksi layt/ (**-lates, -lating, -lated**) to form carboxylic acid by introducing a carboxyl group or carbon dioxide into a compound —**carboxylation** /kaar bóksi láysh'n/ *n*

carboxylic acid /kaár bok síllik-/ *n* any organic acid that contains the carboxyl group

carboxymethylcellulose /kaar bóksi meé thīl séllyoō lōss, -méthil-/ *n* a derivative of cellulose. Use: paper production, food processing, medicines.

carboxypeptidase /kaar bóksi pépti dayz/ *n* a protein-digesting enzyme secreted from the pancreas

carboy /kaár boy/ *n* a large container made of plastic or glass, usually protected by a wooden casing. Use: to hold corrosive liquids such as acids. [Mid-18C. < Persian *karāba* 'large glass flagon'.]

carbuncle /kaár bungk'l/ *n* **1** a multiple-headed boil **2** a red gemstone, especially a garnet, that is smoothly rounded and polished [13C. Via Old French *charbu(n)cle* < Latin *carbunculus* 'small coal' < *carbon-* 'coal'.] —**carbuncled** *adj* —**carbuncular** /kaar búng kyoōlər/ *adj*

carburation /kaárbyoō ráysh'n/, **carburetion** /-résh'n/ *n* the process of mixing the correct proportions of liquid fuel with air to achieve combustion [Late 19C. < CARBURET.]

carburet /kaárbyoō ret, kaárbyoō rét/ (**-rets, -retting, -retted**) *vt* to mix a gas with hydrocarbons in order to increase fuel energy [Early 19C. < obsolete *carburet* 'carbide' < CARBO- + *-uret*, chemical suffix < modern Latin *-uretum*.]

carburetor *n* US = **carburettor**

carburetted /kaár byoō réttid, kaárbə réttid/ *adj* fitted with a carburettor

carburettor /kaár byoō réttər, kaárbə réttər/, **carburetter** *n* a device in an internal combustion engine that mixes liquid fuel and air in the correct proportions, vaporizes them, and transfers the mixture to the cylinders [Mid-19C. < CARBURET.]

carburize /kaár byoō rīz, -bə-/ (**-rizes, -rizing, -rized**), **carburise** (**-rises, -rising, -rised**) *vt* CHEM = **carbonize** *v.* 2 [Mid-19C. < CARBURET.] —**carburization** /kaár byoō rī záysh'n, -bə-/ *n*

carcass /kaárkəss/, **carcase** *n* **1** DEAD BODY OF ANIMAL the dead body of an animal, especially one slaughtered and prepared for use as meat **2** PERSON a living person's body (*humorous*) ○ *Move your carcass!* **3** REMAINS the remains of something decayed or almost totally destroyed **4** BASIC STRUCTURE the basic structure or framework of something [14C. < Anglo-Norman *carcois*, French *carcasse*.]

Carcassonne /kaárkə són/ capital of Aude Department, SW France. Population: 44,991 (1990).

carcass trade *n* the reconstruction of old worn-out pieces of furniture that are then passed off as valuable antiques (*slang*)

Carchemish /kaár kə mísh/ ancient city on the River Euphrates, in present-day N Syria

carcin- *prefix* MED = **carcino-** (*before vowels*)

carcino- *prefix* cancer ○ *carcinogenic* [< Greek *karkinos* 'crab, cancer']

carcinogen /kaar sínnəjən, kaárssinə jen/ *n* a substance or agent that can cause cancer [Mid-19C. < CARCINOMA.]

carcinogenesis /kaárssinō jénnəssiss/ *n* the production of cancerous cells [Early 20C. Blend of CARCINOMA + GENESIS.]

carcinogenic /kaárssinō jénnik/ *adj* capable of causing cancer [Early 20C. < CARCINOMA.] —**carcinogenicity** /kaárssinōjə níssəti/ *n*

carcinoid /kaárssi noyd/ *n* a small benign or malignant tumour on the walls of the small intestine [Early 20C. < CARCINOMA.]

carcinoma /kaárssi nṓmə/ *n* a malignant tumour that starts in the surface layer (**epithelium**) of an organ or body part and may spread to other parts of the body [Early 18C. Via Latin < Greek *karkinōma* < *karkinos* 'crab'; from the pattern of the surrounding blood vessels.] —**carcinomatoid** *adj* —**carcinomatous** *adj*

carcinomatosis /kaárssi nṓmə tṓssiss/ *n* a condition in which cancer has spread widely throughout the body

carcinosarcoma /kaárssinō saar kṓmə/ (*plural* **-mas** *or* **-mata** /-kṓmətə/) *n* a malignant tumour containing elements of both a carcinoma and a sarcoma

carcinosis /kaárssi nṓssiss/ *n* = **carcinomatosis**

car coat *n* an overcoat that ends at mid-thigh

ϟ **card**[1] /kaard/ *n* **1** STIFF PAPER stiff paper or thin cardboard **2** PAPER WITH PICTURES AND GREETINGS a folded piece of stiff paper with illustrations, used to send greetings, e.g., at birthdays **3** PRINTED STIFF PAPER FOR GAMES a small piece of stiff paper, part of a set, that is printed with symbols or figures and used to play games or tell fortunes **4** STIFF PAPER SHOWING IDENTITY a small piece of stiff paper or plastic that shows somebody's identity, business position, or membership in a club or organization **5** PLASTIC CARD HOLDING INFORMATION a small piece of plastic that holds information in a magnetic strip or microprocessor, used in financial activities such as getting cash from cash machines or making phone calls **6** = **postcard** **7** SPORTS = **racecard** **8** AMUSING PERSON an amusing or eccentric person (*dated informal*) **9** COLLECTABLE STIFF PAPER WITH PICTURE a piece of stiff paper with a picture on one side, collected as part of a set of such items **10** PUNCH CARD a punch card **11** PRINTED CIRCUIT BOARD a printed circuit board **12** NAVIG = **compass card** **13** COMPUT = **expansion card** **14 cards** *n* GAME USING CARDS game played using playing cards (+ *singular verb*) ■ *vt* (*informal*) **1** *US* ASK FOR IDENTIFICATION to ask somebody to show identification, usually to check that the person is of legal age to drink alcohol or be admitted somewhere **2** RECORD A GOLF SCORE to record a score after playing a hole or round of golf [15C. Via French *carte* < Latin *c(h)arta* 'papyrus leaf' < Greek *khartēs*.] ◇ **have** *or* **keep a card up your sleeve** to have a secret plan or tactic ready to be used if necessary (*informal*) ◇ **get** *or* **be given your cards** to be dismissed from your job (*informal*) ◇ **on the cards** likely to happen (*informal*) ○ *The collapse of the banking giant had been on the cards for some time.* ◇ **play your cards close to your chest** *or* **vest** to be secretive about plans, thoughts, or feelings (*informal*) ◇ **play your cards right** to take the fullest possible advantage of your chances of success (*informal*) ◇ **put** *or* **lay your cards on the table** to reveal openly what your intentions and plans are (*informal*) ◇ **see how the cards stack up** to find out what are the chances of success or otherwise

card[2] /kaard/ *vt* to comb out and clean wool, cotton, or other fibres before spinning ■ *n* a tool or machine with wire teeth used to comb out or clean wool, cotton, or other fibres before spinning [14C. Via French < late Latin *cardus* 'thistle' < Latin *carduus*.] —**carder** *n*

Card. *abbr* Cardinal

card- *prefix* MED = **cardio-**

cardamom /kaárdəməm/, **cardamon** /-mən/, **cardamum** /-məm/ *n* **1** the aromatic pods and seeds of a tropical plant, used whole or crushed as a spice or flavouring **2** a perennial tropical plant with large hairy leaves that bears cardamom pods. Flowers: small, white, in clusters. *Elettaria cardamomum.* [14C. Directly or via French < Latin *cardamomum* < Greek *kardamōmon* < *kardamon* 'cress' + *amōmon* 'amomum'.]

cardan joint /kaád'n-/ *n* a universal joint that can rotate when out of alignment [Early 20C. After Gerolamo *Cardano* (1501–76), Italian mathematician.]

cardan shaft /kaád'n-/ *n* part of the transmission system in some vehicles [See CARDAN JOINT]

cardboard /kaárd bawrd/ *n* a stiff light material made from wastepaper pulp, often used for making containers or packaging for goods

cardboard city *n* an area in a city where homeless people gather to sleep, often using large cardboard boxes as shelter (*informal*)

card-carrying *adj* officially listed as belonging to an organization and subscribing to its beliefs

card catalog *n* *US* COMM, LIBRARIES = **card index**

card file *n* COMM, LIBRARIES = **card index**

cardholder /kaárd hōldər/ *n* an owner of a card that carries information, especially a credit, debit, bank, or phone card

cardi- *prefix* MED = **cardio-**

cardia /kaárdi ə/ (*plural* **-ae** /-ee/ *or* **-as**) *n* the opening of the oesophagus into the stomach [Late 18C. < Greek *kardia* 'heart'.]

cardiac /kaárdi ak/ *adj* **1** relating to or affecting the heart **2** relating to the upper part of the stomach, where it is connected to the oesophagus [Early 17C. Via French < Latin *cardiacus* < Greek *kardia* 'heart'.]

cardiac arrest *n* the sudden stopping of the heartbeat and therefore of the pumping action of the heart

cardiac compression, cardiac massage *n* rhythmic compression of somebody's heart in order to restore or maintain blood circulation after the person has had a heart attack. ◊ **CPR**

cardiac output *n* the amount of blood pumped by the heart over a given time period

cardialgia /kaárdi álji ə, -áljə/ *n* **1** heartburn (*technical*) **2** pain in or near the heart [Mid-17C. Via modern Latin < Greek *kardialgia* < *kardia* 'heart'.]

cardie /kaárdi/, **cardy** (*plural* **-ies**) *n* a cardigan (*informal*) [Mid-20C. Shortening.]

Cardiff /kaár dif/ capital and largest city of Wales. Population: 315,040 (1996 estimate). Welsh **Caerdydd**

cardigan /kaárdigən/ *n* a long-sleeved knitted jacket that fastens up the front [Mid-19C. After James Thomas Brudenell, 7th Earl of *Cardigan* (1797–1868), British soldier and politician.]

Cardigan Bay /kaárdigən-/ large bay on the coast of W Wales. Length: 105 km/65 mi.

Cardiganshire /kaárdigənshər/ former county of Wales

Cardin /kaár daN/, **Pierre** (*b.* 1922) Italian-born French fashion designer

cardinal /kaárdinəl, -d'nəl/ *n* **1** ROMAN CATHOLIC DIGNITARY in the Roman Catholic Church, one of the group of clergy, next in rank to the pope, who elect the pope from their own number and act as his advisers **2** DEEP RED a deep strong red colour, like that of the robes of a cardinal **3** BRIGHT RED N AMERICAN BIRD a crested finch, the male of which has bright red plumage with a black face. Native to: North America. *Cardinalis cardinalis.* **4** MATH = **cardinal number** **5** WOMAN'S HOODED CAPE a woman's short cape with a hood, originally scarlet in colour, that was worn in the 17th and 18th centuries ■ *adj* **1** IMPORTANT fundamentally important **2** BRIGHT RED bright red in colour [12C. Via French < medieval Latin *cardinalis* < Latin *cardin-* 'hinge'.] —**cardinally** *adv*

cardinalate /kaárdinəl ayt, -d'nəl-/, **cardinalship** /-ship/ *n* **1** ALL CARDINALS the cardinals of the Roman Catholic Church regarded collectively **2** TERM OF OFFICE OF CARDINAL the term of office of a Roman Catholic cardinal **3** OFFICE OF CARDINAL the rank or office of a Roman Catholic cardinal

cardinal flower *n* a perennial lobelia. Flowers: brilliantly coloured, usually red, in clusters. Native to: central and E North America. *Lobelia cardinalis.*

cardinal number *n* a number, such as 4 or 42, used to denote quantity but not order

cardinal point *n* any of the four principal points of the compass, North, South, East, or West

cardinalship *n* RELIG = **cardinalate**

cardinal virtue *n* any of the principal virtues in the classical or Christian traditions

cardinal vowels *npl* a fixed set of vowel sounds, based on the position of the tongue and the shape of the mouth cavity, and spaced at approximately equal acoustic intervals

card index *n* an alphabetical listing of items such as names and addresses or books in a library, with each item on a separate card. US term **card catalog**

cardio- *prefix* heart ○ *cardiopulmonary* [< Greek *kardia*]

cardioaccelerator /kaárdi ō ək séllə raytər/ *n* a drug or other agent that increases the heart rate —**cardioacceleration** /kaárdi ō ək séllə ráysh'n/ *n*

cardiogenic /kaárdi ō jénnik/ *adj* resulting from activity or disease of the heart

cardiogram /kaárdi ə gram/ *n* a graphic record made by a cardiograph, especially an electrocardiogram

cardiograph /kaárdi ə graaf, -graf/ *n* an instrument for recording heart activity, used in the diagnosis of heart disorders —**cardiographer** /kaárdi óggrəfər/ *n* —**cardiographic** /kaárdi ə gráffik/ *adj* —**cardiographical** /-gráffik'l/ *adj* —**cardiographically** *adv* —**cardiography** *n*

cardiology /kaárdi ólləji/ *n* a branch of medicine dealing with the diagnosis and treatment of heart disorders and related conditions —**cardiological** /kaárdi ə lójjik'l/ *adj* —**cardiologist** *n*

cardiomegaly /kaárdi ō méggəli/ *n* pathological enlargement of the heart

cardiomyopathy /kaárdi ō mī óppəthi/ (*plural* **-thies**) *n* a disease of the heart muscle, usually chronic and with an unknown or obscure cause

cardiopathy /kaárdi óppəthi/ (*plural* **-thies**) *n* a heart disease or disorder

cardiopulmonary /kaárdi ō púlmənəri, -pŏŏl-/ *adj* relating to both the heart and the lungs

cardiopulmonary bypass *n* a procedure by which the blood is artificially circulated and oxygenated by a heart-lung machine so that surgery may be carried out on the heart

cardiopulmonary resuscitation *n* an emergency technique to revive somebody whose heart has stopped beating that involves clearing the person's airways and then alternating heart compression with mouth-to-mouth respiration

cardiorespiratory /kaárdi ō rə spírrətəri, -rə spīrətəri, -réspərətəri/ *adj* relating to both the heart and the respiratory system

cardiothoracic /kaárdi ō thaw rássik/ *adj* relating to both the heart and the chest

cardiovascular /kaárdi ō váskyŏŏlər/ *adj* relating to both the heart and the blood vessels

carditis /kaar dītiss/ *n* inflammation of the heart [Late 18C. < Greek *kardia* 'heart'.]

-cardium *suffix* part of the heart ○ *endocardium* [Via modern Latin < Greek *kardia* 'heart']

cardoon /kaar dŏŏn/ (*plural* **-doon** *or* **-doons**) *n* a large perennial plant related to the artichoke with spiny leaves and edible roots and leafstalks. Native to: S Europe. *Cynara cardunculus.* [Early 17C. Via French *cardon* < Latin *carduus* 'thistle'.]

cardphone /kaárd fōn/ *n* a payphone operated by a phonecard

cardsharp /kaárd shaarp/, **cardsharper** /-shaarpər/ *n* a regular cheater at cards —**cardsharping** *n*

card table *n* a small table, usually folding and covered with green baize, used for playing card games

cardy *n* = **cardie**

care /kair/ *v* (**cares, caring, cared**) **1** *vti* BE CONCERNED to be interested or concerned ○ *I said I couldn't care less if he did leave.* **2** *vi* FEEL AFFECTION AND CONCERN to feel affection or love and concern for somebody **3** *vi* LOOK AFTER to look after or supervise somebody or something **4** *vi* LIKE OR WANT to like or be in favour of something (*formal*) ○ *Would you care for dessert, sir?* ■ *n* **1** UPKEEP the process of maintaining something in good condition ○ *a skin care treatment* **2** CAREFUL ATTENTION careful attention to avoid damage or error **3** WORRY a worry or cause for anxiety ○ *without a care in the world* **4** ATTENTIVE TREATMENT the providing of whatever is needed for somebody's well-being, e.g. somebody dependent, or physically or mentally disabled ○ *responsible for the 20 children in her care* ○ *residential care* **5** RESPONSIBILITY OF LOCAL AUTHORITY FOR CHILD the custody and maintenance of a child as the legal responsibility of a local authority after a court order ○ *She went to prison and her children were taken into care.* [Old English *caru* 'sorrow' < Indo-European] ◇ **care of** into the temporary possession of an addressee who will ensure that the specified item will be delivered to the intended recipient ○ *sent the letter to her care of her parents* ◇ **take care 1** to behave prudently, with regard for your own safety **2** used as an affectionate farewell to somebody (*informal*) ◇ **take care of 1** to provide for the needs of somebody or something **2** to deal with somebody or something effectively

SYNONYMS See *worry.*

CARE /kair/ *abbr* Cooperative for American Relief Everywhere

care and maintenance *n* the condition in which a site such as a factory, shipyard, or machinery is kept when it is ready for immediate use at any time

care attendant *n* somebody employed to look after people in a variety of settings such as retirement or nursing homes

careen /kə reén/ *v* **1** *vi* SWAY OR SWERVE WHILE MOVING to move forwards at high speed, swaying, lurching, or swerving from one side to the other ○ *a motorcycle careening around sharp curves* **2** *vi US* RUSH to rush pell-mell ○ *He seemed to careen from one job to the next.* **3** *vti* TURN BOAT ON SIDE to turn over onto the side, or turn a boat over on its side, especially for repairs or cleaning **4** *vi* HEEL IN THE WIND to heel over to one side while sailing [Late 16C. Via French *carène* < Latin *carina* 'keel, nutshell'.] —**careener** *n*

career /kə reér/ *n* **1** LONG-TERM OR LIFELONG JOB a job or occupation regarded as a long-term or lifelong activity **2** PROFESSIONAL PROGRESS somebody's progress in a chosen profession or during that person's working life **3** GENERAL PROGRESS the general path or progress taken by somebody or something ○ *a piece of legislation whose career is rich with conflicting amendments* **4** RAPID FORWARD LURCHING MOTION a rushing onwards while lurching or swaying ■ *adj* PROFESSIONAL FOR LIFE trained for and expecting to work in a particular occupation for an entire working life rather than briefly ○ *a career diplomat* ■ *vi* LURCH RAPIDLY ONWARDS to rush forwards while lurching or swaying [Mid-16C. Via French *carrière* < Latin *carrus* (see CAR).]

LITERARY LINK ***My Brilliant Career,*** a novel (1901) by Australian writer Miles Franklin. It is an account of a young girl's struggle to choose between an independent career and a comfortable life as the wife of a wealthy landowner.

careerism /kə reérizəm/ *n* the behaviour of somebody whose motivation is career advancement —**careerist** *n*

careers officer *n* somebody whose job is to advise secondary pupils on possible careers and jobs as they approach school leaving age

career woman *n* a woman who has a career or who takes her working life seriously

carefree /káir free/ *adj* having no worries or responsibilities —**carefreeness** *n*

careful /káirf'l/ *adj* **1** CAUTIOUS acting with caution and attention **2** PAINSTAKING showing close attention to accuracy and detail **3** NOT OVERSPENDING OR BEING WASTEFUL ensuring that money or resources are not spent or used wastefully or without thought **4** WATCHFUL watchful and protective about something —**carefully** *adj* —**carefulness** *n*

SYNONYMS ***careful, conscientious, scrupulous, thorough, meticulous, painstaking, assiduous, punctilious, finicky, fussy***

CORE MEANING: exercising care and attention in doing something

careful a wide-ranging term, suggesting attention to detail and implying cautiousness in avoiding errors or inaccuracies; **conscientious** showing great care, attention, and industriousness in carrying out a task; **scrupulous** having or showing careful regard for what is morally right; **thorough** extremely careful and accurate; **meticulous** extremely careful and precise; **painstaking** involving or showing great care and attention to detail; **assiduous** undeviating in effort and care; **punctilious** very careful about the conventions of correct behaviour and etiquette; **finicky** concentrating too much on unimportant details; **fussy** tending to worry over details or trivial things.

~~carefull~~ incorrect spelling of **careful**

caregiver /káir givvər/ *n US* **1** SOC WELFARE = **carer 2** a medical or other professional who assists in the management of an illness or disability —**caregiving** *n*

~~careing~~ incorrect spelling of **caring**

care in the community *n* a British government policy of reintegrating people with a history of psychiatric disorders into their communities by moving them from long-stay institutions to their families or community centres

care label *n* a label, sewn onto a piece of clothing or other item, that gives cleaning instructions for the item

careless /káirləss/ *adj* **1** NOT GIVING CAREFUL ATTENTION not giving enough careful attention to the details of something **2** SHOWING NO CONCERN disregarding or showing no concern about something **3** NOT CAREFULLY WORKED ON not carefully worked on or practised, but done or assumed easily and naturally —**carelessly** *adv*

carelessness /káirləssnəss/ *n* **1** LACK OF ATTENTION lack of careful attention to the details of something **2** EXAMPLE OF NEGLIGENCE an example of negligence or of a failure to take enough trouble with something **3** LACK OF CONCERN lack of concern about something

carer /káirər/ *n* the individual who has the principal responsibility of caring for a child or an elderly or dependent adult. US term **caregiver** *n.* 1

caress /kə réss/ *vt* **1** TOUCH OR STROKE AFFECTIONATELY to touch or stroke somebody or something affectionately **2** AFFECT IN SOOTHING WAY to touch, pass over, or affect somebody in a soothing or pleasant way ■ *n* GENTLE TOUCH a gentle affectionate touch or embrace [Mid-17C. Via French *caresse* < Latin *carus* 'dear'.] —**caresser** *n* —**caressive** *adj* —**caressively** *adv*

caressing /kə réssing/ *adj* gentle and soothing —**caressingly** *adv*

caret /kárrət/ *n* a mark (ʌ) made on printed or manuscript material to show where something such as a letter or word should be inserted [Late 17C. < Latin *caret* 'there is lacking', form of *carere* 'to lack'.]

caretaker /káir taykər/ *n* **1** the person who supervises the care of a property such as an office block or a school. ◊ **janitor** *n.* 1 **2** a temporary holder of a post **3** SOC WELFARE = **carer**

caretaker government *n* a government that is in power temporarily after the fall of a previous government, e.g. until an election is held

Carew /kə rŏŏ, káiroo/, **Thomas** (1595?–1645?) English poet, diplomat, and author

ϟ **careware** /káir wair/ *n* software that is made available to users in exchange for a donation to charity

care worker *n* somebody employed to help look after people with physical or mental disabilities in residential accommodation

careworn /káir wawrn/ *adj* exhausted or otherwise badly affected by anxiety or worry

Carey /káiri/, **George** (*b.* 1935) British cleric and archbishop of Canterbury (1991-)

Carey, Peter Philip (*b.* 1943) Australian writer

Carey Street *n* a state of bankruptcy (*dated*) [Because Carey Street in London was the former location of the Bankruptcy Department of the Supreme Court]

carfare /kaár fair/ *n US* the amount charged for a journey on a bus or tram or in a taxi

carfuffle /kər fúff'l/ *n Scotland* a kerfuffle (*informal*)

cargo /kaárgō/ (*plural* **-goes**) *n* **1** goods carried as freight by sea, road, or air **2** a load of something [Mid-17C. Via Spanish < late Latin *car(ri)care* 'to load' < Latin *carrus* (see CAR).]

cargo cult *n* a religion in some SW Pacific islands whose devotees believe that ancestral spirits will return to the island bringing modern consumer goods and wealth

cargo pocket *n* a large pocket with a pleat and a flap, sewn onto the outside of a garment

carhop /kaar hop/ *n US, Can* a server of food to people in parked cars at a drive-in restaurant [Mid-20C. < CAR + BELLHOP.]

cariad /kárri ad/ *n Wales* used as an affectionate form of address (*informal*) [< Welsh]

~~cariage~~ incorrect spelling of **carriage**

Carib[1] /kárrib/ (*plural* **-ibs** *or* **-ib**) *n* **1** a member of a group of Native American people who live in Central America, NE South America, and the Lesser Antilles **2** a Cariban language of the Cariban family spoken in Venezuela and neighbouring countries. Native speakers: 20,000. [Mid-16C. Via Spanish *caribe* < Arawak *carib*.] —**Carib** *adj*

Carib[2] *abbr* Caribbean

Cariban /kárriban/ (*plural* **-bans** *or* **-ban**) *n* **1** PEOPLES = **Carib**[1] *n*. **1 2** a group of about 30 languages spoken in N South America. Native speakers: 40,000. —**Cariban** *adj*

Caribbean[1] /kárri bee an/ *adj* **1** OF CARIBBEAN relating to the Caribbean or its peoples, languages, or cultures **2** OF THE CARIBS relating to the Caribs or their language or culture ■ *n* SOMEBODY FROM CARIBBEAN somebody who comes from a Caribbean island

Caribbean[2] /kárri bee an/ region comprising three main island groups, the Greater Antilles, the Lesser Antilles, and the Bahamas, extending from the southeastern tip of Florida to the coast of Venezuela and separating the Caribbean Sea from the Atlantic Ocean. ◊ **West Indies**

Caribbean Sea arm of the Atlantic Ocean, surrounded by N South America, and E Central America. Area: 1,940,000 sq. km/750,000 sq. mi. Depth: Cayman Trench 7,535 m/24,720 ft.

Caribou

caribou /kárri boo/ (*plural* **-bous** *or* **-bou**) *n* a large deer that lives in large herds and has large branched antlers on both sexes. Native to: northern regions. Genus: *Rangifer*. [Mid-17C. Via Canadian French, < Mi'kmaq *ğalipu* 'snow-shoveller'; because it removes snow to find grass.]

caricature /kárrika choor/ *n* **1** COMIC EXAGGERATION a drawing, description, or performance that exaggerates somebody's or something's characteristics, e.g. somebody's physical features, for humorous or satirical effect **2** TRAVESTY a ridiculously inappropriate or unsuccessful version of or attempt at something **3** ART OF CARICATURES the art of creating caricatures [Mid-18C. < Italian *caricatura* < *caricare* 'exaggerate, load' < late Latin *carricare* < Latin *carrus* (see CAR).] —**caricatural** *adj* — **caricature** *vt* —**caricaturist** *n*

CARICOM /kárri kom/ *abbr* Caribbean Community and Common Market

caries /kaír eez, kaíri eez/ *n* progressive decay of a tooth or, less commonly, a bone [Late 16C. < Latin.] —**carious** /káiri óssəti, kárri-/ *n* —**carious** *adj* —**cariousness** *n*

CARIFTA /ka ríftə/ *abbr* Caribbean Free Trade Association

carillon /kə ríllyən, kárrillyən/ *n* **1** SET OF STATIONARY BELLS a set of chromatically tuned stationary bells, usually hung in a tower and played from a keyboard **2** TUNE PLAYED ON SET OF BELLS a tune played on a keyboard connected to a set of stationary bells **3** ORGAN STOP IMITATING BELLS an organ stop that imitates the sound of a carillon [Late 18C. < French, < assumed Proto-Romance, 'peal of four bells'.] —**carillon** *vi*

carillonneur /kə ríllyə núr, kárrillyə núr/ *n* a player of a carillon [Late 18C. < French.]

carina /kə reénə, kə rínə/ *n* **1** PROJECTING PART OF BIRD'S BREAST-BONE the prominent keel-shaped projection of the breastbone of a bird to which the flight muscles are anchored **2** BOAT-SHAPED FUSED PETALS the boat-shaped part of a pea flower, formed by the two fused lower petals **3** KEEL-SHAPED BODY PART a keel-shaped body part, e.g. the ridge at the base of the windpipe where it divides to form the bronchi [Early 18C. < Latin, 'keel'.] —**carinate** /kárri nayt/ *adj*

Carina /kə reénə, kə rínə/ *n* a constellation of the southern hemisphere containing the star Canopus. See illustration at **constellation**

caring /káiring/ *adj* **1** SHOWING CONCERN compassionate or showing concern for others **2** RELATING TO PROFESSION LOOKING AFTER PEOPLE belonging or relating to a profession such as nursing or social work that involves looking after people's physical, medical, or general welfare ■ *n* PROVISION OF MEDICAL OR SIMILAR CARE provision of medical or other types of care, either professionally or in general —**caringly** *adv*

carioca /kárri ōkə/ *n* **1** a Brazilian dance similar to the samba **2** the music for a carioca [Mid-20C. < Portuguese, < Tupian.]

Cariocan /kárri ōkən/, **Carioca** /-ōkə/ *n* somebody who comes from Rio de Janeiro, Brazil —**Cariocan** *adj*

cariogenic /káiri ō jénnik/ *adj* causing tooth decay [Mid-20C. < CARIES.]

cariole /kárri ōl/, **carriole** *n* a small open carriage or covered cart, the former drawn by one horse [Mid-18C. Via French < Italian *carriuola* 'little car' < *carro* 'car' < Latin *carrus* (see CAR).]

carjacking /kaár jaking/ *n* the crime of holding up a car and either stealing it, robbing the driver, or forcing the driver to drive somewhere for criminal purposes [Late 20C. Blend of CAR + HIJACKING.] —**carjack** *vti* —**carjacker** *n*

cark /kaark/ *vi Aus* to fail, break down, or stop working (*slang*) [Late 20C. < ?]

carline /kaárlin/ (*plural* **-line** *or* **-lines**) *n* a plant that looks like a thistle, with spiny leaves. Flowers: yellow. Native to: Europe, Asia. *Carlina vulgaris*. [Late 16C. Via French < medieval Latin *carlina*.]

carling /kaárling, -lin/ *n* a fore-and-aft wooden beam that supports a boat's deck, especially round an opening in the deck such as a hatchway [14C. < Old Norse.]

Carlisle /kaar líl, kaár líl/ city in NW England. Population: 99,800 (1991).

carload /kaár lōd/ *n* a full complement of people able to get into and ride in a car

carload rate *n* a reduced rate for shipping freight

Carlos /kaár loss/, **Don** (1788–1855) Spanish pretender to the throne. Full name **Carlos Maria Isidro**

Carlovingian *n*, *adj* HIST = **Carolingian**

Carl XVI Gustaf /kaárl gōost af/ (*b.* 1946) king of Sweden (1973–)

Carlyle /kaar líl/, **Thomas** (1795–1881) Scottish historian and essayist

carman /kaármən/ (*plural* **-men** /-mən/) *n* a man who drives a cart or who transports goods

Carmarthen /kar maárth'n/ port in SW Wales. Population: 13,524 (1991). Welsh **Caerfyrddin**

Carmarthenshire /kar maárth'nshər/ county in S Wales. Population: 169,500 (1995). Area: 2398 sq. km/926 sq. mi.

Carme /kaármi/ *n* **1** in Greek mythology, a nymph and mother of the Cretan goddess Britomaris **2** a small satellite of Jupiter that was discovered in 1938

Carmel, Mount /kaárm'l-/ mountain in N Israel, near the Mediterranean Sea, with many biblical associations. Height: 545 m/1,789 ft.

Carmelite /kaármə līt/ *n* a friar or nun belonging to the Roman Catholic order of Our Lady of Mount Carmel [15C. Directly or via French < medieval Latin *Carmelita*, after Mount Carmel.] —**Carmelite** *adj*

Carmichael /kaar mík'l/, **Hoagy** (1899–1981) US singer and songwriter

carmine /kaár mīn, -min/ *n* **1** a deep purplish-red colour **2** a bright red pigment made from cochineal [Early 18C. Via French *carmin* < Arabic *ḳirmiz* 'kermes'.] —**carmine** *adj*

Carnaby Street /kaárnabi-/ a street in Soho, central London, notable in the 1960s as the heart of the new youth-centred fashion trade

Carnac /kaár nak/ village in Brittany, W France, famous for its prehistoric stone monuments

carnage /kaárnij/ *n* widespread and indiscriminate slaughter or massacre, especially of human beings [Early 17C. < Latin *carnaticum* 'flesh (especially as tribute)' < Latin *carn-* 'flesh']

carnal /kaárn'l/ *adj* **1** RELATING TO PHYSICAL NEEDS relating to somebody's physical needs or appetites, especially as contrasted with spiritual or intellectual qualities (*formal*) **2** SENSUAL sensual or sexual **3** RELATING TO BODY relating to or consisting of the body (*formal*) [15C. < Christian Latin *carnalis* < Latin *carn-* 'flesh'.] —**carnalist** *n* —**carnality** /kaar nállati/ *n* —**carnally** *adv*

carnal knowledge *n* sexual intercourse (*formal*)

carnallite /kaárnə līt/ *n* a white or pale hydrous chloride mineral containing magnesium and potassium. Use: source of potassium, fertilizers. [Mid-19C. After Rudolf von *Carnall* (1804–74), German mining engineer.]

carnap /kaár nap/ *vi Philippines* to steal a car (*informal*)

Carnap /kaár nap/, **Rudolf** (1891–1970) German-born US philosopher and logician

carnaptious /kaar nápshass/ *adj Scotland* quarrelsome and liable to snap at people (*informal*)

Carnarvon /kər naárv'n/ coastal town in W Western Australia. Population: 6,357 (1996).

Carnarvon Gorge sandstone canyon in S Queensland, Australia

Carnarvon Range range of mountains in the Little Sandy Desert, Western Australia. Highest peak: Mount Essendon, 907 m/2,975 ft.

carnassial /kaar nássi əl/ *adj* describes the larger sharp cheek teeth in the upper and lower jaw of a carnivore that are adapted for cutting flesh [Mid-19C. < French *carnassier* 'carnivorous' < Latin *carn-* 'flesh'.]

Carnatic /kaar náttik/ linguistic region in south-central India between the Eastern Ghats and the Coromandel coast

carnation /kaar náysh'n/ *n* **1** a perennial plant of the pink family. Flowers: fragrant white, pink, or red with fringed petals, often smelling of cloves. *Dianthus caryophyllus*. **2** a pale reddish-pink colour [Mid-16C. Via French < late Latin *carnation-* 'fleshiness' < Latin *carn-* 'flesh'.] —**carnation** *adj*

carnauba /kaar nówbə, -náwbə/ (*plural* **-ba** *or* **-bas**) *n* **1** a fan palm with an edible root and leaves that yield carnauba wax. Native to: Brazil. *Copernica prunifera*. **2** = **carnauba wax** [Mid-19C. Via Portuguese < Tupi.]

carnauba wax *n* wax obtained from the young leaves of the carnauba tree. Use: the manufacture of polish and candles.

Carné /kaár nay/, **Marcel** (1909–96) French film director

Carnegie /kaar néggi, -náygi, -neégi, kaárnəgi/ usually dry lake in central Western Australia. Area: 1,338 sq. km/517 sq. mi.

Carnegie /kaar neégi gi, kaar néggi/, **Andrew** (1835–1919) Scottish-born US industrialist and philanthropist

Carnegie, Dale (1888–1955) US writer. Born **Dale Carnegey**

carnelian /kaar neéli ən/, **cornelian** /kawr-/ *n* a semi-precious stone that is a hard reddish translucent form of chalcedony. Use: gems. [Late 17C. Alteration (influenced by Latin *carn-* 'flesh') of *cornelian* < obsolete French *corneline*.]

carnet /kaár nay/ *n* **1** a book of travel tickets or coupons costing less than the individual tickets purchased separately **2** a customs document for a car that allows it to be taken across national borders without payment of duty [Early 19C. < French.]

carnitine /kaárni teen/ *n* an amino acid that transports fatty acids into muscle cells for energy production [Early 20C. < Latin *carn-* 'flesh'.]

carnival /kaárnivəl/ *n* **1** a public festive occasion or period, often with street processions, costumes, music, and dancing **2** *US* LEISURE = **fair**[2] *n*. **1** 3 the period just before Lent begins, celebrated with a carnival in some Roman Catholic areas, such as Mardi Gras in New Orleans, Louisiana [Mid-16C. Via Italian *carnevale* < medieval Latin *carnelevamen* 'cessation of meat-eating' < Latin *carn-* 'flesh'.]

carnivore /kaárni vawr/ *n* **1 FLESH-EATING ANIMAL** an animal that eats other animals. ◊ **herbivore, omnivore** *n.* 1 **2** a carnivorous plant **3 SOMEBODY WHO ENJOYS MEAT** a meat eater (*humorous*) [Mid-19C. Via French < Latin *carnivorus* (see CARNIVOROUS).]

carnivorous /kaar nívvərəss/ *adj* **1** feeding mainly on the flesh of other animals **2** able to catch and digest animals such as insects and small invertebrates ○ *a carnivorous plant* [Late 16C. < Latin *carnivorus* 'meat-eating' < *carn-* 'flesh'.] —**carnivorously** *adv* —**carnivorousness** *n*

Carnot cycle /kaárnō-/ *n* a theoretical reversible heat-engine cycle that gives maximum efficiency [After Nicholas Léonard Sadi *Carnot* (1796–1832), French physicist]

carnotite /kaárnə tīt/ *n* a yellow radioactive mineral. Use: source of radium and uranium. [Late 19C. After Marie Adolphe *Carnot*, a French inspector of mines.]

Carnot principle /kaárnō-/ *n* the principle that the efficiency of a reversible heat engine depends on the maximum and minimum temperatures of the working fluid during the operating cycle

carny[1] /kaárni/ (*plural* **-nies**) *n US* (*informal*) **1** a carnival **2** a worker in a fairground or carnival, or such a worker's family member [Mid-20C. Shortening of CARNIVAL.]

carny[2] /kaárni/ (**-nies, -nying, -nied**) *vt* to try to persuade or coax somebody into doing something (*informal*) [Early 19C. < ?]

Caro /kaárō, kárrō/, **Qaro, Joseph ben Ephraim** (1488–1575) Spanish-born Palestinian Talmudic scholar

carob /kárrəb/ (*plural* **-obs** *or* **-ob**) *n* **1 EDIBLE POWDER LIKE CHOCOLATE** an edible powder with a taste similar to that of chocolate, made from the seeds and pods of an evergreen tree **2 EDIBLE POD** a long dark-coloured edible pod that contains a sweet-tasting pulp **3 EVERGREEN TREE WITH EDIBLE PODS** an evergreen tree with edible pods from which carob powder is made. Flowers: red. Native to: Mediterranean. *Ceratonia siliqua.* [Mid-16C. Via obsolete French *car(r)obe* < Arabic *karrūb(a).*]

caroche /kə rósh/ *n* a grand horse-drawn carriage used on ceremonial occasions [Late 16C. Via obsolete French *carroche* < Italian *carraccio* 'large chariot' < Latin *carrum* (see CAR).]

carol /kárrəl/ *n* **JOYFUL HYMN** a joyful religious song or hymn, especially a Christian song celebrating Christmas ■ *v* (**-ols, -olling, -olled**) **1** *vi* **SING CHRISTMAS SONGS** to sing hymns that celebrate Christmas, especially as a group going from house to house **2** *vti* **SING** to sing or call out something in a joyful and lively way (*literary*) ○ *The sun shone, and the birds were carolling.* [13C. < Old French *carole.*] —**caroller** *n*

LITERARY LINK ***A Christmas Carol***, a novella (1843) by Charles Dickens. It recounts the story of an avaricious merchant, Ebenezer Scrooge, who is visited by the ghosts of Christmas Past, Christmas Present, and Christmas Yet to Come. As a result he resolves to become a more generous and charitable person.

Carol II /kárrəl/ (1893–1953) king of Romania (1930–40)

Carolean /kárrə lée ən/ *adj* HIST = **Caroline**

caroli plural of **carolus**

Carolina /kár ə lí nə/ city in NE Puerto Rico. Population: 188,427 (1996).

Caroline /kárrə līn/, **Carolean** /kárrə lée ən/ *adj* **1** relating to the English kings Charles I and Charles II or their reigns **2** relating to any king or emperor called Charles [Early 17C. < medieval Latin *Carolinus* < *Carolus* 'Charles'.]

Caroline Islands /kárrə līn-, -lin-/ archipelago in the W Pacific Ocean, east of the Philippines, comprising the Federated States of Micronesia and the Republic of Palau. Area: 1,165 sq. km/450 sq. mi.

Caroline of Brunswick /kárrə līn əv brúnzwik/ German-born British titular queen consort of George IV (1768–1821)

Carolingian /kárrə línji ən/, **Carlovingian** /kaárlō vínji ən/, **Carolinian** /kárrə línni ən/ *adj* relating to the dynasty of Frankish kings descended from the Emperor Charlemagne that ruled France and Germany from the 8th to the 10th centuries ■ *n* any of the Frankish kings who ruled France and Germany from the 8th to the 10th centuries

Carolinian /kárrə línni ən/ *adj* **1** HIST = **Carolingian** **2** relating to North or South Carolina, or their people, language, or culture

carolus /kárrələss/ (*plural* **caroluses** *or* **caroli** /-lī/) *n* a gold coin named after any king or emperor called Charles, especially Charles I of England [Early 16C. < medieval Latin *Carolus* 'Charles'.]

carom /kárrəm/ *n US, Can* **1** CUE GAMES = **cannon** *n.* 4 **2** a collision that is followed by one of the objects rebounding off at an angle ■ *vi US, Can* **1** CUE GAMES = **cannon** *v.* 3 **2** to rebound off another object or series of objects, or cause this to happen [Late 18thC. Shortening of *carambole* < Spanish *carambola*, probably < *bola* 'ball'.]

carotene /kárrə teen/, **carotin** /-tin/ *n* any of several orange or red physiologically active plant pigments [Mid-19C. < Latin *carota* (see CARROT).]

carotenoid /kə rótti noyd/, **carotinoid** *n* one of a group of orange or red plant pigments that includes the carotenes

carotid /kə róttid/, **carotid artery** *n* a large artery on either side of the neck that supplies blood to the head [Early 17C. Via French *carotide* or modern Latin *carotides* < Greek *karōtides* < *karoun* 'stupefy'.]

carotid body (*plural* **carotid bodies**) *n* a cluster of cells and nerve fibres in each carotid artery that is sensitive to oxygen and acidity levels in the blood and is part of the system that regulates them

carotid sinus *n* a slight bulge in each carotid artery that contains pressure-sensitive nerve endings and forms part of the system that monitors and controls blood pressure

carotin *n* BIOCHEM = **carotene**

carotinoid *n* BIOCHEM = **carotenoid**

carousal /kə rówz'l/ *n* a noisy and boisterous drinking party (*literary*)

carouse /kə rówz/ (**-rouses, -rousing, -roused**) *vi* to drink and become noisy, especially in a group (*literary*) [Mid-16C. < German *gar aus (trinken)* '(drink) right up'.] —**carouser** *n*

carousel /kárrə sél, -zél/ *n* **1** a circular conveyor belt, especially one at an airport displaying luggage for arriving passengers to collect **2** *US* = **merry-go-round** *n.* 1 **3** a circular rotating holder that loads photographic slides into a projector one at a time [Mid-17C. Via French *carrousel* < Italian *carosello* 'tilting match'.]

carousel retaliation *n* retaliation in a trade dispute, especially one between the United States and the European Union, involving the imposition of punitive import tariffs on a list of imports that is changed at regular intervals to spread the effect more widely

carp[1] /kaarp/ *vi* to keep complaining or finding fault ○ *I wish you'd stop carping, I'm doing my best.* [13C. < Old Norse *karpa* 'brag'.] —**carper** *n*

SYNONYMS See ***complain.***

carp[2] /kaarp/ (*plural* **carp** *or* **carps**) *n* **1** a large fish with a single fin on its back, found worldwide in lakes and slow-moving rivers. *Cyprinus carpio.* **2** any fish of the carp family, which includes goldfish and koi. Family: Cyprinidae. [14C. Via French *carpe* < late Latin *carpa.*]

-carp *suffix* part of a fruit ○ *pericarp* [Via modern Latin *-carpium* < Greek *karpos* (see CARPO-)] —**-carpous** *suffix*

carpaccio /kaar páchi ō, -páchō/ *n* a dish of raw beef sliced thinly, moistened with olive oil and lemon juice, and seasoned [Mid-20C. After the Italian painter Vittore *Carpaccio*, who favoured red pigments.]

carpal /kaárp'l/ *adj* relating to the bones in the wrist ■ *n* a bone in the wrist [Mid-18C. < CARPUS.]

carpal tunnel syndrome *n* a condition of pain and weakness in the hand caused by repetitive compression of a nerve that passes through the wrist into the hand

car park *n* an enclosure or building where cars can be parked temporarily

Carpathian Mountains /kaar páythi ən-/ mountain system in E Europe between Slovakia and Poland, extending southwards through Ukraine and E Romania. Highest peak: Gerlachovka 2,655 m/8,711 ft.

carpe diem /kaár pay dée em/ *interj* used as an invocation to enjoy the present and not worry about the future [< Latin, 'seize the day']

carpel /kaárp'l/ *n* a female reproductive organ in a flower, enclosing the fertilized ovules that are developing into seeds [Mid-19C. < French *carpelle* or modern Latin *carpellum* 'little fruit' < Greek *karpos* 'fruit'.] —**carpellary** *adj* —**carpellate** *adj*

Carpentaria, Gulf of /kaárpən táiri ə/ large gulf on the coast of N Australia. Area: 310,000 sq. km/120,000 sq. mi.

carpenter /kaárpintər/ *n* **BUILDER OF WOODEN STRUCTURES OR OBJECTS** a builder or repairer of wooden objects or structures ■ *v* **1** *vi* **BUILD WOODEN STRUCTURES** to build and repair wooden structures (*technical*) **2** *vt* **MAKE SOMETHING WOODEN** to make something by cutting and joining pieces of wood ○ *He had carpentered a series of perfectly fitting dovetail joints.* **3** *vt* **MAKE SOMETHING IN EFFICIENT WAY** to make or devise something efficiently and systematically ○ *They met every day, in the vain attempt to carpenter an agreement that would be acceptable to both sides.* [12C. < Anglo-Norman, Old French *carpentier* < late Latin *carpentarius (artifex)* 'carriage(-maker)' < *carpentum* 'two-wheeled carriage'.]

carpenter ant *n* a large black or brown ant that bores into wood to make its nest. Genus: *Camponotus.*

carpenter bee *n* a bee that bores tunnels into wood to lay its eggs. Families: Xylocopidae and Ceratinidae.

Carpentier /kaar pénti er/, **Alejo** (1904–80) Cuban writer and musicologist

Carpentier /kaar paaNti ay/, **Georges** (1894–1975) French boxer

carpentry /kaárpəntri/ *n* **1** the work or occupation of building and repairing things made of wood, e.g. houses and boats, or the wooden parts of them ○ *a career in carpentry* **2** the work or objects produced by a carpenter ○ *fine carpentry for sale*

carpet /kaárpit/ *n* **1 FLOOR COVERING** thick fabric for covering a floor **2 PIECE OF FLOOR COVERING** a piece of thick heavy fabric covering the floor of a room or area **3 LAYER OR COVERING** a layer or covering (*literary*) ○ *a carpet of snow* ■ *vt* **1 COVER FLOOR WITH CARPET** to cover a floor, or the floor of a room, with a carpet ○ *We could carpet every room in the house with the money she spent on that rug.* **2 COVER** to cover something in a layer (*literary*) ○ *The valley was carpeted with flowers.* **3 REPRIMAND** to reprimand somebody severely (*informal*) [14C. < Old French *carpite* or medieval Latin *carpita* < Latin *carpere* 'to pluck'.] ◇ **roll out the red carpet** to give a special welcome to a distinguished visitor ◇ **sweep something under the carpet** to conceal or ignore something that needs attention

carpetbag /kaárpit bag/ *n* a travelling bag made of a thick fabric such as carpet, commonly used in the United States in the 19th century

carpetbagger /kaárpit baggər/ *n* **1 POST-CIVIL WAR OPPORTUNIST** a Northerner who moved to the S United States after the American Civil War, especially one seeking political or commercial advantage **2 OUTSIDER SEEKING LOCAL VOTE** an outsider whose only interest in coming to a place is to win it as a political seat **3 OPPORTUNIST MEMBER OF BUILDING SOCIETY** a member of a mutual building society or insurance company who campaigns to force it to demutualize, usually for short-term financial gain —**carpetbaggery** *n*

carpetbag steak *n* an Australian dish of a thick beef steak slit horizontally, stuffed with oysters, and grilled

carpet beetle *n* a small beetle whose larvae feed on fabric, furs, or animal remains. Genera: *Anthrenus* and *Attagenus.*

carpet-bomb *vt* **1** to bomb an area intensively **2** *US* to conduct an intensive campaign, especially in the media, to sway public opinion or to destroy somebody's reputation

carpet fitter *n* somebody who cuts and fits wall-to-wall carpet. US term **carpetlayer**

carpet grass *n* a coarse grass that forms a tight matted growth and is widely used in warm humid areas for turf and pasture. Genus: *Axonopus.*

carpeting /kaárpiting/ *n* **1** thick fabric used for covering floors **2** carpets regarded collectively ○ *How much do you want to spend on carpeting?*

carpet knight *n* somebody considered to be lazy or cowardly, especially a soldier who avoids battle and enjoys social and amorous activity (*archaic*) [< time spent in carpeted chambers instead of on the battlefield]

carpetlayer /kaárpit layər/ *n US* = **carpetfitter**

carpet moth *n* a large moth belonging to a group with mottled wings resembling the pattern of a carpet. Family: Tineidae.

carpet shark *n* a shark with a mottled back resembling the pattern of a carpet. Family: Larentidae.

carpet snake *n* a large python with a pattern of scales on its back resembling a traditional carpet. Native to: S Australia. *Morelia variegata*.

carpet sweeper *n* a device for lifting dirt off carpets, with a long handle and revolving brushes in a wheeled casing

carpetweed /kaárpit weed/ *n* a low close-growing weed. Flowers: tiny, greenish-white. Native to: North America. *Mollugo verticillata*.

car phone *n* a mobile phone designed for use in a car

carpi plural of **carpus**

carping /kaárping/ *adj* complaining or finding fault ○ *his usual carping comments* —**carpingly** *adv*

carpo- *prefix* fruit ○ *carpophagous* [< Greek *karpos* < Indo-European, 'gather']

carpology /kaar póllәji/ *n* the branch of botany that deals with the study of fruits and seeds —**carpological** /kaárpә lójjik'l/ *adj* —**carpologist** *n*

car pool *n* **1** a group of associated people sharing the use of their cars, each in turn driving the others **2** a number of motor vehicles kept by an organization for use as needed by its personnel. US term **motor pool**

car-pool *vi* to drive or be driven regularly from one place to another as a small group, with each member sharing driving responsibilities

carpophore /kaárpō fawr/ *n* **1** the part of a flower that bears the carpels and stamens **2** the part of some fungi that contains the spores or supports the part that contains them

carport /kaár pawrt/ *n* an open-sided shelter for a parked car, attached to a house or other building

carpospore /kaárpō spawr/ *n* a spore that forms in some red algae after fertilization

carpus /kaárpәss/ (*plural* **-pi** /-pī/) *n* **1** any bone in the set of eight that form the wrist joint **2** any bone in the set that form the joint between the forelimb of a vertebrate animal and its foot or paw, corresponding to the wrist [Late 17C. Via modern Latin < Greek *karpos*.]

carr /kaar/ *n* an area of marshy land with clumps of willows or other trees [14C. < Old Norse *kjarr* 'brushwood'.]

Carrà /kә raá/, **Carlo** (1881–1966) Italian painter

Carracci /kә raáchi/, **Agostino** (1557–1602) Italian painter and engraver

Carracci, Annibale (1560–1609) Italian painter

Carracci, Lodovico (1555–1619) Italian painter

carrack /kárrәk/, **carack** *n* a large Mediterranean trading ship of the 14th, 15th, and 16th centuries [14C. < French *caraque*.]

carrageen /kárrә geen, kárrә geén/ *n* **1** PLANTS = **Irish moss** **2** FOOD TECH = **carrageenan** [Early 19C. < Irish *carraigín*.]

carrageenan /kárrә geenәn, kárrә geénәn/, **carrageenin, carrageen, carragheen** *n* a complex carbohydrate obtained from edible red seaweeds, especially the seaweed Irish moss. Use: commercial preparation of food and drink. [Late 19C. < CARRAGEEN.]

carragheen /kárrә geen, kárrә geén/ *n* **1** PLANTS = **Irish moss 2** FOOD TECH = **carrageenan**

~~**carraige**~~ incorrect spelling of **carriage**

Carrara /kә raárә/ city in north-central Italy, famous for its marble quarry. Population: 67,197 (1996).

~~**carreer**~~ incorrect spelling of **career**

carrel /kárrәl/, **carrell** *n* a bay, cubicle, or small room where one person can study in private, e.g. in a library [Late 16C. Alteration of CAROL 'circle'.]

Carrel /kә rél, kárrәl/, **Alexis** (1873–1944) French biologist and surgeon

carrell *n* = **carrel**

Carreras /kә rérrәz/, **José** (*b.* 1946) Spanish singer

~~**carress**~~ incorrect spelling of **caress**

carriage /kárrij/ *n* **1 HORSE-DRAWN VEHICLE** a four-wheeled horse-drawn private passenger vehicle, especially one that is large and comfortable **2 RAILWAY COACH** a railway passenger coach **3 WHEELED PLATFORM** a wheeled platform on which something is carried or supported **4 WAY OF HOLDING THE BODY** the way somebody holds his or her head and body when walking (*formal*) ○ *She was a tall woman with a beautiful upright carriage.* **5 TAKING AND DELIVERING GOODS** the transporting and delivering of goods **6 CHARGE FOR TAKING AND DELIVERING GOODS** a charge made for transporting and delivering goods **7 MOVING PART OF MACHINE** a part of a machine that holds and moves another part, e.g. the rotating and sliding paper-holder on a typewriter

carriage bolt *n US* BUILDING = **coach bolt**

carriage clock *n* a small clock set in a case with a handle on top, originally used as a travel clock but now ornamental

carriage horse *n* a horse used to pull carriages

carriage return *n* the key or lever on a typewriter that sends the paper-holding carriage back and rotates it to move the paper upward, ready to begin a new line

carriage trade *n* the most wealthy and prestigious of possible customers ○ *They carry only the highest quality goods, catering to the carriage trade.*

carriageway /kárrij way/ *n* the part of a main road used for vehicles, especially one side of a major two-way road, carrying traffic in one direction only

~~**Carribean**~~ incorrect spelling of **Caribbean**

carrick bend /kárrik-/ *n* an intertwining knot similar to a granny knot, used for tying ropes together [Probably alteration of CARRACK]

carrick bitt /kárrik-/ *n* one of the two posts that support a ship's windlass [See CARRICK BEND]

Carrickfergus /kárrik fúrgәss/ town in NE Northern Ireland. Population: 31,000 (1990).

carrier /kárri әr/ *n* **1 TRANSPORTER OF PEOPLE OR GOODS** a person or company whose function or business is to transport things or people from one place to another ○ *These airlines are among the world's most popular carriers.* **2 TRANSMITTER OF DISEASE** a living creature that is infected with a disease and can pass it to others but does not itself display any of the symptoms **3 TRANSMITTER OF GENETIC DEFECT** an individual carrying a gene for a particular genetic trait or disorder without being affected by it **4 PART OF MACHINE CONVEYING MOTION** a part of a machine that carries and moves something or transmits motion to another part **5 LUGGAGE RACK** a metal frame on which luggage can be tied to a road vehicle or bicycle **6 AIRCRAFT CARRIER** an aircraft carrier **7 MEANS OF TRANSMITTING ACTIVE SUBSTANCE** a neutral substance to which an active ingredient or agent is added as a way of applying or transferring the ingredient or agent ○ *Mix the dye and the carrier in equal proportions.* **8 BEARER OF ELECTRIC CHARGE** something that carries electric current, e.g. an electron or ion **9 RADIO WAVE CARRYING INFORMATION** an electromagnetic wave that is modulated to carry a signal in radio or television transmission **10** = **carrier bag**

carrier air wing *n* a squadron of aircraft operating from an aircraft carrier

carrier bag *n* a large plastic or paper shopping bag with handles, especially one supplied by a shop

carrier pigeon *n* **1** a domestic pigeon trained to deliver messages and return home **2** a large domestic pigeon bred for showing

⚡**carrier wave** *n* TELECOM = **carrier** *n.* **9**

Carrington /kárringtәn/, **Peter, 6th Baron Carrington** (*b.* 1919) British politician

carriole *n* = **cariole**

carrion /kárri әn/ *n* **1** the rotting flesh of a dead animal **2** something that is decaying or disgusting (*literary*) [13C. < Anglo-Norman, Old French *caroi(g)ne* < Latin *caro* 'flesh'.]

carrion crow *n* a medium-sized crow with a greenish tinge to its black plumage. Native to: Europe. *Corvus corone.*

carrion flower *n* **1** a climbing plant with small greenish flowers that smell like rotting flesh. Native to: North America. Genus: *Smilax.* **2** a succulent plant with foul-smelling star-shaped flowers. Native to: tropics. Genus: *Stapelia.*

Carroll /kárrәl/, **Lewis** (1832–98) British writer. Pseudonym of **Charles Lutwidge Dodgson**

carronade /kárrә nayd/ *n* a lightweight iron cannon formerly used on ships [Late 18C. After *Carron*, Scotland.]

carrot /kárrәt/ *n* **1 THIN ORANGE ROOT VEGETABLE** a thin tapering orange-coloured root eaten raw or cooked as a vegetable **2 PLANT WITH EDIBLE ORANGE-COLOURED ROOT** a biennial plant that produces carrots. *Daucus carota.* **3 INCENTIVE** something tempting, offered in order to persuade somebody to do something ○ *They offered us the carrot of a year's free petrol if we'd buy the sports car right then.* [15C. Via French *carotte* < Latin *carota* < Greek *karōton*.]

SPELLCHECK See ***carat***.

carrot-and-stick *adj* relating to or characterized by the use of persuasion involving a combination of rewards and punishments ○ *During the fast-paced negotiations, the diplomats employed a carrot-and-stick strategy.*

carrot fly (*plural* **carrot flies** *or* **carrot fly**) *n* a low-flying insect whose larvae bore into the edible roots of the carrot plant. *Psila rosae.*

carroty /kárrәti/ *adj* **1 TASTING LIKE CARROTS** like carrots in taste **2 RED** describes hair that is red or auburn **3 OF BRIGHT ORANGE COLOUR** of a bright reddish-orange colour

carry /kárri/ *v* (**-ries, -rying, -ried**) **1** *vt* **HOLD AND TRANSPORT** to take somebody or something that you are holding or supporting to another place ○ *The case was too heavy for her to carry.* ○ *a lorry carrying farm produce* **2** *vt* **BE CHANNEL OR ROUTE FOR** to be the means by which something passes or is transmitted from one place to another ○ *The pipeline will carry oil to the coast.* **3** *vt* **TELL OR CONTAIN** to communicate or convey information, an idea, or a feeling by way of content or in an indirect manner ○ *The article carries wider implications than you may think.* **4** *vt* **MOVE ALONG** to take and move somebody or something by a flow or impetus ○ *The current carried them swiftly downstream.* ○ *She could hear children's voices, carried on the light breeze.* **5** *vt* **HAVE TRANSMISSIBLE DISEASE** to be infected with a disease and capable of infecting others ○ *You may be carrying a virus without knowing it.* **6** *vt* **HAVE SOMETHING WITH YOU** to have something with you, e.g. in your pocket or in a handbag ○ *Staff should carry identification at all times.* **7** *vt* **ACCOMMODATE VEHICULAR TRAFFIC** to be able to withstand a particular degree or amount of vehicular traffic ○ *a motorway that can carry hundreds of thousands of vehicles a day* **8** *vt* **YIELD ENOUGH FORAGE FOR** to yield enough forage or grazing crops for animals to survive ○ *fields that can carry llamas as well as cattle* **9** *vt* **BE RESPONSIBLE FOR** to bear the responsibility for something ○ *The Prime Minister carries heavy duties.* **10** *vt* **MAKE SOMEBODY SUCCEED OR ENDURE** to give somebody the incentive, impetus, or encouragement to achieve or deal with something ○ *The audience cheered, carried along on a wave of enthusiasm.* **11** *vt* **PUBLISH, BROADCAST, OR DISPLAY** to feature or include an article, picture, item of news, or piece of information ○ *That evening, all the major networks carried the story.* ○ *Every packet carries a government health warning.* **12** *vt* **INCLUDE OR RESULT IN** to have something as a quality, feature, or consequence ○ *Reckless driving carries a heavy penalty.* **13** *vti* **BE PREGNANT** to be pregnant with a child ○ *She carried the child to term.* **14** *vt* **DEVELOP AN IDEA** to develop an idea in discussion or action ○ *If you carry that argument to its logical conclusion, no one should get married at all.* **15** *vt* **MOVE OR BEHAVE** to move or behave in a particular way, especially with confidence or dignity ○ *He was a handsome man who carried himself with dignity.* ○ *She carried her head high, and looked her accusers in the eye.* **16** *vt* **KEEP FOR SALE** to keep something as stock in a shop ○ *We don't carry household goods.* **17** *vi* **BE HEARD AT A DISTANCE** to be audible at a distance ○ *Sound carries a long way over water.* **18** *vt* **SUPPORT WEAKER ELEMENT** to support or compensate for a weaker element or participant ○ *The rest of the department has to carry him.* **19** *vti* **VOTE FOR** to accept a proposal by voting for it ○ *The nomination was carried, 40–29.* **20** *vt* **GAIN SOMEBODY'S SUPPORT** to win the support or sympathy of a person or group, especially by making a speech or appeal ○ *It looked for a moment as if he would carry the crowd.* **21** *vt US* **WIN VOTES OF AREA** to win support from somebody ○ *The incumbent carried all the cities in her district, and won* **22** *vt* **CAPTURE A PLACE** to capture a place in battle ○ *Their charge carried the hill.* **23** *vt* **STAY IN TUNE WHEN SINGING** to be able to sing and stay in tune ○ *Can you carry a tune?* **24** *vt* **TRANSFER ITEM IN ACCOUNT OR CALCULATION** to transfer a figure from one group or column to another in accounts or in a calculation **25** *vi* **BE HIT A CERTAIN DISTANCE** to reach a certain distance after being struck ○ *Her approach shot didn't carry to the green.* **26** *vt* **MOVE WITH BALL IN SPORT** to bring a ball forward a certain distance in a sport such as American football ○ *Their first rush carried the ball well into the defenders' half.* **27** *vt* **HAVE FIREPOWER RANGE** to have a particular range of fire ○ *an artillery shell that carried for miles* **28** *vt* **SUSTAIN EFFECTS OF ALCOHOL** to be able to drink alcohol without showing adverse effects (*informal*) **29** *vt* **PALM BALL IN BASKETBALL** to keep a hand in illegal contact with the ball in basketball ■ *n* (*plural* **-ries**) **1 DISTANCE COVERED** the distance covered by something struck, thrown, launched, or fired, or the reach of something, e.g. a voice **2 ACT OF RUNNING WITH BALL** a sprint with the ball in American football ○ *a 50-yard carry that won the game* [14C. Directly or via Anglo-Norman < Old French *carier* < *car* (see CAR).]

carry away *vt* to make somebody become less controlled, reasonable, or attentive by arousing his or her emotion or interest (*usually passive*) ○ *I was completely carried away by the beauty of it.*

carry back *vt* to transfer something such as a tax credit so that it is calculated against the previous year's income

carry forward *vt* **1** to transfer an item to the next section or column in accounts or in a calculation **2** to transfer something, such as a tax credit or liability, so that it is calculated against the next year's income

carry off *vt* **1 REMOVE** to take something or somebody away purposefully or by force ○ *carried him off, kicking and screaming, to his crib* **2 WIN** to win a prize (*informal*) ○ *She carried off the award for best newcomer.* **3 DO SOMETHING SUCCESSFULLY OR WELL** to succeed in doing something well or producing a good effect ○ *He was nervous about chairing the meeting, but carried it off in style.* ○ *It's a very sophisticated outfit, but she can't quite carry it off.* **4 KILL** to kill somebody (*usually passive*) ○ *Half the settlers were carried off by smallpox.*

carry on *v* **1** *vti* **KEEP DOING** to continue to do something ○ *Please just carry on with your work and pretend we're not here.* ○ *She carried on the business after her father retired.* **2** *vt* **BE INVOLVED IN** to engage in or be engaged in something ○ *They were carrying on an intense conversation in a corner of the bar.* **3** *vi* **BEHAVE FOOLISHLY OR IMPROPERLY** to behave or talk in a way that is socially awkward or improper (*informal*) ○ *I'm ashamed of the way he's been carrying on in public.* **4** *vi* **HAVE AN AFFAIR** to have a casual affair with somebody (*informal disapproving*)

carry out *vt* **1** to perform or accomplish something ○ *carry out research* **2** to do something that has been ordered, planned, or stated as an aim ○ *We shall carry out your instructions to the letter.*

carry over *v* **1** *vti* **LEAVE SOMETHING TO BE FINISHED LATER** to leave the last part of something to be done at a later date ○ *There were so many candidates that the ceremonies were carried over to the next morning.* **2** *vt* **TRANSFER ITEM IN ACCOUNT OR CALCULATION** to transfer an item to the next group or column in accounts or in a calculation **3** *vt* **TRANSFER SOMETHING TO NEXT YEAR** to transfer an allowance or entitlement from one year or part of a year to the next **4** *vi* **CONTINUE TO EXIST** to continue to exist or produce an effect in changed circumstances ○ *The dislike he always felt for me has obviously carried over into our relationship at work.* **5** *vt* **POSTPONE DEAL ON STOCK EXCHANGE** to postpone a payment or settlement on the Stock Exchange until the next account day

carry through *v* **1** *vt* **DO WHAT WAS PLANNED** to complete or accomplish something planned ○ *We outlined our policy before the election, and we are determined to carry it through.* **2** *vt* **HELP SOMEBODY SURVIVE** to give somebody the support or strength needed to overcome a difficulty ○ *It was my family's support that carried me through.* ○ *Only his determination not to be humiliated carried him through the next five hours.* **3** *vi* **SURVIVE** to continue to exist ○ *It is an old tradition that has carried through into the information age.*

carryall /kárri awl/ *n* **1** US = **holdall** *n*. **2** a covered horse-drawn carriage for four people [Early 18C. Alteration of CARIOLE.]

carryback /kárri bak/ *n* an amount of money, e.g. a tax credit, that is transferred to the accounts for the previous year

carrycase /kárri kayss/ *n* a small case with a handle, used for carrying such items as a laptop computer or documents

carrycot /kárri kot/ *n* a lightweight portable bed for a baby, often detachable from a wheeled base

carrying capacity *n* **1** the number of animals a region can support **2** the number of individuals a region can support in terms of its resources

carrying charge *n* **1** a charge for storing or delivering a customer's goods **2** the cost to a business of holding or storing assets from which it currently earns no income

carrying-on (*plural* **carryings-on**) *n* behaviour regarded as immature or improper (*informal*) ○ *I won't have that kind of carrying-on in my house.*

carryon /kárri on/ *n* a piece of luggage suitable for taking in the cabin of an aircraft ■ *adj* describes or relating to luggage small enough to be carried and stowed aboard the cabin of an aircraft

carry-on *n* an annoying incident involving unwise or overexcited behaviour (*informal*) ○ *I've never heard such a carry-on.*

carryout /kárri owt/ *n* **1** US, Scotland **FOOD EATEN OFF THE PREMISES** an item of ready-to-eat food bought in a shop or restaurant and taken elsewhere to be eaten (*often before nouns*) ○ *a carryout pizza* **2** Scotland **PLACE SELLING FOOD TO TAKE AWAY** a restaurant or shop that sells cooked food to be taken elsewhere to be eaten **3** Scotland **ALCOHOL BOUGHT IN A SHOP** an amount of alcoholic drink bought from a shop and taken elsewhere, especially home, to drink

carryover /kárri övər/ *n* **1** an item transferred to the next group or column in accounts or in a calculation **2** the postponement of a stock market transaction until the next day, in exchange for a fee

carse /kaarss/ *n* Scotland a stretch of flat land beside a river [14C. < ?]

car seat *n* **1** a small seat for children, fitted or strapped inside a car **2** a driver's or passenger's seat in a car

carsick /káar sik/ *adj* feeling sick from the motion of a vehicle you are travelling in —**carsickness** *n*

Carson /kaárss'n/, **Edward Henry, Baron Carson** (1854–1935) Irish-born British politician and lawyer

Rachel Carson

Carson, Rachel (1907–64) US ecologist

Carson City capital of Nevada. Population: 49,301 (1998 estimate).

cart /kaart/ *n* **1 HORSE-DRAWN VEHICLE CARRYING GOODS** an open horse-drawn vehicle, especially one with only two wheels, used for carrying goods or as a farm vehicle **2 HORSE-DRAWN CARRIAGE** a light horse-drawn carriage with two wheels **3 VEHICLE PUSHED BY HAND** a light vehicle or barrow pushed by hand **4** US **WHEELED CARRIER FOR MERCHANDISE OR BAGGAGE** a container or platform on small wheels on which things are pushed along, e.g. supermarket items or airport baggage **5** US **WHEELED TABLE** a small table on wheels, used for taking food and drinks to the table ■ *vt* **1 CARRY SOMETHING ROUGHLY** to take or pull somebody or something roughly or with difficulty (*informal*) ○ *I had to cart the Christmas tree home myself.* ○ *Do you have to cart all those books around?* **2 CARRY OR TRANSPORT SOMETHING OR SOMEBODY** to carry or transport something or somebody, especially in a cart ○ *carting the produce to market* [12C. < Old Norse *kartr*.] —**cartable** *adj* ◇ **put the cart before the horse** to do or say things in the wrong order

cartage /kaártij/ *n* the cost of transporting or delivering goods by cart

Cartagena /kaártə jeènə/ *n* **1** port in NW Colombia. Population: 812,595 (1997 estimate). **2** city and port in SE Spain. Population: 175,628 (1998 estimate).

carte /kaart/ *n* FENCING = **quarte**

carte blanche /kaárt blaánsh/ *n* permission or authority given to somebody to act with freedom or discretion ○ *She's been given carte blanche to make whatever changes she thinks necessary.* [< French, 'white card']

carte du jour /kaárt də zhoòr/ (*plural* **cartes du jour** /kaárt-/) *n* a restaurant menu showing what is available on a particular day [< French, 'card of the day']

cartel /kaar tél/ *n* **1** an alliance of business companies formed to control production, competition, and prices **2** a political alliance among parties or groups having common aims [Mid-16C. Via German *Kartell* < French *cartel* < Italian *cartello* 'placard' < Latin *c(h)arta* (see CARD¹).]

cartelize /kaárti lĩz/ (**-izes, -izing, -ized**), **cartelise** (**-ises, -ising, -ised**) *vti* to form a cartel of business companies or political groups ○ *The market leaders had every incentive to cartelize.*

carter /kaártər/ *n* a user of a cart for transporting goods or for farm work

Carter /kaártər/, **Angela** (1940–92) British writer

Carter, Howard (1873–1939) British archaeologist and draughtsman

The White House

Jimmy Carter

Carter, Jimmy (*b.* 1924) US statesman and 39th president of the United States (1977–81). Full name **James Earl Carter, Jr**

Cartesian /kaar teèzi ən/ *adj* relating to René Descartes or his writings or theories [Mid-17C. < modern Latin *Cartesianus* < *Cartesius*, Latinized form of DESCARTES.] —**Cartesian** *n*

Cartesian coordinate *n* **1** one of a pair of coordinates giving the location of a point on a plane, relative to an origin and two perpendicular axes **2** one of three coordinates giving the location of a point in space, relative to an origin and three mutually perpendicular planes

Cartesianism /kaar teèzi ənizəm/ *n* the philosophy of René Descartes, especially his belief in a distinction between the observing mind and the observed world

Cartesian plane *n* a plane having all points defined by Cartesian coordinates

Cartesian product *n* a set of all the pairs of elements from two sets that have their first element from the first set and the second from the second set

Carthage /kaárthij/ *n* ancient Phoenician city on the coast of N Africa, near present-day Tunis —**Carthaginian** /kaárthə jínni ən/ *n, adj*

carthorse /kaárt hawrss/ *n* a large strong horse bred to pull a cart or for other heavy work

Carthusian /kaar thyoòzi ən/ *n* a member of a contemplative Roman Catholic order of monks and nuns founded in France in the 11th century [Mid-16C. < medieval Latin *Carthusianus* < *Carthusia* 'Chartreuse', France, where the order's first monastery was built.] —**Carthusian** *adj*

Cartier /kaárti ay/, **Jacques** (1491–1557) French navigator

Cartier-Bresson /kaárti ay bréss oN/, **Henri** (*b.* 1908) French photographer

Cartier Island /kaárti ay-/ small uninhabited island off the coast of N Western Australia

cartilage /kaártəlij, kaárt'lij/ *n* the tough elastic tissue that is found in the nose, throat, and ear and in other parts of the body and forms most of the skeleton in infancy, changing to bone during growth [15C. Via French < Latin *cartilago*.]

cartilaginous /kaártə lájjinəss/ *adj* **1** resembling, made of, or relating to cartilage **2** having a skeleton composed mostly of cartilage

cartilaginous fish *n* a fish with a skeleton made entirely of cartilage. Shark, rays, and ratfish are cartilaginous fish. Class: Chondrichthyes.

Cartland /kaártlənd/, **Dame Barbara** (1901–2000) British novelist. Born **Mary Barbara Hamilton**

cartload /kaárt lōd/ n the amount that a cart can carry

cartogram /kaártə gram/ n a diagrammatic map showing the population and other statistics of a region [Late 19C. < French cartogramme < carte 'map'.]

cartographic /kaártə gráffik/, **cartographical** /-k'l/ adj 1 relating to maps ○ cartographic design 2 in the form of a map ○ cartographic representation —**cartographically** adv

cartography /kaar tóggrəfi/ n the science, skill, or work of making maps [Mid-19C. < French cartographie < carte 'map'.] —**cartographer** n

cartomancy /kaártō manssi/ n fortune telling by using playing cards [Late 19C. < French cartomancie < carte (see CARD[1]).]

carton /kaárt'n/ n 1 CARDBOARD BOX a cardboard box in which something, e.g. goods, movable property, or mail, is packaged 2 PLASTIC OR CARD CONTAINER a container made of plastic or waxed card in which food or drink is sold 3 CONTENTS OF CONTAINER the various contents, e.g. juice or milk, contained in a carton 4 TARGET CENTRE the white disc at the centre of a target in competitive shooting ■ vt PUT SOMETHING IN CARTON to put something in a carton ○ Most of our milk is sold cartoned. [Early 19C. Via French < Italian cartone (see CARTOON).]

cartoon /kaar tōon/ n 1 ANIMATED FILM a film made using animation instead of live actors, especially a humorous film intended primarily for children 2 SEQUENCE OF DRAWINGS a sequence of drawings that tell a short story, published in a newspaper or magazine 3 SATIRICAL DRAWING a humorous drawing published in a newspaper or magazine and commenting on a topical event or theme 4 PREPARATORY DRAWING a drawing done, often in great detail, as a preliminary drawing of a painting or other work of art [Late 16C. Via Italian cartone 'pasteboard' (on which artists' preparatory drawings were made) < Latin c(h)arta (see CARD[1]).] —**cartoonist** n

cartoonish /kaar tōonish/, **cartoony** /-tōoni/ adj resembling a humorous or animated cartoon —**cartoonishly** adv

cartoony adj = cartoonish

cartophily /kaar tóffəli/ n collecting cigarette cards as a hobby [Mid-20C. < French carte 'card' or Italian carta.] —**cartophilist** n

cartouche /kaar tōosh/ n 1 CASING FOR GUNPOWDER the paper casing of a firework or cartridge 2 DECORATIVE PANEL a decorative panel in the form of a frame or unrolled scroll, sometimes containing writing, forming an artistic or architectural feature 3 FRAME FOR NAME an oval or oblong shape containing writing, especially one containing a king's name in Egyptian hieroglyphics [Early 17C. Via French < Italian cartoccio 'paper cornet' < carta 'paper'.]

cartridge /kaártrij/ n 1 BULLET'S CASE a cylindrical case holding an explosive charge and a bullet or shot, which is put into a gun 2 CONTAINER FOR LIQUID OR POWDER a container for liquid or powder that is loaded into a device, e.g. a removable ink container for a pen or printer ○ toner cartridges 3 CASE FOR LOADING SOMETHING INTO MACHINE a plastic case containing something that is loaded into a device, e.g. photographic film, a typewriter ribbon, a cassette, or a set of computer disks 4 PART OF HI-FI PICKUP the part of the arm of a record-player that holds the needle [Late 16C. Anglicization of French cartouche (see CARTOUCHE).]

cartridge belt n a belt that holds gun cartridges or cartridge clips

cartridge case n the casing of a gun cartridge

cartridge clip n a container for bullets, loaded directly into an automatic weapon

cartridge paper n thick drawing paper of a good quality with a grained or textured surface

cartridge pen n a pen that holds a replaceable ink cartridge

cart track n a rough track or narrow unsurfaced road used by farm vehicles

cartulary /kaártyŏolari/ n (plural -ies) n 1 a collection of official records, especially those relating to a large estate or a religious community 2 a room or building where official records are kept [Mid-16C. < medieval Latin c(h)artularium < Latin c(h)artula 'document' < c(h)arta (see CARD[1]).]

cartwheel /kaárt weel/ n 1 WOODEN WHEEL OF CART a large wooden spoked wheel for a cart 2 ACROBATIC MOVEMENT an acrobatic movement in which the body is turned sideways onto the hands, then over onto the feet again ■ vi DO CARTWHEEL to perform a cartwheel

cartwright /kaárt rīt/ n a maker of carts

Cartwright /kaárt rīt/, **Edmund** (1743–1823) British inventor and clergyman

caruncle /kə rúngk'l/ n 1 a fleshy growth on the head or body, e.g. a cock's comb 2 a coloured outgrowth of tissue in some types of seed near the point of attachment to the plant [Late 16C. Via obsolete French < Latin caruncula 'small piece of flesh' < caro 'flesh'.] —**caruncular** adj —**carunculate** adj —**carunculated** adj —**carunculous** adj

Caruso /kə rōossō/, **Enrico** (1873–1921) Italian operatic tenor

carvacrol /kaárvə krol/ n an oily liquid with the smell of mint. Source: savory, oregano, thyme. Use: in flavourings, perfumes, as a disinfectant. [Mid-19C. < modern Latin (Carum) carvi 'caraway' + Latin acris 'sharp'.]

carve /kaarv/ (carves, carving, carved) v 1 vti MAKE SOMETHING BY CUTTING AND SHAPING to make an object or design by cutting and shaping a hard material such as wood or stone ○ statues carved from marble ○ I remembered carving her name on a tree, years ago. 2 vt CUT SUBSTANCE to cut and shape a material such as wood or stone in order to make an object or design 3 vti CUT MEAT to cut cooked meat into slices 4 vti MAKE SHAPE BY NATURAL FORCE to make a shape by an eroding action ○ dunes carved into strange shapes by the wind [Old English ceorfan < Germanic, 'to scratch']

carve out vt to make or achieve something through sustained hard work ○ With unrelenting energy and ambition she had carved out a niche for herself in the world of investigative journalism.

carve up vt 1 to divide something, or ownership of something, into rough or crude parts (informal) ○ Their intention was to invade and carve up the kingdom among themselves. 2 to wound somebody with a blade (slang)

carvel n = caravel

carvel-built /kaárv'l-/ adj describes a boat or ship made of planks of wood with their edges flush, not overlapping [Late 18C. Via French < Portuguese caravela < caravela 'small ship' < Greek karabos 'crayfish']

carver /kaárvər/ n 1 MEAT KNIFE a knife for slicing cooked meat 2 SOMEBODY OR SOMETHING THAT CARVES a person or device that carves meat 3 DINING CHAIR WITH ARMS a dining chair with arms designed to stand at the head of the table

carvers /kaárvərz/ npl a large knife and fork for carving meat

carvery /kaárvəri/ n (plural -ies) n a restaurant or buffet where meat is freshly sliced to order for customers, sometimes offering unlimited servings for a fixed price

carving /kaárving/ n 1 an object or design formed by cutting and shaping a material, e.g. wood or stone ○ The walls were covered with carvings depicting gods and heroes. 2 the work or act of carving something ○ The carving of the panels was exquisite.

carving knife n a large knife for slicing meat

car wash n 1 a site, often a tunnel-like building with drive-through conveyors, where motor vehicles are washed automatically by machine or can be washed manually 2 a shed or structure for washing motor vehicles automatically with revolving brushes and jets of water

Cary /káiri/, **Joyce** (1888–1957) Irish-born British novelist

caryatid /kárri áttid/ (plural -ids or -ides /-áttideez/) n a column in the shape of a draped female figure supporting a structure such as the frieze or porch of a classical Greek temple [Mid-16C. Via Latin caryatides < Greek karuatides 'maidens of Karuai (Caryae, Greece), priestesses of Artemis.'] —**caryatidal** adj —**caryatidean** /-átti deè ən/ adj —**caryatidic** /-ə tíddik/ adj

caryopsis /kárri ópsiss/ (plural -ses /-seez/ or -sides /-si deez/) n a dry fruit that looks like a seed, borne by grasses and cereal crops such as wheat [Early 19C. < modern Latin, < Greek karuon 'nut' + opsis 'appearance'.]

carzey n = karzy

Casablanca /kássə blángkə, kázzə-/ largest city in Morocco, on the Atlantic coast. Population: 2,940,623 (1994). Arabic **Dar el-Beida**

Caryatid

Casals /kə sálz/, **Pablo** (1876–1973) Spanish cellist and composer

Casanova /kássə nōvə/ n a charming seducer of women who moves quickly from one casual relationship to another [Early 20C. After Giovanni Jacopo CASANOVA, the Italian adventurer.]

Casanova /kássə nōvə/, **Giovanni Jacopo, Chevalier de Seingalt** (1725–98) Italian adventurer and author

casbah n = kasbah

⚡ **cascade** /ka skáyd/ n 1 WATERFALL a small waterfall or series of waterfalls 2 FLOWING LIQUID a fast downward flow of liquid or small objects 3 HANGING MASS a flowing mass of something that hangs down or lies along a surface ○ The bride carried a cascade of roses and baby's breath. 4 SUCCESSION a succession of things, e.g. chemical reactions or elements in an electrical circuit, each of which activates, affects, or determines the next ■ v (-cades, -cading, -caded) 1 vti FLOW to flow fast and in large amounts, or cause something to flow this way 2 vi HANG OR LIE to hang or lie in a flowing mass (literary) ○ Fine lace ruffles cascaded from his throat and sleeves. 3 vt OVERLAP WINDOWS ON COMPUTER SCREEN to arrange the windows on a computer screen so that they overlap, with the title bar of each visible [Mid-17C. Via French < Italian cascata < Latin cadere 'to fall'.]

Cascade Range /ka skáyd-/ range of mountains in the NW United States and SW Canada. Highest peak: Mount Rainier, 4,392 m / 14,410 ft.

⚡ **cascading menu** /ka skáyding-/ n a menu in a computer program that opens when you select a choice from another menu

cascara /ka skaárə/, **cascara buckthorn** n 1 a bush or small tree of the NW United States. Rhamnus purshiana. 2 TREES = cascara sagrada [Late 19C. Shortening of CASCARA SAGRADA.]

cascara sagrada /-sə graádə/ n the dried bark of the cascara tree. Use: formerly, as a strong laxative. [< Spanish cáscara sagrada 'sacred bark']

case[1] /kayss/ n 1 CIRCUMSTANCE a situation or set of circumstances ○ I don't think the usual rules apply in this case. ○ Sometimes anxiety causes weight loss, but that's not the case here. 2 INSTANCE an instance or example of something ○ This seems to be a case of mistaken identity. 3 SOMETHING EXAMINED OR INVESTIGATED a subject of investigation or scrutiny by a professional person, e.g. a doctor or police officer 4 ACTUAL FACT what happens in reality or fact ○ The case is that the witness has lied under oath. 5 SOMETHING EXAMINED IN LAW COURT a matter examined or judged in a court of law ○ It'll be some weeks before your case comes to trial. 6 ARGUMENTS a set of arguments and evidence that supports a legal claim in court ○ He presented his case calmly and with skill. 7 ARGUMENT FOR OR AGAINST an argument for or against something ○ You can make a case for holding a referendum. 8 GRAMMATICAL FORM OF WORD a form of a noun, pronoun, or adjective that indicates its syntactical relation to surrounding words 9 KIND OF PERSON somebody of a particular kind or in a particular condition, especially an unfortunate one (informal) ○ He's a hopeless case. 10 ODD PERSON an odd or eccentric person (informal) ■ vt (cases, casing, cased) INSPECT PLACE to assess or survey a place with a view to robbing it (slang) ○ He was casing the joint before robbing the place. [13C. Via Old French cas 'event' < Latin casus < cadere 'to fall'.] ◇ **a case in point** a relevant example ○ A case in point is the steady drop in unit sales. ◇ **be on somebody's case 1** to use influence in order to help somebody (slang) **2** to persist in pestering somebody to do something (*slang*) ◇ **get off somebody's case 1** to stop using influence to help somebody (*slang*) **2** to stop pestering somebody to do something (*slang*) ○ *Please get off my case! I'll finish mowing the lawn later.* ◇ **in any case 1** taking into account everything said or done before **2** regardless of that ◇ **in case of something** if something happens ○ *In case of fire, leave by the nearest exit.* ◇ **(just) in case 1** in preparation for an event that may possibly happen ○ *Take your umbrella, just in case.* **2** used to introduce a piece of information and to explain your reason for giving it ○ *In case you're unaware of the fact, this is a nonsmoking area.*

case[2] /kayss/ *n* **1 HOLDER OR OUTER COVERING** something that serves as a container or covering **2 CONTAINER** a container with its contents ○ *bought a case of fizzy drinks* **3 PIECE OF LUGGAGE** an item of luggage, especially a suitcase **4 KIND OF PRINTED CHARACTER** the function of a printed character as a capital or small letter **5 TRAY HOLDING PRINTING TYPE** in hot-metal printing, a tray with compartments in which individual printing blocks are kept **6 PAIR** a pair, especially of pistols **7** = **casing** *n.* 3 ■ *vt* (**cases, casing, cased**) **PUT COVERING ROUND** to enclose something in a covering [13C. Via Old French dialect *casse* < Latin *capsa* 'box' < *capere* 'to hold'.]

⚡**CASE** /kayss/ *abbr* **1** computer-aided software engineering **2** computer-aided systems engineering

casease /káyssi ayss, -ayz/ *n* a bacterial enzyme that aids the breakdown of casein [20C. < CASEIN.]

caseate /káyssi ayt/ (**-ates, -ating, -ated**) *vi* to undergo caseation [Late 19C. Back-formation < CASEATION.] —**caseous** *adj*

caseation /káyssi áysh'n/ *n* the process by which dead tissue decays into a firm and dry mass, characteristic of tuberculosis [Mid-19C. < medieval Latin *caseation-* < Latin *caseus* 'cheese'.]

casebook /káyss bòok/ *n* **1** a record of legal or medical cases and their conduct **2** a collection of academic writings on a subject

casebound /káyss bownd/ *adj* PUBL = **hardback**. ◊ **paperback, softback, clothbound**

cased glass, case glass *n* decorative glass consisting of several coloured layers with some areas cut away in different patterns

casefy /káyssi fī/ (**-fies, -fying, -fied**) *vti* to develop, or cause something to develop, a soft consistency like that of cheese [20C. < Latin *caseus* 'cheese'.]

case glass *n* = **cased glass**

case grammar *n* a system of grammar that analyses sentences in terms of the semantic relation of the noun or noun phrase and other elements to the main verb

case-harden *vt* **1** to harden the surface of an iron alloy by heating and then cooling in water **2** to make somebody unsympathetic or unfeeling as a result of extended dealing with difficult and distressing problems

case history *n* a record of somebody's medical or social history kept by a doctor or social worker

casein /káyssi in, -een/ *n* one of a group of proteins found in milk [Mid-19C. < Latin *caseus* 'cheese'.]

caseinate /káyssi i nayt, -ee nayt/ *n* a compound of casein and calcium or sodium

caseinogen /kay seénajin, káyssi ínn-/ *n* the main protein in milk

case law *n* law established on the basis of previous verdicts according to the doctrine of binding precedent, rather than law established by legislation

caseload /káyss lōd/ *n* the number of cases to be dealt with, e.g. by a doctor or a lawyer, at a particular time

casemate /káyss mayt/ *n* a fortified compartment on an old sailing ship or a rampart where a cannon was mounted [Mid-16C. Directly or via French < Italian *casamatta*.]

casement /káyssmənt/ *n* a window that opens on hinges, as distinct from one that slides up and down [15C. Via Anglo-Latin *cassimentum* < Latin *capsa* (see CASE[2]).]

Casement /káyssmənt/, **Sir Roger** (1864–1916) Irish-born British consular official and rebel

caseose /káyssi ōss, -ōz/ *n* a chemical produced in the digestion of cheese [20C. < Latin *caseus* 'cheese'.]

casern /kə zúrn/, **caserne** *n* a barracks, especially a temporary one [Late 17C. Via French *caserne* < Latin *quarterna* 'hut for four'.]

case shot *n* an old kind of cannon shell containing shrapnel

case stated *n* an outline of the circumstances of a legal case prepared by one court for another court to use in making its decision, e.g. in an appeal hearing or a retrial

case study *n* an analysis of a particular case or situation used as a basis for drawing conclusions in similar situations

case system *n* the teaching of law through the study of important and representative cases rather than by studying theory

casework /káyss wurk/ *n* a system of making a social worker responsible for particular clients on a long-term basis —**caseworker** *n*

caseworm /káyss wurm/ *n* INSECTS = **caddis worm** [Early 17C. < the protective case it builds around itself.]

cash[1] /kash/ *n* **1 COINS AND BANKNOTES** money in the form of coins and notes as distinct from money orders or credit **2 CURRENCY OR CHEQUES** money used as immediate payment in any form, e.g. currency or cheques (*informal*) ■ *vt* **EXCHANGE SOMETHING FOR READY MONEY** to exchange a cheque or money order for coins and banknotes ○ *You can cash your pay cheque at the bank.* [Late 16C. Directly or via obsolete French < Italian *cassa* 'money box' < Latin *capsa* (see CASE[2]).] —**cashable** *adj*

SPELLCHECK See ***cache***.

---

cash in *v* **1** *vt* to withdraw from a business investment such as an insurance policy and take the money that is due **2** *vi* to make large amounts of money (*slang*) ○ *When the stock was sold, she really cashed in.*
cash in on *vt* to exploit a situation in order to get personal benefit, especially money ○ *It seemed that everyone who knew him wanted to cash in on his rise to fame.*
cash out *v* **1** *vti* to sell off an asset that has been held for a long time, e.g. land, in order to profit ○ *He finally decided to cash out and sell the land that had been in his family for three generations.* **2** *vi US* COMM = **cash up 3** *vi US* to commit suicide (*slang*)
cash up *vi* to add up the day's takings of a shop or similar business ○ *shopkeepers cashing up at the end of the day.* US term **cash out**

cash[2] /kash/ (*plural* **cash**) *n* any of several former small Asian coins of low value [Late 16C. Via Portuguese *caixa* < Tamil *kāçu*.]

Cash /kash/, **Martin** (1810–77) Irish-born Australian bushranger

Cash, Pat (*b.* 1965) Australian tennis player. Full name **Patrick Hart Cash**

cash and carry *n* (*plural* **cash and carries**) **1 INEXPENSIVE WHOLESALE STORE** a wholesale store selling inexpensive goods that are paid for in cash and taken away by the buyer **2 POLICY OF SELLING WITHOUT DELIVERY SERVICE** a policy of selling items for cash with no delivery service to customers ■ *adj* **CASH-ONLY AND WITHOUT DELIVERY** sold, or operating, on a basis of cash-only payments by buyers who take their goods away at the time of purchase

cash bar *n* a bar at a large party or reception at which drinks have to be paid for individually

cashbook /kásh bòok/ *n* a book for keeping a record of money spent and received

cash box *n* a lockable box for cash, especially one holding the daily takings of a small business

cash card *n* a coded plastic card that a bank customer uses to access an account by means of a cashpoint

cash cow *n* a profitable business or product with low overheads often used to fund other businesses or investments (*slang*) ○ *The grocery chain has been their cash cow for years.*

cash crop *n* a crop grown for direct sale rather than personal consumption

cash desk *n* a counter for payment of goods in a shop

cash dispenser *n* BANKING = **cashpoint**

cashew /káshoo, ka shóo/ *n* **1 cashew, cashew nut** a kidney-shaped nut **2** an evergreen tree that produces nuts and oil. Native to: South America. *Anacardium occidentale.* [Late 16C. Via Portuguese, < Tupi *acajú*.]

cashew apple *n* the edible swollen stalk by which a cashew nut is attached to its stem, used to make preserves

cash flow *n* **1** the pattern of income and expenses, and its consequences for how much money is available at a given time **2** the prediction or assessment of a company's income and expenditure over a period of time

cashier[1] /ka shéer/ *n* **1 BANK WORKER TAKING AND PAYING MONEY** somebody in a bank who deals directly with customers and handles routine account transactions **2 SOMEBODY RESPONSIBLE FOR FINANCIAL TRANSACTIONS** an official in an organization who is responsible for receiving and paying out money and keeping financial records ■ *vi* **WORK AS CASHIER** to work as a cashier, especially in a place of business such as a restaurant or bar ○ *Who's cashiering tonight?* [Late 16C. Directly or via Dutch *cassier* < French *caissier* < *casse* (see CASH[1]).]

cashier[2] /ka shéer/ *vt* to dismiss somebody from the armed forces because of misconduct [Early 16C. Via Dutch *kasseren* 'disband (soldiers)' < French *casser* 'to break' < Latin *quassare* (see QUASH[1]).]

cashier's cheque *n* a guaranteed cheque issued by a bank against money taken from a customer's account or against cash provided for this purpose

cashless /káshləss/ *adj* using an electronic means of exchanging money instead of dealing in cash

cash machine *n* BANKING = **cashpoint**

cashmere /kásh meer/ *n* **1** the soft wool from a Himalayan goat **2** a woollen fabric made from cashmere [Late 17C. Early spelling of KASHMIR.]

cash method *n* a method of accounting that counts income or expenses at the time they are actually received or paid out, irrespective of when they are earned or incurred. ◊ **accrual method**

cash on delivery *adv* with full payment for ordered goods to be made by the buyer to the one delivering the goods ○ *bought the coat cash on delivery*

cashpoint /kásh poynt/ *n UK* a machine that provides cash and account information on insertion of a machine-readable card. US term **ATM**

cash-poor *adj* financially sound but having little readily available cash

cash ratio *n* the ratio that a bank must maintain between available cash and total deposits

cash register *n* a machine in a shop that records sales, calculates totals, and has a drawer for takings

cash-starved *adj* having very little money or financial support

cash-strapped *adj* having insufficient money (*informal*)

Casimir III /kázzi meer/ (1310–70) king of Poland (1333–70). Known as **Casimir the Great**

casing /káyssing/ *n* **1 OUTER COVERING** an outer covering, e.g. the sheath of an electrical cable or the skin of a sausage **2 FRAME FOR DOOR OR WINDOW** a frame containing a door, window, or stairway **3 LINER PIPE IN WELL** a liner pipe or tube in water, oil, or gas wells

casino /kə séenō/ (*plural* **-nos**) *n* **1** a private club, or a room in a club, hotel, or other establishment, where gambling takes place **2 casino, cassino** a point-scoring card game in which players combine cards exposed on the table with cards in their hands, with the 10 of diamonds being the highest-valued card [Mid-18C. < Italian, 'small house' < Latin *casa* 'house'.]

Casino /kə séenō/ town in N New South Wales, Australia. Population: 9,990 (1996).

casino society *n* a society in which large amounts of money are used and gained in business ventures by a small number of people and organizations while the broad public interest is neglected

cask /kaask/ *n* **1 BARREL CONTAINING ALCOHOL** a wooden barrel containing alcoholic drink **2 CONTAINER LIKE A BARREL** any barrel-like container, whether or not of wood **3 CONTENTS OF BARREL** the contents of a barrel or similar container **4** INDUST = **flask** *n.* 6 [Early 16C. Via French *casque* or Spanish *casco* 'helmet, skull' < Latin *quassare* (see QUASH[1]).]

casket /kaáskit/ *n* **1** a decorative box for valuables **2** *US* = **coffin** [15C. < ?]

Casparian strip /ka spáiri ən-/ *n* a thin impervious band of material in the cell walls of certain plants resembling suberin or lignin [After Robert *Caspary*, 19C German botanist]

Caspian Sea /káspi ən-/ world's largest inland body of water, between SE Europe and Asia. Area: 371,000 sq. km/143,000 sq. mi.

casque /kask/ *n* **1** a helmet from a suit of armour **2** a horny growth on the head of a bird, fish or reptile, resembling a helmet [Late 17C. Via French < Spanish *casco* (see CASK).] —**casqued** *adj*

Cassandra /kə sándrə/ *n* somebody whose warnings of impending disaster are ignored [Early 17C. After *Cassandra*, the daughter of Priam, king of Troy, who was granted the gift of prophecy but was condemned never to be believed.]

cassata /kə saátə/ *n* **1** brightly coloured Italian ice cream containing nuts and candied fruit and layers or streaks of different flavours **2** a Sicilian sponge cake, layered and coated with sweet ricotta, flavoured with candied fruit and chopped chocolate, decorated with candied fruit, and eaten as a celebration cake or dessert [Early 20C. < Italian.]

cassation /ka sáysh'n/ *n* **1** a court of appeal in countries that follow the Napoleonic code of civil law **2** an 18th-century instrumental work similar in form to a divertimento [15C. < Latin *cassare* 'annul'.]

Cassatt /kə sát/, **Mary** (1845–1926) US artist

cassava /kə saávə/ *n* **1** a large thick-skinned tuber that is poisonous when raw and untreated but like the potato when boiled. Use: as a vegetable in many tropical countries, as a source of tapioca. **2** a tropical plant that produces cassava. *Manihot esculenta.* [Mid-16C. < Taino *casávi*.]

Cassegrainian telescope /kássi gráyni ən-/ *n* an astronomical telescope that uses a large concave mirror and a small convex mirror to form an image [Late 19C. After Giovanni *Cassegrain* (1625–1712), French astronomer.]

Cassel = **Kassel**

casserole /kássərōl/ *n* **1** COOKING POT a deep, heavy cooking pot suitable for use in an oven **2** COOKED DISH a stew or other moist food dish, cooked slowly at a low heat in a covered pot or dish **3** LABORATORY CONTAINER a porcelain container used for heating substances in a laboratory ■ *vt* (**-roles, -roling, -roled**) COOK FOOD IN LIQUID to cook food slowly at a low heat with liquid in a covered pot [Early 18C. < French, 'small pan' < *casse* 'pan' < Greek *kuathos* 'cup'.]

cassette /kə sét/ *n* **1** a sealed plastic case containing a length of audio or videotape wound round spools ready for use **2** a sealed plastic case containing material for use in a machine, e.g. photographic film or ribbon for a printer [Late 18C. < French, 'small box' < *casse* (see CASH[1]).]

cassette deck *n* a tape deck that plays or records audio cassettes

cassette player *n* a machine that plays cassettes, but does not record audio

cassette recorder *n* a machine, especially a portable one, that plays and records audio cassettes

cassia /kássi ə/ *n* an evergreen Asian tree with an aromatic bark. *Cinnamomum aromaticum.* [Pre-12C. Via Latin < Hebrew *qᵉṣīʿāh*.]

Cassini division /ka seéni-/, **Cassini's division** *n* the dark area between the two brightest rings, the middle and outermost, of Saturn [Early 20C. After Giovanni Domenico *Cassini* (1625–1712), Italian-born French astronomer.]

cassino *n* CARDS = **casino** *n.* **2**

Cassiopeia /kássi ō peé ə/ *n* a constellation of the northern hemisphere. See illustration at **constellation**

cassis /ka seéss/ *n* a syrupy, usually alcoholic, cordial made in France from blackcurrants [Late 19C. < French, 'blackcurrant', probably < Latin *cassia* (see CASSIA).]

cassiterite /kə síttə rīt/ *n* a dark-coloured mineral consisting of tin oxide. Use: source of tin. [Mid-19C. < Greek *kassiteros* 'tin'.]

Cassius /kássi əss/ (*fl.* 53–42 BC) Roman general and conspirator

cassock /kássək/ *n* a full-length, usually black, robe worn by priests, their assistants, and singers in church choirs [Mid-16C. Via French *casaque* 'long coat' < Italian *casacca* 'riding coat'.] —**cassocked** *adj*

Casson /káss'n/, **Sir Hugh** (1910–99) British architect

cassone /kə sṓni/ *n* a highly decorated Italian chest of the Middle Ages and the Renaissance period [Late 19C. < Italian, < *cassa* (see CASH[1]).]

cassoulet /kássoo láy, kássoo lay/ *n* a French stew of haricot beans cooked in a casserole with meat [Mid-20C. < French, 'small stew-pan' < Greek *kuathos* 'cup'.]

cassowary /kássə wairi/ (*plural* **-ies**) *n* a large black flightless bird that resembles an ostrich or emu. Native to: NE Australia, New Guinea. Genus: *Casuarius.* [Early 17C. < Malay *kesuari*.]

cast /kaast/ *v* (**casts, casting, cast**) **1** *vt* THROW to throw something or somebody, especially something that or somebody who is light in weight **2** *vt* THROW ASHORE to throw something up on the seashore ○ *pieces of driftwood cast up by the incoming tide* **3** *vt* FLING DOWN OR AWAY to throw something away from yourself, usually with force **4** *vt* THROW FISHING LINE INTO WATER to throw a line, baited hook, or fishing net into the water **5** *vt* CAUSE TO APPEAR SOMEWHERE to make something, e.g. light or shadow, appear in a place ○ *The bulb cast an eerie green glow over everything.* **6** *vt* HAVE DISPIRITING EFFECT to reduce the enthusiasm, joy, or happiness of somebody or something ○ *Her mother's absence cast a shadow over the wedding plans.* **7** *vt* CREATE MISTRUST to generate a sense of uncertainty, distrust, or suspicion about something ○ *an accident that has cast doubt over the project's future* **8** *vt* DIRECT A LOOK to direct the eyes or a look towards somebody or something, often in a surreptitious, disapproving, or anxious manner ○ *casting a discreet glance at his watch* **9** *vt* DISMISS FROM THE MIND to remove or banish something from your mind deliberately, decisively, and often with difficulty (*formal*) **10** *vt* PUT SOMEWHERE ROUGHLY to put or throw somebody or something somewhere, especially in a rough or brutal way (*formal*) ○ *cast into the dungeon* **11** *vti* SELECT PARTICIPANTS FOR PERFORMANCE to choose somebody for a particular role in a drama, dance, or other performance, or choose people for all the roles in a production ○ *He was badly cast as Othello.* **12** *vt* DESCRIBE to classify or describe somebody in a particular way ○ *I seem to have been cast as the villain in this affair.* **13** *vt* FORM USING MOULD to pour something such as molten metal or plaster into a mould and allow it to solidify in order to create an object **14** *vt* SHED to shed something, e.g. the skin ○ *a snake that had cast its skin* **15** *vt* DROP to drop or lose something **16** *vt* CALCULATE to add something up, or calculate something **17** *vt Scotland* REPROACH to reproach somebody with something (*informal*) ■ *n* **1** ACT OF THROWING the flinging, hurling, or throwing of something, or an instance of that **2** LENGTH OF THROW the distance that something is thrown ○ *a 20-metre cast of a harpoon* **3** PERFORMERS the actors or other performers in a drama, dance, or other production (*takes a singular or plural verb*) **4** MOULDED OBJECT an object that is made by pouring a molten substance, especially metal, into a mould and leaving it to solidify **5** MOULD a container of a particular shape into which a molten substance, especially metal, is poured and left to solidify **6** SUPPORT FOR BROKEN BONE a stiff plaster of Paris or fibreglass casing that holds a broken bone in place while it is mending ○ *He came back with his leg in a cast.* ◊ **plaster cast** *n.* **1** **7** MOLTEN IMPRESSION an impression formed by pressing soft or molten material over or inside something and letting it harden or dry ○ *a cast of the pianist's hands* **8** PRESERVED SEDIMENT preserved sediment made by the infilling of an impression such as a footprint **9** EMOTIONAL OR PSYCHOLOGICAL TYPE the nature or quality of somebody's character or mind **10** PHYSICAL TYPE the nature or quality of somebody's appearance ○ *I did not trust the sly cast of his face.* **11** SQUINT a defect that causes one eye to look permanently sideways **12** OVERSPREADING OF ONE THING ONTO ANOTHER the overspreading of something, especially an added colour, that results in modification of the hue or general appearance of something else **13** TINGE a general suggestion of something, e.g. a colour ○ *The mud gave a brown cast to the water.* **14** THROW OF LINE OR NET the throwing of a fishing line or net into the water **15** THROWN LINE OR NET a fishing line or net that is thrown into the water **16** DICE THROW a throw of dice, or the number that has been thrown **17** SOMETHING SHED BY ORGANISM a part of an organism, e.g. an insect casing, a snake skin, or worm faeces, that has been shed in a natural recurring process [12C. < Old Norse *kasta* 'to throw'.] —**castability** /kaástə bílləti/ *n* —**castable** *adj*

SYNONYMS See ***throw.***

cast around, cast about *vi* to search for something or try to devise a solution to a problem

cast aside *vt* **1** to reject and abandon somebody or something regarded as no longer interesting or useful ○ *You can't just cast him aside like that!* **2** to abandon something, e.g. a feeling or belief (*formal*) ○ *You must cast your doubts aside and trust in me.*

cast away *vt* to shipwreck somebody, especially on a desert island

cast off *v* **1** *vt* GET RID OF to reject or abandon something or somebody regarded as no longer useful or attractive ○ *I cast off that old coat years ago.* **2** *vti* UNTIE MOORING LINES to untie the ropes securing a boat to its mooring so that it can move away **3** *vti* FINISH KNITTING to make the last row of stitches in a piece of knitting by looping each stitch over the next and removing it from the needle **4** *vti* FIT TEXT to calculate the amount of space a piece of text will take up when it has been typeset

cast on *vti* to make the first row of stitches in a piece of knitting

cast out *v* **1** *vt* to reject, abandon, or eject somebody or something (*formal*) **2** *vi Scotland* to quarrel with somebody (*informal*)

castanet /kástə nét/ *n* either of a pair of small curved pieces of hard wood or plastic that are joined at the top and used to make a rhythmic clicking sound [Early 17C. < Spanish *castañeta* 'small chestnut' < *castaña* 'chestnut' < Latin *castanea*; from their likeness to chestnut shells.]

castaway /kaástə way/ *n* the survivor of a shipwreck —**castaway** *adj*

cast down *adj* experiencing feelings of dejection, depression, or sadness

caste /kaast/ *n* **1** HINDU SOCIAL CLASS any of the four main hereditary classes (**varnas**) into which Hindu society is divided and that dictate the social position and status of people according to their professions **2** HINDU CLASS SYSTEM the Hindu system of organizing society into hereditary classes **3** CLASS SYSTEM a system that divides people into classes according to their rank, wealth, or profession, or that of the family into which they were born **4** SOCIAL CLASS the class and rank or position of somebody in a society, based on birth, occupation, or some other criterion **5** INSECT RANK a group of insects that has a specialized role in a colony or hive of social insects such as ants or bees [Mid-16C. < Spanish, Portuguese *casta* 'pure race' < Latin *castus* 'pure'.] —**casteism** *n*

Castel Gandolfo /káss tel gan dólfō/ village south of Rome, Italy, the site of the pope's summer residence. Population: 6,952 (1993).

Castella /ka stéllə/, **Robert de** (*b.* 1957) Australian marathon runner

castellan /kástilən/ *n* in former times, somebody who governed or managed a castle [14C. Via Old N French *castelain* < medieval Latin *castellanus* < Latin *castellum* (see CASTLE).]

castellated /kástə laytid/ *adj* **1** WITH BATTLEMENTS OR SERRATED TOP EDGE with battlements or a serrated top edge like the walls of a castle **2** INDENTED OR SERRATED LIKE BATTLEMENTS with indented or serrated edges resembling the top of a castle wall ○ *an ornate tablecloth with a castellated edge* **3** WITH CASTLE OR CASTLES with a castle or castles as part of the surroundings or landscape (*literary*) ○ *the castellated French countryside* [Late 17C. < medieval Latin *castellatus* 'having a castle' < Latin *castellum* (see CASTLE).]

caste mark *n* a mark, usually a painted dot on the forehead, that shows a Hindu person's caste

caster /kaástər/ *n* **1** somebody or something that casts something else **2** = **castor**[1] *n.* **1**, **castor**[1] *n.* **2**, **castor**[1] *n.* **3**

caster sugar *n* finely ground white sugar that is often used in baking

castigate /kásti gayt/ (**-gates, -gating, -gated**) *vt* to criticize, rebuke, or punish somebody severely (*formal; often passive*) ○ *They were strongly castigated for their refusal to act.* [Early 17C. < Latin *castigat-*, past participle of *castigare* 'chastise' < *castus* 'chaste'.] —**castigation** /kásti gáysh'n/ *n* —**castigator** *n* —**castigatory** /kásti gáytəri/ *adj*

SYNONYMS See ***criticize.***

Castile /ka steél/ central region of Spain that formed the core of the Kingdom of Castile

Castile soap /ka steél-/ *n* hard white unperfumed soap made from olive oil and soda

Castilian /ka stílli ən/, **Castillian** *n* **1** SPANISH DIALECT the dialect of Spanish that is spoken in the province of Castile **2** SPANISH LANGUAGE the standard form of Spanish, based on the dialect spoken in the province of Castile **3** SOMEBODY FROM CASTILE somebody who comes from the province of Castile in Spain —**Castilian** *adj*

casting /kaásting/ *n* **1** MAKING OF OBJECTS USING MOULDS the making of a solid object by pouring molten metal, glass, or plastic into a mould and allowing it to cool **2** OBJECT MADE WITH MOULD an object made using a mould **3** THROW OF FISHING LINE the throwing out of a fishing line or net **4** SOMETHING THROWN something that is thrown out or thrown off **5** SELECTION PROCESS FOR PERFORMERS the choosing of actors or other performers for a drama, dance, or other production, usually by audition, interview, or screen test **6** CHOICE OF PERFORMERS the choice of actors or other performers for roles in a drama, dance, or other production ○ *The script was very sharp but the casting was terrible.*

casting couch *n* the granting of usually sexual favours in return for work in a film, television, or other production (*informal humorous*)

casting vote *n* the deciding vote in a ballot or debate, cast by the chairperson or presiding officer when votes for and against something are equally divided

cast iron *n* iron with a high carbon content, making it hard but brittle, so that it must be shaped by casting rather than hammering or beating

cast-iron *adj* **1** OF CAST IRON made from cast iron **2** VERY STRONG extremely strong or resistant **3** ALLOWING NO CHANGE not permitting any alteration of its terms ○ *a cast-iron agreement*

castle /kaáss'l/ *n* **1** FORTRESS a large fortified building or complex of buildings, usually with tall solid walls, battlements, and a permanent garrison, built especially during the Middle Ages **2** MANOR HOUSE a large magnificent house built, especially in the 18th and 19th centuries, to resemble the fortified castles of the past **3** PRIVATE REFUGE the building, property, or place to which somebody, especially the owner, turns for privacy or refuge **4** CHESS = **rook**² *n.* ■ *vti* (**-tles, -tling, -tled**) MOVE KING AND ROOK in chess, to move the king two squares to the left or right and move the nearest rook over the king to the adjacent square on the opposite side [Pre-12C. < Latin *castellum* 'fortified village' < *castrum* 'fortified place'.] ◇ **build castles in the air** *or* **in Spain** to have dreams or plans that are extremely unlikely to succeed or be realized

Castlebar /kaáss'l baár/ town in W Ireland. Population: 8,323 (1991).

castled /kaáss'ld/ *adj* ARCHIT = **castellated** *adj.* 1

Castlereagh /kaáss'l ray/ **1** river in N New South Wales, Australia. Length: 550 km/342 mi. **2** district in E Northern Ireland. Population: 60,649 (1991). Area: 85 sq. km/33 sq. mi.

Castlereagh, Robert Stewart, 2nd Marquis of Londonderry (1769–1822) Irish-born British statesman and diplomat

cast net *n* a round or cone-shaped net thrown by anglers and withdrawn by means of lines attached to its opening

castoff /kaást of/ *n* **1** something that or somebody who has been rejected or abandoned because no longer considered useful or attractive (*often plural*) ○ *I don't want your old castoffs!* **2** a calculation of the length of a piece of text made before fitting copy into available space

castor¹ /kaástər/ *n* **1** SMALL WHEEL UNDER FURNITURE a small wheel on a mount that allows it to turn in all directions, attached under the corners of heavy furniture and other objects to make them easier to move **2** SMALL CONDIMENT CONTAINER a small container with a perforated top or open mouth for sprinkling sugar, salt, or other condiments **3** CONDIMENT STAND a small stand that holds condiment containers [Late 17C. Alteration of CASTER; probably associated with CASTOR².]

castor² /kaástər/ *n* **1** BEAVER OIL a brown oily aromatic substance secreted from glands in a beaver's groin. Use: in medicine and perfumes. **2** BEAVER FUR the fur of a beaver **3** BEAVER HAT a hat made of beaver fur or imitation beaver fur [14C. Via French or Latin, < Greek *kastōr* 'beaver'.]

Castor /kaástər/ *n* **1** the second brightest star in the constellation Gemini **2** ◊ **Castor and Pollux**

Castor and Pollux /-ənd pólləks/ *npl* in classical mythology, the twin sons of Leda and the brothers of Helen of Troy and Clytemnestra

castor bean *n* the poisonous seed of the castor-oil plant. Use: source of castor oil

castor oil *n* a thin yellowish oil obtained from the seeds of the castor-oil plant. Use: laxative, lubricant. [< ?]

castor-oil plant *n* a tall tropical plant with large lobed leaves that is cultivated for ornament and for its seeds, from which castor oil is produced. *Ricinus communis.*

castor steering *n* a type of steering found in horse-drawn vehicles, steam wagons, traction engines, and trailers, in which the whole front axle swivels around a central point

castrametation /kástrəmə táysh'n/ *n* the creation and laying out of a military encampment [Late 17C. < French *castramétation* < Latin *castra metari* 'measure or mark out a camp'.]

castrate /ka stráyt/ (**-trates, -trating, -trated**) *vt* **1** REMOVE TESTICLES FROM to remove the testicles of a man or male animal **2** WEAKEN to take away the strength, power, force, or vigour of somebody or something ○ *The department was castrated through heavy budget cuts.* **3** REMOVE OVARIES FROM to remove the ovaries of a woman or female animal [15C. < Latin *castrat-*, past participle of *castrare* 'cut off'.] —**castrater** *n* —**castration** *n*

castration complex /ka stráysh'n-/ *n* according to Freudian psychology, a subconscious fear in men of having their genitals removed as a punishment for wanting to have sexual intercourse with their mother

castrato /ka straátō/ (*plural* **-ti** /-ti/ *or* **-tos**) *n* in the past, a male singer who was castrated before puberty in order to retain a soprano or alto voice [Mid-18C. < Italian, 'castrated one' < Latin *castrat-* (see CASTRATE).]

Castries /ka stréess/ capital of St Lucia in the Caribbean. Population: 11,147 (1991).

Castro /kástrō/, **Cipriano** (1858–1924) Venezuelan national leader

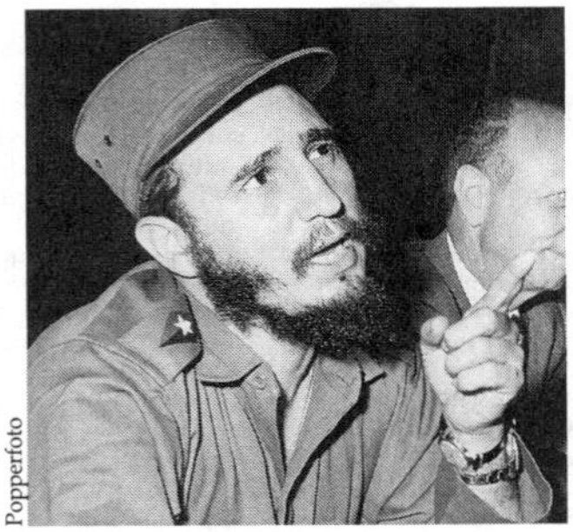

Popperfoto

Fidel Castro

Castro, Fidel (*b.* 1926) Cuban prime minister (1959–76) and president (1976–)

Castroism /kástrō izəm/ *n* the Communist political, social, and economic policies of Fidel Castro and his supporters —**Castroist** *n, adj* —**Castroite** *n, adj*

casual /kázhyoo əl/ *adj* **1** CHANCE OR UNPREMEDITATED happening or done by chance or without prior thought or planning **2** OCCASIONAL OR TEMPORARY relating to or taking on work that is available at irregular intervals or seasonally **3** KNOWN ONLY SLIGHTLY relating to somebody or something known only slightly ○ *a casual acquaintance at work* **4** SUPERFICIAL not involving emotional commitment or loyalty, or lacking in thoroughness or seriousness **5** LENIENT possessing a permissive or lenient approach to things ○ *very casual about enforcing the rules* **6** INDIFFERENT showing little interest or enthusiasm **7** NONCHALANT cool, calm, or nonchalant in manner **8** NOT FORMAL informal and relaxed **9** COMFORTABLE comfortable and suitable for wearing on informal occasions ■ *n* TEMPORARY WORKER an employee who works on a temporary or seasonal basis ■ **casuals** *npl* INFORMAL CLOTHES OR FOOTWEAR informal comfortable clothes or shoes [14C. Directly or via French, < Latin *casualis* < *casus* 'event'.] —**casually** *adv* —**casualness** *n*

casualization /kázhyoo ə lī záysh'n/, **casualisation** *n* the changing of working practices so that workers are employed on a freelance and occasional basis rather than being offered full-time contracts ○ *the increasing casualization of labour*

casualty /kázhyoo əlti/ (*plural* **-ties**) *n* **1** ACCIDENT VICTIM the victim of a fatality or serious injury **2** INJURED OR DEAD SOLDIER a member of the armed forces who is killed or injured during combat **3** VICTIM something or somebody destroyed or suffering as an indirect result of a particular event or circumstances **4** HOSPITAL EMERGENCY DEPARTMENT a hospital department that treats emergency patients who have had accidents or been injured (*often before a noun*) ○ *rushed to casualty with multiple fractures.* US term **emergency room** [15C. Alteration of medieval Latin *casualitas* 'chance' < *casualis* (see CASUAL).]

casualwear /kázhyoo əl wair/ *n* comfortable clothes suitable for wearing on informal occasions

casuarina /kázzyoo ə réenə, kázh-, -rínə/ (*plural* **-nas** *or* **-na**) *n* a tree with needle-shaped leaves that form whorls at the end of short branches. Native to: Australia, parts of Asia. Genus: *Casuarina.* [Late 18C. < modern Latin, < *casuarius* 'cassowary'; from the similarity of its branches to the bird's feathers.]

casuist /kázzyoo ist/ *n* **1** somebody, especially a theologian, who tries to settle questions of ethics and morals by applying general rules and principles to them **2** a subtle, sophisticated, and sometimes deceptive reasoner, especially on moral issues (*disapproving*) [Early 17C. Via French, < modern Latin *casuista* < Latin *casus* 'event'.] —**casuistic** /kázzyoo ístik/ *adj* —**casuistical** *adj* —**casuistically** *adv*

casuistry /kázzyoo istri/ *n* **1** the application of general rules and principles to questions of ethics and morals in order to resolve them **2** the use of sophisticated and subtle argument and reasoning, especially on moral issues, in order to justify something or mislead somebody (*disapproving*)

casus belli /kaássooss béll ee/ (*plural* **casus belli**) *n* a situation or event that causes, or is the pretext for starting, a war or other conflict (*formal*) [< modern Latin, 'occasion of war']

cat /kat/ *n* **1** FURRY ANIMAL THAT PURRS AND MIAOWS a small domesticated mammal that has soft fur, sharp claws, pointed ears, and, usually, a long furry tail **2** ZOOL = **big cat** **3** OFFENSIVE TERM an offensive term for a woman who is regarded as spiteful or malicious (*informal insult*) **4** US MAN a man (*dated slang*) ○ *He's a real cool cat.* **5** ANCHOR TACKLE OR CATHEAD a set of heavy tackle used for raising an anchor to the cathead, or the cathead itself **6** = **cat-o'-nine-tails** **7** ZOOL = **catfish** **8** CATAMARAN a catamaran (*informal*) **9** CATBOAT a catboat (*informal*) **10** CATALYTIC CONVERTER a catalytic converter (*informal*) ■ *v* (**cats, catting, catted**) **1** *vt* RAISE ANCHOR to raise the anchor to the cathead **2** *vi* VOMIT to vomit (*informal*) [Old English *catt(e)* < Germanic] ◇ **bell the cat** to play the leading part in something difficult or dangerous, usually when such action will be of help to a group ◇ **has the cat got your tongue?** used, often to a child, to prompt somebody to speak and to ask the reason for his or her silence ◇ **let the cat out of the bag** to disclose secret or confidential information ◇ **like a cat on hot bricks** extremely nervous or agitated ◇ **play cat and mouse with somebody** to treat somebody who is in your power in such a way that he or she does not know what you are going to do next ◇ **put** *or* **set the cat among the pigeons** to cause trouble ◇ **rain cats and dogs** to rain very heavily (*informal*) ◇ to have an extremely high opinion of yourself ◇ **when the cat's away the mice will play** when somebody in authority is absent, those he or she is in charge of will misbehave

⚡**CAT** *abbr* **1** clear-air turbulence **2** computerized axial tomography **3** College of Advanced Technology **4** computer-aided trading

cata- *prefix* down, apart ○ *catabolism* ○ *catalysis* [< Greek *kata*]

catabolism /kə tábbəlizəm/, **katabolism** *n* the production of energy through the conversion of complex molecules into simpler ones [Late 19C. < Greek *katabolē* 'throwing down' < *ballein* 'to throw'.] —**catabolic** /kàttə bóllik/ *adj* —**catabolically** *adv*

catabolite /kə tábbə līt/ *n* a product of catabolism

catachresis /kàttə kréessiss/ (*plural* **-ses** /-sseez/) *n* the incorrect use of words, e.g. by mixing metaphors or applying terminology wrongly [Mid-16C. Via Latin < Greek *katakhrēsis* < *katakhrēsthai* 'to misuse'.] —**catachrestic** /-kréstik/ *adj* —**catachrestical** *adj* —**catachrestically** *adv*

cataclysm /káttəklizəm/ *n* **1** a sudden and violent upheaval or disaster that causes great changes in society, e.g. a war, earthquake, or drought **2** a terrible and devastating flood [Early 17C. Via French < Greek *kataklusmos* 'deluge' < *kluzein* 'wash'.] —**cataclysmal** /kàttə klízm'l/ *adj* —**cataclysmic** *adj* —**cataclysmically** *adv*

catacomb /káttə koom, -kōm/ *n* (*often plural*) **1** an underground cemetery consisting of passages or tunnels with rooms and recesses leading off them for burial chambers **2** any underground network of passages or tunnels [Pre-12C. Via Old French < late Latin *catacumbas*, subterranean cemetery of St Sebastian in Rome.]

catadromous /kə táddrəməss/ *adj* describes fish that spend most of their lives in fresh water but migrate to salt water to breed, as eels do. ◊ **anadromous**

catafalque /káttə falk/ *n* a raised and decorated platform on which the coffin of a distinguished person lies in state before or during a funeral [Mid-17C. Via French < Italian *catafalco*.]

~~**catagory**~~ incorrect spelling of **category**

Catalan /káttə lan/ *n* **1** the Romance language of Catalonia and the Balearic Islands, Spain, also spoken in Andorra and the French department of Roussillon. Native speakers: 7 million. **2** somebody who comes from Catalonia —**Catalan** *adj*

catalase /káttə layz, -layss/ *n* an antioxidant enzyme in living cells [Early 20C. < CATALYSIS.] —**catalatic** /káttə láttik/ *adj*

catalepsy /káttə lepsi/ *n* actual or apparent unconsciousness during which muscles become rigid and remain in any position in which they are placed [14C. Directly or via French < late Latin *catalepsia* < Greek *katalēpsis* 'seizure' < *katalambanein* 'seize upon' < *lambanein* 'seize'.] —**cataleptic** /káttə léptik/ *adj* —**cataleptically** *adv*

catalexis /káttə léksiss/ *n* the lack of one syllable in the final foot of a line of verse [Mid-19C. < Greek *katalēxis* 'termination' < *katalēgein* 'leave off' < *lēgein* 'cease'.] —**catalectic** /-léktik/ *adj*

catalog *n, vt* US = **catalogue** ■ *n* US = **prospectus** *n.* 1

catalogue *n* (*plural* **-logues**) **1 LIST OF GOODS FOR SALE** a list of priced and illustrated items for sale, presented in book form or in other formats including CD-ROM or video **2 EXHIBITION GUIDE** a booklet that lists and often illustrates the objects on show at an exhibition **3 LIST OF BOOKS** a list of the holdings in a library, usually arranged according to subject, title, or author **4 SERIES OF THINGS** a list of things or events that relate to an issue or person, especially those that are unpleasant or undesirable ○ *a catalogue of disasters* ■ *v* (**-logues, -loguing, -logued**) **1** *vti* **MAKE A CATALOGUE** to classify and list items to form a catalogue **2** *vt* **ENTER SOMETHING IN CATALOGUE** to enter something in a catalogue ○ *I have catalogued all the new additions to the collection.* **3** *vt* **LIST SERIES OF THINGS OR EVENTS** to list or describe a series of related events, items, or qualities ○ *a history of the twentieth century that catalogues many examples of human ingenuity* [15C. Via French < Greek *katalogos* 'list' < *katalegein* 'pick out' < *legein* 'choose'.] —**cataloguer** *n*

catalogue raisonné /káttə log ráyzə náy/ (*plural* **catalogues raisonnés** /káttə log ráyzə náy/) *n* a detailed list of works by a particular artist, especially one produced to accompany an exhibition or collection [< French, 'reasoned catalogue']

Catalonia /káttə lṓni ə/ autonomous region in NE Spain. Capital: Barcelona. Population: 6,226,869 (1995). Area: 32,113 sq. km/12,399 sq. mi. Catalan **Catalunya**. Spanish **Cataluña** —**Catalonian** *adj, n*

Cataluña /káttə lo͞onyə/ ♦ **Catalonia**

Catalunya /káttə lo͞onyə/ ♦ **Catalonia**

catalyse /káttə līz/ (**-lyses, -lysing, -lysed**) *vt* **1** to increase the rate of a chemical reaction by the action or use of a catalyst **2** to cause a particular thing to happen, or bring about a particular state of affairs ○ *The hearings have catalysed the passage of financial reforms.* [Late 19C. < CATALYSIS.] —**catalyser** *n*

catalysis /kə tálləssiss/ (*plural* **-ses** /-seez/) *n* the increase in the rate of a chemical reaction in the presence of a catalyst [Mid-17C. Via modern Latin, 'dissolution' < Greek *katalusis* < *kataluein* 'dissolve' < *luein* 'set free'.]

catalyst /káttəlist/ *n* **1** a substance that increases the rate of a chemical reaction without itself undergoing any change **2** somebody or something that makes a change happen or brings about an event ○ *The quarrel acted as a catalyst for the breakup of their partnership.* [Early 20C. < CATALYSIS.]

catalytic /káttə líttik/ *adj* involving or causing an increase in the rate of a chemical reaction by the use of a catalyst [Mid-19C. < Greek *katalutikos* 'able to dissolve' < *katalusis* (see CATALYSIS).] —**catalytically** *adv*

catalytic converter *n* in the exhaust system of a motor vehicle, a chamber in which gases mix with air so that pollutants such as carbon monoxide can be oxidized

catalytic cracker *n* an oil-refinery device that breaks down large molecules from crude oil into smaller ones that are useful as fuel, using heat and a catalyst to lower the required temperature

catalyze *vt* US = **catalyse**

catamaran /káttəmə rán/ *n* **1** a sailing boat or engine-powered boat that has two identical hulls fixed together by a rigid framework **2** a simple raft made from logs or floats tied together [Early 17C. < Tamil *kaṭṭumaram* 'tied wood'.]

catamite /káttə mīt/ *n* a boy or youth with whom a man has homosexual intercourse (*literary*) [Late 16C. Via Latin *catamitus* < Greek *Ganumēdēs* 'Ganymede'.]

catamount /káttə mownt/, **catamountain** /-mowntin/ *n* ZOOL = **puma** [Mid-17C. From *cat of the mountain*.]

cat-and-mouse *adj* cruel or sadistic, especially in exploiting, compounding, and enjoying somebody else's suffering or fear

cataphora /kə táffərə/ *n* the use of a word or phrase, usually a pronoun, that refers to something mentioned later, as does 'it' in 'It's easy to make mistakes' [Late 20C. < CATA- + ANAPHORA.] —**cataphoric** /káttə fórrik/ *adj*

cataphoresis /káttəfə réessiss/ (*plural* **-ses** /-sseez/) *n* SCI = **electrophoresis** [Late 19C. < CATA- + Greek *phorēsis* 'being carried'.] —**cataphoretic** /-fə réttik/ *adj* —**cataphoretically** *adv*

cataplasia /káttə pláyzi ə/ *n* the degeneration of cells or tissue to a more primitive or embryonic form —**cataplastic** /-plástik/ *adj*

cataplexy /káttə pleksi/ *n* the sudden temporary inability to move, caused by shock, fear, or ecstasy [Late 19C. < Greek *kataplēxis* 'stupefaction' < *kataplēssein* 'strike down' < *plēssein* 'strike'.] —**cataplectic** /káttə pléktik/ *adj*

catapult /káttə pult/ *n* **1 MEDIEVAL WEAPON** a large heavy war machine used in medieval times to hurl large stones at an enemy **2 DEVICE FOR FIRING STONES** a Y-shaped device of wood, plastic, or metal with a piece of elastic stretched between the two top points of the Y, used for firing stones or pellets. US term **slingshot** **3 PLANE OR MISSILE LAUNCHER** a mechanism on an aircraft carrier or warship, used to launch planes or missiles ■ *v* **1** *vt* **HURL** to throw something with great force from a catapult (*often passive*) ○ *The fighters were catapulted from the carrier at 30-second intervals.* **2** *vti* **FLING OR BE FLUNG** to throw somebody or something violently into the air or be thrown in this way ○ *They were catapulted out of their seats by the force of the impact.* **3** *vt* **CHANGE SOMEBODY'S CIRCUMSTANCES** to thrust somebody unexpectedly and suddenly into a particular situation ○ *the hit that catapulted her to fame at the tender age of fifteen* [Late 16C. Directly or via French < Latin *catapulta* < Greek *katapeltēs* < *pallein* 'hurl'.]

cataract /káttə rakt/ *n* **1 EYE DISEASE** an eye disease in which the lens becomes covered in an opaque film that affects sight, eventually causing total blindness **2 FILM OVER EYE LENS** the lens of the eye or the membrane surrounding it (**capsule**) that has become opaque as a result of disease **3 WATERFALL** a series of river rapids and small waterfalls with only moderate vertical drop (*literary*) **4 FLOOD** a heavy downpour of rain or a great flood (*literary*) [15C. < Latin *cataracta* 'portcullis' < Greek *kataraktēs* 'down-dashing' < *katarassein* 'dash down' < *arassein* 'to strike'.]

catarrh /kə taár/ *n* inflammation of a mucous membrane, especially in the nose and throat, causing an increase in the production of mucus, as happens in the common cold [15C. Via French *catarrhe* < Greek *katarrhous* < *katarrhein* 'flow down' < *rhein* 'to flow'.] —**catarrhal** *adj* —**catarrhous** *adj*

catarrhine /káttə rīn/ *adj* describes primates that have nostrils set close together and directed downwards ■ *n* an animal with a catarrhine nose structure, e.g. a human or an ape. Suborder: Catarrhini. [Mid-19C. < CATA- + Greek *rhinos* 'nose'.]

catastrophe /kə tástrəfi/ *n* **1 DISASTER** a terrible disaster or accident, especially one that leads to great loss of life **2 TOTAL FAILURE** an absolute failure, often in humiliating or embarrassing circumstances **3 RESOLUTION OF PLOT** the concluding part of the action in a drama, especially a classical tragedy, when the plot is resolved [Mid-16C. Via Latin *catastropha* < Greek *katastrophē* 'overturning' < *katastrephein* 'overturn' < *strephein* 'turn'.]

catastrophic /káttə strṓffik/ *adj* **1 DISASTROUS** causing or liable to cause widespread damage or death ○ *the uncontrolled spread of an infection that has had a catastrophic effect on livestock* **2 AWFUL** completely unsuccessful or very bad ○ *The party was a catastrophic affair, ending in a riot.* **3** US **LIFE-THREATENING AND REQUIRING EXPENSIVE TREATMENT** so serious in nature as to require extensive, long-term, and expensive medical treatment ○ *cancer, Aids, and other catastrophic illnesses requiring excellent insurance coverage* —**catastrophically** *adv*

catastrophism /kə tástrəfizəm/ *n* **1** a theory, now discarded, that the geological features of the earth were formed by a series of sudden violent catastrophes rather than a gradual evolutionary process **2** an outlook or attitude that foresees disaster as the only possible outcome of any action or situation —**catastrophist** *n*

catatonia /káttə tṓni ə/ *n* a condition, often associated with schizophrenia, characterized by periods of inertia or apparent stupor and rigidity of the muscles [Late 19C. < CATA- + Greek *tonos* 'tone'.]

catatonic /káttə tónnik/ *adj* **1** in a state of inertia or apparent stupor often associated with schizophrenia, characterized by rigidity of the muscles **2** in a stupefied or unconscious state, especially one caused by drunkenness (*informal*) —**catatonically** *adv*

Catawba /kə táwbə/ (*plural* **-ba** *or* **-bas**) *n* **1 MEMBER OF NATIVE N AMERICAN PEOPLE** a member of a Native North American people who once lived along the Catawba and Wateree rivers in North and South Carolina and whose surviving members now live mainly in South Carolina **2 VARIETY OF BLACK GRAPE** a reddish-coloured variety of the N American fox grape **3 RED WINE** a red wine made from the Catawba grape [Early 18C. After the *Catawba* River in North and South Carolina.]

catbird /kát burd/ *n* a songbird whose call resembles the cry of a cat, with dark-grey plumage and a black cap. Native to: North America. *Dumetella carolinensis*.

catbird seat *n* US a position or situation that gives somebody power and an edge over others, especially competitors or opponents (*informal*) [< ?]

catboat /kát bōt/ *n* a sailing boat that is broad across the beam and has a single sail on a forward-stepped mast [Late 19C. < ?]

cat burglar *n* a burglar who, using stealth and agility, breaks into properties, especially through high windows or small openings [< the burglar's catlike agility]

catcall /kát kawl/ *n* a whistle or shout expressing disapproval or dislike, especially at a live performance [Mid-17C. < the resemblance to cats' nocturnal cries.]

catch /kach/ *v* (**catches, catching, caught** /kawt/) **1** *vti* **STOP WITH THE HANDS** to take hold of or stop something that is travelling through the air **2** *vt* **COLLECT FALLING OBJECTS FROM BELOW** to collect something falling, e.g. rain, from below **3** *vt* **GRASP** to take tight hold of somebody or something suddenly ○ *He caught me by the shoulder.* **4** *vt* **CAPTURE ANIMAL** to capture or trap an animal, bird, fish, or other living thing **5** *vt* **CAPTURE CRIMINAL** to capture somebody, especially a criminal or somebody suspected of wrongdoing, after a search or chase ○ *Have they caught the culprit?* **6** *vt* **REACH** to reach or get alongside a person or vehicle moving ahead, usually at speed ○ *trying to catch the car in front* **7** *vt* **GET ON BOARD PUBLIC TRANSPORT** to arrive in time to board a bus, train, or other form of public transport ○ *I have a plane to catch.* **8** *vti* **GET DISEASE** to become infected with a disease **9** *vt* **SURPRISE SOMEBODY DOING WRONG** to surprise or stop somebody who is in the act of doing something illegal or forbidden ○ *He caught her taking money from the till.* **10** *vt* **SURPRISE SOMEBODY DOING SOMETHING EMBARRASSING** to surprise or observe somebody who is doing something considered embarrassing, impolite, or private ○ *I caught him gazing at himself in the mirror.* **11** *vt* **ATTRACT SOMEBODY'S ATTENTION** to attract the interest or attention of others ○ *a campaign that had caught the nation's imagination* **12** *vti* **MANAGE TO HEAR** to manage to hear what is being said ○ *I'm sorry, I didn't quite catch that.* **13** *vt* **UNDERSTAND** to understand the right meaning of something **14** *vt* **NOTICE SOMETHING SUBTLE OR FLEETING** to notice something subtle or fleeting, e.g. something in the way somebody is speaking that tells you how that person really feels ○ *I caught a note of sarcasm in his voice.* **15** *vt* **SEE PERFORMER OR PRODUCTION** to see a particular television programme, a film, or a play, or see a particular person performing in something (*informal*) ○ *If you get the chance, try and catch the new production of 'Hamlet'.* **16** *vt* **MANAGE TO MEET** to manage to meet or talk to somebody, especially somebody who is very busy (*informal*) ○ *I was hoping to catch the doctor before she left.* **17** *vt* **GET SOMETHING YOU NEED** to get food, drink, or rest only hurriedly or in small amounts (*informal*) ○ *We can stop and catch a bite to eat.* **18** *vt* **STRIKE** to strike somebody with a blow ○ *a blow that caught him on the side of the head* **19** *vt* **TAKE IMPACT OF SOMETHING** to receive the impact or force from something such as a blow or the force of somebody's anger or emotions ○ *He caught the full impact of the blast.* **20** *vti* **ENTANGLE** to entangle or hook something such as clothing on something sharp, or become entangled or hooked ○ *She caught her blouse on a nail.* **21** *vti* **TRAP** to trap something in an opening or door, or become trapped ○ *I caught my fingers in the letter box.* **22** *vt* **DELAY** to delay somebody or hold somebody up (*usually passive*) **23** *vr* **STOP YOURSELF FROM DOING SOMETHING** to stop yourself from saying or doing something ○ *He was about to make a sarcastic remark but caught himself just in time.* **24** *vt* **SURPRISE** to take somebody by surprise (*usually passive*) ○ *She got caught in the rain and was absolutely soaked.* **25** *vt* **TRICK** to trick or deceive somebody **26** *vt* **REPRODUCE ASPECTS OF** to reproduce successfully the most typical aspects of somebody or something ○ *a novel that catches the mood of prewar Berlin* **27** *vt* **RECORD ON FILM** to record somebody or something on film or tape ○ *the very first time this elusive bird has been caught on film* **28** *vti* **BE CARRIED BY EMOTION** to be eager to do something, or get caught up in the emotion of the moment **29** *vi* **BEGIN TO BURN** to ignite, become alight, or begin to burn ○ *catch fire* **30** *vi* **PLAY BASEBALL AS CATCHER** to act as catcher on a baseball team ○ *Clevenger will be catching again in the second game of the season.* **31** *vt* **DISMISS BATSMAN** in cricket, to cause the person hitting the ball to be out by catching the ball before it reaches the ground ■ *n* **1** **ACT OF CATCHING** the catching of something such as a ball **2** **SOMEBODY WHO CAN CATCH** a skilled catcher of something ○ *He missed the ball again! He's such a lousy catch!* **3** **BALL GAME** a game in which people throw a ball to each other and catch it **4** **MOVE IN BALL GAMES** a move in ball games such as cricket or rounders in which a player catches a ball hit by another before it touches the ground, forcing that person to retire **5** **NUMBER OF THINGS CAUGHT** the amount or number of things caught, e.g. when fishing ○ *Not much of a catch today, I'm afraid.* **6** **IDEAL OR DESIRABLE PERSON** somebody or something regarded as ideal or particularly desirable, especially as a marriage partner (*informal*) ○ *Her friends regarded Tom as quite a catch.* **7** **DEVICE THAT CLOSES OR FASTENS** a device for fastening something, e.g. a door, window, or piece of jewellery **8** **SNAG** a hidden or unexpected problem, especially one suspected to exist because everything seems too good to be true (*informal*) ○ *Okay, it sounds great: where's the catch?* **9** **BREAK IN VOICE** a brief moment when somebody's voice becomes husky or unclear because of intense emotion ○ *There was a slight catch in his voice as he read out the letter.* **10** **HUMOROUS SONG** a round or canon with humorous, often risqué, words, popular in the 17th and 18th centuries [12C. < Anglo-Norman or Old French *cachier* 'chase' < Latin *captare* 'try to catch' < *capere* 'take'.] —**catchable** *adj* ◇ **catch it** to get into trouble (*informal*) ◇ **catch somebody with his** *or* **her pants** *or* **trousers down** **1** to expose somebody in a very embarrassing situation, especially one that suggests hypocrisy or incompetence **2** to surprise somebody in a state of unpreparedness at a time when alertness is required

catch on *vi* (*informal*) **1** to become popular or widely used **2** to understand a new idea, task, or process ○ *pretty slow to catch on*

catch out *vt* **1** **DEVISE WAY TO SHOW SOMEBODY'S MISTAKES** to find ways of exposing errors or ignorance in order to embarrass somebody or show superiority (*informal*) ○ *He would try to catch me out by asking awkward questions during safety inspections.* **2** **EXPOSE WRONGDOER** to catch somebody doing something wrong or illegal, especially when deliberately setting out to do so (*informal*) **3** **CATCH BALL HIT BY** to catch a ball hit by a player in baseball, rounders, or cricket while it is still in the air, forcing the player or the player's team to retire

catch up *v* **1** *vti* **REACH SOMEBODY OR SOMETHING TRAVELLING AHEAD** to reach or get alongside a person who or vehicle that was moving or had gone ahead **2** *vt* **PICK SOMETHING UP** to quickly pick something or somebody up in the hands or arms ○ *He caught up all the papers and strode off.* **3** *vi* **GET UP TO DATE** to make up for lost time by working harder in order to be up to date ○ *I really must make time to catch up on my reading.* **4** *vt* **ENGROSS** to absorb somebody's attention completely (*usually passive*) ○ *I was so caught up in my work that I didn't have time for lunch.* **5** *vt* **BECOME INVOLVED UNHAPPILY** to become involved in something undesirable (*usually passive*) ○ *They were caught up in the whole messy affair even though they tried to stay out of it.* **6** *vi Malaysia, Singapore* **STAY EVEN WITH** to progress at the same rate as somebody else

catch up on *vt* to have a delayed effect on somebody ○ *Three nights without sleep is beginning to catch up on me.*

catch up with *vt* **1** to find somebody who has committed a crime or done something wrong, especially after a search or chase ○ *By the time the police caught up with him, he had changed his name and moved to Brazil.* **2** to finally have an effect after a period during which somebody seems free from the usual consequences of a particular way of behaving ○ *All those late nights will catch up with you eventually.*

catch-22 *n* a situation or predicament from which it is impossible to extricate yourself because of built-in illogical rules and regulations [After the novel *Catch-22* by Joseph Heller]

LITERARY LINK ***Catch-22***, a novel (1961) by US writer Joseph Heller. The title of this dark satire relates to the skewed military logic that entraps the protagonist, Yossarian, a pilot serving in Italy during World War II. He tries to get himself grounded by being pronounced insane, but is told that only an insane person would want to fly, and his desire not to fly proves that he is, in fact, sane, and so must continue to fly.

catchall /kách awl/ *n* something that covers a wide range of possibilities, meanings, ideas, or situations (*often before nouns*) ○ *one of those catchall phrases that doesn't really mean very much at all*

catch-as-catch-can *n* **NO-HOLDS-BARRED WRESTLING** a style of wrestling in which most holds are permitted, including many that are not allowed in other wrestling styles ■ *adj US* **MAKING DO** making do with whatever is available ○ *We took a catch-as-catch-can approach to our summer holiday.* ■ *adv US* **USING WHAT COMES TO HAND** using whatever happens to be available ○ *The press conference was arranged catch-as-catch-can at very short notice.*

catch basin *n US* **1** CIV ENG = **catch pit** **2** an area or reservoir for catching drainage water or runoff

catch crop *n* a fast-growing crop grown between the harvest and planting of two main crops, between the rows of a main crop, or as a substitute after a crop failure [< catching an opportunity to grow it]

catcher /káchər/ *n* **1** a person, animal, or device that catches things **2** the baseball player who stands behind home plate, signals for pitches, and catches pitched balls that have not been hit by the batter

catchfly /kách flī/ (*plural* **-flies** *or* **-fly**) *n* a plant related to the campion and ragged robin that exudes a sticky substance on the stem beneath each pair of leaves. Genus: *Silene* and *Lychnis*.

catching /káching/ *adj* **1** **INFECTIOUS** describes an illness that can be transmitted to other people because it is contagious or infectious ○ *Don't worry: it's not catching!* **2** **ATTRACTIVE** so attractive as to be memorable **3** **AFFECTING ONE PERSON AFTER ANOTHER** passed from one person to another like an infection ○ *a pessimism that seemed to be catching*

catchment /káchmənt/ *n* **1** **RAINWATER RECEPTACLE** a structure, reservoir, or container for collecting rainwater **2** **COLLECTED RAINWATER** the rainwater that collects in a catchment **3** **COLLECTING OF RAINWATER** the collecting or catching of rainwater

catchment area *n* **1** the area of land that drains rainfall into a river or lake **2** the area from which a particular school, hospital, or doctor will accept pupils or patients

catchpenny /kách penni/ *adj* cheap and made to be sold quickly and easily without much regard for quality (*dated*)

catch phrase *n* a phrase used so frequently by a particular person that it becomes identified with him or her

catch pit *n* a device or receptacle at the entrance of a sewer designed to prevent obstructive material from entering and blocking the sewer. US term **catch basin** *n.* 1

catch points *npl* railway points designed to derail any train or part of a train that might cause a collision by running backwards, or forwards against a signal, to join another track

catchup /kách up/ *n US* = **ketchup**

catchwater drain /kách wawtər-/ *n* a drain cut along the edge of high ground to catch water from it and divert it so that it does not run onto low-lying ground

catchweight /kách wayt/ *adj* describes a sporting contest, e.g. in wrestling or horse-racing, that has no weight restrictions [Early 19C. < ?]

catchword /kách wurd/ *n* **1** **POPULAR WORD** a word or phrase that is so frequently used, often over a short period of time, that it comes to be identified with a particular feeling, quality, or idea ○ *catchwords of the 1980s such as 'upwardly mobile' and 'yuppie'* **2** **WORD MARKING RANGE OF MATERIAL COVERED** a word printed at the top of a page in a dictionary or other reference book, usually the first or last entry for that page. US term **guide word** **3** **BINDER'S CUE** the first word of a page of printed text repeated at the bottom right-hand corner of the previous page, originally placed there to draw the binder's attention to it **4** **ACTOR'S CUE** a cue for an actor to come on stage or to speak

catchy /káchi/ (**-ier, -iest**) *adj* **1** **MEMORABLE** easy to remember because of having a simple and effective melody or wording **2** **ATTRACTING ATTENTION** tending to attract interest or attention because of a notable, unique, or pleasing character or quality ○ *an attempt to come up with a catchy name for a new soft drink* **3** **TRICKY** designed to catch people out or trip them up ○ *There were some catchy questions in the English paper.* **4** **FITFUL** coming in spasmodic or irregular bursts ○ *light rain with catchy squalls of wind* —**catchiness** *n*

cat cracker *n* INDUST = **catalytic cracker**

catechesis /kátti keéssiss/ (*plural* **-ses** /-seez/) *n* oral religious instruction given in advance of baptism or confirmation [Early 17C. Via ecclesiastical Latin < Greek *katēkhēsis* 'instruction by word of mouth' < *katēkhein* (see CATECHIZE).] —**catechetical** /kátti kéttik'l/ *adj*

catechin /káttəkin/ *n* $C_{15}H_{14}O_6$ a yellow crystalline substance. Use: in tanning and dyeing. [Mid-19C. < CATECHU.]

catechise *vt* = **catechize**

catechism /káttəkizəm/ *n* **1** **QUESTION-AND-ANSWER TEACHING** instruction in the principles of Christianity using set questions and answers **2** **RELIGIOUS QUESTIONS AND ANSWERS** the series of questions and answers that are used to test people's religious knowledge in advance of Christian baptism or confirmation **3** **QUESTION-AND-ANSWER BOOK** a book containing questions and answers used to test the religious knowledge of people preparing for Christian baptism or confirmation **4** **BODY OF PRINCIPLES FOLLOWED UNTHINKINGLY** a body of basic beliefs and principles followed unthinkingly **5** **INTERROGATION** a close and intense session of questioning on a particular subject, especially forming part of an examination or an interrogation [Early 16C. Via ecclesiastical Latin *catechismus* < ecclesiastical Greek *katēkhizein* (see CATECHIZE).] —**catechismal** /káttə kízm'l/ *adj*

catechist /káttəkist/ *n* an instructor in the basic principles of Christianity, especially one who teaches people preparing for baptism or confirmation —**catechistic** /káttə kístik/ *adj* —**catechistical** *adj*

catechize /káttə kīz/ (**-chizes, -chizing, -chized**), **catechise** (**-chises, -chising, -chised**) *vt* **1** to instruct somebody in the basic principles of the Christian religion using questions and answers **2** to question somebody closely, e.g. in an examination or interrogation [15C. Via ecclesiastical Latin *catechizare* < ecclesiastical Greek *katēkhizein* < *katēkhein* 'sound through' < *ēkhē* 'sound'.] —**catechization** /káttə kī záysh'n/ *n* —**catechizer** *n*

catechol /kátti kol, -chol/ *n* $C_6H_6O_2$ a colourless crystalline solid. Use: photographic developer, antioxidant, the manufacture of dyes and pharmaceuticals. [Late 19C. < CATECHU.]

catecholamine /káttə kóllə meen/ *n* a compound that acts as a neurotransmitter or hormone

catechu /káttə choo, -shoo/ *n* an astringent water-soluble substance. Source: Asian acacia tree. Use: in medicine, dyeing. [Late 17C. < modern Latin, < Malay *kacu*.]

catechumen /káttə kyóo men, -mən/ *n* a receiver of instruction about Christian baptism or confirmation [14C. Directly or via French, < ecclesiastical Latin *catechumenus* < Greek *katēkhoumenos* 'being instructed', present participle passive of *katēkhein* (see CATECHIZE).] —**catechumenical** /káttəkyoo ménnik'l/ *adj* —**catechumenism** *n*

categorical /káttə górrik'l/, **categoric** /-górrik/ *adj* **1** absolute, certain, and unconditional, with no room for doubt, question, or contradiction ○ *The press office has issued a categorical denial of these allegations.* **2** involving or relating to the use of categories or categorization —**categorically** *adv* —**categoricalness** *n*

categorical imperative *n* according to the moral philosophy of Immanuel Kant, an unconditional moral law applying to all rational beings and independent of all personal desires and motives

categorise *vt* = **categorize**

categorize /káttigə rīz/ (**-rizes, -rizing, -rized**), **categorise** (**-rises, -rising, -rised**) *vt* to place somebody or something in a particular category and define or judge the person or thing accordingly ○ *It was originally categorized as a cactus, but it's actually a succulent.* —**categorizable** *adj* —**categorization** /káttigə rī záysh'n/ *n*

category /káttəgəri/ (*plural* **-ries**) *n* a group or set of things, people, or actions that are classified together because of common characteristics ○ *There are choices available in the following categories: leisure, fitness, health.* [15C. Via late Latin < Greek *katēgoria* 'statement' < *katēgorein* 'speak against' < *agora* 'marketplace'.]

SYNONYMS See ***type***.

catena /kə téenə/ (*plural* **-nae** /-nee/) *n* a series of connected commentaries on or excerpts of writings, especially comments on the Bible written by early Christian theologians [Mid-17C. < Latin, 'chain'.]

catenaccio /káttə náchi ō/ *n* a strongly defensive formation in football, involving one free defender positioned behind his or her team-mates [Late 20C. < Italian, 'door bolt' < Latin *catena* 'chain'.]

catenary /kə téenəri/ (*plural* **-ies**) *n* **1** the curve adopted by a length of heavy cable, rope, or chain of uniform density, hanging between two points, or something with this shape **2** a suspended overhead power cable that supplies current to trolleybuses, trams, and most electric trains [Mid-18C. < modern Latin *catenaria* < Latin *catena* 'chain'.] —**catenary** *adj*

catenate /kátti nayt/ (**-nates, -nating, -nated**) *vt* **1** to form something into a chain or a series of chains **2** to form a chain of atoms of the same element held together by chemical bonds [Early 17C. < Latin *catenat-*, past participle of *catenare* 'chain' < *catena* 'chain'.]

cater /káytər/ *vti* **1** to provide what is wanted or needed in a particular situation or by a particular group of people ○ *We try to cater for all tastes in our bookshop.* **2** to provide food and drink for a number of people, e.g. at a party or meeting ○ *We can cater for up to a hundred people here.* [Late 16C. Shortening of obsolete *acater* 'caterer' < Anglo-Norman *acateor* < *ac(h)ater* 'buy' < Latin *capere* 'take'.] —**caterer** *n*

cater-cornered /káttər kawrnərd/, **cater-corner, catty-cornered** /kátti-/, **catty-corner** *adj US* **DIAGONAL** positioned or arranged diagonally ■ *adv US* **1 DIAGONALLY** in a diagonal position or arrangement ○ *They sit cater-cornered in history class.* **2 OPPOSITE** diagonally opposite something or somebody else ○ *Their office is cater-cornered from the bank.* [*Cater* < dialect, 'diagonally' < French *quatre* 'four']

catering /káytəring/ *n* the provision of food and drink for the people at a social or business function ○ *a career in catering*

caterpillar /káttər pillər/ *n* the larva of a butterfly or moth, with a long soft body, many short legs, and often brightly coloured or spiny skin [15C. Alteration of assumed Old French *catepelose* < assumed late Latin *catta pilosa* 'hairy cat'.]

Caterpillar *tdmk* a trademark for a continuous metal loop or belt made up of hinged links and fitted instead of wheels on tanks, bulldozers, and similar vehicles

~~**caterpiller**~~ incorrect spelling of **caterpillar**

caterwaul /káttər wawl/ *vi* to make a loud howling noise like a cat on heat, or have a noisy argument ○ *a street musician caterwauling in the background while we tried to talk* ■ *n* a loud howl or cry that sounds like a cat on heat [14C. < ?]

catfight /kát fīt/ *n* **1** a fight that takes place among cats **2** a vicious argument or fight, especially between women (*informal*)

catfish /kát fish/ (*plural* **-fish** *or* **-fishes**) *n* a scaleless, usually freshwater, fish with long whiskers (**barbels**) around its mouth that are sensitive to touch, taste, and smell. Order: Siluriformes. [< its barbels, likened to a cat's whiskers]

cat flap *n* a piece of wood or plastic hinged at the top of an opening in a door to enable a pet cat to come and go as it pleases

catgut /kát gut/ *n* a tough thin cord made from the dried intestines of animals. Use: stringing musical instruments, surgical thread. [Late 16C. Probably < CAT (for unknown reasons).]

cath. *abbr* cathode

Cath. *abbr* **1** cathedral **2** Catholic

Cathar /káthər, -aar/ (*plural* **-ars** *or* **-ari** /-ərī, -aarī/) *n* a member of a medieval European heretical Christian sect who believed that salvation lay in the adoption of a spiritual way of life [Late 16C. Via medieval Latin *Cathari* 'Cathars' < Greek *katharoi* 'the pure' < *katharos* 'pure'.] —**Catharism** *n* —**Catharist** *n* —**Catharistic** /káthə rístik/ *adj*

catharsis /kə tháarsiss/ (*plural* **-ses** /-seez/) *n* **1 EMOTIONAL RELEASE** an experience or feeling of spiritual release and purification brought about by an intense emotional experience **2 EMOTIONAL PURGING THROUGH GREEK TRAGEDY** according to Aristotle, a purifying of the emotions that is brought about in the audience of a tragic drama through the evocation of intense fear and pity **3 PSYCHOLOGICAL PURGING OF COMPLEXES** in psychology, the process of bringing to the surface repressed emotions, complexes, and feelings in an effort to identify and relieve them, or the result of this process **4 PURGING OF BOWELS** cleansing or purging of the bowels [Early 19C. Via modern Latin, < Greek *katharsis* < *kathairein* 'to purge' < *katharos* 'pure'.]

cathartic /kə tháartik/ *adj* **1 PURIFYING** producing a feeling of being purified emotionally, spiritually, or psychologically as a result of an intense emotional experience or therapeutic technique ○ *a film that had a truly cathartic effect on me* **2 HAVING PURGATIVE EFFECT ON BOWELS** describes a medicine that causes emptying of the bowels ■ *n* **PURGATIVE MEDICINE** a medicine that causes emptying of the bowels —**cathartically** *adv*

Cathay /ka tháy/ medieval name for China

cathead /kát hed/ *n* a horizontal wooden or iron beam projecting from a ship's bow, where the anchor is carried and hoisted [< CAT 'raise the anchor']

cathect /kə thékt, ka-/ *vt* to concentrate emotional or psychic energy on something, e.g. an object, a person, or an idea [Mid-20C. Back-formation < *cathectic* < CATHEXIS.] —**cathectic** *adj*

cathedra /kə théedrə/ (*plural* **-dras** *or* **-drae** /-dree/) *n* **1** a bishop's official seat or throne. ◊ **ex cathedra** **2** the official rank, office, or jurisdiction of a bishop [15C. Via Latin < Greek *kathedra* < *kata* 'down' + *hedra* 'seat'.]

cathedral /kə théedrəl/ *n* **BISHOP'S CHURCH** a church that contains a bishop's throne and is the most important church in the bishop's diocese ■ *adj* **1 OF BISHOP OR CATHEDRAL** relating to, belonging to, or having a bishop or cathedral **2 LIKE A CATHEDRAL** resembling or appropriate to a cathedral **3 MADE BY BISHOP** describes an official religious announcement made by a bishop or pope [13C. Via Old French < late Latin *cathedralis* < Latin *cathedra* 'bishop's throne'.]

cathepsin /kə thépsin/ *n* an enzyme that digests proteins after cell death [Early 20C. < German *Kathepsin* < Greek *kathepsein* 'to digest', literally 'boil down' < *hepsein* 'to boil'.]

Cather /káthər/, **Willa** (1873–1947) US writer

Catherine (of Aragon) /káth'rin/, **Catherine (of Aragón)** (1485–1536) Spanish-born English queen consort

Catherine (the Great) (1729–96) empress of Russia (1762–96)

Catherine de Médicis /káthrin də méddi chee, -me déechi/, **Catherine de Medici** (1519–89) Italian-born queen of France (1560–63)

Catherine wheel *n* **1** a flat spiral-shaped firework that is fastened to a vertical surface with a central pin, on which it spins, shooting out sparks or flame, after being lit. US term **pinwheel** *n*. 2 **2** in heraldry, a circular window divided by ribs radiating from the centre [Late 16C. After St *Catherine* of Alexandria, executed on a spiked wheel.]

catheter /káthitər/ *n* a thin flexible tube that is inserted into a part of the body to inject or drain away fluid or to keep a passage open [Early 17C. Via late Latin < Greek *kathetēr* < *kathienai* 'send down' < *hienai* 'send'.]

catheterize /káthitə rīz/ (**-izes, -izing, -ized**), **catheterise** (**-ises, -ising, -ised**) *vt* to insert a catheter into a patient or a specific part of the body —**catheterization** *n*

cathexis /ka théksis, kə-/ (*plural* **-es** /-seez/) *n* the concentration of a great deal of psychological and emotional energy on one particular person, thing, or idea [Early 20C. < Greek *kathexis* 'holding' < *katekhein* 'hold fast' < *ekhein* 'to hold'.]

cathode /káthōd/ *n* **1 NEGATIVE ELECTRODE** the negative electrode of an electrolytic cell **2 ELECTRON SOURCE** the negatively charged source of electrons in a valve **3 POSITIVE TERMINAL** the positive terminal of a cell that is producing electrical energy by a chemical process that cannot be reversed [Mid-19C. < Greek *kathodos* 'way down' < *hodos* 'way'.] —**cathodal** /ka thṓd'l/ *adj* —**cathodally** *adv*

cathode ray *n* a stream of electrons that is emitted from a cathode in a vacuum tube

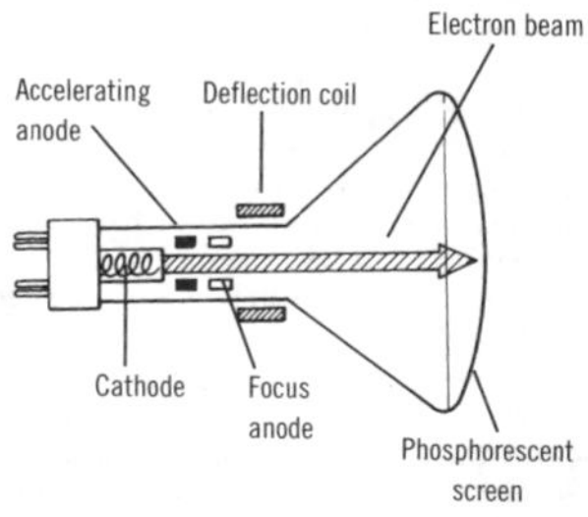

Cathode ray tube

cathode ray tube *n* a vacuum tube in which a stream of electrons is produced and directed onto a fluorescent screen, e.g. in a television or visual display unit, creating images and text

cathodic /ka thóddik, ka thṓdik/ *adj* relating to or involving a cathode —**cathodically** *adv*

cathodic protection *n* the prevention of electrolytic corrosion in something metallic, e.g. an underground pipe or a ship, by making it the cathode in an electrolytic cell

cat hole *n* either of two holes at the stern of a ship through which large ropes are passed

catholic /káthlik, káthəlik/ *adj* **1 ALL-INCLUSIVE** including or concerned with all people **2 USEFUL TO ALL** useful or interesting to a wide range of people **3 ALL-EMBRACING** interested in or sympathetic to a wide range of things [14C. Via Latin *catholicus* < Greek *katholikos* 'universal' < *katholou* 'in general' < *kata* 'in regard to' + *holos* 'whole'.] —**catholically** *adv*

Catholic *adj* **1 ROMAN CATHOLIC** belonging to or characteristic of the Roman Catholic Church **2 CHRISTIAN** belonging to the community of all Christian churches **3 OF THE HISTORICAL UNITED CHURCH** belonging to the united Christian church that existed before its separation into different churches, or to any church that regards itself as continuing the traditions of that united church ■ *n* **CHURCH MEMBER** a member of the Roman Catholic Church [14C. Via ecclesiastical Latin < Greek *katholikē (ekklēsia)* 'universal church' < *katholikos* (see CATHOLIC).]

Catholic Church *n* **1** RELIG = **Roman Catholic Church** **2** any church that regards itself as continuing the traditions of the Christian church before it was divided into separate churches

Catholic Epistles *npl* the New Testament Epistles of James, I and II Peter, I John, and Jude, addressed to the Christian churches as a whole rather than to a local church

catholicise, Catholicise *vti* = **catholicize**

Catholicism /kə thóllisizəm/ *n* **1** the beliefs, doctrines, and rituals of a Catholic church, especially those of the Roman Catholic Church **2** membership of a Catholic church, especially of the Roman Catholic Church

catholicity /káthə líssəti/ *n* **1** wideness of range of tastes or interests **2** the quality of including or applying to everyone or everything

Catholicity /káthə líssəti/ *n* = **Catholicism**

catholicize /kə thólli sīz/ (**-cizes, -cizing, -cized**), **catholicise** (**-cises, -cising, -cised**) *vti* to broaden something, e.g. an idea, classification, or range of things, to include or apply to many or all things or people, or become broader in this way

Catholicize (**-cizes, -cizing, -cized**), **Catholicise** (**-cises, -cising, -cised**) *vti* to convert somebody to Catholicism, or be converted to Catholicism

cathouse /kát howss/ *n US, Can* a brothel (*slang*) [Mid-20C. < CAT 'prostitute'.]

Catiline /káttə līn/ (108?–62 BC) Roman conspirator

cation /kát ī ən/ *n* an ion that has a positive electrical charge and is attracted towards the cathode in electrolysis [Mid-19C. < Greek *kata* 'down' + ION.] —**cationic** /kát ī ónnik/ *adj*

catkin /kátkin/ *n* a long hanging furry cluster of tiny leaves and petal-less flowers, produced by trees such as willows, birches, alders, and poplars [Late 16C. < obsolete Dutch *katteken* 'kitten'.]

Catlins /káttlinz/ scenic area of SE South Island, New Zealand

cat litter *n* absorbent material that is used to fill a box in which a cat can urinate and defecate indoors

catmint /kátmint/ *n* a plant of the mint family with greyish leaves and a strong smell that attracts cats. Flowers: blue or white. Genus: *Nepeta*.

catnap /kát nap/ *n* a short light sleep —**catnap** *vi* —**catnapper** *n*

catnip /kátnip/ *n* PLANTS = **catmint** [Early 18C. < variant of obsolete *nep* 'catmint', via Old English *nepta* < Latin *nepeta*.]

cat-o'-nine-tails (*plural* **cat-o'-nine-tails**) *n* a whip with several, usually nine, strands of knotted rope, formerly used for flogging prisoners and as a punishment in the armed forces

catoptric /kə tóptrik/, **catoptrical** /-trik'l/ *adj* relating to or involving a mirror or reflection [Mid-16C. < Greek *katoptrikos* < *katoptron* 'something that looks back' < *op-* 'see'.]

catoptrics /kə tóptriks/ *n* the branch of optics that deals with mirrors and reflection (+ *singular verb*)

Cato the Elder /káy tō-/, **Marcus Portius** (234–149 BC) Roman general and statesman. Known as **the Censor**

CAT scan *n* MED = **CT scan**

CAT scanner *n* MED = **CT scanner**

cat's cradle *n* a children's game in which a loop of string is threaded between the fingers of both hands in variable complex patterns [< ?]

cat scratch disease, cat scratch fever *n* an illness marked by fever and swollen lymph glands, thought to be caused by a bacterium transmitted to humans by the scratch of a cat

cat's eye *n* **1** a gemstone, especially chrysoberyl or chalcedony, cut so as to reflect a narrow silvery band of light that seems to come from within **2** a clear glass marble with a core or swirl of colour at the centre

Catseye /kats ī/ *tdmk* a trademark for a small reflecting device that is set into a road surface, kerb, or post to assist drivers at night in staying on the road or within lanes

Catskill Mountains /kátskil-/ group of mountains in the Appalachian system in SE New York State. Highest peak: Slide Mountain, 1,281 m/4,204 ft.

cat's meow *n US* = **cat's whiskers**

cat's pajamas *n US* = **cat's whiskers**

cat's paw *n* **1** a victim of trickery who is manipulated into doing something for another person **2** a hitch with two loops, used for attaching a rope to a hook

catsuit /kát soot, -syoot/ *n* a close-fitting one-piece garment that covers the whole body and has long sleeves and trouser legs [Because it gives a sleek outline]

catsup /kátsəp/ *n* = **ketchup**

cat's whiskers *n* an excellent or special person or thing (*dated slang*) US term **cat's pajamas**

cattalo /káttəlō/ (*plural* **-loes** *or* **-los**) *n* = **beefalo** [Late 19C. Blend of CATTLE + BUFFALO.]

cattery /káttəri/ (*plural* **-ies**) *n* a place where cats are bred or boarded

cattish /káttish/ *adj* = **catty** *adj.* **1**, **catty** *adj.* **2** —**cattishly** *adv* —**cattishness** *n*

cattle /kátt'l/ *npl* (+ *plural verb*) **1** large domesticated mammals kept for the production of milk, meat, and hides, and also as draught animals. Cows and oxen are common types of cattle. Genus: *Bos*. **2** people who are regarded as lacking individuality, especially a crowd of people regarded as an undifferentiated mass [13C. Via Anglo-Norman *catel* < Latin *capitale* 'funds'.]

cattle cake *n* a manufactured food for cattle, concentrated and formed into blocks

cattle egret *n* a small, white, yellow-billed egret that often feeds on insects stirred up by cattle. Native to: Africa, S Europe, Asia. *Bubulus ibis*.

cattle grid *n* a grid of metal bars over a shallow pit in a road, designed to stop animals, but not people or vehicles, leaving an enclosed area. US term **cattle guard**

cattle guard *n US* AGRIC = **cattle grid**

cattleman /kátt'lman, -mən/ (*plural* **-men** /-men/) *n* someone who owns, raises, or works with cattle

cattle plague *n* AGRIC = **rinderpest**

cattle prod *n* an electrified rod designed for driving and controlling cattle by giving them mild shocks

cattle stop *n NZ* AGRIC = **cattle grid**

cattle truck *n* a railway wagon for transporting livestock. US term **stock car** *n.* **2**

cattleya /káttli ə/ (*plural* **-yas**) *n* an orchid that is a popular greenhouse plant. Flowers: purple, pink, or white. Native to: tropical America. Genus: *Cattleya*. [Early 19C. < modern Latin, after William *Cattley* (1788–1835).]

catty /kátti/ (**-tier, -tiest**) *adj* **1** saying spiteful or malicious things about somebody, especially in a subtle way **2** resembling a cat, especially in being cautious or secretive —**cattily** *adv* —**cattiness** *n*

catty-cornered, catty-corner *adj US* = **cater-cornered**

Catullus /kə túlləss/, **Gaius Valerius** (84?–54? BC) Roman poet —**Catullan** *adj*

CATV *abbr* community antenna television

catwalk /kát wawk/ *n* **1** a long narrow raised platform along which the models walk in a fashion show **2** a narrow walkway high above the ground, e.g. along the side of a building or behind the stage in a theatre [Because cats can walk safely on narrow surfaces]

Caucasia /kaw káyzi ə, -zhə/ region of SE Europe and SW Asia between the Black Sea and the Caspian Sea, comprising Georgia, Armenia, Azerbaijan, and S Russia. Area: 400,000 sq. km/150,000 sq. mi.

Caucasian /kaw káyzi ən, -zh'n/ *adj* **1 WHITE-SKINNED** relating to people who are light-skinned or of European origin **2 OF FORMER ETHNIC GROUP** belonging to the light-skinned peoples of Europe, N Africa, and W and S Asia, formerly considered a distinct ethnic group (*no longer in technical use*) **3 OF CAUCASIA** relating to Caucasia, or its peoples, languages, or cultures **4 OF LANGUAGES OF CAUCASIA** belonging to two unrelated languages spoken in the area around the Caucasus Mountains ■ *n* **1 WHITE PERSON** somebody light-skinned or of European origin **2 MEMBER OF FORMER ETHNIC GROUP** a member of the people formerly termed Caucasian (*no longer in technical use*) **3 SOMEBODY FROM CAUCASIA** somebody who comes from Caucasia **4 LANGUAGES OF CAUCASIA** either of two unrelated language families spoken in the area around the Caucasus Mountains, Kartvelian or South Caucasian, and North Caucasian

Caucasoid /káwkə soyd, -zoyd/ *adj* = **Caucasian** *adj.* **2** (*no longer in technical use*) ■ *n* = **Caucasian** *n.* **2** (*no longer in technical use*)

Caucasus Mountains /káwkəssəss-/ mountain range extending through Georgia, Armenia, Azerbaijan, and SW Russia, considered a boundary between Europe and Asia. Highest peak: El'brus 5,642 m/18,510 ft.

caucus /káwkəss/ *n* **1 POLITICAL MEETING** a closed meeting of people from one political party, especially a local meeting to select delegates or candidates, or a meeting of party representatives at national level to decide policy **2 SPECIAL-INTEREST GROUP** a group of people, often within a larger group, e.g. a legislative assembly, who unite to promote a particular policy or particular interests ■ *vi* **FORM A CAUCUS** to hold or meet in a caucus [Mid-18C. < ?]

caudal /káwd'l/ *adj* **1** relating to, involving, typical of, or like a tail **2** situated in or extending towards the hind part of the body [Mid-17C. < modern Latin *caudalis* < Latin *cauda* 'tail'.] —**caudally** *adv*

caudate /káw dayt/, **caudated** /-daytid/ *adj* with a tail or an appendage like a tail [Early 17C. < medieval Latin *caudatus* < Latin *cauda* 'tail'.] —**caudation** /kaw dáysh'n/ *n*

caudex /káw deks/ (*plural* **-dices** /-diseez/ *or* **-dexes**) *n* **1** a trunk of a tree that bears leaves only at its apex, as in a palm or tree fern **2** the swollen stem base of certain nonwoody perennial plants that survives over the winter and from which new growth is produced [Late 18C. < Latin, 'tree trunk', variant of *codex* 'block of wood'.]

caudillo /kow deé yō, -lyō/ (*plural* **-los**) *n* a military or political leader, especially a dictator, in a Spanish-speaking country [Mid-19C. Via Spanish, 'leader' < late Latin *capitellum* 'little head' < *caput* 'head'.]

caught past tense, past participle of **catch**

caul /kawl/ *n* **1** the membrane surrounding the amniotic fluid, a part of which sometimes covers a baby's head when it is born **2** ANAT = **omentum** [14C. < ?]

cauldron /káwldrən/, **caldron** *n* a large metal pot in which liquids are boiled [13C. < Anglo-Norman, Old N French *caudron* < late Latin *caldaria* 'cooking pot' < Latin *calidus* 'hot'.]

cauliflower /kólli flowər/ *n* **1** a large solid head of tight white or light-green florets, eaten raw or cooked as a vegetable **2** a plant related to the cabbage that produces cauliflowers. *Brassica oleracea* var. *botrytis*. [Late 16C. Alteration of modern Latin *cauliflora* < Latin *caulis* 'stem' + *flor-* 'flower'.]

cauliflower cheese *n* a hot dish of cauliflower coated in cheese sauce

cauliflower ear *n* an ear that is permanently swollen and misshapen as a result of bleeding into the ear tissues after being repeatedly struck, usually in boxing

caulk /kawk/, **calk** *vt* **1 MAKE BOAT WATERTIGHT** to make a boat or the seams between its planks watertight by filling the seams with waterproof material **2 STOP SOMETHING UP** to stop up the cracks or gaps in something, e.g. a pipe or a window frame, with a waterproof material ■ *n* **SOMETHING USED TO FILL GAPS** material used to make a boat watertight by filling in its seams, or to stop up the cracks or gaps in something [15C. < Old French *cauquer* 'to tread' < Latin *calcare* < *calc-* 'heel'.] —**caulker** *n*

causal /káwz'l/ *adj* **1 BEING OR INVOLVING THE CAUSE** involving or being the cause of something else or the relationship of cause and effect **2 EXPRESSING A CAUSE** expressing or indicating a cause or the relationship of cause and effect ■ *n* **WORD EXPRESSING CAUSE** a word or other grammatical element that expresses the reason or cause of something, or a relationship of cause and effect —**causally** *adv*

causalgia /kaw záljə/ *n* a persistent burning sensation of the skin, caused usually by injury to a peripheral nerve [Mid-19C. < Greek *kausos* 'burning'.] —**causalgic** *adj*

causality /kaw zálləti/ *n* **1** the principle that everything that happens must have a cause **2** the action that causes an effect, or the ability to cause an effect

causation /kaw záysh'n/ *n* **1** the fact that something causes an effect, or the action of causing an effect **2** the relationship between a cause and its effect

causative /káwzətiv/ *adj* **1 INVOLVING CAUSE AND EFFECT** involving being the cause of something or the relationship of the cause and effect **2 EXPRESSING CAUSE** describes verbs that express the action of something causing something else ■ *n* **CAUSATIVE VERB** a causative verb, or a form or class of causative verbs —**causatively** *adv* —**causativeness** *n*

cause /kawz/ *n* **1 WHAT MAKES SOMETHING HAPPEN** something that or somebody who makes something happen or exist or is responsible for a certain result ○ *the cause of all the uproar* **2 REASON** a reason or grounds for doing or feeling something ○ *no cause for complaint* **3 PRINCIPLE** a principle or idea that people believe in or work for **4 INTEREST** the interests and aims of a group of people **5 LEGAL CASE** a lawsuit, or the reason that a suit is brought in a court of law **6 DISCUSSION SUBJECT** something under discussion or to be decided (*archaic*) ■ *vt* (**causes, causing, caused**) **BE THE REASON FOR** to make something happen or exist, or be the reason that somebody does something or that something happens [13C. Via Old French, < Latin *causa* 'reason, motive'.] —**causability** /káwzə bílləti/ *n* —**causable** *adj* —**causeless** *adj* —**causer** *n*

'cause /kəz, koz/ *conj* because (*informal*) [15C. Shortening.]

cause célèbre /kōz sə lébbrə, káwz-/ (*plural* **causes célèbres** /kōz sə lébbrəz, káwz-/) *n* a legal case or public controversy that arouses great interest and becomes famous, because of the issues or the people involved [< French, 'celebrated case']

causerie /kōzəri/ *n* **1** an informal conversation (*literary*) **2** a short piece of writing in a light informal style [Early 19C. < French, via *causer* 'to chat' < Latin *causari* 'discuss' < *causa* 'case'.]

causeway /káwz way/ *n* **1** a raised path or road through a marsh or water or across land that is sometimes covered by water **2** a road or path with a paved or cobbled surface [15C. < CAUSEY + WAY.]

Causeway Coast /káwz way-/ region in NE Northern Ireland that includes the Giant's Causeway

caustic /káwstik/ *adj* **1 CORROSIVE** corrosive or burning by chemical action **2 SARCASTIC** very sarcastic, in a way that is particularly bitter or cutting or causes intensely bad emotions ■ *n* **1 SUBSTANCE THAT CORRODES** a substance that can corrode or burn away other substances by chemical action, especially a strong alkali **2 CURVE FORMED BY REFLECTIONS** a peaked curve formed on a plane by parallel light rays reflected or refracted from a cylindrical or spherical surface [14C. Via Latin < Greek *kaustikos* < *kaustos* 'combustible' < *kaiein* 'to burn'.] —**caustical** *adj* —**caustically** *adv* —**causticity** /kaw stíssəti/ *n* —**causticness** *n*

SYNONYMS See *sarcastic*.

caustic potash *n* CHEM = **potassium hydroxide**

caustic soda *n* CHEM = **sodium hydroxide**

cauterize /káwtə rīz/ (**-izes, -izing, -ized**), **cauterise** (**-ises, -ising, -ised**) *vt* to seal a wound, or destroy abnormal or infected tissue, with a heated instrument, a laser, an electric current, or a caustic substance [14C. < French *cautériser* < Latin *cauterium* (see CAUTERY).] —**cauterization** /káwtə rī záysh'n/ *n*

cautery /káwtəri/ (*plural* **-ies**) *n* **1** an instrument or substance used to seal a wound or to destroy abnormal or infected tissue by burning **2** the process or action of sealing a wound or destroying abnormal or infected tissue by burning [14C. Via Latin *cauterium* < Greek *kautērion* 'branding iron' < *kaiein* 'to burn'.]

caution /káwsh'n/ *n* **1 CAREFULNESS** care, thoughtfulness, lack of haste, and close attention that enable somebody to avoid the risks involved in a task or procedure **2 WARNING** a warning to somebody to be careful about something or in doing something **3 LEGAL WARNING** a formal warning given instead of a penalty to somebody who has done something illegal, advising that punishment will follow if it is repeated **4 POLICE WARNING ABOUT EVIDENCE** a formal warning given by a police officer to somebody who has been arrested that anything he or she says may be used in evidence **5 UNUSUAL PERSON** a surprising or amusing person or thing (*dated*) ■ *vt* **1 WARN** to warn or advise somebody that something is risky or dangerous **2 GIVE LEGAL WARNING** to give somebody who has done something illegal a formal warning, instead of a penalty, advising that punishment will follow if it is repeated **3 GIVE WARNING ABOUT EVIDENCE** to give a formal warning to somebody who has been arrested that anything he or she says may be used in evidence [Late 16C. Via French < Latin *caution-* < *caut-*, past participle of *cavere* 'take heed'.] —**cautioner** *n* ◇ **throw caution to the wind(s)** to be reckless

cautionary /káwsh'nəri/ *adj* involving, giving, or being a warning

caution money *n* money deposited as security for good behaviour, e.g. by a student to cover damage to accommodation, furniture, or equipment

cautious /káwshəss/ *adj* having or showing care, thoughtfulness, restraint, and lack of haste [Mid-17C. < CAUTION.] —**cautiously** *adv* —**cautiousness** *n*

SYNONYMS ***cautious, careful, chary, circumspect, prudent, vigilant, wary, guarded, cagey***
CORE MEANING: attentive to risk or danger
cautious aware of potential risk and behaving accordingly; **careful** taking reasonable care to avoid risks; **chary** cautiously reluctant to act; **circumspect** taking into consideration all possible circumstances and consequences before acting; **prudent** showing good judgment or shrewdness; **vigilant** alert and conscious of possible dangers; **wary** showing watchfulness or suspicion; **guarded** reluctant to share information with others; **cagey** (*informal*) secretive and guarded.

Cauvery /káwvəri/, **Kāveri** river in SW India. Length: 760 km/470 mi.

cava /kaávə/ *n* sparkling white wine produced in Spain

cavalcade /kávv'l káyd/ *n* **1** a procession, especially one of people on horses, in carriages, or in cars **2** a series or procession of things or people, especially a spectacular or dramatic one [Late 16C. Via French < Italian *cavalcata* < *cavalcare* 'ride on horseback' < medieval Latin *caballicare* < Latin *caballus* 'horse'.]

cavalier /kávvə léer/ *adj* **CARELESS** showing an arrogant or jaunty disregard or lack of respect for something or somebody ■ *n* **1 GENTLEMAN** a gallant or chivalrous man, especially one escorting a lady (*formal*) **2 MOUNTED SOLDIER** a knight or soldier in former times who fought on horseback (*archaic*) [Mid-16C. Via French < Italian *cavaliere* 'knight' < medieval Latin *caballarius* 'horseman' < Latin *caballus* 'horse'.] —**cavalierly** *adv*

Cavalier /kávvə léer/ *n* a supporter of King Charles I in the English Civil War. ◊ **Roundhead**

cavalry /kávv'lri/ (*plural* **-ries**) *n* **1** the part of an army made up of soldiers trained to fight on horseback **2** the more mobile part of a modern army, using armoured vehicles and helicopters [Mid-16C. Via French < Italian *cavalleria* 'mounted militia' < *cavallo* 'horse' < Latin *caballus*.] —**cavalryman** *n*

cavalry twill *n* hard-wearing worsted fabric used for making tailored sporting jackets and trousers [< its use in making riding breeches for soldiers]

Cavan /kávv'n/ county in north-central Ireland. Population: 52,903 (1996).

cavatina /kávvə téenə/ (*plural* **-nas** *or* **-ne** /-téeni/) *n* **1** a short and simple operatic song, especially a slow aria of Italian opera of the 18th and 19th centuries, usually followed by a livelier cabaletta **2** a melodious and expressive piece of instrumental music, based loosely on the operatic cavatina [Early 19C. < Italian.]

cave /kayv/ *n* a large, naturally hollowed-out place in the ground, or in rock above ground, that can be reached from the surface or from water [13C. < Old French, < Latin *cavus* 'hollow'.]
cave in *v* **1** *vti* to collapse or cause something to collapse because of pressure or because of being undermined **2** *vi* to yield to persuasion or threats, after trying to resist

caveat /kávvi at, káy-/ *n* **1** something said as a warning, caution, or qualification **2** an official request to a court not to proceed with a case without notice to the person making the request [Mid-16C. < Latin, 'let him or her beware' < *cavere* 'to heed'.]

caveat emptor /-émp tawr, káy-/ *n* the commercial principle that the buyer is responsible for making sure that goods bought are of a reasonable quality, unless the seller is offering a guarantee of their quality [Early 16C. < Latin, 'let the buyer beware'.]

cavefish /káyv fish/ (*plural* **-fish** *or* **-fishes**) *n* a small fish with underdeveloped eyes that lives in subterranean waters. Native to: North America. Family: Amblyopsidae.

cave-in *n* **1 COLLAPSE** a collapse of something caused by pressure or undermining **2 ROOF FALL** a place where something has collapsed because of pressure or being undermined **3 YIELDING** a yielding to persuasion or threats, after trying to resist

Cavell /kávv'l/, **Edith** (1865–1915) British nurse

caveman /káyv man/ (*plural* **-men** /-men/) *n* **1** somebody living in a cave, especially a prehistoric human being of the Palaeolithic period **2** a man who behaves in a brutish or uncivilized way (*informal*)

Cavendish /kávv'ndish/, **Henry** (1731–1810) British chemist and physicist

cave painting *n* a painting made on the wall of a cave by Palaeolithic people

cavern /kávv'n/ *n* **LARGE CAVE** a large underground cave or a large chamber in an underground series of caves ■ *vt* **1 MAKE SOMETHING HOLLOW** to make a mountain, cliff, or area of ground hollow **2 ENCLOSE** to enclose something in a cave or cavern (*literary*) [14C. Directly or via French < Latin *caverna* < *cavus* 'hollow'.]

cavernous /kávvərnəss/ *adj* **1** like or suggestive of a cavern, especially in being large, dark, deep, and hollow **2** with a hollow, resonating sound —**cavernously** *adv* —**cavernousness** *n*

cavesson /kávvissən/ *n* a stiff noseband used in breaking horses [Late 16C. < French *caveçon* < medieval Latin *capitium* 'head covering' < Latin *capit-* 'head'.]

cavetto /kə véttō/ (*plural* **-ti** /-tee/) *n* a concave architectural moulding with a curve that is roughly a quarter circle [Mid-17C. < Italian, diminutive of *cavo* 'hollow' < Latin *cavus*.]

cavewoman /káyv wŏŏmən/ (*plural* **-en** /-wimin/) *n* a woman living in a cave, especially a prehistoric woman of the Palaeolithic period

caviar /kávvi aar, kávvi áar/, **caviare** *n* the salted roe of a large fish, particularly the sturgeon, eaten as a delicacy [Mid-16C. Via French < Italian *caviaro* < Turkish *havyar* < Persian dialect *khāvyār*.]

cavil /kávv'l, kávvil/ *vi* (**-ils, -illing, -illed**) to make objections about something on small and unimportant points ■ *n* a trivial and unreasonable objection [Mid-16C. Via French *caviller* < Latin *cavillari* < *cavilla* 'mockery'.] —**caviller** *n*

caving /káyving/ *n* the activity of exploring and climbing in underground caves and passages for sport —**caver** *n*

cavitand /kávvi tand/ *n* a molecule, especially a synthetic receptor, that is hollow and has one open end [Late 20C. < CAVITY.]

cavitate /kávvi tayt/ (**-tates, -tating, -tated**) *vt* to form bubbles or cavities in a substance [Early 20C. Back-formation < CAVITATION.]

cavitation /kávvi táysh'n/ *n* **1 DISTURBANCE OF LIQUID** the rapid formation and collapse of bubbles in a liquid, caused by the movement of something in the liquid, e.g. a propeller, or by waves of high-frequency sound **2 PITTING OF SURFACE** the pitting of a solid surface as a result of the forces of repeated cavitation in a surrounding liquid **3 FORMATION OF CAVITIES IN TISSUE** the formation of cavities in body tissue, caused by a disease, e.g. as an effect of tuberculosis on the lungs [Late 19C. < CAVITY.]

cavity /kávvəti/ (*plural* **-ties**) *n* **1 HOLLOW PLACE** a hole or hollow space in something **2 HOLE IN TOOTH** a hole in a tooth, caused by decay **3 HOLLOW WITHIN THE BODY** a hollow area inside the body [Mid-16C. Via French *cavité* < late Latin *cavitas* < Latin *cavus* 'hollow'.]

cavity block *n* a concrete construction block made with cavities inside it

cavity wall *n* an external wall of a building that is made up of two leaves of masonry, bricks, or blocks separated by a cavity

cavo-relievo /kaávō ri léevō, káyvō-/ (*plural* **cavo-relievos** *or* **cavo-relievi** /-vi/), **cavo-rilievo** (*plural* **cavo-rilievos** *or* **cavo-rilievi**) *n* a relief sculpture in which even the highest part lies below the level of the original surface, or this style of relief sculpture [Late 19C. < Italian, 'hollow relief'.]

cavort /kə váwrt/ *vi* to behave in a physically lively and uninhibited way [Late 18C. < ?]

Cavour /kə vŏŏr, -váwr/, **Camillo Benso, Conte di** (1810–61) Italian statesman

cavy /káyvi/ (*plural* **-vies**) *n* a short-tailed ground-living rodent of the family that includes the guinea pig. Native to: South America. Family: Caviidae. [Late 18C. Via modern Latin *Cavia* < Galibi *cabiai*.]

caw /kaw/ *vi* to make the loud harsh cry of a crow or a related bird or make a sound like this ■ *n* the loud harsh cry of a crow or a related bird or a sound like this [Late 16C. An imitation of the sound.]

Cawdor /káwdər/ parish in N Scotland, best known for its castle

Cawley /káwli/, **Evonne Fay** (*b.* 1951) Australian tennis player. Born **Evonne Fay Goolagong**

Caxton /kákstən/, **William** (1422?–91) English printer

cay /kee, kay/ *n* a small low island or reef in the sea, made of coral or sand, especially in the Caribbean [Late 17C. < Spanish *cayo* 'shoal'.]

Cayenne /kay én, kī én/ capital of French Guiana, on the N coast of Cayenne Island. Population: 41,000 (1990 estimate).

cayenne pepper, **cayenne** *n* a very hot-tasting red powder. Source: the dried and ground fruit and seeds of several kinds of chilli. Use: in cooking. [Early 18C. Alteration of *kian* < Tupi *kyynha*.]

cayman *n* ZOOL = **caiman**

Cayman Islands /káymən-/ group of three islands in the NW Caribbean Sea, south of Cuba, a British dependency. Capital: George Town. Population: 25,355 (1990). Area: 259 sq. km/100 sq. mi.

Cayuga /kay ōōgə, kī yōōgə/ (*plural* **-ga** *or* **-gas**) *n* a member of an Iroquois people who once lived along Cayuga Lake, and who now live mainly in W New York State, Wisconsin, Ontario, and Oklahoma [Mid-18C. <

Cayuga, 'the place where locusts were taken out'.] —**Cayuga** *adj*

Cayuga Lake /kay oógə-/ one of the Finger Lakes, central New York State. Area: 170 sq. km/66 sq. mi.

Cazaly /kázz'li/, **Roy** (1893–1963) Australian Rules footballer

Cazneaux /káznō/, **Harold Pierce** (1878–1953) New Zealand-born Australian photographer

CB *abbr* 1 Citizens' Band 2 Companion of the (Order of the) Bath (*used as title*)

CBC *abbr* Canadian Broadcasting Corporation

CBD *abbr* 1 **CBD, cbd** cash before delivery 2 central business district

CBE *abbr* Commander of the (Order of the) British Empire (*used as title*)

✦**CBI** *abbr* 1 computer-based instruction 2 Confederation of British Industry

CBS *abbr* Columbia Broadcasting System

✦**CBT** *abbr* computer-based training

CBW *abbr* chemical and biological warfare

cc[1], **c.c.** *abbr* 1 (carbon) copy 2 cubic centimetre 3 cubic capacity (*after a number to indicate the power of an internal-combustion engine*)

✦**cc**[2] *abbr* Cocos Islands (*in Internet addresses*)

CC *abbr* 1 City Council 2 County Council 3 Cricket Club

CC. *abbr* chapters

✦**CCA** *abbr* 1 current-cost accounting 2 cardholder certificate authority (*in e-commerce*)

✦**CCD** *abbr* charge-coupled device

CCF *abbr* Combined Cadet Force

C-clamp *n* a metal clamp shaped like a letter C, with horizontal flat pieces at the ends, that can be adjusted by a screw

C clef *n* a symbol on a musical stave that shows the position of middle C

CCTV *abbr* closed-circuit television

CCU *abbr* coronary care unit

cd *symbol* candela

Cd[1] *symbol* cadmium

Cd[2] *abbr* command (paper) (*before a serial number*)

✦**CD** *abbr* 1 compact disc 2 certificate of deposit 3 Civil Defence 4 Corps Diplomatique (*often displayed on the backs of cars that belong to embassies*)

c/d *abbr* 1 carried down 2 cum dividend

✦**CDE** *n* a compact disc that can have its contents erased and something else recorded onto it. Full form **compact disc erasable**. ◊ **CDR**

cdf *abbr* cumulative distribution function

✦**CDI**, **CD-I** *n* an interactive compact disc containing text, video, and audio and accessed using a self-contained player plugged into a television set. Full form **compact disc interactive**

cDNA *abbr* complementary DNA

Cdr, **CDR** *abbr* Commander

✦**CDR** *n* a compact disc that can be used to record something but cannot be erased. Full form **compact disc recordable**. ◊ **CDE**

Cdre *abbr* Commodore

✦**CD-ROM** /seé dee róm/ *n* a compact disc containing a large amount of data, including text and images, that can be viewed using a computer but cannot be altered or erased. Full form **compact disc read-only memory**

✦**CD-RW** *abbr* CD rewritable

CDT A school subject that can be studied to GCSE level. Full form **Craft, Design, and Technology**

CDU the Christian Democratic Union, a political party in Germany. Full form **Christlich-Demokratische Union**

✦**CDV** *abbr* 1 CD video 2 compact video disc

✦**CD-video** *n* 1 a compact disc used to store and play back video images 2 a player for compact discs that stores and plays back video images

Ce *symbol* cerium

CE *abbr* 1 chemical engineer 2 chief engineer 3 Common Era 4 Church of England 5 civil engineer

C.E. *abbr* 1 civil engineer 2 Common Era

ceanothus /seé ə nóthəss/ *n* a shrub with dark green leaves. Flowers: blue, white, or pink, in clusters. Native to: North America. Genus: *Ceanothus*. [Late 18C. Via modern Latin < Greek *keanōthos* 'thistle'.]

cease /seess/ (**ceases, ceasing, ceased**) *v* 1 *vi* to come to an end 2 *vti* to bring something to an end [14C. Via French *cesser* < Latin *cessare* < *cedere* 'give way'.] ◊ **without cease** without stopping, or without a break

ceasefire /seéss fīr/ *n* 1 an agreement between opposing sides in a conflict that they will stop fighting, usually for a limited time during which they will try to reach a more permanent peace agreement 2 a military order to stop firing

ceaseless /seésslass/ *adj* without pause or end —**ceaselessly** *adv* —**ceaselessness** *n*

Ceauşescu /chow shéskoo/, **Nicolae** (1918–89) Romanian head of state (1967–89)

Cebu /si bóo/ island in the east-central Philippines. Population: 2,646,000 (1990). Area: 4,422 sq. km/1,707 sq. mi.

Cecchetti /che kétti/, **Enrico** (1850–1928) Italian ballet dancer, choreographer, and teacher

Cecilia /sə seéli ə/, **St** (?–230?) Roman Christian martyr

cecropia moth /si krópi ə-/ *n* a large silk moth with red, white, and black wings. Native to: North America. *Hyalophora cecropia*. [Mid-19C. < modern Latin *Cecropia*, after CECROPS.]

Cecrops /seé krops/ *n* in Greek mythology, the first king of Attica and founder of Athens

cecum *n* US = caecum

cedar /seédar/ *n* 1 **TALL EVERGREEN TREE** a tall evergreen tree with spreading branches, needles, and large rounded upright cones. Native to: Europe, Asia, Africa. Genus: *Cedrus*. 2 **TREE LIKE TRUE CEDAR** an evergreen tree that resembles a cedar 3 **WOOD FROM CEDAR** the wood of the cedar tree [Pre-12C. Via Old French *cedre* < Greek *kedros*.]

Cedar City /seédar-/ city in SW Utah. Population: 17,811 (1996).

cedar of Lebanon *n* a tall long-lived cedar with horizontally spreading branches. Native to: Lebanon, Turkey. *Cedrus libani*.

cede /seed/ (**cedes, ceding, ceded**) *vt* to surrender or give up something, e.g. land, rights, or power, to another country, group, or person (*formal*) [Early 16C. Via French *céder* < Latin *cedere* 'give way'.]

SPELLCHECK Do not confuse *cede* with *seed*, which has a similar sound. Beware: your spellchecker will not catch this error.

cedi /seédi/ (*plural* **-di**) *n* see table at **currency** [Mid-20C. < Fanti *sedi* 'small shell'.]

cedilla /sə dílla/ (*plural* **-las**) *n* a mark placed beneath the letters c (ç) and s (ş) in some languages that signals a change in the pronunciation of the letter [Late 16C. < obsolete Spanish, 'little z' < Latin *zeta*.]

CEGEP /sáy zhép/, **cegep** *n* in Quebec, a post-secondary institution offering two-year programmes leading to university and three-year programmes qualifying students in a variety of professions and trades. Full form **Collège d'Enseignement Général et Professionel**

ceiba /sáybə/ (*plural* **-bas**) *n* a large tropical tree that has seed pods containing a silky fibre. Use: production of kapok. *Ceiba pentandra*. US term **silk-cotton tree** [Early 17C. Via Spanish < Arawak, 'giant tree'.]

ceil /seel/ *vt* 1 to construct a ceiling for a room 2 to line a ceiling with a material, e.g. plaster or wood [Early 16C. < ?]

ceilidh /káyli/ *n* 1 a party with singing and dancing to Scottish or Irish traditional music and storytelling 2 *Ireland* an evening visit [Late 19C. Via Irish *céilidhe*, Scots Gaelic *cèilidh* < Old Irish *célide* 'visit' < *céle* 'companion'.]

ceiling /seéling/ *n* 1 **INSIDE TOP OF ROOM** the overhead surface of a room, or the material used to line this surface 2 **UPPER LIMIT** a level above which something is not allowed to rise, e.g. prices, rents, or wages 3 **FLYING HEIGHT** the maximum height at which an aircraft can fly 4 **CLOUD LEVEL** the highest point, usually the base of a layer of clouds, from which the surface of the Earth can be seen [Mid-16C. < CEIL.] —**ceilinged** *adj* ◊ **go through the ceiling** to rise to a very high level ◊ **hit the ceiling** to become very angry

ceiling rose *n* = **rose**[1] *n*. 8

ceilometer /see lómmitar/ *n* an instrument for measuring the height of a cloud ceiling [Mid-20C. < CEILING.]

Cela /séllə, thélla/, **Camilo José** (*b.* 1916) Spanish novelist

celadon /sélladan, -don/ *n* 1 a pale greyish-green colour 2 Chinese porcelain with a greyish-green glaze [Mid-18C. < French *céladon*, after a character in D'Urfé's romance *L'Astrée*.] —**celadon** *adj*

Celaeno /se leénō/ *n* in Greek mythology, one of the Pleiades

Celan /sél an/, **Paul** (1920–70) Romanian-born French poet. Born **Paul Antschel**

celandine /séllan dīn, -deen/ *n* 1 a plant of the buttercup family that has heart-shaped leaves. Flowers: yellow, on individual stems. Native to: woodland, damp locations in Europe and Asia. *Ranunculus ficaria*. US term **lesser celandine** 2 PLANTS = **greater celandine** [Pre-12C. Via Old French *celidoine* < Greek *khelidonion* < *khelidōn* 'swallow'; because it flowered in spring, when swallows returned from migration.]

-cele *suffix* tumour, swelling ○ *varicocele* [< Greek *kēlē*]

celeb /si léb/ *n* a celebrity (*informal*) [Early 20C. Shortening.]

Celebes *n* = Sulawesi

Celebes Sea arm of the W Pacific Ocean surrounded by the Philippines, Borneo and Sulawesi. Area: 427,000 km/165,000 sq. mi.

celebrant /séllabrant/ *n* 1 **OFFICIATING PRIEST** a priest who is officiating at Holy Communion 2 **WORSHIPPER** a participant in a religious ceremony 3 **SOMEBODY CELEBRATING** a celebrator 4 *ANZ* **SOMEBODY WHO OFFICIATES** a secular official who conducts civil ceremonies such as weddings and naming ceremonies [Mid-19C. < Latin *celebrare* (see CELEBRATE).]

celebrate /séllə brayt/ (**-brates, -brating, -brated**) *v* 1 *vti* **SHOW HAPPINESS** to show happiness that something good or special has happened, by doing such things as eating and drinking together or playing music ○ *I told them about my promotion, and we went out to celebrate.* ○ *a noisy crowd of fans celebrating the victory* 2 *vt* **MARK AN OCCASION** to mark a special occasion or day by ceremonies or festivities 3 *vti* **PERFORM A RELIGIOUS CEREMONY** to perform a religious ceremony according to the prescribed forms 4 *vt* **PRAISE** to praise something publicly or make it famous [Mid-16C. < Latin *celebrare* 'attend a festival' < *celeber* 'frequented, famous'.] —**celebration** /séllə bráysh'n/ *n* —**celebrative** /séllabrativ/ *adj* —**celebrator** *n* —**celebratory** /séllabratari, séllə bráytari/ *adj*

celebrated /séllə braytid/ *adj* famous and admired

celebrity /sə lébbrati/ (*plural* **-ties**) *n* 1 a recipient of fame 2 the state of being famous [14C. Directly or via French *célébrité* < Latin *celebritas* < *celeber* 'famous'.]

celebrity skin *n* (*slang*) 1 a photograph showing a well-known person naked or nearly naked 2 an account or profile of a well-known person

celeriac /sə lérri ak/ *n* a type of celery that forms a root like an irregularly shaped turnip, eaten cooked or raw as a vegetable. *Apium graveolens* var. *rapaceum*. [Mid-18C. Alteration of CELERY.]

celerity /sə lérrati/ *n* quickness in movement or in doing something (*literary*) [15C. Via French *célérité* < Latin *celeritas* < *celer* 'swift'.]

celery /séllari/ *n* 1 a plant with long crisp flattish leaf stalks eaten raw or cooked as a vegetable *Apium graveolens* var. *dulce*. 2 the seeds of the celery plant. Use: seasoning. [Mid-17C. < French *céleri* < Greek *selinon* 'parsley'.]

celery pine *n* a tree that has shoots resembling celery and yields timber. Native to: New Zealand. *Phyllocladus trichomanoides*.

celesta /sə léstə/, **celeste** *n* a musical instrument with keys that make hammers strike metal plates, creating a soft tinkling sound [Late 19C. Alteration of French *céleste* 'celestial' < Latin *caelestis* (see CELESTIAL).]

celestial /sə lésti əl/ *adj* 1 belonging to, suitable for, in, or typical of heaven 2 relating to, contained in, or observed in the sky or outer space [14C. < French, < Latin *caelestis* < *caelum* 'sky, heaven'.] —**celestially** *adv*

celestial body *n* an object that is permanently present in the sky, e.g. a star or a planet

celestial equator *n* the great circle in which the plane of the Earth's equator intersects the celestial sphere

celestial globe *n* a globe showing the positions of the celestial bodies

celestial horizon *n* ASTRON = **horizon** *n.* 3

celestial mechanics *n* the branch of astronomy concerned with the motions and positions of celestial bodies in gravitational fields (*+ singular verb*)

celestial navigation *n* the steering of a ship or aircraft by observing the positions of the stars by means of triangulation

celestial pole *n* either of the two points where a line in continuation of the Earth's axis intersects the celestial sphere

celestial sphere *n* the imaginary sphere around the Earth on which the Sun, Moon, stars, and planets appear to be placed

celestite /séllə stīt/, **celestine** /sélləs teen, -stīn/ *n* a white or coloured mineral consisting of strontium sulphate. Use: source of strontium. [Early 19C. < Latin *caelestis* (see CELESTIAL).]

celiac *adj* US = **coeliac**

celibate /sélləbət/ *adj* **1** abstaining from sex **2** unmarried, especially because of a religious vow [Early 19C. < Latin *caelibatus* < *caelebs* 'unmarried'.] —**celibacy** *n* —**celibate** *n* —**celibately** *adv*

Céline /se leén, say-/, **Louis Ferdinand** (1894–1961) French novelist and doctor. Born **Louis-Ferdinand Destouches**

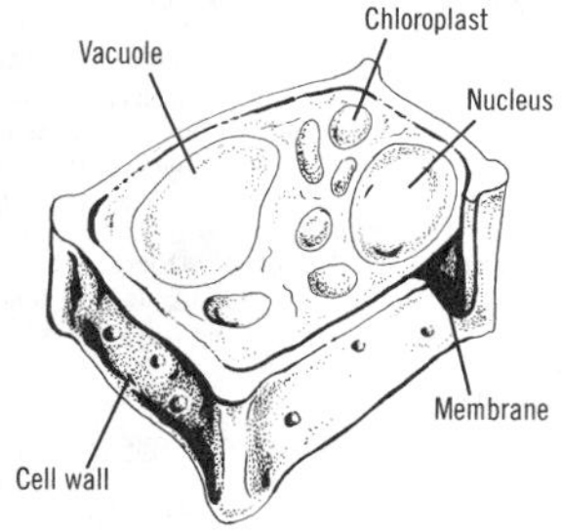

Cell: Structure of a plant cell

cell /sel/ *n* **1 ROOM FOR HOLDING PRISONER** a room in a prison, in which one or more prisoners are confined, or a small room in a police station, used to confine somebody who has been arrested **2 SMALL ROOM** a very small and simple room, especially in a monastery or convent **3 BASIC UNIT OF LIVING THING** the smallest independently functioning unit in the structure of an organism, usually consisting of one or more nuclei surrounded by cytoplasm and enclosed by a membrane **4 SMALL ENCLOSED STRUCTURE** a small contained or hollow unit in a structure, e.g. a compartment in a honeycomb **5 SOMETHING THAT PRODUCES ELECTRICITY** a device that produces electrical energy by the chemical action of electrodes in an electrolyte **6** ELEC = **solar cell** **7 ACTIVIST GROUP** a small group of people who work together and are part of a larger organization, especially members of a political organization who work in secret **8 RANGE OF MOBILE PHONE TRANSMITTER** the area covered by one of the transmitters in a mobile telephone system that automatically switches a travelling user between short-range radio stations **9 SPACE IN TABLE** a space for information in a table, e.g. in a computer spreadsheet, formed where a row and a column intersect **10 DEPENDENT RELIGIOUS HOUSE** a small religious house that is dependent on a larger religious community [Pre-12C. Via Old French *celle* < Latin *cella* 'small chamber'.] —**celled** *adj* —**-celled** *suffix*

cella /séllə/ (*plural* **-lae** /-lee/) *n* the inner room of a classical Greek or Roman temple, which contained the shrine or statue of the god [Late 17C. < Latin, 'small chamber'.]

cellar /séllər/ *n* **1 UNDERGROUND ROOM** a room wholly or partly below ground level that is not suitable as living space and is usually used for storage **2 PLACE FOR STORING WINE** a room where wine is stored **3 STOCK OF WINE** a stock of wine ■ *vt* **STORE WINE** to store something, especially wine, in a cellar [13C. Via Anglo-Norman *celer* < late Latin *cellarium* 'group of storage chambers' < Latin *cella* 'small chamber'.]

cellarage /séllərij/ *n* **1** a fee charged for storing something in a cellar **2** a cellar or cellars, or the amount of space in a cellar

cellarer /séllərər/ *n* a supervisor of food and drink supplies, especially in a monastery

cellaret /séllə rét/ *n* a cabinet or sideboard for storing bottles of wine and glasses

cellarette *n* US = **cellaret**

cellarman /séllərmən/ (*plural* **-men** /séllərmən/) *n* a man who is in charge of the cellar in a pub or restaurant and is responsible for maintaining good storage conditions

cellblock /sél blok/ *n* a group of cells forming a unit in a prison

cell division *n* the process by which a cell divides to form two new cells, either to produce identical cells (**mitosis**) or to produce cells with half the number of chromosomes (**meiosis**)

Cellini /che leéni/, **Benvenuto** (1500–71) Italian sculptor and goldsmith

cellist /chéllist/ *n* a musician who plays the cello

cell membrane *n* the membrane that surrounds the cytoplasm, through which substances pass in and out of the cell

cello /chéllō/ (*plural* **-los**) *n* a large stringed instrument of the violin family that is held upright between a seated player's knees and played with a bow. The cello has a full deep sound. [Late 19C. Shortening of VIOLONCELLO.]

cellobiose /séllō bī ōz/ *n* a sugar obtained by the breakdown of cellulose [Early 20C. < CELLULOSE + BI- + -OSE[2].]

Cellophane /séllə fayn/ *tdmk* a trademark for a thin transparent waterproof material made from wood pulp, used for wrapping and covering things

cellphone /sélfōn/ *n* a mobile telephone operated through a cellular radio network [Late 20C. Contraction of *cellular telephone*.]

cellular /séllyŏolər/ *adj* **1 INVOLVING LIVING CELLS** relating to or consisting of living cells **2 CONTAINING SMALL PARTS OR GROUPS** relating to small parts or groups making up a whole **3 ORGANIZED INTO CELLS** organized as a system of cells, especially for radio communication **4 POROUS** porous in texture and containing many small cavities **5 OPEN-TEXTURED** woven or knitted to produce thick, open-textured cloth [Mid-18C. Via French *cellulaire* < modern Latin *cellularis* < Latin *cellula* (see CELLULE).] —**cellularity** /séllyŏo lárrəti/ *n* —**cellularly** *adv*

cellular phone *n* TELECOM = **cellphone**

cellular radio *n* the type of radio communication used for mobile phones that consists of a network of transmitters, each covering a small area

cellular telephone *n* TELECOM = **cellphone**

cellulase /séllyŏo layz, -layss/ *n* an enzyme that converts cellulose to sugars [Early 20C. < CELLULOSE.]

cellule /séllyool/ *n* a small cell in a living organism [Mid-19C. Via French < Latin *cellula* 'small cell' < *cella* 'small chamber'.]

cellulite /séllyŏol īt/ *n* fatty deposits beneath the skin that give a lumpy or grainy appearance to the skin surface, e.g. on the thighs or buttocks [Mid-20C. < French, < *cellule* (see CELLULE).]

cellulitis /séllyŏo lītiss/ *n* infection and inflammation of the tissues beneath the skin

celluloid /séllyŏo loyd/ *n* **1 COLOURLESS PLASTIC** flammable transparent plastic made from nitrocellulose and a plasticizer such as camphor **2 FILM** the photographic film used for making films **3 CINEMA AS MEDIUM** the cinema as a medium or art form [Mid-19C. < CELLULOSE.] —**celluloid** *adj*

cellulolytic /séllyŏolō líttik/ *adj* describes a process or an organism that can degrade cellulose [Mid-20C. < CELLULOSE.]

cellulose /séllyŏo lōss, -lōz/ *n* the main constituent of the cell walls of plants and algae. Use: plastics, lacquers, explosives, synthetic fibres. [Mid-19C. < French, < Latin *cellula* (see CELLULE).] —**cellulosic** /séllyŏo lóssik, -lózik/ *adj*

cellulose acetate *n* a chemical compound produced by the reaction of acetic or sulphuric acid on cellulose. Use: photographic film, plastics, textile fibres, varnishes.

cellulose nitrate *n* nitrocellulose

cell wall *n* the outermost layer of a cell in plants and certain fungi, algae, and bacteria, providing a supporting framework

celosia /sə lóssi ə/ (*plural* **-sias** or **-sia**) *n* a plant belonging to a genus that includes cockscomb. Flowers: feathery, yellow to purplish-red. Genus: *Celosia*. [Early 19C. < modern Latin, < Greek *kēlos* 'burnt'.]

Celsius /sélssi əss/ *adj* using or measured on an international metric temperature scale on which water freezes at 0° and boils at 100° under normal atmospheric conditions (*generally not in scientific contexts apart from meteorology*) ◊ **Fahrenheit** [Mid-19C. After Anders *Celsius* (1701–44), Swedish astronomer.]

celt /selt/ *n* a prehistoric chisel or axe that has a metal or stone head with a bevelled edge [Early 18C. < medieval Latin *celtis* 'chisel'.]

Celt /kelt, selt/, **Kelt** /kelt/ *n* **1** somebody who speaks or whose ancestors spoke a Celtic language **2** a member of an ancient Indo-European people who lived in central and W Europe [Mid-16C. Via Latin *Celtae* 'Celts' < Greek *Keltoi*.]

Celtic /kéltik, s-/ *adj* relating to the Celts, or their languages or cultures ■ *n* an Indo-European group of languages that includes Irish, Scottish Gaelic, Welsh, and Breton and has Brythonic and Goidelic subgroups. Native speakers: 1.5 million. —**Celticist** *n*

Celtic cross *n* a cross that has a broad ring around the intersection of the upright and crossbar

Celticism /kéltissizəm, s-/ *n* **1** a word or idiom of Celtic origin that has become naturalized in another language **2** a custom or belief of Celtic origin

Celtic Sea /kéltik-, sél-/ extension of the Atlantic Ocean between the Republic of Ireland to the north and SW England to the south

cembalo /chémbəlō/ (*plural* **-li** /-lee/ or **-los**) *n* MUSIC = **harpsichord** [Mid-19C. < Italian, contraction of *clavicembalo* < medieval Latin *clavicymbalum* < Latin *clavis* 'key' + *cymbalum* (see CYMBAL).] —**cembalist** *n*

cement /si mént/ *n* **1 POWDER FOR CONCRETE** a fine grey powder of calcined limestone and clay **2 CONCRETE** a building material that sets hard, made by mixing cement with water, sand, and aggregate **3 GLUE** a glue or similar bonding substance **4 HUMAN BOND** something that unites people or groups **5 SUBSTANCE USED IN DENTISTRY** a substance used in dentistry for filling cavities and anchoring bridgework or crowns. ◊ **amalgam** *n.* **2** **6** ANAT = **cementum** **7 MATERIAL BINDING ROCK** a substance that binds together the particles in sedimentary rocks and fills the spaces ■ *vti* **1 FIX OR BECOME FIXED WITH CEMENT** to fix something in place with cement or a similar substance, or become fixed in this way **2 APPLY CEMENT TO** to cover or fill something with cement or a similar substance **3 STRENGTHEN RELATIONSHIP** to make a relationship between people strong or permanent, or become strong or permanent [14C. Via French *ciment* < Latin *caementum* 'quarry stone', (plural) 'stone chips' < *caedere* 'hew'.] —**cementer** *n*

cementation /seé men táysh'n/ *n* **1 CEMENTING** the application of cement or a similar substance to something **2 CEMENTING OF ROCKS** the injecting of cement into holes or fissures in rocks to make them watertight or strong **3 HEATING METAL WITH POWDER** the modification of a solid, especially a metal, by heating it with one or more other substances that will diffuse into the surface, e.g. the production of steel by heating it with charcoal **4 SEDIMENTARY ROCK FORMATION** the process in which percolating groundwater deposits a cementing material to form a sedimentary rock

cementite /si mén tīt/ *n* Fe_3C a hard brittle compound of iron and carbon that forms in some types of cast iron, in carbon steels, and in alloys of carbon and iron

cement mixer *n* **1** a transportable machine with a revolving drum in which cement powder, water, sand, and other materials can be mixed to make concrete, mortar, or stucco **2** a truck with a large revolving drum for mixing, transporting, and pouring concrete

cementum /si méntəm/ *n* the thin layer of bony tissue that covers the dentine of the roots and neck of a tooth [Mid-19C. < Latin *caementum* (see CEMENT).]

cemetery /sémmətri/ (*plural* **-ies**) *n* an area of ground in which the dead are buried, especially one that is not in the grounds of a church [14C. Via late Latin *coemeterium* < Greek *koimētērion* 'dormitory' < *koiman* 'put to sleep'.]

~~**cemetry**~~ incorrect spelling of **cemetery**

CEN *n* = **CENELEC**

cen. *abbr* 1 central 2 century

-cene *suffix* recent ○ *Pliocene* [< Greek *kainos* 'new']

CENELEC /sénnə lek/, **CEN** /sen/ *n* an EU organization that controls the standard of electrical goods. Full form **Commission Européenne de Normalisation Electrique**

CEng /seè énj/ *abbr* chartered engineer

ceno- *prefix* = **coeno-**

cenobite *n* = **coenobite**

cenogenesis *n* = **caenogenesis**

cenotaph /sénnə taaf, -taf/ *n* a monument erected as a memorial to a dead person or dead people buried elsewhere, especially people killed fighting a war [Early 17C. < Greek *kenotaphion* 'empty tomb' < *kenos* 'empty' + *taphos* 'tomb'.] —**cenotaphic** /sénnə táffik/ *adj*

Cenotaph *n* a monument in London that serves as a memorial to the dead of wars involving British forces since World War I

cenote /si nó tay/ *n* a deep natural hole found in limestone, especially in Yucatán, Mexico [Mid-19C. Via Yucatán Spanish < Maya *tzonot*.]

Cenozoic /seènō zó ik/, **Caenozoic, Cainozoic** /kīnə-, káynə-/ *adj* belonging or relating to the most recent era of geological time, covering the period from the present to about 65 million years ago, during which modern plants and animals evolved [Mid-19C. < Greek *kainos* 'new'.] —**Cenozoic** *n*

cense /senss/ (**censes, censing, censed**) *vt* 1 to burn incense to a deity at an altar or shrine 2 to perfume a place or worshippers with incense [14C. Shortening of French *encenser* < Latin *incendere* 'set fire to' < *candere* 'to glow'.]

censer /sénssər/ *n* a container used for burning incense, especially one that is swung in a religious procession or ceremony [13C. < Old French *censier*, shortening of *encensier* < *encens* 'incense' < ecclesiastical Latin *incensum* < past participle of Latin *incendere* (see CENSE).]

censor /sénssər/ *n* 1 **OFFICIAL REMOVING OBJECTIONABLE MATERIAL** an official who examines plays, films, letters, and publications with a view to removing or banning content considered to be offensive or a threat to security 2 **SOMEBODY WHO SUPPRESSES** somebody who or something that exercises suppressive control 3 **ANCIENT ROMAN OFFICIAL** either of two elected magistrates of ancient Rome who were responsible for holding censuses, overseeing public morals, and controlling aspects of finance and taxation 4 **INHIBITING FORCE IN MIND** in psychology, a mechanism believed to be responsible for what can and cannot emerge from the subconscious to the conscious mind ■ *vt* 1 **REMOVE OFFENSIVE PARTS FROM** to remove or change any part of a publication, play, or film considered offensive or a threat to security 2 **EXERCISE CONTROL OVER** to suppress or control something that may offend or harm others [Mid-16C. < Latin *censere* 'appraise'.] —**censorable** *adj* —**censorial** /sen sáwri əl/ *adj*

USAGE censor or **censure**? Though spelt similarly these two words are pronounced differently and have different meanings. A ***censor*** is a person who suppresses or removes information (*Military censors have excised some of the target photos for security reasons*), while ***censure*** is severe criticism or condemnation (*The angry legislature decided to censure the governor for his fraudulent land deals.*). Both words can work as verbs, and as such they preserve their distinct meanings.

censorious /sen sáwri əss/ *adj* 1 inclined or eager to criticize people or things 2 expressing strong disapproval or harsh criticism —**censoriously** *adv* —**censoriousness** *n*

censorship /sénssər ship/ *n* 1 **SUPPRESSION OF PUBLISHED OR BROADCAST MATERIAL** the suppression of all or part of a publication, play, or film considered offensive or a threat to security 2 **ANY SUPPRESSION** the suppression or attempted suppression of something regarded as objectionable 3 **ANCIENT ROMAN OFFICE** the office, authority, or term of an ancient Roman censor 4 **SUPPRESSION OF MEMORIES** the suppression of potentially harmful memories, ideas, or desires from the conscious mind

censure /sénshər/ *n* 1 **DISAPPROVAL** severe criticism 2 **OFFICIAL CONDEMNATION** official expression of disapproval or condemnation ■ *vt* (**-sures, -suring, -sured**) 1 **CRITICIZE** to subject somebody or something to severe criticism 2 **CONDEMN** to express official disapproval or condemnation of somebody or something [14C. < Latin *censura* 'judgment' < *censere* 'appraise'.] —**censurability** /sənshərə bíllәti/ *n* —**censurable** *adj* —**censurableness** *n* —**censurably** *adv* —**censurer** *n*

SYNONYMS See ***criticize*** and ***disapprove***.

USAGE See ***censor***.

census /sénssəss/ (*plural* **-suses**) *n* 1 **COUNT OF POPULATION** an official count of a population carried out at set intervals 2 **SYSTEMATIC COUNT** a systematic count or survey 3 **REGISTRATION OF ROMANS FOR TAXATION** in ancient Rome, a registration of the population and their property that was used for assessing taxes [Early 17C. < Latin *censere* 'appraise'.]

cent /sent/ *n* see table at **currency** [14C. Directly or via French, 'hundred', or Italian *cento* < Latin *centum*.]

cent. *abbr* 1 centigrade 2 central 3 century

cent- *prefix* = **centi-**

cental /sént'l/ *n* a unit of mass equal to 100 lb (45.3 kg). US term **hundredweight** *n.* 2 [Late 19C. < Latin *centum* 'hundred'.]

centas /sén tass/ (*plural* **-tas**) *n* see table at **currency**

centaur /sén tawr/ *n* in Greek mythology, a wild creature with the head, arms, and torso of a man joined to the body of a horse at its neck [14C. Via Latin *centaurus* < Greek *kentauros*.]

Centaurus /sen táwrəss/ *n* a prominent constellation of the southern hemisphere containing the stars Alpha Centauri and Beta Centauri. See illustration at **constellation**

centavo /sen taávō/ (*plural* **-vos**) *n* see table at **currency** [Late 19C. < Spanish, Portuguese, 'hundredth' < Latin *centum* 'hundred'.]

centenarian /séntə náiri ən/ *n* **100-YEAR-OLD PERSON** a person a hundred years of age or more ■ *adj* 1 **100 YEARS OLD** at least a hundred years of age 2 **OF CENTENARIANS** relating to or characteristic of one-hundred-year-old people

centenary /sen teénəri, -ténnə-/ *n* (*plural* **-ries**) 1 **100-YEAR ANNIVERSARY** an anniversary of a hundred years, or its celebration. US term **centennial** *n.* 2 **CENTURY** a period of one hundred years ■ *adj* 1 **MARKING 100 YEARS** marking an anniversary of 100 years. US term **centennial** *adj.* 3 2 **ONCE-A-CENTURY** occurring every hundred years 3 **OF A CENTURY** relating to or involving a period of one hundred years [Early 17C. < Latin *centenarius* 'containing a hundred' < *centeni* 'hundred each' < *centum* 'hundred'.]

centennial /sen ténni əl/ *adj* 1 relating to or involving a period of a hundred years 2 occurring every hundred years 3 US = **centenary** *adj.* 1 ■ *n* US = **centenary** *n.* 1 [Late 18C. < Latin *centum* 'hundred'.] —**centennially** *adv*

center *n, vti* US = **centre**

centesimal /sen téssim'l/ *adj* 1 **IN 100THS** divided into hundredths 2 **1/100TH** constituting one one-hundredth of something 3 **USING BASE OF 100** describes a number system that uses a base of 100 ■ *n* **100TH PART** one hundredth of something [Late 17C. < Latin *centesimus* 'hundredth' < *centum* 'hundred'.] —**centesimally** *adv*

centesimo /sen téssimō/ (*plural* **-mos** *or* **-mi** /-mi/) *n* see table at **currency** [Mid-19C. < Italian, < Latin *centesimus* (see CENTESIMAL).]

centi- *prefix* 1 hundredth ○ *centipoise* 2 hundred ○ *centipede* [Via French < Latin *centum* 'hundred']

centigrade /sénti grayd/ *adj* a temperature scale, especially Celsius, based on a range of one hundred

centigram /sénti gram/, **centigramme** *n* (*symbol* **cg**) a unit of mass equal to one hundredth of a gram

centilitre /sénti leetər/ *n* (*symbol* **cl**) a unit of volume equal to one hundredth of a litre

centillion /sen tílli ən/ (*plural* **-lions** *or* **-lion**) *n* 1 in the United Kingdom and Germany, the number represented by the figure 1 followed by 600 zeros 2 *US* in the United States, Canada, and France, the number represented by the figure 1 followed by 303 zeros [Mid-19C. < CENTI-.]

centime /són teem, saán-/ *n* see table at **currency** [Early 19C. Via French < Latin *centesimus* (see CENTESIMAL).]

centimetre /sénti meetər/ *n* (*symbol* **cm**) a unit of length equal to one hundredth of a metre

centimetre-gram-second, centimetre-gramme-second *adj* using or relating to a measurement system that uses the centimetre as the basic unit for length, the gram for mass, and the second for time (*In scientific contexts the cgs system has been largely replaced by the SI system*)

centimo /séntimō/ (*plural* **-mos**) *n* see table at **currency** [Late 19C. Via Spanish < French *centime* < Latin *centesimus* (see CENTESIMAL).]

centimorgan /sénti mawrgən/ *n* a unit of measurement used to indicate how closely genes are linked together on the same chromosome [Mid-20C. After Thomas Hunt MORGAN.]

centipede /sénti peed/ *n* a small, fast-moving invertebrate with a long slender body divided into many segments, most of which bear one pair of legs. Class: Chilopoda.

centipoise /sénti poyz/ *n* a unit of measurement for viscosity in the cgs system that is equal to one hundredth of a poise

centner /séntnər/ *n* 1 in the United Kingdom, a unit of mass equal to 45.3 kg/100 lb 2 in some European countries, a unit of mass equal to 50 kg (110.23 lb) [Mid-16C. < German *Zentner* < Latin *centenarius* 'of a hundred'.]

centr- *prefix* = **centro-** (*before vowels*)

centra plural of **centrum**

central /séntrəl/ *adj* 1 **IN THE MIDDLE** in, near, or forming the middle of something 2 **EQUIDISTANT FROM OTHER POINTS** at approximately the same distance from a number of different points or places 3 **IN MAIN PART OF TOWN** in the part of a town or city where the main shops, offices, and other facilities are situated 4 **HAVING CONTROL OVER PARTS** controlling the activities of connected or subordinate parts ○ *a central authority* 5 **HAVING LINKED COMPONENTS** describes a system of linked devices controlled by a single unit or at a single point 6 **CRUCIAL** of critical importance or great influence ○ *the notion is central to their thinking on the subject* 7 **DOMINANT** with a major or the principal role 8 **RELATING TO CENTRUM** relating to the centrum of a vertebra 9 **SAID WITH TONGUE IN MIDDLE POSITION** describes a vowel articulated with the tongue at or near the middle of the hard palate, as is the final vowel in 'cola' [Mid-17C. < Latin *centralis* < *centrum* (see CENTRE).] —**centrally** *adv*

Central /séntrəl/ former administrative region of Scotland

Central African Federation former federation of Nyasaland, Northern Rhodesia, and Southern Rhodesia, present-day Malawi, Zambia, and Zimbabwe

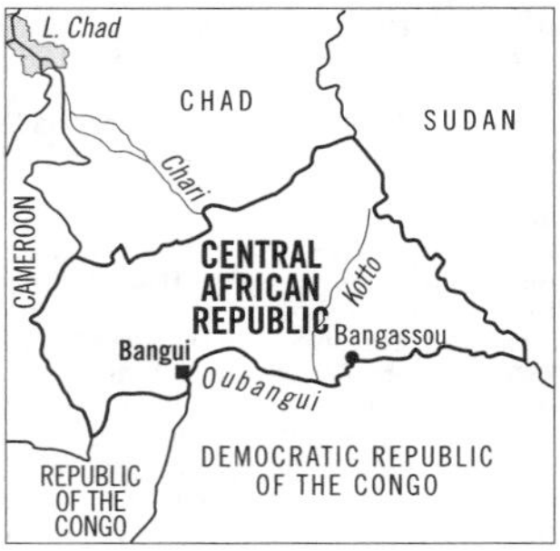

Central African Republic

Central African Republic landlocked country in central Africa. Capital: Bangui. Population: 3,308,198 (1997). Area: 622,436 sq. km/240,324 sq. mi.

Central America southern part of North America, comprising Guatemala, Belize, Honduras, El Salvador, Nicaragua, Costa Rica, and Panama. Population: 31,300,000 (1993). Area: 523,000 sq. km/201,930 sq. mi.

central angle *n* an angle formed in the centre of a circle by the meeting of two radii

central bank *n* a financial institution, e.g. the Bank of England, whose function is to regulate state fiscal and monetary activities —**central banker** *n*

central casting *n US* the department in a film production company whose function is to select appropriate actors to audition for specified parts

Central Committee *n* in a Communist party, the part of the bureaucracy responsible for party policy. ◊ **Politburo, Agitprop**

Central European Time *n* the standard time adopted by most Western European countries, one hour ahead of Greenwich Mean Time

central government *n* the area of government that is concerned with national issues such as taxation, defence, international relations, and trade

central heating *n* a system designed to heat a whole building from a single source of heat by pumping hot water or air to room radiators or vents —**centrally heated** *adj*

Central Intelligence Agency *n* full form of **CIA**

centralise *vti* = **centralize**

centralism /séntrəlizəm/ *n* the concentration of control, especially political control, in a single authority —**centralist** *n, adj* —**centralistic** /séntrə lístik/ *adj*

centrality /sen trállәti/ *n* **1 CRITICAL ROLE** the crucial importance of somebody or something **2 POSITION IN MIDDLE** the location of somebody or something in or near the middle of something **3 LOCATION IN MAIN PART OF TOWN** the location of something in the part of a town or city where the main shops, offices, and other facilities are situated

centralize /séntrə līz/ (**-izes, -izing, -ized**), **centralise** (**-ises, -ising, -ised**) *vti* **1** to remove political or administrative power from local or subordinate levels and concentrate it in a central authority **2** to concentrate or collect something at a single point —**centralization** /séntrə lī záysh'n/ *n* —**centralizer** *n*

central locking *n* a system in which all the doors and the boot of a motor vehicle are automatically locked or unlocked when somebody locks or unlocks one door

Central Lowlands fertile region of central Scotland

Central Mount Stuart mountain in central Australia, considered the geographical centre of the continent. Height: 845 m/2,772 ft.

central nervous system *n* the part of the nervous system, consisting of the brain and spinal cord, that controls and coordinates most functions of the body and mind. ◊ **spinal cord, brain**

Central Park *n* large park on Manhattan Island in New York City

⚡**central processing unit, central processor** *n* the part of a computer that performs operations and executes software commands

central reservation *n UK* a narrow strip of land that separates lanes of traffic travelling in opposite directions on a dual carriageway or motorway. ◊ **median strip**

Central Standard Time, Central Time *n* **1** the standard time in the zone that includes the central states of the United States and the central provinces of Canada. Central Standard Time is six hours behind Greenwich Mean Time. **2** the standard time in the time zone centred on longitude 135° E, which includes the central part of Australia. It is nine-and-a-half hours ahead of Greenwich Mean Time.

central sulcus *n* a deep groove in each of the hemispheres of the brain, separating the frontal and parietal lobes

Central Time *n* = **Central Standard Time**

centre /séntər/ *n* **1 MIDDLE POINT OR AREA** the middle point, area, or part of something that is the same distance from all edges or opposite sides **2 MIDDLE OF CIRCLE OR SPHERE** the interior point that is the same distance from all points on the circumference of a circle or the surface of a sphere or the vertices of a polygon **3 MIDDLE OF LINE** the point on a line that is the same distance from both ends **4 FOOD FILLING** the filling of a chocolate, doughnut, or other food **5 MAIN PART OF TOWN** the part of a town or city where the main shops, offices, and other facilities are situated **6 PLACE FOR PARTICULAR ACTIVITY** a place where a particular activity is carried on ○ *a sports centre* **7 FOCUS OF ATTENTION** the point that is the focus of attention or interest ○ *the issue at the centre of the controversy* **8 INFLUENTIAL PLACE OR ORGANIZATION** a place, area, or group of people exerting control or influence over something or somebody else ○ *a centre of design innovation* **9 CLUSTER OR CONCENTRATION** a place or part where something is concentrated or focused **10 centre, Centre POLITICAL MODERATES** those political parties or the section of a party holding views that are neither left-wing nor right-wing **11 PIVOTAL POINT OR AXIS** the point or line around which something rotates **12 POINT WHERE FORCE ACTS** in physics, the point at or through which a force is considered to act **13 GROUP OF NERVE CELLS REGULATING FUNCTION** a group of nerve cells, especially within the central nervous system, that controls a particular function of the body **14 CONICAL PART OF LATHE** the part of a lathe that supports the work to be turned **15 MARK TO GUIDE DRILL** a dimple made in metal with a pointed tool (**centre punch**) to mark the centre of a larger hole to be drilled **16 ATTACKING PLAYER OR POSITION** in some sports, an attacking player or position in the middle of the field or court **17** BASEBALL = **centre field** ■ *v* (**-tres, -tring, -tred**) **1** *vt* **PUT SOMETHING IN MIDDLE** to position something in the middle of something **2** *vti* **FOCUS ON THEME** to have or cause something to have its focus on a theme or topic ○ *the debate centres on the possible health risks involved* **3** *vti* **CONCENTRATE OR FOCUS** to be concentrated, or cause something to be concentrated, in a particular place or on a particular thing **4** *vt* **PASS BALL TOWARDS MIDDLE** in some sports, to pass, hit, or kick a ball or puck from the edge of the playing area towards the middle [14C. < Latin *centrum* < Greek *kentron* 'point' < *kentein* 'to prick'.]

USAGE ***centre on*** or ***centre around/round?*** If you use the verb ***centre*** to mean 'to focus on something' you can safely use it with the prepositions *on* or *upon*, as in *The court's interpretation of the law centred on* [or *upon*, not *around*] *a recent precedent.* Here, the idea of a specific, narrow focus is implicit. Thus, substitution of *around/round*, which signifies circularity or diffuse movement here and there, is imprecise. ***Centre around/round*** is more acceptable if the idea is to express a generalized focus on a number of things, as in *Discussions centred around the witness's credibility, her previously conflicting statements, and their admissibility.* This usage is well established, but if you wish to avoid ***centre around*** use *revolve around.*

---

centre back *n* a player or position in the middle of the back line in various sports

centre bit *n* a drill attachment or tool for boring or cutting with a pointed projection in the middle and cutters at the sides

centreboard /séntər bawrd/ *n* a keel in a sailing boat that can be retracted upwards in shallow water

centred /séntərd/ *adj* **1** positioned at the same distance from all edges or opposite sides **2** *US* exhibiting confidence, self-awareness, and often a sense of determination —**centredness** *n*

centre field, centre *n* **1** in baseball, the part of the outfield behind second base **2** the position of the baseball player who plays centre field —**centre fielder** *n*

centrefold /séntər fōld/ *n* **1** a single illustration, advertisement, or feature that covers the two facing pages in the middle of a magazine or newspaper, especially a photograph of a nude model **2** the subject of a photograph, especially naked or nearly naked, for a centrefold **3** MEDIA = **centre spread** *n.* 1

centre forward *n* the player or position in the middle of the forward attacking line in sports such as football and hockey

centre half (*plural* **centre halfs**) *n* the player or position in the middle of the half-line in football and hockey

centreline /séntər līn/ *n* **1** a solid or dashed line on a road that marks where traffic should flow, either separating lanes going in opposite directions or multiple lanes going the same way **2** a real or imaginary line through or along the middle of something

centre of curvature *n* the centre of a circle whose radius is perpendicular to a line tangent to any point on the concave side of a smooth curve. ◊ **radius of curvature**

centre of excellence *n* a place where the highest standards of achievement are aimed for in a given sphere of activity

centre of gravity *n* **1** the point through which the sum of gravitational forces on a body can be considered to act **2** PHYS = **centre of mass**

centre of mass *n* the point at which the total mass of a body or system is assumed to be centred and upon which the sum of external forces can be considered to act

centrepiece /séntər peess/ *n* **1** an object placed in the middle of something as decoration or to attract attention **2** the most important part or feature

centre punch *n* a pointed tool used in metalworking for making a dimple to guide a drill bit prior to drilling a hole

centre spread *n* **1** the two pages that face each other in the middle of a magazine or newspaper **2** a magazine or newspaper article featured in the middle to give it prominence

centre stage *n* **1 MIDDLE OF STAGE** the middle area of a theatre stage **2 FOCUS OF INTEREST** the centre of people's attention or interest ■ *adv* **1 IN MIDDLE OF STAGE** in or to the middle area of a theatre stage **2 TO CENTRE OF ATTENTION** at or to the centre of people's attention or interest

centre three-quarter *n* **1** in rugby, either of the two positions at the middle of the three-quarter line **2** in rugby, either of the two people who play in the middle of the three-quarter line

centri- *prefix* = **centro-**

centric /séntrik/, **centrical** /-trik'l/ *adj* **1 AT OR AS THE MIDDLE** at or constituting the middle of something **2 OF OR FROM NERVE CENTRE** issuing from or relating to a nerve centre **3 WITH CONCENTRIC LAYERS OF TISSUE** describes a plant's vascular bundles in which one type of sap-conducting tissue is surrounded by another **4 TAPERING AND CYLINDRICAL** describes leaves that are tapering and cylindrical. ◊ **terete** **5 OF A CLASS OF DIATOMS** relating to a class of diatoms that have radial symmetry. Class: Centrales. —**centrically** /-trikli/ *adv* —**centricity** /sen tríssəti/ *n*

-centric *suffix* **1** having a particular number or kind of centres ○ *hexcentric* ○ *acentric* **2** having as its center ○ *egocentric* **3** having as its focus of attention, interest, or activity ○ *teen-centric* [< medieval Latin *-centricus* < Latin *centrum* (see CENTRE)]

centrifugal /séntri fyóog'l, sen tríffyòog'l/ *adj* **1 AWAY FROM CENTRE** acting, moving, or pulling away from a centre or axis. ◊ **centripetal** *adj.* 1 **2 EMPLOYING CENTRIFUGAL FORCE** using or operated by centrifugal force **3** PHYSIOL = **efferent** **4 DEVELOPING OUTWARDS** describes a plant part or tissue that develops from the centre outwards **5 DECENTRALIZING POWER** tending to disperse political or administrative power away from a central authority ■ *n* **APPARATUS USING CENTRIFUGAL FORCE** an apparatus that uses centrifugal force, or a rotating drum in such an apparatus —**centrifugalism** *n* —**centrifugally** *adv*

centrifugal force *n* an apparent force that seems to pull a rotating or spinning object away from a centre

centrifuge /séntri fyooj, -fyoozh/ *n* **1** a device that rotates rapidly and uses centrifugal force to separate substances of different densities **2** a rotating apparatus used to simulate the effects of gravity or acceleration on humans or animals [Early 18C. < Latin *centrifugus* 'fleeing the centre' < *fugere* 'flee'.] —**centrifugation** /séntri fyoo gáysh'n/ *n* —**centrifuge** *vt*

centriole /séntri ōl/ *n* a two-part rod-shaped structure with the parts lying at right angles to each other, located in pairs near the nucleus of an animal cell. During cell division, centrioles move to opposite ends of the cell and form the poles of the spindle fibres that pull the chromosomes apart. [Late 19C. < modern Latin *centriolum* 'small centre' < *centrum* (see CENTRE).]

centripetal /sen tríppit'l, séntri peét'l/ *adj* **1 TOWARDS CENTRE** acting, moving, or pulling towards a centre or axis. ◊ **centrifugal** *adj.* 1 **2 EMPLOYING CENTRIPETAL FORCE** using or operated by centripetal force **3** PHYSIOL = **afferent** **4 DEVELOPING INWARDS** describes a plant part or tissue that develops from the perimeter inwards **5 CENTRALIZING POWER** tending to concentrate political or administrative power in a central authority [Early 18C. < modern Latin *centripetus* 'seeking the centre' < Latin *petere* (see PETITION).] —**centripetally** *adv*

centripetal force *n* a force that pulls a rotating or spinning object towards a centre or axis

centrism /séntrizəm/ *n* the holding or advocating of moderate political or other views —**centrist** *n, adj*

centro- *prefix* centre ○ *centrosome* [< Latin *centrum* (see CENTRE)]

centroid /sén troyd/ *n* PHYS = **centre of mass** [Late 19C. < CENTRO-.]

centromere /séntrə meer/ *n* the point at which two parts (**chromatids**) of a chromosome join and at which the spindle fibres are attached during cell division (**mitosis**) —**centromeric** /séntrə mérrik, -meérik/ *adj*

centrosome /séntrəsōm/ *n* a small region of cytoplasm near the nucleus of a cell, containing rod-shaped structures (**centrioles**) —**centrosomic** /séntrə sómmik/ *adj*

centrum /séntrəm/ (*plural* **-trums** *or* **-tra** /-trə/) *n* a thick mass of bone in a vertebra that is the point of attachment to the vertebrae above and below [Mid-19C. < Latin (see CENTRE).]

centum /kéntəm/ *adj* describes those ancient Indo-European language groups in which the /k/ sound, when preceding a front vowel, did not palatalize. ◊ **satem** [Early 20C. < Latin, 'hundred'.]

centurion /sen tyóori ən, -chóor-/ *n* in ancient Rome, an officer in charge of a unit of foot soldiers (**century**) [14C. < Latin *centurion-* < *centuria* 'century' < *centum* 'hundred'.] —**centurial** *adj*

century /sénchəri/ (*plural* **-ries**) *n* **1 100 YEARS** a period of a hundred years **2 100-YEAR PERIOD IN DATING SYSTEM** a period of a hundred years in a dating system, from a year numbered 1 or 00, e.g. 1901 or 2000, to one ending in 00 or 99, e.g. 2000 or 2099 **3 100 RUNS** in cricket, 100 runs scored by one batsman **4 UNIT OF ROMAN SOLDIERS** a group of foot soldiers in ancient Rome, originally comprising a hundred men but later between sixty and eighty. ◊ **maniple** *n.* 1 **5 GROUP OF ROMAN VOTERS** a division of citizens in ancient Rome for voting purposes **6 100 THINGS** any group of a hundred similar things **7 LONG TIME** a very long time (*informal; usually plural*) [14C. < Latin *centuria* 'group of a hundred' < *centum* 'hundred'.]

USAGE When does a new century begin? Mathematicians will no doubt insist that a new ***century*** begins on 1 January of a year ending in 01, so that the 22nd century will begin on 1 January 2101. This is because the first century AD began with the year 1 (as did the first century BC – there was no year 0), and if that century is to have contained its requisite hundred years, the first year of any subsequent century must also end in 1. In most contexts, however, a new century is reckoned from the year ending in 00, since this is psychologically the more significant point. Similarly, a new millennium begins for practical purposes on 1 January of the year ending in 000, not 001.

century plant *n* a plant with greyish-green leaves that takes ten to thirty years to mature and flowers just once before dying. Native to: Mexico, S United States. *Agave americana*. [< the length of its maturation]

CEO *abbr* chief executive officer

ceorl /churl/ *n* in Anglo-Saxon England, a freeman of the lowest class [Old English (see CHURL)]

cep /sep/, **cèpe** /sep, seep/ *n* an edible woodland mushroom with a shiny brown cap and a creamy-coloured underside. *Boletus edulis*. [Mid-19C. Via French *cèpe* < Gascon *cep* 'tree trunk, mushroom' < Latin *cippus* 'stake'.]

cephal- *prefix* = **cephalo-** (*before vowels*)

cephalic /sə fállik/ *adj* relating to the head [15C. < Greek *kephalikos* < *kephalē* (see CEPHALO-).] —**cephalically** *adv*

-cephalic *suffix* having a particular number of heads or a particular kind of head ○ *monocephalic* ○ *brachycephalic* [< Latin *cephalicus* < Greek *kephalē* (see CEPHALO-)]

cephalic index *n* the ratio of the width to the length of a human skull, measured at the widest and longest points, and multiplied by 100

cephalin /séffəlin/, **kephalin** /kéff-/ *n* one of a group of chemicals found in all tissues, especially the brain

cephalization /séffəlī záysh'n/, **cephalisation** *n* the tendency for sensory, neural, and feeding organs to be concentrated at the front end of the body, leading to the development of a head in many organisms

cephalo- *prefix* head, skull ○ *cephalometry* [Via modern Latin < Greek *kephalē* < Indo-European]

cephalometry /séffə lómmətri/ *n* the measurement of human heads, especially using X-rays or ultrasound —**cephalometer** *n* —**cephalometric** /séffəlō méttrik/ *adj*

Cephalonia /séffə lóni ə, kéffə-/ the largest of the Ionian Islands in W Greece. Population: 32,474 (1991). Area: 750 sq. km/290 sq. mi.

cephalopod /séffələ pod/ *n* a marine animal with a large head and tentacles, e.g. an octopus, squid, or cuttlefish. Class: Cephalopoda. —**cephalopod** *adj* —**cephalopodan** /séffə lóppədən/ *adj, n* —**cephalopodic** /séffələ póddik/ *adj* —**cephalopodous** /séffə lóppədəss/ *adj*

cephalosporin /séffəlō spáwrin/ *n* a broad-spectrum antibiotic derived from fungi. ◊ **penicillin** [Mid-20C. < modern Latin *Cephalosporium* < sources of CEPHALO- + SPORE.]

cephalothorax /séffəlō tháwraks/ (*plural* **-raxes** or **-races** /-rəsseez/) *n* the fused head and thorax typical of spiders and other arachnids and many crustaceans

-cephalous *suffix* having a particular number of heads or a particular kind of head ○ *dicephalous* ○ *autocephalous* [< Greek *-kephalos* < *kephalē* (see CEPHALO-)]

-cephaly *suffix* a particular condition of the head or skull ○ *microcephaly* [< Greek *kephalē* 'head']

Cepheid /seéfi id/, **Cepheid variable** *n* a star that has regular periods of varying brightness, usually lasting from one to fifty days [Early 20C. < CEPHEUS + -ID.]

Cepheus /seéf yooss, seéfi əss/ *n* a constellation of the northern hemisphere. See illustration at **constellation**

ceraceous /si ráyshəss/ *adj* like wax in appearance or texture (*technical*) [Mid-18C. < Latin *cera* 'wax'.]

ceramal /sə ráym'l/ *n* INDUST = **cermet** [Mid-20C. Blend of CERAMIC + ALLOY.]

ceramic /sə rámmik/ *n* **1** a hard brittle heat-resistant material made by firing a mixture of clay and chemicals at high temperature **2** an object made from ceramic [Early 19C. < Greek *keramikos* 'of pottery' < *keramos* 'pottery'.] —**ceramic** *adj*

ceramic hob *n* a flat cooking surface of ceramic with heating elements underneath

ceramicist *n* = **ceramist**

ceramics /sə rámmiks/ *n* the art, technology, or process of making ceramic objects (+ *singular verb*)

ceramist /sérrəmist/, **ceramicist** /sə rámməsist/ *n* a maker of ceramic objects

Ceram Sea /sə rám-/ sea in the W Pacific Ocean, north of the Moluccas. Area: 51,800 sq. km/20,000 sq. mi.

cerastes /sə ráss teez/ (*plural* **-tes**) *n* a poisonous snake that has a projection like a horn above each eye. Native to: North Africa, SW Asia. Genus: *Cerastes*. ◊ **horned viper** [14C. < Greek *kerastēs* 'horned' < *keras* 'horn'.]

ceratin *n* = **keratin**

ceratopsian /sérrə tópsi ən/, **ceratopsid** /-sid/ *n* a four-footed plant-eating dinosaur of the Cretaceous period, with one or more horns projecting from the head and a bony frill extending from the skull over the neck. Suborder: Ceratopsia. [Early 20C. < modern Latin *Ceratopsia* < Greek *kerat-* 'horn'.] —**ceratopsian** *adj*

Cerberus /súrbərəss/ *n* in Greek mythology, the fierce dog that guards the entrance to Hades, usually represented as having three heads —**Cerberean** /súrbə reé ən, sə beéri ən/ *adj*

-cercal *suffix* having a particular kind of tail ○ *diphycercal* [< French *-cerque* < Greek *kerkos* 'tail']

cercaria /sur káiri ə/ (*plural* **-ae** /-ee/) *n* the tadpole-shaped larva of various parasitic worms (**flukes**) [Mid-19C. < modern Latin, < Greek *kerkos* 'tail'.] —**cercarial** *adj*

cercus /súrkəss/ (*plural* **-ci** /-see/) *n* either of two sensory appendages at the end of the abdomen of the female mosquito and other insects [Early 19C. Via modern Latin < Greek *kerkos* 'tail'.] —**cercal** *adj*

cere /seer/ *n* the thick skin at the base of the upper beak of some birds, e.g. parrots, that contains the bird's nostrils [15C. < Latin *cera* 'wax'.]

cereal /seéri əl/ *n* **1 CROP PLANT WITH EDIBLE GRAIN** a plant belonging to the grass family that is cultivated for its nutritious grains, e.g. oats, barley, rye, wheat, rice, and maize **2 GRAIN OF CEREAL PLANT** the grain produced by a cereal plant **3 BREAKFAST FOOD** food made from cereal grain and eaten especially at breakfast, usually with milk [Early 19C. Directly or via French *céréale* < Latin *cerealis* 'of grain cultivation', after CERES.]

SPELLCHECK Do not confuse ***cereal*** with ***serial***, which has a similar sound. Beware: your spellchecker will not catch this error.

cerebellum /sérrə bélləm/ (*plural* **-lums** or **-la** /-lə/) *n* the part of the brain located directly behind the front part (**cerebrum**), typically consisting of two hemispheres connected by a thin central region, and serving to control and coordinate muscular activity and maintain balance [Mid-16C. < Latin, 'small brain' < *cerebrum* 'brain'.] —**cerebellar** *adj*

cerebra *n* plural of **cerebrum**

cerebral /sérrəbrəl, sə reé-/ *adj* **1 RELATING TO THE FRONT OF BRAIN** relating to or located in the front part of the brain (**cerebrum**) **2 RELATING TO WHOLE BRAIN** relating to or involving the whole brain or any part of it **3 INTELLECTUAL** involving the psychological processes of thinking and reasoning rather than the emotions —**cerebrally** *adv*

cerebral cortex *n* the wrinkled outer layer of the front parts of the brain (**the cerebral hemispheres**). Its functions include the perception of sensations, learning, reasoning, and memory. Technical name **pallium** *n.* 4

cerebral dominance *n* the normal tendency for one of the two sides of the brain (**cerebral hemispheres**) to have stronger control over some functions of the mind and body

cerebral hemisphere *n* either of the two symmetrical halves of the front part of the brain (**cerebrum**)

cerebral palsy *n* a condition caused by brain damage around the time of birth and marked by lack of muscle control, especially in the limbs —**cerebral-palsied** *adj*

cerebral vascular accident *n* = **cerebrovascular accident**

cerebro- *prefix* brain, cerebrum ○ *cerebrovascular* [< CEREBRUM]

cerebroside /sérrəbrō sīd, sə reé-/ *n* a fatty chemical (**lipid**) found in the brain and the covering (**myelin sheath**) of some nerves [Late 19C. < CEREBRO- + -OSE.]

cerebrospinal /sérrəbrō spīn'l/ *adj* relating to or involving the brain and spinal cord

cerebrospinal fluid *n* the colourless fluid in and around the brain and spinal cord that absorbs shocks and maintains uniform pressure

cerebrospinal meningitis *n* inflammation of the membranes (**meninges**) surrounding the brain and spinal cord, causing high fever and sometimes unconsciousness

cerebrovascular /sérrəbrō váskyoolər/ *adj* relating to or involving the blood vessels that supply the brain

cerebrovascular accident *n* any physical event, e.g. cerebral haemorrhage, that may lead to a stroke (*technical*)

cerebrum /sə reébrəm, sérrə-/ (*plural* **-brums** or **-bra** /-brə/) *n* the front part of the brain, divided into two symmetrical halves (**cerebral hemispheres**). In humans, it is where activities including reasoning, learning, sensory perception, and emotional responses take place. [Early 17C. < Latin, 'brain'.]

cerecloth /seér kloth/ *n* fabric coated with melted wax to make it waterproof [Mid-16C. Alteration of *cered cloth* 'waxed cloth', < past participle of *cere* 'to wax' < Latin *cerare* < *cera* 'wax'.]

Ceredigion /kérrə díggi on/ county and local council in Wales. Population: 70,200 (1995).

cerement /seérmənt, sérrə-/ *n* TEXTILES = **cerecloth** ■ **cerements** *npl* burial clothes [Early 17C. < *cere* (see CERECLOTH).]

ceremonial /sérrə móni əl/ *adj* **1 RELATING TO FORMAL OCCASIONS** used on a formal occasion or at a ceremony **2 INVOLVING CEREMONY** involving or done as part of a ceremony ○ *the ceremonial presentation of the awards* **3 NOMINAL** without real power or authority ○ *a largely ceremonial role* ■ *n* **1 FORMAL ETIQUETTE** the correct way to behave on formal occasions **2 RITUAL** a ceremony or set of ceremonies for an occasion **3 ORDER OF SERVICE** the set order of rites or ceremonies in a Christian church, or a book containing this —**ceremonialism** *n* —**ceremonialist** *n* —**ceremonially** *adv*

USAGE ceremonial or **ceremonious**? ***Ceremonial*** is the more neutral word, describing things that involve ceremony or are a part of it, e.g. *ceremonial occasions*. It is not now used of people. ***Ceremonious*** is used of people or their behaviour: a *ceremonious person*, or a person with a *ceremonious manner*, is somebody who likes and adheres to formalities, perhaps even excessively. Avoid using ***ceremonious*** where ***ceremonial*** is appropriate.

ceremonious /sérrə móni əss/ *adj* **1** excessively polite or formal, being careful to observe formalities and behave correctly ○ *He replied with ceremonious dignity.* **2** involving ceremony or consisting of ceremony ○ *ceremonious gestures* —**ceremoniously** *adv* —**ceremoniousness** *n*

USAGE See ***ceremonial***.

ceremony /sérrəməni/ (*plural* **-nies**) *n* **1 RITUAL FOR FORMAL OCCASION** a formal event to celebrate or solemnize something such as a wedding, an official opening, or an anniversary **2 FORMAL ETIQUETTE** the forms of behaviour that are expected or observed on a formal occasion **3 SOCIAL GESTURE** a polite social gesture or ritual performed for the sake of convention [14C. < Latin *caerimonia*.] ◇ **stand on ceremony** to behave in a formal manner or insist on formality

Cerenkov effect /chə réngkof-/, **Cherenkov effect** *n* the emission of light by a charged particle as it passes through a transparent medium at a speed greater than that of light in the same medium [Mid-20C. After Pavel A. *Cherenkov* (1904–90), Soviet physicist.]

Cerenkov radiation, Cherenkov radiation *n* light emitted by a charged particle as it passes through a transparent medium at a speed greater than that of light in the same medium [Mid-20C. See CERENKOV EFFECT.]

Ceres /seér eez/ *n* **1** the Roman goddess of agriculture. Greek equivalent **Demeter** **2** the largest asteroid and the first to be discovered, in 1801, orbiting between Mars and Jupiter [< Latin]

cereus /seéri əss/ *n* **1** a cactus with spiny ribbed stems, especially a Brazilian species that can reach a height of 13 m/40 ft. Genus: *Cereus.* **2** any cactus related to the true cereus, e.g. the night-blooming cereus [Late 17C. < modern Latin, < Latin, 'candle' < *cera* 'wax'.]

ceria /seéri ə/ *n* CHEM = **ceric oxide** [< modern Latin, plural of *cerium* (see CERIUM)]

ceric /seérik/ *adj* relating to or containing cerium with a valency of 4 [Mid-19C. < CERIUM.]

ceric oxide *n* CeO_2 a white crystalline powder. Use: manufacture of ceramics, polishing glass.

cerise /sə reéz, -reéss/ *n* a deep vivid pinkish-red colour [Mid-19C. < French, 'cherry' < Greek *kerasos* 'cherry tree'.] —**cerise** *adj*

cerium /seéri əm/ *n* (*symbol* **Ce**) a grey malleable metallic element, the most abundant of the rare-earth group. Source: bastnaesite, monazite. Use: metallurgy, glass-making, ceramics, cigarette-lighter flints. [Early 19C. < modern Latin, < CERES; because the asteroid was discovered just before this element.]

cermet /súr met, -mit/ *n* a durable substance able to withstand high temperatures. Source: bonding ceramic particles with metal. [Mid-20C. Blend of CERAMIC + METAL.]

CERN /surn/ *n* an EU organization that carries out research into high-energy particle physics, now called the European Laboratory for Particle Physics. Full form **Conseil Européen pour la Recherche Nucléaire**

cero /seérō, sírrō/ (*plural* **-ro** *or* **-ros**) *n* a large edible ocean fish that has silvery sides and large spiny fins. Native to: warm W Atlantic waters. *Scomberomorus regalis*. [Late 19C. Alteration of Spanish *sierra* 'saw' < Latin *serra*.]

cerotic acid /si róttik-/ *n* $CH_3(CH_2)_{24}COOH$ a white fatty acid. Source: natural waxes such as beeswax and carnauba wax. [Mid-19C. < Latin *cerotum* 'wax salve' < Greek *kērōton* 'waxed'.]

cerous /seérəss/ *adj* relating to or containing cerium with a valency of 3 [Mid-19C. < CERIUM.]

cert /surt/ *n* (*informal*) **1** somebody who is certain to do something **2** a foregone conclusion or certain outcome [Late 19C. Shortening of CERTAIN or CERTAINTY.]

⚡**CERT** /surt/ *abbr* computer emergency response team (*in e-mails*)

cert. *abbr* **1** certificate **2** certification **3** certified

certain /súrt'n/ *adj* **1 WITHOUT DOUBT** having no doubts about something ○ *I'm certain he's the man I saw.* **2 KNOWN OR SET** definitely known, fixed, or settled **3 INEVITABLE** guaranteed to happen or to do something ○ *They're certain to lose.* **4 RELIABLE** able to be relied on **5 NOT DEFINED** undeniable but difficult to define, quantify, or express ○ *a certain hesitation in his manner* **6 NOT NAMED** able to be identified but not named ○ *A certain selfish person has used up all the milk.* **7 UNKNOWN OR UNFAMILIAR** used to indicate that only the name of the person, thing, or place mentioned is known ○ *A certain Mr Esposito was involved.* ■ *pron* **SOME** of an imprecise but limited number (*formal*) [13C. < assumed Vulgar Latin *certanus* < Latin *certus* 'determined', past participle of *cernere* 'decide'.] ◇ **certain of** some but not all of (*formal*) ◇ **for certain** without any doubt ◇ **make certain 1** to check that something has been done or is the case **2** to take action to achieve something

certainly /súrt'nli/ *adv* **1 DEFINITELY** without any doubt or qualification on the part of the speaker ○ *It's certainly a big problem.* **2 USED TO CONCEDE POINT** used to concede a point that has been made ○ *That's certainly an area we could improve upon.* **3 YES** used to indicate unreserved assent ◇ **certainly not** used to indicate emphatic denial or refusal

certainty /súrt'nti/ (*plural* **-ties**) *n* **1 CONVICTION** complete confidence in the truth of something or an expected outcome **2 SOMETHING INEVITABLE** a conclusion or outcome that is beyond doubt **3 SOMEBODY OR SOMETHING CERTAIN OF SUCCESS** something that is certain to happen, or somebody assured of a result ◇ **for a certainty** without any doubt

certifiable /súrti fī əb'l/ *adj* **1 DESERVING A CERTIFICATE** authentic or good enough to be given a certificate **2 THAT MUST BE CERTIFIED** requiring to be reported to the appropriate authority (*informal*) ○ *a certifiable disease* **3 REQUIRING PSYCHIATRIC TREATMENT** legally or medically declared to be affected by a psychiatric disorder (*dated*) —**certifiably** *adv*

⚡**certificate** *n* /sər tíffikət/ **1 DOCUMENT PROVIDING OFFICIAL EVIDENCE** an official document that gives proof and details of something, e.g. personal status, educational achievements, ownership, or authenticity **2 DOCUMENT SHOWING CONFORMITY TO STANDARD** an official document awarded to somebody who or something that has passed a test or examination or conforms to a required standard **3 DOCUMENT SHOWING QUALIFICATION** an official document awarded to somebody who has completed a course of study or training **4 DOCUMENT GIVING STATE OF HEALTH** an official document giving details of somebody's state of health **5 ELECTRONIC IDENTIFICATION** an electronic document verifying somebody's relationship, identity, and responsibilities in financial transactions (*in e-commerce*) ■ *vt* /sər tíffi kayt/ (**-cates, -cating, -cated**) **1 GIVE CERTIFICATE TO** to award a certificate to somebody or something **2 AUTHORIZE OR PROVE SOMETHING WITH CERTIFICATE** to authorize or provide evidence of something with a certificate [15C. < medieval Latin *certificatum* < past participle of late Latin *certificare* (see CERTIFY).] —**certification** /súrtifi káysh'n, sər tíffi-/ *n* —**certificatory** /sər tíffikətəri, súrtifi káytəri/ *adj*

⚡**certificate database** *n* in e-commerce, a database storing all certificates issued and used by a certificate authority

certificate of origin *n* an official document stating what country a consignment of goods has come from

Certificate of Secondary Education *n* full form of **CSE**

⚡**certificate walker** *n* a computer software program that reads digital certificates and displays their contents (*in e-commerce*)

certified accountant /súrti fīd ə kówntənt/ *n* an accountant who is a member of the Chartered Association of Certified Accountants and can therefore audit companies' accounts. ◊ **chartered accountant, certified public accountant**

certified cheque *n* a cheque that the issuing bank guarantees to honour because sufficient funds are present to cover the check

certified mail *n US* = **recorded delivery**

certified public accountant *n* a public accountant who has met the requirements of a particular US state and is therefore allowed to practise there

certify /súrti fī/ (**-fies, -fying, -fied**) *v* **1** *vti* **CONFIRM TRUTH OR ACCURACY OF** to state or confirm that something is true or correct **2** *vt* **PROVE QUALITY OF** to declare that somebody or something has passed a test or achieved a certain standard **3** *vt* **ISSUE WITH A CERTIFICATE** to award a certificate to somebody or something **4** *vt* **DECLARE SOMEBODY TO HAVE PSYCHIATRIC DISORDER** to declare somebody officially or legally to have a psychiatric disorder and require confinement in a mental health facility (*dated*) **5** *vt US* **GUARANTEE PAYMENT OF CHEQUE** to indicate on a cheque that there are sufficient funds to guarantee payment [14C. Via French *certifier* < late Latin *certificare* 'make certain' < Latin *certus* (see CERTAIN).] —**certifier** *n*

~~certin~~ incorrect spelling of **certain**

certiorari /súrti ə ráirī, -raári/ *n* a writ issued by a higher court to obtain records on a case from a lower court so that the case can be reviewed. ◊ **mandamus, prohibition** *n.* 3 [15C. < late Latin, 'be informed', passive of Latin *certiorare* 'inform' < *certus* 'sure'; because the word occurs in the writ.]

certitude /súrti tyood/ *n* **1 FEELING OF CERTAINTY** the feeling of conviction about something, especially an opinion or religious faith **2 DEFINITE TRUTH** the definite truth of something **3 SOMETHING THAT IS CERTAIN** something that is certain to happen or about which somebody can feel sure [15C. < late Latin *certitudo* < Latin *certus* (see CERTAIN).]

cerulean /sə roóli ən/ *adj* of a deep blue colour (*literary*) [Mid-17C. < Latin *caeruleus* < *caelum* 'sky'.] —**cerulean** *n*

ceruloplasmin /sə roólō plazmin/, **caeruloplasmin** *n* a copper-transporting protein present in the blood [Mid-20C. < modern Latin *cerulo-* (< Latin *caeruleus*; see CERULEAN) + PLASMA.]

cerumen /sə roómən/ *n* the waxy secretion of glands lining the canal of the external ear (*technical*) [Late 17C. < modern Latin, < Latin *cera* 'wax'.] —**ceruminous** *adj*

ceruse /sə roóss/ *n* **1** a cosmetic used in the past that contained white lead **2** white lead used as a pigment and formerly in cosmetics [14C. Via French < Latin *cerussa*.]

cerussite /seérə sīt/, **cerusite** *n* a lead carbonate mineral forming crystals or aggregates of various colours. Use: source of lead. [Mid-19C. < Latin *cerussa* 'ceruse'.]

Cervantes /sur vánt eez/, **Miguel de** (1547–1616) Spanish novelist and dramatist

cervelat /súrvəlaa, -lat/ *n* a German cured sausage made from pork and beef, usually smoked, with a mild flavour and a fine texture [Early 17C. Via French < Italian *cervellata* < *cervello* 'brain' < Latin *cerebellum* (see CEREBELLUM); because it was made from brains.]

cervical /sər vík'l, súrvik'l/ *adj* relating to or belonging to the neck or any part of the body that resembles a neck, e.g. the cervix of the womb [Mid-19C. < French, < Latin *cervic-* 'neck'.]

cervical cap *n* a small, dome-shaped rubber or plastic contraceptive device for women, placed inside the vagina and fitted tightly over the entrance to the cervix

cervical smear *n* a sample of tissue taken from the cervix of the womb for analysis, to enable early identification of cellular abnormalities that could lead to cervical cancer. US term **Pap smear**

cervices plural of **cervix**

cervicitis /súrvi sítiss/ *n* inflammation of the cervix of the womb [Late 19C. < Latin *cervic-* 'neck'.]

cervid /súrvid/ *n* any ruminant mammal, e.g. a deer, elk, or reindeer, characterized by the presence of antlers in the male or sometimes in both sexes. Family: Cervidae. [Late 19C. < modern Latin *Cervidae* (plural) < Latin *cervus* 'deer'.] —**cervid** *adj*

cervine /súr vīn/ *adj* relating to, resembling, or typical of a deer [Mid-19C. < Latin *cervinus* < *cervus* 'deer'.]

cervix /súrviks/ (*plural* **-vixes** *or* **-vices** /súrvi seez/) *n* **1 NECK OF WOMB** the neck of the womb, consisting of a narrow passage leading to the vagina **2 NECK** the neck (*technical*) **3 PART RESEMBLING NECK** any part of the body that resembles a neck in shape or function [15C. < Latin, 'neck'.]

cesarean /si záiri ən/ *n US* = **Caesarean** *n.*

cesium *n* US = **caesium**

České Budějovice /chésk ay boódə yawvit say/ city in the S Czech Republic. Population: 99,548 (1998 estimate).

cess[1] /sess/ *n* a local tax or levy (*archaic*) [Mid-16C. Variant of *sess* < *assess* 'assessment' < ASSESS.]

cess[2] /sess/ *n Ireland* luck (*informal*) [Mid-19C. Either a shortening of SUCCESS, or < CESS1.]

cessation /se sáysh'n/ *n* a stop, pause, or interruption, especially a permanent discontinuation [15C. < Latin *cessation-* < *cessat-*, past participle of *cessare* 'stop'.]

cession /sésh'n/ *n* the ceding or giving up of something, or something ceded in this way, especially land, property, or a right (*formal*) [14C. Directly or via French < Latin *cession-* < *cess-*, past participle of *cedere* 'yield'.]

Cessnock /séss nok/ town in E New South Wales, Australia. Population: 17,540 (1996).

cesspit /sésspit/ *n* **1** a pit for the collection of waste matter and water, especially sewage **2** a foul and putrid place or situation, especially one linked with moral depravity. US term **cesspool** [Mid-19C. *Cess* < CESSPOOL.]

cesspool /séss pool/ *n* **1** a covered underground tank or well for the collection of waste matter and water, especially sewage **2** = **cesspit** *n.* **2** [Late 17C. Probably alteration of *cesperalle*, variant of *suspiral* 'drainpipe' < Old French *suspirail* 'breathing hole' < *souspirer* 'breathe'.]

cesta /séstə/ *n* a curved wicker basket for catching and throwing the ball in the Basque ball sport jai alai [Early 20C. Via Spanish, 'basket' < Latin *cista* (see CHEST).]

c'est la vie /se laa veé/ *interj* used to express philosophical acceptance of the way things are [Mid-20C. < French, 'that's life'.]

cestode /séss tōd/ *n* a tapeworm (*technical*) [Mid-19C. < modern Latin *Cestoda* (plural) < Latin *cestus* (see CESTUS).]

cestus /séstass/ (*plural* **-ti**), **cestos** (*plural* **-ti** /-tī/) *n* a girdle or belt, especially one worn by women in ancient Greece [Mid-16C. Via Latin < Greek *kestos* 'belt', originally 'stitched'.]

cesura *n* = caesura

CET *abbr* **1** Central European Time **2** Common External Tariff

cetacean /si táysh'n/ *n* a large aquatic mammal, e.g. a whale or a dolphin, that has a streamlined body with forelimbs modified as flippers, no hind limbs, and a blowhole on the back. Order: Cetacea. [Mid-19C. < modern Latin *Cetacea* (plural) < Latin *cetus* 'whale' < Greek *kētos*.] —**cetaceous** /si táyshass/ *adj*

cetane /seé tayn/ *n* $C_{16}H_{34}$ a colourless oily hydrocarbon. Source: petroleum. Use: measuring the ignition quality of diesel fuels, as a solvent. [Late 19C. < *cetyl* (see CETYL ALCOHOL).]

cetane number, cetane rating *n* the performance rating of a diesel fuel, expressed as the percentage of cetane in a mixture with 1-methylnaphthalene that shows the same ignition properties

ceteris paribus /káytariss paáribass, séttariss párrabass/ *adv* used to indicate that something would be the case if everything else under consideration remains the same [Early 17C. < modern Latin, 'other things being equal'.]

cetology /si tólləji/ *n* the branch of zoology concerned with the study of whales, dolphins, and related mammals [Mid-19C. < Latin *cetus* 'whale'.] —**cetological** /seéta lójjik'l/ *adj* —**cetologist** *n*

Cetus /seétass/ *n* a constellation of the celestial equator containing the bright star Mira. See illustration at **constellation**

cetyl alcohol /seétīl-, seét'l-/ *n* a white waxy solid. Use: manufacture of cosmetics, pharmaceuticals, detergents. [< Latin *cetus* 'whale'; because originally isolated from spermaceti]

Cévennes /say vén/ mountain range in S France. Highest peak: Mont Mézenc 1,754 m /5,755 ft.

ceviche /se veéchay/, **seviche** *n* a Latin American dish of raw fish marinated in lemon or lime juice [Mid-20C. < American Spanish *seviche*, probably < Spanish *cebo* 'fish pieces used for bait' < Latin *cibus* 'food'.]

Ceylon /si lón/ former name for **Sri Lanka** (until 1972) — **Ceylonese** *adj, n*

Ceylon moss *n* a red seaweed that is a source of the gelatinous material agar. Native to: East Indian Ocean. *Gracilaria lichenoides*. [Because it grows in CEYLON]

Ceyx /seé iks/ *n* in Greek mythology, a king of Trachis in Thessaly who died in a shipwreck and whose wife, Alcyone, drowned herself in grief

Cézanne /si zán, say-/, **Paul** (1839–1906) French painter

↯ **cf** *abbr* Central African Republic (*in Internet addresses*)

Cf *symbol* californium

CF *abbr* **1** Chaplain to the Forces **2** **CF, cf** cost and freight **3** cystic fibrosis

cf. *abbr* compare

> **USAGE cf. or ff.?** The abbreviation **cf.** means 'compare', as in *Dumas Malone discusses aspects of Jefferson's private life* in Jefferson the Virginian (*cf. Fawn Brodie's* Thomas Jefferson: An Intimate History, *for early reporting on the Sally Hemings matter*). **cf.**, which comes from the Latin imperative verb form *confer*, 'compare', should not be confused with **ff.**, an abbreviation that means 'folios following' and refers to following pages or lines that you are citing or specifying: *See Chapter 21, 'Triangles at Monticello', p. 376 ff. for material on the Hemings family.* Both these abbreviations end with full stops.

C/f *abbr* carried forward

CFA franc *n* a unit of currency used in several francophone African countries [Abbreviation of French *Communauté financière africaine* 'African financial community']

CFC *n* a gas containing carbon, chlorine, fluorine, and fluorine, some forms of which damage the ozone layer in the Earth's atmosphere. Use: refrigerant, aerosol propellant. Full form **chlorofluorocarbon**

CFE *abbr* **1** College of Further Education **2** Conventional Forces in Europe

CFI, cfi *abbr* cost, freight, and insurance. ◊ **c.i.f.**

cg[1] *abbr* US centre of gravity

↯ **cg**[2] *abbr* Congo (*in Internet addresses*)

CG *abbr* **1** captain general **2** coastguard **3** Coldstream Guards **4** Consul General

CGBR *abbr* Central Government Borrowing Requirement

cge *abbr* **1** carriage **2** charge

↯ **CGI** *abbr* common gateway interface

cgm *abbr* centigram

cgs, *abbr* centimetre-gram-second

CGS *abbr* **1** centimetre-gram-second system **2** Chief of General Staff

CGT *abbr* capital gains tax

↯ **ch** *abbr* Switzerland (*in Internet addresses*)

CH *abbr* **1** **CH, c.h.** clearing house **2** Companion of Honour **3** custom house

ch. *abbr* **1** chain **2** chapter **3** check **4** church **5** charge

Ch. *abbr* **1** China **2** channel

C/H *abbr* central heating

chabazite /kábbə zīt/ *n* a pink, yellow, white, or colourless calcium aluminosilicate mineral of the zeolite group. Source: cavities in igneous rocks, hot spring deposits. [Early 19C. < *chabazie* < Greek *khabazie*, misspelling of *khalazie* < *khalaza* 'hail'; from its form and colour.]

Chablis /sháblii/, **chablis** *n* a very dry white Burgundy wine made in the region around Chablis in central France

Chabrier /shábbri ay/, **Alexis Emmanuel** (1841–94) French composer

Chabrol /sha bról/, **Claude** (*b.* 1930) French film director

cha-cha /chaá chaa/, **cha-cha-cha** /chaá chaa chaá/ *n* **1** a fast ballroom dance of Latin American origin consisting of three steps and a hip-swaying shuffle **2** the music for a cha-cha [< American Spanish (Cuban) *cha-cha-cha*, probably an imitation of the musical accompaniment]

chacma /chákmə/ (*plural* **-mas**) *n* a ground-dwelling baboon with a dark-grey coat and naked face with a long muzzle. Native to: Southern Africa. *Papio ursinus*. [Mid-19C. < Khoikhoi.]

chaconia /chə kóni ə/ (*plural* **-as** *or* **-a**) *n* a red flower with large, conspicuous sepals that is the national flower of Trinidad and Tobago. *Warszewiczia coccinea*.

chaconne /shə kón/ *n* **1** an ancient, moderately slow dance, probably of Spanish origin **2** a musical composition consisting of variations on a fixed bass line continually repeated (**ground bass**) [Late 17C. Via French < Spanish *chacona*, probably < Basque *chucun* 'pretty'.]

chacun à son gout /shákuN aa soN goó/ used to express the individuality or peculiarity of somebody's taste or choice [< French, 'each to his or her own taste']

chad /chad/ *n* **1** a small piece of waste paper, card, or tape removed from a sheet by a hole-punching machine or tool **2** *US* a piece removed from a ballot paper by a voter or voting machine in order to register a vote against the name of a candidate [Mid-20C. < ?]

Chad

Chad /chad/ landlocked republic in north-central Africa. Capital: Ndjamena. Population: 7,166,023 (1997). Area: 1,284,000 sq. km/495,755 sq. mi. —**Chadian** *adj, n*

Chad, Lake lake in central Africa, at the junction of Nigeria, Niger, and Chad. Area: 10,000 to 25,900 sq. km/4,000 to 10,000 sq. mi., changing seasonally.

chadar *n* = chador

Chadic /cháddik/ *n* a large group of languages spoken in west-central Africa, that is a branch of the Afro-Asiatic family of languages. Native speakers: 25 million. — **Chadic** *adj*

chador /chúddər/, **chadar, chuddar** *n* **1** a dark traditional garment worn by Muslim and sometimes by Hindu women that covers almost all of the head and body **2** a cloth that is used to cover a Muslim tomb [Early 17C. Directly or via Urdu < Persian *čādar* 'sheet, veil'.]

chaeta /keétə/ (*plural* **-tae** /-teé/) *n* a bristle that occurs singly or in clusters in certain worms, e.g. earthworms and ragworms, and helps them to move [Mid-19C. Via modern Latin < Greek *khaitē* 'long hair'.]

chaetognath /keétəg nath, keétə nath/ *n* a torpedo-shaped marine invertebrate with an almost transparent body and fins running horizontally down both sides of the trunk and tail. Phylum: Chaetognatha. [Late 19C. < modern Latin *Chaetognatha* < Greek *khaitē* 'long hair' + *gnathos* 'jaw'; from the spines on its head.] —**chaetognathous** /kee tógnathass/ *adj*

chafe /chayf/ *v* (**chafes, chafing, chafed**) **1** *vti* BECOME OR MAKE WORN to become sore or worn by rubbing, or make something sore or worn in this way **2** *vt* CAUSE FRICTION to rub something, causing friction **3** *vt* RUB SOMETHING TO WARM IT to warm something, especially the hands or other parts of the body, by rubbing **4** *vti* BECOME ANNOYED OR ANNOY to be or make somebody irritated, annoyed, or impatient ■ *n* **1** SORENESS OR WEAR soreness or wear caused by rubbing **2** FEELING OF IRRITATION a feeling of irritation, annoyance, or impatience [13C. Via Old French *chaufer* < Latin *calefacere* 'make warm' < *calere* 'be warm'.]

chafer[1] /cháyfər/ *n* a large slow-moving scarab beetle, e.g. the cockchafer [Old English *ceafor*, probably < Indo-European, 'jaw, mouth']

chafer[2] /cháyfər/ *n* = chafing dish [15C. Via French *chauffoir* < Latin *calefactorium* < *calefact-*, past participle of *calefacere* (see CHAFE).]

chaff[1] /chaaf, chaf/ *n* **1** SEED COVERINGS REMOVED BY THRESHING the dry coverings (**bracts**) of grains and other grass seeds, that are separated by the process of threshing **2** WORTHLESS THING something that is worthless or irrelevant **3** STRIPS OF METAL TO OBSTRUCT RADAR glass fibres or silvered nylon filaments dispersed into the air as an antiradar measure [Old English *ceaf* < Germanic] —**chaffy** *adj*

chaff[2] /chaaf, chaf/ *v* **1** *vt* TEASE SOMEBODY LIGHT-HEARTEDLY to tease somebody in fun **2** *vi* BANTER to exchange light-hearted teasing or joking remarks ■ *n* JOKING light-hearted joking or teasing [Early 19C. < ?] —**chaffer** *n*

chaffer /cháffər/ *vi* **1** HAGGLE to haggle or bargain about something **2** BANDY WORDS to chatter idly ■ *n* BARGAINING OR HAGGLING bargaining or haggling about something [12C. < Old English *ceap* 'bargain' + *faru* 'faring'.] —**chafferer** *n*

chaffinch /cháffinch/ *n* a finch with white wing bars and a bluish hood. Native to: gardens and farmland of Europe and W Asia. *Fringilla coelebs*. [Old English *ceaffinc* < *ceaf* 'chaff'; because it pecks among farmyard chaff]

chafing dish /cháyfing dish/ *n* a shallow pan with a source of heat beneath it, used for cooking food or keeping food warm at the table

Chagall /sha gál/, **Marc** (1887–1985) Russian-born French painter and designer

Chagas' disease /shaágass-/, **Chagas's disease** /-ssiz-/ *n* an often fatal disease, occurring in South and Central America, that affects the heart and nervous system and is caused by a protozoan parasite transmitted by blood-sucking insects [Early 20C. After Carlos *Chagas* (1879–1934), Brazilian physician.]

chagrin /shággrin, shə grín/ *n* a feeling of vexation or humiliation due to disappointment about something [Early 18C. < French, 'sad, vexed'.] —**chagrin** *vt* —**chagrined** *adj*

chain /chayn/ *n* **1** SERIES OF JOINED METAL RINGS a flexible interlinked series of usually metal links that may be used to support or restrain something, used as an ornament or decoration, or to drive or move something **2** SERIES OF LINKS USED AS ACCESSORY a series of rings, links, or discs used as a necklace, bracelet, or other piece of jewellery **3** BADGE OF OFFICE a chain worn round the neck as a badge of office **4 SOMETHING RESEMBLING CHAIN** a series of things or people linked or joined together for some purpose ○ *They stood hand in hand to form a human chain round the perimeter.* **5 BUSINESSES UNDER ONE OWNERSHIP** a number of shops, hotels, restaurants, or other businesses that are owned by the same company and offer similar goods or services but are found in different locations **6 SEQUENCE OF RELATED EVENTS OR FACTS** a sequence of facts or events that happen one after the other and are connected in some way **7 UNIT OF LENGTH** a unit of length that is now rarely used, equal to 20 m/66 ft **8 SERIES OF ATOMS** a series of atoms, usually of a single element such as carbon, that are joined in a line or ring within a molecule **9 SERIES OF GEOGRAPHIC FORMATIONS** a series of associated geographic features or formations, e.g. mountains, lakes, or islands ■ **chains** *npl* **RESTRAINING CIRCUMSTANCES** feelings or circumstances that restrain or confine somebody (*literary*) ■ *vt* **1 FASTEN WITH A CHAIN** to fasten, tie, or restrain something or somebody with a chain or chains **2 MEASURE WITH A CHAIN** to use a chain or tape to measure something **3 RESTRICT SOMEBODY'S MOBILITY** to restrict or confine somebody's freedom of movement or action ○ *She was chained to the computer all day.* [13C. Via Old French *chaeine* < Latin *catena*.] —**chained** *adj* —**chainless** *adj*

Chain /chayn/, **Sir Ernst Boris** (1906–79) German-born British biochemist

chain drive *n* an endless linked chain that meshes with the teeth of two sprocket wheels to transfer energy and motion from one to the other —**chain-driven** *adj*

chaîné /shə náy/ (*plural* **-nés** /shə náy/) *n* a series of short, usually fast turns made by a ballet dancer moving in a straight line across a floor or stage [Mid-20C. < French, past participle of *chaîner* 'to chain' < Old French *chaeine* (see CHAIN).]

chain ferry (*plural* **chain ferries**) *n* a river ferry that pulls itself along on one or more fixed chains, attached to each bank of the river

chain gang *n* a group of prisoners who work away from prison and are shackled together, usually with leg irons and a series of chains

chain harrow *n* a farm implement, consisting of a horizontal towing bar attached to heavy chains, that is trailed across soil or pasture to break up clods or disperse manure

chain letter *n* a letter sent to a number of people, each of whom is asked to send copies to the same number of new people, sometimes requesting and promising money to recipients

chain lightning *n* METEOROL = **forked lightning**

chainlink fence /cháynlingk fénss/ *n* a fence formed from lengths of strong wire that are interwoven in a diamond pattern —**chainlink fencing** *n*

chain mail *n* interlinked rings of metal forming a flexible piece of armour, worn by knights in medieval times

chain of command *n* a hierarchy of officials in the armed forces or in business, each reporting to and taking orders from the next most senior person

chainplate /cháyn playt/ *n* a metal plate on the hull of a sailing vessel to which the ropes or cables supporting the mast are attached

chain reaction *n* **1 CONNECTED SEQUENCE OF EVENTS** a series of events following on quickly from each other, each of which causes the next one **2 SELF-SUSTAINING NUCLEAR FISSION** a self-sustaining nuclear reaction in which each fission of an atomic nucleus causes neutrons and energy to be emitted, each collision of neutrons with other nuclei causing a further fission **3 SERIES OF CHEMICAL REACTIONS** a series of chemical reactions in which the product from one reaction helps to create the next one —**chain-react** *vi*

chain saw *n* a portable motor-driven saw with cutting teeth made of links that form a continuous chain, used for cutting wood

chain shot *n* two cannonballs or half-balls connected by a chain, formerly used to destroy a ship's rigging

chain-smoke (**chain-smokes, chain-smoking, chain-smoked**) *vti* to smoke cigarettes continuously, often lighting the next from the previous one as it is finished —**chain-smoker** *n*

chain stitch *n* a hand, machine, or crochet stitch in which each stitch forms a loop through the forward end of the previous one to resemble the links of a chain —**chain-stitch** *vti*

chain store *n* one of a series of retail shops, especially department stores or supermarkets, owned by the same company

chair /chair/ *n* **1 SEAT WITH BACK AND SOMETIMES ARMRESTS** a seat with a back support, usually for one person **2 CHAIRPERSON** somebody presiding over something such as a committee, board, or meeting, or the position of such a person **3 PROFESSORSHIP OR PROFESSOR** a university professorship, or the person holding such a position **4 RANKED POSITION OF ORCHESTRAL MUSICIAN** the ranked position of a musician in an orchestra **5 ELECTRIC CHAIR** the electric chair (*informal*) **6** *US* **SUPPORTING DEVICE DURING POURING OF CONCRETE** a device to keep reinforcing rods in place during the pouring of concrete **7 METAL SOCKET ATTACHED TO SLEEPER CAR** a metal socket attached to a railway sleeper car in which a rail is locked into position ■ *vt* **1 PRESIDE OVER** to preside over something such as a committee, board, or meeting **2 CARRY WINNER ON SHOULDERS** to carry a victor or champion on the shoulders in triumph [13C. Via Old French *chaiere* < Latin *cathedra* 'seat'.]

USAGE ***Chair*** has long been used to mean 'the authority or position of chairman', and has been extended to mean 'somebody presiding over a committee or meeting', in order to avoid having to use the gender-specific terms *chairman* or *chairwoman*. An alternative is *chairperson*, though it is disliked by some people.

chairborne /cháir bawrn/ *adj* (*informal*) **1** working at a desk in an office job rather than being more actively engaged **2** *US* working at a desk in an office job in the armed forces, especially the air force, rather than having combat or field duties

chair class *n S Asia* a class of travel on Indian railway trains in which passengers are provided with reclinable seats similar to those in aircraft

chair lift *n* a series of seats suspended from a moving cable, used to carry passengers up or down a mountain or other slope

chairman /cháirmən/ (*plural* **-men** /-mən/) *n* **1** the presiding officer of something such as a committee or meeting **2** the chief presiding officer of a business corporation, elected by its board of directors and responsible for corporate policy and supervision of upper management —**chairmanship** *n*

USAGE See ***chair***.

chairperson /cháir purs'n/ (*plural* **-sons**) *n* the presiding officer of something such as a committee, board, or meeting

USAGE See ***chair***.

chairwoman /cháir wŏŏmən/ (*plural* **-en** /-wimmin/) *n* a woman who is the presiding officer of something such as a committee, board, or meeting

USAGE See ***chair***.

chaise /shayz/ (*plural* **chaises** /shayz/) *n* **1** a light open two-wheeled carriage for one or more people, usually hooded and drawn by one horse **2** TRANSP = **post chaise** [Mid-17C. < French.]

chaise longue /shayz lóng/ (*plural* **chaise longues** /shayz lóng/ *or* **chaises longues**) *n* **1** a chair with an elongated seat, one armrest, and sometimes an adjustable back, designed for lying on **2** *US* a long low foldable chair with an adjustable back, used on a patio or beach [< French, 'long chair']

chakra /chúkrə, chaákrə/ (*plural* **-ras**) *n* in yoga, any of the centres of spiritual power in the body [Late 18C. < Sanskrit *cakra* 'wheel'.]

chalaza /kə láyzə, kə lázzə/ (*plural* **-zas** *or* **-zae** /-zee/) *n* **1** a spiral chord of albumen that is attached at each end of the yolk to the lining membrane inside a bird's egg, holding it in position **2** the base of the immature seed of a plant [Early 18C. Via modern Latin, < Greek *khalaza* 'hail'.] —**chalazal** *adj*

chalazion /kə láyzi ən/ *n* MED = **meibomian cyst** [Early 18C. < Greek *khalazion* 'small lump' < *khalaza* 'hail'.]

Chalcedon /kálssidən/ ancient Greek city on the Bosporus near modern-day Istanbul —**Chalcedonian** /kálssi dṓni ən/ *adj, n*

chalcedony /kal sédd'ni/ *n* a semiprecious stone that is a translucent or greyish form of banded quartz. Use: gems, ornaments. [13C. < Latin *c(h)alcedonius* < Greek *khalkēdōn*, mystical stone.] —**chalcedonic** /kálssi dónnik/ *adj*

chalcid /kálssid/ *n* a small wasp with bright metallic coloration whose larvae are often parasites of other insects. Superfamily: Chalcidoidea. [Late 19C. < modern Latin *Chalcid-* < Greek *khalkos* 'copper'; from its metallic colour.]

chalco- *prefix* copper ○ *chalcopyrite* [< Greek *khalkos*]

chalcocite /kálkə sīt/ *n* a grey to black brittle copper sulphide mineral. Use: source of copper.

chalcography /kal kóggrəfi/ *n* engraving on copper or brass —**chalcographer** *n* —**chalcographic** /kálkə gráffik/ *adj* —**chalcographical** /-gráffik'l/ *adj* —**chalcographist** *n*

chalcolithic /kálkə líthik/ *adj* belonging or relating to the transitional period between the Neolithic and Bronze ages, beginning around 400 BC, when the use of copper became more prevalent

chalcopyrite /kálkə pī́ rīt/ *n* a brassy sulphide mineral containing copper and iron. Use: source of copper.

Chaldea /kal dée ə/ ancient region of Mesopotamia, between the Euphrates and the Persian Gulf, in modern-day S Iraq

Chaldean /kal dée ən/, **Chaldaean** *n* **1** a member of an ancient Semitic people who lived in Chaldea **2** a dialect of the modern Aramaic language, spoken in Iraq and in the United States [Late 16C. < Latin *Chaldaeus* < Assyrian *kaldū*.] —**Chaldaic** *n, adj* —**Chaldean** *adj*

Chaldee /káldee, kal dée/ *n* **1** the Aramaic language (*dated*) **2** PEOPLES = **Chaldean** *n.* 1 [14C. Via Old French < Latin *Chaldaeus* (see CHALDEAN).]

~~**chalenge**~~ incorrect spelling of **challenge**

chalet /shállay/ *n* **1** a house or cottage traditionally made of wood with wide overhanging eaves, in a style originally built in Switzerland **2** a small hut, especially one used for living accommodation in a holiday camp [Late 18C. < Swiss French.]

Chalgrin /shál graN/, **Jean François** (1739–1811) French architect

chalice /chálliss/ *n* **1** a metal drinking cup or goblet (*literary*) **2** a gold or silver cup used in a Christian church for serving the wine at Communion or Mass [14C. Directly or via French < Latin *calic-* 'cup'.]

chalicothere /kállikə theer/ *n* an extinct mammal resembling a horse with clawed feet and forelimbs slightly longer than the hind limbs. Suborder: Chalicotheriidae. [Early 20C. < modern Latin *Chalicotherium* 'animal found in gravel' < Greek *khalik-* 'pebble' + *thērion* 'small animal' < *thēr* 'animal'.]

chalk /chawk/ *n* **1 POWDERY WHITE ROCK** a soft white or grey fine-grained sedimentary rock consisting of nearly pure calcium carbonate that contains minute fossil fragments of marine organisms **2 SOFT MARKER** a piece of chalk or a similar substance, sometimes coloured, used for writing or drawing, e.g. on a blackboard **3 CUBE OF CHALK FOR BILLIARD CUE** a small cube of chalk or similar substance used for rubbing the tip of a billiard or snooker cue to increase friction between the cue and the ball ■ *v* **1** *vti* **DRAW OR MARK WITH CHALK** to draw, write, or mark something with chalk **2** *vi* **BECOME POWDERY** to become powdery **3** *vt* **RUB CHALK ON A CUE** to treat a billiard or snooker cue with chalk [Old English *cealc* 'lime(stone), chalk', via Germanic < Latin *calc-* 'lime(stone)' < Greek *khalix* 'pebble'] ◇ **as like** *or* **different as chalk and cheese** extremely different in important respects (*informal*) ◇ **by a long chalk** by a large margin ◇ **not by a long chalk** not by any means

chalk out *vt* to sketch or outline a plan or proposal

chalk up *vt* **1 SCORE OR KEEP SCORE OF** to score or achieve something, or record a score or victory **2 ATTRIBUTE TO** to credit or ascribe something to something or somebody **3 CHARGE SOMETHING TO** to record the cost of something and charge it to somebody or somebody's account [< the custom at pubs or bars of writing up with chalk an account of credit given]

chalk and talk *n* a traditional method of education in which the teacher addresses the students, using a blackboard to provide examples or illustrations

chalkboard /cháwk bawrd/ *n US, Can* EDUC = **blackboard**

chalkface /cháwk fayss/ *n* teaching in a classroom, as distinct from the other duties of a teacher (*informal*) [After COALFACE]

chalkpit /cháwk pit/ *n* a quarry where chalk is excavated

chalkstone /cháwk stōn/ *n* a piece of chalk taken straight from the ground

chalk talk *n US, Can* an informal lecture during which illustrations or examples are given on a blackboard

chalky /cháwki/ (**-ier, -iest**) *adj* containing or resembling chalk in colour or texture —**chalkiness** *n*

challah /khaálə, haálə/ (*plural* **-lahs** *or* **-loth** /-lōt/), **hallah** (*plural* **-lahs** *or* **-loth** /-lōt/) *n* white bread enriched with eggs, usually in a plaited loaf, traditionally eaten by Jews on Friday evening at the Sabbath meal [Early 20C. < Hebrew *ḥallāh*, probably < *ḥll* 'pierce'; from its original shape.]

challenge /chállənj/ *vt* (**-lenges, -lenging, -lenged**) **1 INVITE SOMEBODY TO CONTEST** to invite somebody to participate in a fight, contest, or competition **2 DARE** to dare somebody to do something **3 CALL SOMETHING INTO QUESTION** to call something into question by demanding an explanation, justification, or proof **4 STIMULATE** to stimulate somebody by making demands on the intellect **5 ORDER SOMEBODY TO PRODUCE IDENTIFICATION** to order somebody to stop and produce identification or a password **6 OBJECT TO INCLUSION OF JUROR** to make a formal objection against the inclusion of a prospective juror on a jury **7 TEST WHETHER SOMETHING PRODUCES ALLERGY** to expose a person or animal to a substance in order to determine whether an allergy or other adverse reaction will occur ■ *n* **1 INVITATION TO TAKE PART IN CONTEST** an invitation to somebody to compete in a fight, contest, or competition **2 STIMULATING TEST OF ABILITIES** a test of somebody's abilities or a situation that tests somebody's abilities in a stimulating way **3 QUESTIONING** a questioning of something by demanding an explanation, justification, or proof **4 DEMAND FOR IDENTIFICATION** an order to somebody to stop and produce identification or a password **5 OBJECTION AGAINST JUROR** an objection against the inclusion of somebody on a jury **6 TESTING FOR ALLERGY** exposure of a person or animal to a substance in order to determine whether an allergy or other adverse reaction will occur [13C. Via Old French *c(h)alengier* 'accuse' < Latin *calumniare* 'accuse falsely' < *calumnia* 'false accusation'.] —**challengeable** *adj*

challenged /chállənjd/ *adj* **1** having a particular physical or mental disability **2** lacking in a particular quality (*humorous; offensive in some contexts*) ○ *judgmentally challenged*

USAGE In euphemisms for personal disabilities, ***challenged*** often appears in combinations such as *physically challenged* (= disabled) and *medically challenged* (= unwell). The intention is to replace a negative-sounding term with a more positive one. But language rarely responds well to such overt manipulation, and in due course a new terminology acquires its own set of context-derived connotations. In British English, ***challenged*** is usually only used jocularly and the expression is ridiculed in such facetious ad hoc formations as *vertically challenged* (= short).

challenger /chállənjər/ *n* **1** the issuer of an invitation to a fight, contest, or competition **2** an opponent of a champion, especially in a boxing match

challenging /chállənjing/ *adj* demanding physical or psychological effort of a stimulating kind —**challengingly** *adv*

challis /shállis, -li/, **challie** /shálli/ *n* a soft lightweight woollen, cotton, or synthetic fabric, often patterned with a small print. Use: clothes. [Mid-19C. < ?]

chalone /káy lōn, kállōn/ *n* a substance produced by cells that inhibits their mitosis [Early 20C. < Greek *khalōn*, present participle of *khalan* 'slacken'.] —**chalonic** /ka lŏnik, kay-/ *adj*

chalumeau /shállyoō mō/ (*plural* **-meaux** /shállyoō mō/) *n* **1** a woodwind instrument of the 17th and 18th centuries that developed into the clarinet **2** the lowest register of a clarinet or its warm tone quality [Early 18C. Via French < late Latin *calamellus* 'small reed' < *calamus* 'reed' < Greek *kalamos*.]

chalutz /khaa loōts/ (*plural* **-lutzim** /khaa loōt seem/), **halutz** (*plural* **-lutzim**) *n* a member of a group of Jewish immigrants to Palestine after 1917 who began or worked in agricultural or forestry projects [Early 20C. < Hebrew *ḥaluṣ* 'pioneer'.]

chalybeate /kə líbbi it/ *adj* **1** containing iron salts **2** having a taste like iron [Mid-17C. < modern Latin *chalybeatus* < Latin *chalybs* 'steel' < Greek *khalups*.]

chalybite /kálli bīt/ *n* MINERALS = **siderite** *n*. 1 [Mid-19C. < Greek *khalub-* 'steel'.]

Cham /kam/ (*plural* **Chams** *or* **Cham**) *n* an Austronesian language spoken in Vietnam and Cambodia. Native speakers: 230,000. —**Cham** *adj*

Chamaeleon /kə meéli ən/, **Chameleon** *n* a faint constellation near the south celestial pole. See illustration at **constellation**

chamaephyte /kámmi fīt/ *n* a perennial plant that produces dormant winter buds on or close to the ground [Early 20C. < Greek *khamai* 'on the ground'.]

chamber /cháymbər/ *n* **1 BEDROOM** a bedroom or other room in somebody's home (*archaic or literary*) **2 OFFICIAL RECEPTION ROOM** a reception room in an official residence or a palace **3 ROOM FOR SPECIFIC PURPOSE** a room used for a designated purpose **4 OFFICIAL ASSEMBLY OR MEETING PLACE** a legislative or judicial assembly, or the place where such a body meets **5 ORGANIZED BODY OF PEOPLE** a body of people organized into a group for a specific purpose **6 COMPARTMENT OR CAVITY** an enclosed space, compartment, or cavity, e.g. one inside a machine, the body, or a plant **7 PLACE IN GUN FOR AMMUNITION** the compartment for a cartridge in a revolver or rifle or for a shell in a cannon **8** HOUSEHOLD = **chamber pot** ■ **chambers** *npl* **1 JUDGE'S PRIVATE OFFICE** a judge's private office for discussing cases or legal matters not taken up in open court **2 LAWYERS' OFFICES** a suite of rooms used by lawyers for consulting with clients **3 FLAT OR SUITE OF ROOMS** a flat or suite of private rooms ■ *adj* **OF CHAMBER MUSIC** relating to, written as, or performing chamber music ■ *vt* **1 ENCLOSE IN OR PROVIDE WITH CHAMBERS** to put something in or provide something with a chamber or chambers **2 PUT AMMUNITION IN WEAPON** to insert a round of ammunition in the breech of a weapon [12C. Via French *chambre* < Latin *camera* 'vault, room' < Greek *kamara* 'vault'.] —**chambered** *adj*

chambered nautilus *n* ZOOL = **pearly nautilus**

chamberlain /cháymbərlin/ *n* **1 MANAGER OF ROYAL OR NOBLE HOUSEHOLD** an official who manages the household of a monarch or member of the nobility **2 TREASURER OF MUNICIPALITY** the treasurer of a municipality **3 PRIEST WHO IS PAPAL ATTENDANT** a priest who is an attendant to the pope, often an honorary position [12C. Via Old French, < assumed Frankish *kamarling* 'little room' < Greek *kamara* 'vault'.]

Chamberlain /cháymbərlin/, **Joseph** (1836–1914) British politician

Chamberlain, Neville (1869–1940) British statesman

Chamberlain, Owen (*b.* 1920) US physicist

chambermaid /cháymbər mayd/ *n* a woman employed to tidy and clean bedrooms in hotels or guest houses

chamber music *n* classical instrumental music written for a small group, e.g., a quartet or trio, and often originally intended for performance in a large room or a small concert hall

chamber of commerce *n* an organization of local business people who work together to promote and protect common interests in trade

chamber of horrors *n* an exhibition depicting macabre or gruesome objects and incidents [< a room in Madame Tussaud's waxwork exhibition in London]

chamber of trade *n* a national organization representing local chambers of commerce

chamber orchestra *n* a small orchestra, usually comprising fewer than 40 players, that performs classical music

chamber pot *n* a large bowl used in a bedroom for urination and defecation

Chambers Pillar /cháymbərz-/ sandstone monolith in S Northern Territory, Australia. Height: 30 km/19 mi.

chambray /shám bray/ *n* a fine lightweight cotton or linen fabric with coloured fibres interlaced with white [Early 19C. Alteration of *Cambrai*, France.]

chameleon /kə meéli ən/ *n* **1** a tree-dwelling lizard with long thin legs, a strong curled tail, a long sticky tongue, and the ability to change colour. Native to: Africa, Madagascar. Family: Chamaeleonidae. **2** a frequent and rapid changer of personality or appearance [14C. Via Latin < Greek *khamaileōn* < *khamai* 'on the ground' + *leōn* 'lion'.] —**chameleonic** /kə meéli ónnik/ *adj*

Chameleon *n* ASTRON = **Chamaeleon**

chametz /khaa méts, kháwmits/, **chometz, hametz, hometz** *n* leavened bread or other food that may not

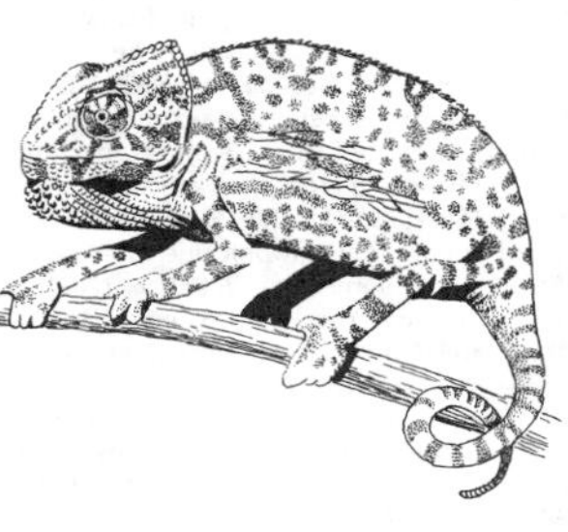

Chameleon

be eaten by Jews during Passover [Mid-19C. < Hebrew *ḥāmēṣ*.]

chamfer /chámfər/ *n* a shallow cut, edge, or groove made in wood, usually at an angle of 45 degrees to a corner [Mid-16C. Back-formation < *chamfering* 'grooving' < French *chanfrein* 'bevelled edge', variant of *chanfreint*, past participle of *chanfraindre* 'bevel' < *chant* 'edge' (< Latin *canthus* 'iron tyre') + *fraindre* 'break'.] —**chamfer** *vt* —**chamfered** *adj*

chamois /shám waa/ (*plural* **-ois** /-waa/ *or* **-oix** /-waa/) *n* **1 EURASIAN GOAT ANTELOPE** an agile goat antelope that has slender backward-curving horns and a tawny coat that darkens in winter. Native to: mountains of Europe and SW Asia. *Rupicapra rupicapra*. **2 chamois, chamois leather SOFT PLIABLE LEATHER** soft pliable leather, originally made from the hide of the chamois. Use: cleaning, polishing. **3 CLOTH FOR POLISHING** a piece of chamois leather, or a natural or synthetic substitute. Use: cleaning, polishing. **4 GREYISH-YELLOW** a greyish-yellow colour, like that of chamois leather [Mid-16C. Via French < late Latin *camox*.] —**chamois** *adj*

chamomile *n* = **camomile**

Chamorro /cha mórrō/, **Violeta Barrios de** (*b.* 1929) Nicaraguan stateswoman

champ[1] /champ/ *n* **1 MASHED POTATOES WITH SPRING ONIONS** an Irish dish of mashed potatoes with milk and spring onions eaten with melted butter **2 BITING, CHEWING, OR GRINDING** the process of biting, chewing, or grinding something vigorously, noisily, or impatiently, or the sound that this makes ■ *v* **1** *vti* **BITE SOMETHING VIGOROUSLY** to bite, chew, or grind something vigorously, noisily, or impatiently **2** *vt Scotland* **MASH FOOD** to mash something, e.g. potatoes (*informal*) [Mid-16C. Probably an imitation of the sound.] —**champer** *n*

champ[2] /champ/ *n* a champion (*informal*) [Mid-19C. Shortening.]

champagne /sham páyn/ *n* **1 WHITE SPARKLING WINE FROM CHAMPAGNE** a dry white sparkling wine produced in the Champagne region of NE France, often drunk at special occasions **2 WHITE WINE RESEMBLING CHAMPAGNE** any dry or semisweet white wine resembling champagne and made by a similar process **3 PALE BROWNISH-GOLD** a very pale brownish-gold colour ■ *adj* **1 EXTRAVAGANT** involving luxury and indulgence ○ *a champagne lifestyle* **2 PALE BROWNISH-GOLD** of the colour champagne

champagne socialist *n* somebody whose luxurious way of life appears to contradict that person's socialist principles (*informal*) —**champagne socialism** *n*

Champaigne /sham páyn/, **Philippe de** (1602–74) Flemish-born French painter

champak /chúmpuk, chámpak/ (*plural* **-paks** *or* **-pak**), **champac** (*plural* **-pacs** *or* **-pac**) *n* an evergreen tree sacred to Hindus and Buddhists. Flowers: fragrant, orange-yellow. Native to: Asia. *Michelia champaca*. [Late 18C. Via Hindi, < Sanskrit *campakā* < Dravidian.]

champers /shámpərz/ *n* champagne (*informal*)

champerty /chámpərti/ (*plural* **-ties**) *n* an agreement between a litigant and somebody who aids or finances litigation in return for a share of the proceeds following a successful outcome [15C. < Anglo-Norman *champartie* < Old French *champart* 'field rent (a portion received by a feudal lord of the produce from land leased)' < *champ* 'field' + *part* 'portion'.] —**champertous** *adj*

champignon /shámpin yoN, cham pínnyən/ *n* a mushroom, especially one cultivated for eating [Late 16C. <

French, 'little country' < *champagne*, via late Latin *campania* < Latin *Campania*, province in Italy.]

champion /chámpi ən/ *n* **1 SUPREME VICTOR IN CONTEST** a person who or team that competes in and wins a contest, competition, or tournament **2 WINNER OF SHOW** something, e.g. an animal or plant, that wins first place in a show **3 DEFENDER** a defender, supporter, or promoter of somebody or something **4 REMARKABLE PERSON** a personal example of excellence or achievement **5 HERO OR WARRIOR** a hero or warrior, especially formerly a knight who fought on behalf of or in defence of a monarch ■ *vt* **DEFEND** to defend, support, or promote a cause or person ■ *adj N England* **EXCELLENT** very good or pleasing ■ *adv N England* **VERY WELL** in a very good or pleasing way [12C. Via Old French, 'combatant' < late Latin *campion-* 'combatant in the arena' < Latin *campus* 'field'.]

championship /chámpi ənship/ *n* **1 CONTEST TO DECIDE A CHAMPION** a contest, competition, or tournament that is held to decide who will be the overall winner **2 TITLE OR TIME OF BEING CHAMPION** the designation or period of being a champion **3 DEFENDING OR SUPPORTING** the defence, support, or promotion of a person or cause

Champlain, Lake /sham pláyn/ lake on the Vermont-New York State border, extending into Quebec, Canada. Area: 1,100 sq. km/430 sq. mi. Depth: 122 m/399 ft.

Champlain, Samuel de (1567?–1635) French explorer

champlevé /shámplə vay, shaàNlə váy/ *n* enamel work in which coloured enamels are used to fill channels cut into a metal base [Mid-19C. < French, < *champ* 'field' + *levé* 'raised'.] —**champlevé** *adj*

Champollion /sham pől yoN/, **Jean François** (1790–1832) French Egyptologist

Champs Élysées /shaàNz ay lèezay/ *n* a broad avenue in Paris leading from the Place de la Concorde to the Arc de Triomphe

Chanc. *abbr* **1** chancellor **2** chancery

chance /chaanss/ *n* **1 LIKELIHOOD THAT SOMETHING WILL HAPPEN** the degree of probability that something will happen (*often plural*) ○ *There's a strong chance we'll win.* **2 OPPORTUNITY OR OPPORTUNE TIME** an opportunity or a set of circumstances that makes it possible for something to happen ○ *I was given no chance to explain.* **3 SUPPOSED FORCE THAT MAKES THINGS HAPPEN** the supposed force that makes things happen in a particular way without any apparent cause **4 UNEXPECTED HAPPENING** an unexpected event **5 SOMETHING CAUSED BY LUCK** something caused by luck or fortune ■ *v* (**chances, chancing, chanced**) **1** *vt* **DO SOMETHING RISKY** to do something knowing that it is risky **2** *vi* **DO SOMETHING UNPLANNED** to do something or happen without a cause or plan [13C. Via Anglo-Norman < late Latin *cadentia* 'falling' < present participle of Latin *cadere* 'to fall'.] ◇ **by any chance** used to enquire if there is any possibility of something ○ *Is there a copy you could lend me, by any chance?* ◇ **by chance** unexpectedly or without plan ◇ **fat chance** something that is highly unlikely (*informal*)

chance on, chance upon *vt* to find or encounter somebody or something unexpectedly

chancel /chaànssəl/ *n* an area of a church near the altar for the use of clergy and choir, often separated from the nave by a screen or steps [14C. Via Old French < Latin *cancelli* 'little lattices' < *cancer* 'lattice'.]

chancellery /chaànssələri, chaànsslәri/ (*plural* **-ies**), **chancellory** (*plural* **-ies**) *n* **1** the official residence of a chancellor **2** the position or rank of a chancellor **3** *US* INTERNAT REL = **chancery** *n.* **3**

chancellor /chaànssələr, chaànsslər/, **Chancellor** *n* **1 HEAD OF GOVERNMENT IN PARLIAMENTARY DEMOCRACY** the chief minister of government in some parliamentary democracies **2 Chancellor** POL = **Chancellor of the Exchequer** **3** *UK, Can* **HONORARY HEAD OF UNIVERSITY** the honorary head of a university **4** *US* **CHIEF ADMINISTRATIVE OFFICER OF UNIVERSITY** the chief administrative officer of some universities **5** *US* **US JUDGE** in some US states, the presiding judge of a court of equity or chancery **6 EMBASSY SECRETARY** the main secretary of an embassy **7 HIGH-RANKING OFFICIAL** a high-ranking government or legal official [Pre-12C. Via Anglo-Norman *c(h)anceler* < Latin *cancellarius* 'court secretary, attendant at the grating' < *cancelli* (see CHANCEL).] —**chancellorship** *n*

Chancellor of the Duchy of Lancaster *n* a honorary title held by a cabinet minister who legally represents a sovereign in matters concerning the Duchy of Lancaster

Chancellor of the Exchequer *n* a member of the British government who is the chief minister of finance

chancellory *n* = **chancellery**

chance-medley *n* **1** the killing of an assailant in self-defence during an unexpected brawl **2** a haphazard event or action, or the randomness of chance [15C. < Anglo-Norman *chance medlee* 'mixed chance'; from the idea of being only partly accidental.]

chancer /chaànssər/ *n* a risk-taker in the interest of personal gain (*informal*)

chancery /chaànssəri/ (*plural* **-ies**), **Chancery** (*plural* **-ies**) *n* **1 LORD CHANCELLOR'S COURT** the Lord Chancellor's court, one of the five divisions of the High Court of Justice in England **2** LAW = **court of chancery** **3 OFFICE ATTACHED TO EMBASSY** an office attached to an embassy or consulate, especially the political section. US term **chancellery** *n.* **3** **4 PUBLIC ARCHIVE** a public archive or record office **5** POL = **chancellery** *n.* **2** [14C. Contraction of CHANCELLERY.]

Chancery Division *n* LAW = **chancery** *n.* **1**

chancre /shángkər/ *n* **1** a small painless highly infectious ulcer or sore that is the first sign of syphilis and certain other infectious diseases **2** a sore or ulcer at the point where a disease-causing organism (**pathogen**) enters the body [Late 16C. Via French < Latin *cancer* 'ulcer'.] —**chancrous** *adj*

chancroid /sháng kroyd/ *n* **1** a sexually transmitted disease that causes a painful ragged ulcer at the site of infection **2** a painful ragged ulcer that is characteristic of the sexually transmitted disease chancroid —**chancroidal** /shang króyd'l/ *adj*

chancy /chaànssi/ (**-ier, -iest**), **chancey** (**-ier, -iest**) *adj* **1** involving risks or danger **2** occurring in a random or haphazard way —**chancily** *adv* —**chanciness** *n*

chandelier /shándə lèer/ *n* a decorative hanging light with several branches and holders for candles or light bulbs [Mid-18C. < French, < *chandelle* 'candle' < Latin *candela*.] —**chandeliered** *adj*

chandelle /shan dél, shaaN-/ *n* a steep climbing turn in which an aircraft almost stalls as it uses momentum to increase the rate of climb ■ *vi* (**-delles, -delling, -delled**) to climb steeply in an aircraft, turning at the same time and almost stalling [Early 20C. < French, 'candle'.]

Chandigarh /chándi gaàr/, **Chandīgarh** joint capital of Punjab and Haryana states, NW India. Population: 574,646 (1991).

chandler /chaàndlər/ *n* **1** a seller of specified supplies and goods ○ *a ship's chandler* **2** a seller or maker of candles [14C. < Anglo-Norman *chaundeler*, Old French *chandelier* < *c(h)andelle* 'candle' < Latin *candela*.]

Chandler /chaàndlər, chánd-/, **Raymond** (1888–1959) US writer

chandlery /chaàndləri/ (*plural* **-ies**) *n* the goods that a chandler deals in, or the place where they are stored or sold

Chandrasekhar limit /chaàndrə sèekə-/ *n* the upper limit for the mass of a white dwarf star beyond which the star collapses to a neutron star or a black hole [After Subrahmanyan *Chandrasekhar* (1910–95), US astrophysicist]

Chanel /shə nél/, **Coco** (1883–1971) French couturier. Full name **Gabrielle Bonheur Chanel**

Chaney /cháyni/, **Lon** (1883–1930) US silent film actor. Full name **Alonso Chaney**

Chang /chang/, **Victor Peter** (1937–91) Chinese-born Australian surgeon

~~**changable**~~ incorrect spelling of **changeable**

Changchun /cháng chŏŏn/ capital of Jilin Province, NE China. Population: 2,110,000 (1991).

change /chaynj/ *v* (**changes, changing, changed**) **1** *vti* **BECOME OR MAKE DIFFERENT** to become different, or make something or somebody different **2** *vt* **SUBSTITUTE OR REPLACE** to exchange, substitute, or replace something ○ *If it doesn't fit, the shop will change it for another size.* **3** *vti* **PASS FROM ONE STATE TO ANOTHER** to pass or make something pass from one state or stage to another ○ *Water changes to ice when it freezes.* **4** *vt* **CONVERT ONE CURRENCY INTO ANOTHER** to replace money of one currency with an equivalent amount in another currency **5** *vt* **EXCHANGE MONEY FOR SMALLER UNITS** to exchange a unit of money for an equal amount of money in lower denominations ○ *Can you change me a £10 note for two fives?* **6** *vti* **MOVE FROM ONE VEHICLE TO ANOTHER** to get out of one vehicle or means of transportation and continue the journey in another **7** *vti* **REMOVE CLOTHES AND PUT ON OTHERS** to remove one or more articles of clothing and replace them with something else ○ *Are you going to change for dinner?* **8** *vt* **REMOVE AND REPLACE** to remove something dirty or used and replace it with another that is clean or unused **9** *vti* **OPERATE GEARS OF VEHICLE** to put a car or other vehicle into a different gear ■ *n* **1 MAKING OR BECOMING DIFFERENT** alteration, variation, or modification, or the result of this ○ *There's been a change of plan.* **2 EXCHANGE OR REPLACEMENT** an exchange, substitution, or replacement of something or somebody **3 MONEY GIVEN BACK** the balance of money given back to a customer who has handed over a larger sum than the cost of the goods or services purchased **4 COINS** coins collectively, especially coins of a small denomination **5 MONEY EXCHANGED FOR HIGHER DENOMINATION** a sum of money given or received as an equivalent of a higher denomination **6 TRANSITION** a shift from one state, stage, or phase to another ○ *a change in attitude* **7 VARIANCE FROM ROUTINE** a variance from a routine or pattern, especially a welcome one ○ *She could do with a change.* **8 FRESH SET** a different, clean, or fresh set of something, especially clothes **9 MENOPAUSE** the menopause (*dated informal*) **10 PROCEDURE FOR RINGING BELLS** the order in which tuned bells are rung. ◊ **change ringing** [12C. Via Old French *changer* < late Latin *cambiare* < Latin *cambire* 'to exchange'.] —**changer** *n* ◇ **ring the changes** to repeat something with variations

SYNONYMS ***change, alter, modify, convert, vary, shift, transform, transmute***

CORE MEANING: to make or become different

change to make or become different in any way; **alter** to change, especially to change an aspect of something; **modify** to make minor changes or alterations, especially in order to improve something; **convert** to change something from one form or function to another; **vary** to change within a range of possibilities, or in connection with something else, with a suggestion of instability; **shift** to change from one position or direction to another; **transform** to make a radical change into a different form; **transmute** to change into another form.

change down *vi* to change into a lower gear in a car or other vehicle. US term **downshift** *v.* **1**

change off *vi US* to alternate tasks, or tasks and work breaks, especially with somebody else

change over *vi* **1 EXCHANGE OR REVERSE PLACES OR POSITIONS** to exchange or reverse places, positions, or roles **2 SUBSTITUTE SOMETHING FOR SOMETHING ELSE** to replace one system, method, or product with another **3 EXCHANGE ENDS OF PLAYING FIELD** in team sports, to switch to opposite ends of a playing field, usually halfway through a match **4 HAND OVER BATON IN RELAY RACE** to pass on the responsibility for participation in a relay race to another team member by handing over a baton or touching

change round *vti* to reverse or alter places, positions, or roles

change up *vi* to change into a higher gear in a car or other vehicle

changeable /cháynjəb'l/ *adj* **1** capable of or liable to change **2** variable in colour according to viewpoint or lighting —**changeability** /cháynjə bíllәti/ *n* —**changeableness** *n* —**changeably** *adv*

changeful /cháynjf'l/ *adj* changing frequently —**changefully** *adv* —**changefulness** *n*

~~**changeing**~~ incorrect spelling of **changing**

changeless /cháynjləss/ *adj* not liable to change —**changelessly** *adv* —**changelessness** *n*

changeling /cháynjling/ *n* in folklore, a child who is secretly substituted for another one by fairies

change of heart *n* a profound change of attitude or opinion

change of life *n* the menopause (*informal*)

change of venue *n* **1** the removal of a trial to another jurisdiction **2** a relocation of a public event, especially a play or concert

changeover /cháynj ōvər/ *n* **1 COMPLETE CHANGE FROM** a conversion, reversal, or complete change from one position, situation, or system to another **2 EXCHANGE OF ENDS IN PLAYING FIELD** in team sports, the switch of teams to opposite ends of a playing field **3 PASSING OF BATON IN RELAY RACE** passing on responsibility for participation in a relay race from one team member to another by handing over the baton or touching, or the point at which this is done

change purse *n US* = **purse** *n.* 1

change ringing *n* the ordered ringing of a peal of bells in various combinations so that none of the combinations is repeated and all possible permutations are rung

changeround /cháynj rownd/ *n* a change to a different or opposite position

changing of the guard *n* the action or ceremony in which one shift of guards takes up duty while another leaves, especially outside Buckingham Palace

changing room *n* an area in a sports or leisure centre where clothes can be changed and showers taken

Chang Jiang /cháng ji áng/ = **Yangtze**

Changsha /cháng shaá/ capital of Hunan Province, SE China. Population: 1,330,000 (1991).

Changzhou /cháng jṓ/ city in E China. Population: 800,000 (1996).

ϟ **channel**[1] /chánn'l/ *n* **1 STRIP OF WATER SEPARATING LAND** a wide passage of water between an island and a larger body of land **2 NAVIGABLE PASSAGE** a navigable route through a river or harbour, especially one that has been deepened by dredging **3 ROUTE OF WATERWAY** the course of a stream, river, canal, or other waterway **4 TUBULAR PASSAGE FOR LIQUID** a long narrow passage or tube along which a liquid can flow ○ *a drainage channel* **5 MEANS OF COMMUNICATION** a course or means of communication or expression (*often plural*) ○ *the proper channels* **6 FREQUENCY SPECTRUM USED IN TRANSMISSION** the portion of a frequency spectrum that is set aside for a specific purpose, e.g. the broadcasting of a television or radio signal **7 TV OR RADIO STATION** a television or radio station broadcasting on a specified band of the frequency spectrum **8 PATH FOR ELECTRICAL CURRENT** a path for an electrical current or signal **9 GROOVE OR TRENCH** a long narrow groove or furrow, e.g. in architecture or sculpture **10 PATH FOR COMPUTER SIGNALS** a path for electronic signals within a computer or between a computer and a peripheral device **11 SUPPOSED SPIRIT MEDIUM** in spiritualism, somebody who is supposed to act as a medium for receiving messages from the spirit world ■ *v* (**-nels, -nelling, -nelled**) **1** *vt* **DIRECT SOMETHING ALONG SPECIFIC ROUTE** to direct, guide, or convey something, e.g. money or information, through or along a specific route ○ *They channelled all their energies into the game.* **2** *vti* **SPEAK WITH SUPPOSED SPIRIT** in spiritualism, to act as a medium for a supposed spirit **3** *vt* **MAKE CHANNEL IN LAND OR WATER** to make a channel in land or water **4** *vt* **MAKE GROOVE OR FURROW IN** to cut a long narrow groove or furrow in a surface [14C. Via Old French *chanel* < Latin *canalis* 'groove' < *canna* 'reed' < Greek *kanna*.] —**channeller** *n*

channel[2] /chánn'l/ *n* a flat piece of wood or metal projecting horizontally from the side of a ship to increase the spread of the ropes or cables (**shrouds**) supporting the mast [Mid-18C. Alteration of *chainwale* < CHAIN + WALE.]

Channel /chánn'l/ = **English Channel**

channel deposit *n* a body of sand deposited by a river, often showing an erratic, sinuous pattern

channel-hop (**channel-hops, channel-hopping, channel-hopped**) *vi* to use a remote control device to move rapidly through many different television channels, either to see whether there is anything worth watching or without searching for anything in particular. US term **channel-surf** —**channel-hopper** *n*

Channel-hop (**Channel-hops, Channel-hopping, Channel-hopped**) *vi* to cross the English Channel for a trip to mainland Europe, usually for shopping or sightseeing, and return on the same day —**Channel-hopper** *n*

channeling *n* US = **channelling**

channel iron *n* an iron or steel bar with a U-shaped cross section

channelise *vt* = **channelize**

Channel Islands group of islands in the English Channel near the French coast, dependencies of the British crown. Population: 143,534 (1991). Area: 195 sq. km/75 sq. mi.

channelize /chánn'l īz/ (**-izes, -izing, -ized**), **channelise** (**-ises, -ising, -ised**) *vt* to make a channel for something, or direct something through a channel —**channelization** /chánn'l ī záysh'n/ *n*

channelling /chánn'ling/ *n* **1 SUPPOSED SPIRITUAL COMMUNICATION THROUGH A MEDIUM** in spiritualism, the practice of acting as a medium for receiving messages believed to come from the spirit world **2 CREATION OF CHANNEL** the making of a channel in or on something **3 TUBING THAT PROTECTS WIRES** a protective casing or container that carries one or more cables or wires inside or outside a building

channel-surf *vi US* BROADCAST = **channel-hop** —**channel-surfer** *n*

Channel Tunnel *n* a railway tunnel, opened in 1994, that runs underneath the English Channel and links Folkestone in England with Coquelles near Calais in France. ◊ **Chunnel**

chanoyu /chaánaw yōō/ *n* a Japanese ceremony in which tea is ritually prepared, served, and consumed [Late 20C. < Japanese, 'hot water for tea'.]

chanson /shaaN sóN, shánssən/ *n* a French song, e.g. a satirical cabaret song of the 20th century or a Renaissance song similar to the madrigal [15C. Via French, 'song' < Latin *cantion-* < *cantare* 'sing'.]

chanson de geste /shaaN sóN də zhést/ (*plural* **chansons de geste** /shaaN sóN də zhést/) *n* a French epic poem written between the 11th and 14th centuries, usually celebrating legendary events and figures [< French, 'song of heroic deeds']

chant /chaant/ *n* **1 PHRASE SPOKEN REPEATEDLY BY CROWD** a phrase or slogan repeatedly and rhythmically spoken, often with a simple singsong intonation, especially in unison by a crowd or group **2 MUSIC FOR RELIGIOUS PASSAGE** a musical passage in which words or syllables are sung on the same note or a single word or syllable is sung on a series of notes **3 HYMN OR PRAYER SUNG TO CHANT** a psalm, hymn, or prayer sung to a chant **4 SOMETHING SPOKEN MONOTONOUSLY OR REPETITIOUSLY** a monotonous or repetitive song or intonation of the voice ■ *vti* **1 REPEAT SLOGAN CONTINUALLY** to speak a slogan repeatedly and rhythmically with a simple singsong intonation **2 SING HYMN OR PRAYER AS CHANT** to sing or intone part of a religious service as a chant **3 UTTER MONOTONOUSLY** to speak or sing something monotonously [14C. Via French, 'song' < Latin *cantus* < past participle of *canere* 'sing'.] —**chantingly** *adv*

chanter /chaántər/ *n* **1 SOMEBODY CHANTING SLOGAN** a chanter of a slogan **2 SOMEBODY CHANTING PSALM OR HYMN** a chanter of a musical passage, e.g. a priest or chorister **3 PIPE WITH FINGER HOLES ON BAGPIPES** on bagpipes, a pipe with finger holes on which the melody is played **4 PIPE FOR PRACTISING BAGPIPES** a pipe used to learn or practise fingering for bagpipes

chanterelle /shaántə rél, chaántə-, shántə-/ *n* an edible mushroom found in temperate woodlands that has a yellow-to-orange trumpet-shaped cap. *Cantharellus cibarius.* [Late 18C. Via French, < modern Latin *cantharellus* 'little cup' < Latin *cantharus* 'drinking vessel' < Greek *kantharos*.]

chanteuse /shaan túrz/ (*plural* **-teuses** /shaan túrz/) *n* a woman singer, especially in a nightclub or cabaret [Mid-19C. < French.]

chantey *n* US = **shanty**[2]

chanticleer /chánti kleer, shánti-/, **chantecler** *n* a cock, especially in fairy tales (*literary*) [13C. < Old French *Chantecler* < *chanter* 'sing' + *cler* 'clear'.]

Chantilly[1] /shan tílli/ *n* **1 Chantilly, Chantilly lace** a delicate black or white ornamental lace with an outlined design. Use: bridal and evening gowns. **2 Chantilly, Chantilly cream** whipped cream, sweetened and often flavoured with vanilla

Chantilly[2] /shan tílli/ town in N France. Population: 10,902 (1999).

chantry /chaántri/ (*plural* **-tries**) *n* **1** an endowment to pay for the saying of masses for the soul of the founder or somebody named by the founder **2 chantry, chantry chapel** a chapel or altar endowed for the performance of chantries [14C. < Anglo-Norman *chaunterie*, Old French *chanterie* < *chanter* 'sing'.]

chanty *n* MUSIC = **shanty**[2]

Chanukah, Chanukkah *n* = **Hanukkah**

chaology /kay ólləji/ *n* the study of chaos theory and chaotic systems —**chaologist** *n*

Chao Phraya /chów prə yaá/ river in Thailand. Length: 365 km/227 mi.

chaos /káy oss/ *n* **1 DISORDER** a state of complete disorder and confusion **2 chaos, Chaos EARLIEST CONDITION OF UNIVERSE** the unbounded space and formless matter supposed to have existed before the creation of the universe **3 APPARENT DISORDER** the unpredictability inherent in a system such as the weather, in which apparently random changes occur as a result of the system's extreme sensitivity to small differences in initial conditions [15C. Directly or via French < Latin, < Greek *khaos* 'void, abyss'.]

chaos theory *n* a theory that complex natural systems obey certain rules but are so sensitive that small initial changes can cause unexpected final results, thus giving an impression of randomness. ◊ **butterfly effect**

QUICK FACTS ON... **CHAOS THEORY**

Key elements: mathematical techniques and theories describing highly complex systems, arising from the study of patterns in natural systems, e.g. the motion of the Sun and planets, the principles determining order in the shapes of clouds and crystals, the complexity of living organisms, and the interactions between synthetic chemicals and natural ecosystems

Key dates: 1963 use of three linked nonlinear differential equations to describe a weather system that exhibited sensitive dependence on initial conditions, 'the butterfly effect': the proposition that a butterfly flapping its wings in Hong Kong can effect the course of a tornado in Texas (Lorenz); 1975 first use of the term 'chaos' in a mathematical application (Li and Yorke)

Key technologies: artificial intelligence, computer modelling, fractal geometry, information theory, neural networks

Key developments: astrophysics, cognitive science, evolutionary and developmental biology, meteorology, particle physics, population dynamics

chaotic /kay óttik/ *adj* **1** completely disordered and out of control **2** describes the state of a system according to chaos theory [Early 18C. < CHAOS.] —**chaotically** *adv*

chap[1] /chap/ *vti* (**chaps, chapping, chapped**) to become, or cause to become sore and cracked by exposure to wind or cold (*refers to skin*) ■ *n* a sore cracked area of skin, caused by exposure to wind or cold [14C. < ?] —**chapped** *adj*

chap[2] /chap/ *n* a man or youth, especially somebody whose name is not known or not relevant (*informal*) [Late 16C. Shortening of *chapman*.]

chap[3] /chap/ *n* the lower exterior half of the jaw, especially the cheek [Mid-16C. < ?]

chap. *abbr* **1** chapter **2** chaplain

chaparral /sháppə rál/ *n* a dense thicket of shrubs or small trees, especially of evergreen oaks in S California [Mid-19C. < Spanish, < *chaparra* 'dwarf evergreen oak'.]

chapati /chə paáti, -pátti/ (*plural* **-tis** *or* **-ties**), **chapatti** (*plural* **-tis** *or* **-ties**) *n* a thin round unleavened bread eaten with Indian dishes [Early 19C. < Hindi *capātī* < *capānā* 'flatten'.]

chapbook /cháp bŏŏk/ *n* a small booklet of poems, ballads, or stories, originally sold by travelling pedlars [Early 19C. Blend of *chapman* + *book*.]

chape /chayp/ *n* **1** the metal tip of a scabbard **2** the tongue of a buckle [14C. Via French, 'cape, hood' < late Latin *cappa* (see CAP).]

chapeau /sha pṓ/ (*plural* **-peaux** /-pṓ, -pṓz/ *or* **-peaus** /-pṓ, -pṓz/) *n* a hat as an item of high fashion or ceremonial dress (*formal*) [15C. Via French < late Latin *cappellum* 'small hooded cloak' < *cappa* (see CAP).]

chapel /chápp'l/ *n* **1 ROOM FOR WORSHIP** a place in a hospital, prison, or other institution, or in a large house, consecrated for Christian worship **2 SEPARATE AREA OF CHURCH** a separate area in a church, having its own altar and intended for private prayer **3 PROTESTANT CHURCH** a place of worship used by a Nonconformist Protestant denomination such as the Methodists or Baptists **4 SERVICE IN CHAPEL** a service held in a chapel, especially in a Nonconformist church **5 SMALL ANGLICAN CHURCH** a small Anglican church that operates as a branch of a parish church **6 TRADE UNION BRANCH** a branch of a trade union in printing and journalism (+ *singular or plural verb*) **7 MEETING OF PRINTERS' CHAPEL** a meeting of a printers' or journalists' chapel ■ *adj* **BELONGING TO NONCONFORMIST CHURCH** belonging to a Nonconformist church [12C. Via Old French *chapele* < medieval Latin *cappella* 'small hooded cloak' < late Latin *cappa* (see CAP).]

chapel of ease *n* a church built for people who live a long distance from a parish church

chapel of rest *n* a place at an undertaker's where bodies are kept and may be visited by family and friends

chaperon /sháppərōn/, **chaperone** *n* **1** somebody, especially an older or married woman, who accompanies and supervises a young single woman at social events **2** a supervisor of young people who accompanies them [12C. < French, < late Latin *cappa* (see CAP).] —**chaperon** *vti* —**chaperonage** *n*

chaplain /chápplin/ *n* a member of the clergy employed to give religious guidance, e.g. to members of the armed services, schoolchildren, or prisoners [12C. Via Anglo-Norman, Old French *chapelain* < medieval Latin *cappellanus* 'guardian of the cloak of St Martin of Tours' < *cappella* (see CHAPEL).] —**chaplaincy** *n* —**chaplainship** *n*

chaplet /chápplət/ *n* **1 HEAD DECORATION** a decorative circle of beads or flowers worn on the head **2 PRAYER BEADS** a string of 55 beads used by Roman Catholics for counting prayers **3 BEADED MOULDING** a small moulding resembling a string of beads [14C. Via French *chapelet* < late Latin *cappa* (see CAP).] —**chapleted** *adj*

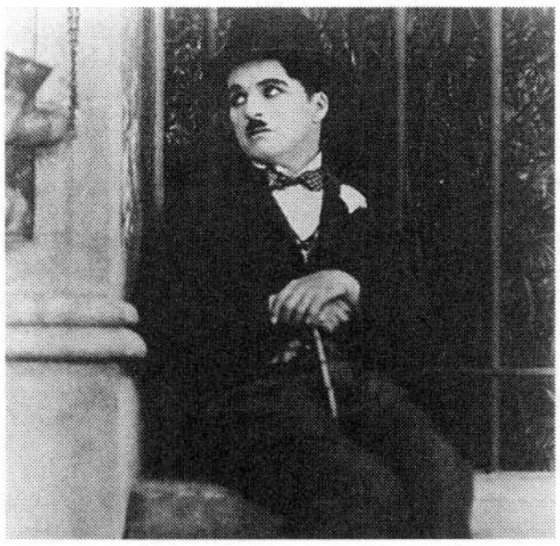

Charlie Chaplin

Chaplin /chápplin/, **Charlie** (1889–1977) British-born US film actor, director, and producer

Chapman /chápmən/, **George** (1559?–1634) English dramatist and translator

Chappell /chápp'l/, **Greg** (*b.* 1948) Australian cricketer

Chappell, Ian Michael (*b.* 1943) Australian cricketer

chappie /cháppi/ *n* a man or youth, especially somebody whose name is not known or not relevant (*informal*)

chaps /chaps/ *npl* protective leather leggings, like a pair of trousers with no seat or crotch, worn on horseback over ordinary trousers by North American ranch workers, rodeo contestants, and cowboys [Late 19C. Shortening of *chaparejos*, alteration of *chaparreras* < *chaparra* (see CHAPARRAL); because worn when riding through chaparral.]

chaptalize /cháptə līz/ (**-izes, -izing, -ized**), **chaptalise** (**-ises, -ising, -ised**) *vt* to increase the alcohol content of wine by adding sugar before or during fermentation [Late 19C. After J. A. *Chaptal* (1756–1832), French chemist.] —**chaptalization** /cháptə lī záysh'n/ *n*

chapter /cháptər/ *n* **1 SECTION OF BOOK** one of the main sections of a text, usually having a title or number as a heading **2 PERIOD OF DEVELOPMENT** an identifiable period in the history or development of something ○ *Their move to France began a new chapter in their lives.* **3 SERIES OF EVENTS** a series of events having a common characteristic ○ *a turbulent chapter in the movements of history* **4 GROUP OF CANONS** the body of canons of a cathedral or collegiate church, or the body of members of an order of knighthood (*+ singular or plural verb*) **5 BRANCH OF A GROUP** a branch of a society or organization (*+ singular or plural verb*) **6 ASSEMBLY OF A CHAPTER** a meeting of a cathedral or church chapter [12C. Via French *chapitre* < Latin *capitulum* 'small head' < *caput* 'head'.] ◇ **give** *or* **quote chapter and verse** to give exact information and detailed references on a topic

Chapter 11 /-i lévv'n/ *n* a section of the US Federal Bankruptcy Code that allows an insolvent company to be reorganized, sometimes providing for repayment of debts or the creation of a new company

chapter book *n US* a book divided into chapters

chapter house *n* **1** a building used for meetings by a religious chapter **2** *US* a building used by a fraternity or sorority at a North American college

Chapultepec /chə pòoltə pek/ rocky hill near Mexico City, Mexico, site of the final battle of the Mexican War in 1847

char[1] /chaar/ (**chars, charring, charred**) *v* **1** *vti* to blacken something or become blackened by burning or scorching **2** *vt* to turn wood into charcoal by partial burning [Late 17C. Back-formation < CHARCOAL.]

char[2] /chaar/ (*plural* **char** *or* **chars**), **charr** (*plural* **charr** *or* **charrs**) *n* a trout with light-coloured spots. Native to: northern waters [Mid-17C. < ?]

char[3] /chaar/ *n* = **charwoman** ■ *vi* (**chars, charring, charred**) to do people's housework, especially cleaning, for pay (*dated informal*) [Old English *cierran* 'to turn' < Germanic]

char[4] /chaar/ *n* tea (*dated informal*) [Early 20C. < Chinese (Mandarin) *chá*.]

charabanc /shárrə bang/ *n* a bus or coach, often open-sided, used for pleasure trips or sightseeing [Early 19C. < French *char-à-bancs* 'carriage with benches'.]

characin /kárrəssin/ (*plural* **-cin** *or* **-cins**), **characid** /-sid/ (*plural* **-cid** *or* **-cids**) *n* a small brightly coloured freshwater fish often kept in aquariums. Native to: Africa, South America. Family: Characidae. [Late 19C. < modern Latin *Characinus* < Greek *kharax* 'pointed stake', also used for a fish.]

⚡**character** /kárrəktər/ *n* **1 DISTINCTIVE QUALITIES** the set of qualities that make somebody or something distinctive, especially somebody's qualities of mind and feeling ○ *It's just not in my character to behave like that.* **2 POSITIVE QUALITIES** qualities that make somebody or something interesting or attractive ○ *an old house full of character* **3 REPUTATION** somebody's public reputation ○ *an attack on his good character that ended in court* **4 SOMEBODY IN BOOK OR FILM** one of the people portrayed in a book, play, or film ○ *None of the central characters is particularly likable.* **5 UNUSUAL PERSON** somebody with an unusual or eccentric personality **6 INDIVIDUAL** somebody considered in terms of personality, behaviour, or appearance ○ *a flamboyant character* **7 LETTER OR SYMBOL** any written or printed letter, number, or other symbol **8 COMPUTER UNIT OF DATA** a single letter, number, or symbol that can be displayed on a computer screen or printer and represents one byte of data **9 GENETICALLY CONTROLLED CHARACTERISTIC** a genetically controlled characteristic of an organism **10 WRITTEN TESTIMONIAL** a written summary of somebody's abilities and personality, written by an employer or other person who knows the person well **11 CAPACITY OR POSITION** a particular role, position, or function that somebody has in society or in an organization (*formal*) ○ *speaking in her character as chairperson* **12 STYLE OF WRITING OR PRINTING** a particular style of handwriting or printing [14C. Via French *caractère* < Greek *kharaktēr* 'tool for marking' < *kharassein* 'engrave' < *kharax* 'pointed stake'.] ◇ **in or out of character 1** typical or untypical of the behaviour of a particular person or thing **2** involved or not involved in the psychological preparations for acting out a particular role in a play, film, or other dramatic work

character actor *n* an actor who specializes in playing the roles of unusual or distinctive characters

character assassination *n* a deliberate and sustained attack on somebody's reputation

character-building, character-forming *adj* creating strength of character, usually as a result of testing and difficult experiences

characterful /kárrəktərf'l/ *adj* having many qualities that are interesting or pleasantly unusual

characterisation *n* = **characterization**

characterise *vt* = **characterize**

characteristic /kárrəktə rístik/ *n* **1 DEFINING FEATURE** a feature or quality that makes somebody or something recognizable **2 WHOLE NUMBER IN LOGARITHM** the whole number (**integer**) found to the left of the decimal point in a common logarithm, e.g. the characteristic of 5.4321 is 5 ■ *adj* **TYPICAL** distinguishing or typical of a particular person or thing —**characteristically** *adv*

characterization /kárrəktər ī záysh'n/, **characterisation** *n* **1** the way in which the writer portrays the characters in a book, play, or film **2** a description of the character or nature of somebody or something

characterize /kárrəktə rīz/ (**-izes, -izing, -ized**), **characterise** (**-ises, -ising, -ised**) *vt* **1** to describe the character or characteristics of somebody or something **2** to be typical of the way a particular person or thing behaves or looks —**characterizable** *adj* —**characterizer** *n*

characterless /kárrəktərləss/ *adj* without any interesting or distinctive features ○ *a characterless view* —**characterlessly** *adv* —**characterlessness** *n*

⚡**character recognition** *n* a magnetic or optical process by which letters, numbers, or symbols are recognized and digitized by a computer

⚡**character set** *n* a complete set of letters, numbers, symbols, and control codes that can be used by a computer

character witness *n* a witness who gives evidence of somebody's good character in a court of law

charade /shə raád, -ráyd/ *n* **1** an absurdly false or pointless act or situation **2** a clue in the game of charades [Late 18C. < French, < modern Provençal *charra* 'to chatter'.]

charades /shə raádz, -ráydz/ *n* a game in which somebody provides a visual or acted clue for a word or phrase, often the title of a book, play, or film, for others to guess (*+ singular verb*)

charas /chaárəss/ *n* DRUGS = **hashish** [Mid-19C. < Hindi *caras*.]

charbroil /chaár broyl/ *vt US* COOK = **chargrill** [Mid-20C. Blend of CHARCOAL + BROIL.] —**charbroiler** *n*

charcoal /chaárkōl/ *n* **1 CARBON** a black or dark grey form of carbon. Source: heating wood or another organic substance in an enclosed space without air. Use: fuel, absorbent, in smelting, in explosives, for drawing. **2 DRAWING IMPLEMENT** sticks of charcoal used for drawing **3 DRAWING USING CHARCOAL** a drawing done with charcoal [14C. < ?]

charcoal grey *adj* of a dark grey colour —**charcoal grey** *n*

charcuterie /shaar kòotəri/ *n* **1** cold cooked, cured, or processed meat and meat products **2** a shop that specializes in charcuterie [Mid-19C. < French, < obsolete *char cuite* 'cooked flesh'.]

chard /chaad/ *n* PLANTS = **Swiss chard** [Mid-17C. Via French *carde* < Latin *cardu(u)s* 'thistle'.]

Chardin /shaar dáN/, **Jean Baptiste Siméon** (1699–1779) French painter

Chardonnay /shaárdə nay, shaar dónnay/, **chardonnay** *n* **1** a white grape used in making wine **2** a dry white wine made from the Chardonnay grape [Early 20C. < French.]

~~**charecter**~~ incorrect spelling of **character**

charge /chaarj/ *v* (**charges, charging, charged**) **1** *vti* **ASK MONEY FOR** to ask somebody for an amount of money as a price or fee **2** *vt* **IMPOSE FEE OR PENALTY ON** to hold a person or organization financially liable for something **3** *vti* **DEBIT** to allow, and enter a record of, a deferred payment for something **4** *vt* **ACCUSE OF CRIME** to accuse somebody formally of having committed a crime **5** *vt* **CRITICIZE** to criticize somebody for doing something wrong ○ *Her boss charged her with being lazy and incompetent.* **6** *vt* **ORDER TO DO** to order or instruct somebody formally to do something ○ *The judge charged the jury to consider all the facts.* **7** *vti* **ATTACK IN A RUSH** to attack somebody or something by rushing forwards, especially in a battle ○ *Police in riot gear charged the lines of demonstrators.* **8** *vi* **RUSH** to run somewhere carelessly or clumsily ○ *He came charging in from the garden.* **9** *vti* **RESTORE POWER IN BATTERY** to restore the power in a battery by connecting it to a supply of electricity **10** *vt* **LOAD OR FILL** to load or fill something, e.g. a gun with explosive, or a glass with drink (*formal*) **11** *vt* **PERVADE** to give an atmosphere of intense interest, excitement, or other strong emotion to a place (*usually passive*) ○ *The concert hall was charged with anticipation.* **12** *vt* **PUT HERALDIC DEVICE ON** to put a heraldic device on something such as a shield or banner ■ *n* **1 AMOUNT OF MONEY ASKED** the price of something that is for sale, or the fee asked for a service or in payment of a financial liability such as a tax ○ *We had to pay several extra charges before getting the vehicle back.* **2 RESPONSIBILITY** the responsibility or duty of looking after somebody or something ○ *He took on the children's welfare as an extra charge.* **3 SOMEBODY BEING TAKEN CARE OF** somebody, especially a child or a member of a minister's congregation, for whom somebody else is responsible (*formal*) ○ *The nanny was keeping a close watch on her little charges.* **4 ACCUSATION** an accusation of wrongdoing, especially an official statement accusing somebody of committing a crime **5 RUSH TO ATTACK** a rush forward to attack, especially in a battle, or the signal for this **6 POWER IN BATTERY** the power stored in a battery **7 ELECTRIC PROPERTY OF MATTER** a fundamental characteristic of matter, responsible for all electric and electromotive forces, expressed in two forms known as positive and negative **8 EXCESS OR LACK OF ELECTRONS** a quantity of electricity caused by an excess or lack of electrons **9 EXPLOSIVE FOR DETONATION** the amount of explosive used to detonate a shell or cartridge **10 ENOUGH TO FILL CONTAINER** the amount required to fill a container or to make a mechanism work **11 INSTRUCTION** a formal order or instruction to do something, e.g. a judge's instructions to a jury **12 SUDDEN BURST OF EXCITEMENT** a sudden burst of excitement or interest **13 HERALDIC DESIGN** a design or image used as part of a coat of arms [12C. Via French *charger* 'to load, charge' < late Latin *car(ri)care* < Latin *carrus* 'carriage'.] ◇ **take charge (of somebody** *or* **something)** to take over control or responsibility for somebody or something

chargeable /chaárjəb'l/ *adj* **1 ABLE TO BE CHARGED** liable or able to be charged **2 LIABLE TO RESULT IN CRIMINAL CHARGE** liable to result in or face a criminal charge **3 SUBJECT TO A CHARGE** describes property or land capable of being subject to a charge —**chargeability** /chaárjə bíllәti/ *n*

charge account *n US FIN* = **credit account**

charge-cap (**charge-caps, charge-capping, charge-capped**) *vt* to put a limit on the amount of flat-rate tax that local authorities in the United Kingdom are allowed to charge people

charge card *n* a card issued to customers by a shop, or other organization, used to charge purchases to an account for later payment

⚡**charge-coupled device** *n* a semiconductor device that converts light patterns into digital signals for a computer, especially in digital cameras and optical scanners

chargé d'affaires /shaár zhay da fáir/ (*plural* **chargés d'affaires** /shaár zhay da fáir, shaár zhayz-/) *n* a diplomat ranking immediately below an ambassador who deputizes in the ambassador's absence or a diplomat who heads a minor diplomatic mission [Mid-18C. < French, 'somebody in charge of affairs'.]

charge density *n* (*symbol* **ρ**) the amount of electric charge per unit of area or volume

charge hand *n* a worker with supervisory responsibilities, ranking below a foreman

charge nurse *n* a nurse in charge of a hospital ward. ◊ **ward manager**

charger[1] /chaárjər/ *n* **1** a large strong cavalry horse **2** *ELEC* = **battery charger 3** somebody or something that charges

charger[2] /chaárjər/ *n* a large flat serving dish of a kind now mainly collected for display [14C. < Anglo-Norman *chargeour* 'something that loads' < Old French *charger* (see CHARGE).]

charge sheet *n* a police document recording criminal charges and court appearances

charge-sheet *vt S Asia* to charge somebody formally with a crime

chargrill /chaár gril/ *vt* to grill food over charcoal on a barbecue or on a ridged pan that produces a similar visual effect. US term **charbroil** [< *char(coal)*]

Chari /shaári/ river flowing from N Central African Republic northwestwards into Lake Chad. Length: 1,400 km/870 mi.

Chari-Nile /chaári nīl/ *n* a Nilo-Saharan group of languages spoken in N Chad, Sudan, Uganda, Kenya, and NE Republic of Congo —**Chari-Nile** *adj*

chariot /chárri ət/ *n* **1** a two-wheeled horse-drawn vehicle used in ancient times in races, warfare, or processions **2** a four-wheeled horse-drawn carriage with rear seats only, used especially on ceremonial occasions [14C. < French, < Latin *carrus* 'carriage'.] —**charioteer** /chárri ə teér/ *n*

charism /kárrizəm/ *n* = **charisma** [15C. < ecclesiastical Latin (see CHARISMA).]

charisma /kə rízmə/ *n* **1** the ability to inspire enthusiasm, interest, or affection in others by means of personal charm or influence **2 charisma** (*plural* **-mata**) a gift or power believed to be divinely bestowed [Mid-17C. Via ecclesiastical Latin < Greek *kharisma* < *kharis* 'favour, grace'.]

charismatic /kárriz máttik/ *adj* **1** possessing great powers of charm or influence **2** describes Christian groups or worship characterized by a quest for inspired and ecstatic experiences such as healing, prophecy, and speaking in tongues —**charismatic** *n* —**charismatically** *adv*

charitable /chárritəb'l/ *adj* **1 GENEROUS** generous to people in need **2 SYMPATHETIC** sympathetic, favourable, or tolerant in judging **3 COLLECTIVELY DISPENSING HELP** dispensing assistance to needy people by means of a group or organization —**charitableness** *n* —**charitably** *adv*

charity /chárrəti/ (*plural* **-ties**) *n* **1 PROVISION OF HELP** the voluntary provision of money, materials, or help to people in need **2 MATERIAL HELP** money, materials, or help voluntarily given to people in need **3 ORGANIZATION PROVIDING CHARITY** an organization that collects money and other voluntary contributions of help for people in need **4 TOLERANT ATTITUDE** the willingness to judge people in a tolerant or favourable way **5 IMPARTIAL LOVE** the impartial love of other people [12C. Via French *charité* < Latin *caritas* < *carus* 'dear'.]

Charity Commission *n* an organization that registers and regulates charities in the United Kingdom —**Charity Commissioner** *n*

charity shop *n* a shop that sells second-hand goods to raise money for a charity

charivari /shaári vaári/ *n* **1** a noisy mock-serenade with the banging of saucepans, kettles, and similar objects, meant to wish newlyweds well. US term **shivaree 2** a noise, commotion, or din (*formal*) [Mid-17C. < French.]

charkha /chaárk ə/, **charka** *n* a spinning wheel, especially for cotton, used in South Asia [Late 19C. Via Urdu *charkạ* < Persian *carḳ(a)*.]

charlady /chaár laydi/ (*plural* **-dies**) *n* = **charwoman** [Late 19C. < CHARWOMAN.]

charlatan /shaárlətən/ *n* a pretender to special skill or expertise [Early 17C. Via French < Italian *ciarlatano* < *ciarlare* 'to babble', an imitation of empty talk.] —**charlatanism** *n* —**charlatanry** *n*

Charlemagne /shaárlə mayn/ (742–814) Frankish king and emperor of the West (800–814)

Charleroi /shaárlə roy, -rwaa/ city in SW Belgium. Population: 203,853 (1998 estimate).

Charles /chaarlz/, **Prince of Wales** (*b.* 1948) British heir apparent

Charles I (1600–49) king of England, Scotland, and Ireland (1625–49)

Charles II (1630–85) king of England, Scotland, and Ireland (1660–85)

Charles V (1500–58) Holy Roman Emperor (1519–58) and, as Charles I, king of Spain (1516–56)

Charles, Bob (*b.* 1936) New Zealand golfer

Charles, Ray (*b.* 1932) US singer and pianist. Born **Ray Charles Robinson**

Charles's law /chaálziz-/ *n* a law that holds that there is a direct relationship between the volume of a gas and its temperature, where its pressure is constant [Late 19C. After J. A. C. *Charles* (1746–1823), French physicist.]

Charles's Wain *n* the Plough (*archaic*)

Charleston[1] /chaárlstən/ *n* a dance, popular in the 1920s, in which the feet are kicked out sideways with the knees kept together [Early 20C. After CHARLESTON[2].]

Charleston[2] /chaárlstən/ port in SE South Carolina. Population: 87,044 (1998 estimate).

Charley *n* = **Charlie 2**

charley horse /chaárli-/ *n US, Can* a severe muscular cramp, especially of the upper leg (*informal*) [< ?]

charlie[1] /chaárli/ *n* cocaine used as an illicit drug (*slang*)

charlie[2] /chaárli/ *n* somebody unintelligent or silly (*informal*) [Early 19C. Pet form of the name *Charles*.]

Charlie /chaárli/ *n* **1** a code word for the letter 'C', used in international radio communications **2 Charlie, Charley** *US, Aus* used to refer to a member of the Viet Cong during the Vietnam War or to the Viet Cong collectively (*slang dated*)

charlock /chaár lok/ (*plural* **-lock** *or* **-locks**) *n* a mustard plant that has hairy stems and leaves and is a common weed. Flowers: yellow. Native to: Europe, Asia. *Brassica kaber.* [Old English *cerlic* < ?]

charlotte /shaárlət/ *n* a sweet, cold or baked dish prepared in a deep straight-sided container and containing fruit surrounded by sponge cake, biscuits, or bread [Late 18C. < French, probably < the name *Charlotte*.]

Charlotte Amalie /shaárlət ə maályə/ capital and main port of the US Virgin Islands, on S St Thomas. Population: 12,000 (1990 estimate).

charlotte russe /-rooss/ (*plural* **charlottes russes** /-rooss/) *n* a cold set dessert made with cream or custard surrounded by sponge fingers [< French, 'Russian charlotte']

Charlottetown /shaárlət town/ capital of Prince Edward Island, Canada. Population: 32,531 (1996).

Charlton /chaárltən/, **Sir Bobby** (*b.* 1937) British footballer. Born **Robert Charlton**

Charlton, 'Boy' (1907–75) Australian swimmer. Born **Andrew Murray Charlton**

Charlton, Jack (*b.* 1935) British footballer and manager. Born **John Charlton**

charm /chaarm/ *n* **1 ATTRACTIVENESS** the power to delight or attract people **2 ATTRACTIVE FEATURE** a feature or quality that delights or attracts (*often plural*) **3 SOMETHING SUPPOSED TO BRING LUCK** something carried or worn because it is believed to bring good luck or ward off evil **4 TRINKET** a miniature metal animal, musical instrument, or similar trinket worn on a bracelet or around the neck **5 MAGIC SPELL** a special phrase or rhyme believed to have magical powers **6 CHARACTERISTIC OF ELEMENTARY PARTICLES** (*symbol* C) a quantum characteristic of elementary particles that accounts for the long lifetime of the J particle, lack of symmetry in hadron interactions, and failure of certain particles to react ■ *v* **1** *vti* **DELIGHT PEOPLE** to delight or attract people **2** *vt* **INFLUENCE PEOPLE** to influence somebody or obtain something from somebody by using powers of persuasion and attraction **3** *vti* **CAST A SPELL** to affect somebody or something by, or as if by, the use of a supposed magic spell [13C. Via French *charme* < Latin *carmen* 'song, incantation' < *canere* 'sing'.] —**charmer** *n*

charmed /chaarmd/ *adj* **1** so pleasant or lucky as to suggest protection by a magic spell **2** describes an elementary particle that has the property of charm

charmed circle *n* a privileged group or elite

charming /chaárming/ *adj* having the power to delight or attract people ○ *a charming village* ○ *a charming young man* ■ *interj* used ironically to express disapproval or distaste at something just done or said (*informal*) —**charmingly** *adv*

charm offensive *n* a campaign, e.g. by a politician, to appear more pleasant, attractive, or reasonable, in order to gain popularity (*informal*)

charm quark *n* a quark with an electric charge of –2/3 and charm of 1

charnel /chaárn'l/ *n* = **charnel house** ■ *adj* suggestive of death or a tomb [14C. Via Old French < medieval Latin *carnale* < Latin *carn-* 'flesh'.]

charnel house *n* a building or vault in which bones or dead bodies are placed

Charolais /shárrə lay/ (*plural* **-lais**), **Charollais** (*plural* **-lais**) *n* a large white cow belonging to a breed originating in France. Kept for: beef. [Late 19C. After Monts du *Charollais*, E France.]

Charon /káirən/ *n* **1** in Greek mythology, a ferryman who took the souls of the dead across the River Styx to Hades **2** the only known satellite of Pluto, discovered in 1978

charoseth, charoset *n JUDAISM* = **haroseth**

Charpentier /shaar paaNti ay/, **Gustave** (1860–1956) French composer

Charpentier, Marc-Antoine (1645?–1704) French composer

charpoy /chaár poy/ *n* a light bedstead of webbing stretched across a frame, commonly used in South Asia [Mid-17C. Via Urdu *chārpāī* < Persian.]

charqui /chaárki/ *n FOOD* = **jerky**[2] *n.* [Early 17C. Via American Spanish < Quechua *cc'arki*.]

charr *n* = **char**[2]

chart /chaart/ *n* **1 DIAGRAM OR TABLE** a diagram or table displaying detailed information **2 MAP TO NAVIGATE BY** a map for navigation by sea or air **3 WEATHER MAP** an outline map that shows weather patterns **4 BASIS FOR HOROSCOPE** a map that shows the relative positions of the planets at the time of somebody's birth on which his or her horoscope is based **5 MUSICAL SCORE** a musical score (*technical*) **6 STITCHING PLAN** a squared grid marked with symbols indicating the placement of stitches in embroidery ■ **charts** *npl* **LIST OF POPULAR RECORDS** a list of the musical recordings that have sold most copies during a specific period ■ *v* **1** *vt* **MAKE A CHART OF** to make a map, graph, or diagram of something **2** *vt* **MAKE A PLAN** to record or describe a plan **3** *vi* **BE IN MUSIC CHARTS** to appear in the music charts [Late 16C. Via French *charte* < Latin *charta* 'paper, papyrus leaf'.] —**chartable** *adj*

charter /chaártər/ *n* **1 FORMAL DOCUMENT OF INCORPORATION** a formal document incorporating an organization, company, or educational institution **2 CONSTITUTION** a formal written statement of the aims, principles, and procedures of an organization **3 STATEMENT OF RIGHTS AND RESPONSIBILITIES** a formal written statement describing the rights and responsibilities of a state and its citizens **4 DOCUMENT OF AUTHORIZATION** a document from an organization or society that authorizes the setting up of a new branch **5 SPECIAL PRIVILEGE** a special privilege, immunity, or exemption, granted to a particular person or group **6 HIRE OR LEASE OF TRANSPORT** the hiring or leasing of transport vehicles for personal or special use, or a contract or agreement for this purpose **7 HIRED OR LEASED TRANSPORT** a vehicle chartered for personal or special use **8** LAW = **charter party** ■ *vt* **1 HIRE OR LEASE TRANSPORT** to hire or lease a vehicle for a personal or special purpose **2 GRANT A CHARTER** to grant a charter of incorporation to a group or organization [12C. Via French *chartre* < Latin *charta* (see CHART).] —**charterer** *n*

chartered /chaártərd/ *adj* **1** that has been granted a charter **2** having membership of a professional body that has been granted a royal charter

chartered accountant *n* an accountant who has passed the examinations of one of the governing professional bodies that has been granted a royal charter

chartered surveyor *n* a surveyor who is a member of the Royal Institution of Chartered Surveyors

charter flight *n* a flight that has been chartered for a specific journey, especially as part of a holiday package

Charterhouse /chaártər howss/ (*plural* **-houses** /-ziz/) *n* a Carthusian monastery [14C. Alteration of Anglo-Norman *Chartrous* or French *Chartreuse* < medieval Latin *Cart(h)usia* (see CARTHUSIAN).]

Charteris /chaártəriss/, **Leslie** (1907–93) British-born US novelist. Born **Leslie Charles Bowyer Yin**

charter member *n* a founding or original member of a society or organization

Charter of Rights *n* a section of the Canadian Constitution stating the rights conferred by Canadian citizenship

charter party *n* a contractual arrangement by which the owner of a ship permits another person to use it to carry goods [Via French < medieval Latin *charta partita* 'divided charter']

Charters Towers /chaártərz tówərz/ town in N Queensland, Australia. Population: 8,893 (1996).

Chartism /chaártizəm/ *n* the principles and practices of a movement advocating political and social reform in England between 1838 and 1848 [Mid-19C. After the *People's Charter*.] —**Chartist** *n, adj*

Chartres /shaártrə/ capital of Eure-et-Loire Department, north-central France. Population: 40,361 (1999).

chartreuse /shaar trúrz/ *n* a bright yellowish-green colour [Early 19C. < French (see CHARTERHOUSE).] —**chartreuse** *adj*

Chartreuse /shaar trúrz/ *tdmk* a trademark for a yellow or green aromatic liqueur, flavoured with herbs and flowers

chart-topping *adj* likely to reach or having reached the top of the list of musical recordings that have sold most copies during a specified period —**chart-topper** *n*

charwoman /chaár wŏŏmən/ (*plural* **-en** /-wimmin/) *n* a woman employed to clean a house or office [Late 16C. < Old English *c(i)err* 'turn (of work)'.]

chary /cháiri/ (**-ier, -iest**) *adj* **1 WARY** cautiously reluctant to do something **2 SPARING** reluctant to share, give, or use something **3 CONCERNED** fussily concerned **4 SHY** showing or characterized by shyness or modesty [Old English *cearig* 'sorrowful' < Germanic] —**charily** *adv* —**chariness** *n*

SYNONYMS See ***cautious***.

Charybdis /kə ríbdiss/ *n* ◊ **Scylla**

chase[1] /chayss/ *v* (**chases, chasing, chased**) **1** *vti* **PURSUE** to try to catch or overtake somebody or something **2** *vt* **MAKE RUN AWAY** to force a person or animal to run away ○ *The kids chased a black cat out of the garden.* **3** *vi* **RUSH ABOUT** to rush about ○ *They chased about all day.* **4** *vt* **INVESTIGATE** to follow up or investigate something that has not been done or somebody who has not done something ○ *We need to chase up the plumber to find out when he's going to come.* **5** *vti* **TRY TO GET** to spend a lot of time and energy trying to acquire something **6** *vti* **PAY PERSISTENT ATTENTION TO** to seek the company of somebody for romantic or sexual purposes, especially in an obvious or unsubtle way ■ *n* **1 PURSUIT** an act or situation in which something or somebody is being pursued **2 HUNTING FOR SPORT** the hunting of animals for sport **3 HUNTING LAND** a privately owned area of land where animals are confined or stocked for hunting purposes **4 RIGHT TO KEEP GAME OR HUNT** the right to keep game or to hunt on a particular area of land **5 SOMETHING PURSUED** the target of a pursuit, especially an animal **6** HORSERACING = **steeplechase** *n.* 1 **7 JAZZ DUET** a jazz duet in which the players play alternate phrases and try to outdo each other in virtuosity and invention [13C. Via Old French *chacier* 'seize' < Latin *captare* 'try to seize' < *capere* 'take'.] ◇ **cut to the chase** *US* to stop wasting time and get on with what needs to be dealt with (*informal*) ◇ **give chase** to pursue something or somebody forcefully (*formal*)

chase[2] /chayss/ *n* **1 PART OF GUN BARREL** the external part of a gun barrel just behind the muzzle **2 GROOVE** a channel, groove, or trench for something such as a pipe to lie in or fit into ■ *vt* (**chases, chasing, chased**) **1 CUT GROOVE IN** to cut or grind a channel, groove, or trench in something **2 CUT THREAD IN SCREW** to cut a metal screw thread with a machine tool (**chaser**) [Late 16C. Via French *châsse* < Latin *capsa* 'box'.]

chase[3] /chayss/ (**chases, chasing, chased**) *vt* to decorate metal or glass by engraving or embossing [15C. Shortening of ENCHASE.]

chase[4] /chayss/ *n* a rectangular frame into which metal type or blocks are fitted so that a page or plate can be printed or made [Early 17C. Via French *chas* 'enclosed space' < Latin *capsum* 'thorax, church nave'.]

chase plane *n* an aeroplane that follows another aircraft carrying an important person such as a head of state

chaser[1] /cháyssər/ *n* **1 SOMEBODY OR SOMETHING THAT CHASES** somebody or something that forcefully pursues another person or thing **2 DIFFERENT DRINK** a second drink, taken with or after one of a different kind, e.g. whisky taken after beer **3** HORSERACING = **steeplechaser 4 NAVAL CANNON** a cannon located at the bow or stern of a vessel and used in pursuing an enemy

chaser[2] /cháyssər/ *n* **1** an engraver or embosser of metal or glass **2** a machine tool for cutting screw threads

Chasid *n* JUDAISM = **Hasid**

chasm /kázzəm/ *n* **1 DEEP HOLE IN EARTH** a deep crack or hole in the ground **2 WIDE DIFFERENCE** a wide difference in feelings, ideas, or interests **3 GAP OR BREAK** a gap or break in the progress or continuity of something [Late 16C. Via Latin *chasma* < Greek *khasma* 'gulf'.]

chassé /shá say/ *n* a gliding step, especially in ballet or square dancing [Early 19C. < French, 'chased'.]

chasseur /sha súr/ *adj* cooked in a rich white-wine and mushroom sauce ■ *n* a soldier in a French special unit equipped and trained for rapid deployment [Mid-18C. < French, 'hunter'.]

Chassid *n* JUDAISM = **Hasid**

chassis /shássi/ (*plural* **-sis** /-siz/) *n* **1 MAIN FRAME OF VEHICLE** the frame and wheels that support the engine and body of a motor vehicle or the frame and wheels of a carriage or wagon **2 MOUNTING FOR ELECTRONIC DEVICE** the mounting or supporting structure for the components of an electronic device, such as a television **3 AIRCRAFT LANDING GEAR** the landing gear of an aircraft **4 MOUNTING FOR GUN CARRIAGE** a frame on which a gun carriage can move back and forth [Mid-17C. < French *châssis* < Latin *capsa* 'box'.]

Chastain /chass táyn/, **Brandi** (*b.* 1968) US soccer player

chaste /chayst/ *adj* **1 ABSTAINING FROM SEX** abstaining from sex on moral grounds **2 SEXUALLY FAITHFUL** not having extramarital sexual relations **3 PURE IN THOUGHT AND DEED** behaving in a pure way, with no immoral thoughts **4 PLAIN** plain, simple, and unadorned in style [13C. Via French < Latin *castus* 'pure'.] —**chastely** *adv* —**chasteness** *n*

chasten /cháyss'n/ *vt* **1 MAKE SOMEBODY SUBDUED** to make somebody less self-satisfied or self-assertive and more subdued **2 DISCIPLINE** to subject somebody to discipline **3 MODERATE INTENSITY OF** to moderate the intensity of something [Early 16C. < obsolete *chaste* (see CHASTISE).] —**chastened** *adj* —**chastener** *n* —**chastening** *adj*

chaste tree *n* a small tree with aromatic hairy leaves and fragrant clusters of light purplish flowers. Native to: Europe, Asia. *Vitex agnus-castus.* [Translation of Latin *agnus castus* < *agnus* 'chaste tree' < Greek *agnos*, confused with *hagnos* 'chaste']

chastise /cha stíz/ (**-tises, -tising, -tised**) *vt* to punish or scold somebody [14C. < obsolete *chaste* 'rebuke', via Old French *chastier* < Latin *castigare* (see CASTIGATE).] —**chastisable** *adj* —**chastisement** *n* —**chastiser** *n*

chastity /chástəti/ *n* **1** the condition or practice of abstaining from sex on moral grounds **2** plainness or simplicity of style

chastity belt *n* a locking device passing round the waist and between the legs, used in medieval times to prevent a woman from having sexual intercourse

chasuble /cházyŏŏb'l/ *n* a loose sleeveless outer garment worn by a Christian priest when celebrating Mass or Holy Communion [13C. Via French < Latin *casula* 'hooded cloak' < *casa* 'house'.]

ϟ **chat** /chat/ *vi* (**chats, chatting, chatted**) **1 TALK INFORMALLY** to talk with somebody in a relaxed informal way **2 EXCHANGE MESSAGES BY COMPUTER** to exchange messages in real time with other computer users ■ *n* **1 INFORMAL TALK** a relaxed informal conversation with somebody **2 EXCHANGE OF MESSAGES BY COMPUTER** an informal exchange of messages in real time with other computer users **3 SONGBIRD** a small songbird related to the thrush with a harsh chattering cry. Subfamily: Turdinae. **4 AUSTRALIAN WREN** any of several wrens. Native to: Australia. Genus: *Ephthianura.* [15C. Shortening of CHATTER.]
chat up *vt* to talk to somebody flirtatiously or flatteringly (*informal*)

chateau /sháttō/ (*plural* **-teaux** /-tōz, -tō/ *or* **-teaus** /-tō, -tōz/), **château** (*plural* **-teaux** /-tō, -tōz/) *n* a castle or large house in France, often one that has a vineyard attached and gives its name to wine produced there [Mid-18C. Via French < Latin *castellum* (see CASTLE).]

Chateaubriand /shátōbri óN/ *n* a thick beefsteak cut from the widest middle part of the fillet [Late 19C. After François René, Vicomte de *Chateaubriand* (1768–1848), French writer and statesman.]

chatelain /sháttə layn/ *n* in former times, a man who owned or controlled a castle or other large house [15C. Via Old French *chastelain* < medieval Latin *castellanus* (see CASTELLAN).]

chatelaine /sháttə layn/ *n* **1** in former times, a woman who owned or controlled a castle or other large house **2** a chain and clasp formerly worn at the waist by a woman to hold keys and other small items [Mid-19C. < French *châtelaine*, feminine of *châtelain* (see CHATELAIN).]

ϟ **chat group** *n* a group of people who exchange messages online, especially people who share a common interest

Chatham /cháttəm/ town in SE England. Population: 71,691 (1991).

Chatham Islands group of islands in the SW Pacific Ocean forming part of New Zealand. Population: 739 (1996). Area: 963 sq. km/372 sq. mi.

chatline /chát līn/ *n* a telephone service allowing a number of people to phone the same number and have a conversation

chatoyant /shə tóy ənt/ *adj* having a changeable iridescent lustre ■ *n* a chatoyant gemstone, e.g. a cat's eye [Late 18C. < French, 'shining like a cat's eyes'.] —**chatoyancy** *n*

ϟ **chat room** *n* a facility in a computer network where participants exchange messages in real time

chat show *n* an informal TV or radio show in which the host interviews celebrities. US term **talk show**

Chattanooga /cháttə nóogə, chátt'n óogə/ port in SE Tennessee. Population: 147,790 (1998 estimate).

chattel /chátt'l/ *n* an item of personal property that is not freehold land and that is not intangible ■ **chattels** *npl* personal possessions (*formal*) [13C. Via Old French *chatel* 'property' < Latin *capitalis* (see CAPITAL[1]).]

chatter /cháttər/ *vi* **1 TALK RAPIDLY** to talk or converse rapidly and informally about unimportant things **2 MAKE HIGH-PITCHED SOUNDS** to make a rapid series of short high-pitched sounds that seem to resemble speech (*refers to animals or machinery*) **3 CLICK TOGETHER** to click together rapidly because of movement of the jaw caused by fear or cold (*refers to teeth*) **4 VIBRATE DURING CUTTING** to vibrate while cutting or being cut by a tool or machine, causing surface flaws (*refers to a sawblade or surface*) ■ *n* **1 TRIVIAL CONVERSATION** rapid and informal talk or conversation, especially about unimportant things **2 HIGH-PITCHED ANIMAL SOUNDS** rapid short high-pitched sounds made by a bird, animal, or machine, that resemble human speech **3 SURFACE FLAWS PRODUCED IN MACHINING** imperfections in a surface, caused by vibration while being cut by a tool or machine [13C. An imitation of the sound.]

chatterbox /cháttər boks/ *n* a chatterer (*informal*)

chatterer /cháttərər/ *n* a talkative person, especially on trivial subjects

chattering classes *npl* educated middle-class people, with an interest in current affairs and culture, who like to make their views known to each other (*disapproving*)

chatter mark *n* **1** a crack or groove on the surface of rock, caused by the abrasive action of a glacier on bedrock or by the collision of fragments in water **2** a mark left on something that has been machined, caused by vibration

Chatterton /cháttərtən/, **Thomas** (1752–70) British poet and journalist. Pseudonym **Thomas Rowley**

chatty /chátti/ (**-tier, -tiest**) *adj* **1** fond of chatting about unimportant things **2** friendly and informal in tone —**chattily** *adv* —**chattiness** *n*

SYNONYMS See ***talkative***.

chat-up line *n* a prepared phrase or topic that somebody uses when trying to initiate a romantic or sexual relationship (*informal*)

Chatwin /cháttwin/, **Bruce** (1940–89) British writer

Chaucer /cháwssər/, **Geoffrey** (1343?–1400) English poet —**Chaucerian** *n, adj*

Chaudhuri /chówdəri/, **Nirad Chandra** (1897–1999) Indian writer

chauffeur /shṓfər/ *n* somebody employed to drive a car ■ *vti* to drive somebody from place to place in a car, or be employed to drive a car for somebody [Late 19C. < French, 'stoker (of a steam car)' < *chauffer* 'to heat'.]

chaulmoogra /chawl moógrə/ *n* a tree with seeds that yield oil. Use: formerly, to treat leprosy. Native to: Southeast Asia. *Hydnocarpus kurzii*. [Early 19C. < Bengali *cāul-mugrā*.]

Chauvel /shṓ vel/, **Charles Edward** (1897–1959) Australian film-maker

chauvinism /shṓvənizəm/ *n* **1** unreasoning, overenthusiastic, or aggressive patriotism **2** an excessive or prejudiced loyalty to a particular gender, group, or cause [Late 19C. < French *chauvinisme*, after Nicolas *Chauvin*, character in the play *La cocarde tricolore* (1831) by the brothers Cogniard.]

chauvinist /shṓvənist/ *n* **1** somebody with an excessive or prejudiced loyalty to a particular gender, group, or cause **2** an unreasoning, overenthusiastic, and aggressive patriot —**chauvinistic** /shṓvə nístik/ *adj* —**chauvinistically** *adv*

Chávez /cha véz/, **César** (1927–93) US trade unionist

chayote /chī ṓti/ *n* **1** a pear-shaped, furrowed green or white gourd, cooked and eaten as a vegetable **2** a climbing plant of the gourd family that bears chayotes. Native to: tropical America. *Sechium edule*. [Late 19C. Via Spanish, < Nahuatl *chayotli*.]

chazan *n* JUDAISM = **hazzan**

ChB *abbr* Bachelor of Surgery [Latin, *Chirurgiae Baccalaureus*]

cheap /cheep/ *adj* **1 COSTING LITTLE** low in price or cost **2 CHARGING LITTLE** charging low prices but offering good value **3 POOR QUALITY** inexpensive and of poor quality **4 WORTH LITTLE** worth little or accorded little value ○ *In times of war, life is cheap.* **5 UNDESERVING OF RESPECT** not deserving of respect **6 UNFAIR** dishonourable, offensive, or unfair, especially in a way that seems obvious or calculated ○ *a cheap trick* **7** *US* **STINGY** stingy or unwilling to give freely [Old English *cēap* 'trade' < Latin *caupo* 'innkeeper'] —**cheap** *adv* —**cheapish** *adj* —**cheaply** *adv* —**cheapness** *n* ◇ **on the cheap** at very low cost (*informal*)

SPELLCHECK Do not confuse ***cheap*** with ***cheep***, which has a similar sound. Beware: your spellchecker will not catch this error.

cheapen /cheépən/ *vti* **1** to make something less expensive, or become less expensive, especially in order to save money or increase profits, rather than to give better value **2** to lower the quality or reputation of somebody or something, or become lower in quality or reputation

cheapie /cheépi/, **cheapy** (*plural* **-ies**) *n US* (*informal*) **1** something that is cheap **2** a mean or ungenerous person

cheapjack /cheép jak/ *n* a seller of inferior goods ■ *adj* inferior in value or quality [< the name *Jack*]

cheapo /cheépō/ *adj* cheap in price or cost (*informal*)

cheapskate /cheép skayt/ *n* a mean or ungenerous person (*informal*)

cheapy *n* = **cheapie**

cheat /cheet/ *v* **1** *vt* **DECEIVE** to deceive or mislead somebody, especially for personal advantage **2** *vi* **BREAK RULES TO GAIN ADVANTAGE** to break the rules in a game, examination, or contest, in an attempt to gain an unfair advantage **3** *vi* **BE UNFAITHFUL** to have a sexual relationship with somebody other than a spouse or regular sexual partner **4** *vt* **ESCAPE** to avoid harm or injury by luck or cunning ■ *n* **1 DECEITFUL PERSON** a deceiver who uses trickery to gain an unfair advantage **2 DISHONEST TRICK** a dishonest or unfair trick **3 DISHONESTLY OBTAINING PROPERTY** the obtaining of somebody else's property by dishonest means **4** *US* PLANTS = **chess**³ *n*. [14C. Shortening of ESCHEAT.] —**cheater** *n*

Chechen /ché chen/ *n* **1** somebody who comes from Chechnya **2** the main language in Chechnya, belonging to the Nakh group of North Caucasian languages. Native speakers: 1 million. —**Chechen** *adj*

Chechnya /chéchni ə/ republic in SW Russia. Capital: Grozny. Population: 1,500,000 (1994). Area: 15,000 sq. km/5,800 sq. mi.

check /chek/ *v* **1** *vti* **EXAMINE** to examine something in order to establish its state or condition ○ *Check the doors and windows to make sure they're locked.* **2** *vti* **CONFIRM TRUTH OR ACCURACY OF** to confirm or establish that something is true or accurate ○ *We need to check with the insurance company to find out whether we're covered.* **3** *vi* **BE CONSISTENT WITH** to be the same as or consistent with something else ○ *What you're telling me now doesn't check with what you told me last week.* **4** *vt* **HALT OR SLOW** to stop or reduce the progress of some unwelcome process **5** *vti* **STOP SUDDENLY** to stop or pause suddenly, or make somebody or something stop suddenly ○ *In mid-sentence, he checked himself abruptly, looking terribly embarrassed.* **6** *vt* **PREVENT SOMETHING BEING EXPRESSED** to prevent or inhibit something from being expressed ○ *Checking the urge to laugh out loud, I buried my head in the newspaper.* **7** *vt* **REPRIMAND** to criticize somebody for a fault or bad behaviour **8** *vt* **BLOCK OPPONENT** in sports such as ice hockey, to move directly into the path of an opponent, usually making physical contact, in order to block his or her progress **9** *vt* = **tick**¹ *v*. 3 **10** *vt US* **HAND OVER BAGGAGE** to hand over something, especially baggage, so that it can be transported separately from passengers, usually in the same aircraft or vehicle ○ *You must check your luggage before boarding.* **11** *vt US* **HAND OVER FOR TEMPORARY KEEPING** to hand over something such as a coat in a restaurant or museum, so that it can be looked after until you need it again ○ *Do you want to check your coat?* **12** *vt* **PUT OPPONENT'S KING IN JEOPARDY** in chess, to put an opponent's king in a situation in which one of your pieces directly threatens it ■ *n* **1 EXAMINATION** an examination or investigation of something, especially to verify its state or condition ○ *Routine checks should have revealed the cracks in the engine housing.* **2 SOMETHING THAT TESTS ACCURACY** something that can be used or referred to in order to test the accuracy, truth, or safety of something else **3 MEANS OF CONTROLLING OR RESTRAINING** a means of controlling or restraining somebody or something ○ *a check on the dog's aggressive tendencies* **4** *US* FIN = **cheque** **5** *US* **RESTAURANT BILL** the bill in a restaurant or bar **6** *US* **NUMBERED TICKET FOR DEPOSITED ITEM** a numbered ticket or token given out when an item is left at a cloakroom **7** *US* = **tick**¹ *n*. 3 **8 PATTERN OF SQUARES** a pattern made up entirely of squares in at least two different colours that are arranged alternately **9 SQUARE IN CHECK PATTERN** a square in a pattern, in which at least two different colours are arranged alternately ○ *Every third check is red.* **10 MOVE ATTACKING KING** a move in chess by which a piece directly threatens the opposing king, or the position resulting from this move ○ *If you move your king there, you'll be in check.* **11 BLOCKING MOVE** in sports, a move directly into the path of an attacking opponent ■ *adj* = **checked** ■ *interj* **WARNING THAT KING IS IN CHECK** in chess, used to announce that an opponent's king is in check [14C. < Old French *eschec* 'check in chess' < Persian *šāh* 'king' (see SHAH).] —**checkable** *adj* ◇ **checks and balances** features in the way a system operates that prevent any one person or group from having too much power or influence ◇ **in check** restrained and under control ○ *managing to keep her anger in check*

check in *v* **1** *vti* **REGISTER AT HOTEL** to register as a guest, or register a guest, on arrival at a hotel ○ *Has my colleague checked in yet?* **2** *vti* **ARRIVE FOR JOURNEY** to register and go through the necessary formalities before beginning a journey, especially by air ○ *All passengers should check in at least one hour before departure.* **3** *vi* **MAKE CONTACT** to make routine contact with a person or organization to exchange information ○ *The patrols are supposed to check in by radio at half-hourly intervals.*

check into *vt* to investigate something in order to get more information about it or to establish its truth or accuracy ○ *When we checked into his background, we found that he had several convictions for fraud.*

check off *vt US* = **tick off** *v*. 1

check out *v* **1** *vi* **LEAVE HOTEL** to pay the bill and leave a hotel or other place ○ *We'll be checking out later this morning.* **2** *vi US* **LEAVE** to leave a particular place or a person (*informal*) **3** *vt* **INVESTIGATE** to establish that something is correct or valid ○ *The date is probably 1961. Check it out, will you?* **4** *vt* **TAKE A LOOK AT** to visit a place briefly to get information about it (*informal*) ○ *Let's check out the new pizza place down the High Street.* **5** *vi* **BE PROVED TRUE** to prove after investigation to be correct or valid ○ *If the DNA checks out, he's our man.* **6** *vti US* **PAY IN SUPERMARKET** to pay for something in a supermarket ○ *When I went to check out, I realized I'd left my purse in the car.* **7** *vt US* **TAKE MONEY FOR GOODS AT SUPERMARKET** to calculate and take payment from a customer in a supermarket ○ *This person's in a hurry, so do you mind if I check her out first?*

check over *vt* **1** to examine something to make sure that it is correct or satisfactory ○ *Could you check over my essay to make sure there are no errors, please?* **2** to examine somebody carefully to establish his or her state of health ○ *I've checked her over, and there are no broken bones.*

check through *vt* to examine or review systematically all the parts of something to make sure that it is satisfactory

check up *vi* to make enquiries to establish a point ○ *I checked up: no one of that name lives at that address.*

checkbook *n US* = **chequebook**

⚡**check box** *n* a small square on a computer screen that, when clicked on with a mouse, displays a small cross or tick to show that an item has been selected

check dam *n* a dam, usually a small one, that interrupts the flow of a stream and builds up a store of water behind itself

⚡**check digit** *n* in computing, a digit derived from and added to the other digits in a sequence, used to ensure that the sequence is correct

checked /chekt/ *adj* with a pattern of small squares ○ *a red-and-white checked tablecloth*

checker /chékər/ *n* **1** somebody who checks something **2** *US* a cashier in a supermarket or large store **3** *US* = **draught** *n*. 7

checkerberry /chékər beri/ (*plural* **-ries**) *n* **1** a low-growing evergreen bush with red berries and fragrant leathery leaves from which an oil (**oil of wintergreen**) is distilled. Native to: E North America. *Gaultheria procumbens*. **2** the edible, red, spicy-flavoured fruit of the checkerberry

checkerboard /chékərbawrd/ *n US* BOARD GAMES = **draughtboard**

checkers /chékərz/ *n US* BOARD GAMES = **draughts**

check-in *n* **1 REGISTRATION AT HOTEL OR AIRPORT** the process of registering on arrival at a hotel or airport **2 REGISTRATION DESK** a place where people check in at a hotel or airport **3** *US* **SOMEBODY CHECKING IN** a traveller who checks in at a facility, e.g. at an airport or hotel ○ *Since the flight was overbooked, the five late check-ins had to wait.*

checking account *n US* BANKING = **current account**

checklist /chék list/ *n* a list of names, items, or points for consideration or action

checkmate /chék mayt/ *n* **1 WINNING POSITION IN CHESS** a move or position in chess, in which a player's king cannot escape check and the other player wins the game **2 MOVE THAT PRODUCES CHECKMATE** a move in chess that produces checkmate, or a game that ends in checkmate ○ *The series was declared a draw with three checkmates apiece.* **3 COMPLETE DEFEAT** a situation of defeat or deadlock ■ *vt* (**-mates, -mating, -mated**) **1 PUT KING IN CHECKMATE** in chess, to put an opponent's king in checkmate **2 THWART** to make it impossible for somebody to succeed or proceed further ■ *interj* **ANNOUNCEMENT OF CHECKMATE** used in chess to announce that an opponent's king is in checkmate [15C. Via Old French *eschec mat* < Persian *šāh māt* 'the king is dead'.]

checkout /chék owt/ *n* **1 SUPERMARKET TILL** a point in a supermarket at which shoppers pay for their purchases ○ *Only three checkouts were open.* **2 DEPARTURE FROM HOTEL** the procedure involved in paying a hotel bill and leaving ○ *We'd like to arrange for a later checkout.* **3** *US* **SOMEBODY CHECKING OUT** a traveller checking out at a facility, e.g. at an airport or a hotel ○ *Apart from a couple of late checkouts, everyone seemed to be ready.*

checkpoint /chék poynt/ *n* a place where police or other officials stop and check vehicles

Checkpoint Charlie *n* a border crossing between East and West Berlin during the Cold War

checkrail /chék rayl/ *n* RAIL = **guardrail** *n.* **2**

checkrein /chék rayn/ *n* **1** *US* RIDING = **bearing rein 2** a rein used when driving a pair of horses, connecting the driving rein of one horse to the mouthpiece of the other

checkroom /chék room, -ro͝om/ *n US* a room in a public building, e.g. a theatre, restaurant, train or bus station where customers can leave belongings

ϟ **checksum** /chék sum/ *n* a value transmitted with a data stream, derived from the other elements in the data stream and used to check for transmission errors in the data

checkup /chék up/, **check-up** *n* a routine examination or inspection, especially one carried out by a doctor or dentist ○ *Regular checkups are required for all pilots.*

check valve *n* a valve designed to allow liquids to flow in one direction only

chedarim plural of **cheder**

cheddar /chéddər/ *n* a hard pale yellow or orange-red cheese with a flavour that ranges from mild to very strong [Mid-17C. After CHEDDAR.]

Cheddar /chéddər/ village in SW England. Population: 4,484 (1991).

Cheddar Gorge deep gorge in SW England, known for its steep limestone cliffs and caves. Height: 137 m/450 ft (cliffs).

cheder /káydər/ (*plural* **-arim** /ke daárim/ *or* **-ers**) *n* classes in Hebrew language and religious knowledge for younger Jewish children [Late 19C. < Hebrew *ḥēḏer* 'room'.]

cheek /cheek/ *n* **1 SOFT PART OF FACE** the soft side area of the face between the nose and ear **2 BUTTOCK** either side of the buttocks (*informal*) **3 BAD MANNERS** impertinent or precocious words or behaviour showing, or appearing to show, disregard for good manners or the feelings of others (*informal*) ○ *He had the cheek to ask me for a lift!* ■ *vt* **SPEAK DISRESPECTFULLY TO** to speak disrespectfully or rudely to somebody (*informal*) [Old English *cēoce* < W Germanic] ◇ **cheek by jowl** side by side or very close together ○ *living cheek by jowl in a tiny unheated flat* ◇ **turn the other cheek** to accept injury or insults without resisting or retaliating

cheekbone /cheék bōn/ *n* an arch of bone in the face, below the eyes and above the cheeks

cheekpiece /cheék peess/ *n* either of the two straps on a bridle that lie along the cheeks of a horse and join the bit to the crownpiece

cheek tooth *n* a premolar or molar of a mammal or any one of the teeth behind the canines

cheeky /cheéki/ (**-ier, -iest**) *adj* **1** insolently or playfully rude or disrespectful **2** amusing or endearing despite offending good manners, especially by being mildly sexually improper (*informal*) ○ *The stories are performed by a raconteur with warmth and a cheeky charm.* —**cheekily** *adv* —**cheekiness** *n*

cheep /cheep/ *n* the high shrill sound made by a young bird [Early 16C. An imitation of the sound.] —**cheep** *vi*

SPELLCHECK See ***cheap***.

cheer /cheer/ *n* **1 SHOUT OF APPROVAL** a shout that expresses happiness, excitement, encouragement, or praise ○ *A huge cheer went up as the band walked onto the stage.* **2 WELL-BEING AND OPTIMISM** a sense of general well-being and optimism ○ *The latest sales figures will bring little cheer.* ■ *v* **1** *vti* **SHOUT ENCOURAGEMENT OR SUPPORT** to shout encouragement, support, or appreciation, especially to people who are performing or competing **2** *vt* **MAKE SOMEBODY FEEL CHEERFUL** to make somebody feel more cheerful, confident, or optimistic (*often passive*) ○ *very cheering news* [13C. Via Anglo-Norman *chere* 'face' < Latin *cara* < Greek *kara* 'head'.] —**cheerer** *n* —**cheeringly** *adv*

cheer on *vt* to give active or vocal support, especially at a sports event ○ *We went to cheer our team on in the championships.*

cheer up *vti* **1** to become, or make somebody feel, less sad ○ *She cheered up a little when I suggested lunch.* **2** to become, or make something, brighter or more attractive and welcoming in appearance ○ *A coat of bright yellow paint will cheer up the dingiest of kitchens.*

cheerful /cheérf'l/ *adj* **1 HAPPY AND OPTIMISTIC** in a happy and optimistic mood, or happy and optimistic by nature ○ *She remained her usual cheerful self despite recent setbacks.* **2 BRIGHT AND PLEASANT** causing people to feel cheerful ○ *a cheerful light blue* **3 WILLING AND UNRESENTFUL** showing willingness or good humour in complying ○ *They set to work cleaning up the mess with cheerful determination.* —**cheerfully** *adv* —**cheerfulness** *n*

cheerio /cheéri ṓ/ *interj* **1** used to say goodbye (*informal*) **2** a word used to express good wishes when drinking (*dated informal*) [Early 20C. Alteration of CHEER.]

cheerleader /cheér leedər/ *n* **1** a uniformed performer in a group that encourages the crowd to support a team at sports events in the United States and other places **2** an uncritically enthusiastic supporter (*disapproving*)

cheerless /cheérləss/ *adj* lacking anything bright, pleasant, or encouraging ○ *a gloomy cheerless day* —**cheerlessly** *adv* —**cheerlessness** *n*

cheers /cheerz/ *interj* **1 GOOD HEALTH** used to express good wishes just before drinking an alcoholic drink (*informal*) **2 GOODBYE** goodbye or farewell **3 THANKS** thank you ○ *Cheers, you've been a big help!*

cheery /cheéri/ (**-ier, -iest**) *adj* happy or in good spirits —**cheerily** *adv* —**cheeriness** *n*

cheese /cheez/ *n* **1** a food made from the pressed curds of the milk of cows, sheep, goats, and some other animals, that can range from hard to semisoft, and from mildly acidic to sharp **2** an individual block of cheese [Old English *cēse* < Germanic, < Latin *caseus*]

cheeseburger /cheéz burgər/ *n* a hamburger covered with melted cheese, served in a roll

cheesecake /cheéz kayk/ *n* **1** a dessert consisting of a layer of sweetened soft cheese mixed with cream and eggs on a biscuit or pastry base **2** photographs of women that highlight their physical appearance, especially in a stereotypical way (*slang*) ◊ **beefcake**

cheesecloth /cheéz kloth/ *n* a light woven cotton material. Use: lightweight clothes, originally, to wrap or strain cheese.

cheese cutter *n* a board to which a piece of wire is attached for cutting cheese

cheesed off /cheézd-/ *adj* feeling annoyed, bored, or frustrated with somebody (*informal*)

cheesemonger /cheéz mung gər/ *n* a supplier of cheese and other dairy products

cheeseparing /cheéz pairing/ *adj* reluctant to spend money [Originally 'a paring of cheese rind', something only the most miserly would save] —**cheeseparing** *n*

cheese powder *n Hong Kong* grated Parmesan cheese, used especially on pasta dishes and soups (*informal*)

cheese straw *n* a long thin biscuit of cheese-flavoured pastry, served as a snack

cheesy /cheézi/ (**-ier, -iest**) *adj* **1** having the flavour or smell of cheese **2** cheap and tawdry (*informal*)

cheetah /cheétə/ (*plural* **-tahs** *or* **-tah**) *n* a large member of the cat family with a yellowish-brown, black-spotted coat, small head, slender body, and long legs that is the fastest land mammal. Native to: Africa, SW Asia. *Acinonyx jubatus.* [Late 18C. Via Hindi *cītā* < Sanskrit *citraka* 'leopard, tiger', literally 'spotted' < *citra-*.]

Cheever /cheévər/, **John** (1912–82) US writer

chef /shef/ *n* a professional cook, especially the principal cook in a hotel or restaurant [Early 19C. < French, shortening of *chef de cuisine* 'head of the kitchen'.]

chef-d'oeuvre /sháy dúrvrə/ (*plural* **chefs-d'oeuvre**) *n* a masterpiece, especially one produced by a musician, writer, or artist ○ *He regarded that particular speech as his chef-d'oeuvre.* [< French, 'chief piece of work']

chef's salad *n US* a tossed green salad with added tomatoes, sliced hard-boiled eggs, and thin strips of meat and cheese

~~**cheif**~~ incorrect spelling of **chief**

Chekhov /chék of/, **Anton Pavlovich** (1860–1904) Russian writer —**Chekhovian** /che kṓvi ən/ *n, adj*

Chekiang /che ki áng/ ◊ **Zhejiang**

chela[1] /keélə/ (*plural* **-lae** /-lee/) *n* the opposable end joint that forms a claw on a limb of a lobster, crab, scorpion, or similar animal (**arthropod**) [Mid-17C. Via modern Latin < Greek *khēlē* 'claw'.]

chela[2] /cháylə/ *n* the pupil or disciple of a Hindu religious teacher [Mid-19C. < Hindi *celā*.]

chelate[1] /kee layt/ *n* **COMPOUND OF METAL AND NONMETAL** a chemical compound in which metallic and nonmetallic, usually organic, atoms are combined ■ *v* (**-lates, -lating, -lated**) **1** *vti* **COMBINE TO FORM CHELATE** to combine, or combine something, with a metal to form a chelate **2** *vt* **TREAT SOMEBODY WITH CHELATING AGENT** to treat somebody with a chelating agent in order to remove a heavy metal such as lead from the bloodstream —**chelatable** *adj* —**chelate** *adj* —**chelation** *n* —**chelator** *n*

chelate[2] /kee layt/ *adj* having or shaped like chelae

chelating agent /kee láyting-/ *n* a chemical that combines with a metal to form a chelate. Use: treatment of metal poisoning.

chelicera /kə líssərə/ (*plural* **-ae** /-rī/) *n* either of the first mouthparts of horseshoe crabs and spiders, resembling fangs or pincers and used to grab or poison prey [Mid-19C. < modern Latin, < *chela* (see CHELA[1]) + Greek *keras* 'horn'.]

chelicerate /kə líssərət/ *n* an invertebrate with feeding appendages shaped like pincers, e.g. a spider or crab. Phylum: Chelicerata. [Early 20C. < modern Latin *chelicerata* < *chelicera* (see CHELICERA).] —**chelicerate** *adj*

Chelmsford /chélmzfərd/ town in SE England. Population: 152,418 (1991).

chelonian /ki lṓni ən/ *n* a reptile, e.g. a turtle or tortoise, that has most of its body enclosed in a hard bony shell. Order: Chelonia. [Early 19C. < modern Latin *Chelonia* < Greek *khelōnē* 'tortoise'.]

Chelsea /chélssi/ former borough of west-central London

Chelsea bun *n* a flat coil-shaped bun, made from yeasted dough, containing currants and sometimes sprinkled with sugar [Early 18C. After *Chelsea*, London.]

Chelsea pensioner *n* a retired soldier who is an inmate of the Chelsea Royal Hospital in London

Cheltenham /chélt'nəm/ town in west-central England. Population: 91,301 (1991).

Chelyabinsk /chel yaábinsk/ city in W Russia. Population: 1,393,608 (1995).

chem. *abbr* **1** chemical **2** chemist **3** chemistry

chem- *prefix* = **chemo-**

chemi- *prefix* = **chemo-**

chemical /kémmik'l/ *adj* **1 RELATING TO CHEMISTRY** produced by or involved in the processes of chemistry **2 COMPOSED OF CHEMICAL SUBSTANCES** composed of or involving the use of substances produced by the process of chemistry ■ *n* **SUBSTANCE USED OR MADE BY CHEMISTRY** a substance used in or produced by the processes of chemistry that has a defined atomic or molecular structure that results from, or takes part in, reactions involving changes in its structure, composition, and properties [Late 16C. < modern Latin *chimicus* 'alchemist', shortening of medieval Latin *alchimicus* < *alchimia* (see ALCHEMY).] —**chemically** *adv*

chemical bond *n* a force resulting from the redistribution of energy contained by orbiting electrons, which tends to bind atoms together to form molecules

chemical dependency *n* addiction to a chemical substance or drug

chemical energy *n* the energy released or absorbed in a chemical reaction during the decomposition or formation of compounds

chemical engineering *n* a branch of engineering that deals with the industrial applications of chemistry and chemical processes —**chemical engineer** *n*

chemical equation *n* a representation, using chemical symbols in a form resembling a mathematical equation, of the process involved in a chemical reaction

chemical free adj US not addicted to drugs or refraining from the use of drugs (informal)

chemical reaction n a process that changes the molecular composition of a substance by redistributing atoms or groups of atoms without altering the structure of the nuclei of the atoms

chemical toilet n a portable toilet containing chemicals to neutralize human waste

chemical warfare n military operations involving the use of weapons containing substances such as nerve gas or poison

chemical weapon n a weapon containing a substance such as nerve gas or poison

chemical weathering n the weathering of a rock surface through chemical processes such as oxidation, solution, and hydrolysis

chemiluminescence /kémmi loŏmi néss'nss/ n emission of light as a result of a chemical reaction, without producing heat —**chemiluminescent** adj

chemin de fer /shə máN də fáir/ n a gambling card game, similar to and derived from baccarat [< French, 'railway'; from the speed at which it is played]

cheminea /chémmi náy ə/ n a large rounded pot with a chimney and an opening in its side, used as a charcoal-burning stove for outdoor heating on patios and at barbecues [< Spanish, 'fireplace']

chemise /shə meéz/ n 1 a long loose dress, sometimes loosely belted at the waist or hip 2 a long loose undergarment shaped like a dress [13C. Via Old French, < late Latin camisia 'shirt'.]

chemisorb /kémmi sawrb/, **chemosorb** /keémō-/ vt to take up a substance by chemisorption [Mid-20C. Back-formation < CHEMISORPTION.]

chemisorption /kémmi sáwrpsh'n/ n the process of coating the surface of a substance rather than being absorbed by it, accompanied by chemical bonding between the surface of the material and the adsorbed substance [Mid-20C. Blend of CHEMI- + ADSORPTION.] —**chemisorptive** adj

chemist /kémmist/ n 1 a shop where medicines, toiletries, and cosmetics are sold, and where prescriptions are dispensed. US term **drugstore** 2 MED = **pharmacist** 3 a scientist who works in the field of chemistry [Mid-16C. Via French chimiste < modern Latin chimista, shortening of medieval Latin alchimista 'alchemist' < alchimia (see ALCHEMY).]

chemistry /kémmistri/ n 1 STUDY OF TRANSFORMATION OF MATTER a branch of science dealing with the structure, composition, properties, and reactive characteristics of substances, especially at the atomic and molecular levels. ◊ **inorganic chemistry, organic chemistry, physical chemistry** 2 CHEMICAL PROPERTIES the chemical composition, structure, and properties of a substance, or the chemical aspects of an activity ○ the chemistry of wine-making 3 REACTION BETWEEN TWO PEOPLE the spontaneous reaction of individuals to each other, especially a mutual sense of attraction or understanding

Chemnitz /kémnits/ n city in east-central Germany. Population: 278,700 (1994).

chemo /keémō/ n chemotherapy (informal) [Mid-20C. Shortening.]

chemo- prefix chemical, chemistry ○ chemoreceptor [< CHEMICAL]

chemoautotroph /keémō áwtətrōf/ n an organism that obtains energy through the oxidation of an inorganic substance, rather than through photosynthesis, e.g. bacteria —**chemoautotrophic** /keémō awtə trófik, -tróffik/ adj

chemokinesis /keémō ki neéssiss, -kī-/ n increased activity of cells or organisms caused by the presence of a chemical agent

chemolithotroph /keémō líthə trōf, -trof/ n a bacterium that obtains its energy from inorganic compounds containing iron, nitrogen, or sulphur, and not from living on decaying organisms —**chemolithotrophic** /keémō líthə trófik, -tróffik/ adj

chemoprophylaxis /keémō profə láksiss/ n the use of chemical agents to prevent disease —**chemoprophylactic** adj

chemoreception /keémō ri sépsh'n/ n the physiological response of an organism or sense organ to a chemical stimulus —**chemoreceptive** adj —**chemoreceptivity** /keémō ree sep tívvəti/ n

chemoreceptor /keémō ri séptər/ n a sense organ, e.g. a taste bud, that responds to a chemical stimulus

chemosensory /keémō sénssəri/ adj involved in or relating to the perception of chemical agents, especially in the sense of smell

chemosorb vt = chemisorb

chemosphere /keémō sfeer, kémmō-/ n a variable region of the atmosphere, approximately 30 to 190 km/20 to 120 mi. above the Earth's surface, where photochemical reactions take place —**chemospheric** /keémō sférrik, kémmō-/ adj

chemostat /keémō stat/ n an apparatus designed to permit the growth of bacterial cultures at controlled rates

chemosurgery /keémō surjəri/ n surgical removal of dead or diseased tissue by chemical means —**chemosurgical** adj

chemosynthesis /keémō sínthəssiss/ n the synthesis of organic molecules by microorganisms using energy derived from chemical reactions —**chemosynthetic** /keémōsin théttik/ adj —**chemosynthetically** adv

chemotaxis /keémō táksiss/ n movement or change in the position of a cell or organism in response to the presence of a chemical agent —**chemotactic** adj —**chemotactically** adv

chemotaxonomy /keémō tak sónnəmi/ n the classification of plants and microorganisms based on their biochemistry —**chemotaxonomic** /keémō taksə nómmik/ adj —**chemotaxonomically** adv —**chemotaxonomist** n

chemotherapy /keémō thérrəpi/ (plural -pies) n the use of chemical agents to treat diseases, infections, or other disorders, especially cancer —**chemotherapeutic** /keémō thérrə pyoótik/ adj —**chemotherapeutically** adv —**chemotherapist** n

chemotropism /kémmō trōpizəm/ n the movement or growth of an organism or part of an organism in response to a chemical stimulus —**chemotropic** /kémmō tróppik/ adj —**chemotropically** adv

Chemulpo /chemool pô/ former name for Inchon

chemurgy /kémmurji/ n US a branch of applied chemistry dealing with the industrial application of organic substances, especially of agricultural origin [Mid-20C. < CHEMICAL.] —**chemurgic** /kem úrjik/ adj —**chemurgical** adj

chemzyme /kém zīm/ n a substance that acts like an enzyme to increase the effectiveness of a drug [Late 20C. Blend of CHEMO- + ENZYME.]

Chen /chen/ n a Chinese dynasty that ruled from AD 557 to 589

Chenab /chi náb/, **Chenāb** river in NW India and E Pakistan. Length: 960 km/600 mi.

Cheney /cháyni/, **Dick** (b. 1941) US statesman and vice president of the United States (2001-)

Chengde /chúng dú/, **Ch'eng-te** city in NE China. Population: 246,799 (1991).

Chengdu /chéng doó/ capital of Sichuan Province, south-central China. Population: 3,347,433 (1991).

Ch'eng-te = Chengde

chenille /shə neél/ n 1 a soft thick cotton or silk fabric with a raised pile. Use: furnishings, clothes. 2 a thick silk, cotton, or worsted cord or yarn. Use: embroidery, fringes, trimmings. [Mid-18C. Via French, 'hairy caterpillar' < Latin canicula 'little dog' < canis 'dog'.]

Chenin Blanc /shə naN blaàN/ n a variety of white grape used for making light dry wine, especially in the Loire region of France and in South Africa [< French]

Chennai /cha nī́/ capital of Tamil Nadu State, SE India. Population: 3,841,396 (1991).

cheongsam /chong sám/ n a straight dress with a small stand-up collar and a slit in the skirt, worn by Chinese women [Mid-20C. < Chinese (Cantonese), 'long gown'.]

Chepstow /chépstō/ n town in S Wales. Population: 9,461 (1991).

cheque /chek/ n a small printed form that, when filled in and signed, instructs a bank to pay a specified sum of money to the person named on it. US term **check** n. 4 [Early 18C. Variant of CHECK.]

chequebook /chékbŏok/ n a book of detachable cheques

chequebook journalism n the payment of large sums of money to secure exclusive rights to a newspaper story

cheque card, **cheque guarantee card** n UK a small plastic card issued by a bank to a customer that guarantees the customer's cheques up to a specified limit

chequer /chéka/ n 1 = check n. 8, check n. 9 2 PIECE USED IN CHINESE CHEQUERS a peg, marble, or other piece used in the game of Chinese chequers ■ vt 1 MARK SOMETHING WITH CHEQUER PATTERN to mark something with a chequer pattern or with alternating areas of light and shade 2 DISRUPT CONTINUOUS SUCCESS OF to affect something adversely from time to time ○ regrettable incidents that will chequer his career [12C. Shortening of EXCHEQUER, which originally denoted the checked chessboard in English.]

chequered /chékərd/ adj 1 = **checked** 2 uneven or inconsistent, and characterized by periods of trouble or controversy as well as periods of success

chequered flag n a flag patterned with black and white squares that is waved as each participant in a motor race crosses the finishing line

Chequers /chékərz/ n a country house in Buckinghamshire that is the official country residence of the prime minister

Cher /shair/ (b. 1946) US entertainer. Full name **Cherilyn LaPierre**

Cherbourg /sháir boorg/ port on the English Channel in NW France. Population: 25,370 (1999).

Cheremis /chérrəmiss/ n LANG, PEOPLES = **Mari** —**Cheremis** adj

Cherenkov effect n PHYS = Cerenkov effect

Cherenkov radiation n PHYS = Cerenkov radiation

cherimoya /chérri móyə/ (plural -as or -a) n 1 a heart-shaped fruit with green skin that turns purple-black when ripe and has creamy-white scented flesh 2 a tropical American tree that bears cherimoyas. Annona cherimola. [Mid-18C. Via Spanish < Quechua chirimuya < chiri 'cold' + muya 'circle'.]

cherish /chérrish/ vt 1 LOVE AND CARE FOR to feel or show great love or care for somebody ○ He cherishes that girl. 2 VALUE HIGHLY to value something highly, e.g. a right, freedom, or privilege ○ I cherish my independence. 3 RETAIN IN MIND to retain a memory or wish in the mind as a source of pleasure or as an ambition [14C. < French chériss-, stem of chérir 'hold dear' < cher 'dear' < Latin carus.] —**cherishable** adj —**cherisher** n —**cherishingly** adv

Chernenko /chur nyéngkō/, **Konstantin** (1911–85) Soviet statesman and President of the Soviet Union (1984–85)

Chernobyl /chər nŏb'l, -nóbb'l/ n the site of a nuclear power plant near Kiev, in Ukraine, where there was a catastrophic accident in 1986

chernozem /chúrnə zem/ n fertile black or brown topsoil that is rich in humus and can support crops for long periods of time without the addition of fertilizers [Mid-19C. < Russian, 'black earth'.] —**chernozemic** /chúrnə zémmik/ adj

Cherokee /chérrə kee/ (plural -kee or -kees) n 1 a member of a Native North American people who once lived in the SE United States and now live mainly in Oklahoma and North Carolina 2 the Iroquoian language of the Cherokee. Native speakers: 10,000. [Late 17C. < obsolete Cherokee tsaraki.] —**Cherokee** adj

cheroot /shə roöt/ n a cigar with two square-cut ends [Late 17C. Via French cheroute < Tamil curuṭṭu 'roll of tobacco'.]

cherry /chérri/ n (plural -ries) 1 SMALL ROUND FRUIT a small round fruit that has a single hard stone and varies in colour from bright red or yellow to dark purplish-black 2 FRUIT TREE a tree that bears cherries. Genus: Prunus. 3 WOOD OF CHERRY TREE the wood of the cherry tree. Use: furniture-making, musical instruments. 4 TABOO TERM a highly offensive term for somebody's virginity, or the hymen as a symbol of a woman's virginity (taboo) ■ adj = **cherry red** [14C. Via Old French cherise (taken as plural) < medieval Latin ceresia < Greek kerasos 'cherry tree'.]

cherry bomb n US a powerful round red firecracker that explodes with a loud bang

cherry laurel n an evergreen shrub with white flowers and shiny leaves. Native to: Europe, Asia. Prunus laurocerasus.

cherry-pick vti to select only the most lucrative or profitable opportunities, especially in business

cherry picker n a mobile crane with an enclosed platform that can be raised to allow somebody to work off the ground, e.g. on an overhead street light or cable

cherry plum *n* a plum tree that produces red or yellow fruit resembling cherries. *Prunus cerasifera.*

cherry red *adj* of a deep vivid pinkish-red colour — **cherry red** *n*

cherrystone /chérri stōn/ *n* a half-grown quahog clam

cherry tomato *n* a small tomato with a strong sweet flavour. *Lycopersicon esculentum.* [< its size and sweetness]

cherrywood /chérriwòod/ *n* INDUST = **cherry** *n.* 3

chersonese /kúrssə neèss/ *n* a peninsula (*archaic*) [Early 17C. Via Latin *chersonesus* < Greek *khersonēsos* < *khersos* 'dry land' + *nēsos* 'island'.]

chert /churt/ *n* a brittle microcrystalline quartz. Source: sedimentary rocks. [Late 17C. < ?] —**cherty** /chúrti/ *adj*

cherub /chérrəb/ *n* 1 (*plural* **-ubim** *or* **-ubs**) ANGEL OF SECOND ORDER an angel, specifically one belonging to the second order of angels in the celestial hierarchy whose distinctive attribute is knowledge 2 DEPICTION OF ANGEL an angel depicted as a chubby-faced child with wings, sometimes simply as a child's head above a pair of wings 3 WELL-BEHAVED CHILD a child whose behaviour, disposition, or appearance is attractively innocent and well-behaved [Pre-12C. Via Latin *cherub*, Greek *kheroub* < Hebrew *kĕrūb*, probably < Akkadian; confused with Aramaic *kĕ-rabyā* 'like a child'.] —**cherubic** /chə róobik/ *adj* —**cherubically** *adv*

Cherubini /kérroo beèni/, **Luigi** (1760–1842) Italian-born French composer

chervil /chúrvil/ *n* 1 a herb with a mild flavour of aniseed. Use: food seasoning. *Anthriscus cerefolium.* 2 any plant related or similar to true chervil. Genera: *Anthriscus* and *Chaerophyllum.* [Pre-12C. Via Latin *chaerephyllum* < Greek *khairephullon.*]

Ches. *abbr* Cheshire²

Chesapeake Bay /chéssa peek-/ inlet of the Atlantic Ocean separating Virginia and Maryland. Area: 8,365 sq. km/3,320 sq. mi.

Cheshire¹ /chéshər/ *n* a mild crumbly cheese that is usually white but sometimes red, originally made in Cheshire

Cheshire² /chéshər/ county in NW England. Population: 978,100 (1995). Area: 2,328 sq. km/900 sq. mi.

Cheshire cat *n* the cat in Lewis Carroll's *Alice's Adventures in Wonderland*, whose broad grin remained suspended in the air after the cat itself had disappeared

Cheshvan *n* = **Heshvan**

Chesil Beach /chézz'l-/, **Chesil Bank** narrow ridge on the coast of S England. Length: 27 km/17 mi.

chess¹ /chess/ *n* a game played on a chequered board by two players, each with 16 pieces, whose object is to capture (**checkmate**) the opponent's king [12C. Shortening of Old French *esches*, plural of *eschec* (see CHECK).]

chess² /chess/ *n* a deck board or floorboard of a pontoon bridge [Early 19C. < ?]

chess³ /chess/ *n US* any one of several types of weedy bromegrass, especially an annual plant, *Bromus secalinus.* [Mid-18C. < ?]

chessboard /chéss bawrd/ *n* a square board divided into 64 alternate light and dark squares, used for playing chess

chessel /chéss'l/ *n* a mould or vat used to make cheese [Late 17C. < ?]

chessman /chéss man/ (*plural* **-men** /-men/) *n* any of the 32 pieces used in a game of chess

chesspiece /chéss peess/ *n* CHESS = **chessman**

chessylite /chéssi līt/ *n US* MINERALS = **azurite** [Mid-19C. After *Chessy*, near Lyons in France.]

chest /chest/ *n* 1 UPPER PART OF BODY the upper part of the body below the neck and above the stomach, covering the ribs and the organs that the ribs enclose 2 FRONT PART OF BODY the front part of the body of a person or animal extending from the neck to the stomach ○ *a dog with a deep chest* 3 STRONG RECTANGULAR BOX a strong rectangular box, usually with a lid and sometimes a lock, used for storage or transport 4 CONTENTS OF CHEST the contents of a chest [Old English *cest* < W Germanic, < Latin *cista* < Greek *kistē* 'basket'] ◇ **get something off your chest** to talk openly about something that has been making you feel guilty, embarrassed, worried, or angry, especially when talking about it helps to reduce or remove those feelings ◇ **keep** *or* **play something** *or* **your cards close to your chest** to be discreet or secretive about current or future plans

Chester /chéstər/ city in NW England. Population: 115,000 (1991).

chesterfield /chéstərfeeld/ *n* 1 SOFA a large sofa with upright armrests at the same height as the back, usually upholstered in leather and with a rolled-over outward curve along the top 2 *Can* COUCH any upholstered couch or sofa with back and arms 3 OVERCOAT a style of overcoat, usually with concealed buttons and a velvet collar [Mid-19C. After a 19C earl of *Chesterfield.*]

Chesterfield /chéstər feeld/ town in north-central England. Population: 101,000 (1994).

Chesterfield, Philip Dormer Stanhope, 4th Earl of (1694–1773) British statesman and writer

Chester-le-Street /chéstər lə streèt/ town in NE England. Population: 35,123 (1991).

Chesterton /chéstərtən/, **G. K.** (1874–1936) British writer. Full name **Gilbert Keith Chesterton**

chestnut /chéss nut/ *n* 1 EDIBLE NUT a glossy brown nut 2 (*plural* **-nuts** *or* **-nut**) TREE WITH PRICKLY FRUIT a tree that has long toothed leaves and bears encased chestnuts in prickly husks. Native to: North America, Europe, Japan, China. Genus: *Castanea.* ◊ **water chestnut, American chestnut** 3 WOOD the coarse-grained durable wood of the chestnut tree 4 REDDISH-BROWN HORSE a horse with a reddish-brown colour 5 CALLUS ON HORSE'S LEG a small hard callus found in several places on the inner surface of a horse's leg and thought to be a vestigial toe 6 DEEP BROWN COLOUR a deep reddish-brown colour 7 STALE JOKE OR STORY a joke or story that has lost its impact through overuse (*informal*) [Early 16C. < obsolete *chesten*, via Old French *chastaine* < Latin *castanea* < Greek *kastanea.*] —**chestnut** *adj*

chestnut blight *n* a disease that kills chestnut trees and is especially destructive to North American chestnuts

chestnut oak *n* a deciduous oak tree with shiny yellow leaves resembling those of a chestnut. Native to: E North America. *Quercus prinus.*

chest of drawers *n* a piece of furniture consisting of a set of drawers in a wooden frame with a flat top, used for storing clothes

chest voice *n* the lowest register of somebody's speaking or singing voice

chesty /chésti/ (**-ier, -iest**) *adj* 1 showing the effects of a chest complaint, such as phlegm in the lungs 2 having a well-developed chest (*informal*) —**chestiness** *n*

cheth *n* = **heth**

Chetnik /chétnik/ (*plural* **Chetniks** *or* **Cetniks**) *n* a Serbian nationalist who was part of a group who fought the Turks before World War I, and was involved in guerrilla warfare in World War I and World War II [Early 20C. < Serbo-Croat *četnik* < *četa* 'band, troop'.]

chetrum /chétrōōm/ (*plural* **-rum** *or* **-rums**) *n* see table at **currency** [Late 20C. < Tibetan.]

cheval-de-frise /shə vál də freèz/ (*plural* **chevaux-de-frise** /-vṓ-/) *n* 1 an obstacle consisting of barbed wire or spikes attached to a wooden frame, used to block an advancing enemy force 2 a line of jagged glass, nails, or spikes set into masonry on top of a wall to deter intruders [< French, 'horse of Friesland'; from its use by the Friesians, who lacked cavalry, during the siege of Groningen (1594)]

chevalet /shə vállay, shévvə láy/ *n* the bridge of a bowed musical instrument [Late 19C. < French, 'small horse' < *cheval* 'horse' < Latin *caballus.*]

cheval glass /shə vál-/ *n* a long mirror that is mounted in a frame so that it can be tilted [< French *cheval* 'frame', literally 'horse']

chevalier /shə válli ər/ *n* 1 used as the title of members of the French Legion of Honour and of other orders 2 a French knight or nobleman of the lowest rank [14C. Via French < medieval Latin *caballarius* < Latin *caballus* 'horse'.]

chevaux-de-frise plural of **cheval-de-frise**

chevet /shə váy/ *n* a complex of elaborate architectural structures at the eastern end of a church, especially a French Gothic church, usually consisting of a semicircular or polygonal apse with radiating chapels and many buttresses [Early 19C. < French, 'pillow'.]

Cheviot /cheèvi ət, chévvi ət/ *n* 1 a hornless sheep of a breed with short thick wool, originally raised in the Cheviot Hills on the border between Scotland and England 2 **Cheviot, cheviot** a woollen fabric with a coarse twill weave, originally made from the wool of Cheviot sheep

Cheviot Hills range of hills along the border of England and Scotland. Highest peak: the Cheviot 816 m/2,676 ft.

chèvre /shévrə/ *n* a soft cheese made from goat's milk [Mid-20C. Via French, 'goat' < Latin *capra*, feminine of *caper.*]

chevron /shévrən/ *n* 1 V-SHAPED SYMBOL a V-shaped symbol, especially one used as a sign of rank on military or police uniforms 2 HERALDIC ORNAMENT a heraldic ornament in the form of a wide inverted V-shape ■ **chevrons** *npl* ROAD SIGN AT BEND a large rectangular road sign with a pattern of horizontal black and white V-shapes, used to indicate a sharp bend [14C. Via French, 'rafter' < Latin *caper* 'goat'.]

chevrotain /shévrə tayn, -tin/ (*plural* **-tains** *or* **-tain**) *n* a small hornless cud-chewing animal similar to a deer, the male of which has projecting canine teeth. Native to: rain forests of west-central Africa and SE Asia. Family: Tragulidae. [Late 18C. < French, 'small goat' < *chèvre* (see CHÈVRE).]

chevy /chévvi/ *v* = **chivvy**

chew /choo/ *v* 1 *vti* GRIND UP FOOD BEFORE SWALLOWING to grind up food or other material with the action of the teeth and jaws 2 *vti* DAMAGE SOMETHING BY BITING to gnaw at something repeatedly, usually causing damage ○ *chewing her nails* 3 *vi US* CHEW TOBACCO to bite into and chew tobacco ■ *n* 1 ACT OF CHEWING the act of chewing something, or a period of chewing 2 SWEET a sweet with a firm texture, which must be chewed before being swallowed ○ *fruit chews* 3 *US* PIECE OF CHEWING TOBACCO a piece of dried tobacco for chewing [Old English *cēowan* < Germanic] —**chewable** *adj* —**chewer** *n*

chew out *vt US* to tell somebody off for doing something wrong (*informal*) ○ *She really chewed me out for being late.*

chew over *vt* to think about or discuss something over a period of time ○ *We chewed the problem over for a couple of days before coming to a decision.*

chew up *vt* 1 to damage or destroy something, especially by passing it through machinery (*informal*) ○ *I'm afraid the machine chewed up your tape.* 2 to destroy something by biting or chewing it

chewie /chóo i/ *n* chewing gum (*informal*) [Early 20C. Shortening.]

chewing gum /chóo ing-/ *n* a sweet flavoured substance that is chewed but not swallowed. ◊ **bubble gum**

chewy /chóo i/ (**-ier, -iest**) *adj* having a consistency or texture that requires chewing —**chewiness** *n*

Cheyenne¹ /shī án/ (*plural* **-enne** *or* **-ennes**) *n* 1 a member of a Native North American people who once lived in the W Great Plains 2 the Algonquian language of the Cheyenne people. Native speakers: 2,000. [Late 18C. Via Canadian French < Dakota *šahíyena.*] —**Cheyenne** *adj*

Cheyenne² /shī án, -én/ 1 river in E Wyoming and South Dakota. Length: 848 km/527 mi. 2 capital of Wyoming, in the southeast of the state. Population: 53,640 (1998 estimate).

Cheyne-Stokes respiration /cháyn stṓks-/ *n* a breathing pattern marked by shallow breathing alternating with periods of rapid heavy breathing [Late 19C. After John *Cheyne* (1777–1836), Scottish physician, and William *Stokes* (1804–78), Irish physician.]

chez /shay/ *prep* at somebody's home or business premises, especially a restaurant [Mid-18C. Via French < Latin *casa* 'cottage'.]

chg. *abbr* 1 change 2 charge

chi¹ /kī/ (*plural* **chis**), **khi** (*plural* **khis**) *n* the 22nd letter of the Greek alphabet [15C. < Greek *khi.*]

chi² /chee/, **ch'i, Chi, Ch'i, qi, Qi** *n* in Chinese medicine and philosophy, the energy or life force of the universe, believed to flow round the body and to be present in all living things [< Chinese *qì* 'air, breath']

Chiang Ch'ing /cháng chíng/ = **Jiang Qing**

Chiang Ching-kuo /cháng ching kwṓ/ (1910–88) Taiwanese statesman

Chiang Kai-shek /cháng kī shék/ (1887–1975) Chinese military leader and president of Taiwan (1949–75)

Chianti /ki ánti/, **chianti** *n* a light Italian red wine produced mainly from the Sangiovese grape in Tuscany, NW Italy [Mid-19C. After the *Chianti* Mountains, Tuscany.]

Chiapas /chi áppəss/ state in SE Mexico. Capital: Tuxtla Gutiérrez. Population: 3,654,000 (1993). Area: 73,724 sq. km/28,465 sq. mi.

chiaroscuro /ki aàrə skoŏrrō/ *n* the use of light and shade in paintings and drawings, or the effect produced by this [Mid-17C. < Italian, < *chiaro* 'bright' + *oscuro* 'dark'.] —**chiaroscurism** *n* —**chiaroscurist** *n*

chiasma /kī ázmə/ (*plural* **-mas** *or* **-mata** /-mətə/) *n* **1** any crossing over of biological tissue, e.g. the intersection of the optic nerves **2** the point at which two chromatids join during the fusion and exchange of genetic material (**crossing-over**) in cell division [Mid-19C. Via modern Latin < Greek *khiasma* 'crosspiece' < *khiazein* 'mark with an X' < *khi* 'the letter chi'.] —**chiasmal** *adj* —**chiasmic** *adj*

chiasmus /kī ázməss/ (*plural* **-mi** /-mī/) *n* a rhetorical construction in which the order of the words in the second of two paired phrases is the reverse of the order in the first. An example is 'grey was the morn, all things were grey'. [Mid-17C. Via modern Latin < Greek *khiasmos* < *khiazein* (see CHIASMA).]

chiastolite /kī ástə līt/ *n* a variety of the mineral andalusite that contains carbon impurities in an X-shape [Early 19C. < Greek *khiastos*, past participle of *khiazein* (see CHIASMA).]

Chiba /cheébə/ capital of Chiba Prefecture, E Honshu, Japan. Population: 5,863,182 (1999).

Chibcha /chíbchə/ (*plural* **-cha** *or* **-chas**) *n* **1** a member of an extinct Native South American people who lived in the Andes Mountains in central Colombia **2** the extinct Chibchan language of the Chibcha [Early 19C. Via American Spanish < Chibcha *zipa* 'chief'.]

Chibchan /chíbchən/ (*plural* **-chan** *or* **-chans**) *n* **1** a group of Native Central American languages spoken in Colombia and Panama. Native speakers: 100,000. **2** a member of any of the peoples who speak a language belonging to the Chibchan group —**Chibchan** *adj*

chic /sheek/ *adj* stylish and elegant ■ *n* fashionable style or elegance [Mid-19C. < French.] —**chicness** *n*

Chicago /shi kaàgō/ city in NE Illinois. Population: 2,802,079 (1998 estimate). —**Chicagoan** *n, adj*

Chicago Board of Trade *n* a major commodities exchange in Chicago, in the United States, that deals in grain and metal futures

Chicana /chi kaánə/ (*plural* **-nas**) *n US* a North American woman or girl of Mexican descent [Mid-20C. < Spanish, feminine of *Chicano* (see CHICANO).]

chicane[1] /shi káyn/ *n* **1** in motor-racing, a sharp double bend created by placing barriers on the circuit **2** a bridge or whist hand without trumps or without cards of one suit [Late 19C. < French, < *chicaner* 'to quibble'.]

chicane[2] /shi káyn/ (**-canes, -caning, -caned**) *vi* to practise chicanery [Late 17C. < French *chicaner* 'to quibble'.] —**chicaner** *n*

chicanery /shi káynəri/ (*plural* **-ies**) *n* deception or trickery, especially by the clever manipulation of language

Chicano /chi kaánō/ (*plural* **-nos**) *n US* a North American man or boy of Mexican descent [Mid-20C. < American Spanish, variant of Spanish *mexicano* 'Mexican' < *México* 'Mexico'.]

Chichester /chíchistər/ city in S England. Population: 104,112 (1996 estimate).

Chichester, Sir Francis Charles (1901–72) British aviator and sailor

chichi /sheé shee/ *adj* trying too hard or too obviously to be chic or modish (*disapproving*) ○ *All this designer furniture – isn't it just a bit chichi?* ■ *n* affected or self-conscious stylishness (*disapproving*) [Mid-20C. < French.]

Chichimec /cheéchi mek/ (*plural* **-mecs** *or* **-mec**) *n* **1** a member of a group of Native Central American peoples who dominated central Mexico from the 11th to the 15th centuries, overthrowing the Toltecs and making way for the Aztecs **2** the Uto-Aztecan language of the Chichimec peoples. Native speakers: 5,000. [Mid-17C. Via Spanish < Nahuatl *chichimecatl*.]

chick /chik/ *n* **1 BABY BIRD** a young bird, especially a young chicken **2** *US* **YOUNG WOMAN** an attractive girl or young woman (*slang; sometimes offensive*) **3 SMALL CHILD** a term of affection used to a baby or small child (*informal*) [14C. Shortening of CHICKEN.]

chickabiddy /chíkə biddi/ (*plural* **-dies**) *n* an affectionate term of address used by adults to children and babies (*archaic*) [Early 19C. < CHICK + BIDDY.]

chickadee /chíkə dee/ (*plural* **-dees** *or* **-dee**) *n* a small tit that has grey plumage, a darker-coloured crown on its head, and a distinctive call. Native to: North America. Genus: *Parus*. [Mid-19C. An imitation of its call.]

chickaree /chíkə ree/ (*plural* **-rees** *or* **-ree**) *n* a squirrel of W North America, related to the red squirrel. *Tamiascurus douglasi*. [Early 19C. An imitation of its cry.]

Chickasaw /chíkə saw/ (*plural* **-saw** *or* **-saws**) *n* **1** a member of a Native North American people who originally lived in NE Mississippi and NW Alabama, and now live mainly in central and S Oklahoma **2** the Muskogean language of the Chickasaw. Native speakers: 10,000. [Late 17C. < Chickasaw *čikaša*.] —**Chickasaw** *adj*

chicken /chíkin/ *n* **1 COMMON DOMESTIC FOWL** a domestic fowl, usually with brown or black feathers and a fleshy crest on its head. Kept for: meat, eggs. *Gallus domesticus*. ◊ **spring chicken 2 MEAT FROM CHICKENS** the flesh of a chicken as food **3 COWARD** a cowardly or timid person (*informal*) ○ *You'll never do it – you're a chicken!* **4 DANGEROUS GAME** a game or challenge in which two or more people attempt a dangerous or daring feat (*informal*) ■ *adj* **COWARDLY** showing a lack of courage (*informal*) ○ *Are you too chicken to do a high dive?* [Old English *cīcen* < Germanic] ◇ **a chicken-and-egg situation** a situation in which it is impossible to know which of two related circumstances occurred first and caused the other

SYNONYMS See ***cowardly***.

chicken out *vi* to fail in or withdraw from something because of a lack of nerve (*slang*)

chicken breast *n* = **pigeon breast** —**chicken-breasted** *adj*

chicken feed *n* an insignificant amount, especially an insignificant sum of money (*informal*)

chicken-fried steak *n US* a cut of beef, usually round steak, that has been tenderized, dredged in flour, and then pan-fried

chicken-hearted, chicken-livered *adj* easily frightened or lacking sufficient courage, boldness, or confidence —**chicken-heartedness** *n*

chickenpox /chíkin poks/ *n* a highly infectious viral disease, especially affecting children, characterized by a rash of small itching blisters on the skin and mild fever. Technical name **varicella** [Mid-18C. < ?]

chickenshit /chíkin shit/ *n US* (*slang*) **1** an offensive term for petty or tedious details or tasks **2** an offensive term for somebody who is regarded as cowardly or timid ■ *adj US* an offensive term meaning petty, unimportant, cowardly, or frightened (*slang*)

chicken wire *n* a lightweight flexible galvanized wire netting, usually made with a hexagonal mesh [< its use as a fence for enclosing chickens]

chickpea /chík pee/ *n* **1** a pale yellow seed about the size of a large pea cooked as a vegetable **2** an annual plant that produces chickpeas. Native to: Asia, the Mediterranean. *Cicer arietinum*. [Early 18C. Alteration of *chich pease* < *chich* 'chickpea' (< French *chiche* < Latin *cicer*) + *pease* (see PEA).]

chickweed /chík weed/ *n* a common weed found on cultivated land. Flowers: small, white. Native to: Europe. *Stellaria media*. [Because chickens eat the plant]

Chiclayo /chi klī ō/ coastal city in NW Peru. Population: 410,486 (1993).

chicle /chík'l/ *n* a gummy substance from the latex of the sapodilla tree. Use: main ingredient of chewing gum. [Late 19C. Via American Spanish < Nahuatl *tzictli*.] —**chicly** *adj*

chicory /chíkəri/ (*plural* **-ries**) *n* **1 LEAVES USED IN SALAD** pale, slightly bitter leaves eaten cooked or raw in salads. US term **endive** *n*. 2 **2 GROUND ROASTED ROOT** a dried, roasted, and ground root, used as a coffee additive or substitute **3 PLANT CULTIVATED FOR LEAVES AND ROOTS** a perennial herb that produces chicory. Flowers: blue. Native to: Europe, N Africa. *Cichorium intybus*. [15C. Via obsolete French *cicoré* 'endive' < medieval Latin *cichorea* < Greek *kikhorion*.]

chide /chīd/ (**chides, chiding, chided** *or* **chid** /chid/, **chided** *or* **chid** *or* **chidden** /chídd'n/) *vti* to reproach or scold somebody (*literary*) [Old English *cīdan*] —**chider** *n* —**chidingly** *adv*

chief /cheef/ *n* **1 LEADER** the person with the most authority or highest rank in a group or organization **2 CHIEFTAIN** the leader or titular head of a people or group **3 CHIEF PETTY OFFICER** a chief petty officer (*informal*) **4 SHIP'S PRINCIPAL ENGINEER** the principal engineer on a ship **5 TOP SECTION OF HERALDIC SHIELD** the upper third of the surface area of a heraldic shield ■ *adj* **1 MOST IMPORTANT** most important, basic, or common **2 HIGHEST IN AUTHORITY** highest in authority, position, or rank [13C. Via French *chef* < Latin *caput* 'head'.] —**chiefdom** *n* —**chiefship** *n* ◇ **the big white chief** the most important person in an organization, often somebody who makes his or her power and influence very obvious (*informal*) ○ *The big white chief says that we all have to work overtime.*

chief constable *n* in Britain, the police officer in overall command of a regional police force

chief education officer *n* the chief administrative officer of a local education authority

chief executive *n* **1 HEAD OF EXECUTIVE BODY** the highest-ranking member of an executive body, e.g. the head of a government or the governor of a US state **2 HIGHEST-RANKING EXECUTIVE** the highest-ranking director of a business or organization who oversees its day-to-day management **3** *US* **US PRESIDENT** the president of the United States

chief executive officer *n* the highest-ranking executive officer within a company or corporation, who has responsibility for overall management of its day-to-day affairs under the supervision of the board of directors

chief justice *n* **1** a judge who presides over a court that has several judges, especially the Supreme Court of the United States **2** the senior judge in the High Courts of Australia and other Commonwealth countries

chiefly /cheéfli/ *adv* **1 ABOVE ALL** above all, especially, or most importantly ○ *We moved to this area of the city chiefly because it's convenient for getting to work.* **2 IN THE MAIN** for the most part ○ *The human body consists chiefly of water.* ■ *adj* **RELATING TO CHIEFS** relating to chiefs

chief master sergeant *n* a noncommissioned officer in the US Air Force of a rank above senior master sergeant

chief minister *n* the leader of a national or provincial government in various countries with a parliamentary system, or a ruler's chief executive official

chief of staff *n* **1** *US* a high-ranking officer in the US Army or Air Force who is a member of the US Joint Chiefs of Staff **2** the senior officer serving on a military staff, who has responsibility for managing it and for advising the commander

chief petty officer *n* a noncommissioned officer in the Royal Navy of a rank above petty officer

Chief Rabbi *n* the senior religious leader of the Jewish community in Great Britain and in some other countries

chieftain /cheéftən/ *n* the leader or titular head of a people or similar group [13C. < Old French *chevetaine*, alteration of late Latin *capitaneus* (see CAPTAIN).] —**chieftaincy** *n* —**chieftainship** *n*

chief technician *n* a noncommissioned officer in the Royal Air Force of a rank below flight sergeant

chief warrant officer *n* **1** an officer in the US armed forces of a rank above warrant officer and below that of second lieutenant or ensign **2** the highest-ranking noncommissioned officer in the Royal Canadian Army or Air Force

chief whip *n* the most senior of a political party's whips, whose role is to maintain party discipline and ensure that party members attend and vote at debates in the Houses of Parliament

chiel /cheel/, **chield** /cheeld/ *n Scotland* a boy or young man (*regional*) [Variant of CHILD]

chiffchaff /chíf chaf/ *n* a small greyish-yellow bird with a characteristic repetitive song. Native to: Europe, Asia. *Phylloscopus collybita*. [Late 18C. An imitation of its call.]

chifferobe *n US* = **chifforobe**

chiffon /shíffon/ *n* **1 FABRIC** a very light sheer nylon, rayon, or silk fabric **2 CLOTHING ACCESSORIES** decorative accessories for women, e.g. laces or ribbons (*often plural*) ■ *adj* **1 MADE OF CHIFFON** made of chiffon or resembling it in lightness and fineness **2 FLUFFY** describes food with a light fluffy texture, usually created by adding whipped egg whites or gelatin [Mid-18C. < French, < *chiffe* 'rag, flimsy stuff'.]

chiffonade /shíffə naád/ *n* vegetables that have been shredded or finely chopped, often used as a garnish for other foods [Late 19C. < French.]

chiffonier /shíffə neér/ *n* **1** a low cabinet or cupboard with shelves above it **2** a relatively tall narrow chest of drawers that often has a mirror attached to the back [Mid-18C. < French.]

chifforobe /shíffə rōb/, **chifferobe** /shíffrōb/, **chiffrobe** n US a tall piece of furniture with drawers and a hanging space for clothes [Early 20C. Blend of CHIFFONIER + WARDROBE.]

Chifley /chíffli/, **Ben** (1885–1951) Australian statesman

chigetai /chígga tī/, **dziggetai** /jíg-/ n a wild ass related to the onager. Native to: Mongolia. *Equus hemionus.* [Late 18C. < Mongolian *chikitei* 'having ears' < *chiki* 'ear'.]

chigger /chíggər/ n 1 ZOOL = harvest mite 2 INSECTS = chigoe n. 1 [Mid-18C. < CHIGOE.]

chignon /shée'ən yon, -yoN/ n a knot or roll of hair, especially when worn at the nape of the neck [Late 18C. < French, 'nape of the neck, chain' < Latin *catena* 'chain'.]

chigoe /chíggō/ n 1 a small tropical flea, the fertilized female of which burrows under the skin causing painful itching sores that easily become infected. *Tunga penetrans.* 2 ZOOL = chigger n. 1 [Mid-17C. < French *chique* < a W African language.]

chihuahua /chi wáawə/ n a very small dog belonging to a breed originally from Mexico that has pointed ears, protruding eyes, and a tiny body with a disproportionately large head [Early 19C. After CHIHUAHUA.]

Chihuahua /chi wáa waa/ n 1 state in N Mexico. Capital: Chihuahua. Population: 2,792,989 (1995). Area: 247,087 sq. km/95,401 sq. mi. 2 capital of Chihuahua State, N Mexico. Population: 627,662 (1995).

Chikamatsu /chíkə mátsoo/, **Monzemon** (1653–1725) Japanese playwright

chilblain /chíl blayn/ n a red itchy swelling on the ears, fingers, or toes, caused by exposure to damp and cold (*often plural*) [Mid-16C. < CHILL + *blain* < Old English *blegen* < Germanic] —**chilblained** adj

child /chīld/ n (plural **children** /chíldrən/) 1 YOUNG HUMAN BEING a young human being between birth and puberty 2 HUMAN OFFSPRING a son or daughter of human parents 3 SOMEBODY NOT YET OF AGE somebody under a legally specified age who is considered not to be legally responsible for his or her actions 4 BABY a baby or infant 5 UNBORN BABY an unborn baby 6 IMMATURE PERSON an adult who behaves in a childish or childlike way 7 DESCENDANT OR MEMBER OF A PEOPLE a descendant of somebody or a member of a people founded by somebody (*often plural*) 8 PRODUCT OR RESULT somebody or something considered to be either produced or strongly influenced by a particular environment, period, or historical figure ○ *a child of nature* ○ *a child of the 1960s* 9 FEMALE CHILD a specifically female child or infant (*regional*) [Old English *cild*] ◇ **with child** pregnant (*archaic or literary*)

SYNONYMS See *youth*.

child abuse n severe mistreatment of a child by a parent, guardian, or other adult responsible for his or her welfare, including physical violence, neglect, sexual assault, or emotional cruelty —**child abuser** n

childbearing /chíld bairing/ n the process of carrying a child in the womb and giving birth to it ○ *Her childbearing years are over.*

childbed /chíld bed/ n the state of a woman in the process of giving birth to a child (*archaic*)

child benefit n in the United Kingdom and New Zealand, a regular payment made by the state to parents towards the maintenance of each child in a family below a certain age

childbirth /chíld burth/ n the act or process of giving birth to a child ○ *natural childbirth methods*

childcare /chíld kair/ n 1 the care and supervision of children by an adult, inside or outside the home and usually for pay, during times when the parents or guardians are at work 2 the care and supervision by a local authority of homeless children or children whose home life is severely disrupted

child-centred adj adapted to the needs and concerns of children as opposed to adults

childe /chīld/ n (plural **childes**) a young person of noble birth (*archaic*) [Variant of CHILD.]

Childe /chīld/, **V. Gordon** (1892–1957) Australian archaeologist. Full name Vere Gordon Childe

Childermas /chíldər mass/ n the religious festival of Holy Innocents' Day. Date: 28 December. (*archaic*) [Old English *cildramæsse* < *childra* 'of children' + *mæsse* 'mass']

Childers /chíldərz/, **Erskine** (1870–1922) British-born Irish nationalist and writer

child guidance n the professional counselling of children who are emotionally disturbed, often also extended to their parents or guardians

childhood /chíld hood/ n 1 the state of being a child, or the period of somebody's life when he or she is a child ○ *heard wonderful stories about her childhood.* 2 an early period or stage in the development or existence of something ○ *Interplanetary travel is still in its childhood.*

childish /chíldish/ adj 1 like that of a child, or suitable for a child ○ *a childish voice* 2 showing a lack of emotional restraint, seriousness, good sense, maturity, or similar adult qualities ○ *I don't have time for your childish tantrums.* —**childishly** adv —**childishness** n

USAGE **childish** or **childlike**? Both words describe people or behaviour that have qualities associated with children. The difference is that **childlike** is complimentary and even affectionate (*childlike innocence*), whereas **childish** is a dismissive and disapproving term: *a childish tantrum.*

child labour n the full-time employment of children, especially of those who are legally too young to work

childless /chíldləss/ adj not having had a child or children —**childlessness** n

childlike /chíld līk/ adj like a child, especially in having a sweet innocent unspoiled quality ○ *childlike innocence*

USAGE See *childish*.

child minder n a person who looks after other people's children in his or her own home, especially when the parents or guardians are working —**child minding** n

child prodigy n a child who possesses extraordinary abilities or talents, often equal to those of adults

childproof /chíld proof/ adj 1 HARD FOR A CHILD TO OPEN designed to be difficult for children to open, tamper with, damage, or break 2 MADE SAFE FOR CHILDREN made safe for young children to use or be in, e.g. through the removal of potential dangers and addition of extra safety devices ○ *Parents with toddlers should have at least one childproof room.* ■ vt MAKE SOMETHING SAFE FOR CHILDREN to make something safe for children to use, or safe against damage or tampering by children ○ *You'll need to childproof your house before the baby is born.*

children plural of **child**

LITERARY LINK *The Man Who Loved Children*, a novel (1891) by Australian writer, Christina Stead. Through the story of the stormy domestic life of Sam and Henny Pollitt and their six children, Stead examines the ways in which human beings attempt, and often fail, to communicate with one other.

Children's Panel n in Scotland, a hearing convened by representatives of the appropriate agencies to deal with a child who has committed a crime or is being mistreated by parents or guardians

child restraint n a seat belt or detachable seat designed to protect a child travelling in a vehicle or a plane

child seat n a detachable seat with a harness, attached to a car seat, used to protect a child too small to wear an adult seat belt

child's play n something that is very straightforward for somebody to do ○ *Skiing these slopes would be child's play for her.*

Child Support Agency n a government-sponsored agency whose task is to ensure that absent parents, usually fathers, are making an adequate contribution to their children's maintenance

child tax benefit n in Canada, an allowance or tax-free benefit given by the federal government or the province of Quebec to assist parents in the expense of rearing children below a specified age. ◇ **family allowance**

Chile /chílli/ republic in SW South America. Capital: Santiago. Population: 14,508,131 (1997). Area: 756,626 sq. km/292,135 sq. mi. —**Chilean** /-ən, adj

Chile nitre n CHEM = Chile saltpetre

Chile pine n TREES = monkey puzzle

Chile saltpetre n $NaNO_3$ a form of sodium nitrate. Source: arid regions, especially in Chile and Peru.

Chile

chili n US = chilli

chiliasm /kílli azəm/ n CHR = millenarianism n. 1 [Early 17C. < Greek *khiliasmos* < *khilias* < *khilioi* 'one thousand'.] —**chiliast** n —**chiliastic** /kílli ástik/ adj

chill /chil/ n 1 MODERATE COLDNESS a moderate but often unpleasant degree of coldness ○ *a chill in the air* 2 SUDDEN SHORT FEVER a sudden short fever with shivering and a sensation of coldness 3 COLDNESS CAUSED BY FEAR a sudden shuddering feeling of coldness caused by fear, anxiety, or excitement ○ *felt a chill run down my spine* 4 DEPRESSING EFFECT a depressing or dampening effect on people or on an occasion ○ *The news cast a chill over the party.* 5 LACK OF WARMTH an emotional coldness or unfriendliness in the atmosphere or in somebody's manner 6 MOULD USED IN CASTING METAL a mould made of a highly conductive material such as iron, used to achieve a rapid even cooling when casting metal ■ adj 1 MODERATELY COLD moderately cold, but usually cold enough to be unpleasant 2 EMOTIONALLY COLD showing no friendliness or emotional warmth ■ v 1 vt MAKE COLD to make somebody or something become cold, usually unpleasantly cold ○ *I was sitting in a freezing draught that chilled me to the bone.* 2 vti COOL OR FREEZE FOOD to cool food or drink, or be left to cool, in a refrigerator 3 vt MAKE FEEL AFRAID to make somebody feel afraid, anxious, or horrified, especially suddenly 4 vt BE DISCOURAGING TO to have a discouraging or dampening effect on somebody or something 5 vi = **chill out** (*slang*) 6 vti HARDEN METAL OR BECOME HARD to harden a metal surface, or become hard, by rapid cooling [Old English *ciele* < Germanic] —**chillness** n

chill out vi (*slang*) 1 to stop behaving stupidly 2 to spend time relaxing

chilled margin /child-/ n the edges of an igneous intrusion as it is cooled by contact with the surrounding colder rocks, marked by a zone of finer-grained crystals

chiller /chíllər/ n 1 a refrigerated cooling or storage compartment 2 a frightening film or story (*slang*)

chill factor n METEOROL = wind-chill factor

chilli /chílli/ n (plural **-lies**) 1 a narrow red or green hot-tasting pod produced by various types of capsicum pepper plant. Use: flavouring sauces and relishes. 2 FOOD = chilli powder 3 FOOD = chilli sauce 4 FOOD = chilli con carne [Early 17C. Via Spanish *chile* < Nahuatl *chilli*.]

SPELLCHECK Do not confuse **chilli** with **chilly**, which has a similar sound. Beware: your spellchecker will not catch this error.

chilli con carne /chílli kon káarni/ n a highly spiced dish made of chopped or minced meat and beans and usually tomatoes [< American Spanish, 'chilli with meat']

chilling /chílling/ adj causing a feeling of dread or horror ○ *a chilling account of his capture* —**chillingly** adv

chilli powder n a seasoning consisting of ground chillies blended with several other seasonings, such as cumin, garlic, and oregano, often added to a dish to give it a hot taste

chillum /chílləm/ n 1 a short straight pipe, usually made of clay, for smoking cannabis or tobacco 2 a quantity of cannabis or tobacco to be smoked [Late 18C. < Hindi *chilam.*]

chilly /chílli/ (**-ier, -iest**) adj 1 MODERATELY COLD moderately or noticeably cold, usually enough to cause discomfort ○ *Bring a sweater to the park; it'll be chilly later.* 2 FEELING RATHER COLD feeling cold enough to be uncomfortable 3 UNFRIENDLY unfriendly or hostile ○ *a chilly reception*

4 SENSITIVE TO COLD prone to feeling cold (*informal*) —**chillily** *adv* —**chilliness** *n*

SPELLCHECK See *chilli.*

chilly bin *n* an insulated container for keeping food from spoiling and drinks cold, often small enough to be carried (*informal*)

chilopod /kílə pod/ *n* an arthropod of the group that includes the centipedes (*technical*) [Mid-19C. < modern Latin *Chilopoda* < Greek *kheilos* 'lip'.]

Chiltern Hills /chíltərn-/ range of chalk hills in south-central England. Highest peak: Combe Hill, 260 m/852 ft.

Chiltern Hundreds *n* a nominal office that Members of Parliament apply for when they want to resign from the House of Commons (+ *singular verb*) Full form **Stewardship of the Chiltern Hundreds** [13C. After the CHILTERN HILLS.]

Chiluba /chi lóobə/, **Frederick** (*b.* 1943) Zambian statesman

Chi-lung /jée lóong/ seaport in N Taiwan. Population: 374,199 (1997 estimate).

chimaera /kī méerə, ki-/ *n* **1** (*plural* **-ras** *or* **-ra**) a deep-sea fish with a skeleton of cartilage, a smooth-skinned tapering body, and a tail that resembles a whip. Family: Chimaeridae. **2** = **chimera** [Early 19C. < Latin (see CHIMERA).]

Chimaera *n* = **Chimera**

chimb *n* = **chime**[2]

Chimborazo /chímbə raázō/ mountain peak in central Ecuador. Height: 6,310 m/20,702 ft.

Chimbote /chim bṓ tay/ port in W Peru. Population: 296,600 (1990).

chime[1] /chīm/ *n* **1** SOUND OF BELL the musical ringing sound made by a bell or bells, or a similar sound made by some other object such as a doorbell **2** DEVICE FOR STRIKING BELL a device for striking a bell or a set of bells in order to make a musical sound or play a tune (*often plural*) **3** NOTES SOUNDED BY CLOCK a series of musical notes sounded by a clock before striking **4** PERCUSSION INSTRUMENT a set of hanging bells, metal bars, or tubes tuned to a scale, used to produce a musical sound when struck (*often plural*) **5** MUSIC = **wind chime** **6** HARMONY an agreement or harmony among people or things (*literary*) ■ *v* (**chimes, chiming, chimed**) **1** *vi* RING HARMONIOUSLY to make a harmonious ringing sound ○ *Did you hear the bells chiming?* **2** *vt* INDICATE BY CHIMING to indicate something, especially the time, by chiming ○ *The clock chimed three o'clock.* **3** *vt* PRODUCE MUSICAL SOUND to strike a bell or bells so as to produce a musical sound **4** *vi* HARMONIZE to harmonize or be in agreement with something else ○ *It was nice to find that her opinion chimed so perfectly with my own.* **5** *vti* SPEAK IN MUSICAL WAY to say or read something aloud in a rhythmical or musical way [13C. < ?] —**chimer** *n*

chime in *vi* **1** to interrupt or join in a conversation between other people, especially in order to voice an opinion **2** to agree or combine harmoniously with something else

chime[2] /chīm/, **chimb, chine** /chīn/ *n* an edge or lip around the rim of a barrel or cask [14C. Probably < assumed Old English *cim*.]

chimera /kī méerə, ki-/, **chimaera** *n* **1** SOMETHING TOTALLY UNREALISTIC OR IMPRACTICAL a figment of the imagination, e.g. a wildly unrealistic idea or hope or a completely impractical plan **2** ORGANISM WITH GENETICALLY DIFFERENT TISSUES an organism, or part of one, with at least two genetically different tissues resulting from mutation, the grafting of plants, or the insertion of foreign cells into an embryo **3** ORGANISM WITH DNA FROM DIFFERENT SOURCES an organism that has genetic material from a variety of sources as a result of the insertion of unspecialized cells (**stem cells**) from other species into an embryo [See CHIMERA] —**chimerism** /kī méerizəm, kímərizəm/ *n*

Chimera /kī méerə, ki-/, **Chimaera** *n* **1** a female fire-breathing monster in Greek mythology, typically represented as a combination of a lion's head, goat's body, and serpent's tail **2** any imaginary monster whose body is a grotesque combination of mismatched animal parts [14C. Via Latin *chimaera* < Greek *khimaira* 'she-goat'.]

chimeric /kī mérrik, ki-/ *adj* describes an organism that is composed of genetically different tissues, either naturally or as a result of a laboratory procedure

chimerical /kī mérrik'l, ki-/ *adj* **1** nonexistent, existing only in somebody's imagination, or wildly improbable or unrealistic **2** having a tendency to indulge in unrealistic fantasies (*literary*) —**chimerically** *adv* —**chimericalness** *n*

chimichanga /chímmi cháng gə/ *n* a dish of the SW United States that consists of a deep-fried burrito containing a spicy filling of meat [Late 20C. < Mexican Spanish, 'trinket'.]

chimney /chímni/ (*plural* **-neys**) *n* **1** STRUCTURE FOR VENTING GAS OR SMOKE a hollow vertical structure, usually made of brick or steel, that allows gas, smoke, or steam from a fire or furnace to escape into the atmosphere **2** PART OF STRUCTURE RISING ABOVE ROOF the part of a chimney that rises above a roof **3** SMOKE-VENTING PASSAGE INSIDE CHIMNEY a passage or pipe inside a chimney through which smoke or steam escapes **4** FUNNEL OF STEAM ENGINE a funnel on a railway engine or steamship. US term **smokestack** *n.* 1 **5** GLASS TUBE PROTECTING LAMP FLAME a tube, usually made of glass, used to enclose the flame of a lamp **6** CLEFT IN ROCK FACE a narrow vertical cleft in a rock face that is large enough for a climber to get inside and use as a means of ascending **7** FIREPLACE a large fireplace or hearth, especially one that is very old (*regional*) [13C. < Old French *cheminée* < late Latin *caminata* < Latin *camera caminata* 'room with a fireplace' < Greek *kaminos* 'oven'.]

chimney breast *n* a projecting section of an interior wall surrounding a chimney or fireplace

chimney corner *n* a recessed seat, beside or within a large old-fashioned open fireplace

chimneypiece /chímni peess/ *n* ARCHIT = **mantelpiece**

chimney pot *n* a short earthenware or metal pipe placed on the top of a chimney in order to increase the draught

chimney stack *n* **1** = **chimney** *n.* 2 **2** a tall, often cylindrical, chimney attached to a factory or other large industrial building

chimney sweep *n* somebody whose job is removing soot from chimneys

chimney swift *n* a small dark swift that nests in chimneys. Native to: North America. *Chaetura pelagica.*

chimp /chimp/ *n* a chimpanzee (*informal*)

chimpanzee /chím pan zée/ *n* a medium-sized ape with long dark-brown hair covering its body except for its naked face and ears. Native to: equatorial Africa. *Pan troglodytes* and *Pan paniscus.* [Mid-18C. < French *chimpanzé* < Kikongo.]

chin /chin/ *n* PART OF FACE the part of the face below the lips, including the usually protruding front portion of the lower jaw ■ *v* (**chins, chinning, chinned**) **1** *vti* RAISE CHIN TO HIGH BAR to pull yourself up by the arms until your chin is level with the horizontal bar you are holding **2** *vt* HIT SOMEBODY ON CHIN to hit somebody on the chin or in the face (*slang*) [Old English *cin* < Germanic] ◇ **keep your chin up** to remain cheerful and hopeful in spite of difficulties or hardships ◇ **take it on the chin** to accept misfortune staunchly, without flinching

Ch'in *n* HIST = **Qin**

china[1] /chínə/ *n* **1** porcelain or a similar high-quality translucent or white ceramic material **2** articles made of china, especially dishes and decorative objects [Late 16C. < Persian *čīnī* 'porcelain from China'.]

china[2] /chínə/ *n* *Cockney* a close and trusted friend (*slang*) [Late19C. < *china plate*, rhyming slang for 'mate'.]

China /chínə/ republic in E and central Asia. Capital: Beijing. Population: 1,226,274,731 (1997). Area: approximately 9,571,300 sq. km/3,695,500 sq. mi.

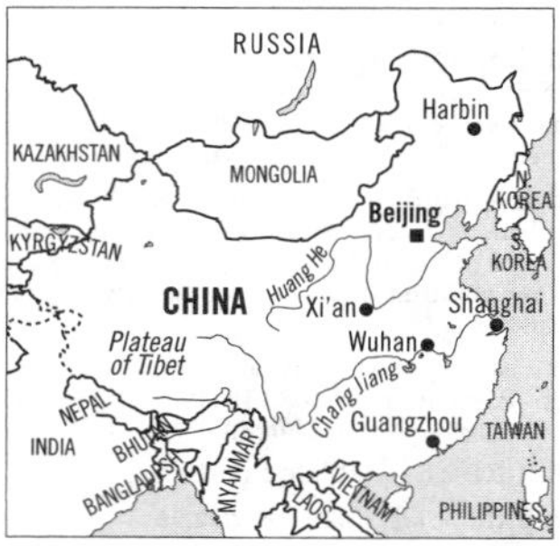

China

chinaberry /chínəbəri/ (*plural* **-ries**) *n* **1** a deciduous tree of the mahogany family. Flowers: white or purple, in clusters. Use: in the United States, as a shade tree. Native to: Asia. *Melia azedarach.* **2** a fruit produced by either the chinaberry or soapberry tree **3** TREES = **soapberry** *n.* 1

china clay *n* = **kaolin**

Chinaman /chínəmən/ (*plural* **-men** /-mən/) *n* **1** an offensive term for a man who was born in or who lives in China (*dated*) **2** in cricket, a slow off-break bowled by a left-handed bowler to a right-handed batsman

Chinan /chée nán/ ♦ **Jinan**

China rose *n* **1** a rose that is the ancestor of many cultivated varieties. Flowers: fragrant pink, red, or white. Native to: China. *Rosa chinensis.* **2** a hybrid garden rose derived from the China rose, especially a dwarf rose with crimson flowers. *Rosa semperflorens.* **3** PLANTS = **hibiscus**

China Sea part of the Pacific Ocean extending from Japan to the southern end of the Malay Peninsula. Area: East China Sea 752,000 sq. km/290,000 sq. mi. Depth: 2,717 m/8,913 ft.

china stone *n* soft white clay formed from partially decomposed granite, used in ceramics and the paper and pharmaceutical industries

China syndrome *n* a hypothetical accident in which the core of a nuclear reactor melts, allowing the radioactive fuel to burn through the floor of its container and straight down into the earth [< the idea of the molten core sinking through the earth and reaching China]

China tea *n* tea produced in China that produces a light-coloured mild brew. China teas are sometimes smoke-cured and flavoured with flower petals.

Chinatown /chínə town/ *n* an area of a city inhabited mainly by Chinese people, and containing businesses owned by them or selling Chinese products

chinaware /chínə wair/ *n* plates, dishes, and other tableware made of china

chincherinchee /chínchə rínchi/ *n* a plant of the lily family. Flowers: large, fragrant. Use: flower arrangements. Native to: southern Africa. *Ornithogalum thyrsoides.* [Early 20C. An imitation of the sound created when stalks are rubbed together.]

chinchilla /chin chíllə/ *n* **1** (*plural* **-las** *or* **-la**) BUSHY-TAILED RODENT a squirrel-sized rodent with a bushy tail and large round ears. Kept for: fur. Native to: South America. *Chinchilla laniger.* **2** CHINCHILLA FUR the fur of the chinchilla **3** WOOLLEN CLOTH a thick woollen fabric. Use: overcoats. [Early 17C. Via Spanish < Aymara or Quechua.]

chin-chin /chín chín/ *interj* used as a greeting, a way of saying goodbye, or as a toast when drinking (*dated informal*) [Late 18C. < Chinese *qing qing*.]

Chindwin /chín dwín/ river flowing from N Myanmar southwards into the River Irrawaddy. Length: 837 km/520 mi.

chine[1] /chīn/ *n* **1** JOINT OF MEAT a cut of meat that includes part of the backbone **2** BOTTOM CORNER OF BOAT the join between the bottom and sides of some boats, especially those with a flat or V-shaped bottom **3** *S England* RAVINE a deep ravine in a cliff wall (*regional*) ■ *vt* (**chines, chining, chined**) CUT MEAT FROM BACKBONE to cut meat along or across the backbone of the carcass [14C. < Old French *eschine* < Germanic ancestor of SHIN + Latin *spina* 'spine'.]

chine[2] *n* = **chime**[2]

Chinese /chī néez/ *npl* PEOPLE OF CHINA people who come from China or whose family came from China ■ *n* (*plural* **-nese**) **1** GROUP OF LANGUAGES SPOKEN IN CHINA a group of related Sino-Tibetan languages spoken across most of China and Taiwan, and by large communities elsewhere **2** OFFICIAL LANGUAGE OF CHINA the standard language of China and Taiwan and an official language of Singapore, also spoken by large communities elsewhere, that belongs to the Chinese group of Sino-Tibetan languages. Native speakers: 800 million. **3** FOOD, MEAL, OR RESTAURANT a restaurant or takeaway run by Chinese people and cooking food in styles from China, or food or a meal from one (*informal*) —**Chinese** *adj*

Chinese boxes *npl* a set of matching boxes graduated in size so that each fits inside the next larger one, and as each opens it reveals another waiting to be opened

Chinese burn *n* a way of inflicting pain that involves grasping somebody's arm and using both hands to twist the skin in opposite directions

Chinese cabbage *n* **1** a plant with a long head of overlapping wrinkled leaves and broad stalks, popular as a salad vegetable. *Brassica pekinensis.* **2** PLANTS, FOOD = **pak choi**

Chinese calendar *n* the traditional calendar used in China that divides the year into 24 fifteen-day periods and is based on both the lunar and solar cycles

Chinese chequers *n* a game played on a board marked with a six-pointed star studded with small holes. Players move or jump marbles hole by hole towards an opposite point of the star. (+ *singular verb*)

Chinese chestnut *n* a chestnut that is resistant to a blight that affects other chestnuts. Native to: China, Korea. *Castanea mollissima.*

Chinese Empire *n* China during the rule of the emperors, beginning with the Qin dynasty in the 5th century BC and ending when the republic was established in 1911–12

Chinese gooseberry *n* FOOD = **kiwi fruit**

Chinese lantern *n* **1** a lantern with a collapsible covering made of thin brightly coloured paper supported by thin wires **2** a plant with papery orange-red seed cases. *Physalis alkekengi.* US term **winter cherry** *n.* 1

Chinese leaves *npl* FOOD = **Chinese cabbage** *n.* 1

Chinese New Year *n* a festival day that introduces two weeks of celebrations marking the new year. Date: 1st day of 1st Chinese month, between January 21 and February 19.

Chinese puzzle *n* a puzzle, either in the form of a game or a problem, that is extremely intricate, ingenious, and difficult to solve

Chinese red *n* a vivid red colour tinged with orange

Chinese restaurant syndrome *n* a group of symptoms, including dizziness, headache, palpitations, and sweating, experienced by some people after eating food containing monosodium glutamate, an ingredient often used in preparing Chinese dishes

Chinese wall *n* **1** a strong or insurmountable barrier, especially one that obstructs the exchange of information **2** a set of strict rules preventing the exchange of confidential information between different departments of a stock exchange business, which might lead to its illegal use for gain

Chinese water torture *n* a method of psychological torture in which water is persistently dripped onto the victim's forehead

Chinese whispers *npl* a game in which people in a circle pass a message by whispering it into the ear of the person next to them, the message becoming increasingly distorted on the way

Chinese wood block *n* a hollow slotted wooden block that, when struck, makes a sound similar to that of horses' hooves striking the ground

Chinese wood oil *n* INDUST = **tung oil**

Ch'ing *n* HIST = **Qing**

chink[1] /chingk/ *n* **NARROW OPENING** a small narrow crack or slit ○ *Sunlight was coming through a chink in the curtains.* ■ *vt US* **1 FILL CRACKS IN** to fill up cracks or holes in something **2 MAKE CRACKS IN** to make cracks in something ○ *A flying pebble chinked my car's windshield.* [Early 16C. < ?] —**chinky** *adj*

chink[2] /chingk/ *n* a short sharp ringing sound such as that made when coins or glasses knock against each other ■ *vti* to make, or cause glass or metallic objects to make, a short sharp ringing sound ○ *We chinked glasses and said a toast.* [Late 16C. An imitation of the sound.]

Chink /chingk/, **Chinky** /chíngki/ (*plural* **-ies**) *n* a highly offensive term for a Chinese person (*taboo*) [Late 19C. < CHINA.]

chinkapin *n* = **chinquapin**

chinless /chínləss/ *adj* **1** having a lower jaw that recedes under the mouth instead of projecting in front of it **2** lacking strength of character

chinless wonder *n* somebody, especially an upper-class man, who is considered weak or ineffectual (*informal insult*)

chino /cheénō/ *n* a durable coarse cotton twill fabric, often khaki-coloured. Use: military uniforms, casual trousers. ■ **chinos** *npl* trousers made of chino [Mid-20C. < American Spanish, 'toasted'; from its original colour.]

chinoiserie /shin wáazəri/ *n* **1** a style of art and interior design that reflects Chinese influence **2** an object or decoration in a style reflecting Chinese influence, or such objects and decorations collectively [Late 19C. < French, < *chinois* 'Chinese'.]

chinook /chi nóok/ *n* **1** a moist warm wind from the sea that affects weather along the coast of the NW United States **2** a dry warm wind that blows down the eastern slopes of the Rocky Mountains

Chinook /chi nóok/ (*plural* **-nook** *or* **-nooks**) *n* **1** a member of a Native North American people who once lived in NW Oregon, and who now live in W Washington State **2** the extinct Penutian language of the Chinook [Early 19C. < Salish *tsinúk*.] —**Chinook** *adj*

Chinook Jargon *n* a pidgin language, once used for trading along the west coast of North America, made up of words borrowed from Chinook, Nootka, various Salishan languages, French, and English

Chinook salmon *n* **1** a large salmon found in the N Pacific Ocean that spawns in the rivers of North America and N Asia. *Oncorhyncus tshawytscha.* **2** the reddish flesh of a chinook salmon used as food

chinquapin /chíngkəpin/, **chincapin, chinkapin** *n* **1 EDIBLE NUT** a variety of chestnut **2 SMALL DECIDUOUS TREE** a small deciduous tree that produces chinquapins. Native to: E United States. *Castanea pumila.* **3 LARGE EVERGREEN TREE** a large evergreen tree bearing chinquapins. Native to: W North America. *Castanopsis chrysophylla.* [Early 17C. < Virginian Algonquian.]

chinstrap /chín strap/ *n* a strap attached to a helmet or hat that passes under the chin and is intended to keep the helmet or hat from falling off

chintz /chints/ *n* a glazed cotton fabric usually printed with a brightly coloured pattern [Early 17C. Alteration of *chints*, plural of *chint* 'calico cloth' < Hindi *chīṭ* 'stain' < Sanskrit *citra* 'variegated'.]

chintzy /chíntsi/ (**-ier, -iest**) *adj* **1 BRIGHTLY COLOURED AND PATTERNED** brightly coloured and patterned, in a style associated with chintz fabric ○ *chintzy curtains* **2 FUSSY OR QUAINT** describes a fussy, quaint, or would-be genteel style of decor (*informal disapproving*) **3** *US* **PENNY-PINCHING** mean and miserly ○ *He's so chintzy about money.* **4** *US* **TRASHY** cheap and gaudy ○ *Don't buy that chintzy suit; it'll fall apart the first time you have it cleaned.*

chin-up *n* an exercise performed by hanging from a horizontal bar and pulling the body up until the chin has been raised above the bar

chinwag /chín wag/ *n* a chat or conversation, especially a long one (*informal*) —**chinwagger** *n* —**chinwagging** *n*

chionodoxa /kī ónnə dóksə/ (*plural* **-as** *or* **-a**) *n* a hardy plant that grows from a bulb and flowers in early spring. Native to: Europe, Asia. Genus: *Chionodoxa.* [Late 19C. < modern Latin, < Greek *khiōn* 'snow' + *doxa* 'glory'.]

~~**chior**~~ incorrect spelling of **choir**

⚡**chip** /chip/ *n* **1 SMALL PIECE BROKEN OR CUT OFF** a small piece that has been broken, chopped, or cut off something hard or brittle **2 CRACK** a space or crack left in something hard or brittle after a small piece has been broken off or out of it ○ *This cup has a chip in it.* **3 LONG PIECE OF FRIED POTATO** a long finger-shaped wedge of potato traditionally fried in deep fat ○ *fish and chips* **4 PIECE OF THIN CRISP SNACK FOOD** a very thin crunchy slice made from a starchy food, usually potato or maize, that has been fried until it is crisp ○ *corn chips* **5 COUNTER USED AS MONEY** a token, often a small round plastic disc, used to represent money in poker and other gambling games **6 WAFER OF SEMICONDUCTOR MATERIAL** a small wafer of semiconductor material, usually silicon, forming the base on which an integrated circuit is laid out, or such a wafer together with its integrated circuit **7 SHORT LOFTED SHOT** in various sports, a short hit, kick, or shot that is lofted into the air over an obstacle or another player's head **8 WOOD CUT AS WEAVING MATERIAL** wood, straw, or other material that has been dried and cut for use in weaving **9** *US* **DRIED DUNG** a piece of dried animal dung, sometimes used for fuel ■ *v* (**chips, chipping, chipped**) **1** *vt* **BREAK OFF SMALL PIECE FROM** to break one or more small pieces from something hard or brittle **2** *vi* **LOSE SMALL PIECES** to become damaged by having a small piece or small pieces break off ○ *paint that will not chip easily* **3** *vt* **HIT IN HIGH ARC IN SPORTS** to hit or kick a ball or puck so that it travels a short distance in a high arc **4** *vi* **PLAY A CHIP SHOT** in golf, to play a chip shot **5** *vt* **CARVE BY REMOVING SMALL PIECES** to carve or shape something by cutting small pieces off or out of it **6** *vt* **CHOP INTO CHIPS** to chop or cut up something, e.g. a potato, to form chips ○ *Will you chip the ice for drinks?* [Pre-12C. < Latin *cippus* 'stake'.] —**chipper** *n* ◇ **a chip off the old block** a person resembling his or her parents (*informal*) ◇ **have a chip on your shoulder** to feel inferior or badly treated and so act in an oversensitive and resentful manner (*informal*) ◇ **have had your chips** to fail, be defeated, or die (*informal*) ◇ **spit chips** *Aus* to be very angry (*slang*) ◇ **when the chips are down** at a time of crisis or when vital matters are at stake (*informal*)

chip away 1 to destroy, reduce, or make something weaker by gradually and persistently attacking it ○ *comments designed to chip away at my self-esteem* **2** to break small pieces off something solid persistently and over a period of time

chip in *v* **1** *vti* **CONTRIBUTE** to contribute something to a common fund or resource (*informal*) ◊ **kick in** *v.* 3 **2** *vi* **INTERRUPT** to interrupt a conversation in order to make a comment (*informal*) **3** *vi* **PUT MONEY INTO POOL IN POKER** in poker and other games, to put chips or money into the pool in order to play

chipboard /chíp bawrd/ *n* a construction material made from compressed wood chips held together by a synthetic resin and produced in the form of hard flat boards

Chipewyan /chíppə wī́ ən/ (*plural* **-an** *or* **-ans**) *n* **1** a member of a Native North American people who live in N Saskatchewan, Manitoba, and the Northwest Territories **2** the Athabaskan language of the Chipewyan. Native speakers: 8,000. [Late 18C. < Cree *cīpwayān* '(wearing) pointed-skin (clothes)'.] —**Chipewyan** *adj*

⚡**chiphead** /chíp hed/ *n* a skilled and enthusiastic user of computers (*slang*)

chip log *n* a wooden chip attached to a line marked off in measured sections that is thrown overboard in order to determine a ship's speed

chipmunk /chíp mungk/ (*plural* **-munks** *or* **-munk**) *n* a striped rodent of the squirrel family that lives on the ground, collects nuts and fruit, and stores food in cheek pouches. Native to: North America, Asia. Genera: *Tamias* and *Eutamias.* [Mid-19C. < Ojibwa *ajidamoonʔ* 'squirrel', literally 'one that comes down trees headlong'.]

chipolata /chíppə láatə/ *n* a small thin sausage, usually made of finely ground pork [Late 19C. Via French < Italian *cipollata* 'with onions' < *cipolla* 'onion' < Latin *cepa*.]

Chipp /chip/, **Don** (*b.* 1925) Australian politician

Chippendale /chíppən dayl/ *adj* describes furniture in an 18th-century English style characterized by graceful flowing lines, cabriole legs, and elaborate ornamentation [After Thomas CHIPPENDALE] —**Chippendale** *n*

Chippendale /chíppən dayl/, **Thomas** (1718–79) British furniture designer

chipper /chíppər/ *adj* (*informal*) **1** cheerful and full of vitality **2** smartly dressed [Mid-19C. < ?]

Chippewa /chíppə waa/ *n, adj* PEOPLES, LANG = **Ojibwa** [Mid-18C. Alteration of OJIBWA.]

chippie *n* = **chippy**[1]

chipping /chípping/ *n* = **chip** *n.* 1 ■ **chippings** *npl* small stones used in surfacing roads

chippy[1] /chíppi/ (*plural* **-pies**), **chippie** *n* (*informal*) **1** a fish and chip shop **2** a carpenter

chippy[2] /chíppi/ (**-pier, -piest**) *adj Can* behaving in an aggressive or belligerent way [< *have a chip on your shoulder*]

⚡**chipset** /chíp set/, **chip set** *n* a group of microchips designed to perform one or more related functions as a unit, e.g. to update a computer screen display

chip shot *n* **1** a short-range kick or shot in which the ball or puck rises sharply into the air **2** a short approach shot in golf, used to loft the ball onto the green

Chirac /sheér ak/, **Jacques** (*b.* 1932) French statesman and Prime Minister (1974–76, 1986–88) and President (1995–) of France

chiral /kī́rəl/ *adj* describes a molecule whose arrangement of atoms is such that it cannot be superimposed on its mirror image [Late 19C. < Greek *kheir* 'hand'.] —**chirality** /kī rálləti/ *n*

Chi-Rho /kī́ rṓ/ *n* a monogram and symbol for Jesus Christ, formed by superimposing the Greek letters *chi* (X) and *rho* (P) [< the first two letters of Jesus Christ's name in Greek]

Chirico /kírrikō/, **Giorgio de** (1888–1978) Greek-born Italian painter

chiro-, cheiro- *prefix* hand ○ *chiromancy* [Via Latin < Greek *kheir*]

chirography /kī róggrəfi/ *n* ARTS = **calligraphy** *n.* 1

chiromancy /kīrō manssi/ *n* PARANORMAL = **palmistry**

Chiron /kīron/ *n* in Greek mythology, the centaur, known for his great wisdom, who was the tutor of Greek heroes such as Hercules, Achilles, and Jason

chironomid /kī rónnəmid/ *n* a small nonbiting midge that gathers in large breeding swarms, especially near water. Family: Chironomidae. [Late 19C. < modern Latin *Chironomidae* < Greek *kheironomos* 'pantomime dancer'.]

chiropody /ki róppədi, shi-/ *n* the branch of medicine concerned with the care and treatment of the feet. US term **podiatry** —**chiropodist** *n*

chiropractic /kīrō práktik/ *n* a medical system based on the theory that disease and disorders are caused by a misalignment of the bones, especially in the spine, that obstructs proper nerve functions [Late 19C. < CHIRO- + Greek *praktikos* 'effective'.] —**chiropractor** /kīrō praktər/ *n*

chiropteran /kī róptərən/, **chiropter** /kī róptər/ *n* a flying mammal, such as the bat, with forelimbs that have evolved as membranous wings (*technical*) [Mid-19C. < modern Latin *Chiroptera* < CHIRO- + Greek *pteron* 'wing'.]

chirp /churp/ *n* **SHORT HIGH-PITCHED SOUND** a short high-pitched sound, especially as made by a bird ■ *v* **1** *vi* **MAKE A CHIRP** to make a short high-pitched sound **2** *vti* **SPEAK IN CHEERFUL MANNER** to speak, or say something, in a cheerful, lively, or pert voice [15C. An imitation of the sound.]

chirpy /chúrpi/ (**-ier, -iest**) *adj* cheerful and lively (*informal*) —**chirpily** *adv* —**chirpiness** *n*

chirr /chur/ *n* a shrill harsh trilled sound made by some insects, e.g. grasshoppers ■ *vi* to make a harsh trilled sound [Early 17C. An imitation of the sound.]

chirrup /chírrəp/ *v* **1** *vi* **TWITTER** to utter a series of chirps **2** *vti* **SPEAK IN HIGH CHEERFUL VOICE** to speak or say something in a high-pitched voice, and in a cheerful and lively fashion **3** *vi* **MAKE CLUCKING SOUND WITH LIPS** to make a clucking sound with the lips, e.g. when encouraging a horse to move faster ■ *n* **CHIRP** a repeated series of chirping or clucking sounds [Late 16C. Alteration of CHIRP.] —**chirrupy** *adj*

chisel /chízz'l/ *n* **1 TOOL WITH FLAT BEVELLED BLADE** a tool for cutting and shaping wood or stone, consisting of a straight flat bevelled blade with a sharp square-cut bottom edge inserted in a handle **2** TECH, DIY = **cold chisel** ■ *v* (**-els, -elling, -elled**) **1** *vti* **CARVE WITH CHISEL** to carve, cut, or work wood or stone using a chisel **2** *vti* **CHEAT** to cheat or swindle somebody (*informal*) **3** *vt* **OBTAIN BY CHEATING** to obtain something by cheating or deception (*informal*) [14C. Via Old French, < Latin *caes-*, stem of *caedere* 'to cut'.]

chiselled /chízzəl'd/ *adj* clear-cut or sharply defined in shape or profile ○ *a finely chiselled face*

chiseller /chízzələr/ *n* **1** a cheat or swindler (*informal*) **2** *Ireland* a child (*slang regional*)

Chisholm /chízzəm/, **Caroline** (1808–77) British philanthropist

Chişinău /kíshi nő/ capital of Moldova, in central Moldova. Population: 667,100 (1992 estimate).

chi-square /kī skwair/ *n* a statistical calculation used to test how well the distribution of a set of observed data matches a theoretical probability distribution

chi-square distribution *n* a probability function widely used in testing a statistical hypothesis, e.g. the likelihood that a given statistical distribution of results might be reached in an experiment

chit[1] /chit/ *n* **1** a note, bill, or any small slip of paper with writing on it, especially a statement of money owed for food or drink (*dated*) **2** an official note or document, usually signed by somebody in authority, e.g. a receipt, order, or requisition form [Late 18C. Shortening of *chitty*, via Hindi *ciṭṭhī* < Sanskrit *citra* 'spot', referring to the writing.]

chit[2] /chit/ *n* a child, girl, or young woman, especially one whose physical slightness seems to be at odds with an impertinent, forceful, or self-confident manner

chit[3] /chit/ *vt* to place a potato in a light place to cause it to produce shoots before planting in the ground

chital /cheét'l/ (*plural* **-tal** *or* **-tals**) *n* = **axis deer** [Late 19C. < Hindi *cītal* < Sanskrit *citrala* 'spotted'.]

chitchat /chít chat/ *n* casual conversation or small talk, or a casual conversation with somebody (*informal*) [Late 17C. Elaboration of CHAT.] —**chitchat** *vi*

chitin /kītin/ *n* a tough semitransparent substance that forms part of the protective outer casing (**cuticle**) of some insects and other arthropods, and the cell walls of some fungi [Mid-19C. Via French *chitine* < Greek *khitōn* 'tunic'.] —**chitinoid** *adj* —**chitinous** *adj*

chitlins /chítlins/, **chitlings** /-lings/ *npl Southern US* = **chitterlings** [Mid-19C. Contraction of CHITTERLINGS.]

chiton /kīt'n, -ton/ *n* **1** a small primitive marine mollusc that lives on rocks and has an elongated body protected by a shell consisting of eight overlapping plates. Class: Polyplacophora. **2** a loose knee-length woollen tunic worn by women and men in ancient Greece [Early 19C. < Greek *khitōn* 'tunic'.]

Chittagong /chíttə gong/ port in SE Bangladesh. Population: 1,566,070 (1991).

chitterlings /chíttərlingz/ *npl* the small intestines of pigs, especially when prepared as food [13C. < ?]

chiv /chiv, shiv/, **chive, shiv** /shiv/ *n* a pocketknife, often a flick knife, or razor (*slang*) ■ *vt* (**chivs, chivving, chivved; chives, chiving, chived; shivs, shivving, shivved**) to slash or stab somebody with a flick knife or razor (*slang*) [Late 17C. < ?]

chivalric /shívv'lrik/ *adj* relating to knights, knighthood, and the knightly code of honour

chivalry /shívv'lri/ (*plural* **-ries**) *n* **1 QUALITIES OF IDEAL KNIGHT** the combination of qualities expected of the ideal medieval knight, especially courage, honour, loyalty, and consideration for others, especially women **2 CHIVALROUS BEHAVIOUR** courteous and considerate behaviour, especially towards women **3 MEDIEVAL KNIGHTHOOD** the medieval concept of knighthood, and the customs, practices, social system, and religious and personal ideals associated with knights and their way of life [13C. Via Old French *chevalerie* < medieval Latin *caballerius* < Latin *caballus* 'horse'.] —**chivalrous** *adj* —**chivalrously** *adv* —**chivalrousness** *n*

chive /chīv/ *n* **1** a long fine hollow leaf with a strong onion flavour. Use: seasoning food. (*usually plural*) **2** a plant that produces chives. Flowers: purple, ball-shaped. *Allium schoenoprasum.* [14C. < Old French dialect, < Latin *cepa* 'onion'.]

chivvy /chívvi/ (**-vies, -vying, -vied**), **chivy** (**-ies, -ying, -ied**), **chevy** /chévvi/ (**-ies, -ying, -ied**) *vt* to urge, pester, or harass somebody, usually in order to make him or her do something or do it more quickly [Late 18C. Probably after *Chevy Chase*, site of a battle (1388) in the Anglo-Scottish border wars.]

chlamydes plural of **chlamys**

chlamydia /klə míddi ə/ *n* **1** a spherical bacterium that causes several eye and urogenital diseases in humans and other animals, and psittacosis in pet birds. Genus: *Chlamydia.* **2** a sexually transmitted disease caused by chlamydia [Mid-20C. Via modern Latin, < Greek *khlamud-* 'mantle'.]

chlamydial /kləmíddi əl/ *adj* describes infections that are caused by a bacterium of the genus *Chlamydia*, e.g. trachoma and sexually transmitted infections such as urethritis

chlamydomonas /klámmidə mṓnəss/ (*plural* **-domonases** *or* **-domonas**) *n* a single-celled organism that lives in fresh water and soil, absorbing its food by photosynthesis. Genus: *Chlamydomonas.* [Late 19C. < modern Latin, < Greek *khlamud-* 'mantle' + *monas* 'unit'.]

chlamydospore /klə míddə spawr/ *n* an asexual thick-walled spore produced by some fungi [Late 19C. < Greek *khlamud-* 'mantle'.]

chlamys /klámmiss, kláy-/ (*plural* **-yses** *or* **-ydes** /klámmi deez/) *n* a short cloak gathered and fastened at the shoulder, worn by men in ancient Greece [Late 17C. < Greek *khlamus* 'mantle'.]

chloasma /klō ázmə/ (*plural* **-mata** /-mətə/) *n* dark coloration on the skin of the face caused by hormonal changes related to pregnancy, liver disease, or the use of birth control pills [Mid-19C. < Greek *khloazein* 'become green'.]

chlor- *prefix* = **chloro-** (*before vowels*)

chloracne /klawr ákni/ *n* a skin eruption resembling acne caused by repeated contact with something containing chlorinated hydrocarbons

chloral /kláwrəl/ *n* CCl_3CHO a colourless oily toxic liquid with a strong odour. Use: manufacture of chloral hydrate and DDT.

chloral hydrate *n* $C_2H_3Cl_3O_2$ a colourless crystalline solid that is soluble in water and is used as a sedative and hypnotic

chloramine /kláwrə meen/ *n* NH_2Cl an unstable colourless liquid with a pungent odour. Use: manufacture of hydrazine.

chloramphenicol /kláwr am fénni kol/ *n* a powerful antibiotic derived from a soil bacterium that sometimes has the side effect of causing the failure of blood cell production [Mid-20C. < CHLOR- + AMIDE + PHEN- + NITRO- + GLYCOL.]

chlorate /kláwr ayt/ *n* any salt of chloric acid [Early 19C. < CHLORIC.]

chlordane /kláwr dayn/, **chlordan** /-dan/ *n* $C_{10}H_6Cl_8$ a thick toxic colourless to amber-coloured liquid that can exist with several different molecular structures (**isomers**). Use: insecticide, fumigant. [Mid-20C. < CHLOR- + INDENE + -ANE.]

chlordiazepoxide /kláwr dī ázzə póksīd/ *n* $C_{16}H_{14}ClN_3O$ a yellow crystalline powder. Use: tranquillizer, treatment for alcoholism. [Mid-20C. < CHLOR- + DI- + AZO- + EPI- + OXIDE.]

chlorella /klə réllə/ *n* a single-celled green alga that is often used in research. Genus: *Chlorella.* [Early 20C. < modern Latin, 'little green (thing)' < Greek *khlōros* 'green'.]

chloric /kláwrik/ *adj* containing chlorine, especially with a valency of 5 [Early 19C. < CHLORINE.]

chloric acid *n* $HClO_3{\cdot}7H_2O$ a toxic unstable acid, known only in solution and as chlorate salts

chloride /kláwr īd/ *n* a compound containing chlorine and one other element [Early 19C. < CHLORINE.] —**chloridic** /klə ríddik/ *adj*

chloride of lime *n* a powder used as a bleach (*technical*)

chloride shift *n* the reversible exchange of bicarbonate and chloride ions from blood serum to red cells during the transport of carbon dioxide

chlorinate /kláwri nayt/ (**-nates, -nating, -nated**) *vt* to combine or treat something with chlorine, especially in order to kill harmful organisms —**chlorinated** *adj* —**chlorination** /kláwri náysh'n/ *n* —**chlorinator** *n*

chlorine /kláwr een/ *n* (*symbol* **Cl**) a gaseous, poisonous, corrosive, greenish-yellow element of the halogen group that is highly reactive. Source: electrolysis of sodium chloride. Use: water purification, disinfectant. [Early 19C. < Greek *khlōros* 'green'.]

chlorite[1] /kláwr īt/ *n* a group of soft, green or black aluminosilicate minerals. Source: metamorphic rocks. [Late 18C. Via Latin *chloritis* < Greek *khlōritis*, green precious stone.]

chlorite[2] /kláwr īt/ *n* any salt of chlorous acid [Mid-19C. < CHLORINE.]

chloro- *prefix* **1** green ○ *chlorophyll* **2** chlorine ○ *chlorobenzene* [< Greek *khlōros* 'green']

chlorobenzene /kláwrō bén zeen/ *n* C_6H_5Cl a combination of chlorine and benzene that produces a colourless flammable liquid with an almond smell. Use: production of solvents and DDT.

chlorofluorocarbon /kláwrō flóorō kaárbən, -fláwrō-/ *n* full form of **CFC**

chloroform /kláwrə fawrm/ *n* $CHCl_3$ a colourless sweet-smelling toxic liquid that rapidly changes to a vapour and causes unconsciousness if inhaled. Use: solvent, cleaning agent, and formerly anaesthetic. ■ *vt* to make a person or animal breathe in chloroform in order to cause unconsciousness [Mid-19C. < CHLORO- + FORMIC.]

chloromethane /kláwrō meé thayn/ *n* = **methyl chloride**

chlorophyll /klórrəfil/ *n* the pigment in plants that captures the light energy required for photosynthesis —**chlorophyllose** /klórrə fílləss/ *adj*

chlorophyte /klórrə fīt/ *n* a green alga found mainly in fresh water. Division: *Chlorophyta.*

chloropicrin /kláwrə píkrin/ *n* CCl_3NO_2 a colourless toxic liquid that causes tears and vomiting. Use: tear gas, insecticide, disinfectant, in dyes. [Mid-19C. < CHLORO- + PICRO-.]

chloroplast /kláwrə plast, -plaast/ *n* a membranous sac (**plastid**) that contains chlorophyll and other pigments and is the place where photosynthesis occurs within the cells of plants and algae —**chloroplastic** /kláwrə plástik/ *adj*

chloroprene /kláwrə preen/ *n* C_4H_5Cl a colourless liquid. Use: manufacture of neoprene. [Mid-20C. < CHLORO- + ISOPRENE.]

chloroquine /kláwrə kween/ *n* a drug used in the treatment of malaria and amoebiasis. [Mid-20C. < CHLORO- + QUINOLINE, from which it is derived.]

chlorosis /klə róssiss/ *n* **1** a yellowing or whitening of a plant's leaves and stems caused by a lack of chlorophyll **2** severe iron-deficiency anaemia that produces a greenish tint in the skin —**chlorotic** /-róttik/ *adj* —**chlorotically** *adv*

chlorothiazide /kláwrō thī́ ə zīd/ *n* a drug that relieves fluid retention. Use: treatment of high blood pressure, swelling, and heart failure.

chlorous /kláwrəss/ *adj* relating to or containing chlorine with a valency of 3 [Mid-19C. < CHLORINE.]

chlorpromazine /klawr prṓmə zeen/ *n* a drug. Use: sedative, tranquillizer, treatment of psychiatric disorders. [Mid-20C. < CHLOR- + PROMETHAZINE.]

chlorpropamide /klawr próppə mīd, -prṓpə-/ *n* a drug that lowers blood sugar. Use: treatment of diabetes. [Mid-20C. < CHLOR- + PROPANE + AMIDE.]

chlortetracycline /klawr téttrə sī́klin, -kleen/ *n* an antibiotic drug. Source: soil bacterium. Use: treatment of infections, stimulation of growth in livestock.

ChM *abbr* Master of Surgery [Latin *Chirurgiae Magister*]

choc /chok/ *n* a chocolate-covered sweet, especially one from a box of chocolates (*informal*) [Shortening]

chocaholic *n* = **chocoholic**

~~**chocalate**~~ incorrect spelling of **chocolate**

choc ice *n* a small block of ice cream coated in a thin layer of chocolate

chock /chok/ *n* **1 BLOCK TO STOP SOMETHING MOVING** a block of wood or metal used to prevent a wheel from turning, an object from moving, or to support something when it is raised off the ground **2 SHIP'S FITMENT FOR SECURING CABLES** a heavy metal fitment attached to the deck of a ship that has two inward-curving horn-shaped projections around which a cable can be secured **3 METAL ANCHOR FOR CLIMBING** a metal device used to provide anchoring systems for climbing or caving ■ *vt* **USE CHOCK FOR BRACE** to keep something from turning, moving, or falling by using a chock to block or brace it ○ *chock the plane's wheels* [14C. Probably < Old French *ço(u)che* 'log'.]

chock-a-block *adj* **1** so crammed with things or crowded with people as to make it virtually impossible to get anything or anybody else in or to move about (*informal*) **2** having the two blocks in a block and tackle tight up against each other [Mid-19C. Alteration of *chock and block* (nautical) 'with pulleys drawn close together'.]

chocker /chókər/, **chocka** /chókə/ *adj* **1 CHOCK-A-BLOCK** chock-a-block (*slang*) **2 COMPLETELY FULL** completely full up after eating (*slang*) **3 VERY FED UP OR IRRITATED** very fed up or irritated (*dated slang*) ○ *I'm chocker with all this work.* [Mid-20C. Shortening of CHOCK-A-BLOCK.]

chock-full *adj* crammed with something (*informal*)

chocoholic /chókə hóllik/, **chocaholic** *n* a lover of chocolate who is apparently addicted to it (*humorous*) [Late 20C. < CHOCOLATE + -AHOLIC.]

chocolate /chóklit/ *n* **1 SMOOTH SWEET BROWN FOOD** a food or flavouring, typically a smooth sweet brown and rather brittle solid, made from roasted and ground cacao seeds usually sweetened and mixed with cocoa butter and dried milk (*often before nouns*) ○ *a bar of chocolate* ○ *chocolate cake* **2 SWEET COVERED IN CHOCOLATE** a small chocolate-coated sweet with a hard or soft centre **3 CHOCOLATE DRINK** a drink, usually served hot or warm, made from sweetened powdered chocolate mixed with water or milk **4 BROWN COLOUR** a deep warm brown colour [Early 17C. Directly or via French < Spanish, < Nahuatl *chocolatl* 'bitter water'.] —**chocolate** *adj* —**chocolatey** *adj*

chocolate-box *adj* depicting pretty scenes or pretty people in a stereotyped and usually sentimental or romanticized way ○ *chocolate-box portraits*

chocolate chip *n* a small piece of chocolate, used especially in making biscuits and desserts ○ *chocolate chip cookies*

chocolate tree *n* TREES = **cacao** *n.* 1

chocolatier /chókə látti ər/ *n* a maker or seller of chocolates

Choctaw /chók taw/ (*plural* **-taw** *or* **-taws**) *n* **1** a member of a Native North American people who once lived in central and S Mississippi, and who now live mainly in Oklahoma and S Mississippi **2** the Muskogean language of the Choctaw. Native speakers: 10,000. [Early 18C. < Choctaw *čahta*.] —**Choctaw** *adj*

choice /choyss/ *n* **1 ACT OF CHOOSING** a decision to choose one thing, person, or course of action in preference to others ○ *Think very carefully before you make a choice.* **2 POWER TO CHOOSE** the chance or ability to choose between different things ○ *They gave us no choice* **3 SELECTION OF THINGS** a variety of things, people, or possibilities from which to choose ○ *a wide choice of styles and colours* **4 CHOSEN OBJECT** a person, thing, or course of action chosen by somebody from among a range of possibilities ○ *Red would not have been my choice.* **5 BEST PART** the best or most desirable part ■ *adj* (**choicer, choicest**) **1 HIGH-QUALITY** being of particularly good quality **2 RUDE OR EMPHATIC** carefully chosen for effectiveness and usually expressing displeasure or dislike in a sufficiently emphatic way (*used euphemistically*) ○ *a few choice words* [13C. < Old French *chois* < *choisir* 'choose' < Germanic.] —**choiceness** *n* ◇ **of choice** chosen from among several as being the best or most suitable ○ *the newspaper of choice*

choir /kwīr/ *n* **1 GROUP OF SINGERS** an organized group of singers who perform together (*takes a singular or plural verb*) **2 AREA WHERE CHOIR SINGS** the part of a church where the choir performs **3 INSTRUMENT GROUP** a group of instruments of the same type **4** = **choir organ** [13C. Via Old French *quer* < Latin *chorus* (see CHORUS).]

choirboy /kwī́r boy/ *n* a boy who sings in a church choir

choirgirl /kwī́r gurl/ *n* a girl who sings in a church choir

choir loft *n* a raised gallery or part of the upper storey in a church, where the choir performs during services

choirmaster /kwī́r maastər/ *n* a trainer and conductor of a choir

choir organ *n* a manual organ or section of a large organ with sets of soft-toned pipes suitable for accompanying a choir. ◊ **great organ**

choir school *n* a school where the members of a cathedral or church choir are educated and attend ordinary lessons as well as receiving special musical training

choke[1] /chōk/ *v* (**chokes, choking, choked**) **1** *vi* **STOP BREATHING THROUGH BLOCKAGE OF THROAT** to stop breathing, or breathe with great difficulty, because of a blockage in or restriction of the throat **2** *vt* **PREVENT BREATHING BY CONSTRICTING THROAT** to prevent somebody from breathing by blocking or squeezing the throat **3** *vt* **BLOCK PASSAGE OR CHANNEL** to form an obstruction in a passage, channel, pipe, or roadway and prevent anything from passing along it **4** *vt* **PREVENT PLANTS FROM GROWING** to prevent plants from developing by growing over them and depriving them of light and air ○ *the bed was choked with weeds* **5** *vti* **BE TOO MOVED TO SPEAK** to be overcome with emotion and unable to speak, or make somebody feel so much emotion that he or she cannot speak (*informal*) **6** *vi US* **LOSE NERVE AND FALTER** to lose nerve or confidence and falter in the middle of saying or doing something (*informal*) ○ *He gets ahead, two sets to one, and then he chokes!* **7** *vi US* **REFUSE TO COOPERATE** to refuse to cooperate when presented with something unacceptable (*informal*) ○ *We choked on their last demand.* ■ *n* **1 NOISE OF CHOKING** a sound or movement made by or resembling somebody choking **2 FUEL MIXTURE REGULATOR FOR ENGINE** a device that controls the ratio of air to fuel in the mixture supplied to an internal-combustion engine ○ *pull the choke out* [Old English *ācēocian* < *cēoce* 'cheek'] —**choking** *adj* —**chokingly** *adv*

choke back *vt* to stop the expression of an emotional response to something by a deliberate effort of self-control ○ *I couldn't choke back my tears any longer.*

choke off *vt* to stop the flow, supply, or development of something, usually abruptly

choke[2] /chōk/ *n* the bristly inner inedible part of an artichoke [Shortening]

chokeberry /chṓkbəri/ (*plural* **-ries**) *n* **1** a small bitter red or purplish fruit **2** (*plural* **-ries** *or* **-ry**) a bush that bears chokeberries. Flowers: small, white or pink. Native to: North America. Genus: *Aronia*. [Late 18C. < the bitterness of the fruit.]

chokebore /chṓk bawr/ *n* **1** a shotgun bore that tapers towards the muzzle to prevent wide scattering of the shot **2** a shotgun with a bore that tapers towards the muzzle

choke chain *n* a chain serving as a collar and short lead that fits in a sliding loop around an animal's neck, so that when the animal pulls away the chain gets tighter

chokecherry /chṓk cheri/ (*plural* **-ries**) *n* **1** a dark red or black bitter fruit of a wild cherry **2** (*plural* **-ries** *or* **-ry**) a wild cherry tree that bears chokecherries. Flowers: small, white, in clusters. Native to: North America. *Prunus virginiana.*

choke coil *n* an induction coil used to limit or suppress the flow of alternating current without stopping the flow of direct current

choke collar *n* = **choke chain**

choked /chōkt/ *adj* overcome by emotion, usually unhappiness, disappointment, or resentment (*informal*) US term **choked up**

chokedamp /chṓk damp/ *n* MIN EXTRACT = **blackdamp**

choked up *adj US* = **choked** (*informal*)

chokehold /chṓk hōld/ *n* a tight hold in which one person restrains another by placing an arm round his or her neck, usually from behind

choke point *n* **1 AREA OF BLOCKAGE** a congested or narrow part where a blockage can occur **2 NARROW SHALLOW SEA CORRIDOR** a place at sea where geography and water depth combine to create a narrow shallow corridor for submarines and surface ships **3** *Can, US* **STICKING POINT** a point or situation that is an obstacle to an agreement or results in an impasse ○ *amnesty being the choke point in the political settlement*

choker /chṓkər/ *n* **1** a short length of cloth or ribbon, or a short necklace, that fastens closely around the neck and is worn as an ornament **2** a high close-fitting collar, e.g. a clerical collar

⚡**choke route** *n* a computer firewall that isolates an internal network from the Internet

chokey *n* = **choky**

choko /chṓkō/ (*plural* **-kos**) *n ANZ* a light- green, pear-shaped tropical fruit of the cayote plant that tastes like a cucumber and is eaten as a vegetable in Australia, New Zealand, and the West Indies [Early 20C. < Brazilian Indian *chuchu*.]

choky /chṓki/, **chokey** *n* prison (*dated slang*) ○ *three months in choky* [Early 17C. < Hindi *caukī* 'lock-up', influenced by CHOKE[1].]

cholangiography /kō lánji óggrəfi/ *n* X-ray examination of the bile ducts to check for obstructions, carried out after the patient has swallowed a substance that shows up on an X-ray [Mid-20C. < CHOLE- + ANGIOGRAPHY.] —**cholangiogram** /kō lánji ə gram/ *n* —**cholangiographic** /-ə gráffik/ *adj*

chole- *prefix* bile, bile ducts, gall bladder ○ *cholelithiasis* [< Greek *kholē* < Indo-European, 'yellow-coloured']

cholecalciferol /kṓlə kal síffərol, kóllə-/ *n* a form of vitamin D found naturally in fish-liver oils and egg yolks. US term **vitamin D_3**

cholecyst /kṓlə sist, kóllə-/ *n* the gall bladder (*technical*)

cholecystectomy /kṓlə si stéktəmi, kóllə-/ (*plural* **-mies**) *n* a surgical operation to remove the gall bladder

cholecystitis /kṓlə si stī́ tiss, kóllə-/ *n* inflammation of the gall bladder, usually caused by a bacterial infection or gallstones

cholecystography /kṓlə si stóggrəfi, kóllə-/ (*plural* **-phies**) *n* X-ray examination of the gall bladder after the patient has swallowed a substance that shows up on an X-ray

cholecystokinin /kṓlə sistə kī́nin, kóllə-/ *n* a hormone secreted by cells at the top of the small intestine that stimulates the gall bladder, making it contract and release bile [Early 20C. < CHOLECYST + KININ.]

cholelithiasis /kṓlə li thī́ əssiss, kóllə-/ *n* the formation or presence of gallstones in the gall bladder or bile ducts

choler /kóllər/ *n* **1** anger or bad temper (*literary or archaic*) **2** one of the four basic fluids (**humours**) of the body according to medieval medicine, thought to make somebody whose body contained too much of it prone to anger and irritability [14C. Via French *colère* < Latin *cholera* 'bile' (see CHOLERA).]

cholera /kóllərə/ *n* an acute and often fatal intestinal disease that produces severe gastrointestinal symptoms and is usually caused by the bacterium *Vibrio* *cholerae* [14C. Via Latin, 'illness caused by bile' < Greek *kholera* < *kholē* 'bile'.] —**choleraic** /kóllə ráy ik/ *adj* — **choleroid** *adj*

choleric /kóllərik/ *adj* showing or tending to show anger or irritation (*literary*) [14C. Directly and via French *cholérique* < Latin *cholericus* 'bilious' < Greek *kholera* (see CHOLERA).] —**cholerically** *adv*

cholestasis /kóli stáysiss, -stássiss, kólli-/ *n* a stoppage or slowing of the flow of bile

cholesteatoma /kóli stee ə tṓmə, kólli-/ *n* a potentially dangerous condition of the middle ear in which a mass of cholesterol and skin scales forms, grows, and invades the local structures, including bone

cholesterol /kə léstə rol/ *n* a steroid alcohol (**sterol**) made by the liver and present in all animal cells that is a precursor of bile and many hormones [Late 19C. < CHOLE- + Greek *stereos* 'stiff'.]

cholestyramine /kóli stéerə meen, kō léstər ámmeen/ *n* a synthetic resin that binds cholesterol with bile acids. Use: to lower blood cholesterol. [Mid-20C. < CHOLE- + STYRENE + -AMINE.]

choli /chṓli/ (*plural* **-lis**) *n* a short fitted top with short sleeves, worn underneath a sari [Early 20C. < Hindi *colī*.]

cholic acid /kṓlik-, kóllik-/ *n* a bile acid made in the liver from cholesterol and secreted in faeces

choline /kṓ leen/ *n* a soluble compound (**amine**) found in animal and plant tissue that is involved in fat transportation and is a precursor of acetylcholine [Mid-19C. < CHOLE-.]

cholinergic /kṓli núrjik/ *adj* **1** describes nerves that are activated by acetylcholine or that release it **2** describes drugs that act like acetylcholine [Mid-20C. < CHOLINE + Greek *ergon* 'work'.] —**cholinergically** *adv*

cholinesterase /kṓlli néstə rayss, -rayz/ *n* BIOCHEM = **acetylcholinesterase** [Mid-20C. < CHOLINE + ESTERASE.]

cholla /chóy ə/ (*plural* **-las** *or* **-la**) *n* a cactus that has cylindrical stem segments and yellow spines. Flowers: vividly coloured in some cultivated types. Native to: SW United States, Mexico. Genus: *Opuntia*. [Mid-19C. Via Mexican Spanish < obsolete Spanish, 'top of the head'.]

chometz *n* = **chametz**

chomp /chomp/, **chump** /chump/ *vti* **CHEW NOISILY** to take big bites of food and chew steadily, noisily, and with obvious satisfaction (*informal*) ■ *n* (*informal*) **1 NOISY BITE** a big noisy bite into something **2 SOUND OF BITE** the sound made by noisy energetic biting or chewing [Mid-17C. Variant of CHAMP[1].]

Chomsky /chómski/, **Noam** (*b.* 1928) US linguist

chon /chōn/ (*plural* **chon**) *n* see table at **currency** [Mid-20C. < Korean.]

chondr- *prefix* = **chondro-**

chondral /kóndrəl/ *adj* relating to or consisting of cartilage

chondri- *prefix* = **chondro-**

chondrify /kóndri fī/ (**-fies, -fying, -fied**) *vti* to change tissue into cartilage, or be changed into cartilage [Late 19C. < Greek *khondros* 'cartilage'.] —**chondrification** /kóndrifi káysh'n/ *n*

chondrite /kón drīt/ *n* a stony meteorite that contains spherical masses (**chondrules**) of mainly silicate minerals [Mid-19C. < Greek *khondros* 'granule'.] —**chondritic** /kon dríttik/ *adj*

chondro-, chondr-, chondri- *prefix* **1** cartilage ○ *chondrocranium* **2** granule ○ *chondrule* [< Greek *khondros*]

chondrocranium /kón drō kráy ni əm/ (*plural* **-ums** *or* **-a** /-ni ə/) *n* the part of an embryo's skull that consists of cartilage that later hardens into bone

chondroma /kon drṓmə/ (*plural* **-mas** *or* **-mata** /-mətə/) *n* a benign abnormal growth of cartilage

chondrule /kón drool/ *n* a small spherical mass of mineral matter from outer space, sometimes found in meteorites [Late 19C. < CHONDRITE.]

Chong /chong/, **Son** (1676–1759) Korean artist

Chongqing /chŏŏng chíng/, **Chungking, Ch'ung-ch'ing** city in SW China. Population: 2,980,000 (1991).

Chonju /jún jŏŏ/, **Chŏnju** capital of North Cholla Province, South Korea. Population: 563,406 (1995).

choo-choo /chŏŏ choo/, **choo-choo train** *n* a railway train or locomotive (*babytalk*) [Early 20C. An imitation of the sound of a steam train.]

chook /chŏŏk, chook/ *n ANZ* **1** a hen or chicken (*informal*) **2** an offensive term that deliberately insults a woman's age or appearance (*slang*) [Mid-20C. An imitation of a clucking sound.]

choose /chooz/ (**chooses, choosing, chose** /chōz/, **chosen** /chōz'n/) *vti* **1** to decide which of a number of different things or people is best or most suitable **2** to make a deliberate decision to do something ○ *Jane has chosen to do the midwifery course.* [Old English *cēosan* < Indo-European] —**chooser** *n*

SPELLCHECK Do not confuse ***choose*** with ***chose***, which has a similar sound and spelling. Beware: your spellchecker will not catch this error.

choose up *vti US* to pick the players wanted in a team for a game

choosy /chŏŏzi/ (**-ier, -iest**) *adj* very precise or discriminating in preferences (*informal*) —**choosily** *adv* — **choosiness** *n*

Cho Oyu /chṓ ṓ yoo/ mountain in the Himalaya range. Height: 8,201 m/26,906 ft.

chop[1] /chop/ *v* (**chops, chopping, chopped**) **1** *vt* **CUT UP WITH SHARP TOOL** to cut something into pieces with downward strokes of an axe, knife, or other sharp-bladed tool ○ *a dish of chopped liver* **2** *vt* **CUT OFF** to use a quick sharp blow or blows to sever or fell something ○ *chopped down the tree* **3** *vi* **MAKE CHOPPING MOVEMENTS** to make downward cutting movements with a tool or with the hand **4** *vt* **FORM BY CHOPPING** to make something such as a hole or path by chopping with an axe or other tool ○ *He chopped his way through the undergrowth.* **5** *vt* **GET RID OF** to get rid of something or somebody, especially jobs or staff, put an end to something, or curtail something drastically (*informal*) ○ *Several junior members of staff have been chopped.* **6** *vt* **HIT BALL WITH SHARP DOWNWARD MOVEMENT IN SPORTS** to hit a ball with a quick sharp downward movement of a racket or bat, often in order to give the ball backspin **7** *vt* **HIT SHARPLY DOWNWARDS** to hit somebody or something with a sharp downward motion ■ *n* **1 SLICE OF MEAT WITH BONE** a small piece of red meat cut from the ribs, loin, or shoulder, usually with the bone still attached ○ *pork chops* **2 SHARP STROKE DOWNWARDS** a sudden strong downward blow with the hand or a cutting tool ○ *a karate chop* **3 DISMISSAL** dismissal from a job (*informal*) ○ *was given the chop* ○ *If the boss finds out, you'll be for the chop.* **4 CLOSEDOWN** the cancellation, closedown, or stoppage of something (*informal*) ○ *Three of our rural offices are to get the chop.* **5 IRREGULAR WAVE MOTION** turbulent irregular motion in waves or water **6 DISTURBED SEA** a stretch of choppy water, especially on the sea [14C. Variant of CHAP[1].]

chop[2] /chop/ (**chops, chopping, chopped**) *vi* to change direction or have a change of mind, especially suddenly or frequently [15C. Variant of CHAP[3].] ◇ **chop and change** to have frequent changes of mind, especially abruptly or in a way that disconcerts or irritates other people

chop[3] /chop/ *n* **1 TRADEMARK IN EAST ASIA** a trademark, official stamp, or mark of quality, especially in East Asia **2** *Malaysia* **PRINTING STAMP** a wooden, metal, or rubber stamp used to frank documents or seal envelopes ■ *vt* (**chops, chopping, chopped**) *Malaysia* **STAMP WITH SEAL** to stamp a letter with an official mark or the date ◇ **not much chop** *ANZ* not very good (*informal*)

chop[4] /chop/ *n W Africa* food [Early 19C. < ?]

chop-chop *interj* used to indicate, often in a bossy or arrogant way, that somebody should hurry or do something quickly or right away (*informal*) [Mid-19C. Repetition of Pidgin English *chop*, alteration of Cantonese Chinese *gap* 'urgent'.] —**chop-chop** *adv*

chophouse /chóp howss/ (*plural* **chophouses** /-howziz/) *n* a restaurant serving grilled meat, e.g. chops and steaks, as its speciality, especially formerly

Chopin /shóp aN, shṓp-/, **Frédéric François** (1810–49) Polish composer and pianist

Chopin, Kate (1850–1904) US novelist, short-story writer, and poet

choplogic /chóp lojik/ *n* the presentation of an argument in a way that is either illogical or pedantic and overcomplicated [Early 16C. < *chop* 'exchange'.]

chopper /chóppər/ *n* **1 SMALL AXE** a small axe **2 CLEAVER** a cutting tool with a handle and a sharp broad blade, used especially for chopping up meat **3 HELICOPTER** a helicopter (*informal*) **4 BIKE WITH HIGH HANDLEBARS** a motorcycle or bicycle with a lowered seat, raised handlebars, and lengthened forks holding the front wheel **5 INTERRUPTING DEVICE** a device that regularly interrupts an electric current, a beam of light, or some other stream of radiation in order to produce a pulsing flow or beam **6 TABOO TERM** a highly offensive term for a penis (*slang taboo*) ■ **choppers** *npl* **TEETH** teeth, especially large or false ones (*slang*) ■ *vti* **GO BY HELICOPTER** to travel or to transport something or somebody by helicopter (*informal*)

chopping board /chópping-/ *n* a piece of wood or plastic used for chopping food on. US term **cutting board**

choppy /chóppi/ (**-pier, -piest**) *adj* rather rough, with the surface of the water broken up into many small waves made by strong winds —**choppily** *adv* —**choppiness** *n*

chops /chops/ *npl* **1** the jaws, or the skin covering the jaws (*informal*) **2** technique or virtuosity in playing an instrument, especially a wind instrument (*slang*)

chop shop *n US* a workshop or garage where stolen vehicles are disguised or broken up for spare parts (*slang*)

chopsocky /chóp soki/ *n* the genre of film in which martial arts, e.g. kung fu, feature prominently ○ *his latest chopsocky extravaganza* [< CHOP[1] + SOCK[2]]

chopstick /chóp stik/ *n* either of a pair of narrow sticks that are held together in one hand and used when eating or preparing East Asian food [Late 17C. < pidgin English (see CHOP-CHOP).]

chop suey /chop sŏŏ i/ *n* a Chinese-style dish made typically of shredded meat and mixed vegetables [Late 19C. < Cantonese Chinese *tsaâp suì* 'mixed bits'.]

choral /káwrəl/ *adj* **1** arranged for or performed by a chorus or choir ○ *choral singing* **2** concerned with choral singing, choruses, or choirs ○ *a choral society* [Late 16C. < medieval Latin *choralis* < Latin *chorus* (see CHORUS).] — **chorally** *adv*

chorale /ko ráal/ *n* **1 LUTHERAN HYMN TUNE** a hymn tune, especially a slow and stately one, originally intended for congregational singing in the Lutheran church **2 PIECE OF MUSIC BASED ON CHORALE** a piece of music, especially a choral work, based on a chorale tune or in a style reminiscent of traditional Lutheran church music **3** *US* **GROUP OF SINGERS** a group of singers specializing in a particular style of music, especially church music [Mid-19C. < German *Choral(gesang)* 'choral (song)'.]

chorale prelude *n* an organ prelude based on a chorale tune, used to introduce congregational singing of the chorale on which it is based or performed as a separate piece

chord[1] /kawrd/ *n* two or more musical notes played or sung simultaneously ○ *an F minor chord* [15C. Shortening and alteration of ACCORD after Latin *chorda*.] —**chordal** *adj* **strike** *or* **touch a chord** to produce an emotional, especially a sympathetic, response in somebody, or jog somebody's memory

USAGE chord or **cord**? In musical contexts the spelling is ***chord***, and this form is also used in figurative expressions that have to do with feelings: *The speech struck the right chord.* In anatomical contexts (*spinal cord, umbilical cord, vocal cords*), ***cord*** is more usual. ***Cord*** is used when referring to thick string.

chord[2] /kawrd/ *n* **1 LINE THROUGH ARC** a straight line connecting two points on an arc or circle **2 AIRFOIL MEASURE** the shortest distance between the leading and trailing edges of an airfoil **3** ANAT = **cord** *n.* **4** **4 HORIZONTAL CONNECTING PART** the horizontal part of a truss designed to absorb tension, e.g. in a roof [Mid-16C. Alteration of CORD, after Latin *chorda*.]

chordate /káwr dayt/ *n* any animal that at some stage in its development has a main dorsal nerve cord, a skeletal rod (**notochord**), and gill slits, including all vertebrates and some primitive invertebrate marine animals. Phylum: Chordata. [Late 19C. < modern Latin *chordata* < *chorda* 'cord'.] —**chordate** *adj*

chordophone /káwrdə fōn/ *n* a stringed instrument (*technical*) [Mid-20C. < CHORD[1].]

chord organ *n* a small electronic organ with special keys to produce chords for accompanying a melody

chore /chawr/ *n* **1** a task, especially an ordinary household task, that has to be done regularly (*often plural*) **2** something that is unpleasant, difficult, awkward, or boring to do [Mid-18C. Alteration of CHAR[3].]

-chore *suffix* a plant distributed by a particular means ○ *anemochore* [< Greek *khōrein* 'spread']

chorea /ko reé ə/ *n* jerky spasmodic movements of the limbs, trunk, and facial muscles, common to various diseases of the central nervous system [Late 17C. Via Latin < Greek *khoreia* 'dance'.] —**choreal** *adj* —**choreic** *adj*

choreograph /kórri ə graaf/ *v* **1** *vti* to plan out dance movements to a piece of music **2** *vt* to plan, coordinate, and supervise an event or activity ○ *His job is to choreograph royal weddings and other state occasions.* [Mid-20C. Back-formation < CHOREOGRAPHY.] —**choreographer** /kórri óggrəfər/ *n*

choreography /kórri óggrəfi/ (*plural* **-phies**) *n* **1 COMPOSING DANCES** the planning of movements for dancing **2 DANCE MOVEMENTS FOR PIECE** the steps and movements planned for a dance, or a written record of them **3 PLANNED MOVEMENT** the carefully planned or executed organization of people, things, or an event [Late 18C. < French *chorégraphie* 'dance writing' < Greek *khoreia* 'dance'.] —**choreographic** /kórri ə gráffik/ *adj* —**choreographically** *adv*

choriamb /kórri amb, -am/ *n* a poetic foot consisting of two short syllables between two long ones or two unstressed syllables between two stressed ones [Early 17C. Via late Latin *choriambus* < Greek *khoriambos* 'iamb of a chorus'.] —**choriambic** /kórri ámbik/ *adj*

choric /kórrik/ *adj* performed by or written for a chorus, especially a chorus in classical Greek theatre [Early 19C. < late Latin *choricus* < Greek *khoros* 'chorus'.]

chorioallantois /kórri ō ə lán tō iss, -állən tō iss/ *n* a membrane surrounding an embryo [Mid-20C. < CHORION + ALLANTOIS.] —**chorioallantoic** /kórri ō állən tṓ ik/ *adj*

chorion /káwri ən/ *n* the outer membrane enclosing the embryo of mammals, reptiles, and birds. ◊ **amnion** *n.* 1 [Mid-16C. < Greek *khorion*.] —**chorionic** /káwri ónnik/ *adj*

chorionic gonadotrophin *n* a hormone that helps maintain a pregnancy

chorionic villus *n* any of the tiny outgrowths from the outer membrane (**chorion**) surrounding an embryo that move into the womb wall to form the placenta (*often plural*)

chorionic villus sampling *n* a prenatal test for birth defects carried out by examining cells from the tiny hairy outgrowths (**villi**) of the outer membrane (**chorion**) surrounding an embryo, which have the same DNA as the foetus

chorister /kórristər/ *n* a member of a chorus, choir, or other group of singers [14C. Via Anglo-Norman < Old French *cueriste* < Latin *chorus* (see CHORUS).]

chorizo /chə reé zō/ (*plural* **-zos**) *n* a very spicy Mexican or Spanish pork sausage [Mid-19C. < Spanish.]

C-horizon, C horizon *n* the lowermost layer of soil immediately above bedrock

chorography /kə róggrəfi/ *n* the preparation of maps in which specific areas or regions are delineated and often highlighted in some way, e.g. by colour-coding [Mid-16C. Directly or via French < Latin *chorographia* < Greek *khōrographia* 'place writing'.] —**chorographer** *n* —**chorographic** /kórrə gráffik/ *adj* —**chorographically** *adv*

choroid /káw royd/ *n* **choroid, choroid coat** a brownish membrane between the retina and the white of the eye in vertebrates that contains blood vessels and large pigmented cells ■ *adj* resembling the chorion in being vascular or membranous [Mid-17C. < Greek *khoroeidēs* < *khorion* 'chorion'.]

choroid plexus *n* a membrane with many small blood vessels in the fluid spaces of the brain that secrets cerebrospinal fluid

chortle /cháwrt'l/ *n* a noisy gleeful laugh [Late 19C. Blend of CHUCKLE + SNORT.] —**chortle** *vi* —**chortler** *n*

chorus /káwrəss/ *n* **1 REPEATED PART OF A SONG** a set of lines that are sung at least twice in the course of a song, usually being repeated after each verse **2 LARGE GROUP OF SINGERS** a large group of singers who perform choral music or opera together (*takes a singular or plural verb*) **3 GROUP OF PERFORMERS** a group of people who appear, sing, and sometimes dance together as a unit in a performance, usually providing backing for the principal performers (*takes a singular or plural verb*) **4 GROUP OF ACTORS IN GREEK DRAMA** a group of actors in ancient Greek drama who sing or speak in unison, generally commenting on the significance of the events that take place in the play **5 VERSE PASSAGE FOR GREEK DRAMA CHORUS** a verse passage in an ancient Greek drama intended to be sung or spoken by the chorus **6 DRAMA ROLE** a role in some Elizabethan and historical dramas for a solo actor, who speaks the introductory prologue, comments on the action, and delivers the epilogue **7 MUSIC FOR GROUP** a musical composition written for a large group of singers ○ *the Hallelujah Chorus* **8 MANY VOICES TOGETHER** the words spoken or feelings expressed by a group of people at the same time ○ *a chorus of complaints* **9 GROUP SPEAKING OR MAKING NOISE TOGETHER** a group of people or animals all speaking or making a noise together ■ *vt* **SAY TOGETHER** to speak at the same time, saying the same thing or expressing the same feeling or opinion [Mid-16C. Via Latin < Greek *khoros*.] ◇ **in chorus** all speaking or making a noise together

chorus boy *n* a man or boy who sings and dances as one of the supporting group of performers in a stage or film production

chorus girl *n* a woman or girl who sings and dances as one of the supporting group of performers in a stage or film production

chorus line *n* the chorus of supporting singers and dancers in a musical or variety show

-chory *suffix* = **-chore**

chose past tense of **choose**

SPELLCHECK See ***choose***.

chosen past participle of **choose** ■ *adj* picked out from or preferred to the rest ○ *one of the chosen few* ■ *npl* RELIG = **elect** *npl.* 1

chosen people *npl* the Jews, who, according to the Bible and their own belief, were selected by God to play a unique role in world history

chott /shot/ *n* a basin in the deserts of North Africa that periodically fills with water but dries out and becomes a salt flat when the weather is warmer

chouette /shoo ét/ *n* a variation of backgammon in which one player plays against two or more opponents in one game [Late 19C. < French, 'barn owl'.]

chough /chuf/ *n* a bird of the crow family with glossy black plumage, red legs and feet, and a red or yellow bill. Native to: Europe, Asia. Genus: *Pyrrhocorax*. [12C. Probably an imitation of its call.]

Chouteau /shōotō/, **René Auguste** (1749–1829) US pioneer

choux pastry /shoō páystri/ *n* a pastry that puffs up into a hollow case when baked

chow[1] /chow/ *n* food (*slang*) [Late 18C. Shortening of Chinese pidgin English *chow-chow* 'food, mixture'.]

chow down *vi US* to eat food enthusiastically (*informal*)

chow[2] /chow/, **chow chow** *n* a stocky thick-coated dog belonging to a breed originally from China, with a tail that curls over its back and a large dark purplish tongue [Late 19C. < pidgin English.]

chow[3] /chow/ *n* FOOD = **chow-chow**

chow chow *n* ZOOL = **chow**[2]

chow-chow, chow *n* **1** a Chinese mixture of fruit and candied peel in syrup, with stem ginger **2** a Chinese mixed vegetable pickle in a yellow sauce, similar to piccalilli

chowder /chówdər/ *n* a thick soup, especially one made with seafood or fish [Mid-18C. Probably via French *chaudière* 'stew pot' < Latin *calidarium* 'hot bath'.]

chowderhead /chówdər hed/ *n US* an unintelligent or irrational person (*informal insult*) [Mid-19C. Alteration of English dialect *jolter-head*.] —**chowderheaded** *adj*

chowhound /chów hownd/ *n US* somebody who is extremely fond of food and eating (*informal*)

chow mein /chów máyn/ *n* a Chinese-style dish of soft fried noodles, usually cooked with chopped meat and vegetables [< Mandarin Chinese *chǎo miàn* 'fried noodles']

Chr. *abbr* **1** Christ **2** Christian **3** Chronicles

chrestomathy /kre stómməthi/ (*plural* **-thies**) *n* a collection of literary passages, especially one assembled for language study [Mid-19C. Directly or via French < Greek *khrēstomatheia* 'useful learning'.] —**chrestomathic** /kréstə máthik/ *adj*

Chrétien /krétti aN/, **Jean** (*b.* 1934) Canadian statesman

Chrétien de Troyes /krétti aN də tróyZ/ (*fl.* 1170) French poet

chrism /krízzəm/ *n* **1** consecrated oil, or a consecrated mixture of balsam and oil, used for anointing people at some ceremonies in the Roman Catholic, Anglican, and Orthodox churches **2** a ceremonial anointing with holy oil, especially at confirmation in the Eastern Orthodox churches [Pre-12C. Via medieval Latin *crisma* < Greek *khrisma* 'an anointing' < *khriein* 'anoint'.] —**chrismal** *adj*

chrismation /kriz máysh'n/ *n* in the Eastern Orthodox tradition, the act of anointing somebody, or of being anointed, with holy oil in a religious ceremony such as confirmation [Mid-16C. < medieval Latin *chrismation-* < *crisma* (see CHRISM).]

chrisom /krízzəm/ *n* a white robe or shawl worn by an infant for his or her baptism [13C. Alteration of CHRISM.]

chrisom child *n* a baby that dies within a month of its baptism (*archaic*)

Chrissie /kríssi/ *n* Christmas (*informal*) [Late 20C. < CHRISTMAS.]

Christ /krīst/ *n* **1** CHR = **Jesus Christ** *n.* 1 **2 THE MESSIAH** according to the Bible, a saviour who will come to deliver God's chosen people **3 PAINTING OF JESUS CHRIST** an artistic representation of Jesus Christ ■ *interj* **TABOO TERM** a highly offensive term used to express surprise, annoyance, exasperation, or alarm (*taboo*) [Pre-12C. Via Latin *Christus* < Greek *Khristos* 'anointed' < *khriein* 'anoint'.] —**Christhood** *n* —**Christly** *adj*

Christadelphian /krístə délfi ən/ *n* a member of a religious group founded by John Thomas in the United States around 1848. Christadelphians reject the doctrine of the Trinity as not in the Bible and believe in the dead being resurrected with the Second Coming of Christ. [Mid-19C. < late Greek *Khristadelphos* 'in brotherhood with Christ'.] —**Christadelphian** *adj*

Christchurch /kríst church/ **1** town in S England. Population: 40,500 (1991). **2** city in the east of the South Island, New Zealand. Population: 339,500 (1998 estimate).

christen /kríss'n/ *vt* **1 BAPTIZE AND NAME** to make somebody, especially a baby, a member of the Christian church in a ceremony that includes a form of baptism and, usually, the giving of a Christian name or names **2 GIVE NAME TO** to give a name to something or somebody, with or without an accompanying ceremony ○ *christen a ship* **3 USE FOR FIRST TIME** to use or wear something for the first time (*informal*) ○ *Shall we christen our new coffeepot?* [Pre-12C. < Old English *cristnian* < *cristen* 'Christian' < Latin *christianus*.] —**christener** *n*

Christendom /kríss'ndəm/ *n* **1** all the areas of the world where Christianity is accepted as the main religion **2** all Christian people considered as a group (*archaic or formal*) ◊ **Christianity** *n.* 3 [Old English *cristendom* 'condition of being Christian' < *cristen* (see CHRISTEN)]

christening /kríss'ning/ *n* a ceremony in a Christian church in which somebody, especially a baby, is baptized and usually given a Christian name or names

Christian /krísschən/ *n* **1 BELIEVER IN JESUS CHRIST AS SAVIOUR** a believer in the historical and divine significance of Jesus Christ and follower of his teaching and example **2** *Malaysia* **PROTESTANT** a Protestant ■ *adj* **1 FROM THE TEACHINGS OF JESUS CHRIST** based on or relating to a belief in Jesus Christ as the Son of God and Messiah, and acceptance of his teachings, contained in the Gospels **2 RELATING TO CHRISTIANITY** relating to Christianity, or belonging to or maintained by a Christian organization, especially a church ○ *Christian theology* ○ *a Christian school* **3 KIND AND UNSELFISH** showing qualities such as kindness, helpfulness, and concern for others (*dated*) [13C. < Latin *Christianus* < *Christus* (see CHRIST).] —**Christianly** *adv*

Christian VIII /krísschən, krísti ən/ (1786–1848) king of Denmark (1839–48)

Christian Democrat *n* a member or supporter of a political party of the moderate right, especially in continental Europe, known as the Christian Democratic Party

Christian Era *n* the period of history dating from the year in which Jesus Christ is believed to have been born

Christianise *vt* = **Christianize**

Christianity /kríss ti ánnəti/ *n* **1 RELIGION THAT FOLLOWS JESUS CHRIST'S TEACHINGS** the religion based on the life, teachings, and example of Jesus Christ **2 HOLDING CHRISTIAN BELIEFS** the fact of holding Christian beliefs or being a Christian **3 CHRISTIANS AS A GROUP** all Christian people considered as a group. ◊ **Christendom**

Christianize /kríschə nīz/ (**-izes**, **-izing**, **-ized**), **Christianise** (**-ises**, **-ising**, **-ised**) vt **1** to change the religious beliefs and practices of a person or group of people from another religion to Christianity **2** to make somebody or something Christian by imbuing him, her, or it with Christian principles or a Christian spirit —**Christianization** /kríschə nī záysh'n/ n —**Christianizer** n

Christian name n a first name, especially one given at christening

Christian Science n a religious group whose members believe that illness should be overcome or managed through religious faith and practice alone, based on the teachings and writings of Mary Baker Eddy

Christian Scientist n a member of the Church of Christ, Scientist, and a believer in the principles of Christian Science

Christian Scriptures npl the New Testament of the Bible as distinct from the Hebrew Scriptures

christie /krísti/, **christy** (plural **-ties**) n in skiing, a type of turn used for stopping or rapidly changing direction, in which the skier twists sharply aside while keeping the skis parallel [Early 20C. Shortening of *Christiania*, former name of Oslo.]

Dame Agatha Christie

Christie /krísti/, **Dame Agatha** (1891–1976) British novelist and playwright

Christie, Linford (b. 1960) Jamaican-born British athlete

Christina /kri steenə/ (1626–89) queen of Sweden (1632–54)

christingle /krísting g'l/, **Christingle** n a Christmas decoration made by children in some Christian churches, consisting of a candle in an orange symbolizing Jesus Christ as the light of the world [Mid-20C. Probably alteration of German *Christkindl* 'Christmas present, Christ-child', after *Kriss Kringle*.]

Christmas /kríssməss/ n **1** FESTIVAL CELEBRATING BIRTH OF JESUS CHRIST a Christian festival marking the birth of Jesus Christ. Date: 25 December. **2** SECULAR HOLIDAY ON 25 DECEMBER an annual public holiday in many countries, when people traditionally exchange presents and greetings. Date: 25 December. **3** CHRISTMAS PERIOD the period around 25 December, or the Christian church season extending from 24 December to 6 January **4** QUARTER DAY in England, Wales, and Ireland, one of the four quarter days, falling on 25 December [Old English *Cristes mæsse* 'mass of Christ']

Christmas box n a gift of money traditionally given at Christmas by a householder or business to workers who have provided a service throughout the year

Christmas bush n any Australian tree whose colourful flowers are used as Christmas decorations

Christmas cactus n a branching cactus cultivated as an ornamental plant. Flowers: red, pink, white, or purplish-red, appearing around December. Native to: Brazil. *Schlumbergera truncata.*

Christmas cake n a rich dark fruit cake traditionally covered with marzipan and white icing

Christmas card n an illustrated greetings card sent at Christmas

Christmas carol n a Christian song celebrating Christmas

Christmas club n a savings account in which money is deposited regularly throughout the year in order to buy gifts and additional food and drink for Christmas

Christmas cracker n = **cracker** n. 1

Christmas Day n = **Christmas** n. 1, **Christmas** n. 2

Christmas disease n a form of haemophilia caused by lack of a protein needed for blood clotting [Mid-20C. After Stephen *Christmas*, who had the disease.]

Christmas Eve n the day or evening of 24 December

Christmas Island /krissməss-/ former name for **Kiritimati**

Christmas pudding n a rich steamed pudding made with dried fruit, spices, and usually candied peel and brandy, prepared and cooked in advance, then reheated for serving at the main Christmas meal

Christmas rose n an evergreen winter-flowering plant. Flowers: drooping, white. Native to: Europe, Asia. *Helleborus niger.*

Christmas stocking n a stocking or large sock hung up on Christmas Eve by children, in the belief that it will be filled with presents by Santa Claus during the night

Christmassy /krissməssi/ adj suggesting the Christmas period or suitable for Christmas ○ *The decorations look really Christmassy.*

Christmastime /krissməss tīm/ n = **Christmas** n. 3

Christmas tree n an evergreen tree, especially a conifer or an artificial version of one, that is decorated with lights and ornaments at Christmas

Christo /krístō/ (b. 1935) Bulgarian-born US artist. Full name **Christo Javacheff**

Christocentric /krístə séntrik, krístō-/ adj **1** assuming, implying, or based on Christian values and beliefs **2** concentrating or based strongly on Jesus Christ and his teachings

Christoff /kríst of/, **Boris** (1919–93) Bulgarian operatic singer

Christology /kri stólləji/ n the branch of theology concerned with the study of the nature, character, and actions of Jesus Christ —**Christological** /krístə lójjik'l/ adj —**Christologist** n

Christopher /krístəfər/, **St** (fl. 3rd century) patron saint of travellers.

Christ's thorn, Christ thorn n a thorny Asian bush or tree, especially a jujube or a Jerusalem thorn, whose branches are popularly believed to have been used for Jesus Christ's crown of thorns

christy n SKIING = **christie**

chroma /krōmə/ n PHYS = **saturation** n. 8 [Late 19C. < Greek *khrōma* 'colour'.]

chromaffin /krōməfin/ adj describes cells in the adrenal medulla that make noradrenaline [Early 20C. < CHROMO- + Latin *affinis* 'related'.]

chromat- prefix = **chromato-** (before vowels)

chromate /krō mayt/ n any salt or ester of chromic acid [Early 20C. < CHROMIC.]

chromatic /krō máttik/ adj **1** RELATING TO CHROMATIC SCALES describes a musical scale that runs through all the semitones in an octave, e.g. using all the keys, black and white, on a keyboard **2** HAVING FREQUENT ACCIDENTALS describes music that is based on the chromatic scale or that makes frequent use of notes that are outside the key in which it is written **3** RELATING TO COLOUR relating to colour and phenomena connected with it [15C. Directly or via French *chromatique* < Greek *chrōmatikos* < *khrōma* 'colour'.] —**chromatically** adv

chromatic aberration n an optical aberration in a lens, caused by a defect and leading to different coloured light being refracted differently

chromaticism /krō máttisizəm/ n the use in music of the chromatic scale or of many notes and harmonies that are foreign to the basic key

chromaticity /krōmə tíssiti/ n the colour quality of light precisely and uniquely defined in terms of three factors (**chromaticity coordinates**)

chromatics /krō máttiks/ n the science or study of colour (+ singular verb) —**chromatist** /krōmatist/ n

chromatid /krōmətid/ n either of the two strands into which a chromosome divides in the process of duplicating itself in cell division [Early 20C. < Greek *khrōmat-* 'colour'.]

chromatin /krōmətin/ n the substance that forms chromosomes and contains DNA, RNA, and various proteins [Late 19C. < Greek *khrōmat-* 'colour'.] —**chromatinic** /krōmə tínnik/ adj

chromato- prefix **1** colour ○ *chromatography* **2** chromatin ○ *chromatolysis* [< Greek *khrōmat-* 'colour']

chromatogram /krə mátta gram, krōmətə gram/ n a pattern formed by substances that have been separated by chromatography

chromatography /krōmə tóggrəfi/ n a method of finding out which components a gaseous or liquid mixture contains that involves passing it through or over something that absorbs the different components at different rates —**chromatograph** /krə mátta graaf, -graf/ n —**chromatographer** n —**chromatographic** /krōmətə gráffik/ adj —**chromatographically** adv

chromatolysis /krōmə tóllississ/ n the breakdown of the substance that forms chromosomes (**chromatin**) within an injured cell nucleus

chromatophore /krə mátta fawr/ n **1** a pigment-containing cell in many animals that, when it expands or contracts, causes a change in the animal's skin colouring. Octopus, squid, and some frogs and lizards contain these cells. **2** PLANT SCI = **chromoplast** —**chromatophoric** /krə mátta fórrik/ adj

chrome /krōm/ n **1** CHEM = **chromium 2** COMPOUND CONTAINING CHROMIUM an alloy, dye, or pigment containing chromium **3** CHROMIUM-PLATED METAL shiny chromium-plated metal. Use: formerly, to trim cars. ■ vt (**chromes, chroming, chromed**) **1** COAT WITH CHROMIUM to electroplate a metal with chromium in order to make it shiny and protect it against corrosion **2** TREAT WITH CHROMIUM COMPOUND to treat a substance with a chromium compound, usually when dyeing or tanning it [Early 19C. Via French < Greek *khrōma* 'colour'; because compounds containing it are often brightly coloured.]

-chrome suffix colour, pigment ○ *phytochrome* [< Greek *khrōma* 'colour']

chrome alum n $CrK(SO_4)_2.12H_2O$ a red-violet crystalline solid. Use: fixing agent in dyeing, tanning, and photography.

chrome green n a brilliant green pigment containing chrome yellow and iron blue. Use: fabric dye.

chrome red n a bright red-orange pigment containing lead chromate and lead oxide. Use: in paints and dyes.

chrome tape n magnetic recording tape that is coated with chromium dioxide

chrome yellow n a yellow pigment containing lead chromate and lead sulphate

chromic /krōmik/ adj relating to or containing chromium with a valency of 3

chromic acid n H_2CrO_4 an unstable oxidizing acid existing only in solution or in the form of a salt

chrominance /krōminənss/ n the part of a television signal that produces the effect of colour or hue, rather than luminance or brightness [Mid-20C. < CHROMO-.]

chromite /krō mīt/ n a brownish-black mineral ore consisting of an oxide of iron and chromium. Use: source of chromium.

chromium /krō mi əm/ n (symbol **Cr**) a hard bluish-white metallic element. Source: chromite. Use: alloys and electroplating to increase hardness and corrosion resistance.

chromium dioxide n CrO_2 a black crystalline solid. Use: to coat recording tape with magnetic properties.

chromo /krō mō/ (plural **-mos**) n a chromolithograph [Mid-19C. Shortening.]

chromo- prefix **1** colour, pigment ○ *chromolithograph* ○ *chromogen* **2** chromium ○ *chromite* [< Greek *khrōma* 'colour']

chromodynamics /krō mō dī námmiks/ n = **quantum chromodynamics**

chromogen /krōməjən/ n **1** any substance that is capable of being converted into a biological pigment or a dye, e.g. through oxidation **2** any microorganism that produces a pigment —**chromogenic** /krōmə jénnik/ adj

chromolithograph /krōmō lítha graaf, -graf/ n a coloured picture produced by making and superimposing multiple lithographs, each of which adds a different colour —**chromolithographer** /krōməli thóggrəfər/ n —**chromolithographic** /krōmō lítha gráffik/ adj —**chromolithography** /krōmōli thóggrəfi/ n

chromomere /krṓmə meer/ *n* a small, dense, bead-shaped granule of chromatin, found at intervals along a chromosome during cell division —**chromomeric** /krṓmə meérik, -mérrik/ *adj*

chromonema /krṓmə neémə/ (*plural* **-mata** /-mətə/) *n* the coiled central filament that forms the core of a chromosome strand (**chromatid**) [Early 20C. < CHROMO- + Greek *nēma* 'thread'.] —**chromonemal** *adj*

chromophore /krṓmə fawr/ *n* a group of atoms in a molecule that produces colour in dyes and other compounds through selective absorption of light, e.g. the azo group —**chromophoric** /krṓmə fórrik/ *adj*

chromoplast /krṓmə plast/ *n* a membrane-surrounded structure (**plastid**) in a plant cell that contains pigment. Red, yellow, or orange chromoplasts contain carotenoid pigments, and green chromoplasts (**chloroplasts**) contain chlorophyll.

chromoprotein /krṓmə prṓ teen/ *n* a protein combined with a pigment

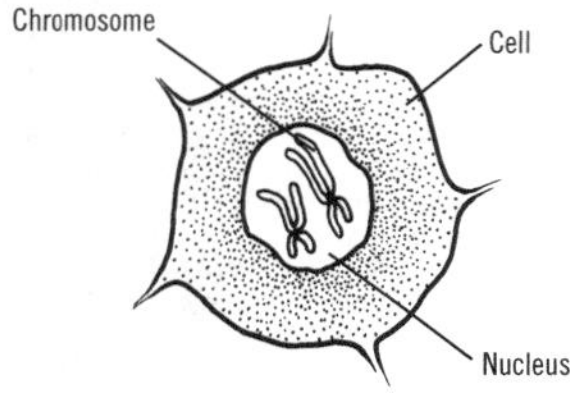

Chromosome

chromosome /krṓmə sōm/ *n* a rod-shaped structure, usually found in pairs in a cell nucleus, that carries the genes that determine sex and the characteristics an organism inherits from its parents [Late 19C. < German *Chromosom* < Greek *khrōma* 'colour' + *sōma* 'body'; because chromosomes readily take up dye.] —**chromosomal** /krṓmə sṓm'l/ *adj*

chromosome band *n* a pattern produced in a chromosome by using a stain, making the chromosome identifiable from other chromosomes

chromosome map *n* = **genetic map**

chromosome number *n* the number of chromosomes present in the cell nucleus of a species of plant or animal

chromosphere /krṓmə sfeer/ *n* **1** the lower region of the Sun's atmosphere, between the photosphere and the corona **2** the lower region of the atmosphere of any star —**chromospheric** /krṓmə sférrik/ *adj*

chromous /krṓməss/ *adj* relating to or containing chromium, especially chromium in its divalent state [Mid-19C. < CHROMIUM.]

chron. *abbr* **1** chronicle **2** chronological **3** chronology

Chron. *abbr* Chronicles

chron- *prefix* = **chrono-** (*before vowels*)

chronic /krónnik/ *adj* **1 LONG-LASTING** describes an illness or medical condition that lasts over a long period and sometimes causes a long-term change in the body **2 WITH LONG-TERM ILLNESS** having a particular long-term illness or condition **3 ALWAYS PRESENT** always present or recurring **4 HABITUAL** repeatedly doing something or behaving compulsively ○ *a chronic liar* **5** ⚠ **DIRE** terrible or appalling (*informal*) [15C. Via French < Greek *khronikos* 'time' < *khronos* 'time'.] —**chronically** *adv* —**chronicity** /krə níssəti/ *n*

USAGE ***Chronic***, used both of illness and in figurative contexts (as in *a chronic problem*), essentially denotes continuation over a long period of time, as its origin in the Greek word for 'time' suggests, rather than severity, although this is often also the case. Its opposite is *acute*, which denotes suddenness and intensity. So a ***chronic*** pain is one that persists whereas an *acute* pain is one that comes on suddenly and may last only a short time. In its informal meaning 'terrible' or 'appalling', ***chronic*** has lost all its sense of time, and for this reason and because of its apparent trivialization of a meaning used in serious contexts, many people dislike it.

chronic fatigue syndrome *n* an illness without a known cause that is characterized by long-term exhaustion, muscle weakness, depression, and sleep disturbances, possibly as a reaction to a viral infection in somebody already debilitated

chronicle /krónnik'l/ *n* **1 HISTORICAL ACCOUNT** an account of events presented in chronological order **2 NARRATIVE** a narrative or fictional account ■ *vt* (**-cles, -cling, -cled**) **MAKE RECORD OF** to record an event or series of events in chronological order [14C. Via Anglo-Norman *cronicle* < Greek *khronika* (plural) 'annals' < *khronos* 'time'.] —**chronicler** *n*

Chronicles /krónnik'lz/ *n* either of two books of the Bible that tell the story of the Israelites from the creation of Adam to the middle of the 6th century BC (+ *singular verb*)

chrono- *prefix* time ○ *chronograph* [< Greek *khronos* 'time']

chronobiology /krónnə bī óllәji, krṓnō-/ *n* the study of recurring cycles of events in the natural world —**chronobiologic** /krónnə bī ə lójjik, krṓnō-/ *adj* —**chronobiologist** *n*

chronograph /krónnə graaf, krṓnə-, krónnə graf, krṓnə-/ *n* an instrument, e.g. a stopwatch, that records time with great accuracy —**chronographic** /krónnə gráffik, krṓnə-/ *adj* —**chronographically** *adv*

chronol., chron. *abbr* **1** chronological **2** chronology

chronological /krónnə lójjik'l, krṓnə-/ *adj* **1** presented or arranged in the order in which events occur or occurred **2** relating to chronology —**chronologically** *adv*

chronological age *n* somebody's real age, as opposed to the age suggested by mental or physical development

chronology /krə nólləji/ (*plural* **-gies**) *n* **1 ORDER OF EVENTS** the order in which events occur, or their arrangement according to this order **2 LIST OF EVENTS** a list or table of events arranged in order of occurrence **3 STUDY OF ORDER IN TIME** the study of, or the science of determining, the order in which things occur [Late 16C. < modern Latin *chronologia* 'discourse of time' < Greek *khronos* 'time'.] —**chronologist** *n*

chronometric /krónnə méttrik, krṓnə-/, **chronometrical** /-méttrik'l/ *adj* relating to or designed for the accurate measurement of time —**chronometrically** *adv*

chronometry /krə nómmətri/ *n* the study or science of the accurate measurement of time —**chronometer** *n*

chronon /krṓ non/ *n* a unit of time equal to the time that it would take for a photon to cross the diameter of an electron, taken as approximately 10^{-24} seconds [< CHRONO- + -ON[1]]

chronoscope /krónnə skōp, krṓnə-/ *n* an electronic instrument that is designed to measure very small intervals of time with extreme precision —**chronoscopic** /krónnə skóppik, krṓnə-/ *adj*

chrysalid /kríssəlid/ *adj* describes the stage between larva and adult in an insect and the protective covering formed at this time ■ *n* (*plural* **chrysalids** *or* **chrysalides**) INSECTS = **chrysalis** [Late 18C. < Latin *chrysa(l)lid-*, stem of *chrysa(l)lis* (see CHRYSALIS).]

chrysalis /kríssəliss/ *n* **1 INSECT BETWEEN LARVA AND ADULT** an insect at the stage of changing from larva to adult, during which it is inactive and encased in a hard cocoon **2 INSECT COCOON** the hard cocoon that protects a butterfly, moth, or other pupa during its change from larva to adult **3 THING DEVELOPING** anything in an early or intermediate stage of development (*literary*) [Early 17C. Via Latin *chrysal(l)is* < Greek *khrūsalis* < *khrūsos* 'gold'; from the colour or sheen of some pupae.]

chrysanthemum /krə sánthiməm, -zán-/ *n* a garden plant with many cultivated varieties. Flowers: brightly coloured, many varied shapes, small densely clustered petals. Genus: *Chrysanthemum*. [Mid-16C. < Greek *khrūsanthemon* 'gold flower'; from the colour of the corn marigold.]

Chryse /krīssi/ lowland plain in the northern equatorial region of Mars where Viking 1 landed in 1976

chryselephantine /kríss eli fántīn/ *adj* describes classical Greek sculptures that are made of or overlaid with gold and ivory [Early 19C. < Greek *khrūselephantinos* < *khrūsos* 'gold' + *elephas* 'elephant, ivory'.]

chryso- *prefix* gold, golden ○ *chrysophyte* [< Greek *khrūsos* 'gold' < Semitic]

chrysoberyl /kríssə berəl/ *n* a form of beryl that is green, yellow, or brown. Use: gems. [Mid-17C. < Latin *chrysoberyllus* < Greek *khrūsos* 'gold' + *bērullos* 'beryl'.]

chrysomelid /kríssə méllid, -meélid/ *n* a small, brightly coloured, leaf-eating beetle. Family: Chrysomelidae. [Late 19C. < modern Latin *Chrysomelidae* (plural) < *Chrysomela* < Greek *khrūsomēlon* 'golden apple'.]

chrysoprase /kríssə prayz/ *n* a semiprecious stone that is a bright green chalcedony. Use: gems. [13C. Via Old French, < Greek *khrūsoprasos* 'golden leek'.]

Chrysostom /kríssəstəm/, **John, St** (349?–407) Syrian theologian and orator

chrysotile /kríssə tīl/ *n* a green, grey, or white fibrous variety of the mineral serpentine. Use: formerly, heat-resistant materials. [Mid-19C. < CHRYSO- + Greek *tilos* 'fibre' < *tillein* 'to pluck'.]

chthonic /thónnik, kthó-/, **chthonian** /thṓni ən, kthṓ-/ *adj* relating to the underworld as described in Greek mythology [Late 19C. < Greek *khthōn* 'earth'.]

chub /chub/ (*plural* **chubs** *or* **chub**) *n* a minnow with a stout rounded body belonging to a family that includes some North American sea and river fishes and the European carp. Family: Cyprinidae. [15C. < ?]

chubby /chúbbi/ (**-bier, -biest**) *adj* pleasantly or charmingly plump, especially in the way that healthy babies and toddlers often are —**chubbily** *adv* —**chubbiness** *n*

chuck[1] /chuk/ *vt* **1 THROW CARELESSLY** to throw something, especially in a careless or casual way (*informal*) **2 GET RID OF** to get rid of something unwanted (*informal*) **3 FORCE TO LEAVE** to eject or remove somebody from a place or a position (*informal*) **4 GIVE UP** to give something up, especially a job (*informal*) **5 END RELATIONSHIP WITH** to end a relationship with a boyfriend or girlfriend (*informal*) **6 TICKLE AFFECTIONATELY UNDER CHIN** to give somebody an affectionate pat or tickle under the chin ■ *n* **1 CARELESS THROW** a throw, especially a careless or casual throw (*informal*) **2 AFFECTIONATE TICKLE UNDER THE CHIN** an affectionate pat or tickle under somebody's chin [Early 16C. < ?]

SYNONYMS See ***throw***.

chuck in *v* (*informal*) **1** *vt* to give something up, especially a job **2** *vi* to contribute to the cost of something

chuck up *vti* to vomit (*informal*) US term **upchuck**

chuck[2] /chuk/ *n* **1** a clamping device with three or four adjustable jaws. Use: to hold a piece of woodwork or metalwork in a lathe or a bit in a drill. **2** a cut of beef that extends from the neck to the shoulder blade [Late 17C. Variant of CHOCK.]

chuck[3] /chuk/ *vi* to cluck [14C. An imitation of the sound.] —**chuck** *n*

chuck[4] /chuk/ *n N England* used as an affectionate way of addressing a man or a woman (*regional*) [Late 16C. Alteration of CHICK.]

chuckhole /chúk hōl/ *n Midwest* a pothole [Mid-19C. < CHUCK[1].]

chuckie /chúki/ *n Scotland* a small stone (*regional*) [Mid-18C. < CHUCK[1]; from its use for throwing in games.]

chuckle /chúk'l/ (**-les, -ling, -led**) *vti* to laugh quietly or to yourself [Late 16C. < CHUCK[3].] —**chuckle** *n* —**chuckler** *n* —**chucklingly** *adv*

chuckwalla /chúk wolə/ (*plural* **-las** *or* **-la**) *n* a large lizard with a dark body and a blunt yellow tail. Native to: deserts of the SW United States and Mexico. *Sauromalus obesus*. [Late 19C. Via Mexican Spanish *chachuala* < Cahuilla *tcàxxwal*.]

chuck-will's-widow *n* a large nightjar with mottled brown markings. Native to: central and S United States. *Caprimulgus carolinensis*. [Late 18C. An imitation of its call.]

chufa /choófə/ *n* a plant of the sedge family with an edible tuber that looks like a nut. Native to: Africa. *Cyperus esculentus*. [Mid-19C. < Spanish, 'fluff, nonsense'.]

chuffed /chuft/ *adj* very pleased or satisfied (*informal*) [Mid-20C. < English dialect *chuff* 'plump, chubby, happy' < ?]

chug[1] /chug/ *vi* (**chugs, chugging, chugged**) **1 MAKE REPEATED THUDDING SOUND** to make a repetitive thudding sound like that of a small engine **2 MOVE WITH CHUGGING SOUND** to move along slowly with a chugging sound under the power of an engine **3 CONTINUE IN STEADY FASHION** to continue steadily doing the usual things (*informal*) ■ *n* **CHUGGING NOISE** the chugging noise that an engine makes [Mid-19C. An imitation of the sound.]

chug[2] /chug/ (**chugs, chugging, chugged**) *vt US* to drink something, especially beer, quickly and in one go (*slang*)

chukar /chu ka'ar, choo kaar/ *n* a greyish-brown partridge with red legs and bill. Native to: S Asia. *Alectoris chukar.* [Early 19C. < Hindi *cakor*, probably an imitation of its cry.]

Chukchi /chúkchi, chookchi/ (*plural* **-chi** or **-chis**), **Chukchee** /chook chee, chúk-/ (*plural* **-chee** or **-chees**) *n* 1 a member of an indigenous people who live in NE Siberia 2 a language spoken in the Chukchi Peninsula of NE Siberia. Native speakers: 12,000. [Early 18C. < Russian.] —**Chukchi** *adj*

Chukchi Sea /chúkchi-, chook-/ part of the Arctic Ocean north of the Bering Strait between Asia and North America

chukka /chúkə/ *n* 1 **chukka, chukka boot** a casual ankle-high lace-up boot, typically made of suede 2 SPORTS = **chukker**

chukker /chúkər/ *n* any of the six periods of continuous play in a polo match, each lasting for approximately 7.5 minutes [Late 19C. < Hindi *cak(k)ar* 'circular course' < Indo-European.]

Chulalongkorn /choolə lóng kawrn/, **Rama V** (1853–1910) Siamese king of Siam (1868–1910)

chum[1] /chum/ *n* (*dated informal*) 1 FRIEND a close friend 2 WAY OF ADDRESSING MAN used as a term of address for a man ■ *v* (**chums, chumming, chummed**) 1 *vi* BE FRIENDS to be friends with somebody or behave in a friendly way towards somebody 2 *vt Scotland* GO WITH to accompany somebody somewhere (*regional*) [Late 17C. Probably shortening of *chamber-fellow*.]

chum[2] /chum/ *n US Canada* 1 FISH BAIT an angler's bait, especially chopped fish, scattered on the water 2 CHEAP TRINKETS inexpensive trinkets such as cuff links and pins bearing, e.g., the US Presidential seal (*slang*) ■ *vti* (**chums, chumming, chummed**) USE FISH CHUM to fish using chum on the water [Mid-19C. < ?]

chum[3] /chum/ (*plural* **chums** or **chum**) *n* ZOOL = **chum salmon** [Early 20C. < Chinook jargon *tzum (samun)* 'spotted (salmon)'.]

chummy /chúmi/ (**-mier, -miest**) *adj* friendly or close (*informal*) —**chummily** *adv* —**chumminess** *n*

chump[1] /chump/ *n* 1 UNWISE PERSON an unwise person, especially somebody whom the person using the term is rather fond of (*dated informal*) 2 THICK END OF MEAT a thick end of a piece of meat, particularly of a leg of lamb or mutton (*often before nouns*) ○ *a chump chop* 3 THICK PIECE OF WOOD a short thick piece of wood 4 HEAD somebody's head or mind (*dated slang*) [Early 18C. < ?]

chump[2] /chump/ *vti, n* = **chomp**

chump change *n US* a small amount of change or an insignificant amount of money (*slang*)

chum salmon *n* a salmon with wavy vertical green streaks and blotches. Native to: N Pacific waters. *Oncorhynchus keta.*

chunder /chúndər/ *vti* to vomit (*slang*) ■ *n* vomit, or the act of vomiting (*informal*) [Mid-20C. Probably shortening of *chunder loo*, rhyming slang for *spew*, after *Chunder Loo of Akim Foo*, cartoon character in Australian boot-polish advertisements.]

Chungking, Ch'ung-ch'ing = **Chongqing**

chunk /chungk/ *n* 1 a thick squarish piece of something, e.g. bread, wood, or meat 2 a large amount or part of something [Late 17C. Alteration of CHUCK[2].]

chunky /chúngki/ (**-ier, -iest**) *adj* 1 WITH LUMPS containing lumps or bits 2 SQUARE AND SOLID solid and squarish ○ *a chunky table* 3 SHORT AND BROAD short, broad, and sometimes overweight (*informal*) 4 MADE OF THICK MATERIAL made from thick material, especially wool —**chunkily** *adv* —**chunkiness** *n*

Chunnel /chúnn'l/ *n* a nickname for the Channel Tunnel (*informal*) [Early 20C. Blend of CHANNEL[1] + TUNNEL.]

chunter /chúntər/ *vi* to say something to yourself in a quiet mumbling voice (*informal*) [Late 17C. Probably an imitation of the sound.]

chuppah /hoopə/ (*plural* **chuppahs** or **chuppot** /-pot/ or **chupoth** /-poth/), **huppah** (*plural* **-pahs** or **-pot** or **-poth**) *n* 1 the canopy under which a Jewish wedding ceremony is performed 2 the Jewish wedding ceremony [Hebrew *ḥuppāh* 'canopy'.]

church /church/ *n* 1 RELIGIOUS BUILDING a building for public worship, especially in the Christian religion 2 RELIGIOUS SERVICES the religious services that take place in a church 3 CLERGY the clergy as distinct from lay people 4 **church, Church** RELIGIOUS AUTHORITY religious authority as

opposed to the authority of the state 5 **church, Church** RELIGION'S FOLLOWERS AS GROUP all the followers of a religion, especially the Christian religion, considered collectively 6 **church, Church** BRANCH OF CHRISTIAN RELIGION a denomination or branch of the Christian religion ■ *vt* GIVE CHURCH BLESSING TO to give somebody, especially a woman who has recently given birth, a blessing in church (*dated; often passive*) [Old English *cir(i)ce* < Germanic, < Greek *kuriakon dōma* 'house of the lord' < *kurios* 'lord']

Church Army *n* a voluntary organization founded by the Church of England in the 19th century to help parish priests evangelize

Church Commissioners *npl* a group of representatives of church and state in England, who are responsible for the administration of the finances and property of the Church of England

church father *n* any of the pre-8th century Christian scholars who set down the doctrines and practices of Christianity

churchgoer /chúrch gō ər/ *n* an attender of a church service or church services —**churchgoing** *n, adj*

Churchill /chúrchil/ 1 port in NE Manitoba, Canada. Population: 1,089 (1996). 2 river in south-central Labrador, Newfoundland, Canada. Length: 856 km/532 mi. 3 river that flows through numerous lakes in Saskatchewan and Manitoba, Canada, into Hudson Bay. Length: 1,609 km/1,000 mi.

Churchill, Charles (1731–64) British poet

Churchill, Randolph, Lord (1849–95) British politician

Sir Winston Churchill

Churchill, Sir Winston (1874–1965) British statesman, writer, and Prime Minister (1940–45, 1951–55)

church key *n US* a metal tool with a sharp-pointed triangular head for opening tins at one end and a bottle opener at the other end

churchly /chúrchli/ *adj* similar to, suitable for, or typical of a church —**churchliness** *n*

churchman /chúrchmən/ (*plural* **-men** /-mən/) *n* 1 a male member of the clergy 2 a man who is a practising member of a church —**churchmanship** *n*

church mode *n* any of the eight scales used for church music in the Middle Ages, e.g. the Dorian, Phrygian, or Lydian modes

Church of Christ, Scientist *n* the official name of the Christian Science Church

Church of England *n* the established church of England, ruled by a system of government by bishops and with the reigning monarch as its titular head

Church of Jesus Christ of Latter-Day Saints *n* a church founded by Joseph Smith in 1830, based on teachings in the Book of Mormon, and centred in Salt Lake City, Utah

Church of Rome *n* CHR = **Roman Catholic Church**

Church of Scotland *n* the established church of Scotland, which is Presbyterian and is administered by selected members of the congregation (**elders**)

church parade *n* a parade, in church, of members of the armed forces or other uniformed organizations as part of a special church service

church school *n* a school that provides children with a general education, and was founded or is supported by the Church of England

Church Slavonic *n* LANG = **Old Church Slavonic**

churchwarden /chúrch wáwrd'n/ *n* 1 a lay person who manages secular matters in an Anglican church 2 a long-stemmed clay tobacco pipe

churchwoman /chúrch woomən/ (*plural* **-en** /-wimin/) *n* 1 a woman member of the clergy 2 a woman who is a practising member of a church

churchy /chúrchi/ (**-ier, -iest**) *adj* 1 zealously, even intolerantly, religious 2 resembling or suggesting a church

churchyard /chúrch yaard/ *n* an area surrounding a church that is usually used as a graveyard

churidars /choori daarz/ *npl S Asia* long, close-fitting trousers worn by both men and women [< Hindi]

churl /churl/ *n* a person with bad manners [Old English *ceorl* 'man, freeman of the lowest rank' < Germanic]

churlish /chúrlish/ *adj* 1 characteristic of somebody who is ill-bred 2 surly, sullen, or miserly —**churlishly** *adv* —**churlishness** *n*

churn /churn/ *n* 1 MILK CAN a large metal container for transporting milk 2 BUTTER MAKER a container or device in which milk or cream is stirred vigorously to produce butter ■ *v* 1 *vt* STIR TO MAKE BUTTER to stir or beat milk or cream vigorously to make butter 2 *vt* MAKE BUTTER to make butter by beating milk or cream 3 *vti* SPLASH VIOLENTLY to move about violently, or cause a liquid or soft solid to move about violently 4 *vi* FEEL UNSETTLED to move unpleasantly, as if in a churn ○ *My stomach was churning.* 5 *vt* TRADE FREQUENTLY FOR COMMISSION to buy and sell stocks and bonds on a frequent basis in order to earn brokerage commissions [Old English *cyrin* < Germanic] —**churner** *n*

churn out *vt* to produce or issue something quickly or regularly and in large quantities

churr /chur/, **chirr** *vi* to make the high-pitched vibrating sound typical of some birds, e.g. the nightjar, and some insects, e.g. the cicada ■ *n* a high-pitched vibrating sound [Mid-16C. An imitation of the sound.]

Churriguera /chúrri gáirə/, **Don José** (1650–1725) Spanish architect

chute[1] /shoot/ *n* 1 SLOPE TO DROP THINGS DOWN an inclined channel or passage that something can slide down 2 CHILDREN'S SLIDE a children's slide in a park or swimming pool 3 SNOW-COVERED SLOPE a snow- or ice-covered slope or channel for sports such as tobogganing or bobsleighing 4 SLOPING PASSAGE FOR ANIMALS a narrow passageway through which animals are driven to be branded, sheared, loaded, dipped, or sprayed 5 SLOPE OR DROP ON WATERCOURSE a waterfall, rapids, or steep descent in a river or stream [Early 19C. < French, 'fall' < Latin *cadere* 'to fall'.]

> SPELLCHECK Do not confuse **chute** with **shoot**, which has a similar sound. Beware: your spellchecker will not catch this error.

chute[2] /shoot/ *n* a parachute (*informal*) [Early 20C. Shortening.] —**chutist** *n*

chutney /chútni/ (*plural* **-neys**) *n* 1 a sweet and spicy relish made from fruit, sugar, and vinegar 2 *Carib* a popular Caribbean form of song with a quick beat, much influenced by calypso in rhythm and choice of subjects [Early 19C. < Hindi *catnī*.]

chutzpah /hootspə, kh-/, **hutzpah, chutzpa** (*informal*) 1 boldness coupled with supreme self-confidence 2 impudent rudeness or lack of respect [Late 19C. Via Yiddish < Aramaic *ḥuspā*.]

Chuvash /choo vaàsh/ *n* a language spoken west of the Urals in central Russia, belonging to the Turkic family of Altaic languages. Native speakers: 2 million. [Via Russian < Chuvash *čǎvaš*] —**Chuvash** *adj*

chyle /kīl/ *n* a milky fluid consisting of lymph and emulsified fat that forms in the small intestine during digestion [15C. Via late Latin < Greek *khūlos* 'animal or plant juice'.] —**chylaceous** /kī láyshəss/ *adj* —**chylous** *adj*

chylomicron /kīlō míkron/ *n* a microscopic particle, containing fats, cholesterol, phospholipids, and protein, formed in the small intestine and absorbed into the blood during digestion

chyme /kīm/ *n* a thick fluid mass of partially digested food and gastric secretions passed from the stomach to the small intestine [Early 17C. Via late Latin < Greek *khūmos* 'animal or plant juice' < Indo-European.] —**chymous** *adj*

chymopapain /kímōpə páy in, -pī in/ *n* an enzyme found in papayas that helps digest proteins. Use: medicines, meat tenderizer.

chymosin /kímәssin/ *n* BIOCHEM = **rennin** [< CHYME + -OSE + -IN]

chymotrypsin /kímō trípsin/ *n* a protein-digesting enzyme in pancreatic juice —**chymotryptic** *adj*

chymotrypsinogen /kímō trip sínnәjәn/ *n* the inactive form of chymotrypsin

chypre /sheépra/ *n* perfume made from sandalwood [Late 19C. < French, 'Cyprus'.]

ci *abbr* Cote d'Ivoire (*in Internet addresses*)

Ci[1] *abbr* cirrus

Ci[2] *symbol* curie

CI *abbr* **1** Channel Islands **2** Cayman Islands

CIA *n* a US federal bureau responsible for intelligence and counterintelligence activities outside the United States. In conjunction with the FBI, it is also involved in domestic counterintelligence. Full form **Central Intelligence Agency**

ciabatta /chә báttә/ (*plural* **-tas** *or* **-te** /-ttay/) *n* a flat white Italian bread made with olive oil [Late 20C. < Italian, 'slipper'; from the shape of the loaf.]

ciao /chow/ *interj* used to say hello or goodbye (*informal*) [Early 20C. < Italian dialect, '(I am your) slave'.]

CIB *abbr* **1** Criminal Investigation Branch **2** Chartered Institute of Bankers

ciborium /si báwri әm/ (*plural* **-a** /-ә/) *n* **1** a canopy that stands on four pillars over the altar in some Christian churches **2** a small container with a lid, used to hold the consecrated wafers for Holy Communion [Mid-16C. Via medieval Latin < Greek *kibōrion* 'seed vessel of a water lily'.]

cicada /si kaádә/ (*plural* **-das** *or* **-dae** /-dee/) *n* a large winged insect that lives in trees and tall grass, the male of which makes a shrill sound. Family: Cicadidae. [15C. < Latin.]

cicatrice *n* = **cicatrix**

cicatrise *vti* = **cicatrize**

cicatrix /síkәtriks/ (*plural* **-trices** /síkә trī seez/), **cicatrice** *n* **1** a scar (*technical*) **2** a scar left on a stem where a leaf used to be attached [Mid-17C. < Latin, 'scar'.] —**cicatricial** /síkә trísh'l/ *adj* —**cicatricose** /si káttrikōss/ *adj*

cicatrize /síkә trīz/ (**-trizes, -trizing, -trized**), **cicatrise** (**-trises, -trising, -trised**) *vti* to heal, or cause a wound to heal, and form a scar (*technical*) [15C. < French *cicatriser* < *cicatrice* 'scar'.] —**cicatrization** /síkә trī záysh'n/ *n*

cicely /síssәli/ *n* PLANTS = **sweet cicely**

cicero /síssәrō/ *n* a size of printed character slightly larger than the pica [< its first use (1458) for an edition of the works of CICERO]

Cicero /síssәrō/, **Marcus Tullius** (106–43 BC) Roman philosopher, writer, and statesman —**Ciceronian** /síssә rṓni әn/ *adj*

cicerone /chíchә rṓni, síssә-/ (*plural* **-nes** *or* **-ni** /-ni/) *n* a guide for tourists [Early 18C. < Italian, after CICERO; from guide's knowledge and eloquence.]

cichlid /síklid/ *n* a tropical freshwater fish with spiny fins, popular as an aquarium fish. Family: Cichlidae. [Late 19C. < modern Latin *Cichlidae* < Greek *kikhlē*, a kind of fish.]

cicisbeo /chíchiz báyō/ (*plural* **-bei** /-báyee/) *n* a married woman's male escort or lover (*archaic or literary*) [Early 18C. < Italian.]

Cid /sid/, **El** (1040?–99) Spanish military leader. Born **Rodriguez Díaz de Vivar**

CID *n* the detective branch of the UK police force. Full form **Criminal Investigation Department**

-cide *suffix* **1** killer ○ *fungicide* **2** killing ○ *tyrannicide* [Via Old French < Latin *-cida* 'killer', *-cidium* 'killing' < *caedere* 'kill'] —**-cidal** *suffix*

cider /sīdәr/ *n* **1** an alcoholic drink made by pressing and fermenting apples. ◊ **cyder 2** *US* a nonalcoholic drink made from freshly-pressed apples [13C. Via Old French *sidre* < Hebrew *šēkār* 'alcoholic drink'.]

LITERARY LINK ***Cider With Rosie***, a memoir (1959) by Laurie Lee. An account of the author's childhood and youth in Gloucestershire, it is noted for its evocative descriptions of rural life and its affectionate portrayal of Lee's family and friends.

ci-devant /see dә vaáN/ *adj, adv* used to indicate that what follows was somebody's former name, office, or title (*formal*) [Early 18C. < French, 'before this'.]

~~**cieling**~~ incorrect spelling of **ceiling**

Cienfuegos /syen fwáy goss/ capital of Cienfuegos Province, central Cuba. Population: 132,038 (1993).

c.i.f., CIF *abbr* cost, insurance, and freight. ◊ **CFI**

c.i.f.c.i. *abbr* cost, insurance, freight, commission, and interest (*in quotes to indicate what is included in the price*)

CIFE *abbr* Colleges and Institutes for Further Education

cig /sig/ *n* a cigarette (*informal*) [Late 19C. Shortening.]

cigar /si gaár/ *n* a cylindrical roll of tobacco leaves for smoking, with thin brown paper or a single tobacco leaf as an outer covering [Early 18C. Directly or via French *cigare* < Spanish *cigarro*, probably < Mayan *sik'ar* 'smoking'.]

cigarette /síggә rét/ *n* **1** a cylindrical roll of shredded tobacco leaves for smoking, with an outer covering of thin, usually white, paper **2** a roll of shredded leaves of any kind for smoking, e.g. marijuana leaves or leaves of herbs [Mid-19C. < French, 'small cigar' < *cigare* (see CIGAR).]

cigarette card *n* a small card with a picture and information on it, formerly given away inside a cigarette packet and now considered a collector's item

cigarillo /síggә rílló/ (*plural* **-los**) *n* a slender cigar about the same size as a cigarette [Mid-19C. < Spanish *cigarillo* 'small cigar' < *cigarro* (see CIGAR).]

ciggy /síggi/ (*plural* **-gies**) *n* a cigarette (*informal*)

cilantro /si lántrō/ *n US* the leaves of the coriander plant, used as a flavourful herb, especially in Latin American and Southwestern US cooking [Early 20C. Via Spanish < Latin *coriandrum* 'coriander'.]

cilia plural of **cilium**

ciliary /sílli әri/ *adj* **1** describes the short threads (**cilia**) projecting from some cells and the beating movement they make **2** describes the tissue and muscle that surrounds the lens of the eye [Late 17C. < CILIUM.]

ciliary body *n* the ring-shaped part at the front of eye that connects the pigmented layer (**choroid**) of the eyeball with the iris diaphragm

ciliate /sílli ayt, -әt/ *n* a simple microscopic organism with projecting threads that thrash to help it to move along. Phylum: Ciliophora. [Mid-18C. < CILIUM.] —**ciliate** *adj* —**ciliated** *adj* —**ciliation** /sílli áysh'n/ *n*

cilice /sílliss/ *n* **1** TEXTILES = **haircloth 2** a garment made of haircloth [Late 16C. Via French < Greek *Kilikia* 'Cilicia', district of Anatolia; because made of goats' hair from Cilicia.]

~~**cilinder**~~ incorrect spelling of **cylinder**

cilium /sílli әm/ (*plural* **-a** /-ә/) *n* **1** a tiny projecting thread, found with many others on a cell or microscopic organism, that beats rhythmically to aid the movement of a fluid past the cell or movement of the organism through liquid **2** an eyelash (*technical*) [Early 18C. < Latin, 'eyelash'.]

Cimarosa /cheémә rṓzә/, **Domenico** (1749–1801) Italian composer

cimbalom /símbәlәm, tsímb-/ *n* a musical instrument resembling a hammered dulcimer. Use: especially in Hungarian folk and gypsy music. [Late 19C. Via Hungarian < Italian *cimbalo* 'dulcimer'.]

cimetidine /sī métti deen/ *n* a drug that decreases production of stomach acid. Use: peptic ulcer treatment. [Late 20C. < CYANO- + METHYL + -IDINE.]

cimex /sīmeks/ (*plural* **cimices** /sīmi seez/) *n* a bedbug or related insect that feeds on birds, humans, and other mammals. Genus: *Cimex*. [Late 16C. < Latin, 'bedbug'.]

Cimmerian /si meéri әn/ *adj* dark and gloomy (*literary*) ■ *n* according to Greek mythology, a member of a people who lived in a land of perpetual darkness [Late 16C. < Latin *Cimmerius* < Greek *Kimmerios*.]

~~**cinamon**~~ incorrect spelling of **cinnamon**

C in C, C-in-C *abbr* Commander in Chief

cinch /sinch/ *n* (*informal*) **1 SOMETHING EASILY DONE** something that can be done or achieved with very little effort **2 SOMETHING CERTAIN** something that is absolutely certain to happen ■ *vt* **1** *US* **GRASP ROUND MIDDLE** to grasp something round the middle, as a belt does (*informal*) **2 MAKE CERTAIN OF** to make certain of something (*dated informal*) [Mid-19C. < Spanish *cincha* 'girth' < Latin *cingere* 'gird'.]

cinchona /sing kṓnә/ *n* **1 cinchona, cinchona bark** the dried bark of a South American tree. Use: source of quinine and some other drugs. **2** an evergreen tree or bush that produces cinchona. Native to: South America. Genus: *Cinchona*. [Mid-18C. < modern Latin, after the Countess of *Chinchón* (1576–1641), vicereine of Peru.] —**cinchonic** /sing kónnik/ *adj*

cinchonine /síng kә neen/ *n* $C_{19}H_{22}N_2O$ a colourless crystalline solid. Source: cinchona bark. Use: treatment of malaria.

cinchonism /síngkәnizәm/ *n* a condition resulting from the excessive use of quinine and other drugs derived from cinchona bark. The symptoms are headache, ringing in the ears, temporary deafness, and dizziness.

Cincinnati /sínssi nátti/ city in SW Ohio. Population: 336,400 (1998 estimate).

cincture /síngkchәr/ *n* a girdle or belt, especially a cord or sash tied round a priest's, monk's, or nun's habit [Late 16C. < Latin *cinctura* 'girdle' < *cingere* 'gird'.]

cinder /síndәr/ *n* **BURNT WOOD OR FUEL** a small piece of charred wood or coal, especially one that continues to glow ■ **cinders** *npl* **1 ASHES** the ashes that remain after a fire has burnt out **2 SLAG** waste material produced by smelting **3 FRAGMENTS OF SOLIDIFIED LAVA** loose fragments of porous solidified lava that is ejected from a volcano and builds up round the crater [Old English *sinder* 'slag' < Germanic] —**cindery** *adj*

cinder block *n US* BUILDING = **breeze block**

Cinderella /síndә réllә/ *n* an object of undeserved neglect ■ *adj* achieving sudden recognition or success, or relating to somebody or something achieving this [Mid-19C. After the fairy-tale character *Cinderella*, who is neglected by her sisters but enabled by her fairy godmother to attend a ball and meet a prince.]

cine- *prefix* film, motion picture ○ *cinephile* [< CINEMA]

cineaste /sínni ast/ *n* **1** a fan of films and film making **2** a maker of films [Early 20C. < French, < *ciné*, shortening of *cinématographe*.]

cine camera /sínni-/ *n* a camera used for taking moving pictures rather than still photographs. US term **movie camera** [Shortening of CINEMATOGRAPHIC]

cine film *n* photographic film used for making moving pictures rather than still photographs. US term **movie film** [Shortening of CINEMATOGRAPHIC]

cinema /sínnәmә, sínni maa/ *n* **1 FILM INDUSTRY** the film industry, or the business of making films **2 FILMS COLLECTIVELY** films considered collectively **3 PLACE TO WATCH FILMS** a building or room where films are shown **4 CINEMAS COLLECTIVELY** cinemas considered collectively [Early 20C. < French *cinéma*, shortening of *cinématographe* 'movement writing' < Greek *kinēma* 'movement'.]

cinemagoer /sínnәmә gō әr, sínni maa-/ *n* somebody who is watching a film at a cinema or who regularly goes to the cinema. US term **moviegoer**

cinematheque /sínnәmә tek/ *n* a small cinema, especially one showing artistic or classic films [Mid-20C. < French, < *cinéma* (see CINEMA).]

cinematic /sínnә máttik/ *adj* **1** typical of the style in which films are made **2** relating to films or film-making —**cinematically** *adv*

cinematography /sínnәmә tóggrәfi/ *n* the art or technique of photographing and lighting films —**cinematographer** *n* —**cinematographic** /sínnә matә gráffik/ *adj* —**cinematographically** *adv*

cinéma vérité /-vérri tay/ *n* a style of film-making characterized by a search for an authentic documentary feel [Mid-20C. < French, 'cinema of truth'.]

cineole /sínni ōl/, **cineol** *n* CHEM = **eucalyptol** [Late 19C. Reversal of modern Latin *oleum cinae* 'wormseed oil'.]

cinephile /sínni fīl/ *n* CINEMA = **cineaste** *n.* 1

cineraria /sínә ráiri ә/ *n* a plant cultivated as a houseplant for its mass of blue, purple, or red flowers resembling daisies. Native to: Canary Islands. *Senecio hybridus*. ■ plural of **cinerarium** [Late 16C. < modern Latin, < Latin *ciner-* 'ashes'; from the fluffy grey leaves of the plant originally called this.]

cinerarium /sínnә ráiri әm/ (*plural* **-a** /-ráiri ә/) *n* a place where the ashes of a corpse are stored [Mid-18C. < late Latin, < Latin *ciner-* 'ashes'.]

cinerary /sínnәrәri/ *adj* relating to ashes, especially human ashes [Mid-18C. < Latin *cinerarius* < *ciner-* 'ashes'.]

cinereous /si néeri əss/ *adj* (*literary*) **1 LIKE OR OF ASHES** resembling or consisting of ashes **2 ASH-GREY** of an ash-grey colour ■ *n* **ASH-GREY** an ash-grey colour (*literary*) [15C. < Latin *cinereus* < *ciner-* 'ashes'.]

cinerin /sínnərin/ *n* an oily liquid compound. Source: pyrethrum. Use: insecticides. [Mid-20C. < Latin *ciner-* 'ashes'.]

cingulum /síng gyŏŏləm/ (*plural* **-la** /-lə/) *n* **1** any part of the body that surrounds or encircles another part **2** a band or stripe that encircles a plant or animal [Early 19C. < Latin, 'girdle' < *cingere* 'gird'.] —**cingulate** /síng gyŏŏlət, -layt/ *adj*

cinnabar /sínnə baar/ *n* **1 MINERAL SOURCE OF MERCURY** a reddish-brown mineral consisting of mercury sulphide. Use: source of mercury. **2 RED PIGMENT** red mercuric sulphide used as a pigment **3 BRIGHT RED** a bright red colour tinged with orange [Via Latin < Greek *kinnabari*] —**cinnabar** *adj* —**cinnabarine** /sínnəbə rīn, -baarin/ *adj*

cinnabar moth *n* a large European moth that has orange-red wings. *Hypocrita jacobaeae.*

cinnamic acid /si námmik-/ *n* $C_9H_8O_2$ a white odourless acid that is insoluble in water. Use: manufacture of perfume. [< its presence in cinnamon oil]

cinnamon /sínnəmən/ *n* **1 SPICE OBTAINED FROM BARK** the dried aromatic bark of any of several Asian trees. Use: as a spice. **2 ASIAN TREE WITH CINNAMON BARK** a tropical evergreen tree that produces cinnamon. Native to: Asia. Genus: *Cinnamomum.* **3 REDDISH-BROWN COLOUR** a warm reddish-brown colour [14C. < French *cinnamome.*] —**cinnamic** /si námmik/ *adj* —**cinnamon** *adj*

cinnamon stone *n* MINERALS = **essonite** [< its colour]

cinque /singk/ *n* the number five on cards or dice, or a throw of five in a dice game [14C. < French, 'five'.]

cinquecento /chíngkwi chéntō/ *n* the 16th century, especially with reference to Italian art and architecture [Mid-18C. < Italian, '500', shortening of *milcinquecento* '1500'.]

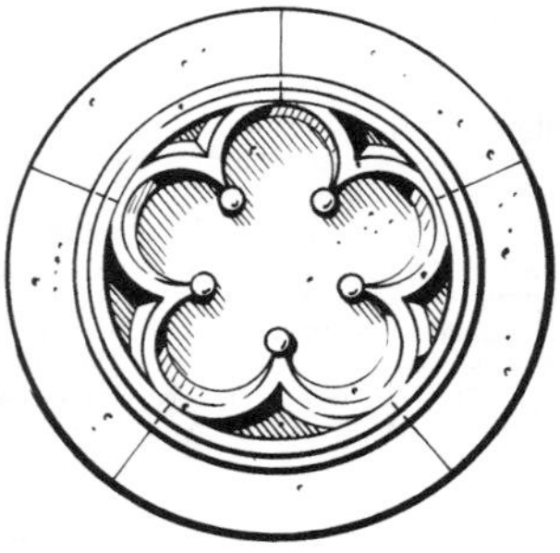

Cinquefoil

cinquefoil /síngk foyl, sángk-/ (*plural* **-foils** *or* **-foil**) *n* **1** PLANTS = **potentilla 2** an architectural design in the form of five arcs joined together [13C. < Latin *quinquefolium* 'five leaves'.]

Cinque Ports /síngk páwrts/ group of seaports in SE England, originally Sandwich, Dover, Hythe, Romney, and Hastings, that historically supplied the monarch with ships in return for special privileges

cioppino /chə péenō/ *n* a thick seafood soup or stew with tomatoes, spices, and herbs, popular in the United States [Mid-20C. < ?]

Cipango /si páng gō/ *n* in medieval mythology, an island off the eastern coast of Asia, perhaps modern-day Japan

cipher /sífər/, **cypher** *n* **1 WRITTEN CODE** a written code in which the letters of a text are substituted according to a system **2 CIPHER KEY** the key to a cipher **3 TEXT IN CIPHER** a text written in cipher **4 DESIGN OF INTERLACING INITIALS** a decorative design consisting of a set of interlaced initials **5 FAULT IN ORGAN VALVE** a fault in an organ valve that causes a pipe to sound continuously without the key having been pressed ■ *v* **1** *vt* **WRITE IN CODE** to write a text or message in cipher **2** *vi* **SOUND OWING TO FAULT** to sound continuously because of a faulty valve (*refers to an organ or organ pipe*) [14C. Via Old French *cif(f)re* < Arabic *ṣifr* 'zero'.]

cipolin /síppəlin/ *n* Italian marble with green and white streaks [Late 18C. Directly or via French, < Italian *cipollino* 'small onion' < *cipolla* 'onion'; because its pattern resembles the layers of an onion.]

cir. *abbr* **1** circle **2** circa **3** circuit **4** circulation **5** circumference

circa /súrkə/ *prep* used before a date to indicate that it is approximate or estimated [Mid-19C. < Latin, < *circus* 'circle'.]

circadian /sur káydi ən/ *adj* describes a pattern repeated approximately every 24 hours [Mid-20C. < Latin *circa* 'about' + *dies* 'day'.]

Circassian /sur kássi ən/ *n* a group of languages spoken in S Russia, N Georgia, and Turkey, belonging to the Abkhaz-Adyghean branch of North Caucasian languages. Native speakers: 1.5 million. [Mid-16C. < *Circassia*, Latinized form of Russian *Cherkes*.] —**Circassian** *adj*

Circe /súrssi/ *n* in Greek mythology, the daughter of Hecate and the Sun, who lured sailors to her island where she made love with them and then turned them into pigs [12C. Via Latin < Greek *Kirkē*.] —**Circean** *adj*

circinate /súrssi nayt/ *adj* describes leaves or fronds that are coiled with the tip in the centre, as in most ferns [Early 19C. < Latin *circinatus*, past participle of *circinare* 'make round' < *circinus* 'pair of compasses' < *circus* 'circle'.] —**circinately** *adv*

Circinus /súrssinəss/ *n* a small inconspicuous constellation in the southern hemisphere [Early 19C. < Latin *circinus* (see CIRCINATE).]

~~**circiut**~~ incorrect spelling of **circuit**

circle /súrk'l/ *n* **1 SHAPE OF PERFECT HOLLOW RING** a curved line surrounding a centre point, every point of the line being an equal distance from the centre point **2 AREA INSIDE CIRCLE** the area enclosed by a circle **3 CIRCLE-SHAPED THING** an area or object in the shape of a circle **4 CIRCLE-SHAPED PATTERN** an arrangement or pattern in the shape of a circle **5 GROUP OF PEOPLE** a group of people who share a common interest, profession, activity, or social background **6 CURVED ROUTE** a course or route that follows a curved path **7 RAISED THEATRE SEATING** a section of tiered seating in a theatre that is above ground level **8 CYCLE** a process or series of events that ends at the point at which it began or that repeats itself continuously **9 FORMATION OF ANCIENT STONES** any ring-shaped formation of large stones that dates from prehistoric times and is thought to have had a religious or astronomical use ■ *v* (**-cles, -cling, -cled**) **1** *vti* **MOVE ALONG CURVING ROUTE** to move or move round something, following a curving route or path that ends where it began and usually repeats its cycle **2** *vt* **MAKE MARK ROUND** to draw a ring round something in order to mark it or draw attention to it **3** *vt* **SURROUND** to surround a place or an area with people [Pre-12C. Via French < Latin *circulus* 'small circle' < *circus* 'circle'.] —**circler** *n* ◇ **come full circle** to return to an earlier or first position or situation after leaving it ◇ **go** *or* **run round in circles** to be very busy without actually achieving anything ◇ **square the circle** to try to do something extremely difficult or impossible

LITERARY LINK ***The Caucasian Chalk Circle***, a play (1948) by German dramatist Bertolt Brecht. The story of a dispute for the custody of a young boy, the work examines traditional values and the need to adapt them to changing historical circumstances.

circlet /súrklət/ *n* **1** a circular decoration, especially a decorative band worn on the head **2** a small circle (*literary*)

circs /surks/ *npl* circumstances (*informal*) [Mid-19C. Contraction.]

circuit /súrkit/ *n* **1 CIRCULAR PATH** a route or path that follows a curved course and finishes at the point at which it began **2 AREA BOUNDED BY CIRCULAR PATH** an area that lies inside a circular route or path **3 SINGLE JOURNEY ROUND CIRCULAR PATH** a single complete journey round a circular route or path **4 REGULAR JOURNEY** a journey that somebody, e.g. a salesperson or circuit judge, regularly makes round an area **5 STOPS ON JOURNEY** the places visited by somebody on a regular circuit **6 ROUND OF EVENTS** a series of events or places regularly attended or visited by the same group of people **7 ONGOING SERIES OF COMPETITIONS** an ongoing series of competitions or tournaments regularly attended by the same group of people **8 ROUTE FOR ELECTRICITY** a route around which an electrical current can flow, beginning and ending at the same point **9 RACE TRACK FOR MOTORSPORTS** a race track for cars or motorcycles **10 CHAIN OF ARTS VENUES** a group of theatres, cinemas, or clubs under the same management or showing the same performances or films in rotation **11 SET OF EXERCISES** a complete round of exercises in circuit training **12 LOCAL GROUP OF METHODIST CHURCHES** a group of Methodist churches that form a local division of the Church's national administration **13 GEOGRAPHICAL DIVISION OF ENGLISH LEGAL SYSTEM** any of the six areas that England is divided into for the purposes of administering the law ■ *vti* **MOVE ROUND ALONG CIRCULAR PATH** to follow a circuit round something (*formal*) [14C. Via French < Latin *circuitus* < *circuire* 'go round' < *ire* 'go'.]

circuit breaker *n* a device that can automatically stop the flow of electricity in a circuit if there is too much current to operate safely

circuit judge *n* a judge who travels from one court to another within a region on a regular basis

circuitous /sur kyŏŏ itəss/ *adj* lengthy because very indirect [Mid-17C. < medieval Latin *circuitosus* < Latin *circuire* (see CIRCUIT).] —**circuitously** *adv* —**circuitousness** *n*

circuit rider *n* *US* formerly, a clergyman who travelled from church to church preaching, especially in rural areas

circuitry /súrkitri/ *n* **1 CIRCUIT COMPONENTS** the components of an electric circuit **2 ELECTRICAL SYSTEM** the system of circuits in an electrical or electronic device **3 ELECTRIC CIRCUIT'S LAYOUT** the design or layout of an electric circuit

circuit training *n* a form of sports training that involves performing different exercises in rotation

circuity /sur kyŏŏ əti/ (*plural* **-ties**) *n* the indirect and lengthy nature of something, especially the way somebody speaks, argues, or reasons [Mid-16C. < French *circuité* < Latin *circuire* (see CIRCUIT).]

circular /súrkyŏŏlər/ *adj* **1 LIKE A CIRCLE** resembling a circle **2 ENDING WHERE BEGINNING** following a curved route or path that ends at the point where it began **3 NOT LOGICAL** describes an argument that does not move logically to a satisfactory conclusion because it assumes as true something that needs to be proved or demonstrated **4 CIRCUITOUS** indirect and complicated **5 WIDELY DISTRIBUTED** intended for distribution to a large number of people ■ *n* **WIDELY DISTRIBUTED NOTICE** a letter, advertisement, or other notice distributed to a large number of people [14C. Via Anglo-Norman < late Latin *circularis* < Latin *circulus* (see CIRCLE).] —**circularly** *adv*

circular breathing *n* the technique of using the cheeks to force air out of the mouth while breathing in through the nose, used by woodwind and brass players to hold long notes

circular function *n* MATH = **trigonometric function**

circularise *vt* = **circularize**

circularity /súrkyŏŏ lárrəti/ *n* **1 CIRCULAR SHAPE** the quality or fact of being circular in shape **2 ILLOGICAL NATURE** the illogical nature of something such as an argument or piece of reasoning **3 COMPLEXITY AND INDIRECTNESS** the indirect and complicated nature of something such as a method or route [Late 16C. < medieval Latin *circularitas* < *circularis* (see CIRCULAR).]

circularize /súrkyŏŏlə rīz/ (**-izes, -izing, -ized**), **circularise** (**-ises, -ising, -ised**) *vt* **1** to publicize something by distributing leaflets or notices widely **2** to ask people for support or to survey public opinion by sending out questionnaires, letters, or leaflets —**circularization** /súrkyŏŏlə rī záysh'n/ *n*

circular measure *n* the measurement of an angle by relating it to the angle formed in the centre of a circle by a sector, in units called radians

circular saw *n* an electrically powered saw with a circular toothed blade that rotates at high speed

circulate /súrkyŏŏ layt/ (**-lates, -lating, -lated**) *v* **1** *vi* **MOVE ROUND CIRCULAR SYSTEM** to move freely through a circuit or to follow a circular route **2** *vti* **PASS ROUND** to distribute or pass something from person to person or from place to place, or be passed in this way **3** *vi* **FLOW** to move or flow freely in an enclosed space or defined area **4** *vi* **MINGLE** to move from person to person or group to group at a social gathering in order to talk with different people (*informal*) [15C. < Latin *circulat-*, past participle of *circulare* < *circulus* 'small circle'.] —**circulatable** *adj* —**circulator** *n*

circulating library *n* = **mobile library**

circulating medium *n* anything used as money, e.g. a valuable commodity, banknotes, or illegal drugs

circulation /súrkyŏŏ láysh'n/ *n* 1 MOVEMENT OF BLOOD ROUND BODY the movement of blood through the body 2 FLOW the free movement of something, e.g. air or water 3 DISTRIBUTION OR COMMUNICATION the passing or communication of something, e.g. news, information, or money, from place to place or from person to person 4 NUMBER DISTRIBUTED OF PUBLICATION the number of copies of a publication that are sold or distributed to readers in a given period 5 USE AS MONEY valid use as currency 6 LIBRARY DEPARTMENT the department of a lending library that oversees the lending and retrieval of books and other items 7 ITEM OR ITEMS BORROWED FROM LIBRARY an item borrowed from a lending library, or the total number of items on loan at a given time

circulatory /súrkyŏŏ láytəri, súrkyŏŏlətəri/ *adj* relating to the circulation of the blood

circulatory system *n* the system consisting of the heart, blood vessels, and lymph vessels that pumps blood and lymph round the body

circum- *prefix* around ○ *circumlunar* [< Latin < *circus* (see CIRCLE)]

circumambient /súrkəm ámbi ənt/ *adj* surrounding (*literary*) —**circumambiently** *adv*

circumambulate /súrkəm ámbyŏŏ layt/ (**-lates, -lating, -lated**) *v* 1 *vti* to walk round something, e.g. round the dead, a tomb, or a sacred site, as part of a ritual (*formal or humorous*) 2 *vi* to avoid the point of a subject or discussion (*literary*) —**circumambulation** /súrkəm ambyŏŏ láysh'n/ *n*

circumcise /súrkəm sīz/ (**-cises, -cising, -cised**) *vt* 1 to remove all or part of the foreskin from the penis, either for hygiene reasons or as part of a religious ritual 2 to cut away the skin (**prepuce**) covering the clitoris, or remove the clitoris, usually as part of a religious ritual [13C. Via Old French < Latin *circumcidere* 'cut round' < *caedere* 'cut'.] —**circumciser** *n*

circumcision /súrkəm sízh'n/ *n* 1 REMOVAL OF MALE'S FORESKIN the removal of all or part of the foreskin from the penis 2 REMOVAL OF CLITORIS OR ITS PREPUCE the cutting away of the skin (**prepuce**) covering the clitoris, or the removal of the clitoris 3 RELIGIOUS CEREMONY WITH CIRCUMCISION a religious ceremony during which a circumcision is performed, especially in Judaism or Islam

Circumcision *n* a Roman Catholic festival held until 1970 marking the circumcision of Jesus Christ. Date: 1 January.

circumference /sər kúmfrənss/ *n* 1 DISTANCE AROUND CIRCLE the distance around the edge of a circle 2 DISTANCE AROUND the distance around the edge of an object or a place that is roughly circular 3 EDGE the edge of a round object or area [14C. < Latin *circumferentia* < *circumferens*, present participle of *circumferre* 'carry round' < *ferre* 'carry'.] —**circumferential** /sər kúmfə rénsh'l/ *adj* —**circumferentially** *adv*

circumflex /súrkəm fleks/, **circumflex accent** *n* a mark ^ placed above a letter to indicate a specific pronunciation or a contraction, usually different from that of the unaccented letter [Late 16C. < Latin *circumflexus*, past participle of *circumflectere* 'bend round' < *flectere* 'bend'.]

circumfluent /sər kúmmflŏŏ ənt/, **circumfluous** /-flŏŏ əss/ *adj* flowing all around a thing or place (*formal*)

circumlocution /súrkəm lə kyŏŏsh'n/ *n* 1 the use of more words than necessary to express something, especially to avoid saying it directly 2 something said using more words than necessary, especially to avoid expressing it directly [15C. Directly or via French < Latin *circumlocution-* 'speaking around' < *locution-* (see LOCUTION).] —**circumlocutory** /súrkəm lókyŏŏtəri/ *adj*

circumlunar /súrkəm lŏŏnər/ *adj* around or surrounding the moon

circumnavigate /súrkəm návvi gayt/ (**-gates, -gating, -gated**) *vt* to sail or fly around something, e.g. an island —**circumnavigable** *adj* —**circumnavigation** /súrkəm navi gáysh'n/ *n* —**circumnavigator** *n*

circumpolar /súrkəm pṓlər/ *adj* located or living near one or both poles of the Earth or some other planet (*technical*)

circumpolar star *n* a star that is always visible above the horizon at a given latitude

circumscribe /súrkəm skrīb/ (**-scribes, -scribing, -scribed**) *v* 1 *vt* to limit the power of something or somebody to act independently (*formal; often passive*) 2 to draw one geometrical figure around another so that they touch at every corner (**vertex**) of the enclosed figure or at every side of the enclosing figure without cutting across each other [14C. < Latin *circumscribere* 'write round' < *scribere* 'write'.] —**circumscribable** /súrkəm skrībəb'l/ *adj* —**circumscriber** *n*

circumscription /súrkəm skrípsh'n/ *n* 1 RESTRICTION OF POWER the limiting of the power of something or somebody to act independently (*formal*) 2 ENCLOSING OF SOMETHING WITHIN GEOMETRICAL SHAPE the act of drawing one geometrical figure around another so that they touch at every corner (**vertex**) of the enclosed figure or at every side of the enclosing figure without cutting across each other 3 DRAWN SHAPE a shape drawn or enclosed by circumscription 4 INSCRIPTION ROUND CIRCULAR EDGE a circular inscription around the edge of a coin or medal —**circumscriptive** *adj* —**circumscriptively** *adv*

circumsolar /súrkəm sṓlər/ *adj* around or surrounding the sun

circumspect /súrkəm spekt/ *adj* showing unwillingness to act without first weighing up the risks or consequences [15C. < Latin *circumspect-*, past participle of *circumspicere* 'look around' < *specere* 'look'.] —**circumspection** /súrkəm spéksh'n/ *n* —**circumspective** /súrkəm spéktiv/ *adj* —**circumspectly** *adv*

SYNONYMS See ***cautious***.

circumstance /súrkəmstənss, -staanss/ *n* 1 CONDITION AFFECTING SITUATION a condition that affects what happens or how somebody reacts in a particular situation (*usually plural*) ○ *Circumstances have arisen that make it impossible to continue.* 2 UNCONTROLLABLE CONDITIONS the conditions that affect somebody's life and that are beyond his or her control 3 EVENT an event or occurrence (*formal*) 4 WAY SOMETHING HAPPENS the way an event happens or develops ○ *Mystery still surrounds the exact circumstances of the accident.* ■ **circumstances** *npl* CONDITIONS the social, financial, material, or spiritual conditions that somebody lives in ○ *Please report any change in your circumstances.* [12C. Directly or via French < Latin *circumstantia* < *circumstant-*, present participle of *circumstare* 'stand around' < *stare* 'stand'.] ◇ **under** *or* **in no circumstances** no matter what the situation might be ○ *You must under no circumstances reveal your name.* ◇ **under** *or* **in the circumstances** taking everything into account ○ *She took it very well under the circumstances.*

circumstanced /súrkəm staanst/ *adj* living in a particular state or set of conditions (*formal*)

circumstantial /súrkəm stánsh'l/ *adj* 1 BASED ON INFERENCE containing or based on facts that allow a court to deduce that somebody is guilty without conclusive proof ○ *circumstantial evidence* 2 SPECIAL related to particular circumstances 3 DETAILED thorough and very detailed (*formal*) 4 FORMAL with a great deal of formality and ceremony —**circumstantiality** /súrkəm stánshi álləti/ *n* —**circumstantially** *adv*

circumstellar /súrkəm stéllər/ *adj* around or surrounding a star

circumterrestrial /súrkəm tə réstri əl/ *adj* around or surrounding the Earth

circumvallate /súrkəm vállayt/ (**-lates, -lating, -lated**) *vt* to protect a town or camp by surrounding it with a rampart or a defensive wall (*archaic or formal*) [Mid-17C. < Latin *circumvallare* 'fortify with a rampart round' < *vallum* 'rampart' < *vallus* 'stake'.] —**circumvallation** /súrkəm və láysh'n/ *n*

circumvent /súrkəm vént/ *vt* 1 to find a way of avoiding restrictions imposed by a rule or law without actually breaking it ○ *an attempt to circumvent the ban* 2 to anticipate and counter somebody's plans [15C. < Latin *circumvent-*, present participle of *circumvenire* 'come round' < *venire* 'come'.] —**circumventer** *n* —**circumvention** *n* —**circumventive** *adj*

circumvolution /súrkəm və lŏŏsh'n/ *n* a turning or winding movement around a central axis [15C. < Latin *circumvolut-*, past participle of *circumvolvere* 'turn around' < *volvere* 'turn'.] —**circumvolutory** /súrkəm və lŏŏtəri/ *adj*

circus /súrkəss/ *n* 1 TRAVELLING SHOW a group of travelling entertainers, including clowns, acrobats, and sometimes animal trainers and their animals 2 SHOW a performance given by circus entertainers, or the place where they perform 3 SELF-IMPORTANT EVENT a confused, noisy, or overwhelming event or situation, especially one that seems full of self-importance (*informal*) ○ *a media circus* 4 ROMAN STADIUM an open stadium built by the ancient Romans to stage chariot races or fights between gladiators 5 ROMAN SHOW a performance staged in a Roman stadium 6 PLACE WHERE STREETS MEET a round or roundish open space where several streets meet ○ *Piccadilly Circus* [14C. < Latin, 'ring, circle'.] —**circusy** *adj*

ciré /séeray/ *adj* SHINY describes fabric with a shiny highly glazed finish ■ *n* 1 SHINY FINISH a very shiny highly glazed finish achieved by treating a fabric with wax or heat 2 SHINY FABRIC a fabric with a shiny finish [Early 20C. < French, < past participle of *cirer* 'to wax' < *cire* 'wax' < Latin *cera*.]

Cirencester /sīrən sestər/ town in west-central England. Population: 15,221 (1991).

cire perdue /seer pair dyŏŏ/ *n* METALL, SCULPTURE = **lost wax** (*technical*) [Late 19C. < French, 'lost wax'.]

cirque /surk/ *n* a semicircular hollow with steep walls formed by glacial erosion on mountains [Mid-19C. Via French < Latin *circus* 'ring'.]

cirrhosis /sə rṓssiss/ *n* a chronic progressive disease of the liver characterized by the replacement of healthy cells with scar tissue [Early 19C. < modern Latin, < Greek *kirrhos* 'orange-coloured'.] —**cirrhotic** /sə róttik/ *adj*

cirri plural of **cirrus**

cirriform /sírr i fawrm/ *adj* shaped like a long slender tendril or tentacle [Early 19C. < Latin *cirrus* 'curl'.]

cirriped /sírri ped/, **cirripede** /sírri peed/ *n* a sea crustacean that lives fixed in one spot and draws food by means of slender hairs (**cirri**). Subclass: Cirripedia. [Mid-19C. < modern Latin *Cirripedia* 'with curly legs' < Latin *cirrus* 'curl'.]

cirrocumulus /sírrō kyŏŏmyŏŏləss/ (*plural* **-li** /-lī/) *n* a high-altitude cloud formed of icy particles that occurs in lines of small rounded clouds often resembling fish scales

cirrose /sírr ōss/ *adj* consisting of thin wisps, as formed by cirrus clouds

cirrostratus /sírrō straátəss/ (*plural* **-ti** /-tī/) *n* a cirrus cloud resembling a transparent white veil high in the sky

cirrus /sírrəss/ (*plural* **-ri** /-rī/) *n* 1 a thin wispy cloud, occurring as narrow bands of tiny ice particles, that forms at the highest and coldest point of the cloud region 2 a slender tentacle with sensory or locomotive function, or a part resembling one [Early 18C. < Latin, 'curl, fringe'.] —**cirrate** /sírrayt/ *adj*

cis /siss/ *adj* having two atoms or groups on the same side of a double bond between carbon atoms [Late 18C. < Latin (see CIS-).]

CIS *abbr* Commonwealth of Independent States

cis- *prefix* on the near side of ○ *cisatlantic* [< Latin *cis* < Indo-European, 'this']

cisalpine /siss álpīn/ *adj* 1 situated south of the Alps 2 relating to a movement in the Roman Catholic Church to limit papal power and encourage the independence of local churches [Mid-16C. < Latin *cisalpinus* 'on this side of the Alps' (as viewed from Rome) < *alpinus* 'alpine'.]

cisatlantic /síss ət lántik/ *adj* situated on the same side of the Atlantic Ocean as the writer or speaker

CISC *abbr* complex instruction set computer

cisco /sískō/ (*plural* **-coes** *or* **-cos**) *n* a silvery freshwater whitefish found in deep lakes. Native to: North America. Genus: *Coregonus*. [Mid-19C. Back-formation < Canadian French *ciscoette*, alteration (influenced by *-ette* 'small') of Ojibwa *bemidewiskawed* 'that which has oily skin'.]

Ciskei /sís kī/ former homeland bordering the Indian Ocean in South Africa

cislunar /siss lŏŏnər/ *adj* situated between the Earth and the Moon

cismontane /siss móntayn/ *adj* on the same side of the mountains as the writer or speaker

cispadane /síss pə dayn/ *adj* situated on the southern side of the River Po [Late 18C. < CIS- + Latin *Padus* 'the Po'.]

cisplatin /siss pláttin/, **cisplatinum** /-tinəm/ *n* a drug that adds an alkyl group to DNA. Use: treatment of ovarian and testicular cancer. [Late 20C. < CIS- + PLATINUM.]

cissing /síssing/ *n* the appearance of marks such as bubbles or pits in paintwork [Late 20C. < ?]

cissy *n, adj* = **sissy** (*informal offensive insult*)

cist /sist/, **kist** /kist/ *n* a wood or stone coffin, dating from the latter part of the Stone Age [Early 19C. < Welsh, 'chest'.]

Cistercian /si stúrsh'n/ *adj* relating to an austere contemplative Christian order of monks and nuns founded by reformist Benedictines in 1098 ■ *n* a member of the Cistercian order of monks and nuns [15C. Via French < Latin *Cistercium* 'Cîteaux', near Dijon, France.]

cistern /sístərn/ *n* 1 a tank for storing water, especially one in the roof of a house or connected to a toilet 2 an underground tank for storing rainwater 3 ANAT = **cisterna** [13C. Via French < Latin *cisterna* < *cista* 'chest' < Greek *kistē*.]

cisterna /si stúrnə/ (*plural* **-nae** /-nee/) *n* a pouch or cavity that contains a body fluid [Late 19C. < Latin *cisterna* (see CISTERN).] —**cisternal** *adj*

cistron /sísstrən, -tron/ *n* a section of DNA containing the genetic code for a short chain of amino acids (**polypeptide**), the smallest functional unit carrying genetic information [Mid-20C. < CIS- + TRANS- + -ON.] —**cistronic** /siss trónnik/ *adj*

cistus /sístəss/ *n* an evergreen bush grown for its white, red, or yellow flowers. Genus: *Cistus*. ◊ **rockrose** [Mid-16C. < Greek *kistos* 'red-flowered bush'.]

cit. *abbr* 1 cited 2 citizen

citadel /síttəd'l, -del/ *n* 1 a fortress or strongly fortified building in or near a city, used as a place of refuge 2 a strong defender of a particular way of life or principle [Mid-16C. Directly or via French < Italian *cittadella* 'little city' < *cittade* 'city' < Latin *civitas* (see CITY).]

citation /sī táysh'n/ *n* 1 OFFICIAL ACKNOWLEDGMENT OF MERIT an official document or speech that praises somebody's actions, accomplishments, or character 2 EXTRACT FROM WORK a quotation from an authoritative source, used, e.g., to support an idea or argument 3 ACT OF CITING the act or process of citing something 4 *US* ORDER TO APPEAR IN COURT a writ for somebody to appear in a court of law 5 REFERENCE TO PREVIOUS DECISION a reference to a previous decision by a court or legal authority 6 USE OF PRECEDENT the legal practice or process of referring to precedent —**citational** *adj* —**citatory** /sítətəri, sī táy-/ *adj*

cite /sīt/ *vt* (**cites, citing, cited**) 1 QUOTE SOMETHING OR SOMEBODY to mention something or somebody as an example to support an argument or help explain what is being said (*formal*) 2 NAME to name somebody officially in a court case 3 *US* ORDER TO APPEAR IN COURT to order somebody officially to appear in court 4 OFFICIALLY PRAISE to praise the actions of a member of the armed services in an official document (*often passive*) ■ *n US* CITATION a citation (*informal*) [15C. < Latin *citare* 'summon repeatedly' < *citus*, past participle of *ciere* 'summon'.]

USAGE cite, site, or **sight**? Though pronounced the same, these three words all mean different things and should not be confused. You ***cite*** your sources in bibliographies and footnotes. Contractors ***site*** buildings on plots of land called building ***sites***. You use your sense of ***sight*** to ***sight*** a ship's sail on the horizon.

cithara /síthərə/, **kithara** /k-/ *n* a stringed musical instrument played in ancient Greece, resembling a lyre [Late 18C. Via Latin < Greek *kithara*.]

citify /sítti fī/ (**-fies, -fying, -fied**) *vt* (*disapproving*) 1 to develop an area and make it more urban 2 to make somebody adopt the customs, behaviour, or dress of those who live in cities —**citification** /sìttifi káysh'n/ *n* —**citified** *adj*

citizen /síttiz'n/ *n* 1 LEGAL RESIDENT a beneficiary of the right to live in a country because of birth in the country, or because of having been legally accepted to live there 2 SOMEBODY WHO LIVES IN A CITY a permanent resident of a city or town 3 CIVILIAN a civilian, rather than a member of the armed forces, a police officer, or a public official [13C. < Anglo-Norman *citezein* < Old French *citeain* < Latin *civitat-* (see CITY).] —**citizenly** *adj*

citizenry /síttiz'nri/ (*plural* **-ries**) *n* the citizens of a place or area collectively (*formal; takes a singular or plural verb*)

citizen's arrest *n* an arrest made by an ordinary citizen rather than by a police officer

citizens band *n* radio frequencies used by the general public to talk to one another over short distances

citizenship /síttiz'nship/ *n* 1 the legal status of being a citizen of a country 2 the duties and responsibilities that come with being a member of a community

Citlaltépetl /seet lal táy pett'l/ volcanic peak in E Mexico, the highest peak in Mexico. Height: 5,700 m/18,700 ft.

citole /síttōl/ *n* MUSIC = **cittern** [14C. < French, probably diminutive of Latin *cithara* (see CITHARA).]

citral /sítrəl/ *n* $C_{10}H_{16}O$ a volatile pale yellow liquid with a pleasant odour. Source: lemon grass oil.

citrate /síttrayt/ *n* a salt or ester of citric acid

citric /síttrik/ *adj* relating to citrus fruit

citric acid *n* a weak colourless acid. Source: lemon, lime, and pineapple juice, fermentation of sugars. Use: flavourings.

citric acid cycle *n* CHEM = **Krebs cycle**

citriculture /síttri kulchər/ *n* the cultivation of citrus fruits [Early 20C. < CITRUS.] —**citriculturist** /síttri kúlchərist/ *n*

citrine /síttrin/ *n* 1 a brownish-yellow semiprecious variety of quartz. Use: gems. 2 a greenish-yellow colour, like that of a lemon [Late 16C. Via French *citrin(e)* 'lemon-coloured' < medieval Latin *citrinus* < Latin *citrus* 'citrus tree'.] —**citrine** *adj*

citron /síttrən/ *n* 1 CITRUS FRUIT LIKE LARGE LEMON a fruit resembling a large lemon with a thick aromatic rind 2 THORNY CITRUS TREE a small thorny evergreen citrus tree that bears citrons. *Citrus medica*. 3 CANDIED RIND the candied rind of a citron fruit. Use: food decoration and flavouring. 4 WATERMELON a small watermelon that has inedible white flesh and a hard rind. *Citrullus lanatus* var. *citroides*. 5 COLOURS = **citrine** *n*. 2 [Early 16C. < French, alteration (influenced by *limon* 'lemon') of Latin *citrus* 'citrus tree'.]

citronella /sìttrə néllə/ *n* 1 **citronella, citronella grass** a tropical grass that has bluish-green lemon-scented leaves and contains oil. Native to: Asia. *Cymbopogon nardus*. 2 **citronella, citronella oil** a pale yellow aromatic oil. Source: a tropical grass. Use: in perfumes, soaps, as insect repellent. [Mid-19C. Via modern Latin < French *citronnelle* 'lemon oil' < *citron* 'citron' < Latin *citrus* 'citrus tree'.]

citronellal /sìttrə nélləl/ *n* $C_{10}H_{18}O$ a colourless liquid, smelling like lemons. Source: citronella oil. Use: perfumes, flavourings.

citronellol /sìttrə néllol/ *n* $C_{10}H_{20}O$ an alcohol. Source: citronellal.

citron wood *n* the wood of the citron tree or of the sandarac tree

citrulline /síttrəlin/ *n* an amino acid formed in the liver during the production of urea [Mid-20C. < medieval Latin *citrullus* 'watermelon' < Latin *citrus* 'citrus tree'.]

citrus /síttrəss/ *n* oranges, lemons, limes, grapefruit, pomelos, and related fruit collectively (*often before nouns*) ○ *citrus flavour* [Early 19C. < Latin, 'citron tree, citrus tree'.]

cittern /síttərn/ *n* a medieval stringed instrument similar to a lute but with wire strings and a flat back [Mid-16C. Probably blend of Latin *cithara* (see CITHARA) + GITTERN.]

city /sítti/ (*plural* **-ies**) *n* 1 VERY LARGE TOWN an extensive built-up area where large numbers of people live and work 2 PEOPLE IN A CITY the inhabitants of a city collectively 3 LARGE BRITISH TOWN a large town in Britain that has received the title of city from the Crown. It is usually the seat of a bishop, and so often has a cathedral. 4 *US* US URBAN CENTRE OF GOVERNMENT an incorporated urban centre in the United States that has self-government, boundaries, and legal rights established by state charter 5 *Can* CANADIAN URBAN AREA a Canadian town or urban area that has been incorporated and given the title of city by the provincial government 6 *US* EXTREME THING a thing, place, or situation that is a good or extreme example of its type (*slang; in combination*) ○ *It was panic city outside.* [12C. Via Old French *cité* < Latin *civitas* 'citizenship, community' < *civis* 'citizen'.]

SYNONYMS ***city, conurbation, metropolis, town, municipality***

CORE MEANING: an urban area where a large number of people live

city originally a town having a cathedral or having such a status conferred on it by the Crown; in the United States, a large municipal centre governed under a charter granted by the state; in Canada, a large municipal unit incorporated by the provincial government, but now used generally for any large urban area; **conurbation** an urban region formed or enlarged by the merging of adjacent cities and towns through expansion or development; **metropolis** a large or important city, sometimes the capital of a country, state, or region; **town** a populated area smaller than a city and larger than a village; **municipality** a city, town, or area with some degree of self-government.

City *n* 1 the important financial institutions of London 2 = **City of London**

City and Guilds (*plural* **City and Guilds**) *n* a technical or craft qualification awarded by the City and Guilds Institute (*informal*)

City and Guilds Institute *n* an examination body that awards qualifications for technical and craft skills

City Code *n* a code established in the United Kingdom in 1968 to control takeover bids and mergers

city council *n* a group of elected officials responsible for the government of a city or other municipality

city desk *n* 1 the newspaper department that deals with financial news 2 *US, Can* a newspaper department that deals with local news

city editor *n* 1 the newspaper editor in charge of financial news 2 *US, Can* the newspaper editor in charge of local news

city father *n* a member of a city or town council or a civil officer who has limited judicial authority

city hall *n* 1 *US* CITY ADMINISTRATORS the administrators and elected officials who run a city 2 *US* BUREAUCRACY the bureaucracy that runs a city, especially when regarded as insensitive or inflexible 3 **city hall, City Hall** CITY COUNCIL BUILDING the building where a city council has its main administrative offices

city manager *n* an administrator appointed by a municipal council to run its affairs

City of London oldest part of London, and its business and financial heart. Population: 4,142 (1991). Area: 2.6 sq. km/1 sq. mi.

cityscape /sítti skayp/ *n* 1 a view of a city or town landscape 2 a photograph or painting of a view of part of a city or town

city slicker *n* a worldly resident of a city (*informal disapproving*)

city-state *n* a independent state consisting of a sovereign city and its surrounding territory

city technology college *n* an inner-city secondary school specializing in technical subjects, with close links to and funding partly provided by private industry

citywide /sítti wīd/ *adj* involving the whole of a particular city ■ *adv* so as to involve the whole of a particular city

Ciudad Bolívar /syoo dád bo lée vaar/ river port and capital of Bolívar State, E Venezuela. Population: 258,112 (1992).

Ciudad Juárez /-hwáa ress/ city in N Mexico, across the Rio Grande from El Paso, Texas. Population: 1,011,786 (1995).

Ciudad Real /-ray aál/ capital of Ciudad Real Province, south-central Spain. Population: 194,996 (1990).

Ciudad Victoria /-vik táwri ə/ capital of Tamaulipas State, NE Mexico. Population: 243,960 (1995).

civet /sívvit/ *n* 1 **civet, civet cat** WILD ANIMAL LIKE CAT a small carnivorous mammal that looks like a cat. Native to: Africa, Asia. Family: Viverridae. 2 SUBSTANCE USED IN PERFUME a yellow or brown greasy substance and smelling strongly of musk, secreted by a civet. Use: perfume manufacture. 3 FUR the fur of a civet [Mid-16C. Via French *civette* < Italian *zivetto* < medieval Latin *zibethum* < Arabic *zabād* 'civet perfume'.]

civic /sívvik/ *adj* 1 related to the government of a town or city ○ *civic reception* 2 connected with the duties and obligations of belonging to a community ○ *civic pride* [Mid-17C. < Latin *civicus* < *civis* 'citizen'.] —**civically** *adv*

civic centre *n* 1 a complex containing the public buildings of a particular town or city, e.g. the town hall, library, and recreational facilities 2 *US* a municipal entertainment complex containing an indoor arena that can be used for sports, concerts, and trade shows

civic-minded *adj* taking an active interest in the community needs and affairs of a town or city —**civic-mindedness** *n*

civics /sívviks/ *n* the study of the rights and duties of citizens (+ *singular verb*)

civil /sívv'l/ *adj* 1 RELATING TO CITIZENS relating to what happens within the state or between different citizens or groups of citizens ○ *civil war* 2 NOT MILITARY connected with ordinary citizens and organizations as opposed to the armed forces ○ *the civil authorities* 3 AS INDIVIDUAL CITIZEN relating to each citizen as an individual rather than as a member of a community or nation 4 NOT RELIGIOUS performed by a state official such as a registrar rather than a member of the clergy ○ *civil marriage* 5 BETWEEN INDIVIDUALS involving individual people or groups in legal action other than criminal proceedings ○ *a civil action* 6 = **civic** *adj.* 2 7 POLITE polite, but in a way that is cold and formal [14C. < Latin *civilis* < *civis* 'citizen'.]

civil code *n* the codified body of statutes in Quebec that derives from Roman and Napoleonic civil law

civil defence *n* 1 the organization and training of civilian volunteers to help the armed forces, police, and emergency services in the event of a war, a national emergency, or a natural disaster 2 civilian volunteers who take part in civil defence

civil disobedience *n* the deliberate breaking of a law by ordinary citizens, carried out as nonviolent protest or passive resistance

civil engineering *n* the branch of engineering concerned with the planning, design, and construction of such things as roads, bridges, and dams —**civil engineer** *n*

civilian /sə vílli ən/ *n* a citizen who is not a member of the armed forces [Early 14C. < Old French *civilien* 'of civil law' < *civil* 'civil' < Latin *civilis* (see CIVIL).] —**civilian** *adj*

civilianize /sə vílli ə nīz/ (-izes, -izing, -ized), **civilianise** (-ises, -ising, -ised) *vt* to change something from military to civilian use —**civilianization** /si vílli ə nī záysh'n/ *n*

civilisation *n* = **civilization**

civilise *vt* = **civilize**

civilised *adj* = **civilized**

civility /sə víllәti/ (*plural* -ties) *n* 1 the rather formal politeness that results from observing social conventions 2 something said or done in a formally polite way

civilization /sívvə lī záysh'n/, **civilisation** *n* 1 HIGHLY DEVELOPED SOCIETY a society that has a high level of culture and social organization 2 ADVANCED DEVELOPMENT OF SOCIETY an advanced level of development in society that is marked by complex social and political organization, and material, scientific, and artistic progress 3 ADVANCED SOCIETY IN GENERAL all the societies at an advanced level of development considered collectively 4 POPULATED AREAS places where people live, rather than uninhabited areas 5 COMFORT the level of material comfort that somebody is used to 6 CIVILIZING PROCESS the process of creating a high level of culture in a particular society or region

civilize /sívvə līz/ (-lizes, -lizing, -lized), **civilise** (-lises, -lising, -lised) *vt* 1 to create a high level of culture in a society or region 2 to teach somebody to behave in a more socially and culturally acceptable way —**civilizable** *adj* —**civilizer** *n* —**civilizing** *adj*

civilized /sívvə līzd/, **civilised** *adj* 1 CULTURALLY ADVANCED having advanced cultural and social development 2 DECENT showing high moral development 3 REFINED refined in tastes

civil law *n* 1 LAW OF CITIZENS' RIGHTS the law of a state dealing with the rights of private citizens 2 ANCIENT ROMAN LAW the law of ancient Rome, especially the part concerned with private citizens 3 LAW BASED ON ROMAN LAW a system of law based on Roman law rather than common law or canon law

civil liberties *npl* the basic rights guaranteed to individual citizens by law, e.g. freedom of speech and action —**civil libertarian** *n*

civil list *n* in the United Kingdom, the money paid each year by the state to support the royal family [Originally for the civil government of the state]

civilly /sívvəli/ *adv* showing politeness in a cold formal way

civil rights *npl* rights that all citizens of a society are supposed to have, e.g. the right to vote or to receive fair treatment from the law

civil servant *n* an employee in a government department

civil service *n* all the government departments of a state and the people who work in them

civil war *n* a war between opposing groups within a country

Civil War *n* 1 the civil war fought between the Royalist supporters of Charles I and the Parliamentarians led by Oliver Cromwell, between 1642 and 1648 2 the civil war fought in the United States from 1861 to 1865 between the North and the slave-owning states of the South

civil year *n* TIME = **calendar year**

civvies /sívviz/ *npl* ordinary clothes as opposed to a military uniform (*informal*) [Late 19C. Shortening and alteration of CIVILIAN, probably after CLOTHES.]

civvy /sívvi/ (*plural* -vies) *n* a civilian (*informal*) [Early 20C. Shortening and alteration.]

civvy street *n* civilian life as referred to by military personnel (*informal*)

⚡ **CIX** *abbr* commercial Internet exchange (*in e-commerce*)

CJ *abbr* 1 Chief Justice 2 *US* Chief Judge

CJD *abbr* Creutzfeldt-Jakob disease

⚡ **ck** *abbr* Cook Islands (*in Internet addresses*)

cl[1] *abbr* 1 centilitre 2 class 3 classification 4 clergy 5 closet 6 cloth 7 carload

⚡ **cl**[2] *abbr* Chile (*in Internet addresses*)

Cl *symbol* chlorine

clachan /klákhən, -kən/ *n Scotland* a small village [15C. < Gaelic, 'village, burying place'.]

clack /klak/ *v* 1 *vti* to cause or make a short hard loud noise, or cause something to make such a noise 2 *vi* to chatter constantly or rapidly (*informal*) 3 *vi* = **cluck** *v.* 1 [13C. An imitation of the sound.] —**clack** *n* —**clacker** *n*

Clackmannan /klak mánnən/ parish and town in central Scotland. Population: 3,420 (1991).

Clackmannanshire /klak mánnənshər/ local government unitary council in Scotland

clack valve *n* a valve with a hinged flap that swings open

Clactonian /klak tṓni ən/ *n* a Lower Palaeolithic culture of NW Europe that made stone chopping tools [After CLACTON-ON-SEA] —**Clactonian** *adj*

Clacton-on-Sea /kláktən-/ seaside town in SE England. Population: 45,065 (1991).

clad[1] /klad/ *adj* 1 wearing particular clothes ○ *clad in blue* 2 covered in a particular thing (*literary; often in combination*) ○ *iron-clad* [13C. < Old English *clāðed*, past participle of *clāðian* (see CLOTHE).]

clad[2] /klad/ (**clads, cladding, clad**) *vt* 1 to cover a wall or building with cladding 2 to cover or plate a metal with a layer of another metal, especially to make armour plating [Mid-16C. Probably < CLAD¹.]

clad- *prefix* = **clado-**

Claddagh ring /kláddəkh-, kláddaak-/ *n* a ring usually in the form of two hands clasping a heart surmounted by a crown, originally given in Ireland as a token of affection [Late 20C. After village in Galway, Ireland.]

cladding /kládding/ *n* 1 OUTER LAYER ON BUILDING a layer of stone, tiles, or wood added to the outside of a building to protect it or improve its insulation or appearance 2 METAL COATING a protective metal coating bonded onto another metal 3 COVERING FOR OPTICAL FIBRE a covering for optical fibre that reflects light back to the core and strengthens the cable

clade /klayd/ *n* a group of organisms, e.g. a species, that are considered to share a common ancestor [Mid-20C. < Greek *klados* 'branch'.]

cladist /kláy dist/ *n* a biologist who classifies organisms according to the principles of cladistics —**cladism** *n*

cladistics /klə dístiks/ *n* a system of biological classification that groups organisms on the basis of their observed shared characteristics in order to deduce the common ancestors (+ *singular verb*) —**cladistic** *adj* —**cladistically** *adv*

clado- *prefix* branch, shoot ○ *cladogram* [< Greek *klados* < Indo-European, 'strike']

cladoceran /klə dóssərən/ *n* a tiny freshwater crustacean such as a water flea. Order: Cladocera. [Early 20C. < modern Latin *Cladocera* < Greek *klados* 'branch' + *keras* 'horn'.] —**cladoceran** *adj*

cladode /kláddōd/ *n* PLANT SCI = **cladophyll** —**cladodial** /klə dṓdi əl/ *adj*

cladogenesis /kláddō jénnəssiss, kláydō-/ *n* evolutionary change regarded as taking place by the splitting of an ancestral species into two or more different descendant species —**cladogenetic** /-jə néttik, -/ *adj* —**cladogenetically** *adv*

cladogram /kláydə gram/ *n* a tree-shaped diagram showing evolutionary relationships and the points where species appear to have diverged from common ancestors

cladophyll /kláydə fil/ *n* a flattened stem similar to a leaf

clafoutis /kláffōōti/ (*plural* -tis) *n* a fruit and batter pastry, typically made with cherries [Late 20C. < French, < dialect *clafir* 'stuff' + standard French *foutre* 'stuff'.]

claim /klaym/ *v* 1 *vt* MAINTAIN SOMETHING IS TRUE to say, without proof or evidence, that something is true ○ *He claims we've already met.* 2 *vt* DEMAND SOMETHING AS ENTITLEMENT to demand officially something that somebody has a right to or owns 3 *vti* RECEIVE STATE MONEY to officially request and receive state money or other benefits 4 *vt* END SOMEBODY'S LIFE to cause the loss of somebody's life 5 *vt* WIN TITLE to take a title, prize, or record 6 *vt* DEMAND ATTENTION to force somebody to give attention ■ *n* 1 SOMETHING THAT MAY BE TRUE an assertion that something is true, unsupported by evidence or proof 2 BASIS FOR ENTITLEMENT the basis for demanding or getting something 3 DEMAND a demand for something somebody has a right to or owns 4 OFFICIAL REQUEST FOR MONEY an official request for money or other benefits from the state or an organization 5 MONEY REQUESTED the amount of money requested in a claim 6 LEGAL RIGHT TO LAND the legal right to own a piece of land and to mine it for minerals 7 PIECE OF LAND the piece of land to which somebody claims a legal right [14C. < Old French *clamer* 'to call' < Latin *clamare*.] —**claimable** *adj* —**claimer** *n* ◇ **lay claim to something** to say that you have a right to something, or take what you think you have a right to

claimant /kláymənt/ *n* 1 a stater of a claim to receive something, e.g. benefits or an inheritance 2 a bringer of a lawsuit in a civil court against somebody (**defendant**)

Clair /klair/, **René** (1898–1981) French film director and scriptwriter. Born **René-Lucien Chomette**

clair de lune /kláir də lōōn/ *n* 1 a pale blue or greyish-blue glaze used on porcelain 2 a pale bluish-grey colour [Late 19C. < French, 'light of the moon'.] —**clair de lune** *adj*

clairvoyance /klair vóyənss/, **clairvoyancy** /-ənssi/ *n* the supposed ability to see things beyond the range of normal human vision [Mid-19C. < French, < *clairvoyant* 'clear-sighted' < *voyant*, present participle of *voir* 'see'.]

clairvoyant /klair vóyənt/ *n* somebody supposedly able to see things beyond the range of normal human vision [Late 17C. < French (see CLAIRVOYANCE).] —**clairvoyant** *adj* —**clairvoyantly** *adv*

clam /klam/ *n* 1 BURROWING SHELLFISH a freshwater or marine mollusc with a muscular foot used to burrow into sand. Class: Pelecypoda. 2 CLAM FLESH the soft edible flesh of the clam 3 *US* SECRETIVE PERSON a shy or secretive person (*informal*) 4 *US* DOLLAR a dollar (*slang*) ■ *vi* (**clams, clamming, clammed**) *US* COLLECT CLAMS to gather clams [Early 16C. < obsolete *clam-shell* 'clamp-shell' < Old English *clamm* 'bond, grip' < Indo-European, 'form into a ball'.]

clam up *vi* to become suddenly secretive or unwilling to talk (*informal*)

clamant /kláymənt/ *adj* demanding attention (*literary*) [Mid-17C. < Latin *clamant-*, present participle of *clamare* 'call'.] —**clamantly** *adv*

clambake /klám bayk/ *n* 1 a picnic in which seafood such as clams and other foods are cooked and eaten 2 *US* a relaxed party or other gathering (*informal*)

clamber /klámbər/ *vi* to climb quickly but awkwardly, using hands and feet ■ *n* a climb that involves clambering [14C. Probably 'climb repeatedly' < *clamb*, former past tense of CLIMB.] —**clamberer** *n*

clam chowder *n* a thick soup made from clams and potatoes

clammy /klámmi/ (-mier, -miest) *adj* 1 slightly damp and unpleasantly cold 2 warm and damp [14C. Probably < *clam* 'to smear', back-formation < *clamde*, past tense of Old English *clǣman* < Germanic, 'clay'.] —**clammily** *adv* —**clamminess** *n*

clamor *vi, n* US = **clamour**

clamorous /klámmərəss/ *adj* 1 **DEMANDING ATTENTION** demanding attention loudly and insistently 2 **LOUD** loud and excited or angry 3 **NOISY** making a loud noise —**clamorously** *adv* —**clamorousness** *n*

clamour /klámmər/ *vi* 1 **DEMAND NOISILY** to demand something noisily or desperately 2 **SHOUT LOUDLY** to shout at the same time as other people, and make a lot of noise ■ *n* 1 **PERSISTENT DEMAND** a persistent demand for something, made in an excited or angry way 2 **LOUD NOISE** a loud noise, especially one made by people shouting together [14C. Via Old French *clamor* < Latin *clamor-* < *clamare* 'call'.] —**clamourer** *n*

clamp /klamp/ *n* 1 **HOLDING DEVICE** a mechanical device with movable jaws. Use: to hold two things firmly together or one object firmly in position. 2 **WHEEL CLAMP** a wheel clamp ■ *vt* 1 **FASTEN THINGS TOGETHER** to fasten two or more things firmly together using a clamp 2 **HOLD FIRMLY** to hold something firmly and tightly in position 3 **PUT CLAMP ON CAR** to fix a clamp to the wheel of an illegally parked car. US term **boot**[1] *v.* 2 [15C. Probably < assumed Middle Dutch or Middle Low German *klampe*.]
clamp down *vi* to take firm action to control or limit something bad or somebody doing something bad ○ *police have clamped down on illegal parking in the area*

clampdown /klámpdown/ *n* firm official action taken to control or limit something bad or somebody doing something bad

clamper /klámpər/ *n* a spiked metal frame fastened under a shoe to avoid slipping on ice or snow

clamshell /klám shel/ *n* 1 **SHELL** the shell of a clam 2 *US* **DREDGING BUCKET** a dredging bucket that has two hinged jaws (*informal*) 3 **HINGED DEVICE** any hinged device that opens like the shell of a clam (*informal*)

clan /klan/ *n* (*takes a singular or plural verb*) 1 **GROUP OF FAMILIES** a group of families related through a common ancestor or marriage 2 **RELATED SCOTTISH FAMILIES** a group of Scottish families with common ancestors and surname and a single chief 3 **LARGE FAMILY** a group of people who are all members of a particular family (*informal*) 4 **GROUP WITH SHARED AIM** a group of people who act together because they have the same interests or aims (*informal*) [15C. < Gaelic *clann* 'offspring' < Old Irish *cland* < Latin *planta* 'sprout'.]

clandestine /klan déstin, klán de stīn/ *adj* secret or furtive, and usually illegal [Mid-16C. < Latin *clandestinus* < *clam* 'secretly'.] —**clandestinely** *adv* —**clandestineness** *n* —**clandestinity** /klán de stínnəti/ *n*

SYNONYMS See *secret*.

clang /klang/ *vti* 1 **MAKE LOUD RINGING NOISE** to make the ringing sound of two metal objects hitting each other 2 **MOVE MAKING CLANGING SOUND** to move or operate with a clanging sound ■ *n* **LOUD RINGING NOISE** a ringing sound made by two metal objects hitting each other [Late 16C. < Latin *clangere* 'emit a ringing sound'.]

clanger /klángər/ *n* an unwise or embarrassing mistake (*informal*) ○ *drop a clanger*

clangor *n* US = **clangour**

clangour /kláng gər/ *n* 1 a clang or repeated loud clanging 2 a din or uproar —**clangorous** *adj* —**clangorously** *adv*

clanjamfry /klán jámfri/ *n Scotland* a rabble or crowd of people

clank /klangk/ *vti* 1 **MAKE METALLIC NOISE** to make the short loud sound of two heavy metal objects hitting each other 2 **MOVE MAKING CLANKING SOUND** to move or operate with a clanking sound ■ *n* **METALLIC NOISE** a short loud noise made by two heavy metal objects hitting each other [Mid-17C. < ?] —**clankingly** *adv* —**clanky** *adj*

clannish /klánnish/ *adj* inclined to stick together as a group and exclude outsiders —**clannishly** *adv* —**clannishness** *n*

clansman /klánzmən/ (*plural* **-men** /-mən/) *n* a male member of a Scottish clan

clap[1] /klap/ *v* (**claps, clapping, clapped**) 1 *vti* **HIT HANDS TOGETHER** to hit the hands together quickly and loudly 2 *vti* **APPLAUD** to hit the hands together repeatedly to express approval 3 *vti* **HIT HANDS IN RHYTHM** to hit the hands together repeatedly in time with a beat 4 *vt* **PUT QUICKLY** to move something to or against something quickly 5 *vt Scotland* **PAT AN ANIMAL** to give a pat to an animal (*informal*) ■ *n* 1 **SUDDEN LOUD SOUND** the sound made by striking the palms together once, or a sound resembling this 2 **EXPRESSION OF APPROVAL THROUGH APPLAUSE** an expression of approval by loud continuous clapping 3 **CLAPPING RHYTHMICALLY** a session of rhythmic clapping 4 *Scotland* **PAT** the act of patting an animal (*informal*) [Old English *clæppan* < Germanic, an imitation of the sound]

clap[2] /klap/ *n* gonorrhoea (*slang*) [Late 16C. < ?]

clapboard /kláp bawrd/ *n* a long narrow wooden board that has one edge thicker than the other. Use: to clad buildings. [Mid-17C. Partial translation of *clapholt* < Low German *klappholt* < *klappen* 'clap, split' + *holt* 'wood'.]

clapped-out *adj* worn out and in very poor condition (*informal; not hyphenated after verbs*)

clapper /kláppər/ *n* 1 **PART MAKING BELL RING** a piece of metal inside a bell that strikes its sides, making it ring 2 **SOMEBODY WHO CLAPS** somebody who claps his or her hands ■ **clappers** *npl* **MUSICAL INSTRUMENT** a musical instrument consisting of two flat pieces of wood that are held between the thumb and forefinger and clapped together ◇ **like the clappers** extremely fast, or as fast as possible (*informal*)

clapperboard /kláppər bawrd/ *n* a pair of hinged boards filmed at the start of each take in a film and clapped together to help to synchronize the soundtrack with the film

Clapton /kláptən/, **Eric** (*b.* 1945) British guitarist, singer, and songwriter

claptrap /kláp trap/ *n* pompous or important-sounding nonsense (*informal*) [Late 18C. Originally, in the theatre, a device or line to elicit clapping.]

claque /klak/ *n* (*takes a singular or plural verb*) 1 a group of people hired to applaud a performance 2 a group of people around a rich or famous person whom they praise and support uncritically [Mid-19C. < French, < *claquer* 'clap', an imitation of the sound.]

claqueur /klákər/ *n* a praiser or applauder who accompanies a rich or famous person [Mid-19C. < French, 'clapper' < *claquer* (see CLAQUE).]

clarabella /klárrə béllə/, **claribella** *n* an eight-foot flute stop on an organ [Mid-19C. < Latin *clara bella* 'clear and beautiful'.]

Clare /klair/ 1 island off the coast of W Ireland. Area: 16 sq. km/6.3 sq. mi. 2 river in the NE of the South Island, New Zealand. Length: 209 km/130 mi.

Clare (of Assisi) /kláir-/, **St** (1194–1253) Italian nun. Born **Clara Offreducia**

Clare /klair/, **John** (1793–1864) British poet and naturalist

clarence /klárrənss/ *n* an enclosed four-wheeled carriage that seats four and has a glass front [Mid-19C. After the Duke of *Clarence*, later William IV.]

Clarence /klárrənss/ 1 river in NE New South Wales, Australia. Length: 394 km/245 mi. 2 river in the NE of the South Island, New Zealand. Length: 209 km/130 mi.

Clarenceux /klárrən sō/ *n* the second King-of-Arms in England [15C. < Anglo-Norman, < English *Clarence*, English dukedom, after *Clare* in Suffolk.]

Clarendon /klárrəndən/ *n* a style of boldface roman type [Mid-19C. Probably after the *Clarendon* Press in Oxford.]

Clarendon /klárrəndən/, **Edward Hyde, 1st Earl of** (1609–74) English statesman and historian

claret /klárrət/ *n* 1 a red wine from the Bordeaux region of France 2 a deep purplish-red colour [Early 18C. < Old French *(vin) claret* 'light-coloured (wine)' < Latin *vinum claratum* 'clarified wine', *claratum* form of *clarare* 'clarify' < *clarus* 'clear'.] —**claret** *adj*

claret cup *n* an iced summer drink made from claret, brandy, lemon, and sugar, sometimes with sherry or curaçao added

clarify /klárri fī/ (**-fies, -fying, -fied**) *v* 1 *vt* **MAKE SOMETHING CLEARER** to make something clearer by explaining it in greater detail 2 *vti* **MAKE BUTTER CLEAR** to make butter or fat clear by gently heating it and removing any impurities, or become clear through this process 3 *vti* **MAKE A LIQUID CLEAR** to make a liquid clear and pure, or become clear and pure, usually by filtering [14C. Via Old French < late Latin *clarificare* 'make clear' < Latin *clarus* 'clear'.] —**clarification** /klárrifi káysh'n/ *n* —**clarifier** *n*

clarinet /klárrə nét/ *n* a musical instrument of the woodwind family, with a straight body and a single reed [Mid-18C. < French *clarinette* 'little clarion' < *clarine* 'clarion' < Latin *clarus* 'clear'.]

clarinettist /klárrə néttist/, **clarinetist** *n* a player of the clarinet

clarion /klárri ən/ *n* 1 a four-foot organ stop that sounds like a trumpet 2 a medieval trumpet with a clear high-pitched tone [14C. < medieval Latin *clarion-* < Latin *clarus* 'clear'.]

clarion call *n* an urgent or inspiring appeal to people to do something [< the use of the clarion as a signal in war]

clarity /klárrəti/ *n* 1 **CLEARNESS OF EXPRESSION** the quality of being clearly expressed 2 **CLEARNESS OF THOUGHT** clearness in what somebody is thinking 3 **CLEARNESS OF REPRODUCTION** the quality of being clear in sound or image 4 **TRANSPARENT QUALITY** the quality of being clear, pure, or transparent ○ *wine of great clarity* [Early 17C. < Latin *claritat-* < *clarus* 'clear'.]

Clark /klaark/, **Helen Elizabeth** (*b.* 1950) New Zealand politician and prime minister (1999–)

Clark, Joe (*b.* 1939) Canadian statesman. Full name **Charles Joseph Clark**

Clark cell *n* a standard battery cell with a mercury anode surrounded by a paste of mercury sulphate, and a zinc cathode immersed in saturated zinc sulphate solution [Late 19C. After Josiah Latimer *Clark* (1822–98), English engineer.]

Clarke /klaark/, **Sir Arthur C.** (*b.* 1917) British writer and scientist. Full name **Arthur Charles Clarke**

Clarke, Austin (1896–1974) Irish poet and playwright

Clarke, Jeremiah (1669?–1707) English composer and organist

Clarke, John (*fl.* 1639) English scholar

Clarke, Marcus Andrew Hislop (1846–81) British-born Australian writer

claro /klaárō/ (*plural* **-ros** *or* **-roes**) *n* a mild light-coloured cigar [Late 19C. Via Spanish, 'light' < Latin *clarus* 'clear'.]

clarsach /klaár sakh, -səkh/ *n* a small harp of ancient Scotland and Ireland [15C. < Irish *cláirseach*, Gaelic *clàrsach*.]

clarts /klaarts/ *npl Scotland, N England* small lumps of mud, especially those stuck to shoes (*informal*) [Early 19C. < ?]

clarty /klaárti/ (**-tier, -tiest**) *adj Scotland, N England* covered in or full of mud or dirt (*informal*)

clary /kláiri/ (*plural* **-ies**) *n* a perennial plant of the mint family. Native to: S Europe. Genus: *Salvia*. [14C. Via obsolete French *clarie* < medieval Latin *sclarea*.]

clash /klash/ *v* 1 *vi* **FIGHT OR ARGUE** to come into verbal or physical conflict with somebody ○ *Demonstrators clashed with police outside the headquarters this morning.* 2 *vi* **BE AT ODDS** to be incompatible ○ *The conclusions clash with the evidence.* 3 *vti* **MAKE LOUD NOISE** to make a loud harsh metallic noise 4 *vi* **NOT HARMONIZE** to look unpleasant or inharmonious when together ○ *The orange of the upholstery clashes with the pink of the paintwork.* 5 *vi* **CONFLICT WITH SOMETHING ELSE** to conflict with something else in terms of timing or appropriateness (*refers to events*) ○ *The final episode of the serial clashes with one of my husband's favourite programmes.* ■ *n* 1 **FIGHT OR ARGUMENT** a verbal or physical conflict with another person or group ○ *There were several clashes between supporters outside the stadium.* 2 **LOUD METALLIC SOUND** a loud harsh metallic noise 3 **LACK OF HARMONY** a jarring or unpleasant juxtaposition of incompatible colours 4 **CONFLICT CAUSED BY DIFFERENCE** a difference of opinions or qualities that causes conflict ○ *a clash of personalities* 5 **COINCIDENCE OF CONFLICTING EVENTS** a conflict between two or more events due to occur at the same time [Early 16C. An imitation of the sound.] —**clasher** *n*

SYNONYMS See *fight*.

clasp /klaasp/ *vt* 1 **HOLD WITH HANDS OR ARMS** to hold somebody or something tightly with the hands or arms ○ *She clasped the baby tightly to herself in the surging crowd.* ○ *I clasped the handrail as the boat lurched.* 2 **FASTEN** to fasten or hold two things together with a device designed for this purpose ■ *n* 1 **SMALL BUCKLE OR FASTENING** a small fastening for holding things, e.g. bags or jewellery, closed or together 2 **TIGHT ARM OR HAND HOLD** a firm tight hold with the arms, a hand, or a device for fastening or holding things together 3 **IDENTIFYING ATTACHMENT ON MILITARY MEDAL** a small metal bar on the ribbon of a medal that identifies the military action or service for which the honour was awarded [14C. < ?]

clasper /klaáspər/ *n* **1** either of a pair of structures located in the anal region of particular male insects and crustaceans and used to grasp a female during copulation **2** either of a pair of elongated reproductive organs on the pelvic fins of male sharks and rays

clasp knife *n* a pocket knife with one or more blades and sometimes other devices that can be folded back into the handle

class /klaass/ *n* **1 GROUP TAUGHT TOGETHER** a group of students or pupils who are taught or study together **2 PERIOD OF TEACHING** a period when students meet to be taught a particular subject ○ *When's our next biology class?* **3 SPECIFIC SUBJECT TAUGHT** a specific course of instruction **4** *US* **STUDENTS WHO GRADUATE TOGETHER** the group of students who leave or graduate from an institution in the same year **5 GROUP WITHIN A SOCIETY** a group of people within a society who share the same social and economic status **6 STRUCTURE OF SOCIETY** the structure of divisions in a society determined by the social or economic grouping of its members **7 ELEGANCE IN STYLE** elegance in appearance, behaviour, or lifestyle (*informal*) **8 EXCELLENCE** admirable skill or excellence in performance (*informal*) ○ *a player of real class* **9 DIVISION ACCORDING TO QUALITY** a categorization of services or goods according to quality ○ *This airline has several classes of seating.* **10 UNIVERSITY HONOURS DEGREE GRADE** a grade assigned to university honours degrees ○ *'What class is your degree?'—'First'.* **11 GROUP OF SIMILAR ITEMS** a group of things with at least one common characteristic **12 SET OF RELATED ORGANISMS** a major category in the taxonomic classification of related organisms, comprising a group of orders ○ *Elephants and dolphins both belong to the class Mammalia.* **13 SOCIAL GROUP WITH SIMILAR OPPORTUNITIES** a category of people who have a similar level of opportunity to obtain economic resources and prestige **14** MATH, LOGIC = **set**^{2} *n.* **8** ■ *vt* **ASSIGN TO A GROUP** to assign somebody or something to a particular category or group ○ *It's not old enough to be classed as a vintage car.* [Mid-16C. < Latin *classis* 'political class'.]

SYNONYMS See ***type***.

class. *abbr* **1** classic **2** classical **3** classification **4** classified

class act *n* a person or thing regarded as an example of excellence (*informal*)

class action *n* a legal action brought by several litigants jointly, usually relying on one another to prove each individual's case

class-conscious *adj* aware of your position in a social class system in relation to members of other classes — **class-consciousness** *n*

classes plural of **classis**

classic /klássik/ *adj* **1 TOP QUALITY** generally considered to be of the highest quality or lasting value, especially in the arts **2 DEFINITIVE** authoritative and perfect as a standard of its kind ○ *a classic example of mixed metaphor English* **3 ALWAYS FASHIONABLE** always fashionable and elegant, usually because of simplicity and restraint in style ○ *the classic 'little black dress'* **4 GENERALLY ACCEPTED** conforming to generally accepted principles or methods **5 EXTREMELY AND USUALLY COMICALLY APROPOS** apropos to an extreme degree, usually with a comical or ironic twist (*informal*) ■ *n* **1 WORK OF THE HIGHEST QUALITY** something created or made, especially a work of art, music, or literature, that is generally considered to be of the highest quality and of enduring value ○ *the novel has become a 20th-century classic* **2 SIMPLE ELEGANT GARMENT** a piece of clothing of a simple and enduring style **3 TOP QUALITY ARTIST OR WRITER** a creator of works of art or literature that have enduring excellence ○ *As a children's book illustrator she's a classic.* **4 MAJOR SPORTING EVENT** a major sporting event, e.g. a horse race or golf tournament **5 SOMETHING COMICALLY APROPOS** something that is comically or ironically apropos (*informal*)

USAGE classic or **classical**? There is some overlap in the meanings of these words, but essentially ***classic*** describes the value or status of something (*a classic example of Art Deco*), whereas ***classical***, although often implying a judgment of value or worth, is a more factual reference to the literature, art, and culture of the ancient world or to the high period of an art form (*a classical education, classical music, classical ballet*). A ***classic*** is something created or made that is of the highest quality, whereas *classics* is the study of the languages and cultures of ancient Greece and Rome.

classical /klássik'l/ *adj* **1 RELATING TO ANCIENT GREECE OR ROME** relating or belonging to the ancient Greeks and Romans or their cultures **2 IN ANCIENT GREEK OR ROMAN STYLE** in the style of ancient Greece or Rome, especially in architecture **3 OF MUSIC CONSIDERED TO BE SERIOUS** describes music that is considered serious or intellectual and is usually written in a traditional or formal style, as opposed to such genres as pop, rock, and folk music **4 OF 18C AND 19C MUSIC** describes the style of music composed in Europe in the 18th and 19th centuries **5 STUDYING LATIN AND GREEK** consisting of or involving the study of the ancient Greek and Latin languages and literature ○ *a classical education* **6 KNOWLEDGEABLE ABOUT ANCIENT GREECE AND ROME** highly knowledgeable about ancient Greek and Roman culture and art ○ *a classical scholar* **7 ORTHODOX OR CONSERVATIVE** considered as the traditional or authoritative form of something ○ *classical Freudianism* **8** = **classic** *adj.* **2 9 EXCLUDING QUANTUM THEORY AND RELATIVITY** not taking into account quantum theoretical or relativistic effects [Late 16C. < Latin *classicus* 'of the first class'.] —**classicality** /klàssi kállәti/ *n* —**classicalness** *n*

USAGE See ***classic***.

classical conditioning *n* the teaching of a response to a new stimulus by pairing it repeatedly with a stimulus for which there is a biological reflex. The best-known example is Pavlov's experiment in which dogs heard a bell ring every time food appeared and eventually started salivating at the sound of the bell alone. ◊ **operant conditioning**

classicalism *n* = **classicism**

classical Latin *n* the form of the Latin language used between the end of the first century BC and the third century AD

classically /klássikli/ *adv* **1 SIMPLY STYLED** in a simple and elegant style **2 AS TRADITIONALLY ACCEPTED OR DONE** in a manner that is traditionally accepted and belongs in the mainstream of the relevant art **3 IN MANNER OF GRAECO-ROMAN CULTURE** in the manner or style of ancient Greece or Rome **4 AS USUALLY OCCURS** used to indicate what usually or typically happens ○ *Classically, cases like this are solved through painstaking investigation.* **5 AS TYPICAL EXAMPLE** as a classic example of something **6 IN CLASSIC WAY** in a classic or classical manner

classicise *vti* = **classicize**

classicism /klássissizәm/, **classicalism** /klássik'lizәm/ *n* **1 RESTRAINED STYLE IN THE ARTS** a style of art and architecture based on Greek and Roman models or principles, characterized by regularity of form and restraint of expression **2 GREEK OR LATIN IDIOM** a Greek or Latin phrase or expression **3 STUDY OF GRAECO-ROMAN CULTURE** the study or knowledge of ancient Greece and Rome

QUICK FACTS ON... **CLASSICISM**

Key dates: early 15th–late 18th centuries
Key locations: Italy, France, England, Germany
Key elements: revival of interest in and imitation of ancient Greek and Roman aesthetics, visual arts, architecture, and literature
Key figures: de' Medici family (patrons); Mantegna, Raphael, Michelangelo, Poussin, Ingres, David (art); Alberti (architecture); Corneille, Racine, Bacon, Jonson, Addison, Pope, Swift, Johnson, Goethe, Schiller (literature); Haydn, Mozart, early Beethoven (music)
Key works: *David* (Michelangelo) 1501–04, *Medée* (Corneille) 1635, *Phèdre* (Racine) 1677, *Arcadia* (Poussin) ?1690, translations of *Iliad* and *Odyssey* (Pope) 1715–25, *Vanity of Human Wishes* (Johnson) 1745

classicist /klássissist/ *n* **1** a scholar of ancient Greek and Latin **2** a supporter of classicism in the arts

classicize /klássi sīz/ (**-cizes, -cizing, -cized**), **classicise** (**-cises, -cising, -cised**) *v* **1** *vt* to imbue something with classical traits, qualities, or characteristics ○ *classicized the design of the windows* **2** *vi* to be in a classic or classical style

classics /klássiks/ *n* the academic study of the language, literature, and history of ancient Greece and Rome (+ *singular verb*) ■ *npl* a body of ancient Greek and Roman literature (+ *plural verb*)

classification /klàssifi káysh'n/ *n* **1 ORGANIZATION INTO GROUPS** the allocation of items to groups according to type ○ *classification of members according to abilities and interests* **2 CATEGORY** a group or category within a system ○ *The classification 'history' can be further subdivided.* **3 CATEGORIZATION OF LIVING THINGS** the categorization of organisms into defined groups on the basis of identified characteristics **4 CATEGORY FOR LIVING THINGS** each of several categories into which biologists organize living things based on structural resemblance or evolutionary relationships ○ *genus and species classifications* **5 DESIGNATION AS SENSITIVE INFORMATION** the restriction of sensitive government or military information to authorized individuals [Late 18C. < French, < *classe* 'class' < Latin *classis* 'political class'.] —**classificational** *adj* —**classificatory** *adj*

classification schedule *n* the complete plan and content of a library's cataloguing system

classified /klássi fīd/ *adj* **1 SECRET OR SENSITIVE** available only to authorized people for reasons of national security. The basic categories of classified information are confidential, secret, and top secret. **2 GROUPED BY TYPE** arranged in groups according to a classification system **3 LISTED IN BRITISH ROAD SYSTEM** classed as a motorway, an A-road, or a B-road in the British system of classifying roads ■ **classifieds** *npl* **GROUP OF ADVERTISEMENTS** classified advertisements printed together in a newspaper or magazine (*informal*)

classified advertisement, classified ad *n* a small advertisement positioned with others of similar content in a newspaper or magazine

classify /klássi fī/ (**-fies, -fying, -fied**) *vt* **1** to assign things or people to classes or groups **2** to designate information as being available only to authorized people for reasons of security [Late 18C. Back-formation < CLASSIFICATION.] —**classifiable** *adj* —**classifier** *n*

class interval *n* any of the intervals into which adjacent discrete values of a variable are divided

classis /klássiss/ (*plural* **-ses** /-seez/) *n* **1** in some Reformed churches, a governing body composed of elders and pastors **2** a district or group of churches governed by a classis [Late 16C. < Latin *classis* 'political class'.]

classism /klaássizәm/ *n* discrimination or prejudice based on social or economic class —**classist** *adj, n*

classless /klaássləss/ *adj* **1** not having social or economic classes **2** not belonging to or associated with a particular social or economic class —**classlessness** *n*

class list *n* a list of the classes of degree awarded in a British university

class mark LIBRARIES = **class number**

classmate /klaáss mayt/ *n* a member of the same school class as another

class number *n* a series of letters and/or numbers on a book or other publication in a library identifying it, the category of its subject matter, and usually its shelf location

classroom /klaáss room, -ro͝om/ *n* a room, especially in a school or college, where classes are held

class struggle *n* the Marxist principle of a continuous struggle for political and economic power between the ruling and working classes

classy /klaássi/ (**-ier, -iest**) *adj* very stylish and elegant (*informal*) —**classily** *adv* —**classiness** *n*

clast /klast/ *n* a fragment of rock produced by the breaking down of larger rocks [Mid-20C. Back-formation < CLASTIC.]

clastic /klástik/ *adj* **1** able to be separated into parts or have parts removed to enable better study ○ *Clastic models are often used to teach anatomy.* **2** describes rock that is composed of fragments of other rocks [Late 19C. < French *clastique* < Greek *klastos* 'broken in pieces'.]

clathrate /kláth rayt/ *n* **CRYSTAL WITH EMBEDDED SUBSTANCE** a solid compound with a physical structure in which molecules of one substance are fully enclosed within the crystal structure of another ■ *adj* **1 WITH CRYSTAL-EMBEDDED SUBSTANCE** having molecules of one substance enclosed fully within the crystal structure of another substance **2 LIKE A LATTICE** resembling a lattice in structure or appearance [Mid-19C. < Latin *clathrare* 'fit with bars' < *clathri* 'lattice' < Greek *klēthra* 'bars'.]

clatter /kláttər/ *v* **1** *vti* **MAKE RATTLING NOISE** to make, or cause something to make, a loud rattling noise ○ *a clattering old lorry* **2** *vi* **CHATTER NOISILY** to chatter or prattle, especially noisily **3** *vt N England, Scotland* **BOX SOMEBODY'S EARS** to hit somebody on the ears, especially as a punishment ■ *n* **1 BANGING METALLIC SOUND** a loud metallic banging or rattling noise ○ *the clatter of pots and pans in the kitchen* **2 NOISY CHATTER** noisy chatter and prattling talk **3 LOUD COMMOTION** a noisy disturbance [Assumed Old

English *clatrian* < Germanic, probably an imitation of the sound] —**clatterer** *n* —**clatteringly** *adv*

Claudel /klō dél/, **Paul Louis Marie** (1868–1955) French writer and diplomat

claudication /kláwdi káysh'n/ *n* **1** limping or impaired walking, especially as a result of reduced blood supply to the leg muscles **2** MED = **intermittent claudication** [15C. < Latin *claudication-* < *claudicare* 'limp' < *claudus* 'lame'.]

Claudius I /kláwdi əss/ (10 BC–AD 54) Roman emperor (AD 41–54)

clause /klawz/ *n* **1** a group of words consisting of a subject and its predicate. A clause usually contains a verb and may or may not be a sentence in its own right. **2** a distinct section of a document, especially a legal document, that is usually separately numbered [13C. < French, < assumed Latin *clausa* 'close of a rhetorical period' < *claudere* 'close'.] —**clausal** *adj*

LANGUAGE NOTE Clauses A ***clause*** is a unit of discourse containing a verb, either explicit or understood. A ***clause*** usually contains the subject of the verb as well, and very often other words such as the object of the verb.
There are two types of clause: *main* (or *independent*) *clauses* and *subordinate* (or *dependent*) *clauses.* Main clauses can be used by themselves as sentences. *Help!* is a main clause. So are: *She left. He finished his drink. The squirrel buried its nuts under the old chestnut tree at the bottom of the garden.* Subordinate clauses cannot be used by themselves; they need to be attached to main clauses. For example, *what the time was* is a subordinate clause. It makes no sense on its own. It has to go with a main clause: *I'd forgotten what the time was.* Another subordinate clause is *although I like chocolate* and it too has to go with a *main clause*: *Although I like chocolate, I can't stand chocolate milk.* Such clauses can be introduced by words such as *what, when* (as in *since when*), *whether, which, who, how,* and *that.* These words are called *relative pronouns,* and the clauses they introduce are known as *relative clauses.* The relative adverbs *when, where,* and *why* introduce *adjectival clauses*; *when everything went wrong* is a *subordinate adjectival clause* in *It was a Monday when everything went wrong.*
There are two types of *relative clause. Defining relative clauses,* also known as *restrictive relative clauses* limit, specify, and define the particular person or thing you are referring to. For instance, in *The team that I support has won all its matches this season,* the defining restrictive clause tells us which team is being talked about: it is the team *which I support. Nondefining relative clauses,* also known as *nonrestrictive relative clauses* add information about a person or thing previously mentioned. They do not limit, specify, or define. For example, in *The team, which I support, has won all its matches this season,* the nondefining relative clause is simply giving us the extra, nonessential, information that the speaker happens to support this particular team. Words such as *when, which,* and *who* can be used in either type of clause, but *that* can be used only in defining relative clauses. Thus, you can say *The team that I support has won all its matches this season,* but not *The team, that I support, has won all its matches this season.* Note that in writing, the nondefining relative clause is marked off with a pair of commas, but the *defining relative clause* is not.

claustrophobe /kláwstrə fōb, klóstrə-/ *n* PSYCHIAT = **claustrophobic** *n.* [Mid-20C. Back-formation < CLAUSTROPHOBIA.]

claustrophobia /kláwstrə fóbi ə, klóstrə-/ *n* an irrational fear of being in a confined or enclosed space [Late 19C. < modern Latin, < *claustrum* (see CLOISTER).]

claustrophobic /kláwstrə fóbik, klóstrə-/ *adj* **1 CONFINED OR CRAMPED** unpleasantly or uncomfortably confined ○ *The room is claustrophobic but painting the walls a light colour might help.* **2 OF OR HAVING CLAUSTROPHOBIA** relating to or having claustrophobia ■ *n* **SOMEBODY WHO FEARS ENCLOSED SPACES** somebody who is affected by claustrophobia —**claustrophobically** *adv*

clavate /kláy vayt/ *adj* with one end thicker than the other ○ *Some protozoa have clavate cilia.* [Early 19C. < modern Latin *clavatus* < Latin *clava* 'club'.] —**clavately** *adv*

clave /klaav, klayv/ *n* either of a pair of hardwood sticks that are hit together to make a clicking sound [Early 20C. Via American Spanish < Spanish, 'keystone' < Latin *clavis* 'key'.]

clavicembalo /klávvi chémbəlō/ (*plural* **-los**) *n* MUSIC = **harpsichord** [Mid-18C. Via Italian < medieval Latin *clavicymbalum* 'key cymbal'.]

clavichord /klávvi kawrd/ *n* a keyboard instrument of the 15th to 19th centuries, a precursor of the modern piano, in which small wedges strike horizontal strings to produce a soft sound [15C. < medieval Latin *clavichordium* < Latin *clavis* 'key' + *chorda* 'string'.] —**clavichordist** *n*

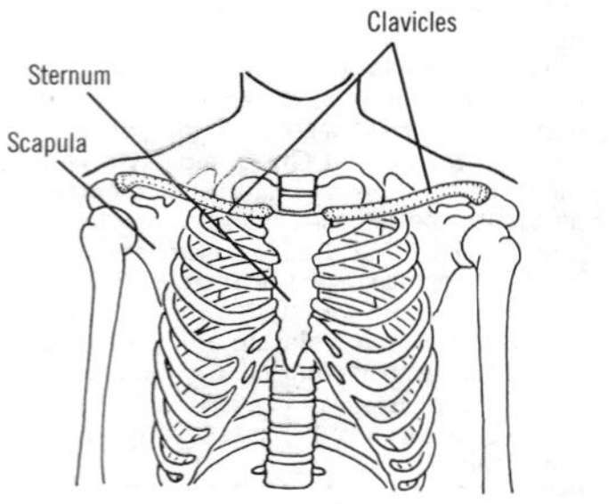

Clavicle

clavicle /klávvik'l/ *n* **1** the long curved bone that connects the upper part of the breastbone with the shoulder blade at the top of each shoulder in humans **2** a bone or structure with a function similar to that of the human clavicle in some other animals [Early 17C. < Latin *clavicula* 'small key' < *clavis* 'key'.] —**clavicular** /klə víkyŏŏlər, kla-/ *adj*

clavier /klə véer, klávvi ər/ *n* **1** a stringed keyboard musical instrument **2** the keyboard of a musical instrument [Early 18C. Directly or via German *Klavier* < French, < medieval Latin *claviarius* 'key-bearer' < Latin *clavis* 'key'.]

Clavius /klaávvi əss/ large walled plain on the Moon near the south pole, approximately 225 km/140 mi. in diameter

claw /klaw/ *n* **1 ANIMAL'S SHARP NAIL** a pointed curved nail on the end of each toe in birds, some reptiles, and some mammals **2 PINCER** an appendage used for grasping in crabs and other invertebrates **3 APPENDAGE RESEMBLING CLAW** something resembling a claw in shape or function, e.g. a mechanical grabbing device ■ *v* **1** *vti* **ATTACK WITH CLAWS** to scratch or dig at something or somebody with claws, fingernails, or something similar ○ *The dogs had clawed at the door.* **2** *vt* **FORM BY SCRATCHING** to form something by digging or scratching with claws or something similar ○ *Using our bare hands we clawed a hole in the sand.* [Old English *clawu* < Germanic] —**clawed** *adj* —**clawless** *adj*
claw back *vt* **1** to get something back with difficulty ○ *She's slowly clawing back some of the status she used to have.* **2** to recover through taxation money paid out, especially in state benefits
claw off *vi* to avoid the dangers of a lee shore or other hazard by sailing as close to the wind as possible on alternate tacks

clawback /kláw bak/ *n* **1** the recovery of money, especially through taxation **2** a sum of money recovered, especially through taxation

claw hammer *n* a hammer with a tapered fork at one end of its head for removing nails

claw setting *n* a jewellery setting in which a stone or similar item is gripped by small prongs

clay /klay/ *n* **1 TYPE OF FINE SOIL OR ROCK** a fine-grained material consisting mainly of hydrated aluminium silicates that occurs naturally in soil and sedimentary rock. Use: in making bricks, ceramics, and cement. **2 MODELLING SUBSTANCE** a substance like clay used for modelling **3 EARTH** earth, especially heavy sticky wet earth **4 HUMAN BODY** the physical body of a human being, particularly the matter of which it is composed (*literary*) ○ *From clay we are made.* **5** TENNIS = **clay court 6** SPORTS = **clay pigeon** *n.* 1 ■ *vt* **COVER WITH CLAY** to cover something with clay [Old English *clǣg* < Indo-European] —**clayey** *adj*

Clay /klay/, **Cassius** ♦ **Muhammad Ali**

Clay, Henry (1777–1852) US statesman

clay court *n* a tennis court with a hard surface made of crushed clay or shale

Claymation /klay máysh'n/ a trademark for an animated film process using clay figurines that are moved and filmed so as to create lifelike imagery and motion

clay mineral *n* hydrated aluminium silicate. Source: clay.

claymore /kláy mawr/ *n* **1** a large double-edged broadsword formerly used by Scottish Highlanders **2** MIL = **claymore mine** [Early 18C. < Gaelic *claidheamh mor* 'great sword'.]

claymore mine *n* a land mine in the shape of a convex disc that is placed above ground and detonates horizontally

claypan /kláy pan/ *n* a layer of impervious clay close to the surface of the ground, which holds water after heavy rain

clay pigeon *n* **1** a clay disc hurled into the air from a machine and used as a target for shooting **2** *US* somebody who is vulnerable to attack (*slang*)

claystone /kláy stōn/ *n* a compact fine-grained rock containing primarily clay particles

cld *abbr* called

clean /kleen/ *adj* **1 NOT DIRTY** free from dirt or impurities ○ *clean hands* **2 UNADULTERATED** containing no foreign matter or pollutants ○ *a clean water supply* **3 FREE OF INFECTION** not infected or diseased ○ *a clean wound* **4 WASHED** freshly laundered or washed after use ○ *fetched some clean shirts* **5 PARTICULAR ABOUT PERSONAL HYGIENE** taking pains over personal hygiene or grooming ○ *He is very clean in his habits.* **6 EMPTY** containing nothing at all (*informal*) ○ *The flat was stripped clean by the previous tenants.* **7 MORALLY UPRIGHT** morally pure and upright **8 HONESTLY FAIR** just and fair ○ *a clean verdict* **9 NOT RUDE** not rude or obscene **10 BLANK** without anything on it, especially anything written ○ *a clean sheet of paper* **11 WITH NO POLICE RECORD** having or showing no record of convictions or penalties, e.g. for driving offences ○ *Don's record is clean.* **12 FREE OF PROBLEMS** without problems or difficulties ○ *The doctor gave me a clean bill of health.* **13 SMOOTH-EDGED** without rough or jagged edges ○ *a clean blow of the axe* **14 STREAMLINED** simple and flowing in design, without projections or additions ○ *the aircraft's clean silhouette* **15 COMPLETE** complete and unqualified ○ *made a clean break with the past* **16 WITH NO FLAWS** describes a gemstone that is free of flaws **17 FREE OF WEEDS** cleared of weeds and unwanted undergrowth **18 NOT HEAVILY CORRECTED** containing relatively few mistakes or corrections **19 PERFORMED PRECISELY** precisely performed and in accordance with the best technique ○ *a clean jump* **20 WITH NO FOULS OR RULE-BREAKING** played, fought, or won by strict compliance with the rules ○ *a clean victory for our team* **21 NOT POLLUTING** producing the least possible pollution ○ *a clean source of energy* **22 MINIMALLY RADIOACTIVE** producing the least possible radioactive fallout or contamination **23 WITH NO CONCEALED ARMS** not carrying concealed weapons (*slang*) ○ *A body search revealed that the suspect was clean.* **24 WITH NO ILLEGAL DRUGS** not containing or possessing illegal drugs (*slang*) **25 UNADDICTED** free from addiction to narcotic drugs or other substances (*slang*) **26 INNOCENT** not guilty of a particular crime (*slang*) **27 RITUALLY UNDEFILED** describes somebody who is ritually undefiled according to Jewish law **28 ABLE TO BE LAWFULLY EATEN** describes food that may be eaten according to Jewish law **29 PURE IN SPIRIT** spiritually pure or purified ■ *v* **1** *vti* **RID SOMETHING OF DIRT** to rid something of dirt or impurities **2** *vt* **ERADICATE UNWANTED DIRT** to remove or eradicate unwanted dirt, stains, or marks ○ *Use this cloth to clean the dust off those books.* **3** *vi* **GET FREE OF DIRT** to become free of dirt, chiefly because of a content or structure that easily repels it ○ *This acrylic rug cleans easily.* **4** *vt* **RID OF CORRUPTION** to free something of dishonest practices ○ *The commissioners were bent on cleaning the council of nepotism.* **5** *vt* **PREPARE DEAD ANIMAL FOR COOKING** to prepare a dead animal for cooking by removing its entrails **6** *vt* **REMOVE CONTENTS** to use up the contents of something ○ *The children cleaned their plates and asked for more.* ■ *n* **SESSION OF CLEANING** a spell of removing unwanted dirt or marks ■ *adv* **1 IN ORDER TO REMOVE DIRT** so as to make something free from dirt **2 IN ORDER TO REMOVE EVIDENCE** so as to rid something of incriminating evidence **3 WITH NO OBSTRUCTION** directly, especially without having any obstruction **4 CLEANLY** in a clean way ○ *Does this type of gas burn clean?* ○ *We wanted to play the game clean.* **5 ENTIRELY** completely or utterly (*informal*) ○ *I clean forgot to call.* [Old English *clǣne* < Germanic, 'pure'] —**cleanability** /kleenə bílləti/ *n* —**cleanable** *adj* —**cleanness** *n* ◇ **come clean** to confess or tell the truth about something (*informal*)
clean out *vt* to use up or steal all of somebody's money or belongings (*informal*) ○ *Buying the new bike cleaned me out.*

clean up *v* 1 *vti* MAKE CLEAN OR TIDY to make somebody or something clean or tidy ○ *Can you just give me a minute to clean up in here?* 2 *vt* ERADICATE SOMETHING UNPLEASANT to rid a place of something unpleasant, e.g. pollution or crime 3 *vi* MAKE MONEY to acquire a large amount of money (*slang*) ○ *They really cleaned up on the stock market last year.*

clean and jerk *n* a movement in weightlifting in which the weight is lifted to shoulder height, held there briefly, and then quickly pushed above the head

clean-cut *adj* 1 distinctly outlined or designed 2 neat in dress or appearance ○ *a clean-cut young officer in a spotless uniform* 3 = **clear-cut** *adj.* 1

cleaner /kléénər/ *n* 1 SOMEBODY EMPLOYED TO CLEAN INSIDE PLACES somebody whose job is to clean the interior of a building 2 SOMETHING USED IN CLEANING a chemical or machine used for cleaning ■ **cleaners** *npl* SHOP PROVIDING DRY-CLEANING SERVICE a shop where clothes and other items are taken to be dry-cleaned ○ *My best suit is at the cleaners.* ◇ **take somebody to the cleaners** to deprive somebody of his or her money or possessions by dishonest means (*slang*)

clean-limbed *adj* having a well-proportioned and youthful-looking body

cleanliness /klénnlinəss/ *n* the degree to which somebody keeps clean or a place is kept clean ○ *a small hotel noted for its cleanliness*

cleanly /kléénli/ *adv* 1 EASILY OR EFFICIENTLY with ease or efficiency ○ *a cleanly executed triple jump on the ice* 2 WITHOUT JAGGED EDGES in a manner that does not leave rough edges ○ *the saw cut cleanly* 3 FAIRLY in a fair manner 4 IN CLEAN WAY in a way that is clean ○ *work cleanly in the kitchen, avoiding spills*

clean room *n* a room maintained with minimal contamination from dust or bacteria

cleanse /klenz/ (**cleanses, cleansing, cleansed**) *vt* 1 MAKE THOROUGHLY CLEAN to remove dirt from somebody or something, especially by washing thoroughly 2 MAKE FREE FROM UNPLEASANTNESS to free a place, person, or society from something wrong or unwelcome ○ *to cleanse the town council of corrupt influences* 3 MAKE FREE FROM SIN to free somebody or something from sin or guilt [Old English *clǣnsian* < *clǣne* (see CLEAN)] —**cleansing** *n*

cleanser /klénzər/ *n* 1 a substance for cleaning something thoroughly, especially cream or another product for cleaning the skin 2 a cosmetic product for cleaning the face

clean-shaven *adj* with the facial hair shaved off

cleanskin /kléén skin/ *n Aus* 1 an unbranded farm animal (*dated*) 2 somebody with no criminal record or record of corruption (*slang*)

cleanup /kléén up/ *n* 1 THOROUGH CLEANING a thorough cleaning ○ *This garage needs a good cleanup.* 2 ELIMINATION OF SOMETHING BAD an elimination of something unpleasant or unwanted 3 *US* LARGE GAIN a large and often illicit acquisition of assets (*slang*)

ϟ **clear** /kleer/ *adj* 1 FREE FROM WHAT DIMS free from anything that darkens or obscures ○ *a clear stream* 2 TRANSPARENT able to be seen through ○ *clear glass* 3 FREE FROM CLOUDS free from clouds, mist, or airborne particles ○ *a clear blue sky* 4 PURE IN HUE pure in colour or hue ○ *a clear red* 5 PERFECT AND UNBLEMISHED free from any defect or impurity ○ *a clear complexion* 6 EASILY HEARD OR SEEN easily heard or seen ○ *clear outlines* 7 SOUNDING PLEASANT having a pleasant sound ○ *a clear singing voice* 8 OUT-AND-OUT completely certain, allowing for no doubt ○ *clear evidence of collusion* 9 UNAMBIGUOUS easy to understand and without ambiguity ○ *clear instructions* 10 UNDERSTOOD PRECISELY understood without confusion or uncertainty ○ *Is it clear what you have to do when the bell rings?* 11 EVIDENT so obvious as to need no further explanation or guidance ○ *After half an hour of trying it was clear that the engine would not work properly.* 12 MENTALLY SHARP AND DISCERNING able to think without confusion ○ *You'll do better in the exam if you keep your mind clear.* 13 WITHOUT GUILT free from feelings of guilt or blame ○ *a clear conscience* 14 UNOBSTRUCTED free from obstructions or hindrances ○ *keep aisles clear* 15 EMPTY empty, with all movable items removed 16 NOT ATTACHED TO OR TOUCHING free of, or freed from, connection or contact ○ *must be clear of any moving parts* 17 NET net of deductions or charges ○ *I earn a clear £500 a week.* 18 NOT FINANCIALLY OBLIGATED not having any debt or financial obligation 19 UNPENALIZED without any penalties being incurred ○ *jumped a clear round* ■ *adv* 1 OUT OF THE WAY completely away from something ○ *Please stand clear of the doors until the vehicle has stopped.* 2 ALL THE WAY totally or completely ○ *they moved clear across the country* ■ *v* 1 *vi* DISSIPATE AND DISPERSE to undergo the process of dissolving or dispersing, thereby disappearing ○ *By noon the fog had finally cleared.* 2 *vi* NO LONGER BE FOGGY OR DULL to brighten and become free of adverse conditions ○ *There will be rain in the morning but the skies will clear by the early afternoon.* 3 *vti* MAKE OR BECOME TRANSPARENT to become or make something transparent or translucent ○ *The water cleared as the particles sank to the bottom.* 4 *vt* RID SOMETHING OF EXTRANEOUS MATTER to free something of impurities or unwanted matter ○ *clear a drain of blockages* 5 *vt* RID THROAT OF OBSTRUCTIONS to rid the throat of phlegm or other obstructions by coughing 6 *vt* CLARIFY THOUGHTS to remove confusion or misunderstanding from the mind ○ *I'd like a few minutes to clear my head before going into the meeting.* 7 *vi* RETURN TO SENSES to become or make the mind free from the dulling effects of alcohol, drugs, illness, or a blow to the head ○ *After my head had cleared I was able to stand up again.* 8 *vt* PROVE SOMEBODY INNOCENT to free somebody from suspicion or blame ○ *anxious to clear her name* 9 *vt* REMOVE OBJECTS OR OBSTRUCTIONS FROM to empty a space of objects or obstructions ○ *the room had been cleared* 10 *vt* FORM SPACE FOR to form a route for somebody or something to pass by removing obstructions 11 *vt* REMOVE PEOPLE FROM A PLACE to empty a building or place of people, e.g. for security reasons ○ *police had to clear the area* 12 *vt* DISENTANGLE to straighten out something that is snarled or otherwise in disarray or disorder ○ *Hurry up and clear that anchor line!* 13 *vt* MOVE PAST WITHOUT TOUCHING to move past or over something and without touching it ○ *If we stay on this course we should clear the buoy.* 14 *vti* ALLOW TO UNLOAD OR DEPART to be allowed to unload or depart, or allow a vehicle or cargo to unload or passengers to depart, after customs and other formalities have been dealt with 15 *vt* AUTHORIZE SOMEBODY TO DO OR GO to authorize somebody to do something or go somewhere ○ *You are now cleared to enter the restricted area.* 16 *vt* GIVE OR GET AUTHORIZATION to give or obtain authorization for an action 17 *vt* GAIN MONEY AS PROFIT to earn or acquire something as profit (*informal*) ○ *We cleared £5,000 on the deal.* 18 *vt* PAY OFF DEBT to settle a debt 19 *vi* MOVE BETWEEN ACCOUNTS to be authorized and credited to the account of the payee ○ *Cheques take three days to clear.* 20 *vti* SETTLE BANKING ACCOUNTS to settle the accounts of a banking transaction through a clearing house 21 *vt* GET BALL OUT OF DEFENCE AREA to get the ball out of the defence area 22 *vt* DELETE DATA to delete data from a computer display or storage device ■ *n* OPEN SPACE an empty or open area or space ○ *The deer were standing in the clear.* [13C. Via Old French *cler* < Latin *clarus* 'clear, bright'.] —**clearable** *adj* —**clearer** *n* —**clearness** *n* ◇ **in the clear** free from suspicion or blame

clear away *vti* to remove unwanted objects from a place and leave it tidy

clear off *vi* to go away (*informal; often a command*) ○ *Clear off and don't come back!*

clear out *v* 1 *vi* LEAVE FAST to leave a place quickly or urgently (*informal*) ○ *We cleared out as fast as we could.* 2 *vt* REMOVE to remove the contents of something, e.g. a room or cupboard, or to tidy something by removing some of its contents ○ *clearing out the attic* 3 *vt* USE ALL OF SOMEBODY'S MONEY to leave somebody without money or other resources (*slang*) ○ *It will clear us out if we have to pay all the legal expenses.*

clear up *v* 1 *vi* BECOME BRIGHTER to become brighter, e.g. after rain 2 *vti* GET OR MAKE BETTER to alleviate or cure something, or be alleviated or cured 3 *vti* PUT SOMETHING IN ORDER to tidy something by removing or arranging disorganized contents ○ *Will you please clear up all this mess before you leave?* 4 *vt* SOLVE MYSTERY OR EXPLAIN MISUNDERSTANDING to solve a mystery or explain a misunderstanding ○ *Here is a big problem that has never been fully cleared up.*

clearance /kléérənss/ *n* 1 REMOVING UNWANTED OBJECTS the removal of obstructions or unwanted objects, e.g. dilapidated buildings or overgrown bushes, before building or cultivating 2 PERMISSION FOR SOMETHING TO HAPPEN permission to do something or for something to take place ○ *several aircraft awaiting clearance to take off* 3 WIDTH OR HEIGHT OF OPENING the width or height of an opening or passage 4 CHEAP SALE OF GOODS a sale of goods at reduced prices in order to clear stock 5 REMOVAL OF PEOPLE FROM LAND the forcible removal from an area of land of the people who have traditionally lived there 6 PASSAGE OF COMMERCIAL DOCUMENTS the passage of commercial documents through a clearing house 7 GETTING BALL OUT OF DEFENCE AREA in games, the process of clearing the ball from the defence area 8 FORESTRY = **clearing** *n.* 1 9 MIL = **security clearance**

clear-cut *adj* 1 so definite as to leave no possibility of ambiguity 2 with a distinct outline or form ○ *a clear-cut silhouette of a naval frigate on the horizon* ■ *vt* (**clear-cuts, clear-cutting, clear-cut**) FORESTRY = **clear-fell**

clear-eyed *adj* 1 DISCERNINGLY PERCEPTIVE able to discern things clearly 2 SHARP-EYED having sharp sight 3 BRIGHT-EYED having bright eyes

clear-fell *vt* to cut down and remove all of the trees from a wood or other area of land. US term **clear-cut** *v.*

clear-headed *adj* able to think clearly and decisively, especially in difficult circumstances —**clear-headedly** *adv* —**clear-headedness** *n*

clearing /kléering/ *n* 1 a space without trees in an area of land that is wooded or overgrown 2 exchange between banks of cheques, drafts, and notes, and the settlement of consequent differences

clearing bank *n* any bank that uses a central clearing house for transferring credits and cheques between itself and other banks

clearing house *n* 1 an institution at which financial transactions between member banks are cancelled against each other, leaving only balances to be paid 2 an agency that collects and distributes information

ϟ **clearing house interbank payment system** *n* an electronic system for international dollar payments and currency exchanges (*in e-commerce*)

clearly /kléérli/ *adv* 1 WITHOUT ANY PROBLEM IN HEARING in a way that is easy to hear 2 WITHOUT ANY PROBLEM IN SEEING in a way that is easy to see 3 WITHOUT ANY PROBLEM IN UNDERSTANDING in a way that is easy to understand ○ *a clearly phrased piece of legislation* 4 LOGICALLY in a logical and unconfused manner ○ *a clearly written legal brief* 5 OBVIOUSLY used to acknowledge that a statement is undeniably true ○ *Clearly, we must take immediate action.*

clear-out *n* a session of removing the contents of something, e.g. a room, or of tidying it by removing some of its contents ○ *We had a great clear-out at the weekend and now we've got room for the new table.*

clear-sighted *adj* 1 having or showing good perception or judgment 2 having sharp vision —**clear-sightedly** *adv* —**clear-sightedness** *n*

clearstory *n* ARCHIT = **clerestory**

clear-up *n* a session of putting something in order

clearway /kléér way/ *n* a section of road where drivers may not normally stop

clearwing /kléér wing/ *n* a moth with scaleless transparent wings that is active during the daytime. Family: Sesiidae.

cleat /kleet/ *n* 1 DEVICE FOR TYING BOAT a device with two projections pointing in opposite directions to which a rope can be tied to secure a boat 2 HARD PIECE FIXED UNDER SHOE a small piece of metal or hard plastic fixed to the sole of a shoe to improve its grip or to reduce wear 3 WEDGE-SHAPED SUPPORT a wooden or other wedge attached to a structure in order to support it 4 DEVICE ON BOOT FOR CLIMBING TREES a device with a blade or set of sharp projections that is attached to a boot to assist in climbing trees or poles ■ *vt* 1 PROVIDE WITH CLEATS to fix a cleat or cleats to something 2 SECURE ROPE TO CLEAT to tie a rope to a cleat 3 SUPPORT WITH CLEAT to support something using a cleat or cleats [14C. Ultimately < W Germanic, 'firm lump'.]

cleavage /kléévij/ *n* 1 ACT OF SPLITTING division or splitting 2 SPLIT MADE a split, division, or separation of something 3 CREASE VISIBLE BETWEEN BREASTS the hollow visible between a woman's breasts when a low-cut garment is worn 4 ROCK OR MINERAL FRACTURE the splitting of minerals or rocks along natural planes of weakness 5 REPEATED DIVISION OF FERTILIZED EGG the repeated division of a fertilized ovum (**zygote**) before formation of the early embryo (**blastula**) 6 SPLITTING OF A MOLECULE the splitting of a molecule into simpler molecules through the breaking of a chemical bond

cleave[1] /kleev/ (**cleaves, cleaving, cleaved** *or* **clove** /klōv/ *or* **cleft** /kleft/, **cleaved** *or* **cloven** /klóv'n/ *or* **cleft**) *vti* 1 SPLIT to split, or make something split, especially along a plane of natural weakness 2 CUT A PATH THROUGH to make a way through something (*literary*) ○ *We watched the bows of the tall ships cleave through the waves.* 3 PENETRATE to penetrate or pierce something deep or dense such as water or heavy undergrowth [Old English *clēofan* < Indo-European] —**cleavable** *adj*

cleave[2] /kleev/ (**cleaves, cleaving, cleaved** *or* **clave** /klayv/, **cleaved**) *vi* to cling closely, steadfastly, or faithfully to something or somebody (*literary*) ○ *Is it wrong to cleave to such fond memories?* [Old English *cleofian* < Indo-European]

cleaver /kleévər/ *n* a heavy knife with a broad blade, used by butchers

cleavers /kleévərz/ *n* PLANTS = **goosegrass** *n.* [Alteration of Old English *clife*, related to CLEAVE[2]; because its bristles stick to whatever they come in contact with]

cleck /klek/ *vi Wales* to gossip about or inform on somebody ■ *n Wales* a piece of gossip [< Welsh *clecan* 'to gossip', *clec* 'gossip']

Cleese /kleez/, **John** (*b.* 1939) British comic actor and writer

Cleethorpes /kleé thawrps/ town in NE England. Population: 67,500 (1991).

clef /klef/ *n* in written or printed music, a symbol placed at the beginning of each staff to indicate the pitch [Late 16C. Via French < Latin *clavis* 'key'.]

cleft[1] /kleft/ *n* **1** a small indentation in a surface, e.g. skin or land **2** a substantial gap or division separating two things (*formal*) ○ *the ever widening cleft between the parties in their approaches to state funding* [Old English *geclyft* < Germanic]

cleft[2] /kleft/ *vti* past tense, past participle of **cleave**[1] ■ *adj* having been separated into two or more sections by division

cleft palate *n* a congenital fissure along the midline of the roof of the mouth

cleg /kleg/ *n N England, Scotland* a horsefly of N Europe and Asia. Genus: *Haematopota.* [15C. < Old Norse *kleggi.*]

Cleisthenes /klīsthə neez/ (570?–507 BC) Greek ruler

cleistogamous /klī stóggəməss/ *adj* relating to or bearing small flowers that do not open, are self-pollinated in the bud, and appear in addition to brighter flowers on the same plant [Late 19C. < Greek *kleistos* 'closed' < *kleiein* 'close'.] —**cleistogamously** *adv* —**cleistogamy** *n*

Cleland /kléllənd/, **John** (1709–89) British government official and writer

clematis /klémmətiss, klə máytiss/ (*plural* **-tises** *or* **-tis**) *n* a climbing plant with fluffy seed heads. Flowers: large, flat, typically blue, purple, pink, or white. Native to: northern temperate regions. Genus: *Clematis.* ◊ **old man's beard** [Mid-16C. Via Latin, 'clematis, periwinkle' < Greek *klēmatis* < *klēma* 'vine branch'.]

Clemenceau /klém aN sō/, **Georges** (1841–1929) French journalist and statesman

clemency /klémmənssi/ *n* **1** an instance of showing mercy or leniency, or the tendency to do this **2** mildness or temperateness, especially in the weather ○ *the clemency of areas affected by the Gulf Stream*

Clemens /klémmənz/, **Samuel Langhorne** ◆ **Mark Twain**

clement /klémmənt/ *adj* **1** showing or experiencing no extremes in weather conditions **2** showing mercy or leniency [15C. < Latin *clement-* 'mild, gentle'.] —**clemently** *adv*

Clement I /klémmənt/, **St** (*d.* AD 101?) Roman pope. Known as **Clement of Rome**

Clement VII (1478–1534) Florentine pope (1523–34). Born **Giulio de' Medici**

clementine /klémmən tīn, -teen/ *n* an orange-coloured citrus fruit, bred by crossing a tangerine with a Seville orange [Early 20C. < French *clémentine.*]

clench /klench/ *v* **1** *vt* HOLD TEETH OR FIST TIGHTLY TOGETHER to close your teeth or fist tightly, e.g. when angry **2** *vt* CLUTCH to hold or grip something tightly ○ *He clenched the rope in his teeth.* **3** *vti* CONTRACT to contract, or cause a muscle to contract, suddenly, often as a result of sudden tension or emotion (*refers to muscles*) ○ *His jaw clenched as he waited.* **4** *vt* NAUT = **clinch** *v.* **4** ■ *n* **1** TIGHT HOLD a tight grasp or hold ○ *She held the steering wheel in a tight clench.* **2** DEVICE THAT GRIPS TIGHTLY a mechanical device that holds or grips something firmly [Old English *beclencan* < Germanic, 'to stick'] —**clenched** *adj*

cleome /kli ṓmi/ *n* an aromatic plant often cultivated for its clusters of white or purplish flowers. Native to: warm regions. Genus: *Cleome.* [Early 19C. Via modern Latin < Greek, a plant.]

Cleon /kleé on/ (*d.* 422 BC) Greek politician and general

Cleopatra /kleé ə páttrə/ (69–30 BC) Egyptian monarch (51–30 BC)

Cleopatra's Needle *n* either of two Egyptian obelisks originally erected at Heliopolis about 1500 BC. One was moved to the Thames Embankment, London (1878), the other to Central Park, New York (1880).

clepsydra /klépsidrə/ (*plural* **-dras** *or* **-drae** /-dree/) *n* an ancient device used for measuring time by noting the amount of water or mercury that passes through a small aperture over a particular period [Mid-17C. Via Latin < Greek *klepsudra* < *kleptein* 'steal' + *hudor* 'water'.]

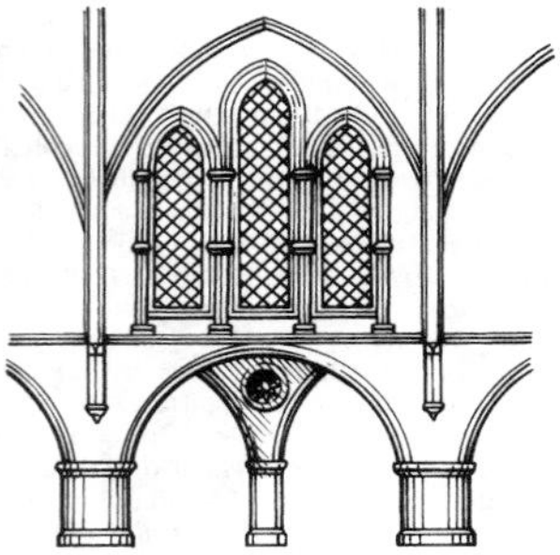

Clerestory

clerestory /kleér stawri, -stəri/ (*plural* **-ries**), **clearstory** (*plural* **-ries**) *n* the upper part of the wall of a church nave that contains windows, or the upper part of a wall in other buildings that contains windows [< earlier spelling of CLEAR]

clergy /klúrji/ (*plural* **-gies**) *n* the body of people ordained for religious service, especially in the Christian church (+ *singular or plural verb*) [13C. Partly < Old French *clergie* (< *clerc* 'cleric'); partly < *clergé* 'body of clerks'; both < ecclesiastical Latin *clericus* (see CLERK).]

clergyman /klúrjimən/ (*plural* **-men** /-mən/) *n* a man who is a member of the clergy

clergywoman /klúrji wŏŏmən/ (*plural* **-en** /-wimin/) *n* a woman who is a member of the clergy

cleric /klérrik/ *n* an ordained priest, minister, or rabbi [Early 17C. < ecclesiastical Latin *clericus* (see CLERK).]

clerical /klérrik'l/ *adj* **1** OF OFFICE WORK relating or belonging to office work, especially of a routine administrative kind **2** OF THE CLERGY relating or belonging to the clergy **3** PROMOTING CLERICALISM advocating or supporting clericalism —**clerically** *adv*

clerical collar *n* a stiff white collar, continuous at the front, worn by some members of the clergy

clericalism /klérrik'lizəm/ *n* **1** a policy of supporting the power or views of the clergy **2** the power or influence of the clergy —**clericalist** *n*

clericals /klérrik'lz/ *npl* the characteristic clothing worn by some members of the clergy

clerihew /klérri hyoo/ *n* a humorous or satirical verse consisting of two rhyming couplets in lines of irregular metre about somebody who is named in the verse [Early 20C. After Edmund *Clerihew* Bentley 1875–1956, British writer.]

clerk /klaark/ *n* **1** GENERAL OFFICE WORKER a worker who performs general office duties such as keeping records or sending out correspondence **2** *US* = **salesclerk** **3** *US* SERVICE DESK WORKER somebody at a service desk who helps and advises other people **4** GOVERNMENT WORKER WHO KEEPS RECORDS an official who keeps transcripts and other records of a legislative or other body **5** ADMINISTRATOR IN COURT OF LAW an administrator of the business of a court **6** COURT LEGAL ADVISER somebody with legal qualifications who advises lay magistrates on points of law in court **7** CLERIC a member of the clergy (*formal*) [Pre-12C. Via ecclesiastical Latin *clericus* 'of the clergy' < Greek *klērikos* < *klēros* 'heritage'.] —**clerk** *vi* —**clerkdom** *n* —**clerkish** *adj* —**clerkship** *n*

clerkly /klaárkli/ *adj* behaving or looking like a clerk ○ *a clerkly attention to detail in the midst of a crisis* —**clerkliness** *n*

clerk of the works *n* an official who inspects the standard of construction of a new building

Clermont-Ferrand /kláir moN fe ráaN/ capital of Puy-de-Dôme Department, south-central France. Population: 137,140 (1999).

cleveite /kleév īt/ *n* a crystalline form of uraninite [Late 19C. After Per T. *Cleve* (1840–1905), Swedish chemist.]

Cleveland /kleévlənd/ **1** former county of NE England **2** port in NE Ohio. Population: 495,817 (1998 estimate).

Cleveland, Grover (1837–1908) US statesman and 22nd and 24th president of the United States (1885–89, 1893–97)

clever /klévvər/ *adj* **1** INTELLIGENT having sharp mental abilities **2** SHOWING INTELLIGENCE demonstrating mental agility and creativity **3** GLIBLY FACILE showing highly capable mental abilities in a showy or superficial way ○ *Don't give me one of your clever answers.* **4** DEXTEROUS highly skilled in using the hands **5** UNUSUAL AND EFFECTIVE produced by skill or ingenuity ○ *a clever idea* ○ *What a clever little gadget!* [13C. < ?] —**cleverly** *adv* —**cleverness** *n*

SYNONYMS See ***intelligent.***

clever-clever *adj* affectedly or ostentatiously clever (*disapproving informal*)

clever clogs (*plural* **clever clogs**) *n* = **clever Dick** (*disapproving informal*)

clever Dick *n* an arrogant or ostentatiously clever person (*informal*)

clevis /klévviss/ *n* a U-shaped device with a hole at the end of each prong through which a pin or bolt can be pushed to secure another part in place [Late 16C. < ?]

clew /kloo/ *n* **1** BALL OF THREAD a wound ball of thread or yarn **2** CORNER OF FORE-AND-AFT SAIL the rear lower corner of a triangular or four-sided sail set along the length of a boat **3** CORNER OF SAIL SET ACROSS BOAT either of the two lower corners of a sail set parallel to the width of a boat, e.g. a square sail or a spinnaker ■ **clews** *npl* HAMMOCK CORDS the cords by which a hammock is suspended ■ *vt* ROLL YARN INTO BALL to roll thread or yarn into a ball [Old English *cliwen*, probably related to CLAW]

clew up *vt* to furl a square sail by pulling on lines attached to its lower corners

clianthus /kli ánthəss, klī-/ (*plural* **-thuses** *or* **-thus**) *n* a plant with drooping clusters of slender scarlet flowers. Native to: Australia, New Zealand. Genus: *Clianthus.* [Mid-19C. < modern Latin, < Greek *kleos* 'glory' + *anthus* 'flower'.]

cliché /kleé shay/ *n* **1** a phrase or word that has lost its original effectiveness or power from overuse **2** an overused activity or notion [Mid-19C. < French, past participle of *clicher* 'stereotype'.]

clichéd /kleé shayd/ *adj* full of clichés

Clichy /kleé shee/ suburb of N Paris, France. Population: 48,204 (1990).

click[1] /klik/ *n* **1** SHORT SHARP SOUND a short sharp sound, often metallic but not resonant **2** MECHANICAL COMPONENT FOR LOCKING POSITION a component of a mechanical device that holds a part in a locking position, or the movement of the part between adjacent positions **3** SOUND PRODUCED BY SUCKING IN AIR a consonant sound produced by sucking in air by movements of the tongue against the soft palate. Technical name **suction stop** **4** PRESS OF COMPUTER MOUSE BUTTON a single action of pressing and releasing a button on a computer mouse ■ *v* **1** *vti* MAKE OR CAUSE SHORT SHARP SOUND to make, or cause something to make, a short sharp sound **2** *vti* PRESS COMPUTER MOUSE BUTTON to press and release a button of a computer mouse ○ *Click on 'yes'.* **3** *vi* BECOME CLEAR FAST to be understood suddenly (*informal*) ○ *The whole thing clicked: they had decided not to hire me.* **4** *vi* EASILY COMMUNICATE OR WORK TOGETHER to communicate or work together easily and readily (*informal*) ○ *It's too bad that the two venture partners in the deal just never clicked.* **5** *vi* BE A SUCCESS to be successful or popular (*informal*) ○ *The new show clicked from the very first performance.* [Late 16C. An imitation of the sound.]

click[2] /klik/ *n* a kilometre (*slang*) [Mid-20C. < ?]

click art *n* computer clip art for use in illustrating electronic documents

click beetle *n* a beetle that can right itself when inverted by springing into the air with a clicking sound. Family: Elateridae.

clicker /klíkər/ *n* **1** a person who or device that clicks **2** a foreman or forewoman at a printing press or shoe factory (*informal*)

⚡**click rate** *n* the number of times that a site in an Internet advertisement is visited, as a percentage of the number of times the advertisement is viewed (*in e-commerce*)

⚡**clicks-and-mortar, click-and-mortar** *adj* describes a hybrid business involved in e-commerce that also markets its products through a traditional store or otherwise incurs the cost of physical structures such as warehouses (*in e-commerce*) ◊ **brick-and-mortar** [After *bricks and mortar*]

⚡**clickstream** /klík streem/ *n* the path of mouse clicks that somebody makes in navigating the World Wide Web, sometimes used in marketing research (*in e-commerce*)

⚡**clickthrough** /klík throo/ *n* a measure of the effectiveness of an Internet advertisement, based on the number of times the viewer accesses the advertisement (*in e-commerce*)

⚡**client** /klī ənt/ *n* **1 SOMEBODY USING PROFESSIONAL SERVICE** a person or organization taking advice from a lawyer, accountant, or other professional person **2 CUSTOMER** a person or organization to whom goods or services are provided and sold **3 USER OF SOCIAL SERVICES AGENCY** the user of services offered by a social services agency **4 PERSON OR ENTITY HELPED BY ANOTHER** a person or entity dependent on the protection or patronage of another person or entity ○ *the former Soviet Union and its clients in the Middle East* **5 COMPUTER PROGRAM THAT REQUESTS DATA** a computer program that obtains data from a program on another computer, often one linked on a network [14C. Via Latin *client-* 'dependent' < *cluere* 'obey'.] —**cliental** *adj* —**clientless** /klī əntləss/ *adj*

client-centred therapy *n* a form of psychotherapy in which the therapist seeks to elicit solutions to problems by gaining the trust of the patient through careful questioning

clientele /klee on tél, -ən-/ *n* the clients or customers of a professional organization or business, considered as a group (*takes a singular verb*) ○ *The clientele of our family law firm consists mostly of big corporations.* [Mid-16C. Directly and via French < Latin *clientela* < *client-* (see CLIENT).]

⚡**client-server, client/server** *adj* used on a computer network in which processing is divided between a client program running on a user's machine and a network server program

client state *n* a country that depends on another for economic, political, or military support

cliff /klif/ *n* a high steep rock or ice face, especially a rock face extending along a coastline [Old English *clif* < Germanic] —**cliffy** *adj*

cliff dweller *n* a member of an Anasazi people who constructed dwellings on ledges of cliffs in the SW United States

cliffhanger /klíf hangər/ *n* **1 ENDING LEFT TEASINGLY UNRESOLVED** an unresolved ending in a serialized drama or book that leaves the audience or reader desperate to know what will happen in the next part **2 DRAMA SERIAL WITH SUSPENSEFUL ENDINGS** a drama serial that has episodes that often end in suspenseful unresolved situations **3 TENSE SITUATION** a situation full of tension or suspense because it is not clear what will happen next [< early serial films in which characters were left hanging off the edge of a cliff at the end of an episode] —**cliffhanging** *adj*

cliff swallow *n* a swallow with a dark throat patch that builds its nest of mud on cliff faces or under eaves. Native to: North America. *Hyrundo pyrrhonota.*

Clift /klift/, **Charmian** (1923–69) Australian writer

climacteric /klī máktərik, klī mak térrik/ *n* **1 PERIOD OF IMPORTANT CHANGE** a period in which critically important changes take place **2 MENOPAUSE** the menopause (*technical*) **3 RIPENING STAGE IN FRUITS** a stage in the ripening of some fruits, e.g. apples, when the rate of respiration increases [Mid-16C. < French, < Greek *klimaktēr* 'rung of a ladder' < *klimax* 'ladder'.] —**climacteric** *adj* —**climacterically** /klī mak térrikli/ *adv*

climactic /klī máktik/ *adj* **1** extremely exciting or decisive **2** forming or relating to a climax [Late 19C. < CLIMAX.] —**climactically** *adv*

> **USAGE climactic** or **climatic**? ***Climactic***, coming from *climax*, means 'exciting or decisive' and 'forming a climax', as in *The hard-fought election was climactic* [not *climatic*]. *In a climactic* [not *climatic*] *passage, the author kills off the heroine.* ***Climatic***, coming from *climate*, means 'relating to weather', as in *severe climatic* [not *climactic*] *changes caused by global warming.*

climate /klīmət/ *n* **1 TYPICAL WEATHER IN REGION** the average weather or the regular variations in weather in a region over a period of years **2 PLACE WITH PARTICULAR WEATHER** a place with a particular kind of weather ○ *I prefer a warm climate.* **3 SITUATION** the situation or atmosphere that prevails at a particular time or place **4 INDOOR ENVIRONMENT** the prevailing conditions or environment in an indoor setting such as an office [14C. Via late Latin < Greek *klimat-* 'slope, region of the earth'.]

climatic /klī máttik/ *adj* relating to, causing, or caused by weather changes —**climatically** *adv*

> **USAGE** See ***climactic***.

climatic zone *n* an area of the earth's surface that possesses a distinct type of climate. There are eight major climatic zones, roughly demarcated by lines of latitude.

climatology /klīmə tólləji/ *n* the scientific study of climates —**climatologic** /klīmətə lójjik/ *adj* —**climatological** *adj* —**climatologically** *adv* —**climatologist** *n*

climax /klī maks/ *n* **1 KEY MOMENT** the most exciting or important moment or point **2 ORGASM** a sexual orgasm **3 EVER-INTENSIFYING SEQUENCE OF PHRASES** a sequence of phrases or sentences, each more forceful or intense than the last, or the conclusion of such a sequence **4 FINAL STAGE IN ECOLOGICAL COMMUNITY'S DEVELOPMENT** a late or final stage in the development of an ecological community in which the composition of plants and animals is relatively stable and well matched to environmental conditions ■ *v* **1** *vti* **REACH THE KEY POINT** to reach the most important or exciting point in something such as an event or a story, or bring something to its most important or exciting point **2** *vi* **HAVE AN ORGASM** to have a sexual orgasm [Mid-16C. Via late Latin < Greek *klimax* 'ladder, progression'.]

climb /klīm/ *v* **1** *vti* **GO UP USING HANDS AND FEET** to move towards the top of something using the hands and feet ○ *climb a ladder* **2** *vti* **MOVE UPWARDS** to move upwards, or move towards the top of something, by any means, and typically through continual or gradual effort ○ *climb the stairs* **3** *vi* **MOVE WITH EFFORT** to manoeuvre the body somewhere with effort or difficulty ○ *I managed to climb out of bed.* **4** *vi* **RISE STEEPLY IN AMOUNT** to rise sharply in value or amount **5** *vi* **BE A MOUNTAINEER** to go up mountains or rocks on foot or using hands and feet as a sport **6** *vti* **MOVE HIGHER SOCIALLY** to move to a higher social or professional position **7** *vti* **GROW CLINGINGLY UPWARDS** to grow upwards by using plants or objects as a support, e.g. by producing shoots or tendrils that cling to the top of them ■ *n* **1 ACT OF CLIMBING** the process of moving to the top of something ○ *It was a steep climb to the top.* **2 HILL OR MOUNTAIN** a route used to go up a hill, mountain, or rock, or the hill, mountain, or rock itself **3 RISE IN VALUE OR AMOUNT** a rise in the value or amount of something [Old English *climban* < W Germanic, 'adhere' < Indo-European, 'form into a ball'] —**climbable** *adj*

> **SPELLCHECK** Do not confuse ***climb*** with ***clime***, which has a similar sound. Beware: your spellchecker will not catch this error.

climb down *vi* to abandon forcefully or publicly expressed views or demands in the face of opposition from other people
climb into *vt* to put on clothes, usually easy-to-wear ones (*informal*)
climb out of *vt* to take off clothes, usually easy-to-wear ones (*informal*)

climb-down *n* an abandonment of forcefully or publicly expressed views or demands

climber /klīmər/ *n* **1 SOMEBODY WHO CLIMBS MOUNTAINS** a climber of rocks or mountains as a sport **2 PLANT THAT CLINGS** a plant that attaches itself to other plants or objects such as posts and walls as it grows **3 SOMEBODY ADVANCING SOCIALLY** a person who steadily gains in rank or status, especially somebody who is unscrupulous and ambitious (*usually in combination*)

climbing /klīming/ *n* the sport of climbing mountains or rocks

climbing frame *n* a framework of interlocking metal, wooden, or plastic bars designed for children to climb on. US term **jungle gym**

climbing iron *n* a spike-covered metal frame that attaches to the sole of a boot to help somebody climb up ice or trees

climbing wall *n* a wall with handholds and footholds, often located indoors, that is designed to provide practice at rock-climbing

clime /klīm/ *n* a place with a particular type of climate (*literary; often plural*) ○ *off to sunnier climes* [Late 16C. Via Latin < Greek *klima* 'slope'.]

> **SPELLCHECK** See ***climb***.

-clinal *suffix* sloping, slanting ○ *isoclinal* [< Greek *klinein* 'to lean']

clinch /klinch/ *v* **1** *vt* **RESOLVE SOMETHING DECISIVELY** to settle the outcome of something that was uncertain, e.g. a business deal or an argument, in a positive way **2** *vt* **FLATTEN NAIL'S END** to bend or flatten the protruding end of a nail or rivet, or fix something together using nails or rivets in this way **3** *vi* **PUT ARMS AROUND OPPONENT** in boxing or wrestling, to put your arms around an opponent's body so as to pin the arms and prevent an exchange of blows **4** *vt* **FASTEN WITH A PARTICULAR KNOT** to fasten or secure something with a knot in a rope that is created by making a half hitch, the rope's end being fastened by seizing it ■ *n* **1 PASSIONATE EMBRACE** a tight passionate embrace between lovers (*informal*) **2 TACTIC OF PINNING OPPONENT'S ARMS** a tactic in boxing and wrestling designed to prevent an exchange of blows by putting your arms around an opponent's body, pinning the arms to the sides **3 BENT END OF NAIL** a nail or rivet with its protruding end bent over, or a fastening made in this way **4 KNOT IN ROPE** a knot in a rope that is created by making a half hitch, the rope's end being fastened by seizing it [Mid-16C. < ?]

clincher /klínchər/ *n* **1 DECIDING FACTOR** the factor that decides the outcome of something, e.g. an argument or a contest (*informal*) **2 NAIL WITH END BENT** a nail or rivet that has its protruding end bent over **3 TOOL FOR BENDING NAIL** a tool for bending the ends of a nail or rivet

cline /klīn/ *n* **1** a continuum between two extremes **2** a gradual variation in the characteristics of a plant or animal species that occurs when it is distributed over an area with differing environmental or geographical conditions [Mid-20C. < Greek *klinein* 'lean'.] —**clinal** *adj* —**clinally** *adv*

Cline /klīn/, **Patsy** (1932–63) US singer. Born **Virginia Patterson Hensley**

-cline *suffix* slope ○ *syncline* [Back-formation < -CLINAL]

cling /kling/ *vi* (**clings, clinging, clung** /klung/) **1 HOLD TIGHTLY** to hold onto somebody or something tightly with the hands or arms **2 STICK** to adhere to something by sticking to it or staying very close to it **3 RETAIN IDEAS OR CUSTOMS** to refuse to give up something, e.g. a belief or tradition, that you have grown fond of or used to **4 NEED SOMEBODY EMOTIONALLY** to have a strong emotional attachment to somebody **5 NOT GO AWAY** to linger, usually in the air, resisting dispersion or dissipation ■ *n* **1 STICKING QUALITY** the tendency of something to stick to surfaces **2** PLANT SCI = **clingstone** [Old English *clingan* 'adhere' < Germanic] —**clinger** *n* —**clingingly** *adv*

cling film *n* a clear plastic film that sticks to itself and to other surfaces. Use: food wrapping.

clingfish /klíng fish/ (*plural* **-fish** *or* **-fishes**) *n* a small fish whose pelvic fins have been modified into a sucking disc that it uses to attach itself to rocks or other objects. Family: Gobiesocidae.

clingstone /klíng stōn/ *n* a fruit with flesh that sticks to the stone. Some varieties of peach, nectarine, and plum have fruit of this type.

clingy /klíngi/ (**-ier, -iest**) *adj* **1** too dependent on the company or emotional support of other people **2** sticking closely to the body (*informal*) ○ *a clingy fabric* —**clinginess** *n*

clinic /klínnik/ *n* **1 MEDICAL CENTRE** a medical centre for outpatients, which may be attached to a hospital or form part of it **2 SPECIALIZED MEDICAL CENTRE** a medical centre that specializes in a particular condition or area of medicine **3 GROUP MEDICAL PRACTICE** a suite of offices or an office where a number of doctors practise general medicine as a partnership **4 PRIVATE HOSPITAL** a hospital that charges patients directly for their treatment, rather than one providing state-funded treatment **5 MEDICINE TAUGHT AT THE BEDSIDE** a teaching session during which student doctors are allowed to examine patients in hospital wards **6 SESSION ATTENDED BY PATIENTS** a session in a hospital that patients attend for specialized treatment or advice **7 SESSION OF PRACTICAL SPORTS INSTRUCTION** a teaching session in which experts in specific sports give practical instruction and advice on improving technique and solving problems [Mid-19C. Via French *clinique* < Greek *klinikē (tekhnē)* '(method of treating) the bedridden' < *klinikos* 'of a bed' < *klinē* 'bed' < *klinein* 'lean'.]

-clinic *suffix* having a particular number of obliquely intersecting axes ○ *triclinic* [< Greek *klinein* 'lean']

clinical /klínnik'l/ *adj* 1 **BASED ON MEDICAL TREATMENT OR OBSERVATION** based on or involving medical treatment, practice, observation, or diagnosis 2 **UNEMOTIONAL** practical and unemotional 3 **SEVERE IN DECOR OR DESIGN** plain and severe in design, usually with the implication of lack of comfort —**clinically** *adv*

clinical ecology *n* the branch of medicine dealing with the supposed effects of the modern technological environment on human health, especially the relationship of allergies to the increase in chemicals in the environment

clinical nurse manager *n* the administrative manager of the nursing staff in a hospital

clinical psychology *n* a branch of psychology that deals with the diagnosis and treatment of psychological and behavioural problems —**clinical psychologist** *n*

clinical thermometer *n* a thermometer used for measuring the temperature of somebody's body, which continues to register the observed temperature until reset

clinician /kli nísh'n/ *n* 1 a medical professional who works directly with patients, as distinct from one working in research 2 a medical professional who conducts or teaches in a clinic

clink[1] /klingk/ *vti* to make or cause something to make the short, high-pitched, slightly ringing sound that metal or glass objects make when they knock against each other [14C. < ?] —**clink** *n*

clink[2] /klingk/ *n* a prison (*dated slang*) [Early 16C. < the *Clink*, former prison in Southwark, borough of London.]

clinker /klíngkər/ *n* 1 **BALL OF COAL RESIDUE** a hard mass of ash and partially fused coal that remains after coal is burnt in a fire or furnace 2 **HARD BRICK** an overhard brick that has been fired in a kiln for too long ■ *vi* **FORM LUMPY BURNT RESIDUE** to form hard lumps of partially fused coal and ash after burning [Mid-17C. Alteration of obsolete *clincard* < obsolete Dutch *klinckaerd* 'brick' < *klinken* 'ring'; from the sound made by a brick when struck.]

clinker-built *adj* describes a boat that has a hull made of overlapping planks [< *clinker* 'clinched nail' < *clink* 'secure a nail', variant of CLENCH]

clinkety-clank /klíngkəti klángk/ *n* the dull short ringing sounds produced when something metallic hits a surface repeatedly [< CLINK[1] + CLANK]

clinkstone /klíngk stōn/ *n* MINERALS = **phonolite** [Translation of German *Klingstein* 'ringing stone'; from its metallic resonance when struck]

clino- *prefix* slope, slant ○ *clinometer* [< Greek *klinein* 'lean']

clinometer /klī nómmitər/ *n* any instrument used in surveying or geology to measure the angle of a slope or incline —**clinometric** /klīnə méttrik/ *adj* —**clinometrical** *adj* —**clinometry** *n*

clinopyroxene /klīnō pī rók seen/ *n* a silicate mineral of the pyroxene group, containing calcium, iron, and magnesium

-clinous *suffix* 1 having stamens and pistils in a particular number of flowers ○ *diclinous* 2 descending from a particular line ○ *matriclinous* [< Greek *klinein* 'lean']

clint /klint/ *n* a limestone block separated from others by cracks, forming a limestone pavement. ◊ **grike** [14C. Via Danish, Swedish *klint* < Old Swedish *klinter* 'rock'.]

Clinton /klíntən/, **Bill** (*b.* 1946) US statesman and 42nd president of the United States (1993–2001). Full name **William Jefferson Clinton**

Clinton, Hillary Rodham (*b.* 1947) US lawyer, first lady, and politician

clintonia /klin tṓni ə/ *n* a broad-leafed perennial plant of the lily family with blue or purple berries. Flowers: white, yellow, or purplish. Genus: *Clintonia*. [Mid-19C. < modern Latin, after De Witt *Clinton* (1769–1828), US politician.]

Clio /klī ō/ *n* in Greek mythology, the muse of history

cliometrics /klī ō méttriks/ *n* the study of economic history using statistics, advanced methods of data processing, analysis of mathematical data, and economic modelling (+ *singular verb*) [Mid-20C. < CLIO.] —**cliometric** *adj* —**cliometrician** /klī ō mə trísh'n/ *n*

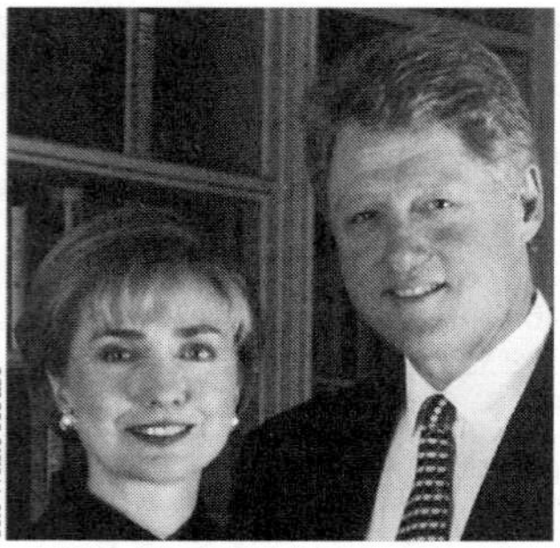
The White House

Hillary Rodham Clinton and Bill Clinton

clip[1] /klip/ *v* (**clips, clipping, clipped**) 1 *vt* **CUT OR TRIM** to cut or trim something, or cut it off, e.g. with scissors or shears 2 *vt* **CUT OUT** to remove something from something else by cutting 3 *vt* **SHORTEN TIME TAKEN FOR** to reduce the time taken to complete something, especially travelling time 4 *vt* **TRUNCATE SPEECH SOUND** to shorten a speech sound 5 *vt* **ABBREVIATE WORD** to shorten a word or other expression by abbreviating it or dropping a syllable 6 *vt* **CURTAIL** to reduce or diminish power or influence 7 *vi* **GO FAST** to move at a brisk pace (*informal*) 8 *vt* **SIDESWIPE** to make physical contact with somebody or something else with a light glancing slapping blow (*informal*) 9 *vt* **SWINDLE** to cheat or swindle somebody, especially by overcharging (*slang*) ■ *n* 1 **FILM OR TV EXTRACT** an extract, especially a short piece from film or television footage 2 **EXTRACT FROM PRINT MEDIA** a news story or other article cut out of a print publication and used, e.g., as a sample of work 3 **THING OR AMOUNT CUT** something cut or removed, especially the amount of wool cut from a flock of sheep at one shearing 4 **GLANCING BLOW** a sideswiping blow 5 **RATE OF MOTION** the speed at which somebody or something moves (*informal*) [13C. Probably < Old Norse *klippa* 'cut short'.]

clip[2] /klip/ *n* 1 **GRIPPING DEVICE** a device that grips or clasps loose things together or that holds things firmly (*often in combination*) 2 **PIECE OF JEWELLERY** a piece of jewellery with a gripping device fitted that attaches to clothing 3 **BULLET-HOLDER** a container for bullets, slotted directly into an automatic firearm ■ *vti* (**clips, clipping, clipped**) **HOLD SOMETHING WITH GRIPPING DEVICE** to hold loose things together, or attach one thing to another, using a clip, or be attached in this way [Old English *clyppan* 'embrace, fasten' < West Germanic]

⚡**clip art** *n* prepackaged artwork, available on software for documents produced on computer [Because it came in the form of *clip sheets*, pages of drawings that graphic designers could cut out]

clipboard /klíp bawrd/ *n* a small portable board with a clip fitted to the top, used for securing papers and providing a hard writing surface for somebody on the move

clip-clop *n, interj* used to represent or imitate the rhythmic sound made by a walking horse's hooves as they strike hard ground ■ *vi* (**clip-clops, clip-clopping, clip-clopped**) to make the sound of hooves striking hard ground [Early 20C. An imitation of the sound.]

clip joint *n* a shop or club that habitually overcharges its customers (*slang*) [< CLIP[1] 'swindle']

clip-on *adj* describes something, especially an item of clothing, that is attached by means of a clip ■ *n* an accessory, e.g. an earring or a tie, that is attached with a clip

clipped /klipt/ *adj* 1 trimmed or cut back neatly 2 spoken with each word pronounced separately and distinctly in a way that sounds terse or upper-class

clipper /klíppər/ *n* 1 **FAST SAILING SHIP** a mid-19th-century tall ship with a sharp bow, designed for fast speeds 2 **USER OF CUTTING TOOL** a cutter or shearer of something 3 ELECTRONICS = **limiter** *n.* 1 ■ **clippers** *npl* **TOOL FOR CLIPPING** a hand tool for cutting or clipping something

clippie /klíppi/ *n* a woman bus or tram conductor (*dated informal*)

clipping /klípping/ *n* MEDIA = **cutting** *n.* 2 ■ **clippings** *npl* pieces of grass or hair that have been cut or clipped off

clique /kleek/ *n* a close group of friends or colleagues having similar interests and goals, and whom outsiders regard as excluding them [Early 18C. < French, < *cliquer* 'click, clap', an imitation of the sound.] —**cliquey** *adj* —**cliquish** *adj* —**cliquishly** *adv* —**cliquishness** *n*

clishmaclaver /klíshmə kláyvər/ *n* *Scotland* casual chat or gossip (*informal*) [Early 18C. < *clish* (probably < Scottish *clish-clash* 'idle gossip') + *claver* '(to) gossip'. < ?]

clitellum /klī téllәm/ (*plural* **-la** /-téllə/) *n* a glandular section, similar in shape to a saddle, in the body wall of some worms, e.g. earthworms and leeches, that secretes a sticky substance during copulation [Mid-19C. Via modern Latin < Latin *clitellae* 'packsaddle' (from its shape), literally 'little litters'.]

clitic /klíttik/ *adj* describes a word that cannot be stressed and is pronounced as part of the word that follows or precedes it, e.g. in 've' in 'I've' [Mid-20C. Back-formation < ENCLITIC, PROCLITIC.] —**clitic** *n*

clitoridectomy /klíttəri déktəmi/ (*plural* **-mies**) *n* the cutting off of all or part of a woman's or girl's clitoris, practised in some societies as a social or cultural rite of passage

clitoris /klíttəriss/ (*plural* **clitorises** *or* **clitorides** /klíttə rí deez/) *n* a highly sensitive erectile organ visible at the front junction of the labia minora in the vulva [Early 17C. Via modern Latin < Greek *kleitoris* 'little hill'.] —**clitoral** *adj*

Clive /klīv/, **Robert, Baron Clive of Plassey** (1725–74) British soldier and colonial administrator. Known as **Clive of India**

Cllr *abbr* Councillor

clm *abbr* column

⚡**CLM** *abbr* career limiting move (*in e-mails*)

cloaca /klō áykə/ (*plural* **-cae** /-kee/) *n* the terminal region of the gut in reptiles, amphibians, birds, and many fishes as well as in some invertebrates. The intestinal, urinary, and genital canals open into it. [Late 16C. < Latin, 'sewer, canal'.] —**cloacal** *adj*

cloak /klōk/ *n* 1 **OUTER GARMENT** a loose sleeveless outer garment that fastens at the neck 2 **ENSHROUDING OBJECT OR FORCE** something that covers or conceals things (*literary*) ■ *vt* **ENSHROUD** to cover or conceal something (*often passive*) [13C. Via Old French *cloque* 'bell, cloak' < medieval Latin *clocca*; from its shape.]

cloak-and-dagger *adj* involving secrecy or intrigue, often as part of an espionage operation [Translation of French *de cape et d'épée* 'of cape and sword', symbols of the rank of characters in dramas of intrigue]

cloakroom /klṓk room, -rŏom/ *n* 1 **PLACE FOR DEPOSITING BELONGINGS** a room in a public building, e.g. a theatre, club, or restaurant, where customers can leave coats, umbrellas, and other belongings during their stay. US term **coat check** 2 **CUPBOARD FOR COATS** a walk-in cupboard in a house, where coats and other outdoor items are stored 3 **LAVATORY** a lavatory, especially one in a public building, or downstairs in a house with an upstairs bathroom. US term **restroom**

clobber /klóbbər/ *vt* (*informal*) 1 **HIT** to hit somebody or something with great force 2 **UTTERLY DEFEAT** to defeat somebody heavily 3 **TREAT HARSHLY** to deal with somebody or something in a harsh or critical way ○ *The scheme has been clobbered in the national press.* ■ *n* **SOMEBODY'S BELONGINGS OR CLOTHES** somebody's belongings or clothes, usually those intended for a particular activity (*informal*) [Mid-20C. < ?]

cloche /klosh/ *n* 1 a small structure made of glass or clear plastic, placed over cold-sensitive garden plants in cold weather 2 a woman's or girl's close-fitting hat with a very narrow brim, or no brim at all, especially popular in the 1920s and 1930s [Late 19C. Via French, 'bell' < medieval Latin *clocca*; from the shape.]

⚡**clock**[1] /klok/ *n* 1 **DEVICE DISPLAYING THE TIME** a freestanding device that measures and records time, which it displays by a pointer on a dial or by a digital read-out 2 **MEASURING INSTRUMENT WITH DISPLAY** a measuring instrument with a dial or a digital display, e.g. any of a vehicle's control gauges, especially the mileometer 3 BUSINESS = **time clock** 4 **SEED HEAD OF DANDELION** the fluffy white seed head of a dandelion 5 **ELECTRONIC CIRCUIT THAT SYNCHRONIZES COMPUTER PROCESSES** an electronic circuit that generates pulses at a constant rate in order to synchronize the internal operations in a computer ■ *vt* 1 **RECORD SOMEBODY'S OR SOMETHING'S TIME** to measure or record the time somebody or something takes, using a stopwatch or an electronic timing device 2 **PUNCH** to punch somebody (*slang*) ○ *He clocked him one.* 3 **NOTICE** to notice something (*slang*) ○ *We clocked him going into the betting shop.* 4 **TAMPER WITH VEHICLE'S MILEOMETER** to turn back the mileometer on a used car so that the mileage appears much lower than it is (*slang*) [14C. Via Middle Dutch, Middle Low German *klocke* < medieval Latin *clocca* 'bell'.] ◇ **against the clock** with limited time to finish something ◇ **around** *or* **round the clock** day and night, without stopping ◇ **turn** *or* **put the clock(s) back** to return to the conditions of an earlier time

clock in, clock on *vi* to arrive for work, or record arrival for work by inserting a personalized card into a time clock

clock out, clock off *vi* to leave work, or record departure from work by inserting a personalized card into a time clock

clock up *vt* to reach a particular total

clock^{2} /klok/ *n* a design on the ankle or side of a stocking or sock [Mid-16C. < ?]

clock golf *n* a putting game in which the ball is played from each of several points on the edge of a circular lawn towards a single hole in the centre

clock radio *n* an electronic device that incorporates a digital clock, an alarm clock, and a radio

ϟ**clock speed** *n* the speed of a microprocessor's internal clock that controls how fast a computer makes calculations, usually measured in megahertz (MHz) or gigahertz (GHz)

clock-watcher *n* an employee who is keen to leave work as soon as possible —**clock-watching** *n*

clockwise /klók wīz/ *adv, adj* in the same direction that the hands of a clock move around a clock face

clockwork /klók wurk/ *n* a mechanism consisting of cogs and a wound spring, used to drive a traditional clock or a moving toy ◇ **like clockwork** with unvarying regularity and predictability ○ *The whole setup ran like clockwork.*

clod /klod/ *n* 1 a large lump of earth or clay 2 an unintelligent and slow-witted person (*insult*) [14C. Variant of CLOT.] —**cloddish** *adj* —**cloddishly** *adv* —**cloddishness** *n* —**cloddy** *adj*

clodhopper /klód hopər/ *n* an unsophisticated or clumsy person (*informal insult*) ■ **clodhoppers** *npl* a pair of large heavy shoes or boots (*informal*) [Early 18C. Originally 'ploughman'; from walking over ploughed land with clods of earth.]

clofibrate /klō fíbbrayt/ *n* a drug. Use: reduction of blood cholesterol, triglycerides, and uric acid. [Mid-20C. < *clofibric acid*.]

clog /klog/ *v* (**clogs, clogging, clogged**) 1 *vti* **BLOCK GRADUALLY** to block a tube or opening gradually with dirt or dust, or become gradually blocked with dirt or dust 2 *vt* **HINDER MOVEMENT IN** to block something such as a road or tunnel, making movement difficult ■ *n* 1 **HEAVY SHOE** a heavy shoe traditionally made of wood, or a shoe with a heavy, traditionally wooden, sole 2 **OBSTRUCTION** something that works against somebody as an obstacle or hindrance 3 **WEIGHT RESTRICTING ANIMAL'S MOVEMENT** a wooden block fastened to an animal's leg to restrict its movement [14C. < ?] ◇ **pop your clogs** to die (*slang*)

clog up *vti* = **clog** *v.* 1

clog dance *n* a dance performed by dancers wearing clogs, who tap or stamp in time to music

cloggy /klóggi/ *adj* sticky or lumpy in texture —**clogginess** *n*

cloisonné /klwaa zónn ay/ *adj* decorated with a pattern formed by pieces of enamel in various colours separated by strips of flattened wire [Mid-19C. < French, 'partitioned', past participle of *cloisonner* < Old French *cloison* 'partition' < Latin *claudere* 'close'.] —**cloisonné** *n*

cloister /klóystər/ *n* 1 **COVERED WALKWAY ROUND COURTYARD** a continuous covered outdoor walkway built against buildings surrounding a central courtyard or quadrangle, especially in a monastery or college 2 **MONASTERY OR CONVENT** a place where people live a life of religious seclusion and contemplation, e.g. a monastery or convent 3 **LIFE OF RELIGIOUS SECLUSION** the life of religious seclusion lived by a monk or nun ○ *He chose the cloister rather than the secular world.* 4 **PLACE OF SECLUSION** a place where people can be private or secluded ■ *vr* **FIND PRIVATE PLACE** to find a quiet private place where you can remain undisturbed [13C. Via Old French *cloistre* < medieval Latin *claustrum* < Latin, 'bar, bolt' < *claudere* 'close'.] —**cloistral** *adj*

cloistered /klóystərd/ *adj* 1 **SECLUDED** secluded from the ordinary life of the world ○ *had led a cloistered life* 2 **IN A MONASTERY** living or occurring in a monastery or convent 3 **WITH A CLOISTER** having a cloister for walking in

clomiphene /klṓmi feen/ *n* a drug that induces ovulation. Use: infertility treatment. [Mid-20C. < CHLORO- + AMINE + PHENYL.]

clomp *n, vti* = **clump**^{2}

Cloncurry /klon kúrri/ town in NW Queensland, Australia. Population: 2,304 (1991).

ϟ**clone** /klōn/ *n* 1 **GENETICALLY IDENTICAL ORGANISM** a plant, animal, or other organism that is genetically identical to its parent, having developed by vegetative reproduction, e.g. from a bulb or a cutting, or experimentally from a single cell 2 **GROUP OF GENETICALLY IDENTICAL PROGENY** a collection of organisms, cells, or molecular segments that are genetically identical direct descendants of a single parent by asexual reproduction, e.g. plant cuttings or grafts 3 **NEAR COPY OF HARDWARE OR SOFTWARE** a hardware device, e.g. a PC, or a piece of software that is a functional copy of another, popular, more expensive product developed by another manufacturer ■ *v* (**clones, cloning, cloned**) 1 *vti* **PRODUCE GENETICALLY IDENTICAL ORGANISMS** to produce an organism that is genetically identical to its parent, by vegetative reproduction or a laboratory technique, or to be produced in this way 2 *vt* **MAKE COPY OF** to produce an exact or near copy of an object or product [Early 20C. < Greek *klōn* 'twig'.] —**clonal** *adj* —**clonally** *adv* —**cloner** *n*

QUICK FACTS ON... **CLONING**

Key elements: production of a group of cells or organisms that are genetically identical because they have developed from the same cell. Occurs naturally, for example, in potatoes, in plants that grow from bulbs, or in primitive organisms that reproduce by dividing

Key dates: 1902 salamander cloned after splitting 2-celled embryo (Spemann); 1952 frogs cloned by transfer of nucleus from one cell to another (Briggs and King); 1958 carrot plant cloned from a root cell (Steward); 1963 the term 'clone' coined (Haldane); 1984 first mammal (sheep) cloned from embryo cells (Willadsen); 1996 Dolly the sheep cloned from adult cells (Wilmut and Campbell); 1997 Polly, genetically modified cloned sheep

Key technologies: cell and tissue culture, nuclear transfer

Key developments: potential medical benefits: source of donor organs for human transplants (xenotransplantation); production of pharmaceutical proteins; research on graft/organ rejection. Potential nonmedical benefits: genetic modification of crop plants for improved characteristics, clonal propagation of plants with desirable traits, micropropagation of potatoes, fruit trees, etc

Key publications: *Clone: The Road to Dolly and the Path Ahead* (Gina Bari Kolata) 1999; *The Human Cloning Debate* (Glenn McGee) 2000

SYNONYMS See ***copy***.

clonidine /klónnə deen, klṓnədin/ *n* a drug that relaxes and widens the arteries. Use: to treat hypertension, migraine headaches, and heart failure. [Late 20C. < CHLORO- + ANILINE + IMIDE + -INE.]

clonk /klongk/ *n, interj* **DULL HOLLOW SOUND** used to represent or imitate the dull hollow sound of something heavy, usually metal, ceramic, or glass, hitting a hard surface ■ *v* 1 *vti* **MAKE THUDDING NOISE** to make a heavy hollow thud 2 *vt* **HIT SOMEBODY HEAVILY** to hit somebody with a heavy blow, usually on a particular part of the body (*informal*) [Mid-19C. An imitation of the sound.]

Clonmel /klon mél/ town in the S Republic of Ireland. Population: 16,000 (1996).

clonus /klṓnəss/ *n* a series of rapid repetitive contractions and relaxations in a muscle during movement, which is characteristic of certain nervous disorders [Early 19C. Via Latin < Greek *klonos* 'turmoil, agitation'.] —**clonic** /klónnik/ *adj* —**clonicity** /klō níssəti/ *n*

Clooney /klóoni/, **George** (*b.* 1961) US film and television actor

cloot /kloot/ *n Scotland* 1 a hoof or either half of a cloven hoof 2 a cloth [Late 18C. Variant of CLOUT.]

clootie dumpling /klóoti-/ *n Scotland* a sweet pudding, full of currants or raisins, that is boiled in a cloth [< CLOOT]

clop /klop/ *n, interj* used to represent or imitate the sound that a walking horse's hooves make when they strike hard ground ■ *vi* (**clops, clopping, clopped**) to make the sound of a walking horse's hooves striking hard ground [Mid-19C. An imitation of the sound.]

cloque /klo káy, klókay/, **cloqué** *n* fabric with a raised woven or embossed pattern that makes it look quilted [Early 20C. < French *cloqué* 'blistered' < dialect *cloque* 'bell, bubble' < medieval Latin *clocca* 'bell'.]

close^{1} /klōss/ *adj* (**closer, closest**) 1 **NEAR** near in space or time ○ *The deadline was getting closer all the time.* 2 **ABOUT TO HAPPEN** about to happen ○ *close to collapse* 3 **KNOWING AND LIKING** knowing somebody very well and liking him or her very much ○ *close friends* 4 **CLOSELY RELATED** being a member of somebody's immediate family 5 **INVOLVING REGULAR CONTACT** involving or having regular contact because of a shared interest in something 6 **THOROUGH** involving great care and thoroughness ○ *give it close inspection.* 7 **DECIDED BY A SMALL MARGIN** decided by, or likely to be decided by, a small margin ○ *a close contest* 8 **ALLOWING LITTLE SPACE BETWEEN** densely packed or woven with only little spaces between ○ *a close weave* 9 **VERY SIMILAR** very similar to an original ○ *a close copy* 10 **NEARLY CORRECT** almost correct, but not exact ○ *You're not quite right, but you're pretty close.* 11 **NEARLY A NUMBER OR QUANTITY** approximately the same as a particular number or quantity ○ *There were close to 300 people at the rally.* 12 **SECRETIVELY SILENT** unwilling to talk about something or to reveal feelings 13 **CUT VERY SHORT** cut so as to be very short 14 **STINGY** unwilling to spend or give money 15 **HARD TO GET** difficult to obtain 16 **CLOSELY GUARDED** kept closely guarded 17 **STUFFY** oppressively hot and airless 18 *US* **DEFENSIVE, WITH SHORT PASSES** in team ball and similar games, involving short passes only, so as to retain possession 19 **PRODUCED WITH TONGUE NEAR PALATE** describes a vowel sound that is produced with the tongue near the palate, e.g. the 'ee' in 'tee' ■ *adv* (**closer, closest**) 1 **NEAR** near in space or time 2 **TIGHTLY** in a snug tight way [13C. Via French *clos* < Latin *clausus*, past participle of *claudere* 'close'.] —**closeness** *n*

ϟ**close**^{2} /klōz/ *v* (**closes, closing, closed**) 1 *vti* **COVER AN OPENING** to move or move something so that an opening or hole is covered or blocked 2 *vti* **COME OR BRING TOGETHER** to come together, or bring the edges or ends of something together, e.g. the eyelids 3 *vti* **SHUT DOWN BUSINESS FOR SHORT TIME** to stop working or operating, or shut a shop or business, for a short period of time or overnight 4 *vti* = **close down** *v.* 1 5 *vt* = **close off** 6 *vti* **TERMINATE** to come to an end, or bring something to an end, e.g. an activity, period of time, or spoken or written text 7 *vti* **REDUCE THE DISTANCE** to reduce the distance between two people or things, especially in a race or chase 8 *vt* **BRING DEAL TO CLOSURE** to complete a transaction successfully, e.g. a business deal or a house purchase 9 *vi* **HAVE AN END-OF-DAY VALUE** to have a particular value at the end of a day's trading on a stock exchange 10 *vt* **DEACTIVATE AND STORE FILE OR PROGRAM** to perform the series of operations necessary to deactivate a computer file or program and store it for later use 11 *vt* **COMPLETE AN ELECTRICAL CIRCUIT** to complete an electrical circuit 12 *vt Malaysia* **SWITCH OFF** to turn or switch something off ■ *n* 1 **END OF AN ACTIVITY** the end of an activity, period of time, or spoken or written text ○ *The applause brought the recital to a close.* 2 MUSIC = **cadence** *n.* 5 [13C. < French *clos-*, stem of *clore* 'close' < Latin *claudere*.] —**closable** *adj* —**closer** *n*

close down *v* 1 *vti* to stop operating or trading permanently, or shut a factory, business, or school so that it stops operating permanently 2 *vi* to stop broadcasting at the end of the day

close in *vi* 1 to move closer and eventually surround somebody or something 2 to become progressively shorter, with fewer hours of daylight

close off *vt* to prevent people from reaching a place or using a route by blocking access to it (*often passive*)

close up *v* 1 *vti* **LOCK BUILDING** to lock the doors of a building at the end of a working or trading session 2 *vti* **MOVE CLOSER TOGETHER** to move closer together, or make people or things move closer together 3 *vti* **BRING TOGETHER** to come together, or bring the ends or edges of something together 4 *vi* **HIDE EMOTIONS** to hide your true emotions deliberately because you do not want somebody to know or understand you

close with *vt* to enter into physical conflict or a fight with somebody ○ *The two boxers closed with one another.*

close^{3} /klōss/ *n* 1 **CUL-DE-SAC** a residential road, often a cul-de-sac in a modern housing estate (*often in street names*) ○ *Brookside Close* 2 **AREA ROUND CATHEDRAL** the area immediately surrounding a cathedral, including the buildings, many of which are often cathedral property 3 *Scotland* **COURTYARD** an outdoor area enclosed by buildings, e.g. a courtyard, or a passageway leading to one (*often in street names*) ○ *Lady Stair's Close* 4 *Scotland* **PASSAGEWAY INSIDE TENEMENT BUILDING** in the West of Scotland, especially Glasgow, a passage inside a tenement building that leads from the street to the common stairway 5 **PARCEL OF LAND** an individual parcel of land, whether marked off by fencing or only having invisible boundaries [13C. Via French *clos* < Latin *clausum* 'enclosure', neuter of *clausus* (see CLOSE[1]).]

Close /klōss/, **Glenn** (*b.* 1947) US stage and film actor

close call *n* a dangerous situation that could have resulted in death or injury, but from which somebody just manages to escape

close company, closed company *n* a company that is controlled by its directors

close-cropped *adj* cut very short

closed /klōzd/ *adj* 1 **WHERE WORK HAS STOPPED** where work, operation, or trading has temporarily or permanently stopped 2 **DENYING ACCESS** where access or passage is denied 3 **NO LONGER TO BE DISCUSSED** about which there is to be no further discussion or investigation ○ *The subject is closed.* 4 **RIGIDLY EXCLUDING OTHERS' IDEAS** rigidly rejecting ideas, beliefs, opinions, and influence from or by others ○ *He has a closed mind to all arguments.* 5 **NOT ADMITTING OUTSIDERS** allowing no outsiders in, or tending not to meet with outsiders 6 **CONFIDENTIAL AND PRIVATE** carried on or conducted in the strictest confidentiality or secrecy 7 **FULLY ENCLOSING AN AREA OR VOLUME** describes a curve, especially a circle, that fully encloses an area, or describes a solid every surface of which is such a curve 8 **HAVING LIMITED NUMBER OF MEMBERS** describes a word class that has a limited number of members, e.g. pronouns or conjunctions 9 **ENDING IN CONSONANT** describes a syllable that ends in a consonant

closed circuit *n* an electrical circuit in which there is an uninterrupted endless path for current to flow when voltage is applied

closed-circuit television, closed-circuit TV *n* a television transmission system in which cameras transmit pictures by cable to connected monitors

closed corporation *n US* = **close corporation**

closed couplet *n* a pair of rhymed lines that form a complete sentence or unit of meaning

closed-door *adj* restricted to members or those directly involved, and not open to the general public or the news media

closed-end fund *n* an investment company with a fixed number of shares trading on the stock exchange

closed-end investment company *n US* a corporation whose capitalization is fixed, whose capital is invested in other companies, and whose own shares are traded by outside investors

closed interval *n* a set consisting of all the numbers between two given numbers (**end points**), including the given numbers

ϟ **closed loop** *n* a system, usually computer-controlled, that adjusts itself to varying conditions by feeding output information back as input

closedown /klṓz down/ *n* 1 a temporary or permanent stopping of work or operations 2 the end of a broadcasting day or period

closed season *n* US = **close season**

closed set *n* a set that includes the limits by which the set is defined, e.g. all the points within and on a circle

closed shop *n* a place of work in which the employer has agreed to employ only members of a particular trade union. ◊ **open shop, union shop**

closed stance *n* a stance, e.g. in baseball or golf, in which the front foot is closer to the line of play than the rear foot

close-fisted *adj* reluctant to spend money (*informal*) —**close-fistedness** *n*

close-fitting *adj* fitting tightly on the body

close-grained *adj* describes wood that has dense fibres and as a result a smooth texture

close harmony *n* the arrangement of chord tones so that they are as close together as possible, used especially in music for vocal ensembles

close-hauled *adj, adv* with the sails set for sailing towards the direction from which the wind is blowing

close-knit *adj* supportive and loyal to the other members of a community or group

closely /klṓssli/ *adv* 1 **CAREFULLY AND THOROUGHLY** in a careful and thorough way ○ *listening closely* 2 **IN A VERY SIMILAR WAY** in a way that is very similar or strongly linked to something ○ *She closely resembles you.* 3 **SO AS TO BE NEAR** in a way that is near something in space or time ○ *We heard a bang, closely followed by another.* 4 **INTIMATELY** in an intimate manner ○ *worked closely with her*

closemouthed /klṓss mówthd, -mówtht/ *adj* unwilling to talk or to reveal anything

close-order drill *n* a formation or movement that is conducted with soldiers at close intervals

closeout /klṓz owt/ *n US* COMM = **closing-down sale**

close punctuation *n* punctuation in which a large number of commas, semicolons, and colons are used

close-run *adj* having a very close result

close season *n* 1 the time of the year when it is illegal to hunt and kill certain animals, birds, or fish 2 the period between the end of one annual seasonal sports competition, e.g. a football season, and the start of the next one

close shave *n* = **close call**

closestool /klṓss stool/ *n* formerly, a stool or chair containing a chamber pot [15C. Literally 'enclosed stool'.]

closet /klózzit/ *n* 1 *US* **LARGE CUPBOARD** a walk-in wardrobe or walk-in cupboard in which clothes and linen are stored 2 **SMALL PRIVATE ROOM** a small private room (*archaic*) 3 **TOILET** a water closet (*archaic*) ■ *adj* **SECRET** having beliefs or behaviour that is not openly acknowledged but kept secret ■ *vt* **PUT SOMEBODY IN PRIVATE PLACE** to put people in a small room where they can have privacy (*often passive*) [14C. < Old French, 'small enclosure' < *clos* (see CLOSE[3]).] —**closetful** *n* ◇ **come out of the closet** to acknowledge openly something previously kept secret, especially the fact of being a homosexual man or woman

closet drama *n US* a play or plays written to be read rather than performed

close thing *n* = **close call**

close-up *n* 1 **CLOSE-RANGE PHOTO OR SHOT** a photograph, film, or television shot taken from a position very close to the subject 2 **DETAILED LOOK** a detailed view or examination of something ■ *adj* **AT CLOSE RANGE** seen from a position very near somebody or something else

closing /klṓzing/ *adj* **FINAL** forming or connected with the final part of an activity or period of time ○ *in the closing stages of the game* ■ *n* 1 **SOMETHING THAT CLOSES** something that closes, e.g. a fastening on clothes 2 *US* **TRANSFER OF PROPERTY OWNERSHIP** a meeting among principals in a real estate transaction, during which legal papers related to the sale and purchase are signed and financial arrangements are made final and binding

closing-down sale *n* a sale of all remaining merchandise, at very low prices. US term **closeout** *n.*

closing price *n* the price of a share or bond on a stock exchange recorded at the official close of trading

closing time *n* the time that an establishment such as a shop, library, or bar closes and people have to leave

clostridium /klo stríddi əm/ (*plural* **-ums** *or* **-a** /-di ə/) *n* a rod-shaped, usually motile, Gram-positive bacterium that can cause serious illnesses including botulism, tetanus, and gas gangrene. Genus: *Clostridium.* [Late 19C. < modern Latin, 'little spindle' < Greek *klōstēr* 'spindle'.] —**clostridial** *adj*

closure /klṓzhər/ *n* 1 **PERMANENT END OF BUSINESS** the permanent ending of a business or activity 2 **BARRING OF ACCESS** blocking the access to a place or blocking a route 3 **SOMETHING THAT CLOSES AN OPENING** a device for closing an opening, e.g. a zip or a cap on a bottle, or the place where the opening closes 4 **CLOSING** an act or process of closing something, e.g. closing an opening or terminating an activity 5 **PROCEDURE FOR CUTTING DEBATE SHORT** a parliamentary procedure that allows a debate to be cut short and a vote to be taken immediately. US term **cloture** *n.* 6 **VERTICAL DISTANCE OF ROCK FORMATION** the distance measured vertically between the top of a rock formation (**anticline**) and the lowest contour 7 **CONTACT BETWEEN VOCAL ORGANS PRODUCING SOUND** a contact made between vocal organs, e.g. the tongue and the soft palate, that produces a speech sound 8 **BEING A CLOSED SET IN MATHEMATICS** the characteristic of a set in which the application of a given mathematical operation to any member of the set always results in another member of that set ■ *vt* (**-sures, -suring, -sured**) **APPLY CLOSURE TO** to apply closure to a debate or speaker in parliament. US term **cloture** *v.*

clot /klot/ *n* 1 **STICKY LUMP** a mass of thickened liquid, especially blood 2 **OFFENSIVE TERM** an offensive term for a person considered to be unintelligent (*informal*) ■ *vti* (**clots, clotting, clotted**) **THICKEN AND FORM LUMPS** to thicken, or make a liquid thicken, and form lumps [Old English *clott* < Indo-European, 'form into a ball'] —**clottish** *adj*

cloth /kloth/ *n* 1 **FABRIC** fabric made by weaving, knitting, or felting thread or fibres 2 **PIECE OF FABRIC** a piece of fabric used for a particular purpose, e.g. a dishcloth (*often in combination*) 3 **CLERGY** the clergy, or the clothes worn by its members 4 **SAIL** a sail of a boat 5 **PIECE OF FABRIC SCENERY** a painted piece of fabric used as scenery [Old English *clāþ* < Germanic]

clothbound /klóth bownd/ *adj* describes a book that has a cloth-lined hardback cover

clothe /klōth/ (**clothes, clothing, clothed** *or* **clad** *literary or archaic* /klad/, **clothed** *or* **clad** *literary or archaic*) *vt* 1 **DRESS** to put clothes on somebody (*often passive*) 2 **PROVIDE CLOTHING FOR** to provide somebody with clothes 3 **COVER** to completely cover an area ○ *The hills were clothed in mist.* 4 **COVER UP** to obscure or conceal something as if wrapping something round it 5 **ENDOW** to endow or invest somebody or something with some quality (*usually passive*) [Old English *clāðian* < *clāþ* (see CLOTH)]

cloth-eared *adj* unable or unwilling to hear (*informal*)

clothes /klōthz/ *npl* 1 garments that cover the body 2 sheets and blankets used to cover a bed (*dated*) [Old English *clāþas*, plural of *clāþ* (see CLOTH)]

clothes hanger *n* HOUSEHOLD = **hanger** *n.* 2

clotheshorse /klṓthz hawrss/ *n* 1 a frame on which clothes are hung to dry indoors 2 a wearer of the latest fashions (*informal*)

clothesline /klṓthz līn/ *n* a cord or wire on which clean laundry is hung to dry

clothes moth *n* any small moth whose larvae feed on wool and fur. Family: Tineidae.

clothes peg *n* a small clip of plastic or wood used to secure laundry to a clothesline. US term **clothespin**

clothespin /klṓthz pin/ *n US* DOMESTIC = **clothes peg**

clothes press *n* a piece of furniture for storing clothes, with hanging space and sometimes drawers or shelves

clothes prop *n* a long pole for holding a clothesline above the ground

clothier /klṓthi ər/ *n* a retailer of clothes or cloth [14C. Alteration of obsolete *clother* < CLOTH.]

clothing /klṓthing/ *n* 1 clothes collectively 2 a covering for something

Clotho /klṓ thō/ *n* one of the three Fates of classical mythology. ◊ **Lachesis, Atropos** [< Greek *Klōthō* 'I spin']

cloth of gold *n* a luxury fabric of the Middle Ages woven from silk, or sometimes wool, intermixed with gold thread

clotrimazole /klō trímə zol/ *n* an antifungal drug

clotted cream /klóttəd kreem/ *n* a thick cream made by removing the cream from the top of heated milk

clotting factor *n* any substance in the blood that is essential for blood to coagulate

cloture /klṓchər/ *n US* POL = **closure** *n.* 5 ■ *vt* (**-tures, -turing, -tured**) *US* POL = **closure** *v.* [Late 19C. < French *clôture* 'closing'.]

ϟ **cloud** /klowd/ *n* 1 **MASS OF WATER IN SKY** a visible mass of water or ice particles in the atmosphere from which rain and other forms of precipitation fall 2 **MASS OF PARTICLES IN AIR** a mass of particles in the air, e.g. dust or smoke ○ *a cloud of smoke* 3 **FLYING MASS** an airborne mass of insects or birds 4 **DARKER PART** a dark or dim area on something such as jewellery 5 **SOMETHING WORRYING** something that causes anxiety or fear ○ *Lack of financial independence was a cloud hanging over our future.* 6 **GLOOMY CONDITION** a condition of gloom or despondency ○ *a cloud of despair* 7 **UNPREDICTABLE PART OF COMPUTER NETWORK** an unpredictable or unidentifiable part of a network through which data passes ■ *v* 1 *vti* **BECOME CLOUDY** to become covered with cloud or mist, or make something cloudy 2 *vt* **CONFUSE** to make something more confusing ○ *cloud the issue* 3 *vt* **DETRACT FROM** to make something appear less good ○ *It clouded their reputation.* 4 *vt* **IMPAIR** to diminish a mental faculty 5 *vti* **LOOK TROUBLED** to become or cause something to become troubled or gloomy ○ *His face clouded with disappointment.* **6** *vti* **BECOME OR MAKE SOMETHING OPAQUE** to become or cause something to become opaque or murky ○ *The water was clouded with particles.* [Old English *clūd* 'mass of rock, hill'] ◇ **on cloud nine** extremely happy (*informal*) ◇ **under a cloud** in disgrace

cloud over, cloud up *vi* **1** to become covered with cloud or mist **2** to become troubled

cloudberry /klówdbəri/ (*plural* **-ries**) *n* a creeping perennial plant with yellowish edible berries. Flowers: white. Native to: Europe, North America, Asia. *Rubus chamaemorus.* [The reason for the name is unknown]

cloudburst /klówd burst/ *n* a sudden heavy rain shower

cloud chamber *n* a device in which the movement of high-energy particles is detected as they pass through a chamber of supersaturated vapour

cloud-cuckoo-land *n* an imaginary place in which problems do not exist [Translation of Greek *Nephelokokkugia*, imaginary city in the air in Aristophanes' *Birds*]

clouded /klówdid/ *adj* **1** appearing troubled **2** opaque or murky

clouded leopard *n* a rare medium-sized cat with short legs and a greyish to yellowish coat with darker irregular markings. Native to: Nepal to Borneo. *Neofelis nebulosa.*

clouded yellow *n* a butterfly that has yellowish wings with brownish or blackish margins and migrates between continental Europe and Britain. *Colias croceus.*

cloud forest *n* a high-altitude tropical forest that is usually covered by cloud

cloudland /klówd land/ *n* = **dreamland** *n.* 1

cloudless /klówdləss/ *adj* **1** bright and sunny without clouds ○ *a cloudless sky* **2** free of trouble —**cloudlessly** *adv* —**cloudlessness** *n*

cloud rack *n* a group of clouds moving across the sky

cloudscape /klówd skayp/ *n* a view or depiction of clouds

cloud seeding *n* the technique or process of scattering substances such as silver iodide into clouds from an aircraft in order to precipitate rain

cloudy /klówdi/ (**-ier, -iest**) *adj* **1 WITH CLOUDS** covered with some clouds, usually a great deal **2 OPAQUE** opaque or murky ○ *a cloudy liquid* **3 RESEMBLING CLOUDS** having the appearance of clouds **4 TROUBLED** seeming troubled or gloomy **5 NOT CLEAR** obscure or difficult to understand —**cloudily** *adv* —**cloudiness** *n*

clough /kluf/ *n* a ravine, or the sloping side of it (*regional*) [Old English *clōh* < Germanic]

clout /klowt/ *n* **1 POWER AND INFLUENCE** the power to direct, shape, or otherwise influence things (*informal*) **2 PUNCH** a blow with the hand or fist **3 ARCHERY TARGET** in archery, a mark or target, especially at a long distance **4 PIECE OF CLOTH** a rag or piece of cloth (*regional*) ○ *a dish clout* ■ *vt* **HIT SOMEBODY WITH HAND** to hit somebody or something hard with the hand [Old English *clūt* 'patch made of cloth']

clove[1] /klōv/ *n* **1** a dried aromatic flower bud. Use: as a spice. **2** an evergreen tree with flower buds that are used dried as a spice and other parts that yield aromatic oil of cloves. Native to: the Moluccas. *Syzgium aromaticum.* [12C. < Old French *clou (de girofle)* 'nail (of the clove tree)' < Latin *clavus* 'nail'; from the resemblance of a clove-tree bud to a nail.]

clove[2] /klōv/ *n* one of the segments of a compound bulb ○ *a clove of garlic* [Old English *clufu* < Germanic]

clove[3] /klōv/ past tense of **cleave**[1]

clove hitch *n* a knot made of two half-hitches. Use: to attach a rope to a post or to another, thicker, rope. [< former past participle of CLEAVE[1]]

Clovelly /klō vélli/ village in SW England. Population: 500 (1989).

cloven /klōv'n/ *v* past participle of **cleave**[1] ■ *adj* split or divided into two parts (*archaic or literary*)

cloven hoof, cloven foot *n* **1** the divided hoof of such animals as cattle, sheep, and pigs. Order: Artiodactyla. **2** an indication of the presence of the Devil, traditionally represented in Christianity with a cloven hoof —**cloven-hoofed** *adj*

clove oil *n* PHARM = **oil of cloves**

clove pink *n* PLANTS = **carnation** *n.* 1 [< CLOVE[1]; from its smell]

clover /klōvər/ (*plural* **-ver** *or* **-vers**) *n* **1** a plant with three-lobed leaves often cultivated as a forage plant, for erosion control, and to provide nectar for bees. Flowers: white or red, rounded. Genus: *Trifolium.* **2** any forage plant similar to clover. Genera: *Meliotus* and *Lespedeza* and *Medicago.* [Old English *clāfre* < Germanic] ◇ **in clover** financially well off

cloverleaf /klōvər leef/ (*plural* **cloverleaves** /-leevz/) *n* **1** the three-lobed leaf of a clover plant (*often before nouns*) ○ *a cloverleaf motif* **2** an arrangement of major roads resembling a four-leaf clover, with entrance and exit roads enabling traffic to change direction at speed without intersections

Clovis /klōviss/ *adj* describes a prehistoric North American culture characterized by leaf-shaped flint points that were used as parts of weapons to hunt game [Mid-20C. After *Clovis*, New Mexico, US.]

clown /klown/ *n* **1 COMIC CIRCUS PERFORMER** a comic performer, usually in a circus, who does not speak and wears an outlandish costume and heavy makeup **2 SOMEBODY FUNNY** somebody who behaves comically **3 PRANKSTER** a prankster or practical joker **4 ILL-MANNERED PERSON** an ill-mannered or ineffectual person (*informal*) ■ *vi* **1 BEHAVE COMICALLY** to behave in a silly or funny way **2 PLAY PRANKS** to play practical jokes **3 PERFORM AS CLOWN** to perform as a circus clown [Mid-16C. < ?] —**clownery** *n*

clown anemone *n* ZOOL = **anemone fish**

clown fish *n* ZOOL = **anemone fish**

clownish /klównish/ *adj* resembling or characteristic of a clown —**clownishly** *adv* —**clownishness** *n*

cloy /kloy/ *vti* to sicken somebody or become sickened with too much sweetness or sensation from something initially pleasing [Mid-16C. Shortening of obsolete *accloy*, via French *encloer* 'drive in a nail' < medieval Latin *inclavare* < Latin *clavus* 'nail'.] —**cloyingly** *adv* —**cloyingness** *n*

clozapine /klōzə peen/ *n* an antipsychotic drug. Use: to treat schizophrenia. [Mid-20C. Contraction of CHLORO- + BENZODIAZEPINE.]

cloze test /klōz-/ *n* a test of comprehension and grammar in which a language student supplies appropriate missing words omitted from a text [alteration of CLOSURE]

club /klub/ *n* **1 THICK STICK USED AS WEAPON** a stout stick used as a weapon **2 STICK FOR HITTING BALL** a stick or bat used in certain sports, especially golf, to hit a ball ○ *a golf club* **3** SPORTS = **Indian club 4 ASSOCIATION FOR PARTICIPATING IN INTEREST** an association of people with a common interest ○ *a gardening club* **5 ORGANIZATION FOR SPORT** an organization formed for the pursuit of a sport on an amateur or a professional basis ○ *a football club* **6 PREMISES OF CLUB** the premises where the activities of a club are pursued ○ *See you at the club tonight!* **7 BUILDING PROVIDING FACILITIES TO MEMBERS** a building that offers facilities and refreshment to members of the organization that owns or occupies it ○ *a gentlemen's club* **8 ORGANIZATION GIVING DISCOUNTS** a scheme or organization in which members receive price reductions in return for regular purchases ○ *a book club* **9 SAVINGS SCHEME** a savings scheme organized as a means of saving for something ○ *a Christmas club* **10 NATIONS SHARING** a group of nations or people who have a particular thing in common ○ *the nuclear club* **11** = **nightclub 12 BLACK SYMBOL ON PLAYING CARD** a black symbol shaped like a three-leaved clover on a playing card ■ *v* (**clubs, clubbing, clubbed**) **1** *vt* **HIT WITH CLUB** to hit somebody or something with a club ○ *She clubbed the ball over the fence.* **2** *vi* **FORM CLUB** to join or form a club for social purposes or to pursue a common interest **3** *vi* **DRIFT WITH ANCHOR LOWERED** to drift with an anchor that drags to reduce the speed of the vessel [12C. < Old Norse *klubba* 'heavy stick', alteration of *klumpa.*] ◇ **in the (pudding) club** pregnant (*informal*) ◇ **join the club!** used to tell somebody that you are in the same position as he or she is

club together *vi* **1** to contribute money collectively for some purpose **2** to collaborate as a group

clubbable /klúbbəb'l/, **clubable** *adj* sociable, and enjoying belonging to clubs —**clubbability** /klúbbə bílləti/ *n*

clubbed /klubd/ *adj* describes an appendage with a swelling at one end, like a club ○ *clubbed antennae*

clubber /klúbbər/ *n* **1 NIGHTCLUB GOER** a regular attender of nightclubs (*informal*) **2 MEMBER OF CLUB** a member of a club **3 CLUB WIELDER** the wielder of a club

clubbing /klúbbing/ *n* **1** the activity of going to nightclubs **2** a medical condition in which the tips of the fingers and toes become thickened, especially at the base of the nail

clubby /klúbbi/ (**-bier, -biest**) *adj* **1 SOCIABLE** enjoying the friendliness associated with clubs **2 TYPICAL OF CLUB** typical of a social club **3 SNOBBISH** socially exclusive and snobbish —**clubbily** *adv* —**clubbiness** *n*

club chair *n* a heavily upholstered chair with a low back and thick arms [< its use in gentlemen's clubs]

club class *n* a class of travel on an aircraft between first class and economy class

clubface /klúbb fayss/ *n* the surface of the head of a golf club with which the player strikes the ball

club foot *n* **1** a congenital condition of the foot, especially one in which the foot is twisted and turned inwards **2** a foot that is affected by club foot —**club footed** *adj*

club hand *n* **1** a congenital condition in which the hand is twisted and turned inwards or outwards **2** a hand affected by club hand —**club handed** *adj*

clubhaul /klúb hawl/ *vti* to force a sailing vessel to change tack by dropping the lee-anchor and hauling in the anchor cable to swing the stern to windward

clubhouse /klúb howss/ *n* the premises of a club, especially a sports club

clubland /klúb land/ *n* an area in a large city such as London in which many exclusive social clubs and nightclubs are located

clubman /klúb mən/ (*plural* **-men** /-mən/) *n* a man who belongs to one or more exclusive social clubs

club moss *n* a nonflowering plant that typically has creeping stems with small overlapping leaves and reproduces by spores, often borne in club-shaped organs (**strobili**). Order: Lycopodiales.

clubroom /klúb room, -rŏŏm/ *n* a room in which members of a club meet

clubroot /klúb root/ *n* a disease affecting plants of the cabbage family, in which the roots become swollen and distorted. *Plasmodiophora brassicae.*

clubs /klubz/ *n* one of the four suits used in cards, with a black shape similar to a three-leaved clover as its symbol (+ *singular or plural verb*)

club sandwich *n* a sandwich consisting of two layers of fillings between three slices of bread [< ?]

club soda *n US, Can* = **soda water** *n.* 1 [< a proprietary name]

cluck /kluk/ *interj* **USED TO REPRESENT HEN'S CALL** used to imitate the short low clicking sound made by a hen ■ *v* **1** *vi* **MAKE HEN'S SOUND** to make natural short low clicking sounds (*refers to hens*) **2** *vti* **EXPRESS SOMETHING WITH CLICKING SOUND** to show disapproval or concern by making short clicking sounds ■ *n* **1 HEN'S CALL** a hen's short low clicking call **2** *US* **UNINTELLIGENT PERSON** a person who is considered mildly unintelligent (*informal*) [15C. An imitation of the sound.]

clucky /klúki/ (**-ier, -iest**) *adj Aus* keen to have children (*slang*) [< the idea of a broody hen]

clue /kloo/ *n* **1 AID IN SOLVING MYSTERY** something that helps to solve a mystery or crime **2 AID IN SOLVING CROSSWORD** one of the numbered items of information used to solve a crossword puzzle **3 EXPLANATION FOR BEHAVIOUR** an explanation or reason for something that is difficult to understand [Late 16C. Alteration of CLEW.] ◇ **not have a clue about something 1** to know nothing about something (*informal*) **2** to be very bad at something (*informal*)

clue in *vt* to provide somebody with useful information ○ *She clued me in about office politics.*

clued-up /klŏŏd úp/ *adj* well-informed about somebody or something (*informal; not hyphenated after verbs*) ○ *She's quite clued up about food additives.* [Alteration of *clewed up* 'furled up' < CLEW 'corner of a sail']

clueless /klŏŏləss/ *adj* incompetent or ignorant (*informal*) —**cluelessness** *n*

Cluj-Napoca /klŏŏzh nə pōkə/ city in NW Romania. Population: 326,017 (1994).

clumber spaniel /klúmbər-/, **clumber** *n* a thickset short-legged spaniel with a dense silky coat belonging to an English breed [After *Clumber* Park, Nottinghamshire]

clumble-fisted /klúmb'l fistid/ *adj W Country* unable to do something gracefully or tactfully

clump[1] /klump/ *n* **1 CLUSTER OF THINGS** a compact cluster or group of growing things ○ *a clump of moss* **2 MASS OF SIMILAR THINGS** an undifferentiated mass of something **3 CLUSTER OF CELLS** a cluster of cells, e.g. bacteria or red blood cells, especially one formed during an immune response or when blood of incompatible blood groups is mixed ■ *v* **1** *vti* **COMBINE THINGS INTO MASS** to be gathered or gather things into a mass **2 CAUSE MASSING OF CELLS** to cause cells, e.g. bacteria or red blood cells, to combine into a mass, especially as part of an immune response [13C. Probably < Low German *klump*.]

clump[2] /klump/, **clomp** /klomp/ *n* **1 THUMPING SOUND** a heavy thumping sound **2 HEAVY BLOW** a heavy blow or punch (*informal*) ■ *v* **1** *vi* **MOVE WITH CLUMP** to walk or move with a heavy thumping sound **2** *vt* **THUMP** to give somebody a heavy thump or punch (*informal*) [Mid-17C. An imitation of the sound.]

clumpy /klúmpi/ (**-ier, -iest**) *adj* **1** large, heavy, and ungainly **2** composed of or growing in clumps —**clumpily** *adv* —**clumpiness** *n*

clumsy /klúmzi/ (**-sier, -siest**) *adj* **1** poorly coordinated physically **2** said or done in an awkward or insensitive way ○ *a clumsy remark* [Late 16C. < ?] —**clumsily** *adv* —**clumsiness** *n*

Clunies-Ross /kloóniz róss/, **Sir Ian** (1899–1959) Australian veterinary scientist

clunk /klungk/ *n* **1 DULL SOUND** a dull sound like that of a heavy piece of metal hitting something **2 BLOW OR SOUND IT MAKES** a blow, or the sound made by a blow (*informal*) ■ *vti* **MAKE DULL SOUND** to make, or cause something to make, a dull heavy sound [Late 18C. An imitation of the sound.]

clunker /klúngkər/ *n US* a dilapidated old motor vehicle or piece of machinery (*informal*)

clunky /klúngki/ (**-ier, -iest**) *adj* solid, bulky, or heavy

Cluny lace /kloóni-/ *n* a strong white lace made of silk, linen, or cotton [Late 19C. After *Cluny*, east-central France.]

clupeid /kloópi id/ *n* a soft-finned bony fish that has oily flesh, a narrow body, and a forked tail. Herrings, sardines, and shad are clupeids. Family: Clupeidae. [Late 19C. < modern Latin *Clupeidae* < Latin *clupea*, a small river fish.]

⚡**cluster** /klústər/ *n* **1 DENSE BUNCH** a small group of people or things that are closely packed together ○ *a cluster of diamonds* ○ *a little cluster of onlookers* **2 STARS THAT APPEAR NEAR EACH OTHER** a group of galaxies or stars that are gravitationally interacting in space and appear to an observer on Earth to be close together **3 GROUP OF CONSONANTS** a group of consecutive consonants in the same syllable **4 SUBSET IN STATISTICAL SAMPLE** a statistically significant subset within a population, used in sampling **5 CHORD OF THREE OR MORE NOTES** a chord consisting of three or more notes spaced a semitone apart **6** *US* **DESIGN INDICATING MILITARY AWARDS** in the US Army, a small metal design indicating that a medal has been awarded before to the same individual **7 GROUP OF BOMBS** a group of bombs dropped together **8 SET OF MINES** a basic unit of mines used in laying a minefield **9 NETWORK OF SMALL COMPUTERS** a network of computers under the control of a larger, more powerful computer ■ *vti* **FORM INTO CLUSTER** to gather something into or form a small group [Old English *clyster* < Germanic] —**clustered** *adj* —**clustery** *adj*

cluster analysis *n* a statistical technique that compares multiple characteristics of a population to determine whether individuals fall into different groups

cluster bomb *n* a canister dropped from an aircraft to release a number of small bombs over a wide area

⚡**cluster controller** *n* a computer that sorts and files data from smaller computers in a network

cluster headache *n* a severe recurring headache associated with the release of histamine in the bloodstream, and marked by sudden sharp pain behind one eye or nostril

clutch[1] /kluch/ *v* **1** *vt* **HOLD TIGHTLY** to grip something tightly **2** *vi* **MAKE GRABBING MOVEMENT** to try to grab hold of something ■ *n* **1 MECHANISM THAT CONNECTS SHAFTS** a device that enables two rotating shafts to be connected and disconnected smoothly, especially one in a motor vehicle that transmits power from the engine to the gearbox **2 PEDAL ACTIVATING CLUTCH** the pedal that activates the clutch in a motor vehicle **3 TIGHT GRIP** a tight grip on something **4 CONTROLLING POWER** control and influence (*often plural*) ○ *We were plainly in his clutches.* [14C. Variant of obsolete *clitch* 'to bend, grasp' < Old English *clyccan* 'to grasp'.]

clutch[2] /kluch/ *n* **1 GROUP OF EGGS HATCHED TOGETHER** the number of eggs hatched by a bird or a pair of birds at one time **2 GROUP OF CHICKENS HATCHED TOGETHER** all the chickens hatched together from one clutch of eggs **3 GROUP OF SIMILAR THINGS** a number of similar people or things (*informal*) [Early 18C. Probably variant of dialectal *cletch* < *cleck* 'hatch' < Old Norse *klekja*.]

Clutha /kloóthə/ longest river in the South Island, New Zealand, in the south east of the island. Length: 336 km/209 mi.

clutter /klúttər/ *n* **1 UNTIDY STUFF** an untidy collection of objects **2 DISORGANIZED MESS** a condition of disorderliness or overcrowding **3 CONFUSING RADAR IMAGES** images on a radar screen that hinder observation ■ *vt* **FILL WITH CLUTTER** to make a place untidy or overfilled with objects [Mid-16C. Probably variant of obsolete *clotter* 'clot repeatedly' < CLOT.]

Clwyd /kloó id/ former county of Wales

Clyde /klīd/ river in SW Scotland. It flows through Glasgow to the Firth of Clyde. Length: 171 km/106 mi.

Clydebank /klīd bangk/ town in W Scotland. Population: 29,171 (1991).

Clydesdale /klīdz dayl/ *n* a strong heavy horse belonging to a breed originally developed in Scotland as draught animals [Late 18C. After an area of the River CLYDE.]

clype /klīp/ *vi* (**clypes, clyping, clyped**) *Scotland* to inform somebody in authority of another's wrongdoings as a way of getting that person into trouble (*informal*) ■ *n Scotland* somebody willing to inform on another person (*informal*) [Early 18C. Probably variant of obsolete *clepe* 'call' < Old English *clipian*.]

clyster /klístər/ *n* an enema (*archaic*) [14C. Directly or via French < Latin *clyster* < Greek *klustēr* 'syringe' < *kluzein* 'wash out'.]

cm[1] *symbol* centimetre

⚡**cm**[2] *abbr* Cameroon (*in Internet addresses*)

Cm *symbol* curium

c.m. *abbr* **1** centre of mass **2** court martial

CMA *abbr* **1** Canadian Medical Association **2** certified medical assistant

Cmdr *abbr* Commander

CMEA *abbr* Council for Mutual Economic Assistance

CMG *abbr* Companion of the Order of St Michael and St George

c'mon /kəm ón/ *contr* come on (*nonstandard*)

⚡**CMOS** /seé moss/ *abbr* complementary metal oxide semiconductor

CMV *abbr* cytomegalovirus

⚡**cn** *abbr* China (*in Internet addresses*)

C/N *abbr* **1** credit note **2** cover note

CNAA *abbr* Council for National Academic Awards

CNAR *abbr* compound net annual rate

CND *abbr* Campaign for Nuclear Disarmament

cnidarian /nī dáiri ən/ *n* any invertebrate sea animal that has tentacles surrounding the mouth, e.g. sea anemones, corals, and jellyfishes. Phylum: Cnidaria. [Early 20C. < modern Latin *Cnidaria* < Greek *knidē* 'nettle' < *knizein* 'cause to itch'.] —**cnidarian** *adj*

CNN *abbr* Cable News Network

CNS *abbr* central nervous system

CN Tower *n* a tall tower in central Toronto, Canada. It is more than 553 m/1800 ft high and was the world's tallest free-standing structure when it was built in 1976.

⚡**co** *abbr* Colombia (*in Internet addresses*)

Co *symbol* cobalt

CO *abbr* **1** Commanding Officer **2** Commonwealth Office **3** conscientious objector **4** Colorado **5** Colombia (*international vehicle registration*)

Co. /kō/ *abbr* **1** Company (*in names of businesses*) **2** County (*in placenames*) **3** Colorado

co- *prefix* **1** together, jointly ○ *coauthor* **2** associate, alternate ○ *copilot* **3** to the same degree ○ *coeternal* **4** complement of an angle ○ *cotangent*

c/o[1] *abbr* care of (*in addresses*)

c/o[2] *abbr* **1** care of **2** carried over

CoA *abbr* coenzyme A

coacervate /kō ássər vayt/ *n* an aggregate of colloidal droplets bound together by electrostatic forces

coach /kōch/ *n* **1 LONG-DISTANCE BUS** a bus designed for long-distance travel or sightseeing **2 HORSE-DRAWN CARRIAGE** a large enclosed horse-drawn carriage **3 RAILWAY CARRIAGE** a railway carriage **4 SOMEBODY WHO TRAINS SPORTS PLAYERS** a trainer of sports players and athletes **5 SOMEBODY WHO TRAINS PERFORMERS** a trainer of actors or singers **6 TUTOR** an instructor of a person in a specified subject **7 TUTOR FOR EXAMINATIONS** a private tutor who prepares students for examinations **8** *US, Can* **INEXPENSIVE TRAVEL CATEGORY** an inexpensive class of passenger accommodation on a bus, train, or aircraft ■ *v* **1** *vt* **TRAIN ATHLETE** to train somebody in a sport **2** *vt* **TRAIN PERFORMER** to train somebody in acting or singing **3** *vt* **TRAIN STUDENT** to give somebody private tuition in a particular subject or towards examinations **4** *vti* **TRANSPORT PEOPLE IN COACH** to carry passengers in a horse-drawn coach, or travel by coach [Mid-16C. Via French *coche* < German *Kutsche* < Hungarian *kocsi (szekér)* '(wagon) of Kocs', after *Kocs*, Hungary.] —**coachable** *adj*

SYNONYMS See ***teach***.

coach bolt *n* a bolt for timber with a shank that at one end is square in section with a rounded head. US term **carriage bolt**

coachbuilder /kṓch bildər/ *n* **1** a person or company that builds the bodies of vehicles such as cars, lorries, or railway carriages **2** a specialist firm that designs and builds or finishes bodywork fitted to motor vehicle chassis —**coachbuilding** *n*

coach-built *adj* **1** made as the body for a vehicle according to an individual specification **2** describes the bodywork of a vehicle when it has been specially made by specialist craftworkers

coaching /kṓching/ *n* training in how to deal with emotional problems and interpersonal relationships

coaching inn *n* a roadside inn, often with stables, that was formerly used by horsedrawn coach services to provide refreshments and accommodation for passengers and to change horses

coachman /kṓchmən/ (*plural* **-men** /-mən/) *n* the driver of a horsedrawn coach or carriage

coach station *n* a long-distance bus station

coachwood /kṓch wòod/ (*plural* **-woods** *or* **-wood**) *n* a medium-sized Australian tree with a straight trunk, small crown, and white flowers that provides a light versatile wood used in cabinetmaking. *Ceratopetalum apetalum.*

coachwork /kṓch wurk/ *n* the painted bodywork of a road vehicle or railway carriage

coaction /kō áksh'n/ *n* joint or reciprocal action [Early 17C. Via French < Latin *coaction-* < *coact-*, past participle of *coagere* 'drive together' < *agere* 'drive'.] —**coactive** *adj* —**coactively** *adv* —**coactivity** /kō ak tívvəti/ *n*

coadaptation /kṓ a dap táysh'n/ *n* the mutually advantageous development of characteristics in two or more species of organisms —**coadapted** *adj*

coadjutant /kō ájjətənt/ *n* a helper of another

coadjutor /kō ájjòotər/ *n* **1** a helper for somebody (*formal*) **2** a bishop who assists a diocesan bishop [15C. Via French < late Latin, 'helper with' < Latin *adjutor* 'helper' < *adjuvare* 'help'.]

coagula plural of **coagulum**

coagulant /kō ággyòolənt/ *n* a substance that coagulates blood —**coagulant** *adj*

coagulase /kō ággyòo layz, -layss/ *n* an enzyme produced by some bacteria that causes coagulation of the blood [Early 20C. < COAGULATE.]

coagulate /kō ággyòo layt/ *vti* (**-lates, -lating, -lated**) **1 MAKE OR BECOME SEMISOLID** to thicken, or cause liquid to thicken, into a soft semisolid mass **2 GROUP TOGETHER IN LARGER MASS** to group together as a mass, or cause the particles in a colloid to group together, as, e.g., egg white does when heated ■ *n* **COAGULATED MASS** a soft semisolid mass produced by coagulation of a colloid [15C. < Latin *coagulat-*, past participle of *coagulare* < *coagere* 'drive together'.] —**coagulability** /kō ággyòolə bíllәti/ *n* —**coagulable** *adj* —**coagulation** /kō ággyòo láysh'n/ *n* —**coagulator** *n*

coagulation factor *n* MED = **clotting factor**

coagulum /kō ággyōōləm/ (*plural* **-la** /-lə/) *n* a clot or coagulated mass of something, especially blood [Mid-16C. < Latin, < *coagere* 'drive together'.]

coal /kōl/ *n* **1 BLACK ROCK USED AS FUEL** a hard black or dark brown sedimentary rock formed by the decomposition of plant material, widely used as a fuel **2 PIECE OF COAL** a piece of coal **3 SMALL PIECE OF BURNABLE MATERIAL** any small piece of combustible material **4** CHEM = **charcoal** *n.* 1 ■ *v* **1** *vt* **CONVERT INTO CHARCOAL** to burn something combustible and convert it into charcoal **2** *vti* **PROVIDE OR TAKE ON COAL** to supply something with coal, or take on coal [Old English *col* < Indo-European, 'glowing ember'] —**coaly** *adj* ◇ **carry** *or* **take coals to Newcastle** to do something superfluous or supply something that is already plentiful ◇ **haul somebody over the coals** to reprimand somebody severely

coal black *adj* **1** completely black **2** very dark black in colour —**coal black** *n*

coaler /kōlər/ *n* a ship or train that transports coal

coalesce /kō ə léss/ (**-lesces, -lescing, -lesced**) *vti* to merge or cause things to merge into a single body or group [Mid-16C. < Latin *coalescere* 'grow up together' < *alescere* 'grow up' < *alere* 'nourish'.] —**coalescence** *n* —**coalescent** *adj*

coalface /kōl fayss/ *n* **1** the newly exposed rock surface in a mine, from which coal is being cut **2** the site of physical or practical work, as opposed to management or administration

coalfield /kōl feeld/ *n* an area with coal deposits

coalfish /kōl fish/ (*plural* **coalfish** *or* **coalfishes**) *n* a black-backed or dark-coloured edible fish, e.g. sablefish or pollack

coal gas *n* **1** a flammable mixture of gases obtained by distilling coal, consisting mainly of methane and hydrogen. Use: fuel. **2** the gas produced when coal is burned

coalification /kōlifi káysh'n/ *n* the process in which coal is formed by the action of pressure and heat on buried plant material

coalition /kō ə lísh'n/ *n* **1** a temporary union between two or more groups, especially political parties **2** the merging of things into one body or mass [Early 17C. < medieval Latin *coalition-* < Latin *coalit-*, past participle of *coalescere* (see COALESCE).] —**coalitionist** *n*

Coalition *n* in Australia, a long-standing political coalition between the Liberal Party and the National Party

coal measures *npl* a series of strata containing economically workable coal deposits, e.g. the upper Carboniferous rocks of NW Europe

coalmine /kōl mīn/ *n* a mine where coal is dug from the ground —**coalminer** *n*

coalminer's lung /kōl mīnərz lúng/ *n* MED = **anthracosis** [Because the disease frequently affects coalminers]

Coalport /kōl pawrt/ *n* a variety of white, strongly patterned bone china made in Coalport, near Shrewsbury, England, in the 19th century

Coalsack /kōl sak/ *n* **1** a dark cloud of interstellar dust (**nebula**), part of the Crux constellation and visible in the southern hemisphere in front of the Milky Way **2** a dark interstellar cloud (**nebula**) of the northern hemisphere near the constellation Cygnus

coal scuttle *n* a metal container for holding and pouring coal for a domestic fire

coal tar *n* a thick black liquid. Source: by-product in the production of coke. Use: in making dyes, drugs, and soap.

coal-tar pitch *n* a by-product of the distillation of coal tar. Use: making road surfaces, in carbon electrodes, in binding fuel briquettes

coal tit, coletit /kōltit/ *n* a small songbird belonging to the tit family, with a black-crowned head, white cheeks, and a white patch on the nape of the neck. Native to: Europe, Asia. *Parus ater.*

coaming /kōming/ *n* a raised edging round the cockpit or hatchway of a boat for keeping out water [Early 17C. < ?]

co-anchor /kō ángkər/ *n* US either of two broadcasters who jointly present a television programme ■ *vti* US to be co-anchor of a television programme, especially a news programme

coapt /kō ápt/ *v* to join or bring displaced parts close together in their correct alignment, e.g. the edges of a wound or broken bone [Late 16C. < late Latin *coaptare* 'fit together' < Latin *aptus* 'fastened, suitable'.] —**coaptation** /kō ap táysh'n/ *n*

coarctate /kō áark tayt/ *adj* **1 CONSTRICTED** describes any vessel or canal in the body that has become constricted, narrowed, or pressed together **2 IN HARD SHELL** describes a pupa that is enclosed in a horny oval case ■ *vi* (**-tates, -tating, -tated**) **CONSTRICT** to become narrow, constricted, or pressed together (*refers to blood vessels or other body passages*) [15C. < Latin *coar(c)tatus*, past participle of *coar(c)tare* 'press close together' < *artare* 'press close' < *artus* 'confined, narrow'.] —**coarctation** /kō aark táysh'n/ *n*

coarse /kawrss/ (**coarser, coarsest**) *adj* **1 ROUGH** harsh or rough to the touch **2 WITH THICK GRAINS OR STRANDS** consisting of large grains or thick strands **3 INDELICATE OR TASTELESS** lacking taste or refinement **4 VULGAR** vulgar or obscene **5 UNREFINED** not refined ○ *coarse metal* **6 INFERIOR** of inferior quality [14C. Originally *corse* 'ordinary' (used of cloth) < ?] —**coarsely** *adv* —**coarseness** *n*

SPELLCHECK Do not confuse *coarse* with *course*, which has a similar sound. Beware: your spellchecker will not catch this error.

---

coarse fish *n* any freshwater fish that does not belong to the salmon family

coarse fishing *n* the sport of fishing for coarse fish

coarse-grained *adj* **1** having a large or rough grain **2** coarse or vulgar in speech or manner

coarsen /káwrss'n/ *vti* to become or make something coarse or coarser

coast /kōst/ *n* **1 LAND NEXT TO SEA** land beside the sea ○ *sailed along the coast* **2** = **seaside** *n.* 3 US, Can **SLOPE FOR SLEDGING** a slope suitable for sledging ■ *v* **1** *vti* **MOVE BY MOMENTUM** to move forwards by momentum, without applying power, or cause something to move in this way **2** *vi* **SUCCEED EFFORTLESSLY** to progress with very little effort **3** *vti* **TRAVEL ALONG SHORE** to sail along a shore [14C. Via Old French *coste* < Latin *costa* 'rib, side'.] —**coastal** *adj* —**coastally** *adv* —**coastwards** *adv*

coaster /kōstər/ *n* **1 SHIP TRADING ALONG COAST** a ship that sails along a coast to trade **2 MAT FOR GLASS** a mat placed under a glass in order to protect a surface **3 TRAY FOR PASSING BOTTLE** a small tray, sometimes on wheels, for passing a bottle or decanter round a table **4 SOMETHING THAT COASTS** something that coasts of its own momentum

coastguard /kōst gaard/ *n* **1** an emergency service that rescues people in difficulties at sea and acts against smuggling **2** a member of the coastguard

Coast Guard *n* a US military service that enforces maritime laws, acts in marine emergencies, and maintains navigational aids, in wartime supplementing the navy

coastline /kōst līn/ *n* the outline of a coast as viewed from the sea or on a map

Coast Mountains /kōst-/ mountain range in W British Columbia, Canada. Highest peak: Mount Waddington, 3,994 m/13,104 ft.

Coast Ranges long narrow mountain ranges on the coast of W North America from S Alaska to NW Mexico. Highest peak: Mount Logan 5,959 m/19,551 ft.

coast-to-coast *adj* from one coast to another of a continent or a nation that is an island ○ *The debate had coast-to-coast coverage on the news media.*

coastwise /kōst wīz/ *adv* US along the coast ■ *adj* US following the direction of the coast

coat /kōt/ *n* **1 WARM OUTER GARMENT** an item of clothing with long sleeves that is usually at least knee-length and is worn outdoors over other clothes **2** US, NZ **SUIT JACKET** a jacket worn as part of a suit, with a skirt or trousers (*dated*) **3 COVERING ON ANIMAL** the fur, wool, or hair that covers an animal **4 THIN COVERING** any thin layer that covers something ■ *vt* **1 COVER SURFACE** to cover a surface with a thin layer of something (*often passive*) **2 PROVIDE SOMEBODY WITH COAT** to provide somebody with a coat (*usually passive*) [14C. < Old French *cote* < Germanic.] —**coater** *n*

Coatbridge /kōt brij/ town in south-central Scotland. Population: 43,617 (1991).

coat check *n* US = **cloakroom** *n.* 1

coat dress *n* a tailored dress that is shaped like a coat and fastened in front from the neck to the hem, usually with buttons

coated /kōtid/ *adj* **1 WITH OUTER LAYER** covered with a layer of something **2 PREPARED FOR WRITING OR PRINTING ON** treated with a fine layer of a mineral to make paper suitable for writing or printing on **3 TREATED AGAINST MOISTURE** with a treated surface or plastic coating that resists moisture ○ *coated fabric*

coatee /kōtee, kō tée/ *n* **1** a baby's knitted coat **2** a military cutaway coat with shortened coat-tails

Coates /kōts/, **Joseph Gordon** (1878–1943) New Zealand statesman

coat hanger *n* a curved frame with a hook, used to hang clothes

coati /kō áati/ (*plural* **-tis** *or* **-ti**), **coatimundi** /kō áati mŏŏndi/ (*plural* **-dis** *or* **-di**) *n* a South or Central American omnivorous mammal related to the raccoon, that has a narrow flexible snout and a striped tail. Genus: *Nasua.* [Early 17C. Via Portuguese < Tupi *kua'ti.*]

coating /kōting/ *n* **1** a thin layer that covers something ○ *a coating of dust* **2** cloth used to make coats

coat of arms *n* **1** a design on a shield that signifies a particular family, university, or city **2** a garment that is decorated with a coat of arms [Translation of French *cote d'armes*]

coat of mail *n* a protective garment of armour worn in medieval times, consisting of linked metal rings

coat-tail *n* the part below the waist at the back of a coat, especially one of the parts when it is divided into two (*usually plural*) ◇ **on somebody's coat-tails** helped by somebody else rather than succeeding alone

coauthor /kō áwthər/ *n* an author who writes something jointly with one or more other authors —**coauthor** *vt*

coax /kōks/ *v* **1** *vti* **PERSUADE GENTLY** to persuade somebody gently to do something **2** *vt* **OBTAIN BY GENTLE PERSUASION** to get something from somebody by gentle persuasion **3** *vt* **GENTLY MAKE SOMETHING WORK** to manipulate something patiently until it moves or works ○ *I finally coaxed the sticky drawers open.* [Late 16C. < obsolete *cokes* 'simpleton' < ?] —**coaxingly** *adv*

coax cable /kō aks-/ *n* ELEC = **coaxial cable** [Shortening]

coaxial /kō áksi əl/ *adj* **1** having a common axis **2** belonging or relating to a coaxial cable —**coaxially** *adv*

coaxial cable *n* a cable consisting of an inner core and outer flexible braided tube, both of conductive material separated by an insulator, used to transmit high-frequency signals at high speeds

cob[1] /kob/ *n* **1 CORE OF MAIZE EAR** the hard core to which individual kernels of maize are attached **2 ROUND BREAD** a rounded loaf of bread **3** FOOD = **cobnut** **4 MALE SWAN** a male swan **5 SHORT-LEGGED RIDING HORSE** a sturdy short-legged riding horse **6 SMALL PIECE** a small lump or mass of something hard, especially coal [15C. < ?]

cob[2] /kob/ *n* a building material consisting of clay, gravel, and straw [Early 17C. < ?]

cob[3] /kob/ *n* a crude often irregularly shaped gold or silver coin that circulated in Spanish colonies in the Americas between the 16th and 18th centuries [< Spanish *cabo de barra* 'end of bar'; from the coin-sized planchets sliced from cast bar]

cobalamin /kə bólləmin/ *n* PHARM = **vitamin B_{12}** [Mid-20C. Blend of COBALT + VITAMIN.]

cobalt /kō bawlt, -bolt/ *n* (*symbol* **Co**) a tough brittle silvery-white metallic element. Source: iron, nickel, copper ores. Use: colouring ceramics, alloys. [Late 17C. < German *Kobalt*, variant of *Kobold* 'harmful goblin'; from miners' belief that cobalt ore was harmful to neighbouring silver ores.]

cobalt 60 *n* a naturally radioactive isotope of cobalt with a mass number of 60, that spontaneously emits strong gamma radiation. Use: in radiotherapy and industry.

cobalt bloom *n* MINERALS = **erythrite** [Translation of German *Kobaltblüte*]

cobalt blue *adj* of a deep greenish-blue colour —**cobalt blue** *n*

cobalt bomb *n* a device containing cobalt 60, used in radiotherapy

cobaltic /kō báwltik, -ból-/ *adj* relating to or containing cobalt, especially with a valency of 3

cobaltite /kō báwl tīt, -ból-/ *n* a rare silvery-white or greyish mineral consisting of cobalt sulphide and arsenide. Use: ceramics.

cobaltous /kō báwltəs, -ból-/ *adj* relating to or containing cobalt, especially with a valency of 2

cobber /kóbbər/ *n ANZ* a friend or companion (*dated informal*) [Late 19C. < ?]

Cobbett /kóbbit/, **William** (1763–1835) British writer, journalist, and reformer

cobble[1] /kóbb'l/ *n* **1** TRANSP = **cobblestone 2** a naturally rounded rock fragment between 64 and 256 mm/2.5 and 10 in in diameter ■ *vt* (**cobbles, cobbling, cobbled**) to pave a road with cobblestones [Early 17C. Shortening of COBBLESTONE.] —**cobbled** *adj*

cobble[2] /kóbb'l/ (**cobbles, cobbling, cobbled**) *vt* to make, mend, or patch footwear [15C. Back-formation < COBBLER[1].] **cobble together** *vt* to assemble or make something roughly and quickly

cobbler[1] /kóbblər/ *n* a maker or mender of footwear [13C. < ?]

cobbler[2] /kóbblər/ *n* **1** a baked fruit dessert with a soft thick crust **2** an iced drink made of wine, rum or whisky, and sugar [Early 19C. Probably < COBBLER[1].]

cobblers /kóbblərz/ *n* an offensive term referring to something perceived as nonsense (*slang*) ■ *npl* an offensive term for the testicles (*slang*) [Mid-20C. Shortening of *cobbler's awls*, rhyming slang for *balls* 'testicles'.]

cobbler's wax *n* a resin used to wax thread

cobblestone /kóbb'l stōn/ *n* a small rounded stone used for paving streets [15C. < COB[1].] —**cobblestoned** *adj*

Cobden /kóbdən/, **Richard** (1804–65) British economist and politician

cobelligerent /kō bə líjjərənt/ *n* a country that or individual who is an ally in a fight or war

cobia /kṓbi ə/ (*plural* **cobia** *or* **cobias**) *n* a large bony dark-striped fish that is related to the perch and sea bass. Native to: tropical and subtropical seas. *Rachycentron canadum*. [Mid-19C. < ?]

coble /kṓb'l/ *n Scotland, N England* a small flat-bottomed boat for fishing, usually used near a coast or in an estuary [Pre-12C. Probably < Celtic.]

cobnut /kób nut/ (*plural* **cobnuts**) *n* a variety of hazelnut [Mid-16C. Alteration of *cobill nut* < COB[1].]

COBOL /kṓ bol/, **Cobol** *n* a high-level computer programming language, widely adopted for corporate business applications [Mid-20C. Acronym < *common business-oriented language*.]

cobra /kṓbrə/ *n* a venomous snake that, when excited, rears up and spreads the skin behind its head to form a hood. Native to: tropical Asia and Africa. Genera: *Naja* and *Ophiophagus*. [Early 19C. Shortening of *cobra de capello* 'snake with a hood' < Portugese; *cobra* < Latin *cubra* 'snake'.]

coburg /kṓburg/ *n* **1** a thin fabric made of wool and cotton or silk, twilled on one surface. Use: dress fabric, lining cloth. **2** a round loaf with a cross cut on the top of the dough before baking [Early 19C. After Prince ALBERT of Saxe-*Coburg*.]

Coburg /kṓ burg/ city in SE Germany. Population: 43,928 (1997).

cobweb /kób web/ *n* **1** DUSTY SPIDER'S WEB a fine thread or web of fine threads spun by spiders, especially when covered with dust **2** SOMETHING RESEMBLING COBWEB something that resembles a cobweb in being flimsy and insubstantial or in acting as a trap or snare ■ **cobwebs** *npl* SLUGGISH MENTAL STATE mental sluggishness and tiredness ○ *I need to blow the cobwebs away.* [14C. *Cob* < obsolete *coppe* 'spider' < Old English *ātorcoppe*, probably 'poison-head'; from the idea that spiders are venomous.] —**cobwebbed** *adj* —**cobwebby** *adj*

coca /kṓkə/ (*plural* **-ca**) *n* **1** the dried leaves of an Andean bush. Use: chewed as a stimulant, processed for cocaine and other alkaloids. **2** a bush whose leaves yield coca. Native to: the Andes. *Erythroxylum coca*. [Late 16C. Via Spanish < Aymara *kuka* or Quechua *koka*.]

cocaine /kō káyn/ *n* $C_{17}H_{21}NO_4$ an addictive narcotic drug obtained from the leaves of the coca plant, taken illegally as a stimulant [Mid-19C. < COCA.]

cocainize /kō káy nīz/ (**-izes, -izing, -ized**), **cocainise** (**-ises, -ising, -ised**) *vt* to anaesthetize somebody using cocaine as a surface (**topical**) application in paste form in the nose —**cocainization** /kō kay nī záysh'n/ *n*

cocarcinogen /kṓ kaar sínnəjən, kō kaársin-/ *n* a substance that does not cause cancer on its own but can increase the effect of carcinogenic factors or substances when acting together with them —**cocarcinogenic** /kō kaárssinə jénnik/ *adj*

cocci plural of **coccus**

coccidia plural of **coccidium**

coccidioidomycosis /kok síddi óydōmī kṓssiss/ *n* a respiratory disease of humans and domestic animals in North America, marked by flu-like symptoms, that is caused by inhalation of spores from the fungus *Coccidioides immitis*.

coccidiosis /kok síddi ṓssiss/ *n* a disease of domestic animals and birds, and occasionally humans, caused by coccidia in the intestines, and causing diarrhoea

coccidium /kok síddi əm/ (*plural* **-a** /-ə/) *n* a parasitic sporozoan that can cause disease in the gut of humans and animals. Order: Coccidia. [Mid-19C. < modern Latin, < Greek *kokkid-* 'little berry' < *kokkos* 'berry'.] —**coccidial** *adj*

coccolith /kókə lith/ *n* a microscopic calcareous platelet that forms the covering for some marine plankton, one form of which makes up chalk deposits [Mid-19C. < modern Latin *Coccolithus* < Greek *kokkos* 'grain' + *lithos* 'stone'.]

coccus /kókəss/ (*plural* **-ci** /kóksī/) *n* **1** a spherical or nearly spherical microorganism, especially a bacterium **2** a subdivision of a fruit that contains a single seed and resembles a berry [Early 19C. Via modern Latin < Greek *kokkos* 'grain, berry'.] —**coccal** *adj* —**coccoid** *adj* —**coccous** *adj*

-coccus *suffix* a spherical microorganism ○ *pneumococcus* [< COCCUS]

coccyx /kók siks/ (*plural* **-cyges** /kok sī jeez/ *or* **-cyxes**) *n* a small triangular bone at the base of the spinal column [Late 16C. Via Latin < Greek *kokkux* 'cuckoo'; from its resemblance to a cuckoo's beak.] —**coccygeal** /kok síjji əl/ *adj*

Cochabamba /kóchə bámbə/ capital of Cochabamba Department, central Bolivia. Population: 448,756 (1993 estimate).

co-channel /kō chán'l/ *adj* relating to a transmission occupying the same frequency band as another

Cochin /kṓ chin/ major port in Kerala State, SW India. Population: 564,589 (1991).

cochineal /kóchi neél/ *n* a red dye obtained from the crushed dried bodies of female cochineal insects. Use: food colouring, fabric dye. [Late 16C. Via French *cochenille* or Spanish *cochinilla* < Latin *coccinus* 'scarlet' < Greek *kokkos* 'berry', because the dried body of the insect was believed to be a berry.]

cochineal insect *n* a small red scale insect that feeds on cacti. Native to: Mexico, Caribbean. *Coccus cacti*.

cochlea /kókli ə/ (*plural* **-ae** /-ī, -ee/ *or* **-as**) *n* a spiral structure in the inner ear that looks like a snail shell and contains over 10,000 tiny hair cells that move in response to sound waves [Mid-16C. Via Latin *coc(h)lea* 'snail shell, screw' < Greek *kokhlias*.] —**cochlear** *adj* —**cochleate** /-li ət, -ayt/ *adj*

cochlear implant *n* a device implanted under the skin that picks up sounds and converts them to impulses transmitted to electrodes placed in the cochlea, restoring some hearing to people with a hearing impairment

Cochran /kókrən/, **Jacqueline** (1910–80) US aviator

cock /kok/ *n* **1** ADULT MALE CHICKEN an adult male of a domestic fowl, normally only kept for breeding **2** MALE BIRD the adult male of a bird **3** MALE ANIMAL an adult male salmon, crab, or lobster **4** PART OF GUN the hammer of a gun that, when released by the action of the trigger, makes the gun fire **5** RAISED POSITION OF HAMMER OF GUN the raised position of the hammer of a gun when it is ready to fire **6** TABOO TERM a highly offensive term for a man's penis (*taboo*) **7** STOPCOCK a stopcock **8** WEATHERCOCK a weathercock **9** TILTED POSITION the tilt or angle in the position of somebody's head or hat, often suggesting that he or she is in a good mood **10** CHUM OR MATE used as a friendly or familiar way of addressing a man, especially among Cockneys (*dated informal regional*) **11** NONSENSE something somebody has said or written that you consider to be nonsense (*dated informal*) ■ *vt* **1** PREPARE GUN FOR FIRING to pull back the hammer of a gun so that it is ready to be fired when the trigger is pulled **2** TURN EARS OR EYES to turn one or both ears or eyes in a particular direction to listen for or look out for somebody or something **3** TILT BACK OR ANGLE to tilt or raise something, often as a way of expressing that you are full of confidence or in good humour **4** RAISE LIMB IN AIR to lift or raise a part of the body **5** SET SOMETHING TO OPERATE to set a device or mechanism so that it will release something, e.g. a camera shutter [Pre-12C. Probably < medieval Latin *coccus*, an imitation of a cock's crow.]

cockade /ko káyd/ *n* a rosette, ribbon, or other ornament worn, usually on a hat, as an identifying badge or as part of a livery [Mid-17C. < French *bonnet à la coquarde* 'bonnet worn proudly' < obsolete *coquard* 'proud' < *coq* 'cock'.] —**cockaded** *adj*

cock-a-doodle-doo /kók ə dood'l dóo/ *n, interj* used as a description or imitation of the sound a cock makes when it crows —**cock-a-doodle-doo** *vi*

cock-a-hoop *adj* **1** extremely happy or excited about something **2** boastful about something that has been achieved [< *set the cock on the hoop* 'celebrate']

cock-a-leekie /kók ə leéki/, **cockieleekie** *n* a Scottish soup made from a whole chicken and leeks and sometimes containing prunes

cockamamie /kókə máymi/, **cockamamy** *adj US* having little or nothing to do with reality (*informal*) ○ *a cockamamie excuse* [Mid-20C. Probably alteration of DECALCOMANIA.]

cock-and-bull story, cock-and-bull *n* a ridiculous and scarcely credible story that somebody tries to convince people is true, usually either to impress them or as an excuse for something [< ?]

cockatiel /kókə teél/, **cockateel** *n* a small grey parrot with a white patch on its wing and a prominent crest that is yellow in males. Native to: Australia. *Nymphicus hollandicus*. [Late 19C. < Dutch *kaktielje*, probably diminutive of *kaketoe* (see COCKATOO).]

cockatoo /kókə tóo/ (*plural* **-toos**) *n* **1** a parrot with a prominent crest, many of which have white or light-coloured plumage. Native to: Australia, New Guinea, South and Southeast Asia, Philippines. Genera: *Cacatua* and *Callocephalon* and *Calyptorhynchus*. **2** *Aus* a farmer who owns a small piece of land [Mid-17C. Via Dutch *kaketoe* < Malay *kakatua*; influenced by COCK.]

cockatrice /kókə triss/ *n* a mythological serpent that was supposed to have hatched from a cock's egg, and to be able to kill with its stare [14C. Via Old French *cocatris* < medieval Latin *calcatrix* 'tracker' < Latin *calcare* 'track' < *calx* 'heel'.]

cockboat /kók bōt/ *n* a small rowing boat, especially one that belongs to a larger ship [15C. *Cock* via Old French *coque* < Latin *codex* 'block of wood'.]

cockchafer /kók chayfər/ *n* a large European beetle with larvae that destroy trees and other plants. Family: Scarabaeidae.

cockcrow /kók krō/ *n* the time of day when the sun begins to show above the horizon (*archaic or literary*)

cocked hat *n* a two- or three-cornered hat with a wide turned up brim, popular in the 18th century ◇ **knock somebody *or* something into a cocked hat** to be much better than somebody or something else (*informal*)

cocker[1] /kókər/ *n* **1** ZOOL = **cocker spaniel 2** somebody involved in cockfighting either as a breeder or trainer of cocks, or as a regular spectator

cocker[2] /kókər/ *vt* to treat somebody in an over-protective or indulgent way ■ *n* used to refer to a close friend (*informal*) [15C. < ?]

cockerel /kókərəl/ *n* a young male chicken, usually one that is less than a year old [15C. Literally 'small cock' < COCK.]

Cockerell /kókərəl/, **Sir Christopher** (1910–99) British radio and marine engineer

cocker spaniel *n* a small dog with long floppy ears and a soft wavy coat, belonging to a breed of spaniel originally bred for flushing out game [< WOODCOCK]

cockeye /kók ī/ *n* an offensive term for an eye that is turned inwards or outwards from the nose, making parallel vision impossible

cockeyed /kók īd/ *adj* **1** FOOLISH not sensible or properly thought out (*informal*) **2** NOT ALIGNED positioned at an awkward or crooked angle **3** OFFENSIVE TERM an offensive term meaning having one eye that turns inwards or outwards from the nose **4** VERY DRUNK so drunk that it is impossible to see straight (*informal*)

cock feather *n* the feather on an arrow positioned at right-angles to the notch into which the bow string fits [< COCK 'stick up']

cockfight /kók fìt/ *n* an organized fight between two cocks, each of which is fitted with sharp metal spurs

cockfighting /kók fìting/ *n* the practice of setting two cocks to fight each other in front of spectators who often make bets on the outcome

cockhorse /kók hawrss/ *n* a rocking horse or a stick with an imitation horse's head on one end

cockieleekie *n* FOOD = **cock-a-leekie**

cockle[1] /kók'l/ *n* **1 MOLLUSC WITH HEART-SHAPED SHELL** a small mollusc with a rounded or heart-shaped ridged shell in two parts. Family: Cardiidae. **2** MARINE BIOL = **cockleshell** *n.* 1 **3** NAUT = **cockleshell** *n.* 2 **4 WRINKLE** a crease or pucker in a piece of material such as paper or cloth ■ *vti* (**-les, -ling, -led**) **BECOME OR MAKE WRINKLED** to become wrinkled or puckered, or make something such as a piece of material wrinkled or puckered [14C. Via French *coquille* 'shell' < Greek *kogkhē* 'conch'.] ◇ **warm the cockles of your heart** to give you a feeling of wellbeing or sentimental contentment

cockle[2] /kók'l/ *n* a weedy plant that belongs to the pink family, especially the corn cockle, which grows in cornfields [Pre-12C. < ?]

cockleboat /kók'l bōt/ *n* NAUT = **cockboat** [Early 17C. *Cockle* < COCKLE[1].]

cocklebur /kók'l bur/ *n* a coarse annual plant with prickly seed husks that attach easily to people's clothes or animals' fur. Genus: *Xanthium*. [Mid-19C. *Cockle* < COCKLE[2].]

cockleshell /kók'l shel/ *n* **1** a shell of a marine cockle, or any similar mollusc **2** a small, light shallow boat

cockloft /kók loft/ *n* a small room beneath the roof of a building

cockney /kókni/ (*plural* **-neys**) *n* **1 cockney, Cockney SOMEBODY FROM LONDON'S EAST END** somebody born in London, traditionally within a two-mile radius of the bells of St Mary-le-Bow church in London's East End **2 cockney, Cockney LONDON DIALECT** the accent or dialect of native Londoners from the East End **3** *Aus* **YOUNG AUSTRALIAN SNAPPER** a young Australian snapper. *Chrysophrys guttulatus*. [14C. < *coken*, genitive plural of *cok* 'cock' + obsolete *ey* 'egg' < Old English *ǣg*.] —**cockneyism** *n*

cock-of-the-rock (*plural* **cocks-of-the-rock**) *n* a bird, the males of which have bright orange or red plumage and crests that extend over the bill. Native to: tropical South America. Genus: *Rupicola*. [Because it nests on rocks]

cockpit /kók pit/ *n* **1 PILOT'S PART OF AIRCRAFT** the compartment in an aircraft or spacecraft where the pilot and other crew members sit **2 AREA FOR DRIVER IN RACING CAR** a space for the driver in a racing car **3 PLACE FOR COCKFIGHTING** an enclosed place where cockfights are held **4 ENCLOSURE FOR WHEEL OR TILLER** an enclosure at the stern of a ship for the wheel or tiller **5 FREQUENT BATTLEGROUND** a place where many battles have been fought

cockroach /kók rōch/ *n* a nocturnal insect with a flat oval body, long antennae, and chewing mouthparts, some species of which are household pests. Order: Blattodea. [Early 17C. By folk etymology < Spanish *cucaracha*.]

cockscomb /kóks kōm/ *n* **1** the red fleshy crest that grows on the top of a domestic cock's head **2** a tropical plant often grown as a houseplant. Flowers: orange or red, appearing as a broad crest or plume resembling a cockscomb. *Celosia cristata*. **3** = **coxcomb** *n.* 1

cockshy /kók shì/ (*plural* **-shies**) *n* (*dated*) **1** a target or mark for throwing things in a contest **2** a throw at a cockshy [Early 19C. Because a cock was formerly the target and prize.]

cockspur /kók spur/ *n* a spur on the foot of some male birds

cocksucker /kóksukər/ *n US* (*taboo offensive insult*) **1** a highly offensive term of abuse for a man **2** a highly offensive term for somebody who performs fellatio

cocksure /kok shóor, -sháwr/ *adj* arrogantly confident and self-assured [Early 16C. < *cock*, euphemism for 'God'.] —**cocksurely** *adv* —**cocksureness** *n*

cockswain *n* = **coxswain**

cocktail /kók tayl/ *n* **1 MIXED BEVERAGE** a drink that is made up of a mixture of different beverages, e.g. fruit juice or soda and usually alcohol, and served iced or chilled **2 LIGHT SNACK** a light appetizer before a main meal, consisting usually of seafood or fruit served with a sauce (*usually in combination*) ○ *a prawn cocktail* **3 MIXTURE OF THINGS** a mixture of different things or elements combined together ○ *a malicious cocktail of lies and gossip* **4 COMBINATION TREATMENT** a combination of two or more drugs or therapeutic agents given as a single treatment ■ **cocktails** *npl* **GATHERING TO CONSUME ALCOHOLIC BEVERAGES** a gathering where alcoholic beverages are consumed, sometimes with light snacks, often taking place early in the evening before another planned event ■ *adj* **SMALL** extra small, designed to be eaten as a snack with the fingers or on a cocktail stick ○ *cocktail sausage* [Early 17C. < COCK.]

cocktail lounge *n* a bar, sometimes a room in a large hotel, where cocktails and other drinks are served

cocktail party *n* a party where cocktails and light snacks are served, often taking place early in the evening before another social event

cocktail stick *n* a small pointed wooden or plastic stick on which olives or cherries are placed in cocktails, or small items of food, e.g. sausages or cubes of cheese, are served

cock-teaser, cock-tease *n* a highly offensive term for somebody who makes sexual advances towards a man without intending to have sex with him (*taboo*)

cockup /kók up/ *n* a blunder, or an instance of mismanagement (*informal*) [Mid-20C. < COCK.]

cocky /kóki/ (**-ier, -iest**) *adj* confident and sure of yourself to the point of being arrogant (*informal*) [Mid-16C. < COCK.] —**cockily** *adv* —**cockiness** *n*

coco /kókō/ (*plural* **-cos**) *n* PLANTS, FOOD = **coconut** [Mid-16C. < Spanish, Portuguese, 'grinning face' (from the appearance of the base of the shell).]

cocoa /kókō/ *n* **1 CHOCOLATE BASE** an unsweetened brown powder made from roasted and ground cocoa beans. Use: making chocolate, cooking, hot drink. **2 HOT DRINK MADE WITH COCOA POWDER** a hot drink made with milk or water, cocoa powder, and sugar **3 LIGHT TO MEDIUM BROWN COLOUR** a light to medium brown colour [Early 18C. Alteration of CACAO.]

cocoa bean *n* the bean-shaped seed of the cacao tree, used to make cocoa powder and chocolate

cocoa butter *n* a thick oily solid obtained from cocoa beans and used in making chocolate, cosmetics, and suntan oils

coco-de-mer /kókō də máir/ (*plural* **cocos-de-mer** /kókō də máir/) *n* **1** a fan palm, now found only in nature reserves in the Seychelles, that produces the largest seed in the world. *Lodoicea maldivica*. **2** an edible two-lobed fruit of a coco-de-mer palm [Early 19C. < French, 'coco from the sea' (because it was first known from nuts found floating in the sea).]

coconut /kókə nut/ (*plural* **-nut** *or* **-nuts**) *n* **1** the fruit of the coconut palm, consisting of a hard fibrous husk around a single-seeded nut with firm white flesh that is eaten raw or dried to make copra, and a hollow core containing sweet-tasting liquid (**coconut milk**). Use: husk: matting, compost. **2** the sweet white flesh of the coconut fruit, used widely in cooking and confectionery in the form of small dried flakes **3** TREES = **coconut palm**

coconut butter *n* solidified coconut oil used in the manufacture of soap and candles

coconut crab *n* a large hermit crab that burrows in the ground and can climb trees. Native to: islands of Pacific and Indian Oceans. *Birgus latro*.

coconut matting *n* coarse floor matting made from the fibres that grow on coconut shells

coconut milk *n* the sweet watery juice that is contained within a coconut and is used in drinks and cookery

coconut oil *n* a thick sweet-smelling oil extracted from the flesh of the coconut and used widely in food and cosmetics

coconut palm *n* a tall tropical palm tree with large fruits. Use: beverages, oil, fibre, utensils, thatch. *Cocos nucifera*.

cocoon /kə kóon/ *n* **1 SHEATH FOR CATERPILLAR** the silky covering with which a caterpillar or other insect larva encloses itself during its transition to an adult state **2 EGG COVERING** a protective covering on the eggs of spiders, leeches, and other invertebrates **3 SHEATH FOR SPIDER'S PREY** a sheath in which spiders wrap their prey **4 COVERING THAT PROTECTS SOMETHING FROM WATER** a cover or protective spray used to seal machinery and make it waterproof, especially military equipment for storage or transport **5 SOMETHING SIMILAR TO COCOON** something that resembles a cocoon in the way that it provides protection or a sense of safety ■ *v* **1** *vt* **WRAP SOMETHING OR SOMEBODY SAFELY** to cover or envelop something or somebody for warmth or protection ○ *cocooned in a pile of bedclothes* **2** *vt* **KEEP SAFE FROM** to protect somebody from unpleasantness or danger **3** *vi US* **WITHDRAW INTO PRIVACY** to withdraw into a state of personal privacy in order to escape stressful everyday life (*informal*) [Late 17C. Via French *cocon* < Latin *coccus* 'berry' < Greek *kokkos*.] —**cocooned** *adj*

coco plum *n* a tropical tree, cultivated for its edible fruit that is usually eaten preserved and, in West Africa, for an oil obtained from its seeds. Native to: tropical America and Africa. *Chrysobalanus icaco*.

Cocos Islands /kókəss-/ dependency of Australia consisting of 27 small islands in the E Indian Ocean. Population: 655 (1996). Area: 14.2 sq. km/5.5 sq. mi.

cocotte /kə kót/ *n* **1** a promiscuous woman or prostitute (*literary*) **2** a heatproof dish in which food can be cooked and served in small portions [Early 20C. Via French *cocasse* < Latin *cucuma* 'cooking-pot'.]

co-counselling *n* a form of counselling in which participants receive training as counsellors and work alternately as counsellor and client

cocoyam /kókō yam/ (*plural* **-yam** *or* **-yams**) *n* a plant with edible tubers. Native to: W Africa. Genus: *Colocasia*. [Early 20C. Probably < coco 'tarot root' (in Caribbean English).]

Cocteau /kóktō/, **Jean** (1889–1963) French writer and film director

cocurricular /kókə ríkyóolər/ *adj US* not forming part of the official curriculum but complementing it

cocuswood /kókəss wòod/ (*plural* **-wood**) *n* **1** hard wood that turns black with age. Use: musical instruments, backs of brushes, and inlays. **2** a tree that yields cocuswood. Native to: Caribbean. *Brya ebenus*. [Mid-17C. < ?]

Cocytus /kō kítəss, -sítəss/ *n* in Greek mythology, one of the tributaries of the river Styx that flowed through the underworld [< Greek *Kōkutos* 'wailing']

cod[1] /kod/ (*plural* **cod** *or* **cods**) *n* **1 MARINE FOOD FISH** a saltwater fish that has three dorsal fins and slender feelers like whiskers (**barbels**) on its jaw and lives close to the seabed. Family: Gadidae. **2 COD AS FOOD** the flesh of a cod used as food **3** *ANZ* **AUSTRALIAN FISH** a fish found in fresh and salt water, including Murray cod (*Maccullochella peeli*) and estuary rock cod (*Epinephelus tauvina*). Native to: Australia. [14C. < ?]

cod[2] /kod/ *n* (*archaic*) **1** a bag **2** a sac of skin that contains the testes of male mammals [Old English *cod(d)* < Germanic]

cod[3] /kod/ *n Ireland* a mildly unintelligent or silly person ■ *vti* (**cods, codding, codded**) *Ireland* to fool around or play a trick on somebody [Late 17C. < ?]

Cod, Cape /kód/ peninsula in SE Massachusetts

COD *abbr* cash on delivery

coda /kódə/ *n* **1** in some pieces of music, a final section that adds dramatic energy to the work as a whole, usually through intensified rhythmic activity **2** an additional section at the end of a text, e.g. a literary work or speech, that is not necessary to its structure but gives additional information [Mid-18C. Via Italian < Latin *cauda* 'tail'.]

coddle /kódd'l/ (**-dles, -dling, -dled**) *vt* **1** to treat somebody in an overprotective and indulgent way **2** to cook an egg in water just below the boiling point [Late 16C. < ?] —**coddler** *n*

ϟ **code** /kōd/ *n* **1 SYSTEM OF LETTERS, NUMBERS, OR SYMBOLS** a system of letters, numbers, or symbols into which normal language is converted to allow information to be communicated secretly, briefly, or electronically **2 INFORMATION SYSTEM OF LETTERS OR NUMBERS** a system of letters or numbers that gives information about something, e.g. postal or telephone areas **3 COMPUTER INFORMATION** a system of symbols, numbers, or signals that conveys information to a computer **4 RULES AND REGULATIONS** a system of accepted laws and regulations that govern procedure or behaviour in particular circumstances or within a particular profession **5 WAY OF BEHAVING** a set of unwritten rules concerning acceptable standards of behaviour ■ *v* (**codes, coding, coded**) **1** *vt* **PUT SOMETHING IN CODE** to put a message or text into code **2** *vi* **PROVIDE**

GENETIC INFORMATION to act as or provide the genetic information that enables a polypeptide, RNA molecule, or one of their constituent groups to be produced (*refers to codons or genes*) **3** *vt* **WRITE COMPUTER PROGRAM** to write a computer program that provides instructions to a computer [Late 16C. < Latin *codex* 'block of wood, book, set of statutes'.] **—coder** *n*

codebook /kódbŏŏk/ *n* a book containing a key to a code or codes

codeine /kô deen/ *n* C₁₈H₂₁NO₃ an opiate drug. Use: to relieve pain and coughing. [Mid-19C. < Greek *kōdeia* 'poppy head'.]

code name *n* a name used to disguise the identity or nature of somebody or something, e.g. a military operation **—code-name** *vt*

code of conduct *n* a set of unwritten rules according to which people in a particular group, class, or situation are supposed to behave

code of practice *n* a set of rules according to which people of a particular profession are expected to behave

codependency /kódi péndǝnsi/, **codependence** /kódi péndǝnss/ *n* **1** the dependence of two people, groups, or organisms on each other, especially when this reinforces mutually harmful behaviour patterns **2** a situation in which one person feels a need to be needed by another person, e.g. the partner of an alcoholic or a parent of a drug-addicted child **—codependent** *n*, *adj*

codetermination /kódi túrmi náysh'n/ *n* cooperation between management and employees in making decisions

code word *n* **1** a secret word or phrase that is used to identify a person, operation, or organization whose true identity is to be kept hidden, or is used as a password in a secret operation **2** a word or phrase used to describe something in a euphemistic way ○ *corporate reengineering is often just a code word for layoffs*

codex /kô deks/ (*plural* **-dices** /-di seez/) *n* a collection of ancient manuscript texts, especially of the Scriptures, in book form [Late 16C. < Latin (see CODE).]

Codex Juris Canonici /kô deks jŏŏriss kǝ nónni sī/ *n* the official body of canon law of the Roman Catholic Church since 1918, when it replaced the Corpus Juris Canonici [< ecclesiastical Latin, 'Code of Canon Law']

codfish /kódfish/ (*plural* **-fish** *or* **-fishes**) *n* ZOOL = **cod**[1] *n*. 1

codger /kójjǝr/ *n* a man, especially a man of advanced years who is seen as slightly eccentric or amusing (*informal*) [Mid-18C. < ?]

codices plural of **codex**

codicil /kódissil/ *n* **1** an additional part of a will that either modifies it or revokes part of it **2** an appendix or supplement to a text [15C. < Latin *codicillus*, diminutive of *codex* (see CODE).] **—codicillary** /kódi síllǝri/ *adj*

codicology /kódi kóllǝji/ *n* the study of manuscripts [Mid-20C. < French *codicologie* < Latin *codic-* 'book'.] **—codicological** /kódikǝ lójjik'l/ *adj*

codify /kódi fī/ (**-fies**, **-fying**, **-fied**) *vt* to arrange things, especially laws, rules, or principles, into an organized system or code **—codification** /kódifi káysh'n/ *n* **—codifier** *n*

codling /kódling/ (*plural* **-lings** *or* **-ling**) *n* a small or young cod

codling moth, **codlin moth** *n* a small stout-bodied moth whose larvae feed on apples, pears, and other fruit. *Laspeyresia pomonella*.

cod-liver oil *n* an oil rich in vitamins A and D that is extracted from the liver of the cod and is often used as a food supplement

codominant /kō dómminǝnt/ *adj* **1** describes genes that each have equal effect in making the character they control appear in offspring **2** determining the kinds of species that exist in an ecological community **—codominance** *n*

codon /kô don/ *n* a unit in messenger RNA consisting of a set of three consecutive nucleotides, which specifies a particular amino acid in protein synthesis [Mid-20C. < CODE + -ON[1].]

codpiece /kód peess/ *n* a decorative pouch attached to the crotch of breeches or hose worn by men in the 15th and 16th centuries [15C. *Cod* < COD[2].]

co-driver *n* a motorist who shares the driving of a motor vehicle

codswallop /kódz wolǝp/ *n*, *interj* nonsense (*informal*) [Mid-20C. < ?]

Coe /kô/, **Sebastian** (*b*. 1956) British athlete and politician

co-ed *n* **1** **SCHOOL FOR BOTH SEXES** a school where boys and girls are educated together (*informal*) **2** US **WOMAN AT MIXED COLLEGE** a woman student who attends a college or university where men and women are educated together (*dated*) ■ *adj* **EDUCATING MEN AND WOMEN TOGETHER** with both male and female students (*informal*) [Late 19C. Shortening of COEDUCATIONAL.]

co-edition *n* a book published by two or more publishers jointly

coeducation /kô eddyŏŏ káysh'n/ *n* the education of both sexes together **—coeducational** *adj* **—coeducationally** *adv*

coef. /kô if/ *abbr* coefficient

coefficient /kô i fish'nt/ *n* **1** the number placed before a letter that represents a variable in algebra, e.g. the '3' of '3x' in the equation '3x = 6' **2** a constant that is a measure of a property of a substance [Mid-17C. < modern Latin *coefficient-* 'combining to produce a result' < Latin *efficient-* (see EFFICIENT).]

coefficient of correlation *n* = **correlation coefficient**

coefficient of expansion *n* the change in length or area of a material per unit length or unit area that accompanies a change in temperature of one degree

coefficient of friction *n* (*symbol* μ) the ratio of the force needed to make two surfaces slide over each other to the force that holds them together

-coel *suffix* cavity, chamber ○ *pseudocoel* [Via modern Latin *-coela* < Greek *koilos* 'hollow' < Indo-European]

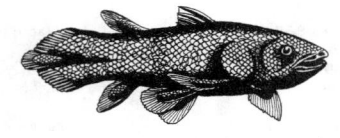

Coelacanth

coelacanth /seélǝ kanth/ *n* a fish that crawls on the sea bottom using its fins to move, formerly thought to be extinct. *Latimeria chalumnae*. [Mid-19C. < modern Latin *Coelacanthus* < Greek *koilos* 'hollow' + *akantha* 'spine' (because its fins have hollow spines).] **—coelacanthine** /seélǝ kán thin/ *adj* **—coelacanthous** *adj*

-coele *suffix* = **-coel**

coelenterate /si léntǝ rayt/ *n* a cnidarian [Late 19C. < modern Latin *Coelenterata* < Greek *koilos* 'hollow' + *enteron* 'intestine'.] **—coelenteric** /seé len térrik/ *adj*

coeliac /seéli ak/ *adj* relating to, involving, or contained in the abdomen [Mid-17C. Via Latin < Greek *koiliakos* < *koilia* 'abdomen' < *koilos* 'hollow'.]

coeliac disease *n* a disorder caused by a sensitivity to gluten that makes the digestive system unable to deal with fat. Symptoms include diarrhoea and anaemia.

coelom /seélǝm, -lōm/ (*plural* **-loms** *or* **-lomata** /si lōmǝtǝ/) *n* the cavity between the body wall and the gut of many animals, formed when the embryonic mesoderm is divided into two layers [Late 19C. Via German *Koelom* < Greek *koilōma* 'a hollow'.] **—coelomic** /si lómmik/ *adj*

coelomate /seélǝ mayt/, si lómit/ *adj* having a cavity between the body wall and the digestive tract **—coelomate** *n*

coelostat /seélǝ stat/ *n* an instrument with a mirror that rotates parallel to the Earth's axis in order to reflect light from a celestial body onto a second mirror aimed at a fixed telescope [Late 19C. < Latin *caelum* 'sky'.]

coemption /kō émpsh'n/ *n* the purchase of all available

supplies of a particular commodity [14C. < Latin *coemption-* 'buying up' < *emere* 'take, buy'.]

Coen /kŏŏn/, **Jan Pieterszoon** (1587–1629) Dutch colonial administrator

coen- *prefix* = **coeno-** (*before vowels*)

coeno- *prefix* general, common ○ *coenocyte* [< Greek *koinos* < Indo-European, 'together']

coenobite /seénō bīt/, **cenobite** *n* a member of a religious community [15C. < French *cénobite* or ecclesiastical Latin *coenobita* < Greek *koinobion* 'common life'.]

coenocyte /seénō sīt/ *n* a cell, part, or organism that contains many nuclei not separated by cell walls, e.g. the threads (**hyphae**) of many fungi or the bodies of some algae **—coenocytic** /seénō síttik/ *adj*

coenosarc /seénō ssaark/ *n* material linking the stems of individuals within a colony of polyps and containing a highly branched canal system with digestive and circulatory functions [Mid-19C. < COENO- + Greek *sark-* 'flesh'.]

coenzyme /kō én zīm/ *n* a nonprotein compound that combines with a specific protein (**apoenzyme**) to form an active enzyme

coenzyme A *n* a complex compound that acts with specific enzymes in energy-producing biochemical reactions

coenzyme Q *n* = **ubiquinone**

coequal /kō eékwal/ *adj* of the same size or belonging to the same rank or status [14C. < Latin *coaequalis* 'of the same age' < *aequalis* (see EQUAL).] **—coequal** *n* **—coequality** /kô i kwólǝti/ *n* **—coequally** *adv* **—coequalness** *n*

coerce /kō úrss/ (**-erces**, **-ercing**, **-erced**) *vt* to force somebody to do something that he or she does not want to do [15C. < Latin *coercere* 'shut in together' < *arcere* 'shut in'.] **—coercer** *n* **—coercible** *adj*

coercion /kō úrsh'n/ *n* **1** the use of force or threats to make people do things against their will **2** force used to make somebody do something against his or her will **—coercionary** *adj* **—coercionist** *n*, *adj*

coercive /kō úrssiv/ *adj* using force, or having the power to use force, to make people do things against their will **—coercively** *adv* **—coerciveness** *n*

coercive force *n* the magnetic force necessary to demagnetize a substance

coercivity /kô ur sívvǝti/ *n* PHYS = **coercive force**

coessential /kô i sénsh'l/ *adj* with the same essence or nature [Late 15C. < ecclesiastical Latin *coessentialis* 'of the same substance' < late Latin *essentialis* (see ESSENTIAL).] **—coessentiality** /kô i senshi állǝti/ *n* **—coessentially** *adv* **—coessentialness** *n*

coeternal /kô i túrn'l/ *adj* existing together throughout eternity (*formal*) [14C. < ecclesiastical Latin *coaeternus* < Latin *aeternus* (see ETERNAL).] **—coeternally** *adv*

coeternity /kô i túrnǝti/ *n* eternal existence with somebody or something else [Late 16C. < late Latin *coaeternitas* < Latin *aeternitas* (see ETERNITY).]

Coetzee /kúrt zee/, **J. M.** (*b*. 1940) South African novelist. Full name **John Michael Coetzee**

coeval /kō eév'l/ *adj* having the same age, duration, or date of origin (*formal*) [Early 17C. < late Latin *coaevus* < Latin *aevum* 'age' < Greek *aion*.] **—coevality** /kô i vállǝti/ *n* **—coevally** *adv*

coevolution /kô eevǝ lŏŏsh'n/ *n* the joint development of two or more interdependent species, e.g. parasites and the animals they live on, such that they adapt to external changes together **—coevolutionary** *adj*

coevolve /kô i vólv/ (**-volves**, **-volving**, **-volved**) *vi* to evolve and adapt together, e.g. in the way that parasites and host organisms do (*refers to two different species*)

coexist /kô ig zíst/ *vi* **1** to exist together at the same time and in the same place **2** to occupy the same place in a peaceful way **—coexistence** *n* **—coexistent** *adj*

coextend /kô ik sténd/ *vti* to extend, or make things extend, in or through the same space or length of time **—coextension** *n*

coextensive /kô ik sténssiv/ *adj* sharing the same limits, boundaries, or scope **—coextensively** *adv*

cofactor /kô faktǝr/ *n* a substance, e.g. a coenzyme or metal ion, that acts with and is essential to the activity of an enzyme

C of C *abbr* chamber of commerce

C of E *abbr* Church of England

coffee /kóffi/ *n* **1 STRONG CAFFEINE-RICH DRINK** a drink made from ground or processed coffee beans that contains caffeine and has a mildly stimulating effect **2 BEANS FOR MAKING COFFEE** the beans used to make coffee **3 BUSH YIELDING COFFEE BEANS** a bush cultivated for the beans used to make coffee. Genus: *Coffea.* **4 PALE BROWN COLOUR** a pale brown colour, like that of milky coffee [Late 16C. Via Turkish *kahve* < Arabic *ḳahwa*.] ◇ **wake up and smell the coffee** *US* used to tell somebody that he or she is wrong about a particular situation and that it is time to acknowledge reality (*informal*)

coffee bag *n* a small porous bag containing ground coffee powder that is steeped in boiling water to make coffee

coffee bar *n* a small café where coffee, other drinks, and snacks are served

coffee bean *n* a seed of the coffee tree that is roasted and ground, or processed in other ways, to make coffee

coffee cake *n* **1** *US* a sweet cake or roll, often containing nuts and raisins, that is eaten with coffee **2** a cake flavoured with coffee

coffee cup *n* a cup intended for drinking coffee, usually smaller than a teacup but sometimes much larger and generally with a saucer underneath

coffee grinder *n* an electrical or hand-operated device for grinding roasted coffee beans

coffeehouse /kóffi howss/ (*plural* **-houses** /-howziz/) *n* a place where coffee and other refreshments are served

coffeemaker /kóffi maykər/ *n* an apparatus, usually an electrical device, for brewing coffee

coffee mill *n* HOUSEHOLD = **coffee grinder**

coffee morning *n* an informal social gathering where coffee and snacks are served, often to raise money for charity or a cause

coffeepot /kóffi pot/ *n* a tall narrow pot with a curved spout and lid designed for serving or brewing coffee

coffee pub *n US* a place where coffee and light meals are sold that also functions as an informal meeting place

coffee shop *n* a place where coffee and snacks are served and coffee beans are sold

coffee table *n* a low table, for use in a living room

coffee-table book *n* a large, typically expensive book with lavish illustrations, usually used for display or casual perusal rather than reading

coffer /kóffər/ *n* **1 STRONGBOX** a strong chest or box used for keeping valuables or money safe **2 CEILING PANEL** an ornamental sunken panel in a ceiling or dome **3** CONSTR = **cofferdam** *n.* 1 ■ **coffers** *npl* **FUNDS** a supply or store of money, often belonging to an organization ■ *vt* **1 STORE SOMETHING VALUABLE IN STRONGBOX** to put money or valuables in a coffer **2 DECORATE CEILING WITH COFFERS** to decorate something, especially a ceiling, with coffers [13C. Via French *coffre* < Latin *cophinus* (see COFFIN).]

cofferdam /kóffər dam/ *n* **1** a temporary watertight structure that is pumped dry to enclose an area underwater and allow construction work on a ship, bridge, or rig to be carried out **2** an empty space that acts as a protective barrier between two floors or bulkheads on a ship

Coffey still *n* INDUST = **patent still**

coffin /kóffin/ *n* **1 BOX FOR CORPSE** a long oblong container, usually made of wood, in which a dead body is placed for burial or cremation **2 PART OF HOOF** the horny part of a horse's hoof that contains the coffin bone **3 TYPE OF PRINTING FRAME** a frame that holds electrotype or stereotype printing plates ■ *vt* **PUT SOMETHING IN A COFFIN** to place somebody or something in a coffin or in something resembling a coffin [14C. < Old French *cof(f)in* 'little basket' < Latin *cophinus* 'basket' < Greek *kophinos*.]

coffin bone *n* the main bone in a horse's hoof

coffin nail *n* a cigarette (*dated slang*)

Coffs Harbour /kófs-/ coastal town in E New South Wales, Australia. Population: 20,315 (1991).

C of S *abbr* chief of staff

cog[1] /kog/ *n* **1** a projection on the edge of a gearwheel that engages with corresponding parts on another wheel to transfer motion from one wheel to the other **2** MECH ENG = **cogwheel** [13C. Probably < N Germanic.] —**cogged** *adj*

cog[2] /kog/ (**cogs, cogging, cogged**) *vti* to cheat in a gambling game by loading the dice (*slang*) [Mid-16C. < ?]

cog[3] /kog/ *n* a piece that projects from the end of a timber beam and is designed to fit into an opening in another beam to form a joint ■ *vt* (**cogs, cogging, cogged**) to join two timber beams with a cog [Early 19C. Probably variant of *cock* 'pamper', shortening of COCKER[2].]

cogeneration /kō jenə ráysh'n/ *n* the production of two types of energy, e.g. heat or electricity, from one source in such a way that both are usable rather than one being treated as waste energy —**cogenerator** /kō jénnə raytər/ *n*

cogent /kṓjənt/ *adj* forceful and convincing to the intellect and reason ○ *a cogent argument* [Mid-17C. < Latin *cogent-*, present participle of *cogere* 'drive together' < *agere* 'drive'.] —**cogency** *n* —**cogently** *adv*

SYNONYMS See ***valid***.

cogitate /kójji tayt/ (**-tates, -tating, -tated**) *vti* to think deeply and carefully about something (*formal*) [Late 16C. < Latin *cogitare* 'disturb together' < *agitare* 'disturb' (see AGITATE).] —**cogitation** /kójji táysh'n/ *n* —**cogitative** *adj* —**cogitatively** *adv* —**cogitativeness** *n*

cognac /kón yak/ *n* a high-quality brandy distilled from white grapes in Cognac, W France

Cognac /kón yak/ town in W France, known for the brandy distilled there. Population: 19,534 (1999).

cognate /kóg nayt/ *adj* **1** having the same linguistic root or origin **2** related by blood or having an ancestor in common (*formal*) [14C. < Latin *cognatus* 'born together' < *gnatus*, past participle of *(g)nasci* 'be born'.] —**cognate** *n* —**cognation** /kog náysh'n/ *n*

cognate object *n* a noun that functions as the object of a verb that is from the same etymological root, as in 'to dream a dream' or 'to think a thought'

cognisable *adj* = **cognizable**

cognisance *n* = **cognizance**

cognisant *adj* = **cognizant**

cognition /kog nísh'n/ *n* **1** the mental faculty or process of acquiring knowledge by the use of reasoning, intuition, or perception **2** knowledge that is acquired through processes such as reasoning, intuition, or perception [15C. < Latin *cognition-* < *cognoscere* 'get to know' < *(g)noscere* 'know'.] —**cognitional** *adj*

cognitive /kógnitiv/ *adj* **1** relating to the process of acquiring knowledge by the use of reasoning, intuition, or perception **2** relating to thought processes [Late 16C. < medieval Latin *cognitivus* < Latin *cognoscere* (see COGNITION).] —**cognitively** *adv*

cognitive dissonance *n* a state of psychological conflict or anxiety resulting from a contradiction between a person's simultaneously held beliefs or attitudes

cognitive map *n* a map of three-dimensional space maintained in the brain

cognitive psychology *n* the branch of psychology concerned with the study of mental states

cognitive science *n* the scientific study of knowledge and how it is acquired, combining elements of philosophy, psychology, linguistics, anthropology, and artificial intelligence

cognitive therapy *n* a treatment of psychiatric disorders such as anxiety or depression that encourages patients to confront and challenge the distorted way of thinking that characterizes their disorder

cognitivism /kógnitivizəm/ *n* the theory that moral judgments are statements of fact and can therefore be classed as true or false

cognizable /kógnizəb'l/, **cognisable** *adj* **1** able to be known or perceived by the human mind (*formal*) **2** falling within the jurisdiction of a particular court of law and therefore able to be tried by that court —**cognizably** *adv*

cognizance /kógnizənss/, **cognisance** *n* **1 KNOWLEDGE** knowledge or awareness of something (*formal*) **2 SOMEBODY'S SCOPE OF KNOWLEDGE** the extent or range of what somebody can know and understand (*formal*) **3 COURT'S RIGHT TO DEAL WITH** the right of a court of law to deal with a particular matter **4 TAKING NOTICE OF A FACT** notice of a fact or facts taken by a court of law **5 DISTINGUISHING SIGN** a badge or other sign that is worn to distinguish the wearer [14C. Via Old French *conis(s)aunce* < Latin *cognoscere* (see COGNITION).]

cognizant /kógnizənt/, **cognisant** *adj* being fully aware or having knowledge of something (*formal*)

SYNONYMS See ***aware***.

cognomen /kog nṓ men/ (*plural* **-nomens** *or* **-nomina** /-nómminə/) *n* **1** a nickname or name that describes somebody, e.g. 'Ethelred the Unready' (*formal*) **2** a surname or family name, especially the third name given to a citizen of ancient Rome, e.g. 'Cicero' in 'Marcus Tullius Cicero' [Early 17C. < Latin, 'added name' < *(g)nomen* 'name'.] —**cognominal** /kog nómmin'l/ *adj*

cognoscenti /kónnyōshénti, kógnə-/ (*singular* **-te** /-tay/) *npl* people who have a refined and superior knowledge of a subject, especially the arts [Mid-18C. < obsolete Italian, 'people who know', < Latin *cognoscent-*, present participle of *cognoscere* (see COGNITION).]

cogon /kṓ gōn/ *n* a coarse tall grass used, especially in the Philippines, as thatching. Genus: *Imperata*. [Late 19C. Via Spanish < Tagalog *kúgon*.]

cog railway *n* TRANSP = **rack railway**

cogwheel /kóg weel/ *n* a wheel with a series of projections around the rim that enable it to engage with projections on another wheel or rack to create traction and so produce motion

cohabit /kō hábbit/ *vi* to live together, especially without being formally married [Mid-16C. < late Latin *cohabitare* < *habitare* (see INHABIT).] —**cohabitant** *n* —**cohabitation** /kṓ habi táysh'n/ *n* —**cohabitational** *adj* —**cohabitee** /kṓ habi teé/ *n* —**cohabiter** *n*

cohen /kṓ in/ (*plural* **-hens** *or* **-hanim** /kṓ ə neém/), **kohen** (*plural* **-hanim**) *n* in Judaism, a person recognized as a descendant of Aaron [< Hebrew *kohein* 'priest']

Cohen /kṓ in/, **Leonard** (*b.* 1934) Canadian poet, novelist, singer, and songwriter

Cohen, Stanley (*b.* 1922) US cell biologist

cohere /kō heér/ (**-heres, -hering, -hered**) *vi* **1 STICK TOGETHER** to stick or hold together in a mass that is not easily separated (*formal*) **2 BE LOGICALLY CONSISTENT** to be logically consistent so that all the separate parts fit together and add up to a harmonious or believable whole (*formal*) **3 BE HELD TOGETHER BY MOLECULAR FORCES** to be held together by the molecular forces of cohesion [Mid-16C. < Latin *cohaerere* < *haerere* 'stick'.]

coherent /kō heérənt/ *adj* **1 LOGICALLY OR AESTHETICALLY CONSISTENT** logically or aesthetically consistent and holding together as a harmonious or credible whole **2 SPEAKING LOGICALLY** able to speak clearly and logically ○ *He was so confused and dazed he was barely coherent.* **3 STICKING TOGETHER** being able to hold together to form an inseparable mass (*formal*) **4 DESCRIBING ELECTROMAGNETIC WAVES** describes electromagnetic waves that have the same wavelength and a fixed phase relationship **5 FORMING UNITS WITHOUT INTRODUCING CONSTANTS** forming a system of units, such as SI units, in which the product or quotient of two units gives the unit of the derived quantity —**coherence** *n* —**coherently** *adv*

cohesion /kō heézh'n/ *n* **1** the state or condition of joining or working together to form a united whole **2** the force of attraction by which the molecules of a solid or liquid tend to remain together [Mid-17C. < Latin *cohaes-*, past participle of *cohaerere* (see COHERE).]

cohesive /kō heéssiv/ *adj* sticking, holding, or working together to form a united whole ○ *She had welded the team into a cohesive unit.* [Early 18C. < Latin *cohaes-*, present participle of *cohaerere* (see COHERE).] —**cohesively** *adv* —**cohesiveness** *n*

cohort /kṓ hawrt/ *n* **1 UNIT OF ROMAN ARMY** an ancient Roman military unit that formed one tenth of a legion and that consisted of 300 to 600 men **2 GROUP OF PEOPLE** a united group of people **3** *US* **SUPPORTER** a supporter, accomplice, or associate of a leader, especially one to whom special treatment and preference is given (*disapproving*) **4 SOLDIERS** a group of soldiers or warriors **5 GROUP WITH STATISTICAL SIMILARITIES** a group of people sharing a common factor, e.g. the same age or the same income bracket, especially in a statistical survey [15C. < Latin *cohort-* 'enclosure'.]

USAGE What is a **cohort**? The common use of ***cohort*** to mean 'a united group of people' has given rise to a use in which a ***cohort*** is a single assistant or supporter: *His most trusted cohort was an Englishman, David Hall* (*The Independent*). This use is more common in US English.

cohosh /kṓ hosh/ *n* a North American plant such as black cohosh or blue cohosh. *Cimicifuga racemosa* and *Caulophyllum thalictroides*. [Late 18C. < Algonquian *kkwàhas*.]

cohune /kō ho͞on/ *n* a palm with feathery leaves that produces a nut yielding an oil similar to coconut oil. Use: in soaps and cosmetics. Native to: Central America. *Orbignya cohune*. [Mid-18C. < Miskito.]

coif *n* /koyf/ **1 TYPE OF SKULLCAP FOR WOMEN** a close-fitting linen cap worn by women in the Middle Ages, and now worn by some nuns under their veils **2 LEATHER SKULLCAP** a thick, close-fitting leather cap formerly worn under a hood of chain mail ■ *vt* /kwaaf/ **1 COVER HEAD WITH COIF** to cover somebody's head with a coif or with something like a coif **2 ARRANGE HAIR** to arrange or style somebody's hair (*formal*) [14C. Via Old French *coife* 'headdress' < late Latin *cofia* 'helmet' < Germanic.]

coiffeur /kwaa fúr/ (*plural* **-feurs**) *n* a male hairdresser (*formal or humorous*) [Mid-19C. < French, < Old French *coife* (see COIF).]

coiffeuse /kwaa fúrz/ (*plural* **-feuses** /kwaa fúrz/) *n* a female hairdresser (*formal or humorous*) [Late 18C. < French, feminine of COIFFEUR.]

coiffure /kwaa fyo͝or/ *n* the way somebody wears his or her hair (*formal or humorous*) [Mid-17C. < French, < *coiffer* 'arrange the hair' < Old French *coife* (see COIF).] —**coiffure** *vt* —**coiffured** *adj*

coign, coigne *n* = **quoin**

coign of vantage /kóyn-/ *n* a good position from which to be able to observe somebody or something or to take action

coil /koyl/ *n* **1 SERIES OF LOOPS** a series of connected loops into which something has been wound or gathered **2 LOOP** one of a series of loops into which something has been wound or gathered **3 SPIRAL** something that curls or is curled into a spiral shape **4 PIPES ARRANGED IN ROWS OR SPIRAL** a series of pipes arranged in rows or in a spiral, e.g. in a radiator or condenser **5 WIRE SPIRAL FOR ELECTRIC CURRENT** a spiral of wire through which an electric current is passed to create a magnetic field or to function as an inductor **6 DEVICE SUPPLYING ELECTRICITY TO SPARKING PLUGS** a device that supplies a high voltage to the sparking plugs in an internal-combustion engine **7 CONTRACEPTIVE DEVICE** a coil-shaped device made of plastic or metal that is placed inside the womb to prevent a woman from becoming pregnant **8 ROLL OF STAMPS** a roll of postage stamps dispensed by a vending machine ■ *v* **1** *vti* **WIND SOMETHING INTO LOOPS** to wind something into a series of connected loops, or form a series of connected loops ○ *The rope had coiled itself around the propeller.* **2** *vi* **CURVE OR BEND** to move in a curving, sinuous way [Early 16C. Via Old French *coillir* 'gather' < Latin *colligere* (see COLLECT[1]).] —**coiler** *n*

coil pot *n* a pot formed from a structure of coils or ropes of clay laid one on top of the other in a spiral

Coimbatore /kóymbə táwr/ town in SE India. Population: 816,321 (1991).

Coimbra /kwímbrə, kwe͞eNbrə/ capital of Coimbra District in west-central Portugal. Population: 96,140 (1991).

coin /koyn/ *n* **1 PIECE OF METAL MONEY** a usually circular flat piece of metal stamped with its value as money **2 METAL MONEY** money in the form of coins rather than banknotes or cheques **3 PAPER OR METAL MONEY** money in whatever form, as opposed to such things as cheques ■ *vt* **1 MINT COINS** to make a coin or coins **2 MAKE METAL INTO COINS** to make a metal, e.g. gold or silver, into coins **3 CREATE EXPRESSION** to invent or devise a word or phrase ■ *adj* **COIN-OPERATED** requiring a coin or coins to be inserted to make it operate (*usually in combination*) [14C. < Old French *coin(g)* 'wedge, (wedge-shaped) die for stamping coins' < Latin *cuneus* 'wedge'.] —**coiner** *n* ◇ **coin it (in)** to earn a great deal of money (*informal*)

coinage /kóynij/ *n* **1 COINS** currency in the form of coins **2 CURRENCY** a system or type of coins in use as currency ○ *decimal coinage* **3 MAKING OF METAL MONEY** the act or process of minting coins **4 INVENTION OF NEW WORD OR PHRASE** the invention of a new word or phrase **5 NEW WORD OR PHRASE** a newly used word or phrase ○ *'Cyberspace' was a popular coinage of the 1980s.*

coin box *n* a box into which coins are inserted to get something from a coin-operated machine

coincide /kṓ in sɪ́d/ (**-cides, -ciding, -cided**) *vi* **1 HAPPEN AT SAME TIME** to happen at or around the same time **2 BE SAME IN POSITION OR FORM** to occupy the same place, or be exactly alike in position or form **3 AGREE** to agree exactly [Early 18C. < medieval Latin *coincidere* 'fall upon together' < Latin *incidere* 'fall upon' < *cadere* 'to fall'.]

coincidence /kō ínssidənss/ *n* **1 CHANCE HAPPENING** something that happens by chance in a surprising or remarkable way **2 HAPPENING WITHOUT PLANNING** the fact of happening by chance ○ *By sheer coincidence, we both ended up at the same restaurant.* **3 HAVING IDENTICAL FEATURES** the fact or condition of happening at the same time or place or being identical (*formal*)

coincident /kō ínssidənt/ *adj* (*formal*) **1** happening at the same time or occupying the same position in space **2** being in exact agreement or matching —**coincidently** *adv*

coincidental /kō ínssi dént'l/ *adj* **1** happening by chance rather than intentionally **2** happening or existing at the same time —**coincidentally** *adv*

coinfection /kṓ in féksh'n/ *n* infection with two or more diseases or viruses at the same time ○ *TB-HIV coinfection*

coir /kóyə/ *n* a coarse fibre that comes from the husk of the coconut. Use: matting, rope. [Late 16C. < Malayalam *kayaṟu* 'cord, coir'.]

coition /kō ísh'n/ *n* MED = **coitus** [Mid-16C. < Latin *coition-* < *coire* (see COITUS).]

coitus /kṓ itəss/ *n* sexual intercourse (*formal or technical*) [Mid-19C. < Latin, past participle of *coire* 'go together' < *ire* 'go'.] —**coital** *adj* —**coitally** *adv*

coitus interruptus /-íntə rúptəss/ *n* during sexual intercourse, the deliberate withdrawal of the penis from the vagina before semen is ejaculated, as an attempted method of contraception [< modern Latin, 'interrupted coitus']

coke[1] /kōk/ *n* a solid residue consisting mainly of carbon, left after the volatile elements have been driven from bituminous coal or other petroleum material. Use: fuel. ■ *vti* (**cokes, coking, coked**) to change something, e.g. bituminous coal, into coke, or to become coke or like coke [Mid-17C. < ?]

coke[2] /kōk/ *n* cocaine used as an illicit drug (*slang*) [Early 20C. Contraction.]

Coke *tdmk* a trademark for a cola-flavoured soft drink

cokehead /kṓk hed/ *n* a frequent user or addict of cocaine (*slang*)

col /kol/ *n* **1** a low point in a ridge of mountains, often forming a pass between two peaks **2** a pattern of atmospheric pressure distribution that develops between two anticyclones and two depressions arranged alternately, characterized by light variable winds and often thundery weather in summer or foggy conditions in winter [Mid-19C. Via French < Latin *collum* 'neck'.]

⚡**COL** *abbr* **1** cost of living **2** computer-oriented language

col. *abbr* **1** college **2** colony **3** colour **4** column

Col. *abbr* **1** Colossians **2** Columbia **3** Columbian **4** Colonel **5 Col., Colo.** Colorado

col-[1] *prefix* = **colo-** (*before vowels*)

col-[2] *prefix* = **com-** (*before l*)

cola[1] /kṓlə/ *n* **1** a sweet carbonated drink flavoured with cola nuts **2** a tropical evergreen tree cultivated for its reddish seeds (**cola nuts**). Genus: *Cola*. [Early 17C. < Temne *k'ola* 'cola nut'.]

cola[2] plural of **colon**[2]

COLA *abbr* cost-of-living adjustment

~~**colaborate**~~ incorrect spelling of **collaborate**

Colac /kṓ lak/ town in central Victoria, Australia. Population: 10,241 (1991).

colander /kúlləndər/ *n* a bowl-shaped dish with holes in it. Use: draining food cooked in water, for washing vegetables or fruit. [14C. < ?]

cola nut, kola nut *n* the small hard seed of the cola tree, which contains caffeine and theobromine. Use: carbonated drinks, medicines.

~~**colateral**~~ incorrect spelling of **collateral**

colatitude /kō látti tyood/ *n* the difference between a latitude and 90°

Colbert /kṓl bair/, **Claudette** (1905–96) French-born US film actor

Colbert, Jean-Baptiste (1619–83) French statesman

colcannon /kəl kánnən/ *n* an Irish dish made of cabbage and potatoes boiled and mashed together [Late 18C. < ?]

Colchester /kṓlchistər/ historic town in Essex. Population: 141,100 (1991).

colchicine /kólchi seen, kólk-/ *n* a poisonous extract of autumn crocus plants. Use: to inhibit cell division and cause chromosome doubling in plants, to treat gout.

colchicum /kólchikəm, kólk-/ *n* a flowering bulb with pink or white flowers that appear separately from the leaves, especially in the autumn. Native to: Europe. Genus: *Colchicum*. [Late 16C. < Greek *kolkhikon* 'product of Colchis' < *Kolkhis* 'Colchis', home of MEDEA; because it was considered poisonous.]

cold /kōld/ *adj* **1 AT LOW TEMPERATURE** at or with a low, relatively low, uncomfortably low, or unusually low temperature ○ *The weather turned colder.* ○ *a cold drink* **2 MAKING PLACE SEEM COOLER** giving a place a feeling of coolness rather than warmth ○ *blue is a cold colour* **3 COOKED HOT THEN COOLED** cooked or prepared as a hot food and then cooled ○ *Serve the pie cold, with ice cream.* **4 TACITURN AND EMOTIONLESS** showing no emotion, sympathy, or kindness **5 UNFRIENDLY AND UNCARING** feeling or exhibiting no friendship or sense of caring **6 STRONG BUT CONTROLLED** intense but expressed or shown in a controlled way ○ *cold fury* **7 SEXUALLY FRIGID** giving or feeling no sexual response **8 HARD TO FOLLOW** no longer recent or fresh and so difficult to track or follow ○ *The trail had gone cold.* **9 NOT NEAR OBJECT OF SEARCH** not close to the correct answer or to something being searched for (*informal*) **10 DEAD** dead, especially from a long time before **11 PROCESSED AT LOW TEMPERATURE** processed at a temperature below that at which recrystallization takes place ■ *n* **1 VIRAL INFECTION OF NOSE AND THROAT** a viral infection of the nose, throat, and bronchial tubes, characterized by coughing, sneezing, headaches, and nasal congestion **2 COLD WEATHER** low-temperature weather or conditions ○ *The cold made me shiver.* **3 CONDITION CAUSED BY LOW TEMPERATURE** the state or condition of being subjected to low temperatures ■ *adv* **1 EXTEMPORANEOUSLY** without any preparation ○ *sang the part cold* **2** US, *Can* **COMPLETELY** completely and without any possibility of a change of mind ○ *turned the proposal down cold* [Old English *c(e)ald* < Indo-European] —**coldness** *n* ◇ **blow hot and cold** to display wide extremes of attitude or mood ◇ **catch a cold** to experience financial loss (*informal*) ◇ **come** *or* **be brought in from the cold** to be allowed to take part in something after being previously excluded ◇ **leave somebody cold** to fail to impress or excite somebody ◇ **left out in the cold** ignored or denied benefits that other people are getting ◇ **out cold** unconscious or in a deep sleep

cold-blooded /-blúddid/ *adj* **1** describes an animal with an internal body temperature that varies according to the temperature of the surroundings **2** showing a total lack of kindness, pity, or care for somebody's suffering —**cold-bloodedly** *adv* —**cold-bloodedness** *n*

⚡**coldboot** /kóld boot/ *vt* to restart a computer by switching it off and on. ◊ **warmboot**

cold call *n* a telephone call or personal visit made to somebody not known to the caller or visitor, in order to try to sell that person goods or services —**cold-call** *vt*

cold chisel *n* a tool consisting of a solid metal shaft with a sharply bevelled point or edge that is struck with a hammer or mallet. Use: break up or shape hard materials such as metal or stone. [Because it can cut cold metal]

cold comfort *n* something intended as encouraging or reassuring that does not help in practice

cold cream *n* a thick cream used for cleaning and softening the skin, especially on the face

cold cuts *npl* slices of cooked meat that are served cold

cold duck *n* a cocktail made with sparkling burgundy and champagne [Translation of German *kalte Ente*, by folk etymology < *kaltes Ende* 'cold end', supposedly because leftover champagne and burgundy were poured into a single bottle]

cold feet *npl* a loss of nerve about something planned, causing a person not to go ahead as originally intended [Because a soldier with cold or frozen feet is prevented from fighting]

cold fish *n* an unfeeling or unfriendly person

cold frame *n* a box with glass or clear plastic sides and an opening roof, used in gardens for protecting seedlings and other plants from cold weather

cold front *n* the boundary zone of an advancing cold-air mass as it replaces warmer air

cold fusion *n* a hypothetical form of nuclear fusion held to take place at room temperature

cold-hearted /-haártid/ *adj* showing no sympathy or warmth to other people —**cold-heartedly** *adv* —**cold-heartedness** *n*

Colditz /kóldits/ site of Colditz Castle, a prisoner-of-war camp in east-central Germany during World War II

cold light *n* light produced from a low-temperature source, e.g. phosphorescence, containing no infrared wavelengths and therefore having no heating effects

coldly /kóldli/ *adv* without emotion, affection, friendliness, or sympathy

cold pack *n* **1** a bag, cloth, or sheet that is soaked with water or filled with something cold and applied to the body to relieve pain or inflammation **2** the packing and sterilization of uncooked food in jars or tins

cold-pressed *adj* describes high-grade olive oil produced from the first pressing of the raw olives

cold-rolled *adj* describes metal that is rolled into sheets under pressure at room temperature in order to retain the crystalline structure of the metal and produce a smooth surface —**cold-rolling** *n*

cold rubber *n* a durable synthetic rubber made through polymerization at low temperature and used for re-treading tyres

cold shoulder *n* a refusal to behave in a friendly or pleasant way towards somebody ○ *He gave me the cold shoulder.* [Because unwelcome guests were formerly given only a cold shoulder of mutton] —**coldshoulder** *v*

cold snap *n* a sudden short period of very cold weather

cold sore *n* a small painful blister on or near the lips, or sometimes the nose, caused by a virus *Herpes simplex* [Because the sores often accompany colds]

cold storage *n* chilled or refrigerated conditions in which perishable items, especially food, are kept to preserve them ◇ **in cold storage** ready to be put into action at some later date, but not currently being acted on

cold store *n* a refrigerated building or area for keeping goods, especially food or furs, in cold conditions to preserve them

Coldstream /kóld streem/ small town in S Scotland. Population: 1,746 (1991).

cold sweat *n* a very nervous, anxious, or frightened state, often with sweating and cold clammy skin

cold turkey *n* **1** a method of stopping drug addiction by not taking any further drugs and not having any other treatment to protect the addict from the withdrawal symptoms **2** the unpleasant symptoms, usually including nausea and shivering, that accompany a sudden withdrawal from an addictive drug [< ?]

cold type *n* typesetting that is done without casting metal

cold war *n* a relationship between two people or groups that is unfriendly or hostile but does not involve actual fighting or military combat. ◊ **hot war**

Cold War *n* the hostile yet nonviolent relations between the former Soviet Union and the United States, and their respective allies, from around 1946 to 1989

cold wave *n* **1** a sudden fall in temperature associated with the passage of air of continental polar origin **2** a permanent wave in hair that is produced using chemicals, rather than heat (*dated*)

cold-weld *vt* to join two metal surfaces using pressure rather than heat —**cold-welding** *n*

cole /kōl/ *n* a member of the cabbage family. Genus: *Brassica*. (*archaic*) [Pre-12C. < Latin *caulis* 'stem, cabbage'.]

Cole /kōl/, **Thomas** (1801–48) British-born US artist

colectomy /kō léktəmi/ (*plural* **-mies**) *n* a surgical operation in which part or all of the colon is removed [Late 19C. < COLON².]

colemanite /kólmən īt/ *n* a white or colourless crystalline mineral consisting of hydrous calcium borate. Use: source of borax. [Late 19C. After William T. *Coleman* (1824–93), US mine owner.]

coleopteran /kólli óptərən/ *n* an insect with modified forewings that function as tough covers for the membranous hind wings, e.g. beetles. Order: Coleoptera. —**coleopterous** *adj*

coleoptile /kólli óp tīl/ *n* the first leaf in some grasses that forms a protective sheath around the stem tip (**plumule**) [Mid-19C. < Greek *koleos* 'sheath' + *ptilon* 'feather'.]

coleorhiza /kólli ə rízə/ (*plural* **-zae** /-zee/) *n* a protective sheath surrounding the young root of a germinating grass seed [Mid-19C. < Greek *koleos* 'sheath' + *rhiza* 'root'.]

Coleraine /kōl ráyn/ city in N Northern Ireland. Population: 20,721 (1991).

Coleridge /kólərij/, **Samuel Taylor** (1772–1834) British poet

coleslaw /kól slaw/ *n* a salad made with shredded raw cabbage and carrot in a mayonnaise dressing [Late 18C. < Dutch *koolsla* < *kool* 'cabbage' + *sla* 'salad'.]

coletit /kól tit/ *n* BIRDS = **coal tit**

Colette /ko lét/ (1873–1954) French novelist. Full name **Sidonie Gabrielle Claudine Colette**

coleus /kó li əss/ *n* a plant grown for its brightly coloured variegated leaves. Genus: *Coleus*. [Mid-19C. Via modern Latin < Greek *koleos* 'sheath'; from the way the plant's filaments are joined.]

coley /kóli/ (*plural* **-ley** *or* **-leys**) *n* an edible white-fleshed fish, especially the coalfish [Mid-20C. Probably < COALFISH.]

coli- *prefix* = **colo-** (*before vowels*)

colic /kóllik/ *n* **1 PAIN IN ABDOMEN** a sudden attack of abdominal pain, often caused by spasm, inflammation, or obstruction **2 CRYING IN BABIES** excessive crying and irritability in infants from a variety of causes, especially stomach or intestinal discomfort **3 SERIOUS DIGESTIVE DISEASE IN HORSES** a serious disease of the digestive system in horses, sometimes leading to fatal intestinal blockage [15C. Via French < Latin *colicus* < Greek *kolikos* 'suffering in the large intestine' < *kolon* 'large intestine'.]

colicky /kólliki/ *adj* experiencing bouts of abdominal pain (**colic**)

coliform /kóli fawrm, kólli-/ *adj* describes rod-shaped bacteria that are normally found in the colons of humans and animals and become a serious contaminant when found in the food or water supply. ◊ **E. coli** [Early 20C. < modern Latin *coli* 'of the large intestine', form of Latin *colon* 'large intestine'.]

colinear /kó línni ər/ *adj* **1** with corresponding parts arranged in a regular linear order **2** MATH = **collinear** [Early 20C. < CO- + LINEAR.] —**colinearity** /kólinni árrəti/ *n*

coliseum /kólli seé əm/, **colosseum** /kóllə-/ *n* a large building used as a theatre or for sports events [Early 16C. Via medieval Latin *coliseum* 'something colossal' < Latin *colosseus* 'colossal' < *colossus* 'colossus'.]

colistin /kə lístin, kō-/ *n* an antibiotic effective against a wide range of organisms. Source: a soil bacterium. Use: to treat gastrointestinal infections. [Mid-20C. < modern Latin (*Bacillus*) *colistinus* < *coli* (see COLIFORM).]

colitis /kə lítiss, ko-/ *n* inflammation of the colon, characterized by lower-bowel spasms and upper abdominal cramps [Mid-19C. < COLON².] —**colitic** /kə líttik, ko-/ *adj*

coll. *abbr* **1** collateral **2** colleague **3** collect **4** collection **5** collector **6** college **7** collegiate **8** colloquial

coll- *prefix* = **collo-** (*before vowels*)

collaborate /kə lábbə rayt/ (**-rates, -rating, -rated**) *vi* **1** to work with another person or group in order to achieve something **2** to betray others by working with an enemy, especially an occupying force [Late 19C. < late Latin *collaborat-*, past participle of *collaborare* 'work together' < Latin *labor* 'toil'.] —**collaborative** *adj* —**collaboratively** *adv* —**collaborator** *n*

collaboration /kə lábbə ráysh'n/ *n* **1** the act of working together with one or more people in order to achieve something **2** the betrayal of others by working with an enemy, especially an occupying force —**collaborationism** *n* —**collaborationist** *n, adj*

collage /ko laázh, kóllaazh/ *n* **1 PICTURE WITH PIECES STUCK ON SURFACE** a picture made by sticking cloth, pieces of paper, photographs, and other objects onto a surface **2 ART OF MAKING COLLAGES** the art of making pictures by sticking cloth, pieces of paper, photographs, and other objects onto a surface **3 COMBINATION OF DIFFERENT THINGS** a combination of different things ■ *vti US* **MAKE COLLAGE** to make a picture by sticking cloth, pieces of paper, photographs, and other objects onto a surface [Early 20C. < French, < *coller* 'glue' < *colle* 'glue' < Greek *kolla*.] —**collagist** *n*

collagen /kólləjən/ *n* a fibrous protein found in skin, bone, and other connective tissues [Mid-19C. < French *collagène* < Greek *kolla* 'glue'.] —**collagenic** /kóllə jénnik/ *adj* —**collagenous** /kə lájjənəss/ *adj*

collagenase /kə lájjə nayz, -nayss/ *n* any enzyme that breaks down collagen

collapsar /kə láp saar/ *n* ASTRON = **black hole** *n.* 1 [Late 20C. < COLLAPSE.]

collapse /kə láps/ *v* (**-lapses, -lapsing, -lapsed**) **1** *vi* **FALL DOWN** to fall down suddenly, generally as a result of damage, structural weakness, or lack of support ○ *A section of cliff had collapsed into the sea.* **2** *vi* **FAIL ABRUPTLY** to fail or come to an end suddenly ○ *Their partnership nearly collapsed under the strain.* **3** *vi* **FALL SUDDENLY** to fall or faint because of illness, exhaustion, or weakness ○ *He collapsed from overwork.* **4** *vi* **SUDDENLY SIT OR LIE DOWN** to sit or lie down suddenly and relax completely, or give way to emotion ○ *I collapsed into an armchair.* **5** *vi* **BEND DOUBLE WITH EMOTION** to bend over double or otherwise contort the body, typically in the throes of emotion such as laughter or crying **6** *vti* **DEFLATE** to fold up or become flat from lack of pressure or loss of air, or cause something such as a parachute to do this ○ *The left lung had collapsed.* **7** *vti* **FOLD SOMETHING TO MAKE SMALLER** to fold something up so that it is smaller or takes up less space, or fold up in this way ■ *n* **1 FAILURE OR END** a failure or sudden end to something ○ *The abrupt collapse of the campaign.* **2 FALLING DOWN** the act of falling down suddenly, generally as a result of damage, structural weakness, or lack of support ○ *The roof was in danger of collapse.* **3 DECREASE IN VALUE** a sudden reduction or decrease in value ○ *the threatened collapse of the yen* **4 SUDDEN ILLNESS** a sudden onset of severe illness, resulting in hospitalization or bed rest ○ *in a state of nervous collapse* [Mid-18C. Back-formation < *collapsed* < Latin *collapsus*, past participle of *collabi* 'fall together' < *labi* 'to fall'.] —**collapsibility** /kə lápsə bílləti/ *n* —**collapsible** *adj*

collar /kóllər/ *n* **1 GARMENT'S NECKBAND** the upright or turned-over neckband of a coat, jacket, dress, shirt, or blouse **2 BAND ROUND NECK OF AN ANIMAL** a leather, plastic, fabric, or metal band placed round the neck of an animal to identify it or attach it to a lead **3 AREA RESEMBLING A COLLAR** an area around the neck of a bird or animal that has a colour or marking different from the rest **4 PART OF A HARNESS** the cushioned ring or other part of a harness that presses against a draught animal's shoulders **5 RING-SHAPED DEVICE OR PART** a ring-shaped device or part on a shaft that guides, seats, or restricts another mechanical part **6 NECKLACE** a close-fitting necklace or one that lies flat over the shoulders **7 ORNAMENTAL INSIGNIA OF OFFICE** an ornamental chain or band worn round the neck as a badge of office or insignia of knighthood **8 MEAT FROM NECK** a cut of meat, especially bacon, taken from an animal's neck **9 POLICE ARREST** an arrest made by a police officer (*slang*) ■ *vt* **1 FIND OR STOP** to find or stop somebody you want to talk to (*informal*) **2 CATCH** to catch somebody and hold him or her to prevent escape (*slang*) **3 MAKE A POLICE ARREST** to arrest a criminal suspect in your capacity as a police officer (*slang*) **4 PUT A COLLAR ON** to put a collar on something, e.g. an animal, a garment, or a machine part **5 PICKLE AND ROLL MEAT** to pickle meat by soaking it in salt or brine with seasonings and flavouring ingredients, then rolling, boiling, and pressing it [14C. Via Old French *colier* < Latin *collare* < *collum* 'neck'.] —**collared** *adj* —**collarless** *adj* ◇ **hot under the collar** angry, irritated, or generally agitated (*informal*)

collarbone /kóllər bōn/ *n* ANAT = **clavicle** *n.* 1

collard /kóllərd/ *n US* a variety of kale with a crown of smooth edible leaves [Mid-18C. Alteration of *colewort*.]

collate /kə láyt, ko-/ (**-lates, -lating, -lated**) *vt* **1 PUT PAGES IN ORDER** to assemble pages in the correct order **2 COMPARE INFORMATION** to bring together pieces of information and compare them in detail **3 EXAMINE SHEETS OR PAGES** to examine sheets or pages so as to put them into the proper sequence prior to binding **4 VERIFY PAGE SEQUENCING** to verify the correct sequencing and completeness of the pages in a book **5 ADMIT CLERIC TO BENEFICE** to admit a member of the clergy to a benefice [Mid-16C. < Latin *collat-*, past participle of *conferre* 'bring together' < *ferre* 'bring'.] —**collator** *n*

collateral /kə láttərəl/ *n* **1 PROPERTY AS SECURITY AGAINST LOAN** property or goods used as security against a loan and forfeited if the loan is not repaid **2 DESCENDANT FROM DIFFERENT LINE** a relative descended from the same ancestor as another person but through a different set of parents, grandparents, and other forebears ■ *adj*

1 **PARALLEL** running side by side in parallel or corresponding in some way, e.g. in size 2 **DESCENDED FROM SAME ANCESTOR** having the same ancestor but descended through a different set of parents, grandparents, and other forebears 3 **ADDITIONAL** additional to and in support of something 4 **ACCOMPANYING** accompanying or additional but secondary 5 **WITH PROPERTY AS SECURITY** obtained by putting up property or goods as security, to be forfeited if the loan cannot be paid [14C. < medieval Latin *collateralis* 'side by side with' < Latin *lateralis* 'on the side' (see LATERAL).] —**collaterality** /kə láttə rálləti/ *n* — **collaterally** *adv*

collateral damage *n* unintended damage to civilian life or property during a military operation

collateralize /kə láttərə līz/ (**-izes, -izing, -ized**) *vt* to pledge property or goods as security for a loan — **collateralization** /kə láttərə lī záysh'n/ *n*

collation /kə láysh'n/ *n* 1 **COMPARISON OF INFORMATION** a detailed comparison between different items or forms of information 2 **ASSEMBLY OF PAGES IN ORDER** the assembling of pieces of paper in the right order, particularly the sections of a book prior to binding 3 **TECHNICAL DESCRIPTION OF BOOK** the technical description of a book, including its bibliographical details and information about its physical construction, or the act of compiling such a description 4 **LIGHT MEAL** a light meal or refreshment ○ *a cold collation* 5 **APPOINTMENT OF CLERGY** the appointment of clergy to a benefice 6 **READING OF RELIGIOUS TEXT** the reading of a religious text to a gathering of monks [14C. < Latin *collation-* 'a bringing together' < *collat-* (see COLLATE).]

collative /kə láytiv/ *adj* describes an ecclesiastical benefice to which a member of the clergy is appointed [Early 17C]

colleague /kólleeg/ *n* a person somebody works with, especially in a professional or skilled job [Early 16C. Via French < Latin *collega* 'person somebody commissions with' < *legare* 'commission, entrust' < *lex* 'law'.] —**colleagueship** *n*

collect[1] /kə lékt/ *v* 1 *vt* **BRING THINGS TOGETHER** to gather things and bring them together ○ *I collected up my belongings and left.* 2 *vt* **KEEP THINGS OF SAME TYPE** to obtain and keep objects of a similar type because of their interest, value, or beauty 3 *vt* **FETCH AND BRING** to fetch people or objects and bring them somewhere ○ *They collected me from the airport.* 4 *vt* **TAKE MONEY OR PRIZE** to take the money or prize to which a person is entitled 5 *vti* **ASK FOR DONATIONS** to ask for money from people for a particular purpose 6 *vti* **ACCUMULATE** to gather and gradually accumulate in a place 7 *vi* **GRADUALLY ASSEMBLE** to come together gradually in a place and form a group or crowd of people ○ *By now an angry crowd had collected.* 8 *vr* **GET CONTROL OF YOURSELF** to gain or regain control of yourself and deliberately calm yourself or prepare yourself psychologically 9 *vi* **GET MONEY** to obtain money that is due, e.g. from an insurance policy 10 *vt ANZ* **COLLIDE** to be in collision with another vehicle (*informal*) ■ *adv US* TELECOM = **reverse charges** ■ *adj US* TELECOM = **reverse-charge** [Mid-16C. Directly or via French < medieval Latin *collectare* < Latin *collect-*, past participle of *colligere* 'gather together' < *legere* 'gather'.]

SYNONYMS ***collect, accumulate, gather, amass, assemble, stockpile, hoard***

CORE MEANING: to bring dispersed things together

collect to bring things together, or to make a collection of similar things as a hobby; **accumulate** to obtain things over a period of time; **gather** to bring together things from various locations; **amass** to obtain a large number of things over an extended period; **assemble** to bring things together in an orderly way; **stockpile** to collect and store things in large amounts for future use; **hoard** to collect and store things in large amounts, often secretly.

collect[2] /kóllekt/ *n* a short formal prayer that can vary according to the day, said before the reading of the epistle in certain Christian church services [13C. Via Old French < late Latin *collecta* 'assembly' < Latin, form of *collectus* (see COLLECT[1]).]

collectable /kə léktəb'l/, **collectible** *n* an object of a type that is valued or sought after by collectors ■ *adj* good for collecting or popular with collectors and much sought after

collectanea /kóllek táyni ə/ *npl* a selection of pieces of writing by an author or by several authors [Mid-17C. < Latin, 'things collected' < form of *collectaneus* 'collected' < *collectus* (see COLLECT[1]).]

collected /kə léktid/ *adj* 1 **CALM AND COMPOSED** calm and in control of yourself 2 **BROUGHT TOGETHER AS WHOLE** gathered together in one book or set of volumes as the whole of an author's work or work of a particular type 3 **CONTROLLED IN GAIT** moving with a controlled gait —**collectedly** *adv* —**collectedness** *n*

collectible *n, adj* = **collectable**

collection /kə léksh'n/ *n* 1 **GROUP OF THINGS OR PEOPLE** a group of things or people together in one place 2 **SEVERAL DIFFERENT WORKS TOGETHER** a number of different pieces of writing or music together in one book, CD, or record 3 **OBJECTS HELD BY COLLECTOR** a set of objects collected for their interest, value, or beauty 4 **PAINTINGS OR OBJECTS IN MUSEUM** all the paintings or objects of one kind held by an art gallery or museum 5 **TAKING OF DONATIONS** the act of taking money due or given ○ *They took up a collection for him when he was in hospital.* 6 **TAKING OF MONEY IN CHRISTIAN CHURCH** the act of accepting money from worshippers in a Christian church service, or the money collected 7 **RANGE OF NEW CLOTHES** a range of newly designed clothes for a particular season ○ *the spring collection* 8 **TAKING** the taking of something on a regular basis, e.g. letters from postboxes by the Post Office, or refuse from buildings 9 **GATHERING TOGETHER** the act of gathering things together (*formal*) [14C. Via Old French < Latin *collection-* < *collect-* (see COLLECT[1]).]

collective /kə léktiv/ *adj* 1 **SHARED BY ALL** made or shared by everyone in a group 2 **COLLECTED TO FORM WHOLE** collected together to form a whole or added up to form a total from different sources or groups 3 **APPLYING TO MANY** applying to a number of individuals taken together ○ *staff training was the collective responsibility of the three personnel officers* 4 **WORKER-RUN UNDER STATE SUPERVISION** describes a business or other enterprise run by the people who work in it but under the jurisdiction of the state ■ *n* 1 **WORKER-RUN ENTERPRISE** an enterprise, such as a farm or factory, that is run by its workers under state control 2 **MEMBERS OF COLLECTIVE** the members of a collective who work in and run the business 3 GRAM = **collective noun** —**collectively** *adv* —**collectiveness** *n*

collective agreement *n* a contract of employment negotiated between a management and union

collective bargaining *n* negotiations between a management and union about pay and conditions of employment on behalf of all the workers in the union

collective farm *n* a farm that is state-supervised but operated by its workers

collective noun *n* a noun that refers to a group of people or things considered as a single unit

USAGE Collective nouns: Examples of collective nouns are *audience, committee, crowd, flock, government, jury,* and *orchestra*, all of which are singular in form but plural in the sense of being made up of a number of individuals or individual things. Nouns that denote a class of objects, for example *furniture* and *luggage*, are always singular: *My luggage is missing.* Other collective nouns can be treated as singular or plural. Thus *The audience was absolutely silent* but *It was so warm the audience were stripping off their jackets.* It is important to avoid inconsistency in your choice of verb and pronoun number when using collective nouns. For instance, this example contains inconsistencies: *The committee has* [singular] *decided to reject the proposal and will give their* [plural: use *its* instead] *reasons in writing tomorrow.* Some people regard the treatment of collective nouns as plural as wrong and it is especially criticized in the United States.

collective security *n* the maintenance of peace and security through the united action of nations

collective unconscious *n* the inherited part of unconscious thought, memories, and instinct, which, according to Jungian principles, is common to members of a people and is observable through dreams and behaviour

collectivise *vt* = **collectivize**

collectivism /kə léktivizəm/ *n* the system of control and ownership of factories and farms and of the means of production and distribution of products by a nation's people [Mid-19C. < COLLECTIVE.] —**collectivist** *n* —**collectivistic** /kə lékti vístik/ *adj* —**collectivistically** *adv*

collectivity /kóllek tívvəti/ (*plural* **-ties**) *n* 1 a state or situation in which people or things are together or work together to form a whole 2 a group regarded as an aggregate, especially a people

collectivize /kə lékti vīz/ (**-izes, -izing, -ized**), **collectivise** (**-ises, -ising, -ised**) *vt* to run or organize something such as a farm according to principles of collective control —**collectivization** /kə lékti vī záysh'n/ *n*

collector /kə léktər/ *n* 1 **SOMEBODY WHO COLLECTS OBJECTS** an accumulator of objects for their interest, value, or beauty ○ *a stamp collector* 2 **SOMEBODY WHO MAKES A COLLECTION** somebody whose job is to collect something, e.g. money owed, tickets, or refuse 3 **CONTAINER WHERE THINGS COLLECT** something in which things are collected intentionally or where unwanted things collect 4 **TRANSISTOR REGION** the region of a transistor towards or through which charge carriers flow 5 *S Asia* **INDIAN ADMINISTRATOR** in India, the chief administrator of a district —**collectorship** *n*

collectorate /kə léktərət/ *n S Asia* in India, the district over which a collector presides

collector's item *n* an object that is sought after or valued highly by collectors

colleen /kə leén, kólleen/ *n* 1 *Ireland* a girl, especially a young girl 2 a girl living or born in Ireland or a girl of Irish descent [Early 19C. < Irish *cailín* 'little girl' < *caile* 'girl'.]

college /kóllij/ *n* 1 **INSTITUTION OF HIGHER LEARNING** an institution of higher or further education, especially one offering courses in specialized or practical subjects 2 **PART OF BRITISH UNIVERSITY** a division of some British universities, e.g. Oxford or Cambridge 3 **SCHOOL** a school for senior students 4 **BRITISH SCHOOL** used as part of the name of some British public schools 5 **COLLEGE BUILDINGS** the building or buildings of a college 6 **COLLEGE STAFF AND STUDENTS** the staff and students of a college 7 **PROFESSIONAL BODY** a group of people, usually of the same profession, who have agreed duties and rights 8 *US* **UNIVERSITY SCHOOL OR DIVISION** a school or a division of a university that usually has its own dean and other administrators and whose faculty teaches and confers degrees in specific academic fields 9 **BODY OF CLERGY** a group or body of clergy who live together [14C. Directly or via Old French < Latin *collegium* 'association, corporation' < *collega* (see COLLEAGUE).]

College of Arms *n* an institution with jurisdiction in England, Wales, and Northern Ireland that specializes in matters relating to heraldry, the granting of arms, and tracing genealogies

College of Cardinals *n* the body of Roman Catholic cardinals who elect popes, assist the pope in church governance, and manage the Holy See in the absence of a living or elected pope [Shortening of *Sacred College of Cardinals*]

College of Heralds *n* HERALDRY = **College of Arms**

College of Justice *n* the Scottish Court of Session, Scotland's highest civil court

collegia plural of **collegium**

collegial /kə leéji əl/ *adj* 1 **OF COLLEGE OR UNIVERSITY** involving, typical of, or belonging to a college or university 2 **POWER-SHARING** with power shared equally between colleagues 3 **OF POWER-SHARING BY BISHOPS** relating to a situation or system in the Roman Catholic Church in which the bishops share equal power [14C. Directly or via Old French < late Latin *collegialis* < Latin *collegium* (see COLLEGE).] —**collegiality** /kə leéji álləti/ *n* —**collegially** *adv*

collegian /kə leéji ən/ *n* a college undergraduate, graduate student, or recent graduate [15C. < medieval Latin *collegianus* < Latin *collegium* (see COLLEGE).]

collegiate /kə leéji ət/ *adj* 1 involving, belonging to, appropriate to, or being a college, including its students and their pursuits 2 consisting of separate university colleges [15C. < medieval Latin *collegiatus* '(member) of a college' < Latin *collegium* (see COLLEGE).] —**collegiately** *adv*

collegiate church *n* 1 **CHURCH WITH CANONS** a Roman Catholic or Anglican church that has a chapter of canons but is not a cathedral 2 **CHURCH WITH TWO MINISTERS** in Scotland, a church with two or more ministers of equal seniority 3 *US* **GROUP OF CHURCHES** a group or association of churches that have pastors in common

collegium /kə leéji əm/ (*plural* **-ums** or **-a** /-ə/) *n* 1 in the former Soviet Union, a committee of equally empowered members in charge of a department or industry 2 CHR = **College of Cardinals** [< Latin (see COLLEGE)]

col legno /kol lég nō, -láy nyō/ *adv* to be played by tapping the strings of a stringed instrument with the back of the bow (*musical direction*) [< Italian, 'with the wood']

collembolan /kə lémbələn/ *n* INSECTS = **springtail** [Late 19C. < modern Latin *Collembola* < Greek *kolla* 'glue' + *embolon* 'peg'.] —**collembolous** *adj*

collenchyma /kə léngkimə/ *n* a layer of supportive plant tissue that consists of elongated living cells that have walls unevenly thickened with cellulose and pectin [Mid-19C. < COLLO-.] —**collenchymatous** /kóllən kímmətəss/ *adj*

Colles' fracture /kólliz-/ *n* a fracture of the radius bone in which a piece broken off at the end is displaced towards the back of the wrist [Late 19C. After Abraham Colles (1773–1843), Irish surgeon.]

collet /kóllit/ *n* 1 CONE-SHAPED MECHANICAL PIECE a slotted cone-shaped piece that encloses and grips a rod or shaft when inserted into the sleeve of a lathe or other machine 2 SETTING FOR GEMSTONE a band or claw that holds a gemstone 3 BAND ATTACHED TO SPRING IN WATCH a ring that holds the hairspring in a watch [16C. < French *collet* 'little collar' < *col* 'collar' < Latin *collum* 'neck'.]

collide /kə líd/ *vi* (**-lides, -liding, -lided**) *vi* 1 to hit a person or object moving towards you or a person or object you are moving towards ◊ *I collided with her in the corridor.* 2 to come into conflict with somebody else or another group [Early 17C. < Latin *collidere* 'shatter', literally 'strike together' < *laedere* 'strike'.]

collider /kə lídər/, **colliding-beam machine** *n* a particle accelerator in which two oppositely moving particle beams are made to collide

collie /kólli/ *n* a dog with a long narrow muzzle, originally bred to herd sheep. There are short-haired (smooth) and long-haired (rough) collies. ◊ **Border collie** [Mid-17C. < ?]

~~**collieflour**~~ incorrect spelling of **cauliflower**

~~**collieflower**~~ incorrect spelling of **cauliflower**

collier /kólli ər/ *n* 1 a coal miner (*dated*) 2 a ship designed to transport coal [13C. < COAL.]

colliery /kóllyəri/ *n* (*plural* **-ies**) *n* a coal mine and the buildings associated with it

collinear /ko línni ər/, **colinear** /kō-/ *adj* lying on or passing through a single straight line [Mid-19C. < COL-2 + LINEAR.] —**collinearity** /ko línni árrəti/ *n*

collins /kóllinz/ *n* an iced drink made with spirits such as gin or vodka and fruit juice such as lemon or lime [Mid-19C. < ?]

Collins /kóllinz/, **Jackie** (b. 1939) British novelist

Michael Collins

Collins, **Michael** (1890–1922) Irish politician

Collins, **Wilkie** (1824–89) British novelist

collision /kə lízh'n/ *n* 1 CRASH the action of two moving vehicles, ships, aircraft, or other objects hitting each other 2 CONFLICT BETWEEN IDEAS a conflict between people or their ideas or beliefs 3 EXCHANGE OF ENERGY BETWEEN PARTICLES an encounter between two or more particles that come together or close to each other, and exchange or transfer energy [15C. < late Latin *collision-* < Latin *collis-*, past participle of *collidere* (see COLLIDE).] —**collisional** *adj* —**collisionally** *adv*

collision course *n* a path or course of action that inevitably leads to conflict ◊ *The two of them were clearly headed on a collision course.*

collision zone *n* an extensive linear feature marking

the collision of two continental plates, characterized by young fold mountains and earthquakes

collo- *prefix* glutinous, gelatinous ◊ *collotype* [Via modern Latin < Greek *kolla* 'glue']

collocate *v* /kólla kayt/ (**-cates, -cating, -cated**) 1 *vi* OCCUR FREQUENTLY WITH ANOTHER WORD to occur frequently in conjunction with another word 2 *vt* PUT SOMETHING NEXT TO to arrange something so that it is next to or close to something else (*formal*) ■ *n* /kólləkət/ WORD THAT OCCURS WITH ANOTHER a word that is frequently or typically used with another word [Early 16C. < Latin *collocat-*, past participle of *collocare* 'place together' < *locare* 'to place'.]

collocation /kólla káysh'n/ *n* 1 the association between two words that are typically or frequently used together 2 an arrangement in which things are placed next to each other or close together —**collocational** *adj*

collodion /kə lódi ən/ *n* a thick colourless solution of pyroxylin, ether, and alcohol. Use: to treat wounds and hold surgical dressings, formerly, to make photographic plates. [Mid-19C. < Greek *kollōdēs* 'gluelike' < *kolla* 'glue'.]

colloid /kólloyd/ *n* 1 SUSPENSION OF SMALL PARTICLES a suspension of small particles dispersed in another substance 2 PARTICLES IN COLLOID the particles that are suspended in a colloid solution 3 SUBSTANCE IN THYROID GLAND a thick gelatinous substance that is produced in the thyroid gland and stores hormones [Mid-19C. < Greek *kolla* 'glue'.] —**colloid** *adj*—**colloidal** *adj*

collop /kólləp/ *n* 1 a slice of meat, especially fried bacon 2 a small piece of something [14C. < N Germanic.]

colloq. *abbr* colloquial

~~**colloquail**~~ incorrect spelling of **colloquial**

colloquia plural of **colloquium**

colloquial /kə lṓkwi əl/ *adj* said more usually in informal conversation than in formal speech or writing [Mid-18C. < Latin *colloquium* (see COLLOQUIUM).] —**colloquiality** /kə lōkwi álləti/ *n* —**colloquially** *adv*—**colloquialness** *n*

colloquialism /kə lṓkwi əlizəm/ *n* an informal word or phrase that is more usual in conversation than in formal speech or writing

colloquium /kə lṓkwi əm/ (*plural* **-ums** or **-a** /-ə/) *n* 1 an academic conference or seminar in which a particular topic is discussed, often with guest speakers 2 an informal meeting to discuss something [Late 16C. < Latin, 'conversation' < *colloqui* 'speak with' < *loqui* 'speak'.]

colloquy /kólləkwi/ (*plural* **-quies**) *n* 1 a formal conversation or discussion (*formal*) 2 a literary or other written work in the form of a dialogue [15C. < Latin *colloquium* (see COLLOQUIUM).]

~~**collosal**~~ incorrect spelling of **colossal**

collotype /kólla tīp/ *n* 1 a process for making lithographic prints 2 a print that is made by use of the collotype process [Late 19C. < Greek *kolla* 'glue'.]

collude /kə lōod/ (**-ludes, -luding, -luded**) *vi* to cooperate with somebody secretly in order to do something illegal or undesirable [Early 16C. < Latin *colludere* 'play with' < *ludere* 'play' < *ludus* 'game'.] —**colluder** *n*

collusion /kə lōozh'n/ *n* secret cooperation between people in order to do something illegal or underhand [14C. Directly or via Old French < Latin *collusion-* < *collus-*, past participle of *colludere* (see COLLUDE).]

collusive /kə lōossiv/ *adj* secretly cooperating or involving secret cooperation in order to do something illegal or underhanded [Late 17C. < Latin *collus-*, past participle of *colludere* (see COLLUDE).] —**collusively** *adv* —**collusiveness** *n*

colluvium /kə lōovi əm/ (*plural* **-a** /-ə/ or **-ums**) *n* loose rock and soil at the base of a cliff or steep slope [Mid-20C. < Latin, < *colluvies* < *colluere* 'wash thoroughly' < *lavere* 'to wash'.] —**colluvial** *adj*

collywobbles /kólli wobb'lz/ *npl* a feeling of nervousness about something (*informal*) [Early 19C. Probably < COLIC + WOBBLE.]

Colo. *abbr* Colorado

colo- *prefix* intestine ◊ *colorectal* [< COLON2]

coloboma /kólla bṓmə/ *n* a structural defect in the retina, iris, or other tissue of the eye, usually present at birth [Mid-19C. Via modern Latin < Greek *koloboma* 'part removed in mutilation' < *kolobos* 'docked'.] —**colobomatous** *adj*

colobus /kólləbəss/ (*plural* **-buses** or **-bi** /-bī/), **colobus monkey** *n* a large slender monkey that has a long tail

and long silky fur but lacks developed thumbs. Native to: Africa. Genus: *Colobus*. [Late 19C. Via modern Latin < Greek *kolobos* 'docked, maimed'.]

⚡**colocation** /kṓ lō kaáysh'n/ *n* the sharing of the facilities of a hosting centre with other Internet clients

colocynth /kólla sinth/ *n* 1 a spongy bitter yellow fruit about the size of a lemon but speckled with green. Use: laxative. 2 a vine related to the pumpkin and squash that bears colocynths. Native to: Europe. *Citrulus colocynthis*. [Mid-16C. Via Latin < Greek *kolokunthis* < *kolokunthē* 'pumpkin, round gourd'.]

cologne /kə lṓn/ *n* a scented liquid that is lighter than perfume [Early 19C. After COLOGNE.]

Cologne /kə lṓn/ port in W Germany. Population: 963,817 (1997).

Colombia

Colombia /kə lúmbi ə, -lóm-/ republic in NW South America. Capital: Bogotá. Population: 37,852,050 (1997). Area: 1,141,748 sq. km/440,831 sq. mi. —**Colombian** *n, adj*

Colombo /kə lúm bō/ commercial capital, largest city and port of Sri Lanka, situated on the W coast. Population: 616,000 (1990 estimate).

colon[1] /kṓlən, -lon/ *n* 1 PUNCTUATION MARK the punctuation mark (:) used to divide distinct but related sentence elements, e.g. clauses in which the second elaborates on the first, or to introduce a list, quotation, or speech, or sometimes to separate numbers 2 MARK (:) USED IN PHONETICS a mark (:) after a vowel in a system of phonetic writing that shows that the vowel is lengthened 3 (*plural* **cola**) UNIT OF CLASSICAL POETRY in Greek or Roman verse, a rhythmic unit consisting of two to six metrical feet with one main accent [Mid-16C. Via Latin < Greek *kōlon*, 'clause', 'limb'.]

PUNCTUATION Use of *colon* The *colon* is used to divide a sentence when the second part explains or elaborates on what has gone before: *They have put forward a different theory: the phenomenon may be caused by movements within the earth's crust.* It is also used to introduce a list: *You will need the following equipment: a rucksack, waterproof clothing, strong walking boots, and a map.* A colon sometimes separates numbers, e.g. in Biblical references, ratios, and clock times: *Genesis 13:8; a ratio of 6:4; the train that departs at 17:42.*

PUNCTUATION See *semi-colon*.

colon[2] /kṓlən, -lon/ (*plural* **-lons** or **-la** /-lə/) *n* the section of the large intestine that runs from the caecum to the rectum [14C. Via Latin < Greek *kolon* 'a large intestine'.]

colón /ko lṓn/ (*plural* **-lóns** or **-lones** /-lṓness/) *n* see table at **currency** [Late 19C. After Cristóbal Colón, Spanish name of Christopher Columbus.]

Colón /ko lṓn/ capital of Colón Province, central Panama. Population: 158,935 (1996 estimate).

colonel /kúrn'l/ *n* 1 MILITARY RANK IN UK an officer in the British Army or Royal Marines of a rank above lieutenant colonel 2 MILITARY RANK IN UNITED STATES an officer in the US Army, Marine Corps, or Air Force of a rank above lieutenant colonel 3 MILITARY RANK IN CANADA an officer in the Canadian army or air force of a rank above lieutenant colonel 4 *US* HONORARY US TITLE an honorary title in a state militia, bestowed by the governor in some US states [Mid-16C. Via obsolete French *coronel* < Italian *colonnella* 'little column' < *colonna* 'column' < Latin *columna* (see COLUMN).] —**colonelcy** *n* —**colonelship** *n*

SPELLCHECK Do not confuse ***colonel*** with ***kernel***, which has a similar sound. Beware: your spellchecker will not catch this error.

Colonel Blimp /-blímp/ *n* = **blimp**[2]

colones plural of **colón**

colonia /kə lṓni ə/ *n US* a poor Hispanic-American community, especially along the border between the United States and Mexico [Late 20C. < Spanish, 'colony'.]

colonial /kə lṓni əl/ *adj* **1 RELATING TO COLONY** possessing, ruling over, living in, or relating to a colony **2 colonial, Colonial RELATING TO BRITISH COLONIES IN AMERICA** relating to the 13 original British colonies in North America before their independence in 1776 **3 colonial, Colonial OF THE BRITISH EMPIRE** relating to the colonies of the former British Empire, or to the Empire as a whole **4 IN STYLE OF AMERICAN COLONIES** dating from or in a style typical of British North America from the late 17th to the early 19th centuries **5 LIVING IN COLONIES** describes animals that live in groups or colonies and are dependent on each other ■ *n* **1 SOMEBODY WHO LIVES IN COLONY** a resident of a colony who comes from the colonizing country **2 SOMEBODY FROM A COLONY** somebody whose native country is a colony [Late 18C. < COLONY.] —**colonially** *adv* —**colonialness** *n*

colonialism /kə lṓni əlizəm/ *n* a policy in which a country rules other nations and develops trade for its own benefit —**colonialist** *n* —**colonialistic** /kə lṓni ə lístik/ *adj*

colonic /kō lónnik/ *adj* relating to or situated in the colon ■ *n* a medical treatment in which fluids are injected through the anus into the colon to clean it out

colonic irrigation, colonic hydrotherapy (*plural* **colonic hydrotherapies**) *n* the injection of fluids through the anus into the colon to clean it out

colonise *vt* = **colonize**

colonist /kóllənist/ *n* **1 SOMEBODY LIVING IN NEW COLONY** an immigrant to a new colony, or one of the founders of it **2 colonist, Colonist EUROPEAN SETTLER OF AMERICA** one of the early European settlers of North America before it became the United States **3 ORGANISM MOVING INTO NEW ECOSYSTEM** an organism, e.g. a plant such as a weed, that moves into and establishes itself in a new ecosystem

colonitis /kóllə nī́tiss/ *n* MED = **colitis**

colonize /kóllə nīz/ (**-nizes, -nizing, -nized**), **colonise** (**-nises, -nising, -nised**) *v* **1** *vti* **ESTABLISH COLONY** to establish a colony in another country or place **2** *vt* **GO TO NEW LAND** to go to and live in a colony or other civilized setting established in a foreign, hitherto sparsely inhabited or virtually unsettled land **3** *vti* **BECOME ESTABLISHED IN NEW ECOSYSTEM** to establish plants or animals, or become established, in a biological colony in a new ecosystem —**colonizable** *adj* —**colonization** /kóllə nī záysh'n/ *n* —**colonizer** *n*

colonnade /kóllə náyd/ *n* a row of columns, usually supporting a roof or arches [Early 18C. < French, < *colonne* 'column' < Latin *columna* (see COLUMN).] —**colonnaded** *adj*

colonoscope /kə lónnə skōp/ *n* a long flexible instrument (**endoscope**) for viewing the interior of the colon, and often equipped with a device that can remove tissue for biopsy

colonoscopy /kóllə nóskəpi/ (*plural* **-pies**) *n* a medical examination of the colon using a colonoscope [< COLON[2]] —**colonoscopic** /kə lónnə skóppik/ *adj*

colony /kólləni/ (*plural* **-nies**) *n* **1 COUNTRY RULED BY ANOTHER** a country or area that is ruled by another country **2 SETTLEMENT IN AMERICA** one of the early settled areas in North America that formed the 13 founding states of the United States after independence (*often plural*) **3 GROUP OF COLONISTS** the group of people who have gone to live in a colony **4 GROUP OF SIMILAR PEOPLE** a group of people of the same nationality or ethnic group, doing the same work, or living in the same circumstances, who reside together or near one another ○ *a colony of artists* **5 AREA WHERE GROUP LIVES** the area, e.g. in a city, where a group of people with shared ethnicity, interests, or occupations lives **6 GROUP OF ANIMALS OR PLANTS** a group of animals, insects, or organisms of the same kind that are living together and dependent on each other, or a group of plants growing in the same place **7 MASS OF ORGANISMS** a localized mass or growth of organisms, e.g. bacteria, in or on a nutrient medium [14C. < Latin *colonia* 'farm, settlement' < *colonus* 'tiller' < *colere* 'cultivate'.]

colophon /kóllə fon/ *n* **1** the symbol or emblem that is printed on a book and represents a publisher or publisher's imprint **2** the details of the title, printer, publisher, and publication date given at the end of a book [Early 17C. Via late Latin < Greek *kolophōn* 'summit, finishing touch'.]

colophony /ko lóffəni/ (*plural* **-ies**) *n* INDUST = **rosin** *n.* [14C. < Latin *colophonia* < *Colophonia resina* 'resin of Colophon', after a city in Lydia, in what is now Turkey.]

color *n, vti* US = **colour**

Colorado /kóllə raádō/ **1** state in the W United States. Capital: Denver. Population: 3,892,644 (1997). Area: 269,618 sq. km/104,100 sq. mi. **2** major North American river, rising in N Colorado and flowing southwest through the Grand Canyon. Length: 2,330 km/1,450 mi.

Colorado beetle *n* a small black-and-yellow striped beetle that is a serious agricultural pest and feeds on the leaves of potato plants. *Leptinotarsa decemlineata.* US term **Colorado potato beetle**

Colorado Desert desert area of SE California

Colorado Springs city in central Colorado, home to the United States Air Force Academy. Population: 344,987 (1998 estimate).

Colorado topaz *n* **1** a brownish-yellow topaz found in the state of Colorado **2** a type of brownish-yellow quartz that resembles true Colorado topaz

coloration /kúllə ráysh'n/, **colouration** *n* **1** the appearance or pattern of colour on an object **2** the pattern of colours naturally occurring on an insect, bird, animal, or plant

coloratura /kóllərə tóórə/ *n* a passage or piece of vocal music characterized by florid and demanding ornamentation, usually consisting of a rapid succession of notes [Mid-18C. < obsolete Italian, 'colouring'.]

coloratura soprano *n* a soprano with a light versatile voice capable of performing coloratura roles

colorectal /kṓlō rékt'l/ *adj* relating to both the colon and rectum

colorific /kúllə ríffik/ *adj* producing or giving colour to something

colorimeter /kúllə rímmitər/ *n* **1** an instrument for measuring and specifying colours by comparison with an established set of standard colours **2** an instrument that determines the concentration of a solution of a coloured substance by reference to standard solutions or standard colour slides [Mid-19C. < Latin *color* (see COLOUR).] —**colorimetric** /kúlləri méttrik/ *adj* —**colorimetrically** *adv* —**colorimetry** *n*

color line *n US* a separation of ethnic groups, physically or socially, either in law or as the result of discrimination

colossal /kə lóss'l/ *adj* **1 VERY LARGE** unusually or impressively large **2 VERY GREAT** very great or impressive ○ *a colossal increase in consumer spending* **3 TWICE LIFE SIZE** describes sculptures that are twice life size. ◊ **heroic** *adj.* **6** —**colossally** *adv*

colosseum *n* = **coliseum**

Colosseum, Rome

Colosseum /kóllə seé əm/ *n* a large amphitheatre in Rome, built in the 1st century AD for sport and entertainment

Colossians /kə lósh'nz/ *n* the twelfth book of the New Testament, a letter from St Paul to the church in the Phrygian city of Colossae written between 55 and 63 AD

colossus /kə lóssəss/ (*plural* **-si** /-sī/ *or* **-suses**) *n* **1** a statue that is several times larger than life size **2** an enormously large or powerful person or thing ○ *a colossus among contemporary fashion designers* [14C. Via Latin < Greek *kolossos*.]

colostomy /kə lóstəmi/ (*plural* **-mies**) *n* **1** a surgical operation that creates an artificial anus through an opening made in the abdomen from the colon **2** an opening surgically created in the abdomen that functions as an anus

colostrum /kə lóstrəm/ *n* a yellowish fluid rich in antibodies and minerals that a mother's breasts produce after giving birth and before the production of true milk [Late 16C. < Latin.]

colour /kúllər/ *n* **1 PROPERTY CAUSING VISUAL SENSATION** the property of objects that depends on the light that they reflect and that is perceived as red, blue, green, or other shades **2 PIGMENT** a pigment used in painting **3 NOT BLACK OR WHITE** a colour such as red or green, as opposed to black, white, or grey **4 SOMETHING THAT ADDS COLOUR** something such as paint, cosmetics, or dye that is used to add colour to something **5 NATURAL SHADE OF COMPLEXION** the natural shade or colour of somebody's skin as characteristic of race, especially of somebody who is not white ○ *a person of colour* **6 NON-WHITE SKIN COLORATION** a skin colour other than that normally described as white ○ *people of colour* **7 HEALTHY LOOK TO SKIN** the normal look of a person's skin, especially in the face, when healthy **8 EXTRA FACIAL REDNESS** an extra redness in somebody's face, e.g. caused by embarrassment or exposure to cold wind **9 VARIETY OF COLOURS** brightness and variety in the colours something such as a room or picture has **10 INTEREST OR VIVIDNESS** a quality in something that gives it interest or immediacy **11 USE OF COLOUR IN PAINTING** the use of colour in painting, as distinct from line, form, or composition ○ *liked her handling of colour* **12 SOUND QUALITY** the quality of a particular sound **13 CLAIM OF LEGALITY** a claim or appearance of legal right ○ *by colour of law* **14 HYPOTHETICAL QUANTUM CHARACTERISTIC** a hypothetical property of quarks that takes three forms designated red, blue, and green **15 ABILITY TO SEE COLOURS** the aspect of visual perception by which an observer recognizes colours **16** *US* **GOLD FOUND IN GRAVEL** a particle of gold found in gravel or sand ■ **colours** *npl* **1 NATIONAL OR MILITARY FLAG** the flag of a nation or military unit **2 COLOURS REPRESENTING TEAM OR GROUP** the colours that are used to represent a team, school, or other group **3 CLOTHING WORN IN SPORT** the clothing worn by a jockey or an athlete that indicates the horse's owner or the team to which the athlete belongs **4 HERALDIC COLOUR** the main heraldic colours (**tinctures**) of azure, vert, sable, gules, and purpure **5 TEAM MEMBERS' BADGE** a badge or other symbol given to members of a sports team ○ *In her second year she got her rowing colours.* **6 SOMEBODY'S REAL SELF** somebody's real beliefs, opinions, ethics, and principles ○ *It showed her up in her true colours.* ■ *v* **1** *vt* **CHANGE OR ADD TO SOMETHING'S COLOUR** to change or add to the colour of something using paint, dye, cosmetics, or a similar agent **2** *vi* **TAKE ON COLOUR** to take on a particular colour or change colour **3** *vi* **BLUSH** to have more red in the cheeks or face than normal, generally because of embarrassment **4** *vt* **SKEW OPINION OR JUDGMENT** to skew the way somebody thinks about something, making an opinion or judgment less objective [13C. Via Old French < Latin *color*.] ◇ **with flying colours** to an excellent standard ◇ **nail your colours to the mast** to make it obvious what your opinions or intentions are ○ *They've nailed their colours to the mast and announced that they will not sell their property for redevelopment.*

colour in *vti* to colour shapes or areas that have been left white or blank, especially in a special book of outline drawings for children ○ *I gave him a box of crayons so he could do some colouring in.*

colour up *vi* to become red in the face because of embarrassment or annoyance ○ *If you so much as look at him he colours up.*

colourable /kúllərəb'l/ *adj* (*formal*) **1** appearing to be reasonable or true, but in fact being neither ○ *a colourable explanation* **2** pretending to be true or valid —**colourability** /kúllərə bílləti/ *n* —**colourableness** *n* —**colourably** *adv*

colourant /kúllərənt/ *n* a dye, pigment, ink, or similar agent that is used to add or change colour

colouration *n* = **coloration**

colour bar *n* the legal, social, and traditional barriers that separate people of different ethnic groups

colour-blind *adj* **1** partially or completely unable to see or to distinguish between certain colours because of a defect in vision **2** not discriminating between people on the grounds of their ethnic group or the colour of their skin —**colour blindness** *n*

colour-code (**-codes, -coding, -coded**) *vt* to classify different types of things by different colours

colour contrast *n* the perceived difference in a colour that occurs when it is surrounded by another colour

coloured /kúllərd/ *adj* **1 HAVING COLOUR** having a particular colour or colours (*often in combination*) ○ *dark coloured* ○ *honey coloured* **2 OFFENSIVE TERM** an offensive term meaning belonging to an ethnic group whose members are predominantly dark skinned (*dated*) **3 DISTORTED OR BIASED** biased or sensationalized ○ *a highly coloured account* ■ *n* **OFFENSIVE TERM** an offensive term for somebody who belongs to an ethnic group that is predominantly dark-skinned (*dated*)

Coloured *adj S Africa* belonging to a group of mixed ethnic origin ■ *n S Africa* somebody whose ancestors were of both African and non-African descent. ◊ **Cape Coloured**

colourfast /kúllər faast/ *adj* containing a dye that will not fade or wash out [Early 20C. < FAST[1].] —**colourfastness** *n*

colour field *adj* relating to the style of painting in abstract impressionism in which the emphasis is on covering the whole canvas with colour so that there is not one focal point

colour filter *n* a filter made of coloured glass or gelatin that absorbs light of a given colour before it reaches the camera lens

colourful /kúllərf'l/ *adj* **1 WITH BRIGHT COLOURS** having bright or varied colours ○ *colourful costumes* **2 INTERESTING** interesting and exciting ○ *one of the most colourful periods in our history* ○ *She has a colourful past.* **3 NOT ORDINARY OR PREDICTABLE** likely to behave in unusual and unexpected ways ○ *The grandfather was certainly a colourful character.* **4 FULL OF SWEARWORDS** characterized by coarse words or obscenities (*informal; used euphemistically*) ○ *colourful language* —**colourfully** *adv* —**colourfulness** *n*

colouring /kúlləring/ *n* **1 ACT OF GIVING COLOUR** the act of giving colour to something ○ *Children often enjoy colouring.* **2 COLOURING SUBSTANCE** a substance that gives colour to something, e.g. a food dye **3 TYPE OF COMPLEXION** the shade of somebody's skin or hair colour **4 CHARACTERISTIC COLOURS** the characteristic colours of a bird's plumage or an animal's coat

colouring book *n* a book with drawings for a child to colour

colouring-in book *n* = **colouring book**

colourise *vt* = **colourize**

colourist /kúllərist/ *n* **1** a painter whose technique involves special use of colour **2** somebody whose work involves colouring things —**colouristic** /kúllə rístik/ *adj* —**colouristically** *adv*

colourize /kúllər īz/ (**-izes, -izing, -ized**), **colourise** (**-ises, -ising, -ised**) *vt* to add colour to a black-and-white film, e.g. by using computer techniques

colourless /kúllərləss/ *adj* **1 WITHOUT COLOUR** lacking colour **2 CHARACTERLESS** not interesting or exciting ○ *a colourless personality* **3 PALE** pale or lacking distinct colour ○ *It looks rather colourless; how about adding some parsley?* —**colourlessly** *adv* —**colourlessness** *n*

colour phase *n* **1** a seasonal variation in the colour of a bird's plumage or an animal's coat **2** a distinct and permanent colour variation shown by a group of animals within a species

colourpoint cat *n* a long-haired cat with the markings of a Siamese cat, bred by crossing a Persian cat with a Siamese cat. US term **Himalayan cat**

colour scheme *n* a combination of colours used in interior decoration

colour subcarrier *n* the component of a television signal that transmits colour information to the receiver

colour supplement *n* a magazine printed in colour and forming a section of a newspaper

colourwash /kúllər wosh/ *n* coloured distemper —**colourwash** *vt*

colourway /kúllər way/ *n* one of range of possible colours available ○ *The shirt comes in three exciting colourways, taupe, red, and navy.*

colour wheel *n* the spectrum represented as a circular diagram that shows how colours are related to one another

colpitis /kol pítiss/ *n* MED = **vaginitis** (*technical*)

colpo- *prefix* vagina ○ *colposcope* [< Greek *kolpos*]

colposcope /kólpəskōp/ *n* a magnifying and photographic instrument used to examine the vagina [Mid-20C. < Greek *kolpos* 'womb'.] —**colposcopic** /kólpə skóppik/ *adj* —**colposcopy** /kol póskəpi/ *n*

colt /kōlt/ *n* a young uncastrated male horse, usually under four years of age ■ **colts** *npl* a team made up of young or inexperienced players, often the junior team representing a club or school [Old English, < ?]

coltish /kóltish/ *adj* energetic and playful in nature —**coltishly** *adv* —**coltishness** *n*

Coltrane /kol tráyn/, **John** (1926–67) US jazz saxophonist and composer

coltsfoot /kóltsfòot/ (*plural* **-foots** *or* **-foot**) *n* a plant with large hoof-shaped leaves. Flowers: yellow. Use: dried leaves and flowers: in herbal medicine to treat coughs. Native to: Europe, Asia, North America. *Tussilago farfara.*

colubrid /kóllyòobrid/ (*plural* **-brid** *or* **-brids**) *n* a snake belonging to a family of mostly nonvenomous snakes. Family: Colubridae. [Late 19C. < modern Latin *Colubridae* < Latin *colubrid-* 'snake'.]

colubrine /kóllyòo brīn/ *adj* **1** resembling a snake **2** belonging or relating to the colubrid snakes [Early 16C. < Latin *colubrinus* < *coluber* 'snake' (see COLUBRID).]

colugo /kə lóogō/ (*plural* **-gos** *or* **-go**) *n* ZOOL = **flying lemur** [Early 18C. < Malay.]

Colum /kólləm/, **Padraic** (1881–1972) Irish poet and dramatist

Columba /kə lúmbə/ *n* a small faint constellation of the southern hemisphere. See illustration at **constellation**

Columba /kə lúmbə/, **St** (521–597) Irish missionary. Alternative names **Colmcille, Columcille, Columbanus**

columbarium /kólləm báiri əm/ (*plural* **-a** /-ə/) *n* **1** a chamber or wall in which urns containing the ashes of the dead are stored **2** one of the niches in a building used to store funeral ashes [Mid-18C. < Latin, < *columba* 'dove'.]

Columbia /kə lúmbi ə/ **1** river that flows through SW Canada and the NW United States into the Pacific Ocean. Length: 2,000 km/1,240 mi. **2** city in central Missouri. Population: 78,915 (1998 estimate). **3** city in central Tennessee. Population: 31,865 (1998 estimate). **4** capital of South Carolina, in the centre of the state. Population: 110,840 (1998 estimate).

Columbian /kəlúmbi ən/ *adj* relating to the United States, or its people or culture. ◊ **pre-Columbian**

columbine[1] /kólləm bīn/ (*plural* **-bines** *or* **-bine**) *n* PLANTS = **aquilegia** [14C. Via Old French < medieval Latin *columbina (herba)* 'dovelike (plant)' < Latin *columbinus* (see COLUMBINE[2]); from its resemblance to a cluster of pigeons.]

columbine[2] /kólləm bīn/ *adj* resembling or relating to doves [14C. Via Old French < Latin *columbinus* 'dovelike' < *columba* 'dove'.]

columbite /kə lúmm bīt/ *n* a black, reddish-brown, or transparent mixed oxide mineral containing niobium, iron, and manganese. Use: source of niobium. [Early 19C. < COLUMBIUM.]

columbium /kə lúmbi əm/ *n* (*symbol* **Cb**) the element niobium (*no longer in technical use*) [Early 19C. < modern Latin *Columbia* 'America'; because discovered in ore from Massachusetts.] —**columbic** *adj* —**columbous** *adj*

Columbus /kə lúmbəss/ **1** capital and largest city of Ohio, in the centre of the state. Population: 670,234 (1998 estimate). **2** city in W Georgia. Population: 182,219 (1998 estimate). **3** city in Indiana. Population: 32,250 (1998 estimate).

Columbus /kə lúmbəss/, **Christopher** (1451–1506) Italian explorer

Columbus Day *n* in the United States, a day marking Christopher Columbus's discovery of the New World in 1492. Date: second Monday in October.

columella /kóllyòo méllə/ (*plural* **-lae** /-lī/) *n* a tiny bone in the middle ear of all land vertebrates that transmits sound waves from the eardrum to the inner ear and corresponds to the stapes in mammals [Late 16C. < Latin, 'little column' < *columna* (see COLUMN).] —**columellar** *adj* —**columellate** *adj*

column /kólləm/ *n* **1 ROUND PILLAR** an upright support shaped like a long cylinder ○ *a Corinthian column* **2 SOMETHING SHAPED LIKE A COLUMN** something compared to a column in form ○ *a column of smoke* **3 LINE OF PEOPLE OR THINGS** a long line of people or vehicles **4 SECTION OF PAGE** one of two or more vertical sections of printed material on a page **5 REGULAR ARTICLE** an item in a newspaper or magazine that is always written by the same person or is always about the same subject **6 VERTICAL ARRANGEMENT OF NUMBERS** a vertical arrangement of figures or mathematical terms **7 PART SHAPED LIKE COLUMN** any long part of a plant or animal ○ *spinal column* [15C. Directly or via Old French < Latin *columna*, probably < *columen* 'top'.] —**columnar** /kə lúmnər/ *adj* —**columned** *adj*

columnar jointing *n* the development of parallel, prismatic columns in contracting intrusive or extrusive rock undergoing cooling

column inch *n* an area on a page one column wide and one inch deep, used to measure the amount of type that would fill that space

columnist /kólləmnist/ *n* a journalist who writes a regular column for a periodical ○ *a gossip columnist*

colure /kə lóor/ *n* either of two great circles on the celestial sphere that intersect at the celestial poles, one of which connects the equinoctial points on the ecliptic while the other connects the solstitial points [14C. Via late Latin *coluri* < Greek *kolourai (grammai)* 'truncated (lines)' < *kolouros* 'truncated' < *kolos* 'docked' + *oura* 'tail'.]

Colwyn Bay /kólwin-/ coastal resort in N Wales. Population: 29,883 (1991).

coly /kō li/ (*plural* **-ies** *or* **-y**) *n* a gregarious bird with soft hairy plumage. Native to: Africa. Family: Coliidae. [Mid-19C. Via modern Latin *Colius* < Greek *kolios* 'green woodpecker'.]

colza /kóllzə/ (*plural* **-zas** *or* **-za**) *n* PLANTS = **rape[2]** [Early 18C. Via French (Walloon) < Low German *kōlsāt*, Dutch *koolzaad* < *kool* 'cabbage' + *zaad* 'seed'.]

colza oil *n* INDUST = **rape oil**

⚡**com[1]** *abbr* commercial organization (*in Internet addresses*)

⚡**com[2]** extension used in a computer file name to show that the file is a program of less than 64 kilobytes ○ *program.com*

⚡**COM** /kom/ *n* a process of converting computer output directly to microfilm. Full form **computer output microfilm**

com. *abbr* **1** comedy **2** comic **3** commerce **4** commercial **5** committee **6** commune[1]

Com. *abbr* **1** Commander **2** Commodore **3** Communist

com- *prefix* together, with, jointly (*before b, n, or p*) ○ *commix* [< Latin,< Indo-European, 'together']

coma[1] /kṓmə/ *n* a prolonged state of deep unconsciousness [Mid-17C. Via modern Latin < Greek *kōma* 'deep sleep'.]

coma[2] /kṓmə/ (*plural* **-mae** /-mee/) *n* **1** a luminous cloud of gas and dust surrounding the head of a comet **2** a lens defect that produces a blurred, comet-shaped image of a point, or the image produced [Early 17C. Via Latin < Greek *komē* 'hair of the head'.] —**comal** *adj*

Coma Berenices /kṓmə bérri nī seez/ *n* a faint constellation of the northern hemisphere. See illustration at **constellation** [Mid-16C. < Latin, 'Berenice's hair', after a 3C BC Egyptian queen whose hair, cut off and dedicated as an offering for her husband's safe return from war, is said to have been placed in the stars.]

Comanche /kə mán chi/ (*plural* **-che** *or* **-ches**) *n* **1** a member of a Native American people who formerly led a nomadic life in areas of Kansas, Oklahoma, and Texas and who now live mainly in Oklahoma **2** the Shoshonean language of the Comanche. Native speakers: 500. [Early 19C. Via Spanish from Southern Paiute or a related language.] —**Comanche** *adj*

Comanchean /kə mán chi ən/ *n US* a part of the early Cretaceous period in North America, which lasted from 140 to 100 million years ago [After *Comanche*, county in Texas] —**Comanchean** *adj*

Comaneci /kómmə néchi/, **Nadia** (*b.* 1961) Romanian-born US gymnast

comatose /kṓmətōss/ *adj* **1** in a coma **2** in a very tired or drunken state (*informal*) [Late 17C. < Greek *kōmat-* 'deep sleep'.] —**comatosely** *adv*

comatulid /kə máttyōōlid/ (*plural* **-lids** *or* **-lid**), **comatula** /kə máttyōōlə/ (*plural* **-lae** /-lee/ *or* **-la**) *n* a marine invertebrate animal that is free-swimming when it reaches maturity, e.g. a feather star. Order: Comatulida. [Late 19C. < modern Latin *Comatulidae* < late Latin *comatulus* 'with neatly curled hair' < Latin *comatus* 'having hair'.]

comb /kōm/ *n* **1** INSTRUMENT FOR NEATENING HAIR an instrument with a row of long thin teeth, used to make hair tidy **2** FASTENING FOR HAIR a piece of plastic or wood with long thin teeth, used to fasten back the hair **3** TOOL FOR CLEANING WOOL a tool or machine part with long slender teeth, used for cleaning wool or other materials **4** RIDING = **currycomb** *n.* **5** NEATENING OF HAIR an act of neatening the hair with a comb (*informal*) **6** CREST OF COCK the fleshy red growth on the head of a cock or other bird **7** HONEYCOMB a honeycomb ■ *vt* **1** NEATEN HAIR WITH COMB to tidy hair or fur with a comb **2** CLEAN OR ARRANGE FIBRES to clean or arrange the fibres of wool or other materials using a comb **3** SEARCH PLACE THOROUGHLY to search an area thoroughly ○ *We combed the house for his keys.* [Old English *camb* < Indo-European, 'tooth'] ◇ **go over** *or* **through something with a fine-tooth(ed) comb** to study or search something extremely carefully

comb. *abbr* **1** combination **2** combining **3** combustion

combat /kóm bat/ *n* **1** FIGHTING fighting between groups or individuals, especially between soldiers (*often before nouns*) ○ *He had never seen combat.* ○ *combat troops* **2** FIGHT OR STRUGGLE a struggle between opposing individuals or forces ○ *a combat between good and evil* ■ *vt* (**-bats, -bating** *or* **-batting, -bated** *or* **-batted**) **1** TRY TO DESTROY SOMETHING DANGEROUS to attempt to destroy or control something harmful ○ *measures to combat pollution* **2** RESIST to resist somebody or something actively [Mid-16C. < French *combattre* 'fight' (literally 'fight with') < Latin *battuere* 'to beat'.] —**combatable** /kom báttəb'l/ *adj* —**combater** /-báttər/ *n*

combatant /kómmbətənt/ *n* **1** a person or group taking part in a war **2** a participant in a struggle or argument

combat fatigue *n* a psychological disorder resulting from the stress of being involved in a battle and characterized by acute anxiety, depression, and loss of motivation

combative /kómmbətiv/ *adj* eager to fight or argue —**combatively** *adv* —**combativeness** *n*

combe /koom/, **coomb, coombe** *n* primarily in S England, a small valley with steep sides that seldom has running water in it [Pre-12C. < Celtic.]

comber /kṓmə/ *n* **1** a person or machine that combs wool or other materials **2** *US* = **beachcomber** *n.* **2**

combination /kómbi náysh'n/ *n* **1** MIXTURE a mixture of different things or factors, or the act of mixing them ○ *We were saved by a combination of skill and good luck.* **2** COMBINED SET two or more things or people that are combined to form a set ○ *The red shirt and navy waistcoat make a striking colour combination.* **3** ALLIANCE an association between groups or individuals established in order to accomplish something **4** NUMBERS THAT OPEN A LOCK a series of numbers or letters needed to open a combination lock **5** ARRANGEMENT OF NUMBERS IN SUBSETS an arrangement of the numbers or symbols in a mathematical set into smaller subsets without regard to the order in which those numbers or symbols appear **6** SUBSET a subset containing a specified number of the elements of a given set, selected without regard to the order in which they were chosen **7** FORMATION OF A COMPOUND the union of substances in the formation of a chemical compound **8** SEQUENCE OF MOVES INVOLVING SEVERAL PIECES a series of tactical moves involving two or more chess pieces **9** SERIES OF PUNCHES in boxing, two or more punches quickly delivered one after the other ■ **combinations** *npl* UNDERWEAR a piece of underwear with long sleeves and legs (*dated*) —**combinational** *adj*

SYNONYMS See ***mixture***.

combination lock *n* a lock that opens only when a set of wheels, each having a sequence of numbers from 0 to 9, are aligned to give a specific sequence of numbers

combinatorial analysis /kómbinə táwr i əl-/ *n* a branch of mathematics dealing with combinations and permutations, especially those relating to probability and statistics

combine *v* /kəm bī́n/ (**-bines, -bining, -bined**) **1** *vti* JOIN OR MIX TOGETHER to be joined or mixed together, or join or mix people or things together ○ *Combine the ingredients in a large mixing bowl.* ○ *All these factors combine to make for a truly successful product.* **2** *vt* DO THINGS SIMULTANEOUSLY to undertake two or more activities at the same time ○ *It can be difficult to combine having a career with being a mother.* **3** *vti* UNITE CHEMICALLY to join together, or make substances join together, to form a chemical compound **4** *vti* HARVEST CROPS WITH MACHINE to harvest crops using a combine harvester ■ *n* /kóm bīn/ **1** ASSOCIATION an association of business organizations **2** AGRIC = **combine harvester** [15C. < late Latin *combinare* 'put two things together' < Latin *bini* 'two at a time' < *bi-* (see BI-).] —**combinable** *adj* —**combinative** /kómbi naytiv, -nətiv/ *adj* —**combiner** *n*

combined /kəm bī́nd/ *n* a skiing event involving competition in downhill and slalom runs that are slightly less arduous than either run as a single event

combine harvester /kóm bīn-/ *n* a large farm machine that is used to harvest crops

combings /kṓmingz/ *npl* small loose pieces of hair, wool, or other fibre that are collected during combing

combo /kómbō/ (*plural* **-bos**) *n* **1** a small jazz or dance band **2** *US* a combination of several people or elements (*informal*) ○ *a burger, fries, and shake combo* [Early 20C. < COMBINATION.]

comb-over *n* a man's hairstyle designed to conceal baldness by allowing the hair to grow long on one side of the head and combing it over the top (*informal*)

combust /kəm búst/ *vti* to react vigorously with oxygen to produce heat and light, seen as a flame [15C. Partly < obsolete *combust* 'burnt' < Latin *combustus* (see COMBUSTION); partly back-formation < COMBUSTION.]

combustible /kəm bústəb'l/ *adj* **1** able or likely to catch fire and burn **2** able to react vigorously with oxygen to produce heat and light, seen as a flame —**combustibility** /kəm bústə bílləti/ *n* —**combustibly** *adv*

combustion /kəm búschən/ *n* **1** the burning of fuel in an engine to provide power **2** a chemical process in which a substance reacts vigorously with oxygen to produce heat and light, seen as a flame [15C. < Latin *combustus*, past participle of *comburere* 'burn up' < *urere* 'to burn'.] —**combustive** *adj*

combustion chamber *n* an enclosed space in which combustion takes place, e.g. in a jet engine or internal-combustion engine

combustor /kəm bústər/ *n* a combustion system in a jet engine or gas turbine, consisting of the fuel injection system, the igniter, and the combustion chamber

Comdr *abbr* Commander

Comdt *abbr* Commandant

come /kum/ (**comes, coming, came** /kaym/, **come**) CORE MEANING: a basic intransitive verb expressing movement towards a specified place or person ○ *Come and sit by me.* ○ *Come to my house tomorrow.*

1 *vi* REACH to reach or extend to a particular point or place ○ *Her hair came down to her waist.* **2** *vi* REACH A STATE to reach or be brought into a particular state or situation ○ *It just came apart in my hands.* **3** *vi* ARRIVE OR HAPPEN to happen or exist at a particular point or time ○ *I never thought this day would come.* **4** *vi* OCCUR IN THE MIND to occur in the mind ○ *An afterthought came to me while I was shaving.* **5** *vi* ORIGINATE FROM to originate from a place or thing ○ *The meat came from Canadian herds.* **6** *vi* RESULT FROM to result from something ○ *We hoped some good would come of it.* **7** *vi* BE PRODUCED to be produced in a particular size, colour, or style ○ *This model also comes in red.* **8** *vi* AMOUNT TO to add up to a particular total ○ *That comes to £14.50.* **9** *vi* HAVE AN ORGASM to reach sexual climax (*slang; sometimes offensive*) **10** *vt* ADOPT BEHAVIOUR to adopt a certain kind of attitude or behaviour (*informal*) ○ *Don't come the smart aleck with me, son.* **11** *prep* by a particular time in the future ○ *Come July there will be an extra fifty cases to deal with.* **12** *n* OFFENSIVE TERM an offensive term for a man's semen (*slang*) ◇ **come again?** used to ask someone to repeat or explain something (*informal*) ◇ **come what may** whatever happens ○ *He swore that, come what may, he would never let her out of his sight again.* ◇ **come to pass** to happen (*archaic or literary*) ◇ **have it coming (to you)** to be about to receive the punishment or retribution that you deserve ○ *He has it coming to him.* ◇ **how come?** used to ask the reason for something (*informal*) ○ *How come you never told me?*

come about *vi* to take place or occur

come across *v* **1** *vt* FIND to find something or meet somebody by chance ○ *I came across a reference to her in the newspaper.* **2** *vi* BE COMMUNICATED to be clearly communicated ○ *The point came across loud and clear: cutbacks are inevitable.* **3** *vi* GIVE AN IMPRESSION to give a particular impression ○ *She comes across as honest and sincere.*

come along *vi* **1** APPEAR to appear or arrive ○ *We'll deal with whatever comes along.* **2** PROGRESS to progress or develop (*only in continuous tenses, usually in questions or with an adverb*) ○ *How's the new recruit coming along?* **3** ACCOMPANY SOMEBODY ELSE to go somewhere with somebody **4** HURRY UP to move or act more quickly ○ *Come along or we'll be late for dinner.* **5** USED TO ENCOURAGE OR REPRIMAND used to encourage or reprimand somebody who is tired, unhappy, unwilling, or uncooperative (*usually imperative*) ○ *Come along, dry your eyes.*

come apart *vi* to tear or disintegrate ○ *The dress just came apart when I washed it.*

come around *vi* US = **come round**

come at *vt* **1** to reach or discover something with difficulty ○ *The only way to come at the facts is to ask pertinent questions.* **2** to set upon and attack somebody ○ *He came at his opponent on a dark side street.*

come away *vi* to become detached from something ○ *The handle came away in my hand.*

come back *vi* **1** BE POPULAR AGAIN to become popular again ○ *Seventies fashions came back briefly during the mid-nineties.* **2** COME INTO SOMEBODY'S MIND to appear or become clear again from somebody's memory ○ *I can't remember the address, but give me a moment and it'll come back to me.* **3** *US* RETORT to reply energetically or aggressively to somebody ○ *She came back at him immediately with a counterblast.*

come back to *vt* **1** to reconsider or refer to something again (*informal*) ○ *I'll come back to that question in a moment.* **2** to speak to somebody again about something at a later time ○ *Do you mind if I come back to you on that one?*

come before *vt* be submitted for consideration or judgment before a group of people with authority ○ *The proposal comes before the committee next week.*

come between *vt* **1** to disrupt a relationship ○ *I won't let anything come between us.* **2** to prevent somebody from having or doing something ○ *He won't let anything come between him and his Saturday football.*

come by *vt* to manage to acquire something ○ *Jobs are not so easy to come by nowadays.*

come down *vi* **1** DECREASE to decrease in value or amount ○ *Prices are coming down.* **2** REACH A DECISION to make a decision or judgment ○ *The judge came down in favour of the plaintiff's motion.* **3** BE HANDED DOWN to be passed down from one generation to another ○ *written records that have come down to us from that period* **4** LEAVE UNIVERSITY to leave a university, especially Oxford or Cambridge **5** RETURN TO NORMAL CONSCIOUSNESS to return to a normal state of consciousness after being affected by drugs (*informal*)

come down on *vt* to punish or criticize somebody severely

come down to *vt* to mean or represent something fundamentally, when all nonessential detail has been disregarded

come down with *vt* to catch a cold, flu, or another minor illness

come for *vt* **1** to arrive at a place to pick somebody or something up **2** to move towards somebody in a threatening way ○ *The dog came for me.*

come forward *vi* to present yourself and show that you are willing to undertake something ○ *She came forward with a rather good suggestion.*

come from *v* **1** *vi* be descended from a particular line, family, or stock **2** *vti* to have a particular place as your original home or a particular source of something ○ *She came from Manchester.*

come in *vi* **1** FINISH IN A PARTICULAR POSITION to finish a race in a particular position ○ *The British yacht came in fifth.* **2** ARRIVE to arrive or be received and become available for use, sale, or communication ○ *The spring fashions will be coming in next month.* **3** BECOME FASHIONABLE to become fashionable ○ *Long hair for men came in during the 1960s.* **4** PARTICIPATE to become involved in something ○ *There are three other companies interested in coming in on the deal.* **5** BEGIN SPEAKING to begin speaking during a discussion or in reply to a radio signal ○ *Perhaps I could ask you to come in on that point, Professor Witz.* **6** PROVE to turn out to have a particular level of usefulness ○ *That little knife came in very handy when we went camping.*

7 **APPROACH DESTINATION** to approach or arrive at a destination 8 **BECOME HIGHER** to become higher, driving water up over the shore (*refers to the tide*)

come in for *vt* to be the object of criticism or scrutiny ○ *The policy has come in for scathing attacks by the media.*

come into *vt* to inherit money or property

come of *vt* to be the result of something

come off *v* 1 *vt* **FALL OFF** to fall from something ○ *She came off at the water jump.* 2 *vt* **COME LOOSE** to become detached or to be detachable from something ○ *The top comes off easily.* 3 *vi* **HAPPEN** to take place as planned or predicted (*informal*) ○ *Let's hope the trip comes off.* 4 *vi* **SUCCEED** to be successful (*informal*) ○ *It was a risky thing to try, but it came off.* 5 *vt* **BE DEDUCTED FROM** to be deducted from something 6 *vt* **STOP TAKING MEDICINE** to stop taking a drug or a medicine ○ *When I came off the painkillers, the doctor put me on aspirin.*

come on *v* 1 *vi* **START TO OPERATE** to become available for use or to begin to function (*refers to a power source or machine*) ○ *The street lights come on at dusk.* 2 *vi* **HURRY** to hurry up (*usually imperative*) ○ *Come on, I haven't got all day!* 3 *vi* **USED TO ENCOURAGE** used to encourage somebody who is tired or unwilling (*usually imperative*) ○ *Come on, you can do it if you try.* 4 *vi* **USED TO SHOW DISBELIEF** used to tell somebody to stop exaggerating or lying ○ *Come on! You don't expect me to believe that, do you?* 5 *vi* **TO TELL SOMEBODY TO STOP PRETENDING** used to tell somebody to drop a pretence or stop behaving in a superior way (*usually imperative*) ○ *Come on! You know you can't afford that car.* 6 *vi* **PROGRESS** to develop well or in the stated way ○ *How's the book coming on?* 7 *vi* **ADVANCE** to move forward, especially in battle ○ *Our cannon fire tore huge holes in their ranks, but still they came on.* 8 *vi* **DEVELOP GRADUALLY** to develop gradually ○ *It grew chilly as night came on.* 9 *vi* **ENTER DURING PLAY** to go onto the stage as part of the action ○ *The villain doesn't come on until Act 2.* 10 *vt* **APPEAR OR SPEAK ON BROADCAST MEDIUM** to appear or speak on television, radio, or the telephone ○ *I noticed her voice when she came on the phone.* 11 *vi* **BEGIN AT SCHEDULED TIME** to begin at a particular time (*refers to radio or television programmes or a stage performer*) ○ *Her favourite show is coming on in an hour, and she never misses it.*

come on to *vt* 1 to begin to deal with something ○ *We now come on to the most controversial item on our agenda.* 2 to make sexual advances to somebody (*slang*)

come out *vi* 1 **REVEAL OR BE REVEALED** to reveal something or be revealed ○ *The true facts only came out when journalists began to dig a little deeper.* 2 **BE PUBLISHED** to be published ○ *Her new novel is coming out next month.* 3 **DECLARE** to state something openly ○ *The majority came out in favour of raising the age limit.* 4 **REVEAL SOMETHING SECRET ABOUT YOURSELF** to reveal to other people something about yourself that you have kept secret 5 **ACKNOWLEDGE SEXUALITY** to declare openly that one is a homosexual man or woman 6 **BECOME ACTIVE IN SAME-SEX RELATIONSHIPS** to become active in sexual relationships with others of the same sex for the first time ○ *I think she came out when she was 17, with her best friend.* 7 **MAKE DEBUT IN SOCIETY** to make a first appearance in society 8 **BE UTTERED** to be uttered involuntarily or with an unintended effect ○ *We had no intention of revealing the story; it came out by accident.* 9 **BECOME VISIBLE IN SKY** to become visible in the sky ○ *The sun came out from behind a cloud.* 10 **BE REMOVABLE** to disappear after cleaning ○ *Even the toughest stains come out with this new detergent.* 11 **STRIKE** to begin a strike ○ *The train drivers came out in sympathy.*

come out in *vt* to have something such as spots or a rash appear on the skin

come out of *vt* 1 to survive a hazard or illness ○ *I'd say she came out of the ordeal in pretty good shape.* 2 to be deducted from an amount of money ○ *The new window will have to come out of your allowance.*

come out with *vt* to say something surprising ○ *never know what children will come out with*

come over *v* 1 *vi* **CHANGE SIDES** to change an opinion or allegiance ○ *She says she'll come over if we guarantee her a seat on the board.* 2 *vi* **BE COMMUNICATED** to be clearly communicated ○ *The message came over loud and clear: he isn't going to change his mind.* 3 *vi* **GIVE IMPRESSION** to give a particular impression ○ *She comes over as much less forceful and ambitious than her sister.* 4 *vt* **AFFECT** to affect or overcome somebody ○ *A feeling of giddiness came over her, and she nearly fell over.* 5 *vi* **BEGIN TO FEEL** to begin to feel a strange sensation (*informal*) ○ *I came over all peculiar and had to sit down.*

come round *vi* 1 **VISIT** to visit somebody ○ *Why don't you come round this evening?* 2 **REGAIN CONSCIOUSNESS** to regain consciousness after being knocked out, e.g. ○ *When I came round, I was in hospital.* 3 **CHANGE YOUR OPINION** to change your opinion to that of somebody else ○ *They soon came round to our way of thinking.* 4 **RECUR** to happen again at the expected time ○ *The same questions come round year after year at these meetings.*

come through *v* 1 *vi* **SURVIVE** to survive a dangerous or unpleasant experience 2 *vi* **BE RECEIVED** to be received or heard, usually through a telecommunications medium ○ *A fax has come through from head office.* 3 *vti* **MOVE THROUGH A PLACE** to move between one place and another ○ *The porch was so crowded, we had to come through the kitchen.* ○ *Coming through! Coming through! These plates are hot!*

come to *v* 1 *vi* **REGAIN CONSCIOUSNESS** to regain consciousness or wake up ○ *The patient came to in the recovery room.* 2 *vi* **SLOW DOWN OR STOP** to slow down or stop (*refers to a ship*) 3 *vt* **TOTAL** to amount to a particular total ◇

come to that used when adding something to what has just been said

come together *vi* 1 to meet or gather together in one place 2 to coalesce successfully from disparate elements ○ *It's all finally starting to come together.*

come under *vt* 1 **BE CLASSIFIED** to be classified under a particular heading ○ *Hawthorne comes under American authors.* 2 **BE UNDER SOMEBODY'S AUTHORITY** to be subject to the authority of somebody or something ○ *Which department do we come under?* 3 **UNDERGO** to be subjected to something ○ *She came under attack from members of her own party.*

come up *vi* 1 **EMERGE FROM WATER** to rise to the surface of water ○ *She'll have to come up for air in a minute.* 2 **APPEAR ABOVE HORIZON** to appear above the horizon ○ *I enjoy watching the sun come up.* 3 **BE MENTIONED** to be mentioned or discussed ○ *a topic that came up in conversation* 4 **OCCUR UNEXPECTEDLY** to happen unexpectedly ○ *I won't be able to make lunch; something's come up at work.* 5 **BE HAPPENING SOON** to be going to happen in the near future ○ *Coming up next, the news.* 6 **APPEAR IN COURT** to be tried by a judge or a court of law ○ *Her case comes up next week.* 7 **BE SELECTED AS WINNER** to win a prize in a game involving luck ○ *if my numbers come up*

come up against *vt* to meet with something that has to be faced or dealt with ○ *He has come up against fierce criticism.*

come up for *vt* to become due for something ○ *The case is coming up for review.*

come upon *vt* to find something or meet somebody by chance

come up to *vt* to be as good as somebody's expectations

come up with *vt* to produce or discover something, in response to a need or challenge ○ *She's come up with a brilliant solution.*

comeback /kúm bak/ *n* 1 **RETURN TO SUCCESS** a return to a successful position or activity ○ *Rumour has it that she's planning a comeback.* 2 **SHARP REPLY** a sharp or witty reply ○ *He's always been one for the quick comeback.* 3 **COMPLAINT OR CLAIM FOR COMPENSATION** a complaint about something, or a claim for compensation ○ *I don't want any comebacks from dissatisfied customers.*

Comecon /kómi kon/, **COMECON** *n* an organization of the former USSR and satellite Communist countries aimed at encouraging economic development. Full form **Council for Mutual Economic Assistance**

comedian /kə méedi ən/ *n* 1 **COMIC ENTERTAINER** a humorous entertainer 2 **COMIC ACTOR** an actor who plays comic roles 3 **AMUSING PERSON** an entertainer who amuses an audience with comedy (*often ironic*) ○ *Some comedian put salt in the sugar bowl.*

comedienne /kə méedi én/ *n* 1 **FEMALE COMIC ENTERTAINER** a female entertainer who tells jokes 2 **COMIC ACTRESS** a female actor who takes comic roles 3 **AMUSING WOMAN** a woman who is or tries to be amusing (*often ironic*)

comedo /kómmidō/ (*plural* **-dones** /-dō neez/ *or* **-dos**) *n* a blackhead (*technical*) [Mid-19C. < Latin, 'glutton, worm' < *comedere* 'devour' (see COMESTIBLE).]

comedogenic /kómmidō jénnik/ *adj* tending to cause or aggravate blackheads

comedown /kúm down/ *n* a decline in status or position (*informal*)

comedy /kómmədi/ (*plural* **-dies**) *n* 1 **FUNNY PLAY, FILM, OR BOOK** a play, film, or book depicting amusing events 2 **COMIC GENRE** comic works, especially plays, considered as a literary genre 3 **COMIC ENTERTAINMENT** entertainment that is amusing 4 **COMIC ELEMENT** the humorous elements of a situation or work of art [14C. Via French *comédie* < Greek *kōmōidia* < *kōmōidos* 'comic actor' < *kōmos* 'revel' + *aoidos* 'singer' < *aeidein* 'sing'.] —**comedic** /kə méedik/ *adj* —**comedically** *adv*

LITERARY LINK ***The Divine Comedy***, an epic poem (1307?–20?) by Italian poet Dante Alighieri. Generally considered to be Dante's masterpiece, it is an account of the poet's journey through Hell, Purgatory, and Paradise, rich in historical, scientific, and philosophical allusion.

comedy of manners *n* a comedy that satirizes the manners and customs of a section of society, especially fashionable society

~~**comeing**~~ incorrect spelling of **coming**

comely /kúm li/ (**-lier, -liest**) *adj* describes a woman who is physically good-looking (*archaic or literary*) [13C. Probably shortening of obsolete *becomely* 'becoming' < BECOME.] —**comeliness** *n*

come-on *n* 1 something that arouses interest or desire, e.g. a free gift intended to encourage purchasers (*informal*) 2 a comment or action intended to indicate somebody's sexual interest in another person

comer /kúmmər/ *n* somebody or something that is likely to succeed (*informal*)

comestible /kə méstəb'l/ *n* something edible, usually a cooked food (*formal*) ■ *adj* edible (*formal*) [15C. Via French < medieval Latin *comestibilis* < Latin *comestus*, past participle of *comedere* 'eat completely' < *edere* 'eat'.]

comet /kómmit/ *n* a celestial body that is composed of a mass of ice and dust and has a long luminous tail produced by vaporization when its orbit passes close to the Sun [12C. Directly or via Old French < Latin *(stella) cometa* 'long-haired (star)' < Greek *(astēr) komētēs* < *komē* 'hair of the head'.] —**cometary** *adj* —**cometic** /kə méttik/ *adj*

comeuppance /kúm úppənss/ *n* something unpleasant, regarded as a just punishment for somebody (*informal*) ○ *He got his comeuppance in the end.* [Mid-19C. < COME UP, probably 'be tried before a court'.]

comfit /kúmfit/ *n* a sweet consisting of a piece of fruit, a seed, or a nut in a sugar coating [14C. Via Old French < Latin *confectum*, *confecta* < *confectus* (see CONFECT).]

comfort /kúmfərt/ *n* 1 **STATE OF BEING COMFORTABLE** conditions in which somebody feels physically relaxed ○ *Enjoy the comfort of your own home.* 2 **COMFORTABLE THING** something that makes you feel physically relaxed (*often plural*) ○ *the comforts of home* 3 **RELIEF FROM PAIN** relief from pain or anxiety ○ *They brought comfort to the wounded.* 4 **SOMETHING PROVIDING RELIEF** somebody or something that provides relief from pain or anxiety ○ *The family has been such a comfort to me since my wife died.* ■ *vt* 1 **CHEER** to bring somebody relief from distress or anxiety ○ *The victim's parents were being comforted at home by relatives.* 2 **MAKE SOMEBODY COMFORTABLE** to make somebody feel pleasantly relaxed ○ *She was comforted by the warmth.* [12C. < Old French *confort* < late Latin *confortare* 'strengthen completely' < Latin *fortis* 'strong'.]

comfortable /kúmftəb'l, -fərtəb'l/ *adj* 1 **RELAXED** feeling comfort or ease ○ *Sit down and make yourselves comfortable.* 2 **MAKING SOMEBODY RELAXED** making somebody feel physically relaxed ○ *I changed into something more comfortable.* 3 **NOT ANXIOUS** free from stress or anxiety ○ *I don't feel comfortable with that idea.* 4 **STABLE PHYSICALLY** in a stable physical condition ○ *The patient is comfortable.* 5 **ADEQUATE OR LARGE** large enough to prevent anxiety or risk ○ *The government won by a comfortable majority.* 6 **WITH ADEQUATE INCOME** having enough income ○ *They're not what you'd call well-off, but they're certainly comfortable.* —**comfortableness** *n*

comfortably /kúmftəbli, -fərtəbli/ *adv* 1 **AT EASE** with a feeling of comfort or ease ○ *Are you sitting comfortably?* 2 **HAVING NO PROBLEMS** having enough of something to stave off worry, especially enough money to live on without worrying about providing essentials ○ *We can manage comfortably on what we earn together.* 3 **EASILY** by a large margin ○ *The home team won comfortably.*

comforter /kúmfərtər/ *n* 1 **SOMEBODY WHO COMFORTS** a reliever of other people's grief or anxieties 2 *US, Can* **QUILT** a warm quilt used as a bed covering 3 **BABY'S DUMMY** a baby's dummy (*dated*)

Comforter *n* the Holy Spirit

comfort food *n* easily prepared unsophisticated food that is psychologically comforting, especially food that is high in carbohydrates (*informal*)

comforting /kúmfərting/ *adj* relieving anxiety or pain —**comfortingly** *adv*

comfortless /kúmfərtləss/ *adj* affording no comfort ○ *a sterile, comfortless room* —**comfortlessly** *adv* —**comfortlessness** *n*

comfort level, comfort zone *n* the set of physical or psychological circumstances in which somebody feels most at ease and free from physical discomfort or stress (*informal*) ○ *He said that the task was outside his workplace comfort zone.*

comfort station *n US* a public toilet (*used euphemistically*)

comfort zone *n* = **comfort level**

comfrey /kúmfri/ (*plural* **-frey** *or* **-freys**) *n* a plant with hairy leaves and stems. Flowers: pink, white, or blue, in clusters. Native to: Europe, Asia. Genus: *Symphytum*. [13C. Via Anglo-Norman, Old French < Latin *conferva* < *confervere* 'heal', literally 'boil together' < *fervere* (see FERVENT).]

comfy /kúmfi/ (**-fier, -fiest**) *adj* comfortable (*informal*) [Early 19C. < Shortening of COMFORTABLE.]

comic /kómmik/ *adj* **1 FUNNY** so amusing that it induces smiles or laughter **2 RELATING TO COMEDY** appearing in or characteristic of comedy ○ *a great comic routine* ■ *n* **1 COMEDIAN** a comedian or comedienne **2 MAGAZINE** a magazine that consists of stories told in a series of coloured panels. US term **comic book** [Late 16C. Via Latin < Greek *kōmikos* < *kōmos* 'revel'.]

comical /kómmik'l/ *adj* so amusing that it elicits smiles or laughter ○ *comical facial expressions* —**comicality** /kómmi kálləti/ *n* —**comically** *adv* —**comicalness** *n*

comic book *n US* = **comic** *n.* **2**

comic opera *n* **1** an opera with a humorous plot and a happy ending **2** comic operas considered as a musical genre

comic strip *n* a series of cartoons that tell a story or a joke

coming /kúmming/ *adj* **1 HAPPENING SOON** about to happen or start ○ *She was dreading the coming winter.* **2 PROBABLY SUCCESSFUL** likely to be successful in the near future ○ *She's the coming power in this company.* ■ *n* **ARRIVAL** the arrival of a person or an event

coming of age *n* **1** the reaching of the official age of adulthood and legal responsibility **2** the reaching of an advanced stage of development ○ *the coming of age of the computer*

comings and goings *npl* busy activity in which people arrive and depart frequently

Comintern /kómmin turn/ *n* an international organization of Communist parties set up by Lenin in 1919 and abolished in 1943 [Early 20C. < Russian *Komintern* < *kommunisticheskii internatsional'nyi* 'communist international'.]

~~**comission**~~ incorrect spelling of **commission**

~~**comitee**~~ incorrect spelling of **committee**

comity of nations /kómmiti-/ *n* the mutual recognition among nations of one another's laws, customs, and institutions

comm. *abbr* **1** commerce **2** commercial **3** committee **4** commonwealth

comma /kómmə/ *n* **1** a punctuation mark (,) that represents a slight pause in a sentence or is used to separate words and figures in a list **2** a short pause or interval in a piece of music [Late 16C. Via Latin < Greek *komma* 'piece cut off' < *koptein* 'to cut'.]

PUNCTUATION *Commas* are used in pairs around text that adds extra information and that can be omitted without affecting the structure of the sentence: *He was staying with his sister, a piano teacher, in Paris. The plant, which thrives in acid soils, is grown for its scented foliage.* A comma may also follow a subordinate clause placed at the beginning of a sentence: *If I miss the train, I will be late for the meeting. Born in 1950, he spent his early childhood in India.* When commas are used to separate items in lists, the final comma (before and/or/etc.) is optional: *We invited Sarah, Jack, Kate, and Tom. You can have coffee, tea, cold milk or hot chocolate. They sell books, paper, envelopes, stamps, etc.* Similarly, a series of adjectives used before a noun may or may not be separated by commas: *It was a long, slow, difficult process. She was wearing a long blue knitted scarf.* Commas may also be inserted at appropriate points to break up a lengthy complicated sentence, but it is often better and clearer to split the sentence up into smaller units. A comma should not, however, be used to separate a long subject from a verb: *The girl I used to know many years ago at school was now unrecognizable* (no comma between *school* and *was*). Never use a comma between sentences.

---

comma butterfly *n* an orange and brown butterfly that has a comma-shaped white mark on the underside of each hind wing. *Polygonia c-album.*

ϟ **command** /kə maánd/ *n* **1 ORDER** an order or instruction given by somebody in authority ○ *On the command to mount up, the crews scrambled into their tanks.* **2 CONTROL** control over somebody or something that is gained by personal power or authority ○ *She sized up the situation and took command.* **3 THOROUGH KNOWLEDGE** thorough knowledge of something, especially a language ○ *a fluent command of French* **4 OPERATING INSTRUCTION TO COMPUTER** an instruction to a computer to carry out an operation **5 AUTHORITY** the authority to control and direct the actions of a group of people, especially a military unit ○ *A new officer arrived to take command of the regiment.* **6 MILITARY CONTROL** the ability to control an area militarily ○ *Our primary objective is to gain command of the high ground.* **7 SOMETHING UNDER OFFICER'S JURISDICTION** troops or a particular area that are controlled by an officer ○ *My new command consists of a mechanized unit.* **8 GROUP OF OFFICERS IN CONTROL** a group of officers who control part of an army ○ *the enemy command* **9 MILITARY GROUP WITH SPECIFIC FUNCTION** a section of an army or air force that has a particular function ■ *v* **1** *vti* **GIVE AN ORDER TO** to give somebody an order or instruction ○ *I command you to let these men go.* **2** *vti* **HAVE AUTHORITY OVER** to control a military unit or a specific area ○ *an officer who commands a special operations battalion* **3** *vt* **CONTROL OR DOMINATE AREA** to control an area using military force ○ *a fort that commanded the single pass through steep mountains* **4** *vt* **BE ABLE TO OBTAIN** to deserve or be entitled to something ○ *With your qualifications you can command a high salary.* **5** *vt* **LOOK OVER** to be in a position that has a wide view over something ○ *The observation deck commands a breathtaking view of San Francisco Bay.* [13C. Via Anglo-Norman, Old French < assumed late Latin *commandare* 'enjoin strongly' < Latin *mandare* (see MANDATE).] —**commandable** *adj*

command and control *n* **1** a system that directs the course of a missile **2** a military commander's exercise of authority and direction of operations

commandant /kómmən dant/ *n* an officer in command of a military establishment

command economy *n* an economy in which resources and business activity are controlled by the government

commandeer /kómən deér/ *vt* **1 SEIZE FOR MILITARY PURPOSES** to take something from its owner for official or military purposes **2 TAKE OVER** to take or use something, sometimes using force (*disapproving*) **3 FORCE INTO MILITARY SERVICE** to force somebody to serve in the armed forces [Early 19C. Via Afrikaans *kommandeer* < Dutch *kommanderen* 'to command' < French *commander* (see COMMAND).]

commander /kə maándər/ *n* **1 MILITARY OFFICER** an officer commanding a military unit **2 NAVAL RANK** an officer in the Royal, Canadian, or US navy or the US Coast Guard of a rank above lieutenant commander **3 SENIOR POLICE OFFICER** an officer in charge of a police district in London **4 MEMBER WITH HIGH RANK** a high-ranking member of a knightly and fraternal order —**commandership** *n*

commander in chief (*plural* **commanders in chief**) *n* an officer who has supreme command of military forces

Commander in Chief *n* used as an honorific title to denote the President of the United States, as commander of the nation's armed forces

Command Group *n* a group of officers and security personnel who accompany a commander

commanding /kə maánding/ *adj* **1 IMPRESSIVE** able to control or dominate ○ *a commanding presence* **2 BEING HIGHER IN POSITION** dominating a landscape or view **3 DOMINATING** demonstrating clear superiority ○ *a commanding lead* —**commandingly** *adv*

commanding officer *n* an officer in command of a military unit or establishment

ϟ **command key** *n* a computer key that gives commands to the computer, expanding the keyboard options

ϟ **command-line** *adj* using letters or words instead of codes to give instructions to a computer [Because such instructions are entered on one line after a particular character]

commandment /kə maándmənt/ *n* a command from God, especially one of the Ten Commandments

command module *n* the part of a spacecraft that houses the controls and the crew's living quarters

commando /kə maándō/ (*plural* **-dos** *or* **-does**) *n* **1 SPECIALLY TRAINED SOLDIER** a member of a military force specially trained to make dangerous raids **2 UNIT** a military unit made up of commandos **3 BOER FIGHTING UNIT** a force of Boer troops during the Boer War [Late 18C. < Portuguese, 'raiding party', < *commandar* 'to command'.]

command paper *n* a government document presented to Parliament, historically by royal command

command performance *n* a performance of a play or film given by command of a ruler or state

command post *n* **1** a military headquarters for a command group and its officers during an operation **2** a temporary headquarters for a team of people involved in an operation

commedia dell'arte /ko máydi ə del aár tay/ *n* an Italian form of popular comedy developed during the 16th and 17th centuries, characterized by the use of stock characters and familiar plots [Late 19C. < Italian, literally 'comedy of art'.]

commemorate /kə mémmə rayt/ (**-rates, -rating, -rated**) *vt* **1** to honour the memory of somebody or something in a ceremony ○ *a service held to commemorate the dead* **2** to serve as a memorial to something [Mid-17C. < Latin *commemoratus*, past participle of *commemorare* 'call to mind clearly' < *memorare* 'remind' < *memor* (see MEMORY).] —**commemorative** *adj, n* —**commemoratively** *adv* —**commemorator** *n* —**commemoratory** *adj*

commemoration /kə mémmə ráysh'n/ *n* **1** a ceremony or religious service to commemorate a person or an event **2** the act of honouring the memory of a person or an event —**commemorational** *adj*

commence /kə ménss/ (**-mences, -mencing, -menced**) *vti* to begin happening, or begin something [14C. < Old French *com(m)encier* < Latin *initiare* (see INITIATE).] —**commencer** *n*

commencement /kə ménssmənt/ *n* **1** the beginning of something (*formal*) ○ *the commencement of open hostilities* **2** *US* a ceremony during which degrees and diplomas are conferred at US high schools, colleges, and universities, or the day on which this ceremony takes place

commend /kə ménd/ *vt* **1 PRAISE** to praise somebody or something in a formal way ○ *She was commended for her bravery.* **2 CAUSE TO BE ACCEPTABLE** to prove something to possess worthwhile qualities ○ *The plan has much to commend it.* **3 ENDORSE** to endorse a person or thing as being worthy of approval ○ *I had no hesitation in commending her to them.* **4 SURRENDER FOR SAFEKEEPING** to entrust somebody, yourself, or your soul to somebody's safekeeping (*archaic or formal*) [14C. < Latin *commendare* 'entrust completely' < *mandare* (see MANDATE).] —**commender** *n*

commendable /kə méndəb'l/ *adj* worthy of praise —**commendableness** *n* —**commendably** *adv*

commendation /kómmen dáysh'n/ *n* **1** praise of somebody's abilities **2** an award or citation given to somebody in recognition of an outstanding achievement —**commendatory** /kə méndətəri/ *adj*

commensal /kə ménss'l/ *adj* describes a relationship between organisms of two different species in which one derives food or other benefits from the association while the other remains unharmed and unaffected [Late 19C. Directly or via French < medieval Latin *commensalis* 'at table together' < Latin *mensa* 'table'.] —**commensal** *n* —**commensality** /kómmen sálləti/ *n* —**commensally** *adv*

commensurable /kə ménshərəb'l/ *adj* **1 RELATED BY MEASUREMENT** related by virtue of sharing the same system of measurement or by being measurable using the same units **2 COMMENSURATE** equal in terms of something else (*formal*) ○ *His salary is commensurable to his ability.* **3 DESCRIBES TWO QUANTITIES** divisible by the same unit an even number of times [Mid-16C. < late Latin *commensurabilis* 'completely measurable' < *mensurabilis* (see MENSURABLE).] —**commensurability** /kə ménshərə bílləti/ *n* —**commensurably** *adv*

commensurate /kə ménshərət/ *adj* **1 EQUAL IN SIZE** of the same size or extent **2 IN PROPORTION** properly or appropriately proportionate ○ *The rewards will be commensurate with the efforts made.* **3 MEASURED USING COMPATIBLE UNITS** measured in or related by units that are compatible [Mid-17C. < late Latin *commensuratus* 'measured with' < Latin *mensura* 'measure'.] —**commensurately** *adv* —**commensurateness** *n* —**commensuration** /kə ménshə ráysh'n/ *n*

⚡**comment** /kómment/ *n* **1 REMARK** a remark that states a fact or expresses an opinion ○ *Comments are invited from all participants.* **2 OBSERVATION** an implied or indirect judgment ○ *The incident attracted a great deal of press comment.* **3 EXPLANATORY NOTE** a note that explains a passage in a text **4 NOTE EXPLAINING PROGRAM CODE** a note embedded in a computer program that describes how the programming code that follows works ■ *vti* **MAKE A COMMENT** to state a fact or give an opinion [14C. < Latin *commentum* 'invention' < *comment-*, past participle of *comminisci* 'invent', literally 'think together'.]

commentary /kómməntəri/ *n* (*plural* **-ies**) **1 SPOKEN DESCRIPTION OF EVENT** a spoken description of an event as it happens, especially of a sporting event being broadcast on radio or television. US term **play-by-play** **2 CLARIFICATION OF A SITUATION** an example illustrating a situation **3 SERIES OF EXPLANATORY NOTES** a series of notes explaining or interpreting a written text **4 EXPLANATORY ESSAY** an essay or book that explains a text ■ **commentaries** *npl* **RECORD OF EVENTS** a record of events, usually written by somebody who participated in them —**commentarial** /kómmən táiri əl/ *adj*

commentary box *n* a booth at a sports stadium where a television or radio commentator broadcasts from

commentate /kómmən tayt/ *vi* to provide a commentary, either in radio or television broadcasting or on texts

commentator /kómmən taytər/ *n* **1** a broadcaster for radio or television who describes events, especially sporting events, as they happen **2** a reporter and analyst of the news for radio, television, or a newspaper

commerce /kómm urss/ *n* **1** the large-scale buying and selling of goods and services **2** the study of the principles and practices of commerce [Mid-16C. < Latin *commercium* 'mutual trade'.]

⚡**commerce service provider** *n* a company that supplies e-commerce services to businesses

⚡**commerce XML** *n* a set of document type definitions used as a meta-language for product information on the Internet (*in e-commerce*) Full form of **cXML**

commercial /kə múrsh'l/ *adj* **1 RELATING TO COMMERCE** relating to the buying and selling of goods or services **2 SUITABLE FOR TRADING** appropriate or sufficient for the purposes of trade **3 FOR INDUSTRIAL USE** produced in bulk for industrial use and often unrefined **4 DONE FOR PROFIT** done with the primary aim of making money **5 PAID FOR WITH ADVERTISING** supported by revenue from advertising ■ *n* **ADVERTISEMENT ON RADIO OR TELEVISION** an advertisement broadcast on radio or television —**commerciality** /kə múrshi álləti/ *n*

commercial art *n* graphic art produced for purposes such as advertising and packaging —**commercial artist** *n*

commercial bank *n* a bank whose primary business is providing financial services to companies

commercial break *n* an interval during a radio or television programme for the purpose of broadcasting advertisements

commercial college *n* a college that teaches primarily business-related subjects

commercialese /kə múrsh'l éez/ *n* the language or jargon used by people who work in business

⚡**commercial Internet exchange** *n* a connection point between commercial Internet service providers (*in e-commerce*)

commercialise *vt* = **commercialize**

commercialism /kə múrsh'lizəm/ *n* **1** the principles and methods of commerce **2** excessive emphasis on profit-making —**commercialist** *n* —**commercialistic** /-ístik/ *adj*

commercialize /kə múrsh'l īz/ (**-izes, -izing, -ized**), **commercialise** (**-ises, -ising, -ised**) *vt* **1** to apply business principles to something or run it as a business **2** to exploit something for financial gain —**commercialization** /kə múrsh'l ī záysh'n/ *n*

commercially /kə múrshəli/ *adv* in commercial terms or from a profit-making point of view

commercial paper *n* short-term negotiable instruments backed only by the good name of the company

commercial traveller *n* a travelling company sales representative (*dated*)

commercial vehicle *n* a road vehicle designed to transport goods or passengers

commère /kómmair/ *n* a woman who introduces acts on a television, radio, or stage show [Early 20C. < French, 'godmother', literally 'mother with' < Latin *mater* 'mother'.]

commie /kómmi/, **commy** (*plural* **-mies**) *n* a Communist (*informal disapproving*) [Mid-20C. < COMMUNIST.] —**commie** *adj*

commination /kómmi náysh'n/ *n* **1 ACT OF DENOUNCING** a formal denunciation of somebody or something (*formal*) **2 THREAT OF PUNISHMENT** a warning of punishment or vengeance, especially punishment by God (*formal*) **3 LIST OF GOD'S WARNINGS** a recital of God's warnings to sinners, read out in the Ash Wednesday service in Anglican churches [15C. < Latin *comminat-*, past participle of *comminari* 'threaten with' < *minari* (see MENACE).] —**comminatory** /kómminətəri/ *adj*

commingle /ko míng g'l/ (**-gles, -gling, -gled**) *v* **1** *vti* to blend or mix two or more things, or become mixed or blended (*literary*) **2** *vt* to put a number of funds or properties into a single fund or stock

comminute /kómmi nyoot/ (**-nutes, -nuting, -nuted**) *v* **1** *vti* **BREAK BONE INTO FRAGMENTS** to break, or cause a bone to break, into small parts **2** *vt* **PULVERIZE** to crush or grind something into a powder **3** *vt* **DIVIDE SOMETHING INTO SMALL PARTS** to divide something, especially property, into small parts (*formal*) [Late 16C. < Latin *comminuere* 'lessen greatly' < *minuere* 'lessen'.] —**comminuted** *adj* —**comminution** /kómmi nyóosh'n/ *n*

comminuted fracture *n* a fracture in which the bone is broken into fragments

commis /kówmi/ (*plural* **-mis** /-mi, -miz/) *n* an agent or deputy [Late 16C. < French, < past participle of *commettre* 'entrust' < Latin *committere* (see COMMIT).]

commis chef *n* a trainee chef who has the most junior position in the kitchen

commiserate /kə mízzə rayt/ (**-ates, -ating, -ated**) *vi* to express sympathy or sorrow [Late 16C. < Latin *commiserari* 'lament with' < *miser* 'miserable'.] —**commiserative** *adj* —**commiseratively** *adv*

commiseration /kə mízzə ráysh'n/ *n* feelings of sympathy or compassion ■ **commiserations** *npl* expressions of sympathy or sorrow

commissar /kómmi saar/ *n* **1** in the former Soviet Union, the chief minister in a government department **2** in the former Soviet Union, a Communist Party official, often attached to a military unit, responsible for providing political education [Early 20C. < Russian *komissar* < medieval Latin *commissarius* 'officer in charge' < Latin *commiss-*, past participle of *committere* (see COMMIT).] —**commissarial** /kómmi sáiri əl/ *adj*

commissariat /kómmi sáiri ət/ *n* **1 ARMY SUPPLY DEPARTMENT** an army department responsible for organizing food and supplies **2 ARMY SUPPLIES** food and other supplies given to soldiers **3 FORMER SOVIET GOVERNMENT DEPARTMENT** a government department in the former Soviet Union before 1946 [Late 16C. < assumed medieval Latin *commissariatus* < *commissarius* (see COMMISSAR).]

commissary /kómmissəri/ (*plural* **-ies**) *n* a deputy or representative, especially of a bishop —**commissaryship** *n*

commission /kə mísh'n/ *n* **1 FEE PAID TO AGENT** a fee paid to an agent for providing a service, especially a percentage of the total amount of business transacted **2 TASK** a job or task given to an individual or group, especially an order to produce a particular product or piece of work **3 GOVERNMENT GROUP** a government agency that has judicial or legislative powers **4 GROUP WITH TASK** a group of people authorized or directed to carry out a duty or task **5 APPOINTMENT AS MILITARY OFFICER** an appointment to the rank of officer in the armed forces **6 AUTHORITY TO ACT AS AGENT** the authority granted to an individual or organization to act as an agent for another **7 AUTHORITY OR INSTRUCTION** the authority or an instruction to do something (*formal*) **8 ACT OF COMMITTING** the committing of a crime or other offence ■ *vt* **1 ASSIGN** to assign a duty or task to somebody **2 ORDER SOMETHING SPECIAL** place an order for something that must be specially made or created ○ *have commissioned a new architectural firm to design the building* **3 MAKE SOMEBODY OFFICER** to confer the rank of officer on somebody in the armed forces **4 BRING INTO OPERATION** to bring equipment or machinery into operation **5 EQUIP SHIP** to bring a ship into active service **6 START UP** to bring a new project or facility such as a nuclear facility into operation [14C. < Latin *commiss-* (see COMMISSAR).] —**commissional** *adj* —**commissionary** *adj* ◇ **in commission** in operational use or in working order ◇ **on commission** with a percentage of the value of sales being full or partial payment for the work of selling ◇ **out of commission** not in operational use or working order

commissionaire /kə míshə náir/ *n* **1** a uniformed attendant or usher at a cinema, hotel, or theatre **2** in Canada, a veteran of the armed forces who belongs to the Corps of Commissionaires, an organization whose uniformed members can be hired to watch or protect buildings and property [Mid-17C. < medieval Latin *commissionarius* < Latin *commission-* 'commission' < *commiss-* (see COMMISSAR).]

commissioned officer *n* a military officer who is appointed by commission

commissioner /kə mísh'nər/ *n* **1 COMMISSION MEMBER** a member of a commission **2 SOMEBODY WORKING FOR COMMISSION** somebody authorized by a commission to carry out prescribed duties or tasks **3 GOVERNMENT OFFICIAL** a government representative in an administrative area —**commissionership** *n*

commissioner for oaths *n* a solicitor authorized to authenticate oaths for people making affidavits

Commission for Racial Equality *n* the official body appointed by the Home Secretary to enforce the Race Relations Act of 1976

commissure /kómmi syoor/ *n* **1 PLACE WHERE CELLS OR ORGANS MEET** a line or point where two cells, organs, or body parts meet or connect **2 LINKING BAND OF NERVE TISSUE** a band of nerve tissue that connects opposite sides of the central nervous system, e.g. the tissue connecting the left and right sides of the brain **3 PLACE WHERE PLANT PARTS JOIN** a junction or seam between two organs or parts, such as that between the carpels of a flower [15C. < Latin *commissura* 'juncture' < *commiss-* (see COMMISSAR).] —**commissural** /kə míssyóorəl, kómmi syóorəl/ *adj*

commit /kə mít/ (**commits, committing, committed**) *v* **1** *vi* **PROMISE DEVOTION** to pledge devotion or dedication to somebody or something ○ *He wasn't yet ready to commit to the relationship.* **2** *vt* **PROMISE RESOURCES** to devote or pledge something, e.g. time or money, to an undertaking **3** *vt* **DO WRONG** to do something wrong or illegal ○ *commit a felony* **4** *vt* **ENTRUST TO** to entrust something or somebody to somebody else for protection **5** *vt* **RECORD FOR THE FUTURE** to consign or record something in order to preserve it **6** *vt* **ASSIGN FOR DESTRUCTION** to give something over for destruction or disposal **7** *vt* **INSTITUTIONALIZE** to confine legally somebody to an institution, e.g. to prison or a mental health facility. ◊ **section 8** *vt* **SEND FOR TRIAL** to send somebody for trial in a higher court **9** *vt* **REFER PROPOSED LAW FOR REVIEW** to refer a bill to a parliamentary committee for review [14C. < Latin *committere* 'put together' < *mittere* 'put, send'.] —**committable** *adj* —**committer** *n*

~~**commited**~~ incorrect spelling of **committed**

~~**commitee**~~ incorrect spelling of **committee**

commitment /kə mítmənt/ *n* **1 RESPONSIBILITY** something that takes up time or energy, especially an obligation **2 LOYALTY** devotion or dedication, e.g. to a cause, person or relationship **3 PREVIOUSLY PLANNED ENGAGEMENT** a planned arrangement or activity that cannot be avoided **4 REFERRAL OF BILL FOR REVIEW** a referral of a bill to a parliamentary committee for review **5 INSTITUTIONALIZING** an act of legally confining somebody to prison or a mental health facility

committal /kə mítt'l/ *n* = **commitment** *n.* 5

committal proceedings *npl* legal proceedings in a magistrates' court to decide whether a case should be tried in a crown court

committed /kə míttid/ *adj* devoted to somebody or something such as a cause or relationship —**committedly** *adv*

committee /kə mítti/ *n* a group of people appointed or chosen to perform a function on behalf of a larger group

committeeman /kə míttimən/ (*plural* **-men** /-mən/) *n* US a man who is a member of one or more committees

committee stage *n* the stage in parliamentary proceedings in which a bill is closely examined by Members of Parliament sitting in relevant committees, between the second and third readings of the bill

committeewoman /kə mítti wòomən/ (*plural* **-en** /-wimən/) *n* US a woman who is a member of one or more committees

~~**committment**~~ incorrect spelling of **commitment**

commode /kə mṓd/ *n* **1 CHAIR WITH CHAMBER POT** a chair or box-shaped piece of furniture holding a chamber pot covered by a lid **2 PORTABLE WASHSTAND** a movable washstand with a cupboard underneath containing a chamber pot or washbasin **3 DECORATED CABINET** a low cabinet or chest of drawers, usually elaborately decorated [Late 17C. < French, originally 'suitable' < Latin *commodus* 'conforming with due measure' < *modus* (see MODE).]

commodious /kə mṓdi əss/ *adj* pleasantly spacious —**commodiously** *adv* —**commodiousness** *n*

commoditization /kə móddi tī záysh'n/ *n* the process by which a product reaches a point in its development where one brand has no features that differentiate it from other brands, and consumers buy on price alone

commodity /kə móddəti/ (*plural* **-ties**) *n* **1** an item that is bought and sold, especially a raw material or manufactured item **2** something that people value or find useful [15C. < Latin *commoditas* (see COMMODE).]

commodore /kómmə dawr/ *n* **1 NAVAL OFFICER** an officer in the navy of a rank above captain **2 MERCHANT NAVY CAPTAIN** a captain in command of a merchant fleet **3 PRESIDENT OF YACHT CLUB** the head of a yacht or boat club [Late 17C. Probably alteration of Dutch *komandeur* 'commander' < French *commandeur* < Old French *comander* (see COMMAND).]

ϟ **common** /kómmən/ *adj* **1 SHARED** belonging to or shared by two or more people or groups ○ *they shared a common goal* **2 OF OR FOR ALL** relating or belonging to the community as a whole ○ *the common good* **3 EVERYDAY** often occurring or frequently seen ○ *a common sight in cities* **4 WIDELY FOUND** describes a widely found species of plant or animal **5 NONSPECIALIST** used by people who have no specialist knowledge ○ *The common name for 'Viscum album' is 'mistletoe'.* **6 GENERAL** done, used, or held by most people ○ *common practice* **7 ORDINARY** without special privilege, rank, or status ○ *the common man* **8 OF AN EXPECTED STANDARD** of the standard that most people expect ○ *common courtesy* **9 VULGAR** considered to be lower-class, ill-bred or vulgar ○ *a common accent* **10 WITH EQUAL MATHEMATICAL RELATIONSHIP** having an equal relationship to two or more mathematical entities **11 OF VARYING STRESS OR LENGTH** describes a syllable that, in a line of poetry, can be either long or short, or stressed or unstressed **12 USEFUL FOR SEVERAL RELIGIOUS FESTIVALS** capable of being used as a service for any of a number of similar religious festivals ■ *n* **1 PIECE OF PUBLIC LAND** an area of land available for anybody to use, e.g. as a public recreation area or as pasture for cattle **2 RIGHT TO USE SOMEBODY'S LAND** the legal right to use somebody else's land or waters in a particular way, usually for grazing or fishing **3 SERVICE FOR SEVERAL RELIGIOUS FESTIVALS** a religious service that can be used for any of a number of similar festivals **4 COMMON SENSE** common sense (*slang*) ■ *npl* **SHARED DATA STORE** data stored in the memory of one computer that is available to all computers linked to it by a network [13C. < Latin *communis* 'duties together' < *munia* (plural) 'duties'.] —**commonness** *n*

commonage /kómmənij/ *n* **1 RIGHT TO USE JOINTLY** the legal right to use something, especially a pasture, in common with other people, or the use that is made of it **2 PUBLIC OWNERSHIP OF LAND** the status of something, usually land, that is publicly owned and available **3 LAND FOR ALL TO USE** land that is publicly owned and available **4** POL = **commonalty** *n.* 1

commonality /kómmə nálləti/ (*plural* **-ties**) *n* **1** the sharing of characteristics or qualities with other individuals **2** a shared characteristic or quality **3** POL = **commonalty** *n.* 1 [Late 16C. Alteration of COMMONALTY.]

commonalty /kómmənəlti/ *n* **1** the ordinary people as distinct from the upper classes, especially when considered as a political class (+ *singular or plural verb*) **2** a group or society or its membership (+ *singular or plural verb*) [13C. Via Old French < medieval Latin *communalitas* < Latin *communis* (see COMMON).]

common bile duct *n* the duct formed by the joining of the duct from the liver and and that from the gall bladder

common blue *n* a common European butterfly, the male of which is blue and the female usually brown with orange markings. *Polyommatus icarus.*

common carrier *n* an individual or company in the business of transporting goods or passengers

common chord *n* a major or minor musical chord of three notes (**triad**) that contains a perfect fifth

common cold *n* = **cold** *n.* 1

common denominator *n* **1** a whole number that can be divided exactly by the lower numbers (**denominators**) of two or more fractions. For example, 8 is a common denominator of $\frac{1}{4}$ and $\frac{1}{2}$. **2** a shared belief or characteristic

common difference *n* the difference between successive terms in an arithmetic series. For example, 3 is the common difference in the series 2, 5, 8, 11.

common divisor *n* MATH = **common factor**

commoner /kómmənər/ *n* **1 ORDINARY PERSON** an ordinary member of society who does not belong to the nobility **2 STUDENT WITHOUT SCHOLARSHIP** in some British universities and colleges, a student who does not receive a college scholarship **3 MEMBER OF HOUSE OF COMMONS** a member of the House of Commons, the lower house in the United Kingdom and Canadian parliaments

Common Era *n* the Christian Era, especially as used in reckoning dates. ◊ **Christian Era, Present Era**

common factor *n* a number that two or more other numbers can be divided by exactly. For example, 4 is a common factor of 8, 12, and 20. US term **common divisor**

common fraction *n* MATH = **simple fraction**

common gender *n* **1** in English, the gender of a noun that can refer to a person or animal of either sex, e.g. 'leader' and 'fox' **2** in some languages, the gender of those nouns that can be either masculine or feminine but not neuter

common good *n* the advantage or benefit of everyone

common ground *n* something mutually agreed upon, especially as a basis for negotiation

common knowledge *n* something that is generally known

common law *n* **1** the body of law developed as a result of custom and judicial decisions, as distinct from the law laid down by legislative assemblies **2** law that is applied consistently throughout a place and is not subject to regional variations

common-law *adj* **1 WITHOUT OFFICIAL CEREMONY** describes a partner in a marriage that is recognized in some jurisdictions when both parties declare themselves married without an official ceremony **2 OF UNMARRIED COUPLE LIVING TOGETHER** describes a partner in a marriage so called because of the length of time the two unmarried people have lived together as husband and wife **3 OF COMMON LAW** based on or relating to common law

common logarithm *n* a logarithm with ten as its base number

commonly /kómmənli/ *adv* by most people or in most circumstances ○ *The measure was commonly held to be a success.*

common market *n* any economic association established, typically between nations, with the aim of removing or reducing trade barriers

Common Market *n* a term used in the 1960s and 1970s to refer to both the European Community and the European Economic Community

common measure *n* **1** MUSIC = **common time** **2** the stanza form used for ballads, with four iambic lines rhymed 'abab' or 'abac' **3** MATH = **common factor**

common metre *n* **1** LITERAT = **common measure** *n.* 2 **2** the verse form used in many hymns, consisting of four-line verses that alternate lines of eight and six syllables

common multiple *n* a number that can be divided exactly by two or more other numbers. For example 12 is a common multiple of 2, 3, and 4.

common noun *n* a noun that refers to any of a class of people or things, e.g. 'singer' and 'place', as distinct from a proper noun, e.g. 'Lennon' or 'Washington'

common or garden *adj* of the ordinary, everyday kind [Originally of a plant]

commonplace /kómmən playss/ *adj* **1 EVERYDAY** encountered or happening often **2 DULL** uninteresting as a result of being unoriginal ■ *n* **1 DULL REMARK** an unoriginal remark **2 SOMETHING ORDINARY** something that occurs, is encountered, or is seen often [Mid-16C. Ultimately translation of Greek *koinos topos* 'general theme'.] —**commonplaceness** *n*

commonplace book *n* a personal notebook used for copying down quotations and memorable passages from other books

Common Pleas *n* LAW = **Court of Common Pleas** (+ *singular verb*)

common prayer, Common Prayer *n* standard prayers for public worship in the Church of England, as recorded in the Book of Common Prayer

Common Riding *n Scotland* a traditional ceremony carried out annually in some towns in Scotland, especially in the Borders, when mounted men inspect the boundaries of the common land

common room *n* **1** a lounge available to everyone living in a residential community or institution **2** a sitting room in a college or university where staff or students can relax

commons /kómmənz/ *n* **1** a dining hall in a college or university (+ *singular verb*) **2 commons, Commons** the common people as distinct from the ruling classes (+ *singular or plural verb*)

Commons *n* (+ *singular or plural verb*) **1** the politicians who are elected to the lower houses of the UK and Canadian parliaments and represent all the people **2** the House of Commons in the parliaments of the United Kingdom and Canada

common salt *n* FOOD = **salt** *n.* 1

common sense *n* sound practical judgment derived from experience rather than study

commonsense /kómmən senss/ *adj* based on common sense —**commonsensical** /-sénssik'l/ *adj* —**commonsensically** *adv*

common stock *n US* FIN = **ordinary shares**

common time *n* a musical metre with four crotchet beats to the bar, commonly referred to as four-four time

common touch *n* the ability of a celebrity or somebody in public life to behave towards members of the general public in a naturally friendly, informal, and uncondescending way

commonwealth /kómmən welth/ *n* **1 NATION OR ITS PEOPLE** a nation or its people considered as a political entity **2 REPUBLIC** a nation or state in which the people govern **3 ASSOCIATION OF STATES** a group of states that have formed an association for the political and economic benefit of all members **4 PEOPLE WITH COMMON INTEREST** a group of people linked by something that they all have in common

Commonwealth /kómmən welth/ *n* **1 ASSOCIATION OF BRITAIN AND SOVEREIGN STATES** a political, educational, and development association of sovereign states, most of which are former British colonies, with the British monarch as its head **2 REPUBLIC IN 17C ENGLAND** the state and republican government in England from the death of Charles I in 1649 until the restoration of the monarchy in 1660 **3 FEDERATED STATES OF AUSTRALIA** the official designation of the federated states of Australia, often used to refer to the federal government as opposed to the state governments **4 TERRITORY ASSOCIATED WITH UNITED STATES** a self-governing territory voluntarily associated with the United States. Puerto Rico and the Northern Mariana Islands are Commonwealths. **5 TITLE FOR SOME US STATES** an official title used by the US states of Kentucky, Massachusetts, Pennsylvania, and Virginia

Commonwealth Day *n* a holiday in some countries of the Commonwealth of Nations. Date: second Monday in March.

Commonwealth Games *npl* a sports contest held every four years involving participants from British Commonwealth countries

Commonwealth of Independent States *n* an association formed in 1991 by most of the republics of the former Soviet Union, with ceremonial headquarters in Minsk, Belarus

Commonwealth of Nations *n* = **Commonwealth** *n.* 1

common year *n* an ordinary year of 365 days, as distinct from a leap year

commotion /kə mṓsh'n/ *n* a scene of noisy confusion or activity [14C. < Latin *commotion-* 'intensive motion' < *motion-* (see MOTION).] —**commotional** *adj*

comms /komz/ *npl* communications, especially in the military sense (*informal*) [Shortening]

communal /kómmyōōn'l, kə myōōn'l/ *adj* **1 SHARED** used or owned by all members of a group or community **2 OF COMMUNITIES** relating to communities or to living in communities **3 OF A COMMUNE** belonging or relating to a commune **4 RELATING TO DIFFERENT SOCIAL GROUPS** relating to or involving different groups within a society [Early 19C. < late Latin *communalis* < Latin *communis* (see COMMON).] —**communally** *adv*

communalise *vt* = **communalize**

communalism /kómmyŏŏn'lizəm/ *n* **1** the principles and practices of communal living or ownership, or support for a communal society **2** a greater loyalty to an ethnic or religious group than to society in general —**communalist** *n* —**communalistic** /kómmyŏŏn'l ístik/ *adj*

communality /kómmyŏŏ nálləti/ *n* **1** shared use or ownership **2** the spirit of cooperation and solidarity that exists among members of a community or commune

communalize /kómmyŏŏn'l īz/ (**-izes, -izing, -ized**), **communalise** (**-ises, -ising, -ised**) *vt* to put something into joint ownership among the members of a community

communard /kómmyŏŏ naard/ *n* somebody living in a commune

Communard /kómmyŏŏ naard/ *n* a member or supporter of the Paris Commune of 1871

commune[1] /kóm yoon/ *n* **1** COMMUNAL GROUP a mutually supportive community in which possessions and responsibilities are shared **2** PEOPLE LIVING IN COMMUNE a group of families or individuals living in a commune **3** SMALLEST ADMINISTRATIVE DISTRICT OF VARIOUS COUNTRIES the smallest administrative district of some countries, e.g. France, Italy, and Switzerland, governed by a mayor and a council [Late 17C. Via French < medieval Latin *communia* < Latin *communis* (see COMMON).]

commune[2] /kə myóon, kóm yoon/ (**-munes, -muning, -muned**) *vi* to experience a deep emotional or spiritual relationship with something [14C. < Old French *comuner* 'share' < *comun* 'common' < Latin *communis* (see COMMON).]

Commune /kóm yoon/ *n* **1** HIST = **Paris Commune 2** the insurrectionary committee that governed Paris at the height of the French Revolution in 1792, originally the driving force behind the executions of members of the previous ruling classes

communicable /kə myóonikəb'l/ *adj* **1** able to be passed from one person, animal, or organism to another ○ *a communicable disease* **2** easily communicated, or capable of being communicated [14C. < late Latin *communicabilis* < Latin *communicare* (see COMMUNICATE).] —**communicability** /kə myóonikə bílləti/ *n* —**communicably** *adv*

communicant /kə myóonikənt/ *n* **1** a taker of the Christian sacrament of Communion **2** somebody or something such as a service that provides information [15C. < Latin *communicant-*, present participle of *communicare* (see COMMUNICATE).]

communicate /kə myóoni kayt/ (**-cates, -cating, -cated**) *v* **1** *vti* EXCHANGE INFORMATION to give or exchange information, e.g. by speech or writing ○ *We communicate by e-mail.* **2** *vt* CONVEY to transmit or reveal a feeling or thought by speech, writing, or gesture so that it is clearly understood **3** *vi* UNDERSTAND ONE ANOTHER to share a good personal understanding **4** *vi* HAVE COMMON ACCESS to be connected or provide access to each other **5** *vt* TRANSMIT DISEASE to pass a disease or infection on to somebody **6** *vi* GIVE OR RECEIVE COMMUNION to give or receive the Christian sacrament of Communion [Early 16C. < Latin *communicare* 'share' < *communis* (see COMMON).] —**communicator** *n* —**communicatory** /-kətəri/ *adj*

communication /kə myóoni káysh'n/ *n* **1** EXCHANGE OF INFORMATION the exchange of information between individuals, e.g. by means of speaking, writing, or using a common system of signs or behaviour **2** MESSAGE a spoken or written message **3** ACT OF COMMUNICATING the communicating of information **4** RAPPORT a sense of mutual understanding and sympathy **5** ACCESS a means of access or communication, e.g. a connecting door —**communicational** *adj*

communication cord *n* a cord or handle in a railway carriage that a passenger can pull to stop a train in an emergency. US term **emergency cord**

communications /kəmyooni káysh'nz/ *npl* **1** SYSTEMS FOR COMMUNICATING the technology and systems used for sending and receiving messages, e.g. postal and telephone networks (+ *plural verb*) **2** EFFECTIVE VERBAL EXPRESSION the effective use of words to convey ideas or information (+ *singular or plural verb*) **3** TRANSPORTATION OF TROOPS a system of routes and transportation for moving troops and supplies (+ *plural verb*) **4** STUDY OF HUMAN COMMUNICATION the study of the different means people use to communicate with each other, e.g. by gesture, speech, telecommunications, and writing (+ *singular or plural verb*)

communications satellite *n* an artificial satellite used to relay data such as radio, telephone, and television signals around the world

communication theory, communications theory *n* the study of all forms of human communication, including branches of linguistics such as semantics, as well as telecommunications and other non-linguistic forms

communicative /kə myóonikətiv/ *adj* **1** TALKATIVE inclined or ready to talk **2** OF COMMUNICATION relating to communication or to systems for communication **3** STRESSING PRACTICAL COMMUNICATION in foreign language teaching, stressing the importance of language as a tool for communicating information and ideas —**communicatively** *adv* —**communicativeness** *n*

communion /kə myóoni ən/ *n* **1** INTIMACY a feeling of emotional or spiritual closeness **2** CONNECTION an association or relationship **3** RELIGIOUS GROUP WITH COMMON FAITH a religious group with its own set of beliefs and practices, especially a Christian denomination **4** FELLOWSHIP BETWEEN RELIGIOUS GROUPS a sense of shared religious identity and fellowship, especially between members of different Christian denominations [14C. < Latin *communion-* < *communis* (see COMMON).] —**communional** *adj* —**communionally** *adv*

Communion /kə myóoni ən/ *n* **1** CHRISTIAN SACRAMENT a Christian sacrament that commemorates Jesus Christ's Last Supper, with the priest or minister consecrating bread and wine that is consumed by the congregation **2** PART OF THE COMMUNION SERVICE the celebration of the sacrament of Communion **3** CONSECRATED BREAD AND WINE the consecrated bread and wine received by worshippers at a Communion service

communiqué /kə myóoni kay/ *n* an official announcement, especially to the press or public [Mid-19C. < French, < past participle of *communiquer* 'communicate' < Latin *communicare* (see COMMUNICATE).]

communise *vt* = **communize**

communism /kómmyŏŏnizəm/ *n* the political theory or system in which all property and wealth is owned in a classless society by all the members of a community [Mid-19C. < French *communisme* < *commun* 'common' < Latin *communis* (see COMMON).]

Communism /kómmyŏŏnizəm/ *n* **1 Communism, communism** the Marxist-Leninist version of a classless society in which capitalism is overthrown by a working-class revolution that gives ownership and control of wealth and property to the state **2** any system of government in which a single, usually totalitarian, party holds power, and the state controls the economy

Communism Peak /kómmyŏŏ nizəm-/ former name for **Ismail Samani Peak**

communist /kómmyŏŏnist/ *n* **1** an advocate or supporter of any type of communism **2** a participant in communal living [Mid-19C. < French *communiste* < *commun* 'common' < Latin *communis* (see COMMON).] —**communist** *adj* —**communistic** /kómmyŏŏ nístik/ *adj*

Communist /kómmyŏŏnist/, **communist** *n* a supporter of Communism or a member of an organization that supports or practises Communism —**Communist** *adj*

communitarian /kə myóoni táiri ən/ *n* a member or supporter of a collectivist or cooperative community or system [Mid-19C. < COMMUNITY.] —**communitarian** *adj* —**communitarianism** *n*

community /kə myóonəti/ (*plural* **-ties**) *n* **1** PEOPLE IN AREA a group of people who live in the same area, or the area in which they live ○ *a close-knit fishing community* **2** PEOPLE WITH COMMON BACKGROUND a group of people with a common background or with shared interests within society ○ *the financial community* **3** NATIONS WITH COMMON HISTORY a group of nations with a common history or common economic or political interests ○ *the international community* **4** SOCIETY the public or society in general ○ *a useful member of the community* **5** INTERACTING PLANTS AND ANIMALS all the plants and animals that live in the same area and interact with one another [14C. Via Old French *communeté* < Latin *communitat-* < *communis* (see COMMON).]

community centre *n* a building used for a range of community activities

community charge *n* a flat-rate tax levied in Britain during the late1980s and until 1993 on all adults to part-finance local government

community chest *n* US a fund raised by voluntary contributions for local charities and social welfare activities (*dated*)

community college *n* **1** EDUC = **village college 2** NZ an adult education college that offers courses in practical or technical subjects

community education *n* educational and recreational programmes provided by local governments for people in their communities

community home *n* a home provided by a local authority or voluntary organization for children who cannot live with relatives or foster parents

community medicine *n* the branch of medicine devoted to the care of public health provision

community policing *n* policing that seeks to integrate officers into the local community in order to reduce crime and foster good community relations

community property *n* US property regarded by law as being jointly owned by husband and wife

community relations *npl* **1** the relationships between different cultural, ethnic, political, or religious groups who live in an area and may come into conflict **2** mediation between different cultural, ethnic, political, or religious groups living in an area

community school *n* a state primary or secondary school for which a local education authority has staffing, premises, and admissions responsibilities. ◊ **foundation school**

community service *n* a penalty requiring that an offender convicted of a relatively minor crime do unpaid work that is beneficial to the community as an alternative to imprisonment

community-service order *n* a court order requiring a convicted offender to do community service for a specified number of hours

communize /kómmyŏŏ nīz/ (**-nizes, -nizing, -nized**), **communise** (**-nises, -nising, -nised**) *vt* **1** to transfer something, e.g. land or property, from private to public ownership **2** to apply communist principles of organization to a government or people [Late 19C. < Latin *communis* (see COMMON).] —**communization** /kómmyŏŏ nī záysh'n/ *n*

commutate /kómmyŏŏ tayt/ (**-tates, -tating, -tated**) *vt* to convert alternating electric current to direct current or vice versa

commutation /kómmyŏŏ táysh'n/ *n* **1** REDUCTION IN SEVERITY OF LEGAL PENALTY the reduction of a prison sentence or other legal penalty to a less severe one **2** CONVERSION OF ELECTRIC CURRENT the converting of an electric current from alternating to direct current or vice versa **3** CONVERSION any exchange or substitution, e.g. the substituting of one kind of payment for another (*formal*) **4** US COMMUTER'S TRAVEL the travelling undertaken by a commuter

commutation ticket *n* US a passenger ticket valid for multiple trips over a given route during a limited period, sold for less than the total cost of tickets purchased separately for each trip

commutative /kə myóotətiv/ *adj* **1** involving or relating to exchanges or substitutions **2** giving the same result in mathematics or logic irrespective of the order in which two or more terms or quantities are placed. For example, addition and multiplication are commutative processes, while subtraction and division are not. —**commutatively** *adv* —**commutativity** /kə myóotə tívvəti/ *n*

commutator /kómmyŏŏ taytər/ *n* a device that maintains the direction of flow of electric current in a generator or reverses it in an electric motor

commute /kə myóot/ *v* **1** *vi* TRAVEL REGULARLY BETWEEN PLACES to travel regularly from one place to another, especially between home and work **2** *vt* REDUCE SEVERITY OF PENALTY to reduce a legal sentence to a less severe one **3** *vti* REPLACE WITH SOMETHING ELSE to be changed or substituted, or change or substitute one thing for another, e.g. one form of payment for another **4** *vi* BE REPLACEMENT to compensate or act as a substitute **5** *vt* ELEC = **commutate 6** *vi* GIVE SAME RESULT WITH DIFFERENT ORDER to give the same mathematical result irrespective of the order in which two or more quantities are placed, e.g. as in addition but not subtraction [15C. < Latin *commutare* 'change altogether' < *mutare* 'to change'.] —**commutability** /kə myóotə bílləti/ *n* —**commutable** *adj*

commuter /kə myóotər/ *n* **1** a regular traveller between places, especially between home and work **2** US an airline that provides short flights between major cities

commuter belt *n* a residential area from which many people commute

commy /kómmi/ *n* = **commie**

Como /kốmō/ capital of Como Province, N Italy, on the southwestern shore of Lake Como. Population: 535,471 (1997 estimate).

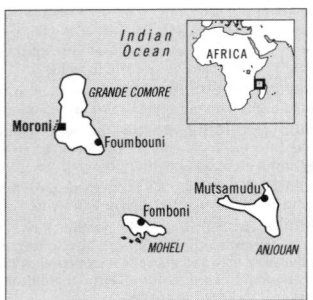

Comoros

Comoros /kómmə rōz, kə máwrōz/ independent state consisting of a group of islands in the Indian Ocean, off the coast of Mozambique. Capital: Moroni. Population: 528,893 (1997). Area: 1,862 sq. km/719 sq. mi. —**Comorian** *n, adj*

comp[1] /komp/ *n* (*informal*) 1 JAZZ ACCOMPANIMENT an accompaniment, especially a jazz accompaniment played on piano or guitar 2 ACCOMPANIST an accompanist ■ *vti* PLAY JAZZ ACCOMPANIMENT to play a musical accompaniment, often improvised, especially in jazz (*informal*) [Mid-20C. Shortening.]

comp[2] /komp/ *n* a competition (*informal*) ■ *vi* to enter a competition (*informal*)

comp. *abbr* 1 companion 2 comparative 3 compare 4 compensation 5 compilation 6 compiled 7 complete 8 composer 9 composite 10 composition 11 compound 12 comprehensive 13 comprising

compact[1] *adj* /kəm pákt/ 1 PACKED TIGHTLY closely clustered or packed together ○ *a compact bundle of papers* 2 SMALL AND EFFICIENTLY ARRANGED small, with efficient use of available space 3 SHORT AND STURDY short and stocky 4 CONCISE brief and concise ■ *v* /kəm pákt/ (**-pacts, -pacting, -pacted, -pacted** *or* **-pact**) 1 *vti* PACK SOMETHING TIGHTLY to become, or make something, more dense or firmly packed 2 *vt* COMPRESS METAL POWDER to compress metal powder in a die so that it bonds into a single component ready for heat-treatment (**sintering**) ■ *n* /kóm pakt/ 1 CASE FOR MAKE-UP a small flat case containing make-up, usually face powder, with a mirror inside the lid 2 COMPACT CAMERA a compact camera 3 *US, Can* SMALLISH CAR a medium-sized car that is economical to run 4 METAL POWDER READY FOR PRESSING a mass of metal powders in a die, ready for the compression and heat-treatment (**sintering**) that will consolidate it into a useable article [14C. < Latin *compactus*, past participle of *compingere* 'fasten together' < *pangere* 'fasten'.] —**compactible** *adj* —**compactly** *adv* —**compactness** *n*

compact[2] /kóm pakt/ *n* an agreement, especially an informal or private agreement [Late 16C. < Latin *compactum* < past participle of *compacisci* 'make an agreement together' < *pacisci* (see PACT).]

compact camera *n* a small camera with an integral lens

compact disc *n* a hard plastic disc approximately 12 cm/4¾ in in diameter on which information, e.g. music or computer data, is digitally encoded in a format readable by laser beam

✦ **Compact Disc-Interactive** *n* full form of **CDI**

compact disc player *n* a machine for playing compact discs

compacter /kəm páktər/ *n US* = **compactor**

compaction /kəm páksh'n/ *n* 1 the pressing together of particles to make a denser mass, or the compressed state of the resulting mass 2 a process in the formation of sedimentary rock in which pressure from overlying sediment forces water from unconsolidated sediment, reducing its volume and yielding solid rock

compactor /kəm páktər/, **compacter** *n US* a machine used in the home to compress rubbish into small bundles for easy disposal

compact video disc *n* a compact disc that plays both sound and pictures

companion[1] /kəm pánnyən/ *n* 1 SOMEBODY TO BE WITH a friend who accompanies or shares time with you 2 SOMEBODY WHOSE JOB IS ACCOMPANYING ANOTHER somebody, usually a woman, employed to live with another, especially in former times 3 MATCHING ARTICLE an article that goes with another to make a pair 4 HANDBOOK a guide or handbook on a particular subject 5 FAINTER OF TWO STARS the fainter of the stars that make up a double-star or multiple-star system [13C. < late Latin *companion-* 'one who shares bread' < Latin *panis* 'bread'.] —**companion** *vt*

companion[2] /kəm pánnyən/ *n* a companionway, or a covering above it [Mid-18C. Alteration of obsolete Dutch *kompanje* 'quarterdeck' < Italian *compagna* '(storeroom for) provisions', < Latin *panis* 'bread'.]

Companion, companion *n* the lowest-ranking member in a British order of knighthood

companionable /kəm pánnyənəb'l/ *adj* friendly, sociable, and good company ○ *They sat in a companionable silence.* —**companionability** /kəm pánnyən bíllati/ *n* —**companionableness** *n* —**companionably** *adv*

companionate /kəm pánnyənət/ *adj* 1 appropriate for a companion 2 right for each other

companionate marriage *n* marriage based on mutual affection and shared interests as opposed to purely economic or dynastic considerations

companion cell *n* in flowering plants, a cell that lies alongside a sap-conducting sieve-tube element, whose function it is thought to influence

companion piece *n* a work, especially of music or literature, that is closely related to another, often by the same composer or author

companion set *n* a set of tools used to tend a fire

companionship /kəm pánnyən ship/ *n* 1 the company of friends and the relationship that exists between them 2 an organized group of people

companionway /kəm pánnyən way/ *n* a stairway or ladder between decks on a boat or ship

company /kúmpəni/ *n* (*plural* **-nies**) 1 BUSINESS a business enterprise 2 BEING TOGETHER being together with others ○ *He didn't feel at ease in company.* 3 GROUP a gathering of people 4 COMPANIONS the people that somebody associates with 5 PARTICULAR TYPE OF COMPANION somebody seen as providing a particular type of companionship ○ *He can be very good company.* 6 GUEST a guest or visitor, especially for a meal or overnight stay ○ *We're having company this weekend.* 7 BUSINESS PARTNERS the partners of a business enterprise whose names are not included in the firm's title 8 TROUPE a group of performing artists, e.g. actors 9 GROUP OF TROOPS a unit of soldiers, usually consisting of two or more platoons 10 SHIP'S CREW the crew and officers of a ship 11 GROUP OF GUIDES a unit of Girl Guides 12 TRADE GUILD a medieval trade guild [13C. < Anglo-Norman *compainie* < late Latin *companion-* (see COMPANION[1]).]

company car *n* a car owned or leased by a business for use by an employee, often as a fringe benefit of a job or position

company doctor *n* 1 a doctor employed by a company to look after the health of its employees 2 a person who specializes in making unprofitable businesses efficient and profitable

company-grade officer *n* = **company officer**

company man *n* an employee who puts loyalty to an employer before friendship or personal beliefs (*disapproving*)

company officer *n* a commissioned officer who holds the rank of captain or below

company town *n US* a town whose residents depend on a single business for employment, housing, and shops

compar. *abbr* comparative

comparable /kómpərəb'l/ *adj* 1 similar enough for a fair comparison to be made ○ *We ate a meal comparable to that of the finest restaurant.* 2 as good as another or each other ○ *They both have comparable skills.* —**comparability** /kómpərə bíllati/ *n* —**comparableness** *n* —**comparably** *adv*

USAGE The most acceptable pronunciation in British English is with the stress on the first syllable, although stress on the second syllable is also heard and is more usual in American usage.

USAGE comparable to or **comparable with**? *Comparable* mimics the verb *compare* in being followed either by *to* or *with*, depending in careful usage on whether unlike or like things are being considered: *The agency provides a service comparable to that of a good library. The air raid was comparable with the ones on Dresden or Hiroshima.*

USAGE See also *compare*.

comparatist /kəm párrətist/ *n* a user of a comparative method, e.g. in the study of linguistics [Mid-20C. < French *comparatiste*, < *comparatif* 'comparative'.]

comparative /kəm párrətiv/ *adj* 1 INVOLVING COMPARISONS based on or using comparisons of different elements or types in the investigation of something ○ *comparative linguistics* 2 COMPARED TO OTHERS considered relative to something known, mentioned, or expected ○ *He passed the test with comparative ease.* 3 IN A FORM EXPRESSING INCREASE describes the form of an adjective or adverb that expresses an increase in quality, quantity, or degree e.g. 'quicker' and 'more importantly' ■ *n* COMPARATIVE FORM OF WORD a comparative form of an adjective or adverb [15C. < Latin *comparat-*, past participle of *comparare* (see COMPARE).] —**comparativeness** *n*

comparatively /kəm párrətivli/ *adv* in comparison to something else ○ *the costs were comparatively high*

comparator /kəm párrətər/ *n* 1 an instrument used for comparing the properties of a system or object, e.g. colour or shape, with those of a standard 2 a circuit used for comparing the difference between two electronic signals

compare /kəm páir/ *v* (**-pares, -paring, -pared**) 1 *vt* EXAMINE FOR SIMILARITIES to examine two or more people or things in order to discover similarities and differences between them 2 *vt* LIKEN to consider or represent somebody or something as similar to another ○ *'Shall I compare thee to a summer's day?'* (William Shakespeare, *Sonnet*; 1564–1616) 3 *vi* BE AS GOOD to be equal or similar in quality or standing, especially to be as good as another ○ *As an athlete she can compare with the best in the sport.* 4 *vi* CONTRAST to have a particular relationship with something or somebody else ○ *Its performance compares badly with that of rival engines.* 5 *vi* MAKE COMPARISON to make a comparison 6 *vt* GIVE ALL ADJECTIVE'S OR ADVERB'S FORMS to give the positive, comparative, and superlative forms of an adjective or adverb ■ *n* COMPARISON comparison (*literary*) ○ *a painting beautiful beyond compare* [15C. < Latin *comparare* < *compar* 'equal with' < *par* 'equal'.] —**comparer** *n*

USAGE Compare to or **compare with**? In careful usage, **compare to** is preferred when two unlike things are being likened: *He compared her skin to ivory.* **Compare with** is used when the comparison is between similar things and implies differences as well as similarities: *Tourists find its hotels poor value compared with those of other European capitals.* When **compare** is used intransitively (i.e. without an object), *with* should always be used: *The new model compares well with others in the same price range.*

comparison /kəm párriss'n/ *n* 1 the act or process of examining two or more people or things in order to discover similarities and differences between them ○ *Journalists continue to draw comparisons between the two systems.* ○ *The initial outlay seems insignificant in comparison with the potential profits.* 2 the quality of being similar ○ *There's no comparison between them.* [14C. Via Old French *comparesoun* < Latin *comparation-* < *comparat-*, past participle of *comparare* (see COMPARE).]

comparison-shop *vi* to compare the prices and features of the same or similar items, especially in different shops, to find the best deal —**comparison shopper** *n* —**comparison shopping** *n*

~~comparitive~~ incorrect spelling of **comparative**

compartment /kəm páartmənt/ *n* 1 PARTITIONED SPACE one of the areas into which an enclosed space is divided 2 TRAIN CARRIAGE SECTION a subdivision of a passenger train carriage, with a door and features such as two facing rows of seats or sleeping accommodation 3 SMALLER PART a separate part of something larger ○ *He liked to divide his life into different compartments.* [Mid-16C. < French *compartiment* < late Latin *compartiri* 'divide* up' < Latin *partiri* 'divide' < *pars* 'part'.] —**compartmental** /kóm paart mént'l/ *adj* —**compartmentally** *adv*

compartmentalize /kóm paart mént'l ɪz/ (**-izes, -izing, -ized**), **compartmentalise** (**-ises, -ising, -ised**) *vt* to divide something into separate areas, categories, or compartments, often in a way that makes the separate parts too isolated ○ *She had to compartmentalize her home life and work.* —**compartmentalization** /kóm paart mént'l ɪ záysh'n/ *n*

compass /kúmpəss/ *n* **1 DIRECTION FINDER** a device for finding directions, usually with a magnetized pointer that automatically swings to magnetic north **2 PERSONAL DIRECTION** a sense of personal direction ○ *a leader who was devoid of moral compass* **3 SCOPE** the scope of something such as a subject or area ○ *beyond the compass of the enquiry* ■ *vt* **1 UNDERSTAND** to understand something fully and completely (*formal*) ○ *far more than the average mind can compass* **2** = **encompass** *v.* 2 **3 ACHIEVE** to achieve or attain something (*literary*) [14C. Via French *compas* 'circle', *compasser* 'to measure' < assumed Vulgar Latin *compassare* 'step off' < Latin *passus* 'step'.] —**compassable** *adj*

compass card *n* the circular diagram in a direction-finding compass over which the needle rotates

compasses /kúmpəssiz/ *npl* a device for drawing circles or measuring distances, e.g. on a map, that consists of two rods, one pointed, the other often holding a pencil, joined by an adjustable hinge

compassion /kəm pásh'n/ *n* sympathy for the suffering of others, often including a desire to help [14C. Via French < Latin *compass-*, past participle of *compati* (see COMPATIBLE).] —**compassionless** *adj*

compassionate /kəm pásh'nət/ *adj* showing feelings of sympathy for the suffering of others, often with a desire to help —**compassionately** *adv* —**compassionateness** *n*

compassionate leave *n* exceptional leave granted to somebody, especially in the armed forces, for personal reasons, e.g. the death of a close relative

compassion fatigue *n* a loss or lessening of sympathy for the misfortune of others because too many demands have been made on your feelings

compass plant *n* a plant with leaves that tend to point north and south. Flowers: yellow, similar to a daisy's. Native to: prairie regions of central United States. *Silphium laciniatum.*

compass rose *n* a circular diagram printed on a chart or map to show the direction of north and other main points of the compass [Because its design was thought to resemble a rose]

compass saw *n* a handsaw with a tapering blade, used for cutting curved shapes

compass sense *n* the ability of certain animals, such as birds, fish, and insects, to use the Earth's magnetic field to guide them across long distances

compass window *n* a semicircular bay window

~~compatable~~ incorrect spelling of **compatible**

⚡**compatible** /kəm páttəb'l/ *adj* **1 HARMONIOUS** able to exist, live, or work together without conflict ○ *a highly compatible couple* **2 CONSISTENT** consistent or in keeping with something else ○ *an observation not compatible with the facts* **3 ABLE TO BE USED TOGETHER** in computing, able to be used together with or substituted for another piece of hardware or software ○ *The software isn't PC-compatible* **4 ABLE TO POLLINATE EACH OTHER** describes plant varieties that are able to pollinate each other successfully **5 ABLE TO BE GRAFTED** describes plants that are able to be grafted onto each other successfully **6 ABLE TO MATE** describes fungal strains that are able to mate successfully **7 ACCEPTABLE TO THE BODY** describes blood, organs, or tissue that can be transplanted or transfused into a person's body without being rejected [Mid-16C. < French < Latin *compati* 'suffer together' < *pati* (see PATIENT).] —**compatibility** /kəm páttə bíllətі/ *n* —**compatibleness** *n* —**compatibly** *adv*

compatriot /kəm páttri ət/ *n* somebody from the same country as another [Late 16C. Via French < late Latin *compatriota* 'fellow countryman' < *patriota* (see PATRIOT).]

compd *abbr* compound

compeer /kóm peer/ *n* (*formal*) **1** the equal or peer of somebody else **2** a person who is a close companion or associate of somebody else [14C. Via Old French *comper* < Latin *compar* (see COMPARE).]

compel /kəm pél/ (**-pels, -pelling, -pelled**) *vt* **1** to force somebody to do something ○ *I felt compelled to listen.* **2** to make something happen by force [14C. < Latin *compellere* 'drive together' < *pellere* (see PULSE[1]).] —**compellable** *adj* —**compellably** *adv* —**compeller** *n*

compelling /kəm pélling/ *adj* **1** attracting strong interest and attention ○ *a compelling account of a major scientific discovery* **2** tending to make somebody do something, make something happen, or be necessary ○ *I felt a compelling need to explain my actions.* —**compellingly** *adv*

compendious /kəm péndi əss/ *adj* containing a wide range of information in a concise form —**compendiously** *adv* —**compendiousness** *n*

compendium /kəm péndi əm/ (*plural* **-ums** *or* **-a** /-ə/) *n* **1 SHORT ACCOUNT** a comprehensive but brief account of a subject, especially in book form **2 TWO BOOKS IN ONE** a book in which two or more previously published books are brought together **3 COLLECTION** a collection of things, especially several different board games in one box [Late 16C. < Latin, < *compendere* 'weigh together' < *pendere* (see PENSIVE).]

compensate /kómpən sayt/ (**-sates, -sating, -sated**) *v* **1** *vt* **PAY SOMEBODY FOR LOSS** to pay somebody for work done or for something lost ○ *adequately compensated for their efforts* **2** *vti* **COUNTERBALANCE** to counterbalance a force or quality **3** *vi* **MAKE AMENDS** to make amends or make up for something ○ *Nothing can compensate for the loss of one's home.* **4** *vi* **STRESS SOMETHING TO MAKE UP DEFICIENCY** to stress the development of one aspect of your personality to make up for deficiency in another [Mid-17C. < Latin *compensat-*, past participle of *compensare* 'weigh together' < *pensare* (see PENSIVE).] —**compensability** /kəm pénssə bílləti/ *n* —**compensable** /kəm pénssəb'l/ *adj* —**compensative** /kómpən saytiv, kəm pénssətiv/ *adj* —**compensator** *n*

compensation /kómpən sáysh'n/ *n* **1 MONEY PAID TO REPAIR A LOSS** an amount of money or something else given to pay for loss, damage, or work done ○ *claimed compensation for loss of earnings* **2 PAYMENT OF MONEY TO COVER LOSS** the giving of something to somebody to pay for work done, loss, or damage **3 AMENDS** something that makes amends or makes up for something else ○ *one of the compensations of living abroad* **4 STRESSING A QUALITY** the stressing of one aspect of the personality to make up for deficiency in another —**compensational** *adj*

compensation order *n* an order from a court instructing somebody convicted of an offence to pay compensation to the victim

compensation time *n US* additional time off work offered by an employer for additional hours worked by an employee

compensatory /kómpən sáytəri/ *adj* serving to offset the negative effects or results of something else

compensatory growth *n* the growth in size of one part or organ of the body to make up for the failure or loss of another

compere /kóm pair/ *n* a host of an entertainment show, especially on television ■ *vti* (**-peres, -pering, -pered**) to act as a compere [Mid-18C. Via French *compère* 'godfather' < medieval Latin *compater* < Latin *pater* 'father'.]

~~competant~~ incorrect spelling of **competent**

compete /kəm péet/ (**-petes, -peting, -peted**) *vi* **1** to do something with the goal of outperforming others or of winning something **2** to be able to put up a contest against somebody or something else and have a chance of winning ○ *This product just can't compete.* [Early 17C. < late Latin *competere* 'strive together' < Latin *petere* (see PETITION).]

competence /kómpitənss/, **competency** /-tənssi/ *n* **1 ABILITY** the ability to do something well or to a required standard ○ *I don't doubt his competence for a moment.* **2 SUFFICIENT INCOME** an income that is enough to live on (*formal*) **3 BEING LEGALLY QUALIFIED** the condition of being accepted by a court as legally qualified to be a party or witness **4 LANGUAGE KNOWLEDGE** a person's internalized knowledge of the rules of a language that enables them to speak and understand it. ◊ **performance** *n.* 8, **parole** *n.* 5 **5 ABILITY OF CELL TO SPECIALIZE** the ability of embryonic cells to respond to an outside stimulus in a way that affects their development into specialized tissue

SYNONYMS See *ability*.

competent /kómpitənt/ *adj* **1 ABLE** having enough skill or ability to do something **2 ADEQUATE** good enough or suitable for something **3 LEGALLY CAPABLE** accepted by a court as credible, legally qualified, or within somebody's capacity **4 FUNCTIONING NORMALLY** able to carry out its normal functions effectively ○ *a competent cervix* [14C. Via French < Latin *competent-*, present participle of *competere* (see COMPETE).] —**competently** *adv*

competition /kómpə tísh'n/ *n* **1 TRYING TO BEAT OTHERS** the activity of doing something with the goal of outperforming others or winning something ○ *several firms are in competition for the contract* **2 CONTEST** an activity in which people try to do something better than others or win something **3 OPPOSITION** those against whom one is competing, or the level of opposition they give ○ *keep one step ahead of the competition* **4 STRUGGLE FOR RESOURCES** the struggle between organisms of the same or different species for limited resources such as food or light [Early 17C. < late Latin *competition-* < Latin *competit-*, past participle of *competere* (see COMPETE).]

competitive /kəm péttitiv/ *adj* **1 INVOLVING BEATING OTHERS** involving or decided by trying to win something or do something better than others ○ *a highly competitive sport* **2 WANTING TO BEAT OTHERS** inclined towards wanting to do something better than others **3 ATTRACTIVE** more attractive than others because of being good value or worth more ○ *competitive prices* —**competitiveness** *n*

competitive exclusion *n* the concept that two or more species with identical requirements cannot coexist on the same limited resources because one will compete more successfully than the other

competitive local exchange carrier *n US* a company that offers an alternative service to the established telephone service provider in a particular area

competitively /kəm péttitivli/ *adv* **1** in a way that involves trying to do something better than others or win something ○ *You will have to play competitively to win.* **2** in an attractive way because of being good value or worth more than something else ○ *competitively priced*

competitor /kəm péttitər/ *n* **1** a person or animal taking part in a competition **2** an opponent that somebody is competing against, especially in a commercial market [Early 16C. < Latin, < *competere* (see COMPETE).]

compilation /kómpi láysh'n/ *n* **1** the activity of gathering things together from various places **2** something created by gathering things together from various places ○ *a compilation of new poems*

⚡**compile** /kəm píl/ (**-piles, -piling, -piled**) *vt* **1 PUT THINGS TOGETHER** to gather things together from various places to form a whole **2 CREATE SOMETHING BY GATHERING THINGS** to create something by gathering things together **3 TRANSLATE COMPUTER LANGUAGE** to convert a computer program written in a high-level language into an intermediate language (**machine language**) using a special program [14C. < French *compiler*, probably < Latin *compilare* 'to plunder', < *pila* (see PILE[1]).]

⚡**compiler** /kəm pílər/ *n* **1** somebody who compiles something **2** a computer program that converts another program from a high-level language into an intermediate language

complacent /kəm pláyss'nt/ *adj* **1** self-satisfied, usually in an unreflective way and without being aware of possible dangers **2** eager to please (*archaic*) [Mid-17C. < Latin *complacent-*, present participle of *complacere* 'please very much' < *placere* (see PLACID).] —**complacency** *n* —**complacently** *adv*

USAGE complacent or **complaisant**? Both words are used of people and their actions. A ***complacent*** smile is a smile of self-satisfaction, whereas a ***complaisant*** smile is one that is intended to please. It is possible for a smile, or for somebody showing the smile, to be both ***complacent*** and ***complaisant***.

complain /kəm pláyn/ *vi* **1 EXPRESS UNHAPPINESS** to express unhappiness about something **2 DESCRIBE SYMPTOMS** to say that you are experiencing something, especially pain or an illness ○ *complaining of chest pains* **3 PROTEST** to accuse somebody of doing something illegal or undesirable, or make a protest about something ○ *The neighbours complained to the police about the noise.* [14C. < French *complaign-*, stem of *complaindre* < Latin *plangere* (see PLAINT).] —**complainer** *n* —**complainingly** *adv*

SYNONYMS ***complain, object, protest, grumble, grouse, carp, gripe, whine, nag***

CORE MEANING: to indicate dissatisfaction with something

complain to express discontent or unhappiness about a situation; **object** to be opposed to something, or express opposition to it; **protest** to express strong disapproval or disagreement; **grumble** to disagree in a discontented way, possibly repeatedly or continually; **grouse** to complain regularly and continually, often in a way that is not constructive;

carp to keep complaining or finding fault, especially about unimportant things; **gripe** (*informal*) to complain continually and irritatingly; **whine** to complain in an unreasonable, repeated, or irritating way; **nag** to find fault with somebody regularly and repeatedly.

complainant /kəm pláynənt/ *n* a person or organization that takes legal action against another

complaint /kəm pláynt/ *n* **1 STATEMENT OF UNHAPPINESS** a statement expressing dissatisfaction with something ○ *If you've any complaints, talk to the manager.* **2 SOMETHING MAKING SOMEBODY UNHAPPY** something that makes somebody unhappy or dissatisfied **3 EXPRESSING OF DISSATISFACTION** the act of expressing dissatisfaction with something ○ *has cause for complaint* **4 AILMENT** a physical disorder, usually something minor **5 STATEMENT** a statement setting out the reasons for a legal action [14C. < French *complainte*, feminine past participle of *complaindre* (see COMPLAIN).]

complaisant /kəm pláyz'nt/ *adj* showing a willingness to please others by carrying out, or allowing them to carry out, their wishes [Mid-17C. < French, present participle of *complaire* 'agree in order to please' < Latin *complacere* (see COMPLACENT).] —**complaisance** *n* —**complaisantly** *adv*

USAGE See ***complacent***.

compleat /kəm pléet/ *adj* having or exhibiting full knowledge of a particular field or skill (*archaic*) [14C. Variant of COMPLETE.]

complement *n* /kómplimənt/ **1 COMPLETING PART** something that completes or perfects something else **2 ONE OF TWO** either of two things that form a unit **3 FULL QUANTITY** a quantity of things or people that is considered complete ○ *the full complement of warships and replenishing vessels* **4 SENTENCE PART** the predicate part of a sentence that refers to the subject, not counting the verb **5 ITEMS EXCLUDED FROM A SUBSET** the elements of a set that are not included in a particular subset of that set **6** MATH = **complementary angle 7 GROUP OF BLOOD PROTEINS** a set of proteins in the bloodstream that, together with antibodies, recognize and attack foreign cells such as bacteria **8 NOTE INTERVAL** an interval that, when added to a given interval, equals an octave ■ *vt* /kómpli ment/ **COMPLETE** to complete, perfect, or accompany something else pleasingly ○ *a light dessert that complements a rich meal* [14C. < Latin *complementum* 'something that fills up' < *complere* (see COMPLETE).] —**complemental** /kómpli mént'l/ *adj* —**complementally** *adv*

USAGE complement or **compliment**? The two words are close in spelling but their meanings are quite different. A ***complement*** is something added to perfect a thing and make it complete, whereas a ***compliment*** is an expression of praise: *A fine wine is the perfect complement to good cooking. The cook received many compliments from the guests that evening.* Both words are also used as verbs, and both have adjectival forms: ***complementary*** and ***complimentary***. ***Complimentary*** has the special meaning 'given free'; and so a ***complimentary*** copy of a book is one given without charge, whereas a ***complementary*** copy is one that completes a set of books.

complementarity /kómpli men tárrəti/ (*plural* **-ties**) *n* **1** the condition of things that complement one another **2** the concept that two different models may be necessary to describe an atomic or subatomic system, e.g. electrons may be regarded as particles or waves in different circumstances

complementary /kómpli méntəri/ *adj* **1 COMPLETING** completing something else **2 INTERDEPENDENT** describes genes that are interdependent and produce their effect only when present together **3 NOT IN SUBSET** describes the elements of a mathematical set that are not included in a particular subset of that set **4** MATH = **complementary angle 5 RELATING TO COMPLEMENTARY MEDICINE** used in or using complementary medicine —**complementarily** *adv* —**complementariness** *n*

USAGE See ***complement***.

complementary angle *n* either of two angles that together make up a right angle

complementary colour *n* a colour or coloured light that, when combined with another, produces white or grey

complementary DNA *n* single-stranded DNA made in a laboratory so that its base sequence is complementary to a messenger RNA template. It is assembled by the enzyme reverse transcriptase, and may be used in gene cloning or as a gene probe.

complementary gene *n* a gene that produces an observable effect in an organism only in conjunction with another gene

complementary medicine *n* a range of therapies based on the holistic treatment of physical disorders, generally addressing the causes of diseases rather than their symptoms and also taking steps in the prevention of disease. ◊ **alternative medicine**

complementation /kómpli men táysh'n/ *n* **1** the action or fact of completing, perfecting, or accompanying something else pleasingly **2** the effect produced when two separate mutations occur together in an organism and partly or wholly cancel out each other's action

complement fixation *n* the process in which a group of blood proteins (**complement**) is bound to a specific combined antibody-antigen pair as part of the immune reaction to foreign cells

complementizer /kómplimən tīzər/ *n* a word introducing a clause that acts as a complement ○ *'For' in 'for Sam to be late is unusual' is a complementizer.*

complete /kəm pléet/ *adj* **1 WHOLE** having every necessary part or everything that is wanted ○ *a complete set of Dickens* **2 FINISHED** having reached the normal or expected end ○ *The washing machine stops when the last spin cycle is complete.* **3 ABSOLUTE** being the greatest degree of something ○ *a complete waste of time* **4 ACCOMPLISHED** having all the necessary qualities or abilities for a particular role ○ *She is the complete diplomat.* **5 HAVING ALL PRINCIPAL FLOWER PARTS** describes flowers that have all the principal flower parts, that is carpels, petals, sepals, and stamens ■ *vt* (**-pletes, -pleting, -pleted**) **1 MAKE WHOLE** to make something whole by including every necessary part or everything that is wanted ○ *one more goblet to complete the set* **2 FINISH** to finish something, or bring something to an end ○ *You have 20 minutes to complete the quiz.* **3 ACCOMPLISH** to carry out or accomplish something ○ *The terms of the sale have been completed.* [14C. Directly or via French < Latin *completus*, past participle of *complere* 'fill up' < *plere* 'fill'.] ◇ **complete with** including a particular thing as a feature

complete blood count *n* a diagnostic test used to identify the levels of all blood-cell types in a quantity of blood

completely /kəm pléetli/ *adv* used to emphasize the extent of something ○ *completely wrong* ○ *I completely forgot about it*

completion /kəm pléesh'n/ *n* **1 FINISHING** the finishing of something or making something whole **2 STATE OF BEING FINISHED** the state of being finished or brought to an end ○ *the building is nearing completion* **3 FINAL STAGE OF SALE** the final stage of the sale of land or real property, when ownership changes hands **4 CAUGHT PASS** a forward pass that has been successfully caught

completist /kəm pléetist/ *n* a collector who wants to obtain everything available in his or her speciality (*informal*)

complex *adj* /kóm pleks, kəm pléks/ **1 COMPLICATED** difficult to analyse, understand, or solve **2 HAVING MANY PARTS** made up of many interrelated parts ■ *n* /kóm pleks/ **1 INTERCONNECTED BUILDINGS** a group of interconnected buildings functioning as a whole ○ *a sports complex* **2 INFLUENCE ON BEHAVIOUR** a set of related feelings, ideas, or impulses that may be repressed but that continues to influence thoughts and behaviour ○ *a guilt complex* **3 EXAGGERATED FEELINGS** an exaggerated or obsessive set of feelings about something (*informal*) ○ *He has a complex about eating in restaurants.* **4 COMPOUND OF NONMETAL AND METAL ATOMS** a compound in which nonmetal molecules or ions form weak bonds (**coordinate bonds**) with a central metal atom [Mid-17C. Directly and via French < Latin *complexus*, past participle of *complecti* 'weave together' < *plectere* (see PLEXUS).] —**complexly** *adv* —**complexness** *n*

complex conjugate *n* a complex number in a pair that have the same real components but opposite imaginary components. The complex conjugate of $a + ib$ is $a - ib$.

complex fraction *n* a fraction with a mixed number or fraction in its numerator or denominator or in both

complexion /kəm pléksh'n/ *n* **1** the quality and colour of the skin, especially of the face **2** the character of something, or the way it appears ○ *This development puts an entirely new complexion on the matter.* [14C. < French, 'bodily constitution' < Latin *complecti* (see COMPLEX).] —**complexional** *adj* —**complexioned** *adj*

complexity /kəm pléksəti/ (*plural* **-ties**) *n* **1** the condition of being difficult to understand or of being made up of many interrelated things ○ *the increasing complexity of computing systems* **2** any one of the interrelated problems or difficulties involved in a complicated matter (*often plural*)

complex number *n* a number in the form $a + ib$, where $i = \sqrt{-1}$, that may be either real or imaginary

complex plane *n* a plane whose coordinates are expressed as single complex numbers

complex sentence *n* a sentence containing one or more subordinate clauses

compliance /kəm plī́ ənss/, **compliancy** /-ənssi/ *n* **1** the state or act of conforming with or agreeing to do something ○ *in compliance with the court order* **2** readiness to conform or agree to do something

compliance documentation *n* the documents that a company issuing shares must publish to comply with regulatory requirements governing new share issues and related matters

compliance legislation *n* legislation enacted to ensure compliance with a legal agreement or requirement, e.g. a treaty or mandate

compliance officer *n* a person employed by a financial organization to ensure that conflicts of interest do not arise in companies with wide-ranging, complex financial dealings and that regulations are not broken

compliant /kəm plī́ ənt/ *adj* **1** ready to conform or agree to do something **2** made or done according to requirements or instructions (*often in combination*) ○ *compliant with the general statutes* —**compliantly** *adv*

complicate /kómpli kayt/ *vt* (**-cates, -cating, -cated**) to make something complex or difficult ○ *Further delay will only complicate matters.* ○ *a complicating factor* ■ *adj* describes things that are folded lengthwise, e.g. leaves or insect wings [Early 17C. < Latin *complicat-*, past participle of *complicare* 'fold together' < *plicare* (see PLY[2]).]

complicated /kómpli kaytid/ *adj* **1** composed of many interrelated parts and so difficult to understand or deal with ○ *a complicated diagram* **2** difficult to deal with because of the need to take different relationships or points of view into consideration ○ *Life is complicated enough as it is.* —**complicatedly** *adv* —**complicatedness** *n*

complication /kómpli káysh'n/ *n* **1 DIFFICULT STATE** a difficult or confused state caused by many interrelated factors **2 DIFFICULTY** something that makes something else more difficult or complex ○ *Far from being helpful, this is just a further complication.* **3 PLOT DEVICE** an event or character whose introduction into a story causes difficulty **4 MEDICAL PROBLEM** a disease or problem that arises in addition to the initial condition or during a surgical operation **5 INTRODUCTION OF DIFFICULTY** the act of making something complex or difficult

complicit /kəm plíssit/ *adj* involved in something illegal or wrong ○ *It was clear that some of the staff were complicit in the attempt to cover up the scandal.* [Late 20C. Back-formation < COMPLICITY.]

complicity /kəm plíssəti/ *n* involvement with another in doing something illegal or wrong [Mid-17C. < complice, via French < Latin *complexus* (see COMPLEX).]

compliment *n* /kómplimənt/ **1 STATEMENT OF PRAISE** something said to express praise and approval **2 ACT OR GESTURE** something done to show respect and honour ■ *vt* /kómpli ment/ **1 SAY SOMETHING NICE TO** to say something that expresses praise and approval to somebody **2 GIVE SOMETHING TO** to give somebody a gift as a sign of respect or affection **3 CONGRATULATE** to congratulate somebody [Mid-17C. Via French < Latin *complere* (see COMPLETE).] ◇ **return the compliment** to respond to a gesture somebody has made towards you with a similar gesture

USAGE See ***complement***.

complimentary /kómpli méntəri/ *adj* **1** expressing praise or approval ○ *a complimentary glance* **2** given free as a courtesy or favour ○ *complimentary seats* —**complimentarily** *adv*

USAGE See ***complement***.

compline /kómplin, -līn/, **complin** /-lin/ *n* the last of the seven separate hours (**canonical hours**) that are set aside for prayer each day in the Roman Catholic Church [12C. Alteration of Old French *complie* < medieval Latin *(hora) completa* 'final (hour)' < Latin *completus* (see COMPLETE).]

comply /kəm plī/ (**-plies, -plying, -plied**) *vi* to obey or conform to something, e.g. a rule, law, wish, or regulation [Late 16C. Via obsolete French *complire* < Latin *complere* (see COMPLETE).] —**complier** *n*

compo[1] /kóm pō/ *n* a material mixed from various ingredients, especially a mix of cement mortar (*slang*) [Early 19C. Shortening of COMPOSITION.]

compo[2] /kómpō/ *n ANZ* compensation, usually that paid to workers for injury or during ill health (*informal*) [Mid-20C. Shortening and alteration of COMPENSATION.]

component /kəm pṓnənt/ *n* **1 PART** a part of something, usually of something bigger ○ *a manufacturer of vehicle components* ○ *one of several major components of our research* **2 ELECTRIC PART** a device, e.g. a resistor or transistor, that is part of an electronic circuit **3 VECTOR** any one of a set of vectors whose combination (**resultant**) is another vector **4 CONSTITUENT SUBSTANCE** any one of the substances necessary to describe each phase of a chemical system ■ *adj* **FORMING PART** forming part of a whole [Mid-16C. < Latin *component-*, present participle of *componere* 'put together' < *ponere* (see POST).] —**componential** /kómpə nénsh'l/ *adj*

compo rations *npl* food in a dried and compressed form, meant for use by soldiers when no fresh food is available

comport /kəm páwrt/ *v* (*formal*) **1** *vr* to behave in a particular way **2** *vi* to agree or be consistent with something ○ *This does not comport with the established facts.* [14C. < Latin *comportare* 'bring together' < *portare* (see PORT[5]).]

comportment /kəm páwrtmənt/ *n* the way in which somebody behaves (*formal*)

compose /kəm pṓz/ (**-poses, -posing, -posed**) *v* **1** *vt* **BE THE PARTS OF** to make something by combining together ○ *fertilizer composed of organic compounds* **2** *vt* **PUT ELEMENTS TOGETHER** to put things together to form a whole ○ *composed a light lunch, using cold meats and salads* **3** *vt* **ARRANGE ITEMS** to arrange things in order to achieve an effect ○ *composing objects for a still life in oils* **4** *vti* **CREATE** to create something, especially a piece of music or writing ○ *She is trying to compose a rather difficult letter to her client.* **5** *vt* **CALM** to make somebody become calm ○ *Please compose yourself.* **6** *vti* **SET TYPE** to set type in preparation for printing [14C. < French *composer*, alteration (influenced by *poser* 'to place') of Latin *componere* (see COMPONENT).] —**composer** *n*

composed /kəm pṓzd/ *adj* not agitated or distracted —**composedly** /kəm pṓzidli/ *adv* —**composedness** /kəm pṓzidnəss/ *n*

SYNONYMS See ***calm***.

composite /kómpəzit/ *adj* **1 COMPOUND** made up of different parts **2 WITH COMPLEX FLOWER HEADS** describes any plant belonging to a large family that has flower heads resembling a single flower but composed of many smaller flowers. Family: Compositae. ■ *n* **1 SOMETHING MADE OF PARTS** something made from different parts ○ *The new law is a composite of previous suggested legislation.* **2** *US* **IMAGE OF SUSPECT** an image of a suspect's face that is created by a police artist or photographer, based on input from witnesses (*informal*) **3 COMPOSITE PLANT** a composite plant **4 BUILDING MATERIAL** any building material made up of different ingredients ■ *vt* (**-posites, -positing, -posited**) **COMBINE PROPOSALS** to combine motions from various local branches of an organization, e.g. a political party or a trade union, for discussion at a higher level [14C. Directly or via French < Latin *compositus*, past participle of *componere* (see COMPONENT).] —**compositely** *adv* —**compositeness** *n*

Composite *adj* belonging to a Classical order of architecture that combines elements of the Ionic and Corinthian orders

composite construction *n* a building technique that combines the use of steel and concrete to make supporting columns, resulting in stronger, lighter, and less costly supports

composite photograph *n* an image or scene made up of two or more original images placed side by side, overlapped, or superimposed

composite school *n* in some Canadian provinces, a secondary school in which academic, business, and vocational programmes are offered

composite volcano *n* GEOL = **stratovolcano**

composition /kómpə zísh'n/ *n* **1 CONSTITUENTS** the way in which something is made, especially in terms of its different parts **2 ARRANGEMENT** the way in which the parts of something are arranged, especially the elements in a visual image ○ *the artist's masterly composition of a group portrait* **3 PUTTING TOGETHER** the act or process of combining things to form a whole, or of creating something such as a piece of music or writing **4 ARTISTIC CREATION** something created as a work of art, especially a piece of music **5 PIECE OF WRITING** a short piece of writing, especially a school exercise **6 PRODUCT** a thing created by combining separate parts **7 SETTLEMENT** a settlement whereby creditors agree to accept partial payment of debts by a bankrupt party, typically in return for a consideration such as immediate payment of a lesser amount **8 WORD FORMATION** the formation of compound words from separate words **9 TYPESETTING** the setting of type in preparation for printing **10 FALLACY** the fallacy of arguing that what is true of parts of a whole is true of the whole [14C. < French < Latin *composit-*, past participle of *componere* (see COMPONENT).] —**compositional** *adj* —**compositionally** *adv*

compositor /kəm pózzitər/ *n* a setter of text in type [Mid-16C. < Latin, 'compiler' < *composit-* (see COMPOSITION).]

compos mentis /kómpəss méntiss/ *adj* sane or of sound mind [< Latin, 'in control of one's mind']

compost /kóm post/ *n* **1 DECAYED PLANT MATTER** a mixture of decayed plants and other organic matter used by gardeners for enriching soil **2 SOIL MIXTURE FOR POT PLANTS** any mixture, e.g. based on peat or soil, used in pots for growing plants ○ *a rich potting compost* ■ *v* **1** *vti* **DECAY** to convert organic matter to compost, or to be converted to compost **2** *vt* **TREAT SOIL** to treat soil or an area of ground by adding compost [14C. Via Old French *composte* 'mixture' < Latin *composita* < *composit-*, past participle of *componere* (see COMPONENT).] —**compostable** *adj*

composter /kóm postər/ *n* a device, often shaped like a box or barrel, used to collect organic materials to be used later in composting

compost heap *n* a pile of organic matter left to rot for use as fertilizer, especially by a gardener or farmer

composure /kəm pṓzhər/ *n* calm and steady control over the emotions

compote /kóm pōt/ *n* fruit cooked in sugar or syrup, served as a hot or cold dessert [Late 17C. Via French, 'mixture' < Old French *composte* (see COMPOST).]

compound[1] *n* /kóm pownd/ **1 MIXTURE** something made by the combination of two or more different things **2 WORD MADE UP OF OTHER WORDS** a word that is formed from two or more identifiable words, e.g. 'blackbird', 'cookbook', or 'bullheaded', or, in some analyses, 'mother-in-law' or 'fire drill' ■ *adj* /kóm pownd/ **1 HAVING PARTS** made by the combination of two or more different things **2 MADE FROM TWO OR MORE WORDS** describes a word that is made up of two or more words or word parts **3 DIVIDED INTO PARTS** describes a leaf that is divided into two or more parts (**leaflets**) attached to a single stalk. ◊ **simple** *adj.* 11 ■ *v* /kəm pównd, kom-/ **1** *vti* **ADD TOGETHER** to add together, or add one thing to another or others, to form a whole ○ *hatred that was compounded with fear and revulsion* **2** *vt* **MAKE SOMETHING BY COMBINING PARTS** to make by the adding together of different parts ○ *a medication compounded from several constituent elements* **3** *vt* **INTENSIFY** to make something more extreme or intense by adding something to it ○ *Further financial reverses compounded his despair.* **4** *vt* **TAKE BRIBE TO IGNORE CRIME** to accept a bribe in return for not prosecuting or informing about a crime **5** *vti* **SETTLE DEBT** to settle a debt by paying a lesser amount owed, typically right away in a lump sum [14C. Past participle of *compoune* 'put together' < Old French *compoun-*, stem of *compondre* < Latin *componere* (see COMPONENT).] —**compoundable** /kəm pówndəb'l/ *adj* —**compounder** /kəm pówndər/ *n*

SYNONYMS See ***mixture***.

compound[2] /kóm pownd/ *n* **1** an enclosed group of buildings for the segregation or restraint of a particular group of people **2** *Malaysia, Singapore* a garden with a fence or wall round it [Late 17C. Alteration of Malay *kampong* 'enclosure, village'.]

Compound eye

compound eye *n* the eye that most insects and some crustaceans have, made up of several separate light-sensitive parts

compound fault *n* a series of geological faults that lie closely together, following the same general direction

compound fraction *n* MATH = **complex fraction**

compound fracture *n* a bone fracture in which a broken bone pierces the skin or comes into contact with an open wound

compound interest *n* interest that is calculated on the combined total of the original sum borrowed (**principal**) and the interest it has already accrued

compound meter *n US* MUSIC = **compound time**

compound microscope *n* a microscope consisting of two lenses or lens systems and an eyepiece, mounted in a tube

compound sentence *n* a sentence containing two or more clauses that can stand independently

compound time *n* musical time in which the number of beats to the bar is a multiple of three. US term **compound meter**

comprehend /kómpri hénd/ *v* **1** *vti* to grasp the meaning or nature of something ○ *It was hard to comprehend the sheer scale of the problem.* **2** *vt* to include something as a part of something else (*formal*) [14C. < Latin *comprehendere* 'grasp fully' < *prehendere* 'seize'.]

comprehensible /kómpri hénssəb'l/ *adj* capable of being understood [15C. Directly or via French < Latin *comprehensibilis* < *comprehens-*, past participle of *comprehendere* (see COMPREHEND).] —**comprehensibility** /kómpri hénssə bílləti/ *n* —**comprehensibleness** *n* —**comprehensibly** *adv*

comprehension /kómpri hénsh'n/ *n* **1 UNDERSTANDING** the grasping of the meaning of something **2 INTELLECTUAL ABILITY** the ability to grasp the meaning of something ○ *It's beyond my comprehension.* **3 SET OF QUESTIONS ON TEXT** an exercise consisting of a set of questions on a short text, designed to test students' understanding of it [15C. Directly or via French < Latin *comprehension-* < *comprehens-*, past participle of *comprehendere* (see COMPREHEND).]

comprehensive /kómpri hénssiv/ *adj* **1 INCLUSIVE** covering many things or a wide area ○ *a comprehensive survey of public opinion* **2 INCLUDING ALL** including everything, so as to be complete ○ *comprehensive knowledge of the subject* **3 COVERING MANY EVENTUALITIES** describes insurance policies that provide coverage or benefit in most areas **4 FOR ALL CHILDREN RELATING TO EDUCATION** for all children of a local area, no matter what their level of ability ■ *n* EDUC = **comprehensive school** [17C. Directly or via French < Latin *comprehensivus* < *comprehens-*, past participle of *comprehendere* (see COMPREHEND).] —**comprehensively** *adv*

comprehensiveness /kómpri hénssivnəss/ *n* the state of including a great deal or everything

comprehensive school *n* a local secondary school for children of all ability levels

ϟ **compress** *v* /kəm préss/ **1** *vti* **SHRINK** to make something smaller by applying pressure or by some analogous process **2** *vt* **PRESS THINGS TOGETHER** to press things, e.g. the lips, together **3** *vt* **MAKE FILES SHORTER** to reduce the size of computer files or transmissions by means of algorithms ■ *n* /kóm pres/ **1 TREATMENT PAD** a cloth pad, often moistened or medicated, pressed firmly against a part of the body as a treatment, e.g. to stop bleeding

2 MACHINE a machine for compressing material, especially cotton that is being packed [14C. Via Old French < late Latin *compressare* 'keep pressing together' < Latin *comprimere* 'press together' < *premere* (see PRESS[1]).] —**compressed** *adj* —**compressibility** /kəm préssə bílləti/ *n* —**compressible** *adj* —**compressibleness** *n*

compressed air *n* air that is kept in a container under pressure, often used to power machines

compression /kəm présh'n/ *n* **1** the reduction of the volume or mass of something by applying pressure, or the state of having been treated in this way **2** a phase in the working of an internal-combustion engine in which a combination of fuel and air is compressed in a cylinder before being ignited [14C. Via French < Latin *compress-*, past participle of *comprimere* (see COMPRESS).] —**compressional** *adj*

compression ratio *n* the ratio between the largest and smallest possible volumes in the cylinder of an internal-combustion engine that contains a combination of fuel and air being compressed

compression sack *n* a tubular bag made of synthetic fabric with special straps to compress the bulk of its contents and make it easier for hikers and mountaineers to carry

compression wave *n* a longitudinal wave created in a fluid by a compressing force, e.g. a sound wave in air

compressive /kəm préssiv/ *adj* having the power or tendency to compress [14C. Via French < Latin *compress-*, past participle of *comprimere* (see COMPRESS).] —**compressively** *adv*

compressor /kəm préssər/ *n* **1** a machine that compresses gas so that the power produced when the gas is released can be used to power another machine, e.g. a pneumatic drill **2** a muscle that compresses or flattens a part of the body

comprimario /kómpri máiri ō/ *n* a secondary role in an opera or ballet, or somebody who performs such a role [< Italian, 'co-primary']

comprise /kəm príz/ *vt* (**-prises, -prising, -prised**) **1 INCLUDE** to incorporate or contain something **2 CONSIST OF** to be made up of something **3 CONSTITUTE** to make up the whole of something. [15C. < French *compris*, past participle of *comprendre* 'include' < Latin *comprehendere* (see COMPREHEND).] —**comprisable** *adj*

compromise /kómprə mīz/ *n* **1 AGREEMENT** a settlement of a dispute in which two or more sides agree to accept less than they originally wanted ○ *After hours of negotiations a compromise was reached*. **2 SOMETHING ACCEPTED RATHER THAN WANTED** something that somebody accepts because what was wanted is unattainable **3 POTENTIAL DANGER OR DISGRACE** exposure to danger or disgrace ■ *v* (**-mises, -mising, -mised**) **1** *vi* **AGREE BY CONCEDING** to settle a dispute by agreeing to accept less than what was originally wanted **2** *vt* **LESSEN VALUE OF** to undermine or devalue something or somebody by making concessions ○ *Don't compromise your integrity by telling half-truths*. **3** *vt* **EXPOSE TO DANGER** to expose somebody or something to danger or risk ○ *This scandal could compromise his chances of re-election*. ○ *drugs that can compromise the immune system* [15C. Via French *compromis* < Latin *compromissum* 'mutual agreement' < past participle of *compromittere* 'make mutual promises' < *promittere* (see PROMISE).] —**compromiser** *n*

compromising /kómprə mīzing/ *adj* liable to expose somebody to disgrace or humiliation —**compromisingly** *adv*

comp time *n US* HR = compensation time

Compton /kómptən, kúmp-/, **Sir Denis** (1918–98) British cricketer and footballer

Compton-Burnett /kómptən bər nét/, **Ivy, Dame** (1884–1969) British novelist

Compton effect *n* the decrease in energy and increase in wavelength experienced by a photon after colliding or interacting with an electron [Early 20C. After A.H. Compton 1892–1962, US physicist.]

comptroller /kən trólər/ *n* FIN = controller *n*. **2** [15C. Variant influenced by *compt*, older spelling of COUNT.] —**comptrollership** *n*

compulsion /kəm púlsh'n/ *n* **1 FORCE** a force that makes somebody do something **2 COMPELLING** an act of compelling or the state of being compelled ○ *You are under no compulsion to leave*. **3 PSYCHOLOGICAL FORCE** a psychological and usually irrational force that makes somebody do something, often unwillingly ○ *felt an irresistible com-*

pulsion [14C. Via French < Latin *compuls-*, past participle of *compellere* (see COMPEL).]

compulsive /kəm púlssiv/ *adj* **1 DRIVEN** driven by an irresistible inner force to do something ○ *a compulsive liar* **2 POWERFULLY INTERESTING** exerting a powerful attraction or interest ■ *n* **SOMEBODY UNDER PSYCHOLOGICAL COMPULSION** somebody whose actions are driven by a usually irrational psychological force —**compulsively** *adv* —**compulsiveness** *n*

compulsory /kəm púlssəri/ *adj* **1 NECESSARY** required by law or an authority ○ *attendance at the lecture is compulsory* **2 FORCED** caused by force, or using force to make somebody do something ■ *n* (*plural* **-ries**) **REQUIRED ROUTINE** an exercise or routine that participants in a sport such as gymnastics or figure skating must perform as part of a competition (*often plural*) [Early 16C. < medieval Latin *compulsorius* < Latin *compuls-*, past participle of *compellere* (see COMPEL).] —**compulsorily** *adv* —**compulsoriness** *n*

compulsory purchase *n* a situation in which somebody is obliged by law to sell property to the government or a local authority because it is wanted for public use

compunction /kəm púngksh'n/ *n* feelings of shame and regret about doing something wrong [14C. Via French *componction* < Latin *compunct-*, past participle of *compungere* 'sting strongly' < *pungere* (see PUNGENT).] —**compunctious** *adj* —**compunctiously** *adv*

compurgation /kóm pur gáysh'n/ *n* formerly, a way of proving that somebody is innocent by collecting oaths from friends and colleagues [Mid-17C. < medieval Latin *compurgation-* < Latin *compurgare* 'cleanse completely' < *purgare* (see PURGE).] —**compurgator** /kóm pur gaytər/ *n*

⚡ **computation** /kómpyōō táysh'n/ *n* **1** the use of a computer, especially for calculation, or something calculated using a computer **2** the calculating of something, or the result of a calculation —**computational** *adj* —**computationally** *adv*

⚡ **compute** /kəm pyōot/ (**-putes, -puting, -puted**) *v* **1** *vt* **CALCULATE** to calculate an answer or result, especially using a computer **2** *vi* **USE COMPUTER OR CALCULATOR** to use a computer or calculator **3** *vi* **YIELD RESULT** to yield a result, especially a correct result, from calculation ○ *These numbers just don't compute*. [Early 17C. < Latin *computare* 'reckon together' < *putare* 'reckon'.] —**computability** *n* —**computable** *adj*

computed tomography *n* a technique for producing images of cross-sections of the body. A computer processes data from X-rays penetrating the body from many directions and projects the results on a screen.

⚡ **computer** /kəm pyōotər/ *n* **1** an electronic device that accepts, processes, stores, and outputs data at high speeds according to programmed instructions **2** a person who calculates figures or amounts using a machine

QUICK FACTS ON... COMPUTERS

Key elements: increase, with each successive generation, in power and speed of computers, in parallel with reduction in size, weight, cost, and environmental requirements of the machines (contrast the room-size first-generation UNIVAC with the fourth-generation handheld personal computer)
Key dates: 1833 the 'Analytical Engine', the first modern computer (Babbage); 1939 first semi-electronic digital computer, ABC (Atanasoff); 1946 first general-purpose electronic digital computer, ENIAC (Eckert and Mauchly); 1951 first computer capable of manipulating both alphabetical and numerical data with equal facility, UNIVAC, becomes commercially available, launching the computer industry's first, or vacuum valve, generation; 1958 first fully transistorized computer, marking the start of the second generation; 1965 first integrated-circuit based, or third-generation, computer; 1970 first microprocessor-based computer, marking the start of the fourth generation of computers; 1981 IBM PC launches the personal computer revolution; 1988 first graphics supercomputers are announced
Key publications: *Before the Computer* (James W. Cortada) 2000; *History of Computing: An Encyclopedia of the People and Machines that Made Computer History* (Mark W. Greenia) 2000

⚡ **computer-aided design** *n* the use of a computer and sophisticated graphics software to design products or systems

⚡ **computer-aided engineering** *n* the use of computers and specialized programs in engineering to automate analysis and testing through simulation of such factors as stress and loads

⚡ **computer conferencing** *n* the use of computers to allow people at distant sites to exchange text and graphic messages as they would at a meeting

⚡ **computer crime** *n* illegal activities carried out on or by means of a computer

⚡ **computer dating** *n* the business or practice of putting people's personal details and preferences into a computer that then matches apparently compatible couples

⚡ **computerese** /kəm pyōōtə reéz/ *n* the technical language used by people involved with computers (*humorous*)

⚡ **computer game** *n* a game in the form of computer software, run on a personal computer or games machine and played by one or more people using a keyboard, mouse, control pad, or joystick

⚡ **computer graphics** *n* the use of a computer and specialized software to produce and manipulate pictorial images for purposes of animation, business presentations, and scientific research (+ *singular verb*) ■ *npl* the images produced by computer graphics

⚡ **computerize** /kəm pyōōtə rīz/ (**-izes, -izing, -ized**), **computerise** (**-ises, -ising, -ised**) *vt* **1** to install or start using a computer system to organize, control, or automate something, such as a mechanical process or calculations **2** to store information in a computer system or process it by computer —**computerization** *adj* —**computerization** /kəm pyōōtə rī záysh'n/ *n* —**computerized** *adj*

computerized axial tomography, **computerized tomography** *n* MED = computed tomography

⚡ **computer language** *n* COMPUT = programming language

⚡ **computer-literate** *adj* having a good understanding and experience of working with a computer or computer system —**computer literacy** *n*

⚡ **computer science** *n* the study of the mathematics and technology of computers and their applications

⚡ **computer virus** *n* COMPUT = virus *n*. 3

⚡ **computing** /kəm pyōōting/ *n* the using or operating of computers or computer software

comrade /kóm rayd, -rid/ *n* **1** a close friend or a companion, often resulting from shared experiences **2 comrade, Comrade** a fellow member of a group, especially a fellow soldier or a fellow supporter of a Communist or Socialist party [Mid-16C. Via French *camerade, camarade* < Spanish *camarada* 'barracks mate' < *camara* 'room' < Latin *camera* (see CAMERA).] —**comradely** *adj* —**comradeship** *n*

comrade-in-arms (*plural* **comrades-in-arms**) *n* somebody who is fighting on the same side in a war, battle, or other armed struggle

Comstockery /kóm stokəri, kúm-/ *n US* the removal of, or strong opposition to, anything that could be seen as immoral or obscene in literary, artistic, or broadcast material [Early 20C. After Anthony *Comstock* 1844–1915, American reformer.]

Comte /komt, koNt/, **Auguste** (1798–1857) French philosopher —**Comtian** /kómti ən, kóNti ən/ *n, adj* —**Comtism** *n*

Comus /kóməss/ *n* the Roman god of revelry

con[1] /kon/ *vt* (**cons, conning, conned**) **1 TRICK** to cheat somebody, usually out of money or property, by first convincing the victim of something that is untrue **2 LIE** to tell somebody something untrue or misleading **3 PERSUADE** to get somebody to agree to something (*informal*) ○ *See if you can con him into babysitting tonight*. ■ *n* **DISHONEST TRICK** a trick or dishonest business ploy that takes advantage of somebody's trust, such as telling lies in order to get money or property unfairly [Late 19C. Shortening of CONFIDENCE TRICK.]

con[2] /kon/ *n* **1** an argument against doing something, or evidence or an opinion stating that something should not be done ○ *the pros and cons* **2** an opponent of something, or a voter against it [Late 16C. Shortening of Latin *contra* 'against'.]

con[3] /kon/ *n* a convict (*slang*) [Late 19C. Shortening.]

con[4] /kon/ (**cons, conning, conned**) *vt* (*archaic*) **1** to study something with great care and attention **2** to learn or memorize something [< Old English *cunnan* 'know how', *cunnian* 'explore' < Indo-European]

con[5] /kon/ *vt* (**cons, conning, conned**) to control or direct the steering of a ship ■ *n* control of the steering of a ship, or the controls so used [Early 17C. Alteration of obsolete *cond* < French *conduire* < Latin *conducere* (see CONDUCE).]

con[6] /kon/ *prep* used to mean 'with' in a musical direction [< Italian, 'with']

con. *abbr* **1** concerto **2** conclusion **3** connection **4** consolidated **5** continued **6** contra

Con. *abbr* **1** Consul **2** Conformist **3** Conservative

Conakry /kónnə kri, kónnə kreé/ capital and main port of Guinea. Population: 705,280 (1983 estimate).

con amore /kón a máwray, -máwri/ *adv* with tender feeling (*musical direction*) [< Italian, 'with love']

conation /kō náysh'n/ *n* in psychology, a mental process involving the will, e.g. impulse, desire, or resolve [Mid-19C. < Latin *conation-* < *conat-*, past participle of *conari* 'try'.] —**conational** *adj* —**conative** /kṓnətiv, kónnə-/ *adj*

con brio /kon breé ō/ *adv* with spirit or vigour (*musical direction*) [< Italian, 'with vigour']

conc. *abbr* **1** concentrated **2** concentration **3** concerning **4** concerto **5** concession

⚡**concatenate** /kon káttə nayt, kən-/ *vt* (**-nates, -nating, -nated**) **1** BRING TOGETHER to connect separate units or items into a linked system **2** LINK UNITS TOGETHER in computing, to link two or more information units, such as character strings or files, so that they form a single unit ■ *adj* LINKED TOGETHER linked together in a sequence or chain [15C. < late Latin *concatenat-*, past participle of *concatenare* 'chain together' < *catena* 'chain'.]

⚡**concatenation** /kon káttə náysh'n, kən-/ *n* **1** the linking of things together or the state of being interconnected **2** the linking of characters, strings, or files in a specified order to form a single entity equal to the sum of the lengths of the original entities

concave /kón kayv, kon káyv/ *adj* **1** curved inward like the inner surface of a bowl or sphere **2** describes a polygon with an interior angle greater than 180° [< Latin *concavus* 'hollowed out' < *cavus* (see CAVE)] —**concavely** *adv* —**concaveness** *n*

concavity /kon kávvəti/ (*plural* **concavities**) *n* **1** the state of being concave **2** a concave part or surface

concavo-concave /kon káyvō kon káyv/ *adj* describes a lens that is concave on both surfaces

concavo-convex /kon káyvō-/ *adj* describes a lens that is concave on one surface and convex on the other

conceal /kən seél/ *vt* **1** to put or keep something or somebody out of sight, or prevent the person or thing from being found ○ *The evidence was carefully concealed.* **2** to keep something secret, or prevent it from being known [13C. Via Old French *conceler* < Latin *concelare* 'hide well' < *celare* 'hide'.] —**concealable** *adj* —**concealment** *n*

concealer /kən seélər/ *n* **1** flesh-coloured makeup that can be applied to the skin to hide blemishes **2** somebody or something that conceals

concede /kən seéd/ (**-cedes, -ceding, -ceded**) *v* **1** *vt* RELUCTANTLY ACCEPT SOMETHING TO BE TRUE to admit or acknowledge something, often grudgingly or with reluctance **2** *vti* ADMIT FAILURE BEFORE END to accept and acknowledge defeat in a contest, debate, election, or fight, often without waiting for the final result **3** *vt* GIVE SOMETHING AWAY to allow your opponent or opposing team to gain something valuable, usually a goal or points **4** *vt* GRANT RIGHTS TO to allow or yield something such as a right or privilege to another person or country [15C. Via French < Latin *concedere* 'yield completely' < *cedere* (see CEDE).] —**conceder** *n*

~~**conceed**~~ incorrect spelling of **concede**

conceit /kən seét/ *n* **1** TOO MUCH PRIDE IN YOURSELF a high opinion of your own qualities or abilities, especially one that is not justified **2** EXAGGERATED COMPARISON IN LITERATURE an imaginative poetic image, or writing that contains such an image, especially a comparison that is extreme or far-fetched **3** WHIMSICAL OBJECT an object created from the imagination **4** IMAGINATIVE IDEA an idea, opinion, or theme, especially one that is fanciful or unusual in some way ■ *vt N England* LIKE to like or tolerate something [14C. < CONCEIVE.]

conceited /kən seétid/ *adj* having or showing an excessively high opinion of your own qualities or abilities —**conceitedly** *adv* —**conceitedness** *n*

SYNONYMS See ***proud***.

conceivable /kən seévəb'l/ *adj* possible to imagine, understand, or believe ○ *We tried every means conceivable to contact her.* —**conceivability** /kən seévə bílləti/ *n* —**conceivableness** *n*

conceivably /kən seévəbli/ *adv* possibly, even if only a remote possibility ○ *You could just conceivably be wrong.*

conceive /kən seév/ (**-ceives, -ceiving, -ceived**) *v* **1** *vti* THINK OF OR IMAGINE to form an idea or concept of something in your mind **2** *vt* INVENT, DEVISE, OR ORIGINATE to think up something that could be put into action such as a plan or an invention ○ *conceived and written by John Sander* **3** START TO EXPERIENCE to produce something from the mind such as an emotion **4** *vti* BECOME PREGNANT to become pregnant with a child or with young **5** *vt* UNDERSTAND to understand something [13C. < Old French *conceiv-*, stem of *concevoir* < Latin *concipere* 'take in' < *capere* (see CAPTURE).] —**conceiver** *n*

concelebrate /kən sélli brayt/ (**-brates, -brating, -brated**) *vti* to celebrate the Christian Mass or Holy Communion jointly with one or more other priests [Late 16C. < Latin *concelebrat-*, past participle of *concelebrare* 'celebrate together' < *celebrare* (see CELEBRATE).] —**concelebrant** *n* —**concelebration** /kən sélli bráysh'n/ *n*

concentrate /kónss'n trayt/ *v* (**-trates, -trating, -trated**) **1** *vti* SILENTLY AND INTENSELY THINK ABOUT to focus all of your thoughts or mental activity on one subject or activity, usually in silence ○ *I found myself unable to concentrate on my work* **2** *vti* DEVOTE EFFORTS TO ONE THING to direct attention, time, and resources to one particular area or activity, usually over a period of time **3** *vti* CLUSTER TOGETHER to bring things to a common centre or close together in the same area **4** *vt* MAKE PURER to make a substance purer by the removal of another substance, especially by removing a liquid **5** *vti* MAKE THICKER OR STRONGER to remove water from a substance, usually a liquid, leaving a smaller quantity that is thicker in consistency and stronger in flavour **6** *vti* ACCUMULATE IN TISSUE to accumulate or be stored, or to cause to accumulate or be stored, in biological tissue over a period of time **7** *vt* PURIFY ORE to remove rock and other material from ore to purify it ■ *n* **1** PURE SUBSTANCE a substance made purer by the removal of another, especially a liquid **2** THICK FOOD SUBSTANCE a food substance, especially a liquid, made thicker or stronger in flavour by the removal of liquid [Mid-17C. < CONCENTRE.] —**concentrated** *adj* —**concentratedly** *adv* —**concentrative** *adj* —**concentratively** *adv*

concentration /kónss'n tráysh'n/ *n* **1** FOCUS OF MIND OR RESOURCES the direction of all thought or effort towards one particular task, idea, or subject **2** CLUSTER OR NUMBER a large number of things or amount of something collected together in one area ○ *the concentration of computing talent in one part of the country* **3** STRENGTH OF SOLUTION (*symbol c*) the amount of a substance dissolved in another **4** MAKING A LIQUID THICKER OR STRONGER the removal of water from something, usually a liquid, to make it thicker or stronger

concentration camp *n* **1** one of the prison camps used for exterminating prisoners under the rule of Hitler in Nazi Germany **2** a prison camp used in war for the incarceration of political prisoners or civilians

⚡**concentrator** /kónss'n traytər/ *n* **1** TELECOMMUNICATIONS DEVICE a telecommunications device that combines outgoing messages into one message or extracts individual messages from one transmission into which they have been combined **2** FACTORY THAT PROCESSES MINERAL ORE an industrial plant that produces purified or concentrated mineral ore **3** MIRROR SYSTEM FOR PRODUCING SOLAR ENERGY a set of mirrors used to concentrate sunlight in the collection of energy from the sun

concentre /kon séntər/ (**-tres, -tring, -tred**) *vti* to direct things to a common centre, or converge at a common centre [Late 16C. < French *concentrer* < *con-* 'together' + *centre* 'centre'.]

concentric /kən séntrik, kon-/ *adj* **1** describes circles and spheres of different sizes with the same middle point **2** with a common axis, as when rotating elements are mounted on shafts that have a common centre line [14C. < medieval Latin *concentricus* 'having the same centre' < Latin *centrum* (see CENTRE).] —**concentrically** *adv* —**concentricity** /kónss'n trísəti/ *n*

Concepción /kən sépsi ón/ capital of Bío-Bío Region, central Chile. Population: 372,252 (1998).

concept /kón sept/ *n* **1** SOMETHING THOUGHT OR IMAGINED something that somebody has thought up, or that somebody might be able to imagine **2** BROAD PRINCIPLE AFFECTING PERCEPTION AND BEHAVIOUR a broad abstract idea or a guiding general principle, e.g. one that determines how a person or culture behaves, or how nature, reality, or events are perceived ○ *the concept of time* **3** UNDERSTANDING OR GRASP the most basic understanding of something **4** WAY OF DOING OR PERCEIVING a method, scheme, or type of product or design [Mid-16C. < late Latin *conceptus* < past participle of Latin *concipere* (see CONCEIVE).] —**conceptual** /kən séptyoo əl/ *adj* —**conceptually** *adv*

conception /kən sépsh'n/ *n* **1** BROAD UNDERSTANDING a general understanding of something **2** SOMETHING CONCEIVED IN THE MIND a result of thought, such as an idea, invention, or plan **3** CONCEIVING OF YOUNG the fertilization of an egg by a sperm at the beginning of pregnancy **4** EMBRYO OR FOETUS an embryo or foetus (*technical*) **5** ORIGIN OR BEGINNINGS the beginnings or origin of something **6** FORMULATION OF IDEA the process of arriving at an abstract idea or belief or the moment at which such an idea starts to take shape or emerge **7** = **concept** *n*. 1 [14C. Via French < Latin *concipere* (see CONCEIVE).] —**conceptional** *adj* —**conceptive** *adj* —**conceptively** *adv*

concept product *n* a highly advanced and innovative product that is not yet in commercial production

concept statement *n* an explanation or summary of the overall aims or nature of a project

conceptual art, concept art *n* art designed to present an idea rather than to be appreciated for its creative skill or beauty, often making use of unconventional media instead of painting or sculpture

QUICK FACTS ON... **CONCEPTUAL ART**

Key dates: mid-1960s–mid-1970s
Key locations: Europe, United States
Key elements: emphasis on concepts rather than objects; presentation of ideas, plans, and instructions as artworks; importance of context; anticommercialism; interest in relationship between art and language; use of wide range of media
Key figures: Joseph Kosuth, Sol LeWitt, Lawrence Weiner, Daniel Buren, Bruce Nauman, Richard Long
Key works: *One and Three Chairs* (Joseph Kosuth) 1965, *Statements* (Lawrence Weiner) 1968, *The True Artist Helps the World by Revealing Mystic Truths* (Bruce Nauman) 1967, *Index 01* (Art & Language) 1972
Key developments: Arte Povera, Land Art, performance art, environmental sculpture, video art

conceptualise *vti* = **conceptualize**

conceptualism /kən séptyoo əlizəm/ *n* **1** the philosophical theory that the existence of something is dependent on our having a mental concept of it **2** a school of art concerned primarily with the ideas behind a work of art rather than the artwork itself —**conceptualistic** /-lístik/ *adj* —**conceptualistically** *adv*

conceptualist /kən séptyoo əlist/ *n* a person who believes in conceptualism

conceptualize /kən séptyoo ə līz/ (**-izes, -izing, -ized**), **conceptualise** (**-ises, -ising, -ised**) *vti* to arrive at a concept or generalization as a result of things seen, experienced, or believed —**conceptualization** /kən séptyoo ə lī záysh'n/ *n* —**conceptualizer** *n*

conceptus /kən séptəss/ (*plural* **-tuses**) *n* an embryo or foetus along with all the tissues that surround it throughout pregnancy, including the placenta, amniotic sac and fluid, and the umbilical cord [Mid-18C. < Latin, 'something conceived' < past participle of *concipere* (see CONCEIVE).]

concern /kən súrn/ *vt* **1** MAKE SOMEBODY WORRIED to give somebody an uneasy or anxious feeling **2** INVOLVE SOMEBODY OR GET INVOLVED to require somebody to be involved with something, or get involved with or interested in something **3** BE INTERESTING OR IMPORTANT TO to have a direct effect on, or be a matter of significance to, somebody or something **4** BE ON THE SUBJECT OF to be about a particular topic ■ *n* **1** WORRY OR SOMETHING CAUSING IT worry, or a cause of worry ○ *His condition is giving rise to concern.* **2** RELEVANT AFFAIR a matter that affects somebody or that somebody has the right to be involved with ○ *It's no concern of yours.* **3** CARING FEELINGS emotions such as worry, compassion, sympathy, or regard for somebody or something **4** BUSINESS a commercial enterprise **5** OBJECT a gadget or trivial object (*dated*) [Late 14C. Via French < late Latin *concernere* 'sift together' < Latin *cernere* 'sift'.]

concerned /kən súrnd/ *adj* 1 **ANXIOUS OR WORRIED** worried or apprehensive, particularly about something such as a situation that is developing or that has newly arisen 2 **INTERESTED** attentive to and interested in something 3 **INVOLVED** having an active role in or related to something ○ *A message was conveyed to the families concerned.* —**concernedly** /-nədli/ *adv*

concerning /kən súrning/ *prep* to do with or involving something or somebody

concert /kónsərt/ *n* 1 **PUBLIC MUSICAL PERFORMANCE** an event where an individual musician or a group of musicians, e.g. a choir or an orchestra, performs in front of an audience 2 **AGREEMENT** harmony or accord, e.g. in purpose or action 3 **UNIFIED PAIR OR GROUP** a combination of people or things in agreement or harmony, especially one resulting from a consensus of opinions and ideas ■ *vti* **ACT IN AGREEMENT OR UNITY** to do or plan something in cooperation or in harmony with another person or group [Late 16C. Via French < Italian *concerto* (see CONCERTO).] ◇ **in concert** 1 playing music or singing at a live concert 2 working or acting together, especially in a united or harmonious way ○ *Jones, in concert with three associates, planned and carried out the attack.*

concertante /kónchər tántay, -ti/ *adj* 1 relating to or resembling a concerto, especially one in the Baroque style 2 relating to a symphonic work that highlights individual instruments within the orchestra [Early 18C. < Italian, present participle of *concertare* 'bring into harmony'.]

concerted /kən súrtid/ *adj* 1 planned or carried out by two or more people working together or with the same aim 2 written for several soloists to perform together in an ensemble or within the context of a larger-scale work —**concertedly** *adv* —**concertedness** *n*

concertgoer /kónssərt gō ər/ *n* an attender of a concert, or somebody who often goes to concerts —**concertgoing** *adj*

concert grand *n* the largest size of grand piano, between 2.74 m/9 ft and 3.66 m/12 ft long, designed for use in a concert hall

concert hall *n* a public building designed for performances of music

concertina /kónssər téenə/ *n* a small accordion with button keys ■ *vi* to collapse in a series of folds like an accordion [Mid-19C. < CONCERT + Italian suffix *-ina*.] —**concertinist** *n*

concertino /kón chər téenō/ (*plural* **-nos** *or* **-ni** /-nee/) *n* 1 the solo instrumental group in a piece of music played by a small group of soloists and a larger ensemble (**concerto grosso**) 2 a small-scale concerto for a single solo instrument [Late 18C. < Italian, 'little concerto' < *concerto* (see CONCERTO).]

concertize /kónssər tīz/ (**-tizes, -tizing, -tized**), **concertise** (**-tises, -tising, -tised**) *vi* to perform in concerts (*refers to a soloist or conductor*)

concertmaster /kónssərt maastər/ *n US* the leader of the first violin section of an orchestra, usually next in rank below the conductor

concertmistress /kónssərt mistrəss/ *n US* a woman who is the leader of the first violin section of an orchestra, usually next in rank below the conductor

concerto /kən cháirtō, -chúrtō/ (*plural* **-tos** *or* **-ti** /-ti/) *n* 1 an instrumental work for orchestra that highlights a soloist or group of soloists 2 in music before 1650, a work for voices with organ or continuo [Early 18C. < Italian, < *concertare* 'bring into agreement'.]

concerto grosso /kən cháirtō góssō/ (*plural* **concerti grossi** /-tee góssee/ *or* **concerto grossos**) *n* a genre of orchestral composition, popular in the 17th century, that contrasts a small group of soloists (**concertino**) with a larger ensemble (**ripieno**) [< Italian, 'big concerto']

concert overture *n* a short orchestral composition similar to an opera overture but intended for concert performance on its own

concert party (*plural* **concert parties**) *n* 1 a small number of performers working together to entertain the public, e.g. in a seaside town (*dated*) 2 a group of people buying shares (*slang*)

concert pitch *n* 1 **STANDARD PITCH TO WHICH INSTRUMENTS TUNED** the internationally agreed standard pitch to which orchestral instruments are tuned, typically using the A above middle C as a reference 2 **PITCH OF NOTE IN TRANSPOSED MUSIC** the sounding pitch of a note played by an instrument when transposing a piece of written music to a different key, as opposed to the written pitch 3 **READINESS** a state of readiness for action

concession /kən sésh'n/ *n* 1 **SPECIAL PRIVILEGE** something such as a particular privilege, right, or kindness, that is allowed or granted to a individual or group, usually in view of special circumstances 2 **CHEAP TICKET** a special reduced price at which tickets for travel or entertainment are sold to some groups of people, such as senior citizens, students, or the unemployed 3 **RELUCTANT YIELDING** an act or an example of conceding, yielding, or compromising in some way, often grudgingly or unwillingly 4 **SOMETHING UNWILLINGLY ADMITTED** something acknowledged or admitted, even if unwillingly or grudgingly 5 **SMALL BUSINESS OUTLET INSIDE ANOTHER ESTABLISHMENT** a branch of a business set up and operating in a place belonging to another commercial enterprise, or a business agreement that grants the right to do this 6 **RIGHT TO USE LAND** an official licence granted by a landowner or government that allows work such as drilling for oil to be carried out in a specified area of land [Early 17C. Directly or via French < Latin *concess-*, past participle of *concedere* (see CONCEDE).] —**concessible** /kən séssəb'l/ *adj* —**concessional** *adj*

concessionaire /kən sésh'n áir/, **concessionnaire, concessioner** /kən sésh'nər/ *n* a holder or operator of a concession [Mid-19C. < French, < *concession* (see CONCESSION).]

concessionary /kən sésh'nəri/ *adj* 1 describes special advantages, particularly price reductions, that exist only for certain groups of people 2 created or executed as a compromise or goodwill gesture, especially within a negotiating process

concessioner, concessionnaire *n* = **concessionaire**

concession road, concession line *n* in Canada, especially in Ontario and Quebec, a rural road running along the line of the survey of Canada that divided farmland into concessions

concessive /kən séssiv/ *adj* 1 relating to a word or part of a sentence that expresses concession, e.g. the word 'although' 2 relating to or containing a concession [Early 18C. < late Latin *concessivus* < Latin *concess-*, past participle of *concedere* (see CONCEDE).] —**concessively** *adv*

conch /kongk, konch/ (*plural* **conches** *or* **conchs**) *n* 1 a tropical marine mollusc with a large, often brightly coloured, spiral shell 2 the large spiral shell of a conch. Use: horn or trumpet, ornament, jewellery. 3 ANAT = **concha** *n.* [14C. Via Latin *concha* < Greek *kogkhē* 'shell, shellfish'.]

conch- *prefix* = **concho-** (*before vowels*)

concha /kóngkə/ (*plural* **-chae** /-ki/) *n* a part of the body shaped like a conch shell, e.g. the external ear or the central cavity of the ear [Late 16C. < Latin (see CONCH).] —**conchal** *adj*

conchi- *prefix* = **concho-**

conchie /kónchi/, **conchy** (*plural* **-chies**) *n* a conscientious objector (*dated disapproving*) [Early 20C. Shortening.]

conchiglie /kon kéeli/ *n* pasta formed into small shell shapes [< Italian, 'little shells' < Latin *concha* (see CONCH)]

conchiolin /kong kí əlin/ *n* a fibrous protein in mollusc shells [Late 19C. < modern Latin *conchiola* 'little shell' < Latin *concha* (see CONCH).]

concho- *prefix* shell ○ *conchology* [< Latin *concha* (see CONCH)]

conchoidal /kong kóyd'l/ *adj* having or being a surface shaped like a bivalve shell with smooth ridges and depressions ○ *conchoidal fracture*

conchology /kong kólləji/ *n* a branch of zoology dealing with sea shells and the animals that inhabit them —**conchological** /kóngkə lójjik'l/ *adj* —**conchologist** *n*

conchy *n* = **conchie** (*dated informal*)

concierge /kónssi airzh, kóN-/ (*plural* **-cierges**) *n* 1 especially in France, somebody whose job is to staff or watch the entrance to a large residential building, and who usually also lives on the premises 2 *US* a person employed at a hotel or apartment building to help the guests or residents, e.g. by dealing with luggage, making travel arrangements, or delivering messages [Mid-16C. Via French < Latin *conservus* 'fellow slave' < *servus* 'slave'.]

~~**concieve**~~ incorrect spelling of **conceive**

conciliar /kən sílli ər/ *adj* belonging to, issued by, or relating to a council, especially a church council [Late 17C. < Latin *concilium* (see COUNCIL).] —**conciliarly** *adv*

conciliate /kən sílli ayt/ (**-ates, -ating, -ated**) *vti* 1 **BRING DISPUTING SIDES TOGETHER** to work with opposing parties with the aim of bringing them to an agreement or reconciliation, especially in an industrial dispute 2 **GET SOMEBODY'S SUPPORT OR FRIENDSHIP BACK** to bring a disagreement with somebody to an end, or overcome somebody's anger, suspicion, or hostility 3 **BE CHARMING** to gain something, especially somebody's friendship, goodwill, or respect, by behaving pleasantly [Mid-16C. < Latin *conciliat-*, past participle of *conciliare* < *concilium* (see COUNCIL).] —**conciliable** *adj* —**conciliation** /kən sílli áysh'n/ *n* —**conciliative** *adj* —**conciliator** *n* —**conciliatorily** *adv* —**conciliatory** *adj*

concinnity /kən sínnəti/ (*plural* **-ties**) *n* 1 a balanced, graceful, polished quality, especially in a literary work 2 a harmonious structuring of all parts of something in terms of the whole [Mid-16C. < Latin *concinnitas* < *concinnus* 'skilfully put together'.] —**concinnous** *adj*

concise /kən síss/ *adj* using as few words as possible to give the necessary information [Late 16C. Directly or via French < Latin *concisus*, past participle of *concidere* 'cut down' < *caedere* 'to cut'.] —**concisely** *adv* —**conciseness** *n* —**concision** *n*

conclave /kóng klayv/ *n* 1 **SECRET MEETING** a private gathering of a select group of people, where discussions are kept secret 2 **MEETING TO SELECT POPE** the secret meeting at which Roman Catholic cardinals elect a new pope 3 **ROOMS WHERE POPE IS ELECTED** the private rooms in which the college of Roman Catholic cardinals assembles to elect a new pope [14C. Via French < Latin, 'locked room' < *clavis* 'key'.] —**conclavist** *n*

conclude /kən klóod/ (**-cludes, -cluding, -cluded**) *v* 1 *vt* **COME TO A CONCLUSION ABOUT** to form an opinion or make a logical judgment about something after considering everything known about it 2 *vti* **FINISH** to come to an end, or bring something to an end 3 *vt* **SETTLE** to make a formal agreement complete and fixed, especially after detailed or prolonged discussions or arrangements 4 *vti US* **DECIDE** to reach a decision about something (*dated*) [13C. < Latin *concludere* 'close completely' < *claudere* 'to close'.] —**concluder** *n*

SYNONYMS See ***deduce***.

conclusion /kən klóozh'n/ *n* 1 **DECISION BASED ON FACTS** a decision made or an opinion formed after considering the relevant facts or evidence 2 **FINAL PART** an ending or the part that brings something to a close (*formal*) 3 **FINAL SETTLEMENT** the completion of a formal agreement or deal, especially after long or detailed discussions and arrangements 4 **PART OF ARGUMENT DEDUCED FROM EVIDENCE** the portion of an argument for which evidence is presented [14C. Via French < Latin *conclus-*, past participle of *concludere* (see CONCLUDE).]

conclusive /kən klóossiv/ *adj* being such that what is specified proves a matter beyond all doubt [Late 16C. < late Latin *conclusivus* < Latin *conclus-*, past participle of *concludere* (see CONCLUDE).] —**conclusively** *adv* —**conclusiveness** *n*

concoct /kən kókt/ *vt* 1 to create something by mixing or combining various ingredients in a new way, especially in cooking 2 to think up a story or plan, especially something ingenious or imaginative [Mid-16C. < Latin *concoct-*, past participle of *concoquere* 'cook together' < *coquere* 'to cook'.] —**concocter** *n* —**concoctive** *adj*

concoction /kən kóksh'n/ *n* 1 **NEW AND UNUSUAL MIXTURE** something that has been concocted, especially a drink or dish created by mixing together ingredients 2 **CONCOCTING A MIXTURE** the act or process of mixing or combining ingredients to create something new and unusual 3 **LIE OR TRICK** something such as a story or plan devised to be deceitful

concomitance /kən kómmitənss/ *n* 1 **EXISTENCE OR OCCURRENCE TOGETHER** the existence or occurrence of something at the same time as, or in connection with, something else 2 **SOMETHING CONNECTED WITH SOMETHING ELSE** something that exists at the same time, or in connection with, something else 3 **CHRISTIAN BELIEF REGARDING COMMUNION** the Christian doctrine that the body and blood of Jesus Christ are embodied in the elements of the Communion

concomitant /kən kómmitənt/ *adj* happening or existing along with or at the same time as something else ○ *parenthood and all its concomitant responsibilities* [Early 17C.

< late Latin *concomitant-*, present participle of *concomitari* 'accompany' < *comit-* 'companion'.] —**concomitant** *n* —**concomitantly** *adv*

concord /kóng kawrd/ *n* **1 PEACEFUL COEXISTENCE** agreement, friendly relations, or peace **2 PEACE TREATY** a peace treaty **3 PLEASING COMBINATION OF SOUNDS** a pleasing sound made when two or more notes are played together **4** GRAM = **agreement** *n.* **5** [13C. Via Old French < Latin *concord-* 'of one heart' < *cor* 'heart'.]

Concord /kóng kawrd/ **1** city in W California. Population: 117,708 (1998 estimate). **2** town in NE Massachusetts. Population: 17,076 (1990). **3** capital of New Hampshire, in the south of the state. Population: 37,444 (1998 estimate). **4** city in SW North Carolina. Population: 34,617 (1998 estimate).

concordance /kən káwrd'nss/ *n* **1** similarity or agreement between two or more things **2** an index of words, e.g. of all the words in a body or bank of text, arranged in alphabetical order [14C. Via French < medieval Latin *concordantia* < Latin *concordant-* (see CONCORDANT).]

concordant /kən káwrd'nt/ *adj* showing harmony, unity, or agreement [15C. Via French < Latin *concordant-*, present participle of *concordare* 'bring into harmony' < *concord-* (see CONCORD).] —**concordantly** *adv*

concordat /kon káwr dat, kən-/ *n* an official agreement, especially a formal contract between the pope and a national government concerning the religious affairs of a country [Early 17C. Via French < Latin *concordatum* < past participle of *concordare* (see CONCORDANT).]

concours /kóng koor/, **concours d'élégance** /-dellay gónss/ *n* a meeting at which classic or vintage cars are exhibited and prizes awarded

concourse /kóng kawrss/ *n* **1 LARGE OPEN SPACE** a large space where people can gather in a public place or building, e.g. at an airport or train station **2 CROWD** a large number of people who have gathered for a special event **3 GATHERING TOGETHER** coming or moving together, or an example of this [14C. Via French < Latin *concursus* 'assembly' < *concurs-*, past participle of *concurrere* (see CONCUR).]

concrescence /kən kréss'nss/ *n* **1** the growing or coming together of body parts or organs, especially in the normal early formation of an embryo **2** MED = **concretion** *n.* **4** [Early 17C. < Latin *concrescent-*, present participle of *concrescere* (see CONCRETE).] —**concrescent** *adj*

concrete /kóng kreet/ *n* **1 HARD CONSTRUCTION MATERIAL** a mixture of cement, sand, aggregate, and water in specific proportions that hardens to a strong stony consistency over varying lengths of time **2 MASS FORMED WHEN PARTICLES COALESCE** a mass formed when particles coalesce ■ *adj* **1 SOLID AND REAL** able to be seen or touched because it exists in reality, not just as an idea **2 DEFINITE** certain and specific rather than vague or general ○ *concrete proposals for reform* **3 SOLIDIFIED** made solid by coalescence ■ *vt* (**-cretes, -creting, -creted**) **COVER WITH CONCRETE** to cover an area with concrete [14C. Via French < Latin *concretus*, past participle of *concrescere* 'grow together' < *crescere* (see CRESCENT).] —**concretely** *adv* —**concreteness** *n*

concrete jungle *n* an urban area completely covered with walkways, roads, and buildings, and perceived as a hostile environment

concrete music *n* electronic music assembled from recordings of live sounds, usually including natural and mechanical sources, manipulated for effect [Translation of French *musique concrète* 'real music']

concrete noun *n* a noun that refers to a physical, and usually visible or touchable, object or substance, e.g. 'clock' or 'elephant'

concrete poetry *n* verse that uses physical arrangement of the words on the page to add to its meaning and effect

concretion /kən kreesh'n/ *n* **1 FORMATION OF WHOLE FROM PARTS** the act or process of separate parts or particles coming together into a solid mass **2 SOLID FORMED BY UNIFICATION OF PARTS** a hard solid mass formed by parts uniting into a whole **3 ROUNDED MASS** a rounded mass of compact concentric layers within a sediment, built up round a nucleus such as a fossil **4 INORGANIC MASS IN BODY** a mass of inorganic material in a body organ or tissue, usually caused by disease [Mid-16C. Via French < Latin *concret-*, past participle of *concrescere* (see CONCRETE).] —**concretionary** *adj*

concretise *vt* = **concretize**

concretism /kóng kreet izəm/ *n* the creation of physical things to represent abstract ideas, especially by the use of concrete poetry —**concretist** *n*

concretize /kóng kreet īz/ (**-tizes, -tizing, -tized**), **concretise** (**-tises, -tising, -tised**) *vt* to make something solid, real, or specific —**concretization** /kóng kree tī záysh'n/ *n*

concubinage /kon kyóobinij, kən-/ *n* the state of being or keeping a concubine

concubine /kóng kyoo bīn/ *n* **1** a woman who is the lover of a wealthy married man but with the social status of a subordinate form of wife, often kept in a separate home, especially in imperial China **2** a woman who lives with a man and has a sexual relationship with him but is not married to him [13C. Via Old French < Latin *concubina* 'bed-mate' < *cubare* 'lie down'.] —**concubinary** /kóng kyoo bīnəri, kon kyóobinəri/ *adj*

concupiscence /kən kyóopiss'nss, kon-/ *n* powerful feelings of physical desire (*formal*) [14C. Via French < late Latin *concupiscere* 'start longing for' < *cupere* 'desire'.] —**concupiscent** *adj*

concur /kən kúr/ (**concurs, concurring, concurred**) *v* **1** *vti* **AGREE** to have the same opinion or reach agreement on a specified point **2** *vi* **COINCIDE** to happen at the same time **3** *vi* **COOPERATE OR COMBINE** to work or act together, especially cooperatively [14C. < Latin *concurrere* 'run together' < *currere* 'run'.] —**concurringly** *adv*

SYNONYMS See ***agree***.

concurrent /kən kúrrənt/ *adj* taking place, existing, or running in parallel at the same time [14C. < Latin *concurrent-*, present participle of *concurrere* (see CONCUR).] —**concurrence** *n* —**concurrently** *adv*

concuss /kən kúss/ *vt* to cause somebody to have concussion, usually by a blow to the head or a jarring fall or jolt [Late 16C. < Latin *concuss-*, past participle of *concutere* 'strike together' < *quatere* 'to strike'.]

concussion /kən kúsh'n/ *n* **1 MILD TO MODERATE BRAIN INJURY** an injury to the brain, often resulting from a blow to the head, that can cause temporary disorientation, memory loss, or unconsciousness **2 INJURY TO A BODILY ORGAN** an injury to an organ of the body, usually caused by a violent blow or shaking **3 SUDDEN JOLT OR SHOCK** any sudden violent jolting or shaking —**concussive** /-kússiv/ *adj*

~~condem~~ incorrect spelling of **condemn**

condemn /kən dém/ *vt* **1 PRONOUNCE AS BAD** to state that something or somebody is in some way wrong or unacceptable **2 GIVE A LEGAL SENTENCE** to make a judicial pronouncement stating what punishment has been imposed on a person found guilty of a crime, especially in the case of a heavy penalty or a death sentence **3 CONSIDER GUILTY** to judge that a person or thing is to blame for something **4 MAKE EXPERIENCE** to force or oblige somebody to experience something very unpleasant, especially something permanent or long-lasting **5 BAN USE OR CONSUMPTION OF** to issue an official order saying that something such as a building is unfit to be used **6 PROVE GUILTY** to serve as proof of the guilt of somebody [14C. Via French *condemner* < Latin *condemnare* 'pass final sentence' < *damnare* (see DAMN).] —**condemnable** *adj* —**condemnation** /kón dem náysh'n, kóndəm-/ *n* —**condemnatory** /kən démnətəri, kón dem náytəri/ *adj*

SYNONYMS See ***criticize***.

condemned cell *n* a prison cell where a person who has been sentenced to death is kept before the execution is carried out

condensate /kón den sayt, kóndən sayt, kən dén sayt/ *n* a substance resulting from condensation, especially a liquid from a vapour

condensation /kón den sáysh'n, kóndən sáysh'n/ *n* **1 CONVERSION OF GAS TO LIQUID** the process by which a vapour loses heat and changes into a liquid **2 FILM OF WATER DROPLETS** tiny drops of water that form on a cold surface such as a window when warmer air comes into contact with it **3 MAKING SOMETHING SHORTER** the state of being compressed or made briefer, or the act or result of summarizing or compressing something **4 FORMATION OF DENSER MOLECULES** the bonding of molecules of a substance to form a larger denser molecule, usually with the release of simpler substances, such as water —**condensational** *adj*

condensation trail *n* AIR = **vapour trail**

condense /kən dénss/ (**-denses, -densing, -densed**) *v* **1** *vti* **CHANGE FROM GAS TO LIQUID** to lose heat and change from a vapour into a liquid, or make a vapour change to a liquid **2** *vt* **MAKE SHORTER** to reduce the length of a text by removing unnecessary words or passages or by expressing the content more concisely **3** *vti* **FORM DENSER MOLECULES** to bond together to form a larger denser molecule, or make molecules undergo this process **4** *vti* **THICKEN BY REMOVING WATER** to make something, especially a food, denser by removing water, or become denser in this way [15C. Via French < Latin *condensare* 'thicken' < *condensus* 'very dense' < *densus* 'thick'.] —**condensability** /kən dénssə bílləti/ *n* —**condensable** *adj*

condensed milk *n* milk thickened by evaporating most of the water content and then sweetened. ◊ **evaporated milk**

condenser /kən dénssər/ *n* **1** a device that converts a gas to a liquid to obtain either the substance or the released heat **2** a lens or mirror used to concentrate light onto, e.g., a transparency or specimen **3** ELEC = **capacitor**

Conder /kóndər/, **Charles Edward** (1868–1909) British painter

condescend /kón di sénd/ *vi* **1** to behave towards other people as though they are less important or less intelligent than you are **2** to do something that you would normally consider yourself too important or dignified to do [14C. Via French *condescendre* < ecclesiastical Latin *condescendere* 'lower oneself' < Latin *descendere* (see DESCEND).] —**condescender** *n*

condescending /kón di sénding/ *adj* behaving towards other people in a way that shows you consider yourself socially or intellectually superior to them, especially when explaining or giving something —**condescendingly** *adv*

condescension /kón di sénsh'n/ *n* behaviour or an example of behaviour that implies that somebody is graciously lowering himself or herself to the level of people less important or intelligent

condign /kən dīn/ *adj* well deserved and completely appropriate (*formal*) [14C. Via French < Latin *condignus* 'wholly worthy' < *dignus* 'worthy'.] —**condignly** *adv*

condiment /kóndimənt/ *n* salt, pepper, mustard, relish, or a similar substance added in small amounts to food to improve or adjust its flavour [15C. Via French < Latin *condimentum* < *condire* 'to preserve'.]

condition /kən dísh'n/ *n* **1 STATE OF REPAIR** the particular state of repair or ability to function of an object or piece of equipment ○ *The meter is still in good condition.* **2 SOMETHING NECESSARY FOR AGREEMENT** something that is necessary for something else to happen, e.g. to bring a situation about or make a contract valid **3 WAY OF BEING** a general state or mode of existence, especially one characterized by hardship or suffering **4 STATUS** position, rank, or social status (*formal*) **5 STATE OF HEALTH** a state of physical fitness or general health ○ *out of condition* **6 DISORDER** a physical disorder **7 STATE OF PREGNANCY** the state of being pregnant (*informal*) ○ *A woman in her condition shouldn't be dancing!* ■ **conditions** *npl* **1 FACTORS AFFECTING PEOPLE** the factors or circumstances that affect the situation somebody is living or working in ○ *poor working conditions* **2 STATE OF WEATHER** the state of the weather ■ *vt* **1 TRAIN** to make people or animals act or react in a certain way by gradually getting them used to a certain pattern of events **2 MAKE STRONG, HEALTHY, OR READY** to give somebody or something a treatment to improve general health, soundness, readiness for use, appearance, or performance **3 IMPROVE HAIR'S CONDITION** to put conditioner or a similar substance on the hair in order to improve its appearance and texture **4 SPECIFY A REQUIREMENT** to state a requirement that must be fulfilled, or to make something dependent on a requirement, especially in a legal contract (*formal*) **5 ADAPT TO** to become accustomed or adapted to specific conditions or activities **6 COOL** to make air cooler ○ *Heat pumps condition the air on the first floor.* [13C. Via Old French < Latin *condition-* 'agreement, stipulation' < *condicere* 'talk together' < *dicere* 'say'.] —**conditionable** *adj*

conditional /kən dísh'nəl/ *adj* **1 DEPENDENT ON SOMETHING ELSE BEING DONE** describes something that will be done or will happen only if and when another thing is done or happens **2 STATING A CONDITION OR LIMITATION** describes a clause, conjunction, verb form, or sentence that expresses a condition or limitation **3 TRUE ONLY FOR CERTAIN MATHEMATICAL VALUES** true only for certain values of one or more variables in a mathematical equation **4 DESCRIBING**

SERIES OF NUMBERS describes a convergent series of numbers that becomes a divergent series when its terms are converted to their absolute values ■ *n* **CONDITIONAL CLAUSE, CONJUNCTION, OR VERB FORM** a conditional clause, conjunction, verb form, or sentence —**conditionality** /kən dísh'n állәti/ *n*

conditional access *n* the coding of television transmissions in order to limit reception to subscribers who have decoding devices

conditional discharge *n* a judgment of a criminal court that finds somebody guilty but lets the person go unpunished subject to certain conditions, e.g. to keep the peace for a year

conditionalization /kən dísh'n'l ī záysh'n/, **conditionalisation** *n* the process of turning a statement into a conditional statement, e.g. changing 'It will rain' into 'If it is cloudy, then it will rain'

conditionally /kən dísh'nәli/ *adv* with the proviso that all valid conditions be met

conditional probability *n* the probability that one event will occur, given that another event has occurred or is certain to occur

ϟ**condition code** *n* a signal, usually in the form of a number, that indicates the status of a previous arithmetic, logic, or input/output operation

conditioned /kən dísh'nd/ *adj* **1** having reached or been brought to a specified or high level of fitness, quality, or performance **2** brought on unconsciously by a stimulus that triggers a reaction because of a learned association with something else

conditioned response, conditioned reflex *n* a response to a new second stimulus as a result of association with a prior stimulus

conditioned stimulus *n* in classical psychological conditioning, an otherwise ineffective stimulus that, when paired with an unconditioned stimulus, is able to evoke a conditioned response

conditioner /kən dísh'nәr/ *n* **1** a liquid or cream applied to hair, either after or with shampoo and usually while the hair is still wet, to make it more manageable or healthier **2** a substance that makes something, e.g. bread dough or soil, easier to manage

conditioning /kən dísh'ning/ *n* **1** a method of controlling or influencing the way people or animals behave or think by using a gradual training process **2** the work or programme used to bring a person or thing to a good physical state

condo /kóndō/ (*plural* **-dos**) *n US* a condominium (*informal*) [Mid-20C. Shortening.]

condole /kən dṓl/ (**-doles, -doling, -doled**) *vi* to express sympathy to somebody who is experiencing grief, loss, or pain, especially over a death [Late 16C. < ecclesiastical Latin *condolere* 'grieve together' < *dolere* 'suffer'.] —**condolatory** *adj* —**condoler** *n* —**condolingly** *adv*

USAGE condole or **console**? These words are easy to confuse because they are both connected with reassuring people in distress. The more common word is ***console***, which takes an object and means 'to provide comfort to somebody': *She tried to console her father when his mother died.* ***Condole*** means 'to express sympathy', and does not take an object but uses *with* instead: *She condoled with her father over the death of his mother.*

condolence /kən dṓlәnss/ *n* an expression of sorrow and sympathy, usually to somebody who is grieving over a death (*often plural*) —**condolent** *adj* —**condolently** *adv*

con dolore /kón do láwray, -ri/ *adv* in a sad or sorrowful way (*musical direction*) [< Italian, 'with sorrow'] —**con dolore** *adj*

condom /kóndәm, -dom/ *n* a close-fitting rubber covering worn by a man over the penis during sexual intercourse to prevent pregnancy or the spread of sexually transmitted disease [Early 18C. < ?]

condominium /kóndә mínni әm/ *n* **1** *US* **INDIVIDUALLY OWNED FLAT** an individually owned unit of real estate, especially a flat or town house, in a building or on land that is owned in common by the owners of the units **2** *US* **BUILDING CONTAINING CONDOMINIUMS** a building or complex containing condominium flats or town houses **3 STATE RULED BY FOREIGN COUNTRIES** a country governed by two or more different countries with joint responsibility **4 JOINT GOVERNMENT OF TERRITORY** the system under which a country or state is ruled by two or more other nations [Early 18C. < modern Latin, 'joint right of ownership' < Latin *dominium* (see DOMINION).] —**condominial** *adj*

condone /kən dṓn/ (**-dones, -doning, -doned**) *vt* to regard something that is considered immoral or wrong in a tolerant way, without criticizing it or feeling strongly about it [Mid-19C. < Latin *condonare* 'give up' < *donare* (see DONATION).] —**condonable** *adj* —**condonation** /kóndә náysh'n, kóndō-/ *n* —**condoner** *n*

Condor

condor /kón dawr, kóndәr/ *n* a large vulture with dull black plumage and white around the neck. Native to: Andes Mountains. *Vultur gryphus.* [Early 17C. Via Spanish *cóndor* < Quechua *kuntur.*]

condottiere /kón doti áiray, -ri/ (*plural* **-ri** /-ri/) *n* **1** a man who led a group of hired soldiers, or one of the hired soldiers in such a group, especially during the period of the Italian Renaissance, between the 13th and 16th centuries **2** a hired soldier [Late 18C. < Italian, 'contractor'.]

conduce /kən dyóoss/ (**-duces, -ducing, -duced**) *vi* to help, contribute, or lead to bringing about an action or event (*formal*) [14C. < Latin *conducere* 'bring together' < *ducere* 'to lead'.] —**conducer** *n* —**conducible** *adj* —**conducingly** *adv*

conducive /kən dyóossiv/ *adj* tending to encourage or bring about a good or intended result ○ *tensions not conducive to a good working relationship*

conduct *v* /kən dúkt/ **1** *vti* **LEAD INSTRUMENTAL OR VOCAL GROUP** to lead a group of musicians or a musical performance by signalling the beat with a baton or hand gestures, giving cues, and offering suggestions for interpretation or expression **2** *vt* **DO OR RUN** to carry out, manage, or control something ○ *Negotiations were conducted in great secrecy.* **3** *vr* **BEHAVE** to behave in a specified way ○ *She conducted herself with great dignity.* **4 TRANSMIT ENERGY** to transmit energy, e.g. heat, light, sound, or electricity **5** *vt* **GUIDE SOMEBODY ALONG** to lead a person or group of people by going along with them ■ *n* /kón dukt/ **1 BEHAVIOUR** the way a person behaves, especially in public ○ *language or conduct likely to offend* **2 HOW SOMEBODY MANAGES** the management or execution of matters such as work or official affairs ○ *criticized for his conduct of the campaign* [15C. Directly and via Old French *conduit* < Latin *conduct-*, past participle of *conducere* (see CONDUCE).] —**conductibility** /kən dúktә bíllәti/ *n* —**conductible** *adj*

conductance /kən dúktәnss/ *n* (*symbol G*) a measure of the ability of an object to transmit electricity. ◊ **conductivity** *n.* 1

conduction /kən dúksh'n/ *n* **1 TRANSMISSION OF ENERGY** the passage of energy through something, particularly heat or electricity **2 TRANSMISSION THROUGH A NERVE FIBRE** the transmission of biochemical or electrical energy through a nerve fibre **3 CONVEYANCE THROUGH PASSAGE** the passage of something through or along something, e.g. water through a pipe

conductive /kən dúktiv/ *adj* **1** transmitting or able to transmit energy, particularly heat or electricity **2** describes a cell that allows a physiological disturbance, e.g. a nerve impulse, to pass through it

conductive education *n* a system of education that teaches children and adults with motor disorders to function independently

conductivity /kón duk tívvәti/ *n* **1** (*symbol σ*) a mathematical relationship between the dimensions of an object and its ability to transmit electricity. ◊ **conductance 2** the ability of tissue to transmit nerve impulses

conductor /kən dúktәr/ *n* **1 SOMEBODY WHO COLLECTS FARES** an employee who takes money for tickets on a bus or tram **2** *US, Can* RAIL = **guard** *n.* 3 **3 DIRECTOR OF ORCHESTRA OR CHOIR** somebody in charge of an orchestra or choir who marks time and signals to musicians or singers when and how to play or sing **4 SOMETHING THAT CONVEYS HEAT OR ELECTRICITY** a substance, body, or medium that allows heat, electricity, light, or sound to pass along it or through it **5** TECH = **lightning conductor** —**conductorial** /kón duk táwri әl/ *adj* —**conductorship** *n*

conduit /kóndyoo it, kóndit/ *n* **1 CHANNEL FOR LIQUID** a pipe or channel that carries liquid to or from a place **2 PROTECTIVE COVER FOR CABLE** a pipe or tube that covers and protects electrical cables **3 CONVEYOR OF INFORMATION** somebody or something that conveys information, especially if in secret [14C. Original form of CONDUCT.]

condyle /kóndil, -dīl/ *n* a rounded part at the end of a bone that forms a moving joint with a cup-shaped cavity in another bone [Mid-17C. Via French < Greek *kondulos* 'knuckle'.] —**condylar** *adj* —**condyloid** /kóndi loyd/ *adj*

condyloma /kóndi lṓmә/ (*plural* **-mas** *or* **-mata** /-mәtә/) *n* a growth resembling a wart on the skin or a mucous membrane, usually of the genitals or anus [14C. Via Latin < Greek *kondulōma* 'callous knob or lump' < *kondulos* 'knuckle'.]

cone /kōn/ *n* **1 POINTED OBJECT WITH ROUND BASE** an object or shape that has a circular base and tapers to a point at the top, or has a circular top and tapers to a point at the bottom **2 POINTED FIGURE WITH CURVED FLAT BASE** a three-dimensional geometric figure formed by straight lines through a fixed point (**vertex**) to the points of a fixed curve (**directrix**) **3 CONE-SHAPED WAFER FOR ICE CREAM** a cone-shaped wafer in which ice cream is sold, or such a wafer with ice cream in it **4 PLASTIC CONE-SHAPED ROAD MARKER** a plastic cone-shaped object used as a temporary road marker or barrier, e.g. to close off part or all of a road during repairs or after an accident **5 SEED-BEARING STRUCTURE OF PINES AND FIRS** a tightly packed cluster of scales that bears the reproductive organs of coniferous plants such as pines and firs. Male cones produce pollen, and female cones bear seeds. Technical name **strobilus** *n.* 1 **6 REPRODUCTIVE PART OF NONFLOWERING PLANTS** a club-shaped, umbrella-shaped, or poker-shaped cluster of fertile leaves that bears the spore-producing organs of a club moss or horsetail **7 LIGHT RECEPTOR CELL IN EYE** a cone-shaped cell sensitive to light and colour in the retina of the eye of a human being or any other vertebrate animal **8 SEA SNAIL WITH CONE-SHAPED SHELL** a sea snail with a cone-shaped, vividly marked shell and a poisonous, sometimes fatal, sting. Native to: South Pacific and Indian oceans. Family: Conidae. **9 VOLCANO** a cone-shaped mountain, especially a volcano ■ *vt* (**cones, coning, coned**) **MAKE SOMETHING INTO CONE SHAPE** to shape something into the form of a cone [15C. Via French < Greek *kōnos* 'pine cone, cone'.]

cone off *vt* to close off a part or all of a road with traffic cones because of road repairs or an accident

~~**conection**~~ incorrect spelling of **connection**

coneflower /kṓn flowәr/ *n* a plant of the daisy family. Flowers: variously coloured with a brown or black cone-shaped centre. Native to: North America. Genera: *Echinacea* and *Rudbeckia.*

cone shell *n* MARINE BIOL = **cone** *n.* 8

con espressione /kón ess pressi ṓni/ *adv* with feeling and expression (*musical direction*) ■ *adj* to be played with great feeling and expression [< Italian, 'with expression']

coney /kṓni/ *n* = **cony**

Coney Island /kṓni-/ amusement area in S Brooklyn, New York City

conf *abbr* **1** confer **2** conference **3** confessor **4** confidential

confab /kón fab/ *n* a chat or casual discussion (*informal*) ■ *vi* (**-fabs, -fabbing, -fabbed**) to have a chat or discussion about something (*informal*) [Early 18C. Shortening of CONFABULATION.]

confabulate /kən fábbyoo layt/ (**-lates, -lating, -lated**) *vi* **1** to discuss or have a chat about something (*formal*) **2** to give fictitious accounts of past events, believing they are true, in order to cover a gap in the memory caused by a medical condition such as dementia or Korsakoff's syndrome [Early 17C. < Latin *confabulat-*, past participle of *confabulari* 'talk together' < *fabula* (see FABLE).] —**confabulation** /kən fábbyoo láysh'n/ *n* —**confabulator** *n* —**confabulatory** /kən fábbyoolәtәri, -fábbyoo láytәri/ *adj*

confect /kən fékt/ *vt* **1** to create something by combining different materials or items ○ *Using scrap lumber, they succeeded in confecting a house of sorts.* **2** to make sweets by combining ingredients such as sugar, fruit, and nuts, or make preserves (*formal*) [14C. < Latin *confect-*, past participle of *conficere* 'put or make together' < *facere* 'make'.]

confection /kən féksh'n/ *n* **1** SOMETHING SWEET a sweet food made by combining ingredients such as fruit, nuts, and sugar **2** COMBINATION a combining of elements or materials or its result ○ *a confection of lies and half-truths* **3** ELABORATE CREATION an often elaborate piece of craftsmanship and skill, e.g. an ornate piece of women's clothing ○ *Her gown was a marvellous confection of lace and tulle.*

confectioner /kən féksh'nər/ *n* a maker or seller of sweets

confectioners' sugar *n US* = **icing sugar**

confectionery /kən féksh'nəri/ (*plural* **-ies**) *n* **1** CONFECTIONS sweets, considered collectively **2** SWEET-MAKING the skill, technique, or practice of making sweets **3** CONFECTIONER'S SHOP a shop where sweets are sold

confed *abbr* **1** confederation **2** confederate

confederacy /kən féddərəssi/ *n* **1** an alliance of people, states, or parties for some common purpose, or the people, states, or parties in an alliance **2** a group of people who have joined together to do something unlawful

Confederacy /kən féddərəssi/ *n* HIST = **Confederate States of America**

confederal /kən féddərəl/ *adj* **1** relating to a confederation **2** relating to the activities of two or more nations —**confederalist** *n*

confederate *n* /kən féddərət/ **1** ALLY one of two or more people, groups, or nations that have formed an alliance for some common purpose **2** ACCOMPLICE a plotter or conspirer ■ *adj* /kən féddərət/ ASSOCIATED joined in common purpose ■ *vti* /kən féddə rayt/ (**-ates, -ating, -ated**) UNITE to form people, groups, or nations into a confederacy, or become part of a confederacy [14C. < late Latin *confoederat-*, past participle of *confoederare* 'league together' < *foeder-* (see FEDERAL).] —**confederative** *adj*

Confederate /kən féddərət/ *n* a supporter or soldier of the Confederate States of America during the American Civil War ■ *adj* relating to the Confederate States of America during the American Civil War

Confederate States of America *n* the confederation of the 11 Southern states that seceded from the United States in 1861, an act that started the American Civil War. Alabama, Arkansas, Florida, Georgia, Louisiana, Mississippi, North Carolina, South Carolina, Tennessee, Texas, and Virginia were the states that seceded.

confederation /kən féddə ráysh'n/ *n* **1** GROUP OF LOOSELY ALLIED STATES a group of states that are allied together to form a political unit in which they keep most of their independence but act together for certain purposes such as defence **2** BODY REPRESENTING INDEPENDENT ORGANIZATIONS a body comprising representatives of independent organizations that wish to cooperate for some common beneficial purpose **3** CONFEDERATING the formation of or state of being a confederation —**confederationism** *n* —**confederationist** *n*

Confederation /kən féddə ráysh'n/ *n* **1** the union of the original 13 states of the United States under the Articles of Confederation from 1781 to 1789 **2** the original union of Ontario, Quebec, New Brunswick, and Nova Scotia in 1867 into the federation of Canada, afterwards joined by the six other provinces

confer /kən fúr/ (**-fers, -ferring, -ferred**) *v* **1** *vi* DISCUSS SOMETHING WITH SOMEBODY to talk to somebody in order to compare opinions or make a decision **2** *vt* GIVE HONOUR OR TITLE to give something such as a title, honour, or favour to somebody (*formal*) ○ *The university conferred an honorary degree on the president.* **3** *vt* GIVE SOMEBODY OR SOMETHING SOME CHARACTERISTIC to give somebody or something a certain status or characteristic ○ *His demeanor conferred a sense of dignity on the whole affair.* ○ *genes that confer resistance to certain infections* [15C. < Latin *conferre* 'bring together' < *ferre* 'bring'.] —**conferment** *n* —**conferrable** *adj* —**conferral** *n* —**conferrer** *n*

SYNONYMS See ***give***.

~~**confered**~~ incorrect spelling of **conferred**

conferee /kónfə reé/, **conferree** *n* **1** a participant in a conference **2** the recipient of a title, honour, or favour

conference /kónfərənss/ *n* **1** MEETING FOR LECTURES AND DISCUSSION a meeting, sometimes lasting for several days, in which people with a common interest participate in discussions or listen to lectures to obtain information **2** MEETING FOR SERIOUS DISCUSSION a meeting to discuss serious matters, e.g. policy or business **3** MEETING OF REPRESENTATIVES OF ORGANIZATION a usually annual gathering of local representatives of an organization, such as a political party, trade union, or church, where policy matters and other issues are discussed or decided ○ *I would ask conference to throw out this motion.* ○ *the Conservative Party Conference* **4** MEETING OF TWO LEGISLATIVE COMMITTEES a meeting of select members or committees from two legislative bodies, for the purpose of settling differences in bills they have passed **5** AREA ORGANIZATION OF CHURCHES in some Protestant churches, a regional or national body to which a number of local churches belong ○ *the Friends General Conference* **6** SPORTS LEAGUE an association or league of athletic teams that compete with each other ○ *the Vauxhall Conference*

Conference *n* a relatively long sweet and juicy variety of pear with a dark green skin

conference call *n* a conversation involving three or more people linked together by telephone

⚡**conferencing** /kónfərənssing/ *n* the holding of a conference, meeting, or discussion in which the participants are linked by telephone (**audioconferencing**), by telephone and video equipment (**video conferencing**), or by computer (**computer conferencing**)

conferree *n* = **conferee**

confess /kən féss/ *v* **1** *vti* ADMIT HAVING DONE SOMETHING WRONG to admit openly a wrongdoing, crime, or error ○ *She confessed to having taken the watch.* ○ *I eventually confessed that I had made the call that night.* **2** *vt* ACKNOWLEDGE TO BE TRUE to admit the truth of something reluctantly, e.g. something that might reflect badly or be embarrassing ○ *I must confess I didn't really want to come here tonight.* ○ *asked me about ley lines but I had to confess my ignorance* **3** *vt* STATE BELIEF ABOUT YOURSELF to say that you believe something to be the case, especially something about yourself and especially something bad ○ *I confess myself quite unworthy of the honour you are bestowing on me.* **4** *vti* ADMIT SINS to reveal sins to a priest or to God and ask for forgiveness ○ *It had been some months since I had confessed.* **5** *vt* HEAR SOMEBODY'S CONFESSION to listen to somebody's confession of sins ○ *A priest visited her to confess her every day.* [14C. Via French *confesser* < Latin *confess-*, past participle of *confiteri* 'acknowledge', literally 'declare utterly' < *fateri* 'declare'.] —**confessable** *adj*

confessant /kən féss'nt/ *n* somebody who confesses sins to a priest

confessedly /kən féssidli/ *adv* used to indicate that something is admitted to be the case

confession /kən fésh'n/ *n* **1** ADMISSION OF WRONGDOING an admission of having done something wrong or embarrassing ○ *a confession of weakness on her part* **2** ADMISSION OF GUILT a voluntary written or verbal statement admitting the commission of a crime ○ *made a full written confession* **3** OPEN ACKNOWLEDGMENT OF FEELINGS a profession of emotions or beliefs such as love, loyalty, or faith **4** DECLARATION OF SINS a formal declaration of sins confidentially to a priest or to God **5** DECLARATION OF BELIEFS OR DOCTRINES a declaration of the beliefs or doctrines of a religious body **6** RELIGIOUS GROUP SHARING BELIEFS a religious group that has a specific set of beliefs and practices

confessional /kən fésh'nəl/ *adj* suited to, typical of, or resembling an act of confession ■ *n* a small wooden stall in a Roman Catholic church with a partition behind which a priest sits to hear confession —**confessionally** *adv*

confessor /kən féssər/ *n* **1** a priest who hears confessions and sometimes acts as a spiritual adviser **2** the maker of a confession

confetti /kən fétti/ *n* small pieces of coloured paper or dried flowers thrown over the bride and groom at a wedding ■ *adj* similar to confetti in shape or colour [Early 19C. < Italian, plural of *confetto* 'small sweet thrown at carnivals' < Latin *conficere* (see CONFECT).]

confidant /kónfi dánt, kónfi dant/ *n* a trusted person with whom personal matters and problems are discussed [Mid-17C. Alteration of CONFIDENT.]

confidante /kónfi dánt, kónfi dant/ *n* a trusted woman with whom personal matters and problems are discussed [Mid-17C. Alteration of CONFIDENT.]

confide /kən fíd/ (**-fides, -fiding, -fided**) *vti* to tell somebody something that is to remain secret or private ○ *He later confided to me that he had not wanted the position at all.* [15C. < Latin *confidere* 'put your trust in' < *fidere* 'to trust' < *fides* 'trust'.] —**confider** *n*

confidence /kónfid'nss/ *n* **1** BELIEF IN OWN ABILITIES a belief or self-assurance in your ability to succeed ○ *lacked the confidence needed to reach the top* **2** FAITH IN SOMEBODY TO DO RIGHT belief or assurance in somebody or something, or in the ability of somebody or something to act in a proper, trustworthy, or reliable manner ○ *I have total confidence in her judgment* **3** SECRET something told to somebody that is to be kept private **4** TRUSTING RELATIONSHIP a relationship based on trust and intimacy ○ *She took me into her confidence.* ○ *But I told you it in confidence!*

confidence game *n US* = **confidence trick**

confidence interval *n* a range of statistical values within which a result is expected to fall with a specific probability

confidence level *n* a measure of how reliable a statistical result is, expressed as a percentage that indicates the probability of the result being correct

confidence limit *n* the highest and lowest values of a confidence interval

confidence trick *n* a fraud in which somebody obtains something of value by first gaining the trust of the victim, then betraying that person. US term **confidence game** —**confidence trickster** *n*

confident /kónfidənt/ *adj* **1** SELF-ASSURED certain of having the ability, judgment, and resources needed to succeed **2** CONVINCED sure about the nature or facts of something ○ *We are confident that the market for our products is expanding.* **3** EXCESSIVELY FORWARD bold and presumptuous in manner [Late 16C. Via French < Latin *confident-*, present participle of *confidere* (see CONFIDE).] —**confidently** *adv*

confidential /kónfi dénsh'l/ *adj* **1** PRIVATE AND SECRET carried out or revealed in the expectation that anything done or revealed will be kept private **2** FOR A SELECT GROUP not available to the public, e.g. because it is commercially or industrially sensitive or concerns matters of national security **3** DEALING WITH PRIVATE AFFAIRS entrusted with somebody's personal or private matters **4** SUGGESTING A CLOSE RELATIONSHIP suggesting familiarity or intimacy that may not exist ○ *a confidential whisper* —**confidentiality** /kónfi denshi álləti/ *n* —**confidentially** *adv*

confiding /kən fíding/ *adj* **1** willing to trust others with the knowledge of private or personal matters **2** in a manner or tone appropriate for telling somebody something secret or that suggests that a secret is being told —**confidingly** *adv*

⚡**configuration** /kən fíggə ráysh'n, -fíggyə-/ *n* **1** ARRANGEMENT OF PARTS the way the parts or elements of something are arranged and fit together ○ *I don't quite grasp the configuration of this engine.* **2** SHAPE OR OUTLINE the shape or outline of something, determined by the way its parts or elements are arranged ○ *Geese fly in a V-shaped configuration.* **3** COMPUTER SYSTEM'S SETUP the way in which the software and hardware components of a computer system are arranged and interconnected **4** ARRANGEMENT OF ATOMS IN MOLECULE the fixed stable spatial arrangement of atoms within a molecule **5** PSYCHOL = **Gestalt** —**configurational** *adj* —**configurationally** *adv* —**configurative** /kən fíggərətiv, -fíggyoo-/ *adj*

configure /kən fíggər/ (**-ures, -uring, -ured**) *vt* to set up, design, or arrange the parts of something for a specific purpose [14C. < Latin *configurare* 'fashion after a pattern', literally 'form together' < *figura* 'shape'.]

confine /kən fín/ *vt* (**-fines, -fining, -fined**) **1** KEEP WITHIN LIMITS to keep somebody or something within certain limits or boundaries ○ *Please confine your comments to the matter in hand.* **2** KEEP IN SOME PLACE to keep somebody or something from leaving an enclosed or limited space such as a prison, room, or bed ■ **confines** *npl* BOUNDARIES the boundaries, limits, or scope restricting somebody or something ○ *seeking emotional fulfilment within the confines of a long-term relationship* [15C. < French *confiner* < *confins* (plural) 'boundaries' < Latin *confinis* 'ending with' < *finis* 'end'.] —**confinable** *adj* —**confiner** *n*

confined /kən fínd/ *adj* small, cramped, and completely enclosed —**confinedness** /kən fínidnəss/ *n*

confined aquifer *n* GEOL = **artesian acquifer**

confinement /kən fínmənt/ *n* **1** the period of time or the process of giving birth, beginning when a woman goes into labour and ending when a child is born (*dated*)

2 restriction or limitation within the boundaries or scope of something

confirm /kən fúrm/ *v* **1** *vt* **PROVE TO BE TRUE** to verify the truth or validity of something thought to be true or valid ○ *Similar findings have been confirmed in recent clinical experiments.* **2** *vti* **MAKE DEFINITE** to make certain that a tentative arrangement or one made earlier is firm ○ *call to confirm the booking* **3** *vt* **LEGALLY APPROVE** to ratify or make something valid with a formal or legal act ○ *confirmed his appointment to the post with a unanimous vote* **4** *vt* **ADMIT INTO RELIGIOUS BODY** in Judaism and Christianity, to admit somebody into full membership of a religious body or community **5** *vt* **STRENGTHEN** to make something stronger (*formal*) [13C. Via Old French *confermer* < Latin *confirmare* 'strengthen together' < *firmare* 'strengthen'.] —**confirmability** /kən fúrmə bílləti/ *n* —**confirmable** *adj* —**confirmatory** /kən fúrmətəri, kónfər máytəri/ *adj* —**confirmer** *n*

confirmation /kónfər máysh'n/ *n* **1 CONFIRMING** verification or ratification ○ *sought confirmation of his suspicions* ○ *the appointment is subject to confirmation by the Senate* **2 SOMETHING THAT CONFIRMS SOMETHING ELSE** something that supports, validates, or verifies something ○ *a confirmation of my worst fears* ○ *Send written confirmation of the date of delivery.* **3 ACCEPTANCE INTO CHURCH** a religious ceremony that marks somebody's formal acceptance into a Christian church **4 CEREMONY MARKING BEGINNING OF RESPONSIBLE ADULTHOOD** in Reform Judaism, a ceremony that marks the completion of somebody's religious training and entry into full adult membership of the community —**confirmational** *adj*

confirmed /kən fúrmd/ *adj* **1 SETTLED AND UNLIKELY TO CHANGE** firmly settled in a particular habit and unlikely to change **2 ESTABLISHED AS TRUE** having been found or shown to be true or definite ○ *confirmed cases of infection* **3 MADE MEMBER OF CHURCH** received into a Christian church as a full member

confirmedly /kən fúrmidli/ *adv* to an extent or in a way that is unlikely to change

confiscate /kónfi skayt/ *vt* (**-cates, -cating, -cated**) **1 TAKE AWAY** to take somebody's property with authority, or appropriate it for personal use ○ *I'll confiscate that ruler if you don't stop playing with it.* **2 TAKE AS LEGAL PENALTY** to seize property legally forfeited to the public treasury as a penalty ○ *The goods were confiscated by customs.* ■ *adj* (*formal*) **1 TAKEN BY AUTHORITY** taken legally, or forfeited **2 HAVING FORFEITED PROPERTY** having had property taken away legally or by forfeiture [Mid-16C. < Latin *confiscare* 'appropriate for the public treasury' < *fiscus* (see FISC).] —**confiscable** /kən fískəb'l/ *adj* —**confiscatable** *adj* —**confiscation** /kónfi skáysh'n/ *n* —**confiscator** *n* —**confiscatory** /kən fískətəri/ *adj*

confit /kón fee/ *n* meat such as goose, duck, or pork that has been cooked and preserved in its own fat [Mid-20C. < French, < Latin *conficere* (see CONFECT).]

Confiteor /kən fítti awr/ *n* a Roman Catholic prayer of confession and plea for forgiveness [13C. < Latin, 'I confess' < the opening words *Confiteor Deo Omnipotenti…* 'I confess to Almighty God…'.]

conflagration /kónflə gráysh'n/ *n* a large fire that causes a great deal of damage [15C. < Latin *conflagration-* < *conflagrare* 'burn up' < *flagrare* 'to blaze'.]

conflate /kən fláyt/ (**-flates, -flating, -flated**) *vti* to join or merge two or more things into a unified whole [15C. < Latin *conflat-*, past participle of *conflare* 'melt together' < *flare* 'to blow'.] —**conflation** *n*

conflict *n* /kón flikt/ **1 WAR** a continued struggle or battle, especially open warfare between opposing forces ○ *news that the conflict had reached the outskirts of the capital* **2 DIFFERENCE** a disagreement or clash between ideas, principles, or people ○ *The two sides came into conflict over the proposed contract.* **3 MENTAL STRUGGLE** a psychological state resulting from the often unconscious opposition between simultaneous but incompatible desires, needs, drives, or impulses **4 PLOT TENSION** opposition between or among characters or forces in a literary work that shapes or motivates the action of the plot ■ *vi* /kən flíkt/ **DIFFER** to be incompatible, in opposition, or in disagreement ○ *The latest findings conflict with those of the original report.* [15C. < Latin *conflictus*, past participle of *confligere* 'strike together, fight' < *fligere* 'strike'.] —**confliction** /kən flíksh'n/ *n* —**conflictive** *adj* —**conflictory** *adj* —**conflictual** *adj*

SYNONYMS See ***fight***.

conflicted /kən flíktid/ *adj* ⚠ *US* confused or ambivalent because of conflicting desires, possibilities, or impulses (*informal*) ○ *I haven't known him when he wasn't conflicted about one thing or another.*

USAGE Since many people dislike ***conflicted***, meaning 'confused or uncertain because of competing desires, possibilities, or impulses', it is wise to avoid using the word in formal writing. It is closely associated with the jargon of psychobabble.

conflicting /kən flíkting/ *adj* **1** inconsistent or contradictory and unable to be reconciled ○ *We've been receiving conflicting reports about the whereabouts of the kidnappers.* **2** not able to be followed or acted on, because each requires different and incompatible actions ○ *In the confusion, the men were given conflicting instructions.* —**conflictingly** *adv*

conflict of interest *n* a conflict between the public and private interests of somebody in an official position, or conflicts between a number of public positions

confluence /kón floo ənss/ *n* **1** a flowing together of two or more streams, a point at which streams combine, or a stream formed by their combining **2** a meeting or gathering together of two or more things, or the place where two or more things meet or join [15C. < late Latin *confluentia* < Latin *confluent-*, present participle of *confluere* 'flow together' < *fluere* 'flow'.] —**confluent** *adj, n*

conflux /kón fluks/ *n* = **confluence** [Early 17C. < Latin *confluxus* 'flowed together' < *confluere* (see CONFLUENCE).]

confocal /kon fṓk'l/ *adj* having the same focus or foci [Mid-19C. < Latin *con-* 'with' + FOCAL.] —**confocally** *adv*

conform /kən fáwrm/ *v* **1** *vi* **BEHAVE ACCEPTABLY** to behave or think in a socially acceptable or expected way ○ *the constant pressure to conform* **2** *vi* **FOLLOW A STANDARD** to comply with a fixed standard, regulation, or requirement ○ *a transformer that doesn't conform to UK standards* **3** *vi* **FIT IN** to be or fit in with a person's idea of what somebody or something should be like ○ *He certainly doesn't conform with my expectations of a diplomat.* **4** *vti* **MATCH** to match, or make somebody or something match, a pattern or sample **5** *vti* **AGREE** to be in accord, or bring something into accord with something else ○ *As soon as possible, the revolutionary government conformed the country's laws with those of the Soviet Union.* **6** *vti* **BE OR MAKE SIMILAR** to be the same as or very similar to something or somebody, or make something similar ○ *The Assyrian account of the great flood conforms closely with the Biblical account.* [14C. Via French *conformer* < Latin *conformare* 'shape after' < *forma* 'shape'.] —**conformer** *n*

conformable /kən fáwrməb'l/ *adj* **1 IN AGREEMENT** consistent with something ○ *This gradual increase in the number of species in a group is conformable with the theory.* **2 SIMILAR** similar in form or shape ○ *I think this software is conformable with what you already have on your system.* **3 COMPLIANT** eager to obey or comply with the wishes of others (*literary*) **4 ABOVE PREVIOUS LAYER** in geology, describes a layer of rock that lies on the stratum that was deposited immediately before it, so there is no break in stratigraphic sequence or intervening erosion —**conformability** /kən fáwrmə bílləti/ *n* —**conformableness** *n* —**conformably** *adv*

conformal /kən fáwrm'l/ *adj* **1** describes a mathematical transformation that leaves the angles between intersecting curves unchanged **2** describes a map that shows the correct shape and scale of a small area

conformance /kən fáwrmənss/ *n* the act of conforming or bringing about accord or compliance

conformation /kón fawr máysh'n/ *n* **1 SOMETHING'S STRUCTURE** the shape, outline, or form of something, especially an animal, determined by the way in which its parts are arranged ○ *the ideal conformation of a young horse suitable as a family mount* **2 SYMMETRY** the symmetrical arrangement of parts or elements of something ○ *That sculpture shows excellent conformation.* **3 MOLECULAR ARRANGEMENT** any of the arrangements of a molecule that result from atoms being rotated about a single bond **4 CREATION OF CONFORMITY** a bringing of one thing into accord with another —**conformational** *adj* —**conformationally** *adv*

conformist /kən fáwrmist/ *n* **1** somebody who behaves or thinks in a socially acceptable or expected way **2** a Christian who belongs to an established national church, especially the Church of England —**conformism** *n* —**conformist** *adj*

conformity /kən fáwrməti/ *n* **1 DOING AND THINKING AS OTHERS** behaving or thinking in a socially acceptable or expected way ○ *a certain lack of conformity in his attitudes* **2 FOLLOWING A STANDARD** compliance with a fixed standard, regulation, or requirement **3 AGREEMENT IN FORM** agreement, correspondence, or similarity in structure, manner, or character **4 COMPLIANCE** acceptance and adherence to the doctrines of an established national church, especially the Church of England

confound /kən fównd/ *vt* **1 MIX UP** to fail to distinguish between two or more things ○ *He often confounds fact and opinion.* **2 BEWILDER** to puzzle or confuse somebody **3 REFUTE** to prove somebody or something to be wrong ○ *confounded the critics and went on to become an international success* **4 MAKE WORSE** to cause a confused situation to become even more confused ○ *Shouting at her like that only confounded the problem.* **5 EXPRESSING ANGER** a word used to express anger at something or somebody ○ *Confound his insolence!* [13C. Via Anglo-Norman *conf(o)undre* < Latin *confundere* 'pour together' < *fundere* 'melt, pour'.] —**confounder** *n* —**confoundingly** *adv*

confounded /kən fówndid/ *adj* **1** used to express annoyance or irritation (*dated informal*) **2** puzzled or confused by something ○ *'I don't know what's happened', he spluttered, completely confounded.* —**confoundedly** *adv* —**confoundedness** *n*

confraternity /kónfrə túrnəti/ (*plural* **-ties**) *n* a group of people united in a common profession or for some purpose, often a group of Christians who have joined together to perform charitable acts [15C. < French *confraternité* < Latin *confrater* 'brother with somebody' < *frater* 'brother'.]

confrère /kón frair/ *n* a fellow member of a professional, charitable, or other group (*formal*) [15C. Via French < Latin *confrater* (see CONFRATERNITY).]

confront /kən frúnt/ *vt* **1 CHALLENGE FACE TO FACE** to come face to face with somebody, especially in a challenge, and usually with hostility, criticism, or defiance **2 MAKE AWARE OF** to bring somebody face to face with something such as contradictory facts or evidence **3 ENCOUNTER DIFFICULTY** to meet something face to face, especially an obstacle that must be overcome ○ *This is just one of the difficulties students confront these days.* **4 BE MET BY DIFFICULTY** to be met face to face by something that must be overcome ○ *The hardships that would confront the settlers were blissfully unknown when they started out.* [Mid-16C. Via French *confronter* < medieval Latin *confrontare* < Latin *front-* 'forehead'.] —**confronter** *n*

confrontation /kón frun táysh'n/ *n* **1 ENCOUNTER** a face-to-face meeting or encounter with somebody or something **2** fighting or a fight or battle **3 HOSTILITY WITHOUT WARFARE** hostility between nations often involving armed forces, yet stopping short of actual warfare **4 CONFLICT BETWEEN IDEAS OR PEOPLE** conflict between ideas, beliefs, or opinions, or between the people who hold them ○ *This country is headed for a confrontation over natural resources and whether exploiting them is a right or a privilege.* **5 FACING UP TO OR ENCOUNTERING** the act or state of facing up to something or encountering something face to face —**confrontational** *adj* —**confrontationist** *n, adj*

Confucian /kən fyóosh'n/ *adj* relating to the teachings of Confucius or his followers, emphasizing personal control, adherence to a social hierarchy, and social and political order —**Confucian** *n* —**Confucianism** *n* —**Confucianist** *n*

Confucius /kən fyóoshəss/ (551?–479? BC) Chinese philosopher, administrator, and moralist

con fuoco /kon foo ṓkō/ *adv* to be played with energy, passion, and fire (*musical direction*) [< Italian, 'with fire'] —**con fuoco** *adj*

confuse /kən fyóoz/ (**-fuses, -fusing, -fused**) *vt* **1 MAKE UNABLE TO THINK INTELLIGENTLY** to make somebody unable to think or reason clearly or act sensibly **2 MAKE HARD TO UNDERSTAND** to make something hard or harder to understand ○ *To call this a 'poem' merely confuses the whole issue.* **3 MIX UP** to mistake one person or thing for another **4 UPSET THE ORDER OF** to cause disorder in something or somebody ○ *The dense fog utterly confused traffic on the motorway.* [14C. Via French *confus* 'perplexed' < Latin *confusus* 'mixed up' < *confundere* (see CONFOUND).] —**confusability** /kən fyóozə bílləti/ *n* —**confusable** *adj*

confused /kən fyóozd/ *adj* **1 UNABLE TO THINK INTELLIGENTLY** unable to think or reason clearly or to act sensibly **2 DISORDERED** in no logical or sensible order ○ *got his grammar hopelessly confused* **3 NOT DIFFERENTIATED** mistaken for each other **4 DISORIENTATED** having impaired psychological capacity to the extent of being forgetful and no longer able to carry out simple everyday tasks —**confusedly** /-fyōōzidli, -fyōōzdli/ *adv* —**confusedness** /-zidnəss/ *n*

confusing /kən fyōōzing/ *adj* unclear and difficult to understand —**confusingly** *adv*

confusion /kən fyōōzh'n/ *n* **1 BEWILDERMENT** the act of confusing somebody or something, or the state of being confused or perplexed ○ *tried to hide his confusion* **2 LACK OF CLARITY** misunderstanding of a situation or the facts **3 MISTAKING ONE FOR ANOTHER** a failure to distinguish between people or things **4 DISORDER** a chaotic or disordered state **5 DISORIENTED STATE OF MIND** a psychological state in which somebody is disoriented and unable to think clearly —**confusional** *adj*

confutation /kónfyōō táysh'n/ *n* (*formal*) **1** proving that somebody is wrong or that something is false, invalid, or faulty ○ *The lawyer's confutation of the witness's testimony was decisive.* **2** a fact, observation, or piece of evidence proving that somebody is wrong or that something is false, invalid, or faulty (*often plural*) —**confutative** /kən fyōōtətiv/ *adj*

confute /kən fyōōt/ (**-futes, -futing, -futed**) *vt* to prove conclusively that somebody is wrong or that something is false, invalid, or faulty (*formal*) [Early 16C. < Latin *confutare* 'restrain, answer conclusively'.] —**confutable** *adj* —**confuter** *n*

cong. *abbr* **1** congress **2** congressional **3** congregational

Cong. *abbr* **1** Congress **2** Congressional **3** Congregational

conga /kóng gə/ *n* **1** a Latin American dance in which people form a line and, holding the waist of the person ahead, move three steps forward, then kick out a leg **2** the music for a conga **3** MUSIC = **conga drum** [Mid-20C. < American Spanish (*danza*) *Conga* 'dance from the Congo' < Spanish *Congo*]

conga drum *n* a tall tapering drum, played with both hands and used in Latin American and African music

congé /kón zhay, kóN-/ (*plural* **-gés**) *n* **1 PERMISSION** formal permission for somebody to leave (*formal*) **2 LEAVE-TAKING** a departure (*formal*) **3 BOW** a formal bow (*formal*) **4 CONCAVE MOULDING** an architectural moulding that is concave in shape [14C. < Old French *congié* < Latin *commeare* 'come and go'.]

congeal /kən jēél/ *vti* **1** to become thick and solid or cause a liquid to thicken and solidify **2** to become, or cause to become, firm and strong ○ *Let's act before opposition to our plan congeals.* [14C. Via French *congeler* < Latin *congelare* 'freeze together' < *gelu* 'frost'.] —**congealer** *n* —**congealment** *n*

congelation /kónji láysh'n/ *n* **1** the process of turning from a liquid into a solid, or the state of being solid as a result of congealing (*formal*) **2** a liquid that has solidified [15C. Directly or via French < Latin *congelation-* < *congelare* (see CONGEAL).]

congener /kən jēénər, kónjinər/ *n* **1** somebody or something that belongs to the same class, group, or type, e.g. an animal or plant of the same genus as another animal or plant, or two elements belonging to the same group **2** a complex organic molecule that develops in wine and spirits during the fermentation and aging processes, thought to be implicated in causing hangovers [Mid-18C. < Latin *congenus* 'of the same race' < *genus* 'race'.]

congeneric /kónji nérrik/ *adj* describes organisms belonging to the same class, group, or type —**congenerous** /kon jénnərəss, kən-/ *adj*

congenial /kən jēéni əl/ *adj* **1 AGREEABLE** pleasant and suited to somebody's character or tastes ○ *found it a very congenial atmosphere* **2 SIMILAR** compatible in tastes, interests, attitudes, or backgrounds ○ *carefree travel with congenial companions* **3 FRIENDLY** having an outgoing pleasant character ○ *Her congenial nature made her well-loved in the town.* [Late 17C. < CON- 'with' + GENIAL.] —**congeniality** /kən jēéni álləti/ *n* —**congenially** *adv* —**congenialness** *n*

congenic /kən jénnik/ *adj* describes animal cells that are genetically identical except for the arrangement of genes in a single restricted chromosome region (**locus**)

congenital /kən jénnit'l/ *adj* **1** describes an unusual condition present at birth **2** firmly established as part of somebody's character or beliefs [Late 18C. < Latin *con-*

genitus 'born with' < *genitus*, past participle of *gignere* 'beget'.] —**congenitally** *adv* —**congenitalness** *n*

congenital anomaly *n* a medically significant condition present at birth and resulting from developmental processes (*technical*)

conger eel /kóng gər-/, **conger** *n* a large scaleless eel. Native to: temperate and tropical coastal waters of the Atlantic Ocean. *Conger oceanicus*. [Via French *congre* < Greek *goggros*]

congeries /kən jeéreez, kónjə reez/ (*plural* **-ries**) *n* a collection or assortment of things (+ *singular verb*) ○ *made a nation of what had been a far-flung congeries of states* [Mid-16C. < Latin, 'heap, pile' < *congerere* (see CONGEST).]

congest /kən jést/ *vti* **1** to overcrowd a street or area, or become overcrowded, so that movement is slow or difficult **2** to accumulate an excessive amount of blood or fluid in an organ or body part, as a result of disease or infection [15C. < Latin *congest-*, past participle of *congerere* 'collect' < *gerere* 'carry'.] —**congested** *adj* —**congestible** *adj* —**congestive** *adj*

⚡**congestion** /kən jéschən/ *n* **1 EXCESSIVE TRAFFIC OR PEOPLE** a state of overcrowding in a street or other area, making movement slow or difficult **2 EXCESSIVE ACCUMULATION OF FLUID** the condition of having an excessive amount of blood or fluid accumulate in an organ or body part, as a result of disease or infection **3 HAVING TOO MUCH INFORMATION TO TRANSFER** in computing, a situation that arises when the amount of information to be transferred is greater than the data communication path can carry

congestive heart failure /kən jéstiv-/ *n* a form of heart failure in which the heart is unable to pump away the blood returning to it fast enough, causing congestion in the veins

conglomerate *n* /kən glómmərət/ **1 BUSINESS ORGANIZATION INVOLVED IN MANY AREAS** a large business organization that consists of a number of companies that deal with a variety of different business, manufacturing, or commercial activities **2 SOMETHING MADE BY COMBINING THINGS** something formed from gathering together a number of dissimilar materials or elements **3 ROCK COMPRISING PIECES OF OTHER ROCKS** in geology, coarse-grained sedimentary rock containing fragments of other rock larger than 2 mm/0.08 in. in diameter, held together with another material such as clay ■ *adj* **FORMED BY COMBINING DIFFERENT THINGS** consisting of a mass or accumulation of dissimilar materials or elements ■ *vti* /kən glómmə rayt/ (**-ates, -ating, -ated**) **BRING THINGS TOGETHER TO FORM MASS** to gather together materials or elements, or be gathered together into a mass [Late 16C. < Latin *conglomeratus* 'wound into a ball' < *glomer-* 'ball'.] —**conglomeratic** /kən glómmə ráttik/ *adj* —**conglomeration** /kən glómmə ráysh'n/ *n* —**conglomerative** *adj* —**conglomerator** *n* —**conglomeritic** /kən glómmə ríttik/ *adj*

conglomerated /kən glómmə raytid/ *adj* made up of and controlling many parts of an industry ○ *a conglomerated corporation*

Congo /kóng gō/ Africa's second longest river, rising in the north of the Democratic Republic of the Congo and emptying into the Atlantic Ocean. Length: 4,374 km/2,710 mi.

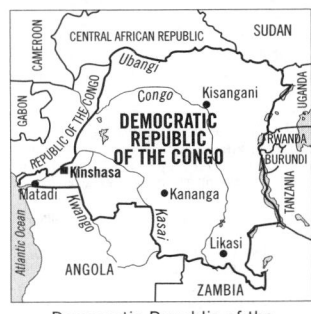

Democratic Republic of the Congo

Congo, Democratic Republic of the large equatorial country of Central Africa with a coastline on the Atlantic Ocean. Capital: Kinshasa. Population: 47,589,551 (1997). Area: 2,344,885 sq. km/905,365 sq. mi. —**Congolese** /kóng gə leéz/ *adj, n*

Congo, People's Republic of the former name for **Republic of the Congo** (1970–62)

Republic of the Congo

Congo, Republic of the republic in west-central Africa. Capital: Brazzaville. Population: 2,599,713 (1997). Area: 342,000 sq. km/132,000 sq. mi. —**Congolese** /kóng gə leéz/ *adj,*

congo dye *n* a dye containing nitrogen, usually derived from benzidine [Because associated with the Congo region or African Americans from there]

Congo eel *n* an amphibian that has a long body with gill slits and two pairs of rudimentary limbs that enable it to travel on land. Native to: SE United States. *Amphiuma means.* [See CONGO DYE]

Congo Free State former name for **Congo, Democratic Republic of the** (1885–1908)

Congo red *n* a dye that is red in alkaline solutions and blue in acid solutions. Use: chemical indicator, biological stain, dye. [See CONGO DYE]

Congo snake *n* = **Congo eel**

congou /kóng goo, kóng gō/ *n* a fine grade of Chinese black tea, made from the largest leaf gathered from the tip of a shoot on a tea plant [Early 18C. Shortening of Cantonese Chinese *kungfûch'a*, Mandarin *gōngfu chá* 'tea made for refined tastes', literally 'effort tea'.]

congrats /kən gráts/ *npl, interj* an expression of congratulations (*informal*) [Early 20C. Shortening.]

congratulate /kən gráttyōō layt, -grächōō-/ (**-lates, -lating, -lated**) *v* **1** *vt* to express pleasure or approval to somebody for an achievement or good fortune or on a special occasion **2** *vr* to feel self-satisfied in having success or good fortune ○ *I was congratulating myself on my driving skills, when I skidded into a snow bank.* [Mid-16C. < Latin *congratulat-*, past participle of *congratulari* 'rejoice with' < *gratus* 'thankful'.] —**congratulative** *adj* —**congratulator** *n* —**congratulatory** *adj*

congratulation /kən gráttyōō láysh'n, -grachoo-/ *n* the expressing of pleasure to somebody for an achievement or good fortune or on a special occasion ○ *made a short speech of congratulation* ■ *npl, interj* **congratulations** an expression of pleasure or acknowledgment of somebody's success or good fortune or on a special occasion

congregant /kóng grigənt/ *n* a member of a religious congregation, especially in a Jewish synagogue [Late 19C. < Latin *congregant-*, present participle of *congregare* (see CONGREGATE).]

congregate *vti* /kóng gri gayt/ (**-gates, -gating, -gated**) **ASSEMBLE PEOPLE OR ANIMALS** to come together in a group, or gather people or animals together in a group ■ *adj* /-gət, -gayt/ (*formal*) **1 HAVING COME TOGETHER** gathered or assembled in a group **2 RELATING TO A GATHERING** relating to an assembled group [15C. < Latin *congregat-*, past participle of *congregare* 'collect together' < *greg-* 'flock'.] —**congregative** *adj* —**congregator** *n*

congregation /kóng gri gáysh'n/ *n* **1 GROUP OF WORSHIPPERS** a group of people who have gathered together for a religious service **2 MEMBERS OF SAME CHURCH** the members of a particular church **3 ROMAN CATHOLIC RELIGIOUS BODY** a Roman Catholic religious body whose members follow a common rule of life and are bound by simple vows (*formal*) **4 DIVISION OF ROMAN CATHOLIC CENTRAL ADMINISTRATION** a section of the central administrative organization (**Curia**) of the Roman Catholic Church **5 COMMITTEE OF ROMAN CATHOLIC RELIGIOUS BISHOPS** a committee of Roman Catholic bishops responsible for handling the business of a general council (*formal*) 6 **GATHERING** a group of people or things gathered together ○ *A congregation of reporters waited outside the courthouse.* 7 **SENIOR MEMBERS OF UNIVERSITY STAFF** an assembly of the senior members of the academic staff of a university 8 **COMING TOGETHER** the act of gathering together or assembling (*formal*) ○ *Congregation in the halls is not allowed.*

congregational /kóng gri gáysh'nəl/ *adj* relating to a congregation

Congregational /kóng gri gáysh'nəl/ *adj* relating to Congregationalism or its followers

Congregational Church *n* a Protestant denomination in which each church is self-governing

congregationalism /kóng gri gáysh'nəlizəm/ *n* a system of church organization in which each church is self-governing —**congregationalist** *n, adj*

Congregationalism *n* a Protestant denomination with a system of government in which each local church governs itself —**Congregationalist** *n, adj*

congress /kóng gress/ *n* 1 **CONFERENCE OR MEETING** a conference or formal meeting of delegates or representatives, e.g. the representatives of a group of nations, to discuss matters of interest or concern 2 **ORGANIZED GROUP** a society or organization of people with common interests and concerns 3 **SEXUAL INTERCOURSE** sexual intercourse (*dated formal*) [15C. < Latin *congressus*, past participle of *congredi* 'go together' < *gradi* 'proceed'.] —**congressional** /kən grésh'nəl/ *adj* —**congressionally** *adv*

Congress *n* 1 **US PARLIAMENT** the national legislative body of the United States, consisting of the House of Representatives and the Senate 2 **SESSION OF CONGRESS** a two-year term of the US Congress, or the members of Congress during such a term ○ *the 22nd Congress* 3 **GOVERNING AND LAW-MAKING BODY** the governing body in some countries ○ *the National People's Congress* 4 **NAME OF CERTAIN POLITICAL PARTIES** the shortened name of a number of political parties whose name includes the word 'Congress', e.g. the African National Congress or the Indian Congress Party —**Congressional** /kən grésh'nəl/ *adj*

congressional district *n* a district within a US state that is entitled to elect one representative to the House of Representatives

Congressional Medal of Honor *n* the highest military decoration in the United States, awarded by Congress for outstanding bravery in action

Congressional Record *n* a government journal in the United States that records and publishes the proceedings of Congress

congressman /kóng gressmən/ (*plural* **-men** /-mən/) *n* a man who is a member of the US Congress, especially of the House of Representatives

Congress of Industrial Organizations *n* a federation of industrial trade unions formed in the United States in 1935 and merged with the American Federation of Labor in 1955 to form the AFL-CIO

congressperson /kóng gress purs'n/ (*plural* **-people** /-peep'l/) *n* a member of the US Congress, especially of the House of Representatives

congresswoman /kóng gress wŏŏmən/ (*plural* **-en** /-wimin/) *n* a woman who is a member of the US Congress, especially of the House of Representatives

Congreve /kóng greev/, **William** (1670–1729) English playwright and poet

congruent /kóng groo ənt/ *adj* 1 **IN AGREEMENT** corresponding to or consistent with each other or something else (*formal*) ○ *culturally congruent education* 2 **WITH THE SAME SHAPE** with identical geometric shapes 3 **DIFFERING BY EXACTLY DIVISIBLE AMOUNT** describes two numbers whose difference is exactly divisible by a third number (**modulus**) [15C. < Latin *congruent-*, present participle of *congruere* 'meet together' < *ruere* 'to fall'.] —**congruence** *n* —**congruency** *n* —**congruently** *adv*

congruity /kən grŏŏ əti/ *n* (*formal*) 1 the state or fact of agreeing or being consistent with each other or with something else 2 the quality or fact of being suitable or appropriate for something

congruous /kóng groo əss/ *adj* 1 appropriate to or suitable for a particular thing or situation (*formal*) 2 corresponding to or consistent with each other or something else [Late 16C. < Latin *congruus* 'suitable' < *congruere* (see CONGRUENT).] —**congruously** *adv* —**congruousness** *n*

conic /kónnik/ *adj* = **conical** ■ *n* = **conic section** [Late 16C. Via modern Latin *conicus* < Greek *kōniko* < *kōnos* 'cone'.]

conical /kónnik'l/ *adj* 1 shaped like a cone 2 relating to or having the form of a geometrical cone

conic projection *n* a method of making a map by projecting the globe onto a surrounding cone whose point is above one of the poles and then flattening the cone, or a map so made

conics /kónniks/ *n* the branch of geometry involving the study of conic sections (*takes a singular verb*)

conic section *n* a curve produced by the intersection of a plane with a circular cone, e.g. a circle, ellipse, hyperbola, or parabola

conidia plural of **conidium**

conidiophore /kō níddi ə fawr/ *n* a simple or branched part (**hypha**) of a fungus that produces spores asexually [Late 19C. < CONIDIUM.] —**conidiophorous** /kō níddi óffərəss/ *adj*

conidium /kō níddi əm/ (*plural* **-a** /-ə/) *n* an asexually produced spore of certain types of fungi [Late 19C. < modern Latin, < Greek *konis* 'dust'.] —**conidial** *adj*

conifer /kónnifər, kṓnifər/ *n* any tree that has thin leaves (**needles**) and produces cones. Many types are evergreen. Order: Coniferales. [Mid-19C. < Latin, 'cone-bearing' < Greek *kōnos* 'cone'.] —**coniferous** /kə níffərəss/ *adj*

coniine /kṓni een, kṓ neen/ *n* $C_8H_{17}N$ a colourless substance with poisonous properties. Source: hemlock. [Mid-19C. < *conium* 'hemlock' < Latin.]

Coniston Water /kónnistən-/ lake in NW England where several water speed records have been set. Area: 7 sq. km/2.75 sq. mi. Depth: 56 m/184 ft.

conj. *abbr* 1 conjugation 2 conjunction 3 conjunctive

conjecture /kən jékchər/ *n* 1 **GUESSWORK** the formation of judgments or opinions on the basis of incomplete or inconclusive information ○ *The origin of this ritual is a matter of conjecture.* 2 **SOMETHING GUESSED** a conclusion, judgment, or statement based on incomplete or inconclusive information 3 a theorem in science or mathematics that has still to be proved [14C. Directly or via French < Latin *conjectura* < *conjicere* 'throw together' < *jacere* 'throw'.] —**conjecturable** *adj* —**conjecturably** *adv* —**conjectural** *adj* —**conjecturally** *adv* —**conjecture** *vti* —**conjecturer** *n*

conjoin /kən jóyn/ *vti* to join two or more things together, or become joined together (*formal*) ○ *conjoined in holy matrimony* [14C. Via French *conjoindre* < Latin *conjungere* 'join together' < *jungere* 'join'.] —**conjoiner** *n*

conjoint /kən jóynt/ *adj* 1 done by, involving, or relating to two or more combined entities ○ *a conjoint project* 2 joined together or combined —**conjointly** *adv*

conjugal /kónjŏŏg'l/ *adj* relating to marriage or to husbands and wives [Early 16C. < Latin *conjugalis* < *conjugare* (see CONJUGATE).] —**conjugality** /kónjŏŏ gálləti/ *n* —**conjugally** *adv*

conjugal rights *npl* the rights that husbands or wives are entitled to in a marriage, especially the right to have sexual relations with their spouse

conjugal visit *n* a visit to a jail by the husband or wife of a prisoner, during which the couple is allowed some privacy, e.g. to allow them to have sexual relations

conjugant /kónjŏŏgənt/ *n* either of a pair of organisms, cells, or gametes in the process of reproducing [Early 20C. < Latin *conjugant-*, present participle of *conjugare* (see CONJUGATE).]

conjugate *v* /kónjŏŏ gayt/ (**-gates, -gating, -gated**) 1 *vti* **STATE FORMS OF VERB** to state systematically the different forms a verb has according to tense, mood, person, and number 2 *vi* **HAVE DIFFERENT GRAMMATICAL FORMS** to have different grammatical forms according to tense, mood, number, and person (*refers to verbs*) 3 *vt* **JOIN SUBSTANCES** to join two substances together in such a way that they can easily be separated again, especially in chemical reactions 4 *vi* **REPRODUCE** to reproduce by physically joining in order to transfer genetic information (*refers to organisms that normally reproduce by division*) ■ *adj* /-gət, -gayt/ 1 **EXISTING TOGETHER IN EQUILIBRIUM** describes a state of chemical equilibrium in which two liquids coexist in separate forms, one being the solute and the other the solvent 2 **DIFFERING BY ONE PROTON** describes substances that have such similar molecular structures that one becomes the other through the gain or loss of a proton 3 **ADDING UP TO 360 DEGREES** describes a pair of angles that together add up to 360 degrees 4 **PAIRED** joined together in pairs (*formal*) ■ *n* /-gət/ 1 **VERB FORM** one of the different forms of a verb according to tense, mood, person, or number 2 **RESULT OF JOINING** a product of joining or union 3 MATH = **conjugate complex number** [15C. < Latin *conjugatus*, past participle of *conjugare* 'yoke together' < *jugum* 'yoke'.] —**conjugable** *adj* —**conjugately** *adv* —**conjugateness** *n* —**conjugative** *adj* —**conjugator** *n*

conjugate complex number *n* either of a pair of complex numbers that are symmetrically located on either side of an x-axis, differing only in the sign of the imaginary component

conjugated /kónjŏŏ gaytid/ *adj* describes a double chemical bond separated by a single bond

conjugated protein *n* a protein attached to a non-protein

conjugation /kónjŏŏ gáysh'n/ *n* 1 **INFLECTION OF VERB** the different patterns of inflection of a given verb 2 **GROUP OF VERBS WITH SAME INFLECTIONS** a group of verbs that use the same patterns of inflection 3 **SET OF VERB INFLECTIONS** the complete set of inflections for a given verb 4 **ACT OF JOINING TOGETHER** the act of joining together or uniting, or the state of being joined together 5 **REPRODUCTION IN SIMPLE ORGANISMS** the simplest form of reproduction, in which two single-celled organisms, e.g. bacteria or protozoans, link together, exchange genetic information, and then separate 6 **FUSION OF NUCLEI** the fusion of the nuclei of a male and a female gamete in algae and fungi 7 **PAIRING OF CHROMOSOMES** the distribution of pairs of chromosomes into the four nuclei produced by the division of a parent nucleus 8 **ALTERNATION OF NUMBER OF BONDS** the occurrence of two or more double or triple bonds in alternation with single bonds in a molecule —**conjugational** *adj* —**conjugationally** *adv*

conjunct /kón jungkt/ *adj* 1 **ATTACHED OR JOINED** attached or joined very close to something 2 **ADJACENT TO CONSONANT** describes consonants that are next to each other within a word without a vowel or vowels between 3 **CONSISTING OF SINGLE STEPS IN SCALE** relating to or consisting of adjacent notes in a musical scale ■ *n* **EITHER PROPOSITION IN CONJUNCTION** either of the two propositions or formulas in a conjunction in logic [15C. < Latin *conjunctus*, past participle of *conjungere* (see CONJOIN).] —**conjunctly** *adv*

conjunction /kən júngksh'n/ *n* 1 **COMBINING OF SEVERAL THINGS** the joining together or combining of two or more things 2 **SIMULTANEOUS OCCURRENCE** a simultaneous occurrence of events or circumstances 3 **CONNECTING WORD** a word that is used to link sentences, clauses, phrases, or words, e.g. 'and', 'but', or 'if' 4 **ALIGNMENT WITH SUN** the position of a planet or the Moon when aligned with the Sun, as seen from Earth 5 **CLOSE PROXIMITY OF PLANETS** the appearance of two planets very close to each other or in the same place on the celestial sphere 6 **ASPECT OF 0° BETWEEN PLANETS** in astrology, an aspect of 0° between two planets 7 **TYPE OF COMPOUND STATEMENT** a proposition in logic of the form 'A and B' that is true only if both A and B are true [14C. < Latin *conjunction-* < *conjunct-*, past participle of *conjungere* (see CONJOIN).] —**conjunctional** *adj* —**conjunctionally** *adv* ◇ **in conjunction with** together with or combined with something

conjunctiva /kón jungk tívə/ (*plural* **-vas** *or* **-vae** /-vee/) *n* a delicate mucous membrane that covers the internal part of the eyelid and is attached to the cornea [14C. < medieval Latin (*tunica*) *conjunctiva* 'connective (membrane)' < Latin *conjunct-*, past participle of *conjungere* (see CONJOIN).] —**conjunctival** *adj*

conjunctive /kən júngktiv/ *adj* 1 **CONNECTIVE** serving to join things together 2 **COMBINED** joined together or combined with something else 3 **OF GRAMMATICAL CONJUNCTIONS** relating to conjunctions or their grammatical function [15C. < late Latin *conjunctivus* < Latin *conjunct-*, past participle of *conjungere* (see CONJOIN).] —**conjunctively** *adv*

conjunctive adverb *n* an adverb or adverbial phrase that is used to connect parts or clauses of a sentence

conjunctive eye movement *n* a simultaneous movement of both eyes in the same direction

conjunctivitis /kən júngkti vítiss/ *n* inflammation of the conjunctiva caused by infection, injury, or allergy

conjuration /kónjŏŏ ráysh'n/ *n* 1 **MAGIC SPELL** a word or phrase that a magician says when casting a spell (*literary*) 2 **INVOCATION OF SUPPOSED SUPERNATURAL FORCE** a summoning or invoking, usually of a supposed supernatural force, by pronouncing a sacred name (*literary*) 3 **SUPPOSED MAGIC TRICK** a supposed magic or supernatural occurrence achieved by pronouncing a spell or chanting

conjure /kúnjər/ (**-jures, -juring, -jured**) *v* **1** *vi* **PERFORM MAGIC TRICKS** to perform illusions and magic tricks that require agile hand movements, usually for entertainment **2** *vti* **INVOKE SUPPOSED SUPERNATURAL FORCES** to call upon or order a supposed supernatural force or being by reciting a spell ○ *He was struck dumb by the very demons he was conjuring.* **3** *vt* **INFLUENCE WITH SPELL** to change or influence something by reciting a spell or invocation **4** *vt* **IMPLORE** to implore somebody to do something (*archaic*) ○ *I conjure you to show me mercy.* [13C. Via Old French < Latin *conjurare* 'bind with an oath', literally 'swear together' < *jurare* (see JURY).]

conjure up *vt* **1 EVOKE** to create something in the mind ○ *This music conjures up images of rural scenes.* **2 PRODUCE AS IF BY MAGIC** to produce or create something difficult or unexpected as if by magic ○ *She conjured up a delicious meal from the most basic ingredients.* **3 SUMMON SUPPOSED SUPERNATURAL BEING** to call upon a supposed supernatural force or being by reciting a spell or chanting magic words

conjurer /kúnjərər/, **conjuror** *n* **1** an entertainer who performs tricks involving manual agility and the illusion of magic **2** a magician or summoner of supposed supernatural forces or beings

conjuring /kúnjəring/ *n* the performance of tricks that involve manual agility or the illusion of magic, as an entertainment

conjuror *n* = **conjurer**

conk /kongk/ *n* (*slang*) **1** the head or the nose **2** a blow, especially on the head or, less commonly, the nose [Early 19C. < ?] —**conk** *vt*

conker /kóngkər/ *n UK* a horse chestnut without its spiny outer casing, used in the game of conkers [Mid-19C. Probably blend of CONCH, CONK + CONQUER.]

conkers /kóngkərz/ *n* a children's game, usually for two people, in which a player has a conker threaded onto a string and uses it to try to smash the opponent's conker (+ *singular verb*)

conk out /kongk/ *vi* (*informal*) **1** to stop operating or break down suddenly ○ *The car conked out at the traffic lights.* **2** to collapse or fall asleep, usually through exhaustion ○ *I conked out the minute I got home.* [Early 20C. < ?]

con man *n* a deceiver who uses persuasive speech and other devices to swindle people (*informal*) [Shortening of CONFIDENCE]

con moto /kon mṓt ō/ *adv* in a lively or brisk way (*musical direction*) [Early 19C. < Italian, 'with movement'.]

Connacht /kónnawt, -nət/, **Connaught** region on the coast of the W Republic of Ireland. Population: 423,031 (1991). Area: 17,122 sq. km/6,611 sq. mi.

connate /kónn ayt/ *adj* **1** describes parts that have grown closely joined to a single structure in a plant or animal **2** describes water, usually very saline, that has been trapped in sedimentary rock since the original deposits were laid down [Mid-17C. < late Latin *connatus*, past participle of *connasci* 'be born with' < Latin *nasci* 'be born'.] —**connately** *adv* —**connateness** *n*

connect /kə nékt/ *v* **1** *vti* **LINK TWO THINGS** to link or join two or more parts, things, or people together ○ *All you have to do is connect these two wires, and it should work.* ○ *A flagstone walk connected the main house with the tool shed.* **2** *vt* **ASSOCIATE WITH SOMETHING ELSE** to make a psychological or emotional association between people, things, or events ○ *She always connected that house with family celebrations.* **3** *vt* **ESTABLISH TELECOMMUNICATION LINK** to set up a communication link between people, organizations, or places ○ *All my friends are connected to the Internet.* **4** *vt* **LINK UP TO UTILITY** to link people or equipment to a source of electricity, water, or gas ○ *Have the gas board connected you yet?* ○ *The appliance should not be connected to the mains.* **5** *vi* **ALLOW TIME FOR PASSENGERS TO TRANSFER** to arrive shortly before another vehicle or vessel departs, or shortly after another arrives, so as to allow passengers to change from one to the other ○ *This train connects with another one going to the city centre.* **6** *vi* **MAKE TRANSPORT CONNECTION** to change from one vehicle or vessel to another ○ *those wishing to connect to a long-haul flight* **7** *vi* **HIT SOMETHING FIRMLY** to strike, punch, or kick firmly, with good contact between the striking surface and the object struck (*informal*) ○ *The punch connected, and he sank to the ground.* **8** *vi* **GET ON WELL** to have a good rapport with somebody ○ *The interview was a disaster – we never really connected.* [15C. < Latin *connectere* 'tie together' < *nectere* 'to bind'.] —**connectible** *adj* —**connector** *n*

connect up *vti* = **connect** *v.* **1**, **connect** *v.* **4**

connected /kə néktid/ *adj* **1 JOINED TOGETHER** joined or linked firmly together **2 WITH BENEFICIAL SOCIAL CONNECTIONS** with useful business or social connections (*often in combination*) **3 LOGICAL AND INTELLIGIBLE** ordered in a logical and intelligible way **4 DESCRIBING MATHEMATICAL RELATION** describes a mathematical relation for which either the relation or its converse is true for any two members in a set —**connectedly** *adv* —**connectedness** *n*

Connecticut /kə néttikət/ **1** southernmost state in New England, NE United States. Population: 3,287,116 (1990). Area: 14,359 sq. km/5,544 sq. mi. **2** longest river of New England, flowing through New Hampshire, Vermont, Massachusetts, and Connecticut. Length: 655 km/407 mi.

connecting rod *n* a rod that transmits motion, especially the rod that connects the crankshaft to the piston in an internal-combustion engine

connection /kə néksh'n/, **connexion** *n* **1 LINKING THINGS TOGETHER** the linking or joining of two or more parts, things, or people **2 PHYSICAL LINK** something that links two or more things ○ *check for a loose connection* **3 LOGICAL LINK** a linking association between people, things, or events ○ *denied any connection with terrorist organizations* **4 CONTEXT** the relationship of something with its context ○ *In this connection, we need to tighten up safety procedures in general.* **5 INFLUENTIAL CONTACT** a friend, relative, or associate who either has or has access to influence or power (*often plural*) ○ *She used her connections to wangle an interview with the lead singer.* **6 RELATION** a relative, usually distantly or by marriage (*often plural*) ○ *The family's English but they have Spanish connections.* **7 TRANSPORT LINK** a place at which passengers may move, choose, or change from one means of transport to another ○ *If we don't hurry, we'll miss our connection in Paris.* **8 VEHICLE SCHEDULED TO PERMIT TRANSFER** a particular bus, train, ferry, or plane that is scheduled to arrive at such a time as to allow passengers to transfer onto it from another scheduled form of transport ○ *Your connection will arrive on platform ten at 9.15.* **9 COMMUNICATION LINK** a communication link, especially between telephones **10 SUPPLIER OF ILLEGAL SUBSTANCES** a supplier of illegal substances, usually drugs (*slang*) ■ **connections** *npl* **CONTROLLERS OF A RACEHORSE** the owners or controllers of a racehorse [14C. < Latin *connexion-* < *connex-*, past participle of *connectere* (see CONNECT).] —**connectional** *adj*

connectionism /kə néksh'nizəm/ *n* the theory that thoughts and behaviour are based on patterns of stimulus and response that have been either inherited or learnt

connective /kə néktiv/ *adj* **LINKING** linking or joining two or more parts, things, or people ■ *n* **1 LINK** something that links or joins two or more parts, things, or people **2 LINKING WORD** a word that links sentences, phrases, clauses, or words **3 STAMEN TISSUE** the tissue that joins the two lobes of an anther in the stamen of a plant —**connectively** *adv*

connective tissue *n* animal tissue that supports, connects, and surrounds organs and other body parts and consists mainly of collagen, elastic and reticular fibres, fatty tissue, cartilage, or bone

ϟ **connectivity** /kónnek tívvəti/ *n* the ability to communicate with another system or piece of hardware or software, or with an Internet site

connect-the-dots *adj US* (*slang*) **1** gathering information or facts from different sources to make a coherent whole ○ *The article was a model of connect-the-dots journalism.* **2** straightforward or obvious ○ *It's a connect-the-dots problem, easily solvable.* [< producing a picture by connecting printed dots]

ϟ **connect time** *n* the period of time a user is logged on to a remote computer

Connemara /kónnə maárə/ mountainous coastal area in W Republic of Ireland

Connery /kónnəri/, **Sir Sean** (*b.* 1930) Scottish film actor

connexion *n* = **connection**

conning tower *n* **1** a structure on the top of a submarine that is used as the navigation bridge and main point of entrance **2** the armoured pilot house in the shape of a low dome found on the deck of a warship [< CON[5]]

conniption /kə nípsh'n/ *n US* a hysterical fit caused by extreme excitement or anger (*informal; often plural*) [Mid-19C. < ?]

connivance /kə nívənss/ *n* **1** secret joint conspiracy or plotting **2** unspoken encouragement of, or consent to, somebody else's wrongdoing

connive /kə nív/ (**-nives, -niving, -nived**) *vi* **1** to plan secretly to do something, usually something wrong or illegal **2** to pretend not to know about or do nothing to stop a wrongful or illegal act, thus showing encouragement of or consent to the act ○ *suspected of conniving in the leaking of a sensitive document* [Early 17C. Via French < Latin *connivere* 'close your eyes'.] —**conniver** *n* —**connivery** *n*

connivent /kə nív'nt/ *adj* describes insect wings and flower petals or stamens that converge and touch but remain separate and not fused

conniving /kə níving/ *adj* devious and scheming —**connivingly** *adv*

~~**connoiseur**~~ incorrect spelling of **connoisseur**

connoisseur /kónnə súr/ *n* an expert in an area of the fine or domestic arts, or with discriminating taste in such a speciality [Early 18C. < French, < *connoistre* 'know' < Latin *cognoscere* (see COGNITION).]

Connolly /kónnəli/, **Maureen** (1934–69) US tennis player. Known as **Little Mo**

Connors /kónnərs/, **Jimmy** (*b.* 1952) US tennis player. Known as **Jimbo**

connotation /kónnə táysh'n/ *n* **1 IMPLIED ADDITIONAL MEANING** an additional sense or senses associated with or suggested by a word or phrase ○ *Patriotism can have some negative connotations for people.* **2 SUGGESTING MEANING FOR WORD** the implying or suggesting of an additional meaning for a word or phrase apart from the literal or main meaning **3 DEFINING CHARACTERISTIC** in logic, the characteristic or set of characteristics that makes up the meaning of a term and thus defines the objects to which a term can be applied —**connotative** /kónnə taytiv, kə nṓtətiv/ *adj* —**connotatively** *adv*

connote /kə nṓt/ (**-notes, -noting, -noted**) *vt* **1** to imply or suggest something in addition to the main or literal meaning ○ *The word 'hearth' often connotes cosiness and warmth.* **2** to imply something else as a condition or a consequence ○ *His reluctance to act connotes cowardice.* [Mid-17C. < medieval Latin *connotare* 'mark along with' < Latin *notare* 'to mark' < *nota* 'sign'.]

connubial /kə nyoōbi əl/ *adj* dealing with or relating to marriage (*literary*) [Mid-17C. < Latin *connubialis* 'concerning marriage' < *connubium* 'marriage' < *nubere* 'marry'.] —**connubially** *adv*

conodont /kṓnə dont, kónnə-/ *n* a very small tooth-shaped fossil thought to be the remains of a marine organism [Mid-19C. < Greek *kōnos* 'cone'.]

conquer /kóngkər/ *vt* **1 SEIZE AREA BY MILITARY FORCE** to take control of a place by force of arms ○ *The Normans conquered England in 1066.* **2 DEFEAT PEOPLE IN WAR** to win a victory over a people in war **3 MASTER SOMETHING DIFFICULT** to overcome a difficulty or problem, e.g. an illness or weakness ○ *conquered his fear of heights* ○ *conquered inflation by controlling public expenditure* ○ *How I Conquered Migraine* **4 CLIMB MOUNTAIN** to make a difficult or dangerous mountain ascent ○ *the first woman to conquer Everest* **5 WIN SOMEBODY'S ADMIRATION** to win somebody's love, affection, or admiration, often through strength of character or seduction, and sometimes somewhat against the person's will ○ *By the end of the last song, she had conquered their hearts.* [13C. < Old French *conquerre* 'seek diligently' < Latin *quaerere* 'seek'.] —**conquerable** *adj*

conqueror /kóngkərər/ *n* **1** a victor at war **2** a victor in a competitive event

conquest /kóng kwest/ *n* **1 SUBJUGATION OF ENEMY** taking control of a place or people by force of arms **2 SOMETHING ACQUIRED BY CONQUERING** something that has been acquired through force of arms, e.g. land, people, or goods **3 ADMIRER** somebody whose love, affection, or admiration has been won, often through strength of character or seduction, and sometimes somewhat against the person's will ○ *boasting about his conquests* [13C. < Old French, literally 'sought diligently' < Latin *quaerere* 'seek'.]

conquistador /kon kwístə dawr/ (*plural* **-dors** *or* **-dores** /-dáwr ayz/) *n* a Spanish conqueror or adventurer, especially one of those who conquered Mexico, Peru, and Central America in the 16th century [Mid-19C. Via Spanish < Latin *conquirere* 'conquer'.]

Conrad /kónn rad/, **Joseph** (1857–1924) Polish-born British writer

Conran /kónnrən/, **Sir Terence** (*b.* 1931) British designer, retailer, and restaurateur

cons. *abbr* 1 consigned 2 consignment 3 consecrated 4 consonant 5 **cons., cons** constitution 6 constitutional

Cons. *abbr* 1 Conservative 2 Constable 3 **Cons** Constitution 4 Consul

consanguinity /kón sang gwínnəti/ *n* 1 relationship by descent from the same ancestor, rather than by marriage or affinity 2 a close relationship or connection —**consanguineous** *adj* —**consanguineously** *adv*

conscience /kónsh'nss/ *n* 1 SENSE OF RIGHT AND WRONG the internal sense of what is right and wrong that governs somebody's thoughts and actions, urging him or her to do right rather than wrong ○ *Let your conscience be your guide.* 2 OBEDIENCE TO CONSCIENCE behaviour in compliance with what your internal sense of right and wrong tells you is right ○ *campaigning on behalf of prisoners of conscience* 3 SHARED MORAL VIEWPOINT a shared concern for moral issues ○ *a social conscience* [13C. Via Old French < Latin *conscientia* 'consciousness' < *conscire* 'be conscious', literally 'know thoroughly' < *scire* (see SCIENCE).] ◇ **in all** *or* **good conscience** while being fair and reasonable ◇ **on somebody's conscience** causing somebody to feel guilty or anxious

conscience clause *n* a clause in an act, law, or contract that exempts those who have moral or religious objections from complying

conscience money *n* money paid voluntarily in compensation for a previous act of wrongdoing by which somebody has been harmed

conscience-stricken, conscience-smitten *adj* feeling guilty or anxious about having done something wrong

conscientious /kónshi énshəss/ *adj* 1 thorough and diligent in performing a task ○ *a conscientious parent* 2 governed by or done according to somebody's sense of right and wrong ○ *a conscientious decision to dedicate an hour a week to charity* [Early 17C. Via French *consciencieux* < Latin *conscientia* (see CONSCIENCE).] —**conscientiously** *adv* —**conscientiousness** *n*

SYNONYMS See ***careful***.

USAGE conscientious or **conscious**? If you are ***conscious*** you are awake or aware: *The patient is conscious; We are conscious of the danger.* ***Conscious*** can also mean 'deliberate, intentional', as in *We made a conscious* [not *conscientious*] *move to win the championship.* If you are ***conscientious*** you are diligent, thorough, and governed by your own sense of ethics: *Conscientious students study diligently. I made a conscientious* [not *conscious*] *effort to contribute to fund-raising events.* Both these adjectives can modify nouns like *decision* and *effort*, but the writer must ensure that the context is clear. A *conscious decision/effort* is one made intentionally and deliberately (*a conscious decision/effort to disregard all risks*); a *conscientious decision/effort* is one involving an ethical judgment (*a conscientious decision/effort to right wrongs when we see them*).

conscientious objector *n* somebody who, for moral or religious reasons, believes it is wrong to wage war and therefore refuses to join any branch of the armed services

conscious /kónshəss/ *adj* 1 AWAKE awake and responsive to stimuli ○ *He's been seriously injured but he's still conscious.* 2 KEENLY AWARE aware of something, and attaching importance to it ○ *I'm conscious of all that you've done for us.* 3 DELIBERATE considered and deliberate ○ *a conscious effort not to lose her temper* 4 AWARE AND WELL-INFORMED aware of issues relating to a particular topic of serious significance (*often with adverbs*) ○ *environmentally conscious* 5 CONCERNED aware of and interested in a particular topic (*often hyphenated in combination*) ○ *fashion-conscious* 6 FUNCTIONING WITH INDIVIDUAL'S KNOWLEDGE concerned with or relating to a part of the mind that is capable of thinking, choosing, or perceiving ■ *n* AREA OF MIND the part of the human mind that is aware of the feelings, thoughts, and surroundings [Late 16C. < Latin *conscius* 'knowing' < *scire* (see SCIENCE).] —**consciously** *adv*

SYNONYMS See ***aware***.

USAGE See ***conscientious***.

consciousness /kónshəssnəss/ *n* 1 BEING AWAKE AND AWARE OF SURROUNDINGS the state of being awake and aware of what is going on around you ○ *feelings of dizziness followed by loss of consciousness* 2 SOMEBODY'S MIND somebody's mind and thoughts ○ *In time, this experience will fade from your consciousness.* 3 SHARED FEELINGS AND BELIEFS the set of opinions, feelings, and beliefs of a group 4 BEING AWARE OF SPECIFIC ISSUES awareness of or sensitivity to issues in a particular field

consciousness-raising *n* 1 the aim of increasing people's awareness of a moral or social issue with a view to encouraging them to take action 2 the increasing of self-awareness, usually through group therapy —**consciousness-raiser** *n*

conscript *vt* /kən skrípt/ to enrol somebody compulsorily in the armed forces or for military service ■ *n* /kón skript/ a recruit who has been compulsorily enrolled, especially in the armed forces [15C. < Latin *conscript-*, past participle of *conscribere* 'enrol' < *scribere* (see SCRIBE).]

conscription /kən skrípsh'n/ *n* obligatory enrolment of citizens for a period of national service, usually in the armed forces

consecrate /kónssi krayt/ (**-crates, -crating, -crated**) *vt* 1 DECLARE HOLY to declare or set apart a building, area of ground, or specific spot as holy or sacred ○ *The cathedral was consecrated in the 12th century.* 2 BLESS BREAD AND WINE to sanctify the bread and wine for use in the Communion service as symbols of the body and blood of Jesus Christ 3 ORDAIN AS BISHOP to ordain a priest as a bishop 4 DEDICATE to dedicate something or somebody to a specific purpose 5 MAKE REVERED to cause a custom to be revered [14C. < Latin *consecrat-*, past participle of *consecrare* 'make sacred' < *sacer* (see SACRED).] —**consecrative** *adj* —**consecrator** *n* —**consecratory** /kónssi kráytəri/ *adj*

consecration /kónssi kráysh'n/ *n* the ceremony in which somebody or something is consecrated

Consecration *n* the process or ceremony of sanctifying the bread and wine during Communion

consecutive /kən sékyòotiv/ *adj* 1 following one after another without interruption or break ○ *He's been off work now for three consecutive days.* 2 following a logical or chronological sequence [Early 17C. Via French < Latin *consecut-*, past participle of *consequi* (see CONSEQUENT).] —**consecutively** *adv* —**consecutiveness** *n*

consensual /kən sénsyòo əl/ *adj* 1 BY MUTUAL CONSENT involving the agreement of all involved 2 REQUIRING CONSENT ONLY requiring only the consent of the parties involved to make it binding 3 RESPONDING INVOLUNTARILY TO INDIRECT STIMULUS describes an involuntary response to a voluntary movement from another body part, e.g. the pupil of one eye constricting when the other eye is exposed to light [Mid-18C. < Latin *consens-*, past participle of *consentire* (see CONSENT).] —**consensually** *adv*

consensus /kən sénsəss/ *n* 1 general or widespread agreement among all the members of a group 2 a concept of society in which the absence of conflict is seen as the equilibrium state of society [Mid-17C. < Latin, < past participle of *consentire* (see CONSENT).]

USAGE The word ***consensus*** is often misspelt *concensus*, probably from the erroneous influence of the word *census*.

USAGE Since ***consensus*** already means 'a view or opinion that is generally shared', expressions such as *general consensus* and *consensus of opinion* are, strictly speaking, tautologies (i.e. they say the same thing twice), and 'general' and 'of opinion' are redundant. However, occasionally a modifier can be justified, as in *There was a consensus of feeling, but no consensus of opinion.* It is always best to begin by considering whether or not the word without modifiers expresses what you mean.

consent /kən sént/ *vi* 1 GIVE PERMISSION to give permission or approval for something to happen ○ *As soon as they met Robert, her parents consented to the marriage.* 2 AGREE to agree to do something ○ *She consented to appear as a witness.* ■ *n* 1 PERMISSION acceptance of or agreement to something proposed or desired by another 2 CONSENSUS agreement on an opinion or course of action ○ *It was by common consent the best.* [13C. Via Old French < Latin *consentire* 'feel with' < *sentire* (see SENTIENT).] —**consenter** *n*

SYNONYMS See ***agree***.

consenting adult *n* somebody who is old enough to be allowed to participate legally in something and is willing to do so, especially in a sexual activity

consequence /kónssikwənss/ *n* 1 RESULT something that follows as a result ○ *This is a direct consequence of your negligence.* 2 RELATION BETWEEN RESULT AND CAUSE the relation between a result and its cause 3 IMPORTANCE importance or significance (*formal; often in negatives*) ○ *Your opinion is of no consequence whatsoever to me.* 4 LOGICAL CONCLUSION a conclusion reached through valid deductive reasoning [14C. Via French < Latin *consequentia* < *consequi* (see CONSEQUENT).] ◇ **in consequence** as a result of something (*formal*)

consequences /kónssikwənssiz/ *npl* the unpleasant or difficult results of a previous action ■ *n* a game in which each player in turn writes down a line of a story about two people, their meeting, and its consequences, without knowing what the previous lines are, thus producing humorous juxtapositions when the completed stories are read out loud (+ *singular verb*)

consequent /kónssikwənt/ *adj* 1 FOLLOWING AS RESULT following as a result or effect ○ *weeks of rain and the consequent flooding* 2 AS LOGICAL CONCLUSION following as a logical conclusion ■ *n* 1 RESULT something that follows as a result 2 SECOND HALF OF CONDITIONAL SENTENCE the part of a conditional sentence that expresses the result and is the q clause in a proposition of the form 'if p then q' 3 SECOND TERM OF RATIO the second term in a mathematical ratio [15C. Via Old French < Latin *consequent-*, present participle of *consequi* 'follow along with' < *sequi* (see SEQUENCE.]

consequential /kónssi kwénsh'l/ *adj* 1 describes costs, loss, or damage beyond the market value of the object lost or damaged, including other indirect costs arising 2 of considerable importance, significance, or value ○ *a consequential figure on the classical music circuit* —**consequentiality** /kónssi kwénshi állәti/ *n* —**consequentially** *adv* —**consequentialness** *n*

consequentialism /kónsi kwénsh'lizəm/ *n* the tenet by which an action is considered right or wrong depending on whether its outcome is good or bad

consequently /kónssikwəntli/ *adv* as a result or in view of this ○ *The joke backfired and the relationship consequently deteriorated.*

~~**consern**~~ incorrect spelling of **concern**

conservancy /kən súrv'nssi/ (*plural* **-cies**) *n* a commission, court, or board with authority to regulate and protect a waterway, port, or area of countryside, and often also its wildlife

conservation /kónssər váysh'n/ *n* 1 the keeping or protecting of something from change, loss, or damage 2 the preservation, management, and care of natural and cultural resources —**conservational** *adj*

conservationist /kónssər váysh'nist/ *n* a supporter of or advocate for the preservation of the environment, especially the natural world

conservation of charge *n* the principle that the total electric charge of an isolated system remains constant no matter what internal changes take place

conservation of energy *n* the principle that the amount of energy in an isolated system remains the same, even though the form of energy may change

conservation of mass, conservation of matter *n* the principle that the total mass of an isolated system remains constant, no matter what physical or chemical changes take place

conservation of momentum *n* the principle that the total linear or angular momentum of an isolated system remains the same

conservatism /kən súrvətizəm/ *n* 1 RELUCTANCE TO ACCEPT CHANGE unwillingness or slowness to accept change or new ideas 2 RIGHT-WING POLITICAL VIEWPOINT a right-of-centre political philosophy based on a tendency to support gradual rather than abrupt change and to preserve the status quo 3 DESIRE TO PRESERVE CURRENT SOCIETAL STRUCTURE an ideology that views the existing form of society as worthy of preservation

Conservatism *n* the principles and practice of Conservative politicians or supporters, e.g. in the United Kingdom or Canada

conservative /kən súrvətiv/ *adj* 1 RELUCTANT TO ACCEPT CHANGE in favour of preserving the status quo and traditional values and customs, and against abrupt change 2 OF CONSERVATISM associated with, characteristic of, or displaying conservatism **3 CAUTIOUS AND ON THE LOW SIDE** cautiously moderate and therefore often less than the final outcome ○ *Several hundred pounds is probably a very conservative estimate.* **4 CONVENTIONAL IN APPEARANCE** conventional or restrained in style and avoiding showiness ○ *a conservative business suit* **5 USING MINIMUM MEDICAL INTERVENTION** designed to help relieve symptoms or preserve health with a minimum of medical intervention ■ *n* **1 TRADITIONALIST PERSON** a supporter or advocate of traditional ideas and behaviour **2 SUPPORTER OF CONSERVATISM** a believer in conservatism, or supporter of it —**conservatively** *adv* —**conservativeness** *n*

Conservative *adj* **1 OF CONSERVATIVE PARTY** supporting, belonging to, or associated with a Conservative Party, e.g. that of the United Kingdom or Canada **2 OF CONSERVATIVE JUDAISM** relating to, associated with, or characteristic of Conservative Judaism ■ *n* **SUPPORTER OF CONSERVATIVE PARTY** a member or supporter of a Conservative Party

Conservative Judaism *n* a form of Judaism that accepts most of the principles and practices of traditional Judaism but supports the modification and relaxing of certain laws

Conservative Party *n* (*+ singular or plural verb*) **1 MAIN UK RIGHT-WING POLITICAL PARTY** in the United Kingdom, the principal right-of-centre political party. It supports low personal taxation, home ownership, and free-market principles. **2 CANADIAN RIGHT-WING POLITICAL PARTY** in Canada, the Progressive Conservative Party, which originally derived its political principles from British Toryism **3 POLITICAL PARTY OPPOSED TO CHANGE** in countries other than the United Kingdom and Canada, a political party that is opposed to change

conservatoire /kən súrvə twaar/ *n* = **conservatory** *n.* 2 [Late 18C. Via French < Italian *conservatorio* < late Latin *conservatorium* (see CONSERVATORY).]

conservator /kən súrvətər/ *n* **1** a preserver or restorer of works of art or other valued objects in a museum or collection **2** a person or institution responsible for protecting the interests of a legal incompetent, e.g. under a protective trust —**conservatorial** /kən súrvə táwri əl/ *adj*

conservatorium /kən súrvə táwri əm/ (*plural* **-ums** *or* **-a** /-ə/) *n* *Australian* MUSIC = **conservatory** *n.* 2 [Mid-19C. Via German < late Latin (see CONSERVATORY).]

conservatory /kən súrvətəri/ (*plural* **-ries**) *n* **1** a room with glass walls and roof where plants are grown or displayed, often built onto the side of a house **2** an institution or school where students are taught one of the arts, most commonly music or drama, to a professional standard [Mid-16C. < late Latin *conservatorium* < Latin *conservare* (see CONSERVE).]

conserve *vt* /kən súrv/ (**-serves, -serving, -served**) **1 PROTECT FROM HARM OR DECAY** to keep something, especially an important environmental or cultural resource, from harm, loss, change, or decay ○ *the importance of conserving our national heritage* **2 USE SPARINGLY** to use something sparingly so as not to exhaust supplies ○ *some drastic measures to conserve water* **3 PRESERVE FOOD IN SUGAR** to preserve food, especially fruit, in sugar **4 KEEP MATTER OR ENERGY CONSTANT** to keep something constant through physical changes or chemical reactions ■ *n* /kón surv, kən súrv/ **FRUIT IN SYRUP** a food consisting of fruit in a thick sugar syrup, like jam but less firmly set and usually containing larger pieces of fruit [14C. Via French < Latin *conservare* 'preserve well' < *servare* (see SERVE).] —**conservable** *adj* —**conserver** *n*

~~**consession**~~ incorrect spelling of **concession**

Consett /kónssit, -set/ town in N England. Population: 20,148 (1991).

consider /kən síddər/ *v* **1** *vti* **THINK CAREFULLY** to think carefully about something ○ *You should consider your next move carefully.* ○ *time to consider whether this is what you really want* **2** *vt* **JUDGE** to have something as an opinion or point of view ○ *He considers himself lucky to be alive.* ○ *I consider it unlikely that they'll accept our proposal.* **3** *vt* **RESPECT** to show respect for or be thoughtful of somebody's feelings or position **4** *vt* **WEIGH UP POSSIBILITIES** to weigh up the pros and cons of situation before making a decision on a course of action ○ *I'm considering my options.* ○ *They're considering buying a new house.* **5** *vt* **EXAMINE** to examine a problem and discuss it in detail ○ *On this week's show, we're going to consider the following question.* **6** *vt* **TAKE INTO ACCOUNT** to take something into account, often in a sympathetic way ○ *We've done rather well, all things considered.* **7** *vt* **LOOK CAREFULLY AT** to look at something carefully and with concentration (*formal*) [14C. Via French *considérer* < Latin *considerare.*] —**considered** *adj* —**considerer** *n*

considerable /kən síddərəb'l/ *adj* **1** large enough in amount or extent to be important ○ *needs a considerable income to afford this flat* **2** worthy of consideration or respect ○ *a considerable figure in the art world*

considerably /kən síddərəbli/ *adv* to a significant degree ○ *He's considerably older than I am.*

considerate /kən síddərət/ *adj* mindful of the needs, wishes, and feelings of others —**considerately** *adv* —**considerateness** *n*

consideration /kən síddə ráysh'n/ *n* **1 CAREFUL THOUGHT** careful thought or deliberation ○ *Your application will be given the fullest consideration.* ○ *the proposal is currently under consideration* **2 RESPECT** thoughtful concern for or sensitivity towards the feelings of others **3 RELEVANT FACTOR IN ASSESSING** something to be taken into account when weighing up the pros and cons before making a decision ○ *Value for money is one of the most important considerations for our customers.* **4 DETAILED EXAMINATION** detailed discussion or scrutiny ○ *The issue for consideration on today's show is cosmetic surgery.* **5 PAYMENT** a payment or fee in return for a service (*formal*) **6 SOMETHING MAKING CONTRACT BINDING** something done by one of the parties as part of a contractual arrangement that makes it binding, e.g. the payment of the price in a contract of sale ◇ **in consideration of 1** because of (*formal*) **2** as payment for (*formal*) ◇ **take something into consideration** to take account of special circumstances, often in a sympathetic way

considering /kən síddəring/ *prep, conj* taking something into account ○ *It's a tremendous bargain, considering the price and how much we need one.* ■ *adv* taking everything into account, often in a sympathetic way (*usually at the end of a phrase or sentence*) ○ *We've done a really good job, considering.*

~~**consience**~~ incorrect spelling of **conscience**

consign /kən sín/ *vt* **1 ENTRUST** to hand somebody or something over to the care of another ○ *The children were consigned to the care of the nanny.* **2 GET RID OF** to dispose of something or somebody, usually for a long time if not permanently ○ *Before fleeing, they consigned the documents to the flames.* **3 DELIVER** to address, deliver, or hand over for later delivery something for sale, safekeeping, or disposal [15C. Via French < Latin *consignare* 'certify with a seal' < *signum* (see SIGN).] —**consignable** *adj* —**consignee** /kón sī neé/ *n* —**consignor** *n*

consignment /kən sínmənt/ *n* **1 DELIVERY** a quantity or package of goods delivered or to be delivered **2 DISPOSAL TO SOMEWHERE DISAGREEABLE** the disposal of somebody or something, or being disposed, usually for a very long time if not forever **3 ENTRUSTING OF SOMEBODY TO ANOTHER'S CARE** the handing over of somebody or something to the care of another ◇ **on consignment** on the understanding that payment will be made only when the goods have been sold and that any remaining unsold articles can be returned

~~**consious**~~ incorrect spelling of **conscious**

consist /kən síst/ *vi* **1** to be made up of diverse elements ○ *This dressing consists of oil, lemon juice, and mustard.* **2** to be based on or defined by something ○ *Her talent consists in her superb musicianship.* [Early 16C. < Latin *consistere* < *sistere* 'make stand' < *stare* 'to stand'.]

~~**consistant**~~ incorrect spelling of **consistent**

consistency /kən sístənssi/ (*plural* **-cies**), **consistence** /kən sístənss/ *n* **1 CONSTANCY** the ability to maintain a particular standard or repeat a particular task with minimal variation ○ *Consistency is important in performing this job.* ○ *'A foolish consistency is the hobgoblin of small minds'.* (Ralph Waldo Emerson *Self-Reliance*; 1841) **2 COHERENCE** reasonable or logical harmony between parts ○ *The plot lacked consistency.* **3 DEGREE OF THICKNESS OR SMOOTHNESS** the degree of thickness or smoothness of a mixture ○ *Blend the mixture until it reaches the consistency of thick cream.*

consistent /kən sístənt/ *adj* **1 COHERENT** reasonably or logically harmonious ○ *The evidence is consistent with the defendant's statement.* ○ *Their accounts of the incident just aren't consistent.* **2 RELIABLE** able to maintain a particular standard or repeat a particular task with minimal variation ○ *He's one of the most consistent strikers in the league.* **3 WITH COMMON SOLUTIONS** with a set of solutions in common, especially for two or more equations or inequalities **4 FREE OF CONTRADICTION** containing no provable contradiction [Late 16C. < Latin *consistent-*, present participle of *consistere* (see CONSIST).] —**consistently** *adv*

consistory /kən sístəri/ (*plural* **-ries**) *n* **1 ASSEMBLY OF CARDINALS AND POPE** in the Roman Catholic Church, an assembly of cardinals convoked and led by the pope **2 ANGLICAN DIOCESAN COURT** in the Anglican Church, the court of any diocese except Canterbury **3 CONGREGATIONAL GOVERNING BODY** in certain Reformed churches, the governing body of a congregation **4 REGULATORY COURT IN LUTHERAN CHURCHES** in Lutheran state churches, a court appointed to regulate ecclesiastical affairs **5 HISTORICAL ASSEMBLY** a council or assembly, e.g. in the Roman Empire [13C. Via Anglo-Norman < late Latin *consistorium* 'place of assembly' < Latin *consistere* (see CONSIST).] —**consistorial** /kónssi stáwri əl/ *adj*

consociate *vti* /kən sṓshi ayt, -sṓssi-/ (**-ates, -ating, -ated**) **JOIN ASSOCIATION** to enter or welcome somebody into a friendly association (*formal*) ■ *adj* /kən sṓshi ət/ **ASSOCIATED** associated or united (*formal*) ■ *n* /kən sṓshi ət/ **PARTNER** an associate or partner (*formal*) [15C. < Latin *consociat-*, past participle of *consociare* 'associate' < *socius* (see SOCIAL).]

consociation /kən sṓshi áysh'n, -sṓssi-/ *n* **1 FRIENDLY ASSOCIATION** a friendly association or alliance (*formal*) **2 ECOLOGICAL COMMUNITY WITH ONE MAIN SPECIES** an ecological community that has one dominant species, e.g. a wood consisting predominantly of beech trees **3 POLITICAL COALITION** a grouping of political parties or pressure groups within a region or country that work together to share power —**consociational** *adj*

consocies /kən sṓsh eez/ (*plural* **-cies**) *n* ECOL = **consociation** *n.* 2 [Early 20C. < CONSOCIATION.]

consolation /kónssə láysh'n/ *n* **1 SOURCE OF COMFORT** a source of comfort to somebody who is upset or disappointed ○ *The fortune she left was little consolation for him.* **2 COMFORT TO SOMEBODY IN DISTRESS** comfort to somebody who is distressed or disappointed ○ *Most of those at the funeral murmured some words of consolation as they left.* **3 GAME FOR EARLIER LOSERS** a game or contest held for people or teams who have lost earlier in a tournament

consolation prize *n* a prize given to comfort the loser or losers in a game or competition

console[1] /kən sṓl/ (**-soles, -soling, -soled**) *vt* to be or provide a source of comfort to somebody who is distressed or disappointed [Mid-17C. Via French < Latin *consolare* < *solari* (see SOLACE).] —**consolable** *adj* —**consolatory** *adj* —**consoler** *n* —**consolingly** *adv*

USAGE See ***condole***.

---

console[2] /kón sōl/ *n* **1 CABINET** a free-standing cabinet, especially one used to house a television or hi-fi system **2 ORGAN CONTROLS** the part of an organ that houses the keyboards or manuals, pedals, and stops **3 ORNAMENTAL BRACKET** an ornamental bracket, often in the shape of a scroll, used for decoration and for supporting wall fixtures **4 CONTROL PANEL** a desk, table, display, or keyboard onto which the controls of an electronic system or some other machine are fixed **5** FURNITURE = **console table** [Mid-17C. < French.]

console table /kón sōl-/ *n* a small table with curved legs designed to stand against a wall

consolidate /kən sólli dayt/ (**-dates, -dating, -dated**) *v* **1** *vti* **UNITE BUSINESS ACTIVITIES** to bring businesses or business activities together, or come together, into a single unit **2** *vti* **STRENGTHEN YOUR POSITION** to increase the strength, stability, or depth of your success or position ○ *This excellent performance has enabled her to consolidate her lead.* **3** *vti* **COMBINE INTO SINGLE MASS** to combine separate items or scattered material into a single whole or mass **4** *vt* **COMBINE ACCOUNTS** to combine several sets of financial accounts in a single set of accounts [Early 16C. < Latin *consolidat-*, past participle of *consolidare* 'make solid' < *solidus* (see SOLID).] —**consolidator** *n*

Consolidated Fund *n* in the United Kingdom, a government fund made up of revenue from taxes, used to cover regular costs, especially interest payments on the national debt

consolidation /kən sólli dáysh'n/ *n* **1 COMBINING OF BUSINESS ACTIVITIES** the bringing together of two or more businesses or business activities into a single unit **2 STRENGTHENING** increasing of the strength, stability, or depth of a person's or group's success ○ *The final six weeks saw a consolidation of their position at the top of the league.* **3 COMBINATION INTO SINGLE MASS** the combination of separate items or scattered material into a single mass

4 COMBINING SEVERAL ACTS INTO SINGLE STATUTE combination of two or more Acts of Parliament into a single statute **5 COMPACTION INTO ROCK** any process by which a loose deposit is compacted into hard rock **6 PSYCHOLOGICAL PROCESS THAT RETAINS MEMORY** the process in the brain that enables somebody to have a lasting memory of a particular event

consols /kón sòlz, kón sәlz/ *npl* in the United Kingdom, government bonds with a fixed interest rate and no date of maturity [Late 18C. Contraction of *consolidated annuities.*]

consommé /kon sómm ay/ *n* a thin clear soup made from meat or chicken stock [Early 19C. < French, < past participle of *consommer* 'use up' < Latin *consummare* (see CONSUMMATE).]

consonance /kónss'nәnss/, **consonancy** /kónss'nәnsi/ (*plural* **-cies**) *n* **1 AGREEMENT** agreement or harmony (*formal*) **2 SIMILARITY BETWEEN CONSONANTS** a close similarity between consonants or groups of consonants, especially at the ends of words, e.g. between 'strong' and 'ring' **3 PLEASANT COMBINATION OF MUSICAL NOTES** a combination of notes that sounds pleasing when played simultaneously

consonant /kónss'nәnt/ *n* **SPEECH SOUND OTHER THAN VOWEL** a speech sound, or the corresponding letter of the alphabet, produced by partly or totally blocking the path of air through the mouth ■ *adj* **1 IN AGREEMENT** in agreement or harmony with something (*formal*) ○ *delighted to learn that their views were consonant with our own* **2 PLEASING IN HARMONY** containing chords or harmonies that are pleasing to hear **3 HAVING SIMILAR SOUNDS** having similar sounds, or showing consonance [14C. Via French < Latin *consonant-* 'sounding together' < *sonare* (see SONANT).] —**consonantal** /kónssә nánt'l/ *adj* —**consonantally** *adv* —**consonantly** *adv*

con sordino /kon sawr deén ō/ *adv* using a mute or the mute pedal (*musical direction*) [Early 19C. < Italian, 'with a mute'.]

consort *vi* /kәn sáwrt/ **ASSOCIATE WITH UNDESIRABLES** to associate with or spend time in the company of undesirable people (*formal*) ○ *consorting with known criminals* ■ *n* /kón sawrt/ **1 consort, Consort SPOUSE OF MONARCH** the husband or wife of a reigning monarch **2 PARTNER** a partner or companion (*formal*) **3 SHIP THAT ESCORTS ANOTHER** a ship that accompanies or escorts another on a journey **4 GROUP SPECIALIZING IN EARLY MUSIC** a small group of musicians specializing in works of the baroque or an earlier period [15C. Via French < Latin *consort-* 'having the same fate' < *sors* 'fortune'.] ◇ **in consort with** in association or together with (*archaic or formal*)

consortium /kәn sáwrti әm/ (*plural* **-a** /-ti ә/) *n* **1** an association or grouping of institutions, businesses, or financial organizations, usually set up for a common purpose that would be beyond the capabilities of a single member of the group **2** the right of husbands or wives to the company, affection, and help of their spouses (*archaic*) [Early 19C. < Latin, 'fellowship' < *consort-* (see CONSORT).] —**consortial** *adj*

conspecific /kónspә síffik/ *adj* of the same species as another organism ■ *n* an organism of the same species as another

conspectus /kәn spéktәss/ *n* **1** a general mental survey or overview of something **2** an overview of something in outline or synopsis (*technical*) [Mid-19C. < Latin, < *conspect-*, past participle of *conspicere* (see CONSPICUOUS).]

conspicuous /kәn spíkyoo әss/ *adj* **1** easily or clearly visible ○ *The building's most conspicuous feature is its dome-shaped roof.* **2** attracting attention through being unusual or remarkable ○ *He felt uncomfortably conspicuous, since he was the only man in evening dress.* [Mid-16C. < Latin *conspicuus* < *conspicere* 'observe carefully' < *specere* (see SPECTACLE).] —**conspicuously** *adv* —**conspicuousness** *n*

conspicuous consumption *n* the practice of spending large quantities of money, often extravagantly, to impress others

conspiracist /kәn spírrәssist/ *n* a believer that a conspiracy caused an event

conspiracy /kәn spírrәssi/ (*plural* **-cies**) *n* **1 PLAN TO COMMIT ILLEGAL ACT TOGETHER** a plan or agreement between two or more people to commit an illegal or subversive act **2 AGREEMENT AMONG CONSPIRATORS** the making of an agreement or plot to commit an illegal or subversive act **3 GROUP OF CONSPIRATORS** a group of conspirators [14C. Via Anglo-Norman *conspiracie* < Latin *conspirat-*, past participle of *conspirare* (see CONSPIRE).]

conspiracy of silence *n* an agreement among a group of people to say nothing in public about a matter of public interest or importance, in order to protect or promote selfish interests

conspiracy theory *n* a belief that a particular event is the result of a secret plot rather than the actions of an individual or chance —**conspiracy theorist** *n*

conspirator /kәn spírrәtәr/ *n* a member of a group of people planning or agreeing to commit an illegal or subversive act

conspiratorial /kәn spírrә táwri әl/ *adj* indicating or betraying knowledge of or involvement in a secret plot —**conspiratorially** *adv*

conspire /kәn spír/ (**-spires, -spiring, -spired**) *vi* **1** to plan or agree in secret with others to commit an illegal or subversive act **2** to combine so as to cause a particular result, often one involving harm, inconvenience, or difficulty ○ *Rain and tears conspired to smudge her carefully applied mascara.* [14C. Via French < Latin *conspirare*, literally 'breathe together' < *spirare* (see SPIRIT).] —**conspiringly** *adv*

conspiriologist /kәn spírri óllәjist/ *n* US a believer in conspiracy theories

con spirito /kon spírritō/ *adv* in a lively or spirited way (*musical direction*) [Late 19C. < Italian, 'with spirit'.]

const. *abbr* **1** constant **2** constitution

constable /kúnstәb'l, kón-/ *n* **1 POLICE OFFICER** in the United Kingdom, Canada, Australia, and New Zealand, a police officer of the lowest rank **2 OFFICER BELOW SHERIFF** a low-ranking law officer in some towns or townships in the United States and, historically, in British towns and boroughs **3 CASTLE WARDEN** the warden of a royal castle or fortress **4 ROYAL HOUSEHOLD OFFICIAL IN MIDDLE AGES** the chief administrative and military officer in a royal household, especially in medieval France and England [12C. < Old French *conestable* < late Latin *comes stabilis* 'count of the stable'.] —**constableship** *n*

Constable /kúnstәb'l/, **John** (1776–1837) British landscape painter

constabulary /kәn stább yoolәri/ *n* (*plural* **-ies**) **1 POLICE FORCE** a police force for a city or a district **2 FORCE OF CONSTABLES** an organized force of constables operating in a city or district ■ *adj* **OF POLICE FORCE OR OFFICERS** relating to a police force or involved in being a police officer

Constance, Lake /kónstәnss/ lake on the borders of Austria, Germany, and Switzerland. Area: 540 sq. km/210 sq. mi. Depth: 252 m/827 ft. Length: 74 km/46 mi. German name **Bodensee**

constant /kónstәnt/ *adj* **1 EVER PRESENT** always present or available ○ *constant whining* ○ *a constant supply of fresh water* **2 HAPPENING OR DONE REPEATEDLY** occurring or made again and again ○ *constant visits to the doctor* **3 NOT CHANGING OR VARYING** remaining the same and not varying with change in other things ○ *kept at a constant pressure* **4 FAITHFUL** faithful and loyal, especially to a husband, wife, or other loved one ■ *n* **1 SOMETHING UNCHANGING** an object, quality, or fact that is invariable ○ *This preoccupation has become a constant in our daily lives.* **2 QUANTITY WITH FIXED VALUE** a mathematical quantity that retains a fixed value in any circumstances or throughout a particular set of calculations **3 UNVARYING PROPERTY** a property, condition, or quantity that is assumed not to vary for the purposes of a theory or experiment, e.g. the speed of light [14C. Via French < Latin *constant-*, present participle of *constare* 'stand together' < *stare* 'to stand'.] —**constancy** *n* —**constantly** *adv*

constantan /kónstәn tan/ *n* an alloy of copper and nickel whose electrical resistance is unaffected by changes in temperature. Use: resistors, thermocouples. [Early 20C. < CONSTANT.]

Constantine II /kónstәn tīn, -teen/ (*b.* 1940) king of Greece (1964–73)

Constantine (the Great) (274–337) emperor of Rome (306–37). Born **Flavius Valerius Aurelius Constantinus**

Constantinople /kón stanti nóp'l/ former name for **Istanbul**

constative /kónstәtiv/ *adj* **1** relating to a statement that conveys information and is capable of being considered as true or false **2** relating to verb forms indicating that something has been completed in the past [Early 20C. < Latin *constat-*, past participle of *constare* (see CONSTANT).]

constellate /kónstә layt/ (**-lates, -lating, -lated**) *vti* to form clusters, e.g. in a constellation (*literary*) [Late 16C. < late Latin *constellatus* 'stars together' < Latin *stella* 'star'.]

constellation /kónstә láysh'n/ *n* **1 GROUP OF STARS FORMING SHAPE** a group of stars visible from Earth that forms a distinctive pattern and has a name, often derived from Greek mythology, linked to its shape **2 AREA OF SKY CONTAINING CONSTELLATION** the area of the sky within and around a constellation **3 GATHERING OF CELEBRITIES** a gathering of famous or important people ○ *a glittering constellation of Hollywood stars* **4 GROUP OF RELATED THINGS** a group of things or circumstances felt to be related to each other in some way ○ *Problems tend to occur not singly, but in constellations.* **5 ASTROLOGICAL ARRANGEMENT OF PLANETS** the arrangement of the planets in the zodiac at a particular time, believed by astrologers to influence human character or events on earth —**constellational** *adj* —**constellatory** /kәn stéllәtәri/ *adj*

consternate /kónstәr nayt/ (**-nates, -nating, -nated**) *vt* to fill somebody with alarm, confusion, or dismay [Mid-17C. < Latin *consternat-*, past participle of *consternare* 'make prostrate with fear' < *sternare* 'lay low'.]

consternation /kónstәr náysh'n/ *n* a feeling of bewilderment and dismay, often caused by something unexpected ○ *The news caused worldwide consternation and a panic on the stock exchange.*

constipate /kónsti payt/ (**-pates, -pating, -pated**) *vt* to cause somebody or something to become constipated [Mid-16C. < Latin *constipat-*, past participle of *constipare* 'cram together' < *stipare* 'to press'.]

constipated /kónsti paytid/ *adj* **1** having difficulty in eliminating solid waste from the body, with faeces being hard and dry **2** unable to flow or produce at the normal rate because of blockage or obstruction

constipation /kónsti páysh'n/ *n* **1** a condition in which a person or animal has difficulty in eliminating solid waste from the body and the faeces are hard and dry **2** a state in which the normal flow of something is blocked or obstructed

constituency /kәn stíttyoo әnssi, -stíchyoo-/ (*plural* **-cies**) *n* **1 ELECTORAL DISTRICT** one of the areas into which a country is divided for election purposes, and from which a representative is elected to serve in a legislative body **2 VOTERS IN A CONSTITUENCY** the voters or residents in a particular electoral district **3 GROUP WITH COMMON OUTLOOK** a group of people thought to have common aims or views, and therefore sometimes appealed to for support ○ *people outside his usual constituency of young married couples* **4 CUSTOMERS CONSIDERED AS A GROUP** a group of people served by an organization, especially a business ○ *enlarging its constituency via a website*

constituent /kәn stíttyoo әnt, -stíchyoo-/ *n* **1 RESIDENT OF CONSTITUENCY** a person living in an electoral district, especially one having the right to vote **2 INGREDIENT** one of the materials or elements that make up something ○ *one of the constituents of cement* **3 WORD, PHRASE, OR CLAUSE** a word, phrase, or clause in a larger construction such as a sentence. ◊ **immediate constituent 4 CLIENT** somebody who appoints another to act on his or her behalf (*formal*) ■ *adj* **1 FORMING A PART** forming a part of something (*formal*) ○ *a constituent part of something* **2 WITH POWER TO DRAW UP CONSTITUTION** having the power to draw up or alter a constitution ○ *a constituent assembly* [15C. Directly or via French < Latin *constituent-*, present participle of *constituere* (see CONSTITUTE).] —**constituently** *adv*

constitute /kónsti tyoot/ (**-tutes, -tuting, -tuted**) *vt* **1 BE** to be, amount to, or have the status of a particular thing ○ *This letter does not constitute an offer of employment.* **2 BE INGREDIENT OF** to make up the whole or a stated part of something ○ *a panel constituted of four individuals* **3 FORMALLY ESTABLISH** to create and establish something formally, especially an official body (*formal*) ○ *constitute an assembly* **4 FORMALLY APPOINT** to appoint somebody formally to a position (*formal*) [15C. < Latin *constitut-*, past participle of *constituere* 'establish' < *statuere* 'set up'.] —**constituter** *n*

constitution /kónsti tyóosh'n/ *n* **1 STATEMENT OF FUNDAMENTAL LAWS** a written statement outlining the basic laws or principles by which a country or organization is governed **2 DOCUMENT CONTAINING FUNDAMENTAL LAWS** the document or statute setting out the fundamental laws or bylaws of a country or organization **3 SOMEBODY'S HEALTH** somebody's general condition of health, especially the body's ability to remain healthy and withstand disease or hardship ○ *has the constitution of an ox* **4 COMPOSITION OF SOMETHING** the parts or members of something, or the way in which they combine to form it **5 ACT OR PROCESS**

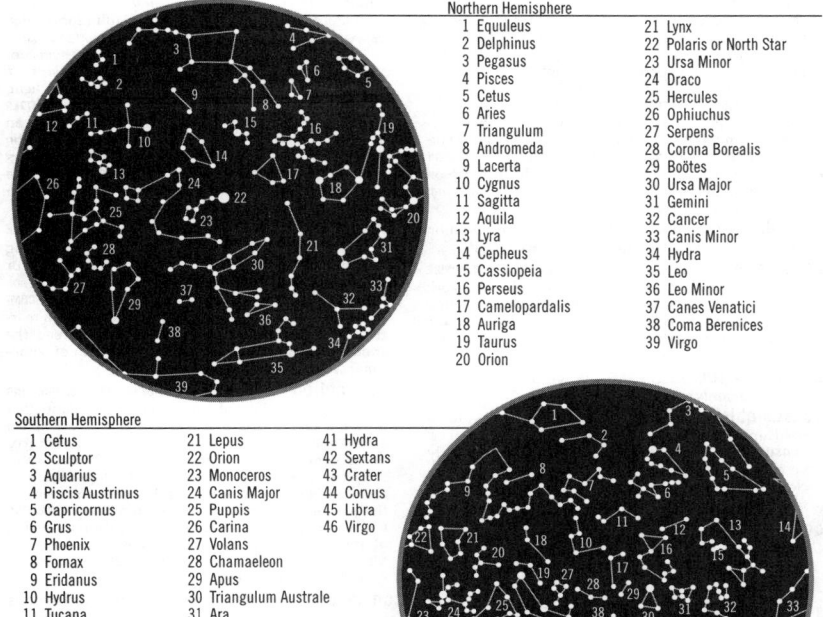

Northern Hemisphere

1	Equuleus	21	Lynx
2	Delphinus	22	Polaris or North Star
3	Pegasus	23	Ursa Minor
4	Pisces	24	Draco
5	Cetus	25	Hercules
6	Aries	26	Ophiuchus
7	Triangulum	27	Serpens
8	Andromeda	28	Corona Borealis
9	Lacerta	29	Boötes
10	Cygnus	30	Ursa Major
11	Sagitta	31	Gemini
12	Aquila	32	Cancer
13	Lyra	33	Canis Minor
14	Cepheus	34	Hydra
15	Cassiopeia	35	Leo
16	Perseus	36	Leo Minor
17	Camelopardalis	37	Canes Venatici
18	Auriga	38	Coma Berenices
19	Taurus	39	Virgo
20	Orion		

Southern Hemisphere

1	Cetus	21	Lepus	41	Hydra
2	Sculptor	22	Orion	42	Sextans
3	Aquarius	23	Monoceros	43	Crater
4	Piscis Austrinus	24	Canis Major	44	Corvus
5	Capricornus	25	Puppis	45	Libra
6	Grus	26	Carina	46	Virgo
7	Phoenix	27	Volans		
8	Fornax	28	Chamaeleon		
9	Eridanus	29	Apus		
10	Hydrus	30	Triangulum Australe		
11	Tucana	31	Ara		
12	Indus	32	Scorpius		
13	Sagittarius	33	Serpens		
14	Aquila	34	Ophiuchus		
15	Corona Australis	35	Lupus		
16	Pavo	36	Centaurus		
17	Octans	37	Crux		
18	Dorado	38	Musca		
19	Pictor	39	Vela		
20	Columba	40	Pyxis		

Constellations

OF ESTABLISHING the formal creation or establishment of something

Constitution *n* the Constitution of the United States, containing seven articles and 26 amendments, that has been in effect since its adoption in 1789

constitutional /kónsti tyóosh'nəl/ *adj* **1 INVOLVING CONSTITUTION** involving the constitution of a country or an organization ○ *constitutional reform* **2 GOVERNED BY CONSTITUTION** governed or regulated by a constitution **3 IN ACCORDANCE WITH A CONSTITUTION** authorized by a constitution ○ *The US Supreme Court has to decide whether such punishments are constitutional.* **4 RELATING TO BODY AND HEALTH** being part of, or a consequence of, a person's physical and sometimes psychological make-up ■ *n* **WALK** a short walk, taken regularly for health reasons

constitutionalise *vt* = **constitutionalize**

constitutionalism /kónsti tyóosh'nəlizəm/ *n* **1** the principles or practice of government regulated by a constitution, especially a written one **2** belief in constitutional government —**constitutionalist** *n, adj*

constitutionality /kónsti tyóosh'n álləti/ *n* validity or permissibility in terms of the provisions or principles of a constitution

constitutionalize /kónsti tyóosh'nə līz/ (**-izes, -izing, -ized**), **constitutionalise** (**-ises, -ising, -ised**) *vt* **1** to incorporate a piece of legislation into a constitution or to authorize a practice through it **2** to make a form of government, a country, or an organization subject to a constitution —**constitutionalization** /kónsti tyóosh'nə lī záysh'n/ *n*

constitutionally /kónsti tyóosh'nəli/ *adv* in accordance with a political constitution

constitutional monarchy *n* **1** a political system in which the head of state is a king or queen ruling to the extent allowed by a constitution **2** a country with a constitutional monarchy —**constitutional monarch** *n*

constitutive /kən stíttyóotiv/ *adj* **1 HAVING POWER TO ESTABLISH INSTITUTION** having the power to create or establish a system of government, legislative body, or other institution, or to appoint members of official bodies **2 FORMING A PART** forming a part of something **3 ESSENTIAL** essential to the particular nature or character of something **4 FORMED CONTINUOUSLY** describes enzymes that are formed continuously without an external stimulus —**constitutively** *adv*

constrain /kən stráyn/ *vt* **1 FORCE TO ACT** to force somebody to do something, especially through pressure of circumstances or a sense of obligation ○ *Many companies have been constrained to lay off workers.* **2 LIMIT** to limit or restrict somebody or something ○ *The industry has been constrained by skill shortages.* ○ *We felt constrained by the presence of the others.* **3 RESTRAIN** to hold somebody or something back from an action (*literary*) [14C. Via Old French *constraindre* < Latin *constringere* 'bind tightly together' < *stringere* 'draw tight'.] —**constrainable** *adj* —**constrainer** *n*

constrained /kən stráynd/ *adj* lacking naturalness or spontaneity because of self-consciousness, reserve, or inhibiting circumstances —**constrainedly** /kən stráynidli/ *adv*

constraint /kən stráynt/ *n* **1 LIMITING FACTOR** something that limits freedom of action ○ *Even in a free society individual liberty must be subject to certain constraints.* ○ *budgetary constraints* **2 LACK OF SPONTANEITY** a lack of warmth and spontaneity in somebody's manner or in the atmosphere on a particular occasion **3 STATE OF RESTRICTION** a state in which freedom of action is severely restricted [14C. < French *constreinte*, feminine past participle of *constraindre* (see CONSTRAIN).]

constrict /kən stríkt/ *v* **1** *vti* **NARROW** to make something, especially a blood vessel, narrower, or to become narrower **2** *vt* **LIMIT OR RESTRICT** to limit the movement of a person or part of the body in an uncomfortable way **3** *vt* **RESTRICT FLOW** to stop or slow down the flow of something, e.g. air, liquid, or blood **4** *vt* **SUFFOCATE PREY**

BY SQUEEZING to squeeze animals caught as prey until they suffocate, as many snakes do [Mid-18C. < Latin *constrict-*, past participle of *constringere* (see CONSTRAIN).] —**constrictive** *adj* —**constrictively** *adv* —**constrictiveness** *n*

constriction /kən stríksh'n/ *n* **1 BECOMING CONSTRICTED** the process of becoming narrower, or of making something narrower, e.g. blood vessels **2 COMPRESSION BY SQUEEZING** the process of squeezing or compressing something, e.g. the prey of a snake **3 NARROW PLACE** a narrow place or part ○ *A constriction in the tube prevents the mercury from returning to the bulb.* **4 FEELING OF TIGHTNESS** a feeling of tightness or pressure, especially in the chest or throat **5 RESTRICTION** something that severely restricts a person's freedom of movement, action, or expression

constrictor /kən stríktər/ *n* **1 SNAKE THAT SQUEEZES PREY TO DEATH** a large non-venomous snake, e.g. an anaconda, boa, or python, that coils itself around its prey and crushes it to death **2 MUSCLE** a muscle that tightens to make a part of the body narrower **3 SOMETHING THAT CONSTRICTS** something that constricts

construct *vt* /kən strúkt/ **1 BUILD** to build or assemble something by putting together separate parts in an ordered way **2 CREATE IN THE MIND** to create something, such as a theory, as a result of systematic thought **3 DRAW ACCURATELY** to draw something accurately using given measurements ■ *n* /kónstrukt/ **CONSTRUCTED THING OR CONCEPT** something that has been systematically put together, usually in the mind, especially a complex theory or subjective notion ○ *sexual identity viewed as a social construct* [15C. < Latin *construct-*, past participle of *construere* 'pile together' < *struere* 'pile, build'.] —**constructible** *adj* —**constructor** *n*

construction /kən strúksh'n/ *n* **1 ACT OR PROCESS OF CONSTRUCTING** the building of something, especially a large structure such as a house, road, or bridge **2 BUILT STRUCTURE** a structure or thing that has been built **3 WORKMANSHIP AND MATERIALS** the way in which something has been built, especially with regard to the type and quality of the structure, materials, and workmanship **4 BUILDING INDUSTRY** the building industry regarded as a whole **5 CREATION OF SOMETHING** the creation of something such as a system or concept from a number of different elements **6 INTERPRETATION** the way in which something is interpreted or explained (*formal*) ○ *put the worst possible construction on the news* **7 COMBINATION OF WORDS** a group of words governed by particular grammatical rules **8 GEOMETRIC SHAPE** a geometric figure drawn accurately in accordance with given measurements **9 WORK OF ART** a visual work of art that is put together from a variety of different materials, abstract in design, and usually three-dimensional —**constructional** *adj* —**constructionally** *adv*

constructionist /kən strúksh'nist/ *n US* an interpreter of a legal text or document

constructive /kən strúktiv/ *adj* **1 USEFUL** carefully considered and meant to be helpful ○ *constructive criticism* **2 BASED ON INFERENCE** based on what somebody infers from other statements or circumstances **3 STRUCTURAL** involved in construction, especially forming part of the basic structure of a building —**constructively** *adv* —**constructiveness** *n*

constructive dismissal *n* action by an employer intended to make continuing in a job intolerable for an unwanted employee, thus forcing the employee to resign

constructive margin *n* a boundary between two tectonic plates at which new crust is formed, e.g. the mid-ocean ridges

constructivism /kən strúktivizəm/ *n* a modern art movement associated with Moscow in the 1920s that produced large non-representational structures made of industrial materials such as plastic, glass, and sheet metal —**constructivist** *n*

QUICK FACTS ON... **CONSTRUCTIVISM**

Key dates: mid-1910s–late 1920s
Key locations: Russia, especially Moscow
Key elements: employment of geometric forms to construct abstract images in two and three dimensions; use of modern, mass-produced materials; rejection of artistic traditions; utilitarianism; functionalism
Key figures: Vladimir Tatlin, El Lissitzky, Aleksandr Rodchenko, Liubov Popova, Naum Gabo, Antoine Pevsner
Key works: *Monument to the Third International* (Vladimir

Tatlin) 1919, *Constructivist Composition* (Liubov Popova) 1921, *Proun Composition* (El Lissitzky) 1922
Key developments: kinetic art, minimalism, abstract expressionism

---

construe (**-strues, -struing, -strued**) *v* /kən stro͞o/ **1** *vt* **INTERPRET** to interpret or understand the meaning of a word, gesture, or action in a particular way ○ *His silence could be construed as an admission of guilt.* **2** *vti* **ANALYSE SYNTAX** to analyse the grammar of a piece of text, such as text that is to be translated **3** *vt* **USE WORD IN PARTICULAR WAY** to use a word in a grammatical structure, e.g. by making it singular or plural ○ *'Folk' is construed as plural, except when it means 'folk music'.* [14C. < Latin *construere* (see CONSTRUCT).] —**construability** /kən stro͞o ə bílləti/ *n* —**construable** *adj* —**construal** *n* —**construer** *n*

consubstantial /kónsəb stánsh'l/ *adj* having the same substance as something else, e.g. another member of the Holy Trinity [14C. < ecclesiastical Latin *consubstantialis* 'substance together' < Latin *substantia* 'substance'.] —**consubstantiality** /kónsəb stánshi álləti/ *n*

consubstantiate /kónsəb stánshi ayt/ (**-ates, -ating, -ated**) *vti* to become united or to unite two things in one single substance, as the body and blood of Jesus Christ are believed to become one with bread and wine in the Christian doctrine of transubstantiation [Late 16C. < late Latin *consubstantiatus* 'united in one substance' < *substantiat-*, past participle of *substantiare* (see SUBSTANTIATE).]

consubstantiation /kónsəb stánshi áysh'n/ *n* **1** the belief of some Christians that the body and blood of Jesus Christ coexist in the bread and wine consecrated at Holy Communion with the natural elements of which bread and wine are made. ◊ **transubstantiation** *n.* 1 **2** the process by which the body and blood of Jesus Christ are believed by some Christians to become present in the bread and wine consecrated at Holy Communion

consuetude /kónswi tyood/ *n* a long-standing custom or right, particularly one that has acquired legal force (*formal*) [14C. Directly or via French < Latin *consuetudo* 'complete accustomedness' < *suescere* 'become accustomed'.] —**consuetudinary** /kónswi tyo͞odinəri/ *adj*

consul /kónss'l/ *n* **1** **GOVERNMENT OFFICIAL WORKING ABROAD** a government official living in a foreign city to promote the commercial interests of the official's own state and protect its citizens **2** **ANCIENT ROMAN MAGISTRATE** one of the two chief magistrates who were elected annually to govern ancient Rome **3** **FORMER FRENCH OFFICIAL** one of the three chief magistrates of the first French Republic between 1799 and 1804 [14C. < Latin.] —**consular** /kónssyo͞olər/ *adj* —**consulship** *n*

consulate /kónssyo͞olət/ *n* **1** **CONSUL'S OFFICE** a consul's office or official residence **2** **SCOPE OF CONSUL'S RESPONSIBILITIES** the political office or period of office of a consul, or the jurisdiction of a consul **3** **ANCIENT ROMAN GOVERNMENT** the ancient Roman government administered by consuls

Consulate /kónssyo͞olət/ *n* **1** the government, consisting of three consuls, that ruled France from 1799 to 1804 **2** the period from 1799 to 1804 during which France was ruled by three consuls

consulate general (*plural* **consulate generals** *or* **consulates general**) *n* the building where a consul general lives or works

consul general (*plural* **consul generals** *or* **consuls general**) *n* a consul of the highest rank, usually based in a major foreign city that is important for trade

consult /kən súlt/ *v* **1** *vti* **ASK FOR SPECIALIST ADVICE** to ask for specialist advice or information, especially from a professional ○ *If symptoms persist, consult a doctor.* **2** *vti* **DISCUSS** to ask for somebody's opinion or permission before taking action ○ *You'd be wise to consult the boss before you make any major changes.* **3** *vt* **REFER TO FOR INFORMATION** to look at something, such as a reference book, in order to get information **4** *vi* **GIVE PROFESSIONAL ADVICE** to provide specialist advice for a fee ○ *After 15 years in computer programming, I now consult from home.* ■ *n* **CONSULTATION** a consultation or discussion about something (*informal*) [Early 16C. Via French *consulter* < Latin *consultare* 'confer' < *consulere* 'seek advice'.] —**consultable** *adj* —**consulter** *n*

consultant /kən súltənt/ *n* **1** an expert who charges a fee for providing advice or services in a particular field **2** a senior doctor who is fully qualified in a particular branch of medicine —**consultancy** *n* —**consultantship** *n*

consultation /kónss'l táysh'n, kónsul-/ *n* **1** **EXCHANGE OF OPINIONS** a discussion, especially in order to ascertain opinions or reach an agreement ○ *After a quick consultation with his wife, he signed the paper.* **2** **MEETING** a meeting with an expert in a particular field to obtain advice ○ *an appointment for a consultation with the heart surgeon* **3** **DISCUSSION FOR ADVICE** the process of discussing something either with experts or with other participants and asking for their opinions or advice ○ *Insufficient time was allowed for consultation before the project began.* **4** **REFERENCE** the act of referring to a book or person for information or advice ○ *Consultation of the manual confirmed the problem was the gearbox.*

consultative /kən súltətiv/ *adj* available for consultation or involved in consultation —**consultatively** *adv*

consulting /kən súlting/ *adj* **1** **PROVIDING SPECIALIST ADVICE** providing specialist advice to other people who work in the same field **2** **OF CONSULTANTS OR CONSULTATION** relating to a consultant or consultation ○ *a consulting fee* ■ *n* **BUSINESS OF CONSULTATION** the business of being a consultant

consulting room *n* the room in which a doctor sees patients, mainly in a hospital

consumable /kən syo͞oməb'l/ *adj* able or intended to be used up or discarded after use rather than saved ■ **consumables** *npl* goods that have to be bought regularly because they wear out or are used up, e.g. food and clothing

~~**consumate**~~ incorrect spelling of **consummate**

consume /kən syo͞om/ (**-sumes, -suming, -sumed**) *v* **1** *vt* **EAT OR DRINK** to eat or drink something, especially in large amounts **2** *vt* **USE UP** to use something in such a way that it cannot be reused or recovered afterwards ○ *The newer models consume less petrol.* **3** *vt* **ENGROSS OR OVERCOME** to fill somebody's mind or attention fully (*usually passive*) ○ *consumed by a desire for new experiences* **4** *vt* **DESTROY COMPLETELY** to destroy something or somebody completely, especially by fire or disease **5** *vti* **BUY FROM OTHERS** to buy goods or services produced by other people [14C. Directly or via French *consumer* < Latin *consumere* 'take up completely' < *sumere* 'to take'.]

consumer /kən syo͞omər/ *n* **1** **BUYER** a buyer of goods or services **2** **SOMEBODY OR SOMETHING THAT CONSUMES** somebody or something that consumes something, by eating it, drinking it, or using it up ○ *The country is one of the largest consumers of paper products.* **3** **ORGANISM THAT FEEDS ON OTHERS** in an ecological community or food chain, an organism that feeds on other organisms, or on material derived from them —**consumership** *n*

consumer credit *n* money lent by financial institutions to enable members of the public to buy consumer goods or services

consumer durables *npl* items such as computers or washing machines that last a relatively long time and are purchased infrequently

⚡**consumer-facing** *adj* involving direct contact with, or able to be directly accessed by, consumers ○ *a consumer-facing website*

consumer goods *npl* goods that are bought by consumers and are not used to produce other goods

consumerism /kən syo͞omərizəm/ *n* **1** **BELIEF IN BENEFITS OF CONSUMPTION** the belief that the buying and selling of large quantities of consumer goods is beneficial to an economy or a sign of economic strength **2** **PROTECTION OF CONSUMERS' RIGHTS** the protection of the rights and interests of consumers, especially with regard to price, quality, and safety **3** **MATERIALISTIC ATTITUDE** an attitude that values the acquisition of material goods (*disapproving*) —**consumerist** *n, adj*

consumer price index *n* a government-issued list of the retail prices of basic household goods and services

consumer society *n* a society in which the consumption of mass-produced goods is encouraged through mass communication

consuming /kən syo͞oming/ *adj* so intense as to take up all of somebody's attention, time, and energy ○ *a consuming interest in horses* —**consumingly** *adv*

consummate *v* /kónssə mayt, kónssyo͞o-/ (**-mates, -mating, -mated**) **1** *vt* **COMPLETE MARRIAGE** to make a marriage legally complete and fully valid by having sexual intercourse **2** *vt* **FULFIL RELATIONSHIP THROUGH SEX** to bring a relationship to completion or to gratify desire, especially by having sexual intercourse (*often passive*) **3** *vti* **CONCLUDE** to bring something such as a business deal to a conclusion, or to be brought to a conclusion (*formal*) ○ *Leaving her business partner to consummate the deal, she boarded a flight for New York.* **4** *vt* **ACHIEVE** to achieve or fulfil something, especially something long sought (*formal; often passive*) ○ *Twelve years of effort and struggle were consummated when the foundation stone for the new theatre was laid.* ■ *adj* /kónssəmət, kən súmmət/ **1** **SUPREME OR PERFECT** excellent, skilful, or accomplished ○ *with consummate ease* **2** **UTTER OR TOTAL** possessing or showing a bad quality to an extreme degree ○ *consummate arrogance* [15C. < Latin *consummat-*, past participle of *consummare* 'accomplish' < *summa* 'the highest thing'.] —**consummately** /kən súmmətli/ *adv* —**consummative** /kən súmmətiv/ *adj* —**consummator** *n* —**consummatory** /kən súmmətəri/ *adj*

consummation /kónsə máysh'n, kónsyo͞o máysh'n/ *n* **1** **PERFECT ENDING** the bringing of something to a satisfying conclusion, or the final satisfying completion or achievement of something ○ *The publication of her book was a consummation of her whole life's work.* **2** **LEGAL COMPLETION OF MARRIAGE BY SEX** the legal completion of a marriage by an act of sexual intercourse between the spouses **3** **COMPLETION OF DEAL** the finalization of something such as a business deal

consumption /kən súmpsh'n/ *n* **1** **ACT OF EATING OR DRINKING** the eating or drinking of something, or the amount that a person eats or drinks ○ *unfit for human consumption* **2** **ACT OF USING SOMETHING UP** the use of natural resources or fuels or the amount of resources or fuels used ○ *consumption of fossil fuels* **3** **CONSUMER EXPENDITURE** the purchase and use of goods and services by consumers, or the quantity of goods and services purchased **4** **WASTING DISEASE** any condition that causes progressive wasting of the tissues, especially tuberculosis of the lungs (*dated*) [14C. Via French *consomption* < Latin *consumption-* < *consumere* (see CONSUME).]

consumptive /kən súmptiv/ *adj* **1** **AFFECTED BY TUBERCULOSIS** affected by a wasting disease, especially tuberculosis of the lungs, or connected with such a disease (*dated*) **2** **ENGAGED IN OR CAUSING CONSUMPTION** engaged in, causing, or encouraging the consumption of food, materials, or goods, especially in a wasteful or destructive way ■ *n* **SOMEBODY WITH TUBERCULOSIS** somebody affected by a wasting disease, particularly tuberculosis of the lungs (*dated*) ○ *a chronic consumptive* [Mid-17C. < medieval Latin *consumptivus* < Latin *consumere* (see CONSUME).] —**consumptively** *adv* —**consumptiveness** *n*

cont. *abbr* **1** containing **2** contents **3** continent **4** continental **5** continued **6** contraction **7** continuous **8** control

contact /kón takt/ *n* **1** **STATE OF COMMUNICATION** a state or relationship in which communication happens or is possible ○ *Our only means of contact with the base was a small radio receiver.* ○ *He made contact with his counterpart in the Tokyo office.* **2** **ACT OF COMMUNICATING** an act of communicating with somebody ○ *All my contacts with her to date have been about business.* **3** **PHYSICAL CONNECTION** a situation or state in which two or more things or people actually touch or strike against one another ○ *White phosphorus ignites on contact with the air.* **4** **INTERACTION** a state in which somebody has access to, and can be affected or influenced by, people, situations, ideas, or information ○ *You'll come into contact with a variety of people.* **5** **SOMEBODY WHO CAN HELP** an acquaintance who may be socially or professionally helpful ○ *I made some very useful contacts at the trade fair.* **6** **DISEASE CARRIER** a person or animal associated with and seen as a possible carrier of an infectious disease **7** **DEVICE MAKING ELECTRICAL CONNECTION** a movable part, such as a component of a switch, that can be made to touch another conductive part in order to enable an electrical current to pass **8** **ELECTRICAL CONNECTION** a connection between, or the connection of, two or more electrical conductors so that current flows between them ■ **contacts** *npl* **CONTACT LENSES** a set of contact lenses (*informal*) ■ *v* **1** *vt* **REACH IN ORDER TO COMMUNICATE** to send a message to somebody, or reach somebody, e.g. by telephone or letter, in order to communicate ○ *You can contact me at this number.* **2** *vti* **TOUCH** to touch or strike against something ■ *adj* **1** **USED FOR COMMUNICATING** used as a means to contact somebody ○ *a contact address* **2** **WORKING BY TOUCHING** working or happening by touching or being touched by something or somebody **3** **CAUSED BY TOUCH** caused by touching something that irritates ○ *contact dermatitis* [Early 17C. < Latin *contactus*, past participle of *contingere* 'touch with' < *tangere* 'to touch'.] —**contactable** /kon táktəb'l/ *adj* —**contactual** /kon táktyo͞o əl/ *adj* —**contactually** *adv*

contact binary *n* a binary star system in which one of the components is transferring matter to its companion star

contact flight, contact flying *n* navigation of an aircraft by observing landmarks and other visible guides without the use of navigational aids

contact group *n* a group of people who are neutral in a dispute and meet both sides to try to resolve disagreements through discussion

contact inhibition *n* the normal cessation of cell division and growth caused by physical contact with other cells

contact language *n* a simplified language variety that retains features of other languages contributing to it, used for communication in places where most speakers do not share a common language

contact lens *n* a small plastic or glass lens placed directly onto the front of the eye to correct defective vision or make the iris appear a different colour

contact print *n* a photographic print made by placing a negative directly on top of photosensitive paper and exposing it to light

contact sport *n* a sport such as boxing, rugby, or ice hockey in which physical contact between players is an integral part of the game

contagion /kən táyjən/ *n* **1 SPREAD OF DISEASE BY PHYSICAL CONTACT** the transmission of disease, especially by physical contact between persons or contact with infected objects such as bedding or clothing **2 DISEASE SPREAD BY PHYSICAL CONTACT** an illness that spreads from one person to another, especially by physical contact between persons or contact with infected objects **3 HARMFUL INFLUENCE** a harmful or corrupting influence with a tendency to spread **4 SPREAD OF FEELING** the spreading of an attitude or emotion from person to person among a number of people (*literary*) ○ *the contagion of happiness* [14C. < Latin *contagion-* < *contingere* (see CONTACT).]

contagious /kən táyjəss/ *adj* **1 ABLE TO BE PASSED BY CONTACT** transmitted from one person to another either by direct contact, such as touching an infected person, or indirect contact **2 CAPABLE OF TRANSMITTING DISEASE** affected by or carrying a disease that can be transmitted by direct or indirect contact **3 LIKELY TO AFFECT OTHERS** quickly spread from one person to another ○ *Laughter is contagious.* [14C. < late Latin *contagiosus* < Latin *contingere* (see CONTACT).] —**contagiously** *adv* —**contagiousness** *n*

contagious abortion *n* a contagious or infectious disease of farm animals, e.g. brucellosis, that is characterized by spontaneous abortion

contain /kən táyn/ *vt* **1 HAVE WITHIN** to have or hold something inside ○ *This pack contains a training video and set of instructions.* **2 INCLUDE OR CONSIST OF** to include something as part of its contents or makeup ○ *The report contains several inaccuracies.* ○ *drinks that contain caffeine* **3 CONTROL EMOTION** to keep an emotion under control ○ *I couldn't contain myself any longer.* **4 HOLD BACK OR RESTRICT** to restrict the movement, spread, or influence of a strong enemy, force, disease, or idea **5 BE DIVISIBLE BY** to be divisible by a number, leaving no remainder **6 FORM SIDES OF ANGLE** to form the boundaries that define an angle [13C. Via French *contenir* < Latin *continere* 'hold together' < *tenere* 'to hold'.] —**containable** *adj*

container /kən táynər/ *n* **1** an object such as a box, jar, or bottle that is used to hold something, especially when it is being stored or transported **2** a large box of a standard size into which goods are packed so that they can be transported securely and efficiently from departure point to destination by road, ship, or rail, without having to be repacked in any way

containerize /kən táynə rīz/ (**-izes, -izing, -ized**), **containerise** (**-ises, -ising, -ised**) *vt* **1** to pack something in freight containers for transportation by sea, road, or rail, especially commercially **2** to convert a port, transport system, or industry so that it can use or handle standard-sized cargo containers —**containerization** /kən táynə rī záysh'n/ *n*

container port *n* a port capable of handling containerized cargo

containment /kən táynmənt/ *n* **1 ATTEMPT TO STOP SPREAD** action taken to restrict the spread of a hostile element such as an enemy or something undesirable such as a disease **2 CONTROL MEASURE IN NUCLEAR REACTIONS** the use of magnetic fields to prevent the reacting particles from touching the containing vessel's walls in a reactor **3 ACT OR PROCESS OF CONTAINING** the act or process of being contained or of containing something

contaminate /kən támmi nayt/ (**-nates, -nating, -nated**) *vt* **1** to make something impure, unclean, or polluted, especially by mixing harmful impurities into it or by putting it into contact with something harmful ○ *contaminate blood products* **2** to make something such as soil unfit for use or exploitation as a result of contact with polluting or harmful substances ○ *land contaminated by heavy industry* [15C. < Latin *contaminare* < *contamen*, literally 'touching with' < *tangere* 'to touch'.] —**contaminable** *adj* —**contaminant** *n* —**contaminative** /-nətiv/ *adj* —**contaminator** *n*

contamination /kən támmi náysh'n/ *n* **1 ACT OF CONTAMINATING** the act or process of contaminating something or becoming contaminated, or the unclean or impure state that results from this **2 SOMETHING THAT CONTAMINATES** something that physically contaminates a substance or that corrupts a person morally ○ *The investigators found considerable contamination in the rivers.* **3 ALTERATION OF WORD OR PHRASE** the process by which a word or phrase changes as a result of mistaken association with another word or phrase

contango /kən táng gō, kon-/ *n* (*plural* **-gos**) **1 INTEREST PAYABLE ON CONTANGO** interest payable by a broker when the delivery of and payment for stock is postponed **2 POSTPONEMENT OF STOCK DELIVERY** formerly, the postponement of the delivery of stock to a broker and payment for it, from one account day to the next ■ *vt* (**-gos, -going, -goed**) **ARRANGE A CONTANGO** to arrange for delivery and payment to be postponed when transferring stock in a stock exchange [Mid-19C. < ?]

contd *abbr* continued

conté /kón tay/ *n* a hard drawing crayon made of clay and graphite [Mid-19C. After the French inventor Nicolas Jacques *Conté* (1755–1805).]

contemn /kən tém/ *vt* to view or treat somebody with contempt (*archaic*) [15C. Directly or via Old French *contemner* < Latin *contemnere* (see CONTEMPT).] —**contemner** *n* —**contemnible** *adj* —**contemnibly** *adv*

contemplate /kóntəm playt, -tem-/ (**-plates, -plating, -plated**) *v* **1** *vt* **LOOK AT THOUGHTFULLY** to look at something thoughtfully and steadily ○ *tourists can now contemplate the restored frescoes* **2** *vt* **CONSIDER** to think about something seriously and at length, especially in order to understand it more fully ○ *I sat there, contemplating what she'd said.* **3** *vt* **HAVE AS POSSIBLE INTENTION** to think about something as a possible course of action ○ *contemplating moving house* **4** *vi* **THINK ABOUT SPIRITUAL MATTERS** to think calmly and at length, especially as a religious or spiritual exercise [Late 16C. < Latin *contemplat-*, past participle of *contemplari* 'observe carefully' < *templum* 'space for observing omens'.] —**contemplation** /kóntəm pláysh'n, -tem-/ *n* —**contemplator** *n*

contemplative /kən témplətiv/ *adj* calm and thoughtful ■ *n* a practitioner of spiritual contemplation such as a monk or nun —**contemplatively** *adv* —**contemplativeness** *n*

contemporaneous /kən témpə ráyni əss, kon-/ *adj* existing, occurring, or beginning at the same time or during the same period of time as something else [Mid-17C. < Latin *contemporaneus* 'time together' < *tempor-* 'time'.] —**contemporaneity** /kən témpərə nee̋ əti, kon-/ *n* —**contemporaneously** *adv* —**contemporaneousness** *n*

contemporary /kən témprəri/ *adj* **1 OF THE SAME TIME** existing or occurring at, or dating from, the same period of time as something or somebody else ○ *The Celts were dismissed by contemporary chroniclers as barbarians.* **2 EXISTING** in existence now ○ *problems of contemporary urban society* **3 MODERN IN STYLE** distinctively modern in style ○ *contemporary dance* **4 OF THE SAME AGE** of the same, or approximately the same, age as somebody else ○ *She and I are more or less contemporary.* ■ *n* (*plural* **-ies**) **1 SOMEBODY OR SOMETHING OF SAME TIME** a person or thing living or existing during the same period of time as another ○ *This 18th-century table is a contemporary of the Shaker furniture in the other room.* **2 SOMEBODY OF SAME AGE** a person of about the same age as somebody else ○ *It was nice to spend time with my Dad's contemporaries.* **3 MODERN PERSON OR THING** somebody or something in existence at the present time [Mid-17C. < medieval Latin *contemporarius* < Latin *tempor-* 'time'.] —**contemporarily** *adv* —**contemporariness** *n*

contemporize /kən témpə rīz/ (**-rizes, -rizing, -rized**), **contemporise** (**-rises, -rising, -rised**) *vt* **1** to make something modern or fashionable **2** to place somebody or something in the same period as somebody or something else [Mid-17C. < late Latin *contemporare* 'make contemporary' < Latin *tempor-* 'time'.] —**contemporization** /kən témpə rī záysh'n/ *n*

~~**contemprory**~~ incorrect spelling of **contemporary**

contempt /kən témpt/ *n* **1** a powerful feeling of dislike towards somebody or something considered to be worthless, inferior, or undeserving of respect **2** LAW = **contempt of court** [14C. < Latin *contemptus* 'scorn' < *contemnere* 'despise utterly' < *temnere* 'to scorn'.]

contemptible *adj* deserving to be treated with contempt —**contemptibility** /kən témptə bílləti/ *n* —**contemptibleness** *n* —**contemptibly** *adv*

contempt of court *n* the crime of deliberately failing to obey or respect the authority of a court of law or legislative body

contemptuous /kən témptyoo əss/ *adj* feeling, expressing, or demonstrating a strong dislike or utter lack of respect for somebody or something [Early 16C. < medieval Latin *contemptuosus* < Latin *contemnere* (see CONTEMPT).] —**contemptuously** *adv* —**contemptuousness** *n*

contend /kən ténd/ *v* **1** *vi* **STATE** to argue or claim that something is true **2** *vti* **COMPETE** to compete for something, especially a prize or trophy ○ *the teams contending for the cup* **3** *vi* **STRUGGLE OR DEAL** to fight with, struggle against, or deal with somebody or something ○ *Their lawyers have a number of awkward issues to contend with.* **4** *vi* **DEBATE** to debate or dispute with somebody (*literary*) [15C. Directly or via French *contendre* < Latin *contendere* 'strive together' < *tendere* 'strive'.]

contender /kən téndər/ *n* a competitor, especially somebody who has a good chance of winning

---

SYNONYMS See ***candidate***.

ϟ **content**[1] /kón tent/ *n* **1 AMOUNT OF SOMETHING IN SOMETHING ELSE** the amount of something contained in something else ○ *fruit with a high vitamin C content* **2 SUBJECT MATTER** the various issues, topics, or questions dealt with in speech, discussion, or a piece of writing ○ *a speech that was highly emotive in both tone and content* **3 MEANING OR MESSAGE** the meaning or message contained in a creative work as distinct from its appearance, form, or style **4 INFORMATION AVAILABLE ELECTRONICALLY** information made available by an electronic medium or product **5 CAPACITY** the capacity of a container ■ **contents** *npl* **1 SOMETHING CONTAINED** everything that is inside a particular container ○ *picked up the file and emptied its contents onto the desk* **2 SUBJECT OF TEXT** the subject matter of a document or publication ○ *revealed the contents of the letter* **3 LIST OF SUBJECT OR CHAPTER HEADINGS** a list at the front of a publication that gives the title and number of the first page of each new chapter, article, or part [15C. < medieval Latin *contentum* 'something contained', a form of Latin *contentus*, past participle of *continere* (see CONTAIN).]

content[2] /kən tént/ *adj* **1 QUIETLY SATISFIED AND HAPPY** reasonably happy and satisfied with the way things are **2 READY TO ACCEPT** willing to accept or comply with a situation or course of action ○ *He had to be content with third place in the race.* ■ *v* **1** *vt* **CAUSE TO FEEL CONTENT** to make somebody feel happy or satisfied with something **2** *vr* **ACCEPT OR MAKE DO** to accept or make do with something, rather than taking further action or making more demands ○ *He contented himself with a few cutting remarks about lack of discipline and did not take the matter further.* ■ *interj* **HOUSE OF LORDS EXPRESSION OF AGREEMENT** used by a member of the House of Lords to express formal agreement to a bill. Disagreement is expressed by the phrase 'not content'. (*formal*) [15C. Via French < Latin *contentus*, past participle of *continere* (see CONTAIN).] —**contently** *adv* —**contentment** *n*

contented /kən téntid/ *adj* peacefully happy and satisfied with the way things are or with what has been done —**contentedly** *adv* —**contentedness** *n*

contention /kən ténsh'n/ *n* **1 ASSERTION IN AN ARGUMENT** an opinion or claim stated in the course of an argument ○ *It is my contention that the scheme was bound to fail.* **2 DISAGREEMENT** angry disagreement between people ○ *a lot of contention over the quality of the goods* **3 RIVALRY** competition between rivals or opponents ○ *fierce contention for the title* [14C. Directly or via French < Latin *contention-* < *contendere* (see CONTEND).]

contentious /kən ténshəss/ *adj* **1 CREATING DISAGREEMENT** causing or likely to cause disagreement and disputes between people with differing views ○ *It should have been possible to word the statement in a less contentious way.* **2 ARGUMENTATIVE** frequently engaging in and seeming to enjoy arguments and disputes 3 SUBJECT TO LITIGATION contested by another interested party ○ *a contentious will* [15C. Via French *contentieux* < Latin *contentiosus* < *contendere* (see CONTEND).] —**contentiously** *adv* —**contentiousness** *n*

content word *n* a word such as a noun, verb, or adjective, that primarily conveys meaning rather than grammatical function. ◊ **function word**

conterminous /kon túrminəss, kən-/, **coterminous** /kō-/ *adj* 1 INSIDE SAME BOUNDARY enclosed inside a common boundary 2 ADJACENT next to and sharing a common boundary with something 3 MEETING IN TIME OR PLACE meeting end to end, so that where or when one finishes the next begins [Mid-17C. < Latin *conterminus* 'boundary with' < *terminus* 'boundary'.] —**conterminously** *adv* —**conterminousness** *n*

contessa /kon téssə/ *n* an Italian countess [Early 19C. Via Italian < medieval Latin *comitissa*, feminine of *comit-* (see COUNT[2]).]

contest *n* /kóntest/ 1 COMPETITION TO FIND THE BEST an organized competition for a prize or title, especially one in which the entrants appear or demonstrate their skills individually and the winner is chosen by a group of judges 2 STRUGGLE FOR CONTROL a struggle between rival or opposing individuals, organizations, or forces for victory or control ■ *vt* /kən tést/ 1 CHALLENGE to challenge or question something 2 TAKE PART IN CONTEST to take part in a contest or competition, especially an election [Late 16C. Directly or via French < Latin *contestari* 'begin a lawsuit by calling witnesses together' < *testari* 'be a witness'.] —**contestable** /kən téstəb'l/ *adj* —**contestably** *adv* —**contester** *n*

contestant /kən téstənt/ *n* 1 a competitor in something 2 a challenger of something, e.g. a will, verdict, or decision

SYNONYMS See ***candidate***.

ϟ **context** /kón tekst/ *n* 1 TEXT SURROUNDING A WORD OR PASSAGE the words, phrases, or passages that come before and after a particular word or passage in a speech or piece of writing and help to explain its full meaning 2 SURROUNDING CONDITIONS the circumstances or events that form the environment within which something exists or takes place ○ *The dispute needs to be viewed in its historical context.* 3 DATA TRANSFER STRUCTURE a data structure used to transfer electronic data to and from a business management system [15C. < Latin *contextus* 'connected' < *contexere* 'weave together' < *texere* 'to weave'.] —**contextless** *adj* —**contextual** /kən tékstyoo əl/ *adj* —**contextually** *adv*

contextualize /kən tékstyoo ə līz/ (**-izes, -izing, -ized**), **contextualise** (**-ises, -ising, -ised**) *vt* to place a word, phrase, or idea within a suitable context —**contextualization** /kən tékstyoo ə lī záysh'n/ *n*

Conti /kónti/, **Tom** (*b.* 1942) Scottish-born British stage and film actor

contiguity /kónti gyoó əti/ (*plural* **-ties**) *n* (*formal*) 1 closeness in space or time to something, or actual contact with it along one side 2 a continuous line, mass, or series ○ *a contiguity of roofs*

contiguous /kən tíggyoo əss/ *adj* (*formal*) 1 ADJOINING sharing a boundary or touching each other physically 2 NEIGHBOURING situated next to something else or to each other 3 CONTINUOUS connected together so as to form an unbroken sequence in time or an uninterrupted expanse in space [Early 16C. < Latin *contiguus* 'touching together' < *contingere* (see CONTACT).] —**contiguously** *adv* —**contiguousness** *n*

continent[1] /kóntinənt/ *n* 1 any of the seven large continuous land masses that constitute most of the dry land on the surface of the Earth. They are Africa, Antarctica, Asia, Australia, Europe, North America, and South America. 2 the part of the Earth's crust that rises above the oceans [Mid-16C. < Latin *terra continens* 'continuous land' < the present participle of *continere* (see CONTAIN).]

continent[2] /kóntinənt/ *adj* 1 able to exercise control over urination and bowel movements 2 restrained, especially abstaining from sexual activity [14C. < Latin *continent-*, present participle of *continere* (see CONTAIN).] —**continence** *n*

Continent *n* the mainland of Europe, not including the British Isles

continental /kónti nént'l/ *adj* 1 relating to, typical of, or belonging to the continents of the earth 2 ■ *n* 1 2 a banknote issued by the Continental Congress during the American War of Independence —**continentalism** *n* —**continentalist** *n* —**continentally** *adv*

Continental *adj* 1 **Continental, continental** OF MAINLAND EUROPE from or relating to mainland Europe 2 OF THE ORIGINAL 13 AMERICAN COLONIES from or relating to the 13 colonies that later became the United States. ◊ **Continental Congress** ■ *n* 1 **Continental, continental** MAINLAND EUROPEAN somebody from mainland Europe (*informal*) 2 AMERICAN SOLDIER DURING REVOLUTION a soldier in the American army during the American War of Independence

continental breakfast *n* a light breakfast usually consisting of fruit juice, a roll, croissant, or pastry with jam and butter, and coffee or tea [Because it is common on the Continent]

continental climate *n* the climate characteristic of the interior of a continent, with hot summers, cold winters, and little rainfall

continental code *n US* = **International Morse code**

Continental Congress *n* the congress of delegates from the American colonies held before, during, and after the American War of Independence

continental crust *n* the part of the outer shell of the solid Earth that constitutes the continents and the rocks beneath them down to the level of the mantle

continental divide *n* a massive area of high ground in the interior of a continent, from either side of which a continent's river systems flow in different directions

Continental Divide series of mountain ridges, running from Alaska to Mexico and including the Rocky Mountains, that forms the main watershed of North America

continental drift *n* a theory that explains the formation, alteration, and extremely slow movement of the continents across the Earth's crust. ◊ **plate tectonics**

continental margin *n* the region of ocean between the deep sea and shore, consisting of the continental rise, slope, and shelf

continental quilt *n* HOUSEHOLD = **duvet** *n.* 1

continental rise *n* the transitional area of the continental margin between the continental slope and abyssal plain

continental shelf *n* the gently sloping undersea area surrounding a continent at depths of up to 200 m/656 ft, at the edge of which the continental slope drops steeply to the ocean floor

continental slope *n* the steep slope from the continental shelf down to the ocean floor

contingence /kən tínjənss/ *n* 1 physical contact between objects 2 = **contingency** *n.* 1

contingency /kən tínjənssi/ (*plural* **-cies**) *n* 1 SOMETHING THAT MAY HAPPEN an event that might occur in the future, especially a problem, emergency, or expense that might arise unexpectedly, needs to be dealt with, and therefore must be prepared for 2 SOMETHING SET ASIDE FOR UNFORESEEN EMERGENCY provision made against future unforeseen events, e.g. an allocation of funds in a budget 3 DEPENDENCE UPON CHANCE dependence upon chance or factors and circumstances that are presently unknown 4 CHANGE IN MEANING PRODUCED BY CLAUSE in systemic grammar, a change in the meaning of the main clause brought about by the addition of a bound clause introduced by 'if', 'when', 'though', or 'since'

contingency fee *n* a payment for professional services, such as those of a lawyer, that is made only if the client receives a satisfactory result

contingency plan *n* a plan designed to deal with a particular problem, emergency, or state of affairs if it should occur

contingent /kən tínjənt/ *adj* 1 DEPENDENT ON WHAT MAY HAPPEN dependent on or resulting from a future and as yet unknown event or circumstance ○ *Payment is contingent upon winning the case.* 2 POSSIBLE BUT NOT CERTAIN possible, but not certain to happen ○ *'. . .all the advantages of a long slow ramble with Elfride, without the contingent possibility of the enjoyment being spoilt by her becoming weary'.* (Thomas Hardy, *A Pair of Blue Eyes*; 1889) 3 CHANCE happening by chance 4 TRUE ONLY UNDER CERTAIN CONDITIONS true only under certain conditions or under existing conditions, and therefore not universally true or valid ■ *n* 1 GROUP OF PEOPLE a group of people representing a particular organization or belief, or from a particular region or country, and forming part of a larger group 2 GROUP OF MILITARY PERSONNEL a group, particularly of soldiers, forming part of a larger force 3 = **contingency** *n.* 1 [14C. < Latin *contingent-*, present participle of *contingere* (see CONTACT).] —**contingently** *adv*

contingent fee *n* = **contingency fee**

contingent worker *n US* a temporary employee, often employed for a specific task

~~**continous**~~ incorrect spelling of **continuous**

continual /kən tínnyoo əl/ *adj* 1 happening again and again, especially regularly 2 ⚠ continuing almost without interruption or ending. [14C. < French *continuel* < *continuer* (see CONTINUE).] —**continually** *adv* —**continualness** *n*

USAGE continual or **continuous**? Something ***continual*** continues, with breaks, over a period of time, whereas something ***continuous*** goes on without stopping. So a ***continual*** noise is one that is constantly repeated, like a dog's barking, and a ***continuous*** noise is one that continues without stopping, like the roar of a waterfall. The same distinction applies to the adverbs ***continually*** and ***continuously***: *The speaker was continually interrupted by hecklers. She drove continuously for three hours.* In popular usage, however, ***continual*** and ***continually*** are now frequently used to mean 'without stopping'.

continuance /kən tínnyoo ənss/ *n* 1 CONTINUATION the fact or quality of continuing to be in a particular situation, to exist, or to occur beyond the present time into the future 2 LENGTH OF TIME SOMETHING LASTS the period of time that something lasts or continues 3 *US* ADJOURNMENT a postponement of legal proceedings until a later date

continuant /kən tínnyoo ənt/ *n* a speech consonant, such as 'l', 'f', or 's', made with the vocal passage partly open for breath to pass through, thus enabling the sound to be prolonged at will. ◊ **stop** *n.* 16

continuation /kən tínnyoo áysh'n/ *n* 1 PROCESS OF CONTINUING the process of continuing something without interruption 2 ADDITION OR EXTENSION an additional part that extends something that already exists or has already begun 3 STARTING AGAIN AFTER INTERRUPTION the renewal of an action, event, or process after it has been interrupted

continuative /kən tínnyoo ətiv/ *adj* 1 AIDING CONTINUITY causing or helping something to continue (*formal*) 2 EXPRESSING CONTINUATION expressing the continuation of an action ■ *n* WORD EXPRESSING CONTINUATION a continuative clause, phrase, or word —**continuatively** *adv*

continuator /kən tínnyoo aytər/ *n* somebody who continues something, especially work started by somebody else, or somebody or something that maintains continuity

continue /kən tínnyoo/ (**-ues, -uing, -ued**) *v* 1 *vti* KEEP GOING to last, or to make something last, beyond the present ○ *pledge to continue campaigning against the ban* 2 *vti* LAST to last or to make something last throughout a particular period of time ○ *Talks between the two sides continued during May.* 3 *vti* NOT STOP to keep up an activity or state already begun ○ *were able to continue broadcasting without interruption* 4 *vti* START SOMETHING AGAIN to start doing something again after an interruption or pause ○ *We'll continue this discussion later.* 5 *vti* UTTER OR BEGIN SPEAKING AGAIN to begin speaking again, or to say something, after an interruption or pause 6 *vti* MAKE SOMETHING LONGER to extend, or to extend something, beyond a particular point or beyond its original length 7 *vi* MOVE FARTHER to move or travel farther in a particular direction ○ *Continue east along the coast path.* 8 *vt US, Scotland* POSTPONE CASE to postpone legal proceedings [14C. Via French *continuer* < Latin *continuare* 'make continuous' < *continere* (see CONTAIN).] —**continuable** *adj* —**continued** *adj* —**continuer** *n*

continued fraction *n* a fraction with a whole number as numerator, and a number plus a fraction as denominator, the denominator in turn having a number plus a fraction as its denominator

continuing /kən tínnyoo ing/ *adj* having existed for some time, currently in existence, and likely to remain so in the future —**continuingly** *adv*

continuing education *n* 1 adult education, usually in the form of short or part-time courses, continuing throughout an individual's life 2 *US* regular courses or training designed to bring professionals up to date with the latest developments in their particular field

continuity /kónti nyoō əti/ (*plural* **-ties**) *n* **1 UNCHANGING QUALITY** the fact of staying the same, of being consistent throughout, or of not stopping or being interrupted ○ *measures to ensure continuity of supply* ○ *the stability and continuity of traditional rural life* **2 CONSISTENT WHOLE** something that remains consistent or uninterrupted throughout ○ *stressed the continuities with the past* **3 CONSISTENCY BETWEEN FILM OR BROADCAST PARTS** consistency in the details from one part of a film or broadcast to another ○ *discrepancies in continuity* **4 SEAMLESSNESS OF NARRATIVE** smoothness in the narrative flow in a film or broadcast **5 DETAILED SCRIPT** a comprehensive script that includes full details of the contents of each shot or scene, including such items as camera positions and settings and costume features **6 SPOKEN LINK IN BROADCASTING** commentary by a television or radio broadcaster that fills the time between the end of one programme or programme segment and the beginning of the next

continuo /kən tínnyoo ō/ (*plural* **-os**) *n* an instrumental bass accompaniment, usually played on a keyboard, with numbers written beneath the notes so that musicians can improvise and provide harmony [Early 18C. < Italian, 'continuous' < Latin *continuus* (see CONTINUOUS).]

continuous /kən tínnyoo əss/ *adj* **1 UNCHANGED OR UNINTERRUPTED** continuing without changing, stopping, or being interrupted ○ *three days of continuous rain* **2 UNBROKEN** having no gaps, holes, or breaks ○ *a continuous line* **3** GRAM = **progressive** *adj.* **6 4 RELATING TO DIFFERENCE OF FUNCTION VALUES** relating to a line or curve along which the difference between function values at any two points within a given interval will approach zero if the interval is decreased sufficiently **5 RELATING TO UNINTERRUPTED CHEMICAL MANUFACTURING** relating to chemical manufacturing in which material is processed in an uninterrupted stream [Mid-17C. < Latin *continuus* 'uninterrupted' < *continere* (see CONTAIN).] —**continuously** *adv* —**continuousness** *n*

USAGE See ***continual***.

continuous creation theory *n* ASTRON = **steady-state theory**

continuous spectrum *n* a sequence of frequencies that is without breaks over a relatively wide range of wavelengths

continuum /kən tínnyoo əm/ (*plural* **-a** /-nyoo ə/ or **-ums**) *n* **1** a link between two things, or a continuous series of things, that blend into each other so gradually and seamlessly that it is impossible to say where one becomes the next ○ *A rainbow forms a continuum of colour.* **2** a set of real numbers between any two of which a third can always be found, and in which there are no gaps [Mid-17C. < Latin, a form of *continuus* (see CONTINUOUS).]

contort /kən táwrt/ *v* **1** *vti* to become so twisted as to take on an unnatural or grotesque shape or to twist something, especially a part of the body, in this way ○ *Fear had contorted their faces.* **2** *vt* to change something so greatly that it becomes unrecognizable [15C. < Latin *contort-*, past participle of *contorquere* 'twist violently' < *torquere* 'to twist'.] —**contortive** *adj*

contorted /kən táwrtid/ *adj* **1** greatly or violently twisted out of shape **2** describes plant parts such as sepals or leaves whose margins overlap in the bud like playing cards in a hand, so that they appear to be twisted —**contortedly** *adv* —**contortedness** *n*

contortion /kən táwrsh'n/ *n* **1** a twisting of something, especially a part of the body, out of its natural shape **2** a bewilderingly complex manoeuvring or manipulation of something ○ *verbal contortions that tie his opponents in knots*

contortionist /kən táwrsh'nist/ *n* **1** somebody who bends his or her own body into unusual shapes as an entertainment ○ *You'd have to be a contortionist to get into those jeans.* **2** a twister or distorter of something, e.g. a statement ○ *a debater skilled as a logical contortionist* —**contortionistic** /kən táwrsh'n ístik/ *adj*

contour /kón toor/ *n* **1 SHAPE'S OUTLINE** an outline, especially of something curved or irregular (*often plural*) ○ *The contours of the hills were characteristically rounded.* **2 GENERAL NATURE** the general character or nature of something ○ *scenes that establish the contour of the play* **3** GEOG = **contour line** ■ *adj* **1 SHAPED OR FITTED** shaped to fit something, especially the shape of somebody's body ○ *contour furniture* **2 FOLLOWING LAND'S SHAPE** following the lie of the land, rather than cutting through or across it ○ *contour farming* ■ *vt* **1 SHAPE TO FIT** to shape one thing so that it fits the outlines of another ○ *furniture that is contoured to the human body* **2 PUT CONTOUR LINES ON** to mark contour lines on something such as a map **3 CAUSE TO FIT LAND'S SHAPE** to build or operate something so that it follows the natural shape of the land ○ *roads that are sensitively contoured* [Mid-17C. Via French < Italian *contornare* 'draw in outline', literally 'turn with' < Latin *tornare* (see TURN).]

contour feather *n* any of the medium-sized feathers of a bird, excluding those on the wings and tail, that make up its external covering and determine its shape

contour interval *n* the interval between contour lines on a map, or the altitude the interval represents ○ *at contour intervals of 10 metres*

contour line *n* a line on a map connecting points on a land surface that are the same elevation above sea level

contour map *n* a map that uses contour lines to show the shapes and elevations of land surfaces

contr. *abbr* **1** contraction **2** contralto **3** control

contra /kóntrə/ *n* a member of the United States-backed counter-revolutionary force opposed to the Nicaraguan government in the 1980s [< Spanish *contrarevolucionario* 'counter-revolutionary']

contra- *prefix* **1** against, opposite, contrasting ○ *contraindicate* **2** lower in pitch ○ *contrabass* [< Latin *contra* 'against' < Indo-European, 'together']

contraband /kóntrə band/ *n* **1 ILLEGAL IMPORTS AND EXPORTS** goods that are illegally imported or exported, e.g. goods that evade duty or are prohibited by law from being taken into or out of a country ○ *dealers in contraband* **2 ILLEGAL TRADE** illegal trade, especially the illegal importing or exporting of goods **3 SUPPLIES FORBIDDEN TO WARRING SIDES** goods that a neutral country must not supply to either side in a war ■ *adj* **1 ILLEGALLY TRADED** bought or sold, especially imported or exported, illegally ○ *truckloads of contraband cigarettes* **2 FORBIDDEN FROM BEING IMPORTED OR EXPORTED** forbidden by law from being traded, especially as an import or export [Late 16C. Via Spanish *contrabanda* < Italian *contrabbando* 'against proclamation' < *bando* 'proclamation' < Germanic.] —**contrabandage** *n* —**contrabandist** *n*

contrabass /kóntrə bayss/ *n* **1 DOUBLE BASS** a double bass **2 INSTRUMENT PITCHED LOWEST OF ITS FAMILY** an instrument pitched an octave below the usual range for that family of instruments **3 CONTRABASSIST** an instrumentalist in an orchestra or band who plays the contrabass ■ *adj* **PITCHED AN OCTAVE BELOW** pitched an octave below the usual range of that instrument ○ *contrabass clarinet* [Early 19C. < Italian *contrabbasso* < *basso* 'bass'.] —**contrabassist** /kóntrə báyssist/ *n*

contrabassoon /kóntrə bə soōn/ *n* **1** a U-shaped woodwind instrument that is the largest in the oboe family and has a pitch an octave below the bassoon **2** an instrumentalist in an orchestra or chamber group who plays the contrabassoon —**contrabassoonist** *n*

contraception /kóntrə sépsh'n/ *n* **1** the prevention of pregnancy using artificial methods such as condoms and contraceptive pills or natural methods such as avoiding sex during the woman's known fertile periods **2** a method or device used to prevent pregnancy [Late 19C. < CONTRA- + CONCEPTION.]

contraceptive /kóntrə séptiv/ *n* **DEVICE PREVENTING FERTILIZATION** a device used to prevent fertilization of an egg, e.g. a condom worn by a man during intercourse or a pill taken regularly by a woman ■ *adj* **1** relating to contraception ○ *contraceptive advice* **2 PREVENTING INSEMINATION** designed to prevent sperm from fertilizing an egg ○ *various contraceptive methods and devices*

contract *n* /kón trakt/ **1 FORMAL AGREEMENT** a formal or legally binding agreement, such as one for the sale of property, or one setting out terms of employment ○ *Such actions would be in breach of contract.* **2 DOCUMENT RECORDING AGREEMENT** a document that records a formal or legally binding agreement ○ *sign a contract* **3 AGREEMENT TO MARRY** a formal agreement to marry (*dated*) **4 PAID ASSASSIN'S ASSIGNMENT** a hiring of an assassin to kill somebody (*informal*) **5 HIGHEST BRIDGE BID IN ONE HAND** a winning bid in a single hand of bridge, in which partners agree regarding the number of tricks they can take **6 NUMBER AND SUIT OF CONTRACT** in bridge, the number and suit of the tricks agreed on by the highest bidders **7** CARDS = **contract bridge 8 contracts BRANCH OF LAW** the branch or category of law and legal education that deals with contracts ○ *She made a career in contracts.* ■ *v* /kən trákt/ **1** *vti* **SHRINK OR LESSEN** to shrink or become smaller, or make something shrink or become smaller ○ *metals expanding and contracting as temperatures change* **2** *vti* **TIGHTEN OR DRAW TOGETHER** to become tighter or draw together, or make something tighter or draw something together ○ *see the muscles contracting under the skin* **3** *vt* **FORMALLY OR LEGALLY AGREE** to make a formal or legally binding agreement with somebody to do something, especially work (*often passive*) ○ *I'm not contracted to work on Sundays.* **4** *vt* **GET ILLNESS** to become affected by an illness or disease **5** *vt* **SHORTEN WORD OR PHRASE** to shorten a word by leaving out letters or syllables or a phrase by leaving out words **6** *vt* **ARRANGE MARRIAGE** to arrange a marriage formally (*dated*) [14C. Directly or via French < Latin *contractus*, past participle of *contrahere* 'draw together' < *trahere* 'to draw'.] —**contractibility** /kən tráktə bílləti/ *n* —**contractible** /kən tráktəb'l/ *adj* —**contractibleness** *n* —**contractibly** *adv*

contract out /kón trakt ówt/ *v* **1** *vt* to offer work to outside companies or individuals **2** *vi* to withdraw from something by making a formal or legally binding declaration ○ *employees contracting out of the state pension scheme*

contract bridge *n* the most common variety of bridge, in which points are awarded only for tricks bid and won

contractile /kən trákt īl/ *adj* able or tending to shrink, tighten, or become narrower —**contractility** /kón trak tílləti/ *n*

contractile vacuole *n* a membrane-surrounded cavity within a cell that regulates the water content of the cell by absorbing water and then contracting to expel it

contraction /kən trácksh'n/ *n* **1 REDUCTION IN SIZE** a shrinking or reducing ○ *alternate expansion and contraction* **2 CONTRACTING OF BODY PART** a tightening or narrowing of a muscle, organ, or other body part **3 TIGHTENING OF WOMB MUSCLES EFFECTING CHILDBIRTH** a tightening of the muscles of the womb that occurs at increasingly frequent intervals immediately before childbirth and eventually pushes the baby out of the womb **4 SHORTENED WORD** a shortened form or shortening of a word or phrase, e.g. 'he'll' for 'he will' —**contractional** *adj* —**contractionary** *adj* —**contractive** *adj*

contractor /kən tráktər/ *n* **1 COMPANY OR PERSON UNDER CONTRACT** a company or individual with a formal contract to do a specific job, supplying labour and materials and providing and overseeing staff if needed **2 THING THAT CONTRACTS** something that contracts, e.g. a muscle **3 SOMEBODY WHO MAKES A CONTRACT** one of the parties to a contract

contractual /kən trákchoo əl/ *adj* contained in, arising from, or in the form of a formal or legally binding agreement ○ *fulfilling your contractual obligations* —**contractually** *adv*

contracture /kən trákchər/ *n* a permanent tightening or shortening of a body part, such as a muscle, a tendon, or the skin, often resulting in deformity

contradance *n* DANCE = **contredanse**

contradict /kóntrə díkt/ *vt* **1** to argue against the truth or correctness of somebody's statement or claim **2** to show that something is not true or that the opposite is true ○ *The results contradicted all previously held theories.* [Late 16C. < Latin *contradict-*, past participle of *contradicere* 'speak against' < *dicere* 'speak'.] —**contradictable** *adj* —**contradicter** *n* —**contradictive** *adj* —**contradictively** *adv* —**contradictiveness** *n*

SYNONYMS See ***disagree***.

contradiction /kóntrə díksh'n/ *n* **1** something that contains parts or elements that are illogical or inconsistent with each other ○ *a contradiction in terms* **2** a statement or the making of a statement that opposes or disagrees with somebody or something ○ *I can say without fear of contradiction that she is our best worker.*

contradictory /kóntrə díktəri/ *adj* **1 INCONSISTENT** inconsistent either within itself or in relation to one or more others **2 OPPOSING** holding or consisting of an opposite view in relation to something **3 ARGUMENTATIVE** fond of or given to taking opposite views —**contradictorily** *adv* —**contradictoriness** *n*

contradistinction /kóntrədi stíngksh'n/ *n* differentiation between two things by identifying their contrasting qualities —**contradistinctive** *adj* —**contradistinctively** *adv*

contraflow /kóntrəflō/ *n* a temporary two-way traffic system on one carriageway of a motorway

contrail /kón trayl/ *n* = **vapour trail** [Mid-20C. Contraction of *condensation trail*.]

contraindicate /kóntrə índi kayt/ (**-cates, -cating, -cated**) *vt* to state something to be inadvisable while taking certain medication because of a likely adverse reaction ○ *Taking aspirin with this drug is contraindicated.* —**contraindicant** *n* —**contraindication** /kóntrə índi káysh'n/ *n* —**contraindicative** /kóntrə in díkətiv/ *adj*

contralateral /kóntrə láttərəl/ *adj* describes a body part on the opposite side of the body or that acts in conjunction with such a part

contralto /kən traáltō/ (*plural* **-tos**) *n* **1** LOWEST FEMALE VOCAL RANGE the lowest vocal range for women's voices, below soprano and mezzo-soprano **2** SOMEBODY WITH CONTRALTO SINGING VOICE a singer, usually a woman, with a contralto voice **3** PART FOR CONTRALTO a singing part for a contralto [Mid-18C. < Italian, 'below alto'.]

contraposition /kóntrəpə zísh'n/ *n* **1** a position opposite to or against something ○ *took up a stand in contraposition to government policy* **2** the relation of a proposition to its contrapositive [Mid-16C. < late Latin *contraposition-* < Latin *contraponere* 'place opposite' < *ponere* 'to place'.]

contrapositive /kóntrə pózzətiv/ *n* a conditional proposition that negates another conditional proposition and also reverses its clauses. The proposition 'if not q then not p' is the contrapositive of the proposition 'if p then q'.

contrapposto /kóntrə póstō/ (*plural* **-tos**) *n* a relaxed asymmetrical pose of the human body in art, especially sculpture, in which the shoulders and hips are turned in different planes [Early 20C. < Italian, past participle of *contrapporre* < Latin *contraponere* (see CONTRAPOSITION).]

contraption /kən trápsh'n/ *n* a device or machine, especially one that appears strange or improvised ○ *They'd rigged up a contraption for opening the door.* [Early 19C. < ?]

contrapuntal /kóntrə púnt'l/ *adj* describes polyphonic music with very active and strongly differentiated parts [Mid-19C. < Italian *contrapunto* 'counterpoint' < *punto* 'point' < Latin *punctum* (see POINT).] —**contrapuntally** *adv*

contrapuntist /kóntrə púntist/ *n* a composer of music in counterpoint or in a contrapuntal style [Late 18C. < Italian *contrapuntista* < *contrapunto* 'counterpoint'.]

contrarian /kən tráiri ən/ *n* **1** a habitual opponent of accepted policies, opinions, or practices ○ *a thoroughgoing contrarian, accepting nothing anyone says* **2** an investor who goes against current market trends, e.g. by buying shares that most other investors are selling

contrariety /kóntrə rī́ əti/ (*plural* **-ties**) *n* **1** OPPOSITENESS the state or quality of opposing or being contrary **2** POINT OF DIFFERENCE a point of difference or inconsistency **3** OBSTACLE TO PROGRESS something that obstructs or hinders progress ○ *battling against the contrarieties of the weather*

contrariwise /kən tráiri wīz/ *adv* **1** IN THE OPPOSITE WAY in the opposite way or direction or on the opposite side **2** ON THE OTHER HAND used to introduce a statement in direct opposition to what has already been said **3** UNHELPFULLY in a way that obstructs or hinders progress ○ *Unfortunately, things turned out contrariwise, and we had to give up the idea.*

contrary /kóntrəri/ *adj* **1** CONFLICTING not at all in agreement with something ○ *Such arrangements were contrary to his moral code.* **2** OPPOSITE opposite in direction **3** OBSTRUCTING OR HINDERING PROGRESS making forward motion extremely hard ○ *slowed by contrary winds* **4** DELIBERATELY DISOBEDIENT wilfully disobedient or uncooperative ○ *a contrary child* **5** UNABLE TO BE TRUE AT ONCE describes a pair of propositions that cannot both be true, though they may both be false ■ *n* THE OPPOSITE the opposite of something ○ *Actually, the contrary is true.* [13C. Via Anglo-Norman *contrarie* < Latin *contrarius* < *contra* 'against'.] —**contrarily** /kən tráirəli/ *adv* —**contrariness** /kən tráirinəss/ *n* ◇ **contrary to** differently from ◇ **on** *or* **to the contrary** quite the reverse is true

contrast *n* /kón traast/ **1** MARKED DIFFERENCE a difference, or something that is different, compared with something else ○ *in stark contrast to the luxury they formerly enjoyed* **2** JUXTAPOSITION OF DIFFERENT THINGS an effect created by placing or arranging very different things, e.g. colours, shades, or textures, next to each other **3** DEGREE OF LIGHTNESS AND DARKNESS the difference or the use of differences between the lightest and the darkest parts of something, e.g. to create a special effect in a painting, photograph, or television image ■ *vti* /kən traást/ BE OR SHOW TO BE DIFFERENT to compare different things or arrange them in a way that highlights their differences, or to be markedly different when compared with something ○ *These poems have a mature voice when contrasted with her earlier work.* [15C. Via French < Italian *contrastare* 'stand against' < Latin *stare* 'to stand'.] —**contrastable** /kən traástəb'l/ *adj* —**contrastably** *adv* —**contrasting** /-ing/ *adj* —**contrastingly** *adv*

contrastive /kən traástiv/ *adj* forming a contrast, or using contrasting colours, tones, or textures —**contrastively** *adv* —**contrastiveness** *n*

contrast medium *n* a substance opaque to X-rays that is used to fill a body cavity, making the outline of the body part easier to see on an X-ray photograph

contrasty /kón traasti/ *adj* showing sharp contrast between the lightest and darkest areas in a photograph or television or movie image

contravene /kóntrə veén/ (**-venes, -vening, -vened**) *vt* **1** to break a rule or law ○ *outdated equipment that contravenes the safety regulations* **2** to disagree with or oppose a statement or decision ○ *There was no question of contravening the committee's findings.* [Mid-16C. < late Latin *contravenire* 'come against' < Latin *venire* 'come'.] —**contravener** *n* —**contravention** /-vénsh'n/ *n*

~~**contraversial**~~ incorrect spelling of **controversial**

contrecoup /kóntrə koo/ *n* an injury to one side of an organ, especially the brain, as a result of a blow that causes it to swing inside the retaining cavity [Mid-18C. < French, 'a blow opposite' < *coup* (see COUP).]

contredanse /kóntrə daanss/, **contradance** *n* **1** a folk dance in which two pairs of partners face each other **2** the music for a contredanse [Early 19C. < French, by folk etymology (influenced by *contre* 'against') < English *country dance*.]

contretemps /kóntrə ton/ *n* **1** a dispute or minor disagreement (*formal*) **2** a mishap, especially an awkward or embarrassing one [Late 17C. < French, 'against the time'.]

contrib. *abbr* **1** contribution **2** contributor

contribute /kən tríbbyoot, kóntri byoot/ (**-utes, -uting, -uted**) *v* **1** *vti* GIVE MONEY FOR SPECIFIC PURPOSE to give money to something, such as a fund or charity, for a specific purpose, along with others ○ *Some organizations contribute thousands to charity.* **2** *vi* BE PARTIAL CAUSE to be one of the factors that causes something ○ *a heart condition that contributed to his early death* **3** *vti* OFFER OPINION to offer opinions or advice in a meeting or discussion ○ *I felt I had nothing new to contribute to the debate on sanctions.* **4** *vti* PROVIDE WORKS FOR PUBLICATION to supply material for a publication or broadcast [Mid-16C. < Latin *contribut-*, past participle of *contribuere* 'bring in together' < *tribuere* 'to grant'.] —**contributive** *adj* —**contributively** *adv* —**contributiveness** *n* —**contributor** *n*

USAGE The traditional pronunciation of ***contribute*** is with the stress on the second syllable; stress on the first syllable is increasingly heard.

contribution /kóntri byoósh'n/ *n* **1** SOMETHING GIVEN something given, such as money or time, especially to a common fund or for a specific purpose **2** REGULAR PAYMENT a regular fixed amount paid, e.g., to a pension fund, often deducted from somebody's wage ○ *national insurance contributions* **3** ROLE PLAYED IN ACHIEVING SOMETHING the part played by somebody or something in causing a particular result ○ *She recognized the contribution of her parents to her success.* **4** MATERIAL SUPPLIED FOR PUBLICATION OR BROADCAST a piece of material that forms part of a publication or broadcast

contributory /kən tríbbyōōtəri/ *adj* **1** HELPING SOMETHING HAPPEN partly responsible for something ○ *Poor diet is often a contributory factor.* **2** GIVEN ALONG WITH OTHERS given with others to a common fund or project **3** REQUIRING EMPLOYEE TO PAY IN PART describes a pension or insurance scheme that requires premiums to be paid by the employee as well as by the employer ■ *n* (*plural* **-ries**) GIVER OF MONEY OR TIME somebody who donates money or effort

contributory negligence *n* a victim's share in the responsibility for an accident, when care to prevent it could have been taken by the victim as well as the other party

con trick *n* a confidence trick (*informal*)

contrite /kón trīt, kən trī́t/ *adj* **1** deeply sorry for behaving wrongly **2** done or said out of a sense of guilt or remorse ○ *full of contrite promises* [13C. Via French *contrit* < Latin *contritus*, past participle of *contrerere* 'rub together' < *terere* 'to rub'.] —**contritely** *adv* —**contriteness** *n*

contrition /kən trísh'n/ *n* **1** deep and genuine feelings of guilt and remorse **2** in the Roman Catholic church, repentance for past sins and a firm resolve not to sin in future ○ *acts of contrition*

contrivance /kən trī́v'nss/ *n* **1** GADGET a cleverly made device or machine to fulfil a particular need ○ *a contrivance for keeping your back straight* **2** DEVIOUS PLOT a plan intended to deceive **3** SCHEMING the making of clever or deceitful schemes

contrive /kən trī́v/ (**-trives, -triving, -trived**) *v* **1** *vti* DO SOMETHING CREATIVELY to accomplish something by being clever and creative ○ *She contrived a meeting between the warring factions.* **2** *vt* MAKE SOMETHING INGENIOUS to make something in a skilful or ingenious way ○ *A tree house had been contrived from bits of scrap.* **3** *vt* MANAGE TO DO to accomplish something difficult or unexpected ○ *She somehow contrived to be both an effective and a well-liked teacher.* **4** *vti* PLOT to formulate clever or deceitful schemes ○ *The gang contrived a way to hack into the main computer system.* [13C. Via Old French *contro(u)ver* 'invent' < medieval Latin *contropare* 'compare' < Latin *tropus* 'turn, manner' < Greek *tropos*.] —**contrivable** *adj* —**contriver** *n*

contrived /kən trī́vd/ *adj* **1** deliberately planned to appear spontaneous or genuine ○ *Her apology was very contrived.* **2** unrealistic and unconvincing ○ *a film with a contrived ending* —**contrivedly** /kən trī́vidli/ *adv*

⚡**control** /kən trṓl/ *vt* (**-trols, -trolling, -trolled**) **1** OPERATE MACHINE to work or operate something such as a vehicle or machine ○ *Computers control many of the safety features on board.* **2** RESTRAIN OR LIMIT to limit or restrict the occurrence or expression of somebody or something, especially to keep it from appearing, increasing, or spreading ○ *The government set out to control inflation.* **3** MANAGE to exercise power or authority over something such as a business or nation ○ *The company is controlled largely by foreign interests.* **4** OVERSEE FINANCIAL AFFAIRS to regulate the financial affairs of a business or other large organization **5** VERIFY ACCOUNTS to examine financial accounts and verify them as correct ■ *n* **1** ABILITY TO MANAGE ability or authority to manage or direct something ○ *circumstances beyond our control* **2** OPERATING SWITCH a mechanical or electronic device used to operate a vehicle or machine ○ *Turn down the heat control* **3** SKILL skill in using something or in performing (*often in combination*) ○ *players with excellent ball control* **4** LIMITS AND RESTRICTIONS the limiting or restricting of something ○ *an era of price and wage control* **5** PLACE OF INSPECTION OR DIRECTION a place at which something is checked or inspected or from which something is directed (*usually in combination*) ○ *passengers filing through passport control* **6** COMPARATIVE STANDARD IN EXPERIMENT a subject taking part in an experiment or survey who is not involved in the procedures affecting the rest of the experiment, thus acting as the standard against which the results are compared **7** SUPERVISING PERSON OR GROUP somebody or a group that supervises or monitors operations or operatives ○ *Their intelligence agents report to control twice a week* **8** COMPUT = **control key** **9** SPIRIT THAT SUPPOSEDLY GUIDES SEANCE a spirit that is believed to help a medium gain access to other spirits being called up in a seance ■ **controls** *npl* **1** MEANS OF CONTROLLING the system by which a machine is operated ○ *nobody at the controls* **2** REGULATIONS a regulatory system ○ *import controls* [15C. Via Anglo-Norman *contreroller* < medieval Latin *contrarotulare* 'check against a duplicate register' < *rotulus* (see ROLL).] —**controllability** /kən trṓlə bílləti/ *n* —**controllable** *adj* —**controllably** *adv*

control freak *n* somebody who exerts an excessive control over others and his or her own life (*slang*)

control gene *n* a gene that regulates the development and specialization of cells

control grid *n* = **grid** *n*. 6

control group *n* in an experiment, the group of test subjects left untreated or unexposed to some procedure and then compared with treated subjects in order to validate the results of the test

⚡**control key** (*plural* **control keys**) *n* a computer key pressed together with other keys to perform particular functions

~~**controll**~~ incorrect spelling of **control**

controlled /kən trṓld/ *adj* **1** DONE WITH SKILL AND DISCIPLINE showing the skill, judgment, and discipline needed in order to achieve a desired result, without doing too little or too much ○ *His controlled performance as Lear was masterful.* **2** CAREFULLY REGULATED carefully measured and regulated, especially in relation to medical treatments or scientific experiments ○ *They tested the effectiveness of controlled doses of the drug.* **3 KEPT UNDER CONTROL** kept in check and not expressed fully or at all ○ *She spoke with scarcely controlled fury.*

controlled substance *n* a substance subject to statutory control, especially a drug that can be obtained legally only with a doctor's prescription

controlled user *n* a drug addict who is able to maintain an otherwise normal way of life

controller /kən trólər/ *n* **1 SOMEBODY WHO CONTROLS OR ORGANIZES** somebody in a managing, supervising, or monitoring position **2 controller, comptroller FINANCIAL SUPERVISOR** somebody whose job is to oversee financial matters in a business or government department **3 CONTROLLING DEVICE** a device or mechanism that controls something, such as part of an operation —**controllership** *n*

controlling interest *n* ownership of enough of a company's shares to allow the holder to control the business

control panel *n* the collection of lights, digital displays, and switches used to monitor and control the operation of a vehicle, device, or machine

control rod *n* a rod or cylinder made of or containing neutron-absorbing material such as graphite, used to control the rate of fission in a nuclear reactor

control surface *n* a movable surface, such as a rudder or elevator, that controls the direction of an aircraft, rocket, or missile

control tower *n* a high building at an airport, from which air-traffic controllers organize the movements of incoming and outgoing aircraft by radioing to their pilots

controversial /kóntrə vúrsh'l/ *adj* **1** provoking strong disagreement or disapproval, e.g. in public debate ○ *The CEO heading the company is a controversial figure.* **2** enjoying or habitually engaging in controversy ○ *a controversial writer* —**controversialism** *n* —**controversialist** *n* —**controversiality** /kóntrə vúrshi állәti/ *n* —**controversially** *adv*

controversy /kóntrə vurssi, kən tróvvərsi/ (*plural* **-sies**) *n* disagreement on a contentious topic, strongly felt or expressed by all those concerned [14C. < Latin *controversia* < *controversus* 'disputed', literally 'turned against' < *vertere* 'to turn'.]

USAGE The traditional pronunciation of ***controversy*** is with the stress on the first syllable (on the analogy of words such as *acrimony* and *matrimony*); stress on the second syllable is increasingly heard.

controvert /kóntrə vúrt/ *vt* to argue strongly against something [Mid-16C. < Latin *contro-* 'against' + *vertere* 'to turn'.] —**controverter** *n* —**controvertible** *adj* —**controvertibly** *adv*

contumacy /kóntyoǒmәssi/ *n* **1** flagrant disobedience or rebelliousness **2** persistent refusal to appear in court or to obey a court order without good reason [13C. < Latin *contumacia* < *contumac-* 'insolent'.] —**contumacious** /kóntyoǒ máyshəss/ *adj* —**contumaciously** *adv* —**contumaciousness** *n*

contumelious /kóntyoǒ meéli əss/ *adj* having or showing an insulting, scornful, or contemptuous attitude (*archaic or literary*) —**contumeliously** *adv* —**contumeliousness** *n*

contumely /kón tyoomli/ (*plural* **-lies**) *n* (*archaic or literary*) **1** insulting, scornful, or contemptuous language or treatment **2** an openly insulting, scornful, or contemptuous remark [14C. Via Old French *contumelie* < Latin *contumelia*.]

contuse /kən tyoóz/ (**-tuses, -tusing, -tused**) *vt* to bruise a body part (*technical*) [14C. < Latin *contus-*, past participle of *contundere* 'beat small' < *tundere* 'to beat'.]

contusion /kən tyoózh'n/ *n* an injury to the body in which skin and bone are not broken, but damage is done to tissues under the skin, causing a bruise or bruises (*technical*)

conundrum /kə núndrəm/ *n* **1** a riddle, especially one with an answer in the form of a play on words **2** something puzzling, confusing, or mysterious [Early 17C. < ?]

conurbation /kón ur báysh'n/ *n* a large urban area created when neighbouring towns spread into and merge with each other [Early 20C. < CON- + Latin *urb-* 'city'.]

SYNONYMS See ***city***.

Conv. *abbr* Conventual

convalesce /kónvə léss/ (**-lesces, -lescing, -lesced**) *vi* to spend time recovering from an illness or medical treatment, especially by resting [15C. < Latin *convalescere* < *valescere* 'grow strong' < *valere* 'be strong'.]

convalescent /kónvə léss'nt/ *n* a patient who is recovering from illness or the effects of medical treatment —**convalescence** *n* —**convalescent** *adj*

convection /kən véksh'n/ *n* **1** circulatory movement in a liquid or gas, resulting from regions of different temperatures and different densities rising and falling in response to gravity **2** heat transfer within the atmosphere involving the upward movement of huge volumes of warm air, leading to subsequent condensation and cloud formation [Mid-19C. < late Latin *convection-* < Latin *convehere* 'bring together' < *vehere* 'carry'.] —**convectional** *adj* —**convective** *adj* —**convectively** *adv*

convector /kən véktər/ *n* a heater that depends on convection of air to transfer heat from the heating element [Early 20C. < CONVECTION.]

convene /kən veén/ (**-venes, -vening, -vened**) *v* **1** *vti* to come together for or arrange a formal meeting ○ *A meeting of the working group has been convened for tomorrow* **2** *vt* to order somebody to appear before a court, tribunal, or other decision-making body [15C. < Latin *convenire* 'come together' < *venire* 'come'.] —**convenable** *adj* —**convener** *n*

~~**conveniant**~~ incorrect spelling of **convenient**

convenience /kən veéni ənss/ *n* **1 QUALITY OF BEING CONVENIENT** the quality of being easy, useful, or suitable ○ *have the convenience of working at home* **2 SOMEBODY'S PERSONAL COMFORT** personal comfort, or circumstances that promote somebody's personal comfort ○ *All rooms have cooking facilities, for our guests' convenience.* **3 SOMETHING PROVIDING EASE OR COMFORT** something that makes life easier or more comfortable, especially a labour-saving device ○ *apartments supplied with every modern convenience* **4 LAVATORY** a lavatory, especially in a public place

convenience food *n* packaged food that can be prepared quickly and easily, e.g. tinned foods and cook-chill meals

convenience store *n* a small shop near a residential area that stocks food and general household goods and is open all or most of the day and night

convenient /kən veéni ənt/ *adj* useful or suitable, because it makes things easier, is close by, or does not involve much effort or trouble ○ *Choose a time convenient for you.* [14C. < Latin *convenient-*, present participle of *convenire* (see CONVENE).] —**conveniently** *adv*

convent /kónvənt/ *n* **1** a community of women who live a life devoted largely to religious worship **2** the building occupied by a community of religious women [13C. Via Anglo-Norman *covent* < Latin *conventus* 'assembly' < *convenire* (see CONVENE).]

conventicle /kən véntik'l/ *n* an unlawful or secret religious gathering or the building where it is held [14C. < Latin *conventiculum* 'small assembly' < *convenire* (see CONVENE).] —**conventicler** *n*

convention /kən vénsh'n/ *n* **1 GATHERING** a gathering of people who have a common interest or profession ○ *He's attending a sales convention in Manchester.* **2 PEOPLE ATTENDING FORMAL MEETING** the people present at a convention **3 FORMAL AGREEMENT** an agreement between groups, especially an international agreement slightly less formal than a treaty ○ *under the terms of the Geneva Convention* **4 USUAL WAY OF DOING THINGS** the customary way in which things are done within a group ○ *designs that flout convention* **5 FAMILIAR DEVICE** a standard technique or well-used device, especially in the arts ○ *Her style does not follow the usual literary conventions.* **6 CODED BID** a bid in bridge intended for a partner to understand differently from its face value, because of a pre-arranged bidding system [15C. Via French < Latin *convention-* < *convenire* (see CONVENE).]

conventional /kən vénsh'nəl/ *adj* **1 SOCIALLY ACCEPTED** conforming to socially accepted customs of behaviour or style, especially in a way that lacks imagination ○ *the conventional white wedding dress* **2 USUAL OR ESTABLISHED** using well-established methods or styles ○ *conventional cooking in an oven rather than a microwave* **3 RELATING TO A GATHERING** relating to a large gathering of people with a common interest or purpose **4 WITHOUT NUCLEAR ENERGY** not involving the use of nuclear weapons or energy **5 BASED ON CONSENT** based or dependent on the consent of the various parties —**conventionalism** *n* —**conventionalist** *n* —**conventionally** *adv*

conventionalise *vt* = **conventionalize**

conventionality /kən vénshənállәti/ (*plural* **-ties**) *n* **1** adherence to social conventions in behaviour, tastes, or methods **2** a socially accepted way of behaving or of doing something ○ *the conventionalities of a formal occasion*

conventionalize /kən vénsh'nə līz/ (**-izes, -izing, -ized**), **conventionalise** (**-ises, -ising, -ised**) *vt* to make conventional, especially in style or taste ○ *His flights of fancy had become conventionalized as the Gothic style.* —**conventionalization** /kən vénsh'nə lī záysh'n/ *n*

conventional wisdom *n* a generally held view, notion, or opinion ○ *Conventional wisdom dictates that such skills merit high rewards.*

convention bounce *n US* an increase in the support for a presidential candidate following nomination at a party convention (*informal*)

conventioneer /kən vénshəneér/ *n US* a participant in a convention

conventual /kən vénchoo əl/ *adj* relating to or resembling a convent in quietness, simplicity, or discipline ○ *living a quiet conventual life* ■ *n* a woman who lives in a convent —**conventually** *adv*

Conventual *n* a member of a branch of a Franciscan order of friars who live a less austere life than in other branches

converge /kən vúrj/ (**-verges, -verging, -verged**) *vi* **1 MEET** to reach the same point coming from different directions ○ *the place where the roads converge* **2 BECOME THE SAME** to become gradually less different and eventually the same ○ *political beliefs that were rapidly converging* **3 ARRIVE AT SAME DESTINATION** to gather or meet at the same destination ○ *Delegates from all over the world are converging on the city of New York.* **4 APPROACH FINITE LIMIT** to approach a finite limit as the number of terms in an infinite series increases **5 DEVELOP SIMILAR CHARACTERISTICS** to develop superficially similar characteristics independently in response to a set of environmental conditions, e.g. the development of wings in birds and insects [Late 17C. < late Latin *convergere* 'lean together' < Latin *vergere* 'to bend'.]

⚡**convergence** /kən vúrjənss/ *n* **1 convergence, convergency COMING TOGETHER** a coming together from different directions, especially a uniting or merging of groups or tendencies that were originally opposed or very different **2 convergence, convergency SERIES WITH CONSTANT OR INCREASING DIFFERENCES** the characteristic of a series or sequence of numbers in which the difference between each term and the following term remains constant or increases. ◊ **divergence** *n.* 7 **3 SIMILAR EVOLUTIONARY DEVELOPMENT** the tendency of different species to develop similar characteristics in response to a set of environmental conditions. ◊ **divergence** *n.* 6 **4 MEETING OF AIR MASSES** the meeting of different air masses, often resulting in vertical air currents **5 TURNING THE EYES INWARDS** the turning inwards of both eyes in order to look at something nearer than the previous object viewed **6 INTEGRATION OF IT SERVICES** automated mapping and integration of information technology environments available to a user —**convergent** *adj*

convergent evolution *n* BIOL = **convergence** *n.* 3

convergent margin *n* a boundary between two tectonic plates that are moving together, one dipping under the other

conversant /kən vúrs'nt/ *adj* knowing about something, or familiar with it, from experience or study ○ *not conversant with local customs* [14C. < French, present participle of *converser* < Latin *conversare* (see CONVERSE[1]).] —**conversance** *n* —**conversantly** *adv*

⚡**conversation** /kónvər sáysh'n/ *n* **1 CASUAL TALK** an informal talk with somebody, especially about opinions, ideas, feelings, or everyday matters ○ *a telephone conversation* **2 TALKING** the activity of talking to somebody informally ○ *in conversation with one of the cleaners* **3 REAL-TIME INTERACTION WITH COMPUTER** an interaction with a computer carried on in real time **4 NONVERBAL EXCHANGE** a nonverbal exchange or interaction ○ *Critics spoke of the conversation between the new building and its neighbours.* [14C. Via French < Latin *conversation-* < *conversari* 'turn yourself about' < *conversare* (see CONVERSE[1]).]

conversational /kónvər sáysh'nəl/ *adj* 1 CONNECTED WITH CONVERSATION relating to informal talking, especially to the ability to say interesting things 2 INFORMAL IN LANGUAGE informal in language and style, and usually dealing with simple subjects ○ *She writes in an easy conversational style.* 3 APPROPRIATE FOR INFORMAL TALK suitable in style and vocabulary for informal talk on simple subjects, usually applied to skill in a foreign language ○ *conversational German* —**conversationally** *adv*

conversationalist /kónvər sáysh'nəlist/, **conversationist** /-sáysh'nist/ *n* a talker who enjoys conversation and can converse in an enjoyable way ○ *Her husband's not much of a conversationalist.*

conversation piece *n* 1 something that attracts people's interest and leads to conversation ○ *I don't think much of the sculpture in their front garden, but it makes a good conversation piece.* 2 a portrait painting of a group of stylish people in a domestic or landscape setting

conversazione /kónvə satsi ṓni/ (*plural* **-ni** /-ṓni/ *or* **-nes**) *n* a social gathering to hear a talk on or discuss a topic related to the arts (*formal*) [Mid-18C. < Italian, 'conversation' < Latin *conversare* (see CONVERSE[1]).]

⚡**converse**[1] *vi* /kən vúrss/ (**-verses, -versing, -versed**) 1 TALK to have a conversation ○ *a place where they can converse uninterrupted* 2 INTERACT WITH COMPUTER to interact with a computer as if engaged in a dialogue ■ *n* /kón vurss/ CONVERSATION conversation (*archaic*) ○ *They were deep in converse with one another.* [14C. Via French *converser* < Latin *conversare* 'live with' < *versari* 'occupy yourself' < *vertere* 'to turn'.] —**converser** *n*

converse[2] /kón vurss/ *n* 1 OPPOSITE the opposite of something ○ *Actually, the converse is true.* 2 REVERSED CATEGORICAL SENTENCE a categorical sentence in which the subject and predicate have been reversed, e.g. 'all dogs are collies' from 'all collies are dogs' ■ *adj* OPPOSITE opposite or reverse [14C. < Latin *conversus*, past participle of *convertere* (see CONVERT).] —**conversely** *adv*

conversion /kən vúrsh'n/ *n* 1 ALTERATION a change in the nature, form, or function of something ○ *a conversion of waste land into a sports field* 2 SOMETHING ALTERED something that has been changed in nature, form, or function, especially a building or room ○ *a loft conversion* 3 CHANGE OF MEASURING SYSTEM a change from one measuring or calculating system to another, or a calculation done to bring about the change ○ *the conversion from miles to kilometres* 4 CHANGING OF SOMEBODY'S BELIEFS an adoption of new opinions or beliefs, especially in religion ○ *his conversion to Islam* 5 KICK FOLLOWING TRY OR TOUCHDOWN in American football or rugby, a kicking of the ball over the crossbar following a try or touchdown, and the score made with a successful kick 6 REVERSING TERMS IN CATEGORICAL SENTENCE the reversing of the subject and predicate in a categorical sentence, forming a new sentence, e.g. 'all dogs are collies' from 'all collies are dogs' 7 UNLAWFUL HOLDING OF ANOTHER'S PROPERTY unlawful treating of somebody else's property as your own 8 CHANGING OF PROPERTY CLASSIFICATION the changing of one type of property to another, e.g. from joint to separate property [14C. Via French < Latin *conversion-* < *convers-*, past participle of *convertere* (see CONVERT).] —**conversional** *adj* —**conversionary** *adj*

conversion disorder *n* a neurosis marked by the appearance of physical symptoms, such as partial loss of muscle function, without physical cause but in the presence of psychological conflict

convert *v* /kən vúrt/ 1 *vti* CHANGE SOMETHING'S CHARACTER to change the nature or form of something, or to be changed in nature or form ○ *a process for converting waste into usable fuel* 2 *vti* CHANGE SOMETHING'S FUNCTION to change the function or use of something, or be able to change in function or use ○ *sofas that convert into beds* 3 *vt* CHANGE MEASURING OR CALCULATING UNITS to change units of one measuring or calculating system into units of another ○ *the formula for converting litres into gallons* 4 *vti* CHANGE SOMEBODY'S BELIEFS to adopt new opinions or beliefs, or to change the opinions or beliefs of another, especially religious beliefs ○ *His wife converted to Judaism.* 5 *vti* KICK TO ADD ON POINTS in rugby, to add to the points awarded for a try by following it with a successful kick of the ball over the crossbar 6 *vt* REVERSE TERMS IN CATEGORICAL SENTENCE reverse the subject and predicate in a categorical sentence, forming a new sentence, e.g. 'all dogs are collies' from 'all collies are dogs' 7 *vt* UNLAWFULLY HOLD ANOTHER'S PROPERTY to treat unlawfully somebody else's property as your own 8 *vt* CHANGE CLASSIFICATION OF PROPERTY to change the classification of property, e.g. from joint to separate property, in the course of certain transactions ■ *n* /kón vurt/ SOMEBODY WITH CHANGED BELIEFS somebody who has chosen a new way of life or a new set of beliefs ○ *ex-conservative converts to liberalism* [13C. Via Old French *convertir* < Latin *convertere* 'turn around' < *vertere* 'to turn'.] ◇ **preach to the converted** to advocate a viewpoint to people who already have it

SYNONYMS See ***change***.

⚡**converter** /kən vúrtər/, **convertor** *n* 1 DEVICE THAT CONVERTS a device that converts something, e.g. an electrical device that converts alternating current into direct current 2 FREQUENCY CHANGER an electronic component for changing one frequency to another 3 FURNACE a furnace for refining molten metal 4 DATA CODE CHANGER in computing, a device for changing data from one form to another, e.g. from analogue to digital 5 INDUST = **converter reactor**

converter reactor *n* a nuclear reactor that converts one nuclear fuel into another, especially fertile into fissile material

convertible /kən vúrtəb'l/ *adj* 1 CAPABLE OF BEING CONVERTED capable of being changed from one form, function, or use to another 2 EXCHANGEABLE FOR GOLD OR ANOTHER CURRENCY able to be legally exchanged for gold or for another currency 3 EXCHANGEABLE FOR STOCK exchangeable for other assets, especially a fixed number of shares in ordinary stock ■ *n* CAR WITH REMOVABLE ROOF a car with a roof that can be folded back or taken off —**convertibility** /kən vúrtə bíllәti/ *n* —**convertibly** *adv*

convertor *n* = **converter**

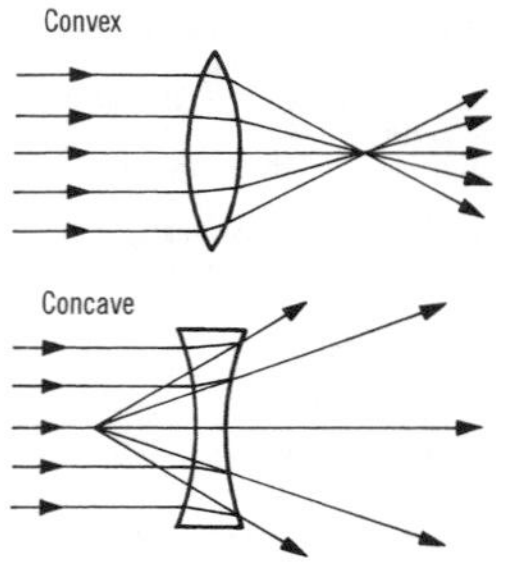

Convex: convex and concave lenses

convex /kón veks, kon véks/ *adj* 1 OUTWARDLY CURVING with a surface that curves outwards rather than inwards 2 SHAPED LIKE A SPHERE'S EXTERIOR shaped like the exterior of a sphere, paraboloid, ellipsoid, or any other outwardly curved surface ○ *a convex lens* 3 CONTAINING NO ANGLE ABOVE 180° describes a polygon with no interior angle greater than 180° ■ *vti* CURVE OUTWARDS to curve outwards, or make something curve outwards [Late 16C. < Latin *convexus* 'vaulted, arched'.] —**convexly** /kón veksli/ *adv*

convexity /kon véksəti/ (*plural* **-ties**) *n* 1 outwardly curving quality 2 an outwardly curving surface or part

convexo-concave /kon véksō konkáyv/ *adj* describes a lens that is convex on one side and concave on the other

convexo-convex *adj* describes a lens that is convex on both sides

convey /kən váy/ (**-veys, -veying, -veyed**) *vt* 1 TAKE SOMEWHERE to take somebody or something somewhere (*formal*) 2 COMMUNICATE to communicate something and make it known ○ *a look that conveyed all the tenderness he felt for her* 3 MEAN have something as a meaning or connotation ○ *'Majesty' conveys grandeur.* 4 TRANSFER THROUGH CARRIER to transfer or transmit something along a wire, pipe, tube, or other carrier 5 TRANSFER OWNERSHIP to transfer ownership of something ○ *The title to the property was conveyed last June.* [14C. Via Old French *conveier* < medieval Latin *conviare* 'go together on the road' < Latin *via* 'road'.] —**conveyable** *adj*

conveyance /kən váyənss/ *n* 1 MOVING the conveying of something, especially the transportation or transmission of something from one place to another ○ *the conveyance of information from the mainland to the islands* 2 VEHICLE a vehicle or other means of transportation (*formal*) ○ *public conveyances* 3 TRANSFER OF OWNERSHIP a document that legally transfers ownership, or the transfer itself —**conveyancer** *n* —**conveyancing** *n*

conveyor /kən váyər/ *n* 1 a device that transports or transmits something, especially a conveyor belt 2 a person or thing that transmits something, especially news ○ *a conveyor of good tidings*

conveyor belt *n* a device that consists typically of a continuous wide flat rubber loop moved by electrically operated rollers, used to move objects from one place to another nearby

convict *v* /kən víkt/ 1 *vt* DECLARE SOMEBODY GUILTY to declare somebody guilty of a crime in a court of law (*often passive*) ○ *had been previously convicted of fraud* 2 *vi* ARRIVE AT GUILTY VERDICT to reach a verdict of guilty ○ *juries who will convict on the slimmest evidence* 3 *vt* SHOW TO BE AT FAULT to show that somebody is in the wrong in some respect ○ *actions that convicted her of selfishness* ■ *n* /kón vikt/ SOMEBODY IN PRISON somebody serving a prison sentence ○ *an escaped convict* [14C. < Latin *convict-*, past participle of *convincere* (see CONVINCE).] —**convictable** *adj*

conviction /kən víksh'n/ *n* 1 FIRMLY HELD BELIEF a belief or opinion that is held firmly ○ *It's my conviction that they are lying.* 2 FIRMNESS OF BELIEF firmness of belief or opinion ○ *said with complete conviction* 3 GUILTY VERDICT the finding or an instance of finding somebody guilty or of being found guilty of a crime ○ *The accused has no previous convictions.* —**convictional** *adj*

USAGE conviction or **persuasion**? ***Conviction*** is 'a firmly held belief' and 'firmness of belief': *It is my conviction* [not *persuasion*] *that the defendant's rights have been violated. I say this with utter conviction* [not *persuasion*]: *we are headed for a recession.* ***Persuasion*** is 'the act or ability to get someone else to accept your opinion, belief, or viewpoint', 'a set of beliefs', and 'a group of people with particular beliefs', as in *used great persuasion in conveying her position to the voters; a politician of the conservative persuasion.*

convince /kən vínss/ (**-vinces, -vincing, -vinced**) *vt* 1 to make somebody sure or certain of something ○ *We are convinced of his guilt.* 2 to persuade somebody to believe or do something ○ *Nothing would convince them to invest in such a scheme.* [Mid-16C. < Latin *convincere* 'prove wrong' < *vincere* 'overcome'.] —**convincer** *n* —**convincible** *adj*

USAGE convince or **persuade**? Traditionally, to ***convince*** somebody is to bring him or her round to an opinion, and to ***persuade*** somebody is to induce him or her to act: *She convinced him that he had talent and persuaded him to study music.* Because of this distinction, some people object to the use of an infinitive after ***convince***, pointing out that *She convinced him to...* will tend to involve action. Nonetheless, the distinction is quickly disappearing by force of widespread usage, and constructions like this one are increasingly seen in the work of reputable writers: *After a long series of tests I was convinced to go ahead with the surgery despite the risks.*

convincing /kən vínssing/ *adj* 1 PERSUASIVE persuading somebody to believe something is true or real ○ *The special effects were very convincing.* 2 ABLE TO PERSUADE PEOPLE skilled at making people believe something ○ *a convincing impostor* 3 BEYOND DOUBT impressively clear or definite ○ *a convincing victory* —**convincingly** *adv*

SYNONYMS See ***valid***.

convivial /kən vívvi əl/ *adj* 1 enjoyable because of its friendliness ○ *spent many a convivial evening at the pub* 2 enjoying the company of others ○ *He was famously convivial.* [Mid-17C. < Latin *convivialis* < *convivium* 'feast' < *vivere* 'live'.] —**convivialist** *n* —**conviviality** /kən vívvi álləti/ *n* —**convivially** *adv*

convocation /kónvə káysh'n/ *n* 1 a large formal assembly, e.g. the senior members of a church or the members of a university council 2 the arranging or calling of a formal meeting [14C. < Latin *convocation-* < *convocare* (see CONVOKE).] —**convocator** /kónvə kaytər/ *n*

convoke /kən vṓk/ (**-vokes, -voking, -voked**) *vt* to call a formal meeting or call people together for such a meeting [Late 16C. < Latin *convocare* 'call together' < *vocare* 'to call'.] —**convocative** /-vókətiv/ *adj* —**convoker** *n*

convolute /kónvə loot/ *vti* (**-lutes, -luting, -luted**) to twist or coil something in folds ○ *The snake's coils were tightly convoluted.* ■ *adj* describes petals or leaves that are rolled from the sides so that one side is wrapped around the other [Late 17C. < Latin *convolut-*, past participle of *convolvere* 'twist round' < *volvere* 'to roll'.] —**convolutely** *adv*

convoluted /kónvə lootid/ *adj* 1 too complex or intricate to understand easily ○ *convoluted sentences* 2 having many twists, coils, or whorls ○ *the brain's convoluted surface* —**convolutedly** *adv* —**convolutedness** *n*

convolution /kónvə lo͞osh'n/ *n* 1 TWISTED SHAPE a curve, coil, or twist 2 TWISTED RIDGE ON BRAIN SURFACE any of the ridges on the brain's surface 3 INTRICACY a complexity or intricacy, especially one of many ○ *The plot had so many convolutions it was difficult to follow.* —**convolutional** *adj* —**convolutionary** *adj*

convolvulus /kən vólvyo͝oləss/ (*plural* **-luses** *or* **-li** /-lī/) *n* a plant of the morning-glory family, many of which have a twining growth habit, including bindweed. Flowers: trumpet-shaped. Genus: *Convolvulus.* [Mid-16C. < Latin, < *convolvere* (see CONVOLUTE).]

convoy /kón voy/ *n* 1 VEHICLES OR SHIPS TRAVELLING TOGETHER a group of vehicles or ships travelling together, often with an escort for protection ○ *travelling in convoy* 2 VEHICLES' OR SHIPS' ESCORT a protective escort for a group of vehicles or ships ■ *vt* ESCORT VEHICLES OR SHIPS to travel as an escort to protect a group of vehicles or ships [14C. < French *convoi* < Old French *conveier* (see CONVEY).]

convulsant /kən vúlss'nt/ *adj* causing convulsions ■ *n* a drug that causes convulsions

convulse /kən vúlss/ (**-vulses, -vulsing, -vulsed**) *v* 1 *vti* SHAKE UNCONTROLLABLY to jerk or shake violently and uncontrollably, or to make a muscle or body part go into repetitive spasm 2 *vt* CAUSE TO SHAKE to make somebody shake with laughter or a strong emotion (*often passive*) ○ *convulsed with panic* 3 *vt* DISRUPT to cause extreme disruption or disturbance in something ○ *Problems in the Asian economies convulsed the London markets.* [Mid-17C. < Latin *convuls-*, past participle of *convellere* 'pull violently' < *vellere* 'to pull'.]

convulsion /kən vúlsh'n/ *n* (*often plural*) 1 UNCONTROLLABLE SHAKING a violent shaking of the body or limbs caused by uncontrollable muscle contractions, which can be a symptom of brain disorders and other conditions 2 DISTURBANCE an extreme disruption or disturbance (*literary*) ■ **convulsions** *npl* LAUGHTER fits of laughter —**convulsionary** *adj*

convulsive /kən vúlssiv/ *adj* 1 sudden, jerky, or uncontrollable 2 undergoing or producing uncontrollable jerking of the body or limbs —**convulsively** *adv* —**convulsiveness** *n*

Conwy /kónwi/ town and local government district in North Wales. Population: town 13,627 (1991); district 111,200 (1995).

cony /kṓni/ (*plural* **-nies**), **coney** (*plural* **-neys**) *n* 1 *US* a rabbit, especially the common domesticated European rabbit 2 rabbit fur used for coats and other articles of clothing 3 ZOOL = **hyrax** 4 ZOOL = **pika** [14C. Via Anglo-Norman < Latin *cuniculus* 'rabbit, burrow'.]

coo /koo/ *v* (**coos, cooing, cooed**) 1 *vi* MAKE SOUND OF PIGEON to make the soft warbling sound that is characteristic of pigeons 2 *vti* SPEAK VERY TENDERLY to speak or say something with affected or exaggerated admiration ■ *n* (*plural* **coos**) BIRD'S SOUND the soft warbling sound that pigeons make ■ *interj* EXPRESSING SURPRISE used to express surprise or wonder (*informal*) ○ *Coo! Look at all that money!* [Mid-17C. An imitation of the sound.]

COO *abbr* Chief Operating Officer

Coober Pedy /ko͞obər péedi/ town in South Australia, noted for its underground dwellings, built by opal miners seeking to escape the heat. Population: 2,492 (1991).

co-occur (**co-occurs, co-occurring, co-occurred**) *vi* 1 to happen at the same time and place 2 to appear together in the same contexts (*refers to linguistic elements, for example sounds*) —**co-occurrence** *n*

cooee /ko͞o ee/ *interj, n* a call used to attract somebody's attention (*informal*) [Late 18C. An imitation of a high-pitched cry used by Australian Aboriginals.]

cook /ko͝ok/ *v* 1 *vti* PREPARE FOOD to prepare food for a meal 2 *vti* MAKE OR BECOME HOT to make food safe and appetizing by heating it, or to undergo heating in order to become ready to eat ○ *The onions have been cooking for a while.* ○ *Cook the beef until it is tender.* 3 *vi* BE UNCOMFORTABLE IN HEAT to feel extreme discomfort in hot conditions (*informal*) ○ *cooking in an overcrowded bus* 4 *vt* CHANGE IN ORDER TO DECEIVE to alter or tamper with information or evidence fraudulently (*informal*) 5 *vi* HAPPEN to be happening or developing (*informal*) ○ *I had the feeling that something was cooking.* 6 *vt* HEAT ILLEGAL DRUG to heat an illegal drug, e.g. heroin (*slang*) ■ *n* SOMEBODY WHO PREPARES FOOD person who prepares and cooks food, usually as a job, or who cooks food in a given way ○ *an uninventive cook* [Pre-12C. Via assumed vulgar Latin *cocus* 'cook' < Latin *coquus* < *coquere* 'to cook'.] —**cookable** *adj*

cook up *vt* 1 to prepare or improvise a meal quickly 2 to invent something untrue or dishonest such as an excuse (*informal*) 3 = **cook** *v.* 6 (*slang*)

Cook, Mount /ko͝ok/ highest mountain in New Zealand, in the Southern Alps on the South Island. Height: 3,754 m/12,316 ft.

Cook, James, Captain (1728–79) British explorer and cartographer

Cook, Sir Joseph (1860–1947) British-born Australian statesman

Cook, Peter (1937–95) British actor and comedian

Cook, Thomas (1808–92) British travel agent

cookbook /ko͝ok bo͝ok/ *n* = **cookery book**

cook-chill *adj* describes food that is cooked, packaged, and refrigerated, and then reheated before serving ■ *n* the preparation of cook-chill food

cooker /ko͝okər/ *n* 1 *UK* APPLIANCE FOR COOKING a box-shaped kitchen appliance for cooking food, powered by electricity, gas, or solid fuel, and including an oven, grill, and hob 2 DEVICE THAT COOKS a device that cooks something, especially in a particular way ○ *a slow cooker* 3 APPLE FOR COOKING a type of apple, usually large and sour, that is more suitable for cooking than for eating raw (*informal*)

cookery /ko͝okəri/ *n* 1 the skill or activity of preparing food 2 a type or style of cooking, such as a national variety or one that meets specific dietary requirements

cookery book *n* a book containing recipes for preparing food

⚡**cookie** /ko͝oki/, **cooky** (*plural* **-ies**) *n* 1 *US* FOOD = **biscuit** *n.* 1 2 a person with a specified characteristic (*informal*) ○ *She's a tough cookie.* 3 a computer file containing information about a user that is sent to the central computer with each request and used to customize data sent back to the user [Early 18C. < Dutch *koekje* 'little cake' < *koek* 'cake'.]

cookie-cutter *adj US* seemingly mass-produced without distinctive features

cooking /ko͝oking/ *n* 1 PREPARATION OF FOOD the skill or practice of preparing food 2 PREPARED FOOD food that has been prepared for eating ○ *She doesn't like my cooking.* ■ *adj* USED IN COOKING intended for use in cooking rather than for consumption on its own

Cook Islands self-governing island group in free association with New Zealand, in the South Pacific Ocean. Population: 18,617 (1991). Area: 237 sq. km/92 sq. mi.

Cookson /ko͝oks'n/, **Dame Catherine Ann** (1906–98) British novelist. Pseudonym **Catherine Merchant, Catherine Fawcett**

Cook's tour /ko͝oks táwr/ *n* a quick tour or survey, with attention only to the main features (*informal*) ○ *The book doesn't aim to give anything more than a Cook's tour of European history.* [After Thomas COOK]

Cookstown /ko͝oks town/ local government district in central Northern Ireland. Population: 31,300 (1995). Area: 622 sq. km/240 sq. mi.

Cook Strait area of ocean separating the North Island and the South Island of New Zealand. At its narrowest, it is 22 km/14 mi. wide.

cooktop /ko͝ok top/ *n US* a flat cooking area on a stove that includes heating units and a surface that can be used for food preparation

Cooktown /ko͝ok town/ coastal town in N Queensland, Australia. Population: 1,344 (1991).

cookware /ko͝ok wair/ *n* utensils, e.g. pots, pans, and dishes, used in cooking

⚡**cooky** *n* = **cookie**

cool /kool/ *adj* 1 COLDISH somewhat cold, usually pleasantly so 2 KEEPING TEMPERATURE LOW made of fabric that keeps the body at a pleasant temperature when it is hot 3 SEEMING COLD giving an impression of coldness ○ *a cool mint green* 4 STAYING CALM staying calm or not showing emotions, especially nervousness or fear 5 UNFRIENDLY unfriendly or unenthusiastic ○ *They gave us a rather cool reception.* 6 FASHIONABLE fashionable and sophisticated (*informal*) ○ *looking cool* 7 EXCELLENT very good (*slang*) ○ *a cool idea* 8 EMPHASIZING SUM OF MONEY used to emphasize how large a sum of money is (*informal*) ○ *a cool £3.2 million* 9 HAVING RELAXED RHYTHM describes a style of jazz, popular in the mid-20th century, characterized by a relaxed rhythm ■ *vti* 1 MAKE OR BECOME LESS WARM to become or cause somebody or something to become less warm ○ *Wait until the mixture cools.* 2 MAKE OR BECOME LESS INTENSE to make somebody or something less intense, or to become less intense ○ *anything that might cool his anger* ■ *n* 1 SLIGHT CHILL moderate coldness, especially in relation to greater heat or coldness ○ *We were glad to come back into the cool of our hotel room.* 2 CALMNESS the ability to remain calm in difficult circumstances (*informal*) 3 STYLISHNESS stylishness that is attractive without being ostentatious (*informal*) ■ *adv* CALMLY in a calm self-controlled way (*informal*) ○ *Just act cool.* ■ *interj* EXPRESSING PLEASURE used to express pleasure or excitement at a prospect or event (*slang*) ○ *You're coming too? Cool!* [Old English *cōl* < Indo-European, 'cold'] —**coolness** *n* ◇ **keep your cool** to remain calm (*informal*) ◇ **lose your cool** to become angry and excitable (*informal*)

cool down *vti* 1 to make somebody or something less warm, or to become less warm ○ *Wait till the engine cools down before you lift the bonnet.* 2 to make somebody or something calm or calmer after strong feeling or excitement, or become calm or calmer ○ *The political situation has cooled down a lot.*

cool off *v* 1 *vi* to become comfortably cool again ○ *I went for a swim to cool off.* 2 *vti* to become calm again after being angry (*informal*)

cool out *vi Carib* to relax (*informal*)

Coolangatta /ko͞olən gáttə/ coastal town in SE Queensland, Australia. Population: 3,778 (1996).

coolant /ko͞olənt/ *n* a substance, usually a liquid, used to prevent overheating in an engine or other mechanism

cool bag, cool box *n* a portable insulated container used to keep food cool outdoors. US term **cooler** *n.* 2

cooldrink /ko͞ol dringk/ *n S Africa* a soft drink

cooler /ko͞olər/ *n* 1 COOL PLACE OR CONTAINER a compartment or container in which something is cooled or kept cool 2 *US* = **cool bag** 3 COLD DRINK a refreshing drink, e.g. an iced mixture of wine, fruit juice, and soda water or a chilled nonalcoholic drink such as an iced coffee 4 PRISON a prison or prison cell (*dated slang*)

Coolgardie /kool gaárdi/ gold-mining town in S Western Australia. Population: 1,258 (1996).

cool-headed *adj* staying calm in tense situations

coolibah /ko͞olə baa/ (*plural* **-bahs** *or* **-bah**), **coolabah** (*plural* **-bahs** *or* **-bah**) *n* a smooth-barked eucalyptus tree with long leaves containing oil glands, that grows near water sources. Native to: Australia. *Eucalyptus microtheca.* [Late 19C. < Kamilaroi *gulubaa.*]

Coolidge /ko͞olij/, **Calvin** (1872–1933) US statesman and 30th president of the United States (1923–29)

coolie /ko͞oli/ *n* an offensive term in India, China, and other parts of Asia for a local man hired cheaply to do manual labour [Mid-17C. < Hindi *kūlī.*]

cooling /ko͞oling/ *adj* making you feel cooler in a pleasant way —**coolingly** *adv*

cooling-off period /ko͞oling-/ *n* 1 an agreed pause in a dispute to allow tempers to cool and peaceful solutions to be examined 2 a period of reflection allowed before making a legally binding commitment

cooling tower *n* a tall open-topped structure in which the steam produced by an industrial process is condensed

cool jazz *n* jazz with a light tone and relaxed character, popular in the mid-20th century, especially on the West Coast of the United States

coolly /ko͞ol li/ *adv* 1 in a calm or relaxed way ○ *She coolly marched up to the desk and demanded to see the manager.* 2 without friendliness or enthusiasm ○ *He greeted her coolly.*

Cooma /ko͞omə/ town in SE New South Wales, Australia. Population: 7,150 (1996).

Coomaraswamy /koo maárə swaámi/, **Ananda Kentish** (1877–1947) Sri Lankan-born Indian Orientalist

Coomassie /koo maássi/ former name for **Kumasi**

coomb /koom/, **coombe** *n* GEOG = **combe**

Coombs /koomz/, **Nuggett** (1906–97) Australian economist. Born **Herbert Cole Coombs**

coon /koon/ *n* a highly offensive term for a Black person (*taboo*) [Mid-19C. < RACCOON.]

Coonabarabran /kòònə bárrə bran/ town in N New South Wales, Australia. Population: 2,946 (1991).

cooncan /kóòn kan/ n a card game from Mexico that is similar to rummy and played with one or two packs [Late 19C. By folk etymology < American Spanish *conquián* < Spanish *con quién?* 'with whom?'.]

coop /koop/ n 1 an enclosure or hut in which poultry is kept 2 a wicker basket used for catching fish [13C. < ?] **coop up** vt to keep somebody in a confined space

co-op /kó op/, **coop** n a cooperative organization or venture, especially a marketing enterprise (*informal*) [Mid-19C. Shortening.]

cooper /kóòpər/ n somebody skilled in making and repairing wooden barrels ■ vti to make or repair wooden barrels [15C. < Middle Dutch *kūper* < *kūpe* 'cask'.]

Cooper /kóòpər/, **Gary** (1901–61) US film actor

Cooper, Henry (b. 1934) British boxer

Cooper, James Fenimore (1789–1851) US writer

Cooper, Samuel (1609–72) English miniaturist

cooperage /kóòpərij/ n 1 **COOPER'S CRAFT** the craft of making and repairing wooden barrels 2 **COOPER'S WORKPLACE** a place where wooden barrels are made and repaired 3 **COOPER'S FEE** the fee charged by a cooper for making or repairing barrels

cooperate /kō óppə rayt/ (**-ates, -ating, -ated**) v 1 vi to work or act together to achieve a common aim 2 to do what is asked or required [Late 16C. < ecclesiastical Latin *cooperat-*, past participle of *cooperari* 'work together' < Latin *operari* 'to work'.] —**cooperator** n

cooperation /kō óppə ráysh'n/ n 1 the act of working together to achieve a common aim ○ *working in cooperation with international aid agencies* 2 doing what is asked or required —**cooperationist** n

cooperative /kō óppərətiv/ adj 1 **WILLING TO HELP** doing, or willing to do, what is asked or required ○ *She's a good worker and very cooperative.* 2 **WORKING TOGETHER** working or acting together with others, or done by people working or acting together ○ *a cooperative effort* 3 **OPERATED COLLECTIVELY** owned jointly by all its members or workers, who share all profits equally ○ *a cooperative farm* ■ n **BUSINESS OWNED BY WORKERS** a business that is jointly owned by the people who run it, with all profits shared equally ○ *a workers' cooperative* —**cooperatively** adv —**cooperativeness** n

cooperative society (*plural* **cooperative societies**) n a commercial organization distributing goods to its members who participate in profit-sharing schemes

Cooper Creek /kóòpər kreèk/ river flowing from central Queensland to Lake Eyre in South Australia. Length: 800 km/500 mi.

Cooper pair n two electrons that are loosely bound together and act dynamically as a pair in a superconducting material [After the L. N. *Cooper* (b. 1930), US physicist.]

co-opt /kō ópt/ vt 1 **APPOINT BY AGREEMENT** to appoint somebody to a body by agreement with the other members 2 **TAKE INTO LARGER GROUP** to absorb an opponent or opposing group into a larger group or society by making promises and concessions 3 **ADOPT OR APPROPRIATE** to adopt or appropriate something, e.g. a political issue or idea, as your own [Mid-17C. < Latin *cooptare* 'choose mutually' < *optare* 'choose'.] —**co-optation** n —**co-option** n —**co-optive** adj

coordinate v /kō áwrdi nayt/ (**-nates, -nating, -nated**) 1 vt **ORGANIZE SOMETHING COMPLEX** to organize a complex enterprise in which numerous people are involved and bring their contributions together to form a unified whole ○ *responsible for coordinating the campaign* 2 vti **MAKE PARTS MOVE TOGETHER** to make moving parts, e.g. parts of the body, work together in sequence or in time with one another, or to work together in this way ○ *hand and eye coordinating perfectly for the overhead shot* 3 vt **PUT TOGETHER** to place or class things together ○ *Before we can proceed, all our files have to be coordinated.* 4 vi **WORK TOGETHER** to work together as a unit ○ *members of the team coordinating brilliantly* 5 vti **GO WELL TOGETHER** to make a pleasing combination or match ○ *outfit and accessories that coordinate stylishly* ■ n /kō áwrdinət/ 1 **NUMBER SPECIFYING POSITION** each of a set of numbers that together describe the exact position of something such as a place on a map with reference to a set of axes ○ *Did you receive the coordinates for your target?* 2 **SOMEBODY OR SOMETHING EQUAL** somebody or something that is equal in rank or importance ○ *We need the faculties of the college as*

coordinates in this endeavour. 3 **VARIABLE** a variable used with others to describe the state of a physical or chemical system ■ **coordinates** npl **MATCHING CLOTHES** clothes that are designed to be worn together ■ adj /kō áwrdinət/ 1 **EQUAL** equal in rank or importance ○ *The district offices should work as coordinate elements of the company.* 2 **INVOLVING SHARE OF VARIABLES** involving the use of coordinates [Mid-17C. < CO- + Latin *ordinare* 'set in order'.] — **coordinated** adj —**coordinately** adv —**coordinateness** n —**coordinative** /kō áwrdinativ/ adj

coordinate bond n a chemical bond between two atoms created by the sharing of a pair of electrons, both supplied by one atom

coordinate clause n any of two or more clauses in a sentence that have the same grammatical function or status, usually joined by a coordinating conjunction such as 'and' or 'but'. ◊ **subordinate clause**

coordinate geometry n MATH = **analytic geometry**

coordinating conjunction n a word such as 'and' or 'but' that joins two words or clauses with the same grammatical function or status

coordination /kō áwrdi náysh'n/ n 1 the combining of diverse parts or groups to make a unit, or the way these parts work together 2 the skilful and balanced movement of different parts, especially parts of the body, at the same time

coordination complex, coordination compound n a chemical compound containing one or more ions, atoms, or molecules bound by coordinate bonds to a central metallic atom

coordination number n the number of ions, atoms, or molecules attached by coordinate bonds to the metallic atom in a complex

coordinator /kō áwrdi naytər/ n 1 somebody responsible for organizing diverse parts of an enterprise or groups into a coherent or efficient whole 2 GRAM = **coordinating conjunction**

Coorong /koo róng/ long narrow salt lagoon on coast of SE South Australia. Area: 4,000 sq. km/1,500 sq. mi.

coot /koot/ (*plural* **coots** or **coot**) n 1 a water bird with long toes, darkish plumage, and a white bill and forehead. Native to: Europe, Asia, North America. Genus: *Fulica*. 2 somebody regarded as odd, eccentric, or unreasonably stubborn (*insult*) [13C. < ?]

Cootamundra /kòòtə múndrə/ city in New South Wales, Australia. Population: 6,389 (1991).

cooter /kóòtər/ n a large freshwater turtle. Native to: E United States. Genus: *Chrysemys.* [Early 19C. < Gullah.]

cop[1] /kop/ n **POLICE OFFICER** a police officer (*slang*) ■ vt (**cops, copping, copped**) 1 **GRAB** to seize or grab something (*slang*) 2 **RECEIVE PUNISHMENT** to receive or undergo something unpleasant, especially punishment (*informal*) 3 **OBTAIN DRUGS** to obtain illegal drugs (*slang*) [Early 18C. 'Police officer': < COPPER[2]. Verb: probably variant of *cap* 'to catch', via French *caper* < Latin *capere* 'seize'.] ◊ **a fair cop** a fair or just arrest (*informal*) ◊ **cop a plea** US to negotiate with a prosecutor in order to avoid prosecution for a serious crime by agreeing to plead guilty to a lesser crime (*slang*) ◊ **not much cop** not very good or useful (*informal*) **cop out** vi to withdraw from an activity because of lack of nerve or inclination (*slang*)

cop[2] /kop/ n a cone-shaped roll of thread on a spindle [Old English *coppe* 'summit']

Copacabana /kópə kə bánnə/ beach resort and residential area in S Rio de Janeiro, Brazil

copacetic /kópə seétik/, **copasetic** adj US, Can excellent or very good (*slang*) [Early 20C. < ?]

copal /kóp'l/ n a hard resin obtained from various tropical trees. Use: making varnish. [Late 16C. Via Spanish < Nahuatl *copalli.*]

Copán /kō pán/ ancient city of the Maya people, in NW Honduras

co-parenting n 1 the care and bringing up of children by two people who have divorced or separated 2 shared responsibility for bringing up children between two people who are not legally married, especially a same-sex couple —**co-parent** n

co-partner n a close partner or associate, especially one who has an equal stake in a company —**co-partnership** n

co-payment n an arrangement by which two or more parties make matching payments on a loan or other financial obligation, or a payment made in this way

cope[1] /kōp/ (**copes, coping, coped**) vi to deal successfully with a difficult problem or situation [14C. < French *couper* 'to strike' < Greek *kolaphos* 'blow'.] —**coper** n

cope[2] /kōp/ n a long sleeveless ceremonial cape worn by priests in some Christian churches [13C. Via medieval Latin *capa* 'cloak, hood' < late Latin *cappa.*] —**coped** adj

cope[3] /kōp/ n BUILDING = **coping** ■ vt (**copes, coping, coped**) 1 to lay a protective top course of brick or stone (**coping**) on a wall 2 to join two pieces of moulded timber [16C. < COPE[2].]

copeck n MONEY = **kopeck**

Copenhagen /kópən háygən, -háàgən/ capital and largest city of Denmark. Population: 487,969 (1998 estimate). Danish **København**

Copenhagen blue adj of a greyish-blue colour —**Copenhagen blue** n

copepod /kópə pod/ (*plural* **-pods** or **-pod**) n a tiny marine or freshwater crustacean that lives among plankton and is an important food source for many fish. Subclass: Copepoda. [Late 19C. < modern Latin *Copepoda* < Greek *kōpē* 'oar' + -POD; from its paddle-shaped feet.]

coper /kópər/ n a trader or merchant, especially one who deals in horses [Mid-16C. < *cope* 'to buy' < Middle Dutch or Low German *kōpen.*]

Copernican system n the theory of Copernicus regarding the mechanics of the solar system, published in 1543, in which he argued that the Earth and other planets revolve around the Sun

Copernicus /kə púrnikəss/ large crater on the Moon in the northwest quadrant, 93 km/58 mi. in diameter. It is the centre of a major system of rays on the lunar surface.

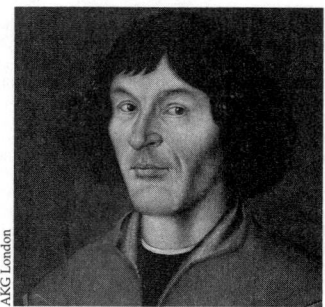

AKG London

Nicolaus Copernicus

Copernicus, Nicolaus (1473–1543) Polish astronomer. Born **Mikołaj Kopernik** —**Copernican** adj

copestone /kóp stōn/ n one of the stones that form the top edge of a wall [Mid-16C. < COPE[3].]

copier /kóppi ər/ n 1 = **photocopier** 2 a device that makes copies of something, e.g. software or recordings

copilot /kó pīlət/ n a second pilot in an aircraft, who shares the flying but is not in command

coping /kóping/ n the top, often sloping, course of brick or stone on top of a wall that forms a protective cap against the weather [Mid-16C. < COPE[3].]

coping saw n a saw with a thin flexible blade held tight in a U-shaped frame that is used for cutting curves in wood

copious /kópi əss/ adj produced or existing in large quantities [14C. Directly or via French < Latin *copiosus* < *copia* 'abundance'.] —**copiously** adv —**copiousness** n

copita /kō peétə/ n a traditional Spanish tulip-shaped sherry glass, or a drink of sherry served in one [Mid-19C. < Spanish, 'little cup'.]

coplanar /kō pláynər/ adj lying in the same plane —**coplanarity** /kō play nárrəti/ n

Aaron Copland

AKG London

Copland /kṓplənd/, **Aaron** (1900–90) US composer

copolymer /kō póllimər/ n a substance with a high molecular weight that results from chemically combining two or more monomers —**copolymeric** /kṓ poli mérrik/ adj

copolymerize /kō póllimə rīz/ (-izes, -izing, -ized), **copolymerise** (-ises, -ising, -ised) vt to unite two or more monomers chemically to form a copolymer —**copolymerization** /kō póllimə rī záysh'n/ n

cop-out n (slang) 1 EVASION OF RESPONSIBILITY a feeble avoidance of a responsibility or commitment 2 EXCUSE FOR NOT TAKING ACTION a feebly transparent excuse or explanation for refusing to face up to something 3 SOMEBODY WHO BACKS OUT a person who avoids an obligation or a commitment ○ What a bunch of cop-outs!

⚡**COPPA** /kóppə/ n an act of the US Congress regulating the collection of data by website operators from children aged under 13. Full form **Children's Online Privacy Protection Act**

copper[1] /kóppər/ n 1 REDDISH-BROWN METAL (symbol **Cu**) a malleable, reddish-brown metallic element that is a good conductor of electricity and heat. Source: ores such as chalcopyrite. Use: wiring, coatings, alloys. 2 REDDISH-BROWN COLOUR a reddish-brown colour, like that of polished copper 3 SMALL COIN a low-value coin made of copper or brass (informal) ○ a pocketful of coppers 4 POT FOR BOILING WATER a large pot used to boil water 5 REDDISH-BROWN BUTTERFLY a small reddish-brown butterfly. Genera: Lycaena and Heodes. ■ vt COVER WITH COPPER to cover or coat something with copper (often passive) [Pre-12C. Via late Latin cuprum < Greek Kupros 'Cyprus', an important ancient source of copper.] —**copper** adj —**coppery** adj

copper[2] /kóppər/ n a police officer (informal) [Mid-19C. < COP[1] (verb).]

copperas /kóppərəss/ n = **ferrous sulphate** [15C. Via French < medieval Latin cuperosa.]

Copper Belt n an area in Central Africa that has rich deposits of copper ore

copper-bottomed adj 1 having a copper coating on the base 2 certain or reliable, especially financially

copper-fasten vt to make an agreement binding [< the use of copper fastenings on ships to prevent corrosion]

copperhead /kóppər hed/ (plural -heads or -head) n 1 a reddish-brown poisonous snake of the viper family. Native to: central and E United States. Agkistrodon contortrix. 2 a large poisonous snake of the cobra family with pale brown to black skin and a copper-coloured band round the back of its head. Native to: Australia. Denisonia superba.

copperplate /kóppər playt/ n 1 PRINTING PLATE a polished copper printing plate with a design etched or engraved on it 2 PRINT a print made from a copperplate 3 NEAT HANDWRITING neat handwriting, especially in the style of copybooks produced from copper plates

copper pyrites n MINERALS = **chalcopyrite**

coppersmith /kóppər smith/ n 1 a maker or repairer of copper objects 2 a small greenish bird with a distinctive metallic call. Native to: SE Asia. Megalaima haemacephala.

copper sulphate n $CuSO_4$ a poisonous blue compound containing copper and sulphur. Use: textile dyeing, electroplating, fungicides, wood preservatives.

coppice /kóppiss/ n an area of densely growing small trees, especially one in which the trees are regularly cut back to encourage more growth ■ vt (-pices, -picing, -piced) to cut back trees periodically to encourage young growth [Mid-14C. < Old French copeiz < coper (see COPE[1]).]

Coppola /kóppələ/, **Francis Ford** (b. 1939) US film director

copra /kóprə/ n the dried flesh of a coconut from which coconut oil is obtained [Late 16C. Via Portuguese < Malayalam koppara.]

Coprates /kóprə teez/ large canyon on Mars running east–west to the equatorial region

copro- prefix dung, excrement ○ coprophilous [< Greek kopros 'dung']

⚡**coprocessor** /kṓ prṓ sessər/ n a second processor in a computer, improving performance by handling specialized tasks

co-produce /kṓ prə dyōoss/ vt to produce a play, film, or television programme jointly with another person or organization ○ The programme was co-produced by British and American companies. —**co-producer** n —**co-production** /-dúksh'n/ n

coprolalia /kóprə láyli ə/ n the uncontrolled use of violent and obscene language, especially as a result of an illness such as Tourette's syndrome

coprolite /kóprə līt/ n fossilized dung from which information about eating patterns in prehistoric times can be discovered —**coprolitic** /kóprə líttik/ adj

coprology /ko próllǝji/ n an obsession with defecation, especially as expressed in art and literature

coprophagy /ko próffǝji/ n the eating of dung by certain species of insects or animals —**coprophagous** /-gǝss/ adj

coprophilia /kóprə fílli ǝ/ n an obsessive and often sexual interest in faeces and defecation —**coprophiliac** n —**coprophilic** adj

coprophilous /kǝ próffilǝss/ adj describes organisms such as some insects or fungi that live on or in dung

copse /kops/ n TREES = **coppice** n. [Late 16C. Alteration of COPPICE.]

Copt /kopt/ n 1 a member of the Coptic Church 2 an Egyptian of non-Arab descent [Early 17C. Via French or modern Latin < Arabic al-kibt 'the Copts' < Coptic Gyptios 'Egyptian' < Greek Aiguptios.]

copter /kóptər/ n a helicopter (informal) [Mid-20C. Shortening.]

Coptic /kóptik/ n a language formerly spoken in Egypt, a later form of ancient Egyptian and one of the Afro-Asiatic languages ■ adj relating or belonging to the Copts, Coptic, or Egyptian Monophysite Christian Church

Coptic Church n the Egyptian Christian Church, established in the 6th century and adhering to the doctrine of the Monophysites

copula /kópp yōolə/ (plural -las or -lae /-lee/) n 1 LINKING VERB a verb such as 'be' or 'seem' that links the subject of a sentence with an adjective or noun phrase (complement) relating to it (technical) 2 LINK BETWEEN SUBJECT AND PREDICATE a form of the verb 'to be' linking the subject and the predicate in certain propositions, such as 'are' in 'Some dogs are poodles' (technical) 3 LINK BETWEEN TWO THINGS anything that provides a link between two things (formal) [Early 17C. < Latin, 'link'.] —**copular** adj

copulate /kóppyōo layt/ (-lates, -lating, -lated) vi to have sexual intercourse [Early 17C. < Latin copulat-, past participle of copulare 'join together' < copula 'link'.] —**copulation** /kóppyōo láysh'n/ n —**copulatory** /-láytəri/ adj

copulative /kóppyōolǝtiv/ adj 1 linking or joining (formal) 2 relating to a verb that links the subject with its complement or to the function of such a verb —**copulatively** adv

copy /kóppi/ n (plural -ies) 1 REPRODUCTION something that is made exactly like something else in appearance or function 2 ONE OF MANY any one of many identical specimens of something produced in large numbers, especially something printed or published 3 WRITTEN TEXT the written text to be published in a book, newspaper, or magazine, as distinct from visual material or graphics ■ v (-ies, -ying, -ied) 1 vt MAKE IDENTICAL VERSION to make another example or specimen that is exactly the same as something else 2 vt DO SAME AS to do exactly what somebody else does 3 vti CHEAT BY DOING SAME to reproduce

the work of another fraudulently [14C. Via French < Latin copia 'abundance'.] —**copyable** adj

SYNONYMS copy, reproduce, duplicate, clone, replicate, re-create
CORE MEANING: to make something that resembles something else to a greater or lesser degree
copy to make another identical version of something; **reproduce** to make a copy by technical means; **duplicate** to create an identical version of something two or more times; **clone** to make a near or exact reproduction, especially of a piece of equipment or an organism; **replicate** to create an identical version of something repeatedly and exactly; **re-create** to make something that appears to be the same as something that no longer exists, or that exists in a different place.

copy down vt to make a written copy of something ○ Journalists copied down his every word.

copybook /kóppi bŏŏk/ n BOOK OF HANDWRITING SPECIMENS a book containing models of handwriting for young students to copy ■ adj 1 EXCELLENT so good that it could be used as a model for others to copy 2 UNORIGINAL following guidelines slavishly and showing no originality ◇ **blot your copybook** to do something that spoils your previously good record or reputation

copycat /kóppi kat/ n somebody, especially a child, who slavishly imitates another (informal) ■ adj done in close imitation of somebody or something else (informal)

copy clothing n Hong Kong clothes that are copies of designer garments, usually passed off as genuine

copy desk n a desk at which written material is edited for publication

copy-edit vti to read written material and correct it for publication

copy editor n a reader and corrector of written texts for publication

copyhold /kóppi hōld/ n a tenure of land held at the will of a landowner, originally a lord [15C. Because it was recorded in a transcript of the manorial court rolls.]

copyholder /kóppi hōldər/ n 1 DOCUMENT STAND a stand that holds documents upright while they are being read or keyed 2 ASSISTANT TO PROOFREADER a reader aloud of written material to a proofreader 3 HOLDER OF ESTATE a holder of a tenement (**copyhold**) that consisted of an estate held at the will of a landowner, originally a lord (dated)

copyist /kóppi ist/ n 1 somebody whose job is making copies of handwritten documents or music 2 a mere imitator of others

⚡**copy protection** n a means of preventing unauthorized duplication of computer software —**copy-protected** adj

copyreader /kóppi reedər/ n US MEDIA = **subeditor** n. 2

copyright /kóppi rīt/ n CREATIVE ARTIST'S CONTROL OF ORIGINAL WORK the legal right of creative artists or publishers to control the use and reproduction of their original works ■ adj PROTECTED BY COPYRIGHT controlled or restricted by a copyright ■ vt GET COPYRIGHT OF to secure the copyright on a creative work —**copyrightable** adj —**copyrighter** n

copyright deposit library, copyright library n a library that receives a free copy of every book published in the British Isles, belonging to a group of six in England, Scotland, Wales and the Republic of Ireland

copy typist n a typist who works from written or typed drafts, rather than from dictation

~~copywrite~~ incorrect spelling of **copyright**

copywriter /kóppi rītər/ n a writer of advertisements or promotional material —**copywriting** n

coq au vin /kók ō váN, -ván/ (plural **coqs au vin** /kók ō váN, -ván/ or **coq au vins**) n a dish of chicken cooked in red wine with other ingredients [< French, 'cock in wine']

coquet /ko két/ (-quets, -quetting, -quetted) vi (literary) 1 to act coyly and flirtatiously 2 to act casually or frivolously [Late 17C. < French, 'little cock' < coq 'cock'.] —**coquetry** /kókitri/ n

coquette /ko két/ n a flirtatious woman [Mid-17C. < French, feminine of coquet (see COQUET).] —**coquettish** adj —**coquettishly** adv —**coquettishness** n

coquille /ko keé/ n 1 SEAFOOD DISH a dish of seafood baked and served in a scallop shell or a scallop-shaped dish 2 SHELL OR SHELL-SHAPED DISH a scallop shell or a scallop-shaped dish 3 GUARD ON FOIL a bell-shaped guard on a fencing foil [< French (see COCKLE[1])]

coquina /kō keénə/ *n* **1** a soft limestone formed largely from crushed shells and coral, used as a building material in the Caribbean and the SE United States **2** a small clam common off the coasts of the E and S United States. Genus: *Donax*. [Mid-19C. < Spanish, 'cockle shell'.]

coquito /ko keétō/ (*plural* **-tos** *or* **-to**) *n* a palm tree with edible nuts and sweet sap that is used to make wine. Native to: Chile. *Jubaea chilensis*. [Mid-19C. < Spanish, 'little coco shell' < Portuguese *cóco* (see COCO).]

cor /kawr/ *interj* used to express amazement or admiration (*informal*) [Mid-20C. Shortening of COR BLIMEY.]

cor. *abbr* **1** corner **2** cornet **3** correction **4** correspondence **5** correspondent

Cor. *abbr* Corinthians

coracle /kórrək'l/ *n* a small round boat made from animal skins stretched over a wicker frame [Mid-16C. < Welsh *corwgl* < Middle Irish *curach* (see CURRACH).]

coracoid /kórrə koyd/ *n* a bony projection on the shoulder blade in most mammals [Mid-18C. Via modern Latin < Greek *korakoeidēs* 'crow-like' (from its resemblance to a crow's beak) < *korax* 'raven, crow'.]

coral /kórrəl/ *n* **1 MARINE ORGANISM** a marine organism that lives in colonies and has an external skeleton. Class: Anthozoa. **2 HARD MARINE DEPOSIT** a hard deposit consisting of coral skeletons, often forming marine reefs **3 SOMETHING MADE OF CORAL** a piece of coral or an article made from it **4 DEEP REDDISH-ORANGE COLOUR** a deep reddish-orange colour **5 LOBSTER'S OR CRAB'S EGGS** the unfertilized eggs of a crab or lobster that turn pinkish-orange when cooked [14C. Via Old French < Greek *korallion*.] —**coral** *adj* —**coralloid** /kórrə loyd/ *adj*

coralberry /kórrəl berri/ (*plural* **-ries** *or* **-ry**) *n* **1** a shrub that produces dark red berries. Native to: North America. *Symphoricarpos orbiculatus*. **2** an evergreen shrub. Native to: E Asia. Genus: *Ardisia*.

coralline /kórrə līn/ *adj* **1 OF OR LIKE CORAL** relating to or resembling coral **2 PINKISH-RED OR PINKISH-ORANGE** of the pinkish-red or pinkish-orange colour of coral ■ *n* **1 CALCIUM-COVERED RED ALGA** a red alga whose fronds are covered or impregnated with calcium deposits. Genus: *Corallina*. **2 ORGANISM THAT RESEMBLES CORAL** a sponge or other organism that resembles coral

coral reef *n* a marine reef composed of the skeletons of living coral, together with minerals and organic matter

coralroot /kórrəl root/ (*plural* **-roots** *or* **-root**) *n* a leafless orchid with small insignificant flowers that feeds through roots that resemble coral. Genus: *Corallorhiza*.

Coral Sea arm of the SW Pacific Ocean bounded by Australia, New Guinea, the Solomon Islands, and Vanuatu

Coral Sea Islands Territory island group and external dependency of Australia in the South Pacific Ocean, east of Queensland

coral snake *n* **1** a poisonous and mainly nocturnal snake that is strikingly marked with red, black, and yellow or white bands. Native to: North and South America. Genera: *Micrurus* and *Micruroides*. **2** a poisonous snake that is red with yellow and black bands. Native to: E Australia. *Brachyurophis australis*.

coral tree *n* a thorny shrub or small tree with brightly coloured seeds growing in long pods. Flowers: large, red or orange, pollinated by birds. Native to: tropical and subtropical regions. Genus: *Erythrina*.

cor anglais /káwr óng glay/ (*plural* **cor anglais** *or* **cors anglais** /káwrz-/) *n* a woodwind instrument like an oboe but larger and lower-pitched. US term **English horn** [< French, 'English horn']

coranto /ko rántō/ (*plural* **-tos**) *n* DANCE = **courante** *n*. **2** [Mid-16C. Alteration of French *courante* 'running'.]

corban /káwr ban/ *n* **1** an offering to God made by the ancient Hebrew people **2** an offering made to the Temple of Jerusalem [14C. Via Greek < Hebrew *qorbān* 'offering' < *qāraḇ* 'approach'.]

corbeil /káwrb'l/, **corbeille** *n* a stone carving of a basket of fruit or flowers as a feature on a building [Mid-18C. Via French < late Latin *corbicula* 'small basket' < Latin *corbis* 'basket'.]

corbel /káwrb'l/ *n* **SUPPORTING STONE BRACKET** a bracket of brick or stone that juts out of a wall to support a structure above it ■ *vt* (**-bels, -belling, -belled**) **1 LAY MASONRY UNITS TO FORM PROJECTION** to lay stones or bricks in layers so that each juts out above the one below to form a supporting bracket **2 SUPPORT WITH CORBELS** to support a cornice or other structure on corbels [14C. < Old French, 'little raven' < *corp* 'raven' < Latin *corvus* (see CORVINE); from its original beak-like profile from being cut slantwise.]

corbelling /káwrbəling/ *n* a structural system using corbels as supports

corbel step *n* ARCHIT = **corbie-step**

Corbett /káwrbit/ *n Scotland* a Scottish mountain between 762 m/2500 ft and 914.4 m/3000 ft [After J. R. *Corbett*.]

Corbett /káwrbit/, **James John** (1866–1933) US boxer. Known as **Gentleman Jim**

corbie /káwrbi/ (*plural* **-bies** *or* **-bie**) *n Scotland* a crow, especially a raven [15C. Via Old French *corbin* < late Latin *corvinus* (see CORVINE).]

corbie gable *n* a gable with top edges shaped like a series of steps [< CORBIE STEP]

corbie step, corbel step *n* each of a series of decorative steps going up the side of a gable [*Corbie* from the idea that only crows can reach them]

cor blimey /káwr blīmi/, **gorblimey** /gáwr blīmi/ *interj* used to express amazement or admiration (*informal*) [Alteration of *God blind me!*]

Corby /káwrbi/ town in central England. Population: 49,053 (1991).

cord /kawrd/ *n* **1 STRING OR ROPE** thick strong string or thin rope ○ *hands and feet tied with cords* **2 FASTENING OR BELT** a length of material used as a fastening or belt **3 ELECTRICAL CABLE** flexible insulated electric cable **4 BODY PART RESEMBLING ROPE** a part of the body resembling cord, e.g. the spinal cord or the umbilical cord **5 RIBBED FABRIC** any fabric with a ribbed surface, especially corduroy **6 UNIT OF VOLUME FOR CUT TIMBER** a unit of volume for cut timber, equal to 128 cu. ft (approximately 3.6 cu. m) ■ **cords** *npl* **TROUSERS** corduroy trousers (*informal*) ○ *a pair of cords* ■ *vt* **1 TIE WITH CORD** to fasten or tie something with cord or rope ○ *Are the packages corded and ready to ship?* **2 STACK WOOD IN CORDS** to stack wood in units with a volume of one cord [13C. Via Old French < Latin *chorda* < Greek *khordē* 'string'.] —**corder** *n*

USAGE See *chord*.

cordage /káwrdij/ *n* **1** ropes or cords collectively, especially the lines and rigging of a ship **2** the amount of wood in a stack, measured in cords

cordate /káwrd ayt/ *adj* describes a leaf that is heart-shaped [Mid-18C. < modern Latin *cordatus* < Latin *cord-* 'heart'.]

Corday /káwrd ay/, **Charlotte** (1768–93) French assassin of Marat during the French Revolution

corded /káwrdid/ *adj* **1 TIED UP** securely tied up with string or rope **2 RIBBED** describes a fabric with a ribbed surface **3 WITH TIGHT MUSCLES** having tensed or well-developed muscles visible as ridges or ripples

Cordelia /kawr deéli ə/ *n* a small natural satellite of Uranus, discovered in 1986 by the Voyager 2 planetary probe

cord grass *n* a coarse grass found on coastal salt marshes or mudflats. Genus: *Spartina*.

cordial /káwrdi əl/ *adj* **1 HOSPITABLY WARM** friendly and affectionate **2 DEEPLY FELT** sincere or profound (*literary*) **3 REFRESHING** stimulating or invigorating (*literary*) ■ *n* **1 FRUIT DRINK** a fruit drink, especially one sold in concentrated form and diluted with water **2 TONIC** a stimulating or medicinal drink [14C. < medieval Latin *cordialis* 'of the heart' < Latin *cord-* 'heart'.] —**cordially** *adv* —**cordialness** *n*

cordiality /káwrdi álləti/ *n* friendliness and affection ○ *We were surprised by the cordiality of their response.*

cordierite /káwrdi ə rīt/ *n* a purplish-blue or grey aluminosilicate mineral containing magnesium and iron. Source: metamorphic rocks. [Early 19C. After Pierre L. *Cordier* (1777–1861), French geologist.]

cordillera /káwdil yáirə/ (*plural* **-ras**) *n* a system of mountain ranges consisting of approximately parallel ridges [Early 18C. < Spanish, < *cordilla* 'small cord' < *cuerda* 'cord' < Latin *chorda* (see CORD).]

cordite /káwrd īt/ *n* a smokeless explosive, usually made of gunpowder and nitroglycerin [Late 19C. < CORD; from its stringy appearance.]

cordless /káwrdləss/ *adj* powered by an internal battery and not needing to be continuously attached by a cable to an external electricity supply

cordless telephone *n* a telephone, powered by a recharging battery, with a portable handset that can be removed from its base unit and has a short-range radio link to it

córdoba /káwrdəbə/ *n* see table at **currency** [Early 20C. After Francisco Fernández de *Córdoba* (1475–1526), Spanish explorer.]

Cordoba /káwrdəbə/, **Córdoba, Cordova** capital of Córdoba Province, S Spain. Population: 300,229 (1991).

cordon /káwrd'n/ *n* **1 PEOPLE OR VEHICLES ENCIRCLING AREA** a chain of police officers or soldiers, or their vehicles, surrounding an area to control access to it **2 RIBBON** a piece of ribbon worn for decoration or as a sign of rank or a mark of honour **3 FRUIT TREE WITH SHORT SIDE SHOOTS** a fruit tree grown as a single stem at an angle against a support, with its side branches pruned back close to the stem **4** ARCHIT = **string course** [Late 16C. < Old French, 'small cord' < *corde* (see CORD).]

cordon off *vt* to surround an area with a line of police officers, soldiers, or their vehicles, to control access to it

cordon bleu /káwr dón blúr/ *adj* **1 OF HIGHEST CLASS** describes a cook or cooking of the highest class **2 WITH CHEESE AND HAM** describes a way of preparing meat, especially veal, by rolling a thin slice around cheese and ham and then coating in breadcrumbs ■ *n* (*plural* **cordon bleus**) **1 MASTER CHEF** a cook of the very highest class, especially a master chef **2 KNIGHT'S RIBBON** a blue ribbon worn by knights of the highest order in Bourbon France [Early 18C. < French, 'blue ribbon'.]

cordon sanitaire /káwr don sani táir/ *n* **1** a barrier erected to control the spread of a disease by restricting movement to and from the infected area **2** a neutral state, or a string of neutral states, lying between two states that are hostile to each other [Mid-19C. < French, 'sanitary line'.]

Cordova /kawr dṓvə/ ♦ **Cordoba**

cordovan /káwrdəvən/ *n* a fine soft leather originally made from goatskin and now usually made from horsehide [Late 16C. < Spanish *cordován*, after CÓRDOBA.]

corduroy /káwdə roy, -dyŏŏ-/ *n* a heavy cotton fabric with a ribbed nap running lengthways ■ **corduroys** *npl* trousers made of corduroy [Late 18C. Probably < CORD + *duroy*, a coarse woollen fabric.]

corduroy road *n* a road made of logs across muddy or swampy ground [Because its surface resembles corduroy fabric]

cordwainer /káwrd waynər/ *n* a maker of shoes and other articles from fine soft leather (**cordovan**) (*archaic*) —**cordwainery** *n*

cordwood /káwrd wŏŏd/ *n* wood in stacks with a volume of one cord, or cut into lengths of 1.2 m/4 ft for stacking in cords

ϟ **core** /kawr/ *n* **1 CENTRAL PART OF FRUIT** the fibrous central part of some fruit, containing the seeds **2 ESSENTIAL PART** the central or most important part of something **3 CENTRE OF EARTH** the central part of the Earth or the corresponding part of another astronomical object **4 CENTRAL PART OF NUCLEAR REACTOR** the central part of a nuclear reactor in which fission takes place **5 IRON IN TRANSFORMER** a block of iron in a coil or transformer, used to intensify and direct the magnetic field produced by a current in surrounding coils **6 SAMPLE OBTAINED BY DRILLING** a tubular segment of rock, ice, or other material obtained as a study sample by drilling **7 STONE USED TO MAKE TOOLS** a block of stone from which tools or flakes are chipped **8 PIECE OF COMPUTER MEMORY** a ring-shaped piece of magnetic material formerly used to store digital data in a computer, each core representing one binary digit (**bit**) **9 COMPUTER MEMORY** the main memory of a computer, which was composed of arrays of ring-shaped magnets before the introduction of semiconductor memories ■ *adj* **ESSENTIAL** of central or fundamental importance ■ *vt* (**cores, coring, cored**) **TAKE CORE OUT OF** to remove the core from a piece of fruit [13C. < ?] —**corer** *n*

CORE /kawr/ *abbr* Congress of Racial Equality

core competency *n* an area of expertise that is fundamental to a particular job or function

core curriculum *n* the subjects that all students are required to study at school

ϟ **core dump** *n* **1** a transfer of data from the main memory of a computer, usually to external storage **2** a long-winded response to a simple question (*informal humorous*)

coreferential /kō refə rénsh'l/ *adj* referring to the same person or thing ○ *In the sentence 'Mary lost her purse', 'Mary' and 'her' are coreferential.*

coreligionist /kō ri líjjənist/ *n* a sharer of a religion

Corelli /kə rélli, ko-/, **Arcangelo** (1653–1713) Italian composer and violinist

ϟ **core memory** *n* COMPUT = **core** *n.* 9 (*technical*)

corepressor /kō ri préssər/ *n* a substance that inhibits gene transfer and protein synthesis by combining with and activating a genetic repressor

coreq /kō rék/ *n US* a corequisite (*informal*)

corequisite /kō rékwizit/ *n US* a course of study that must be taken along with another

~~**corespondence**~~ incorrect spelling of **correspondence**

co-respondent, corespondent /kō rispóndənt/ *n* somebody named in a divorce suit as the alleged adulterous sexual partner of the respondent ■ **co-respondents** *npl* CLOTHES = **co-respondent shoes** —**co-respondency** *n*

co-respondent shoes *npl* men's two-tone shoes, usually black or brown and white (*humorous*)

core subject *n* any of a number of subjects that all students are required to study at school

core time *n* the part of the working day during which workers on flexitime must be present at work

corf /kawrf/ (*plural* **corves** /kawrvz/) *n* a wagon used inside a mine for transporting mined coal or ore [15C. Via Middle Dutch or Middle Low German *korf* 'basket' < Latin *corbis*.]

Corfu /kawr fóō, -fyóō/ most northerly of the Ionian Islands, west of Greece. Population: 107,592 (1991). Area: 641 sq. km/247 sq. mi.

corgi /káwrgi/ (*plural* **-gis**) *n* a small dog with short legs and smooth hair belonging to one of two breeds, the Cardigan Welsh corgi and the Pembroke Welsh corgi [Early 20C. < Welsh, < *cor* 'dwarf' + *ci* 'dog'.]

CORGI /káwrgi/ *abbr* Council for Registered Gas Installers

coriaceous /kórri áyshəss/ *adj* like leather in texture or appearance [Late 17C. < late Latin *coriaceus* < Latin *corium* 'leather'.]

coriander /kórri ándər/ *n* **1** the leaves or seeds of the coriander plant, or a powder made from the crushed seeds. Use: food seasoning. **2** an annual plant grown for its aromatic leaves and seeds. Native to: Asia, the Mediterranean. *Coriandrum sativum.* [13C. Via Old French < Greek *koriandron*.]

Corinth /kórrinth/ ancient city and modern town, S Greece. Population: 29,600 (1995). Greek **Kórinthos**

Corinthian /kə rínthi ən/ *adj* **1 OF CORINTH** relating to the ancient or modern Greek city of Corinth **2 SLENDER AND ORNATE AT TOP** in architecture, describes a slender column with an ornate capital **3 DEBAUCHED** debauched or ostentatiously luxurious (*literary*) **4 OF SPORTS CLUB** used in the name of sports clubs and competitions ○ *The Essex Sunday Corinthian League* ■ *n* **1 SOMEBODY FROM CORINTH** somebody from the Greek city of Corinth **2 WEALTHY SPORTSPERSON** a wealthy amateur sportsperson (*archaic*)

Corinthian order *n* an ancient Greek order of architecture characterized by a slender column with an ornate capital [< its origin in CORINTH]

Corinthians /kə rínthi ənz/ *n* either of two books in the New Testament, originally written as letters by St Paul to the church at Corinth

Coriolanus /kórri ō láynəss/ *n* in Roman legend, the defeater of the Volsci in the 5th century BC

Coriolis effect /kórri óliss-/ *n* the observed deflection of something such as a missile in flight relative to the Earth's surface, caused by the Earth's rotation beneath the object [After Gaspard de *Coriolis* (1792–1843), French mathematician]

Coriolis force *n* an apparent but nonexistent force used to describe the effect of the Earth's rotation on the motion of moving objects

corium /káwri əm/ (*plural* **-a** /-ri ə/) *n* **1** MED = **dermis** **2** the leathery middle part of the forewing of some insects [Early 19C. < Latin, 'hide, leather'.]

cork /kawrk/ *n* **1 OUTER BARK OF CORK OAK** the light, flexible, outer bark of the cork oak tree. Use: for bottle stoppers, as an insulator. **2 BOTTLE STOPPER** a usually cylindrical piece of material used as a bottle stopper **3 FLOAT USED IN ANGLING** a small float used in angling to maintain a hook or net suspended in the water **4 LAYER OF PLANT TISSUE** dead tissue that forms a protective outer layer on plants and is part of the bark in woody plants ■ *vt* **1 SEAL CONTAINER WITH CORK** to stop or seal something, especially a bottle, with a cork **2 RESTRAIN FEELINGS** to restrain feelings, especially strong negative ones such as anger or grief [13C. Probably via Middle Dutch < Arabic dialect *kurk* 'cork-soled sandal'.]

Cork /kawrk/ port in SW Ireland and the second largest city in the republic. Population: 180,000 (1996).

corkage /káwrkij/ *n* a fee charged at some restaurants for serving wine and other alcoholic drinks that customers bring in from elsewhere

corkboard /káwrk bawrd/ *n* a thin sheet made from compressed cork granules, typically used as a floor covering and as wall insulation before plastic was available

corked /kawrkt/ *adj* **1** sealed or stopped with a cork or other object **2** given an unpleasant flavour by substances from a tainted cork ○ *Waiter, this wine's corked!*

corker /káwrkər/ *n* **1** somebody or something particularly striking or special (*dated informal*) ○ *It was a corker of a day.* **2** a person or machine that fits corks, especially into bottles

corking /káwrking/ *adj* excellent or splendid (*dated informal*)

cork oak *n* an evergreen oak whose thick bark is a source of cork. Native to: Mediterranean. *Quercus suber.*

corkscrew /káwrk skroo/ *n* **DEVICE FOR REMOVING CORKS FROM BOTTLES** a device for taking corks out of bottles, usually a pointed spiral of metal attached to a handle or simple lever ■ *v* **1** *vi* **MOVE IN SPIRAL PATH** to move in a spiral path ○ *watched anxiously as the plane corkscrewed towards the ground* **2** *vt* **WIND IN SPIRAL** to wind or twist something in a spiral ■ *adj* **SPIRAL-SHAPED** shaped like a spiral ○ *corkscrew curls*

corkwood /káwrk wŏŏd/ (*plural* **-woods** *or* **-wood**) *n* a deciduous shrub or small tree that grows in wetlands and has light porous wood. Native to: SE United States. *Leitneria floridana.*

corky /káwrki/ (**-ier, -iest**) *adj* **1** made from or resembling cork **2** having the taste or smell of cork —**corkiness** *n*

corm /kawrm/ *n* a short swollen underground stem base in some plants, e.g. crocus and gladiolus, that stores food over the winter and produces new foliage in the spring [Mid-19C. Via modern Latin *cormus* < Greek *kormos* 'lopped-off tree trunk'.] —**cormous** *adj*

Cormorant

cormorant /káwrmərənt/ *n* a large marine diving bird with webbed feet, a hooked bill, and a long neck that can expand to swallow fish. Family: Phalacrocoracidae. [13C. Alteration of Old French *cormaran* 'sea raven' < *corp* 'raven' + *marenc* 'of the sea' (< Latin *marinus*).]

corn[1] /kawrn/ *n* **1** *UK, Ireland* **CEREAL CROP** any cereal crop, especially wheat, barley, or oats **2** *UK, Ireland* **GRAIN OF CORN** the grains produced by corn plants, especially when collected together by harvesting **3** *US* = **maize** *n.* 1 **4** *US* = **maize** *n.* 2 **5** BEVERAGES = **corn whisky** **6 CORNY ITEM OR MATERIAL** something trite or overly sentimental (*informal*) [Old English, < Indo-European, 'grain']

corn[2] /kawrn/ *n* a hardened or thickened, often painful, area of skin, usually on a toe, caused by friction or pressure [Late 14C. Via French < Latin *cornu* 'horn'.]

Corn. *abbr* Cornwall

cornball /káwrn bawl/ *n US* a person regarded as naively sentimental ■ *adj US* trite or overly sentimental ○ *a cornball movie* [Mid-20C. Originally 'ball of popcorn and molasses or syrup', often sold at carnivals.]

corn borer *n* a moth whose larvae bore into and feed on maize. Family: Pyralidae.

corn bread *n US* bread made from maize flour

corn bunting *n* a songbird with brown plumage, a speckled breast, and a strong beak. Native to: Europe, Asia. *Emberiza calandra.*

corn chip *n* a crisp thin piece of fried maize meal batter, eaten as a savoury snack food

corn circle *n* AGRIC = **crop circle**

corncob /káwrn kob/ *n* **1** an ear of sweetcorn or maize **2** the hard core of an ear of maize, on which the kernels grow

corncockle /káwrn kok'l/ (*plural* **-les** *or* **-le**) *n* an annual plant with poisonous seeds, once common as a weed in cornfields. Flowers: reddish-purple. Native to: the Mediterranean. *Agrostemma githago.* [Early 18C. < CORN[1] + COCKLE[2].]

corncrake /káwrn krayk/ *n* a speckled bird with a harsh call, a short bill, and reddish wings. Native to: fields and meadows of Europe and Asia. *Crex crex.*

corncrib /káwrn krib/ *n Can, US* a ventilated building used for the storage and drying of maize ears

corn dog *n US* a hot dog on a stick, coated in maize-flour batter and deep-fried, typically sold at fairs and carnivals

corndogging /káwrn doging/ *n US* a surfing initiation ritual in which a surfer is rolled in sand after surfing by his or her fellow surfers (*slang*)

corn dolly (*plural* **corn dollies**) *n* a small ornamental object made from plaited straw

cornea /káwrni ə, kawr née ə/ (*plural* **-as** *or* **-ae** /-ee/) *n* the transparent convex membrane that covers the pupil and iris of the eye [14C. < medieval Latin *cornea tela* 'horny tissue' < Latin *cornu* 'horn'; from its fibrous consistency.] —**corneal** *adj*

corned /kawrnd/ *adj* cooked and then preserved in salt or brine ○ *corned mutton* [Early 17C. < *corn* 'to preserve with salt' < CORN[1].]

corned beef *n* beef that has been cooked, preserved in salt or brine, and often canned

Corneille /kawr náy/, **Pierre** (1606–84) French playwright

cornel /káwrn'l/ (*plural* **-nels** *or* **-nel**) *n* **1** any plant related to dogwood. Genus: *Cornus.* **2** = **cornelian cherry** [Mid-16C. < French *corneille* or German *Kornelbaum*, < Latin *cornus*.]

cornelian *n* MINERALS = **carnelian**

cornelian cherry /kawrnéeli ən-/ *n* a small deciduous tree cultivated for its clusters of bright yellow spring flowers and small red sour fruits. Use: formerly, in jellies and preserves. Native to: S Europe. *Cornus mas.*

corner /káwrnər/ *n* **1 MEETING OF LINES OR SURFACES** the angle formed where two or more lines or surfaces meet ○ *a corner of the room* **2 AREA ENCLOSED BY CONVERGING LINES** the area enclosed where two lines or surfaces meet **3 PROJECTING PART** a projecting angular part of something **4 PLACE WHERE TWO ROADS MEET** the place where two roads or streets meet **5 DIFFICULT SITUATION** a difficult or embarrassing position, especially one from which there is no easy way of escape ○ *got himself into a corner about his previous statements* **6 QUIET PLACE** a secluded, peaceful, or secret place **7 REMOTE PLACE** an area or place, especially one that is remote **8 OBJECT FITTED OVER CORNER** an object made to fit over a corner of something, especially to protect it ○ *a diary with metal corners* **9 CONTROL OF A MARKET** a monopoly of a particular commodity acquired in order to control its market price **10 PART OF PLAYING FIELD OR SURFACE** in various sports, part of the playing field or surface where two boundaries meet **11 KICK OR SHOT FROM CORNER** in some games, a free kick or shot from a corner of the field given to the attacking team when a defending player plays the ball over the goal line **12 PART OF RING** in boxing and wrestling, any of the four parts of a ring where the ropes are attached to the posts, especially the two where the competitors rest between rounds ■ *adj* **1 LOCATED ON CORNER** situated on a street corner ○ *a corner shop* **2 INTENDED FOR CORNER** intended to be put in a corner ○ *a corner cabinet* **3 SITUATED AT CORNER** at or in a corner of something ○ *sat at a corner table* ■ *v* **1** *vt* **FORCE INTO DIFFICULT POSITION** to force a person or an animal into a position from which escape is difficult **2** *vt* **PUT IN CORNER** to place somebody or something in a corner **3** *vt* **PROVIDE WITH CORNERS** to give corners to something **4** *vt* **ACQUIRE MONOPOLY OF** to acquire a monopoly of a particular commodity and so be able to control its market price ○ *an attempt to corner the soya bean market* **5** *vi* **TURN CORNER** to turn a corner (*refers to vehicles or their drivers*) **6** *vti* **TAKE CORNER** in some games, to take a free kick or hit from a corner of the field on an opponents' goal line [13C. Via Anglo-Norman < Latin *cornua*, plural of *cornu* 'horn, point'.] ◇ **cut corners** to do something in a quicker, cheaper, or less careful way than is desirable or wise ◇ **turn the corner** to get past the worst part of a difficult or dangerous situation

cornerback /káwrnər bak/ *n* in American football, either of two defensive halfbacks placed behind the linebackers and near the sidelines

cornered /káwrnərd/ *adj* **1 IN DIFFICULT POSITION** in a difficult or embarrassing position, especially when there is no easy way of escape **2 WITH PARTICULAR CORNERS** with a particular number or type of corners (*usually in combination*) **3 WITH NUMBER OF CONTENDERS** with a specified number of contenders ○ *a three-cornered struggle for the championship*

corner kick *n* in football, a free kick from a corner of the field given to the attacking team when a defending player plays the ball over the goal line

cornerman /-man/ (*plural* **-men** /-men/) *n US* an advisor, especially to a political candidate (*slang*)

corner shop *n* a small shop, especially one at the corner of two streets, where a limited range of groceries and general goods is sold

cornerstone /káwrnər stōn/ *n* **1 FUNDAMENTALLY IMPORTANT PERSON OR THING** somebody or something fundamentally important **2 STONE AT CORNER OF TWO WALLS** a stone joining two walls where they meet at a corner **3 FIRST STONE OF NEW BUILDING** the first stone laid at a corner where two walls begin and form the first part of a new building

cornerwise /káwrnər wīz/, **cornerways** /-wayz/ *adv, adj* diagonal or diagonally, or with a corner at the front

cornet /káwrnit/ *n* **1 BRASS INSTRUMENT LIKE TRUMPET** a three-valved brass instrument shaped like a compressed trumpet **2** MUSIC = **cornetist 3 CONICAL WAFER FOR ICE CREAM** a wafer shaped into a cone for holding ice cream, or one of these filled with ice cream **4 PAPER CONE FOR HOLDING SWEETS** a piece of paper folded into a cone shape and used to hold small edible things, especially sweets **5 OBSOLETE CAVALRY RANK** formerly, a commissioned officer of the lowest rank in a cavalry regiment **6 WOMAN'S HEADDRESS** a headdress of starched cloth worn by women from the 12th to the 15th centuries **7 NUN'S HEADDRESS** a large white headdress worn by some Christian nuns **8** *S Africa* ARMY = **field cornet** [14C. < French, 'small horn' < *corne* 'horn' < Latin *cornu*.]

cornetfish /káwrnit fish/ (*plural* **-fish** *or* **-fishes**) *n* a sea fish that has a long tubular snout ending in a small mouth and a forked tail with a long trailing extension from its centre. Native to: tropical or subtropical waters. Family: Fistularidae.

cornetist /kawr néttist/, **cornettist** *n* a player of a cornet

cornett /kawr nétt/ *n* Renaissance and Baroque wooden horn with six keys and a cup mouthpiece [Late 19C. Variant of CORNET.]

cornettist *n* MUSIC = **cornetist**

corn exchange *n* a market where corn was bought or sold, or the building where such transactions took place

corn-fed *adj* fed or fattened on cereal grains

cornfield /káwrn feeld/ *n* a field in which cereal crops such as wheat, barley, or oats are growing

cornflakes /káwrn flayks/ *npl* a breakfast cereal consisting of small pieces of toasted maize, usually eaten with cold milk

cornflour /káwrn flowər/ *n* fine-grained starchy flour made from maize, especially used as a thickener in sauces and soups. US term **cornstarch**

cornflower /káwrn flowər/ *n* an annual plant, formerly common as a blue-flowered weed in cultivated fields. Flowers: blue, pink, white, or purple when cultivated. Native to: Europe, Asia, naturalized in North America. *Centaurea cyanus*.

cornflower blue *n* a deep brilliant purplish-blue colour

cornice /káwrniss/ *n* **1 PROJECTING MOULDING ALONG WALL** a projecting horizontal moulding along the top of a wall or building **2 DECORATIVE PLASTER MOULDING** a decorative plaster moulding around a room where the walls and ceiling meet **3 PART OF CLASSICAL BUILDING** the top projecting section of the part of a classical building that is supported by the columns (**entablature**) **4 OVERHANG OF SNOW** an overhanging mass of snow or ice formed by wind action ■ *vt* (**-nices, -nicing, -niced**) **DECORATE WALL WITH CORNICE** to decorate or finish a wall or building with a cornice [Mid-16C. Via French < Italian.]

corniche /kawr neésh/ *n* a coast road, especially one cut into a cliff [Mid-19C. < French (see CORNICE).]

cornification /káwrnifi káysh'n/ *n* the conversion of skin cells into keratin or other horny material, such as nails or scales [Mid-19C. < Latin *cornu* 'horn'.]

Corning /káwrning/ city in S New York State. Population: 11,080 (1998 estimate).

Cornish /káwrnish/ *adj* **OF CORNWALL** relating to Cornwall or its people, language, or culture ■ *npl* **PEOPLE OF CORNWALL** the people of Cornwall ■ *n* (*plural* **-nish**) **EXTINCT CELTIC LANGUAGE** an extinct Celtic language, related to Breton, spoken in Cornwall until the late 18th century

Cornishman /káwrnishmən/ (*plural* **-men** /-mən/) *n* a man who comes from Cornwall

Cornish pasty (*plural* **Cornish pasties**) *n* a baked food made of a circle of pastry filled with beef and vegetables, with the pastry edges pinched together over the filling

Cornishwoman /káwrnish wŏŏmən/ (*plural* **-en** /-wimin/) *n* a woman who comes from Cornwall

Corn Laws *npl* a group of laws introduced in Great Britain in 1804 and repealed in 1846 that were designed to restrict the importation of foreign corn by imposing duty on it

corn lily *n* a plant of the iris family. Flowers: various colours, resembling lilies, on tall, wiry stems. Native to: southern Africa. Genus: *Ixia*.

corn marigold *n* an annual plant that was formerly a common weed in cultivated fields. Flowers: resembling yellow daisies. *Chrysanthemum segetum*. [Because it grows in cornfields]

cornmeal /káwrn meel/, **corn meal** *n* flour made from maize

corn oil *n* oil extracted from maize. Use: cooking, margarine, salad oil, soaps.

corn on the cob *n* an ear of maize that is cooked and served whole

corn pone /-pōn/ *n Southern US* fried or baked bread made with maize meal ■ *adj* **cornpone** *US* typical of country life and people in being simple, unpretentious, and homely (*informal*)

cornrow /káwrn rō/ *n* any of a series of narrow parallel braids of hair lying flat against the scalp ■ *vt* to style hair in cornrows [Late 20C. Because the braids resemble rows of maize.]

corn salad *n* PLANTS = **lamb's lettuce**

corn snow *n US, Can* fallen snow that has a grainy surface because it has thawed and refrozen

cornstarch /káwrn staarch/ *n US* FOOD = **cornflour**

cornstick /káwrn stik/ *n US* a stick of bread made from maize flour

corn syrup *n US, Can* syrup made from cornflour

cornu /káwrnyoo/ (*plural* **-nua** /-nyŏŏ ə/) *n* a part that resembles a horn or has a horn-shaped pattern [Late 17C. < Latin, 'horn'.] —**cornual** *adj*

cornucopia /káwrnyŏŏ kōpi ə/ *n* **1 ABUNDANCE** a great abundance of something **2 GOAT'S HORN OVERFLOWING WITH PRODUCE** a painting or other representation of a goat's horn overflowing with fruits, flowers, and vegetables, used to symbolize plenty or prosperity **3 HORN-SHAPED CONTAINER** an ornament or container shaped like a goat's horn **4 HORN OF GOAT THAT SUCKLED ZEUS** in Greek mythology, the horn of the goat that suckled Zeus [Early 16C. Via late Latin < Latin *cornu copiæ* 'horn of plenty'.] —**cornucopian** *adj*

cornute /kawr nyóot/, **cornuted** /-nyóotid/ *adj* relating to a horn or horns [Early 17C. < Latin *cornutus* 'horned' < *cornu* 'horn'.]

Cornwall /káwrn wəl, -wawl/ county in the extreme southwest of England. Population: 482,700 (1995).

corn whisky *n* whisky distilled from mash made mostly of maize

corny /káwrni/ (**-ier, -iest**) *adj* unsophisticated and trite ○ *a corny love scene* [Late 16C. < CORN[1].] —**cornily** *adv* —**corniness** *n*

corolla /kə róllə/ *n* the petals of a flower collectively, forming a ring around the reproductive organs and surrounded by an outer ring of sepals [Mid-18C. < Latin, 'garland', literally 'little crown' < *corona* 'crown'.]

corollary /kə róllәri/ *n* (*plural* **-ies**) **1 NATURAL CONSEQUENCE** something that is a natural consequence of or accompaniment to something else **2 STATEMENT EASILY PROVED FROM ANOTHER** a proposition that follows, with little or no further reasoning, from the proof of another **3 OBVIOUS DEDUCTION** something that is very obviously or easily deduced from something already proven **4 SOMETHING ADDED** something added to something else, e.g. something appended to a document ■ *adj* **FOLLOWING** following as a consequence or result [14C. < Latin *corollarium* 'money paid for a garland' < *corolla* (see COROLLA).]

coromandel /kórrə mánd'l/ *n* INDUST = **calamander** [Mid-19C. After the COROMANDEL COAST.]

Coromandel Coast /kórə mánd'l-/ SE Indian coast in the states of Tamil Nadu and Andhra Pradesh

Coromandel Peninsula /kóRrə mánd'l-/ peninsula on the coast of the NE of the North Island, New Zealand

corona /kə rṓnə/ (*plural* **-nas** *or* **-nae** /-nee/) *n* **1 RING OF LIGHT AROUND MOON** a ring of light visible around a luminous body, especially the Moon, typically as a result of optical effects caused by thin cloud, water droplets, or ice in the Earth's atmosphere **2 OUTERMOST PART OF SUN'S ATMOSPHERE** the outermost part of the Sun's atmosphere **3 LIP OF FLOWER TRUMPET** the prominent, sometimes frilly lip of the petal tube or trumpet corolla of some flowers such as daffodils and narcissi. ◊ **crown 4 TOP OF BODY PART** the top of a part of the body such as the crown of the head or a tooth **5** PHYS = **corona discharge 6 PART OF CORNICE** the flat vertical surface of a cornice just above the bottom surface (**soffit**) **7 LONG CIGAR** a long cigar with a blunt rounded mouth end **8 CIRCULAR CHANDELIER** a circular hanging chandelier, especially in a church [Mid-16C. < Latin, 'crown'.] —**coronal** /kórrən'l/ *adj*

Corona Australis /-o stráyliss/ *n* a constellation of the southern hemisphere. See illustration at **constellation**

Corona Borealis /-báwri áyliss/ *n* a constellation of the northern hemisphere. See illustration at **constellation**

coronach /kórrənəkh/ *n Scotland, Ireland* a dirge or funeral lament sung or played on bagpipes [Early 16C. < Gaelic *corranach* 'outcry together' < *rànach* 'outcry'.]

corona discharge *n* a luminous discharge from the surface of an object that is highly charged electrically, caused by ionization of the surrounding gas

coronagraph /kə rṓnnə graaf, -graf/, **coronograph** *n* a telescope that masks the bright disc of the Sun so that the Sun's corona can be studied

coronal suture *n* a junction extending side-to-side across the crown of the skull between the two parietal bones and the frontal bone

coronary /kórrənəri/ *n* (*plural* **-ies**) **1** MED = **coronary thrombosis 2 HEART ATTACK** a heart attack (*informal*) ■ *adj* **1 SUPPLYING OR DRAINING BLOOD FROM HEART** describes the arteries that supply blood to the muscle tissue of the heart or the veins that take blood away from it **2 INVOLVING THE CORONARY ARTERIES AND VEINS** relating to disease of the coronary arteries and veins, and conditions associated with it ○ *coronary care* [Early 17C. < Latin *coronarius* 'crownlike' < *corona* 'crown'.]

coronary artery *n* an artery supplying blood to the muscles of the heart, one of a pair arising from the aorta

coronary bypass *n* an operation in which a new blood vessel is grafted onto the heart to replace a blocked coronary artery

coronary thrombosis *n* the blocking of a coronary artery by a blood clot, which obstructs the blood supply to the heart muscle, resulting in death of the muscle and, often, a heart attack

coronary vein *n* any of the veins that drain blood from the muscles and other tissues of the heart

coronation /kórrə náysh'n/ *n* the ceremony or act of crowning a monarch [14C. Via Old French < medieval Latin *coronation-* < Latin *corona* 'crown'.]

coroner /kórrənər/ *n* a public official responsible for investigating deaths that appear not to have natural causes [13C. < Anglo-Norman *coruner* 'officer of the crown' < *coroune* 'crown'.] —**coronership** *n*

coronet /kórrənit/ *n* **1 SMALL CROWN** a small crown, especially one worn by a prince or a peer rather than a reigning monarch **2 WOMAN'S HEAD DECORATION** a circular ornamental band worn by women on the head **3 TOP OF HORSE'S HOOF** the upper part of a horse's hoof, where the horn of the hoof meets the skin of the pastern **4 BASE OF DEER'S ANTLER** the rosette of bone at the base of a deer's antler [14C. < French, 'little crown' < *corone* (see CROWN).]

coronograph *n* ASTRON = **coronagraph**

Corot /kórrō/, **Jean Baptiste Camille** (1796–1875) French landscape and portrait painter

corotate /kō rō táyt/ (**-tates, -tating, -tated**) *vi* to turn in conjunction with another turning object —**corotation** /kō rō táysh'n/ *n* —**corotational** /-táysh'nəl/ *adj*

corp. *abbr* corporation

Corp. *abbr* Corporal

~~**corperation**~~ incorrect spelling of **corporation**

corpora plural of **corpus**

corporal[1] /káwrpərəl/ *adj* relating or belonging to the body ○ *corporal punishment* [14C. Via French < Latin *corporalis* < *corpus* 'body'.] —**corporally** *adv*

USAGE corporal or **corporeal**? ***Corporal*** means 'relating to the body' and is mainly used in the expression *corporal punishment*, in reference to the inflicting of physical hurt. ***Corporeal*** means 'material or physical rather than spiritual': *The gods of antiquity were not just spirits but enjoyed a corporeal existence.*

corporal[2] /káwrpərəl/ *n* **1** a noncommissioned officer in various armed forces, ranking immediately below sergeant, or, in Canada, a master corporal **2** a petty officer in the Royal Navy, immediately junior to the master-at-arms [Mid-16C. Via French < Italian *caporale* 'of the head' < *capo* (see CAPO[2]).] —**corporalcy** *n* —**corporalship** *n*

corporal[3] /káwrpərəl/, **corporale** /káwrpə ráyli/ *n* a white, usually linen, cloth on which the consecrated bread and wine are placed in the Christian sacrament of Communion [14C. Directly or via French < medieval Latin *(pallium) corporale* '(cloth) for the body'.]

corporality /káwrpə rálləti/ *n* the state of being in physical or bodily form rather than spiritual form

Corporal of Horse *n* a noncommissioned officer in the Household Cavalry of a rank above sergeant

corporal punishment *n* the striking of a person's body as punishment

corporate /káwrpərət/ *adj* **1 INVOLVING A CORPORATION** relating or belonging to a corporation **2 OF CORPORATION'S EMPLOYEES** designed for, suitable for, or typical of people who work for large corporations ○ *corporate fashions* **3 INCORPORATED** legally united to form a body that can act as a unit **4 OF GROUP AS A WHOLE** relating to or involving a group as a whole (*formal*) [16C. < Latin *corporatus*, past participle of *corporare* 'form a body' < *corpus* 'body'.] —**corporately** *adv*

⚡ **corporate disaster recovery** *n* the preservation and restoration of computer data and online and telecommunications links of a company whose operations have been compromised

corporate killing *n* a proposed criminal offence under which companies and similar organizations, and their directors, would be held responsible for the deaths of employees, clients, or passengers occurring as a result of the company's negligence

corporate raider *n* a company or person who attempts to take control of a business by acquiring a substantial number of its shares or by manipulating proxies

corporation /káwrpə ráysh'n/ *n* **1 GROUP REGARDED AS INDIVIDUAL BY LAW** a company recognized by law as a single body with its own powers and liabilities, separate from those of the individual members **2 LOCAL GOVERNING AUTHORITY** the governing authority of a municipality, e.g. a city or town ○ *working for the corporation* ○ *corporation transport* **3 GROUP ACTING AS SINGLE ENTITY** a group of people acting as a single entity **4** a paunch, especially a large one (*dated informal humorous*) [15C. < Late Latin *corporation-* < *corporatus* (see CORPORATE).]

corporation tax *n* a tax on the profits of a company

corporatism /káwrpərətizəm/ *n* a system of running a state using the power of organizations like businesses and trade unions that act, or purport to act, for large numbers of individuals —**corporatist** *adj, n*

corporeal /kawr páwri əl/ *adj* **1** relating to or involving the physical body rather than the mind or spirit **2** material or physical rather than spiritual [Early 17C. < late Latin *corporealis* < Latin *corpus* 'body'.] —**corporeality** /kawr páwri álləti/ *n* —**corporeally** *adv*

USAGE See ***corporal***.

corporeity /káwrpə reé əti/ *n* the condition of existing as something material or physical [Early 17C. < French *corporéité* < Latin *corpus* 'body'.]

corps /kawr/ (*plural* **corps**) *n* **1 SPECIALIZED MILITARY FORCE** a military force that carries out specialized duties **2 TACTICAL UNIT** a tactical military unit that is made up of two or more divisions with additional supporting services **3 GROUP OF ASSOCIATED PEOPLE** a group of people who work together or are associated [Late 16C. Via French < Latin *corpus* 'body'.]

corps de ballet /káwr də bállay/ (*plural* **corps de ballet**) *n* the dancers of a ballet company who perform as a group rather than individually [< French, 'dance company']

corps diplomatique /káwr dípplō ma teék/ (*plural* **corps diplomatiques**) *n* INTERNAT REL = **diplomatic corps** [< French]

corpse /kawrps/ *n* a dead body, especially of a human being ■ *vti* (**corpses, corpsing, corpsed**) to become unable to speak lines because of involuntary laughing, or make an actor on stage unable to speak his or her lines because of involuntary laughing (*slang*) [14C. Directly and via French *cors* < Latin *corpus* 'body'.]

corpsman /káwrmən/ (*plural* **-men** /-mən/) *n* US in the US armed forces, an enlisted person with training in giving first aid and basic medical treatment

corpulent /káwrpyŏŏlənt/ *adj* obese (*literary*) [15C. < Latin *corpulentus* < *corpus* 'body'.] —**corpulence** *n* —**corpulency** *n* —**corpulently** *adv*

cor pulmonale /káwr púlmə naáli/ *n* a disease in which the right ventricle of the heart becomes enlarged and fails, caused by disease of the lungs or pulmonary blood vessels [< modern Latin, 'pulmonary heart']

corpus /káwrpəss/ (*plural* **-pora** /-pərə/) *n* **1 BODY OF WRITINGS** a body of writings by a particular person, on a particular subject, or of a particular type ○ *one of the most popular works in the Shakespearean corpus* **2 MAIN PART** the main part of something **3 PART OF ORGAN** the main portion of something, such as an organ or other body part, or a mass of tissue with a distinct function ○ *the corpus of the uterus* **4 CAPITAL** the capital or principal of a sum of money **5 COLLECTION OF LANGUAGE EXAMPLES** a large collection of written, and sometimes spoken, examples of the usage of a language, used for linguistic analysis [Early 18C. < Latin, 'body'.]

corpus callosum /-kə lóssəm/ (*plural* **corpora callosa** /-kə lōsə/) *n* the thick band of nerve fibres that connects the two hemispheres of the brain in higher mammals and allows the hemispheres to communicate [< modern Latin, 'callous body']

Corpus Christi[1] /-krísti/ *n* a mainly Roman Catholic festival honouring the institution of Communion. Date: Thursday after Trinity Sunday. [< medieval Latin, 'body of Christ']

Corpus Christi[2] /-krísti/ city and port in SE Texas. Population: 281,453 (1998 estimate).

corpuscle /káwr puss'l/ *n* **1 UNATTACHED CELL** a small independent body, especially a cell in blood or lymph **2 PARTICLE** a discrete particle, especially a photon **3 SMALL PARTICLE** a very small particle of anything [Mid-17C. < Latin *corpusculum* 'small body' < *corpus* 'body'.] —**corpuscular** /kawr púskyŏŏlər/ *adj*

corpuscular theory *n* the theory, originally introduced by Newton, that light consists of a stream of particles

corpus delicti /-di lík tī/ *n* the body of facts that show that a crime has been committed, including physical evidence such as a corpse [< modern Latin, 'body of the crime']

corpus luteum /-loóti əm/ (*plural* **corpora lutea** /-loóti ə/) *n* a yellow mass of tissue that forms in part of the ovary (**Graafian follicle**) after ovulation in mammals and secretes the hormone progesterone [< modern Latin, 'yellow body']

corpus striatum /-strī áytəm/ (*plural* **corpora striata** /-strī áytə/) *n* a mass of striped grey and white nervous tissue, one of which occurs in each hemisphere of the brain [< modern Latin, 'striated body']

corr. *abbr* **1** correct **2** corrected **3** correction **4** correspondence **5** correspondent

corral /kə raál/ *n* US **1 PLACE FOR KEEPING LIVESTOCK** a fenced area in which livestock or horses are kept **2 CIRCLE OF WAGONS** a temporary defensive enclosure formed by wagons arranged in a circle, formerly used by people travelling through North America ■ *vt* (**-rals, -ralling, -ralled**) US **1 DRIVE ANIMALS INTO CORRAL** to gather animals together and drive them into a corral **2 PUT WAGONS IN CIRCLE** to form wagons into a corral **3 GATHER AND CONTROL** to gather together and take control of people or things ○ *hopes to corral sufficient funding for the project* [Late 16C. < Spanish.]

corrasion /kə ráyzh'n/ *n* the mechanical erosion of a surface by fragments of rock carried by water, wind, or ice [Late 19C. < Latin *corras-*, past participle of *corradere* 'scrape together' < *radere* 'to scrape'.] —**corrasive** /kə ráyssiv/ *adj*

correct /kə rékt/ *vt* **1 REMOVE ERRORS FROM** to take the errors out of something **2 POINT OUT ERRORS IN** to point out or mark the errors in something **3 RECTIFY DEFECT** to rectify a defect in something or counteract something wrong or undesirable ○ *wears glasses to correct his astigmatism* **4 MODIFY** to modify something, e.g. behaviour, to make it acceptable or bring it up to a particular standard ■ *adj* **1 ACCURATE** accurate or without errors ○ *the correct time* **2 ACCEPTABLE** acceptable or meeting a particular standard ○ *correct dress* [14C. < Latin *correct-*, past participle of *corrigere* 'rule completely' < *regere* 'to rule'.] —**correctable** *adj* —**correctly** *adv* —**correctness** *n* —**corrector** *n*

correction /kə réksh'n/ *n* **1 ALTERATION THAT IMPROVES** an alteration that removes an error **2 WRITTEN COMMENT ON ERROR** something written beside an error in a text to point out what should be there instead **3 REMOVING OF ERRORS** the removing of errors from something or the indicating of errors in something **4 MODIFICATION TO CALCULATION** an adjustment made to a calculation or measurement to compensate for an observed deviation from ideal conditions **5 PUNISHMENT MEANT TO IMPROVE** punishment, especially when meant to improve or reform the person punished (*dated*) —**correctional** *adj*

correctional facility *n* US a prison or other institution where criminals are held and treated

correctitude /kə rékti tyood/ *n* the fact of being correct, especially in behaviour and manners [Late 19C. Blend of CORRECT + RECTITUDE.]

corrective /kə réktiv/ *adj* acting to correct or intended to correct something ○ *corrective action* ■ *n* something that corrects or is meant to correct something —**correctively** *adv*

corrective shoe *n* US MED = **surgical boot**

Corregidor /kə réggi dawr/ island at the entrance to Manila Bay in the Philippines. In World War II, the scene of intense fighting between US and Filipino forces against Japanese troops. It was recaptured by US forces in 1945. Area: 5 sq. km/1.93 sq. mi.

correlate /kórrə layt/ *v* (**-lates, -lating, -lated**) **1** *vti* **HAVE OR SHOW MUTUAL RELATIONSHIP** to have a mutual or complementary relationship, or show that two or more things, e.g. a cause and an effect, have a mutual or complementary relationship ○ *How do these results correlate with your findings?* **2** *vt* **GATHER AND COMPARE THINGS** to gather together and compare related things, e.g. results or reports ○ *Her job is to correlate the statistics from a range of sources and prepare a report.* ■ *adj* **HAVING SHARED PROPERTIES** having mutual or complementary properties ■ *n* **1 correlate, correlative COMPLEMENTARY THING** something that shares mutual or complementary properties with something else **2 VARIABLE RELATED TO ANOTHER VARIABLE** either of two variables that are related with the result that a variation in one is accompanied by a linear variation of the other [Mid-18C. Back-formation < CORRELATION.] —**correlatable** *adj* —**correlator** *n*

correlation /kórrə láysh'n/ *n* **1 MUTUAL OR COMPLEMENTARY RELATIONSHIP** a relationship in which two or more things are mutual or complementary or one is caused by another ○ *the close correlation between the two factors* **2 ACT OF CORRELATING** the act of correlating, or the condition of being correlated **3 RELATEDNESS OF VARIABLES** the degree to which two or more variables are related and change together [Mid-16C. < medieval Latin *correlation-* 'mutual relationship' < Latin *relation-* (see RELATION).] —**correlational** *adj*

correlation coefficient *n* a number or function indicating the degree of correlation between two variables

correlative /kə rélləti v/ *adj* **1 BEING CORRELATES** in a mutual or complementary relationship **2 TOGETHER BUT NOT ADJACENT** often used together but not usually adjacent, as are the conjunctions 'either' and 'or' ■ *n* **1** = **correlate** *n.* 1 **2 CORRELATIVE WORD** a word, especially a conjunction, that is often used together with but not usually adjacent to another —**correlatively** *adv* —**correlativeness** *n* —**correlativity** /kə rélla tívvəti/ *n*

correspond /kórri spónd/ *vi* **1 CONFORM OR BE CONSISTENT** to conform, be consistent, or be in agreement with something else **2 BE SIMILAR** to be similar or equivalent **3 WRITE TO ONE ANOTHER** to communicate with somebody by exchanging written messages [Early 16C. Via French < medieval Latin *correspondere* 'respond to each other' < Latin *respondere* (see RESPOND).]

correspondence /kórri spóndənss/ *n* **1 WRITTEN COMMUNICATION** communication by means of exchanged written messages, e.g. letters or e-mail **2 WRITTEN MESSAGES** written messages, especially letters **3 CONFORMITY** conformity, consistency, or agreement between two or more things **4 SIMILARITY** similarity or equivalence between two or more things

correspondence column *n* a part of a newspaper or magazine where letters from readers are printed

correspondence course *n* an educational course in which the teaching organization sends lessons and tests to students by post and students return completed work in the same way

correspondence school *n* an educational organization that carries out teaching by post

correspondent /kórri spóndənt/ *n* **1 SOMEBODY COMMUNICATING BY WRITING** a communicator in writing, or electronically ○ *Most of my correspondents have e-mail now.* **2 SOMEBODY PROVIDING SPECIAL REPORTS** somebody employed by a news organization, especially a newspaper or broadcasting company, to provide reports from a particular place or on a particular subject ○ *our Paris correspondent* **3 BUSINESS DEALING WITH A DISTANT BUSINESS** a person or company that regularly does business with another, especially one that is distant **4 SOMETHING THAT CORRESPONDS** something that conforms or agrees with, or is similar to, something else (*formal*) ■ *adj* = **corresponding**

corresponding /kórri spónding/ *adj* **1 CONSISTENT** consistent, conforming, or in agreement with something else ○ *Line up the prongs on one half with the corresponding sockets on the other.* **2 ANALOGOUS** similar or equivalent to something else in one or more important respects ○ *the corresponding word in her own language* **3 WORKING FROM A DISTANCE** interacting or contributing from a distance, e.g. by post ○ *a corresponding member based in China* **4 DEALING WITH CORRESPONDENCE** handling or assigned to handle correspondence

corresponding angles *npl* the angles formed on the same side of two lines and a third line (**transversal**) that intersects them, each of the four angles at each intersection corresponding to the four angles at the other

correspondingly /kórri spóndingli/ *adv* in a way that is consistent, equivalent, or similar ○ *A large company has correspondingly large problems.*

corrida /ko reédə/ *n* a programme of bullfights [Late 19C. < Spanish, 'running' (of bulls) < Latin *currere* 'to run'.]

corridor /kórri dawr/ *n* **1 PASSAGE INSIDE BUILDING** a passage between parts of a building, often with a series of rooms opening onto it **2 PASSAGEWAY IN RAILWAY CARRIAGE** a passageway in a railway carriage giving access to compartments **3 STRIP OF LAND** a narrow strip of land belonging to one country and projecting through another, e.g. to give a landlocked country access to a port **4 REGION OF AIRSPACE FOR AIR TRAFFIC** a particular region of airspace designated for use by air traffic **5 SPACECRAFT FLIGHT PATH** a predetermined flight path that a spacecraft follows upon re-entry into the Earth's atmosphere [Late 16C. Via French and Italian < Latin *currere* 'to run'.]

corrie /kórri/ *n* GEOG = **cirque** [Mid-16C. Via Scots Gaelic *coire* 'hollow' < Old Irish, 'cauldron'.]

Corriedale /kórri dayl/ (*plural* **-dales** *or* **-dale**) *n* a sheep belonging to a breed without horns developed in New Zealand. Kept for: wool and meat. [Early 20C. After *Corriedale*, estate in New Zealand.]

corrigenda /kórri jén də/ *n* PUBL = **errata** *npl.* (+ *singular or plural verb*)

corrigendum /kórri jéndəm/ (*plural* **-da** /-jéndə/) *n* an error to be corrected [Early 19C. < Latin, 'thing to be corrected'.]

corroborate /kə róbbə rayt/ (**-rates, -rating, -rated**) *vt* to give or represent evidence of the truth of something ○ *The photographs corroborate the verbal account.* [Mid-16C. < Latin *corroborat-*, past participle of *corroborare* 'strengthen together' < *roborare* 'strengthen'.] —**corroboration** /kə róbbə ráysh'n/ *n* —**corroborative** /kə róbbərətiv/ *adj* —**corroboratively** *adv* —**corroborator** *n* —**corroboratory** /kə róbbə ráytəri/ *adj*

corroboree /kə róbbəri/ *n Aus* **1** a gathering of an Aboriginal people **2** any noisy gathering of people, especially a party (*informal*) [Late 18C. < Dharuk *garaabara*.]

corrode /kə rṓd/ (**-rodes, -roding, -roded**) *v* **1** *vti* to destroy something progressively, or be destroyed progressively, by chemical action **2** *vt* to undermine or destroy something gradually [14C. < Latin *corrodere* 'gnaw away' < *rodere* 'gnaw'.] —**corrodant** *n* —**corroder** *n* —**corrodibility** /kə rṓdə bílləti/ *n* —**corrodible** *adj* —**corrosible** *adj*

corrosion /kə rṓzh'n/ *n* **1 DESTRUCTION BY CHEMICAL ACTION** a process by which something, especially a metal, is destroyed progressively by chemical action, as iron is when it rusts **2 MATERIAL PRODUCED BY CORROSION** material produced by corrosion, e.g. rust **3 RESULT OF CORROSION** the condition produced by corrosion [14C. < Old French, or late Latin *corrosion-* < Latin *corros-*, past participle of *corrodere* (see CORRODE).]

corrosive /kə rṓssiv/ *adj* **1 PROGRESSIVELY DESTRUCTIVE** able to destroy something progressively by chemical action **2 DESTROYING GRADUALLY** destroying something gradually **3 VERY SARCASTIC** very strongly sarcastic or bitter ○ *a corrosive review* ■ *n* **DESTRUCTIVE SUBSTANCE** a substance that is able to destroy something progressively by chemical action, e.g. an acid [14C. Via French < Latin *corros-*, past participle of *corrodere* (see CORRODE).] —**corrosively** *adv* —**corrosiveness** *n*

corrosive sublimate *n* = **mercuric chloride**

corrugate /kórrə gayt/ *vti* (**-gates, -gating, -gated**) to become folded into parallel ridges and troughs, or fold something, e.g. a sheet of cardboard, into parallel ridges and troughs ■ *adj* = **corrugated** [Early 17C. < Latin *corrugat-*, past participle of *corrugare* 'wrinkle completely' < *rugare* 'to wrinkle'.] —**corrugation** /kórrə gáysh'n/ *n*

corrugated /kórrə gaytid/ *adj* **1** folded into parallel ridges and troughs **2** made from a corrugated material ○ *a shed with a corrugated roof*

corrugator /kórrə gaytər/ *n* a muscle that wrinkles the skin when it contracts

ϟ **corrupt** /kə rúpt/ *adj* **1 IMMORAL OR DISHONEST** immoral or dishonest, especially as shown by the exploitation of a position of power or trust for personal gain **2 DEPRAVED** extremely immoral or depraved **3 CONTAINING ERRORS** describes computer data or software that is unusable or unreliable because of the presence of errors that have been introduced unintentionally **4 CONTAINING COPYING ERRORS** containing undesirable changes in meaning or errors made in copying ○ *a corrupt transcription of the manuscript* ■ *v* **1** *vti* **MAKE OR BECOME DISHONEST** to become dishonest, or destroy or compromise somebody's morality or honesty **2** *vti* **MAKE OR BECOME DEPRAVED** to become or cause somebody to become immoral or depraved **3** *vt* **INTRODUCE ERRORS INTO COMPUTER DATA** in computing, to introduce unintentional errors into computer data or software, making it unusable or unreliable **4** *vt* **SPOIL TEXT WITH COPYING ERRORS** to make undesirable changes in meaning or errors in a text during copying [14C. < Latin *corruptus*, past participle of *corrumpere* 'break completely' < *rumpere* 'to break'.] —**corrupter** *n* —**corruptibility** /kə rúptə bílləti/ *n* —**corruptible** *adj* —**corruptibleness** *n* —**corruptibly** *adv* —**corruptly** *adv* —**corruptness** *n*

corruption /kə rúpsh'n/ *n* **1 DISHONESTY FOR PERSONAL GAIN** dishonest exploitation of power for personal gain **2 DEPRAVITY** extreme immorality or depravity **3 WORD OR PHRASE ALTERED FROM ORIGINAL** a word or phrase that has been altered from its original form **4 UNDESIRABLE CHANGE** an undesirable change in meaning or error introduced into a text during copying **5 CORRUPTING OF** the corrupting of something or somebody, or the state of being corrupt

corruptive /kə rúptiv/ *adj* having a bad effect on somebody's character or behaviour —**corruptively** *adv*

corsac /káwr sak/ *n* a small yellowish or reddish brown fox. Native to: Central Asia. *Vulpes corsac.* [Mid-19C. Via Russian *korsak* < Turkic *karsak*.]

corsage /kawr saázh, káwrss aazh/ *n* **1** a small bouquet worn on the bodice of a dress or the lapel of a jacket **2** the bodice of a dress (*archaic*) [Early 19C. < French, < Old French *cors* 'body'.]

corsair /káwrss air, kawr sáir/ *n* **1 PIRATE** a pirate, especially one based on the North African coast between the 16th and 19th centuries **2 PIRATE SHIP COMMISSIONED BY GOVERNMENT** a privately owned ship commissioned by a government to attack foreign ships, especially one based on the coast of North Africa **3 OWNER OF PIRATE SHIP** the owner of a ship commissioned by a government to attack ships of other countries [Mid-16C. Via French < medieval Latin *cursarius* < Latin *cursus* 'hostile incursion' < the past participle of *currere* 'to run'.]

corselet /káwrsslət, -it/ *n* **1 corselet, corselette** a garment combining a corset and a bra **2 corselet, corslet** armour covering the upper body [15C. < French, < Old French *cors* 'body'.]

corset /káwrssit/ *n* **1 STIFF GARMENT** a stiffened garment worn by women to shape the waist and breasts **2 STIFF UNDERGARMENT** a stiff undergarment with laces to fasten it tightly, formerly worn to shape and support the body **3 INJURY SUPPORT** a garment similar to a woman's stiff body-shaping undergarment, worn by men or women for support when injured [13C. < French, < Old French *cors* 'body'.] —**corseted** *adj*

Corsica /káwrssikə/ island in the Mediterranean Sea, an administrative region of France. Population: 249,237 (1990). Area: 8,680 sq. km/3,350 sq. mi. —**Corsican** *adj, n*

corslet /káwrsslət/ *n* = **corselet** *n.* 2

Cortázar /káwrtə zaar/, **Julio** (1914–84) Belgian-born Argentinian writer

cortege /kawr táyzh, -tézh/, **cortège** *n* **1** a procession, especially a funeral procession **2** a retinue of servants or attendants [Mid-17C. Via French < Italian *corteggio* < *corteggiare* 'attend court' < *corte* 'court' < Latin *cohort-* 'enclosed space'.]

Cortés, Sea of /káwr tez/ former name for **California, Gulf of**

Cortés, Hernán (1485–1547) Spanish explorer

cortex /káwr teks/ (*plural* **-tices** /-ti seez/ *or* **-texes**) *n* **1** the outer layer of a solid organ or part of the body, e.g. the outer covering of the kidney or brain (**cerebral cortex**) **2** the tissue in plant stems and roots between the outer layer (**epidermis**) and the central core (**stele**) [Mid-17C. < Latin, 'bark'.] —**cortical** /káwrtik'l/ *adj*

cortic- *prefix* = **cortico-** (*before vowels*)

cortico- *prefix* cortex, cortical ○ *corticospinal* [< Latin *cortic-* 'bark']

corticoid /káwrti koyd/ *n* a drug that acts in a similar way to the hormone produced by the outer layer of the adrenal gland

corticospinal /káwrtikō spín'l/ *adj* relating to or connecting the outer covering of the brain (**cerebral cortex**) and the spinal cord

corticosteroid /káwrtikō stérroyd, -steer-/ *n* **1** an adrenal steroid hormone involved in metabolism and immune response **2** a synthetic drug similar to a natural corticosteroid. Use: reduction of inflammation and allergic reactions, prevention of graft rejection.

corticotrophin /káwrtikō trṓfin/, **corticotropin** /-pin/ *n* BIOCHEM = **ACTH** [Mid-20C. Contraction of *adrenocorticotrophic hormone*.]

cortisol /káwrti sol, -zol/ *n* BIOCHEM = **hydrocortisone** *n.* 1 [Mid-20C. < CORTISONE.]

cortisone /káwrti zōn/ *n* a steroid hormone secreted by the adrenal cortex [Mid-20C. Contraction of *corticosterone*, a type of corticosteroid.]

corundum /kə rúndəm/ *n* a hard mineral form of aluminium oxide, that crystallizes in a range of colours. Use: gems, abrasives. ◊ **sapphire** *n.* 1, **ruby** *n.* 1 [Early 18C. < Tamil *kuruntam*.]

coruscate /kórrə skayt/ (**-cates, -cating, -cated**) *vi* (*literary*) **1** to give off flashes of bright light **2** to show brilliance or virtuosity [Early 18C. < Latin *coruscat-*, past participle of *coruscare* 'glitter'.] —**coruscant** /kə rúskənt/ *adj* —**coruscating** *adj* —**coruscation** /kórrə skáysh'n/ *n*

corvée /káwr vay/ *n* **1** a day of unpaid labour required of a serf for a manorial lord **2** a period of labour sometimes required by the state in lieu of taxes, e.g. in pre-Revolutionary France [14C. Via French < Latin *corrogata*, past participle of *corrogare* 'summon together' < *rogare* 'ask'.]

corves plural of **corf**

corvette /kawr vét/ *n* **1** an armed naval escort vessel, smaller than a destroyer **2** a small wooden sailing ship with one tier of guns [Mid-17C. Via French < Dutch *korf* 'small ship', literally 'basket' < Latin *corbis*.]

corvid /káwrvid/ *n* a bird of the family that includes crows, jays, and magpies. Family: Corvidae. [Mid-20C. < modern Latin *Corvidae* < Latin *corvus* 'raven'.]

corvine /káwr vīn/ *adj* relating to crows or the crow family (*literary*) [Mid-17C. < Latin *corvinus* < *corvus* 'raven'.]

Corvus /káwrvəss/ *n* a small constellation of the southern hemisphere. See illustration at **constellation**

Corybant /kórri bant/ (*plural* **-bants** *or* **-bantes** /-bán teez/) *n* **1** in ancient Phrygia, a priest of the goddess Cybele who performed wild ecstatic dances **2** in ancient mythology, any one of the goddess Cybele's attendants [15C. < Latin *Corybant-* < Greek *Korubas*.] —**Corybantic** /kórri bántik/ *adj*

corymb /kórrimb, -im/ *n* a flat flower head (**inflorescence**) consisting of flowers whose stalks grow from different points on the flower stem but reach approximately the same height [Early 18C. Via French < Greek *korumbos* 'summit'.] —**corymbed** *adj* —**corymbose** /kórrimbōss/ *adj* —**corymbous** *adj*

coryphée /kórri fáy/ *n* a leading ballet dancer who usually performs with a small group of other dancers [Early 19C. Via French < Greek *koruphaios* 'chorus leader' < *koruphē* 'head'.]

coryza /kə rīzə/ *n* **1** NASAL CONGESTION severe nasal congestion **2** COLD a common cold (*technical*) **3** BIRD DISEASE a respiratory disease of chickens and turkeys, caused by bacteria [Early 16C. Via Latin < Greek *koruza* 'nasal mucus, catarrh'.] —**coryzal** *adj*

cos[1] /koss/ (*plural* **coses** *or* **cos**) *n* a lettuce with long crisp leaves. US term **romaine** [Late 17C. After Cos.]

cos[2] /koz/ *abbr* cosine

'cos /koz/ *conj* because (*informal*) [Early 19C. Shortening and alteration of BECAUSE.]

Cos /koss/ second largest of the Greek Dodecanese Islands, off the coast of Turkey. Population: 20,350 (1981). Area: 287 sq. km/111 sq. mi. Greek **Kos**

COS /koss/ *abbr* **1** cash on shipment **2** chief of staff

Cosa Nostra /kóssə nóstrə, kṓzə-/ *n* a criminal organization in the United States, linked with the Mafia of Sicily [Mid-20C. < Italian, 'our concern'.]

cosec /kṓ sek/ *abbr* cosecant

cosecant /kō seékənt/ *n* for a given angle in a right-angled triangle, a trigonometric function equal to the length of the hypotenuse divided by that of the side opposite the angle

coseismal /kō sízm'l/ *n* a line on a map that connects places where the effects of an earthquake were felt at the same time

Cosenza /kō zénzə, -zéntsə/ capital of Cosenza Province, S Italy. Population: 76,817 (1997 estimate).

Cosgrave /kóz grayv/, **Liam** (*b.* 1920) Irish statesman and prime minister (1973–77)

Cosgrave, William Thomas (1880–1965) Irish statesman and president of the Irish Free State (1922–32)

cosh /kosh/ *n* a blunt weapon usually made of rubber or metal ■ *vt* to attack somebody using a cosh [Mid-19C. < ?]

COSHH regulations /kósh-/ *npl* legal requirements concerning the storage and use of hazardous chemicals in the workplace [Acronym < *Control of Substances Hazardous to Health*]

cosign /kṓ sīn, kō sín/ *vt* **1** to sign something jointly with one or more other people or representatives of other bodies **2** to sign a loan, lease, or other contractual agreement along with somebody else in order to guarantee that the terms of the contract will be fulfilled by that person —**cosignatory** /kō sígnətəri/ *n* —**cosigner** *n*

cosine /kṓ sīn/ *n* for a given angle in a right-angled triangle, a trigonometric function equal to the length of the side adjacent to the angle divided by the hypotenuse

cosmeceutical /kózmə syoótik'l/ *n* a product that falls between the categories designated as pharmaceuticals and cosmetics, especially in terms of marketing [< COSMETIC + PHARMACEUTICAL]

cosmetic /koz méttik/ *n* (*often plural*) **1** BEAUTIFYING SUBSTANCE a preparation, e.g. lipstick, that is applied to the face or the body to make it more attractive **2** *US* SUPERFICIALLY ATTRACTIVE ASPECT something added or done to something else to cover up defects ■ *adj* **1** BEAUTIFYING intended to improve somebody's physical appearance ○ *cosmetic surgery* **2** ONLY FOR APPEARANCES done to make something seem better but having no real value ○ *The changes to the code of conduct were purely cosmetic, since attitudes remained fundamentally the same.* **3** DECORATIVE designed or added for decorative purposes rather than for any real function [Early 17C. Via French *cosmétique* < Greek *kosmētikos* 'skilled in ornamenting' < *kosmein* 'arrange' < *kosmos* 'order'.] —**cosmetically** *adv*

cosmetician /kózmə tísh'n/ *n* a maker, seller, or applier of cosmetics

cosmetic surgery *n* plastic surgery that is intended to improve the appearance of part of the body, such as the shape of the nose or the size of the breasts

cosmetology /kózmə tólləji/ *n* the study of cosmetics or the art or profession of using them [Mid-19C. < French *cosmétologie* < *cosmétique*.] —**cosmetologist** *n*

cosmic /kózmik/ *adj* **1** OF WHOLE UNIVERSE relating to the whole universe **2** OF UNIVERSE APART FROM EARTH describes outer space or a part of the universe other than the Earth **3** GREAT very great in size or significance ■ *interj* EXPRESSING AMAZEMENT used to express amazement or wonder (*slang*) [Mid-17C. < Greek *kosmikos* < *kosmos* 'universe'.] —**cosmically** *adv*

cosmic dust *n* small particles of solid matter found in outer space, often collected in clouds

cosmic radiation *n* radiation consisting of cosmic rays

cosmic ray *n* a stream of high-energy radiation that reaches the Earth from outer space

cosmic string *n* an extremely long and thin astronomical object theorized to be a space-time defect formed when the universe began

cosmo- *prefix* the universe, space ○ *cosmochemistry* [< Greek *kosmos* 'order, universe']

cosmogony /koz móggəni/ (*plural* **-nies**) *n* **1** the study of the origin of the universe or a part of it **2** a theory that explains the origin of the universe [Late 17C. < Greek *kosmogonia* 'creation of the world' < *kosmos* 'universe'.] —**cosmogonic** /kózmə gónnik/ *adj* —**cosmogonical** *adj* —**cosmogonically** *adv* —**cosmogonist** *n*

cosmography /koz móggrəfi/ (*plural* **-phies**) *n* the study and description or mapping of the entire world or the universe [14C. Via late Latin < Greek *kosmographia* < *kosmos* 'universe'.] —**cosmographer** *n* —**cosmographic** /kózmə gráffik/ *adj* —**cosmographical** *adj* —**cosmographically** *adv*

cosmological argument *n* a logical argument that tries to prove the existence of God from empirical information about the universe

cosmological principle *n* the principle that the universe would look the same to observers at any point in it as it does to us

cosmology /koz mólləji/ (*plural* **-gies**) *n* **1** the philosophical study and explanation of the nature of the universe **2** the scientific study of the origin and structure of the universe [Mid-17C. < modern Latin *cosmologia* < Greek *kosmos* 'universe'.] —**cosmologic** /kózmə lójjik/ *adj* —**cosmological** *adj* —**cosmologically** *adv* —**cosmologist** /koz mólləjist/ *n*

cosmonaut /kózmə nawt/ *n* an astronaut in the space programmes of Russia and the former Soviet Union [Mid-20C. < Russian *kosmonavt* < Greek *kosmos* 'universe' + *nautēs* 'sailor'.]

cosmopolis /koz móppəliss/ *n* a large city where people from many different countries and cultures live [Mid-19C. < Greek *kosmos* 'universe' + *polis* 'city'.]

cosmopolitan /kózmə póllitən/ *adj* **1** WITH FEATURES OF DIFFERENT COUNTRIES composed of or containing people from different countries **2** WELL-TRAVELLED familiar with many different countries and cultures **3** UNPREJUDICED free from national prejudices **4** KNOWLEDGEABLE AND REFINED showing a breadth of knowledge and refinement from having travelled widely **5** OCCURRING WORLDWIDE describes plants or animals growing or occurring in many different parts of the world ■ *n* WELL-TRAVELLED PERSON a sophisticated traveller to many different countries [Mid-17C. < COSMOPOLITE.] —**cosmopolitanism** *n*

cosmopolite /koz móppə līt/ *n* = **cosmopolitan** *n.* [Early 17C. Via French < Greek *kosmopolitēs* 'citizen of the world'.] —**cosmopolitism** *n*

cosmos[1] /kóz moss/ *n* **1** the universe thought of as an ordered and integrated whole **2** an ordered system or harmonious whole [13C. < Greek *kosmos* 'order, universe'.]

cosmos[2] /kóz moss/ (*plural* **-moses** *or* **-mos**) *n* a plant with flowers of various colours that resemble large daisies. Native to: tropical America. Genus: *Cosmos*. [Early 19C. Via modern Latin < Greek *kosmos* 'ornament'.]

cosponsor /kṓ spónssər/ *n* a sponsor who supports a person, organization, or project jointly with others — **cosponsor** *vt* —**cosponsorship** *n*

Cossack /kóss ak/ *n* **1** a peasant of Polish or Russian descent living in SE Russia, Ukraine, or Siberia **2** a member of a Russian army unit whose soldiers are or were Cossacks [Late 16C. Via Russian *kazak* < Turkic, 'nomad, adventurer'.]

cosset /kóssit/ *vt* to give somebody or something excessive care and protection [Mid-16C. < ?]

cossie /kózzi/, **cozzie** *n* a swimming costume (*informal*) [Early 20C. Shortening.]

cost /kost/ *v* (**costs, costing, cost**) **1** *vt* BE PRICED AT to require the payment of a particular sum **2** *vti* BE EXPENSIVE to require payment of a large sum of money (*informal*) **3** *vt* CAUSE LOSS OF to cause somebody or something to lose, sacrifice, or suffer something **4** *vt* CALCULATE MONEY REQUIRED to calculate the price or expense of something ■ *n* **1** AMOUNT PAID the amount of money required to be paid for something **2** MONEY SPENT DOING the amount of money spent in producing or doing something **3** LOSS OR EFFORT the loss, sacrifice, suffering, or effort involved in doing something **4** = **cost price** ■ **costs** *npl* LEGAL EXPENSES the amount of money that is spent pursuing a legal action, especially those expenses that a losing party may be required to pay [14C. Via Old French < Latin *constare* 'stand firm' < *stare* 'to stand'.] —**costless** *adj* —**costlessly** *adv* —**costlessness** *n*

costa /kóstə/ (*plural* **-tae** /-tee/) *n* **1** a rib (*technical*) **2** a part of something, e.g. a leaf or a wing, that resembles a rib [Mid-19C. < Latin, 'rib'.] —**costal** *adj*

Costa Brava /kóstə braávə/ resort region on the Mediterranean coast of NE Spain

cost accountant *n* an accountant who calculates and provides detailed information on the cost of producing something or carrying out some operation in a business, and compares actual costs with expected costs

cost accounting *n* accounting that is concerned with providing detailed information on the cost of producing something or carrying out an operation in a business

Costa del Sol /kóstə del sól/ resort region on the Mediterranean coast of S Spain

costae plural of **costa**

co-star, costar /kṓ staar/ *n* JOINT STAR a star who shares prominence with somebody else in a production ■ *v* (**co-stars, co-starring, co-starred**) **1** *vi* STAR JOINTLY WITH OTHERS to star jointly with another actor or actors in a production **2** *vt* FEATURE AS JOINT STAR to include or feature somebody as a co-star

Costa Rica /kóstə reékə/ republic in S Central America

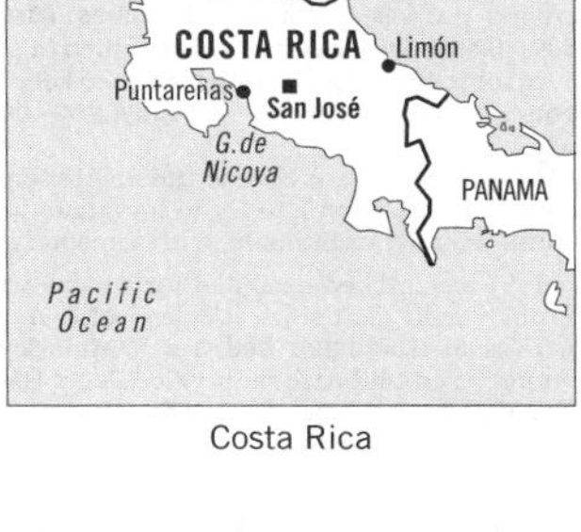

Costa Rica

between the Caribbean Sea and the Pacific Ocean. Capital: San José. Population: 3,534,174 (1997). Area: 51,060 sq. km/19,714 sq. mi. —**Costa Rican** n, adj

costate /kóst ayt/ adj describes a leaf that has ridges or is ribbed [Early 19C. < Latin costatus < costa 'rib'.]

cost-effective adj economically worthwhile in terms of what is achieved for the amount of money spent — **cost-effectively** adv —**cost-effectiveness** n

costermonger /kóstər mung gər/, **coster** /kóstər/ n a seller of fruit and vegetables or other things from a barrow or stall in the street (archaic) [Early 16C. < COSTARD + monger 'seller'.]

costing /kósting/ n 1 the process of calculating the cost involved in undertaking a project 2 the cost that has been calculated for undertaking a project (often plural)

costive /kóstiv/ adj 1 constipated, or causing constipation (technical) 2 slow to act or speak [14C. Via Old French < Latin constipatus, past participle of constipare (see CONSTIPATE).] —**costively** adv —**costiveness** n

costly /kóstli/ (-**lier**, -**liest**) adj 1 EXPENSIVE costing a lot of money to buy 2 LUXURIOUS using expensive and luxurious materials 3 INVOLVING TIME OR EFFORT involving a great deal of effort, time, or sacrifice 4 DAMAGING causing great loss, damage, or suffering —**costliness** n

Costner /kóstnər/, **Kevin** (b. 1955) US film actor and director

cost of living n the amount of money spent on food, clothing, accommodation, and other basic necessities (hyphenated before nouns)

cost-of-living adjustment n an increase in wages or salary to compensate for an increase in the cost of living

cost-of-living index n FIN = consumer price index n.

cost-plus n a pricing system that calculates the price of a product by adding a specified percentage as profit to the production cost

cost price n the price that somebody selling something paid for it

cost-push, **cost-push inflation** n inflation in which price rises result from increased production costs or similar factors rather than from customer demand. ◊ demand-pull

costume /kós tyoom/ n 1 SPECIAL CLOTHES clothes worn to make somebody look like someone or something else, e.g. when performing in a play 2 CLOTHES OF PERIOD OR GROUP the clothes worn during a specific period of time or in a specific location 3 CLOTHES FOR CERTAIN ACTIVITY the clothing appropriate for a particular activity, e.g. swimming 4 WOMEN'S SKIRT SUIT women's clothes comprising a matching jacket and skirt (dated) ■ vt (-**tumes, -tuming, -tumed**) 1 DRESS IN A COSTUME to provide somebody with a costume 2 PROVIDE THEATRICAL ATTIRE to provide attire for a theatrical or dance production [Early 18C. Via French < Italian costume 'custom' < Latin consuetudo (see CUSTOM).]

costume drama n a dramatic production in which the actors wear clothes appropriate for the period during which the drama takes place

costume jewellery n jewellery that is decorative but cheap

costumier /ko styóomi ər, -i ay/, **costumer** /-mər/ n a maker or supplier of costumes for a play, show, or festivity [Mid-19C. < French, < costumer 'provide with a costume'.]

co-survivor n a close relative or friend of somebody who has experienced a traumatizing event, e.g. a rape victim, Aids patient, or victim of a disaster

cosy /kózi/ adj (**cosier, cosiest**) 1 SNUG warm, comfortable, and snug 2 FRIENDLY friendly and intimate 3 UNETHICALLY CLOSE close and friendly, but for mutually beneficial or underhand purposes ■ n (plural **cosies**) COVERING TO KEEP SOMETHING WARM a covering, often knitted or padded, put over something, especially a teapot, to keep it or its contents warm [Early 18C. < ?] —**cosily** adv —**cosiness** n

cosy up v 1 vi to sit or lie as close as possible to somebody for warmth or affection 2 to try to ingratiate yourself, or become friendly or intimate, with somebody

cot[1] /kot/ n 1 a small bed designed for a baby or young child, often with high sides. US term **crib** n. 4 2 US CAMPING, FURNITURE = camp bed 3 a hammock with a stiff frame, used on board ship [Mid-17C. < Hindi khāṭ 'framework strung with rope and used as a bed', via Sanskrit khaṭvā < Tamil kaṭṭu 'tie'.]

cot[2] /kot/ n a cover for an injured finger, shaped like the finger of a glove [Old English, < Germanic]

cot[3] /kot/ abbr cotangent

cot[4] n AGRIC = cote

cotan /kó tan/ abbr cotangent

cotangent /kō tánjənt/ n for a given angle in a right-angled triangle, a trigonometric function equal to the length of the side adjacent to the angle divided by that of the side opposite —**cotangential** /kō tan jénsh'l/ adj

cot case n 1 ANZ an intoxicated person who is capable only of sleep (informal) 2 NZ a patient who must stay in bed because of illness

cot death n the sudden and unexplained death of a baby while sleeping. US term **crib death**

cote /kot/, **cot** /kot/ n a small shelter, especially one for birds or animals (usually in combination) [Old English, < Germanic]

Côte d'Azur /kōt da zyoòr/ part of the French Riviera near the Italian border

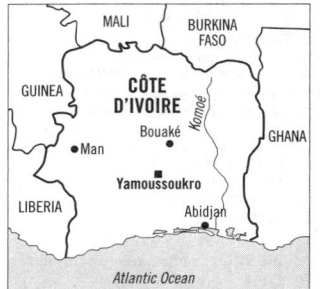

Côte d'Ivoire

Côte d'Ivoire /kōt dee vwaàr/ republic in West Africa, situated north of the Gulf of Guinea. Capital: Yamoussoukro. Population: 15,074,684 (1997). Area: 322,462 sq. km/124,503 sq. mi.

Côte d'Or /-dáwr/ administrative region in E France. Population: 497,917 (1991). Area: 8,765 sq. km/3,384 sq. mi.

coterie /kótəri/ n a small exclusive group of people who share the same interests [Early 18C. Via French < Middle Low German kote 'cottage'.]

coterminous adj = conterminous

Côte-Rôtie /kōt rôti/ (plural **Côte-Rôtie**) n a full-bodied red wine produced in the N Rhône valley, France

Côtes-du-Nord /kōt dyoo náwr/ former department of NW France in Brittany. Area: 6,876 km/2,655 mi.

Côtes du Rhône /kōt dyoo rôn/ n a red or white wine produced in the Rhône valley, France

coth /koth/ abbr hyperbolic cotangent [Late 19C. < cot, shortening of COTANGENT + h for HYPERBOLIC.]

cotidal /kō tíd'l/ adj describes a line that joins together locations on a coastal map where tides occur simultaneously

cotillion /kə tíllyən, kō-/, **cotillon** n 1 FRENCH DANCE a complex French dance popular in the 18th century 2 US BALL a formal ball 3 US DANCE LIKE QUADRILLE a dance similar to a quadrille 4 MUSIC the music for a cotillion [Early 18C. < French cotillon 'petticoat' < cotte < Old French cote (see COAT).]

cotinga /kō tíng gə, kə-/ n a brightly coloured bird. Native to: Central and South America. Family: Cotingidae. [Late 18C. Via French < Tupi cutinga.]

Cotman /kótmən/, **John Sell** (1782–1842) British painter and etcher

cotoneaster /kə tóni ástər/ n a shrub with small oval leaves, cultivated for its red or orange berries that often remain throughout winter. Native to: Europe, Asia. Genus: Cotoneaster. [Mid-18C. < modern Latin, < Latin cotoneum (see QUINCE).]

Cotonou /kōtə noò/ port and capital of Atlantique Province, S Benin. Population: 750,000 (1994 estimate).

Cotopaxi /kōtə páksi/ volcano in the Andes, in central Ecuador. It is the highest active volcano in the world. Height: 5,897 m/19,347 ft.

co-trimoxazole /kō trí móksə zōl/ n an antibiotic. Use: treatment of urinary-tract infections. [Late 20C. < co- + blend of trimethoprim + sulphamethoxazole.]

Cotswold /kóts wold/ n a sheep with fine long wool belonging to a breed originating in the Cotswolds ■ adj relating to the Cotswolds

Cotswolds /kóts woldz/ range of limestone hills in SW England

cotta /kóttə/ n a short surplice reaching to just above the waist, worn by clergy, acolytes, and choristers, in the Roman Catholic Church and in some Anglican and Lutheran churches [Mid-19C. < Italian, < Germanic.]

cottage /kóttij/ n 1 SMALL RURAL HOUSE a small house, usually situated in the country 2 US, Can HOLIDAY HOME in North America, a small holiday home in the country or beside the sea 3 US SMALL RESIDENTIAL UNIT in the United States, a small residential unit, e.g. at a camp, in which residents can be housed in groups 4 PUBLIC TOILET a public toilet, especially one used by homosexuals for sexual encounters (slang) [14C. < Anglo-Norman cotage or Anglo-Latin cotagium, < Germanic.] —**cottagey** adj

cottage cheese n a soft white low-fat cheese with a distinctive lumpy texture and mild flavour

cottage hospital n a small rural hospital that does not have any resident medical staff

cottage industry n a small-scale business involving people who mostly work at home

cottage loaf n a loaf of bread consisting of a large round piece with a smaller one on top

cottage pie n a baked dish made from minced meat in gravy with a topping of mashed potato

cottager /kóttijər/ n 1 OCCUPANT OF COTTAGE a person who lives in a cottage 2 US SOMEBODY WHO HOLIDAYS IN A COTTAGE a holidaymaker at a cottage 3 HOMOSEXUAL WHO HAS SEX IN TOILETS a homosexual who has sex or looks for sexual partners in public toilets (slang)

cottaging /kóttijing/ n homosexual sex or looking for homosexual partners in public toilets, a practice that was especially prevalent in the years when homosexual sex was a criminal offence (slang)

Cottbus /kót bòòss/ city in E Germany. Population: 125,643 (1997).

cotter /kóttər/ n 1 a wedge, key, or bolt used to keep two parts of something, e.g. machinery, together 2 = **cotter pin** [14C. < ?] —**cottered** adj —**cotterless** adj

cotter pin n a split pin inserted through a hole in a machine part and then bent so it holds the part in place

cotton /kótt'n/ n 1 SOFT FIBRE the soft white downy fibre that grows in the seed pods of a cotton plant. Use: textiles. 2 FABRIC MADE FROM COTTON fabric woven or knitted from spun cotton 3 YARN OR THREAD yarn or thread made from cotton or a synthetic substitute 4 SOMETHING MADE OF COTTON something made of cotton fabric (often plural) 5 BUSH PRODUCING DOWNY FIBRE the tropical or subtropical bush that produces cotton. Genus: Gossypium. 6 SUBSTANCE RESEMBLING COTTON a substance that resembles cotton fibre but is produced by another plant, e.g. kapok [14C. Via Italian cotone < Arabic kutun.]
cotton on vi to grasp the meaning of what is being said or done (informal) [< the obsolete verb cotton 'prosper', said to have come from success in raising the nap of cotton and so increasing its value]

Cotton Belt n an extensive agricultural area in SE United States where cotton is the main crop

cotton bud n a short stick with a small amount of cotton wool wound tightly onto one or both ends, used, e.g. to clean ears or apply makeup

cotton cake n compressed cotton seed produced from the residue remaining after the extraction of oil. Use: livestock feed.

cotton candy n US, Can = candy floss

cotton grass n a reed-like bog plant that has white tufted cottony flower heads. Native to: northern temperate areas. Genus: Eriophorum.

cottonmouth /kótt'n mowth/ (plural -**mouths** /-ṯhz, -ṯhs/) n ZOOL = water moccasin n. 1 [Mid-19C. < the whitish colour inside its mouth.]

cotton-picking adj US used to indicate disapproval, annoyance, or emphasis (informal) [Because cotton-picking was done by only the poorest labourers]

cottonseed /kótt'n seed/ n the seed of the cotton plant

cotton stainer *n* an insect that pierces cotton seed pods (**bolls**) and stains the fibres. Genus: *Dysdercus*.

cotton swab *n* US = **cotton bud**

cottontail /kótt'n tayl/ *n* a small rabbit with brown or grey fur and a tail with a white cottony underside. Native to: North America. Genus: *Sylvilagus*.

cotton waste *n* waste cotton yarn. Use: cleaning material.

cottonwood /kótt'n wòod/ (*plural* **-woods** *or* **-wood**) *n* a poplar tree that has seeds with cottony tufts. Native to: North America. *Populus deltoides*.

cotton wool *n* **1** soft fluffy cotton fibre that has been purified and bleached. Use: cleaning wounds, removing makeup. (*hyphenated before nouns*) US term **absorbent cotton 2** raw unprocessed cotton

cottony /kótt'ni/ *adj* looking or feeling like cotton

cottony-cushion scale *n* a small sap-sucking insect that damages citrus crops in California and elsewhere. Native to: Australia. *Icerya purchasi*.

-cotyl *suffix* cotyledon ○ *hypocotyl* [< COTYLEDON]

cotyledon /kótti leéd'n/ *n* **1** the first leaf, or one of the first pair of leaves, produced by the seed of a flowering plant **2** a tuft of projections (**villi**) on the placenta of a mammal [Mid-16C. Via Latin, 'navelwort' < Greek *kotulēdōn* 'cup-shaped cavity' < *kotulē* 'cup'.] —**cotyledonal** *adj* —**cotyledonary** *adj* —**cotyledonous** *adj*

cotylosaur /kóttilə sawr, kə tíllə-/ *n* an extinct reptile with a heavy body and short legs, probably the first land vertebrate. Order: Cotylosauria. [Early 20C. < Greek *kotulē* 'cup' + *sauros* 'lizard'.]

coucal /kóo kal, -k'l/ *n* a tropical bird of the cuckoo family with a large hooked beak and long broad tail. Native to: Africa, S Asia, Australasia. Genus: *Centropus*. [Early 19C. < French, said to be blend of *coucou* 'cuckoo' + *alouette* 'lark'.]

couch[1] /kowch/ *n* **1 LONG SEAT** a piece of upholstered furniture, on which two or more people can sit side by side **2 DOCTOR'S LONG SEAT** a long seat with a headrest that a patient lies on when visiting a doctor, especially a psychiatrist **3 MALTING FRAME** a frame on which barley grain is spread during malting **4 FIRST COAT OF PAINT** a layer of paint or varnish applied to a canvas as a first coat ■ *v* **1** *vt* **PHRASE IN CERTAIN WAY** to express something using a particular style or choice of words **2** *vt* **SPREAD FOR MALTING** to spread barley on a frame for malting **3** *vti* **LIE OR LAY DOWN** to lie down, or lay somebody or something down (*archaic or literary; often passive*) **4** *vt* **LOWER LANCE** to lower a lance into position for an attack **5** *vt* **REMOVE CATARACT** to remove a cataract by pushing down the lens of the eye **6** *vt* **EMBROIDER BY HOLDING DOWN THREADS** to embroider a pattern by holding down threads by means of other threads passed through the material [14C. Noun < French *couche*; verb directly < *coucher* 'lie down' < Latin *collocare* 'place together'.] —**coucher** *n*

couch[2] *n* PLANTS = **couch grass** [Late 16C. Variant of QUITCH.]

couchant /kówchənt/ *adj* used in heraldry to describe an animal lying down with its head raised [15C. < French, present participle of *coucher* (see COUCH[1]).]

couchette /koo shét/ *n* **1** a seat in a compartment on a continental European train that can be converted into a sleeping berth **2** a compartment of a train containing couchettes [Early 20C. < French, 'small bed' < *couche* (see COUCH[1]).]

couch grass /kówch-, kóoch-/, **couch** *n* a grass with rapidly spreading underground roots, that is a troublesome weed in gardens. *Agropyron repens*.

couch potato *n* an inactive person who spends too much time sitting watching television (*disapproving informal*) [< the idea that somebody who watches the 'boob tube' (television) is a 'tuber'; also with reference to potato crisps]

coudé /koo dáy/, **coudé telescope** *n* an astronomical telescope that reflects light from a main mirror onto a detector to one side [Late 19C. < French, past participle of *couder* 'bend at right angles' < *coude* 'elbow' < Latin *cubitum*.]

cougar /kóogər, -aar/ (*plural* **-gars** *or* **-gar**) *n* ZOOL = **puma** [Late 18C. Via French *couguar* < Guarani *cuguaçurana*.]

cough /kof/ *v* **1** *vi* **EXPEL AIR FROM LUNGS NOISILY** to release air through the windpipe and mouth sharply and noisily **2** *vt* **EXPEL BY COUGHING** to expel something from the lungs or windpipe by coughing **3** *vi* **MAKE SHARP NOISE** to make a noise that is similar to the sound of somebody coughing ■ *n* **1 ACT OR SOUND OF COUGHING** a sudden noisy release of air through the windpipe and mouth, often expelling an obstruction **2 ILLNESS CAUSING COUGHING** an illness causing coughing because of an infection in the lungs [14C. < Germanic, an imitation of the sound.] —**cougher** *n*

cough up *vti* to give something such as money or information reluctantly (*informal*)

cough drop *n* a medicated sweet for soothing a cough or sore throat

cough mixture *n* a medicated syrup that soothes or suppresses a cough

⚡**co.uk** *abbr* UK commercial organization (*in Internet addresses*)

could /kòod/ CORE MEANING: a modal verb used to form the past tense of 'can' ○ *My mother did the best she could for my brother and me.* ○ *She could perform on the trapeze.* ○ *His feet were so swollen that he could hardly walk.* ○ *We were so tired we couldn't stay awake.*

vi **1 EXPRESSING POSSIBILITY** used to express that something is possibly true or happening in the future ○ *She thinks that medical technology could be the field for her.* **2 EXPRESSING REQUEST** used when making polite requests ○ *Could you close the window please?* **3 INDICATING A POSSIBLE PAST SITUATION** used to indicate a possible situation in the past that did not happen ○ *We could have gone.* **4 EXPRESSING POLITE OFFER** used to make polite offers and suggestions **5 FOR EMPHASIS** used in questions to emphasize strong feelings about something ○ *How could you do that?* [Old English *cūþe*, past tense of *cunnan* 'know' (see CAN[2]); altered after SHOULD, WOULD]

couldn't /kòodd'nt/ *contr* could not

could've /kòoddəv/ *contr* could have

coulee /kóoli, -lay/ *n* a thick short flow of viscous molten lava [Early 19C. < French, 'flow' < feminine past participle of *couler* 'to flow' < Latin *colare* (see COLANDER).]

coulibiac, coulibiaca *n* FOOD = **koulibiac**

coulis /kóoli/ (*plural* **-lis** /-li/) *n* a thin purée of fruit or vegetables used as a garnish [Late 20C. Via French < Old French *coleïs* 'flowing'.]

coulisse /koo leéss/ *n* in a theatre, a piece of side scenery on a stage or the space between two of these pieces (*often plural*) [Early 19C. < French, < *(porte) coulisse* 'sliding (door)' < Old French *(porte) coleïce* (see PORTCULLIS).]

couloir /kóol waar/ *n* a broad mountain gully, especially one prone to avalanches [Early 19C. < French, 'channel' < *couler* (see COULEE).]

coulomb /kóo lom/ *n* (*symbol* **C**) the SI unit of electric charge equal to the amount of charge transported by a current of one ampere in one second [Late 19C. After Charles Augustin de *Coulomb* (1736–1806), French physicist.]

Coulomb's law *n* a law of electricity stating that the force of attraction or repulsion between two electric charges is proportional to their product and inversely proportional to the square of the distance between them [Mid-19C. See COULOMB.]

coulometry /koo lómmətri/ *n* a means of analysing the results of a process of electrolysis by measuring the amount of electricity used in the process to determine the amount of the substance produced [Mid-20C. < COULOMB.] —**coulometric** /kòolə méttrik/ *adj* —**coulometrically** *adv*

coulter /kóltər/, **colter** *n* a vertical blade attached to a plough that cuts into the soil in front of a ploughshare [Pre-12C. < Latin *culter* 'knife'.]

coumarin /kóomərin/ *n* $C_9H_6O_2$ a fragrant compound. Source: plants or made synthetically. Use: in perfumes and medicine. [Mid-19C. Via French < Tupi *cumarú* 'tonka bean tree', a source of coumarin.] —**coumaric** *adj*

council /kównss'l/ *n* **1 PEOPLE RUNNING LOCAL AFFAIRS** a group of people elected to run the administrative affairs of a local district **2 COMMITTEE** an appointed or elected body of people with an administrative, advisory, or representative function **3 CHURCH ASSEMBLY** an assembly of church representatives who meet to decide matters of discipline and doctrine **4 COUNCIL MEETING** a meeting of a council **5 MEETING FOR DISCUSSION** a meeting to discuss or decide something [Pre-12C. Via Anglo-Norman *cuncile* < Latin *concilium* 'calling together'.]

USAGE council or **counsel**? ***Council*** is a noun only, meaning a body of people, especially in an advisory or administrative context. ***Counsel*** is both a noun and a verb, and has to do with advice, particularly of a professional nature, and the giving of it. The noun ***counsel*** most often means a lawyer or lawyers, whereas a *counsellor* gives some other kind of professional advice. The verb describes the activity of such advisers: *The company psychologist counsels employees having stress problems. International financial analysts counselled caution.*

council area *n* the geographical or administrative area under the control of a particular council

councillor /kównsələr/ *n* **1** a member of a council elected to run the administrative affairs of a local district **2** an elected or appointed member of an advisory council —**councillorship** *n*

councilman /kównss'lmən/ (*plural* **-men** /-mən/) *n US* a man who is a member of a council, especially of a local authority

Council of Europe *n* an organization of European states founded in 1949 to further political unity

Council of Trent *n* a Roman Catholic Church council held in Trento, Italy, from 1545 to 1563 to respond to the threat of Protestantism

council of war *n* **1** a wartime meeting of military officers to discuss a plan of action **2** a meeting called to formulate a plan of action in an emergency

councilor *n* US = **councillor**

council tax *n* in the United Kingdom, a local tax that is levied on the basis of the estimated value of a property

councilwoman /kównss'l wòomən/ (*plural* **-en** /-wimmin/) *n US* a woman member of a council, especially of a local authority

counsel /kównss'l/ *n* **1 COURT LAWYER** a lawyer or group of lawyers who conduct cases in court or give legal advice **2 SOMEBODY WHO GIVES ADVICE** somebody whose advice is sought or who acts as an official adviser (*takes a singular or plural verb*) **3 ADVICE** advice sought from or given by somebody, especially somebody who is wise or knowledgeable (*formal or literary; often plural*) ■ *vt* (**-sels, -selling, -selled**) **1 ADVISE TO DO** to advise somebody on a particular course of action (*formal or literary*) **2 ADVISE ON PERSONAL PROBLEMS** to give somebody advice and support on personal or psychological matters, usually in a professional context [12C. Via Old French *conseil* < Latin *consilium* 'consultation' < *consulere* 'seek advice'.] ◇ **keep your own counsel** to keep your thoughts and intentions secret

USAGE See ***council***.

counseling /kównss'ling/ *n* US = **counselling**

counsellee /kównss' leé/ *n* a receiver of counselling

counselling /kównss'ling/ *n* **1** help with personal or psychological matters usually given by a professional **2** meetings with a counsellor to receive help with personal or psychological problems

counsellor /kównss'lər/ *n* **1 SOMEBODY WHO GIVES ADVICE** somebody, e.g. a friend, who gives advice **2 ADVISER ON PERSONAL PROBLEMS** somebody, usually a professional, who helps others with personal, social, or psychological problems **3 ADVISER ON SPECIAL SUBJECT** a professional who gives advice on such matters as careers, education, or health **4 counsellor, counsellor-at-law** (*plural* **counsellors-at-law**) *US* **LAWYER** a lawyer, especially one who acts for a client in a trial **5 counsellor, counsellor-at-law** (*plural* **counsellors-at-law**) *Ireland* **ADVISORY BARRISTER** in Ireland, a barrister who acts in an advisory capacity **6 SENIOR DIPLOMAT** an officer of senior grade in the diplomatic service **7** *US* **HIGH-RANKING DIPLOMAT** a diplomat ranking below an ambassador or minister **8** *US* **CHILDREN'S SUPERVISOR** a supervisor of young people at a summer camp —**counsellorship** *n*

counselor *n* US = **counsellor**

count[1] /kownt/ *v* **1** *vti* **SAY NUMBERS** to say numbers in order, usually starting at one **2** *vti* **ADD UP** to add things up to see how many there are or to find the value of an amount of money **3** *vt* **INCLUDE** to include somebody or something in a calculation ○ *If you count me and Jodie, there will be 15 people.* **4** *vti* **CONSIDER OR BE CONSIDERED** to consider somebody or something, or be considered, in a particular way or as a particular thing **5** *vi* **BE OF IMPORTANCE** to be of importance or value **6** *vi* **HAVE A VALUE** to have a specific value **7** *vti* **KEEP TIME** to keep musical time by counting beats ■ *n* **1 SAYING OF NUMBERS** an act of saying numbers in order **2 FINDING OF TOTAL** an addition of people or things to find a total **3 TOTAL OF SOMETHING** a total that is reached by adding things up **4 ONE OF MANY POINTS** any one of a number of points, e.g. in a discussion **5 CHARGE AGAINST** a charge against somebody who is on trial **6 BOXING REFEREE'S COUNT** a count to ten by the referee in a boxing match during which a boxer who has been knocked down must stand up or lose the match **7 WRESTLING REFEREE'S COUNT** a count to three by the referee at a wrestling match during which a wrestler being held on the floor must break the hold or lose the point [14C. Noun: < Old French *conte*; verb directly < Old French *co(u)nter* 'reckon' < Latin *computare* 'reckon together'.] ◇ **keep count** to count and remember the number of people or things counted ◇ **lose count** to fail to count accurately or remember the number of people or things counted ◇ **out for the count 1** unconscious or deeply asleep and unlikely to wake again for some time (*informal*) **2** unable to stand up, after being knocked down, within the ten-second count given by the referee in a boxing match, and therefore losing the match

count against *vt* to be damaging to somebody's interests or prospects

count down *vi* to count backwards from a number to zero or from a given time to something such as the launch of a rocket

count in *vt* to include somebody in a plan

count on, count upon *vt* **1** to rely on somebody to do something **2** to be sure that something will happen

count out *vt* **1 COUNT ONE BY ONE** to count something, e.g. money, one item at a time **2 NOT INCLUDE** to exclude somebody from a plan **3 DECLARE BOXER DEFEATED BY COUNTING TEN** to disqualify a boxer who has been knocked down and fails to get up within ten seconds

count towards, count toward *vt* to be included as part of something

count upon *vt* = **count on**

count[2] /kownt/ *n* a nobleman in certain European countries, of a rank equal to that of a British earl [14C. Via Old French *conte* < Latin *comit-* 'companion', literally 'somebody who goes with'.]

countable /kówntəb'l/ *adj* **1** able to be counted **2** describes a noun that can be used with 'a' or 'an' and with a plural verb, usually in a distinct plural form —**countability** /kówntə bíllәti/ *n* —**countably** *adv*

countdown /kównt down/ *n* **1 BACKWARDS COUNT** a count in descending order before an event such as a rocket launch **2 ACTIVITIES BEFORE AN EVENT** the activities carried on during the period of time before something such as a rocket launch **3 PREPARATORY PERIOD** the period immediately preceding an important event

countenance /kówntənənss/ *n* **1 FACE OR EXPRESSION** somebody's face, or the expression on it **2 COMPOSURE** composure or self-control ■ *vt* (**-nances, -nancing, -nanced**) **TOLERATE OR APPROVE** to tolerate, accept, or give approval to something (*formal*) [13C. < Old French *contenance* 'demeanour', literally 'contents' < *contenir* (see CONTAIN).] —**countenancer** *n*

counter[1] /kówntər/ *n* **1 FLAT SURFACE** a flat surface on which food or drink is served, goods are displayed, or business is transacted **2 FLAT SURFACE IN KITCHEN** a kitchen worktop **3 SMALL MARKER** a small object, often a flat disc, used in games to mark a player's position or to keep score **4 IMITATION COIN** an object, usually a flat disc, used as a substitute for a coin [14C. Via Anglo-Norman *counteor* < medieval Latin *computatorium* 'place for counting' < Latin *computare* 'reckon together'.] ◇ **under the counter** secretly and unofficially, usually because there is something illegal about what is being done

counter[2] /kówntər/ *vti* **1 CONTRADICT OR OPPOSE** to say something that contradicts or opposes what somebody has said **2 DO SOMETHING IN OPPOSITION** to do something in opposition to what somebody else is doing, so as to make it less effective **3 PUNCH OPPONENT IN RETURN** to defend yourself against a punch from an opponent, and deliver a punch in return ■ *adj* **CONTRADICTING** contradicting or opposing something ○ *a counter blow* ■ *n* **1 RESPONSE** a response made in retaliation to something that has been said **2 OPPOSITE OF** something that is the opposite of something else or that is done in opposition to something else **3 RETURNING PUNCH** a punch that counters a punch aimed by an opponent **4 FENCING PARRY** in fencing, a parry in which the foils make a circular movement **5 END OF SHIP'S STERN** the part of the stern of a ship or boat that juts out above the waterline **6 HOLLOW PART OF TYPEFACE** a hollow part of a piece of type, such as the inner parts of the letters 'p' and 'd' **7 LEATHER AROUND HEEL OF SHOE** a piece of leather around the heel of a shoe or boot [14C. < COUNTER-.]

counter[3] /kówntər/ *n* **1** a device that counts automatically **2** somebody whose job is to count something, e.g. votes

counter- *prefix* **1** contrary, opposing ○ *counterattack* **2** complementary, corresponding ○ *counterpart* [Via Anglo-Norman *countre-* < Latin *contra* (see CONTRA-)]

counteract /kówntər ákt/ *vt* to prevent something having an effect or lessen its effect —**counteraction** *n* —**counteractive** *adj* —**counteractively** *adv*

counterargument /kówntər aargyŏŏmənt/ *n* a fact or opinion that challenges the reasoning behind somebody's proposal and shows that there are grounds for taking an opposite view

counterattack /kówntər ə tak/ *n* an attack made in response to an attack by an enemy or opponent

counterattraction /kówntər ə tráksh'n/ *n* something set up to draw people away from another attraction

counterbalance /kówntər ballənss/ *vt* (**-ances, -ancing, -anced**) **1 HAVE EQUAL AND OPPOSING EFFECT ON** to be or have an equal and opposing force or effect on something **2 BALANCE WITH EQUAL WEIGHT** to make something balance by putting equal weight on the opposite side ■ *n* **1 COUNTERBALANCING PERSON OR THING** a state of balance with an equal and opposing force or effect **2 WEIGHT THAT BALANCES ANOTHER** a weight that exactly balances another weight

counterbattery fire /kówntər battəri-/ *n* firing weapons with the aim of destroying enemy artillery

counterblast /kówntər blaast/ *n* **1** an attack on somebody in speech or writing, made in response to an attack by that person **2** a blast that counters the effect of a preceding blast

counterchange /kówntər chaynj/ (**-changes, -changing, -changed**) *v* **1** *vti* to interchange the parts or positions of two things **2** *vt* to chequer or dapple something with colours (*literary*)

countercharge /kówntər chaarj/ *n* **1 ACCUSATION AGAINST ACCUSER** an accusation made against the person or group who has accused another of something **2 CHARGE AGAINST AGGRESSORS** a charge made by police or military forces against a group of aggressors ■ *vt* (**-charges, -charging, -charged**) **CHARGE ACCUSER WITH** to bring a charge against an accuser

countercheck /kówntər chek/ *n* **1 SECOND CHECK** a check made to ensure that a previous check was correct **2 RESTRAINT ON** something that acts to block or restrain something else ■ *v* **1** *vti* **CHECK AGAIN** to carry out a second check on something, in order to ensure that the first was accurate **2** *vt* **RESTRAIN** to act in order to block the force or action of something

counterclaim /kówntər klaym/ *n* a claim entered by the defendant in a court of civil law, as a response to the original claim that was entered against the defendant by the plaintiff ■ *vti* to make a claim in response to, or as a defence against, an earlier claim —**counterclaimant** /kówntər kláymənt/ *n*

counterclockwise /kówntər klók wīz/ *adv, adj US, Can* = **anticlockwise**

counterconditioning /kówntər kən dísh'ning/ *n* a process of psychological conditioning that attempts to replace somebody's undesired habitual response to a particular situation with a desired learned response

countercoup /kówntər koo/ *n* a coup made against a group that has seized political power in an earlier coup

counterculture /kówntər kulchər/ *n* a culture that has ideas and ways of behaving that are consciously and deliberately very different from the cultural values of the larger society that it is part of —**countercultural** *adj* —**counterculturist** *n*

countercurrent /kówntər kurrənt/ *n* **CURRENT FLOWING OPPOSITE WAY** a current that flows in the opposite direction to another current ■ *adj* **1 FLOWING IN OPPOSITE DIRECTION** flowing in the opposite direction to another current **2 USING OPPOSING CURRENTS** involving the flow of two currents in opposite directions —**countercurrently** *adv*

counterdemonstration /kówntər demən stráysh'n/ *n* a public demonstration that is held to oppose the purpose of another demonstration that was recently held or is currently being held —**counterdemonstrator** /-démmən straytər/ *n*

counterespionage /kówntər éspi ə naazh/ *n* government activity designed to detect and prevent spying by agents of other countries who are operating against that government's country

counterexample /kówntər ig zaamp'l/ *n* a fact or argument that indicates that a theory, scientific hypothesis, or mathematical theorem is not true

counterfactual /kówntər fákchoo əl/ *adj* **1 CONTRARY TO THE FACTS** not reflecting or taking into account the facts **2 EXPRESSING WHAT MIGHT HAVE HAPPENED** expressing what has not actually happened but might have happened in other circumstances ■ *n* **STATEMENT OF WHAT MIGHT HAVE HAPPENED** a statement expressing something that did not happen but might have

counterfeit /kówntərfit/ *adj* **1 FORGED** made as a copy of something, especially money, in order to defraud or deceive people **2 FALSE** pretended in order to deceive somebody ○ *counterfeit geniality* ■ *vti* **1 FORGE** to make realistic copies of something, especially money, in order to defraud or deceive people **2 PRETEND** to pretend to have an emotion in order to deceive somebody ■ *n* **FORGERY** a copy of something, especially money, made in order to defraud or deceive people [14C. < Anglo-Norman *countrefet*, past participle of *countrefaire* 'counterfeit' < medieval Latin *contrafacere* < Latin *contra-* 'against' + *facere* 'to make'.] —**counterfeiter** *n*

~~**counterfit**~~ incorrect spelling of **counterfeit**

counterfoil /kówntər foyl/ *n* the part of a cheque, ticket, or other paper used in a financial transaction that is detached and kept by the issuer as a record

counterfort /kówntər fawrt/ *n* a buttress that sticks out at right angles from a wall [Late 16C. < French *contrefort* < Old French *contreforcier* 'buttress'.]

counterglow /kówntər glō/ *n* ASTRON = **gegenschein** [Mid-19C. Translation of German *Gegenschein*.]

counterhegemonic /kówntər hejjə mónnik/ *adj US* contrary to the prevailing fashion, especially in intellectual matters

counterinsurgency /kówntər in súrjənssi/ *n* military and political activities undertaken by a government to defeat a rebellion or guerrilla movement —**counterinsurgent** *n*

counterintelligence /kówntər in téllijənss/ *n* government and military activities designed to gather information about enemy spies, thwart their activities, and supply them with false information

counterintuitive /kówntər in tyŏŏ itiv/ *adj* not in accordance with what would naturally be assumed or expected ○ *I know it's counterintuitive, but the highest grade in this system is D and the lowest is A.* —**counterintuitively** *adv*

counterirritant /kówntər írritənt/ *n* a skin cream that produces an irritation to reduce underlying tissue inflammation —**counterirritation** /kówntər írri táysh'n/ *n*

countermand /kówntər maánd, kówntər maand/ *vt* **1 CANCEL A COMMAND** to give an order or instruction that a previous order or instruction should not be followed **2 RECALL** to recall somebody or something sent somewhere by a previous order ■ *n* **ORDER CANCELLING ANOTHER** an order cancelling a previous order [15C. < French *contremander* < Latin *mandare* (see MANDATE).]

countermarch /kówntər maarch/ *n* **1 RETURN MARCH** a march, especially one undertaken by soldiers, back from a position following the same route as that taken on the outward march **2 CHANGE IN MARCHING DIRECTION** a marching manoeuvre in which soldiers change the direction they are marching in while retaining their positions within a formation **3 COMPLETE CHANGE OF APPROACH** a complete change in somebody's behaviour or way of doing things ■ *v* **1** *vti* **MARCH BACK** to return from a position by marching back along the same route, or to make soldiers do this **2** *vi* **CHANGE DIRECTION OF MARCHING** to change the direction of a formation of marching soldiers without altering the positions of the individual soldiers

countermeasure /kówntər mezhər/ *n* something that is done in reaction to and as defence against a hostile action by somebody else or is done in order to deal with a threat

countermine /kówntər mīn/ *v* (**-mines, -mining, -mined**) **1** *vti* **EXPLODE ENEMY'S MINES IN AN AREA** to place explosive mines in an area in order to explode mines placed there by an enemy **2** *vti* **DIG TUNNELS AGAINST ENEMY'S TUNNELS** to dig underground tunnels in order to intercept or destroy tunnels dug by an enemy **3** *vt* **SECRETLY FOIL PLOT** to take secret action against somebody's plans ■ *n* **1 TUNNEL DUG AGAINST ENEMY'S TUNNELS** a tunnel dug to intercept or destroy tunnels dug by an enemy **2 SECRET**

ACTION TO FOIL PLOT a secret action designed to undermine or destroy a plot or scheme

countermove /kówntər moov/ *n* a move made in response to an opponent's move, e.g. in a game ■ *vi* (**-moves, -moving, -moved**) to act in response to an opponent's action, e.g. in a game —**countermovement** *n*

counteroffensive /kówntər ə fenssiv/ *n* a major attack or series of attacks made by a military force in response to the attacks made by an enemy

counteroffer /kówntər ofər/ *n* an offer made by somebody selling something, usually a reduction in what was first asked, made to persuade the buyer to improve a previous unsatisfactory offer

counterpane /kówntər payn/ *n* a cover for a bed and its bedding (*dated*) [15C. Alteration of *counterpoint*, via Old French < medieval Latin *culcita puncta* 'stitched quilt'.]

counterpart /kówntər paart/ *n* **1 SOMEBODY OR SOMETHING CORRESPONDING TO ANOTHER** a person or thing that resembles another or functions similarly in a different system or group **2 MATCHING PART OR THING** either of two parts that fit together or are complementary ○ *I identified bolt A but could not find its counterpart, socket B.* **3 ACTOR PLAYING OPPOSITE ANOTHER** an actor who plays opposite somebody else in a play or film **4 COPY OF LEGAL DOCUMENT** a copy of a lease, contract, or other legal document that is held by one party to a transaction and that duplicates the copy held by the other party

counterplan /kówntər plan/ *n* **1** a plan made to defeat or respond to another plan **2** a plan prepared as an alternative or substitute for the primary plan

counterplea /kówntər plee/ *n* a plea made by the plaintiff in a court of law in response to the plea made by the defendant

counterplot /kówntər plot/ *n* a plot made in order to defeat an enemy's or opponent's plot ■ *vi* (**-plots, -plotting, -plotted**) to make a plot designed to defeat an enemy's or opponent's plot

counterpoint /kówntər poynt/ *n* **1 SOUNDING TOGETHER OF MELODIES** the sounding together of two or more melodic lines in a piece of music, each of which displays an individual and differentiated melodic contour and rhythmic profile **2 MELODY COMBINED WITH ANOTHER** in a piece of music, a melodic line or part that is sung or played at the same time as another **3 CONTRASTING ELEMENT** a theme or element in a work of art that forms a contrast with another ■ *vt* **1 CONTRAST WITH** to make an effective contrast with something, especially in a work of art ○ *Richard's social ease counterpoints his sister's awkwardness.* **2 ARRANGE MUSIC IN COUNTERPOINT** to add one or more melodic lines in counterpoint in a piece of music [15C. Via French < medieval Latin *(cantus) contrapunctus* '(song) with notes marked opposite (the melody)'.]

counterpoise /kówntər poyz/ *n* **1 COUNTERACTING WEIGHT** a weight that balances another weight **2 COMPENSATING FACTOR** something that has the effect of diminishing or compensating for the effect of something else ○ *The government had covertly encouraged the fascists as a counterpoise to the reformers.* **3 BALANCED STATE** a state of balance ■ *vt* (**-poises, -poising, -poised**) **1 OPPOSE AND BALANCE** to counteract or compensate for something by providing an equal force, influence, or weight **2 MAKE BALANCED** to bring something into a state of balance [15C. Alteration of French *contrepeis* 'counterweight'.]

counterproductive /kówntər prə dúktiv/ *adj* producing problems or difficulties instead of helping to achieve a goal ○ *A direct challenge to her authority is likely to be counterproductive.* —**counterproductively** *adv*

counterproof /kówntər proof/ *n* an impression taken from a new print of an engraving while it is still wet, producing a reversed image of the print

counterproposal /kówntər prə pōz'l/ *n* a suggestion made in response to, and with the hope of modifying or replacing, another suggestion in a negotiation

counterpunch /kówntər punch/ *n* a punch made by a boxer in response to an opponent's punch —**counterpunch** *v*—**counterpuncher** *n*

counter-reformation *n* a reform or reform movement that seeks to reverse the effects of earlier reforms

Counter-Reformation *n* the movement of reform and regeneration instituted by the Roman Catholic Church in 1545 to counter the increasing strength of Protestantism in Europe as a result of the Reformation

counter-revolution *n* subversive activity or a revolution with the aim of undoing the effects of a previous revolution and overthrowing the government or social system that it produced —**counter-revolutionist** *n*

counter-revolutionary *n* (*plural* **counter-revolutionaries**) **1 SOMEBODY FIGHTING REVOLUTIONARY GOVERNMENT** somebody, especially a member of a military force, who seeks to overthrow a national government or social system established by a revolution **2 SOMEBODY OPPOSED TO REVOLUTION** an opponent of a revolution as a means of political and social change ■ *adj* **OPPOSED TO REVOLUTION** opposed to a specific revolution or to revolution as a means of political and social change

countersank past tense of **countersink**

counterscarp /kówntər skaarp/ *n* the slope or bank on the outer side of the ditch outside a fort [Late 16C. Via French *contrescarpe* < Italian *controscarpa* < *scarpa* (see SCARP).]

countershading /kówntər shayding/ *n* a pattern of colouring on an animal's skin or coat where the upper parts are darker than the lower, counteracting the effects of sun and shade and camouflaging the animal

countershaft /kówntər shaaft/ *n* an intermediate shaft that transmits power from the main shaft to a working part but rotates in the opposite direction, especially in a belt drive or gear drive

countersign /kówntər sīn/ *vt* to sign a document that somebody else has signed, e.g. as a witness to the signature or to confirm an authorization ■ *n* **1** an agreed and secret sign, word, or signal given as a password to a military sentry in order to pass **2** LAW = **countersignature**

countersignature /kówntər signəchər/ *n* a signature added to a document that has already been signed, e.g. to witness the first signature or to confirm an authorization

countersink /kówntər singk/ *vt* (**-sinks, -sinking, -sank** /-sangk/, **-sunk** /-sungk/) **1 MAKE HOLE TO INCLUDE SCREW HEAD** to widen the top of the hole for a screw or bolt so that the head will fit into the hole and be flush with or below the surface **2 MAKE SCREW HEADS LEVEL WITH SURFACE** to place screws, bolts, or nails in wood or another material so that their heads are level with or below the surface of the material ■ *n* **1 HOLE THAT ACCEPTS SCREW HEAD** a hole for a screw or bolt that is wider at the top so that the head will fit into the hole and be flush with or below the surface **2 COUNTERSINKING TOOL** a special drill bit or other tool for countersinking holes for screws or bolts

counterspy /kówntər spī/ (*plural* **-spies**) *n* a spy who spies on and seeks to thwart enemy spies

counterstain /kówntər stayn/ *n* an additional stain applied to a specimen to be examined under a microscope, in order to bring out features not revealed by the primary stain ■ *vt* to use a counterstain on a microscope specimen

countersubject /kówntər sub jekt/ *n* a second theme or melodic line that contrasts with the main one in a fugue or other piece of music employing counterpoint

countersue /kówntər syoo/ (**-sues, -suing, -sued**) *vti* to bring a lawsuit against somebody who is suing you

countersunk past participle of **countersink**

countertenor /kówntər tenər/ *n* **1** an adult male singing voice that is higher than tenor and covers the alto range, produced by singing in falsetto **2** a man whose singing voice is a countertenor [14C. Via French *contrateneur* < obsolete Italian *contratenore* 'against the tenor'.]

counterterrorism /kówntər térrərizəm/ *n* **1** military or political activities intended to combat or prevent terrorism **2** terrorist activities undertaken in revenge for or in retaliation against terrorism —**counterterrorist** *adj, n*

counter to *prep* **1** in the opposite direction to the movement of something **2** in a contrary manner to something

countertop /kówntər top/ *n US, Can* the surface of a worktop, especially in a kitchen, or of the top of a counter in a shop

countertrade /kówntər trayd/ *n* a system of international trade in which countries exchange goods or services, rather than paying for imports with currency —**countertrader** *n*

countertransference /kówntər transfərənss/ *n* a process that sometimes occurs in psychoanalytic therapy where repressed emotions in the therapist are awakened by identification with the experiences and feelings of the patient

countertype /kówntər tīp/ *n* **1** a type that is the complete opposite of another type **2** a type that corresponds with or is equivalent to another type

countervail /kówntər váyl/ *v* **1** *vti* to exert a counteracting power or influence against something, especially against a harmful force, idea, or influence **2** *vt* to offset or compensate for something [14C. < Anglo-Norman *contrevaloir* 'be worth against'.]

countervailing duty (*plural* **countervailing duties**) *n* an import duty on commodities that can be produced very cheaply in their country of origin, e.g. because of a subsidy, imposed in order to protect domestic producers

counterweigh /kówntər wáy/ *vt* to counterbalance something, or use something to counterbalance something

counterweight /kówntər wayt/ *n* **1** a weight that balances another weight **2** something that counteracts or compensates for something else, e.g. a force, idea, or influence —**counterweighted** *adj*

counterwork /kówntər wurk/ *n* **1** work or action undertaken to counteract other work or another action **2** fortifications against an attack

countess /kówntiss, -ess, kown téss/ *n* **1** the wife or widow of a count or earl **2** a woman who holds the rank of count or earl in her own right [12C. Via Old French *contesse* < medieval Latin *comitissa*, feminine of *comes*, *comit-* (see COUNT[2]).]

counting /kównting/ *prep* taking a particular person or thing into consideration in a total ○ *We were thirteen in all, not counting the children in the party.*

counting house *n* the place where the financial work of a business is done or where its accounts are kept (*archaic*)

countless /kówntləss/ *adj* many more than it is possible or convenient to count ○ *I've told him countless times to be more careful.* —**countlessly** *adv*

count noun *n* a noun referring to one thing rather than a mass of something that can be used with 'a' or 'an', with a number, and in the plural. Examples of English count nouns are 'cat', 'sheep', and 'child'.

count palatine (*plural* **counts palatine**) *n* **1 LOCAL RULER IN HOLY ROMAN EMPIRE** a count who ruled over his own domain (**county palatine**) in the Holy Roman Empire, or an official who ruled an area of the empire as the emperor's representative **2 SOMEBODY WITH JUDICIAL POWER OVER COUNTY** in former times, an earl or other nobleman in England or Ireland who held the highest judicial authority and other supreme powers within his own domain (**county palatine**) **3 ROMAN PALACE OFFICIAL** a palace official with judicial authority in the late Roman Empire

countrified /kúntri fīd/, **countryfied** *adj* **1** having a style or quality appropriate to the country ○ *a pretty, countrified row of houses* **2** not fashionable or sophisticated and of a style or quality considered typical of rural areas

country /kúntri/ *n* (*plural* **-tries**) **1 SEPARATE NATION** a nation or state that is politically independent, or a land that was formerly independent and remains separate in some respects **2 HOMELAND** the nation or state where somebody was born or is a citizen **3 GEOGRAPHICALLY DISTINCT AREA** a large area of land regarded as distinct from other areas, e.g. because of its natural boundaries or because it is inhabited by a particular people ○ *The country was settled by Europeans in the 16th century.* **4 FARMED AND UNDEVELOPED AREA** an area that is farmed or remains in a relatively undeveloped state, as distinct from cities, towns, and other built-up areas ○ *a house in the country* **5 REGION WITH SPECIAL CHARACTER** a region that is distinguished by particular characteristics or is associated with a particular activity, person, or group of people ○ *This was chapel country, and all the pubs were closed.* **6 NATION'S PEOPLE** the people of a nation or state, especially when affected as a group by political or other events ○ *a scandal that rocked the country* **7** = **country music** ■ *adj* **1 CHARACTERISTIC OF RURAL AREAS** characteristic of rural areas or the people living there **2 OF COUNTRY MUSIC** characteristic of, similar to, or performing country music [13C. < Old French *cuntrée* < assumed Vulgar Latin *(terra) contrata* '(land) lying opposite' < Latin *contra* 'against'.] —**countryish** *adj* ◇ **go to the country** to hold a general election

country and western *n* = **country music** (*hyphenated before nouns*)

country bumpkin *n* = **bumpkin**[1] *n.*

country club *n* a club for social and leisure activities with facilities for golf, tennis, or other outdoor sports, usually located in the suburbs or the country

country code *n* a code of conduct for people spending leisure time in the country, suggesting how to respect the natural environment and avoid causing damage or harm

country cousin *n* somebody from the country whose unsophisticated reactions to town life are considered amusing (*dated*)

country dance *n* a folk dance in which several couples move within a square, a circle, or two lines —**country dancing** *n*

countryfied *adj* = **countrified**

country gentleman *n* a man who owns an estate in the country

country house *n* a large house in the country, often with a large area of land attached

countryman /kúntrimən/ (*plural* **-men** /-mən/) *n* **1** a rural resident, especially somebody raised in the country who is familiar with rural life **2** a citizen by birth or adoption of the same nation as somebody else

country music *n* American popular music, based on the traditional music of the rural South and the cowboy music of the West, whose songs express strong personal emotions —**country musician** *n*

country park *n* an area of countryside in the United Kingdom that has been set aside for public recreational use through the agency of the Countryside Commission

country rock[1] *n* rock music that is strongly influenced by American country music

country rock[2] *n* rock that has been intruded by magma or that surrounds veins of mineral ore

country seat *n* an estate or a large house in the country that is the hereditary property of a particular family

countryside /kúntri sīd/ *n* **1** an area of land that is farmed or in a relatively undeveloped state ○ *a village set in wooded countryside* **2** the people who live in a country area ○ *The entire countryside was up in arms against the proposed development.*

Countryside Commission *n* a British organization concerned with the preservation of the countryside in England and Wales and with setting up country parks for public recreation

Countryside Commission for Scotland *n* a British organization concerned with the preservation of the countryside in Scotland and with setting up country parks for public recreation

countrywide /kúntri wíd/ *adj, adv* throughout an entire nation ○ *a countrywide organization for professional women* ○ *rates that were increased countrywide*

countrywoman /kúntri wŏŏmən/ (*plural* **-en** /-wimin/) *n* **1** a woman who lives in the country, especially one brought up there and familiar with rural life and pursuits **2** a woman who was born in or is a citizen of the same nation as somebody else

county /kównti/ *n* (*plural* **-ties**) **1 LOCAL GOVERNMENT AREA** a unit of local government and one of the administrative subdivisions that the states of the United States and, excepting major cities, all of England and Wales are divided into **2 PEOPLE OF A COUNTY** the people who live in a county ■ *adj* **SUGGESTIVE OF RICH COUNTRY FAMILIES** belonging to or typical of long-established British upper-class or wealthy families who live in the country (*informal*) ○ *girls from county families* [13C. Via Anglo-Norman *counté* < Latin *comitatus* 'group of companions' < *comes* (see COUNT[2]).]

county borough *n* any town with a local government that is independent of the surrounding county, including many towns in England and Wales before 1974 and the four largest boroughs in the Republic of Ireland

county council *n* a local government body administering a county in the United Kingdom and some parts of the United States

county court *n* a local court in England and Wales with limited powers to decide civil cases, usually those concerning less than a given amount of money

county palatine (*plural* **counties palatine**) *n* **1** the lands governed by a nobleman or imperial official with the rank of count palatine in the Holy Roman Empire **2** formerly in England and Ireland, the lands administered by an earl or other nobleman who exercised judicial authority

county seat *n US* POL = **county town**

county town *n* a town that is the seat of local government in a county. US term **county seat**

coup /koo/ *n* **1** a success that is unexpected and achieved with exceptional skill ○ *Getting the author to come and speak was quite a coup.* **2** the sudden violent overthrow of a government and seizure of political power, especially by the army [Late 18C. Via French, 'blow' < Greek *kolophos* 'blow with the fist'.]

coup de foudre /kōō də fōōdrə/ (*plural* **coups de foudre** /kōō də fōōdrə/) *n* something that happens suddenly and is overwhelming, especially love at first sight [< French, 'stroke of lightning']

coup de grâce /kōō də graáss/, **coup de grace** (*plural* **coups de grâce** /kōō də graáss/) *n* **1** a final stroke or shot that kills a person or animal, especially one intended to end suffering **2** the final action that assures victory or success, especially in a sporting event [< French, 'stroke of mercy']

coup de main /kōō də máyn/ (*plural* **coups de main** /kōō də máyn/) *n* a sudden, fierce, and successful surprise attack against an enemy [< French, 'blow of the hand']

coup d'état /kōō day taá/ (*plural* **coups d'état** /kōōz day taá/) *n* = **coup** *n.* 2 [< French, 'stroke of state']

coup de théâtre /kōō də tay aátrə/ (*plural* **coups de théâtre** /kōō də tay aátrə/) *n* **1 SURPRISING TURN OF EVENTS** something that occurs in a very dramatic way, especially a sensational and unexpected turn of events **2 EFFECTIVE PIECE OF THEATRE** a strongly dramatic moment in a play or other theatrical production, produced by an exceptional piece of writing, performance, or staging **3 SUCCESSFUL PLAY** a play or other theatrical performance that is very successful [< French, 'stroke of theatre']

coup d'oeil /koo dőy/ (*plural* **coups d'oeil** /koo dőy/) *n* a quick look at something, especially one that provides an overall general impression [< French, 'stroke of the eye']

coupe[1] /koop/ *n* **1** a dessert of ice cream and fruit **2** a small shallow glass bowl, often with a stem, for fruit and ice cream [Late 19C. Via French, 'goblet' < medieval Latin *cuppa* (see CUP).]

coupe[2] /koop, kōō pay/ *n US* CARS = **coupé** *n.* 1 [Early 20C. Variant of COUPÉ.]

coupé /kōō pay/ *n* **1 CAR WITH TWO DOORS** a car with two doors, a sloping back, and a hard fixed roof **2 TWO-SEATER CARRIAGE** a closed four-wheeled carriage that has two inside seats for passengers and a driver's seat outside in the front **3 END COMPARTMENT IN RAILCAR** an end compartment in an old type of European railway carriage, with seats on one side only [Mid-19C. < French *(carrosse) coupé* 'cut-down (carriage)' (because it was smaller than earlier models), past participle of *couper* 'cut' (see COPE[1]).]

Couperin /kōōpə ran, -raN/, **François** (1668–1733) French composer and organist. Known as **Le Grand**

couple /kúpp'l/ *n* **1 TWO SIMILAR THINGS** two things of the same kind that are together or are considered as a pair ○ *found a couple of mugs in the cupboard* **2 SEVERAL** a few things of the same kind ○ *There are a couple of questions I'm not sure about.* **3 TWO PEOPLE SHARING LIVES** two people who are married, are living together, or have an intimate relationship **4 TWO PEOPLE DOING SOMETHING TOGETHER** two people, especially a man and a woman, who are sitting, walking, dancing, or working together ○ *There were only a few couples on the dance floor.* **5 SOMETHING THAT JOINS** something that links or joins two similar things **6 SYSTEM OF OPPOSING FORCES IN MECHANICS** a system of two equal forces that are parallel and in opposite directions **7 PAIR OF DOGS** a pair of hunting dogs attached to each other by a leash, or the double collar and leash on which they are held **8 ELECTRICAL CONTACT** a connection of two dissimilar metals that develops an electric current in the presence of an electrical conductor (**electrolyte**) ■ *v* (**-ples, -pling, -pled**) **1** *vt* **ASSOCIATE TWO THINGS** to associate or combine one person or thing with another ○ *High prices coupled with poor living conditions made their lives difficult.* **2** *vt* **JOIN TWO THINGS** to join or link two things or people ○ *to couple freight cars* **3** *vi* **HAVE SEXUAL INTERCOURSE** to have sexual intercourse (*formal*) [13C. Via Old French < Latin *copula* 'link'.] —**coupledom** *n*

USAGE When ***couple*** refers to two partners or married people, it may be treated as either singular or plural: *The couple wants to be married before the end of the year* but *The couple have not been reconciled, and continue to live apart.* However, if a pronoun refers to the word, it is almost always plural (*they, them, their*), and so the verb should be plural as well: *The couple have repeatedly asked that their privacy be respected.* In other uses, ***couple*** is often followed by *of* and a plural noun, in which case it is treated as plural: *A couple of books were on the table.* In informal uses the strict sense of 'two' may be expanded to 'several'. The use of ***couple*** without *of* in such contexts (*I bought a couple CDs*) is increasingly heard but should be avoided in formal writing.

---

coupler /kúpplər/ *n* **1** a mechanical or electronic device that connects two keyboards on an organ or harpsichord so that all the keys can be played from one keyboard **2** something or somebody that joins or combines two things together **3** ENG = **coupling** *n.* 4 **4** *US, Can* RAIL = **coupling** *n.* 5

couplet /kúpplət/ *n* two lines of verse that form a unit alone or as part of a poem, especially two that rhyme and have the same metre [Late 16C. < French, 'little couple' < *couple* (see COUPLE).]

coupling /kúppling/ *n* **1 SOMETHING THAT JOINS TWO THINGS** something that joins two things, especially a device for connecting two pieces of pipe, hose, or tube **2 JOINING TWO THINGS TOGETHER** a joining together or linking of two persons or things ○ *a disastrous coupling of two very unlike singers* **3 ACT OF SEXUAL INTERCOURSE** an act of sexual intercourse **4 LINK THAT TRANSFERS POWER** a part of a mechanical system by which power is transmitted from one rotating part to another part **5 CONNECTOR FOR RAILWAY CARRIAGES** a device on railway carriages that is used to link them in a train. US term **coupler** *n.* 4 **6 TRUNK OF ANIMAL'S BODY** the part of the body of a four-legged animal between the forequarters and hindquarters **7 CONNECTION OF ELECTRICAL CIRCUITS** a means of connecting two electrical circuits so that power can be passed between them, or the process of connecting electrical circuits in this way

coupon /kōō pon/ *n* **1 VOUCHER REDEEMED BY STORE OR COMPANY** a voucher that entitles somebody to a discount, refund, gift, or place in a draw, typically issued as a sales promotion **2 ORDER FORM** a printed form, e.g. in an advertisement, that may be filled in and returned to order a product or request information **3 FORM FOR PAYMENT BY INSTALMENTS** a form or card showing the payment due on a certain date for something that was bought by hire purchase. The card is returned with the payment. **4 CERTIFICATE OF INTEREST ON BOND** a detachable part of a bond that indicates a date and the amount of interest paid on that date. The holder must present it in order to receive payment of the interest. **5 TICKET IN RATIONING SYSTEM** a ticket issued in a rationing system that entitles somebody to a certain amount of a rationed item and that must be handed over to buy or receive that item **6 ENTRY FORM FOR FOOTBALL POOLS** an entry form for the football pools, with lists of fixtures against which entrants can mark their bets of a draw or a home or away win [Early 19C. < French, 'piece cut off' < *couper* (see COPE[1]).]

couponing /kōōpəning/ *n* the use of coupons as a means of promoting a product's sales or of saving money on purchases

courage /kúrrij/ *n* the ability to face danger, difficulty, uncertainty, or pain without being overcome by fear or being deflected from a chosen course of action ○ *She showed great courage throughout this difficult time.* [13C. < Old French *corage* < Latin *cor* 'heart'.] —**courageous** /kə ráyjəss/ *adj* —**courageously** *adv* —**courageousness** *n*

SYNONYMS ***courage, bravery, fearlessness, nerve, guts, pluck, mettle***

CORE MEANING: personal resoluteness in the face of danger or difficulties

courage the ability to show resoluteness and determination, whether physical, mental, or moral, against a wide range of difficulties or dangers; **bravery** extreme lack of fear; **fearlessness** resoluteness in the face of dangers or challenges; **nerve** coolness, steadiness, and self-assurance; **guts** (*slang*) strength of character and boldness; **pluck** resolution and willingness to continue struggling against the odds; **mettle** spirited determination.

~~**couragous**~~ incorrect spelling of **courageous**

courante /kōō raánt/ *n* **1** a musical composition in quick triple time, often part of a baroque suite **2** a dance of French and Italian origin in triple time with short quick steps [Late 16C. < French, 'running'.]

Courbet /ko͝or bay/, **Gustave** (1819–77) French painter

coureur de bois /koo rúr də bwáa/ (*plural* **coureurs de bois** /koo rúr də bwáa/) *n* somebody of French or French and Native American descent who trapped and traded furs in the 18th and 19th centuries in the north and northwest of what is now Canada [Early 18C. < French, 'woods runner'.]

courgette /kawr zhét/ *n UK* a small vegetable marrow eaten cooked or sometimes raw in salads. US term **zucchini** [Mid-20C. < French, 'small gourd', via Old French *cohourde* < Latin *cucurbita*.]

courier /ko͝ori ər/ *n* **1 SOMEBODY PROVIDING DELIVERY SERVICE** a person or company that delivers documents or small and valuable packages by hand **2 OFFICIAL MESSENGER** a diplomat, soldier, or other person with the responsibility of carrying and delivering official documents **3 SECRET MESSENGER** a smuggler or illicit carrier of something, e.g. illegal drugs **4 TRAVELLERS' GUIDE** a paid guide and helper who accompanies a group of travellers and makes arrangements for them, especially somebody employed by a travel agency to do this ■ *vt* **SEND BY COURIER** to send a document or package by a commercial courier service [14C. < French, 'runner' < Latin *currere* 'to run'.]

Courrèges /ko͝o rézh, -ráyzh/, **André** (*b.* 1923) French fashion designer

course /kawrss/ *n* **1 SEQUENCE OF EVENTS** the progression or development of a sequence of events, especially a development that is normal or expected ○ *events that changed the course of history* **2 PERIOD OF TIME** the progression or development of a period of time ○ *in the course of the afternoon* **3 DIRECTION TRAVELLED** the direction or route along which something travels **4 ACTION CHOSEN** an action or series of actions that somebody decides to take ○ *The simplest course of action would be to say nothing.* **5 PROGRAMME OF STUDY** a programme of study or training, especially one that leads to a qualification from an educational institution **6 UNIT IN EDUCATIONAL PROGRAMME** one of several distinct units that together form a programme of study leading to a qualification such as a degree ○ *a short course in comparative literature* **7 PART OF MEAL** one of two or more different dishes or types of food that are served in sequence during a meal **8 PATH OF RIVER** the route followed by a river or stream or by something very long such as a road or boundary **9 ONWARD MOVEMENT** swift onward movement ○ *Nothing could interrupt his headlong course.* **10 ESTABLISHED SEQUENCE OF TREATMENT** a sequence of treatment, exercise, or medication that is followed over a period of time ○ *on a course of antidepressants* **11 PLACE FOR RACE OR SPORT** an area where a race is run or where a sport in which players progress over the area is played **12 LAYER OF BRICKS** one of the layers of bricks that make up a wall **13 LOWEST SAIL ON SHIP** the lowest sail or row of sails on a square-rigged ship **14 GREYHOUND CHASE** a chase or race by dogs such as greyhounds ■ *v* (**courses, coursing, coursed**) **1** *vi* **RUN FAST** to flow or run swiftly **2** *vti* **HUNT ANIMALS WITH GREYHOUNDS** to hunt animals, especially hares, with greyhounds or other dogs that hunt by sight **3** *vt* **USE GREYHOUNDS FOR HUNTING** to use greyhounds or other dogs that hunt by sight [13C. Via French *cours* < Latin *cursus*, past participle of *currere* 'run'.] ◇ **in due course** after the lapse of an appropriate period of time ◇ **of course 1** without any question or doubt ○ *Of course you must go!* **2** used to show that the speaker has just understood something ○ *'We must tell nobody about this.' 'Of course.'* **3** used to point out a possibility that somebody may not have considered

SPELLCHECK See ***coarse***.

course book *n* a book that is used by students and teachers as the basis of a course of study

courser[1] /káwrssər/ *n* **1** a dog that is trained to hunt its quarry by sight instead of by scent **2** a hunter who uses coursers

courser[2] /káwrssər/ *n* a strong swift horse (*literary*) [13C. < Old French *corsier* < Latin *cursus* (see COURSE).]

courser[3] /káwrssər/ *n* a bird related to the plovers that is a swift runner. Native to: arid regions of Africa and Asia. Subfamily: Cursoriinae. [Mid-18C. Anglicization of modern Latin *Cursorius* < Latin *cursor* (see CURSOR).]

⚡**courseware** /káwrss wair/ *n* software and data used in computer-based training [Late 20C. < COURSE + SOFTWARE.]

coursework /káwrss wurk/ *n* work that is assigned to students as part of an educational course and counts towards the assessment given for the course

coursing /káwrssing/ *n* the sport of hunting with dogs such as greyhounds that follow their quarry using sight instead of scent

court[1] /kawrt/ *n* **1 MEETING WHERE LEGAL JUDGMENTS ARE MADE** a session of an official body that has authority to try cases, resolve disputes, or make other legal decisions ○ *She's threatening to take us to court over this.* **2 JUDGE** the constituted authority presiding over a court of law **3 COURTROOM OR COURTHOUSE** a place where a court of law is held **4 PEOPLE IN COURTROOM** all those present in a courtroom ○ *The court shall rise.* **5 OPEN SPACE WITHIN WALLS** an open space surrounded by buildings and walls, or a roofless area within a building **6 AREA FOR BALL GAME** an area marked out for playing a sport such as tennis or basketball, or a walled area where squash or a similar sport is played **7 MONARCH'S ATTENDANTS** the ministers, courtiers, and officials of the royal household who attend a king or queen **8 MEETING OF MONARCH AND ATTENDANTS** an occasion when a king or queen and the ministers, courtiers, and officials of the royal household are assembled **9 MONARCH'S RESIDENCE** the place where a king or queen and the court are usually in residence **10 IMPORTANT PERSON'S FOLLOWERS** a group of people who devote their time to the service and flattery of a noble, rich, or important person **11 SHORT STREET** a short street of houses that is closed at one end **12 GROUP OF HOUSES** a group of houses built around an open space **13 BLOCK OF FLATS** a large building containing many flats or offices **14 LARGE HOUSE** a large and imposing house and the land surrounding it (*often in placenames*) **15 GOVERNING BODY** the governing body or council of an organization such as a corporation or academic institution [13C. Via Anglo-Norman < Old French *cort* < Latin *cohort-* 'enclosed space'.] ◇ **be laughed out of court** to be ridiculed so severely that what you have to say is not considered seriously ◇ **pay court to somebody 1** to try to win influence with somebody or to win somebody's approval or favour through flattery or attentiveness **2** to try to gain somebody's love ◇ **rule something out of court** to refuse absolutely to allow something to take place

court[2] /kawrt/ *v* **1** *vt* **BE ATTENTIVE TO** to try to win influence with somebody or to win somebody's approval or favour through flattery or attentiveness **2** *vt* **TRY TO GAIN** to try to gain something, e.g. somebody's attention or admiration, by behaving in ways that are intended to attract or encourage it **3** *vt* **RISK EXPERIENCING SOMETHING BAD** to behave in a way that increases the likelihood of failure, injury, or other misfortune **4** *vti* **TRY TO GAIN SOMEBODY'S LOVE** to try to gain somebody's love (*dated*) **5** *vti* **TRY TO ATTRACT MATE** to engage in behaviour that is designed to attract another animal or bird as a mate **6** *vi* **BE SWEETHEARTS** to spend time together in a romantic relationship as a prelude to getting married (*dated*) ○ *We used to come here when we were courting.* [Early 16C. < Old Italian *corteare*, < Latin *cohort-* 'enclosed space'.]

Court /kawrt/, **Margaret Jean** (*b.* 1942) Australian tennis player. Born **Margaret Jean Smith**

court bouillon /káwrt bo͞o yon/ *n* a liquid used for poaching fish, made with water flavoured with vegetables, herbs, and wine or vinegar [< French, 'short broth']

court card *n* any of the kings, queens, and jacks in a pack of playing cards. US term **face card**

court case *n* LAW = **case**[1] *n.* 5

court circular *n* an account of what a country's monarch will be doing that day, along with other news of the royal family, published in a leading national newspaper

court cupboard *n* a sideboard or cabinet with some open shelves for display, used especially in the 16th and 17th centuries

court dress *n* the type and style of clothing that is officially approved for wear at a royal court

Courtenay /káwrtni/, **Bryce** (*b.* 1931) Australian writer

courtesan /káwrti zán, káwrti zan/ *n* a prostitute or mistress, especially one associated with a rich, powerful, or upper-class man who provides her with luxuries and status [Mid-16C. < French *courtisane* < Italian *cortigiana* 'female courtier' < *corte* 'court' < Latin *cohort-* 'enclosed space'.]

courtesy /kúrtəssi/ *n* (*plural* **-sies**) **1 POLITE OR CONSIDERATE BEHAVIOUR** consideration for other people or good manners ○ *He didn't even have the courtesy to offer me a seat.* **2 POLITE OR CONSIDERATE ACTION** something done out of politeness or consideration for another person ○ *We should certainly go, if only as a courtesy to Helen.* ■ *adj* **1 FOR SAKE OF POLITENESS** given or done as a courtesy ○ *a courtesy call* **2 PROVIDED FREE** provided free of charge ○ *Your courtesy limousine will take you to the airport.* [13C. < Old French *curtesie* < *corteis* 'courtly' < Latin *cohort-* 'enclosed space'.] —**courteous** /-ti əss/ *adj* —**courteously** *adv* —**courteousness** *n*

courtesy card *n* a card given to customers of a supermarket or other business that entitles them to special benefits or privileges

courtesy light *n* a light inside the passenger compartment of a vehicle that turns on automatically when the door is opened

courtesy title *n* a personal title that is used to address somebody out of politeness or as a social convention even though the person is not professionally or socially entitled to it

court hand *n* a style of handwriting formerly used by legal clerks

courthouse /káwrt howss/ *n* a building where a court of law is held

courtier /káwrti ər/ *n* **1** an aristocrat who frequents a royal court or attends a king or queen **2** flatterer of a more important person [13C. Alteration of Anglo-Norman *courteour* < Old French *courtoyer* 'be at court' < *cort* (see COURT[1]).]

court leet (*plural* **courts leet**) *n* LAW, HIST = **leet**[1]

courtly /káwrtli/ (**-lier, -liest**) *adj* **1 WITH REFINED MANNERS** showing great delicacy and refinement in behaviour **2 OF THE HIGHEST QUALITY** rich or fine and suitable for a royal court **3 INSINCERELY POLITE** insincerely polite or deferential in order to win somebody's favour —**courtliness** *n*

courtly love *n* a medieval code of behaviour that idealized the love of a knight for a usually married noblewoman and prescribed how they should act towards each other

court martial (*plural* **courts martial** *or* **court martials**) *n* **1** a military court that tries members of the armed forces and others for offences under military law **2** a trial by court martial

court-martial (**court-martials, court-martialling, court-martialled**) *vt* to try somebody by a military court for an offence under military law

Court of Appeal *n* a branch of the Supreme Court in England and Wales that hears civil and criminal appeals from other courts

court of appeals *n* in the United States, a court that has authority to hear appeals against the judgments of lower courts

court of chancery *n* in the United States, a court of equity, ruling on matters not covered by common law

Court of Chancery *n* a division of the High Court in England and Wales, presided over by the Lord Chancellor

court of claims *n* a federal court in the United States that has jurisdiction over claims brought against the government

Court of Common Pleas *n* a former higher court with jurisdiction over civil cases in England and Wales

court of equity *n* a court in England and Wales belonging to a court system organized under the Lord Chancellor that dispenses judgments on the basis of principles of equity, e.g., in cases of wills and trusts

Court of Exchequer *n* a former civil court with jurisdiction over revenue cases

court of first instance *n* a court in which legal proceedings are started, in particular one attached to the European Court of Justice

court of honour *n* a military court that investigates questions involving personal honour

court of inquiry *n* **1** a group specially set up to inquire into a matter of public concern such as the cause of a disaster **2** a military tribunal that investigates a matter of concern, especially in order to determine whether official charges should be brought

Court of Justiciary *n* LAW = **High Court of Justiciary**

court of law *n* a court that hears legal cases and issues rulings based on legal statutes or common law

court of record *n* a court that has its proceedings placed on an official permanent record and has the power to give penalties for contempt of court

Court of Saint James's *n* the court of the monarch of the United Kingdom, to which ambassadors are accredited

Court of Session *n* the highest civil court in Scotland

court order *n* an official order issued by the judge of a court, requiring or forbidding somebody to do something

Courtrai /koor tráy/ city in W Belgium. Population: 75,408 (1998 estimate).

court recorder *n* somebody who records the proceedings of a law court and prepares a verbatim report of them. US term **court reporter**

court reporter *n US* LAW = **court recorder**

courtroom /káwrt room, -ro͝om/ *n* a room used for holding a session of a court of law

courtship /káwrt ship/ *n* **1 TRYING TO GAIN SOMEBODY'S LOVE** the act of paying attention to somebody with a view to developing a more intimate relationship **2 PRELUDE TO MARRIAGE** the period of a romantic relationship before marriage **3 INGRATIATING BEHAVIOUR** friendly and often ingratiating attention for the purpose of winning a favour or establishing an alliance or other relationship **4 MATING BEHAVIOUR** behaviour designed to attract another animal or bird as a mate, or the time during which an animal or bird engages in this

court shoe *n* a woman's shoe that is plain and cut low in front and has a moderately high heel. US term **pump**[2] *n.* 2

courtside /káwrt sīd/ *adj, adv* at the side of an athletic court where a match or game such as tennis or basketball is being played

court tennis *n US* = **real tennis**

courtyard /káwrt yaard/ *n* an area of ground that is surrounded by buildings, lies inside a large building, or is adjacent to a building and enclosed by walls

couscous /ko͝oss kooss/ *n* **1** a food resembling tiny grains, made from semolina and cooked by steaming or briefly soaking in boiling water **2** a North African dish consisting of a spicy stew of meat and vegetables served with couscous [Late 16C. Via French < Arabic *kuskus* < *kaskasa* 'pulverize'.]

cousin /kúzz'n/ *n* **1 UNCLE'S OR AUNT'S CHILD** a child of somebody's uncle or aunt **2 DISTANT RELATIVE** somebody to whom somebody else is related through the brother or sister of a grandparent, great-grandparent, or even older ancestor **3 SOMEBODY WITH MUCH IN COMMON** a person with whom another feels connected because of similar ancestry, ethnic background, or interests ○ *our Canadian cousins* **4 TERM OF ADDRESS BETWEEN SOVEREIGNS** used by European sovereigns as a term of address for another sovereign or a member of a royal family [13C. Via Old French < Latin *consobrinus* 'mother's sister's child' < *sobrinus* 'maternal cousin'.] —**cousinhood** *n* —**cousinly** *adj*

Cousin /koo záN/, **Victor** (1792–1867) French philosopher

cousin german (*plural* **cousins german**) *n* = **cousin** *n.* 1 (*dated*) [14C. < French *cousin germain*; *germain* < Latin *germanus* (see GERMAN).]

Cousteau /ko͞ostō/, **Jacques** (1910–97) French underwater explorer

couth /kooth/ *adj* showing very good manners or great social sophistication (*humorous*) [Late 19C. Back-formation < UNCOUTH.]

couthie /ko͞othi/, **couthy** (**-ier, -iest**) *adj Scotland* **1 FRIENDLY** acting in a friendly or sociable way **2 COMFORTABLE** comfortable and homely **3 HOMESPUN** without pretensions or complications [Early 18C. < COUTH.]

couture /koo tyo͝or/ *n* **1** the design and production of fashionable high-quality custom-made clothes **2** high-quality clothing made to order by a fashion designer [Early 20C. Via French < late Latin *consutura* 'sewing together' < Latin *suere* 'sew'.]

couturier /koo tyo͝ori ay/ *n* a designer of fashionable high-quality custom-made clothes [Late 19C. < French, 'dressmaker' < *couture* (see COUTURE).]

couturière /koo tyo͝ori áir/ *n* a woman designer of fashionable high-quality custom-made clothes [Early 19C. < French, feminine of *couturier* (see COUTURIER).]

couturify /koo tyo͝ori fī/ (**-fies, -fying, -fied**) *vt* to make a garment stylish by using fine fabrics, unusual colours, other elements of designer clothing (*informal*) [Late 20C. < COUTURE.]

couvade /koo vaád/ *n* the mimicking of childbirth by the father while it is taking place, a custom in some Native South American societies [Mid-19C. < French, 'hatching' < *couver* 'hatch' < Latin *cubare* 'lie down'.]

Cov., cov. *abbr* covariance

covalence /kō váylənss/ *n US* CHEM = **covalency**

covalent /kō váylənt/ *adj* describes a chemical bond in which the attractive force between atoms is created by the sharing of electrons —**covalency** *n* —**covalently** *adv*

covalent bond *n* a chemical bond between two atoms created by the sharing of a pair of electrons

covariance /kō váiri ənss/ *n* a statistical measure of the tendency of two variables to change in conjunction with each other

covariant /kō vaíri ənt/ *adj* exhibiting a tendency to change in conjunction with another statistical variable

cove[1] /kōv/ *n* **1 BAY IN SHORELINE** a small bay on the shore of the sea or a lake, especially one that is enclosed by high cliffs **2 NOOK IN CLIFF** a small semicircular recessed valley in the side of a hill or cliff **3 CURVE AT TOP OF WALL** an inwardly curved surface at the point where a wall meets a ceiling **4 CURVED MOULDING** a moulding that curves inwards ■ *vti* (**coves, coving, coved**) **MAKE WITH OR HAVE INWARD CURVE** to have a cove, or design or build a wall with a cove [Old English *cofa* 'bedchamber, alcove' < Germanic, 'hollow place providing shelter']

cove[2] /kōv/ *n* a man (*dated slang*) [Mid-16C. Probably < Romany *kova* 'person, thing'.]

covellite /kō vél īt/ *n* a purple mineral consisting of thin sheets of copper sulphide [Mid-19C. After Niccolò *Covelli* (1790–1829), Italian mineralogist.]

coven /kúvv'n/ *n* a meeting or group of witches, usually 13 in number [Mid-17C. Variant of *covin* 'company, agreement', via Old French < medieval Latin *convenium* < Latin *convenire* (see CONVENE).]

covenant /kúvvənənt/ *n* **1 SOLEMN AGREEMENT** a solemn agreement that is binding on all parties **2 LEGALLY BINDING AGREEMENT** a formal and legally binding agreement or contract such as a lease, or one of the clauses in an agreement of this kind **3 LAWSUIT FOR BREACH OF AGREEMENT** a lawsuit for damages that is brought because of the breaking of a legal covenant **4 MUTUAL PROMISES OF GOD AND ISRAELITES** the promises that were made in the Bible between God and the Israelites, who agreed to worship no other gods ■ *vti* **AGREE IN COVENANT** to promise something in a covenant, especially a legal one promising regular payments of a stated amount to a charity [13C. < Old French, present participle of *convenir* 'agree' (see CONVENE).] —**covenantal** /kúvvə nánt'l/ *adj* —**covenantally** *adv* —**covenanter** *n*

Covenant *n* any of several agreements in the 17th century by which Scottish Presbyterians united to defend their church

covenantee /kúvvənən tée/ *n* somebody to whom something is promised in a covenant

Covenanter *n* a defender of the Scottish Presbyterian church who joined its Covenant during the 17th century

covenant marriage *n US* a form of marriage contract whose statute imposes stricter than usual conditions for couples wishing to marry or get divorced, e.g. premarital counselling and a two-year separation prior to divorce

Coventry[1] /kóvvəntri/ ◇ **send somebody to Coventry** to refuse to speak to or associate with somebody as a punishment or mark of disapproval

Coventry[2] /kóvvəntri/ city in central England. Population: 306,503 (1996 estimate).

co-venture, coventure *vti* to undertake a business venture in partnership with another person or company ■ *n* a business agreement, deal, or partnership involving two or more companies

cover /kúvvər/ *v* **1** *vt* **PUT SOMETHING OVER** to put something over the whole of or the upper surface of something, e.g. in order to hide, protect, or decorate it **2** *vt* **BE ALL OVER** to lie across or in a layer over the whole of or the upper surface of something ○ *rocks covered with seaweed* **3** *vt* **KEEP WARM** to put something such as a blanket over or around somebody for warmth ○ *She covered him with the quilt.* **4** *vt* **BE WRAPPED AROUND** to be lying over or wrapped around somebody to provide warmth ○ *She was covered only by a thin blanket.* **5** *vt* **PUT CLOTHING ON** to put a piece of clothing on part of your own or somebody else's body ○ *Keep your head covered if you are going out.* **6** *vt* **BE WORN ON** to be worn on part of the body **7** *vt* **PUT LID ON** to put a lid or protective covering over something **8** *vt* **TALK OR WRITE ABOUT** to deal with a subject in a discussion, speech, book, or article ○ *His talk covered several aspects of company law.* **9** *vt* **PROVIDE NEWS OF** to be responsible for reporting, video-taping, or photographing an event or a particular class of events for a newspaper or a broadcasting company ○ *We cover everything that has a financial angle.* **10** *vt* **INCLUDE PARTICULAR INSTANCE** to take something into account and provide an adequate treatment of it ○ *Unfortunately, the law does not cover cases of this sort.* **11** *vt* **EXTEND OVER** to include the whole of a particular area, either physically or as a field of operations or responsibility ○ *an office complex covering three blocks* ○ *a police operation that covered the whole of the city* **12** *vt* **TRAVEL CERTAIN DISTANCE** to travel a particular distance **13** *vt* **HIDE STATE OF** to conceal a feeling, action, or situation by presenting a different appearance or directing attention elsewhere ○ *I managed to cover my mistake by changing the subject.* **14** *vt* **INSURE** to provide insurance protection to somebody **15** *vt* **INSURE AGAINST** to provide insurance protection against a type of hazard or risk **16** *vt* **PAY FOR** to be sufficient to pay for something ○ *£20 should cover it.* **17** *vt* **PROTECT FROM ATTACK** to protect somebody, a part of an army, or a piece in chess or another game from attack by occupying a position nearby from which a counterattack can be made **18** *vt* **AIM GUN AT** to have a person or place in the aim or range of a gun, especially in order to provide protection against a possible attack **19** *vt* **PATROL** to maintain a watch on or a patrol of something, e.g. to track somebody's movements ○ *One police officer covered the rear exit while the others knocked at the front door.* **20** *vt* **INFUSE WITH A QUALITY** to bring an overwhelming amount of some quality upon yourself or somebody else (*often passive*) ○ *was covered in confusion* **21** *vi* **DO SOMEBODY'S JOB** to do the work of somebody who is absent for a time **22** *vi* **TELL LIES FOR** to keep people from learning the real truth about somebody ○ *covered for him by lying* **23** *vt* **COPULATE WITH FEMALE** to copulate with a female animal, especially a mare (*refers to male animals, especially stallions*) **24** *vt* **PLAY HIGHER CARD** to play a card that has a higher value than one already played by another person **25** *vti* **BUY REPLACEMENT STOCK** to buy shares of stock or commodities in order to replace others that were borrowed from a broker and sold with the expectation that the price would fall **26** *vt* **MATCH ANOTHER'S BET** to match the amount of money bet by another gambler **27** *vt* **RECORD NEW VERSION OF SONG** to record a new version of a song that was first sung or made popular by another performer **28** *vt* **DEFEND AREA AGAINST OPPONENT** to play in defence against an opponent or in a particular position or area on a playing surface **29** *vt* **SIT ON EGGS** to sit on eggs in a nest to hatch them (*refers to female birds*) ■ *n* **1 SOMETHING THAT COVERS** one thing that hides, protects, or covers something else, or is used to cover something **2 LID** something that covers the top of a container, e.g. a lid **3 BINDING OF BOOK OR MAGAZINE** the protective binding, thick paper, or boards at the front and back of a book or magazine **4 CLOTH THAT COVERS FURNITURE** a cloth or plastic covering for bedding or a piece of furniture **5 SHELTER FROM WEATHER** something that provides shelter from the weather **6 HIDING PLACE** something that provides concealment or protection, especially undergrowth where animals can hide or a shelter from attack ○ *took cover under the trees* **7 VEGETATION** the plants that cover an area of land **8 DEFENCE AGAINST ATTACK** protection provided, especially to an attacking force, by other forces located nearby or in the air ○ *air cover* **9 PROTECTIVE PRETENCE** a false identity or a pretext that provides protection for somebody such as a spy or detective **10 SUBSTITUTES FOR WORKERS** people who are available to do other people's jobs when they are absent ○ *We no longer have enough staff to provide cover in emergencies.* **11 PLACE LAID AT TABLE** a place laid at table, e.g. in a restaurant **12** COMM = **cover charge** **13** CRICKET = **cover point** **14 INSURANCE PROTECTION** the amount or type of protection provided by an insurance policy. US term **coverage** *n.* 2 **15 ENOUGH MONEY** sufficient funds or guaranteed income to meet a liability or cover a planned expenditure **16 NEW RECORDING OF WELL-KNOWN SONG** a recording by a performer of a song that was first sung or popularized by another performer **17 UNDERSTUDY** an understudy for a musical role **18 ENVELOPE** a postmarked envelope ■ **covers** *npl* **1 COVERINGS ON BED** the sheets, blankets, and other coverings on a bed **2 WATERPROOF COVERS PROTECTING SPORTS FIELD** sheets of waterproof material spread over a playing surface to protect it against rain (*usually plural*) **3 OFF-SIDE FIELD** the area of a cricket field in front of the batsman on the off side that is between cover point and extra cover [13C. Via Old French *covrir* < Latin *cooperire* 'cover completely' < *operire* 'to cover'.] —**coverable** *adj* —**coverer** *n* —**coverless** *adj* ◇ **blow somebody's cover** to expose a disguise, lie, or pretence that somebody has been using to conceal something ◇ **under cover of something** hidden or protected by something ◇ **under separate cover** in another envelope or package

cover up *v* 1 *vti* COVER SOMETHING COMPLETELY to cover somebody or something completely 2 *vti* CONCEAL SOMETHING BAD to try to conceal that something illegal, immoral, or undesirable has happened or how or why it happened 3 *vi* PROTECT HEAD AND UPPER BODY to hide the head and upper body behind the arms as protection against another boxer's blows

coverage /kúvvərij/ *n* 1 MEDIA ATTENTION the attention given to an event or topic by newspapers, radio, and television in their reporting 2 US INSUR = **cover** *n*. 14 3 MEDIA AUDIENCE the percentage of all the people in a given area who are reached by a newspaper or radio or television station 4 DEGREE OF COVERING the degree to which something is covered by something else ○ *the coverage of the ground by the snow* 5 AVAILABLE FUNDS the amount of funds available to cover financial liabilities or commitments

coveralls /kúvvər awlz/ *npl* a one-piece outer garment that covers and protects the clothes

cover charge *n* a fixed charge that is added per head to the cost of drinks and food in a nightclub or restaurant, e.g. for bread or entertainment

cover crop *n* a crop planted between main crops to prevent erosion or to plough in to enrich the soil

covered wagon *n US, Can* a large wagon with a canvas roof stretched over arched supports, used by pioneers crossing the plains of North America

cover girl *n* a young woman, usually a glamorous model, whose picture is on the cover of a magazine

cover glass *n* SCI = **cover slip**

covering /kúvvəring/ *n* something that protects, hides, or covers something

covering fire *n* weapon fire used to protect friendly troops from direct fire from the enemy's weapons

covering letter *n* a letter sent with another document or a package, providing necessary or additional information. US term **cover letter**

coverlet /kúvvərlət/ *n* a usually decorative cover for a bed, placed over the other bedclothes when the bed is not being used [13C. < Old French *couvre lit* 'bed cover'.]

cover letter *n US, Can* = **covering letter**

covermount /kúvvər mownt/ *n* a gift fixed to the cover of a magazine, such as a diary or recipe book [Late 20C]

cover note *n* a document given by an insurance company to a person who has taken out a policy, acting as a temporary certificate of insurance until the full policy is issued

cover page, cover sheet *n* a form sent along with a fax that gives information about the sender, e.g. the name, address, telephone number, and fax number

cover point *n* in cricket, a position in the covers to the right of the fielder at point, or a fielder who takes up this position

cover sheet *n* = **cover page**

cover slip *n* a piece of thin glass used to cover a specimen on a microscope slide

cover story *n* 1 a magazine feature that is illustrated on the front cover and is the most important article in the issue 2 a story made up to deceive somebody, e.g. to provide a false identity for an undercover investigator

covert /kúvvərt/ *adj* SECRET not intended to be known, seen, or found out ■ *n* 1 UNDERGROWTH PROVIDING COVER a thicket or undergrowth in which game can shelter or hide 2 SHELTER a shelter or hiding place 3 SMALL FEATHER a small feather around the base of a quill on the wing or tail of a bird 4 **covert, covert cloth** TWILLED CLOTH a hard-wearing twilled cloth. Use: suits. 5 FLOCK OF COOTS a flock of coots (*see* COVER.) —**covertly** *adv* —**covertness** *n*

SYNONYMS See *secret*.

coverture /kúvvərchər/ *n* 1 a shelter or covering 2 the condition of being a married woman [13C. < Old French, < *covrir* (*see* COVER.)]

cover-up *n* 1 a concealment of something illegal, immoral, or undesirable 2 a loose item of clothing worn over another garment, e.g. a wrap over an evening dress or a T-shirt over a swimsuit

cover version *n* RECORDING = **cover** *n*. 16

covet /kúvvət/ *v* 1 *vti* to have a strong desire to possess something that belongs to somebody else 2 *vt* to want to have something very much (*formal*) [13C. < Old French *coveitier* < Latin *cupiditas* 'cupidity'.] —**covetable** *adj* —**coveter** *n* —**covetingly** *adv* —**covetous** *adj* —**covetously** *adv* —**covetousness** *n*

SYNONYMS See *want*.

covey /kúvvi/ (*plural* **-eys**) *n* 1 a small group of game birds such as partridge, grouse, or quail 2 a small group of people or things [14C. < French *covée* 'brood' < Latin *cubare* 'lie down'.]

coving /kốving/ *n* a prefabricated curved moulding used as a decorative cover for the join between a wall and a ceiling

cow[1] /kow/ *n* 1 LARGE FEMALE MAMMAL KEPT FOR MILK an adult female grass-eating quadruped. Kept for: milk, meat, breeding. Genus: *Bos*. 2 MALE OR FEMALE OF DOMESTIC CATTLE a male or female, whether adult or not, belonging to any breed of domestic cattle 3 LARGE FEMALE MAMMAL an adult female of a large mammal species other than cattle, e.g. the whale, elephant, seal, or moose 4 OFFENSIVE TERM an offensive term that deliberately insults a woman (*slang*) [Old English *cū* < Indo-European] ◇ **have a cow** *US* to become suddenly and greatly excited or angry (*slang*) ◇ **till the cows come home** until an extremely long time has elapsed (*informal*)

cow[2] /kow/ *vt* to frighten somebody into submission or obedience [Late 16C. Probably < Old Norse *kúga* 'oppress'.]

Cowan /ków ən/ salt lake in S Western Australia. Area: 940 sq. km/359 sq. mi.

coward /kówərd/ *n* a fearful and uncourageous person [13C. < Old French *cuard* < Latin *cauda* 'tail'.]

Coward /kówərd/, **Sir Noel** (1899–1973) British dramatist, actor, and songwriter

cowardice /kówərdiss/ *n* a lack of courage, or behaviour that shows such a lack

cowardly /kówərdli/ *adj* 1 caused by a lack of courage, or lacking courage 2 showing meanness or cruelty to those who are weaker and fear of those who are equal or stronger —**cowardliness** *n* —**cowardly** *adv*

SYNONYMS **cowardly, faint-hearted, spineless, gutless, pusillanimous, craven, chicken**
CORE MEANING: lacking in courage
cowardly lacking in courage, or caused by a lack of courage; **faint-hearted** timid and lacking in resolve; **spineless** seriously lacking willpower or strength of character; **gutless** seriously lacking in courage and determination; **pusillanimous** (*formal*) showing a contemptible degree of cowardice; **craven** showing a contemptible degree of cowardice and weakness of will; **chicken** (*informal*, often used by children and young people) cowardly.

cowbane /ków bayn/ (*plural* **-bane**) *n* 1 a poisonous Eurasian marsh plant. Native to: Europe, Asia. Genus: *Cicuta*. 2 a poisonous marsh plant. Native to: North America. *Oxypalis rigidior*.

cowbell /ków bel/ *n* 1 a bell fastened to a collar round a cow's neck that clangs as the cow moves, making the animal easier to find 2 a bell without a clapper, played as a percussion instrument by being struck with a drumstick

cowberry /kówbəri/ *n* (*plural* **-ries** or **-ry**) a creeping flowering shrub that produces edible berries. Native to: northern temperate areas. *Vaccinium vitis-idaea*.

cowbird /ków burd/ *n* either of two species of blackbird that lay their eggs in the nests of other birds and often feed alongside grazing cattle. Native to: North America. Genus: *Molothrus*.

cowboy /ków boy/ *n* 1 MAN WHO LOOKS AFTER CATTLE a man employed to look after cattle, especially in the W United States. Cowboys traditionally work on horseback, but now also use motor vehicles. 2 MALE CHARACTER IN WESTERNS a male character in stories and films about the W United States in the late 1800s, often shown fighting Native Americans or outlaws 3 UNRELIABLE WORKER an unskilled or unscrupulous person working in a trade or business who carries out inferior work (*informal*)

cowboy boot *n* a high-heeled boot, like those originally worn by cowboys, usually with pointed toes and ornamental stitching

cowboy hat *n* a hat, usually felt, with a high crown and a wide brim, originally worn by cowboys and now widely worn in the southwestern and midwestern United States

cowboys and Indians *n* a children's game involving two sides pretending to be cowboys and Native Americans fighting against each other (+ *singular verb*)

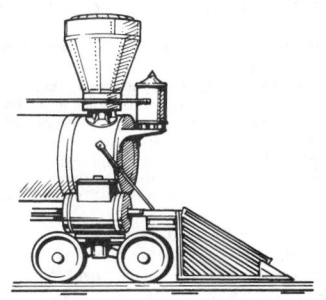

Cowcatcher

cowcatcher /ków kachər/ *n* an angled metal frame formerly fixed to the front of a steam railway engine to clear animals and other obstructions from the track

Cowdrey /kówdri/, **Colin, Baron Cowdrey of Tonbridge** (1932–2000) Indian-born British cricketer

Cowen /ków ən/, **Sir Zelman** (*b.* 1919) Australian lawyer and statesman

cower /kówər/ *vi* to cringe or move backwards defensively in fear [13C. < Middle Low German *kūren* 'lie in wait'.]

Cowes /kowz/ resort and yachting centre on the Isle of Wight, S England. Population: 16,335 (1991).

cowfish /ków fish/ (*plural* **-fish** or **-fishes**) *n* 1 a small brightly coloured warm-water marine fish with spines that resemble horns above the eyes. Family: Ostraciidae. 2 an aquatic mammal, e.g. certain species of dolphin or porpoise, or a manatee

cowgirl /ków gurl/ *n* 1 *US* WOMAN WHO LOOKS AFTER CATTLE a woman employed to look after cattle, especially in the W United States 2 WOMAN CHARACTER IN WESTERNS a woman character in stories and films about the W United States in the late 1800s, usually accompanying or assisting a cowboy in his exploits 3 *US* FEMALE RODEO PERFORMER a woman who performs or competes in shows such as rodeos

cowhand /ków hand/ *n US* somebody employed to look after cattle

cowherd /ków hurd/ *n* a tender of cattle, usually on foot (*archaic or literary*)

cowhide /ków hīd/ *n* 1 SKIN OF COW the skin of a cow or bull, especially removed and processed 2 LEATHER leather made from a cowhide 3 LEATHER WHIP a whip made of braided leather or rawhide ■ *vt* (**-hides, -hiding, -hided**) WHIP to beat somebody with a whip made of braided leather or rawhide

Cowichan sweater /kówichən-/ *n* a heavy homespun jersey, originally black and white and knitted with symbolic designs by Native American peoples of the Pacific Northwest coast [After the *Cowichan* people of Canada]

cowl /kowl/ *n* 1 MONK'S HOOD the hood on a monk's cloak or a monk's hooded cloak 2 CLOTHING = **cowl neck** 3 HOOD FOR CHIMNEY a hood-shaped, sometimes revolving, cover fitted to a chimney or vent to improve ventilation and prevent downward draughts 4 PART OF VEHICLE BODY the part of the body of a motor vehicle to which the windscreen, bonnet, and dashboard are attached 5 ENG = **cowling** [Pre-12C. Via Germanic < Latin *cucullus* 'hood'.]

cowled /kowld/ *adj* fitted with or wearing a hood or hooded cloak

Cowley /kówli/, **Abraham** (1618–67) English poet

cowlick /ków lik/ *n* a tuft of hair growing in a different direction from the rest of the hair on somebody's head and usually sticking up [< its resemblance to a ridge of hair on a cow's hide that is thought to be caused by the animal licking itself]

cowling /kówling/ n a streamlined removable metal covering for an aircraft engine, fuselage, or nacelle

cowl neck n a collar on a woman's garment, e.g. a jersey, that drapes in large folds around the neck (*hyphenated before nouns*)

cowman /kówmən/ (*plural* **-men** /-mən/) n **1** a man who tends cattle, especially somebody responsible for the milking and other aspects of managing a dairy herd **2** *US, Can* a man who owns cattle or a cattle ranch **3** *US AGRIC* = **cowherd**

coworker /kố wurkər/ n a person who shares work with one or more people

cow parsley (*plural* **cow parsley**) n a tall perennial plant that grows along roads and in hedgerows. Flowers: white, in umbrella-shaped clusters. Native to: Europe. *Anthriscus sylvestris.*

cow parsnip n a tall perennial plant with a thick stem. Flowers: tiny, white and purple, in flattened clusters. Native to: northern temperate regions. Genus: *Heracleum.*

cowpat /ków pat/ n a circular flat mass of dung excreted by a cow

cowpea /ków pee/ n PLANTS = **black-eyed bean**

Cowper /koóopər, ków-/, **William** (1731–1800) British poet

Cowper's gland /koóopərz-, ków-/ n either of two small glands, just below the prostate, that secrete into the urethra a lubricant fluid that is released just prior to ejaculation of semen. ◊ **Bartholin's gland** [Mid-18C. After the English anatomist William *Cowper* (1666–1709).]

cowpoke /ków pōk/ n *US, Can* a cowboy or cowgirl (*informal*)

cowpox /ków poks/ n a mild viral skin disease in cattle, usually affecting the udder with a pustular rash. Technical name **vaccinia**

cowpuncher /ków punchər/ n *US, Can* a cowboy or cowgirl (*informal*)

Cowra /kówrə/ town in central New South Wales, Australia. Population: 8,416 (1991).

cowrie /kówri/, **cowry** (*plural* **-ries**) n **1** a tropical marine mollusc that has a glossy brightly coloured shell with a long central toothed opening. Family: Cypraeidae. **2** the shell of a cowrie, formerly used as money in parts of Africa and Asia [Mid-17C. < Hindi *kaurī*.]

cowrite /kố rīt/ (**-writes**, **-writing**, **-written**, **-wrote**) vt to write something, e.g. a screenplay or report, jointly with somebody —**cowriter** n

cowry n = **cowrie**

cowshed /ków shed/ n a building in which cattle are housed

cowslip /kówslip/ n a plant with flowers similar to those of a primrose. Flowers: long-stemmed, drooping, fragrant, yellow. Native to: grassy areas in temperate regions of Europe, Africa, Asia. *Primula veris.* [Old English *cūslyppe* 'cow dung', probably from a belief that it grew where a cowpat had fallen]

cox /koks/ n the member of a rowing crew who faces forward, steers the boat, and directs the speed and rhythm of the rowers ■ vti to act as the cox of a rowing boat, especially in a race [Late 19C. Shortening of COXSWAIN.] —**coxless** adj

Cox /koks/, **David** (1783–1859) British artist

Cox, Paul (b. 1940) Dutch-born Australian film director

Cox, Philip (b. 1939) Australian architect

coxa /kóksə/ (*plural* **-ae** /-see/) n **1** the hipbone or hip joint (*technical*) **2** the base segment of the leg of most insects and other arthropods [Early 19C. < Latin, 'hip'.] —**coxal** adj

coxalgia /kok sálji ə, -jə/ n pain in the hip or a disease of the hip —**coxalgic** adj

coxcomb /kóks kōm/ n (*archaic*) **1** a conceited man with an excessive interest in clothes and fashion **2** the cap worn by a medieval jester, shaped like a cockscomb [Mid-16C. Alteration of COCKSCOMB.] —**coxcombry** /kóks kōmri/ n

Coxsackie virus /kok sáki-, koŏk saáki-/, **coxsackie virus** n an enterovirus belonging to a group that occurs in the human intestinal tract and causes diseases such as viral meningitis and a condition similar to poliomyelitis [Mid-20C. After *Coxsackie*, New York.]

Cox's Orange Pippin n a small variety of eating apple with a yellowish-green skin flecked or patched with red [Mid-19C. After Richard *Cox* (c.1776–1845), an amateur British fruit-grower.]

coxswain /kóks'n, -swayn/, **cockswain** n **1** ROWING = **cox** n. **2** a person who oversees a lifeboat and its crew, and who usually steers it **3** the senior petty officer of a small ship ■ vti ROWING = **cox** v. [14C. < *cock* 'ship's boat' + SWAIN.]

coy /koy/ adj **1** PRETENDING TO BE SHY pretending, in a teasing or provocative way, to be reserved or modest **2** SHY shy or reserved in social situations **3** UNCOMMUNICATIVE unwilling to reveal information about somebody or something, especially in a way that teases or annoys somebody who wants the information [14C. Via French *coi* 'quiet' < Latin *quietus*.] —**coyish** adj —**coyly** adv —**coyness** n

Coy. abbr company

coyote /kóyōt, koy ốti/ (*plural* **-tes** or **-te**) n a carnivorous canine mammal, similar to but smaller than the wolf. Native to: North America. *Canis latrans.* [Mid-18C. Via Mexican Spanish < Nahuatl *coyotl*.]

coyotillo /kŏyŏ teé lyŏ/ (*plural* **-los**) n a thorny shrub with small green flowers and poisonous black berries. Native to: Mexico, SW United States. *Karwinskia humboldtiana*. [Late 19C. < Mexican Spanish, 'little coyote'.]

Coypu

coypu /kóy poo/ (*plural* **-pus** or **-pu**) n a large semiaquatic rodent with webbed feet and a long tail. Kept for: fur. Native to: South America. [Late 18C. < Araucanian.]

coz /kuz/ n a cousin (*archaic*) [Mid-16C. Shortening.]

cozen /kúzz'n/ vti to deceive, cheat, or defraud somebody (*archaic*) [Late 16C. < ?] —**cozener** n

cozy adj, n *US* = **cosy**

cozzie n = **cossie** (*informal*)

CP abbr **1** Canadian Press **2** Cape Province **3** chemically pure **4** command post **5** Communist Party **6** *Aus* Country Party **7** chat post (*in e-mails*)

cp. abbr compare

CPA abbr critical path analysis

cpd abbr compound

Cpl abbr Corporal

CPO abbr Chief Petty Officer

CPR abbr **1** cardiopulmonary resuscitation **2** Canadian Pacific Railway

cps abbr **1** characters per second **2** cycles per second

CPS abbr Crown Prosecution Service

CPSA abbr Civil and Public Services Association

Cpt. abbr Captain

CPU abbr central processing unit

CQ[1] n a set of code letters transmitted at the start of a radio message indicating that the message is meant for all receivers and requesting a response

CQ[2] abbr charge of quarters

Cr abbr Costa Rica (*in Internet addresses*)

Cr[1] symbol chromium

Cr[2] abbr Councillor

CR abbr **1** Community of the Resurrection **2** Costa Rica **3** conditioned reflex **4** conditioned response

cr. abbr **1** credit **2** creditor **3** creek

---

crab[1] /krab/ n **1** FLAT CRUSTACEAN a crustacean with a broad flat shell, antennae, a small abdomen, and five pairs of legs, the front pair of which are in the form of grasping pincers. Suborder: Brachyura. **2** CRUSTACEAN RESEMBLING CRAB an animal similar or related to the true crab, e.g. the hermit crab, horseshoe crab, or king crab **3** FLESH OF CRAB the flesh of a crab when used as food **4** PARASITIC LOUSE IN PUBIC HAIR a parasitic louse resembling a tiny crab that infests the pubic hair of humans, causing inflammation and itching of the skin. *Phthirius pubis.* **5** CRANE a machine similar to a crane designed to lift and move heavy weights **6** FLYING MANOEUVRE a flying manoeuvre in which an aircraft is steered into a crosswind slightly to compensate for drifting off course ■ **crabs** npl LICE INFESTATION an infestation of crab lice (*informal*) ■ v (**crabs**, **crabbing**, **crabbed**) **1** vti SCURRY SIDEWAYS to move sideways as a crab does, or to cause something to move in this way **2** vi CATCH CRABS to go fishing or hunting for crabs **3** vti FLY INTO CROSSWIND to fly an aircraft slightly into a crosswind to compensate for drifting off course **4** vi SAIL WITH SIDEWAYS DRIFT to sail forwards with a slight sideways drift caused by a current [Old English *crabba* < Indo-European, 'scratch'] —**crabber** n **1** catch a crab in rowing, to make a faulty stroke by failing to make contact with the water or plunging the oar blade in too deeply

crab[2] /krab/ n TREES = **crab apple** [15C. < ?]

crab[3] /krab/ n SOMEBODY BAD-TEMPERED somebody regarded as bad-tempered or disagreeable (*informal insult*) ■ v (**crabs**, **crabbing**, **crabbed**) **1** vi CRITICIZE to criticize or grumble about somebody or something **2** vt SPOIL to ruin or spoil something through interference [Late 16C. Probably back-formation < CRABBED.]

Crab n ZODIAC = **Cancer** n. **2**, **Cancer** n. **3**

crab apple n **1** a small sour apple. Use: in preserves. **2** an apple tree that produces small sour fruit. Genus: *Malus.*

Crabbe /krab/, **George** (1754–1832) British poet and clergyman

crabbed /krábbd, krábbid/ adj **1** GROUCHY bad-tempered, irritable, or disagreeable by nature **2** HARD TO READ hard to read, because the words and letters are compressed **3** COMPLICATED complicated and hard to follow (*dated*) ◊ *crabbed logic* [13C. < CRAB[1] because the way crabs threaten with their claws and their sideways walk suggest bad temper; reinforced by the idea of 'sourness' found in CRAB[2].] —**crabbedly** adv —**crabbedness** n

crabbing /krábbing/ n fishing or hunting for crabs

crabby /krábbi/ (**-bier**, **-biest**) adj bad-tempered or irritable in character [Mid-16C. < CRAB[1], CRAB[2].] —**crabbily** adv —**crabbiness** n

crab grass (*plural* **crab grasses** or **crab grass**) n a coarse grass that grows in warm regions, has creeping stems that root freely, and is considered a weed in lawns and gardens. Genus: *Digitaria.*

crab louse n ZOOL = **crab**[1] n. **4**

crabmeat /kráb meet/ n the flesh of a crab when used as food

Crab Nebula n the gaseous remains of an exploded star in the constellation Taurus, about 5,000 light-years from the Earth

crab stick n a stick-shaped piece of processed fish that has been flavoured and coloured to resemble crabmeat

crabstick /kráb stik/ n a stick or club made from the wood of a crab apple

crabwise /kráb wīz/ adv, adj **1** sideways, as crabs usually move **2** in a roundabout and cautious way

crachach /krákh akh/ npl *Wales* upper-class people (*informal*) [Late 20C. < Welsh.]

crack /krak/ v **1** vti BREAK WITHOUT COMING FULLY APART to break, or make something break, in such a way that a fine split or splits appear but the split sections do not come apart ◊ *had cracked a rib in falling* **2** vti BREAK INTO PIECES to break into pieces, or to break something into pieces **3** vti BREAK WITH SHARP NOISE to break, or make something break, with a sudden sharp noise ◊ *cracked some eggs into a saucepan* **4** vti MAKE SHARP NOISE to make a loud sharp sound, or to cause something, e.g. a whip or a rifle, to make such a sound ◊ *thunder cracked overhead* **5** vt HIT HARD to hit somebody or something with a powerful impact **6** vti BREAK OPEN UNDER PRESSURE to break open because of pressure, or to make something, e.g. a nut, break or open by pressure **7** vti FAIL OR MAKE SOMETHING FAIL to fail, give way, or break down, or to make somebody or something do so **8** *vti* BREAK DOWN PSYCHOLOGICALLY to break down psychologically, or to cause somebody to break down psychologically, e.g. under stress or torture **9** *vi* BECOME HOARSE OR CHANGE IN PITCH to become slightly hoarse or suffer from uncontrollable changes in pitch, especially because of emotion or stress (*refers to the voice*) **10** *vt* DECODE OR SOLVE to decipher or solve something, e.g. a code, puzzle, or problem (*informal*) **11** *vt* BREAK INTO to force a way into something, especially a safe (*informal*) **12** *vt* OPEN SOMETHING TO USE to open something, e.g. a tin or book, in order to get access to its contents (*informal*) **13** *vi Scotland* TO CHAT to chat or gossip ○ *We haven't got time to crack with you just now.* **14** *vt* BREAK DOWN INTO SMALLER MOLECULES to break down something, especially the heavier hydrocarbons in petroleum, into smaller molecules by using heat or catalysis ■ *n* **1** THIN BREAK a break or flaw in something, e.g. a mirror, that is visible as a fine line **2** LONG NARROW OPENING a relatively long narrow break, hole, or opening in something ○ *peeked through a crack in the fence* **3** SHARP NOISE a sudden loud sharp noise ○ *the crack of a rifle* **4** WEAKNESS a flaw, defect, or weak spot **5** BLOW a hard blow from somebody or something (*informal*) **6** SARCASTIC COMMENT a sarcastic, funny, or rude remark, especially at somebody else's expense (*informal*) **7** ATTEMPT an attempt at something (*informal*) **8** UNEVEN VOICE TONE a hoarseness or uncontrollable change in pitch in somebody's voice **9** *Scotland, Ireland* CONVERSATION chat, conversation, gossip, or news **10** *Ireland* ENJOYMENT entertainment, fun, or enjoyment, especially when experienced in a group or in a particular place (*informal*) ○ *The crack was fierce in Heraghty's last night!* **11** SOMEBODY OR SOMETHING THAT EXCELS somebody or something that is outstandingly good, talented, or skilled (*informal*) **12 crack** PURIFIED FORM OF COCAINE a purified and extremely addictive form of cocaine (*slang*) ■ *adj* EXCELLENT excellent, expert, or trained to a high degree of efficiency [Old English *cracian* < Germanic, 'make a loud noise'] ◇ **a fair crack of the whip** a reasonable chance to attempt something ◇ **be not all he's** *or* **she's** *or* **it's cracked up to be** to be not as good as promised or reputed ◇ **crack a bottle** to open a bottle of alcoholic drink ◇ **crack a joke** to tell a joke ◇ **crack it** to achieve something or be successful (*informal*) ◇ **paper over the cracks** to try to hide the fact that something is wrong rather than dealing with the problem

crack down *vi* to take strong and decisive action against something undesirable or illegal or against somebody involved in such activity (*informal*)

crack on *vi* to work hard or harder at something (*informal*)

crack up *v* **1** *vi* HAVE BREAKDOWN to experience a psychological or, sometimes, physical breakdown, usually because of stress (*informal*) **2** *vi* BREAK INTO PIECES to crack and break into pieces **3** *vti* LAUGH UNCONTROLLABLY to laugh, or cause somebody to laugh, uncontrollably (*informal*)

crackbrained /krák braynd/ *adj* extremely irrational or eccentric

crack cocaine *n* DRUGS = **crack** *n.* 12

crackdown /krák down/ *n* a strong and decisive measure taken against an undesirable or illegal activity or against somebody involved in such activity

cracked /krakt/ *adj* **1** HAVING CRACKS marked with a crack or cracks ○ *dry, cracked lips* **2** IRRATIONAL extremely irrational (*informal*) **3** COARSELY CRUSHED broken or crushed into coarse pieces ○ *cracked wheat* **4** HOARSE sounding rough or hoarse vocally, often because of emotion or stress

cracked wheat *n* whole grains of wheat that have been chopped into little pieces

cracker /krákər/ *n* **1** DECORATED TUBE WITH TRINKET a cardboard tube, containing a small toy, trinket, joke, or paper hat, and wrapped in coloured paper, that opens with an explosive noise when both its ends are pulled **2** LEISURE = **firecracker 3** FLAT CRISP BISCUIT a thin, crisp biscuit, usually unsweetened and sometimes salted, often eaten with cheese **4** SOMEBODY OR SOMETHING EXCELLENT somebody or something that is excellent or a fine example of its kind (*informal*) **5** DEVICE FOR CRACKING PETROLEUM COMPOUNDS a device in which petroleum oils and tars are broken down to yield more valuable light fuels

cracker-barrel *adj US* expressing unsophisticated but practical sense or wisdom of the kind often associated with a rural community [< the idea of the village store as a social centre]

crackerjack /krákər jak/ *adj* outstanding in quality or ability (*dated informal*) [Late 19C. < CRACKER 'excellent' + JACK[1] 'man'.] —**crackerjack** *n*

crackers /krákərz/ *adj* mildly irrational or eccentric (*informal*)

crackhead /krák hed/ *n* an addict of crack cocaine (*slang*)

crack house *n* a house or flat where crack cocaine is sold to addicts and where, sometimes, it is also made (*slang*)

cracking /kráking/ *adj* (*informal*) **1** QUICK very fast ○ *at a cracking pace* **2** EXCELLENT excellent or impressive ■ *adv* VERY extremely (*informal*) ■ *n* BREAKING DOWN INTO SMALLER MOLECULES the breaking down of something, especially the heavier hydrocarbons in petroleum, into smaller molecules using heat or catalysis ◇ **get cracking** to start moving or doing something quickly or more quickly (informal)

crackle /krák'l/ *v* (**-les, -ling, -led**) **1** *vti* MAKE RAPID SNAPPING NOISE to make, or cause something to make, repeated short sharp snapping or popping noises, such as dry wood makes when burning **2** *vi* SCINTILLATE to be lively, energetic, or scintillating ○ *The play crackles with wit.* **3** *vt* DECORATE WITH CRACKS to decorate a piece of pottery or porcelain with a network of fine cracks in the surface of its glaze ■ *n* **1** REPEATED SNAPPING NOISES a series of repeated short sharp snapping or popping noises **2** FINE DECORATIVE CRACKS a network of fine cracks created as decoration in the surface of the glaze of pottery or porcelain **3 crackle, crackleware** PORCELAIN DECORATED WITH FINE CRACKS pottery or porcelain decorated with a network of fine cracks in the surface of its glaze

crackling /krákling/ *n* **1** SNAPPING OR POPPING NOISES a series of repeated short sharp snapping or popping noises **2** CRISPLY COOKED PORK SKIN the crisp skin of roast pork **3** OFFENSIVE TERM an offensive term for women considered collectively, regarded as sexually desirable or available (*slang*)

crackly /krákli/ (**-lier, -liest**) *adj* **1** brittle or crisp **2** making or consisting of a series of repeated short sharp snapping or popping noises

cracknel /krákn'l/ *n* a hard light brittle biscuit [14C. Via Old French *craquelin* < Middle Dutch *krākeline*, a small cake < *krāken* 'to crack'.]

Cracknell /krákn'l/, **Ruth Winifred** (*b.* 1925) Australian actor

crackpot /krák pot/ *n* an eccentric or wildly imaginative person (*informal insult*) ■ *adj* extremely eccentric or unrealistic (*informal*) ○ *another of his crackpot money-making schemes*

cracksman /kráksmən/ (*plural* **-men** /-mən/) *n* a burglar, especially one who breaks into safes (*slang*)

crack-up *n* (*informal*) **1** a psychological or sometimes physical breakdown **2** a motor vehicle or aircraft crash

Cracow ◆ **Kraków**

-cracy *suffix* rule, government, power ○ *technocracy* [< French *-cratie* < Greek *kratos* 'power, strength' < Indo-European, 'hard']

cradle /kráyd'l/ *n* **1** BABY'S BED a small bed, usually on rockers and with enclosing sides, used for a baby **2** STARTING PLACE the place where something begins or develops in its early stages ○ *the cradle of civilization* **3** MECHANIC'S BOARD ON WHEELS a flat board on wheels or casters on which a mechanic can slide under a vehicle **4** SUPPORTING FRAMEWORK a framework for supporting something, e.g. a ship that is being built or repaired **5** HANGING PLATFORM a movable platform or cage hung on the side of something, e.g. a building or ship, to hold a worker **6** SUPPORT FOR TELEPHONE HANDSET the part of a telephone on which the handset rests or hangs **7** PROTECTIVE FRAME SUPPORTING BEDCLOTHES a frame placed beneath bedclothes covering a patient to keep them from touching a sensitive part of the body, e.g. after injury or an operation **8** PANNING DEVICE a rocking device like a box used in panning for gold ■ *vt* (**-dles, -dling, -dled**) **1** HOLD CAREFULLY to hold or support somebody or something tenderly, carefully, or protectively, especially in a hollow formed with the arms or hands **2** PUT INTO CRADLE to put somebody or something into a cradle or something like a cradle **3** SUPPORT IN FRAMEWORK to support something, e.g. a ship that is being built or repaired, in a framework **4** NURTURE to look after a young child or support something in the early stages of its development **5** HANG UP PHONE to put the handset of a telephone on its cradle **6** WASH SOIL to wash gold-bearing soil in a cradle [Old English *cradol*] —**cradler** *n* ◇ **rob the cradle** *US* to be romantically or sexually involved with somebody who is much younger (*informal*)

cradle cap *n* a skin condition that commonly affects the scalp of young babies, causing thick scaling and flaking

Cradle Mountain /kráyd'l-/ mountain in central Tasmania, Australia. Height: 1,545 m/5,069 ft.

cradle snatcher *n* somebody who has a romantic or sexual relationship with a much younger person (*disapproving*) US term **cradle-robber**

cradlesong /kráyd'l song/ *n* = **lullaby** *n.* 1

cradling /kráydling/ *n* a wooden or iron framework, especially one used to support a ceiling while it is being installed

Crafers-Bridgewater /kráyfərz bríj wawtər/ town in SE South Australia. Population: 11,879 (1991).

craft /kraaft/ *n* **1** SKILFUL CREATIVE ACTIVITY a profession or activity such as weaving, pottery, or wood carving, involving the skilful making of decorative or practical objects by hand (*often in combination*) **2** OBJECT PRODUCED BY SKILFUL HANDWORK something such as a piece of pottery or carving produced skilfully by hand, especially in a traditional manner (*often plural*) **3** SKILL skill in making or doing things, especially by hand **4** SKILLED PROFESSION OR ACTIVITY a profession or activity that requires skill and training, or experience or specialized knowledge (*often in combination*) ○ *his love for the craft of film-making* **5** TRADE ASSOCIATION the people engaged in a skilled trade or profession, considered as a group (*dated*) **6** DEVIOUSNESS skill in trickery or deceiving others **7** (*plural* **craft**) VESSEL a vessel used for travelling, e.g. a boat, ship, aeroplane, or space vehicle (*often in combination*) ■ *vt* MAKE WITH SKILL to produce or create something with skill and care [Old English *cræft* 'strength, power' < Germanic] —**crafter** *n*

craft-brewed *adj US* made by a small-scale brewery in small quantities

craftsman /kraáftsmən/ (*plural* **-men** /-mən/) *n* **1** a man who works at a skilled trade or profession **2** a man who does something with great skill and expertise —**craftsmanlike** *adj* —**craftsmanly** *adj* —**craftsmanship** *n*

craftsperson /kraáfts purss'n/ (*plural* **-people** /-peep'l/) *n* a skilful maker of decorative or practical objects by hand

craftswoman /kraáfts wòomən/ (*plural* **-en** /-wimmin/) *n* **1** a woman who works at a skilled trade or profession **2** a woman who does something with great skill and expertise

craft union *n* a labour union for people who work at a particular skilled trade, as distinct from an organization for everyone employed in a particular industry

craftwork /kraáft wurk/ *n* activity, e.g. weaving, pottery, or wood carving, that involves the skilful making of decorative or practical objects by hand, or the products of this —**craftworker** *n*

crafty /kraáfti/ (**-ier, -iest**) *adj* using or involving cunning or trickery to deceive other people —**craftily** *adv* —**craftiness** *n*

crag /krag/ *n* a steep rough mass of rock forming part of a cliff or mountain peak [14C. < Celtic, probably Welsh *craig* or Gaelic *creagh.*] —**cragged** *adj*

craggy /krággi/ (**-gier, -giest**) *adj* **1** steep and rocky, and forming part of a cliff or mountain peak **2** rugged-looking with strong prominent masculine features —**craggily** *adv* —**cragginess** *n*

cragsman /krágzmən/ (*plural* **-men** /-mən/) *n* a skilled and experienced rock climber

Craig /krayg/, **Sir Edward Gordon** (1872–1966) British actor, director, and stage designer

Craigavon /krayg ávv'n/ administrative district in central Northern Ireland. Population: 77,900 (1995).

Craigieburn /kráygi burn/ town in central Victoria, Australia. Population: 12,919 (1996).

Craiova /krī óvə/ city in SW Romania. Population: 310,838 (1997 estimate).

crake /krayk/ *n* a short-billed long-legged marsh bird of the rail family, e.g. the corncrake or spotted crake. Native to: Europe, Asia. [14C. < Old Norse *kráka* 'crow', *krákr* 'raven' < an imitation of its sound.]

cram /kram/ *v* (**crams, cramming, crammed**) **1** *vt* FORCE INTO to force people or objects into a space or container that is too small to hold them comfortably **2** *vti* EAT GREEDILY to eat food hastily and greedily **3** *vt* FORCE TO EAT to encourage or force a person or animal to eat more than is necessary **4** *vti* **STUDY INTENSIVELY** to study a subject intensively, e.g. for an imminent examination (*informal*) **5** *vt* **TUTOR INTENSIVELY** to tutor somebody intensively for an examination (*informal*) ■ *n* **1 TIGHTLY PACKED STATE** a situation in which a group of people or things are crushed, crowded, or tightly packed together **2 PERIOD OF INTENSIVE STUDY** a period of intensive study, e.g. for an imminent examination (*informal*) [Old English *(ge)crammian* < Germanic]

Cram /kram/, **Steve** (*b.* 1960) British middle-distance runner

cram-full *adj* completely filled with something

crammer /krámmər/ *n* a school or tutor that prepares students intensively for an examination, especially one that they have failed before

cramp¹ /kramp/ *n* **1 PAINFUL MUSCLE CONTRACTION** a sudden painful involuntary contraction of a muscle **2 MUSCLE PARALYSIS** temporary loss of function in a muscle or muscle group caused by repetitive use or overexertion ○ *writer's cramp* ■ **cramps** *npl* **ABDOMINAL PAIN** severe pain in the abdomen or adjoining areas, usually of gastrointestinal or uterine origin ■ *vi* **BE AFFECTED WITH CRAMP** to experience cramp [14C. Via Old French *crampe* < Middle Dutch *krampe*.]

cramp² /kramp/ *n* **1 DEVICE FOR HOLDING THINGS TOGETHER** an adjustable clamp for temporarily holding or pressing objects together **2 RESTRICTION** something that confines, restricts, or restrains, e.g. a set of shackles **3 CONFINED PLACE** a confined or restricted position or place **4 BAR WITH BENT ENDS** a metal bar with ends bent at right angles, used in building to hold objects such as bricks or timbers together ■ *vt* **1 HOLD TOGETHER** to fasten, hold, or press something together with a cramp **2 CONFINE** to confine or enclose somebody or something in a small space (*usually passive*) **3 HAMPER** to hamper or obstruct somebody or something [14C. < Middle Dutch *krampe*.]

cramped /krampt/ *adj* **1 LACKING SPACE** inconveniently or uncomfortably small and confining **2 PACKED IN** packed into too small a space for comfort **3 HARD TO READ** written or printed in small characters that are close together and hard to read

cramp iron *n* BUILDING = **cramp**² *n.* 4

crampon /krám pon, krámpən/ *n* a set of metal spikes fastened to the sole of a boot or shoe to provide better traction on ice or snow (*usually plural*) [13C. Via Old French < Frankish.]

Cranach /kraá nakh/, **Lucas, the Elder** (1472–1553) German painter and engraver. Born **Lucas Müller**

cranage /kráynij/ *n* the use of a crane, or the fee paid for such use

cranberry /kránbəri/ (*plural* **-ries**) *n* **1** a sour red or reddish berry. Use: fruit juice, sauce for roast turkey. **2** a low-growing evergreen plant of the heath family that yields cranberries. Genus: *Vaccinium*. [Mid-17C. < German *Kranbeere* 'crane berry', because the stamens are said to look like a crane's beak.]

Cranborne Chase /krán bawrn-/ ancient forest in S England, still partly wooded. Area: 983 sq. km/379 sq. mi.

Cranbourne /krán bawrn/ town in S Victoria, Australia. Population: 18,886 (1991).

crane /krayn/ *n* **1 LIFTING MACHINE** a large machine used to lift and move heavy objects by means of a hook attached to cables suspended from a supporting, usually movable, beam **2 MOVING SUPPORT FOR CAMERA** a moving platform with a long support for a film or television camera **3 MOVABLE SUPPORT WITH LONG ARM** a device with a long arm for supporting something, e.g. one for swinging and holding a pot or kettle over a fire **4 LONG-LEGGED BIRD** a large long-necked long-legged short-tailed bird that lives on plains and in marshes. Family: Gruidae. ■ *v* (**cranes, craning, craned**) **1** *vti* **STRETCH NECK TO SEE** to stretch the neck in order to get a better view **2** *vt* **MOVE BY CRANE** to lift or move something using a crane [Old English *cran* < Indo-European, probably an imitation of the bird's cry]

Crane /krayn/, **Hart** (1899–1932) US poet

Crane, Stephen (1871–1900) US writer

Crane, Walter (1845–1915) British painter and illustrator

crane fly *n* INSECTS = **daddy longlegs**

cranesbill /kráynz bil/ *n* PLANTS = **geranium** *n.* 2

crani- *prefix* = **cranio-**

crania plural of **cranium**

cranial /kráyni əl/ *adj* relating to, involving, or in the skull, especially the part covering the brain

cranial index *n* ANTHROP = **cephalic index**

cranial nerve *n* each of a pair of nerves that originate in the brain stem and pass out of the skull to the surface of the body. There are 12 pairs of cranial nerves in mammals, birds, and reptiles, and usually 10 in fish and amphibians.

craniate /kráyni it, -ayt/ *adj* having a skull or cranium

cranio- *prefix* cranium, skull ○ *craniofacial* [< CRANIUM]

craniofacial /kráyni ō fáysh'l/ *adj* relating to or involving both the cranium and the face

craniology /kráyni óllәji/ *n* the scientific study of the shapes, sizes, and other characteristics of human skulls —**craniological** /kráyni ə lójjik'l/ *adj* —**craniologically** *adv* —**craniologist** *n*

craniometry /kráyni ómmətri/ *n* the scientific measurement of skulls —**craniometer** *n* —**craniometric** /kráyni ə méttrik/ *adj* —**craniometrical** *adj* —**craniometrically** *adv* —**craniometrist** *n*

craniosacral /kráyni ō sáykrəl, -sák-/ *adj* ANAT = **parasympathetic**

craniosacral therapy *n* gentle manipulation of the bones of the face, skull, and spine, intended to relieve conditions including migraine, sinusitis, and musculoskeletal problems

craniotomy /kráyni óttəmi/ (*plural* **-mies**) *n* cutting open the skull to expose the brain, especially for brain surgery

cranium /kráyni əm/ (*plural* **-ums** *or* **-a** /-ə/) *n* the skull of a vertebrate, especially the part that covers the brain [15C. Via medieval Latin < Greek *kranion*.]

crank¹ /krangk/ *n* **1 MECHANICAL DEVICE FOR TRANSMITTING MOTION** a device consisting of an arm or handle that is connected to a shaft at right angles, enabling the transmission of motion to or from the shaft **2 crank, crank handle HANDLE FOR STARTING MOTOR** a handle with two or four right-angled bends, used to start an engine **3 SOMEBODY ECCENTRIC** a person who holds strong convictions about unusual or eccentric ideas and opinions (*informal insult*) **4** *US* **ILLEGAL DRUG** powdered methamphetamine, used as an illicit drug (*slang*) ■ *v* **1** *vti* **USE CRANK ON** to start, move, or operate something by turning a crank **2** *vt* **FORM INTO CRANK SHAPE** to form something into the shape of a crank ■ *adj* **ECCENTRIC** typical of or done by somebody who has unusual or eccentric, often strongly held, ideas and opinions (*disapproving*) [Old English *cranc* < Germanic, 'crooked']

crank out *vt* to produce something, especially quickly, mechanically, regularly, and in large quantities (*informal*)

crank up *v* **1** *vti* **START WITH CRANK** to start something, especially an engine, with a crank **2** *vt* **INCREASE** to increase the force, volume, or intensity of something (*informal*) **3** *vt* **START** to get something started (*informal*) **4** *vi* **INJECT DRUG** to take or inject an illegal drug (*slang*)

crank² /krangk/ *adj* unsteady on the water and likely to capsize [Early 17C. < ?]

crankcase /krángk kayss/ *n* the metal casing that encloses the crankshaft in some engines, especially internal-combustion engines

crank handle *n* MECH ENG = **crank**¹ *n.* 2

crankpin /krángk pin/ *n* a short cylindrical bearing piece in the arm of a crank, attached to a connecting rod

crankshaft /krángk shaaft/ *n* a shaft driving or driven by a crank, e.g. one attached to a connecting rod in an internal-combustion engine

cranky¹ /krángki/ (**-ier, -iest**) *adj* **1 ECCENTRIC** eccentric or obsessive (*informal*) **2** *US* **GROUCHY** disagreeable and easily irritated (*informal*) **3 NOT IN WORKING ORDER** not in good working order and likely to break down or operate unreliably **4 CROOKED** characterized by turns and twists **5 UNWELL** unwell or infirm (*regional*) —**crankily** *adv* —**crankiness** *n*

cranky² /krángki/ *adj* SAILING = **crank**² *adj.*

Cranmer /kránmər/, **Thomas** (1489–1556) English archbishop

crannog /krànnəg/ *n* an ancient Celtic settlement in Scotland or Ireland, usually fortified, built on a natural or constructed island in a lake or bog [Early 17C. < Irish *crannóg* or Gaelic *crannag* 'timber structure' < *crann* 'tree'.]

cranny /kránni/ (*plural* **-nies**) *n* a small narrow crack, hole, or opening in a wall or rock [15C. < French *crané* 'notched' < popular Latin *crena* 'small notch'.] —**crannied** *adj*

crap¹ /krap/ *n* (*slang*) **1** an offensive term for an act of passing solid waste matter out of the body through the anus **2** an offensive term for rubbish, nonsense, or something worthless or annoying **3** an offensive term for solid waste matter passed out of the body through the anus ■ *adj* an offensive term meaning worthless, useless, or lacking in ability (*slang*) ■ *vti* (**craps, crapping, crapped**) an offensive term meaning to pass solid waste matter out of the body through the anus (*slang*) [15C. Probably < Middle Dutch.]

crap out *vi* (*slang*) to avoid or discontinue an activity, especially out of fear

crap² /krap/ *n* GAMBLING = **craps**

crap out *vi US* to make a losing throw in the game of craps (*slang*)

crape /krayp/ *n* **1** TEXTILES = **crêpe** *n.* 1 **2** black silk formerly used for mourning clothes **3** a band of crape worn as a sign of mourning round the arm or, formerly, round a hat [Early 16C. < French *crêpe* (see CRÊPE).]

crape myrtle *n* a deciduous shrub or tree, cultivated for its white, pink, or red flowers. Native to: Asia. *Lagerstroemia indica*.

crapper /kráppər/ *n* an offensive term for a toilet (*slang*)

crappie /kráppi/ (*plural* **-pies** *or* **-pie**) *n* a freshwater sunfish with equal-sized anal and dorsal fins. Native to: lakes and ponds in North America. Genus: *Pomoxis*. [Mid-19C. < ?]

crappy /kráppi/ (**-pier, -piest**) *adj* an offensive term meaning worthless, useless, of poor quality, or badly made or done (*slang*)

craps /kraps/ *n* **1** a US gambling game played with two dice (+ *singular verb*) **2** *US* a losing throw of the dice in the game of craps (+ *singular or plural verb*) [Early 18C. Probably < French, variant of *crabs* 'score of two ones at dice' < English, plural of CRAB¹.]

crapshoot /kráp shoot/ *n US* **1** a game of craps **2** something that is risky or a matter of chance, the outcome of which cannot be predicted (*informal*)

crapshooter /kráp shootər/ *n US* a player of craps

crapulent /kràpyŏŏlənt/, **crapulous** /-ləss/ *adj* regularly overindulging in both alcoholic drink and food (*dated*) [Mid-17C. < late Latin *crapulentus* 'very drunk' < Greek *kraipalē* 'drunken headache'.] —**crapulence** *n* —**crapulently** *adv* —**crapulousness** *n*

craquelure /kráka loor/ *n* a network of small cracks that sometimes appear on the surface of an oil painting as it ages [Early 20C. < French.]

crash¹ /krash/ *n* **1 VEHICLE COLLISION** a collision involving a moving vehicle or aircraft **2 LOUD NOISE** a loud noise such as that made by thunder or by something breaking violently into pieces **3 COMPUTER BREAKDOWN** a sudden complete failure of a computer system, device, or program, usually with an accompanying loss of data ○ *a system crash* **4 FINANCIAL COLLAPSE** the financial collapse or failure of something such as a stock market, involving a massive drop in share prices, or the collapse of a commercial business ■ *v* **1** *vti* **COLLIDE VIOLENTLY** to strike against something with great force, causing damage or destruction, or cause something, e.g. a car, to strike against something in this way **2** *vti* **MAKE LOUD NOISE** to make a loud noise, or cause something to make such a noise **3** *vti* **BREAK INTO PIECES NOISILY** to break into pieces violently and noisily, or break an object in this way **4** *vti* **MOVE NOISILY** to move, or cause something to move, noisily, destructively, or violently **5** *vti* **HAVE OR CAUSE COMPLETE COMPUTER FAILURE** to experience a sudden complete failure, or cause a computer system to have a sudden complete failure **6** *vi* **COLLAPSE FINANCIALLY** to suffer financial collapse or failure **7** *vi* **DROP SHARPLY** to decrease in value rapidly and steeply **8** *vi* **BE HEAVILY DEFEATED** to be heavily defeated, e.g. in a sports match (*informal*) **9** *vti* **ATTEND UNINVITED** to attend an event, such as a party, without an invitation (*informal*) **10** *vi* **SLEEP** to sleep, especially somewhere other than usual when exhausted, or stay temporarily somewhere other than home (*slang*) ■ *adj* **1 RAPID AND INTENSIVE** done intensively over a short period of time in order to achieve the desired results quickly **2 SUDDEN AND STRONG** abrupt and forceful ○ *a perfectly timed crash tackle* [14C. < ?] —**crasher** *n*

crash out *vi (informal)* **1** = **crash**[1] *v.* **10** **2** to lose consciousness suddenly

crash[2] /krash/ *n* a coarse linen or cotton cloth. Use: towels, curtains, book bindings. [Early 19C. < Russian *krashenina* 'dyed coarse linen'.]

crash-and-burn *adj US* causing or involving spectacular destruction or disastrous consequences *(informal)*

crash barrier *n* a safety barrier, usually metal, at the edge of a road or racetrack or between the carriageways of a motorway

crash box *n* a theatrical sound-effects device consisting of a box filled with various objects that, when shaken or dropped, will simulate the sound of a crash

crash course *n* a course of study or training done intensively over a short period of time in order to learn the basics of a subject, skill, or activity quickly

crash diet *n* a strict and intensive diet carried out over a short period of time in order to lose weight quickly

crash dive *n* a steep rapid dive from the surface of a body of water by a submarine

crash-dive *vti* **1** to dive steeply through the air and crash, or cause an aircraft to do this **2** to make a steep rapid descent from the surface of a body of water, or cause a submarine to do this

crash gearbox *n* a gearbox without synchromesh that demands considerable skill and care by the driver to ensure that engine and wheel speed are aligned during gear changes

crash helmet *n* a hard padded helmet worn by motorcyclists, racing drivers, and others to protect the head in case of an accident

crashing /kráshing/ *adj* complete and utter *(informal)* ○ *a crashing bore*

crash landing *n* an emergency landing by an aircraft, usually causing damage to the aircraft —**crashland** *vti*

crash pad *n* **1** padding inside a vehicle to protect the occupants in a crash **2** a place, other than home, where somebody sleeps or stays temporarily *(dated informal)*

crash-test *vt* **1** to establish the safety and reliability of something by subjecting it to tests, e.g. using heat, pressure, or strain, until it reaches its breaking point **2** to test a vehicle by deliberately crashing it into a wall to learn how it and its occupants will be affected in an accident

crashworthy /krásh wur*th*i/ *adj* able to withstand a crash —**crashworthiness** *n*

crass /krass/ *adj* **1** so thoughtless, vulgar, and insensitive as to lack all refinement or delicacy **2** extreme or flagrant ○ *crass stupidity* [15C. < Latin *crassus* 'thick'.] —**crassitude** *n* —**crassly** *adv* —**crassness** *n*

-crat *suffix* a supporter or member of a particular form of government ○ *technocrat* [< French *-crate* < Greek *kratos* 'strength']

crate /krayt/ *n* **1 BOX OR BASKET** a large basket or a large open sturdy box used to carry or store objects **2 OLD VEHICLE** an old rickety aeroplane, car, or lorry *(dated informal)* ■ *vti* **(crates, crating, crated) PUT IN CRATE** to put or pack something in a crate [14C. < ?]

crater /kráytər/ *n* **1 VOLCANO SUMMIT** a circular funnel-shaped depression produced by volcanic eruption **2 METEORITE IMPACT AREA** a bowl-shaped hole on the surface of the Moon or a planet caused by the impact of a meteorite **3 EXPLOSION HOLE** a large hole in the ground or a surface caused by an explosion **4 ANCIENT GREEK WINE BOWL** in ancient Greece, a large shallow bowl with two handles, used to mix wine and water ■ *vti* **FORM CRATERS** to form craters, or make craters form in something [Early 17C. Via Latin < Greek *kratēr* '(mixing) bowl'.]

Crater *n* a small constellation of the southern hemisphere. See illustration at **constellation**

craton /kráy ton/ *n* the extensive interior of a large block of the Earth's crust that has been relatively stable for many millions of years [Mid-20C. Either alteration of *kratogen* < Greek *kratos* 'strength'; or < German *Kraton*, alteration of Greek *kratos*.] —**cratonic** /krə tónnik/ *adj*

cratur /kráytər/ *n Ireland, Scotland* **1** whisky, often distilled illegally *(informal)* ○ *a drop of the cratur* **2** a person [Variant of CREATURE]

cravat /krə vát/ *n* a scarf or band of fabric worn around a man's neck and tied in front [Mid-17C. < French *cravate* < *Cravate* 'Croatian' < German *Krabat(e)* < Serbo-Croat *Hrvāt* 'a Croat'.]

crave /krayv/ **(craves, craving, craved)** *v* **1** *vti* to have a strong desire for something **2** *vt* to beg or implore something from somebody *(archaic)* [Old English *crafian* 'to demand' < Germanic] —**craver** *n* —**cravingly** *adv*

SYNONYMS See ***want***.

craven /kráyv'n/ *adj* so lacking in courage as to be worthy of contempt ■ *n* a despicable coward *(archaic)* [12C. < ?] —**cravenly** *adv* —**cravenness** *n*

SYNONYMS See ***cowardly***.

craving /kráyving/ *n* a strong desire for something

craw /kraw/ *n* **1** ZOOL = **crop** *n.* **7** **2** INSECTS = **crop** *n.* **8** **3** the stomach of an animal *(informal)* **4** *Ireland* the throat or gullet [14C. Related to Middle Low German *krage* or Middle Dutch *crāghe* 'neck, throat'.]

crawfish /kráw fish/ *(plural* **-fish** *or* **-fishes)** *n US* ZOOL = **crayfish** [Early 17C. Variant of CRAYFISH.]

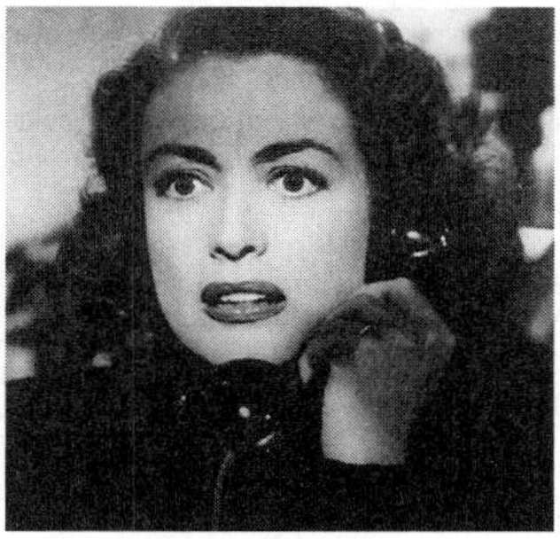

Joan Crawford

Crawford /kráwfərd/, **Joan** (1908–77) US actor. Born **Lucille Le Sueur**

crawl /krawl/ *vi* **1 MOVE CLOSE TO GROUND** to move slowly along on hands and knees or with the body close to the ground or a surface **2 MOVE VERY SLOWLY** to move forward at a slow pace **3 BE SERVILE** to try to please somebody by behaving in a servile way *(informal)* **4 BE OVERRUN** to be filled with large numbers of moving people or things **5 FEEL CREEPY** to feel a sensation of being covered with moving insects, usually in reaction to something frightening or disgusting ■ *n* **1 SLOW SPEED** a very slow pace **2 OVERARM SWIMMING STROKE** a fast swimming stroke in which the swimmer lies face down and uses a flutter kick and an overarm stroke **3 PROGRESS ON HANDS AND KNEES** slow movement on hands and knees or with the body close to the ground [14C. Probably < Old Norse *krafla* 'paw with the hands'.] —**crawlingly** *adv*

crawler /kráwlər/ *n* **1 SOMETHING THAT CRAWLS** an insect or other animal that crawls **2 SOMEBODY ACTING INGRATIATINGLY** a servile or sycophantic person *(informal)* **3 VEHICLE WITH TRACKS** a vehicle that has continuous tracks of linked plates instead of wheels **4 PROGRAM COLLECTING ONLINE DOCUMENTS** a computer program that collects online documents and reference links

crawler lane *n* an extra lane on an uphill section of a main road for slow-moving vehicles

Crawley /kráwli/ town in SE England. Population: 88,203 (1991).

crawling peg *n* a method of controlling exchange rates or prices by limiting their fluctuation for a time and later allowing them to change in small increments

crawl space *n US* a low unfinished space under a floor or above a ceiling in a building that gives access to plumbing, wiring, and ductwork

crawly /kráwli/ **(-ier, -iest)** *adj* causing a shuddery disgust or unease

craw-thumper *n Ireland* an offensive term for somebody who makes a great show of being very pious *(insult)*

Craxi /kráksi/, **Bettino** (*b.* 1934) Italian statesman

crayfish /kráyfish/ *(plural* **-fish** *or* **-fishes)** *n* **1 crayfish, crawfish** a freshwater crustacean with large claws like those of a lobster. Superfamily: Astacoidea. **2** ZOOL = **spiny lobster** [14C. By folk etymology < French *crevice* < Indo-European, 'to scratch'.]

crayon /kráy on/ *n* **1 COLOURED DRAWING STICK** a stick of coloured wax, chalk, or charcoal, sometimes enclosed in wood like a pencil, used for drawing and colouring **2 DRAWING** a drawing made using crayons ■ *vti* **USE CRAYONS** to draw or colour something with crayons [Mid-17C. < French, 'pencil' < *craie* 'chalk' < Latin *creta* 'chalk, clay'.] —**crayonist** *n*

craze /krayz/ *n* **1 FAD** a fashion that is extremely popular for a short time **2 PERSONAL OBSESSION** a short-lived obsession or enthusiasm that somebody has for something **3 FINE CRACK** a fine crack in the glaze of pottery ■ *vti* **(crazes, crazing, crazed) 1 MAKE OR BECOME IRRATIONAL** to become or make somebody become irrational or highly excited *(often considered offensive)* **2 PRODUCE CRACKS IN** to produce fine cracks in the glaze of pottery, or become covered with such cracks [14C. Probably < assumed Old Norse *krasa* 'to shatter'.] —**crazed** *adj*

crazing /kráyzing/ *n* fine cracks in the glaze of a piece of pottery, produced when the glaze cools and contracts at a different temperature from the clay

crazy /kráyzi/ *adj* **(-zier, -ziest) 1 OFFENSIVE TERM** an offensive term meaning affected by a psychiatric disorder **2 RIDICULOUS** not showing good sense or practicality *(informal)* **3 EXCESSIVELY FOND** excessively fond of somebody or something *(informal)* ■ *n (plural* **-zies)** *US* **OFFENSIVE TERM** an offensive term for somebody with a psychiatric disorder —**crazily** *adv* —**craziness** *n*

Crazy Horse (1849?–77) Native North American leader. Born **Tashunca Witco**

crazy paving *n* a pavement of irregularly shaped pieces of paving stone fitted together, often used for garden paths

crazy quilt *n* a quilt made of irregularly shaped and patterned pieces of cloth sewn together

CRE *abbr* Commission for Racial Equality

creak /kreek/ *vi* **1 SQUEAK** to make a prolonged squeaking noise **2 MOVE WITH SQUEAKING** to move along while making prolonged squeaking noises ■ *n* **PROLONGED SQUEAK** a prolonged squeaking noise [14C. An imitation of the sound.] —**creakingly** *adv*

SPELLCHECK Do not confuse ***creak*** with ***creek***, which has a similar sound. Beware: your spellchecker will not catch this error.

creaky /kreéki/ **(-ier, -iest)** *adj* **1 CREAKING** making a prolonged squeaking noise **2 STIFF** not able to move easily, especially as a result of ageing *(informal)* **3 OLD OR OLD-FASHIONED** showing signs of having deteriorated over time or of being old-fashioned *(informal)* —**creakily** *adv* —**creakiness** *n*

cream /kreem/ *n* **1 FATTY PART OF MILK** a high-fat liquid product separated from milk. Use: in cooking, accompaniment to desserts. **2 CREAMY LOTION** a cosmetic or medicinal preparation that has a thick smooth consistency like cream **3 CREAMY FOOD** a food that contains cream or has a consistency like cream **4 SOFT-CENTRED CHOCOLATE** a chocolate with a soft smooth filling **5 BEST PART** the best part of something **6 WHITE TINGED WITH YELLOW** a yellowish-white colour ■ *v* **1** *vt* **MAKE CREAMY** to mix ingredients together to soften and combine them **2** *vt* **PREPARE WITH CREAM** to add cream to something while cooking it or on serving it **3** *vti* **FORM FOAM ON TOP** to form a frothy layer resembling cream on the surface, or to cause something to form in this way **4** *vt* **REMOVE CREAM FROM MILK** to separate the cream from milk **5** *vti* **FORM CREAM** to form cream, or allow milk to form cream **6** *vti* **TABOO TERM** a highly offensive term meaning to ejaculate on something *(taboo)* [14C. < French *creme*, blend of late Latin *cramum* + ecclesiastical Latin *chrisma* 'ointment' (< Greek *khrisma*).] —**cream** *adj*

cream off *vt* **1** to take away the best part of something **2** *US* to take and use something for an illicit or unintended purpose *(informal)*

cream cheese *n* a soft white unmatured cheese with a high fat content

cream cracker *n* a crisp savoury biscuit usually eaten with cheese

creamer /kreémər/ *n* **1** a cream substitute, used especially in coffee or tea **2** a small jug for serving cream

creamery /kréemәri/ (*plural* **-ies**) *n* **1** a place at which milk is processed and dairy products are produced **2** a business that sells dairy products

cream of tartar *n* cooking alternative for potassium bitartrate

cream puff *n* **1** a sweet pastry made of a flaky shell filled with whipped cream and dusted with icing sugar **2** an offensive term that deliberately insults a man's appearance or behaviour (*slang*)

cream sherry *n* a smooth sweet sherry

cream soda *n* a carbonated soft drink flavoured with vanilla

cream tea *n* an afternoon meal of tea served with scones, jam, and thick, traditionally clotted, cream

creamware /kréem wair/ *n* glazed earthenware of a deep creamy colour, first produced in Britain about 1720

creamy /kréemi/ (**-ier, -iest**) *adj* **1** with a texture, colour, taste, or consistency like cream **2** containing a large amount of cream —**creamily** *adv* —**creaminess** *n*

crease /kreess/ *n* **1 FOLD PUT IN FABRIC** a straight line formed in clothing or fabric by pressing **2 UNWANTED FABRIC FOLD** an unwanted line in clothing or fabric that has been crushed or folded **3 SKIN WRINKLE** a line or wrinkle on the skin **4 LINE NEAR WICKET** a line that marks the position of the bowler or batsman in cricket **5 GOAL AREA** the rectangular area in front of an ice hockey goal **6 GOAL AREA** the semicircular area surrounding a lacrosse goal ■ *v* (**creases, creasing, creased**) **1** *vti* **MAKE OR ACQUIRE CREASES** to form lines, folds, or wrinkles in something, or become lined, folded, or wrinkled ○ *This fabric creases badly.* ○ *His face creased into a smile.* **2** *vt* **GRAZE** to graze the skin and inflict a superficial wound [Late 16C. Probably < CREST.] —**creaser** *n* —**creasy** *adj*

crease up *vti* to laugh, or make somebody laugh, uncontrollably (*informal*)

create /kri áyt/ (**-ates, -ating, -ated**) *v* **1** *vt* **MAKE** to bring somebody or something into existence **2** *vt* **GIVE RISE TO** to produce something as a result of action or make something happen **3** *vti* **PRODUCE ART** to use imagination to invent things or produce works of art **4** *vt* **APPOINT** to give somebody a new title, role, or office **5** *vt* **PERFORM FOR FIRST TIME** to be the first person to perform a particular role in a theatrical production **6** *vi* **CAUSE TROUBLE** to become upset and make a fuss (*informal*) [14C. < Latin *creat-*, past participle of *creare* 'bring forth'.]

creatine /kreé ә teen/, **creatin** /-tin/ *n* an amino acid that provides energy to muscles, usually as phosphocreatine [Mid-19C. < assumed Greek *kreat-* 'flesh'.]

creatine kinase *n* an enzyme that breaks down phosphocreatine into creatine and phosphoric acid, releasing energy

creatine phosphate *n* BIOCHEM = **phosphocreatine**

creatinine /kri áttә neen/ *n* a derivative of creatine found in muscle, blood, and urine [Mid-19C. < CREATINE.]

creation /kri áysh'n/ *n* **1 MAKING** the bringing of something into existence **2 EARTH AND ITS INHABITANTS** the world and everything on it **3 SOMETHING CREATED BY** a product of human imagination or invention **4 ELABORATE GARMENT** an elaborate or striking article of clothing —**creational** *adj*

Creation *n* **1** the act of God that, according to the Bible, brought the universe and all living beings into existence **2** the universe as created by God, according to the Bible

creationism /kri áysh'nizәm/ *n* the belief that the Bible's account of the Creation is literally true —**creationist** *adj, n*

creation science *n* the attempt to provide scientific proof for the account of God's creation of the world that is described in the Bible

creative /kri áytiv/ *adj* **1 NEW AND ORIGINAL** using or showing use of the imagination to create new ideas or things ○ *a creative approach to the problem of space* **2 ABLE TO CREATE** able to create things **3 RESOURCEFUL** making imaginative use of the limited resources available **4 INTENTIONALLY DECEPTIVE ABOUT FINANCIAL INFORMATION** employing deceptive methods to distort financial records (*ironic*) ○ *creative accounting* ○ *creative bookkeeping* ■ *n* **IDEAS PERSON** a creator of new ideas and concepts for sales campaigns (*informal*) ○ *ad agency creatives hard at work on a TV infomercial series* —**creatively** *adv* —**creativeness** *n*

creative writing *n* the writing of fiction, poetry, or drama, often as an exercise, or the work written

creativity /kreé ay tívvәti/ *n* **1** the ability to use the imagination to develop new and original ideas or things, especially in an artistic context **2** the quality of being creative

creator /kri áytәr/ *n* an initiator of something —**creatorship** *n*

Creator *n* God regarded as creator of the universe

creature /kreéchәr/ *n* **1 LIVING BEING** any living person or animal **2 UNPLEASANT LIVING BEING** an unpleasant or frightening living thing **3 CREATED THING** somebody or something that has been created ○ *a creature of your imagination* **4 TYPE OF PERSON** somebody of a particular type ○ *He's a harmless creature.* **5 SUBSERVIENT PERSON** a person who owes his or her status or position to another and is thereby subject to undue influence ○ *a creature of his political handlers* [13C. Directly or via French < late Latin *creatura* < Latin *creat-* (see CREATE).] —**creatural** *adj*

creature comforts *npl* things considered necessary to a comfortable life

crèche /kresh, kraysh/ *n* **1** a place where small children are looked after while their parents or guardians are working or doing something else **2** a three-dimensional representation of the scene at the birth of Jesus Christ [Late 18C. Via French, 'crib' < assumed Vulgar Latin *creppia* < Germanic.]

cred /kred/ *n* credibility (*informal*) [Late 20C. Shortening.]

credence /kreéd'nss/ *n* **1 ACCEPTANCE** acceptance based on the degree to which something is believable **2 TRUSTWORTHINESS** the power to inspire belief or trust **3 credence, credence table CHURCH TABLE FOR BREAD AND WINE** a small shelf or table in a church where the bread, wine, and vessels used for Communion are kept [14C. Directly or via French < medieval Latin *credentia* 'belief' < Latin *credent-*, present participle of *credere* 'believe'.]

credential /krә dénsh'l/ *n* **1 PROOF OF ABILITY OR TRUSTWORTHINESS** a certificate, letter, or experience that qualifies somebody to do something **2 AUTHENTICATION** anything that provides authentication for a claim ■ **credentials** *npl* **OFFICIAL IDENTIFICATION** a letter, badge, or other official identification that confirms somebody's position or status [15C. < medieval Latin *credentialis* 'entitling confidence' < *credentia* (see CREDENCE).] —**credentialled** *adj*

credenza /krә dénzә/ *n* a low sideboard, usually without legs [Late 19C. Via Italian < medieval Latin *credentia* (see CREDENCE).]

credibility /kréddә bíllәti/ *n* **1 BELIEVABILITY** the ability to inspire belief or trust **2 WILLINGNESS TO BELIEVE** a willingness to accept something as true **3 STATUS** somebody's status as an acceptable person among a group of people

credibility gap *n* **1 DISTRUST OF OFFICIAL STATEMENTS** a situation in which the public distrusts the accuracy of official statements **2 LACK OF TRUST** any situation in which a lack of trust exists between two groups **3 DISCREPANCY BETWEEN CLAIM AND TRUTH** an apparent difference between what is claimed to be true and what is in fact true

credible /kréddәb'l/ *adj* **1** easy to believe **2** inspiring trust and confidence [14C. < Latin *credibilis* < *credere* 'believe'.] —**credibleness** *n* —**credibly** *adv*

USAGE credible, creditable, or credulous? These three adjectives, and the corresponding nouns *credibility, credit,* and *credulity,* are sometimes confused. Somebody or something is ***credible*** when he, she, or it can be easily or readily believed: *My story may sound barely credible but I assure you it's true.* Somebody is ***credulous*** when he or she is all too ready to believe: *Only the most credulous person would believe such a story.* ***Credible*** also has the newer meaning 'inspiring confidence': *The government needs to develop a credible monetary policy.* ***Creditable*** is connected with the word *credit* and means 'bringing credit': *An excellent squash player, she plays a creditable game of tennis as well.*

credit /kréddit/ *n* **1 DELAYED PAYMENT** an arrangement by which a buyer can take possession of something now and pay for it later or over time ○ *offer credit* ○ *buy on credit* **2 TIME TO PAY** the time allowed for payment of something by credit **3 SPENDING ENTITLEMENT AT SHOP** money that a customer is owed by a shop and is entitled to spend there **4 MONEY PAID INTO ACCOUNT** an amount of money paid into an account **5 AMOUNT BANK WILL LEND** the amount of money that a financial institution is prepared to lend somebody **6 FINANCIAL STATUS** somebody's financial status or reputation **7 RECOGNITION** praise or recognition for something done or achieved **8 SOURCE OF PRIDE** a source of pride or honour **9 ACKNOWLEDGMENT OF SOMEBODY'S ROLE** a mention of the role that somebody played in an endeavour, especially an artistic one **10 DEDUCTION OF PAYMENT FROM OWED AMOUNT** the deduction from a business account of an amount owed that has been paid **11 ACCOUNT PAYMENTS COLUMN** the right-hand side of an account record, where payments to the account are recorded **12 PAYMENT RECORDED** a payment recorded against an amount owed **13 COURSE UNIT** a completed unit of study in a course of higher education **14** *US* **RECOGNITION OF COURSE COMPLETION** official recognition that a student has satisfactorily completed a course of study ○ *get credit for a course* **15 EXAMINATION GRADE** a mark above a basic pass in an exam **16 EXAM MARK** a mark awarded in one examination that usually counts towards an overall grade ■ **credits** *npl* **LIST OF ACKNOWLEDGMENTS** a listing of the people involved in a film or television production, together with their roles or jobs ■ *vt* **1 BELIEVE** to accept that something is true **2 RECOGNIZE** to recognize somebody as the person responsible for an achievement **3 ATTRIBUTE** to ascribe something such as a personal quality to somebody **4 ADD TO BANK ACCOUNT** to add an amount of money to somebody's account **5 RECORD PAYMENT OF** to record an amount of money as a payment in an accounting record **6 RECORD PAYMENT TO** to enter a credit in the record of somebody's account **7 MAKE EDUCATIONAL AWARD TO** to award a credit to a student for successful completion of a course of study [Mid-16C. Via French < Latin *creditum* 'loan' < past participle of *credere* 'entrust, believe'.] ◇ **to somebody's credit** something for which somebody should be commended

creditable /krédditәb'l/ *adj* bringing credit, or worthy of praise —**creditability** /krédditә bíllәti/ *n* —**creditableness** *n* —**creditably** *adv*

USAGE See ***credible.***

credit account *n* an account that allows a customer to buy goods and services and pay for them later

credit bureau *n* US = **credit-reference agency**

credit card *n* a card issued by a bank or business that allows somebody to purchase goods and services and pay for them later, often with interest

ϟ **credit deposit** *n* in e-commerce, the value of the credit card purchases deposited in a merchant's bank account after an acquirer buys the merchant's sales slips

credit line *n* **1** FIN = **line of credit** **2** a printed acknowledgment of the author or source of something that was included in a publication

credit note *n* a slip of paper stating that somebody is owed an amount of money by a shop and is entitled to goods to that value

creditor /krédditәr/ *n* a person or organization owed money by another

credit rating *n* an estimate of somebody's ability to repay money given on credit

credit-reference agency *n* a business that provides information concerning somebody's creditworthiness to companies or banks. US term **credit bureau**

credit squeeze *n* a reduction in the availability of credit or an increase in the interest charged for credit

credit standing *n* the reputation that somebody has for paying off financial obligations

credit transfer *n* a transfer of money between bank accounts

credit union *n* a cooperative savings association that makes loans to its members at reduced interest rates

creditworthy /kréddit wurthi/ *adj* considered to be financially reliable enough to be given credit or lent money —**creditworthiness** *n*

credo /kráydō/ (*plural* **-dos**) *n* a statement of principles or beliefs, especially one that is professed formally [12C. < Latin, 'I believe' (first words of the Apostles' and Nicene creeds), a form of *credere* 'believe'.]

Credo (*plural* **-dos**) *n* **1** the Apostles' Creed or Nicene Creed, both of which are ancient statements of the basic doctrines of Christianity **2** a musical setting, especially in a Mass, of the Credo

credulity /krә dyóolәti/ *n* the tendency to believe something too readily

credulous /kréddyóolәss/ *adj* **1** too easily convinced that something is true **2** resulting from a tendency to believe things too readily [Late 16C. < Latin *credulus* < *credere* 'believe'.] —**credulously** *adv* —**credulousness** *n*

USAGE See ***credible.***

Cree /kree/ (*plural* **Cree** *or* **Crees**) *n* **1** a member of a Native North American people who live in central Canada and Montana **2** the Algonquian language of the Cree. Native speakers: 62,000. [Mid-18C. < Canadian French *Cris*, shortening of *C(h)ristinaux*, alteration of an Algonquian word (modern *kinistiono*).] —**Cree** *adj*

creed /kreed/ *n* **1 STATEMENT OF BELIEFS** a formal summary of the principles of the Christian faith **2 RELIGION** a set of religious beliefs **3 SET OF PRINCIPLES** any set of beliefs or principles [Pre-12C. < Latin *credo* (see CREDO).]

creek /kreek/ *n* **1** a narrow tidal inlet or bay on a sea coast, especially in a salt marsh **2** *US, Can, ANZ* a stream, especially one that flows into a river [15C. Directly or via French *crique* < Old Norse *kriki* 'nook, corner'.] ◇ **up the creek (without a paddle)** in a difficult situation, or in trouble (*informal*)

SPELLCHECK See ***creak***.

Creek (*plural* **Creek** *or* **Creeks**) *n* **1** a member of a Native North American people who once lived in Alabama, Georgia, and Florida, and who now live mainly in central Oklahoma and S Alabama **2** the Muskogean language of the Creek. Native speakers: 50,000. [Early 18C. < CREEK; from the large number of creeks in their country.] —**Creek** *adj*

creel /kreel/ *n* **1 WICKER BASKET FOR FISH** a wicker basket used by anglers for holding fish **2 WICKER FISH TRAP** a wicker trap for catching fish or lobsters **3 BOBBIN HOLDER** a framework in a spinning machine that holds the bobbins [14C. < ?]

creep /kreep/ *vi* (**creeps, creeping, crept** /krept/ *or* **creeped**) **1 MOVE QUIETLY** to move along silently and stealthily **2 MOVE NEAR THE GROUND** to move along with the body close to the ground **3 PROCEED SLOWLY** to move along very slowly **4 GRADUALLY DEVELOP** to appear, approach, or develop gradually **5 SHIVER WITH DISGUST** to tingle uncomfortably as if covered with crawling insects, especially from fear or disgust **6 SPREAD OVER A SURFACE** to grow along a surface by sending out tendrils, suckers, or roots **7 BE DISPLACED SLIGHTLY** to move slightly from the original or proper position **8 BE OBSEQUIOUS** to behave in a servile manner to somebody in authority (*informal*) **9 DEFORM FROM HEAT OR STRESS** to become deformed over a period of time due to stress or heat ■ *n* **1 CREEPING MOVEMENT** a slow or stealthy pace or movement **2 SOMEBODY REPELLENT** somebody considered obnoxious or disliked (*informal*) **3 OBSEQUIOUS PERSON** a person who is servile to those in authority (*informal disapproving*) **4 SLIGHT DISPLACEMENT** the slight movement of something **5 MOVEMENT OF ROCK** a gradual movement of rock and debris down a slope **6 DEFORMATION OF ROCKS UNDER STRESS** a slow deformation of rocks and minerals in response to prolonged stress **7 DEFORMATION OF METAL UNDER STRESS** a gradual deformation of a hard material, especially metal, as a result of heat or stress ■ **creeps** *npl* **UNEASY FEELING** an uneasy or unnerving feeling usually caused by fear or disgust (*informal*) [Old English *crēopan* < Germanic]

creep up on *vt* **1** to approach somebody or something stealthily **2** to enter somebody's consciousness or feelings gradually

creepback /kreep bak/ *n* the tendency for employers to recruit new staff surreptitiously after making unnecessary redundancies

creeper /kreepər/ *n* **1 CLINGING PLANT** any plant that grows by means of tendrils, suckers, or roots that anchor it to a surface **2 SOMEBODY OR SOMETHING THAT CREEPS** a person or animal that moves by creeping **3 SMALL CLIMBING BIRD** a small climbing bird with a slender curved beak and short legs. Native to: forests of North America, Europe, Asia, and Africa. Family: Certhiidae. **4** CARS = **cradle** *n.* 3 **5 UNDERWATER GRAPPLING DEVICE** a device with hooks that is used to drag for submerged objects in deep water

creeping /kreeping/ *adj* **1** developing or advancing gradually over a period of time **2** growing and spreading by sending out tendrils, suckers, or roots

creeping eruption *n* a skin disease caused by hookworm or roundworm larvae, producing itching and eruptions in the form of spreading red lines on the skin

creeping Jennie /-jénni/, **creeping Jenny** *n* an evergreen creeping plant with coin-shaped leaves. Flowers: yellow. Native to: Europe, E North America. *Lysimachia nummularia*. US term **moneywort**

creeping thistle *n* a thistle that grows 90 cm/3 ft tall. Flowers: pinkish-purple to white. *Cirsium arvense*. US term **Canada thistle**

creepy /kreepi/ (**-ier, -iest**) *adj* (*informal*) **1** unsettling because it causes fear, disgust, or uneasiness **2** repellent because of annoying, unpleasant, or disturbing qualities —**creepily** *adv* —**creepiness** *n*

creepy-crawly (*plural* **creepy-crawlies**) *n* a crawling insect or small animal (*informal*)

cremate /krə máyt/ (**-mates, -mating, -mated**) *vt* to burn a corpse until nothing remains but ashes [Late 19C. Either < Latin *cremat-* (see CREMATION), or back-formation < CREMATION.] —**cremator** *n*

cremation /krə máysh'n/ *n* **1** the burning of a dead body until only ashes are left **2** a funeral ceremony during which the body is cremated [Early 17C. < Latin *cremation-* < *cremat-*, past participle of *cremare* 'burn'.]

crematorium /krémmə táwri əm/ (*plural* **-ums** *or* **-a** /-ə/) *n* a building or furnace where corpses are incinerated [Late 19C. < modern Latin, < Latin *cremat-* (see CREMATION).]

crematory /krémmətəri/ *n* (*plural* **-ries**) *US* = **crematorium** ■ *adj* relating to or used for cremation

crème brûlée /krém broo láy/ (*plural* **crème brûlées** /-láyz/ *or* **crèmes brûlées** /-láy/) *n* a rich baked custard with caramelized sugar on top [< French, 'burnt cream']

crème caramel /krém kárrə mél/ (*plural* **crème caramels** /krém kárrə mél/ *or* **crèmes caramel**) *n* a custard cooked in a mould coated with caramelized sugar, which forms a sauce. It is chilled and removed from the mould before serving. [< French, 'caramel cream']

crème de cacao /krém də kə kaá ō/ (*plural* **crème de cacaos** /krém də kə kaá ō/ *or* **crèmes de cacao**) *n* a sweet chocolate-flavoured liqueur [< French, 'cream of cacao']

crème de la crème /krém də la krém/ *n* the very best of a group of people or things [< French, 'cream of the cream']

crème de menthe /krém də maánth/ (*plural* **crème de menthes** /krém də maánth/ *or* **crèmes de menthe**) *n* a sweet mint-flavoured liqueur [< French, 'cream of mint']

crème fraîche /krém frésh/ *n* thickened French soured cream, used in cooking or served with other foods [< French, 'fresh cream']

Cremona /kri mónə/ capital of Cremona Province, N Italy. Population: 332,040 (1997 estimate).

crenate /kree nayt/, **crenated** /-naytid/ *adj* with a scalloped edge or a surface with rounded projections [Late 18C. < modern Latin *crenatus* < Latin *crena* 'small notch'.] —**crenately** *adv*

crenation /kri náysh'n/ *n* **1 ROUNDED PROTRUSION** a rounded protrusion from the edge or surface of something **2 SCALLOPED EDGE OR SURFACE** a scalloped edge or a surface with rounded projections **3 SHRINKAGE OF RED BLOOD CELLS** a medical condition in which the red blood cells shrink and develop multiple indentations and protrusions

crenel /krénn'l/, **crenelle** /krə nél/ *n* **1** any of the rectangular openings in the top of a castle wall or parapet **2** a rounded protrusion from an edge or surface [15C. < Old French, 'small notch' < Latin *crena*.]

crenelate *adj* US = **crenellate**

crenellate (**-lates, -lating, -lated**) *vt* **1** to provide a structure with battlements or decorative features resembling battlements **2** to make something with square indentations like the openings (**crenels**) of a battlement [Early 19C. < French *créneler* < Old French *crenel* (see CRENEL).] —**crenellated** *adj* —**crenellation** *n*

crenelle *n* ARCHIT = **crenel**

crenulate /krénnyoo layt/, **crenulated** /-laytid/ *adj* with a finely scalloped or notched wavy edge [Late 18C. < modern Latin *crenulatus* < *crenula* 'small notch' < Latin *crena*.]

crenulation /krénnyoo láysh'n/ *n* **1** a very small notch or indentation **2** very fine notching or indentation along an edge

creodont /kree ə dont/ (*plural* **-donts** *or* **-donta** /-dóntə/) *n* an extinct carnivorous mammal that lived during the Tertiary period. Suborder: Creodonta. [Late 19C. < modern Latin *Creodonta* 'flesh-toothed ones' < Greek *kreas* 'flesh' + *odont-* 'tooth'.]

creole /kree ōl/ *n* **LANGUAGE OF MIXED ORIGIN** a language that has evolved from the mixture of two or more languages and has become the first language of a group ■ *adj* **1 COOKED AS IN NEW ORLEANS** cooked in a spicy highly-flavoured way typical of the French Creoles of New Orleans **2 OF A CREOLE** relating to or belonging to a creole [Late 19C. < CREOLE.]

Creole *n* **1 SOMEBODY OF FRENCH ANCESTRY** somebody who comes from the S United States, especially S Louisiana, and is descended from early French settlers **2 LANGUAGE OF LOUISIANA** the creolized French language spoken by the Creoles of New Orleans and S Louisiana **3 LANGUAGE OF CARIBBEAN ISLANDS** a group of creolized languages, based on English and French, spoken on some islands of the Caribbean **4 WEST INDIAN OF EUROPEAN ANCESTRY** somebody who comes from a West Indian or Latin American country, and is of European, especially Spanish, descent **5 CREOLE SPEAKER** somebody of both European and African ancestry who speaks a form of Creole [Mid-18C. < French, < Spanish *criollo* 'native' < Portuguese *crioulo* < *criar* 'bring up' < Latin *creare* 'bring forth'.] —**Creole** *adj*

creolize /kree ə līz/ (**-olizes, -olizing, -olized**), **creolise** (**-olises, -olising, -olised**) *vt* to form a new mixed language from two or more other languages —**creolization** /kree ə lī záysh'n/ *n* —**creolized** *adj*

Creon /kree ən/ *n* in Greek mythology, the brother of Jocasta and the successor of Oedipus as king of Thebes

creosol /kree ə sol/ *n* $C_8H_{10}O_2$ a pale yellow or colourless oily liquid. Source: creosote. [Mid-19C. < CREOSOTE.]

creosote /kree ə sōt/ *n* **1 WOOD PRESERVATIVE** a thick yellowish to brown oily substance. Source: coal tar. Use: wood preservative. **2 ANTISEPTIC** a yellow to colourless oily substance. Source: wood tar. Use: antiseptic. ■ *vt* (**-sotes, -soting, -soted**) **APPLY CREOSOTE TO** to apply creosote to wood as a preservative [Mid-19C. < German *Kreosote* < Greek *kreas* 'flesh' + *sōtēr* 'preserver'; from its antiseptic properties.]

creosote bush *n* a resinous evergreen shrub with leaves that smell like creosote. Native to: deserts of SW United States and Mexico. *Larrea tridentata*.

crêpe /krayp/ *n* **1 crêpe, crepe, crape** a light fine fabric with a crinkled surface **2** a thin pancake usually served rolled up or folded with a filling **3** PAPER = **crepe paper** **4** INDUST = **crepe rubber** [Late 18C. < French, < Old French *crespe* 'curled' < Latin *crispus*.] —**crepy** *adj*

crepe de Chine /kráyp də sheen/, **crêpe de Chine** *n* a light smooth silk fabric. Use: delicate articles of clothing. [< French, 'crepe of China']

crepe paper, **crêpe paper** *n* a thin, slightly stretchy, crinkled coloured paper, used for wrapping presents or making decorations (*hyphenated before nouns*)

crepe rubber, **crêpe rubber** *n* rubber in the form of thin crinkled sheets, used especially for the soles of shoes

crêpe suzette /-soo zét/ (*plural* **crêpes suzettes** /kráyp soo zéts/) *n* a pancake prepared with orange sauce and flambéed with an orange-flavoured liqueur or brandy [< French, said to be after the French actress *Suzanne* Reichenberg (1853–1924)]

crepitate /kréppi tayt/ (**-tates, -tating, -tated**) *v* **1** *vi* to make a crackling or grating sound (*formal or literary*) **2** to make the crackling or grating sound of crepitus [Early 17C. < Latin *crepitat-*, past participle of *crepitare* 'crackle' < *crepare* 'to rattle', an imitation of the sound.] —**crepitant** *adj* —**crepitation** /kréppi táysh'n/ *n*

crepitus /kréppitəss/ *n* **1** the grating sound heard when the broken ends of a bone rub together **2** a crackling sound heard in the chest of somebody who has a lung disease, e.g. pneumonia [Early 19C. < Latin, 'rattling' < *crepare* (see CREPITATE).]

crept past tense, past participle of **creep**

crepuscular /kri púskyoolər/ *adj* **1** relating to or resembling the fading light of dusk (*literary*) **2** describes fish and land mammals that are active at dusk and dawn, when the light level is low [Mid-17C. < Latin *crepusculum* 'twilight'.]

Cres. *abbr* Crescent (*in addresses*)

cresc. *abbr* crescendo

crescendo /krə shéndō/ *n* (*plural* **-dos** *or* **-does** *or* **-di** /-dee/) **1 INCREASING LOUDNESS** a gradual increase in the volume of a passage of music **2 MUSIC PLAYED INCREASINGLY LOUD** a passage of music in which there is a gradual increase in volume **3 INTENSIFICATION** an increase in volume or intensity similar to a crescendo in music **4** ⚠ **CLIMAX** the climax of an increase in volume or intensity. ■ *adj* **INTENSIFYING** gradually increasing in volume or intensity ■ *adv* **WITH GREATER VOLUME** with increasing loudness ■ *vi* (**-does, -doing, -doed**) **BECOME LOUDER OR STRONGER** to increase in volume or intensity [Late 18C. < Italian, present participle of *crescere* 'increase' < Latin, 'grow'.]

USAGE A ***crescendo*** is properly a process and not the end of a process. This is usually well understood in musical contexts, where the word is a technical term. In figurative uses, though, it tends to be used as an alternative for *climax*, which is indeed the end point or culmination of a process. In careful usage, noise or feeling can increase *to* a climax but it does so *in* a ***crescendo***. Correct: *The bird's calls rose in a crescendo.* Avoid: *The abusive phone calls reached a crescendo the following week.*

crescent /kréss'nt, krézz'nt/ *n* **1 ARC SHAPE** a curved shape like that of the moon when it is less than half illuminated **2 ARC-SHAPED THING** something shaped like a crescent **3 crescent, Crescent ISLAMIC SYMBOL** the emblem of Islam or Turkey, shaped like a crescent moon **4 crescent, Crescent ISLAMIC OR TURKISH POWER** Islamic or Turkish power **5 crescent, Crescent ARC-SHAPED STREET** a curved street, especially one that opens onto the same street at each end **6 SYMBOL FOR SECOND SON** a crescent moon, used in heraldry to signify a second son ■ *adj* **1 ARC-SHAPED** shaped like a crescent **2 GROWING** gradually increasing in size (*literary*) [14C. Via Anglo-Norman *cressaunt* < Latin *crescent-*, present participle of *crescere* 'grow'.] —**crescentic** /krə séntik, krə zéntik/ *adj*

cresol /kreé sol/ *n* C_7H_8O a colourless compound. Source: wood or coal tar. Use: antiseptic, disinfectant. [Mid-19C. Alteration of CREOSOL.]

cress /kress/ (*plural* **cress** *or* **cresses**) *n* a plant of the mustard family with small pungently flavoured leaves that are used in salads or as a garnish [Old English *cressa* < Germanic]

cresset /kréssit/ *n* a metal cup or basket mounted on a pole and filled with oil or pitch that was burned to give light [14C. < Old French, *cresset* < *craisse* 'oil, grease' < Latin *crassus* 'fat'.]

Cressida[1] /kréssidə/ *n* in medieval retellings of the Trojan War, a Trojan woman captured by the Greeks who is unfaithful to her Trojan lover, Troilus, by giving herself to the Greek Diomedes

Cressida[2] *n* a small natural satellite of Uranus, discovered by the Voyager 2 planetary probe in 1986

crest /krest/ *n* **1 TOP OF CURVE OR SLOPE** the top part of something that slopes or rises upwards, e.g. a wave or a hill **2 CULMINATION** the highest stage or culminating point in an activity or achievement **3 TUFT ON ANIMAL'S HEAD** a tuft or other growth on the top of the head of a bird or other animal **4 SOMETHING RESEMBLING CREST** something resembling the crest of a bird or other animal **5 HELMET ORNAMENT** a plume or other decoration on top of a helmet **6 NECK RIDGE** a ridge along the neck of a horse, lion, or other mammal, from which hair grows **7 SYMBOL OF FAMILY OR OFFICE** a small animal, bird, or other heraldic symbol of a family or office, placed above the shield in a coat of arms or used alone on a helmet ■ *v* **1** *vi* **RISE** to reach or rise to a crest **2** *vt* **REACH TOP OF** to reach the top of something **3** *vt* **TOP** to be at the top of something [14C. Via French *creste* < Latin *crista* 'tuft'.] —**crested** *adj*

crestfallen /krést fawlən/ *adj* disappointed or humiliated, especially after being enthusiastic or confident [< the drooping of somebody's head when disappointed] —**crestfallenly** *adv*

cresting /krésting/ *n* **1** an ornamental ridge on a roof **2** an ornamental carving or rail on the top of a piece of furniture

cresylic acid *n* CHEM = **cresol**

cretaceous /kri táyshəss/ *adj* resembling or consisting of chalk (*technical*) [Late-17C. < Latin *cretaceus* 'chalky' < *creta* 'chalk'.] —**cretaceously** *adv*

Cretaceous *adj* belonging to or dating from the end of the Mesozoic era, 144 to 65 million years ago

Crete /kreet/ the largest Greek island in the S Aegean Sea. Population: 540,054 (1991). Area: 8,335 sq. km/3,218 sq. mi. —**Cretan** *adj, n*

cretic /kreétik/ *n* LITERAT = **amphimacer** [Late 16C. Via Latin *creticus* 'Cretan' < Greek *krētikos* < *Krētē* 'Crete'.]

cretin /kréttin/ *n* **1** an offensive term that deliberately insults somebody's supposed intellectual capacity (*insult*) **2** somebody affected by congenital myxoedema (*dated; sometimes offensive*) [Late 18C. Via French < Swiss French *creitin* 'mentally disabled person' < Latin *Christianus* (see CHRISTIAN).] —**cretinism** *n* —**cretinoid** *adj* —**cretinous** *adj*

cretonne /kre tón/ *n* a heavy cotton, linen, or rayon fabric usually printed with a colourful design. Use: upholstery. [Late 19C. < French, < *Creton*, village in Normandy.]

Creutzfeldt-Jakob disease /króytsfelt yák ob-/ *n* a rare fatal brain disease, a form of spongiform encephalopathy, that develops slowly, causing dementia and loss of muscle control. An abnormal protein (**prion**) is the suspected cause. [Late 20C. After H. G. *Creutzfeldt* (1885–1964) and A. M. *Jakob* (1884–1931), German neurologists.]

crevasse /krə váss/ *n* **1 DEEP CRACK** a deep crack, e.g. in the ice of a glacier **2** *US* **CRACK IN EMBANKMENT** a crack in a river embankment or dyke ■ *vti* (**-vasses, -vassing, -vassed**) **FORM CREVASSES** to develop or make something develop crevasses [Early 19C. < French, < Old French *crevace* (see CREVICE).]

crevice /krévviss/ *n* a narrow crack or opening, especially in rock [14C. < Old French *crevace* 'a burst' < *crever* 'to burst' < Latin *crepare* 'to rattle', an imitation of the sound.] —**creviced** *adj*

crew[1] /kroo/ *n* **1 ONBOARD STAFF** the people who work on a boat, ship, aircraft, or spacecraft **2 SHIP'S STAFF EXCLUDING OFFICERS** the members of a ship's staff who are not officers **3 SPECIALIZED STAFF ON CRAFT** a smaller group within the overall staff of a ship, aircraft, or spacecraft who are assigned a specific task **4 PEOPLE WORKING TOGETHER** a group of people who work together on a project or task **5 GROUP OF FRIENDS** a group of people who spend much time together or are somehow associated with one another (*informal*) **6 ROWERS** the coxswain and oarsmen or oarswomen of a racing boat ■ *v* **1** *vi* **BE ON CREW** to be a member of a crew **2** *vt* **BE ON TRANSPORT STAFF OF** to serve as a member of the personnel of a boat, ship, aircraft, or spacecraft (*often passive*) [15C. < French *creüe* 'increase, recruit' < the past participle of *croistre* 'grow' < Latin *crescere*.]

crew[2] past tense of **crow**

crew chief *n US* a noncommissioned officer in the Air Force who is in charge of the maintenance and ground handling of an aircraft

crew cut *n* a haircut, usually worn by men and boys, with the hair cut close to the head [Probably because adopted by boat crews at the US universities of Harvard and Yale in the mid-20C]

Crewe /kroo/ town and major rail junction in NW England. Population: 63,351 (1991).

crewed /krood/ *adj* operated by onboard personnel ○ *A crewed mission to Mars.*

crewel /kroó əl/ *n* **1** a loosely twisted woollen yarn used in embroidery **2** SEW = **crewelwork** [15C. < ?]

crewelwork /kroó əl wurk/ *n* embroidery work done with crewel yarn

crewmate /kroó mayt/ *n* a fellow member of a crew, especially on board a boat or spacecraft

crew neck *n* **1** a close-fitting round neckline on a sweater, sweatshirt, or other garment **2** a sweater with a close-fitting round neck [< the sweaters with such a neckline worn by boat crews] —**crew-neck** *adj*

crib /krib/ *n* **1 HAY RACK** a trough or box for hay or other fodder from which livestock can feed **2 MODEL OF MANGER** a model of the manger in which Jesus Christ lay after his birth **3 ANIMAL'S STALL** a stall for cattle or horses **4** *US* = **cot**[1] *n.* 1 **5 CRIB SHEET** a crib sheet (*informal*) **6 PLAGIARISM** a theft of material from an intellectual or artistic work **7 PROSTITUTE'S ROOM** a run-down house or room used by a prostitute **8 BASKET** a wicker basket **9 DEALER'S CARDS** the cards used by the dealer in cribbage, consisting of cards discarded by the other players **10 CRIBBAGE** cribbage (*informal*) **11** *ANZ* **SNACK** a light snack (*informal*) ■ *v* (**cribs, cribbing, cribbed**) **1** *vti* **PLAGIARIZE** to steal somebody's ideas or work (*informal*) **2** *vi* **USE CRIB SHEET** to use a crib sheet in an examination (*informal*) **3** *vt* **PUT IN CRIB** to put somebody or something in a crib **4** *vt* **PROVIDE CRIB FOR** to construct or provide a crib for something [Old English *crib(b)* 'manger, trough' < Germanic] —**cribber** *n*

cribbage /kríbbij/ *n* a card game for two to four players in which the score is kept by moving pegs along rows of holes in a small board [Mid-17C. Probably < CRIB + -AGE.]

cribbage board *n* a board with holes in which pegs are placed for scoring in cribbage

cribbing /kríbbing/ *n* **1** using a crib sheet to cheat in an examination (*informal*) **2** the timbers used for a framework, e.g. of a mineshaft or foundation **3** VET = **crib-biting**

crib-biting *n* a behavioural abnormality in horses in which animals kept in stables chew their stalls and salivate excessively —**crib-biter** *n*

crib death *n US, Can* MED = **cot death**

cribellum /kri béllәm/ (*plural* **-la** /-lə/) *n* an oval perforated plate just in front of the silk-secreting organs (**spinnerets**) in some spiders, through which the emerging silk is combed [Late 19C. < late Latin, 'small sieve' < *cribrum* 'sieve'.]

cribriform /kríbbri fawrm/ *adj* with small holes like a sieve (*technical*) [Mid-18C. < Latin *cribrum* 'sieve'.]

crib sheet *n* a list of answers or translation of a foreign text used for cheating in examinations or lessons

cricetid /krī seétid/ (*plural* **-tids** *or* **-tid**) *n* a small rodent of the family that includes the hamster, gerbil, muskrat, and vole. Family: Cricetidae. [Mid-20C. < modern Latin *Cricetidae* < *Cricetus* (genus name of hamsters) < medieval Latin *cricetus* 'hamster'.] —**cricetid** *adj*

crick /krik/ *n* a painful stiffness or muscle spasm in the neck or back ■ *vt* to cause a painful stiffness or muscle spasm in the neck or back [15C. < ?]

Crick /krik/, **Francis H. C.** (*b.* 1916) British biophysicist. Full name **Francis Henry Compton Crick**

cricket[1] /kríkit/ *n* a leaping insect that has biting mouthparts, long legs, and antennae. The male produces a chirping sound by rubbing its forewings together. Family: Gryllidae. [14C. < French *criquet* 'grasshopper, locust' < Old French *criquer* 'to click', an imitation of the sound.]

cricket[2] /kríkit/ *n* an outdoor sport played by two teams of 11 players using a flat bat, a small hard ball, and wickets ■ *vi* to play cricket [Late 16C. < ?] —**cricketer** *n* ◇ **not cricket** unfair and not honourable (*dated informal*)

cricket[3] /kríkit/ *n* a wooden footstool [Mid-17C. < ?]

cricoid /krī́ koyd/ *adj* relating to or in the region of the lowermost cartilage of the larynx [Mid-18C. Via modern Latin *cricoides* 'ring-shaped' < Greek *krikoeidēs* < *krikos* 'ring'.]

cricoid cartilage *n* the lowermost cartilage of the voice box (**larynx**), which has a shape like a signet ring

cri de coeur /kreé də kúr/ (*plural* **cris de coeur** /kreé də kúr/) *n* a heartfelt, usually anguished appeal [< French, 'cry from the heart']

crier /krī́ ər/ *n* **1 SOMEBODY OR SOMETHING THAT CRIES** a person or animal that cries **2** PUBLIC ADMIN = **town crier** *n.* **3 LAW COURT ANNOUNCER** an official who makes public announcements of the orders of a court of law **4 VENDOR SHOUTING WARES** a pedlar who makes public announcements about the goods he or she has for sale (*archaic*)

crim /krim/ *n ANZ* a criminal (*informal*) [Early 20C. Shortening.]

crime /krīm/ *n* **1 ILLEGAL ACT** an action prohibited by law or a failure to act as required by law **2 ILLEGAL ACTIVITY** activity that involves breaking the law **3 IMMORAL ACT** any act considered morally wrong **4 UNDESIRABLE ACT** a shameful, unwise, or regrettable act (*informal*) ○ *It's a crime the way some people waste food.* [13C. Via French < Latin *crimen* (stem *crimin-*) 'judgment' < *cernere* 'decide'.] —**crimeless** *adj*

LITERARY LINK ***Crime and Punishment***, a novel (1866) by Russian writer Fyodor Dostoyevsky. It describes how a young student, Raskolnikov, plans and carries out a murder in order to prove that certain individuals are above the law. Ultimately, however, he confesses.

Crimea /krī meé ə/ peninsula in SE Ukraine between the Black Sea and the Sea of Azov. Area: 25,993 sq. km/10,036 sq. mi. —**Crimean** *n, adj*

crime against humanity *n* a cruel and immoral act, e.g. torture, murder, or expulsion, committed against a large number of people

crime of passion *n* a crime that is motivated by an extreme emotion, especially sexual jealousy

crime passionnel /kreém pássi ə nél/ (*plural* **crimes passionnels** /kreém pássi ə nél/) *n* LAW = **crime of passion** [< French, 'crime of passion']

crime sheet *n* a record that lists somebody's breaches of military regulations

crime wave *n* a period during which more crimes than usual are committed

criminal /krímminəl/ *n* **SOMEBODY ACTING ILLEGALLY** a committer of a crime ■ *adj* **1 PUNISHABLE AS CRIME** punishable as a crime under the law **2 PROSECUTING CRIMINALS** involved in or relating to the prosecution and punishment of people accused of committing crimes **3 RELATING TO CRIMINALS** relating to or typical of criminals **4 MORALLY WRONG** morally wrong whether illegal or not **5 UNWISE OR REGRETTABLE** not showing good sense or fairness (*informal*) [15C. Directly or via French *criminel* < late Latin *criminalis* 'of crime' < Latin *crimin-* (see CRIME).] —**criminally** *adv*

criminal conversation *n* adultery considered as a legal breach of the marriage contract (*technical*)

criminalise *vt* LAW = **criminalize**

criminality /krímmi nálləti/ *n* **1 CRIMINAL QUALITY** a criminal character or quality **2 TENDENCY TO LAWBREAKING** a tendency to commit crimes **3 CRIME** a criminal act or practice (*often plural*)

criminalize /krímminə līz/ (**-izes, -izing, -ized**), **criminalise** (**-ises, -ising, -ised**) *vt* **1** to make an action punishable as a crime under the law **2** to make somebody become or treat somebody as a criminal —**criminalization** /krímminə lī záysh'n/ *n*

criminol. *abbr* criminology

criminology /krímmi nólləji/ *n* the sociological study of crime, criminals, and the punishment of criminals —**criminological** /krímminə lójjik'l/ *adj* —**criminologically** *adv* —**criminologist** *n*

crimp /krimp/ *vt* **1 FOLD OR PRESS TOGETHER** to fold or press the ends or edges of something together **2 PLEAT** to press or gather something into small folds, e.g. a piece of fabric **3 CURL** to make somebody's hair wavy with curling tongs **4 PINCH DECORATIVELY** to pinch or press together the edges of pastry to form a seal or for decoration **5 MOULD** to mould or form leather into a shape **6 JOIN INTO SEAM** to bend or fold the edges of sheet metal to form a seam for a tube or between two pieces ■ *n* **1 CRIMPING ACTION** a pinching, folding, or other action that crimps something **2 TIGHT HAIR WAVE** a tight artificial wave in somebody's hair, usually made with curling tongs **3 PINCHED EDGE** a fold or crease made by pinching together two edges, e.g. of fabric or pastry **4 CREASE FORMED BY BENDING** a fold or crease formed by bending something, e.g. sheet metal **5 CURL OF WOOL FIBRES** the curl or wave of wool fibres [Late 17C. Probably via Dutch or Low German *krimpen* 'shrink, crimp' < Germanic.] —**crimper** *n*

Crimplene /krím pleen/ *tdmk* a trademark for a crease-resistant synthetic clothing fabric

crimpy /krímpi/ (**-ier, -iest**) *adj* with many small waves, folds, or wrinkles

crimson /krímz'n/ *n* **DEEP RICH RED COLOUR** a deep rich purplish-red colour ■ *v* **1** *vti* **MAKE OR BECOME CRIMSON** to become a vivid or deep red colour, or make something become this colour **2** *vi* **BLUSH** to blush, with embarrassment, shyness, or shame [15C. Via Old Spanish *cremesín* < Arabic *ḳirmizī* 'red colour' < *ḳirmīz* 'kermes insect'.]

cringe /krinj/ *vi* (**cringes, cringing, cringed**) **1 CROUCH OR MOVE BACK SUDDENLY** to pull the head and body quickly away from something or somebody in a frightened or servile way **2 BE EMBARRASSED OR UNCOMFORTABLE** to react to something with embarrassment or discomfort, often showing it by physically flinching (*informal*) ○ *We always cringe at his jokes.* **3 ACT HUMBLY** to behave in a very humble or servile way (*disapproving*) ■ *n* **1 COWERING MOVEMENT** a quick pulling away of the head and body from something or somebody in a frightened or servile way **2 EMBARRASSED REACTION** an embarrassed or uncomfortable reaction, often shown by physically flinching (*informal*) [13C. Probably < Old English *crincan* 'to yield'.] —**cringer** *n*

cringe-making *adj* so embarrassing or painful that people wince (*informal*) —**cringe-makingly** *adv*

cringle /kríng g'l/ *n* a piece of rope with a metal ring (**thimble**) in it, fitted into the main rope (**boltrope**) around the edge of a sail [Early 17C. < Low German *kringel* 'small ring'.]

crinkle /kríngk'l/ *vti* **1 CREASE UP** to become, or make something become, finely folded, wrinkled, or wavy, e.g. by crushing or pressing it **2 MAKE SOFT CRACKLING SOUND** to make little crunching or rustling noises, like the sound of paper being crushed, or cause something to make these noises ■ *n* **TINY FOLD OR WAVE** a little fold or wave, especially in paper or cloth [14C. < ?]

crinklecut /kríngk'l kut/ *adj* cut in wavy shapes or with wavy edges

crinkly /kríngkli/ *adj* (**-klier, -kliest**) **1 WAVY OR CREASED UP TIGHTLY** covered in or full of fine creases or folds ○ *made of some kind of crinkly material.* **2 MAKING RUSTLING NOISES** making little crunching or rustling noises ■ *n* (*plural* **-klies**) **OFFENSIVE TERM** an offensive term for a person of advanced years (*slang*) —**crinkliness** *n*

crinoid /krī noyd, krínnoyd/ *n* a primitive marine invertebrate animal (**echinoderm**) with a cup-shaped body and five feathery radiating arms, related to starfish and sea urchins. Class: Crinoidea. [Mid-19C. < Greek *krinoidēs* 'lily-like' < *krinon* 'lily'.] —**crinoid** *adj*

crinoline /krínnəlin/ *n* **1 FABRIC FOR STIFFENING THINGS** a stiff fabric made of horsehair and cotton or linen. Use: formerly, linings, petticoats. **2 STIFF PETTICOAT** a petticoat of crinoline fabric or net, worn to expand a skirt **3 HOOPED SKIRT** a skirt or petticoat containing wire hoops, worn to expand the skirt [Mid-19C. Via French < Italian *crinolino* < *crino* 'horsehair' + *lino* 'flax'.] —**crinolined** *adj*

criollo /kri ólō/ (*plural* **-los**) *n* **1** somebody who comes from a Latin American country, and is of European, especially Spanish, descent **2** a domestic mammal belonging to a Latin American breed [Late 19C. < Spanish (see CREOLE).] —**criollo** *adj*

criosphinx /kreé ō sfingks/ (*plural* **-sphinxes** *or* **-sphinges** /-sfin jeez/) *n* in ancient Egyptian mythology and art, a figure that is like a sphinx in having a lion's body but has the head of a ram rather than a human head [Mid-19C. < Greek *krios* 'ram'.]

cripes /krīps/ *interj* used to express surprise or concern (*slang*) ○ *Cripes! That's torn it!* [Early 20C. Alteration of CHRIST.]

Crippen /kríppin/, **Hawley Harvey** (1861–1910) US-born British dentist and murderer

cripple /krípp'l/ *n* **1** an offensive term for somebody whose use of a limb or limbs is impaired **2** an offensive term for somebody who is impaired in a particular area ■ *vt* (**-ples, -pling, -pled**) **1** an offensive term meaning to impair the ability of somebody to move **2** an offensive term meaning to impair the functioning of something [Old English *crypel* < Germanic, 'bent'] —**crippled** *adj* —**crippling** *adj* —**cripplingly** *adv*

crisis /krī siss/ (*plural* **-ses** /-seez/) *n* **1 DANGEROUS OR WORRYING TIME** a situation or period in which things are very uncertain, difficult, or painful, especially a time when action must be taken to avoid complete disaster or breakdown **2 CRITICAL MOMENT** a time when something very important for the future happens or is decided **3 TURNING POINT IN DISEASE** a point in the course of a disease when the patient suddenly begins to get worse or better [15C. Via Latin < Greek *krisis* 'decisive moment' < *krinein* 'decide'.]

crisis centre *n* a place where people who have suffered emotional or social breakdown or trauma can go to find help and counselling

crisis management *n* the business or process of working through a crisis to solve or cope with problems as they arise

crisp /krisp/ *adj* **1 HARD BUT EASILY BROKEN** dry and firm, and of a texture that breaks easily **2 FRESH AND CRUNCHY** fresh and firm enough to snap when bitten into ○ *nice crisp lettuce* **3 SMOOTH, FIRM, AND CLEAN** with a stiff, uncreased, or unspoilt surface ○ *a crisp white tablecloth* **4 DISTINCT** distinct and clear, without ambiguity or distortion ○ *She was pleased with the crisp image of the print.* **5 SHARP AND CONCISE** sharp and concise, often to the point of brusqueness ○ *crisp responses* **6 INVIGORATING** invigorating and fresh ○ *It was a beautiful crisp frosty morning.* ■ *n* **1 FRIED POTATO SLICE** a very thin slice of fried potato, eaten as a snack, usually salted and often flavoured ○ *cheese-and-onion flavoured crisps* **2** *US* COOK = **crumble** *n.* ■ *vti* **MAKE OR BECOME CRISP** to become or make something crisp or crisper, usually in an oven [Mid-16C. Originally 'curly', < Latin *crispus*.] —**crisply** *adv* —**crispness** *n* ◇ **to a crisp** until it has become hard and crunchy, usually when it should not be (*informal*) ○ *toast burned to a crisp*

crispate /kríss payt/ *adj* describes leaves that have curled or wavy edges [Mid-19C. < Latin *crispatus*, past participle of *crispare* 'curl' < *crispus* 'curled'.]

crispation /kriss páysh'n/ *n* **1** the act of curling, or the condition of being curled (*formal*) **2** a minor convulsive muscle contraction that produces a creeping feeling in the skin [Early 17C. < Latin *crispat-*, past participle of *crispare* (see CRISPATE).]

crispbread /krísp bred/ *n* a flat, crisp, usually rectangular cracker or biscuit made from rye, wheat, corn, or other grain

crisper /kríspər/ *n* a covered compartment in a refrigerator, where fruits and vegetables are placed to keep them fresh and crisp

crispy /kríspi/ (**-ier, -iest**) *adj* with a pleasantly light, crunchy texture ○ *Do you like your bacon crispy?* —**crispily** *adv* —**crispiness** *n*

crissa plural of **crissum**

crisscross /kríss kross/ *n* **CROSS OR LATTICE ARRANGEMENT** a pattern of lines that cross each other ■ *adj* **WITH CROSSED VERTICAL AND HORIZONTAL LINES** running in different directions across each other, or made up of lines like this ■ *adv* **BACK AND FORTH** in a way that makes a crisscross pattern of crossing lines ■ *v* **1** *vti* **MAKE PATTERN OF CROSSED LINES** to create a crisscross pattern on something **2** *vt* **GO TO AND FRO ACROSS** to travel or move backwards and forwards or in all different directions over something [Early 17C. Alteration of *cristcross* 'sign of the cross'.]

crissum /kríssəm/ (*plural* **-sa** /-sə/) *n* the feathers beneath the tail of a bird [Late 19C. < modern Latin, < Latin *crissare* 'wiggle the hips'.] —**crissal** *adj*

crista /krístə/ (*plural* **-tae** /-tee/) *n* **1** a crest or ridge, e.g. the border of a bone **2** a fold in the inner membrane of a mitochondrion, providing a large surface area over which the enzymes responsible for energy metabolism are located [Mid-19C. < Latin, 'tuft of hair, ridge'.] —**cristate** *adj*

cristobalite /kris tṓbəlīt/ *n* a white form of quartz. Source: volcanic rocks. [Late 19C. After the hill of San *Cristóbal*, near Pachuca de Soto, Mexico.]

crit /krit/ *n* a critique (*informal*) ○ *I haven't seen the film but I've read a couple of crits.* [Early 20C. Shortening.]

crit. *abbr* **1** critic **2** critical **3** criticism

criterion /krī teéri ən/ (*plural* **-a** /-ə/) *n* an accepted standard used in making decisions or judgments about something (*often plural*) [Early 17C. < Greek *kritērion* < *kritēs* (see CRITIC).] —**criterial** *adj*

USAGE criterion or **criteria**? ***Criterion*** is singular, and ***criteria*** is plural; it is generally regarded as incorrect to use ***criteria*** as a singular noun (with *criterias* as a bogus plural), although this is commonly seen and heard in the print and electronic media, and in some law contexts as well. The phrase *set of criteria* may be used when a singular expression is required.

critic /kríttik/ *n* **1 SOMEBODY JUDGING** a judge or appraiser of something or somebody ○ *an eminent critic of postwar government* **2 WRITER OF REVIEWS** somebody, especially a journalist, who writes or broadcasts opinions on the quality of things such as drama productions, art exhibitions, and literary works ○ *the newspaper's TV critic* **3 FAULT-FINDER** a person who habitually finds fault [Mid-16C. Via Latin < Greek *kritikos* 'discerning' < *kritēs* 'judge' < *krinein* 'decide'.]

critical /kríttik'l/ *adj* **1 NOT APPROVING** tending to find fault with somebody or something, or with people and things in general **2 GIVING COMMENTS OR JUDGMENTS** containing or involving comments and opinions that analyse or judge something, especially in a detailed way ○ *a critical analysis of modern economic theory* **3 CRUCIAL** extremely important because of being a time or happening at a time of special difficulty, trouble, or danger, when matters could quickly get either worse or better ○ *The decision was a critical one for the country.* **4 ESSENTIAL** absolutely necessary for the success of something ○ *The army's immediate response is critical to our campaign.* **5 LIFE-THREATENING** medically life-threatening or in danger ○ *a patient in critical condition* **6 UNDERGOING CHANGE** relating to a property of a system that is undergoing a sudden change ○ *critical temperature* **7 SUSTAINING NUCLEAR CHAIN REACTION** designed to or having the mass to sustain a nuclear chain reaction —**critically** *adv* —**criticalness** *n*

critical angle *n* **1** the angle between a ray of light and a surface at which the ray will be completely reflected by the surface **2** AEROSP = **stalling angle**

criticality /krítti kálləti/ *n* **1** the condition of being crucial, decisive, or extremely serious **2** the point in an intensifying nuclear reaction at which it becomes self-sustaining

critical mass *n* **1** the smallest amount of fissionable material needed to maintain a nuclear chain reaction **2** the size or amount of something that is required before something can take place ○ *The service fell below the critical mass of subscribers and was suspended.*

critical point *n* **1** a point at which two or more phases of a substance, e.g. liquid and gas, are identical or in equilibrium **2** *US* MATH = **stationary point**

critical region *n* the possible results of a statistical test that are outside the range of acceptable probabilities and, if observed, would lead to their rejection

critical state *n* CHEM = **critical point** *n.* 1

critical temperature *n* the temperature of a substance at the critical point when it is between liquid and vapour phases

critical thinking *n* disciplined intellectual criticism that combines research, knowledge of historical context, and balanced judgment

criticise *vti* = **criticize**

criticism /kríttissizəm/ *n* **1 ACT OF CRITICIZING** a spoken or written opinion or judgment of what is wrong or bad about somebody or something **2 DISAPPROVAL** spoken or written opinions that point out one or more faults of somebody or something **3 ASSESSMENT OF CREATIVE WORK** considered judgment of or discussion about the qualities of something, especially a creative work **4** MEDIA = **critique** *n.* 1

criticize /krítti sīz/ (**-cizes, -cizing, -cized**), **criticise** (**-cises, -cising, -cised**) *vti* **1** to comment on or point out the faults, wrongdoing, or immorality of people or things **2** to make a considered assessment of the qualities of something, especially a creative work —**criticizable** *adj* —**criticizer** *n* —**criticizingly** *adv*

SYNONYMS ***criticize, censure, castigate, blast, condemn, find fault with, pick holes in, nitpick***

CORE MEANING: to express disapproval or dissatisfaction with somebody or something

criticize to point out faults; **censure** to make a formal, often public or official, statement of disapproval; **castigate** (*formal*) to criticize or rebuke severely; **blast** (*informal*) to criticize severely; **condemn** to give an unfavourable judgment on somebody or something; **find fault with** to criticize, often unfairly; **pick holes in** to look for and find mistakes, particularly in an argument; **nitpick** to find fault, often unjustifiably, with insignificant details.

critique /kri teék/ *n* **1** a written or broadcast assessment of something, usually a creative work, with comments on its good and bad qualities **2** MEDIA = **criticism** *n.* 3 ■ *vt* (**-tiques, -tiquing, -tiqued**) to discuss or comment on something, e.g. an artist's work or a political policy, giving an assessment of its good and bad features [Mid-17C. Via French < Greek *kritikē (tekhnē)* 'art of criticism' < *kritikos* (see CRITIC).]

~~**critisism**~~ incorrect spelling of **criticism**

critter /kríttər/ *n US* a living thing, often a child or an animal (*informal or regional*) ○ *That dog was a mean old critter.* [Early 19C. Alteration of CREATURE.]

CRO *abbr* **1** cathode-ray oscilloscope **2** Community Relations Officer **3** Criminal Records Office

Croagh Patrick /krō páttrik/ mountain in the W Republic of Ireland. Height: 765 m/2,510 ft.

croak /krōk/ *n* **CRY OF ANIMAL OR BIRD** a rough, usually low-pitched, vibrating sound, especially made by a frog or a crow, or the rough-sounding voice of somebody with a dry or sore throat ■ *v* **1** *vi* **GIVE HARSH GRATING CALL** to make a rough, usually low-pitched, vibrating call **2** *vti* **SPEAK HOARSELY** to speak or say something in a rough low uneven voice **3** *vti* **DIE OR KILL** to die, or kill somebody (*slang*) **4** *vi* **GRUMBLE** to grumble or mutter gloomily (*informal*) [Mid-16C. Probably an imitation of the sound.] —**croakily** *adv* —**croaky** *adj*

croaker /krṓkər/ *n* **1** a fish that makes croaking or grunting noises. Family: Sciaenidae. **2** a bird or other animal that croaks when it calls

Croat /krṓ at/ *n* **1** somebody who comes from Croatia **2** LANG = **Croatian** *n.* 1 [Mid-17C. Via modern Latin *Croata* < Serbo-Croatian *Hrvāt*.] —**Croat** *adj*

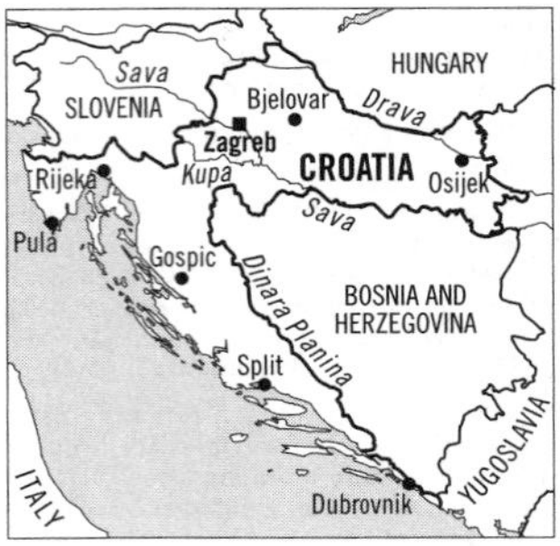

Croatia

Croatia /krō áyshə/ republic in SE Europe, on the Balkan Peninsula, bordering the Adriatic Sea. Capital: Zagreb. Population: 4,664,710 (1997). Area: 56,510 sq. km/21,819 sq. mi.

Croatian /krō áysh'n/ *n* **1** the Slavic language that is the official language of Croatia, closely related to Bosnian and Serbian. Native speakers: 5 million. **2** PEOPLES = **Croat** *n.* 1

croc /krok/ *n* a crocodile (*informal*) ○ *Any crocs in this river?* [Late 19C. Shortening.]

crocein /krṓssi in/ *n* a red or orange acid azo dye [20C. < Latin *croceus* 'saffron-coloured' < *crocus* (see CROCUS).]

crochet /krṓ shay/ *n* a form of needlework used to make clothes or decorative items from wool or thread, by looping it through itself with a hooked needle (**crochet hook**) ■ *vti* (**-chets** /-shayz/, **-cheting** /-shaying/, **-cheted** /-shayd/, **-cheted**) to make things, or a particular item, in crochet work [Mid-19C. < French *crochet* 'little hook' < *croche* 'hook' < Germanic.] —**crocheter** /krṓ shayər/ *n*

crocidolite /krō síddə līt/ *n* a fibrous purplish-blue form of the mineral riebeckite [Mid-19C. < Greek *krokid-* 'nap of woollen cloth'.]

crock[1] /krok/ *n* **1** a pot made of clay **2** a fragment of clay pottery [Old English *crocc* < Germanic]

crock[2] /krok/ *n* a worn-out person, vehicle, or machine (*informal*) ■ *vt* to disable or weaken somebody or something (*slang*) [15C. < ?]

crocked /krokt/ *adj* (*slang*) **1** physically incapacitated by an injury ○ *I'm too crocked to play this week.* **2** *US* drunk [Early 20C. < ?]

crockery /krókəri/ *n* plates, cups, saucers, and other household items made of china or earthenware [Early 18C. < *crocker* 'potter' < CROCK[1].]

crocket /krókit/ *n* a leaf shape carved as a decoration in Gothic architecture [Late 17C. < Old French dialect *croquet* 'shepherd's crook', variant of Old French *crochet* (see CROCHET).]

Crockett /krókit/, **Davy** (1786–1836) US frontiersman. Full name **David Crockett**

crocodile /krókə dīl/ (*plural* **-diles** *or* **-dile**) *n* **1 LARGE REPTILE WITH STRONG JAWS** a large carnivorous reptile that lives near water and has a long, thick-skinned, body and a broad head with strong jaws. Native to: tropical or subtropical regions. Family: Crocodylidae. **2** ZOOL = **crocodilian 3 LEATHER FROM CROCODILE SKIN** leather made from the skin of a crocodile ○ *crocodile shoes* **4 LINE OF CHILDREN** a procession of schoolchildren walking in pairs (*informal*) ○ *A neat crocodile of schoolchildren filed into the museum.* [13C. Via Old French *cocodril* < Greek *krokodilos*, a small lizard.]

crocodile bird *n* a long-legged black-and-white bird that feeds on insects parasitic to the crocodile. Native to: sandy banks of rivers and lakes of Africa. *Pluvianus aegyptius.*

crocodile clip *n* a metal clip with serrated jaws held closed by a spring, used for making temporary electrical connections. US term **alligator clip**

crocodile tears *npl* false tears or an insincere show of grief [Because crocodiles were believed to make sounds like weeping to attract prey, and to shed hypocritical tears over their victims]

crocodilian /krókə dílli ən/ *n* any large predatory reptile belonging to a group that includes the alligator, cayman, crocodile, gavial, and related extinct animals. Order: Crocodylia. —**crocodilian** *adj*

crocoite /krṓkō īt, krṓ kō-/, **crocoisite** /krō kṓ i sīt/ *n* a rare orange or red mineral consisting of lead chromate [Mid-19C. Alteration of French *crocoise* < Greek *krokoeis* 'saffron-coloured' < *krokos* 'saffron'.]

crocosmia /krō kózmi ə/ (*plural* **-as** *or* **-a**) *n* a plant cultivated for its orange-to-red ornamental flower sprays. Native to: southern Africa. Genus: *Crocosmia.*

crocus /krṓkəss/ (*plural* **-cuses** /-kəssiz/ *or* **-ci** /-sī/) *n* **1** a small perennial spring-flowering plant that grows from a corm. Flowers: white, red, purple, or yellow. Genus: *Crocus.* **2** any plant that has a flower like a true crocus, e.g. the autumn crocus **3** *US* CHEM = **jeweller's rouge** [14C. Via Latin < Greek *krokos* 'saffron, crocus'.]

Croesus /kreéssəss/ *n* a very wealthy man [After CROESUS]

Croesus /kreéssəss/ (*fl.* 6th century BC) king of Lydia (560–546 BC) who was proverbially wealthy

croft /kroft/ *n* a small plot of land, often with a house on it, that the owner or occupier works, especially in Scotland [Old English, < ?] —**crofter** *n*

crofting /krófting/ *n* the occupation of working a small plot of land, especially in Scotland, or the system of using land in this way

Crohn's disease /krṓnz-/ *n* a chronic inflammatory disease, usually of the lower intestinal tract, marked by scarring and thickening of the intestinal wall and obstruction [Mid-20C. After B. B. *Crohn* (1884–1983), US pathologist.]

croissant /krwáss oN/ *n* a piece of baked dough or pastry shaped into a crescent, usually moist, flaky, and very rich in fat, originally made in France [Late 19C. < French, 'crescent'.]

Croix de Guerre /krwaa də gáir/ (*plural* **Croix de Guerre**) *n* a French military medal awarded for bravery in war [< French, 'war cross']

Cro-Magnon /krō mágnən, krō mánn yon/ *n* the earliest known form of modern human being found in Europe, dating from about 50,000 to 30,000 years ago [Mid-19C. After the *Cro-Magnon* hill in the Dordogne, France.]

Crome /krōm/, **John** (1768–1821) British landscape painter

cromlech /króm lek/ *n* **1** a group of prehistoric standing stones arranged in a circle **2** an ancient stone burial chamber [Late 17C. < Welsh, < *crwm* 'arched' + *llech* 'flat stone'.]

Crompton /krómptən/, **Samuel** (1753–1827) British inventor

Cromwell /króm wel/, **Oliver** (1599–1658) English soldier and Lord Protector of England (1653–58)

Cromwell, Thomas, Earl of Essex (1485?–1540) English statesman

crone /krōn/ *n* **1** an offensive term that deliberately insults a woman's age, appearance, and temperament (*insult*) **2** *US* a woman aged over 40 (*approving; used by one woman to another*) [14C. < Old N French *carogne* 'withered old woman', literally 'carrion' < Latin *caro* 'flesh'.]

USAGE See ***insult.***

~~**cronic**~~ incorrect spelling of **chronic**

Cronin /krṓnin/, **A. J.** (1896–1981) Scottish novelist and physician. Full name **Archibald Joseph Cronin**

Cronkite /krón kīt, króng-/, **Walter** (*b.* 1916) US broadcast journalist

Cronus /krṓnəss/, **Cronos, Kronos** *n* in Greek mythology, a Titan who ruled the world until his son Zeus dethroned him. Roman equivalent **Saturn**

crony /krṓni/ (*plural* **-nies**) *n* a close friend, sometimes one to whom special treatment and preference is given (*disapproving*) [Mid-17C. < Greek *khronios* 'long-lasting' < *khronos* 'time'.]

cronyism /krṓni izəm/ *n* special treatment and preference given to friends or colleagues, especially the giving of political favours to people (*informal disapproving*)

crook /krŏŏk/ *n* **1 HOOK-SHAPED DEVICE** a curved or hooked tool, instrument, or part in a mechanism **2 SHEPHERD'S HOOKED STICK** a long stick with a curved end used by a shepherd to catch or guide a sheep **3** CHR = **crosier** *n.* 1 **4 DISHONEST PERSON** a thief, cheat, or criminal (*informal*) **5 BEND** a bent or curved part of something, e.g. the curve made by somebody's arm when the elbow is bent **6 TUBE**

INSERTED IN INSTRUMENT a tube inserted into a brass instrument to increase its length and lower its fundamental pitch ■ *vti* **FORM A BEND** to curve, or make something, e.g. a finger, take on a hooked or curved shape ■ *adj ANZ (informal)* 1 **UNWELL** ill or unwell ○ *I'm feeling a bit crook today.* 2 **NOT WORKING PROPERLY** not working properly or in need of repair ○ *It's a bit crook this door; doesn't shut properly.* 3 **UNPLEASANT** nasty or unpleasant ○ *It was real crook that time we had our money stolen.* [12C. < Old Norse *krókr* 'hook'.] —**crookery** *n*

crooked /krŏŏkid/ *adj* 1 **WITH BENT SHAPE** sharply curved, bent, or twisted, often in more than one place 2 **AT ANGLE** not aligned properly ○ *That picture is crooked.* 3 **NOT LEGAL** illegal or dishonest *(informal)* —**crookedly** *adv* —**crookedness** *n*

Crookes /krŏŏks/, **William, Sir** (1832–1919) British chemist and physicist

croon /kroon/ *vti* 1 **SING OR MURMUR GENTLY** to sing or murmur something in a soft, low voice, especially to yourself or to a sleepy child 2 **SING SENTIMENTALLY** to perform a song or songs in a smooth sentimental style ■ *n* **GENTLE SINGING** singing in a soft low way, or something sung in this way [15C. < Middle Dutch *krōnen* 'to lament'.] —**crooner** *n*

crop /krop/ *n* 1 **PLANT GROWN FOR USE** any group of plants grown by people for food or other use, especially on a large scale in farming or horticulture 2 **AMOUNT PRODUCED** the amount harvested from a plant or area of land, during one particular period of time ○ *a good crop of tomatoes* 3 **ANIMALS REARED FOR PRODUCE** a group of animals reared in farming, or something produced from them ○ *a poor crop of lambs* 4 **GROUP OF PEOPLE OR THINGS** a number of things occurring, or people doing or being something, at the same time ○ *last year's crop of students* 5 **WHIP HANDLE** the handle of a whip 6 **SHORT HAIRSTYLE** a short hairstyle, usually for a woman 7 **POUCH IN GULLET OF BIRDS** a pouch in the gullet of many birds in which they store or partially digest food before regurgitating it to feed their young 8 **POUCH IN DIGESTIVE SYSTEM** a pouch in the digestive tract of an insect or earthworm ■ *v* (**crops, cropping, cropped**) 1 *vt* **CUT SOMETHING SHORT** to cut something short, e.g. hair or a lawn 2 *vti* **GRAZE** to eat the top parts of growing plants, especially grass 3 *vti* **GATHER PRODUCE** to cut or gather the produce of plants or of a cultivated area ○ *crop a field* 4 *vti* **PRODUCE CROP** to produce a crop, or make an area of land produce a crop ○ *The tomatoes cropped well this summer.* 5 *vt* **CUT PART OF PHOTO** to cut off or conceal unwanted parts of an image, especially a photograph [Old English *cropp* 'ear of grain' < Germanic, 'round mass']

crop out *vi* GEOL = **outcrop** *v.*

crop up *vi* to appear or arrive, especially unexpectedly or from time to time *(informal)* ○ *Her name keeps cropping up in conversation.*

crop circle *n* an area in a field of crops where the plants have been mysteriously flattened, usually overnight, into the shape of a circle or a more complex pattern

crop-dusting *n* the spraying of powdered fungicide or insecticide onto crops from the air

cropper /króppər/ *n* 1 a plant described in terms of its ability to yield produce ○ *a heavy cropper* 2 *US* AGRIC = **sharecropper** ◇ **come a cropper** 1 to experience a hurtful or embarrassing fall *(informal)* 2 to fail completely *(informal)*

crop rotation *n* a system of farming in which a piece of land is planted with different crops in succession, in order to improve soil fertility and control crop pests and diseases

crop top *n* a piece of clothing for women or girls, covering the upper body but cut short to end above the navel

croquet /krṓ kay, -ki/ *n* 1 **LAWN GAME WITH BALLS AND MALLETS** an outdoor game, usually played on a lawn, in which the players use long-handled wooden mallets to hit large wooden balls through a series of hoops (**wickets**) 2 **STROKE IN CROQUET** a stroke played in the game of croquet whereby a player knocks away an opponent's ball by hitting his or her own ball when the two are touching ■ *vti* (**-quets** /-kayz, -kiz/, **-queting** /-kaying, -ki ing/, **-queted, -queted** /-kayed, -kid/) **KNOCK SOMEBODY'S CROQUET BALL AWAY** to knock away an opponent's ball in the game of croquet by hitting your own ball when the two are touching [Mid-19C. < ?]

croquette /kro két/ *n* a little flat cake, cylinder, or ball of savoury mixture coated in egg and breadcrumbs, and fried [Early 18C. < French, < *croquer* 'to crunch' an imitation of the sound.]

crore /krawr/ (*plural* **crores** *or* **crore**) *n S Asia* ten million, especially ten million rupees [Early 17C. Via Hindi *kroṛ* < Sanskrit *koṭiḥ*.]

Crosby /krózbi/, **Bing** (1904?–77) US singer and actor. Born **Harry Lillis Crosby**

crosier /krṓzi ər, -zhər/, **crozier** *n* 1 a staff with a hooked end like a shepherd's crook, carried by Christian bishops, archbishops, or abbots, symbolizing their roles of caring for their congregations as shepherds tend flocks 2 a part of a plant that has a curled end, e.g. the frond of a fern [13C. < Old French *crosier* 'crook bearer' < *croce* 'crook'.]

cross /kross/ *n* 1 **TWO INTERSECTING LINES** a sign or mark (X) made of two straight lines that bisect each other, used to mark or cancel something, or as a signature by people who cannot write 2 **CHRISTIAN SYMBOL** a long vertical bar intersected at right angles, usually about two-thirds up, by a shorter horizontal bar, used as a symbol of Christianity, or of the Crucifixion 3 **Cross, cross WOODEN STRUCTURE JESUS CHRIST DIED ON** the specific wooden cross on which Jesus Christ was crucified 4 **CROSS-SHAPED DECORATION** a medal or emblem shaped like a cross 5 **WOODEN EXECUTION POST WITH CROSSBAR** an upright wooden post with a shorter post fixed across it at right angles towards the top, on which, formerly, people were nailed or hanged in public executions 6 **STONE MONUMENT** an upright stone or structure in the shape of a cross or holding a cross, erected to commemorate somebody or something *(often in placenames)* 7 **SOMETHING TO BE BORNE** a difficulty in somebody's personal life that is particularly testing, troubling, or painful ○ *What's happened to him is a shame, but we all have a cross to bear.* 8 **MIXTURE** a thing or person that results from blending two different kinds together and is neither one of them nor the other but something in between ○ *a cross between a mystery and a historical novel* 9 **PRODUCTION OF HYBRID** the process of producing a crossbreed or hybrid from genetically different individuals 10 **HYBRID INDIVIDUAL** an animal or plant produced by interbreeding two genetically different individuals 11 **PASSING OF BALL ACROSS PITCH** in football, a kicked pass that sends the ball across the field, usually in the air 12 **SIDEWAYS BLOW IN BOXING** a punch thrown at an opponent from the side, in response to and evading the opponent's jab or lead 13 **PASS ACROSS GOAL** a pass that sends the ball across the field, e.g., in hockey 14 **PIPE CONNECTION** a cross-shaped joint used to connect four pipes 15 **SOMETHING DISHONEST** something dishonest or fraudulent, especially a sports contest in which the outcome has been dishonestly decided before it begins *(slang)* ■ *v* 1 *vt* **MAKE CHEQUE PAYABLE ONLY THROUGH BANK** to draw two parallel lines across the front of a cheque, diagonally or vertically, meaning that it has to be paid into a bank account 2 *vti* **GO ACROSS** to move or move somebody or something from one side of something to the other ○ *We've already crossed the border.* ○ *The river's too swift to cross the horses here.* 3 *vti* **MEET AT ONE POINT** to meet at a particular place or time and then continue separately again ○ *A settlement grew up where two trade routes crossed.* 4 *vt* **PLACE THINGS ONE ACROSS THE OTHER** to put two things so that one lies across the other ○ *crossed her legs* 5 *vi* **BE EN ROUTE AT ONE TIME** to be travelling in opposite directions between the same two correspondents at the same time *(refers to letters and other forms of communication)* 6 *vti* **CONNECT TELEPHONE LINES WRONGLY AND CONFUSINGLY** to make an incorrect connection between telephone numbers or lines, so that two or more conversations intermingle with each other, or to be connected in this way *(often passive)* 7 *vt* **INTERBREED PLANTS OR ANIMALS** to interbreed or hybridize plants or animals that are genetically different 8 *vt* **MAKE CHRISTIAN BLESSING GESTURE WITH HAND** to draw the shape of a Christian cross in the air over somebody or something as a symbol of God's blessing 9 *vti* **PASS BALL ACROSS PITCH** in football and some other games, to make a pass that sends the ball across, rather than up or down, the field 10 *vt* **THWART** to do something that goes against somebody's wishes or that annoys or frustrates somebody ○ *I wouldn't cross her; she angers easily* 11 *vt* **WRITE LINE ACROSS LETTER T** to draw a horizontal line across the vertical line of a letter t, to complete the letter ■ *adj* **ANGRY** angry or indicating anger ○ *exchanged a few cross words* [Pre-12C. Via Old Norse *kross* < Old Irish *cros* < Latin *crux*.] —**crossability** *n* —**crossable** *adj* —**crosser** *n* —**crossly** *adv* —**crossness** *n*

cross off *vt* to remove something, especially a name or item written on a list, by drawing a line through it

cross out *vt* to cancel something, especially a word or item that is wrong or not wanted, by drawing a line through it

cross- *prefix* 1 crossing ○ *crossover* 2 opposing, opposite ○ *crosscurrent* 3 reciprocal, mutual ○ *cross-link* [< CROSS]

cross action *n* a legal proceeding brought by one who has been sued against the one who brought the original action or against a fellow defendant

crossbar /króss baar/ *n* 1 a bar that runs horizontally between two vertical posts, e.g. between goalposts or the uprights of a jump 2 a horizontal metal bar that runs from below the handlebars to below the saddle in a man's or boy's bicycle

crossbeam /króss beem/ *n* a beam that passes between two supports in the structure of a building

crossbearer /króss bairər/ *n* the bearer of a cross in front of a bishop or archbishop in a ceremonial procession

cross bedding *n* 1 layering of geological strata in which deposits were laid down at an angle with respect to those above and below, commonly seen in sandstone deposited as dunes 2 the layering of strata transverse to the main beds of stratified rock —**cross-bedded** *adj*

cross bench *n* one of the benches in a parliament where members sit if they belong to neither the governing party nor one of the main opposition parties *(hyphenated before nouns)* ○ *a cross-bench MP* [Mid-19C. < its position at right angles to the government and opposition benches.] —**crossbencher** /króss benchər/ *n*

crossbill /króss bil/ (*plural* **-bills** *or* **-bill**) *n* a large finch that has a beak with crossed tips that it uses to extract seeds from conifer cones. Native to: coniferous forests. Genus: *Loxia.*

crossbones /króss bōnz/ *npl* a representation of two human thighbones crossing each other in the middle, traditionally placed beneath a skull as a symbol of death. ♦ **skull and crossbones**

crossbow /króssbō/ *n* a medieval weapon, or its modern sports successor, consisting of a bow attached crosswise to a stock with a cranking mechanism and a trigger —**crossbowman** *n*

crossbreed /króss breed/ (**-breeds, -breeding, -bred** /-bred/, **-bred**) *vti* to breed new strains of plants or animals from genetically different individuals —**crossbred** /króss bred/ *adj, n*

cross-buttock *n* a wrestling throw in which the hip is used to pivot an opponent

crosscheck /króss chék/ *vt* 1 to make sure that something such as a fact or figure is correct by looking it up in other sources or asking another person 2 in hockey, ice hockey, and lacrosse, to obstruct an opposing player by using both hands to thrust a playing stick across his or her body —**crosscheck** *n*

cross-claim *n* a claim made against another party on the same side of a lawsuit, e.g. a fellow defendant

cross-country *adj* 1 **NOT ON ROAD OR TRACK** done over fields or hills, or through woods, not on roads or a specially prepared area ○ *a cross-country run* 2 **ACROSS A COUNTRY** from one side of a country to another or throughout a country ○ *The band embarked on a cross-country tour.* 3 **OPERATING OFF ROADS** designed or able to operate without roads ○ *a cross-country vehicle* ■ *n* **RACING OVER FIELDS** running, sporting activity, or a race or event, done off the roads

cross-country skiing *n* skiing on long narrow skis across open countryside on fairly level ground

crosscourt /króss kawrt/ *adj* hit or thrown from one side of a playing court towards the other, especially in tennis or basketball

cross cousin *n* a cousin who is related to somebody through a brother and sister, being either a father's sister's child or a mother's brother's child. ◊ **parallel cousin**

cross-cultural *adj* relating to or comparing two or more different cultures —**cross-culturally** *adv*

crosscurrent /króss kurrənt/ *n* 1 a current that flows across another current, mainly in water but also in air 2 a movement or trend that conflicts with the general one, especially a trend in people's ideas or opinions

crosscut /króss kut/ *adj* 1 **CUT AT ANGLE** describes something such as wood, meat, or fabric that is cut across its main grain 2 **FOR CUTTING ACROSS** made or used for cutting across the grain of wood ■ *vti* (**-cuts, -cutting, -cut**) **MOVE FROM ONE SHOT TO ANOTHER** to alternate repeatedly brief scenes from one filmed sequence with scenes from another to give the impression that the events they show are happening at the same time ■ *n* **1 CUT MADE ACROSS** a cut made across something, e.g. a long piece of timber **2 TUNNEL ACROSS VEIN OF ORE** a tunnel in a mine that cuts across a vein of ore **3 EXAMPLE OF FILM TECHNIQUE** an example of the film technique in which short segments of two or more scenes are alternated **4 SHORT CUT** a shorter and more direct route to place

crosscut saw *n* a saw used for cutting wood across the grain

crosscutting /króss kutting/ *n* repeated alternation between brief film sequences to give the impression that the events they show are happening at the same time

cross-dress *vi* to wear clothes usually worn by somebody of the opposite sex —**cross-dresser** *n* —**cross-dressing** *n*

cross-examine *vt* **1** to question a witness for the opposing side in a hearing or trial **2** to ask somebody a lot of detailed questions in a persistent or aggressive way (*informal*) —**cross-examination** *n* —**cross-examiner** *n*

cross-eyed *adj* an offensive term meaning having an eye alignment that makes one or both eyes turn in towards the nose

cross-fade *vti* in film or television editing, to gradually introduce a new sound or picture while causing another one to disappear

cross-fertilization, cross-fertilisation *n* **1** the fertilization of a female sex cell (**gamete**) of one individual by a male sex cell from a different individual, usually of the same species. ◊ **self-fertilization 2** PLANT SCI = **cross-pollination 3** the exchange of ideas between two groups, especially cultures, that produces benefits for both —**cross-fertile** *adj* —**cross-fertilize** *vti*

crossfield /króss feeld/ *adj* kicked or thrown from one side of a playing field towards the other, especially in football or rugby ○ *a crossfield pass*

crossfire /króss fīr/ *n* **1** shots that come from more than one place, in such a way that the lines of fire converge **2** heated or lively conversation, with different and opposing views and ideas being put forward, or an example of this

cross-grained *adj* **1** with an irregular grain or a grain that runs across the length **2** difficult to deal with because of stubbornness, contrariness, or bad temper (*informal*)

cross hairs, crosshairs /króss hairz/ *npl* a pair of fine lines or wires that cross at right angles inside a lens or sight, used, e.g. in focusing an optical instrument or in aiming a rifle

crosshatch /króss hátch/ *vti* to draw parallel or intersecting lines across part of a drawing or diagram, usually diagonally, especially to give the effect of shadow or different texture —**crosshatching** *n*

crosshead /króss hed/ *n* a sliding metal block securing one end of a piston rod to a connecting rod

cross-index *v* **1** *vt* to give a particular item one or more additional entries in an index, under different headings, as cross-references to it **2** *vti* to supply cross-references in something

crossing /króssing/ *n* **1 SOMEWHERE WHERE SOMEBODY CAN CROSS** a place that has been specially constructed, chosen, or marked out as somewhere where something, e.g. a road or a border, may be crossed **2 POINT WHERE ROUTES CROSS** a place where a railway line and a road, two railway lines, roads, or similar routes go across each other **3 JOURNEY ACROSS WATER** a journey across a body of water **4 CENTRAL AREA OF CROSS-SHAPED CHURCH** the place in a cross-shaped church where the nave and the transept meet

crossing-over *n* the interchange of segments between homologous chromosomes during cell division (**meiosis**), resulting in new combinations of gene types (**alleles**) and therefore variability in inherited characteristics. ◊ **recombination**

crossjack /króss jak/ *n* a sail on the mizzenmast of a ship

cross-legged /-légd, -léggid/ *adj* in a sitting position with the legs bent so that the knees are apart and the ankles are crossed in front ■ *adv* with one leg lying over the other ○ *sitting cross-legged*

crosslet /krósslit/ *n* on coats of arms, a cross that has a smaller cross at the end of each of its arms

cross-link *n* **cross-link, cross-linkage** a transverse connecting element such as an atom, chemical group, or covalent bond between parallel chains of a complex organic molecule, especially a polymer or protein ■ *vt* to join polymer chains by a cross-link

cross matching *n* the process of testing for the compatibility of a donor's and recipient's tissues before blood transfusion or tissue transplantation —**cross-match** *vt*

cross-multiply *vi* to multiply each numerator of two fractions by the denominator of the other —**cross-multiplication** *n*

cross of Lorraine *n* a cross with two horizontal bars, a short bar near the top and a longer one near the bottom [After LORRAINE]

Cross of Valour *n* the highest Canadian decoration for courage

crossopterygian /kro sópta ríjji ən/ (*plural* **-ans** *or* **-an**) *n* a bony fish with paired fleshy pectoral fins like limbs that is thought to be ancestral to amphibians and other land vertebrates. All except the coelacanth are extinct. Subclass: Crossopterygii. [Mid-19C. < modern Latin *Crossopterygii* < Greek *krossoi* 'fringe' + *pterux* 'wing'.] —**crossopterygian** *adj*

crossover /króss ōvər/ *n* **1 CROSSING OR TRANSFER POINT** a place for crossing from one side of something to the other, or from one line, system, or vehicle to another **2** GENETICS = **crossing-over 3 WIDENING OF POPULARITY** the process by which an artistic work becomes popular outside the category in which it originated **4 SOMETHING NOW POPULAR WITH DIFFERENT AUDIENCE** an artist, musician, artistic creation, or piece of music that has become popular outside one original category ■ *adj* **MIXING TWO DIFFERENT STYLES** resulting from a mixture of two different artistic categories or styles or from elements of one category becoming popular in another

cross-party *adj* involving two or more political parties ○ *Members of both government and opposition are arriving for cross-party talks.*

crosspatch /króss pach/ *n* a bad-tempered, touchy person (*dated informal*) [Late 17C. < CROSS 'annoyed' + PATCH 'fool'.]

crosspiece /króss peess/ *n* a piece that crosses a structure or implement from one side to the other, e.g. a beam in a building or part of the handle of a tool

ϟ **cross-platform** *adj* available for more than one type of computer or operating system

cross-ply *adj* used to describe tyres made with the strands of the fabric crossing each other diagonally. US term **bias-ply**

cross-pollination *n* the transfer of pollen from an anther of one flower to the stigma of another —**cross-pollinate** *vti*

cross product *n* MATH = **vector product**

cross-purpose *n* a conflicting or contrary purpose ◇ **at cross-purposes** not understanding each other, usually through not realizing that the other person means or intends something different

cross-question *vt* LAW = **cross-examine** *v.* 1 ■ *n* a lawyer's question to a witness being cross-examined in a court case

cross-reaction *n* the immunological reaction of one antigen with the antibodies developed against another similar antigen —**cross-react** *vi* —**cross-reactive** *adj* —**cross-reactivity** *n*

cross-refer *vti* to give a note that tells a reader of a book, index, or card catalogue to look in another specified part of the same work

cross-reference *n* a note, especially one printed in a book, index, or card catalogue, that tells a reader to look in another specified place for information ■ *v* **1** *vt* to provide a text, index, or card catalogue with cross-references **2** *vti* = **cross-refer**

cross-resistance *n* resistance developed by an organism to the effects of a toxin as a result of being exposed to a similar toxin

crossroad /króssrōd/ *n* US a road that runs across another one or that links two main roads

crossroads /krósstrōdz/ *n* (+ *singular verb*) **1** a place where two or more roads meet or cross each other **2** a time when an important decision must be made

crossruff /króss ruf/ *n* a tactic used in the games of whist and bridge, in which two partners alternately trump each other's first card (**lead**) in each round ■ *vti* to play a crossruff, or trump the card led by your partner or from the dummy in a crossruff [Late 16C. < CROSS- + RUFF[2].]

cross section *n* **1 PLANE CUTTING THROUGH AN OBJECT** a plane surface formed by cutting through an object at right angles to an axis, especially the longest axis **2 SOMETHING CUT IN CROSS SECTION** a piece cut as part of a cross section, or an image of such a piece ○ *draw a cross section of a cone* **3 REPRESENTATIVE SAMPLE** a sample of something that represents all or most of the different elements that the whole contains **4 PROBABILITY OF PARTICLE INTERACTION** a measure of the probability of any specific interaction such as fission or ionization occurring between two elementary particles —**cross-sectional** *adj*

cross-stitch *n* **1 EMBROIDERY STITCH** a stitch made up of two diagonal stitches crossing each other **2 EMBROIDERY IN CROSS-SHAPED STITCHES** pictures, designs, or items of needlework sewn using cross-stitches ■ *vti* **SEW USING CROSS-STITCH** to do embroidery using cross-stitches, or to make something in cross-stitch

crosstalk /króss tawk/ *n* **1** unwanted sounds or other signals picked up by one channel of an electronic communications system from another channel, e.g. between telephones or loudspeakers **2** conversation full of quick and witty lines and replies (*informal*) ○ *He sat quietly at the dinner table, too shy to take part in the scintillating crosstalk that flowed to and fro.*

cross-town, crosstown /króss town/ *adj* travelling or extending across a city or town —**crosstown** *adv*

crosstrainer /króss traynər/ *n* **1** an athlete who trains for more than one competitive sport simultaneously **2** a sports shoe designed for more than one sporting activity —**cross-train** *v*

cross training *n* fitness training in different sports, e.g. running and weightlifting, usually undertaken to enhance performance in one of the sports

cross-training *adj* designed to be used for more than one kind of sporting activity ○ *a cross-training bike*

crosstree /króss tree/ *n* either of a pair of horizontal pieces of wood or metal at the top of a ship's mast to which ropes are fixed to support the mast

cross vault, cross vaulting *n* a ceiling created by the crossing of two or more simple arched vaults (**barrel vaults**)

crosswalk /króss wawk/ *n* US TRANSP = **pedestrian crossing**

crossways /króss wayz/ *adv* **1** = **crosswise** *adv.* 1 **2** from one side or corner to another, in a slanting line

crosswind /króss wind/ *n* a wind that blows across a particular route, flight path, or direction of travel

crosswise /krósswīz/ *adv* **1 SIDEWAYS ACROSS** in such a way as to cross something or be positioned across it **2 IN A CROSS SHAPE** in the shape of a cross ■ *adj* **TRANSVERSE** crossing or lying across something else

crossword /króss wurd/, **crossword puzzle** *n* a puzzle in which numbered clues are solved and words that form the answers entered horizontally or vertically into a correspondingly numbered grid of squares

crostini /kro steéni/ *npl* small canapés made from toasted bread with a savoury topping such as olive paste or mushrooms [< Italian, 'little crusts']

crotch /kroch/ *n* **1 PLACE WHERE LEGS JOIN BODY** the part of the human body where the legs join the trunk **2 PART OF GARMENT COVERING GENITALS** the area of a pair of trousers or underpants that covers the wearer's genitals **3 PLACE WHERE TREE DIVIDES** a part of a tree where it forks into two branches **4 FORKED STICK** a pole or stick with a forked end, or the fork itself. ◊ **crutch** *n.* 4 [Mid-16C. Probably variant of CRUTCH.] —**crotched** *adj*

crotchet /króchit/ *n* **1** a musical note lasting a quarter of the time-length of a semibreve, shown as a black notehead with a stem. US term **quarter note 2** a whim or a perverse idea or opinion (*dated*) [14C. < Old French *crochet* (see CROCHET).]

crotchety /króchəti/ *adj* irritable and difficult to please (*informal*) —**crotchetiness** *n*

croton /krṓt'n/ (*plural* **-ton** *or* **-tons**) *n* **1** a tropical shrub or tree, some types of which are noted for their medicinal properties. Genus: *Croton.* **2** a tropical evergreen plant, grown for its leathery, variegated foliage. *Codiaeum variegatum.* [Mid-18C. Via modern Latin < Greek *krotōn* 'sheep-tick'; from the shape of its seeds (sense 1).]

crotonic acid /krō tónnik-/ *n* $C_4H_6O_2$ a colourless crystalline organic acid. Use: organic synthesis, manufacture of drugs and resins. [< CROTON]

croton oil *n* a yellowish brown oil extracted from the seeds of a croton tree. Use: formerly, as a purgative and counterirritant.

crouch /krowch/ *vi* 1 BEND DOWN LOW to squat down on the balls of the feet with knees bent and body hunched over ○ *I had to crouch to get under the table.* 2 BEND IN PREPARATION TO POUNCE to stay down close to the ground with legs bent, waiting to spring or run forwards (*refers to animals*) ○ *The mountain lion crouched in readiness to pounce.* ■ *n* SQUATTING POSITION the position of a human squatting with back and knees bent or of an animal with the body pressed low to the ground in readiness to spring [14C. Probably < variant of Old French *crochir* 'be crooked' < *croche* (see CROCHET).]

croup[1] /kroop/ *n* an inflammatory condition of the larynx and trachea, especially in young children, marked by a cough, hoarseness, and difficult breathing [Mid-18C. < *croup* 'to croak', probably an imitation of the sound.] —**croupy** *adj*

croup[2] /kroop/, **croupe** *n* the hindquarters of a four-legged animal, especially a horse. ◊ **crupper** *n.* 2 [13C. < Old French *croupe.*]

croupier /kroopi ay, -ər/ *n* somebody in charge of a gaming table who collects and pays out the players' money and chips, and deals the cards or spins the roulette wheel [Mid-18C. < French, 'person who rides behind'.]

crouton /kroo ton/ *n* a small piece, usually a cube, of fried bread used as a garnish for soups, salads, and other dishes (*usually plural*) [Early 19C. < French *croûton*, 'little crust' < *croûte* 'crust' < Latin *crusta* 'rind'.]

crow /krō/ *n* 1 LARGE BLACK BIRD a large bird with shiny black feathers and a raucous cry, of a family whose members are found in most parts of the world, including rooks and ravens. Genus: *Corvus.* 2 OFFENSIVE TERM an offensive term for a woman that deliberately insults the pitch of her voice (*slang*) 3 COCK'S LOUD CRY a long shrill call made by a bird, especially a cock ■ *vi* (**crowed** *or* **crew** /kroo/) 1 CRY LIKE COCK to give the loud shrill cry of a cock 2 CRY OUT HAPPILY to cry out with pleasure in the way that babies do 3 BRAG ABOUT to boast about personal success or celebrate about something another person has failed to do in a noisy and exuberant way [Old English *crāwe* (noun), Old English *crāwan* (verb) < Germanic] ◇ **as the crow flies** in a straight line ◇ **eat crow** *US* to be forced to admit that you have been wrong or have been humiliatingly defeated (*informal*)

Crow /krō/ (*plural* **Crow** *or* **Crows**) *n* 1 a member of a Native North American people who once lived on the plains of North Dakota and who now live in S Montana and Wyoming 2 the Siouan language of the Crow people. Native speakers: 5,000. [Early 19C. Translation of French (*gens de*) *corbeaux* 'raven people', translation of the Native American name.] —**Crow** *adj*

crowbar /krō baar/ *n* an iron or steel bar with one flattened, often bent or forked end that is used to lever things up or off ■ *vt* (**-bars, -barring, -barred**) to prise or force something using a crowbar (*informal*) [Mid-18C. Because the flattened end resembles a crow's foot.]

crowberry /krōbəri/ (*plural* **-ries**) *n* a low-growing evergreen shrub with edible black berries. Native to: colder regions. *Empetrum nigrum.*

crowd[1] /krowd/ *n* 1 PEOPLE GATHERED TOGETHER a large group of people gathered in one place 2 SET OF PEOPLE a group of people with something in common 3 AUDIENCE OR SPECTATORS a group of people attending the same public event or entertainment 4 THE MASSES the mass or majority of people 5 LARGE GROUP OF THINGS a large number of things put or found together ■ *v* 1 *vi* THRONG TOGETHER to assemble or move in large numbers 2 *vt* FILL OR PACK to fill or cover something or a place in large numbers or to capacity 3 *vti* PRESS NEAR to stand or move uncomfortably close to somebody or something 4 *vti* HERD OR CRAM to urge, herd, or force a closely packed group of people, animals, or things into a place 5 *vti* ADVANCE BY SHOVING to move forward by pushing and shoving, or shove past a person or barrier 6 *vt* PRESSURIZE to put pressure on somebody to do something or make somebody feel forced into an act [Old English *crūdan* 'to press'] —**crowded** *adj* —**crowdedness** *n* —**crowder** *n*

crowd out *vt* to exclude or push out somebody or something by force of numbers

crowd[2] /krowd/ *n* an ancient Celtic stringed instrument that was bowed or plucked [14C. < Welsh *crwth.*]

crowd pleaser *n* a person, object, event, or occasion that has great popular appeal —**crowd-pleasing** *adj*

crowd puller *n* a person, object, or event that is popular enough to draw a large audience or body of spectators

Crowe /krō/, **Russell** (*b.* 1964) Australian actor

crowfoot /krō fŏŏt/ *n* 1 PLANT WITH LEAVES LIKE CROW'S FOOT a plant related to the buttercup that has divided leaves resembling the feet of a crow. Flowers: small, yellow or white. Genus: *Ranunculus.* 2 PLANT RESEMBLING CROWFOOT any plant that has leaves resembling a bird's foot 3 (*plural* **-feet**) ROPES SUPPORTING AWNING a set of ropes to support an awning

crown /krown/ *n* 1 HEADDRESS SYMBOLIZING ROYALTY an ornate headdress worn as a symbol of sovereignty, often made of gold and set with gems 2 SYMBOL OF ACHIEVEMENT a wreath or circlet worn on the head as a symbol of victory, success, or high achievement 3 MONARCH the reigning monarch of a country 4 **Crown, crown** MONARCH'S POWER the power or authority vested in a monarch 5 EMBLEM RESEMBLING CROWN an emblem or ornament resembling or representing a crown 6 TOP-RANKING TITLE a title or distinction that signifies victory or supreme achievement 7 PINNACLE the highest point of quality, achievement, or fame 8 UPPERMOST PART the top part of something, especially a hill 9 TOP OF HEAD the top part of the head 10 TOP OF HAT the top part of a hat 11 VISIBLE PART OF TOOTH the visible part of a tooth, covered by enamel 12 ARTIFICIAL TOOTH an artificial replacement for the visible part of a tooth that has decayed or been damaged 13 CENTRE OF ROAD the middle of a road, especially a cambered one 14 BRITISH COIN a former British coin worth five shillings, now issued only to commemorate special events 15 EUROPEAN COIN any European coin, such as the Norwegian and Danish krone or the Swedish krona, whose name is translated as 'crown' 16 UPPER PART OF PLANT the upper part of a tree or shrub, consisting of the foliage and branches 17 ROOTS AND LOWER STEM OF PLANT the roots and lower stem of a plant, or a plant consisting only of these parts, used especially for propagation 18 PLANT SCI = **corona** *n.* 3 19 BIRD'S CREST the crest of a bird 20 TOP OF GEMSTONE the upper part of a cut gemstone 21 JUNCTION OF ANCHOR ARMS AND SHANK the junction where the arms of an anchor join the shank 22 WINDING KNOB ON WATCH a ridged winding knob on a watch 23 SIZE OF PAPER a size of paper equal to 38 by 51 cm/15 by 20 in ■ *vt* 1 CONFER ROYAL STATUS to make a person royal or place a crown on a person's head to symbolize royalty 2 REWARD SOMEBODY WITH CROWN to place a crown on somebody's head, especially in recognition of a victory, success, or achievement 3 RANK HIGHEST to confer the top rank on somebody 4 BE SUMMIT OF to be or form the top of something 5 PUT FINISHING TOUCH TO to complete or be the consummation or confirmation of something 6 FIT CROWN TO TOOTH to fit an artificial crown to a damaged or decayed tooth 7 TOP SOMETHING WITH SOMETHING ELSE to put something on or at the top of something else 8 HIT SOMEBODY ON HEAD to hit somebody over the head (*informal*) 9 MAKE INTO KING IN DRAUGHTS to promote an ordinary draughts piece to the status of king [12C. Via Anglo-Norman *corune* or Old French *corone* < Latin *corona* 'wreath, garland' < Greek *korōnē* 'something curved' < *koronis* 'curved'.]

Crown Agent *n* 1 somebody appointed by the Minister for Overseas Development to sit on a board that provides financial, commercial, and other services to some foreign governments and international organizations 2 a solicitor in Scotland engaged to prepare prosecution cases

Crown attorney *n Can* a lawyer who undertakes criminal prosecutions on behalf of a federal, provincial, or territorial government

crown cap *n* a metal cap with a corrugated edge, used to seal bottles of beer and other drinks

Crown Colony *n* a British colony in which the Crown has a whole or partial governing power

Crown Court *n* a court presided over by circuit judges that hears criminal cases in England and Wales

Crown Derby *n* a soft-paste porcelain manufactured in the city of Derby from 1784–1848 and usually marked with the letter 'D' surmounted by a crown

crowned head *n* a reigning monarch

crown gall *n* a disease of fruit and roses that results in swellings on the roots or stems and is caused by the bacterium *Agrobacterium tumefaciens*

crown glass *n* 1 a traditional window glass made by spinning a bubble of molten glass on the end of a rod until it forms a flat disc 2 high-quality glass with a low refractive index. Use: lenses.

crown green *n* a bowling green that is higher in the middle than it is at the edges

crown imperial (*plural* **crown imperials** *or* **crown imperial**) *n* a garden plant with a strong musky smell that grows from a bulb. Flowers: bell-shaped, orange or yellow, in a cluster at the top of a single tall stem. *Fritillaria imperialis.*

crowning /krówning/ *n* 1 INVESTITURE OF MONARCH the process or ceremony of making somebody a monarch 2 STAGE IN LABOUR the stage in giving birth at which an infant's head passes through the vaginal opening ■ *adj* 1 ULTIMATE IN ACHIEVEMENT representing supreme achievement or the ultimate moment in something 2 FORMING SUMMIT forming a crown or summit

crown jewel *n* 1 a particularly profitable or valuable corporate unit or asset 2 *US* the most valuable part of something, or the most prized asset

Crown jewels *npl* 1 the jewellery and regalia that a monarch wears on state occasions 2 the male genitalia, especially the testicles (*humorous slang*)

crown lens *n* a lens made of crown glass, especially the converging component of an achromatic lens

Crown Office *n* an office of the Queen's Bench Division of the High Court, responsible for administration

crown of thorns *n* 1 SPINY STARFISH a spiny starfish that feeds on live coral. Native to: Pacific. *Acanthaster planci.* 2 SHRUB WITH SCARLET BRACTS a shrub grown as a house plant or as a hedge in tropical areas. Flowers: with scarlet bracts. Native to: Madagascar. *Euphorbia milii.* 3 HEAVY BURDEN a painful or onerous burden [< the biblical accounts of the wreath of thorns placed on the head of Jesus Christ]

crownpiece /krówn peess/ *n* 1 a part that fits over or forms the top of something 2 a bridle strap that fits over a horse's head behind the ears

Crown prince *n* the principal male heir in a monarchy

Crown princess *n* the principal female heir in a monarchy, or the wife of a crown prince

Crown Prosecution Service *n* an independent body set up in 1986 to determine whether cases prepared by the police in England and Wales should be brought to trial

Crown prosecutor *n Can* LAW = **Crown attorney**

crown saw *n* a cylindrical saw with a row of teeth along one edge, designed for cutting round holes

crown vetch *n* a leguminous plant with small pink or white flowers. Native to: Europe. *Coronilla varia.*

crown wheel *n* a wheel in a clock or watch next to the winding knob, formed from two sets of teeth at right angles to each other

crow's feet *npl* a network of wrinkles radiating from the outer corner of the human eye [Because they resemble the footprints of crows]

crow's foot *n* 1 a sewing stitch with three points, used especially for finishing off a seam 2 a set of short ropes, used in airships and ballooning, that redistributes the pull of a single rope 3 MIL = **caltrop** *n.* 2 [< the shape]

crow's-nest *n* 1 a lookout point consisting of a railed platform at the top of a ship's mast or superstructure 2 a high enclosed lookout point on land

crow step *n* ARCHIT = **corbie-step** [Because only a small or perching animal could use it]

Croydon /króyd'n/ borough in South London. Population: 330,900 (1995).

croze /krōz/ *n* 1 a groove at the top of a barrel or cask into which the head is fitted 2 a cooper's tool used to cut grooves at the top of barrels and casks [Early 17C. < French *creux* 'hollow, groove', probably < Celtic.]

crozier *n* CHR, PLANT SCI = **crosier**

CRT[1] *abbr* cathode-ray tube

⚡**CRT**[2] (*plural* **CRTs**) *n* a computer monitor containing a cathode-ray tube

cru /kroo/ *n* 1 a vineyard or wine-growing area in France that meets specified standards of quality 2 an official grade of French wine [Early 19C. < French *crû*, past participle of *croître* 'grow' < Latin *crescere.*]

cruces plural of **crux**

crucial /kro͞osh'l/ *adj* **1 MOST VITAL** most vital and of the greatest significance in determining an outcome **2** ⚠ **IMPORTANT** very important or significant (*informal*) **3 EXCELLENT** great or excellent (*slang*) [Early 18C. < French, < Latin *cruc-* 'cross'.]

USAGE ***Crucial*** has the core meaning of decisive: *Her tie-breaking vote was crucial.* However, ***crucial*** has been trivialized to the point that it often means nothing more than 'important'. This is especially true in media reports: *If proportional representation is adopted, it is crucial (= important) to choose the best method.* Avoid overusing ***crucial*** in formal writing; it is better reserved for something decisive.

crucially /kro͞osh'li/ *adv* in a way that determines the outcome of something or has great impact and importance

crucian /kro͞osh'n/ (*plural* **-cians** *or* **-cian**), **crucian carp** *n* a carp that has a dark-green back, golden-yellow sides, and reddish fins. Native to: Europe, Asia. *Carassius carassius.* [Mid-18C. Alteration of Low German *karu(s)se* < Latin *coracinus*, a black fish of the Nile < Greek *korax* 'raven'.]

cruciate /kro͞oshi ət, -ayt/ *adj* **1** = **cruciform 2** describes insect wings that form a cross shape when at rest [Late 17C. < medieval Latin *cruciata* < Latin *crux* 'cross'.]

crucible /kro͞ossib'l/ *n* **1 CONTAINER FOR MELTING** a heat-resistant container in which ores or metals are melted **2 BOTTOM OF FURNACE** the hollow part at the bottom of a furnace where molten metal collects **3 ORDEAL** a severe trial or ordeal **4 TESTING CIRCUMSTANCES** a place or set of circumstances where people or things are subjected to forces that test them and often make them change [15C. < medieval Latin *crucibulum* 'nightlight, crucible'.]

LITERARY LINK ***The Crucible***, a play (1953) by US dramatist Arthur Miller. Intended as a metaphor for the 'un-American' McCarthy hearings of the 1950s, the play is set in Salem, Massachusetts, in 1692 and describes how the social fabric of a small town is ripped apart when a group of young girls start to denounce townsfolk as witches.

crucible steel *n* a high-grade steel made by mixing steel and additives in a furnace

crucifer /kro͞ossifər/ *n* **1** a plant such as the cabbage, turnip, broccoli, or wallflower, with long narrow seed pods. Flowers: with four petals in the shape of a cross. Family: Cruciferae. **2** a bearer of a cross, especially in a religious ceremony [Mid-16C. < ecclesiastical Latin, < Latin *cruc-* 'cross' + *-fer* 'bearer'.] —**cruciferous** *adj*

~~**crucifiction**~~ incorrect spelling of **crucifixion**

crucifix /kro͞ossifiks/ *n* a model or image of Jesus Christ on the Cross [12C. Via French < ecclesiastical Latin *crucifixus* < Latin *cruci fixus* 'fixed to a cross'.]

crucifixion /kro͞ossi fiksh'n/ *n* **1 EXECUTION BY HANGING ON CROSS** a form of execution used in ancient times that involved binding or nailing the victim to an upright cross until death **2 EXECUTION** an execution involving crucifixion **3 ORDEAL** a painful ordeal or victimization

Crucifixion *n* **1** the agony and death of Jesus Christ on the Cross at Calvary **2** a depiction of Jesus Christ on the Cross

cruciform /kro͞ossi fawrm/ *adj* shaped like a cross [Mid-17C. < Latin *cruc-* 'cross'.] —**cruciformly** *adv*

crucify /kro͞ossi fī/ (**-fies, -fying, -fied**) *v* **1** *vt* **EXECUTE BY CRUCIFIXION** to execute somebody by crucifixion **2** *vt* **TREAT SOMEBODY CRUELLY** to defeat, torment, or victimize somebody in a thorough or cruel way **3** *vr* **SEVERELY DISCIPLINE YOUR BODY** to severely punish your body as a form of self-discipline [14C. Via French *crucifier* < ecclesiastical Latin *crucifigere* < Latin *cruci figere* 'fix to a cross'.] —**crucifier** *n*

cruck /kruk/ *n* one of a pair of curved wooden timbers that supported the roof of some medieval English buildings [Late 16C. Probably variant of CROOK.]

crud /krud/ *n* **1 FILTH** a messy, dirty, or sticky substance (*slang*) **2 WASTE PRODUCT** an unwanted byproduct, especially in the nuclear industry **3 SOMEBODY OR SOMETHING CONTEMPTIBLE** a person or thing that is disgusting or worthless (*slang*) **4 SLUSHY SNOW** slushy snow that is unfit for good skiing (*informal*) **5 NONSENSE** absolute nonsense (*informal*) [14C. Earlier form of CURD.] —**cruddy** *adj*

crude /krood/ *adj* (**cruder, crudest**) **1 IN RAW STATE** in an unprocessed condition ○ *crude ore* **2 APPROXIMATE** not precisely accurate ○ *a crude estimate* **3 UNSKILFUL** roughly or unskilfully made or conceived ○ *a crude model of a ship* **4 UNCORRECTED OR UNEMBELLISHED** describes numerical results or collected data that have not been organized, analysed, adjusted, or altered in any way ○ *crude data* ○ *crude facts* **5 VULGAR** vulgar or obscene ○ *a crude gesture* ■ *n* INDUST = **crude oil** [14C. < Latin *crudus* 'raw, rough'.] —**crudely** *adv* —**crudeness** *n* —**crudity** *n*

crude oil *n* petroleum that has not yet been refined

crudités /kro͞odi tay/ *npl* small pieces of raw vegetables such as carrots and cucumber eaten as an appetizer or snack, often served with a dip [Mid-20C. < French, plural of *crudité* < Latin *cruditas* < *crudus* 'raw'.]

cruel /kro͞o əl/ (**-eller, -ellest**) *adj* **1** deliberately and remorselessly causing pain or anguish, or insensitive to the pain and anguish of others **2** bringing about pain and distress, or painful to bear [12C. Via French < Latin *crudelis*.] —**cruelly** *adv* —**cruelness** *n*

cruelty /kro͞o əlti/ (*plural* **-ties**) *n* **1 DELIBERATELY CRUEL ACT** an act that deliberately causes pain and distress **2 CONDITION OF BEING CRUEL** the quality or condition of being cruel **3 PSYCHOLOGICAL OR PHYSICAL PAIN** the infliction of pain, distress, or anguish, especially when it is long-term and considered extreme enough to be grounds for divorce [13C. Via Old French *crualté* < Latin *crudelitas* < *crudelis* 'cruel'.]

cruelty-free *adj* describes manufactured goods, especially cosmetics, that have been developed without being tested on animals

cruet /kro͞o it/ *n* **1 CONDIMENT CONTAINER** a small container for holding salt, pepper, oil, or vinegar **2 CONDIMENT SET** a set of matching cruets on a stand **3 SMALL BOTTLE USED IN COMMUNION** either of two containers that hold the water and wine used in Communion [13C. < Anglo-Norman, 'little flask' < Old French *crue* 'flask' < Germanic.]

Cruikshank /kro͝ok shangk/, **George** (1792–1878) British caricaturist and illustrator

cruise /krooz/ *v* (**cruises, cruising, cruised**) **1** *vti* **TRAVEL BY SEA** to travel by ship over a sea or other large body of water, usually calling at several places **2** *vi* **TRAVEL AT EASY RATE** to travel at a steady efficient rate, below top speed **3** *vti* **SEEK SEXUAL PARTNER** to go out looking for a sexual partner or frequent a public place in search of one (*slang*) **4** *vi* **PROCEED CASUALLY** to proceed in a leisurely casual way or with no particular destination **5** *vi* **PATROL SEA** to patrol an area of sea on the lookout for enemy vessels ■ *n* **TRIP BY SEA** a journey by ship for pleasure or for naval purposes [Mid-17C. < Dutch *kruisen* 'to cross' < *kruis* 'cross' < Latin *crux*.]

Cruise /krooz/, **Tom** (*b.* 1962) US actor. Born **Thomas Cruise Mapother IV**

cruise control *n* an electronic device in a motor vehicle that allows a selected speed to be maintained consistently

cruise missile *n* a long-range jet-propelled guided missile that flies low

cruiser /kro͞ozər/ *n* **1 SMALL WARSHIP** a fast and easily manoeuvrable warship that is smaller and less heavily armoured than a battleship **2** NAUT = **cabin cruiser 3 SOMETHING OR SOMEBODY THAT CRUISES** a vehicle that cruises, e.g. a ship, aircraft, or motor vehicle, or a person who cruises **4 SOMEBODY SEEKING SEXUAL PARTNER** a seeker of a sexual partner in a public place (*slang*) **5** BOXING = **cruiserweight** [Late 17C. < Dutch *kruiser* < *kruisen* (see CRUISE).]

cruiserweight /kro͞ozər wayt/ *n* a light heavyweight boxer with a maximum weight of 86 kg/190 lb

cruising radius *n* the maximum distance that a vessel or aircraft can travel without needing to refuel

cruller /krúllər/, **kruller** *n US* a small ring-shaped deep-fried cake [Early 19C. < Dutch *kruller* < *krullen* 'curl'.]

crumb /krum/ *n* **1 SMALL FRAGMENT OF BAKED FOOD** a very small fragment of bread, cake, biscuit, or similar food **2 SMALL AMOUNT** a tiny amount of something **3 INNER PART OF LOAF** the soft middle part of a loaf of bread **4 CONTEMPTIBLE PERSON** a contemptible person (*dated slang*) ■ *v* **1** *vt* **PUT CRUMBS ON OR IN FOOD** to coat or thicken food with crumbs, especially breadcrumbs **2** *vti* **CRUMBLE** to break bread, cake, or biscuits into small bits **3** *vt* **CLEAN CRUMBS FROM** to clear away crumbs from something [Old English *cruma* < Germanic]

crumble /krúmb'l/ *v* (**-bles, -bling, -bled**) **1** *vti* **REDUCE TO TINY BITS** to break or make something break into tiny bits **2** *vi* **DISINTEGRATE** to disintegrate or fall apart ■ *n* **PUDDING WITH CRUMB TOPPING** a baked pudding made from fruit topped with a crumbly mixture of flour, fat, and sugar baked until the top is crunchy. US term **crisp** *n.* **2** [15C. Probably < Old English *gecrymmian* 'break into crumbs' < *cruma* (see CRUMB).]

crumbly /krúmbli/ *adj* (**crumblier, crumbliest**) **1 EASILY CRUMBLED** tending to crumble readily **2 WITH MANY CRUMBS** containing or covered with many crumbs ■ *n* (*plural* **crumblies**) **OLDER PERSON** a mildly insulting term for an older person (*informal*) —**crumbliness** *n*

crumbs /krumz/ *interj* used to express dismay or shock (*dated informal*) [Late 19C. Alteration of CHRIST.]

crumby /krúmmi/ (**-ier, -iest**) *adj* **1** full of or covered with crumbs **2** soft and spongy in texture, like the inside of a loaf of bread **3** = **crummy** (*informal*)

crumhorn /krúm hawrn/, **krummhorn** *n* a double-reed medieval woodwind instrument with an upward curving tube [Late 17C. < German, 'crooked horn'.]

crummy /krúmmi/ (**-mier, -miest**) *adj* (*informal*) **1** inferior and of little worth **2** miserable or unwell [Mid-19C. Variant of CRUMBY.]

crump /krump/ *n* **SOUND OF BURSTING BOMB** the thudding sound of an exploding shell or bomb ■ *vi* **1 MAKE THUDDING NOISE** to make a thudding noise like the sound of an exploding shell or bomb **2 MAKE CRUNCHING NOISE** to make a crunching noise like the sound of footsteps in crisp snow [Mid-17C. An imitation of the sound.]

Crump /krump/, **Barry John** (*b.* 1935) New Zealand writer

crumpet /krúmpit/ *n* **1 CAKE COOKED ON GRIDDLE** a griddle cake with a slightly elastic texture and small holes that is made from a batter risen with yeast and is eaten toasted with butter **2** *Scotland* **THIN PANCAKE** a large thin pancake **3 OFFENSIVE TERM** an offensive term for a woman, or women collectively, regarded as sexually desirable or available [Late 17C. < ?]

crumple /krúmp'l/ *v* (**-ples, -pling, -pled**) **1** *vti* **CREASE AND WRINKLE** to become or make something become full of irregular creases and wrinkles **2** *vti* **COLLAPSE** to collapse, or make something collapse **3** *vi* **LOOK UPSET OR DISAPPOINTED** to lose the appearance of equanimity and control, especially when upset or disappointed and close to tears ■ *n* **WRINKLE** a crease or wrinkle in something [14C. < Old English *crump* 'curl up'.] —**crumply** *adj*

crumple zone *n* a part of a motor vehicle designed to absorb the impact of a collision by crumpling easily

crunch /krunch/ *v* **1** *vt* **MUNCH NOISILY** to crush crisp foods audibly with the teeth **2** *vti* **MAKE CRUSHING SOUND** to make or cause something to make a noisy crushing sound **3** *vt* **RAPIDLY PROCESS DATA** to process data or numbers at high speed (*informal*) ■ *n* **1 CRUSHING NOISE** a loud short sound made when something is crushed ○ *the crunch of footsteps on gravel* **2 DECISIVE MOMENT** a critical time or situation, especially one when a decision or action must be taken ○ *when it comes to the crunch* ■ *adj* **NEEDING DECISIVE ACTION** requiring a decision or action [Early 19C. Variant of *cranch*, an imitation of the sound.] —**crunchable** *adj* —**cruncher** *n*

crunchy /krúnchi/ (**-ier, -iest**) *adj* crisp and making a crunching sound when eaten or walked upon —**crunchily** *adv* —**crunchiness** *n*

crupper /krúppər/ *n* **1** a strap that passes under the tail of a horse and is attached to a saddle or harness to prevent it from sliding forwards **2** the hindquarters of a horse. ◊ **croup**² *n.* [14C. < Anglo-Norman *cropere* or Old French *cropiere*.]

crus /kruss, krooss/ (*plural* **crura** /kro͞orə/) *n* **1** the leg between the knee and ankle **2** a body part shaped like a leg or pair of legs [Late 16C. < Latin, 'leg'.] —**crural** /kro͞orəl/ *adj*

crusade /kroo sáyd/ *n* **1 crusade, Crusade RELIGIOUS WAR** a military expedition by European Christians in the 11th to the 13th centuries to retake areas in the Holy Land captured by Muslim forces **2 RELIGIOUSLY MOTIVATED EFFORT** a war or campaign that is religiously motivated, e.g. one with papal sanction **3 CONCERTED EFFORT** a vigorous concerted action to promote or eliminate something ■ *vi* (**-sades, -sading, -saded**) **1 CAMPAIGN** to make a vigorous or concerted effort to promote or eliminate something **2 FIGHT TO RETAKE HOLY LAND** to go on a religious crusade, especially one to retake the Holy Land in the 11th to the 13th centuries [15C. < medieval Latin *cruciata* < Latin *crux* 'cross'.]

crusader /kroo sáydər/ *n* **1 crusader, Crusader** a soldier who took part in any of the crusades **2** a vigorous campaigner for or against something

crusado /kroo sáydō, -zaádō/ (*plural* **-does** *or* **-dos**) *n* a gold or silver coin with a cross imprinted on it that was a unit of currency in Portugal between the 15th and 20th centuries [Mid-16C. < Portuguese *cruzado* (see CRUZADO).]

cruse /krooz/ *n* a small earthenware container used to hold liquids (*archaic*) [Old English *crūse* < Germanic]

crush /krush/ *v* **1** *vti* **COMPRESS** to compress somebody or something, or become compressed, causing injury, damage, or distortion **2** *vti* **CREASE** to crease a fabric or item of clothing, or become creased **3** *vti* **GRIND** to grind something, or become ground, into bits **4** *vt* **QUELL PROTEST** to put down a protest or movement using force **5** *vt* **OVERWHELM** to defeat, subdue, or suppress somebody or something overwhelmingly **6** *vt* **MASH FRUIT** to reduce fruit or vegetables to juice and pulp by pressing **7** *vt* **SQUASH** to exert physical pressure on somebody by hugging, pressing, or pushing **8** *vt* **OPPRESS** to oppress or burden somebody severely **9** *vt* **HUMILIATE** to humiliate somebody by the force of a remark, criticism, or argument **10** *vi* **CROWD TOGETHER** to move in a mass or crowd ■ *n* **1 CROWD OF PEOPLE** a crowd or mass, especially of people **2 CROWDING** a crowded situation or mass, especially of people, or an action that results in this **3 FRUIT DRINK** a drink containing the juice from crushed fruit **4 TEMPORARY ROMANTIC ATTRACTION** a temporary romantic infatuation (*informal*) ○ *a teenage crush* **5 OBJECT OF SOMEBODY'S CRUSH** the person who is the object of somebody's romantic infatuation (*informal*) [14C. < Anglo-Norman *crussier* or Old French *croissir*.] —**crushable** *adj* —**crusher** *n* —**crushing** *adj* —**crushingly** *adv*

SYNONYMS See ***love***.

crush bar *n* a bar in a theatre where drinks are served before performances and during intervals

crush barrier *n* a barrier, especially a temporary one, put up to restrain crowds and prevent people from being crushed

crushed /krusht/ *adj* describes a fabric or material that has been manufactured or treated to create permanent creases in it ○ *crushed velvet*

crushproof /krúsh proof/ *adj* made to resist being crushed, creased, or wrinkled

crust /krust/ *n* **1 OUTER PART OF BREAD** the thin, usually hard or crisp, outer part of a loaf or slice of bread **2 PIECE OF BREAD** a piece of bread that is mostly crust or is stale and dry **3 PASTRY FOR PIE** the pastry that wholly or partly encases a pie or tart **4 HARD UPPER LAYER** a crisp, hard, or thick outer layer or coating that develops on something **5 SCAB** a dry hardened outer layer of blood, pus, or other bodily secretion that forms over a cut or sore **6 SOLID OUTER LAYER OF EARTH** the thin outermost layer of the Earth, approximately one per cent of the Earth's volume, that varies in thickness and has a different composition from the interior **7 LAYER OF POTASSIUM TARTRATE** a thin layer of potassium tartrate that forms on the inside of some wine and port bottles as the contents mature **8 INCOME** a living (*informal*) ○ *just trying to earn a crust* ■ *vti* **1 FORM CRUST** to form into or develop a crust **2 MAKE OR BECOME ENCRUSTED** to cover something or become covered with a crust [14C. Via Old French *crouste* < Latin *crusta* 'rind, shell'.]

crustacean /kru stáysh'n/ *n* an invertebrate animal with several pairs of jointed legs, a hard protective outer shell, two pairs of antennae, and eyes at the ends of stalks. Subphylum: Crustacea. [Mid-19C. < modern Latin *Crustacea* (plural) '(things) having a shell' < Latin *crusta* 'shell'.] —**crustacean** *adj* —**crustaceous** *adj*

crustal /krúst'l/ *adj* describes the crust of the Earth or another astronomical object [Mid-19C. < Latin *crusta* 'shell'.]

crustie *n* = **crusty** *n*.

crustose /krústōss/ *adj* describes lichens or algae that resemble a crust on the surface they adhere to [Late 19C. < Latin *crustosus* < *crusta* 'shell'.]

crusty /krústi/ *adj* (**-ier, -iest**) **1 WITH CRUST** with a crisp crust ○ *crusty bread* **2 CURT** gruff, curt, and candid in speech ■ *n* **crusty, crustie** (*plural* **crusties**) **UNKEMPT PERSON** a dirty, unkempt person who leads an unconventional, unmaterialistic life, often in borrowed or temporary accommodation (*slang informal*) —**crustily** *adv* —**crustiness** *n*

crutch /kruch/ *n* **1 WALKING AID** a staff with a handgrip and a rest for the forearm or armpit, used to help somebody who is lame or injured to walk **2 SOMETHING PROVIDING HELP OR SUPPORT** something that sustains or supports somebody or something liable to collapse, fail, or falter **3** ANAT = **crotch** *n*. 1 **4 FORKED SUPPORT** a forked supporting piece for a boom, oar, or spar ■ *vt* **SUPPORT WITH CRUTCH** to support something with a crutch or similar object [Old English *cryc(c)* < Germanic]

crux /kruks/ (*plural* **cruxes** *or* **cruces** /kroo seez/) *n* **1 CRUCIAL POINT** an essential or deciding point or element in something, e.g. in an argument **2 PUZZLING PROBLEM** an extremely difficult or puzzling problem **3 ARDUOUS PART OF CLIMB** the most demanding part of a climb [Mid-17C. < Latin, 'cross'.]

Crux *n* the Southern Cross

crux ansata /krúks an sáatə/ (*plural* **cruces ansatae** /kroo seez an sáatee/) *n* = **ankh** [< Latin, 'cross with a handle']

Cruyff /kroyf/, **Johan** (*b*. 1947) Dutch footballer

Cruz /krooz/, **Celia** (*b*. 1924) Cuban-born US vocalist

cruzado /kroo zaádō/ (*plural* **-does** *or* **-dos**) *n* **1** a unit of currency used in Brazil between 1986 and 1990, equivalent to 100 centavos **2** a coin or note worth one cruzado **3** MONEY = **crusado** [Mid-16C. < Portuguese, < the past participle of *cruzar* 'mark with a cross' < Latin *crux* 'cross'.]

cry /krī/ *v* (**cries, crying, cried**) **1** *vti* **SHED TEARS** to shed tears as the result of a strongly felt emotion **2** *vti* **SHOUT** to call or shout out loudly **3** *vi* **MAKE DISTINCTIVE SOUND** to make a natural high-pitched call (*refers to a bird or animal*) **4** *vt* **GIVE SOMETHING AS REASON** to plead or profess something as a reason or explanation ○ *cry hardship* ■ *n* (*plural* **cries**) **1 INARTICULATE SOUND** a loud inarticulate expression of rage, pain, or surprise **2 SHOUT** a loud shout or call **3 CALL OF BIRD OR ANIMAL** the natural high-pitched call of a bird or animal **4 PERIOD OF WEEPING** an act or period of shedding tears **5 PUBLIC DEMAND** a public demand, especially an urgent one **6 BAYING OF HOUNDS** the sound of hounds baying as they chase their quarry **7 HOUNDS** a pack of hounds [13C. Via French *crier* < Latin *quiritare* 'raise a public outcry' < *Quirites* 'Roman citizens'.] ◇ **in full cry** in enthusiastic pursuit of something

LITERARY LINK ***Cry, the Beloved Country***, a novel (1948) by South African writer Alan Paton. It tells of a Black man's search for his sister and his son in Johannesburg, where he encounters the underside of life and the racial hatred that divides the country. The novel ends on a note of optimism on the issue of racial harmony.

cry down *vt* to say disparaging or belittling things about somebody or something
cry off *vi* to withdraw from something you had previously agreed to do (*informal*)
cry out *v* **1** *vti* to exclaim loudly because of pain, shock, or fear **2** *vi* to be in obvious and urgent need ◇ **for crying out loud!** used to express annoyance, impatience, frustration, or surprise (*informal*)
cry up *vt* to praise somebody or something highly

crybaby /krī baybi/ (*plural* **-bies**) *n* somebody, especially a child, who cries or complains a lot

crying /krī ing/ *adj* desperate or deplorable and demanding a remedy ○ *a crying shame*

cryo- *prefix* freezing, cold ○ *cryosurgery* [< Greek *kruos* 'icy cold' < Indo-European, 'freeze over']

cryobank /krī ō bangk/ *n* a place where biological material such as semen and body tissues can be stored at extremely low temperatures

cryobiology /krī ō bī óllәji/ *n* the branch of biology that studies how extremely low temperatures affect organisms —**cryobiological** /krī ō bī ə lójjik'l/ *adj* —**cryobiologically** *adv* —**cryobiologist** *n*

cryogen /krī ō jen/ *n* a substance, e.g. liquid nitrogen, used in producing extremely low temperatures

cryogenic /krī ō jénnik/ *adj* having or relating to extremely low temperatures —**cryogenically** *adv*

cryogenics /krī ō jénniks/ *n* a branch of physics that studies the causes and effects of extremely low temperatures (+ *singular verb*)

cryolite /krī ə līt/ *n* an uncommon white fluoride mineral containing sodium and aluminium. Use: source of aluminium. [Early 19C. < CRYO-; because first found in Greenland.]

cryometer /krī ómmitər/ *n* a thermometer that measures very low temperatures —**cryometry** *n*

cryonics /krī ónniks/ *n* the study or practice of keeping a newly dead body at an extremely low temperature in the hope of restoring it to life later with the help of future medical advances (+ *singular verb*) ■ *npl* the collective techniques involved in cryogenics (+ *plural verb*) [Mid-20C. Contraction of CRYOGENICS.] —**cryonic** *adj*

cryophilic /krī ō fíllik/ *adj* capable of living at low temperatures

cryophyte /krī ə fīt/ *n* an organism that can live or grow on snow or ice, e.g. an alga

cryoprecipitate /krī ō pri síppitət/ *n* a substance that is precipitated at low temperatures, especially a precipitate of blood containing a blood-clotting factor

cryopreservation /krī ō prézzər váysh'n/ *n* the process of storing semen, ova, corneas, embryos, or body tissue at extremely low temperatures for future use —**cryopreserve** /krī ō pri zúrv/ *vt*

cryoprobe /krī ō prōb/ *n* an instrument used in cryosurgery for cooling body tissue to low temperatures

cryoprotectant /krī ō prə téktənt/ *n* a substance, e.g. glycerol, used to protect stored living tissue from the effects of freezing

cryoscope /krī ə skōp/ *n* an instrument used for determining the temperature at which a liquid freezes

cryoscopy /krī óskəpi/ *n* the study or practice of determining the freezing point of liquids —**cryoscopic** /krī ə skóppik/ *adj*

cryostat /krī ə stat/ *n* a regulating device for maintaining a constant low temperature

cryosurgery /krī ō súrjəri/ *n* surgery in which low temperatures are applied, e.g. to destroy diseased tissue, or to seal down detached retinas —**cryosurgeon** /krī ō surjən/ *n* —**cryosurgical** *adj*

cryotherapy /krī ō thérrəpi/ (*plural* **-pies**) *n* medical treatment that involves cooling the body, especially by applying ice packs

crypt /kript/ *n* **1** an underground room or vault, often below a church, used as a burial chamber or chapel, or for storing religious artefacts **2** a small recess, tubular gland, or follicle in the body [Late 18C. Via Latin *crypta* < Greek *kruptē* 'vault', feminine of *kruptos* 'hidden'.]

crypt- *prefix* = **crypto-**

cryptanalysis /kríptə nálləsiss/ *n* the process or science of deciphering coded texts or messages —**cryptanalyst** /krip tánnəlist/ *n* —**cryptanalytic** /krípt anə líttik/ *adj* —**cryptanalytical** *adj*

cryptic /kríptik/ *adj* **1 AMBIGUOUS OR OBSCURE** deliberately mysterious and seeming to have a hidden meaning **2 SECRET** secret or hidden in some way **3 INDICATING SOLUTION INDIRECTLY** with an indirect solution or clue, e.g. crosswords, puzzles, or anagrams **4 USING CODES** using or relating to codes and similar techniques **5 PROTECTIVE** describes body markings and colour that camouflage an animal [Early 17C. Via late Latin *crypticus* < Greek *kruptikos* < *kruptē* (see CRYPT).] —**cryptically** *adv* —**crypticness** *n*

SYNONYMS See ***obscure***.

crypto- *prefix* secret, hidden ○ *cryptogram* [< Greek *kruptos* < *kruptein* 'to hide']

cryptococcosis /kríptōkə kóssiss/ *n* an infectious disease that affects parts of the body, especially the brain and central nervous system, with lesions or abscesses caused by the fungus *Cryptococcus neoformans* [Mid-20C. < modern Latin *Cryptococcus*.]

cryptococcus /kríptō kókəss/ (*plural* **-cocci** /-kókī/) *n* a fungus that resembles a yeast, some types of which cause illnesses, e.g. cryptococcosis. Genus: *Cryptococcus*. [Early 20C. < modern Latin, 'hidden coccus'.]

cryptocrystalline /kríptō krístəlīn/ *adj* describes rocks that are composed of crystals too small to be seen with a petrological microscope

cryptogam /kríptə gam/ *n* an organism that reproduces by means of spores instead of seeds, as do ferns, moss, algae, and fungi [Late 18C. Via French < modern Latin *cryptogamus* 'hidden marriage' (because the means of reproduction is not apparent).] —**cryptogamic** /kríptə gámmik/ *adj* —**cryptogamous** /krip tóggəməss/ *adj*

cryptogenic /kríptō jénnik/ *adj* MED = **idiopathic**

cryptogram /kríptə gram/ *n* **1** a text or message that is in code or cipher **2** a symbol with a secret meaning or significance

ϟ **cryptographic key** *n* a parameter that determines the transformation of data to encrypted format, measured in bits (*in e-commerce*)

cryptography /krip tóggrəfi/ n 1 the study or analysis of codes and coding methods 2 coded or secret writing —**cryptograph** /kríptə graaf, -graf/ n —**cryptographer** n —**cryptographic** /kríptə gráffik/ adj —**cryptographical** adj —**cryptographically** adv

cryptology /krip tólləji/ n 1 = cryptography n. 1 2 = cryptanalysis —**cryptologic** /kríptə lójjik/ adj —**cryptological** adj —**cryptologist** n

cryptomeria /kríptō meèri ə/ n a tall coniferous tree with curved needle-shaped leaves arranged in spirals. Native to: China, Japan. *Cryptomeria japonica.* [Mid-19C. < modern Latin, 'hidden part', because its seeds are hidden by scales.]

cryptorchid /krip táwrkid/ n a male human or animal with one or both testicles that have failed to descend into the scrotum [Late 19C. < CRYPTORCHISM.]

cryptorchism /krip táwrkizəm/, **cryptorchidism** /-táwrkidizəm/ n a developmental condition affecting humans or animals in which one or both testicles fail to descend into the scrotum [Late 19C. < CRYPTO- + Latin *orchis* 'testicle' < Greek *orkhis*.]

cryptosporidiosis /kríptōspə ríddi ōssiss/ n an infectious condition of humans and domestic animals, characterized by fever, diarrhoea, and stomach cramps, and spread by a protozoan of the genus *Cryptosporidium* [< CRYPTOSPORIDIUM]

cryptosporidium /kríptōspə ríddi əm/ (*plural* -**a** /-ə/) n a water-borne protozoan parasite that contaminates drinking water supplies, causing intestinal infections in human beings and domestic animals [Late 20C. < modern Latin, < Greek *kruptos* 'hidden' + *sporidium* 'little spore' < *spora* (see SPORE).]

cryptozoic /kríptō zó ik/ adj describes invertebrates that live in dark or concealed places, e.g. under stones or in caves or holes

Cryptozoic adj belonging to a geological time in which only a few very primitive organisms existed —**Cryptozoic** n

cryptozoology /kríptō zoo óllǝji/ n the study of legendary creatures like the Loch Ness monster or the Yeti —**cryptozoological** /kríptō zoo ə lójjik'l/ adj —**cryptozoologist** n

cryst. abbr 1 crystalline 2 crystallography

crystal /kríst'l/ n 1 QUARTZ a clear colourless mineral, especially quartz 2 PIECE OF CRYSTAL a piece of a mineral in crystal form 3 SOLID WITH REPETITIVE INTERNAL STRUCTURE a solid containing an internal pattern of atoms, molecules, or ions that is regular, repeated, and geometrically arranged 4 OBJECT LIKE CRYSTAL something that has the form of a crystal, e.g. a frozen snowflake or a grain of salt 5 HEAVY GLASS a heavy transparent sparkling glass 6 CRYSTAL GLASS OBJECTS things made from crystal 7 ELECTRONIC COMPONENT a crystalline substance that has semiconducting or piezoelectric properties and is used as an electronic component, or the electrical device using it 8 = watch glass n. 1 9 US DRUGS = crank¹ n. 4 (slang) ■ adj VERY CLEAR clear and sparkling [Pre-12C. Via French *cristal* < Latin *crystallum* < Greek *krustallos* 'ice'.]

crystal ball n 1 a clear solid sphere of glass or rock crystal that is used by a fortune teller to predict the future 2 any means used to predict future events

crystal clear adj 1 clean and sparkling 2 clear or obvious to the understanding

crystal gazing n predicting the future by any questionable means, most commonly by staring into a crystal ball in the belief that images of future events will appear —**crystal gazer** n

crystal healing n use of pieces of crystal that are supposed to promote health and increase well-being

crystall- prefix = crystallo- (*before vowels*)

crystal lattice n the regular array of points in space that are occupied by the atoms, ions, or molecules that make up a crystal

crystalliferous /krístə líffərəss/, **crystalligerous** /krístə líjjərəss/ adj forming or containing crystals

crystalline /krístə līn/ adj 1 relating to, made of, containing, or resembling crystals 2 clear and sparkling —**crystallinity** /krístə línnəti/ n

crystalline lens n the transparent lens behind the iris in the eyes of vertebrates

crystallise vti = crystallize

crystallite /krístə līt/ n a tiny rudimentary crystal, e.g. of a type found in some igneous rocks —**crystallitic** /krístə líttik/ adj

crystallize /krístə līz/ (-**lizes, -lizing, -lized**), **crystallise** (-**lises, -lising, -lised**) vti 1 MAKE OR BECOME WELL DEFINED to become or make an idea or feeling become fixed or definite 2 FORM CRYSTALS to form or make something form crystals 3 COAT WITH SUGAR CRYSTALS to coat or impregnate something, or become coated or impregnated, with crystals, especially sugar crystals —**crystallizability** /krístə bíllǝti/ n —**crystallizable** adj —**crystallization** /krístə lī záysh'n/ n —**crystallizer** n

crystallo- prefix crystal, crystalline ○ *crystallography* [< Greek *krustallos* 'ice']

crystallography /krístə lóggrǝfi/ n a branch of science dealing with the formation and properties of crystals —**crystallographer** n —**crystallographic** /krístəla gráffik/ adj —**crystallographically** adv

crystalloid /krístə loyd/ adj LIKE CRYSTAL with the structure, properties, or appearance of a crystal ■ n 1 SUBSTANCE FORMING CRYSTALS a substance that in solution can pass through a semipermeable membrane 2 PROTEIN IN PLANT CELL a mass of protein resembling a crystal that commonly occurs in seeds and other storage organs —**crystalloidal** /krístə lóyd'l/ adj

crystal meth n US DRUGS = crank¹ n. 4 (slang)

Crystal Palace n a large glass building designed for the Great Exhibition in Hyde Park, London, in 1851, later moved to south London and destroyed by fire in 1936

crystal pleat n one of a series of permanently pressed pleats of varying widths, often in a sheer fabric

crystal set n an early form of radio receiver that used a quartz crystal as a detector

crystal violet n a dye derived from gentian violet used as a biological stain and a dermatological antiseptic

Cs symbol caesium

CS abbr 1 civil service 2 chartered surveyor 3 Court of Session 4 capital stock 5 Christian Science 6 Christian Scientist 7 chief of staff

CSA abbr Child Support Agency

csardas n DANCE, MUSIC = czardas

CSB abbr chemical stimulation of the brain

CSC abbr cosecant

CSC abbr Civil Service Commission

CSE n a school-leaving certificate in England and Wales that was replaced in 1988 by the GCSE. Full form **Certificate of Secondary Education**

CSEU abbr Confederation of Shipbuilding and Engineering Unions

CSF abbr cerebrospinal fluid

CS gas n $C_6H_5ClN_2$ a gas that causes tears, salivation, and painful breathing [Abbreviation of *Corson-Stoughton* after B. B. *Corson* (b. 1896) and R. W. *Stoughton* (1906–57), US chemists.]

CSIRO abbr Commonwealth Scientific and Industrial Research Organization

CSM abbr Company Sergeant-Major

CSO abbr Central Statistical Office

CSS abbr Certificate in Social Service

CST abbr 1 Central Standard Time 2 convulsive shock treatment

CSU abbr Civil Service Union

CSYS abbr Scotland Certificate of Sixth Year Studies

ct abbr 1 cent 2 certificate

CT abbr 1 Central Time 2 computerized tomography 3 US Connecticut

Ct. abbr 1 US Connecticut 2 Count (*in titles*)

CTC abbr 1 City Technology College 2 Cyclists' Touring Club

CTD abbr cumulative trauma disorder

ctenidium /ti níddi əm/ (*plural* -**a** /-di ə/) n a gill found in molluscs that has a central axis with a fringe of filaments on either side [Late 19C. Via modern Latin < Greek *ktenidion* 'little comb' < *kteis* 'comb'.]

ctenoid /teèn oyd, ténnoyd/ adj describes fish scales that have tiny projections like the teeth of combs, or fish that have such scales [Mid-19C. < Greek *kten-* 'comb'.]

ctenophore /ténnə fawr, teènə-/ n a marine invertebrate animal resembling a jellyfish but with eight rows of undulating filaments used for swimming. Phylum: Ctenophora. [Late 19C. < modern Latin *ctenophorus* < Greek *kten-* 'comb'.] —**ctenophoran** /ti nóffərən/ adj, n

ctn abbr 1 carton 2 cotangent

⚡**C to C** /seè tə seè/, **C2C** adj relating to Internet transactions between two consumers (*in e-commerce*) Full form **consumer-to-consumer**

⚡**CTRL, Ctrl** abbr control key

⚡**CTRL-ALT-DEL** n a combination of three computer keys, labelled control (CTRL), alternate (ALT), and delete (DEL), that are struck together to reboot a computer

CT scan n a diagnostic medical scan in which cross-sectional images of the body part are formed through computerized axial tomography and shown on a computer screen. US term **CAT scan** n.

CT scanner n a radiological diagnostic scanning machine used to make a CT scan. US term **CAT scanner**

CTV abbr Canadian Television Network Limited

⚡**CU** abbr Cuba (*in Internet addresses*)

Cu symbol copper¹

cu. abbr cubic

cuadrilla /kwaa dreèyə/ n a group of three banderilleros and two picadors who assist a matador in the bullring [Mid-19C. < Spanish, 'little square' (from a formation used) < *cuadra* 'square' < Latin *quadr-*.]

cub /kub/ n 1 YOUNG OF CARNIVOROUS MAMMAL an offspring of some carnivorous mammals, e.g. a bear, lion, or tiger 2 YOUNG PERSON a cheeky young person (*dated*) 3 *Ireland* a boy (*informal regional*) ■ vi (**cubs, cubbing, cubbed**) 1 PRODUCE YOUNG to give birth to an animal cub 2 HUNT FOX CUBS to hunt fox cubs [Mid-16C. < ?] —**cubbish** adj —**cubbishly** adv

Cub /kub/ n YOUTH ORG = Cub Scout

Cuba

Cuba /kyoóbə/ republic in the Caribbean Sea composed of two main islands and over 1,000 islets. Capital: Havana. Population: 10,999,139 (1997). Area: 114,525 sq. km/44,218 sq. mi. —**Cuban** adj, n

cubage /kyoóbij/ n the cubic content or volume of a solid. US term **cubature** n. 2

Cuba libre /kyoóbə leèbray/ n a drink made by mixing rum, cola, ice, and lime juice [< American Spanish, 'free Cuba' (a toast used during the Cuban War of Independence, 1895–98)]

Cuban heel n a straight broad heel of medium height for a shoe

cubature /kyoóbəchər/ n the process of working out the cubic content or volume of a solid [Late 17C. < CUBE¹.]

cubbyhole /kúbbi hōl/, **cubby** (*plural* -**bies**) n 1 a small space or room 2 a small storage compartment

cube¹ /kyoob/ n 1 SOLID FIGURE OF SIX EQUAL SIDES a solid figure of six equal square plane faces, each set at right angles to the four sides adjacent to it 2 CUBE-SHAPED OBJECT a solid shaped like a cube 3 PRODUCT OF THREE EQUAL NUMBERS the product of three equal numbers or quantities multiplied together, usually written in mathematical notation as a raised 3, e.g. 4^3 means $4 \times 4 \times 4$ ■ vt (**cubes, cubing, cubed**) 1 DICE to cut up a shape food into cubes 2 MULTIPLY ITEM BY ITSELF TWICE to multiply a number or quantity by itself twice, e.g. 6 cubed is $6 \times 6 \times 6$ 3 WORK OUT CUBIC CONTENT to calculate the cubic content of something [Mid-16C. Directly or via French < Latin *cubus* < Greek *kubos* 'cube, pelvis'.] —**cuber** n

cube[2] /kyoō bay, koō-/, **cubé** n 1 a root extract containing rotenone. Use: insecticides, fish poison. 2 a leguminous woody plant. Use: source of rotenone. Native to: tropical America. Genus: *Lonchocarpus*. [Early 20C. < American Spanish.]

cubeb /kyoō beb/ n 1 a small unripe spicy berry of a climbing plant. Use: formerly, to treat respiratory and urinary disorders. 2 a climbing plant with heart-shaped leaves, spikes of small flowers, and brownish berries. Native to: SE Asia. *Piper cubeba*. [13C. Via French *cubèbe* < Arabic *kubāba*.]

cube root n a number or quantity that, when multiplied by itself twice, equals a given number or quantity

cubic /kyoōbik/ adj cubic, cubical 1 CUBE-SHAPED shaped like a cube 2 WITH THREE DIMENSIONS with three measurable dimensions 3 DESCRIBING VOLUME BY COMPARING WITH CUBE describes a volume or capacity that is equal to that of a specified cube 4 RELATING TO OR CONTAINING CUBED VARIABLE describes a mathematical expression or equation in which at least one variable is cubed but no variable is to be multiplied by itself more than two times ○ *a cubic equation* 5 WITH THREE EQUAL AXES (*symbol* c) describes a crystal that has three equal perpendicular axes ■ n MATHEMATICAL EQUATION a cubic expression, equation, or curve —**cubically** adv

cubicle /kyoōbik'l/ n a small partitioned area for private use in a larger, more public room, e.g. a changing room or dormitory [15C. < Latin *cubiculum* 'bedroom' < *cubare* 'lie down'.]

cubic measure n a unit or system for measuring volume or capacity

cubic zirconia n a synthetic gemstone resembling a diamond

cubiform /kyoōbi fawrm/ adj shaped like a cube

cubism /kyoōbizəm/, **Cubism** n an artistic style, chiefly in painting and sculpture, that developed in the early 20th century and emphasized the representation of natural forms as geometric shapes seen from several angles [Early 20C. < French *cubisme* < *cube* (see CUBE[1]).] —**cubist** n —**cubistic** /kyoō bístik/ adj —**cubistically** adv

QUICK FACTS ON... CUBISM

Key dates: 1908–late 1910s
Key locations: Paris
Key elements: abandonment of traditional perspective and lighting; representation of objects as series of intersecting planes, suggesting multiple viewpoints; limited palette; shallow pictorial space, unified surface
Key figures: Pablo Picasso, Georges Braque, Juan Gris, Jean Metzinger, Albert Gleizes, Robert Delaunay, Fernand Léger
Key works: *Violin and Palette* (Braque) 1909–10, *The Portuguese* (Braque) 1911, *Ma Jolie* (Picasso) 1911, *Still Life with Chair Caning* (Picasso) 1912, *La Ville de Paris* (Delaunay) 1912, *Still Life (Fantomas)* (Gris) 1915
Key developments: abstraction, collage, orphism, futurism, vorticism, suprematism, constructivism, De Stijl, Dada

cubit /kyoōbit/ n an ancient unit of length, equal to the distance from the elbow to the tip of the middle finger, approximately 43–56 cm / 17–22 in [14C. < Latin *cubitum* 'elbow, forearm'.]

cubital /kyoōbit'l/ adj relating to the elbow, ulnar bone, or forearm [15C. < Latin *cubitalis* < *cubitum* 'elbow'.]

cuboid /kyoō boyd/ n 1 SOLID FIGURE OF SIX RECTANGULAR PLANES a solid figure of six rectangular plane faces, each set at right angles to the four sides adjacent to it 2 BONE IN FOOT the outermost tarsal bone of the foot in vertebrates ■ adj CUBE-SHAPED shaped like a cube —**cuboidal** /kyoō bóyd'l/ adj

cub reporter n a young inexperienced newspaper reporter

Cubs n a Cub Scout meeting (+ *singular verb*) ○ *going to Cubs*

Cub Scout n a member of the branch of the Scout Association for younger children, generally 8 to 11 years of age

cucking stool /kúking-/ n a punishment used in medieval times in which somebody was tied to a stool and pelted with rotting food [< obsolete *cuck* 'defecate' < N Germanic; because a commode was sometimes used]

cuckold /kúkōld/ n a husband whose wife has been unfaithful to him ■ vt to make a cuckold of a husband [Pre-

12C. < Old N French, variant of Old French *cucuault* < *cucu* 'cuckoo'.] —**cuckoldry** n

Cuckoo

cuckoo /koókoō/ n (*plural* -**oos**) 1 BIRD LAYING IN OTHERS' NESTS a songbird that lays its eggs in the nests of other birds, who bring the nestlings up as their own. Native to: Europe. *Cuculus canorus*. 2 RELATED BIRD a bird related to the European cuckoo 3 CUCKOO'S CALL the characteristic two-note call of the European cuckoo 4 ECCENTRIC PERSON an eccentric or extremely unconventional person (*informal*) ■ adj BIZARRE very eccentric or extremely unconventional (*informal*) ■ vi (-**oos**, -**ooing**, -**ooed**) GIVE THE CALL OF THE CUCKOO to make the characteristic two-note call of the cuckoo [13C. < Old French *cucu*, an imitation of its call.]

cuckoo clock n a clock that indicates the hour with the sound of a cuckoo's call and the appearance of a mechanical bird

cuckooflower /koó koo flowər/ n a plant often found in moist meadows. Flowers: light purple or occasionally white, with yellow anthers. *Cardamine pratensis*. [Late 16C. Because the plant is in flower at about the time of year when the European cuckoo is first heard.]

cuckoopint /koó koo pīnt/ n a perennial plant with leaves shaped like arrowheads and flowering stems consisting of a yellowish-green cone around a reddish-purple spike that later carries poisonous scarlet berries. Native to: Europe. *Arum maculatum*. [15C. Shortening of *cuckoo pintle* 'cuckoo penis'; from the shape of the spadix.]

cuckoo spit n a white frothy secretion found on the stems and leaves of plants, produced by the larva of insects like the frog-hopper [Because it was believed to have been spat out by cuckoos]

cuckoo wasp n a solitary wasp known for laying its eggs in the nests of other wasps and bees. Family: Chrysididae.

cucumber /kyoō kumbər/ n (*plural* -**bers** *or* -**ber** US) n 1 a long fruit with dark green peel and crisp white watery flesh that is usually eaten raw in salads and sandwiches or pickled 2 a climbing or trailing annual plant of the gourd family that produces cucumbers. *Cucumis sativus*. ◊ **squirting cucumber** [14C. < Latin *cucumer-*, by association with Old French *cocombre*.] ◊ **cool as a cucumber** calm and composed, especially under pressure

cucurbit /kyoō kúrbit/ n a tropical or subtropical climbing or trailing plant of the gourd family with large, fleshy, tough- or hard-skinned fruits, e.g. cucumber, watermelon, or pumpkin. Family: Cucurbitaceae. [14C. Via French *cucurbite* < Latin *cucurbita* 'gourd'.]

Cúcuta /koókətə/ capital of Norte de Santander Department, NE Colombia. Population: 459,887 (1993).

cud /kud/ n partly digested food that cows and other ruminants return to the mouth, after it has passed into the first stomach, to chew again as an aid to digestion [Old English *cudu* < Indo-European, 'sticky substance']

cuddle /kúd'l/ v (-**dles**, -**dling**, -**dled**) 1 vti TENDERLY HUG OR NESTLE to nestle together or hold somebody or something close for affection, warmth, or comfort 2 vi ASSUME COMFORTABLE POSITION to get into a warm comfortable position ■ n TENDER HUG a prolonged hug or embrace given to comfort or show affection [Early 16C. < ?] —**cuddler** n

cuddle up vi to assume a relaxed comfortable position alone or close to another person

cuddlesome /kúdd'lsəm/ adj = **cuddly** adj. 1

cuddly /kúdd'li/ (-**dlier**, -**dliest**) adj 1 pleasant to hold because of being soft, warm, or endearingly attractive 2 given to or fond of cuddling

cuddy[1] /kúddi/ (*plural* -**dies**) n 1 SMALL CABIN ON BOAT a small cabin or galley on a boat 2 OFFICERS' MESS the officers' mess on a ship 3 SMALL ROOM a small room or closet [Mid-17C. Probably via early modern Dutch *kajute* < French *cahute* 'shanty'.]

cuddy[2] /kúddi/ (*plural* -**dies**) n *Scotland* a donkey or horse (*informal*) [Early 18C. < ?]

cudgel /kújjəl/ n a heavy stick used as a weapon ■ vt (-**els**, -**elling**, -**elled**) to beat somebody with a cudgel [Old English *cycgel* < ?] ◊ **take up the cudgels** to defend or support a person or cause actively and energetically

cudweed /kúd weed/ (*plural* -**weeds** *or* -**weed**) n a plant of the daisy family that has woolly leaves. Flowers: white or yellow, in clusters. Native to: temperate regions worldwide. Genera: *Gnaphalium* and *Filago*.

cue[1] /kyoo/ n 1 SIGNAL TO SPEAK OR ACT something said or done that provides the signal for somebody, especially an actor or performer, to say or do something 2 PROMPT OR REMINDER something that prompts or reminds somebody to do something ○ *I took my cue from my brother and said nothing.* 3 RESPONSE-PRODUCING STIMULUS a stimulus or pattern of stimuli, often not consciously perceived, that results in a specific learned behavioural response ■ vt (**cues, cueing, cued**) GIVE SIGNAL OR PROMPT TO to give somebody, especially an actor or performer, a signal to say or do something [Mid-16C. < ?]

SPELLCHECK Do not confuse *cue* with *queue*, which has a similar sound. Beware: your spellchecker will not catch this error.

cue in vt 1 GIVE SIGNAL TO to signal that it is now time for somebody, especially a performer, to say or do something ○ *The conductor will cue you in.* 2 INSTRUCT OR REMIND to give somebody information, instructions, or a reminder 3 INSERT INTO PERFORMANCE to insert something such as a speech or song into a performance

cue[2] /kyoo/ n 1 STICK USED TO KNOCK BALL a long tapering stick used to strike the cue ball in games such as billiards, snooker, or pool 2 HAIR, HIST = **queue** n. 4 ■ vt (**cues, cueing, cued**) 1 STRIKE WITH CUE to strike a cue ball with a cue in such games as pool, snooker, and billiards 2 TIE IN PLAIT to tie the hair at the back of the head in a plait [Mid-18C. Variant of QUEUE.]

cue ball n the white ball struck with the cue in games such as billiards, snooker, or pool, which strikes the object ball in turn

cue bid n in bridge, a bid made to show a partner that the bidder has either an ace or no cards in a particular suit

cue card n in broadcasting, a large card containing the words that somebody is to say, held up out of sight of the viewing audience

Cuenca /kwéngkə/ capital of Azuay Province, S Ecuador. Population: 247,421 (1996 estimate).

Cuernavaca /kwáirnə vaákə/ capital city of Morelos State, south-central Mexico. Population: 316,782 (1995).

cuesta /kwéstə/ n a ridge with a steep face on one side and a gentle slope on the other, especially in the SW United States [Early 19C. Via Spanish, 'slope' < Latin *costa* 'rib, side'.]

cuff[1] /kuf/ n 1 END OF SLEEVE NEAREST WRIST the part of a sleeve that covers the wrist, either turned back or with a band of fabric attached 2 US, Can, ANZ FOLD AT BOTTOM OF TROUSER a turned-up fold at the bottom of a trouser leg 3 PART OF GLOVE COVERING LOWER ARM the part of a glove or gauntlet that extends up the arm beyond the wrist 4 BAND USED IN MEASURING BLOOD PRESSURE an inflatable band fastened around a patient's arm when measuring blood pressure ■ npl HANDCUFFS a pair of handcuffs (*slang*) ■ vt 1 US, Can, ANZ PUT TURNED-UP FOLDS ON TROUSERS to put turned-up folds on the bottom of a pair of trousers 2 PUT HANDCUFFS ON to put handcuffs on somebody (*slang*) [14C. < ?]

cuff[2] *vt* to hit somebody lightly with an open hand ■ *n* a blow with an open hand [Mid-16C. Probably an imitation of the sound of hitting.]

cuff link *n* one of a pair of ornamental fasteners for shirt cuffs, used as an alternative to buttons (*often plural*)

Cufic *adj* = **Kufic**

Cuiaba /kóoyə baá/ capital of Mato Grosso State, SW Brazil. Population: 389,070 (1990).

cui bono /kwee bṓnō/ *n* **1** the legal principle that somebody who would gain something from a particular action or event is probably responsible for it **2** the usefulness of something used to measure its value [Early 17C. < Latin, 'to whom is the benefit'.]

Cuillin Hills /kóolin-/, **Coolin Hills** range of hills on the Isle of Skye, NW Scotland. Highest peak: Sgurr Alasdair, 1,009 m./3,309 ft.

cuirass /kwi ráss/ *n* **1 ARMOUR FOR UPPER BODY** a piece of body armour made of metal or leather, covering the chest and sometimes the back **2 PROTECTION** a protective covering, or any means of protection **3 ANIMAL'S HARD PROTECTIVE COVERING** a protective outer covering on some animals, e.g. scales or a shell [15C. Via Old French *cuirace* < Latin *coriaceus* 'made of leather' < *corium* 'leather'.]

cuirassier /kwírrə seér/ *n* a mounted soldier wearing a cuirass, especially in 16th-century Europe [Mid-16C. < French, < *cuirasse* < Old French *cuirace* (see CUIRASS).]

cuish *n* MIL = **cuisse**

cuisine /kwi zeén/ *n* **1** a specified style of cooking, especially one that is notable for high quality. ◊ **haute cuisine 2** the range of food prepared by a particular restaurant, country, or individual [Late 18C. Via French, 'kitchen' < Latin *coquina* < *coquere* 'to cook'.]

cuisse /kwiss/, **cuish** /kwish/ *n* a piece of armour formerly worn in battle to protect the thigh [13C. < Old French *cuiss(i)eus*, plural of *cuissel* < late Latin *coxale* < Latin *coxa* 'hip'.]

CUL *abbr* see you later (*in e-mails*)

CUL8R *abbr* see you later (*in e-mails*)

culchie /kúlchi/ *n Ireland* a farm labourer (*informal insult*) [Mid-20C. < ?]

cul-de-sac /kúl də sak, kóol-/ (*plural* **culs-de-sac** *or* **cul-de-sacs**) *n* **1 STREET CLOSED AT ONE END** a road with no exit at one end, often in a residential area **2 IMPASSE** a situation in which further progress is impossible **3 BODY CAVITY RESEMBLING POUCH** a body cavity or tubular structure open at one end only [< French, 'bottom of a sack']

culet /kyóolət/ *n* the flat face at the base of a faceted gemstone [Late 17C. < French, 'little base' < *cul* (see CULOTTES).]

Culiacán /kóolyə kaán/ capital of Sinaloa State, W Mexico. Population: 696,262 (1995).

culinary /kúlli nəri/ *adj* relating to food or cooking [Mid-17C. < Latin *culinarius* < *culina* 'kitchen'.] —**culinarily** *adv*

cull /kul/ *vt* **1 REMOVE FROM HERD** to remove an animal, especially a sick or weak one, from a herd or flock **2 REMOVE AS WORTHLESS** to remove an inferior thing or person from a larger group **3 SELECT** to select or gather things or people, especially those that are good examples of their kind ○ *The following cases are culled from the police reports.* **4 REDUCE BY KILLING MEMBERS** to reduce the size of a herd, flock, or population by killing some of the animals in it ■ *n* **1 SOMETHING WITHOUT VALUE** something regarded as worthless, especially an unwanted or inferior animal removed from a herd **2 REDUCTION OF ANIMAL NUMBERS** a reduction of the numbers of an animal population achieved by killing some of its members [12C. < Old French *coillier* < Latin *colligere* 'gather together' < *legere* 'to gather'.]

cullet /kúlit/ *n* broken or waste glass returned for recycling [Early 19C. Variant of COLLET 'glass left on the end of a blowing iron'.]

Culloden Moor /kə lódd'n-/ stretch of moorland near Inverness, NE Scotland. It was the scene of a battle in 1746 that ended the second Jacobite Rebellion.

cully /kúlli/ (*plural* **-lies**) *n* a friend (*slang*) [Mid-17C. < ?]

culm[1] /kulm/ *n* **1** waste from a coal mine **2** anthracite coal of poor quality [14C. Probably < Old English *col* (see COAL).]

culm[2] /kulm/ *n* the jointed hollow stem of a grass or similar plant [Mid-17C. < Latin *culmus*.]

culminant /kúlminənt/ *adj* **1** describes a planet or other celestial body that is at its highest altitude **2** reaching its climax or point of highest development [Early 17C. < late Latin *culminant-*, present participle of *culminare* (see CULMINATE).]

culminate /kúlmi nayt/ (**-nates, -nating, -nated**) *v* **1** *vti* **COME OR BRING TO HIGHEST POINT** to reach a climax or point of highest development, or to bring something to this point ○ *a general feeling of dissatisfaction that culminated in his resignation* **2** *vti* **FINISH SPECTACULARLY** to come or bring something to a climax ○ *The festivities culminated in a procession through the town.* **3** *vi* **HAVE SOMETHING AT HIGHEST END** to have something at its apex ○ *The tower culminates in a point.* **4** *vi* **REACH HIGHEST OR LOWEST POINT** to reach the highest or, less commonly, the lowest point in the sky relative to an observer's horizon (*refers to astronomical objects*) [Mid-17C. < late Latin *culminat-*, past participle of *culminare* 'exalt' < *culmen* 'summit'.]

culmination /kúlmi náysh'n/ *n* **1 HIGHEST POINT** the highest, most important, or final point of an activity **2 ACT OF CULMINATING** the arrival at, or the bringing of something to, a climax **3 HIGHEST OR LOWEST ALTITUDE** the highest or, less commonly, the lowest point that a celestial body reaches relative to an observer's horizon

culottes /kyoo lóts/ *npl* a pair of women's knee-length shorts, cut to resemble a skirt [Mid-19C. < French, 'knee breeches', literally 'small bottom' < *cul* 'bottom, rump' < Latin *culus*.]

culpable /kúlpəb'l/ *adj* deserving blame or punishment for a wrong [13C. Via French *coupable* < Latin *culpabilis* < *culpare* 'to blame' < *culpa* 'fault, blame'.] —**culpability** /kúlpə bílləti/ *n* —**culpably** *adv*

culpable homicide *n Scotland* the crime of manslaughter

Culpeper /kúl pepər/, **Nicholas** (1616–54) English physician and astrologer

Culpeper, Thomas, 2nd Baron Culpeper (1635–89) English-born colonial governor of Virginia (1680–83)

culprit /kúl prit/ *n* **1 WRONGDOER** the committer of an offence or misdeed **2 ACCUSED PERSON** somebody charged with a crime and awaiting trial, especially somebody who has pleaded not guilty **3 ORIGIN OF PROBLEM** a cause of a problem (*informal*) ○ *A faulty connection proved to be the culprit.* [Late 17C. Probably a misunderstanding of *cul. prist* < Anglo-Norman *Culpable: prest d'averrer* 'You are guilty; we are ready to prove it'.]

cult /kult/ *n* **1 RELIGION** a system of religious or spiritual beliefs, especially an informal and transient belief system regarded by others as misguided or unorthodox **2 RELIGIOUS GROUP** a group of people who share religious or spiritual beliefs **3 IDOLIZATION** extreme or excessive admiration for a person, philosophy of life, or activity ○ *the cult of youth* **4 OBJECT OF IDOLIZATION** a person, philosophy, or activity regarded with extreme or excessive admiration **5 FAD** something popular or fashionable among a devoted group of enthusiasts (*often before nouns*) ○ *cult status* **6 SYSTEM OF SUPERNATURAL BELIEFS** a body of organized practices and beliefs supposed to involve interaction with and control over supernatural powers **7 ELITE GROUP** a self-identified group of people who share a narrowly defined interest or perspective [Early 17C. Directly or via French < Latin *cultus* 'worship' < *colere* 'cultivate'.] —**cultic** *adj* —**cultish** *adj* —**cultism** *n* —**cultist** *n*

culti plural of **cultus**

cultivar /kúlti vaar/ *n* a variety of a cultivated plant that is developed by breeding and has a designated name [Early 20C. Blend of CULTIVATE + VARIETY.]

cultivate /kúlti vayt/ (**-vates, -vating, -vated**) *vt* **1 PREPARE LAND FOR CROPS** to work land or prepare soil for growing crops **2 GROW PLANTS** to grow a plant or crop **3 LOOSEN SOIL** to break up soil with a tool or machine, especially before sowing or planting **4 NURTURE** to improve or develop something, usually by study or education ○ *cultivating her interest in science* **5 DEVELOP, OFTEN SELFISHLY** to develop an acquaintance or intimacy with somebody else, often for personal advantage **6 MAKE CULTURED** to civilize or educate a person or group [Mid-17C. < medieval Latin *cultivat-*, past participle of *cultivare* < *cultivus* 'cultured' < Latin *cult-* (see CULTURE).] —**cultivability** /kúltivə bílləti/ *n* —**cultivable** *adj* —**cultivatability** /kúlti vaytə bílləti/ *n* —**cultivatable** *adj* —**cultivated** *adj*

Cultivated Australian *n* the prestige form of Australian English, spoken with a standard British English accent. ◊ **Broad Australian**

cultivation /kúlti váysh'n/ *n* **1 PREPARATION OF LAND OR GROWING CROPS** planting, growing, and harvesting crops or plants, or preparing land for this purpose **2 IMPROVEMENT** improvement or development, especially through study or education **3 SOPHISTICATION** educated taste or sophistication

cultivator /kúlti vaytər/ *n* a gardening or farm tool or machine for breaking up soil

cultural /kúlchərəl/ *adj* **1** relating to a particular culture or civilization **2** relating to the arts and intellectual activity —**culturally** *adv*

cultural anthropology *n* the scientific study of human culture or the culture of specific societies, including social structure, language, religion, art, and technology. ◊ **social anthropology** —**cultural anthropologist** *n*

cultural cringe *n Aus* a sense of embarrassment caused by a feeling that your national culture is inferior to others

cultural diversity *n* ethnic variety, as well as socioeconomic and gender variety, in a group, society, or institution

cultural lag, culture lag *n* a slower rate of change in one part of a culture or one society compared with another

cultural materialism *n* the anthropological theory that environment, resources, technology, and other material things are the major influences on cultural change

cultural relativism *n* the principle that we should not judge the behaviour of others using the standards of our own culture, and that each culture must be analysed on its own terms

Cultural Revolution *n* a political and cultural reform movement in China from 1965 to 1968 that was intended to revolutionize political opinion and behaviour and was characterized by social upheaval

cultural studies *n* (+ *singular verb*) **1** the study of culture from a sociological rather than an aesthetic viewpoint, drawing on the social sciences, e.g. politics and semiotics, rather than traditional forms of literary, artistic, or musical criticism **2** a wide-ranging educational course, especially at college or university level, covering all aspects of culture, the arts, sciences, and social science, and often intended as a foundation for other courses

cultural weapon *n S Africa* a traditional African weapon sometimes carried by participants at political rallies

culture /kúlchər/ *n* **1 THE ARTS COLLECTIVELY** art, music, literature, and related intellectual activities ○ *Culture is necessary for a healthy society.* ○ *popular culture* **2 KNOWLEDGE AND SOPHISTICATION** enlightenment and sophistication acquired through education and exposure to the arts ○ *They are people of culture.* **3 SHARED BELIEFS AND VALUES OF A GROUP** the beliefs, customs, practices, and social behaviour of a particular nation or people ○ *Southeast Asian culture* **4 PEOPLE WITH SHARED BELIEFS AND PRACTICES** a group of people whose shared beliefs and practices identify the particular place, class, or time to which they belong **5 SHARED ATTITUDES** a particular set of attitudes that characterizes a group of people ○ *The company tries hard to avoid a blame culture.* **6 DEVELOPMENT OF TOOLS AND LANGUAGE** the development and use of artefacts and symbols in the advancement of a society **7 GROWING OF BIOLOGICAL MATERIAL** the growing of biological material, especially plants, microorganisms, or animal tissue, in a nutrient substance in specially controlled conditions for scientific, medical, or commercial purposes **8 BIOLOGICAL MATERIAL GROWN IN SPECIAL CONDITIONS** biological material, especially plants, microorganisms, or animal tissue, grown in a nutrient substance (**culture medium**) in specially controlled conditions for scientific, medical, or commercial purposes **9 TILLAGE** the cultivation of the land or soil in preparation for growing crops or plants **10 IMPROVEMENT** the development of a skill or expertise through training or education ○ *physical culture* ■ *vt* (**-tures, -turing, -tured**) **1 GROW IN SPECIAL CONDITIONS** to grow biological material, especially plants, microorganisms, or animal tissue, in a nutrient substance in specially controlled conditions, for scientific, medical, or commercial purposes **2 CULTIVATE** to cultivate plants or crops [13C. Via French < Latin *cultura* 'tillage' < *cult-*, past participle of *colere* 'inhabit, cultivate'.]

cultured /kúlchərd/ *adj* **1 EDUCATED AND SOPHISTICATED** generally educated and informed about the arts and related intellectual activity **2 GROWN IN NUTRIENT SUBSTANCE** grown in a nutrient substance in a laboratory **3 ARTIFICIALLY PRODUCED** created artificially rather than by natural or organic processes

cultured pearl *n* a pearl created artificially by introducing a foreign body into an oyster or clam shell to attract layers of mother-of-pearl around it

culture lag *n* SOCIOL = **cultural lag**

culture shock *n* the feelings of confusion and anxiety experienced by a person suddenly encountering an unfamiliar cultural environment

culture vulture *n* a strong or obsessive devotee of the arts (*informal*)

cultus /kúltəss/ (*plural* **-tuses** *or* **-ti** /-tī/) *n* a religious group (*formal*) [Early 17C. < Latin *cultus* 'worship' < *cult-* (see CULTURE).]

culverin /kúlvərin/ *n* **1** a long-range cannon used in the 15th to the 17th centuries **2** a musket used in the 15th and 16th centuries [15C. < French *coulevrine* < *couleuvre* 'snake' < Latin *colubra*.]

culvert /kúlvərt/ *n* **1** a covered channel that carries water or cabling underground **2** an arch, bridge, or part of a road that covers a culvert [Late 18C. < ?]

cum /kum/ *prep* together with, along with, in combination with, or functioning as (*informal*) ○ *He lives and works in an apartment cum office.* [Late 19C. < Latin, 'with'.]

Cumb. *abbr* Cumbria

Cumberland /kúmbərlənd/ former county in NW England on the Scottish border

Cumberland Gap pass through the Cumberland Mountains near the meeting point of Tennessee, Virginia, and Kentucky. Height: 503 m/1,650 ft.

Cumberland sausage *n* a large sausage containing coarse-cut pork, originally made in Cumberland

Cumbernauld /kúmbər náwld/ town in central Scotland. Population: 48,762 (1991).

cumbersome /kúmbərsəm/ *adj* **1** awkward to carry or handle because of weight, size, or shape **2** difficult to use or deal with because of length or complexity — **cumbersomely** *adv* —**cumbersomeness** *n*

Cumbria /kúmbri ə/ county in NW England. Population: 490,300 (1995). Area: 6,810 sq. km/2,629 sq. mi. —**Cumbrian** *n, adj*

cumbrous /kúmbrəss/ *adj* large and unwieldy (*archaic or literary*) ○ *'this cumbrous and creaking structure'* (Thomas Hardy, *Tess of the d'Urbervilles;* 1891) —**cumbrously** *adv* —**cumbrousness** *n*

cum div. *abbr* cum dividend

cum dividend /kúm dívvidənd/ *adv* with a right to the current dividend when buying a security. ◊ **cum new**

cumene /kúmmeen/ an oily colourless liquid hydrocarbon. Use: fuel additive, synthesis of chemicals. [Mid-19C. Via French < Latin *cuminum* (see CUMIN).]

cumin /kúmmin/, **cummin** *n* **1** the aromatic seeds of a plant in the carrot family, used whole or ground as a spice **2** a plant of the carrot family with aromatic seeds. Flowers: small, white, pink. Native to: Mediterranean. *Cuminum cyminum*. [Pre-12C. Via Latin *cuminum* < Greek *kuminon* < Semitic.]

cum laude /kúm lów day/ *adv, adj US, Can* with the lowest of the three grades of academic distinction awarded above the general pass. ◊ **magna cum laude, summa cum laude** [< Latin, 'with praise']

cummerbund /kúmmər bund/ *n* a brightly coloured pleated sash worn around the waist by men as part of formal dress [Early 17C. < Urdu *kamar-band* 'loin-band, waistband'.]

cummin *n* PLANTS, COOK = **cumin**

cummings /kúmmingz/, **e. e.** (1894–1962) US poet. Full name **Edward Estlin Cummings**

Cummings /kúmmingz/, **Bart** (*b.* 1927) Australian racehorse trainer. Full name **James Bartholomew Cummings**

cum new *adv* with a right to any shares that may be issued free or on favourable terms to existing shareholders when buying a security. ◊ **cum dividend**

cumquat *n* TREES, FOOD = **kumquat**

cumulate /kyo͞omyo͞o layt/ *v* (**-lates, -lating, -lated**) **1** *vti* = **accumulate** *v.* **2** *vt* to combine two or more items into one ■ *adj* heaped up in a pile or mass [Mid-16C. < Latin *cumulat-*, past participle of *cumulare* 'gather in a heap' < *cumulus* 'heap'.] —**cumulation** /kyo͞o myo͞o láysh'n/ *n*

cumulative /kyo͞omyo͞olətiv/ *adj* **1 GRADUALLY BUILDING UP** becoming successively larger, stronger, or more effective ○ *Many drugs have a cumulative effect on the body.* **2 CREATED BY GRADUAL ADDITIONS** resulting from successive additions **3 ADDED TO NEXT PAYMENT** describes an interest or dividend payment that is added to the next payment rather than being paid out when it falls due **4 ENTITLING SHAREHOLDER TO CLAIM DIVIDEND ARREARS** describes preferred shares whose holder has the right to claim dividend arrears before dividends are distributed to holders of common shares **5 MORE SEVERE FOR REPEAT OFFENDER** describes a more severe punishment imposed on somebody who has previously committed the same crime **6 CONSECUTIVE** following consecutively on from another sentence or term of imprisonment **7 INCLUDING ALL GIVEN VALUES OF VARIABLE** relating to the sum of the number of times a variable has a particular value totalled over all the values of the variable that are less than a given value **8 INCREASING WITH SUCCESSIVE MEASUREMENTS** describes an error that increases as more measurements are taken — **cumulatively** *adv* —**cumulativeness** *n*

cumulative distribution function *n* a procedure that assigns to each possible value of a random variable the probability that this value will be found

cumulative trauma disorder *n US* = **RSI**

cumuli plural of **cumulus**

cumulonimbus /kyo͞omyo͞o lō nímbəss/ (*plural* **-bi** /-bī/ *or* **-buses**) *n* a tall dark cumulus cloud in the shape of an anvil, often bringing thunderstorms

cumulus /kyo͞omyo͞oləss/ (*plural* **-li** /-lī/) *n* **1** a large white or grey cloud with a flat base and a rounded fluffy top, or a mass of such clouds, developing as a result of rising hot air currents **2** a mass or heap [Mid-17C. < Latin, 'heap, pile'.] —**cumulous** *adj*

Cuna /ko͞onə/ (*plural* **-na** *or* **-nas**), **Kuna** (*plural* **-na** *or* **-nas**) *n* **1** a member of a Native Central American people of the isthmus of Panama and NW Colombia **2** the Chibchan language of the Cuna people. Native speakers: 30,000 to 50,000. [Mid-19C. < Cuna.] —**Cuna** *adj*

cuneal /kyo͞oni əl/ *adj* having the shape of a wedge [Late 16C. Directly or via modern Latin < medieval Latin *cunealis* < Latin *cuneus* 'wedge'.]

cuneate /kyo͞oni it, -ayt/ *adj* describes a leaf that is more or less triangular with the narrowest point of the triangle forming the tip [Early 19C. < Latin *cuneus* 'wedge'.] — **cuneately** *adv*

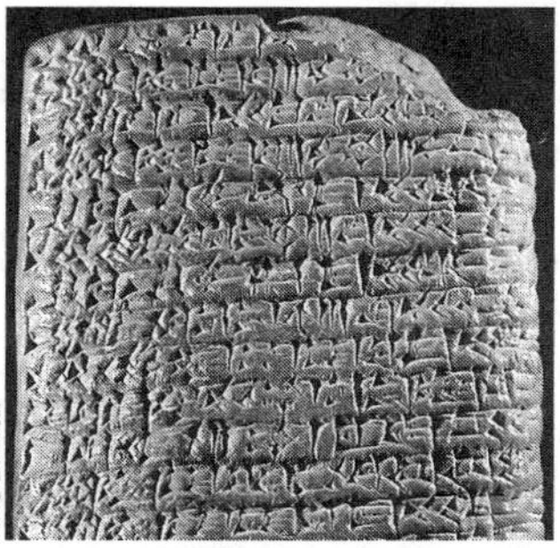

AKG London

Cuneiform: Sumerian clay tablet (18th century BC)

cuneiform /kyo͞oni fawrm/ *adj* **1 USED IN ANCIENT WRITING SYSTEM** relating or belonging to any of several writing systems of ancient SW Asia, e.g. Sumerian or Linear B, in which wedge-shaped impressions were made in soft clay **2 USED FOR CUNEIFORM WRITING** describes the clay tablets on which cuneiform script was written **3 WEDGE-SHAPED** with the narrowly triangular shape of a wedge **4 OF ANKLE** describes any of three wedge-shaped bones of the ankle ■ *n* **1 CUNEIFORM SCRIPT** writing that uses small wedge-shaped characters **2 WEDGE-SHAPED ANKLE BONE** any of the three cuneiform bones of the ankle (*informal*) [Late 17C. < French *cunéiforme* or modern Latin *cuneiformis* < Latin *cuneus* 'wedge'.]

cunjevoi /kúnjə voy/ *n Aus* MARINE BIOL = **sea squirt** [Early 19C. < an Australian Aboriginal language, probably of New South Wales.]

cunner /kúnnər/ (*plural* **-ner** *or* **-ners**) *n* a small fish of the wrasse family. Native to: North Atlantic Ocean. *Tautogolabrus adspersus*. [Early 17C. < ?]

cunnilingus /kúnni líng gəss/ *n* sexual stimulation of a woman's genitals using the tongue and lips [Late 19C. < Latin, 'vulva-licker'.]

cunning /kúnning/ *adj* **1 CRAFTY AND DECEITFUL** clever or artful in a way that is intended to deceive **2 CLEVERLY THOUGHT OUT** showing skill, shrewdness, and ingenuity in planning or doing something **3** *US* **CUTE** attractive in a pleasant delicate way (*informal*) ■ *n* **1 CRAFTINESS AND DECEITFULNESS** the ability to deceive in a clever subtle way **2 SKILFUL PERFORMANCE** skilful ingenuity or grace in doing something [13C. Probably < Old Norse *kunna* 'know'.] —**cunningly** *adv* —**cunningness** *n*

Cunningham /kúnningəm/, **Merce** (*b.* 1919) US dancer and choreographer

cunt /kunt/ *n* **1** a highly offensive term for a woman's genitals (*taboo*) **2** a highly offensive term for a woman (*taboo*) **3** a highly offensive term for somebody who is viewed with great dislike or contempt, especially a man (*taboo insult*) **4** a highly offensive term for sexual intercourse with a woman (*taboo*) [13C. < Germanic.]

cup /kup/ *n* **1 DRINKING CONTAINER** a small container, usually with a handle, used to hold liquids for drinking **2 CONTENTS OF CUP** the contents of a cup ○ *Will you have another cup?* **3 VOLUME MEASURE USED IN COOKING** a unit of volume used especially in cooking, equal to 227 ml/8 fl oz **4 WINNER'S PRIZE IN SPORTS** an ornamental trophy, typically a large two-handled silver goblet, awarded as a prize in a competition **5 SPORTS COMPETITION** a sporting competition in which the winner's prize is a large ornamental goblet **6 BOWL-SHAPED OBJECT** something that has an open hollow rounded shape **7 PART OF BRA** either of the shaped sections of a bra that support and cover the breasts **8 BOWL-SHAPED PLANT OR BODY PART** an open hollow rounded part or structure in a plant or in the body **9 PARTY PUNCH** a mixed drink with a particular ingredient as its base, usually served from a large bowl at parties ○ *a champagne cup* **10 DISH SERVED IN CUP-SHAPED CONTAINER** a dessert or appetizer served in a small bowl or glass dish **11 COMMUNION CHALICE OR WINE** in Christian services, the vessel from which the consecrated wine is drunk during Holy Communion, or the wine itself **12 GOLF HOLE** the hole on a green that is the target in golf, or the metal lining of such a hole **13 SOMEBODY'S LOT IN LIFE** what a person is destined to receive, suffer, or enjoy in life (*literary*) ■ *vt* (**cups, cupping, cupped**) **1 FORM INTO CUP SHAPE** to form one or both of the hands into an open hollow rounded shape, usually to hold or receive something, e.g. water **2 HOLD IN HANDS** to hold something in cupped hands **3 DRAW TO SURFACE OF SKIN** formerly, to use a cupping glass to increase the blood supply to an area of the skin [Pre-12C. < late Latin *cuppa*, probably < Latin *cupa* 'tub'.] —**cupful** *n* ◇ **in your cups** drunk (*archaic*)

cupbearer /kúp bairər/ *n* a servant who pours wine, especially one employed in a royal household

cupboard /kúbbərd/ *n* a piece of furniture, either built-in or freestanding, or a small room used for storing food and other kitchen necessities [14C. Originally 'table on which cups are displayed'.]

cupboard love *n* affection that is motivated by self-interest [< CUPBOARD 'food']

cupcake /kúp kayk/ *n* a small individual iced cake, baked in a paper or foil case or in a cup-shaped mould

cupel /kyo͞op'l/ *n* a small container in which precious metals are refined, especially in which gold and silver are separated from base metals during assaying ■ *vt* (**-pels, -pelling, -pelled**) to separate gold or silver from a base metal using a cupel [Early 17C. < French *coupelle* 'little cup' < *coupe* 'cup' < late Latin *cuppa* (see CUP).] — **cupellation** /kyo͞opə láysh'n/ *n* —**cupeller** *n*

Cup Final, cup final *n* the final match in a knockout sports competition, especially the FA Cup or the Scottish Cup

cup fungus *n* a cup-shaped and often bright red, orange, or yellow fungus with a spore-bearing, often stalkless, structure. Subdivision: *Ascomycotina*.

cupid /kyoópid/ *n* a representation of the god Cupid as a symbol of love in painting or sculpture

Cupid *n* the Roman god of love, the son of Venus, usually represented as a young boy with wings and a bow and arrow. Greek equivalent **Eros** [14C. < Latin *Cupido* 'desire' < *cupere* 'to desire'.]

cupidity /kyoo píddəti/ *n* greed, especially for money or possessions (*formal*) [15C. Directly or via French < Latin *cupiditas* < *cupere* 'to desire'.]

Cupid's bow *n* **1** a double curve, especially the curves of the upper lip **2** a bow with two curves used in archery [< the traditional representation of the bow used by Cupid]

cup of tea *n* **1** what somebody likes or prefers ○ *This is more my cup of tea.* **2** *US* something to be dealt with

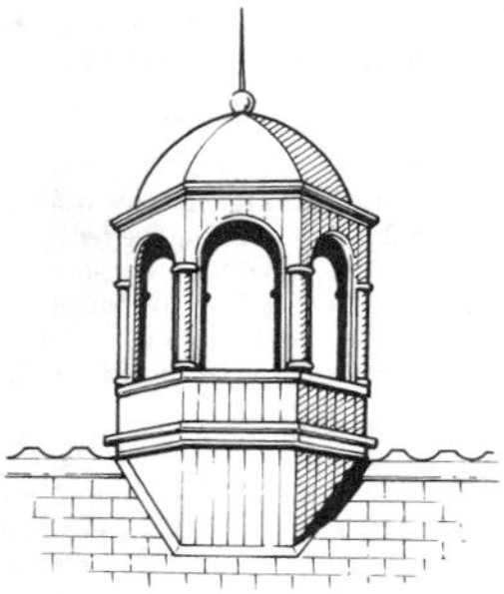

Cupola

cupola /kyoópələ/ *n* **1 DOME-SHAPED ROOF** a roof or ceiling in the form of a dome **2 DOME ON ROOF** a small dome on a roof, sometimes made of glass and providing natural light inside **3 GUN TURRET** a domed structure protecting a gun, e.g. on a warship **4 SMALL OBSERVATION DOME** a glass observation dome on the roof of an armoured vehicle or railway van **5 BLAST FURNACE** a cylindrical blast furnace used in foundries for remelting iron or other metals [Mid-16C. Via Italian < late Latin *cupula* 'little cask, vault' < *cupa* 'cask'.]

cuppa /kúppə/ *n* a cup of tea (*informal*) ○ *Let's have a cuppa.* [Mid-20C. < an informal pronunciation of *cup of*.]

cupped /kupt/ *adj* formed into the open hollow shape of a cup

cupping /kúpping/ *n* a historical medical practice in which a cupping glass was used to increase the blood supply to an area of the skin

cupping glass *n* a glass container in which a partial vacuum is created by heat or suction that is applied to the skin to increase the blood supply in the tissues below

cuppy /kúppi/ (**-pier, -piest**) *adj* **1** with the shape of a cup **2** with many small shallow hollows in the surface

cupr- *prefix* = **cupro-** (*before vowels*)

cuprate /kyoó prayt/ *n* a salt containing an anionic grouping of copper and oxygen

cupreous /kyoópri əss/ *adj* **1** consisting of or containing copper **2** of a reddish-brown colour [Mid-17C. < late Latin *cupreus* < *cuprum* 'copper'.]

cupri- *prefix* = **cupro-**

cupric /kyoóprik/ *adj* containing copper with a valency of 2. ◊ **cuprous** [Late 18C. < late Latin *cuprum* 'copper'.]

cupriferous /kyoo prífférəss/ *adj* having copper as a constituent [Late 18C. < late Latin *cuprum* 'copper'.]

cuprite /kyoó prīt/ *n* a reddish-brown or black mineral that is an ore of copper and consists of copper oxide [Mid-19C. < late Latin *cuprum* 'copper'.]

cupro- *prefix* copper ○ *cupronickel* [< late Latin *cuprum* (see COPPER[1])]

cupronickel /kyoó prō ník'l/ *n* a corrosion-resistant alloy of copper containing up to 40 per cent nickel

cuprous /kyoóprəss/ *adj* containing copper with a valency of 1. ◊ **cupric** [Mid-17C. < late Latin *cuprum* 'copper'.]

cup tie *n* a match in a knockout competition for which the prize is a cup

cup-tied *adj* **1** unable to play in a cup tie for some reason, e.g. disqualification or injury **2** not free to play another fixture because of participation in a cup tie

cupule /kyoó pyool/ *n* a cup-shaped body part or plant part, such as that enclosing the base of an acorn [15C. < late Latin *cupula* 'little cask, vault' < *cupa* 'cask'.]

Cuquenan Waterfall /koó kay nán-/ waterfall in Venezuela, one of the highest in the world. Height: 610 m/2,000 ft.

cur /kur/ *n* **1** a mixed-breed dog, especially one that is ill-natured or in poor condition **2** somebody regarded as mean, cowardly, or otherwise unpleasant (*dated insult*) [12C. Originally in *cur-dog*; < ?]

curable /kyoórəb'l/ *adj* **1** capable of being treated by medical procedures **2** capable of being healed by medical procedures —**curability** /kyoórə bílləti/ *n* —**curably** *adv*

curaçao /kyoórə sow/ *n* an orange-flavoured liqueur that originated on the Caribbean island of Curaçao

Curaçao /koórə sow, -sō, kyoórə-/ largest island of the Netherlands Antilles, in the Caribbean Sea. Area: 444 sq. km/171 sq. mi.

curacy /kyoórəssi/ (*plural* **-cies**) *n* the position or term of office of a curate

curare /kyoo ráari/, **curari** *n* **1** a dark resin from certain South American plants. Use: as a traditional arrow poison, and as a muscle relaxant in medicine. **2** a tropical South American vine from which curare is obtained. Genera: *Strychnos* and *Chondodendron*. [Late 18C. Via Spanish, Portuguese < Carib *kurari*.]

curarize /kyoórə rīz/ (**-rizes, -rizing, -rized**), **curarise** (**-rises, -rising, -rised**) *vt* to treat somebody with curare —**curarization** /kyoórə rī záysh'n/ *n*

curassow /kyoórə sow/ *n* a large crested game bird with a long tail and a brightly coloured bill. Native to: South and Central America. Genus: *Crax*. [Late 17C. Alteration of CURAÇAO.]

curate[1] /kyoórət/ *n* **1** a member of the clergy who assists a vicar, rector, or priest **2** a member of the clergy in charge of a parish [14C. < medieval Latin *curatus* 'somebody who cares for a parish' < Latin *cura* 'care'.]

curate[2] /kyoo ráyt/ (**-rates, -rating, -rated**) *vti* to be the curator of a museum, gallery, or other collection [Early 18C. Back-formation < CURATOR.]

curate's egg *n* something that may be described as only partly bad, especially when this makes the whole thing unacceptable [< a cartoon in *Punch* magazine, 1895, in which a curate, when served a bad egg at the bishop's table, assured his host that 'parts of it are excellent']

curative /kyoórətiv/ *adj* able to restore health ■ *n* a substance or treatment that can restore health —**curatively** *adv* —**curativeness** *n*

curator /kyoo ráytər/ *n* **1** the administrative head of a museum, gallery, or other collection **2** *Scotland* the legal guardian of a minor [14C. < Latin, < *curare* (see CURE).] —**curatorial** /kyoórə táwri əl/ *adj* —**curatorship** *n*

curb /kurb/ *n* **1 IMPOSED LIMITATION** one thing that controls or limits something else **2 HORSE'S BIT AND ATTACHED CHAIN** a horse's bit with a chain or strap attached, passed under the horse's jaw (*often before nouns*) ○ *a curb chain* **3 EDGING FOR LAWN** a line of stones that forms the edge of an area of lawn **4 RAISED PART THAT SURROUNDS** an enclosing frame or raised margin, e.g. around a skylight or a well **5** *US, Can* = **kerb** *n.* ■ *vt* **1 RESTRAIN** to restrain, control, or limit something **2** *US* = **kerb** *v.* [15C. Probably variant of *courb* 'to curve', via French *courber* < Latin *curvare*.]

curb bit *n* a horse's bit attached to a chain or strap

curb roof *n* a roof that has two or more different angles of slope on each side, e.g. a mansard or gambrel roof

curbside /kúrb sīd/ *n US* = **kerbside**

curbstone /kúrb stōn/ *n US* = **kerbstone**

curculio /kur kyoóli ō/ (*plural* **-os**) *n* a weevil that damages fruit trees, vegetables, and other plants. Genus: *Conotrachelus*. [Mid-18C. < Latin, 'corn weevil'.]

curcuma /kúrkyoómə/ *n* a tropical plant from which turmeric and zedoary are obtained. Native to: S Asia. Genus: *Curcuma*. [15C. Via medieval Latin < Arabic *kurkum* 'turmeric' < Sanskrit *kuṇkuma* 'saffron'.]

curd /kurd/ *n* **1 SOLID PART OF SOUR MILK** the solid substance formed when milk coagulates, used to make cheese **2 SUBSTANCE RESEMBLING MILK CURD** a food substance with a consistency similar to milk curd ■ *vti* **CURDLE** to turn something into curd, or to become curd [14C. < ?] —**curdy** *adj*

curd cheese *n* a mild soft cheese made from skimmed milk curds

curdle /kúrd'l/ (**-dles, -dling, -dled**) *vti* **1** to separate, or cause a liquid such as milk, to separate into curds and whey **2** to go bad or wrong, or to spoil something (*informal*) [Late 16C. < CURD.]

cure /kyoor/ *v* (**cures, curing, cured**) **1** *vti* **HEAL** to restore a sick person or animal to health ○ *Six months later she was completely cured.* **2** *vt* **TREAT SUCCESSFULLY** to bring about recovery from an illness, disorder, or injury ○ *Diseases like this are not easily cured.* **3** *vt* **RESOLVE PROBLEM** to solve a problem ○ *curing unemployment* **4** *vti* **PRESERVE FOOD** to preserve food, especially meat or fish, usually by smoking, drying, or salting it, or to be preserved by one of these methods **5** *vt* **PRESERVE BY DRYING** to preserve a substance, especially leather or tobacco, by drying it **6** *vt* **FINISH WITH CHEMICAL PROCESS** to finish a material by applying chemicals **7** *vt* **MAKE RUBBER STRONGER** to strengthen rubber with additives in the presence of heat and pressure **8** *vti* **HARDEN** to make a material, especially concrete or cement, harden ■ *n* **1 SOMETHING THAT RESTORES HEALTH** a medication or treatment that brings about a full recovery from an illness or injury ○ *working to find a cure for the disease* **2 RECOVERY** restoration or return to health ○ *I managed to achieve a complete cure.* **3 PROBLEM'S SOLUTION** something that resolves a problem **4 FOOD PRESERVATION PROCESS** the preservation of meat or fish, especially by smoking, drying, or salting **5 SPIRITUAL CARE** the spiritual and pastoral responsibility of the clergy for laypeople **6** *N Ireland* **FOLK REMEDY** a folk practice supposed to cure an illness, and handed down as a secret in a family [13C. Via Old French < Latin *curare* 'care for' < *cura* 'care'.] —**curer** *n*

curé /kyoóray/ *n* a parish priest in a French-speaking country [Mid-17C. Via French < medieval Latin *curatus* (see CURATE[1]).]

cure-all *n* a treatment or remedy that is believed to be able to cure every ailment or problem

~~**curency**~~ incorrect spelling of **currency**

curet *n, vt* SURG = **curette**

curettage /kyoórə táazh, kyoo réttij/, **curettement** /kyoo rétmənt/ *n* a surgical procedure that involves scraping the inside surface of a body cavity with an instrument shaped like a spoon (**curette**) to remove growths or other unwanted tissue [Late 19C. < French, < *curette* (see CURETTE).]

curette /kyoo rét/, **curet** *n* a spoon-shaped surgical instrument used to remove tissue from the inner surface of a body cavity ■ *vt* (**-rettes, -retting, -retted**) to scrape tissue from the inner surface of a body cavity using a curette [Mid-18C. < French, < *curer* 'clean out' < Latin *curare* 'care for'.]

curettement *n* = **curettage**

curfew /kúr fyoo/ *n* **1 RESTRICTION ON PEOPLE'S MOVEMENTS** an official restriction on people's movements, requiring them to remain indoors after a specified time at night **2 TIME OR SIGNAL FOR CURFEW** the time at which a curfew takes effect, or the signal given at this time **3 LENGTH OF CURFEW** the duration of a curfew **4 MEDIEVAL REMINDER TO EXTINGUISH LIGHTS** in the Middle Ages, the ringing of a bell in the evening as a reminder to put out fires and lights ○ *'The curfew tolls the knell of parting day'* (Thomas Gray, *Elegy written in a Country Churchyard*; 1751) [13C. < Anglo-Norman *coeverfu* or Old French *cuevrefeu* 'cover fire'.]

curia /kyoóri ə/ (*plural* **-ae** /-ri ee/) *n* **1 PAPAL COURT** the administrative body at the Vatican, by which the Pope governs the Roman Catholic Church **2 SUBDIVISION OF ANCIENT ROMAN TRIBE** in ancient Rome, a subdivision of each tribe, or the place where it met **3 ANCIENT ROMAN SENATE** the senate or senate house in an ancient Roman city **4 MEDIEVAL COURT** a medieval monarch's court of justice [Early 17C. < Latin, 'council'.] —**curial** *adj*

curiculum incorrect spelling of **curriculum**

curie /kyooŕi/ n a unit of radioactivity equal to 3.7 times 10^{10} disintegrations per second [Early 20C. After the French physicists Pierre *Curie* (1859–1906) and Marie Curie.]

Marie Curie

AKG London

Curie /kyooŕi/, **Marie** (1867–1934) Polish-born French chemist and physicist. Born **Marja Skłodowska**

Curie point, Curie temperature n the temperature at which in some substances, such as iron, there is a change in the magnetic characteristics, from ferromagnetic to paramagnetic behaviour [After Pierre *Curie* (1859–1906), French physicist]

Curie's law n the law of physics stating that there is an inverse proportionality between the effect of a magnetic field on a paramagnetic material and its absolute temperature [After Pierre *Curie* (1859–1906), French physicist]

Curie temperature n PHYS = **Curie point**

Curie-Weiss law /-vîss-/ n a variation of Curie's law in which the temperature term is reduced by an amount equal to the Curie point [After French physicists Pierre *Curie* (1859–1906) and Pierre Ernest *Weiss* (1865–1940)]

curio /kyooŕi ō/ (*plural* **-os**) n an object that is valued and often collected for its interest or rarity [Mid-19C. Shortening of CURIOSITY.]

curiosa /kyooŕi ōssa, -ōza/ npl 1 books or other texts dealing with unusual topics, especially erotica 2 interesting and unusual objects [Late 19C. < Latin, neuter plural of *curiosus* (see CURIOUS).]

curiosity /kyooŕi óssəti/ (*plural* **-ties**) n 1 DESIRE TO KNOW eagerness to know about something or to get information 2 TENDENCY TO PRY an excessive interest in other people's affairs 3 SOMEBODY OR SOMETHING THOUGHT STRANGE an interesting and unusual object, person, or phenomenon [14C. Via French *curiosité* < Latin *curiositas* < *curiosus* (see CURIOUS).]

curious /kyooŕi əss/ adj 1 EAGER TO KNOW eager to know about something or to get information ○ *I'm curious to know how they found out about the party.* 2 TOO INQUISITIVE excessively eager to know about other people's affairs 3 ODD strange or unusual ○ *several curious events* [14C. Via Old French *curios* < Latin *curiosus* 'careful, inquisitive' < *cura* 'care'.] —**curiously** adv —**curiousness** n

curiousity incorrect spelling of **curiosity**

Curitiba /koóri teéba/ capital of Paraná State, S Brazil. Population: 1,476,253 (1996 estimate).

curium /kyooŕi əm/ n (*symbol* **Cm**) a silvery-white metallic radioactive element. Source: produced artificially from plutonium. [Mid-20C. After Pierre and Marie *Curie* (see CURIE).]

curl /kurl/ v 1 vti MAKE HAIR CURLY to make naturally straight hair curly, usually by twisting it around something while it is damp, or to grow in ringlets naturally 2 vti MAKE OR BECOME CURVED OR COILED to bend, twist, or wind something into a curved or spiral shape, or to become curved or coiled ○ *He curled the silver ribbon into spirals.* ○ *The paper had begun to curl at the edges.* 3 vi MOVE IN A SPIRAL MOTION to move in a curve or spiral ○ *Smoke curled into the sky.* 4 vi PARTICIPATE IN CURLING to play the game of curling ■ n 1 CURVED OR COILED HAIRS a lock of hair curved into a round or spiral shape (*often plural*) 2 TENDENCY TO CURL the tendency for hair to grow or stay in ringlets

○ *My hair doesn't have much curl.* 3 CURVED OR COILED THING something with a curved or coiled shape, e.g. a wood shaving or the crest of a breaking wave 4 ADOPTING CURVED SHAPE the forming of something into a curved or round shape 5 WEIGHTLIFTING MANOEUVRE a weightlifting move in which a barbell is held at thigh height with the underarms facing outwards, then raised to the chest, and lowered without moving the shoulders, upper arms, or legs 6 MARKING ON WOOD a curved or spiral marking in wood grain [14C. < Middle Dutch *krul* 'curly' < Germanic.]

curl up v 1 vi CURVE BODY AND DRAW UP LEGS to sit or lie with the body curved and the legs tucked up, usually in order to relax ○ *curl up in bed with a good novel* 2 vti MAKE OR BECOME CURVED OR COILED to become curved or coiled, or to bend, twist, or wind something into a curved or spiral shape ○ *The paper curled up in the fire before it burst into flames.* 3 vi FEEL EXTREMELY EMBARRASSED to be overcome with embarrassment, revulsion, or some other strong feeling (*informal*) ○ *When I realized my mistake I just wanted to curl up and disappear.*

Curl /kurl/, **Robert Floyd** (b. 1933) US chemist

curled paperwork n ARTS = **rolled paperwork**

curler /kúrlər/ n 1 a roller or other device used to curl hair 2 a player of the game of curling

curlew /kúr lyoo/ n a large shore bird with brownish plumage, long legs, and a long slender bill that curves downwards. Genus: *Numenius*. [14C. < Old French *courlieu*, variant of *courlis*, an imitation of its cry.]

Curlewis /kur loó iss/, **Sir Adrian Herbert** (1901–85) Australian judge

curlicue /kúrli kyoo/ n a curly ornamental twist, especially in calligraphy or design [Mid-19C. < CURLY + CUE[2] 'pigtail'.] —**curlicued** adj

curling /kúrling/ n a team game played on an ice rink, in which a heavy polished stone with a handle is slid towards a circular target (**tee**) [Early 17C. < the curving path of the stone as it reaches the target.]

curling iron n HAIR = **curling tongs**

curling stone n a heavy polished stone with a handle used in the game of curling

curling tongs npl a device consisting of a heated rod round which the hair is twisted to form a curl

curlpaper /kúrl paypər/ n a small piece of paper rolled round a lock of hair, which is then twisted and left to set into a curl

curly /kúrli/ (**-ier**, **-iest**) adj 1 WITH CURLS arranged in curls or curling naturally 2 CURVED OR COILED bent or twisted into a wavy, curved, or spiral shape ○ *The paper has gone all curly.* 3 WITH CURVES IN GRAIN describes wood that has irregular curved or wavy markings in the grain 4 TRICKY difficult to answer or deal with (*informal*) ○ *had to fend off a few curly questions* —**curliness** n

curly endive n PLANTS = **endive** n. 1

curly top n a viral disease of beets, tomatoes, beans, and other plants that makes the leaves curl

curmudgeon /kur mújjən/ n somebody considered to be bad-tempered, disagreeable, or stubborn [Late 16C. < ?] —**curmudgeonly** adj —**curmudgeonry** n

Curnow /kúr now/, **Allen** (b. 1911) New Zealand poet

currach /kúrrakh, -rə/, **curragh** in *Ireland, Scotland* a boat like a coracle, formerly used on Scottish and Irish lakes and rivers [15C. < Irish, Gaelic *curach* 'small boat'.]

currant /kúrrənt/ n 1 SMALL DRIED GRAPE a small dark dried seedless grape. Native to: the Mediterranean. Source: in cookery. Native to: the Mediterranean. 2 FRUIT OF CURRANT BUSH the small round juicy fruit of a currant bush, especially a redcurrant or blackcurrant 3 SMALL FRUIT-BEARING SHRUB a small deciduous shrub cultivated in temperate regions that bears a small round edible fruit, especially the redcurrant or blackcurrant. Genus: *Ribes*. [Early 16C. Shortening of Anglo-Norman *raisins de Corauntz*, variant of Old French *raisins de Corinthe* 'grapes from Corinth', where they originated.]

SPELLCHECK Do not confuse **currant** with **current**, which has a similar sound. Beware: your spellchecker will not catch this error.

currawong /kúrrə wong/ n a large bird with black and white plumage and a strong pointed bill that feeds on carrion and lives in noisy flocks. Native to: Australia.

Genus: *Strepera*. [Early 20C. < Yagara *garrawby* (also found in neighbouring languages).]

currency /kúrrənssi/ (*plural* **-cies**) n 1 MONEY a system of money, or the notes and coins themselves, used in a particular country. See illustration overleaf. 2 ACCEPTANCE OF IDEA OR TERM widespread acceptance or use of an idea, theory, word, or phrase 3 CIRCULATION the transmitting of something, especially money, from person to person 4 TIME WHEN SOMETHING IS CURRENT the period of time during which something is current 5 *Aus* INDIGENOUS AUSTRALIAN an Australian-born resident of Australia, as opposed to a British-born immigrant (*dated slang*) [Mid-17C. < CURRENT.]

current /kúrrənt/ adj 1 EXISTING NOW happening, existing, or in force at the present ○ *In my current job, I am in charge of 25 people.* 2 VALID accepted as legally valid 3 PRESENTLY ACCEPTED widely known, accepted, or believed ○ *The theory is no longer current.* ■ n 1 FLOW OF WATER OR AIR the steady flow of water or air in a particular direction 2 STREAM a mass of water or air flowing steadily in a particular direction 3 FLOW OF ELECTRIC CHARGE the flow of electricity through a cable, wire, or other conductor 4 RATE OF FLOW OF ELECTRICITY the rate of flow of an electric charge through a conductor 5 TENDENCY a trend or tendency ○ *going against the current and moving to a farm* [13C. < Old French *corant*, present participle of *courre* 'run' < Latin *currere*.] —**currentness** n

SPELLCHECK See **currant**.

current account n an account at a bank or building society from which money may be drawn on demand. US term **checking account**

current affairs npl important political and social events or issues of the present time (*often before nouns*)

current assets npl available cash and other assets that could be converted to cash within a year

current-cost accounting n a method of accounting that assesses the value of assets as the cost of replacing them rather than as their original cost

current density n (*symbol j or J*) the ratio of the amount of current flowing through a conductor to the cross-sectional area of the conductor

current efficiency n in an electrolytic process, the mass of the substance liberated by a given current divided by the theoretical mass, as predicted by Faraday's law

current events npl = **current affairs**

current liabilities npl business liabilities that are due to be cleared before the end of the financial year

currently /kúrrəntli/ adv at the present time ○ *They are currently living abroad.*

current ratio n the ratio of current assets to current liabilities

curricle /kúrrik'l/ n a light two-wheeled open carriage drawn by a pair of horses side by side [Mid-18C. < Latin *curriculum* 'racing chariot'.]

curriculum /kə ríkyōoləm/ (*plural* **-la** /-lə/ *or* **-lums**) n the subjects taught at an educational institution or the elements taught in a specific subject [Early 19C. < Latin, 'running, course' < *currere* 'to run'.] —**curricular** adj

curriculum vitae /-veé tī, -ví tee/ (*plural* **curricula vitae**) n a summary of a person's educational qualifications, skills, and professional history [Early 20C. < Latin, 'course of life'.]

currier /kúrri ər/ n a dresser and finisher of leather after it has been tanned [14C. Via Old French *corier* < Latin *coriarius* < *corium* 'leather'.]

currish /kúrish/ adj having a very hostile or disagreeable disposition [15C. < CUR.] —**currishly** adv —**currishness** n

curry[1] /kúrri/ n (*plural* **-ries**) 1 HIGHLY SPICED SAVOURY DISH a dish containing meat, fish, or vegetables in a highly spiced sauce ○ *chicken curry* 2 SEASONING FOR CURRY a mixture of spices in any of various forms, such as sauce, paste, or powder, used to prepare curry (*often before nouns*) ○ *curry paste* ■ vt (**-ries**, **-rying**, **-ried**) COOK IN HIGHLY SPICED SAUCE to cook meat, fish, or vegetables in a highly spiced sauce [Late 16C. < Tamil *kari* 'sauce'.]

curry[2] /kúrri/ (**-ries**, **-rying**, **-ried**) vt 1 to groom a horse 2 to make leather flexible and waterproof as the final

ALPHABETICAL CURRENCY TABLE

See also table at *European Union* for information on Euro

Unit	Country
afghani	Afghanistan
agora	Israel
avo	Macau
baht	Thailand
baisa	Oman
balboa	Panama
ban	Moldova
	Romania
birr	Ethiopia
bolivar	Venezuela
boliviano	Bolivia
butut	Gambia
cedi	Ghana
cent	Antigua and Barbuda
	Australia
	Bahamas
	Barbados
	Belize
	Brunei
	Canada
	Cyprus
	Dominica
	Ecuador
	Eritrea
	Ethiopia
	Fiji
	Grenada
	Guyana
	Hong Kong
	Jamaica
	Kenya
	Kiribati
	Liberia
	Malta
	Marshall Islands
	Mauritius
	Micronesia
	Namibia
	Nauru
	Netherlands
	New Zealand
	Palau
	St Kitts and Nevis
	St Lucia
	St Vincent and the Grenadines
	Seychelles
	Sierra Leone
	Singapore
	Solomon Islands
	Somalia
	South Africa
	Sri Lanka
	Suriname
	Swaziland
	Taiwan
	Tanzania
	Trinidad and Tobago
	Tuvalu
	Uganda
	United States
	Zimbabwe
centas	Lithuania
centavo	Argentina
	Bolivia
	Brazil
	Cape Verde
	Chile
	Colombia
	Cuba
	Dominican Republic
	El Salvador
	Guatemala
	Honduras
	Mexico
	Mozambique
	Nicaragua
	Philippines
	Portugal
centesimo	Panama
	Uruguay
centime	Algeria
	Belgium
	Benin
	Burkina Faso
	Burundi
	Cameroon
	Central African Republic
	Chad
	Comoros
	Congo (Dem. Rep. of the)
	Congo (Rep. of the)
	Côte d'Ivoire
	Djibouti
	Equatorial Guinea
	France
	Gabon
	Guinea
	Guinea-Bissau
	Haiti
	Liechtenstein
	Luxembourg
	Madagascar
	Mali
	Monaco
	Morocco
	Niger
	Rwanda
	Senegal
	Switzerland
	Togo
centimo	Costa Rica
	Paraguay
	Peru
	São Tomé and Príncipe
	Venezuela
CFA franc	Benin
	Burkina Faso
	Cameroon
	Central African Republic
	Chad
	Congo (Rep. of the)
	Côte d'Ivoire
	Equatorial Guinea
	Gabon
	Guinea-Bissau
	Mali
	Niger
	Senegal
	Togo
chetrum	Bhutan
chon	North Korea
	South Korea
colón	Costa Rica
	El Salvador
Congo franc	Congo (Dem. Rep. of the)
cordoba	Nicaragua
dalasi	Gambia
denar	Macedonia, Former Yugoslav Rep. of
Deutschmark	Germany
dinar	Algeria
	Bahrain
	Iraq
	Jordan
	Kuwait
	Libya
	Sudan
	Tunisia
	Yugoslavia
dinar	Iran
dirham	Morocco
	United Arab Emirates
dirham	Libya
	Qatar
dobra	São Tomé and Príncipe
dollar	Antigua and Barbuda
	Australia
	Bahamas
	Barbados
	Belize
	Brunei
	Canada
	Dominica
	Ecuador
	Fiji
	Grenada
	Guyana
	Hong Kong
	Jamaica
	Kiribati
	Liberia
	Marshall Islands
	Micronesia
	Namibia
	Nauru
	New Zealand
	Palau
	St Kitts and Nevis
	St Lucia
	St Vincent and the Grenadines
	Singapore
	Solomon Islands
	Taiwan
	Trinidad and Tobago
	Tuvalu
	United States
	Zimbabwe
dong	Vietnam
drachma	Greece
dram	Armenia
escudo	Cape Verde
	Portugal
eyrir	Iceland
filler	Hungary
fils	Bahrain
	Iraq
	Jordan
	Kuwait
	United Arab Emirates
	Yemen
forint	Hungary
franc	Belgium
	Burundi
	Comoros
	Djibouti
	France
	Guinea
	Liechtenstein
	Luxembourg
	Madagascar
	Monaco
	Rwanda
	Switzerland
gourde	Haiti
groschen	Austria
grosz	Poland
guarani	Paraguay
guilder	Netherlands
	Suriname
halala	Saudi Arabia
haler	Czech Republic
halier	Slovakia
hao	Vietnam
hryvnia	Ukraine
jiao	China
khoum	Mauritania
kina	Papua New Guinea
kip	Laos
kobo	Nigeria
kopek	Russia
kopiyka	Ukraine
koruna	Czech Republic
	Slovakia
krona	Iceland
	Sweden
krone	Denmark
	Norway
kroon	Estonia
kuna	Croatia
kwacha	Malawi
	Zambia
kwanza	Angola
kyat	Myanmar
laari	Maldives
lari	Georgia
lat	Latvia
lek	Albania
lempira	Honduras
leone	Sierra Leone
leu	Moldova
	Romania
lev	Bulgaria
lilangeni	Swaziland
lipa	Croatia
lira	Italy
	Malta
	Turkey
litas	Lithuania
loti	Lesotho
lumma	Armenia
lwei	Angola
manat	Azerbaijan
	Turkmenistan
marka	Bosnia and Herzegovina
markka	Finland
metical	Mozambique
millime	Tunisia
mongo	Mongolia
naira	Nigeria
nakfa	Eritrea
ngultrum	Bhutan
ngwee	Zambia
øre	Denmark
	Norway
öre	Sweden
ouguiya	Mauritania
pa'anga	Tonga
paisa	India
	Nepal
	Pakistan
para	Yugoslavia
pataca	Macau
penni	Finland
penny	Ireland
	United Kingdom
peseta	Andorra
	Spain
pesewa	Ghana
peso	Argentina
	Chile
	Colombia
	Cuba
	Dominican Republic
	Mexico
	Philippines
	Uruguay
pfennig	Germany
piastre	Egypt
	Jordan
	Lebanon
	Syria
poisha	Bangladesh
pound	Cyprus
	Egypt
	Lebanon
	Syria
	United Kingdom
pound	Sudan
pul	Afghanistan
pula	Botswana
punt	Ireland
pya	Myanmar
qindar	Albania
quetzal	Guatemala
rand	South Africa
real	Brazil
rial	Iran
	Oman
	Yemen
riel	Cambodia
ringgit	Malaysia
riyal	Qatar
	Saudi Arabia
rouble	Russia
	Tajikistan
rubel	Belarus
rufiyaa	Maldives
rupee	India
	Mauritius
	Nepal
	Pakistan
	Seychelles
	Sri Lanka
rupiah	Indonesia
santim	Latvia
satang	Thailand
schilling	Austria
sen	Cambodia
	Indonesia
	Japan
	Malaysia
sene	Samoa
seniti	Tonga
sent	Estonia
sente	Lesotho
shekel	Israel
shilling	Kenya
	Somalia
	Tanzania
	Uganda
sol	Peru
som	Kyrgyzstan
	Uzbekistan
stotin	Slovenia
stotinka	Bulgaria
taka	Bangladesh
tala	Samoa
tambala	Malawi
tenge	Kazakhstan
tetri	Georgia
thebe	Botswana
toea	Papua New Guinea
tolar	Slovenia
tughrik	Mongolia
tyiyn	Kyrgyzstan
vatu	Vanuatu
won	North Korea
	South Korea
yen	Japan
yuan	China
zloty	Poland

= main unit
= subunit

stage in its processing [13C. < Old French *correier* 'prepare' < Latin *con* 'with' + Germanic ancestor of READY.]

currycomb /kúrri kōm/ *n* a comb with metal or rubber teeth, used to groom horses ■ *vt* to groom a horse with a currycomb [Late 16C. < CURRY[2].]

curry powder *n* a mixture of finely ground spices, usually turmeric, cumin, coriander, chilli, and ginger, used to make curry

curse /kurss/ *n* **1 SWEARWORD** a swearword, obscenity, or blasphemous oath **2 EVIL PRAYER** a malevolent appeal to a supernatural being for harm to come to somebody or something, or the harm that is thought to result from this **3 SOURCE OF HARM** a cause of unhappiness or harm ○ *the curse of poverty* **4 MENSTRUATION** menstruation or a menstrual period (*dated slang*) **5 RELIGIOUS BAN** an ecclesiastical pronouncement of censure or excommunication ■ *interj* **curses USED AS OATH** used to express irritation or annoyance ■ *v* (**curses, cursing, cursed**) **1** *vi* **SWEAR** to utter swearwords or obscenities **2** *vt* **SWEAR AT** to swear at somebody **3** *vt* **WISH EVIL ON** to appeal malevolently to a supernatural being for harm to come to somebody or something [Old English *curs*] —**curser** *n*

cursed /kúrssid, kurst/ *adj* **1 HAVING BEEN WISHED EVIL** afflicted with harm thought to result from a curse **2 WICKED OR HATEFUL** evil to the point of being despicable **3 ANNOYING OR FRUSTRATING** stubborn to the point of causing irritation or annoyance (*informal*) —**cursedly** *adv* —**cursedness** /kúrssidnəss/ *n*

cursive /kúrssiv/ *adj* **WRITTEN IN FLOWING STYLE** written in a flowing style with the letters joined together ■ *n* **1 FLOWING SCRIPT** cursive writing **2 MANUSCRIPT WRITTEN IN FLOWING STYLE** a piece of flowing handwriting, especially an ancient manuscript **3 TYPEFACE** a cursive typeface [Late 18C. < medieval Latin *cursivus* < Latin *currere* 'to run'.] —**cursively** *adv* —**cursiveness** *n*

⚡ **cursor** /kúrssər/ *n* a moving marker on a computer screen that marks the point at which keyed characters will appear or be deleted ■ *vi* to move the cursor in a particular direction on the screen of a computer or VDU ○ *As we cursor down, the hierarchy changes.* [14C. < Latin (see CURSORY).]

cursorial /kur sáwri əl/ *adj* having a body or body parts that are particularly well-adapted for running [Mid-19C. < Latin *cursor* (see CURSORY).]

cursory /kúrssəri/ *adj* done in a quick or superficial way [Early 17C. < Latin *cursorius* < *cursor* 'runner' < *currere* 'to run'.] —**cursorily** *adv* —**cursoriness** *n*

curt /kurt/ *adj* **1** rude or abrupt **2** using few words [14C. < Latin *curtus* 'cut short'.] —**curtly** *adv* —**curtness** *n*

curtail /kur táyl/ *vt* to reduce the length or duration of something [15C. By folk etymology < *curtal* 'animal with docked tail' < obsolete French *courtault*.] —**curtailment** *n*

curtail step *n* a wider lowest step on some flights of stairs, often rounded at one or both ends

curtain /kúrt'n/ *n* **1 CLOTH HUNG TO COVER** a piece of cloth hung at a window, in a doorway, or round a bed, usually for privacy or to exclude light or draughts **2 CLOTH AT FRONT OF STAGE** in a theatre, a hanging cloth that is raised and lowered or pulled back and forth at the front of the stage **3 BEGINNING OR END OF SHOW** the beginning or end of a performance, act, or scene, as marked by the raising or lowering or opening and closing of the curtain **4 BARRIER OR SCREEN** something that acts as a barrier or screen to divide, protect, or conceal something **5 SOMETHING RESEMBLING CURTAIN** something that resembles a curtain in appearance ○ *a curtain of water* **6 WALL CONNECTING OTHER STRUCTURES** a length of wall, especially one that connects two towers or gates ■ *vt* **1 COVER OR DIVIDE WITH CURTAIN** to surround, separate, or conceal something with a curtain **2 FIT WITH CURTAINS** to provide something, especially a window, with curtains [13C. Via Old French < Latin *cortina* 'cauldron', mistakenly < Greek *aulaia* 'curtain'.] ◇ **ring down the curtain on something** to bring an end to something (*informal*)

curtain call *n* an appearance by actors, dancers, or singers at the front of the stage to receive the audience's applause at the end of a performance

curtain raiser *n* **1** a short performance put on immediately before the main performance **2** a smaller or less important event that takes place before a bigger or more important one

curtain speech *n* **1** a speech addressed to the audience by somebody in front of the curtain after a play has ended **2** the speech before the final curtain of an act or play

curtain wall *n* **1** an external wall that does not bear any of the load of the building it is attached to **2** a low wall outside a castle built for defence

~~**curtesy**~~ incorrect spelling of **courtesy**

curtilage /kúrtəlij/ *n* an enclosed area occupied by a dwelling, grounds, and outbuildings [14C. < Old French *co(u)rtillage* < *co(u)rtil* 'kitchen garden', literally 'small court' < *cort* 'court'.]

Curtin /kúrtin/, **John Joseph** (1885–1945) Australian statesman

Curtiz /kúrtiz/, **Michael** (1888–1962) Hungarian-born US film director

curtsy /kúrtsi/, **curtsey** *vi* (**-sies, -sying, -sied; -seys, -seying, -seyed**) to bend the knees, with one foot behind the other, as a gesture of respect ■ *n* (*plural* **-sies;** *plural* **-seys**) a movement made by a woman as a sign of respect for somebody in which she bends her knees with one foot behind the other [Early 16C. Variant of COURTESY.]

curule /kyŏŏr ool/ *adj* in ancient Rome, having the status to sit on an official chair (**curule chair**) and the privileges associated with this status [Mid-16C. < Latin *curulis* < *currus* 'chariot' < *currere* 'to run'; because the chief Roman magistrate was conveyed in a chariot.]

curule chair *n* a folding chair with heavy legs and no back, used by high officials of ancient Rome

curvaceous /kur váyshəss/ *adj* having an attractive body with rounded hips and breasts —**curvaceously** *adv* —**curvaceousness** *n*

curvature /kúrvəchər/ *n* **1 BEING CURVED** the quality of being curved **2 DEGREE OF CURVE** the degree of curving in a line or surface ○ *the slight curvature of the land* **3 RECIPROCAL OF RADIUS** the reciprocal of the radius of the circle that best matches a curve at a given point [15C. < Latin *curvatura* 'bending' < *curvus* 'curved'.]

curve /kurv/ *n* **1 ROUNDED LINE** a line that bends smoothly and regularly from being straight or flat, like part of a circle or sphere **2 SOMETHING SHAPED IN A CURVE** something with a smooth round shape, such as a rounded part of a woman's body or a bend in a road **3 PLOTTED LINE** a line plotted on a graph from statistical data **4 LINE REPRESENTING EQUATION** a line whose points are defined by an equation and whose coordinates are functions of an independent variable **5** BASEBALL = **curve ball** ■ *v* (**curves, curving, curved**) **1** *vi* **MOVE IN CURVE** to move or bend in a curve **2** *vt* **CAUSE TO CURVE** to make something move or bend in a curve [15C. < Latin *curvus* 'curved, crooked'.] —**curved** *adj* ◇ **ahead of the curve** forward-thinking and ahead of a trend or trends ◇ **behind the curve** reacting, or slow to react, to a trend or trends

curve ball *n* in baseball, a ball that when pitched drifts to the left if thrown by a right-handed pitcher and to the right if thrown by a left-handed pitcher

curvet /kur vét/ *n* a leap by a horse in dressage in which its hind legs are raised just before the forelegs touch the ground ■ *vti* (**-vets, -veting** *or* **-vetting, -veted** *or* **-vetted**) to perform a curvet in dressage or to make a horse perform it [Late 16C. < Italian *corvetta* 'small curve' < *corve* 'curve' < Latin *curvus* 'curved'.]

curvilinear /kúrvi línni ər/, **curvilineal** /kúrvi línni əl/ *adj* **1** being a curve or having a curved part or parts ○ *a curvilinear polygon* **2** moving along a curved path or line ○ *The ball followed a curvilinear trajectory.* [Early 18C. < Latin *curvus* 'curved', after RECTILINEAR.] —**curvilinearity** /kúrvilinni árrəti/ *n* —**curvilinearly** *adv*

curvy /kúrvi/ (**-ier, -iest**) *adj* **1** with a rounded shape **2** having many curves or bends

Curzon /kúrz'n/, **Sir Clifford Michael** (1907–82) British concert pianist

Curzon, Lord George Nathaniel (1859–1925) British statesman

Cusack /kyŏŏss ak, kyŏŏz-/, **Cyril** (1910–93) South African-born Irish actor and stage director

cuscus /kúss kuss/ *n* a tree-dwelling nocturnal mammal with a round head, large eyes, large curved claws, and thick fur. Native to: rain forests of NE Australia and New Guinea. Genus: *Phalanger.* [Mid-17C. Via French *couscous* or modern Latin *cuscus* < Dutch *koeskoes* < a local word in New Guinea.]

cusec /kyŏŏ sek/ *n* a dated unit of flow equal to one cubic foot per second [Early 20C. Shortening of *cubic foot per second*.]

⚡ **CUSeeMe** *n* a computer program, developed at Cornell University, in Ithaca, New York, that enables users to engage in real-time video conferencing over the Internet

Cush /kŏŏsh/, **Kush** *n* **1** in the Bible, the oldest son of Ham and brother of Canaan (Genesis 10:6) **2** a region of NE Africa thought to be where the descendants of Cush settled. It is roughly equivalent to modern Ethiopia, part of N Sudan, and S Egypt.

cushat /kúshət/ *n Scotland* a wood pigeon [Old English *cuscute*]

Cushing /kŏŏshing/, **Peter** (1913–94) British actor

Cushing's disease *n* a form of Cushing's syndrome caused by excessive production of the hormone ACTH by the pituitary gland [Mid-20C. After Harvey *Cushing* (1869–1939), US surgeon.]

Cushing's syndrome *n* a condition caused by excessive production of corticosteroids by the adrenal cortex or pituitary gland and marked by obesity, muscular weakness, hypertension, striated skin, and fatigue [Mid-20C. After Harvey *Cushing*.]

cushion /kŏŏsh'n/ *n* **1 SOFT FILLED BAG FOR SITTING ON** a fabric case filled with soft material, used to sit or lean on **2 SOFT PROTECTIVE PAD** a pad that is used for support, to rest against, to protect against damage, or as a shock absorber **3 SOMETHING SOFT AND YIELDING** something that gives slightly when pressed ○ *a cushion of moss at the foot of the tree* **4 SOMETHING HELPFUL** something that limits the effect of an unpleasant situation ○ *An unexpected legacy provided a cushion when her savings ran out.* **5 BILLIARD TABLE RIM** the raised rim around the top of a billiard table that borders its playing surface **6** TRANSP = **air cushion** *n.* 1 **7 LACEMAKING ACCESSORY** a pillow for supporting the tools used in lacemaking ■ *vt* **1 PROTECT AGAINST IMPACT** to protect somebody or something against the effects of physical impact ○ *A pile of sand cushioned his fall.* **2 REDUCE UNPLEASANT EFFECT OF** to lessen the effect of an unpleasant situation, especially one involving money ○ *a generous pension to cushion the blow of early retirement* **3 SUPPORT OR PLACE ON CUSHION** to support or rest something on a cushion or other soft object **4 PAD** to pad something with cushions or some other soft spongy material [14C. < French *coussin*, literally '(support for the) hip' < Latin *coxa* 'hip'.] —**cushiony** *adj*

Cushitic /kŏŏ shíttik/ *n* a branch of the Afro-Asiatic family of languages spoken in Ethiopia, Somalia, and Kenya [Early 20C. < CUSH.] —**Cushitic** *adj*

cushy /kŏŏshi/ (**-ier, -iest**) *adj* providing a good salary, many perks, and little or no hard work (*informal*) ○ *a cushy job* [Early 20C. < Hindi *khūsh* 'pleasant'.] —**cushily** *adv* —**cushiness** *n*

cusk /kusk/ (*plural* **cusk** *or* **cusks**) *n US* **1** = **torsk** **2** = **burbot** [Early 17C. < ?]

cusp /kusp/ *n* **1 BORDER BETWEEN ZODIAC SIGNS** the border between two astrological star signs **2 POINTED END OF CRESCENT MOON** either of the pointed ends of a crescent moon or of any astronomical object appearing with the same curved shape **3 RIDGE ON MOLAR TOOTH** a ridge on the grinding surface of a molar tooth that helps in grinding and chewing food **4 FLAP OF VALVE** a triangular fold or flap of a valve in the heart or in lymph vessels that allows the flow of blood or lymph in one direction only **5 POINTED END** a pointed end of a leaf or other plant part **6 POINT OF INTERSECTION** a point where two arcs or branches of a curve intersect and the two tangents to the curve coincide **7 POINTED PROJECTION IN GOTHIC ARCHITECTURE** a pointed projection formed by the intersection of two arcs, used especially in Gothic architecture [Late 16C. < Latin *cuspis* 'point'.] —**cusped** *adj* —**cuspidate** /kúspi dayt/ *adj*

cuspid /kúspid/ *n* DENT = **canine** *n.* 1 [Mid-18C. < Latin *cuspid-*, stem of *cuspis* (see CUSP).]

cuspidor /kúspi dawr/ *n US* = **spittoon** [Mid-18C. < Portuguese, < *cuspir* 'to spit' < Latin *conspuere* < *spuere*.]

cuss /kuss/ *vti* **USE BAD LANGUAGE** to use vulgar and offensive language (*informal*) ■ *n* (*informal*) **1 SOMEBODY ANNOYING** somebody with a particular, usually irritating trait ○ *an* *awkward cuss* 2 **VULGAR OATH** an instance of vulgar or offensive language [Late 18C. Variant of CURSE.]

cussed /kússid/ *adj* (*informal*) 1 causing annoyance and anger, especially by being uncooperative 2 cursed [Mid-19C. Variant of CURSED.] —**cussedly** *adv* —**cussedness** *n*

cussword /kúss wurd/ *n US* a swearword (*informal*)

custard /k/ *n* 1 a sweet sauce made with eggs, milk, sugar, and a thickening agent, or with milk and custard powder 2 a cooked mixture of sugar, eggs, and milk [15C. Originally 'open pie of meat or fruit' < Anglo-Norman *crustade* < Old French *crouste* 'crust'.] —**custardy** *adj*

custard apple *n* 1 **HEART-SHAPED GREEN FRUIT** a large heart-shaped fruit with large black seeds and soft whitish flesh inside a green skin 2 **CARIBBEAN TREE** a tree that bears custard apples. Native to: Caribbean. *Annona reticulata.* 3 **FRUIT TREE RELATED TO CUSTARD APPLE** a fruit-bearing tree related to a custard apple tree, e.g. the pawpaw or sweetsop

custard pie *n* a pie filled with custard, whipped cream, or a substance resembling either of these, that is traditionally thrown at people in slapstick comedy routines

Custer /kústər/, **George Armstrong** (1839–76) US military leader

custodial /ku stṓdi əl/ *adj* 1 **INVOLVING DETENTION** involving or consisting of detention in a prison ○ *a custodial sentence* 2 **RELATING TO LEGAL CUSTODY** relating to the legal custody of, and responsibility for, a child ○ *a custodial parent* 3 **RELATING TO A CUSTODIAN** connected with the work of a custodian ■ *n* **SOMEBODY THAT SAFEGUARDS INVESTORS' FUNDS** an organization such as a bank that holds in safekeeping the securities and other assets of an investment company or individual investor

custodian /ku stṓdi ən/ *n* 1 **PERSON RESPONSIBLE FOR SOMETHING VALUABLE** somebody responsible for holding or looking after valuable property on behalf of a company or another person 2 **SAFEGUARDER OF INVESTORS' FUNDS** an organization such as a bank that holds in safekeeping the securities and other assets of an investment company or individual investor 3 **UPHOLDER OF SOMETHING VALUABLE** a protector and upholder of something seen as valuable and endangered, e.g. traditions or moral values 4 **CARETAKER** somebody who looks after a building 5 **PROTECTOR OF VALUABLE COLLECTION** an overseer of the contents of a museum, library, or other public institution [Late 18C. < CUSTODY.] —**custodianship** *n*

custody /kústədi/ *n* 1 **DETENTION** the state of being detained by the police or other authorities ○ *arrested and in custody* ○ *Police have taken a man into custody.* 2 **RIGHTS OVER CHILD** the legal right to look after a child 3 **PROTECTION** the state of being held under the protection of another or being in somebody else's care [15C. < Latin *custodia* 'guarding' < *custos* 'guardian'.]

custom /kústəm/ *n* 1 **TRADITION** something that people always do or always do in a particular way by tradition 2 **HABIT** the way somebody normally or routinely behaves in a situation 3 **REGULAR BUYING FROM A SHOP** the regular buying of goods from a particular shop or business ○ *The manager and staff would like to thank you for your custom.* US term **patronage** 4 **SHOP'S CUSTOMERS** all the customers of a particular shop or business 5 **TRADITION LIKE LAW** a traditional practice that is so long-established and universal that it has acquired the force of law ○ *custom and practice* 6 **FEUDAL RENT** a tribute, rent, or other obligation paid by a feudal vassal to a lord ■ *adj* 1 **MADE TO ORDER** made or built to order 2 **MAKING GOODS TO ORDER** making or selling custom-made goods ○ *a custom tailor* 3 **CHANGED TO SUIT BETTER** altered in order to fit somebody's requirements better [12C. Via Old French *costume* 'habitual practice' < Latin *consuetudin-* < *consuescere*, literally 'accustom completely' < *suescere* 'become accustomed'.]

SYNONYMS See ***habit.***

customable /kústəməb'l/ *adj* liable to import or export duties

customary /kústəməri/ *adj* 1 **USUAL** conforming to what is usual or normal 2 **TYPICAL** usual for somebody or typical of somebody's normal behaviour ○ *his customary good humour* 3 **BY CUSTOM** based on tradition and custom rather than written law ■ *n* (*plural* **-ies**) **BODY OF USUAL PRACTICES** a listing of customary practices that have the force of law —**customarily** *adv* —**customariness** *n*

SYNONYMS See ***usual.***

custom-built *adj* designed and built to meet the requirements of one individual customer —**custom-build** *vt*

custom drug *n* a drug that targets a specific condition, especially one that is tailored to an individual patient's genetic requirements

customer /kústəmər/ *n* 1 a person or company who buys goods or services 2 a person who interacts with others in a characteristic way (*informal*) ○ *a tough customer* [15C. < the idea of 'customary business practice'.]

customer service, customer services *n* a department of a business that deals with complaints from or disputes with customers or that handles routine inquiries from callers ○ *You can call customer service free.*

custom house, customhouse /kústəm howss/, **customs house** *n* an office at a port where customs are collected and where ships are given permission to enter or leave

customize /kústə mīz/ (**-izes, -izing, -ized**), **customise** (**-ises, -ising, -ised**) *vt* to alter something in order to make it fit somebody's requirements better ○ *She has customized the software to suit our needs.* —**customization** /kústə mī záysh'n/ *n* —**customizer** *n*

custom-made *adj* designed and made to meet the requirements of one individual customer ○ *custom-made shoes*

customs /kústəmz/ *n* (+ *singular or plural verb*) 1 **customs, Customs PLACE WHERE DUTIABLE GOODS ARE EXAMINED** the place where goods and baggage are examined on entering a country to see what duty is payable on them and to check for smuggled goods ○ *pass through customs* 2 **customs, Customs GOVERNMENT AGENCY** the government department responsible for collecting taxes on imports and for prevention of illegal imports 3 **DUTIES ON GOODS** taxes payable on imports and exports [14C. < CUSTOM 'customary tax'.]

Customs and Excise *n* the department of the government responsible for collecting customs and VAT and for preventing the import of illegal goods

customs house *n* FIN, SHIPPING = **custom house**

customs union *n* an association of countries that enjoy free trade among themselves and agree on tariffs for nonmembers

ϟ **cut** /kut/ *v* (**cuts, cutting, cut**) 1 *vti* **DIVIDE SOMETHING WITH SHARP TOOL** to divide something into pieces using a knife, scissors, or a similar sharp-edged tool 2 *vt* **SEVER USING SHARP TOOL** to sever something or separate a part of something using a sharp-edged tool such as a knife, scissors, or a saw ○ *cut a slice of bread* 3 *vti* **MAKE HOLE IN** to pierce something or make a hole in something using a sharp instrument 4 *vi* **BE SHARP** to be sharp enough to slice or pierce things easily ○ *These scissors won't cut.* 5 *vt* **INJURE WITH SHARP EDGE** to injure yourself or somebody else with something sharp, usually enough to draw blood 6 *vt* **SHORTEN WITH SHARP TOOL** to make something shorter by removing some of it with a sharp tool such as scissors ○ *I'm having my hair cut this afternoon.* 7 *vt* **FASHION A GARMENT** to shape fabric in a particular way in order to fashion a garment ○ *You can tell a jacket that has been nicely cut.* 8 *vi* **TAKE OR BE A SHORT-CUT** to cross, travel, or make a line through or across an area, especially in order to save time ○ *This path cuts through the woods.* 9 *vt* **REDUCE A QUANTITY** to reduce an amount, e.g. of money or time, or remove an amount from something ○ *The budget cannot be cut any further without reducing services.* 10 *vt* **SHORTEN BY EDITING** to make a film, text, play, broadcast, or speech shorter by removing parts of it, or remove a part to make it shorter 11 *vti* **DELETE DATA** to delete data on a computer from one place, usually with the intention of inserting it in another. ◗ **paste** 12 *vti* **EDIT FILM OR VIDEO** to edit a film or other work intended for performance or broadcast 13 *vi* **STOP FILMING** to stop filming a particular scene (*usually a command*) 14 *vi* **CHANGE SCENE** to switch suddenly from one scene to another when filming or showing a film 15 *vt* **STOP PROVIDING** to stop providing a service or supply of something ○ *cut the food supply to the refugee camps* 16 *vt* **SWITCH OFF** to stop something operating ○ *cut the engine* 17 *vt* **CASTRATE** to castrate or geld a male animal 18 *vti* **DIVIDE PACK OF CARDS** to divide a pack of cards in two, usually after shuffling them 19 *vt* **MAKE A RECORDING** to make a recording of a song or group of songs ○ *The band cut 12 new tracks for the album.* 20 *vti* **REMOVE GRIME** to dissolve something such as dirt or grease from something else in the process of cleaning it 21 *vti* **INTERSECT** to cross something or cross each other at a particular point ○ *The road cuts the river in three places.* 22 *vi* **CHANGE DIRECTION SHARPLY** to make a sharp change in direction ○ *You need to cut to the right here.* 23 *vt* **NOT ATTEND** to not go to a place you are supposed to be, such as school (*informal*) ○ *expelled for cutting classes* 24 *vt* **GROW TEETH THROUGH GUMS** to produce a tooth through the surface of the gums ○ *The baby's cutting a tooth.* 25 *vt* **SNUB ANOTHER** to pay no attention to somebody publicly or obviously or stop a social relationship with somebody 26 *vti* **UPSET** to hurt somebody's feelings ○ *a cruel remark that cut me deeply* 27 *vt* **DILUTE** to add a substance to another, especially to a drug or an alcoholic drink, usually in order to make it weaker or cheaper 28 *vt* **STOP DOING** to stop doing something that is annoying somebody ○ *Cut that racket!* 29 *vt* **HIT A BALL SO IT SPINS** to hit a ball in such a way that it spins as it flies through the air 30 *vt* **HIT WITH BAT HORIZONTAL** to strike a cricket ball square on the offside with the bat more or less parallel to the ground ■ *n* 1 **WOUND IN SKIN** an injury made when something sharp pierces the skin 2 **INCISION** an incision made in something with a knife or other sharp-edged tool 3 **REDUCTION** a reduction in the amount of something ○ *cuts in taxes and interest rates* 4 **HAIRCUT** a haircut or hairstyle 5 **GARMENT STYLE** the way of cutting a garment from fabric that determines its shape and fit 6 **PRUNING OF TEXT** a removal of a section of a film, text, play, broadcast, or speech in order to make it shorter or improve it, or a section removed ○ *The editor advised me to make some cuts in the final chapter.* 7 **VERSION** a particular edited version of a film ○ *the director's final cut of the film* 8 **SHARE** somebody's share from an amount of money or something else to be divided (*informal*) 9 **STOPPING OF SUPPLY** a stopping of a supply, e.g. of electricity or water ○ *power cuts* 10 **PIECE OF MEAT FOR COOKING** a piece of meat cut in a standard way, ready to be cooked ○ *The chef only buys the more expensive cuts.* 11 **CRICKET STROKE** a cricket stroke square on the offside where the bat is swung more or less parallel to the ground 12 **SINGLE RECORDING** a track on a musical recording 13 **SWING OF BASEBALL BAT** a swing of a baseball bat 14 **SPIN ON A BALL** the spin given to a struck ball 15 **DIVIDING OF PACK OF CARDS** the action of dividing a pack of cards in two 16 **ITEMS FOR DRAWING LOTS** one of several pieces of paper or straws used to draw lots 17 **PRINTING DEVICE** a block for printing that has a design engraved, incised, or cut in relief on it (*often in combination*) 18 **HURTFUL WORDS** words or action intended to insult or hurt 19 **CANAL** a stretch of canal or a channel made for a river 20 *Ireland* **LOOKS** somebody's personal appearance (*informal*) 21 *Ireland* **MESS** a messy condition ■ *adj* 1 **INJURED WITH SOMETHING SHARP** injured or damaged by something sharp, usually enough to draw blood ○ *nursing a cut finger* 2 **SEPARATED WITH KNIFE** separated or severed using a knife, scissors, or similar sharp tool 3 **DRUNK** totally drunk (*informal*) 4 **DIVIDED** describes a leaf that is divided into segments [13C. < assumed Old English *cytan.*] —**cuttable** *adj* ◇ **a cut above** somebody or something superior to somebody or something ◇ **cut and run** to leave a place quickly to avoid being caught or detained ◇ **cut both ways** to have both advantages and disadvantages ◇ **cut it fine** to allow barely enough of something, often time, for what has to be done ◇ **cut loose** 1 to behave in an unrestrained and relatively uncontrolled way (*informal*) 2 to break away from the influence or control of somebody or something (*informal*) ◇ **cut somebody dead** to ignore somebody deliberately and completely ◇ **cut something** *or* **somebody short** to end something earlier than expected or desired, or interrupt what somebody is saying ◇ **not (be able to) cut it** to fall short of requirements or be unable to cope with a situation (*informal*) ○ *His usual excuses just don't cut it with me.* ◇ **the cut of somebody's jib** somebody's manner and general appearance

cut across *vt* to affect a widely differing group of people or things equally

cut along *vi* go somewhere promptly (*informal dated; usually a command*)

cut back *v* 1 *vti* to reduce the amount of something ○ *cut back on spending* 2 *vt* to cut the tops or all of the stems or branches off a plant in order to remove dead growth or produce bushier growth

cut down *v* 1 *vti* **REDUCE** to consume, use, or do less of something, especially because it is considered harmful ○ *The doctor says I have to cut down on fried foods.* 2 *vt* **FELL OR CLEAR AWAY PLANTS** to cut through the trunk or stem of a plant so that it can be harvested or removed 3 *vt* **KILL** to kill somebody, especially suddenly or unexpectedly (*informal; usually passive*) 4 *vt* **MAKE CLOTHING SMALLER** to alter a piece of clothing so that it will fit somebody smaller **5** *vt* **REMODEL BY REMOVING EXTRAS** to remodel a car by removing unnecessary extras, especially to make it more suitable for racing

cut in *v* **1** *vti* **INTERRUPT** to interrupt when somebody is speaking **2** *vi* **JOIN TRAFFIC DANGEROUSLY** to join a lane of traffic too close in front of another car so that it has to brake sharply **3** *vti* **JOIN MIDDLE OF QUEUE** to enter a queue of people by pushing in front of others who have been waiting **4** *vt* **START TO OPERATE** to start working as part of a machine or electrical device **5** *vt* **ALLOW TO SHARE** to allow somebody to have a share in something, especially money ○ *cut us in on the profits* **6** *vi* **PARTNER SOMEBODY ALREADY DANCING** to interrupt a dancing couple and take one of them as your own partner **7** *vi* **REPLACE A CARD PLAYER** to take the place of a person who has abandoned a card game **8** *vt* **MIX FAT WITH FLOUR** to mix fat into flour using a metal blade in order to ensure that it is evenly distributed

cut off *v* **1** *vt* **REMOVE PART OF** to remove something that is part of something else by cutting it **2** *vt* **STOP SUPPLY** to stop supplying something ○ *cut off the electricity* **3** *vt* **ISOLATE** to separate a person, place, or group from normal communication or contact ○ *a town cut off by the blizzard* **4** *vt* **STOP SOMEBODY TALKING** to interrupt what somebody is saying and stop him or her talking ○ *cut him off in mid-sentence* **5** *vt* **DISCONNECT TELEPHONE CONNECTION** to disconnect people who are talking on the telephone **6** *vt* **DISINHERIT** to exclude somebody from an inheritance ○ *They cut their son off without a penny.* **7** *vt* **BRING TO ABRUPT END** to bring something to an abrupt end or somebody to an early death (*often passive*) ○ *She was cut off in her prime.* **8** *vi* **CEASE ABRUPTLY** to come to an abrupt end ○ *The noise cut off suddenly.*

cut out *v* **1** *vt* **REMOVE BY CUTTING** to remove part of something using a cutting tool **2** *vt* **CUT SHAPE** to cut a shaped piece from a larger part or whole **3** *vt* **STOP DOING** to stop consuming, using, or doing something, especially because it is considered harmful ○ *I've cut out all dairy products.* **4** *vt* **REMOVE PART FROM TEXT** to remove part of a text or broadcast **5** *vt* **OMIT** to exclude, eliminate, or omit something ○ *I followed the recipe but cut out the walnuts.* **6** *vt* **EXCLUDE** to exclude or eliminate somebody from a group or activity ○ *cut them out of future negotiations* **7** *vt* **DISINHERIT** to change a will so that somebody will no longer inherit **8** *vi* **STOP WORKING** to stop functioning suddenly, especially to stop providing power ○ *The engine cut out.* **9** *vt* **STOP SOMETHING ANNOYING** to stop doing something that is annoying somebody (*informal; often a command*) ○ *Cut out the wisecracks.* **10** *vt* **SEPARATE ANIMAL FROM HERD** to separate an animal or animals, particularly cows, from a herd **11** *vi* **END** to finish or come to an end (*informal*) ○ *The road cuts out at the creek.* ■ *adj* **NATURALLY SUITED** naturally suited for a particular activity or profession ○ *I wasn't cut out to be a driving instructor.*

cut over *vt* to transfer existing data, functions, or users of a system to new facilities or equipment in a synchronized manner, to ensure continuity and minimize disruption

cut through *vt* to deal with an obstacle in a way that reduces or eliminates it ○ *Can't we cut through the formalities?*

cut up *v* **1** *vt* **CUT IN PIECES** to cut something into pieces **2** *vt* **INJURE** to injure somebody, especially enough to draw blood ○ *He was badly cut up after the fight and had to be taken to hospital.* **3** *vt* **UPSET** to upset and distress somebody greatly (*informal; usually passive*) ○ *He was cut up over his mother's death.* **4** *vt* **ENDANGER TRAFFIC** to endanger fellow road users by driving suddenly in front of them or across their path **5** *vi* **US MISBEHAVE** to behave in a humorous and disruptive way (*slang*) ○ *cutting up in class* **6** *vt* **CRITICIZE** to criticize somebody severely (*dated informal*) ◇ **cut up rough** to become very angry or unpleasant

cut-and-cover *adj* describes a method of constructing a tunnel by digging a trench down from ground level and then roofing it

cut-and-dried *adj* **1** clear, settled, and not needing changes or causing further problems **2** obvious or conforming to what is expected ○ *a cut-and-dried press conference* [Originally used of herbs for sale in shops]

⚡ **cut-and-paste** *n* a facility of computers allowing data to be deleted in one place and inserted in another ○ *Use cut-and-paste to move that paragraph into the new document.* —**cut-and-paste** *vt*

cut-and-shut *n* a car created by welding together the bodies of two cars that have been damaged in an accident (*slang*) —**cut-and-shut** *vt*

cut and thrust *n* fast, aggressive, or dramatic exchanges between people ○ *the cut and thrust of parliamentary debate* ■ *adj* describes swords designed for using both the blade and the tip

cutaneous /kyoo táyni əss/ *adj* relating to the skin [Late 16C. < modern Latin *cutaneus* < Latin *cutis* 'skin'.] —**cutaneously** *adv*

cutaway /kútta way/ *n* **1** **MODEL WITH INSIDE VIEW** a drawing or model of something with part of its outside removed to give a view of the inside **2** **SECONDARY SHOT WITH CAMERA** a cut to a camera shot of an action separate from the main action ■ *adj* **1** **GIVING INSIDE VIEW** constructed or represented so as to give a view of the inside **2** **CUT DIAGONALLY** with the front cut diagonally away from the centre, e.g. in the part of a tail coat below the waist

cutback /kút bak/ *n* a reduction in the amount of something ○ *cutbacks in public spending*

cute /kyoot/ (**cuter, cutest**) *adj* **1** **ATTRACTIVE IN CHILDLIKE WAY** endearingly attractive in the way that some children and young animals are **2** *US* **PHYSICALLY ATTRACTIVE** young and physically attractive **3** **PLEASING** smaller than the usual size but nicely arranged or appointed ○ *an apartment with a cute little kitchen* **4** *US* **SHREWD** sharply clever or wily [Early 18C. Shortening of ACUTE.] —**cutely** *adv* —**cuteness** *n* ◇ **get cute (with somebody)** to show insolence to somebody

cutes plural of **cutis**

cutesy /kyóotsi/ (**-sier, -siest**) *adj* too obviously attempting to be charming —**cutesiness** *n*

cutey *n* = **cutie**

cut glass *n* glass with a decorative pattern cut into its surface

cut-glass *adj* **1** made of glass with a decorative pattern cut into its surface **2** sounding extremely upper-class ○ *a cut-glass accent*

Cuthbert /kúthbərt/, **St** (630?–687) English missionary

Cuthbert, Betty (*b.* 1938) Australian sprinter

cuticle /kyóotik'l/ *n* **1** **SKIN AT BASE OF NAILS** an edge of hard skin at the base of a fingernail or toenail **2** ANAT = **epidermis** *n.* **1 3** **DEAD EPIDERMIS** dead or hardened epidermis **4** **PROTECTIVE PLANT LAYER** the thin outermost noncellular layer covering the above ground parts of plants and helping to prevent water loss **5** **HARD COVERING OF INVERTEBRATES** a hardened noncellular layer secreted by and covering the epidermis in many invertebrates [15C. < Latin *cuticula* 'little skin' < *cutis* 'skin'.] —**cuticular** /kyoo tíkyoŏlar/ *adj*

cutie /kyóoti/, **cutey** (*plural* **-eys**) *n* an endearingly attractive person (*informal*)

cutin /kyóotin/ *n* a waxy mixture of fats and soaps forming the protective layer (**cuticle**) of plants [Mid-19C. < CUTIS.]

cut-in *n* a camera shot that focuses in on a smaller portion of a scene already established

cutis /kyóotiss/ (*plural* **-tes** /kyoŏ teez/) *n* ANAT = **dermis** [Early 17C. < Latin, 'skin'.]

cutlass /kútləss/ *n* a short thrusting sword with a flat and slightly curved blade formerly used especially by sailors [Late 16C. Via French *cutelas* 'large knife' < Latin *cultellus* 'small knife' < *culter* (see COULTER).]

cutlass fish *n* ZOOL = **hairtail**

cutler /kútlər/ *n* a maker of cutlery [14C. < French *coutelier* < Old French *coutel* < Latin *cultellus* (see CUTLASS).]

cutlery /kútləri/ *n* **1** knives, forks, and spoons used for eating. US term **flatware 2** knives and other instruments with a blade

cutlet /kútlət/ *n* **1** a piece of lamb or veal taken from the neck of the animal **2** a mixture of chopped meat, fish, nuts, vegetables, or other foods, made into a flat round shape, covered with breadcrumbs, and fried [Early 18C. < French *côtelette* 'little rib' < Latin *costa* 'rib'.]

cutoff /kút of/ *n* **1** **LIMIT** a limit or date, beyond which something is stopped **2** **END OF SUPPLY** an end to the supply of something ○ *a cutoff in oil imports* **3** **VALVE** a valve that controls the flow of fluid or gas through a pipe **4** **BREAK IN MUSIC** the end of a note, passage, or piece of music, especially when indicated by a sign from the conductor **5** **SIGNAL FROM MUSIC CONDUCTOR** a sign given by a conductor to indicate a break in the music **6** **ELECTRICAL THRESHOLD** the value of voltage, frequency, or other variable that represents a minimum or maximum for ef-

fective operation **7** **NEW RIVER CHANNEL** a short channel cut by a river across a bend in the river, forming an oxbow lake ■ **cutoffs** *npl* **SHORTS MADE FROM TROUSERS** shorts made by cutting off the legs of a pair of trousers, especially jeans

cutout /kút owt/ *n* **1** **SILHOUETTE SHAPE** a two-dimensional shape of somebody or something usually made from stiff cardboard **2** **SOMETHING CUT OUT** something that has been cut out from something else **3** **SAFETY DEVICE FOR ELECTRIC CIRCUIT** a device that switches off an electric circuit or supply, e.g. to a machine, as a safety measure **4** **UNORIGINAL PERSON** an unoriginal or characterless person or an unimaginative imitation of somebody (*disapproving*) ○ *a cardboard cutout* **5** **OUTDATED AUDIO RECORDING** a recording sold at a discount because it is out-of-date and supply exceeds demand

⚡ **cutover** /kút ōvər/ *n* the transfer of a system, e.g. a computer network, to new facilities or equipment including the transitional period when old and new systems are operating concurrently

cut-price *adj* **1** on sale for less than the standard price **2** selling goods or services at a cheaper price than is standard ○ *a cut-price chemist*

cutpurse /kút purss/ *n* a pickpocket (*archaic*)

cut-rate *adj* selling for less than the standard price, and often regarded as shoddy

⚡ **CUTS** /kuts/ *abbr* Computer Users' Tape System

Cuttack /kúttək/ *n* city in E India. Population: 403,418 (1991).

cutter /kúttər/ *n* **1** **SHARP TOOL** a tool used to cut through something (*often plural*) ○ *wire cutters* **2** **SOMEBODY WHO CUTS** somebody whose work involves cutting things, e.g. fabrics to be made into clothing **3** **PERSON WHO REDUCES** a person who cuts or reduces something **4** **SINGLE-MASTED SAILING BOAT** a single-masted sailing vessel on which the mast is positioned farther aft than on a sloop **5** **BOAT FOR TRANSPORTING PASSENGERS** a ship's boat, powered by a motor or by oars that is used for transporting passengers and light cargo

cutthroat /kút thrōt/ *adj* **1** **WITH NO HOLDS BARRED** aggressive and merciless in striving for supremacy **2** **FOR 3 PLAYERS** describes games for three players that are adapted from games for four partnered players ○ *cutthroat bridge* ■ *n* **1** **DANGEROUS PERSON** a murderer or a very aggressive dangerous person **2** HOUSEHOLD = **cutthroat razor 3** (*plural* **-throat** *or* **-throats**) ZOOL = **cutthroat trout**

cutthroat razor *n* a razor with a long blade and a handle that the blade can be folded into. US term **straight razor**

cutthroat trout *n* a trout of W North America that resembles the rainbow trout but has reddish-orange markings on either side of the throat. *Salmo clarkii.*

cut time *n* *US* = **alla breve** *n*

cutting /kútting/ *n* **1** **PART OF PLANT FOR PROPAGATION** a piece taken from a stem, leaf, or root that will grow into a new whole plant **2** **ARTICLE CUT FROM NEWSPAPER** an article or photograph that has been cut out of a newspaper or magazine. US term **clipping** *n.* **3** **OPEN TRENCH THROUGH HIGH GROUND** an open trench cut through a hill or high ground to avoid a steep incline for a railway, road, or canal **4** **EDITING PROCESS** the process of editing a text, film, or recording **5** **CHANGING OF SHOTS IN FILM** the technique of changing from one shot to another in the editing of a film ■ **cuttings** *npl* **PILE OF SMALL FRAGMENTS** small fragments that are brought up during rock drilling or that accumulate during coal cutting ■ *adj* **1** **ABRASIVE AND HURTFUL** sharply expressed and likely to upset somebody's feelings ○ *a cutting remark* **2** **VERY COLD** piercingly cold ○ *a cutting wind* —**cuttingly** *adv*

cutting board *n* *US* HOUSEHOLD = **chopping board**

cutting edge *n* the most advanced and modern stage of something (*hyphenated before nouns*)

cutting room *n* a room where cinema film is edited, normally by hand and by being physically cut

cuttlebone /kútt'l bōn/ *n* the white internal shell of a cuttlefish. Use: whole as a mineral supplement for caged birds, in powdered form for polishing. [Late 16C. *Cuttle* < Old English *cudele* (see CUTTLEFISH).]

cuttlefish /kútt'l fish/ (*plural* **-fish** *or* **-fishes**) *n* a marine invertebrate animal that lives on the seabed and has ten arms, a flattened body, and an internal shell. Genus:

Sepia. [Late 16C. *Cuttle* < Old English *cudele* 'cuttlefish', related to COD[2] 'bag'; from its shape.]

cutty /kútti/ (*plural* **-ties**) *n Northern Ireland* an offensive term for a woman [Early 19C. < CUT.]

cutty grass *n* a grass with sharp-edged leaves. Native to: New Zealand. *Cyperus ustulatus*. [< CUT]

cutup /kút up/ *n US* somebody known for telling jokes, showing off, and doing pranks (*informal*)

cutwater /kút wawtər/ *n* **1** the foremost part of a ship's prow **2** a pointed or wedge-shaped upstream face of a bridge pier at water level, designed to minimize the effects of moving water, ice floes, and debris

cutwork /kút wurk/ *n* openwork embroidery in which the design is outlined in buttonhole stitch, then some parts of the fabric within the outlines are cut away

cutworm /kút wurm/ *n* a nocturnal moth caterpillar that feeds on and eats through the base of young plant stems. Family: Noctuidae.

cuvée /koo váy/ *n* a single batch of wine [Mid-19C. < French, 'vatful' < *cuve* 'cask, vat' < Latin *cupa*.]

cuvette /kyoo vét/ *n* a transparent tubular laboratory vessel or dish for holding a liquid [Late 17C. < French, 'small cask' < *cuve* (see CUVÉE).]

Cuvier /kyóovi ay/, **Baron Georges** (1769–1832) French zoologist and anatomist

Cuvilliés /kyoo vílli ay/, **François de** (1695–1768) French architect

Cuzco /kóoss kō, kóoss-/ capital of Cuzco Department, S Peru. Population: 278,590 (1998 estimate).

⚡ **cv** *abbr* Cape Verde (*in Internet addresses*)

CV *abbr* **1** Cape Verde **2** Cross of Valour **3 CV, cv** curriculum vitae

CVA *abbr* cerebrovascular accident

CVO *abbr* Commander of the Royal Victorian Order

CVS *abbr* **1** chorionic villus sampling **2** Council of Voluntary Service

cw *abbr* continuous wave

CW *abbr* **1** chemical warfare **2** chemical weapons **3** continuous wave

cwm /kóom, koom/ *n* **1** *Wales* a valley (*often in placenames*) **2** GEOL = **cirque** [Mid-19C. < Welsh, 'valley'.]

Cwmbran /kóom braán/ town in SE Wales. Population: 46,021 (1991).

CWO *abbr* **1** Chief Warrant Officer **2** chief Web officer

⚡ **c.w.o., CWO** *abbr* cash with order

CWS *abbr* Cooperative Wholesale Society

cwt *abbr* hundredweight [Early 16C. *C* (roman numeral) 'hundred'.]

⚡ **cx** *abbr* Christmas Island (*in Internet addresses*)

⚡ **cXML** *abbr* commerce XML (*in e-commerce*)

⚡ **cy** *abbr* Cyprus (*in Internet addresses*)

-cy *suffix* **1** condition, quality ○ *buoyancy* **2** action ○ *advocacy* **3** rank, office ○ *baronetcy* [Via Old French *-cie*, *-tie* < Latin *-cia*, *-tia*, Greek *-k(e)ia*, *-t(e)ia*]

cyan /sī ən, sī an/ *n* a deep greenish-blue colour that, together with yellow and magenta, is one of the three subtractive colours [Late 19C. < Greek *kuan(e)os* 'dark blue'.] —**cyan** *adj*

cyan- *prefix* = **cyano-** (*before vowels*)

cyanamide /sī ánnə mīd/, **cyanamid** /-mid/ *n* **1** CH_2N_2 a white crystalline caustic compound **2** CHEM = **calcium cyanamide**

cyanate /sī ə nayt/ *n* a salt or ester of cyanic acid

cyanic /sī ánnik/ *adj* of a greenish-blue colour

cyanic acid *n* HOCN a weak colourless unstable acid

cyanide /sī ə nīd/ *n* **1** POISONOUS SALT a poisonous inorganic salt that contains the ion CN^- **2** CHEM = **potassium cyanide** **3** CHEM = **sodium cyanide** ■ *vt* (**-nides, -niding, -nided**) **1** HARDEN METAL WITH CYANIDE to treat something, e.g. a metal surface, with cyanide to increase its hardness **2** TREAT ORE WITH SODIUM CYANIDE to treat ore with a weak solution of sodium cyanide to remove gold or silver [Early 19C. < CYANOGEN.] —**cyanidation** /sī ə nī dáysh'n/ *n*

cyanide process *n* a process for extracting gold or silver from ore by treating the ore with a weak solution of sodium cyanide and recovering the metal particles from the resulting solution

cyanine /sī ə neen/ *n* a chemical belonging to a group of blue dyes. Use: improving the sensitivity of photographic film to green, yellow, red, and infrared light.

cyanite /sī ə nīt/ *n* MINERALS = **kyanite**

cyano- *prefix* **1** blue ○ *cyanosis* **2** containing the –CN group [< Greek *kuanos* 'dark blue']

cyanoacrylate /sī ə nō ákri layt/ *n* a liquid acrylate monomer belonging to a group with adhesive properties. Use: industry and medicine.

cyanobacteria /sī ənō bak téeri ə/ *npl* bacteria belonging to a large group that have a photosynthetic pigment, carry out photosynthesis, and were formerly classified as blue-green algae. Family: Cyanophyta.

cyanocobalamin /sī ə nō kō bállәmin/ *n* BIOCHEM = **vitamin** B_{12}

cyanogen /sī ánnəjən/ *n* **1** C_2N_2 a flammable colourless poisonous gas. Use: organic synthesis. **2 CN** a univalent radical. Source: cyanide compounds. [Early 19C. < French *cyanogène* < Greek *kuan(e)os* 'dark blue'; from its being a constituent of Prussian blue.]

cyanohydrin /sī ə nō hīdrin/ *n* an organic compound containing both cyano and hydroxyl groups, usually linked to the same carbon atom

cyanosis /sī ə nóssiss/ *n* a condition in which the skin and mucous membranes take on a bluish colour because there is not enough oxygen in the blood [Mid-19C. Via modern Latin < Greek *kuanōsis* 'blueness' < *kuan(e)os* 'dark blue'.] —**cyanotic** /sī ə nóttik/ *adj*

cyanotype /sī ánnə tīp/ *n* PRINTING = **blueprint** *n.* 1

Cybele /síbbəli/ *n* the Phrygian goddess of nature. She was worshipped by the Romans as the Great Mother of the Gods.

⚡ **cyber-** *prefix* computers and information systems ○ *cyberlaw* [< CYBERNETICS, CYBERSPACE]

⚡ **cyber age** *n* the present age, thought of as a period characterized by the growth and importance of computer technology and electronic communications

⚡ **cybercafé** /sībər kaffay/ *n* **1** a coffee house where people can browse the Internet for a fee **2** an area on the Internet where people communicate using a chat program or a bulletin board

⚡ **cybercast** /sībər kaast/ *n* a broadcast, in either sound or vision or in both, of an event that is transmitted via the Internet [Blend of CYBER- + BROADCAST] —**cybercast** *vti*

⚡ **cyberfear** /sībər feer/ *n* fear of the damage that can be caused to complex electronic systems by malicious use of computers

⚡ **cyberlaw** /sībər law/ *n* the body of laws relating to computers, information systems, and networks

⚡ **cybernate** /sībər nayt/ (**-nates, -nating, -nated**) *vt* to control a manufacturing process with a servomechanism or computer [Mid-20C. < CYBERNETICS.] —**cybernated** *adj* —**cybernation** /sībər náysh'n/ *n*

⚡ **cybernetics** /sībər néttiks/ *n* (+ *singular verb*) **1** the science or study of communication in organisms, organic processes, and mechanical or electronic systems **2** the replication or imitation of biological control systems with the use of technology [Mid-20C. < Greek *kubernētēs* 'steersman' < *kubernan* 'to steer'.] —**cybernetic** *adj* —**cybernetical** *adj* —**cybernetically** *adv* —**cybernetician** /sībərni tísh'n/ *n*

⚡ **cyberphobia** /sībər fóbi ə/ *n* a pathological fear of computers and information technology

cyberpunk /sībər pungk/ *n* science fiction featuring characters living in a darkly frightening, futuristic world dominated by computer technology

⚡ **cyber-romance** *n* a love affair started or conducted solely on the Internet

⚡ **cyberself** /sībər self/ (*plural* **-selves** /-selvz/) *n* a false identity assumed by somebody in an Internet chat room or in interactive Internet role-play

⚡ **cybersex** /sībər seks/ *n* sexual stimulation involving virtual reality or the Internet

⚡ **cybershopping** /sībər shoping/ *n* shopping for goods and services over the Internet

⚡ **cyberspace** /sībər spayss/ *n* **1** the notional realm in which electronic information exists or is exchanged ○ *an e-mail message lost in cyberspace* **2** the imagined world of virtual reality

⚡ **cybersquatting** /sībər skwoting/ *n* the registering of an Internet domain name containing a trademark with the intention of selling it to the trademark owner

⚡ **cybersurfer** /sībər surfər/, **cybertraveller** /-travvələr/ *n* a user of the Internet who spends much time surfing it (*slang*) —**cybersurfing** *n*

⚡ **cyberterrorism** /sībər térrərizəm/ *n* terrorist activity using the Internet to damage complex electronic systems or the data they contain

⚡ **cyberwar** /sībər wawr/ *n* warfare in which computer systems are used to damage or destroy enemy systems

⚡ **cyberwoozling** /sībər woozling/ *n* the gathering of data from the computer of a visitor to a website without his or her knowledge or authorization (*slang*) [Late 20C. < CYBER- + *woozle*, after the *woozle*, a scary animal in the Winnie the Pooh stories of A. A. MILNE.]

cyborg /sī bawrg/ *n* a fictional being that is part human, part robot [Mid-20C. < CYBERNETICS + ORGANISM.]

⚡ **cybrary** /sībrəri/ (*plural* **-ies**) *n* a guide to the information available on the World Wide Web on a particular topic, or an information-gathering service using the Internet [Late 20C. Blend of CYBER- + LIBRARY.] —**cybrarian** *n*

cycad /sī kad/ *n* a tropical tree that has a thick trunk, sharp-pointed leaves like palm leaves, and cones. Order: Cycadales. [Mid-19C. < modern Latin *Cycad-* < Greek *kukas*, miswriting of *koikas*, plural of *koix*, a palm tree.]

cycl- *prefix* = **cyclo-** (*before vowels*)

Cyclades /síklə deez/ large group of Greek islands in the S Aegean Sea. Population: 257,481 (1991). Area: 2,572 sq. km/993 sq. mi.

cyclamate /síklə mayt/ *n* a salt or ester of cyclamic acid, especially sodium cyclamate. Use: artificial sweetener. [Mid-20C. Contraction of *cyclohexylsulphamate*.]

cyclamen /sīkləmən/ *n* **1** a small plant with heart-shaped leaves that grows wild under trees in parts of Europe, and is also cultivated. Flowers: white, pink. Genus: *Cyclamen*. **2** a bright deep pink colour [Mid-16C. Via Latin *cyclaminos* < Greek *kuklaminos*, probably < *kuklos* 'circle'; from its bulbous root.]

cyclamic acid /síkləmik-/ *n* $C_6H_{13}NO_3S$ a synthetic crystalline acid. Use: production of cyclamates, food additive. [Contraction of *cyclohexylsulfamic acid*]

cyclase /-klayz, -klayss/ *n* an enzyme that aids the formation of hydrocarbon rings (**cyclization**)

⚡ **cycle** /sīk'l/ *n* **1** REPEATED SEQUENCE OF EVENTS a sequence of events that is repeated again and again, especially a causal sequence **2** TIME BETWEEN REPEATED EVENTS a period of time between repetitions of an event or phenomenon that occurs regularly ○ *a seven-year economic cycle* **3** COMPLETE PROCESS a complete process or sequence of processes in a machine or electronic device, or the time that this takes **4** BICYCLE a bicycle or tricycle **5** BICYCLE RIDE a ride on a bicycle or tricycle ○ *go for a cycle* **6** *US* = **motorcycle** *n.* **7** ONE COMPLETE OSCILLATION one complete continuous change in the magnitude of an oscillating quantity or system that brings the system back to its original energy state ○ *running at 100 cycles per second* **8** LINKED ARTWORKS a series of linked songs, poems, stories, plays, or operas that deal with the same story, events, or characters ○ *Wagner's Ring cycle* **9** LONG TIME a very long period of time **10** ORBIT one complete orbit of a celestial body **11** SET OF OPERATIONS a set of instructions completed as a unit by a computer, or the time that completion takes ■ *v* (**-cles, -cling, -cled**) **1** *vi* RIDE BICYCLE to ride a bicycle or tricycle **2** *vti* GO THROUGH CYCLE to put something through or go through a sequence of events ○ *programmed to cycle every hour* [14C. Directly or via French < Latin *cyclus* < Greek *kuklos* 'circle'.]

cycle lane *n* a lane of a road for the use of cyclists

cycle of erosion *n* the development of landforms from mountains to plains

cycle path *n* a route or path for the use of cyclists. US term **bikeway**

cyclic /síklik, sík-/, **cyclical** /síklik'l, sík-/ *adj* 1 IN CYCLES occurring or repeated in cycles 2 ARRANGED IN RING describes organic compounds that are composed of a closed ring of atoms 3 WITH RECURRENT THEME containing a recurrent theme or motif —**cyclicality** /síkli kálləti, sík-/ *n* —**cyclically** *adv* —**cyclicity** /sī klíssəti, si-/ *n*

cyclic AMP *n* a cyclic form of AMP that activates enzymes in many hormone-induced biochemical reactions

cyclic GMP *n* a cyclic form of GMP that is responsible for aspects of cell division and growth

cyclisation *n* CHEM = **cyclization**

cyclist /síklist/ *n* somebody who rides a bicycle or tricycle

cyclization /sī klī záysh'n, síklī-/, **cyclisation** *n* the formation of one or more hydrocarbon rings in an organic compound

cyclo- *prefix* 1 circle, cycle ○ *cyclometer* 2 cyclic compound ○ *cyclopropane* [< Greek *kuklos* 'circle']

cycloaddition /síklō ə dísh'n/ *n* the creation of a ring structure in a chemical compound

cycloalkane /síklō ál kayn/ *n* CHEM = **alicyclic**

cyclo-cross /síklō-/ *n* the sport of racing bicycles across rough country, or a race of this kind [< CYCLE + MOTOCROSS]

cyclogenesis /sī klō jénnəssiss, sí klō-/ *n* the formation and development of a cyclone [Mid-20C. < CYCLONE.]

cyclohexane /sī klō hék sayn, sí klō-/ *n* C_6H_{12} a colourless, pungent, flammable liquid hydrocarbon. Source: benzene. Use: paint thinner, solvent, in organic synthesis.

cyclohexanone /síklō héksənōn/ *n* $C_6H_{10}O$ a colourless liquid ketone. Use: solvent, organic synthesis.

cycloheximide /sī klō héksə mīd/ *n* $C_{15}H_{23}NO_4$ a colourless crystalline compound. Source: the bacterium *Streptomyces griseum*. Use: fungicide.

cycloid /sī kloyd/ *adj* 1 LIKE CIRCLE resembling a circle 2 CIRCULAR describes fish scales that are circular and thin with smooth edges 3 MOODY changing between states of depression and elation (*technical*) ■ *n* 1 GEOMETRIC CURVE a geometric curve formed by a point on the circumference of a circle that rolls along a straight line 2 FISH WITH CYCLOID SCALES a fish with scales that are circular and thin with smooth edges —**cycloidal** *adj* —**cycloidally** *adv*

cyclometer /sī klómmitər/ *n* an instrument that counts the number of a times a wheel rotates and can, therefore, show the distance a vehicle has travelled —**cyclometric** /síklō méttrik/ *adj* —**cyclometry** *n*

cyclone /sī klōn/ *n* 1 LARGE-SCALE STORM SYSTEM a large-scale storm system with winds that rotate anticlockwise in the northern hemisphere and clockwise in the southern hemisphere about and towards a low-pressure centre. ◊ **anticyclone** 2 VIOLENT STORM a violent rotating windstorm or tornado 3 ROTATING DEVICE a device that rotates rapidly, using centrifugal force to separate materials, e.g. particles from a gas [Mid-19C. < Greek *kuklōma* 'wheel, coil' < *kuklos* 'circle'.] —**cyclonic** /sī klónnik/ *adj* —**cyclonical** *adj* —**cyclonically** *adv*

cyclopaedia *n* PUBL = **cyclopedia**

cyclopean /sī klō pée ən, sī klṓpi ən/ *adj* 1 LIKE THE CYCLOPS relating to or resembling the Cyclops 2 MADE OF BIG STONES constructed of massive irregular stone blocks 3 DESCRIBING VISION describes the phenomenon of apparent unity in binocular vision

cyclopedia /sī klō péedi ə/, **cyclopaedia** *n* PUBL = **encyclopedia** [Early 18C. Shortening.] —**cyclopedic** *adj* —**cyclopedist** *n*

cyclopentane /sī klō pén tayn, sí klō pén tayn/ *n* C_5H_{10} a colourless, flammable, pungent, liquid cycloalkane. Use: paint remover, fuel, solvent.

cyclopes plural of **cyclops**

Cyclopes plural of **Cyclops**

cyclophosphamide /síklō fósfə mīd/ *n* a toxic drug that suppresses immunity. Use: treatment of leukaemia, lymphoma, Hodgkin's disease, tumours.

cycloplegia /sī klō pléejə, sí klō-/ *n* loss of movement in the eye muscles that adjust the size of the lens and are used for focusing —**cycloplegic** *adj*

cyclopropane /sī klō prṓ payn, sí klō-/ *n* C_3H_6 a flammable hydrocarbon gas. Use: in medicine as a general anaesthetic, in organic synthesis.

cyclops /sī klops/ (*plural* **-clopes** /sī klṓ peez/ *or* **-clops**) *n* an aquatic crustacean (**copepod**) with a single eye. Genus: *Cyclops*. [Mid-19C. < modern Latin, < Latin, 'Cyclops' (see CYCLOPS).]

Cyclops (*plural* **-clopes** *or* **-clops** *or* **-clopses**) *n* one of a race of giants in Greek mythology who had only one eye in the middle of the forehead [Early 16C. Via Latin < Greek *Kuklōps* < *kuklos* 'circle' + *ōps* 'eye'.]

cyclorama /sī klō ráamə/ *n* 1 a picture painted all the way round the wall of a circular room 2 a large concave curtain or wall behind a stage [Mid-19C. < CYCLO- after PANORAMA.] —**cycloramic** /-rámmik/ *adj*

cyclosis /sī klṓssiss/ *n* the rotary flow of protoplasm within some cells and protozoans [Mid-19C. < Greek *kuklōsis* 'encirclement'.]

cyclosporine /sī klō spáw reen, -spáwrin/, **cyclosporin** /-rin/ *n* a drug obtained from a soil fungus. Use: suppression of tissue rejection following transplant surgery. [Late 20C. < CYCLO- + *polysporum*, the fungus that produces the drug.]

cyclostome /síklə stōm, síklə-/ *n* a jawless fish with a circular sucking mouth and without true teeth. Lampreys and hagfish are cyclostomes. Class: Cyclostomata. [Mid-19C. < CYCLO- + Greek *stoma* 'mouth'.] —**cyclostomate** /sī klóstəmət/ *adj* —**cyclostomatous** /síklō stómmətəss, -stṓmətəss, síklō-/ *adj*

cyclostyle /síklō stīl/ *n* a now obsolete duplication method using perforated stencils, or the special pen used in this process [Late 19C. < CYCLO- + STYLE 'stylus'.] —**cyclostyled** *adj*

cyclothymia /sī klō thīmi ə, sí-/ *n* a psychiatric disorder in which the patient has frequent, relatively mild mood swings between elation and depression [Early 20C. < CYCLO- + Greek *thumos* 'mind, temper'.] —**cyclothymic** *adj*

cyclotron /sī klō tron/ *n* a circular particle accelerator in which charged particles are confined by a vertical magnetic field and accelerated by an alternating high-frequency applied voltage, in order to study the way they interact

cyder /sīdər/ *n* cider (*archaic*) [16C. Variant.]

cygnet /sígnət/ *n* a young or baby swan [15C. Literally 'little swan' < Old French *cigne* 'swan' < Greek *kuknos*.]

Cygnus /sígnəss/ *n* a constellation of the northern hemisphere containing the star Deneb. See illustration at **constellation**

⚡**CYL** *abbr* see you later (*in e-mails*)

cyl. *abbr* 1 cylinder 2 cylindrical

cylinder /síllindər/ *n* 1 TUBE SHAPE a shape with straight sides and circular ends of equal size 2 GEOMETRICAL SOLID a solid bounded by two equal parallel circles and a curved surface formed by moving a straight line so that its ends lie on the circles 3 GEOMETRICAL SURFACE a surface formed by a straight line moving in a circle round and parallel to a fixed straight line, forming a hollow tube shape 4 TUBE-SHAPED OBJECT any object with straight sides and circular ends of equal size 5 LONG THIN CONTAINER a long thin sealed container, such as one in which gas is kept under pressure 6 TANK FOR HOT WATER a closed container, usually insulated, for storing and supplying domestic hot water 7 CHAMBER FOR PISTON a chamber in an internal combustion engine or a pump within which a piston moves back and forth 8 ROTATING PART OF PRINTING PRESS a revolving drum of a printing press that produces or receives the impression 9 ROTATING PART OF REVOLVER the rotating part of a revolver, containing chambers into which cartridges are loaded 10 ANCIENT CYLINDRICAL CLAY OBJECT a hollow barrel-shaped object of baked clay covered in cuneiform script 11 HIST = **cylinder seal** [Late 16C. Via Latin *cylindrus* < Greek *kulindros* 'roller' < *kulindein* 'to roll'.] —**cylindered** *adj*

cylinder barrel *n* a metal casting enclosing a cylinder of an internal-combustion engine

cylinder block *n* a metal casting enclosing the cylinders of an internal-combustion engine. US term **engine block**

cylinder head *n* the closed detachable end of a cylinder in an internal-combustion engine

cylinder press *n* a printing press in which a flat bed holding the type matter moves under a revolving cylinder carrying the paper

cylinder seal *n* an engraved cylindrical clay or stone object used in ancient times, especially in Mesopotamia, as a seal that was rolled in wet clay to leave an impression

cylindrical /si líndrik'l/, **cylindric** /-drik/ *adj* with straight sides, circular ends of equal size, and constant circular cross section —**cylindricality** /si líndri kálləti/ *n* —**cylindrically** *adv*

cyma /sīmə/ (*plural* **-mae** /-mee/ *or* **-mas**) *n* a projecting moulding with an S-shaped profile [Mid-16C. Via modern Latin, < Greek *kuma* 'billow' < *kuein* 'become pregnant'.]

cymbal /símb'l/ *n* a circular brass percussion instrument played with a stick or by striking two of them together [Pre-12C. Directly or via Old French *cymbale* < Latin *cymbalum* < Greek *kumbalon* < *kumbē* 'bowl, cup'.] —**cymbaleer** /símbə léer/ *n* —**cymbaler** *n* —**cymbalist** *n*

SPELLCHECK Do not confuse ***cymbal*** with ***symbol***, which has a similar sound. Beware: your spellchecker will not catch this error.

cymbidium /sim bíddi əm/ (*plural* **-a** /-di ə/ *or* **-ums**) *n* an orchid with long narrow leaves. Flowers: brightly coloured with boat-shaped lower petal. Native to: tropical Asia, Australia. Genus: *Cymbidium*. [Early 19C. < modern Latin, < Greek *kumbē* 'cup'.]

cyme /sīm/ *n* a flower cluster in which each flower stem ends in a single flower and other flower stems form below and to the side [Early 18C. Via French, 'summit' < Latin *cyma* (see CYMA).] —**cymiferous** /sī mífferəss/ *adj* —**cymoid** /sī moyd/ *adj*

cymene /sīmeen/ *n* $(CH_3)_2CHC_6H_4CH_3$ a colourless liquid benzene derivative, existing in three isomers. Use: solvents, manufacture of resins. [Mid-19C. < Greek *kummon* 'cumin'.]

cymophane /sīmə fayn/ *n* an opalescent variety of chrysoberyl. Use: gems. [Early 19C. < Greek *kuma* (see CYMA) + *-phanēs* 'showing'.]

cymose /sī mōss, -mōz, sī mṓss/, **cymous** /sīməss/ *adj* relating to, like, or being a cyme —**cymosely** *adv*

Cymric /kímmrik/ *n* the Welsh language (*dated*) ■ *adj* relating to Wales, or its people, language, or culture [Mid-19C. < Welsh *Cymry* 'the Welsh' < *Cymru* 'Wales'.]

Cymru /kúmri, kóomri/ ♦ **Wales**

Cynewulf /kínniwoolf/, **Cynwulf** /kín-/ (*fl.* 750?) English poet

cynic /sínnik/ *n* 1 a believer that human actions are insincere and motivated by self-interest 2 somebody sneering and sarcastic [Late 16C. < CYNIC.]

Cynic /sínnik/ *n* a member of a group of ancient Greek philosophers who believed that virtue is the only good and that the only means of achieving it is self-control ■ *adj* belonging to, characteristic of, or relating to the Cynics [Mid-16C. Via Latin < Greek *Kunikos*.]

cynical /sínnik'l/ *adj* 1 DISTRUSTFUL OF HUMAN NATURE doubting or contemptuous of human nature or of the motives, goodness, or sincerity of others ○ *Many people have developed a cynical distrust of politicians.* 2 SARCASTIC mocking, scornful, or sneering ○ *cynical remarks to cover up disappointment* 3 IGNORING ACCEPTED STANDARDS OF BEHAVIOUR acting with disregard or contempt for accepted standards of behaviour ○ *a cynical disregard for the welfare of employees* —**cynically** *adv* —**cynicalness** *n*

cynicism /sínnissizəm/ *n* 1 cynical attitude, beliefs, character, or quality 2 a cynical action, comment, or idea

Cynicism *n* the beliefs or philosophy of the ancient Greek Cynics

cynosure /sīnə syoor, sínnə-, -zyoor/ *n* 1 the centre of admiration, attention, or attraction 2 somebody or something acting as a guide or used for direction ○ *Guidebooks are the cynosure of the inexperienced traveller.* [Late 16C. Via Latin *Cynosura* 'Ursa Minor' (which contains the Pole Star) < Greek *kunosoura* 'dog's tail'.] —**cynosural** /sīnə syóorəl, sínnə-, -zyóorəl/ *adj*

Cynthia /sínthi ə/ *n* 1 the Moon personified as a goddess (*literary*) 2 = **Diana** [Late 16C. Because the goddess Diana was supposedly born on Mount *Cynthus* in Delos.]

Cynwulf = **Cynewulf**

cypher *n* COMMUNICATION = **cipher**

⚡ **cypherpunk** /sífər pungk/ *n* an experienced computer hacker who breaks codes and enters secure computer systems [Late 20C. < CYPHER, after CYBERPUNK.]

cy pres /seè práy/ *adv* as nearly as possible to the will or intention of a person whose wishes cannot be executed literally [Via Anglo-Norman < French *si près* 'as near as']

cypress[1] /síprəss/ *n* **1** CONIFER a coniferous evergreen tree with dark green leaves resembling scales and hard wood. Native to: Europe, Asia, North America. Genus: *Cupressus*. **2** TREE OR SHRUB RESEMBLING CYPRESS a coniferous tree or shrub that is similar to the cypress, e.g. a bald or swamp cypress **3** WOOD the hard wood of a cypress tree **4** SYMBOL OF MOURNING the branches of a cypress tree as a symbol of mourning. [12C. Via Old French *cipres* < late Latin *cypressus* < Greek *kuparissos*.]

cypress[2] /síprəss/, **cyprus** *n* a fine silk or cotton fabric, usually black. Use: mourning clothes. [15C. Via Anglo-Norman *cipres* < Old French *Cipre* 'Cyprus'.]

cypress pine *n* a conifer that is grown for timber. Native to: Australia. Genus: *Callitris*.

Cyprian /síppri ən/, **St** (200?–258) African-born Roman lawyer, bishop, and martyr

cyprinid /si prínid, sípprinid/ (*plural* **-nid** *or* **-nids**) *n* a freshwater fish of the family that includes the carps and minnows, typically with rounded scales, soft fins, and toothless jaws. Family: Cyprinidae. [Late 19C. < Latin *cyprinus* 'carp' < Greek *kuprinos*.] —**cyprinid** *adj*

cyprinoid /síppri noyd/ *n* any fish belonging to a large group that includes carp [Mid-19C. < Latin *cyprinus* 'carp' < Greek *kuprinos*.] —**cyprinoid** *adj*

Cypriot /síppri ət/, **Cypriote** *n* SOMEBODY FROM CYPRUS somebody who comes from Cyprus ■ *adj* **1** OF CYPRUS relating to Cyprus, or its peoples, languages, or cultures **2** OF THE LANGUAGES OF CYPRUS relating to the dialects of Greek and Turkish that are spoken on Cyprus [Late 16C. < Greek *Kupriōtēs* < *Kupros* 'Cyprus'.]

cyproheptadine /síprō héptə deen/ *n* an antihistamine drug. Use: treatment of asthma, allergies, skin disorders. [Late 20C. < CYCLIC + PROPYL + HEPTA + PIPERIDINE.]

cyprus *n* TEXTILES = **cypress**[2]

Cyprus

Cyprus /síprəss/ island republic in the E Mediterranean Sea, partitioned between the Greek Cypriot south and the officially unrecognized Turkish Republic of Northern Cyprus. Capital: Nicosia. Population: 752,808 (1997). Area: 9,251 sq. km/3,572 sq. mi.

cypsela /sípsilə/ (*plural* **-lae** /-lee/) *n* a small hard one-seeded fruit with an attached calyx that does not split during seed dispersal, as in the daisy and dandelion. Family: Compositae. [Late 19C. Via modern Latin, < Greek *kupselē* 'hollow vessel'.]

Cyrano de Bergerac /sírrənō də búrzhə rak/, **Savinien** (1619–55) French poet and dramatist

Cyrenaic /sírə náy ik/ *adj* OF THE PHILOSOPHY OF PLEASURE relating to or advocating the philosophical doctrines of Aristippus of Cyrene, who believed pleasure is the supreme good ■ *n* **1** BELIEVER IN CYRENAIC PHILOSOPHY an adherent of the Cyrenaic school of philosophy **2** HEDONIST a believer that pleasure is the sole good in life [Late 16C. Via Latin, < Greek *Kurēnaikos* < *Kurēnē* 'Cyrene'.] —**Cyrenaicism** /sírə náy issizəm/ *n*

Cyrenaica /sírə náy ikə, sírrə-/ historic region settled by the ancient Greeks in present-day NE Libya

Cyrene /sī reèni/ ancient Greek town in present-day NE Libya

Cyril /sírral/, **St** (827–869) Greek missionary.

Cyrillic /si ríllik/ *adj* relating or belonging to the old alphabet derived from Greek script and attributed to St Cyril, or a modified form used in modern Slavonic languages such as Bulgarian and Russian, and in some non-Slavonic languages ■ *n* the Cyrillic alphabet [Early 19C. After ST CYRIL.]

cyst /sist/ *n* **1** SPHERICAL SWELLING a closed, usually spherical, membranous sac that develops in human or other animal tissue and contains fluid or semisolid material **2** HOLLOW ORGAN OR CAVITY a thin-walled bladder, sac, or vesicle in an animal **3** RESTING SPORE a spore that is not undergoing cell division, in some algae and fungi **4** PROTECTIVE SAC ENCLOSING ORGANISM a sac or capsule that encloses and protects some organisms in a dormant or larval stage **5** PROTECTIVE COVERING AROUND PARASITE a protective covering around a parasite, produced by a host or by the parasite itself **6** AIR-FILLED CAVITY IN SEAWEEDS a small air-filled cavity resembling a bladder that occurs in some seaweeds, e.g. the bladder wrack [Early 18C. Via late Latin *cystis* < Greek *kustis* 'bladder, cyst'.] —**cystoid** /sís toyd/ *adj, n*

cyst- *prefix* = **cysto-** (*before vowels*)

cystectomy /si stéktəmi/ (*plural* **-mies**) *n* **1** surgical removal of a cyst **2** surgical removal of the urinary bladder

cysteine /sísti een, sístayn/ *n* a sulphur-containing amino acid that is converted to cystine during metabolism [Late 19C. < CYSTINE + -*eine*, variant of -EIN.]

cystic /sístik/ *adj* **1** RELATING TO CYST describes a cyst or material that forms, contains, or is enclosed in a cyst **2** CONTAINING CYST consisting of or containing a cyst or cysts **3** WITHIN CYST enclosed within a cyst **4** RELATING TO BLADDER relating to a bladder, especially the urinary bladder

cystic duct *n* the duct of the gall bladder that joins the bile duct from the liver to form the common bile duct

cysticercus /sísti súrkəss/ (*plural* **-ci** /-sī/) *n* the larva of some tapeworms that consists of a folded inverted head encapsulated in a fluid-filled sac [Mid-19C. < modern Latin *cysticercus* < Greek *kustis* 'bladder' + *kerkos* 'tail'.]

cystic fibrosis /-fī bróssiss/ *n* a hereditary disease starting in infancy that affects various glands and results in secretion of thick mucus that blocks internal passages, including those of the lungs, causing respiratory infections

cystine /sís teen/ *n* an amino acid found in many proteins, especially keratin [Mid-19C. < Greek *kustis* 'bladder'.]

cystinuria /sísti nyoóri ə/ *n* the excessive excretion of cystine in the urine and the formation of cystine stones in the kidney, characteristic of an inherited disorder of the metabolism

cystitis /si stítiss/ *n* inflammation of the urinary bladder, often caused by infection

cysto- *prefix* hollow structure, sac, cyst ○ *cystocarp* [Via modern Latin *cystis* 'bladder' < Greek *kustis*]

cystocoele /sístə seel/ *n* a hernia of the urinary bladder that protrudes through the vaginal wall

cystography /si stóggrəfi/ *n* X-ray examination of the urinary bladder after the introduction of a liquid that is partially opaque to X-rays

cystolith /sístə lith/ *n* **1** a hard mineral deposit, usually of calcium carbonate, that occurs in the epidermal cells of some plants, e.g. figs or stinging nettles **2** a stone that occurs in the bladder

cystoscope /sístə sköp/ *n* a narrow tubular instrument that is passed through the urethra to examine the interior of the urethra and the urinary bladder —**cystoscopic** /sístə skóppik/ *adj* —**cystoscopy** /si stóskəpi/ *n*

cystostomy /si stóstəmi/ (*plural* **-mies**) *n* the surgical construction of an opening into the urinary bladder to permit the removal of stones

cyt- *prefix* = **cyto-** (*before vowels*)

-cyte *suffix* cell ○ *phagocyte* [Via modern Latin *-cyta* < Greek *kutos* 'hollow vessel']

Cytherea /síthə reè ə/ *n* MYTHOL = **Aphrodite**

Cytherean /síthə reè ən/ *adj* **1** relating to Cytherea **2** relating to the planet Venus

cytidine /sítti deen/ *n* a compound (**nucleoside**) formed from cytosine and ribose [Early 20C. < CYTO- + -IDINE.]

cytidylic acid /sítti díllik-/ *n* a nucleotide derived from cytosine and found in DNA and RNA [Mid-20C. < CYTIDINE + -YL + -IC.]

cyto- *prefix* cell ○ *cytotoxin* [< Greek *kutos* 'hollow vessel' < Indo-European, 'thing that hides']

cytochalasin /sítō kə láyzin/ *n* a substance derived from fungi that inhibits the formation of microscopic filaments within living cells, thereby interfering with various cell activities such as the cleavage of cytoplasm following nuclear division [Mid-20C. < CYTO- + Greek *khalasis* 'dislocation'.]

cytochemistry /sítō kémmistri/ *n* a branch of biochemistry dealing with the chemistry of the cells of organisms —**cytochemical** *adj* —**cytochemically** *adv*

cytochrome /sítō krōm/ *n* any of a group of proteins containing iron that play a role in cell respiration

cytochrome oxidase *n* an enzyme complex that is involved in the electron transport phase of cell respiration

cytogenesis /sítō jénnəssiss/ *n* the origin, development, and variation of cells

cytogenetics /sítō jə néttiks/ *n* the study of the relationship between inheritance and the structure and function of cell components (+ *singular verb*) —**cytogenetic** *adj* —**cytogenetically** *adv* —**cytogeneticist** *n*

cytogeny /sī tójjəni/ *n* BIOL = **cytogenesis**

cytokine /sítō kīn/ *n* any protein secreted by lymph cells that affects cellular activity and controls inflammation [Mid-20C. < CYTO- + Greek *kinein* 'to move'.]

cytokinesis /sítō kī neéssiss, -ki-/ *n* division of the cytoplasm of a cell during mitosis or meiosis —**cytokinetic** /sítō kī néttik, -ki-/ *adj*

cytokinin /sítō kínin/ *n* a plant growth hormone that encourages cell division

cytology /sī tólləji/ *n* **1** a branch of biology dealing with the study of cells, especially their structures and functions **2** the examination of cells obtained from body tissue or fluids, especially to establish if they are cancerous —**cytologic** /sítə lójjik/ *adj* —**cytological** *adj* —**cytologically** *adv* —**cytologist** *n*

cytolysis /sī tólləssiss/ *n* the destruction or dissolution of cells, e.g. by the immune system —**cytolytic** /sítō líttik/ *adj*

cytomegalic /sítō mə gállik/ *adj* characterized by, producing, or relating to enlarged cells [Mid-20C. < CYTO- + MEGALO- + -IC.]

cytomegalic inclusion disease *n* a serious disease of newborn babies affecting the brain, liver, kidneys, and lungs

cytomegalovirus /sítō méggəlō vīrəss/ *n* a virus that causes enlargement of epithelial cells, usually resulting in mild infections but causing more serious disorders in Aids patients and in newborn babies [Mid-20C. < CYTO- + MEGALO- + VIRUS.]

cytopathogenic /sítō pathə jénnik/, **cytopathic** /-páthik/ *adj* relating to or causing damage or disease to cells —**cytopathogenicity** /sítō pathəjə níssəti/ *n*

cytopathology /sítō pə thólləji/ (*plural* **-gies**) *n* **1** a branch of pathology dealing with cell disease and damage **2** the set of features or conditions associated with a diseased cell or cells

cytopathy /sī tóppəthi/ *n* deterioration or disease in a living cell

cytopharynx /sítō fárringks/ (*plural* **-pharynges** /-fə rín jeez/ *or* **-pharynxes**) *n* a tube in some protozoans, extending from the cytoplasm into the endoplasm

cytophotometer /sítō fə tómmitər/ *n* an instrument that utilizes the variations in light intensity produced by stained cell cytoplasm to identify and locate chemical

compounds within cells —**cytophotometric** /sītō fōtō méttrik/ *adj* —**cytophotometrically** *adv* —**cytophotometry** /sītō fə tómmətri/ *n*

cytoplasm /sītō plazəm/ *n* the complex of chemical compounds and structures within a plant or animal cell excluding the nucleus —**cytoplasmic** /sītō plázmik/ *adj* —**cytoplasmically** *adv*

cytoplasmic inheritance *n* the inheritance of genes from the female parent that are not in the nucleus but in organelles such as mitochondria that are found in the cytoplasm

cytoplasmic streaming *n* the movement of cytoplasm within living cells resulting in the transport of nutrients and enzymes, and in the case of one-celled organisms, locomotion of the cell itself

cytoplast /sītō plaast, -plast/ *n* a plant or animal cell that has had the nucleus removed —**cytoplastic** /sītō plástik/ *adj*

cytosine /sītə seen/ *n* (*symbol* C) a pyrimidine base that pairs with guanine in DNA and RNA [Late 19C. < CYTO- + -OSE¹ + -INE.]

cytoskeleton /sītō skéllitən/ *n* the internal network of protein filaments and microtubules in an animal or plant cell that controls the cell's shape and movement —**cytoskeletal** *adj*

cytosol /sītə sol/ *n* the fluid component of a cell's cytoplasm excluding organelles and other structures —**cytosolic** /sītə sóllik/ *adj*

cytosome /sītəsōm/ *n* the cytoplasm in a cell, excluding the nucleus

cytostatic /sītə státtik/ *adj* suppressing cell growth and multiplication ■ *n* a cytostatic agent —**cytostatically** *adv*

cytotaxis /sītō táksiss/ *n* the movement of cells or cell masses in relation to one another

cytotaxonomy /sītō tak sónnəmi/ *n* the classification of organisms according to cell structure, especially the number, structure, and shape of chromosomes —**cytotaxonomic** /sītō taksə nómmik/ *adj*—**cytotaxonomically** *adv*—**cytotaxonomist** /-tak sónnəmist/ *n*

cytotechnologist /sītō tek nólləjist/ *n* somebody trained to prepare cell samples and identify abnormalities —**cytotechnology** *n*

cytotoxic /sītō tóksik/ *adj* **1** describes a drug that prevents cell division **2** describes a type of cell in the immune system that destroys other cells —**cytotoxicity** /sītō tok síssəti/ *n*

cytotoxic T cell *n* a killer cell (*technical*)

cytotoxin /sītō tóksin/ *n* any substance that kills living cells

cytotropic /sītō tróppik/ *adj* describes motile cells that are mutually attracted to each other

cytotropism /sītō trŏpizəm/ *n* the movement or turning of cells or cell masses towards or away from one another

czar *n* HIST = **tsar**

czardas /chaárdash/, **csardas** *n* **1** a Hungarian dance with a slow section followed by a faster one **2** the music for a czardas [Mid-19C. < Hungarian *csárdás* < *csárda* 'inn'.]

czarevitch *n* HIST = **tsarevitch**

czarevna *n* HIST = **tsarevna**

czarina *n* HIST = **tsarina**

czarism *n* HIST = **tsarism**

Czech /chek/ *n* **1** SOMEBODY FROM CZECH REPUBLIC somebody who comes from the Czech Republic **2** SOMEBODY FROM CZECHOSLOVAKIA somebody who came from the former Czechoslovakia **3** OFFICIAL LANGUAGE OF CZECH REPUBLIC the official language of the Czech Republic, belonging to

the West Slavonic group of Indo-European languages. Native speakers: 10 million. [Early 19C. Via Polish < Czech *Čech*.] —**Czech** *adj*

Czechoslovak /chékō slóvak/ *n* somebody who came from the former Czechoslovakia [Early 20C. Back-formation < CZECHOSLOVAKIA.] —**Czechoslovak** *adj*

Czechoslovakia /chékəslə vaàki ə, -vák-, chékō slō váki ə/ former country in central Europe, now divided into the Czech Republic and Slovakia

Czech Republic

Czech Republic /chék-/ republic in central Europe. Capital: Prague. Population: 10,298,324 (1997). Area: 78,864 sq. km/30,450 sq. mi.

Czerny /chúrni/, **Karl** (1791–1857) Austrian pianist and composer

Częstochowa /chéNstə khŏ́və, chénstə kŏ́və/ city in south-central Poland. Population: 259,500 (1995).

Dd

d¹ /dee/ (*plural* **d's**), **D** (*plural* **D's** *or* **Ds**) *n* **1** the fourth letter of the English alphabet, representing a consonant sound **2** the Roman numeral for 500

d² used to refer to the fourth vertical row of squares from the left on a chessboard

d³ *symbol* **1** deci- **2** deuteron **3** relative density

d⁴ *abbr* **1** dam² **2** date **3** daughter **4** day **5** degree **6** denarii (*used of old-style currency in Great Britain before 1971*) **7** denarius (*used of old-style currency in Great Britain before 1971*) **8** departs **9** depth **10** diameter **11** died **12** dollar **13** drachma

'd /d/ *contr* **1 DID** did ○ *Where'd she get that hat?* **2 HAD** had ○ *We'd already finished supper.* **3 SHOULD OR WOULD** should or would ○ *I'd like to stop at the shop.*

D¹ used to refer to the first derivative of a function

D² *n* **1 'D'-SHAPED OBJECT** something shaped like a letter 'D' **2 2ND NOTE IN C MAJOR** the second note of a scale in C major **3 SOMETHING THAT PRODUCES A D** a string, key, or pipe tuned to produce the note D **4 SCALE BEGINNING ON D** a scale or key that starts on the note D **5 WRITTEN SYMBOL OF D** a graphic representation of the tone of D **6 4TH HIGHEST GRADE** the fourth highest grade in a series, e.g. a below-average grade for academic work **7 SEMICIRCLE ROUND HOCKEY GOAL** in hockey, the semicircle surrounding the goal, from which a player may try to score **8 SEMISKILLED OR UNSKILLED WORKER** somebody in a semiskilled or unskilled manual job in the market research system that classifies people according to their employment

D³ *symbol* **1** deuterium **2** dispersion **3** drag

D⁴ *abbr* **1** December **2** Department **3** Deus **4** diameter **5** dinar **6** dioptre **7** Director **8** Dominus **9** Don **10** drive (*on gear levers of automatic transmissions*) **11** Duchess **12** Duke

da *symbol* deca-

DA¹ *abbr* **1** deed of arrangement **2** delayed action **3** digital-to-analog **4** district attorney

DA² *n* a man's hairstyle popular in the 1950s in which the hair is slicked back and drawn into a point at the back of the neck to look like a duck's tail (*informal*)

D/A¹, **d.a.** *abbr* **1** deposit account **2** documents against acceptance

⚡D/A² *abbr* **1** days after acceptance **2** delivery on acceptance **3** digital-to-analogue

dab¹ /dab/ *vti* (**dabs, dabbing, dabbed**) **1 TAP GENTLY** to pat or touch something lightly or gently ○ *She dabbed the tears from her eyes.* **2 APPLY GENTLY** to apply a substance using a quick light tapping action ○ *The nurse dabbed some ointment on the cut.* ■ *n* **1 SMALL QUANTITY** a small quantity, especially of a moist or soft substance ○ *a dab of butter* **2 GENTLE TAP** a light or gentle tap, e.g. with the hand or a soft material **3 FINGERPRINT** a fingerprint, especially of a suspected criminal (*slang; often plural*)

dab² /dab/ (*plural* **dabs** *or* **dab**) *n* **1** a small brown flatfish. Native to: Europe. *Limanda limanda*. **2** the flesh of a dab as food [15C. < ?]

dab³ /dab/ *n* = **dab hand** (*informal*)

dabber /dábbər/ *n* a pad used by engravers and printers to apply ink or colour

dabble /dább'l/ (**-bles, -bling, -bled**) *v* **1** *vi* **SPLASH** to paddle, play, or splash in water **2** *vt* **DIP** to wet something by dipping it in a liquid ○ *We sat by the pool, dabbling our feet in the water.* **3** *vt* **SPLASH WITH LIQUID** to daub, splash, or spatter somebody or something with a liquid **4** *vi*

BECOME INVOLVED SUPERFICIALLY to have a casual or superficial interest in something ○ *He dabbled in local politics for a few years.* **5** *vi* **MOVE UNDER WATER FOR FOOD** to move the bill to the bottom of shallow water in order to reach food (*refers to ducks*) [Mid-16C. Probably < Dutch *dabbelen* 'keep tapping' < *dabben* 'to tap'.] —**dabbler** *n*

dabchick /dáb chik/ *n* a small bird of the grebe family. Family: Podicipedidae.

dab hand *n* somebody with a special ability to perform some activity (*informal*) [Late 17C. < ?]

da capo /daa ka'apō/ *adv* to be played or sung again from the beginning of the passage or piece (*musical direction*) ◊ **dal segno** [Early 18C. < Italian, 'from the head'.] —**da capo** *adj*

Dacca = **Dhaka**

dace /dayss/ (*plural* **dace** *or* **daces**) *n* **1** a small freshwater fish with a slim olive-green body. Native to: Europe. *Leuciscus leuciscus*. **2** a small freshwater fish. Native to: North America. Family: Cyprinidae. [15C. < Old French *dars* 'dace, dart'.]

dacha /dácha/, **datcha** *n* a cottage or house in the suburbs or countryside in Russia [Mid-19C. < Russian, 'grant of land'.]

Dachau /dákow, dákh-/ site of a World War II Nazi concentration camp (1939–45) in SW Germany

dachshund /dáksənd, dásh-, -hŏōnd/ *n* a small dog of a breed that has a long body, short legs, and drooping ears [Late 19C. < German, 'badger dog'.]

~~dachsund~~ incorrect spelling of **dachshund**

dacoit /də kóyt/, **dakoit** *n* a member of a gang of armed robbers in India and Myanmar, especially formerly [Late 18C. < Hindi *dakait* < *dākā* 'gang robbery'.] —**dacoity** *n*

dactyl /dáktil/ *n* **1 dactyl, dactylic** a metrical foot consisting of one long syllable followed by two short syllables in classical verse or one stressed syllable followed by two unstressed syllables in modern verse **2** a finger, toe, or related body part [14C. Via Latin *dactylus* < Greek *daktulos* 'finger'.]

dactyl- *prefix* = **dactylo-** (*before vowels*)

-dactyl *suffix* having fingers or toes of a particular kind or number ○ *polydactyl* [< Greek *daktulos* 'finger'] —**-dactylous** *suffix*

dactylic /dak tíllik/ *adj* relating to a dactyl or containing dactyls ■ *n* LITERAT = **dactyl** *n.* **1** —**dactylically** *adv*

dactylic hexameter *n* a line of verse first used in Greek and roman epic poetry consisting of six feet, the fifth of which is a dactyl, the first four dactyls or spondees, and the sixth a spondee or trochee

dactylo- *prefix* finger, toe ○ *dactylology* [< Greek *daktulos* 'finger']

dactylography /dákti lóggrəfi/ *n* the scientific examination of fingerprints for identification purposes —**dactylographic** /dak tíllə gráffik/ *adj*

dactylology /dákti lólləji/ *n* communication using signs made with the hands, often used by hearing-impaired people

dad /dad/ *n* used as a term of address, to refer to a father (*informal*) [Mid-16C. < ?]

Dada /daa daa/, **dada, Dadaism** /-izəm/, **dadaism** *n* a European artistic and literary movement of the early 20th century whose work was characterized by

anarchy, irrationality, and irreverence [Early 20C. < French, 'hobbyhorse'.] —**Dadaist** *n, adj*

QUICK FACTS ON... DADA

Key dates: mid-1910s–early 1920s
Key locations: W Europe, United States
Key elements: rejection of traditional artistic and cultural values; embracing of the irrational and absurd; nihilism, anarchism; use of unconventional forms and materials
Key figures: Hugo Ball, Tristan Tzara (literature); Jean Arp, Raoul Hausmann, Marcel Duchamp, Francis Picabia, Kurt Schwitters, John Heartfield, George Grosz (art)
Key works: *Fountain* (Duchamp) 1917, *Republican Automatons* (Grosz) 1920, *The Spirit of Our Time* (Hausmann) 1921, *The Bride Stripped Bare by Her Bachelors, Even* (Duchamp) 1915–23, *Merzbau* (Schwitters) 1923–36
Key developments: ready-mades, automatic writing, surrealism, pop art, conceptual art, performance art

---

daddy /dáddi/ (*plural* **-dies**) *n* (*informal*) **1** used as a term of address, especially by a young child, to refer to a father **2** *US, Can, Aus* the earliest or finest example of something ○ *He was a fine trumpet player, the daddy of them all.*

daddy longlegs /-lóng legz/ (*plural* **daddy longlegs**) *n* **1** a long-legged, slender-winged fly. Family: Tipulidae. US name **crane fly 2** *US* a long-legged arachnid with an oval body. Order: Opiliones.

dado /dáydō/ *n* (*plural* **-does** *or* **-dos**) **1** ARCHIT = **die²** *n.* **5 2 LOWER PART OF INTERIOR WALL** the lower part of an interior wall, decorated or faced in a different manner from the upper part, usually with panels, paint, or wallpaper **3 RECTANGULAR GROOVE IN BOARD** a rectangular groove cut into a board so that a matching piece can be fitted into it to form a joint ■ *vt* (**-does, -doing, -doed**) **1 PROVIDE WITH DADO** to fit a wall with a dado **2 CUT DADO IN** to cut a rectangular groove in something so that a matching piece can be fitted into it to form a joint **3 INSERT INTO DADO** to insert something into a rectangular groove to form a joint [Mid-17C. < Italian, 'die (of a pedestal)'.]

daedal /déed'l/, **dedal** *adj* (*literary*) **1 INTRICATE** complex or intricate **2 INGENIOUS** skilful or ingenious ■ *n* **INGENIOUS INVENTOR** an expert or ingenious inventor [Late 16C. Via Latin *dædalus* < Greek *daidalos* 'skilful'.]

Daedalus /déed ələs/ *n* in Greek mythology, a craftsman and inventor who built a labyrinth on the island of Crete to house a half-bull, half-man monster (**Minotaur**). He made wings so that he could escape from Crete with his son (**Icarus**), but his son perished during the flight. —**Daedalian** /di dáyli ən/ *adj*

⚡daemon /déemən, dī-, dáy-/, **daimon** /dī´mōn/ *n* **1 DEMIGOD** a mythological being that is part-god and part-human **2 GUARDIAN SPIRIT** a guardian spirit **3 DEMON** a demon (*archaic*) **4 SOFTWARE** a piece of software that carries out background tasks such as filtering or debugging, at specified intervals or in response to particular events [Variant of DEMON] —**daemonic** /di mónnik/ *adj*

daff /daf/ *n* a daffodil (*informal*) [Early 20C. Shortening.]

daffodil /dáffədil/ *n* **1** a spring-flowering plant with long slender leaves growing from a bulb. Flowers: yellow, trumpet-shaped. Native to: Europe. *Narcissus pseudonarcissus*. **2** a brilliant yellow colour [Mid-16C. < medieval Latin *affodilus* 'asphodel'.] —**daffodil** *adj*

daffy /dáffi/ (**-fier, -fiest**) *adj* silly in an amusing or harmless way (*informal*) [Late 19C. < alteration of DAFT.] —**daffily** *adv* —**daffiness** *n*

daft /daaft/ *adj* (*informal*) **1 NOT SENSIBLE** obviously silly or unreasonable ○ *a daft idea* . **2 VERY ENTHUSIASTIC** extremely enthusiastic about something *Scotland* **THOUGHTLESS OR FRIVOLOUS** thoughtless or frivolous [Old English *gedæfte* 'fitting' < Germanic, 'fit, suitable'] **—daftly** *adv* **—daftness** *n*

Dafydd ap Gwilym /dávvith ap gwíllim/ (1320?–80?) Welsh poet

dag[1] /dag/ *n* **1** ZOOL = **daglock** *n*. **2** a decorative edging on garments, used especially in medieval times ■ *vti* (**dags, dagging, dagged**) to cut off dung-coated wool from a sheep's coat [Early 17C. Shortening of DAGLOCK.]

dag[2] /dag/ *n ANZ* (*informal*) **1 SLOVENLY PERSON** a dirty or untidy person **2 SURPRISING TURN OF EVENTS** a surprising thing or interesting turn of events ○ *I got a real job. What a dag!* **3 UNFASHIONABLE PERSON** a person considered as unfashionable **4 UNUSUAL CHARACTER** somebody who is regarded as odd, often with amusing characteristics or unconventional habits [Early 20C. < DAG[1].]

Dagan /dáagən/ *n* the god of the Earth in Babylonian mythology

Dagestan /dági staan/ republic in the Caucasus region of S Russia. Capital: Makhachkala. Population: 1,953,000 (1994). Area: 50,300 sq. km/19,420 sq. mi.

Dagestanian /dáagə stáyni ən/ *n* a group of North Caucasian languages spoken in Dagestan. Native speakers: 3,000. [< DAGESTAN] **—Dagestanian** *adj*

dagga /dúkhə, dáagə/ *n S Africa* Indian hemp smoked as a narcotic [Late 17C. Via Afrikaans < Nama *daxa*.]

dagger /dággər/ *n* **1 SHORT POINTED KNIFE** a short pointed knife used as a weapon **2 IRRITATION** something that torments or wounds somebody ○ *Such cutting words were a dagger to my heart.* **3 SIGN USED AS REFERENCE MARK** a sign (†) that is used as a reference mark, especially to a footnote ■ *vt* MARK SOMETHING WITH REFERENCE SIGN to mark something with a dagger sign [14C. < ?] ◇ **be at daggers drawn** to be hostile and ready to fight with somebody ◇ **look daggers at somebody** to look at somebody in an angry or hostile way

daggy /dággi/ *adj* (**-gier, -giest**) *adj ANZ* (*informal*) **1 UNFASHIONABLE** describes clothing or behaviour that is considered unfashionable, especially by young people **2 MESSY** untidy, dirty, and unpleasant ○ *Her bedsit was so daggy.* **3 UNCONVENTIONAL** different or unwilling to conform [Early 20C. < DAG[1].]

daglock /dág lok/ *n* a lock of dung-coated wool on a sheep's hindquarters [Early 17C. < *Dag* 'hanging part of something' < ? + LOCK[2].]

dago /dáygō/ *n* (*plural* **-gos** *or* **-goes**), **Dago** (*plural* **-gos** *or* **-goes**) *n* a highly offensive term for somebody of Italian, Spanish, or Portuguese birth or descent (*taboo*) [Mid-19C. Variant of the name *Diego*.]

dagoba /dáagabə/ *n* a dome-shaped shrine that contains Buddhist relics [Early 19C. Via Sinhalese *dāgaba* < Pali *dhātu-gabbha* 'receptacle for relics'.]

Dagomba /də gómbə/ (*plural* **-ba** *or* **-bas**) *n* **1** a member of a people living in NE Ghana and N Togo **2** the language of the Dagomba people, belonging to the Gur branch of Niger-Congo and an official language of Ghana. Native speakers: 500,000. [Mid-20C. < Dagomba.] **—Dagomba** *adj*

Dagon /dáygən/ *n* the chief god in Philistine mythology, often depicted as half man and half fish

Daguerre /da gáir/, **Louis Jacques** (1789–1851) French painter and inventor

daguerreotype /də gérrō tīp/ *n* **1 EARLY PHOTOGRAPHIC PROCESS** an early photographic process in which an image was produced on a light-sensitive silver or silver-coated plate and developed in mercury vapour **2 EARLY PHOTOGRAPH** a photograph produced by the daguerreotype process ■ *vt* (**-types, -typing, -typed**) TAKE PHOTOGRAPH to make a daguerreotype of something or somebody [Mid-19C. < French *daguerréotype*, after L. J. DAGUERRE.] **—daguerreotyper** *n* **—daguerreotypist** *n* **—daguerreotypy** *n*

dah /daa/ *n* the spoken representation of a dash in Morse code and other telegraphic codes [Mid-20C. An imitation of the sound made by a Morse code transmitter.]

dahabeah /dáahə beé ə/, **dahabeeyah, dahabiah, dahabiyeh** *n* a shallow-bottomed passenger boat or houseboat with sails and sometimes an engine, used on the Nile [Mid-19C. < Arabic *dahabiya* 'golden (boat)'.]

Dahl /daal/, **Roald** (1916–90) British writer

dahlia /dáyli ə/ *n* a tall perennial plant with tuberous roots. Flowers: large, brightly coloured. Genus: *Dahlia.* [Early 19C. After Andreas *Dahl*.]

Dahomey /də hómi/ former name for **Benin**

daikon /díkən/ *n* FOOD = **mooli** [Late 19C. < Japanese, 'big root'.]

Dáil Éireann /dóyl áirən, daal-/, **Dáil** *n* the lower house of the parliament of the Republic of Ireland [Early 20C. < Irish, 'Irish Assembly'.]

daily /dáyli/ *adj* **1 DONE EVERY DAY** done or occurring every day **2 FOR EACH DAY** for each day or for a period of a day **3 LASTING A DAY** for the duration of or during a day ■ *adv* **EVERY DAY** on each day ■ *n* (*plural* **-lies**) **NEWSPAPER PUBLISHED EVERY DAY** a newspaper published every day or every day except Sunday (*often plural*) ■ **dailies** *npl* **DAY'S SHOOTING OF FILM SCENES** unedited prints of a day's shooting of scenes from a film, prepared each day for the director to view the following day [15C. < DAY.]

daily double *n* **1** a bet, e.g. in horseracing, won by correctly choosing the winners of two specified races taking place on the same day **2** the two races specified for a daily double bet

daily dozen *n* a set of physical exercises done each day (*informal*)

daimio *n* = **daimyo**

Daimler /dáymlər/, **Gottlieb** (1834–1900) German engineer and inventor

daimon *n* = **daemon**

daimyo /dímyō/ (*plural* **-o** *or* **-os**), **daimio** (*plural* **-o** *or* **-os**) *n* a great Japanese feudal lord who was a vassal of the emperor [Early 18C. < Japanese, 'great name'.]

Daintree /dáyn tree/ river in N Queensland, Australia. Length: 108 km/67 mi.

Daintree River National Park /dáyn tree-/ national park in NE Queensland, Australia. Area: 7,000 sq. km/2,734 sq. mi.

dainty /dáynti/ *adj* (**-tier, -tiest**) **1 PRETTY** delicate and pretty ○ *dainty slippers* **2 TASTY** choice, delicious, or tasty ○ *a dainty morsel* **3 REFINED IN TASTE** having refined taste or manners **4 OVERLY FASTIDIOUS** excessively fastidious or particular ■ *n* (*plural* **-ties**) **DELICACY** something delicious, especially a small piece of food [13C. Via Anglo-Norman *dainte*, *dainte* < Latin *dignitas* (see DIGNITY).] **—daintily** *adv* **—daintiness** *n*

daiquiri /díkəri, dák-/ (*plural* **-ris**) *n* an iced cocktail made from rum, lemon or lime juice, and sugar or syrup [Early 20C. After *Daiquiri*, Cuba.]

dairy /dáiri/ *n* (*plural* **-ies**) **1 PLACE TO STORE MILK AND CREAM** a room or building where milk and cream are stored **2 PLACE TO MAKE BUTTER AND CHEESE** a room or building where butter and cheese are made **3 ESTABLISHMENT THAT SELLS OR PROCESSES MILK** a commercial establishment that processes, sells, or distributes milk and milk products **4 FARM FOR MILK PRODUCTION** a farm that produces milk and milk products **5 DAIRY PRODUCTS** dairy products collectively **6 NZ GROCERY STORE** a small local grocery store that sells milk, newspapers, and other provisions ■ *adj* **1 RELATING TO MILK PRODUCTS** relating to, producing, or containing milk or milk products **2 CONCERNING FOODS IN JEWISH DIETARY LAW** relating to those foods, including milk products, eggs, fish, and vegetables, that Jewish dietary law allows on occasions when milk is consumed [13C. < *Deie* 'woman servant, dairy worker' < Old English *dæge* 'kneader (of bread)'.]

dairying /dáiri ing/ *n* the business of operating a dairy or dairy farm

dairyman /dáirimən, -man/ (*plural* **-men**) *n* an owner or employee of a dairy

dais /dáy iss, dayss/ *n* a raised platform at the end of a hall or large room [13C. Via Old French *deis* < Latin.]

daishiki *n* CLOTHING = **dashiki**

daisy /dáyzi/ (*plural* **-ies**) *n* **1** a low-growing wild plant, with cultivated varieties. Native to: Europe. Flowers: white or pinkish-white petals, yellow centre. *Bellis perennis.* **2** a tall flowering plant. Native to: Europe, Asia, North America. Flowers: large white petals around a yellow centre. *Chrysanthemum leucanthemum.* [Old English *dæges eage* 'day's eye'; because the flower opens in daylight and closes at night]

daisy bush *n* a bush or tree with clusters of white flowers resembling daisies. Native to: Australia, New Zealand, New Guinea. Genus: *Olearia.*

daisy chain *n* **1** a garland made by threading the stems of daisies together **2** a series of connected things, events, or people (*slang*)

daisycutter /dáyzi kuttər/ *n* **1** a ball bowled or struck so that it skims the ground **2** a bomb that detonates just above ground level, used against personnel and to destroy vegetation in order to make a landing zone for helicopters

daisy wheel *n* a wheel with type elements at the ends of spokes radiating from a central hub, used in some electronic typewriters and printers

dak /daak, dak/, **dawk** *n* **1** formerly in India, a system of mail delivery or passenger transport using relays of horses or bearers **2** letters, parcels, and other mail in India [Early 18C. Via Hindi *dāk* < Sanskrit *drāk* 'quickly'.]

Dak. *abbr* Dakota

Dakar /dák aar, -ər/ capital of Senegal, in the west of the country. Population: 1,641,358 (1994 estimate).

dak bungalow *n* a house for travellers, originally on the route of a dak

dakoit *n* = **dacoit**

dakoity *n* = **dacoity**

Dakota /də kṓtə/ (*plural* **-tas** *or* **-ta**), **Dakotan** /də kṓt'n/ *n* **1** a member of the Sioux, especially the Santee branch of this people **2** a Siouan language spoken in the United States and the Canadian province of Manitoba. Native speakers: 10,000–20,000. [Early 19C. < Dakota *Dakhóta* 'allies'.] **—Dakota** *adj*

dal[1] /daal/ *n* = **dhal**

dal[2] *symbol* decalitre

Dalai Lama /dállī láamə/ *n* the highest priest of Tibetan Buddhism and, until the Chinese occupation of Tibet in 1959, the traditional spiritual and secular ruler of Tibet [Late 17C. < Mongolian, 'ocean lama']

dalasi /da láassi/ (*plural* **-sis**) *n* see table at **currency** [Late 20C. < an earlier Gambian coin.]

dale /dayl/ *n* **1** a broad lowland valley, especially in N England ○ *walked over hill and dale* **2 dales, Dales** = **Yorkshire Dales** [Old English *dæl* < Indo-European, 'bend, curve']

Dale /dayl/, **Sir Henry Hallett** (1875–1968) British physiologist and pharmacist

daled *n* = **daleth**

Dalek /dáa lek/, **dalek** *n* an alien creature in a metal casing, similar to a robot and with a harsh monotonous voice, from the British science-fiction television series *Dr Who*

Dales, Yorkshire ♦ **Yorkshire Dales**

dalesman /dáylzmən/ (*plural* **-men** /-mən/) *n* somebody who comes from a dales region, especially the Yorkshire Dales in England

daleth /dáalit/, **daled** /-lid/, **dalet** /-lit/ *n* the fourth letter of the Hebrew alphabet

Daley /dáyli/, **Richard J.** (1902–76) US politician. Full name Richard Joseph Daley

Dalgarno /dal gaàrnō/, **George** (1626?–87) Scottish educator

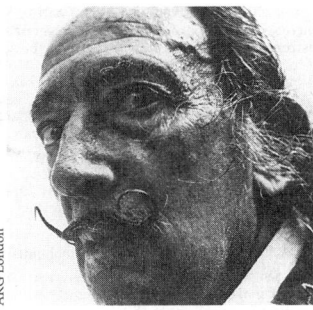

Salvador Dali

Dali /dáali/, **Dalí, Salvador** (1904–89) Spanish surrealist painter **—Daliesque** *adj*

Dalian /dáalyən/ port in NE China. Population: 2,980,513 (1991).

Dalit /daálit/ *n* a member of the lowest caste within the traditional caste system in India

Dallapiccola /dállə píkələ/, **Luigi** (1904–75) Italian composer

Dallas /dálləss/ city in NE Texas. Population: 1,075,894 (1998 estimate).

dalliance /dálli ənss/ *n* **1** the frivolous or idle wasting of time (*literary*) **2** a flirtation or flirtatious episode (*archaic*)

Dall sheep /dáwl-/, **Dall's sheep** *n* a wild mountain sheep with curved horns and a coat varying from white to black. Native to: Alaska, Canada. *Ovis dalli.*

dally /dálli/ (**-lies, -lying, -lied**) *v* **1** *vi* **FLIRT** to act in an amorous, flirtatious, or playful manner **2** *vi* **TOY WITH** to trifle or deal lightly with something or somebody **3** *vti* **WASTE TIME** to dawdle, loiter, or waste time [14C. < Anglo-Norman *dalier* 'amuse yourself'.] —**dallier** *n*

Dalmatia /dal máyshə/ coastal region of Croatia bordering the Adriatic Sea. Area: 12,950 sq. km/5,000 sq. mi.

Dalmatian /dal máysh'n/ *n* **1** **Dalmatian, dalmatian SPOTTED DOG** a dog belonging to a breed that has a white coat with black or brown spots **2** **SOMEBODY FROM DALMATIA** somebody who comes from Dalmatia **3** **EXTINCT ROMANCE LANGUAGE** an extinct Romance language formerly spoken along the Adriatic coast in the region of Dubrovnik —**Dalmatian** *adj*

Dalmatian coast *n* a coastline characterized by chains of islands close to the mainland, formed when rising sea-levels flood a series of valleys and ridges parallel to the coast

dalmatic /dal máttik/ *n* **1** a vestment with slit sides and wide sleeves, worn by a priest or deacon of the Roman Catholic Church **2** a robe with slit sides and wide sleeves, worn by British sovereigns at their coronation [15C. Directly or via Old French *dalmatique* < Latin *dalmatica* '(robe) made of Dalmatian wool' < *Dalmaticus* 'of Dalmatia'.]

d'Alpuget /dal pyoó zhay/, **Blanche** (*b.* 1944) Australian writer

dal segno /dal sényō/ *adv* to be played or sung again from the point marked with the sign 𝄋 to the point marked 'fine' (*musical direction*) ◊ **da capo** [Late 19C. < Italian, 'from the sign'.]

dalton /dáwltən/ *n* = **atomic mass unit** [Mid-20C. After John DALTON.]

Dalton /dáwltən/, **John** (1766–1844) British physicist and meteorologist

daltonism /dáwltənizəm/, **Daltonism** *n* colour blindness, especially an inability to distinguish between red and green [Mid-19C. < French *daltonisme*, after John DALTON, who was affected by this.] —**daltonic** /dawl tónnik/ *adj*

Dalton plan, Dalton system *n* a system of teaching and learning whereby the student is free to continue without interruption on any subject that may arise in the course of his or her study [Early 20C. After *Dalton*, Massachusetts, USA.]

Dalton's law *n* the principle that mixed gases in a given volume exert a pressure equal to the sum of the pressures they would exert individually in the same volume [After JOHN DALTON]

dam[1] /dam/ *n* **1** **BARRIER CONTROLLING FLOW OF WATER** a barrier of concrete or earth that is built across a river or stream to obstruct or control the flow of water, especially in order to create a reservoir **2** **RESERVOIR CONFINED BY DAM** a reservoir of water created, confined, or controlled by a dam **3** **SOMETHING RESEMBLING DAM** a barrier that resembles or acts as a dam ■ *vt* (**dams, damming, dammed**) **1** **CONFINE WITH DAM** to confine, provide, or restrain something with a dam **2** **OBSTRUCT** to block, obstruct, or restrict something [14C. < Middle Dutch.]

dam[2] /dam/ *n* the female parent of an animal, especially of four-legged domestic livestock [14C. Variant of DAME.]

dam[3] *symbol* decametre

Dam /dam/, **Henrik** (1895–1976) Danish biochemist

damage /dámmij/ *n* **1** **HARM OR INJURY** physical harm or injury that makes something less useful, valuable, or able to function ○ *Damage to the vehicle was slight.* ○ *suffered psychological damage as a result of the harassment* **2** **ADVERSE EFFECT** a harmful effect on somebody or something ○ *did untold damage to her standing in the community* **3** **COST** the cost or price of something (*informal*) ○ *What's the damage?* ■ **damages** *npl* **MONEY PAID AS COMPENSATION** money paid or claimed as compensation for harm, loss, or injury ■ *v* (**-ages, -aging, -aged**) **1** *vt* **CAUSE HARM** to cause damage to something or somebody **2** *vi* **BE HARMED** to suffer damage ○ *Soft fruit damages easily.* [13C. < Old French, 'loss through injury' < *dam* 'loss, damage' < Latin *damnum*.] —**damageability** /dámmijə bíllәti/ *n* —**damageable** *adj* —**damager** *n*

damage control *n* **1** shipboard measures to control, contain, and offset damages to a vessel by, e.g. collision, attack, fire, or an explosion **2** containment and neutralization of, e.g. public relations problems caused by a scandal, legal case, or other controversial matter (*informal*) ○ *As soon as the scandal broke, the Party's damage control kicked in.*

damaging /dámmijing/ *adj* causing or capable of causing harm, injury, or loss ○ *a damaging report* —**damagingly** *adv*

damar *n* = **dammar**

Damara /də maárə/ (*plural* **-as** *or* **-a**) *n* a dialect of the Nama language spoken in Namibia. Native speakers: 160,000. [Early 19C. < Nama.] —**Damara** *adj*

Damaraland /də maárə land/ historical region in north-central Namibia

damascene /dámmə seen, -seén/ *vt* (**-cenes, -cening, -cened**) **DECORATE METAL WITH WAVY PATTERNS** to decorate metal such as iron or steel with wavy patterns of etching or inlays of precious metals, especially gold or silver ■ *n* **DESIGN OR OBJECT CREATED BY DAMASCENING** a design or object created by the process of damascening ■ *adj* **1** **RELATING TO DAMASCENING** relating to the art or process of damascening metal **2** **OF OR LIKE DAMASK** made of or resembling damask [< Latin *Damascenus* 'of Damascus' < Greek *damaskēnos*] —**damascener** *n*

Damascus /də máskəss, -maáskəss/ capital of Syria, in the southwest of the country. Population: 1,394,322 (1994). —**Damascene** /dámmə seen, -seén/ *n, adj*

damask /dámməsk/ *n* **1** **PATTERNED FABRIC** a reversible cotton, linen, or silk fabric with a pattern woven into it. Use: table linen. **2** **TABLE LINEN** table linen made from damask **3** **GREYISH-PINK COLOUR** a greyish-pink colour, like that of the damask rose ■ *vt* **DECORATE WITH PATTERN** to decorate or weave a fabric with an elaborate pattern [14C. < Latin *Damascus*.] —**damask** *adj*

damask rose *n* a large hardy rose. Flowers: fragrant, pink or red. Use: essential oil. Native to: Asia. *Rosa damascena.* [< *Damask* 'of Damascus']

Damavand /dámmə vand/ highest mountain in Iran, in the Elburz Mountains in N Iran. Height: 5,771 m/18,934 ft.

Dam Busters *npl* a squadron of the Royal Air Force that bombed dams in Germany during World War II

dame /daym/ *n* **1** *US, Can* **WOMAN OR GIRL** a term for a woman or girl (*often considered offensive*) **2** **WOMAN IN CHARGE OF HOUSEHOLD** the woman in charge of a household (*archaic*) **3** **WOMAN** a married or matronly woman who is no longer young (*archaic*) **4** **SENIOR NUN** used as the formal title of the superior of a nunnery **5** THEATRE = **pantomime dame** [13C. Via Old French and late Latin *domna* < Latin *domina* 'woman in charge of the house'.]

Dame *n* **1** the title of a woman awarded any of various orders of chivalry or merit, e.g. the Order of the British Empire, by a sovereign or government **2** the official title of the wife of a baronet or knight

dame school *n* formerly, a small school, often in a rural area, where children were taught the basics of reading, writing, and arithmetic by a woman of advanced years, usually in her home

dame's rocket *n* = **dame's violet**

dame's violet /dáymz-/ *n* a perennial plant of the mustard family. Flowers: fragrant, purple or white. Native to: Europe, Asia. *Hesperis matronalis.* [Translation of the Latin name in old herbals, *Viola matronalis*]

damiana /dáymi áanə/ *n* a drug extracted from the leaves of the tropical American plant *Turnera diffusa.* Use: stimulant, diuretic. [Late 20C. < American Spanish.]

Damietta /dámmi éttə/ city in the Nile delta, N Egypt. Population: 89,498 (1986).

dammar /dámmər/, **damar, dammer** *n* a hard resin obtained from various trees of Southeast Asia. Use: inks, lacquers, oil paints, and varnishes [Late 17C. < Malay *damar* 'resin'.]

dammit /dámmit/ *interj* used as a swearword to show annoyance [Mid-19C. Variant of *damn it.*]

damn /dam/ *interj* **EXCLAMATION OF ANNOYANCE** used as a mild swearword to emphasize irritation, displeasure, disappointment, or frustration (*informal; sometimes offensive*) ■ *adj, adv* **USED TO EXPRESS ANNOYANCE** used emphatically or as a swearword to express annoyance, disappointment, or frustration with somebody or something (*informal; sometimes offensive*) ■ *v* **1** *vt* **DECLARE TO BE BAD** to express disapproval of something or somebody, especially in public **2** *vt* **DOOM TO FAILURE** to cause somebody or something to fail **3** *vt* **CONDEMN TO HELL** to condemn somebody to hell or to eternal punishment **4** *vti* **CURSE OR SWEAR AT** to curse or swear at somebody or something, using the word 'damn' [13C. Via Old French *damner* 'condemn' < Latin *damnare* < *damnum* 'damage'.] —**damner** *n* ◇ **damn all** nothing at all (*slang*) ◇ **not give** *or* **care a damn** to be not at all concerned or worried about something

damnable /dámnəb'l/ *adj* (*dated*) **1** deserving divine condemnation or damnation **2** detestable, hateful, or extremely bad —**damnably** *adv* —**damnability** /dámnə bíllәti/ *n* —**damnableness** *n*

damnation /dam náysh'n/ *n* **1** **CONDEMNATION** condemnation to hell or eternal punishment **2** **SIN** something that causes condemnation to hell or eternal punishment **3** **PUNISHMENT** eternal punishment in hell ■ *interj* **ANGRY EXCLAMATION** used as a swearword to express anger or disappointment

damnatory /dámnətəri/ *adj* causing, expressing, or threatening condemnation

damned /damd/ *adj* **1** **CONDEMNED** condemned to hell or to eternal punishment **2** **EXPRESSION OF ANNOYANCE** used emphatically or as a swearword to express annoyance (*informal*) ■ *adv* **VERY** extremely (*informal*) ○ *a damned good saxophone player* ■ *npl* **THE CONDEMNED** those condemned to hell or doomed to suffer eternal punishment

damnedest /dámdist/ *adj US* most amazing or extraordinary ○ *It was the damnedest thing I'd ever seen.* ■ *n* everything possible ○ *She did her damnedest to persuade them to stay.*

damnify /dámni fī/ (**-fies, -fying, -fied**) *vt* in law, to cause damage or loss to somebody or something [Early 16C. Via Old French *damnifier* < Latin *damnificare* 'injure, condemn' < *damnare* (see DAMN).] —**damnification** /dámnifi káysh'n/ *n*

damning /dámming/ *adj* **1** very critical or unfavourable **2** proving or showing that somebody or something is guilty, wrong, or very bad —**damningly** *adv* —**damningness** *n*

Damocles /dámmə kleez/ (*fl.* 4th century BC) Syracusan Greek courtier —**Damoclean** /dámmə kleé ən/ *adj*

Damodar /dámmə daar/ river in central Bihar and West Bengal, India. Length: 592 km/368 mi.

damp /damp/ *adj* **1** **MOIST** slightly wet ○ *damp laundry* **2** **HALF-HEARTED** unenthusiastic or indifferent ■ *n* **1** **SLIGHT WETNESS** humidity, moisture, or slight wetness ○ *patches of damp* **2** **HARMFUL GAS** poisonous gas or rank air, especially in a mine **3** **SOMETHING THAT DEPRESSES** a feeling of gloom or melancholy (*archaic*) ○ *The host's low spirits cast a damp over the party.* ■ *vt* **1** **DAMPEN** to make somebody or something slightly wet **2** **EXTINGUISH** to extinguish a fire or make it burn more slowly by reducing its supply of air **3** **STOP** to stop the vibration of a string on a musical instrument **4** **STIFLE** to discourage or stifle somebody or something ○ *Rain damped the picnickers' enthusiasm.* **5** **REDUCE OSCILLATION** to decrease the amplitude of an oscillation or wave **6** **MUFFLE** to deaden or muffle the sound of a musical instrument [14C. < Middle Low German < Germanic.] —**damply** *adv* —**dampness** *n*

damp down, dampen down *vt* **1** **CAUSE TO BURN MORE SLOWLY** to cause a fire to burn more slowly by adding ash or by reducing the flow of air **2** **REDUCE** to control, restrain, or reduce the intensity of something **3** **COVER WITH WATER** to cover a surface with a small quantity of water ○ *Bill damped down his hair.*

damp off, dampen off *vi* to decline in power, wealth, or strength

dampcourse /dámp kawrss/ *n* a layer of waterproof material near the ground in a brick wall that prevents damp from rising

dampen /dámpən/ *vti* **1** to make something slightly wet, or to become slightly wet **2** to deaden or stifle something, or to become deadened or stifled —**dampener** *n*

damper /dámpər/ *n* **1** **SOMEBODY OR SOMETHING DISCOURAGING** somebody or something that causes discouragement or inhibition **2** **PLATE TO CONTROL FIRE** a metal plate that controls the draught in a furnace or stove **3** **PIANO MUTE** a felt-covered block in a piano that stops the vibration of strings **4 HORN OR WOODWIND MUTE** a mute to muffle the sound of a brass or woodwind instrument **5** *Aus* **UNLEAVENED BREAD** traditional Australian bush bread made from a simple flour and water dough and often cooked over an open fire **6 DEVICE TO CONTROL VIBRATION** a device for controlling the excessive vibration of a suspended magnetic needle **7 DEVICE TO REDUCE HUNTING** a piece of copper embedded in or near the poles of an electric motor to reduce any tendency it might have to pulsate to speeds above or below its intended speed ◇ **put a damper on something** to make something less fun and more inhibited ○ *The sudden arrival of the adults put a damper on the kids' party.*

Dampier /dámpi ər/ coastal town in NW Western Australia. Population: 1,819 (1991).

Dampier /dámpi ə/, **William** (1652–1715) English explorer

damping off *n* a fatal disease of seedlings grown under very damp conditions that is caused by various fungi

damp-proof *adj* impervious or resistant to damp or moisture ■ *vt* to make something such as a building damp-proof

damp-proof course *n* = **damp course**

damp squib *n* something that is intended or expected to be effective or impressive but that fails or disappoints (*informal*)

damsel /dámz'l/ *n* a girl or young unmarried woman, originally one of noble birth (*archaic or literary*) [13C. < Old French *dameisele*, alteration (after *dame*) of *donsele* < Vulgar Latin *dominicella* 'little lady' < Latin *domina* 'woman in charge of the house'.]

damselfish /dámz'l fish/ (*plural* **-fish** *or* **-fishes**) *n* a small brightly-coloured marine fish that lives along coral reefs. Family: Pomacentridae.

damselfly /dámz'l flī/ (*plural* **-flies**) *n* a slender insect related to the dragonfly but smaller in size that folds its wings together above its body when resting. Suborder: Zygoptera.

damson /dámz'n/ *n* **1** a small sour dark purple fruit, usually eaten cooked or made into jam **2** a fruit tree related to the plum that bears damsons. *Prunus insititia.* [15C. Alteration of DAMASCENE 'of Damascus'.]

dan[1] /dan/, **Dan** *n* **1** any one of the numbered black-belt levels of proficiency in martial arts such as judo and karate **2** somebody who has achieved a dan [Mid-20C. < Japanese.]

dan[2] /dan/, **dan buoy** *n* a small buoy, often with a flag attached, used as a marker [Late 17C. < ?]

Dan *n* in the Bible, the son of Jacob and Bilhah and the forebear of the tribe of Dan (Genesis 30:6)

Dan. *abbr* **1** Daniel **2** Danish

Dana /dáynə/, **Richard Henry** (1815–82) US writer and lawyer

Danaides /də náy i deez/, **Danaïdes** *npl* in Greek mythology, the fifty daughters of Danaüs, who killed their bridegrooms

dan buoy *n* = **dan**[2]

Danby /dánbi/, **Francis** (1793–1861) Irish-born British painter

dance /daanss/ *v* (**dances, dancing, danced**) **1** *vi* **MOVE RHYTHMICALLY TO MUSIC** to move the feet and body rhythmically, usually in time to music **2** *vt* **DO A DANCE** to perform or participate in a dance ○ *to dance a lively polka* **3** *vt* **CAUSE TO DANCE** to cause somebody to dance ○ *He danced her across the floor.* **4** *vt* **REACH BY DANCING** to arrive at something by dancing ○ *She danced her way to fame and adulation.* **5** *vi* **JUMP UP AND DOWN** to leap or skip, especially in an emotional manner ○ *The children danced with glee.* **6** *vi* **MOVE ABOUT QUICKLY** to bob up and down or move quickly about ○ *The leaves danced across the lawn.* **7** *vi* **FAIL TO ROLL RE-ENTRY NUMBER** in backgammon, to fail to roll a number that re-enters a piece from the bar ○ *He rolled a 6–6 and danced.* ■ *n* **1 RHYTHMICAL BODY MOVEMENTS TO MUSIC** a series of rhythmical steps and movements, usually performed to music **2 PERIOD OF DANCING** a session of dancing **3 OCCASION FOR DANCING** a social gathering for dancing **4 ART OF DANCING** dancing as a performance **5 MUSIC FOR DANCING** a piece of music for a dance **6 PATTERN OF ANIMAL MOVEMENTS** a pattern of animal movements used, e.g. in courtship by birds or by bees to give information about food ■ *adj* **OF OR FOR DANCING** relating to, involving, or created for dancing [13C. < Old French.] —**dancer** *n* —**danceable** *adj*

dance band *n* a band that plays music for dancing

dance floor *n* an area of bare floor for dancing

dance hall *n* **1** an enclosed space where public dances are held **2** *US* electronically produced dance music combining different musical styles with a disc jockey talking or rapping to the rhythm

dance music *n* **1** music suitable for dancing **2** pop music that uses repeated electronic rhythms

dance of death, Dance of Death *n* an allegorical representation in medieval art, literature, and music of a dance in which Death, personified as a skeleton, leads people to the grave

dancercise /da̋anssər sīz/ *n US* aerobic exercise in the form of dance [Mid-20C. Blend of DANCE + EXERCISE.]

dancing /da̋anssing/ *n* performing or taking part in a dance

D and C *n* a gynaecological surgical procedure in which the cervix is widened and some of the womb lining is scraped out, for diagnostic or treatment purposes or in an abortion. Full form **dilatation and curettage**

dandelion /dándi lī ən/ *n* a weed with bright yellow flowers on hollow stalks that produce fluffy white seed heads. Use: leaves: in salads, medicine, winemaking. *Taraxacum officinale.* [15C. < French *dent de lion* 'lion's tooth'.]

Dandenong Ranges /dándə nong-/ forested range of hills in S Victoria, Australia. Highest peak: Mount Dandenong, 634 m./2,080 ft.

dander[1] /dándər/ *n* **1** minute particles or scales shed from the feathers, hair, or skin of various animals. They may be the cause of some allergies, especially asthma. **2** *Ireland* dandruff [Late 18C. < ?] ◇ **get somebody's dander up** to make somebody angry

dander[2] /dándər/, **daunder** /dáwndər/ *n N England, Scotland* a saunter or stroll ■ *vi N England, Scotland* to dawdle, saunter, or stroll [Late 16C. < ?]

Dandie Dinmont /dándi dínmont/, **Dandie Dinmont terrier** *n* a small terrier of a breed from the Scottish Borders with a long body, short legs, drooping ears, and a long wiry greyish or brownish coat [Early 19C. After the fictional owner of such dogs in *Guy Mannering* by Sir Walter Scott.]

dandify /dándi fī/ (**-fies, -fying, -fied**) *vt* to dress somebody as or cause somebody to resemble a dandy or fop —**dandification** /dándifi káysh'n/ *n* —**dandified** *adj*

dandiprat /dándi prat/ *n* **1 16C ENGLISH COIN** a 16th-century English coin **2 BOY** a small boy (*archaic*) **3 INSIGNIFICANT PERSON** an insignificant person (*archaic*) [Early 16C. < ?]

dandle /dánd'l/ (**-dles, -dling, -dled**) *vt* **1** to move a baby or small child gently up and down in your arms or on your knees **2** to fondle or pet somebody or something [Mid-16C. < ?] —**dandler** *n*

dandruff /dándrəf, -druf/ *n* loose dry scales of dead skin that are shed from the scalp [Mid-16C. < *dand-* < ? + *-ruff* < ?] —**dandruffy** *adj*

dandy /dándi/ *n* (*plural* **-dies**) **1 MAN TOO CONCERNED WITH APPEARANCE** a man who is much concerned with his elegant appearance (*dated*) **2** *US* **EXCELLENT PERSON OR THING** a person or thing considered to be very good or the best in its class (*informal dated*) **3 SAILING BOAT** a ketch or yawl **4** PAPER = **dandy roll** ■ *adj* (**-dier, -diest**) **1** *US* **EXCELLENT** very good, excellent, or first-rate (*informal dated*) **2 CHARACTERISTIC OF A DANDY** dressed or acting like a dandy (*dated*) [Late 18C. Shortening of Scottish *Jack-a-dandy* 'affected man'.] —**dandily** *adv* —**dandyish** *adj* —**dandyism** *n*

dandy brush *n* a stiff coarse brush for grooming animals, especially horses

dandy roll, dandy (*plural* **-dies**), **dandy roller** *n* a wire cylinder used in papermaking to produce a watermark

Dane /dayn/ *n* somebody who comes from Denmark [14C. < Old Norse *Danir* (plural) 'Danes'.]

Danegeld /dáyn geld/, **Danegelt** /-gelt/ *n* **1** an annual tax first levied in the 10th century in England to buy off Danish invaders **2** a payment made in order to avoid trouble or to prevent attack from a stronger enemy [Pre-12C. < assumed Old Norse *Danagiald* < *Danir* (plural) 'Danes' + *giald* 'payment'.]

Danelaw /dáyn law/ *n* **1** the body of laws established in the parts of England settled in the 9th century by Danish invaders **2** the parts of Anglo-Saxon England that came under Danish law and where Danish customs were observed [Old English *Dena lagu* 'Danes' law']

dang /dang/ *interj, adj, adv, vti US* = **damn** [Late 18C. Euphemistic alteration.]

danged /dangd/ *adj, adv US* = **damned**

danger /dáynjər/ *n* **1** exposure or vulnerability to harm, injury, or loss ○ *Their lives were in danger.* ○ *His reckless behaviour had put them all in danger.* **2** somebody or something that may cause harm, injury, or loss (*often plural*) [13C. Via Anglo-Norman *daunger* < assumed Vulgar Latin *domniarium* 'power to do harm' < Latin *dominium* 'sovereignty' < *dominus* 'lord'.]

danger money *n* additional payment made for doing a job that involves danger. US term **hazard pay**

dangerous /dáynjərəss/ *adj* **1** likely to cause or result in harm or injury **2** involving risk or difficulty ○ *The business is in a dangerous financial position.* —**dangerously** *adv* —**dangerousness** *n*

dangle /dáng g'l/ *v* (**-gles, -gling, -gled**) **1** *vti* **HANG OR CAUSE TO HANG LOOSELY** to swing or hang loosely or cause something to swing or hang loosely ○ *The children dangled their legs over the side of the swimming pool.* **2** *vt* **OFFER AS INDUCEMENT** to offer or display something as an enticement or inducement ○ *The possibility of promotion was dangled before her.* ■ *n* **DANGLING THING** something that dangles [Late 16C. Thought to suggest the action.] —**dangler** *n* —**dangly** *adj*

dangling participle *n* a participle that is not grammatically linked to the word it is intended to modify. In 'Driving down the street, the house came into view', 'driving' is a dangling participle.

USAGE Dangling participles: Also called 'misplaced' or 'unattached' participles, these typically occur at the beginning of sentences and modify either the wrong thing or nothing in particular: *Startled by the noise, her book fell to the floor* (but it was she, not her book, who was startled). *Lying in the sun, it was hard to imagine the winter back home* (who was lying in the sun?). Correct such mismatches by changing the wording: *Startled by the noise, she dropped her book* and *Lying in the sun, he found it hard to imagine the winter back home.* A number of dangling participles, however, are well established and idiomatic, for example *given, granting,* and *speaking*: *Given that dividends depend on earnings, what determines earnings?* Other similar words, including *considering* and *regarding*, are so well established in such contexts that they are generally thought of as independent of the verbs from which they sprang and are now said to be prepositions.

dan grade *n* MARTIAL ARTS = **dan**[1] *n.* 1

Daniel /dánnyəl/ *n* **1 BIBLICAL PROPHET** a biblical prophet whose faith in God protected him in the lion's den **2 BOOK OF BIBLE** the book of the Bible that tells the story of Daniel **3 WISE PERSON** a wise and honourable person

Daniel /dánnyəl/, **Samuel** (1562–1619) English poet

danio /dáyni ō/ (*plural* **-os**) *n* a brightly-coloured freshwater fish, that is kept as an aquarium fish. Native to: India, Sri Lanka. Genera: *Danio* and *Brachydanio.* [Late 19C. < modern Latin.]

Danish /dáynish/ *adj* **OF DENMARK** relating to Denmark or its people, language, or culture ■ *n* **LANGUAGE OF DANES** the official language of Denmark, also an official language of the Faroe Islands and Greenland, belonging to the North Germanic group of Indo-European languages. Native speakers: 5 million. ■ *npl* **PEOPLE FROM DENMARK** people who come from Denmark ■ *n* **Danish, danish** FOOD = **Danish pastry** [14C. < Anglo-Norman *Danes* (plural) 'Danes' < Old Icelandic *Danir.*]

Danish blue *n* a blue-veined cheese with a strong taste, originally produced in Denmark

Danish pastry *n* a rich puff pastry made from a yeast dough with a sweet filling containing fruit or nuts

dank /dangk/ *adj* unpleasantly damp and cold [14C. Probably < N Germanic.] —**dankly** *adv* —**dankness** *n*

Dankworth /dángk wurth/, **Johnny** (*b.* 1927) British jazz musician, bandleader, and composer

D'Annunzio /da nóonssi ō/, **Gabriele** (1863–1938) Italian novelist, poet, and playwright

danse macabre /da̋anss mə ka̋abrə/ (*plural* **danses macabres** /da̋anss mə ka̋abrə/) *n* = **dance of death** [Late 19C. < French, 'macabre dance'.]

danseur /doN súr, daan súr, daaN sőr/ *n* a male ballet dancer [Early 19C. < French, 'male dancer'.]

danseuse /doN súrz, daan súrz, daaN sőrz/ *n* a female ballet dancer [Early 19C. < French, 'woman dancer'.]

danshiki /dan sheéki/ (*plural* **-kis**) *n* a brightly coloured loose-fitting garment resembling a long shirt without buttons, worn mainly by men in West Africa [Mid-20C. < Hausa.]

Dante Alighieri /dánti alli gyáiri/ (1265–1321) Italian poet —**Dantean** /dánti ən, dan teé ən/ *adj, n*

Dantesque /dan tésk/ *adj* in the style of the works of Dante Alighieri

danthonia /dan thṓni ə/ *n* a perennial tufted grass that has narrow leaves and small flowers growing closely together along the stem. Native to: Australia, New Zealand. Genus: *Danthonia*. [Early 20C. < modern Latin, after Étienne *Danthoine*.]

Danton /dántən, daáN toN/, **Georges Jacques** (1759–94) French lawyer and revolutionary

Danube /dán yoob/ longest river in W Europe, flowing southeastwards from SW Germany into the Black Sea. Length: 2,850 km/1,770 mi. —**Danubian** /də nyoóbi ən/ *adj*

Danzig /dánsig/ ➧ **Gdansk**

dap /dap/ (**daps, dapping, dapped**) *v* **1** *vi* **FISH WITH BOBBING BAIT** to fish by bobbing the bait lightly on the surface of the water **2** *vi* **DIP QUICKLY** to dip gently or quickly into water **3** *vti* **BOUNCE OR SKIP** to bounce or skip, or cause something to bounce or skip, especially across the surface of water **4** *vt* **JOIN WITH A NOTCH** to cut a notch in timber in order to join it to another piece [Mid-17C. Thought to suggest the action.]

daphne /dáfni/ (*plural* **-nes** *or* **-ne**) *n* a cultivated shrub with glossy evergreen leaves. Flowers: fragrant, bell-shaped, pink or purplish. Native to: Europe, Asia. Genus: *Daphne*. [15C. < Greek *daphnē* 'laurel, bay tree'.]

daphnia /dáfni ə/ (*plural* **-as** *or* **-a**) *n* a tiny freshwater flea with a transparent shell and branched antennae. Genus: *Daphnia*. [Mid-19C. < modern Latin, < *Daphne*, nymph in Greek mythology.]

Da Ponte /da pónti/, **Lorenzo** (1749–1838) Italian librettist and poet. Born **Emanuele Conegliano**

dapper /dáppər/ *adj* **1 TRIM** neat and elegant (*refers to men*) **2 LIVELY** alert and lively or brisk **3 NIMBLE** small and active or nimble [15C. < Middle Dutch or Middle Low German 'bold, heavy'.] —**dapperly** *adv* —**dapperness** *n*

dapple /dápp'l/ *vti* (**-ples, -pling, -pled**) **MARK WITH PATCHES OF COLOUR** to mark something with patches or spots of a different colour or with light and shade, or to be marked in this way ○ *Sunlight dappled the path through the trees.* ■ *adj* = **dappled** ■ *n* **1 COLOURED MARKINGS** spots or patches of a different colour, especially on a horse, or of light and shade **2 SPOT OF COLOUR** an individual spot or patch of colour, light, or shade **3 DAPPLED ANIMAL** an animal, especially a horse, with a dappled coat [Late 16C. Back-formation < DAPPLED.]

dappled /dápp'ld/, **dapple** *adj* marked with spots or patches of a different colour or with light and shade ○ *in the dappled shade of the chestnut tree* [15C. < ?]

dapple-grey *adj* describes a horse or pony of a light-grey colour with darker grey spots or patches ■ *n* (*plural* **dapple-greys**) a dapple-grey horse or pony [14C. < ?]

daps /daps/ *npl S W England* light shoes for gymnastics or sport with canvas uppers and rubber soles [Early 20C. < ?]

dapsone /dáp sōn/ *n* an antibacterial drug containing sulphur. Use: treatment of leprosy and dermatitis. [Mid-20C. Contraction of *di(para-amino-phenyl)sulphone*.]

darbies /daárbiz/ *npl* a pair of handcuffs (*archaic slang*) [Late 16C. Shortening of *Father Darby's bands*, a restraint for those arrested for debt.]

Darby and Joan *n* a contented and devoted couple who have long lived together in domestic harmony [Late 18C. < a contented long-married couple in a poem published in the *Gentleman's Magazine* in 1735.]

Darby and Joan club *n* a social club for people of advanced years

Darcy /daárssi/, **Les** (1895–1917) Australian boxer. Full name **James Leslie Darcy**

Dard /daard/ *n* somebody who speaks a Dardic language [Mid-19C. < Dardic.]

Dardanelles /daárdə nélz/ strait in NW Turkey linking the Aegean Sea with the Sea of Marmara. Length: 70 km/43 mi.

Dardic /daárdik/ *n* a subgroup of Indic languages spoken in N India and Pakistan. Native speakers: 7 million. —**Dardic** *adj*

dare /dair/ *vt* (**dares** *or* **dare, daring, dared**) **1 HAVE ENOUGH COURAGE FOR** to have the courage needed to do something (*sometimes used as an auxiliary*) ○ *wanted to ask but then didn't dare* ○ *'We must dare to think about "unthinkable things" because when things have become unthinkable, thinking stops and action becomes mindless'.* (William Fulbright *US Senate Speech*; 27 March, 1965) **2 HAVE AUDACITY TO DO** to do something that angers or outrages somebody (*sometimes used as an auxiliary*) ○ *Don't you dare do that!* ○ *How dare you?* **3 CHALLENGE** to challenge somebody to do something, usually something dangerous or frightening ○ *daring each other to jump first* ■ *n* **CHALLENGE** a challenge to somebody to do something dangerous or frightening, or a response to such a challenge ○ *did it for a dare* [Old English *darr, dearr*, forms of *durran* 'dare' < Germanic] —**darer** *n*

daredevil /dáir devv'l/ *n* **RISK-TAKER** a daring risk-taker, especially somebody who performs dangerous stunts ■ *adj* **1 UNMINDFUL OF DANGER** showing a carefree disregard for risk or danger, especially by performing dangerous stunts **2 DANGEROUS** with a high degree of risk or danger ○ *a daredevil stunt*

daredevilry /dáir devv'lri/, **daredeviltry** /dáir devv'ltri/ *n* **1** a carefree disregard for danger **2** dangerous acts or stunts performed by a daring person

Dar el-Baida /daár el bídə/ ➧ **Casablanca**

daresay /dáir sáy/ ◇ **I daresay, I dare say 1** used, often in an irritable tone, to express the fact that the speaker considers something to be likely or possible **2** used crossly or impatiently to dismiss something that is true but irrelevant

Dar es Salaam /daár ess sə laám/ largest city in Tanzania. Population: 1,734,000 (1995 estimate).

darg /daarg/ *n* **1** *Scotland* a day's work **2** *Aus* a specific amount of work [Mid-16C. Shortening and alteration of *daywork*.]

dargah /daárgə/ *n* **1** a site where a Muslim holy man was buried or cremated **2** a shrine built at a dargah [< Persian]

daring /dáiring/ *adj* **1 BRAVE AND ADVENTUROUS** showing a courageous or reckless disregard for danger ○ *The officer led a daring assault on the enemy machine-gun post.* **2 RISKY** involving an element of risk or danger ○ *a daring move* **3 SHOCKING** unconventional or ahead of its time and therefore likely to shock, upset, or offend ■ *n* **BOLDNESS** courage combined with a willingness to take risks or attempt difficult or unconventional things —**daringness** *n*

daringly /dáiringli/ *adv* in a way that involves taking a risk and is likely to be exciting or shocking ○ *She daringly decided to break with tradition.*

dariole /dárri ōl/ *n* **1 dariole, dariole mould** a small cup-shaped mould in which individual portions of savoury or sweet dishes can be cooked and then served **2** a dish cooked and served in a dariole [14C. < French, 'custard tart'.]

Darius I /də rī́ əss/ (558–486 BC) king of Persia (521–486 BC)

Darjeeling[1] /daar jeéling/ *n* a high-quality black tea grown around Darjeeling in India, or the hot drink made from its leaves

Darjeeling[2] /daar jeéling/ town in NE India, close to the border with Nepal. Population: 73,062 (1991).

dark /daark/ *adj* **1 NOT LIGHT OR LIT** with little or no light ○ *It's getting dark; do you mind if I put the light on?* ○ *It was a dark and stormy night.* **2 NOT LIGHT IN COLOUR** reflecting less light than other colours or shades and therefore appearing deeper, richer, or more sombre ○ *The curtains are dark green.* **3 BROWNISH OR BLACKISH** not pale or fair, but brown to black in hair or eye colour ○ *She has darker eyes than her brother.* **4 MISERABLE** characterized by unhappiness, misfortune, or pessimism ○ *in the dark days of the Depression* **5 ANGRY** suggesting hostility or anger ○ *dark looks* **6 NASTY** evil or wicked ○ *the dark side of his character* **7 MYSTERIOUS** little known or kept hidden from others ○ *dark secrets* **8 UNENLIGHTENED** lacking enlightenment, learning, and artistic or scientific achievement (*formal*) **9 CLOSED** not presenting theatrical performances (refers to a theatre) **10 MELLOW** deep and rich in sound ■ *n* **1 LACK OF LIGHT** a place, time, or situation in which there is too little light to see properly ○ *I don't like driving in the dark.* **2 NIGHTFALL** the beginning of night ○ *We left early to be home before dark.* **3 SHADED AREA** a darker colour or a darker-coloured or shaded part ○ *the contrast between the darks and the lights in the picture* [Old English *deorc* < Indo-European] ◇ **in the dark** ignorant, unaware, or not informed about something ○ *She kept everyone in the dark about her plans.* ◇ **whistle in the dark** to attempt to or pretend to keep up your courage when afraid

Dark /daark/, **Eleanor** (1901–85) Australian writer. Born **Eleanor O'Reilly**

dark adaptation, dark adaption *n* the reflex changes, such as dilation of the pupil and increased sensitivity of the retina, that enable the eye to continue to see in dim light —**dark-adapted** *adj*

dark adaption *n* = **dark adaptation**

Dark-Age *adj* dating from, belonging to, or typical of the Dark Ages

Dark Ages *npl* **1** the period of European history between the fall of the Roman Empire in AD 476 and about AD 1000, for which there are few historical records and during which life was comparatively uncivilized **2** an undeveloped state, way of life, or way of doing things (*informal*) ○ *Computers were in their Dark Ages a few decades ago.*

dark chocolate *n* chocolate that has no added milk and is darker and less sweet than milk chocolate

darken /daárkən/ *vti* **1** to become darker, or to make something darker ○ *I mixed a little blue and brown with the red to darken it.* **2** to become unhappy, less hopeful, or angry, or to cause such a change in somebody or something ○ *The outlook has darkened considerably since the last update.* —**darkener** *n*

ϟ **dark fibre** *n* a fibre optic cable that is not transmitting a signal

dark-field illumination *n* the lighting of a specimen in a microscope from the side so that it can be seen against a dark background

dark-field microscope *n* = **ultramicroscope**

dark glasses *npl* spectacles with dark-tinted lenses, especially sunglasses

dark horse *n* **1 LITTLE-KNOWN PERSON** somebody about whom very little is known or who tends to be reticent, especially somebody who subsequently reveals unexpected talents **2** *US* **UNEXPECTEDLY SUCCESSFUL CANDIDATE** a candidate who gains an unexpected amount of support in an electoral campaign **3 UNEXPECTEDLY SUCCESSFUL CONTESTANT** a little-known competitor who achieves unexpected success in a race or other sporting contest [< the idea of a little-known racehorse making a surprisingly good showing in a race]

darkie /daárki/ *n* = **darky** (*dated taboo offensive*)

darkish /daárkish/ *adj* fairly dark in colour or shading ○ *a woman with darkish hair*

dark lantern *n* a lantern with a sliding panel that is used to dim or hide its light

darkling /daárkling/ *adv* **IN DARKNESS** in the dark (*archaic literary*) ○ *'Darkling I listen, and full many a time…'* (John Keats, *Ode to a Nightingale*; 1820) ■ *adj* (*archaic or literary*) **1 WITHOUT CLARITY** dark, dim, or obscure **2 OCCURRING IN DARKNESS** done or happening in the night [15C. < -LING[2].]

darkling beetle *n* a beetle with a hard black or brown body whose larvae feed on decaying vegetable matter, living plants, and grain. Family: Tenebrionidae.

darkly /daárkli/ *adv* **1** in a way that conveys a threat or a sense of foreboding **2** in or with black or as a dark-coloured shape ○ *trees darkly outlined against the horizon*

dark matter *n* matter postulated to exist in the universe because of observed gravitational effects

dark meat *n* meat from the legs and thighs of poultry, which is a darker colour than the meat of the breast

darkness /daárknəss/ *n* **1 DARK** the absence or lack of light ○ *He flicked a switch and the room was plunged into darkness.* **2 NIGHT** night time **3 DEPTH OF COLOUR** the comparative depth of a colour or its closeness to black

dark reaction *n* the second phase of photosynthesis which does not require light

darkroom /daárk room, -rōōm/ *n* a room from which natural light is excluded so that light-sensitive photographic materials can be safely handled and photographs can be developed

dark rum *n* rum that is brown in colour

darksome /daárksəm/ *adj* without light and gloomy or unpleasant (*archaic or literary*) ○ *doomed to die in a darksome dungeon*

dark star *n* a star that is not visible and is usually detectable only by its radio or infrared emissions or by its gravitational effect on other bodies

darky /daárki/ (*plural* **-ies**), **darkie** *n* a highly offensive term for a Black person (*dated taboo*)

darling /daárling/ *n* **1 LOVING TERM OF ADDRESS** used as an affectionate form of address to a loved one, or as a general, informal, and sometimes slightly affected form of address to social acquaintances **2 SOMEBODY CONSIDERATE** somebody who is kind, helpful, or likable **3 INFORMAL TERM OF ADDRESS** an extremely informal and typically suggestive term of address, often to a stranger (*informal*) **4 FAVOURITE** somebody who is especially popular with somebody else or a group ○ *She's the darling of the literary reviews.* ■ *adj* **1 DEARLY LOVED** loved very much **2 NICE** pretty and charming (*informal*) **3 darling, darlin'** *Ireland* **SWEET-NATURED** lovable, kind, pleasant, or sweet-natured (*informal*) [Old English *deorling* 'dear person, dear one' < DEAR]

Darling /daárling/ river in S Queensland and New South Wales, Australia. Length: 2,739 km/1,702 mi.

Darling, Grace (1815–42) British heroine who rescued shipwrecked mariners

Darling Downs fertile tableland in SE Queensland, Australia. Area: 72,520 sq. km/28,000 sq. mi.

Darling Range range of hills in Western Australia. Highest peak: Mount Cooke, 582 m/1,910 ft.

Darlington /daárlingtən/ town and borough in NE England. Population: 100,600 (1995).

darn[1] /daarn/ *vti* to mend a hole in a piece of clothing or fabric using long interwoven stitches to fill the gap ○ *sat there darning socks.* ■ *n* a repair to a piece of clothing or fabric using long interwoven stitches [Early 17C. Probably < French dialect *darner* 'mend' < *darne* 'piece'.] —**darner** *n*

darn[2] /daarn/ *interj* **EXCLAMATION** used instead of a swearword to express irritation, displeasure, or surprise (*informal*) ■ *adj, adv* **darn, darned EMPHATIC TERM** used instead of a swearword to give emphasis or to indicate irritation or displeasure (*informal*) ○ *a darn good movie* ■ *vt* **CONDEMN** used to express annoyance or frustration (*informal*) ○ *Darn it, I told you not to go in there.* [Late 18C. Alteration of DAMN.]

darned /daarnd/ *adj* used instead of a swearword to express surprise, bafflement, disavowal, or refusal (*informal*) ○ *I'll be darned if I know.* ■ *adj, adv* = **darn**[2] (*informal*)

darnedest /daárndist/ *adj* used to emphasize or draw to somebody's attention something that is unusual or out of the ordinary (*informal*)

darnel /daárn'l/ *n* a grass commonly found growing as a weed in grain fields. Native to: Europe, Asia. Genus: *Lolium*. [Early 14C. < ?]

darning /daárning/ *n* **1** the work of repairing holes in clothes with long interwoven stitches **2** clothes that need to be darned

darning egg, darning mushroom *n* a piece of wood or plastic shaped like an egg or mushroom, used to support the fabric around a hole that is being mended

darning needle *n* a long needle with a large eye, used in darning

Darnley /daárnli/, **Henry Stewart, Lord** (1545–67) Scottish nobleman, husband of Mary, Queen of Scots

darogha /dárrōgə/ *n S Asia* somebody in charge of a group of police officers [Mid-17C. < Persian, Urdu *daroga* 'governor'.]

dart /daart/ *n* **1 MISSILE USED IN DARTS** a short weighted arrow with a long slender point, a tapered tubular body, and plastic or metal fins that is thrown at a dartboard in the game of darts **2 MISSILE USED AS WEAPON** a small arrow with a point at one end and feathers or fins at the other that can be thrown, shot from a blowgun, or scattered by an exploding bomb **3 POINTED PROJECTING PART OR ORGAN** a pointed, projecting body part used, e.g. to penetrate tissue, or, in some species of snail, in mating **4 FAST MOVE** a sudden quick movement ○ *He made a dart for the door.* **5 STITCHED TAPERING FOLD** a tapering fold sewn into a garment to make it fit, e.g. at the waist or bust ■ *v* **1** *vi* **MOVE SWIFTLY** to move suddenly and quickly ○ *The little fish darted under a stone.* **2** *vt* **MAKE SOMETHING MOVE QUICKLY** to move, extend, or direct something quickly and suddenly ○ *She darted a meaningful glance at her husband across the table.* [14C. < Old French < Germanic < Indo-European, 'sharp'.]

dartboard /daárt bawrd/ *n* a round piece of wood or similar material marked with twenty radiating numbered segments and a bull's eye in the centre, used as a target in the game of darts

darter /daártər/ *n* **1 N AMERICAN FISH** a brightly-coloured fast-moving freshwater fish of the perch family. Native to: E North America. Family: Percidae. **2 TROPICAL FISH-EATING BIRD** a fish-eating diving bird with a long neck and sharp bill. Native to: warmer freshwater regions of N and S America, Africa, Asia, and Australia. Family: Anhingidae. US term **anhinga 3 SOMEBODY OR SOMETHING THAT DARTS** somebody or something that moves quickly and suddenly

Dartford /daártfərd/ town in SE England. Population: 59,411 (1991).

darting /daárting/ *adj* swift and sudden ○ *His darting runs down the left flank frequently opened up the Scottish defence.* —**dartingly** *adv*

Dartmoor National Park /daárt moor-/ national park in SW England. Area: 954 sq. km/368 sq. mi.

Dartmoor pony *n* a pony belonging to a hardy long-haired breed. Native to: Dartmoor in Devon.

Dartmouth /daártməth/ town in SW England. Population: 5,676 (1991).

darts /daarts/ *n* an indoor game in which players take turns throwing arrow-shaped missiles (**darts**) from a set distance at a circular board (**dartboard**) placed at about eye level on a wall (+ *singular verb*)

Darwin /daárwin/ capital of Northern Territory, Australia. Population: 70,251 (1996).

Darwin, Charles (1809–82) British naturalist

Darwinian /daar wínni ən/ *adj* relating to the 19th-century British naturalist Charles Darwin or his theory of evolution —**Darwinian** *n*

Darwinian theory *n* the theory, first developed by the 19th-century British naturalist Charles Darwin, that species of living things originate, evolve, and survive through natural selection in response to environmental forces

Darwinism /daárwinizəm/ *n* **1** = **Darwinian theory 2** belief in or advocacy of Charles Darwin's theory of evolution —**Darwinist** *n, adj*

Darwin's finches *npl* the birds of the Galapagos Islands on which Charles Darwin based his theory of evolution through observation of their feeding habits and corresponding differences in bill structure. Subfamily: Geospizinae.

dash /dash/ *n* **1 PUNCTUATION MARK** a short horizontal line (-) used as a punctuation mark, often in place of a comma or colon, or as a sign that certain letters or words have been omitted **2 MORSE SYMBOL** a short horizontal line representing a long sound or flash of light in written transcriptions of Morse code **3 RUSH** a quick purposeful movement by a person or a group of people in any direction ○ *There was a dash for the exit as soon as the alarm was raised.* **4 RACE** a short-distance running race **5 SMALL QUANTITY ADDED** a small quantity of something added to something else, e.g. to improve the flavour of food or drink or to enliven speech or writing ○ *A dash of common sense would make his arguments a lot more convincing.* **6 VIGOUR AND VERVE** a combination of vigour, daring, and style in the way a person acts ○ *She carried it off with a certain amount of dash.* **7 DASHBOARD** the instrument panel of a car (*informal*) **8 QUICK STROKE** a quick and often violent movement, blow, or stroke ○ *with a dash of her arm* ■ *v* **1** *vi* **HURRY** to run, move, or travel fast or hastily ○ *He dashed off to catch his plane.* **2** *vt* **KNOCK OR THROW SOMETHING VIOLENTLY** to knock or throw something with a sudden violent sweep or blow (*formal*) ○ *She dashed the papers down on the desk in anger.* **3** *vti* **SMASH** to break or throw something or to be broken or thrown, usually against a hard surface (*formal*) ○ *The waves were dashing against the sea wall.* **4** *vt* **RUIN** to frustrate or destroy something (*often passive*) ○ *The new crisis has dashed all hopes of a speedy return to democratic government.* **5** *vt* **DISCOURAGE** to make somebody feel discouraged or intimidated (*usually passive*) ○ *I felt more than a little dashed by the ease with which she had refuted my arguments.* **6** *vt* **ADD SMALL AMOUNT** to alter, improve, or flavour with a small amount of another substance (*often passive*) ○ *tonic water dashed with bitters* **7** *vt* **EXPRESS IRRITATION** used to express annoyance or dissatisfaction with something or somebody (*dated informal*) ○ *Dash it, I've already paid the man!* [13C. < ?] ◇ **cut a dash** to be dressed smartly and stylishly so as to attract attention (*dated*)

PUNCTUATION ***Dashes*** are used in pairs around text that adds extra information and can be omitted without affecting the structure of the sentence: *He drives to Glasgow and back – a round trip of 600 miles – at least once a week.* *Commas* and *brackets* can be used for the same purpose, and are often preferable in formal contexts, but dashes (used sparingly) are a stronger means of separating and have the effect of drawing attention to the extra information. Similarly, a dash may be used instead of a *colon* to introduce something that explains or elaborates on what has gone before: *Unemployment in the town has fallen to 3,000 – a drop of almost 20%.* This short dash is called an ***en dash*** and usually has a space on either side; a longer ***em dash*** may be used in the same way but without spaces: *Unemployment in the town has fallen to 3,000—a drop of almost 20%.* An em dash can also be used in place of omitted letters, e.g. to avoid mentioning a person's full name: *Mr J— accused Ms D— of lying.*

dash off *vt* to write, draw, or compose something in a great hurry (*informal*) ○ *She dashed off a note to her secretary before leaving the office.*

dashboard /dásh bawrd/ *n* **1** a panel in front of the driver of a vehicle or the pilot of a small aircraft or boat that contains various indicator dials, switches, and controls **2** a board, panel, or screen to protect the driver of a horse-drawn carriage from being splashed with mud [Mid-19C. < DASH in the obsolete sense 'splash, spatter'.]

dashed /dasht/ past tense, past participle of **dash** ■ *adv* used to add emphasis to an adjective or adverb (*dated informal*) ○ *You see it's dashed awkward, because I've already promised to take Emmy.* ■ *adj* used to express annoyance or dissatisfaction (*dated informal*) ○ *Dashed cartridges got wet, dashed gun wouldn't fire!*

dasheen /da sheén/ *n Carib* **1** = **taro 2** tubers of the dasheen plant, usually boiled for eating [Late 19C. < ?]

dashiki /də sheéki/, **daishiki, dasheki** *n* a brightly coloured loose-fitting garment resembling a long shirt without buttons, worn mainly by men in Africa, the Caribbean, and the United States [Mid-20C. Probably < Yoruba *danshiki*.]

dashing /dáshing/ *adj* **1** smart and stylish ○ *That's a rather dashing outfit, if I may say so.* **2** confident and full of bravado and spirit (*dated*) ○ *a dashing young officer* —**dashingly** *adv* —**dashingness** *n*

dashpot /dásh pot/ *n* a device consisting of a piston inside a fluid-filled cylinder that absorbs or dampens vibrations in a mechanism

dassie /dássi/ *n* ZOOL = **hyrax** [Late 18C. Via Afrikaans < Dutch *dasje* 'small badger' < *das* 'badger'.]

dastardly /dástərdli/ *adj* used to refer humorously or melodramatically to somebody or something mean, treacherous, and cowardly ○ *a dastardly deed* [Late 16C. < *dastard*, probably < *dast*, a past participle of DAZE.] —**dastardliness** *n*

dasyure /dássi yoor/ *n* a small usually carnivorous marsupial. Native to: Australia, Tasmania, neighbouring islands. Subfamily: Dasyurinae. [Mid-19C. Via French, < modern Latin *dasyurus* < Greek *dasus* 'rough, hairy' + *oura* 'tail'.]

DAT /deé ay teé, dat/ *abbr* digital audio tape

ϟ **data**[1] /dáytə, daátə/ *n* (+ *singular or plural verb*) ⚠ **1** information, often in the form of facts or figures obtained from experiments or surveys, used as a basis for making calculations or drawing conclusions **2** information, e.g. numbers, text, images, and sounds, in a form that is suitable for storage in or processing by a computer [Mid-17C. < plural of Latin *datum*, neuter past participle of *dare* 'give, grant'.]

USAGE Data – singular or plural? Use of the term ***data*** has grown apace with the use of computer technology and statistical methods. Because the word's meaning is much like that of the singular noun *information*, and because its Latin *-a* plural announces the word's plural status less plainly than a final *s* would, it is often treated as if it were singular. This use is extremely common, and few perceive it as wrong these days, especially given the word's connotation of a collection or single unit made up of many informational subunits. All the same, in formal English, *Our data have been assembled over a number of years* would be regarded as correct, and constructions such as *very little data, the data* *shows...*, and *a great deal of data* would be regarded as incorrect.

data[2] plural of **datum**

ϟ **data bank** *n* 1 a large store of information, especially kept in or available to a computer, sometimes consisting of several databases 2 = **database**

ϟ **database** /dáytə bayss/ *n* a systematically arranged collection of computer data, structured so that it can be automatically retrieved or manipulated

ϟ **database management system** *n* a computer program devised to create, store, and manipulate databases

ϟ **data capture** *n* the collecting and entering of data in a computer, or the conversion of data into a form compatible with computers

ϟ **data centre** *n* a place at which large amounts of data or information are stored, usually the main storage facility for data relating to a particular field of knowledge

ϟ **data compression** *n* the encoding of data so that it requires less disk space for storage and time for transmission

ϟ **data element** *n* the smallest meaningful piece of information in an electronic business transaction (*in e-commerce*)

ϟ **dataglove** /dáytə gluv/ *n* a glove with sensors that feed spatial and tactile data to a computer, allowing the wearer to manipulate and explore virtual reality

ϟ **data mining** *n* the locating of previously unknown patterns and relationships within data using a database application

ϟ **data processing** *n* the entering, storing, updating, and retrieving of information, using a computer

ϟ **data protection** *n* 1 legal safeguards to prevent misuse of information stored on computers, particularly information about individuals 2 the adoption of administrative, technical, or physical deterrents to safeguard computer data

ϟ **data warehouse** *n* a database used in analysing overall business strategy rather than routine operations

datcha /dáchə/ *n* ARCHIT = **dacha**

date[1] /dayt/ *n* 1 **DAY, MONTH, AND YEAR** a phrase or string of numbers that denotes a particular day of the month or year 2 **TIME OF AN EVENT** a date used to locate a past or future event in time ○ *The concert has been postponed to a later date.* 3 **VISUAL REPRESENTATION OF DATE** the words or numbers of a date in the form of a written statement or inscription, e.g. on a document or coin ○ *There's no date on this letter.* 4 **PERIOD** the period during which something such as a work of art was created ○ *This has much in common with other artefacts of the same date.* 5 **APPOINTMENT** an appointment to meet somebody for a social or business activity ○ *I've got a dinner date with a client.* 6 **ROMANTIC APPOINTMENT** a social or romantic engagement with somebody ○ *I thought we had a date tonight.* 7 **PARTNER ON DATE** somebody with whom a date has been arranged ○ *My date stood me up.* 8 **COMMITMENT TO PERFORM** an engagement to give a performance ○ *Our band has a date to play at the Coliseum.* ■ **dates** *npl* **DATES OF BIRTH AND DEATH** the years of somebody's birth and death ○ *Do you happen to know Van Gogh's dates?* ■ *v* (**dates, dating, dated**) 1 *vt* **PUT DATE ON** to mark something with a date, usually the current date ○ *Please sign and date the contract.* 2 *vt* **ASSIGN DATE TO** to find out or state the time or period when something was made ○ *The early works of Shakespeare are rather difficult to date precisely.* 3 *vi* **ORIGINATE** to have an origin in a particular time in the past ○ *We have records dating back to the 16th century.* 4 *vi* **GO OUT OF STYLE** to become old-fashioned ○ *This is a classic style and won't date.* 5 *vt* **MAKE SOMEBODY OR SOMETHING SEEM OLD** to reveal the age of somebody or something, or to make somebody or something seem old-fashioned ○ *The shape of the headlights dates the car.* 6 *vti* **GO ON DATES WITH** to go out regularly with somebody as a social or romantic partner ○ *We dated for a few months.* [14C. < medieval Latin *data* < past participle of Latin *dare* 'give, grant'; from uses such as *(epistola) data Romae* '(letter) given at Rome', with the day and month appended.] —**dateable** *adj* ◇ **to date** up to the present time

date[2] /dayt/ *n* 1 a dark-coloured oval fruit that has sweet flesh and a single hard narrow seed 2 TREES = **date palm** [13C. Via Old French, < Greek *daktulos* 'finger or toe, date'.]

datebook /dáyt bo͝ok/ *n US* a diary in which social engagements and other things to be remembered are noted

dated /dáytid/ *adj* 1 no longer used or in vogue, often having been current or fashionable in the recent past 2 with a date marked or written on it

dateless /dáytləss/ *adj* unlikely to become old-fashioned or obsolete

dateline /dáyt līn/ *n* a line at the head of a newspaper article or similar item giving the date and place of writing

Date Line *n* = **International Date Line**

date palm *n* a tall palm tree with feathery fronds, cultivated for its fruit. Native to: North Africa, West Asia. *Phoenix dactylifera.*

date rape *n* an act of rape committed on somebody during or after a date

date-rape (**date-rapes, date-raping, date-raped**) *vt* to rape somebody after a date

date stamp *n* a rubber stamp used to mark the date on something, or the date marked by such a stamp —**date-stamp** *vt*

Datin /daátin/ *n* the title of a woman member of a senior order of chivalry in Malaysia

dating agency /dáyting-/ (*plural* **dating agencies**) *n* an agency whose business is to establish personal contacts between similar or compatible people

dative /dáytiv/ *n* 1 a grammatical form (**case**) that identifies the source, agent, or instrument of action of the verb in some inflected languages and that affects nouns, pronouns, and adjectives 2 a word or phrase in the dative [15C. < Latin *dativus* 'of giving' < *dat-*, past participle of *dare* 'give, grant'.]

dative bond *n* CHEM = **coordinate bond** [Because one atom gives up electrons to another]

datolite /dáttə līt/ *n* a hydrated silicate containing calcium and boron. Source: igneous rocks. [Early 19C. < Greek *dateisthai* 'divide'; from the divisions between its crystals.]

Datuk /daátək/ *n* the title of a man member of a senior order of chivalry in Malaysia [Mid-19C. < Malay *datok*.]

datum /dáytəm, daá-/ (*plural* **-ta** /-tə/) *n* 1 **ITEM OF INFORMATION** a single piece of information 2 **GIVEN FACT** a known or assumed fact that is used as the basis for a theory, conclusion, or inference 3 **POINT OF REFERENCE** a point, line, or surface used as a basis for measurement or calculation in mapping or surveying [Mid-18C. < Latin (see DATA[1]).]

datum line, datum level, datum plane *n* the horizontal plane or line from which all other heights and depths are measured or calculated on a map or chart

DATV *abbr* digitally assisted television

daub /dawb/ *v* 1 *vt* **APPLY BLOTCHILY** to put or spread a semi-liquid substance, e.g. mud, paint, or cream, on a surface in a crude, hurried, or irregular way ○ *They had daubed slogans all over the walls.* 2 *vti* **PAINT CRUDELY** to paint or apply paint crudely and inexpertly ■ *n* 1 **BLOTCH** a crude patch, splash, or smear of a semiliquid substance on something 2 **BAD PAINTING** a painting that is considered to be badly or inexpertly done ○ *'When he first came to Rome he painted worthless daubs and gave no promise of talent'.* (Henry James, *Roderick Hudson*; 1876) 3 **SUBSTANCE FOR DAUBING** a mixture of clay, lime, and chopped straw plastered onto interwoven rods or twigs to make a wall. ◊ **wattle and daub** [14C. Via Old French *dauber* < Latin *dealbare* 'whiten over, plaster' < *albare* 'whiten' < *albus* 'white'.] —**dauby** *adj* —**dauber** *n*

daube /dōb/ *n* a dish of braised meat or vegetables [Early 18C. < French, via Italian *dobba* < Catalan *a la adoba* 'stewed' < Germanic, 'to strike'.]

Daubigny /dṓbinyi/, **Charles-François** (1817–78) French painter and etcher

daud /dawd/ *n Scotland* a lump, chunk, or stiff dollop of something ■ *vt Scotland* to knock or thump something [Late 16C. Probably an imitation of a thumping sound.]

Daudet /dṓ day/, **Alphonse** (1840–97) French writer

daughter /dáwtər/ *n* 1 **FEMALE CHILD** somebody's female child 2 **WOMAN OR GIRL CONNECTED WITH PLACE** a woman or girl considered as a product of a place or institution (*formal*) ○ *Daughters of the American Revolution* 3 **PRODUCT OF SOMETHING** something produced by or issuing from something else (*literary*) ○ *Truth is the daughter of time.* 4 **DESCENDANT** a woman or girl descendant (*literary*) ○ *a daughter of Eve* 5 **NUCLIDE FORMED BY RADIOACTIVE DECAY** a nuclide formed from an element by radioactive decay ■ *adj* 1 **FORMED FROM SOMETHING ELSE** formed by or from a similar thing, usually retaining close links with it and sometimes remaining subordinate to it 2 **BEING AN OFFSPRING** produced by a process of reproduction, replication, or division [Old English *dohtor* < Indo-European] —**daughterless** *adj*

ϟ **daughterboard** /dáwtər bawrd/ *n* a printed circuit board that plugs into a motherboard, usually to improve the performance of a system or add function

daughter cell *n* either of the identical cells produced when a living cell divides

daughter-in-law (*plural* **daughters-in-law**) *n* the wife of somebody's son

daughterly /dáwtərli/ *adj* typical or expected of a daughter ○ *She came to regard the distinguished professor with an almost daughterly affection.* —**daughterliness** *n*

Daughters of the American Revolution *npl* in the United States, a women's patriotic society founded in 1890 by descendants of those who fought in the War of American Independence

Daumier /dṓ mi ay/, **Honoré** (1808–79) French painter and caricaturist

daunder *n, vi N England, Scotland* = **dander**[2]

daunt /dawnt/ *vt* to make somebody feel anxious, intimidated, or discouraged (*usually passive*) ○ *The scale of the task would have daunted even the most experienced organizer.* [13C. Via Anglo-Norman *daunter* < Latin *domitare* 'to tame'.] —**daunter** *n*

daunting /dáwnting/ *adj* likely to discourage, intimidate, or frighten somebody ○ *You'll find the task less daunting if you divide it up into manageable sections.* —**dauntingly** *adv*

dauntless /dáwntləss/ *adj* unlikely or unable to be frightened or discouraged ○ *We remember with admiration their dauntless courage and optimism.* —**dauntlessly** *adv* —**dauntlessness** *n*

dauphin /dáwfin, dṓ-/ *n* in former times, the eldest son of the king of France and the direct heir to the throne [15C. < French, in Old French *daulphin* (see DOLPHIN); because of dolphins on a relevant coat of arms.]

dauphine /dáw feen, dṓ-/, **dauphiness** /dáwfinəss/ *n* the wife of the dauphin [Mid-19C. < French, feminine form of *dauphin* (see DAUPHIN).]

daven /daá ven/ *vi* 1 to recite prayers from the Jewish liturgies 2 to lead Jewish prayers [Mid-20C. < Yiddish *davnen* 'pray'.]

Davenant /dávv'nənt/, **Sir William** (1606–68) English poet and dramatist

davenport /dávv'n pawrt/ *n* 1 an ornamental writing desk with a sloping top and drawers in its sides 2 *US* a large well-upholstered sofa, especially one that can be converted into a bed [Mid-19C. < ?]

David /da veéd/, **St** (520?–589?) patron saint of Wales

David /dáyvid/ (*d.* 962 BC) king of Judah (1000–962 BC)

David /da veéd/, **Sir Edgeworth** (1858–1934) Welsh-born Australian geologist and explorer

David, Elizabeth (1913–92) British food researcher and writer

David, Jacques-Louis (1748–1825) French painter

David-and-Goliath *adj* describes a situation in which a much smaller and apparently weaker person or organization is pitted against one that is very large and powerful [See GOLIATH]

Davies /dáyviss/, **Paul Charles William** (*b.* 1946) British-born Australian physicist

Davies, Sir Peter Maxwell (*b.* 1934) British composer and conductor

Davies, Robertson (1913–95) Canadian novelist, essayist, and playwright

Davies, W. H. (1871–1940) British poet. Full name **William Henry Davies**

Bette Davis

Davis /dáyviss/, **Bette** (1908–89) US film actor. Full name **Ruth Elizabeth Davis**

Davis, **Jefferson** (1808–89) US statesman

Davis, **Davys, John** (1550?–1605) English navigator

Davis, **Judy** (b. 1955) Australian actor

Davis, **Miles** (1926–91) US trumpet player and band leader

Davis Cup n 1 an annual international men's tennis competition for which a trophy is awarded to the winning nation 2 the trophy awarded to the winning nation in the Davis Cup competition [Early 20C. After Dwight Filley *Davis*,who donated the trophy.]

Davison /dáyviss'n/, **Emily** (1872–1913) British suffragette

Davis Strait body of water separating Baffin Island, Canada, from Greenland, and forming the entrance to Baffin Bay. Depth: 3,660 m/11,900 ft.

davit /dávvit/ n a small crane at the side of a ship's deck, especially one of a pair of curved metal posts with tackle attached for suspending and lowering a lifeboat [15C. < Anglo-Norman *daviot, daviet* < the name *Davi* 'David'.]

Davitt /dávvit/, **Michael** (1846–1906) Irish nationalist leader

Davos /dávvoss/ mountain resort in E Switzerland. Population: 11,325 (1998).

Davy /dáyvi/, **Sir Humphry** (1778–1829) British chemist

Davy Jones n the personification of the sea

Davy Jones's locker n the bottom of the sea, especially considered as the final resting place of drowned sailors or sunken ships (*informal*)

Davy lamp /dáyvi-/ n a portable oil-burning lamp, formerly used by miners, in which the flame is protected by metal gauze to prevent it from igniting explosive gases underground [Early 19C. After Sir Humphry *Davy*.]

Davys = Davis, John

daw /daw/ n a jackdaw (*archaic or regional*) [15C. Probably < assumed Old English *dawe* < Germanic.]

dawdle /dáwd'l/ (-dles, -dling, -dled) vi 1 to walk or move slowly and reluctantly or idly ○ *We'll get there in time if you don't dawdle.* 2 to spend far more time than is necessary in doing something ○ *We dawdled over lunch and it was three o'clock before we left the restaurant.* [Mid-17C. < ?] —**dawdler** n —**dawdling** n, adj —**dawdlingly** adv

Dawkins /dáwkinz/, **Richard** (b. 1941) British evolutionary biologist

dawn /dawn/ n 1 DAYBREAK the first appearance of light in the sky as the sun rises at the beginning of a new day 2 BEGINNING the beginning of something, especially a period of time or history ○ *the dawn of the industrial era* ■ vi 1 BEGIN to begin, as the sun rises and light appears in the sky ○ *The day dawned cloudy and wet.* 2 BECOME APPARENT to begin to be perceived ○ *The realization dawned that few of them would survive.* 3 START TO EXIST to begin to develop or exist (*literary*) [15C. Back-formation (as verb) < DAWNING.]

dawn on vt to come into somebody's mind or consciousness ○ *It was some time before the seriousness of the situation dawned on them.*

dawn chorus n 1 the loud singing of many birds as the first light of day appears in the sky 2 any loud sound, especially from a number of different sources, occurring very early in the morning (*humorous*) ○ *a dawn chorus of power drills and hammering*

dawning /dáwning/ n the beginning of a new day or of a new period of time or history ○ *with the dawning of the computer age* ■ adj beginning to appear, develop, or be perceived [13C. Alteration of obsolete *dawing* < Old English *dagian* 'dawn, become day' < Germanic.]

dawn raid n 1 a surprise attack on enemy troops at dawn 2 a surprise attempt to buy a large number of a company's shares at the start of a day's trading, especially as a first stage in a takeover bid

dawn redwood n a deciduous tree with flat leaves and small round cones, widely grown as an ornamental. Native to: China. *Metasequoia glyptostroboides.*

Dawson river in E Queensland, Australia. Length: 640 km/398 mi.

DAX n a share index on the Frankfurt Stock Exchange. Full form **Deutsche Aktienindex**

day /day/ n 1 24 HOURS a period of 24 hours, usually beginning and ending at midnight 2 SUNRISE TO SUNSET the part of a 24-hour period when it is light, between sunrise and sunset 3 TIME OF ACTIVITY the part of a 24-hour period when somebody is working or active ○ *I work an 8-hour day.* 4 INDEFINITE PERIOD OR POINT IN TIME a time or period of time in the past, present, or future ○ *One of these days we'll get round to painting the house.* 5 TIME OF FAME the time when a particular person or thing is well known, popular, successful, or effective ○ *In her day she was one of our best-known Shakespearean actors.* 6 LIFE OR EXISTENCE the time when a particular person or thing is active or in existence ○ *In my day we had to work on Saturday mornings.* 7 PERIOD OF EARTH'S ROTATION ABOUT AXIS a unit of time equal to the Earth's period of rotation about its axis, measured either relative to the Sun (**solar day**) or the stars (**sidereal day**) 8 PERIOD OF PLANET'S ROTATION ABOUT AXIS the period of time in which a planet revolves once on its axis [Old English *dæg* < Indo-European] ◇ **call it a day** to finish work or stop doing something ◇ **carry** or **win the day** to gain a victory ◇ **day after day** for several or many days in a row ◇ **day by day 1** each consecutive day **2** progressively ◇ **day in, day out** every day without exception and all day long ◇ **have seen better days** to be in a less prosperous or less good condition than previously ◇ **in this day and age** nowadays, as opposed to past times and customs ◇ **it's early days** things are at an early stage and it is uncertain how they will develop or turn out ◇ **make somebody's day** to make somebody very happy ◇ **name the day** to set a date for something, typically a wedding ◇ **save the day** to prevent defeat or disaster ◇ **somebody's** or **something's days are numbered** somebody or something will not survive much longer ◇ **that'll be the day!** expresses the opinion that something is most unlikely to happen (*informal*) ○ *You think they'll offer me Mike's job? That'll be the day!* ◇ **the other day** not long ago ◇ **those were the days!** expresses affection and nostalgia for past times

Day /day/, **Doris** (b. 1924) US film actor and singer. Born Doris von Kappelhoff

Dayak /dí ak/ (*plural* -**aks** /dí ak/ or -**ak**) n = Dyak

Dayan /dī án/ n the title of the judge of the Beth Din, a Jewish religious court [Late 19C. < Hebrew, < *dān* 'to judge'.]

Dayan /dī án/, **Moshe** (1915–81) Israeli general and statesman

day bed n a couch or bed for reclining on during the day

day blindness n the inability to see clearly in bright light with comparatively good vision in dim light. Technical name **hemeralopia**

daybook /dáy bŏŏk/ n a book in which financial transactions are recorded day by day

dayboy /dáy boy/ n a boy who is a pupil at a residential school but lives at home

daybreak /dáy brayk/ n the time when light first appears in the sky at the beginning of a day

daycare /dáy kair/ n daytime supervision and recreational, training, or medical facilities for preschool children, disabled people, or elderly people wanting special assistance

day centre n a place providing nonresidential care or recreation for senior citizens, people with physical disabilities, or people with psychiatric disorders

daydream /dáy dreem/ n 1 DREAM EXPERIENCED WHILE AWAKE a series of often distracting and usually pleasant thoughts and images that pass through the mind while awake 2 UNREALIZABLE HOPE OR FANTASY a pleasant wish or hope that is unlikely to be fulfilled ■ vi (-dreams, -dreaming, -dreamt or -dreamed /-dremt/, -dreamt or -dreamed) THINK DISTRACTING THOUGHTS to have or indulge in daydreams —**daydreaming** n —**daydreamy** adj

daydreamer /dáy dreemər/ n an inattentive or unrealistic person

dayflower /dáy flowər/ n a tropical plant with narrow pointed leaves. Flowers: blue or purplish, soon wilting. Genus: *Commelina.* [Late 17C. Because the flowers last for only one day.]

dayfly /dáy flī/ (*plural* -**flies**) n INSECTS = mayfly n. 1 [Early 17C. Because it lives for only one day.]

daygirl /dáy gurl/ n a girl who is a pupil at a residential school but lives at home

Day-Glo /dáy glō/ tdmk a trademark for fluorescent dyes and colouring agents

day hospital n a nonresidential hospital or part of a hospital where patients go for treatment or therapy during the daytime

day job n a job that somebody does merely to earn an income while trying to achieve success in another field, especially the arts

day labourer n a manual worker who is hired and paid on a day-to-day basis

Day-Lewis, **Cecil** /dáy loō iss/, **Cecil** (1904–72) Irish-born British poet and novelist

Day-Lewis, **Daniel** (b. 1957) British-born Irish stage and film actor

daylight /dáy līt/ n 1 SUNLIGHT natural light from the sun ○ *Open the curtains and let in a bit of daylight.* 2 DAYTIME the part of the day when it is light 3 DAYBREAK the time when light first appears in the sky at the beginning of a day 4 PUBLIC AWARENESS public knowledge, notice, or scrutiny ○ *There are some secrets that they would prefer not to have exposed to daylight.* 5 VISIBLE GAP a visible gap between competitors in a race, showing the lead that one has over the other ○ *There's definitely daylight now between the two boats as they approach the halfway mark.* ◇ **in broad daylight** in the daylight hours for all to see

daylight lamp n a lamp that gives light with a range of wavelengths similar to natural light

daylight robbery n charging prices that seem far too high (*informal*) US term **highway robbery**

daylight-saving time n an adjustment of clock time to allow more hours of normal daylight

day lily n a perennial summer flowering plant with long slender leaves. Flowers: large yellow, red, or orange, resembling those of the lily, usually dying after one day. Genus: *Hemerocallis.*

daylong /dáy long/ adj, adv throughout the entire day

day-night match n a one-day cricket match that begins in the early afternoon in natural light and continues into the evening under artificial light

day nursery n a place where preschool children are looked after during the daytime, usually while their parents are at work

Day of Atonement n = Yom Kippur

day off (*plural* **days off**) n a day on which somebody does not have to work

Day of Judgment n = Judgment Day

day of reckoning n a time when somebody is made to answer for crimes or mistakes

day one n the first day or the very beginning of something ○ *It's day one of the electoral campaign.*

day out (*plural* **days out**) n a day of leisure spent away from home

daypack /dáy pak/ n a small rucksack or bag for carrying things needed during the day

day release n a system that allows employees to take days off work without loss of pay to continue their education or training (*hyphenated before nouns*)

day return n a ticket, or the fare charged, to travel to a place and back again on the same day, usually at a reduced price ○ *Two day returns to Glasgow, please.*

day room n a communal recreation room in an institution such as a hospital or barracks

days /dayz/ adv during the day or every day ○ *I work days one week and nights the next.*

day sailer *n* a small sailing boat without sleeping accommodation

day school *n* 1 a private school that does not take boarders 2 a school that holds classes during the daytime but not during the evening

day shift *n* 1 a shift that is worked during the day or part of the day 2 a group of employees who work during the day at a place where others work during the night

dayside /dáy sīd/ *n* the side of a planet that faces the sun

Days of Awe *npl* JUDAISM = **High Holidays**

days of grace *npl* the extra days, customarily three, allowed for the settlement of a note or bill after it falls due

dayspring /dáy spring/ *n* the first light of day (*literary*)

daystar /dáy staar/ *n* = **morning star** (*literary*)

daytime /dáy tīm/ *n* the part of the day when there is natural light ■ *adj* occurring, done, or used during the daytime

day-to-day *adj* 1 occurring or tending to be the same every day ○ *the day-to-day business of earning a living* 2 planning or providing for one day at a time ○ *We do everything on a day-to-day basis – we can never plan ahead.*

Dayton /dáyt'n/ city in SW Ohio. Population: 167,475 (1998 estimate).

Daytona Beach /day tṓnə-/ coastal city in NE Florida. Population: 65,136 (1998 estimate).

Dayton Accords *npl* an agreement signed by the presidents of Bosnia, Croatia, and Serbia in 1995, containing measures to end hostilities [< DAYTON, where the agreement was reached]

day trading *n* the purchase and subsequent sale of securities on the same day, used as a way of making quick profits on price movements —**day trader** *n*

day trip *n* a journey or outing to and from a place within a day —**day tripper** *n*

daywear /dáy wair/ *n* clothes for wearing during the day

daze /dayz/ *n* **CONFUSED STATE** a state of confusion and unclear thinking, often the result of a blow or shock ○ *Things happened so quickly I was left in a daze.* ■ *vt* (**dazes, dazing, dazed**) 1 **STUN** to leave somebody wholly or partly unconscious or unable to think clearly, especially as a result of a blow or shock ○ *The blow seemed to have dazed her.* 2 **BEWILDER** to leave somebody feeling confused or amazed [14C. Back-formation < *dazed* < Old Norse *dasaðr* 'weary from cold or exertion'.] —**dazed** *adj* —**dazedly** /dáyzidli/ *adv*

dazzle /dázz'l/ *vti* (**-zles, -zling, -zled**) 1 **DEPRIVE OF SIGHT TEMPORARILY** to make somebody temporarily unable to see ○ *The glare of the oncoming headlights dazzled me.* 2 **AMAZE** to amaze somebody with brilliance or skill or with a wonderful spectacle or display (*often passive*) ○ *She dazzled the spectators with a triple somersault.* ■ *n* **LIGHT THAT DAZZLES** very bright light that deprives somebody of sight temporarily ○ *a lot of dazzle from the white-painted walls of the house* [15C. < DAZE.]

dazzle up *vt* to make something more attractive and colourful (*informal*)

dazzling /dázzling/ *adj* 1 bright enough to deprive somebody of sight temporarily 2 spectacularly skilful or impressive ○ *a dazzling line-up of stars* —**dazzlingly** *adv*

Db *symbol* dubnium

DB, D/B *abbr* daybook

DBA[1], **DBA** *abbr* Doctor of Business Administration

ϟ **DBA**[2] *abbr* doing business as (*in e-mails*)

ϟ **DB connector** *n* a connector that facilitates serial and parallel input and output. Full form **data bus connector**

DBE *abbr* Dame Commander of the Order of the British Empire

ϟ **DBMS** *abbr* database management system

DBS *abbr* 1 direct broadcasting by satellite 2 direct broadcasting satellite

DC *abbr* 1 da capo 2 direct current. ◊ **AC** 1 3 District Commissioner 4 Detective Constable

D.C. *abbr* District of Columbia

DCB *abbr* Dame Commander of the Order of the Bath

DCC *abbr* digital compact cassette

DCL *abbr* Doctor of Civil Law

DCM *abbr* Distinguished Conduct Medal

DCMG *abbr* Dame Commander of the Order of St Michael and St George

DCVO *abbr* Dame Commander of the Royal Victorian Order

dd *abbr* 1 delivered 2 dated

DD *abbr* 1 demand draft 2 direct debit 3 dishonourable discharge 4 Doctor of Divinity

D/D *abbr* direct debit

D-day *n* 1 6 June, 1944, the day on which Allied forces landed in N France to begin the liberation of occupied Europe in World War II 2 a day chosen for the beginning of a military operation or other major venture

DDR *abbr* Deutsche Demokratische Republik

DDS *abbr* 1 Dewey Decimal System 2 Doctor of Dental Science 3 Doctor of Dental Surgery

DDSc *abbr* Doctor of Dental Science

DDT *n* $C_{14}H_9Cl_5$ an insecticide effective especially against malaria-carrying mosquitoes that has been banned in many countries since 1974 because of its toxicity, its persistence in the environment, and its ability to accumulate in living tissue. Full form **dichlorodiphenyltrichloroethane**

ϟ **de** *abbr* Germany (*in Internet addresses*)

DE *abbr* Delaware[2]

de- *prefix* 1 opposite, reverse ○ *decertify* 2 remove ○ *decaffeinate* ○ *delist* 3 derived from ○ *denominative* 4 reduce ○ *declass* 5 get off ○ *deplane* 6 formed by removing one or more atoms from a particular element ○ *deoxy-* [Via Old French *de-*, *des-* < Latin *de-*, *dis-* 'apart, away']

deaccession /dée ək sésh'n/ *vti* to remove a book or work of art from the collection of a library or museum and sell it

deacidify /dée ə síddi fī/ (**-fies, -fying, -fied**) *vt* to remove the acid from something or reduce the acid content of something —**deacidification** /dee ə síddifi káysh'n/ *n*

deacon /déekən/ *n* 1 in the Roman Catholic, Orthodox, and Anglican Churches, an ordained member of the clergy who ranks below a priest 2 in many Protestant churches, a lay person who is appointed or elected to assist the minister [Pre-12C. Via Latin *diaconus* < Greek *diakonos* 'servant, messenger'.]

deaconess /déekənəss/ *n* a woman who ranks below a priest or who is appointed to assist a minister

deaconry /déekənri/ (*plural* **-ries**) *n* 1 the position or rank of deacon 2 deacons considered as a group

deactivate /dee ákti vayt/ (**-vates, -vating, -vated**) *vt* 1 **MAKE SOMETHING INACTIVE** to prevent something that is active or live, especially an explosive device, from operating 2 **STOP ACTIVE COMPOUND FROM WORKING** to render a biologically active compound, e.g. an enzyme, inactive or ineffective 3 *US* **END ACTIVE MILITARY STATUS** to make a military unit no longer active —**deactivation** /dee akti váysh'n/ *n* —**deactivator** *n*

dead /ded/ *adj* 1 **NO LONGER ALIVE** having passed from the living state to being no longer alive ○ *a dead bird* 2 **INANIMATE** never having been alive and having none of the characteristics of a living thing 3 **WITHOUT LIVING THINGS** having no living things, or unable to support life 4 **WITHOUT PHYSICAL SENSATION** having lost normal sensitivity to touch or pain, e.g. from the effects of cold, disease, or anaesthesia ○ *My fingers have gone completely dead.* 5 **INSENSITIVE** unable or unwilling to respond to, understand, or appreciate something 6 **LACKING ANY SIGNS OF LIFE** showing little indication of feeling or vitality ○ *His eyes were dead.* 7 **LIKE CORPSE** having the appearance of a dead person 8 **LACKING ACTIVITY OR INTEREST** without human activity or anything interesting or entertaining ○ *This town is dead after seven o'clock at night.* 9 **NO LONGER CURRENT** no longer in use, or no longer relevant, appropriate, or important ○ *That issue is now well and truly dead, despite attempts to revive it.* 10 **BROKEN DOWN** no longer able to operate because of a fault, breakdown, or loss of power ○ *The phone went dead.* 11 **NOT BURNING** no longer burning or able to burn 12 **NONRESONANT** not resonant or producing sounds that are not resonant ○ *'... To where Saint Mary Woolnoth kept the hours / With a dead sound on the final stroke of nine ...'* (T. S. Eliot, *The Waste Land*; 1922) 13 **TOTALLY QUIET** unbroken by any sound or movement ○ *There was dead silence for a few seconds; then everyone started cheering.* 14 **TOTAL** sudden, abrupt, and complete ○ *came to a dead stop in the middle of the road* 15 **EXACT** precise or exact in position or character ○ *dead centre* 16 **EXHAUSTED** very tired or completely without energy (*informal*) 17 **DOOMED** certain to face a very unpleasant fate (*informal*) ○ *If I don't get this report in by tomorrow, I'm dead.* 18 **EMPTY** empty and ready to be cleared away (*informal*) 19 **WITH NO RETURN** producing or yielding no return 20 **OUT OF PLAY** in some sports describes a ball that has crossed the boundary of the playing area 21 **LANDING CLOSE TO GOLF HOLE** describes a golf shot in which the ball comes to rest so close to the hole that the next shot cannot miss ■ *npl* **DEAD PEOPLE** people who have died or been killed (+ *plural verb*) ○ *respect for the dead* ■ *adv* 1 **PRECISELY** emphasizes that an approximate-sounding description or instruction, e.g. concerning a time, a position, or a straight line, is in fact precise or to be followed precisely ○ *Keep going dead ahead for another 300 yards.* 2 **ENTIRELY** completely or absolutely ○ *You can be dead sure that he won't make the same mistake again.* 3 **WITH SUDDENNESS** abruptly or immediately ○ *stopped dead in her tracks* 4 **VERY** used in informal contexts to add emphasis to an adjective or adverb (*informal*) ○ *I was dead scared.* [Old English *dēad* <Germanic, 'died'] —**deadness** *n*
◇ **the dead of night** *or* **winter** the most extreme point of night or winter

SYNONYMS ***dead, deceased, departed, late, lifeless, defunct, extinct***

CORE MEANING: no longer living, functioning, or in existence

dead describes organisms that are no longer alive, physical objects that no longer function or exist, and abstract entities that are no longer valid or relevant; **deceased** (*formal*, restricted to people, especially in legal or other technical contexts, or as a euphemism) no longer living; **departed** (*formal or literary*, restricted to people) no longer living; **late** (restricted to people) having died recently or within living memory; **lifeless** not living, or apparently not living; **defunct** no longer operative, valid, or functional; **extinct** no longer in existence, or no longer active.

dead air *n* an unintentional period of silence during a broadcast

dead-air space *n* a space that is sealed or has no ventilation

dead-and-alive *adj* without any interest or vitality (*informal*) ○ *something more than this dead-and-alive existence*

dead beat *adj* completely exhausted (*informal*)

deadbeat /déd beet/ *n* 1 **LOAFER** somebody regarded as irresponsible, lazy, and disreputable (*slang insult*) 2 *US* **SOMEBODY WHO DOES NOT PAY DEBTS** a debtor who does not repay money that is owed (*slang*) ■ *adj* **DAMPED AND NOT OSCILLATING** describes an instrument that gives a true reading without oscillation

dead bolt, deadbolt /déd bōlt/ *n* a bolt that is operated directly by the turning of a key or knob and not by a spring mechanism

dead cat bounce *n* an apparent recovery from a major decline in share prices resulting from speculators re-buying stock that they previously sold rather than from a genuine upturn in the market (*slang*)

dead centre *n* 1 **MIDDLE** the exact centre of something 2 **TOP OR BOTTOM OF A PISTON STROKE** the position at the top or bottom of a piston stroke in a reciprocating engine or pump, at which point the piston and the connecting rod are in a straight line 3 **POINTED ROD IN A LATHE** a non-rotating pointed shaft mounted at both ends or one end of a lathe to support the workpiece and hold it in place

dead duck *n* something or somebody with no chance of success or survival (*slang*)

deaden /dédd'n/ *vt* 1 **MAKE SOMETHING LESS INTENSE** to lessen the intensity of something, such as pain or sound ○ *The snow deadened the sound of their footsteps.* 2 **DESENSITIZE** to make something or somebody less sensitive to pain or other stimuli ○ *A local anaesthetic will deaden the nerves.* 3 **MAKE SOMETHING LESS RESONANT** to make an area sound-proof or less resonant —**deadener** *n*

dead end *n* 1 **POINT AT WHICH SOMETHING ENDS ABRUPTLY** an end of a street, path, road, or passage beyond which it is impossible to proceed 2 **PASSAGE THAT ENDS ABRUPTLY** a street, path, or passage beyond which somebody or something cannot proceed ○ *Our road is a dead end, so we don't get much traffic.* 3 **SITUATION THAT LEADS NOWHERE** a situation or course of action in which further progress or development is impossible ○ *a line of research that proved to be a dead end*

dead-end *adj* 1 **WITH CLOSED END** with no exit at one end 2 **WITHOUT PROSPECTS** offering no prospects of progress, development, or improvement ○ *stuck in a dead-end job*

3 *US* **ROWDY AND TOUGH** describes young people, usually from underprivileged backgrounds, whose behaviour makes them unlikely to succeed in life (*informal*)

deadening /dédd'ning/ *n* material used to make a room or building soundproof or less resonant

deadeye /déd ī/ *n* **1** a rounded block of wood, pierced by three holes with a groove around its edge, used to tighten shrouds on sailing vessels **2** *US* a skilled marksman or markswoman (*informal*)

deadfall /déd fawl/ *n* a simple trap consisting of a heavy weight that falls on and crushes its victim when a support is removed

dead fingers *n* a condition that can affect people who work with pneumatic drills, causing loss of sensation and reduced blood circulation in the fingers (+ *singular verb*)

dead hand *n* **1** a negative or oppressive influence or control exerted over an activity or a group of people ○ *remove the dead hand of bureaucracy* **2** = **mortmain**

deadhead /déd hed/ *n* **1 SOMEBODY INCOMPETENT** somebody regarded as unintelligent, useless, or ineffectual (*informal insult*) **2 SOMEBODY WITH A FREE TICKET** a person who uses a free ticket for travel or to attend an event (*informal*) **3** *US* **VEHICLE WITH NO PASSENGERS** a vehicle or aircraft that is carrying no passengers or freight (*informal*) ■ *v* **1** *vt* **REMOVE DEAD FLOWERS FROM PLANT** to remove dead flower heads from a plant to improve its appearance or stimulate further flowering **2** *vti US* **DRIVE EMPTY VEHICLE** to drive or pilot a vehicle or aircraft that is carrying no passengers or freight ○ *Williams deadheaded it from New Jersey to California last weekend.*

dead heat *n* a race or other competition in which two or more contestants finish together or with the same score

dead-heat *vi* to finish a race or other competition together or with the same score

dead letter *n* **1 LETTER THAT CANNOT BE DELIVERED** a letter that the postal service cannot deliver, usually because the address is inadequate or the addressee does not claim it **2 UNENFORCED OR INEFFECTIVE RULE** a law or regulation that still applies but is not enforced or uniformly obeyed **3 SOMETHING NOW IRRELEVANT OR UNIMPORTANT** something that is no longer considered relevant or important

dead letter box, dead letter drop *n* a place where a message or other item can be left in secret by one person and collected later by another, so that the two people do not meet

dead lift *n* a weightlifting event in which a weight is raised from the floor to the level of the hips and lowered again in a controlled manner

deadlight /déd līt/ *n* **1** a protective shutter or plate fastened over a porthole or cabin window in bad weather **2** a thick glass window set in the deck or side of a ship to let light into a cabin

deadline /déd līn/ *n* **1** the time by which something must be done or completed **2** in former times, a line in a prison or prison camp marking a boundary beyond which prisoners were forbidden to go on pain of death

dead load *n* the permanent weight of a structure, e.g. a bridge, exclusive of its load

deadlock /déd lok/ *n* **1 STALLED SITUATION** a situation in which no further progress is possible in a dispute, usually because the people involved are unwilling to change their positions or to compromise ○ *try to break the deadlock in negotiations* **2 DRAW** in sport, a draw **3 TYPE OF LOCK** a lock that can only be opened or closed with a key —**deadlock** *vti*

dead loss *n* **1** something or somebody that is completely useless and not worth spending any further time, effort, or money on (*informal*) **2** a complete loss for which no form of compensation is available

deadly /déddli/ *adj* (**-lier, -liest**) **1 CAUSING DEATH** able or likely to cause death **2 PRECISE** very accurate, especially in shooting **3 EXTREMELY HOSTILE** involving or having an intense desire for the defeat, downfall, or death of somebody ○ *deadly enemies* **4 CAUSING OFFENCE** causing or intended to cause great offence to another person **5 COMPLETE** emphasizes the intensity of something ○ *in deadly earnest* **6 DULL** extremely boring (*informal*) ○ *back to the deadly routine of daily life* ■ *adv* **1** = **deathly** **2 COMPLETELY** to the greatest extent possible ○ *I was being deadly serious when I made that suggestion.* —**deadliness** *n*

SYNONYMS ***deadly, fatal, mortal, lethal, terminal***

CORE MEANING: causing death

deadly likely or designed to cause death; **fatal** describes accidents or illnesses that result in death; **mortal** causing, continuing until, or relating to death; **lethal** certain to or intended to cause death; **terminal** describes illnesses that result in death.

deadly nightshade *n* a poisonous plant with small black berries, commonly found in hedgerows. Flowers: drooping, purplish. Native to: Europe, Asia. *Atropa belladonna*. US term **belladonna** *n.* 1

deadly sins *npl* the sins that lead to damnation according to some Christian beliefs, specifically the seven deadly sins of anger, avarice, envy, gluttony, lechery, pride, and sloth

deadman /déd man/ (*plural* **-men** /-men/) *n* **1** a heavy block or plate buried in the ground that serves as an anchor to a connected structure such as a retaining wall **2** a belaying point for use in firm snow, consisting of a metal plate with a wire loop attached to it [Mid-19C. Because buried securely, like a coffin.]

dead man's float *n* a floating position in which a swimmer is face down with arms extended forward and legs kept together

dead man's handle, dead man's pedal *n* a safety device on an electric or diesel train that automatically cuts off the power and applies the brakes when the driver releases pressure on it

dead march *n* a piece of solemn music played to accompany a procession at a funeral

dead men's shoes *npl* a situation in which the only prospect of promotion is the death or retirement of more senior employees

dead nettle *n* a flowering plant that resembles a nettle but does not sting. Genus: *Lamium*.

dead-on *adj* very accurate or correct (*informal; not hyphenated after verb*) ○ *a dead-on prediction*

deadpan /déd pan/ *adj* **PURPOSELY IMPASSIVE** deliberately expressing no emotion ■ *adv* **EXPRESSIONLESS** without showing any expression or emotion ○ *delivered the line absolutely deadpan* ■ *n* **EXPRESSIONLESS FACE OR PERFORMER** an expressionless face or somebody with an expressionless face ■ *vti* (**-pans, -panning, -panned**) **SPEAK OR ACT IN DEADPAN MANNER** to speak or do something in a deliberately expressionless way [Early 20C. < US slang *pan* 'face'.]

dead reckoning *n* a simple method of determining the position of a ship or aircraft by charting its course and speed from a previously known position

dead ringer[1] *n* somebody or something that exactly resembles another (*informal*)

dead ringer[2] *n* an automatically dialled telemarketing call that cuts off when answered because there is nobody at the sender's end available to deal with it

Dead Sea /déd-/ salt lake on the Israel-Jordan border that is 400 m/1,312 ft below sea level, the lowest point on earth. Area: 1,020 sq. km/394 sq. mi.

Dead Sea Scrolls *npl* a collection of ancient manuscripts, discovered in caves near the Dead Sea between 1941 and 1956, that provide important evidence for biblical scholars and historians

dead set *n* the rigid motionless position of a hunting dog pointing with its muzzle at game

dead shot *n* an expert shooter

dead spot *n* an area within the range of a radio transmitter where reception of the signal is weak or dead

⚡**deadstart** /déd staart/ *vti* COMPUT = **coldboot**

dead time *n* an interval during which an electrical device or component, having just responded to one stimulus, is unable to respond to another

dead weight *n* **1 A HEAVY WEIGHT** a heavy motionless weight bearing down on something or somebody ○ *a foundation slab carrying the dead weight of the building* **2 OPPRESSIVE BURDEN** somebody or something that weighs somebody else down or hinders progress **3 TOTAL WEIGHT** the total weight of everything carried on a ship, equal to the difference between the laden and unladen weight **4** CIV ENG = **dead load**

Dead White European Male, Dead White Male *n* a conventionally important historical figure, especially one of the writers and thinkers whose works have traditionally formed the basis of academic study in Europe and North America (*informal disapproving*)

deadwood /déd wòod/ *n* **1 DEAD TREE PARTS** dead trees and branches **2 SOMEBODY OR SOMETHING UNNECESSARY** useless or superfluous people or things **3 PLANKS BETWEEN KEEL AND STERN** vertical planks filling the gap between the keel and the stern of a sailing vessel

deaf /def/ *adj* **1 HEARING-IMPAIRED** completely or partially unable to hear in one or both ears **2 UNRESPONSIVE OR INDIFFERENT** unwilling to respond to something ○ *They remained deaf to all our entreaties.* ■ *npl* **HEARING-IMPAIRED PEOPLE** people who cannot hear [Old English *dēaf* < Indo-European] —**deafness** *n*

deaf aid *n* a hearing aid

deafblind /déf blīnd/ *adj* unable either to hear or to see

deafen /déff'n/ *vt* **1** to make somebody temporarily or permanently unable to hear ○ *I was momentarily deafened by the noise of the explosion.* **2** to soundproof a room, wall, or building

deafening /déff'ning/ *adj* extremely or unbearably loud ○ *She turned up the volume until the noise was absolutely deafening.* —**deafeningly** *adv*

deaf-mute *adj* an offensive term meaning unable to hear or speak (*dated*) ■ *n* an offensive term meaning somebody who is unable to hear or speak (*dated*)

deaf without speech *adj* hearing-impaired and able to utter sounds but not words, usually because of being born hearing-impaired or having become so before learning how to talk

Deák /dáy aak/, **Ferenc** (1803–76) Hungarian statesman

Deakin /deékin/, **Alfred** (1856–1919) Australian statesman

deal[1] /deel/ *n* **1 BUSINESS TRANSACTION** an agreement, arrangement, or transaction, usually one that benefits all the parties involved **2 BARGAIN** something offered for sale on favourable terms (*informal*) **3 TREATMENT** the particular treatment given to somebody or received from somebody (*informal*) ○ *They got a pretty raw deal from their employer.* **4 DISTRIBUTION OF CARDS** the distribution of the cards needed to play a card game **5 PLAYER'S TURN TO DISTRIBUTE CARDS** a particular player's right or turn to distribute the cards for a card game ○ *Whose deal is it?* **6 ROUND OF GAME** a round of a card game following a particular distribution of the cards **7 CARDS DISTRIBUTED OR RECEIVED** the cards distributed or received for a particular round of a card game ■ *v* (**deals, dealing, dealt** /delt/) **1** *vti* **DISTRIBUTE CARDS** to distribute the cards for a round of a card game ○ *You deal seven cards to each player.* **2** *vti* **GIVE OUT A PARTICULAR CARD** to give a particular card or cards to a player when distributing them ○ *I was dealt five clubs and no hearts.* **3** *vti* **SELL ILLEGAL DRUGS** to sell something, especially illegal drugs **4** *vt* **MAKE SOMEBODY EXPERIENCE** to cause somebody to experience or suffer something, often as a reward or punishment ○ *The latest opinion poll has dealt a severe blow to her hopes of re-election.* [Old English *dǣl* 'part, share, amount', *dǣlan* 'divide' < Germanic] ◇ **cut a deal** to negotiate an agreement ◇ **a done deal** something that has already been settled or finalized ◇ **make a big deal out of something** to make a fuss about something unimportant (*informal*)

deal in *vt* **1** to buy and sell something as a business ○ *We deal mainly in second-hand goods.* **2** to let somebody join in a card game or some other form of joint activity (*informal*) ○ *Deal me in.*

deal out *vt* to give something, or a share of something, to each of a number of people ○ *She dealt out compliments to all the actors.*

deal with *vt* **1 HANDLE** to take action with regard to something or somebody, e.g. to solve a problem or to help somebody **2 BE ABOUT** to write or speak about something or to have something as the subject of written or spoken material ○ *I was intending to deal with the Metaphysical poets in my next lecture.* **3 TREAT SOMEBODY IN PARTICULAR WAY** to treat or behave towards somebody in a specified way, especially in a business context ○ *People who break the regulations will be dealt with severely.* **4 HAVE BUSINESS DEALINGS WITH** to do business with somebody or an organization

deal[2] *n* **1** fir or pine wood, especially when cut to a standard size **2** a plank or board of deal [15C. < Middle Low German or Middle Dutch *dele* 'plank'.]

Deal /deel/ port in SE England. Population: 28,504 (1991).

dealcoholize /dee álkə hol īz/ (**-izes, -izing, -ized**), **dealcoholise** (**-ises, -ising, -ised**) *vt* to remove some or all of the alcohol from a drink —**dealcoholization** /di álkə hol ī záysh'n/ *n*

dealer /deeler/ n **1 SELLER OR TRADER** an individual or company whose business is buying and selling, especially a particular commodity **2 SELLER OF DRUGS** a seller of illegal drugs **3 SOMEBODY WHO DEALS CARDS** a dealer of cards in a card game

dealer plates npl US CARS = trade plates

dealership /deelership/ n **1** a franchise to sell a particular brand of product or service **2** the premises from which a dealer, especially a car dealer, operates

dealfish /deel fish/ (plural -fish or -fishes) n a deep-sea Atlantic fish with a long flat silvery body. Genus: Trachipterus. [Mid-19C. < DEAL², because it resembles a thin plank.]

dealing /deeling/ n conduct towards or treatment of other people, especially in business matters ○ The firm's reputation for fair dealing is at stake. ■ **dealings** npl contact and interaction with other people or organizations for business purposes

dealmaker /deel mayker/ n an arranger of deals, especially in business or politics —**dealmaking** n

dealt /delt/ past tense, past participle of **deal¹**

deaminase /di ámmə nayss, -nayz/ n an enzyme that breaks down amino compounds

deaminate /dee ámmə nayt/ (-**nates**, -**nating**, -**nated**), **deaminize** (-**nizes**, -**nizing**, -**nized**), **deaminise** (-**nises**, -**nising**, -**nised**) v to remove an amino group from a molecule —**deamination** /dee ámmə náysh'n/ n —**deaminization** /dee ámmə nī záysh'n/ n

dean /deen/ n **1 ACADEMIC ADMINISTRATOR** a senior member of the academic staff of a university or college who manages the whole institution or a department, faculty, or group of students **2 COLLEGE ADVISER OR RULE-ENFORCER** a member of the academic staff of a university or college responsible for the counselling and welfare of students, and sometimes, as at Oxford and Cambridge universities, for discipline **3 SENIOR CLERIC** a senior member of the clergy who holds an administrative position in a cathedral or collegiate church, or in a division in a diocese [14C. Via Old French deien < late Latin decanus 'person in charge of ten others' < Latin decem 'ten'.] —**deanship** n

Dean, Forest of /deen/ wooded area and national park in west-central England. Population: 75,400 (1995).

Dean, Christopher (b. 1958) British ice dancer

Dean, James (1931–55) US film actor

Deane /deen/, **Sir William Patrick** (b. 1931) Australian judge and statesman

deanery /deenəri/ (plural -**ies**) n **1** a dean's jurisdiction, office, or residence **2** a group of parishes administered by a rural dean

Dean of Faculty n **1** the president of the Faculty of Advocates in Scotland **2** the administrator of a university or college faculty

dean's list n in the United States, a list of students who have achieved a high standard in their work at a secondary school, college, or university

dear /deer/ adj **1 BELOVED** loved or especially valued ○ a dear friend **2 COSTLY** high in price ○ Prices are dear at that shop. **3 CHARGING A LOT** charging high prices ○ That's a dear place for food. ■ n **1 SOMEBODY BELOVED** a loved or valued person, especially for being kind or thoughtful **2 TERM OF ENDEARMENT** used as an affectionate term of address ■ interj **EXPRESSES SHOCK** expresses shock or consternation ■ adv **DEARLY** at a high cost ○ This will cost you dear. [Old English deore < Germanic] —**dearness** n ○ **dear knows!** expresses ignorance about something

SPELLCHECK Do not confuse **dear** with **deer**, which has a similar sound. Beware: your spellchecker will not catch this error.

Dear adj used before a name or title to begin a letter

dearie /deeri/, **deary** (plural -**ies**) n used to address somebody in an affectionate way (informal)

Dear John letter, Dear John n a letter from a woman ending a romantic or sexual relationship [< the salutation opening such a letter, John being a common man's forename]

dearly /deerli/ adv **1** with great affection or intensity **2** at a high cost ○ He paid dearly for his mistake.

dearth /durth/ n a scarcity or lack of something ○ a dearth of new ideas [13C. < DEAR.]

SYNONYMS See lack.

---

deasil /déss'l, dyésh'l/ adv Scotland in a clockwise direction [Late 18C. < Gaelic deiseil.]

death /deth/ n **1 END OF BEING ALIVE** the ending of all vital functions or processes in an organism or cell **2 WAY OF DYING** a way of dying ○ an easy death **3 SOMEBODY'S DYING** an instance of somebody's dying **4 END OF** the destruction or extinction of something ○ Losing the job marked the death of his ambitions. **5 CONDITION OF BEING DEAD** the condition or quality of being dead ○ In death she looked peaceful and composed. [Old English déap < Germanic] ◇ **be in at the death** to be present at the end or culmination of something ◇ **be the death of somebody** to cause somebody's death ◇ **catch your death (of cold)** to get a very bad cold ◇ **flog something to death** to repeat something, such as a story or idea, so often that people become bored with it ◇ **hold on for grim death, hang on like grim death** to keep hold of somebody or something very tightly and determinedly (informal) ◇ **like death warmed up** looking very ill ◇ **put somebody to death** to execute somebody ◇ **sick to death of something** tired of hearing about something or having to deal with it ◇ **to death 1** until somebody or something dies **2** used to add emphasis ○ bored to death ◇ **to the death** until one opponent in a fight is killed

Death n a personification of death, usually represented as a ghostly form or skeleton holding a scythe

death adder n a poisonous Australian snake with a body like an adder. Acanthophis antarcticus.

death angel n FUNGI = death cap

deathbed /déth bed/ n the bed on which somebody dies ■ adj said, done, or made by somebody while near death ○ deathbed confessions

death benefit n a sum of money that is paid to the beneficiary of a life insurance policy after the death of the insured

deathblow /déth blō/ n **1** an action or event that destroys or ends something **2** a blow that kills somebody

death camp n a place where prisoners are systematically killed or where harsh conditions make survival unlikely

death cap n a poisonous fungus of European and North American woodlands that has a pale cap and a structure resembling a cup at its base. Amanita phalloides.

death cell n a prison cell in which somebody who has been sentenced to death is kept before execution

death certificate n an official document completed and signed by a doctor, stating that somebody is dead and giving the cause of death if known

death chamber n a room where prisoners condemned to death are executed

death-dealing adj causing or liable to cause death

death-defying adj taking the risk of being killed

death duty (plural **death duties**) n the former name for a tax paid in the United Kingdom on inherited property. Now called **inheritance tax**

death futures npl a financial investment in the form of the purchase at a reduced rate of the life insurance of somebody who has a terminal illness, which provides necessary income for the dying person to meet medical costs and guarantees a good return for the purchaser (hyphenated before nouns)

death grant n a sum of money formerly paid under the British National Insurance scheme when somebody died, in order to cover funeral expenses

death house n a building where prisoners condemned to death are housed prior to execution

death instinct n an inherent and unconscious tendency, proposed in some theories of the mind, towards self-destruction

death knell n **1** a sign that something is dead, destroyed, or coming to an end ○ The bankruptcy notice was the company's death knell. **2** the ringing of a bell to announce that somebody has died

deathless /déthləss/ adj immortal, usually because of being excellent —**deathlessly** adv —**deathlessness** n

deathly /déthli/ adj **1 LIKE DEATH** resembling death or somebody who is dead ○ deathly pallor **2 EXTREME** high in degree or intensity ○ a deathly hush ■ adv **EXTREMELY** extremely or intensely —**deathliness** n

---

Death mask: 'Mask of Agamemnon', discovered in a grave at Mycenae, Greece, in 1876

death mask n a cast made of somebody's face soon after death

death metal n heavy metal music characterized by satanic and horror film iconography

death penalty n = capital punishment

death rate n the proportion of deaths to the population of a particular area or group

death rattle n a rough gurgling noise that sometimes comes from somebody's throat at the moment of death, caused by breath passing through mucus

death ray n an imaginary power beam that can kill

death row n a row of prison cells, or an area in a prison, housing prisoners that have been sentenced to death

death sentence n **1** the punishment of death, received in a court of law **2** an event or decision that has a fatal effect

death's head n a human skull or its representation in art, often a symbol of mortality

death's head moth, death's head hawkmoth n a large European hawkmoth with pale markings on the back of its thorax that look like a human skull. Acherontia atropos.

death squad n an unofficial but organized group of people who seek out and murder political opponents or other people they consider as enemies (takes a singular or plural verb)

death stroke n = deathblow

deathtrap /déth trap/ n a building, structure, or vehicle that is extremely unsafe (informal)

Death Valley National Park /déth válli-/ national park in SE California and SW Nevada. Area: 13,765 sq. km/8,554 sq. mi.

death warrant n **1** an official document that authorizes somebody's execution **2** something that ends hope or expectation

deathwatch /déth woch/ n **1** a vigil near a dead or dying person, sometimes a traditional or religious custom **2** ZOOL = deathwatch beetle

deathwatch beetle n a small beetle whose larva bores into wood and makes a ticking sound. Xestobium rufovillosum.

death wish n a desire to die or, less commonly, a desire for the death of somebody else

deattribution /di áttri byoósh'n/ n a change in an official or agreed opinion about the attribution of a work of art

deave /deev/ vt (informal) **1** Scotland, N England, Ireland to weary or confuse somebody, especially by making a lot of noise or fuss **2** to cause somebody to be unable to hear, especially temporarily [Old English déafian 'deafen' < DEAF]

deb /deb/ n a debutante (informal) [Early 20C. Shortening.]

deb. abbr **1** debenture **2** debit

debacle /day baàk'l, di-/ n **1** a sudden disaster, defeat, or humiliating failure **2** a sudden breakup of river ice in the spring thaw, causing a violent rush of flow water and ice [Early 19C. < French, < débâcler 'unbar' (of ice breaking on a river) < Latin bacculus 'stick'.]

debag /dee bág/ (**-bags, -bagging, -bagged**) *vt* to take off somebody's trousers by force as a joke or humiliation (*slang*) [Early 20C. < BAGS 'trousers'.]

debar /di baár/ (**-bars, -barring, -barred**) *vti* to exclude somebody from entering or taking part in something [15C. < Old French *desbarrer* < *barrer* 'to bar'.] —**debarment** *n*

debark[1] /di baárk/ *v* **1** *vi* TRANSP = **disembark** *v.* 1, **disembark** *v.* 2 **2** *vt US* to take something off a vehicle after transporting it (*formal*) [Mid-17C. < French *débarquer* 'get out of a boat'.] —**debarkation** /dée baar káysh'n/ *n*

debark[2] /dée baárk/ *vt* to remove the bark from wood

debase /di báyss/ (**-bases, -basing, -based**) *vt* **1** to reduce something in value or quality **2** to reduce somebody in status, significance, or moral worth —**debasedness** /di báyssidnəss/ *n* —**debaser** *n* —**debasement** *n*

debatable /di báytəb'l/ *adj* **1** liable to be questioned or disputed ○ *Whether it's actually an improvement is debatable.* **2** claimed by more than one country or party (*formal*)

debatably /di báytəbli/ *adv* used to show that the speaker or writer is aware that some people might disagree with the statement about to be made ○ *He was, debatably, the best orator of his generation.*

USAGE See ***arguably***.

debate /di báyt/ *vti* (**-bates, -bating, -bated**) **1** TALK OR ARGUE ABOUT to talk about something at length and in detail, especially as part of a formal exchange of opinion **2** THINK ABOUT to ponder something carefully ■ *n* **1** PUBLIC MEETING FOR DISCUSSION an organized or public discussion of something **2** CONSIDERATION a prolonged consideration of something **3** ARGUMENT argument or prolonged discussion ○ *The matter is not open to debate.* [13C. < Old French *debat* < Latin *battere* 'to fight'.] —**debater** *n*

debating society *n* an organization whose main purpose is to hold regular formal debates on various topics

debauch /di báwch/ *vt* (*formal*) **1** LEAD SOMEBODY INTO IMMORAL BEHAVIOUR to persuade somebody to behave in an immoral way **2** SEDUCE to seduce somebody ■ *n* EPISODE OF DISSIPATION a period of indulgence in drunkenness or immoral behaviour (*formal*) [Late 16C. < French *débaucher.*] —**debaucher** *n*

debauched /di báwcht/ *adj* unrestrainedly and immorally self-indulgent —**debauchedly** /di báwchtli, -chidli/ *adv* —**debauchedness** /di báwchtnəss, -chidnəss/ *n*

debauchee /débbaw chée/ *n* an immoral, unrestrained, and self-indulgent person

debauchery /di báwchəri/ (*plural* **-ies**) *n* unrestrained self-indulgent behaviour, or an instance of this

de Beauvoir /də bo vwaár/, **Simone** ➧ **Simone de Beauvoir**

debenture /di bénchər/ *n* **1 debenture, debenture bond** BOND BACKED ONLY BY CREDIT RATING a bond backed only by the credit standing of the issuer, sometimes convertible into stock **2** CERTIFICATE OF DEBT a certificate that acknowledges the existence of a debt of a specified amount owed to somebody **3** CUSTOMS REFUND CERTIFICATE a certificate issued by customs officials to somebody that provides for a refund of a duty previously paid [15C. < Latin *debentur* 'they are owed', form of *debere* 'owe'.] —**debentured** *adj*

debilitate /di bílli tayt/ (**-tates, -tating, -tated**) *vt* to sap the strength of somebody or something [Mid-16C. < Latin *debilitat-*, past participle of *debilitare* 'weaken' < *debilitas* 'weakness' (see DEBILITY).] —**debilitation** /di bílli táysh'n/ *n* —**debilitative** *adj*

debilitated /di bílli taytid/ *adj* with diminished strength and energy

SYNONYMS See ***weak***.

debilitating /di bílli tayting/ *adj* reducing somebody's strength or energy

debility /di bílləti/ (*plural* **-ties**) *n* a general lack of energy and strength [15C. Via French *débilité* < Latin *debilitas* < *debilis* 'weak'.]

debit /débbit/ *n* **1** RECORDED DEBT OR EXPENSE an entry showing a debt or expense in a record of accounts **2** SUM OF MONEY DEDUCTED an amount of money taken out of an account **3** TOTAL OF DEBTS OR EXPENSES the total of individual debit entries in an account **4** COLUMN FOR RECORDING DEBTS OR EXPENSES a column on the left of an accounting statement where debts and expenses are recorded **5** DRAWBACK something that is disadvantageous or unfavourable ○ *The pay's better, but on the debit side there's a lot more work to do.* ■ *vt* **1** RECORD DEBIT to make, enter, or record a debit in an account **2** CHARGE SOMEBODY MONEY to remove a sum of money from somebody's account in payment for something [15C. < Latin *debitum* 'debt' (see DEBT).]

debit card *n* a plastic card that the holder can use to pay for purchases, the money being transferred directly from the holder's account to the seller

debonair /débbə náir/ *adj* **1** looking well-dressed, sophisticated, and at ease **2** showing ease of manner, elegance, or sophistication [13C. < Old French < *de bon aire* 'of good disposition'.] —**debonairly** *adv* —**debonairness** *n*

debone /dée bṓn/ (**-bones, -boning, -boned**) *vt* to remove the bones from meat or fish

de Bono /də bṓ nō/, **Edward** (*b.* 1933) Maltese-born British psychologist

debouch /di bówch, di bóosh, dee-/ *vi* **1** to move from an enclosed or confined area into more open terrain **2** to widen out, or flow out, from a valley or ravine into a wider area (*refers to a valley or a flow of water*) [Mid-18C. < French *déboucher* 'come out of the mouth' < Latin *bucca* 'cheek, mouth'.] —**debouchment** *n*

débouché /débboo sháy/ *n* an exit or outlet for troops in fortifications [Mid-18C. < French, < past participle of *déboucher* (see DEBOUCH).]

Debrecen /débbrə tsen/ capital of Hajdú-Bihar County, E Hungary. Population: 206,882 (1998 estimate).

Debrett /də brét/, **Debrett's Peerage** *n* a publication that lists members of the British aristocracy [Mid-19C. After John *Debrett* (1705–1822), publisher.]

débridement /di bréedmənt, day bréed moN/ *n* the removal of dead, damaged, or infected tissue from a wound in order to expose healthy tissue and allow the wound to heal [Mid-19C. < French, 'unbridling'.]

debrief /dée bréef/ *v* **1** *vt* to question somebody closely, or to supply information, about a task, mission, or event after it has ended

debriefing /dee bréefing/ *n* an interview in which somebody is asked about or reports on an event or mission after it has ended

debris /déb ree, dáy bree/ (*plural* **-bris**), **débris** (*plural* **-bris**) *n* fragments of something that has been destroyed or broken down [Early 18C. Via French *débris* 'broken up' < Old French *brisier* 'break'.]

de Broglie wavelength /də brṓgli-, də brṓli-/ *n* the wavelength of the wave associated with the motion of an atomic or subatomic particle (**de Broglie wave**) that produces diffraction [Early 20C. After French physicist Louis Victor *de Broglie* (1892–1987).]

debt /det/ *n* **1** SOMETHING THAT IS OWED an amount of money, a service, or an item of property that is owed to somebody **2** OBLIGATION an obligation or borrowing ○ *the criminal must repay his debt to society* **3** STATE OF OWING the condition of owing something to somebody [13C. Via French *dette* < Latin *debitum* < past participle of *debere* 'owe'.] —**debtless** *adj*

debt of honour *n* a debt that somebody is morally, but not legally, obliged to pay

debtor /déttər/ *n* a person who owes a debt

debt swap *n* an exchange of financial obligations with somebody or something in order to gain profit or a more convenient repayment schedule

debud /dée búd/ (**-buds, -budding, -budded**) *vt* PLANT SCI = **disbud** *v.* 1

⚡**debug** /dée búg/ (**-bugs, -bugging, -bugged**) *vt* **1** FIND AND REMOVE ERRORS to find and remove errors in something, especially a computer program or system **2** REMOVE SECRET LISTENING DEVICES to find and take away any electronic listening devices that are concealed in a place **3** CLEAR PLACE OF INSECTS to remove or destroy insects that are in a place (*informal*)

⚡**debugger** /dee búggər/ *n* **1** a computer utility program that helps find software errors by allowing the user to access the source code **2** a remover of something unwanted

debunk /dee búngk/ *vt* to show that something is wrong or false [Early 20C. < BUNK[2].] —**debunker** *n*

deburr /dée búr/ *vt* to remove rough edges (**burrs**) from a piece of machined metal

debus /dée búss/ (**-busses** *or* **-buses, -bussing** *or* **-busing, -bussed** *or* **-bused**) *vti* to leave a bus or unload people or supplies from it

Debussy /də byóozsi/, **Claude** (1862–1918) French composer

debut /dáybyoo, débb-/ *n* **1** FIRST PUBLIC APPEARANCE the first public appearance or presentation of a performer, programme, or performance **2** YOUNG WOMAN'S FIRST OFFICIAL SOCIAL ENGAGEMENT a young woman's first appearance in public at a formal social event ■ *vti* MAKE FIRST FORMAL PUBLIC APPEARANCE to show or perform something formally and publicly for the first time [Mid-18C. < French, < *débuter* 'lead off' < *de-* 'from' + *but* 'goal, target'.]

debutante /débbyoo taant/ *n* a young woman who is being introduced formally into society by appearing at a public event such as a dance or party [Early 19C. < French, 'leading off' < present participle of *débuter* (see DEBUT).]

debye /də bī́/ *n* a unit of electric dipole moment [After Peter J. *Debye* (1884–1966), US chemical physicist.]

dec. *abbr* **1** deceased **2** declaration **3** declension **4** declination **5** decrease

Dec. *abbr* December

dec- *prefix* = **deca-**. symbol **da** (*before vowels*)

deca-, deka- *prefix* (*symbol* **da**) ten ○ *decagram* [< Greek *deka* < Indo-European, 'ten']

decade /dék ayd, di káyd/ *n* **1** a period of ten years **2** a group, set, or series of ten [15C. Via French < late Latin *decad-* < Greek *deka* 'ten'.] —**decadal** /dékəd'l/ *adj*

USAGE The pronunciation of ***decade*** with a stress on the second syllable is increasingly heard, but the traditional pronunciation puts the stress on the first syllable.

decadence /dékədənss/, **decadency** /-dənssi/ *n* **1** PROCESS OF CIVILIZATION'S DECLINE a process of decline or decay in a society, especially in its morals **2** STATE OF DECLINE the condition of a civilization in decline **3** IMMORALITY a state of uninhibited self-indulgence [Mid-16C. Via French *décadence* < medieval Latin, <Latin *decidere* 'fall down or away' (see DECAY).]

decadent /dékədənt/ *adj* **1** IN DECLINE undergoing a process of decline or decay, especially in morals **2** IMMORAL showing uninhibitedly self-indulgent behaviour ■ *n* DEGENERATE PERSON a self-indulgent or immoral person [Mid-19C. < French *décadent*, back-formation < *décadence* (see DECADENCE).] —**decadently** *adv*

decaf /dée kaf/ *n* a decaffeinated drink, especially coffee, tea, or a soft drink (*informal*) ■ *adj* decaffeinated (*informal*) [Late 20C. Shortening.]

decaffeinated /dee káffi naytid, di-/ *adj* with all or most of the caffeine taken out ■ *n* a drink from which all or most of the caffeine has been removed —**decaffeinate** *vt*

decagon /dékəgən, -gon/ *n* a polygon with ten straight sides and ten angles [Mid-17C. Via medieval Latin < Greek *dekagōnos* 'ten-angled'.] —**decagonal** /də kággən'l/ *adj* —**decagonally** *adv*

decahedron /dékə héedrən/ *n* a solid geometrical figure with ten flat outer surfaces —**decahedral** *adj*

decal /di kál, dée kal/ *n* **1** *US* a decorative paper or plastic sticker **2** a picture or design on specially treated paper that allows it to be transferred to a surface such as glass, wood, or metal [Mid-20C. Shortening of DECALCOMANIA.]

decalcify /dee kálssi fī/ (**-fies, -fying, -fied**) *vti* to lose calcium or a calcium compound from the bones or teeth —**decalcifier** *n* —**decalcification** /dee kálssifi káysh'n/ *n*

decalcomania /di kálkə máyni ə/ *n* **1** the process of fixing a design to the surface of something, e.g. glass or pottery, by transferring it from a prepared type of paper **2** = **decal** [Mid-19C. < French *décalcomanie* < *décalquer* 'transfer a tracing' + *-manie* 'mania, craze'; from its popularity in the 19C.]

decalescence /déekə léssənss/ *n* the absorption of heat without temperature increase at specific conditions during the heating of a metal, caused by changes in the crystalline composition [Late 19C. < *calescence* 'increasing warmth or heat'.] —**decalescent** *adj*

decaliter *n* US = **decalitre**

decalitre /dékə leetər/ *n* (*symbol* **dal**) a unit of volume equal to ten litres [Early 19C. < French *décalitre*.]

Decalogue /dékə log/ *n* = **Ten Commandments** [14C. Directly or via French < ecclesiastical Latin *decalogus* < Greek *dekalogos (biblos)* '(book of) ten pronouncements' < *deka* 'ten' + *logos* 'word, pronouncement'.]

decameter *n* US = **decametre**

decametre /dékə meetər/ *n* (*symbol* **dam**) a unit of length equal to 10 metres [Early 19C. < French *décamètre*.]

decametric /dékə méttrik/ *adj* having radio waves of high frequency, between 10 and 100 metres

decamp /di kámp/ *vi* **1** to leave a place abruptly or secretly **2** to pack up and leave a camp or camping site [Late 17C. < French *décamper* < *camp* 'camp'.] —**decampment** *n*

decanal /di káyn'l, dékənəl/ *adj* relating to a dean or deanery (*formal*) [Early 18C. < medieval Latin *decanalis* < late Latin *decanus* (see DEAN).]

decani /di káyn ī/ *adj* connected with or sung by the half of a choir that sits on the south side of the chancel. ◊ **cantoris** [Mid-18C. < late Latin, form of *decanus* (see DEAN), referring to the side of the church the dean usually sits on.]

decanoic acid /dékə nṓ ik-/ *n* = **capric acid**

decant /di kánt/ *vt* **1** to pour a liquid gently and carefully from one container to another so as not to disturb sediment **2** to move people temporarily from their houses or areas to another to allow work to be done on their own houses [Mid-17C. < medieval Latin *decanthare* < Latin *canthus* 'lip of a jug' < Greek *kanthos* 'corner of the eye' (from the supposed similarity in shape).]

decanter /di kántər/ *n* a decorative bottle with a stopper, used for holding and serving drinks, especially wine

decapitate /di káppi tayt/ (**-tates, -tating, -tated**) *vt* to cut off the head of somebody or something [Early 17C. < late Latin *decapitat-*, past participle of *decapitare* < Latin *caput* 'head'.] —**decapitator** *n* —**decapitation** /di káppi táysh'n/ *n*

decapod /dékə pod/ *n* **1** an invertebrate animal with stalked eyes and five pairs of legs, one or more with pincers, attached to the thorax, e.g. marine crustaceans such as shrimps, lobsters, and crabs. Order: Decapoda. **2** a marine mollusc with ten tentacles, e.g. a cuttlefish or squid. Class: Cephalopoda. [Early 19C. Via French *décapode* < modern Latin, 'ten legs'.] —**decapodal** /də káppəd'l/ *adj* —**decapodan** /-dən/ *adj* —**decapodous** /-dəss/ *adj*

decapsulate /dee kápsyoo layt/ (**-lates, -lating, -lated**) *vt* to remove a capsule from a body part or organ such as the kidney —**decapsulation** /dee kápsyoo láysh'n/ *n*

decarbonate /dee kaárbə nayt/ (**-ates, -ating, -ated**) *vt* to remove carbon dioxide or carbonic acid from something —**decarbonation** /dee kaárbə náysh'n/ *n* —**decarbonator** *n*

decarbonize /dee kaárbə nīz/ (**-izes, -izing, -ized**), **decarbonise** (**-ises, -ising, -ised**) *vt* to remove the carbon from something, e.g. the carbon deposits from an internal-combustion engine —**decarbonization** /dee kaárbə nī záysh'n/ *n* —**decarbonizer** *n*

decarboxylase /dee kaar bóksi layz, -layss/ *n* an enzyme that removes a carboxyl group from a molecule

decarboxylation /dee kaar bóksi láysh'n/ *n* the removal or loss of a carboxyl group

decarburize /dee kaárbyoo rīz, -kaárbə-/ (**-rizes, -rizing, -rized**), **decarburise** (**-rises, -rising, -rised**) *vt* = **decarbonize**

decastyle /dékə stīl/ *n* a portico that has ten columns ■ *adj* consisting of or having ten columns [Early 18C. < Greek *dekastulos* 'having ten columns'.]

decasyllable /dékə silәb'l/ *n* a line of verse, or sometimes a word, made up of ten syllables —**decasyllabic** /dékə si lábbik/ *adj*

decathlete /di káth leet/ *n* an athlete who competes in the decathlon

decathlon /di káth lon, -lən/ *n* a contest for men in which the athletes compete in ten different events and are awarded points for each to find the best all-round athlete. The events are long jump, high jump, pole vault, shot put, discus, javelin, 110 metre hurdles, and running over 100 metres, 400 metres, and 1500 metres. ◊ **heptathlon, pentathlon** *n.* **2**, **triathlon** [Early 20C. < DECA- + Greek *athlon* 'contest'.]

decay /di káy/ *v* **1** *vti* **GO ROTTEN OR DETERIORATE** to decompose, or make something decompose, and become soft, crumbly, or liquefied **2** *vti* **DECLINE OR CAUSE SOMETHING TO DECLINE** to decline in quality gradually and steadily, or cause something to undergo such a decline **3** *vi* **DISINTEGRATE** to undergo spontaneous disintegration (*refers to radioactive material*) **4** *vi* **DECREASE** to decrease gradually in magnitude (*refers to a physical quantity or effect*) **5** *vi* **DESCEND** to decrease gradually in altitude (*refers to an artificial satellite in orbit*) ■ *n* **1 DECLINE** a decline in quality ○ *'A state too extensive in itself, or by virtue of its dependencies, ultimately falls into decay'.* (Simón Bolívar, *Letter from Jamaica*; 1815) **2 PROCESS OF BIOLOGICAL DETERIORATION** the process of rotting and decomposition that affects plant material and the bodies of animals after they die and are invaded by bacteria or fungi **3 ROTTEN OR SPOILED PART** the areas of something that are decomposed or rotted ○ *cut out the decay* **4 DISINTEGRATION OF RADIOACTIVE MATERIAL** the spontaneous disintegration of a radioactive material along with the emission of one or more elementary particles or radiation **5 GRADUAL DECREASE** a gradual decrease in the magnitude of a physical quantity or effect, such as current, stored charge, or phosphorescence **6 DESCENT OF ARTIFICIAL SATELLITE** the gradual decrease in altitude of an orbiting artificial satellite **7 DECLINE IN SOUND OF NOTE** the fading away of a musical note [15C. Via French *decair* < Latin *decidere* 'fall off or away' < *cadere* 'fall'.] —**decayable** *adj*

decay constant *n* the probability that an unstable radioactive nucleus will decay in a standard unit of time

Deccan /dékən/ triangular plateau in S India between the Eastern and Western Ghats

decease /di seéss/ *n* death, especially the death of somebody (*formal*) ■ *vi* (**-ceases, -ceasing, -ceased**) to die (*formal*) [14C. Via French *décès* < Latin *decessus* 'death, departure' < past participle of *decedere* 'go away' < *cedere* 'give way'.]

deceased /di seést/ *n* somebody who has died recently (*formal*) ■ *adj* no longer living (*formal*)

SYNONYMS See ***dead***.

deceit /di seét/ *n* **1** the act or practice of deceiving or misleading somebody **2** something that is done to trick or mislead somebody [13C. < Old French, < *deceveir* (see DECEIVE).]

deceitful /di seétf'l/ *adj* intentionally misleading or fraudulent in not telling the whole truth —**deceitfully** *adv* —**deceitfulness** *n*

deceive /di seév/ (**-ceives, -ceiving, -ceived**) *v* **1** *vt* **INTENTIONALLY TRICK OR MISLEAD** to mislead somebody or hide the truth deliberately **2** *vr* **FOOL YOURSELF** to convince yourself of something that is not true **3** *vt* **BE SEXUALLY UNFAITHFUL TO** to be sexually unfaithful to a spouse or sexual partner [13C. Via Old French *deceveir* < Latin *decipere* 'ensnare, take in' < *capere* 'take, seize'.] —**deceivability** /di seévə bíllәti/ *n* —**deceivable** *adj* —**deceiver** *n*

deceiving /di seéving/ *adj* liable or meant to mislead —**deceivingly** *adv*

decelerate /dee séllə rayt/ (**-ates, -ating, -ated**) *vti* to reduce speed, or make something go more slowly [Late 19C. < DE- + ACCELERATE.] —**deceleration** /dee séllə ráysh'n/ *n* —**decelerator** *n*

December /di sémbər/ *n* the 12th month of the year in the Gregorian calendar, made up of 31 days [13C. Via French *décembre* < Latin *december* < *decem* 'ten', because the tenth month of the Roman year.]

Decembrist /di sémbrist/ *n* a member of a group of Russian officers who tried unsuccessfully to overthrow Tsar Nicholas I of Russia in December 1825

decemvirate /di sémvərәt/ *n* a group of ten people who hold power or office together

decency /deéss'nssi/ *n* (*plural* **-cies**) **1 CONFORMITY WITH MORAL STANDARDS** behaviour or an attitude that conforms to the commonly accepted standards of what is right and respectable **2 MODESTY** modesty or propriety ■ **decencies** *npl* **MORAL BEHAVIOUR** the commonly accepted standards of good behaviour (*formal*)

decennary /di sénnəri/ *n* (*plural* **-ries**) a ten-year period (*formal*) ■ *adj* = **decennial** *adj.* [Early 19C. < DECENNIUM.]

decennial /di sénni əl/ *adj* lasting for, consisting of, or happening every ten years ■ *n* an anniversary celebrated ten years after something or every ten years —**decennially** *adv*

decennium /di sénni əm/ (*plural* **-ums** *or* **-a** /-ni ə/) *n* a ten-year period [Late 17C. < Latin < *decennis* < *decem* 'ten' + *annus* 'year'.]

decent /deéss'nt/ *adj* **1 MORAL** conforming to accepted standards of moral behaviour **2 GOOD** above average in quality or quantity ○ *one of the few decent restaurants around here* **3 QUITE GOOD** adequate or sufficient in quality ○ *did a decent job* **4 SUFFICIENTLY DRESSED** fully dressed, as opposed to being naked or wearing underwear only (*informal*) ○ *Don't come in; I'm not decent!* **5 KIND** kind, considerate, or generous [Mid-16C. Directly or via French *décent* < Latin *decent-*, present participle of *decere* 'be fitting'.] —**decentness** *n*

decently /deéss'ntli/ *adv* in a way that conforms to accepted standards of conduct or appearance

decentralize /dee séntrə līz/ (**-izes, -izing, -ized**), **decentralise** (**-ises, -ising, -ised**) *vti* to reorganize something such as a political unit so that power is shifted from a central or upper location to another less central place —**decentralization** /dee sentrə lī záysh'n/ *n*

deception /di sépsh'n/ *n* **1** the practice of deliberately making somebody believe things that are not true **2** an act, trick, or device intended to deceive somebody [15C. Directly or via French < Latin *deception-* < *decept-*, past participle of *decipere* (see DECEIVE).]

Deception Bay /di sépsh'n-/ coastal town in SE Queensland, Australia. Population: 13,163 (1996).

deceptive /di séptiv/ *adj* **1** liable or meant to mislead somebody **2** capable of being mistaken for something else ○ *a deceptive barking noise* [Early 17C. Directly or via French < late Latin *deceptivus* < Latin *decept-* (see DECEPTION).] —**deceptiveness** *n*

deceptively /di séptivli/ *adv* in a way that misleads people or is contrary to appearances ○ *a deceptively easy task*

USAGE Although *deceptively simple* almost invariably means 'complex despite apparent simplicity', that is not a model from which to generalize about the meaning of ***deceptively***. When people are asked whether, for example, *a deceptively dangerous place to stand* is a place that is more or less dangerous than it appears, they respond variously, with a substantial minority admitting they have no idea what ***deceptively*** is intended to convey. Sometimes context clarifies the meaning: *It was a small house, but it had deceptively large rooms.* Unless the context makes the meaning clear, ***deceptively*** is best avoided.

decerebrate /dee sérri brayt/ *adj* having lost all cerebral function, vision, hearing, and other senses, and voluntary motor activity, e.g. as a result of a severe stroke ■ *vt* (**-brates, -brating, -brated**) to remove the cerebrum or brain stem from an animal surgically [Late 19C. < DE- + CEREBRUM.] —**decerebration** /dee sérri bráysh'n/ *n*

decern /di súrn/ *vti* in Scots law, to make a binding decree ○ *They decern and decree the said John Smith to be returned to prison.* [15C. Via French *décerner* < Latin *decernere* 'decide, pronounce a decision' < *cernere* 'separate, sift'.]

decertify /dee súrti fī/ (**-fies, -fying, -fied**) *vt* to withdraw certification from somebody or something —**decertification** /dee súrtifi káysh'n/ *n*

dechannelize /dee chánn'l īz/ (**-izes, -izing, -ized**), **dechannelise** (**-ises, -ising, -ised**) *vt* to reroute a river to its original location and configuration of flow

deci- *prefix* (*symbol* **d**) a tenth ○ *decigram* [< French, < Latin *decimus* (see DECIMAL)]

decibel /déssi bel, déssib'l/ *n* (*symbol* **dB**) a unit of relative loudness, electric voltage, or current equal to ten times the common logarithm of the ratio of two readings

decide /di sīd/ (**-cides, -ciding, -cided**) *v* **1** *vti* **CHOOSE** to make a choice or come to a conclusion about something ○ *We decided not to go in the end.* **2** *vt* **LEAD SOMEBODY TO CHOOSE** to make somebody choose what to do or come to a conclusion about something (*informal*) ○ *His encouraging letter decided me against giving up the course.* **3** *vt* **END SOMETHING CLEARLY** to bring something to an end in a definite or obvious way **4** *vi* **ARRIVE AT VERDICT** to come to a verdict or judgment [14C. Directly or via French *décider* < Latin *decidere* 'cut off' < *caedere* 'cut'.] —**decidable** *adj*

decided /di sīdid/ *adj* **1** clearly seen, felt, or noticed **2** free of uncertainty or doubt —**decidedness** *n*

decidedly /di sīdidli/ *adv* without any doubt or question

decider /di sīdər/ *n* something that settles the outcome of a contest or argument, especially, in sport, a game played to determine the ultimate winner

deciding /di sīding/ *adj* acting to settle the result of a contest or debate, or to make clear what must be done next

decidua /di síddyoo ə/ (*plural* **-as** *or* **-ae** /-ee/) *n* a specialized part of the mucous membrane (**endometrium**) that lines the womb during pregnancy and is shed with the placenta at birth [Late 18C. < modern Latin *decidua (membrana)* 'deciduous (membrane)'.] —**decidual** *adj* —**deciduate** *adj*

deciduous /di síddyoo əss/ *adj* **1** SHEDDING LEAVES IN AUTUMN describes trees and shrubs that shed their leaves in the autumn **2** OF DECIDUOUS TREES describes a forest or wood that is composed mostly of deciduous trees **3** SHED AFTER DEVELOPMENTAL STAGE shed after a stage of development, as are the teeth, antlers, or wings of animals and birds, or shed easily or at intervals, as are the scales of fish [Mid-17C. < Latin *deciduus* < *decidere* 'fall down' < *cadere* 'fall, die'.] —**deciduously** *adv* —**deciduousness** *n*

deciduous tooth *n* = **milk tooth**

~~**decieve**~~ incorrect spelling of **deceive**

decile /déss īl, -il/ *n* **1** any one of ten groups containing an equal number of the items that make up a frequency distribution **2** any of the nine values that divide the total number of items in a frequency distribution into ten groups, each containing an equal number of items

deciliter *n* US = **decilitre**

decilitre /déssi leetər/ *n* (*symbol* **dl**) a unit of volume equal to 0.1 litre [Early 19C. < French *décilitre*.]

decimal /déssim'l/ *adj* relating to the number 10 as a base and counted or ordered in units of 10 ■ *n* a number expressed in a counting system that uses units of 10, especially a decimal fraction [Early 17C. < modern Latin *decimalis* < Latin *decimus* 'tenth' < *decem* 'ten'.] —**decimally** *adv*

decimal classification *n* = **Dewey Decimal System**

decimal currency *n* currency based on units of ten or multiples of ten, now used in most countries

decimal fraction *n* a numerical fraction with ten as its denominator, written showing the fractional elements after a decimal point

decimalize /déssimə līz/ (**-izes, -izing, -ized**), **decimalise** (**-ises, -ising, -ised**) *vti* to convert something, e.g. a country's currency or measurement system, into a decimal or metric system, or convert to this —**decimalization** *n*

decimal place *n* the place or a specific number of digits to the right of the decimal point in a line of numbers

decimal point *n* a printed or written dot in a decimal number that divides the whole numbers from the tenths, hundredths, and smaller divisions of ten

decimal system *n* a numerical system that has the number ten as the basic unit from which the other counting units are formed as multiples

decimate /déssi mayt/ (**-mates, -mating, -mated**) *vt* **1** ⚠ DESTROY LARGE PROPORTION OF to kill off or remove a large proportion of a group of people, animals, or things, or of the population of a place. **2** VIRTUALLY DESTROY to inflict so much damage on something that it is seriously reduced in effectiveness ○ *Current prices will decimate the present level of service provision.* **3** KILL ONE PERSON IN 10 to kill one out of every ten people, especially in a body of mutinous soldiers (*archaic*) [Late 16C. < Latin *decimat-*, past participle of *decimare* 'take a tenth' < *decimus* (see DECIMAL).] —**decimator** *n* —**decimation** /déssə máysh'n/ *n*

USAGE The popular meaning of ***decimate***, 'to destroy', now predominates because the need for a word meaning 'to kill one person in ten' has greatly diminished. Even so, the popular meaning is not accepted by everyone, and it is often better to use *annihilate*, *exterminate*, *destroy*, or *devastate*.

decimeter *n* US = **decimetre**

decimetre /déssi meetər/ *n* (*symbol* **dm**) a metric unit of length equal to 0.1 metre

decipher /di sīfər/ *vt* **1** to succeed in establishing what a word or piece of writing says when it is difficult or almost impossible to read **2** to study something that is written in code or in an unknown form of writing until it can be understood and read normally —**decipherability** /di sīfərə bílləti/ *n* —**decipherable** *adj* —**decipherer** *n* —**decipherment** *n*

decision /di sízh'n/ *n* **1** SOMETHING SOMEBODY HAS SETTLED ON something that somebody chooses or makes up his or her mind about, after considering it and other possible choices ○ *It was a tough decision to make.* **2** FIRMNESS IN CHOOSING the ability to choose or decide about things in a clear and definite way without too much hesitation or delay ○ *a man of decision* **3** PROCESS OF CHOOSING the process of coming to a conclusion or determination about something **4** BOXING VICTORY DECIDED ON POINTS a win in a boxing match that is awarded to the fighter who is given the higher total of points by the judges ○ *He won a 10-round decision.* [15C. Directly or via French < Latin *decision-* < past participle of *decidere* (see DECIDE).] —**decisional** *adj*

decision-making *n* the process of making choices or reaching conclusions, especially on important political or business matters —**decision-maker** *n*

decision theory *n* the study of the best possible outcomes for decisions made under varying conditions

decision tree *n* a diagram set out like the branches of a tree that shows the consequences of a decision, each decision entailing a course of action that requires various other decisions

decisive /di sīssiv/ *adj* **1** settling or ending something, e.g. a debate, controversy, or contest ○ *a decisive victory* **2** showing an ability to make decisions quickly, firmly, and clearly [Early 17C. Via French < medieval Latin < Latin *decidere* (see DECIDE).] —**decisiveness** *n*

decisively /di sīssivli/ *adv* in a way that brings a clear and definite decision or a recognizable end

deck /dek/ *n* **1** FLOOR SURFACE ACROSS SHIP a level surface that runs from one side of a ship to the other and along all or part of its length, forming a floor **2** VEHICLE SECTION ON ONE LEVEL a floored, self-contained area of a ship or a passenger vehicle such as a bus or tram **3** AUDIO UNIT a wide flat piece of audio equipment that contains a player for tapes, records, cassettes, or compact discs **4** *US* LEVEL OF STRUCTURE a tier or level of a building or other structure **5** FLOOR OF ROADWAY OR BRIDGE the floor or platform of a roadway or bridge **6** *US, Can* PACK OF CARDS a pack of playing cards **7** *US, Can* TERRACE OF HOUSE an open unroofed area of floor extending from the back of a house ○ *They had a barbecue on the deck.* **8** GROUND the ground or floor (*informal*) ■ *vt* **1** DECORATE to decorate or ornament something or somebody (*literary*) ○ *deck the hall with boughs of holly* **2** KNOCK DOWN to strike and knock somebody down deliberately (*informal*) **3** BUILD DECK FOR to make a deck for a ship or other structure [15C. < Middle Dutch *dec* 'roof, covering, cloak' < Germanic.] —**decker** *n* —**decked** *adj* ◇ **clear the deck** *or* **decks** to get rid of all obstacles, especially pending work, prior to beginning a new task ◇ **hit the deck 1** to fall on the floor or ground, often as self-protection (*informal*) **2** *US* to get out of bed ◇ **on deck 1** on the top external surface of a ship or boat **2** *US* scheduled to appear next ◇ **play with a full deck** *US* to be sane and reasonably intelligent (*slang*)

deck out *vt* to decorate something, or dress somebody up in fancy clothes

deck over *vt* to complete the construction of an upper deck on a ship or boat

deck bridge *n* a bridge designed so that the roadway or track is supported by the upper horizontal part of the structural framework

deck chair *n* a collapsible adjustable outdoor chair with a wooden framework and a seat made from strong fabric

deck hand *n* a labourer on a ship, yacht, or other vessel

deckhouse /dék howss/ (*plural* **-houses** /-howziz/) *n* a structure built on the main deck of a ship or other vessel, used as a room or several rooms

decking /déking/ *n* planking or other flooring material used for the deck of a ship or a seating area in a garden

deckle /dék'l/ *n* **1** a metal frame used to contain pulp in a mould during the making of handmade paper **2** = **deckle edge** [Mid-18C. < German *Deckel* 'little covering' < *Decke* 'covering'.]

deckle edge *n* a rough, irregular, or feathery edge on handmade paper —**deckle-edged** *adj*

deck officer *n* an officer responsible for tasks such as navigation that take place on a ship's main deck

deck tennis *n* a game based on lawn tennis, using a small court with a net and a ring made of rubber or rope that the players throw back and forth

declaim /di kláym/ *v* **1** *vti* to make a dramatic or formal speech or statement about something **2** *vi* to deliver a recitation [14C. Directly or via French *déclamer* < Latin *declamare* 'cry out' < *clamare* 'cry, call'.] —**declaimer** *n*

declamation /déklə máysh'n/ *n* **1** a speech or presentation spoken in a formal and theatrical style **2** the art or process of declaiming ○ *'The air of the New World seems favourable to the art of declamation'.* (Joseph Conrad, *Nostromo*; 1904)

declamatory /di klámmətəri/ *adj* **1** formal and dramatic in public speech **2** loud and rhetorical but without very meaningful content —**declamatorily** *adv*

declarant /di kláirənt/ *n* the maker of a formal, often legal, statement [Late 17C. < French *déclarant*, present participle of *déclarer* 'declare'.]

declaration /déklə ráysh'n/ *n* **1** FORMAL STATEMENT a formal document giving explicit details, e.g. the terms of a business agreement or plan, or information on goods or assets for tax purposes **2** OFFICIAL PROCLAMATION an emphatic formal public statement, especially by a government or public body **3** PROCESS OF MAKING A DECLARATION the process or act of declaring something in an official or public way **4** UNSWORN BUT SOLEMN EVIDENCE a formal statement of facts that is allowed in a legal case in place of a statement made under oath **5** PLAINTIFF'S OFFICIAL WRITTEN CLAIM a formal document in which a plaintiff lays out precise details of the circumstances leading to the legal action being taken **6** RULING ON QUESTIONS OF LAW a ruling by a judge or court on the legal position of contesting parties **7** ANNOUNCEMENT OF BID the act of naming a particular suit as trumps, or of declaring no-trumps, by the player who makes the final bid of a hand of bridge

Declaration of Human Rights *n* a United Nations document approved on 10 December, 1948 by the General Assembly, affirming the dignity of all human beings

declaration of independence *n* a proclamation by which a country, group, or people asserts firmly and publicly that it has become independent of a governing power

Declaration of Independence *n* a written statement issued and adopted by the Continental Congress in 1776 proclaiming that the 13 North American colonies henceforward would govern themselves rather than be ruled by Great Britain. The Declaration of Independence was adopted by the Congress on 2 July, 1776 and formally endorsed on 4 July. ○ *'If the American Revolution had produced nothing but the Declaration of Independence, it would have been worthwhile'.* (Samuel Eliot Morison, *The Oxford History of the American People*; 1965)

declarative /di klárrətiv/ *adj* containing a statement, or in the form of a statement —**declaratively** *adv*

declarator /di klárrətər/ *n* a legal action brought in Scotland by somebody who wants a particular right or status to be clarified and stated judicially

declaratory /di klárrətəri/ *adj* **1** stating and clarifying something, especially a legal right, status, decree, or judgment **2** = **declarative** —**declaratorily** *adv*

declare /di kláir/ (**-clares, -claring, -clared**) *v* **1** *vti* ANNOUNCE CLEARLY OR LOUDLY to state something in a plain, open, or emphatic way **2** *vt* STATE FORMALLY OR OFFICIALLY to make an official or public announcement about somebody or something, especially on a legal or medical matter ○ *The doctors declared her fit to work.* ○ *The chairperson declared the meeting open.* **3** *vti* REVEAL AS DUTIABLE OR TAXABLE to inform customs or tax authorities about goods on which duty is owed or about income that is taxable **4** *vt* ANNOUNCE ACTION OR STATUS to make an official statement that a particular course of action or status is in effect ○ *to declare independence* **5** *vi* MAKE DECISION KNOWN to announce a choice or decision formally and publicly (*formal*) **6** *vti* SAY WHICH SUIT IS TRUMPS to announce to the other players in bridge the suit that has been chosen as trumps or no-trumps for the next hand **7** *vi* CHOOSE TO END INNINGS to end an innings in cricket before all the batsmen have been dismissed, having decided, as the batting side or the captain of it, that the team has probably made enough runs **8** *vti* LAY CARDS ON TABLE to show that you have a particular score in a card game such as bezique by displaying the cards face up on the table and claiming your score **9** *vr* PROPOSE MARRIAGE to make a formal or open statement of love for and a wish to marry somebody (*dated*) [14C. < Latin *declarare* 'make clear' < *clarus* 'clear'.] —**declarable** *adj*

declass /dee klaàss/ *vt* to give somebody a lower status or class in society

déclassé /day kláss ay, -klaàss-, dáy kla sáy/ *adj* reduced to a lower class or status in society [Late 19C. < French, past participle of *déclasser* 'declass'.]

declassify /dee klássi fī/ (**-fies, -fying, -fied**) *vt* to remove something from an official list of confidential or top-secret material so that anyone may see it —**declassifiable** *adj* —**declassification** /dee klássifi káysh'n/ *n*

declaw /deè kláw/ *vt* to remove the claws from an animal's paws, often to prevent it from injuring or catching other animals, or from scratching or climbing

declension /di klénsh'n/ *n* **1** SET OF WORDS THAT BEHAVE SIMILARLY a group of nouns, adjectives, or pronouns that all change their form or word-endings in the same way according to gender, number, or grammatical case **2** PROCESS OF ENDING WORDS the process by which some sets of nouns, adjectives, and pronouns vary in form to show gender, number, or grammatical case **3** WORSENING OR FALLING AWAY the process of gradually declining or deteriorating (*formal*) **4** DOWNWARD SLOPE a downward slope, especially of terrain [15C. Via French *déclinaison* < Latin *declination-* < *declinare* 'bend away' (see DECLINE), from the idea of inflections deviating from the pure form.] —**declensional** *adj* —**declensionally** *adv*

declination /dékli náysh'n/ *n* **1** the angular distance of an astronomical object measured in degrees from the celestial equator along the great circle passing through it and the celestial poles **2** PHYS, GEOG = **magnetic declination** —**declinational** *adj*

decline /di klīn/ *v* (**-clines, -clining, -clined**) **1** *vti* REFUSE INVITATION to give a polite refusal to an invitation **2** *vt* REFUSE PARTICIPATION to refuse to respond or take part in something **3** *vi* DIMINISH to become fewer or less ○ *shares declining in value* **4** *vi* GET WEAKER to become physically or mentally less vigorous, especially because of illness or mature years ○ *His health had declined.* **5** *vti* SHOW VARIOUS FORMS to state the grammatical forms of a noun, adjective, or pronoun, or have various grammatical forms **6** *vti* SLOPE DOWN to bend something downwards, or slope downwards ■ *n* **1** DETERIORATION a deterioration in quality, strength, or degree, or a reduction in amount **2** PERIOD NEAR END the terminal period of somebody or something, ending in death or disappearance ○ *at the decline of the empire* **3** DOWNWARD SLOPE a downward slope or movement [14C. Directly and via French *décliner* < Latin *declinare* 'turn aside, bend away' < *clinare* 'bend'.] —**decliner** *n* ◇ **be on the decline 1** to show a gradual lessening of quality, amount, or degree **2** to show a gradual worsening of health

declinometer /dékli nómmitər/ *n* an instrument that measures the difference between magnetic north or south and true north or south at a particular point on the Earth's surface [Mid-19C. < DECLINATION.]

declivitous /di klívvətəs/ *adj* sloping downwards

declivity /di klívvəti/ (*plural* **-ties**) *n* **1** a surface, especially a piece of land, that slopes downwards **2** a downward inclination, especially of a piece of land [Early 17C. < Latin *declivitas* < *clivus* 'slope'.]

declutch /deè klúch/ *vi* to disengage the clutch of a motor vehicle (*technical*)

Deco /dékō/, **deco** *adj* = **art deco**

decoct /di kókt/ *vt* to extract the essence or active ingredient from a substance by boiling it [15C. < Latin *decoct-*, past participle of *decoquere* 'boil down' < *coquere* 'cook'.]

decoction /di kóksh'n/ *n* **1** the extraction of an essence or active ingredient from a substance by boiling **2** a concentrated substance that results from decoction

decode /dee kōd/ (**-codes, -coding, -coded**) *v* **1** *vt* DECIPHER CODE to transform an encoded message or signal into a usable form **2** *vt* INTERPRET MEANING to find the direct meaning of cryptic or indirect language **3** *vti* TRANSLATE FOREIGN LANGUAGE to understand the meaning of a word or phrase in a foreign language —**decodable** *adj* —**decoder** *n*

decoke /deè kōk/ (**-cokes, -coking, -coked**) *vt* to remove the carbon deposits from an internal-combustion engine

decollate /deè kə láyt, dékə layt/ (**-lates, -lating, -lated**) *vt* **1** to separate continuous paper into single sheets **2** to decapitate (*archaic*) —**decollation** /deèkə láysh'n, dékə-/ *n* —**decollator** *n*

décolletage /dáy kol taàzh, day kóllə taazh/ *n* **1** the top front part of a woman's low-cut garment **2** a piece of women's clothing with a décolletage [Late 19C. < French < *décolleté* (see DÉCOLLETÉ).]

décolleté /day kól tay, -kóllə tay/ *n* CHEST AREA the upper part of a woman's chest, below the neck ○ *a décolleté moisturizing treatment* ■ *adj* **1** WITH LOW NECKLINE having a low-cut front neckline ○ *a décolleté dress* **2** WEARING LOW-CUT GARMENT wearing a décolleté garment [Mid-19C. < French, past participle of *décolleter* 'lower the neckline' < *collet* 'collar' < Latin *collum* 'neck'.]

decolonize /dee kóllə nīz/ (**-nizes, -nizing, -nized**), **decolonise** (**-nises, -nising, -nised**) *vt* to grant a colony its independence —**decolonization** /dee kóllə nī záysh'n/ *n*

decolorant /dee kúllərənt/ *n* a chemical that removes the colour from a fabric or other substance —**decolorant** *adj*

decolorize /dee kúllə rīz/ (**-izes, -izing, -ized**), **decolorise** (**-ises, -ising, -ised**) *vt* to remove the colour from a fabric or other substance, e.g. by chemical means —**decolorization** /dee kúllə rī záysh'n/ *n*

decolour /dee kúllər/ *vt* = **decolorize** —**decoloration** /dee kúllə ráysh'n/ *n*

decommission /deè kə mísh'n/ *vt* to remove something, e.g. a ship, nuclear power station, machinery, or weapons, from service

decompensation /deè kom pen sáysh'n/ *n* **1** the failure of the heart to maintain adequate circulation because of various stresses upon it **2** the deterioration of existing psychological defences in a patient already exhibiting pathological behaviour

ϟ **decompiler** /deèkəm pīlər/ *n* a computer program that translates basic machine code back into high-level source code

decompose /deèkəm pōz/ (**-poses, -posing, -posed**) *vti* **1** ROT to break down organic matter from a complex to a simpler form, mainly through the action of fungi and bacteria, or undergo this process **2** BREAK DOWN INTO PIECES to break something down, or be broken down, into smaller or simpler parts **3** BREAK DOWN INTO CONSTITUENT PARTS to separate or cause something to separate into constituent parts —**decomposability** /deèkəm pōzə bílləti/ *n* —**decomposable** *adj* —**decomposition** /deè kompə zísh'n/ *n* —**decomposer** *n*

ϟ **decompress** /deèkəm préss/ *vti* **1** REDUCE PRESSURE to cause or experience a reduction in the atmospheric pressure of an enclosed space **2** ALLOW EXPANSION to allow a substance to expand to normal dimensions or volume by the removal of pressure, or to undergo this process **3** EXPAND DATA to expand compressed data to its normal extent, or to undergo this process —**decompressive** *adj*

ϟ **decompression** /deèkəm présh'n/ *n* **1** PRESSURE DECREASE a decrease in surrounding or inherent pressure, especially the controlled decrease in pressure that divers undergo to prevent decompression sickness **2** DATA EXPANSION the expansion to full size of compressed computer data ○ *decompression must precede installation* ○ *decompression software* **3** SURGERY TO REDUCE PRESSURE IN ORGAN a surgical procedure to reduce pressure in an organ or part of the body caused, e.g. by fluid on the brain, or to reduce the pressure of tissues on a nerve

decompression chamber *n* a sealed room where decompression is carried out

decompression sickness, decompression illness *n* a condition experienced by divers and workers in caissons who emerge too quickly from a pressurized environment, it is caused by the formation of nitrogen bubbles in the blood and tissues

decon /deè kon/ (**-cons, -conning, -conned**) *vt* to decontaminate something (*informal*)

decondition /deèkən dísh'n/ *vt* to cause or teach a person or animal to stop exhibiting a conditioned response

decongest /deè kənjést/ *vt* **1** to loosen mucus in the nasal passages, sinuses, or bronchi **2** to increase the flow in something that is compacted or congested

decongestant /deè kənjéstənt/ *n* an agent that relieves nasal congestion —**decongestant** *adj*

deconsecrate /dee kónssi krayt/ (**-crates, -crating, -crated**) *vt* to convert a sacred place, building, or object to secular use —**deconsecration** /deè konssi kráysh'n/ *n*

deconstruct /deèkən strúkt/ *vt* to subject a text to critical analysis using the theories of deconstruction

deconstruction /deèkən strúksh'n/ *n* a method of analysing texts based on the ideas that language is inherently unstable and shifting and that the reader rather than the author is central in determining meaning. It was introduced by the French philosopher Jacques Derrida in the late 1960s. —**deconstructionist** *n*

deconstructionism /deè kən strúksh'n izəm/ *n* the methods or beliefs of deconstruction

QUICK FACTS ON... **DECONSTRUCTIONISM**

Key dates: late 20th century
Key locations: France, United States
Key elements: rejection of traditional metaphysical assumptions, theories, and conceptual systems based on stable and logical meaning; meaning is socially constructed, and close reading of texts reveal them to be unstable and illogical; the concealed, unconscious, and ignored in texts emphasized; reliance on interplay with other texts and use of puns and wordplay as a means of devaluing logic
Key figures: Jacques Derrida, Paul de Man
Key publications: *Of Grammatology* (Derrida) 1967, *Allegories of Reading* (de Man) 1979

decontaminate /deèkən támmi nayt/ (**-nates, -nating, -nated**) *vt* to remove unwanted chemical, radioactive, or biological impurities or toxins from land or a person or object —**decontamination** /deè kən támmi náysh'n/ *n*

decontrol /deèkən trṓl/ (**-trols, -trolling, -trolled**) *vt* to remove official restraints or regulations on something, especially rents

decor /dáy kawr, dék-/, **décor** *n* **1** the style of furniture and furnishings chosen for a room or house **2** the scenery of a stage [Late 19C. < French, < *décorer* 'decorate' < Latin *decorare* (see DECORATE).]

decorate /dékə rayt/ (**-rates, -rating, -rated**) *v* **1** *vt* MAKE SOMETHING ATTRACTIVE to make something more attractive by adding ornate or stylish elements to it **2** *vti* CHANGE APPEARANCE OF ROOM to paint or wallpaper a building or a room **3** *vt* AWARD SOMEBODY A MEDAL to give a medal or other honour or award to somebody to acknowledge bravery, dedication, or achievement [Mid-16C. < Latin *decoratus*, past participle of *decorare* 'beautify' < *decus* 'ornament'.]

Decorated architecture, Decorated style *n* the second, more ornate stage of English Gothic architecture that is characterized by an increased use of geometric tracery and floral motifs

decoration /dékə ráysh'n/ *n* **1** ATTRACTIVE ITEM an item, usually one of a group, attached to something to make it look more attractive or to mark a special occasion **2** ORNAMENTATION the addition of ornaments to make something more attractive **3** PAINTING AND PAPERING the painting and wallpapering in a room or building **4** AWARD a medal or other honour or award given to somebody to acknowledge bravery, dedication, or achievement

decorative /dékərətiv/ *adj* **1** ATTRACTIVE serving merely to look attractive rather than having a functional purpose **2** OF DECORATION relating to the decoration of a room or home ○ *added some nice decorative touches* **3** ORNAMENTAL serving to make something look more attractive, especially by the addition of nonfunctional embellishments —**decoratively** *adv* —**decorativeness** *n*

decorative art *n* art concerned with the design and production of functional but decorative items for home use, e.g. ceramics, furniture, and fabrics (*often plural*)

decorator /dékə raytər/ *n* **1** somebody whose job is painting and wallpapering houses and other buildings **2** somebody whose job is to decorate something (*often in combination*)

decorous /dékərəss/ *adj* **1** conforming to what is acceptable or expected in formal or solemn settings, especially in dress or behaviour ○ *'They began to talk politely, in decorous half-completed sentences, with little gasps of agreement'.* (William Faulkner, *Sanctuary*; 1931) **2** understated and dignified [Mid-17C. < Latin *decorus* 'seemly' < *decor* 'attractiveness'.] —**decorously** *adv* —**decorousness** *n*

decorticate /dee káwrti kayt/ *vt* (**-cates, -cating, -cated**) **1** REMOVE OUTER LAYER FROM A PLANT to remove an outer layer such as bark, rind, or a husk from a plant or part of a plant **2** REMOVE SOMETHING FROM AN ORGAN to remove surgically the outer layer of an organ or structure such as the brain or kidney ■ *adj* **WITHOUT CORTEX FUNCTION** describes a brain that has lost the function of its cerebral cortex as a result of disease or surgery [Early 17C. < Latin *decorticare* < *cortex* (see CORTEX).] —**decortication** /dee káwrti káysh'n/ *n* —**decorticator** *n*

decorum /di káwrəm/ *n* **1** dignity or good taste that is appropriate to a particular occasion **2** the compatibility of an element in a literary or artistic work, e.g. character, form, style, or plot, with the work as a whole [Mid-16C. < Latin, < *decorus* (see DECOROUS).]

decoupage /dáy koo paázh/, **découpage** *n* **1** a technique for decorating something in which a design is made of cut-out pieces of printed paper glued onto a flat base and then varnished **2** a picture or other form of decoration, made using decoupage [Mid-20C. < French, < *découper* 'cut up, cut out' < *couper* 'cut'.]

decouple /deé kúpp'l/ (**-ples, -pling, -pled**) *vt* **1** to separate or disengage one thing from another **2** to remove or weaken the interaction between two electronic circuits, subsystems, or systems so that there is little or no transfer or feedback of energy between them —**decoupler** *n*

decoy /deé koy, di kóy/ *n* **1 HUNTING LURE** a bird or animal, or a realistic replica, used by hunters to attract an animal or bird to a place for trapping or shooting **2 DISTRACTER** something or somebody used to deceive or divert attention, especially in order to lure somebody into a trap **3 ENTRAPMENT AREA** an enclosed area or stretch of water that game or fowl are driven or lured into so that they can be easily shot or captured **4 FAKE EQUIPMENT** a fake tank, ship, aircraft, or other military apparatus meant to deceive the enemy ■ *vt* **DECEIVE** to deceive or entrap a person or animal by using a decoy [Mid-16C. < Dutch *de kooi* 'the cage' < Latin *cavea* 'cage'.] —**decoyer** *n*

decoy duck /deé koy-/ *n* **1** a wild duck that has been tamed so it can be used for attracting other ducks **2** a model duck, typically carved from wood, for use as a decoy or decoration

decrease /di kreéss/ *vti* (**-creases, -creasing, -creased**) **DIMINISH** to lessen or cause something to lessen in size, strength, or amount ■ *n* **1 PROCESS OF DECREASING** the process of becoming less, fewer, or smaller ○ *street crime is on the decrease* **2 REDUCTION** a reduction in the amount or rate of something ○ *a 2% decrease in revenue* [14C. Via Old French *decreiss-* < Latin *decrescere* < *crescere* 'grow'.] —**decreasing** *adj* —**decreasingly** *adv*

decree /di kreé/ *n* **1 OFFICIAL ORDER** an order with the power of legislation issued by a ruler or other person or group with authority **2 COURT RULING** a ruling given by a court, especially a divorce court **3 DIVINE WILL** the will or purpose of God, interpreted through events considered to be God's doing ■ *vt* **MAKE ORDER** to make an official order, pronouncement, or legal ruling to effect something [14C. Via Old French *decré* < Latin *decretum*, neuter past participle of *decernere* 'decide, pronounce a decision'.] —**decreeable** *adj* —**decreer** *n*

decree absolute (*plural* **decrees absolute**) *n* the final divorce court ruling that officially ends a marriage, leaving both parties free to marry again

decree nisi /-ní sī/ (*plural* **decrees nisi**) *n* an interim ruling of a divorce court that will become absolute in the absence of objections arising

decreet /di kreét/ *n* in Scots law, the final judgment in a court case

decrement /dékrimənt/ *n* **1** the amount by which a quantity or quality gradually decreases **2** the process of becoming less or fewer (*formal*) [Late 16C. < Latin *decrementum* < *decrescere* (see DECREASE).] —**decremental** /dékri mént'l/ *adj* —**decrementally** *adv*

decrepit /di kréppit/ *adj* in poor condition, especially old, overused, or not working efficiently [15C. < Latin *decrepitus* < *crepitus*, past participle of *crepare* 'crack, creak'.] —**decrepitly** *adv* —**decrepitude** *n*

SYNONYMS See *weak*.

decrepitate /di kréppi tayt/ (**-tates, -tating, -tated**) *vti* to heat a substance, especially a salt, until it crackles or stops crackling, or to be heated in this way [Mid-17C. < DE- + Latin *crepitare* 'crackle' < *crepitus* 'cracked' (see DECREPIT).] —**decrepitation** /di kréppi táysh'n/ *n*

decresc. *abbr* decrescendo

decrescendo /deékrə shéndō/ *adv* MUSIC = **diminuendo** *adv.* ■ *n* (*plural* **-dos**) MUSIC = **diminuendo** *n.* [Early 19C. < Italian, 'decreasing'.] —**decrescendo** *adj*

decrescent /di kréss'nt/ *adj* describes the moon when it is waning (*technical*) [Early 17C. < Latin *decrescere* (see DECREASE).] —**decrescence** *n*

decretal /di kreét'l/ *n* a papal decree or edict that relates to an aspect of church law or doctrine [14C. Via late Latin *decretale* < Latin *decret-*, past participle of *decernere* (see DECERN).] —**decretal** *adj*

decretory /di kreétəri/ *adj* relating to or having the force of a decree [Late 16C. < Latin *decretorius* < *decret-*, past participle of *decernere* (see DECERN).]

decriminalize /dee krímminə līz/ (**-izes, -izing, -ized**), **decriminalise** (**-ises, -ising, -ised**) *vt* to make legal an action or substance that was formerly illegal —**decriminalization** /deé krimminə lī záysh'n/ *n*

SYNONYMS See *legal*.

decry /di krí/ (**-cries, -crying, -cried**) *vt* to express strong disapproval of or openly criticize somebody or something ○ *critics decrying lowered standards in education* [Early 17C. After French *décrier* 'cry down'.] —**decrial** *n* —**decrier** *n*

decrypt /dee krípt/ *v* **1** *vt* = **decode** *v.* **1 2** *vt* = **decode** *v.* **2** [Mid-20C. < DE- + CRYPTOGRAM.] —**decryption** *n*

decubitus /di kyoóbitəss/ *n* the particular position of somebody's body when he or she is lying down, usually on the front, back, or side (*technical*) [Late 19C. < modern Latin, < Latin *decumbere* 'lie down'.] —**decubital** *adj*

decubitus ulcer *n* a bedsore (*technical*)

decumbent /di kúmbənt/ *adj* **1** describes plants that lie along the ground but have a tip growing upwards **2** describes hair or bristles that lie or grow flat along a surface [Early 17C. < Latin *decumbere* 'lie down' < *cubare* 'lie down'.] —**decumbence** *n* —**decumbently** *adv*

decurrent /di kúrrənt/ *adj* describes plant leaves that curve down at the edges, or trees with a rounded shape [15C. < Latin *decurrere* 'run down' < *currere* 'run'.] —**decurrently** *adv*

decussate /di kússayt/ *adj* **1** having the shape of a cross **2** describes leaves that form pairs opposite each other and at right angles to the pair above and the pair below, as in the horse chestnut [Early 19C. < Latin *decussatus*, past participle of *decussare* 'divide crosswise' < *decussis*, the numeral ten (written 'X') < *decem* 'ten' + *assis*, a coin.] —**decussately** /-aytli, -ətli/ *adv* —**decussation** /deé ku sáysh'n/ *n*

dedans /də daáN/ *n* (*plural* **-dans**) in real tennis, the open end of the court just behind the serving area where spectators can watch the match ■ *npl* the spectators who watch from the dedans [Early 18C. < French, 'inside, interior'.]

Dedham Vale /déddəm-/ Area of Outstanding Natural Beauty in E England. Area: 90 sq. km/35 sq. mi.

dedicate /déddi kayt/ (**-cates, -cating, -cated**) *vt* **1 DEVOTE ATTENTION TO** to spend time or energy doing something **2 COMMIT YOURSELF TO** to commit yourself or your life to something **3 SET SOMETHING ASIDE AS SPECIAL** to set something aside for a particular purpose ○ *an entire TV series dedicated to birds* **4 ADDRESS WORK OF ART TO** to associate a book, piece of music, or other art form with somebody as a token of friendship or esteem or as an acknowledgment of help received **5 SET SOMETHING APART AS HOLY** to set something apart for a sacred purpose or to the memory of a holy person, saint, or god, especially in a ceremony for this purpose ○ *'We cannot dedicate – we cannot consecrate – we cannot hallow – this ground. The brave men... who struggled here have consecrated it'.* (Abraham Lincoln, *Gettysburg Address*; 19 November, 1863) **6 PLAY MUSIC ADDRESSED TO** to play a piece of music, or request the playing of a piece of music, as a tribute, especially on the radio [15C. < Latin *dedicare* 'consecrate' < *dicare* 'proclaim'.] —**dedicatee** /déddikə teé/ *n* —**dedicative** /déddikətiv, -kaytiv/ *adj* —**dedicator** *n* —**dedicatory** /déddikətəri, -kaytəri/ *adj*

dedicated /déddi kaytid/ *adj* **1** wholeheartedly devoted or committed to an aim, cause, or job **2** designed to carry out only one task or set aside for a specific purpose ○ *relayed via a dedicated satellite link* —**dedicatedly** *adv*

dedication /déddi káysh'n/ *n* **1 DEVOTION** the quality of being devoted or committed to something ○ *her dedication to duty* **2 INSCRIPTION** a short printed text at the beginning of a written or musical work associating it with somebody esteemed by the author **3 PIECE OF MUSIC** a piece of music played or requested as a tribute, especially on the radio **4 SETTING ASIDE** an act or process of setting something aside for a particular purpose, especially in a ceremony that achieves this —**dedicational** *adj*

dedifferentiation /deé difə renshi áysh'n/ *n* BIOL = **anaplasia**

deduce /di dyoóss/ (**-duces, -ducing, -duced**) *vt* **1** to come to a conclusion, often without all the necessary or relevant information, but using what is known in a logical way **2** to come to a conclusion by inference from a general principle [15C. < Latin *deducere* 'lead out' < *ducere* 'to lead'.] —**deducibility** /di dyoóssə bílləti/ *n* —**deducible** *adj* —**deducibleness** *n*

SYNONYMS *deduce, infer, assume, reason, conclude, work out, figure out*

CORE MEANING: to reach a logical conclusion on the basis of information

deduce to reach a conclusion using available knowledge; **infer** to draw a conclusion from specific circumstances or evidence; **assume** to take a premise or information as true without checking or confirming it; **reason** to consider information and use it to reach a conclusion in a logical way; **conclude** to form an opinion or make a judgment after much consideration; **work out** to find a solution or explanation by careful thought or reasoning; **figure out** to find a solution or reach a conclusion by careful thought or reasoning.

deduct /di dúkt/ *vt* to subtract an amount for some purpose [15C. < Latin *deduct-*, past participle of *deducere* (see DEDUCE).]

deductible /di dúktəb'l/ *adj* **1** capable of being, or liable to be, subtracted from something for some purpose **2** *US, Can* allowed by tax authorities as a legitimate expense not liable to tax ■ *n US* INSUR = **excess** *n.* **4** —**deductibility** /di dúktə bílləti/ *n*

deduction /di dúksh'n/ *n* **1 CONCLUSION DRAWN** a conclusion drawn from available information **2 DRAWING A CONCLUSION** the process of drawing a conclusion from available information **3 LOGICAL CONCLUSION** a conclusion reached by applying the rules of logic to a premise **4 AMOUNT DEDUCTED** an amount that is subtracted from something, especially as an allowance against tax **5 SUBTRACTION OF AN AMOUNT** the subtracting of an amount for some particular purpose **6 REASONING** the forming of conclusions by applying the rules of logic to a premise

deductive /di dúktiv/ *adj* based on logical or reasonable deduction —**deductively** *adv*

deed /deed/ *n* **1 SOMETHING DONE** an intentional act ○ *'The last temptation is the greatest treason / To do the right deed for the wrong reason'.* (T.S. Eliot, *Murder in the Cathedral*; 1935) **2 NOTEWORTHY ACTION** an action that is outstanding in a particular way **3 DOCUMENT** a signed document that outlines the terms of an agreement, especially one that details a change in ownership of property **4** LAW = **title deed** ■ **deeds** *npl* **ACTIONS** action in general, especially as contrasted with speech ■ *vt US* **TRANSFER PROPERTY TO** to sign over or transfer something, especially property, to another person [Old English *dēd* < Germanic, 'a doing' < Indo-European]

deed box *n* a lockable strongbox where deeds and other important documents can be safely kept

deed of covenant *n* a signed document by which somebody formally agrees to make payments for a period of several years to a charity or other organization

deed poll *n* an official document, especially one that makes a change in somebody's name, that is signed and executed by one person only [< POLL 'cut off cleanly', as opposed to notched at the edge as with a contract drawn up in multiple copies]

deejay /deé jay/ *n* a disc jockey (*informal*) [Mid-20C. Respelling of DJ.] —**deejay** *vi*

deem /deem/ *vt* to judge or consider something in a particular light (*formal; often passive*) ○ *a plan that was deemed impractical from the very start* [Old English *dēman* < Germanic, 'to judge']

de-emphasize /dee émfə sīz/, **de-emphasise** (**de-emphasises, de-emphasising, de-emphasised**) *vt* to make something seem or be less important or central —**de-emphasis** /-fəssiss/ *n*

deemster /deémstər/, **dempster** /démpstər/ *n* the title given to either of the two justices serving on the Isle of Man —**deemstership** *n*

de-energize /dee énnər jīz/ (**de-energizes, de-energizing, de-energized**), **de-energise** (**de-energises, de-energising, de-energised**) *v* **1** *vt* to cut off an electrical circuit from its source of power **2** *vti* to have or cause somebody to have less energy or vitality —**de-energization** /deè ennər jī záysh'n/ *n*

deep /deep/ *adj* **1** DOWN FROM SURFACE extending from a surface downwards or inwards ○ *a deep wound* **2** FAR FROM TOP TO BOTTOM extending a long way from top to bottom ○ *a deep well* ○ *'The deep dark-shining / Pacific leans on the land'*. (Robinson Jeffers, *Night*; 1925) **3** FAR FROM FRONT TO BACK extending a long way from front to back ○ *a cupboard with deep shelves* **4** FAR FROM EDGE extending a long way from a surface or boundary inwards ○ *deep wood* **5** MADE UP OF UNITS standing or lining up in a particular number of rows ○ *people six deep on the pavement* **6** FAR DOWN OR IN relatively far down, in, or inside something ○ *a nagging pain deep in his chest* **7** COMING FROM OR REACHING INSIDE BODY coming from or reaching far down inside the body ○ *take a deep breath* **8** LOW IN PITCH low in pitch and rounded in tone ○ *a deep booming voice* **9** DARK IN COLOUR relatively dark, rich, or intense in colour ○ *deep purple* **10** EXTREME extreme, severe, or intense ○ *deep suspicion* **11** PROFOUND intellectually profound ○ *no evidence of deep thinking* ■ *adj, adv* **1** NEAR OWN GOAL in sports such as football, nearer to the goal a team is defending than the goal it is attacking ○ *Aberdeen played with two deep defenders.* ○ *deep in their own territory* **2** NEAR BOUNDARY in cricket, playing or played near the boundary of the playing area, relatively far from the batsman ○ *deep mid-on* ■ *adv* FAR far, especially from a surface or point of entry ○ *The expedition went deep into the jungle.* ■ *n* **1** SEA the ocean depths **2** POSITION FAR FROM BATSMAN in cricket, the fielding position relatively far from the batsman **3** INTENSE PART the middle or most intense part of something (*literary*) ○ *the deep of night* [Old English *dēop* < Indo-European, 'deep, hollow'] —**deepness** *n* ◇ **deep down (inside)** in your innermost being ◇ **deep in something** completely overwhelmed by or absorbed in something ○ *She sat silent, deep in thought.* ◇ **in deep** very involved

deep-discount bond *n* a bond sold at a large discount because it bears little or no interest although it provides a capital gain on redemption

deep-dish *adj* baked in a deep dish and so thicker than normal ○ *deep-dish pizza*

deep-dyed *adj* **1** describes fabric that has been dyed with a concentrated fade-resistant dye **2** = **dyed-in-the-wool** *adj.* 1

deepen /deèpən/ *vti* **1** to become or make something deep or deeper **2** to become or make something more intense ○ *the recession was deepening* —**deepener** *n*

deep end *n* the part of a swimming pool, lake, or other body of water where the water is deepest ◇ **be thrown in at the deep end** to have to learn something new or difficult with very little experience or warning ◇ **go off (at) the deep end** to fly into a rage or lose your emotional equilibrium

deep-fat fryer *n* = **deep fryer**

deep-freeze (**deep-freezes, deep-freezing, deep-froze, deep-frozen**) *vt* **1** FREEZE SOMETHING QUICKLY to freeze something such as food quickly in order to prolong its freshness or nutritional value **2** KEEP SOMETHING VERY COLD to store something at very low temperatures **3** SUSPEND ACTIVITY to put off or suspend activity (*informal*) —**deep-frozen** *adj*

deep-fry (**deep-fries, deep-frying, deep-fried**) *vt* to cook food in fat or oil that is deep enough to cover the food completely —**deep-fried** *adj*

deep fryer, deep-fat fryer *n* an electrical appliance for deep-frying food

deep-laid *adj* carefully worked out and highly confidential ○ *a deep-laid plan*

deep-litter *adj* **1** using a thick layer of straw or other natural material for farm animals, especially poultry, to move about in **2** from or produced by animals raised in deep-litter conditions

deeply /deèpli/ *adv* **1** profoundly or intensely ○ *deeply offended* **2** far down inside ○ *breathe deeply* ○ *deeply felt pain*

deep-pan *adj* describes a pizza with a deep filling baked in a dish with raised sides

deep-rooted *adj* **1** firmly held or established, usually over a long period of time, and so unlikely to change **2** having roots that grow deep in the soil

deep-sea *adj* relating to the deep waters of the ocean far away from land

deep-seated *adj* firmly established and difficult to change or eradicate ○ *deep-seated fear*

deep-set *adj* describes eyes with deep sockets

Deep South region in the SE United States, usually considered to comprise Alabama, Georgia, Louisiana, Mississippi, and South Carolina, and regarded as the heartland of traditional Southern culture

deep space *n* space beyond the Earth's gravitational influence or beyond the orbit of the Moon

deep structure *n* the underlying form of a language, conceived as containing all the information needed to make any sentence in that language. ◊ **surface structure**

deep-water *adj* describes a harbour or anchorage that is deep enough to accommodate large ocean-going vessels

deer /deer/ (*plural* **deer**) *n* a mammal distinguished by the branched antlers on males. Family: Cervidae. [Old English *dēor* 'animal' < Germanic, 'breathing creature' < Indo-European, 'breath, vapour']

SPELLCHECK See ***dear***.

deer fly *n* a biting fly that infests deer and other animals, sucking blood and spreading the infectious disease tularemia. Genus: *Chrysops.*

deergrass /deèr graass/ (*plural* **-grass**) *n* a perennial flowering grassy plant that grows in thick tufts. Native to: temperate peat bogs. *Trichophorum caespitosum.*

deerhound /deèr hownd/ *n* a large long-legged dog with a very shaggy coat, belonging to a breed developed in Scotland as a hunting dog from a Mediterranean strain of greyhound

deer lick *n* a naturally occurring or artificial salty patch of ground where deer come to lick

deer mouse *n* an agile mouse. Native to: North and Central America. Genus: *Peromyscus.* ◊ **white-footed mouse**

deerskin /deèr skin/ *n* the treated hide of a deer used as a fabric

deerstalker /deèr stawkər/ *n* **1** **deerstalker, deerstalker hat** a tweed hat with peaks at the front and back and earflaps that can either be tied together on its crown or fastened under the chin **2** a deer hunter on foot

deerstalking /deèr stawking/ *n* the activity of hunting wild deer by stealthily following them on foot

de-escalate /dee éskə layt/ (**de-escalates, de-escalating, de-escalated**) *vt* to reduce the level or intensity of a difficult or dangerous situation —**de-escalation** /deè eskə láysh'n/ *n*

Deeside and Lochnagar /deè sīd ənd lókhnə gaár/ National Scenic Area in E Scotland. Area: 400 sq. km/250 sq. mi.

deet /deet/ *n* $C_{12}H_{17}NO$ an oily colourless insect repellent. Full form **diethyl toluamide** [Mid-20C. Probably from the initial letters of its chemical name.]

def /def/ *adj* excellent (*slang*) [Late 20C. Shortening of DEFINITIVE.]

def. *abbr* **1** defence **2** defendant **3** deferred **4** definite **5** definition

deface /di fáyss/ (**-faces, -facing, -faced**) *vt* to spoil the appearance of something, especially intentionally [14C. < French *défacer* < *face* (see FACE).] —**defaceable** *adj* —**defacer** *n* —**defacement** *n*

de facto /day fáktō/ *adv* IN FACT in fact, whether with a legal right or not ■ *adj* AS THOUGH RIGHTFUL acting or existing in fact but without legal sanction ○ *the de facto rules of the country* ■ *n* (*plural* **de factos**) *ANZ* PARTNER somebody not married to somebody else but living with the person as if they are married (*informal*) [Early 17C. < Latin, 'in fact', literally 'from what is done'.]

defaecate *vi* = **defecate**

defalcate /deè fal kayt, -fawl-/ (**-cates, -cating, -cated**) *vt* to misuse something, especially money or property, that belongs to somebody else and is held in trust [Mid-16C. < medieval Latin *defalcare* 'deduct' < Latin *falx* 'scythe'.] —**defalcator** *n* —**defalcation** /deè fal káysh'n, -fawl-/ *n*

defame /di fáym/ (**-fames, -faming, -famed**) *vt* to attack somebody or somebody's reputation, character, or good name by making slanderous or libellous statements [14C. Via Old French *deffamer* < Latin *diffamare* 'spread about as an insulting report' < *fama* 'talk, report, reputation'.] —**defamation** /déffə máysh'n/ *n* —**defamatory** /di fámmətəri/ *adj* —**defamer** *n*

SYNONYMS See ***malign***.

defang /deè fáng/ *vt* to remove the fangs from a snake or other animal

defat /deè fát/ (**-fats, -fatting, -fatted**) *vt* to remove the fat or fats from something

ϟ **default** /di fáwlt/ *n* **1** PRESET OPTION an option that will automatically be selected by a computer if the user does not choose one **2** FAILURE TO DO a failure to meet an obligation, especially a financial one **3** NONAPPEARANCE IN COURT a failure to make a summoned court appearance **4** NONPARTICIPATION IN COMPETITION a failure to appear for or complete a competition ■ *vi* **1** FAIL TO PAY to fail to pay a debt or other financial obligation **2** FAIL TO APPEAR IN COURT to fail to make an appearance in court although summoned to do so **3** FAIL TO COMPETE to fail to appear for a match or contest **4** USE PRESET OPTION to use a device, command, or file when no other is specified [13C. < Old French *defaute*, past participle of *defaillir* 'fail' < *faillir* (see FAIL).] ◇ **by default** **1** having come about because some other thing, often something expected, did not happen **2** having come about because somebody failed to appear as expected **3** according to a computer's preset configuration ◇ **in default of something** *or* **somebody** because of a lack of or the absence of something or somebody (*formal*)

defaulter /di fáwltər/ *n* **1** NONPAYER a debtor who defaults on a financial obligation **2** ABSENTEE FROM COURT a person who fails to respond to a court summons **3** ABSENTEE FROM COMPETITION a person or team failing to appear for a match or contest **4** MILITARY OFFENDER a soldier who commits a military offence

defeasance /di feèz'nss/ *n* **1** MAKING VOID the declaration of something as null and void **2** LEGAL CLAUSE a clause in a legal document that states that, in the event of a condition being fulfilled, the document will become null and void **3** LEGAL DOCUMENT a document containing a defeasance [15C. < Old French *defesance* < *defaire* < medieval Latin *disfacere* (see DEFEAT).]

defeasible /di feèzəb'l/ *adj* **1** capable of being made or declared null and void **2** liable to be forfeited —**defeasibility** /di feèzə bíllәti/ *n* —**defeasibleness** *n*

defeat /di feèt/ *vt* **1** BEAT ENEMY to win a victory over enemy forces in a battle or war **2** BEAT COMPETITOR to win a victory over a competitor, e.g. in sport or business **3** WIN A VOTE to win a victory over another in a debate or vote **4** CAUSE FAILURE OF to cause something to fail or to fall short of realization ○ *The truck defeated all my attempts to get it to start.* **5** BAFFLE to leave somebody in a baffled or uncomprehending state ○ *His logic defeats me.* **6** MAKE SOMETHING VOID to make or declare something null and void ■ *n* **1** LOSING TO AN OPPONENT the fact or an instance of losing to an enemy in battle or an opponent in a competition ○ *the home team's humiliating defeat* **2** FAILURE failure to win or to realize a goal ○ *She refused to admit defeat and appealed.* [14C. Via Anglo-Norman *defeter* 'disfigure, destroy' < medieval Latin *disfacere* 'unmake' < Latin *facere* 'do, make'.] —**defeater** *n* ◇ **defeat the object** *or* **purpose of something** make the desired or expected outcome ridiculous or possible

defeatist /di feètist/ *adj* showing a tendency to expect failure or accept it too readily ■ *n* a person who consistently expects or accepts failure —**defeatism** *n*

defecate /déffə kayt/ (**-cates, -cating, -cated**), **defaecate** (**-cates, -cating, -cated**) *v* **1** *vi* to expel faeces from the bowel through the rectum (*formal or technical*) **2** *vt* to remove impurities from a solution, especially a solution that contains sugar [15C. < Latin *defaecare* 'remove waste' < *faex* 'dregs, waste'.] —**defecation** /déffə káysh'n/ *n* —**defecator** *n*

defect *n* /deè fekt/ **1** FLAW a failing, blemish, or flaw, especially one that still allows the affected thing to function, however imperfectly **2** PERSONAL FLAW a personal failing, weakness, or shortcoming, especially in character **3** IMPERFECTION IN CRYSTAL an imperfection in the internal structure of a crystal, e.g. an atom of a different substance ■ *vi* /di fékt/ **1** REJECT HOMELAND to leave your native country or the country you are living in and refuse to return there, usually for political or moral reasons **2** ABANDON ALLEGIANCE to abandon allegiance to a cause or party, especially when this also involves supporting something previously opposed [15C. < Latin *defect-*, past participle of *deficere* 'be wanting, desert' < *facere* 'do, make'.] —**defection** *n* —**defector** /di féktər/ *n*

SYNONYMS See *flaw*.

defective /di féktiv/ *adj* **1 FAULTY** imperfect or faulty, so not functioning properly or at all **2 OFFENSIVE TERM** an offensive term that means having learning difficulties or problems in coping with emotions (*insult*) **3 INCOMPLETE** lacking the usual or expected range of grammatical inflections ■ *n* **OFFENSIVE TERM** an offensive term meaning somebody who has learning difficulties or problems in coping with emotions (*insult*) —**defectively** *adv* —**defectiveness** *n*

USAGE ***defective*** or ***deficient***? ***Defective*** is normally used in reference to processes, machines, or to other functional things such as the human senses: *If the workmanship is defective, they'll replace the shoes with a new pair. As he grew older his hearing became defective.* ***Deficient*** describes things that lack a quality, element, or ingredient, without this amounting to actual failure to work or function: *Her voice is beautiful but a little deficient in power. Their diet is deficient in vitamin D.*

defeminize /dee fémmi nīz/ (**-nizes, -nizing, -nized**), **defeminise** (**-nises, -nising, -nised**) *vt* to remove or diminish characteristics of somebody or something that are traditionally regarded as associated with women or girls

defence /di fénss/ *n* **1 PROTECTION** the protection of something, especially from attack by an enemy **2 SOMETHING THAT PROTECTS** a method or object for protecting something ○ *a castle with strong defences* **3 ARMED FORCES** a country's armed forces **4 JUSTIFICATION** an excuse or justification for something ○ *spoke in defence of the motion* **5 REASONS OFFERED** the set of reasons that a defendant offers in court in denial of a charge **6 DEFENDANT'S CASE** the facts and their presentation as they relate to the defendant in a court case **7 LAWYER AND DEFENDANT** the lawyer or lawyers and the defendant in a court case **8 DEFENSIVE PLAY** in sports, the method or manoeuvres that prevent the other team from scoring **9 DEFENSIVE PLAYERS** the sports team members who have responsibility for defence ■ **defences** *npl* **1 PROTECTIVE QUALITIES** the qualities of the body or mind that protect somebody from attack, injury, or illness **2 FORTIFICATIONS** the fortifications that protect a place from enemies or the forces of nature ○ *Roman defences that are now a tourist attraction* ○ *sea defences* [14C. Via Old French < Latin *defens-*, past participle of *defendere* (see DEFEND).]

defenceless /di fénssləss/ *adj* lacking any form of protection and therefore vulnerable ■ *npl* people who are unable to defend themselves and their interests ○ *working as a shield for the defenceless* —**defencelessly** *adv* —**defencelessness** *n*

defenceman /di fénss man/ (*plural* **-men** /-men/) *n US* a team member who plays in a defensive position, especially in ice hockey

defence mechanism *n* **1** any means of avoiding emotional distress, destructive impulses, or a threat to self-esteem, especially by the suppression of unwanted thoughts or memories **2** any of the natural protective responses to danger or attack used by an organism, e.g. when faced with a predator or invaded by a disease agent

defence-minded *adj* giving emphasis to building a team with strong defensive skills

defend /di fénd/ *v* **1** *vt* **PROTECT** to protect somebody or something from attack, harm, or danger **2** *vti* **REPRESENT IN COURT** to represent and speak on behalf of an accused person in court **3** *vt* **SUPPORT POSITION** to offer support for something or somebody, especially by arguing against the objections or criticism of others **4** *vi* **RESIST OPPONENT** in sports, to resist the attacks of an opposing side and try to prevent from scoring **5** *vt* **TRY TO KEEP A TITLE** to try to retain a title, especially a sporting one, by competing in the relevant competitions **6** *vt* **PROTECT GOAL** in sports, to protect the goal and goal area from the attacks of the opposition [13C. Via French *défendre* < Latin *defendere* 'ward off' < Indo-European, 'strike, kill'.] —**defendable** *adj*

SYNONYMS See *safeguard*.

defendant /di féndənt/ *n* a person, party, or company required to answer criminal or civil charges in a court

~~**defendent**~~ incorrect spelling of **defendant**

defender /di féndər/ *n* **1 PROTECTOR** a protector of a person or place against attack **2 SUPPORTER** a supporter or justifier of something or somebody **3 DEFENSIVE PLAYER** in sports, somebody whose role is to try to prevent the opposition from scoring or getting into a scoring position **4 HOLDER OF TITLE** a holder of a title that is challenged recurrently

Defender of the Faith *n* a title given by Pope Leo X in 1521 to King Henry VIII and held by English and British monarchs ever since

defending /di fénding/ *adj* holding a title that is subject to recurring competition ○ *the defending champions*

defenestrate /dee fénni strayt/ (**-trates, -trating, -trated**) *vt* to throw something or somebody out of a window (*formal or humorous*) [Early 17C. < DE- + Latin *fenestra* 'window'.] —**defenestration** /dee fénni stráysh'n/ *n*

defense *n US* = **defence**

defensible /di fénssəb'l/ *adj* **1** capable of being protected from attack **2** able to be explained, justified, or excused —**defensibility** /di fénssə bílləti/ *n* —**defensibleness** *n* —**defensibly** *adv*

defensin /di fénssin/ *n* any of three peptides present in human white blood cells that appear to play a role in the prevention or elimination of infection

defensive /di fénssiv/ *adj* **1 QUICK TO JUSTIFY** aiming to deflect or avoid perceived criticism **2 SERVING TO PROTECT** designed or intended for protection or defence **3 FAVOURING DEFENCE AS PLAYING STRATEGY** concentrating more on preventing an opponent from gaining an advantage than on scoring **4** *US* **OF A DEFENCE PLAYER** relating to those players who have responsibility for defence —**defensiveness** *n* ◇ **on the defensive 1** expecting criticism or aggression and prepared to respond **2** having assumed a position that indicates readiness to play defensively

defensively /di fénssivli/ *adv* **1** in a defensive way **2** as regards defence, especially defensive play ○ *Defensively they played well, but they couldn't manage to score.*

defensive medicine *n US* medical treatment that involves carrying out extensive diagnostic testing in order to minimize the chances of a patient's suing the doctor or hospital for negligence

defer[1] /di fúr/ (**-fers, -ferring, -ferred**) *vti* to put something off until a later time [14C. < French *différer* 'put aside, differ'.] —**deferment** *n* —**deferrable** *adj* —**deferrer** *n* —**deferral** *n*

defer[2] /di fúr/ (**-fers, -ferring, -ferred**) *vi* to give way to, and usually acknowledge the merit of, somebody else's judgment, opinion, wishes, or action ○ *I defer to your superior knowledge.* [15C. Via French *déférer* < Latin *deferre* 'carry away' < *ferre* 'carry' (see FERTILE).] —**deferrer** *n*

deference /déffərənss/ *n* **1** polite respect, especially putting another person's interests first **2** submission to the judgment, opinion, or wishes of another person [Mid-17C. < DEFER[2].] ◇ **in deference to** out of respect or courtesy to somebody or something

deferent[1] /déffərənt/ *adj* = **deferential**

deferent[2] /déffərənt/ *adj* describes a duct, nerve, or vessel in the body that is capable of carrying impulses or fluid away, down, or outwards

deferential /déffə rénsh'l/ *adj* showing or expressing polite respect or courtesy —**deferentially** *adv*

deferred annuity *n* an investment that does not pay out until at least one year after the final premium has been paid

deferred sentence *n* a sentence that is not passed until a specified period has elapsed in order to allow the court time to assess the behaviour of the convicted person

defervescence /deefər véss'nss/ *n* **1** a decrease in a fever **2** the stage of an illness during which fever subsides [Early 18C. < Latin *defervescere* 'stop boiling' < *fervere* 'be hot, boil'.] —**defervesce** *vti* —**defervescent** *adj*

defiance /di fí ənss/ *n* open, bold, or hostile refusal to obey or conform ◇ **in defiance of** with complete disregard for a rule, law, or person in authority

defiant /di fí ənt/ *adj* **1** tending to confront and challenge **2** deliberately and openly disobedient [Late 16C. < French *défiant*, present participle of *défier* < assumed Vulgar Latin *disfidare* 'renounce your faith'.] —**defiantly** *adv*

defibrillate /dee fíbbri layt/ (**-lates, -lating, -lated**) *vt* to apply an electric shock to the chest, or sometimes directly to the heart itself, in order to restore a regular heartbeat after a critically irregular beat has developed —**defibrillation** /dee fíbbri láysh'n/ *n*

defibrillator /dee fíbbri laytər/ *n* a machine that administers a controlled electric shock to the chest or heart to correct a fluttering heartbeat that cannot drive the circulation

deficiency /di físh'nssi/ (*plural* **-cies**) *n* **1** a lack or shortage of something **2** the amount by which something falls short of being complete

SYNONYMS See *lack*.

deficiency disease *n* a disease resulting from lack of a nutrient or other substance required by a human or other animal or plant for growth, development, or general health

deficient /di físh'nt/ *adj* **1** lacking a particular quality, element, or ingredient, especially one that is expected or necessary ○ *deficient in tact* **2** inadequate or not good enough [Late 16C. < Latin *deficient-*, present participle of *deficere* 'leave undone, fail' < *facere* 'do, make'.] —**deficiently** *adv*

USAGE See *defective*.

deficit /déffəssit/ *n* **1** the amount by which expenditure exceeds income or budget **2** the amount by which a total is less than it should be [Late 18C. Via French *déficit* < Latin *deficit* 'it is lacking' < *deficere* (see DEFICIENT).]

SYNONYMS See *lack*.

deficit financing *n* the practice of deliberately allowing government spending to exceed its revenues in order to try to boost economic activity and lower unemployment

deficit spending *n* government spending that is financed by borrowing money rather than through money raised by taxation

defilade /déffi láyd/ *n* fortifications or protection against enemy gunfire that might be aimed at a line of troops. ◊ **enfilade** *n.* 1 ■ *vt* (**-lades, -lading, -laded**) to set up protective fortifications to protect troops or a position [Early 19C. < French *défiler* (see DEFILE[2]), after ENFILADE.]

defile[1] /di fíl/ (**-files, -filing, -filed**) *vt* **1 CORRUPT** to corrupt or ruin something (*formal*) ○ *'The dust is his original sin and inward corruptions, that have defiled the whole man'.* (John Bunyan, *Pilgrims Progress*; 1678) **2 DAMAGE REPUTATION** to damage somebody's reputation or good name **3 DESTROY SANCTITY OF** to make a holy or sacred thing or place no longer fit for ceremonial use **4 POLLUTE** to make something dirty or polluted (*formal*) **5 DEPRIVE WOMAN OF VIRGINITY** to be the first man to have sexual intercourse with a woman, usually outside marriage (*archaic*) [14C. Alteration of French *defouler* 'trample' < *fouler* 'trample under foot'.] —**defilement** *n* —**defiler** *n*

defile[2] /di fíl/ *n* **1 NARROW MOUNTAIN PASS** a narrow pass between mountains **2 NARROW PASSAGE** a passage only wide enough for people to pass single-file ■ *vi* (**-files, -filing, -filed**) **MARCH SINGLE-FILE** to march or go in single file, especially when the way is too narrow to march in any other formation [Late 17C. < French *défiler* 'march in a line' < *file* (see FILE[1]).]

~~**definate**~~ incorrect spelling of **definite**

~~**definately**~~ incorrect spelling of **definitely**

define /di fín/ (**-fines, -fining, -fined**) *v* **1** *vti* **GIVE MEANING OF WORD** to give the precise meaning of a word or expression **2** *vt* **STATE** to state or describe something exactly ○ *clearly defined objectives* **3** *vt* **CHARACTERIZE** to identify somebody or something by a distinctive characteristic quality or feature ○ *The age we live in is defined by a deep sense of uncertainty.* **4** *vt* **SHOW SOMETHING CLEARLY** to show something clearly, especially in shape or outline (*usually passive*) ○ *The tyre marks were clearly defined in the snow.* **5** *vt* **MARK** to mark a boundary, edge, or limit ○ *That row of trees defines the eastern boundary of the estate.* [14C. Via Old French *definer* < Latin *definire* 'limit, determine' < *finis* 'final moment, end'.] —**definability** /di fínə bílləti/ *n* —**definable** *adj* —**definably** *adv* —**definer** *n*

definiendum /di fínni éndəm/ (*plural* **-da** /-də/) *n* the word or expression defined by a definition, e.g. in a dictionary or glossary (*technical*) [Late 19C. < Latin, 'thing to be defined' < *definire* (see DEFINE).]

definiens /di fínni enz/ (*plural* **-entia** /-énshə/) *n* the words used to define a particular word or expression, e.g. in a dictionary or glossary (*technical*) [Late 19C. < medieval

Latin, 'something that defines' < present participle of Latin *definire* (see DEFINE).]

defining /di fíning/ *adj* giving a distinctive character to something or encapsulating its character ○ *That was the defining act of his election campaign.*

definite /déffənət/ *adj* 1 **WITH CLEAR LIMITS** precise and distinct in describing the limits of something ○ *with a definite age range for the junior chess club* 2 **WITH CLEAR OUTLINE** having a clearly distinct shape or outline ○ *the definite outline of a building amongst the trees* 3 **OBVIOUS** unquestionable and unmistakable ○ *a definite turn for the better* 4 **FIXED** fixed, certain, and not to be altered ○ *Have we got a definite date for the meeting?* 5 **ABSOLUTELY SET ON** certain about something and unlikely to have a change of mind ○ *I'm definite about this.* 6 **WITH TERMINAL FLOWER** describes a flower head in which the first-formed flower is at the stalk's end with subsequent flowers developing lower down on one or both sides of the stalk [Mid-16C. < Latin *definitus*, past participle of *definire* (see DEFINE).] —**definiteness** *n*

USAGE definite or **definitive**? ***Definite*** describes something as being distinct or precise without making any strong judgment about it: *He has definite ideas on the subject.* ***Definitive*** denotes something authoritative, conclusive, or decisive, and is therefore a more evaluative word: *She wrote the definitive book on the subject.*

definite article *n* a word, e.g. 'the' in English, that designates a noun as being specific and identifiable

definite integral *n* a determination of the difference in values of an integral between two specified limits, expressed using symbols

definitely /déffənətli/ *adv* 1 **CERTAINLY** without a doubt ○ *He definitely had a Swedish accent.* 2 **FINALLY AND UNCHANGEABLY** as a conclusion after some thought or hesitation ○ *Once she had definitely decided to go, she started packing.* 3 **EXACTLY** in a precise way ○ *Without knowing definitely what it was, he just felt that something was wrong.* 4 **CLEARLY** in a distinct and unmistakable way ○ *Her attitude suddenly became more definitely critical.* 5 **ABSOLUTELY** with no exceptions ○ *The notice said 'Definitely no bikers'.* ■ *interj* **YES** used to say 'yes' in an emphatic and enthusiastic way ○ *'Are you going to come to the party?' 'Definitely!'*

definition /déffə nísh'n/ *n* 1 **MEANING OF WORD** a brief precise statement of what a word or expression means, e.g. in a dictionary 2 **ACT OF DEFINING WORD** the act or process of defining what a word or expression means, e.g. in writing a dictionary 3 **CLARIFICATION** the act of describing or stating something clearly and unambiguously 4 **CLARITY** the clarity of an image or sound 5 **EMBODIMENT** somebody or something believed to represent or embody a particular idea or quality (*formal*) ○ *His behaviour has always seemed to me the very definition of courtesy.* [14C. Via French < Latin, < *definire* (see DEFINE).] —**definitional** *adj* ◇ **by definition** emphasizes that somebody or something is considered to have a particular intrinsic quality

definitive /di fínnətiv/ *adj* 1 **CONCLUSIVE AND FINAL** providing a final decision that will not be questioned or changed ○ *We need a definitive answer.* 2 **MOST AUTHORITATIVE** recognized as being the most authoritative and of the highest standard ○ *the definitive study of the subject* 3 **SOLD FOR LONG TIME** describes postage stamps sold for an extended or indefinite period, often as part of a set sharing common design elements 4 **FULLY GROWN** fully formed or completely developed ■ *n* **DEFINITIVE STAMP** a postage stamp sold for an extended or indefinite period [14C. < French *définitif* < Latin *definire* (see DEFINE).] —**definitively** *adv* —**definitiveness** *n*

USAGE See ***definite***.

definitive host *n* the plant or animal in or on which a parasitic organism reaches sexual maturity. ◊ **intermediate host**

~~**definitly**~~ incorrect spelling of **definitely**

deflagrate /défflə grayt/ (**-grates, -grating, -grated**) *vti* to burn or make something burn violently (*technical*) [Early 17C. < Latin *deflagrare* 'burn up' < *flagrare* 'burn'.] —**deflagration** /défflə gráysh'n/ *n*

deflate /di fláyt/ (**-flates, -flating, -flated**) *v* 1 *vti* **LET AIR OUT** to let out or lose air or gas from an inflatable object with the result that it shrinks or collapses 2 *vt* **MAKE SOMEBODY LESS CONFIDENT** to destroy somebody's confidence or make somebody less self-assured or conceited 3 *vt* **DESTROY THEORY** to show that a theory or argument is wrong 4 *vt* **CAUSE DEFLATION** to bring about deflation in the economy or the money supply [Late 19C. < DE- + INFLATE.] —**deflator** *n* —**deflated** *adj*

deflation /di fláysh'n/ *n* 1 **COLLAPSE BECAUSE OF AIR LOSS** the releasing or escaping of air or gas from something, resulting in its shrinking or collapsing 2 **LOSS OF SELF-ESTEEM** a sudden loss of confidence, self-assurance, or conceit 3 **REDUCED ECONOMIC ACTIVITY** the reduction of general economic activity, including lower prices and a reduced supply of money and credit 4 **EROSION** the erosion of land by wind

deflationary /di fláysh'nəri/ *adj* undergoing or creating a lower level of general economic activity

deflationist /di fláysh'nist/ *adj* in favour of economic deflation —**deflationist** *n*

deflect /di flékt/ *v* 1 *vti* **CHANGE COURSE** to change course because of hitting something, or change something's course by coming into contact with it 2 *vt* **DIRECT ATTENTION AWAY FROM** to direct people's attention or criticism away from a particular subject or issue to something else 3 *vt* **FORCE ALTERATION OF PLANS** to force somebody to change from what he or she usually does or planned to do [Mid-16C. < Latin *deflectere* 'bend away' < *flectere* 'bend'.] —**deflectable** *adj* —**deflective** *adj* —**deflector** *n*

deflection /di fléksh'n/, **deflexion** *n* 1 **CHANGING OF COURSE** a change of course after hitting somebody or something, or a changing of something's course by being hit by it 2 **AMOUNT SOMETHING DEFLECTS** the amount or distance by which something is deflected 3 **DIVERTING OF ATTENTION** the act of directing people's attention or criticism away from something 4 **MOVEMENT OF NEEDLE AWAY FROM ZERO** a definite movement of the indicator on a measuring instrument 5 **MOVEMENT OF STRUCTURE UNDER LOAD** the movement of a structure or a part of a structure when it is bearing a load

deflexed /di flékst, dée-/ *adj* describes petals or leaves that bend sharply downwards [Late 18C. < Latin *deflexus*, past participle of *deflectere* (see DEFLECT).]

deflexion *n* = **deflection**

defloration /dée flaw ráysh'n, défflə-/ *n* ending of a woman's or girl's virginity (*literary*) [14C. Via French < late Latin *deflorare* (see DEFLOWER).]

deflower /dee flówər/ *vt* 1 to end the virginity of a girl or woman (*literary*) 2 to remove some or all of the flowers from a plant [14C. Via Old French *deffleurer* < late Latin *deflorare* < Latin *flos* 'flower'.] —**deflowerer** *n*

defocus /dee fókəss/ *v* (**-cuses** *or* **-cusses, -cusing** *or* **-cussing, -cused** *or* **-cussed**) 1 *vt* **SOFTEN PICTURE BY SHIFTING FOCUS** to soften or blur an image by focusing away from the exact plane of focus of the object in the image 2 *vti* **STOP FOCUSING** to stop focusing on something ■ *n* **CONDITION OF DEFOCUSING** the condition or state caused by defocusing, e.g. the blurring of a photographic image

Defoe /di fó/, **Daniel** (1660?–1731) English novelist and journalist. Born **Daniel Foe**

defog /dée fóg/ (**defogs, defogging, defogged**) *vti* 1 *US* CARS = **demist** 2 to remove condensation from the lens of a camera or other optical equipment, especially by allowing it to warm up, or lose condensation in this way —**defogger** *n*

defogger *n US* CARS = **demister**

defoliant /dee fóli ənt/ *n* a chemical that strips trees and plants of their leaves

defoliate /dee fóli ayt/ (**-ates, -ating, -ated**) *vti* to strip trees and plants of their leaves, e.g. by using chemicals or through pollution or attack by pests, or to lose leaves in any of these ways [Late 18C. < late Latin *defoliare* < *folium* 'leaf, page'.] —**defoliation** /dee fóli áysh'n/ *n* —**defoliator** *n*

deforce /dee fáwrss/ (**-forces, -forcing, -forced**) *vt* to keep the rightful owner of property away from it, or keep the property away from its owner, by force or violence (*formal*) [14C. < Anglo-Norman *deforcer* 'force away from' < *forcier* < Latin *fortis* 'strong'.] —**deforcement** *n*

deforest /dee fórrist/ *vt* to remove the trees from an area of land —**deforestation** /dee fórri stáysh'n/ *n* —**deforester** *n*

deform /di fáwrm/ *vti* 1 **DISTORT** to become, or make something become, distorted, damaged, or disfigured 2 **SPOIL** to spoil the appearance of something and make it ugly, or become spoiled and ugly ○ *The new office buildings have deformed the whole area.* 3 **CHANGE SHAPE** to change the shape of something through stress, or become changed in this way [15C. Via Old French *deformer* < Latin *deformare* < *forma* 'mould, shape, beauty'.] —**deformability** /di fáwrmə bílləti/ *n* —**deformable** *adj* —**deformed** *adj* —**deformedness** *n* —**deformer** *n*

deformation /dée fawr máysh'n/ *n* 1 **ACT OF DEFORMING OR BEING DEFORMED** the act or process of damaging, disfiguring, or spoiling the look of something, or the condition of being damaged, disfigured, or spoiled 2 **CHANGE IN SHAPE** a change in the shape of something, especially one that suggests damage or disfigurement 3 **UNPLEASANT RESULT OF CHANGE** the harmful or disfiguring result of a change in form 4 **CHANGE IN SHAPE BECAUSE OF STRESS** a change in shape resulting from the application of stress

deformity /di fáwrməti/ (*plural* **-ties**) *n* 1 **DISFIGUREMENT** the condition of being disfigured or badly formed ○ *the deformity of the pine trees at such a high altitude in the mountains* 2 **STRUCTURAL CHANGE FROM NORMAL** a permanent change from normal body structure 3 **SOMETHING WITH SHAPE FAR FROM NORMAL** something that has a shape not normal for its kind or nature

ϟ **defrag** /dée frag/ (**-frags, -fragging, -fragged**) *vt* to defragment something (*informal*)

ϟ **defragment** /dée frag mént/ *vt* to reorganize the storage space on a hard disk by consolidating similar files

defraud /de fráwd/ *vt* to deprive somebody of money or property by dishonest means [14C. Directly or via Old French < Latin *defraudare* < *fraudare* 'to cheat'.] —**defraudation** /dée fraw dáysh'n/ *n* —**defrauder** *n* —**defraudment** *n*

defray /di fráy/ *vt* to provide money to pay for part or all of the cost of something ○ *The company will defray the cost of your training course.* [Mid-16C. < French *défrayer* < *frais* 'expenses'.] —**defrayable** *adj* —**defrayal** *n* —**defrayer** *n* —**defrayment** *n*

defrock /dée frók/ *vt* to take away the status, job, and authority of a priest or other member of the clergy, especially as a punishment for wrongdoing [Early 17C. < French *défroquer* < *froc* 'frock'.]

defrost /di fróst, dee-/ *vti* 1 to remove frost or ice from something, or become free of frost or ice 2 to thaw frozen food, or become thawed

deft /deft/ *adj* 1 moving or acting in a quick, smooth, and skilful way 2 showing good sense and skill in achieving or acquiring things [13C. Variant of DAFT.] —**deftly** *adv* —**deftness** *n*

defunct /di fúngkt/ *adj* 1 no longer operative, valid, or functional 2 no longer alive or in existence [Mid-16C. < Latin *defunctus*, past participle of *defungi* 'finish' < *fungi* 'perform'.] —**defunctness** *n*

SYNONYMS See ***dead***.

defuse /dee-/ (**-fuses, -fusing, -fused**) *vt* 1 to make a bomb or mine harmless by removing its detonating device 2 to make a situation less tense, dangerous, or uncomfortable ○ *The diplomats tried to defuse the escalating crisis.*

defy /di fí/ (**-fies, -fying, -fied**) *vt* 1 **OPENLY RESIST** to challenge openly somebody's or something's authority or power by refusing to obey a command or regulation ○ *He defied all orders from head office.* 2 **CHALLENGE** to challenge or dare somebody to do something ○ *I defy you to find a better deal than this.* 3 **NOT BE EXPLAINED BY** to fail to be explained or clarified by something such as logic or analysis ○ *a decision that defies all logic* [14C. Via French *défier* < assumed Vulgar Latin *disfidare* 'renounce your faith' < Latin *fides* 'trust, belief'.] —**defier** *n*

dégagé /dáy gaa zháy/ *adj* (*formal*) 1 casual and relaxed 2 detached and without emotional involvement [Late 17C. < French, 'disengaged'.]

degas /dee gáss/ (**degases** *or* **degasses, degassing, degassed**) *vt* to remove gas from a liquid or solid or from a vacuum system

Degas /dáy gaa/, **Edgar** (1834–1917) French painter and sculptor

De Gaulle /də gól/, **Charles, General** (1890–1970) French statesman and president of France (1959–69)

degauss /dée gówss/ *vt* to remove or counteract a magnetic field in something, e.g. electrical equipment or a ship's hull —**degausser** *n*

degenderize /dee jéndə rīz/ (**-izes, -izing, -ized**), **degenderise** (**-ises, -ising, -ised**), **degender** /dee jéndər/ *vt* to remove references to people's gender from language or a text in order to make it more neutral or less biased —**degenderization** /dee jéndə rī záysh'n/ *n*

degeneracy /di jénnərəssi/ *n* **1 WORSENING OF CONDITION** the process of becoming physically, morally, or mentally worse **2 WORSENED CONDITION** a condition that is worse than normal or worse than before **3** (*plural* **-cies**) **BAD BEHAVIOUR** immoral, depraved, or corrupt behaviour **4 STATE OF EQUAL ENERGY** the condition of two or more quantum states that have the same energy

degenerate /di jénnə rayt/ *vi* (**-ates, -ating, -ated**) **1 BECOME WORSE** to develop into a condition that is worse than before, worse than normal, or not as good as it should be **2 BECOME USELESS** to become less specialized or lose the ability to function (*refers to organisms or body parts*) ■ *adj* **1 IN WORSENED CONDITION** in a condition that is worse than normal or worse than before **2 INFERIOR** in a condition that is worse than an original or previous state **3 EQUAL IN ENERGY** describes a system in which different quantum states have equal energy **4 WITH REDUCED OR ABSENT PART** describes a part, or an organism with a part, that has become reduced in size or function or lost completely during the history of its species or compared to related species ■ *n* **SOMEBODY IMMORAL** an immoral or corrupt person [15C. < Latin *degenerare* 'depart from your own kind' < *genus* 'race, kind'.] —**degenerately** *adv* —**degenerateness** *n*

degenerate matter *n* highly compressed matter consisting of elementary particles that are not combined to form atoms, occurring in the final stage of a star's development into a white dwarf

degeneration /di jénnə ráysh'n/ *n* **1 WORSENING OF CONDITION** the process of becoming physically, morally, or mentally worse **2 DETERIORATION** a disease process that causes a gradual deterioration in the structure of a body part with a consequent loss of the ability to function **3 BIOLOGICAL LOSS OVER GENERATIONS** the gradual loss of the biological function, specialization, or adaptation of a part of the body over many generations

degenerative /di jénnərətiv/ *adj* causing or showing a gradual deterioration in the structure of a body part with a consequent loss of the part's ability to function

degenerative joint disease *n* MED = **osteoarthritis**

deglamorize /dee glámmə rīz/ (**-izes, -izing, -ized**), **deglamorise** (**-ises, -ising, -ised**) *vt* to make something less attractive or exciting than it sometimes appears — **deglamorization** /dee glámmə rī záysh'n/ *n*

deglutinate /dee glóoti nayt/ (**-nates, -nating, -nated**) *vt* to remove the gluten from cereal or flour [Late 19C. < DE- + Latin *glutin-*, stem of *gluten* 'glue'.] —**deglutination** /dee glóoti náysh'n/ *n*

deglutition /deè gloo tísh'n/ *n* the act or process of swallowing (*technical*) [Mid-17C. < French *déglutition* < Latin *degluttire* 'swallow down' < *gluttire* (see GLUTTON).]

degradable /di gráydəb'l/ *adj* **1** able to undergo chemical or biological decomposition **2** able to be degraded in any way —**degradability** /di gráydə bílləti/ *n*

degradation /déggrə dáysh'n/ *n* **1 GREAT HUMILIATION** great humiliation brought about by loss of status, reputation, or self-esteem ○ *suffered the degradation of overwhelming defeat at the polls* **2 HUMILIATING** the humiliating of somebody, causing him or her a loss of status, reputation, or self-esteem ○ *the constant degradation and undermining of other members of staff* **3 BAD LIVING CONDITIONS** a way of life without dignity, health, or social comforts **4 LOSS OF QUALITY** a decline in something's quality or performance ○ *a rapid degradation in the engine's horsepower* **5 PROCESS OF DECLINE** the process by which a decline in quality or performance is brought about **6 EROSION** erosion of the Earth's land surface by water, wind, or ice **7 BREAKDOWN OF COMPOUND** the breakdown of a chemical compound into atoms or simpler compounds **8 DECREASE OF ENERGY** the process by which the energy available for doing work is irreversibly decreased

Charles De Gaulle

degrade /di gráyd/ (**-grades, -grading, -graded**) *v* **1** *vt* **TREAT HUMILIATINGLY** to cause somebody a humiliating loss of status, self-esteem, or reputation **2** *vt* **LOWER IN GRADE** to lower somebody in rank, grade, or level **3** *vti* **WORSEN** to become worse, or make something become worse, especially in quality or performance ○ *Using the wrong fuel had significantly degraded the engine's power.* **4** *vti* **ERODE** to erode the land surface or a river bed, or be eroded by the action of wind, ice, or water. ◊ **aggrade 5** *vt* **DESTROY OR DAMAGE** to cause damage or destruction to part of the environment as a result of human activity **6** *vti* **REDUCE AVAILABLE ENERGY IN** to reduce irreversibly the energy available in matter, or be reduced irreversibly [14C. Via French *dégrader* < ecclesiastical Latin *degradare* 'reduce in rank' < Latin *gradus* 'step, stage'.] — **degraded** *adj* —**degradedly** *adv* —**degradedness** *n* — **degrader** *n*

degrading /di gráyding/ *adj* causing somebody to feel shame and humiliation —**degradingly** *adv*

degrease /dee greéss/ (**-greases, -greasing, -greased**) *vt* to remove grease from something such as an engine, especially using chemicals —**degreaser** *n*

degree /di greé/ *n* **1 EXTENT OR AMOUNT** the relative extent, amount, intensity, or level of something, especially when compared with other things ○ *showed a high degree of awareness of the issues* **2 EDUCATIONAL QUALIFICATION** a qualification awarded by a university or college following successful completion of a course of study or period of research, or a similar qualification granted as an honour **3 UNIT OF TEMPERATURE MEASUREMENT** a unit of measurement for temperature on a scale such as Celsius or Fahrenheit **4 UNIT FOR MEASURING ANGLES** a unit of measurement for planar angles, equal to 1/360 of a full revolution **5 UNIT OF LATITUDE OR LONGITUDE** a unit of latitude or longitude, equal to 1/360 of a circle, used to locate and designate places on the Earth ○ *27 degrees north* **6** *US* **CLASSIFICATION OF MURDER** a level of classification of murder according to its seriousness, in which first-degree murder is the most serious **7 SEVERITY OF BURNS ON BODY** a level of classification of the seriousness of the damage to tissue caused by a burn, in which third-degree burns are the most serious **8 UNIT OF MEASUREMENT ON SCALE** a unit on any of various measurement scales, e.g. that used to measure specific gravity or that used to specify the alcohol content of drinks **9 STATE OF ADJECTIVE OR ADVERB** a state of an adjective or adverb, either the positive, the comparative, or the superlative **10 CLOSENESS OF RELATIONSHIP** an indication of the genealogical closeness of a relationship within a family ○ *second-degree relatives* **11 STATUS** rank, position, or status in society (*formal or literary*) ○ *of high degree* **12 POSITION OF NOTE ON MUSICAL SCALE** the relative position of a note on a musical scale **13 HIGHEST EXPONENT OF DERIVATIVE** in a differential equation, the exponent of the derivative of highest order, e.g. $4x^2y^2$ is of degree four **14 SUM OF POLYNOMIAL VARIABLE EXPONENTS** in a polynomial equation, the sum of the exponents of the variables in the term with the highest power, e.g. $4x^3y^2 + 3y^2 + 2$ is of degree five [13C. Via French *degré* < assumed Vulgar Latin *degradus* 'step down' < Latin *gradus* 'step, stage'.]

degree day *n* the day on which students receive their degrees at a university award ceremony

degree-day *n* a unit of measurement for heating systems, used to estimate fuel requirements and representing one degree of variation from the mean daily temperature out of doors

degree of freedom *n* **1 INDEPENDENT VARIABLE** an independent variable in a statistical measure or frequency distribution **2 VARIABLE SPECIFYING ENERGY** an independent variable needed to specify the energy state of an atom, molecule, or system **3 VARIABLE SPECIFYING STATE** any of the independent variables such as pressure that are needed to specify the state of a system according to the phase rule

degression /di grésh'n/ *n* **1** a gradual decrease or downward movement (*formal*) **2** a gradual lowering of the tax rate on sums below a specified amount [15C. < medieval Latin, < Latin *degress-*, past participle of *degredi* 'step down' < *gradus* 'step, stage'.] —**degressive** *adj*

De Havilland /də hávvilənd/, **Sir Geoffrey** (1882–1965) British aviation pioneer and aircraft designer

De Havilland, Olivia (*b*. 1916) British-born US film actor

dehisce /di híss/ (**-hisces, -hiscing, -hisced**) *vi* **1** to burst open, releasing seeds, pollen, or spores (*refers to dry fruits, seed pods, anthers, or spore-bearing structures*) **2** to open along the joined edges (*technical; refers to a wound that has been stitched*) [Mid-17C. < Latin *dehiscere* 'open up' < *hiscere* 'begin opening' < *hiare* 'gape'.] —**dehiscence** *n* —**dehiscent** *adj*

dehorn /dee háwrn/ *vt* to remove or prevent the growth of an animal's horns by surgery or cauterization — **dehorner** *n*

Dehra Dūn /dáirə dóon/ city in N India. Population: 270,159 (1991).

dehumanize /dee hyóomə nīz/ (**-izes, -izing, -ized**), **dehumanise** (**-ises, -ising, -ised**) *vt* **1** to take away somebody's individuality, the creative and interesting aspects of his or her personality, or his or her compassion and sensitivity towards others **2** to take away the qualities or features of something that make it able to meet human needs and desires or enhance people's lives ○ *The very design of these tower blocks dehumanizes them.* —**dehumanization** /dee hyóomə nī záysh'n/ *n* — **dehumanized** *adj* —**dehumanizing** *adj*

dehumidifier /deè hyoo míddi fīr/ *n* an electrical appliance for removing excess humidity from the air in a room or building —**dehumidify** *vt*

dehydrate /dee hī drayt, deè hī dráyt, deè hī drayt/ (**-drates, -drating, -drated**) *v* **1** *vt* **PRESERVE FOOD BY DRYING** to remove moisture from food as a way of preserving it **2** *vti* **LOSE BODY FLUIDS** to remove or lose water or fluids from the body or its tissues **3** *vti* **TAKE AWAY WATER FROM** to deprive a chemical compound of water or of the proportion of hydrogen and oxygen atoms that are present in water —**dehydrated** *adj*

dehydration /deè hī dráysh'n/ *n* **1 REMOVAL OF MOISTURE FROM FOOD** the removal of moisture from food as a way of preserving it **2 LOSS OF BODY FLUID** a dangerous lack of water in the body resulting from inadequate intake of fluids or excessive loss through sweating, vomiting, or diarrhoea **3 LOSS OF WATER BY CHEMICAL COMPOUND** the process by which a chemical compound loses water molecules or the proportion of hydrogen and oxygen atoms that would be present in water

dehydrator /dee hī draytər, deè hī dráytər, deè hī draytər/ *n* an electrical appliance for drying food, consisting of a stack of interlocking trays through which heated air is circulated

dehydrochlorinase /dee hī drō kláwri nayz, -nayss/ *n* an enzyme that removes hydrogen and chlorine from compounds

dehydrochlorinate /dee hīdrō kláwri nayt/ (**-ates, -ating, -ated**) *vt* to chemically remove hydrogen and chlorine or hydrogen chloride from a substance —**dehydrochlorination** /dee hīdrō kláwri náysh'n/ *n*

dehydrogenase /deè hī drójjə nayz, -nayss, dee hīdrəjə-/ *n* an enzyme that speeds up the transfer of hydrogen between compounds

dehydrogenate /deè hī drójjə nayt, dee hīdrəjə nayt/ (**-ates, -ating, -ated**) *vt* to remove hydrogen from a compound —**dehydrogenation** /deè hī drójjə náysh'n, dee hīdrəjə-/ *n*

dehydrogenize /deè hī drójjə nīz, dee hīdrəjə nīz/ (**-izes, -izing, -ized**), **dehydrogenise** *vt* = **dehydrogenate** — **dehydrogenization** /deè hī drójjə nī záysh'n, dee hīdrəjə nī-/ *n*

dehypnotize /dee hípnə tīz/ (**dehypnotizes, dehypnotizing, dehypnotized**), **dehypnotise** (**-tises, -tising, -tised**) *vt* to bring somebody out of a hypnotic state —**dehypnosis** /deè hip nóssiss/ *n* —**dehypnotization** /dee hípnə tī záysh'n/ *n*

de-icer *n* a device or chemical substance that removes ice or prevents it forming, e.g. on the windscreen of a motor vehicle or the wings of an aircraft —**de-ice** *vt*

deicide /deè i sīd, dáy-/ *n* **1** the act of killing a god or goddess **2** a killer of a god or goddess [Early 17C. Partly < ecclesiastical Latin *deicida* 'god-killer', partly < Latin *deus* 'god' + -CIDE.] —**deicidal** /dáy i sīd'l, deè i-/ *adj*

deictic /dīktik/ *adj* depending for its full meaning on the context in which it is used, e.g. 'you', 'this', 'now', and 'there' [Early 19C. < Greek *deiktikos* < *deiknunai* 'to show'.] —**deictically** *adv*

deid /deed/ *adj Scotland* dead [15C. Variant.]

deify /dée i fī, dáy-/ (**-fies, -fying, -fied**) *vt* **1** to make somebody into a god **2** to honour or adore somebody or something as if he, she, or it were divine [14C. Via French *déifier* < Latin *deus* 'god'.] —**deifier** *n* —**deification** /dée ifi káysh'n, dáy ifi káysh'n/ *n*

Deighton /dáyt'n/, **Len** (*b.* 1929) British writer. Full name **Leonard Cyril Deighton**

deign /dayn/ *vti* to do something in a way that shows that you consider it a great favour and almost beneath your dignity to do it ○ *I don't suppose he'll deign to accept our invitation.* [13C. Via Old French *deignier* < Latin *dignare* 'deem worthy' < *dignus* 'worthy'.]

Dei gratia /dáy i graáti ə, dée ī gráyshə/ *adv* by the grace of God [< Latin]

deil /deel/ *n Scotland* a devil [15C. Variant.]

Deimos /dáy moss/ *n* the outermost of the two natural satellites of Mars. ◊ **Phobos**

deindustrialise *vti* = **deindustrialize**

deindustrialization /dée in dústri ə lī záysh'n/, **deindustrialisation** *n* the removal or reduction of industrial activity in a country or region, especially heavy industry or manufacturing industry

deindustrialize /dée in dústri ə līz/ (**deindustrializes, deindustrializing, deindustrialized**), **deindustrialise** (**deindustrialises, deindustrialising, deindustrialised**) *vti* to take away or lose industries, especially the heavy industries and manufacturing industries, that a particular country or region has

deinstitutionalize /dée insti tyoósh'nə līz/ (**-izes, -izing, -ized**), **deinstitutionalise** (**-ises, -ising, -ised**) *vt* to discharge somebody from institutional care, often in order to treat him or her in the community where he or she lives —**deinstitutionalization** /dée insti tyoósh'nə lī záysh'n/ *n*

deionize /dee ī ə nīz/ (**deionizes, deionizing, deionized**), **deionise** (**-ises, -ising, -ised**) *v* to remove ions from a solution —**deionization** /dee ī ə nī záysh'n/ *n* —**deionizer** *n*

deism /dée izəm, dáy-/ *n* a belief in God based on reason rather than revelation, and involving the view that God has set the universe in motion but does not interfere with how it runs [Late 17C. < Latin *deus* 'god'.] —**deist** *n* —**deistic** /dee ístik, day-/ *adj* —**deistically** *adv*

deity /dée i ti, dáy-/ (*plural* **-ties**) *n* **1 GOD OR GODDESS** a god, goddess, or other divine being **2 SOMEBODY OR SOMETHING LIKE GOD** somebody or something that is treated like a god **3 DIVINE STATE** the condition or status of a god or goddess [14C. Via French *déité* < ecclesiastical Latin *deitas* 'divine nature' < Latin *deus* 'god'.]

Deity /dée i ti, dáy-/ *n* God in monotheistic belief

deixis /dīksiss/ *n* the use of a word such as 'he', 'that', 'now', or 'here', whose full meaning depends on the context in which it is used [Mid-20C. < Greek, 'reference' < *deiknunai* 'to show'.]

déjà vu /dáy zhaa voó/ *n* **1** a feeling of having experienced something before although in fact it is the first time that it has been experienced **2** a state of boring familiarity [Early 20C. < French, 'already seen'.]

USAGE Extension of meaning: ***déjà vu*** once referred exclusively to the illusion of having experienced something before: *Entering the house for the first time, she had an eerie sense of déjà vu.* Recently, however, it has come to encompass as well the reality of repetitiveness in events or actions: *As they began to discuss which route was best, he had a distinct sense of déjà vu.*

dejected /di jéktid/ *adj* feeling or showing sadness and lack of hope, especially because of disappointment [Late 16C. < *deject* < Latin *deject-*, past participle of *dejicere* 'throw down' < *jacere* 'throw'.] —**dejectedly** *adv* —**dejectedness** *n*

dejection /di jéksh'n/ *n* **1 GREAT UNHAPPINESS** unhappiness and lack of hope, especially caused by disappointment **2 DEFECATION** the act of passing solid waste matter out of the anus (*technical*) **3 EXCREMENT** solid waste matter that is passed out through the anus (*technical*)

de jure /dee joóri, day yoó ray/ *adv, adj* by right according to the law [Mid-16C. < Latin, 'from the law'.]

deka- *prefix* = **deca-**

Dekker /dékər/, **Thomas** (1572?–1632) English dramatist and pamphleteer

dekko /dékō/ (*plural* **-kos**) *n* a quick look or glance (*informal*) ○ *Come and have a dekko at this!* [Late 19C. < Hindi *dekho* 'look!'.]

de Klerk /də klúrk/, **F. W.** (*b.* 1936) South African statesman and president of South Africa (1989–94). Full name **Frederick Willem de Klerk**

de Kooning /də kóoning/, **Willem** (1904–97) Dutch-born US artist

del *abbr* delete

del. *abbr* **1** delegate **2** delegation **3** delete

Del. *abbr* Delaware[2]

Delacroix /déllə krwaa/, **Eugène** (1798–1863) French painter and lithographer

Delagoa Bay /déllə gō ə-/ bay on the S Mozambique coast

delaine /di láyn/ *n* a fine woollen or woollen and cotton fabric resembling muslin [Mid-19C. Shortening of MOUSSELINE DE LAINE.]

de la Mare /də la máir/, **Walter** (1873–1956) British poet, anthologist, and novelist

delaminate /dee lámmi nayt/ (**delaminates, delaminating, delaminated**) *vti* to separate or peel off in thin layers, or cause something to do this —**delamination** /dee lámmi náysh'n/ *n*

de la Roche /déllə rósh/, **Mazo** (1885–1961) Canadian writer

Delaroche /déllə rósh/, **Paul** (1797–1856) French painter

Delaunay /də láw nay/, **Robert** (1885–1941) French painter

Delaunay, Sonia (1885–1980) Russian-born French painter and designer. Born **Sonia Terk**

Delaware[1] /déllə wair/ (*plural* **-ware** *or* **-wares**) *n* a member of a group of Native North American peoples who once lived between the Delaware and Hudson rivers, and now live mostly in Oklahoma, Wisconsin, Kansas, Ontario, and in Canada [Early 18C. After the *Delaware* River, E United States.] —**Delawarean** /déllə wáiri ən/ *n, adj*

Delaware[2] /déllə wair/ state of the E United States. Capital: Dover. Population: 731,581 (1997). Area: 6,206 sq. km/2,396 sq. mi.

De La Warr /déllə waár/, **Thomas West, 3rd Baron** (1577–1618) English-born colonial governor. Known as **Lord Delaware**

delay /di láy/ *v* **1** *vti* **PUT OFF UNTIL LATER** to postpone something or wait until later before doing something **2** *vt* **MAKE LATE** to make somebody or something late or slow ○ *I was delayed at the office.* **3** *vi* **PROCRASTINATE** to hesitate or fail to do something quickly enough ○ *Don't delay, book today.* ■ *n* **1 LATENESS** a situation in which something does not happen or start at the time it was meant to ○ *All services are subject to delay or cancellation.* **2 EXTENT OF LATENESS** the extent of the period of time by which somebody or something is made late or slowed down ○ *long delays on the M1* **3 PROCRASTINATION** procrastination or failure to do something quickly enough ○ *This must be done without delay.* [13C. < Anglo-Norman *delaier* 'leave off' < *laier* 'leave'.] —**delayer** *n*

delay action *n* = **delayed action** *n.* 1

delayed /di láyd/ *adj* **1 MADE LATE** made to happen, start, arrive, or leave later than intended or later than usual **2 LATER THAN USUAL** happening at some time after the usual or expected time ○ *delayed language development* **3 HAPPENING LATER** happening after a period of time ○ *causing delayed damage to the kidneys*

delayed action *n* **1** the activation of a mechanism a short time after it has been set (*hyphenated before nouns*) **2** a mechanism used to produce delayed action

delayering /dee láy ə ring/ *n* the process of simplifying the structure of an organization to make it more efficient —**delayer** *vti*

delaying action, delaying operation *n* a manoeuvre used to gain time or allow a retreat when there are not enough resources to confront an opponent directly

delaying tactic *n* a deliberate attempt to delay something in order to gain time or some other advantage

delay line *n* a device designed to cause a delay in transmitting an electronic signal

Delbrück /déll broók/, **Max** (1906–81) German-born US biologist

dele /deéli/ *n* a mark used in the margin of printed material to show that something is to be deleted (*informal*) ■ *vt* (**-les, -leing, -led**) to mark a passage of printed material for deletion (*informal*) [Early 18C. < Latin, 'delete!'.]

delectable /di léktəb'l/ *adj* **1 DELICIOUS** with a delicious taste **2 DELIGHTFUL** absolutely delightful, very pleasing, or very attractive ■ *n* **SOMETHING VERY TASTY** an appetizing food or dish [14C. < French *délectable* < Latin *delectare* (see DELIGHT).] —**delectability** /di léktə bílləti/ *n* —**delectableness** *n* —**delectably** *adv*

delectation /dée lek táysh'n/ *n* pleasure or enjoyment (*formal*) [14C. < Old French, < Latin *delectare* (see DELIGHT).]

delegate *n* /délligət, délli gayt/ **1 REPRESENTATIVE OR DEPUTY** somebody chosen to represent or given the authority to act on behalf of another person, group, or organization, e.g. at a meeting or conference **2 MEMBER OF HOUSE OF DELEGATES** a member of a US House of Delegates, the lower house of the legislature in Maryland, Virginia, or West Virginia **3 REPRESENTATIVE OF US TERRITORY** a representative of a territory in the US House of Representatives, who may speak on issues but not vote ■ *v* /délli gayt/ (**-gates, -gating, -gated**) **1** *vti* **GIVE TASK TO** to give a task to somebody else with responsibility to act on your behalf **2** *vti* **GIVE POWER OR AUTHORITY TO** to give somebody the power to act, make decisions, or allocate resources on your behalf ○ *an executive who was unafraid to delegate* **3** *vt US* **SEND DEBTOR TO CREDITOR** to appoint one of your debtors to represent you to your creditor [15C. < Latin *delegare* 'send away' < *legare* 'send'.] —**delegable** *adj* —**delegator** *n*

delegation /déllə gáysh'n/ *n* **1 GROUP REPRESENTING OTHERS** a group of people chosen to represent or act on behalf of others **2 GIVING OF RESPONSIBILITY TO SOMEBODY ELSE** the giving of some power, responsibility, or work to somebody else **3 BEING GIVEN TO SOMEBODY ELSE** the condition of being given to somebody else as a duty or responsibility **4 STATE REPRESENTATIVES** all the members of the US Congress who represent one state

delegitimize /deélə jíttə mīz/ (**-mizes, -mizing, -mized**), **delegitimise** (**-mises, -mising, -mised**) *vt* to take away the legitimacy or legal status of somebody or something —**delegitimization** /deélə jíttə mī záysh'n/ *n*

delete /di leét/ *vt* (**-letes, -leting, -leted**) to remove or score out something that is printed or written, or erase something from a computer file or disk ■ *n* = **delete key** ○ *Click on the icon for that file and then hit delete.* [15C. < Latin *delere* 'blot out, efface'.]

delete key *n* a computer key that moves the cursor to erase characters, or removes highlighted text

deleterious /délli teéri əss/ *adj* with a harmful or damaging effect on somebody or something [Mid-17C. Via medieval Latin < Greek *dēlētērios* 'noxious'.] —**deleteriously** *adv* —**deleteriousness** *n*

deletion /di leésh'n/ *n* **1 REMOVING SOMETHING OR SCORING SOMETHING OUT** the action or process of removing or erasing something or scoring something out **2 SOMETHING REMOVED OR SCORED OUT** something removed or scored out from a text or erased from a computer file **3 ABSENCE OF GENETIC MATERIAL** the loss or absence of part of a chromosome, ranging from a pair of chemicals (**base pair**) to a whole chromosomal arm

deleverage /dee leévərij/ (**-ages, -aging, -aged**) *vti* to reduce the amount of debt that a company owes, usually by laying off workers, selling off unprofitable divisions, and other cost-cutting measures

delft /delft/, **Delft, delftware** /délft wair/, **Delftware** *n* earthenware with an opaque white glaze, usually with blue decoration [Late 17C. After DELFT.]

Delft /delft/ city in W Netherlands. Population: 96,370 (2000).

delftware, Delftware *n* = **delft**

Delgado, Cape /del gaádō/ cape in NE Mozambique

Delhi /délli/ city in N India and capital of the Union Territory of Delhi. Population: 7,206,704 (1991). ◊ **New Delhi**

deli /délli/ (*plural* **-is**) *n* a delicatessen (*informal*) [Mid-20C. Shortening.]

Delian League /deéli ən leég/ *n* an alliance of Greek states set up in 477 BC to oppose Persia

deliberate *adj* /di líbbərət/ **1 INTENTIONAL** carefully thought out and done intentionally **2 CAREFUL** slow, careful, and methodical ■ *vti* /di líbbə rayt/ (**-ates, -ating, -ated**) **THINK** to consider something carefully and in detail [15C. < Latin *deliberare* 'weigh carefully' < *librare* 'weigh' < *libra* 'balance'.] —**deliberateness** *n* —**deliberator** *n*

deliberately /di líbbərətli/ *adv* **1** in a way that is intentional and thought out in advance ○ *The police believe that the fire was started deliberately.* **2** with care and thought ○ *He spoke slowly and deliberately.*

deliberation /di líbbə ráysh'n/ *n* (*formal*) **1 CAREFUL THOUGHT** long careful consideration of something **2 DISCUSSION** formal or official discussion or debate ○ *The planning committee's deliberations seemed to last all night.* **3 CARE** slowness and methodical carefulness

deliberative /di líbbərətiv/ *adj* (*formal*) **1** involved in or organized for careful discussion and debate **2** relating to or resulting from discussion and debate —**deliberatively** *adv* —**deliberativeness** *n*

Delibes /də leéb/, **Léo** (1836–91) French composer

delicacy /déllikəssi/ (*plural* **-cies**) *n* **1 SOMETHING NICE TO EAT** a delicious, rare, or highly prized item of food **2 SENSITIVITY** sensitivity to the feelings of others **3 NEED FOR TACT** the quality of requiring great tact or sensitivity ○ *a matter of extreme delicacy* **4 GREAT SENSITIVITY IN FEELINGS** extreme and perhaps unnecessary fussiness or squeamishness in the way somebody responds to something offensive or embarrassing ○ *his delicacy on matters of a medical nature* **5 SUBTLETY AND REFINEMENT** pleasing subtlety in something, e.g. taste, smell, or colour ○ *the delicacy of her perfume* **6 FINENESS** fineness and subtlety of feeling, observation, or execution ○ *the delicacy of the brushwork in his later paintings* **7 FRAGILITY** the quality of being easily damaged or broken **8 LACK OF PHYSICAL STRENGTH** lack of physical strength or health **9 SENSITIVITY OF RESPONSE IN EQUIPMENT** sensitivity in the way something, e.g. scientific equipment or a musical instrument, responds to use

delicate /déllikət/ *adj* **1 FRAGILE** easily damaged or broken **2 FRAIL** without much resistance to illness or injury ○ *in delicate health* **3 SUBTLE** mild, gentle, pale, or soft, and pleasant to the senses ○ *a delicate shade of blue.* **4 FINE** finely made and with small parts or detail in its design **5 SKILFUL** showing somebody's skill or craft, especially in producing finely detailed intricate work or gentle or adroit movements ○ *a filigree of delicate, shimmering brushstrokes* **6 NEEDING TACT** needing to be dealt with using tact and sensitivity ○ *The negotiations were at a delicate stage.* **7 REFINED** having or showing a refined and sensitive taste **8 EASILY OFFENDED** easily shocked or upset by offensive or embarrassing things **9 ACCURATE** describes instrumentation that is very precise and able to give exact readings **10 NOT WELL** uncomfortable as the result of over-indulgence (*humorous*) ○ *I'm feeling a bit delicate this morning.* ■ **delicates** *npl* **CLOTHES NEEDING SPECIAL WASHING AND DRYING** clothes that need careful washing and drying, e.g. using a special washing machine programme [14C. Directly or via French *délicat* < Latin *delicatus*, related to *delicere* (see DELIGHT).] —**delicateness** *n*

SYNONYMS See ***fragile***.

delicately /déllikətli/ *adv* **1 FINELY** in a way that shows skill in producing fine detail **2 SUBTLY** in a pleasingly mild and subtle way ○ *delicately flavoured* **3 GENTLY AND CAREFULLY** gently and carefully, with no rough or sudden movements **4 WITH TACT** tactfully and sensitively ○ *a matter that must be handled very delicately* **5 PRECARIOUSLY** in a way that seems precarious or sensitive to even a slight change or disturbance ○ *delicately balanced on its edge*

delicatessen /déllikə téss'n/ *n* **1** a shop specializing in imported or unusual foods and ingredients **2** prepared food sold in a delicatessen [Late 19C. Via German and French < Italian *delicatezza* 'delicacy' < Latin *delicatus* (see DELICATE).]

delicious /di líshəss/ *adj* **1** with an appealing or enjoyable taste or smell **2** highly amusing, pleasing, or enjoyable [13C. < Old French, < Latin *delicia* 'pleasure' < *delicere* (see DELIGHT).] —**deliciousness** *n*

deliciously /di líshəssli/ *adv* **1 TASTILY** in a way that appeals to the sense of taste or smell ○ *a deliciously sweet and crunchy apple* **2 APPETIZINGLY** in an appetizing way ○ *king prawns sizzling away deliciously on the barbecue* **3 VERY SATISFYINGLY** to a great and very satisfying degree ○ *a deliciously ironic twist of fate* **4 ENJOYABLY** in an enjoyable and pleasant way

delict /di líkt/ *n* in Scottish civil law, a wrong or injury done to somebody [Early 16C. < Latin *delictum*, neuter past participle of *delinquere* 'offend' (see DELINQUENT).]

delight /di lít/ *n* **1 JOY** great enjoyment and pleasure ○ *To my delight, he accepted.* **2 SOMEBODY OR SOMETHING GIVING JOY** somebody or something that brings somebody great joy and pleasure ○ *That's one of the delights of having children.* ■ *v* **1** *vti* **GIVE JOY TO** to give somebody great joy and pleasure **2** *vi* **GAIN ENJOYMENT FROM** to gain great enjoyment or pleasure from something ○ *She delighted in outwitting her competitors.* [13C. < Old French *delit* < Latin *delectare* 'keep enticing' < *delicere* 'allure' < *lacere* 'entice'.] —**delighted** *adj* —**delightedly** *adv* —**delightedness** *n* —**delighter** *n*

delightful /di lítf'l/ *adj* giving great pleasure and joy, especially by being pleasant, good to look at, or amusing —**delightfulness** *n*

DeLillo /də leélō/, **Don** (*b.* 1936) US novelist

delimit /di límmit/, **delimitate** /di límmi tayt/ (**-tates, -tating, -tated**) *vt* to set out or establish the limits or boundaries of something [Mid-19C. Via French *délimiter* < Latin *delimitare* < *limit-* (see LIMIT).] —**delimitation** /di límmi táysh'n/ *n* —**delimitative** *adj*

⚡**delimiter** /di límmitər/ *n* a character or space marking the beginning or end of a data element

delineate /di línni ayt/ (**-ates, -ating, -ated**) *vt* **1 DESCRIBE** to describe or explain something in detail (*formal*) **2 DRAW** to sketch or draw something in outline **3 PORTRAY VISUALLY** to represent something visually using something such as a chart or graph **4 DEMARCATE** to indicate the physical boundaries of something [Mid-16C. < Latin *delineare* 'sketch out' < *linea* (see LINE[1]).] —**delineable** *adj* —**delineation** /di línni áysh'n/ *n* —**delineative** *adj*

delineator /di línni aytər/ *n* **1** an adjustable pattern that a tailor uses to cut garments of different sizes **2** somebody or something that outlines or describes something

delinquency /di língkwənssi/ *n* **1 UNLAWFUL BEHAVIOUR** antisocial or illegal behaviour or acts, especially by young people **2 NEGLECT OF OBLIGATION** failure to fulfil an obligation, commitment, or pledge (*formal*) **3** *US* **SOMETHING OVERDUE** something that is overdue, e.g. a debt or tax (*formal*)

delinquent /di língkwənt/ *n* **LAWBREAKER, ESPECIALLY YOUNG OFFENDER** somebody, especially a young person, who has acted antisocially or broken the law ■ *adj* **1 ANTISOCIAL OR UNLAWFUL** relating to antisocial behaviour or lawbreaking **2 IGNORING DUTY** neglecting a duty, commitment, or responsibility (*formal*) **3 UNPAID** with unpaid sums of money due [15C. < Latin *delinquere* 'offend' < *linquere* 'leave'.] —**delinquently** *adv*

deliquesce /délli kwéss/ (**-quesces, -quescing, -quesced**) *vi* **1 ABSORB MOISTURE** to dissolve gradually by absorbing moisture from the air **2 FORM BRANCHES** to form many branches without a main stem **3 BECOME LIQUID** to become soft or liquid after the release of spores [Mid-18C. < Latin *deliquescere* 'start melting away' < *liquere* 'be liquid'.] —**deliquescence** *n* —**deliquescent** *adj*

delirious /di lírri əss/ *adj* **1** irrational as a temporary result of a physical condition, e.g. fever, poisoning, or brain injury. ◊ **delirium 2** extremely excited or emotional ○ *delirious with joy* [Late 16C. < DELIRIUM.] —**deliriousness** *n*

deliriously /di lírri əssli/ *adv* **1** as a result of being delirious, e.g. due to poisoning, fever, or brain injury ○ *muttering and shouting out deliriously* **2** in an almost uncontrollably excited or emotional way ○ *deliriously happy at passing her driving test*

delirium /di lírri əm/ (*plural* **-ums** *or* **-a** /-ri ə/) *n* **1** a state marked by extreme restlessness, confusion, and sometimes hallucinations, caused by fever, poisoning, or brain injury **2** a condition of extreme excitement or emotion [Mid-16C. < Latin, < *delirare* 'be deranged', literally 'be out of your track' < *lira* 'ridge between furrows'.]

delirium tremens /di lírri əm trémmenz, -treé menz/ *n* agitation, tremors, and hallucinations caused by alcohol dependence and withdrawal [< Latin, 'trembling delirium']

delish /di lísh/ *adj* very delicious (*slang*) [Early 20C. Shortening.]

delist /dee líst/ *vt* **1** to remove somebody or something from an official list **2** *US* to remove a security from a listing on a stock exchange

Delius /deéli əss/, **Frederick** (1862–1934) British composer

deliver /di lívvər/ *v* **1** *vti* **CARRY SOMETHING TO** to take something, e.g. mail, goods that have been bought, or a message, to a particular person or address **2** *vt* **ASSIST DURING BIRTH** to give medical help when a baby or other offspring is being born **3** *vt* **PRODUCE BABY** to give birth to a baby (*often passive*) **4** *vt* **MAKE SPEECH** to make a speech or give a talk to an audience **5** *vt* **ANNOUNCE** to announce something formally, e.g. an opinion, decision, or judgment ○ *The jury delivered its verdict.* **6** *vt* **THROW BALL OR PUNCH** to toss or throw a ball or aim a punch at somebody or something **7** *vti* **DO AS PROMISED** to do what has been promised ○ *He has yet to deliver anything that was promised in his speeches.* **8** *vt US* **ACHIEVE SUPPORT FOR** to organize and produce the support of a place or people for somebody (*informal*) **9** *vt* **PRODUCE** to provide or produce something ○ *Note the total dosage of antibiotics delivered.* **10** *vt* **RELEASE** to free or save somebody from captivity or hardship (*literary*) **11** *vt* **GIVE SOMEBODY** to hand somebody or something over to somebody else ○ *You have 48 hours to deliver the payment.* [13C. Via Old French *délivrer* < Latin *deliberare* 'free completely' < *liberare* (see LIBERATE).] —**deliverability** /di lívvərə bílləti/ *n* —**deliverer** *n*

deliverable /di lívvərəb'l/ *adj* able to be delivered as promised ■ *n* something that has been promised to a customer or client, especially work that forms part of a larger project or a piece of software (*usually plural*)

deliverance /di lívvərənss/ *n* **1** rescue from captivity, hardship, or domination by evil (*formal*) ○ *He sought deliverance from his imprisonment.* **2** a formal announcement of a decision, judgment, or opinion

delivery /di lívvəri/ (*plural* **-ies**) *n* **1 TAKING SOMETHING TO** the carrying of something to a particular person or a particular address ○ *We can arrange delivery of any items purchased.* **2 VISIT BY SOMEBODY BRINGING SOMETHING** one of the regular visits made to a person, address, or area by a postal worker or a vendor's vehicle ○ *We only get one delivery a day.* **3 ITEM BROUGHT TO** something brought by a postal worker or a vendor, e.g. the post or goods that have been bought **4 GIVING BIRTH** the process of giving birth to a baby **5 MANNER OF SPEAKING** the action or manner in which somebody speaks to an audience ○ *She needs to work on her vocal delivery.* **6 RESCUE** the rescue or saving of somebody from captivity, hardship, or evil ○ *He prayed for delivery from his oppressors.* **7 WAY OF PUTTING BALL IN MOTION** the action or manner of throwing, tossing, or rolling a ball or aiming a punch **8 ACTION NEEDED TO EFFECT PROPERTY TRANSFER** a formal action needed to accomplish a transfer of property

delivery room *n* a specially equipped room in a hospital where women give birth

dell /del/ *n* a small, usually wooded, valley or hollow (*literary*) [Old English, < Germanic]

Della Robbia /déllə róbbi ə/, **Luca** (1400?–82) Italian sculptor and ceramicist

Delmarva Peninsula /del maárvə-/ peninsula in the US states of Delaware, Maryland, and Virginia. Length: 290 km/180 mi.

delocalize /dee lṓkə līz/ (**-izes, -izing, -ized**), **delocalise** (**-ises, -ising, -ised**) *vt* to remove something from its locality —**delocalization** /dee lṓkə lī záysh'n/ *n*

Delon /də lóN/, **Alain** (*b.* 1935) French actor, producer, director, and screenwriter

Delors /də láwr/, **Jacques** (*b.* 1925) French statesman

Delos /deé loss/ smallest of the Greek Cyclades islands. Area: approximately 3 sq. km/1 sq. mi. —**Delian** *adj, n*

delouse /dee lówss/ (**-louses, -lousing, -loused**) *vt* to give a person or animal treatment to remove lice

Delphi /délfi/ ancient Greek town in central Greece, the site of the Temple of Apollo and the Delphic oracle

Delphic /délfik/ *adj* **1 Delphic, Delphian** relating to Delphi or its temple or oracle **2 Delphic, delphic** obscure and open to more than one interpretation

Delphic oracle *n* the oracle of great authority and notorious ambiguity at Delphi, where it was believed the god Apollo spoke through a priestess

delphinium /del fínni əm/ (*plural* **-ums** *or* **-a** /-ni ə/) *n* a tall ornamental plant. Flowers: blue or white in long spikes. Genus: *Delphinium.* [Early 17C. Via modern Latin < Greek *delphinion* 'larkspur' < *delphis* 'dolphin' (because of the shape of the flower).]

Delphinus /del fínəss/ *n* a small faint constellation of the northern hemisphere. See illustration at **constellation**

delt /delt/ *n US* a deltoid (*informal*) [Shortening]

delta /déltə/ *n* **1 TRIANGULAR LAND AREA AT RIVER MOUTH** a triangular deposit of sand and soil at the mouth of a river or inlet **2 delta, Delta AREA IN RIVER DELTA** an area in or around the delta of a river **3 4TH LETTER OF GREEK ALPHABET** the fourth letter of the Greek alphabet **4 SOMETHING LIKE DELTA** something shaped like a triangle or delta **5 CHANGE IN VARIABLE** (*symbol* Δ) a change in the value of a variable [Pre-12C. Via Latin < Greek, < Phoenician.]

Delta /déltə/ *n* **1 FOURTH BRIGHTEST STAR** the fourth brightest star in a constellation **2 US ROCKET** a rocket used by the United States to launch satellites into orbit above the Earth **3 CODE WORD FOR LETTER 'D'** a code word for the letter 'D', used in international radio communications

Delta Force *n* the US Army 1st Special Forces Operational Detachment, a military and counter-terrorist force similar to the SAS

delta ray *n* a low-energy particle such as an electron, emitted by matter when subjected to ionizing radiation

delta wave, delta rhythm *n* a slow brain wave that is produced by adults in deep sleep

delta wing *n* an aeroplane wing that has a triangular, swept-back shape

deltiology /délti óllәji/ *n* the collection and study of postcards [Mid-20C. < Greek *deltion* 'little writing tablet' < *deltos* 'writing tablet'.] —**deltiologist** *n*

deltoid /dél toyd/ *n* a thick triangular muscle that covers the shoulder joint ■ *adj* triangular in shape (*technical*) [Mid-18C. Directly or via French *deltoïde* < modern Latin *deltoides* 'delta-shaped' < Greek *delta*.]

delude /di lóod/ (**-ludes, -luding, -luded**) *vt* to persuade somebody to believe in something that is untrue or unreal [15C. < Latin *deludere* 'play to your detriment' < *ludere* 'play' (see LUDIC).] —**deludable** *adj* —**deluder** *n* —**deludingly** *adv* —**deluded** *adj*

deluge /déllyooj/ *n* **1 SUDDEN HEAVY DOWNPOUR** a sudden heavy downpour of rain or torrent of water **2 VAST QUANTITY** an overwhelming amount of something ■ *vt* (**-uges, -uging, -uged**) **1 OVERWHELM WITH** to inundate somebody suddenly with a large amount of something **2 OVERWHELM WITH WATER** to flood or soak somebody or something with heavy rain or a sudden torrent of water [15C. < Old French, < Latin *diluere* 'wash away' < *lavare* 'wash'.]

Deluge *n* BIBLE = **Flood**

delusion /di lóozh'n/ *n* **1** a persistent false belief held in the face of strong contradictory evidence, especially as a symptom of psychiatric disorder **2** a false or mistaken belief or idea about something [15C. < Latin *delusion-* < past participle of *deludere* (see DELUDE).] —**delusional** *adj*

USAGE See *allusion*.

delusions of grandeur *npl* gross and false overestimation of personal worth, importance, powerfulness, or attractiveness

delusive /di lóossiv/ *adj* leading to a belief in something untrue or unreal [Early 17C. < Latin *delus-*, past participle of *deludere* (see DELUDE).] —**delusively** *adv* —**delusiveness** *n*

delusory /di lóossәri/ *adj* so deceptive in nature or character as to be likely to mislead or delude somebody [15C. < late Latin *delusorius* < past participle of Latin *deludere* (see DELUDE).]

deluxe /dә lúks/, **de luxe** *adj* of a luxurious standard and surpassing all others in its class [Early 19C. < French *de luxe* 'of luxury'.]

delve /delv/ (**delves, delving, delved**) *v* **1** *vi* **DIG INTO SOMETHING AND SEARCH AROUND** to thrust your hand deeply into something to find a hidden or hard-to-reach item or items **2** *vi* **DIG FOR INFORMATION** to investigate or research something thoroughly to obtain information **3** *vt* **EXCAVATE** to dig something such as a ditch, hole, or burrow (*archaic*) [Old English *delfan* < Germanic] —**delver** *n*

Dem /dem/ *n* a member of the Democratic Party in the United States (*informal*) [Late 19C. Shortening.]

dem. *abbr* demonstrative

Dem. *abbr* **1** Democrat **2** Democratic

demagnetize /dee mágnә tīz/ (**-izes, -izing, -ized**), **demagnetise** (**-netises, -netising, -netised**) *vt* to remove the magnetic properties from something —**demagnetization** /dee mágnә tī záysh'n/ *n* —**demagnetizer** *n*

demagogic /démmә góggik/, **demagogical** /démmә góggik'l/ *adj* making an appeal to people's emotions, instincts, and prejudices in a way that is considered to be politically manipulative and dangerous [Mid-19C. < Greek *dēmagōgikos* < *dēmagōgos* (see DEMAGOGUE).] —**demagogically** *adv*

demagogue /démmә gog/ *n* **1** a political leader who gains power by appealing to people's emotions and prejudices rather than their rationality **2** in ancient times, a popular leader who represented the ordinary people [Mid-17C. < Greek *dēmagōgos* 'leader of the people' < *agōgos* 'leader' < *agein* 'lead'.] —**demagoguery** /démmә goggәri/ *n*

de Man /dә mán/, **Paul** (1919–83) Belgian philosopher and theorist

demand /di maánd/ *n* **1 FORCEFUL REQUEST** a clear and firm request that is difficult to ignore or deny **2 CUSTOMER INTEREST IN ACQUIRING** the level of desire or need that exists for particular goods or services ○ *Demand for that particular model is outstripping supply.* **3 NEED FOR RESOURCES OR ACTION** an urgent requirement for time, facilities, resources, or action **4 LEGALLY ENFORCEABLE REQUEST** a formal request that must be complied with by law ■ *v* **1** *vt* **ASK FORCEFULLY** to request something firmly in a way that is difficult to ignore or deny **2** *vt* **ASK TO KNOW AT ONCE** to ask a question in an extremely forceful way **3** *vti* **CALL FOR RESOURCES** to require something such as time, resources, facilities, or action in order to function or succeed [14C. Via Old French *demander* < Latin *demandare* 'entrust completely' < *mandare* 'entrust, order' (see MANDATE).] —**demandable** *adj* —**demander** *n* ◇ **in demand** wanted or sought by many people ◇ **on demand** promptly, whenever a request is received

demand deposit *n* a bank deposit that can be withdrawn at any time without notice

demand feeding *n* the practice of feeding a baby when it cries to be fed, rather than at set times

demanding /di maánding/ *adj* requiring a lot of time, attention, energy, or resources

demandingly /di maándingli/ *adv* in a highly insistent manner

demand loan *n* FIN = **call loan**

demand note *n* a bill or draft stating that a particular amount of money will be paid when it is asked for

demand-pull, demand-pull inflation *n* inflation caused by demand for goods and services outstripping supply. ◊ **cost-push**

demand-side *adj* relating to an economic policy that emphasizes the importance of demand and consumption

demantoid /di mán toyd/ *n* a transparent green variety of garnet. Use: gems. [Late 19C. < German, 'diamond-shaped' < *Demant* 'diamond'.]

demarcate /dée maar kayt/ (**-cates, -cating, -cated**) *vt* **1** to decide on and fix land boundaries **2** to state in a clear way where something begins and ends [Early 19C. Back-formation < DEMARCATION.] —**demarcator** *n*

demarcation /dée maar káysh'n/ *n* **1 SETTING OF BORDERS** the process of deciding on and fixing land boundaries **2 IDENTIFIABLE SEPARATION OF THINGS** the division of something so that its divided parts are separate and identifiable **3 CLEAR DIVISION OF WORK DUTIES** the division of work duties into clearly identifiable parts to be carried out by different workers [Early 18C. < Spanish *demarcación* 'marking off' < *marcar* 'to mark' < Germanic.]

demarcation dispute *n* **1** a disagreement over where a land boundary lies **2** in industrial relations law, a dispute as to which workers are to perform which tasks, especially when different trade unions are involved

démarche /dáy maarsh/ (*plural* **-marches** /dáy maarsh/) *n* **1 DIPLOMATIC REPRESENTATION** a diplomatic representation, especially a move, manoeuvre, or protest made orally **2 CITIZENS' PROTEST STATEMENT** a statement of protest made by or on behalf of the citizens of a nation to their government or to a controlling authority **3 MOVE OR COUNTERMOVE** a move, step, or countermove [Mid-17C. < French *démarcher* 'take steps' < *marcher* 'march'.]

De Maria /dә ma rée ә/, **Walter** (*b.* 1935) US artist

dematerialize /déemә téeri ә līz/ (**-izes, -izing, -ized**), **dematerialise** (**-ises, -ising, -ised**) *vti* to disappear or cause something to disappear physically or apparently —**dematerialization** /déemә téeri ә lī záysh'n/ *n*

deme /deem/ *n* **1** a township in Attica in ancient Greece **2** a local population of closely related interbreeding species [Mid-19C. < Greek *dēmos* (see DEMOS).]

demean /di méen/ *vt* to reduce somebody to a much lower status in a humiliating way [Early 17C. < DE- 'down' + MEAN² 'inferior in rank'.] —**demeaning** *adj*

demeanor *n* US = **demeanour**

demeanour /di méenәr/ *n* somebody's behaviour, manner, or appearance, especially as it reflects on character

demented /di méntid/ *adj* **1** completely unreasonable or without any sense of consequences (*informal*) **2** affected by the loss of intellectual functions that is associated with dementia [Mid-17C. Past participle of obsolete *dement* 'deprive of reason' < Latin *dementare* < *ment-* 'mind'.] —**dementedly** *adv* —**dementedness** *n*

dementia /di ménshә/ *n* the usually progressive deterioration of intellectual functions such as memory that can occur while other brain functions such as those controlling movement and the senses are retained. ◊ **senile dementia** [Late 18C. < Latin, < *dement-* < *de-* 'away' + *ment-* 'mind'.]

dementia praecox /-prée koks/ *n* schizophrenia (*archaic*) [< Latin, 'premature loss of mind']

demerara /démmә ráirә/, **demerara sugar** *n* sugar with yellowish-brown crystals that feel slightly moist [Mid-19C. < *Demerara*, region of Guyana.]

demerger /dée múrjәr/ *n* a merger between two or more companies that is dissolved, or the separation of one company from a larger company or group —**demerge** *vti*

demerit /dee mérrit/ *n* **1** a negative feature or disadvantage of something, especially when contrasted with its positive features or advantages (*often plural*) **2** *US* a mark against somebody such as a student or cadet for a deficiency or misconduct [14C. Directly or via Old French *desmerite* < Latin *demeritum* < *demereri* 'deserve thoroughly' < *mereri* 'deserve'.] —**demeritorious** /dee mérri táwri әss/ *adj* —**demeritoriously** *adv*

demersal /di múrss'l/ *adj* living or found in the deepest part of a body of water [Late 19C. < Latin *demersus*, past participle of *demergere* 'submerge' < *mergere* 'plunge'.]

demesne /di máyn/ *n* **1 POSSESSION OF OWN LAND** possession and use of your own land, as opposed to ownership of land that is occupied by tenants (*formal*) ◊ **domain** *n.* **5 2 PRIVATE GROUNDS WITH MANSION** the estate attached to a mansion for the private use of the owner (*archaic*) **3 FEUDAL MANORIAL LAND** manorial land that a feudal lord kept for his own private use (*formal*) **4 ESTATE** an extensive landed property (*formal*) **5 REALM OF MONARCH** the realm under the rule of a monarch (*formal*) [14C. Via Old French *demeine* 'belonging to a lord' < Latin *dominicus* < *dominus* 'lord'.]

Demeter /di méetәr/ *n* in Greek mythology, the goddess of corn and the harvest, daughter of Cronus and Rhea and mother of Persephone. Roman equivalent **Ceres**

demi- *prefix* **1** half ○ *demirep* **2** partly ○ *demigod* [Via Old French < Latin *dimidius* 'split in two' < *dis-* 'apart' + *medius* 'half']

demibastion /démmi básti әn/ *n* a two-sided fortification that consists of a wall facing forward and a wall facing a flank

demigod /démmi god/ *n* **1 SOMEBODY TREATED LIKE GOD** an important or revered man who is treated like a god **2 HUMAN WITH POWERS OF A GOD** a mythological being who is half human and half god **3 MINOR GOD** a god regarded as minor in a hierarchy of other gods

demigoddess /démmi goddess/ *n* **1** an important or revered woman who is treated like a goddess **2** a mythological being who is half woman and half goddess

demijohn /démmi jon/ *n* a large bottle that has a short narrow neck and is often used for making wine [Mid-18C. By folk etymology < French *dame-jeanne* 'Lady Jane', its popular name in France.]

demilitarize /dee míllitә rīz/ (**-rizes, -rizing, -rized**), **demilitarise** (**-rises, -rising, -rised**) *vt* to remove or prohibit the presence of soldiers, weapons, and military installations in an area after an agreement has been made to stop fighting —**demilitarization** /dée millitә rī záysh'n/ *n*

demilitarized zone, demilitarised zone *n* an officially recognized area from which all soldiers, weapons, and military installations have been removed after an agreement to stop fighting

DeMille /dә míl/, **Cecil B.** (1881–1959) US film director and producer

demimondaine /démmi mon dáyn/ *n* a woman who is financially supported by a wealthy lover [Late 19C. < French, < *demi-monde* 'half world'.]

demimonde /démmi mónd/ *n* (*literary*) **1** people who are not considered to be completely respectable **2** a class of women who were financially supported by wealthy lovers, especially in the 19th and early 20th centuries [Mid-19C. < French *demi-monde* 'half world'.]

demineralize /dee mínnərə līz/ (**-izes, -izing, -ized**), **demineralise** (**-ises, -ising, -ised**) *vt* to remove minerals or mineral salts from something such as bone or a liquid —**demineralizer** *n* —**demineralization** /dee mínnərə lī záysh'n/ *n*

demi-pension /démmi paáN syoN/ *n* = **half board**

Demirel /démmi rél/, **Süleyman** (*b.* 1924) Turkish statesman and president (1993–)

demirelief /démmiri leef/ *n* SCULPTURE = **half relief**

demise /di míz/ *n* (*formal*) **1** SOMEBODY'S DEATH the death of somebody, especially when it happens slowly and predictably **2** END the end of something that used to exist, especially one that happens slowly and predictably ■ *vti* (**-mises, -mising, -mised**) BE LEGALLY TRANSFERRED to transfer something or undergo transfer through a line of descent or according to a will (*formal*) [15C. < Anglo-Norman, < Old French *demis* 'sent away' < Latin *dimittere* (see DEMIT).] —**demisable** *adj*

demi-sec /démmi sék/ *adj* describes champagne or sparkling wine that is more sweet than dry [< French, 'half dry'] —**demi-sec** *n*

demisemiquaver /démmi semi kwayvər/ *n* a note with the time value of one thirty-second of a semibreve. US term **thirty-second note**

demission /di mísh'n/ *n* resignation from an important official post [Mid-16C. Via French *démission* < Latin *dimission-* 'dismissal' < past participle of *dimittere* (see DEMIT).]

demist /dee míst/ *vti* to remove mist or condensation from something, especially a car windscreen. US term **defog**

demister /dee místər/ *n* a piece of equipment that clears away mist or condensation, especially a device that channels warm air over the inside of a car windscreen. US term **defogger**

demit /di mít/ (**-mits, -mitting, -mitted**) *vti* to resign from or give up an important official post [15C. Via Old French *desmettre* < Latin *dimittere* 'send away' < *mittere* 'send'.]

demitasse /démmi tass/ *n* a small cup of strong black coffee, or the cup in which such coffee is served [Mid-19C. < French, 'half cup'.]

demiurge /démmi urj/ *n* **1** a very strong, driving, and influential force or personality (*formal*) **2** a public magistrate in some ancient Greek states [Early 17C. Via ecclesiastical Latin *demiurgus* < Greek *dēmiourgos* 'skilled person' < *dēmios* 'of the people' + *-ergos* 'working'.] —**demiurgeous** *adj* —**demiurgic** *adj* —**demiurgical** *adj* —**demiurgically** *adv*

Demiurge /démmi urj/ *n* in Gnostic and Platonic philosophies, the creator and controller of the material world

demivierge /démmi vi áirzh/ *n* a young woman who takes part in sexual activity without ending her virginity [Early 20C. < French, 'half virgin'.]

demivolte /démmi volt/, **demivolt** *n* in dressage, a half turn made by a horse with its forelegs raised [Mid-17C. < French, 'half turn'.]

demiworld /démmi wurld/ *n* = **demimonde** *n*. 1

⚡**demo** /démmō/ *n* (*plural* **demos**) **1** PUBLIC PROTEST a public event in which people protest against something, often by marching through the streets (*informal*) **2** TRIAL SOFTWARE a trial version of software that demonstrates its principle features (*informal*) **3** MUSIC SAMPLE a recorded sample of music produced for promotional purposes (*informal*) **4** *US* = **demonstrator** *n*. 3 **5** DEMONSTRATION OF PRODUCT a demonstration, especially of a new product (*informal*) ■ *vt* (**demos, demoing, demoed**) SHOW HOW SOMETHING WORKS to explain, describe, or give a demonstration of how something works or how to do something (*informal*) [Mid-20C. Shortening of DEMONSTRATION.]

demob /dee mób/ (**-mobs, -mobbing, -mobbed**) *vti* to demobilize armed forces (*informal*) [Early 20C. Shortening.]

demobilize /di mṓbə līz/ (**-izes, -izing, -ized**), **demobilise** (**-ises, -ising, -ised**) *vti* to discharge personnel from the armed forces and send them home, usually after a war —**demobilization** /di mṓbə lī záysh'n/ *n*

democracy /di mókrəssi/ (*plural* **-cies**) *n* **1** REPRESENTATION OF PEOPLE the right to a form of government in which power is invested in the people as a whole, usually exercised on their behalf by elected representatives ○ *'Democracy is like the experience of life itself – always changing, infinite in its variety, sometimes turbulent and all the more valuable for having been tested for adversity'.* (Jimmy Carter, *Speech to Parliament of India*; 2 June, 1978) **2** DEMOCRATIC NATION a country with a democratically elected government **3** DEMOCRATIC GOVERNMENTAL SYSTEM a system of government based on the principle of majority decision-making **4** ORGANIZATIONAL CONTROL BY MEMBERS the control of an organization by its members, who have a right to participate in decision-making processes [Late 16C. Directly and via Old French *democratie* < medieval Latin *democratia* < Greek *dēmokratia* 'rule of the people' < *dēmos* 'people' + *kratos* 'rule'.]

democrat /démmə krat/ *n* a believer in democracy who argues in favour of it

Democrat /démmə krat/ *n* **1** a member of the Democratic Party, one of the two major political parties in the United States **2** a member of the Australian Democrats, a centre-left minority political party

democratic /démmə kráttik/ *adj* characterized by democracy in government or in the decision-making processes of an organization or group —**democratically** *adv*

Democratic *adj* relating to or associated with the Democratic Party of the United States or the Australian Democrats

democratic deficit *n* a situation in which political structures, organizations, or decision-making processes lack democratic legitimacy, especially as discussed in the European Union

Democratic Party *n* one of the two major political parties in the United States, formed after a split in the former Democratic-Republican Party under Andrew Jackson in 1828

democratize /di mókrə tīz/ (**-tizes, -tizing, -tized**), **democratise** (**-tises, -tising, -tised**) *vt* **1** GIVE GOVERNMENT CONTROL TO THE PEOPLE to make a country into a democracy **2** INTRODUCE DEMOCRACY TO STATE to take steps towards establishing the features of liberal democracy in a state **3** GIVE ORGANIZATIONAL CONTROL TO MEMBERS to put an organization under the control of its members by giving them free and equal decision-making powers **4** GIVE SOMETHING POPULAR APPEAL to make something accessible to everybody —**democratization** /di mókrə tī záysh'n/ *n*

Democritus /di mókritəss/ (460?–370? BC) Greek philosopher

démodé /day mṓd ay/ *adj* no longer fashionable [Late 19C. < French, past participle of *démoder* 'go out of fashion' < *mode* 'fashion'.]

demodulate /dee móddyoo layt/ (**-lates, -lating, -lated**) *vt* to extract a signal carrying information from a radio wave (**carrier**) —**demodulator** *n* —**demodulation** /dee modyoo láysh'n/ *n*

demographic /démmə gráffik/ *adj* relating to demography or demographics —**demographical** *adj* —**demographically** *adv*

demographics /démmə gráffiks/ *npl* the characteristics of a human population or part of it, especially its size, growth, density, distribution, and statistics regarding birth, marriage, disease, and death (+ *plural verb*)

demography /di móggrəfi/ *n* **1** the study of human populations, including their size, growth, density, and distribution, as well as statistics regarding birth, marriage, disease, and death **2** the makeup of a particular population [Late 19C. < Greek *dēmos* 'people'.] —**demographist** *n* —**demographer** *n*

demoiselle /dém waa zél/ *n* **1** **demoiselle, demoiselle crane** a small crane with a slender grey body, black plumes, and white ear tufts. Native to: N Africa, Asia. *Anthropoides virgo*. **2** a young woman or girl, especially one who is French (*literary*) **3** ZOOL = **damselfish** **4** INSECTS = **damselfly** [Early 16C. < French, 'damsel' < Old French *dameisele* (see DAMSEL).]

demolish /di móllish/ *vt* **1** WRECK to destroy a building or other structure completely **2** DAMAGE IRREPARABLY to damage something so severely that it cannot be repaired or restored **3** BEAT SOUNDLY to beat an opponent very convincingly, especially in sport or debate (*informal*) **4** EAT FAST AND GREEDILY to eat a large amount of food very quickly (*informal*) [Mid-16C. < Old French *démoliss-*, stem of *démolir* < Latin *demolire* 'undo construction of a mass' < *moles* 'mass'.] —**demolisher** *n*

demolition /démmə lísh'n/ *n* **1** WRECKING OF BUILDING the total destruction of a building or other structure ○ *The old hospital is scheduled for demolition.* **2** DESTRUCTION OR ANNIHILATION the destruction or annihilation of something or somebody ■ **demolitions** *npl* EXPLOSIVES explosives, especially those used by the military [Mid-16C. Via French *démolition* < Latin *demolition-* < *demolire* (see DEMOLISH).]

demolition derby *n US* an entertainment and sporting event held at a fair or on a speedway, during which drivers crash old cars, the winner being the driver of the last car running

demolitionist /démmə lísh'nist/ *n* a person or company whose job it is to demolish buildings

demon /deémən/ *n* **1** EVIL SPIRIT an evil supernatural being such as a ghost or spirit **2** PERSONAL FEAR OR ANXIETY a fear or anxiety that torments somebody **3** EXPERT a person who is very skilled at something (*informal*) [13C. Via Latin *daemon*, medieval Latin *demon* 'evil spirit' < Greek *daimōn* 'divine power, guiding spirit'.]

demonetize /dee múnni tīz/ (**-tizes, -tizing, -tized**), **demonetise** (**-tises, -tising, -tised**) *vt* **1** to stop using a particular metal to make coins **2** to withdraw units of money from circulation [Mid-19C. < French *démonétiser* 'refrain from using money' < Latin *moneta* 'money'.] —**demonetization** /dee múnni tī záysh'n/ *n*

demoniac /di mṓni ak/, **demoniacal** /deemə nī ək'l/ *adj* **1** RESEMBLING A DEMON resembling or characteristic of an evil spirit **2** EVIL OR WICKED evil or wicked in character or nature **3** INTENSE OR FRANTIC intense, frantic, or wild, as if driven or possessed by a demon [14C. < late Latin *daemoniacus* < Latin *daemon* (see DEMON).]

demonic /di mónnik/ *adj* **1** relating to or resembling a demon, especially in wickedness **2** intense, frantic, or wild, as if driven or possessed by a demon —**demonically** *adv*

demonise *vt* = **demonize**

demonism /deémənizəm/ *n* **1** the worship of or belief in demons **2** = **demonology** —**demonist** *n*

demonize /deémə nīz/ (**-izes, -izing, -ized**), **demonise** (**-ises, -ising, -ised**) *vt* to cause somebody or something to appear evil or wicked in the eyes of others —**demonization** /deémə nī záysh'n/ *n*

demonolatry /deémə nóllətri/ *n* worship of demons or of the devil —**demonolater** *n*

demonology /deémə nólləji/ *n* the study of demons, especially those that are frequent in folklore of certain societies —**demonological** /deémənə lójjik'l/ *adj* —**demonologist** *n*

demonstrable /di mónstrəb'l/ *adj* **1** so obvious as to be readily provable **2** capable of being shown to exist or be true [14C. Directly or via Old French < Latin *demonstrabilis* < *demonstrare* (see DEMONSTRATE).] —**demonstrability** /di mónstrə bílləti/ *n* —**demonstrableness** *n* —**demonstrably** *adv*

demonstrate /démmən strayt/ (**-strates, -strating, -strated**) *v* **1** *vt* EXPLAIN WORKINGS to explain or describe how something works or how to do something **2** *vt* SHOW CONVINCINGLY to show or prove something clearly and convincingly **3** *vi* PROTEST OR SUPPORT to make a public show as a group for or against an issue, cause, or person, often by marching through the streets [Mid-16C. < Latin *demonstrat-*, past participle of *demonstrare* < *monstrare* 'show' < *monstrum* 'omen'.]

demonstration /démmən stráysh'n/ *n* **1** DISPLAY SHOWING HOW TO DO a display given to others of how something is done or how something works **2** CONCLUSIVE PROOF evidence or proof that allows no doubt as to its validity or soundness **3** GROUP DISPLAY OF OPINION a public show as a group for or against an issue, cause, or person **4** ATTACK OR SHOW OF FORCE a show of military force or a movement towards an enemy —**demonstrational** *adj* —**demonstrationist** *n*

demonstration sport *n* a sport that is contested in the Olympics on a trial basis even though it is not a permanent medal sport

demonstrative /di mónstrətiv/ *adj* **1** OBVIOUSLY AFFECTIONATE unrestrained in showing love and affection towards somebody **2** PROVING serving to show proof of truth **3** SPECIFYING WHICH PERSON OR THING referring to a particular person or thing, e.g. 'this', 'that', 'these', and 'those' ■ *n* WORD SPECIFYING WHICH PERSON OR THING a demonstrative word or phrase, e.g. 'this', 'that', 'these', or 'those' —**demonstratively** *adv* —**demonstrativeness** *n*

demonstrator /démmən straytər/ *n* **1 SUPPORTER OR PROTESTER** a public protester or supporter of something, usually a member of a group **2 EXPLAINER OF DEVICES** a person who shows or explains how to do something, or how something works **3 SOMETHING DEMONSTRATING FEATURES** something such as a motor vehicle, electrical appliance, or power tool made available for testing by potential buyers. US term **demo** *n.* 4

demoralize /di mórrə līz/ (**-izes, -izing, -ized**), **demoralise** (**-ises, -ising, -ised**) *vt* **1 ERODE MORALE OF** to erode or destroy the courage, confidence, or hope of a person or group **2 CAUSE DISORDER IN** to throw something into disorder or chaos **3 CORRUPT MORALS OF** to corrupt somebody's morals —**demoralization** /di mórrə lī záysh'n/ *n* —**demoralizer** *n* —**demoralizingly** *adv*

demos /déemoss/ *n* **1** the ordinary people of a community or nation (*formal*) **2** the common people in an ancient Greek city-state [Late 18C. < Greek *dēmos* 'district, people living in a district'.]

demote /dee mṓt/ (**-motes, -moting, -moted**) *vt* to reduce somebody or something to a lower rank, status, or position [Late 19C. Blend of DE- + PROMOTE.]

demotic /di móttik/ *adj* **1** relating to or involving ordinary people (*formal*) **2** relating to a simplified form of Egyptian hieroglyphics [Early 19C. < Greek *dēmotikos* 'popular, common' < *dēmos* 'people'.]

Demotic *n* **1** the colloquial form of modern Greek, adopted as the official variety of the language **2** the later form of the ancient Egyptian language, written in the demotic script that was current in the first millennium BC —**Demotic** *adj*

Demotike /di móttikə/ *n* Demotic Greek, used in conversation and in literature, and now adopted as the official variety of the language [< modern Greek, < Greek *dēmotikos* (see DEMOTIC)] —**Demotike** *adj*

demotion /dee mṓsh'n/ *n* a reduction in the rank, status, or position of somebody or something

demotivate /dee mṓti vayt/ (**-vates, -vating, -vated**) *vt* to make somebody feel less keen to work or study effectively —**demotivation** /dee mṓti váysh'n/ *n*

demount /dee mównt/ *vt* **1** to take a piece of equipment away from its supports **2** to take something apart, usually with the intention of reassembling it later —**demountable** *adj*

Dempsey /démpsi/, **Jack** (1895–1983) US professional boxer. Full name **William Harrison Dempsey**. Known as **the Manassa Mauler**

dempster *n* = **deemster**

demulcent /di múls'nt/ *n* a substance that soothes irritated or inflamed skin or mucous membranes [Mid-18C. < Latin *demulcent-*, present participle of *demulcere* 'soothe down' < *mulcere* 'soothe'.] —**demulcent** *adj*

demulsify /di múlssi fī/ (**-fies, -fying, -fied**) *vti* to break an emulsion down permanently into its components, or be broken down permanently —**demulsification** /di múlssifi káysh'n/ *n* —**demulsifier** *n*

demur /di múr/ (**-murs, -murring, -murred**) *v* **1** *vi* **SHOW RELUCTANCE** to delay or try to avoid doing something because of personal reservations or objections ○ *'While I acknowledged it might come to that [the use of force in the Persian Gulf], I demurred, saying it was too early to contemplate such action'.* (George Bush, *A World Transformed*; 1998) **2** *vi* **OBJECT MILDLY** to object mildly to something that you do not want to do but have been asked to do **3** *vti* **MAKE LEGAL OBJECTION** to admit the facts of an opposing argument, but object that those facts alone are not by themselves adequate to make the case [13C. < Old French *demorer* 'delay, stay' < Latin *demorare*.] —**demurrable** *adj* —**demurral** /di múrrəl/ *n*

SYNONYMS See ***object***.

demure /di myóor/ (**-murer, -murest**) *adj* **1** looking or behaving in a modest manner, with reserve or seriousness **2** acting in an affectedly shy or modest way [14C. < past participle of Old French *demorer* (see DEMUR).] —**demurely** *adv* —**demureness** *n*

demurrage /di múrrij/ *n* **1** detention or delay of a cargo carrier during its loading or unloading process, beyond its scheduled time of departure **2** compensation paid when there is a delay in loading or unloading a carrier causing a delay in the carrier's departure [Mid-17C. < Old French *demo(u)rage* < *demorer* (see DEMUR).]

demurrer /di múrrər/ *n* a legal objection that admits the facts of an opposing argument but asserts that those facts alone are not adequate to make the case [Early 16C. < French *demorer* (see DEMUR).]

demutualization /dee myóochoo ə lī záysh'n/, **demutualisation** *n* the conversion of a mutual organization such as a building society or an insurance company to a public company

demutualize /dee myóochoo ə līz/ (**-izes, -izing, -ized**), **demutualise** (**-ises, -ising, -ised**) *vti* to convert a mutual organization such as a building society or an insurance company to a public company, or be converted in this way

demy /di mī/ *adj* describes printing paper that is 444.5 mm/17.5 in by 571.5 mm/22.5 in or writing paper that is 393.7 mm/15.5 in by 508 mm/20 in [15C. Alteration of DEMI-.]

demyelination /dee mī əli náysh'n/ *n* the loss of the fatty covering (**myelin**) of nerve fibres —**demyelinate** /dee mī əli nayt/ *vt*

demystify /dee místi fī/ (**-fies, -fying, -fied**) *vt* to remove the mystery surrounding something, e.g. by explaining it in simple language —**demystification** /dee místifi káysh'n/ *n* —**demystifier** *n*

demythologize /deemi thóllə jīz/ (**-gizes, -gizing, -gized**), **demythologise** (**-gises, -gising, -gised**) *vt* to reveal and understand the true character, nature, or meaning of something by ridding it of all mythical or mysterious aspects —**demythologization** /deemi thóllə jī záysh'n/ *n* —**demythologizer** *n*

den /den/ *n* **1 WILD ANIMAL'S LAIR** the hidden home of a wild animal **2 PLACE OF CRIME** a place where illegal or secret activities take place **3 CHILDREN'S HIDEOUT** a secret place where children play **4 QUIET ROOM** a small quiet retreat in a house, especially a study (*dated*) **5** *US* **ROOM FOR RELAXING** a room in a house where family members and guests relax **6 SQUALID ROOM** a squalid small room or place to live **7** *US* **CUB SCOUT GROUP** a group of Cub Scouts typically made up of eight to ten youths [Old English *denn* 'wild animal's lair' < Indo-European, 'flat surface']

DEN *abbr* District Enrolled Nurse

denar /déenər/ *n* see table at **currency** [See DINAR]

denarius /di náiri əss/ (*plural* **-i** /-ri ī/) *n* **1** an ancient Roman silver coin originally worth ten asses **2** an ancient Roman gold coin worth 25 silver denarii [14C. < Latin, 'containing ten' < *deni* 'ten at a time'.]

denary /déenəri/ *adj* relating to a number system, or a number belonging to it, that has ten as its base, as in the decimal system [Mid-19C. < Latin *denarius* (see DENARIUS).]

denationalize /dee násh'nə līz/ (**-izes, -izing, -ized**), **denationalise** (**-ises, -ising, -ised**) *vt* **1** to sell industries or other major assets owned by the state to private corporations **2** to deprive a people or nation of national rights or characteristics —**denationalization** /dee násh'nə lī záysh'n/ *n*

denaturalize /dee náchərə līz/ (**-izes, -izing, -ized**), **denaturalise** (**-ises, -ising, -ised**) *vt* **1** to take away a naturalized citizen's citizenship, e.g. for illegal entry into the country **2** to take away the original nature of something ○ *once verdant jungles that were denaturalized by defoliants* —**denaturalization** /dee náchərə lī záysh'n/ *n*

denature /dee náychər/ (**-tures, -turing, -tured**) *vt* **1 MAKE UNPALATABLE** to make food or drink, especially alcohol, unsuitable for human consumption, by adding poison, dye, or unpleasant flavours **2 MODIFY MOLECULAR STRUCTURE** to change the molecular structure and characteristics of a molecule by chemical or physical means **3 REMOVE WEAPON POTENTIAL OF NUCLEAR MATERIAL** to make nuclear material unsuitable for use in a weapon by adding an isotope that cannot be split —**denaturant** *n* —**denaturation** /dee náychə ráysh'n/ *n*

denazify /dee naátsi fī/ (**-fies, -fying, -fied**) *vt* to remove something or somebody connected to Nazis or Nazism —**denazification** /dee naátsifi káysh'n/ *n*

Denbighshire /dénbishər/ county in NE Wales. Population: 91,600 (1995).

Dench /dench/, **Dame Judi** (*b.* 1934) British actor. Full name **Dame Judith Olivia Dench**

dendr- *prefix* = **dendro-**

dendri- *prefix* = **dendro-**

dendrite /dén drīt/ *n* **1** a mineral crystallized in the shape of a tree **2** a branched extension of a nerve cell (**neuron**) that receives electrical signals from other neurons and conducts those signals to the cell body [Early 18C. Directly or via French < Greek *dendritēs* 'of a tree' < *dendron* 'tree'.] —**dendritic** /den dríttik/ *adj* —**dendritical** *adj* —**dendritically** *adv*

dendro- *prefix* tree, resembling a tree ○ *dendrology* ○ *dendrite* [< Greek *dendron* < Indo-European, 'be solid']

dendrochronology /déndrō krə nólləji/ *n* the study of the annual growth rings in trees or wooden objects, especially as a way of dating wooden remains or determining past climatic conditions —**dendrochronological** /déndrō krónnə lójjik'l/ *adj* —**dendrochronologist** *n*

dendrogram /déndrə gram/ *n* a diagram showing the relationships of items arranged like the branches of a tree

dendroid /dén droyd/, **dendroidal** /den dróyd'l/ *adj* **1 WITH STEM RESEMBLING TREE TRUNK** describes plants with an erect main stem like a tree trunk **2 MULTIBRANCHED** describes plants with many branches, like a tree **3 RESEMBLING A TREE** generally resembling a tree in shape or form

dendrology /den drólləji/ *n* the study of trees and other woody plants —**dendrologic** /déndrə lójjik/ *adj* —**dendrological** *adj* —**dendrologist** *n* —**dendrologous** *adj*

dendron /dén dron/ *n* a dendrite (*dated*) [Late 19C. < DENDRITE + -ON² *suffix*.]

dene /deen/ *n* a narrow wooded valley (*often in placenames*) [Old English *denu* < Germanic]

Dene /dénni, dénnay/ *npl* a group of Athapaskan-speaking Native North Americans who live in N Canada, chiefly in the Northwest Territories [Late 19C. Via Canadian French < Athabaskan.]

denervate /dee núr vayt, dénnər vayt/ (**-vates, -vating, -vated**) *vt* to deprive an organ or body part of nerves, either by cutting them or by blocking them with drugs, e.g. to control pain —**denervation** /dee nur váysh'n/ *n*

Deneuve /də nṓv/, **Catherine** (*b.* 1943) French film actor. Born **Catherine Dorléac**

dengue /déng gi, -gay/, **dengue fever** *n* a tropical disease caused by a virus that is transmitted by mosquitoes and marked by high fever and severe muscle and joint pains [Early 19C. < W Indian Spanish.]

Deng Xiaoping /dúng shów píng/ (1904–97) Chinese political leader and national leader of China (1976–97)

deni /dénee/ (*plural* **-ni**) *n* see table at **currency**

deniable /di nī əb'l/ *adj* referring to something that can be disclaimed or declared untrue —**deniably** *adv*

denial /di nī əl/ *n* **1 DISAVOWAL** a statement saying that something is not true or not correct **2 REFUSAL TO GRANT** a refusal to allow people to have something that they want or that they believe they have a right to **3 REFUSAL TO ACKNOWLEDGE EXISTENCE OF** an inability or a refusal to admit that something exists **4 REFUSAL TO FACE UNPLEASANT FACTS** a state of mind marked by a refusal or an inability to recognize and deal with a serious personal problem ○ *She's in denial.* **5 OPPOSITION TO AN ALLEGATION** in a court of law, saying that you did not do something that you are accused of

⚡ **denial-of-service attack** *n* an illegal attempt to put a computer system out of action by overloading it with data from many sources simultaneously

denier /dénni ər/ *n* **1** a unit of fineness of silk and some artificial fibres, such as nylon, equal to one gram per 9,000 metres of yarn **2** /də neer/ a silver coin, formerly used in several European countries [15C. Via Old French < Latin *denarius* (see DENARIUS).]

denigrate /dénni grayt/ (**-grates, -grating, -grated**) *vt* **1** to defame somebody's character or reputation **2** ⚠ to disparage or criticize somebody or something, or to make something seem unimportant [15C. < Latin *denigrat-*, past participle of *denigrare* 'blacken completely' < *niger* 'black'.] —**denigration** /dénni gráysh'n/ *n* —**denigrator** *n*

USAGE In its best-established sense ***denigrate*** means 'ruin a reputation'. However, it is now often found in sentences like *I don't mean to denigrate the problem*, where its meaning has become closer to 'disparage or belittle'. In this, it is following in the footsteps of *deprecate*, whose traditional meaning is 'express condemnation of somebody or something', but which in *self-deprecating* has taken on the additional sense of 'belittle'.

denim /dénnim/ *n* a hard-wearing woven cotton cloth. Use: clothing, especially jeans. ■ **denims** *npl* clothes made of denim, especially jeans, jackets, shirts, or skirts [Late 17C. < French *(serge) de Nîmes* '(serge) of Nîmes', France.]

De Niro /də neérō/, **Robert** (*b.* 1943) US actor

denitrate /dee nī trayt/ (**-trates, -trating, -trated**) *vti* to remove a nitro or nitrate group, nitrogen compound, or nitrous acid from a chemical compound, or lose such components —**denitration** /deè nī tráysh'n/ *n*

denitrify /dee nītri fī/ (**-fies, -fying, -fied**) *vt* **1** to remove nitrogen or a nitrogen compound from a substance **2** to convert nitrates into nitrites and ammonia —**denitrification** /dee nītrifi káysh'n/ *n*

denizen /dénniz'n/ *n* **1 RESIDENT OF PLACE** a resident of a specific country or area **2 HABITUAL VISITOR TO PLACE** a habitual visitor to a place ○ *denizens of cyberspace chat rooms* **3 FOREIGNER WITH RIGHTS OF RESIDENCE** a new resident in a foreign country who is given some legal rights there **4 NONNATIVE PLANT OR ANIMAL** a nonnative plant or animal that grows or lives in an area [15C. < Anglo-Norman *deinzein* < Old French *deinz* 'inside' < Latin *de intus* 'from inside'.]

Denmark

Denmark /dén maark/ southernmost country in Scandinavia, comprising the Jutland peninsula and about 480 islands. Capital: Copenhagen. Population: 5,305,048 (1997). Area: 43,094 sq. km/16,639 sq. mi.

Denning /dénning/, **Alfred, Baron Denning of Whitechurch** (1899–1999) British judge

Dennis /dénniss/, **C. J.** (1876–1938) Australian writer. Full name **Clarence Michael James Dennis**

denom. *abbr* denomination

denominal /di nómminəl/ *adj* describes parts of speech that are formed from or have the same form as a noun, e.g. the verb 'to butter'

denominate /di nómmi nayt/ (**-nates, -nating, -nated**) *vt* **1** to define something in terms of a specific unit of currency **2** to give something a particular name or description (*formal*) [Mid-16C. < Latin *denominat-*, past participle of *denominare* 'name completely' < *nominare* 'to name'.] —**denominable** *adj*

denomination /di nómmi náysh'n/ *n* **1 RELIGIOUS GROUPING** a religious grouping within a faith that has its own system of organization **2 UNIT OF VALUE OR MEASURE** a unit in the scale of value (especially monetary value), weight, measure, or size **3 NAME OR DESIGNATION** a name or designation given to a class, group, or type —**denominational** *adj* —**denominationally** *adv*

denominative /di nómminətiv/ *adj* denominal —**denominative** *n* —**denominatively** *adv*

denominator /di nómmi naytər/ *n* **1 NUMBER BELOW LINE IN FRACTION** the number below the line in a fraction, which indicates the number of parts making up the whole **2 COMMON CHARACTERISTIC** something held in common **3 AVERAGE LEVEL** an average standard, degree, or level of quality or taste

de nos jours /də nō zhoór/ *adj* of our time [< French]

denotation /deènō táysh'n/ *n* **1** the most specific or literal meaning of a word, as opposed to its figurative senses or connotations **2** the reference of a term in logic

denote /di nót/ (**-notes, -noting, -noted**) *vt* **1 MEAN** to have something as a specified meaning ○ *The name actually denotes 'lightning bolt' in Italian.* **2 REFER TO** to designate or refer to somebody or something specified ○ *The term 'caregiver' will be used to denote those providing unpaid family care.* **3 SIGNIFY** to be a sign or representation of something ○ *The specks of light denote planets.* [Late 16C. Via French *dénoter* < Latin *denotare* 'mark completely' < *notare* 'to mark'.] —**denotative** *adj* —**denotatively** *adv* —**denotive** *adj*

USAGE denote or **represent**? Use ***denote*** when you want to say 'to mean', 'to refer to', or 'to signify': *That word denotes 'life' in Spanish. For our purposes, the word 'corporation' will denote the XYZ Foundation. The tiny points of light in the sky denote the Plough.* It is preferable to use ***represent*** when you mean 'to symbolize something else': *The red maple leaf represents* [not *denotes*] *Canada.*

denouement /day noó moN/ (*plural* **-ments**) *n* **1** a final part of a story or drama in which everything is made clear and no questions or surprises remain **2** the final stage or climax of a series of events ○ *the gripping denouement of the championship* [Mid-18C. < French, < *dénouer* 'untie' < *nouer* 'to tie' < Latin *nodus* 'knot'.]

denounce /di nównss/ (**-nounces, -nouncing, -nounced**) *vt* **1 CRITICIZE PUBLICLY AND HARSHLY** to express harsh criticism or condemnation of something or somebody, usually in public **2 ACCUSE PUBLICLY** to accuse somebody publicly of something such as disloyalty, or inform against somebody **3 ANNOUNCE TERMINATION OF** to make a formal announcement of the end of a treaty or other agreement (*formal*) [14C. Via Old French *denoncier* < Latin *denuntiare* < *nuntiare* 'proclaim, announce' < *nuntius* 'messenger'.] —**denouncement** *n* —**denouncer** *n*

SYNONYMS See ***disapprove.***

de novo /di nṓvō/ *adv* anew, afresh, or over again from the beginning [Mid-16C. < Latin, 'from new'.]

Denpasar /den paá saar/ capital of Bali, Indonesia. Population: 373,272 (1997 estimate).

dense /denss/ (**denser, densest**) *adj* **1 TIGHTLY PACKED** so close together that there is not much sense of room or open space **2 VERY THICK** so thick that it is difficult or impossible to see through **3 WITH HIGH MASS** with a relatively high mass per unit volume **4 HARD TO PENETRATE INTELLECTUALLY** so complex and intricate that it is difficult to assimilate and understand **5 SLOW TO LEARN OR UNDERSTAND** lacking the ability to learn or understand quickly (*informal insult*) [15C. Directly or via French < Latin *densus* 'thick, dense'.] —**densely** *adv* —**denseness** *n*

densimeter /den símmitər/ *n* an instrument that measures density or specific gravity [Mid-19C. < Latin *densus* 'dense'.] —**densimetric** /dénssi méttrik/ *adj* —**densimetry** /-símmətri/ *n*

densitometer /dénssi tómmitər/ *n* **1** an instrument for measuring optical density, e.g. that of a photographic negative **2** = **densimeter** [Early 20C. < DENSITY.] —**densitometric** /dénssitə méttrik/ *adj* —**densitometry** /-tómmətri/ *n*

density /dénssəti/ (*plural* **-ties**) *n* **1** concentration of people or things within an area in relation to its size **2** (*symbol* **ρ**) a measure of a quantity such as mass or electric charge per unit volume **3** ELEC = **charge density** **4** ELEC = **current density**

density function *n* STATS = **probability density function** *n.* **2**

dent /dent/ *v* **1** *vti* **MAKE DEPRESSION IN BY HITTING** to make a shallow depression in the surface of something by hitting it or putting pressure on it **2** *vt* **HARM SOMETHING ABSTRACT** to do nonphysical, usually minor, damage to something ○ *His reputation was somewhat dented.* ■ *n* **1 AREA IN DEPRESSED SURFACE** a shallow depression in the surface of something that is made by hitting it or putting pressure on it **2 NONPHYSICAL DAMAGE** nonphysical, usually minor, damage, e.g. to somebody's reputation **3 ADVANCE** progress in reaching a goal (*informal*) ○ *make a dent in the backlog* **4 REDUCTION** a reduction in an amount of something such as resources (*informal*) ○ *a dent in the budget* [13C. Variant of DINT.]

dent. *abbr* **1** dental **2** dentistry

dent- *prefix* = **denti-** (*before vowels*)

dental /dént'l/ *adj* **1 OF DENTISTRY** relating to or used in dentistry **2 OF TEETH** relating or belonging to the teeth **3 NEAR TOOTH** affecting or located in or near a tooth ○ *dental abscess* **4 MADE BY TONGUE AND TEETH** describes a consonant that is formed by placing the tongue against the back of the top front teeth [Late 16C. < late Latin *dentalis* < Latin *dent-* 'tooth'.]

dental caries *n* decay of teeth that is caused by the action of acid-forming bacteria and improper dental care

dental floss *n* thread that is used to remove food and plaque from between the teeth

dental hygiene *n* the care people take of their teeth and gums to prevent tooth and gum disease

dental hygienist *n* somebody who provides certain kinds of dental care under the supervision of a dentist, especially cleaning and scaling teeth

dental surgeon *n* = **dentist**

dental technician *n* somebody trained to make dental appliances such as caps, dentures, and bridges

dentate /dén tayt/ *adj* edged with pointed or tooth-shaped projections [15C. < Latin *dentatus* < *dent-* 'tooth'.] —**dentately** *adv* —**dentation** /den táysh'n/ *n*

denti- *prefix* tooth, dental ○ *dentiform* [< Latin *dent-*, stem of *dens* 'tooth' < Indo-European]

denticle /déntik'l/ *n* **1** a small tooth or tooth-shaped projection **2** a small tooth-shaped scale with a projecting spine, typical of cartilaginous fish [15C. < Latin *denticulus* 'small tooth' < *dent-* 'tooth'.] —**denticular** /den tíkyoolər/ *adj*

denticulate /den tíkyoolət, -layt/ *adj* **1** with fine teeth or pointed projections **2** decorated with small rectangular blocks (**dentils**) that look like a row of teeth [Mid-17C. < Latin *denticulatus* < *denticulus* (see DENTICLE).] —**denticulately** *adv*

dentifrice /déntifriss/ *n* a paste or similar compound for cleaning teeth [15C. Via French < Latin *dentifricium* < *dent-* 'tooth' + *fricare* 'rub'.]

dentil /déntil/ *n* a rectangular block that is arranged with others to look like a row of teeth, used as a form of architectural decoration [Late 16C. < Italian *dentello* or obsolete French *dentille* 'small tooth' < Latin *dent-* 'tooth'.]

dentilingual /dénti líng gwəl/ *adj* pronounced or articulated with the tongue touching the teeth on the top jaw

dentine /dén teen/, **dentin** /-tin/ *n* the hard part of a tooth that lies underneath the enamel and surrounds the pulp and root canals [Mid-19C. < Latin *dent-* 'tooth'.] —**dentinal** /-tin'l/ *adj*

dentist /déntist/ *n* somebody trained and licensed to practise general dentistry or a branch of dentistry such as orthodontics or dental surgery [Mid-18C. < French *dentiste* < *dent* 'tooth' < Latin *dent-*.]

dentistry /déntistri/ *n* the medical science concerned with the prevention and treatment of tooth and gum disorders and diseases

dentition /den tísh'n/ *n* **1** the type, number, and arrangement of a set of teeth **2** the process of developing and cutting new teeth [Late 16C. < Latin *dent-* 'tooth'.]

Denton /déntən/ city in N Texas. Population: 76,933 (1998 estimate).

denture /dénchər/ *n* a partial or complete set of artificial teeth for the upper or lower jaw, usually attached to a plate [Late 19C. < French, < *dent* 'tooth' (see DENTIST).]

denturist /dénchərist/ *n US, Can* a dental technician who makes and fits dentures that are sold directly to the public rather than through a dentist

denuclearize /dee nyoókli ə rīz/ (**-izes, -izing, -ized**), **denuclearise** (**-ises, -ising, -ised**) *vt* to remove, ban, or eliminate nuclear weapons or nuclear power sources from a place, industry, or organization —**denuclearization** /dee nyoókli ə rī záysh'n/ *n*

denude /di nyoód/ (**-nudes, -nuding, -nuded**) *vt* **1 STRIP BARE** to strip somebody or something bare **2 STRIP AWAY GROUND COVER** to strip away the vegetation that covers an area **3 STRIP BY EROSION** to remove soil from an area or expose underlying layers of rock by weathering and erosion [15C. < Latin *denudare* 'strip away' < *nudare* 'strip' < *nudus* 'nude'.] —**denudation** /deè nyoo dáysh'n/ *n* —**denuder** *n*

denumerable /di nyoómərəb'l/ *adj* able to form a one-to-one correspondence with the positive integers [Early 20C. < late Latin *denumerare* 'count out' < Latin *numerare* (see NUMERATE).] —**denumerability** /di nyoómərə bíllәti/ *n* —**denumerably** *adv*

denunciation /di núnssi áysh'n/ *n* a public accusation or condemnation of something or somebody

Denver /dénvər/ capital of Colorado, in the north-central part of the state. Population: 499,055 (1998 estimate).

Denver boot *n US* CARS = **wheel clamp** [After DENVER, Colorado]

deny /di nī/ (**-nies, -nying, -nied**) *v* **1** *vt* **SAY SOMETHING IS NOT TRUE** to declare that something is not true or not the case **2** *vt* **REFUSE** to refuse something to somebody **3** *vt* **REFUSE TO ACKNOWLEDGE** to refuse to acknowledge somebody **4** *vr* **NOT ALLOW YOURSELF** to refuse to gratify your needs or desires [13C. Via Old French *deneier* < Latin *denegare* 'negate completely' < *negare* 'deny'.]

deoch an doruis /dyókh-/, **doch an doris** /dókh ən dórriss/ *n Scotland* a parting drink [< Scots Gaelic *deoch an doruis* 'a drink at the door']

deodar /dée ō daar/ (*plural* **-dars** *or* **-dar**) *n* **1** a cedar with dark blue-green leaves and drooping branches. Native to: Himalayas. *Cedrus deodara.* **2** the hard sweet-smelling wood of the deodar tree. Use: timber. [Early 19C. Via Hindi *deodār* < Sanskrit *devadāru* 'divine wood'.]

deodorant /di ṓdərənt/ *n* **1** a spray, cream, or liquid that people apply under their arms to mask body odour **2** a substance that is used to disguise unpleasant smells

deodorize /di ṓdə rīz/ (**-izes, -izing, -ized**), **deodorise** (**-ises, -ising, -ised**) *vt* to disguise or eliminate unpleasant smells —**deodorization** /di ṓdə rī záysh'n/ *n* —**deodorizer** *n*

Deo gratias /dáy ō graáti əss/ *interj* thanks be to God (*used in various Christian choral and liturgical contexts*) [< Latin]

deontic /di óntik/ *adj* relating to the concept of moral obligation [Mid-19C. < Greek *deont-*, present participle of *dein* 'be wanting, be needful'.]

deontological /di óntə lójjik'l/ *adj* relating to philosophical theories that state that the moral content of an action is not wholly dependent on its consequences —**deontologically** *adv*

deontology /dée on tólləji/ *n* the study of what is morally obligatory, permissible, right, or wrong [Early 19C. < Greek *deont-* (see DEONTIC).] —**deontologist** *n*

deorbit /dee áwrbit/ *vti* to put something out of orbit or go out of orbit

Deo volente /dáy ō və lénti/ *interj* God willing [< Latin]

deoxidize /dee óksi dīz/ (**-dizes, -dizing, -dized**), **deoxidise** (**-dises, -dising, -dised**) *vt* **1** to remove the oxygen from a compound or molecule **2** CHEM = **reduce** *v.* 12 —**deoxidization** /dee óksi dī záysh'n/ *n* —**deoxidizer** *n*

deoxy- *prefix* containing less oxygen than a related compound ○ *deoxyribose* [< DE- + OXY-]

deoxygenate /dee óksijə nayt/ (**-ates, -ating, -ated**) *vt* to remove dissolved oxygen from a substance —**deoxygenation** /dee óksijə náysh'n/ *n*

deoxygenize /dée óksijə nīz/ (**-izes, -izing, -ized**), **deoxygenise** (**-ises, -ising, -ised**) *vt* = **deoxygenate**

deoxyribonuclease /dée oksi rībō nyoókli ayz/ *n* full form of **DNAase** [Mid-20C. < DEOXYRIBONUCLEIC ACID.]

deoxyribonucleic acid /dée oksi rībō nyoo kláyik-, -kláy-/ *n* full form of **DNA** [Mid-20C. < DEOXYRIBOSE.]

deoxyribonucleotide /dée oksi rībō nyoókli ə tīd/ *n* a nucleotide containing deoxyribose that is a component of DNA [Mid-20C. < DEOXYRIBOSE.]

deoxyribose /dée oksi rībōss/ *n* a five-carbon simple sugar that is a structural component of DNA

dep. *abbr* **1** department **2** departs **3** departure **4** deponent **5** deposed **6** deposit **7** depot **8 dep., Dep.** deputy

Depardieu /dé paar djö/, **Gérard** (*b.* 1948) French actor

depart /di paárt/ *v* **1** *vi* **SET OFF** to leave, especially at the beginning of a journey **2** *vi* **CHANGE** to change or vary from a pattern **3** *vt* **DIE** to end your life (*formal*) ○ *depart this life* [13C. < French *départir* 'end your life' < Latin *partire* 'divide into parts' < *pars* 'part'.]

departed /di paártid/ *adj* having died (*formal or literary*) ■ *n* (*plural* **-ed**) a person who has died, especially recently (*formal or literary*)

SYNONYMS See ***dead***.

department /di paártmənt/ *n* **1** **SECTION OF ORGANIZATION** a specialized section of a large organization such as a university or store **2** **PART OF GOVERNMENT** a major division of government that is responsible for dealing with a particular area of policy or administration **3** **SPECIALITY** somebody's speciality or particular area of responsibility (*informal*) **4** **CATEGORY** a specified quantifiable or qualifiable category (*informal*) **5** **FRENCH DISTRICT** an administrative district in France

departmental /dée paart mént'l/ *adj* relating to or for a department in a government or an organization —**departmentally** *adv*

departmentalise *vt* = **departmentalize**

departmentalism /dée paart mént'lizəm/ *n* **1** the division of organizations into departments, particularly as a deliberate policy that is taken to excess **2** the tendency of government departments to follow their own interests

departmentalize /dée paart mént'l īz/ (**-izes, -izing, -ized**), **departmentalise** (**-ises, -ising, -ised**) *vt* to divide an organization into departments, especially as a policy or to an excessive extent —**departmentalization** /dée paart mént'l ī záysh'n/ *n*

department store *n* a large store that sells a wide range of goods in separate departments

departure /di paárchər/ *n* **1** **SETTING OFF** the action of setting off on a journey **2** **CHANGE FROM USUAL** a change from the usual or expected way **3** **COURSE** a course of action or the beginning of one **4** **EAST OR WEST TRAVEL** the distance travelled due east or west by a ship

departure lounge *n* an area where departing passengers can wait until their aircraft or other transport is ready

depasture /dée paáschər/ (**-tures, -turing, -tured**) *vt* **1** = **overgraze** **2** to allow animals to graze on a particular area

depauperate /di páwpərət/ *adj* **1** less than fully grown or developed **2** lacking or depleted in the variety of plant or animal species [Mid-19C. < medieval Latin *depauperatus*, past participle of *depauperare* 'impoverish' < Latin *pauper* (see PAUPER).]

depend /di pénd/ *vi* **1** **BE CONTINGENT** to be affected or decided by other factors **2** **VARY** to vary according to the circumstances **3** **HANG DOWN** to hang down or be suspended from something (*archaic*) [15C. Via French *dépendre* < Latin *dependere* 'hang down' < *pendere* 'hang'.]

depend on, depend upon *vt* **1** to need something in order to exist or survive **2** to have complete confidence in somebody or something

dependable /di péndəb'l/ *adj* able to be trusted to act in the way required or expected —**dependability** /di péndə bílləti/ *n* —**dependably** *adv*

dependably /di péndəbli/ *adv* **1** used to indicate that the way somebody or something is behaving as expected **2** in a way that inspires confidence that whatever is required or promised will be done

dependant /di péndənt/ *n* a family member or other person who is supported financially by another, especially one living in the same house. US term **dependent** *n.*

dependence /di péndənss/ *n* **1** a need for something or somebody to be available in order to exist or survive ○ *financial dependence* ○ *dependence on public transport* **2** a physical or psychological need to use a drug or other substance regularly, despite the fact that it is likely to have a damaging effect

dependency /di péndənssi/ (*plural* **-cies**) *n* **1** a country or state that belongs to another non-adjacent country **2** a building near to and associated with a larger main building **3** = **dependence**

dependency theory *n* a theory of international relations holding that major states influence other states though their economic power

dependent /di péndənt/ *adj* **1** **NOT SELF-RELIANT** not able to live without support from other people, especially financial support from a parent or child **2** **NEEDING** needing to use something, especially a drug (*usually in combination*) **3** **CONTINGENT** affected or decided by stated factors or circumstances (*often in combination*) ○ *age-dependent* ■ *n US* = **dependant** —**dependently** *adv*

dependent clause *n* = **subordinate clause**

dependent variable *n* an element in a mathematical expression that changes its value according to the value of other elements present

depersonalize /dée púrss'nəl īz/ (**-izes, -izing, -ized**), **depersonalise** (**-ises, -ising, -ised**) *vt* **1** to take away or omit personal qualities from somebody or something **2** to make somebody lose his or her sense of personal identity and external reality —**depersonalization** /dee púrss'nəl ī záysh'n/ *n*

depict /di píkt/ *vt* **1** to describe or portray something in words **2** to show something in a picture, painting, or sculpture [15C. < Latin *depict-*, past participle of *depingere* 'portray' < *pingere* 'to paint'.] —**depicter** *n* —**depictive** *adj*

depiction /di píksh'n/ *n* a picture, description, or other representation of something

depigmentation /dée pígmən táysh'n/ *n* partial or total absence of the body colouring pigment melanin, especially in the skin, hair, and eyes

depilate /déppi layt/ (**-lates, -lating, -lated**) *vti* to remove hair from the body, usually from the legs or underarms [Mid-16C. < Latin *depilare* < *pilus* 'hair'.] —**depilator** *n*

depilation /déppi láysh'n/ *n* the removal of hair, including its roots, from the body or from hides or leather

depilatory /di píllətəri/ *adj* used for removing hair from the body ■ *n* (*plural* **-ries**) a substance that removes hair from the body

deplane /dée pláyn/ (**-planes, -planing, -planed**) *vi US, Can* to disembark from an aeroplane

deplete /di pléet/ (**-pletes, -pleting, -pleted**) *vt* **1** to use up or reduce something, e.g. supplies, resources, or energy **2** to empty something [Early 19C. < Latin *deplet-*, past participle of *deplere* 'empty out' < *plere* 'fill'.] —**depletable** *adj* —**depletion** *n* —**depletive** *adj*

depletion layer *n* a layer in a semiconductor that has few charge carriers transporting electric charge between zones of different conductivity

deplorable /di pláwrəb'l/ *adj* **1** worthy of severe condemnation **2** wretched because of neglect, poverty, or other misfortune —**deplorability** /di pláwrə bílləti/ *n* —**deplorableness** *n* —**deplorably** *adv*

deplore /di pláwr/ (**-plores, -ploring, -plored**) *vt* **1** to condemn something or disapprove of it strongly **2** to regret or feel grief about something [Mid-16C. Via French *déplorer* or Italian *deplorare* < Latin *deplorare* 'lament, regret' < *plorare* 'wail'.] —**deplorer** *n* —**deploringly** *adv*

SYNONYMS See ***disapprove***.

deploy /di plóy/ *v* **1** *vti* to position troops, weapons, or resources in a specific area in readiness for action, or take up position in this way **2** *vt* to put something to use [15C. Via French *déployer* < Latin *displicare* 'unfold' < *plicare* 'to fold'.] —**deployable** *adj* —**deployer** *n* —**deployment** *n*

deplume /dee ploóm/ (**-plumes, -pluming, -plumed**) *vt* to remove the feathers from a bird [15C. Via French *deplumer* < medieval Latin *deplumare* < Latin *pluma* 'down, feather'.] —**deplumation** /dée ploo máysh'n/ *n*

depolarize /dee pṓlə rīz/ (**-izes, -izing, -ized**), **depolarise** (**-ises, -ising, -ised**) *vti* to remove or lose polarization or polarity —**depolarization** /dee pṓlə rī záysh'n/ *n* —**depolarizer** *n*

depoliticize /déepə lítti sīz/ (**-cizes, -cizing, -cized**), **depoliticise** (**-cises, -cising, -cised**) *vt* to remove the political aspect of something —**depoliticization** /déepə lítti sī záysh'n/ *n*

depollution /déepə loósh'n/ *n* the removal of pollution from something —**depollute** *vt*

depolymerize /dee póllimə rīz/ (**-izes, -izing, -ized**), **depolymerise** (**-ises, -ising, -ised**) *vti* to break down a polymer into simpler monomers or to undergo this process —**depolymerization** /dee póllimə rī záysh'n/ *n*

depone /di pṓn/ (**-pones, -poning, -poned**) *vti* to testify or declare something under oath [15C. < medieval Latin *deponere* 'testify' (see DEPOSE).]

deponent /di pṓnənt/ *n* **1** **TESTIFYING WITNESS** a signer of an affidavit or testifier under oath **2** **DEPONENT VERB** a deponent verb ■ *adj* **PASSIVE AND ACTIVE** inflecting like a passive verb but active in meaning

depopulate /dee póppyoǒ layt/ (**-lates, -lating, -lated**) *vt* to cause a reduction in the number of residents in an area through, e.g. disease, war, famine, or enforced relocation [Mid-16C. < Latin *depopulare* 'ravage completely, reduce in population' < *populari* 'lay waste' < *populus* 'people'.] —**depopulation** /dee póppyoǒ láysh'n/ *n* —**depopulator** *n*

deport[1] /di páwrt/ *vt* **1** to force a foreign national to leave a country **2** to expel or banish somebody from their own country [Mid-17C. Via French *déporter* < Latin *deportare* 'carry off' < *portare* 'carry'.] —**deportation** /dée pawr táysh'n/ *n* —**deportable** *adj*

deport[2] /di páwrt/ *vr* to conduct yourself in a particular way [15C. < Old French *deporter* 'behave, conduct yourself' < *porter* < Latin *portare* 'carry'.]

deportee /dee pawr tée/ *n* a person subject to deportation

deportment /di páwrtmənt/ *n* the way that you stand, sit, or move, especially whether you have a straight back, move smoothly, and carry yourself well [Early 17C. < French *déportement* < Old French *deporter* (see DEPORT[2]).]

depose /di pṓz/ (**-poses, -posing, -posed**) *v* **1** *vt* to remove somebody from office or from a position of power **2** *vti* to give evidence or testify on oath, either in a written or verbal form [13C. < French *déposer*, alteration (influenced by *poser* 'put') of Latin *deponere* 'put down', in medieval Latin 'testify' < *ponere* 'to place'.] —**deposable** *adj* —**deposal** *n* —**deposer** *n*

deposit /di pózzit/ *v* **1** *vt* PUT SOMETHING SOMEWHERE to put or drop something somewhere ○ *She deposited her coat on the couch.* **2** *vti* FORM LAYER to form a layer of sand, sediment, or other substance, as a gradual process in one place ○ *layers of silt deposited by the river* **3** *vt* PUT MONEY IN BANK to pay money into a bank or other financial institution **4** *vt* LEAVE SAFELY to leave something somewhere for safekeeping ○ *deposit valuables in the hotel safe* **5** *vt* GIVE AS SECURITY to give a sum of money as part-payment or security ○ *deposited £500 as a down payment* ■ *n* **1** PUTTING MONEY IN BANK an act of placing money or a valuable item in a bank or other institution ○ *make a monthly deposit* **2** MONEY IN BANK an amount of money or a valuable item that is paid into or left in a bank or other institution ○ *Deposits made after 2 pm are credited the following day.* **3** SECURITY MONEY a partial payment or security on something you wish to buy ○ *You need to pay a deposit.* **4** SURETY MONEY money that is given as security against possible damage or loss, e.g. on something rented **5** ACCUMULATION OF NATURAL MATERIALS an accumulation of sand, sediment, minerals, or other substances that has built up over a period of time through a natural process ○ *a land rich in mineral deposits* **6** ELECTION CANDIDATE'S MONEY money that candidates in a parliamentary election must deposit to show that their standing is serious and which they forfeit if they fail to win a given percentage of votes **7** COATING a coating or crust that is left on a surface by a process such as evaporation or electrolysis **8** DEPOSITED THING something put or left in a place [Late 16C. < Latin *depositum* < *deposit-*, past participle of *deponere* (see DEPOSE).] —**depositor** *n*

deposit account *n* a bank account that earns interest

depositary /di pózzitəri/ (*plural* **-ies**) *n* **1** a person or institution that is entrusted with something for safekeeping **2** = **depository** *n.* 1

deposition /déppə zísh'n, deépə-/ *n* **1** WITNESS'S TESTIMONY testimony that is given under oath, especially a statement given by a witness that is read out in court in the witness's absence **2** OUSTING FROM OFFICE the act of removing somebody from high office or power **3** DEPOSIT something that has been deposited somewhere **4** BUILD-UP OF DEPOSITS the accumulation of natural materials by a gradual process [14C. Via French *déposition* < Latin *deposition-* < *deponere* (see DEPOSE).] —**depositional** *adj*

depository /di pózzitəri/ (*plural* **-ries**) *n* **1** a place where something is kept for safekeeping or storage, such as a warehouse or store for furniture or valuables **2** = **depositary** *n.* 1

deposit slip *n US* BANKING = **paying-in slip**

depot /déppō/ *n* **1** WAREHOUSE a warehouse or other place used for storing things **2** VEHICLE BASE a building where buses, trains, or lorries are based and serviced **3** *US, Can* STATION a railway or bus station **4** MILITARY STORE a place where military supplies are stored **5** MILITARY TRAINING BASE a place where military recruits are gathered together and trained [Late 18C. Via French *dépôt* < Latin *depositum* (see DEPOSIT).]

deprave /di práyv/ (**-praves, -praving, -praved**) *vt* to have a morally bad influence on somebody (*often passive*) [14C. Directly or via French, < Latin *depravare* 'corrupt' < *pravus* 'crooked'.] —**depraver** *n*

depraved /di práyvd/ *adj* showing great moral corruption or wickedness —**depravedly** /di práyvidli, -práyvd-/ *adv* —**depravedness** /di práyvidnəss, -práyvd-/ *n*

depravity /di právvəti/ (*plural* **-ties**) *n* **1** a state of moral corruption **2** a morally corrupt or wicked act [Mid-17C. Alteration (after DEPRAVE) of obsolete *pravity* < Latin *pravitas* < *pravus* 'crooked'.]

deprecate /déppri kayt/ (**-cates, -cating, -cated**) *vt* **1** DEPLORE to express condemnation of something or somebody ○ *The spokesman deprecated the use of violence* **2** ⚠ BELITTLE to speak disparagingly about something of somebody. **3** DECLARE OBSOLESCENT to state that a method or feature is superseded [Early 17C. < Latin *deprecari* 'pray against' < *precari* (see PRAY).] —**deprecation** /déppri káysh'n/ *n* —**deprecator** *n*

USAGE deprecate or **depreciate**? To ***deprecate*** something is to condemn it as wrong in itself: *We deprecate the use of public money for nonessential purposes.* To ***depreciate*** something is to belittle or disparage it, even though it may not be wrong or bad in itself: *They were constantly depreciating our attempts to speak Italian.* This use is increasingly rare. Admittedly, *self-deprecate* goes a long way towards blurring the distinction, for it means 'belittle yourself', not 'condemn yourself'; in this sense it is well established, but it may be best regarded as the exception rather than the rule. Both words have more common synonyms: *condemn, deplore,* and *disapprove of* for ***deprecate***, and *belittle, disparage,* and *decry* for ***depreciate***. ***Depreciate*** is also commonly used intransitively (without an object), in financial contexts, to mean 'lose value': *The value of the yen has depreciated 20 per cent in real terms.*

deprecating /déppra kayting/ *adj* showing or expressing disapproval —**deprecatingly** *adv*

deprecatory /déppri kaytəri, -kətəri/, **deprecative** /-kətiv/ *adj* **1** disapproving and critical **2** showing or expressing apology —**deprecatorily** *adv*

depreciate /di preéshi ayt/ (**-ates, -ating, -ated**) *v* **1** *vti* LOSE VALUE to lessen in value or to become less valuable **2** *vt* DECREASE VALUE FOR TAX PURPOSES to consider something as having less value each year over a fixed period, for the calculation of income tax **3** *vt* BELITTLE to speak critically or disparagingly about something or somebody [15C. < late Latin *depreciare*, alteration of Latin *depretiare* 'lower the price of' < *pretium* 'price, money'.] —**depreciatingly** *adv* —**depreciator** *n* —**depreciable** *adj*

USAGE See ***deprecate***.

depreciation /di preéshi áysh'n/ *n* **1** DROP IN VALUE the decrease in value of an item over time **2** AMOUNT OF DECREASE the amount or percentage by which something decreases in value over time, usually one year **3** BELITTLEMENT critical commentary or strong disparagement of somebody or something

depreciative /di preéshi ətiv/ *adj* **1** reducing or tending to reduce something in value **2** losing or tending to lose value

depreciatory /di preéshi ətəri/ *adj* **1** FIN = **depreciative** **2** belittling or critical

depredation /déppra dáysh'n/ *n* an attack involving plunder and pillage

depress /di préss/ *vt* **1** MAKE SAD to make somebody feel very sad or hopeless ○ *'There's nothing that depresses me more than seeing a planet being destroyed'.* (Douglas Adams, *Life, The Universe, and Everything;* 1982) **2** WEAKEN to weaken something or make something less active **3** REDUCE to decrease the value of something **4** PRESS to press something, e.g. a button or lever [14C. Via Old French < Latin *depress-*, past participle of *deprimere* 'press down' < *premere* 'press'.] —**depressible** *adj*

depressant /di préss'nt/ *n* a drug or agent that slows the body's vital functions ■ *adj* able to sedate or lower the rate of the body's vital functions

depressed /di prést/ *adj* **1** UNHAPPY unhappy or hopeless **2** HAVING DEPRESSION having the psychiatric disorder depression **3** ECONOMICALLY LACKING lacking economic resources or activities **4** WEAK less active or strong than usual **5** LOWER lower than the surrounding area **6** FLATTENED flattened, as if from downward pressure

depressing /di préssing/ *adj* making somebody feel sad or disheartened —**depressingly** *adv* —**depressingness** *n*

depression /di présh'n/ *n* **1** UNHAPPINESS a state of unhappiness and hopelessness **2** PSYCHIATRIC DISORDER a psychiatric disorder showing symptoms such as persistent feelings of hopelessness, dejection, poor concentration, lack of energy, inability to sleep, and, sometimes, suicidal tendencies **3** ECONOMIC SLUMP a period in which an economy is greatly affected by unemployment, low output, and poverty **4** REDUCED ACTIVITY a lowering of activity, quality, vitality, or force **5** HOLLOW an area on the surface of something that is lower than the surface surrounding it **6** LOW PRESSURE AREA an area of low barometric pressure that often brings rain

depressive /di préssiv/ *adj* **1** CAUSING DEPRESSION relating to or causing depression ○ *the depressive atmosphere of a grey, cold marshland* **2** HAVING DEPRESSION experiencing or with a history of depression ■ *n* DEPRESSED PERSON a habitually depressed person —**depressively** *adv* —**depressiveness** *n*

depressor /di préssər/ *n* **1** MEDICAL INSTRUMENT a medical or surgical instrument that is used to move aside or press down an organ or part of the body **2** PULLING MUSCLE a muscle that acts to pull down a part of the body **3** SOMEBODY OR SOMETHING THAT PRESSES DOWN somebody or something that presses down

depressor nerve *n* a nerve that, when stimulated, decreases activity in an organ, lowers blood pressure, or slows the heart

depressurize /dee préshə rīz/ (**-izes, -izing, -ized**), **depressurise** (**-ises, -ising, -ised**) *vt* to reduce the pressure of air or gas within a container, cabin, or other enclosed space —**depressurization** /de préshə rī záysh'n/ *n*

deprivation /déppri váysh'n/ *n* **1** the state of being without or denied something, especially of lacking adequate food or shelter **2** the act of taking something away from somebody or preventing somebody from having something

deprive /di prīv/ (**-prives, -priving, -prived**) *vt* to prevent somebody from having something [14C. Via Old French < medieval Latin *deprivare* 'deprive completely' < Latin *privare* (see PRIVATION).] —**deprivable** *adj* —**depriver** *n*

deprived /di prīvd/ *adj* lacking adequate food and shelter

de profundis /dáy prə fŏŏndiss/ *adv* out of the depths of misery or despair [13C. < Latin, 'out of the depths', first words of Psalm 130.]

deprogramme /deé prṓ gram/ (**-grammes, -gramming, -grammed**) *vt* to undo the effects of indoctrination on an individual, especially somebody under the influence of a religious group —**deprogrammer** *n*

dept *abbr* department

depth /depth/ *n* **1** HOW DEEP SOMETHING IS the distance or measurement from the top of something to its bottom, from front to back, or from the outside in **2** BEING DEEP the quality of being deep **3** INTENSITY the intensity or strength of a feeling or emotion **4** COMPLEXITY complexity or profundity of character ○ *a woman of great depth* ○ *hidden depths of knowledge* **5** BREADTH wideness in scope **6** COLOUR QUALITY the intensity or richness of a colour **7** LOWNESS the low tone or pitch of a sound ■ *npl* **1 depths** LOWEST POINT the lowest or worst point or moment ○ *the depths of despair* **2 depths** DEEP PART a deep or remote part of something ○ *the ocean depths* **3 depths** MIDDLE PART the middle part of something long, monotonous, and possibly unpleasant ○ *in the depths of tedious research* **4** DEBASEMENT a state of great moral debasement ○ *having fallen to such depths* [14C. < DEEP.] ◇ **hidden depths** interesting or serious aspects of a somebody's character that are not immediately obvious ○ *He has hidden depths.* ◇ **out of your depth 1** unable to stand because the water is too deep **2** unable to understand or do something because it is outside the range of your knowledge or skills

depth charge, depth bomb *n* a bomb that is designed to explode at a particular depth under water, often used against submarines

depth gauge, depth finder *n* an instrument that measures the depth of water or other liquid

depth of field *n* the total focused area in front of and behind an object held in the focus of a camera or lens

depth of focus *n* the distance that a camera lens can be moved closer to or further from the film, without the resulting image being blurred

depth perception *n* the ability to perceive objects and their spatial relationship in three dimensions

depth psychology *n* the study and psychology of the unconscious mind

depth sounder *n* an ultrasonic instrument that measures the depth of water under a ship

depurate /déppyŏŏ rayt/ (**-rates, -rating, -rated**) *vt* to cleanse or purify something, especially by removing toxins [Early 17C. < medieval Latin *depurare* < Latin *purus* 'pure'.] —**depuration** /déppyŏŏ ráysh'n/ *n* —**depurator** *n* —**depurative** *adj*

deputation /déppyŏŏ táysh'n/ *n* **1** a group of people who have been chosen to represent a larger group of people and act on their behalf **2** the act of appointing a deputy or deputation

depute /di pyŏŏt/ *vt* (**-putes, -puting, -puted**) (*formal*) **1** CHOOSE REPRESENTATIVE to choose somebody to be your agent, substitute, or representative **2** DELEGATE to delegate one's work, authority, or duties to somebody else ■ *adj Scotland* **DEPUTY** acting as deputy (*formal*) ○ *headmaster depute* [14C. Via French *députer* < Latin *deputare* 'assign' < *putare* 'consider'.]

deputize /déppyoo tīz/ (**-tizes, -tizing, -tized**), **deputise** (**-tises, -tising, -tised**) *v* **1** *vi* to act as somebody's deputy **2** *vt* to choose somebody to act as a deputy to somebody —**deputization** /déppyoo tī záysh'n/ *n*

deputy /déppyooti/ (*plural* **-ties**) *n* **1 SOMEBODY'S REPRESENTATIVE** a person fully authorized or appointed to act on behalf of somebody else **2 SECOND-IN-COMMAND** an assistant who is authorized to act in a superior's place **3 MEMBER OF PARLIAMENT** a parliamentary representative in some countries, e.g. France, Germany, or Italy **4** *US* LAW = **deputy sheriff** [15C. < French *député*, past participle of *députer* (see DEPUTE).]

deputy head *n* a senior member of a school staff, second in status to the head teacher

deputy sheriff *n* a sheriff's assistant in the United States, authorized to take charge when the sheriff is absent

De Quincey /də kwínssi/, **Thomas** (1785–1859) British essayist and critic

deracinate /dee rássi nayt/ (**-nates, -nating, -nated**) *vt* to remove somebody or something from a natural environment, especially people from their native culture (*literary*) [Late 16C. < French *déraciner* < *racine* 'root', via late Latin *radicina* < Latin *radix*.] —**deracination** /dee rássi náysh'n/ *n*

derail /dee ráyl/ *vti* **1** to make a train or tram come off the rails, or to come off the rails **2** to send something off course, or to go off course [Mid-19C. < French *dérailler* < *rail* (see RAIL[1]).] —**derailment** *n*

derailleur /di ráylyər/ *n* a device for changing gears on a bicycle that lifts the chain from one sprocket wheel to another [Mid-20C. < French *dérailleur* < *dérailler* (see DERAIL).]

Derain /də ráN/, **André** (1880–1954) French painter, illustrator, and stage designer

derange /di ráynj/ (**-ranges, -ranging, -ranged**) *vt* **1 MAKE IRRATIONAL** to make somebody irrational or extraordinarily angry **2 DISTURB** to disturb the normal way in which something works **3 THROW INTO DISORDER** to throw something into disorder and confusion [Late 18C. < French *déranger* 'put out of line' < *rang* 'line'.] —**derangement** *n* —**deranged** *adj*

derate /dee ráyt/ (**-rates, -rating, -rated**) *vt* **1** to lower the rated capability of an electrical apparatus **2** to lower or abolish the rates on a property

deration /dee rásh'n/ *vt* to stop rationing a commodity, usually because the supply has become adequate

derby /daárbi/ (*plural* **-bies**) *n* **1** a horserace run annually, usually for three-year-olds **2** a race or contest, open to qualified competitors **3** *US, Can* CLOTHING = **bowler hat** [Late 19C. After DERBY[1].]

Derby[1] /daárbi/ *n* a flat horserace for three year olds, run annually at Epsom Downs, Surrey, England or one held each spring at Churchill Downs in Louisville, Kentucky, in the United States [Early 19C. After the 12th Earl of *Derby*, who founded the English race.]

Derby[2] /daárbi/ (*plural* **-by** *or* **-bies**) *n* a close-textured pale-coloured cheese, sometimes flavoured with sage [After DERBYSHIRE, where most of it is made]

Derby[3] /daárbi/ **1** city in north-central England. Population: 225,400 (1997). **2** port in NW Australia. Population: 11,942 (1998 estimate).

Derby, 14th Earl of (1799–1869) British statesman and prime minister (1852, 1858–59, and 1866–68). Full name **Edward George Geoffrey Smith Stanley**

Derbyshire /daárbishər/ county in north-central England. Population: 726,000 (1995).

derecognize /dee rékəg nīz/ (**-nizes, -nizing, -nized**), **derecognise** (**-nises, -nising, -nised**) *vt* to stop accepting the legitimacy of something, especially a trade union or diplomatic mission —**derecognition** /dee rekəg nísh'n/ *n*

deregister /dee réjjistər/ *vti* to remove something or somebody from a register or official list —**deregistration** /dee réjji stráysh'n/ *n*

deregulate /dee réggyoo layt/ (**-lates, -lating, -lated**) *vt* to free something such as an organization or industry from regulation —**deregulation** /dee réggyoo láysh'n/ *n* —**deregulator** *n* —**deregulatory** *adj*

derelict /dérrəlikt/ *adj* **1 DESERTED** no longer lived in **2 NEGLECTED** in poor condition because of neglect **3 ABANDONING DUTY** neglectful of your duty or obligations ■ *n* **1 HOMELESS PERSON** a person without a home or employment **2 ABANDONED BUILDING** a building, ship, or other property that has been abandoned or deserted **3 NEGLECTFUL PERSON** a person who is neglectful of duty or obligations [Mid-17C. < Latin *derelictus*, past participle of *derelinquere* 'abandon utterly' < *relinquere* (see RELINQUISH).]

dereliction /dérrə líksh'n/ *n* **1 NEGLECT OF DUTY** deliberate neglect of duty or obligations **2 ABANDONMENT** the act of abandoning or deserting a building **3 STATE OF NEGLECT** a state of abandonment or neglect **4 LAND GAINED FROM THE SEA** land gained because water has receded from it

derepress /dee ri préss/ *vt* to activate a gene by deactivating the repressor —**derepression** *n*

derepressor /dee ri préssər/ *n* an agent, e.g. a protein, that begins or enhances gene transcription by removing the repression of an operon —**derepression** *n*

derequisition /dee rékwi zísh'n/ *vt* to return something to civilian use that was earlier requisitioned by the military or a government

derestrict /dee ri stríkt/ *vt* to remove the restrictions from something —**derestriction** *n*

Derg, Lough /durg/ stretch of water in W Ireland, in counties Tipperary, Galway, and Clare. Area: 96 sq. km/37 sq. mi. Depth: 36 m/118 ft. Length: 32 km/20 mi.

deride /di ríd/ (**-rides, -riding, -rided**) *vt* to ridicule or show contempt for somebody or something [Mid-16C. < Latin *deridere* 'laugh down' < *ridere* 'laugh'.] —**derider** *n* —**deridingly** *adv*

~~**de rigeur**~~ incorrect spelling of **de rigueur**

de rigueur /də ri gúr/ *adj* strictly required by the current fashion or by etiquette [Mid-19C. < French, 'of strictness'.]

derision /di rízh'n/ *n* contempt and mockery [14C. < French *dérision* < Latin *deridere* (see DERIDE).] —**derisible** /di rízzəb'l/ *adj*

derisive /di ríssiv, -zív/ *adj* showing contempt or ridicule [Mid-17C. < DERISION.] —**derisively** *adv* —**derisiveness** *n*

USAGE ***derisive*** or ***derisory***? ***Derisive*** means 'showing contempt or ridicule': *He gave a derisive laugh.* ***Derisory*** means 'deserving contempt or ridicule': *a derisory offer*, though it sometimes is used as a synonym of ***derisive***, as in *looked at me with a derisory smile.* Careful writers do try to maintain the distinction and the use of ***derisory*** where ***derisive*** is appropriate is best avoided.

derisory /di ríssəri, -ríz-/ *adj* **1** so small or inadequate for the purpose intended that it is ridiculous **2** ⚠ contemptuous. [Early 17C. < late Latin *derisorius* < Latin *deridere* (see DERIDE).]

USAGE See ***derisive***.

deriv. *abbr* **1** derivation **2** derivative

derivate *n, adj* = **derivative** [15C. < Latin *derivatus*, past participle of *derivare* (see DERIVE).]

derivation /dérri váysh'n/ *n* **1 SOURCE** the origin or source of something, e.g. a word or someone's name **2 WORD FORMATION** the formation of a word or term from another word or from a basic form **3 PROOF** a mathematical or logical argument whose steps show that the conclusion follows necessarily from initial assumptions **4 ACT OF DERIVING** the act of obtaining something from a source or issuing from a source —**derivational** *adj*

SYNONYMS See ***origin***.

derivative /di rívvətiv/ *adj* **UNORIGINAL** copied from somewhere and not original ■ *n* **1 DERIVED THING** an idea, language, term, or other thing that has developed from something else that is similar to it **2 DERIVED WORD** a word that is formed from another word, e.g. 'quickly' from 'quick' **3 RELATED CHEMICAL PRODUCT** a chemical substance that is formed from a related substance **4 CHANGE OF FUNCTION** the limit approached in the ratio of a function and its variable, as the variable is changed ever more infinitesimally **5 FINANCIAL PRODUCT** a tradable financial product whose value depends on the value of some other asset or combination of assets —**derivatively** *adv* —**derivativeness** *n*

derive /di rív/ (**-rives, -riving, -rived**) *v* **1** *vti* **GET OR COME FROM** to obtain something or come from a source **2** *vt* **DEDUCE** to reach a conclusion about something by reasoning **3** *vt* **MAKE COMPOUND** to create a chemical substance from another **4** *vti* **COME FROM SOURCE** to develop from another word or a source word or term **5** *vt* **OBTAIN FUNCTION** to obtain a function by differentiation [14C. Directly or via French *dériver* < Latin *derivare* 'draw off water through a channel' < *rivus* 'stream'.] —**derivable** *adj* —**deriver** *n*

derived unit *n* a unit of measurement that is a multiple or fraction of a base unit

derm- *prefix* = **derma-** (*before vowels*)

-derm *suffix* skin ○ *ectoderm* [< Greek *derma*]

derma- *prefix* skin ○ *dermatome* [Early 18C. Via modern Latin < Greek, 'skin'.]

dermabrasion /dúrmə bráyzh'n/ *n* a surgical process that removes scars or other imperfections of the skin by scraping the skin's surface with wire brushes or very fine sandpaper [Mid-20C. < Greek *derma* 'skin' + ABRASION.]

dermal /dúrm'l/, **dermic** /-mik/ *adj* involving, located in, or made up of skin or its main layer (**dermis**) [Early 19C. < Greek *derma* 'skin'.]

dermapteran /dur máptərən/ *n* an insect, e.g. an earwig, that has strong sharp sensory appendages coming from the end of its abdomen [Late 19C. < modern Latin *Dermaptera* < Greek *derma* 'skin' + *pteron* 'wing'.] —**dermapteran** *adj*

dermat- *prefix* = **dermato-** (*before vowels*)

dermatitis /dúrmə títiss/ *n* inflammation of the skin from any cause, resulting in a range of symptoms such as redness, swelling, itching, or blistering

dermato- *prefix* skin ○ *dermatoplasty* [< Greek *dermat-*, stem of *derma* 'skin']

dermatoglyphics /dúrmətō glíffiks/ *npl* the lines that form a pattern on the skin, e.g. on the fingers and palms of the hands ■ *n* the study of dermatoglyphics (+ *singular verb*) [Early 20C. < DERMATO- + Greek *gluphē* 'carving' (see GLYPH).] —**dermatoglyphic** *adj*

dermatoid /dúrmə toyd/ *adj* resembling skin

dermatology /dúrmə tólləji/ *n* the branch of medicine that deals with the skin and diseases affecting the skin —**dermatological** /dúrmətə lójjik'l/ *adj* —**dermatologically** *adv* —**dermatologist** *n*

dermatome /dúrmətōm/ *n* **1** an area of skin that has nerve fibres coming from a single spinal nerve **2** an instrument used to slice thin layers of skin for skin grafting —**dermatomic** /dúrmə tómmik/ *adj*

dermatophyte /dur máttə fīt/ *n* a parasitic fungus that affects the skin, hair, or nails —**dermatophytic** /dur máttə fíttik/ *adj*

dermatophytosis /dúrmətō fī tóssiss/ *n* a fungal infection of the skin, hair, or nails

dermatoplasty /dúrmətō plasti/ *n* any operation on the skin, especially skin grafting (*technical*) —**dermatoplastic** /dúrmətō plástik/ *adj*

dermatosis /dúrmə tóssiss/ (*plural* **-ses** /-seez/) *n* any disease affecting the skin

-dermatous *suffix* having a particular kind of skin ○ *sclerodermatous* [< Greek *dermat-* (see DERMATO-)]

dermestid /dur méstid/ *n* a beetle with clubbed antennae that eats organic materials, e.g. cabinet and carpet beetles. Family: Dermestidae. [Late 19C. < modern Latin *Dermestidae* < Greek *derma* 'skin' + *esthiein* 'eat'.]

dermic /dúrmik/ *adj* = **dermal** [Mid-19C. < Greek *derma* 'skin'.]

dermis /dúrmiss/ *n* the thick sensitive layer of skin or connective tissue beneath the epidermis that contains blood, lymph vessels, sweat glands, and nerve endings [Mid-19C. < modern Latin, back-formation < EPIDERMIS.]

-dermis *suffix* skin ○ *endodermis* [Back-formation < EPIDERMIS]

dermoid /dúr moyd/, **dermoid cyst** *n* a benign tumour that contains skin or skin derivatives, found in the ovaries or on the face, especially round the eyes [Early 19C. < Greek *derma* 'skin'.]

dernier cri /dúrni ay kréé/ *n* the latest thing in fashion [Late 19C. < French, 'latest cry'.]

derogate /dérrə gayt/ (**-gates, -gating, -gated**) *v* **1** *vi* **DEVIATE FROM CONDITIONS** to deviate from a norm, rule, law, or set of conditions, e.g. by refusing to be bound by part of a treaty **2** *vi* **MAKE SEEM INFERIOR** to make something seem inferior or less significant (*formal*) ○ *conduct that will derogate from your good name* **3** *vt* **CRITICIZE** to criticize somebody or something **4** *vt* **REPEAL PARTIALLY** to repeal or abolish part of a law or decree [15C. < Latin *derogare* 'repeal a law, detract from, impair' < *rogare* 'ask, propose a law'.]

derogation /dérrə gáysh'n/ *n* **1 DEVIATION** a deviation from a rule or law, especially one specifically provided for **2 EXEMPTION FROM RULE** an exemption from a law or ruling given to a state **3 DISPARAGEMENT** the act of belittling or criticizing somebody or something —**derogative** /di róggətiv/ *adj* —**derogatively** *adv*

derogatory /di róggətəri/ *adj* expressing a low opinion or criticism —**derogatorily** *adv* —**derogatoriness** *n*

derrick /dérrik/ *n* **1** a simple crane that is typically used for moving cargo onto or from a ship **2** a structure placed over an oil well that is used to raise and lower piping, drills, and other boring equipment [Early 17C. Originally 'hangman, gallows', after a London hangman called *Derrick*.]

Derrida /de réedа/, **Jacques** (*b.* 1930) Algerian-born French philosopher

derrière /dérri air, dérri áir/ *n* somebody's bottom (*humorous*) [Late 18C. < French, 'behind'.]

derring-do /dérring dóo/ *n* boldness or acts of great daring (*dated*) [Late 16C. Alteration and misinterpretation of *dorring don* 'daring to do'.]

derringer /dérrinjər/ *n* a pocket-sized, short-barrelled, large-calibre pistol [Mid-19C. After Henry *Deringer*.]

derris /dérriss/ *n* **1** an insecticide made from a tropical plant, which contain the natural toxin rotenone **2** a woody climbing plant with a tuberous root that produces derris. Native to: SE Asia. Genus: *Derris*. [Mid-19C. Via modern Latin < Greek, 'leather covering'.]

derry /dérri/ (*plural* **-ries**) *n* a derelict house (*dated slang*) [Mid-20C. Shortening.]

Derry /dérri/ district council in NW Northern Ireland. Population: 72,334 (1991).

derv /durv/ *n* diesel oil used as a fuel for road vehicles [Mid-20C. Acronym < *diesel-engined road vehicle*.]

dervish /dúrvish/ *n* **1** a member of any of several ascetic Muslim religious groups, some of which are known for their practices of very energetic dancing, whirling, chanting, or singing **2** a very energetic person [Late 16C. Via Turkish *derviş* < Persian *darvīš* 'poor, mendicant'.]

Derwent /dúrwent/ river in S Tasmania, Australia. Length: 190 km/118 mi.

Derwentwater /dúrwənt wawtər/ lake in NW England. Length: 4.8 km/3 mi.

⚡**DES** *abbr* **1** data encryption standard **2** diethylstilboestrol

desacralize /dee sákrə līz/ (**-izes, -izing, -ized**), **desacralise** (**-ises, -ising, -ised**) *vt* to remove the sacred, religious, or supernatural qualities or status from something

Desai /de sí/, **Morarji Ranchhodji** (1896–1995) Indian statesman and prime minister of India (1977–79)

desalinate /dee sálli nayt/ (**-nates, -nating, -nated**) *vt* to remove the salt from something —**desalinator** *n* —**desalination** /dee sálli náysh'n/ *n*

desalinize /dee sálli nīz/ (**-nizes, -nizing, -nized**), **desalinise** (**-nises, -nising, -nised**) *vt* = **desalinate** —**desalinization** /dee sálli nī záysh'n/ *n*

desalt /dee sáwlt, -sólt/ *vt* = **desalinate** —**desalter** *n*

desaturation /dee sáchə ráysh'n/ *n* the addition of white to a saturated colour in order to achieve a paler shade

descale /dee skáyl/ (**-scales, -scaling, -scaled**) *vt* to remove the limescale that has accumulated in a household appliance such as a kettle

descant /déss kant, díss-/, **discant** /díss-/ *n* **1 HIGH MELODY** a melody that is sung or played above the basic melody of a piece of music **2 COMMENT** a comment, remark, or criticism on a particular subject ■ *vi* **DISCOURSE ON** to comment at length on a particular subject (*literary*) [14C. Via Anglo-Norman *descaunt* < medieval Latin *discantus* 'part song, refrain' < Latin *cantus* 'song'.] —**descanter** /de skántər, di-/ *n*

Descartes /dáy kaart/, **René** (1596–1650) French philosopher and mathematician

descend /di sénd/ *v* **1** *vti* **GO DOWN** to go down a staircase, hill, valley, or other downward incline **2** *vi* **COME NEARER GROUND** to come nearer the ground, especially in an aircraft in preparation for landing **3** *vi* **SLOPE** to slope downwards **4** *vti* **BE RELATED** to be connected by blood to an ancestor ○ *Our family descends from French royalty.* ○ *be descended from* **5** *vi* **BE INHERITED** to be inherited from or passed down by parents or ancestors **6** *vi* **LOWER ONESELF** to behave in a way that is disappointing and below somebody's normal standards **7** *vi* **ARRIVE SUDDENLY** to arrive at a place suddenly, especially in large numbers ○ *tourists descending on unspoilt areas* **8** *vi* **BECOME ESTABLISHED** to become more evident or established, suddenly or by degrees ○ *An atmosphere of gloom descended on the assembled crowd.* [14C. Via French *descendre* < Latin *descendere* 'climb down' < *scandere* 'climb'.] —**descendable** *adj*

descendant /di séndənt/ *n* **1** a person, animal, or plant related to one that lived in the past **2** something that is based in design, form, or concept on an earlier thing ■ *adj* = **descendent**

SPELLCHECK Do not confuse ***descendant*** with ***descendent***, which has a similar sound. Beware: your spellchecker will not catch this error.

descendent /di séndənt/, **descendant** *adj* **1** moving downwards **2** descending from an ancestor

SPELLCHECK See ***descendant***.

descender /di séndər/ *n* **1** the tail part of a letter, e.g. on a 'y' or 'g', that extends below the baseline of other letters **2** somebody or something that descends

descendeur /déssaaN dúr/ *n* a mechanical device that can be tightened or loosened on a rope, enabling a climber to control the speed of his or her descent [Late 20C. < French, 'descender' < *descendre* (see DESCEND).]

descendible /di séndəb'l/ *adj* **1** able to be inherited **2** allowing descent or downward movement

descending /di sénding/ *adj* going or arranged from highest to lowest, greatest to smallest, or latest to earliest ○ *in descending order*

descent /di sént/ *n* **1 GOING DOWN** an act of going from the top to the bottom or from a higher position to a lower position **2 WAY DOWN** a path or other way down something, e.g. a mountain **3 DECLINE** a decline or change from something better to something worse **4 ANCESTRAL BACKGROUND** the connection somebody has to an ancestor or group of ancestors **5 SUDDEN ARRIVAL** the sudden arrival of a person or group of people **6 INHERITED DEVELOPMENT** characteristics or developments that can be traced to an earlier source **7 ONE GENERATION** a step of one generation in a lineage **8 INHERITANCE** the transmission of property by inheritance [13C. < French *descente* < *descendre* (see DESCEND).]

SPELLCHECK Do not confuse ***descent*** with ***dissent***, which has a similar sound. Beware: your spellchecker will not catch this error.

Deschamps /day shaáN/, **Eustache** (1340?–1407?) French poet

deschool /dee skóol/ *v* **1** *vt* to remove children from school to educate them at home **2** *vti* to reduce somebody's involvement with education within the school system, or to undergo this process —**deschooling** *n*

descramble /dee skrámb'l/ (**-bles, -bling, -bled**) *vt* to make intelligible a message transmitted in code form —**descrambler** *n*

describe /di skríb/ (**-scribes, -scribing, -scribed**) *vt* **1 EXPLAIN** to give an account of something by giving details of its characteristics **2 LABEL** to label or typify somebody or something **3 DRAW SHAPE** to make a shape or outline in the air (*formal*) ○ *The plane described a perfect figure of eight.* **4 REPRESENT** to represent something pictorially or with a model [15C. < Latin *describere* 'write down' < *scribere* 'write'.] —**describable** *adj* —**describer** *n*

description /di skrípsh'n/ *n* **1 EXPLANATION** a written or verbal account, representation, or explanation of something **2 PROCESS OF DESCRIBING** the process of giving an account or explanation of something **3 SORT** a kind or variety of something ○ *cars of every description* [14C. Via French < Latin *description-* < *descript-*, past participle of *describere* (see DESCRIBE).]

descriptive /di skríptiv/ *adj* **1 BEING DESCRIPTION** containing or consisting of description **2 CLASSIFYING** serving mainly to label, describe, or classify **3 ATTRIBUTIVE** expressing an attribute or quality of a noun [Mid-18C. < late Latin *descriptivus* < Latin *describere* (see DESCRIBE).] —**descriptively** *adv* —**descriptiveness** *n*

descriptive clause *n* = **nonrestrictive clause**

descriptive linguistics *n* the study of a language limited to a comprehensive account of its grammar at a given time, omitting historical or comparative features and not attempting to formulate prescriptive rules

descriptivism /di skríptivizəm/ *n* **1** adherence to the practices and tenets of descriptive linguistics **2** the notion or thesis that descriptive statements can be true and accurate reflections of phenomena —**descriptivist** *n, adj*

⚡**descriptor** /di skríptər/ *n* a word or phrase used to categorize records in a database so that all records containing the key can be retrieved together [Mid-20C. < Latin, 'describer' < *describere* (see DESCRIBE).]

descry /di skrí/ (**-scries, -scrying, -scried**) *vt* to catch sight of something (*literary*) [14C. < Old French *descrier* 'cry out, proclaim' < *crier* (see CRY).] —**descrier** *n*

Desdemona /dézdi mṓnə/ *n* a small satellite of Uranus, discovered in 1986 by Voyager 2

~~**desease**~~ incorrect spelling of **disease**

desecrate /déssi krayt/ (**-crates, -crating, -crated**) *vt* to damage something sacred or do something that is offensive to the religious nature of something [Late 17C. < DE- + CONSECRATE.] —**desecrater** *n* —**desecration** /déssi kráysh'n/ *n* —**desecrator** /déssi kraytər/ *n*

desegregate /dee séggri gayt/ (**-gates, -gating, -gated**) *vti* to put an end to a customary or enforced separation of ethnic or racial groups, e.g. in a workplace or school —**desegregation** /dee seggri gáysh'n/ *n* —**desegregationist** *n*

⚡**deselect** /dee si lékt/ *vt* **1 REJECT MP** to refuse to select a serving MP, councillor, or party member for re-election **2 REMOVE SELECTION** to remove selection status from an option or data on a menu or list on a computer monitor **3** *US* **LET TRAINEE GO** to end the training of an unsuitable trainee before the training program is completed —**deselection** *n*

desensitize /dee sénssə tīz/ (**-tizes, -tizing, -tized**), **desensitise** (**-tises, -tising, -tised**) *vt* **1 MAKE LESS SENSITIVE** to make somebody or something insensitive or less sensitive **2 MAKE LESS ALLERGIC** to make somebody less sensitive to a known allergen by injecting increasing amounts of the allergen over time, building up resistance **3 MAKE LESS SENSITIVE TO FEAR** to make somebody less responsive to an overwhelming fear by repeated exposure to the feared situation or object, either in natural or artificial circumstances —**desensitization** /dee sénssə tī záysh'n/ *n* —**desensitizer** *n*

desert[1] /dézzərt/ *n* **1 ARID AREA** an area of land, usually in very hot climates, that consists only of sand, gravel, or rock with little or no vegetation, no permanent bodies of water, and erratic rainfall. See chart overleaf. **2 DEPRIVED PLACE** a place or situation that is devoid of some desirable thing or overwhelmed by an undesirable thing ○ *a cultural desert* **3 LIFELESS PLACE** a place devoid of life [12C. Via French *désert* < late Latin *desertum* 'abandoned place' < Latin *desert-* (see DESERT[2]).]

desert[2] /di zúrt/ *v* **1** *vt* **ABANDON PLACE** to leave a place with no one staying behind **2** *vt* **ABANDON PERSON** to leave or abandon somebody, especially when you have some kind of duty or obligation towards him or her **3** *vti* **LEAVE ARMY WITHOUT PERMISSION** to run away from an armed force or military post without permission and intending never to go back **4** *vt* **LEAVE** to be absent when needed ○ *Her sense of humour appeared to have deserted her.* [14C. Via French *déserter* < Latin *desert-*, past participle of *deserere* 'abandon' < *serere* 'join'.] —**deserted** *adj* —**deserter** *n*

USAGE desert or **dessert**? ***Dessert*** is a noun, is pronounced with the stress on the second syllable, and has only one modern meaning: 'a sweet course eaten at the end of a meal'. ***Desert*** is pronounced with the stress on the first syllable when it is a noun meaning 'an arid area', and with the stress on the second syllable when it is a noun meaning 'something somebody deserved', in *just deserts* and similar expressions. The stress is also on the second syllable when ***desert*** is used as a verb, meaning 'abandon something' or 'run away'.

desert[3] /di zúrt/ *n* something deserved, either punishment or reward (*usually plural*) ○ *He'll get his just deserts.* [13C. < Old French, 'what is deserved' < past participle of *deservir* (see DESERVE).]

WORLD'S LARGEST DESERTS

1 Sahara Desert	
Area	[3.5 million sq. mi. / 9.1 million sq. km]
Location	North Africa
2 Rub' al-Khali Desert	
Area	[0.9 million sq. mi. / 2.3 million sq. km]
Location	Southwestern Asia /Arabia
3 Gobi Desert	
Area	[0.5 million sq. mi. / 1.3 million sq. km]
Location	Central Asia / Mongolia
4 Patagonian Desert	
Area	[0.3 million sq. mi. / 0.8 million sq. km]
Location	South America / Argentina
5 Kalahari Desert	
Area	[0.27 million sq. mi. / 0.71 million sq. km]
Location	Southwestern Africa
6 Great Victoria Desert	
Area	[0.25 million sq. mi. / 0.65 million sq. km]
Location	Australia
7 Great Basin Desert	
Area	[0.2 million sq. mi. / 0.5 million sq. km]
Location	North America
8 Great Sandy Desert	
Area	[0.15 million sq. mi. / 0.4 million sq. km]
Location	Australia
9 Sonoran Desert	
Area	[0.12 million sq. mi. / 0.31 million sq. km]
Location	North America
10 Garagum Desert	
Area	[0.11 million sq. mi. / 0.28 million sq. km]
Location	Central Asia / Turkmenistan

desertification /di zúrtifi káysh'n/ n a process by which land becomes increasingly dry until almost no vegetation grows on it, making it a desert

desertion /di zúrsh'n/ n the act or an instance of deserting from the armed forces

desert island n a small isolated unpopulated tropical island

desert pavement n a layer of gravel that remains when the finer-grained particles of a desert soil have been blown away

desert pea n a trailing plant with bright red flowers. Native to: Australia. *Clianthus formosus*.

desert rat n 1 any rodent that lives in a desert 2 a soldier who served in the British 7th Armoured Division in North Africa during World War II (*informal*)

desert varnish n a very thin dark surface coating of iron and manganese oxides that forms on exposed rock surfaces in deserts

deserve /di zúrv/ (-serves, -serving, -served) vt to have earned or be worthy of something [13C. Via Old French *deservir* < Latin *deservire* 'serve well' < *servire* (see SERVE).] —**deserved** adj —**deservedness** n —**deserver** n

deservedly /di zúrvidli/ adv in a way that is justly and fully earned or merited ○ *She was deservedly popular as a teacher.*

deserving /di zúrving/ adj worthy to receive something because of need, merit, or justice ○ *The charity was thought to be a deserving cause.* —**deservingly** adv —**deservingness** n

desex /dee séks/ vt 1 to remove the sex organs from an animal or person 2 = **desexualize**

desexualize /dee séksho ə līz/ (-izes, -izing, -ized), **desexualise** (-ises, -ising, -ised) vt to suppress or diminish the sexual characteristics of an animal or person —**desexualization** /dee séksho ə lī záysh'n/ n

deshabille /dáysə beél/, **dishabille** /díssə-/ n a state in which somebody is partially undressed or dressed very casually or incompletely (*formal*) [Late 17C. < French *déshabillé*, past participle of *déshabiller* 'undress' < *habiller* 'dress'.]

De Sica /də seékə/, **Vittorio** (1901–74) Italian film director and actor

desiccant /déssikənt/ n a substance that absorbs water. Use: removal of moisture. [Late 17C. < Latin *desiccant-*, present participle of *desiccare* (see DESICCATE).]

desiccate /déssi kayt/ (-cates, -cating, -cated) v 1 to remove the moisture from something or become free of moisture 2 vt to preserve food by removing its moisture [Late 16C. < Latin *desiccat-*, past participle of *desiccare* 'dry out' < *siccus* 'dry'.] —**desiccation** /déssi káysh'n/ n —**desiccative** adj —**desiccator** n

desiccated /déssi kaytid/ adj 1 dried and often pulverized 2 lacking in energy or vitality

SYNONYMS See **dry**.

desiderata plural of **desideratum**

desiderative /di zíddərətiv, -sídd-/ adj 1 having a desire for something (*formal*) 2 describes a verb that, in some languages, expresses a desire to perform the action indicated by a related verb

desideratum /di zíddə ráátəm, -síddə-/ (*plural* **-ta** /-tə/) n something that is desired or felt to be essential [Mid-17C. < Latin, neuter past participle of *desiderare* 'desire, wish for'.]

design /di zín/ v 1 vti CREATE DETAILED PLAN OF to make a detailed plan of the form or structure of something, emphasizing features such as its appearance, convenience, and efficient functioning ○ *a well-designed car interior* 2 vti PLAN AND MAKE to plan and make something in a skilful or artistic way 3 vt INTEND FOR A USE to intend something for a particular purpose ○ *The scholarship was designed to aid foreign students.* 4 vt INVENT to contrive, devise, or plan something ○ *They designed a scheme to get rich quick.* ■ n 1 PICTURE OF SOMETHING'S FORM AND STRUCTURE a drawing or other graphical representation of something that shows how it is to function or be made 2 WAY SOMETHING IS MADE the way in which something is planned and made ○ *the elegant design of the aircraft's wings* 3 DECORATIVE PATTERN a pattern or shape, sometimes repeated, used for decoration ○ *a geometric design* 4 PROCESS OF DESIGNING the process, techniques, or art of designing things ○ *studied architecture and design* 5 INTENTION an underlying sense of purpose or planning ■ **designs** npl SELFISH OR DISHONEST PLAN a secretive plan undertaken for selfish or dishonest motives [14C. < Latin *designare* (see DESIGNATE).] —**designable** adj ◇ **by design** intentionally or on purpose

designate /dézzig nayt/ vt (-nates, -nating, -nated) 1 DESCRIBE FORMALLY to give somebody or something a formal description or name (*often passive*) 2 CHOOSE FOR A USE to choose something for a particular purpose (*usually passive*) 3 NAME TO A POSITION to formally choose somebody for a job, position, or duty 4 MARK to mark or indicate something ○ *Coloured pins on the map designated the new buildings.* ■ adj CHOSEN FOR FUTURE POST chosen for a particular position, while not yet actually in office [Late 18C. < Latin *designat-*, past participle of *designare* 'mark out' < *signum* 'mark'.] —**designative** /dézzig naytiv/ adj —**designator** n —**designatory** /dézzig náytəri, -nətəri/ adj

designated driver n a driver of a motor vehicle who abstains from alcoholic drinks on a social occasion in order to drive people home safely

designated hitter n a player in baseball who does not play defensively but substitutes for a pitcher in the batting order

designation /dézzig náysh'n/ n 1 a name, label, or description given to something or somebody 2 the act or process of being named or specified

designedly /di zínidli/ adv intentionally or on purpose

designer /di zínər/ n SOMEBODY WHO DESIGNS a maker of designs ■ adj 1 FASHIONABLE describes something to suggest that it is trendy and popular ○ *designer foods* 2 DESIGNED BY SOMEBODY FAMOUS created or produced by a famous designer

designer baby n a baby preselected at the embryo stage for desirable characteristics (*informal*)

designer drug n a drug that has been chemically altered to enhance its properties or to evade a legal prohibition

designer gene n a gene that is introduced into an organism to control the presence or absence of a specific characteristic

designer stubble n beard growth that is kept deliberately short to look as if the person has not shaved recently rather than as if trying to grow a beard (*informal*)

designing /di zíning/ adj tending to scheme and make secret plans for personal benefit —**designingly** adv

desinence /déssinənss/ n an ending or suffix of a word (*technical*) [Late 16C. Via French *désinence* < medieval Latin *desinentia* < Latin *desinere* 'leave off, end' < *sinere* 'leave'.] —**desinential** /déssi nénsh'l/ adj

desirable /di zírəb'l/ adj 1 WORTHY OF DESIRE worth having or doing 2 ATTRACTIVE sexually attractive or pleasing ■ n SOMEBODY OR SOMETHING DESIRED somebody who or something that is desired —**desirability** /di zírə bílləti/ n —**desirably** adv

desire /di zír/ vt (-sires, -siring, -sired) 1 WISH FOR to want something very strongly 2 FIND SEXUALLY ATTRACTIVE to want to have sexual relations with somebody 3 REQUEST to wish for and request something (*formal*) ■ n 1 CRAVING a wish, craving, or longing for something 2 SOMETHING WISHED FOR something that or somebody who is wished for (*formal*) 3 SEXUAL CRAVING a strong wish for sexual relations with somebody (*formal*) ○ *'Is it not strange that desire should so many years outlive performance?'* (William Shakespeare, *Henry IV, Part 2*) [13C. Via Old French < Latin *desiderare*.] —**desirer** n

SYNONYMS See **want**.

desirous /di zírəss/ adj seeking or wishing for something very much (*formal*) —**desirously** adv —**desirousness** n

desist /di síst, -zíst/ vi to cease or stop doing something [15C. Via Old French < Latin *desistere* < *sistere* 'bring to a standstill' < *stare* 'stand'.] —**desistance** n

desk /desk/ n 1 TABLE USED FOR WORK a table with a broad flat or sloping top, often with drawers and compartments, used for writing, reading, drawing, or computing 2 COUNTER OFFERING SERVICE TO CUSTOMERS a counter where a service is provided, e.g. in a hotel or an airport 3 DEPARTMENT OF ORGANIZATION a division of a communications company or other organization that specializes in a particular area of interest 4 STAND FOR SUPPORTING MUSIC a stand for supporting a musical score that is shared by two players in an orchestra, or the two players who share it 5 BOOK STAND IN CHURCH a stand for the book from which a service is read in church ■ adj OF A DESK at, for, done on, or taking place at a desk [14C. Via medieval Latin *desca* < Latin *discus* 'disc, dish, tray' (see DISH).]

deskbound /désk bownd/ adj working at a desk rather than at a physically active or practical task

desk dining n eating lunch at your desk at your place of work, in order to save time (*informal*)

desk editor n a preparer of text for typesetting or publishing

deskill /deé skíl/ vt to remove the need for skill or judgment in the performance of a task, often because of increasingly sophisticated production methods

desk sergeant n a police sergeant who works in administration at a police station

⚡**desktop** /désk top/ n 1 SURFACE OF DESK the working surface of a desk 2 GRAPHICAL COMPUTER REPRESENTATION OF OFFICE DESK a display on a computer screen comprising background and icons representing equipment, programs, and files ■ adj USABLE ON TOP OF DESK small and compact enough for the top of a desk, especially a piece of computer equipment

⚡**desktop publishing** n the use of a personal computer and specialist software to lay out and produce typeset-quality documents for printing

desm- *prefix* = **desmo-** (before vowels)

desman /déssman/ n 1 an amphibious mammal resembling a mole that has dense fur, webbed feet, and a flat scaly tail. Native to: Pyrenees. *Galemys pyrenaicus*. 2 an amphibious mammal related to the Pyrenean desman. Native to: Russia. *Desmana moschata*. [Late 18C. Shortening of Swedish *desmanrátta* 'muskrat' < *desman* 'musk' + *rátta* 'rat'.]

desmid /déssmid, déz-/ n a green, usually one-celled, freshwater alga composed of two symmetrical halfcells. Family: Desmidiaceae. [Mid-19C. < modern Latin *Desmidium* < Greek *desmos* 'bond, chain'.] —**desmidian** /dess míddi ən, dez-/ adj

desmo- *prefix* ligament, bond ○ *desmosome* [< Greek *desmos* < *dein* 'bind']

Des Moines /di móyn/ capital of Iowa, in the south-central part of the state. Population: 191,293 (1998 estimate).

desmosome /dézmə sōm/ *n* a small patch of interlocking fibres between the outer membranes of adjacent cells that helps to hold cells together in tissues such as skin

Desmoulins /dáy moo láN/, **Camille** (1760–94) French revolutionary and journalist

desolate *adj* /déssələt/ **1 EMPTY** bare, uninhabited, and deserted **2 ALONE** solitary, joyless, and without hope ○ *'And I was desolate and sick of an old passion'* (Ernest Dowson, *Non Sum Qualis Eram Bonae Sub Regno Cynarae*; 1896) **3 GRIM** dismal and gloomy ■ *vt* /déssə layt/ (**-lates, -lating, -lated**) **1 DEVASTATE PLACE** to make a place barren or deserted **2 MAKE WRETCHED** to make somebody feel sad and lonely [14C. < Latin *desolatus*, past participle of *desolare* 'leave alone' < *solus* 'alone'.] —**desolater** *n* —**desolately** *adv* —**desolateness** *n* —**desolation** /déssə láysh'n/ *n*

desorption /dee sáwrpsh'n, -záwrp-/ *n* the action or process of releasing an absorbed substance from something, e.g. gas from rocks [Early 20C. < DE- + ABSORPTION.]

De Soto /də sṓtō/, **Hernando** (1500?–42?) Spanish explorer

despair /di spáir/ *n* **1 FEELING OF HOPELESSNESS** a profound feeling that there is no hope **2 CAUSE OF HOPELESSNESS** somebody or something that makes somebody feel hopeless or exasperated ■ *vi* **LOSE HOPE** to feel that there is no hope [13C. Via Old French, < Latin *desperare* 'stop hoping' < *sperare* 'to hope' < *spes* 'hope'.]

despairing /di spáiring/ *adj* feeling or showing loss of hope ○ *a despairing look* —**despairingly** *adv*

~~**desparate**~~ incorrect spelling of **desperate**

despatch *vti, n* = **dispatch**

desperado /déspə raádō/ (*plural* **-does** *or* **-dos**) *n* a reckless and violent criminal [Early 17C. Alteration of obsolete *desperate* 'desperate person', after Spanish *desesperado*.]

desperate /déssparət/ *adj* **1 DESPAIRING** overwhelmed with urgency and anxiety, to the point of losing hope ○ *Desperate because of his financial situation, he took his own life.* **2 AS LAST RESORT** so drastic or reckless as to be suitable only for a last resort ○ *The firefighters made a last desperate attempt to rescue the children.* **3 EXTREME** extremely difficult, serious, or dangerous ○ *a desperate shortage of food and water* **4 IN GREAT NEED** wanting or needing something very much ○ *Desperate for an answer, she phoned again.* **5 BEYOND HOPE** so wicked as to allow no hope of redemption **6 AWFUL** extremely bad or deplorable [14C. < Latin *desperatus*, past participle of *desperare* (see DESPAIR).] —**desperately** *adv* —**desperateness** *n*

desperation /déspə ráysh'n/ *n* **1** recklessness brought on by great urgency and anxiety ○ *In desperation people were jumping from the windows of the blazing building.* **2** a condition of being without hope

~~**desperatly**~~ incorrect spelling of **desperately**

despicable /di spíkəb'l/ *adj* fully deserving of contempt [Mid-16C. < late Latin *despicabilis* < Latin *despicari* 'look down on'.] —**despicability** /di spíkə bílləti/ *n* —**despicableness** *n* —**despicably** *adv*

Despina /de speénə/ *n* a small natural satellite of Neptune, discovered in 1989 by the Voyager 2 planetary probe

despise /di spíz/ (**-spises, -spising, -spised**) *vt* to look down on and feel contempt for somebody or something [13C. < Old French *despis-*, stem of *despire* < Latin *despicere* 'look down on' < *specere* 'look'.] —**despiser** *n*

despite /di spít/ *prep* **1** notwithstanding or regardless of something ○ *A mission to investigate the rings of Saturn blasted off today despite bad weather.* **2** indicates that something is done unexpectedly or unintentionally ○ *She blushed deeply despite herself.* [13C. Via Old French *despit* 'spite' < Latin *despect-*, past participle of *despicere* (see DESPISE).]

despoil /di spóyl/ *vt* to rob a place, often using force, of everything of value ○ *Thieves had despoiled the palace.* [13C. Via Old French *despoillier* < Latin *despoliare* 'strip entirely of booty' < *spolium* 'booty'.] —**despoiler** *n* —**despoilment** *n* —**despoliation** /di spṓli áysh'n/ *n*

despond /di spónd/ *n* a feeling of extreme unhappiness and hopelessness (*archaic or literary*) [Mid-17C. < Latin *despondere* 'give up (your vitality)' < *spondere* 'to promise'.] —**despondingly** *adv*

despondent /di spóndənt/ *adj* extremely unhappy and discouraged —**despondence** *n* —**despondency** *n* —**despondently** *adv*

despot /déss pot, -pət/ *n* **1 POWERFUL RULER** a tyrant or ruler with absolute powers **2 TYRANNICAL PERSON** somebody who behaves in a tyrannical way towards other people **3 ROMAN, BYZANTINE, OR OTTOMAN RULER** a minor emperor or prince of the later Roman, Byzantine, or Ottoman empires [Mid-16C. Via French *despote* < Greek *despotēs* 'absolute ruler'.]

despotic /di spóttik/, **despotical** /-k'l/ *adj* relating to, typical of, or behaving like a despot —**despotically** *adv*

despotism /déspətizəm/ *n* **1** rule by a despot or tyrant **2** cruel and arbitrary use of power

despumate /di spyoó mayt, désspyoo-/ (**-mates, -mating, -mated**) *v* **1** *vi* to form froth or scum on the surface of a liquid **2** *vt* to remove the scum or froth on the surface of a liquid [Mid-17C. < Latin *despumat-*, past participle of *despumare* 'skim off (scum)' < *spuma* 'foam, scum'.] —**despumation** /désspyoo máysh'n/ *n*

desquamate /déskwə mayt/ (**-mates, -mating, -mated**) *v* **1** *vi* to flake or peel off naturally in small pieces (*refers especially to skin*) **2** *vt* to remove a thin layer of skin, especially as a treatment for acne [Early 18C. < Latin *desquamat-*, past participle of *desquamare* 'scale off' < *squama* 'scale'.] —**desquamation** /déskwə máysh'n/ *n*

des res /déz réz/ *n* a house or flat that is considered, especially by an estate agent, as highly desirable (*informal*) [Late 20C. Shortening of *desirable residence*.]

Dessau /déssow/ city in east-central Germany. Population: 97,800 (1990).

dessert /di zúrt/ *n* a sweet course eaten at the end or towards the end of a meal [Mid-16C. < French, '(course following) clearing the table' < past participle of *desservir* 'remove what has been served' < *servir* (see SERVE).]

USAGE See *desert*[2].

dessertspoon /di zúrt spoon/ *n* **1** a medium-sized spoon, larger than a teaspoon but smaller than a tablespoon and used for eating dessert **2 dessertspoon, dessertspoonful** the amount a dessertspoon contains

dessert wine *n* a sweet wine served with dessert or after a meal

~~**dessicated**~~ incorrect spelling of **desiccated**

destabilize /dee stáybə līz/ (**-lizes, -lizing, -lized**), **destabilise** (**-lises, -lising, -lised**) *vt* to make something, particularly a government or economy, unstable in order to impair its functioning or bring about its collapse —**destabilization** /dee stáybə lī záysh'n/ *n*

destination /désti náysh'n/ *n* **1 PREDETERMINED END OF TRIP** the place to which somebody or something is going or must go **2 INTENDED OR DESTINED END** a purpose for which somebody or something is intended ■ *adj* **INVOLVING A PARTICULAR PLACE** involving or relating to an establishment such as a restaurant or shop that people make a point of going to, usually because of its reputation (*informal*) ○ *destination dining* [14C. < Latin *destination-* 'appointment' < *destinare* (see DESTINE).]

destination wedding *n* a wedding for which the couple travel to an exotic location to have their marriage ceremony

destine /déstin/ (**-tines, -tining, -tined**) *vt* to preordain or intend somebody or something for a particular fate or use [14C. Via French < Latin *destinare* 'set up, decree, determine' < *-stinare* 'cause to stand'.]

destined /déstind/ *adj* **1** sure, preordained, or intended ○ *From an early age he was destined to follow his father in the family business.* **2** bound or travelling towards a particular destination

destiny /déstini/ (*plural* **-nies**) *n* **1 SOMEBODY'S PREORDAINED FUTURE** the apparently predetermined and inevitable series of events that happen to somebody or something ○ *No one could have foreseen that the child's destiny was to rule an empire.* **2 INNER REALIZABLE PURPOSE OF A LIFE** the inner purpose of a life that can be discovered and realized ○ *He decided that his destiny was to go into show business.* **3 destiny, Destiny SOMETHING THAT PREDETERMINES EVENTS** a force or agency that predetermines what will happen ○ *Destiny had decided her future.* [14C. < Old French *destinee* < Latin *destinare* (see DESTINE).]

destitute /désti tyoot/ *adj* **1** lacking all money, resources, and possessions necessary for subsistence **2** lacking or without something [14C. < Latin *destitutus*, past participle of *destituere* 'set down, abandon' < *statuere* 'set' < *status* 'position'.] —**destituteness** *n*

destitution /désti tyoósh'n/ *n* lack of the necessary means of subsistence

destrier /déstri ər/ *n* a warhorse or charger, especially of a medieval knight (*archaic*) [14C. Via Anglo-Norman *destrer*, Old French *destrier* < Latin *dexter* 'right' (because led by the right hand).]

destroy /di stróy/ *v* **1** *vti* **DEMOLISH** to demolish or reduce something to fragments **2** *vti* **RUIN** to ruin or make something useless **3** *vti* **ABOLISH** to abolish, rescind, or end something **4** *vt* **DEFEAT** to defeat somebody in a crushing way **5** *vt* **KILL ANIMAL** to kill something or somebody, especially an animal (*usually passive*) ○ *Afterwards, the dog could not be cured and so had to be destroyed.* [12C. Via Old French *destruire* < Latin *destruere* 'undo results of building' < *struere* 'build'.] —**destroyable** *adj*

destroyer /di stróyər/ *n* **1** a fast highly manoeuvrable warship, smaller than a cruiser and bigger than a frigate, that is used to escort convoys and attack submarines **2** somebody or something that causes destruction

destroying angel *n* a highly poisonous large white mushroom with a frill near the top of its stalk. *Amanita virosa.*

destruct /di strúkt/ *n* the intentional destruction of a malfunctioning missile or rocket after its launch ■ *vti* to intentionally destroy a malfunctioning missile or rocket after its launch, or be destroyed in this way [Mid-20C. Back-formation < DESTRUCTION.]

destructible /di strúktəb'l/ *adj* capable of being destroyed or liable to be destroyed [Mid-18C. Via French < late Latin *destructibilis* < Latin *destruct-* (see DESTRUCTION).] —**destructibility** /di strúktə bílləti/ *n*

destruction /di strúksh'n/ *n* **1 PROCESS OF DESTROYING** the act or process of destroying something **2 DESTROYED STATE** the condition of having been destroyed **3 MEANS OF DESTROYING** a cause or means of destroying something [13C. < Latin *destruction-* < *destruct-*, past participle of *destruere* (see DESTROY).]

destructive /di strúktiv/ *adj* **1** causing or capable of causing destruction **2** intended to damage or hurt rather than be helpful or instructive [15C. Via French, < late Latin *destructivus* < Latin *destruct-* (see DESTRUCTION).] —**destructively** *adv* —**destructiveness** *n* —**destructivity** /di strúk tívvəti, dee struk-/ *n*

destructive distillation *n* the process of heating solid substances in the absence of air to decompose them in order to obtain useful products from the vapour and residues

destructor /di strúktər/ *n* **1** an incinerator used to burn rubbish **2** an onboard explosive device used to destroy a missile or rocket if it malfunctions dangerously after its launch

desuetude /désswi tyood/ *n* the condition of not being in use (*formal*) [Early 17C. Via French *désuétude* < Latin *desuetudo* < *desuescere* 'become unaccustomed' < *suescere* 'be accustomed'.]

desulfurize *vti* US = **desulphurize**

desulphurize /dee súlfə rīz/ (**-izes, -izing, -ized**), **desulphurise** (**-phurises, -phurising, -phurised, -phurised**) *vti* to remove sulphur and its compounds from something, typically from petroleum products or from flue gases when coal or another fuel is burned, or to lose sulphur in this way —**desulphurization** /dee súlfə rī záysh'n/ *n* —**desulphurizer** *n*

desultory /déss'ltəri/ *adj* **1** aimlessly passing from one thing to another **2** happening in a random, disorganized, or unmethodical way ○ *The soldiers were subject to desultory fire from the enemy position.* [Late 16C. < Latin *desultorius* 'leaping' < *desilire* 'leap down' < *salire* 'leap'.] —**desultorily** *adv* —**desultoriness** *n*

det., **det** *abbr* determiner

detach /di tách/ *v* **1** *vti* to separate, disconnect, or unfasten something, or become separated, disconnected, or unfastened **2** *vt* to separate a military unit or an individual from the normal, larger unit for special duties [Late 17C. Via French *détacher* < Old French *destachier* < *attachier* (see ATTACH).] —**detachability** *n* —**detachable** *adj* —**detacher** *n*

detached /di tácht/ *adj* **1 NOT ATTACHED** not attached to something **2 SEPARATE** standing on its own and not joined to another building **3 FREE FROM EMOTIONAL INVOLVEMENT** unaffected by emotional involvement or any form of bias —**detachedly** /di táchidli, di táchtli/ *adv* —**detachedness** /di táchtnəss/ *n*

detached retina *n* an eye condition in which the retina becomes separated from the eyeball, causing loss of vision

detachment /di táchmənt/ *n* **1 ALOOFNESS** lack of interest in or involvement with other people or with worldly concerns **2 DISINTERESTEDNESS** a lack of bias, prejudice, or emotional involvement **3 SEPARATION** the condition of being separated from something, or the process of separating one thing from another **4 MILITARY UNIT** a military unit separated from its normal, larger unit for special duties **5 SPECIALIZED GROUP** any specialized and separately employed unit of a group or organization

detail /dée tayl/ *n* **1 INDIVIDUAL PART** an individual separable part of something, especially one of several items of information ○ *No details of the proposed legislation are available yet.* **2 EACH AND EVERY ELEMENT** all of the individual elements that together make up a whole **3 INCLUSION OF ALL ELEMENTS** treatment of and inclusion of all of the individual elements that make up something ○ *Your description of the item needs more detail.* **4 INSIGNIFICANT PART** something that is insignificant or a minor part of something else ○ *Safety in the sport is not a mere detail.* **5 SMALL ELEMENT OF ART OR STRUCTURE** a small element of a work of art or building structure, considered separately **6 GROUP WITH SPECIAL TASK** a group of people, especially in the armed services, given a specific task ■ **details** *npl* **PERSONAL FACTS** facts about somebody, e.g. his or her name and address ■ *vt* **1 LIST THINGS** to list or enumerate a series of items or events ○ *Please detail all the things that were stolen.* **2 DECORATE** to add refinements or decorations to something **3 CLEAN CAR COMPLETELY** to clean and polish a motor vehicle so thoroughly inside and out that it is spotless **4 GIVE MILITARY UNIT SPECIALIZED ASSIGNMENT** to assign a military unit to a specialized task (*often passive*) [Early 17C. < French *détail* 'piece cut off' < *détaillir* 'cut up' < *taillier* 'cut'.] ◇ **go into detail** to be very specific and include all of the particulars ◇ **in detail** covering every item or particular

detail drawing *n* a large-scale drawing that shows part of a machine, device, or building

detailed /dée tayld/ *adj* including all or many of the particular elements of something

detain /di táyn/ *vt* **1** to hold back or delay somebody or something **2** to restrain or keep somebody or something in custody [15C. Via Old French *detenir* < Latin *detinere* 'hold back' < *tenere* 'hold, keep'.] —**detainable** *adj* —**detainment** *n*

detainee /dée tay née, di-/ *n* a person who is held in custody

detainer /di táynər/ *n* **1** a writ authorizing that somebody in custody may be confined for a further period **2** the wrongful withholding of somebody's property or freedom

detect /di tékt/ *vt* **1** to notice or discover the existence of something **2** ELECTRONICS = **demodulate** [15C. < Latin *detect-*, past participle of *detegere* 'uncover' < *tegere* 'cover'.] —**detectable** *adj* —**detectably** *adv*

detection /di téksh'n/ *n* **1** the act of noticing or discovering the existence of something, or the state of having been detected **2** the work of a detective in investigating crime or wrongdoing

detective /di téktiv/ *n* somebody who investigates and gathers evidence about possible crimes or wrongdoing ■ *adj* acting to detect something ○ *detective devices*

detector /di téktər/ *n* **1** a device for sensing the presence of or changes in something, e.g. radiation or pressure **2** somebody who or something that detects

detent /di tént/ *n* a locking device, e.g. a lever or spring-loaded catch, that permits movement of a machine part in one direction only [Late 17C. < French *détente* 'release' < Latin *tendere* 'to stretch'.]

détente /day tónt, -taánt/ *n* a relaxation of tension or hostility between nations [Early 20C. < French, 'relaxation' (see DETENT).]

detention /di ténsh'n/ *n* **1** the act keeping somebody in custody, or the state of being kept in custody **2** a form of punishment for school students in which they are made to stay in class at a break or at school after normal hours [15C. < late Latin *detention-* < Latin *detinere* (see DETAIN).]

detention centre *n* a place where young people can be confined for a brief period by order of a court

detention home *n US* CRIME = **remand home**

deter /di túr/ (**-ters, -terring, -terred**) *vti* to discourage somebody from taking action or prevent something happening, especially by making people feel afraid or anxious ○ *New laws to deter speeding will be enforced at the end of the month.* [Mid-16C. < Latin *deterrere* 'scare off' < *terrere* 'scare'.] —**determent** *n*

deterge /di túrj/ (**-terges, -terging, -terged**) *vt* to cleanse something, especially a wound (*technical*) [Early 17C. Directly or via French *déterger* < Latin *detergere* 'wipe off' < *tergere* 'wipe'.]

detergent /di túrjənt/ *n* a cleansing substance, especially a synthetic liquid that dissolves dirt and oil ■ *adj* with the properties of a detergent —**detergency** *n*

deteriorate /di téeri ə rayt/ (**-rates, -rating, -rated**) *vti* to become or make something worse in quality, value, or strength [Late 16C. < late Latin *deteriorat-*, past participle of *deteriorare* < Latin *deterior* 'worse'.] —**deteriorative** *adj* —**deterioration** /di téeri ə ráysh'n/ *n*

determinable /di túrminəb'l/ *adj* **1** able to be worked out, decided, or found **2** subject to being terminated —**determinability** /di túrminə bílləti/ *n* —**determinably** *adv*

determinant /di túrminənt/ *n* **1 CAUSE** a factor that causes or influences something **2 ARRAY OF MATHEMATICAL ELEMENTS** a square array of elements that is used in various mathematical processes, e.g. solving simultaneous equations and studying linear transformations, and that itself has a numerical value ■ *adj* **CAUSAL** influencing or causing something

determinate /di túrminət/ *adj* **1 LIMITED** with exact and definite limits **2 DETERMINED** determined (*formal*) **3 WITH STEMS ENDING IN A BUD** describes a pattern of flowering in which primary and secondary stems end in a flower bud and stop growing. ◊ **indeterminate** *adj.* **6** —**determinately** *adv* —**determinateness** *n* —**determinacy** *n*

determination /di túrmi náysh'n/ *n* **1 FIRMNESS OF PURPOSE** firmness of purpose, will, or intention ○ *full of ambition and determination* **2 FIXED PURPOSE** a fixed purpose or resolution ○ *her determination to succeed* **3 ACT OF DISCOVERING** an act of finding out or ascertaining something, especially as a result of investigation or research (*formal*) ○ *determination of the cause of death* **4 DECISION ON COURSE OF ACTION** decision-making on, or the establishment of, a course of action (*formal*) ○ *They were entrusted with the determination of future policy.* **5 SETTLEMENT OF DISPUTE OR CONTEST** the authoritative settlement of a dispute, especially by a judicial body **6 END OF ESTATE, INTEREST, OR RIGHT** the conclusion or termination of an estate, interest, or right **7 QUALIFYING OF CONCEPT** the qualifying of a concept or proposition by defining its attributes **8 STAGE IN DEVELOPMENT OF EMBRYONIC TISSUE** the stage in the development of embryonic tissue after which it can only develop as one specific type of tissue and no longer has the potential to develop into different types

determinative /di túrminətiv/ *adj* able to determine something ■ *n* **1** a factor that determines something **2** GRAM = **determiner** *n.* **1** —**determinatively** *adv* —**determinativeness** *n*

determine /di túrmin/ (**-mines, -mining, -mined**) *v* **1** *vt* **DECIDE** to decide or settle something conclusively **2** *vt* **FIND OUT** to find out or ascertain something, usually after investigation **3** *vt* **INFLUENCE** to influence or give form to something **4** *vt* **FIX LIMITS** to fix the limits or form of something **5** *vti* **ADOPT OR CAUSE TO ADOPT PURPOSE** to adopt a set purpose, or make somebody do this ○ *determined to leave as soon as possible* **6** *vti* **END** to end something, or come to an end [14C. Via Old French < Latin *determinare* 'set the limits of' < *terminus* 'limit, boundary'.]

determined /di túrmind/ *adj* feeling or showing firmness or a fixed purpose —**determinedly** *adv* —**determinedness** *n*

determiner /di túrminər/ *n* **1** a word such as 'a', 'the', 'this', 'each', 'some', 'either', 'my', and 'your' that appears before any descriptive adjective and decides the kind of reference that a noun has **2** something that or somebody who determines

determining /di túrmining/ *adj* causing or deciding something

determinism /di túrminizəm/ *n* the doctrine or belief that everything, including every human act, is caused by something and that there is no real free will —**determinist** *n* —**deterministic** /di túrmi nístik/ *adj*

deterrent /di térrənt/ *adj* **ACTING TO DETER** capable of deterring somebody or something ■ *n* **1 SOMETHING THAT DETERS** something that deters somebody or something **2 WEAPONS THAT DETER AN ATTACK** weapons, particularly nuclear weapons, held as a retaliatory threat —**deterrence** *n*

detest /di tést/ *vt* to dislike somebody or something very much [15C. Via French *détester* < Latin *detestari* 'bear witness against, denounce' < *testis* 'witness'.] —**detester** *n*

detestable /di téstəb'l/ *adj* causing or deserving intense dislike —**detestability** /di téstə bílləti/ *n* —**detestably** *adv*

detestation /dée te stáysh'n/ *n* **1** an intense loathing or hatred **2** something that or somebody who is detested ○ *Apples are a real detestation for him.*

dethrone /dee thrṓn/ (**-thrones, -throning, -throned**) *vt* **1** to remove a ruler, especially a monarch, from power **2** to remove somebody from a high or powerful position —**dethronement** *n* —**dethroner** *n*

detinue /détti nyoo/ *n* a legal action to reclaim wrongfully withheld personal property [15C. < Old French, 'detention' < *detenir* (see DETAIN).]

detonate /déttə nayt/ (**-nates, -nating, -nated**) *vti* to explode, or make something explode [Early 18C. < Latin *detonat-*, past participle of *detonare* 'thunder down' < *tonare* 'to thunder'.] —**detonative** /déttə naytiv/ *adj*

detonation /déttə náysh'n/ *n* **1** an explosion, or an act of making something explode **2** a premature spontaneous burning of a fuel-air mixture inside an internal-combustion engine

detonator /déttə naytər/ *n* a device or small quantity of explosive used to make a bomb or larger quantity of explosive explode

detour /dée toor, day tóor/ *n* **1** a deviation from a shorter, more direct route **2** *US* TRANSP = **diversion** *n.* **2** ■ *vti* to deviate or make somebody or something deviate from a shorter route [Mid-18C. < French *détour* < Old French *destorner* 'turn away' < *torner* < Latin *tornare* (see TURN).]

detox /dée toks/ *n* the detoxification of an alcoholic or drug addict ■ *vti* to detoxify an alcoholic or drug addict [Late 20C. Shortening.]

detoxicate /dee tóksi kayt/ (**-cates, -cating, -cated**) *vt* MED = **detoxify** *v.* **2** —**detoxicant** *n, adj*

detoxify /dee tóksifī/ (**-fies, -fying, -fied**) *v* **1** *vt* to remove a poison from something **2** *vti* to subject somebody to withdrawal of a toxic or addictive substance [Early 20C. < DE- + TOXIC.] —**detoxification** /dee tóksifi káysh'n/ *n*

detract /di trákt/ *vti* to reduce the quality, value, or importance of something by taking something away [15C. < Latin *detract-*, past participle of *detrahere* 'take or pull away' < *trahere* 'pull'.] —**detractingly** *adv* —**detractive** *adj* —**detractively** *adv* —**detractory** *adj*

detraction /di tráksh'n/ *n* **1** the act of damaging somebody's reputation, especially by making discrediting comments (*formal*) **2** somebody or something that detracts from the quality, value, or importance of something

detractor /di tráktər/ *n* a belittler of something or somebody

detrain /dee tráyn/ *vti* to get out of or remove people from a railway train —**detrainment** *n*

detribalize /dee trībə līz/ (**-izes, -izing, -ized**), **detribalise** (**-ises, -ising, -ised**) *vti* to abandon or make people abandon tribal practices, usually by exposure to another culture —**detribalization** /dee trībə lī záysh'n/ *n*

detriment /déttrimənt/ *n* **1** damage, harm, or disadvantage **2** something that causes harm or injury (*formal*) [15C. Via French < Latin *detrimentum* < *deterere* 'wear away' < *terere* 'rub, wear'.]

detrimental /déttri mént'l/ *adj* causing harm or damage —**detrimentally** *adv*

detrition /di trísh'n/ *n* the process of wearing something away by friction [Late 17C. < medieval Latin *detrition-* < Latin *deterere* (see DETRIMENT).]

detritivore /di trītə vawr/, **detritovore** *n* an organism that feeds on decaying animal or plant material, e.g. an earthworm [Mid-20C. < DETRITUS.]

detritus /di trītəss/ *n* **1 DEBRIS** debris or discarded material **2 ROCK FRAGMENTS** fragments of rock that have been worn away **3 ORGANIC MATTER** organic debris formed by the decomposition of plants and animals [Late 18C. < Latin, < past participle of *deterere* (see DETRIMENT).] —**detrital** *adj*

Detroit /di tróyt/ city in SE Michigan. Population: 970,196 (1998 estimate).

de trop /də trṓ/ *adj* superfluous or excessive [Mid-18C. < French, 'excessive'.]

detumescence /dèe tyoo méss'nss/ *n* a gradual reduction in a swelling, especially of a penis [Late 17C. < Latin *detumescere* 'stop swelling' < *tumere* 'swell'.] —**detumesce** *vi* —**detumescent** *adj*

deuce[1] /dyooss/ *n* **1** in tennis, badminton, and other racket games, a situation in which a player must score two successive points to win after the score is tied **2** a playing card with two pips or the face of a die with two spots [15C. Via Old French *deus* 'two' < Latin *duos*.]

deuce[2] /dyooss/ *interj* used instead of a swearword to show displeasure, irritation, or surprise (*dated slang*) [Mid-17C. Via Dutch or Low German *duus* 'throw of two on two dice' (the lowest score) < Latin *duos* 'two'.]

deuced /dyóossid, dyoost/ *adj* used instead of a swearword to give emphasis or to show irritation or displeasure (*dated slang*) ■ *adv* decidedly or extremely (*dated slang*) —**deucedly** *adv*

Deus /dáyooss/ *n* God [13C. < Latin.]

deus ex machina /dáyooss eks mákinə/ *n* **1** in ancient Greek and Roman theatre, a god introduced to resolve a complicated plot **2** an improbable character or unconvincing event used to resolve a plot [< modern Latin, 'god from the machinery' (used in Greek theatre to lower actors onto the stage)]

Deut. *abbr* Deuteronomy

deuter- *prefix* = **deutero-** (*before vowels*)

deuteragonist /dyootə rággənist/ *n* a character second in importance to the leading character (**protagonist**) in ancient Greek drama [Mid-19C. < Greek *deuteragōnistēs* < *deuteros* 'second' + *agōnistēs* 'actor' (see PROTAGONIST).]

deuteranopia /dyootərə nṓpi ə/ *n* colour blindness in which red and green are confused —**deuteranopic** /-nóppik/ *adj*

deuterate /dyootə rayt/ (**-ates, -ating, -ated**) *vt* to add deuterium to a chemical compound [Mid-20C. < DEUTERIUM.] —**deuteration** /dyootə ráysh'n/ *n*

deuteride /dyootə rīd/ *n* a compound of hydrogen (**hydride**) in which hydrogen has been replaced by its heavier isotope deuterium [Mid-20C. < DEUTERIUM.]

deuterium /dyoo téeri əm/ *n* (*symbol* **D**) an isotope of hydrogen that has double the mass of ordinary hydrogen because it contains a neutron in its nucleus. Use: tracer in experiments. [Mid-20C. < Greek *deuteros* 'second'.]

deuterium oxide *n* = **heavy water**

deutero- *prefix* second, secondary ○ *deuteroplasm* [< Greek *deuteros*]

deuterocanonical /dyootərōkə nónnik'l/ *adj* part of secondary, less well regarded, or disputed collection of religious scripture, especially the Apocrypha and the Antilegomena, or constituting or relating to one of these secondary canons

deuteron /dyootə ron/ *n* (*symbol* **D⁺**) the nucleus of a deuterium atom, consisting of one proton and one neutron [Mid-20C. < DEUTERO-, after PROTON.]

Deuteronomist /dyootə rónnəmist/ *n* one of the authors of Deuteronomy, the fifth book of the Bible

Deuteronomy /dyootə rónnəmi/ *n* the fifth book of the Bible [14C. Via late Latin < Greek *Deuteronomion* 'second law' (because the book contains a repetition of the Decalogue and of parts of *Exodus*).] —**Deuteronomic** /dyootərə nómmik/ *adj*

deuterostome /dyootərō stōm/ *n* an animal whose mouth develops from a second opening in the early embryo, opposite to the initial opening (**blastopore**) of the rudimentary gut

deutoplasm /dyootə plazzəm/ *n* nutrient matter contained in certain reproductive cells, e.g. the yolk in a bird's egg —**deutoplasmic** /dyootə plázmik/ *adj*

Deutschmark /dóychə maark/, **Deutsche Mark** *n* symbol **DM**. see table at **currency** [Mid-20C. < German, 'German mark' < *deutsch* 'German' + *Mark* (see MARK[2]).]

deutzia /dyootsi ə/ (*plural* **-as** *or* **-a**) *n* a shrub with clusters of white to pink or lavender flowers. Native to: Asia, Central America. Genus: *Deutzia*. [Mid-19C. < modern Latin, after Johann van der *Deutz*.]

deva /dáyvə/ *n* a Hindu or Buddhist god [Early 19C. < Sanskrit, 'god'.]

De Valera /dévvə láirə/, **Eamon** (1882–1975) US-born Irish statesman

de Valois /də vál waa/, **Dame Ninette** (1898–2001) Irish-born British ballet dancer and choreographer. Born **Edris Stannus**

devaluate /dee vályoo ayt/ (**-ates, -ating, -ated**) *vti* = **devalue** *v.* 1

devalue /dee vállyoo/ (**-ues, -uing, -ued**) *v* **1** *vti* to lower the value of a nation's currency by a governmental action, or to become lowered in value **2** *vt* to cause the value or importance of somebody or something to be reduced, or to become reduced in value or importance —**devaluation** /dee valyoo áysh'n/ *n*

Devanagari /dáyvə naágəri/ *n* the alphabet that is used to write many modern languages of India as well as ancient Sanskrit [Late 18C. < Sanskrit, < *deva* 'god' + *Nāgarī*, earlier name for the script.]

devastate /dévvə stayt/ (**-tates, -tating, -tated**) *vt* **1** to cause severe or widespread damage to something ○ *an area devastated by floods* **2** to shock or upset somebody enormously, producing a feeling of being overwhelmed or helpless (*often passive*) ○ *We were devastated by the news of his death.* [Mid-17C. < Latin *devastat-*, past participle of *devastare* 'lay waste completely' < *vastare* 'lay waste' < *vastus* 'waste'.] —**devastation** /dévvə stáysh'n/ *n* —**devastative** *adj* —**devastator** *n*

devastating /dévvə stayting/ *adj* **1 DAMAGING** causing severe or widespread damage ○ *policies that have a devastating effect on economic growth* **2 VERY UPSETTING** causing enormous shock or upset ○ *The news was devastating.* **3 SHARPLY CRITICAL** containing criticism that is very sharp and very effective or damaging, often as a result of its precise detail or caustic wit **4 REMARKABLE** startlingly impressive or attractive (*informal*) ○ *the devastating speed of her forehand return* —**devastatingly** *adv*

develop /di vélləp/ *v* **1** *vti* **CHANGE AND GROW** to change, or cause to change, and become larger, stronger, or more impressive, successful, or advanced ○ *The business has developed from humble beginnings into a multinational concern.* **2** *vi* **ARISE AND INCREASE** to arise and then increase or progress to a more complex state ○ *Tension was developing between the two nations.* **3** *vt* **ACQUIRE FEATURE, HABIT, OR ILLNESS** to acquire a particular feature, habit, or illness that then becomes more marked or extreme ○ *The baby is developing a cold.* **4** *vt* **ENLARGE ON** to add details to a basic plan or idea **5** *vti* **PRESENT OR BE REVEALED IN STAGES** to present the sequential events or successive stages of a story or argument, or to have such events or stages revealed ○ *The theory is developed at length in her new book.* **6** *vt* **USE RESOURCES FOR HUMAN PURPOSES** to use or make available land, minerals, or other natural resources for human purposes such as housing **7** *vt* **BUILD STRUCTURES** to plan and construct buildings, roads, or other technological structures ○ *develop a global communications system* **8** *vt* **TURN FILM INTO NEGATIVES OR PRINTS** to treat photographic film with chemicals in order to produce a negative or print (*often passive*) ○ *Send the films off to be developed.* **9** *vi* **ACHIEVE SEXUAL MATURITY** to become sexually mature **10** *vt* **BRING PIECE INTO PLAY** to bring a chess piece into play **11** *vt* **VARY MUSICAL THEME** to add to a musical theme by using variation or ornamentation [Mid-17C. < French *développer* 'unwrap' < Old French *voloper* 'wrap'.] —**developable** *adj*

~~**develope**~~ incorrect spelling of **develop**

developed /di vélləpt/ *adj* wealthy and technologically advanced, with sophisticated manufacturing and service industries

~~**developement**~~ incorrect spelling of **development**

developer /di vélləpər/ *n* **1 SOMEBODY WHO DEVELOPS** somebody who or something that develops something ○ *the developer of a new manufacturing process* **2 BUYER OF LAND FOR BUILDING** a person or company that buys land in order to build on it or sell it to others who want to build on it **3 CHEMICAL FOR MAKING NEGATIVES OR PRINTS** a chemical used to turn exposed film into negatives or prints

developing /di vélləping/ *adj* using or involving small-scale agriculture and industry of the kind that characterized the earlier economic stages of technologically advanced nations

developing agent *n* PHOTOGRAPHY = **developer** *n.* 3

development /di vélləpmənt/ *n* **1 EVENT CAUSING CHANGE** an incident that causes a situation to change or progress (*often plural*) ○ *Have there been any political developments since last week?* **2 DEVELOPING OF** the process of developing, developing something, or of being developed, e.g. by growth, change, or elaboration ○ *sustained economic development* **3 BEING DEVELOPED** a state in which the developing of something is not yet completed ○ *The prototype is in development.* **4 GROUP OF BUILDINGS** a group of buildings of the same kind that are built as a single construction project **5 ELABORATION OF MUSICAL THEME** the process of varying and elaborating the rhythm and melody of a musical theme **6 MUSICAL SECTION WHERE THEME IS DEVELOPED** one of the three main sections of the sonata form, in which the musical themes presented in the exposition are rhythmically and melodically elaborated —**developmental** /di vélləp mént'l/ *adj* —**developmentally** *adv*

developmental psychology *n* the branch of psychology that deals with the ways that personality, cognitive ability, and behaviour change during a person's life span, concentrating particularly on childhood development

development area *n* an area of high unemployment that receives government money to help develop new industry there

développé /dáyvəllə pay, di véll/ *n* a ballet movement in which the foot of one leg is drawn up to the knee of the other and then extended slowly out into the air [Early 20C. < French, past participle of *développer* (see DEVELOP).]

deverbative /dee vúrbətiv/, **deverbal** /dee vúrb'l/ *adj* derived from a verb, such as the noun 'driver', which is derived from the verb 'drive', and the adjective 'clingy', from the verb 'cling'

Devi /dáyvi/ *n* the supreme Hindu goddess, wife of the god Shiva, manifested in the different forms and characters of Durga, Kali, Parvati, and Sati [Late 20C. < Sanskrit, 'goddess'.]

deviance /déevi ənss/, **deviancy** /-ənssi/ *n* behaviour that is sharply different from the norm or the accepted standard

deviant /déevi ənt/ *adj* diverging sharply from a customary or traditional norm or accepted standard ○ *abstract paintings, once thought deviant, now worth millions* ■ *n* somebody whose behaviour is different from the norm or from accepted standards [14C. < late Latin *deviant-*, present participle of *deviare* (see DEVIATE).]

deviate *vi* /déevi ayt/ (**-ates, -ating, -ated**) **1 BE DIFFERENT** to be different or behave differently **2 TURN FROM** to turn off from a course or path ■ *adj* /déevi ət/ **BEHAVING DIFFERENTLY OR UNACCEPTABLY** exhibiting behaviour that diverges sharply from a norm or accepted standards ■ *n* /déevi ət/ **SOMEBODY BEHAVING DIFFERENTLY FROM TRADITIONAL NORM** somebody whose behaviour differs sharply from the customary or traditional norm or accepted standards [Mid-17C. < late Latin *deviat-*, past participle of *deviare* 'depart from the way' < Latin *via* 'way, road'.] —**deviator** *n* —**deviatory** *adj*

deviation /déevi áysh'n/ *n* **1 CHANGE OR DIFFERENCE** a change or difference from what is normal, accepted, expected, or planned ○ *These rituals represented a deviation from established practices.* **2 UNACCEPTABLE BEHAVIOUR OR ATTITUDE** behaviour or an attitude that is sharply different from what is normal or acceptable **3 DIFFERENCE FROM STATISTICAL AVERAGE** the difference between any particular value and a fixed value, such as the average of all the other values in its series **4 COMPASS ERROR** an error in a compass reading caused by local magnetic fields, especially on a ship at sea

deviationism /déevi áysh'nizəm/ *n* departure from accepted or established political views, especially from orthodox communism —**deviationist** *n, adj*

device /di vīss/ *n* **1 TOOL OR MACHINE** a tool or machine designed to perform a particular task or function **2 PLOY** a way of achieving something, especially a clever or dishonest way **3 BOMB** a bomb or something that causes an explosion or fire **4 LITERARY OR DRAMATIC TOOL** something designed to create a particular effect in a story or drama or to evoke a particular response from a reader, listener, or viewer ○ *a familiar cinematic device* **5 EMBLEM OR MOTTO** an emblem or motto, or a combination of the two, especially when used in heraldry ○ *a heraldic device* **6 ORNAMENTAL DESIGN** an ornamental pattern or design, e.g. in embroidery [13C. < Old French *devis* 'division, contrivance', *devise* 'plan', < Latin *dividere* (see DIVIDE).] ◇ **leave somebody to his** *or* **her own devices** to let somebody do as he or she wishes, instead of giving the person direction or assistance

~~**devide**~~ incorrect spelling of **divide**

devil /dévv'l/ *n* **1 devil, Devil GOD'S ENEMY** in Christianity and some other religions, the enemy of God, who rules Hell, tempts people to sin, and personifies the spirit of evil as Satan **2 EVIL SPIRIT** an evil spirit, particularly a subordinate of Satan **3 EVIL PERSON OR ANIMAL** an unpleasant, violent, or evil person or animal **4 MISCHIEVOUS PERSON OR ANIMAL** a mischievous, troublesome, or high-spirited person or animal **5 PERSON OR ANIMAL** a person or animal of the sort described ○ *You lucky devil!* **6 NAME FOR TOOL** a name given to various tools or machines, especially ones that cut or tear **7** METEOROL = **dust devil** **8 DIFFICULT OR UNPLEASANT CASE** an extremely difficult or unpleasant instance of something (*informal*) **9 INTENSIFIER** used as an intensifier in questions and exclamations (*slang*) ○ *Who the devil does he think he is, talking to his boss like that?* ■ *vt* (**-ils, -illing, -illed**) **1 MAKE FOOD SPICY** to cook or prepare a food with spicy seasonings **2** *US* **PESTER** to annoy, worry, or pester somebody, especially by making repeated requests for something (*informal*) ○ *He's been devilling me with requests for an interview.* [Old English *dēofol*, via Latin *diabolus* < Greek *diabolus* 'devil, Satan'] ◇ **between the devil and the deep blue sea** faced with two equally undesirable choices

devilfish /dévv'l fish/ (*plural* **-fish** *or* **-fishes**) *n* a fish that is thought to have an evil or frightening appearance, such as a manta ray or octopus

devilish /dévv'lish/ *adj* **1 SINISTER OR CRUEL** so sinister, cruel, or evil as to be considered like or worthy of the devil ○ *some devilish scheme to get what they want* **2 MISCHIEVOUS** full of or indicating mischievousness ○ *a devilish grin* **3 GREAT** extremely great or intense (*informal*) ○ *the devilish midday heat* ■ *adv* **VERY** extremely (*informal*) —**devilishly** *adv* —**devilishness** *n*

devil-may-care *adj* **1** foolishly lighthearted about risk or danger **2** tending to enjoy the present and not think or worry about the future

devilment /dévv'lmənt/ *n* troublesome, mischievous, or devilish behaviour ○ *always getting up to some devilment or other*

devilry /dévv'ltri/ (*plural* **-ries**) *n* **1** cruel or evil behaviour or actions **2** evil act or acts supposedly performed by calling on the powers of the devil or evil spirits

devil's advocate *n* **1** a person who argues about something merely to provoke discussion **2** a Roman Catholic official appointed to argue against the canonization or beatification of a candidate

devil's coach-horse *n* a large fierce black beetle with long jaws. Family: Staphylinidae. ◊ **rove beetle** [< the rearing and defiant attitude that it assumes when disturbed]

devil's darning needle *n* a damselfly (*informal*) [< its long thin body]

devil's food cake *n* a rich dark chocolate cake [< the contrast with the paleness of ANGEL FOOD CAKE]

Devil's Island /dévv'lz-/ rocky islet in the Atlantic Ocean off the coast of French Guiana, formerly the site of a penal colony

Devil's Marbles /-maárb'lz/ mound of granite boulders and sacred Aboriginal site in central Northern Territory, Australia

devious /deévi əss/ *adj* **1 SECRETIVE AND CALCULATING** not straightforward, sincere, and honest in or about your intentions or motives **2 UNFAIR OR UNDERHAND** not adhering to the right or usual course, procedures, or standards **3 RAMBLING** circuitous and roundabout, usually changing direction many times ○ *got here by a devious route* [Late 16C. < Latin *devius* 'out of the way' < *via* 'way, road'.] —**deviously** *adv* —**deviousness** *n*

devisal /di vīz'l/ *n* **1** the inventing or contriving of something **2** the handing down of property through a will

devise /di vīz/ *vt* (**-vises, -vising, -vised**) **1 THINK UP** to conceive of the idea for something and work out how to make it or put it into practice **2 PASS ON PROPERTY** to pass on property through a will ■ *n* **1 CLAUSE BEQUEATHING PROPERTY** a clause in a will stating that an item of property is to be given to somebody or something **2 BEQUEATHING PROPERTY** the bequeathing of an item of property **3 PROPERTY BEQUEATHED** an item of property bequeathed through a will [13C. < French *deviser* 'divide, order, form a plan' < Latin *dividere* (see DIVIDE).] —**devisable** *adj* —**deviser** *n*

devisee /di vī zeé/ *n* somebody to whom property has been bequeathed in a will

devisor /di vízər/ *n* a person who bequeaths property in a will [15C. < Anglo-Norman *devisour*, Old French *deviseor* < Old French *deviser* (see DEVISE).]

devitalize /dee vítə līz/ (**-izes, -izing, -ized**), **devitalise** (**-ises, -ising, -ised**) *vt* to deprive something of its strength or vigour —**devitalization** /dee vítə lī záysh'n/ *n*

DeVito /də veétō/, **Danny** (*b.* 1944) US film actor and director. Full name **Daniel Michael DeVito**

devitrify /dee vítri fī/ (**-fies, -fying, -fied**) *vti* to change, or cause a material to change, from a glassy to a crystalline state and become brittle and opaque —**devitrification** /deè vitrifi káysh'n/ *n*

Devizes /di vīziz/ town in S England. Population: 13,205 (1991).

devocalize /dee vṓkə līz/ (**-izes, -izing, -ized**), **devocalise** (**-ises, -ising, -ised**) *vt* = **devoice** —**devocalization** /deèvōkə lī záysh'n/ *n*

devoice /dee vóyss/ (**-voices, -voicing, -voiced**) *vt* to make a usually voiced speech sound without vibration of the vocal cords

devoid /di vóyd/ *adj* completely lacking in or without something ○ *a house devoid of charm* [14C. < past participle of obsolete *devoid* 'remove, vacate' < Old French *devoidier* 'empty out' < *vuidier* 'to empty' < Latin *vacare* 'be empty'.]

devoirs /də vwaá/ *npl* expressions or acts of courtesy and respect (*archaic or literary*) [15C. < Old French *deveir* 'owe' < Latin *debere*.]

devolatilize /dee vóllətə līz/ (**-izes, -izing, -ized**), **devolatilise** (**-ises, -ising, -ised**) *vt* to remove volatile material from a substance, usually by means of heat or a vacuum and sometimes by both —**devolatilization** /dee vóllətə lī záysh'n/ *n*

devolution /deèvə lóosh'n/ *n* **1 DELEGATING OF RESPONSIBILITIES** the delegation of responsibilities from a superior to a subordinate, deputy, or substitute **2 DELEGATING POWER** the transfer of power from a central to a subordinate level or organization, particularly from a central government to regional or local governments **3 INHERITANCE OF PRIVILEGES** the transfer or inheritance of authority, rights, or property, e.g. from a monarch to his or her successors **4** BIOL = **degeneration** *n.* 3 [15C. < late Latin *devolution-* < Latin *devolvere* (see DEVOLVE).] —**devolutionary** *adj*

devolutionist /deèvə lóosh'nist/ *n* an advocate of transferring power from a central government to smaller political units —**devolutionist** *adj*

devolve /di vólv/ (**-volves, -volving, -volved**) *v* **1** *vti* **TRANSFER OR BE TRANSFERRED TO ANOTHER** to transfer power, responsibility, or rights to somebody or something, e.g. from a central government to a regional government, or to be transferred in this manner ○ *the government's pledge to devolve powers to local communities* **2** *vi* **BECOME ANOTHER PERSON'S OBLIGATION** to become the duty or responsibility of another person ○ *Many child-care responsibilities have devolved on husbands.* **3** *vi* **RELY OR DEPEND** to be decided by something or depend on something for its validity (*formal*) ○ *Their case devolved on witnesses' willingness to testify.* **4** *vi* **BE GIVEN OR BEQUEATHED** to be given to somebody under the terms of a will or other legal instruction [15C. < Latin *devolvere* 'roll down' < *volvere* 'roll'.] —**devolvement** *n*

USAGE devolve on or **to**? The traditional distinction is that powers, authority, etc., ***devolve*** or are ***devolved*** *on* (or *upon*) somebody, whereas a right or benefit ***devolves*** *to* somebody. However, this is not widely observed in current usage. The two constructions are used more or less interchangeably, though the use of *to* is somewhat more common: *The point of devolving power to provincial assemblies . . . was to give these provinces some control over their own affairs* (*Economist*). *On* or *upon* is used when the right or authority is regarded as a kind of inheritance (actually or figuratively): *In 1912 the leadership of the expedition's remnant at Cape Evans devolved upon Atkinson, the sole remaining officer* (*Dictionary of National Biography*).

Devon /dévv'n/ county in SW England. Population: 378,900 (1995). Area: 6,711 sq. km/2,591 sq. mi.

Devonian /de vṓni ən/ *n* **1 Devonian, Devonian period GEOLOGICAL PERIOD** the geological period that extended from 410 to 360 million years ago, when forests and amphibians first appeared and fish became abundant **2 SOMEBODY FROM DEVON** somebody who comes from the county of Devon ■ *adj* **1 BELONGING TO GEOLOGICAL PERIOD** belonging or relating to the geological period that extended from 410 to 360 million years ago **2 CHARACTERISTIC OF DEVON** relating to Devon, or its people or culture [Early 17C. < medieval Latin *Devonia* < Old English *Defenascīr* 'Devonshire', former name of DEVON.]

Devonport /dévv'n pawrt/ city in N Tasmania, Australia. Population: 22,299 (1996).

Devonshire cream /dévv'nshər-/ *n* FOOD = **clotted cream** [Because a speciality of DEVON, formerly *Devonshire*]

devoré /də váw ray/, **dévoré** *n* **1** the use of a chemical paste to create patterns in fabrics such as velvet by dissolving the natural fibres and revealing the synthetic warp and weft threads **2** fabric created using the devoré technique [< French *dévorer* (see DEVOUR)]

devote /di vṓt/ (**-votes, -voting, -voted**) *vt* to commit yourself to, or allot or use something for, a particular activity, aim, or purpose ○ *She devoted her whole life to the cause.* [Late 16C. < Latin *devot-*, past participle of *devovere* 'dedicate by a vow' < *vovere* 'to vow'.]

devoted /di vṓtid/ *adj* **1** feeling or showing great love, commitment, or loyalty to somebody or something, especially over a long period of time **2** feeling or showing great dedication to something —**devotedly** *adv* —**devotedness** *n*

devotee /dévvō teé/ *n* **1** a very keen enthusiast or follower of something **2** a dedicated member of a religious or spiritual group

devotion /di vṓsh'n/ *n* **1 COMMITTED LOVE** deep love and commitment **2 DEDICATION** great dedication and loyalty **3 ENTHUSIASM** strong enthusiasm and admiration for somebody or something **4 RELIGIOUS FERVOUR** fervent religious or spiritual feeling **5 ACT OF DEVOTING** the act of devoting something or being devoted to a particular purpose ■ **devotions** *npl* **PRAYERS** prayers or other religious observances, especially somebody's private prayers or observances —**devotional** *adj* —**devotionality** *n* —**devotionally** *adv* —**devotionalness** *n*

devour /di vówər/ *vt* **1 EAT QUICKLY** to eat something quickly and hungrily ○ *They devour in minutes what it's taken you all afternoon to prepare.* **2 TAKE IN EAGERLY** to read, look at, watch, or listen to something eagerly ○ *Young children seem to devour her stories.* **3 DESTROY** to destroy something rapidly and completely (*literary; often passive*) ○ *a house devoured by the flames* **4 WASTE** to use up something unwisely or wastefully (*literary*) **5 OVERWHELM** to become an overwhelming and destructive passion or obsession for somebody (*literary; usually passive*) [14C. Via Old French *devour-*, stressed stem of *devorer* < Latin *devorare* 'swallow down' < *vorare* 'swallow'.] —**devourer** *n* —**devouring** *adj* —**devouringly** *adv*

devout /di vówt/ *adj* **1 VERY RELIGIOUS** deeply and faithfully religious **2 VERY SINCERE** deeply and sincerely felt or meant (*formal*) **3 DEVOTED TO CAUSE** devoted to a particular personal interest or cause ○ *a devout sports fan* [12C. Via French *dévot* < Latin *devotus*, past participle of *devovere* (see DEVOTE).] —**devoutly** *adv* —**devoutness** *n*

De Vries /də vreéss/, **Hugo** (1848–1935) Dutch botanist and geneticist

dew /dyoo/ *n* **1 WATER DROPLETS ON COOL OUTDOOR SURFACES** moisture from the air that has condensed as tiny drops on outdoor objects and surfaces that have cooled, especially during the night **2 SMALL DROPS** drops of moisture of any kind, e.g. tears or sweat (*literary*) **3 FRESHNESS AND PURITY** a fresh and pure or refreshing quality in something (*literary*) ■ **dews** *npl* **DEWDROPS** drops of dew (*literary*) ■ *vt* **COAT WITH DEW** to coat or moisten something with drops of dew (*literary*) [Old English *dēaw* < Germanic]

SPELLCHECK Do not confuse ***dew*** with ***due***, which has a similar sound. Beware: your spellchecker will not catch this error.

Dewar /dyóo ər/, **Donald** (1937–2000) Scottish politician and first First Minister of Scotland (1999–2000)

Dewar flask /dyóo ər-/, **Dewar vacuum flask** /dyóo ər-/ *n* a double-walled silvered glass or metal flask with a vacuum between the walls, providing thermal insulation [Mid-20C. After Sir James *Dewar* (1824–1923).]

dewater /dee wáwtər/ *vt* to remove water from a substance, especially sewage or crude oil, or from a place

dewberry /dyóobəri/ (*plural* **-ries**) *n* **1** a variety of the blackberry bramble with trailing stems and bluish-black fruit. Genus: *Rubus*. **2** the edible blue-black fruit of a dewberry plant

dewclaw /dyóo klaw/ *n* a functionless shorter digit or claw on the foot of a dog or other mammal [Late 16C. < ?] —**dewclawed** *adj*

dewdrop /dyóo drop/ *n* **1** a drop of water that has condensed on a cool outdoor surface **2** a drop of mucus hanging from somebody's nostril (*informal; used euphemistically*)

Dewey /dyoó i/, **John** (1859–1952) US philosopher, psychologist, and educator

Dewey, Melvil (1851–1931) US librarian and educator

Dewey Decimal System, Dewey decimal classification *n* a system of classifying library books that divides them into ten main classes, divided in turn into categories with three-digit numbers and subcategories with numbers after a decimal point [Late 19thC. After Melvil DEWEY.]

dewfall /dyoó fawl/ *n* **1** the formation of dew, or the time when dew begins to form **2** the amount of dew that has condensed on objects and surfaces

de Wint /də wínt/, **Peter** (1784–1849) British painter

De Witt /də wít/, **Jan** (1625–72) Dutch statesman

dewlap /dyoó lap/ *n* **1** a loose fold of skin hanging from the neck of certain animals such as cows **2** a loose fold of skin on somebody's throat, often forming later in life [14C. < obsolete *dewe* < ? + LAP[1] 'loose piece'.] —**dewlapped** *adj*

DEW line /dyoó-/ *n* a line of radar stations across the Arctic regions of North America, designed to give an early warning of approaching enemy aircraft and missiles [Acronym < *distant early warning*]

deworm /dee wúrm/ *vt* to cure an animal of an infestation of worms —**dewormer** *n*

dew point *n* the temperature at which the air cannot hold all the moisture in it and dew begins to form

dew pond *n* a small shallow pond on high ground that is regularly refreshed by heavy rainfall and condensing fog

dew worm *n US, Can* a common earthworm used as fishing bait

dewy /dyoó i/ (**-ier, -iest**) *adj* **1 COVERED WITH DEW** covered with dew or characterized by the presence of dew **2 MOIST** moist or moist-looking **3 LIKE DEW** like dew, especially in having a fresh, pure, or refreshing quality (*literary*) —**dewily** *adv* —**dewiness** *n*

dewy-eyed *adj* childishly innocent, inexperienced, or trusting ○ *full of dewy-eyed optimism*

dex /deks/ *n* dextroamphetamine or a tablet containing it (*slang*) [Mid-20C. Shortening.]

dexamethasone /déksə méthəsōn/ *n* a synthetic steroid. Use: treatment of inflammatory conditions and hormonal imbalances. [Mid-20C. < *dexa-* (blend of HEXA- + DECA-) + METHYL + CORTISONE.]

dexie /déksi/ *n* a tablet containing dextroamphetamine (*slang*) [Mid-20C. Shortening.]

dexter /dékstər/ *adj* placed on the right-hand side of a coat of arms, that is, on the left from the point of view of somebody looking at it (*technical; usually after the noun*) [Mid-16C. < Latin, 'on the right'.]

dexterity /dek stérrəti/ *n* **1** ease and skill in physical movement, especially in using the hands and manipulating objects ○ *manual dexterity* **2** sharpness or quickness of mind

dexterous /dékstərəss/, **dextrous** /dékstrəss/ *adj* **1** characterized by ease and skill in movement, especially in the use of the hands to carry out tasks **2** mentally sharp or quick [Early 17C. < Latin *dexter* 'skilful, on the right'.] —**dexterously** *adv* —**dexterousness** *n*

dextr- *prefix* = **dextro-** (*before vowels*)

dextral /dékstrəl/ *adj* (*technical*) **1 ON THE RIGHT** on or relating to the right-hand side, especially of the body **2 RIGHT-HANDED** right-handed **3 SPIRALLING TO THE RIGHT** describes the clockwise spiralling of the shell of a marine invertebrate animal [Mid-17C. < medieval Latin *dextralis* < Latin *dextra* 'right hand' < *dexter* 'on the right'.] —**dextrality** /dek strálləti/ *n* —**dextrally** *adv*

dextran /dékstrən/ *n* a branched polysaccharide produced by the action of bacteria on sucrose. Use: blood plasma substitute, food additive. [Late 19C. < DEXTRO- + -AN[1].]

dextrin /dékstrin/, **dextrine** /-streen, -strin/ *n* $(C_6H_{10}O_5)_n$ a product that is an intermediate in the formation of maltose. Source: heating of starch. Use: adhesive, size, in syrups and beers. [Mid-19C. < DEXTRO-.]

dextro /dékstrō/ *adj* = **dextrorotatory** [Early 20C. Shortening.]

dextro- *prefix* **1** right, on the right ○ *dextrocardia* **2** dextrorotatory ○ *dextroglucose* [< Latin *dexter* 'on the right']

dextroamphetamine /dékstrō am féttə meen/ *n* a form of amphetamine. Use: stimulant, antidepressant.

dextrocardia /dékstrō kaárdi ə/ *n* a medical condition in which the heart inclines to the right side of the centre of the chest instead of the left, often with a similar reversal of all abdominal organs

dextroglucose /dékstrō gloókōz/ *n* = **dextrose**

dextrorotary *adj* = **dextrorotatory**

dextrorotation /dékstrō rō táysh'n/ *n* a rotation to the right, particularly of the plane of polarization of light passing through a crystal or solution

dextrorotatory /dékstrō rō táytəri/, **dextrorotary** /-rṓtəri/ *adj* rotating the plane of polarization of light passing through it to the right or clockwise

dextrose /dékstrōz/ *n* ◆ **glucose**

dextrous *adj* = **dexterous**

DF *abbr* **1** Defender of the Faith **2** direction finder

D/F *abbr* direction finder

DFC *abbr* Distinguished Flying Cross

DfEE *abbr* Department for Education and Employment

DFID *abbr* Department for International Development

DFM (*plural* **DFMs**) *n* a medal awarded to members of the RAF below officer rank for bravery while flying but not in combat. Full form **Distinguished Flying Medal**

dg *abbr* decigram

DG *abbr* **1** Deo gratias **2** director-general

DH *abbr* **1** Department of Health **2 DH, dh** *US* designated hitter

DHA *abbr* District Health Authority

Dhaka /dákə/, **Dacca** capital of Bangladesh, in the centre of the country. Population: 3,368,940 (1991).

dhal /daal/, **dal** *n* a thick Indian stew made from pulses, onions, and spices

dhansak *n* an Indian curry that is made from meat or vegetables mixed with lentils [Late 20C. < Gujarati.]

dharma /daármə/ *n* **1** in Hinduism, somebody's duty to behave according to strict religious and social codes, or the righteousness earned by performing religious and social duties **2** in Buddhism, the truth about the way things are, and will always be, in the universe or in nature, especially when contained in scripture [Late 18C. < Sanskrit, 'something established, decree, custom'.] —**dharmic** *adj*

dharna /daárnə/, **dhurna** /dúrnə/ *n* in India, the practice of protesting against an injustice by sitting and fasting outside the door of the offender [Late 18C. < Hindi, 'placing, act of sitting in restraint'.]

Dharuk /dúrrook/ (*plural* **-uk** *or* **-uks**) *n* **1** a member of an Australian Aboriginal people that formerly inhabited the area around present-day Sydney **2** the language of the Dharuk people, now extinct [Probably < an Aboriginal language] —**Dharuk** *adj*

Dhaulagiri /dówlə geéri/ one of the world's highest mountains, in the Himalayas in N Nepal. Height: 8,172 m/26,811 ft.

dhobi /dṓbi/ *n* in India, some other parts of Asia, and East Africa, somebody who washes laundry [Mid-19C. < Hindi, < *dhob* 'washing'.]

dhobi itch /dṓbbee-/ *n* a fungal infection of the skin in the groin area, especially in men in the tropics. Technical name **tinea cruris**. US term **jock itch**

dhobiwallah /dṓbi wolə/ *n S Asia* a person whose job is to wash clothes

dhole /dōl/ *n* a wild dog that has a reddish coat and bushy tail, and hunts large animals in packs. Native to: South Asia. *Cuon alpinus*. [Early 19C. < ?]

dhoti /dṓti/, **dhootie** /doóti/, **dhotie** /dṓti/, **dhuti** /doóti/ *n* **1** a loincloth worn by some men in India **2** the cotton cloth used in India to make the loincloths called dhotis [Early 17C. < Hindi.]

dhow /dow/ *n* a low-sided, one- or two-masted ship with triangular curving sails, used by Arab sailors in the Indian Ocean [Late 18C. Probably < Persian.]

Dhu al-Hijjah /doó əl híjjaa/ *n* in the Islamic calendar, the 12th lunar month of the year during which the holiday of Yom Arafat is celebrated [Late 18C. < Arabic, 'the one of the pilgrimage'.]

Dhu al-Qa'dah /doó əl kaá daa/ *n* in the Islamic calendar, the 11th lunar month of the year, made up of 30 days [Late 18C. < Arabic, 'the one of the sitting'.]

Dhurga /dúrgə/ *n* an Australian Aboriginal language of New South Wales, now extinct or almost extinct [Mid-20C. < Dhurga.] —**Dhurga** *adj*

dhurna *n* = **dharna**

dhurrie /dúrri/, **durrie** *n* **1** a flat-woven cotton rug made in India **2** a heavy woven cotton rug, traditionally from India [Late 19C. < Hindi *darī*.]

di-[1] *prefix* **1** two, twice, double ○ *dicephalous* **2** containing two atoms, radicals, or groups ○ *dimethyl* [< Greek. Ultimately from a form of the Indo-European word for 'two' that is also the ancestor of English *twin, twilight*, and *bi-*.]

di-[2] *prefix* = **dia-** (*before vowels*)

dia. *abbr* diameter

dia- *prefix* through, across ○ *diachronic* ○ *diadromous* [< Greek *dia*]

diabase /dí ə bayss/ *n US* GEOL = **dolerite** [Mid-19C. < French.] —**diabasic** /dí ə báyssik/ *adj*

diabetes /dí ə beé teez/ *n* a medical disorder that causes the body to produce an excessive amount of urine, especially diabetes mellitus [Mid-16C. Via Latin < Greek, 'passer through, siphon' < *diabainein* 'go through'.]

diabetes insipidus /-in síppidəss/ *n* a disorder of the pituitary gland that causes the body to produce large amounts of urine [< modern Latin, 'bland diabetes']

diabetes mellitus /-mə lítəss/ *n* a disorder in which there is no control of blood sugar, through inadequate insulin production (Type 1) or decreased cellular sensitivity to insulin (Type 2), causing kidney, eye, and nerve damage [< modern Latin, 'honey-sweet diabetes']

diabetic /dí ə béttik/ *adj* **1 HAVING DIABETES** having diabetes, especially diabetes mellitus **2 RELATING TO DIABETES** relating to or caused by diabetes, especially diabetes mellitus ○ *diabetic symptoms* **3 INTENDED FOR DIABETICS** made without sugar and therefore suitable for people who have diabetes mellitus ■ *n* **SOMEBODY WITH DIABETES** a person affected by diabetes

diablerie /di aáblə ri/ *n* **1 MAGIC** witchcraft or magic **2 THINGS CONNECTED WITH WITCHCRAFT OR EVIL** stories, traditions, and practices associated with magic or devil worship **3 MISCHIEF** mischief (*literary*) [Mid-18C. < French < *diable* 'devil' < Latin *diabolus* (see DEVIL).]

diabolical /dí ə bóllik'l/ *adj* **1 diabolical, diabolic OF DEVIL** connected with the devil or devil worship **2 diabolical, diabolic EVIL** extremely cruel or evil **3 VERY BAD** extremely bad or unpleasant (*informal*) **4 USED FOR EMPHATIC DISAPPROVAL** used for emphasis when disapproving of something, especially somebody's behaviour (*slang*) [14C. < French *diabolique* < late Latin *diabolicus* < Greek *diabolos* 'devil'.] —**diabolically** *adv* —**diabolicalness** *n*

diabolise *vt* = **diabolize**

diabolism /dí ábbəlizəm/ *n* **1** worship of the devil or devils **2** evil behaviour or character (*literary*) —**diabolist** *n*

diabolize /dí ábbə līz/ (**-lizes, -lizing, -lized**), **diabolise** (**-lises, -lising, -lised**) *vt* **1** to cause somebody or something to appear evil **2** to make somebody or something evil

diabolo /dí ábbəlō/ (*plural* **-los**) *n* **1** the game of spinning a top with a narrow waist and two heads on a string tied to two sticks held in the hands **2** a top designed to be used in the game of diabolo [Early 20C. Via Italian *diabolo* 'devil' < Latin *diabolus* (see DEVIL).]

diacetylmorphine /dí ássətil máwr feen/ *n* heroin (*technical*)

diachronic /dí ə krónnik/ *adj* involving, or relating to the study of, or the development of something, especially a language, through time ○ *diachronic linguistics*. ◊ **synchronic** [Mid-19C. < DIA- + Greek *khronos* 'time'.] —**diachronically** *adv*

diachrony /dí ákrəni/ *n* change or development over time

diacid /dí ássid/ *adj* having two acidic hydrogen atoms that may be replaced by metal or acid ions to form a salt or an ester ■ *n* an acid that has two acidic hydrogen atoms

diaconal /dí ákənəl/ *adj* relating to a deacon or deaconess or to the position of deacon or deaconess [Early 17C. < late Latin *diaconalis* < Latin *diaconus* (see DEACON).]

diaconate /dí ákə nayt/ *n* the position of deacon or deaconess, or the period of time during which it is held by a particular person [Early 18C. < late Latin *diaconatus* < Latin *diaconus* (see DEACON).]

COMMON DIACRITICAL MARKS

Name	Mark	Word/Phrase
grave	À à	à la mode
acute	Á á	Cádiz
circumflex	Â â	château
tilde	Ã ã	São Paulo
umlaut	Ä ä	Fräulein
angstrom	Å å	smörgåsbord
cedilla	Ç ç	façade
grave	È è	crèche
acute	É é	purée
circumflex	Ê ê	fête
umlaut	Ë ë	noël
grave	Ì ì	Forlì
acute	Í í	Valparaíso
circumflex	Î î	maître d'hôtel
umlaut	Ï ï	faïence
eth	Ð ð	Hamðir
tilde	Ñ ñ	mañana
acute	Ó ó	Kraków
circumflex	Ô ô	maître d'hôtel
umlaut	Ö ö	danke schön
Danish/Norwegian O	Ø ø	øre
haček	Ř ř	Dvořák
acute	Ú ú	Setúbal
circumflex	Û û	croûtons
umlaut	Ü ü	gemütlich

diacritic /dī ə krĭttik/ adj = **diacritical** ■ n **diacritical mark** a mark above or below a printed letter that indicates a change in the way it is to be pronounced or stressed [Late 17C. < Greek diakritikos 'that distinguishes or separates' < krinein 'separate, decide'.] —**diacritically** adv

diacritical /dī ə krĭttik'l/, **diacritic** adj indicating a change or modification in something, especially in the way a printed letter is to be pronounced or stressed

diacritical mark n = diacritic n.

diacylglycerol /dī ássil glíssə rol/ n an intermediate signalling molecule produced during intracellular processes

diadelphous /dī ə délfəss/ adj describes stamens or flowers that have the stamen filaments grouped into two bundles [Early 19C. < DI-1 + Greek adelphos 'brother'.]

diadem /dī ə dem/ n 1 **CROWN** a jewelled headband used as a royal crown 2 **JEWELLED HEADBAND** any jewelled headband 3 **REGAL POWER** royal power or dignity (literary) [14C. Via Old French, < Greek diadēma '(regal) headband' < diadein 'bind around' < dein 'bind'.]

diadem spider n a harmless spider common in Europe and Asia. Araneus diadematus. [< its orb webs]

Diadochi /dī áddəkī/ npl the six Macedonian generals who divided up and then fought over the empire of Alexander the Great after his death

diadochy /dī áddəki/ n the replacement of one element by another within the structure of a crystal [Early 18C. < Greek diadokhē 'succession' < diadekhesthai 'succeed' < dekhesthai 'take, accept'.]

diadromous /dī áddrəməss/ adj describes fish that migrate between fresh and salt water

diaeresis /dī eérəssiss/ (plural -ses /-seez/), **dieresis** (plural -ses) n 1 **MARK MAKING ADJACENT VOWEL SEPARATE SYLLABLE** a mark consisting of two dots, printed above the second of two adjacent vowels to show that it

should be pronounced as a separate syllable, as in the word 'naïve' 2 **MARK CHANGING PRONUNCIATION OF VOWEL** a mark consisting of two dots, placed above certain vowels in some languages to show that they are to be pronounced in a particular way 3 **PAUSE IN POETRY** a pause in a line of poetry that occurs when the end of a metrical foot coincides with the end of a word [Late 16C. Via Latin < Greek diairesis < diairein 'separate, divide' < hairein 'take'.] —**diaeretic** /dī ə réttik/ adj

diag. abbr 1 diagonal 2 diagram

diagenesis /dī ə jénnəssiss/ n the changes that take place in a sediment as a result of increased temperatures and pressures, causing solid rock to form, e.g. as sand becomes sandstone —**diagenetic** /dī ə je néttik/ adj

Diaghilev /dī ággə lef/, **Sergei** (1872–1929) Russian ballet impresario

diagnose /dī əgnōz/ (-noses, -nosing, -nosed) vt 1 to identify an illness or disorder in a patient through an interview, physical examination, and medical tests and other procedures ○ The doctor diagnosed rheumatism. 2 to identify the nature or cause of something, especially a problem or fault [Mid-19C. Back-formation < DIAGNOSIS.] —**diagnosable** /dī əg nōzəb'l/ adj

diagnosis /dī əg nóssiss/ (plural -ses /-seez/) n 1 **IDENTIFICATION OF ILLNESS** the identifying of an illness or disorder in a patient through physical examination, medical tests, or other procedures ○ a doctor with vast experience of diagnosis 2 **IDENTIFICATION OF PROBLEM** the identifying of the nature or cause of something, especially a problem or fault ○ mechanics specializing in fault diagnosis 3 **DECISION REACHED BY DIAGNOSIS** a decision or conclusion reached by medical or other diagnosis ○ The diagnosis is flu. [Late 17C. Via modern Latin, < Greek diagnosis < diagignōskein 'distinguish' < gignōskein 'know, perceive'.]

SPELLCHECK Do not confuse **diagnosis** with **diagnoses**, which has a similar sound and spelling. Beware: your spellchecker will not catch this error.

diagnostic /dī əg nóstik/ adj identifying, or used in identifying, the nature or cause of an illness, disorder, or problem ■ n a test, procedure, or instrument used to identify the nature or cause of an illness, disorder, or problem —**diagnostically** adv —**diagnostician** /dī əg no stísh'n/ n

diagnostics /dī əg nóstiks/ n the art of, or procedures for, identifying illnesses or disorders in patients through diagnosis (+ singular verb)

diagonal /dī ággənəl/ adj 1 **SLANTING OR OBLIQUE** running from one side to another in a slanting or oblique way 2 **WITH SLANTING LINES** having slanting lines or markings 3 **JOINING ANGLES OR CORNERS** describes a line that joins two opposite or nonadjacent angles or corners of a straight-sided geometric figure ■ n 1 **SLANTING LINE** a slanting line or direction 2 **LINE JOINING ANGLES** a line that joins two opposite or nonadjacent angles or corners of a straight-sided geometric figure 3 **PRINTING** = **slash** n. 6 [Mid-16C. < Latin diagonalis < Greek diagōnios 'from angle to angle' < gōnia 'angle'.] —**diagonally** adv

diagram /dī ə gram/ n 1 **SIMPLE EXPLANATORY DRAWING** a simple drawing showing the basic shape, layout, or workings of something 2 **CHART** a chart or graph that illustrates something such as a statistical trend 3 **MATHEMATICAL DRAWING** a line drawing that presents mathematical information ■ vt (-grams, -gramming, -grammed) **ILLUSTRATE** to make a diagram that represents or illustrates something [Early 17C. Via Latin, < Greek diagramma 'geometrical figure, written list, scale in music' < diagraphein 'mark out by lines, draw' < graphein 'write'.] —**diagrammable** adj

diagrammatic /dī əgrə máttik/ adj in the form of an explanatory drawing or chart —**diagrammatically** adv

diagraph /dī ə graf, -graaf/ n a mechanical instrument used for producing scale copies of diagrams and maps [Late 19C. < French diagraphe < Greek diagraphein (see DIAGRAM).]

diakinesis /dī əki neéssiss, -kī-/ n the final stage in cell reduction division (**meiosis**), during which the paired chromosomes begin to shorten, thicken, and separate [Early 20C. Via modern Latin, < German Diakinese < Greek kinēsis 'motion' (see KINESIS).] —**diakinetic** /-néttik/ adj

dial /dī əl/ n 1 **INDICATOR WITH MOVABLE POINTER** an instrument with a movable pointer that displays a measurement, e.g. the current speed of a vehicle or the level of steam pressure inside a boiler 2 **CONTROL KNOB** a round control

knob or disc turned with the fingers to adjust a piece of electrical or mechanical equipment, such as a radio 3 **STATION INDICATOR ON RADIO** a numbered panel with a movable pointer on a radio, used for tuning in to different stations 4 **CLOCK FACE** the round face of a traditional clock 5 **DISC WITH HOLES ON TELEPHONE** a disc with numbered finger holes on the front of an old telephone, turned with a finger to select the required telephone number ■ vti (-als, -alling, -alled) **CONTACT ON TELEPHONE** to contact a number or person by telephone ○ She must have dialled the wrong number. [14C. < Old French, 'wheel in clockwork that makes a revolution once a day' < Latin dies 'day'.] —**dialler** n

dial. abbr 1 dialect 2 dialectal

dial-a-ride n a bus service that can be called to the door by telephone, generally intended for people in need of assistance in moving about

dialect /dī ə lekt/ n 1 **REGIONAL VARIETY OF LANGUAGE** a regional variety of a language, with differences in vocabulary, grammar, and pronunciation 2 **LANGUAGE SPOKEN BY CLASS OR PROFESSION** a form of a language spoken by members of a particular social class or profession 3 **NONSTANDARD SPEECH** nonstandard spoken language 4 **MEMBER OF LANGUAGE FAMILY** one of a family of related languages ○ Romance dialects such as French and Italian [Mid-16C. Directly or via French < Latin dialogus 'way of speaking, dialect' < Greek dialektos 'conversation, language, local speech' < dialegesthai (see DIALOGUE).] —**dialectal** /dī ə lékt'l/ adj —**dialectally** adv

dialectic /dī ə léktik/ n 1 **TENSION BETWEEN CONFLICTING IDEAS** the tension that exists between two conflicting or interacting forces, elements, or ideas 2 **INVESTIGATION OF TRUTH THROUGH DISCUSSION** the investigation of the truth through discussion, or the art of investigating truths through discussion 3 **dialectic, dialectics** **DEBATE RESOLVING CONFLICT** debate intended to resolve a conflict between two contradictory or apparently contradictory ideas or elements logically, establishing truths on both sides rather than disproving one argument (+ singular verb) 4 **HEGELIAN PROCESS** the process, in Hegelian and Marxist thought, in which two apparently opposed ideas, the thesis and antithesis, become combined in a unified whole, the synthesis 5 **SOCRATIC METHOD FOR REVEALING TRUTH** the methods used in Socratic philosophy to reveal truth through disputation [Late 16C. Via Latin dialectica < Greek dialektikē (tekhnē) '(art) of discussion or debate' < dialektikos 'of conversation' < dialektos (see DIALECT).] —**dialectician** /dī ə lek tísh'n/ n

dialectical /dī ə léktik'l/ adj 1 **ACHIEVED BY DIALECTIC** achieved or attempted by dialectic 2 **INVOLVING DIALECTIC** involving or depending upon dialectic 3 **RELATING TO DIALECT** relating to or belonging to a dialect —**dialectically** adv

dialectical materialism n the Marxian concept of reality in which material things are in the constant process of change brought about by the tension between conflicting or interacting forces, elements, or ideas —**dialectical materialist** n

dialectics n = dialectic n. 3

dialectology /dī ə lek tóllaji/ n the study of language dialects —**dialectological** /dī ə lektə lójjik'l/ adj —**dialectologically** adv —**dialectologist** /dī ə lek tóllajist/ n

dial gauge n a sensitive measuring device that indicates small displacements of a plunger by means of a pointer moving over a circular scale

dialling code /dīaling-/ n digits indicating a particular area or country that are dialled before the local number in calls made from outside that area or country

dialling tone n a continuous sound that is heard when a telephone receiver is lifted, signalling that a number can be dialled. US term **dial tone**

⚡ **dialog box** n a small rectangular window on a computer screen that conveys information to, or requires a response from, the user

dialogic /dī ə lójjik/ adj 1 written in the form of a conversation 2 relating to dialogues

dialogise vi = **dialogize**

dialogist /dī álləjist/ n 1 a writer of dialogue for films, television, or radio 2 a participant in a dialogue —**dialogistic** /dī ələ jístik/ adj

dialogue /dī ə log/ n 1 **CHARACTERS' WORDS** the words spoken by characters in a book, a film, or a play, or a section of a work that contains spoken words ○ pages of dialogue 2 **FORMAL DISCUSSION** a formal discussion or negotiation, especially between opposing sides in a political or international context 3 **CONVERSATION** talk of any kind between two or more people (*formal*) **4 LITERARY WORK IN CONVERSATION FORM** a work of literature in the form of a conversation ■ *vi* (**-logues, -loguing, -logued**) ⚠ **TAKE PART IN TALK** to take part in a conversation, discussion, or negotiation. [12C. Via Old French < Greek *dialogos* < *dialegesthai* 'speak with each other' < *legein* 'speak'.] —**dialoguer** *n*

USAGE Avoid using ***dialogue*** as a verb meaning 'to negotiate or discuss', as this usage may be criticized. Instead of writing *Towards the end of 1787 Thomas Jefferson dialogued with the French ministers of state in order to persuade them to improve trade with the United States*, say *Towards the end of 1787 Thomas Jefferson engaged in diplomatic dialogue with the French ministers of state in order to persuade them to improve trade with the United States*. Some people regard this functional shift of the word from noun to verb as political and journalistic jargon. See Language Note at ***functional shift***.

dial tone *n US, Can* TELECOM = **dialling tone**

ϟ **dial-up** *adj* requiring a computer modem and telephone line to establish communication with another computer or a network

dialyse /dí ə līz/ (**-lyses, -lysing, -lysed**) *vti* **1** to remove the accumulated waste products of metabolism from the blood of a patient whose kidneys are not functioning, or to undergo such a procedure **2** to separate dissolved substances from a solution by diffusing it through a semi-permeable membrane, or to be subjected to this process [Mid-19C. < DIALYSIS, after ANALYSE.] —**dialysability** /dí ə līzə bíllәti/ *n* —**dialysable** *adj* —**dialysation** /dí ə lī záysh'n/ *n* —**dialyser** *n*

dialysis /dī állәssiss/ *n* **1** the process of filtering the accumulated waste products of metabolism from the blood of a patient whose kidneys are not functioning properly, using a kidney machine **2** the separation of dissolved substances from a solution by allowing the solution to diffuse through a semi-permeable membrane [Mid-19C. Via Latin, 'set of propositions without a connecting conjunction' < Greek *dialusis* 'separation, loosening' < *luein* 'loosen'.] —**dialytic** /dí ə líttik/ *adj* —**dialytically** *adv*

dialyze *v* US = **dialyse**

diamagnet /dí ə magnәt/ *n* a substance that is repelled by magnetic fields, such as noble gases, halogens, and alkali and alkaline earth metals —**diamagnetic** /dí ə mag néttik/ *adj* —**diamagnetically** *adv*

diamagnetism /dí ə mágnәtizәm/ *n* a tendency in materials with a relative permeability of less than one to be repelled by a magnetic field and align themselves at right angles to it

diamanté /dée ə mónt ay, dí ə-/ *adj* decorated with colourless imitation gems (**rhinestones**) that look like diamonds ■ *n* colourless imitation gems that look like diamonds. Use: jewellery. [Early 20C. < French, past participle of *diamanter* 'set with diamonds' < *diamant* (see DIAMOND).]

Diamantina /dí әmәn téenә/ river flowing from central Queensland to Lake Eyre in South Australia. Length: 800 km/500 mi.

diamantine /dí ə mán tīn/ *adj* **1** resembling diamonds **2** made of diamond or consisting of diamonds [Early 17C. < French *diamantin* < *diamant* (see DIAMOND).]

diameter /dī ámmitәr/ *n* **1** a straight line running from one side of a circle or other rounded geometric figure through the centre to the other side, or the length of this line **2** the width or thickness of something, especially something circular or cylindrical ○ *in diameter* [14C. Via Old French *diametre* < Latin, < Greek *diametros (grammē)* '(line) that measures through' < *metron* 'measure'.] —**diametral** *adj* —**diametrally** *adv*

diametric /dí ə méttrik/, **diametrical** /dí ə méttrik'l/ *adj* complete in respect of being opposite or different

diametrically /dí ə méttrikli/ *adv* used to emphasize that a difference or contrast is as great as it can be ○ *diametrically opposite concepts*

diamine /dí ə meen/ *n* an organic chemical compound that contains two amino (**nitrogen-containing**) groups

diamond /dí әmәnd/ *n* **1 HARD COLOURLESS MINERAL** a hard transparent precious stone that is a form of carbon. Use: gems, abrasives, cutting tools. **2 SHAPE LIKE SQUARE RESTING ON CORNER** a four-sided shape like a square standing on one of its corners **3 CARD WITH DIAMOND-SHAPED SYMBOL** a playing card with a diamond-shaped symbol on it. ◊ **diamonds 4 PART OF PLAYING AREA IN BASEBALL** the area of a baseball field bounded by home plate and the three bases **5 BASEBALL PLAYING AREA** an area for playing baseball including the infield and the outfield **6** *N Ireland* **IRISH MARKET SQUARE** the market square of a town in Northern Ireland (*regional*) ■ *vt* **DECORATE WITH DIAMONDS** to decorate something with diamonds or similar gemstones [13C. Via Old French *diamant* 'hardest metal' < medieval Latin *diamant-*, alteration of Latin *adamant-* (see ADAMANT).]

diamond anniversary *n* an anniversary celebrating 60, or sometimes 75, years of something, e.g. marriage [< custom of marking the occasion with gifts containing diamonds]

diamondback /dí әmәnd bak/ *n* **1** a large poisonous rattlesnake with diamond-shaped markings on its back. Native to: SW United States, Mexico. *Crotalus adamantus* and *Crotalus atrox*. **2** a terrapin with diamond-shaped markings on its shell. Native to: salt marshes of the Atlantic and the Gulf coasts of North America. Genus: *Malaclemys*.

diamondback moth *n* a brightly coloured moth with diamond-shaped markings on the underside of the front wings, visible when the wings are folded. Family: Plutellidae.

diamondiferous /dí әmәn díffәrәss/ *adj* containing diamond or diamonds

diamond in the rough *n US* = **rough diamond** *n.* 2

diamond jubilee *n* = **diamond anniversary**

diamond point *n* a cutting tool in which two cutting edges meet at an acute angle, forming a diamond shape

diamond python *n* a greenish-yellow python with yellow diamond-shaped markings along its side. Native to: Australia, New Zealand, New Guinea. *Morelia argus*.

diamonds /dí әmәndz/ *n* one of the four suits used in cards, with a red diamond shape as its symbol (+ *singular or plural verb*)

diamond wedding *n* the celebration of 60 years of marriage [< custom of marking the occasion with gifts containing diamonds]

diamorphine /dí ə máwr feen/ *n* heroin (*technical*) [Early 20C. Contraction of DIACETYLMORPHINE, its chemical name.]

Diana /dī ánnә/ *n* in Roman mythology, the goddess of hunting, virginity, and the moon. Greek equivalent **Artemis**

Barnaby's

Diana, Princess of Wales

Diana, Princess of Wales (1961–97) British princess. Born **Diana Frances Spencer**

dianthus /dī ánthәss/ *n* a flowering plant belonging to the group that includes carnations, pinks, and sweet william. Genus: *Dianthus*. [Late 18C. < modern Latin, < Greek *Dios* 'of Zeus' + *anthos* 'flower'.]

diapason /dí ə páyz'n, -páyss'n/ *n* **1 PIPE ORGAN'S MAIN STOP** one of two main stops on a pipe organ that control the organ's tone and characteristic sound **2 RANGE OF SINGER OR MUSICAL INSTRUMENT** the range of a musical instrument or somebody's singing voice (*technical*) **3 TUNING DEVICE** a tuning fork or pitch pipe (*technical*) [14C. Via Latin, < Greek *dia pasōn khordōn* 'across all the notes of the scale'.] —**diapasonal** *adj* —**diapasonic** /dí ə pay zónnik, -sónnik/ *adj*

diapause /dí ə pawz/ *n* a period during which the metabolism of certain animals or insects slows down, temporarily suspending their bodily development and growth

diapedesis /dí әpә déesiss/ *n* a condition in which blood leaks through the apparently unruptured walls of blood vessels into surrounding tissue, as a reaction to severe inflammation or injury [Early 17C. < modern Latin, < Greek *dia-* 'through' + *pēdan* 'to leap'.] —**diapedetic** /-déttik/ *adj*

diaper /dí әpәr/ *n* **1** *US, Can* = **nappy 2 PATTERN OF SMALL MOTIFS** a pattern woven into or printed on fabric, consisting of a small motif, often a diamond, repeated to cover an entire surface **3 FABRIC WITH DIAPER PATTERN** cotton or linen fabric with a diaper pattern woven into or printed on it ■ *vt* **1** *US, Can* **PUT NAPPY ON BABY** to put a nappy on a baby **2 DECORATE WITH DIAPER PATTERN** to decorate something, especially fabric, with a diaper pattern [14C. Via Old French *diapre* 'ornamental cloth' < medieval Greek *diaspros* 'thoroughly white'.]

diaphanous /dī áffәnәss/ *adj* **1** delicate or gauzy, so as to be transparent ○ *the insect's diaphanous wings* **2** fragile or insubstantial because extremely faint or slight (*literary*) ○ *diaphanous imaginings* [Early 17C. Via Latin *diaphanus* < Greek *diaphanēs* 'shown through' < *phainein* 'show'.] —**diaphaneity** /dí әfә née әti/ *n* —**diaphanously** *n* —**diaphanousness** *adv*

diaphone /dí ə fōn/ *n* **1** a set of all the different ways that a particular speech sound is pronounced in all the dialects of a language, or a member of this set **2** a foghorn with a two-note sound

diaphoresis /dí әfә réessiss/ *n* sweating, especially sweating induced for medical reasons (*technical*) [Late 17C. < late Latin, < Greek *diaphorein* 'dissipate by sweating' < *phorein* 'carry'.]

diaphoretic /dí әfә réttik/ *adj* describes agents that induce sweating, or their effect —**diaphoretic** *n*

diaphragm /dí ə fram/ *n* **1 MUSCULAR WALL BELOW RIB CAGE** a curved muscular membrane in humans and other mammals that separates the abdomen from the area around the lungs **2 DOME-SHAPED CONTRACEPTIVE** a dome-shaped rubber or plastic contraceptive device for women, placed inside the vagina over the entrance to the womb to prevent sperm from entering **3 CAMERA'S MECHANISM CONTROLLING OPENING FOR LIGHT** a disc with a fixed or variable opening that controls the amount of light that enters a camera or other optical instrument **4 VIBRATING DISC IN SOUND EQUIPMENT** a thin disc in a microphone, telephone receiver, or other sound device that vibrates in response to sound waves or electrical signals, converting one into the other **5 THIN MEMBRANE** any thin separating membrane, e.g. the porous plate dividing the sections of an electrolytic cell or the plate of cells across the stems of some water plants [14C. < late Latin *diaphragma* < Greek *diaphrassein* 'to barricade' < *phrassein* 'fence in'.] —**diaphragmatic** /dí ə frag máttik/ *adj* —**diaphragmatically** *adv*

~~**diaphram**~~ incorrect spelling of **diaphragm**

diaphysis /dī áffәssiss/ (*plural* **-ses** /-seez/) *n* the central section of a long bone, between the growth areas at each end. ◊ **epiphysis** *n.* 1 [Mid-19C. < Greek *diaphusis* 'growing through' < *phusis* 'growth'.] —**diaphysial** /dí ə fízzi әl/ *adj*

diapir /dí ə peer/ *n* a dome-shaped body of rock that migrates upwards through denser overlying rock, e.g. a salt deposit [Early 20C. < Greek *diapeirainein* 'pierce through' < *peirainein* 'pierce'.] —**diapiric** /dí ə pírrik/ *adj*

diapositive /dí ə pózzitiv/ *n* a photographic slide

diarchy /dí aarki/ (*plural* **-chies**), **dyarchy** (*plural* **-chies**) *n* **1** a form of government in which power is held by two supreme rulers or two governing bodies **2** a country ruled or run by two supreme rulers or two governing bodies [Mid-19C. < DI-[1] after MONARCHY.] —**diarchal** /dī áark'l/ *adj* —**diarchic** *adj* —**diarchical** *adj*

~~**diarhea**~~ incorrect spelling of **diarrhoea**

diarist /dí әrist/ *n* the writer of a diary, especially one that is published

~~**diarrea**~~ incorrect spelling of **diarrhoea**

diarrhoea /dí ə rée ә/, **diarrhea** *n* **1** frequent and excessive discharging of the bowels producing abnormally thin watery stools, usually as a symptom of gastro-intestinal upset or infection **2** abnormally thin watery faeces [Early 16C. Via Latin, < Greek *diarrhoia* < *diarrhein* 'flow through' < *rhein* 'to flow'.] —**diarrhoeal** *adj* —**diarrhoeic** *adj*

diarthrosis /dí aar thróssiss/ (*plural* **-ses** /-seez/) *n* **1** a joint of the body that is able to move freely in various directions, e.g. the shoulder, hip, knee, or elbow **2** the ability of some joints of the body to move in several directions [Late 16C. < Greek, < *diarthroun* 'fasten by a joint' < *arthroun* 'fasten'.] —**diarthrodial** *adj*

diary /dī́ əri/ (*plural* **-ries**) *n* **1 PERSONAL RECORD OF LIFE'S EVENTS** a personal record of events in somebody's life, often including personal thoughts and observations **2 BLANK BOOK** a book with blank or lined paper for keeping a diary in **3 BOOK FOR APPOINTMENTS** a book, usually with pages labelled according to the days of a given year, in which people keep notes of appointments ○ *a desk diary* ○ *I'll check my diary to see if I'm free.* US term **appointment book 4 LIST OF EVENTS** a list of events taking place in a particular place during a particular period of time ○ *a diary of October's events* [Late 16C. < Latin *diarium* < *dies* 'day'.]

diaspora /dī áspərə/ *n* a dispersion of a people, language, or culture that was formerly concentrated in one place ○ *the African diaspora* [Late 19C. < Greek, < *diaspeirein* 'disperse' < *speirein* 'sow, scatter'.]

Diaspora /dī áspərə/ *n* **1** the dispersion of the Jews from Palestine following the Babylonians' conquest of the Judean Kingdom in the 6th century BC and again following the Romans' destruction of the Second Temple in AD 70 **2** the Jewish communities living outside either the present-day state of Israel or the ancient biblical kingdom of Israel

diaspore /dī́ ə spawr/ *n* **1** a white, grey, or pink form of aluminium oxide mineral. Source: bauxite. Use: abrasives, heat-resistant materials. **2** a seed or spore that is dispersed from a plant [Early 19C. < Greek *diaspora* (see DIASPORA); from its dispersion when heated.]

diastase /dī́ ə stayz, -stayss/ *n* now called **amylase** [Mid-19C. < modern Latin *diastasis* (see DIASTASIS) + -ASE.] —**diastasic** /dī́ ə stáyzik, -stáysik/ *adj*

diastasis /dī ástəssiss/ (*plural* **-ses** /-seez/) *n* the dislodging of the end **(epiphysis)** of a long bone from its shaft without a fracturing of the bone itself (*technical*) [Early 18C. Via modern Latin < Greek, 'separation' < *stasis* 'placing'.] —**diastatic** /dī́ ə státtik/ *adj*

diastema /dī́ ə steemə/ (*plural* **-mata** /-mətə/) *n* a larger than usual gap between two adjacent teeth (*technical*) [Mid-19C. Via late Latin, < Greek, 'gap' < *diistanai* 'place apart' < *histanai* 'to place'.] —**diastematic** /dī́ əstə máttik/ *adj*

diastereoisomer /dī́ ə stérri ō íssəmər/, **diastereomer** /dī́ ə stérriəmər/ *n* a molecule that has the same formula and structure as another **(stereoisomer)**, but is arranged differently in space and is therefore not a mirror image of the other **(enantiomer)**

diastole /dī ásstəli/ *n* the rhythmic expansion of the chambers of the heart at each heartbeat, during which they fill with blood [Late 16C. Via late Latin, < Greek, 'separation, expansion' < *diastellein* 'to place apart' < *stellein* 'to place'.] —**diastolic** /dī́ ə stóllik/ *adj*

diastyle /dī́ ə stīl/ *adj* describes classical buildings with columns set at intervals equal to three or sometimes four times the diameter of a column, slightly farther apart than in the Doric order ■ *n* a diastyle building or colonnade [Mid-16C. Directly or via Latin < Greek *diastulos* 'between columns' < *stulos* 'column'.]

diathermia /dī́ ə thúrmi ə/ *n* MED = **diathermy** [Early 20C. < modern Latin, 'heat across' < Greek *thermē* 'heat'.]

diathermic /dī́ ə thúrmik/ *adj* **1** relating to diathermy **2** able to conduct or transmit heat or infrared radiation [Early 20C. < French *diathermique* < Greek *thermē* 'heat'.]

diathermy /dī́ ə thurmi/ *n* the treatment of organs or tissues by passing high-frequency electric currents through them in order to generate heat, thus increasing circulation [Early 20C. < modern Latin *diathermia* (see DIATHERMIA).]

diathesis /dī áthississ/ (*plural* **-ses** /dī áthisseez/) *n* a susceptibility to a particular disease or set of diseases, e.g. allergies or gout [Mid-17C. < modern Latin, < Greek *diatithenai* 'arrange, dispose' < *tithenai* 'put'.] —**diathetic** /dī́ ə théttik/ *adj*

diatom /dī́ ə tom/ *n* a microscopic one-celled alga that has silica-filled cell walls or shells divided into two halves. Diatoms are responsible for the formation of diatomite in water. Class: Bacillariophyceae. [Mid-19C. < modern Latin *Diatoma* < Greek *diatomos* 'cut in two' < *diatemnein* 'to cut through' < *temnein* 'to cut'.] —**diatomaceous** /dī́ ətə máyshəss/ *adj*

diatomaceous earth *n* **1** = **diatomite 2** a form of unrefined diatomite. Use: insecticide.

diatomic /dī́ ə tómmik/ *adj* having two atoms per molecule —**diatomicity** /dī́ atə míssəti/ *n*

diatomite /dī áttə mīt/ *n* a soft powdery porous rock. Source: accumulated shells of diatoms. Use: in fireproof cements, insulating materials, dynamite.

diatonic /dī́ ə tónnik/ *adj* relating to or based on musical scales consisting of five tones and two semitones, e.g. the major or minor scale, with no sharps or flats added ■ *n* the interval between any two notes of a diatonic scale [Early 17C. Via French *diatonique* or late Latin *diatonicus* < Greek *diatonikos* 'at intervals of a tone' < *tonos* 'tone'.] —**diatonically** *adv* —**diatonicism** /-tónnissizəm/ *n*

diatribe /dī́ ə trīb/ *n* a bitter verbal or written attack on somebody or something ○ *a diatribe against falling standards* [Late 16C. Via French < Greek *diatribē* 'act of spending time (in discourse)'.]

diaz- *prefix* = **diazo-** (*before vowels*)

diazepam /dī áyzə pam, -ázzə-/ *n* a tranquillizing drug. Use: treatment of anxiety and tension, muscle relaxant, sedative. [Mid-20C. < shortening of BENZODIAZEPINE + shortening of AMIDE.]

diazine /dī́ ə zeen/, **diazin** /-zin, dī ázzin/ *n* $C_4N_2H_4$ a chemical compound in which the molecules contain a hexagonal ring of four carbon atoms and two nitrogen atoms, existing in three isomeric forms

diazo /dī áy zō/ *adj* describes any organic compound containing two adjacent nitrogen atoms, e.g. an azo compound or a diazonium salt. ◊ **azo** ■ *n* (*plural* **-azos** *or* **-azoes**) a photograph or photocopy made using the diazotype process

diazo- *prefix* containing a pair of carbon atoms bonded to an aromatic hydrocarbon ○ *diazonium*

diazole /dī áy zōl/ *n* an organic chemical compound with a five-sided ring structure containing three carbon atoms and two nitrogen atoms

diazotize /dī áyzə tīz/ (**-tizes, -tizing, -tized**), **diazotise** (**-tises, -tising, -tised**) *vt* to use nitrous acid to transform an amine into a diazo compound —**diazotization** /dī áyzə tī záysh'n/ *n*

diazotype /dī áyzə tīp/ *n* a printing or photographic process that exploits the light-sensitive properties of diazo compounds

dib /dib/ (**dibs, dibbing, dibbed**) *vi* to fish by causing the bait to bob on the surface of the water [Early 17C. Alteration of DAB[1].]

dibasic /dī báyssik/ *adj* **1** describes an acid that has two replaceable hydrogen atoms **2** describes a salt or an acid that is formed with two atoms of a univalent metallic element —**dibasicity** /dī bay síssəti/ *n*

dibber /díbbər/ *n* a small pointed gardening tool used to make holes in the soil for planting seeds, bulbs, or seedlings [Mid-18C. < *dib*, related to DIBBLE.]

dibble /díbb'l/ *n* = **dibber** ■ *vt* (**-bles, -bling, -bled**) to make planting holes in soil with a pointed tool, or put plants or seeds in such holes [14C. < ?] —**dibbler** *n*

dibbuk *n* JUDAISM = **dybbuk**

dibromide /dī brō mīd/ *n* a chemical compound whose molecules contain two bromine atoms

dibs /dibz/ *npl* **1** money, especially in small amounts (*dated informal*) **2** = **jacks 3** a claim of exclusive rights to take or use something (*informal*) ○ *called dibs on the front seat* [Early 19C. < shortening of *dibstones* 'game played with pebbles'.]

dicarboxylic acid /dī kaar bok síllik-/ *n* any acid that contains two carboxyl groups

dice /dīss/ *n* (*plural* **dice**) **1 NUMBERED CUBE USED IN GAMES** a small cube with the numbers 1 to 6 marked in dots on the sides, used in gambling and in a wide variety of games of chance **2 GAMBLING GAME PLAYED WITH DICE** a gambling game played with dice, e.g. craps (*+ singular or plural verb*) ■ *npl* **CHUNKS** cube-shaped pieces, especially of meat ■ *v* (**dices, dicing, diced**) **1** *vt* **CUT INTO CUBES** to cut food into cubes ○ *diced carrots* **2** *vti* **GAMBLE WITH DICE** to gamble using dice **3** *vi* **TAKE RISKS** to challenge or take risks with somebody or something dangerous ○ *dicing with death* **4** *vt* **DECORATE WITH SQUARE PATTERN** to decorate something with a pattern of squares or cubes **5** *vt Aus* **ABANDON** to abandon or discard something (*informal*) [14C. < French *dé* (plural *dés*) < Latin *datum*, past participle of *dare* 'give, play'.] —**dicer** *n* ◇ **load the dice 1** to manipulate a situation unfairly in order to obtain a desired result **2** to add weight to a dice so that it always falls on a particular side (*informal*) ◇ **no dice** used to indicate that there is no chance of something happening

USAGE Dice – singular or plural? The singular form *die*, of which ***dice*** was originally the plural, is now seldom used other than in the idiom *The die is cast.* ***Dice***, used with a singular verb, means 'a small cube with the numbers 1 to 6 marked in dots on its sides used in gambling' (its plural in this use is ***dice***), or a gambling game in which these cubes are used. ***Dice*** (plural) can also refer to cube-shaped pieces, especially of food.

dicentra /dī séntrə/ *n* a perennial plant that grows best in shade. Flowers: small, drooping, in arching sprays. Genus: *Dicentra.* [Mid-19C. Via modern Latin, < Greek *dikentros* 'two-pointed' < *kentron* 'centre, point'; from the shape of its leaves.]

dicey /díssi/ (**-ier, -iest**), **dicy** (**-ier, -iest**) *adj* uncertain and involving danger or risk (*informal*)

dich- *prefix* = **dicho-** (*before vowels*)

dichlorodifluoromethane /dī kláwr ō dī flóor ō meeth ayn/ *n* CCl_2F_2 a colourless, nonflammable, gaseous CFC. Use: propellant in aerosols, refrigerant, in fire extinguishers.

dichlorodiphenyltrichloroethane /dī kláwr ō dī feen īl trī kláwr ō ee thayn/ *n* full form of **DDT**

dichloroethene /dī kláwrō é theen/ *n* $C_2H_2Cl_2$ a colourless liquid that exists in three structurally different forms **(isomers)** and is used as a solvent

dichloromethane /dī kláwr ō meeth ayn/ *n* CH_2Cl_2 a colourless, nonflammable, toxic gas. Use: in paint strippers, degreasing, and plastics processing.

dichlorophenoxyacetic acid /dī kláwrō fə nóksi ə seetik ássid/ *n* CHEM = **2,4-D**

dicho- *prefix* having two parts ○ *dichogamy* [< Greek *dikha* 'in two']

dichogamy /dī kóggəmi/ *n* a plant's production of male and female parts at different times, in order to prevent self-pollination and ensure cross-fertilization [Mid-19C. < Greek *dikho-* 'apart' + *gamos* 'marriage'.] —**dichogamic** /dī kō gámmik/ *adj* —**dichogamous** /dī kóggəməss/ *adj*

dichotic /dī kóttik/ *adj* involving or relating to the simultaneous stimulation of each ear with different sounds [Mid-20C. < Greek *dikho-* 'apart' + *ōt-* 'ear'.]

dichotomize /dī kóttə mīz/ (**-mizes, -mizing, -mized**), **dichotomise** (**-mises, -mising, -mised**) *vti* to divide something, or become divided, into two classes or groups —**dichotomization** /dī kóttə mī záysh'n/ *n*

dichotomy /dī kóttəmi/ (*plural* **-mies**) *n* **1 SEPARATION OF DIFFERENT OR CONTRADICTORY THINGS** a separation into two divisions that differ widely from or contradict each other **2 BRANCHING OF PLANTS** the division of each of a plant's branches into two more branches **3 MOON PHASE WHEN HALF VISIBLE** the phase of the Moon or a planet when half of its surface appears illuminated by the Sun [Late 16C. Via modern Latin, < Greek *dikhotomia* 'cutting in two' < *dikho-* 'apart, in two' + *temnein* 'to cut'.] —**dichotomic** /dī kō tómmik/ *adj* —**dichotomous** *adj* —**dichotomously** *adv*

dichroic /dī krō ik/, **dichroitic** /dī krō íttik/ *adj* describes a crystal that appears to be a different colour when viewed along a different axis [Mid-19C. < Greek *dikhroos* 'two-coloured' < *khrōs* 'colour'.] —**dichroism** *n*

dichroite /dī krō īt/ *n* = **cordierite**

dichroitic *adj* CHEM = **dichroic**

dichromate /dī krō mayt/ *n* a salt of dichromic acid, characteristically orange-red in colour

dichromatic /dī krō máttik/ *adj* **1 WITH TWO COLOURS** having two colours **2 dichromatic, dichromic PARTIALLY COLOUR-BLIND** able to distinguish only two of the three primary colours and their combinations **3 WITH DIFFERENT COLOUR PHASES** describes animals, especially birds, that have two different colours in phases that are not associated with the normal variations in colour that occur with sex and age

dichromatism /dī krómatizəm/ *n* **1** the presence of only two colours in something **2** colour-blindness in which only two of the three primary colours and their combinations can be distinguished

dichromic /dī krómik/ *adj* = **dichromatic** *adj.* **2** [Mid-19C. < Greek *dikhrōmos* 'two-coloured' < *khrōma* 'colour'.]

dichromic acid *n* $H_2Cr_2O_7$ an unstable acid found only in solution and in the form of dichromate salts

dichromism /dī króm izəm/ *n* = **dichromatism** *n.* **2**

dicht /dikht/ *vti Scotland* to wipe or rub dirt or dust from something ■ *n Scotland* a wipe or rub to clean dirt or dust away [Late 17C. Variant of DIGHT.]

~~**dicision**~~ incorrect spelling of **decision**

dick¹ /dik/ *n* (*slang*) **1** an offensive term for the penis **2** an offensive term for a very thoughtless boy or man [Mid-16C. < the male first name *Dick*.]

dick² /dik/ *n US* a detective (*dated slang*) [Early 20C. < ?]

Dick and Jane /dík ənd jáyn/ *npl US* the stereotypes of middle-class white Americans (*informal; hyphenated before nouns*)

dickens /díkinz/ *n* used for emphasis in a variety of expressions, especially expressions of surprise or annoyance (*informal*) ○ *What the dickens is going on here?* ○ *scared the dickens out of me* [Late 16C. Probably < the surname *Dickens*.]

Dickens /díkinz/, **Charles** (1812–70) British novelist

Dickensian /di kénzi ən/ *adj* **1 OF CHARLES DICKENS** relating to the 19th-century British author, Charles Dickens, his writing, or the times he lived in **2 FULL OF TWISTS AND AMAZING COINCIDENCES** full of twists and remarkable coincidences, like the plots of some of the novels of Dickens ○ *an episode too Dickensian for most modern audiences to swallow* **3 REMINISCENT OF POVERTY-STRICKEN VICTORIAN BRITAIN** typical or reminiscent of the harsh poverty-stricken living conditions described in the works of Dickens **4 JOLLY AND GENIAL** jolly and cordial, like some of the scenes and characters featured in the novels of Dickens

dicker /díkər/ *vi* to bargain for goods or services (*informal*) ○ *collectors dickering at antique sales* ■ *n* bargaining in general, or something settled, achieved, or obtained through bargaining [Early 19C. Probably < Latin *decuria* 'group of ten, ten hides for sale' < *decem* 'ten' + *vir* 'man'.]

dickey *n* = **dicky**¹

dickeybird *n* = **dicky bird**

dickhead /dík hed/ *n* an offensive term for a man who is regarded as unintelligent or inattentive (*slang offensive insult*)

Dickinson /díkinss'n/, **Emily** (1830–86) US poet

dicky¹ /díki/ (*plural* **-ies**), **dickey** *n* **1 FALSE SHIRT FRONT OR NECK** a garment that is only the front or neck of a shirt, worn under a shirt, jacket, or jumper **2 DONKEY** a donkey, especially a male **3 OUTSIDE CAR SEAT** a folding outside seat on the back of some early cars [Mid-18C. < ?]

dicky² /díki/ (**-ier, -iest**) *adj* (*informal*) **1** not well in health **2** faulty or unreliable ○ *The doctor says I have a dicky heart.* [Late 18C. < ?]

dicky bird, dickeybird /díki burd/ *n* **1** a small bird (*babytalk*) **2** a single word (*slang*) ○ *did not say a dicky bird* [In sense 2, rhyming slang]

dicky bow *n* a bow tie (*informal*) [< ?]

diclinous /díklinəss, dī klínəss/ *adj* describes plants that have stamens and pistils in separate flowers, rather than in the same flower [Early 19C. < modern Latin *diclines* 'two beds' < Greek *klinē* 'bed'.] —**diclinism** /dī klinnizəm/ *n* —**dicliny** *n*

dicot /dī kot/ *n* PLANTS = **dicotyledon** [Late 19C. Shortening.]

dicotyledon /dī kotti léed'n/ *n* a flowering plant that produces two seed leaves (**cotyledons**) when it germinates and whose subsequent leaves have a network of veins. Most herbaceous plants, trees, and bushes are dicotyledons. Subclass: Dicotyledonae. [Early 18C. < modern Latin *Dicotyledonae* 'two cotyledons'.] —**dicotyledonous** *adj*

dicrotism /díkrətizəm/ *n* a physiological condition in which each heartbeat produces a double pulse, as occurs, e.g., in typhoid fever [Mid-19C. < Greek *dikrotos* 'double-beating'.] —**dicrotal** *adj* —**dicrotic** /dī króttik/ *adj*

dict. *abbr* **1** dictation **2** dictator **3** dictionary

dicta plural of **dictum**

Dictaphone /díktəfōn/ *tdmk* a trademark for a small hand-held tape recorder used for dictation

dictate *v* /dik táyt/ (**-tates, -tating, -tated**) **1** *vti* **SPEAK ALOUD WORDS TO BE WRITTEN** to speak the words of a text or letter to be written, either to somebody writing it down as it is spoken, or into a tape recorder for later transcription **2** *vti* **RULE OR CONTROL OTHER PEOPLE** to rule over or make decisions for others with absolute authority, or attempt to do so ○ *dictates their every move* **3** *vt* **CONTROL** to have control over something (*usually passive*) ○ *The possibility of play today will be dictated largely by the weather.* ■ *n* /dík tayt/ **1 COMMAND GIVEN** an order telling people what they must do ○ *dictates received from their superiors* **2 GOVERNING PRINCIPLE** a rule or principle that governs how people behave ○ *the dictates of fashion* [Late 16C. < Latin *dictat-*, past participle of *dictare* 'say often' < *dicere* 'to say'.]

dictation /dik táysh'n/ *n* **1** the act of dictating a text or letter, or of writing down what is being dictated **2** a test or exercise of language comprehension in which pupils write down words spoken aloud by a teacher ○ *a French dictation* —**dictational** *adj*

dictator /dik táytər/ *n* **1 POWERFUL RULER** a leader who rules a country with absolute power, usually by force **2 BOSSY PERSON** a person who behaves in an autocratic or domineering way **3 AUTHORITY ON SUBJECT** somebody whose opinions on a subject are listened to and followed by society at large ○ *one of the great dictators of modern music* **4 TEMPORARY ROMAN RULER** in ancient Rome, a temporary appointed leader with absolute power to deal with a crisis or an emergency

dictatorial /díktə táwri əl/ *adj* **1** fond of telling others what to do or of using power or authority to make them do it **2** relating to or ruled by dictators —**dictatorially** *adv*

dictatorship /dik táytər ship/ *n* **1 DICTATOR'S POWER OR RULE** a dictator's power or authority, or the period of time during which a dictator rules **2 GOVERNMENT BY DICTATOR** government by a dictator **3 COUNTRY RULED BY DICTATOR** a state ruled by a dictator **4 ABSOLUTE AUTHORITY** absolute power or authority

diction /díksh'n/ *n* **1** the clarity with which somebody pronounces words when speaking or singing **2** choice of words to fit their context ○ *'a tendency to identify the poetic impulse with melancholy moods and sonorous diction'* (Northrop Frye, *The Bush Garden*; 1972) [Mid-16C. < Latin *diction-* < *dicere* 'to say'.] —**dictional** *adj* —**dictionally** *adv*

ϟ**dictionary** /díksh'nəri/ (*plural* **-ies**) *n* **1 BOOK OF WORD MEANINGS** a reference book that contains alphabetically ordered words, with explanations of their meanings, often with information about grammar, pronunciation, and etymology **2 FOREIGN-LANGUAGE REFERENCE BOOK OF WORDS** a reference book that alphabetically arranges and translates words and phrases in two or more languages ○ *a Spanish-English dictionary* **3 SPECIALIZED REFERENCE BOOK** a reference book that alphabetizes and explains terms relating to a particular subject or topic ○ *a dictionary of music* **4 LIST OF INFORMATION** a book that lists examples or information arranged alphabetically or in some other way, e.g. by author ○ *a dictionary of quotations* **5 ALPHABETICAL LIST OF COMPUTER CODES** an alphabetized list of keys or code names used in a program, each briefly defined **6 WORD-PROCESSING REFERENCE** a file used as a reference by a word-processing program for correct spelling and hyphenation [Early 16C. < medieval Latin *dictionarius* 'of words' < Latin *diction-* (see DICTION).]

dictum /díktəm/ (*plural* **-tums** *or* **-ta** /-tə/) *n* **1** an authoritative saying, statement, or pronouncement (*formal*) **2** a popular saying **3** LAW = **obiter dictum** *n.* 1 [Late 16C. < Latin, < past participle of *dicere* 'to say'.]

dictyopteran /díkti óptərən/ *n* an insect with, typically, a flattened body, long legs, and leathery front wings held flat over the membranous hind wings, e.g. cockroaches and mantises. Order: Dictyoptera.

dicumarol /dī kyóomə rol/ *n* a synthetic agent that inhibits coagulation [< DI-¹ + COUMARIN + -OL¹]

dicy *adj* = **dicey**

dicynodont /dī sínnə dont/ *n* an extinct plant-eating reptile with teeth like tusks. Suborder: Dicynodontia. [Mid-19C. < modern Latin *Dicynodontia* 'two canine teeth' < Greek *kun-* 'dog' + *odont-* 'tooth'.]

did past tense of **do**¹

DID *abbr* dissociative identity disorder

didactic /dī dáktik, di dáktik/ *adj* **1** containing a political or moral message ○ *didactic theatre* **2** tending to give instruction or advice, even when it is not welcome or not needed [Mid-17C. < Greek *didaktikos* < *didaskein* 'teach'.] —**didactically** *adv*

didacticism /dī dáktisizəm, di-/ *n* the instructional quality of something, e.g. a piece of writing, or the attitude of somebody who likes to instruct others or give them advice ○ *the welcome absence of didacticism in modern poetry*

didactics /dī dáktiks, di dáktiks/ *n* the science or profession of teaching (*+ singular verb*)

ϟ**diddle**¹ /dídd'l/ (**-dles, -dling, -dled**) *vt* (*informal*) **1 CHEAT** to cheat or swindle somebody (*often passive*) **2 MANIPULATE DATA ILLEGALLY** to manipulate computer data illegally **3 MANIPULATE PROGRAM** to manipulate a computer program in an informal or a not particularly serious manner [Early 19C. < ?] —**diddler** *n*

diddle² /dídd'l/ (**-dles, -dling, -dled**) *v* **1** *vi* **SPEND TIME IDLY** to spend time doing nothing in particular (*informal*) ○ *spent the morning diddling about* **2** *vt US* **OFFENSIVE TERM** an offensive term meaning to have sexual intercourse with a woman (*slang*) **3** *vt* **JERK REPEATEDLY** to jerk something up and down or back and forth (*informal*) [Mid-17C. < ?] —**diddler** *n*

diddlysquat /díddli skwot/, **diddly** *n US* nothing at all (*informal*) ○ *And what did I get? Diddlysquat!* [Mid-20C. Probably alteration of *doodlysquat* < ?]

diddy /díddi/ (**-dier, -diest**) *adj* very small (*informal*) ○ *a diddy little travelling manicure set* [Mid-20C. Probably alteration of *tiddy* 'small'.]

Diderot /déedərō/, **Denis** (1713–84) French encyclopedist and philosopher

didgeridoo /díjjəri dóo/ (*plural* **-doos**), **didjeridoo** (*plural* **-doos**) *n* an Aboriginal musical instrument with a long thick wooden pipe that is blown to create a deep reverberating humming sound [Early 20C. < an Aboriginal language, an imitation of the sound.]

didn't /díd'nt/ *contr* did not ○ *I didn't want to go.*

Dido /dīdō/ in Roman mythology, the queen and founder of Carthage who killed herself when abandoned by her lover, Aeneas

didst /didst/ *contr* second person present singular of 'did', used with 'thou' (*archaic*)

didymium /dī dímmi əm/ *n* a mixture of metallic elements from the rare-earth, or lanthanide, series of elements, consisting chiefly of neodymium and praseodymium. Use: production of coloured glass and optical filters. [Mid-19C. < Greek *didumos* 'twin'.]

die¹ /dī/ (**dies, dying, died**) *v* **1** *vi* **STOP LIVING** to cease to be alive (*refers to a person, plant, or animal*) **2** *vi* **STOP EXISTING** to cease to exist, especially gradually ○ *feelings I thought had died long ago* **3** *vi* **STOP WORKING** to stop functioning ○ *The engine suddenly died.* **4** *vti* **DIE AS STATED** to cease to live in a particular way ○ *The villain, of course, dies a gruesome death.* **5** *vi* **EMPHASIZING DESIRE OR WISH** used to indicate how strongly the speaker wishes to do or have something ○ *I'm dying to tell them!* [12C. Probably < Old Norse *deyja* < Indo-European.] ◇ **die hard** to give up or come to an end only after long, difficult, and sustained resistance. ◊ **diehard** ◇ **to die for** highly desirable and hence worth sacrificing something to obtain

---

SPELLCHECK Do not confuse ***die*** with ***dye***, which has a similar sound. Beware: your spellchecker will not catch this error.

USAGE A person can *die of* an illness, or *die in* an earthquake or a fire. In careful usage, *die from* should be reserved for indirect causes of death, such as stubbornness or failure to wear a seat belt.

---

die away *vi* to fade or grow faint

die back *vi* to wither or die from the tips of new shoots back to the established stem or old wood of the plant, as a result of disease, seasonal change, or poor conditions

die down *vi* to become quieter, weaker, or less intense

die off *vi* to die gradually one by one, till none are left (*refers to plants or animals*)

die out *vi* **1** to become extinct or cease to exist gradually ○ *entire species that have died out in our century* **2** to fade and finally disappear gradually ○ *Over the years, opposition to the plan had died out.*

die² /dī/ *n* **1** (*plural* **dice**) **NUMBERED CUBE USED IN GAMES** a small cube with the numbers 1 to 6 marked in dots on the sides, used in gambling and in a wide variety of games of chance (*formal*) **2 STAMPING OR PRESSING TOOL** the metal tool on a stamping or pressing machine that gives the finished article its shape and design **3 MOULD** a tool for moulding substances such as metal or plastic **4 TOOL FOR CUTTING** a tool that cuts screw threads on metal rods **5 PART OF PEDESTAL** the part of a pedestal that lies between the base and the cornice, especially when it is cubic in shape [12C. < French *dé* (see DICE).] ◇ **as straight as a die** completely honest and trustworthy (*informal*)

dieback /dī bak/ *n* gradual decay that sets in at a plant's young shoots then works back to established stems or old wood, as a result of disease, seasonal change, or poor conditions

die-cast (**die-casts, die-casting, die-cast**) *vt* to make a metal or plastic object by pouring or forcing molten metal or plastic into a mould —**die-cast** *adj*

diecious *adj* = **dioecious**

Diefenbaker /deéfən baykər/, **John George** (1895–1979) Canadian statesman and prime minister (1957–63)

dieffenbachia /deéf'n báki ə/ *n* an evergreen plant with poisonous sap, widely cultivated as a house plant for its large many-coloured leaves. Native to: tropical America. Genus: *Dieffenbachia*. [Late 19C. < modern Latin, after Ernst *Dieffenbach* (1794–1855).]

~~diegn~~ incorrect spelling of **deign**

diehard /dí haard/ *adj* resistant to any kind of change, and reluctant to give up beliefs, positions, or attitudes ○ *diehard fans* ■ *n* a resister of change who stubbornly persists in a belief or opinion ○ *with the old diehards holding out to the bitter end* —**diehardism** *n*

~~dieing~~ incorrect spelling of **dying**

dieldrin /deéldrin/ *n* $C_{12}H_{10}OCl_6$ a contact insecticide based on a chlorinated naphthalene derivative, now widely banned [Mid-20C. After Otto *Diels* (1876–1954) + ALDRIN.]

dielectric /dī iléktrik/ *adj* not able to conduct direct electric current, and therefore useful as an insulator [Mid-19C. < DIA-.] —**dielectric** *n* —**dielectrically** *adv*

dielectric constant *n* PHYS = **relative permittivity**

dielectric heating *n* the heating of an insulating material by placing it in a rapidly changing electric field. The technique is used in the manufacture of foam rubber, plastics, and other materials.

dielectric lens *n* a lens made of insulating material that deflects radio waves passing through it in the way that a glass lens deflects light

Diels-Alder reaction /deélz áwldər-/ *n* a chemical reaction in which an organic compound with two double bonds between carbon atoms (**diene**) and a compound containing a double or triple bond, combine to form a ring compound [Mid-20C. After Otto *Diels* (see DIELDRIN) and Kurt *Alder* (see ALDRIN).]

Diem /dyem/, **Ngo Dinh** (1901–63) Vietnamese statesman and president of South Vietnam (1955–63)

diencephalon /dí en séffə lon/ *n* the area in the centre of the brain just above the brain stem that includes the thalamus and hypothalamus [Late 19C. < DIA- + Greek *enkephalos* 'brain'.] —**diencephalic** /dí enssə fállik/ *adj*

diene /dí een/ *n* an unsaturated hydrocarbon (**alkene**) containing two carbon-to-carbon double bonds

Dieppe /di ép/ port on the English Channel in NW France. Population: 34,653 (1999).

dieresis *n* LANG, LITERAT = **diaeresis**

Dieri /deéri/, **Diyari** *n* an Aboriginal language of South Australia, now almost extinct [Late 19C. < Dieri.] —**Dieri** *adj*

diesel /deéz'l/ *n* **1** = **diesel engine 2** a vehicle such as a car or train that is powered by a diesel engine **3** AUTOMOT = **diesel oil** [Late 19C. After Rudolf *Diesel* (1858–1913).]

diesel-electric *n* a locomotive in which a diesel engine drives an electric generator that provides current to the traction motors driving the wheels

diesel engine, diesel *n* an internal combustion engine that ignites diesel oil using compression alone, rather than using an electrical spark

diesel fuel *n US* = **diesel oil**

diesel-hydraulic *n* a locomotive primarily powered by a diesel engine but with power transmitted through an oil-filled torque converter or infinitely variable gear

diesel oil *n* a thick oily fuel that is obtained from the distillation of petroleum. It has an ignition temperature of 540°C and is ignited by the heat of compression. US term **diesel fuel**

Dies Irae /deé ayz eér ī/ *n* **1** a 13th century Latin hymn that describes the Last Judgment, used in a Christian Mass for the dead **2** a musical setting of the Dies Irae, usually as part of a Requiem Mass [< Latin, 'day of wrath']

diesis /dí əsiss/ (*plural* **-ses** /-seez/) *n* PRINTING = **double dagger**

dies non /dí eez nón/ *n* a day on which no legal business is done [Early 19C. Shortening of Latin *dies non juridicus* 'day not judicial'.]

diestock /dí stok/ *n* a device for holding the dies that are used for cutting threads on screws

diestrus *n* US = **dioestrus**

diet[1] /dí ət/ *n* **1** WHAT A PERSON OR ANIMAL EATS the food that a person or animal usually consumes **2** CONTROLLED INTAKE OF FOOD a controlled intake of food and drink designed for weight loss, for health or religious reasons, or to control or improve a medical condition ○ *a wheat-free diet* **3** REGULAR INTAKE OF a continuous or daily experience of, or indulgence in, something other than food ○ *living on a diet of soap operas and game shows* ■ *adj* DESIGNED OR PROMOTED FOR WEIGHT LOSS describes a food or drink that is intended for people trying to lose weight, usually because it is low in calories or fat, or contains a sugar substitute ○ *a diet soda* ■ *vi* EAT LESS to follow a restricted pattern of eating or drinking in order to lose weight [Pre-12C. Via Old French *diete* < Greek *diaita* 'course of life'.] —**dietary** *adj* —**dieter** *n*

diet[2] /dí ət/ *n* **1** PARLIAMENT a legislative assembly in certain countries, e.g. Japan **2** COURT SESSION IN SCOTLAND in Scotland, a session of a court, or the date fixed for a court hearing **3** ASSEMBLY IN HOLY ROMAN EMPIRE a general assembly of the estates of the Holy Roman Empire [15C. < medieval Latin *dieta* 'day's journey, work', (by association with Latin *dies* 'day') 'day for a meeting (of legislators)', probably < Greek *diaita* 'course of life'.]

dietary fibre *n* = **fibre** *n.* 7

dietary laws *npl* the rules governing which items of food practising Jewish people are permitted to eat, derived from Leviticus 11 and Deuteronomy 14

dietetic /dí ə téttik/ *adj* **1** relating to what people eat and drink **2** specially prepared to suit the requirements of a particular diet —**dietetically** *adv*

dietetics /dí ə téttiks/ *n* the study of food and nutrition and its relation to people's health (+ *singular verb.*)

diethylcarbamazine /dī éthil kaar bámmə zeen, dī eé thīl-/ *n* a white water-soluble substance in the form of crystals. Use: to treat worms in humans, dogs, and cats. [< DI- + ETHYL + CARBO- + AMIDE + AZINE]

diethyl ether /dī éthil-/ *n* CHEM = **ether** *n.* 1

diethylstilbestrol *n* US = **diethylstilboestrol**

diethylstilboestrol /dī éthil stil béstrol, dī eé thīl-/ *n* a synthetic oestrogen. Use: formerly, for hormone replacement. [Mid-20C. < DI-[1] + ETHYL + STILBENE + OESTRUS + -OL.]

diethyl toluamide /dī éthil tóllyoō ámmīd, dī eé thīl-/ *n* full form of **deet**

dietitian /dí ə tísh'n/, **dietician** *n* a specialist in the study of food and nutrition in relation to health

Dietrich /deé trik/, **Marlene** (1901–92) German-born US singer and film actor. Full name **Maria Magdalene Dietrich von Losch**

Dieu et mon droit /dyő ay mon drwaá/ *n* 'God and my right', the motto written under the coat of arms of the British Royal Family [< French]

~~diferent~~ incorrect spelling of **different**

diff. *abbr* **1** difference **2** different

differ /díffər/ *vi* **1** to be dissimilar or unlike ○ *new models that differ greatly from the early prototypes* **2** to have different opinions about something ○ *We agreed to differ.* [14C. Via French *différer* 'differ, defer' < Latin *differre* 'differ' < *ferre* 'carry'.]

SYNONYMS See *disagree*.

difference /díffrənss/ *n* **1** STATE OF BEING UNLIKE OTHERS the quality of being different from or unlike something or somebody else ○ *There's no real difference between going by train and going by car.* **2** DISTINGUISHING FEATURE a feature that distinguishes one person or thing from another ○ *Can you spot the differences between the two?* **3** SIGNIFICANT CHANGE a change that has an effect ○ *a noticeable difference in her moods* **4** DISAGREEMENT a disagreement, argument, or divergence of opinions ○ *settle our differences* **5** ANSWER TO SUBTRACTION EQUATION the amount by which one quantity is greater or smaller than another ○ *What's the difference between 16 and 6?* **6** DEFINING FEATURE a distinguishing feature that marks out a thing that is being defined or discussed, from others that are more general ○ *being divisible by two is the difference between even numbers and other whole numbers* **7** ADDITION TO COAT OF ARMS an addition to a family's coat of arms that represents a younger branch of the family ◇ **make all the difference** have an enormous, usually positive, effect or influence ◇ **make no difference** be of no importance or not matter ◇ **split the difference** take the average of two amounts, or agree on something that is halfway between two extremes ◇ **tell the difference** distinguish or figure out the particular features that make things unlike each other

USAGE difference or **differentiation**? These two words do not share a single meaning, so careful writers avoid using them interchangeably. *My paper explores the difference* [not *differentiation*] *between the world of the adult and the world of the child.* Conversely, do not use ***difference*** when ***differentiation*** is called for: *studied the history of the differentiation* [not *difference*] *of Latin into vernaculars.* ***Difference*** denotes dissimilarity or an instance of it. ***Differentiation*** denotes becoming different in the course of development.

different /díffrənt/ *adj* **1** UNLIKE SOMETHING OR SOMEBODY ELSE not the same as something or somebody else ○ *This is certainly different from anything I've ever experienced before.* **2** DISTINCT separate or distinct from another or others ○ *She wore a different pair of shoes every day.* **3** UNUSUAL contrary to norms or expectations ○ *What do you think of my hat? – Well, it's certainly different.* [14C. Via French < Latin *different-*, present participle of *differre* (see DIFFER).] —**differently** *adv*

USAGE Different from or **different than**? No one objects to ***different from*** (on the analogy of *differ from*: *His attitude towards women was quite different from that of his contemporaries*). *Different to* is not so generally accepted, although it is commonly used in British English. *Different than* is also seen and heard, especially in US English. Although some object to it as a matter of principle and it should be avoided in formal writing, it can at times serve as a useful shortcut. Compare *The book has a title different from the one that I thought it had* with *The book has a different title than I thought.*

differentia /díffə rénshi ə/ (*plural* **-ae** /-shi ee/) *n* an element that separates one thing from another, especially a trait that distinguishes one subclass from another, e.g. one species from another in the same genus

differential /díffə rénsh'l/ *n* **1** DIFFERENCE BETWEEN POINTS ON A SCALE a difference between two values on a scale, e.g. a difference in the rates of pay for different jobs in the same line of work **2** AUTOMOT = **differential gear 3** INFINITESIMAL CHANGE IN VARIABLE an infinitesimal change in a variable ■ *adj* **1** OF DIFFERENCES relating to or based on differences **2** RELATING TO INFINITESIMAL CHANGES relating to a function of one or more variables that exhibits an infinitesimal change as a consequence of a small change in the variables

differential calculus *n* the branch of mathematics dealing with continuously varying quantities, with applications in the determination of maximum and minimum points, and with rates of change through the use of derivatives and differentials

differential coefficient *n* MATH = **derivative** *n.* 4

differential equation *n* a mathematical equation that relates functions and their derivatives

differential gear *n* an arrangement of gears that allows two shafts driven by a third to turn at different speeds, e.g. in a motor vehicle

differentiate /díffə rénshi ayt/ (**-ates, -ating, -ated**) *v* **1** *vti* SEE DIFFERENCES BETWEEN THINGS to see or show the differences between two or more things **2** *vt* BE A DIFFERENCE to establish a difference between two things or among several things **3** *vti* MAKE OR BECOME DIFFERENT to make something different or specialized by modifying it, or to become different or specialized by being modified **4** *vti* PROVIDE ACTIVITIES MATCHED TO ABILITY to provide school work and activities that are suited to the individual abilities of each student **5** *vi* BECOME SPECIALIZED to change from a generalized form into a form specialized for a certain tissue, organ, or other body part (*refers to embryo cells*) **6** *vt* CALCULATE DERIVATIVE to calculate the mathematical derivative of a function [Early 19C. < medieval Latin *differentiat-*, past participle of *differentiare* < Latin *differre* (see DIFFER).] —**differentiability** /díffə renshə bílləti/ *n* —**differentiable** *adj* —**differentiator** *n*

differentiation /díffə renshi áysh'n/ *n* **1** DEVELOPMENT FROM ONE INTO MANY a developmental process from a single unit or whole into many other derived things, or from a simple to a complex state **2** VISIBLE DIFFERENCES the complex of visible differences exhibited among two or more things **3** ESTABLISHMENT OF DIFFERENCES the establishment of differences or a difference among two or more things **4** SPECIALIZATION change from a generalized form to another, specialized, form for a certain tissue, organ, or other body part **5 CALCULATION OF DERIVATIVE** calculation of the derivative of a mathematical function

USAGE See ***difference***.

difficult /díffik'lt/ *adj* **1 HARD TO DO** requiring a lot of planning or effort to accomplish ○ *a difficult job* **2 FULL OF PROBLEMS** full of problems, trouble, or aspects that are hard to endure ○ *a difficult birth* **3 HARD TO UNDERSTAND** hard to understand, learn, or solve ○ *a difficult subject* **4 HARD TO ANSWER** hard to answer, deal with, or fulfil ○ *a difficult question* **5 HARD TO MANAGE** hard to cope with or control ○ *a difficult plant to grow indoors* **6 HARD TO PLEASE** hard to please or satisfy ○ *a difficult audience* **7 HARD TO CONVINCE** hard to convince or persuade ○ *If they're difficult, offer them more.* **8 FULL OF HARDSHIP** containing great hardship, especially of a financial kind [14C. Back-formation < DIFFICULTY.] —**difficultness** *n*

SYNONYMS See ***hard***.

difficulty /díffik'lti/ *n* (*plural* **-ties**) **1 QUALITY OF BEING DIFFICULT** the quality of being hard to do, understand, or deal with **2 SOMETHING NOT EASILY DONE** something that is hard to do, understand, or deal with **3 EFFORT** a great effort or struggle to do something **4 A DISPUTE** a dispute or controversy ■ **difficulties** *npl* **1 TROUBLE** a situation full of trouble, danger, or embarrassment ○ *Even a strong swimmer can get into difficulties in this river.* **2 OBJECTIONS** objections or attempts to prevent the progress of something ○ *You're supposed to be here to help, not make difficulties.* [14C. < Latin *difficultas* < *difficilis* 'not easy' < *facilis* (see FACILE).]

diffident /díffidənt/ *adj* **1** lacking self-confidence and rather shy **2** reserved or restrained in the way you behave [15C. < Latin *diffident-*, present participle of *diffidere* 'distrust' < *fidere* 'trust'.] —**diffidence** *n* —**diffidently** *adv*

diffract /di frákt/ *vti* to produce or undergo diffraction [Early 19C. < Latin *diffract-*, past participle of *diffringere* 'break apart' < *frangere* 'break'.] —**diffractive** *adj* —**diffractively** *adv* —**diffractiveness** *n*

diffraction /di fráksh'n/ *n* the bending or spreading out of waves, e.g. of sound or light, as they pass round the edge of an obstacle or through a narrow aperture

diffraction grating *n* a glass plate or metal mirror engraved with a large number of parallel lines or grooves, used to produce a spectrum by diffraction or interference

diffraction ring *n* a circular pattern of light that surrounds a particle under a microscope, resulting from diffraction

diffractometer /díffrak tómmitər/ *n* an instrument that uses diffraction, typically of X-rays or electrons by crystals, to investigate the atomic structure of a material

~~**diffrent**~~ incorrect spelling of **different**

diffuse[1] /di fyóoz/ (**-fuses, -fusing, -fused**) *v* **1** *vti* **SPREAD THROUGH** to spread something throughout something else, or to become spread throughout something else **2** *vti* **SCATTER OR BECOME SCATTERED** to scatter something over an area, or become scattered over an area **3** *vt* **MAKE LESS INTENSE** to make something, especially light, less bright or intense **4** *vti* **UNDERGO OR SUBJECT TO DIFFUSION** to undergo or subject something to diffusion [14C. < Latin *diffus-*, past participle of *diffundere* 'pour in every direction' < *fundere* 'pour'.] —**diffusibility** /di fyóozə bíllәti/ *n* —**diffusible** *adj*

diffuse[2] /di fyóoss/ *adj* **1** spread throughout a wide area **2** lacking organization and conciseness, especially in writing or speech [15C. Directly or via French *diffus* < Latin *diffusus* 'spread out', past participle of *diffundere* (see DIFFUSE[1]).] —**diffusely** *adv* —**diffuseness** *n*

SYNONYMS See ***wordy***.

diffuser /di fyóozər/, **diffusor** *n* **1 DEVICE THAT DIFFUSES LAMP LIGHT** a piece of translucent or reflective material fixed to a light source, such as a lamp, in order to soften or spread the light over a wide area **2 DEVICE THAT SOFTENS LIGHT** a cloth screen, piece of frosted glass, or other material that is used to soften the brightness of the lighting in photography or cinematography **3 HAIR DRYER ATTACHMENT** an attachment for a hair dryer that slows down and spreads the air flow, making the drying action gentler **4 CONE TO DISPERSE SOUND WAVES** a device, such as a cone or wedge, fixed inside a loudspeaker to diffuse sound waves

diffusion /di fyóozh'n/ *n* **1 PROCESS OF DIFFUSING** a process during which something diffuses or is diffused **2 RESULT OF DIFFUSING** the result of something diffusing or being diffused, or a situation in which something is diffused **3 SPREAD OF CULTURAL FEATURES** the spread of tools, practices, or other features from one culture to another **4 SCATTERING OF LIGHT** the scattering of light in many directions as the result of reflection from an uneven surface or passage though a translucent material **5 INTERMINGLING OF SUBSTANCES** the random movement of atoms, molecules, or ions from one site in a medium to another, resulting in complete mixing —**diffusional** *adj*

diffusionism /di fyóozh'nizəm/ *n* the theory that similarities in tools, practices, or other features between cultures, result from their being spread from one culture to another rather than being arrived at independently —**diffusionist** *adj, n*

diffusive /di fyóossiv/ *adj* **1** involved in diffusion **2** in which diffusion is important or characteristic **3** = **diffuse**[2] *adj.* **2** —**diffusively** *adv* —**diffusiveness** *n*

diffusor *n* = **diffuser**

dig /dig/ *v* (**digs, digging, dug** /dug/, **dug**) **1** *vti* **BREAK UP OR REMOVE EARTH** to break up, turn, or remove something, especially earth, with the hands, paws, a tool, or a machine ○ *The excavator dug the rock out of the hole.* **2** *vt* **CREATE BY DIGGING** to make something by removing material, especially earth, with the hands, paws, a tool, or a machine ○ *digging a hole* **3** *vti* **OBTAIN OR FREE BY DIGGING** to obtain, uncover, or free something by removing the material covering it using a shovel, the hands, paws, a tool, or a machine **4** *vi* **SEARCH BY DIGGING** to try to find something by digging ○ *dig for buried treasure* **5** *vi* **MOVE THROUGH SOMETHING BY DIGGING** to move through something by digging a way through it **6** *vt* **DISCOVER BY RESEARCH** to find out something by research or questioning ○ *See what you can dig up about her past.* **7** *vi* **SEARCH CAREFULLY** to search something carefully or persistently ○ *digging through the papers in a file* **8** *vti* **PUSH INTO SOMETHING FORCEFULLY** to push something into something else with force, or be pushed forcefully into something ○ *He dug his teeth into the steak.* **9** *vti* **POKE** to push somebody with something fairly sharp ○ *She dug her elbow into my side.* **10** *vti* **UNDERSTAND** to understand something fully or with sympathy (*dated slang*) ○ *I dig what you're saying.* **11** *vt* **LIKE** to like or appreciate something (*dated slang*) ○ *They don't dig jazz.* ■ *n* **1 PROD** a push with something fairly sharp ○ *a dig in the ribs* **2 CUTTING REMARK** a remark that is meant to hurt or make fun of somebody ○ *a dig about her new hairstyle* **3 ARCHAEOLOGICAL EXCAVATION** an archaeological or palaeontological excavation ○ *a dig in Egypt* **4 POWERFUL BLOW** a powerful blow, especially a kick at a football (*slang*) ○ *It was a well-placed free kick and he really gave it quite a dig.* **5 ACT OF DIGGING** the act of digging or excavating something ■ **digs** *npl* **LODGINGS** a room or rooms that somebody rents in another person's house (*dated informal*) [12C. < ?]

dig in *v* **1** *vti* **TAKE UP POSITIONS** to prepare trenches or other defensive structures, or to establish a force or equipment in a defensive position **2** *vi* **RESIST ATTACK** to put up a stubborn resistance to an attack **3** *vi* **FIGHT STUBBORNLY** to stick to an established position, e.g. in an argument, and fight stubbornly to maintain it **4** *vi* **START EATING** to start eating, especially in an enthusiastic way (*informal*) **5** *vt* **BURY PLANTS** to cover plants or the remains of a crop by turning over the soil in which they are growing and burying them

dig out *vt* **1** to obtain, uncover, or free something by removing the material covering it using a shovel, the hands, paws, a tool, or a machine **2** to retrieve something from where it is kept, or find out something by research or questioning (*informal*)

dig up *vt* **1 TAKE OUT OF GROUND** to dig for something that is buried in the ground and remove it **2 TURN OVER EARTH** to dig into and turn over the earth in an area **3 INVESTIGATE** to find out something by research or investigation (*informal*)

digamma /dī gamə/ *n* a letter of the ancient Greek alphabet that became obsolete in the classical period [Late 17C. Via Latin < Greek, 'double gamma'; from its resemblance to two capital gammas, one above the other.]

digamy /díggəmi/ (*plural* **-mies**) *n* a second marriage that, unlike bigamy, is legal because the first husband or wife is dead or has been divorced (*formal*) [Early 17C. Via late Latin *digamia* < Greek, < *digamos* 'married to two people' < *gamos* 'marriage'.] —**digamous** *adj*

digastric /dī gástrik/ *adj* describes a muscle, especially the muscle on either side of the lower jaw, in which two fleshy parts are connected by a tendon [Early 18C. < modern Latin *digastricus* < *gastricus* (see GASTRIC); from an analogy between 'fleshy parts' and 'stomachs'.]

ϟ **digerati** /díjjə raáti/ *npl* people with expertise in computers, the Internet, and the World Wide Web [Late 20C. < DIGITAL after LITERATI.]

digest *v* /dī jést, di jést/ **1** *vti* **PROCESS FOOD** to process food in the body into a form that can be absorbed and used or excreted **2** *vt* **ABSORB MENTALLY** to think about something and come to understand or appreciate what it means **3** *vt* **ORGANIZE SYSTEMATICALLY** to organize something into a system, often through selective condensing of the various items, so that essential information is readily available **4** *vt* **ABRIDGE** to make a summary of something, often a written work **5** *vti* **BREAK DOWN** to soften or break down a substance through exposure to heat, water, or chemicals, or to be broken down in this way ■ *n* /dí jest/ **1 SUMMARY** a shortened version of a work that contains the most important or interesting information from the original version **2 COLLECTION OF ABRIDGED PIECES** a magazine, book, or broadcast that contains shortened versions of articles or stories originally from different sources **3 COLLECTION OF LEGAL OPINIONS** a systematic compilation of laws or legal opinions [14C. < Latin *digest-*, past participle of *digerere* 'carry apart' < *gerere* 'carry'.]

digestate /dī jést ayt/ *n* a material, e.g. compost, produced by a process of biodegradation

digester /dī jéstər, di-/ *n* **1** somebody or something that digests something **2** a vessel or device in which chemical digestion takes place

digestible /dī jéstəb'l, di-/ *adj* easily digested —**digestibility** /dī jéstə bíllәti, di-/ *n* —**digestibly** *adv*

digestif /di zhe stéef/ *n* an alcoholic drink, e.g. a brandy or liqueur, drunk after a meal supposedly to help the digestion of food [Early 20C. < French, 'digestive' < Latin *digestivus* < *digerere* (see DIGEST).]

digestion /dī jéschən, di-/ *n* **1 PROCESSING OF FOOD IN BODY** the breaking down of foodstuffs in the body into a form that can be absorbed and used or excreted **2 ABILITY TO DIGEST FOOD** the ability to process food in the body into a form that can be absorbed and used or excreted **3 ABILITY TO ABSORB IDEAS** the ability to think about something and come to understand or appreciate its content, or the process of doing so **4 BREAKING DOWN** the softening or breaking down of a substance through exposure to heat, water, chemicals, enzymes, or bacteria —**digestional** *adj*

digestive /dī jéstiv, di-/ *adj* associated with or aiding in the digestion of food ■ *n* **1** something that aids or promotes the digesting of food **2** = **digestive biscuit** —**digestively** *adv*

digestive biscuit *n* a semisweet round biscuit that is made from wholemeal flour

digestive gland *n* any gland that secretes digestive enzymes, e.g. the pancreas in vertebrates

digestive tract *n* ANAT = **alimentary canal**

digger /díggər/ *n* **1** somebody or something that digs **2** a tool, machine, or part of a machine that is used for digging or excavation

Digger /díggər/, **digger** *n* (*informal*) **1 SOMEBODY FROM AUSTRALIA OR NEW ZEALAND** somebody from Australia or New Zealand, especially a soldier who served in World War I **2** *Aus* **MAN IN LATER LIFE** a man who has lived for a long time **3 FORM OF ADDRESS** used as a friendly form of address between men

diggings /díggingz/ *n* **MINING LOCATION** a place where something is mined, especially precious metals or gems ■ *npl* **1 MATERIAL EXCAVATED** material that has been dug out of a hole or mine **2 LODGINGS** a room or rooms that somebody rents in somebody else's house (*dated informal*)

dight /dīt/ (**dights, dighting, dight** *or* **dighted**) *vt* to equip, dress, or adorn somebody (*archaic*) [Old English *dihtan*, via Germanic < Latin *dictare* 'say often', (see DICTATE)]

digit /díjjit/ *n* **1 NUMERAL IN DECIMAL SYSTEM** any of the ten Arabic numerals, 0 to 9, that are used to represent numbers in the decimal system **2 NUMERAL IN ANY NUMBER SYSTEM** a symbol that represents a number in any number system, such as the hexadecimal system **3 HUMAN FINGER OR TOE** a finger or toe of a human **4 ANIMAL FINGER OR TOE** a finger, toe, or similar part on a terrestrial vertebrate [14C. < Latin *digitus* 'finger, toe'.]

⚡**digital** /díjjit'l/ *adj* 1 **REPRESENTING DATA AS NUMBERS** processing, storing, transmitting, representing, or displaying data in the form of numerical digits, as in a digital computer. ◊ **analogue** *adj.* 2 **REPRESENTING SOUND/LIGHT WAVES AS NUMBERS** representing a varying physical quantity, such as sound or light waves, by means of discrete signals interpreted as numbers, usually in the binary system, as in a digital recording or digital television 3 **LIKE FINGER** like a finger or toe 4 **DONE WITH FINGERS** using the fingers, or operated by a finger or fingers [15C. < Latin *digitalis* < *digitus* 'finger, toe'.] —**digitally** *adv*

⚡**digital audio tape** *n* a magnetic tape used in the digital recording of music

⚡**digital cash** *n* credit in the form of an encoded bank authorization that can be used for buying on the Internet

⚡**digital coins** *npl* electronic payment in small denominations (*in e-commerce*)

⚡**digital computer** *n* a computer that stores and performs a series of mathematical and logical operations on data expressed as discrete signals interpreted as numbers, usually in the form of binary notation

⚡**digital display** *n* a video display that renders a limited number of colours and shades of grey

⚡**digital encryption standard** *n* a standard for private key data encryption that uses 56-bit encryption (*in e-commerce*)

⚡**digital forensics** *n* the examination of computer data and computer networks in order to obtain legal evidence (*+ singular verb*)

⚡**digital imagery, digital imaging** *n* the process of altering a digital image on a computer

⚡**digitalize** /díjjitə līz/ (**-izes, -izing, -ized**), **digitalise** (**-ises, -ising, -ised**) *vt* 1 COMPUT = **digitize** 2 to treat somebody with digitalis —**digitalization** /díjjitə lī záysh'n/ *n*

⚡**digital logic** *n* the use of digital circuitry to determine if a condition is true or false

⚡**digital object identifier** *n* an identifying symbol for a Web file that redirects users to any new Internet location for that file

digital recording *n* 1 audio recording in which sounds are stored as numbers, producing purer sound 2 a recording made using the digital method

⚡**digital signature** *n* a digital signal or pattern that identifies the user or the user's habits

⚡**Digital Subscriber Line** *n* a high-speed telephone line that can supply television, video, Internet access, and video telephoning, often over standard copper wire

⚡**digital tablet** *n* COMPUT = **graphics tablet**

digital television *n* 1 television broadcasting in which the picture is transmitted as discrete signals represented as numbers 2 a television set specially constructed or adapted for receiving such signals

⚡**digital-to-analog converter** *n* an electronic circuit that changes digital information into an analogue signal

⚡**digital video disc, digital versatile disc** *n* full form of **DVD**

⚡**digital video disc-ROM** *n* full form of **DVD-ROM**

digital watch *n* a watch that shows the time in numerical form, rather than by hands on a dial

digitate /díjji tayt/, **digitated** /-taytid/ *adj* 1 having fingers or toes, or having parts that are like fingers or toes 2 having divisions or parts arrayed from a central point like the spread fingers of a hand, e.g. in the leaves of certain trees —**digitately** *adv* —**digitation** /díjji táysh'n/ *n*

digiti- *prefix* finger or toe ○ *digitigrade* [< Latin *digitus* 'finger, toe']

digitigrade /díjjiti grayd/ *adj* describes the gait of those animals that walk with only the tips of the digits touching the ground, the rest of the foot being raised, e.g. cats and deer ■ *n* an animal, such as a deer or cat, that walks with its weight on its digits and the back of its foot raised [Mid-19C. < French, < Latin *digitus* 'finger, toe' + *gradus* 'step'.]

⚡**digitize** /díjji tīz/ (**-tizes, -tizing, -tized**), **digitise** (**-tises, -tising, -tised**) *vt* to convert an image, graph, or other data into digital form for processing on a computer —**digitization** /díjji tī záysh'n/ *n* —**digitizer** *n*

⚡**digitizing tablet** *n* COMPUT = **graphics tablet**

⚡**digizine** /díjji zeen/ *n* a magazine that is delivered in digital form either on the Internet or on a CD-ROM (*informal*) ◊ **e-zine** [Blend of DIGITAL + MAGAZINE]

diglossia /dī glóssi ə/ *n* the existence of a formal literary form of a language, considered higher and more prestigious, along with a colloquial form used by most speakers and considered of lower status [Mid-20C. < Greek *diglōssos* 'bilingual' < *glōssa* 'language'.]

dignified /dígni fīd/ *adj* showing self-respect or behaving in a proper and respectable way —**dignifiedly** *adv*

dignify /dígni fī/ (**-fies, -fying, -fied**) *vt* 1 **GIVE DISTINCTION TO** to give honour or a sense of importance to something 2 **GIVE UNDESERVED ATTENTION TO** to treat somebody or something as honourable or worthy of attention when this treatment is undeserved 3 **MAKE NOBLE** to award an honour to somebody, or raise a person to noble rank [15C. Via obsolete French *dignifier* < late Latin *dignificare* 'make worthy' < Latin *dignus* 'worthy'.]

dignitary /dígnitəri/ (*plural* **-ies**) *n* a person who holds a high rank or position

dignity /dígnəti/ (*plural* **-ties**) *n* 1 **PRIDE AND SELF-RESPECT** a proper sense of pride and self-respect 2 **SERIOUSNESS IN BEHAVIOUR** seriousness, respectfulness, or formality in somebody's behaviour and bearing 3 **WORTHINESS** the condition of being worthy of respect, esteem, or honour 4 **DUE RESPECT** the respect or honour that a high rank or position should be shown 5 **HIGH OFFICE** a high rank, position, or honour [12C. Via Old French *digneté* < Latin *dignitas* < *dignus* 'worthy'.]

digoxin /dī jóksin/ *n* a glycoside extracted from foxglove leaves. Use: heart stimulant. [Mid-20C. Contraction of *digitoxin*, a similar glycoside.]

digraph /dī graaf, -graf/ *n* 1 a pair of letters that represents a single speech sound, such as 'ng' in 'ring' or 'ch' in 'child' 2 PRINTING = **ligature** *n.* 5 —**digraphic** /dī gráffik/ *adj* —**digraphically** *adv*

digress /dī gréss/ *vi* to move away from the central topic or line of argument in speaking or writing, usually temporarily [Early 16C. < Latin *digress-*, past participle of *digredi* 'step aside' < *gradus* 'step'.]

digression /dī grésh'n/ *n* 1 an act or instance of departing from the central topic or line of argument while speaking or writing 2 a part of something spoken or written that departs from the central topic or line of argument —**digressional** *adj* —**digressionary** *adj*

digressive /dī gréssiv/ *adj* tending to depart from the main subject or line of argument —**digressively** *adv* —**digressiveness** *n*

dihedral /dī heédrəl/ *n* 1 **dihedral, dihedral angle** the angle contained between two planes that intersect, measured by the angle made by any two lines at right angles to the two planes 2 the angle between an upwardly inclined aircraft wing and a horizontal line [Late 18C. < DI- + Greek *hedra* 'seat, base'.]

dihybrid /dī hībrid/ *n* an organism that is heterozygous for two genes, so that each gene is represented by two variant forms (**alleles**) —**dihybridism** *n*

dihydric /dī hīdrik/ *adj* containing two hydroxyl groups

Dijon /deé zhoN/ capital of Côte d'Or Department, east-central France. Population: 149,867 (1999).

dik-dik /dík dik/ (*plural* **dik-diks** *or* **dik-dik**) *n* a small long-muzzled antelope. Native to: arid regions of E Africa. Genus: *Madoqua*. [Late 19C. An imitation of the animal's cry.]

dike[1] *n, vt* = **dyke**

dike[2] *n* = **dyke**[2] (*slang offensive*)

dike swarm *n* a series of parallel or linear dikes

diktat /dík taat/ *n* 1 a statement or order that cannot be opposed 2 a harsh settlement imposed on a defeated opponent or enemy [Mid-20C. Via German, < Latin *dictatum* < past participle of *dictare* (see DICTATE).]

dilapidate /di láppi dayt/ (**-dates, -dating, -dated**) *vti* to become or make something become partially ruined or decayed, especially through neglect [Early 16C. < Latin *dilapidat-*, past participle of *dilapidare* 'squander' < *lapis* 'stone'.]

dilapidated /di láppi daytid/ *adj* in a condition of disrepair or partial decay

dilatancy /dī láyt'nssi, di-/ *n* the tendency of a substance to become more viscous or solid when affected by an outside force or agitation

dilatant /dī láyt'nt, di-/ *adj* 1 **ABLE TO EXPAND** able or likely to expand 2 **BECOMING MORE VISCOUS** tending to become more viscous or solid when affected by an outside force or agitation ■ *n* **SUBSTANCE CAUSING EXPANSION** a substance that causes another to expand

dilatation /dīlə táysh'n, dillə-/ *n* 1 **PROCESS OF EXPANDING** the act or process of widening or being widened, stretching or being stretched, or enlarging or being enlarged 2 **EXPANDED CONDITION** a condition in which something is enlarged, expanded, or stretched 3 **DILATED THING** something, especially a part of something else, that has become enlarged, expanded, or stretched 4 **LENGTHY EXPLANATION** a lengthy detailed explanation or discussion of a subject by a speaker or writer 5 MED = **dilation** *n.* 3 —**dilatational** *adj*

dilatation and curettage *n* full form of **D and C**

dilatator /dīlə taytər, dillə-/ *n* = **dilator** *n.* 1

dilate /dī láyt, di-/ (**-lates, -lating, -lated**) *v* 1 *vti* to become or cause something to become wider or larger 2 *vi* to talk or write about something at great length [14C. Via French *dilater* < Latin *dilatare* 'spread widely apart' < *latus* 'wide'.] —**dilatability** /dī láytə bílləti, di-/ *n* —**dilatable** *adj* —**dilatableness** *n* —**dilative** *adj*

dilation /dī láysh'n, di-/ *n* 1 **EXPANDING OF** the act or process of widening or being widened, stretching or being stretched, or enlarging or being enlarged 2 **DILATED CONDITION** a condition in which something is enlarged, expanded, or stretched 3 **dilation, dilatation ENLARGEMENT OF BODY PART** the stretching or enlargement of a hollow organ or body cavity

dilatometer /dillə tómmitər/ *n* an instrument used to measure expansion, e.g. in the volume of a liquid —**dilatometric** /dillətə méttrik/ *adj* —**dilatometry** *n*

dilator /dī láytər, di-/ **dilatator** *n* 1 something that makes something else wider or larger, especially a medical instrument used to widen a body passage 2 a muscle or muscle group that expands a part of the body

dilatory /díllətəri/ *adj* 1 tending to waste time or move slowly 2 intended to cause a delay or waste time [15C. < late Latin *dilatorius* < Latin *dilat-*, past participle of *differre* 'delay'.] —**dilatorily** *adv* —**dilatoriness** *n*

dildo /díl dō/ (*plural* **-dos**), **dildoe** (*plural* **-does**) *n* an object shaped like a penis, used in sexual activity [Late 16C. < ?]

~~**dilema**~~ incorrect spelling of **dilemma**

dilemma /di lémmə, dī-/ *n* 1 a situation in which somebody must choose one of two or more unsatisfactory alternatives 2 in logic, a form of reasoning that, though valid, leads to two undesirable alternatives [Early 16C. < Greek *dilēmma* 'double proposition' < *lēmma* 'proposition'.]

dilettante /dílli tánti, -taánti/ *n* (*plural* **-tantes** *or* **-tanti** /-ti/) 1 **DABBLER IN ART OR KNOWLEDGE** somebody who takes up a subject or interest in a superficial or desultory way 2 **ART LOVER** an admirer of the fine arts (*dated*) ■ *adj* **SUPERFICIAL** typical of somebody who has only a superficial understanding of something [Mid-18C. < Italian, < *dilettare* 'to delight' < Latin *delectare* (see DELIGHT).] —**dilettantish** *adj* —**dilettantism** *n*

diligence[1] /díllijənss/ *n* 1 persistent and hard-working effort in doing something 2 the care or attention expected by the law in doing something, such as fulfilling the terms of a contract [14C. Via French < Latin *diligentia* < *diligent-* (see DILIGENT).]

diligence[2] /dílliјənss/ *n* a stagecoach, especially in France (*literary*) [Late 17C. < French, shortening of *carrosse de diligence* 'coach of speed'.]

diligent /díllijənt/ *adj* showing persistent and hard-working effort in doing something [14C. Via French, < Latin *diligent-*, present participle of *diligere* 'value highly, love' < *legere* 'choose'.] —**diligently** *adv*

dill /dil/ *n* 1 a herb with fine feathery leaves and flat flower heads, that produces dill. *Anethum graveolens.* 2 the leaves or seeds of an aromatic herb, used as a flavouring or garnish [Old English *dile* < ?] —**dilly** *adj*

dill pickle *n* a cucumber that has been pickled in dill-flavoured vinegar or brine, or a portion of it. ◊ **gherkin**

dilly bag /dílli-/ *n Aus* a bag traditionally made of plaited grass or reeds, used by Aborigines for carrying food and other belongings [< Aboriginal *dili* 'coarse grass']

dilly-dally /dílli-/ (**dilly-dallies, dilly-dallying, dilly-dallied**) *vi* to waste time by being too slow, doing nothing, or being unable to decide what to do [Doubled < DALLY]

diluent /díllyoo ənt/ *n* a substance that dilutes another substance ■ *adj* used for diluting something [Early 18C. < Latin *diluent-*, present participle of *diluere* (see DILUTE).]

dilute /dī lóot, -lyóot/ *vti* (**-lutes, -luting, -luted**) **1 MAKE THINNER** to make something thinner or weaker by adding water or another liquid, or to become thinner or weaker by the addition of water or another liquid **2 LESSEN STRENGTH** to lessen the strength or effect of something, or to become weaker in strength or effect ■ *adj* **THINNED** thinner or weaker than at full concentration because of the addition of water or another liquid [Mid-16C. < Latin *dilut-*, past participle of *diluere* 'wash away' < *lavare* 'wash'.] —**diluteness** *n* —**diluter** *n*

dilution /dī lóosh'n, -lyóosh'n/ *n* **1 A THINNING OR WEAKENING** a thinning or weakening of a substance, usually a liquid, by the addition of another substance, such as water **2 LESSENING OF STRENGTH** a lessening of the strength or effect of something **3 THINNED OR WEAKENED STATE** a thinned or weakened condition **4 LESS CONCENTRATED LIQUID** a substance, especially a liquid, that has been made thinner or weaker by the addition of water or another liquid

diluvial /dī lóovi əl, di-/, **diluvian** /-vi ən/ *adj* relating to the great Flood described in the Bible [Mid-17C. < late Latin *diluvialis* < Latin *diluvium* 'flood' < *diluere* (see DILUTE).]

dim /dim/ *adj* (**dimmer, dimmest**) **1 NOT WELL LIT** not easy to see in or into because of inadequate light **2 PRODUCING LITTLE LIGHT** not producing very much light, or less bright than is usual **3 DULL IN COLOUR** dull or subdued in colour or brightness **4 NOT CLEARLY VISIBLE** not clearly visible or distinct **5 NOT EASY TO PERCEIVE** difficult to understand or perceive with the senses **6 NOT CLEAR TO THE MIND** not clearly recalled **7 NOT SEEING CLEARLY** not able to see clearly **8 IMPROBABLE** unlikely to be successful or fulfilled **9 UNINTELLIGENT** lacking in intelligence or mental sharpness (*informal insult*) ■ *v* (**dims, dimming, dimmed**) **1** *vti* **MAKE OR BECOME DIM** to make or become less bright, clear, or keen **2** *vt US* CARS = **dip** *v.* 7 [Old English < Germanic] —**dimly** *adv* —**dimmable** *adj* —**dimness** *n*

⚡**DIM** *abbr* do it myself (*in e-mails*)

dim. *abbr* **1** dimension **2** diminuendo **3** diminutive

DiMaggio /di májji ō/, **Joe** (1914–99) US baseball player. Full name **Joseph Paul DiMaggio**. Known as **Joltin' Joe, Yankee Clipper**

Dimbleby /dímb'lbi/, **Richard** (1913–65) British broadcaster and journalist

dime /dīm/ *n US* a US or Canadian coin worth ten cents [14C. Via French, 'tithe, tenth part' < Latin *decima*, form of *decimus* 'tenth' < *decem* 'ten'.] ◇ **a dime a dozen** *US* very numerous or common, and therefore of little value

dimenhydrinate /dī men hídri nayt/ *n* an antihistamine drug. Use: treatment of travel sickness. [Mid-20C. < DIMETHYL + AMINE + HYDR- + AMINE.]

dimension /di ménsh'n, dī-/ *n* **1 MEASUREMENT OF THE SIZE OF** a measurement of something in one or more directions, e.g. its length, width, or height **2 SIZE** the size or extent of something (*usally used in the plural*) **3 ASPECT** a feature or distinctive part of something **4 LIFE-LIKE QUALITY** a roundedness that gives a convincingly life-like quality **5 LEVEL OF REALITY** a level of consciousness, existence, or reality **6 COORDINATE FOR SPACE AND TIME** a coordinate used with others to locate a point in space and time **7 PROPERTY DEFINING PHYSICAL QUANTITY** any of a group of properties or magnitudes, such as mass or time, that collectively define a physical quantity ■ *vt US* **1 MAKE TO REQUIRED DIMENSIONS** to cut or make something to a specified size **2 INDICATE THE DIMENSIONS OF** to specify the size of something [14C. Via Old French < Latin *dimension-* < *dimetiri* 'measure out' < *metiri* 'measure'.] —**dimensional** *adj* —**dimensionality** /di ménshə nálləti, dī-/ *n* —**dimensionally** *adv* —**dimensionless** *adj*

dimensional analysis *n* **1** the procedure of checking or ensuring that the terms in a physical equation have the same dimensions **2** the application of knowledge of the physical dimensions of a system to infer information mathematically too complex to calculate

dimer /dīmər/ *n* a molecule made up of two simpler identical molecules —**dimeric** /dī mérrik/ *adj*

dimercaprol /dīmər ká prol/ *n* an antidote to heavy metal poisoning [Mid-20C. < DI-[1] + MERCAPTAN + PROPANE.]

dime store *n US* a shop that sells a range of inexpensive goods [the maximum price of goods sold there being, originally, one dime]

dime-store *adj US* **1** not costing very much money **2** of low or second-rate quality

dimeter /dímmitər/ *n* **1** a line of poetry consisting of two metrical feet **2** verse made up of lines consisting of two metrical feet [Late 16C. Via late Latin, Greek *dimetros* 'having two measures' < *metron* 'measure'.]

dimethoate /dī méthō ayt/ *n* $C_5H_{12}NO_3PS_2$ a white crystalline compound. Use: insecticide. [Mid-20C. < DIMETHYL + THIO-.]

dimethyl /dī meé thīl, -méth'l/ *adj* with two methyl groups in a molecule

dimethylamine /dī meé thīl áy meen, -méth'l-/ *n* a soluble flammable gas with an odour like ammonia. Use: solvent, in drugs, synthesis of chemicals.

dimethylglyoxime /dī meé thīl glī ók seem, -méth'l-/ *n* a white powdery or crystalline substance soluble in alcohol. Use: reagent, biochemical research.

dimethylnitrosamine /dī meé thīl nītrṓsə meén, dī méth'l-, dī meé thīl nī tróss áy meen/ *n* $C_2H_6N_2O$ a yellow carcinogenic compound. Source: tobacco smoke, certain foods.

dimethylsulphoxide /dī meé thīl sul fók sīd, -méth'l-/ *n* full form of **DMSO**

dimidiate /di míddi it, -ayt/ *adj* **1 DIVIDED IN TWO** divided into halves **2 ASYMMETRICAL** with one part or side developed more than, or differently from, the other ■ *vt* (**-ates, -ating, -ated**) **HALVE HERALDIC EMBLEM** to halve each of two heraldic emblems so that both can appear on one shield [Late 16C. < Latin *dimidiat-*, past participle of *dimidiare* 'halve' < *dimidium* 'half' < *medium* 'middle'.] —**dimidiation** /di míddi áysh'n/ *n*

dimin. *abbr* **1** diminuendo **2** diminutive

diminish /di mínnish/ *v* **1** *vti* **MAKE OR BECOME SMALLER** to make something smaller or less important, or to become smaller or less important **2** *vti* **APPEAR SMALLER** to appear smaller or to make something appear smaller **3** *vti* **TAPER FROM BOTTOM TO TOP** to taper or make something taper from the lower part to the upper part **4** *vt* **CONTRACT MUSICAL INTERVAL** to contract a perfect or minor musical interval by one semitone [15C. Blend of obsolete *diminue* (< Latin *minuere* 'lessen') + *minish* 'diminish' (< Latin *minutia* 'smallness').] —**diminishable** *adj* —**diminishingly** *adv* —**diminishment** *n*

diminished /di mínnisht/ *adj* **1** reduced in quantity, size, or importance **2** describes a musical interval or chord reduced by one semitone

diminished responsibility *n* a partial defence in criminal law where the defendant seeks to argue reduced culpability on the grounds that a psychiatric disorder reduced responsibility for his or her actions

diminishing returns *npl* additional increases in something produced, e.g. profits or benefits, that do not rise in proportion to the additional effort or investment necessary to produce them

diminuendo /di mínnyoo éndō/ *adv* having a gradual decrease in volume (*used as a musical direction*) US term **decrescendo** *adv.* ■ *n* (*plural* **-dos**) a piece of music, or a section of a piece, played diminuendo. US term **decrescendo** *n.* [Late 18C. < Italian, present participle of *diminuire* 'diminish' < Latin *deminuere* (see DIMINUTION).] —**diminuendo** *adj*

diminution /dímmi nyóosh'n/ *n* **1** a lessening, decreasing, or reduction of something, or the result of such a reduction **2** the repetition of a musical phrase, using notes that are of a shorter duration than in the original phrase [14C. < Latin *diminut-*, past participle of *diminuere* 'break into small pieces' < *minuere* 'lessen'.] —**diminutional** *adj*

diminutive /di mínnyootiv/ *adj* **1 VERY SMALL** very small or much smaller than is usual **2 INDICATING SMALLNESS** describes a suffix that indicates small size, youth, familiarity, or fondness, e.g. '-ette' or '-let' ■ *n* **1 WORD INDICATING SMALLNESS OR FONDNESS** a word or name that indicates small size, youth, familiarity, or fondness, e.g. 'kitchenette' or 'booklet' **2 SUFFIX INDICATING SMALLNESS OR FONDNESS** a suffix, e.g. '-ette', or '-let' that indicates small size, youth, familiarity, or fondness **3 VERY SMALL PERSON OR THING** a person or thing that is very small or much smaller than is usual [14C. < French *diminutif* < Latin *diminut-* (see DIMINUTION).] —**diminutively** *adv* —**diminutiveness** *n*

dimity /dímmiti/ (*plural* **-ties**) *n* a thin cotton fabric with a striped or checked texture produced by weaving together yarn of different thicknesses [15C. < medieval Latin *dimitum* < Greek *dimitos* 'of double thread' < *mitos* 'warp thread'.]

⚡**DIMM** /dim/ *n* a plug-in module that adds random-access memory to a computer. Full form **dual in-line memory module**

dimmer /dímmər/ *n* **1 dimmer, dimmer switch** a device, such as a variable resistor, that can be used to vary the brightness of a light by regulating the amount of current supplied to it **2** *US* CARS = **dip switch** *n.* 1

dimorphism /dī máwrfizəm/ *n* **1 DIFFERENT FORMS WITHIN SINGLE BIOLOGICAL SPECIES** the existence of two or more different forms within a biological species. In sexual dimorphism, male and female may vary in colour, size, or some other trait. **2 DIFFERENT FORMS OF THE SAME ORGAN** the existence of two different forms of the same organ or part in a plant, such as leaves or flower forms **3 DIFFERENT CRYSTALLINE FORMS** the existence of a substance in two different crystalline forms —**dimorphic** *adj* —**dimorphous** *adj*

dimple /dímp'l/ *n* **1 INDENTED AREA IN SKIN** a naturally occurring slightly indented area in the skin and flesh of the cheek, chin, or other part of the body **2 INDENTED SURFACE AREA** an indented, hollowed, or depressed area in the surface of something ■ *v* (**-ples, -pling, -pled**) **1** *vti* **FORM DIMPLE** to form or have a dimple ○ *This mould dimples the surface of the golf ball.* **2** *vt* **PRODUCE DIMPLES IN** to smile, causing dimples to appear in the cheeks [14C. < assumed Old English *dympel* < Germanic.] —**dimply** *adj*

dimpled chad *n* a chad on a ballot paper that bulges as if pressed down on by a voter's stylus, but that remains attached to the paper with none of its perforations broken through

dim sum /dím súm/ *n* dumplings, spring rolls, and various other traditional Chinese dishes served in small portions as a meal (*takes a singular or plural verb*) [< Chinese (Cantonese) *tím sam* 'small centre']

dimwit /dím wit/ *n* an unintelligent or unresponsive person (*informal insult*) —**dimwitted** /dím wíttid/ *adj* —**dimwittedly** *adv* —**dimwittedness** *n*

din /din/ *n* **LOUD PERSISTENT NOISE** a loud persistent noise, especially one composed of confused sounds ■ *v* (**dins, dinning, dinned**) **1** *vi* **MAKE LOUD NOISE** to make a loud persistent noise **2** *vt* **SUBJECT TO LOUD NOISE** to subject somebody to a loud persistent noise **3** *vt* **INSTIL THROUGH REPETITION** to fix something in somebody's mind by repeating it over and over again [Old English *dyne* < Indo-European]

din *symbol* dinar

DIN /din/ *n* **1** a system of numbers used to express the speed of a photographic film **2** a system of standard electrical connections, especially used with television and audio equipment [Acronym < German *Deutsche Industrie-Norm* 'German industry standard']

Dinant /deé naaN/ town in S Belgium. Population: 12,461 (1995).

dinar /deé naar/ *n* **1** see table at **currency** **2** a former Middle Eastern coin, usually gold [Mid-17C. Via late Greek *dēnarion* < Latin *denarius* (see DENARIUS).]

Dinaric Alps /di nárrik-, dī-/ range of the Eastern Alps, extending from NE Italy southeastwards along the Adriatic coast of the Balkan Peninsula to Bobotov Kuk. Highest peak: 2,522 m/8,274 ft.

DIN connector *n* a multi-pin electrical connection compatible with the DIN system

D'Indy /dáN dee/, **Vincent** (1851–1931) French composer, teacher, and writer

dine /dīn/ (**dines, dining, dined**) *v* **1** *vi* **EAT DINNER** to eat dinner ○ *We dine early.* **2** *vi* **EAT** to eat or have a particular food or type of food in a meal ○ *We dined on vegetables and rice.* **3** *vt* **PROVIDE DINNER FOR** to provide dinner for somebody or take somebody out to dinner (*informal*) ○ *wined and dined their guests* [13C. < Old French *di(s)ner*.]

dine out *vi* to eat dinner somewhere other than at home, especially in a restaurant

diner /dīnər/ *n* **1** somebody eating a meal, especially dinner **2** *US* a small inexpensive restaurant where customers eat at the counter or in booths

Dinesen /dínniss'n/, **Isak** (1885–1962) Danish writer. Born **Karen Christence Dinesen**

dinette /dī nét/ *n* an alcove or part of a room where meals are eaten, especially in or near a kitchen

ding[1] /ding/ *v* **1** *vti* **RING OR MAKE RING** to ring or make something ring with a high-pitched sound **2** *vi* **TALK REPEATEDLY** to talk repeatedly or wearyingly about something ■ *n* **RINGING** a ringing sound, especially made by a bell [Mid-16C. An imitation of the sound.]

ding[2] /ding/ *v* (*informal*) **1** *vti regional* **STRIKE** to strike something or strike against something **2** *vt US, Aus* **MAKE A DENT IN** to make a dent or cause other surface damage in something ■ *n US, Aus* **DENT** a dent or other surface damage in something (*informal*) [14C. Probably < Old Norse.]

ding-a-ling *n* **1** the sound of a bell, especially a small hand-held bell, being rung **2** somebody regarded as having very odd, irrational ideas or behaviour (*informal insult*) [Late 19C. An imitation of the sound.]

dingbat /díng bat/ *n* **1 SILLY PERSON** a person with very odd, irrational ideas or behaviour (*informal*) **2** *US* **THING WHOSE NAME IS NOT KNOWN** an object whose name has been forgotten or is not known (*slang*) **3 PRINTER'S SYMBOL** a symbol or ornamental character, such as a star or pointing hand, used in a printed work [Mid-19C. < ?]

dingbats /díng bats/ *n Aus* delirium tremens (*slang*) ■ *adj* behaving in a way thought to be strange or irrational (*slang*) [Mid-20C. Plural of DINGBAT.] ◇ **give somebody the dingbats** *Aus* to make somebody nervous or annoyed (*slang*)

ding-dong *n* **1 SOUND OF BELL** a sound of a bell being struck two or more times **2 SOUND IMITATIVE OF BELL SOUND** any ringing or repeated sound that is similar to that made by a bell **3 ARGUMENT** a fierce argument (*informal*) ■ *adj* **FIERCELY CONTESTED** fiercely contested, with advantage shifting continually from one side to another (*informal*) ○ *a ding-dong battle of wills* ■ *vi* **MAKE RINGING SOUND** to make a ringing sound like a bell [Mid-16C. An imitation of the sound.]

dinghy /díngi, díng gi/ (*plural* **-ghies**) *n* **1** any small boat, especially one that is towed behind or carried on a larger boat **2** an inflatable life raft [Early 19C. < Hindi *dīgī* 'small boat' < *dēgā* 'boat'.]

dingle /díng g'l/ *n* a wooded valley (*literary*) [13C. < ?]

dingleberry /díng g'l berri/ (*plural* **-ries**) *n* a small piece of dried faeces that clings to the hair or fur near the anus (*slang*) [Mid-20C. < ?]

dingo /díng gō/ (*plural* **-goes**) *n* an Australian wild dog with a reddish brown coat. *Canis dingo.* [Late 18C. < Aboriginal *dingu*.]

Dingo /díng gō/, **Ernie** (*b.* 1956) Australian actor and television presenter

dingy /dínji/ (**-gier, -giest**) *adj* **1** dirty-looking, discoloured, or faded **2** shabby and uninviting [Mid-18C. < ?] —**dingily** *adv* —**dinginess** *n*

dining car *n* RAIL = **restaurant car**

dining room *n* a room where meals are eaten, especially in a home or hotel

dinitrobenzene /dī nī trō bén zeen/ *n* $C_6H_4(NO_2)_2$ a yellow crystalline compound that occurs in three isomeric forms. Use: manufacture of dyes and plastics.

dink /dingk/ *n* SPORTS = **drop shot** [Mid-20C. An imitation of the sound of the ball being hit.]

DINK /dingk/, **dink** *n US* = **dinky**[2] *n.* (*informal*) [Late 20C. Acronym < *dual* (or *double*) *income, no kids.*]

Dinka /díngkə/ (*plural* **-kas** *or* **-ka**) *n* **1** a member of a people who live in the Nile Valley in S Sudan **2** a language of the Nilo-Saharan family, spoken in S Sudan. Native speakers: 1.4 million. [Mid-19C. < Dinka *Jieng* 'people'.] —**Dinka** *adj*

dinkie *n* = **dinky**[2]

dinkum /díngkəm/ *adj ANZ* believed to be genuine, real, or honest (*informal*) ◊ **fair dinkum** [Late 19C. < ?]

dinky[1] /díngki/ (**-kier, -kiest**) *adj* small and compact or neat (*informal*) [Late 18C. < Scots dialect *dink* 'finely dressed, trim' < ?]

dinky[2] (*plural* **-kies**), **dinkie** *n* a member of a couple who both have careers, usually in well-paid fields, and who have no children (*informal*) US term **DINK** [Late 20C. < DINK.]

dinky-di /-dī/ *adj Aus* believed to be genuine, real, or typical (*informal*) [Early 20C. Alteration of DINKUM.]

dinna /dínnə/, **dinnae** /dínni/ *vi regional* do not [Early 18C. Contraction.]

dinner /dínnər/ *n* **1 MAIN MEAL** the main meal or one of the main meals of the day, eaten either at midday or in the evening **2 BANQUET** a formal evening meal given in honour of somebody or something **3 FULL-COURSE RESTAURANT MEAL** a meal that is eaten in a restaurant and consists of several courses, often offered together for a set price **4 FOOD SERVED FOR DINNER** the food served during or for a dinner [13C. < Old French *di(s)ner* 'dine'.]

dinner-dance *n* a formal social occasion at which dancing follows a dinner

dinner jacket *n* a man's jacket without tails that is worn on formal occasions, especially in the evening. US term **tuxedo**

dinner lady *n* a woman who serves food and supervises children during the midday meal break in a school (*informal*)

dinner party *n* a social gathering where dinner is served at somebody's home

dinner service, **dinner set** *n* a matching set of all the plates, dishes, cups, and saucers needed to serve a meal to a number of people

dinnertime /dínnər tīm/ *n* the time of the day when dinner is usually eaten ○ *Will you be home by dinnertime?*

DIN number *n* a number that indicates the speed of a photographic film, as expressed in the DIN system

dinoflagellate /dī nō flájjələt/ *n* a tiny single-celled sea organism with two long slender appendages (**flagella**), occurring in large numbers in plankton. *Dinoflagellata.* [Late 19C. < modern Latin *Dinoflagellata* < Greek *dinos* 'a whirling' + Latin *flagellum* 'whip' (see FLAGELLUM).]

dinosaur /dínə sawr/ *n* **1** an extinct, chiefly terrestrial reptile that lived in the Mesozoic Era. Order: Ornithischia and Saurischia. **2** a person or thing that is hopelessly out of date or incapable of adapting to change [Mid-19C. < modern Latin *dinosaurus* < Greek *deinos* 'terrible' < Indo-European.] —**dinosaurian** /dínə sáwri ən/ *adj*

dint /dint/ *n* a dent ■ *vt* to make a dent in something [Old English *dynt* 'blow, stroke (especially of a weapon)' < Germanic] ◇ **by dint of** using something, or by the force of something

diocese /dī əssiss/ *n* the churches that are under the authority of one bishop, or the district containing them [14C. < Greek *dioikēsis* 'administration' < *dioikein* 'manage' < *oikos* 'house'.] —**diocesan** /dī óssiss'n/ *adj*

Diocletian /dī ə kleesh'n/ (245–313) emperor of Rome (284–305)

diode /dī ōd/ *n* an electronic device that has two electrodes and is used to convert alternating current to direct current

dioecious /dī eeshəss/, **diecious, dioicous** /dī óykəss/ *adj* having male and female flowers on different plants of the same species [Mid-18C. < modern Latin *Dioecia*, literally 'two houses' < Greek *oikos* 'house'.] —**dioeciously** *adv* —**dioeciousness** *n* —**dioecism** /-eesizəm/ *n*

dioestrus /dī eestrəss/ *n* a stage of the oestrous cycle, following oestrus, in which the ovary is functional and the predominant ovarian hormone produced is progesterone —**dioestrous** *adj*

Diogenes /dī ójjə neez/ (412?–323 BC) Greek philosopher

diol /dī ol/ *n* an alcohol with two hydroxyl groups in each molecule

Dione /dī ōni/ *n* a natural satellite of Saturn discovered in 1684. It has a radius of 560 km/348 mi. and the surface exhibits several distinct terrain types.

Dionysiac *adj* = **Dionysian**

dionysian /dī ə nízzi ən, -níssi-/ *adj* **1** involving drunkenness and sexual activity **2** in the philosophical writings of Nietzsche, spontaneous and intuitive rather than rational

Dionysian /dī ə nízzi ən, -níssi-/, **Dionysiac** /dī ə nízzi ak, -níssi-/ *adj* **1** relating to the Greek god Dionysus **2** connected with the worship of the Greek god Dionysus [Early 17C. < Greek *Dionusos* 'Dionysus'.]

Dionysius Exiguus /dī ə níssi əss eg zíggyoo əss/ (500?–556) Scythian Roman scholar

Dionysius the Areopagite /-árri óppə gīt/ (*fl.* 1st century AD) Greek religious leader

Dionysus /dī ə nīssəss/ *n* ◆ **Bacchus**

Diophantine equation /dī ō fán tīn-/ *n* an algebraic equation that contains two or more variables, has only whole-number (**integral**) coefficients, and has integral solutions for the variables [After DIOPHANTUS]

Diophantus /dī ə fántəss/ (*fl.* 3rd century AD) Greek mathematician

diopside /dī óp sīd/ *n* a pale green mineral consisting of calcium magnesium silicate. Source: igneous rocks. [Early 19C. < DI-[1] + Greek *opsis* 'aspect'.]

dioptre /dī óptər/ *n* (*symbol* **D.**) a unit of measurement for the power of a lens, especially a spectacle lens, equal to the reciprocal of the focal length of the lens in metres [Late 19C. Via French < Latin *dioptra* 'instrument for measuring angles' < Greek, < *dia-* 'through' + *optos* 'visible'.] —**dioptral** *adj*

dioptric /dī óptrik/, **dioptrical** /-óptrik'l/ *adj* **1** relating to the study of how images are formed by lenses **2** relating to the refractive powers of light or the measurement of the refractive power of a lens [Mid-17C. < Greek *dioptrikos* < *dioptra* (see DIOPTRE).] —**dioptrically** *adv*

dioptrics /dī óptriks/ *n* the branch of optics that studies the refraction of light by lenses or within the eye

Dior /dee awr/, **Christian** (1905–57) French couturier

diorama /dī ə raamə/ *n* **1** a three-dimensional representation of a scene, e.g. in a museum, in which objects or models are arranged in a natural setting against a realistic background **2** a representation of a scene that is made to appear three-dimensional, e.g. one in which the viewer looks through a hole at objects painted on layers of translucent material [Early 19C. < French, 'sight through'; < Greek *dia-* 'through' after *panorama*.] —**dioramic** /-rámmik/ *adj*

diorite /dī ə rīt/ *n* a dark granular igneous rock that consists of plagioclase and a ferromagnesian mineral such as hornblende. Use: surfacing roads. [Early 19C. < Greek *diorizein* 'distinguish' < *orizein* 'to limit'.] —**dioritic** /dī ə ríttik/ *adj*

Dioscuri /dī óskyoori, -óskyoo rī, dī o skyoori, -skyoor ī/ *npl* the twin gods Castor and Polydeuces, or Pollux, who in Greek mythology were the sons of Zeus and Leda [Early 20C. < Greek *Dioskouroi* < *Dios* 'of Zeus' + *kouros* 'boy, son'.]

dioxane /dī ók sayn/, **dioxan** /dī óks'n/ *n* $C_4H_8O_2$ a toxic flammable colourless liquid. Use: solvent for waxes and resins, paints, lacquers, cosmetics, deodorants, textile manufacture.

dioxide /dī ók sīd/ *n* an oxide that has two oxygen atoms in each molecule

dioxin /dī óksin/ *n* any derivative of dibenzo-*p*-dioxin, a carcinogen and toxic environmental pollutant. Source: byproduct of combustion processes, manufacture of herbicides and bactericides, chlorine bleaching of paper.

dip /dip/ *v* (**dips, dipping, dipped**) **1** *vt* **PUT BRIEFLY IN LIQUID** to put something briefly into a liquid and take it out again ○ *She dipped her fingers in the water.* **2** *vi* **MOVE DOWNWARDS** to sink to a lower level ○ *The plane dipped and then flew on.* **3** *vt* **LOWER** to lower something and raise it again ○ *The horse dipped its head.* **4** *vi* **BECOME LESS** to fall to a lower level or amount, especially for a short time ○ *Prices dipped at the beginning of October.* **5** *vti* **PUT YOUR HAND IN** to put your hand into something in order to take something out ○ *He dipped his hand into his pocket.* **6** *vt* **SCOOP** to take up liquid or small pieces of a substance with something such as a spoon or cup ○ *She was dipping soup from the pot.* **7** *vt* **LOWER HEADLIGHTS** to alter a car's headlights so that they shine downwards and slightly towards the kerb in order to avoid dazzling oncoming vehicle drivers ○ *driving with dipped headlights.* US term **dim** *v.* **2 8** *vt* **DISINFECT ANIMAL** to put an animal such as a sheep or dog into a bath of disinfectant **9** *vi* **SLOPE DOWNWARDS** to slope downwards from the horizontal **10** *vt* **MAKE FROM WAX** to make a candle by repeatedly putting a wick into melted wax ○ *dip a candle* ■ *n* **1 LOWERING** an act of sinking lower, of lowering something, or of putting something in liquid ○ *She acknowledged him with a dip of her head.* **2 PUTTING HAND IN** the action of putting the hand into something to take something out or of scooping up liquid or small pieces of a substance **3 SWIM** a quick swim ○ *There's time for a dip before lunch.* **4 SLIGHT DECREASE** a temporary decrease in the amount or level of something ○ *a dip in sales* **5 LOWER PLACE** a place where the ground slopes, especially to form a hollow ○ *We came to a dip in the road.* **6 MIXTURE FOR DIPPING FOOD INTO** a creamy mixture into which pieces of food can be dipped ○ *an avocado dip* **7 DISINFECTANT FOR ANIMALS** a mixture of chemicals used to disinfect animals ○ *sheep dip* **8 LIQUID CHEMICAL PREPARATION** a chemical mixture in which something can be immersed, e.g. a dye or preservative **9** *US* **UNINTELLIGENT PERSON** somebody regarded as unintelligent or unsophisticated (*slang insult*) **10 ANGLE OF MAGNETIC NEEDLE** the angle that a magnetic needle makes with the horizontal plane **11 ANGLE OF ROCK LAYER** the angle a sloping rock layer makes to the horizontal ○ *The rock bed has a dip of ten degrees.* **12 CANDLE** a candle made by dipping a wick repeatedly in wax **13 PARALLEL BARS EXERCISE** an exercise on parallel bars in which the elbows are bent until the gymnast's chin is level with the bars, and the body is raised by straightening the arms **14 PICKPOCKET** a pickpocket (*slang*) [Old English *dyppan* < Germanic]

dip into *vt* **1** to read parts of a text, such as a book or magazine, rather than the whole of it **2** to use some of the money that has been saved

Dip., dip. *abbr* diploma

DipEd /dip éd/ *abbr* Diploma in Education

dipeptidase /dī pépti dayz, -dayss/ *n* an enzyme that breaks down dipeptides in the final stage of protein digestion

dipeptide /dī pép tīd/ *n* a compound composed of two amino acids

diphenyl /dī feen'l, -fénn'l/ *n* $C_{12}H_{10}$ a white crystalline substance. Use: fungicide, in organic synthesis, as a heat transfer agent.

diphenylamine /dī feen'l ə meen, -fénn'l-/ *n* $(C_6H_5)_2NH$ a colourless toxic crystalline substance. Use: in solid rocket propellants, dyes, manufacture of plastics.

diphenylketone /dī feen'l keetōn, -fénn'l-/ *n* CHEM = **benzophenone**

diphosgene /dī fóz jeen/ *n* $ClCOOCCl_3$ a colourless oily liquid with an extremely poisonous vapour. Use: in gas warfare during World War I.

diphosphate /dī fóss fayt/ *n* a chemical compound that contains two phosphate groups per molecule

diphosphoglyceric acid /dī fósfō gli sérrik-/ *n* a compound in red blood cells that allows the release of oxygen from haemoglobin

diphtheria /dif theeri ə, dip-/ *n* a serious infectious disease, caused by a bacterium *Corynebacterium diphtheriae*, that attacks the membranes of the throat and releases a toxin that damages the heart and the nervous system [Mid-19C. < modern Latin < Greek *diphthera, diphtheris* 'hide, skin', indicating the tough membrane developed in the throat.] —**diphtherial** *adj* —**diphtheric** /-thérrik, dip thérrik/ *adj* —**diphtheritic** /dífthə ríttik, díp-/ *adj* —**diphtheroid** /dífthə royd, díp-/ *adj*

diphthong /díf thong, díp-/ *n* **1** a complex vowel sound in which the first vowel is gradually raised by a second vowel so that both vowels form one syllable, such as 'a' and 'i' in 'rail' **2** a character formed by joining the two letters 'a' and 'e' as 'æ' or the two letters 'o' and 'e' as 'œ' [15C. Via French < Latin *diphthongus* 'two sounds' < Greek *phthoggos* 'sound'.] —**diphthongal** /dif thóng g'l, dip-/ *adj*

diphthongize /díf thong īz, díp-/ (**-izes, -izing, -ized**), **diphthongise** (**-ises, -ising, -ised**) *vti* to become a diphthong or make a vowel into a diphthong —**diphthongization** /díf thong ī záysh'n, díp-/ *n*

diphycercal /díffi súrk'l/ *adj* describes a fish's tail fin that is divided into two equal parts [Mid-19C. < Greek *diphu-* 'of double form' + *kerkos* 'tail'.]

dipl. *abbr* **1** diplomat **2** diplomatic

dipl- *prefix* = **diplo-** (*before vowels*)

diplegia /dī pleejə/ *n* inability to move corresponding parts on both the right and left sides of the body [Late 19C. < DI-[1] after PARAPLEGIA.] —**diplegic** *adj, n*

diplex /dí pleks/ *adj* capable of simultaneously transmitting or receiving two signals in the same direction along a telecommunications channel [Late 19C. Alteration of DUPLEX.] —**diplexer** *n*

diplo- *prefix* **1** double, twin ○ *diplopod* **2** having twice the basic number of chromosomes ○ *diplont* [< Greek *diploos* 'double']

diplococcus /dípplō kókəss/ (*plural* **-ci** /-kók sī/) *n* a spherical or ovoid bacterium that typically occurs in pairs, e.g. the pneumococcus responsible for pneumonia —**diplococcal** /-kók'l/ *adj* —**diplococcic** /-kóksik/ *adj*

diplodocus /di plóddəkəss, dípplō dōkəss/ *n* a large herbivorous dinosaur of the late Jurassic Period that had four legs and a very long neck and tail. Genus: *Diplodocus*. [Late 19C. < modern Latin, < Greek *diploos* 'double' + *dokos* 'beam'.]

diploë /dípplō ee/ *n* a layer of spongy bone tissue found between the harder inside and outside bone layers of the cranium [Late 16C. < Greek *diploē* 'doubling' < *diploos* 'double'.]

diploid /díp loyd/ *adj* possessing two matched sets of chromosomes in the cell nucleus, one set from each parent —**diploidic** /di plóydik/ *adj* —**diploidy** /díp loydi/ *n*

diploma /di plṓmə/ *n* **1** a certificate given by a college, university, or professional organization, indicating that somebody has completed a course of education or training and reached the required level of competence **2** a written document or charter, especially one that confers specific rights or privileges [Mid-17C. Via Latin < Greek, 'folded paper' < *diploun* 'fold, make double' < *diploos* 'double'.]

diplomacy /di plṓməssi/ *n* **1 INTERNATIONAL RELATIONS** the management of communication and relationships between nations by members and employees of each nation's government **2 SKILL IN INTERNATIONAL DEALINGS** skill in managing communication and relationships between nations **3 TACT** skill and tact in dealing with other people

diplomat /dípplə mat/ *n* **1** a member or employee of a government who represents his or her country in dealings with other nations, especially by working in an embassy or consulate abroad **2** somebody who is tactful and sensitive to other people [Early 19C. < French *diplomate*, back-formation < *diplomatique* 'diplomatic'.]

diplomate /dípplə mayt/ *n* a holder of a professional diploma

diplomatic /dípplə máttik/ *adj* **1 INVOLVING DIPLOMACY** concerned with or involving international diplomacy or the work of diplomats **2 TACTFUL** showing tact and skill in dealing with people **3 COPIED ACCURATELY** accurately reproducing an original document or printed text [Early 18C. < French *diplomatique* and modern Latin *diplomaticus* < Latin *diploma* (see DIPLOMA).] —**diplomatically** *adv*

diplomatic bag *n* a bag in which official correspondence travels between a government office and an embassy of that government in another country, carried by a special messenger

diplomatic corps *n* all the diplomats from other countries who reside in another nation

diplomatic immunity *n* the legal status of diplomats, who are not subject to the legal and taxation systems of a country in which they are resident as accredited representatives

diplomatics /dípplə máttiks/ *n* the study and verification of very old documents (+ *singular verb*)

diplomatist /di plṓmətist/ *n* a professional diplomat

diplont /díp plont/ *n* an organism whose cells, other than reproductive cells, have a diploid number of chromosomes in their nuclei —**diplontic** /di plóntik/ *adj*

diplopia /di plṓpi ə/ *n* double vision (*technical*) —**diplopic** /di plóppik/ *adj*

diplopod /dípplə pod/ *n* a millipede that has two pairs of legs on each body segment. Class: Diplopoda. [Mid-19C. < modern Latin *Diplopoda* < Greek *diploos* 'double' + *pod-* 'foot'.] —**diplopodous** /di plóppədəss/ *adj*

diplotene /dípplō teen/ *n* a stage in the first part of reproductive cell division (**meiosis**) in which paired chromosomes start to move apart from one another [Early 20C. < DIPLO- + Greek *tainia* 'band, ribbon'.]

dipody /díppədi/ (*plural* **-dies**) *n* a unit of poetry that consists of two stressed units or feet [Late 19C. < Greek *dipod-* 'two-footed'.]

dipole /dí pōl/ *n* two equal and opposite magnetized or electrically charged poles that are separated by a short distance —**dipolar** /dī pṓlər/ *adj*

dipole moment *n* **1** the product of one of the equal but opposite charges on two atoms in a molecule, and the distance separating them **2** the product of two equal and opposite magnetic poles or electric charges that are separated by a short distance

dipper /díppər/ *n* **1 SCOOP** a cup or ladle for dipping into liquid **2 SMALL WATER BIRD** a small plain-coloured bird that lives beside rivers and can swim and dive. Family: Cinclidae. **3 SOMETHING THAT DIPS** somebody or something, such as a machine, that dips objects in a liquid, e.g. in an industrial process

dippy /díppi/ (**-pier, -piest**) *adj* silly or eccentric, especially in an amusing or harmless way (*informal*) [Early 20C. < ?] —**dippily** *adv* —**dippiness** *n*

dipropellant /dīprə péllənt/ *n* AEROSP = **bipropellant**

diprotic /dī próttik/ *adj* with two transferable hydrogen protons [< DI-[1] + PROTON]

diprotodont /dī prṓtə dont/ *adj* describes a mammal that has the first pair of incisor teeth in each jaw enlarged ■ *n* a marsupial with enlarged incisors, e.g. kangaroos and wallabies. Order: Diprotodontia.

dipshit /díp shit/ *n* an offensive term for somebody who is regarded as unintelligent or unworthy of respect (*slang insult*)

dipso /díp sō/ (*plural* **-sos**) *n* a dipsomaniac (*slang insult*) [Late 19C. Shortening.]

dipsomania /dípsō máyni ə/ *n* a habitual and uncontrollable craving for alcohol (*dated*) [Mid-19C. < Greek *dipsa* 'thirst'.]

dipsomaniac /dípsō máyni ak/ *n* somebody with a habitual and uncontrollable craving for alcohol (*dated*) —**dipsomaniacal** /dípsō mə nī ək'l/ *adj*

dipstick /díp stik/ *n* **1** a measuring rod that is dipped into a container to indicate the depth of liquid in it, especially one used to measure the amount of oil in a car's engine **2** an unintelligent and incompetent person (*informal insult*)

⚡**dip switch** /díp-/ *n* **1** a control used to dip a car's headlights or raise them to full beam. US term **dimmer** *n.* **2** **2** = **DIP switch**

⚡**DIP switch, dip switch** *n* a switch that turns optional settings on or off on a computer component. Abbr of **dual in-line package**

dipteran /díptərən/, **dipteron** /-ron/ *n* a two-winged fly. Order: Diptera. [Mid-19C. < modern Latin *Diptera* < Greek *dipteros* 'two-winged'.] —**dipteral** *adj*

dipterous /díptərəss/ *adj* characteristic of or relating to the order Diptera of two-winged insects that includes flies, gnats, mosquitoes, and midges

~~diptheria~~ incorrect spelling of **diphtheria**

~~dipthong~~ incorrect spelling of **diphthong**

diptych /díptik/ *n* **1** a pair of paintings, especially religious paintings on two hinged panels **2** a pair of writing tablets joined by a hinge and having wooden backs and waxed writing surfaces, used especially in ancient Greece and Rome [Early 17C. Via late Latin *diptycha* < late Greek *diptukha* 'pair of writing tablets', plural of *diptukhos* 'folded in two' < *ptukhē* 'fold'.]

dipyridamole /dī pī ríddə mōl/ *n* a drug that widens the blood vessels. Use: treatment of angina, to prevent formation of blood clots. [Mid-20C. < DI-[1] + PYRIMIDINE + PIPERIDINE + AMINO- + -OL.]

diquat /dī kwot/ *n* a biodegradable herbicide used to control weeds in water [Mid-20C. < DI-[1] + QUATERNARY; because based on a quaternary amine.]

Dirac /di rák/, **Paul** (1902–84) British theoretical physicist

Dirac constant *n* a constant used in quantum mechanics that is Planck's constant divided by 2π

Dirac equation *n* an equation in quantum mechanics that describes the wave behaviour of an electron in an electromagnetic field, in a manner consistent with special relativity

dire /dīr/ (**direr, direst**) *adj* **1** characterized by severe, serious, or desperate circumstances **2** warning of a future disaster or serious consequences [Mid-16C. < Latin *dirus* 'fearful, awful, boding ill'.] —**direly** *adv* —**direness** *n*

direct /di rékt, dī-/ *v* **1** *vt* **SUPERVISE** to organize and control the work of an organization or a group of people ○ *I found her directing the efforts of a team of rescue workers.* **2** *vt* **INSTRUCT** to tell somebody to do something (*formal*) ○ *The medicine should be taken only as directed.* **3** *vt* **FOCUS ATTENTION ON** to focus attention or concentrate activities on something ○ *Please direct your attention towards the figures at the right of the screen.* **4** *vt* **AIM** to aim, point, or send something in a particular direction ○ *Direct the extinguisher at the base of the flames.* **5** *vt* **ADDRESS LETTER** to write an address on something to be delivered ○ *The envelope was directed to our offices.* **6** *vt* **GIVE DIRECTIONS** to tell somebody how to get to a place ○ *Can you direct me to the station?* **7** *vt* **ADDRESS** to say something to somebody specifically ○ *The remarks were directed to his sister.* **8** *vti* **SUPERVISE FILMS OR PLAYS** to be responsible for supervising the creative aspects of a film, play, or television programme, giving instructions and guidance to the actors and other people involved ○ *He has directed several films.* **9** *vt US* MUSIC = **conduct** *v.* 1 ■ *adj* **1 NOT STOPPING OR DEVIATING** going straight from one place or point to another ○ *a direct flight from Paris to Miami* **2 IMMEDIATE** lacking the influence of any other factors ○ *No direct link between the two events has been established.* **3 PERSONAL** not having a person, action, or process intervene ○ *We are in direct contact with them.* **4 STRAIGHTFORWARD** easy to understand or respond to ○ *The author makes a direct appeal to our emotions.* **5 PRECISE** having the characteristics of accuracy and precision ○ *a direct quotation* **6 IMMEDIATELY RELATED** connected by a straight and unbroken line of descent from parent to child ○ *a direct descendant of George Washington* **7 COMPLETE OR EXACT** showing complete contradiction or opposition ○ *Their conclusions were in direct contradiction to ours.* **8 DIRECTLY INVOLVING THE ELECTORATE** involving participation in government from the electorate rather than through electoral representatives ○ *direct democracy* **9 WORKING FROM PREMISE TO CONCLUSION** working immediately from the premise to the conclusion in proving something **10 MOVING WEST TO EAST** moving from west to east as observed from celestial north ■ *adv* **1 STRAIGHT WITHOUT DIVERSION** straight from one place or person to another, without a stop or diversion ○ *You can fly direct from Amsterdam to Chicago.* **2 DIRECTLY** by an immediate connection, without somebody or something intervening ○ *You can dial Calcutta direct.* [14C. < Latin *directus*, past participle of *dirigere* 'set straight, guide'.] —**directness** *n*

ϟ**direct access** *n* the ability to retrieve information directly from any part of a storage device without referring to the preceding data

direct action *n* a political or industrial action, such as a strike, a boycott, or civil disobedience, intended to have an immediate and noticeable effect that will influence a government or employer

direct coupling *n* direct connection of one part of a circuit to another without the use of transformers or capacitors, allowing both direct current and alternating current to flow along the connection —**direct-coupled** *adj*

direct current *n* electrical current that flows in only one direction and has a fairly constant average value. ◊ **alternating current**

direct debit *n* an arrangement by which sums of varying amounts that are owed at regular intervals, such as bills, are paid to the creditor directly from the payer's bank account

direct discourse *n US* GRAM = **direct speech**

direct dye *n* a dye that can be used directly on a fabric without needing an extra chemical (**mordant**) to fix the colour

direct evidence *n* evidence, such as a photograph, a document, or a witness's account, that provides direct factual information in a trial

direct free kick *n* a free kick in football that is awarded as compensation for a foul and can be taken as a direct shot at the opponent's goal

direct injection *n* the injection of fuel in liquid form into the cylinders of an internal-combustion engine, without previously passing it through a carburettor

direction /di réksh'n, dī-/ *n* **1 MANAGEMENT** the management or control of somebody or something by providing instructions **2 WAY** the way in which somebody or something goes, points, or faces ○ *They shook hands and walked off in opposite directions.* **3 SUPERVISION OF** the control and supervision of a group, person, or organization **4 DEVELOPMENT** the way in which something develops ○ *The organization has begun to take a new direction.* **5 ART OF DIRECTING** the art or practice of directing a film or play **6 SENSE OF PURPOSE** a feeling of having a definite goal or purpose ○ *He's a nice boy, but seems to lack a sense of direction.* **7 INSTRUCTION IN MUSIC** an instruction in a piece of music that shows how it should be played **8 CONDUCTING PERFORMERS** the process of conducting an orchestra or choir ■ **directions** *npl* **INSTRUCTIONS** instructions on how to get to a place or how to do something ○ *I need to stop the car and ask for directions.* —**directionless** *adj*

directional /di réksh'nəl, dī-/ *adj* **1 RELATING TO DIRECTION** showing, concerned with, or dependent on direction ○ *Use your directional lights to indicate the way you plan to turn.* **2 MORE EFFICIENT IN ONE DIRECTION** more efficient in a specific direction for transmitting and receiving sound waves, nuclear particles, light, or radio waves **3 RELATING TO CONTROL OF** showing or relating to the management or control of somebody's work, behaviour, or way of thinking **4 INDICATING TREND** showing the future direction in which something might go —**directionality** /di rékshə nálləti, dī-/ *n*

directional antenna *n* an antenna in which the transmitting and receiving characteristics are concentrated in certain directions, used when transmitting or receiving over very long distances, e.g. when receiving signals from space

directional drilling *n* a method of drilling for oil or gas in which special assemblies are used to turn a drill hole in the required direction

direction finder *n* a device used especially in navigation to determine the direction of a transmitted radio signal —**direction finding** *n*

directive /di réktiv, dī-/ *n* **1 ORDER** an order or official instruction **2 EU LAW PASSED IN MEMBER COUNTRIES** a law passed by the European Union that is then applied through the domestic law of its member states ■ *adj* **1 PROVIDING GUIDANCE** giving explicit guidance or instructions ○ *directive utterances* **2 SHOWING DIRECTION** indicating a direction ○ *directive signals*

direct labour *n* labour that is directly involved in the production of goods or the provision of services rather than, e.g. in administration or sales

direct lighting *n* a method of lighting in which a large percentage, usually not less than 90 per cent, of the emitted light is directed downwards

directly /di réktli, dī-/ *adv* **1 STRAIGHT** straight to a place or a person, or straight in a particular direction ○ *She went directly to the filing cabinet.* ○ *Your letter was sent directly to me.* **2 WITH NOTHING IN BETWEEN** without any person, thing, or event intervening ○ *I prefer to deal directly with senior management.* **3 COMPLETELY** in every respect ○ *I am directly opposed to everything that they stand for.* **4 CLEARLY** in a clear and unambiguous manner ○ *She refuses to say directly what the trouble is.* **5 IMMEDIATELY** at once ○ *I'll deal with it directly.* **6** *US* **SOON** in a short while (*regional*) ○ *Please take a seat, and I'll be with you directly.* ■ *conj* **IMMEDIATELY AFTER** as soon as something happens ○ *I left directly I heard the news.*

direct mail, direct mail shot *n* the use of mail addressed to potential customers as a way of advertising, or the promotional material that is mailed —**direct mailer** *n*

direct marketing, direct selling *n* methods of marketing by which a company deals directly with its end customers, including mail order by catalogue, direct mail, telephone sales, or the advertising of goods

direct object *n* the word or phrase in a sentence that indicates somebody or something directly affected by the action of the verb, such as 'cat' in 'she fed the cat'

director /di réktər, dī-/ *n* **1 HEAD OF MANAGEMENT** a manager of an organized group or a programme of activity **2 SOMEBODY WHO RUNS COMPANY** a member of the board that controls the affairs of a company **3 FILMMAKER** a supervisor of the actual making of a film or television programme **4 MUSICAL CONDUCTOR** a supervisor of the work of a group of musicians, especially an orchestra conductor [15C. Via Anglo-Norman < late Latin, < Latin *directus* (see DIRECT).] —**directorial** /dī rek táwri əl, di rék-/ *adj* —**directorially** *adv* —**directorship** *n*

directorate /di réktərət, dī-/ *n* a board of directors, e.g. of a company

director-general (*plural* **directors-general**) *n* the title given to the head of some large public organizations, such as the BBC in Britain

Director of Public Prosecutions *n* **1** the head of the Crown Prosecution Service, which is responsible for the conduct of all criminal prosecutions in England and Wales **2** in Australian states and at a federal level, the government official responsible for prosecutions on behalf of the Crown

director's chair *n* **1** the chair used by the director on the set of a film **2** a light folding chair with a wooden or metal frame with arms, and a canvas back and seat

ϟ**directory** /di réktəri, dī-/ *n* (*plural* **-ries**) **1 BOOK OF NAMES** a book alphabetically listing persons and organizations, usually with information about how to contact them **2 LIST OF TENANTS** a listing in the lobby of a building of those who live or work in the building, with their floor or room numbers **3 INDEX OF COMPUTER FILES** an index of files stored on a computer disk **4 RULE BOOK** a book of rules or instructions **5 GROUP OF DIRECTORS** a board of directors ■ *adj* **GIVING DIRECTION** providing direction or advice

directory enquiries *n* a service provided by a telephone company that provides the telephone number of anyone in the country who has agreed to have his or her number listed. US term **information** *n.* 3

direct primary *n* a primary election in the United States, in which the candidates who will seek office as nominees of a political party are chosen directly by popular vote

direct question *n* **1** a question directed to a specific person and requiring a response **2** a question repeated in the exact words that were spoken, placed inside quotation marks in writing

direct-reading *adj* allowing the immediate reading of a measurement, without intervening calculations

directrix /di rékt riks, dī-/ (*plural* **-trixes** *or* **-trices** /-seez/) *n* a fixed line used in constructing a curve or conic section, the distance from the line divided by the distance from a fixed point being identical for all points on the figure [Early 16C. < medieval Latin, feminine form of late Latin *director* (see DIRECTOR).]

direct selling *n* = **direct marketing**

direct speech *n* the repeating of speech by giving the exact words that were spoken, and in writing, conventionally shown inside quotation marks. US term **direct discourse**

direct tax *n* a tax that is levied directly on the income or capital of a person or organization rather than as part of the price of goods or services

dire straits *npl* a situation of emergency or desperate need

dire wolf *n* a large extinct mammal of the Pleistocene Epoch, similar to a wolf. Native to: North America. Latin name: *Canis dirus.*

dirge /durj/ *n* **1 FUNERAL HYMN** a song of mourning or lament, especially one about death or intended for a funeral **2 MOURNFUL MUSIC** a song or piece of music that sounds sad or depressing **3 FUNERAL SERVICE** a funeral service that is sung [Early 15C. < Latin *dirige* 'guide!' (first word of the antiphon in the funeral service, Psalm 5:8).]

dirham /déer ram, déerrəm/ *n* see table at **currency** [Late 18C. Via Arabic < Greek *drachmē* 'number of coins one hand can hold'.]

dirigible /dírrijəb'l/ *n* AIR = **airship** ■ *adj* able to be steered or navigated [Late 16C. < Latin *dirigere* 'direct, guide'; because an airship (unlike a balloon) can be steered.] —**dirigibility** /dírrijə bílləti/ *n*

dirigisme /dírri zhízəm/ *n* full and direct state control of a country's economy and social institutions [Mid-20C. < French, < *diriger* 'to direct' < Latin *dirigere*.] —**dirigiste** /dírri zhéest/ *adj*

diriment /dírrimənt/ *adj* invalidating a marriage in canon law [Mid-19C. < Latin *diriment-* < *dirimere* 'take apart'.]

dirk /durk/ *n* a dagger with a long straight blade, formerly used by Scottish Highlanders ■ *vt* to stab somebody with a dagger [Mid-16C. < ?]

Dirk Hartog Island /dúrk háar tog-/ uninhabited island off W Australia, the westernmost point on the continent. Area: 613 sq. km/234 sq. mi.

dirndl /dúrnd'l/ *n* **1 dirndl, dirndl skirt** a full skirt that is gathered at the waist **2** a dress with a full gathered skirt and a tight, low bodice that is worn over a short-sleeved blouse [Mid-20C. < German dialect, 'little girl'.]

dirt /durt/ *n* **1 UNCLEAN SUBSTANCE** a substance that spoils the cleanness of somebody or something ○ *There was a smear of dirt on his shirt.* **2 EARTH** earth, soil, or mud ○ *Children were playing in the dirt by the side of the road.* **3 HARD-PACKED EARTH** earth packed down to make a firm surface, especially mixed with gravel and cinders to make a racetrack for motor cycles or for horse racing ○ *dirt floors.* **4 SCANDALOUS FACTS** scandalous or damaging facts about somebody ○ *The local paper may have some dirt on the candidates.* **5 CORRUPTING INFLUENCE** something such as pornography or bad language that is considered to have a corrupting influence [13C. < Old Norse *drit* 'excrement' < Germanic.] ◇ **dig the dirt on somebody** *or* **something** to search for scandalous information about somebody or something in order to make it public

dirt bike *n* a motorcycle designed to be ridden across country or on dirt roads

dirt-cheap *adj, adv* extremely cheap or cheaply (*informal*)

dirt-poor *adj* having so little money that the basic needs of life can scarcely be satisfied

dirt track *n* **1** a narrow road or path that is not surfaced, but consists of earth **2** a track of earth mixed with gravel and cinders that is used for horse racing or motorcycle racing

dirty /dúrti/ *adj* (**-ier, -iest**) **1 NOT CLEAN** marked by dirt or covered in dirt ○ *dirty fingernails* **2 CAUSING DIRT** creating dirt or pollution ○ *a battered truck with a dirty engine* **3 MAKING SOMEBODY GRIMY** likely to cause somebody to be filthy or grimy ○ *Working on cars is a dirty job.* **4 NOT KEPT UP** lacking care and maintenance **5 NOT HONEST OR LEGAL** lacking honesty or moral integrity, especially if the rules of a game or law have been broken ○ *dirty tactics* **6** *US* **RELATING TO ILLEGAL DRUGS** relating to the use or sale of illegal drugs by somebody (*slang*) **7 MALICIOUS** characterized by extreme meanness and cruelty ○ *a dirty lie* **8 SEXUALLY SUGGESTIVE** concerned with sex, especially in a way that is rude or suggestive **9 ANGRY** expressing anger, displeasure, or disapproval ○ *a dirty look* **10 DESPICABLE** immoral or behaving in a despicable way (*informal*) **11 LACKING BRIGHTNESS OR CLARITY** lacking in lustre or clarity (*often in combination*) ○ *The walls were a dirty green.* **12 STORMY** characterized by heavy rain and strong winds ○ *dirty weather* **13 RADIOACTIVE** producing radioactive contamination ■ *adv* (**-ier, -iest**) **1 UNFAIRLY** in an unfair or dishonest way ○ *You have to fight dirty if you want to win.* **2 SUGGESTIVELY** in a sexually suggestive or indecent way ■ *v* (**-ies, -ying, -ied**) **1** *vti* **MAKE DIRTY** to make something or somebody dirty, or become dirty ○ *He wouldn't want to dirty his hands with that kind of work.* **2** *vt* **DISHONOUR** to make something seem less honest or honourable ○ *to dirty their reputation* —**dirtily** *adv* —**dirtiness** *n* ◇ **get your hands dirty 1** to perform menial or manual labour or work very hard **2** to perform or participate in a degrading or unpleasant act

SYNONYMS ***dirty, filthy, grubby, grimy, soiled, squalid, unclean***

CORE MEANING: not clean

dirty stained or marked with dirt; **filthy** extremely or disgustingly dirty; **grubby** slightly dirty; **grimy** heavily ingrained with accumulated dirt; **soiled** stained or marked, especially during normal use; **squalid** insanitary and unpleasant; **unclean** dirty or impure, especially in moral or religious contexts.

dirty linen, dirty laundry *n* personal matters that it would be embarrassing or disadvantageous to let other people know about ○ *Don't wash your dirty linen in public.*

dirty old man *n* an older man who shows an interest in sex that is perceived as immoral, perverted, or generally unpleasant (*informal insult*)

dirty trick *n* **UNFAIR ACTION** something unfair or dishonest that is done to gain an advantage ■ **dirty tricks** *npl* **1 UNFAIR POLITICAL TACTICS** tactics used in a political campaign to discredit an opponent in a way that is not completely fair or honest **2 SPY TACTICS** secret activities carried out by the spies of one government in order to disrupt or destroy the internal functioning of another nation (*informal*) **3 COMMERCIAL ESPIONAGE** the activity of stealing secret products or processes from one company and selling them to rival companies (*informal*)

dirty word *n* **1** a swearword or offensive word **2** something that is disapproved of ○ *Delay seems to be a dirty word in this office!*

dirty work *n* something that somebody wants to be done that is unpleasant, unfair, unkind, dishonest, or illegal

dis /diss/ (**disses, dissing, dissed**), **diss** *vt* (*slang*) **1** to treat somebody without respect, e.g. by talking back to somebody in authority, or by being purposely rude or inconsiderate **2** to criticize somebody or something [Late 20C. < ?]

Dis /diss/ *n* **1** = **Pluto** *n.* 1 **2** in Roman mythology, the underworld, or region of the dead. Greek equivalent **Hades**

dis- *prefix* **1** to undo, do the opposite ○ *disapprove* **2** opposite or absence of ○ *discourtesy* **3** to deprive of, remove from ○ *dishonour* **4** not ○ *disobedient* **5** to free from ○ *disburden* **6** completely ○ *dissever* [Directly and via Old French *des-* < Latin *dis-* < *dis* 'apart']

disability /díssə bílləti/ (*plural* **-ties**) *n* **1 RESTRICTED CAPABILITY TO PERFORM PARTICULAR ACTIVITIES** an inability to perform some or all of the tasks of daily life **2 MEDICAL CONDITION RESTRICTING ACTIVITIES** a medically diagnosed condition that makes it difficult to engage in the activities of daily life **3 LEGAL DISQUALIFIER** something that causes somebody to be regarded in law as ineligible to perform a particular transaction

disability clause *n* a clause in a life insurance policy, indicating the conditions that will apply if the holder becomes unable to work, including release from payment of further premiums

disable /di sáyb'l/ (**-bles, -bling, -bled**) *vt* **1 RESTRICT IN CERTAIN ACTIVITIES** to make somebody unable to perform the activities needed to earn a living or to carry out the basic tasks of daily life without difficulty **2 STOP FROM WORKING** to prevent a machine, weapon, system, or device from working by disconnecting a part of it **3 DISQUALIFY LEGALLY** to make somebody ineligible in law to perform a particular transaction —**disablement** *n*

disabled /di sáyb'ld/ *adj* **1 UNABLE TO PERFORM PARTICULAR ACTIVITIES** describes somebody with a condition that makes it difficult to perform some or all the basic tasks of daily life **2 UNABLE TO OPERATE** incapable of performing or functioning ■ *npl* **DISABLED PEOPLE** people with disabilities

disabuse /díssə byóoz/ (**-buses, -busing, -bused**) *vt* to tell somebody or make somebody realize that an idea is not true ○ *I was quickly disabused of my idealistic notions about the campaign.* ○ *She disabused him of many old prejudices.* [Early 17C. < ABUSE in the obsolete sense 'a delusion'.] —**disabusal** *n*

disaccharide /dī sákə rīd/ *n* a sugar consisting of two linked monosaccharide units

disaccord /díssə káwrd/ *n* lack of harmony or agreement (*formal*) ■ *vi* to disagree or not be in accordance with one another (*formal*)

disadvantage /díssəd vaántij/ *n* **1 BAD INFLUENCE** something that makes a situation less good or that makes somebody or something less effective or desirable **2 BAD SITUATION** a situation that is unfavourable to somebody ○ *He was at a disadvantage, having only received the documents that morning.* **3 LOSS** injury, loss, or damage (*formal*) ■ *vt* (**-tages, -taging, -taged**) **COUNT AGAINST** to put somebody or something at a disadvantage

disadvantaged /díssəd vaántijd/ *adj* **1** in a worse position than somebody else or other people **2** unable to perform well in a competitive or military endeavour

disadvantageous /díss advən táyjəss, diss ádvən-/ *adj* not helpful or favourable —**disadvantageously** *adv* —**disadvantageousness** *n*

disaffect /díssə fékt/ *vt* to make somebody dissatisfied with somebody or something, especially somebody to whom respect or loyalty is owed —**disaffected** *adj* —**disaffectedly** *adv* —**disaffectedness** *n* —**disaffection** *n*

disaffiliate /díssə fílli ayt/ (**-ates, -ating, -ated**) *vti* to end the connection or affiliation of one group with another, or to withdraw a personal association from a group or organization formally ○ *The group was formally disaffiliated from its parent body at the end of 1985.* —**disaffiliation** /díssə fílli áysh'n/ *n*

disaffirm /díssə fúrm/ *vt* **1** to say that something is not true or that the opposite is true (*formal*) **2** to alter a legal decision or to refuse to recognize or acknowledge something formally —**disaffirmance** *n* —**disaffirmation** /díss affər máysh'n/ *n*

disaggregate /diss ággrəgət, -gayt/ (**-gates, -gating, -gated**) *vti* to separate something into its component parts, or to break apart —**disaggregation** /díss agrə gáysh'n/ *n*

disagree /díssə grée/ *v* **1** *vt* **NOT AGREE** to have or put forward a different view or opinion from somebody or from each other **2** *vi* **NOT MATCH** to fail to be in accordance with something, or to show a different result **3** *vi* **AFFECT BADLY** to have an unpleasant effect on somebody ○ *I love oysters, but they disagree with me.* **4** *vi* **DISAPPROVE OF** to be opposed to a rule, law, or idea [15C. < French *désagréer* < *agréer* 'agree'.]

SYNONYMS ***disagree, differ, argue, dispute, take issue with, contradict, agree to differ, be at odds***

CORE MEANING: to have or express a difference of opinion with somebody

disagree to have or put forward a different view or opinion from somebody; **differ** to have different opinions about something; **argue** to express disagreement with somebody, especially continuously or angrily; **dispute** to have a heated argument; **take issue with** to disagree strongly with somebody or something; **contradict** to argue against the truth or correctness of somebody's statement or claim; **agree to differ** to stop arguing and accept that the opposing viewpoints are irreconcilable; **be at odds** to be in disagreement, especially over a period of time or about a particular issue.

disagreeable /díssə grée əb'l/ *adj* **1** causing feelings that are not enjoyable **2** lacking courtesy or constantly finding a reason to disagree with somebody —**disagreeability** /díssə gree ə bílləti/ *n* —**disagreeableness** *n* —**disagreeably** *adv*

disagreement /díssə gréemənt/ *n* **1 FAILURE TO AGREE ABOUT** the fact of having or expressing a different opinion and failing to agree about something **2 SLIGHT ARGUMENT** a situation in which a number of people or groups argue **3 DIFFERENCE** failure to be in accordance with something

disallow /díssə lów/ *vt* **1** to refuse to accept something because it is not true, valid, or correctly done **2** to cancel a privilege or entitlement, or refuse to allow something that was previously allowed —**disallowable** *adj* —**disallowance** *n*

~~**disallusion**~~ incorrect spelling of **disillusion**

disambiguate /díss am bíggyoo ayt/ (**-ates, -ating, -ated**) *vt* to establish the true meaning of an expression, regulation, or ruling that is confusing or that could be interpreted in more than one way —**disambiguation** /díss am bíggyoo áysh'n/ *n*

~~**disapear**~~ incorrect spelling of **disappear**

~~**disapointed**~~ incorrect spelling of **disappointed**

disappear /díssə péer/ *v* **1** *vi* **VANISH FROM SIGHT** to cease to be seen, e.g. by moving away, or going behind or into something **2** *vi* **NOT BE FOUND** to be gone from or no longer be seen in a place without any explanation **3** *vi* **CEASE TO EXIST** to no longer exist **4** *vt* **CAUSE OPPONENT TO DISAPPEAR** to make a political opponent disappear by arresting or killing them without any process of law —**disappearance** *n*

disappeared /díssə péerd/ *npl* people who have been arrested by a regime that they opposed and whose subsequent fate is not known [Late 20C. Translation of Spanish *desaparecido*.]

disapplication /díss appli káysh'n/ *n* a special exemption from the National Curriculum given to a school

disappoint /díssə póynt/ *v* **1** *vi* to be less good, attractive, or satisfactory than was hoped or expected **2** *vt* to let somebody down by not doing something or by something not happening as hoped or expected [15C. < French *désappointer* 'deprive of an appointment'.]

disappointed /díssə póyntid/ *adj* unhappy because something was not as good, attractive, or satisfactory as expected, or because something hoped for or expected did not happen —**disappointedly** *adv*

disappointing /díssə póynting/ *adj* not as good, attractive, or satisfactory as was expected or hoped —**disappointingly** *adv*

disappointment /díssə póyntmənt/ *n* **1 FEELING OF BEING LET DOWN** a feeling of sadness or frustration because something was not as good, attractive, or satisfactory as expected, or because something hoped for did not happen **2 SOMETHING DISAPPOINTING** something or somebody that disappoints **3 FRUSTRATION** the frustration of somebody's hopes or wishes

Disappointment, Lake /díssə póyntmənt/ dry salt lake in Western Australia. Area: 330 sq. km/130 sq. mi.

disapprobation /diss áppra báysh'n/ *n* the expression of moral or social disapproval (*formal*)

disapproval /díssə próov'l/ *n* dislike or condemnation of somebody or something immoral or bad in some way

disapprove /díssə próov/ (**-proves, -proving, -proved**) *v* **1** *vi* to dislike, look down on, or condemn somebody or something as being immoral or bad in some way **2** *vt* to refuse to give approval or agree to something (*formal*) —**disapproving** *adj* —**disapprovingly** *adv*

SYNONYMS ***disapprove, frown on, object, criticize, condemn, deplore, denounce, censure***

CORE MEANING: to have an unfavourable opinion of something or somebody

disapprove to judge somebody or something negatively based on personal standards; **frown on** to dislike or disapprove of something; **object** to be opposed to something, or express opposition; **criticize** to point out flaws or faults; **condemn** to give an unfavourable judgment on somebody or something; **deplore** to disapprove of something strongly; **denounce** to criticize or condemn publicly and harshly;

censure to make a formal, often public or official, statement of disapproval.

disarm /diss aárm/ *v* **1** *vti* **GIVE UP WEAPONS** to give up a supply of weapons or reduce the strength of armed forces, or to force another nation to do this **2** *vt* **DEFUSE BOMB** to make a bomb unable to explode, or to make a weapon incapable of being fired **3** *vt* **WIN OVER** to make somebody less hostile or suspicious and more inclined to act in a friendly way ○ *They disarmed us with their confidence and skill.* —**disarmer** *n*

disarmament /diss aármәmәnt/ *n* **1** the process of reducing a nation's supply of weapons or the strength of its armed forces ○ *a believer in negotiated mutual disarmament* **2** the condition of having given up weapons ○ *Disarmament brought peace to the troubled region.*

disarming /diss aárming/ *adj* making somebody feel more friendly or trusting —**disarmingly** *adv*

disarrange /díssә ráynj/ (**-ranges, -ranging, -ranged**) *vt* to disturb or spoil the order or arrangement of something —**disarrangement** *n*

disarray /díssә ráy/ *n* **1** **DISORGANIZED STATE** a disorganized and confused state ○ *The meeting was thrown into disarray by the surprise announcement.* **2** **UNTIDINESS** a state of untidiness, especially in dress ■ *vt* **1** **MAKE DISORGANIZED** to make something confused and disorganized **2** **UNDRESS** to remove somebody's clothes (*archaic*)

disarticulate /díss aar tíkyoo layt/ (**-lates, -lating, -lated**) *vti* to separate something at the joints, or to become separated at the joints —**disarticulation** /díss aar tíkyoo láysh'n/ *n* —**disarticulator** *n*

disassemble /díssә sémb'l/ (**-bles, -bling, -bled**) *vt* to take something apart, e.g. a piece of machinery —**disassembly** *n*

disassociate /díssә sṓshi ayt, -sṓssi-/ (**-ates, -ating, -ated**), **dissociate** *vt* **1** to end an association or relationship with another person or group ○ *She had disassociated herself from that clique years ago.* **2** to deny any connection or involvement with somebody or something ○ *In a press conference, the MP attempted to disassociate himself from the scandal.*

disassociation /díssә sōshi áysh'n, -sōssi-/, **dissociation** *n* **1** the termination of an association or relationship with another person or group **2** the denial of any connection or involvement with somebody or something else

USAGE disassociation or **dissociation**? Both these words, and the verbs (*disassociate, dissociate*) from which they come, share the meaning 'separation from a relationship or union with another', and in this sense they are interchangeable: *sought disassociation/dissociation from the scandal; sought to dissociate/disassociate themselves from the scandal.* ***Dissociation***, however, does have two senses not shared by ***disassociation***: 'in psychology and psychiatry, separation of emotions as a defence mechanism' and 'in chemistry, the breaking up of a molecule into simpler components'. Do not confuse the two words.

disaster /di zaástәr/ *n* **1** an event that causes serious loss, destruction, hardship, unhappiness, or death **2** somebody or something that fails completely, especially in a way that is distressing, embarrassing, or laughable (*informal*) [Late 16C. Via French *désastre* < Italian *disastro* 'ill-starred' < Latin *astrum* 'star' < Greek *astron*.]

disaster area *n* **1** a place that is officially declared to be in a state of emergency and in need of special assistance after a natural disaster ○ *The southern half of the state has been declared a disaster area.* **2** a very messy, untidy, or disorganized place or situation (*informal*)

disaster movie *n* a film that deals with a disaster such as an earthquake or plane crash in a dramatic and spectacular way

~~**disasterous**~~ incorrect spelling of **disastrous**

disastrous /di zaástrәss/ *adj* **1** having seriously damaging results **2** performed in an incompetent or awkward way [Late 16C. < French *désastreux* < Italian *disastro* (see DISASTER).] —**disastrously** *adv* —**disastrousness** *n*

~~**disatisfied**~~ incorrect spelling of **dissatisfied**

disavow /díssә vów/ *vt* to deny any knowledge of, responsibility for, or association with somebody or something —**disavowable** *adj* —**disavowal** *n* —**disavowedly** /díssә vówidli/ *adv* —**disavower** *n*

disband /diss bánd/ *vti* to break up as a group or organization, or to cause a group or organization to break up —**disbandment** *n*

disbar /diss baár/ (**-bars, -barring, -barred**) *vt* to take away officially the right of a barrister to practise law —**disbarment** *n*

disbelief /díss bi leéf/ *n* the feeling of not believing or of not being able to believe somebody or something

disbelieve /díss bi leév/ (**-lieves, -lieving, -lieved**) *v* **1** *vt* to think that something somebody has said is untrue **2** *vi* to have no belief in something, especially in God or religion —**disbeliever** *n* —**disbelieving** *adj* —**disbelievingly** *adv*

disbenefit /diss bénnifit/ *n* something that makes a situation disadvantageous or unfavourable

disbud /diss búd/ (**-buds, -budding, -budded**) *vt* **1** to remove buds or shoots from a plant so that the remaining ones will be larger and stronger **2** to remove the horns from a young animal

disburden /diss búrd'n/ *vt* **1** to gain relief by telling somebody about something that is causing anxiety or guilt **2** to free somebody or something from a burden or constraint —**disburdenment** *n*

disburse /diss búrss/ (**-burses, -bursing, -bursed**) *vt* to pay out money, especially from a fund [Mid-16C. < Old French *desbourser* 'remove from the purse' < *bourse* 'purse'.] —**disbursable** *adj* —**disbursement** *n* —**disburser** *n*

disc[1] /disk/, **disk** *n* **1** **ROUND FLAT OBJECT** object that is, or appears to be, thin, flat, and circular **2** **BRAKE PART** a circular piece of metal around the hub of a vehicle wheel, against which the pads of a disc brake press **3** **STEEL BLADE** a circular steel blade with a sharpened edge that is used on a disc harrow or plough **4** **PART BETWEEN BONES OF SPINE** a flat round structure in the skeleton of a person or animal that separates the bones of the spine **5** **CENTRE OF FLOWER HEAD** the central part of the flower head of a composite plant, made up of tiny tubular flowers [Mid-17C. Directly or via French *disque* < Latin *discus* 'dish, quoit' < Greek *diskos* (see DISH).]

disc[2] /disk/ *n* a record (*informal dated*)

disc. *abbr* **1** discount **2** discovered

disc- *prefix* = **disco-** (*before vowels*)

discalced /diss kálst/ *adj* wearing sandals or going barefoot in accordance with the rules of some orders of monks, friars, or nuns [Mid-17C. Shortening of obsolete *discalceated* 'with shoes removed' < Latin *calceare* 'to shoe' < *calceus* 'shoe'.]

discant /díss kant/ *n, vi* MUSIC = **descant** —**discanter** *n*

discard /diss kaárd/ *v* **1** *vt* **THROW AWAY** to get rid of something that is not wanted or needed **2** *vt* **REJECT CARD** in some card games, to put down a card from a hand and not play it **3** *vti* **PLAY CARD** in a card game such as bridge or whist, to play a card so that it has no value, because it is neither in the required suit nor a trump ■ *n* **1** **ACT OF DISCARDING** the act of discarding a playing card **2** **SOMETHING DISCARDED** somebody or something that has been discarded —**discardable** *adj* —**discarder** *n*

discarnate /diss kaárnәt, -nayt/ *adj* lacking a physical body [Mid-17C. < DIS- + Latin *carn-* 'flesh'.]

disc brake *n* a brake that works by the friction of a caliper or pads against a rotating disc

disc camera *n* a camera that uses film on a disc rather than a spool or cartridge

discern /di súrn, -zúrn/ *v* **1** *vt* **SEE OR NOTICE SOMETHING UNCLEAR** to see something that is not very clear or obvious **2** *vt* **UNDERSTAND** to understand something that is not immediately obvious **3** *vti* **DISTINGUISH** to be able to tell the difference between two or more things [14C. Directly or via French *discerner* < Latin *discernere* 'separate off' < *cernere* 'separate, determine'.] —**discernably** *adv* —**discerner** *n* —**discernible** *adj*

discernibly /di súrnәbli, -zúrnәbli/, **discernably** *adv* in an obvious way or to a noticeable extent ○ *not discernibly different*

discerning /di súrning, -zúrning/ *adj* showing good judgment and good taste —**discerningly** *adv*

discernment /di súrnmәnt, -zúrnmәnt/ *n* good taste and judgment

disc flower, **disc floret** *n* a tiny tubular flower that is one of the group that forms the centre disc of the flower head of certain composite plants, e.g. the daisy

discharge *v* /diss chaárj/ (**-charges, -charging, -charged**) **1** *vti* **EMIT OR DUMP LIQUID OR GAS** to emit, give off, or dispose of a gas or liquid **2** *vt* **DISMISS FROM INSTITUTIONAL SETTING** to allow or write the orders for somebody to leave an institution, especially a hospital, or to make the decision yourself to leave such a place after being an inpatient **3** *vt* **CARRY OUT** to carry out a duty, responsibility, or promise (*formal*) **4** *vt* **FREE OR RELEASE FROM DUTY** to excuse or release somebody from a duty or obligation **5** *vt* **DISMISS EMPLOYEE** to dismiss somebody from a job (*formal*) **6** *vt* **PAY DEBT** to pay a debt in full (*formal*) **7** *vti* **SHOOT OR BE SHOT FROM** to fire a weapon or to be fired from a weapon (*formal*) **8** *vt* **BE RELEASED FROM ARMED FORCES** to be formally released from service in the armed forces **9** *vt* **RELEASE OR ACQUIT** to release a prisoner or acquit somebody in a court of law **10** *vt* **CANCEL COURT ORDER** to cancel or annul a court order **11** *vti* **OFFLOAD SHIP'S CARGO** to unload cargo from a ship **12** *vti* **LOSE ELECTRIC CHARGE** to lose or release electric charge by the addition or loss of electrons from a stationary body, such as in static electricity **13** *vi* **SPARK** to give off electricity suddenly in the form of a spark or arc **14** *vti* **DRAIN ELECTRICITY** to drain slowly, or make the electricity in a battery drain slowly **15** *vt* **RELEASE PRESSURE ON BUILDING** to release the pressure on part of a building by spreading it over adjacent parts **16** *vt* **BLEACH FABRIC** to remove the colour from fabric by bleaching it **17** *vi* **RUN OR BLUR** to undergo a running or blurring of dyes ■ *n* /diss chaarj/ **1** **DISMISSAL FROM INSTITUTION** permission or orders to leave an institution, especially a hospital, after being a patient **2** **SEPARATION FROM ARMED FORCES** formal and official release of somebody from the armed forces, or a document certifying this **3** **MUCUS** a flow of fluid from the body, especially an unusual or large flow of mucus from the bodily orifices or pus from a wound **4** **EMISSION OF SUBSTANCES** the emission, giving off, or dumping of gases, liquids, or chemicals **5** **RATE OF EMISSION** the rate at which a gas or liquid is being emitted **6** **PERFORMANCE OF DUTY** the carrying out of a duty, obligation, responsibility, or promise (*formal*) **7** **DEBT PAYMENT** the payment of a debt (*formal*) **8** **FIRING** the firing of a gun (*formal*) **9** **PRISONER'S RELEASE** the release of a prisoner from custody **10** **PRODUCTION OF ELECTRICITY** the process of converting chemical energy into electrical energy, e.g. in a battery **11** **CONTINUOUS FLOW OF ELECTRICITY THROUGH AIR** the continuous flow of electric energy through air or a gas as a result of ionization, as occurs when a spark jumps a gap, or at a reduced pressure, as in a fluorescent lamp **12** **CARGO OFFLOADING** the unloading of cargo **13** **VOLUME OF RIVER WATER FLOW** the volume of water in a river flowing past a particular point during a specific time interval [14C. Via Old French *descharger* < late Latin *discar(r)icare* 'unload' < Latin *car(ri)care* 'to load'.] —**dischargeable** *adj* —**discharger** *n*

discharged bankrupt *n* somebody whose period of bankruptcy has come to an end and who is no longer bound by the restrictions that apply to people who have been declared bankrupt

discharge lamp *n* an electric lamp that glows as a result of electricity passing through a gas

discharge tube *n* a tube filled with low-pressure gas that glows when it conducts electricity at a given voltage. Use: neon and fluorescent lights.

disc harrow *n* a harrow with a series of discs set at an angle on one or more axles that loosen the soil when moved over ploughed land

disci plural of **discus**

disci- *prefix* = **disco-** (*before vowels*)

disciple /di sīp'l/ *n* **1** a strong believer in the teachings of a leader, a philosophy, or a religion, who tries to follow them **2** **disciple, Disciple** one of the 12 original followers of Jesus Christ, according to the Bible [Pre-12C. < Latin *discipulus* 'learner' < *discere* 'learn'.] —**discipleship** *n* —**discipular** /di sípyoolәr/ *adj*

Disciple *n* a member of the Disciples of Christ

Disciples of Christ *n* a Protestant denomination of the Christian Church, founded in the United States in 1809 by Thomas and Alexander Campbell

disciplinarian /díssәpli náiri әn/ *n* an enforcer of strictly defined rules who punishes people who break them

disciplinary /díssәplinәri/ *adj* **1** relating to the enforcing of rules and the punishing of people who break them **2** relating to an academic subject ○ *Teachers tried to cut across traditional disciplinary boundaries in their lessons.* —**disciplinarily** *adv* —**disciplinarity** /díssәpli nárrәti/ *n*

discipline /díssəplin/ *n* 1 **MAKING PEOPLE OBEY RULES** the practice or methods of ensuring that people obey rules by teaching them to do so and punishing them if they do not 2 **ORDER AND CONTROL** a controlled orderly state, especially in a class of schoolchildren 3 **CALM CONTROLLED BEHAVIOUR** the ability to behave in a controlled and calm way even in a difficult or stressful situation 4 **CONSCIOUS CONTROL OVER LIFESTYLE** mental self-control used in directing or changing behaviour, learning something, or training for something 5 **ACTIVITY OR SUBJECT** a subject or field of activity, e.g. an academic subject 6 **PUNISHMENT** punishment designed to teach somebody to obey rules 7 **CHURCH RULES** the system of rules and punishment used in a particular religious denomination ■ *v* (**-plines, -plining, -plined**) 1 *vr* **MAKE YOURSELF DO SOMETHING REGULARLY** to make yourself act or work in a controlled or regular way 2 *vt* **PUNISH** to punish somebody because he or she has broken the rules 3 *vt* **TEACH OBEDIENCE OR ORDER TO** to teach somebody to obey rules or to behave in an ordered or controlled way [13C. Directly or via French *descepline* < Latin *disciplina* 'instruction given to a learner' < *discipulus* (see DISCIPLE).] —**disciplinable** *adj* —**disciplinal** /díssə plín'l/ *adj* —**disciplined** *adj* —**discipliner** *n*

disc jockey *n* MUSIC = **DJ** *n.* 1

disclaim /diss kláym/ *v* 1 *vt* **DENY A CONNECTION WITH** to deny that you know about something or that you are responsible for something 2 *vt* **DENY VALIDITY OF** to refuse to accept the validity or authority of something 3 *vti* **RENOUNCE LEGAL RIGHT** to renounce a legal claim or right to something [15C. < Anglo-Norman *disclaimer* 'not to claim' < Old French *clamer* 'to claim'.] —**disclamation** /dísklə máysh'n/ *n*

disclaimer /diss kláymər/ *n* 1 **REFUSAL TO ACCEPT RESPONSIBILITY** a statement refusing to accept responsibility for something, e.g. a written warning stating a possible hazard associated with a product or service and denying legal liability for any injury 2 **STATEMENT RENOUNCING LEGAL RIGHT** a statement saying that somebody gives up a legal right or claim to something, e.g. damages arising from an accident 3 **DENIAL OF KNOWLEDGE** a statement denying knowledge of something

disclose /diss klṓz/ (**-closes, -closing, -closed**) *vt* 1 to reveal something that has been kept a secret 2 to reveal something that has been covered or hidden [15C. < Old French *desclos-*, present stem of *desclore* < medieval Latin *disclaudere* 'to open' < Latin *claudere* 'to close'.] —**disclosable** *adj* —**discloser** *n*

disclosing agent *n* a dye in liquid or tablet form that colours something, especially the teeth to show plaque

disclosure /dis klṓzhər/ *n* the revealing of information that was previously kept secret, or the information that is revealed

disco /dískō/ *n* 1 **disco, discotheque CLUB OR PARTY WITH DANCING** a club or party where people dance to recorded pop music, often introduced by a DJ 2 **STEADY-BEAT POP MUSIC FOR DANCING** a style of pop music, popular in the 1970s for dancing, with a steady, pronounced beat 3 **STYLE OF DANCING TO DISCO MUSIC** popular dancing with hips and arms moving to the repetitive beat of disco music 4 **EQUIPMENT PLAYING RECORDED MUSIC FOR DANCERS** the audio equipment used to play records for crowds of people to dance to, usually consisting of amplifiers, speakers, and a record, tape, or CD deck, often with lighting equipment ■ *vi* (**-cos, -coing, -coed**) **TAKE PART IN DISCO DANCING** to dance to disco music (*informal*) [Mid-20C. Shortening of DISCOTHEQUE.]

disco- *prefix* 1 disk ○ *discoid* 2 phonograph record ○ *discography* [Via Latin < Greek *diskos* (see DISH)]

discobolus /diss kóbbələss/ (*plural* **-li** /-lī/), **discobolos** (*plural* **-li**) *n* a discus thrower in ancient Greece [Early 18C. Via Latin < Greek *diskobolos* 'disc-throwing' < *diskos* (see DISH) + *-bolos* 'throwing' < *ballein* 'throw'.]

discography /diss kóggrəfi/ (*plural* **-phies**) *n* a list of the recordings made by a performer, group, or recordings of a specific category of music —**discographer** *n* —**discographic** /dískə gráffik/ *adj*

discoid /dísk oyd/ *n* a disc-shaped object or part ■ *adj* **discoid, discoidal** shaped like a disc [Late 18C. < Greek *diskoeidēs* < *diskos* (see DISH).]

discolour /diss kúllər/ *vti* to change, or make something change, from the original or proper colour and take on an unpleasant, faded, darkened, or dirty appearance [14C. Directly or via Old French *descolorer* < medieval Latin *discolorare* < Latin *colorare* 'to colour'.] —**discolouration** *n* —**discoloured** /dis kúllərd/ *adj* —**discolourment** *n*

discombobulate /dískəm bóbbyōō layt/ (**-lates, -lating, -lated**) *vt US, Can* to throw somebody into a state of confusion (*informal; often passive*) [Mid-19C. Probably alteration of DISCOMPOSE or DISCOMFIT.] —**discombobulation** /dískəm bóbbyōō láysh'n/ *n*

discomfit /dis kúmfit/ *vt* 1 to make somebody feel confused, uneasy, or embarrassed 2 to frustrate somebody's plans (*formal*) [13C. < Old French *desconfit*, past participle of *desconfire* 'destroy' < *confire* 'make' < Latin *conficere* (see CONFECT).] —**discomfiter** *n* —**discomfiture** *n*

discomfort /dis kúmfərt/ *n* 1 **STATE OF PHYSICAL UNEASE** very mild pain or a feeling of being physically uncomfortable 2 **EMBARRASSMENT** feelings of awkwardness and embarrassment 3 **CAUSE OF UNEASE** something that causes physical or mental uneasiness 4 **CAUSE OF LACK OF COMFORT** something that makes somebody feel physically uncomfortable or inconvenienced ■ *vt* **MAKE UNCOMFORTABLE** to make somebody feel physically or mentally uncomfortable [14C. < Old French *desconfort* < *desconforter* 'deprive of comfort' < *conforter* 'to comfort'.] —**discomfortable** *adj* —**discomforting** *adj* —**discomfortingly** *adv*

discommode /dískə mṓd/ (**-modes, -moding, -moded**) *vt* to cause problems or inconvenience to somebody (*formal*) [Early 18C. < obsolete French *discommoder* 'deprive of convenience' < Latin *commodus* 'suitable'.] —**discommodious** *adj* —**discommodiously** *adv*

discompose /dískəm pṓz/ (**-poses, -posing, -posed**) *vt* to make somebody lose his or her composure —**discomposedly** /dískəm pṓzidli/ *adv*

discomposure /dískəm pṓzhər/ *n* the state of being anxious, confused, or physically disordered

disconcert /dískən súrt/ *vt* 1 to make somebody feel ill at ease, slightly confused, or taken aback 2 to prevent somebody from carrying out plans or arrangements and therefore create confusion [Mid-17C. < French *desconcerter* 'bring out of agreement' < Old Italian *concertare* 'bring into agreement'.] —**disconcerted** *adj* —**disconcertedly** *adv* —**disconcertion** *n* —**disconcertment** *n*

disconcerting /dískən súrting/ *adj* making somebody feel uneasy confusion and dismay —**disconcertingly** *adv*

disconfirm /dískən fúrm/ *vt* to show that something such as a theory cannot be right —**disconfirmation** /díss konfər máysh'n/ *n*

disconformity /dískən fáwrməti/ (*plural* **-ties**) *n* a break in the sedimentary record in which the rock layers remain parallel

disconnect /dískə nékt/ *v* 1 *vti* **DETACH POWER SOURCE FROM APPLIANCE** to break the connection between an appliance and its source of power 2 *vt* **SHUT OFF SUPPLY OF PUBLIC UTILITY** to shut off the telephone line or the supply of water, gas, or electricity to a building 3 *vt* **BREAK TELEPHONE CONNECTION** to break or lose the connection between two people who were speaking on the telephone (*usually passive*) 4 *vt* **DETACH ONE PART FROM ANOTHER** to detach something that was connected to something else 5 *vti* **BREAK OFF EMOTIONAL OR SPIRITUAL RELATIONSHIP** to end, forget, or lose an emotional or spiritual connection with something or somebody ■ *n* **DISCONNECTION** a disconnection of joined parts or things ○ *a disconnect between his words and his acts* —**disconnecter** *n* —**disconnective** *adj*

disconnected /dískə néktid/ *adj* showing no logical connection or relationship ○ *rambling disconnected prose* —**disconnectedly** *adv* —**disconnectedness** *n*

disconnection /dískə néksh'n/, **disconnexion** *n* 1 the disconnecting of a telephone line or a supply of gas, water, or electricity 2 the separation of things that were formerly linked or connected

disconsolate /diss kónssələt/ *adj* miserable or disappointed and unable to be cheered up [15C. < medieval Latin *disconsolatus* 'comfortless' < Latin *consolatus*, past participle of *consolare* (see CONSOLE[1]).] —**disconsolately** *adv* —**disconsolateness** *n* —**disconsolation** /diss kónssə láysh'n/ *n*

discontent /dískən tént/ *n* 1 **DISSATISFIED UNHAPPINESS** unhappiness or dissatisfaction 2 **RESTLESS LONGING FOR BETTER THINGS** a restless desire for something better (*literary*) 3 **SOMEBODY WHO IS DISCONTENTED** somebody who is dissatisfied and unhappy about something (*literary or formal*) ■ *adj* = **discontented** —**discontentment** *n*

discontented /dískən téntid/ *adj* feeling unhappy or dissatisfied with a situation —**discontentedly** *adv* —**discontentedness** *n*

discontinue /dískən tínnyoo/ (**-ues, -uing, -ued**) *v* 1 *vti* to come to an end after happening regularly, or end something that has been happening regularly 2 *vt* to stop manufacturing something, usually a particular model or type of product [15C. Via French *discontinuer* < medieval Latin *discontinuare* 'not to continue' < Latin *continuare* 'continue'.] —**discontinuance** *n* —**discontinuation** /dískən tínnyoo áysh'n/ *n* —**discontinued** *adj* —**discontinuer** *n*

discontinuity /díss konti nyōō əti/ (*plural* **-ties**) *n* 1 **BREAK IN OTHERWISE CONTINUOUS PROCESS** a break or gap in a process that would normally be continuous 2 **POINT OF CHANGE** the point or value of a variable at which a curve or mathematical function shows an abrupt change as the variable smoothly increases or decreases 3 **LACK OF MATHEMATICAL CONTINUITY** the characteristic of being discontinuous 4 **MATHEMATICAL VALUE** a value of a variable for which a function is not continuous 5 **BOUNDARY BETWEEN ROCK TYPES** a boundary between rock types deep within the Earth's crust that is detected as a change in the speed of seismic waves

discontinuous /dískən tínnyoo əss/ *adj* 1 having breaks or gaps in an otherwise continuous process or line 2 with a mathematical discontinuity (*refers to variables and functions*) —**discontinuously** *adv* —**discontinuousness** *n*

discord /díss kawrd/ *n* 1 disagreement or strife between people, things, or situations 2 unpleasant or harsh sounds clashing with each other, usually musical notes that produce a disagreeable combination [13C. Via Old French *discorde* < Latin *discordia* < *discord-*, stem of *discors* < *cors* 'heart'.]

discordant /diss káwrd'nt/ *adj* 1 in disagreement 2 consisting of sounds, usually musical notes, that are harsh, unpleasant, or clashing —**discordance** *n* —**discordancy** *n* —**discordantly** *adv*

discotheque /dískə tek/ *n* = **disco** *n.* 1 [Mid-20C. < French *discothèque* < *disque* 'disc, record' + *-thèque* 'library'.]

discount *n* /díss kownt/ 1 **REDUCTION IN PRICE** a reduction in the usual price of something 2 FIN = **discount rate** 3 **INTEREST DEDUCTED FROM FINANCIAL INSTRUMENT** the interest deducted from the face value of a financial instrument or promissory note before a sale or loan is completed 4 **DEDUCTION FROM PAR VALUE OF SHARES** the amount by which the (**par value**) of shares exceeds the market price actually paid by purchasers ■ *v* /diss kównt/ 1 *vt* **DISMISS AS UNTRUE OR TRIVIAL** to decide that something can be disregarded as unimportant, irrelevant, or untrue ○ *We had already discounted the theory that they were involved.* 2 *vt* **REDUCE IN PRICE** to reduce the price of something by a particular amount or percentage 3 *vt* **ANTICIPATE THEN ADJUST** to foresee something and make adjustments to lessen or absorb its impact ○ *Tax cuts in the next budget have already been discounted by the City.* 4 *vt* **TRADE INVESTMENT AT REDUCED PRICE** to buy or sell a financial instrument at a reduced price that is calculated according to the interest rate and risk on the investment 5 *vti* **MAKE SECURED LOAN AT REDUCED RATE** to lend money on a negotiable long-term financial instrument at a reduced price that is calculated according to the instrument's risk and the interest due before its maturity ■ *adj* /díss kownt/ **WITH REDUCED PRICE** less than the usual price, or selling goods for less than the usual price ○ *a discount warehouse* [Early 17C. < French *descompte* and Italian *discontare* < medieval Latin *discomputare* 'count away' < Latin *computare* 'reckon together'.] —**discountable** /diss kówntəb'l, díss kowntəb'l/ *adj* —**discounter** /diss kówntər, díss kowntər/ *n*

discount broker *n* 1 *US* a stockbroker who executes trades for customers, but who in exchange for low commissions offers little advice or investment research 2 an agent who buys and sells bills or other commercial paper at a discount —**discount brokerage** *n*

discounted cash flow *n* a method of valuing an investment by calculating what future cash returns will be worth at the time they are received, based on estimates of future inflation and interest rates

discountenance /diss kówntinənss/ *vt* (**-nances, -nancing, -nanced**) (*formal*) 1 **EMBARRASS** to make somebody embarrassed 2 **DISAPPROVE OF** to discourage or disapprove of somebody or something ■ *n* **DISFAVOUR** disapproval of somebody or something (*formal*)

discounter *n* = **discount store**

discount house *n* a financial institution that buys and sells negotiable bills of exchange at discounted rates

discount market *n* the part of the financial market trading in discounted commercial bills, including banks, brokers, and discount houses

discount rate, discount *n* the rate at which expected cash returns from a security are converted into the security's market price

discount store, discounter *n* a shop that sells goods at prices that are reduced from those recommended by the manufacturers

discourage /dis kúrrij/ (**-ages, -aging, -aged**) *vt* **1 TRY TO STOP SOMEBODY'S ACTIONS** to try to stop somebody from doing something **2 TEND TO STOP** to tend to prevent something from happening by making it more difficult or unpleasant ○ *dirty beaches that discourage sunbathing* **3 MAKE LESS OPTIMISTIC** to make somebody feel less motivated, confident, or optimistic [15C. < Old French *descoragier* 'deprive of courage' < *corage* 'courage'.] —**discouragement** *n* —**discourager** *n*

discouraging /dis kúrrijing/ *adj* making somebody feel less motivation, confidence, or optimism about something —**discouragingly** *adv*

discourse *n* /díss kawrss/ **1 SERIOUS SPEECH OR PIECE OF WRITING** a serious and lengthy speech or piece of writing about a topic **2 SERIOUS CONVERSATION** serious discussion about something between people or groups **3 LANGUAGE** language, especially the type of language used in a particular context or subject **4 MAJOR UNIT OF LANGUAGE** a unit of language, especially spoken language, that is longer than the sentence ■ *vi* /diss káwrs/ (**-courses, -coursing, -coursed**) **1 SERIOUSLY SPEAK OR WRITE ON TOPIC** to speak or write about a subject in a formal context and at length ○ *In the second part, the author discourses on ethics.* **2 CONVERSE** to have a conversation (*formal*) [15C. < Latin *discursus* 'running to and fro' < *discurrere* 'run apart' < *currere* 'run'.] —**discourser** /diss káwrssər/ *n*

discourtesy /diss kúrtəssi/ (*plural* **-sies**) *n* behaviour or an action that is bad-mannered or impolite —**discourteous** /diss kúrti əss/ *adj* —**discourteously** *adv* —**discourteousness** *n*

discover /diss kúvvər/ *vt* **1 FIND OUT ABOUT** to find out information that was not previously known ○ *We discovered she'd known all along.* **2 BE FIRST TO FIND OR LEARN** to be the first person to find or learn something previously unknown ○ *researchers discovered a new genetic link to the causes of the disease* **3 FIND** to find somebody or something unexpectedly or after a search ○ *The missing child was finally discovered in the town centre.* **4 FIRST NOTICE INTEREST IN** to realize for the first time that you enjoy or have a talent for a particular thing ○ *Having discovered painting in her 50s, she ended up making a living by it.* **5 RECOGNIZE SOMEBODY'S TALENT OR BEAUTY** to realize that a musician, actor, performer, or everyday citizen has exceptional talent or unusual beauty, and help to bring him or her to prominence [14C. Via Old French *descovrir* < late Latin *discooperire* 'uncover' < Latin *cooperire* 'cover'.] —**discoverable** *adj* —**discoverer** *n*

discovered check *n* a move in chess that creates a check previously blocked by the piece moved

discovery /diss kúvvəri/ (*plural* **-ies**) *n* **1 SOMETHING LEARNT OR FOUND** something new that has been learnt or found ○ *These dinosaur remains were one of the most important discoveries of the century.* **2 PROCESS OF LEARNING SOMETHING PREVIOUSLY UNKNOWN** the fact or process of finding out about something for the first time ○ *the discovery of DNA* ○ *a voyage of discovery* **3 PROCESS OF FINDING** the process or act of finding something or somebody unexpectedly or after searching ○ *The discovery of the abandoned car provided new clues.* **4 RECOGNITION OF UNUSUAL TALENT OR BEAUTY** the recognition of somebody's exceptional talent or beauty, leading to that person's fame, or the person who is recognized in this way **5 MUTUAL DISCLOSING OF DATA OR DOCUMENTS** the stage of a legal proceeding during which each side must provide data and documents to the other side **6 DISCLOSABLE DATA AND DOCUMENTS** data or materials that a party in a legal proceeding must disclose to another party before or during the proceeding

Discovery Bay /di skúvvəri-/ bay on the coast of Victoria, Australia. It is 80 km/50 mi. wide.

disc plough *n* an agricultural implement with a cutting disc fixed in a frame that is drawn by a tractor that cuts furrows in the soil and turns it up

discredit /dis kréddit/ *vt* **1 HARM REPUTATION OF** to make somebody or something appear untrustworthy or wrong **2 CAUSE TO SEEM DOUBTFUL** to cast doubt on the validity or accuracy of something **3 NOT BELIEVE** to not accept that something is accurate or true ○ *Scientists generally discredit the theory of canals on Mars.* ■ *n* **1 LOSS OF REPUTATION** the loss of somebody's or something's good name or reputation, or the person or thing that causes its loss ○ *Their conduct is regarded as a discredit to the whole industry.* **2 DOUBT OR SUSPICION** doubt about the validity or accuracy of something —**discreditable** *adj* —**discreditably** *adv*

discreet /di skréet/ *adj* **1 CAREFUL TO AVOID OFFENDING PEOPLE** careful to avoid embarrassing or upsetting others **2 GOOD AT KEEPING SECRETS** careful not to speak about anything that should be secret or confidential **3 CIRCUMSPECTLY SUBTLE AND CAREFUL** subtle and circumspect, ensuring that no undue attention is attracted **4 MODEST** modest, and not ostentatious or flashy [14C. Via French *discret* < Latin *discretus* 'distinct', past participle of *discernere* 'distinguish' (see DISCERN).] —**discreetness** *n*

SPELLCHECK Do not confuse ***discreet*** with ***discrete***, which has a similar sound. Beware: your spellchecker will not catch this error.

discreetly /di skréetli/ *adv* taking care to avoid upsetting or embarrassing people, giving away anything confidential, or appearing immodest or flashy

discrepancy /di skréppənssi/ (*plural* **-cies**) *n* a distinct difference between two things, e.g. sets of figures, that should match or correspond [Early 17C. < Latin *discrepantia* < *discrepare* 'differ' < *crepare* 'to rattle'.] —**discrepant** *adj* —**discrepantly** *adv*

discrete /diss kréet/ *adj* **1** completely separate and unconnected **2** describes elements or variables that are distinct, unrelated, and have a finite number of values [14C. < Latin *discretus* (see DISCREET).] —**discretely** *adv* —**discreteness** *n*

SPELLCHECK See ***discreet***.

discretion /di skrésh'n/ *n* **1 ABILITY TO AVOID OFFENCE** the good judgment and sensitivity needed to avoid embarrassing or upsetting others **2 FREEDOM TO DECIDE** the freedom or authority to judge something or make a decision about it ○ *Tipping is left to the customer's discretion.* **3 CONFIDENTIALITY** the ability to keep sensitive information secret [14C. Via French *discrétion* < Latin *discretion-* 'separation, discernment' < *discret-*, past participle of *discernere* (see DISCERN).]

discretionary /di skrésh'nəri/ *adj* **1 GIVING SOMEBODY AUTHORITY TO DECIDE** giving somebody the freedom to make a decision according to individual circumstances **2 GIVEN OR REFUSED ACCORDING TO CIRCUMSTANCES** given according to the merits of an individual case, rather than being provided or awarded automatically **3 USABLE AS WANTED** able to be used as desired without any stipulations —**discretionarily** *adv*

discretionary account *n* a securities account in which the broker has been given the authority to make decisions about buying and selling without the customer's prior permission

discretionary income *n* income that is left over after necessary expenditure

discretionary trust *n* a trust in which somebody other than its founder, e.g. a trustee, determines the beneficiaries' shares

discriminant /di skrímminənt/ *n* a relation between the coefficients *a*, *b*, and *c* of a mathematical expression of the form $ax^2 + bx + c = 0$, used in the study of roots and other properties of the expression [Mid-19C. < Latin *discriminant-*, present participle of *discriminare* (see DISCRIMINATE).]

discriminant function *n* a statistical method used to place an item that could belong to any of two or more sets of variables in the correct set, with a minimal probability of error

discriminate /di skrímmi nayt/ *v* (**-nates, -nating, -nated**) **1** *vi* **TREAT GROUP UNFAIRLY BECAUSE OF PREJUDICE** to treat one person or group worse than others or better than others, usually because of a prejudice about race, ethnic group, age group, religion, or gender **2** *vti* **DISCERN DIFFERENCE** to recognize or identify a difference ○ *could not discriminate between red and green* **3** *vi* **BE AWARE OF DIFFERENCES** to pay attention to subtle differences and exercise judgment and taste ■ *adj* **SHOWING DISCRIMINATION** showing the ability to appreciate quality or notice differences [Early 17C. < Latin *discriminat-*, past participle of *discriminare* 'divide' < *discrimin-* 'division' < *discernere* (see DISCERN).] —**discriminability** *n* —**discriminable** *adj* —**discriminably** *adv* —**discriminately** *adv* —**discriminative** *adj* —**discriminatively** *adv*

discriminating /di skrímmi nayting/ *adj* **1** able to identify subtle differences and appreciate good quality or taste ○ *Discriminating customers prefer these handmade linens.* **2** describes tariffs that are set at different rates for different importers —**discriminatingly** *adv*

discrimination /di skrímmi náysh'n/ *n* **1 TREATING PEOPLE DIFFERENTLY THROUGH PREJUDICE** unfair treatment of one person or group, usually because of prejudice about race, ethnic group, age group, religion, or gender **2 ABILITY TO NOTICE AND VALUE QUALITY** the ability to appreciate good quality or taste **3 ATTUNEMENT TO SUBTLE DIFFERENTIATION** the ability to notice subtle differences **4 SIGNAL SELECTION** the selection of a transmitted signal with a particular characteristic, such as frequency, by elimination of signals with other characteristics, using a discriminator —**discriminational** *adj*

discriminator /di skrímmi naytər/ *n* a device or circuit that translates phase or frequency variations into amplitude variations in a modulated signal, e.g. a radio signal, and is used to select signals with particular characteristics

discriminatory /di skrímminətəri/ *adj* **1** treating a person or group unfairly, especially because of prejudice about race, ethnicity, age, or gender **2** describes a statistical test that is unbiased because the sampling procedure avoided the systematic distortion that could be introduced by an unrepresentative population —**discriminatorily** *adv*

~~**discription**~~ incorrect spelling of **description**

disc sander *n* an electrically powered tool with a revolving abrasive disc, used for sanding, grinding, and polishing irregular surfaces

discursive /diss kúrssiv/ *adj* **1** lengthy and including extra material that is not essential to what is being written or spoken about ○ *One book is concise and snappy, while the other has a more relaxed, discursive style.* **2** using logic rather than intuition to reach a conclusion [Late 16C. < medieval Latin *discursivus* < *discurs-*, past participle of *discurrere* (see DISCOURSE).] —**discursively** *adv* —**discursiveness** *n*

discus /dískəss/ (*plural* **-cuses** *or* **-ci** /-ī/) *n* **1 DISC THROWN IN ATHLETICS** a weighted disc thrown in competitions by an athlete who spins with outstretched arms to launch it from the flat of his or her hand **2 EVENT OF THROWING DISCUS** the event or sport in which athletes compete to throw a discus as far as possible **3 COLOURFUL AQUARIUM FISH** a small colourful South American freshwater fish that has a compressed disc-shaped body and is popular as an aquarium fish. *Symphysodon discus.* [Mid-17C. Via Latin < Greek *diskos* (see DISH).]

discuss /di skúss/ *vt* **1** to talk about a subject with others ○ *need to discuss it with them first* **2** to consider a particular topic in speaking or writing ○ *Chapter 3 discusses the events leading up to the War of Independence.* [14C. < Latin *discuss-*, past participle of *discutere* 'dash to pieces' < *quatere* 'shake'.] —**discussant** *n* —**discusser** *n* —**discussible** *adj*

discussion /di skúsh'n/ *n* **1** talk or a talk between two or more people about a subject **2** a detailed consideration or examination of a topic in writing or speech —**discussional** *adj*

disc wheel *n* a car wheel with a continuous flat outer surface instead of spokes

disdain /diss dáyn/ *n* extreme contempt or disgust for something or somebody ■ *vt* to regard somebody or something as not worthy of respect [14C. Probably < Old French *desdeignier* 'treat as unworthy' < late Latin *dedignare* < *dignare* 'treat as worthy'.] —**disdainful** *adj* —**disdainfully** *adv* —**disdainfulness** *n*

disease /di zéez/ *n* **1 MEDICAL CONDITION IN HUMANS** a condition that results in medically significant symptoms in a human **2 MEDICAL CONDITION IN PLANTS OR ANIMALS** a condition in plants or animals that causes medically significant symptoms **3 PARTICULAR DISORDER** a disorder with recognizable signs and often having a known cause **4 PROBLEM IN SOCIETY** a serious problem in society or with a particular group of people [14C. < Old French *desaise* 'lack of ease' < *aise* 'ease'.] —**diseased** *adj*

diseconomy /díssi kónnəmi/ (*plural* **-mies**) *n* something that contributes to increased costs

disembark /díssim baárk/ *v* **1** *vi* to get off a passenger vehicle, especially a ship, aircraft, or train **2** *vt* to let passengers off a ship, bus, train, or aircraft, or to unload cargo (*formal*) [Late 16C. < French *désembarquer*, Spanish *desembarcar*, or Italian *disimbarcare*, < French *embarquer* or the equivalent (see EMBARK).] —**disembarkation** /diss ém baar káysh'n, díss im-/ *n* —**disembarkment** *n*

disembarrass /díssim bárrəss/ *vt* to free somebody from something embarrassing, unpleasant, or burdensome (*formal*) —**disembarrassment** *n*

disembodied /díssim bóddid/ *adj* coming from somebody who cannot be seen, often regarded as eerie or frightening ○ *a disembodied voice whispering in the darkness*

disembody /díssim bóddi/ (**-ies, -ying, -ied**) *vt* to free the soul or spirit from the body —**disembodiment** *n*

disembowel /díssim bówəl/ (**-els, -elling, -elled**) *vt* **1** to cut open the stomach of a person or animal and remove the internal organs, especially the intestines **2** to remove the internal substance, elements, or parts of something (*literary*) —**disembowelment** *n*

disembroil /díssim bróyl/ *vt* to free yourself or somebody else from a difficult situation

disempower /díssim pów ər/ *vt* to take power or influence away from somebody or from yourself —**disempowerment** *n*

disenable /díssi náyb'l/ (**-bles, -bling, -bled**) *vt* to prevent something or make something unable to operate or perform a function ○ *disenabled the weapons system on the aircraft prior to landing* —**disenablement** *n*

disenchant /díssin chaánt/ *vt* **1** to make somebody stop believing that something or somebody is worthwhile, right, or deserving of support **2** to free somebody from an enchantment or magic spell (*literary*) [Late 16C. < French *désenchanter* 'undo enchantment' < *enchanter* 'enchant'.] —**disenchanted** *adj* —**disenchantedly** *adv* —**disenchanter** *n* —**disenchanting** *adj* —**disenchantingly** *adv* —**disenchantment** *n*

disencumber /díssin kúmbər/ *vt* to relieve somebody or something of a burden or problem —**disencumberment** *n*

disendow /díssin dów/ *vt* to withdraw an endowment, especially a gift of money —**disendower** *n* —**disendowment** *n*

disenfranchise /díssin fránch īz/ (**-chises, -chising, -chised**) *vt* to deprive a person or organization of a privilege, immunity, or legal right, especially the right to vote —**disenfranchisement** /-fránchizmənt/ *n*

disengage /díssin gáyj/ (**-gages, -gaging, -gaged**) *v* **1** *vti* **PHYSICALLY DISCONNECT OR BECOME DISCONNECTED** to disconnect one thing from another, or to become disconnected from something **2** *vt* **MENTALLY DISCONNECT OR BECOME UNINVOLVED** to mentally separate yourself or somebody else from, or to become uninvolved in, a situation or difficulty **3** *vti* **STOP FIGHTING IN WAR** to bring troops out of, or end involvement in, a war or combat **4** *vti* **MOVE SWORD IN FENCING** to move the point of your sword around an opponent's sword in order to open a new line of attack

disengagement /díssin gáyjmənt/ *n* **1** the process or action in which something or somebody is released from a physical or mental attachment **2** the withdrawal of troops or an army from a war or combat

disentail /díssin táyl/ *vt* to lift the restrictions on who may inherit somebody's property —**disentailment** *n*

disentangle /díssin táng g'l/ (**-gles, -gling, -gled**) *vt* **1 UNTANGLE** to untangle and free things that are muddled, tied, or knotted together **2 DISTINGUISH, ANALYSE, OR UNDERSTAND** to clarify something confusing ○ *It was hard to disentangle fact from fiction in his account.* **3 BREAK OFF RELATIONSHIP** to free somebody or yourself from a relationship or connection —**disentanglement** *n*

disentomb /díssin tóom/ *vt* to take a body out of a tomb or from a place like a tomb. ◊ **exhume** *v.* 1

disequilibrium /díss eekwi líbbri əm/ *n* a state of instability or imbalance, usually in the economy

disestablish /díssi stáblish/ *vt* **1** to undo or change something that has been established for a long time **2** to end the official relationship between the state and a nation's official church or religion —**disestablishment** *n* —**disestablishmentarian** /díssi stáblishmən táiri ən/ *n*

disesteem /díssi stéem/ *vt* to have a low opinion of somebody or something (*formal*) ■ *n* lack of respect or esteem (*formal*) ○ *held in disesteem*

diseur /dee zúr/ *n* a man, usually an actor, who is an accomplished reciter of dramatic monologues [< French, 'talker' < *dire* 'say' < Latin *dicere*]

diseuse /dee zúrz/ *n* a woman, usually an actor, who is an accomplished reciter of dramatic monologues [Late 19C. < French, feminine of *diseur* (see DISEUR).]

disfavour /diss fáyvər/ *n* **1 CONDITION OF DISAPPROVAL** the state of being disapproved of ○ *This fell into disfavour years ago.* **2 NO RESPECT OR APPROVAL** disapproval or lack of respect ○ *They were looked on with disfavour.* ■ *vt* **NOT LIKE OR APPROVE OF** to dislike or disapprove of something (*formal*)

disfigure /diss fíggər/ (**-ures, -uring, -ured**) *vt* to mar the appearance of somebody or something [14C. < Old French *desfigurer* 'deprive something of its figure' < Latin *figura* 'figure'.] —**disfiguration** /diss fíggə ráysh'n/ *n* —**disfigurement** *n*

disforest /diss fórrist/ *vt* FORESTRY = **deforest**

disfranchise /dis fránch īz/ (**-chises, -chising, -chised**) *vt* POL = **disenfranchise**

disfrock /dis frók/ *vt* CHR = **defrock**

disgorge /dis gáwrj/ (**-gorges, -gorging, -gorged**) *vt* **1 POUR SUBSTANCES OUT** to pour out liquid, gas, or other contents in a gushing stream **2 LET PEOPLE OUT** to let a large number of people come out of a building or vehicle at the same time ○ *a cruise ship disgorging thousands of passengers* **3 REGURGITATE OR VOMIT** to vomit or regurgitate food that has been eaten or partly eaten, as some birds and mammals do to feed their young [15C. < Old French *desgorger* 'expel from the throat' < *gorge* 'throat'.] —**disgorgement** *n*

disgrace /diss gráyss/ *n* **1 STATE OF BEING DISAPPROVED OF** shame or loss of respect arising from bad behaviour ○ *She was sent home in disgrace.* **2 CAUSE OF SHAME OR DISRESPECT** a cause of shame or loss of respect ○ *She's a disgrace to the family.* ■ *vt* (**-graces, -gracing, -graced**) **CAUSE FEELINGS OF SHAME TO** to bring shame on yourself or others who are associated with you by bad behaviour ○ *He disgraced himself by forgetting the wedding.* [Mid-16C. Via French *disgracier* < Italian *disgrazia* 'disfavour' < Latin *gratia* (see GRACE).] —**disgracer** *n*

disgraceful /diss gráyssf'l/ *adj* so bad or unacceptable that it is something to be ashamed of ○ *The way they were treated was disgraceful.* —**disgracefully** *adv* —**disgracefulness** *n*

disgruntle /diss grúnt'l/ (**-tles, -tling, -tled**) *vt* to make somebody feel dissatisfied and irritated [Mid-17C. < obsolete *gruntle* 'grumble, grunt' < GRUNT[1].] —**disgruntled** *adj* —**disgruntlement** *n*

disguise /diss gīz/ *vt* (**-guises, -guising, -guised**) **1 CHANGE SOMEBODY'S APPEARANCE FOR CONCEALMENT** to make changes in the appearance of somebody or something to avoid being recognized ○ *He fled the besieged city disguised as a woman.* **2 HIDE SOMETHING TO PREVENT OTHERS KNOWING** to hide feelings or facts from other people ○ *She couldn't disguise her horror.* **3 CHANGE SOMETHING TO PREVENT RECOGNITION** to change something so that it cannot be recognized ○ *His voice has been disguised during the interview to conceal his identity.* ■ *n* **1 SOMETHING DONE TO PREVENT RECOGNITION** something worn or done in order to change somebody's appearance and prevent recognition ○ *Anyone would have seen through such a flimsy disguise.* **2 ALTERATION OR CONCEALMENT TO PREVENT RECOGNITION** the alteration or concealment of something in order to prevent it being seen or recognized by others ○ *a plot that relies on disguise* **3 STATE OF ALTERED APPEARANCE** an altered appearance intended to conceal somebody's identity or make somebody look like somebody else ○ *The film star must be travelling in disguise.* [14C. < Old French *desguis(i)er* 'remove your appearance' < *guise* 'appearance'.] —**disguisable** *adj* —**disguised** *adj* —**disguisedly** /diss gīzidli/ *adv* —**disguiser** *n*

disgust /diss gúst/ *n* **1 STRONG DISAPPROVAL OR REVULSION** a feeling of horrified or sickened distaste for something ○ *viewed the tawdry scandal with unconcealed disgust* **2 IMPATIENT IRRITATION** a feeling of impatient irritation ○ *Much to my disgust, I was compelled to hand over the documents.* ■ *vt* **MAKE SOMEBODY FEEL REVOLTED** to make somebody feel sickened or revolted [Late 16C. < French *desgoust* or Italian *disgusto* 'have a distaste for' < Latin *gustus* 'taste'.] —**disgusted** *adj* —**disgustedly** *adv* —**disgustedness** *n* —**disgustful** *adj*

SYNONYMS See ***dislike***.

---

disgusting /diss gústing/ *adj* **1** tending to repel and sicken people ○ *a disgusting smell* **2** completely unacceptable or disgraceful ○ *a disgusting waste of money* —**disgustingly** *adv* —**disgustingness** *n*

dish /dish/ *n* **1 CONTAINER FOR SERVING FOOD** a container for serving food **2 SERVING OF FOOD** a serving or plateful of food, especially one that forms only part of a larger meal **3 FOOD PREPARED TO RECIPE OR STYLE** food prepared to a particular recipe or in a particular style **4 SHALLOW OPEN CONTAINER** a shallow open container used, e.g., in laboratories or hospitals **5 RADIO OR TELEVISION AERIAL** a dish-shaped aerial transmitting and receiving radio or television signals, used, e.g. in radar and satellite broadcasting **6 HOLLOW PLACE** a shallow depression, e.g. in rock **7 GOOD-LOOKING PERSON** a good-looking person (*slang*) ■ **dishes** *npl* **DIRTY PLATES, CUTLERY, AND PANS** the plates, eating utensils, and pans that are dirtied during the cooking and eating of a meal ○ *my turn to wash the dishes* ■ *vt* **1 RUIN** to ruin or thwart something ○ *The rejection letter dished her hopes of a university place.* **2 HOLLOW OUT** to make or form a concave shape in something [Pre-12C. Via Latin *discus* 'dish, platter' < Greek *diskos* 'disc, quoit, platter' < *dikein* 'throw'.]

dish out *vt* **1** to give something out freely, especially criticism, money, punishment, or advice (*informal*) **2** to serve food to people ○ *dishing out mashed potatoes*

dishabille *n* = **deshabille**

dish aerial *n* a transmitting and receiving aerial in the form of a dish-shaped reflector, used, e.g. in radar and in satellite broadcasting. US term **dish antenna**

dish antenna *n* US ELECTRONICS = **dish aerial**

disharmony /diss haármәni/ *n* **1 CONFLICT BETWEEN PEOPLE** disagreement or conflict between people or groups who cannot get along with each other **2 LACK OF MUSICAL HARMONY** lack of agreement in music or sounds, resulting in unpleasant sound combinations **3 IMBALANCE** lack of balance in something such as the body or the environment —**disharmonious** /díss haar mṓni əss/ *adj* —**disharmoniously** *adv*

dishcloth /dísh kloth/ *n* **1** = **tea towel 2 dishcloth, dishrag** a cloth used for washing dishes

dishearten /diss haárt'n/ *vt* to make somebody lose hope and enthusiasm —**disheartenment** *n*

disheartening /diss haárt'ning/ *adj* making somebody lose hope or enthusiasm —**dishearteningly** *adv*

dished /disht/ *adj* **1 CONCAVE** hollowed out in a shape like a dish **2 POINTING IN TOWARDS EACH OTHER** describes pairs of vehicle wheels that are set at an angle so that the bottoms are closer together than the tops **3 DEFEATED** completely exhausted, beaten, or thwarted

dishevel /di shévv'l/ (**-els, -elling, -elled**) *vt* to disarrange somebody's clothes or hair [Late 16C. Probably back-formation < DISHEVELLED.] —**dishevelment** *n*

disheveled *adj* US = **dishevelled**

dishevelled *adj* **1** with untidy hair or clothes **2** disordered and untidy [14C. < Old French *deschevelé*, past participle of *descheveler* 'disarrange the hair' < *des-* 'apart' + *chevel* 'hair'.]

dishonest /diss ónnist/ *adj* meaning or meant to deceive, defraud, or trick people [14C. Via Old French *deshoneste* < Latin *dehonestus* < *honestus* 'honourable'.]

dishonestly /diss ónnistli/ *adv* in a lying or deceitful way

dishonesty /diss ónnisti/ (*plural* **-ties**) *n* **1** the use of lies or deceit or the tendency to be deceitful **2** a dishonest act or action

dishonor *n, vt* US = **dishonour**

dishonour *n* **1 LOSS OF OTHER PEOPLE'S RESPECT** the loss of a good reputation **2 CAUSE OF SHAME** a cause of shame or loss of respect **3 FAILURE TO PAY CHEQUE** failure or refusal by a bank or other financial institution to pay a cheque, bill of exchange, or other financial document ■ *vt* **1 BRING SHAME ON** to do something that brings shame on yourself or on people associated with you **2 BREAK AGREEMENT** to fail to keep a promise or agreement **3 TREAT DISRESPECTFULLY** to treat somebody without any respect (*formal*) **4 FAIL TO PAY CHEQUE** to fail to pay a cheque, bill of exchange, or other financial document (*formal*) **5 DISGRACE WOMAN BY SEDUCTION OR RAPE** to bring shame on a woman by having sexual intercourse with her before marriage or by raping her (*archaic*) [14C. Via Old French *deshonorer* < medieval Latin *dishonorare* 'not to honour' < *honorare* 'to honour'.] —**dishonourer** *n*

dishonourable /diss ónnərəb'l/ *adj* **1** morally unacceptable and liable to make somebody lose the respect of others **2** behaving in a dishonest or morally unacceptable way —**dishonourableness** *n* —**dishonourably** *adv*

dishonourable discharge *n* dismissal from the armed forces as punishment for a serious offence such as desertion

dishpan /dísh pan/ *n US* a large pan or plastic tub used for washing dishes

dishpan hands *npl* a condition of the hands in which the skin is dry, scaly, and reddened because of sensitivity or overexposure to cleaning materials such as detergent (*+ singular or plural verb*)

dishrag /dísh rag/ *n* = **dishcloth** *n.* 2

dishtowel /dísh towəl/ *n US, Can* = **tea towel**

dishwasher /dísh woshər/ *n* **1** an electrically operated machine that washes, rinses, and dries crockery and kitchen utensils **2** a washer of dishes, especially in a restaurant

dishwashing liquid *n US* = **washing-up liquid**

dishwater /dísh wawtər/ *n* **1** water that is or has been used for washing crockery or kitchen utensils **2** a weak or tasteless drink

dishy /díshi/ (**-ier, -iest**) *adj* good-looking (*informal*)

~~**disign**~~ incorrect spelling of **design**

disillusion /díssi lóozh'n/ *vt* to destroy or undermine an ideal, illusion, or mistaken belief that is held by somebody (*often passive*) ■ *n* = **disillusionment** —**disillusioned** *adj* —**disillusive** *adj*

disillusionment /díssi lóozh'nmənt/ *n* disappointment caused by a frustrated ideal or belief

disincentive /díssin séntiv/ *n* something that deters somebody from taking a particular action

disinclination /díssinkli náysh'n/ *n* a reluctance to do something

disincline /díssin klín/ (**-clines, -clining, -clined**) *vt* to make somebody reluctant or unwilling to do something (*often passive*)

disincorporate /díssin káwrpə rayt/ (**-rates, -rating, -rated**) *vti* to remove the corporate status of a company or organization, or to undergo such a process —**disincorporation** /díssin káwrpə ráysh'n/ *n*

disinfect /díssin fékt/ *vt* to clean something so as to destroy disease-carrying microorganisms and prevent infection [Late 16C. < French *désinfecter* < *infecter* 'infect'.] —**disinfection** *n* —**disinfector** *n*

disinfectant /díssin féktənt/ *n* a chemical that destroys or inhibits the growth of microorganisms that cause disease

disinfest /díssin fést/ *vt* to free a place, person, or animal of small pests such as rodents or insects —**disinfestation** /díssin fe stáysh'n/ *n*

disinflation /díssin fláysh'n/ *n* a slowdown in the rate at which prices increase, e.g. during a recession —**disinflationary** *adj*

disinformation /díssinfər máysh'n/ *n* false or deliberately misleading information, often put out as propaganda

disingenuous /díssin jénnyoo əss/ *adj* **1** withholding or not taking account of known information **2** giving a false impression of sincerity or simplicity —**disingenuously** *adv* —**disingenuousness** *n*

disinherit /díssin hérrit/ *vt* **1** to change a will so as to deprive somebody of an inheritance **2** to deprive somebody of a natural or established right or privilege —**disinheritance** *n*

disinhibit /díssin híbbit/ *vt* to free somebody from inhibitions (*technical*)

disinhibition /díssinhi bísh'n/ *n* **1 LOSS OF INHIBITION** a loss of inhibition, e.g. through the influence of alcohol or drugs (*technical*) **2 TEMPORARY LOSS OF INHIBITION** a temporary loss of inhibition caused by an outside stimulus, e.g. a loud noise **3 REMOVAL OF INHIBITOR** the removal of a substance that slows or stops a chemical reaction

disintegrate /diss ínti grayt/ (**-grates, -grating, -grated**) *v* **1** *vti* **BREAK INTO FRAGMENTS** to break into components or fragments, or break something into small pieces or constituent parts **2** *vti* **LOSE WHOLENESS** to destroy the cohesion, unity, or wholeness of something, or undergo such destruction **3 SPLIT ATOMS** to split the nuclei of atom or cause the nuclei of atoms to split —**disintegrable** *adj* —**disintegrative** *adj*

disintegration /diss ínti gráysh'n/ *n* **1 BREAKING INTO PIECES** irreversible breaking into components or fragments **2 LOSS OF UNITY** the loss of unity, cohesion, or integrity **3 BREAK-UP OF NUCLEUS** the break-up of an atomic nucleus or an unstable elementary particle into smaller parts, either by radioactive decay or through bombardment with high-energy particles

disintegration constant *n* PHYS = **decay constant**

disintegrator /diss ínti graytər/ *n* **1** a machine in which atoms are split as a result of being hit by accelerated particles **2** a person, machine, or force that destroys or disintegrates something

disinter /díssin túr/ (**-ters, -terring, -terred**) *vt* **1** to dig up or remove a dead body from a grave or tomb **2** to expose something that was hidden (*formal*) [Early 17C. < French *désenterrer* < *enterrer* 'inter'.] —**disinterment** *n*

disinterest /diss íntrəst/ *vt* to cause somebody to lose interest or partiality ■ *n* lack of bias or self-interest

disinterested /diss íntrəstid/ *adj* **1** free from bias or self-interest **2** ⚠ indifferent, not interested, or no longer interested. —**disinterestedly** *adv* —**disinterestedness** *n*

USAGE disinterested or **uninterested**? ***disinterested*** means 'impartial or objective' and also has a widely used but much criticized meaning, 'indifferent or not interested'. In formal writing you should avoid using the meaning 'not interested'.

disintermediation /díssintər meedi áysh'n/ *n* the elimination of intermediaries, e.g. wholesalers or retailers, in business transactions between producers and consumers

disintoxicate /díssin tóksi kayt/ (**-cates, -cating, -cated**) *vt* = **detoxify** *v.* 2 —**disintoxication** /díssin tóksi káysh'n/ *n*

disinvent /díssin vént/ *vt* to undo the invention of something ○ *Nuclear weapons cannot be disinvented.*

disinvest /díssin vést/ *vti* to withdraw an investment in something —**disinvestment** *n*

disinvite /díssin vít/ (**-vites, -viting, -vited**) *vt* to withdraw an invitation to somebody (*humorous*)

~~**disipline**~~ incorrect spelling of **discipline**

disjoin /diss jóyn/ *vti* to disconnect parts, things, or ideas, or become separated [15C. < Old French *desjoign-*, stem of *desjoindre* < Latin *disjungere* < *jungere* 'join'.] —**disjoinable** *adj*

disjoint /diss jóynt/ *v* **1** *vti* **SEPARATE AT JOINTS** to separate something at the joints, or be separated in this way **2** *vti* **DISLOCATE** to force or move something out of its usual position, or undergo such a change **3** *vt* **DESTROY UNITY** to destroy the unity or coherence of something **4** *vt* = **disjoin** [15C. < Old French *desjoint*, past participle of *desjoindre* (see DISJOIN).] —**disjoint** *adj* —**disjointed** *adj* —**disjointedness** *n*

disjointedly /diss jóyntidli/ *adv* in a way that makes connections or order unclear

disjunct /diss júngkt/ *adj* **1 SEPARATED** discontinuous or separated in time or space **2 DESCRIBING NOTES A SECOND APART** relating to two consecutive notes that are separated by an interval of a second **3 DESCRIBING A LEAPING MELODY** relating to a melody in which leaps are the dominant feature rather than smooth progression ■ *n* **disjunct, disjunction CLAUSE** either the p clause or the q clause in a logical proposition of the form 'p or q' [15C. < Latin *disjunctus*, past participle of *disjungere* (see DISJOIN).]

disjunction /diss júngksh'n/ *n* **1 disjunction, disjuncture DISCONNECTION** a disconnection of joined parts or things **2 disjunction, disjunctive PROPOSITION WITH 'OR'** a proposition of the form 'p or q' that is false if both p and q are false, but true if at least one of them is true **3** LOGIC = **disjunct** *n.* **4 CHROMOSOME SEPARATION** the separation of like chromosomes during cell division

disjunctive /diss júngktiv/ *adj* **1 DIVIDING** serving to divide or having the effect of dividing (*technical*) **2 SHOWING CONTRAST** describes a word, e.g. 'or', that establishes a contrast between two words or linguistic elements **3 CONTAINING OR RELATED TO A DISJUNCTION** relating to or having the form of a proposition of the type 'p or q' ■ *n* **1 CONTRAST WORD** a conjunction or other word that establishes a contrast **2** LOGIC = **disjunction** *n.* 2 —**disjunctively** *adv*

disjuncture /diss júngkchər/ *n* = **disjunction** *n.* 1

⚡**disk** /disk/ *n* **1** a device consisting of one or more magnetically or optically etched thin plates, used in a computer to store information **2** = **disc**

⚡**disk drive** *n* a computer device that reads data from and writes data to spinning magnetic or optical disks

⚡**diskette** /di skét/ *n* = **floppy disk**

⚡**disk operating system** *n* an operating system for personal computers that uses disks and diskettes for storage of programs and data

⚡**disk pack** *n* a removable data storage device used in minicomputers and mainframes, consisting of a stack of magnetic or optical disks

dislike /diss lík/ *vt* (**-likes, -liking, -liked**) **CONSIDER DISAGREEABLE** to consider something or somebody disagreeable or unpleasant ■ *n* **1 DISAPPROVING FEELING** an attitude or feeling of aversion, disapproval, or distaste **2 SOMETHING PERSONALLY DISAGREEABLE** something that you do not like —**dislikable** *adj*

SYNONYMS ***dislike, distaste, hatred, hate, disgust, loathing, repugnance, abhorrence, animosity, antipathy, aversion, revulsion***

CORE MEANING: not liking somebody or something

dislike a feeling or attitude of disapproval; **distaste** mild dislike, mainly of behaviour and activities; **hatred** *or* **hate** intense dislike or hostility; **disgust** a feeling of horrified and sickened disapproval; **loathing** intense dislike; **repugnance** strong disgust, mainly of behaviour and activities; **abhorrence** a feeling of aversion or intense disapproval, mainly of behaviour and activities; **animosity** a feeling of hostility and resentment; **antipathy** a deep-seated dislike or hostility; **aversion** a strong feeling of dislike; **revulsion** a sudden violent feeling of disgust.

dislocate /dísslə kayt/ (**-cates, -cating, -cated**) *vt* **1 PUT OUT OF PLACE** to put or force something out of its usual place or position **2 DISPLACE BODY PART** to move or force a bone out of the joint into which it fits **3 THROW INTO CONFUSION** to disrupt, upset, or disturb the order of something [Late 16C. Probably a back-formation < DISLOCATION.] —**dislocated** *adj*

dislocation /dísslə káysh'n/ *n* **1 DISLOCATING OR BEING DISLOCATED** the displacement of something from its usual or proper position **2 DISPLACEMENT OF BODY PART** the displacement of a body part, especially of a bone, from its usual fitting in a joint **3 IMPERFECTION IN CRYSTAL** an irregularity in the fine structure (**lattice**) of an otherwise normal crystal [14C. Directly or via Old French < medieval Latin *dislocation-* < Latin *locat-* (see LOCATE).]

dislodge /diss lój/ (**-lodges, -lodging, -lodged**) *vti* to force something or somebody from a previously fixed or secure position, or leave such a position [15C. < Old French *dislogier* < *logier* < *loge* 'hut'.] —**dislodgment** *n*

disloyal /diss lóyəl/ *adj* showing a lack of faith in or loyalty to somebody or something [15C. < Old French *desloial* < *loial* (see LOYAL).] —**disloyally** *adv*

disloyalty /diss lóyəlti/ (*plural* **-ties**) *n* **1** a lack of loyalty to a person, vow, organization, or state **2** a disloyal or unfaithful act

dismal /dízzm'l/ *adj* **1 DEPRESSING** depressing to the spirit or outlook **2 HOPELESS** showing a lack or failure of hope **3 OF POOR QUALITY** very poor or inadequate ○ *a dismal performance* [14C. Via Anglo-Norman *dismal* 'unlucky days' < medieval Latin *dies mali*.] —**dismally** *adv* —**dismalness** *n*

dismal science *n* political economy (*humorous*)

dismantle /diss mánt'l/ (**-tles, -tling, -tled**) *v* **1** *vt* **TAKE APART** to take something apart in a way that causes it to stop working **2** *vi* **COME APART** to be able to be separated into components **3** *vt* **DESTROY SOMETHING BY REMOVING KEY ELEMENTS** to destroy something, e.g. an institution or system, by removing essential elements **4** *vt* **REMOVE EQUIPMENT** to strip a room or building of furniture or equipment [Late 16C. < Old French *desmanteler* 'tear down a fortress wall' < *emmanteler* 'shelter, fortify' < *mantel* 'cloak' (see MANTLE).] —**dismantlement** *n* —**dismantler** *n*

dismast /diss maást/ *vt* to break off or remove the mast or masts of a boat or ship —**dismastment** *n*

dismay /diss máy/ *vt* (*usually passive*) **1 DISCOURAGE** to cause somebody to feel discouraged or disappointed **2 ALARM** to fill somebody with alarm, apprehension, or distress ■ *n* **1 FEELING OF DISCOURAGEMENT** a feeling of hopelessness, disappointment, or discouragement **2 LOSS OF COURAGE** a sudden loss of courage or confidence [14C. < assumed Anglo-Norman *desmaiier*.] —**dismayingly** *adv*

dismember /diss mémbər/ *vt* **1 REMOVE LIMB FROM BODY** to cut off or remove a limb or other part of a person or animal **2 DIVIDE SOMETHING UP** to cut or tear something into pieces **3 DESTROY SOMETHING BY TAKING IT APART** to destroy something by taking it apart so that its parts no longer work together ○ *dismembered the alliance* [14C. Via Old French < assumed Vulgar Latin *dismembrare* < Latin *membrum* 'limb, part'.] —**dismemberer** *n* —**dismemberment** *n*

dismiss /diss míss/ *vt* **1 END EMPLOYMENT OF** to stop employing somebody, e.g. because of unsatisfactory work or wrongdoing **2 SEND AWAY** to give somebody permission to leave **3 REFUSE TO CONSIDER** to refuse to give consideration to something **4 REJECT WITH REASON** to consider somebody or something as unsuitable for a particular reason ○ *dismissed the idea as ridiculous* **5 REFUSE FURTHER HEARING IN COURT** to refuse to give further hearing to a case in court **6 PUT PLAYER OR TEAM OUT** to end the innings of a batsman or a team [15C. < medieval Latin *dismiss-*, past participle of *dismittere* 'send away' < Latin *mittere* 'send off'.] —**dismissible** *adj*

dismissal /diss míss'l/ *n* **1 ENDING OF SOMEBODY'S EMPLOYMENT** the removal of somebody from employment **2 NOTICE OF DISCHARGE** an order or notice of discharge from employment or service **3 SENDING AWAY** the formal sending away of a person or group **4 REJECTION** the rejection of something from consideration **5 PUTTING PLAYER OR TEAM OUT** the ending of a batsman's or team's innings

dismissive /diss míssiv/ *adj* indicating rejection, especially showing contempt or indifference —**dismissively** *adv* —**dismissiveness** *n*

dismount /diss mównt/ *v* **1** *vi* **GET OFF ANIMAL** to get down from the back of an animal, e.g. a horse or camel **2** *vi* **GET OFF CYCLE** to get off a bicycle or motorcycle **3** *vt* **REMOVE FROM FRAME** to remove something from a frame, mounting, stand, or support **4** *vt* **THROW SOMEBODY OFF** to remove somebody from a mounted position ○ *The horse dismounted its rider.* ■ *n* **ACT OF DISMOUNTING** an act of dismounting or of being dismounted —**dismountable** *adj*

CORBIS/Bettmann

Walt Disney

Disney /dízni/, **Walt** (1901–66) US animator and producer. Full name **Walter Elias Disney**

Disneyesque /dízni ésk/ *adj* reminiscent of, or in the style of, the sometimes whimsical films and cartoons created by Walt Disney or the Disney studios

disobedience /díssə beédi ənss/ *n* refusal or failure to obey

disobedient /díssə beédi ənt/ *adj* refusing or failing to obey, especially habitually [15C. Via Old French < assumed Vulgar Latin *desobedient-* < Latin *oboedient-*, present participle of *oboedire* (see OBEY).] —**disobediently** *adv*

disobey /díssə báy/ (**-beys, -beying, -beyed**) *vti* to refuse or fail to obey a rule, instruction, or authority, or somebody giving an instruction or in authority [14C. Via French *désobéir* < assumed Vulgar Latin *desobedir* < Latin *oboedire* (see OBEY).] —**disobeyer** *n*

disobliging /díssə blíjing/ *adj* selfishly or rudely unwilling to help —**disobligingly** *adv* —**disobligingness** *n*

~~**disolve**~~ incorrect spelling of **dissolve**

disomic /dī sṓmik/ *adj* with chromosomes occurring in pairs [Early 20C. < DI- + -SOME[1].] —**disomy** *n*

disorder /diss áwrdər/ *n* **1 LACK OF ORDER** a lack of systematic or orderly arrangement **2 UNTIDINESS** a state of untidiness ○ *found the room in complete disorder* **3 UNRULY BEHAVIOUR** a public disturbance or breach of the peace **4 ILLNESS** a medical condition involving a disturbance to the normal functioning of the mind or body ■ *vt* **UPSET ARRANGEMENT** to disarrange or disturb the order of something

disordered /diss áwrdərd/ *adj* **1** marked by confusion or disarray **2** having lost normal physical functioning or thought processes ○ *disordered sleep*

disorderly /diss áwrdərli/ *adj* **1 LACKING ORDER** lacking order or organization **2 UNRULY** unruly and resisting authority **3 DISTURBING THE PEACE** disturbing the peace or violating public order —**disorderliness** *n*

disorderly conduct *n* any one of several minor offences likely to cause a breach of the peace

disorderly house *n* an establishment such as a brothel or gaming club where activities take place that may become unruly or violate public order or decency (*formal or archaic*)

disorganisation *n* = **disorganization**

disorganise *vt* = **disorganize**

disorganization /diss áwrgə nī záysh'n/, **disorganisation** *n* **1** a lack of organization or orderly arrangement **2** the destruction of an order or system

disorganize /diss áwrgə nīz/ (**-izes, -izing, -ized**), **disorganise** (**-ises, -ising, -ised**) *vt* to destroy or disrupt the organization, system, or unity of something [Late 18C. < French *désorganiser* < *organiser* (see ORGANIZE).] —**disorganized** *adj* —**disorganizer** *n*

disorientate /diss áwriən tayt/ (**-orientates, -orientating, -orientated**), **disorient** /diss áwri ənt/ *vt* **1** to cause somebody to feel lost or confused, especially with regard to direction or position **2** to confuse somebody by giving misleading information —**disorientated** *adj* —**disorientation** /diss áwri ən táysh'n/ *n*

disown /diss ṓn/ *vt* to refuse or no longer acknowledge a connection with somebody or something —**disowner** *n* —**disownment** *n*

~~**dispair**~~ incorrect spelling of **despair**

disparage /di spárrij/ (**-ages, -aging, -aged**) *vt* to refer disapprovingly to somebody or something —**disparagement** *n* —**disparager** *n*

disparaging /di spárrijing/ *adj* showing or expressing contempt or disapproval —**disparagingly** *adv*

disparate /díspərət/ *adj* describes things or people so completely unlike each other that they cannot be compared [15C. < Latin *disparatus*, past participle of *disparare* 'separate' < *parare* 'prepare'.] —**disparately** *adv* —**disparateness** *n*

~~**disparitry**~~ incorrect spelling of **disparity**

disparity /di spárrəti/ (*plural* **-ties**) *n* **1** lack of equality between things or people **2** dissimilarity or incongruity [Mid-16C. Via French *disparité* < late Latin *disparitas* < *paritas* (see PARITY[1]).]

dispassion /diss pásh'n/ *n* absence of prejudicial feeling ○ *viewed the chaos round her with dispassion*

dispassionate /dis pásh'nət/ *adj* not influenced by emotion or personal feelings —**dispassionately** *adv* —**dispassionateness** *n*

dispatch /di spách/, **despatch** *vt* **1 SEND** to send off something, e.g. a letter or parcel, to a particular destination **2 SEND SOMEBODY AWAY TO DO** to instruct somebody to go somewhere to carry out a task **3 DEAL WITH SOMETHING QUICKLY** to complete or deal with something quickly or efficiently **4 EAT UP** to eat food quickly (*informal*) **5 KILL** to kill a person or animal ■ *n* **1 SENDING OFF** the sending of something or somebody such as a letter or a messenger **2 SPEED** speed and efficiency ○ *carried out her duties with dispatch* **3 OFFICIAL MESSAGE** a message or report, especially an official communication from a diplomat or an officer in the armed forces **4 NEWS REPORT** a news item or report sent by a journalist or news agency ○ *dispatches from the scene of the fire* **5 ACT OF KILLING** the killing of a person or animal [Early 16C. Via Italian *dispacciare* < negative form of assumed Vulgar Latin *impactare* 'impede' < Latin *impact-*, past participle of *impingere* (see IMPINGE).] —**dispatcher** *n*

dispatch box *n* **1** a case for carrying documents, especially a red case of the kind used by British government ministers **2** either of two boxes in each side of the chamber in the House of Commons that are used as lecterns by ministers when they address Parliament

dispatch case *n* a case for carrying papers or documents (*dated*)

dispel /di spél/ (**-pels, -pelling, -pelled**) *vt* **1** to rid somebody's mind of a particular thought or idea, especially an erroneous one **2** to disperse or drive away something ○ *clouds and mist that the sun soon dispelled* [15C. < Latin *dispellere* 'drive away' < *pellere* 'beat'.] —**dispeller** *n*

dispensable /di spénssəb'l/ *adj* able to be dispensed with or replaced —**dispensability** /di spénssə bílləti/ *n* —**dispensableness** *n*

dispensary /di spénssəri/ (*plural* **-ries**) *n* **1** a place where medical supplies are stored and distributed to patients by a pharmacist **2** a place where temporary medical treatment is provided

dispensation /díspən sáysh'n/ *n* **1 EXEMPTION** exemption or release from a rule or obligation, especially a religious one **2 DOCUMENT GIVING EXEMPTION** an official document authorizing dispensation, especially religious dispensation **3 RELIGIOUS SYSTEM** in Christian belief, a divinely ordained religious system **4 DIVINE ORDERING** in Christian belief, a divine ordering or management of affairs and events in the world **5 RELIGIOUS EPOCH** the time during which a religious doctrine or practice is believed to be in force **6 DISPENSING** the distribution or giving out of something ○ *dispensation of emergency supplies* —**dispensational** *adj* —**dispensatory** /di spénsətəri/ *adj*

dispense /di spénss/ (**-penses, -pensing, -pensed**) *v* **1** *vt* **PROVIDE** to distribute something to several recipients **2** *vt* **SELL** to sell something at more than one location or to more than one customer **3** *vt* **SUPPLY MEDICINES** to supply medicine according to a prescription **4** *vt* **ADMINISTER JUSTICE** to be an agent of the administration of justice **5** *vi* **GRANT DISPENSATION** to grant a religious dispensation [14C. Via Old French < Latin *dispensare* < *dispendere* 'weigh out' < *pendere* 'weigh'.]

dispense with *vt* **1** to manage without something ○ *Since it's sunny, we can dispense with the rain gear.* **2** to get rid of something not wanted or needed ○ *Let's dispense with all these convoluted rules and regulations.*

dispenser /di spénssər/ *n* **1 DEVICE FOR DISPENSING GOODS** a device that releases its contents in convenient or measured quantities when operated (*usually in combination*) **2 PROVIDER OF** a distributor of something **3 MEDICINE SUPPLIER** a retail supplier of prescription medicine

dispensing optician *n* OPHTHALMOL = **optician** *n.* 2

dispersal /di spúrss'l/ *n* **1 DISTRIBUTION** the distribution or scattering of people or things over an area **2 NATURAL SPREAD OF SEED** the natural distribution of plant seeds and the offspring of nonmobile organisms over a wide area by various methods **3 MOVEMENT OF ORGANISMS** the movement of organisms away from their place of birth or from centres of population density **4 DISAPPEARANCE** disappearance as a result of scattering or going away in different directions

dispersant /di spúrss'nt/ *n* a liquid or gas that facilitates or improves the dispersion of small particles or droplets, e.g. in an aerosol —**dispersant** *adj*

disperse /di spúrss/ (**-perses, -persing, -persed**) *vti* **1 SCATTER** to cause something to scatter or go away in different directions **2 DISTRIBUTE** to distribute something over a wide area, or become widespread **3 CAUSE TO DISAPPEAR** to cause something to disappear, or disappear **4 DISTRIBUTE EVENLY** to distribute particles evenly throughout a medium, or become distributed in this way **5 SEPARATE INTO COLOURS** to separate white light into the component colours of the spectrum, or undergo this process [14C. < Old French *disperser* < Latin *dispers-*, past participle of *dispergere* 'scatter around' < *spargere* 'scatter'.] —**disperser** *n*

dispersion /di spúrsh'n/ *n* **1 DISPERSING** the scattering or distribution of something within an area or space **2 BEING DISPERSED** the fact or state of being spread, scattered, or distributed **3 DISTRIBUTION OF VALUES** the distribution of a statistical frequency distribution about an average or median **4 MEDIUM WITH DISPERSED PARTICLES** a chemical system consisting of a gas, liquid, or colloid containing dispersed particles

Dispersion *n* JUDAISM = **Diaspora** *n.* 1

dispersive /di spúrssiv/ *adj* tending to cause dispersion —**dispersively** *adv* —**dispersiveness** *n*

dispirit /di spírrət/ *vt* to discourage or dishearten somebody —**dispirited** *adj* —**dispiritedly** *adv* —**dispiritedness** *n*

dispiriting /di spírriting/ *adj* depressing or disheartening —**dispiritingly** *adv*

displace /diss pláyss/ (**-places, -placing, -placed**) *vt* **1 MOVE FROM USUAL PLACE** to move something from its usual or correct place **2 FORCE TO LEAVE HOME** to force somebody to leave his or her home or country, e.g. because of war **3 REMOVE FROM POST** to discharge or remove somebody from an office, position, or job **4 REPLACE** to take the place of somebody or something **5 TAKE PLACE OF ATOM** to take the place of another atom or group in a compound **6 REPLACE FLUID WITH OBJECT** to replace a volume of fluid with a floating or submerged object, forcing the original fluid to move elsewhere —**displaceable** *adj* —**displacer** *n*

displaced person *n* a refugee from war or political oppression

displacement /diss pláyssmənt/ *n* **1 DISPLACING OR BEING DISPLACED** the moving or movement of something from its usual or correct place **2 FLUID DISPLACED** the fluid, e.g. water, that is forced to move by an object floating or submerged in it, often used as a measure of a ship's size **3 AMOUNT OF MOVEMENT IN PARTICULAR DIRECTION** the amount of movement of an object measured in a particular direction **4 CHEMICAL REPLACEMENT** a chemical reaction in which one atom or chemical group takes the place of another in a compound **5 TRANSFER OF EMOTIONS OR BEHAVIOUR** transfer of emotion from the original focus to another less threatening object or person, or the substitution of one response or piece of behaviour for another **6 MOVEMENT OF GEOLOGICAL FAULT** the distance that a point on one side of a geological fault has moved, relative to a corresponding point on the other side **7 ENGINE VOLUME** the total volume displaced by the pistons in an internal combustion engine

displacement ton *n* a unit of measure for the displacement of a floating ship, equivalent to 2240 lb

ϟ**display** /di spláy/ *v* **1** *vt* **MAKE VISIBLE** to make something visible or available for others to see **2** *vt* **MAKE EVIDENT** to reveal or make evident a quality or feeling **3** *vti* **SHOW DATA** to show messages, data, or graphics on a monitor, or appear on a monitor **4** *vti* **SHOW STYLIZED BEHAVIOUR** to show a particular pattern of animal behaviour, e.g. to attract a mate or defend a territory ■ *n* **1 VISUAL ARRANGEMENT** a collection of things arranged or done for others to see, especially something considered attractive, interesting, or entertaining (*often in combination*) **2 BEING VISIBLE OR ARRANGED FOR VIEWING** the act of being clearly and easily visible or placed for people to view ○ *new work on display* **3 EVIDENT FEELING OR QUALITY** an evident feeling or quality ○ *a display of courage* **4 GRAPHIC ADVERTISING** printed advertising that uses attractive pictures, typography, and other features **5 ELECTRONIC SCREEN** an electronic device that presents visual information **6 INFORMATION ON A SCREEN** the information shown on a computer monitor or other electronic device **7 STYLIZED BEHAVIOUR** a particular pattern of animal behaviour used to produce a response in other animals, especially of the same species, e.g. when courting or defending territory ■ *adj* **FOR ADVERTISING** relating to typefaces that are designed for prominent use in advertising [Late 16C. Via Old French *despleier* < Latin *displicare* 'unfold' < *plicare* 'fold'.] —**displayer** *n*

display cabinet, display case *n* a case or stand with glass panels, used for showing items of interest

displease /diss pléez/ (**-pleases, -pleasing, -pleased**) *vti* to annoy or dissatisfy somebody [14C. < Old French *desplais-*, stem of *desplaire* < assumed Vulgar Latin *displacere* < Latin *placere* 'please'.] —**displeased** *adj*

displeasing /diss pléezing/ *adj* causing annoyance or dissatisfaction —**displeasingly** *adv*

displeasure /diss plé<u>zh</u>ər/ *n* a feeling of annoyance or dissatisfaction [15C. < Old French *desplaisir* 'displease, displeasure' < *plaisir* 'pleasure'.]

disport /di spáwrt/ *vi* to behave in a playful manner (*archaic or humorous*) ■ *n* a form of lively entertainment or diversion [14C. < Old French *desporter* 'divert' < *des-* 'apart' + *porter* 'carry'.]

disposable /di spṓzəb'l/ *adj* **1 THROWAWAY** designed to be thrown away after use **2 AVAILABLE FOR USE** describes money or assets that are available for use ■ *n* **SOMETHING TO BE USED ONLY ONCE** something that is designed to be thrown away after use, e.g. a paper cup (*often plural*) —**disposability** /di spṓzə bíllәti/ *n* —**disposableness** *n*

disposable income *n* **1** income that remains available for spending after deductions for taxes and other obligations **2** the total amount of money that a country or community has available for spending

disposal /di spṓz'l/ *n* **1 PROCESS OF GETTING RID OF** the process of throwing away or getting rid of something **2 disposal, disposition ORDERLY ARRANGEMENT** an orderly arrangement, distribution, or placement **3 disposal, disposition TRANSFERRING SOMETHING TO ANOTHER** the transferring of something valuable to another by sale or gift **4** *US* **GARBAGE DISPOSAL** the disposing of domestic rubbish (*informal*)

dispose /di spṓz/ (**-poses, -posing, -posed**) *v* **1** *vt* **PUT IN PLACE** to arrange or position something for use or for a particular purpose (*formal; often passive*) **2** *vti* **SETTLE** to settle a matter by putting it into its correct or definitive form **3** *vt* **INCLINE** to make somebody likely to experience something **4** *vt* **MAKE WILLING** to make somebody willing or receptive to something (*often passive*) [14C. < French *disposer*, alteration (after *poser* 'to place') of Latin *disponere* 'set out' < *ponere* 'to place'.] —**disposer** *n*

dispose of *vt* **1 GET RID OF** to throw away or get rid of something **2 TRANSFER** to transfer something to another's ownership, by sale or other means **3 ATTEND TO** to deal with a matter in order to settle it (*formal*) **4 KILL** to kill a person or animal

disposition /díspə zísh'n/ *n* **1 PERSONALITY** somebody's usual mood or temperament **2 BEHAVIOURAL TENDENCY** an inclination or tendency to act in a particular way **3 SETTLEMENT** settlement of a business or legal matter **4** = **disposal** *n.* **2, disposal** *n.* **3** [14C. Via French < Latin *disposition-* < *disponere* (see DISPOSE).] —**dispositional** *adj*

dispositive /diss pózzətiv/ *adj* deciding the final outcome of a court case [Early 17C. Directly or via French < medieval Latin *dispositivus* < *disposit-*, past participle of Latin *disponere* (see DISPOSE).]

dispossess /díspə zéss/ *vt* to take away possession or occupancy of something, especially property, from somebody (*archaic or formal*) [15C. < Old French *despossesser* < *possesser* (see POSSESS).] —**dispossessor** *n* —**dispossessory** *adj*

dispossessed /díspə zést/ *adj* deprived of property or rights ■ *npl* people who have been deprived of their property or rights

dispossession /díspə zésh'n/ *n* **1** the act of depriving somebody of what he or she owns, usually land or money **2** the state of being deprived of everything you have, especially land or money

dispraise /diss práyz/ *vt* (**-praises, -praising, -praised**) to express disapproval of somebody (*archaic or literary*) ■ *n* the expression of disapproval (*archaic*) —**dispraiser** *n*

disproof /diss próof/ *n* **1** the disproving of a legal argument or point **2** evidence that disproves something

disproportion /díspra páwrsh'n/ *n* something that is out of proportion or unequal ■ *vt* to make something disproportionate —**disproportionable** *adj* —**disproportionableness** *n* —**disproportionably** *adv*

disproportionate /díspra páwrsh'nət/, **disproportional** /-sh'nəl/ *adj* unequal or out of proportion in quantity, shape, or size —**disproportionately** *adv* —**disproportionateness** *n*

disproportionation /díspra páwrsh'n áysh'n/ *n* a chemical reaction in which a single substance acts as both oxidizing and reducing agent, resulting in the production of dissimilar substances

disprove /diss próov/ (**-proves, -proving, -proved**) *vt* to show that something is incorrect [14C. < Old French *desprover* & *prover* (see PROVE).] —**disprovable** *adj* —**disproval** *n*

disputable /di spyóotəb'l/ *adj* not definitely true or valid and therefore debatable or open to argument —**disputability** /di spyóotə bíllәti/ *n* —**disputableness** *n*

disputably /di spyóotəbli/ *adv* used to suggest that the speaker or writer thinks something is true and could defend that view against those who disagree

USAGE See ***arguably***.

disputation /díspyoo táysh'n/ *n* **1** arguing or disagreement (*formal*) **2** a formal academic debate in defence of a thesis

disputatious /díspyoo táyshəss/, **disputative** /di spyóotətiv/ *adj* tending to argue or disagree without adequate cause —**disputatiously** *adv* —**disputatiousness** *n*

dispute /di spyóot, díss pyoot/ *v* (**-putes, -puting, -puted**) **1** *vti* **QUERY** to question or doubt the truth or validity of something **2** *vi* **DISAGREE** to disagree or argue about something **3** *vt* **CONTEST** to fight for or strive to win something (*formal*) **4** *vt* **OPPOSE** to strive against or resist something (*formal*) ■ *n* **1 ARGUMENT** serious argument or disagreement **2 INDUSTRIAL DISAGREEMENT** a prolonged disagreement between management and workers or a trade union, often involving industrial action [Late 16C. Via Old French < Latin *disputare* 'argue out' < *putare* 'consider'.] —**disputant** *adj, n* —**disputer** *n*

SYNONYMS See ***disagree***.

USAGE The traditional pronunciation of both the noun and the verb uses of ***dispute*** is with the stress on the second syllable. More recently, a stress on the first syllable has been increasingly heard.

disqualification /diss kwóllifi káysh'n/ *n* **1 INELIGIBILITY** being or becoming ineligible to do or take part in something **2 ACT OF BEING DISQUALIFIED** an instance of being disqualified **3 SOMETHING THAT DISQUALIFIES** something that makes somebody ineligible to do or take part in something

disqualify /diss kwólli fī/ (**-fies, -fying, -fied**) *vt* **1** to make or declare somebody unfit, unqualified, or ineligible to do or take part in something **2** to deprive somebody of a legal or other right or privilege —**disqualifiable** *adj* —**disqualified** *adj* —**disqualifier** *n*

disquiet /diss kwī ət/ *n* a lack of inner peace resulting from anxiety

disquieting /diss kwī əting/ *adj* causing discomfort, worry, or doubt to arise —**disquietingly** *adv*

disquietude /diss kwī ə tyood/ *n* = **disquiet**

disquisition /dískwi zísh'n/ *n* a long formal essay or discussion on a subject [Early 17C. Via French < Latin *disquisition-* < *disquirere* 'inquire' < *quaerere* 'seek, ask'.] —**disquisitional** *adj*

Disraeli /diz ráyli/, **Benjamin, 1st Earl of Beaconsfield** (1804–81) British statesman and novelist

disrate /díss ráyt/ (**-rates, -rating, -rated**) *vt* to demote somebody in the military to a lower rank

disregard /díssri gaárd/ *vt* **1 IGNORE** to ignore or pay no attention to somebody or something **2 TREAT WITHOUT RESPECT** to treat somebody or something with contempt or without respect ■ *n* **NEGLECT** lack of attention or respect —**disregarder** *n* —**disregardful** *adj* —**disregardfully** *adv* —**disregardfulness** *n*

disremember /díssri mémbər/ *vti* to forget or fail to remember something (*informal*)

disrepair /díssri páir/ *n* poor working order or condition as a result of neglect

disreputable /diss réppyootəb'l/ *adj* **1** lacking respectability on the basis of past or present actions **2** untidy, dirty, or worn in appearance (*humorous*) —**disreputability** /diss réppyootə bíllәti/ *n* —**disreputableness** *n* —**disreputably** *adv*

disrepute /díssri pyóot/ *n* a lack or loss of good reputation or respect

disrespect /díssri spékt/ *n* a lack of respect ■ *vt* to show a lack of respect for somebody or something —**disrespectable** *adj* —**disrespectableness** *n* —**disrespectful** *adj* —**disrespectfully** *adv*

disrobe /dis rṓb/ (**-robes, -robing, -robed**) *vti* to remove your own or somebody else's clothing (*formal*) [Late 16C. < Old French *desrober* < *robe* (see ROBE).] —**disrobement** *n* —**disrober** *n*

disrupt /dis rúpt/ *vt* **1** to interrupt the normal course of a process or activity **2** to destroy the order or orderly progression of something [15C. < Latin *disrupt-*, past participle of *disrumpere* 'break apart' < *rumpere* 'break'.] —**disrupter** *n*

disruption /dis rúpsh'n/ *n* **1 UNWANTED BREAK** an unwelcome or unexpected break in a process or activity **2 SUSPENSION** the interruption or suspension of normal activity or progress **3 STATE OF DISORDER** a state of disorder caused by outside influence **4 Disruption** *Scotland* **SPLIT IN CHURCH OF SCOTLAND** a split in the Church of Scotland in 1843, leading to the formation of the Free Church

disruptive /dis rúptiv/ *adj* interrupting normal order or progress —**disruptively** *adv* —**disruptiveness** *n*

ϟ**disruptive technology** *n* new and advanced technology that is incompatible with traditional business methods and requires large-scale changes or a new approach

diss *vt* = **dis** (*slang*)

~~**dissapear**~~ incorrect spelling of **disappear**

~~**dissapointed**~~ incorrect spelling of **disappointed**

dissatisfaction /díss satiss fáksh'n, di sáttiss-/ *n* a state or feeling of not being satisfied

dissatisfactory /díss satiss fáktəri/ *adj* not satisfactory

dissatisfy /díss sáttiss fī/ (**-fies, -fying, -fied**) *vt* to displease or fail to satisfy somebody —**dissatisfied** *adj* —**dissatisfiedly** *adv*

dissect /dī sékt, di-/ *v* **1** *vti* to cut and separate the parts of animal or plant specimens for scientific study **2** *vt* to examine or analyse a person or subject in detail [Late 16C. < Latin *dissect-*, past participle of *dissecare* 'cut apart' < *secare* 'cut'.] —**dissectible** *adj* —**dissector** *n*

dissected /dī séktid, di-/ *adj* **1** describes a leaf that is divided into narrow lobes or segments **2** describes a landscape that has been eroded into hills and valleys

dissection /dī séksh'n, di-/ *n* **1 CUTTING AND EXAMINING** the cutting and separating of the constituent parts of animal or plant specimens for scientific study **2 DISSECTED SPECIMEN** something that has been dissected, e.g. an anatomical specimen **3 EXAMINATION** a thorough and detailed analysis or examination

disseise /diss séez/ (**-seises, -seising, -seised**), **disseize** (**-seizes, -seizing, -seized**) *vi* to deprive somebody wrongfully of possession of land [14C. < Anglo-Norman *disseisir*, variant of Old French *dessaisir* 'dispossess' < *saisir* (see SEIZE).] —**disseisor** *n*

disseize *vt* = **disseise**

dissemble /di sémb'l/ (**-bles, -bling, -bled**) *v* **1** *vi* **PUT ON FALSE APPEARANCE** to put on a false appearance in order to conceal facts, feelings, or intentions **2** *vt* **GIVE APPEARANCE** to put on the appearance of something not actually felt or true (*formal*) **3** *vt* **HIDE BY PRETENCE** to hide real beliefs or intentions through misleading speech or behaviour (*formal*) [15C. < Old French *dessembler* 'be different' < *sembler* 'seem'.] —**dissemblance** *n* —**dissembler** *n*

dissembling /di sémbling/ *n* creation or adoption of a false appearance so as to elicit a false impression on the part of somebody else ■ *adj* feigning or pretending —**dissemblingly** *adv*

disseminate /di sémmi nayt/ (**-nates, -nating, -nated**) *vti* to distribute or spread something, especially information, or become widespread [15C. < Latin *disseminat-*, past participle of *disseminare* 'sow abroad' < *semin-* 'seed'.] —**dissemination** /di sémmi náysh'n/ *n* —**disseminative** *adj* —**disseminator** *n*

SYNONYMS See ***scatter***.

dissension /di sénsh'n/ *n* disagreement or difference of opinion, especially when leading to open conflict [14C. Via French < Latin *dissension-* < *dissentire* (see DISSENT).]

dissensus /diss sénsəss/ *n* a preponderance of disagreement [Mid-20C. Blend of DISSENT + CONSENSUS.]

dissent /di sént/ *vi* **1 DISAGREE** to disagree with a widely held or majority opinion **2 NOT SUPPORT RELIGIOUS PRACTICES** to refuse to conform to the authority, doctrines, or practices of an established church **3 WITHHOLD ASSENT** to withhold assent or approval ■ *n* **1 DISAGREEMENT** disagreement from a widely held or majority opinion **2 RELIGIOUS NONCONFORMITY** refusal to conform to the authority, doctrines, or practices of an established church **3 MINORITY OPINION** an opinion of a judge that is not in agreement with that of other judges **4 REFUSAL TO ACCEPT POLITICAL RULES** opposition to the laws, norms, and structures of a political regime, especially on moral grounds [15C. < Latin *dissentire* 'feel differently' < *sentire* 'feel'.]

SPELLCHECK See ***descent***.

dissenter /di séntər/ *n* an opponent of the beliefs or opinions of a majority

Dissenter *n* somebody who rejects the authority, doctrines, or practices of an established church, especially a Protestant who did not accept the Church of England in the 17th and 18th centuries

dissentient /di sénshi ənt/ *adj* showing or expressing disagreement with the beliefs or opinions of a majority [Early 17C. < Latin *dissentient-*, present participle of *dissentire* (see DISSENT).] —**dissentience** *n* —**dissentiency** *n* —**dissentient** *n* —**dissentiently** *adv*

dissenting /di sénting/ *adj* **1 EXPRESSING OR SHOWING DISAGREEMENT** disagreeing with the beliefs or opinions of a majority **2 dissenting, Dissenting OF DISSENTERS** relating or belonging to a group of religious nonconformists, especially an English Protestant denomination of the 17th or 18th centuries **3 DISAGREEING WITH OTHER JUDGES** disagreeing with the majority verdict or opinion of other judges —**dissentingly** *adv*

dissepiment /di séppimənt/ *n* a dividing wall or membrane separating an organ, e.g. a plant ovary, into distinct chambers [Early 18C. < Latin *dissaepimentum* < *dissaepire* 'make separate' < *saepire* 'divide off' < *saepes* 'hedge'.] —**dissepimental** /di séppi mént'l/ *adj*

dissertation /díssər táysh'n/ *n* **1** a lengthy and formal written treatment of a subject, especially a long essay submitted as a requirement for a university degree **2** a formal spoken or written discourse —**dissertational** *adj* —**dissertationist** *n*

disservice /diss súrviss/ *n* an action that causes harm or difficulty

dissever /di sévvər/ *v* (*formal*) **1** *vt* **SEPARATE** to separate or sever something **2** *vt* **BREAK UP** to break up or divide something **3** *vi* **COME APART** to come apart or become disunited [13C. Via Anglo-Norman *deseverer* < late Latin *disseparare* 'split apart' < Latin *separare* (see SEPARATE).] —**disseverance** *n* —**disseveration** /díss sevə ráysh'n/ *n* —**disseverment** *n*

dissidence /díssidənss/ *n* disagreement with authority or with prevailing opinion

dissident /díssidənt/ *n* a public opponent of an established political or religious system or organization [Mid-16C. < Latin *dissident-*, present participle of *dissidere* 'sit apart' < *sedere* 'sit'.] —**dissident** *adj* —**dissidently** *adv*

dissimilar /di símmilər/ *adj* differing in one or more respects —**dissimilarly** *adv*

dissimilarity /díssimi lárrəti/ (*plural* **-ties**) *n* **1** the fact or state of being different in one or more respects **2** a point of difference or distinction

dissimilate /di símmi layt/ (**-lates, -lating, -lated**) *vti* **1** to make something dissimilar, or become dissimilar **2** to undergo linguistic dissimilation, or to change a consonant or consonants by this process [Mid-19C. < DIS- + ASSIMILATE.] —**dissimilative** *adj* —**dissimilatory** *adj*

dissimilation /di símmi láysh'n/ *n* **1** the process of becoming dissimilar **2** the development of a dissimilarity between two consonant sounds in a word that are originally identical

dissimilitude /díssi mílli tyood/ *n* the condition or quality of differing or of being different to something else or others (*formal*) [15C. < Latin *dissimilitudo* < *dissimilis* 'unlike' < *similis* 'like, similar'.]

dissimulate /di ssímmyoo layt/ (**-lates, -lating, -lated**) *vti* to disguise or hide your true feelings, thoughts, or intentions [15C. < Latin *dissimulat-*, past participle of *dissimulare* 'disguise completely' < *simulare* (see SIMULATE).] —**dissimulation** /di símmyoo láysh'n/ *n* —**dissimulative** *adj* —**dissimulator** *n*

dissipate /díssi payt/ (**-pates, -pating, -pated**) *v* **1** *vti* **CAUSE TO DIMINISH** to cause something to fade or disappear, or to undergo such a process **2** *vt* **WASTE** to spend or use something wastefully **3** *vi* **OVERINDULGE** to indulge excessively or extravagantly in the pursuit of pleasure by physical methods [15C. < Latin *dissipat-*, past participle of *dissipare* 'scatter around'.] —**dissipater** *n* —**dissipative** *adj* —**dissipator** *n*

dissipated /díssi paytid/ *adj* overindulging in the pursuit of pleasure by physical methods —**dissipatedly** *adv* —**dissipatedness** *n*

dissipation /díssi páysh'n/ *n* **1 OVERINDULGENCE** overindulgence in the pursuit of physical pleasures by physical methods **2 WASTEFUL USE** the use or squandering of resources, e.g. money or fuel (*formal*) **3 DISAPPEARANCE** disappearance through being scattered or dispersed **4 REMOVAL** the disappearing of a feeling or emotion, e.g. anger or anxiety

dissociate /di sóshi ayt, -sóssi-/ (**-ates, -ating, -ated**) *v* **1** *vt* **REGARD AS DISTINCT** to treat somebody or something as distinct from or unconnected with somebody or something else **2** *vt* = **disassociate** *v.* 2 **3** *vt* = **disassociate** *v.* 1 **4** *vti* **SPLIT INTO SIMPLER PARTS** to cause the molecules of a compound to break down into simpler molecules, atoms, or ions, usually in a reversible reaction, or break down in this way **5** *vi* **SEPARATE OFF AREAS OF THE MIND** to separate a group of mental processes from the rest of the mind, causing them to lose their normal relationship with it [Mid-16C. < Latin *dissociare* 'separate from fellowship' < *sociare* 'join together' < *socius* 'companion'.] —**dissociability** *n* —**dissociable** *adj* —**dissociableness** *n* —**dissociative** *adj*

dissociation /di sóshi áysh'n, -sóssi-/ *n* **1 TREATMENT OF SOMETHING AS UNCONNECTED** the treatment of somebody or something as distinct or unconnected, or the fact of being regarded in this way **2** = **disassociation** *n.* 2 **3** = **disassociation** *n.* 1 **4 DIVISION OF MOLECULE** a breaking up of a molecule into simpler components **5 SEPARATION OF EMOTIONS** the separation of a group of normally connected mental processes, e.g. emotion and understanding, from the rest of the mind as a defence mechanism

USAGE See ***disassociation***.

dissoluble /di sóllyoob'l/ *adj* able to be dissolved, separated, or ended [Mid-16C. Directly or via French < Latin *dissolubilis* < *dissolvere* (see DISSOLVE).] —**dissolubility** /di sóllyoo bíllati/ *n* —**dissolubleness** *n*

dissolute /díssə loot/ *adj* overindulging in physical pleasures in a way or to an extent that is considered immoral or harmful [14C. < Latin *dissolutus*, past participle of *dissolvere* (see DISSOLVE).] —**dissolutely** *adv* —**dissoluteness** *n*

dissolution /díssə lóosh'n/ *n* **1 BREAKING DOWN OF SOMETHING INTO PARTS** the separating, decomposing, or disintegrating of something into smaller or more basic constituents **2 BREAKING UP OF** the breaking up or destruction of an organization or institution ○ *the dissolution of parliament* **3 FORMAL CLOSING** the bringing to an end of a meeting or assembly, especially the formal ending of the current parliament's jurisdiction before a general election **4 ENDING OF LEGAL RELATIONSHIP** the termination of a legal relationship, e.g. a business partnership or a marriage **5 DEMISE** somebody's death (*formal*)

dissolve /di zólv/ *v* (**-solves, -solving, -solved**) **1** *vti* **BECOME ABSORBED IN LIQUID** to become absorbed in a liquid solution, or cause this process to occur to a solid ○ *Dissolve two tablets in a glass of water.* **2** *vti* **DISAPPEAR** to fade away gradually and disappear, or make something gradually fade away and disappear ○ *All his fears dissolved.* **3** *vti* **BREAK UP** to break up, or break something up, into smaller or more basic parts **4** *vi* **START LAUGHING OR CRYING** to begin to laugh or cry uncontrollably **5** *vt* **CLOSE FORMALLY** to bring something such as a meeting or a political assembly to a formal close, especially to end the jurisdiction of a current parliament before a general election **6** *vt* **END LEGAL RELATIONSHIP** to bring a legal relationship, e.g. a business partnership or a marriage, formally to an end **7** *vi* **SIMULTANEOUSLY FADE OUT AND IN** to fade out slowly as a second image fades in, briefly merging one with the other ■ *n* **SIMULTANEOUS FADING OUT AND IN** a change from one scene to another, with the first scene gradually fading out and the next one gradually fading in over it [14C. < Latin *dissolvere* 'loosen asunder' < *solvere* 'loosen'.] —**dissolvability** /di zólvə bíllati/ *n* —**dissolvable** *adj* —**dissolvent** *adj* —**dissolver** *n*

dissonance /díssənənss/ *n* **1 UNPLEASANT NOISE** a combination of sounds that is unpleasant to listen to **2 INCONSISTENCY** lack of consistency or compatibility between actions or beliefs **3 UNSTABLE COMBINATION OF MUSICAL NOTES** a combination of notes that, when played simultaneously, sounds displeasing and needs to be resolved to a consonance

dissonant /díssənənt/ *adj* **1 UNPLEASANT TO HEAR** making or involving a combination of sounds that is unpleasant to listen to **2 CONFLICTING** incompatible or inconsistent (*formal*) **3 CONTAINING UNSTABLE CHORDS** containing unstable chords or harmonies that need to be resolved to a consonance [15C. < Latin *dissonant-*, present participle of *dissonare* 'be apart in sound' < *sonare* 'to sound'.] —**dissonantly** *adv*

dissuade /di swáyd/ (**-suades, -suading, -suaded**) *vt* to persuade somebody not to do something or not to believe, think, or feel something [Early 16C. < Latin *dissuadere* 'advise against' < *suadere* 'advise, persuade'.] —**dissuadable** *adj* —**dissuader** *n*

dissuasion /di swáyzh'n/ *n* persuasion not to do something or not to believe, think, or feel something [15C. Directly or via French < Latin *dissuasion-* < *dissuas-*, past participle of *dissuadere* (see DISSUADE).]

dissuasive /di swáyssiv/ *adj* convincing enough to persuade somebody not to do something or not to believe, think, or feel something [Early 16C. < the Latin past participle stem *dissuas-* of *dissuadere* (see DISSUADE).] —**dissuasively** *adv* —**dissuasiveness** *n*

dissyllable *n* = **dissyllable**

dissymmetric /díss si méttrik, díssi-/, **dissymmetrical** /-méttrik'l/ *adj* 1 = **asymmetric** *adj.* 1 2 showing the sort of symmetry possessed by things that are mirror images of each other —**dissymmetrically** *adv*

dissymmetry /diss símmitri, di-/ (*plural* **-tries**) *n* 1 = **asymmetry** *n.* 1 2 the kind of symmetry that exists between things that are mirror images of each other

dist. *abbr* 1 distance 2 district

distaff /dí staaf/ (*plural* **-taffs** *or* **-taves** /-stayvz/) *n* 1 women's work, or any other matters traditionally considered to be the concern of women (*literary*) 2 a rod on which wool or flax is wound for somebody to use when spinning by hand, or the corresponding rod on a spinning wheel [Old English *distæf* < Germanic, 'bunch of flax' + STAFF[1]]

distaff side *n* a wife's or mother's side of a family (*literary*) ◊ **spear side**

distal /díst'l/ *adj* describes a body part situated away from a point of attachment or origin. ◊ **proximal** [Early 19C. < DISTANT + -AL[1].] —**distally** *adv*

distance /dístənss/ *n* 1 **LENGTH BETWEEN THINGS** the length of the space separating two people, places, or things ○ *What's the distance between Paris and New York?* 2 **FAR-OFF PLACE** a place or position far away or not very close ○ *It's best seen from a distance.* 3 **CLOSENESS ALLOWING SOME ACTIVITY** the space between two people, places, or things with regard to activity carried on between the two ○ *We can do nothing until they're within hailing distance.* 4 **AMOUNT OF SEPARATION** the amount by which two places are separated, especially when thought of in terms of the time or inconvenience of a journey between the two ○ *She lives some distance away.* 5 **ALOOFNESS** a cool or slightly aloof response to another person or group 6 **INTERVAL OF TIME** the interval between one point in time and another, especially a long interval ○ *You can't expect to remember all the details at a distance of more than 20 years.* 7 **AMOUNT OF PROGRESS** the amount of progress that has been made or that is still to be made ○ *still some distance to go before we can reach an agreement* 8 **IDEOLOGICAL GULF** difference of opinion or ideology ○ *There's still some distance between us with regard to the basic issues.* 9 **SPACE GREATER THAN 20 LENGTHS** a space of more than twenty lengths between two racehorses, usually the winner and the horse finishing second ■ *v* (**-tances, -tancing, -tanced**) 1 *vr* **AVOID EMOTIONAL INVOLVEMENT** to avoid becoming emotionally involved in something ○ *Try to distance yourself from past experiences.* 2 *vt* **AVOID SUPPORTING** to avoid giving or deny that you provide support to or are involved with somebody or something ○ *He was trying to distance himself from the allegations.* 3 *vt* **WIN BY A DISTANCE** to beat another racehorse by more than twenty lengths [13C. Directly or via French < Latin *distantia* < *distant-* 'standing apart' (see DISTANT).] ◇ **go the distance** to continue until you have completed something

distance learning *n* education for students working at home, with little or no face-to-face contact with teachers and with material provided remotely, e.g. by e-mail, television, or post

distant /dístənt/ *adj* 1 **FAR AWAY** situated, living, or happening far away ○ *a distant galaxy* 2 **FAR AWAY IN TIME** remote in time, either in the future or the past ○ *They hope to meet again in the distant future.* 3 **ALOOF** showing that somebody does not want to be friendly or intimate 4 **FAINT** so slight as to be hard to discern ○ *a distant resemblance* [14C. Directly or via French < Latin *distant-*, present participle of *distare* 'stand apart' < *stare* 'stand'.] —**distantness** *n*

distantly /dístəntli/ *adv* 1 **FAR AWAY** from far away and therefore usually not clear or loud ○ *We could distantly make out figures dancing in the village square.* 2 **FAR AWAY MENTALLY** not concentrating on the immediate surroundings 3 **ALOOFLY** in a detached, cold, or formal way ○ *He smiled at her distantly as she walked past.* 4 **NOT CLOSELY** not closely in terms of family or blood relations ○ *distantly related*

distaste /diss táyst/ *n* a feeling of dislike, disapproval, or mild disgust

SYNONYMS See ***dislike***.

distasteful /diss táystf'l/ *adj* provoking dislike, disapproval, or mild disgust —**distastefully** *adv* —**distastefulness** *n*

distemper[1] /dis témpər/ *n* a viral disease that affects various animals, especially dogs and cats [Mid-16C. < late Latin *distemperare* 'combine awry' (referring to an imbalance of bodily 'humours') < Latin *temperare* (see TEMPER).]

distemper[2] /dis témpər/ *n* 1 paint in which the colouring material is mixed with water and a substance such as glue or size rather than with oil 2 the use of distemper in painting posters and murals [14C. Directly or via Old French *destremper* 'soak, mix' < late Latin *distemperare* (see DISTEMPER[1]).] —**distemper** *vt*

distend /di sténd/ *vti* to expand, swell, or inflate as if by pressure from within [14C. < Latin *distendere* 'stretch apart' < *tendere* 'stretch'.] —**distender** *n* —**distensibility** /di sténssə bílləti/ *n* —**distensible** /-sténssəb'l/ *adj* —**distension** /-sténsh'n/ *n*

distich /dí stik/ *n* two lines of poetry, sometimes rhyming, that form a complete unit in themselves [Early 16C. Via Latin < Greek *distikhon*, form of *distikhos* 'of two rows or verses' < *stikhos* 'row, line of verse'.] —**distichal** *adj*

distichous /dístikəss/ *adj* describes leaves that grow in vertical rows on opposite sides of a stem —**distichously** *adv*

distil /di stíl/ (**-tils, -tilling, -tilled**) *v* 1 *vti* **PURIFY LIQUID WITH HEAT** to purify a liquid by heating it and then condensing its vapour, or undergo purification in this way 2 *vt* **MAKE ALCOHOLIC SPIRITS** to produce alcoholic spirits using the process of heating liquid and condensing its vapour 3 *vt* **CREATE FROM ESSENTIAL ELEMENTS** to create something from the essential or most important elements of something larger or longer 4 *vi* **EMERGE SLOWLY** to be emitted slowly or in small quantities ○ *'Then slowly from the silence there distilled drops of music'* (John Buchan, *Greenmantle*; 1916) [14C. < Latin *distillare*, alteration of *destillare*, literally 'drip apart' < *stillare* 'to drip' < *stilla* 'drop'.] —**distillable** *adj*

distill *vti* US = **distil**

distillate /dístələt, -ayt/ *n* 1 **distillate, distillation** a concentrated liquid produced by heating a liquid mixture and condensing the vapour 2 the concentrated essence of something

distillation /dístə láysh'n/ *n* 1 the process of separating, concentrating, or purifying liquid by boiling it and condensing the resulting vapour 2 something that consists of the essential points, aspects, or implications of something larger or longer 3 CHEM = **distillate** *n.* 1 —**distillatory** /di stíllətəri/ *adj*

distillation column *n* a hollow vertical column, fitted inside with perforated trays or packing material, in which liquid mixtures are separated into their components by heating the mixture and condensing the vapour produced

distilled /di stíld/ *adj* 1 derived from or encapsulating a wider experience or larger set of ideas 2 describes liquids that have been purified or concentrated by distillation

distiller /di stíllər/ *n* a company that or person who produces alcoholic spirits such as whisky, vodka, and gin

distillery /di stílləri/ (*plural* **-ies**) *n* a place where strong alcoholic drinks such as whisky, vodka, and gin are made by distilling

distinct /di stíngkt/ *adj* 1 **SEPARATE** clearly different and separate ○ *The word has two distinct senses.* 2 **APPARENT TO THE SENSES** easy to hear, see, smell, or understand ○ *I have a very distinct memory of that day.* 3 **CERTAIN** definite or undeniable ○ *I had the distinct impression they'd been arguing.* 4 **NOTICEABLE** strong enough, large enough, or definite enough to be noticed ○ *There's a distinct smell of petrol in the car.* 5 **EMPHATIC** very great in degree, e.g. as an honour felt or experienced ○ *a distinct privilege* [14C. Directly or via French < Latin *distinctus*, past participle of *distinguere* 'to separate' (see DISTINGUISH).] —**distinctly** *adv* —**distinctness** *n*

distinction /di stíngksh'n/ *n* 1 **DIFFERENCE** a difference, or the recognition of a difference, between two or more things or people 2 **HIGH QUALITY** excellence in quality or talent ○ *tailors of distinction* 3 **SOMETHING TO BE PROUD OF** something done or given as a mark of respect or honour ○ *I had the distinction of giving the opening address.* 4 **DISTINGUISHING FEATURE** something that characterizes or singles out something or somebody ○ *She has the dubious distinction of being the government's most slavish defender.* 5 **HIGH EXAMINATION GRADE** a high mark in an examination

distinctive /di stíngktiv/ *adj* 1 uniquely characteristic of a particular person, group, or thing 2 relating to the features of a phoneme that distinguish it from other similar phonemes, e.g. the fact that it is labial, fricative, or nasal —**distinctively** *adv* —**distinctiveness** *n*

distingué /di stáng gay/ *adj* having the confidence and dignity of somebody who is used to being respected [Early 19C. < French, past participle of *distinguer* (see DISTINGUISH).]

distinguish /di stíng gwish/ *v* 1 *vti* **RECOGNIZE DIFFERENCES** to be aware of a difference between two or more people, groups, or things, or show that they are different from each other ○ *to distinguish between fact and fiction* 2 *vt* **BE THE DIFFERENCE BETWEEN** to be the feature or characteristic that shows that one person, group, or thing is different from another ○ *What distinguishes dogs from wolves?* 3 *vt* **MAKE OUT** to be able to recognize or identify something ○ *I could barely distinguish people's faces in the fog.* 4 *vr* **DO SOMETHING WELL** to attract attention and praise in a particular field ○ *He distinguished himself on the field of battle.* [Late 16C. < French *distinguer* or Latin *distinguere* 'to separate' < *stinguere* 'quench'.] —**distinguishability** /di stíng gwishə bílləti/ *n* —**distinguishable** /di stíng gwishəb'l/ *adj* —**distinguisher** *n*

distinguished /di stíng gwisht/ *adj* 1 **RECOGNIZED FOR EXCELLENCE** well known and respected for a particular achievement, skill, knowledge, or talent ○ *a distinguished composer* 2 **CONFIDENT AND DIGNIFIED** showing the confident and dignified appearance and manners of somebody who is used to respect 3 **SUCCESSFUL** showing or involving a great deal of skill, talent, or success

Distinguished Conduct Medal *n* a medal awarded to noncommissioned officers, warrant officers, and ordinary soldiers and airmen and women in the British Army and Royal Air Force for distinguished conduct in action

Distinguished Flying Cross *n* 1 a Royal Air Force medal awarded to noncommissioned and warrant officers for distinguished conduct when flying in action 2 a US military medal awarded for extraordinary achievement or for heroism in air combat

Distinguished Service Cross *n* 1 a British medal awarded in all branches of the armed forces for distinguished service in action 2 a US Army medal awarded for extraordinary heroism against an enemy

Distinguished Service Medal *n* a British medal awarded for distinguished conduct in action to noncommissioned officers and ordinary seamen and women in the Royal Navy and Royal Marines

Distinguished Service Order *n* a British medal awarded to commissioned officers in all armed forces for distinguished service in action

distinguishing /di stíng gwishing/ *adj* allowing one person, group, or thing to be told apart from another ○ *distinguishing characteristics*

distort /di stáwrt/ *v* 1 *vt* **GIVE AN INACCURATE REPORT OF** to describe or report something in a way that is inaccurate or misleading 2 *vti* **ALTER SHAPE** to bend, twist, stretch, or change from a normal or natural shape, or make something do this 3 *vt* **MAKE UNNATURAL OR UNCLEAR** to change something such as an image in such a way that it becomes unclear or unrecognizable 4 *vt* **REPRODUCE INACCURATELY** to amplify or reproduce something, e.g. a radio signal, inaccurately [15C. < Latin *distort-*, past participle of *distorquere* 'twist completely' < *torquere* 'twist'.] —**distorted** *adj* —**distortedly** *adv* —**distortedness** *n* —**distorter** *n* —**distortive** *adj*

distortion /di stáwrsh'n/ *n* 1 **MISLEADING ALTERATION** the altering of information in such a way that people are misinformed or misled 2 **CHANGING FROM CORRECT SHAPE** the bending or twisting of something out of its normal or natural shape 3 **MISSHAPEN PART** a part of something that has been bent, twisted, stretched, or forced out of its normal or natural shape 4 **MAKING SOMETHING UNCLEAR** the altering of something, e.g. a radio or television signal, to the extent that it becomes unclear or unrecognizable 5 **ALTERATION IN OPTICAL IMAGE** an alteration in an image in which the original proportions are changed, resulting from a defect in a lens or optical system —**distortional** *adj* —**distortionary** *adj*

distr. *abbr* 1 distribution 2 distributor

distract /di strákt/ *vt* 1 **CATCH SOMEBODY'S ATTENTION** to take somebody's attention away from what he or she is doing or thinking or from what is happening 2 **AMUSE** to amuse or entertain somebody, especially as a means of taking his or her mind off something unpleasant 3 **MAKE UNEASY** to unsettle somebody's mind with disturbing, confusing, or conflicting emotions (*archaic*) ○ *'O Husband, Husband, my Heart long'd to see thee; but to see thee thus distracts me'.* (John Gay, *The Beggar's Opera*; 1728) [14C. < Latin *distract-*, past participle of *distrahere* 'draw away' < *trahere* 'draw, drag'.] **—distracter** *n* **—distractibility** /di strắktə bíllәti/ *n* **—distractible** *adj* **—distractive** *adj* **—distractively** *adv*

distracted /di stráktid/ *adj* **1** showing a lack of concentration **2** so worried or upset as to be unable to think clearly or act sensibly **—distractedly** *adv* **—distractedness** *n*

distracting /di strákting/ *adj* **1** taking somebody's attention away from what he or she wants to do or ought to be doing **2** helping somebody to relax and forget work or worries **—distractingly** *adv*

distraction /di stráksh'n/ *n* **1 SOMETHING THAT DIVERTS ATTENTION** something that interferes with concentration or takes attention away from something else **2 AMUSEMENT** something providing entertainment or amusement, especially something that takes the mind off work or worries and helps relaxation **3 EMOTIONAL UPSET** a state of great mental or emotional upset

distractor /di stráktər/ *n* **1** any of the incorrect options shown as possible answers to a multiple-choice question **2** a person or thing that distracts people's attention

distrain /di stráyn/ *vt* to take and hold somebody's property as a pledge for something such as unpaid rent [14C. < Old French *destreign-*, present stem of *destreindre* < Latin *distringere* 'draw asunder'.] **—distrainable** *adj* **—distrainee** /di stráy neé/ *n* **—distrainer** *n* **—distrainment** *n*

distraint /di stráynt/ *n* the seizing of somebody's movable property either in lieu of payment of a debt or in order to force the person to pay. US term **distress** *n.* **5** [Mid-18C. < DISTRAIN; after CONSTRAINT.]

distrait /di stráy, dí stray/ *adj* inattentive and slightly distracted or absent-minded (*literary*) [14C. < French, < past participle of Old French *destraire* 'distract' < Latin *distrahere* (see DISTRACT).]

distraught /di stráwt/ *adj* extremely upset and distressed [14C. Alteration of archaic *distract* 'perplexed' < Latin *distractus*, past participle of *distrahere* (see DISTRACT).] **—distraughtly** *adv*

distress /di stréss/ *n* **1 MENTAL SUFFERING** mental suffering, e.g. that caused by grief, anxiety, or unhappiness **2 HARDSHIP** difficulty or hardship caused by a lack of basic necessities **3 PHYSICAL PAIN** physical pain or discomfort **4 DANGER** great danger or difficulty, with a need for immediate assistance ○ *a ship in distress* **5 distress, distraint** LAW = **distraint** ■ *vt* **1 UPSET** to make somebody extremely upset, anxious, or alarmed **2 MAKE FURNITURE OR FABRIC LOOK OLD** to give a new piece of furniture or fabric an old or worn appearance [13C. Via Old French *destresce* < assumed Vulgar Latin *districtia* < Latin *district-*, past participle of *distringere* 'draw asunder'.]

distressed /di strést/ *adj* **1 VERY UPSET** extremely upset, anxious, or unhappy **2 LACKING MONEY** not having enough money to live on **3 MADE TO LOOK OLDER** artificially given an old or worn appearance **4** *US* **REPOSSESSED FROM BAD DEBTOR** repossessed by a bank or other lender from the borrower and offered for sale at a reduced price ○ *a distressed loan*

distressing /di stréssing/, **distressful** /-stréssf'l/ *adj* causing somebody to feel extremely upset **—distressingly** *adv*

distress signal *n* a signal, e.g. a radio message or a flare, sent by a ship or aircraft in urgent need of assistance

distributary /di stríbbyŏŏtəri/ (*plural* **-ies**) *n* a channel leading water away from a main single channel

distribute /di stríbbyoot/ (**-utes, -uting, -uted**) *v* **1** *vt* **GIVE OUT** to deliver or share things out to people ○ *distribute prizes* **2** *vt* **SHARE OUT** to share something out among a number of people **3** *vt* **SPREAD** to scatter something about or spread it throughout a particular area or place **4** *vt* **DIVIDE INTO CLASSES** to divide something up into different classes or categories **5** *vt* **MAKE TERM APPLY TO ALL** to apply a term to all the members of the class it designates **6** *vti* **MAKE OPERATION APPLY THROUGHOUT** to apply or make an operation, e.g. multiplication or division, apply to each part of a mathematical expression [15C. < Latin *distribut-*, past participle of *distribuere* 'assign separately' < *tribuere* (see TRIBUTE).] **—distributable** *adj*

SYNONYMS See *scatter*.

ϟ **distributed** /di stríbbyŏŏtid/ *adj* describes computer systems in which two or more computers have a telecommunications link to each other but can also operate independently

distributer *n* = **distributor**

distribution /dístri byoósh'n/ *n* **1 GIVING OUT** the sharing out or delivery of things to a number of people **2 SHARING OUT** the process of dividing up and giving out something, e.g. money, when it is shared by a number of people **3 SCATTERING** the scattering or spreading of something over an area **4 ENTIRE AREA WHERE SPECIES IS FOUND** the area or areas taken together where something is located or where a species lives and reproduces **5 SPREAD OF STATISTICS** the spread of statistics within known or possible limits, especially in relation to the norm or to expectations **6 SHARING OUT OF SOMEBODY'S ESTATE** the dividing up of the estate of somebody who has died intestate among people who are entitled to receive a share **7 RECOMBINING OF TWO PROPOSITIONS** the recombining of two operations from one proposition in another equivalent proposition, e.g. 'p and (q or r)' is equivalent to '(p and q) or (p and r)' **—distributional** *adj*

distributive /di stríbbyŏŏtiv/ *adj* **1 INVOLVING DISTRIBUTION** relating to or involving the handing out, sharing out, or scattering about of things **2 REFERRING TO EACH MEMBER** referring to each member of a set or group individually and separately **3 REFERRING TO INDIVIDUALS** referring to an individual member of a class **4 PRODUCING EQUAL RESULTS** describes a mathematical expression with two operators whose expansion produces the same results whether operated on as a whole or as a sum of the parts ■ *n* **DISTRIBUTIVE WORD** a word that refers to every member of a set or group individually and separately **—distributively** *adv* **—distributiveness** *n*

distributor /di stríbbyŏŏtər/, **distributer** *n* **1 SOMEBODY WHO DISTRIBUTES** a person who or an organization or thing that distributes something **2 WHOLESALER** a wholesaler who sells goods to retailers, usually within a specified geographic area **3 DEVICE CONVEYING ELECTRICITY TO SPARK PLUGS** the device in a motor vehicle's engine that transfers electric current from the induction coil to the spark plugs **4 ORGANIZATION ARRANGING SCREENING OF FILMS** an organization that advertises films and arranges with exhibitors, who own the cinemas, to have them shown

district /dístrikt/ *n* **1** an area of a town or country, especially one with a particular distinguishing feature or one that is an administrative division ○ *a fruit-growing district* **2** the area around a particular place, e.g. the area around somebody's home or around a town [Early 17C. Via French < medieval Latin *districtus* '(area of) jurisdiction' < Latin *district-* (see DISTRESS).]

district attorney *n US* in the United States, the prosecuting officer of a particular jurisdiction

district court *n* **1 SCOTTISH MAGISTRATES' COURT** in Scotland, a magistrates' court dealing with minor offences, e.g. parking fines and nonpayment of debts **2 US DISTRICT TRIAL COURT** in the United States, the trial court in either a state or a federal district **3 AUSTRALIAN LOWER COURT** in some states of Australia, a court that deals with cases that are not important enough to be tried in a high court

district nurse *n* a community nurse

District of Columbia federal district of the E United States, coextensive with the city of Washington, D.C. Area: 176 sq. km/68 sq. mi.

distringas /di stríng gəss, -gass/ *n* in former times, a court order instructing a sheriff to repossess somebody's property [15C. < medieval Latin, 'you shall distrain' (opening word of the writ), form of *distringere* 'draw asunder'.]

~~**distroy**~~ incorrect spelling of **destroy**

distrust /diss trúst/ *n* a feeling that somebody or something is dishonest or unreliable and does not deserve to be trusted **—distrust** *vt* **—distruster** *n* **—distrustful** *adj* **—distrustfully** *adv* **—distrustfulness** *n*

disturb /di stúrb/ *vt* **1 INTERRUPT** to interrupt or distract somebody when he or she is busy **2 UPSET** to make somebody feel anxious or slightly troubled **3 CHANGE SHAPE OR POSITION** to move something so that it is not in its normal, expected, or correct shape or position ○ *Nothing had been disturbed.* **4 SPOIL PEACE AND QUIET** to spoil the quietness, stillness, or peacefulness of something **5 AWAKEN** to waken somebody or something [12C. Directly or via Old French *desto(u)rber* < Latin *disturbare* 'disturb completely' < *turbare* 'disturb'.] **—disturber** *n* **—disturbing** *adj* **—disturbingly** *adv*

SYNONYMS See *bother*.

disturbance /di stúrbənss/ *n* **1 DISRUPTION OF PEACE** the disruption of a peaceful or ordered environment, or something that causes such disruption **2 DISRUPTION OF CONCENTRATION** the disruption of somebody's concentration, or something that disrupts somebody's ability to get on with a task **3 COMMOTION** noisy and violent behaviour in a public place, or an incident involving such behaviour **4 MENTAL UPSET** psychological or emotional upset **5 EARTH TREMOR** a minor movement of the earth that falls short of an earthquake **6 INTERFERENCE WITH SOMEBODY'S RIGHTS** any act that causes disruption to others or hinders them from pursuing normal legal activities **7 LOW-PRESSURE AREA** a small area of low pressure

disturbance of the peace *n* a violation of public order that disrupts or destroys public tranquillity

disturbed /di stúrbd/ *adj* **1 ANXIOUS** worried or concerned **2 TROUBLED** unsettled and unhappy, with many troubles and upsets **3 NOT IN MENTAL HEALTH** affected by or displaying symptoms of psychiatric disorder

disulfide *n* US = **disulphide**

disulfiram /dī súlfi ram/ *n* a drug used in the treatment of alcoholism [Mid-20C. < DISULFIDE + THIOUREA + AMYL.]

disulphide /dī súlfīd/ *n* a chemical compound that has two atoms of sulphur combined with one or more other elements

disunion /diss yoónyən/ *n* **1** disagreement or discord **2** the splitting up of something into separate smaller parts or groups

disunite /díssyoo nít/ (**-nites, -niting, -nited**) *v* **1** *vt* to create or be a source of disagreement between different people or factions within a group **2** *vti* to divide something, or become divided, into smaller parts or groups **—disunited** *adj* **—disuniter** *n* **—disunity** *n*

disuse /diss yoóss/ *n* the fact or condition of not being used, applied, or followed, especially for a long time

disused /díss yoózd/ *adj* no longer in use ○ *a disused airfield*

disutility /díssyoo tíllәti/ (*plural* **-ties**) *n US* a state of causing inconvenience, counterproductivity, or harm (*formal*)

disyllable /dī síllәb'l, di-/, **dissyllable** *n* **1** a word composed of two syllables **2** a two-syllable unit of rhythm in poetry **—disyllabic** /dī si lábbik, dí-/ *adj*

dit /dit/ *n* the spoken form of the short sound used in Morse and other telegraphic codes. ◊ **dah** [Mid-20C. An imitation of the sound.]

ditch /dich/ *n* **1 NARROW CHANNEL** a long narrow channel dug in the ground, usually used for drainage or irrigation but sometimes used as a boundary marker **2 SMALL BROOK** a small natural stream or brook ■ *v* **1** *vt* **ABANDON** to abandon something or somebody as no longer wanted, liked, or needed (*informal*) **2** *vti* **MAKE EMERGENCY LANDING ON WATER** to land, or make an aircraft land, on water in an emergency (*informal*) **3** *vti* **DIG DITCHES** to enclose, drain, or irrigate an area with ditches, or dig ditches for this purpose [Old English *dīc* < Germanic, 'hole and mound produced by digging'] **—ditcher** *n*

ditchwater /dích wawtər/ *n* the dirty stagnant water found in ditches

ditheism /díthi izəm, dī theé-/ *n* **1** belief in two equal gods **2** the belief that the world is ruled by two equal and opposing forces or gods, one good and one evil **—ditheist** *n* **—ditheistic** /díthi ístik/ *adj*

dither /díthər/ *vi* **1 BE AGITATED** to behave in a nervous and indecisive way **2 TREMBLE** to tremble or quiver, e.g. with cold (*regional*) ■ *n* **AGITATED STATE** a state of nervous agitation or indecisiveness [Mid-17C. Alteration of obsolete *didder* 'tremble, shake' < ?] **—ditherer** *n* **—dithery** *adj*

ϟ **dithering** /díthəring/ *n* **1** nervously confused indecisiveness in the face of alternative possible actions **2** the mixing of pixels of several colours on a computer display to create the illusion of extra colours or shading

dithyramb /díthi ram, -ramb/ *n* **1** a passionately emotional speech or piece of writing (*formal*) **2** in ancient Greece, a wild and impassioned choral hymn, originally directed to the god Dionysus [Early 17C. Via Latin < Greek *dithurambos*.]

dithyrambic /díthi rámbik/ *adj* **1** passionately emotional or wildly enthusiastic **2** involving or relating to a dithyramb **—dithyrambically** *adv*

ditsy /dítsi/ (**-sier, -siest**), **ditzy** (**-zier, -ziest**) *adj US* silly or scatterbrained (*informal*) [Late 20C. < ?]

dittany /díttəni/ (*plural* **-nies** *or* **-ny**) *n* **1** an aromatic plant related to oregano and marjoram and cultivated as an ornamental and for its medicinal properties. Flowers: pink. Native to: S Europe. *Origanum dictamnus*.

2 an aromatic plant, cultivated in the United States as a kitchen herb. *Cunila origanoides.* 3 PLANTS = **gas plant** [12C. < Old French *ditain*, medieval Latin *ditaneum* < Greek *diktamnon*.]

ditto /díttō/ *interj* **SAME HERE** used instead of repeating something that has just been said to indicate that the same thing applies to you (*informal*) ■ *adv* **THE SAME THING APPLIES ELSEWHERE** indicating that whatever has just been said about one person or thing applies equally to somebody or something else ○ *The car will need to be cleaned; ditto the children* ■ *n* (*plural* **-tos**) **SYMBOLS REPRESENTING REPEATED MATTER** a pair of symbols (") that together represent matter that is repeated directly from what appears above them but that is unstated ■ *vt* (**-tos, -toing, -toed**) **REPEAT** to repeat or imitate something that somebody else has said or done [Early 17C. Via Tuscan dialect variant of Italian *detto* 'said' < Latin *dictus*, past participle of *dicere* 'say'.]

ditty /dítti/ (*plural* **-ties**) *n* a short simple popular song [14C. Via Old French *dité* 'composition' < Latin *dictatum* 'thing dictated' < *dictat-* (see DICTATE).]

ditty bag *n* 1 a small canvas or leather bag used by men for holding small personal belongings 2 *US* = **sponge bag**

ditzy *adj* = **ditsy**

diuresis /dīyōō reéssiss/ *n* abnormally increased excretion of urine caused by excessive intake of fluids, a drug, or a disease [Late 17C. < modern Latin, 'urination through' < Greek *ourēsis* 'urination'.]

diuretic /dīyōō réttik/ *adj* causing increased flow of urine [14C. Via late Latin *diureticus* < Greek *diourētikos* < *diourein* 'urinate through' < *ourein* 'urinate'.] —**diuretic** *n* —**diuretically** *adv*

diurnal /dī úrn'l/ *adj* 1 **IN THE DAYTIME** happening during the day as opposed to at night 2 **EVERY DAY** happening every day 3 **VARYING WITHIN A DAY** varying within the course of a single day 4 **OPEN ONLY IN DAYTIME** describes flowers that open during the day and close at night 5 **ACTIVE IN DAYTIME** describes animals that are active during the day rather than at night ■ *n* **WORSHIP BOOK** in the Roman Catholic Church, a book containing the prayer and worship material for all the set daily services except matins [14C. < late Latin *diurnalis* < Latin *diurnus* 'daily' < *dies* 'day'.] —**diurnally** *adv*

diurnal parallax *n* the change in an astronomical object's apparent position caused by the change in the observer's position because of the motion of the Earth in a day

diuron /dī́ ə ron/ *n* $C_9H_{10}Cl_2N_2O$ a long-lasting agricultural herbicide. Use: killing annual weeds. [Mid-20C. < DICHLOR- + UREA.]

div /div/ *n* an offensive term for somebody thought to be unintelligent (*slang insult*)

div. *abbr* 1 diversion 2 divide 3 dividend 4 division 5 divorced

diva /deévə/ (*plural* **-vas** *or* **-ve** /-vay/) *n* 1 a distinguished woman singer, especially one who sings in operas 2 an extremely arrogant or temperamental woman [Late 19C. Via Italian < Latin, 'goddess'.]

divagate /dīvə gayt/ (**-gates, -gating, -gated**) *vi* (*literary*) 1 to wander off the subject under discussion 2 to wander about somewhere [Mid-16C. < Latin *divagat-*, past participle of *divagari* 'wander about' < *vagari* 'wander'.] —**divagation** /dīvə gáysh'n/ *n*

divalent /dī váylənt/ *adj* having a valency of 2

Divali *n* RELIG = **Diwali**

divan /di ván/ *n* 1 **KIND OF BED** a bed with no headboard or footboard, especially one with, instead of legs, solid sides fitted with feet or castors 2 **BACKLESS SOFA** a sofa without a back, and sometimes without arms 3 **ISLAMIC COURTROOM OR OTHER CHAMBER** a courtroom, council chamber, or other official hall in some Islamic countries 4 **SMOKING ROOM** in former times, a smoking room attached to a coffee shop or cigar shop 5 **ARABIC POEMS** a collection of poems written in Persian or Arabic, often by a single poet [Late 16C. Via French or Italian *divano* < Turkish *dīvān* < Persian *dīvān*.]

divaricate /dī várri kayt, di-/ (**-cates, -cating, -cated**) *vi* to branch or fork at a wide angle [Early 17C. < Latin *divaricat-*, past participle of *divaricare* 'stretch apart' < *varicus* 'straddling'.] —**divaricate** *adj* —**divaricately** *adv* —**divaricatingly** *adv*

divarication /dī várri káysh'n, di-/ *n* 1 separation into widely spread parts or branches, or the point at which something forks or branches 2 a difference of opinion (*formal*)

dive /dīv/ *v* (**dives, diving, dived**) 1 *vi* **JUMP HEAD FIRST INTO WATER** to jump or throw yourself into water head first, especially with your arms stretched out above your head 2 *vi* **SWIM UNDER WATER** to swim below the surface of a stretch of water, often with special breathing apparatus 3 *vi* **GO TOWARDS BOTTOM OF WATER** to go down steeply and quickly in the direction of the bottom of a body of water, sometimes in search of something ○ *dive for treasure* 4 *vi* **DESCEND STEEPLY AND RAPIDLY** to fly or make an aircraft fly steeply and rapidly in the direction of the ground or the sea 5 *vi* **THROW YOURSELF TO THE GROUND** to jump quickly to one side or throw yourself forwards or sideways to the ground ○ *dive out of the way* 6 *vi* **MOVE FAST** to move quickly and in a rush in a particular direction ○ *dive for the door* 7 *vti* **PUT HAND IN** to put your hand or hands quickly into something, e.g. a pocket, a bag, or a cupboard, in order to get something out of it 8 *vi* **BEGIN ENTHUSIASTICALLY** to undertake or start on some activity with great enthusiasm ○ *He dived into the project.* 9 *vi* **PERFORM JUMPS INTO WATER** to perform a pattern of acrobatic movements in the air ending in a headfirst plunge into water, or do this regularly as a sport 10 *vi* **GO UNDER WATER** to cause something such as a submarine to go below the surface of the sea 11 *vi* **DROP IN VALUE** to fall sharply in value ■ *n* 1 **HEADLONG JUMP INTO WATER** a jump into water head first, especially with your arms stretched out above your head 2 **ACROBATIC PLUNGE** an acrobatic plunge into water performed as a sport or in a competition 3 **ACT OF SWIMMING UNDER WATER** a swim below the surface of a stretch of water, often with special breathing apparatus 4 **DESCENT TOWARDS BOTTOM OF WATER** a steep and usually rapid descent in the direction of the bottom of a body of water 5 **SUBMARINE'S DESCENT** a submarine's descent below the surface of the sea 6 **STEEP DESCENT** a bird's or aircraft's rapid and steep fall or flight in the direction of the ground or the sea 7 **QUICK MOVEMENT SIDEWAYS OR DOWN** a quick jump or movement to one side, forwards, or sideways to the ground 8 **FAST MOVEMENT** a rapid movement in a particular direction 9 **DISREPUTABLE ESTABLISHMENT** a dirty, shabby, or disreputable place, e.g. a bar or club (*informal*) 10 **SHARP FINANCIAL DROP** a sharp fall in value 11 **FOOTBALLER'S FALL** a feigned dramatic fall by a player to try to gain a free kick or penalty, or a goalkeeper's attempt to stretch horizontally to save a shot (*informal*) 12 **BOXER'S FEIGNED FALL** a fall or injury feigned by a boxer in order to lose a fight dishonestly (*slang*) [Old English *dūfan* 'sink', *dȳfan* 'dip' < Germanic]

dive in *vi* to begin eating quickly and with gusto (*informal*)

dive-bomb *vt* to descend steeply in a military aircraft and deliver bombs onto a target —**dive-bomber** *n* —**dive-bombing** *n*

dive brake *n* AIR FORCE = **air brake** *n.* 2

diver /dīvər/ *n* 1 **SOMEBODY WHO DIVES IN WATER** a person who goes under the surface of water for work or recreation 2 **DIVING WATER BIRD** a water bird belonging to a family that is skilled in swimming and diving. Native to: the N hemisphere. Family: Gaviidae. US term **loon**[1] *n.* 3 **WATER BIRD** any water bird noted for its diving skills

diverge /dī vúrj, di-/ (**-verges, -verging, -verged**) *vi* 1 **SEPARATE** to separate and go in a different direction or different directions 2 **DIFFER** to differ to some extent 3 **NOT MATCH** to deviate from or not fit in with or conform to something, e.g. a typical pattern or expressed wish [Mid-17C. < medieval Latin *divergere* 'bend apart' < Latin *vergere* 'bend'.] —**diverging** *adj*

divergence /dī vúrjənss/, **divergency** /-jənssi/ (*plural* **-cies**) *n* 1 **DIFFERENCE OR DISPARITY** a difference between two or more things, e.g. opinions or attitudes 2 **FAILURE TO CONFORM OR MATCH** deviation from something, e.g. a typical pattern or expressed wish 3 **MOVING APART** the process of separating or moving apart to follow different paths or different courses 4 **AMOUNT OF DIFFERENCE** the amount by which something differs from something else, especially where such a difference is not expected 5 **DEVIATION OF EYE FROM SIGHT LINE** a condition in which only one eye is directed at the object of interest and the other is directed outwards 6 **DIFFERENT DEVELOPMENT** the development of different characteristics by organisms that come from the same ancestor, caused by the influence of different environments. ◊ **convergence** *n.* 3 7 **SEQUENCE OF NUMBERS WITHOUT LIMIT** the characteristic of a series or sequence of numbers in which the value of the last term and the sum of the series are without limit. ◊ **convergence** *n.* 2 8 **MOVEMENT OF AIR CURRENTS** a set of meteorological conditions in a given area in which the air expands and the net flow of air is out of the area, usually resulting in fair, dry conditions

divergent /dī vúrjənt/ *adj* 1 **MOVING APART** following paths or courses that become increasingly different or separate 2 **DIFFERING** showing or having differences 3 **NOT MATCHING** deviating from something, e.g. a typical pattern or an expressed wish 4 **INCREASING WITHOUT LIMIT** describes a series or sequence of numbers in which each term is equal to or greater than the preceding term, and the value of the last term and the sum of the series are without limit 5 **RADIATING FROM A POINT** describes lines radiating from a single point —**divergently** *adv*

diverging lens *n* a lens, usually concave, that causes a parallel beam of light to spread

divers /dīvərz/ *adj* more than one, and of various types (*literary*) [13C. Via French < Latin *diversus*, past participle of *divertere* 'separate' (see DIVERT).]

diverse /dī vúrss, dī vurss/ *adj* 1 made up of many different elements or kinds of things 2 very different or distinct from one another [13C. Variant of DIVERS.] —**diversely** *adv* —**diverseness** *n*

diversify /dī vúrssi fī/ (**-fies, -fying, -fied**) *vti* 1 to become more varied, or make something more varied 2 to expand, or expand a commercial organization, into new areas of business [15C. Via Old French *diversifier* < medieval Latin *diversificare* 'make unlike' < Latin *diversus* (see DIVERS).] —**diversifiability** /dī vúrssi fī ə bílləti/ *n* —**diversifiable** *adj* —**diversification** /dī vúrssifi káysh'n/ *n* —**diversified** *adj* —**diversifier** *n*

diversion /dī vúrsh'n/ *n* 1 **DISTRACTION** something that takes somebody's attention away from something else, especially from more routine activities ○ *a welcome diversion from housework* 2 **ALTERNATIVE ROUTE** a route to be taken by traffic as an alternative to the normal route, when the normal route cannot be used. US term **detour** *n.* 2 3 **CHANGE OF PURPOSE** a change in the purpose or use of something from what was intended or from what something was previously 4 **CHANGE OF DIRECTION** a change in the direction or path of something 5 **PASTIME** an activity or interest that takes somebody's mind off more routine or serious things 6 **MOCK ATTACK** a mock attack aimed at drawing enemy attention and troops away from the place of the intended main attack [15C. Directly or via French < late Latin *diversion-* 'turning away' < Latin *diversus* (see DIVERS).] —**diversional** *adj*

diversionary /dī vúrsh'nəri/ *adj* designed or carried out to divert somebody's attention away from something

diversity /dī vúrssəti/ (*plural* **-ties**) *n* 1 a variety of something such as opinion, colour, or style ○ *a city of great cultural diversity* 2 discrepancy, or a difference from what is normal or expected [14C. Via French < Latin *diversitas* < *diversus* (see DIVERS).]

divert /dī vúrt/ *vt* 1 **CHANGE SOMETHING'S PATH** to change the route or path taken by something, e.g. traffic or a river 2 **DRAW ATTENTION FROM** to take somebody's mind off something and draw attention to something else 3 **CHANGE PURPOSE OR USE** to change the purpose or use of something from what it was previously 4 **AMUSE** to amuse or entertain somebody [15C. Via French *divertir* < Latin *divertere* 'turn aside' < *vertere* 'turn'.] —**diverter** *n* —**divertible** *adj* —**divertive** *adj*

diverticula plural of **diverticulum**

diverticulitis /dīvər tikyōō lītiss/ *n* inflammation of abnormal protrusions (**diverticula**) of the lining of the large intestine, causing severe abdominal pain, often with fever and constipation

diverticulosis /dīvər tikyōō lóssiss/ *n* the presence of abnormal protrusions (**diverticula**) in the bowel, caused when the bowel muscles rupture the bowel wall

diverticulum /dīvər tíkyōōləm/ (*plural* **-la** /-lə/) *n* a pouch or sac in the lining of the mucous membrane of a hollow organ, especially one produced in the bowel when the bowel muscle ruptures the bowel wall. ◊ **hernia** [Mid-17C. < medieval Latin, 'byway', variant of Latin *deverticulum* < *vertere* 'turn'.] —**diverticular** *adj*

divertimento /di vúrti méntō/ (*plural* **-ti** /-ti/) *n* a piece of light classical instrumental music composed in several movements for an ensemble [Mid-18C. < Italian, 'diversion' < *divirtire* 'divert' < Latin *divertere* (see DIVERT).]

diverting /dī vúrting/ *adj* amusing or entertaining, and acting as a temporary distraction from more routine or serious matters —**divertingly** *adv*

divertissement /di vúrtiss moN/ *n* **1 SERIES OF UNTHEMED DANCES** in a ballet, a dance highlighting a dancer's skill rather than developing the story **2 DANCE INTERLUDE** a dance interlude in a play or opera **3 TUNES DERIVED FROM FAMOUS MELODIES** a set of tunes that are based on well-known melodies [Early 18C. < French, < *divertiss-*, stem of *divertir* 'divert' < Latin *divertere* (see DIVERT).]

divest /dī vést/ *vt* **1 TAKE AWAY FROM** to take away something, especially status or power, from somebody or something (*often passive*) **2 TAKE OFF** to remove something, usually clothes (*formal or humorous*) **3 GIVE UP** to give up or get rid of something, especially a belief or idea **4 GIVE AWAY PROPERTY RIGHTS** to lose or give away rights to the possession of property, or deprive somebody of them [Early 17C. Alteration of obsolete *devest* 'deprive' < Old French *de(s)vester* 'undress' < *vestir* 'clothe' < Latin *vestire*.] —**divestible** *adj* —**divestment** *n* —**divesture** *n*

divestiture /dī véstichər/ *n* **1** the removal or deprivation of something **2** *US* the sale of one or more of a company's subsidiaries, divisions, or holdings, or of its stock in those holdings

divi /dívvi/ (*plural* **-vis**) *n* FIN = **divvy**[2] *n.* 2

divide /di vīd/ *v* (**-vides, -viding, -vided**) **1** *vti* **SPLIT INTO PARTS** to separate or split something, or be separated or split, into two or more parts ○ *a dormitory divided into cubicles* **2** *vti* **SHARE** to share something, or be shared, between two or more people or groups ○ *Her inheritance was divided equally among the children.* **3** *vi* **GO IN DIFFERENT DIRECTIONS** to split into two or more parts that go off in different directions **4** *vti* **SEPARATE TWO PLACES** to be a barrier or boundary between one place or thing and another ○ *The river divides the north of the island from the south.* **5** *vt* **CAUSE DISAGREEMENT BETWEEN** to be the cause or subject of disagreement between people **6** *vti* **CALCULATE OCCURRENCE OF ONE NUMBER IN ANOTHER** to calculate how many times one number contains another **7** *vt* **MARK OFF** to mark units or sections of a particular size on a measuring instrument, e.g. a ruler **8** *vi* **VOTE** to vote on an issue by separating into two groups, one for and one against, inside a legislative chamber such as Parliament ■ *n* **1 BOUNDARY** a boundary or gap that stands between two things, conditions, or groups **2** GEOG = **watershed** *n.* 1 [14C. < Latin *dividere* 'separate apart' < *-videre* 'to separate'.] —**dividable** *adj*

divided /di vīdid/ *adj* **1 SEPARATED** separated into two or more parts or groups **2 IN TWO MINDS** drawn towards two or more different and often incompatible purposes or groups **3 IN DISAGREEMENT** in a state of internal discord, strife, or disagreement **4 SEPARATED INTO SECTIONS** describes leaves that are divided into separate sections —**dividedly** *adv* —**dividedness** *n*

divided highway *n US* TRANSP = **dual carriageway**

dividend /dívvi dend/ *n* **1 BONUS** something good or desirable that is gained as a bonus along with something else **2 SHAREHOLDER'S SHARE OF PROFIT** company profits paid pro rata to shareholders, either in cash or in more shares **3 PAYMENT TO COOPERATIVE'S CUSTOMER** a payment made periodically to the customer-members of a cooperative commercial organization, usually in proportion to the amount the member spends **4 NUMBER DIVIDED BY ANOTHER** a number or quantity that is to be divided by another number or quantity. ◊ **divisor** **5 PROPORTION OF A BANKRUPT'S ESTATE** the proportion of a bankrupt party's estate that is to be divided among the creditors [15C. Via Anglo-Norman < Latin *dividendum* 'thing to be divided', form of *dividere* (see DIVIDE).]

divider /di vīdər/ *n* a device that separates something into sections, e.g. a screen that partitions a room or a sheet of card that separates the sections of a loose-leaf binder

dividers /di vīdərz/ *npl* an instrument with two movable pointed legs hinged at one end, used for measuring distances on maps and charts and for transferring measurements from one chart to another

dividing line *n* something that marks a change or distinction between two states or qualities

divi-divi /dívvi dívvi/ (*plural* **divi-divis** *or* **divi-divi**) *n* **1** a long seed pod that has a high tannin content. Use: tanning leather. **2** a small tropical American tree that bears divi-divis. *Caesalpinia coriaria.* [Mid-19C. Via American Spanish < Carib.]

divination /dívvi náysh'n/ *n* **1 SEEKING KNOWLEDGE BY SUPERNATURAL MEANS** the methods or practice of attempting to foretell the future or discovering the unknown through omens, oracles, or supernatural powers **2 PROPHECY** a prophecy or prediction **3 PREMONITION** a premonition or feeling of foreboding about something that is going to happen —**divinatory** /di vínnətəri/ *adj*

divine /di vīn/ *adj* **1 HAVING GODLIKE NATURE** being God or a god or goddess **2 RELATING TO GOD** connected with, coming from, or caused by God or a god or goddess **3 CONNECTED WITH WORSHIP** connected with the worship or service of God or a god or goddess **4 LOVELY** pleasing or attractive (*informal or humorous*) ■ *v* (**-vines, -vining, -vined**) **1** *vt* **REALIZE** to come to understand or realize something **2** *vt* **DISCOVER AS IF SUPERNATURALLY** to learn or discover something by intuition, inspiration, or other apparently supernatural means **3** *vt* **PREDICT AS IF SUPERNATURALLY** to predict something by apparently supernatural means **4** *vti* **SEARCH WITH DIVINING ROD** to search for underground water, metal, or minerals using something such as a divining rod ■ *n* **1 THEOLOGIAN** a member of the clergy, especially one who is knowledgeable about theology **2 Divine, divine GOD** God or an underlying creative and sustaining force in the universe [14C. Via Old French < Latin *divinus* < *divus* 'god'.] —**divinable** *adj* —**divineness** *n* —**diviner** *n*

divinely /di vīnli/ *adv* **1** well, pleasingly, or attractively (*informal or humorous*) **2** by God or a god or goddess

divine right *n* the belief that the monarch's authority comes directly from God rather than from the people

diving beetle *n* a predatory water beetle adapted for swimming that has flattened hind legs and the capacity to breathe air trapped under its wings. Family: Dytiscidae.

diving bell *n* a metal bell-shaped device used for working underwater, with an open bottom and a supply of compressed air

diving board *n* a raised board at the edge of a swimming pool from which to dive into the water

diving dress *n* SWIMMING = **diving suit**

diving duck *n* a duck, e.g. the bufflehead, pochard, or scaup, that dives for food and swims under water

diving reflex *n* a reflex in mammals in which the heart rate slows and skin blood vessels narrow on immersion in cold water to conserve oxygen

diving suit *n* a waterproof suit, often including a helmet and an air supply, worn by divers

divining rod *n* a forked stick used as a device for sensing underground water sources or minerals

divinise *vt* = **divinize**

divinity /di vínnəti/ (*plural* **-ties**) *n* **1 THEOLOGY** the study of religion, especially the Christian religion **2 QUALITY OF BEING GOD, A GOD, OR GODDESS** the quality associated with being God, a god, or a goddess **3 divinity, Divinity GOD** God, a god, or a goddess [13C. Via French *divinité* < Latin *divinitat-* 'godhead, divinity' < *divinus* (see DIVINE).]

divinize /dívvi nīz/ (**-izes, -izing, -ized**), **divinise** (**-ises, -ising, -ised**) *vt* to regard a person, being, or object as a god or goddess —**divinization** /dívvi nī záysh'n/ *n*

divisible /di vízzəb'l/ *adj* **1** able to be divided, especially without leaving a remainder **2** capable of being separated into different parts [15C. Directly or via French < late Latin *divisibilis* < Latin *divis-* (see DIVISION).] —**divisibility** /di vízzə bíllәti/ *n* —**divisibleness** *n* —**divisibly** *adv*

division /di vízh'n/ *n* **1 SPLITTING INTO PARTS** the act of separating or splitting something into parts, or an instance of this ○ *the division of the region into smaller administrative districts* **2 SHARING OUT** the separation of something into parts to be shared out among people or groups ○ *The division of work between members of the group should be equal.* **3 DIVIDING ONE NUMBER BY ANOTHER** an operation used to calculate the number of times one number is contained in another **4 DISAGREEMENT** a disagreement or strong difference of opinion, especially when this leads to a split in a group ○ *Deep divisions exist within senior management itself as to the best way of dealing with the problem.* **5 SOMETHING SEPARATING** something that separates things by forming a boundary between them **6 SEPARATE PART** one of the parts created when something is split **7 SECTION OF ORGANIZATION** a section of a large organization that has a particular task or function ○ *the sales division of a large firm* **8 GROUP OF TEAMS** a group of teams of roughly similar standard in a sports league **9 ARMY UNIT** a self-contained military unit in an army capable of sustained operations, including a headquarters and two or more brigades or, in the Marines, several regiments **10 NAVAL UNIT** a self-contained unit in a navy including a group of ships of the same class **11 AIR FORCE UNIT** a self-contained unit in an air force including two or more fighter wings **12 SMALL UNIT OF GOVERNMENT** a small unit of government, or an area administered by such a unit **13 PARLIAMENTARY VOTE** a vote in the British Parliament or a similar legislative body **14 CATEGORY IN PLANT CLASSIFICATION** a major category in the taxonomic classification of plants, comprising a group of classes. ◊ **phylum** *n.* 1 **15 SPLITTING ROOTS FOR PROPAGATION** the process of separating the root mass of a perennial plant into smaller pieces that are used to grow new plants **16 LOGICAL FALLACY** a fallacy in which it is argued that what is true of a whole collectively is true of any of its parts. An example would be arguing that because a car is expensive so is its windscreen wiper. ◊ **composition** *n.* 10 **17 GROUP OF ORGAN STOPS** a group of organ stops played on the same manual [14C. Via Old French < Latin *division-* < *divis-*, past participle of *dividere* (see DIVIDE).] —**divisional** *adj* —**divisionally** *adv* —**divisionary** *adj*

division bell *n* a bell rung in the British House of Commons when it is time for Members of Parliament to vote

divisionism /di vízhənizəm/ *n* **1** = **pointillism** *n.* 1 **2** a late-19th-century style of painting in which unmixed colour is applied to the canvas in small dots that from a distance form recognizable shapes and colour tones —**divisionist** *n, adj*

division lobby *n* POL = **lobby** *n.* 3

division of labour *n* a system of organizing production by giving separate tasks to separate workers or groups of workers

division sign *n* a sign (÷) placed between two numbers to show that the first number is divided by the second

divisive /di víssiv/ *adj* causing disagreement or hostility within a group so that it is likely to split [Late 16C. < late Latin *divisivus* < Latin *divis-* (see DIVISION).] —**divisively** *adv* —**divisiveness** *n*

divisor /di vízər/ *n* a number divided into another number. ◊ **dividend** *n.* 4 [15C. Directly or via French < Latin, < *divis-* (see DIVISION).]

divorce /di váwrss/ *n* **1 OFFICIAL ENDING OF A MARRIAGE** the ending of a marriage by an official decision in a court of law **2 SEPARATION** a complete separation or split ■ *v* (**-vorces, -vorcing, -vorced**) **1** *vti* **OFFICIALLY END A MARRIAGE** to end a marriage to somebody by an official decision in a court of law **2** *vt* **SEPARATE** to separate or distinguish something from something else [14C. Via French < Latin *divortium* < *divortere*, variant of *divertere* 'part, turn aside'.] —**divorceable** *adj* —**divorced** *adj* —**divorcer** *n* —**divorcive** *adj*

divorcé /di váwr sée, -váwrss ay/ *n* a man who is divorced [Late 19C. < French, < past participle of *divorcer* 'to divorce' < Latin *divortium* (see DIVORCE).]

divorcée /di váwr sée/ *n* a woman who is divorced [Early 19C. Partly < French, < feminine of *divorcé* (see DIVORCÉ); partly < DIVORCE + -EE[1].]

divot /dívvət/ *n* a small lump of grass and earth accidentally dug out of the ground while playing a sport, especially golf [Early 16C. < ?]

divulge /dī vúlj/ (**-vulges, -vulging, -vulged**) *vt* to reveal information, especially information that was previously secret [15C. < Latin *divulgare* 'make widely known to the masses' < *vulgus* 'masses'.] —**divulgement** *n* —**divulgence** *n* —**divulger** *n*

divvy[1] /dívvi/ (*plural* **-vies**) *n* an offensive term for somebody thought to be unintelligent (*slang offensive insult*) [Late 20C. < ?]

divvy[2] /dívvi/ *vt* (**-vies, -vying, -vied**) **DIVIDE SOMETHING UP** to divide something up and share it out among a group of people (*informal*) ■ *n* (*plural* **-vies**) (*informal*) **1** *US, Can* **PORTION** a person's share of something **2 divvy, divi COOPERATIVE DIVIDEND** a dividend or share of the profits given to members of a cooperative [Late 19C. Shortening of DIVIDEND.]

Diwali /di wáali/, **Divali** *n* a Hindu festival associated with Lakshmi, the goddess of prosperity, during which lamps are lit. Date: autumn. [Late 17C. Via Hindi *diwālī* < Sanskrit *dīpāvalī* 'row of lights' < *dīpa* 'light, lamp'.]

Dix /diks/, **Otto** (1891–1969) German painter and etcher

dixie /díksi/ *n* a metal cooking pot used for making tea in the British army [Early 20C. < Hindi *degcī*.]

Dixie *n* **1** *US* the southern states that were members of the Confederacy during the American Civil War (*informal*) **2** the popular name for a song used as a

Confederate marching tune during the American Civil War [Mid-19C. < ?]

Dixieland /díksi land/, **dixieland** n a style of jazz, originally from New Orleans, characterized by a fast two-beat rhythm and simultaneous improvization [Early 20C. < Original Dixieland Jazz Band, the first jazz band to record commercially.]

Dixon /díks'n/, **Sir Owen** (1886–1972) Australian lawyer

DIY, **d.i.y.** abbr do-it-yourself

Diyarbakir /di yaàr bu keer/ capital of Diyarbakir Province, SE Turkey. Population: 375,800 (1990).

Diyari n, adj LANG = **Dieri**

dizygotic /dí zī góttik/, **dizygous** /dī zígass/ adj describes twins derived from two separately fertilized eggs (zygotes). ◊ **monozygotic**

dizzy /dízzi/ (**-zier**, **-ziest**) adj **1** UNSTEADY unsteady, as if about to lose balance, and slightly giddy **2** BEWILDERED confused, overwhelmed, and unable to think clearly **3** FUN-LOVING BUT THOUGHTLESS fun-loving and rather silly or empty-headed (informal) **4** FAST extremely fast ○ dizzy speeds **5** EXTREME so high as to make somebody giddy ○ the dizzy height of the tower [Old English dysig 'foolish, stupid' < Germanic] —**dizzily** adv —**dizziness** n —**dizzy** vt

⚡ **dj** abbr Djibouti (in Internet addresses)

DJ n **1** a player of records or other recorded music, e.g. at a live dance or on the radio **2** a dinner jacket (informal)

djebel n = **jebel**

djellaba /jə laàba/, **djellabah** n a long loose-fitting robe with sleeves and a hood, worn especially in Islamic countries [Early 19C. < Moroccan Arabic jellāb(a), jellābiyya.]

Djerba /júrba/ island off SE Tunisia, in the Gulf of Gabes in the Mediterranean Sea. Population: 92,269 (1984). Area: 510 sq. km/197 sq. mi.

Djibouti

Djibouti /ji boòti/ **1** republic in NE Africa, on the Gulf of Aden. Capital: Djibouti. Population: 434,116 (1997). Area: 23,200 sq. km/8,958 sq. mi. **2** capital of the Republic of Djibouti. Population: 383,000 (1995 estimate).

djinn, **djinni** n ◊ **jinni**

dk[1] abbr **1** dark **2** deck **3** dock[1]

⚡ **dk**[2] abbr Denmark (in Internet addresses)

DK abbr Denmark (international vehicle registration)

dl symbol decilitre

D/L abbr demand loan

D layer n **1** METEOROL = **D region** n. **1 2** the lower layer of the Earth's mantle, from 720 km/450 mi. deep down to the boundary with the core

DLitt /dee lit/, **DLit** abbr **1** Doctor of Letters **2** Doctor of Literature

dm[1] symbol decimetre

⚡ **dm**[2] abbr Dominica (in Internet addresses)

DM abbr Deutschmark

DMAC n a coding system used for broadcasting colour television programmes via satellite. Full form **duobinary multiplexed analogue component**

D-mark, **D-Mark** abbr Deutschmark

DMD abbr Doctor of Dental Medicine

DMK n a political party in Tamil Nadu, India. Full form **Dravida Munnetra Kazgham**

⚡ **DMS** abbr **1** Diploma in Management Studies **2** data management system

DMSO n ($CH_3)_2SO$ a clear odourless liquid compound. Use: solvent, in medicine to enable drugs applied to the skin to penetrate. Full form **dimethylsulphoxide**

DMus /dee múz/ abbr Doctor of Music

DMZ abbr demilitarized zone

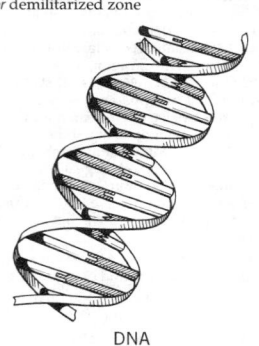

DNA

DNA n a nucleic acid molecule in the form of a twisted double strand (**double helix**) that is the major component of chromosomes and carries genetic information. Full form **deoxyribonucleic acid**

DNAase /dèe en áyz/, **DNase** n an enzyme that aids the hydrolysis of DNA into smaller molecules. Full form **deoxyribonuclease**

DNA fingerprinting n the analysis and use of DNA patterns from body tissues such as blood, saliva, or semen in order to establish somebody's identity

QUICK FACTS ON... **DNA FINGERPRINTING**

Key elements: use of genetic variation between individuals as a means of identification, based on unique SNPs (single nucleotide polymorphisms) that occur approximately once in every 1,000 nucleotides in DNA sequences of individual humans
Key dates: 1985 DNA fingerprinting developed (Jeffreys); 1986 first commercial use of DNA fingerprinting in paternity testing; 1999 SNP Consortium established
Key technologies: DNA sequencing, polymerase chain reaction (PCR), restriction digests, gel electrophoresis, Southern blots
Key developments: Medical benefits: genome mapping, transplantation medicine, tumour biology, medical microbiology, pharmacogenomics. Non-medical benefits: forensic science, evolutionary genetics, paternity testing
Key publications: Individual-specific 'fingerprints' of human DNA (Jeffreys et al.) 1985, Nature 316: 76–79; DNA Fingerprinting (Schmidtke and Krawczak) 1999

DNA ligase n an enzyme (**ligase**) that joins two DNA strands during replication, repair, and recombination

DNA polymerase n an enzyme that uses single-stranded DNA to reproduce and repair DNA

DNase n = **DNAase**

DNA sequencing n the process of determining the exact sequence of the bases along a section length of DNA

DNA virus n a virus with a genome containing DNA

Dnestr = **Dniester**

Dnieper /neèpar, dn-/, **Dnepr** river flowing through W Russia, Belarus, and Ukraine into the Black Sea. Length: 2,290 km/1,420 mi.

Dniester /neèstar, dn-/, **Dnestr** river flowing through Ukraine and Moldova into the Black Sea. Length: 1,400 km/870 mi.

D-notice n an official government communication to news editors advising them against publishing specified information for security reasons [< its administrative classification letter]

⚡ **DNS** abbr domain name system

do[1] /doo/ (**does** (stressed) /duz/; (unstressed) /daz/, **doing**, **did** /did/, **done** /dun/) CORE MEANING: a verb indicating that somebody performs an action, an activity, or a task ○ He usually did the cleaning on a Sunday morning. ○ Why won't you let me do your hair for you? ○ Assuming that your

terminal is properly set, here is what you have to do to connect it.

1 vt USE to use something in a particular way ○ She's done absolutely nothing with the money she inherited. **2** vt TAKE ACTION to take action in a particular situation in order to change it or solve a problem ○ Companies must decide what to do about their chemical waste. **3** vt CAUSE to cause or produce a particular effect or result ○ These disputes do little to help the peace process. ○ I could see what the divorce was doing to him. **4** vt WORK AT to work at something, particularly as a job or profession, or as a course of study ○ What does your mother do at the bank? **5** vt BE OCCUPIED WITH to be occupied or busy with something ○ Are you doing anything this evening? **6** vt CONDUCT SELF to behave in a particular manner ○ Do what you want. **7** vi FARE to be successful or unsuccessful to a particular extent ○ Automobile insurance firms are doing well this year. **8** vt PROVIDE to prepare or provide something ○ I'm sorry but we don't do a lunch menu. **9** vt ACHIEVE A SPEED OR RATE to achieve a particular speed or rate ○ We were doing 55 down the motorway. ○ We did about 400 miles a day. **10** vt STUDY to study or work at doing something ○ Have you done Nabokov yet? ○ I've never been able to do algebra. **11** vt PERFORM to perform or act a particular play, role, or accent ○ They're doing 'Macbeth'. ○ I'm not very good at doing accents. **12** vt VISIT PLACE to visit or explore a country or city as a tourist (informal) ○ We're doing London tomorrow. **13** vt BE ADEQUATE to be adequate in quantity or quality ○ A paper cup does just as well. ○ Just an orange juice will do me. **14** vt SERVE TIME IN PRISON to serve a period of time in prison (slang) **15** vt EXHAUST to wear somebody out (informal) ○ After slaving in the garden for six hours, I'm done! **16** vt ADAPT to translate or adapt a play, book, or other work ○ The novel was done into a feature film. **17** vt CHEAT to cheat or trick somebody (informal) ○ They did her out of her lunch money. **18** vt ROB to rob a person or place (slang) ○ They got caught while they were doing the post office. **19** vt ARREST to arrest somebody (slang) **20** vt CONVICT to prosecute and convict somebody of a crime (slang) ○ He got done for breaking and entering. **21** vt SPEND MONEY to spend or lose all your money (slang) ○ Have you done your money? **22** vt TAKE DRUGS to take or use a narcotic drug (slang) **23** vt HAVE SEX WITH to have sexual intercourse with somebody (slang) **24** vt MURDER to kill somebody deliberately (slang) **25** vt FORMS QUESTIONS AND NEGATIVES used with simple present and simple past tenses in the formation of questions and negative sentences. 'Do' and 'did' are often contracted to 'don't' and 'didn't' in negative structures. ○ What did he want? ○ Don't sit there! ○ It doesn't matter if you can't come. **26** vi GIVES EMPHASIS used to emphasize a positive statement or command, often as a way of politely inviting or persuading somebody to do something ○ Yes, I do realize you can't finish the work today. ○ Please do be quiet! **27** vt CHANGES THE EMPHASIS used to form inverted sentences in order to change the emphasis of a statement ○ She hopes to go to college, as do her brothers. **28** vt REPLACES ANOTHER VERB used to replace an earlier verb or verb phrase to avoid repetition, usually when comparing two things ○ I want to have a break just as much as you do. **29** n SOCIAL GATHERING a formal social gathering, e.g. a wedding reception (informal) **30** n EXCREMENT excrement (informal; euphemistic) ○ a pile of doggy do [Old English dōn < Indo-European, 'to place'] ◇ **could do with** be sure to benefit from something ○ I could do with some help. ◇ **have to do with 1** be connected with somebody or something **2** concern somebody or something **3** involve contact or a relationship with something or somebody ◇ **to do with** related to or about something or somebody ○ The lecture was to do with road safety.

USAGE **do have** or **have got**? Both these constructions are used in questions and in negative statements: Do you have change for a ten pound note? or Have you got change for a ten pound note? I don't have any change or I haven't got any change. Some consider the first wording in each pair to be more correct, perceiving **have got** as colloquial and even redundant, and pointing out that have alone is sufficient to signify possession. But Have you change? is not idiomatic, and **do have** has just as many syllables as **have got**. Therefore, it is hard to see what reasonable basis exists for preferring **do have** to **have got**.

USAGE **did you** or **have you**? A distinction that arises in connection with questions and negative statements is represented by the wordings Did you see the show? or Have you seen the show? I didn't see the show or I haven't seen the show. In informal conversation, the two are used almost interchangeably. In strict usage, however, there is a difference in time perspective: the first wording in each pair (*Did you...?*) refers to a particular point in the past, whereas the second wording (*Have you...?*) has to do with any time in the past (thus, *ever* could be added to the second sentence in each pair without substantially changing its meaning).

do away with *vt* **1** to abolish something so that it no longer happens or exists **2** to kill somebody (*informal*)
do down *vt* **1** to suggest that somebody or something is insignificant or unimportant (*informal*) **2** to treat somebody unfairly in order to gain an advantage
do for *vt* **1 CHARGE OR CONVICT SOMEBODY OF OFFENCE** to charge somebody with an offence, or convict somebody of a crime (*informal*) **2 KILL** to kill somebody (*informal*) **3 HARM** to cause serious damage to something or serious difficulties to somebody (*dated informal*) **4 EXHAUST** to make somebody feel so exhausted that he or she has no more energy or enthusiasm to continue (*dated informal*) **5 WORK AS DOMESTIC CLEANER FOR** to be employed to clean and tidy a house for somebody (*dated informal*)
do in *vt* (*informal*) **1** to kill or severely beat somebody **2** to make somebody feel exhausted
do out *vt* to clean or tidy a place, e.g. a room or cupboard (*informal*)
do over *vt* **1** to clean or redecorate a place, e.g. a house or room (*informal*) **2** to subject somebody to a violent beating (*slang*)
do up *vt* **1 FASTEN** to fasten something, e.g. with string or ribbons **2 MAKE SOMETHING USABLE AGAIN** to make something fit to use again by repairing or decorating it **3 GIVE SOMETHING DECORATIVE WRAPPING** to wrap or cover something in something decorative (*often passive*) **4 DRESS SMARTLY** to dress somebody or yourself in smart clothes (*informal*)
do without *vti* to manage or survive without something that you want, need, or normally have

do2 /dō/ *n* MUSIC = **doh**

ϟ **do**3 *abbr* Dominican Republic (*in Internet addresses*)

DO *abbr* **1** Doctor of Optometry **2** Doctor of Osteopathy

D/O *abbr* **1** delivery order **2** direct order

DOA *abbr* dead on arrival

doable /dóo əb'l/ *adj* able to be done or achieved

DOB, d.o.b *abbr* date of birth

dobbin /dóbbin/, **Dobbin** *n* a horse, especially a large heavy working horse [Late 16C. < *Dobbin*, personal name, alteration of *Robin*.]

dobby /dóbbi/ (*plural* **-bies**) *n* a part of a loom that allows small figures to be woven on it [Late 17C. < ?]

Dobell /dō bél/, **Sir William** (1899–1970) Australian painter

Doberman pinscher /dṓbərmən pínshər/, **Dobermann pinscher, Doberman** *n* a medium-sized to large powerful dog with a smooth black or dark brown coat, often used as a guard dog or for police work and belonging to a breed originating in Germany [Early 20C. After Ludwig *Dobermann*, *pinscher* < German, breed name.]

dobra /dṓbrə/ *n* see table at **currency** [Late 20C. Via Portuguese < Latin *duplus* 'double'.]

dobsonfly /dóbsən flī/ (*plural* **-flies**) *n* **1** *US, Can* a very large winged North American insect that has long slender mouthparts in the male. Genus: *Corydalus cornutus*. **2** a large stout-bodied flying insect with two pairs of delicately veined wings, occurring virtually worldwide. The larvae (**hellgrammites**) are voracious predators of small aquatic animals. Family: Corydalidae.

doc /dok/ *n* a doctor (*informal*)

DOC *n* a certification for Italian wine that guarantees its origin [< Italian *Denominazione di Origine Controllata*]

doc. *abbr* document

docent /dṓss'nt/ *n US* **1** a lecturer or teacher in a US university, especially one who is not a full-time member of the faculty **2** a tourist guide working in some museums or cathedrals in the United States [Late 19C. < obsolete German, < Latin *docent-*, present participle of *docere* 'teach'.] —**docentship** *n*

Docetism /dō sèetizəm, dṓsit-/ *n* in Christianity, an early heresy that claimed that Jesus Christ was not a real person [Mid-19C. < *Docete* 'Docetist', via medieval Latin *Docetae* (plural) 'Docetists' < patristic Greek *Dokētai* < Greek *dokein* 'seem, appear'.] —**Docetist** *n*

DOCG *n* a certification for Italian wine that guarantees its origin and verifies that it meets production regulations [< Italian *Denominazione di Origine Controllata e Garantita*]

doch an doris *n Scotland* BEVERAGES = **deoch an doruis**

docile /dṓ sīl/ *adj* quiet, easy to control, and unlikely to cause trouble [15C. < Latin *docilis* < *docere* 'teach'.] —**docilely** *adv* —**docility** /dō sílləti/ *n*

dock1 /dok/ *n* **1 PLACE FOR SHIPS** an area of water between two piers or next to a pier, where ships can be moored safely for loading and repair **2 BUILDINGS CONNECTED WITH SHIPPING** all the offices, workshops, and other buildings associated with the loading and repair of ships, together with the nearby areas of water (*usually plural*) US term **dockyard** **3** *US* **WHARF** a long narrow structure stretching out into a body of water, or a raised area of land alongside water where ships can load and unload **4 ENCLOSED AREA OF WATER** an enclosed area of water for a ship in which the water level can be adjusted **5** = **dry dock** ■ *vti* **1 MOOR** to steer a ship into a dock and tie it up, or be steered in and tied up there **2 LINK UP WITH SPACECRAFT** to link up with another spacecraft in space [14C. < Middle Low German *docke* or Middle Dutch *docke*.]

dock2 /dok/ *n* the area in a law court where the accused person stands during a trial [Late 16C. Probably < Flemish *dok* 'fowl pen, rabbit hutch'.]

dock3 /dok/ (*plural* **docks** *or* **dock**) *n* **1** a plant of the buckwheat family with long broad leaves and a long taproot. Flowers: greenish or reddish. Genus: *Rumex*. **2** any broad-leafed weedy plant [Old English *docce* < Germanic]

dock4 /dok/ *vt* **1 REMOVE TAIL** to remove the tail of a dog, sheep, or other animal, leaving a short stump **2 REDUCE WAGES** to deduct a sum of money from somebody's wages, especially as a punishment ■ *n* **1 SOLID PART OF TAIL** the solid part of an animal's tail **2 STUMP OF TAIL** the stump left when an animal's tail has been docked [14C. < ?]

dockage /dókij/ *n* **1 MOORING CHARGE** a charge payable for mooring at a dock **2 FACILITIES FOR MOORED SHIPS** the facilities for ships moored at a dock **3 DOCKING PROCESS** the process of docking a ship

docken /dókən/ (*plural* **-ens** *or* **-en**) *n Scotland* a dock plant [Old English *doccan*, form of *docce* (see DOCK3)]

docker /dókər/ *n* somebody whose job is to load and unload ships. US term **longshoreman**

docket /dókit/ *n* **1 DOCUMENT LISTING CONTENTS OF PARCEL** a short document listing the contents of a parcel or the goods being delivered, often also acting as a receipt **2 SUMMARY OF COURT CASE** a summary of the proceedings of a court case **3** *US* **LIST OF FUTURE COURT CASES** a list of pending cases in a court **4** *US* **LIST OF THINGS TO DO** a list of things to do **5 DOCUMENT SUMMARY** a summary of a document **6 CUSTOMS CERTIFICATE** a customs certificate confirming payment of duty ■ *vt* **1** *US* **PUT A LEGAL CASE IN THE CALENDAR** to enter a legal case in the calendar of future cases **2 SUMMARIZE A COURT CASE** to summarize a court case and enter the summary in the appropriate register **3 LABEL A PACKAGE** to label a package with a document giving the contents or delivery details **4 SUMMARIZE** to attach or give a summary of something [15C. < ?]

ϟ **docking station** *n* a piece of hardware that a portable computer is inserted into for recharging or expanded operations

dockland /dók land/ *n* the area surrounding a city's docks or port (*often plural*)

dockside /dók sīd/ *n* the area of ground alongside the moorings in a dock or harbour

dockworker /dók wurkər/ *n* SHIPPING = **docker**

dockyard /dók yaard/ *n* SHIPPING = **dock**1 *n.* **2**

doctor /dóktər/ *n* **1 SOMEBODY MEDICALLY QUALIFIED** somebody qualified and licensed to give people medical treatment **2** *US, Can* **DENTIST, VET, OR OSTEOPATH** a title used before the names of health professionals such as dentists, vets, and osteopaths **3 SOMEBODY WITH THE HIGHEST UNIVERSITY DEGREE** a title given to somebody who has been awarded a doctorate, the highest level of degree awarded by a university **4 ROMAN CATHOLIC THEOLOGIAN** in the earlier history of the Roman Catholic Church, an eminent and influential theologian **5 SOMEBODY WHO CAN MEND THINGS** a skilled practitioner of something, especially mending or improving something **6 TEACHER OR SCHOLAR** a teacher, or somebody very knowledgeable (*archaic*) ■ *v* **1** *vt* **CHANGE TO DECEIVE** to change something in order to make it appear different from the facts or the truth ○ *doctored the figures* **2** *vt* **ADD TO A SUBSTANCE** to add something, especially a drug, alcohol, or poison, to food or drink **3** *vt* **REMOVE SEX ORGANS** to spay or castrate an animal to prevent it from producing young **4** *vti* **TREAT ILL PEOPLE** to treat people when they are ill **5** *vt* **MEND** to mend something, especially in a rather rough or hurried way [14C. Via Old French < Latin, 'teacher' < *doct-*, past participle of *docere* 'teach'.] —**doctorly** *adj*

doctor-assisted suicide *n* the suicide of somebody with an incurable disease carried out with the help of a doctor. Doctor-assisted suicide is illegal in most countries. US term **physician-assisted suicide**

doctorate /dóktərət/ *n* the highest level of university degree, usually awarded for a lengthy piece of original research but sometimes for other outstanding achievements —**doctoral** /dóktərəl/ *adj*

Doctor of Philosophy *n* **1** the highest level of university degree that can be studied for, awarded to somebody who has successfully completed a lengthy piece of original research **2** a recipient of the degree of Doctor of Philosophy

doctrinaire /dóktri náir/ *adj* determined to use a particular theory or method and refusing to accept that there might be a better approach —**doctrinaire** *n* —**doctrinarian** *n* —**doctrinairism** *n*

doctrine /dóktrin/ *n* **1** a rule or principle that forms the basis of a belief, theory, or policy **2** a body of ideas, particularly in religion, taught to people as truthful or correct [14C. Directly or via French < Latin *doctrina* 'teaching, learning' < *doctor* (see DOCTOR).] —**doctrinal** /dok trín'l/ *adj* —**doctrinality** /dóktri nálləti/ *n* —**doctrinally** /dok trín'li/ *adv*

docudrama /dókyoo draamə/ *n* a dramatized film or television version of a true story [Mid-20C. Blend of DOCUMENTARY + DRAMA.] —**docudramatic** /dókyoodrə máttik/ *adj*

ϟ **document** /dókyoomənt/ *n* **1 FORMAL PIECE OF WRITING** a formal piece of writing that provides information or that acts as a record of events **2 OBJECT CONTAINING INFORMATION** an object such as a film, photograph, or audio recording that contains information and can be used as evidence **3 COMPUTER FILE** a computer file created using an applications program, e.g. a database, spreadsheet, illustration, or text file ■ *vt* **1 RECORD INFORMATION IN OR ON** to make a record of something by writing about it or by filming or photographing it **2 SUPPORT WITH EVIDENCE** to provide evidence for a statement or claim by supplying supporting information [15C. Via French < Latin *documentum* 'lesson, example' (in medieval Latin, 'instruction, official paper') < *docere* 'teach'.] —**documentable** /dókyoo méntəb'l/ *adj* —**documental** /dókyoo mént'l/ *adj* —**documenter** /dókyoo mentər/ *n*

documentalist /dókyoo mént'list/ *n* a specialist in documentation

documentary /dókyoo méntəri/ *n* (*plural* **-ries**) **FACTUAL FILM OR TV PROGRAMME** a film or TV programme presenting facts and information, especially about a political, historical, or social issue ■ *adj* **1 CONSISTING OF DOCUMENTS** in the form of documents, or collected from documents **2 GIVING FACTS** giving facts and information rather than telling a fictional story —**documentarily** *adv*

ϟ **documentation** /dókyoo men táysh'n/ *n* **1 EVIDENTIAL OR REFERENCE DOCUMENTS** documents provided or collected together as evidence or as reference material **2 PROCESS OF PROVIDING WRITTEN INFORMATION** the process of providing written details or information about something **3 COMPUTER SOFTWARE INFORMATION** the instructions, tutorials, and reference information provided to explain how to install and use software or a computer system

document feeder *n* the part of a printer, scanner, or fax machine that holds a stack of papers and feeds them through the machine to be printed

document holder *n* a stand that holds papers in a vertical position so that they can be read easily by somebody working at a desk

docusoap /dókyoo sōp/ *n* a television programme that combines documentary style with elements of soap opera, e.g. by showing the personal lives of people at their workplace [Blend of DOCUMENTARY + SOAP OPERA]

docutainment /dókyoo táynmənt/ *n US* MEDIA = **infotainment**

Dodd /dod/, **Charles Harold** (1884–1973) Welsh biblical scholar

dodder1 /dóddər/ *vi* **1** to tremble or shake slightly as a result of age **2** to walk slowly and unsteadily with shaking limbs as a result of age [Early 17C. Variant of obsolete and dialect *dadder* 'quake, tremble' < ?] —**dodderer** *n*

dodder[2] /dóddər/ (*plural* **-ders** *or* **-der**) *n* a leafless rootless parasitic plant of the morning glory family that lacks chlorophyll and has a reddish twining stem. Flowers: small, white. Genus: *Cuscuta*. [14C. < ?]

doddering /dóddəring/, **doddery** /-əri/ *adj* walking unsteadily, especially as a result of age —**dodderingly** *adv*

doddle /dódd'l/ *n* something very easy to do (*informal*) ○ *I'm sure I'll past the test – it'll be a doddle.* [Mid-20C. < ?]

dodeca- *prefix* twelve ○ *dodecahedron* [< Greek *dōdeka* < *duō* 'two' + *deka* 'ten']

dodecahedron /dṓ deka heédrən/ (*plural* **-drons** *or* **-dra** /-drə/) *n* a solid figure with 12 equal pentagonal faces meeting in threes at 20 vertices [Late 16C. < Greek *dodekaedron* < *dōdeka* 'twelve' + *hedra* 'seat, face'.] —**dodecahedral** *adj*

Dodecanese /dṓ dekə neéz/ group of islands in the SE Aegean Sea that form a department of Greece. Capital: Rhodes. Population: 163,476 (1991). Area: 2,663 sq. km/1,028 sq. mi.

dodecanoic acid /dṓ dekə nṓ ik-/ *n* = **lauric acid** [Mid-20C. < *dodecane* '(kind of) paraffin' < DODECA-.]

dodecaphonic /dṓ dekə fónnik/ *adj* = **twelve-tone** —**dodecaphonism** *n* —**dodecaphonist** *n* —**dodecaphony** *n*

dodecasyllable /dṓ dekə sílləb'l/ *n* a line of verse of 12 syllables —**dodecasyllabic** *adj*

dodge /doj/ *v* (**dodges, dodging, dodged**) **1** *vti* MOVE QUICKLY TO AVOID to move quickly and suddenly to one side to avoid being caught or hit ○ *He dodged the punch.* **2** *vt* AVOID SOMETHING UNPLEASANT to avoid doing something regarded as unpleasant **3** *vt* MASK AREA OF PRINT to mask an area of a print during exposure to prevent light reaching it ■ *n* **1** TRICK TO AVOID DOING a clever trick or tactic to avoid doing something ○ *a tax dodge* **2** QUICK AVOIDING MOVEMENT a sudden quick movement to one side to avoid being caught or hit [Mid-16C. < ?]

dodge ball *n* a children's game in which opponents try to avoid being hit by a large rubber ball

Dodge City /dój-/ city in S Kansas. Population: 22,456 (1998 estimate).

Dodgem /dójjəm/ *tdmk* a trademark for a bumper car

dodger /dójjər/ *n* **1** SOMEBODY AVOIDING DUTY a shirker of duty or responsibility, especially by using dishonest or deceitful methods **2** SOMEBODY DISHONEST somebody cunning and untrustworthy **3** SHELTERING SCREEN ON SHIP a canvas screen on a ship or yacht to protect the person at the helm from spray

dodgy /dójji/ (**-ier, -iest**) *adj* (*informal*) **1** SUSPECT OR DISHONEST suspect, dishonest, or untrustworthy **2** RISKY dangerous or risky **3** LIKELY TO BREAK DOWN unreliable and likely to break down or stop working —**dodgily** *adv* —**dodginess** *n*

Dodo

dodo /dṓdō/ (*plural* **-dos** *or* **-does**) *n* **1** EXTINCT BIRD a large extinct flightless bird that once inhabited Mauritius and neighbouring islands in the Indian Ocean. *Raphus cucullatus.* **2** THOUGHTLESS PERSON somebody regarded as thoughtless or unintelligent (*informal insult*) **3** OLD-FASHIONED PERSON somebody regarded as old-fashioned and unprogressive person (*informal insult*) [Early 17C. < Portuguese *doudo* 'fool, simpleton'.] —**dodoism** *n* ◇ **(as) dead as a dodo** no longer existing, functioning, flourishing, or popular

Dodoma /dṓdəmə/ capital of Tanzania, in the centre of the country. Population: 203,833 (1988).

doe /dō/ *n* a mature female of several mammals, including the deer, kangaroo, rabbit, hare, and goat [Old English *dā* < ?]

SPELLCHECK Do not confuse ***doe*** with ***dough***, which has a similar sound. Beware: your spellchecker will not catch this error.

Doenitz = **Dönitz**

doer /dóo ər/ *n* **1** a person who does something (*often in combination*) ○ *wrongdoer* **2** person who takes action rather than just thinking or talking about it

doeskin /dṓ skin/ *n* **1** SKIN OF DEER the skin of various animals, including a doe, deer, and goat **2** LEATHER light supple leather made from doeskin that is particularly suitable for gloves **3** SMOOTH WOOLLEN CLOTH a densely woven smooth woollen cloth

doesn't /dúzz'nt/ *contr* does not

~~**does'nt**~~ incorrect spelling of **doesn't**

doest /dóo əst/ 2nd person present singular of **do**[1] (*archaic*)

doeth /dóo əth/ 3rd person present singular of **do**[1] (*archaic*)

doff /dof/ *vt* **1** to take off a hat or lift and tilt it as a greeting or a mark of respect **2** to take off a coat or another piece of clothing [14C. Contraction of archaic *do off* 'take off'.] —**doffer** *n*

dog /dog/ *n* **1** DOMESTIC ANIMAL a domestic carnivorous animal that typically has a long muzzle, pointed ears, a fur coat, and a long fur-covered tail, and whose characteristic call is a bark. *Canis familiaris.* **2** WILD ANIMAL any wild animal that resembles a domestic dog and belongs to the same family, e.g. a wolf, fox, dingo, or coyote. Family: Canidae. **3** MALE DOG a male dog, wolf, fox, or other member of the dog family **4** CONTEMPTIBLE PERSON an unpleasant or contemptible person (*insult*) **5** OFFENSIVE TERM an offensive term for somebody who is regarded as not good-looking (*slang insult*) **6** MAN a man of the particular type described (*informal*) ○ *You lucky dog!* **7** *US, Can* SOMETHING USELESS OR INFERIOR something useless or of a very poor standard (*informal*) **8** *Aus* BETRAYER a betrayer of his or her associates (*informal*) **9** HOUSEHOLD = **andiron** **10** METEOROL = **seadog** **11** GRIPPING TOOL a device for gripping or holding things ■ **dogs** *npl* **1** DOG RACING greyhound racing in general, or a greyhound race meeting (*informal*) **2** FEET somebody's feet (*dated informal*) ■ *vt* (**dogs, dogging, dogged**) **1** BOTHER PERSISTENTLY to bother or trouble somebody persistently (*often passive*) ○ *dogged by bad luck* **2** FOLLOW CLOSELY to follow somebody closely in a determined way ○ *dogging her footsteps* **3** GRIP WITH MECHANICAL DEVICE to grip or hold something firmly with a mechanical device [Old English *docga* < ?] —**dog-like** *adj* ◇ **a dog in the manger** a person who tries to prevent somebody else from having or doing something that he or she cannot have or do ◇ **a dog's breakfast** *or* **dinner** something that is messy, disorganized, or badly done (*informal*) ◇ **a dog's life** a wretched existence ◇ **dog eat dog** ruthlessly competitive ◇ **go to the dogs** be in the final stages of a gradual decline in standards (*informal*) ◇ **let sleeping dogs lie** take no action in a situation that is currently peaceful but potentially troublesome ◇ **put on the dog** *US, Aus* make a display of wealth or knowledge ostentatiously or pretentiously (*dated informal*)

dog-and-pony show *n US* an elaborate business presentation or promotional event (*informal*)

dogbane /dóg bayn/ *n* a plant that bears dogberries with pungent milky juice and a bitter root. Flowers: small, bell-shaped, white or pink. Genus: *Apocynum.*

dogberry[1] /dóg beri, -bəri/ (*plural* **-ries**) *n* **1** a berry of any of various plants, including dogwood **2** a plant that bears dogberries

dogberry[2] /dóg beri, -bəri/ (*plural* **-ries**), **Dogberry** (*plural* **-ries**) *n* an unintelligent but self-important official [Mid-19C. After *Dogberry*, constable in *Much Ado About Nothing* by Shakespeare.] —**dogberryism** *n*

dog biscuit *n* a hard biscuit made for dogs to eat

dogcart /dóg kaart/ *n* a two-wheeled vehicle drawn by a horse and seating two people back to back

dogcatcher /dóg kachər/ *n US* = **dog warden**

dog chew *n* a hard piece of leather or compressed edible material given to a dog to chew on, either as a treat or to keep its teeth in good condition

dog collar *n* **1** COLLAR FOR DOG a piece of leather or fabric worn around a dog's neck, often with the dog's name attached to it **2** CLERICAL COLLAR a clerical collar (*informal*) **3** CLOSE-FITTING NECKLACE a necklace that fits closely round the neck

dog days *npl* **1** the hottest period of the summer **2** a lazy or inactive period of time [Because in ancient times heralded by the simultaneous rising of the Dog Star and the Sun]

doge /dōj, dōzh/ *n* the chief magistrate in Renaissance Venice and Genoa [Mid-16C. Via French < Venetian Italian *doze* < Latin *ducem* 'leader'.] —**dogeship** *n*

dog-eared *adj* **1** having worn and well-thumbed pages that have been creased or folded over to mark the place reached in reading **2** shabby or well-used

dog-end *n* the discarded end of a cigarette after the rest of it has been smoked (*informal*)

dogey *n US, Can* = **dogie**

dogfight /dóg fīt/ *n* **1** COMBAT BETWEEN FIGHTER PLANES an aerial combat involving two or more fighter planes **2** FIERCE FIGHT a fierce violent fight **3** FIGHT INVOLVING DOGS a fight between dogs —**dogfighting** *n*

dogfish /dóg fish/ (*plural* **-fishes** *or* **-fish**) *n* **1** a small, long-tailed shark, either spiny or smooth-skinned. Native to: Pacific, Atlantic, Mediterranean waters. Families: Squalidae and Carcharhinidae and Scyliorhinidae. **2** = **bowfin**

dogged /dóggid/ *adj* determined to continue without giving up in spite of difficulties —**doggedly** *adv* —**doggedness** *n*

dogger[1] /dóggər/ *n* a Dutch fishing vessel [14C. < Middle Dutch.]

dogger[2] /dóggər/ *n* a large mass of calcium-containing sandstone or ironstone occurring in sedimentary rock [Late 17C. < ?]

doggerel /dóggərəl/, **doggrel** /dóggrəl/ *n* **1** poetry that does not scan well and is often not intended to be taken seriously **2** something that is badly written or makes no sense at all [14C. Probably < DOG (with its pejorative connotations).]

Doggett /dóggit/, **Thomas** (1660?–1721) Irish actor and playwright

doggie *n* = **doggy**

doggie bag *n* = **doggy bag**

doggish /dóggish/ *adj* **1** resembling a dog, or possessing the qualities of a dog **2** bad-tempered and aggressive —**doggishly** *adv* —**doggishness** *n*

doggo /dóggō/ *adv* not moving or making any sound in order not to be discovered ○ *lying doggo* [Late 19C. Because dogs can lie in this manner.]

doggone /dóggon/, **doggoned** *adv, adj US, Can* used to emphasize how bad or annoying something is (*informal*) ■ *interj US* used to express annoyance or irritation (*informal*) [Early 19C. Probably alteration of *God damn*.]

doggy /dóggi/, **doggie** *n* (*plural* **-gies**) DOG a dog (*babytalk*) ■ *adj* **1** RESEMBLING A DOG resembling or typical of a dog's behaviour or appearance **2** FOND OF DOGS fond of or interested in dogs (*informal*)

doggy bag *n* a bag that can be used by a customer at a restaurant to take home any leftover food from his or her meal [< giving the food to a dog]

doggy paddle *n* a swimming stroke in which the swimmer lies face down and makes rapid downward movements with the arms and legs underneath the body. US term **dog paddle** *n.* ■ *vi* (**doggy paddles, doggy paddling, doggy paddled**) to swim using the doggy paddle. US term **dog paddle** *v.*

dog handler *n* a police officer or security guard who is in charge of a specially trained working dog

doghouse /dóg howss/ (*plural* **-houses** /-howziz/) *n US, Can* = **kennel** *n.* 1 ◇ **in the doghouse** in disgrace (*informal*)

dogie /dṓgi/, **dogy** (*plural* **-gies**), **dogey** (*plural* **-geys**) *n US, Can* a calf with no mother [Late 19C. < ?]

dog Latin *n* Latin that is incorrect in some way, especially a word or phrase that is falsely made to look or sound like Latin for humorous or satirical effect

dogleg /dóg leg/ *n* **1** a sharp bend or angle in something, especially in a road **2** a hole in golf in which the fairway contains a gentle or sharp bend [< the bent form of a dog's hind leg] —**dogleg** *vi* —**doglegged** /dóg léggid, dóg légd/ *adj*

dogma /dógmə/ (*plural* **-mas** *or* **-mata** /-mətə/) *n* **1** a belief or set of beliefs that a religion holds to be true **2** a belief or set of beliefs that a political, philosophical, or moral group holds to be true [Mid-16C. Via late Latin < Greek *dogma, dogmat-* 'opinion, tenet' < *dokein* 'seem good, think'.]

dogmatic /dog máttik/, **dogmatical** /-ik'l/ *adj* **1** prone to expressing strongly held beliefs and opinions **2** relating to or expressing a religious, political, philosophical, or moral dogma —**dogmatically** *adv*

dogmatics /dog máttiks/, **dogmatic theology** *n* the study of religious dogmas, especially Christian dogmas (+ *singular verb*)

dogmatise *vti* = **dogmatize**

dogmatism /dógmətizəm/ *n* the tendency to express strongly held opinions in a way that suggests they should be accepted without question

dogmatist /dógmətist/ *n* **1** an expresser of strongly held opinions who expects them to be accepted without question **2** a deviser of a new dogma

dogmatize /dógmə tīz/ (**-tizes, -tizing, -tized**), **dogmatise** *vi* to express strongly held opinions in a way that suggests they should be accepted without question —**dogmatization** /dógmə tī záysh'n/ *n* —**dogmatizer** *n*

dognap /dóg nap/ (**-naps, -napping, -napped**) *vt* to steal a dog, especially in order to sell it for use in medical research —**dognapper** *n*

do-gooder /-gŏŏdər/ *n* a person who sincerely tries to help others, but whose actions may be unwelcome (*informal*) —**do-goodery** *n* —**do-gooding** *n, adj*

dog paddle *n US* = **doggy paddle** *n.* ■ *vi* (**dog paddles, dog paddling, dog paddled**) *US* = **doggy paddle** *v.*

dog racing *n* the sport of greyhound racing in which dogs chase a mechanical hare round a track and spectators may bet on which dog will win

dog rose *n* a wild rose. Flowers: delicate, pink or white. Native to: Europe. *Rosa canina.*

dogsbody /dógz bodi/ (*plural* **-ies**) *n* a worker who does boring tasks that others do not want to do (*informal*)

dogsled /dóg sled/ *n* a vehicle mounted on runners and pulled by dogs, designed to travel over snow and ice

dog's-tail *n* a European grass that has flowers along a narrow spike. Genus: *Cynosurus.*

Dog Star *n* ASTRON = **Sirius**

dog's-tooth check *n* TEXTILES = **houndstooth check**

dog tag *n* **1** a metal disc, attached to a dog's collar, that gives the name and address of the dog's owner **2** *US* a metal identification tag for a member of the military, worn on a chain around the neck (*informal*)

dogteeth /-teeth/ plural of **dogtooth**

dog-tired *adj* completely exhausted (*informal*)

dogtooth /dóg tooth/ (*plural* **-teeth**) *n* **1** a canine tooth (*informal*) **2** in 13th-century English architecture, a small raised ornamental feature on a building consisting of four leaf-shaped parts arranged to form an X-shape

dog-tooth check *n* TEXTILES, CLOTHING = **houndstooth check**

dogtooth violet *n* a small spring-flowering bulbous plant with red-speckled leaves. Flowers: drooping, yellow or purple, like small lilies. Genus: *Erythronium.* [< the toothed inner segments of the perianth]

dogtrot /dóg trot/ *n* a gentle trot at a steady pace

dog violet *n* a type of violet. Flowers: blue and yellow. Native to: Europe, Asia. *Viola canina.*

dog warden *n* somebody employed to catch stray dogs. US term **dogcatcher**

dogwatch /dóg woch/ *n* on a ship, the late afternoon watch from 4:00 P.M. to 6:00 P.M. or the early evening watch from 6:00 P.M. to 8:00 P.M.

dogwood /dóg wŏŏd/ (*plural* **-woods** *or* **-wood**) *n* a tree or bush with clusters of small white flowers surrounded by four large white or reddish leaves (**bracts**). Genus: *Cornus.*

dogy *n US, Can* = **dogie**

doh /dō/ *n* a syllable that represents the first note in a scale when singing solfeggio. US term **do**[2] [Mid-18C. < Italian *do.*] ◇ **be up to high doh** *Scotland* to be extremely agitated or anxious (*informal*)

DoH, DOH *abbr* Department of Health

Doha /dṓ haa, dṓ ə/ capital and largest city of Qatar, on the Persian Gulf. Population: 392,384 (1995 estimate).

DOI *abbr* digital object identifier

doily /dóyli/ (*plural* **-lies**), **doyly** (*plural* **-lies**) *n* a decorative lacy mat that is put on plates under cakes or party food to display the food attractively [Late 18C. After *Doiley* or *Doyley,* 17C London draper.]

doing /dóo ing/ present participle of **do**[1] ■ *n* **1** CARRYING OUT OF the act of performing or carrying out something ○ *It's all your doing.* **2** BEATING OR REBUKE a beating or rebuke given as a punishment (*dated informal*) ■ **doings** *npl* **1** DEEDS OR ACHIEVEMENTS the things that somebody has done **2** SOCIAL ACTIVITIES social activities

doings /dóo ingz/ *n* something whose name has been forgotten or is not known (*informal; + singular or plural verb*)

doit /doyt/ *n* a small low-value silver coin that was a Dutch unit of currency between the 15th and 17th centuries [Late 16C. < Middle Low German *doyt.*]

doited /dóytid/, **doitit** /-tit/ *adj Scotland* an offensive term meaning behaving unreasonably or childishly, especially when the behaviour is thought to result from advanced age (*insult*) [15C. < ?]

do-it-yourself *n* the activity of doing repairs and alterations in the home yourself, especially as a hobby, instead of employing tradespeople to do the work —**do-it-yourselfer** *n*

dojo /dṓjō/ (*plural* **-jos**) *n* a school or room for practising judo [Mid-20C. < Japanese, < *dō* 'way, art' + *-jō* 'ground'.]

dol. *abbr* dollar

dolce /dólchi/ *adv* sweetly and gently (*musical direction*) [Early 19C. Via Italian, 'sweet' < Latin *dulcis.*] —**dolce** *adj*

dolce far niente /-faar nyén ti/ *n* pleasant idleness and relaxation [Early 19C. < Italian, 'sweet doing nothing'.]

Dolcelatte /dól chay látt ay/ *n* a soft creamy Italian blue cheese with a mild flavour

dolce vita /-véetə/ *n* a life of luxury and idle self-indulgence [Mid-20C. < Italian, 'sweet life'.]

doldrums /dóldrəmz, dṓl-/ *npl* **1** STAGNATION a sluggish state in which something fails to develop or improve **2** GLOOMINESS a state of gloominess or very low energy **3** AREA NORTH OF EQUATOR an area with no wind or light variable winds just north of the equator in the Atlantic and Pacific oceans, situated between the trade winds **4** WEATHER CONDITIONS IN DOLDRUMS the weather conditions prevailing in the doldrums that caused sailing ships to become becalmed [Late 18C. < ?]

dole[1] /dōl/ *n* **1** CHARITY the giving of clothes, money, or food to people who are in need **2** SOMEBODY'S FATE somebody's fate in life (*archaic*) ■ *vt* (**doles, doling, doled**) DISTRIBUTE SOMETHING AS CHARITY to distribute something as charity to people who are in need [Old English *dāl* 'portion' < Germanic]
dole out *vt* to give something to each of a group of people (*informal*)

dole[2] /dōl/ *n* grief, sadness, or misery (*archaic*) [13C. Via Old French *dol* 'mourning' < Vulgar Latin *dolus* < Latin *dolere* 'grieve, suffer pain'.]

dole bludger *n Aus* a person who lives on benefit payments and makes no obvious effort to find work (*disapproving*)

doleful /dṓlf'l/ *adj* very sad and mournful —**dolefully** *adv* —**dolefulness** *n*

dolente /do lénti/ *adv* in a sorrowful manner (*musical direction*) [< Italian, present participle of *dolere* 'feel grief' < Latin] —**dolente** *adj*

dolerite /dóllə rīt/ *n* a medium-grained basic igneous rock typically forming a minor intrusion such as a sill or dyke. US term **diabase** *n.* [Mid-19C. < French *dolérite* < Greek *doleros* 'deceptive' < *dolos* 'deceit' (because difficult to distinguish from diorite).] —**doleritic** /dóllə ríttik/ *adj*

dolichocephalic /dóllikō si fállik/, **dolichocephalous** /-séffələss/ *adj* having a head disproportionately longer than it is wide, specifically one with a cephalic index of less than 75 [Mid-19C. < Greek *dolikhos* 'narrow'.] —**dolichocephalism** /dóllikō séffəlizəm/ *n*

dolichosaurus /dóllikō sáwrəss/ *n* an extinct aquatic long-necked reptile that was common 65 million years ago [< Greek *dolikhos* 'narrow']

Dolin /dóllin/, **Sir Anton** (1904–83) British dancer and choreographer. Pseudonym of **Sydney Francis Patrick Chippindall Healey Kay**

doline /də léenə/, **dolina** *n* a large, often roughly circular basin of valley-sized proportions formed as a result of water dissolving surface limestone [Late 19C. Via German < Slovene *dolina* 'valley'.]

D'Oliviera /dólli véerə/, **Basil Lewis** (*b.* 1931) South African-born British cricketer

doll /dol/ *n* **1** a child's toy in the shape of a person or baby **2** a woman or girl who is pleasant to look at (*informal; sometimes offensive*) [Mid-16C. < form of the woman's name *Dorothy.*] —**dollish** *adj* —**dollishly** *adv* —**dollishness** *n*
doll up *vt* to make yourself or somebody else, e.g. a child, look particularly smart and stylish, usually for a special occasion (*informal*)

dollar /dóllər/ *n* **1** see table at **currency** **2** a former British coin worth five shillings (*informal*) [Mid-16C. Via early Flemish *daler* or Low German < German *Taler,* shortening of *Joachimst(h)aler,* after the silver mine of *Joachimsthal,* now Jáchymov, Czech Republic.]

dollarbird /dóllər burd/ *n* a blue-grey bird with pale round patches on its wings the size of a dollar coin. Native to: Indonesia and New Guinea, migrating to Australia. *Eurystomus orientalis.*

dollar cost averaging *n* the periodic and systematic purchase of a security regardless of the security price

dollar diplomacy *n US* **1** in the United States, a policy aimed at encouraging and protecting American investment abroad **2** the use of financial resources to facilitate foreign relations

dollars-and-cents *adj US* considering finance as the determining factor

dollar sign *n* the symbol ($) that represents a dollar

Dollfuss /dól fŏŏss/, **Engelbert** (1892–1934) Austrian statesman

dollhouse /dól howss/ (*plural* **-houses** /-howziz/) *n US* = **doll's house**

dollop /dólləp/ *n* a spoon-sized quantity of a thick liquid or a soft solid such as ice cream or cream (*informal*) ■ *vt* to spoon a quantity of a thick liquid or a soft solid (*informal*) [Late 16C. < ?]

doll's house *n* a toy house containing miniature furniture. US term **dollhouse**

dolly /dólli/ *n* (*plural* **-lies**) **1** DOLL a toy doll (*babytalk*) **2** MOVING PLATFORM FOR CAMERA OPERATOR a platform with wheels on which a camera operator and camera are placed in order to film moving shots for a film or television programme **3** PLATFORM ON WHEELS FOR MOVING THINGS a platform on wheels used to move heavy weights **4** WEIGHT DROPPED ON POST a heavy weight dropped on a stake or pile to force it into the ground **5** TOOL FOR HOLDING RIVET an anvil that holds one end of a rivet while the other end is being hammered **6** HEAVY BLOCK HELD BEHIND HAMMERED METAL a heavy block held behind sheet metal that is being hammered **7** EASY CATCH an easy catch ■ *vti* (**-lies, -lying, -lied**) MOVE CAMERA ON A DOLLY to move a camera on a dolly

dolly bird *n* a young woman thought to be good-looking (*dated informal; sometimes offensive*)

dolly drop *n* in cricket, a ball bowled high and slowly that reaches the batsman without touching the ground

dolly mixtures *npl* a variety of small coloured sweets sold as a mixture

dolly shot *n* a shot filmed from a camera mounted on a wheeled platform

Dolly Varden /dólli vaárd'n/ *n* **1** a woman's hat with a large brim, usually with one side turned down, and decorated with flowers **2** (*plural* **Dolly Varden**) a trout or char with red spots found in lakes and streams. Native to: W North America, E Asia. *Salvelinus malma.* [Late 19C. After a woman of colourful dress in the novel *Barnaby Rudge* by Charles Dickens.]

dolma /dólmə/ (*plural* **-mas** *or* **-mades** /-maá deez/) *n* a vine or cabbage leaf with a savoury stuffing usually containing meat and rice, a speciality of Greek and Turkish cooking [Late 17C. < Turkish, 'something stuffed'.]

dolman /dólmən/ *n* **1** a woman's coat with large sleeves cut in one piece with the body of the garment **2** a long Turkish robe [Late 16C. Via French *dol(i)man* < Turkish *dolama(n)* 'robe'.]

dolman jacket *n* a style of riding jacket, usually worn like a cloak over the shoulders with the sleeves hanging loose

dolman sleeve *n* a sleeve cut in one piece with the body of a garment such as a jacket or dress, particularly one fitting tightly at the wrist and wide at the armhole

dolmen /dólmən/ *n* a prehistoric structure that consists of a large horizontal slab of stone supported by two or more vertical slabs and is thought to have been used as a tomb [Mid-19C. < French.]

dolomite /dóllə mīt/ *n* **1** a white, reddish, or greenish mineral consisting of calcium magnesium carbonate. Source: sedimentary rocks. Use: building stone, cement, fertilizers. **2** a sedimentary rock consisting mainly of the mineral dolomite [Late 18C. < French, after Déodat de *Dolomieu*.]

Dolomites /dóllə mīts/ mountain group in the NE Italian Alps. Highest peak: Marmolada, 3,342 km/10,964 ft.

dolor *n* US = **dolour**

doloroso /dóllə róssó/ *adv* to be played with sadness (*musical direction*) [Early 19C. Via Italian < late Latin *dolorosus* (see DOLOROUS).] —**doloroso** *adj*

dolorous /dóllərəss/ *adj* showing, causing, or involving sorrow or pain (*literary*) [14C. Via Old French < late Latin *dolorosus* < Latin *dolor* (see DOLOUR).] —**dolorously** *adv* —**dolorousness** *n*

dolostone /dóllə stōn/ *n* a form of limestone having more than 50% dolomite [Mid-20C. < DOLOMITE.]

dolour /dóllər/ *n* intense sadness (*literary*) [13C. Via Old French < Latin *dolor* 'pain, grief, sorrow' < *dolere* 'feel pain'.]

dolphin /dólfin/ (*plural* **-phins** *or* **-phin**) *n* **1** an intelligent marine mammal (**cetacean**) that resembles a large fish and has teeth and a snout similar to a beak. Family: Delphinidae. **2** a large sea fish of the perch family, popular as a game fish, that has a long dorsal fin, high blunt forehead, and a brilliant green, blue, and yellow body. *Coryphaena hippurus* and *Coryphaena equisetis*. [14C. Via Old French *daulphin* < Greek *delphin*.]

dolphinarium /dólfi naíri əm/ (*plural* **-ums** *or* **-a** /-ri ə/) *n* a large pool in which dolphins are kept, either for research or for public displays

dolphinfish /dólfin fish/ (*plural* **-fish** *or* **-fishes**) *n* = **dolphin** *n*. 2

dolphin striker *n* a strut that helps to prevent upward movement of a spar extending from the front of a sailing vessel

dolt /dōlt/ *n* somebody considered as being without intelligence (*dated informal insult*) [Mid-16C. < ?]

doltish /dóltish/ *adj* of low intelligence or showing lack of intelligence (*dated informal*) —**doltishly** *adv* —**doltishness** *n*

Dom /dom/, **dom** *n* **1** a title used before the name of some Roman Catholic monks, especially Benedictines **2** a title formerly used before the names of certain members of the aristocracy and royalty in Portugal and Brazil [Late 17C. Shortening of Latin *dominus* 'lord'.]

DOM *abbr* to God, the best, the greatest [< Latin *Deo Optimo Maximo*]

dom. *abbr* **1** domestic **2** dominant

-dom *suffix* **1** status, condition ○ *martyrdom* **2** people associated with a particular status or rank ○ *fandom* **3** office, rank, domain ○ *dukedom* [Old English *-dōm* < Indo-European, 'put, place']

⚡**domain** /dō máyn, də-/ *n* **1** PURVIEW the scope of a subject **2** SPHERE OF INFLUENCE an area of activity over which somebody has influence **3** TERRITORY GOVERNED territory ruled by a government or a leader **4** LAND OWNED an area of land owned and controlled by a person, family, or organization **5** RIGHTS OF OWNERSHIP rights relating to the ownership of land. ◊ **demesne** *n*. **6** REGION OF UNIFORM MAGNETISM a region in a ferromagnetic material within which all the atoms are magnetically oriented in the same direction **7** SET OF VALUES OF VARIABLE the set of possible values specified for a given mathematical function **8** *ANZ* PUBLIC SPACE a public recreation area **9** ONLINE = **domain name** [15C. < French *domaine*, alteration of *demeine* (see DEMESNE).]

⚡**domainist** /dō máynist/ *n* a computer user who snobbishly judges other people by the domain names on their e-mail

---

INTERNET DOMAINS

Top-level domains in Internet addresses are the final letters of the address. They indicate the country – except for the United States, where no country code is used – or type of organization, or both.

Selected Organization Domains

Domain	Organization
.aero	aviation industry
.biz	business
.com	commercial organization
.coop	non-profitmaking cooperative
.edu	educational organization
.gov	government organization
.info	general use
.int	international organization
.mil	military organization
.museum	museum
.name	private individual
.net	networking organization
.org	non-commercial organization
.pro	professional practice

For countries other than the United States, country domains can be combined with organization domains, for example:

.co.uk	United Kingdom organization
.edu.au	Australian educational organization

Selected Country Domains

Domain	Country
.au	Australia
.bd	Bangladesh
.ca	Canada
.gh	Ghana
.hk	Hong Kong
.id	Indonesia
.ie	Ireland
.in	India
.ke	Kenya
.my	Malaysia
.nz	New Zealand
.ng	Nigeria
.pk	Pakistan
.sg	Singapore
.za	South Africa
.lk	Sri Lanka
.ug	Uganda
.uk	United Kingdom
.zm	Zambia
.zw	Zimbabwe

⚡**domain name**, **domain** *n* the sequence of words, phrases, abbreviations, or characters that serves as the Internet address of a computer or network

dome /dōm/ *n* **1** HEMISPHERICAL ROOF a hemispherical roof, e.g. on a palace or cathedral **2** HEMISPHERICAL TOP something that resembles a dome in shape and position, e.g. the cover of a furnace or the top of somebody's head ○ *the dome of the sky* **3** HEMISPHERICAL BUILDING STRUCTURE a hemispherical or convex structure, especially a building ○ *the Millennium Dome* **4** CRYSTAL FORMATION RESEMBLING A ROOF a crystal form in which two inclined surfaces intersect to form an edge like a roof **5** LARGE STATELY BUILDING a large grand building (*archaic*) **6** CURVED ROCK LAYER a hemispherical topographic feature that slopes in all directions from a central point, formed by upward folding of sediments **7** LAVA MASS a mass of solidified viscous lava formed above the vent of a volcano by the build-up of magma ■ *v* (**domes, doming, domed**) **1** *vti* FORM A HEMISPHERICAL SHAPE to rise in a hemispherical shape, or form something into this shape **2** *vt* COVER WITH A DOME to cover something with a dome [Mid-17C. Via French *dôme* < Italian *duomo* 'house, house of God, cathedral' < Latin *domus* 'house'.] —**domed** *adj*

domesday /dóomz day/ *n* doomsday (*archaic*)

Domesday Book, **Doomsday Book** *n* a record of all the land in England, its value and its ownership, commissioned by William the Conqueror in 1085 [Because the ultimate authority]

domestic /də méstik/ *adj* **1** RELATING TO HOME relating to or used in the home or everyday life within a household **2** RELATING TO FAMILY relating to or involving the family or people living together within a household **3** NOT WILD kept as a farm animal or as a pet **4** NOT FOREIGN produced, distributed, sold, or occurring within a country ○ *domestic oil producers* **5** OF A NATION'S INTERNAL AFFAIRS relating to the internal affairs of a nation or country ○ *domestic issues such as elections* **6** ENJOYING HOME enjoying home and family life ■ *n* **1** HOUSEHOLD SERVANT somebody employed to do housework in somebody else's home

or other duties in a large household **2** PRODUCT NOT ORIGINATING ABROAD a product manufactured within a country [15C. Via French *domestique* < Latin *domesticus* < *domus* 'house'.] —**domestically** *adv*

domesticate /də mésti kayt/ (**-cates, -cating, -cated**) *vt* **1** TAME AN ANIMAL to accustom an animal to living with or near people, usually as a farm animal or pet **2** ACCUSTOM TO HOUSEHOLD LIFE to accustom somebody to home life or housework (*humorous*) **3** ADAPT PLANTS AND ANIMALS FOR HUMANS to cultivate plants or raise animals, selectively breeding them to increase their suitability for human requirements [Mid-17C. < medieval Latin *domesticat-*, past participle of *domesticare* < Latin *domesticus* (see DOMESTIC).] —**domesticable** *adj* —**domesticated** *adj* —**domestication** /də mésti káysh'n/ *n* —**domesticator** *n*

domesticity /dōm e stíssəti, dóm-/ *n* **1** HOME LIFE life as it is lived at home **2** FONDNESS FOR HOME LIFE a liking for or familiarity with home life ■ **domesticities** *npl* HOUSEHOLD MATTERS the concerns of the home and family

domestic prelate *n* a Roman Catholic priest with honorary membership of the papal household

domestic violence *n* physical violence between members of a family, especially between spouses

Domett /dómmit/, **Alfred** (1811–87) British-born New Zealand statesman and poet

domette /dō mét/ *n* a soft fleecy wool and acrylic fabric. Use: lightweight interlining. [Early 19C. < ?]

domical /dómmik'l/ *adj* **1** shaped like a dome **2** having a dome or domes

domicile /dómmi sīl/ *n* **1** SOMEBODY'S HOME the house, flat, or other place where somebody lives (*formal*) **2** SOMEBODY'S PLACE OF RESIDENCE somebody's true, fixed, and legally recognized place of residence, especially in cases of prolonged absence that require them to prove a continuing and significant connection with the place **3** PLACE FOR PAYMENT the place at which a bill of exchange is to be paid ■ *vt* (**-ciles, -ciling, -ciled**) GIVE A HOME to establish somebody in or provide somebody with a place of residence [15C. Directly or via French < Latin *domicilium* < *domus* 'house'.]

domiciliary /dómmi sílli əri/ *adj* **1** relating to a home or homes **2** provided for or attending to people in their own homes ○ *domiciliary care* [Late 19C. Via French *domiciliare* < medieval Latin *domiciliarius* < Latin *domicilium* (see DOMICILE).]

domiciliary care *n* personal, domestic, or nursing care provided for people at home rather than in an institution

domiciliate /dómmi sílli ayt/ (**-ates, -ating, -ated**) *vt* = **domicile** v. [Late 18C. < Latin *domicilium* (see DOMICILE).]

dominance /dómmmnanss/ *n* **1** POWER EXERTED OVER OTHERS control or command wielded over others **2** FIRST IMPORTANCE prime importance, effectiveness, or prominence **3** EXPRESSION OF GENETIC FEATURE the property of a gene that causes a parental characteristic it controls to occur in any offspring **4** PREPONDERANCE OF ONE SPECIES the preponderance of a single plant or animal species in a specific community or over a specific period

dominance hierarchy BIOL = **hierarchy** *n.* 3

dominant /dómminənt/ *adj* **1** IN CONTROL in control or command over others **2** MORE IMPORTANT more important, effective, or prominent than others **3** EXPRESSING SAME CHARACTERISTIC IN OFFSPRING describes a gene that causes a parental characteristic it controls to occur in an offspring, or the characteristic itself **4** PREPONDERANT IN A COMMUNITY OR PERIOD relating to a single plant or animal species that is preponderant within a specific community or over a specific period **5** RELATING TO 5TH NOTE OF SCALE relating to the fifth note of a musical scale or the harmony based around that note ■ *n* **1** 5TH NOTE OF SCALE the fifth note of a musical scale **2** CHORD BASED ON 5TH NOTE a chord or key based on the fifth note of a musical scale [15C. Via French < Latin *dominant-*, present participle of *dominari* (see DOMINATE).] —**dominantly** *adv*

dominant estate *n* US LAW = **dominant tenement**

dominant hemisphere *n* the half of the brain that tends to exercise greater control over certain functions, e.g. language or movement of the left or right side of the body

dominant tenement *n* property that gives its owner certain rights over other property, e.g. the right to cross land belonging to somebody else in order to reach your own house. US term **dominant estate**

dominate /dómmi nayt/ (**-nates, -nating, -nated**) *vti* **1** CONTROL to have control, power, or authority over somebody or something **2** BE PROMINENT to be the most important aspect or element of something **3** BE INFLUENTIAL to have a prevailing influence on somebody or something **4** TOWER ABOVE to overlook an area from a prominent and usually elevated position [Early 17C. < Latin *dominat-*, past participle of *dominari* 'be lord, rule' < *dominus* 'lord'.] —**domination** /dómmi náysh'n/ *n* —**dominative** *adj* —**dominator** *n*

dominatrix /dómmi náytriks/ (*plural* **-trices** /-tri seez/) *n* a dominant woman partner in a sadomasochistic relationship [Mid-16C. < Latin, 'woman ruler' < *dominari* (see DOMINATE).]

dominee /dómmi neè/ *n S Africa* CHR = **predikant** [Mid-20C. Via Afrikaans or Dutch < Latin *dominus* 'lord'.]

domineer /dómmi neèr/ *vi* to rule tyrannically or behave in an overbearing way [Late 16C. Via Dutch *domineren* < Latin *dominari* (see DOMINATE).]

domineering /dómmi neèring/ *adj* showing a desire or tendency to exercise excessive control or authority over others —**domineeringly** *adv*

Domingo /də míng gō/, **Plácido** (*b.* 1941) Spanish opera singer

Dominica /dómmi neèkə, də mínnikə/ island republic in the Leeward Islands, in the E Caribbean Sea. Capital: Roseau. Population: 666,633 (1997). Area: 751 sq. km/290 sq. mi. Length: 47 km/29 mi.

dominical /də minnik'l/ *adj* (*formal*) **1** relating to Jesus Christ as the Lord **2** relating to Sunday as the day of the Lord [15C. Directly or via French < late Latin *dominicalis* < Latin *dominus* 'lord'.]

Dominican[1] /də mínnikən/ *n* **1** somebody who comes from the Dominican Republic **2** somebody who comes from Dominica —**Dominican** *adj*

Dominican[2] /də mínnikən/ *n* a member of the order of friars founded by St Dominic in 1215 ■ *adj* relating or

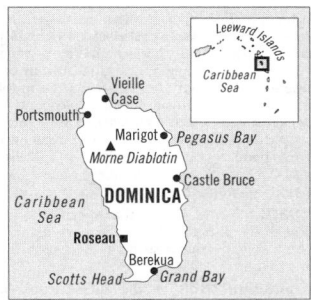

Dominica

belonging to St Dominic or his order of friars [Late 16C. < medieval Latin *Dominicanus* < founder's name.]

Dominican Republic

Dominican Republic /də mínnikən-/ republic on Hispaniola Island in the N Caribbean Sea. Capital: Santo Domingo. Population: 7,868,731 (1997). Area: 48,734 sq. km/18,816 sq. mi. Length: 380 km/235 mi.

dominion /də mínnyən/ *n* **1** RULING CONTROL ruling power, authority, or control **2** SPHERE OF INFLUENCE somebody's area of influence or control **3** LAND RULED the land governed by a ruler (*often plural*) ○ *the monarch's dominions beyond the sea* **4** dominion, Dominion SELF-GOVERNING TERRITORY a self-governing part of the British Commonwealth or, formerly, the British Empire [15C. Via Old French < medieval Latin *dominion-* < Latin *dominium* 'property, right of ownership' < *dominus* 'lord'.]

dominium /də mínnyəm/ *n* the right of ownership of property, especially land and buildings [Mid-18C. < Latin (see DOMINION).]

domino /dómminō/ (*plural* **-noes**) *n* **1** SMALL OBLONG TILE any one of a set of small oblong blocks with its face divided into two sections, each section either blank or marked with a number of spots **2** HOODED CLOAK AND MASK a hooded cloak and eye mask formerly worn as a disguise at a party (**masquerade**), the cloak or mask alone, or the wearer of any of these **3** COUNTRY AFFECTED BY DOMINO THEORY a country thought likely to be affected by political events in another country, particularly by the spread of Communism [Late 17C. < French, 'priest's winter hood, masked cloak worn at masquerades'.]

domino effect *n* an inevitable succession of related and usually undesirable events, each caused by the preceding one. ◊ **domino theory** [Because dominoes set up in a row fall in sequence once the first has fallen]

domino theory *n* a theory that political events are interrelated and that one can trigger off a chain of others. ◊ **domino effect**

don[1] /don/ *n* **1** UNIVERSITY OR COLLEGE TEACHER a university or college teacher, especially one at Oxford or Cambridge **2** SPANISH MAN OF RANK a Spanish gentleman or aristocrat **3** LEADER OF ORGANIZED CRIME FAMILY a head of an organized crime family, especially in the Mafia [Late 16C. Via Spanish < Latin *dominus* 'lord'.]

don[2] /don/ (**dons, donning, donned**) *vt* to put on a garment [14C. Contraction of *do on* 'put on'.]

Don[1] *n* a title used before a man's name in Spain and other Spanish-speaking countries [Early 16C. < Spanish (see DON[1]).]

Don[2] /don/ river in W Russia, flowing into the Sea of Azov. Length: 1,870 km/1,160 mi.

Dona /dónnə/ *n* a title used before a married woman's name in Portugal and other Portuguese-speaking countries [Early 17C. Via Portuguese < Latin *domina* 'lady'.]

Doña /dónnyə/ *n* a title used before a married woman's name in Spain and other Spanish-speaking countries [Early 17C. Via Spanish < Latin *domina* 'lady'.]

Donaldson /dónn'lds'n/, **Roger** (*b.* 1945) Australian-born New Zealand filmmaker

donate /dō náyt/ (**-nates, -nating, -nated**) *v* **1** *vt* GIVE OR PRESENT to give or present something, especially to a charitable organization or other good cause **2** *vt* GIVE BODY PART to give your own blood, tissue, organs, or reproductive material to be used in the treatment of another person, either while you are alive or after your death **3** TRANSFER ELECTRONS to transfer electrons to another atom or molecule in a chemical reaction [Late 18C. Back-formation < DONATION.]

SYNONYMS See *give*.

Donatello /dónnə tél ō/ (1386?–1466) Italian sculptor. Full name **Donato di Niccolò di Betto Bardi**

donation /dō náysh'n/ *n* **1** a gift or contribution, especially a sum of money given to a charity ○ *All donations will be gratefully received.* **2** the act of giving something, especially money to a charity [15C. Via French < Latin *donation-* < Latin *donare* 'give' < *donum* 'gift'.]

Donatism /dónətizəm/ *n* the beliefs of the Donatists

Donatist /dónətist/ *n* a member of a Christian group of the 4th and 5th centuries, originating in North Africa, that placed great emphasis on sanctity [Late 16C. < late Latin *Donatista*, after *Donatus*, regarded by Donatists as the first bishop of Carthage.]

donative /dónətiv/ *n* **1** OFFICIAL DONATION a donation, especially a formal or official one **2** CHURCH POSITION GIVEN AS GIFT a church office (**benefice**) that is or can be presented as a gift without reference to the bishop, as opposed to one received as a right ■ *adj* MADE AS GIFT given or presented as a gift (*formal*) [15C. < Latin *donativum* < *donare* 'give' (see DONATION).]

Doncaster /dóngkəstər/ town in N England. Population: 292,900 (1995).

done /dun/ past participle of **do**[1] ■ *adj* **1** CONCLUDED completed or finished **2** COOKED THROUGH cooked as thoroughly as required ○ *I like my steak well done.* **3** US PREORDAINED having been decided already, therefore permitting no alterations or changes (*slang*) ○ *It's a done deal, and you can't fight it.* **4** SOCIALLY ACCEPTABLE acceptable to the established rules and expectations of a society **5** CHEATED cheated or tricked (*informal*) ■ *interj* AGREED used to confirm acceptance of a deal ■ *v Carib, Southern US* ALREADY used as an auxiliary verb to express the sense of 'already' (*nonstandard*) ○ *He done leave.* ◊ **have done with it** to be finished with something and never return to it ○ *Why don't we just sell the house and have done with it?* ◊ **the done thing** the polite and proper thing to do in accordance with social etiquette (*informal*) ◊ **well done** used to express praise or approval of something somebody has done

USAGE done or **finished**? It is sometimes maintained that *done* is the wrong word to indicate that you have completed something. Certainly, *I have finished reading the newspaper* is more formal than *I'm done with the paper.* Not only does the first of these sentences use *finished* instead of *done*, but *done* in the second example is being used after *be* rather than *have*. *Finished*, too, can be used in this way, emphasizing the state arrived at rather than the process of achieving it: *I'm finished with the paper.* Such uses are very common in casual speech and writing. In formal contexts *finished* is preferable to *done*, and if used with *be* should modify what has been completed (*The job is finished*), rather than the person who has completed something (*I am finished*).

Done /dōn/, **Ken** (*b.* 1940) Australian painter and graphic designer. Full name **Kenneth Stephen Done**

donee /dō neè/ *n* the recipient of a gift [Early 16C. < DONOR.]

done for *adj* (*informal*) **1** NEAR DEATH close to the point of dying **2** EXHAUSTED extremely tired **3** ABOUT TO BE RUINED facing defeat, ruin, or destruction

Donegal /dónni gawl/ county in NW Ireland. Population: 129,435 (1996). Area: 4830 sq. km/1865 sq. mi. Irish **Dœn Na nGall**

Donegal tweed *n* a rough tweed characterized by white flecks [Early 20C. After County DONEGAL, Ireland.]

doneness /dún nəss/ *n US* the state of being fully cooked or ready to serve

doner kebab /dónnər-/, **donner kebab** *n* pitta bread filled with slices cut from a block of spiced meat, usually lamb, grilled on a spit. US term **gyro** [< Turkish *döner kebap* 'rotating kebab']

Donets /də néts/ river in SW Russia and SE Ukraine. Length: 1,020 km/631 mi.

Donets Basin industrial region in SE Ukraine

Donets'k /də nyétsk/ city in SE Ukraine. Population: 1,102,000 (1995).

done with *adj* completely finished and no longer an issue of importance

dong[1] /dong/ *n* **1 DEEP TOLL** a deep ringing sound **2** *ANZ* **PUNCH** a heavy blow or punch (*informal*) ■ *vi* **TOLL DEEPLY** to make a deep ringing sound [Late 16C. An imitation of the sound.]

dong[2] /dong/ *n* a highly offensive term for a penis (*taboo slang*) [Mid-20C. < ?]

dong[3] /dong/ *n* see table at **currency** [Early 19C. < Vietnamese.]

dongle /dóng g'l/ *n* a small hardware device that, when plugged into a computer, enables a specific copy-protected program to run [Late 20C. Probably arbitrary.]

Dongola /dóng gələ/ town on the River Nile in N Sudan. Population: 5,626 (1973).

Dong Yuan /dóng yŏŏ án/ (*fl.* late 10th century) Chinese artist

Dönitz /dőnits/, **Doenitz, Karl** (1891–1980) German naval commander

Donizetti /dónni zétti/, **Gaetano** (1797–1848) Italian composer

donjon /dónjən, dúnj-/ *n* a fortified central tower in a medieval castle [14C. Form of DUNGEON.]

Don Juan /dón jŏŏ ən, -waán/ *n* a man who has a reputation for having casual sexual relationships with numerous women [Mid-19C. After *Don Juan* Tenorio, legendary Spanish nobleman.]

donkey /dóngki/ (*plural* **-keys**) *n* **1** a small domesticated member of the horse family with a grey or brown coat, long ears, and a large head. *Equus asinus.* **2** somebody thought of as lacking intelligence (*informal insult*) [Late 18C. < ?] ◇ **donkey's years** a very long time (*informal*) ○ *I haven't seen Jack for donkey's years.*

donkey derby (*plural* **donkey derbies**) *n* a race for people riding on donkeys, usually as a fundraising event or amusement, e.g. at a country fête

donkey engine *n* a small auxiliary engine used either to start a larger engine or independently, e.g. for pumping water on steamships

donkey jacket *n UK* a dark blue heavy woollen jacket, typically worn by people working outdoors

donkeywork /dóngki wurk/ *n* **1** hard or boring work (*informal*) **2** basic preparation or groundwork

Donleavy /don leévi/, **J. P.** (*b.* 1926) US-born Irish novelist, short-story writer, and playwright. Full name **James Patrick Donleavy**

Donna /dónnə/ *n* a title used before a married woman's name in Italy [Early 17C. Via Italian < Latin *domina* 'lady'.]

Donne /dun/, **John** (1572–1631) English poet, prose writer, and clergyman

donnée /dónnay/, **donné** *n* **1** a basic fact or assumption on which something else, e.g. a literary or theatrical work, is based and from which it develops or moves forward **2** a theme or subject, e.g. of a literary or theatrical work [Late 19C. < French, form of *donner* 'give'.]

donnert /dónnərt/ *adj Scotland* **1** an offensive term meaning unintelligent (*insult*) **2** very surprised [Early 18C. < past participle of Scots dialect *donner* 'daze, stun' < ?]

donnish /dónnish/ *adj* resembling the stereotypical image of a university professor, e.g. in displaying erudition or being absent-minded —**donnishly** *adv* —**donnishness** *n*

donnybrook /dónni brŏŏk/ *n* a riotous brawl [Mid-19C. After *Donnybrook*, a suburb of Dublin, Ireland.]

donor /dṓnər/ *n* **1 SOMEBODY WHO GIVES** a giver of something, especially money **2 SOMEBODY GIVING BLOOD OR BODY ORGAN** a voluntary giver of a substance or part from his or her body for the medical treatment of somebody else, e.g. blood for transfusion, or an organ or tissue for transplantation **3 IMPURITY ADDED TO SEMICONDUCTOR** an impurity (**dopant**), e.g. antimony, that is deliberately added to a pure semiconductor material, e.g. silicon, in order to increase its conductivity by increasing the number of free electrons, carriers of negative electrical charge **4 ATOM PROVIDING ELECTRONS FOR A BOND** an atom, molecule, or group that provides the pair of electrons necessary to form a chemical bond. ◊ **acceptor** *n.* 2 [15C. Via Anglo-Norman, Old French < Latin *donator* < *donare* 'give' (see DONATION).] —**donorship** *n*

donor card *n* a card stating that specified organs, or sometimes the entire body, of the person carrying it may be used for the treatment of others after the donor's death

donor insemination *n* the introduction into a woman's vagina of sperm from a man who is not the woman's sexual partner as a method of assisted conception

do-nothing *n* a person regarded as lazy or idle (*informal insult*)

Don Quixote /dón kwíksət, -kee hṓti/ *n* an impractical idealist who champions hopeless causes [Mid-17C. After the hero of the satirical romance *Don Quixote de la Mancha* (1605, 1615) by Cervantes.]

don't /dōnt/ *contr* do not

don't know *n* a voter or respondent who is undecided about an issue, e.g. during an election campaign or in an opinion survey (*informal*)

doo /doo/ (*plural* **doos**) *n Scotland* **1** a dove (*informal*) **2** used as a term of endearment [14C. Variant of DOVE[1].]

doocot /dŏŏkit, dŏŏ-/, **dooket** *n Scotland* a dovecote

doodad /dŏŏ dad/ *n US* = **doodah** (*informal*) [Early 20C. < ?]

doodah /dŏŏ daa/ *n* a thing whose name somebody cannot remember or does not know (*informal*) US term **doodad** *n.* [Early 20C. Probably < *dooda(h)* in the refrain to the song *Camptown Races.*]

doodle /dŏŏd'l/ (**-dles, -dling, -dled**) *vti* to draw aimlessly or absent-mindedly, usually while doing something else such as having a telephone conversation or attending a meeting [Early 17C. < Low German *dudel-* in *dudeltopf* 'fool'.] —**doodle** *n* —**doodler** *n*

doodlebug /dŏŏd'l bug/ *n* **1** the V-1 flying bomb (*informal*) **2** *US* the large-jawed larva of an antlion or a similar insect larva

doo-doo /dŏŏ doo/ *n US* human or animal excrement (*slang humorous*) [Mid-20C. Probably < repetition of DO.]

doofer /dŏŏfər/ *n* an object or gadget whose name you cannot remember or do not know (*slang*) [Mid-20C. Probably < *do for.*]

doohickey /dŏŏhiki/ (*plural* **-eys**) *n US, Can* an unspecified gadget (*informal*) [Early 20C. Blend of DOODAD + HICKEY.]

dook /dŏŏk/ *n Scotland* a wooden plug that is forced into a wall to provide loadbearing support for a nail or screw ■ *vt Scotland* to force a wooden plug into a wall to support a nail or screw [Early 19C. < ?]

doolally /doo lálli/ *adj* an offensive term meaning irrational (*informal insult*) [Early 20C. Alteration of *Deolali*, town near Mumbai (Bombay), India.]

Doolittle /dŏŏlitt'l/, **Hilda** (1886–1961) US poet. Pseudonym **H. D., Imagiste**

doom /doom/ *n* **1 DISASTROUS DESTINY** a dreadful fate, especially death or utter ruin **2 OFFICIAL JUDGMENT** an official judgment on somebody (*formal*) **3 doom, Doom LAST JUDGMENT** the Last Judgment (*archaic*) ■ *vt* **DESTINE TO DISASTER** to condemn somebody or something to a dreadful fate [Old English *dōm* 'judgment, sentence, law' < Indo-European, 'set, put']

doomed /doomd/ *adj* **1** condemned to suffer a dreadful fate, especially one that is imminent and inescapable ○ *With our best player hurt, we were doomed to lose.* **2** bound to fail or suffer something unpleasant ○ *The partnership was doomed from the start.*

doom-laden *adj* suggesting impending disaster or ruin

doomsayer /dŏŏm sayər/ *n* a frequent predicter of disasters

doomsday /dŏŏmz day/ *n* **1 doomsday, Doomsday** a day of final reckoning, especially, in Christian theology, the day of the Last Judgment **2** the final destruction or dissolution of the world

Doomsday Book *n* = **Domesday Book**

doomster /dŏŏmstər/ *n* a frequent predictor of disasters (*informal*)

doomwatch /dŏŏm woch/ *n* the expectation or prediction of imminent disaster, especially environmental disaster [< *Doomwatch*, television series] —**doomwatcher** *n*

doomy /dŏŏmi/ (**-ier, -iest**) *adj* (*informal*) **1** not hopeful about the future **2** causing feelings of imminent disaster

door /dawr/ *n* **1 MOVABLE PANEL AT AN ENTRANCE** a movable barrier used to open and close the entrance to a building, room, cupboard, or vehicle, usually a solid panel, hinged to or sliding in a frame **2 GAP FORMING AN ENTRANCE** the gap that forms the entrance to a building or room **3 BUILDING OR ROOM** a building or room considered in relation to those on either side ○ *She live two doors down the street.* [Old English *duru* 'door', *dor* 'gate' < Indo-European, 'entrance to the enclosure around a house'] ◇ **close** *or* **shut the door on something** to disallow the possibility of something happening ◇ **lay something at somebody's door** to blame something on somebody ◇ **out of doors** in the open air ◇ **show somebody the door** to tell somebody to leave

doorbell /dáwr bel/ *n* a bell placed on or beside a door, to be rung by visitors as a sign of their arrival

door bundle *n* a bundle of equipment pushed out of an aircraft by hand before parachutists exit

doorcase /dáwr kayss/ *n* BUILDING = **doorframe**

do-or-die *adj* involving the determination to risk everything in an effort to succeed

doorframe /dáwr fraym/ *n* the frame constructed around the entrance to a building or room and into which a door is set

door furniture *n* all the fittings used on doors, e.g. handles, locks, knockers, and letter boxes

doorjamb /dáwr jam/ *n* either of the vertical side pieces of a doorframe

doorkeeper /dáwr keepər/ *n* somebody on duty at a door or gate, especially somebody who guards the entrance

doorknob /dáwr nob/ *n* a round handle used to open or close a door

doorman /dáwrmən/ (*plural* **-men** /-mən/) *n* somebody on duty at the door of a building such as a nightclub or hotel, usually employed to assist customers, e.g. by calling cabs

doormat /dáwr mat/ *n* **1** a mat to wipe your shoes on immediately before or after entering a building **2** a passive person who submits to being treated inconsiderately (*informal*)

~~**doormouse**~~ incorrect spelling of **dormouse**

doornail /dáwr nayl/ *n* a nail with a large head formerly used to decorate or reinforce a door

doorplate /dáwr playt/ *n* a plate or plaque attached to the door of a building or room, usually giving information about the person associated with the building or room. ◊ **nameplate**

doorpost /dáwr pōst/ *n* = **doorjamb**

doorsill /dáwr sil/ *n* = **threshold** *n.* 1

doorstep /dáwr step/ *n* **1 STEP IN FRONT OF DOOR** a step at the entrance to a building **2 THICK BREAD** a very thick slice of bread or a sandwich made from thickly cut bread (*informal*) ■ *v* (**-steps, -stepping, -stepped**) **1** *vti* **CANVASS ALL HOUSES IN AREA** to make door-to-door visits to members of the public to ask for their support during an election campaign **2** *vt* **WAIT AT DOOR OF FAMOUS PERSON** to wait outside the home or workplace of politicians or celebrities in the hope of interviewing them —**doorstepping** *n* ◇ **on your (own) doorstep** very near where you live

doorstop /dáwr stop/ *n* **1** a movable device such as a wedge or heavy object used to hold a door open **2** a rubber stud or rubber-tipped projection on a wall, floor, or door that prevents damage to the wall when the door is opened

door to door *adv* **1** going from one house to the next, usually in order to sell things, to collect money for charity, or to canvass support in an election **2** from the place of departure to the place of arrival ○ *The trip took three hours door to door.*

door-to-door *adj* (*not hyphenated after verbs*) **1** done or going from one house to the next **2** from the point of departure to the point of arrival

doorway /dáwr way/ n **1** an entrance to a building or room, especially one that has a door **2** a means of achieving or escaping from something

doo-wop /dóò wop/ n harmonized singing of nonsense syllables, with a rhythm-and-blues melody on top, popularized by street singers in the 1950s [Mid-20C. An imitation of the sound.]

dop /dop/ n S Africa a small drink (slang) [Late 19C. < ?]

dopa /dópə/ n a natural precursor of adrenaline and dopamine. Use: in synthetic form, treatment of Parkinson's disease. [Early 20C. Acronym < DI-1 + OXY- + PHENYL + ALANINE.]

dopamine /dópə meen/ n a neurotransmitter that is also a precursor of adrenaline [Mid-20C. Blend of DOPA + AMINE.]

dopant /dópənt/ n a substance, e.g. arsenic or antimony, that is added in small quantities to a semiconductor material in order to change its electrical characteristics

dope /dop/ n **1** ILLEGAL DRUG an illegal drug, especially cannabis (slang) **2** DRUG AFFECTING PERFORMANCE a drug given illegally, e.g. to racehorses or athletes, to affect performance **3** INSIDE INFORMATION confidential information about somebody or something (slang) **4** VISCOUS LIQUID a viscous liquid. Use: lubrication, waterproofing and strengthening fabrics, coating aircraft wings, improving the combustion of engine fuels. **5** ABSORBENT MATERIAL an absorbent material. Use: manufacture of dynamite. **6** ELECTRONICS = dopant ■ vt (dopes, doping, doped) **1** ADD DRUG TO FOOD OR DRINK to add a drug to somebody's food or drink secretly in order to adversely affect the person's performance or consciousness adversely **2** ADD IMPURITY TO SEMICONDUCTOR to add a substance, e.g. arsenic or antimony, to a semiconductor material like silicon or germanium during the manufacturing process in order to increase its conductivity [Early 19C. < Dutch doop 'thick dipping sauce' < doopen 'dip, mix'.] — **doper** n

dope up vt to make somebody drowsy or semiconscious by administering a drug (slang)

dope dog n US a dog specially trained to locate by scent contraband narcotics hidden in luggage or packages or concealed on a person's body (informal)

dope sheet n a booklet that gives information about the horses entered for races (slang)

dopey /dópi/ (-ier, -iest), **dopy** (-ier, -iest) adj showing a lack of good sense or intelligence (informal insult) — **dopily** adv — **dopiness** n

dopiaza /dópi aza/ n in Indian cookery, a mildly spiced dish of meat or fish cooked with onions and tomatoes [< Hindi do 'two' + pyāz 'onion']

doping agent n ELECTRONICS = dopant

doppelgänger /dópp'l gangər, -geng-/ n an apparition in the form of a double of a living person [Mid-19C. < German, 'double-goer'.]

Doppler effect /dóppler-/, **Doppler shift** n a perceived change in the frequency of a wave as the distance between the source and the observer changes. For example, the sound of a siren on a moving vehicle appears to change as it approaches and passes an observer. ◊ **blueshift, red shift** [Early 20C. After Christian J. Doppler (1803–53), Austrian physicist.]

Doppler radar n a means of detecting a moving target that uses electromagnetic radiation and relies on a change in the frequency of microwave signals reflected from the target [Mid-20C. < its use of the DOPPLER EFFECT.]

Doppler shift n = Doppler effect

dopy adj = dopey

dor /dawr/ n a European dung beetle that makes a droning sound as it flies. Geotrupes stercorarius. [Old English dora 'bumblebee' < ?]

dorado /də raádò/ (plural **-dos** or **-do**) n **1** ZOOL = dolphin n. **2** a South American fish resembling a salmon. Genus: Salminus. [Early 17C. Via Spanish, literally 'gilded' < late Latin deaurare (see DORY2).]

Dorado /də raádò/ n an inconspicuous constellation of the southern hemisphere containing part of the Large Magellanic Cloud. See illustration at **constellation**

Doráti /də raáti/, **Antal** (1906–88) Hungarian-born US conductor and composer

dorbeetle /dáwr beet'l/ n = dor

Dorcas society /dáwrkəss-/ n a Christian women's charitable organization that gives clothes to the poor [Mid-

19C. After a Christian woman in the Bible (Acts 9:36, 39) who made clothes for the poor.]

Dorchester /dáwrchistər/ town in S England. Population: 15,037 (1991).

Dordogne /dawr dóyn, -dónnyə/ river in SW France. Length: 483 km/300 mi.

Dordrecht /dáwr drekt, -drekht/ port in the SW Netherlands. Population: 119,811 (2000).

Doré /dáw ray/, **Gustave** (1833–83) French illustrator, painter, and sculptor

Dorian /dáwri ən/ n a member of a Greek-speaking people who overthrew the Mycenaean civilization on mainland Greece about 1,100 BC [Mid-16C. Via Latin Dorius 'of Doris' (region of ancient Greece) < Greek Dōrios < Dōris 'Doris'.] — **Dorian** adj

Dorian mode n a scale of notes originating in ancient Greek music and consisting of the eight notes of the diatonic scale rising from D to D

Doric /dórrik/ n **1** ANCIENT GREEK DIALECT a dialect of ancient Greek spoken mainly in the area of the modern Peloponnese **2** DIALECT OF ENGLISH a rural dialect of Scots spoken in parts of NE Scotland ■ adj **1** IN SIMPLE CLASSICAL ARCHITECTURAL STYLE relating to or built in a style of architecture characterized by fluted columns with a rounded moulding at the top and no base **2** OF DORIANS relating to the Dorians of ancient Greece, or their language or culture **3** OF DORIC DIALECT relating to a Doric dialect [Mid-16C. Via Latin Doricus 'of Doris' (region of ancient Greece) < Greek Dōrikos < Dōris 'Doris'.]

Doric order n the first of the five classical orders of architecture, characterized by fluted columns with a rounded moulding at the top and no base

dork /dawrk/ n an offensive term deliberately insulting somebody's physical appearance or social skills (slang insult) [Mid-20C. < ?]

Dorking[1] /dáwrking/ n a heavy domestic fowl belonging to a breed originating in England. Kept for: food. [Late 18C. After DORKING2.]

Dorking[2] /dáwrking/ town in SE England. Population: 15,658 (1991).

dorky /dáwrki/ (-ier, -iest) adj regarded as being unintelligent or useless (slang)

dorm /dawrm/ n a dormitory (informal) [Early 20C. Shortening.]

dormant /dáwrmənt/ adj **1** NOT ACTIVELY GROWING in an inactive state, when growth and development slow or cease, in order to survive adverse environmental conditions **2** TEMPORARILY INACTIVE temporarily inactive or not in use **3** NOT ERUPTING describes a volcano that is not erupting, but not extinct **4** LATENT latent and able to be aroused ◊ dormant feelings of uneasiness **5** SLEEPING in a heraldic device, portrayed in a sleeping posture [14C. < French, present participle of dormir 'to sleep' < Latin dormire.] — **dormancy** n

dormer /dáwrmər/, **dormer window** n a window for a room within the roof space that is built out at right angles to the main roof and has its own gable [Late 16C. < Old French dormēor 'sleeping room' < dormir (see DORMANT).]

dormice plural of **dormouse**

dormie /dáwrmi/ adj in golf, as many holes up on an opponent as there are holes left to play ◊ dormie four [Mid-19C. < ?]

dormitory /dáwrmitəri/ (plural **-ries**) n **1** a large room in which many people sleep, e.g. at a boarding school or in a hostel **2** US EDUC = hall of residence [15C. < Latin dormitorium < dormire 'to sleep'.]

dormitory town n a small town whose residents commute to work in a nearby city. US term **bedroom community**

Dormobile /dáwrmō beel/ tdmk a trademark for a motor vehicle equipped for living and sleeping in as well as travelling

dormouse /dáwr mowss/ (plural **-mice** /-mīss/) n a small nocturnal rodent resembling a mouse with reddish-brown fur and a bushy tail. Family: Gliridae. [15C. < ?]

Dornoch Firth /dáwr nok-, -nəkh-/ inlet of the North Sea in NE Scotland

Dorothy bag /dórrəthi-/ n a small handbag tied by drawstrings that are looped over the wrist [Early 20C. < the woman's name Dorothy.]

dorp /dawrp/ n a village or small country town in South Africa, especially one perceived as backward or unappealing [Mid-19C. < Dutch.]

Dors. abbr Dorset

dors- prefix = dorso-

dorsa plural of **dorsum**

dorsal /dáwrss'l/ adj **1** relating to or situated on the back of the body **2** describes the underside of a leaf or other surface that faces away from the stem [15C. Directly or via French < late Latin dorsalis, < dorsum (see DORSUM).] — **dorsally** adv

dorsal fin n a single fin on the back of a fish or other aquatic animal e.g. a dolphin that gives it stability while swimming. ◊ **ventral fin**

Dorset /dáwrssit/ county on southern coast of England. Population: 673,000 (1994). Area: 2,654 sq. km/1,025 sq. mi.

Dorset Down n a sheep belonging to a sturdy domestic breed with dense wool and a broad head. Kept for: lamb production.

Dorset Horn n a sheep belonging to a domestic breed with large horns and dense fine-textured wool

dorsiflexion /dáwrssi fléksh'n/ n the bending back of a hand or foot or of the fingers or toes

dorsiventral /dáwrssi véntrəl/ adj **1** flat, with distinct upper and lower surfaces **2** ANAT = dorsoventral adj. **2** — **dorsiventrality** /-ven tráləti/ n — **dorsiventrally** adv

dorso- prefix back, upper surface ◊ dorsolateral [< Latin dorsum]

dorsolateral /dáwrssō láttərəl/ adj relating to or involving both the back and the side — **dorsolaterally** adv

dorsoventral /dáwrssō véntrəl/ adj **1** PLANT SCI = dorsiventral adj. **1** **2** extending from the back of the body to the front

dorsum /dáwrssəm/ (plural **-sa** /-sə/) n the back or upper surface of a part of the body, e.g. the hand or foot (technical) [Late 18C. < Latin, 'the back'.]

Dortmund /dáwrtmənd, -mŏŏnd/ inland port in NW Germany. Population: 600,918 (1997).

dory[1] /dáwri/ (plural **-ries**) n **1** a small boat used for various purposes e.g. patrolling a harbour or transporting people from a larger vessel to the shore **2** US, Can a narrow flat-bottomed fishing boat with high sides [Early 18C. < ?]

dory[2] /dáwri/ (plural **-ries**) n a fish with a deep flattened body, spiny fins, and an extendable mouth, found near the ocean bottom. Family: Zeidae. [14C. < French dorée < form of dorer 'gild' < late Latin deaurare 'gild over' < Latin aurum 'gold'.]

dos-à-dos /dó zaa dō, dóssi dō/ n a seat on which two or more people can sit back to back, or a vehicle fitted with such a seat (dated) ■ n, interj DANCE = do-si-do [Mid-19C. < French, 'back to back'.]

dosage /dóssij/ n **1** DOSE OF DRUG the amount and frequency of drug administration ◊ Do not exceed the recommended dosage. **2** ADMINISTRATION OF DOSE the administration of a measured amount of a drug, or the determination of the correct amount **3** ADDING OF EXTRA INGREDIENT the addition of an extra ingredient to something, especially wine

dose /dōss/ n **1** PRESCRIBED AMOUNT OF MEDICATION a measured quantity of medication administered once or at stated intervals **2** SHORT PERIOD OF SOMETHING UNPLEASANT a bout of something unpleasant, especially a minor illness (informal) **3** VENEREAL DISEASE an infection with a sexually transmitted disease (slang) **4** EXPOSURE TO RADIATION the amount of radiation to which somebody or something is exposed during a specified time **5** EXTRA INGREDIENT an additional ingredient, e.g. syrup added to wine to fortify it ■ vt (doses, dosing, dosed) **1** GIVE MEDICINE TO to administer medication to somebody ◊ I've been dosing myself up with flu remedies all week. **2** MEASURE OUT MEDICATION to prescribe or administer the required amount of medication **3** ADD EXTRA INGREDIENT to add an extra ingredient to something [15C. Via French < Greek dosis 'prescribed portion' < didonai 'give'.] ◊ **go through something like a dose of salts** to do and finish something very quickly (informal)

dosemeter /dóss meetər/ *n* = **dosimeter**

dosh /dosh/ *n* money (*slang*) [Mid-20C. < ?]

do-si-do /dóssi dó/ *n* (*plural* **do-si-dos**) a movement in square dancing in which two dancers pass each other and circle back to back ■ *interj* used to instruct dancers to perform a do-si-do [Early 20C. Alteration of DOS-À-DOS.] —**do-si-do** *vi*

dosimeter /dō símmitər/ *n* an instrument for measuring the amount of radiation absorbed by somebody or something, often fixed in a working area or worn by personnel who might be exposed to radiation [Late 19C. < DOSE.] —**dosimetric** /dóssi méttrik/ *adj* —**dosimetrician** /-mə trísh'n/ *n* —**dosimetrist** *n* —**dosimetry** /-símmətri/ *n*

Dos Passos /doss páss oss/, **John** (1896–1970) US writer

doss /doss/ *vi* **SLEEP ON MAKESHIFT BED** to sleep or settle down to sleep, especially on an improvised bed (*slang*) ○ *Can I doss down on your floor tonight?* ■ *n* **1 IMPROVISED OR BASIC BED** a bed for the night or a place to sleep, especially a makeshift one or one in a dosshouse **2 PERIOD OF SLEEP** a period of sleep (*slang*) **3 EASY TASK** an easy job or activity (*slang*) [Late 18C. < ?]

dossal /dóss'l/, **dossel** *n* a rich hanging for the back of an altar or the sides of a chancel in a church [Mid-17C. < medieval Latin *dossale* < Latin *dorsum* 'the back'.]

dosser /dóssər/ *n* **1** an offensive term for somebody who sleeps on the street or in a cheap lodging house because he or she has no private dwelling (*slang insult*) **2** *Ireland* an offensive term for somebody perceived as lazy and unwilling to work (*insult*)

dosshouse /dóss hówss/ *n* a cheap and very basic lodging house for homeless people (*informal*) US term **flophouse**

dossier /dóssi ay, -ər/ *n* a collection of documents relating to a particular person or topic [Late 19C. < French (originally 'bunch of papers with a label on the back') < *dos* 'the back' < Latin *dorsum*.]

dost /dust/ 2nd person present singular of **do**[1] (*archaic*)

Fyodor Dostoyevsky

Dostoyevsky /dóst oy éfski/, **Fyodor** (1821–81) Russian novelist

⚡**dot**[1] /dot/ *n* **1 WRITTEN OR PRINTED POINT** a small round written or printed mark, e.g. that placed above the body of the lower case letter 'i' or one of a set of three replacing missing text **2 SPOT OR SPECK** a small round mark, spot, or speck ○ *The ship was just a dot on the horizon.* **3 SMALL AMOUNT** a very small amount, especially of butter used for basting **4 INTERNET PUNCTUATION MARK** a punctuation mark used to separate the various components of an Internet address **5 MARK USED IN MORSE CODE** the shorter of the two signalling elements used in Morse code, represented as a small round mark **6 SYMBOL PLACED AFTER NOTE IN MUSIC** in written or printed music, a small round mark placed after a note or rest to increase its value by half **7 MARK INDICATING LOGICAL CONJUNCTION** a small round mark used in logic to join compound sentences when both elements are true ■ *v* (**dots, dotting, dotted**) **1** *vt* **MARK WITH DOT** to mark something with a dot ○ *dot your i's* **2** *vt* **SPRINKLE WITH DOTS** to scatter or sprinkle something with spots, specks, or small amounts of something ○ *Dot the surface with butter.* **3** *vi* **MAKE SMALL ROUND MARK** to make a small round mark [Old English *dott* 'head of a boil', probably < Germanic, 'lump, plug'] —**dotter** *n* ◇ **on the dot (of)** exactly at the specified time ○ *arrived on the dot* ○ *was expected to get here on the dot of nine*

dot[2] /dot/ *n* in law, a woman's dowry [Mid-19C. Via Old French < Latin *dot-*, stem of *dos* 'dowry'.] —**dotal** /dót'l/ *adj*

dotage /dótij/ *n* an offensive term for the lack of strength or concentration sometimes believed to be characteristic of old age [14C. < DOTE.]

dotard /dótərd/ *n* an offensive term for somebody who is thought to be unable to think clearly, especially when the inability is attributed to the person's age (*insult*) [14C. < DOTE.] —**dotardly** *adj*

⚡**dot.com**, **dot-com** *n* a company that does business on the Internet or that provides Internet services [< the domain identification *.com* of company Internet addresses.] —**dot-com** *adj*

⚡**dot-comer** /dot kómmər/, **dotcomer, dot.comer** *n* somebody who does business on the Internet or who consistently buys high-tech shares

dote /dōt/ (**dotes, doting, doted**) *vi* to be excessively fond of somebody or something ○ *They dote on their grandchildren.* [12C. < ?] —**doter** *n*

dotgov /dót guv/ *n* a government official (*informal*) [After .gov ending of government domain names on the Internet.]

doth /duth/ 3rd person present singular of **do**[1] (*archaic*)

doting /dóting/ *adj* expressing and demonstrating great love and fondness for somebody or something ○ *doting parents of two new babies* —**dotingly** *adv*

⚡**dot matrix** *n* a grid of dots selectively lighted or coloured to display or print letters, numbers, and other symbols

⚡**dot pitch** *n* a measure of the clarity of a computer image, based on the amount of white space between the pixels or dots forming the image. The smaller the dot pitch, the greater the clarity.

dot product *n* MATH = **scalar product**

⚡**dots per inch** *n* full form of **dpi**

dotted /dóttid/ *adj* **1 WITH DOTS** marked or patterned with dots **2 INCREASED IN VALUE BY HALF** describes a note or rest in written or printed music increased in value by half **3 COVERED WITH SPECKS** scattered or sprinkled with small things or larger things seen from a distance ○ *a sky dotted with stars* **4 RANDOMLY ARRAYED** spread randomly over a wide area ○ *a lawn dotted with hoop-skirted belles*

dotted line *n* a printed line formed from dots or dashes, especially one on which somebody is to write something such as a signature

dotted swiss *n* a cotton fabric patterned with raised dots [Shortening of *Swiss muslin*]

dotterel /dóttərəl/ (*plural* **-els** *or* **-el**), **dottrel** (*plural* **-trels** *or* **-trel**) *n* **1 EURASIAN BIRD** a reddish-brown bird of the plover family with white markings on the head and neck. Native to: Europe, Asia. *Eudromias morinellus*. **2 BIRD FOUND IN WETLANDS** a bird found mainly in marshy areas or on seashores. Native to: Australia. Family: Charadriidae. **3** (*plural* **-terels** *or* **-trels**) **GULLIBLE PERSON** an easily deceived person [15C. < DOTE + *-rel* (< Old French *-erel*); because the Eurasian plover is easy to catch.]

dottle /dótt'l/ *n* the plug of tobacco that is left in a pipe after it has been smoked [15C. < DOT[1].]

dottrel *n* = **dotterel**

dotty /dótti/ (**-tier, -tiest**) *adj* (*informal*) **1 SILLY** regarded as being irrational or impractical, often endearingly so **2 UNCONVENTIONAL** behaving in a manner that seems amusingly strange to others **3 ABSURD** illogical, impractical, or absurd **4 INFATUATED** very fond of or passionately interested in somebody or something [Late 19C. < ?] —**dottily** *adv* —**dottiness** *n*

Douai /doo áy/ city in NW France. Population: 42,796 (1999).

Douala /doo áalə/, **Duala** largest port in Cameroon, in the western part of the country. Population: 1,500,000 (1997 estimate).

Douay Bible /doó ay-/, **Douay Version** *n* **1** a Roman Catholic translation of the Latin Vulgate version of the Bible into English, written in the early 17th century **2** a copy of the Douay Bible [Mid-19C. After *Douay* (modern DOUAI).]

double /dúbb'l/ *adj* **1 BEING TWICE AS MUCH OR MANY** being twice as much in size, number, or value **2 HAVING TWO LIKE PARTS** consisting of two identical, similar, or equal parts **3 MEANT FOR TWO PEOPLE** designed or intended for two people ○ *booked a double hotel room* **4 FITTING A DOUBLE BED** describes bedding of a size that will fit onto a double bed **5 TWO-LAYERED** consisting of two layers **6 FOLDED OVER ONCE** folded in two **7 OF TWO ELEMENTS** consisting of two different elements **8 ACTING IN OPPOSING WAYS** acting one way while feeling very differently, especially when this involves hypocrisy or deceit **9 HAVING EXTRA PETALS** describes flowers that have more petals than normal or plants that have flowers of this type **10 SOUNDING AN OCTAVE BELOW** sounding an octave of a musical instrument lower than the written music indicates ■ *adv* **1 TWICE AS MUCH** twice as much as normal ○ *had to pay double to get in* **2 IN TWO LAYERS** so as to form two layers ■ *n* **1 TWO TOGETHER** two viewed or regarded together **2 TWICE THE NORMAL AMOUNT** twice the normal or standard amount ○ *He offered me double.* **3 TWO MEASURES OF DRINK** a drink containing two single measures, especially of spirits (*informal*) **4 DUPLICATE IN APPEARANCE** somebody or something that looks very like another, especially a living person bearing a strong resemblance to somebody else **5 GHOST IDENTICAL TO LIVING PERSON** an apparition that closely resembles a living person **6 STAND-IN FOR FILM STAR** a replacement for a film actor in scenes that, e.g., involve danger, special skill, or nudity **7 BET ON TWO RACES** a bet on two races, in which any winnings from the first become the stake for the second (*informal*) **8 SUCCESS IN TWO EVENTS** success in two events or competitions in the same year or series or against the same opponent **9 DART THAT LANDS IN OUTER RING** a throw of a dart that lands within the narrow outer ring of the dartboard, scoring twice the nominal value **10 CALL INCREASING SCORE** in an auction at bridge, a call that increases the score for succeeding or failing in a contract **11 STROKE THAT MAKES BALL REBOUND** in cue games, a stroke that makes the ball rebound against a cushion and land in the opposite pocket **12 DOUBLE FAULT** a double fault (*informal*) **13 FAST MARCHING PACE** a fast marching pace at twice the usual speed **14 ABRUPT DIRECTIONAL CHANGE** a sharp change of direction **15** PRINTING = **doublet** *n.* 3 ■ *v* (**-bles, -bling, -bled**) **1** *vti* **INCREASE TWOFOLD** to make something twice as large or numerous, or become twice as much or many ○ *We doubled our profits the following year.* **2** *vt* **FOLD IN TWO** to fold or bend something in two **3** *vt* **MAKE A FIST** to clench the fist (*informal*) **4** *vi* **HAVE SECOND FUNCTION** to have a second or secondary function ○ *His felt hat doubled as a water pail.* **5** *vi* **ACT AS STAND-IN** to replace a film actor in certain scenes, e.g. those that include danger, special skill, or nudity **6** *vi* **PLAY SECOND ROLE** to play an additional part in the same performance **7** *vt* **DUPLICATE A MUSICAL PART** in music, to duplicate a part, either at the same pitch or an octave above or below **8** *vi* **PLAY MORE THAN ONE MUSICAL INSTRUMENT** to play one or more musical instruments, in addition to the principal one ○ *a violinist who doubles on cello* **9** *vi* **ANNOUNCE BRIDGE DOUBLE** to announce a double as a bid in an auction at bridge **10** *vti* **REBOUND** in cue games, to rebound, or make a ball rebound, off a cushion **11** *vt* **PLACE PIECES NEXT TO EACH OTHER** to place two chess pieces of the same type and colour together ○ *double your opponent's pawns* **12** *vi* **MAKE TWO-BASE HIT** to make a hit in baseball that gives the batter time to run to second base **13** *vt* **ROUND A HEADLAND** to sail around a headland [12C. Via Old French *do(u)bler* < Latin *duplare* < *duplus* 'twofold' < *duo* 'two'.] —**doubleness** *n* ◇ **at** *or* **on the double** straight away and as quickly as possible ○ *told the children to get into lines at the double*

double back *vi* to turn around and retrace your steps
double over *vi* to bend from the waist in response to pain or laughter
double up *vi* **1** to share something with somebody else ○ *There weren't enough beds, so some of the children had to double up.* **2** to bend the body over sharply

double act *n* two entertainers who regularly perform together

double-acting *adj* **1** with one or more pistons that move in both directions, giving two strokes per cycle **2** acting in opposite directions from a central point

double agent *n* a spy for one government who supplies secret information about that government to its rival

double bar *n* a symbol, ‖, that marks the end of a piece of music or the end of its principal sections

double-barrelled *adj* **1 WITH TWO BARRELS** describes a gun that has two barrels **2 WITH TWO NAMES TOGETHER** formed from two names, usually hyphenated **3 WITH TWO PURPOSES OR INTERPRETATIONS** serving two purposes, or open to two possible interpretations

double bass *n* the largest and lowest in pitch of the instruments of the violin family, used in the modern symphony orchestra

double-bass *adj* describes an instrument that is larger and lower in pitch than others of its group

double bassoon *n* MUSIC = **contrabassoon** *n.* 1

double bed *n* a bed intended for two people

double bill *n* a programme of entertainment that has two main items, especially a cinema programme showing two full-length films

double bind *n* **1** an unresolvable situation from which there is no escape without undesirable consequences **2** a situation in which conflicting demands make it impossible to do the right thing

double-blind *adj* describes an experiment in which neither the experimenters nor the subjects know which of two similar treatments is genuine and which is a control procedure

double boiler *n* a pair of cooking pots, one fitting on top of and partly inside the other

double bond *n* a chemical bond in which two atoms share two pairs of electrons

double-breasted *adj* describes a coat or jacket that has a large overlap at the front, usually with two sets of buttons

double bridle *n* a bridle with four reins and a bit with two rings on each side

double check *n* **1** a second examination to make sure **2** a situation in chess in which a king is in check from two pieces at once

double-check *vti* to check something twice or for a second time ○ *I double-checked that the windows were locked.*

double chin *n* a fold of flesh or loose skin under the chin —**double-chinned** *adj*

⚡**double-click** *vti* to press and release a mouse button twice in rapid succession, often to invoke a specific command

double-clutch *vi US CARS* = **double-declutch**

double concerto *n* a concerto for two solo instruments

double cream *n UK* cream with a high fat content that can be whipped to make it thicker

double cross *n* a genetic cross in which a new hybrid is produced from parents each of which is a first-generation hybrid of pure strains

double-cross *vt* to betray or cheat somebody who believes that he or she is a partner or associate in the same, often criminal, enterprise ■ *n* an act of double-crossing a partner or associate —**double-crosser** *n* —**double-crossing** *adj*

double dagger *n* the printed character (‡), used to mark a cross-reference, especially to a footnote

double date *n* an arrangement for two couples to go out together socially as a foursome

double-date (**double-dates, double-dating, double-dated**) *vi* to go out socially as a couple with another couple

double-dealing *n* deliberately deceitful behaviour, especially involving the betrayal of a partner or associate —**double-dealer** *n* —**double-dealing** *adj*

double-decker *n* **1** a bus with an upper and a lower deck **2** something that has two layers, levels, or tiers ○ *a double-decker sandwich*

double-declutch *vi* to use the clutch twice when changing gear in a motor vehicle, first to put the gear lever into neutral and rev the engine, then to engage the new gear. US term **double-clutch**

double decomposition *n* a chemical reaction in which two compounds exchange one or more of their components so that two new compounds are formed

⚡**double density** *adj* describes a floppy or hard disk that can hold twice the amount of information as standard disks

double descent *n* the use in some societies of sometimes mother's and sometimes father's ancestry in establishing different features of social identity or status

double digging *n* the process of digging a plot of ground to twice the normal depth and transferring soil from the lower level to the top in order to revitalize it before planting

double-digit *adj* being between 10 and 99 ○ *double-digit inflation*

double dipping *n ANZ* the fraudulent practice of receiving income from a pension fund as well as social security payments (*informal*) —**double dipper** *n*

double dissolution *n* the dissolution of both houses of the Australian federal parliament by the Governor-General when the upper house repeatedly refuses to pass legislation already passed by the lower house

double doors *npl* two full-length doors that meet in the middle of the doorway when closed

double-dotted *adj* **1** describes a musical note or rest that has two dots following it to indicate that its length is to be increased by three quarters **2** characterized by the use of double-dotted notes

double dribble *n* an illegal move in basketball, in which the player dribbles the ball with both hands simultaneously or, having stopped, starts to dribble again

double Dutch *n* speech or writing that cannot be understood (*informal*)

double-dyed *adj* **1** completely and permanently imbued with a particular characteristic or opinion (*literary*) **2** describes fabrics that are dyed twice in order to make sure that the colour does not run when they are wet

double eagle *n* **1** a former US gold coin worth 20 dollars **2** *US GOLF* = **albatross**. **3**

double-edged *adj* **1** AMBIGUOUS having two possible meanings or interpretations, especially one that is apparently innocuous and another that is intentionally cutting or malicious **2** DOING TWO THINGS achieving two purposes or having two effects **3** HAVING TWO CUTTING EDGES having a blade sharpened on both edges

double effect *n* the ethical principle that intentionally doing wrong is impermissible, even if the action has good consequences, and that intentionally doing right is permissible, even if the action has bad consequences

double entendre /doobʹl on tóndrə/ *n* **1** a remark that is ambiguous and sexually suggestive **2** ambiguity in which one meaning is sexually suggestive [Late 17C. < obsolete French, 'double understanding'.]

double entry *n* a bookkeeping system that records each transaction as a credit to one account and a debit from another (*hyphenated when used before a noun*)

double exposure *n* **1** the exposure of two separate images on a single piece of photographic film **2** a photograph that contains one image superimposed on another

double-faced *adj* **1** FINISHED ON BOTH SIDES describes fabrics that are finished on both sides **2** HAVING TWO USABLE SIDES having two faces or sides that can both be used ○ *a double-faced tape* **3** TWO-FACED behaving insincerely or deceitfully

double fault *n* in tennis, two consecutive serves that land outside the service box or in the net, with the result that the server loses a point

double-fault *vi* in tennis, to make two consecutive faulty serves, and lose a point as a result

double feature *n US* a programme consisting of two full-length films shown consecutively

double figures *npl* the numbers with two digits, from 10 to 99 (*hyphenated when used before a noun*)

double first *n* a first-class honours degree in two subjects studied simultaneously

double flat *n* **1** a symbol, ♭♭, placed in front of a musical note to indicate that the pitch of the note is to be lowered by two semitones (*hyphenated when used before a noun*) **2** a musical note marked with a double flat

double glaze (**double glazes, double glazing, double glazed**) *vt* to fit a window or building with double glazing

double glazing *n* windows consisting of two layers of glass separated by a space, designed to provide improved heat and sound insulation (*hyphenated when used before a noun*)

Double Gloucester *n* a hard English cheese that is slightly orange in colour [< production in Gloucestershire]

double-header *n* a train pulled by two engines coupled together

double helix *n* the molecular structure of DNA, consisting of a pair of polynucleotide strands connected by a series of hydrogen bonds and wound in opposing spirals

double-hung *adj* describes a window that has two sashes, each sliding vertically in its own grooves

double indemnity *n US, Can* the guaranteed payout of

double the face value of a life insurance policy if the policyholder dies in an accident

double jeopardy *n US* the prosecution of somebody a second time for something that he or she has already been tried for. It is prohibited by the US Constitution.

double-jointed *adj* describes a joint or limb that has unusual flexibility and can bend in the opposite direction to the normal one, or somebody with such joints —**double-jointedness** *n*

double knit *n* a thick knitted fabric (*hyphenated before a noun*)

double knitting *n* knitting wool of medium thickness (*hyphenated before nouns*)

double life *n* a situation in which somebody is simultaneously involved in two sets of circumstances or relationships and keeps each completely separate, and usually secret, from the other

double magnum *n* a wine bottle containing the equivalent of four standard bottles, used mainly for Bordeaux

double negation *n* in logic, the principle that a proposition and the negation of its negation mean one and the same thing

double negative *n* a phrase containing two negatives

USAGE *Double negatives* of the type *I don't know nothing*, in which two negatives close together are intended to reinforce each other, are considered poor style in current standard English, acceptable though they were in earlier usage. These are to be distinguished from the acceptable, if somewhat uncommon, construction *That's not a good idea, I don't think*, in which the reinforcing negatives appear in different clauses. The more usual type of acceptable double negative is seen in *It is not impossible* (= it is distinctly possible), in which the negatives are intended to cancel each other out. This is a figure of speech called *litotes*.

double obelisk *n* PRINTING = **double dagger**

double occupancy *n* the use of a hotel room or other accommodation by two people (*hyphenated before nouns*)

double or nothing *n US* = **double or quits**

double or quits *n* a bet in gambling where a player who owes money has the debt doubled or cancelled depending on the outcome of the next play

double-page spread *n* a feature or article that fills two facing pages of a newspaper or magazine

double-park *vti* to park a vehicle alongside another already parked and so cause an obstruction —**double-parker** *n* —**double-parking** *n*

double play *n* a baseball play in which two players are put out

double pneumonia *n* pneumonia affecting both lungs

double-quick *adj, adv* extremely fast (*informal*)

double quote *n* a quotation mark that consists of two marks ("), not one

doubler /dúbblʹər/ *n* an electronic device that doubles an input frequency or voltage

double reed *n* **1** a reed in the oboe, cor anglais, or bassoon consisting of two halves that vibrate against each other when air passes through them (*hyphenated before nouns*) **2** a woodwind instrument that has a double reed

double refraction *n* the splitting of one ray of light into two in an anisotropic medium. US term **birefringence**

double rhyme *n* a two-syllable rhyme e.g. 'cooking' and 'looking'

doubles /dúbb'lz/ (*plural* **-bles**) *n* a racket game played between two pairs of players

double salt *n* a salt such as alum that dissolves in solution as two substances but crystallizes as one

double saucepan *n* = **double boiler**

double sculls *n* a race between boats for two rowers who sit one behind the other and pull two oars each

double sharp *n* **1** a symbol, ♯ placed in front of a musical note to indicate that the pitch of the note is to be raised by two semitones (*hyphenated when used before a noun*) **2** a musical note marked with a double sharp

double-sided *adj* used or usable on both sides

double-space (**double-spaces, double-spacing, double-spaced**) *vt* to type or print text with a blank line between typed or printed lines

doublespeak /dúbb'l speek/ *n* = **double talk** *n.* 1

double spread *n* PUBL = **double-page spread**

double standard *n* a principle, rule, or expectation that is applied unfairly to different groups, one group usually being condemned for the slightest offence while the other is treated far more leniently

double star *n* 1 = **binary star** 2 = **optical double star**

double-stop *vi* (**double-stops, double-stopping, double-stopped**) to draw the bow of a stringed instrument simultaneously across two strings, producing two tones ■ *n* a musical chord of two notes played on a stringed instrument —**double-stopping** *n*

doublet /dúbblət/ *n* 1 MAN'S JACKET a man's close-fitting jacket, with or without sleeves, popular in Europe between the 15th and 17th centuries 2 WORD WITH SAME ROOT either of two similar words in a language that have the same historical root but have arrived at their current forms via different languages, e.g. 'mood' and 'mode' 3 REPEATED PRINTED LETTER a repeated letter, word, or line that is printed in error 4 PAIR OF LENSES a pair of lenses designed to be used together so that one lens cancels out the distortions in the other 5 FAKE GEM a fake gem made by sticking a coloured layer between two pieces of glass or by sticking a thin layer of a gem on a glass base ■ **doublets** *npl* 1 DICE WITH SAME NUMBER THROWN a pair of dice thrown simultaneously, each showing the same number of spots 2 WORD GAME a word game in which one word is transformed into another by substituting letters, the object being to achieve this in the minimum number of substitutions [14C. < French, 'something doubled'.]

double tackle *n* a pair of double pulleys for lifting or pulling

double take *n* a reaction of surprise or astonishment after an initial hesitation

double talk *n* 1 intentionally ambiguous or confusing talk 2 speech that includes a mixture of real words and nonsense syllables

double-team *vt US* in various team games, to use two players to mark an opponent, e.g. in basketball or American football —**double team** *n*

doublethink /dúbb'l thingk/ *n* the conscious or unconscious holding of two opposing beliefs at the same time [Coined by George Orwell in *1984* (1949)]

double time *n* 1 DOUBLE PAY double the usual rate of pay 2 DOUBLY FAST MUSICAL TEMPO a tempo twice as fast as the basic tempo of a piece of music, or a passage played at that speed 3 *US* FAST MARCHING PACE a fast marching pace of 180 steps per minute

double-time *vi* (**double-times, double-timing, double-timed**) *US* to march at the fast pace of 180 steps per minute

doubleton /dúbb'ltən/ *n* two cards of the same suit that are the only cards of that suit dealt to a player [Early 20C. After SINGLETON.]

double-tonguing *n* the production of a rapid series of staccato notes on a wind or brass instrument by using rapid movements of the tongue —**double-tongue** *vi*

double top *n* in darts, a score of double 20

doubletree /dúbb'l tree/ *n* a bar used to harness two horses to a carriage or other vehicle [After SINGLETREE]

double vision *n* a condition in which two images of the same object are seen simultaneously because the eyes are not focusing properly. Technical name **diplopia**

double whammy *n* two setbacks or unpleasant experiences occurring very close together (*slang*)

double yellow line *n* two lines painted in yellow at the edge of a road, indicating that parking is not permitted at most times of the day. ◊ **yellow line**

double-zero option *n* an offer to limit the number of intermediate- and short-range nuclear missiles or remove them altogether if an opposing side agrees to do the same

doubloon /du bloón/ *n* a former Spanish gold coin [Early 17C. < Spanish *doblón* < *dobla* 'double' < Latin *duplus*.]

doublure /də bloór, doo-/ *n* a lining, especially one made of leather or highly decorated, inside the cover of a book [Late 19C. < French, 'lining'.]

doubly /dúbb li/ *adv* 1 in two different ways 2 to twice the usual degree or extent

doubt /dowt/ *vt* 1 THINK UNLIKELY to feel unconvinced or uncertain about something, or think that something is unlikely 2 NOT TRUST to suspect that something is not true, likely, or genuine, or that somebody is not sincere or trustworthy 3 *Scotland* EXPECT to tend to believe something ■ *n* 1 UNCERTAINTY a feeling or state of uncertainty, especially as to whether something is true, likely, or genuine, or as to whether somebody is sincere or trustworthy 2 METHOD OF PHILOSOPHICAL QUESTIONING the method of questioning claims to knowledge, especially in the philosophy of Descartes [13C. Via Old French *doter* < Latin *dubitare* 'be uncertain' < *dubius* 'uncertain'.] —**doubtable** *adj* —**doubtably** *adv* —**doubter** *n* —**doubtingly** *adv* ◇ **beyond doubt** completely certain ◇ **no doubt** almost definitely ◇ **open to** *or* **in doubt** not certain, settled, foreseeable with confidence, or finally proved

SYNONYMS See ***doubtful***.

USAGE doubt whether, if, or **that**? The verb ***doubt*** is normally followed by *whether* or *if*, or by *that* if it is in the negative: *I doubt whether/if it's true* but *I don't doubt that it's true.* In recent usage, *that* has been used in positive contexts too: *I doubt that it's true.* This use remains disputed.

doubtful /dówtf'l/ *adj* 1 UNSURE unsure or undecided about something 2 UNLIKELY not likely to happen or be successful 3 INVITING SUSPICION probably not true, honest, reputable, or genuine —**doubtfulness** *n*

SYNONYMS ***doubtful, uncertain, unsure, in doubt, dubious, sceptical***

CORE MEANING: feeling doubt or uncertainty

doubtful undecided or feeling hesitant; **uncertain** or **unsure** lacking certainty or confidence; **in doubt** still undecided and liable to change; **dubious** doubtful and, often, suspicious; **sceptical** questioning the truth or likelihood of something.

doubtfully /dówtf'li/ *adv* with or expressing doubt

doubting Thomas *n* a person who doubts something, especially until given proof [< Jesus Christ's apostle who doubted (John 20:24–9)]

doubtless /dówtləss/ *adv* 1 CERTAINLY certainly or almost certainly ○ *That was doubtless their intention, as these documents show.* 2 PROBABLY probably or presumably ○ *You would doubtless have been informed in due course.* ■ *adj* (*formal*) 1 CERTAIN impossible to doubt or deny 2 HAVING NO DOUBT having no doubts or suspicions —**doubtlessly** *adv* —**doubtlessness** *n*

douc /dook/ *n* a rare yellow-faced monkey of the langur family. Native to: Southeast Asia. *Pygathrix nemaeus.* [Late 18C. < Vietnamese.]

douce /dooss/ *adj* quiet, serious, and undemonstrative in character or expression (*regional*) [13C. < French (see DOUCEUR).] —**doucely** *adv* —**douceness** *n*

douceur /doo súr/ *n* something given as a tip or a bribe [14C. < French, 'sweetness, favour' < *douce* 'sweet' < Latin *dulcis*.]

douche /doosh/ *n* 1 CLEANING BODY BY SQUIRTING WATER a cleaning of part of the body, with a jet of water or air 2 EQUIPMENT PRODUCING CLEANSING WATER JET a piece of equipment that produces a jet of water or air for a douche ■ *vti* (**douches, douching, douched**) CLEAN BODY WITH WATER JET to clean a part of the body or body cavity with a jet of water or air [Mid-18C. Via French < Italian *doccia* 'water pipe' < Latin *duction-* 'leading (through a pipe)'.]

dough /dō/ *n* 1 MIXTURE OF FLOUR AND WATER a soft elastic mixture of flour and water, often with other ingredients such as yeast, oil, butter, salt, and sugar, that becomes bread or pastry when baked 2 MONEY cash and other financial assets (*slang*) 3 SOFT MASS a soft elastic substance similar to baking dough, used, e.g., as children's modelling clay [Old English *dāg* < Indo-European, 'to form']

SPELLCHECK See ***doe***.

doughboy /dṓ boy/ *n* a ball of bread dough boiled, steamed, or fried as a dumpling

dough boy, Dough Boy *n* a US infantryman in World War I

doughnut /dṓ nut/ *n* 1 ROUND CAKE WITH HOLE OR FILLING a small sugar-coated cake of sweet dough, fried or baked, and either spherical with a filling of cream or jam, or ring-shaped with no filling 2 RING-SHAPED OBJECT an object in the shape of an inflated ring, e.g. an accelerating tube in a nuclear reactor or a baby's floor cushion for sitting in ■ *vt* (**-nuts, -nutting, -nutted**) 1 CROWD AROUND MP BEING FILMED to surround a Member of Parliament who is speaking and being filmed for television in order to give the impression that the chamber is fuller than it really is 2 CROWD TELEVISION STUDIO AUDIENCE TOGETHER to crowd members of a television studio audience together to give viewers the impression that the audience is much larger than it really is

doughty /dówti/ (**-tier, -tiest**) *adj* brave and determined (*archaic*) [Old English *dohtig, dyhtig* 'worthy, virtuous' < Indo-European, 'be fit, prosper'] —**doughtily** *adv* —**doughtiness** *n*

Doughty /dówti/, **Charles Montagu** (1843–1926) British travel writer and poet

doughy /dṓ i/ (**-ier, -iest**) *adj* 1 soft, sticky, and elastic, like dough 2 unhealthily pale and a bit flabby —**doughiness** *n*

Douglas /dúggləss/ capital of the Isle of Man. Population: 20,368 (1991).

Douglas, Lord Alfred (1870–1945) British writer and poet

Douglas, Gawin (1474?–1522) Scottish poet and bishop

Douglas, Sir James, 4th Earl of Morton (1516?–81) Scottish courtier

Douglas, Kirk (*b.* 1916) US film actor. Born **Issur Danielovitch**

Douglas, Michael (*b.* 1944) US television and film actor

Douglas, Norman (1868–1952) British writer

Douglas, William O. (1898–1980) US jurist

Douglas fir *n* 1 a tall pine tree with distinctive rough bark and shaggy-looking cones. Use: timber, Christmas trees. Native to: NW North America. *Pseudotsuga menziesii.* 2 the strong durable wood of the Douglas fir tree [After David *Douglas* (1798–1834), Scottish botanist]

Douglas-Home /-hyoóm/, **Sir Alec, 14th Earl of Home** (1903–95) British statesman and prime minister (1963–64)

Douglas spruce *n* TREES = **Douglas fir** *n.* 1

doula /doólə/ *n* a woman who is experienced in childbirth and who provides physical, emotional, and informational assistance and support to a mother before, during, or after childbirth [< Greek *doule* 'enslaved woman']

doum /doom/, **doum palm, doom palm** *n* an Egyptian palm tree with egg-shaped fruits that have a gingery taste. *Hyphaene thebaica.* [Early 18C. < Arabic *dūm*.]

douma *n* HIST, POL = **duma**

dour /door/ *adj* 1 SEVERE OR UNFRIENDLY severe or gloomy, and unfriendly and unresponsive towards other people 2 DETERMINED grimly and stubbornly determined ■ *Scotland* SOLEMN solemn, obstinate, unyielding [14C. Probably via Gaelic *dūr* 'obstinate' < Latin *durus* 'hard'.] —**dourly** *adv* —**dourness** *n*

Douro /doórō/, **Duero** river in N Spain and N Portugal. Length: 895 km/556 mi.

douroucouli /doó roo koóli, doórə-/ (*plural* **-lis**) *n* a fairly small, large-eyed, nocturnal monkey with an inflatable sac under its neck that amplifies its calls. Native to: South America. Genus: *Aotus.* [Mid-19C. Probably < language of a people in S Venezuela.]

douse[1] /dowss/, **dowse** *vt* (**douses, dousing, doused; dowses, dowsing, dowsed**) 1 IMMERSE SOMETHING IN WATER to plunge or submerge somebody or something in water 2 PUT LIQUID ON to put a lot of water or other liquid on somebody or something 3 EXTINGUISH to put out a light, fire, or flame, especially with water ■ *n* DRENCHING a thorough wetting or soaking [Early 17C. < ?] —**douser** *n*

douse[2] /dowss/ (**douses, dousing, doused**) *vt* to lower a sail, especially at speed [Mid-16C. < ?]

DOVAP /dṓ vap/ *n* a system for measuring the speed and position of objects in flight that is based on the frequency of sound waves. Full form **Doppler velocity and position**

dove[1] /duv/ *n* 1 BIRD OF PIGEON FAMILY a bird of the pigeon family with a heavy body, a small head, and a cooing call. Family: Columbidae. 2 SUPPORTER OF PEACE a supporter of peaceful measures against confrontation or war. ◊ **hawk**[1] *n.* 2 3 TERM OF ENDEARMENT used as an affectionate name for a loved one ■ *adj, n* COLOURS = **dove grey** [Assumed Old English *dūfe*, originally 'dark-coloured bird' < Indo-European, 'darken']

dove[2] *US* past tense of **dive**

Dove /duv/ *n* in Christianity, a manifestation or representation of the Holy Spirit

dovecote /dúvkōt/, **dovecot** /-kot/ *n* a building or structure, e.g. mounted on a pole or set into a wall, with many separate entrances and compartments, used for housing domestic pigeons

dove-grey *adj* of a mid-grey colour with a tinge of pink or blue —**dove grey** *n*

dovekie /dúvki/ (*plural* **-kies**), **dovekey** (*plural* **-keys**) *n* BIRDS = **little auk** [Early 19C. Diminutive.]

Dover /dṓvər/ **1** port in SE England. It is England's busiest port and the one nearest to France. Population: 102,600 (1991). **2** capital of Delaware, in the central part of the state. Population: 30,369 (1998 estimate). **3** city in SE New Hampshire. Population: 25,953 (1998 estimate).

Dover, Strait of narrowest part of the English Channel, between Dover, England, and Calais, France. Length: 34 km/21 mi.

Dover sole *n* **1 EUROPEAN FLATFISH** a flat-bodied fish. Native to: Europe. *Solea solea.* **2 FLATFISH OF N AMERICAN PACIFIC** a brownish mottled flat-bodied fish. Native to: Pacific coast of North America. *Microstomus pacificus.* **3 DOVER SOLE AS FOOD** the flesh of a Dover sole used as food [Early 20C. Probably after *Dover*, England.]

dovetail /dúv tayl/ *v* **1** *vti* **FIT TOGETHER** to fit neatly together or combine smoothly and efficiently, or to fit or combine things in this way **2** *vt* **JOIN PIECES OF WOOD** to join wooden boards with interlocking V-shaped tenons ■ *n* **1 V-SHAPED TENON** a V-shaped projection on the end of a piece of wood that fits into a similarly shaped opening in another piece to form a strong joint **2 dovetail, dovetail joint JOINT WITH DOVETAILS** a joint made using dovetails [< its shape]

dovetail saw *n* a small saw with a reinforced back, slightly smaller than a tenon saw and used for fine woodworking

Dovzhenko /dov zhéngkō/, **Aleksandr** (1894–1956) Ukrainian film director

dowager /dówəjər/ *n* **1** a woman who has inherited a title or property from her deceased husband **2** a rich-looking or respected woman of advanced years [Mid-16C. < Old French *douagere* < Latin *dos* 'dowry'.]

dowager's hump *n* a marked abnormal curving of the spine around the area of the shoulder blades, caused by osteoporosis and found among women, often as the result of age

dowdy /dówdi/ (**-dier, -diest**) *adj* **1** unattractively plain and unfashionable in style **2** wearing plain unfashionable clothes [Late 16C. < *dowd* 'poorly dressed woman' < ?] —**dowdily** *adv* —**dowdiness** *n*

dowel /dówəl/ *n* **dowel, dowel pin** a short wooden or metal peg used to join two pieces of wood or metal by fitting tightly at each end into specially drilled holes in the two pieces to be joined ■ *vt* (**dowels, dowelling, dowelled**) to join pieces of wood or metal using dowels [13C. < ?]

Dowell /dów əl/, **Anthony** (*b.* 1943) British ballet dancer

dower /dówər/ *n* **1 WIDOW'S INHERITANCE** a dead man's estate, or part of his estate, inherited by his widow **2 NATURAL GIFT** something, especially a skill or talent, with which somebody is endowed (*literary*) ■ *vt* **ENDOW** to endow somebody with something (*literary*) [13C. < Old French *douaire* < Latin *dotare* 'endow' < *dos* 'marriage portion'.]

dower house *n* a house originally built by a rich landowner for his widow to live in after his death, especially a house on a country estate

Dow Jones Averages *tdmk* a trademark for an index of the prices of selected industrial, transportation, and utilities stocks that is based on a formula developed and revised periodically by Dow Jones & Company, Inc.

Dowland /dówlənd/, **John** (1562–1626?) English composer and musician

ϟ **down**[1] /down/ CORE MEANING: a grammatical word used to indicate movement or position towards a lower level or the ground ○ (prep) *He ran down the stairs and opened the door.* ○ (prep) *The sheep was caught in brambles 50 ft down the hillside.* ○ (prep) *Tears were pouring down her cheeks.* ○ (adv) *I was numb from the waist down.* ○ (adv) *They all watched the sun go down.* ○ (adv) *She pressed a button and the window slid down.*

1 *prep* **TO LOWER LEVEL IN** towards or at a lower level in something ○ *I dropped my keys down a hole.* **2** *prep* **ALONG** towards or at a position farther along the length of something and usually at a somewhat lower level ○ *halfway down the street* **3** *adv* **AT OR TO LOWER LEVEL** at or to a physically lower level or position ○ *down in the basement* **4** *adv* **ONTO SURFACE** out of the hand and onto a surface ○ *She calmly put her fork down.* **5** *adv* **AWAY FROM PRESENT LOCATION** to another place away from your present location or base **6** *adv* **TO MORE SOUTHERLY PLACE** to a place in the south, or to the south of your present location ○ *going down to Spain for the summer* **7** *adv* **TO OR AT LOWER AMOUNT** to or at a lower amount or price ○ *to get interest rates down* **8** *adv* **SHORT BY SPECIFIED AMOUNT** short of, having lost, or losing by a specified amount ○ *They were two goals down at half time.* **9** *adv* **HAVING ONLY SPECIFIED AMOUNT LEFT** having only a specified amount left ○ *I'm down to my last pound.* **10** *adv* **IN PART PAYMENT** in part payment for something or as a deposit ○ *You put 5% down, and pay the rest in instalments.* **11** *adv* **INCLUDING EVERYONE OR EVERYTHING** including everyone or everything, from highest to lowest, within a specified group or hierarchy of people or things, or even including the particular person or thing mentioned ○ *everyone from the managing director down* ○ *account for everything down to the last farthing* **12** *adv* **TO LATER PERIOD** from an earlier to a later time or person ○ *The piano had been handed down to him by his grandmother.* **13** *adv* **IN INFERIOR POSITION** in or to an inferior, less free, or less privileged position or condition ○ *holding political opponents down* **14** *adv* **TO REDUCED CONDITION** to a lower level of intensity or activity ○ *wind down after work* **15** *adv* **INTO LESS SOLID STATE** into a different and less solid state **16** *adv* **ON PAPER** in writing on paper, as a record **17** *adv* **CHOSEN OR ARRANGED** chosen or detailed for something, or arranged or scheduled for a particular time or date ○ *We're down for two sessions next month.* **18** *adv* **VERTICALLY IN A CROSSWORD** in a vertical position in a crossword ○ *the solution to 10 down.* ◊ **across 8 19** *adv* **AWAY FROM UNIVERSITY** away from, or no longer at, a university ○ *down from Cambridge* **20** *adv* **TO WINDWARD** having the rudder to windward **21** *adj* **UNHAPPY** unhappy and gloomy **22** *adj* **NOT IN OPERATION** of a computer system, temporarily not in operation **23** *adj* **MADE IN PART PAYMENT** made or given in part payment for something or as a deposit ○ *a down payment on the car* **24** *adj* **NOT IN PLAY** no longer in play **25** *adj* **PUT OUT** eliminated from a game **26** *adj* **ON THE GROUND** lying on the ground ○ *a down tree* **27** *interj* **INSTRUCTION TO DOG** used as an instruction to a dog to stop jumping up or to lie or sit ○ *Down boy!* **28** *vt* **EAT OR DRINK** to eat food or drink liquid, especially quickly or greedily **29** *vt* **MAKE FALL TO THE GROUND** to cause somebody or something to fall to the ground through being hurt or damaged **30** *vt* **DECLARE BALL OUT OF PLAY** in American football, to declare a ball as no longer in play **31** *n* **MOVE MADE IN AMERICAN FOOTBALL** one of four consecutive plays within which an American football team must either score or advance the ball at least ten yards [Old English *dūn(e)*, shortened < *adūn(e)* 'from the hill' < *dūn* (see DOWN[3])] ◇ **be down on somebody, have a down on somebody** to show dislike or hostility towards somebody or something, often giving him, her, or it unfair treatment (*informal*) ◇ **be down to somebody** to be the responsibility of somebody ◇ **be down to something** to be the result of something ◇ **be** *or* **go down with something** to be *or* become ill with something ◇ **down under** to or in Australia or New Zealand (*informal*) ◇ **down with somebody** *or* **something!** used to express disapproval of, opposition to, or a desire to get rid of somebody or something

down[2] /down/ *n* **1 SOFT FLUFFY FEATHERS** the soft fluffy feathers that are a young bird's first plumage or that lie beneath the outer feathers in some adult birds **2 FEATHERS AS STUFFING** the soft breast feathers of a duck or goose, especially the female eider duck. Use: filling for pillows and quilts. **3 COVERING OF SOFT HAIRS** a covering of fine fluffy hairs, e.g. on a child's skin or on the skin of some kinds of fruit [14C. < Old Norse *dúnn*.]

down[3] /down/ *n* a grassy treeless hill or ridge (*often in placenames*) ■ **downs** *npl* an area of gently rolling, treeless, grassy upland, used mainly as pasture [Old English *dūn* < ?]

Down /down/ former county in SE Northern Ireland

down-and-dirty *adj US* crude and often unpleasant (*slang*) ○ *the down-and-dirty truth*

down-and-out *adj* **1 JOBLESS AND POOR** having no money or job, often no home, and little hope of things getting better **2 UNABLE TO CARRY ON** completely incapacitated and unable to carry on ■ *n* **JOBLESS POOR PERSON** a person who lacks money, a job, or a home

down-at-heel *adj* shabbily dressed through poverty

downbeat /dówn beet/ *adj* **1 PESSIMISTIC** showing or expressing pessimism and hopelessness **2 CASUAL** deliberately casual and relaxed (*informal*) **3 UNDERSTATED** carefully or deliberately understated or restrained ■ *n* **1 FIRST BEAT IN BAR** the first beat in a bar of music **2 CONDUCTOR'S DOWNWARD GESTURE** the downward movement made by a conductor to indicate the downbeat of a bar of music

down-bow *n* the action of drawing a bow from its heel towards its point across a stringed instrument

downburst /dówn burst/ *n* a powerful downward wind, often part of a thunderstorm system, that creates strong horizontal winds in all directions when it strikes the earth and is a danger to aircraft

downcast /dówn kaast/ *adj* **1** sad and pessimistic **2** looking or directed towards the ground ○ *with downcast eyes*

downcourt /dówn kawrt/ *adj, adv* in, to, or towards the opposite end of a basketball or similar court

downdraft *n US* = **downdraught**

downdraught /dówn draaft/ *n* a downward movement of air, e.g. on the lee side of a mountain range or down a chimney

downer /dównər/ *n* **1 SEDATIVE DRUG** a drug, especially a barbiturate, that induces calmness or sleepiness (*slang*) **2 GLOOMY PERSON OR THING** a gloomy person, situation, or experience (*informal*) **3 GLOOMY MOOD** a gloomy and pessimistic mood (*informal*) ○ *was on a real downer*

downfall /dówn fawl/ *n* **1 FAILURE OR RUIN** the failure or ruin of a previously successful person, group, or organization **2 CAUSE OF RUIN** an action or situation responsible for the failure or ruin of a previously successful person, group, or organization **3 FALL OF RAIN OR SNOW** a sudden heavy fall of rain or snow

downfield /dówn feeld/ *adj, adv US* in, to, or towards the opponents' half of a field of play

downgrade /dówn grayd/ *vt* (**-grades, -grading, -graded**) **1 LOWER STATUS** to lower the status, value, or rating of something ○ *The hurricane was downgraded to a tropical storm.* **2 MOVE SOMEBODY TO LESS IMPORTANT JOB** to move somebody from one post or job to another with less responsibility, status, or pay **3 DISPARAGE** to speak or write about somebody or something disparagingly ■ *n US, Can* **DOWNWARD SLOPE** a downward slope on a road

downhaul /dówn hawl/ *n* a rope for pulling down or holding down a sail or a spar

downhearted /dówn haártid/ *adj* discouraged and unhappy —**downheartedly** *adv* —**downheartedness** *n*

downhill *adv* /down híl/ **TOWARDS BOTTOM OF HILL** towards the bottom of a slope or hill ■ *adj* /dówn hil/ **SLOPING DOWN** sloping down or taking place on a downward slope ■ *n* /dówn hil/ **RACE DOWN LONG MOUNTAINSIDE COURSE** a skiing race against the clock down a long mountainside course with several hundred yards between marker flags ◇ **go downhill** to decline or deteriorate

downhole /down hṓl/ *adj* describes equipment used inside an oil well

downhome /down hṓm/ *adj US* appealingly simple, informal, and unpretentious, and therefore considered typical of ordinary people, especially the country people of the S United States (*informal*) ○ *downhome cooking*

Downing Street /dówning-/ *n* **1** the street off Whitehall in Westminster, central London, where the official residences of the British prime minister and chancellor of the exchequer are located **2** the British prime minister or the British government ○ *Downing Street sources*

downland /dówn land/ *n* undulating grass-covered hills in S England or similar, often flatter grassland in Australia and New Zealand

downlight /dówn līt/ *n* a lamp or bulb whose light is directed straight downwards

downlink /dówn lingk/ *n* a path for the transmission of signals and data between a vehicle or satellite in space and the Earth —**downlink** *vti*

ϟ **download** /down lṓd/ *vti* **TRANSFER DATA** to transfer or copy data from one computer to another, or to a disk or peripheral device, or be transferred or copied in this way ■ *n* **1 INSTANCE OF DOWNLOADING** an instance or the process of downloading data **2 DOWNLOADED DATA** data that has been downloaded in a single operation

downmarket /dówn maarkit/ *adj* cheap, appealing to mass taste, and regarded as being of low quality ■ *adv* towards the part of the market that deals in cheaper, lower-quality goods for mass consumption

Downpatrick /down páttrik/ town in SE Northern Ireland, where St Patrick is traditionally believed to be buried. Population: 10,257 (1991).

down payment *n* a part of the full price of something paid at the time it is bought, with the remaining part to be paid later

downpipe /dówn pīp/ *n* a pipe that carries rainwater from a roof gutter down to a drain or to the ground. US term **downspout**

downplay /down pláy/ *vt* to make something seem less important, significant, or serious than it really is

downpour /dówn pawr/ *n* a heavy and sustained fall of rain

down quark *n* a quark with an electric charge of $-\frac{1}{3}$, zero strangeness, and zero charm

downrange /down ráynj/ *adj, adv* away from where a missile was fired

downright /dówn rīt/ *adj* **1** ABSOLUTE complete and utter ○ *a downright lie* **2** STRAIGHTFORWARD frank in expressing opinions ■ *adv* POSITIVELY positively and undeniably ○ *downright unfair* —**downrightly** *adv* —**downrightness** *n*

downriver /dówn rívvər/ *adv, adj* towards or nearer the mouth of a river or following the direction of its current

Downs /downz/ either of two chalk uplands in S England

downscale /down skáyl/ *adj US* = **downmarket** *adj.* ■ *vti* (**-scales, -scaling, -scaled**) *US* to reduce the scale or extent of something, especially a business

downshift /dówn shift/ *vi* **1** *US* CARS = **change down 2** to change a highly paid but stressful job for one that makes it possible to improve quality of life in other respects — **downshift** *n*

downside /dówn sīd/ *n* a negative side to something that also has positive aspects

downsize /dówn sīz/ (**-sizes, -sizing, -sized**) *vti* to reduce the size of a business or organization, especially by cutting the workforce

downslide /dówn slīd/ *n* a downwards trend or course

downspout /dówn spowt/ *n US* CONSTR = **downpipe**

Down's syndrome /dównz-/ *n* a genetic disorder characterized by a broad skull, blunt facial features, short stature, and learning difficulties [Mid-20C. After J. H. L. *Down* (1828–96), English physician.]

downstage /dówn stáyj/ *adv, adj* towards or at the front of a theatre stage ■ *n* the front half of a theatre stage

downstairs /dówn stáirz/ *adv* TO LOWER FLOOR down the stairs or to a lower floor ■ *adj* ON LOWER FLOOR on a lower or the lowest floor ○ *a downstairs bathroom* ■ *n* **1** LOWER FLOOR the lower floor of a building **2** HOUSE'S SERVANTS all the servants of a household (*informal*) ◊ **upstairs** *n.* **2**

downstate /dówn stáyt/ *adj, adv US* **1** in or to the southerly part of a US state **2** away from the big cities and in or into the more rural parts of a US state whose major metropolitan area is to the north ○ *downstate Illinois* — **downstate** *n* —**downstater** *n*

⚡**downstream** /dówn stréem/ *adj* **1** OF LATER PRODUCTION STAGES relating to or occurring in the later stages of production **2** SITUATED TOWARDS MOUTH OF RIVER situated towards or nearer the mouth of a river ■ *adv* **1** FURTHER FORWARD ON DNA MOLECULE further forward on a DNA molecule, in the direction in which the sequence is being read during replication **2** TOWARDS MOUTH OF RIVER towards or nearer the mouth of a river, or following the direction of the current ■ *n* TRANSMISSION AWAY FROM CENTRAL NETWORK transmission of data on a network away from a central distribution point

downstroke /dówn strōk/ *n* a stroke moving or made in a downwards direction

downswing /dówn swing/ *n* **1** a downwards trend or course **2** the downwards part of a golfer's swing

Down syndrome /dówn-/ *n US* = **Down's syndrome**

down-the-line *adj US* unwavering in support of or adherence to rules or policy

downthrow /dówn thrō/ *n* the relative vertical displacement of rocks on one side of a fault

downtime /dówn tīm/ *n* time during which work or production is stopped, e.g. because machinery is not working

down-to-earth *adj* practical and realistic

downtown /dówn tówn/ *adj, adv US, Can, NZ* in or to the centre of a city, especially its business centre ■ *n US* the centre of a city, especially its business centre — **downtowner** *n*

downtrend /dówn trend/ *n* a downward trend or tendency

downtrodden /-trod'n/, **downtrod** /-trod/ *adj* made submissive by constant harsh treatment

downturn /dówn turn/ *n* a period or trend in which business or economic activity is reduced or is less successful

downward *adj, adv* = **downwards**

downwardly mobile *adj* moving to a lower status, social class, or income bracket

downward mobility *n* movement to a lower status, social class, or income bracket

downwards /dównwərdz/, **downward** /dównwərd/ *adj* **1** MOVING LOWER IN SPACE moving or directed to the ground or to a lower place **2** MOVING TO LOWER LEVEL moving to a lower level or condition **3** COMING FROM ORIGIN OR SOURCE descending from a source, origin, or beginning ■ *adv* **1** TOWARDS LOWER PLACE towards the ground or a lower place **2** TO LOWER LEVEL to a lower level or condition **3** TO AND INCLUDING EVERYONE to and including all the members of an organization, even the most junior ○ *everyone from the managing director downwards* **4** TO LATER TIME to a later time or generation —**downwardly** *adv* —**downwardness** *n*

downwash /dówn wosh/ *n* a downwards wind, e.g. the wind created by an aircraft wing

downwind /dówn wínd/ *adv, adj* **1** in the direction that the wind is blowing **2** in or into a position further along the line of the direction of the wind

downy /dówn i/ (**-ier, -iest**) *adj* **1** SOFT soft and fluffy **2** COVERED WITH SOFT HAIRS covered with soft fine hairs **3** FEATHER-FILLED filled with feathers —**downiness** *n*

downy mildew *n* a disease of plants that produces grey velvety patches on lower leaf surfaces, caused by various fungi. Family: Peronosporaceae.

downy woodpecker *n* a small black and white woodpecker with a white back, the male of which has a red head patch. Native to: North America. *Picoides pubescens.*

dowry /dówri/ (*plural* **-ries**) *n* **1** BRIDE'S FAMILY'S GIFT TO BRIDEGROOM an amount of money or property given in some societies by a bride's family to her bridegroom or his family when she marries **2** MAN'S GIFT TO BRIDE an amount of money or property transferred by a man to his bride when they marry **3** MONEY PAID TO ENTER NUNS' ORDER a sum of money required for a woman to enter some monastic orders **4** TALENT a natural talent (*literary*) **5** DOWER a dower (*archaic*) [14C. Via Anglo-Norman *dowarie* < Old French *douaire* (see DOWER).]

dowry death *n S Asia* the death of a married woman by murder or suicide arising from a dispute over her dowry

dowse[1] /dowss/ (**dowses, dowsing, dowsed**) *vi* to use a divining rod to search for underground water or minerals [Late 17C. < ?] —**dowser** *n*

dowse[2] *vt, n* = **douse**[1]

dowse[3] /dowz/ *vt* = **douse**[2]

dowsing rod *n* = **divining rod**

Dowson /dówss'n/, **Ernest** (1867–1900) British poet

Dow theory /dów-/ *n* a theory that states that stock-market prices can be forecast on the basis of the movements of a selected group of stocks

doxastic /dok sástik/ *n* the branch of logic that deals with belief [Early 19C. < Greek *doxa* 'opinion'.] —**doxastic** *adj*

doxie *n* RELIG = **doxy**

doxology /dok sóllə ji/ (*plural* **-gies**) *n* in Christian religious services, a hymn, prayer, or formula of worship in praise of God [Mid-17C. < medieval Latin *doxologia* 'science of opinion' < Greek *doxa* 'opinion'.] —**doxological** /dóksə lójjik'l/ *adj* —**doxologically** *adv*

doxorubicin /dóksō róobissin/ *n* an antibiotic obtained from a bacterium. Use: treatment of some tumours. [Late 20C. < DE + OXY + Latin *rubus* 'red' + MYCIN.]

doxy /dóksi/ (*plural* **-ies**), **doxie** *n* a set of beliefs, especially religious beliefs (*informal*) [Mid-18C. Extracted < such words as ORTHODOXY, HETERODOXY.]

doxycycline /dóksi sī kleen/ *n* a tetracycline-derived antibiotic. Use: treatment of many diseases. [Mid-20C. Contraction of *deoxytetracycline*.]

doyen /dóyən/ *n* a man who is the most experienced and respected member of a group or profession [15C. Via French < Latin *decanus* 'person in charge of ten others' (see DEAN).]

doyenne /doy énn/ *n* a woman who is the most experienced and respected member of a group or profession [Mid-19C. < French, form of *doyen* (see DOYEN).]

Doyle /doyl/, **Sir Arthur Conan** (1859–1930) Scottish-born British writer and physician

Doyle, Roddy (*b.* 1958) Irish novelist, playwright, and screenwriter

doyly *n* = **doily**

D'Oyly Carte /dóyli kaárt/, **Richard** (1844–1901) British theatre agent, manager, and producer

doz. *abbr* dozen

doze[1] /dōz/ (**dozes, dozing, dozed**) *vi* **1** to sleep lightly for a short time, especially during the day **2** to spend time lazily or in a daydream [Mid-17C. Probably < N Germanic.] —**doze** *n* —**dozer** *n*

doze off *vi* to fall into a light sleep, especially unintentionally

doze[2] /dōz/ (**dozes, dozing, dozed**) *vt* to bulldoze something (*slang*) [Mid-20C. Back-formation < DOZER.]

dozed /dōzd/ *adj Ireland* describes wood that is rotten or rubber that is perished [Late 18C. Past participle of DOZE[1].]

dozen /dúzz'n/ *n* (*plural* **-en**), *det* GROUP OF 12 a group of 12 objects or people ■ *det* (*informal*) **1** MANY a large number of ○ *I've told you a dozen times already!* **2** **dozens** LOTS a large quantity or a great many [13C. Via Old French *dozeine* < Latin *duodecim* 'twelve' < *duo* 'two' + *decem* 'ten'.] —**dozenth** *adj* ◇ **by the dozen** in large quantities ◇ **daily dozen** a regular regime of physical exercises

dozer /dṓzər/ *n* a bulldozer (*slang*) [Mid-20C. Shortening of BULLDOZER.]

dozy /dṓzi/ (**-zier, -ziest**) *adj* **1** half asleep or tending to fall asleep or doze **2** slow in understanding something or things in general (*informal*) —**dozily** *adv* —**doziness** *n*

⚡**DP** *abbr* **1** **DP, dp** data processing **2** **DP, dp** dew point **3** displaced person

D/P *abbr* **1** documents against payment **2** documents against presentation

DPhil /dee fíl/, **DPh** *abbr* Doctor of Philosophy

⚡**dpi** *n* a measure of the density of the image produced by a computer screen or printer. Full form **dots per inch**

DPP *abbr* Director of Public Prosecutions

DPS *abbr* dividends per share

dpt *abbr* **1** department **2** deponent

DPT *abbr* diphtheria, pertussis, tetanus (vaccine)

dr *abbr* **1** debtor **2** dram[1] **3** **dr, DR** dining room (*in advertisements*) **4** drawer

Dr *abbr* **1** doctor **2** drachma **3** *US* Drive (*in addresses*)

DR *abbr* **1** dead reckoning **2** dry riser

dr. *abbr* **1** debit **2** drachma **3** dram[1]

drab[1] /drab/ *adj* (**drabber, drabbest**) **1** LACKING COLOUR OR BRIGHTNESS uninteresting to look at because of a lack of colour or brightness **2** BORING lacking interest, enthusiasm, or excitement **3** OF PALE GREYISH-BROWN COLOUR of a dull pale greyish-brown colour ■ *n* **1** PALE GREYISH-BROWN COLOUR a dull pale greyish-brown colour **2** DULL-COLOURED FABRIC a grey or brown fabric [Early 16C. < Old French *drap* 'cloth' (see DRAPE).] —**drably** *adv* —**drabness** *n*

drab[2] /drab/ *n* **1** an offensive term that insults a woman's appearance or cleanliness (*archaic insult*) **2** an offensive term for a prostitute (*archaic*) [Early 16C. < ?]

drabbet /drábbit/ *n* coarse undyed linen fabric [Early 19C. < DRAB[1].]

drabble /drább'l/ (**-bles, -bling, -bled**) *vti* to become, or make something, wet and dirty [14C. < Low German *drabbeln* 'splash in water'.]

Drabble /drább'l/, **Margaret** (*b.* 1939) British novelist, editor, and critic

dracaena /drə séenə/, **dracena** *n* **1** a member of a genus of tropical evergreen plants that have long, strap-shaped, often variegated leaves and are popular as house plants. Genus: *Dracaena.* **2** a plant with long narrow leaves resembling a true dracaena. Genus: *Co-*

rdyline. [Early 19C. Via modern Latin < Greek *drakaina*, feminine of *drakōn* 'dragon'; from the supposed resemblance of the juice of one of the species to dragon's blood.]

drachm /dram/ *n* **1** a unit of liquid capacity in the apothecary system, equal to $\frac{1}{8}$ of a fluid ounce. US term **fluid dram 2** MONEY = **drachma** [14C. Via Old French < Greek *drakhmē* 'number of coins one hand can hold' < assumed *drakh-* 'grasp'.]

drachma /drákmə/ (*plural* **-mas** *or* **-mae** /-mī/) *n* see table at **currency** [Early 16C. Via Latin < Greek *drakhmē* (see DRACHM).]

Draco /dráykō/ *n* a large faint constellation of the northern hemisphere. See illustration at **constellation**

draco lizard *n* ZOOL = **flying lizard**

dracone /drákōn/ *n* a large flexible container for transporting liquids by towing them on the surface of the sea

Draconian /drə kṓni ən/, **draconian, Draconic** /-kónnik/, **draconic** *adj* **1** unjustly harsh or severe **2** relating to the Athenian statesman Draco of the 7th century BC or to his wide-ranging and harsh code of laws [Late 19C. < Greek *Drakōn-* 'Draco'.] —**Draconianism** *n* —**Draconically** *adv*

draconic /drə kónnik/ *adj* relating to or like a dragon or dragons —**draconically** *adv*

draff /draf/ *n* a residue left in brewing after the grain has been fermented, used as food for cattle [13C. < ?] —**draffy** *adj*

draft /draaft/ *n* **1 PRELIMINARY VERSION** a preliminary version of a piece of writing such as a speech, essay, or report **2 PRELIMINARY SKETCH** a preliminary sketch or plan **3** US = **call-up 4 LEVELLING LINE ON STONE** a line chiselled on the surface of a building stone as guide to laying it level ■ *n, adj* US = **draught** ■ *vt* **1 WRITE PRELIMINARY VERSION OF SOMETHING** to write a preliminary version of something such as a speech or report **2 MAKE PLAN** to make a preliminary plan or sketch of something, before all the required information is to hand **3 TRANSFER SOMEBODY SOMEWHERE FOR DUTY** to move or send somebody somewhere to carry out a particular task or general work and duties **4** US = **call up** *v.* 1 **5** *ANZ* **SORT LIVESTOCK INTO SMALLER GROUPS** to divide or sort livestock into smaller groups according to age, sex, or a particular characteristic [Mid-16C. Form of DRAUGHT.] —**drafter** *n*

draft dodger *n US* a person who seeks to avoid being called up for military service

draftee /draaf tée/ *n US* a person who has been drafted for military service

draftsman *n* US = **draughtsman**

draftsperson *n* US = **draughtsperson**

draftswoman *n* US = **draughtswoman**

drafty *adj* US = **draughty**

ϟ **drag** /drag/ *v* (**drags, dragging, dragged**) **1** *vt* **PULL ALONG WITH EFFORT** to move something, especially something that is too large, heavy, or cumbersome to carry, by pulling it along the ground or across a surface **2** *vt* **PULL BY FORCE** to move or remove somebody or something that resists, usually by pulling at the person or object with considerable force or violence ○ *They dragged the fallen tree out of the road.* **3** *vt* **PERSUADE TO COME AWAY** to cause, persuade, or force somebody to stop doing something or to leave a place unwillingly ○ *I'm sorry to drag you away from your work.* **4** *vti* **TRAIL ALONG THE GROUND** to be in continuous contact with the ground while moving across it, or allow something such as the foot or the bottom of a garment to do this ○ *He dragged his feet as he walked.* **5** *vti* **MOVE** to move, or move yourself or your feet, slowly and with difficulty or great reluctance ○ *I was so tired that I could scarcely drag myself up the stairs.* **6** *vi* **PASS SLOWLY** to pass or proceed at a very slow and boring pace ○ *The afternoon was beginning to drag.* **7** *vt* **MOVE ICON WITH MOUSE** to move an icon or other selected item on a computer screen by clicking on it with the mouse and pulling it to a new location **8** *vt* **SEARCH** to search a river bed, pond, or other area of water using a net or hook in an attempt to find something or somebody that is missing **9** *vi* **PUFF ON SMOKING MATERIAL** to put a cigarette, pipe, or cigar to the mouth and suck in the smoke (*informal*) ■ *n* **1 HINDRANCE** a person or thing that slows down physical movement or progress in an area or activity ○ *These measures have been a drag on our economy.* **2 RESISTANCE TO MOTION** (*symbol* **D**) the resistance experienced by a body moving through a fluid medium, especially by an aircraft when travelling through the air **3 SOMEBODY OR SOMETHING BORING** a person, task, duty, or event that is held to be extremely boring and irritating (*informal*) ○ *It was such a drag having to take our heavy coats and hats with us.* **4 SLOW AND LABORIOUS MOVEMENT** an action or movement carried out slowly and with great effort or difficulty **5 DRAGGING MOVEMENT** a sound, movement, or act of dragging **6 CLOTHING OF OPPOSITE SEX** clothing characteristic of one sex worn by a member of the other, especially women's clothing when worn by men (*slang*) **7 PUFF** a puff on a cigarette, pipe, or cigar (*informal*) **8 LINE USED FOR DRAGGING RIVER** a line, chain, or hook that is used for searching or dredging the bottom of an area of water such as a river or pond **9 VEHICLE THAT IS DRAGGED** a vehicle such as a cart, sledge, or other vehicle that is pulled along the surface of the ground **10 BRAKING DEVICE** a braking device, especially a horseshoe-shaped piece of metal fitted on the underside of the wheel of a horse-drawn vehicle **11 FOX SCENT** the scent left by a fox or other animal that is hunted by dogs **12 ARTIFICIAL SCENT** an artificial scent put on the ground for hunting dogs to follow **13** FIELD SPORTS = **drag hunt 14** MOTOR SPORTS = **drag race 15 HORSE-DRAWN COACH** a large coach, similar to a stagecoach but privately owned, with seats inside and on top and usually drawn by four horses [14C. < either a form of DRAW or < related Old Norse *draga* < Germanic.] ◇ **drag your feet** *or* **heels** to be slow to act, usually because you would prefer to avoid doing anything if possible ○ *The Administration has been dragging its feet on the new budget proposals.*

SYNONYMS See *pull*.

drag down *vt* **1** to reduce somebody or something to a lower level or an inferior status by force or pressure of some kind ○ *Don't allow yourself to be dragged down by a timid banker.* **2** to make somebody feel listless, uninterested, or physically weak and tired ○ *Sitting at home all week really dragged me down.*

drag in *vt* to involve somebody or something in something when it is not necessary or appropriate to do so, especially to insist on mentioning something that is not relevant in a conversation ○ *Mention music and he's bound to drag in a reference to the song he's just written.*

drag into *vt* to involve somebody in something dishonest, disreputable, or otherwise undesirable ○ *What are you trying to drag me into?* ○ *They were dragged into the scandal.*

drag on *vi* to continue for a very long time, especially past the expected or desired finishing time

drag out *vt* to make something last longer than is necessary or desirable

drag out of *vt* to force somebody to reveal or admit something ○ *Are you going to tell me, or do I have to drag it out of you?*

drag up *vt* **1** to mention something that somebody does not want to be discussed or known because it is unpleasant, upsetting, or embarrassing, especially something from that person's past **2** to bring somebody up in a lazy or undisciplined way (*informal humorous; usually passive*) ○ *Where were you dragged up?*

ϟ **drag and drop** *vt* to click onto an item on a computer screen, move it with the mouse, and release it on a particular icon

dragée /dra <u>zh</u>áy/ *n* **1 HARD-COATED SWEET** a sweet consisting of a nut, piece of fruit, or other centre covered in a hard sugar coating **2 TINY CONFECTIONERY BALL** a tiny silver-coated ball used for decorating cakes **3 SWEETENED PILL** a medicinal pill covered with a sugar coating to make it taste better [Late 17C. < French, variant of Old French *dragie* (see DREDGE[2]).]

draggle /drágg'l/ (**-gles, -gling, -gled**) *v* **1** *vti* to make something wet and dirty by trailing it along the ground, or become wet and dirty by being trailed along the ground **2** *vi* to follow along behind somebody else in a slow and usually undisciplined or slovenly fashion [Early 16C. Probably < DRAG.]

draggy /drág gi/ (**-gier, -giest**) *adj* (*informal*) **1** slow-moving ○ *a draggy musical* **2** boring or otherwise annoying ○ *spent a draggy afternoon weeding the garden*

draghound /drág hownd/ *n* a hound used in a drag hunt to follow an artificial scent trail

drag hunt *n* a hunt in which a pack of hounds follows an artificial scent trail

drag-hunt *vti* to hunt prey with a pack of hounds that follow an artificial scent trail

draglift /drág lift/ *n* a ski lift with metal bars or ropes that people hold onto as they are pulled up to the top of a slope on their skis

dragline /drág līn/ *n* **1** an excavating machine with a digging bucket attached by cables to a long jib and operated by being dragged back towards the machine by another cable **2** a line that is used for dragging, e.g. when hauling a load or dragging a river or pond

drag link *n* a link that conveys motion from one point to another

dragnet /drág net/ *n* **1 WEIGHTED NET** a net with weights on it used when trawling for fish at sea or when searching for something at the bottom of a river or pond **2 GAME NET** a net that is drawn across the ground and used to trap small game **3 POLICE HUNT FOR A CRIMINAL** a systematic and coordinated search for a wanted person made by police

dragoman /drággəmən/ (*plural* **-mans** *or* **-men** /-mən/) *n* a guide or interpreter in certain Arabic-, Turkish-, or Persian-speaking countries (*archaic*) [16C. Via French, Italian, and medieval Greek < Arabic *targumān* < Aramaic *tūrgemānā* < Akkadian *targumānu* 'interpreter'.]

dragon /drággən/ *n* **1 SCALY GREEN MONSTER** a large and usually ferocious fire-breathing creature in myths, legends, and fairy tales that has green scaly skin, a long tail, and wings **2 LARGE LIZARD** a large lizard, e.g. the Komodo dragon **3 INSULT FOR FORMIDABLE WOMAN** a woman who is regarded as fierce and formidable (*insult*) [13C. Via Old French < Latin *draco* < Greek *drákōn* 'snake'.] ◇ **chase the dragon** to take heroin by heating it and breathing in the fumes (*slang*)

Dragon *n* ASTRON = **Draco**

dragon boat *n* a long narrow boat decorated like a dragon, used especially by Chinese people when taking part in boat races during a festival held every 5th May of the lunar year

dragonet /drággənit/ (*plural* **-ets** *or* **-et**) *n* a small brightly coloured spiny marine fish belonging to a family with flat heads, narrow bodies, and large pectoral fins, living near the bottom of warm shallow waters. Family: Callionymidae. [14C. < DRAGON.]

dragonfly /drággən flī/ (*plural* **-flies**) *n* an insect with a large head and eyes, a long thin body, and two pairs of iridescent often blue wings that usually remain outstretched when the insect is at rest. Suborder: Anisoptera.

dragonroot /drággən root/ (*plural* **-roots** *or* **-root**) *n* **1** a tuberous, foul-smelling, and poisonous perennial plant belonging to the arum family. *Dracunculus vulgaris.* **2** PLANTS = **green dragon**

dragon's blood *n* a red resinous substance. Source: various trees including the dragon tree. Use: colouring varnishes and lacquers.

dragon tree *n* an evergreen tree that has a trunk that grows very thick clusters of spiky leaves, orange fruit, and resin that is a source of dragon's blood. Native to: Canary Islands. *Dracaena draco.*

dragoon /drə góon/ *n* **1 MOUNTED INFANTRYMAN** in European armies of the 17th and 18th centuries, a mounted infantryman armed with a carbine **2 CAVALRYMAN** in armies of the late 18th and 19th centuries, a cavalryman, especially a heavily armed cavalryman ■ *vt* **1 FORCE** to involve somebody in an activity, or force somebody to do something, against his or her will ○ *He was dragooned into joining the chorus for the show.* **2 SUBJUGATE** to persecute or subjugate somebody using military troops [Early 17C. < French *dragon* 'carbine, musket', literally 'dragon'.]

drag queen *n* a man who dresses as a woman, especially a performer who dresses in a flamboyant women's costume and traditionally affects feminine mannerisms for comic effect (*slang*)

drag race *n* a race between cars with specially modified bodies and engines on a straight track over a distance of a quarter of a mile to discover which has the fastest acceleration —**drag racer** *n* —**drag racing** *n*

dragster /drágstər/ *n* **1** a car that is specially designed for and used in drag racing **2** a driver who takes part in a drag race

drag strip *n* a short straight track, usually a quarter of a mile in length, used for drag racing

drain /drayn/ *n* **1 SEWAGE PIPE** a pipe or channel that carries water or sewage away from a place **2 SOMETHING THAT USES UP RESOURCES** something that diminishes or uses up resources or energy ○ *a serious drain on our financial resources* **3 LOSS OR DIMINISHING** the gradual loss, withdrawal, or diminishing of something regarded as an important resource ○ *the drain of trained personnel from the industry* **4** DEVICE TO REMOVE FLUID FROM WOUND a tube or other device placed in a wound or incision to draw off fluids such as blood, pus, or water **5** ARTIFICIAL WATERWAY an artificial waterway that allows for land drainage ■ *v* **1** *vti* FLOW OUT to flow out of something, often leaving it empty or dry, or allow a liquid to do this **2** *vti* EMPTY to empty or dry something by allowing the water to flow out of or off it, or become empty or dry in this way ○ *The water drained slowly from the bath.* **3** *vt* DRY OUT LAND to make marshy land drier by laying pipes, digging ditches or channels, or by any other means that removes the excess water **4** *vt* CHANNEL WATER AWAY FROM to be a channel for leading water off land ○ *The river Loire drains most of central France.* **5** *vi* DISCHARGE to discharge water from its surface or channel into a river or lake (*refers to a geographical area or a smaller watercourse*) **6** *vt* DRINK UP to empty a cup, glass, or other container by drinking all its contents ○ *He drained his tea in one gulp and left.* **7** *vt* USE UP to use up or deplete something gradually, especially somebody's energy and resources, by making constant demands on it ○ *These payments are draining the country dry.* **8** *vi* WANE to disappear gradually, or become less strong or intense ○ *The colour drained from her cheeks.* **9** *vt* EXHAUST to leave somebody feeling physically or emotionally exhausted ○ *Caring for six active youngsters five days a week drains all my energies.* [Old English *drēahnian* < Germanic] —**drainable** *adj* ◇ **down the drain 1** wasted or squandered with no hope of retrieval (*informal*) **2** towards or in a state of total failure or ruin, especially financial failure (*informal*)

drainage /dráynij/ *n* **1** DRAINING PROCESS the process of draining liquid from something **2** SEWAGE SYSTEM a system of pipes or channels that carries water or sewage away from a place **3** FLUID REMOVAL FROM BODY the removal of fluid such as water, blood, or pus from a wound or part of the body, usually by means of a tube **4** FLUID REMOVED BY DRAINING water, sewage, or any other fluid removed by draining

drainage basin, drainage area *n* GEOG = **catchment area** *n.* 1

drainboard /dráyn bawrd/ *n US* = **draining board**

drainer /draynər/ *n* a rack or container in which things are put so that liquid can drain off them

draining board *n* a slightly sloping metal, wooden, or plastic surface next to a sink, with shallow grooves on it to allow water to drain off drying dishes into the sink. US term **drainboard**

drainpipe /dráyn pīp/ *n* a pipe that carries off rainwater, waste water, or sewage to or through the drains, especially a downpipe attached to the side of a house ■ **drainpipes, drainpipe trousers** *npl* trousers with very narrow legs that were particularly popular in the 1950s, and again in the 1970s and 1980s in punk fashion

drake /drayk/ *n* a male duck [13C. Probably < Germanic.]

Drake /drayk/, **Sir Francis** (1540?–96) English navigator and admiral

Drakensberg /draákənz burg/ mountain range in SE South Africa and Lesotho. Highest peak: Thabana Ntlenyana, 3,482 m/11,424 ft.

Drake Passage /dráyk-/ stretch of water between South America and the Antarctic Peninsula that separates the South Atlantic and South Pacific oceans. Length: 800 km/500 mi.

dram[1] /dram/ *n* **1** a unit of mass in the avoirdupois system equal to 1/16 of an ounce (or approximately 1.77 grams) **2** a small amount of an alcoholic drink, particularly whisky or brandy ○ *How about a wee dram before you go?* [15C. Via Old French *drame* or medieval Latin *drama* < Greek *drakhmē* 'handful'.]

dram[2] /dram/ *n* see table at **currency**

dram[3] *abbr* dramatic

ϟ **DRAM** /dram/ *abbr* dynamic random access memory

drama /draámə/ *n* **1** PERFORMED PLAY a serious play written for performance on stage, television, or radio **2** PLAYS AS GENRE works written for performance on the stage, radio, or television considered as a literary genre ○ *17th-century French drama* **3** PRODUCING OR PERFORMING PLAYS the performance, production, or writing of plays considered as a job, activity, or subject to be studied **4** EXCITING EVENT a real-life event or situation that is particularly exciting or emotionally involving **5** DRAMATIC EVENTS OR QUALITY exciting, tense, and gripping events and actions, or an exciting, tense, and gripping quality, either in a work of art or in a real-life situation ○ *an evening full of drama* [Early 16C. Via late Latin < Greek, 'play, deed' < *dran* 'do'.]

drama documentary (*plural* **drama documentaries**) *n* a documentary work, usually on television or radio, in which real events are re-enacted by actors, or in which real events and characters are mingled with fictional ones

drama queen *n* a person who likes to make a drama out of a situation by acting in an emotional way (*informal*)

dramatic /drə máttik/ *adj* **1** FOR THE THEATRE written for the theatre, or relating to the theatre, plays, or acting **2** EXCITING AND INTENSE characterized, in real life or in art, by the kind of intense and gripping excitement, startling suddenness, or larger-than-life impressiveness associated with drama and the theatre ○ *the dramatic sequence of events leading to his escape* **3** SUDDEN AND MARKED large in degree or scale, and often occurring with surprising suddenness ○ *a dramatic jump in prices* **4** STRIKING bold, vivid, or strikingly impressive in appearance, colour, or effect ○ *a dramatic view of the Alps* **5** HAVING POWERFUL EXPRESSIVE VOICE having a powerful singing voice especially suited to the expression of intense emotion, e.g. in tragic or villainous roles in opera [Late 16C. Via Late Latin *dramaticus* < Greek *drāmatikos* < *drama* (see DRAMA).]

dramatically /drə máttikli/ *adv* **1** in a way that grabs the attention and causes an excited, shocked, or startled reaction **2** to a very noticeable degree and often with surprising suddenness ○ *Things have improved dramatically since your last visit.*

dramatic irony *n* a situation, or the irony arising from a situation, in which the audience has a fuller knowledge of what is happening in a drama than a character does

dramatic monologue *n* a poem or other literary work consisting of words supposedly spoken by a character, often in a specific situation, either directly to the reader or to a listener

dramatics /drə máttiks/ *n* the performance and production of plays for the theatre, especially in a non-professional context (+ *singular or plural verb*) ■ *npl* theatrical and exaggerated behaviour (+ *plural verb*) ○ *Spare us the dramatics, for goodness sake, and tell us what happened!*

dramatise *vt* = **dramatize**

dramatis personae /draámətiss pər sṓ nī/ *n* a list of the names of the characters that appear in a play, usually printed at the beginning of the text of a play or, sometimes, in a theatre programme ■ *npl* the characters who appear in a drama or the people involved in a situation (*formal*) [< Latin, 'persons of the drama']

dramatist /drámmətist/ *n* a writer of plays for the stage, television, or radio

dramatize /drámmə tīz/ (**-tizes, -tizing, -tized**), **dramatise** (**-tises, -tising, -tised**) *v* **1** *vt* to turn a literary work or a real event into a drama for presentation on the stage, television, or radio **2** *vti* to make something more dramatic, especially to exaggerate the importance or seriousness of a situation in an attention-seeking and theatrical way —**dramatizable** *adj* —**dramatization** /drámmə tī záysh'n/ *n* —**dramatizer** *n*

dramaturge /drámmə turj/ *n* **1** **dramaturge, dramaturgist** /- turjist/ a playwright, particularly one who works with a specific theatre or company **2** **dramaturge, dramaturg** a member of the staff of a theatre with mainly literary responsibilities such as choosing the plays for performance, editing and adapting texts where necessary, and writing programme notes [Mid-19C. Via French < Greek *dramatourgos* 'worker in drama' < *drama* (see DRAMA).]

dramaturgy /drámmə turji/ *n* the art of the theatre, especially with regard to the techniques involved in writing plays —**dramaturgic** /drámmə túrjik/ *adj* —**dramaturgical** *adj* —**dramaturgically** *adv*

Drammen /drámmən/ port in S Norway. Population: 53,680 (1998).

drank past tense of **drink**

drape /drayp/ *v* (**drapes, draping, draped**) **1** *vt* PLACE FABRIC OVER to hang a piece of fabric over something so that it falls in folds around it or covers it ○ *draped a scarf over her shoulders* **2** *vt* COVER OVER WITH FABRIC to cover something with a piece of fabric, usually so that the fabric hangs down around it in folds ○ *a chair draped in a dust sheet* **3** *vi* HANG IN FOLDS to hang or be able to hang in loose folds on or over something ○ *a heavy fabric that will drape well* **4** *vt* LAY CASUALLY to place part of the body on or over something, e.g. the back of a chair, in a relaxed and casual way ○ *She draped herself elegantly over the sofa.* ■ *n* **1** *US* HOUSEHOLD = **curtain** *n.* 1 **2** PIECE OF DRAPING FABRIC a piece of fabric used to drape over something **3** WAY FABRIC HANGS the way in which fabric hangs and forms folds, especially when made into a garment ○ *adjusting the drape of the dress* [15C. < Old French *draper* < *drap* 'cloth' < late Latin *drappus* < Celtic.]

draper /dráypər/ *n* a dealer in fabric and sewing materials (*dated*) [14C. < Old French *drapier* < *drap* (see DRAPE).]

Draper /dráypər/ city in N Utah. Population: 12,478 (1996).

drapery /dráypəri/ (*plural* **-ies**) *n* **1** CLOTH ARRANGED TO HANG IN FOLDS cloth or clothing that has been arranged to hang in elegant or decorative folds **2** PIECE OF ELEGANTLY HANGING FABRIC a piece of fabric used as a decorative cover or garment and usually hanging in loose elegant folds **3** *US* HOUSEHOLD = **curtain** *n.* 1 **4** FABRICS AND SEWING MATERIALS fabrics and sewing materials collectively, especially as goods sold in a shop ○ *the drapery department.* US term **dry goods** **5** DRAPER'S OCCUPATION the occupation of selling fabrics and sewing materials (*dated*) [14C. < Old French *draperie* < *drap* (see DRAPE).]

drastic /drástik/ *adj* **1** having a powerful effect or far-reaching consequences ○ *a crisis calling for drastic remedies* **2** very noticeable, significant, and usually worrying because of its amount or degree [Late 17C. < Greek *drastikos* 'effective, active' < *dran* 'do'.]

drastically /drástikli/ *adv* to a very great and usually very worrying degree

drat /drat/ *interj* used to express annoyance or frustration (*informal*) [Early 19C. Alteration of *od rot*, shortening of *God rot*.]

dratted /dráttid/ *adj* used to express annoyance or frustration with something or somebody (*informal*) ○ *Where is that dratted pen?*

draught /draaft/ *n* **1** CURRENT OF COLD AIR a current of uncomfortably cold air penetrating a room or other space **2** CURRENT OF AIR IN ENCLOSED SPACE a current of air, especially one that is moving through an enclosed space such as a chimney or tunnel **3** REGULATING DEVICE a valve that regulates the flow of air to or from a pipe, e.g. a chimney **4** MOUTHFUL the amount of air, liquid, or smoke taken in in a single breath or swallow **5** DOSE OF LIQUID MEDICINE a dose of medicine in liquid form (*dated*) **6** BEER IN BARRELS beer that is stored in and served from barrels or casks rather than bottles **7** QUANTITY OF FISH the amount of fish found in a net when it is hauled in **8** DRAUGHT PIECE any one of the 24 flat round pieces used in the game of draughts. US term **checker** *n.* 3 **9** DEPTH NEEDED BY SHIP the distance between the water line of a ship and the lowest part of its hull, which is the minimum depth of water it requires in order to float ■ *adj* **1** SERVED FROM BARREL stored in and served from a barrel rather than a bottle **2** PULLING HEAVY LOADS used to pull heavy loads ○ *a draught animal* [12C. < Old Norse *dráttr* < Germanic.] —**draughter** *n* ◇ **feel the draught** to be exposed to dangers or difficulties, especially through a shortage of money (*informal*) ◇ **on draught** available for serving from the barrel

draughtboard /draáft bawrd/ *n* a game board with eight rows of eight alternate black and white squares on it, used for playing draughts. US term **checkerboard**

draughts /draafts/ *n* a game played with 12 black and 12 white pieces on a chequered board. Pieces can only move diagonally, and are taken when enemy pieces jump over them. (*takes a singular verb*) US term **checkers**

draughtsman /draáftsmən/ (*plural* **-men** /-mən/) *n* **1** a man who makes detailed plans or drawings for buildings, ships, aircraft, or machines before they are built **2** a man who is skilled at drawing —**draughtsmanship** *n*

draughtswoman /draáfts wŏŏmən/ (*plural* **-en** /-wimmin/) *n* **1** a woman who makes detailed plans or drawings for buildings, ships, aircraft, or machines before they are built **2** a woman who is skilled at drawing

draughty /draáfti/ (**draughtier, draughtiest**) *adj* chilly and uncomfortable because of flowing currents of cold air —**draughtily** *adv* —**draughtiness** *n*

Drava /draávə/ river flowing through N Italy, Austria, and Slovenia, and forming part of Croatia's frontier with Hungary before joining the Danube. Length: 719 km/447 mi.

Dravidian /drə víddi ən/ *n* **1** a family of languages spoken in S India and NE Sri Lanka. Native speakers: 200 million. **2** a member of an ancient people who were the indigenous inhabitants of India and who moved southwards during the influx of Indo-European peoples from the North [Mid-19C. < Sanskrit *drāvida* 'relating to the Tamils' < *Dravida* 'Tamil'.] —**Dravidian** *adj*

draw /draw/ *v* (**draws, drawing, drew** /droo/, **drawn** /drawn/) **1** *vti* **MAKE A PICTURE** to make a line, picture, or plan on a surface using a pencil, pen, or crayon rather than paints ○ *She drew a picture of a flower.* **2** *vt* **DESCRIBE** to depict or describe something in words ○ *He drew a vivid picture of life in 18th-century London.* **3** *vi* **MOVE** to move in a particular direction, often alongside, towards, or away from something else, and with a smooth steady motion ○ *Another car drew alongside ours.* **4** *vi* **APPROACH** to approach through time, or move towards a particular point or stage in something, especially its end ○ *The meeting was drawing to a close.* **5** *vt* **PULL TOWARDS OR AWAY** to pull something or lead or pull somebody in a particular direction, especially towards or away from something ○ *She drew him towards the door.* **6** *vt* **PULL A VEHICLE** to pull a vehicle along ○ *a carriage drawn by six white horses* **7** *vt* **OPEN OR CLOSE A CURTAIN** to pull a curtain or blind across a window so that it covers or uncovers it **8** *vt* **PULL ON A STRING** to pull on a string, rope, or cord, usually in order to tighten it around something **9** *vt* **PULL BACK THE STRING OF A BOW** to pull back the string of a bow prior to shooting an arrow **10** *vt* **TAKE OUT** to take or pull an object out of something in which it has been enclosed or embedded ○ *He drew his hand from his pocket.* **11** *vti* **PULL WEAPON FROM SHEATH** to pull a weapon from a holster or sheath in order to use it **12** *vt* **REMOVE LIQUID** to remove liquid from a large container such as a barrel by means of a tap **13** *vt* **DRAIN A WOUND** to drain a liquid such as blood, pus, or water from a wound or incision **14** *vt* **HAUL UP WATER** to haul up water from a well or other source using a bucket on a rope **15** *vt* **ELICIT A RESPONSE** to cause somebody or something to make a particular type of response or sound ○ *The speech had drawn hoots of derision from the crowd.* **16** *vt* **OBTAIN FROM SOURCE** to obtain a physical or a moral resource from a particular place or thing ○ *They drew courage from our example.* **17** *vt* **OBTAIN INFORMATION FROM** to obtain information, a secret, or an opinion from somebody by questioning or persuasion (*often passive*) ○ *She refused to be drawn on the subject.* **18** *vt* **CAUSE TO BE DIRECTED TOWARDS** to cause somebody's attention, eye, or interest to be directed towards somebody or something **19** *vt* **ATTRACT PEOPLE** to attract somebody or arouse people's interest or curiosity so that they come to see something or somebody ○ *The performance had drawn a huge crowd of onlookers.* **20** *vt* **SUCK IN** to suck something in, especially air into the lungs ○ *I drew a long breath.* **21** *vi* **ALLOW AIR THROUGH** to allow a current of air to flow through, removing smoke or gases **22** *vt* **WITHDRAW MONEY** to take money out of a bank or savings account or a similar source ○ *You can draw up to £200 a day with this card.* **23** *vt* **RECEIVE MONEY** to receive money regularly from a particular source **24** *vt* **WRITE A CHEQUE** to write a cheque, bill of exchange, or promissory note on an account so that somebody can receive money from that account **25** *vt* **WRITE OUT A LEGAL DOCUMENT** to compose or write out a legal document in the proper form **26** *vt* **ARRIVE AT A CONCLUSION** to arrive at a particular conclusion or inference by examining the evidence for something ○ *You'll have to draw your own conclusions.* **27** *vt* **FORMULATE** to formulate or state a distinction, comparison, or parallel between two or more different things ○ *There are certain parallels that may be drawn between the two cases.* **28** *vt* **CHOOSE AT RANDOM** to choose or be given something at random, usually in order to ensure that all participants are treated fairly ○ *They drew lots to see who would have to go.* **29** *vt* **TAKE A CARD** to take a card from a stack, the pack, or the dealer during a card game **30** *vt* **MAKE PLAYERS PLAY PARTICULAR SUIT** to make the other players in a card game play the cards they have in a particular suit by repeatedly leading that suit ○ *drew all the trumps early in the hand* **31** *vti* **FINISH EQUAL** to finish a game with the scores for the opposing sides level or with neither side having won ○ *Finland and Holland drew 1–1 in the semifinal.* **32** *vt* **NEED PARTICULAR DEPTH OF WATER** to need a particular depth of water in which to float **33** *vti* **STEEP IN BOILING WATER** to steep tea leaves, or allow tea leaves to steep, in boiling water ○ *Let the tea draw for five minutes.* **34** *vt* **MAKE WIRE** to make wire by pulling a length of metal through a conical hole **35** *vt* **REMOVE INNARDS FROM CARCASS** to remove the innards from a carcass before cooking it **36** *vt* **DISEMBOWEL** to disembowel a hanged person, especially in former times **37** *vt* **GIVE BACKSPIN TO A BALL** to give a backward spin to a ball when making a stroke, especially in billiards **38** *vt* **MAKE THE BALL CURVE** to hit a golf ball so that it curves in flight following the direction of the golfer's swing (to the left for a right-handed player) instead of travelling straight **39** *vt* **SEND BOWL IN A CURVE** in bowling, to make the bowl travel along a curved path to the point aimed at ■ *n* **1 ACT OF DRAWING** the act of pulling or sucking on something or otherwise drawing something **2 LOTTERY** a lottery, raffle, or other competition where the winner is decided by selecting a ticket at random **3 CHOOSING LOTTERY WINNER** the choosing of a winner in a lottery, raffle, or other competition by selecting a ticket at random ○ *The draw will be held next Wednesday.* **4 SELECTION OF OPPONENTS** the act of selecting at random which contestants are to play each other in a sporting contest, or the resulting list of matches to be played ○ *the draw for the third round of the competition* **5 SOMETHING CHOSEN AT RANDOM** something chosen at random, e.g. a ticket in a lottery or a card or cards taken from a stack or the dealer **6 ATTRACTION** something or somebody that interests a lot of people and attracts them as spectators, visitors, or customers ○ *The rock band will be a huge draw for the local fair.* **7 CONTEST THAT NEITHER SIDE WINS** a contest that ends with both sides having the same score or with neither side having won **8 DRAWING A GUN** the action of pulling a gun from its holster in order to fire it, especially in a gunfight **9 SECOND OR FURTHER DEAL** in draw poker, the deal made to improve the players' hands after they have discarded [Old English *dragan* < Germanic, 'carry'] —**drawable** *adj*

SYNONYMS See *pull*.

draw back *vi* to decide not to continue with some contemplated, planned, or agreed action ○ *They drew back from the deal at the last moment.*
draw in *v* **1** *vi* **BEGIN EARLIER** to begin earlier, causing it to become darker sooner (*refers to nights or evenings in autumn*) **2** *vi* **BECOME SHORTER** to become shorter, so that it gets dark sooner (*refers to days in autumn*) **3** *vt* **INVOLVE** to get somebody involved in something unwillingly (*often passive*) ○ *I got drawn in before I realized what the argument was really about.*
draw off *vt* to remove a small amount of liquid from a larger amount by means of a tube or pipe
draw on *v* **1** *vt* **USE** to make use of a resource of some kind for personal benefit ○ *The novel draws on her experiences in Alaska.* **2** *vi* **ENTER A LATER STAGE** to enter a later stage or move towards its end ○ *As the day drew on I grew worried that they would not come.* **3** *vt* **TAKE IN SMOKE** to inhale the smoke from a cigarette or pipe ○ *He drew on his pipe.*
draw out *v* **1** *vt* **PROLONG** to make something continue longer than is usual, necessary, or desirable ○ *I drew the conversation out as long as I could.* **2** *vi* **GROW LONGER** to have more hours of daylight (*refers to days*) **3** *vt* **GET SOMEBODY TO TALK** to encourage a shy, hostile, or reserved person to talk at length or in detail, or to become more forthcoming in a social or legal situation ○ *The prosecutor took great pains to draw the hostile witness out during cross-examination.*
draw up *v* **1** *vt* **WRITE SOMETHING OUT** to prepare or write out a plan, list, or other document ○ *The lawyers are drawing up the terms of the contract as we speak.* **2** *vti* **COME TO A STOP** to arrive at a particular point or place in a vehicle or on a horse and stop, or bring a vehicle or horse to a halt ○ *A car drew up outside.* **3** *vt* **BRING SOMETHING NEARER** to place a chair or seat near something or somebody and sit down on it **4** *vr* **STRAIGHTEN** to straighten the body in order to reach full height and look as imposing or dignified as possible ○ *She drew herself up to her full height, then spoke.*

drawback /dráw bak/ *n* something that causes problems or is a disadvantage or hindrance ○ *The only drawback is the size of the machine.*

drawbar /dráw baar/ *n* a strong metal bar fitted across the back of a tractor, locomotive, or other vehicle, with a coupling on it to which machinery or a trailer can be hitched

drawbridge /dráw brij/ *n* a bridge that is hinged at one end or in the middle and can be lifted up to cut off access to a place or allow something to pass beneath it

drawdown /dráw down/ *n* a lowering of the level of the water in a reservoir

drawee /draw ée/ *n* the person or organization from whose account money is taken when a cheque or other order for payment is drawn

drawer /drawr/ *n* **1 PLACE TO STORE THINGS** a storage compartment in a piece of furniture such as a desk, chest, or table that slides in and out and is usually shaped like a shallow rectangular box **2 SOMEBODY WHO WRITES A CHEQUE** a person who draws a cheque or money order **3 SOMEBODY OR SOMETHING THAT DRAWS** somebody or something that draws, especially somebody who draws pictures or plans

drawers /drawrz/ *npl* large old-fashioned underpants with short legs, worn by men or women

drawgate *n* a barrier that can be raised or lowered to control the flow of water in a sluice

draw gear *n* the couplings and other equipment used to join railway carriages and trucks together

drawing /dráwing/ *n* **1** a picture of something made with a pencil, pen, or crayon, usually consisting of lines, often with shading, but generally without colour **2** the art, activity, or practice of making pictures using a pencil, crayon, or pen ○ *I never was very good at drawing.*

drawing board *n* a large flat board used for drawing and design work, usually attached to a frame with legs and adjustable to different heights and angles ◇ **back to the drawing board** back to the beginning or the planning stage of a failed operation or project, ready to start all over again (*informal*) ○ *Since all else has failed, we're now back to the drawing board.*

drawing pin *n* a short pin with a wide round top used for pinning paper or cardboard to a noticeboard, wall, or other surface. US term **thumbtack** *n.*

drawing room *n* a large formal room in a house, in which guests are entertained [Mid-17C. Shortening of *withdrawing-room*.]

drawknife /dráw nīf/ (*plural* **-knives** /-nīvz/) *n* a tool for shaving the surface of wood, consisting of a narrow rectangular blade with a handle at either end fixed at right angles to it

drawl /drawl/ *vti* to draw out the vowel sounds and pronounce words with a slow inflection when speaking ■ *n* a way of speaking in which the speaker draws out the vowel sounds and pronounces words slowly [Late 16C. Probably < Middle Dutch *dralen* 'linger, delay' < *dragan* 'draw'.] —**drawler** *n* —**drawlingly** *adv* —**drawly** *adj*

drawn[1] /drawn/ *adj* appearing tired and careworn, usually as a result of anxiety, grief, or illness ○ *He looked pale and drawn.*

drawn[2] /drawn/ past tense of **draw**

drawn-out *adj* continuing longer than is intended or desired

drawn-thread work, drawn work *n* embroidery in which some threads are pulled from the fabric and stitches are worked on the remaining threads to produce decorated open areas

drawplate /dráw playt/ *n* a plate pierced by conical holes through which metal is drawn in wire-making

draw poker *n* a form of poker in which each player is dealt five cards face down and after the first round of betting can draw replacements for any discards

drawshave /dráw shayv/ *n* WOODWORK = **drawknife**

draw shot *n* in cue games, a shot in which the cue ball is hit below centre so that the backspin makes it bounce back when it hits another ball

drawstring /dráw string/ *n* a cord threaded through a hem, piping, or eyelets around the opening in a bag or a garment so that it can be drawn tight and the opening closed

drawtube /dráw tyoob/ *n* a tube that slides inside another tube, e.g. one of the extending tubes in a telescope

dray /dray/ *n* a large low horsedrawn cart with no fixed sides, designed for heavy loads, or a similar motorized vehicle, used especially by breweries [14C. < Old English *dragan* 'draw'.]

drayhorse /dráy hawrss/ *n* a large horse used for pulling a dray

Drayton /dráyt'n/, **Michael** (1563–1631) English poet

dread /dred/ *vti* **1 FEEL EXTREMELY FRIGHTENED** to feel extremely frightened or worried about something that may happen in the future **2 BE RELUCTANT** to be reluctant or frightened to do something because it is unpleasant, upsetting, or annoying ■ *n* **1 TERROR** a feeling of great fear or terror, especially at the thought of experiencing or encountering something unpleasant **2 SOURCE OF DREAD** something that is dreaded ■ *adj* (*literary*) **1 FEARED** causing fear and extreme anxiety ○ *The dread day arrived.* **2 AWE-INSPIRING** inspiring fear and respect or awe in equal measure [12C. Shortened < Old English *adrǣdan, ondrǣdan* 'counsel against' < *rǣdan* (see REDE).]

dread disease *n* a serious and potentially fatal disease ○ *dread disease insurance*

dreaded /dréddid/ *adj* inspiring great fear (*sometimes used humorously*)

dreadful /dréddf'l/ *adj* 1 EXTREMELY BAD extremely unpleasant, harmful, or serious in its effects ○ *a dreadful mistake* 2 EXTREME extreme in character or degree ○ *a dreadful shame* 3 AWE-INSPIRING inspiring awe (*literary*) —**dreadfulness** *n*

dreadfully /dréddf'li/ *adv* 1 to a very great extent 2 in a very unsatisfactory or unpleasant way ○ *He behaved dreadfully.*

dreadlocks /dréd loks/ *npl* long strands of hair that have been twisted closely from the scalp down to the tips in a style made popular by Rastafarians [Mid-20C. Because of a supposed fear of the power of faithful Rastafarians.]

dreadnought /dréd nawt/, **dreadnaught** *n* a heavily armed battleship whose main guns are all of the same calibre [Early 20C. After the British battleship *Dreadnought*.]

dreads /dredz/ *npl* HAIR = **dreadlocks** [Late 20C. Contraction.]

dream /dreem/ *n* 1 IMAGININGS WHILE ASLEEP a sequence of images that appear involuntarily to the mind of somebody who is sleeping, often a mixture of real and imaginary characters, places, and events 2 WAKING IMAGININGS a series of images, usually pleasant ones, that pass through the mind of somebody who is awake 3 SOMETHING HOPED FOR something that somebody hopes, longs, or is ambitious for, usually something difficult to attain or far removed from present circumstances 4 IDLE HOPE an idea or hope that is impractical or unlikely ever to be realized 5 VAGUE STATE a state of inattention owing to preoccupation with thoughts or fantasies 6 SOMETHING BEAUTIFUL somebody or something that seems particularly good-looking or wonderful ■ *v* (**dreams, dreaming, dreamt** /dremt/ *or* **dreamed, dreamt** *or* **dreamed**) 1 *vti* HAVE A DREAM WHILE SLEEPING to experience vivid mental images while sleeping 2 *vi* DAYDREAM to let the mind dwell on pleasant scenes and images while awake, often resulting in inattention 3 *vi* WISH to want something very much and imagine having or doing it, though it may be unlikely ○ *For years I'd dreamed of living abroad.* 4 *vi* CONSIDER to think of or consider doing something regarded as wrong or inappropriate ○ *How could you even dream of doing such a thing?* ■ *adj* 1 OCCURRING IN A DREAM occurring in or reminiscent of a dream ○ *a dream sequence* 2 IDEAL perfect and wonderful in every way [13C. < ?] —**dreamful** *adj*

dream up *vt* to devise or invent something, especially a complicated, ingenious, or ridiculous plan

dreamboat /dreém bōt/ *n* somebody considered to be very good-looking (*informal*)

dreamer /dreémər/ *n* 1 somebody who dreams 2 somebody who is absorbed by fantasies or unrealistic plans

dreamland /dreém land/ *n* 1 an imaginary, very pleasant or perfect sphere of existence that exists only in dreams 2 a state of sleep or unconsciousness (*informal*)

dreamless /dreémləss/ *adj* deep, peaceful, and undisturbed by dreams ○ *a dreamless sleep* —**dreamlessly** *adv* —**dreamlessness** *n*

dreamlike /dreém līk/ *adj* resembling a dream or the images in a dream, especially in seeming unreal and strange

dreamscape /dreém skayp/ *n* a scene, setting, or picture that has the unreal or strange qualities usually associated with images in dreams

dreamt past tense, past participle of **dream**

dream team *n* the best possible combination of people to perform a task (*informal*)

dream ticket *n* candidates standing as a team for associated political offices who seem to have between them all the qualities needed for electoral success (*informal*)

Dreamtime /dreém tīm/ *n* in the mythology of Australian Aboriginals, the period during which the earth was formed, the landscape shaped, and living things created

dream world *n* a world that bears little resemblance to reality and exists only in the mind

dreamy /dreémi/ (**dreamier, dreamiest**) *adj* 1 VAGUE caused by dreaming or by thinking about something very pleasant and absorbing 2 GIVEN TO DAYDREAMING having a tendency to spend time daydreaming or lost in thought 3 UNREAL strange, vague, or ethereal, like an image in a dream 4 GORGEOUS extremely good-looking or desirable (*informal*) —**dreamily** *adv* —**dreaminess** *n*

drear /dreer/ *adj* dark, foreboding, and gloomy (*literary*) ○ *It was a cold, drear day.* [Mid-16C. Back formation < DREARY.]

dreary /dreéri/ (**drearier, dreariest**) *adj* gloomy, unexciting, and certain to have a wearying and depressing influence ○ *the dreary routine of prison life* [Old English *drēorig* 'dripping with blood' < Germanic] —**drearily** *adv* —**dreariness** *n*

dreck /drek/ *n US* worthless trashy stuff, especially low-quality merchandise [Early 20C. < Yiddish *drek* 'filth, dung' < Middle High German *drec*.] —**drecky** *adj*

dredge[1] /drej/ *n* 1 MACHINE FOR DIGGING UNDERWATER a machine equipped with a continuous revolving chain of buckets, a scoop, or a suction device for digging out and removing material from under water 2 SHIPPING = **dredger**[1] *n.* 1 3 SHELLFISH NET a net on a frame dragged along the bottom of the sea or a river to gather shellfish ■ *v* 1 *vt* DIG SOMETHING UP WITH A DREDGE to remove or recover material from under water by means of a dredge 2 *vti* CLEAR A CHANNEL to clear, deepen, or widen a waterway, especially one intended for shipping, using a dredge 3 *vti* SEARCH WITH A DREDGE to search something, or search for something, using a dredge or a similar device [Early 16C. < ?]

dredge up *vt* to bring something to light from an obscure source, e.g. to recall something bad that happened long ago or unearth some scandalous information

dredge[2] /drej/ (**dredges, dredging, dredged**) *vt* to sprinkle or cover food with a coating of icing sugar, flour, or sugar [Late 16C. Via Old French *dragie* 'sugarplum, sugar almond' < Latin *tragemata* < Greek *tragēmata* 'spices, sweets'.]

dredger[1] /dréjjər/ *n* 1 a boat or barge with a dredge on it, used mainly for clearing or deepening waterways 2 = **dredge**[1] *n.* 1

dredger[2] /dréjjər/ *n* a container with small holes in the top used for sprinkling icing sugar, flour, or sugar onto food

dree /dree/ (**drees, dreeing, dreed**) *vt Scotland* to bear something unpleasant [Old English *drēogan* 'work, suffer' < Germanic] ◇ **dree your (own) weird** *Scotland* to live your own life, accepting or making your own destiny

dreg /dreg/ *n* a small amount, especially a small remainder of something ○ *not a dreg of sympathy for them* [14C. Probably < Old Norse *dregg* 'sediment'.]

D region *n* 1 the lowest part of the ionosphere above the Earth's surface 2 a short sequence of various amino acids in an immunoglobulin that contributes to antibody diversity

dregs /dregz/ *npl* 1 GRITTY PARTICLES IN LIQUID small solid particles found in liquids such as coffee or wine that sink to the bottom of a container and are most in evidence when the container is nearly empty 2 LEAST VALUABLE PART the least valuable or most unpleasant part of something, especially a group of people ○ *the dregs of society* 3 LAST REMAINING PART the last remaining, and often least attractive part of something (*literary*) ○ *sat through the dregs of a long boring evening*

dreich /dreekh/ *adj Scotland* describes weather that is dull and depressing [Old English *gedrēog* 'patient, serious' < Germanic]

dreidel /dráyd'l/, **dreidl** *n* a toy that looks like a spinning top, used to play games during Hanukkah [Mid-20C. < Yiddish *dreydl* < Middle High German *dræhen* 'turn'.]

Dreiser /drīssər, drīzər/, **Theodore** (1871–1945) US novelist and journalist

drench /drench/ *vt* 1 SOAK to make somebody or something completely wet ○ *I got absolutely drenched going out in the storm.* 2 GIVE AN ANIMAL LIQUID MEDICINE to give an animal a large dose of medicine in liquid form by mouth ■ *n* DOSE OF ANIMAL MEDICINE a large oral dose of medicine given to an animal in liquid form [Old English *drencan* 'give to drink' < Germanic] —**drencher** *n* —**drenching** *adj, n*

Dresden /drézdən/ capital of the state of Saxony, east-central Germany. Population: 474,443 (1997).

Dresden china *n* fine and delicate porcelain as made in Meissen near Dresden in Germany since the early 18th century. US term **Meissen**[1]

dress /dress/ *v* 1 *vti* PUT CLOTHES ON to put clothes on somebody 2 *vi* WEAR PARTICULAR CLOTHING to wear clothes of a particular type, or wear them in a particular way ○ *She usually dresses in black.* 3 *vi* PUT ON APPROPRIATE CLOTHES to put on clothes appropriate to a particular occasion, especially formal clothes ○ *We need to dress for the theatre.* 4 *vt* DECORATE to make a place or thing look festive by putting special decorations on it ○ *They dressed the big house for the holidays.* 5 *vt* ARRANGE GOODS IN A WINDOW DISPLAY to arrange goods in a shop window so that they look attractive ○ *windows that were dressed for spring* 6 *vt* COVER A WOUND to put a bandage or other protective covering on a wound 7 *vt* PUT SAUCE ON SALAD to put mayonnaise, vinaigrette, or a similar type of sauce on a salad 8 *vt* CLEAN FISH AND GAME to clean and prepare fish, poultry, or meat for cooking or selling 9 *vt* ARRANGE HAIR to arrange hair, e.g. by combing, clipping, or oiling it 10 *vti* COME INTO ALIGNMENT to come, or bring troops, into a correct alignment with one another for a parade formation 11 *vt* SPREAD FERTILIZER ON SOIL to spread manure or fertilizer over the surface of an area of land 12 *vt* FINISH A MATERIAL to apply a finishing process to a material such as stone or timber, usually in order to give it a smooth and good-looking surface ■ *n* 1 WOMAN'S ONE-PIECE GARMENT a one-piece garment for women and girls combining a bodice, with or without sleeves, and a skirt, and covering most of the body 2 TYPE OF CLOTHES clothes of a particular type or style 3 CLOTHES clothes and clothing in general, considered, e.g. as an item in a budget or from the point of view of somebody's taste in them ○ *He has no interest in matters of dress.* 4 CLOTHING FOR PARTICULAR OCCASION the clothing required for a particular occasion 5 OUTWARD APPEARANCE the outward appearance or covering of a thing, especially a living thing, or the way in which something is presented (*literary*) 6 DRESS REHEARSAL a dress rehearsal (*informal*) ■ *adj* 1 FORMAL worn on formal occasions ○ *dress uniform* 2 REQUIRING FORMAL ATTIRE requiring formal clothes to be worn ○ *a dress banquet* [14C. Via Old French *dresser* 'arrange, prepare' < Vulgar Latin *directiare* < Latin *directus* 'straight' (see DIRECT).] ◇ **dressed to kill** dressed in very glamorous clothes, especially when intending to impress somebody (*informal*)

dress down *v* 1 *vi* to dress in a deliberately understated or casual way for an occasion (*informal*) 2 *vt* to scold somebody severely

dress up *v* 1 *vi* DRESS FORMALLY to put on formal or especially elegant clothes, usually for a special occasion such as a party 2 *vi* PUT ON COSTUMES to put on a special costume or different clothes from those normally worn so as to look like or pretend to be somebody else 3 *vt* DISGUISE to disguise something unpleasant and try to make it look more pleasant

dressage /dréssaazh/ *n* 1 the training of a horse to carry out a series of precise controlled movements in response to minimal signals from its rider 2 a competitive event in which horse and rider are judged on the elegance, precision, and discipline of the horse's movements [Mid-20C. < French, 'training' < *dresser* (see DRESS).]

dress circle *n* a separate raised section of the auditorium in a theatre, concert hall, or opera house, usually the first seating gallery above ground level

dress coat *n* a coat, forming part of a man's full evening dress, that is usually black with a cutaway skirt and tails

dress code *n* a set of requirements as to how people should dress when attending a function or visiting a place

dress-down day *n* a day, typically a Friday, or days during the summer months, on which office workers wear casual clothing to work

dresser[1] /dréssər/ *n* 1 a piece of furniture consisting of a set of shelves on top of a chest containing cupboards and drawers, often used for storing crockery and cutlery in traditional kitchens ○ *a Welsh dresser* 2 *US* a chest of drawers used in a bedroom for storing clothes sometimes with a mirror on top [Early 15C. < Old French *dresseur* < *dresser* (see DRESS).]

dresser[2] /dréssər/ *n* 1 SOMEBODY WHO DRESSES IN PARTICULAR WAY somebody who wears clothes in a specific way 2 ACTOR'S ASSISTANT a stage employee who helps an actor to put on or change a costume 3 PERSONAL GROOMING ASSISTANT somebody whose job it is to ensure that somebody else's wardrobe is in order 4 SURGEON'S ASSISTANT an assistant of a surgeon during operations

dress form *n* an adjustable tailor's dummy

dressing /dréssing/ *n* 1 WOUND COVERING a bandage, plaster, or other sterile covering that is put on a wound to protect it from infection or further damage 2 SALAD SAUCE a sauce used on salads, usually with an oil and vinegar or mayonnaise base **3** *US* **STUFFING** stuffing for poultry or meat **4 FERTILIZER** natural or artificial fertilizer for spreading on the soil **5 STIFFENING FOR FABRIC** size used to stiffen fabrics

dressing-down *n* a scolding or severe reprimand, often in public

dressing gown *n* a coat made of soft light material that is worn over nightclothes, before or after taking a bath, or in the early stages of getting formally or smartly dressed

dressing room *n* **1** a room in a theatre where actors can prepare for a performance by putting on their make-up and costumes **2** a small room or alcove in a house, hotel suite, or other place that people can use when putting on or changing their clothes

dressing station *n* a first-aid station near a combat area

dressing table *n* a low table with drawers and a mirror on top, usually placed in a bedroom so that a woman can sit at it when putting on her make-up

dressmaker /dréss maykər/ *n* a maker of women's clothes, especially professionally —**dressmaking** *n*

dress parade *n* a military parade in which the soldiers wear formal dress uniform

dress rehearsal *n* **1** the final rehearsal of a play, in full costume and with lights, music, and effects, before it is given its first public performance **2** a full-scale practice before any important event

dress sense *n* the ability to choose clothes well and coordinate colours and styles effectively

dress shield *n* a small fabric pad worn around the armpits of a piece of clothing to prevent sweat from showing or staining it

dress shirt *n* a man's shirt worn with formal evening wear, usually white and with either a stiff collar or a ruffle down the front

dress suit *n* a man's suit worn as part of formal evening wear, especially with a tail coat

dress uniform *n* a ceremonial uniform worn by members of the armed forces for formal occasions

dressy /dréssi/ (**-ier, -iest**) *adj* **1 ELEGANT** stylish and elegant **2 AT WHICH GUESTS DRESS FORMALLY** at which stylish and elegant clothes are worn ○ *a very dressy buffet luncheon* **3 OVERDRESSED** dressed in an inappropriately elaborate or showy way —**dressily** *adv* —**dressiness** *n*

drew past tense of **draw**

Drewe /droo/, **Robert Duncan** (*b.* 1943) Australian writer

drey /dray/ *n* a squirrel's nest [Early 17C. < ?]

Dreyer /dráy ər/, **Carl Theodor** (1889–1968) Danish film director and screenwriter

Dreyfus /dráyfəss/, **Alfred** (1859–1935) French soldier

drib /drib/ *n* a very small amount, usually a tiny drop of liquid or a fragment of material ○ *just a drib of paint on the porch floor* [Early 18C. < ?] ◇ **in dribs and drabs** in very small amounts or stages, and usually in a rather haphazard way ○ *Wedding presents are beginning to arrive in dribs and drabs.*

dribble /drĭbb'l/ *v* (**-bles, -bling, -bled**) **1** *vi* **PRODUCE SALIVA** to let saliva spill out of the mouth **2** *vti* **SPILL DROPS** to flow, or allow a liquid to flow or spill out, in drops or a small stream **3** *vti* **MOVE BALL** to move a ball along using small repeated movements of the foot, the hand, or a stick **4** *vti* **BOUNCE A BALL ON COURT** in basketball, to propel the ball in any direction on the court by bouncing it with the hands ■ *n* **1 TINY AMOUNT OF LIQUID** a small amount of liquid that is falling or has fallen in drops or a thin stream **2 MOVEMENT WHILE DRIBBLING BALL** a movement or run made while dribbling a ball, especially in basketball or football ○ *a hard, fast dribble to centre court* [Mid-16C. < *drib*, alteration of DRIP.] —**dribbler** *n* —**dribbly** *adj*

driblet /drĭbblət/, **dribblet** *n* a tiny amount of a liquid [Late 16C. < *drib*, alteration of DRIP.]

drier /drī́ə/ comparative of **dry** ■ *n* = **dryer**

driest /drī́ist/ superlative of **dry**

drift /drift/ *v* **1** *vi* **BE CARRIED ALONG** to be, or allow something to be, carried along by the flow of water or air **2** *vi* **MOVE AIMLESSLY** to move in a slow, smooth, gentle, and unforced way, usually without any direction or purpose ○ *The crowd gradually drifted away.* **3** *vi* **WANDER AIMLESSLY** to go from one place to another, never staying anywhere for very long and seemingly with little purpose **4** *vi* **WANDER FROM A SET COURSE OR POSITION** to deviate from a set course or move gradually away from a fixed position **5** *vi* **CHANGE GRADUALLY** to change or develop gradually, or move slowly from one point or position to another ○ *Prices have drifted downwards in recent weeks.* **6** *vti* **FORM HEAPS** to build up and form heaps as a result of the action of the wind or water currents, or cause something such as snow, sand, or leaves to form heaps ■ *n* **1 PILED-UP DEPOSITS** a heap, pile, or bank of something such as snow, sand, or leaves created by the action of the wind or water currents **2 DRIFTING MOVEMENT** a slow gentle movement in which something is, or seems to be, carried along on a current of air or water **3 MATERIAL CARRIED ALONG** an amount of something carried along by the flow of air or water ○ *drifts of smoke coming from the chimneys* **4 MOVEMENT OF PEOPLE** a gradual movement over a period of time of groups of people or animals towards or away from a place ○ *the drift of young people away from rural areas* **5 GRADUAL CHANGE** a broad and gradual change or development, e.g. in people's opinions or behaviour ○ *a drift back to larger cars* ○ *a downward drift in prices* **6 GENERAL MEANING** the general meaning of an argument, opinion, or statement ○ *She used a lot of technical jargon but I managed to get the drift of her argument.* **7 INACTIVITY** a state of inactivity or indecision in which a person or group is carried along by events **8 DEVIATION** the distance or extent to which a ship or aircraft deviates from its set course due to the action of wind or water currents **9 DEPOSIT OF GRAVEL** a loose deposit of sand, gravel, or rock left by a glacier or ice sheet **10 CURRENT** the motion of a river or broad ocean current **11 HORIZONTAL MINESHAFT** a horizontal or virtually horizontal mineshaft that follows a vein of ore **12 CONNECTING PASSAGE IN MINE** a small passage in a mine connecting two main shafts or tunnels **13 UNCONTROLLED CHANGE IN A SETTING** a slow uncontrolled change in a previously adjusted setting, e.g. in the frequency to which an electronic device has been set **14 TAPERING STEEL TOOL** a tapering steel tool used to enlarge or align holes in pieces of metal before they are bolted or riveted **15 CONTROLLED SKID** a controlled slide used by racing drivers as a method of cornering at high speed **16** *S Africa* **FORD** a shallow part of a river, or a ford across it [14C. < Old Norse *drift* 'snowdrift' < Germanic.] —**drifty** *adj*

driftage /drĭfftij/ *n* **1** material that has drifted along on, and been deposited by, air or water currents **2** the distance by which a ship or aircraft has deviated from its set course owing to winds or currents

drifter /drĭftər/ *n* **1** a habitual wanderer, apparently without aim **2** a fishing vessel that fishes with a drift net

drift ice *n* large areas of ice that float in the open sea

drift net *n* a large fishing net supported by floats that is allowed to drift along with the current or is attached to a vessel

driftwood /drĭft wŏŏd/ *n* broken pieces of wood that are found washed up on a beach or riverbank or floating in the sea or a river

drill[1] /dril/ *n* **1 PART OF TOOL THAT BORES HOLES** a long pointed piece of metal that is held in a machine and rotated at high speed to bore holes in hard substances such as wood, metal, masonry, or rock **2 BORING TOOL WITH DRILL** a tool or machine that holds, drives, and bores holes with a drill **3 TRAINING BY REPETITION** a type of military training, particularly in marching manoeuvres and weapons handling, that involves the constant repetition of a set pattern of movements or tasks **4 REPEATED EXERCISE** a sequence of tasks, exercises, or words repeated over and over until they can be performed faultlessly, as used in teaching military skills, languages, or basic arithmetic **5 SAFETY ROUTINE** a sequence of actions practised repeatedly so that people know what to do in an emergency to ensure their safety **6 ROUTINE** a set procedure or routine for doing something (*informal*) **7 PREDATORY MOLLUSC** a marine mollusc that preys on oysters by boring into their shells. *Urosalpinx cinerea.* ■ *v* **1** *vti* **BORE WITH A DRILL** to bore a hole in something with a drill **2** *vti* **PRACTISE MARCHING** to practise marching manoeuvres repeatedly on a parade ground as a form of military training and discipline **3** *vt* **TEACH BY ROTE** to make somebody repeat a sequence of exercises or procedures over and over again in order to learn it **4** *vt* **SHOOT** to shoot somebody with bullets or shoot bullets into something (*informal*) **5** *vt* **THROW A BALL HARD** to throw or hit a ball with great force in a straight line towards somebody or something (*informal*) [Early 16C. < Middle Dutch *drillen* 'make a hole, whirl'.] —**drillable** *adj* —**driller** *n*

SYNONYMS See ***teach***.

drill[2] /dril/ *n* **1 FURROW FOR SEEDS** a shallow furrow in which seeds are sown **2 SEED-PLANTING MACHINE** a machine for planting seeds in furrows **3 PLANTED ROW OF SEEDS** a row of seeds planted along a small furrow ■ *vt* **PLANT WITH DRILL** to plant seeds with a drill [Early 18C. < ?]

drill[3] /dril/ *n* tough cotton twill. Use: working clothes, uniforms. [Mid-18C. < German *Drillich* < Latin *trilix* 'with three threads' < *licium* 'thread'.]

drill[4] /dril/ *n* a baboon with a black face and brown fur, similar to a mandrill though smaller in size. Native to: West Africa. *Papio leucophaeus.* [Mid-17C. < West African name.]

drilling platform *n* a structure used in offshore oil drilling that supports drilling equipment and is either fixed to the seabed or floats independently

drilling rig /drĭlling-/ *n* INDUST = **rig**[1] *n.* 1

drill instructor *n* *US* MIL = **drillmaster** *n.* 1

drillmaster /drĭll maastər/ *n* **1** a noncommissioned officer who trains soldiers in drill. US term **drill instructor** **2** a strict and militaristic trainer of people

drill pipe *n* INDUST = **drill string**

drill press *n* a machine consisting of a powered drill on a vertical stand that is brought down onto the work automatically or by a hand lever

drill sergeant *n* MIL = **drillmaster** *n.* 1

drillstock /drĭll stok/ *n* the part of a drilling tool or machine that holds the shank of the drill

drill string *n* a long metal pipe, progressively built up from lengths of steel tubing, that is attached above the drill when drilling for oil or gas and eventually forms the bore of the well

drily /drī́li/, **dryly** *adv* with subtle and almost imperceptible irony or humour

drink /dringk/ *vti* (**drinks, drinking, drank** /drangk/, **drunk** /drungk/) **1 SWALLOW LIQUID** to take in liquid through the mouth **2 DRINK ALCOHOL** to drink an alcoholic beverage, especially habitually ○ *Don't drink and drive.* **3 TOAST BY RAISING A GLASS** to raise a glass and then drink from it as a sign that you wish somebody or something happiness, luck, success, or good health ■ *n* **1 DRINKABLE LIQUID** liquid that can be drunk, usually in a container ○ *There isn't much food or drink in the house.* **2 AMOUNT OF LIQUID** an amount of liquid that somebody drinks ○ *Could I have a drink of water?* **3 ALCOHOLIC BEVERAGE** alcoholic drink, especially an individual serving in a glass, bottle, or can **4 EXCESSIVE CONSUMPTION OF ALCOHOL** excessive consumption of alcohol **5 BODY OF WATER** the sea or a large body of water, e.g. a lake or swimming pool (*informal*) ○ *in the drink* ■ **drinks** *npl* **INFORMAL PARTY WITH DRINKS** an informal party with alcoholic or other drinks served but not a meal [Old English *drincan* < Germanic]

drink in *vt* **1** to absorb as much liquid as is available ○ *The plants drank in the welcome rain.* **2** to absorb eagerly every aspect of something with the mind and senses ○ *She stood silently on the beach, drinking in the beauty.*

drink up *vt* **1** to drink all of something **2** to absorb a liquid completely ○ *The dry earth drank up the rain.*

drinkable /dríngkəb'l/ *adj* **1** safe for humans or animals to drink **2** pleasant or enjoyable to drink ○ *a very drinkable local fruit juice* —**drinkability** /dríngkə bĭlləti/ *n* —**drinkableness** *n*

drink-driving *n* the offence of driving a vehicle while having a higher blood-alcohol content than the law allows. US term **drunk-driving** —**drink-driver** *n*

drinker /dríngkər/ *n* **1** person who drinks a specific type of beverage (*in combination*) ○ *I'm not a coffee drinker.* **2** a person who drinks alcoholic beverages, especially to excess

drinking fountain *n* a device attached to a wall that produces a jet of water that people can drink

drinking song *n* a song, often rowdy or suggestive, sung by people drinking alcohol together

drinking-up time *n* a period allowed in a public house after official closing time, when drinks already bought may be finished

drinking water *n* water intended for people to drink, especially when free of harmful elements such as industrial waste, chemicals, or animal waste

drink problem *n* an addiction to alcoholic beverages that requires outside assistance to help control it

drinks cabinet *n* an upright piece of furniture, usually made of wood and consisting of shelves and compartments for storing alcoholic beverages

Drinkwater /dríngk wawtər/, **John** (1882–1937) British playwright, poet, and actor

drip /drip/ *v* (**drips, dripping, dripped**) **1** *vti* FALL OR LET FALL IN DROPS to fall as drops of liquid, or let liquid fall as drops ○ *The tap is dripping.* **2** *vt* LET SOMETHING OUT COPIOUSLY to let out something, particularly an emotion, in great quantity ○ *His voice positively dripped malice.* ■ *n* **1** SMALL AMOUNT OF LIQUID a drop of liquid or moisture ○ *a bucket to catch the drips* **2** DRIPPING OF LIQUID an instance or the process of a liquid falling in drops ○ *Our ceiling has developed a drip.* **3** SOUND OF FALLING DROPS the sound of drops of liquid falling onto something ○ *the steady drip of a leaking tap* **4** MEDICAL PROCEDURE FOR INJECTING LIQUID a medical procedure whereby considerable quantities of a therapeutic fluid, e.g. blood, plasma, saline, or glucose, are injected directly into somebody's vein at an adjustable rate. US term **drip feed** *n.* 1 **5** FLUID USED IN A DRIP the therapeutic fluid used in a drip ○ *Add 2 cc of morphine to the drip.* US term **drip feed** *n.* 2 **6** EQUIPMENT USED TO ADMINISTER A DRIP the equipment used to administer a drip (*informal*) US term **drip feed** *n.* 3 **7** SOCIALLY INEPT PERSON somebody regarded by others as socially inept, inadequate, or uninteresting (*slang insult*) **8** PROTECTIVE GROOVE a protective groove cut in a sill or other overhang of a wall or building to cause water to drip freely [Old English *dryppan* < Indo-European, 'to drop']

drip with *vt* **1** HAVE DROPS FALLING CONTINUOUSLY to have liquid falling in a continuous stream of drops ○ *dripping with sweat* **2** HAVE TOO MUCH OF to have too much of something, especially some kind of adornment, usually in a way that is considered to be bad taste **3** GIVE VENT TO EMOTION to give continuous expression to an emotion, especially a negative one such as spite, malice, or sarcasm ○ *Her voice dripped with sarcasm.*

drip-dry *adj* not wrinkling or creasing as it dries, and thus not needing ironing ○ *a drip-dry shirt* ■ *vti* (**drip-dries, drip-drying, drip-dried**) to dry without creases when hung up wet, or cause something to dry in this way

drip feed *n* **1** = **drip** *n.* 4 **2** = **drip** *n.* 5 **3** = **drip** *n.* 6 (*informal*)

drip-feed /dríp feed/ (**drip-feeds, drip-feeding, drip-fed**) *vt* **1** ADMINISTER A DRIP TO to pass a liquid, especially a sugar solution, directly into somebody's vein using a drip **2** PROVIDE PLANTS WITH A CONTINUOUS WATER SUPPLY to provide water, and sometimes nutrients, to indoor plants or field crops continuously in small quantities **3** PROVIDE MONEY IN INSTALMENTS to give money to a new business in instalments at various stages of its development instead of giving the entire sum at the beginning (*informal*)

dripless /dríplәss/ *adj US* designed or made not to drip ○ *This teapot has a dripless spout.*

dripping /drípping/ *n* FAT FROM COOKING MEAT the fat that melts off meat when it is being cooked and hardens when cold, used for frying, basting, and making pastry ■ **drippings** *npl US* JUICES FROM COOKING MEAT the juices, including melted fat, produced by roasting or frying meat ■ *adj* **dripping wet** THOROUGHLY WET thoroughly wet ○ *She hurried in, cold and dripping wet from the storm.*

dripping wet *adj* = **dripping** *adj.*

drippy /dríppi/ (**-pier, -piest**) *adj* **1** regarded as weak and ineffectual (*slang insult*) **2** silly and extremely sentimental (*slang*) —**drippily** *adv* —**drippiness** *n*

dripstone /dríp stōn/ *n* **1** a stone drip used to protect a projection over a door or window **2** calcium carbonate deposits in the form of stalactites or stalagmites

drissy /drísssi/ *adj Wales* frantic (*informal*)

⚡**drive** /drīv/ *v* (**drives, driving, drove** /drōv/, **driven** /drívv'n/) **1** *vti* CONTROL MOVEMENT OF A VEHICLE to operate a vehicle, controlling its speed and direction, or be operated so as to move in a particular direction ○ *He's learning to drive.* **2** *vti* TRAVEL OR CONVEY IN VEHICLE to travel somewhere in a vehicle, or take somebody somewhere in a vehicle ○ *I'll drive you to the airport.* **3** *vt* PROVIDE POWER FOR to supply the power that makes something work (*often passive*) ○ *The lawn mower is driven by a petrol engine.* **4** *vt* STEER THE PROGRESS OF to provide momentum towards the successful operation or functioning of something ○ *This company is driven by a concern for quality.* **5** *vt* FORCE INTO A CONDITION to force somebody or something into a particular state or condition, often an extremely negative one ○ *Her son's behaviour drove her to despair.* **6** *vt* COMPEL TO ACT to supply the emotional or physical energy that leads somebody to act or behave in an extreme way ○ *Driven by fear, the elephants stampeded.* **7** *vr* FORCE YOURSELF TO WORK to force yourself to work too hard or for too long at something ○ *You drive yourself too hard.* **8** *vt* FORCE TO MOVE to force people or animals to go somewhere ○ *Rain drove them indoors.* **9** *vt* FORCE IN OR OUT to push, knock, or hammer something forcefully into a particular position ○ *He drove the stakes into the ground.* **10** *vti* MOVE OR PROPEL FORCEFULLY to move or be blown or thrown with great force against something, or provide the force that does this ○ *The wind drove the snow into huge drifts.* **11** *vt* MAKE A HOLE to make a hole or tunnel in something using great force **12** *vt* HIT A BALL HARD to kick or hit a ball forcefully when playing a sport **13** *vti* HIT A LONG SHOT to hit a long shot in golf, from either a tee or a fairway, when covering the principal distance between holes ○ *He drove into the rough.* **14** *vti* DRIBBLE DIRECTLY TOWARDS THE BASKET in basketball, to dribble the ball through a particular area of the court towards the basket ○ *She's unstoppable when she drives the baseline.* **15** *vt* STRIKE BALL WITH FORCE in cricket, to strike the ball very hard and straight with the bat held vertically **16** *vt* CHASE GAME INTO THE OPEN to chase a hunted animal into the open where it can be killed **17** *vt NZ* FELL TREES BY CUTTING ONE DOWN to cut down a tree in such a way that it falls on other trees and makes them fall ■ *n* **1** RIDE TAKEN IN A VEHICLE a trip in a car or other vehicle ○ *go for a drive* **2** ROAD LINKING HOUSE TO STREET a paved area or private road that goes between a house or garage and the street. US term **driveway** **3** WIDE ROAD any street or road that can be used for vehicles, especially one that has pleasant views (*often in placenames*) **4** TRANSMISSION OF POWER the means of converting power into motion in a machine, e.g. a motor vehicle (*often in combination*) ○ *a car with four-wheel drive* **5** COMPUT = **disk drive** **6** HARD HIT OF BALL in some sports, a forceful shot or stroke in hitting a ball ○ *She has a good backhand drive.* **7** LONG SHOT a long shot in golf, played from either a tee or fairway, when covering the main portion of the distance between the tee and green **8** FAST MOVEMENT TOWARDS BASKET in basketball, a fast direct run towards the basket while dribbling the ball ○ *Our players are having trouble scoring off drives.* **9** FOCUSED ENERGY energy and determination that helps somebody achieve what he or she wants to do ○ *Do you have the drive to achieve your ambitions?* **10** MOTIVATING NEED a powerful need or instinct, e.g. hunger or sex, that motivates behaviour **11** MAJOR PLANNED EFFORT an organized effort made by a lot of people working together to achieve a particular goal ○ *a recruitment drive* **12** PARTY FOR PLAYING CARD GAME a social event for the purpose of playing a game, e.g. whist, often organized in order to raise funds (*in combination*) ○ *a beetle drive* **13** SUSTAINED MILITARY ATTACK a major sustained attack on an enemy, usually including armoured vehicles and large guns **14** VOLTAGE voltage applied to the grid of a transmitting or amplifying valve or to the base of a transistor **15** FORWARD POSITION IN AUTOMATIC TRANSMISSION in an automatic transmission, the principal shift position that moves the vehicle forwards [Old English *drīfan* < Indo-European] —**drivability** *n* —**drivable** *adj*

drive-by *n* a drive-by shooting (*informal*)

drive-by shooting *n* an act of firing a firearm from a moving vehicle

drive chain *n* an endless chain that transmits power from one toothed wheel to another in a mechanical system

drive-in *n* a commercial establishment, e.g. a cinema, that provides services or products to customers while they remain in their cars (*often before nouns*) —**drive-in** *n*

drivel *n* **1** SILLY TALK silly and irrelevant or inaccurate talk ○ *They're talking drivel.* **2** DROOLED SALIVA saliva dribbling from the mouth ■ *vi* (**-els, -elling, -elled**) **1** TALK NONSENSE to talk silly and irrelevant or inaccurate nonsense **2** DROOL to let saliva dribble from the mouth [Old English *dreflian* < ?] —**driveller** *n* —**drivelling** *n*

driven past participle of **drive** ■ *adj* **1** striving to achieve because of a strong need or inner compulsion ○ *Driven people are often overachievers.* **2** having a particular thing as its principal cause (*in combination*) ○ *a demand-driven economy*

⚡**driver** /drívər/ *n* **1** SOMEBODY WHO CAN DRIVE somebody who operates a motor vehicle, or who is capable of operating one **2** CHAUFFEUR somebody who drives a car or limousine for other people **3** GOLF CLUB a golf club with a wide wooden head, deep face, and a long shaft, used to drive the ball from the tee down the fairway **4** PART THAT TRANSMITS a part of a machine that causes another part to move **5** TOOL THAT APPLIES PRESSURE a tool, e.g. a screwdriver or drill, that exerts heavy pressure on something else **6** ELECTRONIC CIRCUIT an electronic circuit that produces an output used to control another circuit **7** CONTROLLING SOFTWARE computer software that controls the input and output of a device ○ *a printer driver* **8** STRONG FORCE something that provides impetus or motivation, e.g. within an organization

driver ant *n* INSECTS = **army ant**

driverless /drívərləss/ *adj* **1** LACKING A DRIVER WHILE MOVING moving out of control because the driver is missing **2** HAVING NO DRIVER not having a driver on a specific occasion ○ *Looks like we're driverless tonight.* **3** NEEDING NO DRIVER having no driver because of being automatically operated

driver's license *n* US = **driving licence**

driver's seat *n* US = **driving seat**

driver's side *n* the side of a car on which the steering wheel is located, where the driver sits when operating a vehicle

drive shaft *n* **1** a rotating shaft that transmits the power from a motor or engine to another part of the machine, e.g. from the engine to the propeller of an aircraft **2** the shaft that transmits power from the transmission to the differential in a rear-wheel drive vehicle

drive-through *n US* a business, e.g. a fast-food restaurant or bank, that provides goods or services through a special window to customers who remain in their cars (*often before nouns*)

drive time *n* a time during the morning or afternoon when commuters are driving to and from work in their cars and listening to the radio

drive train *n* a mechanical part of a vehicle, including the drive shaft and universal joint, that connects the transmission with the axles and transmits power, torque, and motion

drive-up *n US* a place in a commercial establishment such as a restaurant or bank where customers are served while remaining in their cars (*often before nouns*)

driveway /drív way/ *n* TRANSP = **drive** *n.* 2

driving /dríving/ *adj* **1** FALLING HARD falling or being blown very hard and forcefully ○ *driving rain* **2** ABLE TO MAKE SOMETHING HAPPEN having the ability or influence to make something new or different happen ○ *She is the driving force behind the new development.* ○ *driving ambition* ■ *n* PROCESS OF OPERATING VEHICLE the act or process of operating a motor vehicle, especially with regard to how skilful somebody is ○ *Your driving is even worse than usual today.* —**drivingly** *adv*

driving chain *n* MECH ENG = **drive chain**

driving examiner *n* an official who conducts the test of somebody's ability to drive, which people must pass to obtain a driving licence

driving iron *n* an iron golf club that can be used instead of a driver

driving test *n* a test of driving skills and knowledge, usually consisting of both a written and a practical test that people must pass before driving without supervision on public roads

driving wheel *n* a wheel that causes other wheels to rotate

drizzle /drízz'l/ *n* LIGHT RAIN light steady rain ■ *v* (**-zles, -zling, -zled**) **1** *vi* RAIN LIGHTLY to rain lightly and steadily **2** *vt* DRIBBLE LIQUID OVER FOOD to pour very small quantities of a liquid in a thin stream over food ○ *Lightly drizzle the dressing over the vegetables.* [Mid-16C. < ?] —**drizzly** *adj*

⚡**DRM** *abbr* digital rights management (*in e-commerce*)

drogue /drōg/ *n* **1** NAUT = **sea anchor** **2** AEROSP, AIR = **drogue parachute** **3** TARGET TOWED BY AN AIRCRAFT a cylindrical target towed behind an aircraft, used for firing practice **4** RECEPTACLE ON A TANKER AIRCRAFT a funnel-shaped receptacle attached to the refuelling hose of a tanker aircraft that locates the probe of the receiving aircraft and fits over it, ensuring firm connection during refuelling **5** WINDSOCK a windsock (*technical*) [Early 18C. < ?]

drogue parachute *n* **1** a small parachute, used on a spacecraft or satellite re-entering the atmosphere, that is released before a larger one to slow the object and stabilize it **2** a small parachute used to release a larger one from its pack

droit /drwaa/ *n* a right or claim, either legal or moral, that is due to somebody and must be acknowledged [15C. Via French < late Latin *directum* 'rule' < Latin *directus* 'straight' (see DIRECT).]

droit de seigneur /drwaá də say nyúr/, **droit du seigneur** /-dyoo-/ *n* the supposed former legal right of a feudal lord to have sexual intercourse with the bride or daughter of an inferior, usually a serf, on the night of her wedding [< French, 'lord's right']

droll /drōl/ *adj* amusing in a wry or odd way [Early 17C. < French *drôle* 'buffoon, comical'.] —**drollness** *n* —**drolly** *adv*

drollery /drṓləri/ (*plural* **-ies**) *n* **1 QUIRKY HUMOUR** slightly odd or wry humour **2 TALKING OR BEHAVING AMUSINGLY** talking or acting in a wryly or oddly amusing way ○ *Such drollery is inappropriate in a formal context.* **3 SOMETHING FUNNY** an act or story that is wryly funny ○ *Whoever would have guessed that he was capable of such drolleries?*

-drome *suffix* racecourse, field ○ *hippodrome* ○ *cosmodrome* [Via Latin < Greek *dromos* 'racecourse' < Indo-European, 'walk, run']

Dromedary

dromedary /drómmədəri, drúmm-/ (*plural* **-ies**) *n* a camel with one hump. Kept for: working, racing. Native to: North Africa, SW Asia. *Camelus dromedarius.* [13C. < Old French *dromedaire*, late Latin *dromedarius* < Latin *dromad-* 'dromedary' < Greek *dromad-* 'running'.]

dromond /drómmənd, drúmm-/, **dromon** /-ən/ *n* a sailing galley used during the Middle Ages [14C. Via Anglo-Norman *dromund* < late Latin *dromon-* < Greek *dromō* 'swift ship' < *dromos* 'running'.]

-dromous *suffix* moving, migrating ○ *catadromous* [< modern Latin *-dromus* < Greek *dromos* 'running']

drone[1] /drōn/ *v* (**drones, droning, droned**) **1** *vi* **MAKE A LOW HUMMING SOUND** to make a continuous low humming sound **2** *vti* **TALK IN A BORING VOICE** to talk for a long time in a boring voice ○ *I could hear his voice droning on in the background.* ■ *n* **1 HUMMING SOUND** a continuous low sound **2 UNCHANGING NOTE HELD DURING MELODY** a single note or chord that is held through a melodic part **3 PIPE IN BAGPIPES PRODUCING CONTINUOUS NOTE** one of the pipes in a bagpipe that produces a single continuous note [Early 16C. < DRONE[2].] —**droningly** *adv*

drone[2] /drōn/ *n* **1 NONWORKER MALE BEE** a male bee that has no sting, does not gather pollen, and exists only to mate with the queen bee **2 LAZY PERSON** a lazy worker or contributor to something who relies on the work or energy of others **3 PILOTLESS AIRCRAFT** an aircraft whose flight is controlled from the ground [Old English *drān* < Indo-European, 'to buzz'] —**dronish** *adj*

drone fly *n* INSECTS = **hoverfly**

drongo /dróng gō/ (*plural* **-gos**) *n* **1 drongo** (*plural* **-gos** *or* **-go**), **drongo shrike** (*plural* **drongo shrikes** *or* **drongo shrike**) a tropical bird that is usually black with a strong beak, glossy feathers, and a long forked tail. Native to: Africa, Asia, Australia. Family: Dicruridae. **2** somebody regarded as unintelligent or slow to learn (*informal insult*) [Mid-19C. < Malagasy.]

droob /droob/ *n ANZ* an offensive term for somebody who is thought to be ineffectual (*informal insult*) [Mid-20C. < ?]

drool /drool/ *v* **1** *vi* **SHOW EXAGGERATED APPRECIATION** to show excessive appreciation of something or somebody really liked or wanted **2** *vi* **DRIBBLE SALIVA** to let saliva dribble from the mouth ○ *The dog lay drooling at his feet.* **3** *vti* **TALK NONSENSE** to talk nonsense or foolishness ■ *n* **SALIVA DRIBBLING FROM THE MOUTH** saliva dribbling from the mouth [Early 19C. < ?] —**droolingly** *adv*

droop /droop/ *v* **1** *vti* **HANG OR BEND DOWN LIMPLY** to move lower, hang down, or sag limply, or make something sag limply ○ *Her eyelids drooped with weariness.* **2** *vi* **BE DISPIRITED** to become discouraged or dejected ○ *His spirits drooped at the prospect of the long and arduous journey.* ■ *n* **SAGGING** a lowered, sagging, or slumped position ○ *The droop of her shoulders suggested her disappointment.* [13C. < Old Norse *drūpa.*] —**droopily** *adv* —**droopiness** *n* —**droopingly** *adv* —**droopy** *adj*

droop nose, droop snoot *n* an aircraft nose section that can be tilted downward to increase the pilot's range of vision during landing and takeoff

drop /drop/ *v* (**drops, dropping, dropped**) **1** *vt* **LET GO OF** to allow something to fall, sometimes intentionally ○ *He dropped the bowling ball on my foot.* ○ *Somebody had dropped a glove in the street.* **2** *vi* **FALL** to fall from a higher place to a lower place **3** *vti* **MOVE TO A LOWER POSITION** to move into a lower position ○ *He dropped into a chair.* **4** *vti* **FALL IN DROPS** to fall or make something fall in drops of liquid ○ *We listened to the rain dropping on the roof.* **5** *vti* **LESSEN** to decrease, or reduce something, to a lower level, rate, or number ○ *The temperature dropped sharply overnight.* **6** *vi* **SLOPE DOWNWARDS** to slope downwards, often in a particular way **7** *vti* **LOWER THE VOICE** to lower the voice to a quieter level ○ *She dropped her voice to a whisper.* **8** *vt* **TAKE SOMEBODY OR SOMETHING SOMEWHERE** to take somebody or something to a place, usually by car, and leave the person or thing there ○ *Can you drop me at the bus station?* **9** *vt* **WRITE TO** to write and send an informal message or greeting to somebody ○ *Drop me a line when you get there.* **10** *vt* **STOP DOING OR PLANNING** to abandon a plan or course of action ○ *The council have dropped plans to build a major new leisure centre.* **11** *vti* **STOP TALKING ABOUT** to stop talking about something, or stop being talked about ○ *Can we drop the subject please?* **12** *vt* **END RELATIONSHIP WITH** to end a close or intimate relationship with somebody (*informal*) **13** *vt* **REMOVE** to remove somebody from a group of which she or he was formerly a member ○ *She may be dropped from the team.* **14** *vt* **OMIT LETTER OR WORD** to leave out a letter, word, or phrase ○ *You can drop the 'Sir': just call me Max.* **15** *vi* **COLLAPSE FROM EXHAUSTION** to collapse in a state of complete exhaustion ○ *I'm ready to drop.* **16** *vi* **COLLAPSE** to lose consciousness or die, especially suddenly or unexpectedly (*informal*) ○ *People were dropping like flies from the extreme heat.* **17** *vt* **LOSE A MATCH OR GAME** to lose a match, game, or part of a game ○ *He got through to the finals without dropping a set.* **18** *vt* **SAY SOMETHING CASUALLY** to say something with an air of pretended casualness ○ *She's dropping hints about what she wants for her birthday.* **19** *vt US* **SPEND OR LOSE MONEY** to spend or lose a particular amount of money on something expensive or in gambling (*informal*) **20** *vti* **HIT A BALL INTO THE TARGET HOLE** to make the ball go into a target, e.g. a hole or net, or go into a target hole or net **21** *vt* **GIVE BIRTH TO** to give birth to young, especially a foal **22** *vt* **TAKE ILLEGAL DRUGS** to take an illegal drug by mouth, especially in pill form (*slang*) **23** *vt* **LOWER A HEM** to lower the hem of something, e.g. a garment or curtain **24** *vt* **DELIVER SOMETHING BY PARACHUTE** to deliver somebody or something by parachute from an aircraft, e.g. soldiers or supplies **25** *vt* **UNLOAD** to unload something from a ship or vehicle ■ *n* **1 SMALL ROUND PORTION OF LIQUID** a very small amount of liquid that becomes a rounded or pear shape as it falls **2 SMALL AMOUNT OF LIQUID** any small amount of a liquid ○ *There's not a drop of milk in the house.* **3 TINIEST AMOUNT** the least amount of sympathy or other feeling (*in negatives*) ○ *I swear there isn't a drop of sympathy in that man.* **4 DECREASE IN** a decrease in quantity or amount ○ *a drop in salary* **5 DISTANCE BETWEEN A HIGH POINT AND THE GROUND** the distance between a higher level and a lower level or the ground **6 DESCENT** a slope or discontinuity in ground level, usually sharp or sudden **7 SMALL ROUND SWEET** a small round or oval sweet (*in combination*) ○ *cough drops* **8 ROUND EARRING OR PENDANT** an earring or pendant, typically round or pear-shaped **9 DESCENT BY PARACHUTE** a descent from an aircraft by parachute **10 DELIVERY** a delivery ○ *make a drop every two weeks* **11 GOODS DELIVERED BY PARACHUTE** goods, e.g. equipment, that an aircraft delivers by parachute, or people dropped by parachute (*often in combination*) **12 SECRET REPOSITORY FOR DANGEROUS MESSAGES** a secret place where somebody leaves dangerous letters or messages to be picked up by somebody else **13 ACT OF LEAVING SECRET COMMUNICATION** the act of leaving a dangerous letter, message, or goods at a prearranged location ○ *It's too dangerous to make the drop tonight.* **14** THEATRE = **drop curtain** *n.* 1 **15 CONNECTION ON LINE** a point on a transmission line where data can be put in or taken out **16 SHORT SPUR** a short line that feeds signals to an individual house from a cable television trunk line **17 TRAPDOOR UNDER GALLOWS** a trapdoor on which somebody who is to be hanged stands under the gallows **18 CURTAIN LENGTH** the measured length for a curtain, from the top of a window to its sill or to the floor ■ **drops** *npl* **LIQUID MEDICINE APPLIED IN SMALL QUANTITIES** liquid medicine delivered by a dropper to the ear, nose, or eye [< Old English *dropa* (noun), *droppian* (verb) < Indo-European] ◇ **a drop in the ocean** just a tiny part of the full quantity that is required, and thus insignificant ◇ **at the drop of a hat** without needing persuasion or prompting ◇ **drop a clanger** *or* **brick** to say something tactless, inappropriate, or mistaken that will cause embarrassment (*informal*) ◇ **let something drop** to reveal information to somebody, often casually or accidentally

drop away *vi* **1** = **drop** *v.* 6 **2** to leave a group or formation gradually, either on purpose or not ○ *One by one, each jet banked and dropped away from the formation.* **3** to disappear gradually

drop back, drop behind *vi* to move more slowly than other people and gradually fall farther behind them

drop by *v* **1** *vi* to visit somebody casually or without having agreed on a time **2** *vt* to deliver something or somebody to a specific place ○ *Just drop the laundry by some time this afternoon.*

drop in *vi* to visit somebody casually or without having agreed on a time

drop into *vt* to go from a more active into a less active state of consciousness

drop off *v* **1** *vi* **DOZE OFF** to fall asleep (*informal*) **2** *vi* **DECREASE** to decline or fall to a lower level (*informal*) ○ *Sales tend to drop off during the summer.* **3** *vt* **TAKE SOMEBODY OR SOMETHING SOMEWHERE** to take somebody or something to a place, usually by car, and leave the person or thing there

drop out *vi* **1** to abandon a project or activity without finishing it ○ *He dropped out of college in his final year.* **2** to reject conventional society and live in an alternative way (*informal*)

drop over, drop round *vi* to visit somebody casually and without agreeing on a time ○ *Drop round any time.*

drop cloth *n* **1** *US* = **dustsheet** **2** THEATRE = **drop curtain** *n.* 1

drop curtain *n* **1** an unframed curtain that can be lowered to a theatre stage from the flies, usually providing background scenery **2** a theatre curtain that is raised or lowered on stage, rather than being opened or closed by moving sideways

drop forge *n* a machine used to shape or stamp molten metal by placing it between two dies and dropping a weight on it —**drop-forge** *vt*

drop front *n* a part of a writing desk that can be lowered to provide a writing surface and then raised to conceal the inner part of the desk (*hyphenated before nouns*) ○ *a drop-front desk*

drop goal *n* a goal in rugby scored by dropping the ball and then kicking it

drop hammer *n* METALL = **drop forge**

drop handlebars *npl* on a racing bicycle, handlebars that curve downwards, enabling the rider to adopt a more aerodynamic posture

drophead coupé /dróp hed-/ *n* a two-door car that has a folding top and a sloping back and seats four people

drop-in centre *n* a place that people can visit without an appointment to get advice, information, or to meet others

drop kick *n* **1** a way of kicking a football by dropping it first and then kicking it just as it bounces up from the ground **2** in amateur wrestling, an illegal move in which one wrestler attacks another by leaping into the air and striking an opponent with both feet —**drop-kick** *vti*

drop leaf *n* an extension on the end of a table that can be folded down when not needed (*hyphenated before nouns*) ○ *a drop-leaf table*

droplet /dróplət/ *n* a very small drop of liquid

droplight /dróp līt/ *n* an electric light that can be raised or lowered by using a rope, cord, or pulley

drop lock *n* in international financial markets, a variable-rate bank loan that is automatically converted to a fixed-rate bond when long-term interest rates fall to a specified level

drop-off *n* a fall in the level of something

⚡ **dropout** /dróp owt/ *n* **1 SOMEBODY WHO LEAVES WITHOUT COMPLETING A COURSE** a person who withdraws from an educational course, usually at a college or university **2 UNCONVENTIONAL PERSON** somebody who chooses an unconventional way of life (*informal*) **3 DROP KICK BY DEFENDERS TO RESTART** a drop kick performed by a defending rugby team in order to restart a game, e.g. after a goal has been scored **4 SECTION WITHOUT DATA** a small section on a magnetic tape or disk that is missing data

dropper /dróppər/ *n* **1** a small glass or plastic tube with a rubber bulb at one end that is used to suck up liquid and release it one drop at a time (*often in combination*) ○ *an eye dropper* **2** a short piece of monofilament line, used by anglers to attach a fly above the tail fly

droppings /dróppingz/ *npl* animal or bird excrement left on the ground or another surface

drop scone *n* a small round flat cake made by dropping a spoonful of batter onto a heated pan or griddle

drop shipment *n* a consignment of goods shipped directly from the manufacturer to the retailer but billed to a third party

drop shot *n* a shot in a racket game in which the ball drops abruptly to the ground just after crossing over the net or hitting the wall

dropsided lorry /dróp sĭdid-/ *n* an open lorry with hinged sides that can be lowered to allow loading or unloading

dropsonde /dróp sond/ *n* an instrument, dropped from an aircraft and carried down by a parachute, that transmits information about temperature, pressure, and humidity [Mid-20C. < DROP + RADIOSONDE.]

dropsy /drópsi/ *n* oedema (*dated*) [13C. Shortening of *hydropsy*, via Old French < medieval Latin *hydropsia* < Greek *hudrōps* 'somebody with oedema' < *hudōr* 'water'.] —**dropsied** *adj*

drop tank *n* on fighter and bomber planes, an extra tank of fuel that enables the aircraft to fly longer and farther and can be jettisoned when empty

drop volley *n* a softly hit volley in a racket game in which the ball drops abruptly to the ground before an opponent can reach it

dropwort /dróp wurt/ (*plural* **-worts** *or* **-wort**) *n* **1** a plant with finely divided leaves. Flowers: small, white or red, in clusters. Native to: Europe, Asia. *Filipendula vulgaris*. **2** an umbelliferous marsh plant. Genus: *Oenanthe*. [Because of its tuberous root fibres]

drop zone *n* an area where troops or goods such as military equipment or medical supplies are to be landed, usually by parachute

droshky /dróshki/ (*plural* **-kies**), **drosky** (*plural* **-kies**) *n* an open four-wheeled carriage drawn by horses, formerly used in Russia and Poland [Early 19C. < Russian *drozhki* 'small wagon' < *drogi* 'wagon'.]

drosometer /dro sómmitər/ *n* a device for measuring dew deposits [Early 19C. < Greek *drosos* 'dew'.]

drosophila /dro sóffilə, drə-/ (*plural* **-las** *or* **-la** *or* **-lae** /-lee/) *n* a small two-winged fruit fly that is frequently used in genetic research. Genus: *Drosophila*. [Early 19C. < modern Latin, < Greek *drosos* 'dew' and *-philos* 'loving'.]

dross /dross/ *n* **1 SOMETHING WORTHLESS** something that is worthless or of a low standard or quality ○ *I considered her early fiction to be pure dross.* **2 SCUM ON METAL** the scum formed on molten metals, usually caused by oxidation **3** *Scotland* **SMALL COALS** small coals or coal dust [Old English *drōs* < Indo-European, 'dark, muddy'] —**drossiness** *n* —**drossy** *adj*

drought *n* **1** a long period of extremely dry weather when there is not enough rain for the successful growing of crops **2** a lengthy serious lack of something ○ *She experienced a period of creative drought.* [Old English *drūgaþ* 'dryness' < Germanic, 'dry'] —**droughty** *adj*

drouth /drowth, drooth/ *n* **1** *Scotland, Ireland* a drought **2** thirst (*regional*) —**drouthy** *adj*

drove[1] /drōv/ past tense of **drive**

drove[2] /drōv/ *n* **1 GROUP OF ANIMALS MOVING** a large number of animals, especially cattle, moving in the same direction, especially when being driven **2 TYPE OF STONE CHISEL** a broad-edged chisel used for dressing stone ■ **droves** *npl* **CROWDS OF PEOPLE** very large numbers of people ○ *They came out of the football ground in droves.* ■ *vti* (**droves, droving, droved**) **MOVE ANIMALS ALONG** to move a herd or flock of animals from one place to another, usually over long distances, e.g. to new pastures or to market [Old English *drāf* < *drīfan* (see DRIVE)] —**drover** *n*

drove road *n Scotland* a road or track along which cattle or sheep were formerly driven on foot to market

drown /drown/ *v* **1** *vti* to die, or kill a person or animal, by immersion and usually suffocation in a liquid, normally water ○ *death by drowning* **2** *vt* = **drown out 3** *vt* to cover or soak something, usually an item of food, with too much liquid ○ *He served us pancakes drowned in syrup.* [13C. Probably < a N Germanic language.] —**drowned** *adj* —**drowner** *n*

drown out *vt* to make so much noise that it is impossible to hear another sound (*often passive*)

drowse /drowz/ (**drowses, drowsing, drowsed**) *vi* to be in a state partway between sleeping and waking [Late 16C. Back-formation < *drowsy* < Old English *drūsian* 'be sluggish' < Germanic.] —**drowse** *n*

drowsy /drówzi/ (**-ier, -iest**) *adj* **1 ALMOST ASLEEP** almost asleep or very lightly asleep **2 CAUSING SLEEPINESS** tending to make somebody feel sleepy ○ *a drowsy summer afternoon* **3 SLUGGISH** sluggish and dull [15C. < ?: ultimately < Old English *drūsian* 'be sluggish' < Germanic that is also the ancestor of English *drop* and *droop*.] —**drowsily** *adv* —**drowsiness** *n*

drub /drub/ *vt* (**drubs, drubbing, drubbed**) **1 BEAT WITH A STICK** to beat somebody using a heavy stick or club **2 DEFEAT** to defeat an opponent comprehensively ○ *Their team really drubbed us last year.* **3 STAMP YOUR FEET** to stamp the feet hard on the ground ■ *n* **BLOW WITH A STICK** a blow made using a heavy stick or club [Early 17C. < ?] —**drubber** *n*

drudge /druj/ *n* a worker who performs dull and laborious tasks [15C. < ?] —**drudge** *vi* —**drudger** *n* —**drudgingly** *adv*

drudgery /drújjəri/ *n* exhausting, boring, unpleasant work

drug /drug/ *n* **1 SUBSTANCE GIVEN AS MEDICINE** a natural or artificial substance given to treat or prevent disease or to lessen pain **2 ILLEGAL SUBSTANCE** an often illegal and sometimes addictive substance that causes changes in behaviour and perception and is taken for the effects **3 MEDICAL SUBSTANCE** a substance given to treat or prevent illness that is officially listed in a medical pharmacopoeia ■ *vt* (**drugs, drugging, drugged**) **1 GIVE A DRUG** to give a drug to somebody **2 ADD DRUG TO** to mix a drug with food or a drink and give it to somebody to make him or her fall asleep or become unconscious [14C. < French *drogue*.]

drug abuse *n* = **drug misuse**

drug baron *n* = **drug lord**

drugged /drugd/ *adj* **1** heavily asleep, unconscious, or unable to function after being given drugs **2** extremely tired and unable to concentrate ○ *drugged with sleep*

drugget /drúggit/ *n* **1 CARPETING FABRIC** a thick heavy woollen or cotton and wool blend fabric. Use: floor coverings. **2 RUG** a coarse rug made of wool or cotton and wool **3 WOOLLEN FABRIC** a woollen or woollen mix fabric. Use: formerly, clothing. [Mid-16C. < French *droguet*.]

druggie /drúggi/, **druggy** (*plural* **-gies**) *n* a drug addict (*slang*)

druggist /drúggist/ *n US, Can* a pharmaceutical chemist

druggy /drúggi/ *adj* (**-gier, -giest**) typical of somebody who takes drugs regularly and often (*slang*) ○ *a druggy stupor.* ■ *n* = **druggie**

drug holiday *n* a period when somebody does not take medication normally given every day

drug lord *n* a controller of an international network for the production, processing, and sale of illegal drugs (*informal*)

drug misuse *n* deliberate use of an illegal drug or of too much of a prescribed drug

drug pusher *n* a seller of illegal drugs

drug runner *n* a smuggler of illegal drugs, usually by ship or plane

drugs squad *n* the department of a police force that investigates the use and sale of illegal drugs

drugstore /drúg stawr/ *n US, Can* = **chemist** *n.* 1

drug tsar *n* in the UK, a senior official appointed to supervise the detection and suppression of illegal drug dealing (*informal*)

Druid /droō id/, **druid** *n* **1 PRIEST IN ANCIENT CELTIC RELIGION** a priest of an ancient religion practised in Britain, Ireland, and Gaul until the people of those areas were converted to Christianity **2 MODERN FOLLOWER OF ANCIENT CELTIC RELIGION** a man who worships and celebrates the forces of nature **3 OFFICER OF WELSH GORSEDD** an officer of the Gorsedd, who administers eisteddfods in Wales [Mid-16C. Directly or via French < Latin *druides* 'Druids' < Celtic.] —**druidic** /droo íddik/ *adj* —**druidical** *adj*

Druidess /droō idəss/ *n* **1** a woman priest of an ancient religion practised in Britain, Ireland, and Gaul until the people of those areas were converted to Christianity **2** a woman who worships and celebrates the forces of nature

Druidism /droō idizəm/ *n* an ancient Celtic religion in which the forces of nature were worshipped, and the priests were also prophets and poets, or the modern religion said to derive from it

drum /drum/ *n* **1 PERCUSSION INSTRUMENT** a musical instrument usually consisting of a membrane stretched across a hollow frame and played by striking the stretched membrane **2 TAPPING SOUND** a regular tapping sound made by something striking a surface ○ *the drum of rain on the roof* **3 CYLINDRICAL CONTAINER** a large cylindrical container used for storing liquids, e.g. oil or chemicals **4 SPOOL** a large spool around which wire, cable, or rope is wound for storage **5 PART IN A MACHINE** a cylindrical hollow part in a machine, e.g. a washing machine **6** ANAT = **eardrum 7 FISH THAT MAKES A RHYTHMIC SOUND** a large bony saltwater or freshwater fish that emits a repeated rhythmic sound. Family: Sciaenidae. **8 CYLINDRICAL STONE BLOCK** one of the cylindrical stone blocks used to make a column **9 SUPPORT FOR A DOME** a band or other structure around the bottom of a dome or circular ceiling that supports it ■ *vi* (**drums, drumming, drummed**) **1 PLAY A DRUM** to play a drum or drums **2 TAP A SURFACE** to tap repeatedly and rhythmically on a surface ○ *The rain was drumming on the roof.* **3 MAKE SOUND WITH THE BILL OR WINGS** to make a repeated sound with the bill or wings (*refers to birds*) [Mid-16C. Probably < Middle Dutch *tromme* 'instrument making a loud noise', an imitation of the sound.] —**drumming** *n* ◇ **bang** *or* **beat the drum (for somebody** *or* **something)** to try to attract support and favourable attention for somebody or something that you favour (*informal*)

drum into *vt* to tell somebody something repeatedly and persistently until the person has learned it or will always remember it (*often passive*)

drum out *vt* (*usually passive*) **1** to force somebody to leave a group or an organization, usually in disgrace **2** to force somebody to stop doing something

drum up *vt* **1** to try actively to get more of something such as business or support **2** to create or think up an explanation ○ *What excuse can I drum up this time?*

drum and bass *n* popular music originating in the United Kingdom in the 1990s that has a fast rhythm, complex percussion, and very low bass lines

drumbeat /drúm beet/ *n* heavy unending criticism, typically public criticism ○ *a steady drumbeat of accusations*

drum brake *n* a brake on vehicles that operates by applying pressure to the inner part of the wheel (**brake drum**)

drum corps *n* a marching band, with percussion instruments and sometimes bugles or fifes, that performs precisely choreographed field drills

drumfire /drúm fīr/ *n* continuous heavy gunfire

drumfish /drúm fish/ (*plural* **-fish** *or* **-fishes**) *n* ZOOL = **drum** *n.* 7

drumhead /drúm hed/ *n* **1** the membrane, usually made of calfskin or plastic, that is stretched over the frame of a drum **2** the round topmost part of a capstan that holds the capstan bars in position for turning

drumhead court-martial *n* an informal brief trial held during military operations to hear charges of serious offences committed by soldiers while in action [Because an upturned drum serves as the magistrate's bench]

drum kit *n* a set of percussion instruments used in bands, usually consisting of one or more snare drums, tom-toms, bass drums, and various cymbals. US term **drum set**

drumlin /drúmlin/ *n* a long narrow ridge of gravel and rock deposited by a moving glacier, one end of which is blunt and the other end tapering [Mid-19C. < *drum* 'ridge' < Irish *druim* 'back, ridge'.]

drum machine *n* an electronic synthesizer that can reproduce drum and percussion sounds in various rhythms and combinations

drum major *n* a leader and conductor of a marching band who moves a baton up and down and twirls it rhythmically

drum majorette *n US* MUSIC = **majorette**

drummer /drúmmər/ *n* **1** DRUM PLAYER a player of a drum **2** *US* TRAVELLING SALESPERSON a travelling salesperson **3** (*plural* **-mers** *or* **-mer**) AUSTRALIAN FISH a fish that frequents rocky shores. Native to: Australia. Family: Kyphosidae.

Drummond /drúmmənd/, **William** (1585–1649) Scottish poet. Known as **Drummond of Hawthornden**

drum roll *n* a very fast regular beating on a drum that sounds like one long sound

drum set *n US* MUSIC = **drum kit**

drumstick /drúm stik/ *n* **1** the stick used to beat a drum **2** the lower half of the leg of a bird such as a chicken when prepared for eating

drunk /drungk/ past participle of **drink** ■ *adj* **1** INTOXICATED WITH ALCOHOL having drunk too much alcohol and lost control over behaviour, movement, and speech **2** EMOTIONALLY INTOXICATED overwhelmed with and judgmentally impaired by an intense emotion ○ *drunk with power* **3** LONG-SOAKED describes a meat dish in Chinese cooking in which the meat, usually chicken, has been immersed in a liquid and boiled or marinated overnight ○ *drunk chicken* ■ *n* **1** = **drunkard** **2** DRINKING BOUT a bout of drinking too much alcohol (*slang*) ○ *One more drunk, and I divorce you.*

drunkard /drúngkərd/ *n* a habitual drinker of too much alcohol

drunk-driver *n* a driver of a motor vehicle who drives after having drunk more than the legal limit of alcohol

drunk-driving *n US* = **drink-driving**

drunken /drúngkən/ *adj* **1** INVOLVING ALCOHOL involving too much alcohol, or occurring while people have had too much alcohol ○ *a drunken quarrel* **2** INTOXICATED overly excited by or as if by having consumed too much alcohol **3** AFFECTED BY ALCOHOL drunk or frequently drunk [Old English, old past participle of DRINK] —**drunkenly** *adv* —**drunkenness** *n*

drupe /droop/ *n* a fruit with a thin outer skin, soft pulpy middle, and hard stony central part that encloses a seed [Mid-18C. Via modern Latin < Latin *drupa* 'overripe olive' < Greek *druppa* 'olive'.]

drupelet /dróoplət/, **drupel** /dróop'l/ *n* a small fruit enclosing a single seed that, with many other small sections, makes up a compound fruit such as a blackberry or raspberry

Druze /drooz/ (*plural* **Druze** *or* **Druzes**), **Druse** (*plural* **Druse** *or* **Druses**) *n* a member of a religion similar to Islam that is found mainly in Israel, Lebanon, and Syria [Late 18C. Directly or via French < Arabic *durūz*, plural of *durzī* < the religion's founder, Muḥammad ibn Ismā'īl *ad-Darazī* (d. 1019).] —**Druzean** *adj*

dry /drī/ *adj* (**drier** *or* **dryer**, **driest** *or* **dryest**) **1** NOT WET not or no longer wet **2** LACKING MOISTURE IN THE AIR having very little or no rain or moisture in the air **3** NOT WET AND THUS COMFORTABLE not wet and therefore comfortable to wear ○ *dry clothes* **4** LACKING IN APPROPRIATE MOISTURE lacking in normal levels of natural oiliness or moisture ○ *dry skin* **5** DRAINED OF WATER no longer having water because it has evaporated or been exhausted ○ *The spring has been dry for years.* **6** LACKING CUSTOMARY MOISTURE not producing or accompanied by associated moisture, in the form of phlegm, tears, or vomit ○ *a dry cough* **7** NOT REQUIRING LIQUID FOR USE manufactured so as to be usable without water ○ *dry shampoo* **8** WITHOUT FLESH ATTACHED no longer having the meat attached ○ *dry bones* **9** THIRSTY thirsty and dehydrated **10** LACKING SWEETNESS not sweet because the sugar has been broken down during the process of fermentation ○ *dry sherry* **11** SERVED WITHOUT FAT OR LIQUID lacking the usual moist spread such as butter or jam ○ *dry toast* **12** UNAPPETIZINGLY LACKING MOISTNESS lacking in appetizing moistness, e.g. because of being stale or overcooked **13** SHREWDLY AMUSING witty in a shrewd, subtle, or sarcastic way **14** BORING AND ACADEMIC dense and academic in style **15** MATTER-OF-FACT plain and without unnecessary ornamentation ○ *a dry, matter-of-fact account of the incident* **16** NOT ALLOWING ALCOHOL SALES not allowing legal sale of alcoholic beverages **17** NO LONGER GIVING MILK describes a female animal that no longer produces milk **18** CONTAINING NO MOISTURE from which the liquid or moisture has been removed ○ *dry weight* **19** NOT CONDUCTING ELECTRICITY describes a current-carrying path that cannot conduct electricity because the solder at the joint has not completely adhered to a surface ○ *a dry joint* ■ *v* (**dries, drying, dried**) **1** *vti* MAKE SOMETHING DRY to make something dry, or become dry ○ *It's your turn to dry the dishes.* **2** *vi* FORGET LINES IN PERFORMANCE to forget lines during a performance or rehearsal **3** *vt* PRESERVE FOOD BY EXTRACTING MOISTURE to preserve food, especially fruit, vegetables, and meat, by extracting most of the moisture from it ■ *n* **1** DRY PLACE a place that is dry or sheltered from the rain (*informal*) ○ *stay in the dry* **2** *Aus* DRY SEASON the dry season (*informal*) **3** RIGHT-WING POLITICIAN a politician who is a member of the right wing of the British Conservative Party (*dated*) [Old English *drȳge* < Germanic] —**dryable** *adj* —**dryness** *n*

SYNONYMS *dry, dehydrated, desiccated, arid, parched, shrivelled, sere*

CORE MEANING: lacking moisture

dry having little or no moisture; **dehydrated** experiencing fluid loss, or preserved by drying; **desiccated** (used of products, especially food) free from moisture, or preserved by drying; **arid** (used of land) dry from lack of rain; **parched** dry from excessive heat or lack of rain; **shrivelled** dry, shrunken, and wrinkled; **sere** (*literary*) dry and withered.

---

dry off *vti* to become drier, or make something drier

dry out *vti* **1** to become completely dry, or make something completely dry ○ *It will take a while for the plaster to dry out.* **2** to purge alcohol or other drugs from the body, or put somebody through such a process (*informal*)

dry up *v* **1** *vti* LOSE OR REMOVE MOISTURE to lose water or moisture over a period, or make a river or pool lose its water over a period ○ *The river dried up centuries ago.* **2** *vi* STOP BEING AVAILABLE to stop being available as a resource ○ *Our project ended because our sources of funding dried up.* **3** *vt* DRY DISHES to dry plates, dishes, pans, and cutlery with a cloth after they have been washed **4** *vi* STOP TALKING to stop talking, or forget lines during a performance or rehearsal (*informal; often a command*) ○ *Oh, just dry up, will you? I'm trying to think!* **5** *vi* RUN OUT OF IDEAS to be unable to perform as usual or as expected ○ *His ideas have dried up.*

dryad /drī ad, -əd/ (*plural* **-ads** *or* **-ades** /-ə deez/) *n* in Greek mythology, a spiritual being believed to live in trees and forests [14C. Via Latin < Greek *Druad-* < *drus* 'tree'.] —**dryadic** /drī áddik/ *adj*

dry battery (*plural* **dry batteries**) *n* an electric battery that has more than one dry cell

dry-bone ore *n* a type of smithsonite that has many holes, found near the surface of the Earth's crust

dry cell *n* a current-generating electric cell that cannot be regenerated and contains an electrolyte in the form of a paste or within a porous material to keep it from spilling. ◊ **wet cell**

dry-clean *vt* to clean clothes or fabrics with a chemical solvent

dry-cleaner's (*plural* **dry-cleaner's**) *n* a shop that cleans clothes and household fabrics using a chemical solvent

dry-cleaning *n* **1** the professional cleaning of clothes and fabrics using a chemical solvent **2** clothes and other fabrics that require dry-cleaning or have just been dry-cleaned

dry cough *n* a cough that does not produce phlegm

Dryden /drīd'n/, **John** (1631–1700) English poet, dramatist, and critic

dry distillation *n* CHEM = **destructive distillation**

dry dock *n* an enclosed dock from which the water can be removed so that construction or repairs can be carried out below the water line of a boat or ship —**dry-dock** *vti*

dryer /drī ər/, **drier** comparative of **dry** ■ *n* **1** a machine or device for drying things **2** a substance added to paint or ink to speed up the drying process

dry-erase *adj US* able to be wiped away or erased without the use of liquids, or suitable for writing on with dry-erase markers ○ *a dry-erase board*

dryest /drī ist/ superlative of **dry**

dry-eyed /-īd/ *adj* unable or unwilling to shed tears ○ *He remained dry-eyed throughout the trial.*

dry farming *n* a method of growing crops in dry areas by selecting plants that are drought-resistant and using mulch to retain moisture in the soil, so making irrigation unnecessary —**dry farmer** *n*

dry fly *n* an artificial lure used in fly-fishing that remains on the surface of the water instead of sinking. ◊ **wet fly**

dry goods *npl US* COMM = **drapery** *n.* **4**

dry hole *n* an oil well that has been drilled but that produces no oil, or not enough to make it economically profitable

dry ice *n* cold solid carbon dioxide at the temperature of –78.5°C/–110°F. Use: refrigeration, production of an artificial fog effect.

drying oil *n* an organic oil, e.g. linseed or cottonseed oil, used as a base in paints and varnishes because it reduces drying time

dry kiln *n* a large oven used to season cut timber

dry land *n* the land as distinct from the sea or a body of water

dryland /drī land/ *n* areas prone to severe drought, such as deserts and savannas (*often plural*) —**dryland** *adj*

dryly *adv* = **drily**

dry measure *n* a system of units used to measure dry products such as grains and fruits by volume, or a unit in such a system

dry nurse *n* a nurse employed to look after somebody's young baby but not to breast-feed it (*archaic*) ◊ **wet nurse** —**dry-nurse** *vt*

dryopithecine /drī ō pítha seen/ (*plural* **-cines** *or* **-cine**) *n* an extinct ape of the Miocene and Pliocene epochs, believed by some scientists to be the ancestor of modern apes and humans. Genus: *Dryopithecus*. [Mid-20C. < modern Latin *Dryopithecus* < Greek *drus* 'tree' + *pithēkos* 'ape'.]

dry point *n* **1** METHOD OF ENGRAVING a technique of engraving in intaglio on a metal, usually copper, plate that produces a feathery effect in the lines of the print **2** STEEL NEEDLE a hard steel needle used to engrave a metal plate **3** PRINT MADE BY DRY POINT an engraving or print made by using dry point

dry riser *n* a waterless pipe that runs vertically, with connections on different levels of a building to which a firefighter's hose can be attached in case of fire

dry rot *n* **1** CRUMBLING DECAY IN WOOD dry crumbling decay in wood caused by various fungi. ◊ **wet rot** **2** PLANT DISEASE a disease caused by various fungi that invade plant stems, bulbs, and fruits, causing them to dry out and decay **3** DESTRUCTIVE FUNGUS a fungus that causes dry rot. Genus: *Merulius*.

dry run *n* a rehearsal of a planned action or activity ○ *Let's have a dry run to make sure it's going to work.*

dry-salt *vt* to use salt to dry and preserve food

dry-salter *n* a dealer in chemical products, e.g. dyes, and also salted, dried, and tinned foods (*archaic*) —**dry-saltery** *n*

Drysdale /drīz dayl/, **Sir Russell** (1912–81) British-born Australian landscape painter

dry socket *n* a painful condition caused when the blood left by an extracted tooth fails to clot or the clot is dislodged

dry-stone *adj* built with pieces of stone that are fitted together without mortar ○ *a dry-stone wall*

drywall /drī wawl/, **dry wall** *n US* **1** CONSTR = **plasterboard** **2** a wall constructed with sheets of plasterboard **3** a wall constructed of stone or masonry without mortar —**dry-wall** *vt*

DS, ds *abbr* dal segno

d.s. *abbr* **1** days after sight **2** document signed

DSc *abbr* Doctor of Science

DSC *abbr* Distinguished Service Cross

⚡ **DSL** *abbr* Digital Subscriber Line

DSM *abbr* Distinguished Service Medal

DSO *abbr* Distinguished Service Order

dsp *abbr* died without issue

DSS[1] *abbr* Director of Social Services

DSS[2] *abbr* Department of Social Security

DST *abbr* daylight-saving time

DTI *abbr* Department of Trade and Industry

ϟ **DTP** *abbr* desktop publishing

DTs *n* delirium tremens (*informal*)

DTV *abbr* digital television

DU *abbr* depleted uranium

dual /dyoó əl/ *adj* 1 **HAVING TWO SIMILAR ELEMENTS** having two parts, functions, aspects, or items of a similar kind ○ *dual citizenship* 2 **HAVING TWO DISTINCT ASPECTS** made up of two distinct, often opposite, elements ○ *serve a dual purpose* 3 **SPECIFYING TWO** in various languages, used to describe or relating to a grammatical number category, in addition to singular and plural, that specifies two people or things ■ *n* **DUAL NUMBER OR INFLECTED FORM** dual number, or, in various languages, the inflected form of a noun, pronoun, adjective, or verb that refers to dual number [Early 17C. < Latin *dualis* < *duo* 'two'.] —**dually** *adv*

SPELLCHECK Do not confuse ***dual*** with ***duel***, which has a similar sound. Beware: your spellchecker will not catch this error.

Duala /doó aalə, doó aa laa/ *n* (*plural* **-la** *or* **-las**) 1 a member of an African people who live in Cameroon 2 the language of the Duala people, belonging to the Bantu group of Niger-Congo languages —**Duala** *adj*

dual carriageway *n* a road with two or more lanes of traffic in each direction divided by a central reservation or barrier. US term **divided highway**

ϟ **dual in-line package** *n* a package consisting of a printed circuit board and a series of switches, used to control optional settings for electronic devices

dualism /dyoó əlizəm/ *n* 1 **STATE OF HAVING TWO PARTS** a state in which something has two distinct parts or aspects, which are often opposites 2 **THEORY OF TWO OPPOSING CONCEPTS** a philosophical theory based on the idea of opposing concepts, especially the theory that human beings are made up of two independent constituents, the body and the mind or soul 3 **DOCTRINE OF OPPOSING PRINCIPLES** the religious doctrine that two opposed and antagonistic forces of good and evil determine the course of events 4 **DUAL NATURE OF PEOPLE** the religious idea that people are inherently dual in nature, both spiritual and physical —**dualist** *n* —**dualistic** /dyoó ə lístik/ *adj* —**dualistically** *adv*

duality /dyoo állәti/ (*plural* **-ties**) *n* 1 **SOMETHING CONSISTING OF TWO PARTS** a situation or nature that has two states or parts that are complementary or opposed to each other 2 **THEORY OF MATTER** in microphysics, the theory that both wave and particle theory account for the behaviour of matter and energy under different conditions 3 **MATHEMATICAL SYMMETRY OF OBJECTS OR OPERATIONS** a mathematical symmetry in which certain objects or operations to be interchanged without invalidating a relationship, e.g. the interchange of points and lines in a plane in projective geometry

dual-purpose *adj* capable of performing two functions satisfactorily ○ *a dual-purpose cleaner*

ϟ **dual signature** *n* the linking of two discrete parts of a single message allowing a cardholder to communicate with a merchant and a payment gateway simultaneously (*in e-commerce*)

Duarte /dwaár tay/, **José Napoleón** (1925–90) Salvadorean statesman and president (1980–82, 1984–89)

dub[1] /dub/ *vt* (**dubs, dubbing, dubbed**) 1 **GIVE DESCRIPTIVE NICKNAME** to give a descriptive nickname to somebody or something ○ *The press dubbed him the King of Chess.* 2 **CONFER A KNIGHTHOOD ON** to give somebody a knighthood by tapping the person on the shoulder with a sword as part of a formal ceremony 3 **MAKE SOMETHING SMOOTH OR EVEN** to dress a material, e.g. leather or timber, to make it smooth or even 4 **DECORATE AN ARTIFICIAL FLY** to add material such as hair or fur to an artificial fly, to give body and a natural look ■ *n* **SOUND OF A DRUM** the sound a drum makes [Pre-12C. < Anglo-Norman *duber*, variant of Old French *adober* 'equip with armour'.] —**dubber** *n*

dub[2] /dub/ *vt* (**dubs, dubbing, dubbed**) 1 **ADD A SOUNDTRACK IN A DIFFERENT LANGUAGE** to add a new soundtrack to a film or television show with the dialogue in a different language but synchronized as closely as possible with the actors' lips ○ *The film was dubbed into Italian.* 2 **COPY SOMETHING ONTO NEW MEDIUM** to copy something already recorded onto a different recording medium 3 **COPY** to make a copy of a record or tape 4 **ADD SOUNDS TO A FILM** to add sounds that have been recorded separately to a film soundtrack ■ *n* 1 **SOMETHING ADDED BY DUBBING** new sounds added by dubbing 2 **COPY OF RECORDING** a copy made of a tape or recording 3 **STYLE OF MUSIC** a style of popular music, originating in reggae in the 1970s, involving remixing records to bring certain instruments into the foreground and causing others to echo [Early 20C. Shortening of DOUBLE.] —**dubber** *n*

dub[3] /dub/ *n Scotland, N England* a puddle or small pool of water on the ground, especially in the road [15C. < ?]

Dubai /doo bí/, **Dubayy** capital of Dubai state in the NE United Arab Emirates. Population: 674,100 (1995).

dubbin /dúbbin/ *n* a mixture of oil and tallow rubbed into leather to soften it and make it waterproof [Early 19C. Alteration of *dubbing*, present participle of DUB[1].]

dubbing /dúbbing/ *n* 1 **PROCESS OF ADDING NEW SOUNDTRACK** the process of providing a new soundtrack for a film or television show with the dialogue in a different language but synchronized as closely as possible with the actors' lips 2 **SOUNDTRACK** a soundtrack recorded for a film or television show after the photography is finished 3 **FINAL SOUNDTRACK** a final mix of all the soundtracks for a film

Dubbo /dúbbō/ town in central New South Wales, Australia. Population: 28,040 (1991).

Dubček /doóp chek, doób-/, **Alexander** (1921–92) Czech statesman

dubiety /dyoo bí əti/ (*plural* **-ties**) *n* (*formal*) 1 a feeling of uncertainty about something 2 something about which you are unsure [Mid-18C. < late Latin *dubietas* < Latin *dubius* 'doubtful'.]

dubious /dyoóbi əss/ *adj* 1 **UNSURE ABOUT AN OUTCOME** uncertain about an outcome or conclusion ○ *I was a little dubious about whether or not to trust him.* 2 **POSSIBLY DISHONEST OR IMMORAL** likely to be dishonest, untrustworthy, or morally worrying in some way ○ *It's a dubious proposition.* 3 **OF UNCERTAIN QUALITY** of uncertain quality, intention, or appropriateness ○ *The thesis is based on several dubious theories.* [Mid-16C. < Latin *dubius* 'doubtful'.] —**dubiously** *adv* —**dubiousness** *n*

SYNONYMS See ***doubtful***.

dubitable /dyoóbitəb'l/ *adj* causing or leading to doubt or uncertainty (*formal*) [Early 17C. < Latin *dubitabilis* < *dubitare* 'be uncertain'.] —**dubitably** *adv*

Dublin /dúbblin/ capital of the Republic of Ireland. Population: 953,000 (1996). Irish **Baile Átha Cliath** —**Dubliner** *n*

dubnium /dúbni əm/ *n* (*symbol* **Db**) an extremely rare, unstable element. Source: high-energy bombardment of californium.

Du Bois /doó bóyss/, **W. E. B.** (1868–1963) US historian, sociologist, and civil rights leader. Full name **William Edward Burghardt Du Bois**

dub poetry *n* performance poetry using the rhythms and speech styles of Caribbean English [< disc jockeys dubbing their own words onto records]

Dubrovnik /doó bróvnik/ coastal city in SE Croatia. Population: 49,728 (1991).

Dubuffet /dyoó boó fay/, **Jean** (1901–85) French painter and sculptor

ducal /dyoók'l/ *adj* belonging to, relating to, or like a duke or dukedom ○ *a ducal palace* [15C. < French, < *duc* (see DUKE).] —**ducally** *adv*

ducat /dúkət/ *n* a gold or silver coin formerly used in European countries, e.g. Italy and the Netherlands ■ **ducats** *npl* money or cash (*dated informal*) [14C. Via Old French < medieval Latin *ducatus* 'duchy' (see DUCHY); because the word appeared on early coins.]

Duccio di Buoninsegna /dúchi ō di bwónnin sényə/ (1260–1320) Italian painter

duce /doó chay, doóchi/ *n* an Italian term for 'leader'. The Italian Fascist leader Mussolini was called 'Il Duce'. [Early 20C. Via Italian < Latin *dux* 'leader'.]

Duchamp /dyoó shaaN/, **Marcel** (1887–1968) French-born US artist

Duchenne muscular dystrophy /doo shén-/, **Duchenne's muscular dystrophy** /doo shénz-/, **Duchenne dystrophy, Duchenne's dystrophy** *n* a form of muscular dystrophy that attacks the muscles of the upper respiratory and pelvic areas, usually affecting boys and causing death before maturity [Late 19C. After G. B. A. *Duchenne* (1806–75), French neurologist.]

duchess /dúchəss/ *n* 1 a noblewoman of high rank 2 the wife or widow of a duke [14C. Via Old French *duchesse* < medieval Latin *ducissa*, feminine form of *dux* 'leader'.]

duchesse satin /dyoo shéss-/ *n* a firm heavy satin with a glossy finish. Use: formal gowns.

duchy /dúchi/ (*plural* **-ies**) *n* the territory over which a duke or duchess has jurisdiction [14C. Via Old French *duche* < medieval Latin *ducatus* < Latin *duc-*, stem of *dux* 'leader'.]

duck[1] /duk/ *n* 1 (*plural* **ducks** *or* **duck**) **COMMON WATER BIRD** a common water bird with webbed feet, short legs, and a broad flat bill. Order: Anseriformes. 2 **FEMALE DUCK** a female duck. ◊ **drake** 3 **DUCK AS FOOD** the flesh of a duck when eaten as a food 4 **duck, ducks DEAR** used when addressing somebody in a friendly way (*informal regional*) ○ *Can I help you, ducks?* 5 **ODD PERSON** a mildly unconventional person [Old English *dūce* < ?] ◇ **take to something like a duck to water** to have a natural talent for something

duck[2] /duk/ *v* 1 *vti* **BEND QUICKLY** to bend or move the head down quickly, especially to avoid being hit by something 2 *vi* **MOVE QUICKLY** to move somewhere very quickly, often to avoid being seen ○ *I ducked behind a desk and kept as still as possible.* 3 *vti* **PLUNGE UNDER WATER** to push somebody under water, or move quickly so as to go below the surface of the water 4 *vt* **AVOID** to avoid dealing with something that ought to be dealt with ○ *The candidate ducked all the questions about her past.* 5 *vi* **DELIBERATELY LOSE A TRICK** to play a card lower than an opponent's on purpose in order to lose a trick ■ *n* **QUICK DOWNWARD MOVEMENT** a movement downwards with the head, especially to avoid being hit by something [13C. Probably < assumed Old English *dūcan* < W Germanic, 'dive, dip'.] —**ducker** *n* ◇ **duck and run** to avoid meeting somebody face to face

duck out *vi* to avoid or dodge doing something ○ *She's trying to duck out of paying her part of the bill.*

duck[3] /duk/ *n* strong, fairly stiff, closely-woven cotton or canvas cloth. Use: protective clothing, furnishings. ■ **ducks** *npl* a pair of trousers, usually white, or like those worn by sailors

duck[4] /duk/ *n* a score of zero by a batsman or batswoman [Shortening of *duck's egg*, a zero] ◇ **break your duck** have your first success or victory after several failures ◇ **have your ducks in a row, have your ducks lined up in a row** 1 *US* to have all the relevant facts or material ready for presentation 2 to have everything prepared and organized

Duck-billed platypus

duck-billed platypus *n* an egg-laying aquatic mammal with a snout shaped like a duck's bill and webbed feet. Native to: Australia. *Ornithorynchus anatinus.*

duckboard /dúk bawrd/ *n* a temporary walkway made of wooden boards laid over a wet or muddy area to form a raised path

duck-egg blue *n* a pale greenish-blue colour —**duck-egg blue** *adj*

ducking and diving *n* erratic moving or running, in order to avoid being shot or hit

ducking stool *n* formerly, in Europe and New England, a chair or stool in which an offender was tied and then immersed in water as a punishment

duckling /dúkling/ *n* a duck that has not reached maturity

ducks *n* ◆ **duck**[1] *n.* 4

dune buggy *n* TRANSP = **beach buggy**

Dunfermline /dun fúrmlin/ town in E Scotland. Population: 55,083 (1991).

dung /dung/ *n* **1** the solid excrement of animals, especially large animals such as cattle or horses **2** AGRIC = **manure** *n.* 1 ■ *vt* to cover land with dung or manure [Old English < ?] —**dungy** *adj*

Dungannon /dun gánnən/ town in S Northern Ireland. Population: 9,420 (1991).

dungaree /dúng gə reé/ *n* a sturdy hard-wearing blue-denim fabric [Late 17C. < Hindi *dungrī* 'kind of coarse cloth', after a village near Mumbai (Bombay).]

dungarees /dúng gə reéz/ *npl* **1** a garment made from strong material consisting of loose-fitting trousers with an attached bib and shoulder straps, intended to be worn over ordinary clothing for protection while working. ◊ **overall** *npl.* 2 **2** a casual garment of trousers and bib front, usually made from denim and worn especially by women and children

dung beetle *n* a scarab beetle that rolls large balls of dung into tunnels to feed the larvae that hatch from the eggs it lays there. Subfamily: Coprinae.

Dungeness /dúnjə néss/ shingle headland on the coast of SE England, site of two nuclear power stations

dungeon /dúnjən/ *n* a prison cell, often underground, especially beneath a castle [14C. Via Old French *donjon* 'castle keep' (later 'secure underground cell') < Latin *dominus* 'lord'.]

dunghill /dúng hil/, **dungheap** /-heep/ *n* a pile of solid animal excrement

dunite /dúnīt/ *n* a coarse-grained dark igneous rock consisting mainly of a magnesium-rich olivine [Mid-19C. After Mt *Dun*, New Zealand.] —**dunitic** /də nÍttik/ *adj*

dunk /dungk/ *vt* **1** to dip food into a liquid before eating it **2** to submerge something in liquid, especially quickly and for a short time ■ *n US* BASKETBALL = **dunk shot** [Early 20C. Via Pennsylvanian German *dunke* 'dip' < Old High German *dunkōn*.] —**dunker** *n*

Dunker /dúngkər/, **Dunkard** /-ərd/ *n* a member of a group of German-American Baptists, the German Baptist Brethren [Mid-18C. < Pennsylvanian German, < *dunke* 'dip'.]

Dunkirk /dun kúrk/ port in NE France. In World War II over 330,000 Allied troops were evacuated from the town by sea, under constant enemy fire. Population: 71,071 (1990).

Dunk Island /dúngk-/ island off the E coast of Queensland, Australia

dunk shot *n US* a shot in basketball made by jamming or slamming the ball through the hoop from above

Dún Laoghaire /dun leéri, doon-/ port on Dublin Bay on the E coast of the Republic of Ireland. Population: 55,540 (1991).

dunlin /dúnnlin/ (*plural* **-lins** *or* **-lin**) *n* a small wading bird with a slightly downcurved bill and a black belly. Native to: North America, Europe, Africa, Asia. *Calidris alpina.* [Mid-16C. < DUN[1].]

Dunlop /dún lop/, **John Boyd** (1840–1921) British inventor

Dunlop, Weary (1907–93) Australian surgeon and war hero. Born **Sir Ernest Edward Dunlop**

dunnage /dúnnij/ *n* packing material used to cushion cargo on a ship [14C. < ?]

Dunnet Head /dúnnət-/ peninsula and northernmost point of mainland Scotland

dunnite /dúnnīt/ *n* an explosive that contains ammonium picrate [Early 20C. After Col. B. W. *Dunn* (1860–1936).]

dunno /də nṓ, du-/ *contr* (I) don't know (*nonstandard*) ○ *'Who broke the glass'? 'Dunno'.*

dunnock /dúnnək/ *n* a woodland bird distinguished from the house sparrow by its thin bill and grey head and breast. Native to: Europe. *Prunella modularis.* [15C. Probably < DUN[1].]

Dunoon /də nóon/ resort town on the Firth of Clyde, W Scotland. Population: 9,038 (1991).

Dunsinane /dun sínnən/ hill in central Scotland, site of Macbeth's castle in Shakespeare's play *Macbeth.* Height: 308 m/1,012 ft.

Duns Scotus /dúnz skṓtəss/, **John** (1266?–1308) Scottish philosopher and theologian

Dunstable /dúnstəb'l/ town in central England. Population: 49,666 (1991).

Dunstable, Dunstaple /dúnstəp'l/, **John** (1390?–1453) English composer and mathematician

Dunstan /dúnstən/, **St** (909?–988) Anglo-Saxon prelate and reformer

dunt /dunt/ *n* (*regional*) **1** INJURY FROM BLOW the injury or damage caused by a hit or a blow **2** ACT OF HITTING a hit or blow ■ *vt* HIT to strike somebody or something (*regional*) [15C. Variant of DINT.]

Duntroon /dun tróon/ suburb of North Canberra, Australian Capital Territory, Australia. Population: 1,906 (1996).

duo /dyóo ō/ (*plural* **-os**) *n* **1** DUET a duet, especially one for two instruments **2** PLAYERS OF A DUET a pair of musicians who play together **3** PAIR OF CLOSELY ASSOCIATED PEOPLE two people who are considered to be closely connected in some way **4** SET OF TWO CLOSELY RELATED THINGS a set of two items considered closely connected [Late 16C. Via Italian, 'two' < Latin.]

duo- *prefix* two ○ *duopoly* [< Latin, < Indo-European]

duodecimal /dyóo ō déssim'l/ *adj* BASED ON 12 using units of 12 as a basis for counting or ordering ■ *n* **1** DUODECIMAL NUMBER a number used to count or order in units of 12 **2** 12TH a 12th part [Early 18C. < Latin *duodecimus* 'twelfth'.] —**duodecimally** *adv*

duodecimo /dyóo ō déssi mō/ (*plural* **-mos**) *n* a book size in which each leaf is formed by folding the printing sheet twelve times, or a book of this size [Mid-17C. < Latin *in duodecimo* 'in twelfth'.]

duodenum /dyóo ō deé nəm/ (*plural* **-na** /-nə/ *or* **-nums**) *n* the first short section of the small intestine immediately beyond the stomach [14C. < medieval Latin *intestinum duodenum digitorum* 'intestine 12 finger-breadths long' < Latin *duodecim* 'twelve'.] —**duodenal** *adj*

duologue /dyóo ə log/ *n* **1** a play or part of a play in which only two actors speak **2** a dialogue between two actors, or a conversation between two people [Mid-18C. Blend of DUO + MONOLOGUE.]

duomo /dwṓmō/ (*plural* **-mos** *or* **-mi** /-mi/) *n* a cathedral in Italy [Mid-16C. Via Italian < Latin *domus* 'house'.]

duopoly /dyoo óppəli/ (*plural* **-lies**) *n* an economic situation in which two powerful groups or organizations concentrate or dominate commerce in one business market or commodity [Early 20C. After MONOPOLY.] —**duopolistic** /dyoo óppə lístik/ *adj*

duopsony /dyoo ópsəni/ (*plural* **-nies**) *n* a situation in which two competing buyers exert controlling influence over many sellers [< DUO + *-opsony* < Greek *opsōnía* 'purchasing of food']

Dupain /dyoo páyn/, **Max** (1911–92) Australian photographer. Full name **Maxwell Spencer Dupain**

dupe /dyoop/ *vt* (**dupes, duping, duped**) to persuade or induce somebody to do something by trickery or deception ○ *He was duped into thinking that they intended to pay.* ■ *n* an object of trickery or deceit [Late 17C. < French.] —**dupability** /dyóopə bílləti/ *n* —**dupable** *adj* —**duper** *n* —**dupery** *n*

dupion /dyóopi on/ *n* a rough silk fabric woven from threads of a double cocoon [Early 19C. Via French *doupion* < Italian *doppione* < *doppio* 'double'.]

duple /dyóop'l/ *adj* consisting of two beats to the bar or measure [Mid-16C. < Latin *duplus* 'double'.]

Duplessis /dyoo pléssi/, **Maurice Le Noblet** (1890–1959) Canadian statesman

duplet /dyóoplət/ *n* **1** a pair of electrons shared between two atoms that are joined in a chemical bond **2** a group of 2 notes played in the time usually required by three [Mid-17C. After DOUBLET.]

duple time *n* a musical metre in which there are two beats to the bar, e.g. 2/4 or 6/8

duplex /dyóo pleks/ *n* **1** *Aus, Can, US* 2-FAMILY DWELLING a house that is divided into two halves and is inhabited by two separate families or tenants with separate entrances and exits **2** TRANSMISSION IN BOTH DIRECTIONS transmission of signals along a communications channel in both directions at the same time, e.g. over a telephone line ■ *adj* **1** TWOFOLD consisting of two parts, especially two identical or equivalent parts **2** HAVING TWO PARTS PERFORMING ONE OPERATION consisting of pairs of units or components that perform the same machine function but operate independently [Mid-16C. < Latin, 'twofold' < *plicare* 'to fold'.] —**duplexity** /dyoo pléksəti/ *n*

duplicate *vt* /dyóopli kayt/ (**-cates, -cating, -cated**) **1** COPY to make an exact copy of something **2** REPEAT to do something more than once, especially unknowingly or unnecessarily ■ *n* /-kət/ **1** COPY MADE an exact copy, especially of a document **2** ANOTHER OF THE SAME a spare of the same kind **3** THING REPEATED a repeat of an earlier action or achievement ■ *adj* /-kət/ **1** COPIED EXACTLY being an exact copy of something ○ *a duplicate key* **2** HAVING 2 CORRESPONDING PARTS consisting of or existing in two corresponding parts [15C. < Latin *duplicare* 'make twofold, double' < *duplus* 'twofold'.] —**duplicability** /dyóoplikə bílləti/ *n* —**duplicable** /dyóoplikəb'l/ *adj* —**duplicately** /dyóoplikətli/ *adv* —**duplicative** /-kətiv/ *adj* ◇ **in duplicate** so as to create or consist of two exact copies

SYNONYMS See ***copy***.

duplicate bridge *n* contract bridge in which the same hand is played by different consecutive players

duplication /dyóopli káysh'n/ *n* **1** REPEATING OR COPYING the action or an act of duplicating something **2** EXACT COPY an exact copy of something **3** REPETITION OF GENES a chromosome mutation in which a section of a chromosome, along with the genes it carries, occurs twice

duplicator /dyóopli kaytər/ *n* something that makes copies, especially a machine for copying printed matter

duplicity /dyoo plíssəti/ *n* **1** the fact of being deceptive, dishonest, or misleading **2** the state of being double or in a pair (*formal*) ○ *the duplicity of the stars of the constellation* [15C. Directly or via French *duplicité* < late Latin *duplicitas* < Latin *duplic-*, stem of *duplex* (see DUPLEX).] —**duplicitous** /dyoo plíssitəss/ *adj* —**duplicitously** *adv* —**duplicitousness** *n*

duppy /dúppi/ (*plural* **-pies**) *n Carib* a ghost or spirit [Late 18C. < ?]

du Pré /dyoo práy/, **Jacqueline** (1945–87) British cellist and teacher

Dupré /dyoo práy/, **Marcel** (1886–1971) French musician and composer

durable /dyóorəb'l/ *adj* lasting for a long time, especially without sustaining damage or wear ○ *durable materials* ○ *a durable peace* [14C. Via Old French < Latin *durabilis* < *durare* 'last, harden'.] —**durability** /dyóorə bílləti/ *n* —**durableness** *n* —**durably** *adv*

durable goods *npl* long-lasting products, e.g. motor vehicles and large appliances such as cookers and refrigerators. US term **durables**

durables /dyóorəb'lz/ *n* COMM = **durable goods**

Durack /dyóor ak/ river in Western Australia. Length: 230 km/143 mi.

Durack, Dame Mary (1913–94) Australian writer

dura mater /dyóorə máytər/ *n* the tough outermost membrane of the three that cover the brain and spinal cord [14C. < medieval Latin, 'hard mother', translation of Arabic *al-'umm al-jāfiya* 'coarse mother'.] —**dural** /dyóorəl/ *adj*

duramen /dyoo ráymən/ *n* heartwood (*technical*) [Mid-19C. < Latin, 'hardness' < *durare* 'last, harden'.]

durance /dyóoranss/ *n* forcible confinement or imprisonment (*archaic or literary*) [15C. < Old French, < Latin *durare* 'last, harden'.]

Durance /dyoo raánss/ river in SE France. Length: 505 mi./813 km.

Durango /dyoo ráng gō/ capital of Durango State, central Mexico. Population: 413,835 (1990).

Durante /də ránti/, **Jimmy** (1893–1980) US comic entertainer. Full name **James Francis Durante**

Duras /dyoo raa/, **Marguerite** (1914–96) Vietnamese-born French novelist, playwright, film director, and screenwriter

duration /dyoo ráysh'n/ *n* the period of time that something lasts or exists ○ *an interval of 15 minutes' duration* [14C. Via Old French < medieval Latin *duration-* < Latin *durare* 'last, harden'.] —**durational** *adj* ◇ **for the duration** for the entire period of time that something is going on or will continue to go on

durative /dyóorətiv/ *adj* describes a verb in a continuous tense or aspect or a verb indicating a continuous action

Durban /dúrbən/ port in E South Africa. Population: 715,669 (1991).

durbar /dúr baar/ *n* formerly, an official reception held by a local prince or British governor in colonial India, or by a local chief or British official in colonial Africa [Early 17C. < Urdu *darbār* < Persian *dar* 'door' + *bār* 'court'.]

Dürer /dyóorər/, **Albrecht** (1471–1528) German painter and engraver

duress /dyoo réss/ *n* **1** the use of force or threats to make somebody do something **2** illegal force or coercion used, e.g., against a criminal suspect or a prisoner in lawful custody before trial [14C. Via Old French *duresse* < Latin *duritia* 'hardness' < *durus* 'hard'.]

Durex /dyóor eks/ *tdmk* **1** *UK* a trademark for a brand of condom **2** *Aus* a trademark for a type of transparent adhesive tape

Durga /dóorgə/ *n* a goddess who is one of the most important Hindu deities, embodying for many the supreme manifest form of godhead

Durgapur /dúrgə poor/, **Durgāpur** city in NE India. Population: 425,836 (1991).

Durham[1] /dúrrəm/ city in NE England. Population: 85,800 (1991).

Durham[2] /dúrrəm/ *n* a shorthorn beef or dairy cow belonging to a hardy breed originating in NE England

Durham[3] /dúrrəm/ county in NE England. Population: 507,100 (1995). Area: 2,435 sq. km/940 sq. mi.

durian /dyóori ən/ *n* **1** a foul-smelling but deliciously flavoured fruit **2** the tree that bears durians. Native to: tropical rain forests of SE Asia. *Durio zibethinus.* [Late 16C. < Malay, < *duri* 'thorn, prickle'.]

duricrust /dyóori krust/ *n* a hard crust formed on the surface of the soil by the precipitation of soluble minerals from mineral waters, particularly during the dry season in semiarid climates [Early 20C. < Latin *durus* 'hard'.]

during /dyóoring/ *prep* **1** throughout a particular period or event, either continuously or several times between the beginning and the end ○ *There was not even a whisper during the service.* **2** at some point or moment within a particular period or event ○ *I can't remember the date, but it was during the winter.* [14C. Present participle of obsolete *dure* 'last' < Old French *durer* < Latin *durus* 'hard'.]

Durkheim /dúrk hīm/, **Émile** (1858–1917) French social theorist

durmast oak /dúr maast/, **durmast** *n* an oak tree that has lobed leaves and yields a heavy flexible wood. Use: cabinet-making. Native to: Europe, Asia Minor. *Quercus petraea.* [Late 18C. < ?]

durn /durn/ *interj, adj, adv, vt Southern US* used to indicate frustration or mild anger (*informal*) [Variant of DARN[2]]

duro /dóorō/ (*plural* **-ros**) *n* in some Latin American countries and formerly in Spain, a coin worth a peso or a dollar [Late 18C. < Spanish *peso duro* 'hard or solid piastre'.]

durra /dóorrə/, **dourra** *n* a sorghum grown for its grain and as animal feed, especially in tropical and warm arid areas. *Sorghum bicolor.* [Late 18C. < Arabic *dura.*]

Durrell /dúrrəl/, **Gerald** (1925–95) British naturalist and writer

Durrell, Lawrence (1912–90) British novelist, poet, and travel writer

Dürrenmatt /dyóorrən mat/, **Friedrich** (1921–90) Swiss writer

Durrës /dúrrəss/ port in W Albania. Population: 85,400 (1990 estimate).

durrie *n* TEXTILES = **dhurrie**

durst /durst/ past tense of **dare** (*archaic*)

durum wheat /dyóorəm/, **durum** *n* a wheat that produces glutinous flour. Use: pasta. *Triticum durum.* [Early 20C. < Latin, form of *durus* 'hard'.]

Duryea /dóoryay, dóor i ay/, **Charles Edgar** (1861–1938) US car manufacturer and inventor

Duse /dóoz ay/, **Eleonora** (1859–1924) Italian actress

Dushanbe /doo shaánbi/ capital of Tajikistan, in the western part of the country. Population: 602,000 (1990 estimate).

dusk /dusk/ *n* **1 PERIOD AFTER DAY BUT BEFORE NIGHT** the period of the day after the sun has gone below the horizon but before the sky has become dark **2 ABSENCE OF DAYLIGHT** partial or almost complete darkness (*literary*) ■ *adj* **DIM** having little or insufficient light (*literary*) ■ *vti* **DARKEN** to become or make something dark (*literary*) [Old English *dox* 'dark in colour' < Indo-European]

dusky /dúski/ (**-ier, -iest**) *adj* **1 DARK-COLOURED** rather dark in colour **2 DIM** having little or insufficient light **3 OFFENSIVE TERM** an offensive term meaning having a rather dark skin or complexion (*dated*) —**duskily** *adv* —**duskiness** *n*

Dusky Sound /dúski-/ coastal inlet in the SW part of the South Island, New Zealand

Düsseldorf /dóoss'l dawrf/ capital of North Rhine-Westphalia, west-central Germany. Population: 572,638 (1997).

dust /dust/ *n* **1 SMALL DRY PARTICLES** very small dry particles of a substance such as sand or coal, either in the form of a deposit or a cloud **2 HOUSEHOLD DIRT** the small pieces of dirt that accumulate in a layer on horizontal surfaces in buildings **3 REMOVAL OF DUST** an act of removing small particles of dirt from something, usually by wiping with a cloth **4 REMAINS FROM DECAY** the small particles that something, especially a human body, is thought to be reduced to by decay after death **5 EARTH AS A BURIAL PLACE** dirt or soil, particularly that of somebody's grave (*literary*) **6 RUBBISH** household rubbish **7 MINERS' DISEASE** silicosis or another respiratory disease affecting miners (*informal*) ■ *v* **1** *vti* **CLEAN OFF DIRT PARTICLES** to remove small particles of dirt from something, usually by wiping with a cloth **2** *vt* **SPRINKLE** to sprinkle a powdery substance over something ○ *Dust the board with flour to stop the dough sticking to it.* [Old English *dūst* < Germanic] —**dustless** *adj* ◇ **(as) dry as dust** so scholarly and devoid of humour as to be arid in tone and content ◇ **bite the dust 1** to die, especially in or as a result of a fight (*informal*) **2** to suffer total failure (*informal*) ◇ **gather dust** to remain unused over a period of time ◇ **kick up** *or* **raise a dust** to cause a controversy or loud disturbance (*informal*) ◇ **shake the dust (of something) from your feet** to leave somewhere for ever, especially when glad to do so ◇ **throw dust in somebody's eyes** to attempt to deceive or mislead somebody

dust down *vt* **1 dust down, dust off RECYCLE SOMETHING OLD** to prepare something for reuse or further consideration **2 WIPE OR BRUSH** to clean something, especially by wiping or brushing it **3 REPRIMAND** to tell somebody off severely (*dated*)

dust up *vt* to attack somebody verbally or physically (*slang*)

dust-bath *n* a form of grooming behaviour in animals, especially birds, that consists in rolling or making agitated movements in the dust on the ground in order to remove parasites

dustbin /dúst bin/ *n* a large lidded usually cylindrical container for household rubbish, kept outdoors. US term **garbage can**

dustbin man *n UK* = **dustman**

dust bowl *n* an area in a semiarid environment in which the topsoil is exposed and dust storms are likely to occur

Dust Bowl *n* a large area in the southern part of the central United States that suffered badly from wind erosion during the 1930s

dustcart /dúst kaart/ *n UK* a large motor vehicle used to collect and compact waste materials left bagged or in containers outside buildings. ◊ **garbage truck**

dust cloth *n US* = **duster** *n.* **1**

dust cover *n* **1** a cover, often made from transparent plastic, for protecting a piece of equipment **2** PUBL = **dust jacket 3** = **dustsheet**

dust devil *n* a rising or travelling funnel of dust, dirt, or sand that occurs on hot days, especially in desert or arid areas

duster /dústər/ *n* **1 CLEANING CLOTH** a piece of cloth used for removing dust, especially from household objects and surfaces. US term **dust cloth 2 DUST REMOVER** a cloth or pad that removes household dust **3** CLOTHING = **dust coat 4 DEVICE FOR SPREADING AGROCHEMICALS** a machine or device for spreading powdered fungicide, insecticide, or fertilizer over crops or other plants **5 WOMAN'S LONG LOOSE COAT** a woman or girl's long loose coat, sometimes one without buttons or lapels

dustily /dústili/ *adv* in an abrupt and impolite manner

dustiness /dústinəss/ *n* **1** the state of being covered with or containing dust **2** curtness and impoliteness

dusting /dústing/ *n* **1 REMOVAL OF DUST** the act of removing small particles of dirt from something, usually by wiping with a cloth **2 THIN POWDERY COVERING** a thin, sometimes patchy covering of a powdery substance ○ *a dusting of snow on the ground* **3 DEFEAT** a defeat or setback (*slang*) ○ *a candidate who took a real dusting at the polls*

dusting down *n* a severe telling-off

dusting powder *n* fine powder such as talcum powder, especially for use on the skin

dust jacket *n* a paper book cover that protects the hardbound binding and that can be discarded

dustman /dústmən/ (*plural* **-men** /-mən/) *n UK* somebody employed to remove rubbish, especially from dustbins outside people's houses. ◊ **garbage man**

dustpan /dúst pan/ *n* a container with a flat base and an open front into which dirt and dust can be swept

dustsheet /dúst sheet/ *n* a large piece of cloth placed over furniture or furnishings to protect them from dust, dirt, or paint. US term **drop cloth**

dust storm *n* a strong hot dry wind laden with dust

dust-up *n* a violent argument or physical altercation, often one that starts and stops quickly (*slang*)

dusty /dústi/ (**-ier, -iest**) *adj* **1 FULL OF DUST** covered with or containing dust **2 TINGED WITH GREY** containing tinges of grey ○ *dusty pink* **3 BORING** boring, especially because of being obscure or outdated ○ *dusty political slogans* **4 LIKE DUST** resembling dust ○ *a dusty gold powder* ◇ **not so dusty** all right (*dated informal; in answer to a query about somebody's health*)

Dusty /dústi/, **Slim** (*b.* 1927) Australian singer and songwriter. Born **David Gordon Kirkpatrick**

dusty answer *n* a reply that is unhelpful and curt or impolite (*dated*)

dusty miller *n* **1** a plant with grey or white leaves covered with a down resembling dust. *Senecio cineraria* and *Cerastium tomentosum.* **2** = **rose campion**

dutch /duch/ *n Cockney* somebody's wife (*slang*) [Late 19C. Shortening of DUCHESS.]

Dutch /duch/ *n* the official language of the Netherlands and the Republic of Suriname, belonging to the West Germanic group of Indo-European languages. Native speakers: 20 million. ■ *npl* the people of the Netherlands [14C. < Middle Dutch *dutsch* < Germanic, 'people'.] —**Dutch** *adj* ◇ **go Dutch** to pay for your own part of the cost of a meal or entertainment

Dutch auction *n* an auction in which the price is lowered gradually until somebody makes a bid

Dutch barn *n* a farm building with a curved roof and open sides and two levels. Hay, straw, and grain are stored on the upper level and animals are kept below.

Dutch cap *n* a contraceptive diaphragm with triangular flaps, of a type no longer used (*informal*)

Dutch courage *n* the temporary confidence supposedly obtained from drinking alcohol (*informal*)

Dutch doll *n* a wooden doll with jointed limbs and body

Dutch East Indies former name for **Indonesia**

Dutch elm *n* a cultivated hybrid elm tree introduced to Great Britain from the Netherlands in the 17th century and now common in NE France and parts of W Great Britain and Ireland. *Ulmus x hollandica.*

Dutch elm disease *n* a disease of elm trees caused by a fungus, *Ceratocystis ulmi,* carried by a bark beetle [Because identified by Dutch scientists]

Dutch Guiana /dúch gi aánə/ former name for **Suriname** (until 1948)

Dutch hoe *n* a hoe used for weeding that is pushed instead of pulled

Dutchman /dúchmən/ (*plural* **-men** /-mən/) *n* **1** a man who comes from the Netherlands **2** a piece of building material used to repair or conceal a fault in a construction ◇ **I'm a Dutchman** you may assert something but even if you do, I do not believe you ○ *If that's a genuine antique, I'm a Dutchman.*

Dutchman's breeches (*plural* **Dutchman's breeches**) *n* a woodland plant that has creamy white flowers with two spurs. Native to: E United States. *Dicentra cucullaria.*

Dutchman's pipe *n* a woody climbing vine that has mottled greenish-brown flowers shaped like the bowl and stem of an old-fashioned tobacco pipe. Native to: E United States. *Aristolochia sipho.*

Dutch oven *n* **1** an iron or earthenware container with a lid, used for cooking stews or casseroles **2** a metal box with an open front placed beside an open fire so that food can be cooked inside it

Dutch treat *n* an outing, e.g. to a restaurant or theatre, at which each person pays for himself or herself (*informal*)

Dutch uncle *n* somebody, typically a mentor, who criticizes or advises in a frank, sometimes harsh manner (*informal*)

Dutch wife *n* a firm bolster or framework used in bed to support the upper knee while somebody is sleeping on his or her side

Dutchwoman /dúch wŏŏmən/ (*plural* **-en** /-wimmin/) *n* a woman who comes from the Netherlands

duteous /dyóoti əss/ *adj* obedient or submitting to duty (*archaic*) —**duteously** *adv* —**duteousness** *n*

dutiable /dyóoti əb'l/ *adj* subject to customs or other duties —**dutiability** /dyóoti ə bílləti/ *n*

dutiful /dyóotif'l/ *adj* **1** done to fulfil obligations, often with little enthusiasm ○ *made a dutiful attempt at conversation* **2** acting according to obligations ○ *a dutiful and hard-working employee* —**dutifully** *adv* —**dutifulness** *n*

Dutton /dútt'n/, **Geoffrey Piers Henry** (*b.* 1922) Australian writer and editor

duty /dyóoti/ (*plural* **-ties**) *n* **1 OBLIGATION** something that somebody is obliged to do for moral, legal, or religious reasons ○ *your duties as a parent* **2 ALLOCATED TASK** a task or service allocated to somebody, especially in the course of work **3 NEED TO MEET OBLIGATIONS** the urge to meet moral or religious obligations ○ *a strong sense of duty* **4 TAX** a tax on goods, especially imports and exports **5 QUALITY** suitability for a particular grade of use (*usually in combination*) ○ *heavy-duty shoes* ○ *medium-duty carpet* **6 MACHINE'S WORKLOAD** the amount of work that a machine is designed to do, or a measure of a machine's efficiency **7 VOLUME OF WATER FOR IRRIGATION** the volume of water that is needed in order to irrigate an area of land so as to cultivate a crop from planting to harvest time [13C. < Anglo-Norman *dueté* < Old French *deu* 'owed' (see DUE).] ◇ **off duty** not at work (*hyphenated before nouns*) ○ *an off-duty police officer* ◇ **on duty** at work

duty-free *adj* **EXEMPTED FROM EXCISE DUTIES** on or at which no customs or excise duties have to be paid ■ *adv* **WITHOUT CUSTOMS AND EXCISE DUTIES** without paying or charging customs or excise duties ■ *n* **SHOP SELLING DUTY-FREE GOODS** a shop, especially at an airport or on board ship, that sells duty-free goods ■ **duty-frees** *npl* **DUTY-FREE GOODS** duty-free goods, especially the allowance of duty-free goods that an individual is allowed to bring into his or her own country

duty of care *n* the legal duty of everyone who has control of waste to ensure that it is managed safely and transferred only to somebody authorized to take it

duty officer *n* an officer who is present in an office or headquarters and responsible for handling situations that may arise during a given period, especially a period when others are off duty

duumvir /dyoo úmvər/ (*plural* **-virs** *or* **-viri** /-və reel/) *n* **1** either of two people who share a position of authority equally between them **2** a joint holder of any of the paired posts in the ancient Roman government or judiciary [Early 17C. < Latin, < *duo* 'two' + *vir* 'man'.] —**duumvirate** *n*

Duvalier /dyŏŏ válli ay/, **François** (1907–71) Haitian national leader and doctor. Known as **Papa Doc**

Duvalier, Jean-Claude (*b.* 1951) Haitian national leader. Known as **Baby Doc**

duvet /dŏŏ vay, dyŏŏ-/ *n* **1** a bed quilt made up of broad channels stuffed with down or synthetic material, usually used inside a removable washable cover in place of or together with sheets and blankets **2 duvet, duvet jacket** a quilted jacket constructed from channels filled with down, intended for outdoor wear in severe weather conditions [Mid-18C. < French, 'down' < Old Norse *dūnn*.]

duvet day *n* any one of an agreed number of days that an employee can take as leave at short notice in addition to his or her official holiday allowance [From the idea of wanting to remain under the duvet rather than go to work]

duvetyn /dyŏŏvə teen/, **duvetyne, duvetine** *n* a soft velvety silk, cotton, woollen, or rayon fabric with a nap [Early 20C. < French *duvetine* < *duvet* 'down'.]

du Vigneaud /doo véenyō, dyoo-/, **Vincent** (1901–78) US biochemist

dux /duks/ *n Scotland* the student whose academic achievements are highest in a school, subject, or class [Mid-18C. < Latin, 'leader'.]

duyker /dīkər/ *n* ZOOL = **duiker**

DV *abbr* Deo volente

dvandva /dvaán dvaa/ *n* a compound word made up of two elements of equal status which would make sense if joined by 'and' instead of being compounded, e.g. 'push-pull' and 'Marxist-Leninist' [Mid-19C. < Sanskrit, doubling of *dva* 'two'.]

⚡**DVD** *n* a high-capacity optical compact disc that can store a large quantity of video, audio, or other information. Full form **digital video disc**

⚡**DVD-ROM** *n* a high-capacity optical disc on which data can be stored but not altered. Full form **digital video disc read only memory**

⚡**DVI** *abbr* digital video imaging

Dvina /dvéenə/ river in W Russia, W Belarus, and Latvia. Length: 1,768 km/1,090 mi.

DVLA *abbr* Driving and Vehicle Licensing Agency

DVM *abbr* Doctor of Veterinary Medicine

Dvořák /dváwr zhak/, **Antonín** (1841–1904) Bohemian Czech composer

⚡**Dvorak keyboard** *n* a keyboard with frequently used keys placed near the centre for quicker typing [After August *Dvorak*]

dwaal /dwaal/ *n S Africa* a state of inattention or confusion and bewilderment (*informal*) [< Afrikaans]

dwam /dwaam/ (**dwams, dwamming, dwammed**) *vi Scotland* to become ill, especially suddenly, or feel faint [Early 16C. Ultimately < Germanic.]

dwarf /dwawrf/ *n* (*plural* **dwarves** /dwawrvz/ *or* **dwarfs**) **1 SMALL HUMANOID CREATURE IN FOLKLORE** in fairy tales and folklore, a small creature with a mainly human appearance, associated with mountains, mines, and buried treasures. Fictional dwarves were often believed to have magic powers and to be sometimes malevolent. **2 PERSON SMALL FOR MEDICAL REASONS** a person of small stature for medical reasons, usually somebody with an average-sized body but unusually short limbs, or somebody with growth hormone deficiency **3 SMALL PLANT OR ANIMAL** a plant or animal that is much smaller than others of its species, usually as a result of selective breeding (*often before nouns*) ○ *a dwarf conifer* **4** ASTRON = **dwarf star** ■ *vt* **1 MAKE SOMEBODY OR SOMETHING SEEM SMALL** to make somebody or something else seem very small or very unimportant, by comparison ○ *The cathedral is dwarfed by the enormous tower blocks surrounding it.* **2 STUNT SOMEBODY'S OR SOMETHING'S GROWTH** to stunt the growth of somebody or something [Old English *dweorg* < Germanic] —**dwarfish** *adj* —**dwarfishly** *adv* —**dwarfishness** *n*

dwarf bean *n* **1** a thin green edible bean pod from a type of French bean **2** a short bushy type of French bean plant. *Phaseolus vulgaris*. US term **bush bean**

dwarf cornel *n* **1** a widely cultivated arctic–alpine plant with scarlet berries that grows only about 20 cms/8 in high. Flowers: purple, surrounded by white bracts resembling petals. *Cornus suecica*. **2** *US* PLANTS = **bunchberry**

dwarfism /dwáwrfizəm/ *n* the condition of being a dwarf

dwarf star, dwarf *n* a star with relatively low mass, size, and luminosity. The Sun is a dwarf star. ◊ **giant star**

dwarves plural of **dwarf**

dweeb /dweeb/ *n US* a boring, silly, or socially inept person (*slang insult*) [Late 20C. < ?]

dwell /dwel/ *vi* (**dwells, dwelling, dwelt** /dwelt/ *or* **dwelled, dwelt** *or* **dwelled**) to live and have a home in a particular place (*literary*) ■ *n* a regular pause in the operation of a machine [Old English *dwellan* 'lead astray' < Indo-European, 'rise in a cloud'] —**dweller** *n*

dwell on, dwell upon *vt* to think, write, or talk about something at considerable length

dwelling /dwélling/ *n* a house or other building or place in which somebody lives (*formal*) ■ *adj* living in a specified type of place or environment (*usually in combination*)

dwelt past tense, past participle of **dwell**

DWEM /dwem/, **dwem** *abbr* dead white European male (*slang offensive*)

dwindle /dwínd'l/ (**-dles, -dling, -dled**) *vti* to decrease little by little in size, number, or intensity and approach zero, or reduce something in this way ○ *Supplies were dwindling.* [Late 16C. < obsolete *dwine* 'waste away' < Indo-European, 'become exhausted'.]

dwt *abbr* dead weight tonnage

DX *symbol* long-distance

Dy *symbol* dysprosium

dyad /dī ad/ *n* **1 COUPLE** two individual units, things, or people linked as a pair (*formal*) **2 ATOM WITH VALENCY OF TWO** an atom or chemical group with a valency of two **3 VECTOR OPERATOR** a mathematical operator consisting of two vectors expressed without a multiplication sign between them **4 TWO-NOTE CHORD** a musical chord consisting of two notes [Late 17C. Via late Latin < Greek *duad-* < *duo* 'two'.] —**dyadic** /dī áddik/ *adj* —**dyadically** *adv*

Dyak /dī ak/ (*plural* **-aks** *or* **-ak**), **Dayak** (*plural* **-aks** *or* **-ak**) *n* a member of a Malaysian people who live in the interior of Borneo [Mid-19C. < Malay, 'up-country'.]

dyarchy *n* POL = **diarchy**

dybbuk /díbbək/ (*plural* **-buks** *or* **-bukim** /-kim/), **dibbuk** *n* in Jewish folklore, a malevolent spirit of a dead person, believed able to take over a living person's body and control his or her behaviour unless exorcised [Early 20C. Via Yiddish *dibek* < Hebrew *dibbūq* < *dābaq* 'cling'.]

Dyck /van dīk/, **Sir Anthony van** (1599–1641) Flemish painter

dye /dī/ *v* **1** *vt* **COLOUR BY SOAKING** to colour or stain something, e.g. fabric or hair, by soaking it in a colouring solution so that it takes on the new colour permanently or semi-permanently **2** *vi* **COLOUR WELL OR BADLY** to respond to being treated with a colouring agent and take its colour in a particular way ■ *n* **1 COLOURING AGENT** a natural or synthetic substance that can be used to colour something such as a textile or hair and is most often applied as a liquid **2 COLOURING SOLUTION** a colouring solution containing a dye **3 COLOUR PRODUCED BY A DYE** the colour produced on something by a dye [Old English *dēah* 'colour, colour that hides'] —**dyable** *adj* —**dyer** *n*

SPELLCHECK See *die*.

dyed-in-the-wool *adj* **1** wholeheartedly and stubbornly attached to a set of beliefs, political party, or philosophy and totally convinced of its merits **2** dyed before weaving into cloth

dyeline /dī līn/ *adj* CHEM = **diazo** *n.*

dyestuff /dī stuf/ *n* INDUST = **dye** *n.* **1**

dyewood /dī wŏŏd/ *n* any wood that can be used as a dye

Dyfed /dúvvid/ former county in SW Wales

dying /dī ing/ *adj* **1 ABOUT TO DIE** on the point of death **2 OCCURRING JUST BEFORE DEATH** carried out, spoken, or occurring at or just before the point of death **3 FINAL** occurring as something is about to reach its end ○ *in the dying seconds of the game*

dyke[1] /dīk/, **dike** *n* **1 EMBANKMENT TO PREVENT FLOODS** an embankment built along the shore of a sea or lake or beside a river to hold back the water and prevent flooding **2 BARRIER** a barrier or obstacle meant to keep something out **3 CAUSEWAY** a raised roadway across a swamp or body of water **4** *US* **DITCH** a drainage ditch or other artificial watercourse **5** *Scotland* **DRY-STONE WALL** an enclosing or dividing wall, usually made of stone, often without mortar **6 LONG MASS OF IGNEOUS ROCK** a vertical or near-vertical mass of igneous rock that has forced its way upwards through overlying strata **7** *ANZ* **LAVATORY** a lavatory (*informal*) ■ *vt* (**dykes, dyking, dyked; dikes, diking, diked**) **1 PROTECT WITH DIKES** to enclose or protect an area of land with a dyke or series of dykes **2 DRAIN WITH DITCHES** to drain an area of land using ditches [13C. Probably < Old Norse *dík* < Germanic, 'hole and mound resulting from digging'.] —**dyker** *n*

dyke[2] /dīk/, **dike** *n* an offensive term for a lesbian (*slang*)

Dylan /díllən/, **Bob** (*b.* 1941) US folk singer. Born **Robert Zimmerman.** See illustration overleaf.

dyn *symbol* dyne

⚡**dynamic** /dī námmik/ *adj* **1 VIGOROUS AND PURPOSEFUL** full of energy, enthusiasm, and a sense of purpose and able both to get things going and to get things done **2 ACTIVE AND CHANGING** characterized by vigorous activity and producing or undergoing change and development ○ *a dynamic economy* **3 RELATING TO ENERGY** involving or relating to energy and forces that produce motion **4 RELATING TO DYNAMICS** involved in or connected with the study of dynamics **5 RELATING TO LOUDNESS IN MUSIC** relating to or indicating variations in the loudness of musical sounds **6 CHANGING OVER TIME** describes any system that

Bob Dylan

changes over time ■ *n* **DRIVING FORCE** a driving or energizing force, especially one involved in a process of social or psychological change ■ *adj* **WHILE PROGRAM IS RUNNING** performed while a program or system is running [Early 19C. Via French *dynamique* < Greek *dunamikos* < *dunamis* 'force'.] —**dynamical** *adj* —**dynamically** *adv*

dynamic markings, dynamic marks *npl* the symbols and words that indicate the degree of loudness or softness with which a piece, passage, or note of music should be played

dynamic range *n* **1** the range of volume used within a single piece of music **2** the range over which an electronic audio system can operate to a set standard of performance based on given limits for noise and distortion

dynamics /dī námmiks/ *n* **1** **CHANGE-PRODUCING FORCES** the forces that tend to produce activity and change in any situation or sphere of existence (+ *plural verb*) **2** **LOUDNESS AND SOFTNESS IN MUSICAL PIECE** the different levels of loudness and softness in a piece of music, and the way in which a performer reproduces them in performance (+ *plural verb*) **3** **MUSIC** = **dynamic markings** (+ *plural verb*) **4** **STUDY OF MOTION** the study of motion and the way in which forces produce motion (+ *singular verb*)

dynamism /dínimizəm/ *n* **1** a vigorously active, forceful, and energizing quality, especially as the hallmark of somebody's personality or approach to a task **2** a philosophical or scientific theory stressing the role of dynamic forces in explaining phenomena, especially by interpreting events as an expression of forces residing within the object or person involved —**dynamist** *n* —**dynamistic** /dínə místik/ *adj*

dynamite /dínə mīt/ *n* **1** **POWERFUL EXPLOSIVE** a powerful explosive consisting of a porous material, e.g. wood pulp or sawdust, combined with ammonium or sodium nitrate, or nitroglycerine, and an antacid, e.g. calcium carbonate. Use: blasting. **2** **VERY EXCITING THING** something that or somebody who is exceptionally exciting or has an extremely powerful effect (*slang*) ○ *This music is absolute dynamite.* **3** **VERY HARMFUL THING** something that or somebody who is potentially very dangerous or harmful (*slang*) ○ *news stories that were political dynamite* ■ *vt* (**-mites, -miting, -mited**) **BLAST SOMETHING WITH DYNAMITE** to blast or explode something with dynamite [Mid-19C. < Greek *dunamis* 'force'.] —**dynamiter** *n*

dynamo /dínə mō/ (*plural* **-mos**) *n* **1** a machine that converts mechanical energy into electrical energy, usually in the form of direct current **2** a hard-working, tirelessly energetic person (*informal*) [Late 19C. Shortening of *dynamo-electric machine*.]

dynamo- *prefix* power, energy ○ *dynamometer* [< Greek *dunamis* (see DYNAMIC)]

dynamoelectric /dínəmō i léktrik/, **dynamoelectrical** /-trik'l/ *adj* involved in or relating to the production of electrical energy from mechanical energy, and vice versa

dynamometer /díni mómmitər/ *n* an instrument used to measure mechanical force or power, e.g. the power output of an engine —**dynamometric** /dínəmō méttrik/ *adj* —**dynamometry** *n*

dynamotor /dínə mōtər/ *n* an electrical device combining

a motor and generator. Use: to convert alternating current to direct current, and vice versa. [Early 20C. < Greek *dunamis* 'force'.]

dynast /dínn ast, -əst/ *n* **1** a ruler, especially a hereditary monarch (*literary*) **2** a member or founder of a dynasty [Mid-17C. Via Latin < Greek *dunastēs* 'lord' < *dunasthai* 'be able'.]

dynasty /dínnəsti/ (*plural* **-ties**) *n* **1** a succession of rulers from the same family **2** a prominent and powerful family or group of people whose members retain their power and influence through several generations [14C. Directly or via French < late Latin *dynastia* < Greek *dunastēs* 'lord' (see DYNAST).] —**dynastic** /di nástik/ *adj* —**dynastically** *adv*

dyne /dīn/ *n* (*symbol* **dyn**) the unit of force in the cgs system equal to the force that will accelerate a mass of one gram one centimetre per second per second [Late 19C. < Greek *dunamis* 'force'.]

dys- *prefix* bad, impaired, abnormal ○ *dysplasia* [Via Latin < Greek *dus-*]

dysarthria /diss aàrthri ə/ *n* difficulty in speech articulation due to lack of muscle control caused by damage to the central nervous system [Late 19C. < modern Latin, < Latin *dys-* 'bad' + Greek *arthron* 'joint'.]

dyscrasia /diss kráyzi ə/ *n* any abnormal condition of blood cells [14C. Via late Latin < Greek *dyskrasia* 'bad mixture' < *krasis* 'mixing'.]

dysentery /díss'ntəri/ *n* the disease of the lower intestine caused by infection with bacteria, protozoa, or parasites and marked by severe diarrhoea, inflammation, and the passage of blood and mucus [14C. Directly or via Old French < Latin *dysenteria* < Greek *dusenteros* 'bad intestines' < *enteron* 'intestine'.] —**dysenteric** /díss'n térrik/ *adj*

~~dysentry~~ incorrect spelling of **dysentery**

dysfluency /diss floò ənssi/ (*plural* **-cies**) *n* an impairment of a person's ability to speak, such as a stammer

dysfunction /diss fúngksh'n/ *n* a medical abnormality in the functioning of an organ or other part or system of the body

dysfunctional /diss fúngksh'nəl/ *adj* **1** **NOT PERFORMING ITS FUNCTION PROPERLY** failing to perform the function that is normally expected ○ *counselling a dysfunctional family* **2** **RELATING BADLY** unable to function emotionally as a social unit **3** **NOT FUNCTIONING NORMALLY** unable to function as a result of disease or impairment

dysgenic /diss jénnik/ *adj* involving or causing the inheriting of detrimental characteristics

dysgenics /diss jénniks/ *n* the study of factors relating to or causing a decrease in the survival of the hereditarily well-adapted members of a line of descent (+ *singular verb*)

dysgraphia /diss gráffi ə/ *n* impairment of writing ability, arising from brain injury or disease

dyskinesia /diski neèzi ə/ *n* impairment of the control over ordinary muscle movement, often resulting in spasmodic movements or tics [Early 18C. Via modern Latin < Greek *duskinēsia* 'difficulty in moving' < *kinēsis* 'movement'.]

dyslexia /diss léksi ə/ *n* a learning disorder marked by a severe difficulty in recognizing and understanding written language, leading to spelling and writing problems [Late 19C. < DYS- + Greek *lexis* 'speech' < *legein* 'speak'.] —**dyslexic** *adj, n*

dysmenorrhoea /díss menə reè ə/ *n* severe pain or cramps in the lower abdomen during menstruation —**dysmenorrhoeal** *adj* —**dysmenorrhoeic** *adj*

dyspareunia /díspar yoòni ə/ *n* pain occurring during sexual intercourse

dyspepsia /diss pépsi ə/ *n* acid indigestion (*technical*) [Early 18C. Via Latin < Greek *duspepsia* 'difficult digestion' < *peptein* 'cook, digest'.]

dyspeptic /diss péptik/ *adj* **1** having acid indigestion **2** bad-tempered [Late 17C. < Greek *duspeptos* 'difficult of digestion' < *peptein* 'cook, digest'.] —**dyspeptic** *n*

dysphagia /diss fáyji ə/ *n* difficulty in swallowing, with a variety of possible causes —**dysphagic** /-fájjik/ *adj*

dysphasia /dis fáyzi ə/ *n* difficulty in speaking and understanding spoken or written language, caused by brain injury or disease —**dysphasic** *adj*

dysphemism /dísfimizəm/ *n* **1** the deliberate substitution of an offensive expression for a neutral one **2** an offensive expression deliberately substituted for a neutral one [Late 19C. < DYS- after *euphemism*.] —**dysphemistic** /dísfə místik/ *adj*

dysphonia /diss fóni ə/ *n* hoarseness or difficulty in speaking as a result of dysfunction of the vocal cords caused by brain injury, brain disease, or chemical poisoning [Early 18C. Via modern Latin < Greek *dusphōnia* 'roughness of sound' < *phōnē* 'sound'.] —**dysphonic** /-fónnik/ *adj*

dysphoria /diss fáwri ə/ *n* a state of feeling acutely hopeless, uncomfortable, and unhappy [Mid-19C. < Greek *dusphoria* 'discomfort' < *pherein* 'to bear'.] —**dysphoric** /-fórrik/ *adj*

dysplasia /diss pláyzi ə/ *n* medically abnormal development or growth of a part of the body, e.g. an organ, bone, or cell, including the total absence of such a part —**dysplastic** /-plástik/ *adj*

dyspnea *n* US = **dyspnoea**

dyspnoea /disp neè ə/ *n* difficulty in breathing caused, e.g., by heart disease or overexertion [Mid-17C. Via Latin < Greek *duspnoia* 'difficulty of breathing' < *pnein* 'breathe'.] —**dyspnoeal** *adj* —**dyspnoeic** *adj*

dyspraxia /diss práksi ə/ *n* **1** poor coordination displayed by some children, diagnosed by illegible handwriting and inability to catch a ball and clap while the ball is in the air **2** MED = **apraxia** *n*. [< Greek *duspraxia* 'ill success' < *praxis* 'action'] —**dyspraxic** *adj*

dysprosium /diss prözi əm/ *n* (*symbol* **Dy**) a soft silvery element of the rare-earth group that is paramagnetic and highly reactive. Source: monazite, bastnasite. Use: laser materials, nuclear research. [Late 19C. < Greek *dusprositos* 'difficult to approach' < *ienai* 'go'.]

dysrhythmia /diss ríthmi ə/ *n* an irregularity in an otherwise normal rhythm, especially of heartbeats or brain waves [Early 20C. < modern Latin, 'bad rhythm' < Greek *rhuthmos* 'rhythm'.]

dystocia /diss tôsha/ *n* abnormally difficult childbirth [Early 18C. < Greek *dustokia* 'difficult childbirth' < *tokos* 'childbirth'.] —**dystocial** *adj*

dystopia /diss tôpi ə/ *n* an imaginary place where everything is as bad as it possibly can be, or a vision or description of such a place [Mid-20C. < DYS- + UTOPIA.] —**dystopian** *adj*

dystrophia /diss trôfi ə/ *n* = **dystrophy**

dystrophic /diss tróffik/ *adj* **1** relating to or affected by dystrophy **2** describes a pond or lake containing abnormally acidic brown water and lacking in oxygen

dystrophin /dístrəfin/ *n* a protein found in normal muscle that is missing in muscular dystrophy

dystrophy /dístrəfi/ (*plural* **-phies**), **dystrophia** /diss trôfi ə/ *n* **1** progressive degeneration of a body tissue, e.g. muscle, as a result of inadequate nourishment of the affected part, due to some unknown cause **2** a condition in which pond or lake water is unable to support animal or plant life because of excessive humus content

dysuria /diss yoòri ə/ *n* pain or difficulty in urinating —**dysuric** *adj*

Dyula /dee oòla, dyoòla/ (*plural* **-la** or **-las**) *n* a Mande language spoken in the Ivory Coast, Burkina Faso, and Ghana. Native speakers: 1 million. —**Dyula** *adj*

⚡ dz *abbr* Algeria (*in Internet addresses*)

Dzerzhinsk /dur zhínsk/ *city* in central European Russia. Population: 286,000 (1990).

dzo /zō/ (*plural* **dzos** or **dzo**), **zo** (*plural* **zos** or **zo**), **zho** (*plural* **zhos** or **zho**) *n* an animal belonging to a breed developed from a hybrid between a cow and a yak [Mid-19C. < Tibetan *mdso*.]

Dzongkha /zóngka/, **Dzongka** *n* the official language of Bhutan, a dialect of Tibetan. Native speakers: 1 million. [Early 20C. < Tibetan, 'language of the fortress'.] —**Dzongkha** *adj*

Dzungaria /júng gáiri ə/ *n* ♦ **Junggar Pendi**

e¹ /ee/ (plural **e's**), **E** (plural **E's** or **Es**) n the fifth letter of the English alphabet, representing a vowel sound

e² symbol electron

e³ /ee/ **1** used to refer to the transcendental number 2.718 282... **2** used to refer to the fifth vertical row of squares from the left on a chessboard

e⁴ abbr **1** engineer **2** engineering

E¹ (plural **E's** or **Es**) n **1** 'E-SHAPED OBJECT something shaped like a letter 'E' **2** 3RD NOTE IN C MAJOR the third note of a scale in C major **3** SOMETHING THAT PRODUCES AN E a string, key, or pipe tuned to produce the note E **4** SCALE BEGINNING ON E a scale or key that starts on the note E **5** WRITTEN SYMBOL OF E a graphic representation of the tone of E **6** 5TH HIGHEST GRADE the fifth highest grade in a series, e.g. a grade indicating that a student's work is of very low quality **7** ECSTASY the drug ecstasy or a tablet of the drug (slang) **8** CASUAL WORKER a casual worker or somebody who is dependent on the state, in the market research system that classifies people according to their employment

E² symbol **1** electric field strength **2** electromotive force (usually written italicized) **3** energy **4** exa- **5** internal energy **6** a negative categorical proposition

E³ abbr **1** earl **2** earth **3** east **4** eastern **5** English

e- prefix **1** electronic ○ e-mail **2** electronic data transfer via the Internet ○ e-commerce [Shortening]

E111 n a form that entitles citizens of the EU to free health care when visiting other EU countries

ea. abbr each

EAC abbr East African Community

each /eech/ det, pron, adv used to refer to every member of a group of people or things, considered individually ○ With each victory we get closer to the championship. ○ Is a VCR that can be connected to more than one TV better than buying one for each? ○ Environmental health officers were assessed an average of 40 cases each. [Old English ǣlc < Germanic, 'ever alike']

> **USAGE each** or **every**? In some contexts these two words are nearly interchangeable, as in I examined each puppy in the litter and I examined every puppy. Here the only difference is a slight shift in perspective from considering the animals individually, with **each**, to considering them collectively, with **every**. Either of the words, placed before the noun, requires the noun and the verb to be singular: Each puppy is affectionate. Every puppy is affectionate. **Each**, though not **every**, may also be placed after a plural noun, and then the plural governs the verb: The puppies each have their own toys. **Each** can also refer to two or more, whereas **every** must refer to three or more. **Each** can be an adjective or determiner (each puppy), a pronoun (each of them), and an adverb (Give them a bowlful each), whereas **every** is an adjective or determiner only (every puppy). The expression each and every, a so-called emphatic modifier, relates to a singular noun only, and therefore takes a singular verb only: Each and every passenger is required to present two photo IDs. Avoid use of this expression in formal writing, for it is objected to by some people as unnecessarily wordy.

each other pron each one of two or more persons or things reciprocally

> **USAGE each other** or **one another**? The traditional rule is that **each other** refers to two items and **one another** refers to more than two: Joe and Lee respect each other deeply. All the people at the party knew one another already. However,

this distinction is not supported by the weight of usage, and there is no good reason to reject the alternatives Joe and Lee respect one another deeply and All the people at the party knew each other already.

each way adv on the same horse to come first or be placed in the first three in a race ○ had £5 each way on number 6 —**each-way** adj

eager /éegər/ adj **1** enthusiastic and excited about something and impatiently waiting to do or get it ○ eager to help ○ eager for praise **2** expressing enthusiastic interest and expectation or an impatient desire to do something ○ eager face [13C. Via Anglo-Norman egre < Latin acer 'sharp'.] —**eagerly** adv —**eagerness** n

USAGE See anxious.

eager beaver n an enthusiastic worker or volunteer (informal) [< the perceived industriousness of beavers]

eagle /éeg'l/ n **1** LARGE BIRD OF PREY a large bird of prey with a hooked bill and broad wing span that hunts by day and is noted for its keen eyesight and soaring flight. Subfamily: Buteoninae. **2** EAGLE AS A SYMBOL the figure of an eagle used as a symbol of military or political power, e.g. on the standards carried by the Roman legions **3** SCORE OF 2 UNDER PAR a score of two under par for a single hole in golf ■ vti (**-gles**, **-gling**, **-gled**) SCORE 2 UNDER PAR to complete a hole in two strokes under par in golf [14C. Via Anglo-Norman egle < Latin aquila.]

eagle eye n extremely keen eyesight, or the ability to notice what other people might miss —**eagle-eyed** adj

eagle owl n a large owl, the largest species of owl in the world, with brownish plumage and tufts of feathers on its head that look like horns. Native to: Europe, Asia. Bubo bubo.

eagle ray n a large ray with a projecting snout, massive jaws, and pectoral fins shaped like wings that propel it with a soaring motion. Native to: tropical and subtropical seas. Family: Myliobatidae.

eaglet /éeglət/ n a young eagle, especially before it leaves the nest

eaglewood /éeg'l wŏod/ n (plural **-woods** or **-wood**) **1** a tree with fragrant resinous timber. Use: perfumes. Native to: Asia. Aquilaria agallocha. **2** INDUST = **aloes** n. **2**

eagre /éegər/ n GEOG = **bore³** n. [Early 17C. < ?]

Eakins /áykinz/, **Thomas** (1844–1916) US artist

Ealing /éeling/ borough in W London, England. Population: 275,257 (1991).

Ealing comedy n a British comedy film made at Ealing Studios between the 1930s and 1950s

Ealing Studios n the film studios in Ealing, London, where a number of popular and highly regarded British comedy films were made from the 1930s to 1950s

Eames /eemz/, **Charles** (1907–78) US designer

ear¹ /eer/ n **1** ORGAN OF HEARING the organ of hearing and balance in vertebrates that, in mammals, is divided into three parts, the external, middle, and inner ear **2** EXTERNAL PART OF HEARING ORGAN the external part of an ear, visible in humans and most mammals on each side of the head as a flap of cartilage with skin surrounding or covering it **3** INVERTEBRATE SENSORY ORGAN any sensory organ in invertebrates that is able to sense vibrations and perform a similar function to a vertebrate ear **4** BIRDS = **ear tuft** **5** EAR SHAPE something shaped like an

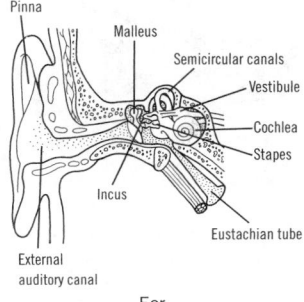

Pinna
Malleus
Semicircular canals
Vestibule
Cochlea
Stapes
Incus
Eustachian tube
External auditory canal

Ear

ear, especially a handle on a jug or jar **6** ABILITY TO TELL SOUNDS APART the ability to distinguish accurately between different sounds, e.g. in speech or music ○ She has an ear for other languages. **7** ATTENTION somebody's attention, especially somebody's sympathetic or favourable attention [Old English ēare < Indo-European, 'ear'] ◇ **all ears** listening, or ready to listen, attentively or enthusiastically to something (informal) ◇ **go in one ear and out the other** to be forgotten as soon as heard and so have absolutely no effect on somebody ◇ **have somebody's ear** to be a trusted adviser to somebody, especially somebody powerful or influential ◇ **have** or **keep your ear to the ground** to remain continuously alert to discover new developments or information ◇ **out on your ear** unceremoniously thrown out or dismissed from a place or position you previously occupied (informal) ○ You'll be out on your ear if you're late again. ◇ **play it by ear** to improvise or adapt your response to a situation as it occurs rather than make plans in advance ◇ **prick up your ears** to begin listening or paying attention to something ◇ **set something** or **somebody by the ears** to cause conflict or disagreement among people or within an organization ◇ **set somebody on his** or **her ear, set something on its ear** to send somebody or something into a state of excited agitation, shock, or confusion ◇ **wet behind the ears** very inexperienced or naive

ear² /eer/ n the grain-bearing part at the top of the stalk of a cereal plant such as wheat, maize or sweetcorn, or barley ■ vi to form the part of a cereal plant that contains the grains [Old English ēar < Indo-European, 'sharp']

earache /éer ayk/ n pain in the middle or inner ear. Technical name **otalgia**

earbash /éer bash/ v ANZ (informal) **1** vi to talk nonstop ○ Will you two stop earbashing and give me a hand? **2** vt to nag or harangue somebody ○ always earbashing me about the state of the garden —**earbasher** n

earbashing /éer bashing/ n ANZ a lengthy scolding or reprimand (informal) ○ copped a right earbashing for getting home late

ear clip n **1** an ornament, e.g. a metal band, clipped to the upper part of the ear **2** a clip-on earring

eardrop /éer drop/ n a pendant earring ■ **eardrops** npl liquid medicine for the ear, usually inserted with a dropper

eardrum /éer drum/ *n* a membrane of thin skin and fibrous tissue that vibrates in response to sound waves, located between the external and the middle ear. Technical name **tympanic membrane**

eared seal *n* a seal with conspicuous external ears and independent hind limbs or flippers that are used to walk on land. Sea lions and fur seals are eared seals. Family: Otariidae.

earflap /éer flap/ *n* a piece of fabric or fur on a hat that can be let down to keep the ear warm (*often plural*)

earful /éer fòol/ *n* **1** a severe scolding or lecture from somebody (*informal*) **2** a large quantity of sound, conversation, or gossip that somebody hears or overhears

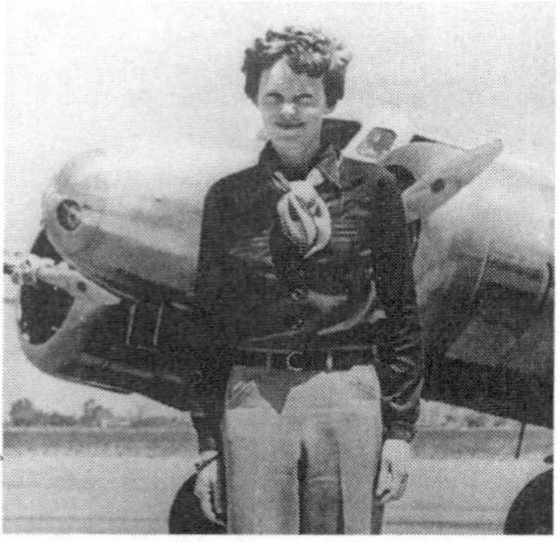

Barnaby's

Amelia Earhart

Earhart /áir haart/, **Amelia** (1898–1937) US aviator

earhole /éer hōl/ *n* the opening in the side of the head that leads into the ear or the ear itself (*informal*)

earing /éering/ *n* a small rope that attaches the upper corner of a sail to a yard [Early 17C. < ?]

earl /url/ *n* a British nobleman ranked above a viscount and below a marquess [Old English *eorl* 'warrior, nobleman' < ?] —**earldom** *n*

Earle /url/, **Augustus** (1793–1838) British painter

earless seal /éerləss-/ *n* a seal that does not have conspicuous external ears and has short front and hind flippers that are adapted for swimming rather than walking on land. Family: Phocidae.

Earl Grey *n* a tea flavoured with bergamot to produce a lighter-coloured brew with a rather musky taste [Said to be named for Charles *Grey*, the second Earl Grey (1764–1845), British statesman and prime minister]

Earl Marshal *n* an officer of the English peerage who presides over the College of Heralds and organizes important ceremonial occasions

earlobe /éer lōb/ *n* the soft fleshy lower part of the outer ear

early /úrli/ *adv* (**-lier, -liest**) **1 BEFORE THE EXPECTED TIME** before the expected or arranged time ○ *They arrived early.* **2 NEAR THE BEGINNING** at or near the beginning of a specified period, process, or event that is experienced over a period of time ○ *early in the interview* **3 DURING THE FIRST STAGES** at a time when something was not far advanced or developed or when somebody was at a comparatively young age ○ *She decided early that she wanted to become a teacher.* **4 SOON** promptly or soon ○ *Post early for Christmas.* **5 BEFORE OTHER VARIETIES** before other varieties of the same plant or animal ■ *adj* (**-lier, -liest**) **1 OCCURRING NEAR THE BEGINNING** occurring at or near the beginning of a period of time, process, or sequence of events ○ *Early reports indicate a high level of interest.* **2 OCCURRING BEFORE THE EXPECTED TIME** occurring before the expected or arranged time ○ *early retirement* **3 PRODUCED NEAR THE BEGINNING** produced at, characteristic of, or representing a not very advanced stage in the development of something or somebody ○ *looking forward to an early end to the deadlock* **4 IN THE NEAR FUTURE** due, expected, or requested to happen in the very near future **5 RIPENING BEFORE OTHERS** ripening before other varieties of the same type ○ *early peaches* [Old English *ǣrlīce* < Indo-European, 'day'] —**earliness** *n* ◇ **early on** at the beginning or start of something such as a chain of events or a period of time ○ *We should have realized early on that financing would be a major problem.*

USAGE The expression ***early on***, derived from *earlier on*, is a 20th-century use, as in the example *The BBC recognized early on that there was money to be made from selling archive programmes on video (New Scientist).*

early bird *n* an early riser, or somebody who arrives earlier than the expected or arranged time (*informal*) [< the proverb *The early bird catches the worm*]

early closing *n* the regular closing of most of the shops in a town or part of a town on one particular afternoon in the week

early day motion *n* a parliamentary motion tabled for future discussion in the British Parliament on an unspecified day when business finishes early. Its main purpose is to draw Parliament's attention to a particular topic.

Early English *adj* belonging to or typical of the style of early Gothic architecture used in the late 12th to late 13th centuries in England, characterized by sharply pointed arches and lancet windows —**Early English** *n*

early music *n* music written during the Medieval and Renaissance periods, sometimes also including the music of the Baroque and early Classical periods ■ *adj* typical of a way of performing early music that aims to be as authentic as possible, using period instruments, the contemporary performing style, and a carefully researched score

early retirement *n* retirement from work before the usual age, often offered, with special inducements, by employers as a way of reducing staff numbers

early riser *n* a person who gets up early, especially on a regular basis

early warning *n* advance notice that something, especially something dangerous or threatening, is going to happen

early warning system *n* a network of radar, satellites, or other sensing devices designed to give advance warning of an enemy attack, especially in time to take countermeasures

earmark /éer maark/ *vt* **1 DESIGNATE FOR PARTICULAR PURPOSE** to select and reserve something to be used for a particular purpose ○ *That money's already been earmarked for upgrading the computer system.* **2 PUT AN IDENTIFICATION MARK ON AN ANIMAL'S EAR** to mark the ear of a farm animal with an identifying symbol, notch, or hole ■ *n* **1 IDENTIFYING CHARACTERISTIC** something enabling recognition of the nature or origins of something (*often plural*) ○ *The crime seemed to have all the earmarks of an inside job.* **2 IDENTIFICATION MARK ON AN ANIMAL'S EAR** an identifying symbol, hole, or notch in the ear of a farm animal

earmuffs /éer mufs/ *npl* ear covers attached to an adjustable headband, worn in cold weather

earn /urn/ *v* **1** *vti* **MAKE MONEY BY WORKING** to receive money or payment of some other kind in return for work done ○ *earn enough to live on* **2** *vt* **DESERVE** to acquire something as a result of your actions or behaviour ○ *earn praise* ○ *The remark earned him a stern rebuke.* **3** *vt* **PRODUCE DIVIDENDS** to produce interest or dividends from money invested [Old English *earnian* < Germanic, 'harvest']

Earn /urn/ river in Tayside, central Scotland. Length: 74 km/46 mi.

earned income /urnd-/ *n* income from paid employment as opposed to income from investments

earner /úrnər/ *n* **1** somebody who earns a particular level of income ○ *tax incentives for high earners* **2** an activity, job, or transaction that generates income ○ *This line is one of the company's best earners.* ◇ **a nice little earner** a job or activity that earns somebody a lot of money (*informal*)

earnest[1] /úrnist/ *adj* **1 INTENSELY SERIOUS AND SINCERE** intensely, or even excessively, serious and sincere in manner or attitude **2 DONE IN A DEEPLY SINCERE WAY** undertaken or made in a spirit of deep seriousness and sincerity, or with deep feeling **3 DESERVING SERIOUS ATTENTION** of a serious nature, or worthy of serious attention (*formal*) [Old English *eornost* < Germanic] —**earnestly** *adv* —**earnestness** *n* ◇ **in earnest 1** serious and sincere in your actions, words, or intentions **2** more intensely or in a determined and purposeful way

earnest[2] /úrnist/ *n* **1 earnest, earnest money** a small advance payment that confirms a contract **2** a sign, foretaste, or pledge of something to come (*literary*) [13C. Probably alteration of Old French *erres* 'pledges' < Latin *arra*, via Greek *arrabōn* 'pledge' < Hebrew *'ērābhôn* < *'ārab* 'to pledge'.]

earnings /úrningz/ *npl* money earned, either through paid employment, as profit, or from investments

EAROM /ée rom/ *abbr* electrically alterable read-only memory

Earp /urp/, **Wyatt** (1848–1929) US frontiersman and law enforcement officer

earphone /éer fōn/ *n* a device that converts electric signals into audible sound and is worn on or held close to the ear (*often plural*)

earpiece /éer peess/ *n* **1** the part of a device such as a telephone, radio, or hearing aid that is held in, or close to, the ear **2** the part of the frame of a pair of spectacles that fits over and round the ear

ear-piercing *n* the making of a hole through the earlobe with a sterilized needle, so that an earring can be attached through the hole ■ *adj* extremely or painfully loud and shrill

earplug /éer plug/ *n* a piece of something soft such as wax or foam rubber that is placed in the ear to keep out noise, water, or cold (*often plural*)

earring /éer ring/ *n* a piece of jewellery worn on the ear, usually either clipped to the earlobe or attached through a hole pierced in it (*often plural*)

ear shell *n* MARINE BIOL = **abalone**

earshot /éer shot/ *n* the distance within which sound is audible to somebody ○ *within earshot* [Early 17C. After words such as BOWSHOT.]

earsplitting /éer spliting/ *adj* extremely loud or shrill —**earsplittingly** *adv*

earth /urth/ *n* **1** ASTRON = **Earth 2 LAND** the solid dry land surface of the Earth, as opposed to the sea or sky **3 SOIL** the soft workable material in which plants grow **4 HUMAN INHABITANTS OF EARTH** all the human inhabitants of the Earth (*formal*) **5 PURSUITS OF EVERYDAY LIFE** the pursuits of everyday human life, especially as opposed to matters of the spirit **6 BURROW** the hole or underground lair of a fox or other burrowing animal **7 ELECTRICAL CONNECTION TO GROUND FOR SAFETY** an electrical connection to the ground intended to carry current safely away from a circuit in the event of a fault, or a wire that makes such a connection. US term **ground**[1] *n.* 13 **8** COLOURS = **earth colour 9 ONE OF THE FOUR ELEMENTS** in ancient and medieval philosophy, one of the four elements, earth, air, fire, and water, from which it was believed everything was made ■ *vt* **CONNECT APPLIANCE SAFELY TO GROUND** to equip an electrical circuit or appliance with a connection to the ground so that current is carried away safely in the event of a fault. US term **ground**[1] *v.* 10 [Old English *eorþe* < Germanic] ◇ **come** *or* **be brought back (down) to earth** to come back to reality after a period of happiness or unrealistic hopes ◇ **cost** *or* **charge the earth** to cost *or* charge a great deal of money ◇ **on earth** used to add intensity to a question, often indicating surprise or disbelief on the part of the questioner (*informal*) ○ *What on earth have you done to the computer now?* ◇ **run somebody** *or* **something to earth** to find somebody or something after a long and difficult search

earth up *vt* to cover part of a plant, especially the lower stem, with soil, in order to protect it against frost or light, or to prevent it from turning green

Earth, earth *n* the third planet in order from the Sun with an orbital period of 365.26 days, a diameter of 12,756 km/7,926 mi., and an average distance from the sun of 149,600,000 km/93,000,000 mi. See table at **planet**

earthborn /úrth bawrn/ *adj* born on or originating from the Earth, and therefore human, mortal, or earthly (*literary*)

earthbound /úrth bownd/ *adj* **1** exclusively concerned with or confined to ordinary everyday or worldly matters and lacking in imagination or spirituality **2** heading or moving towards Earth

earth closet *n* a toilet in which earth is used to cover the faeces, often consisting of a seat placed over a deep hole in the ground inside a small outdoor building

earth colour *n* any pigment obtained from the earth, e.g. umber or ochre

earthed /urtht/ *adj* connected to the ground by an electrical earth

earthen /úrth'n/ *adj* made of earth or baked clay

earthenware /úrth'n wair/ *n* pottery made of fairly coarse-textured baked clay that is fired at a very low temperature

earthlight /úrth līt/ *n* ASTRON = **earthshine**

earthling /úrthling/ *n* especially in science fiction, a human being as contrasted with an extraterrestrial or supernatural being

earthly /úrthli/ (**-lier, -liest**) *adj* 1 belonging to or characteristic of this world, especially as opposed to the spiritual realm or heaven 2 imaginable or possible

earthman /úrth man/ (*plural* **-men** /-men/) *n* especially in science fiction, a resident of Earth as referred to by an extraterrestrial

earth mother *n* 1 DEVOTEE OF NATURAL WAY OF LIFE a woman who is dedicated to nature and to natural, organic, and environmentally-friendly ways of doing things, often rejecting social conventions (*informal*) 2 SENSUAL AND MOTHERLY WOMAN a woman who conveys a warm earthy combination of sensuality and motherliness 3 THE EARTH PERSONIFIED AS MOTHER the Earth personified as a mother 4 GODDESS SYMBOLIZING EARTH a goddess symbolizing earth and worshipped as a source of life and fertility

earthmover /úrth moovər/ *n* a vehicle such as a bulldozer that is designed to move earth, especially in large quantities —**earthmoving** *adj*

earthnut /úrth nut/ *n* a plant, e.g. the peanut, that has underground pods

earth pillar *n* a pillar of soft material capped by a boulder of more resistant rock that protects it from erosion

earth tone *n* a colour with an element of deep rich brown in it, e.g. gold or russet

earthward /úrthwərd/ *adj* directed or facing towards the Earth ■ *adv* **earthward, earthwards** in the direction of the Earth or the ground

earthwork /úrth wurk/ *n* 1 a fortification made of earth 2 construction work involving excavating, earthmoving, and building embankments

earthworm /úrth wurm/ *n* a worm that burrows in the soil and helps to aerate and improve it. Family: Lumbricidae.

earthy /úrthi/ (**-ier, -iest**) *adj* 1 LIKE SOIL relating to or consisting of soil 2 NOT SQUEAMISH OR PRETENTIOUS having or showing a hearty, cheerful, no-nonsense acceptance of the realities and facts of life 3 CRUDE crude and coarse —**earthily** *adv* —**earthiness** *n*

ear trumpet *n* an early type of hearing aid consisting of a trumpet-shaped device that was held to the ear

ear tuft /eer tuft/ *n* a tuft of feathers above the eyes of some owls and other birds, causing the bird to look larger or blend in with foliage but not used in hearing

earwax /eer waks/ *n* a yellowish waxy substance secreted by glands in the external ear to protect the delicate lining of the outer ear. Technical name **cerumen**

earwig /eer wig/ *n* SLENDER INSECT WITH PINCERS a common insect with a slender shiny body, small forewings, an-

MEASURING EARTHQUAKES USING THE RICHTER SCALE

The Richter scale measures the magnitude of an earthquake based on how much the ground shakes at a distance of 100 km (60 miles) above the epicentre of the earthquake (the site on the Earth's surface directly above its origin). Other systems used by seismologists to measure earthquakes include the Modified Mercalli scale, a 12-point scale that measures intensity at different locations.

Richter number	Increase in the motion of the ground	Results
1	1	Generally not felt, but recorded on seismometers
2	10	Generally not felt, but recorded on seismometers
3	100	Generally not felt, but recorded on seismometers
4	1,000	Felt by many people; trees sway
5	10,000	Poorly built structures damaged
6	100,000	Specially designed structures damaged; others collapse
7	1,000,000	Many structures destroyed; cracks in ground
8+	10,000,000	Severe destruction; very wide cracks in ground

earthquake /úrth kwayk/ *n* 1 a violent shaking of the Earth's crust that may cause destruction to buildings and installations and results from the sudden release of tectonic stress along a fault line or volcanic activity 2 an event that causes an upheaval in society, politics, or somebody's life

earthrise /úrth rīz/ *n* the rising of the Earth above the Moon's horizon, as seen from space or from the Moon itself

earth science *n* a science that deals with the Earth's physical properties, structure, or development, e.g. geology

earthshattering /úrth shàttəring/, **earthshaking** /úrth shayking/ *adj* extremely great or important or having an extremely powerful effect —**earthshatteringly** *adv*

earthshine /úrth shīn/ *n* sunlight reflected from the Earth that illuminates the part of the Moon not receiving light directly from the Sun

earth sign *n* any of the three signs of the zodiac, Taurus, Virgo, or Capricorn, associated with stability and consistency

earthstar /úrth staar/ *n* a woodland fungus with a round outer surface that splits open in a star-shaped pattern to release spores. Genus: *Geastrum*.

earth station *n* a system for relaying radio signals between one or more satellites and other communications networks. Earth stations may be on the ground, at sea, or in aircraft.

tennae, and pincers at the end of its abdomen. Order: Dermaptera. ■ *v* 1 *vi* EAVESDROP to eavesdrop (*humorous*) 2 *vt* TRY TO INFLUENCE to try to influence somebody, e.g. a judge, privately or clandestinely [Old English *ēarwicga* < *ēare* 'ear' + *wicga* 'insect']

ease /eez/ *n* 1 LACK OF DIFFICULTY lack of difficulty in doing or achieving something ○ *defeated the challenger with ease* 2 LACK OF AWKWARDNESS lack of awkwardness, stiffness, or self-consciousness in social situations ○ *He felt totally at ease with her.* 3 COMFORT AND AFFLUENCE a comfortable and leisured state free from problems and restrictions, especially those caused by poverty ○ *a life of ease* 4 RELAXATION a state of comfort and relaxation 5 RELIEF FROM WORRY OR PAIN freedom or relief from worry or pain ■ *v* (**eases, easing, eased**) 1 *vt* MAKE LESS UNPLEASANT to make something less unpleasant, difficult, or restrictive 2 *vt* RELIEVE FROM PAIN to relieve somebody's mind or body from pain or discomfort 3 *vi* ABATE to become less strong or intense ○ *The rain eased.* 4 *vti* MANOEUVRE GENTLY to manoeuvre gently and carefully, especially in a tight space, or manoeuvre something in this way ○ *eased the truck into the space* 5 *vt* LOOSEN to slacken something that is tied or fitted tightly 6 *vt* MAKE EASIER to enable something to take place more easily ○ *This would certainly ease the measure's passage through Parliament.* [12C. < Old French *aise* 'comfort'.]

ease off *v* 1 *vi* to lessen in intensity ○ *The rain had begun to ease off.* 2 *vt* to slacken a rope or cable

easeful /eezf'l/ *adj* giving relief from pain, suffering, or distress (*literary*) —**easefully** *adv* —**easefulness** *n*

easel /eez'l/ *n* a freestanding upright support for a painter's canvas or a school blackboard, usually made of wood and having movable clamps [Late 16C. Via Dutch *ezel* 'donkey' < Latin *asinus* 'ass'.]

easement /eezmənt/ *n* a limited right to make use of a property owned by another, e.g. a right of way across the property [14C. < Old French *aisement* < *aise* 'comfort'.]

easily /eezili/ *adv* 1 WITHOUT DIFFICULTY in an easy manner and without difficulty or strain ○ *We can easily be there by lunchtime.* 2 QUICKLY quickly and after comparatively little effort, stress, or provocation ○ *She doesn't give up easily.* 3 BY FAR without doubt and by a large margin ○ *She's easily the best.* 4 PROBABLY used to show that something might probably or could almost certainly happen ○ *He could easily have forgotten, so I'd better check.* 5 AT LEAST certainly not less and probably far more than a particular number or amount ○ *There were easily 200 people at the meeting.* 6 CALMLY in a relaxed and untroubled way

east /eest/ *n* 1 DIRECTION IN WHICH THE SUN RISES the direction that lies directly ahead of somebody facing the rising sun or that is located towards the right-hand side of a conventional map of the world 2 COMPASS POINT OPPOSITE WEST the compass point that lies directly opposite west 3 east, East AREA IN THE EAST the part of an area, region, or country that is situated in or towards the east 4 ALTAR END OF CHURCH the end of a church where the altar is situated 5 east, East POSITION EQUIVALENT TO EAST the position equivalent to east in any diagram consisting of four points at 90 degree intervals ■ *adj* 1 IN THE EAST situated in, facing, or coming from the east of a place, region, or country 2 BLOWING FROM THE EAST blowing from the east ■ *adv* TOWARDS THE EAST in or towards the east [Old English *ēast-* < Indo-European, 'to shine']

East Africa region in east-central Africa, usually including Burundi, Kenya, Rwanda, Somalia, Tanzania, and Uganda —**East African** *n, adj*

East Anglia /-áng gli ə/ mainly agricultural region in E England —**East Anglian** *n, adj*

East Asia *n* the countries, territories, and regions of China, Hong Kong SAR, Japan, North Korea, South Korea, Macau, Mongolia, parts of Russia, and Taiwan. ◊ **Far East**

East Ayrshire council area in west-central Scotland. Area: 1,252 sq. km/483 sq. mi.

East Bengal former region of British India that became East Pakistan in 1947 and Bangladesh in 1971

eastbound /eest bownd/ *adj* going or leading towards the east

Eastbourne /eest bawrn/ seaside resort in SE England. Population: 88,600 (1995).

east by north *n* the direction or compass point midway between east and east-northeast —**east by north** *adj, adv*

east by south *n* the direction or compass point midway between east and east-southeast —**east by south** *adj, adv*

East Cape peninsular region in the E of the North Island, New Zealand

East China Sea arm of the NW Pacific Ocean between the coast of E China and the Ryukyu Islands. Area: 752,000 sq. km/290,000 sq. mi.

East Coast *n* the easternmost part of the United States, consisting of the states along its eastern seaboard from Maine to Florida, especially the oldest, most urban part of this area: New England, New York, New Jersey, Pennsylvania, Maryland, Virginia, and Washington, D.C.

East Dunbartonshire council area in central Scotland. Area: 172 sq. km/66 sq. mi.

East End *n* a densely populated area in the east of London, England —**East Ender** *n*

Easter /eestər/ *n* 1 CHRISTIAN FESTIVAL a Christian festival marking the resurrection of Jesus Christ. Date: the Sunday following the full moon on or after 21 March. 2 DAY OF THE EASTER FESTIVAL the Sunday on which Easter is celebrated 3 EASTER WEEKEND the period from Good Friday to Easter Monday [Old English *Ēastre* < Germanic dawn-goddess whose festival was celebrated at the vernal equinox < Indo-European, 'to shine']

Easter bonnet *n* a woman's hat, often elaborately decorated, traditionally worn for the first time at Easter

Easter Day *n* CALENDAR = **Easter** *n.* 2

ϟ**Easter egg** *n* 1 a chocolate egg given as a gift to children at Easter 2 a secret message, graphic, animation, or sound effect hidden in a computer program and activated by a specific undocumented sequence of keystrokes

Easter Island /éestər-/ island in the South Pacific Ocean belonging to Chile. Population: 2,095 (1989). Area: 117 sq. km/45 sq. mi. —**Easter Islander** *n*

Easter lily *n* a cultivated, spring-blooming lily. Flowers: white.

easterly /éestərli/ *adj* 1 IN THE EAST situated in or towards the east 2 BLOWING FROM THE EAST describes a wind that blows from the east ■ *n* (*plural* **-lies**) WIND FROM THE EAST a wind blowing from the east —**easterly** *adv*

Easter Monday *n* the Monday after the Christian festival of Easter

eastern /éestərn/ *adj* 1 IN THE EAST situated in the east of a region or country 2 FACING EAST situated in or facing the east 3 EAST OF GREENWICH MERIDIAN lying east of the Greenwich meridian 4 BLOWING FROM THE EAST describes a wind that blows from the east 5 **eastern, Eastern** RELATING TO THE EAST relating to or native to the east of a geographical region

Eastern *adj* 1 relating to the Eastern Orthodox Church 2 relating or belonging to the countries of Asia as viewed from Europe or North America

Eastern Cape province in SE South Africa. Capital: Bisho. Population: 6,481,300 (1995). Area: 169,580 sq. km/65,475 sq. mi.

Eastern Empire *n* HIST = **Byzantine Empire**

easterner /éestərnər/ *n* a person who comes from the eastern part of a geographical area

Eastern European Time *n* the standard time in the time zone centred on longitude 30° E, which includes Finland and Greece. It is two hours later than Universal Coordinated Time.

Eastern Ghats mountain range in SE India, with an average elevation of 600m/2,000 ft

eastern hemisphere *n* 1 the half of the Earth that lies east of the Greenwich meridian and contains Asia, Australasia, and most of Europe and Africa 2 the countries within the eastern hemisphere, especially the countries of Asia

easternmost /éestərn mōst/ *adj* 1 farthest to the east 2 located at the most eastern extreme of a county, state, or country

Eastern Orthodox Church *n* the self-governing Orthodox Christian churches that originated in the Byzantine Empire and recognize the Patriarch of Constantinople as primate

Eastern Standard Time *n* 1 the standard time in the time zone centred on longitude 75° W, which includes the eastern part of North America. It is five hours earlier than Universal Coordinated Time. 2 the standard time in the time zone centred on longitude 150° E, which includes the eastern part of Australia. It is ten hours later than Universal Coordinated Time.

Eastern Townships group of settlements in S Quebec Province, Canada

Eastern Transvaal former name for **Mpumalanga**

Easter Rising *n* an armed rebellion against British rule that took place in Dublin on Easter Day in 1916

Easter Sunday *n* CALENDAR = **Easter** *n.* 2

Easter term *n* the term at the High Court that follows Hilary term

Eastertide /éestər tīd/, **Eastertime** /-tīm/ *n* the period around Easter [12C. < Old English *eastertīd*.]

East Germanic *n* a group of extinct languages that were formerly spoken in parts of E Europe. It is one of the three groups that form the Germanic branch of Indo-European. —**East Germanic** *adj*

East Germany former republic of central Europe that reunited with the rest of Germany in 1990. Area: 108,178 sq. km/41,768 sq. mi. —**East German** *n, adj*

East India Company *n* a trading company established in England in 1600 to trade with the East Indies, and later with India, which it effectively governed for many years

East Indies /-ín deez/ name formerly applied to India, Southeast Asia, and the Malay Archipelago, especially Indonesia —**East Indian** *adj, n*

easting /éesting/ *n* 1 DISTANCE TRAVELLED EAST the net distance eastwards that a vessel travels when making for the east 2 PART OF A MAP REFERENCE the first part of a map reference that shows how far east a point lies from a reference line running from north to south 3 NORTH-SOUTH GRID LINE ON MAP a grid line on a map running north to south

East Kilbride /-kil brīd/ town in south-central Scotland. Population: 70,422 (1991).

East London city in SE South Africa. Population: 102,325 (1991).

East Lothian council area in SE Scotland. Area: 678 sq. km/262 sq. mi.

Eastman /éestmən/, **George** (1854–1932) US inventor and philanthropist

east-northeast *n* the direction or compass point midway between east and northeast ■ *adj, adv* in, from, facing, or towards the east-northeast —**east-northeasterly** *adv*

East Pakistan area of Pakistan that became Bangladesh in 1971

East Prussia former German province on the Baltic Sea that was divided between Poland and Russia in 1945 —**East Prussian** *n, adj*

East Renfrewshire council area in central Scotland. Area: 173 sq. km/67 sq. mi.

East Riding of Yorkshire /-rīding-/ 1 historic division of Yorkshire in NE England 2 council area in NE England. Area: 1819 sq. km/704 sq. mi.

East River strait in SE New York State. Length: 24 km/15 mi.

East Sea = **Japan, Sea of**

east-southeast *n* the direction or compass point midway between east and southeast ■ *adj, adv* in, from, facing, or towards the east-southeast —**east-southeasterly** *adv*

East Stewartry Coast /-styoō ərtri-/ National Scenic Area in SW Scotland. Area: 45 sq. kms/17 sq. mi.

East Sussex county in SE England. Area: 1,795 sq. km/693 sq. mi.

East Timor disputed territory on the eastern half of the island of Timor in Southeast Asia. Capital: Dili. Population: 839,700 (1995). Area: 14,874 sq. km/5,743 sq. mi.

eastward /éestwərd/ *adj* towards or in the east ■ *n* a direction towards or a point in the east ■ *adv* = **eastwards** —**eastwardly** *adj, adv*

eastwards /éestwərdz/ *adv* in an easterly direction

Eastwood /éestwŏŏd/, **Clint** (*b.* 1930) US film actor and director

easy /éezi/ *adj* (**-ier, -iest**) 1 NOT DIFFICULT not causing problems or difficulty or requiring much effort, work, or thought ○ *Answer the easy questions first.* ○ *It's easy to see why they chose him.* 2 INAPPROPRIATELY EFFORTLESS requiring less effort, thought, or emotional involvement than is appropriate or right ○ *always taking the easy way out* ○ *easy answers* 3 RELAXED AND INFORMAL relaxed, informal, and without awkwardness or self-consciousness, especially in social situations ○ *an easy manner* 4 GOOD-NATURED good-natured and tolerant ○ *an easy disposition* 5 FINANCIALLY PROSPEROUS characterized by financial prosperity and security and the comfort and peace of mind that goes with them 6 NOT HARSH not severe or harsh ○ *She's always claiming that easy discipline makes people soft.* 7 EASY TO TAKE ADVANTAGE OF not difficult to catch, acquire, take advantage of, or exploit ○ *unscrupulous sellers looking for easy targets* 8 LOOSE not tight or close-fitting ○ *jeans that are an easy fit* 9 UNHURRIED comfortable, unhurried, and not too fast ○ *took an easy pace up the trail* 10 NOT STEEP not steep or difficult to climb up or down ○ *It's an easy slope to the top.* 11 PLEASANT TO EXPERIENCE pleasant to experience through one of the senses, especially good to look at or soothing to listen to ○ *easy on the eyes* 12 LACKING PREFERENCES having no strong preferences (*informal*) ○ *We can do either; I'm easy.* 13 NOT ANXIOUS free from unpleasant feelings such as anxiety, guilt, or worry ○ *Rest easy; we'll be there soon.* 14 READILY OBTAINABLE readily obtainable, because demand is lower than usual 15 MARKED BY LOW DEMAND AND PRICES characterized by low demand or overproduction and hence low prices 16 OFFENSIVE TERM an offensive term meaning sexually promiscuous or too willing to become sexually involved (*slang*) ■ *adv* 1 EASILY without difficulty or the need for hard work ○ *Everything comes easy to her.* 2 WITHOUT PUNISHMENT without punishment or suffering ○ *Considering what they did, they got off easy.* ■ *interj* USED TO CALM used to try to make a person or animal calm down or slow down (*informal*) [12C. < Old French *aisié*, past participle of *aisier* 'put at ease' < *aise* 'comfort'.] —**easiness** *n* ◇ **go easy on somebody** to treat or deal with somebody gently, leniently, or without harsh criticism or reproaches (*informal*) ◇ **go easy on something** to avoid using, eating, or drinking too much of something (*informal*) ◇ **take it easy** 1 to relax, avoid effort, or not work too hard 2 to calm down and avoid becoming upset or angry

easy-care *adj* easy to wash and iron

easy chair *n* a comfortably upholstered chair, especially an armchair

~~**easyer**~~ incorrect spelling of **easier**

easy game *n* = **easy meat**

easygoing /éezi gō ing/ *adj* 1 relaxed, informal, and tolerant in attitude and reluctant to make heavy demands or enforce strict discipline on people 2 unhurried and comfortable

easy listening *n* popular music in an undemanding style, usually with a lyrical or romantic tune, gentle rhythms, and soft soothing orchestration

~~**easyly**~~ incorrect spelling of **easily**

easy mark *n* a person who can easily be taken advantage of (*informal*)

easy meat, easy game *n* a person who can be easily taken advantage of (*informal*)

easy money *n* 1 money made with little effort, and often dishonestly 2 money that can be borrowed at a low rate of interest

easy-peasy /-péezi/ (**easy-peasier, easy-peasiest**) *adj* extremely easy (*informal*) [Reduplication]

easy terms *npl* a form of credit involving payment by instalments

easy virtue *n* lax sexual morals and promiscuous sexual habits (*dated*)

eat /eet/ (**eats, eating, ate** /et, ayt/, **eaten** /éet'n/) *v* 1 *vti* CONSUME AS SUSTENANCE to take something into the mouth as food and swallow it ○ *They hadn't eaten for three days.* 2 *vt* CONSUME USUALLY to include something as a usual or fundamental part of a diet ○ *Do dogs eat fish?* 3 *vi* DINE to have a meal ○ *Are you ready to eat?* 4 *vt* BOTHER to bother or annoy somebody (*slang*) ○ *What's eating her?* 5 *vt* USE A LOT OF to use or consume something in large quantities (*slang*) ○ *a car that eats petrol* 6 *vti* PENETRATE to penetrate the surface of something by corrosive or mechanical action ○ *Rust had eaten into the chrome.* 7 *vt* TABOO TERM a highly offensive term meaning to perform fellatio or cunnilingus on somebody (*taboo*) [Old English *etan* < Indo-European] —**eater** *n*

eat away *vt* to consume or destroy something gradually ○ *eaten away in parts by acid rain*

eat away at *vt* 1 to worry or be a continual source of distress to somebody ○ *Guilt had been eating away at him all day.* 2 to deplete or use up something gradually by taking small amounts regularly ○ *medical expenses eating away at our income*

eat in *vi* to consume a meal at home ○ *Would you rather eat in or go to a restaurant?*

eat into *vt* to use up part of something, especially in a wasteful or nonproductive way

eat out *vi* to consume a meal away from home, usually in a restaurant or similar establishment ○ *Let's eat out tonight.*

eat up *v* 1 *vti* EAT COMPLETELY to consume food completely or with great appetite 2 *vt* OBSESS to absorb or obsess somebody (*usually passive*) ○ *eaten up by envy* 3 *vt* RECEIVE ENTHUSIASTICALLY to receive something with enthusiasm or pleasure (*informal*) ○ *The reading public eats up everything she writes.* 4 *vt* CONSUME QUICKLY to consume or deal with something quickly (*informal*)

eatable /éetəb'l/ *adj* fit, suitable, or pleasant to eat ■ *n* something that is fit or suitable for eating (*informal; usually plural*) ○ *buy some bread and other eatables*

USAGE eatable or **edible**? ***Eatable*** is used to refer to food that can be eaten with enjoyment, whereas ***edible*** refers to any substance in respect of its suitability as food. If something is ***eatable*** it is also ***edible***, but a substance can be ***edible*** without being ***eatable*** (for example, raw potatoes). Informally, however, ***edible*** is often used to mean ***eatable*** (though not usually the other way round): *The vegetables were overcooked but just about edible.* The same distinction applies to the negative forms of these words: *The meal was uneatable. Toadstools are inedible.*

eaten past participle of **eat**

eatery /éetəri/ (*plural* **-ies**) *n* a place where food is cooked and sold (*informal*)

eating /éeting/ *n* **FOOD** food, especially of a particular quality ○ *These apples are good eating.* ■ *adj* **1 SUITABLE FOR EATING** suitable for human consumption, especially uncooked **2 INVOLVING FOOD** relating to or used for the consumption of food

eating disorder *n* any emotional disorder, e.g. bulimia, that manifests itself in an irrational craving for or avoidance of food

eats /eets/ *npl* food (*slang*) ○ *What do you do for eats around here?* [Late 19C. < EAT.]

Eau Claire /ō kláir/ city in W Wisconsin. Population: 56,856 (1990).

eau de cologne /ṓ də kə lṓn/ *n* = **cologne** [Early 19C. < French, 'water of Cologne'.]

eau de nil /ṓ də neél/ *adj* of a pale yellowish-green colour [Late 19C. < French, 'water of the Nile'.] —**eau de nil** *n*

eau de toilette /ṓ də twaa lét/ *n* = **toilet water** [< French, 'toilet water']

eau de vie /ṓ də veé/ *n* a strong alcoholic spirit, especially brandy [Mid-18C. < French, 'water of life'.]

eaves /eevz/ *npl* the part of a roof that projects beyond the wall that supports it [Old English *efes* < Germanic]

eavesdrop /éevz drop/ (**-drops, -dropping, -dropped**) *vi* to listen to a conversation without the speakers being aware of it [Early 17C. Probably back-formation < *eavesdropper* < obsolete *eavesdrop* 'ground on which rainwater thrown off by eaves falls'; from standing in this area trying to hear private conversations.] —**eavesdropper** *n*

Eban /eé ban/, **Abba** (*b.* 1915) South African-born Israeli statesman. Born **Aubrey Solomon**

ebb /eb/ *vi* **1 RECEDE FROM THE SHORE** to recede from the land, as the tide falls (*refers to the sea or tidal water*) **2 DIMINISH** to diminish or lessen in intensity ○ *The pain gradually ebbed away.* ■ *n* **1 TIDAL MOVEMENT AWAY FROM LAND** the movement of a receding tide away from the land **2 DIMINUTION** diminution or lessening ○ *the ebb and flow of the company's fortunes* [Old English *ebbian* < Germanic] ◇ **at a low ebb** lacking hope and energy, or in a depleted condition

ebb tide *n* a receding tide, or the time when this happens

Ebbw Vale /ébboo-/ town in SE Wales. Population: 24,100 (1996).

⚡**EBCDIC** /éb see dik/ *n* a binary computer character code, representing 256 standard letters, numbers, symbols, and control characters by means of eight binary digits. Full form **extended binary coded decimal interchange code**

⚡**e-blocker** *n* an employer who uses special software to prevent employees from visiting particular websites while at work

E-boat *n* a fast torpedo boat used by the German navy in World War II [Abbreviation of ENEMY]

Ebola /i bṓlə/, **Ebola virus** *n* a contagious virus transmitted by blood and body fluids that causes the linings of bodily organs and vessels to leak blood and fluids, usually resulting in death [Late 20C. After the River *Ebola*, Democratic Republic of the Congo.]

ebon /ébbən/ *n, adj* ebony (*literary*) [14C. Via Old French < Greek *ebenos* < Semitic.]

Ebonics /e bónniks/ *n* LANG = **African American Vernacular English** [Late 20C. Blend of EBONY + PHONICS.]

ebonise *vt* = **ebonize**

ebonite /ébbənīt/ *n* MANUF = **vulcanite**

ebonize /ébbə nīz/ (**-izes, -izing, -ized**), **ebonise** (**-ises, -ising, -ised**) *vt* to stain something black so as to resemble ebony

ebony /ébbəni/ (*plural* **-ies**) *n* **1 DARK HARD WOOD** a hard blackish wood **2 ASIAN TREE** a tree that yields ebony. Native to: tropical Asia. Genus: *Diospyros*. **3 BROWNISH-BLACK COLOUR** black tinged with olive or brown —**ebony** *adj*

⚡**e-book** *n* a battery-powered portable reading device displaying text on a high-resolution screen

Eboracum /i bórrəkəm, eé baw raákəm/ Roman name for the city of York

EBRD *abbr* European Bank for Reconstruction and Development

Ebro /eébrō/ river in NE Spain. Length: 909 km/565 mi.

ebullient /i búl yənt, i bóoll-/ *adj* **1** full of cheerful excitement or enthusiasm **2** boiling vigorously (*formal*) [Late 16C. < Latin *ebullient-*, present participle of *ebullire* 'bubble out' < *bullire* 'to bubble'.] —**ebullience** *n* —**ebulliently** *adv*

ebullioscopy /i búlli óskəpi, i bóolli-/ *n* a process for determining the molecular weight of a substance by measuring the change it produces in the boiling point of a solution [Early 20C. < Latin *ebullire* (see EBULLIENT).] —**ebullioscope** /i búlli ə skōp/ *n*

ebullition /ébbə lísh'n/ *n* **1** a state of bubbling up or boiling (*formal*) **2** a sudden outbreak of violent emotion (*literary*) [14C. Via French < late Latin *ebullition-* < Latin *ebullire* (see EBULLIENT).]

eburnation /eébər náysh'n, ébbər-/ *n* an abnormal hardening of the surfaces of bones in a joint that have lost their cartilage covering, as occurs in such conditions as osteoarthritis [Mid-19C. < Latin *eburnus* 'made of ivory'.]

⚡**e-business** *n* **1** the conduct of business using Internet technology to create links between customers, suppliers, employees, and business partners (*in e-commerce*) **2** a company engaged in e-business

EBV *abbr* Epstein-Barr virus

EB virus *n* MED = **Epstein-Barr virus**

EC *abbr* **1** European Community **2** European Commission

écarté[1] /ay kaár tay/ *n* a card game for two people played with 32 cards in which cards may be discarded in exchange for others [Early 19C. < French, 'discarded'.]

écarté[2] /ay kaár tay/ *n* a ballet position in which the arm and leg on one side of the body are extended [Early 20C. < French, 'spread out'.]

⚡**e-cash** *n* E-COMMERCE = **electronic cash**

ecce homo /ékay hṓmō, éksi-/ *n* a portrayal of Jesus Christ crowned with thorns [< Latin, 'behold the man' (John 19:5)]

eccentric /ik séntrik, ek-/ *adj* **1 UNCONVENTIONAL** unconventional, especially in a whimsical way ○ *an eccentric mode of dress* **2 AWAY FROM THE CENTRE** away from the centre or axis **3 HAVING DIFFERENT CENTRES** describes circles with different centres **4 ELLIPTICAL** describes an orbit that is elliptical rather than circular ■ *n* **1 UNCONVENTIONAL PERSON** an unconventional person who has odd, sometimes endearing habits **2 MECHANICAL DEVICE** a mechanical device with an off-centre axis of revolution that converts the rotary motion of one component of a mechanism to reciprocating motion in another [Mid-16C. < late Latin *eccentricus* < Greek *ekkentros* 'out of centre' < *kentron* (see CENTRE).] —**eccentrically** *adv*

eccentricity /ék sen tríssəti/ (*plural* **-ties**) *n* **1 ECCENTRIC QUALITY** unconventionality, especially of a whimsical sort **2 ECCENTRIC ACT** an example or instance of unconventional whimsical behaviour **3 DISTANCE BETWEEN A MAIN AND SECONDARY AXIS** the distance between the axis about which an object rotates and a secondary axis on the object at which a device such as a rod could be attached **4 DEVIATION** the deviation of the path of an orbiting body from a true circle **5 GEOMETRIC CONSTANT** a constant that describes the shape of a conic section

ecchymosis /éki mṓssiss/ (*plural* **-moses** /-seez/) *n* bleeding into surrounding tissue caused by bruising (*technical*) [Mid-16C. Via modern Latin < Greek *ekkhumōsis* < *ekkhumonothai* 'pour out'.]

Eccles /ék'lz/, **Sir John** (1903–97) Australian physiologist

Eccles cake *n* a pastry filled with dried fruit [< town in NW England]

ecclesia /i kleézi ə/ (*plural* **-ae** /-zi ee/) *n* a church or congregation (*formal*) [Late 16C. Via Latin < Greek *ekklēsia* 'assembly' < *ekkalein* 'call to come out, summon' < *kalein* 'call'.]

Ecclesiastes /i kleézi ás teez/ *n* a book in the Bible that discusses the futility of life and how to be a God-fearing person

ecclesiastic /-ástik/ *n* a member of the clergy

ecclesiastical /i kleézi ástik'l/ *adj* belonging to or involving the Christian church or clergy —**ecclesiastically** *adv*

ecclesiasticism /i kleézi ástisizəm/ *n* **1** all-absorbing regard for the principles and customary practices of the Christian Church **2** the principles or body of thought constituting organized Christianity

Ecclesiasticus /i kleézi ástikəss/ *n* a book of teachings in the Jerusalem Version of the Bible

ecclesiology /i kleézi ólləji/ *n* **1** the study of the history and theology of the Christian Church **2** the study of the architecture and decoration of Christian churches

eccremocarpus /ékrəmə kaárpəss/ *n* a climbing, widely-cultivated, evergreen plant. Flowers: brightly-coloured tubular. Native to: Chile, Peru. [< modern Latin, < Greek *ekkremēs* 'suspended' + *karpos* 'fruit']

eccrine /ékrīn, ékrin/ *adj* describes sweat glands that are distributed all over the body, especially on the hands and feet, that do not secrete organic matter, and that are important in regulating body temperature [Mid-20C. < German *Ekkrin* < Greek *ekkrinein* 'secrete'.]

ecdysiast /ek dízzi ast/ *n* a performer of striptease (*humorous*) [Mid-20C. < ECDYSIS, after *gymnast*.]

ecdysis /ékdississ, ek dī́-/ *n* the regular moulting of an outer layer by arthropods, e.g. insects and crustaceans, and by reptiles [Mid-19C. < Greek *ekdusis* < *ekduein* 'put off, shed'.]

ecdysone /ékdi sōn/ *n* a hormone that promotes metamorphosis and ecdysis in insects and crustaceans

ecesis /i seéssiss/ *n* the successful establishment of a plant or animal species in a new environment [Early 20C. < Greek *oikēsis* 'an inhabiting' < *oikos* 'house'.]

Ecevit /échəvit/, **Bülent** (*b.* 1925) Turkish statesman and prime minister (1974, 1978–79, 1999–)

ECG *abbr* **1** echocardiograph **2** electrocardiogram **3** electrocardiograph

ECGD *abbr* Export Credits Guarantee Department

Echegaray y Eizaguirre /éch ay ga rī́ ee ay tha gírray/, **José** (1832–1916) Spanish playwright and politician

echelon /éshə lon/ *n* **1 LEVEL IN A HIERARCHY** a level of authority or rank in an organization or system ○ *the lower echelons of society* **2 FORMATION WITH OFFSET POSITIONS** a formation in which individuals or units are positioned behind and to one side of those in front to give a stepped effect and allow each a clear view ahead **3 AIRCRAFT FORMATION WITH OFFSET POSITIONS** a group of aircraft flying in positions behind and to one side of the aircraft in front **4 DEVICE FOR STUDYING SPECTRA** a series of glass plates of equal thickness arranged like steps, used in spectroscopy for studying the fine structure of spectral lines ■ *vti* **FORM AN ECHELON** to arrange something in or form an echelon [Late 18C. < French, 'rung' < *échelle* 'ladder' < Latin *scala* 'stair'.]

echeveria /échə veéri ə/ *n* a usually stemless cultivated plant with rosettes of fleshy leaves. Flowers: tubular, bell-shaped. Native to: tropical America. Genus: *Echeveria*. [Mid-19C. < modern Latin, after Atanasio *Echeverria*.]

echidna /i kídnə/ *n* a spiny insect-eating mammal with a long snout and strong claws. Native to: Australia, Tasmania, New Guinea. Family: Tachyglossidae. [Mid-19C. Via modern Latin, 'viper' < Greek, < *ekhis* 'viper'.]

echin- *prefix* = **echino-** (*before vowels*)

echinacea /éki náyssi ə/ *n* **1** a herbal remedy prepared from the pulverized leaves and stems of purple coneflowers, thought to bolster the immune system **2** PLANT SCI = **coneflower** [< modern Latin, < Greek *ekhinos* 'hedgehog, sea urchin']

echinate /éki nayt/, **echinated** /-naytid/ *adj* describes plant and animal parts that have spines or similar outgrowths [Late 17C. < Latin *echinatus* < Greek *ekhinos* 'hedgehog, sea urchin'.]

echini plural of **echinus**

echino- *prefix* **1** spine ○ *echinoderm* **2** echinoderm ○ *echinoid* [Via Latin *echinus* < Greek *ekhinos* 'hedgehog, sea urchin']

echinoderm /i kī́nə durm/ *n* a marine invertebrate animal that has a radially symmetrical body, tube feet, and a system of calcareous plates under the skin. Phylum: Echinodermata. [Mid-19C. < ECHINO- + Greek *derma* 'skin'.] —**echinodermal** /i kī́nə dúrm'l/ *adj* —**echinodermatous** /-mətəss/ *adj*

echinoid /i kī́ noyd, ékə-/ *n* a marine invertebrate animal with a hard ovoid body and movable spines. Class: Echinoidea. —**echinoid** *adj*

echinus /i kínəss/ (*plural* **-ni** /-nī/) *n* **1** a rounded moulding beneath the flat upper part (**abacus**) of a Doric or Tuscan column **2** MARINE BIOL = **sea urchin** [14C. Via Latin < Greek *ekhinos* 'hedgehog, sea urchin'.]

echium /éki əm/ *n* a plant with oblong or lance-shaped leaves. Flowers: funnel-shaped spikes. Native to: Europe, W Asia, Africa. Genus: *Echium*. [Late 19C. < modern Latin, < Greek *ekhis* 'viper'; from the spotted markings on its stem.]

⚡**echo** /ékō/ *n* (*plural* **-oes**) **1 REPEATED SOUND** the repetition of a sound caused by the reflection of sound waves from a surface **2 SYMPATHETIC REACTION** a reaction of agreement or sympathy ○ *Her songs found an echo in the hearts of thousands.* **3 SOMETHING REPEATED** something repeated or imitated rather than original ○ *echoes of the boss's ideas* **4 REMINDER** something that looks back to an earlier period or is reminiscent of it ○ *the current style with its echoes of the 1920s* **5 EFFECT** a lingering effect of an earlier event **6 IMITATOR** a close imitator of somebody else, especially in repeating his or her opinions (*dated*) **7 RETURNED SIGNAL** the signal reflected by an object struck by a radar transmission, or the image of this on a radar screen **8 REPETITION OF SOUNDS** the repetition of sounds within a sequence of verse or prose **9 REPEATED MUSIC** the repetition, usually quieter, of a phrase or note in music **10 ELECTRONIC SOUND REPETITION** the repetition of sound created electronically for effect or by accident ○ *The echo on the guitar riff was added in the studio.* **11 ORGAN CONTROL** a device on some organs that gives the effect of an echo coming from a distance ■ *v* (**-oes, -oing, -oed**) **1** *vt* **MAKE REPEAT** to make a sound repeat by the reflection of sound waves ○ *The surrounding peaks echoed the eagle's cry.* **2** *vt* **REPEAT** to repeat a statement or opinion, especially in agreement or imitation ○ *The completed report echoed the initial assessment.* **3** *vt* **IMITATE** to imitate or incorporate parts of something earlier ○ *The building's design echoes the surrounding Georgian terraces.* **4** *vt* **DISPLAY AS A CHECK** to return a character back to its source after a computer or communications device receives it, as an accuracy check **5** *vi* **RESOUND** to resound by the reflection of sound waves ○ *Their footsteps echoed down the tunnel.* **6** *vi* **BE FULL OF SOUND** to be full of echoes of a sound ○ *The auditorium echoed with cheering.* [14C. Via Old French or Latin < Greek *ēkhō* 'echo'.] —**echoingly** *adv*

Echo /ékō/ *n* a code word for the letter 'E', used in international radio communications

echocardiogram /ékō kaárdi ə gram/ *n* the visual record produced by an echocardiograph

echocardiograph /ékō kaárdi ə graaf, -graf/ *n* an ultrasound device used to examine the working heart and display moving images of its action —**echocardiographic** /ékō kaárdi ə gráffik/ *adj* —**echocardiographically** /-gráffikli/ *adv* —**echocardiography** /ékō kaárdi óggrəfi/ *n*

echo chamber *n* a room with sound-reflecting walls, used in making acoustic measurements or generating sound effects

echoencephalogram /ékō en séffələ gram/ *n* the visual record produced by an echoencephalograph

echoencephalograph /ékō en séffələ graaf, -graf/ *n* an ultrasound device used to examine the structures of the brain —**echoencephalographic** /ékō en séffələ gráffik/ *adj* —**echoencephalographically** *adv* —**echoencephalography** /ékō en séffə lóggrəfi/ *n*

echogram /ékō gram/ *n* PHYS = **sonogram**

echography /e kóggrəfi/ *n* PHYS = **ultrasonography**

echoic /e kṓ ik/ *adj* **1** resembling or relating to an echo **2** LITERAT = **onomatopoeic**

echoic memory *n* the ability to remember and reproduce a sound in the two or three seconds after it is heard

echoism /ékō izəm/ *n* **1** LITERAT = **onomatopoeia 2** a process by which the sound of a vowel changes to imitate the sound of a preceding vowel

echolalia /ékō láyli ə/ *n* the compulsive repetition of words spoken by somebody else, often a sign of psychiatric disorder

echolocation /ékō lō káysh'n/ *n* a means of locating an object using an emitted sound and the reflection back from it, used naturally by animals such as bats and electronically by humans

echo plate *n* an electromechanical device used in broadcasting or recording to create the effect of reverberation or echo

echopraxia /ékō práksi ə/, **echopraxis** /-siss/ *n* the compulsive imitation of the actions of others, often a sign of psychiatric disorder [Early 20C. < modern Latin, < Greek *ēkhō* 'echo' + *praxis* 'action'.]

echo quilting *n* a quilting stitch that follows the outlines of an appliquéd design

echo sounder *n* a device used to ascertain water depth or to locate underwater objects by measuring the time taken for emitted sound waves to return from the bottom or from the object

echovirus /ékō vīrəss/ *n* a virus found in the gastrointestinal tract that belongs to a group of retroviruses associated with intestinal and respiratory infections and meningitis [Mid-20C. Acronym < *enteric cytopathogenic human orphan*.]

Echuca /e choókə/ town in N Victoria, Australia. Population: 6,486 (1991).

Eckert /ékərt/, **John Presper** (1919–95) US electronics engineer

Eckhart /ék haart/, **Meister** (1260?–1328?) German philosopher and Christian theologian. Born **Johannes Eckhart**

éclair /ay kláir, i-/ *n* **1** a long thin cylinder of choux pastry filled with whipped cream and topped with chocolate icing **2** a hard toffee sweet with a soft filling, usually chocolate [Mid-19C. < French, 'lightning'.]

éclaircissement /ay kláir seess maaN/ *n* a clearing up of something puzzling [Mid-17C. < French, 'clearing up'.]

eclampsia /i klámpsi ə/ *n* an illness that sometimes occurs during the later stages of pregnancy and involves high blood pressure and convulsions sometimes followed by a coma [Mid-19C. Via modern Latin < French *éclampsie* < Greek *eklampsis* 'sudden development' < *eklampein* 'shine out'.] —**eclamptic** *adj*

éclat /ay klaá, áy klaa/ *n* **1 SUCCESS** brilliant success ○ *The show came off with éclat.* **2 DISPLAY** ostentatious display **3 RENOWN** renown based on achievement [Late 17C. < French, 'splinter, fragment'.]

eclectic /i kléktik/ *adj* **1** choosing what is best or preferred from a variety of sources or styles ○ *an eclectic taste in music* **2** made up of elements from various sources ○ *an eclectic collection of paintings* [Late 17C. < Greek *eklektikos* 'picking out, selecting' < *eklegein* 'pick out' < *legein* 'choose'.] —**eclectic** *n* —**eclectically** *adv*

eclecticism /i klékti sizəm/ *n* the theory or use of an eclectic approach

eclipse /i klíps/ *n* **1 OBSCURING OF A CELESTIAL BODY** the partial or complete hiding from view of a celestial body, e.g. the Sun or Moon, when another celestial body comes between it and the observer **2 LOSS OF LIGHT** a loss or blocking of light **3 DECLINE** a loss of status, power, or favour ○ *the eclipse of the aristocracy* ■ *vt* (**eclipses, eclipsing, eclipsed**) **1 OBSCURE CELESTIAL BODY** to cause a total or partial obscuring of another celestial body **2 SHADOW** to block the light falling on something, or cast a shadow on it **3 OUTDO** to outdo in achievement or become more powerful or popular than something or somebody ○ *a performance that eclipsed all the others* [13C. Via Old French and Latin < Greek *ekleipsis* < *ekleipein* 'no longer to appear or be present' < *leipein* 'leave'.] —**eclipser** *n*

eclipse plumage *n* dull plumage grown for a short period by some birds, especially male ducks, after the brightly coloured breeding plumage has been shed

eclipsing binary *n* **1** a binary star whose orbit places it between its companion and the observer, resulting in an eclipse **2** a system in which one star's orbit periodically brings it between the Earth and the other star of the pair

eclipsing variable *n* ASTRON = **eclipsing binary** *n.* 2

ecliptic /i klíptik/ *n* the apparent path of the Sun's annual motion relative to the stars, shown as a circle passing through the centre of the imaginary sphere (**celestial sphere**) containing all astronomical objects ■ *adj* relating to, involving, or typical of an eclipse [14C. Via Latin < Greek *ekluptikos* < *ekleipein* (see ECLIPSE); because eclipses of the Sun or Moon can occur only when the Moon crosses the ecliptic.]

eclogue /ék log/ *n* a pastoral poem, usually in the form of a dialogue between shepherds [15C. Via Latin *ecloga* < Greek *eklogē* 'selection (of poems)' < *eklegein* (see ECLECTIC).]

eclosion /i klṓzh'n/ *n* the emergence of an insect from its pupal case, or the hatching of a larva from an egg [Late 19C. < French *éclosion* < *éclore* 'hatch, open' < Latin *excludere* 'hatch'.]

⚡**ECML** *abbr* electronic commerce modelling language (*in e-commerce*)

Eco /ékō/, **Umberto** (*b.* 1932) Italian novelist and academic

eco- *prefix* environment, ecology ○ *ecofriendly* [Shortened < ECOLOGY]

ecocatastrophe /eékōkə tástrəfi, ékō-/ *n* an event, usually caused by human actions, that results in very severe damage to the environment

ecofreak /eékō freek, ékō-/ *n* a person who is preoccupied or obsessed with the state of the environment (*slang insult*)

ecofriendly /eékō frendli, ékō-/ *adj* intended or perceived to have no harmful effect on the natural environment and its inhabitants

ecol. *abbr* **1** ecological **2** ecology

E. coli /ee kō lī/ *n* a bacterium found in the colon of human beings and animals that becomes a serious contaminant when found in the food or water supply. Full form **Escherichia coli** [Late 20C. Abbreviated < modern Latin *Escherichia coli*, after the German physician T. *Escherich* (1857–1911); *coli* 'of the colon'.]

ecology /i kólləji/ (*plural* **-gies**) *n* **1** the study of the relationships and interactions between living organisms and their natural or developed environment ○ *'A land ethic ... should be as honest as Thoreau's Walden, and as comprehensive as the sensitive science of ecology'.* (Stewart Udall, *The Quiet Crisis*; 1963) **2** the relationships between individual organisms and between organisms and their environment **3** SOC SCI = **human ecology** [Late 19C. < Greek *oikos* 'house, habitation'.] —**ecological** /eékə lójjik'l, ékə-/ *adj* —**ecologically** *adv* —**ecologist** *n*

⚡**e-commerce** *n* transactions conducted over the Internet, either by consumers buying goods and services, or between businesses

econ. *abbr* **1** economy **2** economics **3** economist

econometrics /i kónnə méttriks/ *n* the application of mathematical and statistical techniques to economic data and problems (+ *singular verb*) —**econometric** *adj* —**econometrically** *adv* —**econometrician** /i kónnəmə trísh'n/ *n*

economic /ékə nómmik, eékə-/ *adj* **1 OF ECONOMY OR ECONOMICS** relating to economics, the economy of a country, or money in general **2 PROFITABLE** producing or capable of producing a profit **3 MATERIAL** relating to or affecting material goods and resources **4** = **economical** *adj* 3 [Late 16C. Directly or via French < Latin *oeconomicus* < Greek *oikonomikos* < *oikonomos* (see ECONOMY).]

USAGE economic or **economical**? The adjective ***economic*** denotes economics or the economy, and is concerned with aspects of the production, distribution, and consumption of goods and services: *a Nobel Laureate's economic theories.* The adjective ***economical***, on the other hand, has to do with the prudent management of resources and attempts to reduce expenditure: *It is much more economical to buy in bulk. Public transport is economical, compared with hiring a limousine.* But the two adjectives can overlap in one sense, 'efficient in terms of avoiding unnecessary expenditure': *an economical* [or *economic*] *use of electricity.*

economical /ékə nómmik'l, eékə-/ *adj* **1 RESOURCEFULLY FRUGAL** careful in making the best use of resources ○ *an economical cook* **2 INEXPENSIVE** costing relatively little in comparison with other things in the same class ○ *a home that's economical to run* **3 EFFICIENT** efficient in terms of avoiding unnecessary expenditure of time or energy ○ *an economical gesture*

USAGE See ***economic***.

economically /ékə nómmikli, eékə-/ *adv* **1 WITH REGARD TO ECONOMY OR ECONOMICS** with regard to economics, the economy of a country, or financial matters in general ○ *economically and socially developing societies* **2 PROFITABLY** in such a way as to produce a profit **3 FRUGALLY** in a thrifty, sparing, or careful manner

economic determinism *n* the belief that the economic organization of a society determines the nature of all other aspects of its life

economic geography *n* a branch of geography that deals with the distribution and use of an area's economic resources

economic geology *n* the study of geological deposits from the viewpoint of their value as resources

economic indicator *n* a quantity expressed statistically and taken as a measure of an economic variable

economic migrant *n* a travelling or migrant worker who goes to an area where work or an easier life is available

economic rent *n* **1** a payment for use of a factor of production that is enough to make it profitable for the owner **2** a level of housing rent that is enough to make letting profitable for the owner

economics /éekə nómmiks, eékə-/ *n* **1** the study of the production, distribution, and consumption of goods and services (+ *singular verb*) **2** the financial element of something (+ *plural verb*) ◊ *the economics of running a business* [Late 18C. Probably < French *économique*.]

economic union *n* a merging of the economies of two or more states to function as a unit that shares a common financial policy and currency

economise *vi* = **economize**

economism /i kónnə mizəm/ *n* **1** the belief that economics is the most important element in a society **2** the belief that bringing about an improvement in the living standards of its members is the chief goal of a political organization or trade union organization

economist /i kónnəmist/ *n* a student or expert in the field of economics

economistic /i kónnə místik/ *adj* showing bias towards economic factors

economize /i kónnə mīz/ (**-mizes, -mizing, -mized**), **economise** (**-mises, -mising, -mised**) *vi* to reduce expenditure or use resources less wastefully ◊ *We had to economize on fuel.* —**economizer** *n*

economy /i kónnəmi/ *n* (*plural* **-mies**) **1** THRIFT the prudent managing of resources to avoid extravagant expenditure or waste **2** SAVING a saving or attempt to reduce expenditure **3** SPARING USE a sparing, controlled, or efficient use of something ◊ *a graceful economy of effort* **4** FINANCIAL AFFAIRS the production and consumption of goods and services of a community regarded as a whole ◊ *a gradual shift from an agricultural to an industrial economy* **5** TRANSP = **economy class 6** SYSTEM a system of interacting elements, especially when seen as being harmonious ◊ *the economy of the natural world* ■ *adj* CHEAPER intended to be cheaper or give better value for money [15C. Via French or Latin < Greek *oikonomiā* < *oikonomos* 'steward of a household' < *oikos* 'house' + *nemein* 'manage'.]

economy class *n* a class of travel, especially on airlines, that is relatively low in price and carries the majority of passengers

economy class syndrome *n* thrombosis believed to be caused by a prolonged period of restricted movement and dehydration, such as occurs during air travel

economy drive *n* an organized attempt to reduce expenditure and waste

economy of scale *n* a reduction in unit cost achieved by increasing the amount of production

écorché /é kawr shay/ (*plural* **-chés**) *n* an anatomical model of part or all of the human body with the skin removed, to allow study of the muscle structure [Mid-19C. < French, past participle of *écorcher* 'flay'.]

ecospecies /éekō spee sheez, ékō spee sheez/ (*plural* **-cies**) *n* a species made up of several subgroups (**ecotypes**) and characterized by its ecological traits

ecosphere /éekō sfeer, ékō-/ *n* ECOL = **biosphere**

écossaise /áy ko sáyz/ *n* a lively folk dance in 2/4 time [Mid-19C. < French, 'Scottish'.]

ecosystem /éekō sistəm, ékō-/ *n* a localized group of interdependent organisms together with the environment that they inhabit and depend on

ecoterrorism /éekō térrə rizəm, ékō-/ *n* the sabotage of the activities of individuals or corporations, e.g. industrial companies, considered to be polluting or destroying the natural environment —**ecoterrorist** *n*

ecotone /éekə tōn, ékə-/ *n* a zone of transition between two different ecosystems, e.g. where the sea meets the land [Early 20C. < ECO- + Greek *tonos* 'tension'.]

ecotourism /éekō tōŏrizəm, ékō-/ *n* a form of tourism that strives to minimize ecological or other damage to areas visited for their natural or cultural interest

ecotoxicology /éekō tóksi kólləji, ékō-/ *n* the study of how organisms are affected by chemicals released into the environment by human activities

ecotype /éekō tīp, ékō-/ *n* a subgroup of a species of plant or other organism whose members show genetically determined adaptations to certain environmental conditions in their habitat

ecowarrior /éekō worri ər, ékō-/ *n* an activist who takes direct, often unlawful action on an environmental issue

ecru /ékroo, áy-/ *adj* of a pale brown colour, like unbleached linen [Mid-19C. Via French, 'raw, unbleached' < Latin *crudus* 'raw'.] —**ecru** *n*

ECS *abbr* European Communications Satellite

ECSC *abbr* European Coal and Steel Community

~~ecstacy~~ incorrect spelling of **ecstasy**

ecstasy /ékstəssi/ (*plural* **-sies**) *n* **1** INTENSE DELIGHT a feeling of intense delight **2** INTENSE FEELING OR ACTIVITY a feeling or activity characterized by its extreme intensity ◊ *an ecstasy of remorse* **3** LOSS OF SELF-CONTROL a mental state, usually caused by intense religious experience, sexual pleasure, or drugs, in which somebody is so dominated by an emotion that self-control and sometimes consciousness are lost **4 ecstasy, Ecstasy** ILLEGAL DRUG $C_{11}H_{15}NO_2$ a drug used illicitly as a stimulant and relaxer of inhibitions [14C. Via Old French < Greek *ekstasis* < *existanai* 'displace, drive out (of your mind)' < *histanai* 'put'.]

ecstatic /ik státtik, ek-/ *adj* **1** DELIGHTED showing or feeling great pleasure or delight **2** DOMINATED BY EMOTION completely dominated by an intense emotion ■ *n* SOMEBODY SUBJECT TO A TRANCE a person who experiences spells of intense emotion —**ecstatically** *adv*

ECT *abbr* electroconvulsive therapy

ectasia /ek táyzi ə/, **ectasis** /éktəssiss/ *n* a swelling or dilation of a part of the body (*technical*) [Late 19C. < modern Latin, < Greek *ektasis* < *ekteinein* 'stretch out'.]

ecto- *prefix* external, outside ◊ *ectotherm* [< Greek *ektos* < *ek* 'out']

ectocommensal /éktə kə méns'l/ *n* a harmless parasitic plant or animal that lives on the outer surface or skin of another organism

ectoderm /éktə durm/ *n* the outermost of three cell layers of an embryo, from which the epidermis, nervous tissue, and sense organs develop

ectogenesis /éktō jénnisiss/ *n* the development of an organism in an artificial environment, outside the body in which it would normally be found —**ectogenous** /ek tójjənəss/ *adj*

ectomere /éktə meer/ *n* a cell (**blastomere**) produced during the division of a fertilized egg that develops with others into the outer cell layer (**ectoderm**) of an embryo

ectomorph /éktə mawrf/ *n* somebody belonging to a physiological type that is tall with long lean limbs. ◊ **endomorph** *n*. **1**, **mesomorph** —**ectomorphic** /éktə máwrfik/ *adj*

-ectomy *suffix* surgical removal of a part of the body ◊ *iridectomy* [< modern Latin *-ectomia* 'cutting out' < Greek *ek-* 'out' + *-tomia* (see -TOMY)]

ectoparasite /éktə párrə sīt/ *n* a parasite that lives on the outside of its host, e.g. on the skin or in the hair —**ectoparasitic** /éktə parə síttik/ *adj* —**ectoparasitism** /-párrəsitizəm/ *n*

ectophyte /éktə fīt/ *n* a parasitic plant that lives on the outer surface of its host —**ectophytic** /éktə fíttik/ *adj*

ectopia /ek tópi ə/ *n* a change from the normal positioning of an organ or body part [Mid-19C. < modern Latin < Greek *ektopos* 'out of place' < *topos* 'place'.]

ectopic /ek tóppik/ *adj* describes an organ or body part occurring in a position or form that is not usual or normal

ectopic pregnancy *n* the development of a fertilized egg outside the womb, e.g. in a fallopian tube

ectoplasm /éktə plazəm/ *n* **1** the dense outer layer of the substance (**cytoplasm**) that surrounds the nucleus of a cell **2** the substance believed by spiritualists to issue from a medium who is communicating with spirits —**ectoplasmic** /éktə plázmik/ *adj*

ectotherm /éktə thurm/ *n* an animal that maintains its body temperature by absorbing heat from its environment. ◊ **poikilotherm** [Mid-20C. < ECTO- + Greek *thermē* 'heat'.] —**ectothermic** /éktə thúrmik/ *adj*

Ecuador

Ecuador /ékwə dawr/ republic in NW South America bordering the Pacific Ocean. Capital: Quito. Population: 12,105,124 (1997). Area: 272,045 sq. km/105,037 sq. mi. —**Ecuadorian** /ékwə dáwri ən/ *n*, *adj*

ecumenical /éekyōŏ ménnik'l/, **ecumenic** /-ménnik/ *adj* **1** relating to, involving, or promoting the unity of Christian Churches around the world **2** involving all people or groups [Late 16C. Via late Latin *oecumenicus* 'general, universal' < Greek *oikoumenikos* < *oikoumenē* (*gē*) 'inhabited (world)' < *oikos* 'house, habitation'.] —**ecumenically** *adv*

ecumenical council *n* a gathering of leaders and representatives from the Christian Churches of the world

ecumenicalism *n* CHR = **ecumenism**

ecumenical patriarch *n* the Archbishop of Constantinople, the most senior dignitary of the Eastern Church

ecumenicism *n* CHR = **ecumenism**

ecumenics /éekyōŏ ménniks/ *n* the study of the aims and development of unity between different Christian denominations (+ *singular verb*)

ecumenism /i kyoŏmə nizəm/, **ecumenicism** /éekyōŏ ménnisizəm/, **ecumenicalism** /éekyōŏ ménnik'lizəm/ *n* a movement in the Christian Church aiming at unity between different denominations on basic issues

eczema /éksəmə/ *n* an inflammation of the skin characterized by reddening and itching and the formation of scaly or crusty patches that may leak fluid [Mid-18C. Via modern Latin < Greek *ekzema* 'eruption' < *zein* 'to boil' < Indo-European.]

ed. *abbr* **1** edited **2** edition **3** editor **4** education

-ed[1] *suffix* **1** used to form the past participle of regular verbs ◊ *wasted* **2** used to form the past tense of regular verbs ◊ *nicked* ◊ *landed* [Old English *-ed*, *-od* < Germanic]

-ed[2] *suffix* having, characterized by, like ◊ *redheaded* ◊ *bigoted* [Old English *-ede*, *-ode* < Germanic]

edacious /i dáyshəss/ *adj* voracious or devoted to gluttony (*formal*) [Early 19C. < Latin *edac-* 'voracious, gluttonous' < *edere* 'eat'.] —**edacity** /i dássəti/ *n*

Edam[1] *n* a mild Dutch cheese with a slightly rubbery texture, typically formed into balls covered with red wax [Early 19C. After EDAM[2].]

Edam[2] /ée dam/ town in the W Netherlands. Population: 25,603 (1994).

edaphic /i dáffik/ *adj* describes the effect of soil characteristics, especially chemical or physical properties, on plants and animals [Late 19C. < Greek *edaphos* 'floor, ground, soil'.]

edaphic climax *n* a stable ecological community (**climax**) that results from the content or properties of the soil rather than the climate

Edberg /éd burg/, **Stefan** (*b.* 1966) Swedish tennis player

EDC *abbr* **1** electronic data capture **2** European Defence Community

Edda /éddə/ *n* **1** a 12th-century collection of Old Norse poems **2** a 13th-century collection compiled by Snorri Sturluson containing Norse myths, poems, and a treatise on poetry [Late 17C. Probably < Old Norse *ōðr* 'spirit, mind, passion, song, poetry'.] —**Eddic** *adj*

Eddington /éddingtən/, **Sir Arthur** (1882–1944) British astronomer

eddo /éddō/ (*plural* **-does**) *n* PLANTS = **taro** [Late 17C. Of W African origin.]

eddy /éddi/ *n* (*plural* **-dies**) **1** SMALL WHIRL a movement in a flowing stream of liquid or gas in which the current doubles back to form a small whirl ○ *a pleasing pattern of eddies in the river* **2** DIVERGENCE a relatively unimportant divergence from or movement contrary to the mainstream of something ○ *negotiated a few political eddies* ■ *vti* (**-dies, -dying, -died**) FLOW CONTRARY to flow or make something flow contrary to the main current ○ *He waded out, the stream eddying around his legs.* [15C. < ?]

Eddy /éddi/, **Mary Baker** (1821–1910) US religious leader. Born **Mary Baker**

eddy current *n* an electric current set up by an alternating magnetic field

Eddystone Rocks /édistən-/ dangerous rocks in the English Channel, near Plymouth, England

edelweiss /áyd'l vīss/ *n* a small plant with white woolly leaves. Flowers: small, yellow with white brachts. Native to: Alps, mountains of Asia. *Leontopodium alpinum.* [Mid-19C. < German, 'noble white'.]

edema *n* US = **oedema**

Eden[1] /eéd'n/ *n* **1** in the Bible, the garden where Adam and Eve first lived **2** any place seen as being perfect, highly pleasing, or happy ○ *The first explorers saw America as an Eden.* —**Edenic** /ee dénnik/ *adj*

Eden[2] /eéd'n/ coastal town in S New South Wales, Australia. Population: 3,280 (1991).

Eden, Anthony, 1st Earl of Avon (1897–1977) British statesman and prime minister (1955–57)

edentate /ee dén tayt/ *n* any placental mammal that has few or no teeth, e.g. a sloth or armadillo. Native to: tropical America. Order: Edentata. [Early 19C. < Latin *edentatus* < *dent-* 'tooth'.]

edentulous /ee déntyŏŏləss/, **edentulate** /-lət, -layt/ *adj* without any teeth [Early 18C. < Latin *edentulus* < *dent-* 'tooth'.]

Edgar /édgər/ (944–975) king of the English (959–975). Known as **The Peaceful**

Edgbaston /éj bastən/ district in Birmingham, England

edge /ej/ *n* **1** BORDER a line or area that is the outermost part or the part farthest away from the centre of something ○ *a tablecloth with embroidered edges* **2** PART ABOVE A DROP the area where land suddenly falls away steeply ○ *the cliff edge* **3** BRINK the point or moment just before a marked change or event ○ *on the edge of victory* **4** MEETING SURFACES the line where two surfaces of something solid meet ○ *A cube has 6 faces and 12 edges.* **5** SHARP SIDE the cutting side of a blade ○ *a razor's edge* **6** SHARPNESS sharpness of a blade ○ *a knife with a fine edge* **7** SHARP QUALITY a piercing, cutting, or wounding quality, e.g. of language or expression ○ *There was an unmistakable edge to her remarks.* **8** VIGOUR noticeable vigour and energy ○ *After the time-out there was a new edge to the team's play.* **9** ADVANTAGE an advantage over somebody, e.g. a competitor (*informal*) **10** RIDGE a ridge, crest, or cliff (*often in placenames*) ■ *v* (**edges, edging, edged**) **1** *vt* ADD A BORDER TO to add a border to something, especially a decorative one ○ *a handkerchief edged with lace* **2** *vt* TRIM to cut, shape, or trim the border of something ○ *a tool for edging the lawn* **3** *vt* SHARPEN to sharpen or give a sharp edge to a blade **4** *vi* MOVE GRADUALLY to move gradually sideways, or make something move in this direction by pushing it ○ *just room enough to edge through* **5** *vt* STRIKE WITH SIDE to strike a ball or other object with the side of something, e.g. a cricket bat or football boot ○ *The batsman edged the first ball for four.* **6** *vt* LEAN A SKI to lean a ski over so that its edge cuts the snow [Old English *ecg* 'corner, edge, sword' < Indo-European, 'be sharp or pointed'] —**edger** *n* ◇ **live on the edge** to be habitually in highly stressful and demanding situations, often involving physical risk and danger ◇ **on edge** in an irritated or nervous state ◇ **take the edge off something** **1** to reduce the intensity or strength of something ○ *The snack took the edge off my hunger.* **2** to do something that makes a tense situation less so

edge out *vt* **1** to move somebody or something gradually out of position ○ *trying to edge him out of the presidency* **2** to defeat a competitor by a narrow margin (*informal*) ○ *She was edged out of the championship.*

edge city *n* **1** a small city or urban development that exists next to a major conurbation **2** *US* a highly urbanized, yet officially unincorporated community adjacent to a major established city, with homes, varied businesses, entertainment districts, and large shopping areas (*informal*) ○ *'Edge City ... is the creation of a new world, being shaped by the free in a constantly reinvented land'.* (Joel Garreau, *Washington Post*; September 19, 1991)

Edgehill /éj híl/ ridge in central England, where the first battle of the English Civil War was fought in 1642

edge tool *n* an implement that has at least one cutting edge

edgeways /éj wayz/, **edgewise** /éj wīz/ *adv, adj* with the edge or side foremost ○ *fit in edgeways* ○ *with an edgeways motion*

Edgewood /éjwŏŏd/ town in NE Maryland. Population: 23,903 (1990).

Edgeworth /éj wurth/, **Maria** (1767–1849) British novelist

edging /éjjing/ *n* **1** BORDER something used as a border or trim, usually for decoration or protection **2** FORMING OF AN EDGE the formation of an edge ■ *adj* USED TO FORM EDGES used in forming an edge

edgy /éjji/ (**-ier, -iest**) *adj* **1** ON EDGE nervous and irritable **2** INTENSE having an intense or energetic quality or atmosphere ○ *an edgy district* **3** STYLISH unusually smart or stylish ○ *edgy clothes* —**edgily** *adv* —**edginess** *n*

edh /eth/ (*plural* **edhs**), **eth** (*plural* **eths**) *n* a character (ð) used in the runic alphabet and in modern phonetics to represent the 'th' sound in the English words 'this' and 'other' [Mid-19C. < Danish.]

edible /éddəb'l/ *adj* fit or suitable for eating by human beings ■ **edibles** *npl* things to eat [Early 17C. < Latin *edibilis* 'eatable' < *edere* 'eat'.] —**edibility** /éddə bílləti/ *n* —**edibleness** *n*

USAGE See ***eatable***.

edict /eédikt/ *n* **1** a formal proclamation, especially one issued by a government, ruler, or other authority **2** a formal or authoritative command [15C. < Latin *edictum* < past participle of *edicere* 'proclaim' < *dicere* 'say'.]

Edict of Nantes /-naánt/ *n* a law signed by Henry IV in 1598 and revoked by Louis XIV in 1685 that allowed civil and religious tolerance to French Protestants

edification /éddifi káysh'n/ *n* instruction or enlightenment, especially when it is morally or spiritually uplifting

edifice /éddifiss/ *n* **1** a building, especially a large or impressive one **2** a large or complex structure or organization ○ *the edifice of government* [14C. Via French < Latin *aedificium* < *aedificare* 'build' (see EDIFY).]

edify /éddifī/ (**-fies, -fying, -fied**) *vt* to improve the morals or knowledge of somebody [14C. Via French *édifier* < Latin *aedificare* 'build, construct, instruct' < *aedis* 'building, temple' + *facere* 'make'.] —**edifier** *n*

edifying /éddi fī ing/ *adj* providing morally useful knowledge or information

Edinburgh /éddinbərə/ capital of Scotland. Population: 447,600 (1995).

Edinburgh, Duke of ➧ **Prince Philip**

Edinburgh rock *n* a Scottish confectionery in the form of pastel-coloured sticks with a powdery texture, made of sugar, cream of tartar, and flavourings

Edirne /e deérnə/ city of NW Turkey. Population: 102,300 (1990).

Edison /éddiss'n/, **Thomas Alva** (1847–1931) US inventor

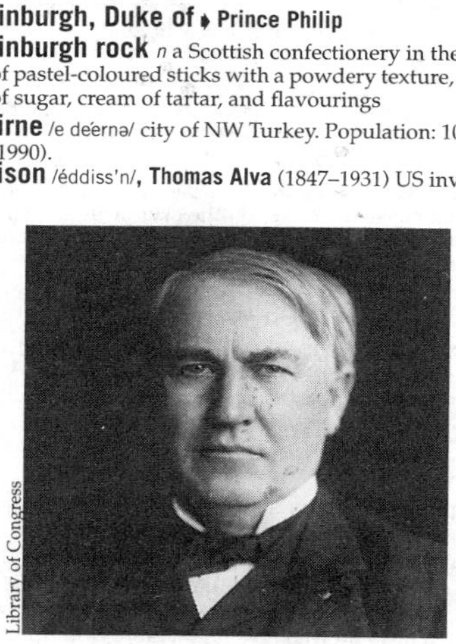

Thomas Alva Edison

edit /éddit/ *vt* **1** PREPARE FOR PUBLICATION to prepare a text for publication by correcting errors and ensuring clarity and accuracy **2** DECIDE THE CONTENT OF A PUBLICATION to be in overall charge of the publication of a newspaper or magazine **3** DECIDE THE CONTENT OF A PROGRAMME to be in overall charge of the content of a broadcast programme **4** CUT A FILM OR TAPE to cut and arrange a film or recording, deciding its final order and content ○ *The show was edited down from hours of live recording.* **5** CUT MATERIAL to remove material from something, such as a publication or broadcast item, e.g. because it is lengthy or offensive ■ *n* EDITING the preparation of a text for publication or release, or a stage in this process ○ *Look out for errors missed in the first edit.* [Late 18C. Back-formation < EDITOR.] —**edited** *adj*

edit out *vt* to delete an unwanted part of a text, film, or recording ○ *Her walk-on part was eventually edited out.*

edit. *abbr* **1** edited **2** edition **3** editor

edition /i dísh'n/ *n* **1** PRINTED VERSION one version of a publication issued serially, periodically, or in multiple formats ○ *the morning edition of the newspaper* **2** BROADCAST VERSION a version or instalment of a broadcast for a particular time or purpose ○ *last week's edition of the show* **3** PRINTED BATCH a batch of identical copies of a publication all printed at the same time **4** BATCH OF ITEMS a batch or number of items all produced at the same time **5** SIMILAR THING a version or copy of something [15C. < Latin *edition-* < *edit-*, past participle of *edere* 'give out' < *dare* 'give'.]

editio princeps /i díshi ō prín seps/ (*plural* **editiones principes** /i díshi ō neez prínssi peez/) *n* the first printed edition of a piece of writing (*literary*) [< modern Latin, 'first edition']

⚡**editor** /édditər/ *n* **1** PUBLISHING SUPERVISOR the overall supervisor of content for a book, newspaper, or magazine **2** CHIEF JOURNALIST the supervisor of content in a part of a newspaper or magazine **3** TEXT CORRECTOR a preparer of a text for publication **4** CONTROLLER OF PROGRAMME CONTENT a supervisor of the content in a broadcast programme **5** SOMEBODY WHO EDITS FILM a preparer of the final version of a film, who determines the length and order of shots and scenes **6** COMPUT = **text editor** [Mid-17C. < late Latin, 'producer, publisher' < Latin *edit-* (see EDITION).] —**editorship** *n*

editorial /éddi táwri əl/ *adj* relating to, involving, or concerned with the editing of something such as a text or broadcast ○ *made lots of editorial comments in the margins* ■ *n* an article in a newspaper or magazine that expresses the opinion of its editor or publisher —**editorialist** *n* —**editorially** *adv*

editorialize /éddi táwri ə līz/ (**-izes, -izing, -ized**), **editorialise** (**-ises, -ising, -ised**) *vi* **1** to express an opinion or view in an editorial **2** to introduce personal opinions or views, especially inappropriately ○ *He couldn't resist the opportunity, when reporting on a burglary, to editorialize on security systems.*

editor in chief (*plural* **editors in chief**) *n* the executive editor of a publication, publishing house, or set of publications

Edmonton /édməntən/ capital of Alberta, Canada, in the centre of the province. Population: 616,306 (1996).

Edmund /édmənd/ (841?–870) saint and king of East Anglia (855–70)

Edmund I (921–946) king of the English (939–46)

Edmund II (981?–1016) king of the English (1016). Known as **Edmund Ironside**

Edmund (of Abingdon), St (1175?–1240) English priest and scholar

Edo /éddō/ (*plural* **-o** *or* **-os**) *n* **1** a member of a people living in the Benin region of Nigeria **2** the language of the Edo people, belonging to the Kwa branch of the Niger-Congo family of languages. Native speakers: 1 million. [Late 19C. < Edo name for BENIN CITY.] —**Edo** *adj*

Edom /eédəm/ ancient country south of the Dead Sea

Edomite /eédə mīt/ *n* **1** a member of an ancient people who lived in the kingdom of Edom in pre-Christian times **2** an extinct language formerly spoken in the ancient kingdom of Edom in the Middle East —**Edomitic** /eédə míttik/ *adj*

⚡**EDP** *abbr* electronic data processing

⚡**EDT** *abbr* **1** Eastern Daylight Time **2** electronic depository transfer (*in e-commerce*)

EDTA *n* $C_{10}H_{16}N_2O_8$ a colourless compound that reacts with metals. Use: food preservative, anticoagulant, treatment of lead poisoning. Full form **ethylene diamine tetra-acetate**

⚡**edu** *abbr* US educational organization (*in Internet addresses*)

educ. *abbr* **1** education **2** educational

educate /éddyoŏ kayt/ (**-cates, -cating, -cated**) *v* **1** *vti* **TEACH** to give knowledge to or develop the abilities of somebody by teaching ○ *educated at a state school* ○ *highly educated* **2** *vt* **ARRANGE SCHOOLING FOR** to arrange or provide schooling for somebody ○ *They educated their daughters at home.* **3** *vt* **DEVELOP** to develop or improve a faculty or sense **4** *vt* **TRAIN** to train or instruct somebody in a particular field [15C. < Latin *educat-*, past participle of *educare* 'bring up, rear', related to *educere* 'lead out' < *ducere* 'lead'.] —**educability** /éddyoŏkə bíllәti/ *n* —**educable** *adj* —**educative** *adj* —**educatory** /éddyoŏkə tawri, éddyoŏ káytəri/ *adj*

SYNONYMS See ***teach***.

educated /éddyoŏ kaytid/ *adj* **1** **WELL-TAUGHT** having had a good education ○ *This is the writing of an educated person.* **2** **CULTURED** showing good taste, expert knowledge, or cultivation ○ *cast an educated eye over the antiques* **3** **KNOWLEDGEABLE** having the benefit of experience or knowledge

educated guess *n* a guess that is based on a degree of experience, knowledge, or information

education /éddyoŏ káysh'n/ *n* **1** **EDUCATING** the imparting and acquiring of knowledge through teaching and learning, especially at a school or similar institution ○ *'After all, what is education but a process by which a person begins to learn how to learn?'* (Peter Ustinov, *Dear Me*; 1977) **2** **KNOWLEDGE** the knowledge or abilities gained through being educated **3** **INSTRUCTION** training and instruction in a particular subject, e.g. health matters **4** **STUDY OF TEACHING** the study of the theories and practices of teaching ○ *a degree in education* **5** **SYSTEM FOR EDUCATING PEOPLE** the system of educating people in a community or society ○ *jobs in education* **6** **LEARNING EXPERIENCE** an informative experience ○ *Spending a weekend in their house was a real education.*

education action zone *n* in England, a cluster of about 20 primary and secondary schools that work together to meet educational targets for improvement

educational /éddyoŏ káysh'nəl/ *adj* **1** giving knowledge, instruction, or information **2** relating to, involving, or concerned with education —**educationally** *adv*

educationalist /éddyoŏ káysh'nəlist/, **educationist** /-káysh'nist/ *n* an expert in the theories or administration of education

educational psychology *n* a branch of applied psychology that studies children in an educational setting and is concerned with the assessment of ability and aptitude and the evaluation of teaching and learning methods —**educational psychologist** *n*

Educational Welfare Officer *n* somebody employed by a local education authority to investigate the home background of children with difficulties at school, identify any problems there, and help to find solutions

educationist /éddyə káyshənist/ *n* **1** = **educationalist** **2** a theorist on educational topics (*disapproving*)

educator /éddyoŏ kaytər/ *n* **1** a professional teacher **2** an expert in the theories or administration of education

educe /i dyoŏss/ (**educes, educing, educed**) *vt* (*formal*) **1** to elicit or derive something, e.g. a conclusion **2** to make something latent develop or appear [15C. < Latin *educere* 'lead out' < *ducere* 'lead'.]

educt /ée dukt/ *n* a substance extracted from another substance without chemical alteration [Late 17C. < Latin *eductum* < past participle of *educere* (see EDUCE).]

eduction /i dúksh'n/ *n* **1** the derivation or development of something, or something derived or developed (*formal*) **2** the exhaust of an engine, especially an internal-combustion or steam engine (*technical*) [Mid-17C. < Latin *eduction-* < *educere* (see EDUCE).]

edulcorate /i dúlkə rayt/ (**-rates, -rating, -rated**) *vt* to remove soluble impurities from something by washing (*technical*) [Mid-17C. < medieval Latin *edulcorat-*, past participle of *edulcorare* 'sweeten' < Latin *dulcis* 'sweet'.]

⚡**edutainment** /éddyoŏ táynmənt/ *n* television programmes, computer software, or other media content intended both to entertain and educate users [Late 20C. Blend of EDUCATION + ENTERTAINMENT.]

Edward I /éddwərd/ (1239–1307) king of England (1272–1307). Known as **Edward Longshanks**

Edward II (1284–1327) king of England (1307–27). Known as **Edward of Caernarvon**

Edward III (1312–77) king of England (1327–77)

Edward IV (1442–83) king of England (1461–83)

Edward V (1470–83?) king of England (1483)

Edward VI (1537–53) king of England (1547–53)

Edward VII (1841–1910) king of the United Kingdom (1901–10)

Edward VIII (1894–1972) king of the United Kingdom (January–December 1936)

Edward (the Black Prince) (1330–76) prince of Wales and father of Richard II

Edward (the Confessor) (1002?–66) saint and king of the English (1042–66)

Edward (the Martyr) (963?–978) saint and king of the English (975–978)

Edward, Lake lake in the Great African Rift Valley straddling the border between the Democratic Republic of Congo and Uganda. Area: 2,150 sq. km/830 sq. mi.

Edwardian /ed wáwrdi ən/ *adj* relating to, belonging to, or typical of British society during the reign of Edward VII in the first decade of the 20th century ■ *n* a person who was alive or active during Edward VII's reign or who specializes in this historical period

Edwin /éddwin/ (585?–633) saint and king of Northumbria (617–633)

ee[1] /ee/ (*plural* **een** /een/) *n Scotland* an eye [Variant of EYE]

⚡**ee**[2] *abbr* Estonia (*in Internet addresses*)

EE *abbr* **1** electrical engineer **2** electrical engineering **3** Early English

-ee[1] *suffix* **1** one who receives or benefits from an action ○ *consignee* **2** one who receives a thing ○ *biographee* **3** one who performs an action ○ *attendee* [Via Anglo-Norman < Latin *-atus*]

-ee[2] *suffix* **1** one that resembles ○ *coatee* **2** a kind of, especially a small one ○ *vestee* **3** one connected with ○ *bargee* [Variant of -Y]

EEC *abbr* European Economic Community

⚡**EECA** *abbr* end entity certificate authority (*in e-commerce*)

EEG *abbr* **1** echoencephalograph **2** electroencephalogram **3** electroencephalograph

eejit /ée jit/ *n Scotland, Ireland* an offensive term that deliberately insults somebody's intelligence or foresight (*informal insult*) [Late 19C. Representing a pronunciation of IDIOT.]

eel /eel/ (*plural* **eels** *or* **eel**) *n* **1** **LONG THIN FISH** a fish with a long thin body resembling that of a snake, smooth skin without scales, and reduced fins. Native to: shallow marine waters. Order: Apodes. **2** **FISH RESEMBLING AN EEL** any fish similar to a true eel in appearance, e.g. an electric eel **3** **DEVIOUS PERSON** an untrustworthy or evasive person [Old English *ǣl* < Germanic]

eelgrass /éel graass/ *n* **1** a perennial plant with long narrow dark-green leaves that grows submerged in shallow seawater. Genus: *Zostera*. **2** PLANTS = **tape grass**

eelpout /éel powt/ (*plural* **-pouts** *or* **-pout**) *n* **1** a marine fish with a long thin body like an eel. Family: Zoarcidae. **2** = **burbot**

eelworm /éel wurm/ (*plural* **-worms** *or* **-worm**) *n* ZOOL = **nematode**

een *Scotland* plural of **ee**

e'en /een/ *n* evening (*literary*) ■ *adv* even (*literary*)

e'er /air/ *adv* ever (*literary*) [Late 16C. Contraction.]

-eer *suffix* a person engaged in or concerned with ○ *auctioneer* ○ *charioteer* [Via Old French *-ier* < Latin *-arius*]

eerie /éeri/ (**-rier, -riest**) *adj* unnerving or unusual in a way that suggests a connection with the supernatural ○ *an eerie old house* [13C. Probably < Old English *earg* 'cowardly'.] —**eerily** *adv* —**eeriness** *n*

~~eery~~ incorrect spelling of **eerie**

EFA *abbr* essential fatty acid

eff /ef/ *vti* an offensive term meaning to express strong feelings by similarity in sound to other offensive terms (*slang*) [Mid-20C. Spelling of first letter of FUCK.] ◇ **eff and blind** to swear or use offensive language (*slang*)

efface /i fáyss/ (**-faces, -facing, -faced**) *v* **1** *vt* to remove or obliterate something by or as if by wearing away or rubbing out **2** *vr* to act in an inconspicuous manner, especially because of shyness or modesty [15C. < French *effacer* 'wipe out, destroy' < *face* 'face, appearance'.] —**effaceable** *adj* —**effacement** *n* —**effacer** *n*

effect /i fékt/ *n* **1** **RESULT** a change or changed state occurring as a direct result of action by somebody or something else ○ *showing the effects of prolonged malnutrition* **2** **POWER TO INFLUENCE** success in bringing about a change in somebody or something, or the ability to achieve this ○ *I've told her again and again, but it has no effect on her.* **3** **BEING IN FORCE OR OPERATION** the state of being in force, in operation, or the case, often from a particular point in time ○ *The new law doesn't come into effect until next month.* ○ *Much-needed changes were now being put into effect.* ○ *You have to wait for the medicine to take effect.* **4** **IMPRESSION** an impression produced in the mind of somebody who sees, hears, or reads something, especially one that is deliberately intended or engineered **5** **CAUSE OR PRODUCTION OF AN IMPRESSION** something that produces an impression, or the actual process of causing a special feeling or impression ○ *a grand little speech made merely for effect* **6** **SPECIAL SOUND, LIGHTING** something done to produce a desired response or to add to the realism or theatricality of a film, play, or broadcast (*often plural*) **7** **MEANING** the intent or essential meaning conveyed, often in other words, by a statement, or words to that effect **8** **SCIENTIFIC PHENOMENON** a scientifically observed and described phenomenon ■ **effects** *npl* **BELONGINGS** somebody's personal belongings, or the things that somebody is carrying about him or her (*formal*) ○ *Her personal effects consisted of not much more than the clothes on her back.* ■ *vt* **DO OR MAKE** to succeed in making or doing something (*formal*) ○ *They effected their escape through a rear window.* [14C. Directly or via Old French < Latin *effectus* < *efficere* 'accomplish' < *facere* 'make, do'.] —**effecter** *n* —**effectible** *adj* ◇ **in effect** used to indicate that what is being said represents the truth of the matter, even though the words used may not be those that other people would choose ○ *In effect, this means that the program is shut down.*

USAGE See ***affect***.

effective /i féktiv/ *adj* **1** **PRODUCING A RESULT** causing a result, especially the desired or intended result ○ *an effective remedy for headaches* **2** **HAVING A STRIKING RESULT** successful, especially in producing a strong or favourable impression on people ○ *The painting had the characteristics of a winner, including effective colour use.* **3** **ACTUAL** actual or in practice, even if not officially or theoretically so ○ *He was effective ruler during the monarch's last illness.* **4** **OFFICIALLY IN FORCE** officially in force, operative, or applicable ○ *a regulation effective as from next month* **5** **READY FOR ACTION** fully equipped and ready for action ■ *n* **MILITARY PERSONNEL OR EQUIPMENT** a soldier, military unit, or piece of military equipment that is ready for action —**effectiveness** *n* —**effectivity** /éffek tívvəti/ *n*

SYNONYMS ***effective, efficient, effectual, efficacious***
CORE MEANING: producing a result
effective causing the desired or intended result; **efficient** capable of achieving the desired result with the minimum use of resources, time, and effort; **effectual** (*formal*) potentially successful in producing a desired or intended result; **efficacious** (*formal*) having the power to achieve the desired result, especially an improvement in somebody's physical condition.

effectively /i féktivli/ *adv* **1** in a way that produces a desired result **2** in fact or in practical terms, though not usually directly or technically ○ *She was effectively barred from seeking another position with the firm.*

effector /i féktər/ *n* **1** a body part, e.g. a muscle or organ, that is activated by a stimulus, particularly a nerve impulse **2** a substance, procedure, or agent that produces an effect, e.g. a nerve ending activating a muscle or a molecule affecting enzyme activity

effectual /i fékchoo əl/ *adj* (*formal*) **1** potentially successful in producing a desired or intended result **2** valid, or legally in force [14C. < medieval Latin *effectualis* < Latin *effectus* (see EFFECT).] —**effectuality** /i fékchoo állәti/ *n* —**effectually** *adv* —**effectualness** *n*

SYNONYMS See ***effective***.

effectuate /i fékchoo ayt/ (**-ates, -ating, -ated**) *vt* to do, cause, or accomplish something (*formal*) [Late 16C. <

medieval Latin *effectuat-*, past participle of *effectuare* < Latin *effectus* (see EFFECT).] —**effectuation** /i fékchoo áysh'n/ *n*

effeminate /i fémminət/ *adj* (*disapproving*) **1** similar to or imitating a woman or girl, or the behaviour, appearance, or speech traditionally associated with women and girls (*refers to men*) **2** weak through over-refinement or an absence of vigorous qualities [14C. < Latin *effeminatus*, past participle of *effeminare* 'make feminine' < *femina* 'woman'.] —**effeminacy** *n* —**effeminate** *n* —**effeminately** *adv* —**effeminateness** *n*

effendi /e féndi/ (*plural* **-dis**) *n* **1** in Middle Eastern countries, an important or well-educated man **2** a title of respect that is the Turkish equivalent of such terms as 'Mr' and 'Sir' [Early 17C. Via Turkish *efendi* < modern Greek *aphentēs* < Greek *authentēs* 'lord, master'.]

efferent /éffərənt/ *adj* conducting outwards or directing away from an organ, especially the brain or spinal cord. ◊ **afferent** [Mid-19C. < Latin *efferent-*, present participle of *effere* 'bring out' < *ferre* 'bring, carry'.] —**efferent** *n*

efferent neuron *n* ANAT = **motor neuron**

effervesce /éffər véss/ (**-vesces, -vescing, -vesced**) *vi* **1 PRODUCE TINY GAS BUBBLES** to give off gas in small bubbles, often producing foam and a hissing sound (*refers to a liquid*) **2 ESCAPE AS TINY BUBBLES** to be given off by a liquid in the form of small bubbles (*refers to gas*) **3 BE LIVELY** to behave in a lively, high-spirited, or highly excited way [Early 18C. < Latin *effervescere* < *fervescere* 'come to the boil' < *fervere* 'be hot, boil'.] —**effervescence** *n* —**effervescent** *adj* —**effervescently** *adv*

effete /i feet/ *adj* **1** characterized by decadence, over-refinement, or overindulgence **2** no longer able to reproduce [Early 17C. < Latin *effetus* 'worn out by bearing young' < *fetus* 'breeding'.] —**effetely** *adv* —**effeteness** *n*

efficacious /éffi káyshəss/ *adj* having the power to produce the desired result, especially a cure or an improvement in somebody's physical condition (*formal*) [Early 16C. < Latin *efficac-* < *efficere* (see EFFECT).] —**efficaciously** *adv* —**efficaciousness** *n*

SYNONYMS See ***effective***.

efficacy /éffikəssi/, **efficacity** /éffi kássəti/ *n* ability to produce the necessary or desired results [Early 16C. < Latin *efficacia* < *efficac-* (see EFFICACIOUS).]

efficiency /i físh'nssi/ (*plural* **-cies**) *n* **1** the ability to do something well or achieve a desired result without wasted energy or effort, or the degree to which this ability is used **2** the ratio of the amount of energy used by a machine to the amount of work done by it **3** *US* = **efficiency apartment**

efficiency apartment *n US* a small, usually furnished, flat consisting of one room that includes kitchen facilities, and a bathroom

efficient /i físh'nt/ *adj* **1 WELL-ORGANIZED** performing tasks in an organized and capable way **2 ABLE TO FUNCTION WITHOUT WASTE** able to function well or achieve a desired result without waste ○ *an efficient use of fuel* **3 ACTING DIRECTLY TO PRODUCE AN EFFECT** acting directly to bring something into being or produce changes in it ○ *efficient cause* [14C. < Latin *efficient-*, present participle of *efficere* (see EFFECT).] —**efficiently** *adv*

SYNONYMS See ***effective***.

effigy /éffiji/ (*plural* **-gies**) *n* **1** a dummy, often roughly made and intentionally amusing or insulting, representing somebody or something disliked or despised **2** a carved representation of somebody, used, e.g., as an architectural decoration or a monument [Mid-16C. < Latin *effigies* < *effingere* 'portray, form' < *fingere* 'fashion, shape'.]

effing /éffing/ *adj* an offensive term expressing strong feelings by similarity in sound to other offensive terms (*slang*)

effloresce /éfflə réss/ (**-resces, -rescing, -resced**) *vi* **1 LOSE WATER FROM CRYSTAL** to lose water (**water of crystallization**) from a crystal **2 BLOOM** to bloom or develop, like a flower coming into blossom (*literary*) **3 PRODUCE FINE POWDER** to become covered with a layer of fine powder **4 BECOME ENCRUSTED WITH POWDERY DEPOSIT** to become encrusted with a powdery deposit or crystals as a result of a process of chemical change or the evaporation of a solution [Late 18C. < Latin *efflorescere* < *florescere* 'come into flower' < *flos* 'flower'.]

efflorescence /éfflə réss'nss/ *n* **1 LOSS OF WATER FROM CRYSTAL** the loss of water (**water of crystallization**) from a crystal **2 UNFOLDING AND FLOURISHING** a process or time of development and unfolding, or the culmination of this (*literary*) **3 POWDERY SUBSTANCE ON ROCK SURFACE** a powdery substance that forms on the surface of some rocks —**efflorescent** *adj*

effluence /éffloo ənss/ *n* **1** the act or process of flowing out **2** something, often an immaterial substance or intangible influence, that flows out from a source (*literary*)

effluent /éffloo ənt/ *n* **1** liquid waste discharged from a sewage system, factory, nuclear power station, or other industrial plant **2** a stream or river that flows out of a larger body of water such as a lake or a larger stream [15C. < Latin *effluent-*, present participle of *effluere* 'flow out' < *fluere* 'flow'.]

effluvium /i flóovi əm, e-/ (*plural* **-a** /-ə/) *n* an unpleasant smell or harmful fumes given off by something, usually waste or decaying matter (*often plural*) [Mid-17C. < Latin, < *effluere* (see EFFLUENT).] —**effluvial** *adj*

efflux /éff luks/ *n* **1 INSTANCE OR ACT OF FLOWING OUT** the act or process of flowing out **2 SOMETHING THAT FLOWS OUT** something that flows out of something else (*formal*) **3 PASSING AWAY OF** a passing away of something, e.g. time (*formal*) [Mid-16C. < medieval Latin *effluxus* < Latin *efflux-*, past participle of *effluere* (see EFFLUENT).] —**effluxion** /i flúksh'n, e-/ *n*

effort /éffərt/ *n* **1 ENERGY** mental or physical energy that is exerted in order to achieve a purpose ○ *I wish they'd put a bit more effort into it.* **2 USE OF ENERGY** the use of physical or mental energy, often in considerable quantities, in order to achieve a particular goal or overcome a particular difficulty ○ *With an effort, he managed to get himself out of the bed.* **3 ATTEMPT** an attempt to do something, especially one that involves a considerable amount of exertion, work, or determination ○ *He can at last make an effort to improve things.* **4 SOMETHING DONE** something that somebody has made or done, especially for the first time ○ *It's not bad for a first effort.* **5 APPLIED FORCE** the force (**input force**) applied to a simple machine that produces an effect (**output force**) on the load [15C. < French, < Old French *esforcier* 'exert power' < Latin *fortis* 'strong'.] —**effortful** *adj* —**effortfully** *adv*

effortless /éffərtləss/ *adj* involving or appearing to involve little or no effort —**effortlessly** *adv* —**effortlessness** *n*

effrontery /i frúntəri/ (*plural* **-ies**) *n* behaviour or an attitude that is so bold or arrogant as to be insulting [Late 17C. < French *effronterie* < late Latin *effrons* 'barefaced' < *frons* 'forehead'.]

effulgence /i fúljənss, -fóol-/ *n* brightness or a brilliant light radiating from something (*literary*) [Mid-17C. < late Latin *effulgentia* < Latin *effulgere* 'shine brightly' < *fulgere* 'shine'.] —**effulgent** *adj*

effuse *v* /i fyóoz/ (**-fuses, -fusing, -fused**) **1** *vti* **POUR OUT** to flow out, or produce a flow of something such as a liquid, gas, or light (*formal*) **2** *vti* **POUR OUT WORDS AND IDEAS** to pour out words and ideas, or speak profusely about something, generally in an excited way (*formal*) **3** *vi* **RADIATE** to spread out or radiate from something ■ *adj* /i fyóoss/ **IRREGULARLY SPREAD** tending to spread loosely or irregularly ○ *effuse lichens* [15C. < Latin *effus-*, past participle of *effundere* 'pour out' < *fundere* 'pour'.]

effusion /i fyóozh'n/ *n* **1 UNRESTRAINED OUTPOURING OF FEELINGS** an extravagant and sometimes excessive expression of feelings in speech or writing **2 ACT OF POURING OUT** the pouring out of something such as a liquid or light **3 SOMETHING POURED OUT** something, e.g. a liquid, that is poured out **4 MOVEMENT OF BODY FLUIDS** the oozing of fluids from blood or lymph vessels into body cavities or intercellular tissue spaces as a result of inflammation, or the presence of excess blood or tissue fluid **5 FLOW OF GAS THROUGH A SMALL APERTURE** the flow of a gas through a small aperture under pressure, particularly when the aperture is so small that the distance between molecules is significant

effusive /i fyóossiv/ *adj* giving or involving an extravagant and sometimes excessive expression of feelings in writing or speech ○ *effusive thanks* —**effusively** *adv* —**effusiveness** *n*

~~eficient~~ incorrect spelling of **efficient**

Efik /éffik/ (*plural* **-ik** *or* **-iks**) *n* **1** a member of an Ibibio people who live in SE Nigeria **2** a Niger-Congo language spoken in Nigeria. Native speakers: 4 million. [Mid-19C. < Efik.] —**Efik** *adj*

EFL *abbr* English as a Foreign Language

⚡**EFRA** *abbr* electronic forms routing and approval (*in e-commerce*)

eft /eft/ *n* an immature newt in the terrestrial phase, usually reddish-orange in colour. *Notophthalmus viridescens*. [Old English *efeta* < ?]

⚡**EFT** *abbr* electronic funds transfer

EFTA /éftə/ *abbr* European Free Trade Association

⚡**EFTPOS** /éft poss/ *abbr* electronic funds transfer at point of sale

⚡**EFTS** /efts/ *abbr* electronic funds transfer system

⚡**eg** *abbr* Egypt (*in Internet addresses*)

e.g., eg, eg. *abbr* for or as an example [Abbreviation of Latin *exempli gratia*]

USAGE e.g. or **i.e.**? Do not confuse these two abbreviations, which mean different things and have different origins. The abbreviation ***i.e.*** meaning 'that is, that is to say', comes from the Latin expression *id est* ('that is'). Use it when you want to specify or define one thing only: *The tribunal, i.e.* [not *e.g.*] *the industrial tribunal, is set for noon on Friday.* The abbreviation ***e.g.,*** meaning 'for or as an example', comes from another Latin expression, *exempli gratia* ('for example'). Use it when you want to list a few items out of many: *I have the laboratory equipment, e.g.* [not *i.e.*] *beakers, thermometers, and test tubes, that we need.* Do not end a list that starts with ***e.g.*** with ***etc.*** Two full stops punctuate e.g. and i.e. in US English, whereas they may be unpunctuated in British English.

⚡**EGA** *abbr* enhanced graphics adapter

egad /i gád, ee-/ *interj* used as an exclamation, generally to express surprise (*archaic*) [Late 17C. < Alteration of AH + *gad*, euphemism for GOD.]

egalitarian /i gálli táiri ən/ *adj* maintaining, relating to, or based on a belief that all people are, in principle, equal and should enjoy equal social, political, and economic rights and opportunities [Late 19C. < French *égalitaire* < *égal* 'equal' < Latin *aequalis* (see EQUAL).] —**egalitarian** *n* —**egalitarianism** /i gálli táiri ənizəm/ *n*

Egeria /i jéeri ə/ *n* a woman who acts as a trusted adviser or loyal companion (*literary*) [Early 17C. < Roman goddess and adviser to the early Roman king Numa Pompilius.]

egesta /i jéstə/ *npl* waste materials excreted from a cell or organism [Early 18C. < Latin, neuter plural of *egestus*, past participle of *egerere* 'carry out' < *gerere* 'carry'.]

egg /eg/ *n* **1 ANIMAL REPRODUCTIVE STRUCTURE** a large sex cell produced by birds, fish, insects, reptiles, or amphibians, enclosed in a protective covering that allows the fertilized embryo to continue developing outside the mother's body until it hatches **2 HARD-SHELLED OBJECT LAID BY HEN** the hard-shelled, oval, cream- or light-brown egg produced by a hen or similar fowl, used as food **3 SOMETHING SHAPED LIKE A HEN'S EGG** something that resembles a hen's egg in shape, e.g. a carved or moulded ornament or chocolate made in an egg shape **4 FEMALE REPRODUCTIVE CELL** a female reproductive cell **5 PERSON** a person (*dated informal*) ○ *All in all, he's not a bad egg.* [14C. < Old Norse.] —**eggy** *adj* ◇ **have egg on your face** to be left in an embarrassing or humiliating situation, especially because of having made an obvious mistake ◇ **put all your eggs in one basket** to rely entirely on one thing or person, or on the outcome of one plan or course of action

egg-and-dart *n* an ornamental pattern, commonly used in mouldings on buildings or furniture, in which egg-shaped figures alternate with slightly tapered bars, arrows, or anchors

eggar *n* ZOOL = **egger**

eggbeater /ég beetər/ *n* **1** a kitchen utensil used for beating or blending such ingredients as raw eggs or cream, especially one with two sets of spaced vertical blades rotated by turning a handle **2** *US* a rotary-wing aircraft (*slang*)

eggcup /ég kup/ *n* a small bowl-shaped container, often with a short neck and wide base below the bowl, used for holding a boiled egg while it is being eaten

egg custard *n* FOOD = **custard** *n.* **2**

egger /éggər/, **eggar** *n* a moth with a brown body and wings whose larvae spin egg-shaped cocoons in the branches of trees. Family: Lasiocampidae. [Early 18C. Probably because of its egg-shaped cocoon.]

egg flip *n* a drink made by mixing beaten egg, sugar, and an alcoholic beverage, usually sherry, brandy, or port

egg foo yung *n US* FOOD = **foo yung**

egghead /ég hed/ *n* an intellectual or bookish person (*informal*) [Early 20C. < the idea that a high forehead indicates brains.] —**eggheaded** /ég héddid/ *adj*

eggnog /égg nóg, ég nog/ *n* a drink made of milk or cream, eggs, sugar, spice, and sometimes an alcoholic beverage such as brandy or rum, traditionally served in the winter, especially at Christmas [Early 19C. < *nog*, a strong beer < ?]

egg on *vt* to encourage somebody to do something, especially something wrong, foolish, or dangerous ○ *She never would have done it herself, but the girls were egging her on.* [12C. < Old Norse *eggja* 'urge' < Germanic.]

eggplant /ég plaant/ *n* **1** *US, Can, ANZ* EDIBLE FRUIT a large oval fleshy usually purple fruit, eaten cooked as a vegetable. ◊ **aubergine** *n.* 1 **2** *US, Can, ANZ* PLANT WITH LARGE EDIBLE FRUIT a plant of the nightshade family that produces eggplants. Native to: S and E Asia. *Solanum melongena.* ◊ **aubergine** *n.* 2 **3** *ANZ, Can, US* BLACKISH PURPLE a very dark purple colour. ◊ **aubergine** *n.* 3

egg roll *n US* a Chinese-American snack similar to a spring roll

egg sac *n* the pouch or cocoon that a female spider spins to protect its eggs

eggs Benedict *n* ham and a poached egg in hollandaise sauce on a slice of toast or a split toasted muffin (+ *singular or plural verb*) [Late 19C. < ?]

eggshell /ég shel/ *n* **1** HARD COVER OF AN EGG the hard brittle protective outer cover of the egg of a bird **2** PALE WHITISH COLOUR a pale yellowish-white colour ■ *adj* **1** OF YELLOWISH-WHITE of the colour eggshell **2** SLIGHTLY GLOSSY having a slight sheen, giving a finish between that of gloss and matt paint **3** FRAGILE as fragile, thin, or delicate as an eggshell ◇ **walk on eggshells** to proceed with extreme wariness, caution, and tact

eggshell blue *adj* of a delicate pale blue colour —**eggshell blue** *n*

egg slice *n* a flat-bladed kitchen utensil for lifting fried eggs or omelettes out of a frying pan

egg timer *n* a small hourglass or clockwork timing device used to time the boiling of an egg, usually capable of timing intervals of three to five minutes

egg tooth *n* a small projection on the beak of a baby bird or the upper jaw of a baby reptile, used to cut through the eggshell when hatching and later shed

egg white *n* the clear viscous liquid found in an egg that turns solid and white when cooked

eglantine /égglən tīn/ (*plural* **-tines** *or* **-tine**) *n* PLANTS = **sweetbriar** [14C. Via French *églantine* < Latin *aculentus* 'spiny' < *acus* 'needle'.]

EGM *abbr* extraordinary general meeting

Egmont, Mount /ég mont/ dormant volcano in the SW of the North Island, New Zealand. Height: 2,518 m/8,261 ft.

ego /éegō, éggō/ (*plural* **egos**) *n* **1** APPROPRIATE SELF-ESTEEM somebody's idea of his or her own importance or worth, usually of an appropriate level **2** INFLATED OPINION OF YOURSELF an exaggerated sense of your own importance and a feeling of superiority to other people **3** PART OF THE MIND CONTAINING CONSCIOUSNESS in Freudian psychology, one of three main divisions of the mind, containing consciousness and memory and involved with control, planning, and conforming to reality ○ *'The poor ego has a still harder time of it; it has to serve three harsh masters, and has to do its best to reconcile the claims and demands of all three'.* (Sigmund Freud, *The Anatomy of the Mental Personality, Lecture 31*) ◊ **id, superego 4** THE SELF the individual self, as distinct from the outside world and other selves [Early 19C. < Latin, 'I'.]

egocentric /éegō séntrik, éggō-/ *adj* **1** SELFISH interested only in the needs and wants of the self and not caring about other people **2** LIMITED OR CONFINED IN OUTLOOK limited in outlook or confined to things mainly relating to yourself **3** MORE CONCERNED WITH THE INDIVIDUAL THAN SOCIETY concerned with the individual rather than, or at the expense of, society as a whole **4** CENTRED ON THE SELF centred on the individual self, and considering it to be the hub of all experience —**egocentric** *n* —**egocentrically** *adv* —**egocentricity** /éegō sen trísəti, éggō-/ *n* —**egocentrism** *n*

ego ideal *n* an ideal image of what you could or should be, built up from observation of parents or other admired people

egoism /éegō izəm, éggō-/ *n* **1** = **egotism** *n.* 1 **2** making personal welfare and interests your primary or only concern, sometimes at the expense of others **3** the belief that the correct basis for a moral code is every person's concern for his or her own best interests, or the doctrine supporting this belief

USAGE **egoism** or **egotism**? These two words, which are equally common, are often used interchangeably, though a distinction can be made between them. ***Egoism*** refers, in terms of philosophy, to theories in which self-interest is regarded as the principal motivating factor. And so an *egoist* believes an individual should seek as an end only his or her own welfare: *His conduct was characterized by ruthless egoism.* ***Egotism*** implies a vain and selfish absorption with the self as a matter of behaviour rather than an ethical principle, and an *egotist* is somebody who behaves in a selfish or self-centred way: *Her egotism makes her oblivious to other people's concerns.*

egoist /éegō ist, éggō-/ *n* **1** a believer that the correct basis for morality is each person's concern for his or her best interests **2** = **egotist** —**egoistic** /éegō ístik, éggō-/ *adj* —**egoistical** *adj* —**egoistically** *adv*

egomania /éegō máyni ə, éggō-/ *n* a dangerously obsessive preoccupation with the self —**egomaniac** *n* —**egomaniacal** /-mə nī́ ək'l/ *adj* —**egomaniacally** /éegō mə nī́ əkli, éggō mə nī́ əkli/ *adv*

ego surfing *n* the practice of searching for your own name on the Internet

egotism /éegōtizəm, éggō-/ *n* **1** INFLATED SENSE OF SELF-IMPORTANCE the possession of an exaggerated sense of self-importance and superiority to other people **2** PREOCCUPATION WITH SELF the tendency to speak or write too much about the self **3** SELFISHNESS selfishness or self-centredness [Early 18C. < EGO + *t* + -ISM.]

USAGE See ***egoism***.

egotist /éegōtist, éggō-/ *n* **1** somebody with an exaggerated sense of his or her self-importance, especially somebody who tends to speak or write about himself or herself all the time **2** a selfish and self-centred person —**egotistic** /éegō tístik, éggō-/ *adj* —**egotistical** *adj*

ego trip *n* a course of action or an experience, the main effect of which is to boost somebody's own sense of self-importance (*slang*) —**ego-trip** *vi* —**ego-tripper** *n*

egregious /i gréejəss, -ji əss/ *adj* bad, blatant, or ridiculous to an extraordinary degree (*formal*) [Mid-16C. < Latin *egregius* 'illustrious' < *greg-* 'flock'.] —**egregiously** *adv* —**egregiousness** *n*

egress /ée gress/ *n* **1** COMING OR GOING OUT the act of coming or going out from or of leaving a place (*formal*) **2** RIGHT TO LEAVE the right to leave or go out from a place (*formal*) **3** EXIT an exit from a place (*formal*) **4** ASTRON = **emersion** *n.* 2 ■ *vi* COME OUT to come out from or leave a place (*formal*) [Mid-16C. < Latin *egressus* < *egredi* 'go out' < *gradi* 'proceed, step'.]

egression /i grésh'n/ *n* = **egress** *n.* 1

egret /éegrət/ *n* a heron that produces long drooping ornamental feathers on the lower part of the back at the start of the breeding season. Family: Ardeidae. [14C. Via Anglo-Norman *egrette* < Provençal *aigreta* < *aigron* 'heron' < Germanic.]

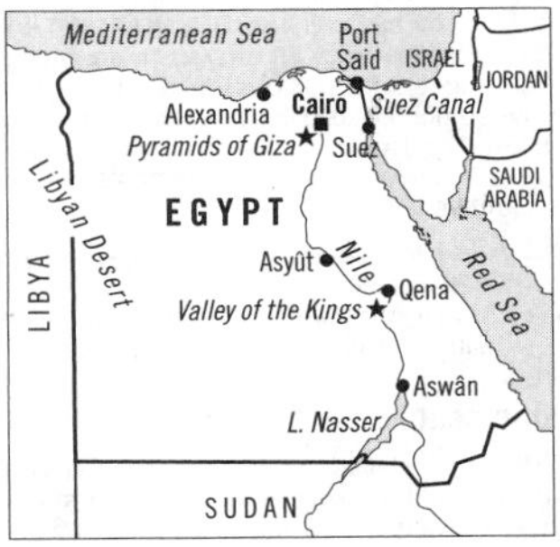

Egypt

Egypt /éejipt/ republic in NE Africa bordering the Mediterranean Sea and the Red Sea. Capital: Cairo. Population: 63,575,100 (1996). Area: 997,739 sq. km/385,229 sq. mi.

Egyptian /i jípsh'n/ *n* **1** NATIVE OR CITIZEN OF EGYPT somebody who comes from Egypt **2** LANGUAGE OF ANCIENT EGYPT the extinct Afro-Asiatic language of ancient Egypt that developed into Coptic around AD 200 **3** DIALECT OF ARABIC SPOKEN IN EGYPT the dialect of Arabic spoken in modern Egypt. Native speakers: 65 million. —**Egyptian** *adj*

Egyptology /éejip tólləji/ *n* the study of the history, archaeology, culture, and language of ancient Egypt —**Egyptologist** *n*

eh[1] /ay, e/ *interj* (*informal*) **1** PARDON? used to ask somebody to repeat something **2** WHAT? used to express surprise at something that has been said **3** ISN'T THAT SO? used to invite somebody to respond to something that has been said, especially to agree with it or confirm that it is correct or accurately sums up a previous statement **4** *Can* ARE YOU WITH ME? used to maintain or regain a listener's interest or to establish that what is being said is understood [Mid-16C. Natural exclamation.]

eh[2] *abbr* Western Sahara (*in Internet addresses*)

Ehrlich /áirlik, -likh/, **Paul** (1854–1915) German bacteriologist and immunologist

EIA *abbr* environmental impact assessment

EIB *abbr* European Investment Bank

Eichendorff /īkən dawrf, īkhən-/, **Joseph, Freiherr von** (1788–1857) German poet

Eichmann /īkmən, īkh-/, **Adolf** (1906–62) German Nazi official and war criminal

Eid /īd/ *n* ISLAM = **Eid-ul-Adha, Eid-ul-Fitr** [Late 17C. < Arabic *'īd* 'festival' < Aramaic.]

eider /īdər/ (*plural* **-ders** *or* **-der**), **eider duck** *n* a large sea duck, the male of which has distinctive black-and-white plumage while the female, the source of eiderdown, has mottled brown plumage. Native to: N hemisphere. Genus: *Somateria.* [Late 17C. Via Icelandic *æður* < Old Norse *æðr*.]

eiderdown /īdər down/ *n* **1** a warm bed covering consisting of a fabric container filled with feathers or artificial fibres **2** the soft fluffy breast feathers of the female eider duck. Use: stuffing for pillows and bed coverings.

eider duck *n* = **eider**

eidetic /ī déttik/ *adj* (*formal*) **1** recalled or reproduced with startling accuracy, clarity, and vividness ○ *eidetic images* **2** able to recall or reproduce things previously seen with startling accuracy, clarity, and vividness ○ *an eidetic memory* [Early 20C. < Greek *eidētikos* < *eidos* 'form'.] —**eidetically** *adv*

eidolon /ī dṓlən, ī dṓ lon/ (*plural* **-lons** *or* **-la** /-lə/) *n* (*literary*) **1** a ghostly figure or image **2** an idealized image of something or somebody [Mid-17C. < Greek *eidōlon* 'idol' (see IDOL).]

Eid-ul-Adha /éed ŏŏl aadə/ *n* an Islamic festival marking the sacrifice made by Abraham and the end of the annual pilgrimage to Mecca, traditionally celebrated by the sacrifice of sheep

Eid-ul-Fitr /éed ŏŏl feetər/ *n* an Islamic festival marking the end of Ramadan

Eiffel /īf'l/, **Gustave** (1832–1923) French engineer

Eiffel Tower *n* a 300-metre-/984-foot-high iron tower in central Paris [After Gustave EIFFEL]

eigenfrequency /īgən freekwənssi/ (*plural* **-cies**) *n* in quantum mechanics, a frequency at which a system will vibrate [Mid-20C. < German *eigen* 'own' + FREQUENCY, after German *Eigenfrequenz*.]

eigenvalue /īgən valyoo/ *n* a value of a variable in an equation giving a solution that complies with the conditions that exist at a system's boundaries [Early 20C. < German *eigen* 'own' + VALUE, after German *Eigenwert*.]

eigenvector /īgən vektər/ *n* a vector whose value is not zero corresponding to a particular eigenvalue in the equation giving rise to the eigenvalue [Mid-20C. < German *Eigenvektor* < *eigen* 'own'.]

Eiger /īgər/ mountain peak in the Bernese Alps, southeast of Bern, Switzerland. Height: 3,970 m/13,025 ft.

Eigg /eg/ island of the Inner Hebrides, NW Scotland. Population: 69 (1991). Area: 67 sq. km/26 sq. mi.

eight /ayt/ *n* **1** see table at **number 2** a crew of eight rowers **3** a long narrow rowing boat crewed by eight rowers [Old English *e(a)hta* < Indo-European] —**eight** *adj*, *pron* ◇ **have one over the eight** to have too much to drink and get drunk (*informal*)

eight ball *n* **1** *US, Can* in pool, the black ball, because it has the number 8 on it **2** a form of pool in which a player must pocket a given 7 of the 15 balls, and then pocket the eight ball, before his or her opponent does ◇ **behind the eight ball** *US* in a difficult or awkward position (*slang*)

eighteen /ay teén, áyt een/ *n* **1** see table at **number 2** *Aus* a team of eighteen players in Australian Rules football [Old English *e(a)hatēne* < Germanic] —**eighteen** *adj, pron*

18 certificate *n* a certificate designating a motion picture that has been classified as suitable only for people aged 18 or over because it contains scenes showing sex and violence

eighteenmo /ay teén mō/ (*plural* **-mos**) *n* PRINTING = **octodecimo**

eighteenth /ay teénth/ *n* **1** see table at **number 2** the birthday of somebody who has just reached 18 years of age —**eighteenth** *adj, adv*

eightfold /áyt fōld/ *adj* **1 MULTIPLYING BY 8** multiplying the original figure by eight **2 CONSISTING OF 8 PARTS** consisting of eight parts ■ *adv* **BY A FACTOR OF 8** by eight, or to an amount eight times greater than the original

eighth *n* see table at **number** —**eighth** *adj, adv*

eighth note *n US* MUSIC = **quaver** *n.* **2**

eighth rest *n US* MUSIC = **quaver rest**

eightieth /áyti əth/ *n* see table at **number** —**eightieth** *adj, adv*

eightsome reel /áytsəm-/ *n* a Scottish dance performed by sets of four couples in circles

eightvo /áyt vō/ (*plural* **-vos**) *n* PRINTING = **octavo** [< *8vo*, written abbreviation of OCTAVO]

eighty /áyti/ *n* (*plural* **-ies**) see table at **number** ■ **eighties** *npl* **1** the numbers 80 to 89, especially as a range of fahrenheit temperatures **2** the years from 80 to 89 in a century or somebody's life [13C. Shortening of Old English *hundeahtatig* < *hund-* 'hundred' + *e(a)hta* 'eight' + *-tig* 'group of ten'.] —**eighty** *adj, pron*

Eighty-Mile Beach /áyti mīl-/ beach in NW Western Australia. Length: 137 km/85 mi.

eighty-six, 86 (**86es, 86ing, 86ed**) *vt US* (*slang*) **1** to dispose of somebody or something **2** to refuse to serve somebody in a restaurant or bar [Mid-20C. < ?]

~~**eigth**~~ incorrect spelling of **eight**

Eijkman /íkmən, íkh-/, **Christiaan** (1858–1930) Dutch physician

Eilat /ay laát/, **Elat** seaport in S Israel, at the head of the Gulf of Aqaba. Population: 33,300 (1993).

Eildon and Leaderfoot /eéldən and leédərfòot/ National Scenic Area in S Scotland. Area: 36 sq. kms/14 sq. mi.

-ein *suffix* a chemical compound related to one whose name ends in '-in' or '-ein' ○ *fluorescein* [Alteration of -IN]

Einstein /ínst īn/, **Albert** (1879–1955) German-born US physicist

einsteinium /īn stíni əm/ *n* (*symbol* **Es**) a synthetic radioactive element. Source: irradiation of plutonium and other elements. [After Albert EINSTEIN]

Einthoven /ínt hōv'n/, **Willem** (1860–1927) Dutch physiologist

eirenicon /ī reéni kon/, **irenicon** *n* a proposal made in order to achieve peace or harmony (*formal*)

ϟ**EISA** *abbr* extended industry standard architecture

Eisenhower /íz'n howər/, **Dwight D.** (1890–1969) US soldier, statesman, and 34th president of the United States (1953–61). Known as **Ike**

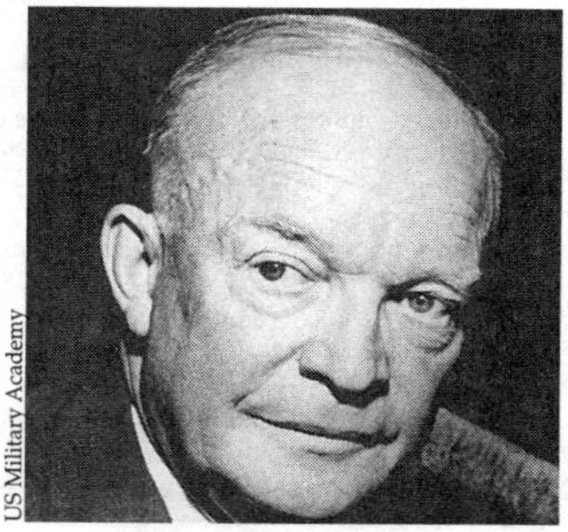
US Military Academy

Dwight D. Eisenhower

Eisenstein /íz'n stīn/, **Sergey** (1898–1948) Soviet film director

eisteddfod /ī stédfəd, ī stéth vod/ (*plural* **-fods** *or* **-fodau** /áy steth vóddī, ī-/) *n* a traditional Welsh festival at which competitions are held for performers and composers of music and poetry [Early 19C. < Welsh, 'session, sitting'.]

eiswein /íss vīn/ *n* a sweet white wine produced in Germany and Austria from grapes that have frozen on the vine, concentrating the sugar content

either /ī̄thər, eéthər/ CORE MEANING: a grammatical word that introduces two situations, one of which may include or exclude the other ○ (det) *It won't make much difference either way.* ○ (pron) *I refuse to meet either of them.* ○ (conj) *Either there's a problem or there isn't.*

1 *det, pron* **ONE OR THE OTHER** one or the other, when it does not matter which ○ (det) *You can execute commands on either machine.* ○ (pron) *If either fell behind, the other would help him to catch up.* ○ (pron) *You can get this information from either of the two addressees.* **2** *det, pron* **INDICATES A NEGATIVE** used to refer negatively to each of two situations where the negative includes them both ○ (det) *You cannot send e-mails to either address at the moment.* ○ (pron) *I'm not interested in either of them.* **3** *det* **BOTH** both of two things ○ *The red and yellow patches on either side of the sun are radiation from the dust ring.* **4** *conj* **INDICATES ALTERNATIVES** used to indicate that there is a choice between two or more options ○ *The only way to get round the city was either by the super freeways or by the canals and the gondolas.* ○ *Data sources may be either digital or analog.* **5** *adv* **INDICATES CONNECTION** used in a negative statement that indicates a connection or a partial agreement with a previous statement (*at the end of a second statement*) ○ *You won't find really bad conditions, but you won't find luxury hotels either.* [Old English *ǣgþer*, contraction of *ǣg(e)hwæþer* < Germanic, 'always each of two']

USAGE Singular or plural after **either**? ***Either*** is normally used with a singular verb: *Has either of you been to Paris? Either Lee or David is responsible.* Informally, however, the plural is used when the choices are regarded collectively rather than individually, and it is quite natural to say *Have either of you been to Paris?*, which caters for the possibility that both the people addressed have done so. When ***either . . . or . . .*** occurs with a mixture of singular and plural subjects, the verb traditionally agrees with the one that is closer to it: *Either David or his parents are at home.*

either-or *adj* offering a choice strictly limited to two options ○ *It's an either-or situation – either you accept or you refuse.*

ejaculate *v* /i jákyoo layt/ (**-lates, -lating, -lated**) **1** *vti* **EJECT SEMEN DURING ORGASM** to eject semen from the penis during an orgasm **2** *vt* **EXCLAIM SOMETHING SUDDENLY** to exclaim something suddenly and usually forcefully (*literary*) ■ *n* /i jákyoolət/ **EJACULATED SEMEN** semen that has been ejected from the penis during orgasm [Late 16C. < Latin *ejaculat-*, past participle of *ejaculari* 'throw out' < *jacere* 'throw'.] —**ejaculation** /i jákyoo láysh'n/ *n* —**ejaculatory** /i jákyoolətəri/ *adj*

eject /i jékt/ *v* **1** *vt* **PUSH SOMETHING OUT WITH FORCE** to cause something to burst out from something else with considerable force **2** *vt* **REMOVE SOMEBODY FROM A PLACE OR POSITION** to force somebody to leave a place or give up a position, e.g. a job or membership ○ *They were forcibly ejected from the meeting.* **3** *vi* **LEAVE AN AIRCRAFT IN AN ESCAPE DEVICE** to escape from an aircraft in an emergency by means of an ejector seat or special capsule **4** *vt* **EVICT** to remove somebody, especially a tenant, from a property by taking legal action [15C. < Latin *eject-*, past participle of *e(j)icere* < *jacere* 'throw'.] —**ejectable** *adj* —**ejection** *n* —**ejective** *adj*

ejecta /i jéktə/ *n* substances ejected from something, especially the material thrown out by a volcanic eruption or from a star (*formal; + singular or plural verb*) [Late 19C. < Latin, a plural of past participle of *e(j)icere* (see EJECT).]

ejection seat *n US* AIR = **ejector seat**

ejectment /i jéktmənt/ *n* **1** the process of ejecting somebody or something, or of being ejected from somewhere (*formal*) **2** a legal action brought by somebody to recover possession of land that is being held by somebody else

ejector /i jéktər/ *n* **1** a device for ejecting something from something else, especially a mechanism for ejecting an empty cartridge or shell from a gun **2** a jet pump device that uses water, steam, or air to remove a gas, fluid, or powder from a space

ejector seat *n* a seat in the cockpit of an aircraft that in an emergency propels the occupant clear of the craft by means of a rocket or explosive device. US term **ejection seat**

eke out /eék-/ (**ekes out, eking out, eked out**) *vt* **1 MAKE LAST WITH SPARING USE** to make a supply of something last by using it as slowly and economically as possible **2 SUPPLEMENT** to supplement something that is insufficient or inadequate, usually with difficulty and by hard work **3 GET ONLY WITH EFFORT** to manage to get or achieve something but only on a small scale and with a great deal of effort ○ *eked out a bare existence* [Late 16C. Later form of Old English *ēacan, ēacian* < Germanic.]

ekistics /i kístiks/ *n* the study of human settlements in all their aspects, including, e.g. the origin and development of towns and town planning (*+ singular verb*) [Mid-20C. < Greek *oikistikos* < *oikizein* 'settle' < *oikos* 'house'.] —**ekistic** *adj* —**ekistician** /éki stísh'n/ *n*

el /el/ *n US* an elevated railway in a city (*informal*)

el. *abbr* elevation

elaborate *adj* /i lábbərət/ **1 COMPLEX** having many different parts or a lot of detail and being organized in a complicated way **2 FINELY OR RICHLY DECORATED** made with a lot of intricate detail or extravagant ornamentation ○ *an elaborate headdress* **3 DETAILED AND THOROUGH** thought out or organized with thoroughness and careful attention to detail ■ *v* /i lábbə rayt/ (**-rates, -rating, -rated**) **1** *vi* **GIVE MORE DETAIL ABOUT** to go into greater detail about something that has already been spoken about or described in broad terms ○ *Would you care to elaborate on that?* **2** *vt* **WORK SOMETHING OUT IN DETAIL** to work out the details of something **3** *vti* **MAKE OR BECOME MORE COMPLEX** to make something more complex or ornate, or become more complex or ornate [15C. < Latin *elaborat-*, past participle of *elaborare* 'produce by effort or labour' < *labor* 'labour'.] —**elaborately** *adv* —**elaborateness** *n* —**elaboration** /i lábbə ráysh'n/ *n* —**elaborator** *n*

Elam /eéləm/ ancient state in SW Iran

Elamite /eéləm īt/ *n* **1** somebody who came from the ancient Middle Eastern kingdom of Elam **2** an extinct language formerly spoken in the ancient kingdom of Elam —**Elamite** *adj* —**Elamitic** /eélə míttik/ *adj*

élan /ay lóN, ay lán/, **elan** *n* vigour and enthusiasm, often combined with self-confidence and style [Mid-19C. < French, < *élancer* 'dart, throw' < *lance* (see LANCE).]

eland /eélənd/ (*plural* **elands** *or* **eland**) *n* the largest of living antelope having humped shoulders, a dewlap, and tightly spiralling horns. Native to: central and southern Africa. Genus: *Taurotragus*. [Late 18C. Via Afrikaans < Dutch, 'elk' < Lithuanian *élnis*.]

élan vital /ay lóN vee taál, ay lán-/ *n* in the philosophy of Henri Bergson, a creative life force present in all living things and responsible for evolution [< French]

elapid /élləpid/ *n* a venomous snake that has its short fangs at the front of the upper jaw. Family: Elapidae. [Late 19C. < modern Latin *Elapidae* < Greek *elaps*, variant of *el(l)ops*, kind of fish and sea serpent.] —**elapid** *adj*

elapse /i láps/ *vi* (**elapses, elapsing, elapsed**) to pass or go by, especially in a gradual, slow, or imperceptible way ○ *several hours elapsed* ■ *n* the passing of a certain period of time (*formal*) [Late 16C. < Latin *elaps-*, past participle of *elabi* 'slip away' < *labi* 'glide, fall'.]

Elara /éllərə/ *n* a small natural satellite of Jupiter, discovered in 1905

elasmobranch /i lássmə brangk, -lázmə-/ *n* a fish with a cartilaginous skeleton, e.g. a shark, ray, or skate. Subclass: Elasmobranchii. [Late 19C. < modern Latin *Elasmobranchii* < Greek *elasmos* 'beaten metal' + *bragkhia* 'gills'.] —**elasmobranch** *adj*

elastic /i lástik/ *n* **1 STRETCHY MATERIAL** a strip or thread of rubber or similar stretchable material **2** *US* = **rubber band** ■ *adj* **1 STRETCHY AND FLEXIBLE** able to return quickly to its original shape and size after being bent or stretched **2 EASILY CHANGED** able to incorporate changes or adapt to new circumstances easily **3 OF ELASTIC** made of elastic **4 SPRINGY** light and springy, especially in movement **5 RETURNING TO ITS ORIGINAL SHAPE** describes a substance that is capable of returning to its original shape after undergoing stress or deformation [Mid-17C. Via modern Latin < Greek *elastikos* 'driving, propelling' < *elaunein* 'drive'.] —**elastically** *adv*

SYNONYMS See *pliable*.

elasticate /i lásti kayt/ (**-cates, -cating, -cated**) *vt* to put strips or threads of rubber or a similar material into a fabric in order to make it stretchy. US term **elasticize** *v*.

elastic band *n* = rubber band

elastic collision *n* a collision between two perfectly elastic bodies such that the final kinetic energy of the system is the same as the initial kinetic energy of the system

elastic fibre *n* a smooth, long, thin fibre in connective tissue, composed mainly of the fibrous protein elastin

elasticity /èe lass tíssəti/ *n* **1 ABILITY TO RETURN TO SHAPE** the ability of an object or substance to return quickly to its original shape and size after being bent, stretched, or squashed **2 FLEXIBILITY** the ability to incorporate changes or adapt to new circumstances easily **3 ABILITY TO REGAIN DIMENSIONS AFTER STRESS** the property that makes a material return to its original dimensions after being stressed or deformed, or the degree to which this is exhibited **4 RELATIVE CHANGE IN AN ECONOMIC VARIABLE** the relative change in an economic variable, e.g. demand, that occurs in reaction to changes in other variables, e.g. price or advertising input

elasticize /i lásti stíz/ (**-cizes, -cizing, -cized**), **elasticise** (**-cises, -cising, -cised**) *vt* **1** US = **elasticate 2** to make something elastic or more elastic

elastic limit *n* the maximum stress that can be applied to a material without the material becoming permanently deformed

elastic wave *n* a wave propagated in a medium in which particles are temporarily displaced, transfer motion to other particles, and then return to their original state

elastin /i lástin/ *n* a fibrous protein resembling collagen that is the main constituent of the elastic fibres of connective tissue [Late 19C. < ELASTIC.]

elastomer /i lástəmər/ *n* a natural material, e.g. rubber, or a synthetic material, e.g. polyvinyl, that has elastic properties [Mid-20C. < ELASTIC.] —**elastomeric** /i lástə mérrik/ *adj*

Elat = Eilat

elate /i láyt/ (**elates, elating, elated**) *vt* to make somebody very happy and excited [Late 16C. < Latin *elat-*, used as past participle of *effere* 'carry up' < *ferre* 'carry'.] —**elate** *adj* —**elated** *adj* —**elatedly** *adv* —**elatedness** *n*

elater /éllatər/ *n* a beetle that belongs to the click beetle family. Family: Elateridae. [Mid-17C. < Greek *elatēr* 'driver' < *elaunein* 'drive'.]

elaterid /i láttərid/ *n* INSECTS = **elater** ■ *adj* belonging or relating to the click beetle family

elation /i láysh'n/ *n* a feeling of extraordinary happiness and excitement

Elba

Elba /élbə/ island off the coast of W Italy, the place of Napoleon's first period of exile (1814–15)

Elbe /elb/ river in central Europe that rises in the N Czech Republic and flows northwest to the North Sea. Length: 1,170 km/724 mi.

Elbert, Mount /élbərt/ highest peak in Colorado, in the centre of the state, and the highest of the Rocky Mountains. Height: 4,399 m/14,433 ft.

elbow /élbō/ *n* **1 JOINT IN THE ARM** the joint between the upper and lower parts of the human arm **2 PART OF A SLEEVE** the part of a sleeve that covers the elbow **3 JOINT IN AN ANIMAL LEG** the joint in an animal's forelimb corresponding to the elbow in humans **4 BEND** a bend in something such as a river, road, or pipe **5 SOMETHING BENT** something, especially a piece of pipe, made with a bend in it ■ *vti* **PUSH WITH THE ELBOW** to push or hit somebody or something with the elbow, or progress through a crowd by pushing with the elbow or elbows [Old English *el(n)boga* 'arm bend' < Germanic] ◇ **bend the** *or* **your elbow** to drink alcohol often (*informal*) ◇ **get** *or* **be given the elbow** to be dismissed or rejected (*informal*) ◇ **out at elbow, out at the elbows** poorly dressed, or short of money

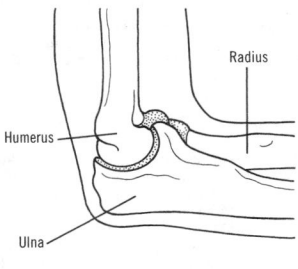

Elbow

elbow grease *n* hard physical effort or work with the arms, especially scrubbing or polishing (*informal*)

elbowroom /élbō room, -rōōm/ *n* (*informal*) **1** space to move around or work in comfortably **2** freedom from restriction for a time, especially to move or develop in a new area or direction

Elbrus, Mount /il brōoss/, **El'brus** the highest mountain in Europe, in the Caucasus Mountains in S Russia. Height: 5,642 m/18,510 ft.

Elburz Mountains /el bōōrz-/ mountain range in N Iran. Highest peak: Damavand 5,604 m/18,386 ft.

elder[1] /éldər/ *adj* **1 BORN EARLIER** born before another, especially within a family, or having more seniority **2 SUPERIOR** superior to others, either by rank or experience ■ *n* **1 PERSON BORN EARLIER** somebody who was born before somebody else, or is higher in rank ◇ *She is five years my elder.* **2 SENIOR MEMBER OF A CHURCH** a senior lay member in some Christian churches with responsibility for aspects of church administration, the pastoral care of church members, and sometimes for teaching and preaching **3 SENIOR MEMBER OF A COMMUNITY** a member of a family, tribal group, or village who is respected for advanced years and has some influence and authority within the community [Old English *(i)eldra* < Germanic] —**eldership** *n*

USAGE elder or **older**? *Elder* and *eldest* are used only of people, and usually in the context of family relationships: *She is the elder of Ruth's daughters. Mark is my eldest son. Older* and *oldest* can apply to things as well as people, and can be used in a wider range of grammatical constructions: *I am older than David. It is the oldest church in Paris.* When *eldest* (or less commonly, **elder**) is used after a verb (for example *be*), it has to be preceded by *the: Who is the eldest?* not *Who is eldest?*

elder[2] /éldər/ *n* a bush or tree with flat clusters of white flowers and purplish-black berries. *Sambucus nigra.* [Old English *ellærn* < ?]

elderberry /éldər berri, -bəri/ (*plural* **-ries**) *n* **1** the purplish-black fruit of the elder tree, sometimes used to make wine **2** PLANT SCI = **elder**[2]

elderly /éldərli/ *adj* **1 PAST MIDDLE AGE** past middle age and approaching the rest of life (*sometimes offensive*) **2 CHARACTERISTIC OF OLDER PEOPLE** characteristic of or relating to older people **3 OLD-FASHIONED** old and somewhat old-fashioned ■ *npl* **OLDER PEOPLE AS A GROUP** older people, considered as a group (*sometimes offensive*) —**elderliness** *n*

elder statesman *n* a person, advanced in years and experience, especially a politician or former politician,

who is respected for his or her wisdom and whose advice is still valued and unofficially sought

eldest /éldist/ *adj* first, either in age or seniority [Old English *(i)eldest* < Germanic]

USAGE See *elder*.

ELDO /éldō/ *abbr* European Launch Development Organization

Eldon /éldən/, **1st Earl of** (1751–1838) British judge and statesman. Born **John Scott**

El Dorado /élda raádō/ *n* **1** a legendary place in South America where the streets were said to be paved with gold and wealth and riches were to be had in abundance **2** a place that has great wealth or where great riches can be acquired [< Spanish, 'the gilded']

Eleatic /élli áttik/ *adj* relating to an ancient Greek school of philosophy that flourished in the 5th and 6th centuries BC. It advocated philosophical reflection over sensory observation. [Late 19C. < Latin *Eliaticus* < *Elea*, ancient Greek city in SW Italy.] —**Eleatic** *n* —**Eleaticism** /-áttisizəm/ *n*

elec. *abbr* **1** electric **2** electrical **3** electricity

elecampane /élli kam páyn/ (*plural* **-panes** *or* **-pane**) *n* a tall perennial plant related to daisies and dandelions having large toothed hairy leaves. Flowers: yellow. Use: herbal remedy for coughs and fevers made from roots. *Inula helenium.* [14C.< Contraction of medieval Latin *enula campana* 'elecampane of the fields' < *enula* 'elecampane', via Latin *inula* < Greek *helenion*.]

elect /i lékt/ *v* **1** *vt* **CHOOSE SOMEBODY BY VOTE** to choose somebody by a vote, e.g. for public office, an official role, or membership of some group ◇ *She was elected leader of the commission.* **2** *vt* **DECIDE TO DO** to make a decision to do something **3** *vt* **CHOOSE SOMEBODY FOR SALVATION** to choose somebody by divine will for salvation **4** *vti* US **CHOOSE SOMETHING** to choose or select something, particularly a subject or course of study at university ■ *adj* **1 CHOSEN BUT NOT YET IN OFFICE** chosen by a vote but not yet formally installed in office (*after a noun*) ◇ *the president-elect* **2 CHOSEN BY GOD** specially chosen by God for favour, salvation, or a task ◇ '*Samson has assumed that, as an elect instrument, he must be always actively engaged in God's service*'. (John Spencer Hill, *John Milton: Poet, Priest, and Prophet;* 1979) ■ *npl* **1 PEOPLE CHOSEN BY GOD** people specially chosen or favoured by God, e.g. those chosen by God for salvation **2 SELECT GROUP** a specially privileged or gifted group (*literary*) ◇ *World-class opera singers are among today's elect.* [15C. < Latin *electus* < *eligere* 'pick out' < *legere* 'choose'.] —**electability** *n* —**electable** *adj*

election /i léksh'n/ *n* **1 EVENT FOR CHOOSING BY VOTE** an organized event at which somebody is chosen for something, especially a public office, by vote **2 CHOOSING OR BEING CHOSEN BY VOTE** the process of choosing somebody or of being chosen by vote ◇ *He stood for election.* **3 SELECTION** the act or process of choosing something, e.g. a course of action or subject (*formal*) **4 SELECTION BY GOD** the fact of being chosen by God, or God's act of choosing somebody for salvation, a task, or special favour

Election Day *n* in the United States, a day designated by law for the election of people to public office

electioneer /i léksha neèr/ *vi* **1 CAMPAIGN IN AN ELECTION** to take an active part in an election campaign, especially as, or on behalf of, a candidate for political office **2 DO SOMETHING JUST TO WIN VOTES** to attempt to win votes in an election by being insincere and unscrupulous (*disapproving*) ■ *n* **electioneer, electioneerer** CAMPAIGN WORKER a worker on behalf of a candidate or party in an election

elective /i léktiv/ *adj* **1 REQUIRING ELECTION** chosen by a vote, or whose holder is chosen by a vote ◇ *The monarchy at that time was elective not hereditary.* **2 NOT COMPULSORY** optional rather than essential or compulsory **3 RELATING TO VOTING** involving or concerned with voting **4 VOTING** empowered to vote ■ *n* OPTIONAL SUBJECT OF STUDY an optional course that a student may select from among several alternatives —**electively** *adv* —**electiveness** *n*

elector /i léktər/ *n* **1 SOMEBODY WHO VOTES** a voter in an election **2 Elector** GERMAN RULER WHO ELECTED THE EMPEROR any one of the rulers of the German states within the Holy Roman Empire who was entitled to vote in the election of the emperor (*often used as a title*) **3 MEMBER OF AN ELECTORAL COLLEGE** a member of an electoral college or the Electoral College

electoral /i léktərəl/ *adj* relating to or involving elections or electors —**electorally** *adv*

electoral college *n* a select body of people who elect somebody to an office

Electoral College *n* in the United States, the formal body elected by voters to choose the President and Vice President

electoral quota *n* in Australia, the number of representatives of a state or territory that can be elected to the House of Representatives

electoral roll, electoral register *n* an official list of the names and addresses of the people in a given area who are entitled to vote in an election

electorate /i léktərət/ *n* **1** all the officially qualified voters within a given country or area or for a given election **2** *ANZ* an area represented by a Member of Parliament

electr- *prefix* = **electro-** (*before vowels*)

Electra /i léktrə/ *n* in Greek mythology, the daughter of Agamemnon and Clytemnestra [< Greek *Ēlektra* 'bright, beaming' < *ēlektōr* 'sun']

Electra complex *n* in psychoanalysis, a daughter's unconscious unresolved sexual attraction to her father

Electra paradox *n* a logical paradox arising from the possibility of somebody knowing that something is true when it is described in one way but not when it is described in another [< a Greek myth in which Electra is said to know her brother Orestes when he is described but not when she encounters him as a stranger]

electress /i léktrəss/, **Electress** *n* the wife of an elector of a German state within the Holy Roman Empire (*often used as a title*)

electret /i léktrit/ *n* a piece of insulating material that is permanently polarized and has a permanent electric field, used in microphones and telephones [Late 19C. Blend of ELECTRICITY + MAGNET.]

electric /i léktrik/ *adj* **1** INVOLVING OR CAUSED BY ELECTRICITY involving, relating to, or caused by electricity **2** FOR ELECTRICITY carrying or conveying electricity **3** USING ELECTRICITY powered or operated by electricity ○ *an electric guitar* **4** TENSE OR EXCITED full of tension or excitement and anticipation **5** BRIGHT extremely bright in colour ○ *electric blue* ■ *n* **1** ELECTRICITY electricity, or the electricity supply, e.g. to a house (*informal*) **2** SOMETHING OPERATED BY ELECTRICITY a vehicle, machine, or other device that is powered by electricity ■ **electrics** *npl* ELECTRICAL EQUIPMENT OR PARTS the parts of a device or system that are operated by, carry, or generate electricity, or electrically powered equipment [Mid-17C. < modern Latin *electricus* < *electrum* 'amber' < Greek *ēlektron*.] —**electrically** *adv*

USAGE **electric** or **electrical**? ***Electric*** is the word more commonly used to describe a device that works by electricity or is involved in producing or carrying electricity: *an electric oven; an electric socket.* ***Electrical*** is applied to more general things and to areas of study or activity that are concerned with electricity: *electrical appliances; electrical engineering.* ***Electric*** is usual in the figurative meaning 'tense or excited': *The atmosphere at the meeting was electric.*

electrical /i léktrik'l/ *adj* **1** = **electric** *adj.* 1 **2** = **electric** *adj.* 2 **3** = **electric** *adj.* 3 **4** INVOLVING THE APPLICATION OF ELECTRICITY involved in or involving the application of electricity in technology **5** RELATING TO ELECTRIC FUNCTIONING involving or concerned with electric cables or circuits, or parts powered by electricity ○ *You'll need an electrician for the electrical work.* **6** CAUSED BY ELECTRICITY caused by electricity or something that uses or conveys electricity ■ **electricals** *npl* ELECTRICITY COMPANY SHARES shares in electricity companies

USAGE See ***electric***.

electrical engineering *n* a branch of engineering that studies the practical applications of electricity in science and technology —**electrical engineer** *n*

electric blanket *n* a blanket containing an insulated electric heating element, used to warm a bed

electric-blue *adj* of a bright metallic blue colour —**electric blue** *n*

electric chair *n* **1** a specially designed chair used especially in the United States to execute people sentenced to death by electrocuting them **2** a sentence of death by electrocution in an electric chair

electric eel *n* a long air-breathing fish resembling a true eel that can release a strong discharge of electricity from specialized organs in the tail region. Native to: South American rivers. *Electrophorus electricus*.

electric eye *n* a device that converts light into electrical energy or uses it to regulate a flow of current, often incorporated into automatic control systems for doors and lighting

electric fence *n* a wire fence carrying an electric current that gives a mild electric shock to any person or animal that touches it

electric field *n* a field of force surrounding a charged body or associated with a fluctuating magnetic field, with which charged particles interact

electric fire *n* a heater for a room with an element that is made hot by an electric current passing through it

electric guitar *n* an electrically operated guitar, often with a solid body, that has a device for picking up sound fitted below the strings and connected to an amplifier and loudspeaker

electrician /i lek trísh'n, éllek-/ *n* somebody who installs, maintains, or repairs electrical wiring or electrical goods

electricity /i lek tríssəti, éllek-/ *n* **1** ENERGY CREATED BY MOVING CHARGED PARTICLES a fundamental form of kinetic or potential energy created by the free or controlled movement of charged particles such as electrons, positrons, and ions **2** ELECTRIC CURRENT electric current, especially when used as a source of power **3** ANTICIPATION OR TENSION a feeling or atmosphere of excited anticipation or tension

electric jazz *n* jazz produced using electronic instruments or other electronic devices

electric light *n* **1** a light operated by electricity, e.g. one with an electric bulb or a fluorescent tube **2** the illumination produced by electricity

electric motor *n* a machine that converts energy from electricity into mechanical energy

electric organ *n* **1** an organ whose sound is produced or amplified by means of electricity **2** a specialized muscle tissue in some fish that creates an electric field used for finding enemies, obstacles, and food in murky water, and, in some species, for defence against attack

electric piano *n* an electronic keyboard instrument that produces sound similar to that of a piano

electric potential *n* (*symbol V*) the work required to bring a unit of positive electric charge from infinity to a specified point in an electric field

electric ray *n* a fish that can emit a strong electric discharge from organs in its enlarged pectoral fins. Native to: tropical or temperate seas. Family: Torpedinidae.

electric razor *n* a small electrically powered device used for shaving hair on the face or body

electric shock *n* a sudden painful physical reaction consisting of nerve stimulation and muscle contraction caused by an electric current flowing through the body

electrify /i léktri fī/ (**-fies, -fying, -fied**) *vt* **1** CONVERT TO USING ELECTRICITY to convert something, e.g. a railway line or a piece of machinery so that it can operate on electric power **2** CHARGE ELECTRICALLY to charge something with electricity **3** THRILL to cause somebody to feel a sudden and surprising shock, thrill, or sense of excitement **4** ELECTRICALLY AMPLIFY to amplify electrically the sounds produced by a musical instrument —**electrifiable** *adj* —**electrification** /i léktrifi káysh'n/ *n* —**electrifier** *n*

electro- *prefix* **1** electricity, electric, electronic ○ *electromyogram* **2** electrolysis ○ *electrometallurgy* **3** electron ○ *electropositive* [Via modern Latin < Greek *ēlektron* 'amber']

electroacoustic /i léktrō ə kóostik/ *adj* describes a device that converts sound into electrical signals or vice versa

electroacoustics /i léktrō ə kóostiks/ *n* a branch of electronics that is concerned with how electricity is converted into sound (+ *singular verb*) —**electroacoustically** *adv*

electroanalysis /i léktrō ə nálləssiss/ (*plural* **-ses** /-seez/) *n* the use of electrolysis to perform chemical analysis —**electroanalytic** /i léktrō ánnə líttik/ *adj* —**electroanalytical** *adj* —**electroanalytically** *adv*

electrocardiogram /i léktrō kaárdi ə gram/ *n* a visual record of the heart's electrical activity made using an electrocardiograph

electrocardiograph /i léktrō kaárdi ə graaf, -graf/ *n* a device that records the electrical activity of the heart muscle via electrodes placed on the chest, and displays it as a visual record —**electrocardiographic** /i léktrō kaárdi ə gráffik/ *adj* —**electrocardiographically** /-gráffikli/ *adv* —**electrocardiography** /i léktrō kaárdi óggrəfi/ *n*

electrocautery /i léktrō káwtəri/ *n* the process of destroying unwanted tissue, e.g. warts and polyps, or sealing blood vessels, by means of an electrically heated needle

electrochemical series *n* a series in which the chemical elements are arranged in order of decreasing tendency to lose electrons

electrochemistry /i léktrō kémmistri/ *n* a branch of chemistry that studies chemical change associated with electrons and electricity —**electrochemist** *n*

electrocoagulation /i léktrō kō ággyoo láysh'n/ *n* the use of an electrical device that burns tissue to stop bleeding from small blood vessels during surgery or to destroy small tumours

electroconvulsive therapy /i léktrō kən vúlssiv-/ *n* the passing of a small electric current through the brain to induce a seizure, used in the treatment of severe psychiatric disorders

electrocute /i léktrə kyoot/ (**-cutes, -cuting, -cuted**) *vt* **1** to cause injury or death with an electric shock **2** to execute somebody by means of the electric chair [Late 19C. Blend of ELECTRO- + EXECUTE.] —**electrocution** /i léktrə kyóosh'n/ *n*

electrode /i lék trōd/ *n* either of the two conductors through which electricity enters or leaves something such as a battery or a piece of electrical equipment

electrodeposit /i léktrō di pózzit/ *vt* to deposit a substance, especially a metal, on an electrode by using electrolysis ■ *n* a substance deposited by using electrolysis —**electrodeposition** /i léktrō dépə zísh'n/ *n*

electrode potential *n* the potential difference existing between an electrode and the solution in which it is immersed

electrodialysis /i léktrō dī álləssiss/ (*plural* **-ses** /-seez/) *n* **1** the removal of unwanted ions from a solution by applying a direct electric current to electrodes inserted in a dialysis system **2** the desalination of salt water by electrolysis through a series of semipermeable membranes

electrodynamics /i léktrō dī námmiks/ *n* a branch of physics that studies how electric currents interact with magnetic and mechanical forces (+ *singular verb*) —**electrodynamic** *adj*

electrodynamometer /i léktrō dīnə mómmitər/ *n* a device for measuring the strength of an electric current by the magnetic force it induces in a coil

electroencephalogram /i léktrō in séffələ gram/ *n* the record of the electrical activity of the brain that is produced by an electroencephalograph

electroencephalograph /i léktrō in séffələ graaf, -graf/ *n* a machine that uses electrodes placed on the scalp to monitor the electrical activity of different parts of the brain, recording these as complex tracings —**electroencephalographic** /-in séffələ gráffik/ *adj* —**electroencephalography** /-in séffə lóggrəfi/ *n*

electroform /i léktrə fawrm/ *vt* to form something, e.g. a medal, by using electrolysis to coat the surface of the mould or matrix with a metal

electrograph /i léktrō graaf, -graf/ *n* **1** ELECTROMETER an electrometer that produces a graphical record of the measurements it makes **2** GRAPH FROM AN ELECTROMETER the visual record produced by an electrometer **3** ELECTRICAL ENGRAVING DEVICE an electrical device for engraving a design on a metal plate. Use: printing patterns on fabrics or wallpaper. **4** ELECTRICAL PICTURE TRANSMISSION DEVICE an apparatus used to transmit pictures by electrical means, e.g. by fax **5** TRANSMITTED PICTURE a printed picture produced by an electrograph

electrohydraulic /i léktrō hī drólik/ *adj* using, or relating to the use of, electrical and hydraulic components —**electrohydraulically** *adv*

electrokinetics /i lék trōki néttiks, -kī-/ *n* a branch of physics that deals with the motion of electrically charged particles (+ *singular verb*) —**electrokinetic**

adj —**electrokinetically** *adv* —**electrokineticist** /-néttissist/ *n*

electroluminescence /i léktrō lòomi néss'nss/ *n* the emission of light by something such as a gas or phosphor resulting from a high-frequency electrical discharge —**electroluminescent** *adj*

electrolyse /i léktrə līz/ (**-trolyses, -trolysing, -trolysed**) *vt* to use electrolysis to decompose a chemical compound [Mid-19C. Blend of ELECTROLYSIS + ANALYSE.]

electrolysis /i lek tróllәssiss, éllek-/ *n* **1** the conduction of electricity through something melted or dissolved in order to induce decomposition of the melted or dissolved chemical into its components **2** the use of an electric current applied though a needle to remove body hair for cosmetic purposes, or to destroy warts, moles, or tumours for medical reasons

electrolyte /i léktrō līt/ *n* **1 COMPOUND SEPARABLE INTO IONS IN SOLUTION** a chemical compound that separates into ions in a solution or when molten and is able to conduct electricity **2 ION** an ion in an electrolyte **3 ION NEEDED BY CELL** any ion in cells, blood, or other organic material

electrolytic /i léktrō líttik/ *adj* **1** involved in or relating to electrolysis **2** relating to, containing, or consisting of electrolytes —**electrolytically** *adv*

electrolytic cell *n* **1** a device in which electrolysis can be produced, usually consisting of an electrolyte, its container, and electrodes **2** a device consisting of an electrolyte, its container, and two electrodes, in which a chemical reaction between the electrolyte and the electrodes produces electricity

electrolyze *vt* US = **electrolyse**

electromagnet /i léktrō mágnit/ *n* a magnet consisting of a core, often made of soft iron, that is temporarily magnetized by an electric current in a coil that surrounds it

electromagnetic /i léktrō mag néttik/ *adj* created by or relating to electromagnetism —**electromagnetically** *adv*

electromagnetic field *n* a field of force associated with a moving electric charge and consisting of electric and magnetic fields that are generated at right angles to each other

electromagnetic force *n* the force resulting from the interaction of charged particles and their electric and magnetic fields

electromagnetic interference *n* the interference in a circuit, e.g. disturbance on a television set, caused by the radiation of an electric or magnetic field or the operation of a nearby electric motor

electromagnetic radiation *n* electromagnetic energy such as gamma rays, X-rays, ultraviolet light, visible light, infrared rays, microwaves, and radio waves

electromagnetic spectrum *n* the complete range of electromagnetic radiation from the shortest waves (**gamma rays**) to the longest (**radio waves**)

electromagnetic unit *n* any unit in the centimetre-gram-second system of units for measuring electricity and magnetism that gives a value of 1 to the magnetic constant, e.g. the abampere or the abvolt

electromagnetic wave *n* a wave of energy with a frequency within the electromagnetic spectrum, generated by the periodic fluctuation of an electromagnetic field resulting from the acceleration or oscillation of an electric charge

electromagnetism /i léktrō mágnə tizəm/ *n* **1** magnetism produced by an electric current **2** the branch of physics concerned with the interaction of electric and magnetic fields and with electromagnetism

electromechanical /i léktrō mi kánnik'l/ *adj* relating to or used to describe a mechanical device that is powered or controlled by electricity —**electromechanically** *adv*

electrometallurgy /i léktrō mi tállərji, -métt'l urji/ *n* the range of metallurgical processes in which electricity has a key role, e.g. electroplating and the use of arc furnaces

electrometer /i lek trómmitər, éllek-/ *n* a sensitive device for measuring extremely low voltages by means of the forces of attraction and repulsion between charged bodies on plates or wires

electromotive /i léktrō mṓtiv/ *adj* relating to or producing an electric current

electromotive force *n* **1** a force that causes the flow of electricity from one point to another **2** (*symbol E*) the energy available in a source such as a battery for conversion into electricity from a chemical, mechanical, or other nonelectric form, measured in volts per unit of electric charge

electromyogram /i léktrō mī́ ə gram/ *n* a graphical tracing of the electrical activity in a muscle at rest or during contraction, used to diagnose nerve and muscle disorders

electromyograph /i léktrō mī́ ə graaf, -graf/ *n* a machine for producing an electromyogram from electrical activity picked up via electrodes inserted into muscle tissue

electron /i lék tron/ *n* a stable negatively charged elementary particle with a small mass that is a fundamental constituent of matter and orbits the nucleus of an atom

electron affinity *n* the amount of energy needed to remove an electron from a negatively charged ion

electronegative /i léktrō néggətiv/ *adj* ◊ **electropositive** **1** with negative electric charge, and so tending to move towards a positive electric pole **2** tending to gain electrons to form a bond in a chemical reaction

electronegativity /i léktrō neggə tívvəti/ *n* a measure of the tendency of an atom in a molecule to attract the electrons in a chemical bond

electron gun *n* a device such as one used in a cathode-ray tube, that directs a steady stream of electrons in a desired direction

ϟ **electronic** /íllek trónnik, éllek-/ *adj* **1 INVOLVING A CONTROLLED FLOW OF ELECTRONS** relating to, or produced or operated by, the controlled flow of electrons through a semiconductor, a gas, or free space **2 USING VALVES, TRANSISTORS, OR SILICON CHIPS** relating to devices, systems, or circuits that employ components such as valves, integrated circuits, or transistors in their design **3 BY COMPUTER** relating to a computer or computer network ○ *electronic banking* **4 OF ELECTRONS** relating to electrons ○ *electronic spectrum* —**electronically** *adv*

electronic configuration *n* the three-dimensional arrangement within an atom or molecule of atoms in their orbitals

ϟ **electronic data processing** *n* computer-based tasks involving the input and manipulation of data, usually using database programs

ϟ **electronic depository transfer** *n* the transfer of funds between bank accounts using the automated clearing house system (*in e-commerce*)

electronic flash *n* a flash device used in high-speed photography that produces a very bright light by passing an electric charge through a gas-filled tube

ϟ **electronic funds transfer at point of sale** *n* a system of paying for goods at the point of sale by the direct computerized transfer of money from the buyer's bank or building society account to the seller's

ϟ **electronic journalism** *n* news coverage that is transmitted electronically, e.g. by television or over the Internet

ϟ **electronic magazine** *n* a magazine that is distributed online over a computer network rather than being printed on paper

ϟ **electronic mail** *n* full form of **e-mail**

electronic music *n* music produced or modified by electronic means, often with the aid of a computer

electronic newsgathering *n* television news coverage made at the time and place of the event or incident by means of video equipment

ϟ **electronic office** *n* an office in which traditional office equipment has been replaced by telecommunications gear and computers running integrated programs

electronic organ *n* an electric organ

ϟ **electronic point of sale** *n* a computerized checkout system in shops that records sales by scanning bar codes, automatically updates the retailer's stock lists, and provides a printout of the customer's purchases

ϟ **electronic publishing** *n* the production of documents in computer-readable form for distribution over a computer network or in other formats such as CD-ROMs

ϟ **electronic purse** *n* a method of prepayment used in e-commerce, in which cash is stored electronically on a microchip (*in e-commerce*)

electronics /i lek trónniks, éllek-/ *n* the branch of technology concerned with the design, manufacture, and maintenance of electronic devices (*+ singular verb*) ■ *npl* the electronic parts of a piece of equipment or electronic devices and equipment generally

ϟ **electronic shopping** *n* the ordering and purchase of goods and services over a computer network, especially over the Internet

ϟ **electronic signature** *n* an encoded attachment to an electronic message, verifying the identity of its sender

electronic smog *n* nonionizing radiation produced in the atmosphere by sources such as radar, radio and television broadcasting, considered by some people to pose a general health risk

ϟ **electronic superhighway** *n* ONLINE = **information superhighway**

electronic surveillance *n* the gathering of information, especially in crime detection and prevention or in espionage, using electronic devices such as video cameras and wiretaps

electronic tagging *n* the supervision of an offender by means of an electronic tracking device such as a bracelet, used as an alternative to prison confinement

ϟ **electronic transfer of funds** *n* the transfer of money from one account to another by computer

electron lens *n* a device that creates an electric or magnetic field around the path of an electron beam so that the beam may be focussed

electron micrograph *n* a photograph of a specimen taken using an electron microscope

electron microscope *n* a high-powered microscope that uses beams of electrons focussed by an electron lens to create a magnified image on a fluorescent screen or photographic plate —**electron microscopy** *n*

electron multiplier *n* a device for amplifying a very small current using the effects of secondary emission

electron optics *n* the science that deals with the direction, deflection, or focussing of beams of electrons by electric and magnetic fields, e.g. in electron lenses (*+ singular verb*)

electron sea *n* a model for the electron state in metals in which a regular array of cations is surrounded by a group of loosely bound electrons

electron shell *n* PHYS = **shell** *n.* **19**

electron transport *n* a process in which electrons are transferred from one compound to another with a release of energy used in the production of ATP

electron tube *n* a device that consists of a sealed glass vessel containing a gas or a vacuum, within which electrons flow between electrodes

electron volt /i léktron vṓlt/ *n* **1** (*symbol* **eV**) a unit of energy equal to the energy gained by an electron accelerated through a potential difference of one volt and equal to 1.602×10^{-19} joule **2** the unit of mass of elementary particles, measured as a function of energy and usually expressed in terms of mega electron volts (**MeV**)

electro-osmosis *n* the movement of a liquid through a membrane under the effect of an electric field

electrophile /i léktrō fīl/ *n* an atom, molecule, or chemical group that is attracted to electrons or accepts them —**electrophilic** /i léktrō fíllik/ *adj*

electrophonic /i léktrə fónnik/ *adj* producing sound by means of electronic equipment

electrophoresis /i léktrō fə réessiss/ *n* the movement of charged particles in a colloid or suspension when an electric field is applied to them [Early 20C. < ELECTRO- + Greek *phorēsis* 'being carried' (see PHORESIS).] —**electrophoretic** /-fə réttik/ *adj*

electrophorus /i lek tróffərəss, éllek-/ (*plural* **-ri** /-rī/) *n* a device that produces electric charges from the friction between a disc and a metal plate [Late 18C. < ELECTRO- + *-phorus*, Latinization of -PHORE.]

electrophotography /i léktrōfə tóggrəfi/ *n* any form of photography, e.g. xerography, that uses electricity to transfer an image onto paper —**electrophotographic** /i léktrō fōtə gráffik/ *adj*

electrophysiology /i léktrō fízzi ólləji/ *n* the branch of medicine or biology dealing with the study of electrical activity in human or animal bodies —**electrophysiologic** /-fizi ə lójjik/ *adj* —**electrophysiological** *adj* —**electrophysiologically** *adv* —**electrophysiologist** /i léktrō fizi óllәjist/ *n*

electroplate /i léktrō playt/ *vt* (**-plates, -plating, -plated**) to use electrolysis to coat the surface of an object with metal ■ *n* objects coated with metal by means of electrolysis

electroporation /i léktrō pō ráysh'n/ *n* a method of introducing DNA from one organism into a protoplast of another using an electric pulse [< ELECTRO- + PORE[1]]

electropositive /i léktrō pózzitiv/ *adj* ◊ **electronegative** **1** with positive electric charge, and so tending to move towards a negative electric pole **2** tending to release electrons to form a bond in a chemical reaction

electroreception /i léktrō ri sépsh'n/ *n* the detection of changes in an electric field using either special sense organs, e.g. as fish do, or by electronic means

electroreceptor /i léktrōri septər/ *n* an organ in fish such as sharks, electric eels, and catfish that detects electrical charges

electroretinogram /i léktrō réttinō gram/ *n* **1** a record of the electrical currents induced in the retina by exposure to flashes of light, used to distinguish disorders of the light-sensitive cells and the retinal rods and cones **2** the use of electrodes placed on the eye to obtain a record of the electrical activity of the retina

electroscope /i léktrō skōp/ *n* a device that detects and measures an electric charge, usually consisting of a rod holding two strips of gold foil that separate when a like charge is applied to each —**electroscopic** /i léktrō skóppik/ *adj*

electroshock /i léktrō shok/ *n* *US* PSYCHIAT = **electroconvulsive therapy** ■ *vt US* to administer electroconvulsive therapy to a patient

electroshock therapy *n* PSYCHIAT = **electroconvulsive therapy**

electrostatic /i léktrō státtik/ *adj* **1** produced by or relating to static electricity **2** relating to electrostatics —**electrostatically** *adv*

electrostatic generator *n* PHYS = **Van de Graaff generator**

electrostatic precipitator *n* a device that removes small particles of smoke, dust, or oil from air by electrostatically charging them and then attracting them to an oppositely charged collector plate or surface —**electrostatic precipitation** *n*

electrostatic printing *n* a photocopying or printing process in which images are reproduced on a surface using electrostatic charges

electrostatics /i léktrō státtiks/ *n* a branch of physics dealing with electric charges at rest (**static electricity**) (*+ singular verb*)

electrostatic unit *n* a unit for measuring the magnitude of forces of repulsion between static electrical charges in the centimetre-gram-second system, e.g. the statampere and the statvolt

electrosurgery /i léktrō súrjəri/ *n* the use of an electrical device or current during surgery, e.g. to cut or cauterize tissue —**electrosurgical** *adj* —**electrosurgically** *adv*

electrotechnology /i léktrō tek nólləji/, **electrotechnics** /-tékniks/ *n* the technological application of electrical and electronic engineering —**electrotechnic** /i léktrō téknik/ *adj* —**electrotechnical** *adj*

electrotherapy /i léktrō thérrəpi/ *n* any form of medical treatment that uses electricity as a cure or relief, e.g. as a way of stimulating nerves and the muscles they are connected to —**electrotherapeutic** /i léktrō therə pyoótik/ *adj*

electrothermal /i léktrō thúrm'l/ *adj* relating to electricity and heat, especially to the production of heat by electricity ○ *electrothermal energy conversion*

electrotype /i léktrō tīp/ *n* **1** DUPLICATE PRINTING PLATE MADE BY ELECTROPLATING a duplicate of a block of type or engraving made by electroplating a wax, lead, or plastic mould of the original **2** PRINTED ITEM something printed from an electrotype ■ *vt* (**-types, -typing, -typed**) PRINT USING AN ELECTROTYPE to print something from an electrotype —**electrotyper** *n* —**electrotypic** /i léktrō típpik/ *adj*

electrovalency /i léktrō váylənss/, **electrovalence** (*plural* **-lencies** /-lənssi/) *n* the combining power of an element, measured by the number of electrons one atom of it acquires from or transfers to another atom during the formation of a chemical compound —**electrovalent** *adj*

electrovalent bond *n* a chemical bond that is created during the formation of a compound by transfer of one or more electrons from one atom to another, the resulting oppositely charged ions being held together by attraction

electroweak /i léktrō week/ *adj* describes a type of fundamental interaction uniting electromagnetic forces with the weak interaction

electrum /i léktrəm/ *n* a pale-coloured alloy of silver and gold used in jewellery and ornaments [14C. Via Latin, 'amber' < Greek *ēlektron*.]

electuary /i léktyoo əri/ (*plural* **-ies**) *n* a sweet-tasting paste made by mixing a drug with syrup or honey, administered by being applied to the teeth, tongue, or gums [14C. < late Latin *electuarium*, probably < Greek *eleikton* < *eleikhein* 'lick up'.]

eleemosynary /élli ee mόssinəri, -mózzinəri, éllee-/ *adj* (*formal*) **1** relating to charity **2** supported by or depending on charitable gifts [Late 16C. < medieval Latin *eleemosynarius* < *eleemosyna* 'alms' < Greek *eleos* 'mercy'.]

elegance /élligənss/ *n* **1** GRACE AND DIGNITY a combination of graceful stylishness, distinction, and good taste in appearance, behaviour, or movement **2** CONCISENESS a satisfying or admirable neatness, ingenious simplicity, or precision in something ○ *the elegance of the solution* **3** SOMETHING ELEGANT an elegant thing or quality [Early 16C. Via French *élégance* < Latin *elegantia* < *elegans* 'choice' (see ELEGANT).]

elegant /élligənt/ *adj* **1** STYLISH AND GRACEFUL stylishly graceful, and showing sophistication and good taste in appearance or behaviour **2** SHOWING SKILL AND GRACE executed or made with a combination of skill, ease, and grace ○ *an elegant forehand return* **3** CONCISE pleasingly and often ingeniously neat, simple, or concise ○ *an equation elegant in its simplicity* [15C. Via French *élégant* < Latin *elegans* 'choice' < *eligire* (see ELECT).] —**elegantly** *adv*

elegiac /élli jī́ ək/, **elegiacal** /-jī́ ək'l/ *adj* **1** expressing sorrow or regret (*formal or literary*) ○ *'The same elegiac and lonely tone continues to haunt the later poetry'.* (Northrop Frye, *The Bush Garden*; 1971) **2** resembling or characteristic of a poetic elegy in form or content [Late 16C. Via French or late Latin < Greek *elegeiakos* < *elegos* 'song'.] —**elegiacally** *adv*

elegiac couplet *n* a two-line unit of classical Greek and Latin poetry in which the first line comprises six dactylic feet and the second line five

elegiac stanza *n* a four-line unit of verse in which each line comprises five iambic feet and alternate lines rhyme

~~**elegible**~~ incorrect spelling of **eligible**

elegise *vti* = **elegize**

elegist /éllijist/ *n* a writer or speaker of an elegy

elegit /i léejit/ *n* a writ against a debtor's property that permits a creditor to keep it until the debt is paid [Early 16C. < medieval Latin, 'he or she has chosen' (occurring in the writ), form of Latin *eligire* (see ELECT).]

elegize /élli jīz/ (**-gizes, -gizing, -gized**), **elegise** (**-gises, -gising, -gised**) *v* **1** *vti* to write or speak about somebody or something in a mournful sorrowful way ○ *He elegized his lost comrade.* **2** *vi* to write, read, or recite an elegy

elegy /élliji/ (*plural* **-gies**) *n* **1** a mournful or reflective poem **2** a poem written in elegiac couplets or stanzas [Early 16C. Directly or via French *élégie* < Latin *elegia* < Greek *elegos* 'song'.]

LITERARY LINK ***Elegy Written in a Country Churchyard***, a poem (1750) by Thomas Gray. Inspired by a churchyard at Stoke Poges, Buckinghamshire, England, it is a reflection on rural life, human ambitions, friendship, and mortality.

element /éllimənt/ *n* **1** SEPARATE PART OR GROUP a separate identifiable part of something, or a distinct group within a larger group ○ *Landowners were the most stable element of society.* **2** LITTLE BIT a small amount of something ○ *There was an element of revenge in what she did.* **3** FACTOR a cause or factor leading to something ○ *Surprise was the key element in ensuring the success of the operation.* **4** BASIC UNIT OF MATTER any substance that cannot be broken down into a simpler one by a chemical reaction **5** SUPPOSED BASIC UNIT OF MATTER any of the four primary substances, earth, air, fire, and water, that were formerly thought to be the materials from which all matter is constructed **6** HABITAT a natural habitat or environment **7** HEATING PART OF APPLIANCE a part of an electric heater, cooker, or other appliance that heats up when an electric current is passed through it **8** CONSTITUENT OF GEOMETRICAL FIGURE a point, line, plane, or other part of which a geometrical figure is composed **9** COMPONENT OF ELECTRIC CIRCUIT any component of an electrical circuit **10** PART OF MATHEMATICAL QUANTITY a part of a given mathematical or geometric quantity, e.g. a number in an array or an angle in a triangle **11** MEMBER OF SET a member of a set **12** COMPONENT OF OPTICAL SYSTEM any lens or other component of an optical system **13** PARAMETER-DEFINING ORBIT any one of the parameters required to define the nature of an orbit and to determine the position of a planetary body within it **14** GRAMMATICAL UNIT a word, part of a word, or sequence of words that retains the same meaning in various contexts ■ **elements** *npl* **1** FORCES OF WEATHER the forces of the weather, e.g. wind, cold, rain, or sunshine, especially when thought of as harsh and damaging ○ *We're rather exposed to the elements up here on the hilltop.* **2** BASIC PRINCIPLES the basic and most important things to be learned when studying a subject ○ *She was endeavouring to teach us the elements of a good prose style.* **3** BREAD AND WINE IN CHRISTIAN CEREMONY the bread and wine used by Christians to celebrate the ceremony known as the Eucharist, Communion, or the Lord's Supper [14C. Via Old French < Latin *elementum* 'rudiment'.] ◇ **in your element** in the situation or environment to which you feel most suited or where you feel particularly happy

elemental /élli mént'l/ *adj* **1** FUNDAMENTAL basic and essential **2** RELATING TO NATURAL FORCES relating to or caused by powerful natural forces ○ *elemental passions* **3** reduced to, or reducing something to, a stark simplicity ○ *classic, elemental sculptures* **4** OF CHEMICAL OR ANCIENT ELEMENTS relating to the chemical elements, or to the elements of earth, air, fire, and water that were once supposed to be the basic units of matter

elementary /élli méntəri/ *adj* **1** RUDIMENTARY involving or encompassing only the most simple and basic facts or principles ○ *Anyone with an elementary knowledge of computing could have pointed that out to you.* **2** SIMPLE TO DO OR UNDERSTAND requiring little skill or knowledge **3** *US* OF AN ELEMENTARY SCHOOL relating to an elementary school or the education provided there —**elementarily** *adv* —**elementariness** *n*

elementary particle *n* any one of the basic constituents of which matter and energy are composed, e.g. electrons, leptons, photons, or hadrons, held to be indivisible

elementary school *n* **1** *US* in the United States, a school that provides the first four to eight years of basic education **2** formerly in the United Kingdom, a school of a type that was attended by children from the age of 5 until they left at 14

elemi /éllimi/ *n* a fragrant resin obtained from various tropical trees. Use: varnishes, inks, ointments, perfumes. [Mid-16C. Via modern Latin < Arabic *al-lāmī*.]

elenchus /i léngkəss/ (*plural* **-chi** /-kī/) *n* an argument that refutes a proposition by proving the opposite of its conclusions [Mid-17C. Via Latin < Greek *elegkhos* 'refutation'.] —**elenctic** *adj*

elephant /éllifənt/ (*plural* **-phants** *or* **-phant**) *n* **1** LARGE GREYISH ANIMAL WITH LONG TRUNK a very large grey or greyish-brown animal with a long flexible trunk, prominent ears, thick legs, and pointed tusks. Native to: Africa, South Asia. *Loxodonta africana* and *Loxodonta cyclotis* and *Elephas maximus*. **2** SOMETHING VERY LARGE somebody or something that is extremely large or much larger than average **3** LARGE SIZE OF SHEET OF PAPER a size of drawing or writing paper, 584 × 711 mm/23 × 28 in [13C. Via Old French < Latin *elephantus* < Greek *elephās* 'elephant, ivory'.]

Elephanta Island /élli fántə-/ island in Mumbai harbour, W India. Area: 5 sq. km/2 sq. mi.

elephant bird *n* BIRDS = **aepyornis**

elephant folio *n* a book size from 61 to 63.5 cm/24 to 25 in in height

elephant garlic *n* a mild-flavoured variety of garlic with very large bulbs, often roasted as a vegetable. *Allium ampeloprasum*.

elephant grass *n* tall coarse grass or a similar plant. Native to: tropical Africa, S Asia. Genera: *Typha* and *Pennisetum*.

elephant gun *n* a large-calibre gun, typically .410 or more, used in hunting big game.

elephantiasis /éllifən tī́ əssiss/ *n* **1** a chronic disease in which parasitic worms obstruct the lymphatic system, causing enlargement of parts of the body such as the legs and scrotum and hardening of the surrounding skin 2 excessive and unreasonable growth or development of something [Mid-16C. Via Latin, < Greek, *elephās* 'elephant'.]

elephantine /élli fán tīn/ *adj* **1 SLOW AND HEAVY** moving in a slow, heavy, and often clumsy or awkward way ○ *the heavy, elephantine tread of his feet* **2 ENORMOUS** very large or very great **3 LIKE AN ELEPHANT'S** resembling that of an elephant [Early 16C. Via Latin < Greek *elephantinos* < *elephās* 'elephant'.]

elephant seal *n* a large earless seal, the male of which has a long inflatable snout resembling an elephant's trunk. *Mirounga angustirostris* and *Mirounga leonina*.

elephant's ear *n* **1** = **taro 2** any bergenia with large showy leaves

elephant's foot (*plural* **elephant's foots**) *n* an ornamental climbing or trailing plant of the yam family with a large above-ground tuber that is sometimes used for food. Native to: South Africa. *Dioscorea elephantipes*.

Eleusinian mysteries /éllyoo sínni ən-/ *npl* an ancient Greek festival held annually at Eleusis and Athens that honoured and celebrated Persephone, Demeter, and Dionysus

elev. *abbr* elevation

elevate /élli vayt/ (**-vates, -vating, -vated**) *vt* **1 RAISE SOMETHING UP** to raise something to a higher level or position **2 RAISE SOMEBODY TO HIGHER RANK** to raise or promote somebody or something to a high or higher status, rank, or office **3 INCREASE** to increase the amount or intensity of something ○ *This was one factor that elevated interest rates.* **4 RAISE SOMEBODY'S MIND OR SPIRIT** to lift somebody's mind or spirit to a more enlightened or exalted level (*formal*) **5 MAKE GUN BARREL POINT HIGHER** to make the barrel of a field gun point at a higher angle **6 LIFT UP HOST OR CHALICE** to lift up the Host or the chalice in front of the congregation during a Mass [14C. < Latin *elevatus* < *levare* 'lighten'.]

elevated /élli vaytid/ *adj* **1 AT A HIGH LEVEL OR POSITION** raised above ground level or situated at a higher level than something else ○ *elevated track* **2 HIGH OR HIGHER IN RANK** high or higher in rank or status **3 INCREASED** increased in amount ○ *elevated levels of cholesterol* **4 AT A HIGH MORAL OR INTELLECTUAL LEVEL** set at a high moral or intellectual level ○ *Milton's elevated conception of the role of the poet*

elevated railway *n* a rail system operating on a raised structure, usually above or over a street

elevation /élli váysh'n/ *n* **1 HEIGHT ABOVE A LOCATION** the height above a specific reference point, especially sea level ○ *at an elevation of 1,000 metres above sea level* **2 RAISING SOMETHING, OR BEING RAISED** the act of raising somebody or something in height or status or the process of being raised in height or status ○ *They congratulated him on his elevation to the cardinalship.* **3 DEGREE OF BEING RAISED** the degree or amount by which somebody or something is raised or elevated ○ *a figure skater who is able to get tremendous elevation in her triple jumps* **4 INCREASE** an increase in something (*technical*) ○ *Among the effects was an elevation in the level of dopamine.* **5 ARCHITECTURAL DRAWING OF A SIDE OF BUILDING** a scale drawing of any side of a building or other structure ○ *the front elevation of the proposed new wing* **6 ANGLE IN SURVEYING** the angle between a horizontal line and the line from a surveying instrument to a point above the horizontal, e.g. between eye level and a line to a nearby rooftop **7 ANGLE OF A GUN BARREL ABOVE HORIZONTAL** the angle to which the barrel of a large gun is raised above the horizontal **8 RAISING OF THE HOST AND CHALICE** the raising up and showing to the people of the Host or chalice by a priest immediately after their consecration in a Mass **9** ASTRON = **altitude** *n.* 4 **10 ABILITY TO JUMP, OR THE HEIGHT REACHED** the ability of a ballet dancer to jump high and hold the position briefly, or the height a dancer can reach in jumping —**elevational** *adj*

elevator /élli vaytər/ *n* **1** *US, Can, ANZ* **PLATFORM FOR TAKING UP OR DOWN** a platform, cage, or enclosed compartment that is raised or lowered mechanically and used to take people or things to a higher or lower level in a building **2** *Can, US* **GRAIN STOREHOUSE** a storehouse for grain, equipped with a mechanism for taking in, lifting, and discharging the grain **3 HOISTING MACHINE** a machine with scoops or similar devices for hoisting something to a higher level **4 AIRCRAFT DEVICE CONTROLLING CLIMB AND DESCENT** a hinged flap, either of a pair on the rear portion of the horizontal stabilizing surface or tail plane of an aircraft, used to control the aircraft's up-and-down movement **5 AIRCRAFT PLATFORM ON CARRIER** on an aircraft carrier, a mechanized platform that transports aircraft from a below-the-deck hangar up to the flight deck and vice versa **6 MUSCLE THAT LIFTS PART OF THE BODY** a muscle that contracts to lift a part of the body

elevator music *n US* bland instrumental background music played over loudspeakers in lifts, shops, and other public places (*informal*)

eleven /i lévv'n/ *n* **1** see table at **number 2** a team of 11 players, e.g. a football team, a hockey team, or a cricket team [Old English *endleofan* 'one over (ten)' < Germanic] —**eleven** *adj, pron*

eleven-plus *n* an examination formerly taken by all children in the United Kingdom in their last year of primary school, used to determine what sort of secondary education they would receive

elevenses /i lévv'nziz/ *n* a mid-morning snack (+ *singular or plural verb*)

eleventh /i lévv'nth/ *n* see table at **number** —**eleventh** *adj, adv*

eleventh hour *n* the last moment before something happens ○ *'Time after time you'll find solutions are reached at the 59th minute of the eleventh hour'.* (John Major, *Guardian Weekly*; 3 April, 1994) —**eleventh-hour** *adj*

elevon /élli von/ *n* a hinged flap on an aircraft, especially one with a delta wing or no tail, that functions both as an elevator and an aileron [Mid-20C. Blend of ELEVATOR + AILERON.]

elf /elf/ (*plural* **elves** /elvz/) *n* **1** in folklore, a small lively creature resembling a human being, often considered to have a mischievous nature and magical powers **2** any small person, especially a child, who plays pranks or tricks [Old English < Germanic]

ELF *abbr* extremely low frequency

elfin /élfin/ *adj* **1 OF OR LIKE AN ELF** like, characteristic of, or associated with elves **2 BY ELVES** caused or made by elves **3 DELICATE** small and delicate ○ *elfin features* **4 SMALL AND LIVELY** small, delicate, and charmingly sprightly, lively, or mischievous **5 MAGICAL OR CHARMING** having a magical or delicately charming quality

elfish /élfish/, **elvish** /élvish/, **elflike** /élf līk/ *adj* **1** like or relating to an elf **2** full of lively mischief —**elfishly** *adv*

elflock /élf lok/ *n* a tangled coil of hair (*often plural*)

Elgar /él gaar/, **Sir Edward** (1857–1934) British composer

Elgin /élgin/ city in NE Scotland. Population: 19,027 (1991).

Elgin Marbles *npl* Greek sculptures from the Parthenon in Athens, brought to Britain in 1806 by Thomas Bruce, seventh earl of Elgin, and now in the British Museum in London

Elia /éeli ə/ pseudonym of **Lamb, Charles**

elicit /i líssit/ *vt* **1** to cause or produce something as a reaction or response to a stimulus of some kind ○ *His jokes failed to elicit even the faintest of smiles from her.* **2** to bring to light, or cause somebody to disclose, something hidden or not immediately obvious, especially by a process of questioning or research ○ *What were their chances of eliciting any worthwhile information from such an obstinately uncooperative witness?* [Mid-17C. < Latin *elicitus* 'drawn out' < *lacere* 'deceive'.] —**elicitation** /i líssi táysh'n/ *n* —**elicitor** *n*

SPELLCHECK Do not confuse ***elicit*** with ***illicit***, which has a similar sound. Beware: your spellchecker will not catch this error.

elide /i līd/ (**elides, eliding, elided**) *vt* **1** to omit a vowel, consonant, or syllable of a word, or leave out part of a sentence or phrase **2** to omit, delete, or ignore something (*formal*) [Late 16C. < Latin *elidere* 'strike out' < *laedere* 'strike'.]

eligible /éllijəb'l/ *adj* **1 QUALIFIED** entitled or qualified to do, be, or get something ○ *She is eligible to run for office.* **2 MARRIAGEABLE** considered a good candidate for marriage ○ *the most eligible bachelor in town* **3** *US* **ALLOWED BY RULES TO CATCH FOOTBALL** permitted by the rules to catch a forward pass during a play in American football ■ *n* **SOMEBODY OR SOMETHING ELIGIBLE** a person or thing that meets a set of requirements ○ *We've separated the eligibles from the nonstarters.* [15C. Via French *éligible* 'fit to be chosen' < late Latin *eligibilis* 'that may be chosen' < Latin *eligere* (see ELECT).] —**eligibility** /éllijə bíllәti/ *n* —**eligibly** *adv*

eliminate /i límmi nayt/ (**-nates, -nating, -nated**) *vt* **1 TAKE SOMEBODY OR SOMETHING AWAY** to remove something or somebody from a list or group, or decide to disregard somebody or something as irrelevant or unimportant ○ *The police eliminated him from the list of suspects.* **2 END** to put an end to something, usually something undesirable ○ *They are pledged to eliminate poverty by the end of the century.* **3 PUT SOMEBODY OUT OF A COMPETITION** to defeat and put a player or team out of a competition ○ *The local team was eliminated in the first round.* **4 DESTROY** to kill somebody, destroy something, or make somebody or something ineffective ○ *The pills eliminated the dog's worms.* **5 DEFECATE OR URINATE** to expel waste from the body (*technical*) **6 REMOVE A MATHEMATICAL VARIABLE** to remove variables from two or more simultaneous mathematical equations by combining the equations [Mid-16C. < Latin *eliminare* 'turn out of doors' < *limen* 'threshhold'.] —**elimination** /i límmi náysh'n/ *n* —**eliminative** *adj* —**eliminatory** *adj*

eliminator /i límmi naytər/ *n* a round in a competition or a question in a quiz, after which competitors who are defeated are removed

ELINT /éllint/, **elint** *n* the gathering of information by electronic means, e.g. from aircraft or ships, or the section of the military intelligence service involved in this [Mid-20C. < shortenings of ELECTRONIC + INTELLIGENCE.]

George Eliot

Eliot /élli ət/, **George** (1819–80) British novelist, pseudonym of **Mary Ann Evans**

Eliot, Sir John (1592–1632) English politician

Eliot, T. S. (1888–1965) US-born British poet, critic, and dramatist. Full name **Thomas Stearns Eliot**

ELISA /i līzə/ *n* a widely used technique for determining the presence or amount of protein in a biological sample, using an enzyme that bonds to an antibody or antigen and causes a colour change. Full form **enzyme-linked immunosorbent assay**

elision /i lízh'n/ *n* **1** the omission of a vowel, consonant, or syllable while pronouncing or writing something **2** the suppression, omission, or deletion of something, or what has been suppressed, omitted, or deleted (*formal*) [Late 16C. < Latin *elision-* < *elidere* 'strike out' (see ELIDE).]

elite /i léet, ay-/ *n* **1 PRIVILEGED MINORITY** a small group of people within a larger group who have more power, social standing, wealth, or talent than the rest of the group (+ *singular or plural verb*) **2 SIZE OF PRINTING TYPE** a 10-point type that has about 12 characters to the inch or just under 5 characters to the centimetre ■ *adj* **1 RICHEST, BEST, OR MOST POWERFUL** belonging to an elite, especially in being more talented, privileged, or highly trained than the rest ○ *elite troops* **2 FOR RICH OR PRIVILEGED PEOPLE** with a membership that is restricted, especially to the rich or privileged [Late 18C. < French, < Latin *eligere* 'pick out' (see ELECT).]

elitism /i léetizəm, ay-/ *n* **1 BELIEF IN CONCEPT OF SUPERIORITY** the belief that some people or things are inherently superior to others and deserve preeminence, preferential treatment, or higher rewards because of their superiority **2 BELIEF IN CONTROL BY SMALL GROUP** the belief that government or control should be in the hands of a small group of privileged, wealthy, or intelligent people, or the active promotion of such a system **3 CONTROL BY SMALL GROUP** government or control by a small, specially qualified or privileged group —**elitist** *n, adj*

elixir /i líksər/ *n* **1 SWEETENED DRUG** a sweetened solution of a drug in alcohol and water **2 elixir, elixir of life MIRACULOUS SUBSTANCE** a substance once believed to prolong life indefinitely, or to transform base metals into gold **3 CURE-ALL** a panacea or a quick or magical cure [14C. Via medieval Latin < Arabic *al-iksir* < Greek *xērion* 'dry powder for treating wounds' < *xēros* 'dry'.]

Elizabeth /i lízzəbath/, **queen consort of the United Kingdom** (b. 1900) mother of Queen Elizabeth II. Born **Lady Elizabeth Bowes-Lyon**

Elizabeth I (1533–1603) queen of England and Ireland (1558–1603)

Elizabeth II (b. 1926) queen of the United Kingdom (1952–)

Elizabethan /i lízza beéth'n/ adj 1 relating to or characteristic of the life and times of Elizabeth I, queen of England and Ireland, who reigned from 1558 to 1603 2 suggesting or embodying a style of English Renaissance building from the reign of Elizabeth I that emphasized symmetrical layouts and moulded or sculptured decoration with a German or Flemish influence

Elizabethan sonnet n LITERAT = **Shakespearean sonnet**

Elizabethville /i lízzəbath vil/ former name for **Lubumbashi**

elk /elk/ (plural **elk** or **elks**) n 1 a large thin-legged heavy-bodied deer with a long head and a bulbous pliable muzzle, the male of which has huge antlers. Native to: N Europe, Asia, North America. *Alces alces*. US term **moose 2** US = **wapiti** [Old English *eolh*]

Elk n a member of a North American men's social and charitable organization, the Benevolent and Protective Order of Elks

elkhound /élk hownd/ n a medium-sized sturdy dog belonging to a breed developed in Norway to hunt elk and other game. It has pointed ears, a broad head, and a thick grey coat. US term **Norwegian elkhound**

ell[1] /el/ n 1 an extension of a building, usually at right angles to the main part 2 something L-shaped or with a right-angled bend [Late 18C. Spelling of the letter *L*.]

ell[2] /el/ n an obsolete English unit of length equal to about 1.14 m/45 in, used mainly for measuring cloth [Old English *eln* 'length of the forearm' < Indo-European, 'to bend']

Ella /éllə/, **Mark Gordon** (b. 1959) Australian rugby player

ellagic acid /i lájjik-/ n $C_{14}H_6O_8$ a yellow crystalline compound. Source: oak galls, tannins. Use: reduction of bleeding.

Ellef Ringnes Island /éllef ríng ness-/ uninhabited island of the Canadian Sverdrup Island group, in the Arctic Ocean. Area: 13,310 sq. km/5,139 sq. mi.

Ellesmere Island /élzmeer/ uninhabited island in Nunavut Territory, Canada, in the Arctic Ocean near NW Greenland. Area: 212,690 sq. km/82,120 sq. mi.

Ellesmere Island National Park Reserve former name for **Quttinirpaaq National Park**

Ellesmere Port /élz meer-/ town in NW England. Population: 64,504 (1991).

Ellice Islands /éllis-/ former name for **Tuvalu** (until 1975)

Barnaby's

Duke Ellington

Ellington /éllingtən/, **Duke** (1899–1974) US jazz pianist, composer, and band leader. Born **Edward Kennedy Ellington**

Elliott /élli ət/, **Herb** (b. 1938) Australian athlete. Full name **Herbert James Elliott**

ellipse /i líps/ n 1 a shape like a stretched circle with slightly longer flatter sides 2 the shape formed by the intersection of a right cone and an oblique plane that does not intersect the base of the cone [Mid-18C. Via French < Latin *ellipsis* < Greek *elleipsis* 'defect, omission' < *elleipein* 'leave out, fall short'.]

ellipsis /i lípsis/ (plural **-ses** /-seez/) n 1 the omission of one or more words from a sentence, especially when what is omitted can be understood from the context 2 a printed mark, usually three dots (...) or, less often, asterisks (***), used to indicate that something has been omitted from a text [Early 17C. < Latin (see ELLIPSE).]

PUNCTUATION The *ellipsis* in the form of three dots is used when text is omitted from the beginning, middle, or end of a quotation: *Shakespeare wrote, 'When sorrows come, they come...in battalions'*. (The full quotation is *When sorrows come, they come not single spies,/But in battalions*). Any punctuation that precedes or follows the omitted text may or may not be shown before or after the ellipsis: *You can fool all the people some of the time...but you cannot fool all the people all of the time.* When the ellipsis comes at the end of a sentence, it is usually followed by a full stop. Dots are also used in direct speech to show that the speaker is hesitating or has left something unsaid: *'I don't know... I'll try...I can't promise anything'.* In some styles of writing, asterisks are used when part of a word is omitted, usually part of a swearword.

ellipsoid /i líp soyd/ n a geometric surface or a solid figure shaped like a rugby ball ■ adj in the shape of an ellipsoid —**ellipsoidal** /íllip sóyd'l, éllip-/ adj

elliptical /i líptik'l/, **elliptic** /i líptik/ adj 1 LIKE ELLIPSE in the shape or pattern of a geometrical ellipse 2 RELATING TO ELLIPSIS relating to ellipsis or containing an example of ellipsis 3 HIGHLY ECONOMICAL IN SPEECH OR WRITING extremely concise in speech or writing, sometimes so concise as to be difficult or impossible to understand —**elliptically** adv

elliptical galaxy n a galaxy with an overall elliptical or spherical shape and no arms or internal structure

ellipticity /íllip tíssati, éllip-/ (plural **-ties**) n the deviation or degree of deviation of an ellipse or ellipsoid from a perfect circle or sphere

Ellis /élliss/, **Havelock** (1859–1939) British psychologist

Ellis Island /élliss-/ island in upper New York Bay near Manhattan. From 1892 to 1954 it served as a chief entry point for immigrants to the United States. Area: 0.11 sq. km/0.04 sq. mi.

Ellsworth Land /élz wurth-/ plateau in W Antarctica. Highest peak: Vinson Massif 5,140 m/16,863 ft.

elm /elm/ n 1 a deciduous tree with serrated leaves and winged fruits. Native to: Northern temperate regions. Genus: *Ulmus*. 2 the hard dense wood of the elm tree. Use: fuel, furniture, boats, construction. [Old English < Indo-European]

El-Mahallah el-Kubra /el mə haàlə al kō braá/ city in N Egypt, in the Nile delta. Population: 408,000 (1992).

elm bark beetle n the beetle that spreads the fungus causing Dutch elm disease. Family: Scolytidae.

El Niño /el neènyō/ n a periodic change occurring every 5 to 8 years in Pacific Ocean currents off South America, often bringing severe climate disruption to countries in and beside the Pacific [< Spanish, shortening of *El Niño de Navidad* 'the Christmas Child'; from the time of year when the currents change]

elocution /élla kyoòsh'n/ n the art of speaking clearly and well, with correct enunciation [15C. < Latin *elocution-* < *eloqui* (see ELOQUENT).] —**elocutionary** adj —**elocutionist** n

elodea /ə lōdi ə/ n a plant that grows submerged in ponds and ditches. Use: oxygenating aquariums. Genus: *Elodea*. [Late 19C. < modern Latin, < Greek *helōdēs* 'marshy'.]

Elohim /e lō him, éllō heèm/ n in the Bible, a Hebrew word for God [Late 16C. < Hebrew *elōhīm*, plural of *elōah* 'God'.]

elongate /eè long gayt/ vti (**-gates, -gating, -gated**) LENGTHEN to make something longer, or become longer ■ adj 1 LONG long and narrow or slender (*technical*) 2 MADE LONGER lengthened or stretched out (*formal*) [Mid-16C. < late Latin *elongat-*, past participle of *elongare* 'length-en' < Latin *longus* 'long'.] —**elongated** adj

elongation /eè long gáysh'n/ n 1 LENGTHENING the act of lengthening something, or the condition of being lengthened 2 SOMETHING LENGTHENED something that has become or been made longer 3 ANGLE BETWEEN SUN AND CELESTIAL OBJECT the angle between the Sun and either the Moon or a planet, as seen from Earth or a point in space

elope /i lōp/ (**elopes, eloping, eloped**) vi to go away suddenly without telling anyone, especially in order to get married without the knowledge or consent of parents or guardians, 'or to live with a lover [Late 16C. < Anglo-Norman *aloper* 'run away'.] —**elopement** n —**eloper** n

eloquence /éllakwanss/ n 1 the ability to speak forcefully, expressively, and persuasively 2 forceful, expressive, and persuasive language

eloquent /éllakwant/ adj 1 said or saying something in a forceful, expressive, and persuasive way 2 expressing a feeling or thought clearly, memorably, or movingly [14C. Via French < Latin *eloquent-*, present participle of *eloqui* 'speak out' < *loqui* 'speak'.] —**eloquently** adv —**eloquentness** n

El Paso city in W Texas on the Rio Grande. Population: 579,307 (1994).

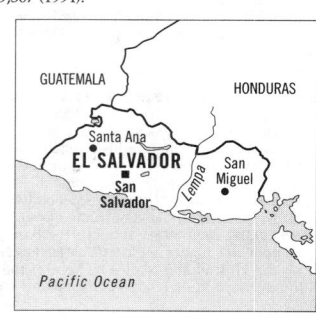

El Salvador

El Salvador /el sálva dawr/ republic on the Pacific coast of Central America. Capital: San Salvador. Population: 5,661,827 (1997). Area: 21,041 sq. km/8,124 sq. mi. —**Salvadoran** /sálva dáwran/ adj, n

else /elss/ adj, adv 1 used to refer in a vague way to another person, place, or thing ○ (adj) *Something else I'd like to see is more jobs for skilled workers.* ○ (adj) *What else did she say?* ○ (adv) *I didn't go anywhere else.* 2 used to refer in a vague way to somebody or something other or different ○ (adj) *Let's try something else.* ○ (adv) *He was unhappy and considered working somewhere else.* [Old English *elles* < Indo-European] ◇ **or else 1** otherwise ○ *Go away, or else I'll call the police.* 2 used to make a threat ○ *Have it ready by tomorrow or else!*

USAGE The word *else* should not be combined with *besides*, *but*, *except*, and other prepositions of this type. Do not write: *No one else except the guard saw the intruder.* Write: *No one but the guard saw the intruder.* When *else* follows an indefinite pronoun such as *anyone*, *nobody*, and *someone* in a possessive construction, attach an apostrophe + *s* to *else*, not to the preceding indefinite pronoun: *We will not accept anyone else's offer.* *Else* works possessively with the pronouns *who* and *whose* as follows: *Who else's mistakes could these be?* and *Whose else are these boots but yours?*

elsewhere /élss wáir/ adv at, in, or to another place ○ *If you're calling from elsewhere, please press 2 to contact reception.* ○ *They stock books that may be hard to find elsewhere.*

ELT n the teaching of English to non-native speakers of English. Full form **English Language Teaching**

eluant n = eluent

Éluard /élloo aar/, **Paul** (1895–1952) French poet. Pseudonym of **Eugène Grindel**

eluate /éllyoo ayt/ n the liquid left after the process of elution, consisting of dissolved matter and the solvent used [Mid-20C. < Latin *eluere* (see ELUTE).]

elucidate /i loòssi dayt/ (**-dates, -dating, -dated**) vti to explain or clarify something [Mid-16C. < late Latin *elucidat-*, past participle of *elucidare* 'make clear' < Latin *lucidus* 'clear'.] —**elucidation** /i loòssi dáysh'n/ n —**elucidative** adj —**elucidator** n —**elucidatory** adj

elude /i loòd/ (**eludes, eluding, eluded**) vt 1 to escape from or avoid somebody or something by cunning, skill, or resourcefulness 2 to be beyond somebody's understanding or be unable to be recalled [Mid-16C. <

Latin *eludere* 'deceive, escape from, win from somebody at play' < *ludere* 'play'.]

SPELLCHECK See ***allude***.

USAGE See ***avoid***.

eluent /éllyoo ənt/, **eluant** *n* a solvent used to remove something from a substance [Mid-20C. < Latin *eluent-*, present participle of *eluere* (see ELUTE).]

Elul /e loól/ *n* in the Jewish calendar, the 12th month of the civil year and the 6th month of the religious year [Mid-16C. < Hebrew *elūl*.]

elusive /i loóssiv/ *adj* **1 HARD TO FIND** difficult to find or catch **2 HARD TO PIN DOWN** difficult to understand, define, or identify **3 HARD TO REMEMBER** not easily called to mind or memory —**elusively** *adv* —**elusiveness** *n*

SPELLCHECK Do not confuse ***elusive*** with ***illusive***, which has a similar sound. Beware: your spellchecker will not catch this error.

elusory /i loóssəri/ *adj* **1 HARD TO FIND** difficult to find or catch (*formal*) **2 EVASIVE** avoiding the issue in an evasive or deceitful way **3 HARD TO GRASP** not easy to understand

elute /i loót/ (**elutes, eluting, eluted**) *vt* to remove one substance from another, usually an adsorbed material from an adsorbent surface, by washing it out with a solvent (*technical*) [Mid-18C. < Latin *elut-*, past participle of *eluere* 'wash out' < *luere* 'wash'.] —**elution** *n*

elutriate /i loótri ayt/ (**-ates, -ating, -ated**) *vt* to purify or separate something from a mixture by washing, decanting, or straining it (*technical*) [Mid-18C. < Latin *elutriat-*, past participle of *elutriare* 'wash out' < *lutriare* 'wash'.] —**elutriation** /i loótri áysh'n/ *n*

eluvia plural of **eluvium**

eluvial deposit *n* a concentration of an ore deposit formed as a result of the removal of less dense host material

eluviation /i loóvi áysh'n/ *n* a process by which material dissolved or suspended in water within soil moves down or sideways as rainwater moves through the soil

eluvium /i loóvi əm/ (*plural* **-a** /-ə/) *n* an accumulated mass of soil, sand, silt, or rock debris resulting from weathering or drifting [Late 19C. < Latin *eluere* (see ELUTE) after ALLUVIUM.] —**eluvial** *adj*

elver /élvər/ *n* a young freshwater eel, especially one that migrates from salt water [Mid-17C. < English dialect *ellfare*, literally 'eel-journey'.]

elves plural of **elf**

elvish *adj* = **elfish**

Ely /eéli/ city in east-central England, noted for its cathedral. Population: 11,760 (1994).

Elysian /i lízzi ən/ *adj* **1** relating to or typical of Elysium **2** full of or giving great pleasure and delight (*literary*) [Mid-16C. < ELYSIUM[1].]

Elysian Fields *npl* = **Elysium**[1] *n.* 1

Elysium[1] /i lízzi əm/ *n* **1** in Greek mythology, the home of the blessed after death **2** any ideally delightful or blissful place or condition

Elysium[2] /i lízzi əm/ extensive low bulge on the surface of Mars in the northern hemisphere. Highest peak: 5 km/3 mi.

elytron /élli tron/ (*plural* **-tra** /-trə/), **elytrum** /-trəm/ (*plural* **-tra**) *n* a tough front wing, occurring in pairs on beetles and some other insects, that acts as a protective covering for the rear wings [Mid-18C. < Greek *elutron* 'sheath'.]

em /em/ *n* **1** a unit of measurement of print size, equal to the point size of the typeface being used **2** = **pica**[1] *n.* 1

'em /əm/ *contr* them (*informal*) [14C. Originally variant of Old English *hem* 'them'; now regarded as shortening.]

EM *abbr* **1** electromagnetic **2** electron microscope

E.M. *abbr* Engineer of Mines

em- *prefix* = **en-** (*before m, b, or p*)

emaciate /i máyssi ayt/ (**-ates, -ating, -ated**) *vti* to become, or make somebody or something become, extremely thin [Early 17C. < Latin *emaciat-*, past participle of *emaciare* 'make lean, waste away' < *macer* 'lean'.] —**emaciation** /i máyssi áysh'n/ *n*

emaciated /i máyssi aytid/ *adj* extremely thin, especially because of starvation or illness

SYNONYMS See ***thin***.

e-mail /eé mayl/, **email** *n* **1 COMPUTER-TO-COMPUTER COMMUNICATION SYSTEM** a system for transmitting messages and data from one computer to another, using a telephone connection and modems. Full form **electronic mail 2 E-MAIL MESSAGE** a communication sent by e-mail ■ *vt* **COMMUNICATE SOMETHING BY E-MAIL** to send a message to somebody by e-mail

emalangeni plural of **lilangeni**

emanate /émmə nayt/ (**-nates, -nating, -nated**) *v* **1** *vi* to come from or come out of somebody, something, or somewhere **2** *vt* to emit, send out, or give out something such as rays or information (*formal*) [Mid-18C. < Latin *emanat-*, past participle of *emanare* 'flow out, arise' < *manare* 'flow'.] —**emanative** *adj*

emanation /émmə náysh'n/ *n* **1 ACT OF SENDING OUT** the act of emitting, sending out, or giving out something **2 SOMETHING SENT OUT** something that issues or is sent out or given out from somebody or something **3 RADIOACTIVE GAS** any gas produced by radioactive decay, e.g. radon —**emanational** *adj*

emancipate /i mánssi payt/ (**-pates, -pating, -pated**) *vt* **1** to free somebody from slavery, serfdom, or bondage **2** to free somebody from restrictions or conventions (*often passive*) [Early 17C. < Latin *emancipat-*, past participle of *emancipare* 'free from parental power' < *mancipium* 'ownership'.] —**emancipation** /i mánssi páysh'n/ *n* —**emancipative** *adj* —**emancipator** *n* —**emancipatory** *adj*

EMAS /eé mass/ *n* a voluntary scheme of the European Union in which commercial and other organizations are encouraged to assess their approach to environmental matters against a given set of criteria. Full form **Eco-Management and Audit Scheme**

emasculate /i máskyoo layt/ (**-lates, -lating, -lated**) *vt* **1 CASTRATE** to remove the testicles of a male human being or animal (*formal or literary*) **2 WEAKEN** to deprive somebody or something of effectiveness, spirit, or force (*formal; sometimes offensive*) **3 REMOVE STAMENS FROM** to remove the male reproductive organs (**stamens**) from a flower, e.g. to prevent self-pollination [Early 17C. < Latin *emasculat-*, past participle of *emasculare* 'remove the male glands of, castrate' < *masculus* 'male'.] —**emasculation** /i máskyoo láysh'n/ *n* —**emasculative** *adj* —**emasculator** *n* —**emasculatory** *adj*

embalm /im baám/ *vt* **1 PRESERVE DEAD BODY** to treat a dead body with a preservative substance in order to stop it decaying **2 KEEP SOMETHING INTACT** to preserve something from change or oblivion (*formal*) **3 PERFUME** to give a sweet scent to something (*literary*) [14C. < French *embaumer* < *baume* 'balm'.] —**embalmer** *n* —**embalmment** /im baám mənt, em-/ *n*

embank /im bángk/ *vt* to surround or line a road, canal, or other area with an embankment

embankment /im bángkmənt/ *n* a ridge or raised platform built of earth or stone to confine a waterway or support a road or railway line

~~embarass~~ incorrect spelling of **embarrass**

embargo /em baárgō/ *n* (*plural* **-goes**) **1 ORDER STOPPING TRADE** a government restriction or restraint on commerce, especially an order that prohibits trade in a given commodity or with a particular nation **2 PROHIBITION** any official restraint or prohibition **3 ORDER HALTING MOVEMENT OF SHIPS** a government order that prohibits commercial ships from entering or leaving its ports, often as a measure during war ■ *vt* (**-goes, -going, -goed**) **1 PROHIBIT OR FORBID** to place an embargo on something **2 SEIZE** to confiscate or seize something for government use [Late 16C. < Spanish, < *embargar* 'restrain, seize'.]

embark /em baárk/ *vti* to go on board, or put or take somebody or something on board a ship or aircraft [Mid-16C. < French *embarquer* < *barque* 'ship'.] —**embarkation** /ém baar káysh'n/ *n* —**embarkment** *n*

embark on, embark upon *vti* to start or engage in an undertaking

~~embarras~~ incorrect spelling of **embarrass**

embarras de richesses /ómba raá də ree shéss/ *n* an overabundance of desirable things that makes choice among them difficult [< French, 'embarrassment of wealth']

embarrass /im bárrəss, em-/ *v* **1** *vti* to become or cause somebody to become painfully self-conscious, ashamed, humiliated, or ill at ease **2** *vt* to hinder or impede somebody or something (*archaic; often passive*) [Late 17C. Via French *embarrasser* 'impede, disconcert' < Portuguese *embaraçar* < *baraço* 'halter'.] —**embarrassable** *adj*

embarrassed /im bárrəst, em-/ *adj* **1** painfully self-conscious, ill at ease, ashamed, or humiliated **2** in financial difficulties because of a lack of money —**embarrassedly** *adv*

embarrassing /im bárrəssing, em-/ *adj* causing painful self-consciousness, uncomfortableness, shame, or humiliation —**embarrassingly** *adv*

embarrassment /im bárrəssmənt/ *n* **1 ACUTE SELF-CONSCIOUSNESS** a feeling of painful self-consciousness, uncomfortableness, shame, or humiliation **2 SOMETHING THAT CAUSES SELF-CONSCIOUSNESS** something that causes a feeling of painful self-consciousness, uncomfortableness, shame, or humiliation **3 LACK OF MONEY** a state of financial difficulty

embassy /émbəssi/ (*plural* **-sies**) *n* **1 AMBASSADOR'S HEADQUARTERS** the residence and place of business of an ambassador **2 EMBASSY STAFF** an ambassador with his or her ambassadorial staff **3 AMBASSADOR'S POSITION AND RESPONSIBILITIES** the mission, rank, or function of an ambassador [Late 16C. Via Old French *ambassé* < assumed Vulgar Latin *ambactiare* 'go on a mission'.]

embattle /im bátt'l/ (**-tles, -tling, -tled**) *vt* **1** to arrange forces in readiness for battle **2** to fortify something such as a building, village, or position in battle (*archaic; usually passive*) [14C. < Old French *embataillier* < *bataille* 'battle'.]

embattled /im bátt'ld/ *adj* **1 UNDER ASSAULT** under attack or subject to controversy **2 FIGHTING OR READY TO FIGHT** ready for or engaged in battle **3 WITH BATTLEMENTS** with battlements provided (*archaic*) **4 LIKE BATTLEMENTS** in heraldry, used to describe a design with an edge resembling battlements

embayment /im báymənt/ *n* **1** a bay in a coastline (*technical*) **2** the process by which a bay is formed in a coastline

Embden-Myerhof pathway /émdən mí ərhof-/ *n* BIOCHEM = **glycolysis**

embed /im béd/ (**-beds, -bedding, -bedded**), **imbed** (**-beds, -bedding, -bedded**) *v* **1** *vti* **PLACE OR BE PLACED SOLIDLY** to fix something or become fixed in a surrounding mass **2** *vt* **SURROUND** to surround or cover something closely (*usually passive*) **3** *vt* **FIX SOMETHING IN MIND** to fix something deeply in the mind or memory (*often passive*) **4** *vi* **BECOME LODGED** to become deeply and solidly lodged in something

embellish /im béllish/ *vt* **1 BEAUTIFY** to increase the beauty of something by adding ornaments or decorations **2 ADD FICTITIOUS OR EXAGGERATED DETAILS TO** to make an account or description more interesting by inventing or exaggerating details **3 ADD TO MELODY** to add extra notes, accents, or trills to a melody to make it more beautiful or interesting [14C. < Old French *embelliss-*, stem of *embellir* 'make beautiful' < *bel* 'beautiful' < Latin *bellus*.] —**embellishment** *n*

ember /émbər/ *n* **BURNING FRAGMENT** a small piece of glowing or smouldering material from a dying fire ■ **embers** *npl* **1 REMAINS OF FIRE** the glowing or smouldering remains of a dying fire **2 REMAINS OF PASSION** the dying but not yet extinguished remains of a great emotion, especially love (*literary*) [Old English *myrge* < Indo-European, 'burn']

Ember Days *npl* days of prayer and fasting in Roman Catholic and Anglican Churches, comprising the Wednesday, Friday, and Saturday following Pentecost, the first Sunday after Lent, 14 September, and 13 December [< Old English *ymbryne* 'circuit' < *ryne* 'course, running'; because they 'come round' four times a year]

embezzle /im bézz'l/ (**-zles, -zling, -zled**) *vti* to take for personal use money or property that has been given on trust by others, without their knowledge or permission [15C. < Anglo-Norman *embesiler* 'steal' < Old French *besillier* 'gouge, destroy'.] —**embezzlement** *n* —**embezzler** *n*

SYNONYMS See ***steal***.

embitter /im bíttər/ *vt* **1** to make somebody feel bitter or aggrieved **2** to make something more bitter or acrimonious —**embittered** *adj* —**embitterment** *n*

emblazon /im bláyz'n/ *vt* **1 DECORATE FLAG OR SHIELD** in heraldry, to decorate or adorn a shield or flag by depicting something, especially a coat of arms **2 ADD DESIGN TO** to decorate or adorn something such as clothing with bright colours or a symbol or picture 3 **MAKE SOMEBODY OR SOMETHING FAMOUS** to celebrate somebody or something or make somebody or something famous (*literary; often passive*) —**emblazoner** *n* —**emblazonment** *n*

emblazonry /im bláyz'nri/ (*plural* **-ries**) *n* 1 the act or process of putting heraldic decorations on something such as a shield or flag 2 heraldic decorations on such things as shields and flags

emblem /émbləm/ *n* 1 **SYMBOL** something that visually symbolizes an object, idea, group, or quality 2 **BADGE** a badge or sign that represents a person, group, or organization 3 **ALLEGORICAL IMAGE** an allegorical picture, often with a motto, used to illustrate a moral lesson [15C. Via Latin, 'inlaid design' < Greek *emblēma* 'insertion' < *emballein* 'insert' < *ballein* 'throw'.]

emblematic /émblə máttik/, **emblematical** /-máttik'l/ *adj* relating to, consisting of, or acting as an emblem or symbol —**emblematically** *adv*

emblematize /em blémmə tīz/ (**-tizes, -tizing, -tized**), **emblematise** (**-tises, -tising, -tised**) *vt* to serve as a symbol of something (*formal*)

embodiment /im bóddimənt/ *n* 1 a tangible or visible expression of an idea or quality 2 the act or process by which something is made tangible or visible

embody /im bóddi/ (**-ies, -ying, -ied**) *vt* 1 **MAKE SOMETHING TANGIBLE** to give a tangible or visible form to something abstract 2 **PERSONIFY** to express or exemplify something abstract in bodily form 3 **INCORPORATE THINGS INTO ORGANIZED WHOLE** to gather and organize a number of things into a whole

embolden /im bṓld'n/ *vt* to give somebody courage or boldness

embolectomy /émbə léktəmi/ (*plural* **-mies**) *n* the surgical removal of an embolus, usually a blood clot or other obstruction in a blood vessel

emboli plural of **embolus**

embolic /em bóllik/ *adj* relating to or caused by an embolus or embolism

embolisation *n* = **embolization**

embolism /émbəlizəm/ *n* 1 **BLOCKAGE OF ARTERY** a condition in which an artery is blocked by an embolus, usually a blood clot formed at one place in the circulation and then lodging in another 2 **EMBOLUS** an embolus (*informal*) 3 **INSERTION OF DAY OR DAYS** the insertion of a day or days into a calendar 4 **PRAYER DURING ROMAN CATHOLIC MASS** in the Roman Catholic Church, a prayer for deliverance from evil inserted in a Mass after the Lord's Prayer [14C. Via late Latin < Greek *embolismos* < *emballein* 'insert' (see EMBLEM).]

embolization /émbə lī záysh'n/, **embolisation** *n* the process or condition in which a blood vessel is blocked by a blood clot or other obstruction (**embolus**)

embolus /émbələss/ (*plural* **-li** /-lī/) *n* an abnormal mass, most commonly a blood clot, that becomes lodged in a blood vessel and obstructs it [Mid-17C. Via Latin < Greek *embolos* 'peg, stopper, wedge' < *emballein* 'insert' (see EMBLEM).]

embonpoint /om boN pwaaN/ *n* a body weight that is above average and causes an impression of roundness (*humorous*) ○ *'She was slightly inclined to embonpoint'.* (J. M. Barrie, *Peter Pan*; 1904) ■ *adj* having a body weight that is above average and causes the impression of roundness (*humorous dated; sometimes offensive*) [Late 17C. < French *en bon point* 'in good condition'.]

embosom /im bóozəm/ *vt* (*archaic*) 1 to surround or envelop somebody or something, especially in a protective way 2 to take somebody into your arms and hold him or her to your bosom

emboss /im bóss/ *vt* 1 to decorate or mark a surface with a slightly raised design or lettering 2 to make something as a raised pattern on a surface ○ *The title was embossed in gold lettering on the cover.* [14C. < Old French *embocer* < *boce* 'protuberance'.] —**embosser** *n* —**embossment** *n*

embouchure /ómboo shoor/ *n* 1 **RIVER MOUTH** the mouth of a river 2 **VALLEY MOUTH** the mouth of a valley where it becomes a plain 3 **POSITION OF LIPS AND TONGUE** the adjustment of the lips and tongue in playing a wind instrument 4 **MOUTHPIECE** the mouthpiece of a wind instrument [Mid-18C. < French, < *emboucher* 'put to your mouth' < *bouche* 'mouth'.]

embourgeoisement /om boor zhwaaz maaN/ *n* the process by which a social group becomes middle-class in manners and attitudes [Mid-20C. < French, < *bourgeois* (see BOURGEOIS).]

embowed /im bṓd, em-/ *adj* shaped like a vault or arch

embowel /im bówəl/ *vt* to disembowel somebody or something (*archaic*)

embower /im bówər/ *vt* to shelter or enclose somebody or something in a bower or a place or structure resembling a bower (*literary*)

embrace /im bráyss/ *v* (**-braces, -bracing, -braced**) 1 *vti* **HUG** to hug somebody in your arms fondly, or hug each other fondly 2 *vt* **MAKE USE OF** to welcome and take advantage of something eagerly or willingly 3 *vt* **ADOPT** to adopt or take up something, especially a belief or way of life 4 *vt* **COMPRISE** to include something as part of a whole 5 *vt* **SURROUND** to surround or enclose something (*literary; often passive*) ■ *n* **HUG GIVEN** an affectionate or passionate hug [14C. < Old French *embracer* 'take into your arms' < Latin *bracchium* 'arm'.] —**embraceable** *adj* —**embracement** *n* —**embracer** *n*

embracery /im bráyssəri/ *n* the offence of trying to influence a judge or jury, e.g. by bribery, threats, or promises

embranchment /im bránchmənt/ *n* 1 an act of branching out by a feature of the natural landscape, e.g. a river or mountain range 2 a branch of something such as a river or mountain range [Mid-19C. < French *embranchement* < *branche* (see BRANCH).]

embrasure /im bráyzhər/ *n* 1 a slanted opening in the wall or parapet of a fortification, designed so that a defender can fire through it on attackers 2 an opening in the wall of a building for a door or window, tapered so as to be wider on the inside than on the outside [Early 17C. < French, < obsolete *embraser* 'widen (a door or window)'.]

embrittle /im brítt'l/ (**-tles, -tling, -tled**) *vti* to become or make something become brittle

embrocate /émbrə kayt/ (**-cates, -cating, -cated**) *vt* to rub lotion or liniment onto a part of the body [Early 17C. < Latin *embrocat-*, past participle of *embrocare* 'treat with healing liquid' < late Latin *embroc(h)a* < Greek *embrokhē* 'lotion'.]

embrocation /émbrə káysh'n/ *n* a liniment that relieves muscle or joint pain

embroider /im bróydər/ *v* 1 *vti* **SEW PATTERN INTO** to decorate something with needlework 2 *vt* **MAKE SOMETHING BY SEWING** to use needlework to make a decoration 3 *vti* **EMBELLISH STORY** to add exaggerated or fictitious details to an account of something to make it more interesting [14C. < Anglo-Norman *enbrouder* < Old French *brouder* 'embroider' < Germanic.] —**embroiderer** *n*

embroidery /im bróydəri/ (*plural* **-ies**) *n* 1 **ACT OF MAKING DECORATIVE NEEDLEWORK** the craft of using needlework to make decorative designs 2 **SOMETHING WITH DECORATIVE NEEDLEWORK** something produced by or ornamented with decorative needlework 3 **ADDITION OF FICTITIOUS DETAILS** elaboration or embellishment in somebody's account of something to make it more interesting

embroil /im bróyl/ *vt* 1 to involve somebody or yourself in trouble, disagreement, or conflict 2 to make something confused or over-complicated [Early 17C. < French *embrouiller* 'confuse, confound' < *brouiller* 'mix confusedly' < Germanic.]

embrue /im bróo/ *vt* = **imbrue**

embryo /émbri ō/ (*plural* **-os**) *n* 1 **HUMAN OFFSPRING IN INITIAL DEVELOPMENTAL STAGE** a human offspring in the early stages following conception up to the end of the eighth week, after which it is classified as a foetus 2 **ANIMAL IN INITIAL DEVELOPMENTAL STAGE** the developing young of an animal from the earliest stages after conception up to birth or hatching 3 **PLANT IN INITIAL DEVELOPMENTAL STAGE** a plant in its earliest stages of development. In seed-bearing plants, the embryo is contained within the seed. 4 **EARLY FORM** an early form or rudimentary stage of something ○ *the embryo of an exciting new invention* [14C. Via Latin < Greek *embruon* < *bruein* 'swell, grow'.]

embryogenesis /émbri ō jénnəssiss/, **embryogeny** /-ójjini/ *n* the formation and growth of an embryo —**embryogenetic** /-jə néttik/ *adj* —**embryogenic** *adj*

embryology /émbri óllәji/ *n* 1 the scientific study of embryos and their development 2 the study of the growth and development of the human embryo and foetus from conception to birth —**embryologic** /émbri ə lójjik/ *adj* —**embryologically** *adv* —**embryologist** *n*

embryonic /émbri ónnik/, **embryonal** /-ən'l/, **embryotic** /émbri óttik/ *adj* 1 relating to or characteristic of an embryo 2 **embryonic, embryotic** in an initial or rudimentary stage of development —**embryonically** *adv*

embryonic membrane *n* any membranous structure, e.g. the amnion, chorion, or yolk sac, that comes from a fertilized ovum but does not become part of the embryo

embryo sac *n* a large oval cell found inside a female reproductive organ (**ovule**) of a flowering plant, that contains the egg cell, which gives rise to the embryo and the endosperm nuclei

embryotic *adj* = **embryonic**

embryo transfer *n* the transplanting of an embryo from one female animal into the womb of a surrogate mother

embus /im búss/ (**-busses** *or* **-buses, -bussing** *or* **-busing, -bussed** *or* **-bused**) *vti* to put somebody, especially troops, on a bus, or to get on a bus

emcee /ém sée/ *n* a master of ceremonies (*informal*) ■ *vti* to act as a master of ceremonies for an event (*informal*) [Mid-20C.< MC 'master of ceremonies'.]

em dash *n* in printing, a dash that is one em long

-eme *suffix* a distinctive unit of linguistic structure ○ *lexeme* [< French *-ème* < *phonème* (see PHONEME)]

emend /i ménd/, **emendate** *vt* to correct or alter a text in order to improve it [15C. < Latin *emendare* 'take out a fault' < *menda* 'fault, blemish'.] —**emendation** /ée men dáysh'n/ *n* —**emender** *n*

USAGE See *amend*.

---

emerald /émmərəld/ *n* a precious stone that is a form of beryl coloured green by chromium. Use: gems. ■ *adj, n* COLOURS = **emerald green** [13C. Directly or via Old French *emeraude* < medieval Latin *esmeraldus*, alteration of Latin *smaragdus*, via Greek *smaragdos* 'green gem' < Semitic, 'shine'.]

Emerald /émmərəld/ town in SE Queensland, Australia. Population: 9,345 (1996).

emerald cut *n* a rectangular multifaceted cut for gemstones, especially emeralds and diamonds

emerald green *n* a bright green colour, like that of an emerald —**emerald-green** *adj*

Emerald Isle *n* Ireland, so called because of its vividly green countryside and because the wearing of green was associated with the struggle for national sovereignty

emerge /i múrj/ (**emerges, emerging, emerged**) *v* 1 *vi* **COME OUT** to appear out of or from behind something 2 *vi* **SURVIVE** to come out of an experience, condition, or situation, especially a difficult one 3 *vti* **BECOME KNOWN** to become known or apparent ○ *It emerged that I had been wrong all along.* 4 *vi* **APPEAR OR HAPPEN** to arise, appear, or occur [Late 16C. < Latin *emergere* 'rise out or up' < *mergere* 'dive, plunge'.] —**emergence** *n*

emergency /i múrjənssi/ *n* (*plural* **-cies**) 1 **SUDDEN CRISIS REQUIRING ACTION** an unexpected and sudden event that must be dealt with urgently 2 *ANZ* **RESERVE PLAYER** a reserve player who replaces a member of a team who is injured or who has to pull out at the last minute ■ *adj* 1 **USED IN EMERGENCY** used or suitable for use in an emergency 2 **FOR IMMEDIATE TREATMENT** requiring, providing, or given immediate medical attention

emergency brake *n US* TRANSP = **handbrake** *n.* 1

emergency cord *n* = **communication cord**

emergency exit *n* an exit from a building or vehicle that is designed and designated as an escape route in an emergency such as a fire

emergency medicine *n* a branch of medicine dealing with the treatment of patients whose condition requires immediate action

emergency powers *npl* special powers given to a government or other authority to take extraordinary actions in order to cope with a crisis

emergency room *n US* MED = **casualty** *n.* 4

emergency services *npl* the fire brigade, the police, and the ambulance service collectively, especially when mobilized to deal with emergencies

emergency vehicle *n* an ambulance, fire engine, police car, or other vehicle used by the emergency services

emergent /i múrjənt/ *adj* 1 **NEWLY INDEPENDENT** newly or recently independent as a nation. US term **emerging** *adj.* 2 2 **NEW** appearing, arising, occurring, or developing, especially for the first time ■ *n* 1 **PLANT WITH UPPER PARTS**

ABOVE WATER a plant that has its roots under water but its upper part above the surface **2 TALL TREE** a forest tree that stands taller than surrounding trees

emergent evolution *n* the theory of evolution in which new organisms and characteristics appear at crises not predictable from those already in existence

emerging /i múrjing/ *adj* **1** starting to appear, arise, occur, or develop **2** *US* POL = **emergent** *adj.* 1

emerita /i mérritə/ *adj* retired but retaining professional title, especially as a woman professor ○ *She's a professor emerita of biology.* ■ *n* (*plural* **-tae** /-tee/) a woman who has retired from a post but retains her former professional title, especially as a professor [Early 20C. < Latin, form of *emeritus* (see EMERITUS).]

emeritus /i mérritəss/ *adj* retired but retaining a professional title, especially as a professor ○ *He's a professor emeritus of chemistry.* ■ *n* (*plural* **-ti** /-tī/) a man who has retired from a post but retains his former professional title, especially as a professor [Early 17C. < Latin, past participle of *emerere* 'serve out, earn, deserve' < *merere* 'serve, earn'.]

emersion /i múrsh'n/ *n* **1** the act or process of emerging **2** the reappearance of a celestial body after it has been eclipsed or occulted

Emerson /émmərss'n/, **Ralph Waldo** (1803–82) US essayist, lecturer, and poet —**Emersonian** /émmər sṓni ən/ *adj*

emery /émməri/ *n* a variety of the mineral corundum. Use: abrasives. [15C. Via French *émeri* < Italian *smeriglio* < Greek *smuris* 'abrasive powder'.]

emery board *n* a small strip of card or thin wood coated with powdered emery and used for filing the fingernails

emery paper *n* a strong paper coated with powdered emery and used as an abrasive and for polishing

emery wheel *n* a wheel coated with powdered emery and used as an abrasive and for polishing

emesis /émmississ/ *n* vomiting (*technical*) [Late 19C. < Greek, < *emein* 'to vomit'.]

emetic /i méttik/ *adj* causing a person or animal to vomit [Mid-17C. < Greek *emetikos* < *emein* 'to vomit'.] —**emetic** *n* —**emetically** *adv*

emetine /émmə teen, -tin/ *n* an alkaloid extracted from a South American shrub (**ipecacuanha**). Use: formerly, as an emetic.

EMF *abbr* **1 EMF, emf** electromotive force **2** European Monetary Fund

EMG *abbr* **1** electromyogram **2** electromyograph

-emia *suffix* = **-aemia**

emic /éemik/ *adj* **1** relating to the analysis of structural and functional elements of language or behaviour **2** relating to the organization and interpretation of data that makes use of the categories of the people being studied. ◊ **etic** [Mid-20C. Shortening of PHONEMIC.]

emigrant /émmigrənt/ *n* a person who leaves a place, especially his or her native country, to go and live elsewhere —**emigrant** *adj*

emigrate /émmi grayt/ (**-grates, -grating, -grated**) *vi* to leave a place, especially a native country, to go and live in another country [Late 18C. < Latin *emigrat-*, past participle of *emigrare* 'move away from a place' < *migrare* 'move from place to place'.] —**emigration** /émmi gráysh'n/ *n*

émigré /émmi gray, áymi-/ *n* somebody who has had to leave his or her native country, usually for political reasons, especially somebody who fled abroad after the French or Russian revolutions [Late 18C. < French, past participle of *émigrer* < Latin *emigrare* (see EMIGRATE).]

Emilia-Romagna /i méeli ə rō máanyə/ region in northern Italy, on the Adriatic Sea. Capital: Bologna. Population: 3,984,055 (1991). Area: 22,124 sq. km/8,542 sq. mi.

eminence /émminənss/, **eminency** /émminənssi/ (*plural* **-cies**) *n* **1 HIGH POSITION** a position or rank of distinction or superiority **2 HILL** a high or raised area of ground (*formal*) **3 BODY PROJECTION** a projecting area of the body, especially a bone

Eminence, Eminency (*plural* **-cies**) *n* in the Roman Catholic Church, a title and form of address for a cardinal

éminence grise /áymi noNss gréez/ (*plural* **éminences grises** /áymi noNss gréez/) *n* a person who exerts great power or influence secretly or unofficially [< French, 'grey eminence', originally nickname of Père Joseph, secretary to Cardinal Richelieu]

eminency *n* = **eminence**

Eminency *n* = **Eminence**

eminent /émminənt/ *adj* **1 OF HIGH STANDING** superior in position, fame, or achievement **2 CLEAR** easy to see or notice **3 HIGH** in a high or raised position [15C. < Latin *eminent-*, present participle of *eminere* 'stand out, project' < *minere* 'stand, project'.]

eminent domain *n* the power of a government to take private property for public use, usually with compensation paid to the owner

eminently /émminəntli/ *adv* to a great degree ○ *He is eminently qualified to be a corporate officer.*

emir /e méer/, **amir** *n* **1** an independent ruler, commander, or governor in some Islamic countries **2** a title for a descendant of the prophet Muhammad [Early 17C. Via French < Arabic *amīr* 'commander'.]

emirate /émmirət, e méerət/ *n* **1** the rank or office of an emir **2** an area ruled by an emir

emissary /émmissəri/ (*plural* **-ies**) *n* **1** an agent or representative sent on a particular mission **2** a secret agent or spy (*dated*) [Early 17C. < Latin *emissarius* 'somebody sent out' < *emiss-*, past participle of *emittere* (see EMIT).]

emission /i mísh'n/ *n* **1 LETTING SOMETHING OUT** the act or process of letting something out or giving something out **2 SOMETHING GIVEN OUT** something that is produced or given out **3 RELEASED ENERGY** energy released from a source, usually in the form of electromagnetic radiation **4 SOMETHING RELEASED FROM BODY** a bodily discharge, especially of semen [15C. < Latin *emission-* 'a sending out' < *emiss-*, past participle of *emittere* (see EMIT).]

emission nebula *n* a cloud of interstellar gas and dust that emits light when electrons recombine with protons to form hydrogen atoms

emissivity /ímmi sívvəti, émmi-/ (*plural* **-ties**) *n* (*symbol* *υ*) the ability of a surface to emit radiation, measured as the ratio of the energy radiated by a surface to that radiated by a black body at the same temperature

emit /i mít/ (**emits, emitting, emitted**) *vt* **1 PRODUCE** to send or give out something **2 UTTER** to utter something as a sound **3 PUT MONEY INTO CIRCULATION** to put currency in circulation [Early 17C. < Latin *emittere* 'send out' < *mittere* 'send'.]

emitter /i míttər/ *n* **1** a person who or thing that emits something **2** a layer of semiconductor material in a transistor from which charge carriers such as electrons originate and control the current flow

Emmanuel *n* = **Immanuel**

Emmental /émmən taal/, **Emmenthal, Emmenthaler, Emmentaler** *n* a hard cheese of Swiss origin with large holes and a mild nutty flavour [Early 20C. After *Emmental*, region in Switzerland.]

emmer /émmər/ *n* a wheat grown chiefly for fodder. Native to: Europe, Asia. *Triticum dicoccum.* [Early 20C. < German.]

emmet /émmit/ *n* an ant (*archaic regional*) [Old English *mete*, variant of *æmette* (see ANT)]

Emmet /émmit/, **Robert** (1778–1803) Irish patriot

emmetropia /émmi trṓpi ə/ *n* the normal condition of the eye in which vision is accurate [Mid-19C. < Greek *emmetros* 'in measure' + *ōps* 'eye'.] —**emmetropic** /-tróppik/ *adj*

Emmy /émmi/ (*plural* **-mys**) *n* a statuette awarded annually by the American Academy of Television Arts and Sciences for excellence in television programming, production, or performance [Mid-20C. < ?]

emollient /i mólli ənt/ *adj* **1 SOOTHING TO SKIN** softening or soothing, especially to the skin **2 CALMING** trying to avoid anger and argument by using a calming manner ■ *n* **SOOTHING SUBSTANCE** a substance that softens or soothes something, especially the skin [Mid-17C. < Latin *emollient-*, present participle of *emollire* 'soften' < *mollis* 'soft'.]

emolument /i móllyoōmənt/ *n* any payment for work (*formal*) [15C. < Latin *emolumentum* 'profit, gain', literally 'fee paid for grinding grain' < *emolere* 'grind out'.]

SYNONYMS See ***wage***.

emote /i mṓt/ (**emotes, emoting, emoted**) *vi* to make an exaggerated show of emotions, e.g. in the playing of a dramatic part (*humorous*) [Early 20C. Back-formation < EMOTION.]

:-) Happy	:-(Sad	|-| Asleep	;-) Winking
:-)) Very happy	:-~) User has a cold	:-* Blowing a kiss	:-& Tongue tied
(:+(Scared	(-D Laughing	:-() Talking	:-O Shocked
:-X Mute	~:-) Baby	|-O Yawning	@->- Rose
{:V Duck	3:-) Cow	<:3 Mouse	:8) Pig

Emoticon

⚡**emoticon** /i mṓti kon/ *n* an arrangement of keyboard characters intended to be viewed sideways as a symbolic picture conveying emotions [Late 20C. Blend of EMOTION + ICON.]

emotion /i mṓsh'n/ *n* **1** a strong feeling about somebody or something **2** agitation or disturbance caused by strong feelings [Late 16C. < French, < *émouvoir* 'stir up the feelings of' < Latin *emovere* 'move out, remove' < *movere* 'to move'.]

emotional /i mṓsh'nəl/ *adj* **1 EXPRESSING EMOTION** relating to or expressing emotion **2 EASILY AFFECTED BY EMOTIONS** being by nature easily affected by or quick to express emotions **3 AFFECTED BY EMOTION** openly affected by emotion, especially sadness **4 STIRRING EMOTIONS** arousing or affecting the emotions **5 INSPIRED BY EMOTION** inspired or governed by emotion rather than reason or willpower ○ *one of the more emotional issues before the public this decade* —**emotionality** /i mṓshə nálləti/ *n* —**emotionally** *adv*

emotionalise *vt* = **emotionalize**

emotionalism /i mṓsh'nəlizəm/ *n* **1** a tendency to be easily swayed by the emotions **2** an exaggerated or undue display of strong feelings

emotionalist /i mṓsh'nəlist/ *n* **1** somebody whose thoughts or actions are greatly influenced by the emotions **2** an overly demonstrative person

emotionalize /i mṓsh'nə līz/ (**-alizes, -alizing, -alized**), **emotionalise** (**-ises, -ising, -ised**) *vt* to present or treat something emotionally

emotionless /i mṓsh'n ləss/ *adj* not having or showing emotions —**emotionlessly** *adv* —**emotionlessness** *n*

emotive /i mṓtiv/ *adj* **1** causing or intended to cause emotion ○ *emotive delivery of the last lines of the play* **2** showing or characterized by emotion ○ *an emotive plea for outlawing land mines* [Mid-18C. < Latin *emotus*, past participle of *emovere* (see EMOTION).] —**emotively** *adv* —**emotiveness** *n*

emotivism /i mṓtivizəm/ *n* the theory that ethical terms are not statements but instead reflect the feelings of the user

Emp. *abbr* **1** Emperor **2** Empire **3** Empress

empale (**-pales, -paling, -paled**) *vt* = **impale**

empanada /émpə naádə/ *n* a Spanish, Filipino, or Latin American turnover with a spicy savoury or sweet filling [Mid-20C. < Spanish, < past participle of *empanar* 'bake or roll in pastry' < *pan* 'bread'.]

empanel *vt* = **impanel**

empathize /émpə thīz/ (**-thizes, -thizing, -thized**), **empathise** (**-thises, -thising, -thised**) *vi* to identify with and understand another person's feelings or difficulties

empathy /émpəthi/ *n* **1** the ability to identify with and understand another person's feelings or difficulties **2** the transfer of your own feelings and emotions to an object such as a painting [Early 20C. < Greek *empatheia* 'affection, passion'.] —**empathetic** /émpə théttik/ *adj* —**empathetically** *adv* —**empathic** /empáthik/ *adj* —**empathically** *adv*

Empedocles /em péddə kleez/ (490?–430BC) Sicilian-born Greek philosopher, poet, and statesman. Known as **Empedocles of Akragas**

empennage /em pénnij, ómpə naázh/ *n* the tail portion of an aircraft, including the stabilizer, elevator, vertical fin, and rudder [Early 20C. < French, 'feathering (of an arrow)' < *empenner* 'feather in' < *penne* 'feather'.]

emperor /émpərər/ *n* **1** a man who rules an empire **2** INSECTS = **emperor moth 3** INSECTS = **emperor butterfly** [12C. Via French < Latin *imperator* 'commander' < *imperare* 'to command' < *parare* 'prepare'.]

emperor butterfly *n* a brightly coloured butterfly that typically has mottled purple and brownish markings. Family: Nymphalidae. [From imperial associations of purple]

emperor moth *n* a large brightly coloured moth with distinctive markings resembling eyes on its wings. Native to: Europe, asia. *Saturnia pyri.* [From its large size]

emperor penguin *n* a penguin with bluish-grey and black plumage, a white chest, and yellowish-orange neck markings. Native to: Antarctica. *Aptenodytes forsteri.* [From its large size]

emphasis /émfəssiss/ (*plural* **-ses**) *n* **1** IMPORTANCE special importance, significance, or stress **2** FORCEFULNESS OF EXPRESSION forcefulness of expression to indicate the importance of something **3** EXTRA SPOKEN STRESS ON IMPORTANT WORD extra stress of voice put on a syllable, word, or phrase, usually to show its significance [Late 16C. Via Latin, < Greek, 'significance, appearance' < *emphainein* 'show, indicate' < *phainein* 'to show'.]

emphasize /émfə sīz/ (**-sizes, -sizing, -sized**), **emphasise** (**-sises, -sising, -sised**) *vt* to stress or give importance to something

emphatic /im fáttik/ *adj* **1** WITH EMPHASIS expressed, thought, or done with emphasis **2** DEFINITE forcible and definite **3** SHOWING EMPHASIS GRAMMATICALLY describes a grammatical form that shows emphasis, e.g. the auxiliary 'do' in the statement 'I do like apples' [Early 18C. Via late Latin < Greek *emphatikos* < *emphasis* (see EMPHASIS).]

emphatically /im fáttikli, em-/ *adv* **1** with great force or definiteness **2** used to reinforce the accuracy or appropriateness of a description ○ *It might be entertainment, but it is emphatically not education.*

emphysema /émfə seémə, -zeémə/ *n* **1** a chronic medical disorder of the lungs in which the air sacs are dilated or enlarged and lack flexibility, resulting in breathing impairment and sometimes infection **2** an abnormal enlargement of an organ or body tissue caused by retention of air or other gas [Mid-17C. Via late Latin < Greek *emphusēma* 'swelling' < *emphusan* 'inflate' < *phusan* 'blow'.] —**emphysematous** /émfə sémmətəss, -seém-, -zémm-, -zeém-/ *adj* —**emphysemic** *adj*

empire /émpīr/ *n* **1** LANDS RULED BY SINGLE AUTHORITY a group of nations, territories, or peoples ruled by a single authority, especially an emperor or empress **2** MONARCHY HEADED BY EMPEROR OR EMPRESS a monarchy that has an emperor or empress as its ruler **3** PERIOD OF EMPIRE'S EXISTENCE the period during which an empire exists **4** LARGE FAR-FLUNG BUSINESS a very large, powerful, and extensive industrial or commercial organization **5** PART OF ORGANIZATION SOMEBODY PERSONALLY CONTROLS a part of an organization controlled by a single person, especially somebody who is keenly protective of personal power **6** ABSOLUTE POWER supreme or absolute power (*formal or literary*) [13C. Via Old French < Latin *imperium* 'command' < *imperare* (see EMPEROR).]

Empire *adj* relating to a style of architecture, furniture, and clothing popular during the French First Empire (1804–15) during the reign of Napoleon I ■ *n* a variety of red eating apple

empire-building *n* the tendency to acquire power and authority within an organization, especially by adding extra staff or subordinates —**empire-builder** *n*

Empire Day *n* the former name for Commonwealth Day, used before 1958

Empire State Building *n* a skyscraper on Fifth Avenue in New York City built between 1930 and 1931

empiric /em pírrik, im-/ *n* **1** a person who exclusively relies upon observation and experiment to determine the truth about something **2** a charlatan or quack, especially in medicine (*archaic*) [Mid-16C. < Latin *empiricus* < Greek *empeirikos* 'experienced' < *empeiros* 'skilled' < *peira* 'trial'.]

empirical /em pírrik'l, im-/ *adj* **1** BASED ON OBSERVATION AND EXPERIMENT based on or characterized by observation and experiment rather than theory **2** BASED ON PRACTICAL MEDICAL EXPERIENCE based on practical experience in the medical treatment of real cases rather than on applied theory or scientific proof **3** DERIVED SOLELY FROM EXPERIENCE derived as knowledge from experience, particularly from sensory observation, rather than from the application of logic —**empirically** *adv*

empirical formula *n* a chemical formula showing the relative proportion of elements in a compound instead of their structural arrangement or molecular weights, e.g. the formula H_2O

empiricism /em pírrissìzəm/ *n* **1** PHILOSOPHICAL BELIEF REGARDING SENSE-DERIVED KNOWLEDGE the philosophical belief that all knowledge is derived from the experience of the senses **2** APPLICATION OF OBSERVATION AND EXPERIMENT the application of observation and experiment, rather than theory, in determining something **3** MEDICINE BASED SOLELY ON EXPERIENCE medicine that is based on practical experience rather than on theory and scientific proof —**empiricist** *n*

QUICK FACTS ON... **EMPIRICISM**

Key dates: late 17th to mid-20th centuries
Key locations: Britain, United States
Key elements: opposition to philosophical rationalism; theory that knowledge is exclusively based on experience, especially sensory perceptions
Key figures: John Locke, David Hume, John Stuart Mill, Auguste Comte, William James, John Dewey, C. S. Peirce, Bertrand Russell, G. E. Moore, Ludwig Wittgenstein, A. J. Ayer
Key works: *Essay Concerning Human Understanding* (Locke) 1690, *A Treatise of Human Nature* (Hume) 1739–40, *Utilitarianism* (Mill) 1863, *Pragmatism* (James) 1907, *Tractatus Logico-Philosophicus* (Wittgenstein) 1921, *Language, Truth, and Logic* (Ayer) 1936
Key developments: positivism, philosophy of science, behaviourism

emplace /im pláyss/ (**-places, -placing, -placed**) *vt* to put something into place or position [Mid-19C. Back-formation < EMPLACEMENT.]

emplacement /im pláyssmənt/ *n* **1** a position that is specially prepared for a large gun or group of guns **2** the act of putting something into place, or the condition of being in place [Early 19C. < French, 'placing in' < *place* 'place'.]

emplane /im pláyn/ (**-planes, -planing, -planed**) *vti* to board or allow somebody to board an aircraft. US term **enplane**

employ /im plóy/ *vt* **1** GIVE PAID WORK TO to hire somebody to work in exchange for money **2** KEEP BUSY to keep somebody occupied doing something **3** USE to make use of something ■ *n* **1** EMPLOYED STATE the condition of working for pay (*formal*) ○ *I was in his employ.* **2** JOB a job or occupation (*archaic*) [15C. Via French *emploier* 'apply' < Latin *implicare* 'involve, enfold' < *plicare* 'fold'.] —**employability** /im plóyə bílləti/ *n* —**employable** *adj*

SYNONYMS See ***use***.

employee /im plóy ee, ém ploy eé/ *n* a paid worker

employee association *n* a social or professional organization of employees who have the same employer

employer /im plóyər/ *n* **1** a person, business, or organization that engages and pays one or more workers **2** a user of something

employers' association *n* an organization of employers, usually working in a similar area, that provides support for its members and negotiates in industrial disputes

employment /im plóymənt/ *n* **1** WORKING FOR PAY the condition of working for pay **2** WORK OR JOB DONE BY SOMEBODY the work, especially paid work, that somebody does **3** NUMBER OF PAID WORKERS IN POPULATION the total number or level of people that work for pay in a given population **4** USE the use or practice of something

employment agency *n* a commercial organization that finds jobs for people or people for jobs

emporium /em páwri əm/ (*plural* **-ums** *or* **-a** /-ri ə/) *n* a shop, usually a large shop, that offers a wide selection of goods (*humorous*) [Late 16C. Via Latin, < Greek *emporion* < *emporos* 'merchant, traveller' < *poros* 'journey'.]

empower /im pówər/ *vt* **1** to give somebody power or authority (*often passive*) **2** to give somebody a sense of confidence or self-esteem —**empowerment** *n*

empress /émprəss/ *n* **1** a woman who rules an empire **2** the wife or widow of an emperor

empressement /oN préss moN/ *n* great attentiveness or cordiality (*literary*) [Early 18C. < French, < *empresser* 'urge, be eager' < *presser* 'press' (see PRESS[1]).]

emprise /em príz/ *n* (*formal*) **1** a chivalrous, brave, or daring undertaking **2** chivalrous skill or daring [13C. < French, < Old French *emprendre* 'seize into' < Latin *prendere* 'seize'.]

empty /émpti/ *adj* (**-tier, -tiest**) **1** CONTAINING NOTHING not containing or holding anything ○ *a heap of empty packets* **2** UNOCCUPIED unoccupied or uninhabited ○ *There's an empty office next door.* **3** WITH NO PASSENGERS OR LOAD without passengers, a load, or cargo ○ *The bus goes back to the depot empty.* **4** INSINCERE lacking sincerity or truthfulness ○ *another empty promise* **5** MEANINGLESS without value, meaning, or purpose ○ *contemplating his empty existence* **6** DULL devoid of vitality ○ *an empty look* **7** UNFED hungry or lacking food ○ *can't work on an empty stomach* **8** WITHOUT MEMBERS OF SET describes a set that has no elements or members ■ *v* (**-ties, -tying, -tied**) **1** *vti* REMOVE CONTENTS OF to remove or pour out the contents of something **2** *vti* DISCHARGE OR TRANSFER to discharge or transfer something, or be discharged and transferred **3** *vr* UNBURDEN YOURSELF to unburden or free yourself of something ■ *n* (*plural* **-ties**) CONTAINER WITHOUT CONTENTS a bottle or other container that has nothing in it [Old English *ǣmtig* 'unoccupied, at leisure' < *ǣmetta* 'rest, leisure' < ?] —**emptiable** *adj* —**emptily** *adv* —**emptiness** *n*

SYNONYMS See ***vacant***. See ***vain***.

empty-handed *adj* **1** holding nothing in the hands **2** with nothing gained or achieved

empty-headed *adj* silly or lacking in intelligence

empty nester *n* a parent whose children have grown up and moved away from home (*informal*)

empty-nest syndrome *n* distress, especially a lack of energy or an emotional letdown, experienced by parents whose grown children have moved away from home

empyema /ém pī eémə/ *n* an accumulation of pus in a body cavity, e.g. the chest [Early 17C. Via late Latin < Greek *empuēma* < *empuein* 'put pus in' < *puon* 'pus'.] —**empyemic** *adj*

empyreal /ém pī reé əl, em pírri əl/ *adj* **1** relating to the sky, the celestial sphere, or heaven **2** glorious and sublime (*literary*) [15C. < medieval Latin *empyreus* (see EMPYREAN).]

empyrean /ém pī reé ən, em pírri ən/ *n* **1** the sky or celestial sphere (*literary*) **2** the highest part of heaven, believed in ancient Greek and Roman times to contain pure fire or light and believed by some Christians to be the dwelling place of God (*archaic*) ■ *adj* = **empyreal** *adj.* **2** [15C. < medieval Latin *empyreus* < Greek *empurios* 'in fire' < *pur* 'fire'.]

EMS *abbr* **1** Emergency Medical Services **2** European Monetary System

emu[1] /eé myoo/ (*plural* **emus** *or* **emu**) *n* a large flightless bird that is related to the ostrich and has three-toed feet and loose shaggy feathers. Native to: Australia. *Dromaius novaehollandiae.* [Early 17C. < Portuguese *ema.*]

emu[2], **EMU** *abbr* electromagnetic unit

EMU /eé em yoó, eé myoo/ *abbr* European Monetary Union

emu bush *n* a shrub whose fruit is eaten by emus. Native to: Australia. Genus: *Eremophila.*

⚡**emulate** /émyoo layt/ (**-lates, -lating, -lated**) *vt* **1** TRY TO EQUAL to try hard to equal or surpass somebody or something, especially by imitation **2** COMPETE SUCCESSFULLY WITH to be successful in competing with or rival somebody or something **3** MAKE BEHAVE LIKE ANOTHER COMPUTER SYSTEM to modify a computer system so that it appears to behave like another computer system, and can thereby accept data and run programs that are designed for the system being emulated [Late 16C. < Latin *aemulat-*, past participle of *aemulari* 'to rival' < *aemulus* 'rival'.] —**emulation** /émyoo láysh'n/ *n* —**emulative** *adj* —**emulatively** *adv*

SYNONYMS See ***imitate***.

⚡**emulator** /émyoo laytər/ *n* **1** somebody or something that emulates another person or thing **2** hardware or software that permits a computer system to run programs written for, and process data originating from, a different type of computer system. ◊ **simulator** *n.* 1

emulous /émyŏŏləss/ *adj* **1** seeking to match or rival another's achievement or performance **2** motivated or characterized by rivalry or imitation [14C. < Latin *aemulus* 'rival'.] —**emulously** *adv* —**emulousness** *n*

emulsifier /i múlssi fī ər/ *n* a chemical agent that maintains or creates an emulsion

emulsify /i múlssi fī/ (**-fies, -fying, -fied**) *vti* to convert two or more liquids into an emulsion or become an emulsion —**emulsible** *adj* —**emulsifiable** *adj* —**emulsification** /i múlssifi káysh'n/ *n*

emulsion /i múlsh'n/ *n* **1 SUSPENSION OF LIQUID WITHIN ANOTHER LIQUID** a suspension of one liquid in another, e.g. oil in water or fat in milk **2 LIGHT-SENSITIVE PHOTOGRAPHIC COATING** a thin light-sensitive coating of silver bromide or silver halide in a medium such as gelatin on a photographic plate, paper, or film **3 WATER-BASED PAINT WITH MATT FINISH** a water-based paint that is mainly used for interior decorating and usually has a matt finish [Early 17C. < Latin *emuls-*, past participle of *emulgere* 'milk out' < *mulgere* 'to milk'.] —**emulsive** *adj*

emunctory /i múngktəri/ (*plural* **-ries**) *n* a body part or organ that removes waste products from the body, e.g. the kidneys, lungs, or skin [14C. < medieval Latin *emunctorius* < Latin *emungere* 'blow the nose thoroughly' < *mungere* 'blow the nose'.]

en /en/ *n* a measure of printing width, half that of an em

EN *abbr* enrolled nurse

en- *prefix* **1** to put or go into, or cover with ○ *entomb* ○ *encamp* ○ *enfold* **2** to provide with **3** to cause to be ○ *enlarge* **4** thoroughly ○ *enmesh* **5** in, within, into ○ *enzootic* [Via Old French < Latin *in* 'in']

-en *suffix* **1** to cause to be or have ○ *brighten* ○ *strengthen* **2** to come to be or have ○ *tauten* ○ *lengthen* **3** made of or resembling ○ *wooden* [Old English, < Germanic]

enable /in áyb'l/ (**-bles, -bling, -bled**) *vt* **1** to provide somebody with the resources, authority, or opportunity to do something **2** to make something possible or feasible —**enablement** *n* —**enabler** *n*

-enabled *suffix* made capable of using or operating with a particular system ○ *WAP-enabled*

enabling /in áybling/ *adj* conferring new legal powers

enact /in ákt/ *vt* **1** to perform or relate something using acting **2** to make proposed legislation into law —**enactable** *adj* —**enactive** *adj* —**enactor** *n* —**enactory** *adj*

enactment /in áktmənt/ *n* **1** the act or process of enacting something **2** something that is enacted, especially a law

enamel /i námm'l/ *n* **1 GLASSY DECORATIVE OR PROTECTIVE COATING** a glassy decorative or protective coating, usually coloured and opaque, that is fused onto metal, glass, or ceramics **2 SOMETHING WITH ENAMEL COATING** something that is coated with enamel **3 PAINT WITH HARD SHINY FINISH** a paint that gives a shiny smooth finish when dry **4 SHINY SMOOTH TOUGH COATING** any coating that is shiny, smooth, and durable ○ *nail enamel* **5 HARD LAYER ON TOOTH CROWN** a hard thin calcium-containing layer that covers and protects the crown of a tooth ■ *vt* (**-els, -elling, -elled**) **1 COAT SOMETHING WITH ENAMEL** to decorate or coat all or part of an object with enamel **2 APPLY BRIGHT SHINY SURFACE TO** to apply a shiny brightly coloured surface to something [14C. < Anglo-Norman *enamailler* 'enamel in' < Old French *esmail* 'enamel' < Germanic, 'melting'.] —**enameller** *n*

enamelling /i námm'ling/ *n* **1** the process of applying enamel to something **2** the surface of something coated with enamel

enamelware /i námm'l wair/ *n* household utensils coated with enamel

enamelwork /i námm'l wurk/ *n* = **enamelling** *n.* 2

enamor *vt* US = **enamour**

enamour /in ámmər/ *vt* (*formal or literary*) **1** to inspire somebody with love or passion **2** to charm, fascinate, or captivate somebody [13C. < Old French *enamourer* < *en-* 'cause to' + *amour* 'love'.]

enantiomorph /i nánti ə mawrf/, **enantiomer** /-əmər/ *n* either of a pair of molecules that are mirror images of each other in structure but cannot be superimposed [Late 19C. < Greek *enantios* 'opposite'.] —**enantiomorphic** /i nánti ə máwrfik/ *adj* —**enantiomorphism** /-máwrfizəm/ *n* —**enantiomorphous** /-máwrfəss/ *adj*

enarch *vt* = **inarch**

enate /ée nayt/ *adj* related through the mother ■ *n* somebody related on the mother's side [Mid-17C. < Latin *enatus*, past participle of *enasci* 'issue out, be born'.]

enatic /ee náttik/ *adj* = **enate** *adj.*

enation /ee náysh'n/ *n* a small outgrowth on an organ, especially on a leaf, caused by a virus infection [Mid-19C. < Latin *enation-* < *enasci* 'issue out, be born'.]

en bloc /oN blók, on blók/ *adv* all together at the same time [Mid-19C. < French, 'in a lump'.]

enc *abbr* **1** enclosed **2** enclosure

encaenia /en séeni ə/ *n* an event commemorating or dedicating an institution or community, e.g. a university, church, or city (*formal*) [14C. Via Latin < Greek *egkainia* 'dedication festival' < *en* 'in' + *kainos* 'new'.]

encage /in káyj/ (**-cages, -caging, -caged**) *vt* to confine somebody or something in or in something resembling a cage (*literary*)

encamp /in kámp/ *vti* to lodge in a camp, or provide somebody with a camp

encampment /in kámpmənt/ *n* **1** a place occupied by a camp **2** residence in a camp, or the setting up of a camp

encapsulate /in kápsyŏŏ layt/ (**-lates, -lating, -lated**), **incapsulate** (**-lates, -lating, -lated**) *v* **1** *vt* to express something in concise form **2** *vti* to enclose something or be enclosed completely —**encapsulation** /in kápsyŏŏ láysh'n/ *n* —**encapsulator** *n*

encapsulated /in kápsyŏŏ laytid/ *adj* describes an organ or tumour covered by a thin protective membrane

encase /in káyss/ (**-cases, -casing, -cased**), **incase** (**-cases, -casing, -cased**) *vt* to surround something completely with a case or cover —**encasement** *n*

encash /in kásh/ *vt* to convert a cheque or bond into cash —**encashable** *adj* —**encashment** *n*

encaustic /in káwstik, -kóstik/ *adj* having pigments mixed with wax applied to a surface by heat ■ *n* an object or work of art whose colours are fused to a surface by the application of heat, especially an earthenware tile decorated with an inlaid design in the style of medieval floor tiles [Late 16C. Via Latin, < Greek *egkaustikos* < *egkaiein* 'burn in'.]

enceinte[1] /on sánt/ *adj* having a child developing in the womb (*used euphemistically*) [Early 17C. Via French < medieval Latin *incincta* 'ungirded' < *cincta* 'girded'.]

enceinte[2] /on sánt/ *n* **1** a defensive wall or enclosure **2** a place protected by a defensive wall or enclosure [Early 18C. Via French < Latin *incincta*, past participle of *incingere* 'gird in'.]

Enceladus /en sélladəss/ *n* a small natural satellite of Saturn, discovered in 1789

encephal- *prefix* = **encephalo-** (*before vowels*)

encephalic /én si fállik, -ki-/ *adj* related to the brain or its location within the cranium [Mid-19C. < Greek *egkephalos* 'brain' (see ENCEPHALO-).]

encephalin *n* MED = **enkephalin**

encephalitis /en séffə lítiss, -kéffə-/ *n* inflammation of the brain, usually caused by a viral infection —**encephalitic** /-líttik/ *adj*

encephalitis lethargica /-li thaárjikə/ *n* sleeping sickness (*technical*) [< modern Latin, 'sleepy encephalitis']

encephalo- *prefix* brain ○ *encephalogram* [Via modern Latin, < Greek *egkephalos* 'brain' < *en* 'in' + *kephalē* 'head']

encephalogram /en séffələ gram, -kéffələ-/ *n* **1** an X-ray photograph of the brain **2** MED = **electroencephalogram**

encephalograph /en séffələ graaf, -graf, -kéffə-, -graf/ *n* **1** MED = **encephalogram** *n.* 1 **2** MED = **electroencephalograph** —**encephalographic** *adj* —**encephalographically** *adv* —**encephalography** /en séffə lóggrəfi, -kéffə-/ *n*

encephalomyelitis /en séffəlō mī ə lītiss, -kéffə-/ *n* inflammation of the brain and spinal cord —**encephalomyelitic** /-mī ə líttik/ *adj*

encephalon /en séffə lon, en kéffə-/ (*plural* **-la** /-lə/) *n* the brain of a vertebrate [Mid-18C. < Greek *egkephalon* 'what is inside the head' < *kephalē* 'head'.] —**encephalous** *adj*

encephalopathy /en séffə lóppəthi, -kéffə-/ *n* any disease of the brain —**encephalopathic** /en séffələ páthik, -kéffələ-/ *adj*

enchain /in cháyn, en-/ *vt* **1** to bind somebody or something with chains (*formal or literary*) **2** to dominate somebody's attention or thoughts (*literary*) [14C. < French *enchainer* < Latin *catenare* 'to chain'.] —**enchainment** *n*

enchant /in chaánt/ *vt* **1** to charm, delight, or captivate somebody **2** to cast a spell on somebody or something [14C. Via Old French, < Latin *incantare* 'chant a magic formula upon' < *cantare* 'sing'.] —**enchanted** *adj* —**enchanter** *n*

enchanter's nightshade *n* a woodland plant having bristly fruits. Flowers: white, small. Genus: *Circaea.*

enchanting /in chaánting/ *adj* captivating or delightful —**enchantingly** *adv*

enchantment /in chaántmənt/ *n* **1 STATE OF BEING ENCHANTED** the act or condition of being enchanted **2 CHARM** something that delights or captivates **3 SPELL** a magic spell

enchantress /in chaántrəss/ *n* **1** a woman who is charming or delightful **2** a woman who casts spells

enchase /in cháyss/ (**-chases, -chasing, -chased**) *vt* **1** to set jewellery or other decorative objects with gems **2** to emboss, engrave, or carve designs on metal [15C. < French *enchasser* 'set (gems), encase' < *chasse* 'case, box'.]

enchilada /én chi laádə/ *n* a fried tortilla rolled around a savoury filling and served hot with a usually spicy sauce [Late 19C. < Mexican Spanish, form of past participle of *enchilar* 'season with chilli'.] ◆ **whole enchilada**

enchiridion /én kī ríddi ən/ (*plural* **-ons** *or* **-a** /-di ə/) *n* a manual or handbook (*archaic*) [Mid-16C. Via late Latin < Greek *egkheiridion* 'small thing in the hand' < *kheir* 'hand'.]

-enchyma *suffix* cellular tissue ○ *aerenchyma* [< PARENCHYMA]

encipher /in sífər/ *vt* to convert a text into code or cipher —**encipherer** *n* —**encipherment** *n*

encircle /in súrk'l/ (**-cles, -cling, -cled**) *vt* **1** to form a circle around somebody or something **2** to go in a circle around somebody or something —**encirclement** *n* —**encircling** *adj*

Encke /éngkə/, **Johann Franz** (1791–1865) German astronomer

encl. *abbr* **1** enclosed **2** enclosure

enclasp /in klaásp/ *vt* to embrace or hold somebody or something tightly (*formal*)

enclave /én klayv, ón-/ *n* **1** a small country or territory that is culturally or ethnically different from a surrounding larger and distinct political unit. ◊ **exclave 2** a distinct group that lives or operates together within a larger community [Mid-19C. < French, < Old French *enclaver* 'enclose' < Latin *in* 'in' + *clavis* 'key'.]

enclitic /in klíttik/ *adj* depending on a preceding word for its formation or pronunciation [Mid-17C. Via late Latin < Greek *egklitikos* < *egklinein* 'lean on'.] —**enclitic** *n*

enclose /in klṓz/ (**-closes, -closing, -closed**), **inclose** (**-closes, -closing, -closed**) *vt* **1 SURROUND** to surround or shut in something **2 SURROUND LAND OR BUILDING WITH BOUNDARY** to surround land or a building with a fence, wall, or other boundary **3 INSERT SOMETHING IN ENVELOPE OR PACKAGE** to add something to the contents of an envelope or package **4 HOLD** to hold or contain something [14C. < Old French *enclos*, past participle of *enclore* < Latin *includere* 'shut in' (see INCLUDE).] —**enclosable** *adj*

enclosed order *n* a Christian religious community whose members remain physically within it

enclosure /in klṓzhər/, **inclosure** *n* **1 LAND SURROUNDED BY A BOUNDARY** an area of land surrounded by a fence, wall, or other boundary **2 BOUNDARY FENCE** a fence, wall, or other boundary surrounding something **3 SOMETHING INSIDE A LETTER** something added to a letter or package **4 RESERVED AREA AT SPORTS EVENT** an area of ground at a sports event set aside for particular spectators or competitors **5 ACT OF ENCLOSING** the act or process of enclosing something **6 COMMON LAND TAKEN AS PRIVATE PROPERTY** between the twelfth and nineteenth centuries, the appropriation of land in England and Scotland, especially common land, so it could be fenced or hedged as private property **7 RESTRICTED PART OF CONVENT OR MONASTERY** the part of a convent or monastery, especially the living quarters, that is restricted to members

ϟ**encode** /in kṓd/ (**-codes, -coding, -coded**) *vt* **1 CONVERT TEXT TO CODE** to convert a message from plain text into code **2 CONVERT COMPUTER CHARACTERS INTO DIGITAL FORM** to convert input data, e.g. analogue signals, characters, and commands, into a digital form recognizable by a computer **3 PROVIDE GENETIC INFORMATION** to provide the genetic information that enables a polypeptide, RNA molecule, or one of their constituent groups to be produced (*refers to codons and genes*) —**encodement** *n*

encomiast /en kṓmi ast/ *n* a speaker or writer of an encomium (*formal*) [Early 17C. < Greek *egkōmiastēs* < *egkōmiazein* 'to praise' < *egkōmion* (see ENCOMIUM).]

encomium /en kṓmi əm/ (*plural* **-ums** *or* **-a** /-mi ə/) *n* (*formal*) **1** a formal text that expresses high praise for somebody **2** an expression of high praise [Mid-16C. Via Latin < Greek *egkōmion* 'eulogy' < *kōmos* 'revel'.]

encompass /in kúmpəss/ *vt* **1 INCLUDE IN ENTIRETY** to include the entirety of something **2 ENCIRCLE** to surround, envelop, or encircle something **3 CAUSE SOMETHING TO OCCUR** to cause or bring about something (*formal*) — **encompassment** *n*

encore /óng kawr/ *n* **EXTRA OR REPEATED PERFORMANCE** an additional or repeated performance of something in response to a demand from an audience ■ *interj* **USED TO DEMAND REPEAT PERFORMANCE** used to demand an additional or repeated performance of something ■ *vti* (**-cores, -coring, -cored**) **ADD TO OR REPEAT PERFORMANCE OF** to give an additional or repeated performance of something [Early 18C. < French, 'still, again'.]

encounter /in kówntər/ *vt* **1 MEET UNEXPECTEDLY** to meet somebody or something, usually unexpectedly **2 MEET IN CONFLICT** to confront somebody or something with hostility or aggression **3 COME UP AGAINST** to be faced with or come up against somebody or something ■ *n* **1 UNEXPECTED MEETING** a meeting with somebody or something, usually unexpected and brief **2 CONFRONTATION** a hostile confrontation or contest [13C. < Old French *encontrer* 'confront' < late Latin *incontra* 'in front of' < Latin *in-* 'in' + *contra* 'against'.]

encounter group *n* a small group of people, often guided by a leader, who meet in order to achieve personal growth, self-awareness, and social skills by means of emotional expression and interaction

encourage /in kúrrij/ (**-ages, -aging, -aged**) *vt* **1 GIVE SOMEBODY HOPE OR COURAGE** to give somebody hope, confidence, or courage **2 BE SUPPORTIVE OF** to urge somebody in a helpful way to do or be something **3 FOSTER** to assist something to occur or increase [15C. < French *encoragier* < *en-* 'cause' + *corage* 'courage'.] —**encourager** *n*

encouragement /in kúrrijmənt/ *n* **1** support of a kind that inspires confidence and a will to continue or develop **2** somebody who or something that encourages

encouraging /in kúrrijing/ *adj* giving hope, confidence, or courage —**encouragingly** *adv*

encroach /in krṓch/ *vi* **1** to intrude gradually or stealthily, often taking away somebody's authority, rights, or property **2** to exceed the proper limits of something [14C. < Old French *encrochier* 'seize' < *croc* 'hook' < Old Norse *krókr*.] —**encroacher** *n* —**encroachingly** *adv* — **encroachment** *n*

en croute /oN kroŏt/ *adj, adv* enclosed in a pastry crust ○ *salmon en croute* [Late 20C. < French.]

encrust /in krúst/, **incrust** *vt* (*often passive*) **1** to cover something with a hard thick coating **2** to embellish something richly, especially with jewels [Early 17C. Via French, < Latin *incrustare* < *in-* 'upon' + *crusta* 'crust'.]

encrustation /in krust áysh'n/, **incrustation** *n* **1** the act of encrusting something or the state of being encrusted **2** a hard thick coating or covering

encrypt /in krípt/ *vt* **1** to convert a text into code or cipher **2** to convert computer data and messages into something incomprehensible using a key, so that only a holder of the matching key can reconvert them — **encryption** *n*

enculturation /en kúlchə ráysh'n/ *n* SOC SCI = **socialization** —**enculturative** /en kúlchərətiv/ *adj*

encumber /in kúmbər/, **incumber** *vt* **1 HINDER** to hamper or impede somebody or something **2 LOAD DOWN** to burden or weigh down somebody or something (*often passive*) **3 FILL WITH SUPERFLUOUS THINGS** to fill something with superfluous matter or objects (*often passive*) [14C. < Old French *encombrer* 'obstruct' < *combre* 'barrier'.]

encumbrance /in kúmbrənss/ *n* **1** a hindrance or burden to somebody **2** a lien, charge, or claim on property, especially a mortgage

encumbrancer /in kúmbrənssər/ *n* somebody who has a legal claim on property, especially a mortgage

encyclical /en síklik'l/ *n* in the Roman Catholic Church, a formal statement issued by the pope to bishops, often on matters of doctrine [Mid-17C. < Greek *egkuklios* 'circular, general' < *kuklos* 'circle'.]

encyclopaedia *n* = **encyclopedia**

encyclopaedic *adj* = **encyclopedic**

encyclopaedism *n* = **encyclopedism**

encyclopaedist *n* = **encyclopedist**

encyclopedia /in sīklə peedi ə/, **encyclopaedia** *n* a reference work offering comprehensive information on all or specialized areas of knowledge [Mid-16C. < Greek *egkuklopaideia* 'general education' < *egkuklios* (see ENCYCLICAL) + *paideia* 'education' < *pais* 'boy, child'.]

encyclopedic /in sīklə peédik/, **encyclopaedic** *adj* covering or including a broad range of detailed knowledge such as is found in an encyclopedia — **encyclopedically** *adv*

encyclopedism /in sīklə peédizəm/, **encyclopaedism** *n* comprehensive learning or knowledge

encyclopedist /in sīklə peédist/, **encyclopaedist** *n* a compiler of or contributor to an encyclopedia

Encyclopedist /in sīklə peédist/ *n* a writer or editor of the *Encyclopédie* (1751–72), a French reference work in which the advanced secular, technical, and political ideas of the period were articulated

encyst /en síst/ *vti* to enclose or be enclosed in a cyst — **encystation** /énsiss táysh'n/ *n* —**encysted** *adj* —**encystment** *n*

end /end/ *n* **1 FINAL PART** the final part or finishing point of a period of time or of an event or of a book, film or other work ○ *His address is at the end of the article.* **2 EXTREMITY OF OBJECT** the tip or extremity of a long narrow object ○ *I'm surprised he knows which end to hold the mike.* **3 LIMIT OR BOUNDARY** the limit, extent, or boundary of something ○ *They walked the valley from end to end.* **4 STOPPING** the act or result of stopping something ○ *a scandal that brought his career to an abrupt end* **5 EXTREMITY OF A SCALE** either of the extreme points on a scale ○ *at both ends of the political spectrum* **6 GOAL** a goal, object, or purpose ○ *for purely political ends* **7 PART OF COMMUNICATIONS LINK** either of the places connected by a communications link ○ *Pick up the phone and find out who's on the other end.* **8 DEATH** the experience of death ○ *an untimely end* **9 LEFTOVER PIECE** a piece or part of something that is left over **10 SHARE OF JOINT RESPONSIBILITY** a part or portion of shared responsibility ○ *Are you sure they'll honour their end of the deal?* **11 AREA ON PLAYING FIELD** the area at either end of a playing field **12 PLAYER POSITIONED AT END OF LINE** in American football, a player positioned at either end of the offensive or defensive line ■ *v* **1** *vti* **STOP** to reach, or bring something to, a close or a final point ○ *She abruptly ended the meeting.* ○ *The meeting ended without an agreement being made.* **2** *vi* **RESULT** to have an ultimate consequence or result ○ *The holiday ended in tragedy.* **3** *vi* **STOP AT A PLACE** to reach a particular place and stop there ○ *The road ends at a little village called Monkton.* **4** *vi* **HAVE A TIP** to have a particular kind of tip or extremity ○ *The dog's tail ends in a tuft of hair.* [Old English *ende* < Indo-European, 'front'] ◇ **an end in itself** something that is worth having or doing although it may not lead to anything ○ *A friendship should be satisfying; it is an end in itself and not a means to an end.* ◇ **at a loose end** having no purpose or occupation ○ *With all her work done, she found herself at a loose end.* ◇ **at loose ends** US at a loose end ◇ **at the end of the day** after everything has been taken into consideration ○ *You can give them as much advice as you like, but at the end of the day they'll have to decide for themselves.* ◇ **come to** *or* **meet a sticky** *or* **bad end** to have an unpleasant or unfortunate outcome, especially a violent death (*informal*) ◇ **end for end** US reversed or inverted ○ *They turned the boxes end for end.* ◇ **end it all** commit suicide ◇ **end to end** in a row with the ends adjacent ○ *The beds of flowers were arranged end to end.* ◇ **get (hold of) the wrong end of the stick** to misunderstand what somebody is saying ◇ **in the end** finally ○ *In the end, I had to admit he was right.* ◇ **look like the back end of a bus** an offensive term meaning to lack appealing physical features (*informal*) ◇ **make ends meet** to be able to afford to pay for the expenses of daily living ◇ **no end** very much indeed (*informal*) ◇ **no end of something** a great deal of something (*informal*) ○ *The old photocopier gave us no end of trouble.* ◇ **on end 1** for an uninterrupted period ○ *The rain continued for weeks on end.* **2** in a vertical position ○ *We left the table standing on end against the wall.* ◇ **the end of the line** *or* **road** the point beyond which somebody or something can no longer continue or survive ○ *The coming of the supermarkets was the end of the line for many small independent grocers.* ◇ **the ... to end all ...** something that is so impressive or important that nothing else of the same kind will ever rival it ○ *the war to end all wars* ◇ **the thin end of the wedge** something bad or disadvantageous that seems quite minor but may well lead to something worse ◇ **to no end** without success or achieving useful results (*formal*) ◇ **to the end** for as long as is possible, however unpleasant the situation becomes ○ *The company's policy was to fight to the bitter end all consequent damage suits.* ◇ **until the end of time** forever

---

USAGE Avoid using the expression *to no end* (meaning 'pointlessly') when *no end* (meaning 'to a great extent') is called for, as in *He annoyed her to no end*, where *He annoyed her no end* is the correct wording.

---

end up *vi* **1** to become something eventually **2** to arrive at a destination at long last

end- *prefix* = **endo-** (*before vowels*)

-end *suffix* person or thing to be treated in a particular way ○ *adherend* [< Latin *-endus, -endum*]

endamoeba /éndə meébə/ (*plural* **-moebae** *or* **-moebas** /-bee/ *or* **-mebas**) *n* a parasitic protozoan found in the digestive tracts of some invertebrates, especially cockroaches and termites. Genus: *Endamoeba.*

endanger /in dáynjər/ *vt* to expose somebody or something to danger —**endangered** *adj* —**endangerment** *n*

endangered species *n* a species of animal, plant, or other organism, whose numbers are so few, or declining so quickly, that it may soon become extinct

endarterectomy /én daartə réktəmi/ (*plural* **-mies**) *n* the surgical removal of material that is wholly or partially obstructing blood flow in an artery [Mid-20C. < END- + ARTERY.]

en dash *n* in printing, a dash that is one en in length

endear /in deér/ *vt* to make somebody or something affectionately loved or greatly liked

endearing /in deéring/ *adj* producing feelings of affection or fondness —**endearingly** *adv*

endearment /in deérmənt/ *n* **1** an expression of affection, especially if spoken **2** the act or condition of being endeared

endeavor *vt, n* US = **endeavour**

endeavour /in dévvər/ *vt, n* **TRY TO DO** to make an effort to achieve something ■ *n* **1 EFFORT** an earnest exertion in order to achieve something **2 ENTERPRISE** an enterprise or directed activity [15C. < obsolete *put in dever*, partial translation of French *mettre en devoir* 'put in duty'.] — **endeavourer** *n*

endemic /en démmik/ *adj* **1 OCCURRING IN PARTICULAR PLACE** describes a disease occurring within a specific area, region, or locale **2 RESTRICTED TO PARTICULAR AREA** describes a species of organism that is confined to a particular geographical region, e.g. an island or river basin **3 CHARACTERISTIC OF AREA** characteristic of a particular place, or among a particular group, or area, of interest or activity ■ *n* **ENDEMIC DISEASE** an endemic disease [Mid-17C. < Greek *endēmos* 'native' < *dēmos* 'people'.] —**endemically** *adv* — **endemicity** /én de míssəti, éndə-/ *n* —**endemism** /éndəmizəm/ *n*

endergonic /éndər gónnik/ *adj* describes a reaction that requires energy [Mid-20C. < END- + Greek *ergon* 'work'.]

~~**endevour**~~ incorrect spelling of **endeavour**

endgame /énd gaym/ *n* **1** the final stage of a chess game in which only a few pieces are left on the board **2** the final stage of a process or contest ○ *As the trial neared its close, reporters watched closely to see what the prosecutors' endgame would be.*

ending /énding/ *n* **1 FINAL PART** the final or concluding part of something, e.g. a book or film **2 WAY SOMETHING IS FINISHED** the manner in which something is ended **3 END PART OF WORD** the terminating part of a word, e.g. an inflection or suffix **4** CHESS = **endgame** *n.* 1 **5 PROCESS OF CONCLUDING A RELATIONSHIP** the process of concluding a relationship with another person, especially a therapist

endive /én dīv, éndiv, óN deev/ (*plural* **-dives** *or* **-dive**) *n* **1** a plant grown for its tightly packed curly leaves. Use: in salads, as a garnish. *Cichorium endivia.* **2** US FOOD *Cichorium intybus.* = **chicory** [14C. Via French < Latin *endivia* < medieval Greek *entubia.*]

endless /éndləss/ *adj* **1** having no end or limit **2** made continuous by joining the ends —**endlessly** *adv* —**endlessness** *n*

end line *n* a line at the end of a court or field that marks the boundary of a playing area

end matter *n* PUBL = **back matter**

end moraine *n* a ridge of rock, gravel, and soil at the terminal end of a glacier or ice field

endmost /énd mōst/ *adj* **1** nearest or at the end **2** last or most distant

endnote /énd nōt/ *n* a note of comment or reference placed at the end of a chapter, book, or essay

endo- *prefix* in, within, inside ○ *endotracheal* [< Greek *endo* < Indo-European, 'in']

endoblast *n* **1** = **endoderm** **2** = **hypoblast** *n.* 1 —**endoblastic** *adj*

endocardial /éndō kaárdi əl/ *adj* **1** located within the heart **2** concerned with the membranous lining of the heart's cavities (**endocardium**)

endocarditis /éndō kaar dítiss/ *n* inflammation of the membranous lining of the heart's cavities (**endocardium**) —**endocarditic** /-díttik/ *adj*

endocardium /éndō kaárdi əm/ (*plural* **-a** /-di ə/) *n* the thin membranous lining of the heart's cavities

endocarp /éndə kaarp/ *n* the innermost of the three layers of the wall (**pericarp**) of a fruit. It may be toughened or hardened, as in a cherry stone or peach stone. (*technical*) —**endocarpal** /éndə kaárp'l/ *adj*

endocranium /éndō kráyni əm/ (*plural* **-a** /-ni ə/) *n* ANAT = **dura mater** —**endocranial** *adj*

endocrine /éndō krīn, -krin/ *adj* relating to glands that secrete hormones directly into the lymph or bloodstream. ◊ **exocrine** [Early 20C. < ENDO- + Greek *krinein* 'to separate'.]

endocrine gland *n* any gland of the body that secretes hormones directly into the blood or lymph, e.g. the thyroid, pituitary, pineal, and adrenal glands

endocrinology /éndō kri nólləji, -krī-/ *n* a branch of medicine dealing with disorders of the endocrine glands —**endocrinologic** /éndō krinə lójjik/ *adj* —**endocrinological** *adj* —**endocrinologist** *n*

endocytosis /éndō sī tóssiss/ *n* the process by which a cell membrane folds inwards to take in substances bound to its surface

endoderm /éndō durm/ *n* the innermost layer of an animal embryo that develops into the lining of the respiratory and digestive tracts [Mid-19C. < ENDO- + Greek *derma* 'skin'.] —**endodermal** /éndō dúrm'l/ *adj*

endodermis /énd ō dúrmiss/ *n* a layer of cells that marks the boundary between the inner core (**stele**) and outer surrounding tissue (**cortex**) of a plant root [Late 19C. < ENDODERM, after *epidermis*.]

endodontics /éndō dóntiks/, **endodontia** /-dónti ə/ *n* the branch of dentistry that deals with diseases of the dental pulp (+ *singular verb*) [Mid-20C. < ENDO- + ORTHODONTICS.] —**endodontic** *adj* —**endodontist** *n*

endoenzyme /énd ō én zīm/ *n* an enzyme that is produced and functions inside cells

endoergic /énd ō úrjik/ *adj* relating to a nuclear reaction in which energy is consumed [Mid-20C. < ENDO- + Greek *ergon* 'work'.]

endogamy /en dóggəmi/ *n* **1** the social practice of marrying another member of the same clan, people, or other kinship group **2** pollination between the flowers of the same plant —**endogamous** *adj*

endogenic /éndō jénnik/ *adj* formed, located, or happening beneath the Earth's surface. ◊ **exogenic**

endogenous /en dójjənəss/ *adj* **1** with no apparent external cause ○ *endogenous depression* **2** originating or growing within an organism or tissue ○ *endogenous secretions.* ◊ **exogenous** —**endogenously** *adv* —**endogeny** *n*

endolymph /éndō limf/ *n* the fluid inside the membranous labyrinth of the ear —**endolymphatic** /éndō lim fáttik/ *adj*

endometria plural of **endometrium**

endometriosis /éndō meétri óssiss/ *n* a medical condition in which the mucous membrane (**endometrium**) that normally lines only the womb is present and functioning in the ovaries or elsewhere in the body

endometrium /éndō meétri əm/ (*plural* **-a** /-tri ə/) *n* the mucous membrane that lines the womb and increases in thickness in the latter part of the menstrual cycle [Late 19C. < ENDO- + Greek *mētra* 'womb'.] —**endometrial** *adj*

endomitosis /éndō mī tóssiss/ *n* a process by which chromosomes divide within a cell but the nucleus does not, so that an increase in chromosome number results —**endomitotic** /-mī tóttik/ *adj*

endomorph /éndō mawrf/ *n* **1** somebody whose body has a stocky build and a prominent abdomen. ◊ **ectomorph, mesomorph** **2** a mineral surrounded by another. ◊ **perimorph** —**endomorphic** /éndō máwrfik/ *adj* —**endomorphy** *n*

endonuclease /éndō nyoókli ayz/ *n* an enzyme that splits DNA or RNA

endoparasite /éndō párrə sīt/ *n* a parasite, e.g. a tapeworm, that lives inside its host —**endoparasitic** /éndō párrə síttik/ *adj* —**endoparasitism** /éndō párrə sītizəm/ *n*

endopeptidase /éndō pépti dayz, -dayss/ *n* an enzyme that splits proteins into peptides

endophyte /éndō fīt/ *n* a plant or fungus that lives inside another plant —**endophytic** /éndō fíttik/ *adj*

endoplasm /éndō plazəm/ *n* the inner, more fluid layer of cytoplasm in a cell —**endoplasmic** /éndō plázmik/ *adj*

endoplasmic reticulum *n* an intricate system of tubular membranes in the cytoplasm of a cell

end organ *n* the specialized end of a sensory or motor nerve

endorphin /en dáwrfin/ *n* a substance in the brain that attaches to the same cell receptors that morphine does. Endorphins are released when severe injury occurs, often abolishing all sensation of pain. [Late 20C. Blend of ENDOGENOUS + MORPHINE.]

endorse /in dáwrss/ (**-dorses, -dorsing, -dorsed**), **indorse** (**-dorses, -dorsing, -dorsed**) *vt* **1 APPROVE FORMALLY** to give formal approval or permission for something ○ *This practice is not endorsed by head office.* **2 SUPPORT** to give public support to somebody or something, especially during an election ○ *decided to endorse the mayor as a candidate for higher office* **3 PROMOTE** to give public approval of a product for advertising purposes ○ *a brand endorsed by a popular TV star* **4 SIGN CHEQUE TO OBTAIN CASH** to sign the back of a cheque or postal order in order to cash it **5 SIGN SOMETHING TO ASSIGN PAYMENT** to sign the back of a negotiable document in order to make it payable to a specified payee **6 SIGN RECEIPT** to sign a document to acknowledge receipt of a payment **7 WRITE ON BACK OF DOCUMENT** to write a comment on the back of a document ○ *a fitness report that had been endorsed on the back by its recipient* **8 RECORD CONVICTIONS ON LICENCE** to record details of convictions for motoring offences on a driving licence ○ *You will pay a fine and have your licence endorsed with three penalty points.* [15C. < medieval Latin *indorsare* < Latin *dorsum* 'back'.] —**endorsable** *adj* —**endorsee** /in dáwr seé/ *n* —**endorser** *n*

endorsement /in dáwrssmənt/, **indorsement** *n* **1 ACT OF ENDORSING** an act or instance of endorsing something or somebody ○ *make an endorsement of a cheque* **2 SIGNATURE OR WRITTEN COMMENT** something, especially a signature, written on the back of a document to make it payable, approve it, or comment on it **3 OFFICIAL APPROVAL OR PERMISSION** official approval of or permission for something **4 PUBLIC SUPPORT** public support for somebody or something **5 ADVERTISING TESTIMONIAL** an instance of public approval of a product for advertising purposes **6 RECORD OF OFFENCE** details of a conviction for a motoring offence recorded on a driving licence **7 POLICY ALTERATION** a clause added to an insurance policy that changes the coverage

endoscope /éndə skōp/ *n* a medical instrument consisting of a long tube inserted into the body, usually through a small incision —**endoscopic** /éndə skóppik/ *adj* —**endoscopically** *adv* —**endoscopy** /en dóskəpi/ *n*

endoskeleton /éndō skéllitən/ *n* the internal skeleton of an animal, especially of a vertebrate —**endoskeletal** *adj*

endosmosis /énd oz mόssiss/ *n* osmosis in which fluid is absorbed from a surrounding fluid into a cell —**endosmotic** /énd oz móttik/ *adj* —**endosmotically** *adv*

endosperm /éndō spurm/ *n* the tissue that surrounds the embryo inside a plant seed and provides nourishment for it —**endospermic** /éndō spúrmik/ *adj*

endospore /éndō spawr/ *n* **1** an asexual spore that is formed inside the cells of certain bacteria and algae **2** the inner layer of the wall of a spore —**endosporous** /en dóspərəss/ *adj*

endosteum /en dósti əm/ (*plural* **-a** /-ti ə/) *n* a layer of vascular tissue lining the inside of certain bones, e.g. the femur [Late 19C. < ENDO- + Greek *osteon* 'bone'.] —**endosteal** *adj*

endosulfan /éndō súlfən/ *n* $C_9H_6Cl_6O_3S$ a toxic organochlorine compound. Use: insecticide, acaricide. [Mid-20C. < ENDO- + SULFUR.]

endosymbiont /éndō símbi ont, -bī-/ *n* an organism that lives inside another organism to the benefit of both

endosymbiosis /éndō sím bi óssiss/ *n* symbiosis in which one organism lives inside the body of another —**endosymbiotic** /éndō símbi óttik/ *adj*

endosymbiotic hypothesis *n* a theory holding that the mitochondria and chloroplasts of eukaryotic cells originated as free-living prokaryotic organisms

endothecium /éndō theéshi əm, -theéssi əm/ (*plural* **-a** /-shi ə, -si ə/) *n* **1** the inner tissue of the spore-producing capsule of a moss **2** the tissue of the inner wall of an anther in a flower [Mid-19C. < ENDO- + Greek *thēkion* 'little case' < *thēkē* 'chest'.]

endothelia plural of **endothelium**

endothelioma /éndō theeli ṓmə/ (*plural* **-mas** *or* **-mata** /-ṓmətə/) *n* a tumour of cells that line internal body surfaces

endothelium /énd ō theéli əm/ (*plural* **-a** /-li ə/) *n* a layer of cells that lines the inside of certain body cavities, e.g. blood vessels [Late 19C. < modern Latin, < Greek *endon* 'within' + *thēlē* 'nipple'.] —**endothelial** *adj* —**endothelioid** *adj*

endotherm /éndō thurm/ *n* an animal that is able to maintain a constant body temperature despite changes in the temperature of its environment [Mid-20C. < ENDO- + Greek *thermē* 'heat'.]

endothermic /éndō thúrmik/, **endothermal** /-thúrm'l/ *adj* **1** describes a reaction that absorbs heat (*the preferred term in nuclear physics is 'endoergic'*) **2** maintaining a constant body temperature despite changes in the temperature of the environment —**endothermy** /éndō thurmi/ *n*

endotoxin /éndō tóksin/ *n* a toxin produced within certain bacteria that is released only when the bacteria disintegrate —**endotoxic** *adj*

endotracheal /éndōtrə keé əl/ *adj* located in or passed through the windpipe ○ *an endotracheal tube*

endow /in dów/ *vt* **1** to provide a person or institution with income or property **2** to provide somebody or something with desirable qualities, abilities, or characteristics ○ *Nature has endowed the area with a perfect climate.* [14C. Via Anglo-Norman *endouer* < Latin *dotare* 'provide with a dowry' < *dos* 'dowry'.]

endowment /in dówmənt/ *n* **1 FUNDS OR PROPERTY** an amount of income or property that has been provided to a person or institution, especially an educational institution **2 GIVING OF ENDOWMENT** the giving of an endowment, or an instance of this **3 NATURAL QUALITY** a natural ability or quality ○ *A sharp mind was one of her many endowments.*

endowment assurance, endowment insurance *n* life insurance that pays a set amount to the policyholder when the policy matures or to a beneficiary if the policyholder dies before maturity

endowment mortgage *n* a mortgage in which the borrower pays the lender interest and repays the capital to a life assurance policy that repays the loan at maturity or when the borrower dies

endozoic /éndō zṓ ik/ *adj* **1** describes organisms that live inside an animal **2** describes a method of seed dispersal in which the seeds are eaten by an animal and then passed out in the animal's faeces

endpaper /énd paypər/ *n* a sturdy sheet of paper pasted to the inside of a book's front or back cover and to the spine edge of the first or last page

end pin *n* the adjustable spike-shaped leg at the bottom of a cello or double bass that the instrument rests on while being played

endplay /énd play/ *n* in bridge, a play in which an opponent is forced to lead near the end of the hand, with the result that he or she loses a trick that would otherwise have been won —**endplay** *vt*

end point *n* **1** the point at which something is complete or comes to an end **2** the point, marked by a colour change or other indicator, at which a titration is complete

endpoint /énd poynt/ *n* the point located at either end of a line segment or at the end of a ray

end product *n* the final result of a process or series of events or operations

end rhyme *n* the use of rhyme at the ends of lines of poetry, or an example of this

endrin /éndrin/ *n* $C_{12}H_8Cl_6O$ a poisonous white crystalline chlorinated hydrocarbon. Use: insecticide. [Mid-20C. < ENDO- + DIELDRIN.]

end-stopped /-stopt/ *adj* describes poetry containing a pause in meaning at the end of a line or couplet, instead of continuing into the next line or couplet

endue /in dyóo/ (**-dues, -duing, -dued**), **indue** (**-dues, -duing, -dued**) *vt* to endow somebody or something with an ability or quality ○ *His successes have endued him with an aura of invincibility.* [14C. < French *enduire* < Latin *ducere* 'to lead'.]

endurance /in dyóorənss/ *n* **1 ABILITY TO BEAR PROLONGED HARDSHIP** the ability or power to bear prolonged exertion, pain, or hardship ○ *an endurance race* **2 TOLERATION OF HARDSHIP** an act or example of toleration of prolonged suffering or hardship ○ *an unflinching endurance of pain* **3 PERSISTENCE OVER TIME** the survival or persistence of something despite the ravages of time ○ *the endurance of ancient traditions* [15C. < French, < *endurer* (see ENDURE).]

endure /in dyóor/ (**-dures, -during, -dured**) *v* **1** *vti* **BEAR HARDSHIP** to experience exertion, pain, or hardship without giving up ○ *The nation endured years of war to create a lasting peace.* **2** *vt* **TOLERATE DISAGREEABLE THINGS** to tolerate or accept somebody or something that is extremely disagreeable (*formal*) ○ *I cannot endure that song.* **3** *vi* **SURVIVE** to last or survive over a period of time, especially when faced with difficulties ○ *The philosophical ideas of the ancient Greeks endure to this day.* [14C. Via French *endurer* < Latin *indurare* 'harden' < *durus* 'hard'.] —**endurability** *n* —**endurable** *adj* —**endurableness** *n* —**endurably** *adv*

enduring /in dyóoring/ *adj* **1** persisting or surviving in the face of difficulties **2** patient or tolerant despite many difficulties —**enduringly** *adv* —**enduringness** *n*

enduro /in dyóorō/ (*plural* **-os**) *n* a long race, especially one involving motorcycles or cars, in which the emphasis is on endurance rather than speed [Mid-20C. Alteration of ENDURANCE.]

end user *n* a person or group that is one of the ultimate consumers or users that a product has been designed for ○ *a survey that is designed to assess what the end user really needs*

endways /énd wayz/, **endwise** *adv* **1 WITH END UP** with an end up or forwards **2 TOWARDS ENDS** towards the ends **3 WITH ENDS TOUCHING** with one end next to another end

Endymion /en dímmi ən/ *n* in Greek mythology, a handsome man loved by the moon goddess Selene

end zone *n* either of the two areas at the ends of an American football field between the goal line and the end line where a touchdown is scored

ENE *abbr* east-northeast

-ene *suffix* an unsaturated organic compound ○ *butene* [< Greek *-ēnē*, form of *-ēnos*, adjective suffix]

enema /énnəmə/ (*plural* **-mas** *or* **-mata** /-mətə/) *n* **1** the insertion of a liquid into the bowels via the rectum as a treatment, especially for constipation, or as an aid to diagnosis **2** the liquid used in an enema ○ *a barium enema* [Late 17C. Via late Latin < Greek, < *enienai* 'send or put in' < *hienai* 'send'.]

enemy /énnəmi/ (*plural* **-mies**) *n* **1 UNFRIENDLY OPPONENT** a person who hates or seeks to harm somebody or something **2 MILITARY OPPONENT** a person or group, especially a military force, that fights against another in combat or battle **3 HOSTILE POWER** a hostile nation or power **4 HARMFUL THING** something that harms or opposes something else ○ *In a case like this, time is the enemy.* [13C. Via French < Latin *inimicus* 'enemy, unfriendly' < *amicus* 'friend'.]

energetic /ènnər jéttik/ *adj* **1** displaying great vigour or force **2** requiring great vigour or stamina [Mid-17C. < Greek *energētikos* 'active' < *ergon* 'work'.] —**energetically** *adv*

energetics /ènnər jéttiks/ *n* the branch of physics that studies energy and its transformations (+ *singular verb*)

energize /énnər jīz/ (**-gizes, -gizing, -gized**), **energise** (**-gises, -gising, -gised**) *v* **1** *vt* **GIVE SOMEBODY OR SOMETHING ENERGY** to supply somebody or something with strength or power ○ *He felt energized by his nap.* **2** *vti* **MAKE OR BECOME ACTIVE** to become or cause something to become vigorously active **3** *vt* **SUPPLY WITH ELECTRICAL POWER** to supply something with a source of electrical power —**energization** /ènnər jī záysh'n/ *n* —**energizer** *n*

energy /énnərji/ (*plural* **-gies**) *n* **1 VIGOUR** liveliness and forcefulness ○ *She gave a speech that was full of energy.* **2 ABILITY TO DO THINGS** the ability or power to work or make an effort ○ *His illness left him feeling drained of energy.* **3 FORCEFUL EFFORT** a vigorous effort or action ○ *We must concentrate our energies on the task in hand.* **4 POWER SUPPLY OR SOURCE** a supply or source of electrical, mechanical, or other form of power **5 CAPACITY TO DO WORK** (*symbol E*) the capacity of a body or system to do work [Mid-16C. Via French < Greek *energeia* < *ergon* 'work'.]

energy audit *n* a survey of the use of energy in a building or organization, undertaken in order to make energy use as efficient as possible

energy balance *n* a mathematical relationship, using the principle of the conservation of energy, that shows the energy inputs and outputs of a process or system

energy band *n* PHYS = **band**[2] *n.* **9**

energy bar *n* a bar-shaped snack made of ingredients intended to boost a person's physical energy

energy crisis *n* a situation in which available sources of energy are not sufficient to meet the demand

energy efficient *adj* using electrical or other energy in an economical way (*hyphenated before nouns*)

energy level *n* one of the discrete stable energy values that can be assumed by a physical system, e.g. the electrons in an atom or an atomic nucleus

energy recovery *n* the extraction of energy from synthetic materials, e.g. using the heat from incineration of solid waste to generate electricity

energy tax *n* a tax on an energy source intended to discourage environmentally unfriendly sources and encourage energy conservation or use of alternative sources

enervate (**-vates, -vating, -vated**) *vt* /énnər vayt/ to weaken somebody's physical, mental, or moral vitality ○ *I was feeling quite enervated by the strain of moving house.* [Early 17C. < Latin *enervat-*, past participle of *enervare* 'extract the sinews of, weaken' < *nervus* 'sinew'.] —**enervation** /ènnər váysh'n/ *n*

Enewetak /énnə wée tok, ə née wi tok/ atoll in the NW Marshall Islands in the N Pacific Ocean, a former testing ground for nuclear weapons. Population: 715 (1988). Area: 5 sq. km/2 sq. mi.

enface /in fáyss/ (**-faces, -facing, -faced**) *vt* to mark something on the face of a document by writing, stamping, or printing —**enfacement** *n*

en famille /oN fa mée/ *adv* **1** with the members of your family, especially at home **2** in an informal, relaxed, or casual way [Early 18C. < French, 'in the family'.]

enfant terrible /óN foN te réeblə/ (*plural* **enfants terribles** /óN foN te réeblə/) *n* **1** somebody whose unconventional behaviour, attitudes, or remarks are shocking to others **2** a young person, especially in the arts, who has become successful because of work that is radically innovative or extremely avant-garde [< French, 'terrible child']

enfeeble /in féeb'l/ (**-bles, -bling, -bled**) *vt* to reduce the strength of somebody or something to the point of weakness [14C. < Old French *enfiblir* < *feble* (see FEEBLE).] —**enfeeblement** *n*

enfeoff /in féef/ *vt* to invest somebody with the freehold possession of a piece of land [14C. < Anglo-Norman *enfeoffer* < Old French *fief* (see FIEF).] —**enfeoffment** *n*

Enfield *n* ARMS = **Enfield rifle**

Enfield musket /én feeld-/ *n* a muzzle-loading rifled musket used by British forces in the 19th century and by American troops in the American Civil War [After ENFIELD]

Enfield rifle, Enfield *n* **1** a .303-calibre bolt-action breech-loading rifle, used by British forces in World War I and until the 1930s. **2** a .30-calibre bolt-action breech-loading rifle used by US forces in World War I. **3** = **Enfield musket** [After ENFIELD]

enfilade *n* /énfi layd/ **1 VULNERABLE POSITION** a position in which troops are exposed to gunfire along the length of their formation. ◊ **defilade** *n.* **2 RAKING FIRE** gunfire that strikes a body of troops along its whole length ■ *vt* /énfi láyd/ (**-lades, -lading, -laded**) **1 FIRE AT SOMETHING ALONG ITS LENGTH** to attack a position or body of troops with gunfire along its whole length **2 POSITION FOR FIRING ALONG WHOLE LENGTH** to place guns or troops in a position from which they can fire on the whole length of an enemy position or body of troops [Early 18C. < French, < *fil* 'thread' < Latin *filum*.]

enfleurage /óN flur raázh/ *n* a process used in making perfume in which oils acquire fragrance by being exposed to the scent of flowers [Mid-19C. < French, < *enfleurer* 'saturate with the scent of flowers' < *fleur* 'flower'.]

~~**enflict**~~ incorrect spelling of **inflict**

enfold /in fṓld/, **infold** *vt* **1 ENVELOP** to wrap, or wrap something, completely around somebody or something **2 EMBRACE** to hold somebody or something in an embrace **3 ENCLOSE OR SURROUND** to enclose or surround somebody or something ○ *enfold a child in your love* —**enfolder** *n*

~~**enforcable**~~ incorrect spelling of **enforceable**

enforce /in fáwrss/ (**-forces, -forcing, -forced**) *vt* **1 MAKE PEOPLE OBEY** to compel obedience to a law, regulation, or command **2 IMPOSE** to impose something by force **3 STRENGTHEN** to give strength or emphasis to something ○ *enforce an argument* [13C. < French *enforcir* < Latin *fortis* 'strong'.] —**enforceability** /in fáwrssə bílləti/ *n* —**enforceable** *adj* —**enforcement** *n*

enforcer /in fáwrssər/ *n* **1** an enforcer of a rule, law, or order **2** *US* a member of a criminal gang who uses physical violence to intimidate and enforce compliance (*slang*)

enfranchise /in frán chīz/ (**-chises, -chising, -chised**) *vt* **1 GIVE SOMEBODY RIGHT TO VOTE** to give somebody the right to vote in an election **2 SET FREE** to set somebody free, especially from slavery **3 ALLOW REPRESENTATION TO** to grant political representation to a town or city [Early 16C. < Old French *enfranchir* < *franc* 'free' < Latin *francus*.] —**enfranchisement** /-chiz-/ *n*

ENG *abbr* electronic newsgathering

eng. *abbr* **1** engine **2** engineer **3** engineering

Eng. *abbr* **1** England **2** English

engage /in gáyj/ (**-gages, -gaging, -gaged**) *v* **1** *vti* **INVOLVE OR BECOME INVOLVED** to involve somebody in an activity, or become involved or take part in an activity **2** *vt* **HIRE** to hire somebody for a job or to do some work **3** *vt* **RESERVE** to reserve or rent something for personal use (*dated*) **4** *vt* **REQUIRE USE OF** to require the use or devotion of something **5** *vt* **HOLD ATTENTION OF** to attract and hold somebody's attention **6** *vt* **ATTRACT SOMEBODY BY PLEASING** to attract or win the affection of somebody by pleasing that person ○ *He was engaged by the child's charm.* **7** *vti* **PROMISE** to commit yourself or something to an obligation ○ *She engaged to meet them tomorrow.* **8** *vti* **FIGHT** to fight or begin a battle with an enemy **9** *vti* **INTERLOCK** to become interlocked, or bring something together and cause something to interlock **10** *vti* **ACTIVATE OR BECOME ACTIVATED** to activate something or bring something into operation, or become activated or operational [Early 16C. < French *engager* < *gage* 'pledge'.] —**engager** *n*

engagé /óng ga zháy/ *adj* committed to a political cause or ideology, usually a left-wing one [Mid-20C. < French, past participle of *engager* (see ENGAGE).]

engaged /in gáyjd/ *adj* **1 HAVING AGREED TO MARRY** having agreed to be married ○ *the newly engaged couple* **2 OCCUPIED** busy doing something ○ *The Minister is otherwise engaged this afternoon.* **3 FIGHTING BATTLE** fighting a military battle **4 WITH PARTS INTERLOCKED** with teeth or other parts interlocked and often in operation **5 CURRENTLY BEING USED FOR TELEPHONE CALL** used to describe a telephone line that is currently being used to make a telephone call. US term **busy** *adj.* **6** **6 BUILT INTO OR ATTACHED TO WALL** describes a part of a building that is built into or attached to a wall

engaged tone *n* a series of repeated short tones heard through a telephone when the line belonging to the number dialled is already being used. US term **busy signal**

engagée /óng ga zháy/ *adj* describes a woman who is committed to a political cause or ideology, usually a left-wing one [Mid-20C. < French, form of past participle of *engager* (see ENGAGE).]

engagement /in gáyjmənt/ *n* **1 AGREEMENT TO MARRY** an agreement to get married ○ *announce our engagement* **2 COMMITMENT TO ATTEND** an arrangement to be present at an event, especially a business or social appointment **3 PLEDGE** something, e.g. a promise, that is freely made and that carries an obligation to do something **4 SHORT JOB** a job that lasts for a short period of time, especially one for an entertainer in a club or theatre ○ *a week-long engagement in Las Vegas* **5 BATTLE** a battle or other conflict involving military forces ○ *a minor engagement on the frontier* **6 ACTIVE OR OPERATIONAL STATE** an act or condition of being activated or becoming operational

SYNONYMS See *fight*.

engagement ring *n* a ring given by a man to his fiancée to mark their engagement to marry

engaging /in gáyjing/ *adj* charming or pleasing in a way that attracts and holds the attention —**engagingly** *adv*

en garde /oN gaárd/ *interj* used to warn a fencer to assume the prescribed stance for the start of a match [< French, 'on guard']

Engels /éng g'lz/, **Friedrich** (1820–95) German political thinker and revolutionary

engender /in jéndər/ *v* **1** *vti* to arise or come into existence, or cause something to do so ○ *Secrecy engenders suspicion.* **2** *vt* to cause offspring to be conceived or born (*formal*) [14C. Via French < Latin *ingenerare* < *generare* 'produce'.] —**engenderer** *n*

engine /énjin/ *n* **1 MACHINE FOR POWERING EQUIPMENT** a machine that converts energy into mechanical power or motion ○ *an oil-fired engine* **2 RAILWAY LOCOMOTIVE** a railway locomotive **3 DRIVING FORCE OR ENERGY SOURCE** something that supplies the driving force or energy to a movement, system, or trend ○ *a political movement that was seen as a great engine of social change* **4 BATTLEFIELD MACHINE** a battering ram, catapult, or other device used in warfare (*archaic*) ○ *a siege engine* [14C. Via French < Latin *ingenium* 'talent, clever device'.] —**engined** *adj* —**engineless** *adj*

engine block *n US* MECH ENG = **cylinder block**

engine driver *n* somebody who operates a railway locomotive. US term **engineer** *n.* **2**

engineer /énji neér/ *n* **1 ENGINEERING PROFESSIONAL** a person who is trained as a professional engineer **2** *US, Can* RAIL = **engine driver 3 MECHANIC** an operator or servicer of machines **4 SHIP'S OFFICER** an officer on a ship who is in charge of the engines **5 CONSTRUCTION SOLDIER** a member of a unit of the armed forces that specializes in building and sometimes destroying bridges, fortifications, and other large structures **6 PLANNER** a planner, initiator, or supervisor of something, especially something that is achieved with ingenuity or secretiveness ○ *the engineer of the overthrow of the government* ■ *vt* **1 CONTRIVE** to plan something or bring it about, especially in an ingenious or secretive manner **2 USE ENGINEERING SKILL TO DESIGN** to use professional engineering skill to design or create something ○ *This car was engineered in Italy.* **3 USE GENETIC ENGINEERING ON** to use the techniques of genetic engineering on something [14C. < Old French *engigneor* 'contriver' < Latin *ingenium* 'talent, clever device'.]

engineering /énji neéring/ *n* **1 APPLICATION OF SCIENCE TO DESIGNING THINGS** the application of science in the design, planning, construction, and maintenance of buildings, machines, and other manufactured things ○ *leading the world in engineering* **2 PROFESSION INVOLVING TECHNICAL DESIGNING** any one of various branches of engineering pursued as a profession, e.g. civil engineering or electronic engineering **3 CONTRIVANCE** the planning or bringing about of something, especially when done with ingenuity or secretiveness

engine room *n* the place on board a ship where the engines are housed

enginery /énjinri/ (*plural* **-ries**) *n* a group of engines

engirdle /in gúrd'l/ (**-girdles, -girdling, -girdled**) *vt* to surround or encircle something (*literary*)

englacial /in gláysh'l/ *adj* describes material or processes occurring within a glacier

England /íng glənd/ country forming the southern and largest part of Great Britain and of the United Kingdom. Capital: London. Population: 48,903,000 (1995). Area: 130,410 sq. km/50,352 sq. mi.

Englified /íng gli fīd/ *adj Scotland* anglicized (*informal disapproving*)

English /íng glish/ *n* **1 LANGUAGE OF UK, US, AND CANADA** an official language of the United Kingdom of Great Britain and Northern Ireland, the Republic of Ireland, the United States, Canada, Australia, New Zealand, South Africa, and several other countries. Native speakers: 350 million. Other speakers: 375 million. **2 PEOPLE FROM ENGLAND** people who come from England **3 STUDY OF ENGLISH** the English language, together with literature written in it, as a subject of study **4 UNDERSTANDABLE ENGLISH** clear, understandable spoken or written English **5 English, english** *US* CUE GAMES = **side** *n.* **20** ■ *adj* **1 OF THE LANGUAGE ENGLISH** relating to the language of English **2 OF THE ENGLISH** relating to the English or England [Old English *Englisc* < *Engle* 'the Angles'] —**Englishness** *n*

English bond *n* an arrangement of bricks in a wall in which layers (**courses**) of bricks laid end to end (**stretchers**) alternate with layers of bricks laid side to side (**headers**)

English breakfast *n* a breakfast usually consisting of cereal or fruit, followed by cooked bacon, eggs, sausages, and tomatoes, and then toast and marmalade or jam ○ *a choice of continental or full English breakfast*

English Channel area of water between England and France linking the North Sea with the Atlantic Ocean. Length: 560 km/350 mi. French **La Manche**

English disease *n* recurring industrial unrest marked by many strikes, formerly regarded by non-British commentators as endemic in and damaging to British industry

English Heritage *n* a body partly funded by government that is responsible for maintaining buildings and monuments of historical interest in England

English horn *n* MUSIC = **cor anglais**

Englishman /íng glishmən/ (*plural* **-men** /-mən/) *n* a man who comes from England

English Nature *n* the English division of the Nature Conservancy Council, a government agency responsible for various nature-conservation functions including national nature reserves, and for advising central government

English setter *n* a hunting dog of a medium-sized breed of setter that has a silky white coat with brown or black markings

Englishwoman /íng glish wòòmən/ (*plural* **-en** /-wimmin/) *n* a woman who comes from England

engobe /én gōb/ *n* liquid clay used to decorate a ceramic piece before it has been fired and usually applied before the piece has dried [Mid-19C. < French.]

engorge /in gáwrj/ (**-gorges, -gorging, -gorged**) *v* **1** *vti* **FILL WITH BLOOD** to fill something with blood until it is congested, or become filled with blood **2** *vti* **EAT GREEDILY** to eat something greedily **3** *vr* **GORGE YOURSELF** to gorge or fill yourself with food [15C. < French *engorger* < Old French *gorge* 'throat' (see GORGE).] —**engorgement** *n*

engr. *abbr* **1** engraved **2** engraver **3** engraving

engraft /in graáft/, **ingraft** *vt* **1 GRAFT PLANT PART** to graft a bud or other plant part from one plant onto another (*technical*) **2 GRAFT ANIMAL TISSUE** to graft animal tissue from one part of the body onto another part or onto another animal (*technical*) **3 ATTACH SOMETHING PERMANENTLY** to attach something permanently to something else by a process resembling grafting **4 IMPLANT SOMETHING PERMANENTLY** to implant something permanently or deeply in something else —**engraftment** *n*

engrailed /in gráyld/ *adj* **1** edged with a series of concave indentations **2** edged with a row of raised dots ○ *an engrailed gold coin* [14C. < Old French *engresler* 'make thin' < *gresle* 'thin' < Latin *gracilis*.]

engrain *vt* = **ingrain**

engram /én gram/ *n* a hypothetical physical impression made in neural tissue by a mental stimulus, suggested as an explanation of the persistence of memory [Early 20C. < German *Engramm* < Greek *gramma* 'something written'.]

engrave /in gráyv/ (**-graves, -graving, -graved**) *vt* **1 CARVE OR ETCH MATERIAL** to carve or etch a hard surface with a design or lettering for decoration or printing ○ *engraved a silver cup* **2 CARVE OR ETCH DESIGN** to carve or etch a design or lettering into a hard surface for decoration or printing ○ *engraving a dedication on a watch* **3 PRINT IMAGE** to print an image, especially a raised image, from an engraved printing plate **4 IMPRESS** to impress something deeply, e.g. a memory on the mind —**engraver** *n*

engraving /in gráyving/ *n* **1 ENGRAVED PRINT** a print of an image that was made using an engraved plate or block **2 ENGRAVED DESIGN** a design or lettering engraved into a hard surface for decoration or printing **3 CUTTING OR ETCHING OF IMAGES** the art or process of cutting or etching images into a hard surface **4 PRINTING SURFACE** a plate, block, or other hard surface on which an image has been engraved for printing

engross[1] /in grṓss/ *vt* **1** to take up somebody's whole attention ○ *The children were engrossed by the story.* **2** to buy all of a commodity or enough of it to control its market [14C. < Old French *en gros*, medieval Latin *in grosso* 'in bulk, wholesale' < late Latin *grossus* 'bulky, coarse'.] —**engrosser** *n*

engross[2] /in grṓss/ *vt* **1** to write or print the final version of a legal document **2** to copy a document in large clear handwriting (*dated*) [14C. < Anglo-Norman *engrosser*, medieval Latin *ingrossare* < late Latin *grossus* 'bulky, coarse'.] —**engrosser** *n*

engrossing /in grṓssing/ *adj* engaging somebody's whole attention —**engrossingly** *adv*

engrossment /in grṓssmənt/ *n* **1 COMPLETELY ABSORBED STATE** the complete absorption of somebody's attention with something **2 FINAL LEGAL COPY** a formally prepared copy of a deed or other document for legal use **3 DOCUMENT PREPARATION** the preparation of the final legal copy or a clean copy of a document (*dated*) **4 CORNERING OF MARKET** the purchasing of enough of a commodity to control the market in it

engulf /in gúlf/, **ingulf** *vt* **1** to surround, cover over, and swallow up somebody or something, as floodwaters do **2** to overwhelm somebody or something with a great amount or number of something (*often passive*) ○ *The attacking hordes engulfed the undefended town.* —**engulfment** *n*

ϟ **enhance** /in haánss/ (**-hances, -hancing, -hanced**) *vt* **1** to improve or add to the strength, worth, beauty, or other desirable quality of something **2** to increase the clarity, degree of detail, or another quality of an electronic image by using a computer program [13C. < Anglo-Norman *enhauncer* 'raise up' < Latin *altus* 'high'.] —**enhancement** *n* —**enhancer** *n* —**enhancive** *adj*

enharmonic /én haar mónnik/ *adj* describes notes, e.g. A♯ and B♭, that are spelt differently in a score but have the same pitch in a tempered scale, e.g. on the piano —**enharmonically** *adv*

ϟ **ENIAC** /énni ak/ *abbr* Electronic Numerical Integrator And Computer

enigma /i nígmə/ *n* somebody or something that is not easily explained or understood [Mid-16C. Via Latin < Greek *ainigma* < *ainos* 'fable'.]

enigmatic /énnig máttik/, **enigmatical** /-máttik'l/ *adj* difficult to interpret, understand, or explain —**enigmatically** *adv*

SYNONYMS See *obscure*.

enisle /in íl/ (**-isles, -isling, -isled**) *vt* (*literary*) **1** to isolate somebody or something from other people or things **2** to make something into an island

enjambment /in jám mənt/, **enjambement** *n* the continuation of meaning, without pause or break, from one line of poetry to the next [Mid-19C. < French *enjambement* < *jambe* 'leg' (see JAMB).] —**enjambed** *adj*

enjoin /in jóyn/ *vt* **1 COMMAND** to command somebody to do something or behave in a certain way (*formal*) **2 IMPOSE** to urge or impose a condition or course of action upon others ○ *She enjoined secrecy upon all of us.* **3 FORBID OR COMMAND LEGALLY** to forbid or command somebody to do something by means of a legal injunction —**enjoiner** *n* —**enjoinment** *n*

enjoy /in jóy/ *v* **1** *vt* **FIND PLEASING** to take pleasure in something ○ *She really enjoys ballet.* **2** *vt* **HAVE USE OF** to have the full and satisfying use or benefit of something ○ *He enjoys sole possession of the estate.* **3** *vt* **BENEFIT FROM** to benefit from a desirable condition or situation ○ *The resort enjoys months of uninterrupted sunshine.* **4** *vr* **HAVE GOOD EXPERIENCE** to have a pleasurable experience ○ *They all enjoyed themselves at the party.* [14C. < Old French *enjoïr* < Latin *gaudere* 'rejoice'.] —**enjoyer** *n*

enjoyable /in jóyəb'l/ *adj* providing or capable of providing pleasure ○ *The food is always enjoyable.* —**enjoyableness** *n* —**enjoyably** *adv*

enjoyment /in jóymənt/ *n* **1 PLEASURE** pleasure that results from using or experiencing something ○ *eating with great enjoyment* **2 EXPERIENCING OF SOMETHING THAT PROVIDES PLEASURE** the experiencing of something that provides pleasure ○ *He wished his enjoyment of the concert would never end.* **3 SOURCE OF PLEASURE** something that gives pleasure ○ *Fishing is one of her chief enjoyments.* **4 USE OR BENEFIT** the use or benefit of something, especially as a legal right ○ *the enjoyment of his rights as a landowner*

enkephalin /en kéffəlin/, **encephalin** /en kéffəlin, -séffə-/ *n* either of two chemicals with opiate qualities that are secreted in the brain and spinal cord and act to relieve pain [Mid-20C. < Greek *egkephalos* 'brain' (see ENCEPHALO-).]

enkindle /in kínd'l/ (**-dles, -dling, -dled**) *v* **1** *vt* to spark an emotional or intellectual response in somebody **2** *vti* to set something on fire, or start burning —**enkindler** *n*

enl. *abbr* **1** enlarged **2** enlisted

enlace /in láyss/ (**-laces, -lacing, -laced**), **inlace** (**-laces, -lacing, -laced**) *v* **1** *vt* to wrap something round with laces or something similar **2** *vti* to intertwine with something, or become intertwined —**enlacement** *n*

enlarge /in laárj/ (**-larges, -larging, -larged**) *v* **1** *vti* MAKE OR BECOME LARGER to increase the size, amount, or extent of something, or become larger **2** *vti* BROADEN IN SCOPE to broaden the scope of something, or become broader in scope ○ *the need for the investigation to be enlarged* **3** *vi* GIVE MORE DETAIL to speak or write at greater length or in more detail about something **4** *vt* MAKE LARGER PHOTOGRAPH to make a photographic print or image that is larger than the original negative, print, or slide —**enlarger** *n*

SYNONYMS See ***increase***.

enlargement /in laárjmənt/ *n* **1** PROCESS OF ENLARGING OR BEING ENLARGED the process of increasing, broadening, or enlarging something, or of being increased, broadened, or enlarged **2** ADDITION something added to something else to make it larger ○ *an enlargement to a house* **3** ENLARGED CONDITION the increased, broadened, or enlarged state of something **4** ENLARGED PHOTOGRAPH a photographic print or image that is larger than the negative, print, or slide from which it was made

enlighten /in lít'n/ *vt* **1** GIVE INFORMATION TO to give clarifying information to somebody ○ *Let me enlighten you about our problems.* **2** FREE SOMEBODY FROM IGNORANCE to free somebody from ignorance, prejudice, or superstition ○ *an article written to enlighten his critics* **3** TEACH SOMEBODY RELIGION to teach religious beliefs to an unbeliever —**enlightener** *n* —**enlightening** *adj*

enlightened /in lít'nd/ *adj* **1** RATIONAL free of ignorance, prejudice, or superstition ○ *an enlightened age* **2** WELL-INFORMED having a sound and open-minded understanding of all the facts, or based on such an understanding ○ *an enlightened piece of legislation* **3** HAVING ACHIEVED GREAT SPIRITUALITY having achieved the realization of a spiritual or religious understanding, especially when it results in the transcendence of human suffering and desire

enlightenment /in lít'nmənt/ *n* **1** ENLIGHTENING the enlightening of somebody or a cause of the enlightening of somebody **2** ENLIGHTENED STATE the condition of somebody who has been enlightened **3** TRANSCENDENCE OF DESIRE AND SUFFERING a state attained when the cycle of reincarnation ends and desire and suffering are transcended, or the achievement of this state

Enlightenment *n* an 18th-century intellectual movement in W Europe that emphasized reason and science in philosophy and in the study of human culture and the natural world

enlist /in líst/ *vti* **1** to enrol somebody in a branch of the armed forces, or join the armed forces **2** to gain the cooperation or support of somebody or something, or become actively involved in an effort ○ *May I enlist your help in this?* —**enlistment** *n*

enlisted person *n US* somebody serving in the US armed forces, especially of a rank below non-commissioned officer

enliven /in lív'n/ *vt* **1** to make somebody or something more lively or interesting ○ *We felt enlivened after our walk in the fresh air.* **2** to make something brighter or more cheerful ○ *A few more pictures on the wall would enliven this room.* —**enlivener** *n* —**enlivenment** *n*

en masse /óN máss/ *adv* as a body or in a group ○ *people rising from their seats en masse, starting to cheer* [Late 18C. < French, 'in a mass'.]

enmesh /in mésh/, **inmesh, immesh** /i mésh/ *vt* **1** to entangle somebody or something in something from which it is difficult to be extricated or separated ○ *a government enmeshed in scandal* **2** to catch somebody or something in the mesh of a net —**enmeshment** *n*

enmity /énmiti/ (*plural* **-ties**) *n* the extreme ill will or hatred that exists between enemies ○ *trying to resolve age-old enmities* [Via Old French *enemistie* < Latin *inimicus* (see ENEMY)]

ennage /énnij/ *n* in printing, the number of ens calculated as being in a piece of text for typesetting

Ennerdale Water /énnər dayl-/ lake in NW England. Area: 5 sq. km/2 sq. mi.

Enniskillen /énniss kíllən/ town in Northern Ireland, on an island in the River Erne. Population: 11,436 (1991).

Ennius /énni əss/, **Quintus** (239–169? BC) Roman poet and dramatist

ennoble /i nób'l/ (**-bles, -bling, -bled**) *vt* **1** to make somebody or something more noble or more dignified (*formal*) ○ *Your presence ennobles this gathering.* **2** to confer a noble title on somebody ○ *ennobled for his services to his country* —**ennoblement** *n* —**ennobler** *n*

ennui /ón wee/ *n* weariness and dissatisfaction with life that results from a loss of interest or sense of excitement [Mid-18C. < French, < Latin *in odio (est)* '(it is) hateful'.]

ENO *abbr* English National Opera

enoki /e nóki/, **enoki mushroom** *n* a white edible mushroom with a small cap and long thin stem. Native to: E Asia, North America. *Flammulina velutipes*. [Late 20C. < Japanese.]

enol /ée nol/ *n* an organic compound that has a hydroxyl group bonded to a carbon atom that is attached to another carbon atom by a double bond —**enolic** /ee nóllik/ *adj*

enolase /éenō layz, -layss/ *n* an enzyme involved in the metabolism of carbohydrates

enology /ee nólləji/ *n* US = **oenology**

enormity /i náwrməti/ (*plural* **-ties**) *n* **1** WICKEDNESS extreme wickedness or moral offensiveness ○ *the enormity of his crimes against humanity.* **2** EXTREMELY WICKED DEED an extremely wicked or morally offensive deed **3** ⚠ IMMENSITY an extreme greatness of size, amount, or degree that is overwhelming ○ *the enormity of the budget deficit* **4** GREAT SIGNIFICANCE great importance and consequence ○ *the enormity of the social change wrought by the Industrial Revolution* [15C. Via French < Latin *enormitas* < *enormis* 'irregular' (see ENORMOUS).]

USAGE enormity or **enormousness**? ***Enormity*** is the older word, and after several changes in usage over several centuries it settled down in the 19th century in the meanings associated with wickedness or moral offensiveness. It is used in this way both as a concept or attribute and as a specific instance with a plural form: *We were shocked by the enormity of the crime. The regime committed many enormities to suppress opposition.* ***Enormousness*** has the more neutral meaning in relation to size, so that *the enormousness of the task* implies only a great or difficult task. Although ***enormity*** is commonly used informally in this neutral sense, in formal writing a better course may be to find an alternative such as *immensity* or *vastness*.

enormous /i náwrməss/ *adj* unusually large or great in size, amount, or degree [Mid-16C. < Latin *enormis* 'irregular' < *norma* 'rule'.] —**enormously** *adv*

enormousness *n* the quality of being huge in size, scope, or significance

USAGE See ***enormity***.

enough /i núf/ *adj* **1** ADEQUATE as much as is needed ○ *enough time to go shopping* **2** AS MUCH AS BEARABLE as much or as many as can be tolerated ○ *in enough trouble already* ■ *adv* **1** IN THE RIGHT AMOUNT to an extent that is as much as is needed ○ *I couldn't run fast enough to catch the cat.* **2** USED FOR EMPHASIS used to give emphasis to adverbs ○ *Oddly enough, our husbands had met each other just the day before.* **3** SUFFICIENTLY to an extent that is as much as can be tolerated ○ *She was arrogant enough before the promotion.* **4** PASSABLY to a moderate or satisfactory extent ○ *speaks the language well enough* ■ *pron* NEEDED OR TOLERATED AMOUNT the amount that is needed or that can be tolerated ○ *take more cash because we never have enough* ■ *interj* STOP THAT! used to tell somebody firmly to stop doing something (*informal*) ○ *Enough! There will be no more teasing in the car.* [Old English *genōg* < Germanic] ◇ **enough is enough** used by a speaker to indicate that he or she will tolerate no more of something

enounce /i nówns/ (**enounces, enouncing, enounced**) *vt* **1** to pronounce a word clearly and definitely **2** to state something in an official way (*formal*) [Early 19C. Via French *énoncer* < Latin *enuntiare* 'tell' (see ENUNCIATE).] —**enouncement** *n*

en passant /ón páss on, óN pa saánt/ *adv* **1** in passing rather than as the full focus of somebody's attention (*formal*) ○ *He mentioned it en passant.* **2** used when a pawn that has moved two squares is captured by an enemy pawn as if it had only moved one square ○ *capture a pawn en passant* [Mid-17C. < French, 'in passing'.]

enplane /in pláyn/ *vti* US = **emplane**

enprint /én print/ *n* a photographic print in standard size, usually 15 cm x 10 cm/6 in x 4 in, enlarged from a negative [Mid-20C. < *enlarged print*.]

en prise /oN préez/ *adj* describes a chess piece positioned in such a way that it could be captured if it is not moved [Early 19C. < French, 'in (position for) capture'.]

enquire *vti* = **inquire**

USAGE See ***inquire***.

enquiring *adj* = **inquiring**

enquiry *n* = **inquiry**

enrage /in ráyj/ (**-rages, -raging, -raged**) *vt* to make somebody furiously angry —**enragement** *n*

enrapt /in rápt/ *adj* in a state of delight or ecstasy (*formal*)

enrapture /in rápchər/ (**-tures, -turing, -tured**) *vt* to fill somebody with delight —**enrapturement** *n*

enrich /in rích/ *vt* **1** IMPROVE to improve the quality of something **2** IMPROVE NUTRITIONAL CONTENT OF FOOD to add substances such as vitamins or minerals to a food to improve its nutritional value ○ *calcium-enriched orange juice* **3** MAKE WEALTHIER to increase the amount of wealth that somebody or something has **4** ADD MORE OF CONSTITUENT TO SUBSTANCE to boost the amount of an active substance in a mixture, e.g. in a fuel **5** IMPROVE SOIL to improve the nutrient value of soil by adding natural or artificial fertilizers **6** MAKE MORE BEAUTIFUL to add to the beauty of something with decoration (*literary*) —**enricher** *n* —**enrichment** *n*

Enright /én rīt/, **D. J.** (*b.* 1920) British poet, author, and critic. Full name **Dennis Joseph Enright**

enrobe /in rób/ (**-robes, -robing, -robed**) *v* **1** *vti* to put ceremonial robes on somebody (*formal*) **2** *vt* to invest somebody with a grand or noble quality (*literary*)

enrol /in ról/ (**-rols, -rolling, -rolled**) *v* **1** *vti* ENTER ON REGISTER to enter your own or somebody else's name on an official register or list of members ○ *enrol the children in school* **2** *vt* MAKE SURE OF AVAILABILITY OF to make sure that something, especially somebody's help, will definitely be available **3** *vt* ROLL OR WRAP UP to form something into a roll **4** *vt* WRITE OUT OFFICIAL COPY OF to produce the final version of something, usually a formal document or record [14C. < Old French *enroller* 'put on a roll' < *rolle* (see ROLL).] —**enrollee** /in ró lée/ *n*

enrolment /in rólmənt/ *n* **1** SIGNING UP FORMALLY the official act or process of entering your own or another person's name on a register or membership list **2** NUMBER OF REGISTERED the number of people registered for something, e.g. a class ○ *a sharp increase in student enrolments* **3** LIST OF REGISTERED a list of people registered for or enrolled in something

en route /ón ròot/ *adv* during the journey to a destination [Late 18C. < French, 'on (the) way'.]

ens /enz/ (*plural* **entia** /énshi ə, énti ə/) *n* an actual entity, as distinct from a quality or characteristic [Mid-16C. < late Latin, present participle (after Latin *absens* 'absent') of Latin *esse* 'be'.]

Ens. *abbr* ensign

ENSA /énssə/ *n* a British organization formed to provide entertainment for Allied forces during World War II. Full form **Entertainments National Service Association**

ensconce /in skónss/ (**-sconces, -sconcing, -sconced**) *vt* to make somebody or yourself comfortably established, as though ready to stay a long while (*often passive*) ○ *ensconced on the sofa*

ensemble /on sómb'l/ *n* **1** GROUP OF PERFORMERS a group of musicians, dancers, or actors who perform together with roughly equal contributions from all members (*takes a singular or plural verb*) **2** OUTFIT OF CLOTHES a number of different items of clothing and accessories, put together to create an outfit **3** SOMETHING FORMED BY SEVERAL ITEMS something created from a number of individual parts put together deliberately **4** PART PERFORMED BY WHOLE GROUP a section of a larger work, e.g. a ballet or opera, that all the cast perform together ■ *adj* COLLABORATIVE performed collaboratively, with no performer given prominence [Mid-18C. < French, 'together' < Latin *insimul* 'in at the same time' < *simul* 'at the same time'.]

enshrine /in shrín/ (**-shrines, -shrining, -shrined**), **inshrine** (**-shrines, -shrining, -shrined**) *vt* **1** to protect something from change, e.g. in a formal constitution

○ *principles enshrined in law* **2** to keep or cherish something in a shrine or other special place —**enshrinement** *n*

enshroud /in shrówd/ *vt* **1** to cover or obscure something (*usually passive*) ○ *towers enshrouded in mist* **2** to cover somebody in a shroud

ensiform /énssi fawrm/ *adj* long and narrow with a pointed tip ○ *ensiform leaves* [Mid-16C. Via French < modern Latin *ensiformis* < Latin *ensi-* 'sword' + *forma* 'form, shape'.]

ensign /én sīn, énss'n/ *n* **1** FLAG INDICATING ALLEGIANCE a flag that shows the nationality of the ship or aircraft flying it or what military unit it belongs to **2** FLAG WITH UNION FLAG IN CORNER a naval flag bearing a small Union Flag in the upper corner next to the staff (**canton**) **3** US NAVY RANK a US Navy or Coast Guard commissioned officer of the lowest rank **4** BADGE OF OFFICE an emblem or sign that indicates authority or command **5** FLAG-BEARER a bearer of a national emblem or a standard (*dated*) **6** FORMER RANK IN BRITISH ARMY before 1871, a British infantry commissioned officer of the lowest rank [14C. < Old French *enseigne* < Latin *insignia* (plural) 'badges' < *signum* 'mark'.]

ensilage /énssilij/ *n* **1** the harvesting and preservation of green fodder crops for future use by fermentation in a silo **2** green fodder preserved in a silo

ensile /en sīl/ (**-siles, -siling, -siled**) *vt* to preserve green fodder, e.g. grass, as silage by allowing it to ferment and become acidified in a silo [Late 19C. Via French < Spanish *ensilar* < *en* 'in' + *silo* (see SILO).]

enslave /in sláyv/ (**-slaves, -slaving, -slaved**) *vt* **1** to subject somebody to a dominating influence that takes away his or her freedom **2** to take somebody prisoner and claim legal ownership of that person and his or her labour —**enslavement** *n* —**enslaver** *n*

ensnare /in snáir/ (**-snares, -snaring, -snared**), **insnare** (**-snares, -snaring, -snared**) *vt* **1** to lure somebody into a bad situation from which it is difficult to escape **2** to catch an animal in a trap —**ensnarement** *n* —**ensnarer** *n*

ensnarl /in snaárl/ *vt* to involve somebody or something in a situation that causes delay (*often passive*)

Ensor /én sawr, óN-/, **James Sydney, Baron** (1860–1949) Belgian painter and engraver

ensoul /in sṓl/, **insoul** *vt* (*literary*) **1** to endow somebody with a soul **2** to cherish deeply something such as a feeling or memory

ensphere /in sféer/ (**-spheres, -sphering, -sphered**), **insphere** (**-spheres, -sphering, -sphered**) *vt* **1** to enclose something in a sphere or in something like a sphere (*literary*) **2** to make something sphere-shaped (*formal*)

enstatite /énstə tīt/ *n* a brown, grey, or yellowish magnesium iron silicate mineral of the pyroxene group. Source: igneous rocks, meteorites. [Mid-19C. < German *Enstatit* < Greek *enstat-* 'adversary' (from its refractoriness).]

ensue /in syóō/ (**-sues, -suing, -sued**) *vi* **1** to follow closely after something **2** to be a consequence of something [14C. < Old French *ensu-*, stem of *ensuivre* < assumed Vulgar Latin *insequere* 'follow in' < Latin *sequi* 'follow'.]

ensuing /in syóō ing/ *adj* happening next or as a result

en suite /óN swéet/ *adj, adv* LEADING OFF forming part of a larger unit or set of rooms ○ *an en suite bathroom* ■ *n* (*informal*) **1** ADJOINING BATHROOM a bathroom leading off the bedroom **2** HOTEL ROOM WITH OWN BATHROOM a hotel bedroom with an en suite bathroom [Late 18C. < French, 'in succession'.]

ensure /in shóor, in shawr/ (**-sures, -suring, -sured**) *vt* **1** to make sure that something will happen **2** to protect something or somebody from harm

USAGE See ***assure***.

enswathe /in swáyth/ (**-swathes, -swathing, -swathed**) *vt* to wrap somebody or something in bandages or cloth (*literary*)

ENT *abbr* ear, nose, and throat

-ent *suffix* **1** performing a particular action ○ *acquiescent* **2** one that performs a particular action ○ *respondent* [< Latin *-ent-*, stem of *-ens*, present participle ending] —**-ence** *suffix* —**-ency** *suffix*

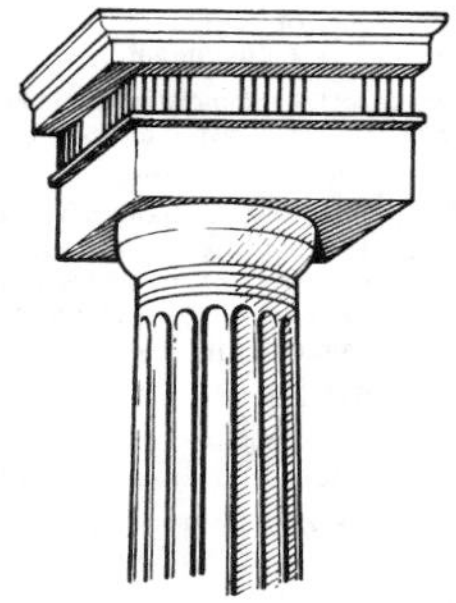

Entablature

entablature /en tábbləchər/ *n* in classical architecture, the section that lies between the columns and the roof [Early 17C. Via obsolete French < Italian *intavolatura* 'boarding' < *intavolare* 'board up, put on a table' < *tavola* 'table'.]

entablement /in táyb'lmənt/ *n* a plinth (*technical*) [Mid-17C. < French, < *table* 'table'.]

entail /in táyl/ *vt* **1** HAVE AS CONSEQUENCE to involve or result in something inevitably **2** RESTRICT OWNERSHIP OF BEQUEST to restrict the future ownership of property to particular descendants, through instructions written into a will ■ *n* **1** RESTRICTION OF FUTURE OWNERSHIP the limiting of the future ownership of bequeathed property to particular descendants **2** ENTAILED PROPERTY a property that has been entailed **3** FUTURE OWNERS OF ENTAILED PROPERTY the line of descendants who own an entailed property [14C. < EN- + Old French *taille* 'limitation' < *taillier* 'to cut' (see TAILOR).] —**entailment** *n*

entangle /in táng g'l/ (**-gles, -gling, -gled**) *vt* **1** TANGLE UP to make something become twisted up in a mass of strands, e.g. netting or hair (*usually passive*) **2** PUT INTO DIFFICULT SITUATION to involve somebody or something in a muddle that will be difficult to escape from (*usually passive*) ○ *entangled in corporate politics* **3** COMPLICATE to make something complicated —**entanglement** *n*

entasis /éntəssiss/ *n* a slight bulge in the shaft of a column, designed to counter the visual impression of concavity that a perfectly straight column would give [Mid-18C. < Greek, 'straining' < *teinein* 'to stretch'.]

Entebbe /en tébbi/ city of S Uganda on the shore of Lake Victoria. Its airport was the scene of a successful Israeli raid on a hijacked commercial aircraft in 1976. Population: 41,638 (1991 estimate).

entelechy /in télləki/ *n* **1** the real existence of a thing, not merely its theoretical existence **2** in some philosophies, a life-giving force believed to be responsible for the development of all living things [Early 17C. Via late Latin < Greek *entelekheia* 'having completeness' < *entelēs* 'complete' < *telos* 'end'.]

entente /on tónt/ *n* **1** a state of friendly agreement or understanding that exists or is declared between two or more countries **2** the parties involved in an entente [Mid-19C. < French, 'understanding' < *entendre* (see INTEND).]

entente cordiale /-káwrdi aál/ (*plural* **ententes cordiales** /on tónt káwrdi aál/) *n* amicable relations between countries or states, especially the agreement formed between France and Britain in 1904 [< French, 'friendly understanding']

⚡**enter** /éntər/ *v* **1** *vti* GO IN to go or come into a place **2** *vt* WRITE OR TYPE IN to write or type something in a book or on a computer ○ *The names and addresses are entered into a database.* **3** *vt* PUT IN FOR FORMAL CONSIDERATION to submit something, e.g. a proposal, complaint, or bid, officially **4** *vti* BECOME COMPETITOR to take part in a competition **5** *vt* BECOME MEMBER OF to join or become officially involved in something, especially a body such as a college or company **6** *vi* WALK ON to come on stage during a play ○ *She enters stage right.* **7** *vti* MAKE HOLE to force a way into something, or be pushed or inserted into something, especially the human body ○ *The bullet entered through the anterior abdominal wall.* **8** *vt* TAKE OWNERSHIP OF LAND LEGALLY to go onto land and take legal possession of it ■ *n* COMPUT = **enter key** [13C. Via Old French < Latin *intrare* 'go in, enter' < *intra* 'inside, within'.] —**enterable** *adj*

enter into *v* **1** *vt* TAKE PART ENTHUSIASTICALLY to get actively involved in something ○ *Enter into the spirit of things.* **2** *vt* BE RELEVANT TO to be one of the factors that are relevant to something ○ *Money doesn't enter into it.* **3** *vt* SIGN UP TO to become one of the parties bound by a contract **4** *vi* TAKE PART IN to become involved in something **5** *vt* CONSIDER FORMALLY to go into a discussion or investigation about something ○ *I do not propose to enter into the issue of who is responsible.*

enter on, enter upon *vt* to start out on something, e.g. an important task or a significant period

enter- *prefix* = **entero-** (*before vowels*)

enteral feeding /énteral-/ *n* direct infusion into the intestines of nutrients in liquid form [Partly < ENTERIC, partly back-formation < PARENTERAL]

enteric /en térrik/ *adj* relating to or situated in the intestine [Mid-19C. < Greek *enterikos* < *enteron* 'intestine'.]

enteric fever *n* MED = **typhoid** *n.*

enteritis /éntə rītiss/ *n* inflammation of the intestine, most commonly of the small intestine

⚡**enter key** *n* **1** a key on a numeric keypad for entering calculations **2** = **return key**

entero-, enter- *prefix* intestine ○ *enterotomy* [< Greek *enteron* < Indo-European, 'in, inside']

enterobiasis /éntərō bī əssiss/ *n* infestation of the large intestine with pinworms, especially in children

enterocolitis /éntərō kə lītiss/ *n* inflammation of the small and large intestine as a result of infection

enterokinase /éntərō kī nayz/ *n* a duodenal enzyme that converts trypsinogen to trypsin

enteron /éntə ron/ *n* **1** the alimentary canal, especially of an embryo **2** the intestine of marine invertebrates, e.g. sea anemones and jellyfish, with one opening that serves as both mouth and anus [Mid-19C. < Greek, 'intestine'.]

enteropathy /éntər óppəthi/ (*plural* **-thies**) *n* any disease of the intestines

enterostomy /éntə róstəmi/ (*plural* **-mies**) *n* the surgical creation of a permanent opening into the intestine through the abdominal wall —**enterostomal** *adj*

enterotomy /éntə róttəmi/ (*plural* **-mies**) *n* a surgical incision into the intestine

enterotoxin /éntərō tóksin/ *n* any toxin produced by bacteria that causes the vomiting and diarrhoea associated with food poisoning

enterprise /éntər prīz/ *n* **1** BUSINESS a commercial company or firm **2** DARING PROJECT a new, often risky, venture that involves confidence and initiative **3** ENERGETIC CONFIDENCE readiness to put effort into new, often risky, ventures or activities **4** HIGHLY MOTIVATED INDUSTRY organized business activities aimed specifically at growth and profit [15C. < Old French *entreprise* < past participle of *entreprendre* 'undertake' < *prendre* 'take' (see PRIZE[2]).]

Enterprise Allowance Scheme *n* formerly, a government scheme to help the unemployed set up in business by providing an allowance

⚡**enterprise resource planning** full form of **ERP**

⚡**enterprise software** *n* computer software designed to integrate and automate all of a company's functions

enterprise zone *n* an economically depressed urban area where the government encourages new business ventures by offering financial incentives

enterprising /éntər prīzing/ *adj* showing initiative and a willingness to undertake new, often risky, projects —**enterprisingly** *adv*

entertain /éntər táyn/ *v* **1** *vti* AMUSE OR INTEREST to engage a person or audience by providing amusing or interesting material **2** *vti* OFFER HOSPITALITY to offer hospitality, especially by providing food and drink for people in your home **3** *vt* CONSIDER to turn something over in your mind, looking at it from various points of view ○ *He would never entertain such an idea!* [15C. < Old French *entretenir* 'hold together, support' < assumed Vulgar Latin *intertenere* 'hold between' < Latin *tenere* 'hold'.]

entertainer /éntər táynər/ *n* a provider of entertainment, especially a professional one

entertaining /éntər táyning/ *adj* enjoyable to watch, read, or listen to —**entertainingly** *adv*

entertainment /éntər táynmənt/ *n* **1** ART OF KEEPING PEOPLE ENTERTAINED the various ways of amusing people, especially by performing for them **2** ENJOYMENT the amount of pleasure or amusement you get from something **3** PERFORMANCE OR EXHIBITION something that is produced or performed for an audience ○ *chief among the evening's entertainments*

enthalpy /én thəlpi, en thálpi/ *n* (*symbol* **H**) a thermodynamic property equal to the sum of the internal energy of a system and the product of its pressure and volume [Early 20C. < Greek *enthalpein* 'to warm within' < *thalpein* 'to heat'.]

enthral /in thráwl/ (**-thrals, -thralling, -thralled**), **inthrall** *vt* **1** to delight or fascinate somebody thoroughly, engaging that person's attention completely **2** to make somebody a prisoner and claim legal ownership of that person (*literary*) [Late 16C. < EN- + THRALL.] —**enthralment** *n*

enthrall *vt* US = **enthral**

enthrone /in thrṓn/ (**-thrones, -throning, -throned**), **inthrone** (**-thrones, -throning, -throned**) *vt* **1** to install a monarch or bishop, especially in a ceremony that involves seating the person on a throne (*formal*) **2** to regard somebody as being worthy of adoration (*literary*) —**enthronement** *n*

enthuse /in thyóoz/ (**-thuses, -thusing, -thused**) *vti* **1** to have, or make somebody feel, great excitement or interest **2** to express enthusiasm about something or say something enthusiastically ○ *enthusing about the new restaurant* [Early 19C. Back-formation < ENTHUSIASM.]

enthusiasm /in thyóozi azəm/ *n* **1** passionate interest in or eagerness to do something **2** something that arouses a consuming interest [Late 16C. Via late Latin < Greek *enthousiasmos* 'possession by (a) god' < *enthous* 'inspired' < *theos* 'god'.]

enthusiast /in thyóozi ast/ *n* a person who is enthusiastic about something, especially a hobby [Early 17C. < Greek *enthousiastēs* 'somebody inspired (by a god)' < *enthous* (see ENTHUSIASM).]

enthusiastic /in thyóozi ástik/ *adj* showing passionate interest in something or eagerness about something —**enthusiastically** *adv*

enthymeme /énthə meem/ *n* an argument that assumes the truth of one or more premises and therefore omits them from the logical sequence [Late 16C. Via Latin < Greek *enthumēma* '(something) in mind' < *thumos* 'mind'.]

entia plural of **ens**

entice /in tíss/ (**-tices, -ticing, -ticed**) *vt* to make a person or animal do something by offering something desirable [13C. Via Old French *enticier* < assumed Vulgar Latin *intitiare* 'set on fire' < Latin *titio* 'firebrand'.] —**enticement** *n* —**enticer** *n*

enticing /in tíssing/ *adj* very desirable and hard to resist —**enticingly** *adv*

entire /in tír/ *adj* **1 WHOLE** as a whole, from beginning to end, or including everything **2 ABSOLUTE** in every way, without doubt or question ○ *The day was an entire fiasco.* **3 IN ONE PIECE** not damaged or broken up (*literary*) ○ *'with strength entire, and free Will arm'd'* (John Milton, *Paradise Lost*; 1667) **4 UNGELDED** describes a male animal, especially a stallion or dog, that has not been castrated **5 SMOOTH-EDGED** describes leaves with smooth edges that are not lobed or indented ■ *n* **STALLION** a stallion [14C. Via Old French *entier* < Latin *integrum*, form of *integer* 'whole, intact'.] —**entireness** *n*

entirely /in tírli/ *adv* **1** in every sense **2** exclusively or individually

entirety /in tírəti/ *n* the whole extent of something

entitle /in tít'l/ (**-tles, -tling, -tled**) *vt* **1 ALLOW TO CLAIM** to give somebody the right to have or to do something (*often passive*) **2 GIVE TITLE TO** to assign a title to something such as a book (*usually passive*) **3 GIVE SPECIAL TITLE TO** to confer an official position or honour on somebody that brings a particular title with it [14C. Via Old French < late Latin *intitulare* < Latin *titulus* 'inscription'.] —**entitlement** *n*

entitlement program *n US* in the United States, a government programme that targets a particular section of the population to receive certain benefits

entity /éntəti/ (*plural* **-ties**) *n* **1 OBJECT** something that exists as or is perceived as a single separate object **2 EXISTENCE** the state of having existence **3 ESSENTIAL NATURE** the essence or character of something [Late 16C. < medieval Latin *entitas* < late Latin *ent-*, stem of *ens* (see ENS).]

entoderm /éntō durm/ *n* BIOL = **endoderm**

entomb /in tóom/ *vt* **1 PUT IN TOMB** to put a corpse into a tomb **2 PUT IN DEEP PLACE** to put something in a place that is hidden or very deep ○ *the secret vaults where the treasures were entombed* **3 SERVE AS TOMB** to serve as a tomb for somebody or something ○ *the collapsed mine that entombed them* —**entombment** *n*

entomo- *prefix* insect ○ *entomophilous* [Via French < Greek *entomon* < *entomos* 'cut in two' < *temnein* 'cut'; because of insects' distinctly segmented bodies]

entomology /éntə mólləji/ *n* the branch of zoology that deals with the study of insects [Mid-18C. < French *entomologie* or modern Latin *entomologia* 'science of insects' < Greek *entomon* (see ENTOMO-).] —**entomological** /éntəmə lójjik'l/ *adj* —**entomologically** *adv* —**entomologist** *n*

entomophagous /éntə móffəgəss/ *adj* feeding on insects

entomophilous /éntə móffiləss/ *adj* describes flowering plants that are pollinated by insects —**entomophily** *n*

entourage /ón too raazh/ *n* **1** a group of special employees who go with a high-ranking or famous person on visits and engagements **2** the surroundings or environment (*literary*) [Mid-19C. < French, < *entourer* 'surround' < *tour* 'circuit'.]

entr'acte /ón trakt/ (*plural* **-actes**) *n* **1** an interval between the acts of a play or opera **2** an additional piece of entertainment during the break between the acts of a play or opera [Mid-18C. < obsolete French, 'between the act(s)' < *acte* 'act'.]

entrails /én traylz/ *npl* **1 INTERNAL ORGANS** an animal's or person's internal organs **2 SOMETHING'S INSIDES** the various working parts inside something, especially something complex **3 ANIMAL'S INSIDES USED FOR ROMAN DIVINATION** the internal organs of a sacrificial animal, used by the ancient Romans to try to determine the will of the gods [13C. Via Old French *entrailles* < medieval Latin *intralia*, alteration of Latin *interanea* 'intestines' < *inter* 'between'.]

entrain[1] /in tráyn/ *vti* to board or to put somebody or something aboard a train —**entrainer** *n* —**entrainment** *n*

entrain[2] /in tráyn/ *v* **1** *vt* to cause something to happen as a consequence of an action **2** to draw solid particles, air bubbles, or liquid drops into a moving fluid and carry them along in the flow [Mid-16C. < Old French *entraîner* 'drag away' < *traîner* 'drag'.] —**entrainment** *n*

entrance[1] /éntrənss/ *n* **1 WAY IN** a door or gate through which people enter **2 COMING ONTO THE SCENE** the occasion or act of entering a place ○ *a highly theatrical entrance* **3 RIGHT OF ENTRY** the right to go into a place or to enter an institution [15C. < Old French, < *entrer* (see ENTER).]

entrance[2] /in traánss/ (**-trances, -trancing, -tranced**) *vt* **1** to hold somebody's attention and produce a sense of wonder in that person **2** to make somebody go into a trance —**entrancingly** *adv*

entrant /éntrənt/ *n* a person who enters a competition, contest, or examination [Mid-17C. < French, present participle of *entrer* (see ENTER).]

SYNONYMS See ***candidate***.

entrap /in tráp/ (**-traps, -trapping, -trapped**) *vt* **1** to lead somebody into doing something wrong or into danger **2** to catch something such as an animal in a trap —**entrapment** *n*

entreat /in treét/ *vti* to beg somebody for something, often repeatedly [14C. < Old French *entraitier* 'treat in (a certain way)' < *traitier* (see TREAT).] —**entreatingly** *adv*

entreaty /in treéti/ (*plural* **-ies**) *n* a serious and passionate request

entrechat /óntrə shaa/ *n* in ballet, a leap in which the dancer's legs are crossed rapidly in the air and the heels are beaten together [Late 18C. Via French < Italian *(capriola) intrecciata* 'intricate (caper)'.]

entrecôte /óntrə kōt/, **entrecôte steak** *n* a piece of beef without any bone, cut from between the ribs [Mid-19C. < French, 'between (the) rib(s)'.]

entrée /ón tray/ *n* **1 MAIN COURSE** a dish served as the main part of a meal **2 DISH BEFORE MAIN COURSE** in a formal dinner, a light dish served before the main course **3 RIGHT OF ENTRY** something that permits entry into something, especially to an exclusive group or place [Late 18C. < French (see ENTRY).]

entremets /óntrə may/ (*plural* **-mets**) *n* **1** in a formal dinner, a light dish served between the main course and the dessert **2** a sweet dish, especially one served after cheese in a multi-course dinner [15C. < Old French, 'between the course(s)' < *mes* 'course'.]

entrench /in trénch/, **intrench** *v* **1** *vt* **DIG DITCH ROUND** to defend something by surrounding it with trenches **2** *vt* **PROTECT** to take action to protect an argument or position **3** *vi* **ENCROACH** to encroach upon or trespass on somebody else's property or things (*archaic*) —**entrenchment** *n*

entrenched /in trénch t/ *adj* **1** firmly held and hard to change ○ *deeply entrenched political views* **2** firmly established and unlikely to change

entre nous /óntrə nóo/ *adv* in confidence [Late 17C. < French, 'between ourselves'.]

entrepôt /óntrə pō/ *n* **1** COMM = **free port** *n*. 2 **2** a bonded warehouse [Early 18C. < French, < *entreposer* 'place in, store' < *poser* 'to place'.]

entrepreneur /óntrəprə núr/ *n* an initiator or financier of new commercial enterprises [Late 19C. < French, 'somebody who undertakes' < *entreprendre* (see ENTERPRISE).] —**entrepreneurial** *adj* —**entrepreneurialism** *n* —**entrepreneurism** *n* —**entrepreneurship** *n*

entresol /óntrə sol/ *n* ARCHIT = **mezzanine** *n*. 1 [Early 18C. Via French < Spanish *entresuelo* 'between-level' < *suelo* 'level' < Latin *solea* 'sole'.]

entropy /éntrəpi/ (*plural* **-pies**) *n* **1 MEASURE OF DISORDER** a measure of the disorder that exists in a system **2 MEASURE OF UNAVAILABLE ENERGY** (*symbol* S) a measure of the energy in a system or process that is unavailable to do work **3 MEASURE OF COMMUNICATIONS SYSTEM EFFICIENCY** a measure of the random errors (**noise**) occurring in the transmission of signals, and from this a measure of the efficiency of transmission systems [Mid-19C. < Greek *en-* 'in' + *tropē* 'change', after ENERGY.] —**entropic** /en tróppik/ *adj* —**entropically** *adv*

entrust /in trúst/, **intrust** *vt* to give something to another person to be responsible for —**entrustment** *n*

ϟ **entry** /éntri/ (*plural* **-tries**) *n* **1 GOING IN** an act or instance of somebody entering **2** = **entrance**[1] *n*. 3 **3 SINGLE WRITTEN ITEM** an item or piece of data included in a list or a book **4 INCLUDING AN ITEM ON LIST** the process of recording something in writing or on a computer ○ *data entry* **5 WAY IN** a way into a place **6 SOMEBODY OR SOMETHING ENTERED IN CONTEST** a person, animal, or item entered in a contest, or the total number entered ○ *the winning entry* **7 APPEARANCE ON STAGE** the occasion when an actor comes on stage **8 WINNING CARD** in some games, a card that can win a trick and thus gain the lead for a player **9 PASSAGE BETWEEN HOUSES** a passage between the backs of two rows of houses, or leading into a block of flats, or to the backs of houses in a terrace (*regional*) [13C. Via French *entrée* < Latin *intrata*, form of past participle of *intrare* (see ENTER).]

entryism /éntri izəm/ *n* the tactic of joining an existing political party in large numbers with the purpose of changing its policies and direction —**entryist** *n*

entry-level *adj* at the lowest level and suitable for somebody who is new to a job, field, or subject

Entryphone /éntri fōn/ *tdmk* a trademark for an intercom system that links each flat in a building with the main door and allows the occupant to open the door remotely

entwine /in twín/ (**-twines, -twining, -twined**), **intwine** (**-twines, -twining, -twined**) *vti* to twist things together or to twist something round something else (*often passive*) —**entwinement** *n*

entwist /in twíst/, **intwist** *vti* = **entwine**

enucleate /i nyóokli ayt, -kli ət/ *vt* (**-ates, -ating, -ated**) **1 TAKE OUT THE NUCLEUS** to remove the nucleus of a cell **2 SURGICALLY REMOVE WITHOUT DAMAGE** to remove something surgically, such as a tumour, from its capsule while keeping it intact ■ *adj* **WITHOUT A NUCLEUS** describes a cell without a nucleus [Mid-16C. < Latin *enucleat-*, past participle of *enucleare* 'remove the pit from (olives, fruit)' < *nucleus* 'kernel' (see NUCLEUS).] —**enucleation** /i nyóokli áysh'n/ *n*

E number *n* **1** a code by which a given additive is identified on food labels, consisting of the letter E followed by a number **2** a food additive (*informal*) [Abbreviation of EUROPEAN]

enumerate /i nyóomə rayt/ (**-ates, -ating, -ated**) *vt* **1** to name a number of things on a list one by one **2** to count how many things there are in something [Mid-17C. < Latin *enumerat-*, past participle of *enumerare* 'count out' < *numerus* 'number'.] —**enumerable** *adj* —**enumeration** /i nyóomə ráysh'n/ *n* —**enumerative** *adj* —**enumerator** *n*

enunciate /i núnssi ayt/ (**-ates, -ating, -ated**) *v* **1** *vti* to pronounce something distinctly **2** *vt* to give a speech or statement that explains something clearly [Early 17C. < Latin *enuntiat-*, past participle of *enuntiare* 'announce' < *nuntius* 'message, messenger'.] —**enunciation** /i núnssi áysh'n/ *n* —**enunciative** *adj* —**enunciatively** *adv* —**enunciator** *n*

enure /i nyo͝or/ *vt* = **inure**

enuresis /ènnyo͞o réessiss/ *n* involuntary discharge of urine, especially while asleep (*technical*) [Late 18C. < modern Latin, < Greek *enourein* 'urinate in' < *ouron* 'urine'.] —**enuretic** /-réttik/ *adj*

envelop /in véllәp/ *vt* **1 WRAP UP** to enclose somebody or something completely (*often passive*) **2 HIDE** to conceal something or somebody (*often passive*) **3 SURROUND AN ENEMY** to surround an enemy completely [14C. < Old French *envoluper* 'wrap in'.] —**enveloper** *n* —**envelopment** *n*

SPELLCHECK See ***envelope***.

envelope /énvә lōp, ónv-/ *n* **1 PAPER COVER FOR A LETTER** a flat pocket of paper with a sealable flap for holding letters **2 ENCLOSING CASE** something that surrounds or encloses something else ○ *seafood sauce in filo pastry envelopes* **3 ENCLOSING STRUCTURE** a covering that encloses and protects an animal's body or a biological structure, such as a shell or membrane **4 CURVE FORMING A TANGENT** a curve or surface that forms a tangent to each of the members of a set of curves or surfaces, such as circles with a common centre but different radii **5 BALLOON** the bag of an airship or balloon that contains the gas **6 PERFORMANCE LIMITS OF AN AIRCRAFT** the performance limits of a piece of equipment, particularly of an aircraft [Early 18C. < French *enveloppe* < *envelopper* 'wrap in'.] ◇ **push the envelope** to try to accomplish more than is theoretically possible (*informal*)

SPELLCHECK Do not confuse ***envelope*** with ***envelop***, which has a similar spelling. Beware: your spellchecker will not catch this error.

envenom /in vénnәm/ *vt* **1** to make something poisonous (*technical*) **2** to cause somebody to become malicious or hostile (*formal*) —**envenomization** *n*

Enver Pasha /énvәr páshә/ (1881–1922) Turkish general and statesman

enviable /énvi әb'l/ *adj* likely to evoke feelings of envy ○ *in the enviable position of having two job offers to choose from* —**enviably** *adv*

envious /énvi әss/ *adj* wanting to have somebody's else's success, good fortune, qualities, or possessions —**enviously** *adv* —**enviousness** *n*

~~**enviroment**~~ incorrect spelling of **environment**

environ /in vīrәn/ *vt* to surround somebody or something. ◊ **environs** [14C. < Old French *environer* 'make a circle around' < *viron* 'circle' < *virer* 'to turn'.]

environment /in vīrәnmәnt/ *n* **1 NATURAL WORLD** the natural world, within which people, animals, and plants live **2 SURROUNDING INFLUENCES** all the external factors influencing the life of organisms, such as light or food supply **3 SOCIAL AND PHYSICAL CONDITIONS** the conditions that surround people and affect the way they live ○ *the nurturing environment a child needs*

Environment Agency *n* the government agency responsible for environmental protection in England and Wales

environmental /in vīrәn mént'l/ *adj* **1** relating to the natural world, especially to its conservation ○ *environmental groups* **2** relating to, or caused by, a person's or animal's surroundings

environmental art *n* creative art, usually on a grand scale, that is meant to invite the viewer's participation by interacting with it

environmental assessment *n* the identification of the likely environmental effects of a proposed development. ◊ **environmental impact statement**

environmental health *n* the local government functions concerned with minimizing risks to public health and the local environment, including the monitoring of water and air quality, hygiene in restaurants and shops, and pest control

environmental impact *n* the indirect and direct consequences of human actions on the natural environment

environmental impact statement *n* a written statement of the likely environmental effects of a proposed development based on a scientific assessment or study ○ *'After the public comment period, the NRC will issue a final environmental impact statement by November'.* (*Washington Post*; April 1999) ◊ **environmental assessment**

environmentalism /in vīrәn mént'lizәm/ *n* **1** the movement, especially in politics and consumer affairs, that works towards protecting the natural world from harmful human activities **2** a theory stating that a person's environment is more influential than heredity in determining his or her development

environmentalist /in vīrәn mént'list/ *n* **1** somebody involved in issues relating to the protection of the natural world, especially a member of a political group campaigning against the perceived harmful effects of industrialized societies **2** a supporter of the theory that a person's environment is more influential than heredity in determining his or her development. ◊ **hereditarian**

environmentally /in vīrәn mént'li/ *adv* with regard to the natural world and its vulnerability to destructive influences ○ *the environmentally aware consumer*

environmentally friendly, environment-friendly *adj* designed to minimize harmful impact on the natural world, e.g. by using biodegradable ingredients

environmentally sensitive area *n* a rural area designated by the government as in need of protection from certain modern farming practices

environmental studies *n* a course of academic study including a range of disciplines that relate to the environment (+ *singular or plural verb*)

Environmental Sustainability Index *n* a figure intended to represent the overall status of a country or region with respect to the environmental sustainability of its industries and lifestyle

environment-friendly *adj* ECOL = **environmentally friendly**

environs /in vīrәnz/ *npl* the land or area surrounding a place [Mid-17C. < French, plural of *environ* 'surroundings' < *viron* (see ENVIRON).]

envisage /in vízzij/ (**-ages, -aging, -aged**) *vt* (*formal*) **1 FORESEE** to conceive of and contemplate a future possibility ○ *Do you envisage being able to avert a crisis?* **2 IMAGINE** to form a mental picture of something or somebody **3 CONSIDER** to regard something in a particular way [Early 19C. < French *envisager* '(to cause to be) in the face' < *visage* 'face' (see VISAGE).]

USAGE envisage or **envision**? In the sense of 'imagine', ***envisage*** is more common in British English, and ***envision*** in American English.

envision /in vízh'n/ *vt* to form a mental picture of something, typically something that may occur or be possible in the future

USAGE See ***envisage***.

envoi *n* LITERAT = **envoy** *n.* 3

envoy /én voy/ *n* **1 OFFICIAL REPRESENTATIVE** somebody acting as a diplomat on behalf of a national government or sent as its official messenger **2 envoy, envoy extraordinary** (*plural* **envoys extraordinary**) **DIPLOMATIC MINISTER** a minister in the Diplomatic Service of a rank above chargé d'affaires **3 envoy, envoi CONCLUDING PART OF A POEM** the final section of a book or play, or a short stanza at the end of a poem, used for summing up or as a dedication [Mid-17C. < French *envoyé*, past participle of *envoyer* 'send' < assumed Vulgar Latin *inviare* 'put on the way' < Latin *via* 'way'.]

envy /énvi/ *n* the resentful or unhappy feeling of wanting somebody else's success, good fortune, qualities, or possessions ■ *vt* (**-vies, -vying, -vied**) to desire something possessed by somebody else ○ *It would be churlish of me to envy them their success.* [13C. Via Old French *envie* < Latin *invidia* < *invidere* 'look askance at' < *videre* 'see'.] —**envyingly** *adv* ◇ **be the envy of somebody** to be the object of somebody's envy

enwind /in wínd/ (**-winds, -winding, -wound** /in wównd/, **-wound**) *vt* to wind or coil something around somebody or something (*literary*)

enwomb /in wo͞om/ *vt* to hold something or somebody in a warm safe place (*literary*)

enwound past participle, past tense of **enwind**

enwrap /in ráp/ (**-wraps, -wrapping, -wrapped**), **inwrap** (**-wraps, -wrapping, -wrapped**) *vt* **1** to involve or engross somebody or something thoroughly (*formal; often passive*) **2** to wrap something or somebody up

enwreathe /in re͞eth/ (**-wreathes, -wreathing, -wreathed**), **inwreathe** (**-wreathes, -wreathing, -wreathed**) *vt* to encircle something, especially with decorations (*literary*)

Enzed /en zéd/ *n ANZ* New Zealand (*informal*) [Early 20C. Representing the initial letters of NEW ZEALAND.]

Enzedder /en zéddәr/ *n ANZ* a person from New Zealand (*informal*)

enzootic /én zō óttik/ *adj* describes an animal disease that occurs only within a specific geographic area —**enzootic** *n*

enzyme /én zīm/ *n* any complex chemical produced by living cells that is a biochemical catalyst [Late 19C. < German *Enzym* < modern Greek *enzumos* 'leavened' < Greek *zumē* 'leaven'.] —**enzymatic** /én zī máttik, énzi-/ *adj* —**enzymic** /en zímik, -zímmik/ *adj* —**enzymically** *adv*

enzymology /énzi móllәji/ *n* the study of enzymes

eo- *prefix* oldest, earliest ○ *eolithic* [< Greek *ēōs* 'dawn'. Ultimately < Indo-European.]

EOC *abbr* Equal Opportunities Commission

Eocene /ée ō seen/ *n* the epoch of geological time when mammals first appeared, 56.5 to 35.4 million years ago —**Eocene** *adj*

⚡**EOF** *abbr* end of file

eohippus /ée ō híppәss/ (*plural* **-puses**) *n* a small prehistoric horse that lived in North America [Late 19C. < modern Latin, < Greek *ēōs* 'dawn' + *hippos* 'horse'.]

eolian *adj* US = **aeolian**

Eolic *adj, n* LANG = **Aeolic**

⚡**e.o.m.** *abbr* **1** end of the month **2** end of message (*in e-mails*)

eon *n* = **aeon**

eosin /ée ōssin/ *n* $C_{20}H_6Br_4O_5K_2$ a red crystalline solid. Use: biological stain, dye in cosmetics. [Mid-19C. < Greek *ēōs* 'dawn' + -IN; so called because of its colour.]

eosinophil /ée ō sínnōfil/ *n* a granular white blood cell that stains with the dye eosin and is thought to play a part in allergic reactions and the body's response to parasitic diseases —**eosinophilic** /ée ō sínnә fíllik/ *adj* —**eosinophilous** /ée ōsi nóffilәss/ *adj*

eosinophilia /ée ō sínnә fílli ә/ *n* an increase in the number of granular white blood cells that stain with the dye eosin, occurring in some allergies and parasitic diseases

-eous *suffix* = **-ous** [< Latin *-eus*, suffix forming adjectives of material]

EP *n* a gramophone record that is the size of a single but contains a longer recording and is designed to be played at 33 1/3 revolutions per minute rather than 45 [Mid-20C. Abbreviation of *extended play*.]

Ep. *abbr* Epistle

e.p. *abbr* en passant

ep- *prefix* = **epi-** (*before vowels or h*)

EPA *n* a cholesterol-reducing fatty acid found in some types of fish oil. Full form **eicosapentaenoic acid**

epact /ée pakt/ *n* a period of about 11 days that represents the difference between the lunar year and the solar year [Mid-16C. Via Old French < late Latin, < Greek *epaktē (hēmera)* 'added (day)' < *agein* 'to lead'.]

eparch /éppaark/ *n* **1** a bishop in the Greek Orthodox Church **2** the governor of a modern Greek province [Mid-17C. < Greek *eparkhos* 'ruler over' < *arkhos* 'ruler' (see -ARCH).]

eparchy /éppaarki/ (*plural* **-chies**) *n* **1** a bishop's diocese in the Greek Orthodox Church **2** a political subdivision of a province in modern Greece [Late 18C. < Greek *eparkhia* 'prefecture, province' < *eparkhos* (see EPARCH).]

epaulet *n* US = **epaulette**

epaulette /éppә lét/ *n* a decoration on the shoulder of a jacket, especially on a military uniform [Late 18C. < French, < *épaule* 'shoulder' < Latin *spatula* 'broad piece, shoulder blade' (see SPATULA).]

épée /éppay/ (*plural* **épées**) *n* **1** a fencing sword that has a narrow triangular blade with a blunted end and a large guard for the hand, heavier than a foil **2** the sport of fencing using épées [Late 19C. < French, 'sword' < Latin *spatha* 'broad double-edged sword' (see SPATHE).] —**épéeist** *n*

epeirogeny /éppī rójjәni/, **epeirogenesis** /e pīrō jénnәssiss/ *n* the slow movements of the Earth's crust that lead to the formation of features such as continents [Late 19C. < Greek *ēpeiros* 'mainland, continent'.] —**epeirogenic** /e pīrō jénnik/ *adj* —**epeirogenically** *adv*

epenthesis /i pénthəssiss/ *n* insertion of an extra sound into a word, as happens in some dialect pronunciations or in a word's development over time. The 'b' in 'crumble' is an example of epenthesis. [Mid-17C. Via late Latin < Greek, < *epentithenai* 'place in also' < *tithenai* 'to place'.] —**epenthetic** /éppen théttik/ *adj*

epergne /i púrn/ *n* a large elaborate centrepiece for a table with containers for fruit or confectionery [Mid-18C. Probably < French *épergne* 'savings, treasury' < Old French *espargnier* < Germanic.]

epexegesis /e péksi jeéssiss/ (*plural* **-ses** /-jeéss eez/) *n* **1** the addition of words or phrases to a text to clarify its meaning **2** a word or phrase added to help explain the sense of a text [Early 17C. < Greek *epexēgēsis* < *epi* 'in addition' + *exēgēsis* (see EXEGESIS).] —**epexegetic** /-jéttik/ *adj* —**epexegetical** *adj* —**epexegetically** *adv*

Eph. *abbr* Ephesians

eph- *prefix* = **epi-**

ephebe /i feéb, éffeeb/, **ephebus** /i feébəss/ (*plural* **-bi** /i feébī/), **ephebos** (*plural* **ephebi** /i feébī/) *n* in ancient Greece, a young man aged between 18 and 20 who had just reached manhood or full citizenship and was undergoing military training [Mid-19C. Via Latin < Greek *ephēbos* 'somebody approaching manhood' < *hēbē* 'early manhood'.] —**ephebic** *adj*

ephedra /i féddrə/ (*plural* **-dras** *or* **-dra**) *n* a bush found in warm temperate regions that has slender green jointed stems and whorls of small scaly leaves. It is a source of the drug ephedrine. Genus: *Ephedra.* [Early 20C. Via the modern Latin genus name < Greek < *ephedros* 'a sitting upon'.]

ephedrine /éffi dreen/, **ephedrin** /-drin/ *n* an alkaloid that dilates the air passages. Use: asthma, nasal congestion. [Late 19C. < modern Latin *Ephedra* < Latin *ephedra* 'horsetail' < Greek, plant of a genus including some that contain this substance.]

ephemera[1] plural of **ephemeron**

ephemera[2] /i fémmərə, i feémərə/ *n* (*plural* **-ae** /i fémməree, i feéməree/ *or* **-as**) **1** something that is transitory and without lasting significance **2** INSECTS = **mayfly** *n.* 1 ■ *npl* a range of collectable items that were originally designed to be short-lived ○ *He's a collector of ticket stubs, theatre programmes, and other ephemera.* [14C. < medieval Latin, < form of late Latin *ephemerus* 'lasting only a day' < Greek *ephēmeros* < *hēmera* 'day'.]

ephemeral /i fémmərəl, i feé-/ *adj* lasting for only a short period of time ○ *the ephemeral nature of slang* ■ *n* a plant or insect that lives for only a short period of time —**ephemerality** /i fémmə rálləti, i feémə-/ *n* —**ephemerally** *adv* —**ephemeralness** *n*

ephemerid /i fémmərid, i feé-/ *n* an insect of the mayfly family that emerges in the summer from a long aquatic larval stage and lives only a matter of hours as an adult. Family: Ephemeridae. [Late 19C. < modern Latin *Ephemeridae* < Greek *ephēmeros* (see EPHEMERA[2]).]

ephemeris /i fémməriss, i feé-/ (*plural* **ephemerides** /éffi mérrideez/) *n* a table listing the future positions of the Sun, Moon, and planets over a given period of time [Early 16C. Via Latin < Greek, < *ephēmeros* (see EPHEMERA).]

ephemeris time *n* a system of time measurement based on the Earth's orbit round the Sun and therefore independent of the irregularities of the Earth's rotation

ephemeron /i fémməron, i feéməron/ (*plural* **-a** /-mərə/ *or* **-ons**) *n* a short-lived thing (*usually plural*) [Late 16C. < Greek *ephēmeron*, form of *ephēmeros* (see EPHEMERA[2]).]

Ephesians /i feézh'nz/ *n* one of the books of the Bible, consisting of a letter from the Apostle Paul to the early Christians (+ *singular verb*) [15C. < Latin *ephesius* 'of Ephesus' < Greek *ephesios* < *Ephesos* 'Ephesus'.]

Ephesus /éffəssəss/ ancient Greek city on the coast of W Asia Minor, in present-day Turkey. An important centre for early Christianity, it was also the site of the temple of Artemis, one of the Seven Wonders of the World.

ephor /eé fawr, éffawr/ (*plural* **-ors** *or* **-ori** /eéfə rī/) *n* in ancient Greece, one of five magistrates elected in any of various Dorian states, especially Sparta, to supervise the king [Late 16C. Directly or via Latin < Greek *ephoros* 'overseer' < *horan* 'see'.] —**ephoral** /eéfərəl, éffərəl/ *adj* —**ephorate** *n*

epi- *prefix* **1** on, over, above ○ *epiphyte* ○ *epipelagic* **2** around, near ○ *epicalyx* **3** after, in addition ○ *epiphenomenon* [< Greek *epi* 'upon']

epiblast /éppi blast/ *n* the outer layer of cells in an early embryo (**blastula**). It develops into ectoderm. —**epiblastic** /éppi blástik/ *adj*

epiboly /i píbbəli/ *n* the growth of a layer of rapidly dividing cells over a layer of more slowly dividing cells during embryo development in the eggs of birds and reptiles [Late 19C. < Greek *epibolē* 'throwing on' < *epiballein* < *ballein* 'to throw'.] —**epibolic** /éppi bóllik/ *adj*

epic /éppik/ *n* **1** LONG NARRATIVE POEM a lengthy narrative poem in elevated language celebrating the adventures and achievements of a legendary or traditional hero, e.g. Homer's *Odyssey* **2** EPIC POETRY epic poetry as a genre ○ *This term we'll cover epic, romance, and allegory.* **3** LARGE-SCALE PRODUCTION a work of literature, cinema, television, or theatre that is large-scale and expensively produced and often deals with a historical theme **4** LONG SERIES OF EVENTS a long series of events characterized by adventures or struggle ○ *Our trek across town turned out to be an epic.* ■ *adj* **1** ABOUT AN EPIC relating to or being an epic ○ *Milton's 'Paradise Lost' is an epic poem.* **2** LIKE AN EPIC having some of the characteristics of an epic ○ *an epic story of true love and adventure* **3** VERY LARGE OR HEROIC impressive by virtue of greatness of size, scope, or heroism ○ *a scandal of epic proportions* [Late 16C. Via Latin < Greek *epikos* < *epos* 'word, song', from *ep-*, stem of *eipein* 'say'.] —**epical** *adj* —**epically** *adv*

epicalyx /éppi káyliks, -kálliks/ (*plural* **-lyxes** *or* **-lyces** /-li seez/) *n* a ring of modified leaves (**bracts**) at the base of a flower that resemble an extra calyx, found in the carnation, hibiscus, and mallow

epicanthic fold /éppi kánthik-/ *n* a fold of skin from the eyelid that partially covers the part of the eye nearest the nose

epicanthus /éppi kánthəss/ (*plural* **-thi** /-thī/) *n* ANAT = **epicanthic fold**

epicardium /éppi kaárdi əm/ (*plural* **-dia** /-di ə/) *n* the inner layer of the fibrous sac (**pericardium**) that surrounds the heart [Mid-19C. < EPI- + Greek *kardia* 'heart', after PERICARDIUM.]

epicarp /éppi kaarp/ *n* PLANT SCI = **exocarp**

epicene /éppi seen/ *adj* **1** HAVING CHARACTERISTICS OF BOTH SEXES having both male and female characteristics **2** NEITHER MALE NOR FEMALE of neither male nor female sex **3** WITH FEMALE CHARACTERISTICS describes a male having typically female characteristics (*literary*) **4** WEAK lacking vigour and strength **5** SAME FOR MASCULINE AND FEMININE having only one grammatical form for both masculine and feminine in languages where nouns have genders ■ *n* **1** SOMEBODY OR SOMETHING EPICENE an epicene person or thing (*literary*) **2** NOUN WITH SAME MASCULINE AND FEMININE FORM a noun with the same grammatical form for both masculine and feminine in languages where nouns have genders [15C. Via late Latin < Greek *epikoinos* 'in common' < *koinos* 'common'.] —**epicenism** /éppi seénizəm/ *n*

epicenter /éppi sentər/ *n* US = **epicentre**

epicentre /éppi sentər/ *n* **1** the exact location on the Earth's surface directly above the focus of an earthquake or underground nuclear explosion **2** the very centre or focal point ○ *Paris is the epicentre of the fashion world.* [Mid-19C. < Greek *epikentron*, form of *epikentros* 'situated on a centre' < *kentros* 'centre'.] —**epicentral** /éppi séntrəl/ *adj*

epicotyl /éppi kóttil/ *n* the tip of a plant embryo above the embryonic leaves (**cotyledons**) that gives rise to the stem of the new plant [Late 19C. < EPI- + Greek *kotulē* 'cup, socket'.]

epic simile *n* a lengthy simile developed over a number of lines of verse in narrative poetry

epicure /éppi kyoor/ *n* **1** a consumer of food who has a refined appetite **2** a person who loves sensual pleasure and luxury [14C. < medieval Latin *epicurus* < EPICURUS.] —**epicurism** *n*

epicurean /éppi kyoŏ reé ən/ *adj* **1** devoted to sensual pleasures and luxury, especially good food **2** suitable for or pleasing to an epicure ○ *led an epicurean life* ■ *n* = **epicure** *n.* 2 [14C. Directly or via French *épicurien* < Latin *epicureus* < EPICURUS.] —**epicureanism** *n*

Epicurean /éppi kyoŏ reé ən/ *adj* relating to the philosophy of Epicureanism ■ *n* a follower of Epicureanism

Epicureanism /éppi kyoŏreé ənizəm/ *n* the school of philosophy founded by Epicurus and its teachings

Epicurus /éppi kyoŏrəss/ (341–270 BC) Greek philosopher

epicuticle /éppi kyoŏtik'l/ *n* the waxy outer layer of the protective body covering (**cuticle**) for the exoskeleton of an insect

epicycle /éppi sīk'l/ *n* **1** in the Ptolemaic theory of the solar system, a circle that is followed by a planet, the circle itself being centred on a larger circle within which is the Earth **2** a circle that rolls around the circumference of another circle, either inside or outside [14C. Via French or late Latin < Greek *epikuklos* 'on a circle' < *kuklos* 'circle'.] —**epicyclic** /éppi sīklik, -síklik/ *adj* —**epicyclical** *adj*

epicyclic train *n* a system of gears arranged such that one or more gears engage with and revolve around a fixed or moving part

epicycloid /éppi sī kloyd/ *n* a mathematical curve traced by a point on the circumference of a circle that rolls around the outside of the circumference of another circle —**epicycloidal** /-sī klóyd'l/ *adj*

epidemic /éppi démmik/ *n* **1** FAST-SPREADING DISEASE an outbreak of a disease that spreads more quickly and more extensively among a group of people than would normally be expected **2** RAPID DEVELOPMENT a rapid and extensive development or growth, usually of something unpleasant ○ *an epidemic of civil unrest and rioting* ■ *adj* SPREADING UNUSUALLY QUICKLY AND EXTENSIVELY spreading more quickly and more extensively among a group of people at the same time than would normally be expected ○ *Influenza was epidemic.* [Early 17C. < French *épidémique* < *épidémie* 'an epidemic' < Greek *epidēmia* 'disease prevalent among the people' < *dēmos* 'people'.] —**epidemically** *adv* —**epidemicity** /éppidə míssəti/ *n*

SYNONYMS See ***widespread***.

epidemiology /éppi deémi ólləji/ *n* **1** the scientific and medical study of the causes and transmission of disease within a population **2** the origin and development characteristics of a particular disease [Late 19C. < Greek *epidēmia* (see EPIDEMIC).] —**epidemiological** /-deémi ə lójjik'l/ *adj* —**epidemiologically** *adv* —**epidemiologist** *n*

epidermis /éppi dúrmiss/ *n* **1** OUTER LAYER OF THE SKIN the thin outermost layer of the skin, itself made up of several layers, that covers and protects the underlying dermis **2** OUTER LAYER OF INVERTEBRATES' CELLS the outer layer of cells of invertebrates that secretes the protective waxy cuticle **3** OUTER CELL LAYER OF A PLANT the outermost layer of cells on a plant [Early 17C. Via late Latin < Greek, 'above skin' < *derma* 'skin'.] —**epidermal** *adj* —**epidermic** *adj* —**epidermoid** *adj*

epidiascope /éppi dī əskōp/ *n* a device for projecting an enlarged image of an opaque or transparent object onto a screen

epididymis /éppi díddimiss/ (*plural* **-mides** /éppidi dímmədeez/) *n* a coiled tube attached to the back and upper side of the testicle that stores sperm and is connected to the vas deferens [Early 17C. < Greek *epididumis* < *didumis* 'testicle, twin' < *duo* 'two'.] —**epididymal** *adj*

epidote /éppi dōt/ *n* a shiny green, yellow, or black hydrous aluminosilicate mineral containing calcium and iron. Source: metamorphic rocks. [Early 19C. < French *épidote* < Greek *epididonai* 'give in addition' < *didonai* 'give'; from its very long crystals.] —**epidotic** /éppi dóttik/ *adj*

epidural /éppi dyoŏrəl/ *n* a local anaesthetic injected into the space between the outer membrane covering the spinal cord and the overlying bones of the spine ■ *adj* located on or outside the outermost membrane covering the brain and spinal cord (**dura mater**) [Late 19C. < EPI- + *dura* < DURA MATER.]

epifauna /éppi fawnə/ *npl* animals that live on the sea floor or attached to other animals or objects under water —**epifaunal** /éppi fáwn'l/ *adj*

epigamic /éppi gámmik/ *adj* describes a trait or behaviour that attracts a mate, such as large antlers or bright colours [Late 19C. < EPI- + Greek *gamos* 'marriage'.]

epigastrium /éppi gástri əm/ (*plural* **-a** /-tri ə/) *n* the upper middle part of the abdomen [Late 17C. Via late Latin < Greek *epigastrion*, form of *epigastrios* 'over the stomach' < *gaster* 'stomach'.]

epigeal /éppi jeé əl/ *adj* **1** living or growing on or right above the surface of the ground. ◊ **hypogeal** *adj.* 2 **2** describes seed germination in which the embryo elongates so that the seed leaves (**cotyledons**) are carried above the soil to form the first leaves of the new plant [Mid-19C. < Greek *epigeios* 'on the earth' < *gē* 'earth'.]

epigene /éppi jeen/ *adj* formed or occurring at the Earth's surface, especially with reference to weathering, erosion, and deposition [Early 19C. Via French *épigène* < Greek *epigenēs* 'born on or after' < *-genes* 'born'.]

epigenesis /éppi jénnəssiss/ *n* **1** the theory that the development of tissues and organs during embryonic development proceeds by successive gradual change **2** change in the mineral content or structure of a rock through external influences, such as the injection of a vein of ore into existing rock —**epigenesist** *n* —**epigenetic** /éppijə néttik/ *adj* —**epigenetically** *adv* —**epigenist** /i píjjənist/ *n*

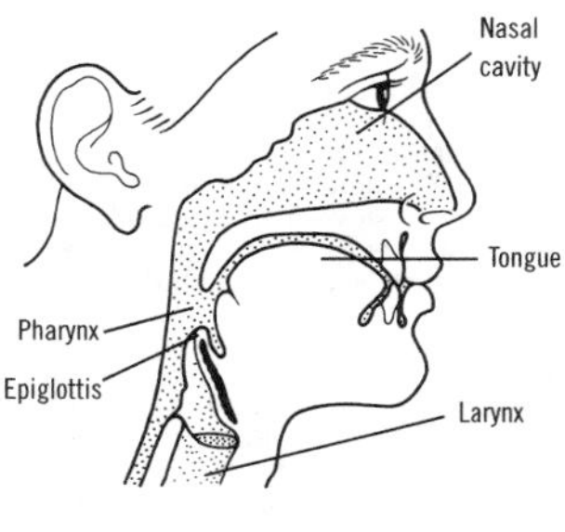

Epiglottis

epiglottis /éppi glóttiss/ (*plural* **-tises** *or* **-tides** /éppi glóttideez/) *n* a flap of cartilage situated at the base of the tongue that covers the opening to the air passages when swallowing, preventing food or liquids from entering the windpipe (**trachea**) [Early 16C. < Greek *epiglōttis* 'on the tongue' < *glōtta* (see GLOTTIS).] —**epiglottal** *adj* —**epiglottic** *adj*

epigone /éppi gōn/, **epigon** /-gon/ *n* a follower, especially of an important artist or philosopher, who is a mediocre imitator (*literary*) [Mid-18C. Via French (plural) < Greek *epigonoi*, plural of *epigonos* 'offspring' < *gignesthai* 'be born'.] —**epigonic** /éppi gónnik/ *adj* —**epigonism** /i píggənizəm/ *n* —**epigonous** /e píggənəss/ *adj*

epigram /éppi gram/ *n* **1 WITTY SAYING** a concise, witty, and often paradoxical remark or saying **2 SHORT POEM** a short poem, often expressing a single idea, that is usually satirical and has a witty ending **3 WITTY EXPRESSION** a written or spoken mode of expression that is witty or concise like an epigram [15C. Directly or via French < Latin *epigramma* < Greek, 'writing upon' < *graphein* 'write'.] —**epigrammatism** /éppi grámmətizəm/ *n* —**epigrammatist** *n*

epigrammatic /éppigrə máttik/, **epigrammatical** /-máttik'l/ *adj* **1** containing or in the form of an epigram **2** tending to use epigrams —**epigrammatically** *adv*

epigrammatize /éppi grámmə tīz/ (**-matizes, -matizing, -matized**), **epigrammatise** (**-ises, -ising, -ised**) *vti* to create a short and witty poem or saying about something

epigraph /éppi graaf, -graf/ *n* **1** a quotation at the beginning of a book, chapter, or section of a book, usually related to its theme **2** an inscription on something, e.g. a statue or building [Late 16C. < Greek *epigraphē* < *epigraphein* 'write on' < *graphein* 'write'.] —**epigraphic** /éppi gráffik/ *adj* —**epigraphical** *adj* —**epigraphically** *adv*

epigraphy /e píggrəfi/ *n* **1** inscriptions or introductory quotations as a whole **2** the study and deciphering of ancient inscriptions —**epigrapher** *n* —**epigraphist** *n*

epilation /éppi láysh'n/ *n* COSMETICS = **depilation** [Late 19C. < French *épilation* < *épiler* 'remove hair' < Latin *pilus* 'hair'.]

epilepsy /éppi lepsi/ (*plural* **-sies**) *n* a medical disorder involving episodes of abnormal electrical discharge in the brain and characterized by periodic sudden loss or impairment of consciousness, often accompanied by convulsions [Mid-16C. Via French < Greek *epilēpsia* 'seizure' < *epilambanein* 'seize' < *lambanein* 'to grasp'.]

epileptic /éppi léptik/ *adj* relating to or affected by epilepsy ■ *n* an offensive term for somebody who has epilepsy [Early 17C. Via French < Greek *epilēptikos* < *epilēpsia* (see EPILEPSY).] —**epileptically** *adv*

epileptiform /éppi lépti fawrm/ *adj* resembling epilepsy

epileptogenic /éppi léptə jénnik/ *adj* causing or able to cause an epileptic episode

epileptoid /éppi lép toyd/ *adj* **1** MED = **epileptiform** **2** showing symptoms similar to those of epilepsy

epilimnion /éppi límni ən/ *n* the uppermost circulating layer of warm water in a lake with different temperatures at different levels in summer [Early 20C. < EPI- + Greek *limnion* 'small lake' < *limnē* 'lake'.]

epilogue /éppi log/ *n* **1 CONCLUDING SPEECH** a short speech, usually in verse, that an actor addresses directly to the audience at the end of a play **2 ACTOR GIVING A SHORT SPEECH** the actor who addresses a short speech, usually in verse, directly to the audience at the end of a play **3 SHORT SECTION AT THE END OF A BOOK** a short chapter or section at the end of a literary work, sometimes detailing the fate of its characters **4 FINAL PROGRAMME** a short programme, usually of religious content, that used to be broadcast at the end of the day [15C. Via French *épilogue* < Greek *epilogos* 'additional speech' < *logos* 'speech'.] —**epilogist** /e píllәjist/ *n*

epimysium /éppi mízzi əm/ (*plural* **-a** /-zi ə/) *n* the covering of connective tissue surrounding a muscle [Early 20C. < modern Latin, < Greek *mus* (see MUSCLE).]

epinephrine /éppi néf reen/, **epinephrin** /-frin/ *n* synthetic adrenaline. Use: to relax the airways, constrict blood vessels. [Late 19C. < EPI- + Greek *nephros* 'kidney'.]

epineurium /éppi nyoór ri əm/ (*plural* **-a** /-ri ə/) *n* a sheath of connective tissue around a nerve [Late 19C. < modern Latin, < Greek *neuron* 'nerve'.] —**epineurial** *adj*

epipelagic /éppipə lájjik/ *adj* relating to or living in the upper zone of the ocean, from the surface to a depth of about 200 m

Epiph. *abbr* Epiphany

epiphany /i píffəni/ (*plural* **-nies**) *n* **1** the manifestation of a divine being **2** a sudden intuitive leap of understanding, especially through an ordinary but striking occurrence ○ *It came to him in an epiphany what his life's work was to be.* [17C. Via French *épiphanie* < Greek *epiphaneia* 'manifestation' < *epiphanein* 'to manifest' < *phanein* 'to show'.] —**epiphanic** /éppi fánnik/ *adj* —**epiphanous** /i píffənəss/ *adj*

Epiphany *n* a Christian festival marking the divine manifestation of Jesus Christ through the Three Wise Men's visit or, in the Eastern Orthodox Church, the baptism of Jesus Christ. Date: 6 January.

epiphenomenalism /éppifi nómminəlizəm/ *n* the view that consciousness is merely an aftereffect of physical processes in the brain and nervous system —**epiphenomenalist** *n*

epiphenomenon /éppifi nómminən/ (*plural* **-na** /nə/) *n* **1** a secondary phenomenon resulting from another **2** a secondary incidental condition or symptom that appears during the course of an illness —**epiphenomenal** *adj* —**epiphenomenally** *adv*

epiphysis /e píffəssiss/ (*plural* **-ses** /-seez/) *n* **1** the end of a long bone that fuses with the shaft of the bone at the point where it was previously separated by cartilage. ◊ **diaphysis** **2** a pineal gland (*archaic*) [Mid-17C. Via modern Latin < Greek *epiphusis* 'growing on' < *phusis* 'growth'.] —**epiphyseal** /éppi fízzi əl/ *adj*

epiphyte /éppi fīt/ *n* a plant that grows on top of or is supported by another plant but does not depend on it for nutrition —**epiphytic** /éppi fíttik/ *adj* —**epiphytically** *adv*

epiphytotic /éppi fī tóttik/ *adj* describes an outbreak of disease that rapidly affects many plants in a given area ■ *n* a plant disease that suddenly and rapidly affects many plants in a given area

Epis. *abbr* **1 Epis., Episc.** Episcopal **2 Epis., Episc.** Episcopalian **3** Epistle

episcopacy /i pískəpəssi/ (*plural* **-cies**) *n* **1** church government by bishops, as in the Roman Catholic, Eastern and Anglican Churches **2** CHR = **episcopate** *n.* **3** [Mid-17C. < ecclesiastical Latin *episcopatus* (see EPISCOPATE).]

episcopal /i pískəp'l/ *adj* **1** relating to a bishop or bishops **2** involving or recognizing church government by bishops [15C. < French *épiscopal* or ecclesiastical Latin *episcopalis* < *episcopus* (see BISHOP).] —**episcopally** *adv*

Episcopal /i pískəp'l/ *adj* relating to or being the Protestant Episcopal Church

Episcopal Church *n* an independent branch of the Anglican Church in North America and Scotland

episcopalian /i pískə páyli ən/ *adj* adhering to or practising church government by bishops ■ *n* a supporter of church government by bishops —**episcopalianism** *n*

Episcopalian *adj* relating to or belonging to the Episcopal Church ■ *n* a member of the Episcopal Church of North America or Scotland —**Episcopalianism** *n*

episcopalism /i pískəpəlizəm/ *n* the belief that authority in a church government should lie in a group of bishops

episcopate /i pískəpət/ *n* **1 OFFICE OR POSITION OF BISHOP** the office, position, or term of office of a bishop **2 DIOCESE** a bishop's diocese or jurisdiction **3 BISHOPS** bishops as a group [Mid-17C. < ecclesiastical Latin *episcopatus* < *episcopus* (see BISHOP).]

episcope /éppi skōp/ *n* a device for projecting an enlarged image of an opaque object such as a printed page or a photograph onto a screen using reflected light. US term **opaque projector**

episiotomy /i pízzi óttəmi/ (*plural* **-mies**) *n* an incision sometimes made to enlarge the vaginal opening in the late stages of labour to prevent tearing and facilitate the birth [Late 19C. < Greek *epision* 'pubic region'.]

episode /éppi sōd/ *n* **1 SIGNIFICANT INCIDENT** an event that is a part of but distinct from a greater whole and that often has some kind of significance ○ *Let's try to put this unfortunate episode behind us, shall we?* **2 PART OF SERIALIZED WORK** a part of a serialized work that is published or broadcast separately **3 EVENT IN A NARRATIVE** an incident, description, or series of events in a narrative that is part of the whole but may digress from the main plot ○ *The episode in the library reveals a lot about the main character.* **4 OCCURRENCE OF ILLNESS** an occurrence of a particular illness or symptom of an illness, usually one of a connected series, often repeated over a period of time ○ *episodes of breathlessness and chest pain* **5 SECTION OF GREEK TRAGEDY** a section of an ancient Greek tragedy between two choruses **6 DIGRESSIVE MUSICAL PASSAGE** a digressive passage between two musical themes, e.g. in a rondo or fugue [Late 17C. < Greek *epeisodion* 'addition', form of *epeisodios* 'coming in besides' < *eisodos* 'coming in' < *hodos* 'road'.]

episodic /éppi sóddik/, **episodical** /-sóddik'l/ *adj* **1 OF AN EPISODE** relating to an episode **2 DIVIDED INTO EPISODES** divided into or composed of closely connected but independent sections **3 SPORADIC** happening at irregular intervals ○ *episodic pain in the lower back* **4 TEMPORARY** of a limited duration ○ *episodic wind squalls* —**episodically** *adv*

episome /éppi sōm/ *n* a genetic unit that can multiply independently in host cells or when integrated with a chromosome [Mid-20C. < EPI- + Greek *sōma* 'body'.] —**episomal** /éppi sṓm'l/ *adj* —**episomally** *adv*

Epist. *abbr* Epistle

epistasis /i pístəssiss/ (*plural* **-ses** /-seez/) *n* the nonappearance of a characteristic determined by one gene because it has been suppressed or masked by the activity of another gene [Early 19C. < Greek, 'stoppage' < *ephistanai* 'to stop' < *histanai* 'put'.] —**epistatic** /éppi státtik/ *adj*

epistaxis /éppi stáksiss/ (*plural* **-staxes** /-seez/) *n* a bleeding from the nose (*technical*) [Late 18C. Via modern Latin < Greek, < *epistazein* 'to drip at (the nose)' < *stazein* 'to drip'.]

epistemic /éppi steémik/ *adj* involving or relating to knowledge [Early 20C. < Greek *epistēmē* 'knowledge' < *epistasthai* 'know' < *histasthai* 'to stand'.] —**epistemically** /-steémikli, -stémmikli/ *adv*

epistemics /éppi steémiks/ *n* the use of logic, philosophy, psychology, and linguistics to study knowledge and how it is processed by humans (+ *singular verb*)

epistemology /i písti mólləji/ *n* the branch of philosophy that studies the nature of knowledge, in particular its foundations, scope, and validity [Mid-19C. < Greek *epistēmē* (see EPISTEMIC).] —**epistemological** /i pístimə lójjik'l/ *adj* —**epistemologically** *adv* —**epistemologist** *n*

epistle /i píss'l/ *n* **1** a long formal letter that often serves to instruct (*formal*) **2** a literary work in the form of a letter [12C. Directly or via Old French < Latin *epistola* < Greek *epistolē* 'something sent' < *stellein* 'send'.]

Epistle *n* **1** any letter written by the apostle Paul or other early Christian writers and included as a book of the Bible **2** an excerpt from one of the Epistles read as part of the service in a Christian church

epistle side, Epistle Side *n* the right side of a Christian church as you face the altar [Because an extract from one of the Epistles is traditionally read from there as part of the Communion service]

epistolary /i pístələri/, **epistolatory** /-tələtəri, i pístə láytəri/ *adj* 1 associated with, conducted by, or suitable for letters (*formal*) 2 taking the form of a letter or a series of letters [Mid-17C. Directly or via French *épistolaire* < Latin *epistolaris* < *epistola* (see EPISTLE).]

epistrophe /i pístrəfi/ *n* repetition of a word or phrase at the end of consecutive clauses or sentences for rhetorical effect [Late 16C. < Greek, < *epistrephein* 'turn about' < *strephein* 'to turn'.]

epistyle /éppi stīl/ *n* ARCHIT = **architrave** *n.* 1 [Mid-16C. Directly or via French < Latin *epistylium* < Greek *epistulion* 'on a column' < *stulos* 'column'.]

epitaph /éppi taaf, -taf/ *n* 1 an inscription on a tombstone or monument commemorating the person buried there 2 a short speech or piece of writing celebrating the life of a recently deceased person [14C. Via French *épitaphe* < Greek *epitaphion* 'something above a tomb or burial' < *taphos* 'funeral ceremonies, tomb'.] —**epitaphic** /eppi táaffik, -táffik/ *adj*

epitasis /i píttəssiss/ (*plural* **-ses** /-seez/) *n* in classical drama, the middle part of a play that develops the main action [Late 16C. Via modern Latin < Greek, < *epiteinein* 'intensify, stretch upon' < *teinein* 'to stretch'.]

epitaxy /éppi taksi/, **epitaxis** /éppi táksiss/ *n* growth of a layer of crystal on a single crystal of another substance [Mid-20C. < French *épitaxie* 'growth on' < Greek *taxis* 'growth'.] —**epitaxial** /-táksi əl/ *adj*

epithalamium /éppithə láymi əm/ (*plural* **-a** /-mi ə/), **epithalamion** (*plural* **-a** /-mi ə/) *n* a poem or song written or performed in celebration of a wedding [Late 16C. < Greek *epithalamion* '(song sung) at the bridal chamber' < *thalamos* 'bridal chamber'.] —**epithalamic** /-lámmik/ *adj*

epithelia plural of **epithelium**

epithelial /éppi théeli əl/ *adj* describes tissue that forms a thin protective layer on exposed bodily surfaces and forms the lining of internal cavities, ducts, and organs

epithelialisation *n* = **epithelialization**

epithelialise *vti* = **epithelialize**

epithelialize /éppi théeli ə līz/ (**-izes, -izing, -ized**), **epithelialise** (**-ises, -ising, -ised**), **epithelize** /éppi théelīz/ (**-izes, -izing, -ized**), **epithelise** (**-ises, -ising, -ised**) *vti* to become or cause to become covered with epithelial tissue, as in the healing of a wound —**epithelialization** /eppi théeli ə lī záysh'n/ *n*

epithelise *vti* = **epithelialize**

epithelium /éppi théeli əm/ (*plural* **-a** /-li ə/ *or* **-ums**) *n* a thin layer of tightly packed cells lining internal cavities, ducts, and organs of animals and covering exposed bodily surfaces, especially in healing wounds [Mid-18C. < modern Latin, < Greek *thēlē* 'teat, nipple'.]

epithelize /éppi théelīz/ *vti* MED = **epithelialize** —**epithelization** /éppi théeli záysh'n/ *n*

epithermal /éppi thúrm'l/ *adj* describes veins of gold or silver originally formed deep within the Earth's crust from ascending hot solutions

epithet /éppi thet/ *n* 1 DESCRIPTIVE WORD ADDED TO SOMEBODY'S NAME a descriptive word or phrase added to or substituted for the name of somebody or something, highlighting a feature or quality ○ *easy to see how she earned herself the epithet 'The All-Knowing'* 2 INSULT an abusive insulting word or phrase 3 PART OF TAXONOMIC NAME in biological classification, the species name that follows the genus name [Late 16C. Directly or via French *épithète* < Latin *epitheton* 'something added' < Greek *epitheto*, past participle of *epitithenai* 'put on' < *tithenai* 'to place'.] —**epithetic** /éppi théttik/ *adj* —**epithetical** *adj*

epitome /i píttəmi/ *n* 1 a highly representative example of a type, class, or characteristic ○ *Isn't she just the epitome of elegance?* 2 a brief summary of a piece of written work (*formal*) [Early 16C. Via Latin < Greek, < *epitemnein* 'to cut short' < *temnein* 'to cut'.]

epitomise *vt* = **epitomize**

epitomize /i píttə mīz/ (**-mizes, -mizing, -mized**), **epitomise** (**-ises, -ising, -ised**) *vt* 1 to be a highly representative example of something ○ *This incident epitomizes all that is wrong with modern society.* 2 to write a brief summary of a piece of writing (*formal*) —**epitomization** /i píttə mī záysh'n/ *n* —**epitomist** *n*

~~**epitomy**~~ incorrect spelling of **epitome**

epitope /éppi tōp/ *n* an immunologically active binding site on an antigen to which an antibody or a B- or T-cell receptor becomes attached [Mid-20C. < EPI- + Greek *topos* 'place'.]

epizoic /éppi zō ik/ *adj* 1 describes a nonparasitic animal or plant that lives on the external surface of a living animal 2 describes plants whose seeds or spores are dispersed by being attached to the coats of animals —**epizoism** *n*

epizoon /éppi zō on/ (*plural* **-a** /-ə/), **epizoite** /-zō īt/ *n* an organism that lives on the external surface of a living animal [Mid-19C. < modern Latin, 'on an animal' < Greek *zōion* 'animal'.] —**epizoan** *adj*

epizootic /éppi zō óttik/ *adj* describes an outbreak of disease that rapidly affects many animals in a given area at the same time ■ *n* a disease that rapidly affects a large number of animals in a given area at the same time [Late 18C. < French *épizootique* 'at animals' < Greek *zōion* 'animal'.] —**epizootically** *adv*

e pluribus unum /áy plóor ribəss óonəm, -yóonəm/ one out of many (*used as the motto of the United States*) [Latin]

EPNS *abbr* electroplated nickel silver

EPO *abbr* erythropoietin

epoch /ée pok/ *n* 1 SIGNIFICANT PERIOD a significant period in history or in somebody's life 2 START OF HISTORICALLY SIGNIFICANT PERIOD the beginning of a long period of history considered particularly significant ○ *The invention of the telephone marked an epoch in the development of international communication.* 3 UNIT OF GEOLOGICAL TIME a unit of geological time that is a division of a period and is characterized by rock formation ○ *the Holocene and Pleistocene epochs of the Quaternary period* 4 MOMENT IN TIME AS REFERENCE POINT a precise moment in time arbitrarily chosen as a reference point for defining the position of celestial bodies [Early 17C. Via modern Latin *epocha* < Greek *epokhē* 'pause (in time)' < *ekhein* 'to hold'.] —**epochal** /éppok'l, ée pok'l/ *adj*

epoch-making *adj* having great importance or momentous significance ○ *Galileo's epoch-making discoveries*

epode /éppōd/ *n* 1 the part of a lyric ode in classical Greek drama that follows the strophe and the antistrophe 2 a lyric ode characterized by couplets made up of a long line followed by a shorter one [Early 17C. Directly or via French *épode* < Latin *epodos* < Greek *epōidos* 'sung after' < *ōidē* 'song'.]

eponym /éppə nim/ *n* 1 PERSON AFTER WHOM SOMETHING IS NAMED the name of a person or mythical character from which another name or term is derived 2 MEDICAL NAME FROM A PERSON a medical name, e.g. of a disease, derived from the name of a person 3 NAME DERIVED FROM A PERSON a name derived from the name of a person or mythical character [Mid-19C. < Greek *epōnumos* 'given as a name' < *onuma* 'name'.] —**eponymic** /éppə nímmik/ *adj*

eponymous /i pónniməss/ *adj* having the name that is used as the title or name of something else, especially the title of a book, play, or film ○ *the eponymous hero* —**eponymously** *adv*

⚡**EPOS** /ée poss/ *abbr* electronic point of sale

epoxide /i póksīd/ *n* a chemical compound containing a three-membered ring consisting of an oxygen atom bonded to each of two carbon atoms

epoxide resin *n* CHEM = **epoxy resin**

epoxy /i póksi/ *adj* relating to an epoxide or epoxy resin ■ *n* (*plural* **-ies**) CHEM = **epoxy resin** ■ *vt* (**-ies, -ying, -ied**) to stick one thing to another using epoxy resin

epoxy resin, epoxide resin *n* a tough synthetic resin, containing epoxy groups, that sets after the application of heat or pressure. Use: adhesives, surface coatings.

Epping Forest /épping-/ region of ancient woodland in SE England

⚡**EPROM** /ée prom/ *n* an integrated circuit that can be reprogrammed by a user to correct an error in the program or add a function. Full form **erasable-programmable read-only memory**

eps *abbr* earnings per share

epsilon /ep sílən, épsilon/ *n* the fifth letter of the Greek alphabet [Early 18C. < Greek *e psilon* 'short e' (literally 'bare e').]

Epsom /épsəm/ city in SE England, site of a racecourse on Epsom Downs. Population: 90,437 (1991).

Epsom salts *n* a bitter-tasting preparation of hydrated magnesium sulphate. Use: formerly, as a purgative and to reduce swelling. (+ *singular verb*) [Because originally obtained from a mineral spring at Epsom]

Epstein /ép stīn/, **Sir Jacob** (1880–1959) US-born British sculptor

Epstein-Barr virus /ép stīn báar-/ *n* a virus believed to cause glandular fever and associated with Burkitt's lymphoma and some carcinomas [Mid-20C. After M. A. *Epstein* (b. 1921) and Y. M. *Barr* (b. 1932), British virologists.]

EQ *n* the ratio of educational attainment to chronological age. Full form **educational quotient**

eq. *abbr* 1 equal 2 equation 3 equivalent

equable /ékwəb'l/ *adj* 1 calm and not easily disturbed ○ *She maintained the most equable of temperaments despite her financial problems.* 2 free from variation and marked extremes [Mid-16C. < Latin *aequabilis* < *aequare* (see EQUATE).] —**equability** /ékwə bílləti/ *n* —**equableness** *n* —**equably** *adv*

equal /éekwəl/ *adj* 1 IDENTICAL identical in size, quantity, value, or standard ○ *equal quantities of flour and sugar* 2 WITH THE SAME RIGHTS having the same privileges, rights, status, and opportunities as others 3 WITH AN EVEN BALANCE evenly balanced between opposing sides ○ *hoping for a more equal match in the second game* 4 EQUIPPED WITH THE NECESSARY QUALITIES equipped with the necessary qualities or means to accomplish something ○ *didn't think he would be equal to the task* 5 EQUIVALENT having the same effect, value, or meaning as another ■ *n* SOMEBODY OR SOMETHING EQUAL somebody or something equal in quality to another ○ *As a defender he has no equal in the Premiership.* ■ *v* (**equals, equalling, equalled**) 1 *vt* HAVE SAME VALUE AS to be equal to, usually in value ○ *Two plus two equals four.* 2 *vt* DO SOMETHING EQUAL TO SOMETHING ELSE to do, produce, or achieve something to the same standard or of the same value as something else ○ *And with that jump, she has equalled the world record.* 3 *vi* BECOME EQUAL to become identical or the same ○ *It will all equal out in the end.* [14C. < Latin *aequalis* < *aequus* 'equal, even'.] ◇ **first among equals** the most powerful or influential person in a group whose members are supposed to have equal status

equal-area *adj* on a map projection, accurately representing the relative sizes of regions that are of equal area, although distorting shape and direction

equalise *vti* = **equalize**

equaliser *n* = **equalizer**

equalitarian /i kwólli táiri ən/ *n, adj* SOC WELFARE = **egalitarian** —**equalitarianism** *n*

equality /i kwólləti/ (*plural* **-ties**) *n* 1 rights, treatment, quantity, or value equal to all others in a given group ○ *full equality under the law* 2 an equation in which the quantities on each side of an equal sign are the same

equalize /éekwə līz/ (**-izes, -izing, -ized**), **equalise** (**-ises, -ising, -ised**) *v* 1 *vt* to make things uniform or equal ○ *You must equalize the liquid levels in each bottle.* 2 *vi* to score a point or goal that brings a score level with that of an opponent ○ *They equalized just before half-time.* —**equalization** /éekwə lī záysh'n/ *n*

equalizer /éekwə līzər/, **equaliser** *n* 1 SOMEBODY OR SOMETHING THAT EQUALIZES somebody or something that makes things uniform or equal 2 ELECTRONIC SOUND ADJUSTER an electronic device used to reduce distortion in a sound system by internally adjusting the system's response to different audio frequencies 3 GOAL OR POINT THAT LEVELS SCORES a goal or point that brings a person's or team's score level with that of an opponent 4 *US* WEAPON a dangerous weapon, e.g. a knife or gun (*slang*)

equally /éekwəli/ *adv* 1 IN SAME WAY in an identical or uniform way ○ *treat people equally* 2 TO SAME EXTENT to the same degree or extent ○ *This issue is equally important.* 3 IN SAME-SIZED AMOUNTS in parts or amounts of the same size ○ *Divide it equally between four people.* 4 AT THE SAME TIME used to introduce a second statement that is of equal importance to the first but may contrast or balance it ○ *I want the business to succeed, but equally, I don't want to be working all the time.*

USAGE ***Equally*** and ***as*** cannot be used together. You can say *She is a brilliant pianist, and her brother is equally talented* or *She is a brilliant pianist, and her brother is as talented*, but not *She is a brilliant pianist, and her brother is equally as talented.*

equal opportunity *n* the availability of the same rights, position, and status to all people, regardless of gender, sexual preference, age, race, ethnicity, or religion (*often* *used in the plural*) ○ *the implementation of an equal opportunities policy*

equal sign, equals sign *n* a mathematical symbol (=) used to indicate that two or more numbers, symbols, or terms have the same value as each other

equal temperament *n* the division of a musical octave into 12 equal half steps in the tuning of an instrument

equanimity /ékwə nímməti, éekwə-/ *n* evenness of temper even under stress ○ *faced his critical constituents with equanimity* [Early 17C. < Latin *aequanimitas* < *aequus* 'even' + *animus* 'mind'.] —**equanimous** /i kwánniməss, i kwónni-/ *adj*

equate /i kwáyt, ee-/ (**equates, equating, equated**) *v* **1** *vt* **CONSIDER AS EQUIVALENT** to treat, show, or consider something as equivalent to something else ○ *equating money with happiness* **2** *vt* **FORM AN EQUATION** to form an equation involving an equality **3** *vi* **APPEAR TO BE EQUAL** to be or appear to be the same (*formal*) ○ *Their two accounts of the incident seem to equate.* [15C. < Latin *aequat-*, past participle of *aequare* 'make equal' < *aequus* 'equal, even'.] —**equatability** /i kwáytə bílləti, ee-/ *n* —**equatable** *adj*

equation /i kwáyzh'n/ *n* **1 STATEMENT OF EQUALITY** a mathematical statement that two expressions, usually divided by an equals sign, are of the same value **2 ACT OF REGARDING AS EQUAL** the act or process of making things equal or considering them to be equal **3 STATE OF BEING EQUAL** the state of being the same or equivalent ○ *bring the balance of power into equation* **4 SITUATION INVOLVING MANY VARIABLE FACTORS** a situation that has two or more variable elements to be considered ○ *The selling option just does not enter into the equation.* **5 REPRESENTATION OF A CHEMICAL REACTION** a written representation of the reactants and products in a chemical reaction —**equational** *adj* —**equationally** *adv*

equation of state *n* an equation that states the relationship between the pressure, temperature, and volume of a gas or liquid

equation of time *n* the difference between apparent solar time and mean solar time, usually expressed as a correction to the apparent time, and varying in a complex annual pattern between maxima of about fifteen minutes in February and November

equator /i kwáytər/ *n* **1 IMAGINARY CIRCLE AROUND EARTH** the imaginary great circle around the Earth that is the same distance from the North and South Poles and divides the Earth into the northern and southern hemispheres **2 IMAGINARY CIRCLE AROUND AN ASTRONOMICAL OBJECT** the imaginary great circle around an astronomical object that is everywhere the same distance from the poles **3 CIRCLE DIVIDING A SPHERE INTO TWO** a circle that divides a sphere or other surface into two equal parts **4** ASTRON = **celestial equator** [14C. Directly or via French < medieval Latin *aequator*, in *aequator diei et noctis* 'equalizer of day and night' < *aequare* (see EQUATE).]

equatorial /ékwə táwri əl, éekwə-/ *adj* **1** relating to or present near the equator **2** situated in the plane of an equator —**equatorially** *adv*

equatorial current *n* a current that moves in a westerly direction near the surface of an ocean at the equator

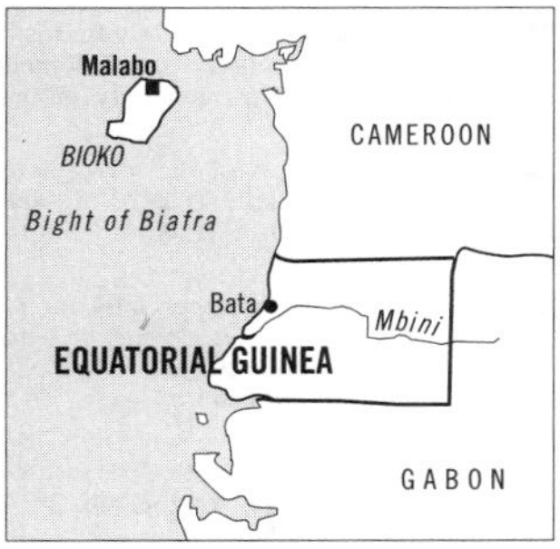

Equatorial Guinea

Equatorial Guinea /ékwə táwri əl-/ republic in W Africa bordering the Atlantic Ocean and comprising a mainland section, Río Muni, and several islands. Capital: Malabo. Population: 442,516 (1997). Area: 28,051 sq. km/10,831 sq. mi.

equatorial plate *n* the area midway between the poles of the spindle of a dividing cell, where chromosomes are aligned

equatorial telescope *n* an astronomical telescope mounted so that it allows an astronomical object to be kept in view without adjustment as the Earth rotates

equerry /i kwérri, ékwəri/ (*plural* **-ries**) *n* **1** an officer who is the personal attendant of the British monarch or a member of the royal family **2** formerly, an officer in an aristocratic or royal household who was responsible for the supervision of the horses [Early 16C. Via obsolete French *escurie* < Old French *escuierie* 'company of squires, prince's stables' < *escuier* 'squire' (see ESQUIRE).]

equestrian /i kwéstri ən/ *adj* **1 OF HORSES** relating to horses or riding **2 DEPICTING SOMEBODY ON HORSEBACK** depicting somebody mounted on a horse ○ *an equestrian statue* **3 OF MOUNTED SOLDIERS** composed of soldiers on horseback ■ *n* **SKILLED RIDER** a skilled rider or performer on horseback [Mid-17C. < Latin *equester* 'of a horse-rider' < *eques* 'horse-rider, knight' < *equus* 'horse'.] —**equestrianism** *n*

equestrienne /i kwéstri én/ *n* a woman who is skilled at riding horses or performing on horseback [Mid-19C. < EQUESTRIAN after French feminine nouns ending in *-enne*.]

equi- *prefix* equal ○ *equimolar* [< Latin *aequus*]

equiangular /éekwi áng gyŏolər, ékwi-/ *adj* describes a geometric figure in which all the angles are equal [Mid-17C. < late Latin *equiangulus* < Latin *angulus* 'corner'.]

equid /ékwid/ *n* a member of the family of animals that includes horses, donkeys, and zebras. Family: Equidae. [Late 19C. < modern Latin *Equidae* < Latin *equus* 'horse'.]

equidistant /éekwi dístənt, ékwi-/ *adj* situated at the same distance from two or more places or points ○ *Birmingham is equidistant from Leeds and London.* [Late 16C. < French *équidistant* or medieval Latin *equidistant-* < Latin *distant-* (see DISTANT).] —**equidistance** *n* —**equidistantly** *adv*

equilateral /éekwi láttərəl, ékwi-/ *adj* **WITH EQUAL SIDES** describes a geometric figure in which all the sides are of equal length ■ *n* **1 EQUILATERAL FIGURE** a geometric figure with all of its sides of equal length **2 SIDE OF AN EQUILATERAL FIGURE** any side of a geometric figure that is the same length as the other sides [Late 16C. Directly or via French *équilatéral* < late Latin *aequilateralis* < Latin *lateralis* (see LATERAL).] —**equilaterally** *adv*

equilibrant /i kwíllibrənt/ *n* a force able to balance out another force and produce an equilibrium [Late 19C. < French *équilibrant* < *équilibre* 'balance' < Latin *aequilibrium* (see EQUILIBRIUM).]

equilibrate /éekwi lī́ brayt, i kwílli brayt/ (**-brates, -brating, -brated**) *vti* to be evenly balanced, or counterbalance something, or bring something into a state of balance [Mid-17C. < late Latin *aequilibrare* < *libra* 'balance'.] —**equilibration** /éekwi lī bráysh'n, i kwílli-/ *n* —**equilibrator** /i kwílli braytər/ *n* —**equilibratory** /i kwílli bráytəri/ *adj*

equilibrist /i kwíllibrist/ *n* a performer skilled in the art of balancing, especially tightrope walking (*archaic*)

equilibrium /éekwi líbbri əm, ékwi-/ (*plural* **-ums** *or* **-a** /-ri ə/) *n* **1 SITUATION OF BALANCE** a state or situation in which opposing forces or factors balance each other out and stability is attained **2 EMOTIONAL STABILITY** a mental state of calmness and composure **3 BALANCE BETWEEN FORCES** a static or dynamic state in which all forces or processes are in balance and there is no resultant change **4 BODILY BALANCE** a physical state or sense of being able to maintain bodily balance [Early 17C. < Latin *aequilibrium* 'equal balance' < *libra* 'balance'.]

equilibrium constant *n* the constant value that relates the concentration of products and starting materials in a reversible chemical reaction at equilibrium

equimolar /éekwi mṓlər, ékwi-/ *adj* with an equal concentration of moles in one litre of solution

equimolecular /éekwimə lékyŏolər, ékwimə-/ *adj* describes a substance or mixture that has the same number of molecules as another

equine /é kwīn, ée kwīn/ *adj* **1 OF HORSES** relating to, belonging to, or affecting horses **2 RESEMBLING A HORSE** characteristic of or similar to a horse in appearance or behaviour **3 BELONGING TO THE HORSE FAMILY** belonging to or characteristic of the family of mammals that includes horses, zebras, and donkeys ■ *n* **HORSE OR HORSE'S RELATIVE** a horse or other member of the horse family [Late 18C. < Latin *equinus* < *equus* 'horse'.]

equinoctial /éekwi nóksh'l, ékwi nóksh'l/ *adj* **1 OCCURRING AT AN EQUINOX** happening at or near either of the two equinoxes **2 WITH FLOWERS OPEN AT DEFINITE TIMES** describes a plant whose flowers open and close at specific times of day **3 OF THE CELESTIAL EQUATOR** relating to the celestial equator ■ *n* **1 STORM AT AN EQUINOX** a storm or strong wind that occurs at a time when day and night are the same length (**equinox**) **2** ASTRON = **celestial equator** [14C. < French *équinoctial* < Latin *aequinoctium* (see EQUINOX).]

equinoctial circle *n* ASTRON = **celestial equator**

equinoctial point *n* either of the two points on the celestial sphere where the Sun crosses the celestial equator

equinoctial year *n* ASTRON = **solar year**

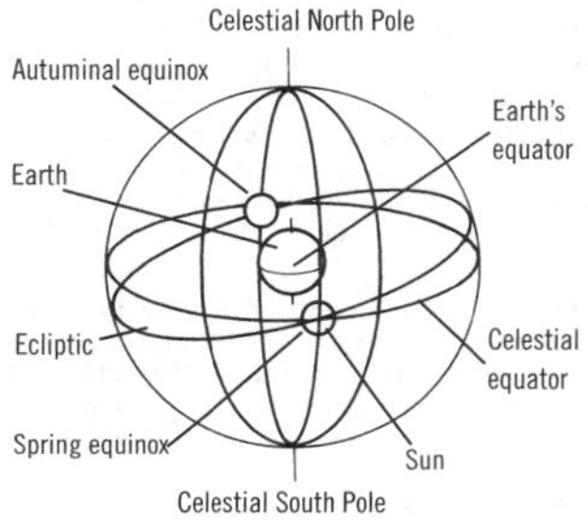

Equinox: Diagram showing positions of Sun and Earth at spring and autumnal equinoxes

equinox /éekwi noks, ékwi-/ *n* **1** either of the two annual crossings of the equator by the Sun, once in each direction, when the length of day and night are approximately equal everywhere on Earth **2** ASTRON = **equinoctial point** [14C. Directly or via French < Latin *aequinoctium* 'equal night' < *nox* 'night'.]

equip /i kwíp/ (**equips, equipping, equipped**) *vt* **1** to provide somebody or something with what is needed for a particular activity or purpose, e.g. with the appropriate tools, supplies, parts, or clothing ○ *a computer equipped with a modem and a CD-ROM drive* ○ *They equipped themselves with the most up-to-date camping gear.* **2** to prepare somebody with the necessary education, training, or experience to succeed at a task or role in life (*often passive*) ○ *I'm sorry, but I don't feel equipped to answer that question.* [Early 16C. < French *équiper*, probably < Old Norse *skipa* 'fit out a ship' < *skip* 'ship'.] —**equipper** *n*

equipage /ékwipij/ *n* **1** a horse-drawn carriage, especially a luxurious one, or a carriage together with its horses and attendants **2** the equipment and supplies needed for an undertaking, especially a military expedition or ship's journey

equipartition /éekwi paar tísh'n, ékwi-/ *n* the equal distribution of energy among the components of motion, such as linear movement and rotation, of the gas molecules in a system

~~**equiped**~~ incorrect spelling of **equipped**

equipment /i kwípmənt/ *n* **1 NECESSARY ITEMS** the tools, clothing, or other items needed for a particular purpose or activity ○ *camping equipment* **2 PROVIDING SOMEBODY WITH EQUIPMENT** the equipping of somebody or something with what is necessary for a particular purpose or activity **3 PERSONAL RESOURCES FOR SUCCESS** the intellectual and emotional resources that enable a person to succeed at a task or role in life

equipoise /ékwi poyz, éekwi-/ *n* (*formal*) **1 BALANCED STATE** a condition where weights are in balance or there is a balance between different social, emotional, or intellectual influences **2 SOMETHING CAUSING BALANCE** something that creates a balanced state, usually by counterbalancing some other force or thing ■ *vt* (**-poises, -poising, -poised**) **COUNTERBALANCE** to counterbalance a weight or influence (*formal*)

equipollent /éekwi póllənt, ékwi-/ *adj* having the same weight, influence, validity, or effect as another, or as each other (*formal*) [14C. < Old French *equipolent* < Latin *pollere* 'be strong'.] —**equipollence** *n* —**equipollency** *n* —**equipollently** *adv*

equipotential /èekwipə ténsh'l, ékwi-/ *adj* describes a surface that has the same electric or gravitational potential at all points —**equipotentiality** /-ténshi állәti/ *n*

equiprobable /èekwi próbbəb'l, ékwi-/ *adj* equally likely to be true or to occur according to logic or mathematics

equisetum /ékwi seétəm/ (*plural* **-tums** *or* **-ta** /-tə/) *n* a nonflowering plant with a hollow jointed stem, tiny thin leaves, and spore-producing cones borne at the top of the stems. Genus: *Equisetum.* [Late 17C. < Latin *equisaetum* 'horse bristle'.]

equitable /ékwitəb'l/ *adj* **1** characterized by justice or fairness and impartiality towards those involved (*formal*) **2** applicable under the law of equity as distinguished from common or statute law [Mid-16C. < French *équitable* < *équité* (see EQUITY).] —**equitableness** *n* —**equitably** *adv*

equitation /ékwi táysh'n/ *n* the skill and theory of riding horses (*formal*) [Mid-16C. Directly or via French < Latin *equitation-* < *equitare* 'to ride on horseback' < *equus* 'horse'.]

equites /ékwi teez/ *npl* **1** the cavalry of ancient Rome **2** a privileged class of ancient Romans of a rank above the common people, whose members served as cavalry [Early 17C. < Latin, plural of *eques* 'horse-rider' (see EQUESTRIAN).]

equity /ékwiti/ *n* (*plural* **-ties**) **1 FAIRNESS** actions, treatment of others, or a general condition characterized by justice, fairness, and impartiality (*formal*) **2 MODIFICATION OF COMMON LAW** the system of jurisprudence that supplements common and statutory law, when those bodies of law are inadequate in the attainment of justice **3 JUSTICE TEMPERED BY ETHICS** justice applied in conformity with the law, but influenced at the same time by principles of ethics and fair play **4 FAIR CLAIM** a claim that is judged to be just and fair **5 PART OF VALUE PAID** the value of a piece of property over and above any mortgage or other liabilities relating to it ■ **equities** *npl* **SHARES ENTITLING HOLDER TO PROFITS** shares of stock in a corporation that pay the holder some of the company's profits [14C. Via French < Latin *aequitas* < Latin *aequus* 'equal, even'.]

Equity *n* the trade union for actors

equity capital *n* funds for a business raised by selling shares or by retaining earnings

equity of redemption *n* the right of a mortgagor to redeem mortgaged property by paying the sum owed within a reasonable time after the date on which payment was due

equivalence /i kwívvələnss/, **equivalency** /-lənssi/ *n* **1** the fact of being the same, effectively the same, or interchangeable with something else **2** the relationship between two statements, both of which are either true or false, and each of which can be proved from the other

equivalence relation *n* the relation between members of a set that is reflexive, symmetrical, and transitive, e.g. if 'a' equals 'b' and 'b' equals 'c', then 'a' equals 'c'

equivalency *n* = **equivalence**

equivalent /i kwívvələnt/ *adj* **1 EQUAL** being the same, or effectively the same, in effect, value, or meaning as something and usually interchangeable with it ○ *That's equivalent to the amount of energy needed to power a single light bulb.* **2 OF THE SAME SIZE BUT DIFFERENT SHAPE** describes geometric figures that have different shapes but equal areas, e.g. a circle and a square, or equal volumes, e.g. a cylinder and a cube **3 WITH THE SAME SOLUTION** describes equations that share a common solution or solutions, e.g. for both $2x-3 = x+2$ and $x-5 = 0$ the solution is $x = 5$ **4 IN AN EQUIVALENCE RELATION** describes members of a set that are in a reflexive, symmetrical, and transitive relation with each other ■ *n* **1 SOMETHING CONSIDERED THE SAME** something that is considered to be equal to or have the same effect, value, or meaning as something else ○ *He's the Italian equivalent of the Chancellor of the Exchequer.* **2** CHEM = **equivalent weight** [15C. < French *équivalent* < late Latin *aequivalere* 'be of equal value' < Latin *valere* 'be strong'.] —**equivalently** *adv*

equivalent weight *n* the mass of a substance that will combine with or replace 8 parts by weight of oxygen or 1.008 parts of hydrogen

equivocal /i kwívvək'l/ *adj* **1 AMBIGUOUS** open to more than one interpretation, especially in being deliberately expressed in an ambiguous way in an attempt to mislead somebody ○ *an equivocal reply to a tough question* **2 DIFFICULT TO INTERPRET** difficult to interpret, understand, or respond to ○ *Their stance on this issue is equivocal and nobody knows how they are likely to react.* **3 RAISING DOUBTS** arousing doubts and suspicions, especially about somebody's honesty or sincerity ○ *To arrive at the peace talks with an armed guard was an equivocal gesture.* [Mid-16C. < late Latin *aequivocus* (see EQUIVOCATE).] —**equivocality** /i kwívvə kálləti/ *n* —**equivocally** *adv* —**equivocalness** *n*

equivocate /i kwívvə kayt/ (**-cates, -cating, -cated**) *vi* to speak vaguely or ambiguously, especially in order to mislead ○ *When pressed for a firm answer, she equivocated.* [15C. < late Latin *aequivocat-*, past participle of *aequivocare* < *aequivocus* 'ambiguous' < Latin *vox* 'voice'.] —**equivocatingly** *adv* —**equivocator** *n* —**equivocatory** *adj*

equivocation /i kwívvə káysh'n/ *n* **1 USE OF AMBIGUITY** the use of vague or ambiguous and sometimes misleading language ○ *What we ask for is facts: what we get is equivocation or downright lies.* **2 AMBIGUOUS STATEMENT** an expression or statement that is vague or ambiguous and often deliberately misleading ○ *Their equivocations could not disguise the fact that corruption was rife in the committee.* **3 WRONG LOGICAL CONCLUSION** an invalid conclusion based on statements in which one term has two different meanings

equivoque /ékwi vōk, èekwi-/, **equivoke** *n* (*formal*) **1 PLAY ON WORDS** an amusing use of an ambiguous word **2 AMBIGUOUS WORD OR PHRASE** a word or phrase with a double meaning **3 AMBIGUITY** ambiguity, double meaning, or misleading words and expressions [Early 17C. Directly or via French *équivoque* < late Latin *aequivocus* (see EQUIVOCATE).]

Equuleus /e kwóoli əss/ *n* constellation of the northern hemisphere, the second-smallest of the constellations. See illustration at **constellation**

er[1] /ur/ *interj* used to express hesitation [Mid-19C. An imitation of the sound.]

⚡ **er**[2] *abbr* Eritrea (*in Internet addresses*)

Er *symbol* erbium

ER *abbr* **1** Eduardus Rex **2** Elizabetha Regina **3** *US* emergency room

-er[1] *suffix* **1** somebody or something that performs or undergoes a particular action ○ *adjuster* ○ *fryer* **2** somebody connected with, often as an occupation ○ *trucker* **3** somebody or something that has a particular characteristic, quality, or form ○ *fore-and-after* **4** somebody from a particular place ○ *Londoner* ○ *foreigner* [Partly Old English *-ere* < Germanic; partly via Anglo-Norman < Latin *-arius*; partly < Old French *-eor* (see OR[1])]

-er[2] *suffix* more ○ *greener* ○ *slower* [Old English *-re, -ra* < Germanic]

era /eérə/ *n* **1 DISTINCTIVE PERIOD OF HISTORY** a period of time made distinctive by a significant development, feature, event, or personality ○ *during the postwar era* **2 PERIOD WITH OWN CHRONOLOGICAL SYSTEM** a time period within which years are consecutively numbered from a particular significant event that provides its starting point ○ *the Christian era* **3 DATE THAT BEGINS PERIOD** a significant date or event that is regarded as the beginning of a new period of time ○ *The agreement marked an era in US-Soviet relations.* **4 DIVISION OF EARTH'S HISTORY** a division of geological time composed of several periods [Mid-17C. < late Latin *aera* 'number used as a basis for counting'.]

ERA *abbr* **1** *US* Equal Rights Amendment ■ **2** a law passed by Parliament in 1988, covering the publication of information on schools, open enrolment, and grant-maintained schools. Full form **Education Reform Act**

eradicate /i ráddi kayt/ (**-cates, -cating, -cated**) *vt* to destroy or get rid of something completely, so that it can never recur or return [15C. < Latin *eradicat-*, past participle of *eradicare* 'pull up by the roots' < *radix* 'root'.] —**eradicable** *adj* —**eradicably** /-kəbli/ *adv* —**eradication** /i ráddi káysh'n/ *n* —**eradicative** *adj* —**eradicator** *n*

⚡ **erase** /i ráyz/ (**erases, erasing, erased**) *vt* **1 REMOVE WRITTEN MATERIAL** to remove written, typed, or printed material by rubbing it out, or to obliterate it with something such as correction fluid **2 DELETE RECORDED DATA** to delete data or recorded material from a computer's memory, a magnetic tape, or other storage media **3 REMOVE OR DESTROY** to remove or destroy something completely ○ *an ancient civilization, all traces of which had been erased over time* [Late 16C. < Latin *eras-*, past participle of *eradere* 'scrape out' < *radere* 'to scrape'.] —**erasability** /i ráyzə bíllәti/ *n* —**erasable** *adj*

eraser /i ráyzər/ *n* = **rubber**[1] *n.* 7

Erasmus /i rázməss/, **Desiderius** (1466?–1536) Dutch scholar and writer

Erastianism /i rásti ənizəm/ *n* the theory that the state, not a church, should have the ultimate authority in ecclesiastical matters [Late 17C. After *Erastus*.] —**Erastian** *n, adj*

erasure /i ráyzhər/ *n* **1** the complete removal or destruction of something ○ *an erasure of data from a hard drive* **2** the place where something has been rubbed out, or the mark left behind

Erato /érrətō/ *n* in Greek mythology, the muse of lyric poetry. ◊ **Muse**

Eratosthenes /érrə tósthə neez/ prominent deep crater on the Moon, 58 km/36 mi. in diameter, located at the southern edge of Mare Imbrium

Eratosthenes (276?–196? BC) Greek astronomer and mathematician

erbium /úrbi əm/ *n* (*symbol* **Er**) a soft silvery metallic element of the rare-earth group. Source: monazite, bastnaesite. Use: alloys, pigment. [Mid-19C. After *Ytterby*, town in Sweden.]

ere /air/ *prep, conj* before or earlier in time than (*literary or archaic*) [Old English *ǣr* < Germanic]

SPELLCHECK See ***air***

Erebus, Mount /érribəss/ active volcano on the eastern coast of Ross Island, Antarctica. Height: 3,794 m/12,448 ft.

erect /i rékt/ *adj* **1 STRAIGHT AND VERTICAL** in an upright position ○ *an erect plant stem* **2 FIRM AND RIGID** stiff and swollen as a result of being filled with blood, e.g. when sexually aroused **3 RIGHT SIDE UP** describes an optically produced image that is the correct way up and not inverted ■ *v* **1** *vt* **CONSTRUCT** to build a structure from basic parts and materials ○ *The building was erected in 1885.* **2** *vt* **PUT TOGETHER** to fit something together and put it into position so that it is ready for use **3** *vt* **SET UPRIGHT** to fix something in an upright position **4** *vt* **ESTABLISH** to bring an organization, system, or theory into being ○ *The corporation erected a new legal department to deal with mergers and acquisitions.* **5** *vt* **DRAW FIGURE ON BASE** to draw or construct a line or figure on a given base **6** *vti* **BECOME OR MAKE RIGID** to become, or cause an organ to become, stiff and swollen by being filled with blood [14C. < Latin *erectus*, past participle of *erigere* 'to set up' < *regere* 'to direct, rule'.] —**erectable** *adj* —**erectly** *adv* —**erectness** *n*

erecter *n* = **erector**

erectile /i rék tīl/ *adj* capable of filling with blood under pressure, swelling, and becoming stiff —**erectility** /i rék tíllәti/ *n*

erectile dysfunction *n* a medical condition that prevents a man from achieving an erection or maintaining one throughout sexual intercourse

erection /i réksh'n/ *n* **1 PUTTING SOMETHING UP** the construction or setting up of something **2 SWELLING OF TISSUE** the swollen and stiffened state of erectile tissue, especially that of the penis, usually as a result of sexual arousal **3 STRUCTURE** something that has been built or constructed (*formal*)

erector /i réktər/, **erecter** *n* **1** a muscle that is capable of raising or holding up a body part **2** somebody or something that erects things, generally things made elsewhere

E region *n* the middle part of the ionosphere, lying approximately 80 to 110 km/50 to 70 mi. above the Earth's surface, that reflects medium-length radio waves

eremite /érrə mīt/ *n* a hermit, especially for religious reasons (*literary*) [13C. < Old French *eremite* or late Latin *eremita* (see HERMIT).] —**eremitic** /érrə míttik/ *adj* —**eremitical** /-míttik'l/ *adj* —**eremitism** *n*

erethism /érrithizəm/ *n* excessive sensitivity of a body part to stimuli (*technical*) [Early 19C. < French *éréthisme* < Greek *erethizein* 'irritate'.] —**erethismic** /érri thízmik/ *adj* —**erethistic** *adj* —**erethitic** *adj*

erf /urf/ (*plural* **erfs** *or* **erven** /úrvən/) *n* *S Africa* a small plot of land on which to build, usually in urban areas [Late 17C. < Dutch, 'land, yard'.]

erg[1] /urg/ *n* the unit of energy or work in the cgs system equal to the work done by a force of one dyne acting through a distance of one centimetre. 1 erg is equivalent to 10^7 joule. [Late 19C. < Greek *ergon* 'work'.]

erg[2] /urg/ (*plural* **ergs** *or* **areg** /ə rég/) *n* a large, relatively flat area of desert covered with shifting wind-swept sand, especially in the Sahara [Late 19C. Via French < Arabic 'irk, 'erg.]

ergative /úrgətiv/ *adj* **1 ALLOWING OBJECT TO BE SUBJECT** describes a class of verbs in which the object of the transitive form can be used as the subject of the intransitive form with an equivalent meaning, e.g. 'open' in 'I opened the door' and 'The door opened' **2 INDICATING DOER OF ACTION AS OBJECT** describes a case of nouns in languages such as Inuit and Basque indicating that the object of the verb acts, while the subject is affected by the action ■ *n* ERGATIVE WORD an ergative verb or a noun in the ergative case [Mid-20C. < Greek *ergatēs* 'worker' < *ergon* 'work'.]

ergo /úrgō/ *adv, conj* therefore [14C. < Latin.]

ergocalciferol /úrgō kal síffə rol/ *n* BIOCHEM = **vitamin D**₂ [Mid-20C. < ERGOSTEROL.]

ergometer /ur gómmitər/ *n* an instrument for measuring muscle power or work done by muscles, e.g. when exercising [Late 19C. < Greek *ergon* 'work'.] —**ergometric** /úrgə méttrik/ *adj*

ergonomic /úrgə nómmik/ *adj* designed for maximum comfort, efficiency, safety, and ease of use, especially in the workplace —**ergonomically** *adv*

ergonomics /úrgə nómmiks/ *n* the study of how a workplace and the equipment used there can best be designed for comfort, safety, efficiency, and productivity (+ *singular verb*) ■ *npl* those factors or qualities in the design of something, especially a workplace or equipment used by people at work, that contribute to comfort, safety, efficiency, and ease of use [Mid-20C. < Greek *ergon* 'work' after ECONOMICS.] —**ergonometric** /úrgənə méttrik/ *adj* —**ergonomist** /ur gónnəmist/ *n*

ergosterol /ur góstə rol/ *n* a sterol present in yeast and moulds that is converted to vitamin D₂ by UV light [Early 20C. < ERGOT.]

ergot /úrgət, úrgot/ *n* **1** a disease of cereals caused by the parasitic fungus *Claviceps purpurea* that grows in dense black masses (**sclerotia**) in the grains of the ear **2** the dried sclerotia of an ergot fungus containing physiologically active substances. Use: treatment of migraine, initiation of labour. [Late 17C. < French, 'cock's spur', because the diseased grain resembles a cock's claw.] —**ergotic** /ur góttik/ *adj*

ergotamine /ur góttə meen/ *n* C₃₃H₃₅N₅O₅ an alkaloid drug derived from ergot that causes constriction of blood vessels. Use: treatment of migraine.

ergotism /úrgətizəm/ *n* a severe toxic reaction to food containing ergot-contaminated grain or excessive amounts of drugs containing ergot derivatives

Erhard /áir haard/, **Ludwig** (1897–1977) German statesman

erica /érrikə/ (*plural* **-cas** *or* **-ca**) *n* an evergreen bush or small tree of the heath family with small leathery leaves. Flowers: bell-shaped. Genus: *Erica*. [Early 17C. Via modern Latin < Greek *ereikē* 'heath'.]

ericaceous /érri káyshəss/ *adj* **1** belonging or relating to the heath family, a group of evergreen bushes and small trees that includes the heath, heather, rhododendron, azalea, and arbutus **2** describes potting compost that is suitable for ericaceous and other acid-loving or lime-hating plants

Ericson /érriks'n/, **Leif** (975–1020) Icelandic explorer

Eric the Red /érrik-/ (950?–1000?) Norwegian explorer. Born **Eric Thorvaldson**

Eridanus /e riddənəss/ *n* a large faint constellation of the southern hemisphere. See illustration at **constellation**

Erie, Lake /éeri/ one of the Great Lakes in the United States and Canada. Area: 25,667 sq. km/9,910 sq. mi.

Erie Canal artificial inland waterway between Buffalo, on Lake Erie, and Albany, New York, where it links with the River Hudson. Length: 547 km/340 mi.

Erigena /érri jéenə, -gáynə/, **Johannes Scotus** (815?–877?) Irish-born scholar

erigeron /i ríjjə ron/ (*plural* **-ons** *or* **-on**) *n* a plant of the daisy family, many species of which are cultivated as ornamentals. Genus: *Erigeron*. [Early 17C. Via Latin < Greek, 'early old man'; from its former application to the groundsel, an early-flowering plant with fluffy white seed heads.]

Erikson /érrikss'n/, **Erik** (1902–94) German-born US psychoanalyst

Erin /érrin/ *n* the country of Ireland (*literary*)

Erin go bragh /érrin gō braá/ *interj* Ireland an expression meaning 'Ireland forever' [< ERIN + Irish *go brách, go bráth* 'till doomsday']

Erinyes /i rínni eez/ *npl* MYTHOL = **Furies**

eristic /e rístik/ *adj* **eristic, eristical** ARGUMENTATIVE fond of or characterized by argument or controversy (*formal*) ■ *n* (*formal*) **1 ART OF DISPUTING** the skill or practice of debating, especially in a manner involving subtle logic and specious argument **2 DEBATER** somebody who is an expert or delights in argument and controversy [Mid-17C. < Greek *eristikos* < *eris* 'strife'.] —**eristically** *adv*

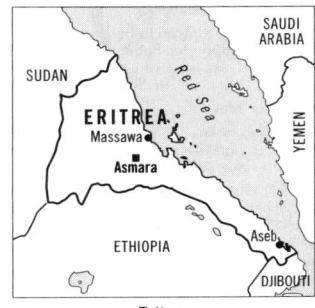
Eritrea

Eritrea /érri tráy ə/ republic on the Red Sea coast in NE Africa. Capital: Asmara. Population: 3,714,963 (1997). Area: 121,144 sq. km/46,774 sq. mi. —**Eritrean** *n, adj*

erk /urk/ *n* **1 LOW-RANKING MEMBER OF RAF** an aircraftman or -woman or other low-ranking member of the Royal Air Force (*slang*) **2 SEAMAN** a noncommissioned sailor in the Royal Navy (*slang*) **3 OFFENSIVE TERM** an offensive term for somebody who is disliked or despised (*dated slang insult*) [Early 20C. < ?]

Erlenmeyer flask /úrlən mī ər-/ *n* a cone-shaped laboratory flask with a narrow neck and broad flat bottom [Late 19C. After Emil *Erlenmeyer* (1825–1909), German chemist.]

ERM *abbr* Exchange Rate Mechanism

Ermine

ermine /úrmin/ (*plural* **-mines** *or* **-mine**) *n* **1 STOAT** a stoat, especially in its white winter coat **2 WHITE FUR OF ERMINE** the white fur of an ermine, once valued as a symbol of wealth, nobility, or high rank **3 OFFICE REPRESENTED BY ERMINE FUR** the rank or office of a dignitary whose robe is trimmed in ermine fur [12C. < Old French (*h*)*ermine*, probably < medieval Latin (*mus*) *Armenius* 'Armenian (mouse)'.]

erne /urn/ (*plural* **ernes** *or* **erne**), **ern** (*plural* **erns** *or* **ern**) *n* a long-winged sea eagle. Native to: Europe. *Haliaetus albicilla*. [Old English *earn* < Indo-European]

Erne /urn/ river in the Republic of Ireland and Northern Ireland, emptying into Donegal Bay. Along its route it broadens into two large lakes, Upper and Lower Lough Erne.

Ernie /úrni/, **ERNIE** in the United Kingdom, the machine used for drawing winning premium bond numbers [Mid-20C. Acronym < *electronic random number indicating equipment.*]

Ernst /airnst, urnst/, **Max** (1891–1976) German-born French artist

erode /i rōd/ (**erodes, eroding, eroded**) *v* **1** *vti* WEAR AWAY LAND to wear away outer layers of rock or soil, or to be gradually worn away by the action of wind or water **2** *vti* FORM BY WEATHERING to form a land feature such as a valley or gully by the action of wind or water **3** *vti* BREAK DOWN GRADUALLY to diminish or destroy something such as a relationship or feeling gradually over time, or to be gradually diminished or destroyed ○ *Deceit will erode any friendship.* **4** *vti* EAT AWAY to eat into or destroy something by corrosion or chemical action, or to be damaged or destroyed in this way **5** *vt* WEAR TISSUE AWAY to cause tissue to wear away as a result of decay, cancer, ulceration, or the chemical processes associated with inflammation [Early 17C. Directly or via French < Latin *erodere* 'gnaw off' < *rodere* 'gnaw'.] —**erodent** *n, adj* —**erodibility** /i rōdə bílləti/ *n* —**erodible** *adj*

erogenous /i rójjənəss/, **erogenic** /érrə jénnik/, **erotogenic** /i róttə jénnik/ *adj* **1** sensitive and arousing sexual feelings when touched or stroked **2** stimulating sexual desire [Late 19C. < EROS.]

erogenous zone *n* an area of the body that is sensitive to sexual stimulation

Eros /éer oss/ *n* **1 GREEK GOD OF LOVE** the god of love in ancient Greece. Roman equivalent **Cupid 2 Eros, eros SEXUAL LOVE** sexual love or desire **3 INSTINCT FOR SELF-PRESERVATION** in psychoanalytic theory, the instincts for self-preservation, pleasure, and procreation considered as a group [Late 17C. Via Latin < Greek, 'sexual love'.]

erosion /i rōzh'n/ *n* **1 WEARING AWAY OF ROCK** the gradual wearing away of rock or soil by physical breakdown, chemical solution, and transportation of material, as caused, e.g. by water, wind, or ice **2 GRADUAL BREAKING DOWN** the gradual destruction or reduction and weakening of something such as a relationship or somebody's power ○ *The erosion of profits was due to careless management.* **3 WEARING AWAY OF TISSUE** the wearing away of surface tissue by disease, ulceration, cancer, or the chemical processes associated with inflammation **4 LOSS OF TOOTH ENAMEL** loss of tooth enamel caused by excessive intake of acidic citrus juices or through repeated contact with stomach acid, as in bulimia [Mid-16C. < French *érosion* < Latin *eros*-, past participle of *erodere* (see ERODE).] —**erosional** *adj* —**erosionally** *adv*

erosive /i rōssiv/ *adj* causing the gradual breaking down or wearing away of something, especially rock or soil —**erosiveness** *n* —**erosivity** /irō sívvəti/ *n*

erotic /i róttik/ *adj* **1** arousing, or designed to arouse, feelings of sexual desire **2** characterized by or arising out of sexual desire [Mid-19C. Via French < Greek *erōtikos* < *erōs* 'sexual love'.] —**erotically** *adv*

erotica /i róttikə/ *n* art or literature intended to arouse sexual desire by portraying sex in an explicit way. ◊ **pornography** [Mid-19C. < Greek *erōtika*, neuter plural of *erōtikos* (see EROTIC).]

eroticise *vt* = **eroticize**

eroticism /i rótti sizəm/, **erotism** /érrə tizəm/ *n* **1 EROTIC QUALITY** an erotic quality in something, especially an erotic style or subject in literature or art ○ *the eroticism of her poetry* **2 SEXUAL DESIRE** feelings of sexual desire **3 EXCESSIVE SEXUAL EXCITEMENT** unusually persistent or frequent sexual interest or desire —**eroticist** *n*

eroticize /i rótti sīz/ (**-cizes, -cizing, -cized**), **eroticise** (**-cises, -cising, -cised**), **erotize** /érrə tīz/ (**-tizes, -tizing, -tized**), **erotise** (**-tises, -tising, -tised**) *vt* to make something erotic, especially by giving a sexual quality to something not usually regarded in that way ○ *The paintings were thought to eroticize flowers.* —**eroticization** /i rótti sī záysh'n/ *n*

erotise *vt* = **eroticize**

erotism *n* = **eroticism**

erotize /érrə tīz/, **erotise** *vt* = **eroticize**

erotogenic *adj* = **erogenous**

erotology /érrə tólləji/ *n* the study of erotic material and the stimulation of sexual desire —**erotological** /érrətə lójjik'l/ *adj* —**erotologist** *n*

erotomania /i róttō máyni ə/ *n* **1** excessive and insatiable feelings of sexual desire **2** the delusion of being loved by and romantically involved in a relationship with a person, especially somebody famous or of high social position —**erotomaniac** *n*

⚡ERP *n* software that enables all the departments in an organization to be integrated on a single computer system. Full form **enterprise resource planning**

err /ur, air/ *vi* (*formal*) **1** to make a mistake or do an incorrect thing ○ *The committee erred in interpreting the contract in this way.* **2** to behave badly and do something that is morally wrong ○ *'To err is human, to forgive, divine'.* (Alexander Pope, *Essay On Criticism*; 1711) [13C. Via Old French < Latin *errare* 'wander'.] ◇ **err on the side of something** to show a particular quality, e.g. caution or generosity, to a greater extent than is strictly necessary in order to avoid the risks involved in its opposite

SPELLCHECK See ***air***.

errancy /érranssi/ *n* (*formal*) **1** incorrect or morally wrong behaviour **2** the propensity for making mistakes or acting improperly

errand /érrand/ *n* **1** a short trip somewhere to do something on behalf of somebody else, e.g. to buy something or deliver a message ○ *She sometimes runs errands for me if I'm not well enough to go out.* **2** the task that somebody goes on an errand to carry out ○ *My errand was to collect her suit from the dry cleaners.* [Old English *ǣrende* 'message, mission' < ?]

errant /érrant/ *adj* **1 BEHAVING BADLY** behaving in an unacceptable manner **2 GOING ASTRAY** wandering from an intended course or not reaching an intended destination **3 LOOKING FOR ADVENTURE** wandering in search of adventure and romance (*literary*) **4 MOVING IRREGULARLY** with no regular or purposeful pattern of motion [14C. < Latin *errant-*, present participle of *errare* 'wander'.] —**errantly** *adv*

errantry /érrantri/ *n* the wandering, romantic, and adventurous life of a knight errant

errata /e raáta/ plural of **erratum** ■ *npl* a list of mistakes noticed after a book was printed, often included as a separate sheet in the book

erratic /i ráttik/ *adj* **1 INCONSISTENT** not predictable, regular, or consistent, especially in being likely to depart from or fall below expected standards at any time ○ *His driving tends to be rather erratic.* **2 OFTEN CHANGING DIRECTION** often changing direction and not following any definite course **3 CARRIED AND DEPOSITED BY ICE** describes a rock or boulder that was carried from its source by ice and deposited when the ice melted ■ *n* **1 SOMEBODY BEHAVING UNPREDICTABLY** a person who behaves unpredictably **2 ROCK MOVED BY ICE** a piece of rock that was carried from its source by ice and deposited when the ice melted [14C. < Old French *erratique* < Latin *errare* 'wander'.] —**erratically** *adv* —**erraticism** /i ráttissizam/ *n*

erratum /e raátam/ (*plural* **-ta** /-ta/) *n* a mistake in printing or writing, especially one on a list that is included with a printed book [Mid-16C. < Latin, form of past participle of *errare* 'wander'.]

erroneous /i róni ass/ *adj* incorrect, based on an incorrect assumption, or containing something that is incorrect [14C. < Old French *erroneus* < Latin *erron-* 'truant' < *errare* 'wander'.] —**erroneously** *adv* —**erroneousness** *n*

ϟ **error** /érrar/ *n* **1 MISTAKE** something unintentionally done wrong, e.g. as a result of poor judgment or lack of care ○ *The report blames the crash on human error.* **2 WRONG BELIEF** a belief or opinion that is contrary to fact or to established doctrine ○ *Errors and superstitions were to be banished by the pure light of science.* **3 STATE OF BELIEVING OR ACTING WRONGLY** a state in which somebody holds incorrect beliefs or opinions or acts wrongly or misguidedly **4 BEING WRONG** incorrectness, inappropriateness, or unacceptability ○ *He's seen the error of his ways and has decided to apologize.* **5 PROBLEM DETECTED BY PROGRAM** the failure of a computer program, subroutine, or system to produce an anticipated result, such as the result of a calculation not falling within an expected range **6 MATHEMATICAL DIFFERENCE** a variation between the true value of a mathematical quantity and a calculated or measured value [13C. < Old French *err(o)ur* < Latin *errare* 'wander'.] —**errorless** *adj* ◇ **in error 1** by mistake **2** mistaken or acting on the basis of a false assumption or belief

SYNONYMS See ***mistake***.

ϟ **error code** *n* a combination of characters printed or displayed by a computer uniquely identifying an error or problem in operation

ϟ **error message** *n* an alert message indicating that a computer has encountered a problem, often suggesting alternative action

ersatz /áir zats/ *adj* imitating or presented as a substitute for something of superior quality (*disapproving*) [Late 19C. < German, 'replacement'.]

Erse /urss/ *n* LANG = **Gaelic** *n.* ■ *adj* relating to the Gaelic language, especially Irish Gaelic [14C. Early Scots variant of IRISH.]

Ershad /úrsh ad, ur shád/, **Hossain Mohammad** (*b.* 1930) Indian-born Bangladeshi soldier and statesman

Erskine /úrskin/, **Ralph** (*b.* 1914) British architect

Erskine, Thomas, 1st Baron Erskine (1750–1823) British advocate and politician

erst /urst/ *adv* in the past or a long time ago (*archaic*) [Old English *ǣrest* 'first' < Germanic]

erstwhile /úrst wīl/ *adj* who in the past was something, e.g. a friend or supporter, but now no longer is ○ *Since leaving the bank, she has been ostracized by her erstwhile colleagues.* ■ *adv* at a time in the past (*archaic*) ◊ **erewhile**

erub *n* JUDAISM = **eruv**

erucic acid /i roóssik-/ *n* a soft colourless solid fatty acid. Source: rape seeds. Use: manufacture of plastics. [< Latin *eruca* 'rape plant']

eruct /i rúkt/, **eructate** /i rúk tayt/ (**-tates, -tating, -tated**) *vti* to expel stomach gases through the mouth (*technical*) [Mid-17C. < Latin *eructare* 'belch or vomit up' < *ructare* 'belch'.] —**eructation** /i rúk táysh'n, eé ruk-/ *n*

erudite /érroō dīt/ *adj* having or showing great knowledge gained from study and reading ○ *scholars erudite in Sanskrit* [15C. < Latin *eruditus*, past participle of *erudire* 'instruct' < *rudis* 'untrained'.] —**eruditely** *adv* —**eruditeness** *n*

erudition /érroō dísh'n/ *n* knowledge acquired through study and reading ○ *a work of great erudition*

erupt /i rúpt/ *v* **1** *vti* **VIOLENTLY RELEASE MATERIAL** to eject material such as gas, steam, ash, or lava, usually violently, from within ○ *The volcano last erupted in 1935.* **2** *vi* **BURST OUT** to burst out suddenly or violently ○ *Tired of her comments, he suddenly erupted into a fit of temper.* **3** *vi* **APPEAR ON SKIN** to appear as a rash or blemish on the skin or a mucous membrane **4** *vi* **COME THROUGH GUM** to break through and emerge from a gum (*technical; refers to growing teeth*) [Mid-17C. < Latin *erupt-*, past participle of *erumpere* 'break out' < *rumpere* 'break'.] —**eruptible** *adj* —**eruptive** *adj* —**eruptively** *adv*

eruption /i rúpsh'n/ *n* **1 VIOLENT RELEASE OF MATERIAL** the violent ejection of material, such as gas, steam, ash, or lava from a volcano **2 OUTBURST** a sudden outburst or occurrence of something **3 RASH OR BLEMISH ON SKIN** a rash or blemish or the appearance of it on the skin or a mucous membrane **4 EMERGENCE OF TOOTH** an emergence of a growing tooth from a gum

eruv /érroōv/, **erub** *n* the physical boundary within which certain relaxations of the rules concerning the Jewish Sabbath are allowed [Early 18C. < Hebrew *'ērūbh* 'mixture'.]

erven *S Africa* plural of **erf**

Erving /úrving/, **Julius** (*b.* 1950) US basketball player. Known as **Dr J**

-ery, -ry *suffix* **1** place for ○ *brewery* **2** activity or behaviour ○ *trickery* **3** collection of ○ *crockery* **4** qualities or character of ○ *buffoonery* **5** state, condition ○ *drudgery* [< Old French *-erie* < *-er* '-er, -or' + *-ie* '-y']

erysipelas /érri síppalass/ *n* a severe skin rash accompanied by fever and vomiting and caused by a streptococcal bacterium. ◊ **Saint Anthony's fire** [14C. Via Latin < Greek *erusipelas* 'red skin'.] —**erysipelatous** /érrissi péllatass/ *adj*

erythema /érri theéma/ *n* redness of the skin as a result of a widening of the small blood vessels near its surface [Late 18C. < Greek *eruthēma* < *eruthros* 'red'.] —**erythematous** /érri theématass, -thémma-/ *adj* —**erythemic** *adj*

erythr- *prefix* = **erythro-** (*before vowels*)

erythrism /érri thrizam, i ríth rizam/ *n* unusual redness of plumage or hair, often with a ruddy complexion in humans [Late 19C. < Greek *eruthros* 'red'.] —**erythrismal** /érri thrízm'l/ *adj*

erythrite /érri thrīt, i ríth rīt/ *n* a pale red cobalt arsenate mineral. Use: glass colourant. [Mid-19C. < Greek *eruthros* 'red'.]

erythro- *prefix* **1** red ○ *erythrocyte* **2** erythrocyte ○ *erythroblast* [< Greek *eruthros* 'red' < Indo-European]

erythroblast /i ríthra blast/ *n* an immature red blood cell that is found in bone marrow —**erythroblastic** /i ríthra blástik/ *adj*

erythroblastosis /i ríthrō bla stṓssiss/ *n* the abnormal presence of immature red blood cells in the bloodstream that occurs especially in erythroblastosis fetalis

erythroblastosis fetalis /-fi tálliss/ *n* a serious blood disease of foetuses and newborn babies, in which the antibodies produced by a rhesus-negative mother destroy the red blood cells of a rhesus-positive foetus [*Fetalis* < modern Latin, 'foetal']

erythrocyte /i ríthrō sīt/ *n* BIOL = **red blood cell** —**erythrocytic** /i ríthrō síttik/ *adj*

erythromycin /i ríthrō míssin/ *n* a broad-spectrum antibiotic derived from the bacterium *Streptomyces erythreus*

erythropoiesis /i ríthrō poy eéssiss/ *n* the formation of red blood cells, a process that begins with stem cells in the bone marrow and ends with the release of mature red blood cells (**erythrocytes**) into circulation [Early 20C. < ERYTHROCYTE.] —**erythropoietic** /-éttik/ *adj*

erythropoietin /i ríthrō poy eétin, -éttin/ *n* a kidney hormone that stimulates the development of red blood cells in the bone marrow [Mid-20C. < ERYTHROPOIESIS.]

ϟ **es** *abbr* Spain (*in Internet addresses*)

Es *symbol* einsteinium

ES *abbr* **1** El Salvador (*international vehicle registration*) **2** Eastern States

-es *suffix* used to form the plural of regular nouns ending in -s,-ss, -x, -sh, or -ch ○ *buses* ○ *birches.* ◊ **-s**

ESA *abbr* **1** environmentally sensitive area **2** European Space Agency

ϟ **Esc** *abbr* escape (key)

escadrille /éskadril, éska dríl/ *n* a squadron of usually six aircraft, especially a French air squadron of World War I [Early 20C. Via French < Spanish *escuadrilla* 'little squadron' < *escuadra* 'squadron'.]

escalade /éska láyd/ *n* an attack involving the use of ladders to scale the walls of a fortified place ■ *vt* (**-lades, -lading, -laded**) to scale the walls of a fortification using ladders [Late 16C. Directly or via French < Spanish *escalada*.] —**escalader** *n*

escalate /éska layt/ (**-lates, -lating, -lated**) *vti* to become or cause something to become greater, more serious, or more intense [Early 20C. Back-formation < ESCALATOR.] —**escalation** /éska láysh'n/ *n* —**escalatory** /éska láytari/ *adj*

USAGE No one uses ***escalate*** now to mean 'travel on an escalator', and the figurative meaning has taken over completely. Its earliest and still most common uses are in connection with military activity and conflicts: *Officials killed by mine as terrorist attacks escalate.* It is used most effectively when it describes a development that proceeds in stages, rather than as a simple synonym for *increase* or *mount*.

escalator /éska laytar/ *n* **1** a set of moving steps attached to a continuously circulating belt, that carries people up or down between different levels in a building **2 escalator, escalator clause** a stipulation in a contract that makes an increase or decrease in something conditional on a change in something else [Early 20C. < ESCALADE, after ELEVATOR.]

escallop /éska lop, e skóllap/ *n* HANDICRAFT = **scallop** *n.* 6 [15C. < Old French *escalope* 'shell'.]

escalope /éska lop, e skóllap/ *n* a slice of boneless lean meat, especially veal or poultry, that is beaten flat for cooking quickly or rolling around a stuffing. US term **scallop** *n.* 7 [Early 19C. < French, 'shell'; probably because it curls into a shell shape in cooking.]

escapade /éska payd/ *n* something exciting or adventurous that somebody does or is involved in, especially something showing recklessness or disregard for authority [Mid-17C. Via French < Spanish *escapada* 'an escape' < assumed Vulgar Latin *excappare* (see ESCAPE).]

ϟ **escape** /i skáyp/ *v* (**-capes, -caping, -caped**) **1** *vti* **BREAK FREE FROM CAPTIVITY** to free yourself and get away from captivity or confinement ○ *prisoners who attempted to escape* **2** *vt* **AVOID BAD SITUATION** to avoid danger, harm, or involvement in an unpleasant situation ○ *There's no escaping the fact that the house needs painting.* **3** *vi* **LEAK OUT** to leak out from a container **4** *vt* **BE TEMPORARILY UNKNOWN TO** to fail to be noticed, remembered, or understood by somebody ○ *a little village whose name escapes me for the moment* **5** *vti* **BE UTTERED** to be uttered by somebody unintentionally ○ *A muffled curse escaped his lips.* **6** *vi*

SPREAD FROM GARDEN INTO THE WILD to spread from a garden or other cultivated area and become established in the wild (*refers to cultivated plants*) **7** *vi* **EXIT COMPUTER PROCEDURE** to exit from a computer program or file, cancel a command or operation, or return from the currently active menu to a previous one ■ *n* **1 BREAKING FREE FROM CAPTIVITY** an act of getting free from captivity or confinement ○ *He made his escape while the guard was asleep.* **2 AVOIDANCE OF BAD SITUATION** the avoidance of a dangerous, harmful, or unpleasant situation ○ *an escape from danger* **3 MEANS OF GETTING AWAY** a method, means, or route by which somebody can escape from a place or situation **4 DISTRACTION** something that takes your mind off routine or serious matters ○ *an escape from the humdrum of daily life* **5 GAS OR LIQUID LEAK** a leak of gas or liquid from a container **6 WILD PLANT ONCE CULTIVATED** a plant that has spread from a garden or other cultivated area and is growing wild **7 COMPUTER KEY** the key on a computer keyboard that allows a user to exit a program, cancel a command, or return to a previous menu ○ *Press escape to exit the program.* **8** COMPUT = **escape code** [13C. Via Old Northern French *escaper* < assumed Vulgar Latin *excappare* 'throw off your cloak' < *cappa* 'cloak'.] —**escapable** *adj* —**escaper** *n*

escape artist *n* **1** a performer who is skilled at escaping from restraints or confinement **2** a person who is skilled at escaping from difficulty or danger

escape clause *n* a clause in a contract that sets out the conditions under which a party to the contract can be released from his or her obligations under it

⚡**escape code** *n* a character or characters instructing a device that what follows is not data but a command

escapee /i skáy peé, éskay peé/ *n* a person who has escaped

escape hatch *n* a small opening providing a way out of an enclosed space, such as a submarine, through which people can escape in an emergency

escapement /i skáypmənt/ *n* **1 CLOCK MECHANISM** a mechanism in a clock or watch that allows power from a spring or falling weight to turn gears connected to the hands **2 PIANO MECHANISM** a mechanism in a piano that allows the hammer to rebound from a string after striking it **3 TYPEWRITER MECHANISM** a mechanism in a typewriter or printer that regulates the relative movement between the paper carrier and the typing or printing position on a line [Late 18C. < its allowing a cogwheel to 'escape' or be released repeatedly.]

escape road *n* a road branching off from a steep hill or sharp bend into which a vehicle can turn if it gets into difficulties

escape velocity *n* the minimum speed at which an object must travel to escape a planet's or moon's gravitational field in order to orbit around it or move off into space

escape wheel *n* a toothed wheel in the mechanism of a watch or clock, designed to regulate the movement of the pendulum or balance wheel and so move the hands at regular intervals

escapism /i skáypizəm/ *n* **1** something such as fantasy or entertainment that makes it possible to forget about the ordinary or unpleasant realities of life for a while **2** the act of indulging in daydreams or fantasies to escape from everyday reality

escapist /i skáypist/ *adj* providing a means of forgetting about everyday or unpleasant realities for a while ■ *n* a daydreamer or fantasist who tries to avoid reality

escapologist /éskə póllәjist/ *n* ARTS = **escape artist** *n.* 1

escapology /éskə póllәji/ *n* the skill of escaping from restraints or confinement as a form of entertainment

escargot /e skaárgō/ *n* a snail that is cooked and eaten [Late 19C. Via French < Old Provençal *escaragol*.]

escarole /éskәrōl/ *n US* FOOD = **endive** *n.* 1 [Early 20C. Via French < Italian *scariola* < Latin *esca* 'food' (see ESCULENT).]

escarp /i skaárp/ *n* the inner side of a ditch dug as a fortification [Late 17C. Via French *escarpe* < Italian *scarpa* 'slope'.]

escarpment /i skaárpmәnt/ *n* **1** a steep slope or cliff that marks the boundary of a flat or gently sloping upland area such as a plateau, often formed by faulting or erosion **2** a steep slope constructed in front of a fortification

-escent *suffix* **1** beginning or inclined to be, becoming, slightly ○ *acquiescent* ○ *alkalescent* **2** having a particular kind of lustre ○ *adularescent* **3** resembling, having ○ *arborescent* [Via French < Latin *-escent-*, present participle ending of verbs in *-escere*, expressing the beginning of action] —**-escence** *suffix*

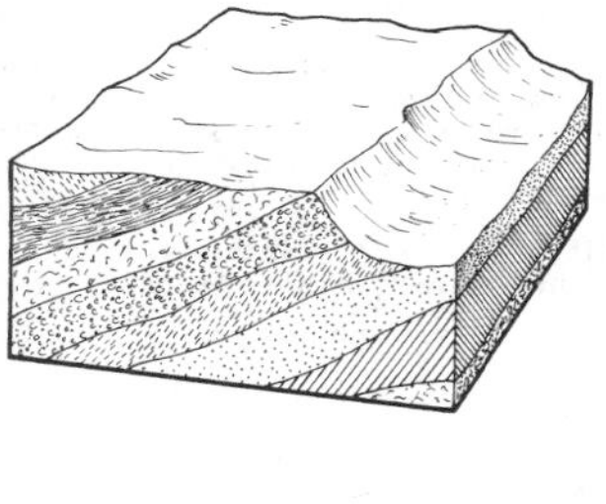

Escarpment

eschar /és kaar/ *n* a dry scab formed on skin that has been burned or cauterized [15C. Directly or via Old French *escare, escharre* < late Latin *eschara* 'scab' < Greek *askhara* (see SCAR[1]).]

eschatology /éskə tóllәji/ *n* the body of religious doctrines concerning the human soul in its relation to death, judgment, heaven, and hell [Mid-19C. < Greek *eskhatos* 'last'.] —**eschatological** /éskәtə lójjik'l/ *adj* —**eschatologically** *adv* —**eschatologist** *n*

escheat /iss cheét/ *n* **1 REVERSION OF PROPERTY TO STATE** the reversion of the property of a deceased person to the state in the United States, or to the Crown in England before 1926, when there are no legal heirs **2 REVERSION OF PROPERTY TO FEUDAL LORD** in medieval England, the reversion to a feudal overlord of the property of a deceased person when there was no legal heir or when a tenant was outlawed **3 PROPERTY AFFECTED BY ESCHEAT** property that reverts by escheat [13C. < Old French *eschete* and Anglo-Latin *escheta* < assumed Vulgar Latin *excadere* 'fall away' < Latin *cadere* 'to fall'.] —**escheatable** *adj*

Escher /éshәr/, **M. C.** (1898–1972) Dutch graphic artist

eschew /iss chóō/ *vt* to avoid doing or using something on principle or as a matter of course [14C. < Old French *eschiver*.] —**eschewal** *n*

eschscholzia /i shóltsi ə, ish-/, **eschscholtzia** *n* = **California poppy** [Late 19C. < modern Latin, after J. F. *Eschscholtz*.]

Escoffier /i skóffi ay/, **Auguste** (1846–1935) French chef and cookery author

escolar /éskə laár/ *n* a fish with a slim bony body, jutting lower jaw, and sharp teeth. Native to: tropical and temperate deep seas. Family: Gempylidae. [Late 19C. Via Spanish, 'student' (because of the rings around its eyes resembling spectacles) < late Latin *scholaris* (see SCHOLAR).]

Escondido /éss kon deédō/ city in SW California. Population: 120,578 (1998 estimate).

escort *n* /éss kawrt/ **1 SOMEBODY ACCOMPANYING** one or more persons accompanying somebody or something as a guard or guide or as a mark of honour **2 ACCOMPANYING MILITARY VESSEL OR AIRCRAFT** one or more warships or fighter aircraft accompanying a larger, more vulnerable ship or aircraft as protection **3 MAN AS SOCIAL PARTNER** a man accompanying a woman on a social occasion **4 HIRED SOCIAL PARTNER** a man or woman who is hired to accompany another person as a companion, especially to a social event or entertainment **5 PROTECTION OR SECURITY FOR JOURNEY** protection or restraint provided by an escort ○ *The prisoner will proceed under escort to the guardhouse.* ■ *vt* /i skáwrt/ **GO WITH AS ESCORT** to accompany somebody or something as an escort ○ *The butler will escort you to the door.* [Late 16C. Via French *escorte* < Italian *scorta* < *scorgere* 'to guide', via assumed Vulgar Latin *excorrigere* < Latin *corrigere* (see CORRECT).]

escritoire /éskri twaár/ *n* a writing desk, often with a hinged flap that conceals drawers and pigeonholes [Late 16C. Via Old French, 'writing box' < medieval Latin *scriptorium* (see SCRIPTORIUM).]

escrow /éskrō, e skrṓ/ *n* **1 SOMETHING HELD INDEPENDENTLY UNTIL CONDITION MET** an amount of money or property granted to somebody but held by a third party and only released after a condition has been met **2 STATE OF BEING AN ESCROW** the condition of being held as an escrow ■ *vt* **PUT IN ESCROW** to place something in escrow [Mid-17C. < Anglo-Norman *escrowe* 'scroll', variant of Old French *escroe* (see SCROLL).]

escudo /i skóōdō/ (*plural* **-dos**) *n* see table at **currency** [Early 19C. Via Spanish and Portuguese < Latin *scutum* 'shield'; because early coins resembled heraldic shields.]

esculent /éskyōōlәnt/ *adj* fit to be eaten (*formal*) ■ *n* something edible, especially a plant (*formal*) [Early 17C. < Latin *esculentus* < *esca* 'food' < *edere* 'eat'.]

escutcheon /i skúchәn/ *n* **1 HERALDIC SHIELD** a shield, especially one used in heraldry to display a coat of arms **2 PROTECTIVE SHIELD** a plate or shield fixed around something, e.g. a light switch or keyhole, as an ornament or to protect the surrounding surface **3 NAME PLATE ON VESSEL** a panel on the stern of a vessel on which the vessel's name is shown [15C. Via Anglo-Norman *escuchon* < Latin *scutum* 'shield'.] —**escutcheoned** *adj*

Esdraelon, Plain of /éss dray eé lon/ plain in N Israel between the River Jordan and the Mediterranean Sea. It is approximately 60 km/35 mi. long and has an average width of 24 km/15 mi.

Esdras /éz drass/ *n* **1** either of two books in the Apocrypha **2** either of two books of the Roman Catholic version of the Bible (**Douay Bible**), equivalent to the books of Ezra and Nehemiah in the Authorized Version

ESE *abbr* east-southeast

-ese *suffix* **1** from, of, native to, or inhabiting a particular place ○ *Taiwanese* **2** the language of a particular place ○ *Faeroese* **3** style or jargon ○ *officialese* [Via Old French *-eis*, Italian *-ese* < Latin *-ensis* 'originating in']

~~**esential**~~ incorrect spelling of **essential**

eserine /éssə reen, -rin/ *n* PHARM = **physostigmine** [Mid-19C. < French *ésérine* < Efik *esere* 'Calabar bean'.]

Eshkol /ésh kol/, **Levi** (1895–1969) Russian-born Israeli statesman. Born **Levi Shkolnik**

⚡**e-signature** *n* E-COMMERCE = **electronic signature**

esker /éskәr/, **eskar** /és kaar, éskәr/ *n* a long narrow winding ridge of sand or gravel, deposited by a stream flowing under a glacier [Mid-19C. < Irish *eiscir*.]

Eskimo /éski mō/ (*plural* **-mos** *or* **-mo**) *n* **1** a member of a people indigenous to N Canada, Alaska, Greenland, and Siberia, comprising the Inuit and Yupik (*sometimes considered offensive*) **2** the language group comprising Inuit and Yupik [Late 16C. < French *Esquimaux* < Algonquian.] —**Eskimo** *adj*

USAGE See ***Inuit***.

Eskimo-Aleut *n* a family of languages spoken in Greenland, Alaska, N Canada, Siberia, and the Aleutian Islands

Eskimo dog *n* a large powerful thick-coated dog with erect ears that is used to pull sleds in Arctic regions

Eskimo roll *n* a process or procedure by which a capsized kayak is rolled over underwater in order to come up righted

Eskişehir /ess keé she heer/ city in W Turkey. Population: 413,300 (1990).

Esky /éski/ *tdmk Aus* a trademark for an insulated portable container for keeping food and beverages cool

ESL *abbr* English as a second language

ESOL /eé sol/ *abbr* English for speakers of other languages

esophagus *n* US = **oesophagus**

esoteric /éssō térrik, eéssō-/ *adj* **1 RESTRICTED TO INITIATES** intended for or understood by only an initiated few **2 ABSTRUSE** difficult to understand **3 SECRET** secret or highly confidential [Mid-17C. < Greek *esōterikos* 'belonging to an inner circle' < *esōterō* 'inner' < *esō* 'within'.] —**esoterically** *adv*

esoterica /éssō térrikə, eéssō-/ *npl* things that are for initiates only or are difficult or secret [Early 20C. < Greek *esōterika* < *esōterikos* (see ESOTERIC).]

esotericism /éssō térrissizəm, eéssō-/ *n* **1** beliefs or practices that are arcane, mysterious, or secret **2** the condition or quality of being esoteric

ESP *abbr* **1** English for special purposes **2** extrasensory perception

esp. *abbr* especially

espadrille /éspə dríl, éspədril/ *n* a light shoe with a fabric upper and a sole made of twisted cord [Late 19C. Via French < Provençal *espardilho* < *espart* 'esparto' (from which originally made) < Latin *spartum* (see ESPARTO).]

espalier /i spálli ay, -li ər/ *n* a plant, especially a fruit tree, trained to grow flat against a wall or other upright support [Mid-17C. Via French < Italian *spalliera* 'shoulder support' < *spalla* 'shoulder' < Latin *spatula* (see SPATULA).]

esparto /e spaár tō/ (*plural* **-tos**), **esparto grass** *n* a coarse grass. Use: paper, ropes, mats. Native to: S Europe, N Africa. *Stipa tenacissima*. [Mid-19C. Via Spanish < Latin *spartum* < Greek *sparton* 'rope'.]

especial /i spésh'l/ *adj* (*formal*) **1** unusual or exceptional **2** particular or specific [13C. Via Old French < Latin *specialis* 'of a specific kind' < *species* (see SPECIES).]

especially /i spésh'li/ *adv* **1 EXCEPTIONALLY** to an unusual or exceptional degree **2 PARTICULARLY** used to single out one among a range **3 CHIEFLY** in most cases **4** ⚠ **SPECIALLY** for a particular or specific purpose.

USAGE ***especially*** or ***specially***? Although traditionally there is a clear difference in meaning, the two words are often used interchangeably: *The car is designed especially for people with disabilities.* (Some would say ***specially*** is better here because the car is designed 'for a special purpose'.) *The buildings are not specially large.* (Some would say ***especially*** is better here because the buildings are not 'exceptionally' large.) In rapid conversation, the first syllable of ***especially*** tends to be slurred or omitted, which may be why the words are not always distinguished when written.

~~especialy~~ incorrect spelling of **especially**

Esperance /éspərənss/ port on the southwestern coast of Western Australia. Population: 7,064 (1991).

Esperanto /éspə rántō/ *n* an artificial language invented in 1887, based on the root forms of certain words common to the major European languages [Late 19C. After Doctor *Esperanto* 'somebody who hopes', Esperanto pseudonym of Ludwik Zamenhof (1859–1917), Polish inventor of the language.] —**Esperantist** *n*

espial /i spí əl/ *n* (*archaic*) **1** the action of sighting or discovering something **2** the action of noticing or detecting something [14C. < Old French *espialle* < *espier* (see SPY).]

espionage /éspi ə naazh, éspi ə naázh/ *n* the use of spying or spies to gather secret information [Late 18C. < French *espionnage* < *espionner* 'to spy' < *espion* 'spy'.]

esplanade /ésplə náyd, ésplə naád, ésplə nayd/ *n* **1** a long level area, especially by the sea, for walking or driving along **2** a wide level area outside a fortification, where attackers will be exposed to fire from defenders [Late 17C. < French, < Latin *explanare* 'flatten out' (see EXPLAIN).]

espousal /i spówz'l/ *n* **1** the adoption of something as a belief or cause **2** a betrothal or wedding (*formal; often plural*)

espouse /i spówz/ (**-pouses, -pousing, -poused**) *vt* **1** to adopt or support something as a belief or cause **2** to marry somebody or give somebody in marriage (*archaic*) [15C. Via Old French *espouser* < Latin *sponsare* < *spons-* (see SPONSOR).] —**espouser** *n*

espressivo /éspre seé vō/ *adv* played in a expressive way (*musical direction*) [Late 19C. < Italian, 'expressively'.]

espresso /es préssō/, **expresso** /iks préssō/ *n* **1 STRONG COFFEE MADE IN A SPECIAL MACHINE** dark strong-tasting coffee made by using a special machine to pass steam under pressure or boiling water through finely ground coffee beans **2 CUP OF ESPRESSO** a serving of espresso coffee, usually in a small cup ○ *Two espressos and a cappuccino.* **3 MACHINE FOR MAKING ESPRESSO** a machine for making espresso coffee ○ *the hiss of the espresso* [Mid-20C. < Italian *(caffè) espresso* 'pressed-out (coffee)' < past participle of *esprimere* 'press out' < Latin *exprimere* (see EXPRESS).]

esprit /e spreé/ *n* lively intelligence or wit [Late 16C. Via French < Latin *spiritus* (see SPIRIT).]

esprit de corps /-də káwr/ *n* a feeling of pride in belonging to a group and a sense of identification with it [< French, 'group spirit']

espy /i spí/ (**-pies, -pying, -pied**) *vt* to catch sight of or detect something (*literary*) [14C. < Old French *espier* (see SPY).]

Esq. *abbr* Esquire (*in correspondence*)

-esque *suffix* in the style of, like ○ *Pythonesque* [Via French < assumed Vulgar Latin *-iscus* < Germanic]

Esquimalt /éski mawlt/ seaport and naval station on SE Vancouver Island, British Columbia, Canada. Population: 16,192 (1991).

esquire /i skwír/ *n* a youth serving as an attendant or shield bearer to a medieval knight, especially as a stage in his own training for knighthood [14C. Via Old French *escuier* < late Latin *scutarius* 'shield bearer' < Latin *scutum* 'shield'.]

Esquire /i skwír/ *n* a courtesy title placed after a man's full name, especially in correspondence

ESR *abbr* **1** electron spin resonance **2** erythrocyte sedimentation rate

ESRC *abbr* Economic and Social Research Council

ess /ess/ *n* **1** the letter s or S **2** something shaped like an S [Mid-16C. < Latin *es*.]

-ess *suffix* woman or girl ○ *heiress* [Via Old French and Latin < Greek *-issa*]

essay /éssay/ *n* **1 SHORT NONFICTION PROSE PIECE** a short analytical, descriptive, or interpretive piece of literary or journalistic prose dealing with a particular topic, especially from a personal and unsystematic viewpoint **2 SET WRITTEN PIECE** a short piece of written work set as an assignment for a student **3 WORK RESEMBLING A WRITTEN ESSAY** an artistic or journalistic work resembling a written essay but in another medium ○ *not so much a short film as a cinematographic essay* **4 ATTEMPT** an attempt to accomplish something (*formal*) **5 TEST** a test or trial of something (*formal*) ■ *vt* **1 ATTEMPT TO DO** to try out or attempt something (*formal*) ○ *Shall we essay a walk on the promenade?* **2 TEST OUT** to make a test of something ○ *essay his theory* [15C. Via Old French *essaier* 'to try' < assumed Vulgar Latin *exagiare* 'weigh out' < Latin *agere* 'do'.]

essayist /éssayist/ *n* a writer of literary or journalistic essays

essayistic /éssay ístik/ *adj* resembling or styled like a literary or journalistic essay

essay question *n* a question in an examination that must be answered in a prose piece of a specified length

Essen /éss'n/ city in west-central Germany. Population: 626,100 (1990).

essence /éss'nss/ *n* **1 IDENTIFYING NATURE** the quality or nature of something that identifies it or makes it what it is **2 BASIC FEATURE** the most basic element or feature of something ○ *Lack of time is the essence of the problem.* **3 PERFECT FORM** the perfect or idealized form of something, especially when embodied in a person ○ *She is the essence of tact.* **4 SPIRITUAL ENTITY** a spiritual entity **5 CHEMICAL CONSTITUENT OF PLANT** a purified plant extract **6 CONCENTRATED PLANT EXTRACT** a concentrated plant extract containing its unique flavour and fragrance ○ *peppermint essence* [14C. Via French < Latin *essentia* < *essent-*, present participle of *esse* 'be'.] ◇ **in essence** fundamentally or intrinsically ◇ **of the essence** of the highest importance for achieving something

essential /i sénsh'l/ *adj* **1 NECESSARY** of the highest importance for achieving something ○ *It is essential that we arrive on time.* **2 BASIC** being the most basic element or feature of something or somebody ○ *We wanted the biography to tell us the essential nature of the man.* **3 PERFECT** being the pure or perfect form or embodiment of something **4 REQUIRED IN DIET** describes a nutrient that is not made by the body and is required in the diet for normal function **5 DEFINING** constituting the property or characteristic of something that makes it what it is ○ *Being three-sided is essential to being a triangle.* **6 WITHOUT KNOWN CAUSE** describes a disease that has no known cause ■ *n* **SOMETHING ESSENTIAL** something that is necessary or fundamental ○ *Having your own computer is an essential for this kind of work.* ○ *She soon picked up the essentials of the subject.* [14C. < late Latin *essentialis* < Latin *essentia* (see ESSENCE).] —**essentiality** /i sénshi állәti/ *n* —**essentially** *adv* —**essentialness** *n*

SYNONYMS See ***necessary.***

essential amino acid *n* any amino acid that the body cannot make and must be obtained from food to maintain growth

essential element *n* a chemical element that is necessary to the healthy growth of an organism

essential fatty acid *n* a natural fat or oil found in whole grains, seeds, nuts, and oily fish, required in the diet to make prostaglandins

essentialism /i sénsh'lizəm/ *n* the doctrine that things have an essence or ideal nature that is independent of and prior to their existence —**essentialist** *n*

essential oil *n* an oil extracted from plant material

Essex /éssiks/ county in E England. Area: 3,674 sq. km/1,419 sq. mi.

Essex, David (*b.* 1947) British singer, songwriter, and actor. Pseudonym of **David Albert Cook**

Essex, Robert Devereux, 2nd Earl of (1566–1601) English soldier and courtier

Essex girl *n* an offensive term stereotyping a young woman from the Essex area as brash, lower-class, unintelligent, materialistic, and sexually promiscuous (*informal insult*)

Essex man *n* an offensive term stereotyping a man from the Essex area as vulgar in appearance and habits, with disposable income but no taste (*informal insult*)

essonite /éssə nīt/ *n* a yellow to brown garnet [Early 19C. < Greek *hēssōn* 'inferior' (because less hard than other garnets).]

EST *abbr* Eastern Standard Time

-est *suffix* most ○ *hardest* ○ *sloppiest* [Old English, < Germanic]

establish /i stábblish/ *v* **1** *vt* **FIX PERMANENTLY** to place something securely and permanently in a position, situation, or condition ○ *A settlement was established here two hundred years ago.* **2** *vt* **INAUGURATE** to start or set up something that is intended to continue or be permanent ○ *The firm was established in 1954.* **3** *vt* **PROVE** to investigate something and prove or confirm its truth or validity ○ *Have we established who gave the instruction?* **4** *vt* **CAUSE TO BE RECOGNIZED** to cause something or somebody to become generally accepted or recognized ○ *The victory established his superiority.* ○ *Her first novel established her on the literary scene.* **5** *vt* **MAKE A CHURCH NATIONAL AND OFFICIAL** to make a church an official national institution **6** *vti* **CAUSE A PLANT TO GROW SUCCESSFULLY** to grow, or cause a plant to grow, successfully in a new place ○ *The new owners established an avenue of poplars.* ○ *Keep the area well weeded to allow the seedlings to establish.* [14C. < Old French *establiss-*, stem of *establir* < Latin *stabilire* 'make stable' < *stabilis* (see STABLE[1]).] —**establisher** *n*

established *adj* **1 ACCEPTED AS TRUE** generally recognized as being true or valid ○ *an established fact* **2 SUCCESSFUL** having gained public recognition in a particular sphere of activity ○ *an established author* **3 GROWING SUCCESSFULLY** growing strongly ○ *an established garden* **4 LEGALLY RECOGNIZED** legally recognized and sometimes financially supported as an official national institution, especially the Church of England ○ *an established church*

establishing shot /i stábblishing-/ *n* a shot in a film that introduces a new scene

establishment /i stábblishmənt/ *n* **1 ESTABLISHING** the act of establishing something or the condition of being established **2 SOMETHING ESTABLISHED** something that is established as a business, institution, or successful undertaking ○ *The establishment hired several new managers.* **3 BUSINESS PREMISES** a place of business ○ *The restaurant manager told them they were now barred from the establishment.* **4 establishment, Establishment PEOPLE IN POWER** a group of people who hold power in a society or social group and dominate its institutions ○ *One period's avant-garde becomes the next's artistic establishment.* **5 PERMANENT STAFF** the staff of a permanent organization, institution, or department, especially in the military or government **6 HOUSEHOLD** a place of residence or the household that occupies it —**establishmentarian** /i stábblishmən táiri ən/ *n* —**establishmentarianism** *n*

estaminet /e stámmi náy/ *n* a small and simple café, bar, or bistro, especially in France [Early 19C. < French.]

estancia /e stánssi ə/ *n* a large landed estate, especially a cattle ranch, in South America [Mid-17C. Via Spanish, 'station' < medieval Latin *stantia* < Latin *stant-*, present participle of *stare* 'to stand'.]

estate /i stáyt/ *n* **1 RURAL PROPERTY WITH A RESIDENCE** an area of rural privately owned property that includes a large residence **2 COMMERCIAL OR INDUSTRIAL AREA** a large area set aside for industrial or commercial use **3 ALL OF SOMEBODY'S PROPERTY** the whole of somebody's property, possessions, and capital **4 PROPERTY OF DEAD OR BANKRUPT PERSON** the assets and liabilities of somebody who is dead or bankrupt **5 CAR** an estate car (*informal*) **6 SOMEBODY'S OVERALL SITUATION** the circumstances, period, or condition in which somebody lives **7 SECTOR OF SOCIETY**

especially formerly in Europe, any of three traditional ranks or sectors of society with some political power, broadly the clergy, the nobility, and the middle class **8 DIVISION OF PARLIAMENT** any of three divisions of parliament or constitutional government, either the Lords Temporal, Lords Spiritual, and the Commons, or the Crown, the House of Lords, and the House of Commons **9** AGRIC = **plantation** n. 1 [13C. < Old French estat (see STATE).]

estate agent n 1 a person or business that sells or leases houses and other buildings and land on behalf of the owners. ◊ **real-estate agent 2** a manager of a landed property on behalf of its owner —**estate agency** n

estate-bottled adj bottled by the same vineyard at which the wine was made

estate car n UK a car with extra carrying space behind the seats, a rear seat that folds down, and a hinged rear door [< its ability to hold the owner's possessions]

estd, est'd abbr established

esteem /i steem/ vt 1 **VALUE HIGHLY** to value somebody or something highly **2 REGARD AS** to consider or regard something or somebody as being in a particular category ○ I esteem him a friend. ■ n 1 **HIGH REGARD** high valuation of somebody or something ○ It was a relationship founded on mutual esteem. **2 VALUATION** judgment or estimation of the worth of somebody or something [Early 16C. Via Old French estimer 'to value' < Latin aestimare 'estimate, assess'.]

SYNONYMS See **regard**.

ester /éstər/ n an organic, often fragrant compound formed in a reaction between an acid and an alcohol with the elimination of water [Mid-19C. < German, contraction of Essigäther 'acetic ether'.]

esterase /ésta rayz, ésta rayss/ n any enzyme that catalyses the hydrolysis of an ester

esterify /e stérri fI/ (**-fies, -fying, -fied**) vti to change or make a substance change into an ester —**esterification** /e stérrifi káysh'n/ n

Esth. abbr Esther

Esther /éstər/ n 1 in the Bible, the Jewish queen of Persia who is described as having rescued her Jewish subjects from massacre **2** a book in the Bible that tells the story of Esther

esthesia n US MED = **aesthesia**

esthete n US ARTS, PHILOS = **aesthete**

esthetic adj, n US ARTS, PHILOS = **aesthetic**

estheticize vt US ARTS, PHILOS = **aestheticize**

esthetics n US ARTS, PHILOS = **aesthetics**

estimable /éstiməb'l/ adj deserving respect or admiration [15C. < Old French, < Latin aestimare 'estimate, assess'.] —**estimableness** n —**estimably** adv

estimate /ésti mayt/ vti (**-mates, -mating, -mated**) **1 CALCULATE ROUGHLY** to make an approximate calculation of something ○ Can you estimate the time it will take? **2 SUBMIT A PRICE** to assess something, such as an item to be bought or a job to be done, and to state a likely price for it ○ Ask at least two firms to estimate the job. **3 ASSESS** to form an opinion or judgment about somebody or something ○ How would you estimate that performance? ■ n 1 **ROUGH CALCULATION** an approximate calculation. **2 APPROXIMATE PRICE** an assessment of the likely price of something, such as an item to be bought or a job to be done ○ Their estimate is the lowest. [Late 16C. < Latin aestimare 'estimate, assess'.] —**estimative** adj —**estimator** n

USAGE estimate or estimation? Broadly speaking, **estimation** refers to a thinking or valuing process and **estimate** to the result of such a process. An estimate of the time needed is the figure produced by working out how long something will take, whereas an estimation of the time needed is the calculation process that produces that figure. **Estimation** also has the special meaning 'judgment or opinion', which **estimate** does not have: What, in your estimation, is the cause of the problem? She went down in their estimation when the truth came out.

estimation /ésti máysh'n/ n 1 a judgment or opinion about somebody or something ○ Her behaviour bore out his estimation of her. **2** the act of estimating something, or the result of this

USAGE See **estimate**.

---

estival adj US = **aestival**

estivate vi US = **aestivate**

estivation n US = **aestivation**

Estonia

Estonia /e stóni ə/ republic in NE Europe on the Gulf of Finland. The smallest of the Baltic States, it gained its independence from the former Soviet Union in 1991. Capital: Tallinn. Population: 1,437,000 (1997). Area: 45,227 sq. km/17,462 sq. mi.

Estonian /e stóni ən/ n 1 somebody who comes from Estonia **2** the official language of Estonia, belonging to the Finnic group of the Finno-Ugric branch of Uralic. Native speakers: 1.7 million. —**Estonian** adj

estop /i stóp/ (**-tops, -topping, -topped**) vt to use the legal rule of estoppel to prevent something [15C. < Anglo-Norman, Old French estopper 'plug up' < Latin stuppa 'tow, broken flax' (used for plugging gaps).] —**estoppage** n

estoppel /i stópp'l/ n a legal rule that prevents somebody from stating a position inconsistent with one previously stated, especially when the earlier representation has been relied upon by others [Mid-16C. < Old French estouppail 'stopper' < estopper (see ESTOP).]

estradiol n US = **oestradiol**

estrange /i stráynj/ (**-tranges, -tranging, -tranged**) vt to cause somebody to stop feeling friendly or affectionate towards somebody else or sympathetic towards a tradition or belief (usually passive) ○ He managed to become estranged from all of his friends. [15C. Via Old French estrangier 'alienate' < Latin extraneare 'treat as a stranger' < extraneus (see STRANGE).] —**estrangement** n —**estranger** n

estranged /i stráynjd/ adj no longer living with a husband or wife

estreat /i stréet/ n a true extract from or copy of a legal record ■ vt to make a copy from a legal record in order to prosecute somebody [15C. < Anglo-Norman estrete, past participle of estraire 'extract' < Latin extrahere (see EXTRACT).]

estriol /éstri ol, eéss-/ n US = **oestriol**

estrogen n US = **oestrogen**

estrogen-replacement therapy n US MED = **hormone replacement therapy**

estrone n US = **oestrone**

estrous adj US = **oestrous**

estrus /éstrəss, eés-/ n US = **oestrus**

estuarine /éstyoō rīn, éstyo rin/ adj relating to, formed in, or found in an estuary

estuary /éstyoō ri/ (plural **-ies**) n the wide lower course of a river where the tide flows in, causing fresh and salt water to mix [Mid-16C. < Latin aestuarium < aestus 'heat, surge, tide'.] —**estuarial** /éstyoō áiri əl/ adj

Estuary English n a variety of standard English influenced by Cockney, spoken by people in London and SE England along the Thames Estuary (informal)

e.s.u., ESU abbr electrostatic unit

esurient /i syoóri ənt/ adj very hungry or greedy (archaic or formal) [Late 17C. < Latin esurient-, present participle of esurire 'be hungry' < edere 'eat'.] —**esurience** n —**esuriency** n

↯ et abbr Ethiopia (in Internet addresses)

ET abbr 1 Eastern Time **2** extraterrestrial

-et suffix 1 small one ○ falconet **2** something worn on ○ anklet [< Old French]

---

eta /eétə/ n the seventh letter of the Greek alphabet [15C. < Greek ēta.]

ETA[1] abbr estimated time of arrival

ETA[2] /éttə/, **Eta** n a Basque nationalist guerrilla group that seeks separation and independence from Spain for the Basque region [Mid-20C. < Basque, acronym < Euzkadi ta Askatsuna 'Basque Nation and Liberty'.]

étagère /áy taa zháir/ n a piece of furniture made up of open shelves, used to hold small objects [Mid-19C. Via French < Old French estagiere 'scaffold' < estage (see STAGE).]

et al.[1] /et ál/ and others (used of joint authors of a book or article) [Latin, et alii]

USAGE etc. or **et al.**? The abbreviation **etc.** (from the full form etcetera/et cetera) came into English from the Latin expression et cetera ('and the rest'). Do not use **etc.** as a substitute for the adverb **et al.**, which came into English from another Latin expression, et alii ('and others'). Use **etc.** when you list some, or a few, of many, as in We will discuss the Plymouth Colony, the Puritans, the witchcraft trials, etc., in our early American literature seminar. (Never write 'and etc.' or '& etc.', as these are redundant). Use **et al.** when you mention one person or a few people out of several or many, as in bibliographies, footnotes, or textual references: In the October issue of the medical journal, Smith, Jones, Roe, Doe, et al. [not etc.] discuss correct insertion of artificial airways.

et al.[2] /et ál/ adv and elsewhere [Shortening of Latin et alibi, 'and elsewhere']

etalon /étta lon/ n a spectroscopic device that has two flat parallel reflecting surfaces and is used to measure wavelengths [Early 20C. < French étalon 'standard' < Old French estal 'standing place'.]

etamine /étta meen/ n a light, loosely woven cotton or worsted fabric [Early 18C. Via French < Latin stamineus 'made of threads' < stamen 'thread in the warp of a loom'.]

etc. abbr et cetera

USAGE See **et al.**[1].

et cetera /it séttərə/, **etcetera** adv used to indicate that a list contains other unspecified items ○ an urgent request for clothes, food, medicines, etc. ■ n one of several or many unspecified things or people [< Latin, 'and the rest']

etch /ech/ v 1 vti **CUT A DESIGN INTO SOMETHING WITH ACID** to create a design or drawing on the surface of something, especially a printing plate, by the action of an acid **2** vti **CUT MARKS WITH SOMETHING SHARP** to cut a design or mark into the surface of something using a sharp point or laser beam **3** vt **MAKE CLEARLY VISIBLE** to leave a clear and distinct impression of something (usually passive) ○ His sorrow was etched on his face. [Mid-17C. Via Dutch etsen < Old High German ezzen 'eat away'.] —**etcher** n

etching /éching/ n 1 **CREATION OF CUT DESIGNS** the art or process of creating etched designs or making prints from etched surfaces **2 PRINT FROM AN ETCHED PLATE** a print made from an etched plate **3 PRINTING PLATE FOR ETCHING** a printing plate with an etched design

ETD abbr estimated time of departure

eternal /i túrn'l/ adj 1 **EXISTING THROUGH ALL TIME** lasting for all time without beginning or end ○ eternal life **2 UNCHANGING** unaffected by the passage of time ○ eternal truths **3 SEEMINGLY EVERLASTING** seeming to go on forever or recur incessantly (informal) ○ an eternal student ■ n **WHAT LASTS FOREVER** something that exists everlastingly [14C. Via Old French, < late Latin aeternalis < Latin aeternus < aevum 'age'.] —**eternality** /eétər nálləti/ n —**eternally** adv

Eternal /i túrn'l/ n God as a universal spirit

Eternal City n Rome, the capital of Italy

eternalize /i túrn'l īz/ (**-izes, -izing, -ized**), **eternalise** (**-ises, -ising, -ised**) vt 1 to make something eternal **2** to make something so famous as to become immortal

eternal triangle n a sexual or romantic relationship among three persons that involves jealousy or other emotional conflicts [Because known throughout history]

eternise vt = **eternize**

eternity /i túrnəti/ n 1 **INFINITE TIME** time without beginning or end ○ lost for all eternity **2 TIMELESSNESS** the condition, quality, or fact of being without beginning or end **3 TIMELESSNESS AFTER DEATH** a timeless state conceived as being experienced after death **4 VERY LONG TIME** a very long or seemingly very long period of time ○ *It will take an eternity to put it together again.* ■ **eternities** *npl* TRUTHS SAID TO BE ETERNAL beliefs or ideas about life that are conceived as being timeless [14C. Via Old French < Latin *aeternitas* < *aeternus* (see ETERNAL).]

eternity ring *n* a ring with gemstones set round its whole circumference

eternize /i túr nīz/ (**-nizes, -nizing, -nized**), **eternise** (**-nises, -nising, -nised**) *vt* = **eternalize** [Mid-16C. < French *éterniser* < Latin *aeternus* (see ETERNAL).]

etesian wind /i téezhi ən-/ *adj* an annual summer wind that blows from the northwest in the Aegean Sea and other parts of the E Mediterranean [Early 17C. < Latin *etesius* 'annual' < Greek *etēsios* < *etos* 'year'.]

ϟ **ETF** *abbr* electronic transfer of funds

eth *n* LING = **edh**

ethambutol /e thámbyoǒ tol/ *n* an antimicrobial substance. Use: in tuberculosis treatment. [Mid-20C. < ETHYL + AMINE + BUTANOL.]

ethanal /éethə nal, éthə-/ *n* CHEM = **acetaldehyde**

ethanamide /i thánnə mīd/ *n* CHEM = **acetamide**

ethane /ée thayn, é thayn/ *n* C_2H_6 a colourless odourless gas that is highly flammable. Source: petroleum, natural gas. Use: fuel, in refrigeration. [Late 19C. < ETHYL.]

ethanedioic acid /ée thayn dī ó ik-, é thayn-/ *n* CHEM = **oxalic acid**

ethanoate /éthə nō ət/ *n* CHEM = **acetate**

ethanoic acid /éethənō ik-, éthə-/ *n* = **acetic acid**

ethanoic anhydride CHEM = **acetic anhydride**

ethanol /éethə nol, éthə nol/ *n* C_2H_5OH a colourless liquid with a pleasant smell. Source: fermentation by yeasts and other microorganisms. Use: in alcoholic beverages, as solvent, in the manufacture of other chemicals.

ethanolamine /éethə nóllə meen, éthə-/ *n* any of three colourless solid or viscous substances. Use: manufacture of antibiotics, cosmetics, detergents, and herbicides.

Ethelbert /éth'l burt/ (552?–616) king of Kent (560–616)

Ethelred I /éth'l red/ (830?–871) king of the West Saxons and Kentishmen (866–71)

Ethelred II (968–1016) king of the English (978–1016). Known as **Ethelred the Unready**

ethene /é theen/ *n* ethylene (*technical*) [Mid-19C. < ETHYL.]

ether /éethər/ *n* **1** LIQUID SOLVENT AND ANAESTHETIC $C_2H_5OC_2H_5$ a volatile colourless liquid with a pleasant smell. Use: solvent, formerly as an anaesthetic. **2** ORGANIC COMPOUND WITH LINKED HYDROCARBON GROUPS any organic compound containing two hydrocarbon groups linked by an oxygen atom **3 ether, aether** HYPOTHETICAL ELECTROMAGNETIC MEDIUM a medium formerly believed to fill the atmosphere and outer space and to carry electromagnetic waves ○ *send a message across the ether* **4 ether, aether** SKY the sky or upper reaches of the atmosphere (*literary*) **5 ether, aether** AIR air (*literary*) [14C. Via Latin < Greek *aithēr* 'upper air' < Indo-European, 'to burn'.] —**etheric** /ee thérrik, i thérrik/ *adj*

ethereal /i théeri əl/ *adj* **1** EXQUISITE very delicate or highly refined ○ *ethereal beauty* **2** AIRY very light, airy, or insubstantial ○ *Her fragrance lingered in the room, an ethereal reminder of her presence.* **3** HEAVENLY belonging to the heavens or the celestial sphere **4** OF ETHER consisting of, containing, or relating to ether [Early 16C. < Latin *aetherius* < Greek *aithēr* (see ETHER).] —**ethereality** /i théeri állәti/ *n* —**ethereally** *adv* —**etherealness** *n*

etherealize /i théeri ə līz/ (**-izes, -izing, -ized**), **etherealise** (**-ises, -ising, -ised**) *vt* **1** to make something very delicate or refined **2** to turn something into ether —**etherealization** /i théeri ə lī záysh'n/ *n*

Etherege /éthərij/, **Sir George** (1635?–91) English playwright

etherify /éethəri fī, i thérri fī/ (**-fies, -fying, -fied**) *vt* to convert a substance, especially an alcohol, into ether (*technical*) —**etherification** /i thérrifi káysh'n/ *n*

etherize /éethə rīz/ (**-izes, -izing, -ized**), **etherise** (**-ises, -ising, -ised**) *vt* CHEM = **etherify** —**etherization** /éethə rī záysh'n/ *n* —**etherizer** *n*

ethic /éthik/ *n* a system of moral standards or principles ○ *the Protestant work ethic* ■ *adj* = **ethical** *adj.* **2** [Late 19C. Via French *éthique* < Greek *ēthikos* 'ethical' < *ēthos* (see ETHOS).]

ethical /éthik'l/ *adj* **1** CONFORMING TO ACCEPTED STANDARDS consistent with agreed principles of correct moral conduct ○ *While such activities are not strictly illegal, they are certainly not ethical.* **2** OF ETHICS relating to or involving ethics **3** AVAILABLE BY PRESCRIPTION ONLY describes a prescription drug —**ethicality** /éthi kállәti/ *n* —**ethically** *adv* —**ethicalness** *n*

ethicist /éthissist/ *n* a student of ethics or a devotee of ethical ideals

ethics /éthiks/ *n* **1** the study of moral standards and how they affect conduct (+ *singular verb*) **2** a system of moral principles governing the appropriate conduct for an individual or group (+ *plural verb*) [15C. Via Old French *ethiques* < Greek *ēthika* < *ēthikos* 'ethical' (see ETHIC).]

ethinyl *n* PHARM = **ethynyl**

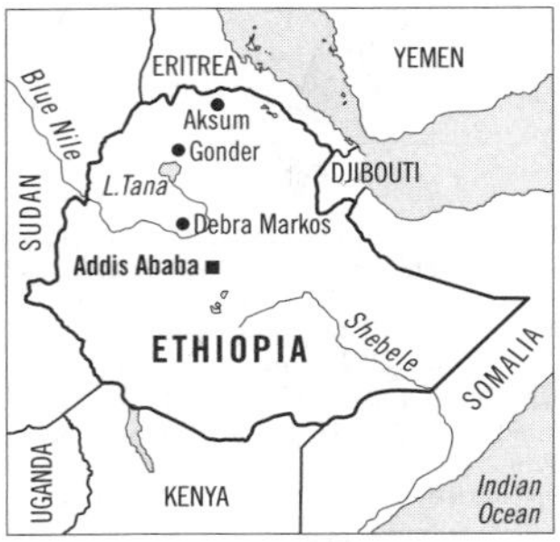

Ethiopia

Ethiopia /éethi ṓpi ə/ landlocked country in NE Africa. Capital: Addis Ababa. Population: 57,098,762 (1997). Area: 1,133,380 sq. km/437,600 sq. mi. —**Ethiopian** *adj, n*

Ethiopic /éethi óppik, -ṓpik/ *n* LANG = **Ge'ez** [Mid-17C. Via Latin < Greek *aithiopikos* < *Aithiop-* 'Ethiopian' < *aithein* 'burn' + *ōps* 'face'.]

ethmoid bone /éth moyd-/ *n* a perforated bone in the skull whose outer surfaces form part of the outer wall of the nasal cavity and the inner wall of the eye socket [Mid-18C. < Greek *ēthmoeidēs* 'like a sieve' < *ēthmos* 'sieve'.] —**ethmoidal** /eth móyd'l/ *adj*

ethnic /éthnik/ *adj* **1** SHARING CULTURAL CHARACTERISTICS sharing distinctive cultural traits as a group in society ○ *ethnic minorities* **2** OF A GROUP SHARING CULTURAL CHARACTERISTICS relating to a group or groups in society with distinctive cultural traits ○ *ethnic origins* **3** OF SPECIFIED ORIGIN OR CULTURE relating to a person or to a large group of people who share a national, racial, linguistic, or religious heritage, whether or not they reside in their countries of origin **4** CULTURALLY TRADITIONAL belonging to or typical of the traditional culture of a social group, especially a non-Western one ○ *ethnic clothing* ■ *n US, Can* MEMBER OF AN ETHNIC GROUP a member of an ethnic group within a society [14C. Via late Latin, 'heathen' < Greek *ethnikos* < *ethnos* 'people, nation' < Indo-European, 'self'.] —**ethnically** *adv*

ethnic cleansing *n* the violent elimination or removal from an area of people attacked because of their ethnic backgrounds, by means of genocide or forced expulsion

ethnicity /eth níssəti/ (*plural* **-ties**) *n* ethnic affiliation or distinctiveness

ethnic minority *n* an ethnic group that is a minority within a nation or society

ethno- *prefix* people, culture ○ *ethnohistory* [< Greek *ethnos* 'people, nation' (see ETHNIC)]

ethnobotany /éthnō bóttəni/ *n* the scientific study of the traditional classification and uses of plants in different human societies —**ethnobotanical** /éthnōbə tánnik'l/ *adj* —**ethnobotanically** *adv* —**ethnobotanist** *n*

ethnocentrism /éthnō séntrizəm/ *n* a belief in or assumption of the superiority of your own social or cultural group (*disapproving*) —**ethnocentric** *adj* —**ethnocentrically** *adv* —**ethnocentricity** /éthnō sen tríssəti/ *n*

ethnogenesis /éthnō jénnəssiss/ *n* the creation of a new ethnic group identity

ethnography /eth nóggrəfi/ *n* a branch of anthropology concerned with the description of ethnic groups —**ethnographer** *n* —**ethnographic** /éthnə gráffik/ *adj* —**ethnographically** *adv*

ethnohistory /éthnō hístəri/ *n* the scientific study of how cultures have developed through history —**ethnohistorian** /éthnō hi stáwri ən/ *n* —**ethnohistoric** /-hi stórrik/ *adj*

ethnolinguistics /éthnō ling gwístiks/ *n* the scientific study of the relationship between language and culture (+ *singular verb*) —**ethnolinguist** /éthnō líng gwist/ *n* —**ethnolinguistic** *adj* —**ethnolinguistically** *adv*

ethnology /eth nólləji/ *n* **1** the scientific comparison of different cultures **2** ANTHROP = **cultural anthropology** —**ethnologic** /éthnə lójjik/ *adj* —**ethnologically** *adv* —**ethnologist** *n*

ethnomethodology /éthnō méthə dólləji/ *n* the study of how people interact in ways that maintain the social structure of the situations in which they find themselves —**ethnomethodologist** *n*

ethnomusicology /éthnō myoozi kólləji/ *n* the study of the music of non-Western cultures —**ethnomusicological** /éthnō myoozikə lójjik'l/ *adj* —**ethnomusicologist** *n*

ethology /i thólləji/ *n* **1** the study of the behaviour of animals in their natural habitat, usually proposing evolutionary explanations **2** ANTHROP = **human ethology** [Mid-17C. < Latin *ethologia* < Greek *ēthos* (see ETHOS).] —**ethological** /éethə lójjik'l/ *adj* —**ethologist** *n*

ethos /ée thoss/ *n* the fundamental and distinctive character of a group, social context, or period of time, typically expressed in attitudes, habits, and beliefs [Mid-19C. < Greek *ēthos* 'custom, disposition' < Indo-European, 'self'.]

ethoxy /ee thóksi/ *adj* CH_3CH_2O forming or containing a chemical group composed of ethyl and oxygen [Late 19C. < ETHYL + OXY-.]

ethoxyethane /ee thóksi ée thayn/ *n* ether (*technical*)

ethoxyl /ee thóksil/ *adj* CHEM = **ethoxy**

ethyl /ée thīl, éth'l/ *n* CH_3CH_2 a chemical group containing carbon and hydrogen, deriving from ethane [Mid-19C. < ETHER.]

ethyl acetate *n* $C_4H_8O_2$ a volatile colourless liquid with a pleasant fruity smell. Use: manufacture of perfumes, solvent.

ethyl alcohol *n* CHEM = **ethanol**

ethylamine /éthilə méen/ *n* $C_2H_5NH_2$ a colourless volatile liquid. Use: oil refining, detergents.

ethylate /éthi layt/ (**-ates, -ating, -ated**) *vt* to attach an ethyl group to a molecule or to one of the molecules of a compound —**ethylation** /éthi láysh'n/ *n*

ethyl carbamate *n* CHEM = **urethane** *n.* 1

ethylene /éthi leen/ *n* C_2H_4 a colourless flammable gas. Source: petroleum, natural gas, ripening fruit. Use: manufacture of polymers and other chemicals, in metallurgy, to ripen and colour harvested fruit. —**ethylenic** /éthi léenik/ *adj*

ethylene glycol *n* $C_2H_6O_2$ a viscous colourless liquid with a sweet taste. Use: antifreeze, manufacture of polyester.

ethylene oxide *n* a soluble colourless gas. Use: synthesis of chemicals especially ethylene glycol, fumigant, sterilant.

ethyl ethanoate *n* CHEM = **ethylacetate**

ethyl mercaptan *n* C_2H_5SH a strong-smelling colourless liquid. Use: added to odourless fuels to make leaks detectable.

ethyne /ée thīn, éth īn/ *n* CHEM = **acetylene**

ethynyl /éthi nīl, -nil/, **ethinyl** *n* a radical derived from acetylene by the removal of one hydrogen atom

etic /éttik/ *adj* making use of preestablished categories for organizing and interpreting anthropological data, rather than categories recognized within the culture being studied. ◊ **emic** *adj.* **2** [Mid-20C. < PHONETIC.]

-etic *suffix* used to form adjectives from nouns ending in *-esis* ○ *geodetic* [Via Latin < Greek *-ētikos* < *-etos*]

etiolated /éeti ə laytid/ *adj* describes a plant that is abnormally tall and spindly and deficient in green pigment owing to lack of light [Late 18C. < French *étioler*.] —**etiolation** /éeti ə láysh'n/ *n*

etiology *n* = **aetiology**

etiquette /étti ket/ *n* the rules and conventions governing correct or polite behaviour in society in general or in a particular social or professional group or situation ○ *Etiquette dictates that wedding invitations should be acknowledged in writing.* [Mid-18C. < French, literally 'ticket'.]

Etna, Mount /étnə/ volcano in E Sicily, Italy. Height: 3,323 m/10,902 ft.

Eton /éet'n/ town in SE England. Population: 3,523 (1991).

Eton collar *n* a broad stiff white collar turned down over the collar and lapels of a coat or jacket, especially one worn as part of the Eton College uniform

Eton College, Eton *n* a public school in the town of Eton, in Buckinghamshire, SE England —**Etonian** /ee tṓni ən/ *n, adj*

Eton crop *n* a hairstyle in which the hair is cut short and lies flat, fashionable among women in the 1920s [From its resemblance to a schoolboy's haircut]

Eton jacket *n* a short black jacket with wide lapels and an open front, formerly worn by the pupils of Eton College

Etosha National Park /e tóshə-/ national park in Namibia, SW Africa, containing the Etosha Pan, a salt desert that was once a lake. Area: 20,700 sq. km/8,000 sq. mi.

étrier /áytri ay/ *n* a short rope ladder using in mountain climbing [Mid-20C. < French, 'stirrup, rope ladder'.]

Etruria /e tróori ə/ ancient region on the coast of NW Italy, where the Etruscan civilization flourished in the first millennium BC —**Etrurian** *n, adj*

Etruscan /i trúskən/ *n* **1** a member of an ancient people who lived in Etruria and were overcome by the Romans during the 2nd century BC **2** an extinct language spoken in ancient Etruria that has no relation to Indo-European languages [Early 18C. < Latin *Etruscus* 'of Etruria'.] —**Etruscan** *adj*

et seq. *abbr* **1** and another following, especially the next page in a book. Full form **et sequens 2 et seq., et seqq.** and others following, especially the next pages in a book. Full form **et sequentia** [Shortening of Latin *et sequens, et sequentia* 'and the following one(s)']

-ette *suffix* **1** small ○ *diskette* **2** female ○ *usherette* **3** imitation ○ *leatherette* [< Old French, form of *-et*]

étude /áy tyood/ *n* a short musical composition for a solo instrument intended to develop a point of technique or to display the performer's skill, but often played for its artistic merit [Mid-19C. < French, 'study' < Latin *studium*.]

étui /ay twée/ *n* a small ornamental case for needles or other small items [Early 17C. < French, < Old French *estui* 'prison' < *estuier* 'to keep'.]

ety., etym. *abbr* **1** etymological **2** etymology

etyma plural of **etymon**

etymol. *abbr* **1** etymological **2** etymology

etymologize /étti móllə jīz/ (**-gizes, -gizing, -gized**), **etymologise** (**-gises, -gising, -gised**) *vti* to study, trace, or describe the origin and development of a word, or make a suggestion as to its possible origin and development

etymology /étti mólləji/ (*plural* **-gies**) *n* **1** the study of the origins of words or parts of words and how they have arrived at their current form and meaning **2** the origin of a word or part of a word, or a statement of this and how it has arrived at its current form and meaning ○ *The words have the same spelling but different etymologies.* [14C. Via Old French < Greek *etumologia* < *etumon* (see ETYMON).] —**etymological** /éttimə lójjik'l/ *adj* —**etymologically** *adv* —**etymologist** *n*

etymon /étti mon/ (*plural* **-mons** *or* **-ma** /-mə/) *n* **1** an earlier form of a word or part of a word, especially the first recorded form in any language **2** a word or part of a word from which another word is derived [Late 16C. Via Latin < Greek *etumon* 'true sense of a word' < *etumos* 'true, original'.]

Eu *symbol* europium

EU *abbr* European Union

eu- *prefix* good, well, true, easily ○ *euphonious* ○ *euplastic* [Via Latin < Greek *eus*]

eubacteria /yóo bak téeri ə/ *npl* in modern biological classification, all those bacteria considered to be the true bacteria, characterized by their rigid cell walls

eucalyptol /yóokə líp tol/, **eucalyptole** /-tōl/ *n* $C_{10}H_{18}O$ a colourless oily liquid. Source: eucalyptus oil. Use: in pharmaceuticals, perfumes, and flavourings.

eucalyptus /yóokə líptəss/ (*plural* **-tuses** *or* **-ti** /-tī/), **eucalypt** /yóokə lipt/ *n* an evergreen tree that has aromatic leaves and produces timber, resin, and a medicinal oil. Native to: Australia. Genus: *Eucalyptus.* [Early 19C. < modern Latin, < Greek *eu-* 'well' + *kaluptos* 'covered'; from the covering on the tree's buds.]

eucaryote *n* BIOL = **eukaryote**

Eucharist /yóokərist/ *n* **1** a ceremony in many Christian churches during which symbolic or consecrated bread and wine are consumed, to commemorate the last meal of Jesus Christ with his disciples before his death. ◊ **Communion** *n.* 1 **2** the symbolic or consecrated bread and wine eaten and drunk during the ceremony of the Eucharist [14C. Via Old French < Greek *eukharistia* 'giving of thanks' < *eukharistos* 'grateful' < *kharizesthai* 'show favour'.] —**Eucharistic** /yóokə rístik/ *adj*

euchre /yóokər/ *n* **1 CARD GAME OF WINNING TRICKS** a card game played with the highest 32 cards in the pack in which each player receives five cards and must take at least three tricks to win **2 THWARTING OF AN OPPONENT AT EUCHRE** an instance of preventing another player from making the three tricks needed to win a game of euchre ■ *vt* (**-chres, -chring, -chred**) **1 THWART AN OPPONENT AT EUCHRE** to prevent another player from taking the three tricks needed to win a game of euchre **2** *ANZ, Can, US* **TRICK** to cheat, trick, or deceive somebody [Early 19C. < ?]

euchromatin /yoo krṓmətin/ *n* an expanded form of the material of which chromosomes are composed, occurring when DNA is being actively copied. ◊ **heterochromatin** —**euchromatic** /yóokrə máttik/ *adj*

Euclid /yóoklid/ (*fl.* 300 BC) Greek mathematician —**Euclidean** /yoo klíddi ən/ *adj*

Euclidean geometry *n* geometry according to the principles of Euclid, as described in his *Elements*, in which only one line parallel to another given line may pass through a given point

eudemon /yoo déemən/, **eudaemon** *n* a benevolent supernatural being [Early 17C. < Greek *eudaimōn* 'having a guardian spirit, fortunate, happy' < *daimōn* 'spiritual being, guardian'.]

eudemonism /yoo déemənizəm/, **eudaemonism** *n* an ethical doctrine that characterizes the value of life in terms of happiness —**eudemonist** *n* —**eudemonistic** /yoo déemə nístik/ *adj*

eudiometer /yóodi ómmitər/ *n* an instrument used to measure the volume changes that take place in chemical gas reactions [Late 18C. < Greek *eudios* 'fine (weather)' < *eu-* 'good' + *dios* 'heavenly'.] —**eudiometric** /yóodi ə méttrik/ *adj* —**eudiometrically** *adv* —**eudiometry** *n*

Eudoxus of Cnidus /yoo dóksəss əv kníddəss/ (408?–355? BC) Greek astronomer and mathematician

eugenics /yoo jénniks/ *n* the proposed improvement of the human species by encouraging or permitting reproduction of only those individuals with genetic characteristics judged desirable. It has been regarded with disfavour since the Nazi period. (+ *singular verb*) —**eugenic** *adj* —**eugenically** *adv* —**eugenicist** /yoo jénnissist/ *n* —**eugenist** /yóojənist/ *n*

eugenol /yóoji nol/ *n* $C_{10}H_{12}O_2$ a colourless oily liquid. Source: cloves. Use: in dentistry to reduce pain, in perfumes. [Late 19C. < modern Latin *Eugenia*, former genus name of the clove tree, after Prince *Eugene* of Savoy.]

euglena /yoo gléenə/ *n* a single-celled freshwater organism that has appendages (**flagella**) for locomotion and produces its food by photosynthesis. Genus: *Euglena.* [Mid-19C. < modern Latin, < Greek *eu-* 'well' + *glēnē* 'eyeball'.] —**euglenoid** /yoo gléen oyd/ *adj*

euhemerism /yoo héemərizəm/ *n* the theory that mythology has its origins in history, the gods being deified heroes of the past [Mid-19C. < Latin *Euhemerus* < Greek *Euēmeros*, Greek writer (4C BC) who maintained this.] —**euhemerist** *n* —**euhemeristic** /yoo héemə rístik/ *adj* —**euhemeristically** *adv*

eukaryote /yoo kárri ot/, **eucaryote** *n* any organism with one or more cells that have visible nuclei and organelles [Mid-20C. < EU- + Greek *karuōtos* 'having nuts' < *karuon* 'nut'.] —**eukaryotic** /yoo kárri óttik/ *adj*

eulachon /yóolə kon/ (*plural* **-chons** *or* **-chon**) *n* ZOOL = **candlefish** [Mid-19C. < Lower Chinook *úłxan*.]

Euler /óylər, yóolər/, **Leonhard** (1707–83) Swiss mathematician

eulogia[1] /yoo lṓji ə/ *n* bread blessed and given after the liturgy in the Eastern Orthodox Church to those not present at the Eucharist [Mid-18C. Via late Latin, 'consecrated bread' < Greek (see EULOGIUM).]

eulogia[2] plural of **eulogium**

eulogise *vt* = **eulogize**

eulogistic /yóolə jístik/ *adj* full of praise for somebody or something —**eulogistically** *adv*

eulogium /yoo lṓji əm/ (*plural* **-a** /-ji ə/ *or* **-ums**) *n* a eulogy (*formal*) [Early 17C. < medieval Latin, probably blend of *eulogia* 'praise' (< Greek, < *eu-* 'well' + *-logia* 'speaking') + Latin *elogium* 'epitaph'.]

eulogize /yóolə jīz/ (**-gizes, -gizing, -gized**), **eulogise** (**-gises, -gising, -gised**) *vti* to praise somebody or something very highly —**eulogizer** *n*

eulogy /yóoləji/ (*plural* **-gies**) *n* **1** a speech or piece of writing that praises somebody or something very highly, especially a tribute to somebody who has recently died **2** great praise (*formal*) [15C. < medieval Latin *eulogium* (see EULOGIUM).] —**eulogist** *n*

Eumenides /yoo ménni deez/ *n* three sister goddesses in Greek mythology. They were originally fertility goddesses, but were later identified with the Furies. [Late 17C. Via Latin < Greek, < *eumenēs*, 'kindly, friendly' < *menos* 'spirit'.]

eunuch /yóonək/ *n* **1** a man or boy whose testicles have been removed or do not function **2** a man who is regarded as lacking power or effectiveness (*informal insult*) [15C. Via Latin < Greek *eunoukhos* 'attendant of a bedroom or harem' < *eunē* 'bed' + *ekhein* 'keep'.] —**eunuchism** *n*

eunuchoid /yóonə koyd/ *adj* lacking fully developed male sexual organs or characteristics

euonymus /yoo ónniməss/ *n* a tree or bush grown for its decorative evergreen foliage and clusters of orange or red fruits. Native to: Northern temperate regions. Genus: *Euonymus.* [Mid-19C. Via modern Latin < Greek *euōnumos* 'of good name, lucky'.]

eupatrid /yoo páttrid/ (*plural* **-ridae** /-dee/ *or* **-rids**) *n* somebody belonging to the hereditary class of nobles and landowners in ancient Athens [Mid-19C. < Greek *eupatridēs* 'somebody of noble ancestry' < *patēr* 'father'.]

eupepsia /yoo pépsi ə/ *n* good or efficient digestion [Early 18C. < Greek, 'digestibility' < *eupeptos* (see EUPEPTIC).]

eupeptic /yoo péptik/ *adj* **1** relating to or producing good digestion **2** with a cheerful manner or disposition [Late 17C. < Greek *eupeptos* 'easy to digest, having good digestion' < *peptein* 'digest'.] —**eupeptically** *adv*

euphemise *vti* = **euphemize**

euphemism /yóofəmizəm/ *n* **1** a word or phrase used in place of a term that might be considered too direct, harsh, unpleasant, or offensive ○ *The phrase 'collateral damage' is a euphemism for injury to civilians during a military operation.* **2** the use of a word or phrase that is more neutral, vague, or indirect to replace a direct, harsh, unpleasant, or offensive term [Late 16C. < Greek *euphēmismos* < *euphēmizein* 'speak with pleasing words' < *phēmē* 'speech'.] —**euphemist** *n* —**euphemistic** /yóofə místik/ *adj* —**euphemistically** *adv*

LANGUAGE NOTE ***Euphemisms*** make the unpalatable more palatable. People use euphemisms chiefly to conceal feared things, such as death; to conceal the reality of unthinkable crimes; to conceal references to sex, body parts and fluids, and excrement; and to elevate otherwise lowly-sounding or derogatory occupational titles and institutional names. For instance, there are hundreds of euphemisms used on a daily basis for *to die*, a few of which are *pass on/away, go to one's final rest, depart/depart this life*, and *meet one's Maker.* Two of the most notorious euphemisms for genocide are, of course, *the Final Solution* and *ethnic cleansing.* Euphemistic references to sex and physiology are legion: *sleep with* for *have sex with* and *break wind* for *fart* are typical, as is *social disease* for *sexually transmitted disease.* Euphemisms that elevate the language of occupational titles include, for example, *sanitation engineer* for *garbage collector*, and those that elevate rather harsh-sounding institutional names include *correctional facility* for *prison.* The capacity of a euphemism to conceal tends to diminish over the years, as it becomes more and more closely associated with its referent, and if the taboo against talking about the referent remains in force, a fresh euphemism needs to be found for it. For instance, *toilet* was once a euphemism (it had previously referred to a dressing-room with washing facilities), but it has long since become a plainly understood neutral term for 'a place of urination and defecation', a term now needing its *own* euphemism: *rest room* and *powder room* for the room itself, and *commode* for the plumbing fixture. Euphemisms tend to turn into *dysphemisms*, their opposite, because the inescapable fact is that if something is feared or despised, the vocabulary used to refer to it will become tainted by those feelings, even if originally it was intended to disguise them.

euphemize /yoófə mīz/ (**-mizes, -mizing, -mized**), **euphemise** (**-mises, -mising, -mised**) *vti* to avoid saying or writing something direct, harsh, unpleasant, or offensive by using milder or more indirect language —**euphemizer** *n*

euphonious /yoo fṓni əss/ *adj* **1** having a pleasant sound **2** made easier to pronounce by a change in speech sounds —**euphoniously** *adv* —**euphoniousness** *n*

euphonise *vt* = **euphonize**

euphonium /yoo fṓni əm/ *n* a brass instrument similar to, but smaller than, a tuba, used mainly in military and brass bands [Mid-19C. < Greek *euphōnos* (see EUPHONY).]

euphonize /yoófə nīz/ (**-nizes, -nizing, -nized**), **euphonise** (**-ises, -ising, -ised**) *vt* **1** to make something sound pleasant **2** to change speech sounds to make something easier to pronounce

euphony /yoófəni/ (*plural* **-nies**) *n* **1** a pleasant sound, especially in speech or pronunciation **2** changing of speech sounds to make something easier to pronounce [15C. < French *euphonie* < Greek *euphōnos* 'sweet-voiced' < *phōnē* 'sound'.] —**euphonic** /yoo fónnik/ *adj* —**euphonically** *adv*

euphorbia /yoo fáwrbi ə/ *n* a plant with milky juice, e.g. spurge or poinsettia. Flowers: green. Genus: *Euphorbia*. [12C. < Latin *euphorbea* < *Euphorbus* (1C BC), physician to Juba, king of Mauretania, who supposedly discovered it.] —**euphorbiaceous** /yoo fáwrbi áyshəss/ *adj*

euphoria /yoo fáwri ə/ *n* a feeling of great joy, excitement, or well-being ○ *She was in a state of euphoria after her win.* [Late 17C. Via modern Latin < Greek, < *euphoros* 'borne well, healthy'.]

euphoriant /yoo fáwri ənt/ *n* a drug or other substance that induces euphoria —**euphoriant** *adj*

euphoric /yoo fórrik/ *adj* extremely happy or excited ○ *She'll be euphoric when she hears these results.* —**euphorically** *adv*

euphotic /yoo fṓtik, -fóttik/ *adj* describes the upper layer of a body of water that allows the penetration of enough light to support photosynthetic, or green, plants

Euphrates /yoo fráyteez/ river in SW Asia, rising in Turkey and flowing through Syria and Iraq before joining the River Tigris near the Persian Gulf. Length: 2,700 km/1,700 mi.

Euphrosyne /yoo frózzi nee/ *n* in Greek mythology, one of the three Graces who lived on Mount Olympus and were attendants of the goddess Aphrodite

euphuism /yoó fyoo izəm/ *n* **1** a literary style of the 16th and 17th centuries characterized by excessive use of devices such as alliteration, antithesis, and simile **2** an affected or pompous expression or use of language (*formal*) [Late 16C. After *Euphues*, fictional character in the works of John *Lyly*.] —**euphuist** *n* —**euphuistic** /yoó fyoo ístik/ *adj* —**euphuistically** *adv*

euplastic /yoo plástik/ *adj* healing readily

euploid /yoó ployd/ *adj* with a chromosome number that is an even multiple of the basic chromosome set for the species ■ *n* a euploid cell or organism —**euploidy** *n*

Eur. *abbr* **1** Europe **2** European

Eur- *prefix* = **Euro-** (*before vowels*)

Eurasia /yoor áyshə, yoor áyzhə/ the land mass consisting of the continents of Europe and Asia

Eurasian /yoor áyzh'n, yoor áysh'n/ *n* somebody of both European and Asian descent —**Eurasian** *adj*

Euratom /yoor áttəm/ *n* a body formed in 1957 to coordinate the development and use of atomic energy in Europe, later incorporated into the European Community [Mid-20C. Contraction of the first two words of its full name, European Atomic Energy Commission.]

eureka /yoo réekə/ *interj*, *n* used to express delight on finding, discovering, or solving something or finally succeeding in doing something ○ *I rolled back the carpet and eureka – there it was!* [Early 17C. < Greek *heurēka* 'I have found (it)' < *heuriskein* 'find', supposedly exclaimed by Archimedes when he discovered the principle of water displacement.]

eurhythmic /yoo ríthmik/, **eurythmic, eurhythmical** /-ríthmik'l/, **eurythmical** *adj* **1** having an aesthetically pleasing rhythm or structure **2** relating to eurhythmics or eurhythmy

eurhythmics /yoo ríthmiks/, **eurythmics** *n* a system of physical exercise, therapy, and musical training in which the body moves rhythmically and gracefully in interpretation of a piece of music (+ *singular or plural verb*)

eurhythmy /yoo ríthmi/, **eurythmy** *n* **1** harmony of proportion or structure **2** a system of rhythmical movement performed to verse or music for artistic or therapeutic purposes [Late 16C. Via Latin < Greek *eurhuthmia* 'good proportion' < *rhuthmos* 'proportion, rhythm'.]

Euripides /yoo ríppi deez/ (480?–406? BC) Greek dramatist

euro /yoórō/ (*plural* **-ros** *or* **-ro**) *n Aus* ZOOL = **wallaroo** [Mid-19C. < an Aboriginal language.]

Euro /yoórō/ (*plural* **-ros**) *n* the currency unit of 11 countries in the European Union, introduced in 1999 as part of economic and monetary union, which by 2002 will have replaced local currency in the participating member states. ◊ **ECU** [Late 20C. Shortening of EUROPEAN.]

Euro- *prefix* Europe, European ○ *Eurocurrency* [< EUROPE]

euro-ad *n* an advertisement that is designed or suitable for use in all countries of the European Union

Eurobeach /yoórō beech/ *n* a bathing beach in any of the countries of the European Union that meets the EU regulations for safe levels of bacteria in the water

Eurobond /yoórō bond/ *n* a bond measured in dollars or other currency and sold to investors from a country other than that whose currency is specified in the bond

Eurocentric /yoórō séntrik/ *adj* focusing on Europe or its people, institutions, and cultures, sometimes in an arrogant way (*disapproving*) —**Eurocentrism** *n*

Eurocheque /yoórō chek/ *n* a cheque that can be written in the currency of any European and some other countries, drawing on the writer's personal bank account in any of the participating countries

Eurocommunism /yoórō kómmyoōnizəm/ *n* a Communist movement in W Europe that advocated independent Communist parties for individual countries

Eurocrat /yoórə krat/, **eurocrat** *n* an administrative official of the European Union, especially one in a senior post [Mid-20C. Blend of EURO- + BUREAUCRAT.]

Eurocurrency /yoórō kurənssi/ (*plural* **-cies**) *n* money deposited by companies and governments in banks outside the home country

Eurodollar /yoórō dolər/ *n* a United States dollar on deposit in a bank outside the United States, especially a European bank (*usually plural*)

Euroland /yoórō land/, **euroland** *n* the countries in the European Union committed to adopting the common European currency, the euro

Euromarket /yoórō maarkit/ *n* **1** the European Union considered as a single market **2** the European financial markets collectively, especially when considered as a finance source for international trade

Euro-MP *n* a member of the European Parliament

Europa /yoo rṓpə/ *n* **1** in Greek mythology, a Phoenician princess who is abducted by Zeus and taken to the island of Crete **2** a large natural satellite of Jupiter, discovered in 1610 by Galileo. It is 3,130 km/1,880 mi in diameter and thought to have a thin icy crust.

Europe /yoórəp/ the second smallest continent after Australia, lying west of Asia, north of Africa, and east of the Atlantic Ocean. Population: 728 million. Area: 10,525,000 sq. km/4,065,000 sq. mi.

European /yoórə pée ən/ *adj* **1 OF EUROPE** relating to Europe or its peoples, languages, or cultures **2 OF THE EUROPEAN UNION** relating to the European Union ■ *n* **1 SOMEBODY FROM EUROPE** somebody who comes from Europe or is of European descent **2 ADVOCATE OF EUROPEAN UNION** a supporter of the principles and ideals of the European Union

European appointment *n W Africa* a high-level, white-collar position in a company or an organization

European Commission *n* the executive arm of the European Union, which formulates community policy and drafts most community legislation

European Community *n* an economic and political union of 12 European countries that developed from the European Economic Community and was itself replaced in 1993 by the European Union

European Currency Unit full form of **ECU**

European Economic Community *n* the alliance of six European countries begun in 1957 to promote free trade in Europe, and subsequently expanded in both numbers and areas of interest, and called the European Union

European Free Trade Association *n* a union of W European countries, established in 1960 to eliminate trade tariffs between member states

Europeanise *vt* = **Europeanize**

Europeanism /yoórə pée ənizəm/ *n* support for the European Union and its further development

Europeanize /yoórə pée ə nīz/ (**-izes, -izing, -ized**), **Europeanise** (**-ises, -ising, -ised**) *vt* **1** to make somebody or something part of European culture, or change somebody or something to fit in with European life, customs, or ideas **2** to make a country part of the European Union or make something conform to the regulations or specifications of it —**Europeanization** /yoórə pée ə nī záysh'n/ *n*

European Monetary System *n* a system for stabilizing currency exchange rates within the European Union, using the ERM. The introduction of a single European currency is its ultimate goal.

European Parliament *n* the primarily advisory legislature of the European Union

European Union *n* the economic and political alliance of 15 European nations, including the United Kingdom

europium /yoo rṓpi əm/ *n* (*symbol* **Eu**) a soft silvery-white metallic element of the rare-earth group. Source: monazite, bastnasite. Use: lasers. [Early 20C. < modern Latin, < Latin *Europa* 'Europe'.]

Eurosceptic /yoórō skeptik/ *n* a British person, especially a politician, who is not in favour of closer links between Britain and the European Union —**Euroscepticism** /yoórō sképtisizəm/ *n*

Eurovision song contest *n* an annual competition, broadcast on television, in which singers from primarily European countries perform a specially composed song and the participating nations vote for their favourite

eury- *prefix* wide, broad ○ *euryphagous* [< Greek *eurus*]

eurybathic /yoóri báthik/ *adj* describes aquatic organisms that tolerate a wide range of depths [Early 20C. < EURY- + Greek *bathos* 'depth'.] —**eurybath** /yoóri baath/ *n*

Eurydice /yoo ríddissi/ in Greek mythology, the wife of Orpheus

euryhaline /yoóri háy leen, -háy līn/ *adj* describes aquatic organisms that tolerate a wide range of salinity [Late 19C. < EURY- + Greek *halinos* 'of salt'.]

euryphagous /yoo ríffəgəss/ *adj* describes organisms that feed on a variety of different things

eurypterid /yoo ríptərid/ *n* an extinct invertebrate animal that was common in fresh or brackish water during the Palaeozoic era. Order: Eurypterida. [Late 19C. < modern Latin *Eurypterida* < Greek *eury-* 'wide' + *pteron* 'wing'.]

eurythermal /yoóri thúrm'l/, **eurythermic** /-thúrmik/, **eurythermous** /-thúrməss/ *adj* describes organisms that tolerate a wide range of temperatures —**eurytherm** /yoóri thurm/ *n*

eurythmic, eurythmical *adj* MUSIC, FITNESS = **eurhythmic**

eurythmics *n* FITNESS, MUSIC = **eurhythmics**

eurythmy *n* FITNESS, MUSIC = **eurhythmy**

eurytopic /yoóri tóppik/ *adj* describes organisms that tolerate a wide range of environmental conditions [Mid-20C. < EURY- + Greek *topos* 'place'.]

Eusebius (of Caesarea) /yoo séebi əss/ (260?–340?) bishop and Christian scholar, probably born in Palestine. Known as **Eusebius Pamphili**

Eusebius (of Nicomedia) (*d.* 342?) Syrian bishop and Christian theologian

eusocial /yoo sṓsh'l/ *adj* living as a species in a highly complex form of social organization [Late 20C]

Eustachian tube /yoo stáysh'n-/ *n* a bony passage extending from the middle ear to the nasopharynx that has a role in equalizing air pressure on both sides of the eardrum [Mid-18C. After Bartolomeo *Eustachio*.]

eustasy /yoóstəssi/ (*plural* **-sies**) *n* a worldwide change

MEMBERS OF THE EUROPEAN UNION

State	Capital	Population	Area (sq. km)	Area (sq. mi.)
Austria	Vienna	8,054,000	83,858	32,378
Belgium	Brussels	10,165,059	30,528	11,787
Denmark	Copenhagen	5,305,048	43,094	16,639
Finland	Helsinki	5,137,269	338,145	130,559
France	Paris	58,609,285	543,965	210,026
Germany	Berlin	82,071,765	356,970	137,827
Greece	Athens	10,493,000	131,957	50,949
Ireland	Dublin	3,606,952	70,273	27,133
Italy	Rome	56,830,508	301,323	116,341
Luxembourg	Luxembourg City	420,415	2,586	998
Netherlands	Amsterdam	15,451,000	41,526	16,033
Portugal	Lisbon	9,865,114	92,345	35,655
Spain	Madrid	39,181,114	504,782	194,897
Sweden	Stockholm	8,858,000	449,964	173,732
United Kingdom	London	58,784,000	244,101	94,248

The number of member countries in the European Union (currently 15) is expected to increase, with applications for membership from several countries in eastern and southern Europe. Of these, the Czech Republic, Estonia, Hungary, Poland, and Slovenia come closest to meeting the criteria for membership. Other countries that have applied for membership include Bulgaria, Cyprus, Latvia, Lithuania, Malta, Romania, Slovakia, and Turkey.

From January 2002 the Euro becomes the main currency of the following EU states: Austria, Belgium, Finland, France, Germany, Greece, Ireland, Italy, Luxembourg, the Netherlands, Portugal, and Spain.

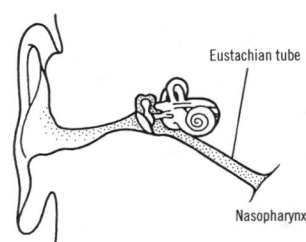

Eustachian tube

Nasopharynx

Eustachian tube

in sea level, as a result of melting glaciers or earth movements [Mid-20C. < EUSTATIC.]

eustatic /yoo státtik/ *adj* relating to a global change in sea level [Mid-20C. < Greek *eu* 'well' + *statikos* 'static'.]

eutectic /yoo téktik/ *adj* describes a mixture, especially an alloy, that has the lowest freezing point of all combinations or constituents, or to refer to the temperature at which this occurs ■ *n* a substance or mixture that is eutectic [Late 19C. < Greek *eutēktos* 'easily melting' < *tēkein* 'melt'.]

Euterpe /yoo túrpi/ *n* in Greek mythology, the muse of lyric poetry and music. ◊ **Muse**

euthanasia /yóotha náyzi ə, -náyzhə/ *n* the act or practice of killing somebody who has an incurable illness or injury or assisting that person to die [Early 17C. < Greek, 'easy death' < *thanatos* 'death'.]

euthanize /yóotha nīz/ (**-izes, -izing, -ized**), **euthanatize** /yoo thánnə tīz/ (**-tizes, -tizing, -tized**) *vt US* to kill an incurably ill or injured person or animal to relieve suffering

euthenics /yoo thénniks/ *n* the study of ways of improving people's environment and living standards in order to improve their health and well-being (+ *singular verb*) [Early 20C. < Greek *euthēnein* 'thrive'.] —**euthenist** /yoóthənist/ *n*

eutherian /yoo theéri ən/ *adj* describes a mammal whose young develop to an advanced stage within the womb surrounded by a placenta ■ *n* a mammal whose young develop within the womb surrounded by a placenta. Subclass: Eutheria. (*technical*) [Late 19C. < modern Latin *Eutheria* < Greek *thērion* 'wild animal'.]

eutrophic /yoo trófik, -tróffik/ *adj* describes a body of water whose oxygen content is depleted by organic nutrients (**eutrophication**) [Mid-20C. < Greek *eutrophia* 'good nutrition' < *trephein* 'nourish'.] —**eutrophy** /yoótrəfi/ *n*

eutrophication /yoo trófi káysh'n, -tróffi-/ *n* the process by which a body of water becomes rich in dissolved nutrients, thereby encouraging the growth and decomposition of oxygen-depleting plant life and resulting in harm to other organisms

EVA *abbr* extravehicular activity

evacuant /i vákyoo ənt/ *adj* describes a drug that empties the bowels

evacuate /i vákyoo ayt/ (**-ates, -ating, -ated**) *v* 1 *vt* MAKE EVERYONE LEAVE A PLACE to empty a dangerous or potentially dangerous place of people ○ *Towns near the nuclear plant were evacuated as a precautionary measure.* 2 *vti* MOVE TO SAFETY to leave or cause people to leave a place of danger and go somewhere safer ○ *The government has evacuated all its embassy officials from the city.* 3 *vti* EMPTY BOWELS OR BLADDER to discharge faeces or urine from the body (*technical*) 4 *vt* EMPTY to empty something by removing all its contents (*formal*) 5 *vt* CREATE VACUUM IN to remove a gas from something, leaving a vacuum [14C. < Latin *evacuat-*, past participle of *evacuare* 'empty (the bowels)', in late Latin 'clear out' < *vacuus* 'empty'.] —**evacuative** *adj* —**evacuator** *n*

evacuation /i vákyoo áysh'n/ *n* 1 CLEARING OF A DANGEROUS PLACE an emptying of a dangerous or potentially dangerous place 2 MOVING PEOPLE TO SAFETY a removal of people from a dangerous or potentially dangerous place 3 DISCHARGE OF BODILY WASTE elimination of faeces or urine from the body (*technical*) 4 BODILY WASTE faeces or urine eliminated from the body (*technical*) 5 CREATION OF A VACUUM the making of a vacuum by the removal of gas from something

evacuee /i vákyoo eé/ *n* a person who is taken from a dangerous place and sent somewhere safer, especially during a war [Early 20C. < French *évacué* < past participle of *évacuer* 'cease to occupy' < Latin *evacuare* (see EVACUATE).]

evade /i váyd/ (**evades, evading, evaded**) *v* 1 *vt* CLEVERLY ESCAPE to escape or avoid somebody or something, usually by ingenuity or guile 2 *vt* AVOID SOMETHING UNPLEASANT to avoid doing something unpleasant, especially something that is a moral or legal obligation 3 *vti* GIVE INDIRECT RESPONSE to avoid dealing with or responding directly to something 4 *vt* BE UNATTAINABLE to be difficult or impossible for somebody to find, obtain, or achieve (*formal*) [Early 16C. Via French < Latin *evadere* 'to escape' < *vadere* 'go, walk'.] —**evadable** *adj* —**evader** *n*

USAGE See *avoid*.

evaginate /i vájji nayt/ (**-nates, -nating, -nated**) *vt* to turn a hollow structure or bodily organ inside out [Mid-17C. < Latin *evaginat-* past participle of *evaginare* 'unsheathe' < *vagina* 'sheath'.] —**evagination** /i vájji náysh'n/ *n*

evaluate /i vállyoo ayt/ (**-ates, -ating, -ated**) *vt* 1 EXAMINE AND JUDGE to consider or examine something in order to judge its value, quality, importance, extent, or condition ○ *We evaluated the situation carefully.* 2 PUT A VALUE ON to estimate the monetary value of something ○ *The appraiser evaluated the property at £100,000* 3 FIND NUMERICAL VALUE to calculate a numerical value for a mathematical expression ○ *evaluate an expression* [Mid-19C. Back-formation < EVALUATION.] —**evaluator** *n*

evaluation /i vállyoo áysh'n/ *n* 1 the act of considering or examining something in order to judge its value, quality, importance, extent, or condition 2 a spoken or written statement of the value, quality, importance, extent, or condition of something [Mid-18C. < French *évaluation* < *évaluer* 'find the value of' < *value* (see VALUE).]

evaluative /i vállyoo ətiv/ *adj* 1 relating to or based on examination and judgment of the value, quality, or importance of something 2 expressing a judgment about something, or assigning a value to it, as opposed to describing a fact

evan. *abbr* 1 evangelical 2 evangelist

evanesce /évvə néss/ (**-nesces, -nescing, -nesced**) *vi* to grow less until completely gone (*literary*) ○ *His cares evanesced.* [Mid-19C. < Latin *evanescere* 'vanish' < *vanus* 'empty'.]

evanescent /évvə néss'nt/ *adj* disappearing after only a short time ○ *an evanescent moment* —**evanescence** *n* —**evanescently** *adv*

evang. *abbr* 1 evangelical 2 evangelist

evangel /i vánjəl/ *n* (*archaic*) 1 the Christian gospel 2 evangel, Evangel any of the four Christian Gospels: Matthew, Mark, Luke, or John [14C. Via Old French *evangile* < Greek *euaggelion* 'good news' < *euaggelos* 'bringing good news' < *eu* 'good' + *aggelein* 'announce'.]

evangelic, Evangelic *adj* CHR = evangelical

evangelical /eé van jéllik'l/ *adj* 1 evangelical, Evangelical, evangelic, Evangelic OF PARTICULAR PROTESTANT CHURCHES relating or belonging to any Protestant Christian church whose members believe in the authority of the Bible and salvation through the personal acceptance of Jesus Christ 2 evangelical, evangelic WITH STRONG BELIEFS enthusiastic or zealous in support of a particular cause and very eager to make other people share its beliefs or ideals 3 evangelical, evangelic RELATING TO THE CHRISTIAN GOSPELS relating to or based on the Christian Gospels: Matthew, Mark, Luke, or John ■ *n* evangelical, Evangelical MEMBER OF EVANGELICAL CHRISTIAN CHURCH a member of an evangelical Christian church or movement —**evangelically** *adv*

evangelicalism /eé van jéllik'lizəm/, **Evangelicalism** *n* a Protestant movement of the Christian church whose members believe in the authority of the Bible and salvation through the personal acceptance of Jesus Christ

evangelise *vti* = **evangelize**

evangelism /i vánjəlizəm/ *n* **1** the spreading of Christianity, especially through the activities of evangelists **2** great enthusiasm, fervour, or zeal for a particular cause

evangelist /i vánjə list/ *n* **1** a Christian who tries to persuade other people to become Christian, especially at public gatherings or in broadcasts **2 evangelist, Evangelist** any of the writers of the first four Christian Gospels: Matthew, Mark, Luke, or John —**evangelistic** /i vánjə lístik/ *adj* —**evangelistically** *adv*

evangelize /i vánjə līz/ (**-izes, -izing, -ized**), **evangelise** (**-ises, -ising, -ised**) *vti* **1** to convert somebody or the people of an area to Christianity, especially by preaching or missionary work **2** to try to persuade other people to share enthusiasm for particular beliefs and ideals —**evangelization** /i vánjə lī záysh'n/ *n* —**evangelizer** *n*

Evans, Mount /évv'nz/ mountain in north-central Colorado. Height: 4,348 m/14,264 ft.

Evans, Sir Arthur John (1851–1941) British archaeologist

Evans, Dame Edith (1888–1976) British actor

Evans, Sir Geraint (1922–92) Welsh singer and teacher

Evans-Pritchard /évv'nz príchərd/, **E.E., Sir** (1902–73) British anthropologist. Full name **Sir Edward Evan Evans-Pritchard**

Evansville /évənz vil/ city in SW Indiana. Population: 122,779 (1998 estimate).

evaporate /i váppə rayt/ (**-rates, -rating, -rated**) *v* **1** *vti* **CHANGE LIQUID TO VAPOUR** to change a liquid into a vapour, usually by heating to below its boiling point, or to change from a liquid to vapour in this way **2** *vt* **REMOVE LIQUID FROM** to remove liquid from something, usually by heating, to produce a more concentrated or solid substance **3** *vi* **VANISH** to disappear gradually or fade away to nothing **4** *vt* **DEPOSIT A FILM** to deposit something such as a metal film on a surface through the condensation of a vaporized substance [15C. < Latin *evaporat-*, past participle of *evaporare* 'go out in vapour' < *vapor* 'steam, heat'.] —**evaporability** *n* —**evaporable** *adj* —**evaporative** *adj*

evaporated milk /i váppə raytəd-/ *n* milk that has been thickened by removing some of the water by evaporation

evaporation /i váppə ráysh'n/ *n* a process in which something is changed from a liquid to a vapour without its temperature reaching the boiling point

evaporator /i váppə raytər/ *n* **1** the vaporization portion of a refrigeration system **2** a vaporizing device that removes water or other solvents to obtain the dried or concentrated residue, as in the preparation of powdered milk from milk

evaporite /i váppə rīt/ *n* a sedimentary rock or deposit that results from the evaporation of salt water in lagoons and saline lakes [Early 20C. < EVAPORATION.]

evapotranspiration /i váppō tránspə ráysh'n/ *n* the return of moisture to the air through both evaporation from the soil and transpiration by plants [Mid-20C. < EVAPORATION.]

evasion /i váyzh'n/ *n* **1 AVOIDANCE** avoidance of something unpleasant, especially a moral or legal obligation **2 MEANS OF AVOIDANCE** a means of escaping or avoiding something, especially one that involves cunning or deceit **3 AVOIDING AN ISSUE** not giving a direct answer to a direct question, usually in order to conceal the truth [15C. Via Old French < Latin *evasion-* < *evadere* (see EVADE).]

USAGE See *avoidance*.

evasive /i váyssiv/ *adj* **1** not giving a direct answer to a direct question **2** intended to avoid something unpleasant, e.g. trouble or an attack ○ *took evasive action* —**evasively** *adv* —**evasiveness** *n*

Evatt /évvət/, **Herbert Vere** (1894–1965) Australian judge and politician

eve /eev/ *n* **1 eve, Eve DAY BEFORE FESTIVAL** the day, evening, or night before a religious festival or public holiday **2 PERIOD BEFORE EVENT** the day or days immediately before an important event or special occasion ○ *He died on the eve of his 100th birthday.* **3 EVENING** an evening (*literary*) ○ *on a cold winter's eve* [12C. Variant of EVEN².]

Eve /eev/ *n* in the Bible, the first woman created by God, and Adam's companion in the Garden of Eden

evection /i véksh'n/ *n* a periodic irregularity in the motion of the Moon caused by the variation in the gravitational attraction of the Sun as the Moon orbits the Earth [Mid-17C. < Latin *evection-* < *evect-*, past participle of *evehere* 'carry out, elevate' < *vehere* 'carry'.] —**evectional** *adj*

Evelyn /éevlin/, **John** (1620–1706) English writer and government official

even[1] /éev'n/ *adj* **1 NOT SLOPING, ROUGH, OR IRREGULAR** having no slope, roughness, or irregularities **2 AT THE SAME HEIGHT** at the same distance above the ground or other point of reference **3 ALIGNED** lining up along the same horizontal or vertical line and usually with equal spaces between **4 NOT CHANGING OR FLUCTUATING** not changing or fluctuating in level or strength **5 THE SAME THROUGHOUT** the same all over or throughout ○ *an even consistency* **6 EQUAL IN AMOUNT** equal in amount, number, or extent ○ *At the end of the first round, the score was even.* **7 WELL-BALANCED** between competitors of equal strength or skill, and therefore fair or well-balanced **8 NOT OWING ANYTHING** not or no longer owing anything to each other (*informal*) ○ *Give me five pounds, and we'll call it even.* **9 EXACTLY DIVISIBLE BY TWO** describes a number or quantity that can be exactly divided by two with nothing left over, e.g. 2, 6, 30, or 518. ◊ **odd** *adj.* **2 10 WITH AN EVEN NUMBER** having a number that can be exactly divided by two ○ *on the even pages* **11 CALM AND STEADY** calm and controlled **12 EXACT IN AMOUNT** exact in amount, number, or extent ○ *an even dozen* ■ *vti* **LEVEL OR EQUALIZE** to make something more level or equal, or become more level or equal ○ *Atlanta scored three quick runs to even the score.* [Old English *efen* < Germanic] —**evener** *n* —**evenly** *adv* —**evenness** *n* ◇ **get even (with somebody)** to take revenge on somebody ○ *They took advantage of me, and I was determined to get even.*

even out *vti* **1** to become or make something more flat, smooth, or level **2** to make two or more different things more equal, or become more equal

even up *vti* to become or make something more equal, fair, or well-balanced

even[2] /éev'n/ *n* evening (*literary*) ○ *at even, when the sun was set* [Old English *æfen* (see EVENING)]

even[3] /éev'n/ CORE MEANING: used for emphasis to indicate something surprising, unlikely, or extreme ○ *Even I know how to repair a puncture!*

adv **1 SO MUCH AS** used after a negative for emphasis to indicate something unexpected and usually annoying or disappointing ○ *She couldn't even remember my name.* **2 TO A GREATER EXTENT** used for emphasis in comparisons to indicate the degree to which something exists ○ *His writing is even more untidy than hers, and hers is barely legible.* **3 FURTHERMORE** used to indicate that the description that follows applies in addition to and more strongly or precisely than the preceding one ○ *She is careful with her money, even miserly.* [Old English *efne* < Germanic] ◇ **even so** regardless of anything else ○ *It sounds unlikely; even so, it could be true.*

even break *n* an equal opportunity for winning or losing

even chance *n* an equal likelihood that something will or will not happen

evenhanded /éev'n hándid/ *adj* treating everyone fairly, without favouritism or discrimination ○ *an evenhanded distribution of the profits* —**evenhandedly** *adv* —**evenhandedness** *n*

evening /éevning/ *n* **1 LATE PART OF DAY** the part of the day between afternoon and night, as daylight begins to fade **2 TIME BEFORE BEDTIME** the part of the day between sunset or the last main meal of the day and bedtime ○ *We went out for the evening.* **3 EVENING'S ACTIVITY** a social gathering, meeting, or entertainment held in the evening ○ *Thank you for an enjoyable evening.* **4 PERIOD AT END** the final part of a period of time, e.g. somebody's life or a historical era (*literary*) ○ *the evening of the British Empire* **5 AFTERNOON** the afternoon (*regional*) ■ *interj* **GOOD EVENING** good evening (*informal*) [Old English *æfnung* < *æfen* < Indo-European, 'lateness']

evening class *n* a course or session of adult education held between approximately 7pm and 10pm, usually once a week throughout the school year

evening dress *n* **1** clothing worn by men or women for formal social events held in the evening **2** a woman's dress suitable for formal social events held in the evening, usually a full-length dress of elegant design. US term **evening gown**

evening gown *n* US = **evening dress** *n.* **2**

evening prayer, Evening Prayer *n* CHR = **evensong** *n.*

evening primrose *n* a biennial plant with hairy leaves and seeds that yield an oil used especially in treatments for menstrual problems. Genus: *Oenothera.* [Because it has yellow flowers that open in the evening]

evenings /éevningz/ *adv* US in the evening, especially regularly

evening star *n* a bright planet that can be seen in the western sky around sunset, usually Venus but occasionally Mercury

Evenki /i véngki/ (*plural* **-ki** *or* **-kis**), **Ewenki** (*plural* **-ki** *or* **-kis**) *n* **1** a member of a people who live mainly in E Asiatic Russia and NW China **2** a Tungusic language spoken in E Asiatic Russia and NW China that belongs to the Mongolian branch of Altaic. Native speakers: 30,000. [Via Russian, 'Evenki people' < Evenki] —**Evenki** *adj*

even money *n* a betting situation in which the odds of winning or losing are equal and the winnings equal the stake ■ *adj* equally likely or unlikely ○ *It's even money she'll forget.*

evens /éev'nz/ *adj, adv* with equal odds of winning or losing a bet

evensong /éev'n song/ *n* the daily evening worship service of the Anglican Church

even-steven /stéevən/, **even Stevens** /stéevənz/ *adj* (*informal*) **1** with all debts or grievances mutually settled **2** with equal scores or chances of winning ○ *At the end of the first round the two teams were even-steven.* [Probably arbitrary]

ϟ **event** /i vént/ *n* **1 IMPORTANT INCIDENT** an occurrence, especially one that is particularly significant, interesting, exciting, or unusual ○ *the events leading up to the strike* **2 ORGANIZED OCCASION** an organized occasion such as a social function or sporting competition ○ *She has competed in many international events.* **3 INDIVIDUAL SPORTING CONTEST** a race or other competition that forms part of a larger sporting occasion, e.g. the Olympic Games ○ *The 100 metres is his best event.* **4 OCCURRENCE IN PHILOSOPHY** a happening or occurrence **5 SINGLE POINT IN SPACE-TIME** an occurrence defined in the theory of relativity as a single point in space-time **6 OCCURRENCE AFFECTING COMPUTER PROGRAM** an occurrence or happening of significance to a computer program, e.g. the clicking of a mouse button or the completion of a write operation to a disk ■ *vi* **COMPETE IN EVENTING** to compete in equestrian competitions, especially eventing [Late 16C. < Latin *eventus* < past participle of *evenire* 'happen' < *venire* 'come'.] ◇ **be wise after the event** to know with hindsight what should have been done or said in a situation ◇ **in the event** contrary to what was expected ◇ **in the event of something** if something should happen

ϟ **event-driven** *adj* describes a computer program with a main loop that waits for an event and then passes the details along

even-tempered *adj* not easily angered or upset —**even-temperedly** *adv* —**even-temperedness** *n*

eventer /i véntər/ *n* a horse or rider that regularly competes at eventing

eventful /i véntf'l/ *adj* **1** full of important, interesting, or exciting occurrences **2** having a major effect on somebody's life —**eventfully** *adv* —**eventfulness** *n*

event horizon *n* the theoretical boundary surrounding a black hole, within which gravitational attraction is so great that nothing, not even radiation, can escape because the escape velocity is greater than the speed of light

eventide *n* evening (*literary*)

eventide home *n* a home for senior citizens (*dated*)

eventing /i vénting/ *n* an equestrian competition that includes dressage, cross-country riding, and stadium jumping, usually over three days

eventless /i véntləss/ *adj* having no significant events

eventual /i vénchoo əl/ *adj* happening in the course of time or events, usually much later ○ *her eventual fall from power* [Early 17C. < French *éventuel* < Latin *eventus* (see EVENT).]

eventuality /i vénchoo álləti/ (*plural* **-ties**) *n* a possible occurrence or result, especially something undesirable or unexpected ○ *We must be prepared for all eventualities.*

eventually /i vénchoo əli/ *adv* **1** after a long time, especially after many problems or setbacks ○ *We eventually managed to open the door.* **2** at some later time after a series of events ○ *She hopes eventually to study.*

eventuate /i vénchoo ayt/ (**-ates, -ating, -ated**) *vi* to happen as a final result (*formal*)
eventuate in *vt* to cause or result in something, especially after an extended period of time (*formal*) ○ *The oil spill eventuated in the destruction of wildlife habitats along the coast.*

evenweave /éevən weev/ *n* a fabric with warp and weft threads that are equally thick and tense and in equal numbers in any square measurement

ever /évvər/ *adv* **1 AT ANY TIME** used for emphasis in indicating any time in the past or future ○ *This is the most fascinating book I've ever read.* ○ *Will I ever see you again?* ○ *It's his biggest blunder ever.* **2 USED TO INDICATE SURPRISE** used for emphasis to indicate surprise, shock, or incomprehension at something ○ *Where ever can it be?* **3 INCREASINGLY** to an increasing degree (*formal*) ○ *The questions were becoming ever more technical.* **4 USED AS INTENSIFIER** used to emphasize a particular quality, especially to express enthusiasm (*informal*) ○ *It'll be ever such fun!* **5 ALWAYS** showing at all times a particular quality ○ *He is ever anxious to please.* [Old English *æfre* < Indo-European, 'eternity']

USAGE *The best book* **ever**: Some people object to this use of ***ever*** because they maintain that ***ever*** should include the future as well as the past. However, the future can rarely be accounted for, and the idiom is well established in conversational use, although it would not normally be used in more formal spoken or written English.

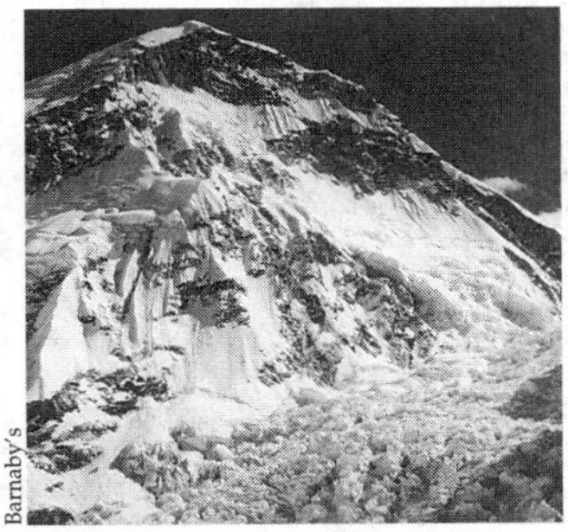
Barnaby's
Mount Everest: western shoulder of the mountain

Everest, Mount /évvərist/ mountain in the Himalayas on the border between Nepal and China. It is the highest mountain in the world. Height: 8,848 m/29,028 ft.

everglade /évvər glayd/ *n US* a stretch of marshy grassland usually covered with water for at least part of the year

Everglades National Park /évvər glaydz-/ national park in S Florida. Area: 6,105 sq. km/2,357 sq. mi.

evergreen /évvər green/ *adj* **1 WITH LEAVES THROUGHOUT THE YEAR** describes a tree or bush that retains its foliage throughout the year **2 REMAINING FRESH OR POPULAR** describes people or things that always seem fresh, lively, or interesting, and that remain popular despite their age ■ *n* **1 EVERGREEN TREE** a tree or bush that keeps its foliage throughout the year **2 EVERGREEN PERSON OR THING** somebody or something that remains fresh, lively, interesting, or popular

everlasting /évvər laásting/ *adj* **1 LASTING FOR EVER** never failing or coming to an end **2 LASTING A LONG TIME** continuing indefinitely or for a long time **3 INCESSANT** going on for too long and becoming tedious or annoying ○ *everlasting grumbling* ■ *n* **1 INFINITY** infinite time **2 everlasting, everlasting flower FLOWER THAT LOOKS FRESH WHEN DRIED** a plant with flowers that keep their shape and colour when dried —**everlastingly** *adv* —**everlastingness** *n*

Everlasting *n* God

evermore /évvər máwr/ *adv* from now until the end of time or the end of somebody's life (*literary*) ○ *I will be evermore in your debt.*

eversion /i vúrsh'n/ *n* **1** the process or condition of being turned inside out ○ *eversion of the bladder* **2** a condition of being turned outwards ○ *an eversion of the feet* [Mid-18C. Directly or via French < Latin *eversion-* < *evers-*, past participle of *evertere* (see EVERT).] —**eversible** *adj*

evert /i vúrt/ *vt* to turn an organ or other body part outwards or inside out [Mid-16C. < Latin *evertere* 'turn out' < *vertere* 'to turn'.]

Evert /évvərt/, **Chris** (*b.* 1954) US tennis player

every /évvri/ CORE MEANING: used to indicate each member of a group without exception ○ *dangers to health with which every citizen is familiar* ○ *Every life has value.* ○ *The press have been scrutinizing his every decision.*
det **1** used to emphasize that there is all there could be of a particular quality ○ *The government has every intention of exploring this issue.* **2** used to indicate each occurrence in recurrent or intermittent groups of things ○ *We intend to meet every two weeks.* ○ *Take this medicine every three hours.* [13C. < Old English *ǣfre ǣlc* 'ever each'.]
◇ **every other** each alternate thing, person, or occasion

USAGE See ***each***.

everybody *pron* = **everyone**

everyday /évvree day/ *adj* **1 ORDINARY AND UNREMARKABLE** having no remarkable feature to set it apart ○ *an everyday story of city life* **2 HAPPENING OR DONE EACH DAY** happening or done each day ○ *an everyday occurrence* **3 USED ON ORDINARY OCCASIONS** suitable for use on ordinary days or for routine tasks, rather than on special occasions ■ *n* **ORDINARY OCCASIONS** routine or daily life —**everydayness** *n*

USAGE everyday or **every day**? When you intend using either of these words as an adjective or a noun meaning 'ordinary occasions', as in *everyday life* or *part of the everyday*, the one-word version is correct. Adverbial uses, as in *We should eat fruit every day*, and the noun use meaning 'each day', as in *Every day is different*, call for the two-word version. Thus *everyday in every way* means 'ordinary in all respects', whereas *every day in every way* means 'daily and completely'.

Everyman /évvri man/ *n* **1 Everyman, everyman** somebody, usually a man, considered to be typical or representative of all human beings **2** the hero of a medieval morality play who represents the whole of the human race

every man jack, every man Jack *n* every single member of a group of people, without exception (*informal*) ○ *They ran away, every man jack of them.*

everyone /évvri wun/, **everybody** /évvri bodi/ *pron* every person, whether of a defined group or in general ○ *Everyone is going to come to the office party.* ○ *This is not just for one area; it will affect everyone around the country.*

everything /évvri thing/ *pron* **1** all the items, actions, or facts in a given situation ○ *We used to sit in front of his mother's house and talk about everything.* ○ *Everything I do is for my family.* ○ *Is everything all right?* **2** used to emphasize that somebody or something is the most important person or thing there is ○ *To them, family is everything.*

everywhere /évvri wair/ *adv* in or to all conceivable places ○ *Children everywhere play these games.* ○ *Her cat followed her everywhere she went.*

Everywoman /évvri wòomən/, **everywoman** *n* a woman considered to be typical or representative of woman generally

Eve's pudding *n* a baked pudding of apples topped with sponge [< the apple eaten by Eve in the Garden of Eden]

eve-teasing *n South Asia* the harassment of young women —**eve-teaser** *n*

evict /i víkt/ *vt* **1 EJECT FROM A PROPERTY** to force a tenant to leave a property, especially the tenant's residence, usually because he or she has failed to comply with the terms of the letting contract **2 THROW OUT OF A PLACE** to force somebody to leave a place, usually because of bad behaviour ○ *She was evicted from the game for insulting the referee* **3 GET BACK PROPERTY** to recover property or title to property from somebody by legal means [15C. < Latin *evict*, past participle of *evincere* (see EVINCE).] —**evictee** /i vík tée/ *n* —**eviction** *n* —**evictor** *n*

evidence /évvidənss/ *n* **1 SIGN OR PROOF** something that gives a sign or proof of the existence or truth of something, or that helps somebody to come to a particular conclusion ○ *There is no evidence that the disease is related to diet.* **2 PROOF OF GUILT** the objects or information used to prove or suggest the guilt of somebody accused of a crime ○ *The police have no evidence.* **3 STATEMENTS OF WITNESSES** the oral or written statements of witnesses and other people involved in a trial or official inquiry ■ *vt* **DEMONSTRATE OR PROVE** to demonstrate or prove something (*usually passive*) ○ *Their unwillingness to participate is evidenced by their failure to contact us.* ◇ **turn King's** *or* **Queen's evidence** to give evidence against a partner in crime so as to receive a less severe sentence

evident /évvidənt/ *adj* easy or clear to see or understand ○ *The full extent of her injuries did not become evident until they tried to move her.* [14C. Via Old French < Latin *evident-* 'clear' < *videre* 'see'.]

evidential /évvi dénsh'l/ *adj* relating to, consisting of, or based on evidence ○ *statements with no evidential value.* US term **evidentiary** —**evidentially** *adv*

evidentiary /évvi dénshəri/ *adj US* LAW = **evidential**

evidently /évvidəntli/ *adv* **1** used to indicate that something is undoubtedly true, often because it is there to be seen ○ *Evidently, you have not grasped all the ramifications of this proposal.* **2** used to indicate that something may be true based on available evidence ○ *He then completely ignored her, evidently intent on hurting her feelings even more.*

evil /éev'l/ *adj* **1 MORALLY BAD** profoundly immoral or wrong **2 HARMFUL** deliberately causing great harm, pain, or upset ○ *This evil act is clearly the work of terrorists.* **3 DEVILISH** connected with the devil or other powerful destructive forces ○ *evil spirits* **4 CAUSING MISFORTUNE** characterized by, bringing, or signifying bad luck ○ *an evil omen* **5 MALICIOUS** characterized by a desire to cause hurt or harm ○ *an evil mood* **6 DISAGREEABLE** very unpleasant ○ *What an evil smell!* ■ *n* **1 WICKEDNESS** the quality of being profoundly immoral or wrong **2 evil, Evil FORCE CAUSING HARMFUL EFFECTS** the force held to bring about harmful, painful, or unpleasant events ○ *a struggle between good and evil* **3 SOMETHING EVIL** a situation or thing that is very unpleasant, harmful, or morally wrong [Old English *yfel* < Indo-European, 'exceeding due limits'] —**evilly** *adv* —**evilness** *n*

evildoer /éev'l doo ər, éev'l dòo ər/ *n* a person who does evil acts —**evildoing** *n*

evil eye *n* **1** a piercing look that conveys strong feelings of hatred, disapproval, jealousy, or malice, or that supposedly can cause harm **2** a supernatural or magical power that some people believe can bring harm or cause bad luck ○ *an amulet to protect children from the evil eye*

Evil One *n* the devil

evince /i vínss/ (**evinces, evincing, evinced**) *vt* **1** to show a feeling or a quality clearly ○ *She evinced her disapproval of the production by leaving the auditorium.* **2** to indicate something by action or implication [Late 16C. < Latin *evincere* 'win out' < *vincere* 'conquer'.] —**evincible** *adj* —**evincive** *adj*

eviscerate /i víssə rayt/ (**-ates, -ating, -ated**) *vt* **1 DISEMBOWEL** to remove the internal organs or entrails of a person or an animal **2 REMOVE IMPORTANT PART OF** to remove an essential part of something and so weaken it **3 REMOVE THE CONTENTS OF AN ORGAN** to remove the contents of the eyeball or another organ or body cavity [Late 16C. < Latin *eviscerare* < *viscera* 'internal organs, entrails'.] —**evisceration** /i víssə ráysh'n/ *n* —**eviscerator** *n*

Evita /i véetə/ ➧ **Perón, Eva de**

evocation /éevō káysh'n, évvō-/ *n* **1** a recreation of something not present, especially an event or feeling from the past ○ *an accurate evocation of that period* **2** the transfer of a case from a lower to a higher court for review

evocative /i vókətiv/ *adj* prompting vivid memories or images of things not present, especially things from the past ○ *an outfit evocative of the 1960s* —**evocatively** *adv* —**evocativeness** *n*

evoke /i vṓk/ (**evokes, evoking, evoked**) *vt* **1 STIMULATE MEMORIES FROM PAST** to bring to mind a memory or feeling, especially from the past ○ *evoke childhood memories* **2 CAUSE REACTION OR FEELING** to provoke a particular reaction or feeling ○ *Her question evoked a bitter retort.* **3 CAUSE TO APPEAR** to make beings appear who are normally invisible ○ *evoke a spirit* [Early 17C. < Latin *evocare* 'call out' < *vocare* 'to call'.] —**evocable** /évvəkəb'l, i vṓkəb'l/ *adj* —**evocator** /évvə kaytər/ *n* —**evoker** *n*

evolute /éevə loot, évvə-/ *n* the curve formed by the set of points that are the centres of curvature of another geometric curve (**involute**) [Mid-18C. < Latin *evolutus*, past participle of *evolvere* (see EVOLVE).]

evolution /eévə loósh'n, évvə-/ *n* **1 THEORY OF DEVELOPMENT FROM EARLIER FORMS** the theoretical process by which all species develop from earlier forms of life **2 DEVELOPMENTAL PROCESS** the natural or artificially induced process by which new and different organisms develop as a result of changes in genetic material **3 GRADUAL DEVELOPMENT** the gradual development of something into a more complex or better form ○ *the evolution of democracy in Western Europe* **4 GIVING OFF HEAT OR GAS** the emission of heat, gas, or vapour **5 PATTERN CAUSED BY MOVEMENT** a pattern formed by a series of movements **6 FINDING ROOT OF NUMBER** an algebraic operation in which the root, e.g. the square root or cube root, of a number is found. ◊ **involution** *n.* 6 **7 MILITARY EXERCISE** a military exercise or manoeuvre carried out according to a plan [Early 17C. < Latin *evolut-*, past participle of *evolvere* (see EVOLVE).] —**evolutional** *adj* —**evolutionally** *adv*

evolutionary /eévə loósh'nəri, évvə-/ *adj* **1 OF EVOLUTION** relating to the theory of evolution **2 FROM EVOLUTION** resulting from or conferred by evolution ○ *evolutionary advantage* **3 GRADUAL** developing in small increments that accumulate to bring about significant change ○ *an evolutionary process* —**evolutionarily** *adv*

evolutionary psychology *n* a general approach to psychology, influenced by evolutionary biology, that stresses the links between the psychological processes of modern humans and those of their ancient ancestors

evolutionism /eévə loósh'nizəm, évvə-/ *n* **1** the theory of biological evolution **2** belief in the theory of biological evolution —**evolutionist** *n*

evolve /i vólv/ (**evolves, evolving, evolved**) *v* **1** *vti* **DEVELOP GRADUALLY** to develop something gradually, often into something more complex or advanced, or undergo such development **2** *vti* **DEVELOP VIA EVOLUTIONARY CHANGE** in evolutionary theory, to develop from an earlier biological form **3** *vt* **EMIT HEAT OR GAS** to give off heat, gas, or vapour [Early 17C. < Latin *evolvere* 'roll out' < *volvere* 'roll'.] —**evolvable** *adj* —**evolvement** *n* —**evolver** *n*

EW *abbr* enlisted woman

ewe /yoo/ *n* a female sheep, especially when fully grown [Old English *ēowu* < Indo-European]

Ewe /é way, áy-/ (*plural* **Ewe** *or* **Ewes**) *n* **1** a member of a West African people living in coastal regions of Ghana, Togo, and Benin **2** the language of the Ewe people, belonging to the Kwa branch of the Niger-Congo family [Mid-19C. < Ewe.] —**Ewe** *adj*

ewe-neck *n* a thin concave neck in a horse or dog, considered to be a defect —**ewe-necked** *adj*

ewer /yoó ər/ *n* a large jug or pitcher with a wide spout [15C. Via Anglo-Norman < Old French *aiguière* < Latin *aquarius* 'of water' < *aqua* 'water'.]

ewt /yoot/ *n S England* a newt (*informal*) [14C. Variant of EFT.]

ex[1] /eks/ *n* the letter X [Late 19C. From the pronunciation.]

ex[2] /eks/ *n* a former spouse, boyfriend, or girlfriend (*informal*) [Early 19C. < EX-[1].]

ex[3] /eks/ *prep* **1** not including or participating in ○ *ex dividend* **2** sold directly from with no charge before collection ○ *ex works* [Mid-19C. < Latin (see EX-[1]).]

Ex. *abbr* Exodus

ex-[1] *prefix* **1** out, outside, away ○ *exclave* ○ *explant* **2** not, without **3** former ○ *ex-convict* [< Latin, 'out of' < Indo-European, 'out']

ex-[2] *prefix* = **exo-** (*before vowels*)

exa- (*symbol* E) one million million million (10^{18}) [< HEXA-]

exacerbate /ig zássər bayt/ (**-bates, -bating, -bated**) *vt* to make an already bad or problematic situation worse [Mid-17C. < Latin *exacerbat-*, past participle of *exacerbare* 'make thoroughly harsh' < *acerbus* 'harsh, bitter'.] —**exacerbation** /ig zássər báysh'n/ *n*

exact /ig zákt/ *adj* **1 CORRECT** accurate and correct in all important details ○ *an exact account* **2 PRECISE** precise and not allowing for any variation ○ *a cheque for the exact amount* **3 THIS AND NO OTHER** used to emphasize that what is being referred to is one precise and often significant thing and not any other ○ *on this exact spot* **4 STRICT** rigorous and thorough ○ *an exact argument* **5 FUNCTIONING ACCURATELY** characterized by precise measurements ○ *exact instruments* ■ *vt* **1 OBTAIN** to demand and obtain something, especially payment ○ *exacted a heavy tribute from their defeated enemies* **2 INFLICT AS SUFFERING** to make somebody endure something unpleasant (*formal*) ○ *I was already thinking how I could exact revenge for what he had done.* **3 REQUIRE** to call for something as a matter of necessity or urgency [15C. < Latin *exactus*, past participle of *exigere* 'to demand' < *agere* 'to drive'.] —**exactable** *adj* —**exactness** *n* —**exactor** *n*

exacta /ig záktə/ (*plural* **-as**) *n US* GAMBLING = **perfecta** [Mid-20C. < American Spanish *quiniela exacta* 'exact quinella', game of chance.]

exacting /ig zákting/ *adj* **1** demanding hard work and great effort ○ *an exacting boss* **2** requiring concentration and strict attention to detail ○ *an exacting job* —**exactingly** *adv* —**exactingness** *n*

exaction /ig záksh'n/ *n* **1 ACT OF DEMANDING AND OBTAINING** the act of forcing somebody to give something, especially payment **2 UNFAIR DEMAND** an unfair or excessive demand for something, especially money (*formal*) **3 PAYMENT OBTAINED BY FORCE** a sum of money or a payment that has been forcibly demanded and obtained (*formal*)

exactitude /ig zákti tyood/ *n* the quality or state of being exact, precise, or accurate ○ *'The children were drilled in their parts with a military exactitude; obedience and punctuality became cardinal virtues'.* (Frank Norris, *McTeague – A Story of San Francisco*; 1899)

exactly /ig záktli/ *adv* **1 PRECISELY** used to emphasize that a particular quality or quantity is stated precisely ○ *One circuit of the park is exactly two miles.* **2 FULLY** used to emphasize that what is stated is true in all details or to the fullest extent ○ *He did exactly what I said he would.* **3 SHOWING AGREEMENT** used to indicate agreement that what has just been said is true or correct ○ *'We need to give this more thought.' 'Exactly.'* **4 SHOWING DISAPPROVAL** used in questions to ask for precise information, often implying suspicion or disapproval ○ *So exactly what are you doing?*

exact science *n* a science such as physics that deals with precise quantifiable measurements

~~**exagerate**~~ incorrect spelling of **exaggerate**

exaggerate /ig zájjə rayt/ (**-ates, -ating, -ated**) *v* **1** *vti* to state that something is better, worse, larger, more common, or more important than is true or usual **2** *vt* to make something appear more noticeable or prominent than is usual or desirable [Mid-16C. < Latin *exaggerat-*, past participle of *exaggerare* 'heap up' < *agger* 'heap' < *gerere* 'carry'.] —**exaggeratedly** *adv* —**exaggeratingly** *adv* —**exaggeration** /ig zájjə ráysh'n/ *n* —**exaggerative** /ig zájjərətiv, -raytiv/ *adj* —**exaggerator** *n*

exalt /ig záwlt, -zólt/ *vt* (*formal*) **1 PROMOTE** to raise somebody or something in rank, position, or esteem **2 PRAISE** to praise or worship somebody or something **3 INTENSIFY** to increase the intensity or effect of something [15C. < Latin *exaltare* 'put up high' < *altus* 'high'.] —**exalter** *n*

exaltation /ég zawl táysh'n, ég zol-/ *n* **1 FEELING OF EXTREME HAPPINESS** a feeling of intense or excessive happiness or exhilaration (*formal*) ○ *the miseries and exaltations of romance* **2 RAISING UP** the act of raising or holding something up (*formal*) **3 FLOCK** a flock of larks (*literary*)

exalted /ig záwltid, -zóltid/ *adj* (*formal*) **1 ELEVATED** high in rank, position, or esteem **2 NOBLE** grand or noble in character **3 HIGH-SPIRITED** in very high spirits —**exaltedly** *adv* —**exaltedness** *n*

exam /ig zám/ *n* **1** a test designed to assess somebody's ability or knowledge in a particular subject or field ○ *a chemistry exam* **2** *US* MED = **examination** *n.* 3 [Mid-19C. Shortening of EXAMINATION.]

examen /ig záymən/ *n* in the Roman Catholic Church, an examination of conscience [Early 17C. < Latin (see EXAMINE).]

examination /ig zámmi náysh'n/ *n* **1 INSPECTION** the process of looking at and considering something carefully with the aim of learning something ○ *Their applications are currently under examination.* **2** EDUC= **exam** *n.* 1 **3 MEDICAL INSPECTION OF PATIENT** a medical inspection carried out on a patient. US term **exam 4 STUDY OF SAMPLES FOR MEDICAL DIAGNOSIS** the study of laboratory samples from a patient in order to diagnose an illness **5 INTERROGATION IN LAW COURT** an interrogation of a witness or party to a case in a court of law

examination paper *n* EDUC = **exam paper**

examine /ig zámmin/ (**-ines, -ining, -ined**) *vt* **1 STUDY** to inspect or study somebody or something in detail ○ *examine the scene for fingerprints* **2 INVESTIGATE** to analyse something in order to understand or expose it ○ *examine your conscience* **3 TEST** to test the knowledge or ability of somebody by setting written, oral, or practical examinations **4 INSPECT CONDITION OF A PATIENT** to inspect a patient in order to determine his or her condition or health ○ *examined by a doctor* **5 INTERROGATE A WITNESS** to ask questions of a witness or other party to a case in a court of law [14C. Via French < Latin *examinare* 'weigh' < *examen* 'weighing out' < *exigere* (see EXACT).] —**examinable** *adj* —**examinee** /ig zámmi neé/ *n* —**examiner** *n*

examine-in-chief (**examines-in-chief, examining-in-chief, examined-in-chief**) *vt* to ask questions of a witness or other person in a court of law who is giving primary evidence in support of the case being presented by the questioner. ◊ **cross-examine** —**examination-in-chief** *n*

exam paper, examination paper *n* the printed set of questions used to test somebody's knowledge in an exam

example /ig zaámp'l/ *n* **1 SAMPLE** something that is representative by virtue of having typical features of the thing it represents ○ *a fine example of baroque carving* **2 MODEL** a person, action, or thing taken as a model to be copied or avoided by others ○ *Her achievement is an example to us all.* **3 ILLUSTRATION SUPPORTING SOMETHING** an illustration that supports or provides more information on an opinion, theory, or principle ○ *The prosecutor then listed several examples of the accused's mismanagement of funds.* **4 LEARNING AID** an exercise or description that illustrates a principle, method, or problem ○ *Each chapter contains easy-to-follow examples.* ■ *vt* (**-ples, -pling, -pled**) **EXEMPLIFY** to exemplify (*archaic; usually passive*) [14C. Via Old French < Latin *exemplum* < *eximere* 'take out' < *emere* 'take'.] ◇ **for example** used to introduce a typical instance of somebody or something ◇ **make an example of somebody** to punish somebody as a warning to others who might be inclined to offend in the same way

exanthema /ék san theémə/ (*plural* **-themata** /-mətə/ *or* **-themas**), **exanthem** /ek sánthəm/ *n* **1** a skin rash appearing as a sign of some infectious diseases, such as measles **2** a disease characterized by the appearance of a skin rash, e.g. measles or scarlet fever [Mid-17C. Via late Latin < Greek *exanthēma* 'eruption' < *anthein* 'to blossom' < *anthos* 'flower'.] —**exanthematic** /ek sánthi máttik/ *adj* —**exanthematous** /ék san thémmətəss/ *adj*

exarch /éks aark/ *n* **1** a bishop in the Eastern Orthodox Church of a rank above a metropolitan **2** the ruler of a province in the Byzantine Empire [Late 16C. Via ecclesiastical Latin *exarchus* < Greek *exarkhos* 'leader' < *exarkhein* 'lead' < *arkhein* 'rule'.] —**exarchal** /ek saárk'l/ *adj*

exarchate /éks aar kayt, ek saárk-/, **exarchy** /éks aarki/ (*plural* **-chies**) *n* the office, domain, or term of an exarch

exasperate /ig záspə rayt, -zaásp-/ (**-ates, -ating, -ated**) *vt* **1** to make somebody very angry or frustrated, often by repeatedly doing something annoying (*usually passive*) **2** to make an unpleasant condition or feeling worse (*literary*) [Mid-16C. < Latin *exasperat-*, past participle of *exasperare* 'irritate, roughen' < *asper* 'rough'.] —**exasperatedly** *adv* —**exasperating** *adj* —**exasperatingly** *adv* —**exasperation** /ig záspə ráysh'n, -zaáspə-/ *n*

~~**exaust**~~ incorrect spelling of **exhaust**

Excalibur /ek skállibər/ *n* in Arthurian legend, King Arthur's magic sword that was given to him by the mysterious Lady of the Lake [15C. Alteration of medieval Latin *Caliburnus* < Middle Welsh *Caletuwlch* or Middle Irish *Caladbolg*, sword of Irish legend.]

ex cathedra /éks kə theédrə/ *adj, adv* with the authority of status or rank ○ *imposed the decisions ex cathedra* [< Latin, 'from the (teacher's) chair']

excavate /ékskə vayt/ (**-vates, -vating, -vated**) *v* **1** *vti* **REMOVE EARTH** to remove earth or soil by digging or scooping out **2** *vti* **HOLLOW SOMETHING OUT** to make a hole or cavity in something by removing the material inside ○ *excavate a tooth* **3** *vt* **FORM BY HOLLOWING** to form a shape or cavity by hollowing ○ *excavates a hollow in the sand as its nest* **4** *vti* **DIG FOR ARTEFACTS** to dig in a place carefully and methodically, taking notes about procedures, conditions, and finds, with a view to uncovering objects of archaeological interest **5** *vti* **UNCOVER SOMETHING WITH DIFFICULTY** to discover or uncover something valuable by effort [Late 16C. < Latin *excavat-*, past participle of *excavare* 'hollow out' < *cavus* 'hollow'.]

excavation /ékskə váysh'n/ *n* **1** the act or process of digging, removing earth, hollowing something out, or excavating an archaeological site ○ *recent excavations in Sumatra* **2** a hole that has been made by digging or hollowing something out, or part of an archaeological site that has been excavated

excavator /ékskə vaytər/ *n* **1** a large machine with a hinged metal bucket attached to a hydraulic arm, used to move large quantities of earth or soil or for lifting **2** a person or animal that digs or hollows something out, especially somebody engaged in archaeological excavation

~~**exeede**~~ incorrect spelling of **exceed**

exceed /ik séed/ *vt* **1 BE GREATER THAN** to be greater than something in quantity, degree, or scope ○ *The cost of the film is reported to exceed 20 million dollars.* **2 GO BEYOND LIMITS** to go beyond the limits of something in quantity, degree, or scope ○ *He was fined for exceeding the speed limit.* ○ *You've exceeded your authority.* **3 OUTDO** to be better than something or somebody ○ *descriptions of nature that far exceed in merit anything else we've heard* [14C. Via Old French < Latin *excedere* 'go beyond, depart' < *cedere* 'go'.]

SPELLCHECK See ***accede***.

exceeding /ik séeding/ *adj* very great (*literary*) ○ *exceeding joy* ■ *adv* to an unusually high degree (*archaic*)

exceedingly /ik séedingli/ *adv* to an unusually high degree ○ *You've been exceedingly generous.*

excel /ik sél/ (**-cels, -celling, -celled**) *v* **1** *vti* to do very well, or do better than all others or than a given standard **2** *vi* to be outstanding or have a particular talent in something ○ *excels in marketing* [15C. < Latin *excellere* 'rise above' < assumed *cellere* 'rise'.]

excellence /éksələnss/ *n* **1** the quality or state of being outstanding and superior ○ *an award for excellence in photography* **2** a feature or respect in which somebody or something is superior and outstanding

Excellency /éksələnssi/ (*plural* **-cies**), **Excellence** /-lənss/ *n* a title and form of address for some high officials, e.g. governors, ambassadors, and high-ranking Roman Catholic clergy

excellent /éksələnt/ *adj* of a very high quality or standard ■ *interj* used to show wholehearted approval or agreement —**excellently** *adv*

excelsior /ek sélssi awr, ik-/ *n US* packing material made from wood shavings [Mid-19C. Originally proprietary, < Latin, 'higher'.]

except /ik sépt/ CORE MEANING: a grammatical word indicating the only person or thing that does not apply to a statement just made, or a fact that modifies the truth of that statement ○ (prep) *Every house in the street except ours is painted white.* ○ (conj) *He dislikes the game except when he wins.*

1 *vt* to leave out or exclude somebody or something (*formal; usually passive*) ○ *'Hazel eyes excepted, two years more might make her all that he wished'.* (Jane Austen, *Emma*; 1816) **2** *conj* unless (*archaic*) [14C. < Latin *exceptus*, past participle of *excipere* 'take out' < *capere* 'take'.] ◇ **except for** apart from ○ *He had always been healthy except for an irregular heartbeat.*

USAGE except, except for, or **excepting**: Often the question of whether to use ***except*** or ***except for*** is a matter of indifference: *We'd all seen the play except* [or *except for*] *Joe.* Where the exception is closely paired with what it is an exception to, ***except*** is more usual: *All of us except Joe had seen the play.* ***Except for*** is used where the connection to what is being excepted is indirect, and is also more common at the beginning of a sentence: *Except for that, we were in agreement.* ***Excepting*** is the correct choice after *not*: *She was the most important person in his life, not excepting his mother.*

USAGE See ***accept***.

excepted /ik séptid/ *adj* with the exception of a particular person or thing ○ *present company excepted*

excepting /ik sépting/ *prep, conj* used to indicate the only person or thing excluded from a statement just made (*formal*)

USAGE See ***except***.

exception /ik sépsh'n/ *n* **1 SOMEBODY OR SOMETHING EXCLUDED** somebody or something that is not included in or does not fit into a general rule, pattern, or judgment ○ *make an exception for family members* **2 EXCLUSION** the act or condition of being excluded **3 CRITICISM** a criticism, usually a negative one (*formal*) **4 LEGAL CLAUSE** a clause in a legal document that limits the effect of a part or the whole of it ○ *read through and approved all the exceptions* ◇ **take exception (to something)** to be annoyed or offended by something ◇ **the exception that proves the rule** something that, by being an exception, shows that a general rule exists

exceptionable /ik sépsh'nəb'l/ *adj* causing or liable to cause objection or offence (*formal*)

USAGE See ***exceptional***.

exceptional /ik sépsh'nəl/ *adj* **1** not conforming to a general rule or pattern ○ *exceptional circumstances* **2** having or showing intelligence or ability well above average ○ *an exceptional talent* —**exceptionality** /ik sépshə nálləti/ *n* —**exceptionally** *adv* —**exceptionalness** *n*

USAGE exceptional or **exceptionable**? ***Exceptional*** is the more common word and refers, often favourably, to a person or thing unusual in some way: *She has exceptional powers of concentration.* However, ***exceptional*** is also used in a factual or neutral way: *Expenses can be reimbursed only in exceptional cases.* ***Exceptionable***, despite its similar sound, has a very different meaning, referring to something that arouses disapproval or offence: *There was something in his manner that we found exceptionable.* More often, it is used in the negative form *unexceptionable*, meaning 'good enough to provide no reason for criticism or objection'.

exceptive /ik séptiv/ *adj* relating to or of the nature of an exception

excerpt *n* /éks urpt/ a section or passage taken from a longer work, e.g. a book, film, musical composition, or document ■ *vt* /ek súrpt/ to select a section or passage from a longer work (*usually passive*) [Mid-16C. < Latin *excerptus*, past participle of *excerpere* 'pluck out' < *carpere* 'pluck'.] —**excerptible** /ik súrptəb'l/ *adj* —**excerption** *n* —**excerptor** *n*

excess *n* /ik séss, éks ess/ **1 SURPLUS** an amount or quantity beyond what is considered normal or sufficient ○ *leaped up in an excess of enthusiasm* **2 EXTRA** the amount by which one quantity exceeds another **3 UNRESTRAINED BEHAVIOUR** behaviour or activity that goes beyond what is socially or morally acceptable, or beyond what is good for somebody's health or well-being ○ *led a life of excess* **4** *UK, Carib* **MONEY PAID TOWARDS INSURANCE CLAIM** a particular amount of money that a policy-holder must pay towards the cost of any insurance claim made ○ *an insurance policy with a £50 excess.* US term **deductible** *n.* ■ *adj* /éks ess, ek séss/ **1 MORE THAN ENOUGH** more than is usual, required, or allowed ○ *excess capacity* **2 REQUIRED IN ADDITION** that constitutes or is required as an additional payment ○ *excess postage* ■ *vt US* **DISMISS FROM EMPLOYMENT** to dismiss an employee as part of a programme of redundancies ○ *excessed in the most recent downsizing* [14C. Via French < Latin *excessus* < past participle of *excedere* (see EXCEED).] ◇ **to excess** beyond what is considered normal, sufficient, or healthy

SPELLCHECK See ***access***.

excess baggage *n* luggage that is heavier than the amount a passenger is allowed to take on a flight without an extra charge

excess demand *n* demand for a product or service that outstrips the supply and so pushes the price up

excessive /ik séssiv/ *adj* beyond what is considered acceptable, proper, usual, or necessary ○ *excessive hilarity* —**excessively** *adv* —**excessiveness** *n*

excess luggage *n* AIR = **excess baggage**

excess supply *n* supply of a product or service that outstrips the demand and so pushes the price down

exch. *abbr* **1 exch., ex.** exchange **2 exch., Exch.** exchequer

exchange /iks cháynj/ *v* (**-changes, -changing, -changed**) **1** *vt* **GIVE AND GET** to give something and receive something different in return ○ *exchange land for peace* ○ *exchange tokens for cash* **2** *vti* **SWAP** to give something and receive another of the same or an equivalent in return ○ *exchange glances* **3** *vt* **REPLACE** to hand something over and receive as a replacement something more suitable or more satisfactory ○ *exchanged her coat for one a size smaller* **4** *vt* **TAKE A PIECE OF SIMILAR VALUE** in chess, to take a piece in return for a piece of your own, usually of similar value, that your opponent has just taken or will soon take ■ *n* **1 GIVING AND RECEIVING** the action or process or an instance of exchanging something for something else or for something the same ○ *an exchange of compliments* **2 ARGUMENT** a short conversation, usually between two people or groups who are angry ○ *a bitter exchange* **3 SOMETHING GIVEN OR RECEIVED** something given or received in place of another **4 ARRANGEMENT TO VISIT ANOTHER COUNTRY** an arrangement between families, schools, or organizations in different countries for stays in each other's country **5 BUILDING USED FOR COMMERCIAL ACTIVITIES** a building used as a centre for the trading of commodities, securities, or other assets **6** TELECOM = **telephone exchange 7 MONEY TRANSFER BETWEEN TWO CURRENCIES** the transferring or a transfer of equal amounts of money between two currencies **8 SYSTEM OF PAYMENTS** a system of payments in which commercial documents, e.g. bills of exchange, are used instead of money **9 FEE FOR PAYMENT** the percentage or fee that is charged when paying in commercial documents instead of money **10 TAKING OF CHESS PIECES** the taking of chess pieces of similar value by each player in consecutive or nearly consecutive moves **11 TRADE OF A ROOK FOR A MINOR PIECE** in chess, taking a rook just before or after your opponent takes your knight or bishop or vice versa **12 TRANSFER OF PARTICLE** in physics, the transfer of a particle between two others [14C. Via Old French < assumed Vulgar Latin *excambiare* < late Latin *cambiare* 'barter' (see CHANGE).] —**exchangeability** /iks cháynjə bílləti/ *n* —**exchangeable** *adj* —**exchanger** *n*

exchange force *n* a force existing between particles due to the transfer of another particle

exchange particle *n* a virtual particle that travels between elementary particles undergoing one of the four fundamental interactions, strong, weak, electromagnetic, and gravitational

exchange rate *n* the rate at which a unit of the currency of one country can be exchanged for a unit of the currency of another

Exchange Rate Mechanism *n* a system of controlling the exchange rate between some countries in the European Union that sets an agreed limit on the extent to which rates can fluctuate in relation to one another

exchange student *n* a student who studies in another country as part of a programme in which students change places for a year or more

exchequer /iks chékər/, **Exchequer** *n* **1** formerly in the United Kingdom and some other countries, the government department responsible for collecting taxes and managing public spending **2** a national treasury or account, especially the UK government's account at the Bank of England, or the assets in it **3 Exchequer** = **Court of Exchequer** [13C. < Old French *eschequier* 'counting table, chessboard' < *eschec* 'check'; from the custom of counting royal revenue on a checked tablecloth.]

excimer /ék sīmər/ *n* a stable atomic pair (**dimer**) in which one of the two bound atoms is in a higher energy state [Mid-20C. Contraction of *excited dimer.*]

excipient /ik síppi ənt/ *n* an inert substance combined with a drug [Early 18C. < Latin *excipient-*, present participle of *excipere* 'take out' (see EXCEPT).]

excise[1] *n* /ék sīz/ **1 TAX ON GOODS FOR THE HOME MARKET** taxation of or a tax imposed on goods for a domestic market only **2 LICENSING CHARGE** a tax paid for a licence, e.g. one required to use a vehicle on public roads or to engage in certain commercial activities ■ *vt* /ik sīz/ (**-cises, -cising, -cised**) **IMPOSE TAX ON** to impose an excise on somebody or something [15C. Via Middle Dutch < Old French *acceis*, partly < assumed Vulgar Latin *accensum* < Latin *census* 'tax', partly < Old French *assise* (see ASSIZE).] —**excisable** /ik sīzəb'l/ *adj*

excise[2] /ik sīz/ (**-cises, -cising, -cised**) *vt* **1** to edit or delete a part of something, e.g. a text (*formal*) **2** to remove something by cutting, especially in surgery [Late 16C. < Latin *excis-*, past participle of *excidere* 'to cut out' < *caedere* 'to cut'.] —**excision** /ik sízh'n/ *n*

excise duty *n* tax imposed on goods intended for a domestic market only

exciseman /ék sīz man/ (*plural* **-men** /-men/) *n* formerly, somebody hired by the government to collect excise duty and prevent smuggling

excitable /ik sītəb'l/ *adj* **1** nervous and liable to become quickly excited **2** describes a nerve or tissue that is able to respond to a stimulus —**excitability** /ik sītə bílləti/ *n* —**excitableness** *n* —**excitably** *adv*

excitant /ik sītənt, éksitənt/ *adj* tending to excite or stimulate ■ *n* (*plural* **-tants**) a drug that stimulates or augments a response

excitation /éksi táysh'n, éks ī-/ *n* **1 EXCITING** the act or process of exciting something (*formal*) **2 BEING EXCITED** the state of being excited **3 ACTIVITY CAUSED BY STIMULATION** the activity or altered condition produced in a cell, tissue, or organ as a result of stimulation **4 PRODUCTION OF MAGNETIC FIELD** the production of a magnetic field in a generator or motor by passing electricity through the coil **5 RAISING ENERGY OF ATOM FROM LOWEST** the addition of sufficient energy to an electron, atom, atomic nucleus, or molecule, to raise it from its lowest energy level (**ground state**) to a higher energy level **6 APPLICATION OF SIGNAL MAKING TRANSISTOR OPERATE** the application of an electrical signal to a device such as a transistor causing it to operate —**excitatory** *adj*

excite /ik sīt/ (**-cites, -citing, -cited**) *v* **1** *vti* **STIMULATE FAVOURABLY** to cause somebody to feel enjoyment or pleasurable anticipation ○ *an exciting story* **2** *vt* **STIMULATE UNFAVOURABLY** to make a person or animal feel nervous apprehension or an unpleasant state of heightened emotion ○ *Don't excite the dog or he'll bite.* **3** *vt* **AROUSE AN EMOTION** to cause somebody to feel a particular emotion or reaction ○ *excite suspicion* **4** *vt* **EVOKE A THOUGHT** to cause a memory, thought, or other response to form in the mind ○ *an image that excited a memory* **5** *vt* **AROUSE PHYSICALLY** to cause somebody to feel physical desire **6** *vt* **INCREASE SOMETHING'S ACTIVITY** to stimulate or increase the rate of activity of an organ, tissue, or other body part **7** *vt* **RAISE A PARTICLE TO A HIGHER ENERGY LEVEL** to raise a particle or system of particles, e.g. an electron, atom, atomic nucleus, or molecule, above its lowest energy level (**ground state**) to a higher energy level **8** *vt* **PRODUCE MAGNETIC FIELD IN ELECTRIC MACHINE** to produce a magnetic field in a generator or motor by supplying electricity to the coil **9** *vt* **APPLY SIGNAL CAUSING DEVICE TO OPERATE** to apply an electrical signal that will cause a device, such as a transistor, to operate [14C. Directly or via French < Latin *excitare* 'rouse' < *ciere* 'summon, set in motion'.] —**excited** *adj* —**excitedly** *adv* —**excitedness** *n* —**exciting** *adj* —**excitingly** *adv*

excited state *n* the condition of a physical system, especially of atoms and atomic nuclei, that has an energy level higher than the lowest possible level (**ground state**)

excitement /ik sītmənt/ *n* **1 BEING EXCITED** the feeling or condition of lively enjoyment or pleasant anticipation ○ *finding it difficult to contain her excitement* **2 EXCITING EVENT** something that engages people's attention or emotions in a lively and compelling way ○ *Going in a helicopter was a great excitement for the children.* **3 EXCITING** the act or process of exciting something ○ *excitement of electrons*

exciter /ik sītər/ *n* **1 CAUSE OF EXCITEMENT** somebody or something that causes excitement **2 SMALL AUXILIARY GENERATOR** a small generator or transmitter that provides the necessary energy to run a larger device or amplifier **3 ELECTRICAL OSCILLATOR** an oscillator for supplying a radio transmitter with the basic wave that is modified to carry a radio signal

exciton /éksi ton, ék sī ton/ *n* a mobile neutral combination of an electron in an excited state and a hole in a crystal. Exciton activity is important in semiconductors. [Mid-20C. < EXCITATION + -ON[1].]

excl. *abbr* **1** exclamation **2** exclusive

exclaim /ik skláym/ *vti* to speak or cry out loudly and suddenly, often through surprise, anger, or excitement [Late 16C. Directly or via French < Latin *exclamare* 'call out' < *clamare* 'to call'.] —**exclaimer** *n*

exclamation /éksklə máysh'n/ *n* **1** a word, phrase, or sentence that is shouted out suddenly, often through surprise, anger, or excitement ○ *an exclamation of horror* **2** the act of crying out suddenly —**exclamational** *adj*

exclamation mark *n* **1** a punctuation mark (!) used after an exclamation or interjection, and sometimes after a command **2** a mark (!) used to indicate a road hazard or a mistake or point of note in a text or as a mathematical or logical symbol

exclamation point *n* US = **exclamation mark**

exclamatory /ik sklámmətəri/ *adj* using, of the nature of, or relating to an exclamation or exclamations —**exclamatorily** *adv*

exclaustration /éks klaw stráysh'n/ *n* the return of a monk or nun to lay life after relinquishing vows [Mid-20C. < modern Latin *exclaustration-* 'putting out of the enclosed space' < Latin *claustrum* (see CLOISTER).]

exclave /éks klayv/ *n* a part of a country that is isolated from the main body of the country, being surrounded by foreign territory [Late 19C. < EX-[1] + ENCLAVE.]

exclosure /eks klṓzhər/ *n* an area fenced in to keep out animals or intruders

exclude /ik sklóod/ (**-cludes, -cluding, -cluded**) *vt* **1 KEEP OUT** to prevent somebody or something from entering or participating **2 REJECT** to prevent somebody or something from being considered or accepted ○ *cannot exclude the possibility of treason* **3 OMIT** to fail to include something or somebody ○ *Three names were inadvertently excluded from the list.* **4 BAN SCHOOLCHILD** to ban a child from attending school on disciplinary grounds for a temporary, indefinite, or permanent period [14C. < Latin *excludere* 'to shut out' < *claudere* 'to shut'.] —**excludability** /ik sklóodə bíllәti/ *n* —**excludable** *adj* —**excluder** *n*

exclusion /ik sklóozh'n/ *n* **1 EXCLUDING** the act of excluding something or somebody **2 BEING EXCLUDED** the state of being excluded, especially from mainstream society and its advantages ○ *addressing the issue of social exclusion* **3 EXCLUDED PERSON OR THING** somebody or something that has been excluded [15C. < Latin *exclusion-* < *exclus-*, past participle of *excludere* (see EXCLUDE).] —**exclusionary** *adj*

exclusionary rule *n* a law that prevents illegally obtained evidence from being used in a criminal trial

exclusionist /ik sklóozh'nist/ *adj* US **1 DISCRIMINATORY** describes a policy that excludes individuals or groups from areas or rights and privileges **2 PROTECTIONIST** describes a policy that excludes specific imports or forms of commerce ■ *n* US **EXCLUSION ADVOCATE** a supporter of exclusionist policies —**exclusionism** *n* —**exclusionistic** /ik sklóozh'n ístik/ *adj*

exclusion principle *n* QUANTUM PHYS = **Pauli exclusion principle**

exclusion zone *n* **1** an area where an authority has banned a particular activity **2** an area that is out of bounds to people because a hazardous substance has been released ○ *the Chernobyl exclusion zone*

exclusive /ik sklóossiv/ *adj* **1 HIGH-CLASS** limited to a group of people, especially one considered fashionable or wealthy ○ *an exclusive club* **2 SELECTIVE** excluding or intending to exclude many from participation or consideration **3 RESTRICTED IN USE** only available to or used by one person, group, or organization ○ *Members have exclusive use of the pool.* **4 APPEARING IN ONE PLACE** published or broadcast in only one place ○ *exclusive coverage* **5 SOLE** being the only one **6 CONFINED TO ONE THING** limited to one thing and excluding everything else ○ *exclusive attention* **7 NOT INCLUDING THE STATED NUMBERS** not including the numbers, dates, or other series members mentioned immediately before ○ *from 8 July to 17 July exclusive* **8 RESTRICTING TRADE** restricting trade in certain goods or services only to those who have signed the contract or agreement **9 WHERE BOTH CANNOT BE TRUE** describes a proposition (**disjunction**) where one alternative rules out the other, e.g. being an odd number rules out the possibility of being an even number. ◊ **inclusive** *adj.* **4** ■ *n* **REPORT IN ONE PUBLICATION OR PROGRAMME** a news report or article that is printed in only one publication or broadcast on only one channel ○ *an exclusive on the wedding* [15C. < medieval Latin *exclusivus* < Latin *exclus-*, past participle of *excludere* (see EXCLUDE).] —**exclusively** *adv* —**exclusiveness** *n* —**exclusivity** /ék skloo sívvəti/ *n* ◇ **exclusive of** not including ○ *The price covers all your vacation costs, exclusive of travel insurance.*

exclusivism /ik sklóossivizəm/ *n* the practice or policy of being exclusive or excluding others —**exclusivist** *n, adj*

excogitate /eks kójji tayt/ (**-tates, -tating, -tated**) *vt* to consider or think about something carefully and thoroughly (*formal*) [Early 16C. < Latin *excogitat-*, past participle of *excogitare* 'think out' < *cogitare* 'think' (see COGITATE).] —**excogitable** *adj*

excommunicate *vt* /ékskə myóoni kayt/ (**-cates, -cating, -cated**) **EXCLUDE SOMEBODY FROM THE CHRISTIAN COMMUNITY** to exclude a baptized Christian from taking part in Communion because of doctrine or moral behaviour that is adjudged to offend against God or the Christian community ■ *adj* /ékskə myóonikət, -kayt/ **EXCOMMUNICATED** having been officially excluded from taking part in the Eucharist ■ *n* /ékskə myóonikət, -kayt/ **EXCOMMUNICATED PERSON** a person who has been formally excluded from taking part in the Eucharist [15C. < late Latin *excommunicare* 'put out of the community' < Latin *communis* 'common'.] —**excommunicable** *adj* —**excommunication** /ékskə myóoni káysh'n/ *n* —**excommunicative** *adj* —**excommunicator** *n*

ex-convict, ex-con *informal n* somebody who has served time in prison, having been convicted of a crime

excoriate /ik skáwri ayt, -skórri-/ (**-ates, -ating, -ated**) *vt* **1 DENOUNCE** to criticize somebody or something very strongly (*formal*) ○ *The paper excoriated the government's conduct in this case.* **2 TEAR SOMEBODY'S SKIN OFF** to tear the skin off a person or animal (*formal*) **3 REMOVE SKIN LAYER** to destroy or remove an area of skin, often through abrasion or chemical action [15C. < Latin *excoriat-*, past participle of *excoriare* 'strip off the hide' < *corium* 'hide, skin'.] —**excoriation** /ik skáwri áysh'n, -skórri-/ *n* —**excoriator** *n*

excrement /ékskrimənt/ *n* waste material, particularly faeces, discharged from the body (*technical*) [Mid-16C. < Latin *excrementum* < *excretus*, past participle of *excernere* (see EXCRETE).] —**excremental** /ékskri mént'l/ *adj* —**excrementitious** /ékskri men tíshəss/ *adj*

excrescence /ik skréss'nss/ *n* **1** a growth that sticks out from the body of a human, animal, or plant, especially an abnormal or diseased one **2** an ugly addition or extension to something, e.g. a building

excrescent /ik skréss'nt/ *adj* **1 SUPERFLUOUS** added or growing out unnecessarily (*formal*) **2 RELATING TO AN OUTGROWTH** relating to or like an outgrowth on an organism **3 ADDED IN SPEAKING** describes a speech sound that occurs in a word to allow ease of pronunciation [15C. < Latin *excrescent-*, present participle of *excrescere* 'grow out' < *crescere* 'grow'.] —**excrescently** *adv*

excreta /ik skréetə/ *npl* any waste matter discharged from the body, e.g. faeces or urine (*technical*) [Mid-19C. < Latin, 'things excreted' < form of past participle of *excernere* (see EXCRETE).] —**excretal** *adj*

excrete /ik skréet/ (**-cretes, -creting, -creted**) *vt* **1** to isolate and discharge waste matter generated during metabolism, e.g. through urinating or defecating (*formal*) **2** to eliminate waste matter from leaves and roots [Early 17C. < Latin *excret-*, past participle of *excernere* 'separate out, discharge' < *cernere* 'to separate'.] —**excreter** *n* —**excretory** *adj*

excretion /ik skréesh'n/ *n* **1** the act or process of discharging waste matter from the tissues or organs **2** waste matter that has been discharged from an animal or a plant

excruciate /ik skróoshi ayt/ (**-ates, -ating, -ated**) *vt* (*formal*) **1** to inflict severe mental and emotional distress on somebody **2** to inflict physical pain on somebody [Late 16C. < Latin *excruciare* 'torture thoroughly' < *cruciare* 'torture, crucify' < *cruc-* 'cross'.] —**excruciation** /ik skróoshi áysh'n/ *n*

excruciating /ik skróoshi ayting/ *adj* **1** extremely painful, physically or emotionally **2** intolerably embarrassing, tedious, or irritating ○ *The first act was bad enough, but the second was just excruciating.* —**excruciatingly** *adv*

exculpate /éks kul payt, iks kúl payt/ (**-pates, -pating, -pated**) *vt* to free somebody from blame or accusation of guilt (*formal*) [Mid-17C. < medieval Latin *exculpare* 'remove from blame' < Latin *culpa* 'blame'.] —**exculpable** /ik skúlpəb'l/ *adj* —**exculpation** /ék skul páysh'n/ *n*

exculpatory /ik skúlpətəri/ *adj* tending to prove that somebody is free from guilt or blame (*formal*) ○ *exculpatory evidence*

excursion /ik skúrsh'n, -skúrzh'n/ *n* **1 SHORT TRIP** a short trip to a place and back, for pleasure or a purpose **2 GROUP ON A SHORT TRIP** a group of people who are on an excursion **3 DIGRESSION** a temporary change of direction ○ *After an unsuccessful excursion into banking, he returned to public life.* **4 ALTERNATING MOTION** an oscillating or alternating motion away from a point of equilibrium and back **5 DISTANCE COVERED** the distance traversed by an oscillating excursion away from a point of equilibrium and back **6 MOVEMENT OF A BODY PART** the movement of a part or organ of the body, e.g. the lungs, from the resting position to another position [Late 16C. < Latin *excursion-* < *excurs-*, past participle of *excurrere* 'run out' < *currere* 'to run'.]

excursionist /ik skúrsh'nist, -skúrzh'n-/ *n* a taker of an excursion, especially for pleasure (*dated*)

excursus /ek skúrssəss/ (*plural* **-suses** *or* **-sus**) *n* a lengthy digression from the main topic (*formal*) [Early 19C. < Latin, 'excursion' < *excurs-* (see EXCURSION).]

excusatory /ik skyóozətəri/ *adj* tending or serving to excuse somebody or something (*formal*)

excuse v /ik skyóoz/ (**-cuses, -cusing, -cused**) 1 vt FORGIVE to release somebody from blame or criticism for a mistake or wrongdoing 2 vt OVERLOOK to make allowances for somebody or something ○ *Please excuse my spelling.* 3 vt RELEASE FROM AN OBLIGATION to release somebody from an obligation or responsibility ○ *excused from games because of a sprained ankle* 4 vt JUSTIFY to provide a reason or explanation for somebody's behaviour that makes it appear more acceptable or less offensive ○ *That doesn't excuse the way he acted last night.* 5 vt ALLOW TO LEAVE to allow somebody to leave or say politely that somebody should leave ○ *asked if he could be excused* 6 vr APOLOGIZE FOR LEAVING to leave with a polite apology or explanation ○ *excused herself and left the room* ■ n /ik skyóoss/ 1 JUSTIFICATION a reason or explanation, not necessarily true, given in order to make something appear more acceptable or less offensive ○ *There can be no excuse for laziness.* 2 FALSE REASON a false reason that enables somebody to do something he or she wants to do or avoid something he or she does not want to do ○ *the perfect excuse to do nothing* 3 BAD EXAMPLE an inept performer of an action or task (*informal*) ○ *a poor excuse for a cook* 4 US HR = **sick note** [15C. Via Old French < Latin *excusare* 'remove from accusation' < *causa* 'accusation'.] —**excusable** *adj* —**excusableness** *n* —**excusably** /-əbli/ *adv*—**excuser** *n* ◇ **excuse me** 1 used to attract attention politely, e.g. when asking somebody to move aside or when interrupting somebody 2 used to apologize for doing something rude or embarrassing, such as belching 3 used to indicate politely that you disagree with something or think that it is incorrect 4 US used to ask somebody to repeat what he or she has just said because you did not hear it properly or did not understand it

excuse-me, excuse-me dance *n* a dance in which participants interrupt other pairs to invite a change of partner

ex-directory *adj UK* not listed in the telephone directory by request

ex dividend *adv, adj* without the right to the current dividend on purchase

ϟ **exe** /eks/ *suffix* an extension used in a computer file name to show that the file is a program ○ *program.exe*

exeat /éksi at/ *n* 1 a short leave of absence from a boarding school or similar institution, usually lasting a day or a weekend 2 formal leave to move to a new diocese, granted by a bishop to a priest [Early 18C. < Latin, 'let him or her go out', form of *exire* (see EXIT).]

exec /ig zék/ *n* an executive or executive officer (*informal*) [Late 19C. Shortening.]

execrable /éksikrəb'l/ *adj* 1 extremely bad or of very low quality ○ *has execrable taste* 2 deserving to be detested ○ *execrable behaviour* [14C. Via Old French < Latin *execrabilis* < *execrari* (see EXECRATE).] —**execrableness** *n* —**execrably** *adv*

execrate /éksi krayt/ (**-crates, -crating, -crated**) *v* (*literary or formal*) 1 vt DETEST to feel loathing for somebody or something 2 vt DENOUNCE to declare somebody or something to be loathsome 3 vti CURSE to curse or put a curse on somebody or something [Mid-16C. < Latin *execrari* 'undo consecration' < *sacrare* (see SACRED).] —**execrative** *adj* —**execrator** *n*

execration /éksi kráysh'n/ *n* (*literary or formal*) 1 CURSE a curse ○ *'With an execration the thoroughly terrified robber threw down the pocketbook, and the relieved owner hastened forward to pick it up'.* (Horatio Alger, Jr., *Struggling Upward*; 1868) 2 SOMETHING CURSED something that is cursed or detested 3 EXECRATING the act of execrating somebody or something, or the state of being execrated

ϟ **executable** /éksi kyootəb'l/ *adj* describes a file, often carrying the extension .exe, that can be run as a program on a computer —**executable** *n*

executant /ig zékyootənt/ *n* a usually skilled performer of a musical, dance, or theatre piece (*formal*)

ϟ **execute** /éksikyoot/ (**-cutes, -cuting, -cuted**) *v* 1 vt CARRY OUT to put an instruction or plan into effect 2 vt PERFORM to complete or perform an action or movement, especially one requiring skill 3 vt CREATE to produce or create something, usually a work of art, to a specific design ○ *execute a drawing* 4 vt KILL to put somebody to death as part of a judicial or extrajudicial process 5 vti RUN ON COMPUTER to run a computer file or program in response to a command or instruction 6 vt SIGN A LEGAL DOCUMENT BEFORE WITNESSES to sign a will or other legal document in the presence of witnesses in order to make it binding 7 vt CARRY OUT TERMS OF A LEGAL DOCUMENT to carry out the terms laid out in a will, legal document, or legal decision ○ *execute a sentence* [14C. < Latin *executus*, past participle of *exsequi* 'follow out' < *sequi* 'follow'.] —**executer** *n*

execution /éksi kyóosh'n/ *n* 1 KILLING the killing of somebody as part of a judicial or extrajudicial process 2 PERFORMING the carrying out of an action, instruction, command, or movement ○ *a plan that failed in execution* 3 MANNER OF PERFORMANCE the style or manner in which something is carried out or accomplished 4 ENFORCEMENT OF A COURT JUDGMENT the carrying out or enforcing of a judgment made in court 5 CARRYING OUT OF LEGAL PROVISIONS the carrying out of the provisions of a legal document such as a will or contract 6 WRIT a legal writ that orders the carrying out of a judgment or decision

executioner /éksi kyóosh'nər/ *n* 1 an official who puts to death somebody who has been sentenced to capital punishment 2 a hired assassin

ϟ **execution time** *n* the amount of time needed for a complete run of a computer program

executive /ig zékyootiv/ *n* 1 SENIOR MANAGER a senior manager in a company or organization, whose job it is to make and implement major decisions 2 GOVERNMENT SECTION RESPONSIBLE FOR DECISIONS the section of a country's government responsible for implementing legislative decisions 3 COMMITTEE THAT MAKES DECISIONS a committee or group in a political organization that makes decisions and has the authority to implement them ○ *the executive of the Transport Union* ■ *adj* 1 OF POLICYMAKING responsible for or relating to the making and implementing of general decisions in a company, organization, or government ○ *a meeting of the executive committee* 2 FOR BUSINESSPEOPLE restricted to or designed to be used by businessmen and businesswomen 3 VERY EXPENSIVE very expensive and so only affordable by those who earn high salaries ○ *executive homes* [15C. < Old French *executif* < *executer* 'carry out' < Latin *execut-* (see EXECUTE).] —**executively** *adv*

executive agreement *n* an agreement between a US president and a foreign head of state that has not been given approval by the Senate

Executive Council *n* 1 in Canada, the cabinet of a provincial government 2 in Australia and New Zealand, a body made up of the Governor-General or Governor and government ministers

executive director *n* a director of a company who is employed by the company in a senior management position

executive jet *n* a small jet aircraft designed for private use, especially one used to transport corporate executives

Executive Mansion *n* = **White House** *n*. 1

executive officer *n* 1 an officer who is second in command of a military or naval unit 2 somebody in a senior management position in an organization

executive privilege *n* in the United States, the right of the President and other government officials in the executive branch to refuse to reveal confidential material if this would interfere with the administration's ability to govern

executive producer *n* 1 the head producer in charge of other producers at a film or television studio 2 the producer who handles the finances for a film

executive secretary *n* 1 a senior official who handles an organization's business affairs 2 a secretary who reports to a senior manager or executive in a company

executive session *n* a meeting of the US Senate, closed to the public, to discuss confidential government business such as judicial appointments or the ratification of treaties

executive toy *n* a small but usually sophisticated and expensively produced toy, e.g. a Newton's cradle, marketed as suitable for an executive's desk where it may aid concentration or relieve stress

executor /ig zékyootər/ *n* 1 somebody named in a will or appointed by a court to carry out the instructions contained in a will 2 a person who performs an action or task [13C. Via Anglo-Norman < Latin, < *execut-* (see EXECUTE).] —**executorial** /ig zékyoo táwri əl/ *adj* —**executorship** *n*

executory /ig zékyootəri/ *adj* 1 coming into effect at a future time or in accordance with circumstances 2 relating to the task or process of carrying out laws, policies, or instructions [15C. < late Latin *executorius* < Latin *executor* (see EXECUTOR).]

exedra /éksidrə, ek séedrə/ *n* 1 CONVERSATION ROOM a room for relaxation or conversation in ancient Greece and Rome, especially a semicircular recess in a larger hall with a continuous bench along the wall 2 LONG CURVED OUTDOOR BENCH a long curved or semicircular outdoor bench, usually with a high back 3 RECESS any kind of recess or niche (*technical*) [Early 18C. Via Latin < Greek, 'outside seat' < *hedra* 'seat'.]

exegesis /éksi jéessiss/ (*plural* **-ses** /-seez/) *n* the explanation or interpretation of texts, especially from the Bible, or an explanation or interpretation of a particular text [Early 17C. < Greek *exēgēsis* < *exēgeisthai* 'interpret' < *hēgeisthai* 'to guide'.]

exegete /éksi jeet/ *n* a student and interpreter of texts, especially religious writings [Mid-18C. < Greek *exēgētes* < *exēgeisthai* (see EXEGESIS).]

exegetic /éksi jéttik/, **exegetical** /-jéttik'l/ *adj* 1 relating to the study and interpretation of texts, especially religious writings 2 intended to explain or interpret something, especially a written text (*formal*) [Early 17C. < Greek *exēgetikos* < *exēgeisthai* (see EXEGESIS).] —**exegetically** *adv*

exegetics /éksi jéttiks/ *n* the branch of theology dealing with the study and interpretation of scripture (+ *singular verb*)

exegetist /éksi jéetist/ *n* = **exegete**

~~**exellent**~~ incorrect spelling of **excellent**

exempla plural of **exemplum**

exemplar /ig zémplaar, -lər/ *n* 1 IDEAL an ideal example of something, worthy of being copied or imitated (*literary*) ○ *Michelangelo's David is an exemplar of Renaissance sculpture.* 2 TYPICAL EXAMPLE a typical example or instance of something (*literary*) 3 COPY OF A BOOK a copy of a book or text, especially one from which further copies have originated [15C. Directly or via French < late Latin *exemplarium* < Latin *exemplum* (see EXAMPLE).]

exemplary /ig zémpləri/ *adj* 1 SETTING AN EXAMPLE so good or admirable that others would do well to copy it ○ *the child's exemplary conduct* 2 SERVING AS AN EXAMPLE designed to serve as a warning to others ○ *exemplary punishment* 3 GIVING AN EXAMPLE serving as an illustration or example of something (*formal*) [Late 16C. < late Latin *exemplaris* < Latin *exemplum* (see EXAMPLE).] —**exemplarily** *adv* —**exemplariness** *n* —**exemplarity** /ég zem plárrəti/ *n*

exemplary damages *npl* damages well above the value of the loss suffered, awarded to punish the offender and deter others

exemplify /ig zémpli fī/ (**-fies, -fying, -fied**) *vt* 1 BE AN EXAMPLE OF to show or illustrate something by being a typical or model example of it ○ *He exemplified all the qualities of a natural leader.* 2 GIVE AN EXAMPLE OF to give an example or examples in order to make something clearer or more convincing ○ *Perhaps you could exemplify your point with a few statistics.* 3 MAKE A COPY OF DOCUMENT to make an official copy of a legal document [15C. < medieval Latin *exemplificare* < Latin *exemplum* (see EXAMPLE).] —**exemplifiable** *adj* —**exemplification** /ig zémplifi káysh'n/ *n* —**exemplifier** *n*

exempli gratia /eg zém plī gráati aa/ *adv* full form of **e.g.** [Mid-17C. < Latin, 'for example's sake'.]

exemplum /ig zémpləm/ (*plural* **-pla** /-plə/) *n* 1 a brief story told to illustrate a moral point or support an argument 2 an example or illustration (*literary*) [Late 19C. < Latin (see EXAMPLE).]

exempt /ig zémpt/ *adj* NOT SUBJECT freed from or not subject to something such as a duty, tax, or military service that others have to do or pay ○ *tax-exempt savings accounts* ■ *vt* 1 FREE SOMEBODY FROM AN OBLIGATION to allow or entitle somebody not to do something that others are obliged to do 2 RELEASE SOMETHING FROM A RULE to release something from a rule that applies to others ○ *a law that exempts certain capital gains from taxes* ■ *n* EXEMPT PERSON OR THING somebody or something that is exempt from something [14C. Directly or via French < Latin *exemptus*, past participle of *eximere* (see EXAMPLE).] —**exemptible** *adj*

exemption /ig zémpsh'n/ *n* 1 permission or entitlement not to do something that others are obliged to do 2 somebody who or something that is exempt, e.g. income that is not taxed ○ *a range of tax exemptions*

exenterate /ig zéntə rayt/ (**-ates, -ating, -ated**) *vt* to remove surgically all the organs and other contents of a body cavity, usually to minimize the spread of cancer [Early 17C. < Latin *exenterat-*, past participle of *exenterare*, after Greek *exenterizein* 'remove the intestine' < *enteron* 'intestine'.] —**exenteration** /ig zéntə ráysh'n/ *n*

~~**exept**~~ incorrect spelling of **except**

exequies /éksikwiz/ *npl* a funeral ceremony (*formal*) [14C. Via Old French < Latin *exsequias* 'funeral procession, obsequies' < *exsequi* (see EXECUTE) 'accompany to the grave'.]

exercise /éksər sīz/ *n* **1 PHYSICAL ACTIVITY** physical activity and movement, especially when intended to keep a person or animal fit and healthy **2 PHYSICAL MOVEMENT** a physical movement or action, or a series of them, designed to make the body stronger and fitter or to show off gymnastic skill (*often plural*) **3 PRACTICE OF A SKILL OR PROCEDURE** a series of actions, movements, or tasks performed repeatedly or regularly as a way of practising and improving a skill or procedure (*often plural*) **4 PIECE OF WORK** a piece of work intended to test somebody's knowledge or skill **5 MILITARY TRAINING OPERATIONS OR MANOEUVRES** a set of extensive operations or manoeuvres, usually under simulated combat conditions, intended to train military personnel, test their equipment, and assess their capabilities **6 ACTIVITY INTENDED TO ACHIEVE A PARTICULAR PURPOSE** an action, activity, or undertaking intended to achieve a particular purpose ○ *The object of the exercise is to make money fast.* **7 CARRYING OUT OR USING** the carrying out or making use of something such as a choice, duty, responsibility, or right (*formal*) ○ *We urge the exercise of patience and restraint.* ■ *v* (**-cises, -cising, -cised**) **1** *vi* **TAKE EXERCISE** to undertake physical exercise in order to keep fit and healthy **2** *vt* **SUBJECT TO PHYSICAL EXERTION** to subject the body, or part of it, to repetitive physical exertion or energetic movement in order to strengthen it or improve its condition ○ *a routine designed to exercise your back and thigh muscles* **3** *vt* **EXERT AN ANIMAL PHYSICALLY** to make an animal exert itself physically in order to keep it healthy and fit **4** *vt* **DO EXERCISES TO DEVELOP A SKILL** to develop a particular faculty or skill by carrying out specific tasks or procedures repeatedly or systematically **5** *vt* **PUT SOMETHING TO PRACTICAL USE** to make use of a right or responsibility ○ *They have the power to prevent the merger, if they choose to exercise it.* **6** *vt* **SHOW A TYPE OF BEHAVIOUR** to adopt a type of behaviour or quality of character when dealing with a situation ○ *Exercise extreme care in your dealings with them.* **7** *vt* **OCCUPY OR WORRY** to be a cause for serious thought, worry, or anxiety to somebody (*formal*) ○ *It is not a question that has exercised me greatly in the past.* **8** *vti* **TAKE PART IN MILITARY TRAINING OPERATIONS** to take part in, or make troops take part in, large-scale operations or manoeuvres as part of combat training [14C. Via French < Latin *exercitium* < *exercere* 'keep busy' < *arcere* 'restrain'.] —**exercisable** *adj*

exercise bike, exercise bicycle *n* a fitness machine in the form of a stationary bicycle that is pedalled vigorously for exercise

exercise book *n* **1** a book containing exercises in a particular subject for students to complete **2** a book containing blank pages for school students to write or draw on

exercise price *n* the price at which the holder of stock options or warrants has the right to buy or sell

exerciser /éksər sīzər/ *n* **1** a piece of equipment used to exercise all or part of the body **2** a person who performs physical exercises or who exercises something, especially somebody hired to exercise racehorses

~~**exercize**~~ incorrect spelling of **exercise**

exergonic /éksər gónnik/ *adj* describes a spontaneous biochemical reaction that releases energy [Mid-20C. < EX-[1] + Greek *ergon* 'work'.]

exergue /ek súrg, éks urg/ *n* the part of a coin or medal that carries details such as the date and place of minting [Late 17C. Via French < medieval Latin *exergum* < Greek *ex-* 'outside' + *ergon* 'work'.]

~~**exerpt**~~ incorrect spelling of **excerpt**

exert /ig zúrt/ *v* **1** *vt* to apply influence, pressure, or authority in an attempt to have a powerful effect on a situation **2** *vr* to make a strenuous physical or mental effort [Mid-17C. < Latin *ex(s)ert-*, past participle of *ex(s)erere* 'thrust out, put forth' < *serere* 'join, plait, entwine'.]

exertion /ig zúrsh'n/ *n* **1 STRENUOUS EFFORT** strenuous physical exercise or effort **2 STRENUOUS ACTION** an action that involves strenuous physical effort (*often plural*) ○ *After his exertions in the garden, he felt he deserved a rest.* **3 BRINGING SOMETHING TO BEAR** the application of pressure or influence (*formal*) ○ *the exertion of pressure on unsuspecting clients*

Exeter /éksitər/ city in SW England, noted for its historic cathedral. Population: 107,729 (1996 estimate).

exeunt /éksi unt, -ay ənt/ *vi* used as a stage direction in a text in place of 'exit' when more than one person is to leave the stage. ◊ **exit** *v.* 3 [15C. < Latin, 'they go out', form of *exire* (see EXIT).]

exfoliate /eks fṓli ayt/ (**-ates, -ating, -ated**) *v* **1** *vi* **FALL OFF IN FLAKES** to come off the outer surface of something in thin flakes, scales, or layers **2** *vti* **REMOVE THIN OUTER LAYER** to remove or shed a thin outer layer from something, e.g. skin, a mineral, or a bone in surgery **3** *vti* **SCRUB SKIN** to scrub skin with a gritty substance to remove the dead surface layer **4** *vti* **SPLIT INTO THIN LAYERS** to split, or split a mineral, into thin layers [Mid-17C. < late Latin *exfoliat-*, past participle of *exfoliare* 'take leaves from' < Latin *folium* 'leaf'.] —**exfoliation** /eks fṓli áysh'n/ *n* —**exfoliative** *adj* —**exfoliator** *n*

exfoliating scrub *n* a cosmetic preparation designed to refresh the skin of the face or body by removing a surface layer of dead cells

ex gratia /eks gráyshə/ *adj, adv* given as a gift, favour, or gesture of goodwill, rather than because it is owed ○ *an ex gratia payment* [Mid-18C. < Latin, 'out of kindness'.]

exhalation /éks hə láysh'n/ *n* **1 BREATH FROM THE LUNGS** a breath exhaled from the lungs **2 BREATHING OUT** the act of breathing out **3 SCENT OR VAPOUR GIVEN OFF** a scent, a vapour, or fumes given off by something (*literary*)

exhale /eks háyl, eg záyl/ (**-hales, -haling, -haled**) *vti* **1** to breathe out, or breathe something out **2** to give off something such as a smell or a vapour, or be given off (*literary*) [14C. Via French < Latin *exhalare* < *halare* 'breathe'.]

exhaust /ig záwst/ *v* **1** *vt* **TIRE SOMEBODY OUT** to make somebody feel very tired or weak **2** *vt* **USE SOMETHING UP** to use up all that is available of something ○ *Our supplies of fuel were now exhausted.* **3** *vt* **TRY OUT ALL POSSIBILITIES** to try out or consider every one of a number of possibilities **4** *vt* **SAY EVERYTHING ABOUT SOMETHING** to say or write everything about something, so that nothing is left to be discussed **5** *vt* **DRAIN SOMETHING OF ITS RESOURCES** to draw off or use up all the resources contained within something ○ *over-grazing that has exhausted the pasture* **6** *vti* **LET OUT WASTE GASES** to escape, or allow steam or waste gases to escape, at the end of an industrial process ○ *Waste gases are exhausted through the flue.* **7** *vt* **REMOVE GAS TO CREATE A VACUUM** to remove all of the air or gas from a container in order to create a vacuum inside it ■ *n* **1 DISCHARGE OF WASTE GASES** the discharge of waste gases, vapour, and fumes created by and released at the end of a process, especially from the working of an internal-combustion engine **2 ESCAPE SYSTEM FOR WASTE GASES** a pipe or other piece of apparatus through which waste gases escape [Mid-16C. < Latin *exhaust-*, past participle of *exhaurire* 'draw out' < *haurire* 'draw (water) out or up, drain'.] —**exhausted** *adj* —**exhaustedly** *adv* —**exhauster** *n* —**exhaustibility** /ig záwstə bílləti/ *n* —**exhaustible** *adj*

exhaustion /ig záwsch'n/ *n* **1** a state of extreme physical or mental tiredness or collapse ○ *He was close to exhaustion.* **2** the process of using up the entire stock or contents of something (*formal*) [Early 17C. < Latin *exhaustion-* < *exhaust-* (see EXHAUST).]

exhaustive /ig záwstiv/ *adj* involving or dealing with everything relevant to the matter in hand ○ *an exhaustive account of the author's life* —**exhaustively** *adv* —**exhaustiveness** *n* —**exhaustivity** /ig záwss tívvəti/ *n*

exhaust pipe *n* a pipe that allows waste gases to escape from a vehicle's engine. US term **tailpipe**

exhibit /ig zíbbit/ *v* **1** *vti* **DISPLAY ART** to display something, especially a work of art, in a public place such as a museum or gallery **2** *vt* **SHOW SOMETHING TO OTHERS** to show something off for others to look at or admire ○ *She decided it was a good time to exhibit her skills as a solver of business disputes.* **3** *vt* **REVEAL A QUALITY** to show the outward signs of something, especially an emotion or a physical or mental condition (*formal*) ○ *The wings exhibited signs of metal fatigue.* **4** *vt* **GIVE SOMETHING AS EVIDENCE** to present something to be used as evidence in a court of law ■ *n* **1 OBJECT ON DISPLAY** an object displayed in public, especially in a gallery or museum or for a show or competition **2** ARTS = **exhibition** *n.* 1 **3 PIECE OF EVIDENCE** an object or document presented or identified as evidence in a court of law [15C. Partly < Latin *exhibere* 'hold out, display' < *habere* 'hold'; partly back-formation < EXHIBITION.] —**exhibiter** *n* —**exhibitor** *n* —**exhibitory** *adj*

exhibition /éksi bísh'n/ *n* **1 PUBLIC DISPLAY OF WORKS OF ART** a public display, usually for a limited period, of a collection of works of art or objects of special interest **2 DISPLAYING** the displaying of something in public ○ *one or two of the works on exhibition* **3 DEMONSTRATION OF SKILL** a demonstration of a particular skill or craft ○ *a karate exhibition* **4 DISPLAY OF BEHAVIOUR** a display of a particular type of behaviour, usually bad behaviour ○ *What did she mean by that little exhibition, I wonder?* **5 SCHOOL'S GRANT TO STUDENT** a sum of money, usually of lower value than a scholarship, that a school or university awards a student to help with the cost of his or her studies [14C. Directly or via French < late Latin *exhibition-* 'handing over, display' < Latin *exhibere* (see EXHIBIT).] ◇ **make an exhibition of yourself** to behave embarrassingly in public and attract attention to yourself

exhibitioner /éksi bísh'nər/ *n* a student who has been awarded an exhibition by a school or university

exhibition game *n* a sports contest played purely as a display of skill and an entertainment for spectators, with no prizes or competition points at stake

exhibitionism /éksi bísh'nizəm/ *n* **1** loud, exaggerated, or boastful behaviour designed to attract attention **2** a psychological disorder causing a compulsion to show the genitals in public —**exhibitionist** *n* —**exhibitionistic** /éksi bíshə nístik/ *adj*

exhibition match *n* SPORTS = **exhibition game**

exhibitive /ig zíbbitiv/ *adj* displaying or demonstrating something (*formal*) —**exhibitively** *adv*

exhilarate /ig zíllə rayt/ (**-rates, -rating, -rated**) *vt* to make somebody feel happy, excited, and more than usually vigorous and alive [Mid-16C. < Latin *exhilarat-*, past participle of *exhilarare* 'gladden thoroughly' < *hilarare* 'gladden' < Greek *hilaros* 'cheerful, glad'.] —**exhilarating** *adj* —**exhilaratingly** *adv* —**exhilaration** /ig zíllə ráysh'n/ *n* —**exhilarative** /ig zíllərətiv/ *adj* —**exhilarator** *n*

~~**exhilerating**~~ incorrect spelling of **exhilarating**

~~**exhileration**~~ incorrect spelling of **exhilaration**

exhort /ig záwrt/ *v* (*formal*) **1** *vt* to urge somebody strongly and earnestly to do something **2** *vi* to give somebody urgent or earnest advice [14C. Directly or via French < Latin *exhortari* 'encourage thoroughly' < *hortari* 'encourage, urge'.] —**exhortative** /ig záwrtətiv/ *adj* —**exhorter** *n*

exhortation /égz awr táysh'n/ *n* (*formal*) **1** something said or written in order to urge somebody strongly to do something **2** the giving of earnest advice or encouragement

exhume /eks hyoóm, ig zyoóm/ (**-humes, -huming, -humed**) *vt* **1** to dig up a corpse from a grave. ◊ **disentomb 2** to reveal, re-establish, or refer again to something long forgotten or neglected ○ *Cultures are re-invented and dead traditions exhumed for the tourists.* [15C. < medieval Latin *exhumare* < *humare* 'bury' < Latin *humus* 'ground, earth'.] —**exhumation** /éks hyoo máysh'n, ég zyoo-/ *n* —**exhumer** *n*

~~**exibition**~~ incorrect spelling of **exhibition**

exigency /éksijənssi, ig zíjjənssi/ (*plural* **-cies**), **exigence** /éksijənss/ *n* (*formal*) **1** something that a situation demands or makes urgently necessary and that puts pressure on the people involved (*often plural*) ○ *unable to cope with the exigencies of political life* **2** a difficult situation requiring urgent action [Late 16C. < late Latin *exigentia* < Latin *exigent-*, present participle of *exigere* 'to demand' (see EXACT).]

exigent /éksijənt/ *adj* (*formal*) **1** needing immediate action **2** making heavy demands on somebody ○ *suffered at the hands of an exigent schoolmaster* [Early 17C. < Latin *exigent-* (see EXIGENCY).] —**exigently** *adv*

exiguous /ig zíggyoo əss, ik sígg-/ *adj* scanty or meagre (*formal*) ○ *eking out their exiguous supplies* [Mid-17C. < Latin *exiguus* < *exigere* 'weigh precisely, measure' (see EXACT).] —**exiguity** /éksi gyoó əti/ *n* —**exiguously** *adv* —**exiguousness** *n*

exile /égz īl, éks-/ *n* **1 ABSENCE FROM YOUR OWN COUNTRY** unwilling absence from your own country or home, whether enforced by a government or court as a punishment, or imposed for political or religious reasons **2 SOMEBODY LIVING OUTSIDE HIS OR HER OWN COUNTRY** a citizen of one country who is forced to live in another **3 BANISHMENT FROM HOME OR COUNTRY** official expulsion from a home country or area, sometimes to a specified place, as a punishment ■ *vt* (**-iles, -iling, -iled**) **BANISH SOMEBODY FROM HOME OR COUNTRY** to order somebody to leave and stay away from his or her own country or home as a punishment [14C. Via French < Latin *exilium* 'banishment' < *exul* 'banished person'.] —**exilic** /eg zíllik, ek síllik/ *adj*

exine /éksin, ék sīn/ *n* the outer layer of a pollen grain or other spore [Late 19C. < ?]

exist /ig zíst/ *vi* **1 BE** to be, especially to be a real, actual, or current thing, not merely something imagined or written about ○ *Does life exist on other planets?* **2 LIVE** to be alive or continue to live ○ *Humans need water and food to exist.* **3 OCCUR** to be present or found in a particular place or situation ○ *Shortages on products in high demand exist.* **4 SURVIVE** to manage to survive or stay alive ○ *The lost hikers existed for two days on berries.* **5 LIVE AN UNSATISFACTORY LIFE** to live an unsatisfactory, joyless, or humdrum life, as opposed to an exciting or meaningful one [Early 17C. Probably back-formation < EXISTENCE.]

~~**existance**~~ incorrect spelling of **existence**

existence /ig zístənss/ *n* **1 BEING REAL** the state of being real, actual, or current, rather than imagined, invented, or obsolete ○ *evidence for the existence of other worlds* **2 PRESENCE IN A PLACE OR SITUATION** the presence or occurrence of something in a particular place or situation ○ *discovered the existence of the bacterium in sheep* **3 WAY OF LIVING** a way of living, especially a life of severe hardship ○ *scratch out a pitiable existence* **4 EVERYTHING** all living things (*literary*) ○ *hymns that celebrate the wonder of existence* **5 SINGLE LIVING THING** something that lives or exists (*literary or archaic*) [14C. Directly or via French < late Latin *existentia* < Latin *ex(s)istere* 'emerge, come into being' < *sistere* 'cause to stand firm'.]

existent /ig zístənt/ *adj* (*formal*) **1 REAL** real or actual, not imagined or invented **2 CURRENT** currently existing or in operation ■ *n* **REAL THING** a real or living thing (*formal*)

existential /égzi sténsh'l, éksi-/ *adj* **1 RELATING TO HUMAN EXISTENCE** concerned with or relating to existence, especially human existence **2 CRUCIAL IN SHAPING INDIVIDUAL DESTINY** in the context of existentialism, involved in or vital to the shaping of an individual's self-chosen mode of existence and moral stance with respect to the rest of the world **3 GOVERNED BY THE EXISTENTIAL QUANTIFIER** governed by the existential quantifier and thus asserting the existence of something by saying that there is at least one object that possesses the properties specified ■ *n* **EXISTENTIAL PROPOSITION** a proposition governed by the existential quantifier —**existentially** *adv*

existentialism /égzi sténsh'l izəm, ékzi-/ *n* a 19th- and 20th-century philosophical movement that denies that the universe has any in-built meaning or purpose and requires individuals to take responsibility for their own actions and shape their own destinies [Mid-20C. < German *Existentialismus*, translation of Danish *existents-forhold* 'condition of existence'.] —**existentialist** *adj, n*

QUICK FACTS ON... **EXISTENTIALISM**

Key dates: early 19th to mid-20th centuries
Key locations: France, Germany
Key elements: emphasis on subjective, individual freedom; notion of absurdity of human existence in a meaningless universe; rejection of metaphysics, systematic reasoning, and objective standards of judgment; notion that existence precedes essence
Key figures: Søren Kierkegaard, Fyodor Dostoyevsky, Friedrich Nietzsche, Martin Heidegger, Jean-Paul Sartre, José Ortega y Gasset, Albert Camus
Key works: *Fear and Trembling* (Kierkegaard) 1846, *Notes from the Underground* (Dostoyevsky) 1864, *Thus Spake Zarathustra* (Nietzsche) 1883–85, *Being and Time* (Heidegger) 1927, *The Myth of Sisyphus* (Camus) 1942, *Being and Nothingness* (Sartre) 1943
Key developments: expressionism, deconstructionism, nihilism, Dada

existential quantifier *n* the logical constant, frequently symbolized as 'Ex', that is a prefix to another clause and that is read as saying 'there is at least one object such that'. ◊ **universal quantifier**

existing /ig zísting/ *adj* currently present, in operation, or available ○ *Existing legislation is inadequate to cover these cases.*

ϟ **exit** /éksit, égzit/ *n* **1 MEANS OF LEAVING A PLACE** a door or other means of leaving a room or building **2 DEPARTURE** an act of leaving a room, building, or gathering **3 DEATH** departure from life (*formal*) **4 ACTOR'S LEAVING OF THE STAGE** an actor's departure from the stage **5 PLACE FOR LEAVING A MOTORWAY** a slip road by which a vehicle can leave a motorway or other main road with limited access **6 TERMINATION OF A COMPUTER OPERATION** an act of terminating a computer operation ■ *v* **1** *vti* **LEAVE** to leave something such as a room, building, or gathering ○ *In the event of a fire, exit the building at the rear.* **2** *vi* **DIE** to cease to live (*literary*) **3** *vi* **GO OFFSTAGE** to leave the stage during a performance of a play (*refers to an actor*) ◊ **exeunt 4** *vti* **TERMINATE A COMPUTER PROGRAM** to terminate the running of a computer operating system, program, or routine in a program [Mid-16C. < Latin *exitus* 'departure' < past participle of *exire* 'go out' < *ire* 'go'.]

exit permit *n* a permit granted to a banned person in South Africa during apartheid rule, allowing the person to leave the country without right of return

exit poll *n* a poll designed to give an early indication of the result of an election, conducted by asking people how they voted as they leave the place of voting

ex libris /éks leébriss/ *adv* from the library of the person whose name follows (*on bookplates*) [< Latin, 'from the books (of)']

Exmoor /éks moor, -mawr/ *n* **1** = **Exmoor pony 2** = **Exmoor sheep**

Exmoor National Park /éks moor-, éks mawr-/ national park in a moorland region of SW England. Area: 692 sq. km/267 sq. mi.

Exmoor pony *n* a small sturdy pony with a long thick mane and a light brown muzzle, belonging to a breed originating on Exmoor

Exmoor sheep *n* a sheep with horns and short wool, belonging to a breed originating on Exmoor

Exmouth /éksməth/ **1** port at the mouth of the River Exe, in SW England. Population: 28,414 (1991). **2** town overlooking Exmouth Gulf on the coast of Western Australia. Population: 3,128 (1991).

Exmouth Gulf inlet of the Indian Ocean in NW Western Australia. Area: 3,000 sq. km/1,158 sq. mi.

ex nihilo /eks nīhilō/ *adv, adj* from or out of nothing (*formal*) [Late 16C. < Latin.]

exo- *prefix* outside, external ○ *exothermic* [< Greek *exō* < *ex* 'out' < Indo-European]

exobiology /éksō bī óllәji/ *n* a branch of biology concerned with the possibility that life forms exist on other planets and with the problems of adapting the Earth's life forms to alien environments —**exobiological** /-bī ə lójjik'l/ *adj* —**exobiologist** *n*

exocarp /éksō kaarp/ *n* the outer layer of the fruit wall (**pericarp**)

Exocet /éksō set/ *tdmk* a trademark for a French-manufactured surface-to-surface guided missile with a high-explosive warhead, used by Argentinian forces against the British task force in the Falklands War of 1982

exocrine /éksō krīn, -krin/ *adj* describes glands such as sweat glands or salivary glands that release a secretion through a duct to the surface of an organ. ◊ **endocrine** [Early 20C. < EXO- + Greek *krinein* 'to separate'.]

exocrine gland *n* a gland that releases a secretion through a duct to the surface of an organ

exocyclic /éksō sīklik, -síklik/ *adj* situated outside a chemical ring structure ○ *an exocyclic bond*

exocytosis /éksō sī tóssiss/ *n* the release of substances contained in a sac (**vesicle**) within a cell by a process in which the membrane surrounding the sac unites with the membrane forming the outer wall of the cell —**exocytotic** /-sī tóttik/ *adj*

exodontics /éksō dóntiks/, **exodontia** /éksō dónshə/ *n* the branch of dentistry concerned with extracting teeth (+ *singular verb*) [Early 20C. < EXO- + Greek *odont-* 'tooth'.] —**exodontist** *n*

exodus /éksədəss/ *n* a departure or going out or away from a place that involves large numbers of people [Pre-12C. Via ecclesiastical Latin, '(biblical Book of) Exodus' < Greek, 'way out' < *hodos* 'way, road'.]

Exodus *n* **1** the second book of the Bible, which describes the flight of the Israelites from Egypt and Moses receiving the Ten Commandments on Mount Sinai **2** the flight of Moses and the Israelites from Egypt, as described in the second book of the Bible

exoenzyme /éksō én zīm/ *n* an enzyme that acts outside the cell that secretes it

exoergic /éksō úrjik/ *adj* PHYS = **exothermic** [Mid-20C. < EXO- + Greek *ergon* 'work'.]

ex officio /éks ə físhi ō/ *adv, adj* as a result of the official position somebody holds ○ *Heads of state are often ex officio heads of the armed forces* [Mid-16C. < Latin, 'out of duty, on account of office'.]

exogamy /ek sóggəmi/ *n* **1** the custom in some societies of marrying outside their people's own tribe, clan, or social group **2** the fusion of sex cells (**gametes**) of organisms not closely related, as occurs in cross pollination and outbreeding —**exogamous** *adj*

exogenic /éksō jénnik/ *adj* formed, located, or happening on the Earth's surface. ◊ **endogenic**

exogenous /ek sójjənəss/ *adj* originating outside an organism or system. ◊ **endogenous** *adj.* **2** [Mid-19C. < modern Latin *exogena* 'growing on the outside' < Greek *genēs* 'born'.] —**exogenously** *adv*

exon[1] /éks on/ *n* a discontinuous sequence of DNA that codes for protein synthesis and carries the genetic code for the final messenger RNA molecule. ◊ **intron** [Late 20C. < shortening of *expressed*.]

exon[2] /éks on/ *n* any of four officers who command the Yeomen of the Guard in London [Mid-18C. Representing pronunciation of French *exempt* 'exempt' (from ordinary military duties).]

exonerate /ig zónnə rayt/ (**-ates, -ating, -ated**) *vt* **1** to declare officially that somebody is not to blame or is not guilty of wrongdoing **2** to relieve somebody from an obligation or responsibility [15C. < Latin *exonerat-*, past participle of *exonerare* 'take off a burden' < *onus* 'burden'.] —**exoneration** /ig zónnə ráysh'n/ *n* —**exonerative** *adj*

exonuclease /éksō nyóokli ayz, -ayss/ *n* an enzyme that breaks down a nucleic acid by detaching the terminal nucleotides from the end of a chain

exophthalmos /éks of thálməss/, **exophthalmus, exophthalmia** /-thálmi ə/ *n* abnormal protrusion of the eyeball, sometimes resulting from an aneurysm [Early 17C. Directly or via modern Latin < Greek *exophthalmos* '(condition of) the eye being outside' < *ophthalmos* 'eye'.] —**exophthalmic** *adj*

exor. *abbr* executor

exorbitant /ig záwrbitənt/ *adj* **1** far greater or higher than is reasonable ○ *exorbitant prices* **2** going beyond what is reasonable, proper, or manageable [15C. < ecclesiastical Latin *exorbitant-*, present participle of *exorbitare* 'go out of the track' < Latin *orbita* 'track' < *orbis* 'circle'.] —**exorbitance** *n* —**exorbitantly** *adv*

exorcise *vt* = **exorcize**

exorcism /éks awr sizəm/ *n* **1 DRIVING OUT OF EVIL SPIRITS** the use of prayer or religious ritual to drive out evil spirits **2 CEREMONY TO DRIVE OUT EVIL SPIRITS** a religious ceremony in which somebody endeavours to drive out an evil spirit believed to be possessing a person or place **3 THING DONE TO EXPEL EVIL** a special ritual or spoken formula used with the intention of driving out evil spirits **4 CLEARING THE MIND OF OPPRESSIVE FEELINGS** the act of ridding the mind of oppressive feelings or memories [14C. Via ecclesiastical Latin < ecclesiastical Greek *exorkismos* < *exorkizein* (see EXORCIZE).] —**exorcist** *n*

exorcize /éks awr sīz, éksər-/ (**-cizes, -cizing, -cized**), **exorcise** (**-cises, -cising, -cised**) *vt* **1 FREE A PERSON OR PLACE FROM EVIL** to use prayers and religious rituals with the intention of ridding a person or place of the presence or influence of evil spirits **2 SEND EVIL AWAY** to use prayers and religious rituals with the intention of driving away an evil spirit believed to have been possessing a person or place **3 GET RID OF AN OPPRESSIVE FEELING** to clear the mind of a painful or oppressive feeling or memory [15C. Directly or via French < ecclesiastical Latin *exorcizare* < Greek *exorkizein* 'swear out (an evil spirit)' < *orkos* 'oath'.] —**exorcizer** *n*

exordium /ek sáwrdi əm/ (*plural* **-ums** *or* **-a** /-di ə/) *n* an opening section, especially of a lecture or a piece of scholarly writing (*formal*) [Late 16C. < Latin, < *exordiri* 'begin'.] —**exordial** *adj*

exoskeleton /éksō skéllitən/ *n* a hard covering on the outside of many organisms such as crustaceans, insects, turtles, and armadillos that provides support and protection —**exoskeletal** *adj*

exosmosis /éks oz mósiss/ *n* movement of fluid towards a solution of lower concentration, as is the case when water percolates through a cell membrane into the medium surrounding the cell [Mid-19C. < French *exosmose* < Greek *ōsmos* 'act of pushing'.] —**exosmotic** /-móttik/ *adj*

exosphere /éksō sfeer/ *n* the outermost region of the atmosphere of the Earth or another planet —**exospheric** /éksō sférrik/ *adj*

exostosis /éksō stóssiss/ (*plural* **-ses** /-seez/) *n* an abnormal benign bony growth on the surface of a bone or a tooth root, caused by inflammation or repeated trauma [Late 16C. < Greek, 'bony outgrowth' < *osteon* 'bone'.]

exoteric /éksō térrik/ *adj* capable of being understood by most people, not just an informed or select minority (*formal*) [Mid-17C. Via Latin < Greek *exōterikos* < *exōterō* 'outer' < *exō* 'outside'.] —**exoterically** *adv*

exothermic /éksō thúrmik/, **exothermal** /-thúrm'l/ *adj* describes a reaction that produces heat (*preferred term in nuclear physics is 'exoergic'*) [Late 19C. < French *exothermique* < Greek *thermē* 'heat'.] —**exothermically** *adv*

exotic /ig zóttik/ *adj* **1** STRIKINGLY DIFFERENT strikingly unusual and often very colourful and exciting or suggesting distant countries and unfamiliar cultures **2** FROM DISTANT COUNTRY from or relating to distant, especially tropical, places ○ *exotic fruits* **3** FROM ELSEWHERE introduced from another place or region ○ *an exotic species* ■ *n* EXOTIC PERSON OR THING a person or thing that is foreign and unusual, especially a plant or animal [Late 16C. Via Latin *exoticus* < Greek *exōtikos* < *exō* 'out, outside'.] —**exotically** *adv* —**exoticism** /ig zóttissizəm/ *n* —**exoticness** *n*

exotica /ig zóttikə/ *npl* exotic or extraordinary things, especially when forming a collection [Late 19C. < Latin, form of *exoticus* (see EXOTIC).]

exotic dancer *n* a striptease artist

exotoxin /éksō tóksin/ *n* a highly potent soluble toxin produced by a bacterium and released into its infected host, often affecting the central nervous system

exp *symbol* exponential function

exp. *abbr* **1** experiment **2** experimental **3** expired **4** expires **5** export **6** exported **7** express

expand /ik spánd/ *v* **1** *vti* MAKE OR BECOME LARGER to become or cause something to become larger in size, scope, or extent, or greater in number or amount **2** *vti* INCREASE IN SIZE OR VOLUME to increase or cause something to increase in size or volume as a result of a rise in temperature or decrease in pressure **3** *vti* OPEN OUT to open out or open something out wider after being kept folded in **4** *vti* DESCRIBE SOMETHING MORE FULLY to explain or describe something more fully, usually by giving more detail ○ *If you expanded that argument a little, it would fill another chapter.* ○ *The film expands on themes familiar from her earlier work.* **5** *vt* GIVE THE FULL FORM OF ABBREVIATION to give the full form of something such as the abbreviation of a word **6** *vi* RELAX to relax and become friendlier and more talkative (*formal*) **7** *vt* REWRITE A MATHEMATICAL EXPRESSION to rewrite a mathematical expression as the sum or product of its terms, e.g. $(x+1)(x-1)+2x$ expands to x^2+2x-1 [15C. Directly or via Anglo-Norman < Latin *expandere* 'spread out' < *pandere* 'spread'.] —**expandability** /ik spándə bílləti/ *n* —**expandable** *adj* —**expander** *n* —**expansibility** *n* —**expansible** /ik spánssəb'l/ *adj*

SYNONYMS See ***increase***.

expanded /ik spándid/ *adj* **1** MADE LARGER extended, unfolded, or outstretched **2** MADE INTO FOAM describes plastics made into a lightweight solid foam by the introduction of gas during the manufacturing process ○ *expanded polyurethane* **3** WIDER THAN USUAL describes typefaces or printed characters that are wider than usual in relation to their height

expanded metal *n* strong metal mesh made by cutting slits in sheet metal and stretching it out of shape, used as a reinforcing material in construction

expanse /ik spánss/ *n* a wide area or surface, especially of sea, land, or sky [Mid-17C. < modern Latin *expansum* 'firmament' < past participle of Latin *expandere* (see EXPAND).]

expansile /ik spán sīl/ *adj* **1** relating to expansion or the ability to expand **2** able to expand or be expanded

expansion /ik spánsh'n/ *n* **1** PROCESS OF BECOMING ENLARGED the process of increasing, or increasing something, in size, extent, scope, or number ○ *This site does not give us enough room for expansion.* **2** INCREASE an increase, or the amount by which something increases, in size, extent, or scope ○ *Geologists measured the expansion of the volcanic island.* **3** INCREASE IN DIMENSIONS an increase in the dimensions of something as a result of a rise in temperature or decrease in pressure **4** GROWTH BY ACQUISITION the increase of a country's size by the acquisition of new territory ○ *westward expansion* **5** FULLER TREATMENT a fuller or more detailed treatment or version of something ○ *The expansion of 'Dr' is 'Doctor'.* **6** COMBUSTION STAGE IN AN ENGINE a stage in an engine cycle during which the fuel and air mixture explodes, thereby increasing in volume and providing power **7** EXPANDED MATHEMATICAL EXPRESSION the result of expanding a mathematical expression

expansionary /ik spánsh'nəri/ *adj* bringing about expansion, especially economic or territorial expansion

⚡**expansion board** *n* COMPUT = **expansion card**

expansion bolt *n* a bolt with an attachment on the screw end that expands as the bolt is tightened, thereby securing it

⚡**expansion card** *n* a printed circuit board adding features or capability to a computer

expansionism /ik spánsh'nizəm/ *n* a policy of expanding a country's economy or territory —**expansionist** *n*, *adj* —**expansionistic** /ik spánshə nístik/ *adj*

expansion joint *n* a gap between adjacent parts or surfaces, e.g. between the concrete sections that form the road surface of a bridge, to prevent buckling when they expand under heat

⚡**expansion slot** *n* a receptacle for an expansion card that interfaces with a computer's internal circuitry

expansive /ik spánssiv/ *adj* **1** COMMUNICATIVE willing to talk openly and at some length, usually in a relaxed and jovial way ○ *He gradually became more expansive once he got to know us.* **2** EXTENSIVE covering a wide area or broad in scope (*formal*) ○ *a large house with expansive grounds* **3** EXPANDING capable of, having a tendency to, or typically undergoing expansion ○ *polymers with expansive capability* **4** WITH OUTSTRETCHED ARMS with the arms stretched out and open wide ○ *an expansive gesture* **5** LAVISH generous, lavish, or extravagant in scale ○ *an expansive lifestyle* **6** HAVING EXAGGERATED FEELINGS OF SELF-WORTH characterized by extreme feelings of euphoria and delusions of grandeur or self-importance —**expansively** *adv* —**expansiveness** *n* —**expansivity** /ék span sívvəti/ *n*

ex parte /eks paárti/ *adj*, *adv* made or undertaken on behalf of only one of the parties involved in a court case [Early 17C. < Latin, 'from a (or the) side'.]

expat /éks pát/ *n* an expatriate (*informal*) [Mid-20C. Shortening.]

expatiate /ek spáyshi ayt/ (**-ates, -ating, -ated**) *vi* to speak or write about something at length ○ *We had to listen to him expatiating on the shortcomings of our system.* [Mid-16C. < Latin *ex(s)patiat-*, past participle of *ex(s)patiari* 'walk out' < *spatiari* 'walk' < *spatium* 'space'.] —**expatiation** /ek spáyshi áysh'n/ *n*

expatriate *n* /eks páttri ət, -páytri-, -ayt/ **1** SOMEBODY WHO HAS MOVED ABROAD a citizen who has left his or her own country to live in another, usually for a prolonged period **2** SOMEBODY WITHOUT CITIZENSHIP a citizen who has renounced or has had repealed his or her citizenship ■ *adj* /eks páttri ət, -páytri-, -ayt/ RELATING TO THOSE LIVING ABROAD relating to people who live abroad ■ *v* /eks páttri ayt, -páytri-/ (**-ates, -ating, -ated**) **1** *vi* SETTLE ABROAD to settle in another country **2** *vti* TAKE AWAY SOMEBODY'S CITIZENSHIP to deprive somebody of native citizenship, or renounce native citizenship voluntarily **3** *vt* EXPEL SOMEBODY FROM HIS OR HER OWN COUNTRY to send somebody away from his or her own country as a punishment [Mid-18C. < Latin *expatriat-*, past participle of *expatriare* 'leave your native land' < *patria* 'native land' < *pater* 'father'.] —**expatriation** /eks páttri áysh'n, -páytri-/ *n*

expect /ik spékt/ *v* **1** *vti* CONFIDENTLY BELIEVE to believe with confidence, or think it likely, that an event will happen in the future ○ *A few setbacks along the way were only to be expected.* **2** *vt* WAIT FOR AN ANTICIPATED THING to wait for, or look forward to, something that you believe is going to happen or arrive ○ *We'll expect you late morning, then.* ○ *I'm expecting a visit from them any day now.* **3** *vt* DEMAND SOMETHING AS A RIGHT OR DUTY to demand or anticipate receiving something because of a perceived right to it or because it is due or appropriate ○ *They expect you to abide by their rules.* **4** *vti* BE GOING TO HAVE A BABY to be pregnant with or look forward to the birth of a child (*informal; only in progressive tenses*) ○ *She is expecting her third in July.* [Mid-16C. < Latin *ex(s)pectare* 'look out for' < *spectare* 'look at' < *specere* 'to look'.] —**expectable** *adj* —**expectably** *adv* —**expectedly** *adv* —**expectedness** *n*

USAGE See ***envisage***.

expectancy /ik spéktənssi/ (*plural* **-cies**), **expectance** /ik spéktənss/ *n* **1** excited awareness that something is about to happen ○ *An air of expectancy hung over the crowd.* **2** something expected, especially an amount or length of time expected on the basis of statistical calculations

expectant /ik spéktənt/ *adj* **1** EXCITEDLY ANTICIPATING excitedly aware that something is about to happen **2** EXPECTING A BABY expecting the birth of a baby **3** EXPECTING SOMETHING FAVOURABLE expecting something, especially something that will bring success or wealth (*formal*) [14C. Directly or via French < Latin *ex(s)pectant-*, present participle of *ex(s)pectare* (see EXPECT).]

expectantly /ik spéktəntli/ *adv* in the expectation that something interesting, exciting, or pleasurable will happen

expectation /éks pek táysh'n/ *n* **1** ANTICIPATION OF SOMETHING HAPPENING a confident belief or strong hope that a particular event will happen **2** NOTION a mental image of something expected, often compared to its reality (*often plural*) ○ *All our expectations of a quiet evening at home were dashed by the arrival of guests.* **3** EXPECTED STANDARD a standard of conduct or performance expected by or of somebody (*often plural*) ○ *Her work wasn't up to expectations so she was dismissed.* **4** = **expectancy** *n.* 1 ■ **expectations** *npl* PROSPECTS FOR THE FUTURE somebody's likely prospects of wealth or success in the future

LITERARY LINK ***Great Expectations***, a novel (1861) by Charles Dickens. It is the story of the orphan Pip, his early encounter with the convict Magwitch, and his love for the beautiful Estella, who lives with her eccentric guardian Miss Havisham. Pip subsequently receives a fortune from an unknown benefactor and moves to London, but is forced to return penniless to the humble blacksmith's home where he grew up.

expected value *n* the value of a random variable that is most likely to occur, calculated by taking the sum of every possible value multiplied by a factor representing the probability of its occurrence

expectorant /ik spéktərənt/ *adj* causing phlegm to be coughed up ■ *n* a medicine that stimulates the production of phlegm. Use: treatment of coughs.

expectorate /ik spéktə rayt/ (**-rates, -rating, -rated**) *vti* to cough up and spit out phlegm, thus clearing the bronchial passages [Early 17C. < Latin *expectorat-*, past participle of *expectorare* 'get out of the chest' < *pectus* 'chest, breast'.] —**expectoration** /ik spéktə ráysh'n/ *n*

expediency /ik speédi ənssi/ (*plural* **-cies**), **expedience** /-ənss/ *n* **1** the use of methods that bring the most immediate benefits, based on practical rather than moral considerations **2** the usefulness, appropriateness, or advisability of something, especially of a particular action or type of behaviour in a particular situation ○ *doubts about the expediency of such a course in the present crisis* **3** = **expedient** *n.*

expedient /ik speédi ənt/ *adj* **1** APPROPRIATE appropriate, advisable, or useful in a situation that requires action **2** ADVANTAGEOUS advantageous for practical rather than moral reasons ○ *She changed her vote because it was expedient for her to do so.* ■ *n* SOMETHING ACHIEVING AIMS QUICKLY something done or a method used to achieve an aim quickly, regardless of whether it is fair, right, or wise in the long term [14C. Directly or via French < Latin *expedient-*, present participle of *expedire* (see EXPEDITE).] —**expediently** *adv*

expedite /ékspə dīt/ (**-dites, -diting, -dited**) *vt* (*formal*) **1** to insure that something takes place or is dealt with more quickly than usual **2** to deal with something, especially a business transaction, swiftly and efficiently [15C. < Latin *expedit-*, past participle of *expedire* 'set free' < *pes* 'foot'.] —**expediter** *n*

expedition /ékspə dísh'n/ *n* **1** ORGANIZED JOURNEY BY A GROUP a journey made by a group of people for a specific purpose, e.g. to explore unknown territory, to do scientific study, or to achieve a military objective ○ *a scientific expedition to the ocean floor* **2** PEOPLE MAKING EXPEDITION a group of people who go on an expedition together ○ *The expedition returned at the end of the month.* **3** OUTING a short journey, usually for a pleasurable purpose **4** PROMPTNESS speed, promptness, or efficiency in doing something ○ *carried out our errand with expedition* [15C. Directly or via French < Latin *expedition-* < *expedire* (see EXPEDITE).]

expeditionary /ékspə dísh'nəri/ *adj* sent to fight or do military service in another country ○ *an expeditionary force*

expeditious /ékspə díshəss/ *adj* speedy or carried out

promptly and efficiently —**expeditiously** *adv* —**expeditiousness** *n*

expel /ik spél/ (**-pels, -pelling, -pelled**) *vt* **1** to compel somebody to leave or give up membership of an institution such as a school, political party, or club ○ *expel a child from school* **2** to push or drive something out with force ○ *Air is expelled under pressure from outlets under the hovercraft's apron.* [14C. < Latin *expellere* 'drive out' < *pellere* 'beat, drive'.] —**expellable** *adj* —**expellee** /ik spél eé, éks pel eé/ *n* —**expeller** *n*

expellant /ik spéllənt/, **expellent** *adj* capable of expelling something, especially from the body ■ *n* a medicine that causes the body to get rid of something undesirable, especially intestinal worms

expellent *adj, n* MED = **expellant**

expence incorrect spelling of **expense**

expend /ik spénd/ *vt* **1** to use up time, energy, effort, or some other resource **2** to spend money or an amount of money (*formal*) [15C. < Latin *expendere* 'weigh out (money in payment)' < *pendere* 'weigh'.] —**expender** *n*

expendable /ik spéndəb'l/ *adj* **1 NOT WORTH PRESERVING** not worth preserving or saving for reuse **2 DISPENSABLE** easily sacrificed or dispensed with if the need arises or in order to achieve an aim ■ *n* **EXPENDABLE ITEM** an expendable person or thing —**expendability** /ik spéndə bíllәti/ *n*

expenditure /ik spéndichər/ *n* **1** an amount of money spent, as a whole or on a particular thing ○ *when income exceeds expenditure* **2** the consuming or using up of something ○ *the huge expenditure of time and human resources on this scheme* [Mid-18C. After *expenditor* 'somebody in charge of expenditure'.]

expense /ik spénss/ *n* **1 MONEY SPENT** the amount of money spent in order to buy or do something **2 VALUE OF RESOURCE USED** the value of a resource that has been used during the current accounting period and can be charged against revenues for that period **3 SOMETHING EXPENSIVE TO BUY** something that costs money, usually a lot of money, to buy, keep, or run **4 USING UP** the using up or loss of something ○ *preserved his integrity at the expense of his job* ■ **expenses** *npl* **BUSINESS EXPENDITURES** an amount of money that somebody spends for business purposes that is reimbursable by an employer or deductible from income tax [14C. Via Anglo-Norman < late Latin *expensa* < Latin *expendere* (see EXPEND).]

expense account *n* **1** a facility given by an employer that entitles an employee to be repaid for some or all of the expenses incurred in the course of his or her employment **2** the amount or a record of an employee's expenses during a particular period

expensive /ik spénssiv/ *adj* **1 COSTING A LOT** costing a lot of money **2 CHARGING A LOT** charging high prices **3 VERY DISADVANTAGEOUS** involving serious losses or disadvantage to a particular person or group ○ *an expensive first half for the home team* —**expensively** *adv* —**expensiveness** *n*

experiance incorrect spelling of **experience**

experience /ik speéri ənss/ *n* **1 INVOLVEMENT IN SOMETHING OVER TIME** active involvement in an activity or exposure to events or people over a period of time, leading to an increase in knowledge and skill **2 KNOWLEDGE AND SKILL ACQUIRED** the knowledge of and skill in something gained through being involved in it or exposed to it over a period of time ○ *Paper qualifications are no substitute for real-life experience.* **3 SOMETHING THAT HAPPENS** something that happens to somebody or an event that somebody is involved in ○ *an experience that changed his life* **4 DIRECT PERSONAL AWARENESS** direct personal awareness of or contact with a particular thing ○ *Very few of us remember our first experience of pain.* **5 SUM TOTAL OF AN INDIVIDUAL'S EXPERIENCES** the sum total of the things that have happened to an individual and of his or her past thoughts and feelings ○ *Nothing quite like this has ever been done before, at least not in my experience.* **6 KNOWLEDGE FROM OBSERVATION** knowledge acquired through the senses rather than through abstract reasoning ■ *vt* (**-ences, -encing, -enced**) **1 HAVE EXPERIENCE OF** to be exposed to, involved in, or affected by something ○ *the most thrilling ride I've ever experienced* **2 FEEL** to feel a particular sensation or emotion ○ *You might experience a tingling sensation in your face.* [14C. Via French < Latin *experientia* < *experiri* 'try out'.]

LITERARY LINK ***Songs of Experience***, a collection of poems (1794) by William Blake. Blake's *Songs of Innocence* (1789) described the world from the optimistic viewpoint of an innocent child. In this, its adult counterpart, he portrays a world of disease, poverty, and irredeemable corruption.

experienced /ik speéri ənst/ *adj* possessing knowledge and skill acquired through involvement in or exposure to something over a period of time ○ *an experienced pilot*

experiential /ik speéri énsh'l/ *adj* derived from or relating to experience as opposed to other methods of acquiring knowledge [Mid-17C. After a word such as INFERENTIAL.] —**experientially** *adv*

experiment *n* /ik spérrimənt/ **1 SCIENTIFIC TEST** a test, especially a scientific one, carried out in order to discover whether a theory is correct or what the results of a particular course of action would be ○ *experiments in parapsychology* **2 DOING SOMETHING NEW** an attempt to do something new or to see what will happen ○ *We switched to decaffeinated coffee as an experiment.* **3 USING OF REPEATED TRIALS AND TESTS** the use of tests and trials in order to make discoveries ○ *The most efficient way of working was developed by experiment.* ■ *vi* /ik spérrimənt, -ment/ **1 TRY NEW THINGS** to try out new methods of doing or using things ○ *a reluctance to experiment with new ingredients* **2 CARRY OUT A SCIENTIFIC TEST** to carry out a scientific test of a theory or process [14C. Directly or via Old French < Latin *experimentum* 'trial, test' < *experiri* 'try out'.] —**experimentation** /ik spérri men táysh'n/ *n* —**experimenter** *n*

experimental /ik spérriméntʼl/ *adj* **1 RELATING TO SOMETHING NEW AND UNTRIED** employing ideas, methods, or materials that have not been tried before ○ *a new, experimental form of treatment* **2 RELATING TO SCIENTIFIC EXPERIMENTS** relating to, involving, or based on scientific experiments **3 BASED ON EXPERIENCE AND EVIDENCE** based on experience and practical evidence rather than on ideas —**experimentally** *adv*

experimentalism /ik spérri mént'lizəm/ *n* the use of new techniques in artistic, literary, and musical works —**experimentalist** *n*

experimental psychology *n* the branch of psychology that studies the basic mechanisms of the mind, e.g. perception, thinking, learning, and memory, often using experiments with individuals in controlled situations

expert /éks purt/ *n* **SKILLED OR KNOWLEDGEABLE PERSON** somebody with a great deal of knowledge about, or skill, training, or experience in, a particular field or activity ○ *a medical expert* ■ *adj* **1 SKILFUL OR KNOWLEDGEABLE** having a great deal of knowledge about, or skill, training, or experience in, a particular field or activity ○ *an expert pizza maker* **2 GIVEN OR DONE BY AN EXPERT** given or done by somebody who is very knowledgeable or highly skilled, trained, or experienced [14C. Via French < Latin *expertus*, past participle of *experiri* 'try out'.] —**expertly** *adv* —**expertness** *n*

expertise /éks pur teéz/ *n* the skill, knowledge, or opinion of somebody who is an expert [Mid-19C. < French, < *expert* (see EXPERT).]

expert system *n* a computer program that applies artificial-intelligence methods to problem-solving

expert witness *n* an expert called to answer questions on the stand in a court of law in order to provide specialized information relevant to the case being tried

expiate /ékspi ayt/ (**-ates, -ating, -ated**) *vt* to make amends, show remorse, or suffer punishment for having done something wrong [Late 16C. < Latin *expiat-*, past participle of *expiare* 'atone completely' < *pius* 'dutiful'.] —**expiation** /ékspi áysh'n/ *n* —**expiator** *n* —**expiatory** /ékspi ətəri, ékspi áytəri/ *adj*

expiration date *n US* **1** = **expiry date** *n.* 1 **2** = **expiry date** *n.* 2

expiratory /ik spírətəri/ *adj* relating to the process of breathing out

expire /ik spír/ (**-pires, -piring, -pired**) *vi* **1 END OR BE NO LONGER VALID** to come to an end or be no longer valid or in operation ○ *My visa has expired.* **2 BREATHE OUT** exhale (*technical*) **3 DIE** to die or release a last breath (*formal or literary*) [14C. Via French < Latin *exspirare* 'breathe out' < *spirare* 'breathe'.] —**expiration** /ékspi ráysh'n/ *n*

expiry /ik spíri/ (*plural* **-ries**) *n* **1** the fact of coming to an end and being no longer valid after a certain period of time ○ *two weeks before the date of expiry* **2** death, especially the death of a person (*formal or literary*)

expiry date *n* **1** a date printed on the packaging of food and medicines that indicates the time after which they should not be used. US term **expiration date** *n.* 1 **2** the date after which a credit card is no longer valid. US term **expiration date** *n.* 2

explain /ik spláyn/ *v* **1** *vti* **GIVE DETAILS** to give an account of something with enough clarity and detail to be understood by somebody else ○ *I explained to him that we had no option.* **2** *vt* **CLARIFY MEANING OF** to make the meaning of something clear to somebody ○ *Can you explain this sentence to me?* **3** *vti* **GIVE REASON** to give the reason for something, often as justification for something that has happened **4** *vr* **OFFER JUSTIFICATION** to give reasons to justify personal behaviour or actions ○ *You'll have to explain yourself to the head teacher.* **5** *vr* **CLARIFY IDEAS** to express ideas or thoughts in a way that is easily understood ○ *I'm sorry, I'm not explaining myself very well.* [Early 16C. < Latin *explanare* 'flatten out, unfold' < *planus* 'flat, clear'.] —**explainable** *adj* —**explainer** *n*

explain away *vt* to give excuses, reasons, or explanations for something in an attempt to show that it is less serious, important, or problematic than it seems

explanation /éksplə náysh'n/ *n* **1 STATEMENT EXPLAINING SOMETHING** a statement giving reasons for something or details of something ○ *an explanation of how the machine works* **2 GIVING OF DETAILS OR REASONS** the giving of details about something or reasons for something **3 DISCUSSION TO END A MISUNDERSTANDING** a mutual discussion or clarification of something that removes misunderstandings or reconciles the parties [14C. < Latin *explanation-* < *explanare* (see EXPLAIN).]

explanatory /ik splánnətəri/, **explanative** /ik splánnətiv/ *adj* giving reasons or details that explain something ○ *an explanatory leaflet is enclosed* [Early 17C. < late Latin *explanatorius* < Latin *explanare* (see EXPLAIN).] —**explanatorily** *adv*

explant /ek spláant/ *vt* to remove living tissue from an organism and place it in a culture medium ■ *n* tissue removed from an organism and placed in a culture medium [Early 20C. After IMPLANT.] —**explantation** /éks plaan táysh'n/ *n*

expletive /ik spleétiv/ *n* **1 SWEARWORD** an exclamation, especially a swearword **2 WORD WITH NO MEANING** a word that carries no meaning but has a grammatical function in a sentence **3 MEANINGLESS WORD IN A LINE OF POETRY** a word added to a line of verse in order to fill it out, usually for the sake of the metre ■ *adj* **USED AS AN EXPLETIVE** functioning as an expletive in a sentence or poem [Early 17C. < late Latin *expletivus* < *explet-*, past participle of *explere* 'fill up' < *plere* 'fill'.]

expletory /ik spleétəri/ *adj* GRAM, LITERAT = **expletive** *adj.* [Late 17C. < Latin *explet-* (see EXPLETIVE).]

explicable /ik splíkəb'l, éksplik-/ *adj* able to be explained —**explicably** *adv*

explicate /ékspli kayt/ (**-cates, -cating, -cated**) *vt* **1** to explain something, especially a literary text, in a detailed and formal way **2** to explain and develop an idea or theory and show its implications [Early 16C. < Latin *explicat-*, past participle of *explicare* 'unfold' < *plicare* 'to fold'.] —**explication** /ékspli káysh'n/ *n* —**explicative** *adj* —**explicatively** *adv* —**explicator** *n* —**explicatory** /ik splíkətəri/ *adj*

explicit /ik splíssit/ *adj* **1 CLEAR AND OBVIOUS** expressing all details in a clear and obvious way, leaving no doubt as to the intended meaning ○ *explicit instructions* **2 DEFINITE** definite and unqualified rather than implied or guessed at ○ *I didn't have explicit knowledge of what was going on, but I knew that something was happening.* **3 SHOWING SEX** portraying nudity or sexual activity in an open and direct way **4 WITH ONLY INDEPENDENT VARIABLES** describes a mathematical function that contains only variables whose value is independent of the value of the other variables in the function [Early 17C. Directly or via French < Latin *explicitus*, past participle of *explicare* (see EXPLICATE).] —**explicitly** *adv* —**explicitness** *n*

USAGE explicit or **implicit**? ***Explicit*** means 'clear, obvious, and definite': *explicit directions; had explicit knowledge of the plot because of being a co-conspirator.* ***Implicit*** means 'implied or unstated but understood', 'absolute', and 'present as a necessary component': *nodding and smiling that signified implicit agreement with our position; implicit faith; the implicit confidentiality between physician and patient.*

explode /ik splód/ (**-plodes, -ploding, -ploded**) *v* **1** *vti* **BLOW UP OR BURST** to blow up or burst with a sudden release of chemical or nuclear energy and a loud noise, or cause something to blow up or burst explosively **2** *vti* **BURST OR SHATTER** to burst like a bomb or shatter into many pieces, or cause something to burst or shatter **3** *vi*

EXPRESS EMOTION to give vent to an emotion, suddenly or violently ○ *He exploded into roars of laughter.* **4** *vi* INCREASE DRAMATICALLY to increase suddenly in extent or severity in an uncontrolled way ○ *The growth rate in home ownership exploded.* **5** *vi* PRODUCE A VIVID DISPLAY to produce a vivid, often sudden display of light or colour ○ *Her late paintings explode with intense reds and oranges.* **6** *vi* COME SUDDENLY to appear or start as suddenly and forcefully as an explosion ○ *The band exploded onto the pop scene late last year.* **7** *vt* DISPROVE A THEORY to show that a belief or theory is completely wrong [Mid-16C. < Latin *explodere* 'drive off the stage by clapping' < *plaudere* 'clap'.] —**exploder** *n*

exploded /ik splṓdid/ *adj* showing the parts of something as separate items in a diagram, but with their relative positions maintained ○ *an exploded diagram*

exploit *vt* /ik splóyt/ **1** TAKE ADVANTAGE OF to take selfish or unfair advantage of a person or situation, usually for personal gain **2** USE FOR BENEFIT to use or develop something in order to gain a benefit ■ *n* /éks ployt/ NOTABLE ACT an interesting or daring action or achievement [Mid-16C. Via Old French, 'accomplishment' < Latin *explicitum*, past participle of *explicare* (see EXPLICATE).] —**exploitable** *adj* —**exploitative** *adj* —**exploitatively** *adv* —**exploitativeness** *n* —**exploiter** *n* —**exploitive** *adj* —**exploitively** *adv* —**exploitiveness** *n*

exploitation /éks ploy táysh'n/ *n* **1** unfair treatment or use of somebody or something, usually for personal gain **2** the use or development of something to produce a benefit

exploration /éksplə ráysh'n/ *n* **1** TRAVEL FOR DISCOVERY travelling to discover what a place is like or where it is ○ *polar exploration* **2** STUDY OR CONSIDERATION an investigation of something such as data or the consideration and testing of something such as possible courses of action **3** SEARCHING FOR NATURAL RESOURCES the testing of a number of places for natural resources, e.g. drilling or boring for samples that will be examined for possible mineral deposits **4** EXAMINATION FOR DIAGNOSIS the examination of a part of the body for the purpose of diagnosis

exploratory /ik splórrətəri, -spláwrə-/ *adj* involving exploration ○ *an exploratory mission* ○ *exploratory surgery*

explore /ik spláwr/ (**-plores, -ploring, -plored**) *v* **1** *vti* TRAVEL FOR DISCOVERY to travel to or in a place in order to discover what it is like or what is there **2** *vti* INVESTIGATE OR STUDY to make a careful investigation or study of something ○ *The committee is exploring all possible avenues of research.* **3** *vti* SEARCH A PLACE FOR NATURAL RESOURCES to make a search of an area for natural resources such as mineral deposits **4** *vt* EXAMINE SOMETHING FOR DIAGNOSIS to examine a part of the body in order to make a diagnosis [Mid-16C. Via French < Latin *explorare* 'search out' < *plorare* 'cry out'.] —**explorer** *n*

Explorer /ik spláwrər/ *n US* a Scout aged between 14 and 21 taking part in a programme run by the Boy Scouts of America that enables young people to gain work experience in a career in which they are interested

explosion /ik splṓzh'n/ *n* **1** SUDDEN NOISY RELEASE OF ENERGY the sudden loud release of energy and a rapidly expanding volume of gas that occurs when a bomb detonates or gas explodes **2** BURSTING OR SHATTERING a bursting with a loud noise, or a shattering of something into many pieces **3** SUDDEN BURST OF EMOTION a sudden release of intense feeling such as anger ○ *an explosion of rage* **4** DRAMATIC INCREASE a sudden and dramatic increase in the extent or severity of something, e.g. a population or an activity ○ *the explosion in e-mail subscriptions* **5** SUDDEN APPEARANCE the sudden and forceful appearance of somebody or something or sudden and forceful beginning of something **6** INTENSE DISPLAY a vivid, often sudden display of light or colour **7** PHON = **plosion** [Early 17C. < Latin *explosion-* < *explos-*, past participle of *explodere* (see EXPLODE).]

explosive /ik splṓssiv, -splṓz-/ *adj* **1** LIABLE TO EXPLODE able or serving to explode **2** OPERATED BY EXPLODING designed to explode or operated by means of something that explodes **3** LIKELY TO GENERATE VIOLENT ANGER likely to cause or erupt suddenly into angry disagreement or violence ○ *an explosive temperament* **4** SUDDEN AND DRAMATIC happening or appearing suddenly and dramatically ○ *The company capitalized on the explosive increase in the popularity of their new game.* **5** PHON = **plosive** *adj* ■ *n* **1** SOMETHING THAT EXPLODES any substance or device that suddenly produces a volume of rapidly expanding gas **2** PHON = **plosive** *n* —**explosively** *adv* —**explosiveness** *n*

expo /ékspō/ *n* a large exhibition or internationally sanctioned exposition [Mid-20C. Shortening of EXPOSITION.]

exponent /ik spṓnənt/ *n* **1** ADVOCATE a supporter or promoter of a cause **2** EXPLAINER an explainer or interpreter of something ○ *an exponent of Kant's philosophy* **3** PRACTITIONER OF AN ART OR SKILL a performer or practitioner of some art or skill, especially somebody who is regarded as an excellent example of how something should be done **4** INDICATOR OF THE TIMES TO MULTIPLY A NUMBER a number or variable placed to the upper right of a number or mathematical expression that indicates the number of times the number or expression is to be multiplied by itself, as in 2^3, which equals 8 [Late 16C. < Latin *exponent-*, present participle of *exponere* (see EXPOUND).]

exponential /ékspə nénsh'l, ékspō-/ *adj* **1** RELATING TO EXPONENT describes a mathematical entity such as a curve, function, equation, or series that contains, is expressed as, or involves numbers or quantities raised to an exponent **2** USING A BASE OF NATURAL LOGARITHMS describes a mathematical entity that involves the transcendental number *e*, the base of natural logarithms, raised to an exponent **3** RAPIDLY DEVELOPING rapidly becoming greater in size ○ *an exponential increase in sales* —**exponentially** *adv*

exponential function *n* (*symbol* **exp**) a mathematical expression with the formula e^x, in which *e* is the base of natural logarithms

exponential notation *n* SCI = **scientific notation**

exponentiation /ékspə nénshi áysh'n, ékspō-/ *n* the multiplication of a number or quantity by itself a given number of times, the number of times being the power to which the number or quantity is to be raised

⚡**export** *v* /ik spáwrt, éks pawrt/ **1** *vti* SEND GOODS ABROAD to send goods for sale or exchange to other countries **2** *vt* SPREAD CULTURE TO ANOTHER SOCIETY to cause the spread of ideas, values, or a way of life from one society, culture, or nation to another **3** *vt* ALTER THE FORMAT OF COMPUTER DATA to convert data from a computer program into a form suitable for a different program or environment ■ *n* /éks pawrt/ **1** SELLING OF GOODS ABROAD the selling of goods to other countries **2** PRODUCT SOLD ABROAD a product sold and transported to another country **3** TYPE OF SCOTTISH BEER a strong brown beer brewed in Scotland [15C. < Latin *exportare* 'carry away' < *portare* 'carry'.] —**exportability** /ik spáwrtə bílləti, éks pawrtə-/ *n* —**exportable** *adj* —**exportation** /éks pawr táysh'n/ *n* —**exporter** *n*

expose /ik spṓz/ (**-poses, -posing, -posed**) *v* **1** *vt* LET SOMETHING BE SEEN to uncover something or turn it over with the result that it can be seen ○ *expose the wound to the air* **2** *vt* PUT SOMEBODY IN AN UNPROTECTED SITUATION to put somebody or something in a vulnerable or potentially dangerous situation ○ *financially exposed* **3** *vt* MAKE SOMEBODY EXPERIENCE SOMETHING to cause somebody to have a personal and often enlightening experience of something **4** *vt* REVEAL SOMEBODY'S WRONGDOINGS to reveal that somebody has done something wrong, especially by publishing or broadcasting the information **5** *vr* REVEAL THE BODY INDECENTLY to uncover a part of the body, especially the genitals, in public in an indecent way **6** *vt* ALLOW LIGHT ONTO A FILM to allow light to fall on light-sensitive material such as photographic film **7** *vt* LEAVE A BABY TO DIE OUTSIDE especially in earlier societies, to abandon a baby to die in the open air, e.g. because it was not healthy **8** *vt* SHOW SOMETHING TO BE REVERED to display something for religious veneration, e.g. the Eucharist in a Roman Catholic service [15C. Via French *exposer* < (after *poser* 'to place') < Latin *exponere* 'set out' (see EXPOUND).] —**exposal** *n* —**exposer** *n*

exposé /ek spṓz ay/ (*plural* **-sés**) *n* **1** a book or article that reveals details of a scandal or crime **2** a formal and systematic statement giving facts about something [Early 19C. < French, past participle of *exposer* (see EXPOSE).]

exposed /ik spṓzd/ *adj* **1** VISIBLE OR UNPROTECTED uncovered and therefore visible or without protection ○ *Cover any exposed areas of skin liberally with sunscreen.* **2** WITH NO SHELTER unprotected from wind and weather by shelter from trees or higher ground **3** UNPROTECTED FROM HARM vulnerable to danger or harm **4** CARRIED OUT ON OPEN ROCK FACE carried out on a high, sheer, and open rock face ○ *an exposed ascent* —**exposedness** /ik spṓzidnəss, -spṓzd-/ *n*

exposition /ékspə zísh'n/ *n* **1** DETAILED DESCRIPTION OR DISCUSSION a detailed description of a theory, problem, or proposal discussing the issues involved, or a commentary on a written text discussing its meaning and implications **2** ACT OF DESCRIBING OR DISCUSSING the act of describing and discussing a theory, problem, or proposal or commenting on a written text **3** EXHIBITION OR FAIR a large exhibition, e.g. of industrial achievements, sometimes international in scope **4** OPENING SECTION OF A PIECE OF MUSIC the opening section of a piece of music, especially of a sonata or fugue, in which the principal themes are introduced **5** DISPLAYING SOMETHING TO THE PUBLIC the act of showing or displaying something such as a relic or the host for veneration **6** FACTUAL BACKGROUND OF NOVEL OR PLAY the basic facts of setting, period, character, or other relevant parts of a literary work, usually fictional or meant for the theatre [14C. Directly or via French < Latin *exposition-* < *exposit-*, past participle of *exponere* (see EXPOUND).] —**expositive** /ik spózzitiv/ *adj* —**expositor** *n* —**expository** *adj*

ex post facto /éks pōst fáktō/ *adj, adv* applying to events that have already occurred as well as to subsequent events [Mid-17C. < Latin *ex postfacto* 'from what is done afterwards'.]

expostulate /ik spóstyoo layt/ (**-lates, -lating, -lated**) *vi* to express disagreement or disapproval or attempt to dissuade somebody from doing something [Late 16C. < Latin *expostulat-*, past participle of *expostulare* 'demand from' < *postulare* 'to demand'.] —**expostulation** /ik spostyoo láysh'n/ *n* —**expostulator** *n* —**expostulatory** *adj*

SYNONYMS See ***object***.

exposure /ik spṓzhər/ *n* **1** CONTACT OR EXPERIENCE the experience of coming into contact with some environmental condition or social influence that has an effect, either harmful or beneficial **2** HARMFUL EFFECTS OF WEATHER the harmful effects of cold or other extreme weather conditions **3** PUBLICITY reporting of events by the broadcast or print media **4** REVELATION OF A SCANDAL OR IDENTITY the revelation of a scandal or of somebody's secrets or private information **5** TIME AND INTENSITY OF LIGHT an amount of light permitted to fall on light-sensitive material such as film or paper coated with emulsion **6** TAKING OF A PHOTOGRAPH the act or process of taking a photograph **7** FILM OR PLATE EXPOSED FOR PHOTOGRAPH a section of film or a photographic plate exposed to light in taking a photograph **8** POSITION OF A ROOM OR BUILDING the direction something faces or the way it is sited relative to sunlight or wind direction ○ *This room has a southern exposure.* **9** RISK OF FINANCIAL LOSS the state of being at risk of financial loss or the amount of possible financial loss involved **10** DEGREE EXPOSED TO THE WEATHER the extent to which a rock face is exposed to the weather **11** LEAVING OF A BABY TO DIE OUTDOORS the former practice in some societies of leaving a baby in the open to die, e.g. because it was not healthy **12** ROCKY OUTCROPPING the outcropping of bare rock in a landscape, enabling mapping of the underlying geology

exposure meter *n* a device for measuring the intensity of light for photography, often giving the value as a combination of shutter speed and lens aperture

expound /ik spównd/ *vti* to give a detailed description and explanation of a theory or viewpoint or an explanation of the meaning and implications of a written text [13C. Via Old French < Latin *exponere* 'explain, set out' < *ponere* 'to place'.] —**expounder** *n*

express /ik spréss/ *v* **1** *vt* SAY to state thoughts or feelings in words ○ *I'd like to express my gratitude to everyone.* **2** *vt* SHOW MEANING SYMBOLICALLY to convey meaning by gesture, behaviour, representation in art or drama, or in some other symbolic way **3** *vr* REVEAL THOUGHTS to make thoughts and feelings known to others ○ *able to express herself through her music* **4** *vt* REPRESENT SOMETHING AS A SYMBOL to use a symbol, figure, or formula to represent something such as a quantity in a different way ○ *Express the fractions as decimal numbers.* **5** *vt* SQUEEZE SOMETHING OUT to force a liquid out of something by squeezing or pressing (*formal*) **6** *vt* SEND SOMETHING BY SPECIAL FAST DELIVERY to send a package or message using a special rapid-delivery service **7** *vt* PRODUCE AN INHERITED CHARACTERISTIC to produce an observable inherited characteristic (*refers to genes*) ○ *Some genes are only expressed in adults.* ■ *adj* **1** DONE OR TRAVELLING VERY QUICKLY travelling, moving, or delivered quickly and directly to the destination **2** OF BRIEF TRANSACTIONS relating to purchases or other transactions that can be completed quickly and easily, e.g. because only one item or cash is involved **3** EXPLICIT stated in a clear unambiguous way ○ *his express wish* **4** SPECIFIC definitely, and usually exclusively, intended or specified ○ *formed for the express purpose of making a profit* ■ *adv* BY EXPRESS DELIVERY OR TRANSPORT by a special high-speed delivery service or an express train, bus, or similar mode of transport ■ *n* 1 FAST TRAIN OR BUS a fast train or bus that travels to its destination directly, making few or no stops on the way 2 FAST DELIVERY SERVICE a special fast delivery service or the organization providing it [14C. < medieval Latin *expressare* 'press out' and Latin *expressus* 'clearly evident' < Latin *exprimere* 'press out' < *premere* 'to press'.] —**expresser** *n* —**expressible** *adj*

expression /ik sprésh'n/ *n* 1 LOOK ON SOMEBODY'S FACE a look on somebody's face, conveying a thought or feeling 2 WORD OR PHRASE a word or phrase that communicates an idea 3 CONVEYING OF THOUGHTS OR FEELINGS the communication of thoughts or feelings, e.g. directly to another person ○ *a heart-rending expression of sorrow* 4 WAY OF COMMUNICATING something done or given as a means of communicating a feeling or thought to somebody else 5 INFLECTION IN THE VOICE somebody's intonation or tone of voice 6 INTERPRETIVE ELEMENT OF MUSIC the interpretive element of music, including tempo, dynamics, articulation, and phrasing, by which a player or singer evokes emotions 7 MATHEMATICAL REPRESENTATION a combination of constants, operators, and variables representing numbers or quantities 8 EXTRACTION OF LIQUID the pressing out of a liquid from a substance 9 EFFECT OR ACTION OF A GENE the effect or action produced by a gene —**expressional** *adj*

expressionism /ik sprésh'nizəm/ *n* 1 an artistic movement that flourished in Germany between 1905 and 1925 whose adherents sought to represent feelings and moods rather than objective reality, often distorting colour and form 2 a literary movement of the early 20th century, especially in the theatre, that represented external reality in a highly stylized and subjective manner, attempting to convey a psychological or spiritual reality rather than a record of actual events —**expressionist** *n, adj* —**expressionistic** /ik spréshə nístik/ *adj* —**expressionistically** *adv*

QUICK FACTS ON... **EXPRESSIONISM**

Key dates: 1905–25
Key locations: N Europe, especially Germany
Key elements: subjectivity; primacy of emotional expression; rejection of naturalism; use of simplified forms, compositional distortion, bright colours, bold brushwork
Key figures: Ernst Ludwig Kirchner, Emil Nolde, Franz Marc, August Macke, Paul Klee, Wassily Kandinsky, Oskar Kokoschka
Key works: *Self-Portrait with Model* (Kirchner) 1907, *Cossacks* (Kandinsky) 1910, *The Fate of the Animals* (Marc) 1913, *The Tempest, or The Bride of the Wind* (Kokoschka) 1914
Key developments: Die Brücke, Der Blaue Reiter, abstract expressionism, neoexpressionism

expressionless /ik sprésh'nləss/ *adj* showing no emotion or interest by the tone of voice or by the look on the face —**expressionlessly** *adv* —**expressionlessness** *n*

expression mark *n* a symbol or written direction, often in Italian, that indicates the expression to be used in performing a piece of music

expressive /ik spréssiv/ *adj* 1 FULL OF EXPRESSION expressing a great deal of feeling and meaning ○ *an expressive face* 2 CONVEYING MEANING communicating a particular meaning ○ *a gesture expressive of the utmost contempt* 3 OF SPEAKING AND WRITING relating to disorders involving the expression of ideas in speech and writing as opposed to the interpretation of what is heard or read —**expressively** *adv* —**expressiveness** *n*

expressivity /éks pre sívvəti/ (*plural* **-ties**) *n* 1 the ability or the extent to which somebody has the ability to communicate emotion or meaning 2 the extent to which a gene affects the observable characteristics (**phenotype**) of an organism

express lane *n US* TRANSP = **fast lane** *n.* 1

expressly /ik spréssli/ *adv* 1 having a deliberate and specific intention or purpose or somebody specific in mind 2 in a clear and unambiguous way ○ *He expressly rejected my offer.*

expresso *n* BEVERAGES = **espresso**

expressway /ik spréss way/ *n US* a limited-access road with several lanes in each direction, designed for fast direct travel especially through or round a city

expropriate /ik sprṓpri ayt/ (**-ates, -ating, -ated**) *vti* to take property or money from somebody, either legally for the public good or illegally by theft or fraud [Late 16C. < medieval Latin *expropriat-*, past participle of *expropriare* 'take away and make your own' < Latin *proprius* 'your own'.] —**expropriation** /ik sprṓpri áysh'n/ *n* —**expropriator** *n* —**expropriatory** *adj*

expulsion /ik spúlsh'n/ *n* 1 the act of compelling somebody to give up membership in or leave an institution such as a school, political party, or club, usually as a punishment 2 the forcing out of something or somebody from something ○ *expulsion of air from the lungs* [15C. < Latin *expulsion-* < *expuls-*, past participle of *expellere* (see EXPEL).] —**expulsive** *adj*

expunge /ik spúnj/ (**-punges, -punging, -punged**) *vt* 1 to delete or blot out something unwanted 2 to destroy or put an end to something [Early 17C. < Latin *expungere* 'prick out' < *pungere* 'mark with a point'; from the placing of points next to text to be deleted.] —**expunction** /ik spúngksh'n/ *n* —**expunger** *n*

expurgate /ékspər gayt/ (**-gates, -gating, -gated**) *vt* to remove words or passages considered offensive or unsuitable from a book before publication [Late 17C. < Latin *expurgat-*, past participle of *expurgare* 'cleanse out' < *purgare* 'purify'.] —**expurgation** /ékspər gáysh'n/ *n* —**expurgator** *n* —**expurgatorial** /ik spúrgə táwri əl/ *adj* —**expurgatory** /ek spúrgətəri/ *adj*

exquisite /ik skwízzit, ékskwizit/ *adj* 1 FINELY BEAUTIFUL very beautiful and delicate or intricate ○ *exquisite workmanship* 2 EXCELLENT perfect and delightful 3 SENSITIVE AND DISCRIMINATING sensitive and capable of detecting subtle differences ○ *exquisite taste in dress* 4 INTENSE felt with a sharp intensity ○ *exquisite pain* [Mid-16C. < Latin *exquisitus*, past participle of *exquirere* 'seek out' < *quaerere* 'seek, ask'.] —**exquisitely** *adv* —**exquisiteness** *n*

exsert /ek súrt/ *vt* to thrust out or project something ○ *A bee exserts its sting.* ■ *adj* **exsert, exserted** projecting beyond an enclosing or adjoining part ○ *an exsert stamen* [Early 19C. < Latin *exsert-*, past participle of *exserere* (see EXERT).] —**exsertion** *n*

ex-service *adj* 1 formerly enlisted in the armed forces 2 provided for or concerned with people who have served in the armed forces

ex-serviceman *n* a man formerly in the armed forces

ex-servicewoman *n* a woman formerly in the armed forces

ex silentio /éks si lénshō/ *adv* from or based on a lack of evidence to the contrary [Early 20C. < Latin, 'from silence'.]

ext. *abbr* 1 extension 2 exterior 3 external 4 extract

extant /ek stánt, ékstənt/ *adj* still in existence ○ *Three copies of the document are extant.* [Mid-16C. < Latin *exstant-*, present participle of *exstare* 'exist' < *stare* 'to stand'.]

SYNONYMS See ***living***.

~~**extasy**~~ incorrect spelling of **ecstasy**

extemporaneous /ik stémpə ráyni əss/, **extemporary** /ik stémpərəri/, **extemporal** /ik stémpərəl/ *adj* 1 DONE UNREHEARSED performed without any preparation 2 PREPARED BUT SAID WITHOUT NOTES prepared in advance but delivered without notes 3 SPEAKING UNREHEARSED speaking without preparation or notes 4 MAKESHIFT done as a temporary measure [Mid-17C. < late Latin *extemporaneus* < *ex tempore* 'out of the moment'.] —**extemporaneity** /ik stémpərə neé əti, -náy əti/ *n* —**extemporaneously** *adv* —**extemporaneousness** *n*

extempore /ik stémpəri/ *adj, adv* with little or no preparation [Mid-16C. < Latin *ex tempore* 'out of the moment'.]

extemporize /ik stémpə rīz/ (**-rizes, -rizing, -rized**), **extemporise** (**-rises, -rising, -rised**) *vti* 1 PERFORM SOMETHING WITHOUT PREPARATION to perform or speak without having made any preparation 2 IMPROVISE MUSIC to compose or perform a piece of music by improvising 3 HANDLE IN A MAKESHIFT WAY to do or devise something in a makeshift fashion [Mid-17C. < EXTEMPORE.] —**extemporization** /ik stémpə rī záysh'n/ *n* —**extemporizer** *n*

extend /ik sténd/ *v* 1 *vi* OCCUPY DISTANCE OR SPACE to continue for a distance or occupy a space, often within a particular range ○ *The city centre extends for another mile in both directions.* 2 *vi* CONTINUE FOR A TIME to last or continue for a period of time, usually a particular one 3 *vti* APPLY to affect or apply to somebody or something, or make something affect or apply ○ *The offer extends to new readers too.* 4 *vt* INCREASE SIZE to make something larger or longer ○ *extend the driveway* 5 *vt* INCREASE TIME SPAN to increase the length of time something lasts or the length of time before something applies or ceases to apply 6 *vt* INCREASE LIMITS to broaden or expand the range, influence, or scope of something ○ *a vital research project that will extend our knowledge of the disease* 7 *vt* INCREASE AN AMOUNT BY ADDING to increase the amount of something by adding something else to it ○ *There's not much stew left, but we could always extend it by adding more potatoes and vegetables.* 8 *vti* OPEN OUT INTO SPACE to stretch out into space, or stretch something out 9 *vt* OFFER OR GIVE to offer or provide something to somebody ○ *to extend the hand of friendship* 10 *vt* MAKE AN EXTRA EFFORT TO DO to work or make somebody or something work as hard as possible to achieve the best possible result ○ *They had to extend themselves to finish on time* 11 *vt* CALCULATE THE LINE TOTAL ON INVOICE to calculate the total on the line of an invoice by multiplying quantity by price [14C. < Latin *extendere* 'stretch out' < *tendere* 'hold out, stretch'.] —**extendability** /ik sténdə bílləti/ *n* —**extendable** *adj* —**extensibility** /ik sténssə bílləti/ *n* —**extensible** /ik sténssəb'l/ *adj* —**extensibly** /ik sténssəbli/ *adv* —**extensile** /ik stén sīl/ *adj*

SYNONYMS See ***increase***.

extended /ik sténdid/ *adj* 1 LENGTHIER THAN USUAL lasting longer than expected or planned 2 MADE LONGER OR LARGER stretched or pulled out, lengthened, enlarged, or expanded 3 HAVING A WIDER RANGE having wider influence, effect, or application 4 PRINTING = **expanded** *adj.* 3 —**extendedly** *adv*

ϟ**Extended Binary Coded Decimal Interchange Code** *n* full form of **EBCDIC**

extended family *n* the family as a unit embracing parents and children together with grandparents, aunts, uncles, cousins, and sometimes more distant relatives. ◊ **nuclear family**

extended-play *adj* (*not hyphenated after verbs*) 1 describes a video tape format that can record four or six hours of material on a two-hour tape 2 describes a vinyl record of the same size as a single but with two tracks on each side rather than one

extender /ik sténdər/ *n* 1 a substance that is added to a product to dilute it, add body to it, or modify it in other ways 2 the part of a lower-case letter such as 'p' or 'h' that projects above or below the body of the letter

extensimeter *n* MEASURE = **extensometer**

ϟ**extension** /ik sténsh'n/ *n* 1 ADDITION TO A BUILDING a room or area added to an existing building ○ *We're having an extension built onto the kitchen.* 2 ADDITIONAL PIECE a piece that has been or can be added, or that can be pulled out, to enlarge or lengthen something 3 ADDITIONAL TELEPHONE LINE an additional telephone line or telephone connected to the main line in a building or organization, often having its own number 4 TELEPHONE NUMBER OF AN EXTENSION the number used to contact a telephone extension within a building or organization 5 ELEC = **extension lead** 6 ADDITIONAL PERIOD OF TIME an additional period of time allowed for completion of work or payment of a debt ○ *You'll never finish that essay on time; why don't you ask for an extension?* 7 EXTENDED DRINKS LICENCE permission to serve alcoholic drinks until a later time than usual 8 EXTENDING OR BEING EXTENDED the act or process of increasing the size, scope, range, or application of something, or the fact of being increased in size, scope, range, or application 9 RANGE the range or sphere over which something extends 10 OFF-CAMPUS UNIVERSITY TEACHING PROGRAM courses or facilities provided by a college or university for people who are unable to attend classes on the campus or during scheduled class periods 11 MED = **traction** *n.* 1 12 STRAIGHTENING OF A LIMB the stretching out of a limb after it has been bent, or the position attained by a limb after stretching it 13 BROADER SENSE OF AN EXPRESSION the broad range of meaning of an expression, as opposed to its precise meaning 14 SET INCLUDING TWO SIMILAR SETS a mathematical set that includes as subsets all the members of a given set and of another similar set 15 COMPUT = **file extension** ■ **extensions** *npl* EXTRA HAIR ATTACHED TO YOUR OWN HAIR lengths of real or synthetic hair attached to the hair to create a longer hairstyle [Early 16C. < late Latin *extension-* < Latin *extens-*, past participle of *extendere* (see EXTEND).] —**extensional** *adj* —**extensionally** *adv*

extension cable *n* a cable that can be used to attach an extension lead to an electric supply when the lead itself is too short to reach it

extension lead *n* a length of electrical lead with a plug at one end and a socket at the other, used to connect an appliance when the electrical supply is some distance away

extensive /ik sténssiv/ *adj* **1 VAST** covering a large area ○ *a hotel set in extensive grounds* **2 BROAD IN SCOPE** great in extent, range, or application ○ *extensive research into a subject* **3 LARGE IN AMOUNT** great in amount or number **4 USING LOW TECHNOLOGICAL INPUT** relating to a farming practice in which a large area of land is cultivated using little labour and expense, resulting in a relatively small crop. ◊ **intensive** [Early 17C. Directly or via French < late Latin *extensivus* < Latin *extens-* (see EXTENSION).] —**extensively** *adv* —**extensiveness** *n*

extensometer /ék sten sómmitər/, **extensimeter** /-símmitər/ *n* a device for measuring small changes of length in a sample, especially those caused by stress or thermal expansion in a metal [Late 19C. < Latin *extens-* (see EXTENSION).]

extensor /ik sténssər, ik stén sawr/ *n* a muscle that straightens or extends a part of the body such as an arm or leg [Early 18C. < modern Latin, < Latin *extens-* (see EXTENSION).]

extent /ik stént/ *n* **1 RANGE OR SCOPE** the area or range covered or affected by something ○ *a technique for determining the location and extent of brain damage* **2 DEGREE** the degree to which something applies ○ *To what extent should we allow newspaper reporters into people's private lives?* **3 REGION** an area of land or water ○ *a vast extent of fertile land* **4 WRIT ALLOWING SEIZURE OF PROPERTY** a writ that authorizes somebody to take possession of the property of somebody who owes him or her money [Late 16C. Via Anglo-Norman, 'valuation of land' < medieval Latin *extenta* < Latin *extendere* (see EXTEND).]

extenuate /ik sténnyoo ayt/ (**-ates, -ating, -ated**) *vt* to make a mistake or wrongdoing seem less serious than it first appeared, or to provide a mitigating excuse for something that has happened [Early 16C. < Latin *extenuat-*, past participle of *extenuare* 'thin out' < *tenuis* 'thin'.] —**extenuating** *adj* —**extenuatingly** *adv* —**extenuation** /ik sténnyoo áysh'n/ *n* —**extenuative** *adj* —**extenuator** *n* —**extenuatory** *adj*

exterior /ik stéeri ər/ *adj* **1 ON THE OUTSIDE** on or for the outside of something ○ *the exterior walls of the building* **2 COMING FROM OUTSIDE** coming from outside or beyond something or somebody ○ *There must be some exterior cause for this.* **3 OUTDOOR** taken out of doors or depicting an outdoor scene ○ *an exterior shot* ■ *n* **1 OUTSIDE** the outside surface, appearance, or coating of something **2 OUTWARD APPEARANCE** somebody's outward appearance as distinct from his or her inner thoughts **3 SCENE OUTSIDE** an outdoor scene, especially as represented in the visual arts [Early 16C. < Latin, 'more outward' < *exter* 'outward, on the outside'.] —**exteriority** /ik stéeri órrəti, éks teeri órrəti/ *n*

exterior angle *n* **1** an angle on the outside of a polygon, formed between a side and an extension of an adjacent side **2** any of four angles formed on the outside of a pair of lines that are crossed by a third line

exteriorize /ik stéeri ə rīz/ (**-izes, -izing, -ized**), **exteriorise** (**-ises, -ising, -ised**) *vt* **1** = **externalize 2** to remove an internal organ from the body, e.g. to perform surgery on it —**exteriorization** /ik stéeri ə rī záysh'n/ *n*

exterminate /ik stúrmi nayt/ (**-nates, -nating, -nated**) *vt* to kill or destroy somebody or something completely ○ *a species nearly exterminated by hunting* [Late 16C. < Latin *exterminat-*, past participle of *exterminare* 'drive beyond the boundaries' < *termen* 'boundary'.] —**extermination** /ik stúrmi náysh'n/ *n* —**exterminator** *n* —**exterminatory** *adj*

extern /ék sturn/, **externe** *n US* a nonresident doctor or other staff member attached to a hospital [Early 17C. Via French < Latin *externus* (see EXTERNAL).] —**externship** *n*

external /ik stúrn'l/ *adj* **1 OUTSIDE** situated on, happening on, or coming from the outside ○ *The sudden collapse of the empire should not be put down to external forces alone.* **2 FOR USE ON THE OUTSIDE** suitable or designed for use only on the outside or surface of something, especially the body **3 OUTSIDE SOMETHING'S SCOPE** existing outside the body or mind, or the limits of something ○ *What real evidence is there for the existence of the external world?* **4 VISIBLE FROM OUTWARD APPEARANCE** conveyed by somebody's or something's outward appearance, as opposed to what is inside or underneath **5 OUTSIDE AN ORGANIZATION** relating to, forming, or from a separate or independent organization ○ *The investigation must be carried out by members of an external body.* **6 RELATING TO FOREIGN COUNTRIES** dealing with or involving relations with foreign countries ■ *n* **1 SOMETHING'S EXTERIOR** the outer surface of something **2** *Aus* **EXTRAMURAL STUDENT** an extramural student ■ **externals** *npl* **1 OUTWARD APPEARANCES** the outward appearance of somebody or something, especially when it is not considered to be a true indication of the person's or thing's real nature **2 SURROUNDINGS** somebody's or something's circumstances or environment [Late 16C. Partly < French *externe*, partly < Latin *externus* < *exter* 'outward, on the outside'.] —**externally** *adv*

external-combustion engine *n* an engine that converts into power heat generated from fuel consumed outside the engine, e.g.a steam engine. ◊ **internal-combustion engine**

external degree *n* a degree for which the candidate does not follow a formal course of study within a university, but sits the required examinations to gain the qualification

external ear *n* the outside part of the ear, consisting of the auricle and auditory canal

external examination *n* an examination set and marked by an authority outside a candidate's own school, college, or university —**external examiner** *n*

externalism /ik stúrn'lizəm/ *n* **1** excessive concern about outward forms and appearances, especially in religious matters **2** the view that the content of thoughts depends at least partly on relationships with objects outside the mind —**externalist** *n*

externality /ékstur nálləti/ (*plural* **-ties**) *n* **1 QUALITY OF BEING EXTERNAL** the fact or quality of being external **2 SOMETHING OUTSIDE OR EXTERNAL** an outward form or appearance **3 CONSEQUENCE OF PRODUCTION IGNORED IN PRICING** a factor, e.g. environmental damage, that results from the way something is produced but is not taken into account in establishing the market price of the goods or materials concerned **4 EXISTENCE INDEPENDENT OF THE MIND** the quality something has of existing independently of the mind that perceives it

externalize /ik stúrnə līz/ (**-izes, -izing, -ized**), **externalise** (**-ises, -ising, -ised**) *vt* **1 GIVE OUTWARD EXPRESSION TO** to express ideas or feelings in some visible or perceptible way in order to communicate them to others **2 PERCEIVE SOMETHING AS EXTERNAL** to attribute something to causes in the outside world **3 ATTRIBUTE FEELINGS TO OUTSIDE CAUSES** to attribute emotions or inner conflicts to outside causes, sources, or surroundings —**externalization** /ik stúrnə lī záysh'n/ *n*

externe /ék sturn/ *n* MED = **extern**

exteroceptor /ékstərō séptər/ *n* a body part or sensory organ such as the eye, ear, or any of the nerve endings in the skin that is able to receive outside stimuli [Early 20C. < Latin *exter* 'outward, on the outside' + RECEPTOR.] —**exteroceptive** *adj*

exterritorial *adj* POL, LAW = **extraterritorial**

extinct /ik stíngkt/ *adj* **1 HAVING NO LIVING MEMBERS** having no members of the species or family in existence, as is the case with many organisms known only from fossils **2 NO LONGER IN EXISTENCE** having died out or ceased to exist ○ *relics of extinct and forgotten civilizations* **3 NO LONGER ERUPTING** no longer active or likely to erupt ○ *an extinct volcano* **4 NOT NOW VALID** no longer valid or practised ○ *This custom has for many years been almost extinct.* **5 EXTINGUISHED** extinguished, quenched, or no longer burning [15C. < Latin *exstinctus*, past participle of *exstinguere* (see EXTINGUISH).]

SYNONYMS See ***dead***.

extinction /ik stíngksh'n/ *n* **1 THE FACT OF BECOMING EXTINCT** the gradual process of a group of related organisms dying out **2 OBSOLESCENCE** the process or fact of disappearing completely from use ○ *'Dominant languages and dialects spread widely, and lead to the gradual extinction of other tongues'.* (Charles Darwin, *The Descent of Man*; 1871) **3 PROCESS OF BECOMING INACTIVE** the permanent ceasing of eruptions in a volcano **4 BEING NO LONGER USED** the state of no longer being valid or practised, or the process of ceasing to be valid or practised **5 DESTRUCTION** the destruction or killing off of somebody or something ○ *the extinction of self and ego through meditation* **6 LOWERING OF RADIATION INTENSITY** reduction of radiation intensity because of absorption or scattering as it passes through matter **7 REDUCTION IN RESPONSE** the decreasing or dying out of a behavioural response created by conditioning because of lack of reinforcement —**extinctive** *adj*

extinguish /ik stíng gwish/ *vt* **1 PUT OUT A FIRE OR LIGHT** to put out something that is burning or giving off light ○ *The lamps along the terrace had not been extinguished.* **2 END** to take away or bring to an end something such as a hope, feeling, custom, or practice ○ *As the days went by, hope for more survivors was extinguished.* **3 DESTROY** to kill or destroy somebody or something completely (*literary*) ○ *They came with a large army in order to be certain of extinguishing the enemy by force of numbers.* **4 OUTSHINE** to outshine or eclipse something or somebody by having greater brilliance ○ *Beauty that extinguishes all others by comparison.* **5 PAY DEBT** to pay off a debt **6 MAKE SOMETHING INVALID** to make something no longer valid or applicable **7 DECREASE RESPONSE** to cause a decrease in a conditioned response through lack of reinforcement [Early 16C. < Latin *exstinguere* 'quench completely' < *stinguere* 'quench, prick'.] —**extinguishable** *adj* —**extinguishment** *n*

extinguisher /ik stíng gwishər/ *n* **1** EMERGENCIES = **fire extinguisher 2** somebody or something that puts an end to something else or eliminates its effects

extirpate /ék stur payt/ (**-pates, -pating, -pated**) *vt* **1** to completely get rid of, kill off, or destroy something or somebody considered undesirable (*formal*) **2** to remove something surgically [Mid-16C. < Latin *exstirpat-*, past participle of *exstirpare* 'root out' < *stirps* 'stem, root'.] —**extirpation** /ék stur páysh'n/ *n* —**extirpative** *adj* —**extirpator** *n*

extol /ik stṓl/ (**-tols, -tolling, -tolled**) *vt* to praise somebody or something with great enthusiasm and admiration (*literary*) [Early 16C. < Latin *extollere* 'raise up' < *tollere* 'raise'.] —**extoller** *n* —**extolment** *n*

extort /ik stáwrt/ *vt* to obtain something, such as money or information, from somebody by using force, threats, or other unacceptable methods [15C. < Latin *extort-*, past participle of *extorquere* 'twist out' < *torquere* 'to twist'.] —**extorter** *n* —**extortive** *adj*

extortion /ik stáwrsh'n/ *n* **1 OBTAINING SOMETHING BY ILLEGAL THREATS** the crime of obtaining something such as money from somebody using illegal methods of persuasion **2 EXCESSIVE CHARGING** the charging of an excessive amount of money for something (*informal*) **3 GETTING SOMETHING BY FORCE** the acquiring of anything through the use of force or threats —**extortionary** *adj* —**extortioner** *n* —**extortionist** *n*

extortionate /ik stáwrsh'nət/ *adj* **1** highly excessive, especially in price **2** involving or using extortion —**extortionately** *adv*

extra /ékstrə/ *adj* **1 MORE THAN USUAL** added to, or over and above, the usual, original, or necessary amount **2 MORE AND BETTER** greater in degree and of better quality than is normal **3 CHARGED FOR IN ADDITION** charged for in addition to the basic cost ○ *You get one free drink with the meal; further drinks are extra.* ■ *adv* **EXCEPTIONALLY** to a greater extent than is usual or expected ○ *Be extra careful at that crossing.* ■ *pron* **MORE** more than the usual amount or price ○ *The hotel charges extra for satellite television.* ■ *n* **1 SOMETHING ADDITIONAL** something additional or unexpected ○ *The remaining items are optional extras.* **2 SOMETHING CHARGED IN ADDITION** something for which an additional charge is made, or the additional charge itself ○ *Make sure there are no hidden extras.* **3 NONSPEAKING FILM ACTOR** somebody employed in a minor, usually nonspeaking, part in a film, e.g. in a crowd scene **4 SPECIAL EDITION OF NEWSPAPER** a special edition of a newspaper or magazine, often reporting later news or concentrating on a particular subject ○ *a sports extra* **5 RUN SCORED WITHOUT HITTING BALL** in cricket, a run added to a team's score but not credited to an individual batsman, e.g. as a result of the bowler bowling a no-ball or a wide [Mid-17C. Probably shortening of EXTRAORDINARY.]

extra-, **extro-** *prefix* beyond or outside something ○ *extraterrestrial* ○ *extracurricular* [< Latin *extra* 'outside, beyond' < *exter* 'outer']

extracellular /ékstrə séllyŏŏlər/ *adj* situated or happening outside a cell or cells —**extracellularly** *adv*

extrachromosomal /ékstrə krṓmə sṓm'l/ *adj* describes an inheritance of characteristics that is controlled by factors that are not carried on chromosomes

extracorporeal /ékstrə kawr páwri əl/ *adj* situated or happening outside the body —**extracorporeally** *adv*

extra cover *n* **1** in cricket, a fielding position that lies between cover and mid-off **2** in cricket, a player fielding in the position of extra cover

extracranial /ékstrə kráyni əl/ *adj* situated or happening outside the skull

extract /ik strákt/ *vt* **1 PULL SOMETHING OUT** to pull something out, often using force ○ *have a tooth extracted* **2 OBTAIN SOMETHING FROM SOURCE** to obtain something from a source, usually by separating it out from other material ○ *a few snippets of information that I managed to extract from the conversation* **3 GET SOMETHING BY FORCE** to obtain something from somebody who is unwilling to give it, often by using force or threats ○ *After a lengthy interrogation the police extracted a confession from him.* **4 COPY SOMETHING OUT FROM** to copy or remove a passage from a text ○ *This passage is extracted from the author's memoirs.* **5 DERIVE PLEASURE FROM** to obtain pleasure or enjoyment from something **6 TAKE SOMETHING OUT OF COMPOUND** to obtain a substance from a compound, in solid, liquid, or gas form, by using an industrial or chemical process **7 FIND THE ROOT OF NUMBER** to calculate the value of the root, e.g. the square root or cube root, of a number ■ *n* **1 PASSAGE** a passage taken from a publication, film, or play ○ *The novelist read a few extracts from her forthcoming book.* **2 SOMETHING SEPARATED FROM A COMPOUND** a substance obtained from a compound by an industrial or chemical process ○ *mineral extracts* **3 PURIFIED SUBSTANCE** a concentrated or purified substance obtained by first using a solvent to dissolve this substance when present in a mixture and then evaporating the solvent ○ *vanilla extract* **4 CONCENTRATED SOLUTION** an alcohol solution of the pharmaceutically active agents in a natural product [15C. < Latin *extract-*, past participle of *extrahere* 'pull out' < *trahere* 'pull'.] —**extractable** *adj*

extraction /ik stráksh'n/ *n* **1 TAKING OUT** the process of extracting something or of being extracted, or a thing that has been extracted **2 REMOVAL OF A TOOTH** the removal of a tooth or teeth **3 SEPARATION OF SUBSTANCES** the separation of a substance from a mixture by dissolving one or more of the components in a solvent **4 ETHNIC ORIGIN** the original nationality of somebody's ancestors ○ *of Spanish extraction*

extractive /ik stráktiv/ *adj* **1 EXTRACTABLE** capable of being extracted **2 USED IN AN EXTRACTION PROCESS** used in the process of extraction **3 OBTAINED BY EXTRACTION** obtained as a result of extraction ■ *n* **1 SOMETHING EXTRACTABLE** something that can be extracted **2 PART OF A CHEMICAL EXTRACT** the insoluble part of a chemical extract —**extractively** *adv*

extractor /ik stráktər/ *n* **1 SOMEBODY OR SOMETHING THAT EXTRACTS** somebody who or something that extracts something **2 DEVICE FOR TAKING OUT LIQUID** a device that removes a liquid from a solid, e.g. the juice out of a fruit **3** = **extractor fan 4 PART OF GUN** a part of a firearm that removes spent cartridges from the chamber

extractor fan *n* an electric fan, often set into a window, used to remove steam, fumes, or stale air from a room or building

extracurricular /ékstrə kə ríkyŏŏlər/ *adj* **1 OUTSIDE CURRICULUM** done or happening outside the normal curriculum of a school, college, or university **2 OUTSIDE NORMAL DUTIES** not part of the normal duties of a job or profession **3 WITH SOMEBODY OTHER THAN A PARTNER** involving somebody other than a spouse or partner (*informal*)

extraditable /ékstrə dītəb'l/ *adj* **1** describes a crime for which somebody may be extradited, or a person who has committed such a crime **2** able to be extradited

extradite /ékstrə dīt/ (**-dites, -diting, -dited**) *vt* to return somebody accused of a crime by a different legal authority to that authority for trial or punishment [Mid-19C. Back-formation < EXTRADITION.]

extradition /ékstrə dísh'n/ *n* the handing over by a government of somebody accused of a crime in a different country for trial or punishment there [Mid-19C. < French, < Latin *ex-* 'out' + *tradition-* 'deliverance' (see TRADITION).]

extrados /ek stráy doss/ (*plural* **-dos** *or* **-doses**) *n* the outer curve of an arch [Late 18C. < French, < Latin *extra* 'outside' + French *dos* 'back'.]

extraembryonic membrane /ékstrə émbri onik mém brayn/ *n* a membrane derived from embryonic tissue that lies outside the embryo, e.g. the yolk sac, amnion, and chorion

extragalactic /ékstrəgə láktik/ *adj* existing, originating, or happening outside the Milky Way, the galaxy that contains the solar system

extrajudicial /ékstrə joo dísh'l/ *adj* **1** happening or originating outside the normal course of legal proceedings **2** outside the jurisdiction of a court —**extrajudicially** *adv*

extralegal /ékstrə lēeg'l/ *adj* not permitted by or subject to the law —**extralegally** *adv*

extralimital /ékstrə límmit'l/ *adj* describes a species or group of organisms found outside a given area, e.g. a population of lions outside a national park

extramarital /ékstrə márrit'l/ *adj* involving sexual relations with somebody other than a marriage partner

extramundane /ékstrə mun dáyn/ *adj* not belonging to the physical world [Mid-17C. < late Latin *extramundanus* < *extra mundum* 'outside the world or universe'.]

extramural /ékstrə myŏŏrəl/ *adj* **1** outside or additional to the usual courses of study at a university, college, or other educational institution, though usually connected with them **2** outside the walls or boundaries of something, e.g. a castle, town, or organization [Mid-19C. < Latin *extra muros* 'outside the walls'.]

extraneous /ik stráyni əss/ *adj* **1 NOT RELEVANT** not relevant or applicable **2 NOT ESSENTIAL** not essential or important **3 COMING FROM OUTSIDE** existing or coming from outside [Mid-17C. < Latin *extraneus* 'foreign, strange' < *extra* 'outside' (see EXTRA-).] —**extraneously** *adv* —**extraneousness** *n*

extranet /ékstrə net/ *n* an extension of the intranet of a company or organization, giving authorized outsiders controlled access to the intranet

extranuclear /ékstrə nyŏŏkli ər/ *adj* **1** existing in or affecting parts of a cell outside the nucleus **2** existing, happening, or originating outside the nucleus of an atom

extraordinaire /ik stráwdi náir/ *adj* excellent or outstanding ○ *a piano player extraordinaire* [Mid-20C. Via French < Latin *extraordinarius* (see EXTRAORDINARY).]

extraordinary /ik stráwrd'nəri, ékstrə áwrd'nəri/ *adj* **1 VERY UNUSUAL** very unusual and deserving attention and comment because of being wonderful, excellent, strange, or shocking ○ *For a ten-year-old, her mathematical abilities are quite extraordinary.* **2 ADDITIONAL** additional and having a special purpose **3 EMPLOYED FOR SPECIAL PURPOSE** employed for a special purpose or to do additional work ○ *ambassador extraordinary* **4 ADDITIONAL AND GREATER** additional to and going beyond the scope of something in ordinary or established use ○ *Extraordinary measures are necessary in these highly unusual circumstances.* [15C. < Latin *extraordinarius* < *extra ordinem* 'out of order, exceptionally'.] —**extraordinarily** *adv* —**extraordinariness** *n*

extraordinary general meeting *n* a meeting of a company or any formally constituted association, specially called by the board or a group of shareholders or members, to discuss a specified, and usually important, piece of business

extra point *n* in American football, a point scored by kicking the field goal awarded after a touchdown

extrapolate /ik stráppə layt/ (**-lates, -lating, -lated**) *v* **1** *vti* to use known facts as the starting point from which to draw inferences or conclusions about something unknown ○ *If we extrapolate from the data, we can come up with a reasonable prediction.* **2** *vt* to estimate a value that falls outside a range of known values, e.g. by extending a curve on a graph [Mid-19C. < EXTRA- + INTERPOLATE.] —**extrapolation** /ik stráppə láysh'n/ *n* —**extrapolative** *adj* —**extrapolator** *n*

extrasensory /ékstrə sénssəri/ *adj* relating to or involving powers of perception other than the normal five senses

extrasensory perception *n* the apparent ability of some people to become aware of things by means other than the normal senses, e.g. through clairvoyance or telepathy

extrasystole /ékstrə sístəli/ *n* a heart contraction occurring too soon after the previous beat and followed by a longer pause than normal between heartbeats, caused by heart disease or excessive caffeine or nicotine

extraterrestrial /ékstrətə réstri əl/ *adj* existing or coming from somewhere outside the Earth and its atmosphere ■ *n* a supposed living creature that comes from outside the Earth

extraterritorial /ékstrə térri táwri əl/, **exterritorial** /éks térri-/ *adj* **1** situated or coming from outside a country's territorial boundary **2** relating to or involving exemption from the legal jurisdiction of a country of residence —**extraterritorially** *adv*

extraterritoriality /ékstrə térri táwri állәti/ *n* exemption from the legal jurisdiction of a country of residence, as granted e.g. to foreign diplomats

extra time *n* an additional fixed period played at the end of a match if the scores are equal at full time and a decisive result is needed. US term **overtime** *n.* 3

extrauterine /ékstrə yŏŏtə rīn, -rin/ *adj* occurring or situated outside the womb ○ *extrauterine pregnancy*

extravagance /ik strávvəgənss/, **extravagancy** /-gənssi/ (*plural* **-cies**) *n* **1 WASTEFUL SPENDING** excessive or wasteful spending of money ○ *condemned to poverty by their father's extravagance* **2 EXPENSIVE THING** something that is expensive or wasteful ○ *A car like that is an extravagance in today's economic climate.* **3 EXTRAVAGANT NATURE** the exaggerated, excessive, or extremely flamboyant nature of something, e.g. a wild unreasonableness in somebody's speech or behaviour

extravagant /ik strávvəgənt/ *adj* **1 SPENDING TOO MUCH** characterized by spending excessively or wastefully ○ *I think it's extravagant to spend £250 on a shirt.* **2 BEYOND WHAT IS REASONABLE** exaggerated or unreasonable ○ *The scientific community has dismissed these claims as wildly extravagant.* **3 UNREASONABLY HIGH IN PRICE** unreasonably high in price or cost **4 FLAMBOYANT** profusely or exaggeratedly decorated, decorative, or showy **5 ABUNDANT** extremely abundant [14C. < medieval Latin, < Latin *extra* 'outside' + *vagari* 'wander'.] —**extravagantly** *adv* —**extravagantness** *n*

extravaganza /ik strávvə gánzə/ *n* **1** a lavish and spectacular entertainment **2** any spectacular or fanciful display [Mid-18C. < Italian *estravaganza* 'peculiar behaviour' < *estravagante* 'extravagant'.]

extravasate /ik strávvə sayt/ (**-sates, -sating, -sated**) *vti* to leak, or cause blood or other fluid to leak, from a vessel into the surrounding tissue, following injury, burns, or inflammation [Mid-17C. < EXTRA- + Latin *vas* 'vessel'.] —**extravasation** /ik strávvə sáysh'n/ *n*

extravascular /ékstrə váskyŏŏlər/ *adj* not contained in the body's blood vessels or lymph vessels

extravehicular /ékstrə vi híkyŏŏlər/ *adj* happening or for use outside a spacecraft

extravehicular activity *n* an activity undertaken by an astronaut outside the spacecraft during a mission, e.g. a repair to the craft, or an experiment on the surface of the Moon

extraversion *n* PSYCHOL, MED = **extroversion**

extravert *n, adj* PSYCHOL = **extrovert**

extra virgin olive oil *n* the highest quality of olive oil, made from the first cold pressing of ripe olives

extreme /ik strēem/ *adj* **1 HIGH IN DEGREE OR INTENSITY** highest in intensity or degree ○ *will withstand extreme pressure* **2 NOT REASONABLE** going far beyond what is reasonable or normal ○ *an extreme reaction* **3 FARTHEST OUT** farthest out, especially from the centre ○ *the extreme north of the country* **4 SEVERE** very strict or severe **5 SENSATION-SEEKING** denoting an activity in which participants actively seek out dangerous or even life-threatening experiences ○ *extreme skiing* ■ *n* **1 FURTHEST LIMIT** the furthest limit or highest degree of something ○ *the extreme of bad taste* **2 END OF SCALE** something or somebody that represents either of the two ends of a scale or range, e.g. the highest or lowest degree of something, or a quality and its polar opposite ○ *Between these two extremes there must be a middle way.* **3 FIRST OR LAST TERM** the first or last term in a mathematical proportion or series ■ **extremes** *npl* **DRASTIC MEASURES** drastic or unreasonable measures ○ *The authorities have been driven to extremes by the widespread popular unrest.* [15C. Via French < Latin *extremus* 'farthest, last' < *ex* 'out'.] —**extremeness** *n*

extremely /ik strēemli/ *adv* to a very high degree ○ *She plays the violin extremely well.*

extremely high frequency *n* a radio frequency in the range between 30,000 and 300,000 megahertz

extremely low frequency *n* a radio frequency below 30 hertz

extreme unction *n* the sacrament of anointing the sick in the Roman Catholic Church (*dated*)

extremism /ik strēemizəm/ *n* the holding of extreme political or religious views or the taking of extreme actions on the basis of those views

extremist /ik strēemist/ *n* a holder of extreme or radical political opinions or religious beliefs —**extremist** *adj*

extremity /ik strémmәti/ *n* (*plural* **-ties**) **1 FARTHEST POINT** a point that is the farthest out, especially from the centre ○ *the southernmost extremity of the continent* **2 HIGHEST DEGREE** the highest degree or greatest intensity of something ○ *in the extremity of her grief* **3 DANGER** a situation of great danger or distress ○ *They prayed for help in their extremity.* **4 LIMB** a limb of a person or animal, or the part of a limb that is farthest from the body, especially somebody's hand or foot ○ *Frostbite attacks the extremities first.* **5 STATE OF BEING EXTREME** the state of being extreme, especially extremely dangerous or severe ○ *You don't seem to understand the extremity of the situation.* ■ **extremities** *npl* **DRASTIC MEASURES** drastic or unreasonable measures (*formal*) ○ *There was no need for such extremities.*

~~**extremly**~~ incorrect spelling of **extremely**

extricate /ékstri kayt/ (**-cates, -cating, -cated**) *vt* to release somebody or something with difficulty from a physical constraint or an unpleasant or complicated situation [Early 17C. < Latin *extricat-*, past participle of *extricare* 'remove from perplexities' < *tricae* 'perplexities'.] —**extricable** /ik stríkәb'l, ékstrik-/ *adj* —**extrication** /ékstri káysh'n/ *n*

extrinsic /ek strínssik, -zik/ *adj* **1** that is not an essential part of something ○ *It's a good point, but extrinsic to the argument.* **2** coming or operating from outside something ○ *the importance of extrinsic influences on a nation's literature* [Mid-16C. < late Latin *extrinsecus* 'outer' < Latin *exter* 'external' + adverb-forming ending *-im* + *secus* 'alongside of'.] —**extrinsically** *adv*

extro- *prefix* = **extra-** [Alteration, after INTRO-]

~~**extrordinary**~~ incorrect spelling of **extraordinary**

extrorse /ik stráwrss/, **extrorsal** /ik stráwrss'l/ *adj* facing or turning outwards or away from a centre [Mid-19C. < late Latin *extrorsus* 'in an outward direction' < Latin *extra* 'outside' + *versus* 'towards', past participle of *vertere* 'turn'.]

extroversion /ékstrә vúrsh'n/, **extraversion** *n* **1** interest in and involvement with people and things outside the self **2** the turning inside out of an organ or other body part, especially the womb [Mid-17C. < EXTRO- + Latin *version-* 'turning' < *vertere* 'turn'.] —**extroversive** *adj* —**extroversively** *adv*

extrovert /ékstrә vurt/, **extravert** *n* **1** a sociable and self-confident person **2** a person whose interests are directed outside the self [Early 20C. < EXTRO- + Latin *vertere* 'to turn'.] —**extrovert** *adj* —**extroverted** *adj*

USAGE The original spelling is ***extravert***, which is still more common in American usage. In British English, however, the form ***extrovert***, influenced by *introvert*, is now standard.

extrude /ik stróod/ (**-trudes, -truding, -truded**) *v* **1** *vt* to force or squeeze something out **2** *vt* to make something by forcing a semi-soft material such as plastic or molten metal through a specially shaped mould or nozzle **3** *vi* = **protrude** [Mid-16C. < Latin *extrudere* 'thrust out' < *trudere* 'to thrust'.]

extrusion /ik stróozh'n/ *n* **1 SOMETHING FORMED BY BEING EXTRUDED** something formed by forcing semi-soft material through a specially shaped mould or nozzle **2 PROCESS OF EXTRUDING** the process or an instance of making something by forcing semi-soft material through a specially shaped mould or nozzle **3 IGNEOUS ROCK** an igneous rock formed by the emission of molten material (**magma**) through cracks in the Earth's surface where it forms a lava flow **4 MOVEMENT OF MOLTEN ROCK** the movement of molten material (**magma**) from a volcano or through cracks in the Earth's surface to form solidified igneous rock [Mid-16C. < medieval Latin *extrusion-* < Latin *extrudere* (see EXTRUDE).]

extrusive /ik stróossiv/ *adj* describes rock formed from molten material (**magma**) that has flowed out of cracks in the Earth's surface

exuberant /ig zyóob'rәnt/ *adj* **1 FULL OF ENTHUSIASM** full of happy high spirits and vitality **2 ABUNDANT** growing in great abundance or profusion **3 LAVISH** lavish or elaborate, often to the point of being excessive [15C. Via French < Latin *exuberant-*, present participle of *exuberare* 'be very fruitful' < *uberare* 'be fruitful' < *uber* 'fertile'.] —**exuberance** *n* —**exuberantly** *adv*

exudate /éksyoo dayt, égz-/ *n* a substance such as sweat or a cellular waste product that is exuded from a cell or organ

exudation /éksyoo dáysh'n, égz-/ *n* **1** the release of a substance through pores or a surface cut, e.g. the release of sweat from the body or resin from a tree **2** BIOL = **exudate** —**exudative** /éksyoo daytiv, égz-/ *adj*

exude /ig zyóod/ (**-udes, -uding, -uded**) *v* **1** *vt* to communicate a particular quality or feeling in abundance and very clearly, usually through general behaviour and body language ○ *a voice that exuded confidence* **2** *vti* to release something such as a liquid or an odour slowly from a gland, pore, membrane, or cut, or ooze out slowly [Late 16C. < Latin *ex(s)udare* 'ooze out like sweat' < *sudare* 'to sweat'.]

exult /ig zúlt/ *vi* **1** to be extremely happy or joyful about something ○ *exulted in his new-found freedom* **2** to be very happy or triumphant about something unpleasant that happens to somebody else ○ *The victors exulted over their enemies' annihilation.* [Late 16C. Via French *exulter* < Latin *exsultare* 'keep leaping up' < *exsalire* 'leap out' < *salire* 'leap'.] —**exultance** *n* —**exultation** /ég zul táysh'n, ék sul-/ *n* —**exultingly** *adv*

exultant /ig zúltәnt/ *adj* extremely happy, joyful, or triumphant ○ *an exultant roar from the crowd* —**exultantly** *adv*

exurb /éks urb/ *n US* a prosperous residential area outside a city, beyond the suburbs [Mid-20C. Back-formation < *exurban* (< Latin *ex* 'out of' + *urbs* 'city'), after SUBURB.] —**exurban** /eks úrbәn/ *adj* —**exurbanite** /eks úrbә nīt/ *n* —**exurbia** *n*

exuviae /ig zyóovi ee/ *npl* a skin, shell, or other body covering cast off by an animal [Mid-17C. < Latin, 'things cast off' < *exuere* 'divest yourself of'.] —**exuvial** *adj*

ex works *adv* excluding any costs incurred after an item leaves the factory, such as delivery charges and retailer's profit ○ *I know where I can buy one ex works* — **ex-works** *adj*

-ey *suffix* = **-y**[1] [Variant]

eyas /ī әss/ *n* a young hawk or falcon, especially one bred for falconry [15C. Alteration of obsolete *nias* < French *niais* 'bird taken from the nest' < Latin *nidus* 'nest'.]

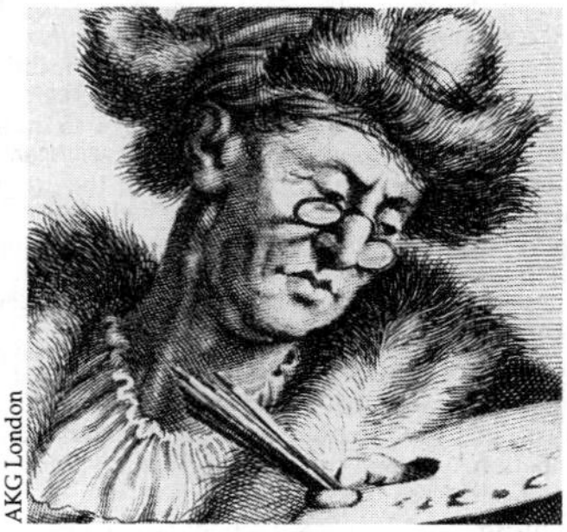
AKG London

Jan van Eyck: Portrait engraving by Joachim von Sandrart

Eyck /īk/, **Jan van** (1390?–1441) Flemish painter

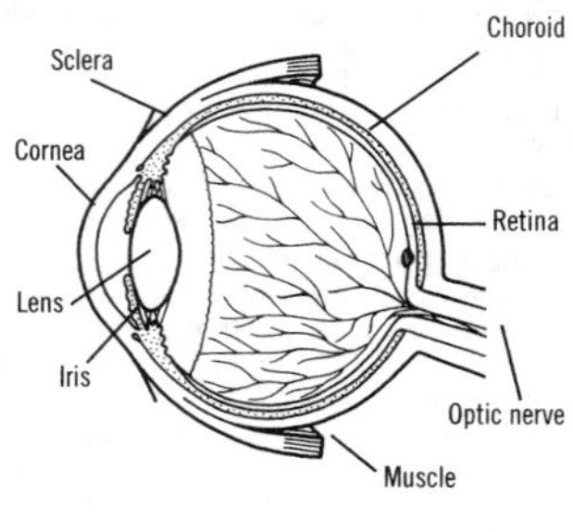
Sclera
Choroid
Cornea
Retina
Lens
Iris
Optic nerve
Muscle

Cross-section of a human eye

eye /ī/ *n* **1 ORGAN OF VISION** the organ of sight or light sensitivity in vertebrates, usually occurring in pairs **2 VISIBLE AREA OF THE EYE** the externally visible part of the eye, and the area of face around it, including the orbit, eyelid, and eyelashes **3 POWER OF SIGHT** the ability to see (*often plural*) ○ *If my eyes get any worse I'll have to wear glasses.* **4 ATTENTION** somebody's attention or gaze ○ *He took his eye off the prisoners at the wrong moment.* **5 EXPRESSION** a look, or the facial expression of a person looking ○ *She looked me over with a cold eye.* **6 APPRECIATION** an ability to recognize and appreciate something ○ *He's got a good eye for talent.* **7 OPINION** a point of view or way of thinking ○ *He can do no wrong in her eyes.* **8** ZOOL = **eyespot** *n.* 2 **9 NEW SHOOT ON POTATO** a dark round patch on a potato tuber, from which a new shoot grows **10 HOLE IN NEEDLE** a hole in the top of a needle for passing a thread through **11 LOOP PART OF FASTENER** a loop into which a small hook fits, used as a means of fastening two parts of a garment together **12 CENTRE OF STORM** a calm area at the centre of a storm ■ *vt* (**eyes, eyeing** *or* **eying, eyed**) **1 LOOK AT** to look at something or somebody inquisitively ○ *She quickly eyed the building up and down.* **2 OGLE** to give somebody a look that signals sexual interest (*informal*) ○ *A man was eyeing her from across the room.* [Old English *eage* < Indo-European] —**eyeless** *adj* ◇ **close** *or* **shut your eyes to something** to ignore or overlook something obvious ◇ **cry your eyes out** to cry bitterly ◇ **eyes out on stalks** wide-eyed in extreme astonishment or shock (*informal*) ◇ **give somebody the (glad) eye** to look at somebody in a way that signals sexual interest ◇ **have eyes in the back of your head** to be aware of what is happening when unable to see it (*informal; usually in negative context*) ◇ **keep your eye on the ball** **1** to watch somebody or something closely **2** to take care of somebody or something, especially for a short time ◇ **see eye to eye (with somebody)** to have a similar outlook or viewpoint to somebody else ◇ **turn a blind eye (to something)** to pretend not to be aware of something ◇ **with an eye to something** having something as a purpose or objective ◇ **with your eyes (wide) open** fully aware of all that is involved in what you are doing

ϟ**eyeball** /ī bawl/ *n* **ROUND MASS OF THE EYE** the round mass of the eye within its bony socket ■ **eyeballs** *npl* **WEBSITE VISITORS** users of the Internet who visit a particular site or use a particular product (*slang*) ○ *sites competing for eyeballs* ■ *vt* **STARE AT** to stare at somebody or something intently (*informal*)

eye bank *n* a place where human corneas taken from people who have recently died are stored for use in corneal transplants

eyebolt /ī bōlt/ *n* a bolt with an eye or ring at the end instead of the usual head, used for pulling, lifting, or fastening

eyebright /ī brīt/ *n* a plant of the snapdragon family. Flowers: white and purple, small. Genus: *Euphrasia.* [Because formerly used for treating eye diseases]

eyebrow /ī brow/ *n* **1** the arched line of hair above each eye socket **2** the upper bony ridge of the eye socket. Technical name **supraorbital ridge**

eyebrow pencil *n* a soft cosmetic pencil used to darken the eyebrows

ϟ**eye candy** *n* **1** something visually pleasing but intellectually undemanding (*slang*) **2** ornamental visual elements on a computer monitor or a web page

eye-catching *adj* that attracts people's attention easily —**eye-catcher** *n* —**eye-catchingly** *adv*

eye chart *n* a sheet printed with different sizes of letters, used to test eyesight

eye contact *n* the act of looking directly into the eyes of another person

eyecup /ī kup/ *n US* MED = **eyebath**

eye dialect *n* the use of spellings that represent the sound of dialectal or nonstandard forms, e.g. 'enuff' or 'wimmin'

eye drops *npl* liquid medication for the eyes, usually applied with a dropper

eyeful /ī fōol/ *n* **1** a long steady look at something or somebody (*informal*) ○ *Get an eyeful of this!* **2** an offensive term for somebody or something that is very beautiful, especially a woman who has a pleasing appearance (*slang*)

eyeglass /ī glaass/ *n* **1** a single framed lens for correcting defective vision, e.g. a monocle **2** OPHTHALMOL = **eyepiece** ■ **eyeglasses** *npl US* a pair of glasses (*formal*)

eyehole /ī hōl/ *n* **1** = **eyelet** *n.* 1 **2** = **peephole** *n.* 2

eyehook /ī hōok/ *n* a hook that is fixed to a ring at the end of a rope or chain

eyelash /ī lash/ *n* **1** any of the short hairs that grow out of the edge of the eyelid **2** the row of short hairs that grow out of the edge of the eyelid

eyelet /ílət/ *n* **1 HOLE FOR CORD** a small hole, especially in fabric, for a lace or cord to be passed through **2 METAL REINFORCEMENT FOR EYELET** a small ring of metal or stiff fabric fixed to an eyelet to strengthen its edges **3 ORNAMENTED HOLE IN EMBROIDERY** a small hole with ornamental stitched edges in embroidered fabric **4 = peephole** *n.* **2** [14C. Anglicization of Old French *oillet* 'little eye' < *oil* 'eye' < Latin *oculus*.]

eyelevel /í levv'l/ *adj* positioned approximately at the same height as a person's eyes ○ *a cooker with an eyelevel grill*

eyelid /ílid/ *n* a protective fold of skin and muscle that can be closed to cover the front of the eyeball ◇ **not bat an eyelid** to show no sign of emotion, especially of surprise

eyelift /ílift/ *n* a surgical operation to improve the appearance of the area around the eyes, e.g. by removing wrinkles

eyeliner /í línər/ *n* a cosmetic worn along the edges of the eyelids to emphasize the eyes

eye opener *n* a surprising or revealing experience or piece of information —**eye-opening** *adj*

eye patch *n* a covering worn over one eye to protect it or as concealment

eyepiece /í peess/ *n* the lens or group of lenses in an optical instrument on the side that the user looks through

eye-popping *adj* so striking or unusual that eyes widen in amazement (*informal*) ○ *an eye-popping crimson dress* —**eye-popper** *n*

eye rhyme *n* the use of rhymes as words that, because they are similarly spelt, look as if they rhyme but are in fact pronounced differently, e.g. 'bough' and 'enough'

eyeshade /í shayd/ *n* a tinted or opaque visor worn round the head above the eyes to protect them from glare

eye shadow *n* a coloured cosmetic for the area around the eyes, especially the eyelids

eyeshot /í shot/ *n* the range over which the eye can see

eyesight /í sít/ *n* the power of sight

eye socket *n* either of the two bony recesses in the skull that contain the eyeballs

eyes-only *adj* intended to be seen only by the person to whom it is addressed ○ *an eyes-only memo from the chief*

eyesore /í sawr/ *n* an offensively ugly building or place ○ *That old office block is a real eyesore and ought to be pulled down.*

eyespot /í spot/ *n* **1** a small pigmented area or organelle that is sensitive to light, found in some algae and simple multicellular organisms, including some flatworms, and jellyfish **2** a marking shaped like an eye, e.g. on the wings of some butterflies or on a peacock's tail

eyestalk /í stawk/ *n* a flexible stalk with a compound eye at the tip found in crustaceans and some molluscs

eyestrain /í strayn/ *n* tiredness or irritation in the eyes caused, e.g. by an uncorrected visual defect or by prolonged close work

Eyetie /í tí/ *n* a highly offensive term for an Italian person (*taboo*) [Early 20C. < *Eyetalian*, representing a nonstandard pronunciation of ITALIAN.] —**Eyetie** *adj*

eyetooth /í tooth/ (*plural* **-teeth** /-teeth/) *n* a canine tooth found on each side of the upper jaw [Because directly below the eye] ◇ **give your eyeteeth for something** to be prepared to do anything to be able to do or have something

eyewash /í wosh/ *n* **1** a liquid used to cleanse or soothe the eyes **2** pretentious nonsense that is intended to flatter or deceive (*informal*) ○ *The official version is just so much eyewash.*

eyewear /í wair/ *n* something worn over the eyes to protect them or correct sight, e.g. glasses, goggles, or contact lenses

eyewitness /í witnəss, í witnəss/ *n* a witness of an event who can give evidence about it

eyot /ayt, áyət/ *n* = **ait** (*regional*)

eyra /áirə/ *n* a jaguarundi in its reddish-brown seasonal colour phase. *Felis yagouaroundi.* [Early 17C. Via Spanish < Tupi-Guarani *(e)irára.*]

Eyre, Lake /air/ largest salt lake in Australia, in central South Australia. Area: 9,300 sq. km/3,600 sq. mi.

Eyre, Edward John (1815–1901) British explorer and colonial official

Eyre Peninsula peninsula in S South Australia that separates the Great Australian Bight from the Spencer Gulf. Area: 55,000 sq. km/21,236 sq. mi.

eyrie /eéri, áiri, íri/ *n* **1 EAGLE'S NEST** the nest of a bird of prey, especially an eagle, in a high and inaccessible place **2 HIGH INACCESSIBLE PLACE** any high and inaccessible place, often a fortified one **3 BROOD OF BIRD OF PREY** the brood of a bird of prey [15C. < medieval Latin *aeria*, probably via Old French *aire* < Latin *area* 'level ground, garden bed', later 'bird of prey's nest'.]

eyrir /áy reer/ (*plural* **aurar** /ö raar/) *n* see table at **currency** [Early 20C. < Icelandic, probably < Latin *aureus* 'gold coin'.]

Eysenck /í zengk/, **H. J.** (1916–97) German-born British psychologist

Ez. *abbr* Ezra

Ezek. *abbr* Ezekiel

Ezekiel /i zéeki əl/ *n* **1** a Hebrew priest and prophet who lived in the 6th century BC **2** the book of the Bible that tells the story of the Jews' exile in Babylon in the 6th century BC, traditionally attributed to Ezekiel

⚡**e-zine** /eé zeen/ *n* a website with contents and layout modelled on a print magazine [< *e(lectronic)* (*maga)zine*]

Ezr. *abbr* Ezra

Ezra /ézzrə/ *n* **1** a Hebrew high priest who lived in the 5th century BC. He led the Jews back to Jerusalem from their exile in Babylon and founded a Jewish nation. **2** the book of the Bible that tells the story of the rebuilding of the Jewish state in Palestine 536–432 BC after the Babylonian captivity, traditionally attributed to Ezra

Ff

f¹ /ef/ (plural **f's**), **F** (plural **F's** or **Fs**) n the sixth letter of the English alphabet, representing a consonant sound

f² used to refer to the sixth vertical row of squares from the left on a chessboard

f³ symbol **1** femto- **2** f-number **3** focal length **4** force **5** frequency n. 4. **6** function

f⁴ abbr **1** folio **2** following (page) **3** forte² adv (musical direction) **4** foul

F¹ symbol **1** farad **2** faraday (usually italicized) **3** force¹ n. 9.

F² abbr **1** fail (used as grade on a piece of work) **2** false **3** Fellow **4** farad **5** Fahrenheit **6** fathom **7** February **8** female **9** feminine **10** fine¹ adj. 12. **11** folio **12** Friday

F³ (plural **F's** or **Fs**) n **1** 'F'-SHAPED OBJECT something shaped like a letter 'F' **2** 4TH NOTE IN C MAJOR the fourth note of a scale in C major **3** SOMETHING THAT PRODUCES AN F a string, key, or pipe tuned to produce the note F **4** SCALE BEGINNING ON F a scale or key that starts on the note F **5** WRITTEN SYMBOL FOR F a graphic representation of the tone of F **6** LOWEST GRADE the sixth lowest grade in a series, also used to indicate a 'fail' in grading a student's work

F- prefix fighter (plane)

f/ symbol f-number

⚡F2F abbr face-to-face (in e-mails)

fa n MUSIC = **fah**

FA abbr **1** field artillery **2** financial adviser **3** Football Association **4** freight agent

fab /fab/ adj fabulous (informal) ○ It was a fab party! [Mid-20C. Shortening.]

Fabergé /fábbər zhay/, **Peter Carl** (1846–1920) Russian goldsmith and jeweller. Born **Karl Gustavovich Fabergé**

Fabian /fáybi ən/ adj **1** RELATING TO FABIAN SOCIETY relating to, belonging to, or typical of the Fabian Society **2** CAUTIOUS using delaying tactics and avoiding direct confrontation ■ n MEMBER OF FABIAN SOCIETY a member or supporter of the Fabian Society [Late 16C. < Latin *Fabianus* 'of Fabius' (see Quintus FABIUS MAXIMUS).]

Fabianism /fáybi ənizəm/ n the beliefs or tactics of the Fabian Society —**Fabianist** n

Fabian Society n a political organization founded in Britain in 1884 with the aim of bringing about socialism by gradual and lawful means rather than by revolution

Fabius Maximus /fáybi əss máksiməss/, **Quintus** (275?–203 BC) Roman commander and statesman. Known as **Fabius Cunctator (the 'Delayer')**

fable /fáyb'l/ n **1** STORY THAT TEACHES A LESSON a short story with a moral, especially one in which the characters are animals **2** FALSE ACCOUNT a false or improbable account of something ○ His version of events turned out to be a complete fable. **3** LEGEND a story about supernatural, mythological, or legendary characters and events **4** MYTHS AND LEGENDS myths and legends collectively ○ a character out of fable ■ vt (**-bles, -bling, -bled**) TELL IN FABLE to tell a story or describe something in a fable (usually passive) [13C. Via Old French < Latin *fabula* 'story' < *fari* 'speak'.] —**fabler** n

fabled /fáyb'ld/ adj **1** famous from being described or recounted in legends ○ Eldorado, the fabled city of gold **2** made-up or fictitious

fabliau /fábbli ō/ (plural **-aux** /-ōz/) n a comic and often bawdy story in verse, especially of a kind popular in 12th- and 13th-century France [Early 19C. < French, < plural of Old French *fablel* 'little story' < *fable* (see FABLE).]

Fabre /fábbrə/, **Jean Henri** (1823–1915) French entomologist

Fabriano /fábri a′ànō/, **Gentile da** (1370–1427) Italian painter

fabric /fábbrik/ n **1** CLOTH any type of cloth made from woven, knitted, or felted thread or fibres **2** TEXTURE the particular texture or quality of a kind of cloth **3** SUBSTANCE the fundamental structure or make-up of something ○ the fabric of her being **4** STRUCTURAL MATERIAL the material from which something is constructed, especially a building, or the physical structure of something ○ damage to the fabric of the church **5** ROCK COMPOSITION the texture of a rock with respect to its macroscopic and microscopic arrangement of minerals and particles [15C. Via Old French < Latin *fabrica* 'trade, manufactured object' < *faber* 'worker in metal or stone, artisan'.]

fabricate /fábbri kayt/ (**-cates, -cating, -cated**) vt **1** INVENT to make up something that is not true ○ The evidence against him has been fabricated. **2** CONSTRUCT to make something from different parts **3** FORGE to make a fraudulent imitation of a signature or document [15C. < Latin *fabricat-*, past participle of *fabricare* 'make' < *fabrica* (see FABRIC).] —**fabricator** n

fabrication /fábbri káysh'n/ n **1** UNTRUTH something that is not true but has been made up ○ This story is a mere fabrication. **2** CONCOCTING LIES the invention of something that is not true ○ engaged in the fabrication of stories to discredit him **3** ACT OF MAKING the construction of something, or something that has been constructed or made **4** COUNTERFEIT a fraudulent imitation of a signature or document

SYNONYMS See *lie*.

fabulist /fábbyo͞olist/ n **1** a writer or reciter of fables **2** a teller of fanciful stories

fabulous /fábbyo͞oləss/ adj **1** EXCELLENT extremely good, pleasant, or enjoyable (informal) **2** AMAZING amazingly or almost unbelievably great or wonderful **3** TYPICAL OF A FABLE described in or typical of myths and legends [15C. Directly or via French < Latin *fabulosus* 'celebrated in fable' < *fabula* (see FABLE).] —**fabulously** adv —**fabulousness** n

façade /fə sa'àd/, **facade** n **1** the face of a building, especially the principal or front face showing its most prominent architectural features **2** the way something or somebody appears on the surface, especially when that appearance is false or meant to deceive ○ Her geniality is just a façade. [Mid-17C. < French, < face (see FACE), after Italian *facciata*.]

face /fayss/ n **1** FRONT OF HEAD the front of the human head, where the eyes, nose, mouth, chin, cheeks, and forehead are **2** PERSON a person being looked at (informal) ○ It's nice to see so many familiar faces here today. **3** COUNTENANCE a facial expression or look of a specified kind ○ an unhappy face **4** UNPLEASANT FACIAL EXPRESSION an expression in which the face is distorted, e.g. to show distaste or as a way of being rude to somebody ○ The children made faces at him behind his back. **5** WAY SOMETHING LOOKS the general or outward appearance of something ○ The arrival of the motor car changed the face of the modern city. **6** FALSE APPEARANCE an outward appearance that does not show the true nature of somebody's feelings or is intended to deceive ○ Even after a third defeat he was still putting on a brave face. **7** REPUTATION personal prestige or reputation ○ a way of enabling her to back down without losing face **8** BOLDNESS impudence or self-assurance (informal) ○ How can he have the face to come back here after what he said? **9** FACE MAKE-UP make-up for the face (informal) **10** SURFACE OF OBJECT a plane surface or side of a three-dimensional object, e.g. a geometric figure or gem, that is presented towards a particular direction **11** OUTSIDE OF BUILDING the exterior of the front or side of a large building **12** SIDE OF CLIFF the steep exposed side of a cliff **13** SIDE OF MOUNTAIN a steep mountainside, often named after the direction it faces ○ the north face of the Eiger **14** WORKING AREA IN A MINE an area in a mine from which a mineral such as coal is being extracted **15** TYPEFACE a typeface, or the area of a printing character that actually prints **16** DIAL ON CLOCK OR INSTRUMENT the surface of a timepiece or similar instrument that displays the time or other data **17** SIDE OF CARD SHOWING VALUE the side of a playing card that is marked with numbers and symbols **18** WORKING SURFACE OF IMPLEMENT the functional side of something such as a tool or golf club **19** SIDE OF COIN either surface of a coin, especially one with somebody's head on it **20** CELEBRITY a well-known or important person (informal) ○ We get a few faces in the club at the weekend. ■ v (**faces, facing, faced**) **1** vti TURN TOWARDS to be positioned or turn so that the face or front side is directed a particular way or towards something or somebody ○ The largest bedroom faces south. **2** vt BE LOOKING AT to be in a position opposite somebody or something **3** vt COME UP AGAINST to meet or confront somebody or something directly and bravely **4** vt ACCEPT THE FACTS to accept the reality of a difficult or unpleasant situation ○ Let's face it, our chances of being on time are slim. **5** vt HAVE TO CONTEND WITH to have to deal with or undergo something unpleasant or difficult ○ She was faced with the task of breaking the news to her family. **6** vt BE ENCOUNTERED BY to be met and overcome by somebody ○ the difficulties facing the new administration **7** vt EXPECT SOMETHING BAD to have the prospect of experiencing something unpleasant, usually within a short period of time ○ They face ruin if the bank calls in the loan. **8** vt LINE OR DECORATE to line or trim the edge of something with a contrasting material **9** vt SMOOTH to put a smooth surface on a piece of stone [13C. Via French < Latin *facies* 'appearance, aspect, form, face'.] —**faceable** adj ○ **face to face 1** in the actual presence of another person **2** in direct contact with, or having first-hand knowledge of, an unpleasant fact or situation ◇ **fly in the face of something** to defy something deliberately or recklessly ◇ **in (the) face of something** when confronted by or in spite of something (slang) ◇ **not just a pretty face** having more to offer than an attractive appearance ◇ **set your face against something** to oppose something with determination ◇ **show your face (somewhere or at something)** to put in an appearance somewhere ○ He won't dare show his face at her house again.

face about vti to turn to face the other way, or turn somebody or something to face the other way

face down vt to prevail against somebody in a direct confrontation

face off v **1** vti to start or restart play in ice hockey, lacrosse, and other sports by dropping the puck or ball between two opposing players **2** vi to confront each other or somebody else (informal)

face out *vt* to endure something such as criticism or misfortune bravely

face up to *vt* 1 to accept having to deal with something unpleasant 2 to confront somebody or something bravely

faceache /fáyss ayk/ *n* an offensive term for somebody who is thought to be ugly or who looks unhappy (*slang insult*)

face angle *n* an angle between two flat surfaces on a polyhedron

face card *n US* = **court card**

face-centred *adj* describes a crystal lattice with an atom in the centre of each unit cell face as well as at the corners

facecloth /fáyss kloth/ *n* a small cloth used in washing the face and hands. US term **washcloth**

-faced *suffix* 1 having a specified number of faces 2 having a face of a specified kind

facedown /fáyss down/ *n* a determined confrontation between two adversaries

face flannel *n* = **facecloth**

faceless /fáyssləss/ *adj* lacking character or distinction as an individual —**facelessly** *adv* —**facelessness** *n*

facelift /fáyss lift/ *n* 1 a surgical operation in which the skin of the face is pulled back and up to tighten it and remove wrinkles 2 a renovation or refurbishment of something e.g. an area or a building ○ *The whole dockside area could do with a facelift.*

facemail /fáyss mayl/ *n* ordinary person-to-person conversation (*slang*)

face mask *n* 1 = **face pack** 2 a covering for the whole head or the face alone, used either to protect or to disguise the face

face-off *n* 1 a start or restart of play in ice hockey, lacrosse, and other sports in which the referee drops the puck or ball between two opposing players 2 a direct confrontation

face pack *n* a cosmetic preparation that cleanses the pores of the face and removes dead layers of skin

faceplate /fáyss playt/ *n* 1 PART OF LATHE a perforated metal disc at the end of the spindle or headstock of a lathe for holding a workpiece in place 2 SEE-THROUGH PART OF HEADGEAR the transparent part of a piece of protective headgear that protects the face while allowing the wearer to see 3 FRONT OF CATHODE-RAY TUBE the front of a cathode-ray tube, on which an image is seen

face powder *n* a flesh-coloured cosmetic powder applied to the face to make it look smoother or less shiny

facer /fáyssər/ *n* 1 a lathe tool used to smooth a surface 2 something that is astonishing or very difficult to deal with (*dated informal*) ○ *This latest development is a facer, and no mistake!*

face-saving *adj* intended to preserve somebody's reputation and dignity ○ *find a face-saving compromise* —**face-saver** *n*

facet /fássit/ *n* 1 ASPECT a part or possible aspect of something 2 FACE OF A GEMSTONE any surface of a cut gemstone 3 PART OF INSECT EYE a lens segment in the compound eye of an insect or other arthropod 4 FLAT AREA a smooth flat area on a hard surface such as a bone or a tooth ■ *vt* (**facets, faceting** *or* **facetting, faceted** *or* **facetted**) CUT FACETS IN to cut facets in something, especially a gemstone [Early 17C. < French *facette* 'little face' < *face* (see FACE).]

facetiae /fə séeshi ee/ *npl* (*archaic*) 1 witty or humorous remarks 2 coarsely humorous books [Early 16C. < Latin, 'jokes', plural of *facetia* (see FACETIOUS).]

⚡**face time** *n* 1 *US* TIME SPENT FACE-TO-FACE time spent dealing face-to-face with other people (*informal*) ○ *The schedule calls for weekly e-mail reports as well as some actual face time between team members.* 2 TIME SPENT ON TELEVISION the amount of time that somebody spends appearing on television ○ *We need more face time to sway public opinion on this issue.* 3 EXTRA TIME AT PLACE OF EMPLOYMENT the amount of time somebody spends at his or her place of employment, especially beyond normal working hours ○ *What is she trying to prove with all this face time?*

facetious /fə séeshəss/ *adj* 1 intended to be humorous but often silly or inappropriate 2 not to be taken seriously ○ *a facetious suggestion* [Late 16C. < French *facétieux* < *facétie* 'joke' < Latin *facetia* < *facetus* 'graceful, witty'.] —**facetiously** *adv* —**facetiousness** *n*

face-to-face *adj, adv* 1 in the physical presence of somebody else (*not hyphenated after verbs*) 2 in direct contact or confrontation ○ *We came face-to-face with the situation.*

face value *n* 1 the value that is stated on something, especially a note, coin, or stamp 2 what something seems to mean or be worth, which may be better than its true worth or meaning ○ *We'd be unwise to take his promises at face value.*

Facey /fáyssi/, **Albert Barnett** (1894–1982) Australian writer

facia *n* = **fascia** *n.* 1, **fascia** *n.* 2, **fascia** *n.* 3, **fascia** *n.* 5

facial /fáysh'l/ *adj* relating to the face ○ *an unhappy facial expression* ■ *n* a beauty treatment for the face, usually consisting of a facial massage followed by cleansing and makeup —**facially** *adv*

facial nerve *n* a nerve of the seventh cranial pair that controls the muscles of the face and jaw, and the sensory abilities of the palate, front of the tongue, and nose

facial scrub *n* a slightly abrasive cream or lotion used on the face to remove a layer of dead skin and improve the complexion

-facient *suffix* causing, making ○ *febrifacient* [< Latin *facient-*, present participle of *facere* 'do, make']

facies /fáyshi eez, -shiz/ (*plural* **-es**) *n* 1 GENERAL APPEARANCE the general characteristic appearance of something, e.g. a plant or animal species 2 ROCK FEATURES INDICATING FORMATION the combined physical and chemical features of a rock that indicate the manner of its formation or deposition 3 FACIAL APPEARANCE LINKED TO DISEASE the appearance of somebody's face as a characteristic of a particular disease or condition [Early 18C. < Latin (see FACE).]

facile /fáss īl/ *adj* 1 SUPERFICIAL made or arrived at without any serious thought or depth of feeling and therefore of little value or significance 2 FLUENT BUT INSINCERE produced, spoken, or speaking so fluently and easily as to seem insincere or superficial 3 EASY TO DO requiring little effort 4 WORKING EASILY working or acting smoothly and easily [15C. Via French, 'easy' < Latin *facilis* 'easy to do, pliant, courteous' < *facere* 'do, make'.] —**facilely** *adv* —**facileness** *n*

facilitate /fə síllə tayt/ (**-tates, -tating, -tated**) *vt* to make something easy or easier to do [Early 17C. Via French < Italian *facilitare* 'make easy' < *facile* 'easy' < Latin *facilis* (see FACILE).] —**facilitative** *adj*

facilitation /fə síllə táysh'n/ *n* 1 the process of making something easy or easier 2 a decrease in the resistance to a nerve impulse in a neural pathway, brought about by prior or repeated stimulation

facilitator /fə síllə taytər/ *n* 1 an enabler of a process, especially by encouraging people to find their own solutions to problems or tasks 2 an organizer and provider of services for a meeting, seminar, or other event

facility /fə sílləti/ *n* (*plural* **-ties**) 1 SKILL an ability to do something easily 2 EFFORTLESSNESS ease in doing something or in being done 3 SOMETHING WITH A FUNCTION something designed or created to provide a service or fulfill a need (*often plural*) ○ *A wide range of facilities is available at the sports centre.* ■ **facilities** *npl* TOILET a toilet

facing /fáyssing/ *n* 1 LINING THAT FINISHES EDGE a lining that finishes the edge of something, especially a piece of fabric sewn inside a garment to neaten the edges 2 WALL SURFACE a layer of material that covers the outer surface of a wall to decorate or protect it ■ **facings** *npl* CUFFS AND COLLAR OF JACKET contrasting coverings on the cuffs and collar of a jacket, especially a military jacket

-facing *suffix* pointing in the specified direction

~~**facism**~~ incorrect spelling of **fascism**

façonné /fássə nay/, **faconne** *n* 1 a fabric with a pattern or design woven into it 2 the woven pattern on a façonné fabric [Late 19C. < French, 'fashioned'.]

facsimile /fak símməli/ *n* 1 COPY an exact copy of something, e.g. a document, a coin, or somebody's handwriting 2 FAX a fax (*dated*) ■ *vt* (**-iles, -ileing, -iled**) MAKE COPY OF to make an exact copy or reproduction of something [Late 16C. < modern Latin, < Latin *facere* 'do, make' + *simile* 'similar'.]

facsimile edition *n* a book or print that is reprinted in exactly the same style as an earlier edition, often being a photographic reproduction of the original

fact /fakt/ *n* 1 SOMETHING KNOWN TO BE TRUE something that can be shown to be true, to exist, or to have happened 2 TRUTH OR REALITY the truth or actual existence of something, as opposed to the supposition of something or a belief about something 3 PIECE OF INFORMATION a piece of information such as a statistic or a statement of the truth 4 ACTUAL COURSE OF EVENTS the circumstances of an event or state of affairs, rather than an interpretation of its significance ○ *Matters of fact are issues for a jury, while matters of law are issues for the court.* 5 SOMETHING BASED ON EVIDENCE something that is based on or concerned with the evidence presented in a legal case [15C. < Latin *factum* 'deed' < *fact-*, past participle of *facere* 'do, make'.] ◇ **after the fact** after something, especially a criminal act, has been done ◇ **before the fact** before something, especially a criminal act, has been done ◇ **in fact, in actual fact** used to correct a previous misunderstanding or false impression

USAGE The phrase ***in fact***, as in *You are, in fact, wrong*, is spelled as two words, never as *infact*.

fact-finding *adj* intended to find out information about something ■ *n* activity that is intended to find out information about something —**fact-finder** *n*

faction[1] /fáksh'n/ *n* 1 a group that is a minority within a larger group and has specific interests or beliefs that are not always in harmony with the larger group 2 conflict or dissension within a group [15C. Via French < Latin *faction-* 'act of making' < *fact-* (see FACT).] —**factional** *adj* —**factionally** *adv*

faction[2] /fáksh'n/ *n* 1 writing or film-making that portrays real people or events by dramatizing the facts using the techniques of fiction 2 a piece of writing, a film, or a television programme that portrays real people or events in a dramatized way [Mid-20C. Blend of FACT + FICTION.] —**factional** *adj*

-faction[1] *suffix* the making or production of something ○ *liquefaction*

-faction[2] *suffix* making, producing ○ *rarefaction* [Via Old French < Latin *-faction-* < *fact-* (see FACT)]

factionalise *vti* = **factionalize**[1], **factionalize**[2]

factionalism /fáksh'nəlizəm/ *n* the existence of or conflict between groups within a larger group —**factionalist** *n*

factionalize[1] /fáksh'nə līz/ (**-izes, -izing, -ized**), **factionalise** (**-ises, -ising, -ised**) *vti* to split, or cause something to split, into factions

factionalize[2] *vt* to dramatize actual events

factious /fákshəss/ *adj* liable to cause, taking part in, or typical of conflict within a group [Mid-16C. Directly or via French < Latin *factiosus* < *factio*, *faction-* (see FACTION[1]).] —**factiously** *adv* —**factiousness** *n*

factitious /fak tíshəss/ *adj* 1 contrived and insincere rather than genuine 2 not real or natural but artificial or invented (*formal*) [Mid-17C. < Latin *factitius* < *fact-* (see FACT).] —**factitiously** *adv* —**factitiousness** *n*

factitive /fáktətiv/ *adj* describes a verb that takes a direct object and a complement [Mid-19C. < modern Latin *factitivus* < Latin *factitare* 'do again' < *fact-* (see FACT).] —**factitively** *adv*

fact of life *n* an unavoidable truth, especially an unpleasant one ■ **facts of life** *npl* basic information on sexual matters and reproduction

factoid /fákt oyd/ *n* 1 something that may not be true but is widely accepted as true because it is repeatedly quoted, especially in the media 2 a small and often unimportant bit of information

factor /fáktər/ *n* 1 INFLUENCE something that contributes to or has an influence on the result of something ○ *Access to emergency exits is an important factor when planning the layout of a public building.* 2 LEVEL a quantity or level of something 3 AMOUNT BY WHICH SOMETHING IS MULTIPLIED an amount by which something is multiplied to give a specific result ○ *The number of visitors to the museum has increased by a factor of three.* 4 QUANTITY MULTIPLIED WITH OTHERS one of two or more numbers or quantities that can be multiplied together to give a specified number or quantity ○ *3 and 5 are factors of 15.* 5 SOMEBODY TRADING FOR COMMISSION a person who or organization that buys and sells goods for a commission 6 BUSINESS AGENT an agent or transactor of business for somebody else 7 *Scotland* MANAGER OF ESTATE a person who or firm that manages an estate or property on behalf of the owner 8 BIOLOGICAL SUBSTANCE a biological substance that has a physiological effect ■ *v* 1 *vi* ACT AS FACTOR to work as a factor 2 *vt* MATH = **factorize** [15C. Via French < Latin, < *fact-* (see FACT).] —**factorability** /fáktərə bílləti/ *n* —**factorable** *adj*

factor in *vt* to include or consider something as contributing to or influencing something else, e.g. when making a decision

factorage /fáktərij/ *n* **1** the fees or commission charged by a factor **2** the business of working as a factor

factor analysis *n* a statistical technique used to determine the relative strength of various influences on an outcome

factor VIII *n* a protein substance, one of a number that promote clotting of blood. Its inherited absence causes haemophilia.

factorial /fak táwri əl/ *n* **PRODUCT OF MULTIPLICATION** (*symbol* **!**) the number resulting from multiplying a whole number by every whole number between itself and 1 inclusive ■ *adj* **1 RELATING TO FACTORIAL** relating to or involving a factorial **2 INVOLVING FACTOR** involving or typical of a commercial factor or the work of such a factor —**factorially** *adv*

factoring /fáktəring/ *n* **1** the work of a commercial factor **2** the business of buying debts at a discount so as to make a profit from collecting them

factorize /fáktə rīz/ (**-izes, -izing, -ized**), **factorise** (**-ises, -ising, -ised**) *vti* to find out or calculate the factors of a given integer or equation. US term **factor** *v.* **2** —**factorization** /fáktə rī záysh'n/ *n*

factorship /fáktərship/ *n* the position or business of being a factor for another person or business

factory /fáktəri/ (*plural* **-ries**) *n* **1 BUILDING WHERE GOODS ARE MANUFACTURED** a building or complex of buildings where goods are manufactured on a large scale (*often before nouns*) ○ *a factory worker* **2 PRODUCTIVE PLACE** a place where a lot of things of a particular kind are produced (*informal*) ○ *As far as popular music was concerned, it was a hit factory.* **3 PLACE ABROAD WHERE AGENTS DID BUSINESS** formerly, a place where business was carried out abroad by commercial agents (**factors**), especially a trading station

factory farm *n* a farm where animals are reared by intensive methods and on a large scale using modern industrial equipment —**factory farming** *n*

factory floor *n* the area of a factory where the manufacturing process is carried out, as opposed to the administration areas

factory ship *n* a large fishing vessel equipped to process and freeze its own catch, or a whole fleet's catch

factotum /fak tṓtəm/ *n* somebody employed to do a variety of jobs for somebody else [Mid-16C. < Latin, 'do everything!' < *fac*, imperative of *facere* 'do, make' + *totum* 'all'.]

fact sheet *n* a printed sheet or booklet giving information about something, especially a subject covered in a broadcast programme

factual /fákchoo əl/ *adj* **1** involving, containing, or based on facts **2** consisting of the truth or including only those things that are actual [Mid-19C. After ACTUAL.] —**factuality** /fákchoo álləti/ *n* —**factually** *adv* —**factualness** *n*

factualism /fákchoo əlizəm/ *n* a strict devotion to or adherence to facts —**factualist** *n*

facula /fákyŏŏlə/ (*plural* **-lae** /-lee/) *n* a large bright extremely hot region on the Sun's surface, usually occurring near a sunspot [Early 18C. < Latin, 'little torch'.] —**facular** *adj*

facultative /fák'ltətiv/ *adj* **1 NOT REQUIRED** optional rather than obligatory **2 ALLOWING SOMETHING TO HAPPEN** enabling or capable of permitting something to happen or be done, but not able to force its occurrence **3 ASSOCIATED WITH A VARIETY OF CONDITIONS** able to live or take place under a range of external conditions ○ *a facultative parasite.* ◊ **obligate** *adj.* —**facultatively** *adv*

faculty /fák'lti/ (*plural* **-ties**) *n* **1 MENTAL POWER** a mental power or ability that somebody has, e.g. reason or memory **2 ABILITY** any capacity or ability that somebody is born with or learns ○ *have a great faculty for learning languages* **3 DIVISION OF UNIVERSITY** a department or group of departments dealing with a particular subject in a university or college **4 TEACHING STAFF FOR PARTICULAR UNIVERSITY DIVISION** the teaching staff of a particular faculty in a university or college **5** *US, Can* EDUC = **staff**[1] *n.* **3** **6 ALL MEMBERS OF PROFESSION** all of the people who practise a particular profession, especially medicine **7 POWER GRANTED BY AUTHORITY** a power or right given by an authority [14C. Via French < Latin *facultas* < *facilis* 'easy'.]

Faculty of Advocates *n Scotland* the professional association for advocates in the Scottish legal system

FA Cup *n* **1** a yearly competition in which teams are gradually eliminated, open to football teams that belong to the Football Association of England **2** the trophy awarded to the winning team in the FA Cup

fad /fad/ *n* **1** something that is very popular but only for a short time **2** something that is important only to a particular person [Mid-19C. < ?]

Fadden /fádd'n/, **Sir Arthur William** (1895–1973) Australian statesman

faddish /fáddish/ *adj US* = **faddy** —**faddishly** *adv* —**faddishness** *n*

faddism /fáddizəm/ *n* the existence of or participation in briefly popular fashions —**faddist** *n*

faddy /fáddi/ (**-dier, -diest**) *adj* tending to have strongly held likes and dislikes about food ○ *a faddy eater.* US term **faddish** *adj.* —**faddily** *adv* —**faddiness** *n*

fade /fayd/ *v* (**fades, fading, faded**) **1** *vti* **GRADUALLY BECOME LESS** to lose or make something lose brightness, colour, or loudness gradually **2** *vi* **BECOME TIRED** to lose strength, freshness, and vigour **3** *vi* **DISAPPEAR SLOWLY** to die away or vanish gradually **4** *vi* **LOSE EFFECTIVENESS** to become less effective temporarily **5** *vti* **STRIKE GOLF BALL SO IT CURVES** to hit a golf ball deliberately so that, in a right-handed shot, it curves slightly from left to right ■ *n* **1 GRADUAL LESSENING** an instance of something gradually becoming quieter, less bright, or less distinct **2 GRADUAL DISAPPEARANCE OF IMAGE** a gradual disappearance of an image in a film or television show **3** *US* **OFFENSIVE TERM** an offensive term for a Black person who has adopted white friends and attitudes (*slang*) **4 GOLF SLICE** a golf shot in which the ball spins slightly from left to right in the air [14C. < French *fade* 'weak, pale'.] —**fadable** *adj* —**fadedness** *n*

fade away *vi* **1** to become gradually fainter or weaker and finally disappear **2** to become thin and unhealthy

fade in *vti* to gradually make a sound audible or an image visible, or become gradually audible or visible

fade out *vti* to gradually make an image or sound fainter until it disappears, or become gradually fainter before disappearing

fade up *vti* BROADCAST, CINEMA = **fade in**

fade-in *n* the gradual introduction of a sound until it is audible or of an image until it is visible and clear

fadeless /fáydləss/ *adj* not fading in sunlight or after washing —**fadelessly** *adv*

fade-out *n* **1** a gradual decrease in loudness or brightness as a sound or image becomes fainter and less distinct until it disappears **2** a gradual reduction in the strength of a broadcast television or radio signal, especially with temporary loss of reception, often because of interference in transmission

fader /fáydər/ *n* a control on technical equipment that makes a sound or picture fade in or out

fade-up *n* BROADCAST, CINEMA = **fade-in**

fado /faá doo/ (*plural* **-dos**) *n* a sad Portuguese folk song [Early 20C. < Portuguese, 'fate'.]

faeces /feésseez/ *npl* the body's solid waste matter, composed of undigested food, bacteria, water, and bile pigments and discharged from the bowel through the anus [14C. < Latin, plural of *faex* 'sediment, dregs'.] —**faecal** /feék'l/ *adj*

faena /fa áynə/ *n* a series of manoeuvres in the final stages of a bullfight, leading up to the killing of the bull by the matador [Early 20C. < Spanish, 'task'.]

faerie /fáyəri, fáiri/, **faery** (*plural* **-ies**) *n* (*literary*) **1** the world of the fairies **2** a fairy [Late 16C. Mock-medieval alteration of FAIRY.]

Faeroe Islands /fáyrō ílandz/ = **Faroe Islands**

Faeroese *n, adj* LANG, PEOPLES = **Faroese**

faery *n* LITERAT = **faerie**

faff about /faff-/, **faff around** *vi* to waste time by being indecisive or fussing unnecessarily (*informal*) [< *faff* 'blow as a light blustery wind', probably suggestive of the action]

FAFSA *abbr* Free Application for Federal Student Aid

fag[1] /fag/ *n* **1 SOMETHING BORING** something that is tedious or that makes somebody weary (*informal*) **2** *UK* **ERRAND BOY** a schoolboy at a public school who has to do menial jobs and run errands for an older schoolboy (*dated*) ■ *v* (**fags, fagging, fagged**) **1** *vti US* **EXHAUST THROUGH WORK** to tire out, or cause to become exhausted, through drudgery or hard labour **2** *vi* **ACT AS ERRAND BOY** to do menial jobs and run errands for an older schoolboy (*dated*) [Mid-16C. < ?]

fag[2] /fag/ *n* a cigarette (*informal*) [Late 19C. Shortening of FAG END.]

fag[3] /fag/ *n US* an offensive term for a homosexual man (*slang*) [Early 20C. Shortening of FAGGOT[2].] —**faggy** *adj*

fag end *n* **1 CIGARETTE STUB** the remaining part of a cigarette that has been smoked (*informal*) **2 LAST AND WORST PART OF** the last part of something after the best of it has been used ○ *the fag end of the day* **3 REMNANT OF CLOTH** the remaining part of a piece of cloth, most of which has been used

fagged /fagd/, **fagged out** *adj* feeling very tired or worn out (*informal*)

faggot[1] /fággət/ *n* **1 BUNDLE OF STICKS FOR FIREWOOD** a bundle of sticks or twigs, especially wood to be burnt as fuel **2 BUNDLE OF PIECES OF METAL** a bundle of pieces of metal, especially pieces of iron or steel for welding **3 OFFAL MEATBALL** a ball of chopped meat, usually pork offal, mixed with bread and herbs, that is baked in the oven ■ *vt* **1 COLLECT SOMETHING AND TIE INTO BUNDLE** to collect things, especially sticks, and tie them into a bundle or bundles **2 STITCH WITH FAGGOTING** to sew something using faggoting [13C. Via Old French < Italian *faggotto* < Greek *phakelos* 'bundle'.]

faggot[2] /fággət/ *n US* an offensive term for a homosexual man (*slang*) [Early 20C. < FAGGOT[1] as an offensive term for a woman.] —**faggoty** *adj*

faggoting /fággəting/ *n* **1** a decorative way of sewing two hemmed pieces of fabric together, filling the gap between them with an insertion stitch **2** an embroidery technique in which lengthwise threads are pulled out and the cross threads tied into bundles, producing a decorative openwork effect

fag hag *n US* an offensive term for a woman who enjoys socializing with homosexual men (*slang*)

fagot *n* US = **faggot**[2] (*slang offensive*)

fagoting *n* US = **faggoting**

fah, **fa** *n* a syllable that represents the fourth note in a scale, used for singing solfeggio

Fahd /faad/ (*b.* 1922) king of Saudi Arabia (1982–)

fahlband /faál band/ *n* a thin bed of rock that contains metal sulphide minerals, although not in sufficient quantity to be used as an ore [Late 19C. < German, 'pale (ash-coloured) band'.]

Fahr. *abbr* Fahrenheit

Fahrenheit /fárrən hīt/ *adj* using or measured on a temperature scale on which water freezes at 32° and boils at 212° under normal atmospheric conditions. ◊ **Celsius** [Mid-18C. After Gabriel *Fahrenheit* (1686–1736) German physicist.]

faience /fī óNss, -aánss/, **faïence** *n* earthenware decorated with coloured opaque metallic glazes (*often before nouns*) ○ *a faience bowl* [Late 17C. < French, after *Faïence* 'Faenza', town in N Italy.]

fail /fayl/ *v* **1** *vi* **BE UNSUCCESSFUL** to be unsuccessful in trying to do something ○ *This plan can't fail.* **2** *vi* **BE UNABLE TO DO** to be incapable of doing something or unwilling to do it ○ *She failed to see what the problem was.* **3** *vti* **NOT PASS EXAM OR COURSE** to fall short of the standard required to pass an examination or course ○ *He failed English.* **4** *vt* **JUDGE STUDENT NOT GOOD ENOUGH** to judge a student not good enough to pass an examination or a course **5** *vi* **STOP FUNCTIONING OR GROWING** to stop working or not perform or grow as expected ○ *The brakes on the car failed.* **6** *vi* **COLLAPSE FINANCIALLY** to collapse financially, becoming insolvent or bankrupt ○ *The business failed after six years.* **7** *vt* **LET SOMEBODY DOWN** to abandon, forsake, or let somebody down by not doing what is expected or needed ○ *My courage failed me.* **8** *vi* **BECOME WEAKER** to lose strength, loudness, or brightness ○ *The light began to fail.* ■ *n* **FAILURE** an instance of falling short of the standard required to pass an examination or course, especially if given as an essay or examination grade [13C. Via Old French *faillir* < Latin *fallere* 'deceive somebody's hopes, disappoint'.] ◇ **without fail** for certain

failing /fáyling/ *n* a fault or weakness ■ *prep* if something does not happen ○ *Failing a resolution of the dispute by this afternoon, we will suspend you.*

SYNONYMS See *flaw.*

failing school *n* a school judged by the Secretary of State for Education, on the advice of inspectors, to be in need of special attention to bring it up to the required standard

faille /fayl/ *n* a closely woven, slightly ribbed, silk, cotton, or rayon fabric [Mid-16C. < French.]

fail-safe *adj* 1 **SWITCHING TO SAFE CONDITION** designed to switch equipment or a system to a safe condition if there is a fault or failure, e.g. as a thermostat turns something off if it overheats 2 **SURE TO SUCCEED** not capable of failing ■ *n* **SOMETHING THAT SAFEGUARDS** a fail-safe device or procedure

ϟ**fail-soft** *adj US* describes electronic equipment that can operate at a reduced level after the failure of a component or power supply

failure /fáylyər/ *n* 1 **LACK OF SUCCESS** a lack of success in or at something 2 **SOMETHING LESS THAN THAT REQUIRED** something that falls short of what is required or expected ○ *Failure will not be tolerated.* 3 **SOMETHING THAT FAILS** an unsuccessful person or thing 4 **BREAKDOWN** a breakdown or decline in the performance of something, or an occasion when something stops working or stops working adequately ○ *engine failure* 5 **LACK OF DEVELOPMENT OR PRODUCTION** inadequate growth, development, or production of something ○ *crop failure* 6 **BANKRUPTCY** a financial collapse, usually leading to bankruptcy

failure to thrive *n* pronounced lack of growth in a child due to inadequate absorption of nutrients or a serious heart or kidney condition, resulting in below-average height and weight

fain /fayn/ *adv* **HAPPILY** with gladness or eagerness (*archaic*) ■ *adj* (*archaic*) 1 **EAGER** willing or eager 2 **COMPELLED** forced by an obligation or circumstances [Old English *faegen* 'glad' < Germanic]

fainéant /fáyni ənt/ *adj* unwilling to do anything (*literary*) ■ *n* a lazy person (*literary*) [Early 17C. < French, alteration of *fait-nient* 'does nothing' < *faignant* 'shirker'.]

faint /faynt/ *adj* 1 **DIM** not bright, clear, or loud 2 **UNENTHUSIASTIC** feeble and done without conviction ○ *damned him with faint praise* 3 **DIZZY** dizzy or weak, as if about to become unconscious ○ *All of a sudden he felt faint.* 4 **SLIGHT** remote or slight ■ *vi* 1 **LOSE CONSCIOUSNESS BRIEFLY** to become unconscious, especially for a short time, because of a reduction in the flow of blood to the brain 2 **WEAKEN** to become weak or lose courage (*archaic*) ■ *n* **SUDDEN LOSS OF CONSCIOUSNESS** a sudden, usually brief, loss of consciousness, caused by a reduction in the flow of blood to the brain. Technical name **syncope** *n.* 1 [13C. < Old French, < *faindre* 'pretend, shirk'.] —**fainter** *n* —**faintish** *adj* —**faintly** *adv* —**faintness** *n*

SPELLCHECK Do not confuse ***faint*** with ***feint***, which has a similar sound. Beware: your spellchecker will not catch this error.

faint-hearted *adj* lacking courage, boldness, or enthusiasm —**faint-heartedly** *adv* —**faint-heartedness** *n*

SYNONYMS See ***cowardly***.

fainting fit *n* an attack of dizziness, often leading to unconsciousness

fair[1] /fair/ *adj* 1 **REASONABLE OR UNBIASED** not exhibiting any bias, and therefore reasonable or impartial 2 **DONE PROPERLY** according to the rules ○ *fair and free elections* 3 **LIGHT-COLOURED** light-coloured especially with light-coloured hair or skin 4 **SIZEABLE** reasonably large in size or quantity ○ *They had a fair number of responses to the advertisement.* 5 **BETTER THAN ACCEPTABLE** moderately good or reasonable ○ *a fair understanding* 6 **ACCEPTABLE** no more than acceptable or average ○ *Your performance this year has only been fair.* 7 **PLEASING TO LOOK AT** beautiful or pleasing to the eye 8 **NOT STORMY OR CLOUDY** sunny or clear, and without much wind 9 **NOT BLOCKED** clear and unobstructed ○ *a fair view of the enemy's forces* 10 **UNSULLIED** not marred by any blemish or stain 11 **FALSE DESPITE APPEARANCES** seemingly good or true, but actually false or insincere 12 **GOOD FOR SAILING** favourable for sailing or travel by ship ○ *a fair wind* ■ *adv* 1 **PROPERLY** in accordance with the rules or what is expected ○ *He's always played fair with me.* 2 **DIRECTLY** in a direct or straight way, and squarely ○ *hit fair in the centre of the board* 3 **QUITE** quite or rather (*informal regional*) ○ *I'm getting fair sick of this.* ■ *v* 1 *vi Scotland* **IMPROVE** to become bright after cloud or rain (*refers to the weather or sky*) 2 *vt* **MAKE SMOOTH AND EVEN** to smooth or streamline the surface of something, e.g. of an airplane wing or tabletop [Old English *faeger* 'beautiful' < Germanic, 'suitable'] ◇ **fair and square** justly, fairly, or according to the rules ◇ **fair do's** used to call for fairness or justice, especially as a warning that an injustice may be occurring (*informal*) ◇ **fair enough** 1 used to say that you accept something, though you would probably have been happier with something better (*informal*) 2 acceptable and understandable, but not ideal ◇ **fair's fair** used to urge or appeal for just or even treatment (*informal*) ◇ **fair to middling** reasonably good or reasonably well (*informal; hyphenated before nouns*) ◇ **no fair** *US* something that is unfair or against the rules (*informal*)

SPELLCHECK Do not confuse ***fair*** with ***fare***, which has a similar sound. Beware: your spellchecker will not catch this error.

fair[2] /fair/ *n* 1 **OUTDOOR EVENT WITH AMUSEMENTS** a temporary outdoor entertainment with amusements such as machines to ride on, sideshows, and food stands, usually set up on open ground and moving from place to place. US term **carnival** *n.* 2 2 **LIVESTOCK MARKET** a large market selling a wide range of goods including livestock, sometimes with amusements and sideshows 3 **COMMERCIAL EXHIBITION** an exhibition, often held annually, at which companies show their products to potential buyers 4 **SALE TO RAISE MONEY** a sale of goods to raise money for something, especially a charity 5 *US* LEISURE, AGRIC = **show** *n.* 4 6 *Scotland* **TRADES HOLIDAY** an annual two-week trades holiday observed in summer at different times in various towns, especially the Glasgow Fair, which occupies the last two weeks in July [13C. Via Old French < late Latin *feria* 'holiday' < Latin *feriae* (plural).]

Fairbanks /fáir bangks/ town in E Alaska. Population: 33,295 (1998 estimate).

Fairbanks, Douglas (1883–1939) US silent film actor. Born **Douglas Elton Ullman**

Fairburn /fáir burn/, **A. R. D.** (1904–57) New Zealand journalist and writer. Full name **Arthur Rex Dugant Fairburn**

fair copy *n* an unmarked version of a document that has been corrected and retyped or printed out again

fair dinkum *adj Aus* **GENUINE** true or genuine (*informal*) ■ *adv* (*informal*) 1 *Aus* **REALLY** used to emphasize or query the truthfulness or accuracy of what is being said 2 *ANZ* fair play

Fairfax /fáir faks/, **John** (1804–77) British-born Australian newspaper proprietor

Fairfax, Thomas, 3rd Baron Fairfax of Cameron (1612–71) English general, commander of the Parliamentary army during the Civil War

fair game *n* a permissible object of pursuit, ridicule, or attack

fair green *n* GOLF = **fairway** *n.* 1

fairground /fáir grownd/ *n* a large open outdoor space where fairs or exhibitions may be held ○ *fairground attractions*

fair-haired *adj* with light-coloured hair

fair-haired boy *n US* = **blue-eyed boy** (*informal*)

fairing[1] /fáiring/ *n* a streamlined structure added to an aircraft, car, or other vehicle to reduce drag. ◊ **cowling**

fairing[2] /fáiring/ *n* 1 a sweet buttery biscuit 2 a gift, especially one brought back from, or given at, a fair (*archaic*)

fairish /fáirish/ *adj* 1 reasonably good or large ○ *a fairish amount* 2 quite light in colour

Fair Isle[1] /fáyr īl/ *n* 1 any traditional Shetland Islands knitting design, used especially for sweaters, that incorporates bands of repeated multicoloured geometrical motifs 2 a technique of knitting designs with two or more colours in which any colours not actually being knitted are woven into the back of the work [Mid-19C. After FAIR ISLE[2].]

Fair Isle[2] /fáir īl/ the southernmost of the Shetland Islands, off the coast of NE Scotland. Population: 70. Area: 15 sq. km/8 sq. mi.

fairlead /fáir leed/, **fairleader** /-leedər/ *n* a ring, hole, or other device through which a rope is guided in order to reduce friction and prevent chafing, or to keep it in place

fairly /fáirli/ *adv* 1 **HONESTLY** in a just and honest, proper, or legitimate way 2 **MODERATELY** to a reasonable or moderate degree ○ *a fairly easy decision* 3 **CONSIDERABLY** to a considerable degree ○ *The ground fairly shook with the impact.*

fair-market value *n US* a price for something that both buyer and seller willingly agree to when neither party is under undue pressure to complete the transaction

fair-minded *adj* able to make impartial and just judgments or resulting from such a judgment —**fair-mindedly** *adv* —**fair-mindedness** *n*

fairness /fáirnəss/ *n* 1 the condition of being just or impartial 2 the condition of being pleasing to look at ◇ **in (all) fairness** being just and impartial

fair play *n* 1 the playing of a game without cheating or breaking the rules 2 conduct that is just and equitable ◇ **fair play to somebody** *Ireland* used to express general good wishes to somebody (*informal*)

fair sex *n* women and girls collectively (*literary*)

fair shake *n* just treatment or a reasonable chance to attempt something (*informal*)

fair-skinned *adj* having pale skin of a type that is easily burned by the sun

fair-spoken *adj* speaking in a pleasant and polite way —**fair-spokenness** *n*

fair-trade agreement *n US* an agreement between a manufacturer of a product and distributors or retailers that the product will not be sold for less than a price set by the manufacturer

fairway /fáir way/ *n* 1 the closely mown area on a golf hole that forms the main avenue between a tee and a green 2 a navigable channel or the usual course followed by vessels in a river, harbour, or other body of water

Fairweather, Mount /fáir wethər/ mountain in the St Elias Mountains on the border between SE Alaska and W British Columbia, Canada. Height: 4,663 m/15,300 ft.

Fairweather, Ian (1891–1974) Scottish-born Australian painter

fair-weather *adj* 1 suitable, done, or taking part only when the weather is fine 2 able to be relied upon only when things are going well

Fairweather Cape /fáir wethər-/ cape on the coast of SE Alaska

fairy /fáiri/ *n* (*plural* **-ies**) 1 **SMALL SUPERNATURAL CREATURE** an imaginary supernatural being, usually resembling a small person, with magic powers 2 **OFFENSIVE TERM** an offensive term for a homosexual man (*slang*) ■ *adj* **OF FAIRIES** relating to, belonging to, or typical of fairies ○ *the fairy folk* [14C. < Old French *faerie* 'enchantment' < *fae* 'fairy' < Latin *fata* 'the Fates', plural of *fatum* 'fate'.] —**fairy-like** *adj*

fairy cycle *n* a small children's bicycle or tricycle

fairyfloss /fáiri floss/ *n Aus* candyfloss

fairy godmother *n* 1 in some fairy stories, a kind fairy in the form of a woman who gives vital help to somebody, especially to the hero or heroine 2 somebody, especially a woman, who gives generous help, often anonymously

fairyland /fáiri land/ *n* 1 the imaginary country where fairies live 2 any enchanting place, e.g. a fantasy world existing in somebody's imagination

fairy lights *npl* a long string of small, often coloured, electric lights, used on Christmas trees and for other types of decoration

fairy ring *n* a ring of grass darker than the surrounding grass, traditionally thought to be associated with dancing fairies but actually marking the outer edge of growth of various underground perennial fungi

fairy ring champignon *n* a buff-coloured edible fungus, often growing in a ring-shaped cluster. *Marasmius oreades.*

fairy shrimp *n* a tiny soft-bodied crustacean found in fresh or brackish water, with an elongated body and eleven pairs of appendages. Order: Anostraca.

fairy tale, fairy story *n* 1 a story for children about fairies or other imaginary beings and events, often containing a moral message 2 an improbable invented account of something, often a false excuse

LITERARY LINK *Grimm's Fairy Tales*, a collection of folk tales (1812–15) compiled and edited by German scholars Jacob and Wilhelm Grimm. Based on written sources dating back to the 16th century and on German folk tales, it includes many stories now famous worldwide, including 'Cinderella', 'Hansel and Gretel', and 'Rumpelstiltskin'.

fairy-tale *adj* 1 derived from or typical of a fairy tale 2 like something from a fairy tale, especially in being fortunate, happy, or extravagantly beautiful

fairy thorn *n N Ireland* a hawthorn bush left growing in the middle of a field through fear that misfortune would befall whoever chopped it down

fairy wren *n* a wren, the male of which has colourful breeding plumage. Native to: Australia. Genus: *Malurus.*

Faisal /físs'l/ (1905–75) king of Saudi Arabia (1964–75)

Faisal I (1885–1933) king of Iraq (1921–33)

Faisal II (1935–58) king of Iraq (1939–58)

Faisalabad /fízələ bad/, **Faisalābād** city in NE Pakistan. Population: 1,977,246 (1998).

fait accompli /fáyt ə kóm plee/ (*plural* **faits accomplis** /fáyt ə kóm plee/) *n* something that is already done or decided and seems unalterable [Mid-19C. < French, 'accomplished fact'.]

faites vos jeux /fáyt vō zhō/ *v* used by a croupier in roulette and other gambling games to ask people to place their bets [< French]

faith /fayth/ *n* 1 **BELIEF OR TRUST** belief in, devotion to, or trust in somebody or something, especially without logical proof ○ *I wouldn't put my faith in him to sort things out.* 2 **RELIGION OR RELIGIOUS GROUP** a system of religious belief, or the group of people who adhere to it 3 **TRUST IN GOD** belief in and devotion to God ○ *Her faith is unwavering.* 4 **SET OF BELIEFS** a strongly held set of beliefs or principles ○ *people of different political faiths* 5 **LOYALTY** allegiance or loyalty to somebody or something [13C. Via Old French *feid* < Latin *fides* 'trust, belief'.] ◇ **keep faith with somebody** *or* **something** to be loyal or true to a person or promise ◇ **on faith** without demanding proof

faithful /fáythf'l/ *adj* 1 **CONSISTENTLY LOYAL** consistently trustworthy and loyal, especially to a person, a promise, or duty 2 **NOT ADULTEROUS OR PROMISCUOUS** not having sexual relations with somebody other than a spouse or partner 3 **CONSCIENTIOUS** displaying or resulting from a sense of responsibility or devotion to duty 4 **CORRECT** accurate and true ○ *a faithful account of the events* 5 **WITH UNWAVERING BELIEF** believing firmly in something or somebody, especially a religion ■ *n* **SOMEBODY OR SOMETHING RELIABLE** a person who or thing that can be trusted and relied upon ■ *npl* 1 **faithful, Faithful RELIGIOUS BELIEVERS** the believers in a religion considered as a group, especially Muslims or Christians 2 **LOYAL SUPPORTERS** people who believe in or follow somebody or something, especially the loyal members of a political party ○ *the party faithful* —**faithfulness** *n*

faithfully /fáythf'li/ *adv* in a loyal, true, or accurate way ◇ **yours faithfully** used immediately before the signature to end a letter that is not addressed to somebody by name

faith healer *n* a healer who treats illness or disorders through prayer, sometimes also by touching the affected person —**faith healing** *n*

faithless /fáythləss/ *adj* 1 **DISHONEST** dishonest, or disloyal to somebody or something, e.g. in not keeping a promise or performing a duty 2 **UNTRUSTWORTHY** not to be trusted or relied on 3 **NOT RELIGIOUS** not believing in a religious faith —**faithlessly** *adv* —**faithlessness** *n*

fajitas /fə heétəss/ *npl* a Mexican dish consisting of beef or other meat that has been marinated, grilled, cut into strips, and served in a soft flour tortilla [Late 20C. < Mexican Spanish, 'little strips, belts'.]

fake[1] /fayk/ *n* **SOMETHING NOT GENUINE** a person or thing that appears or is presented as being genuine but is not ■ *adj* **NOT GENUINE** not genuine, but meant to be taken for genuine ■ *v* (**fakes, faking, faked**) 1 *vt* **FALSELY PRESENT SOMETHING AS GENUINE** to make or produce something and claim it is genuine when it is not 2 *vti* **PRETEND FEELING OR KNOWLEDGE** to pretend to have, feel, or know something 3 *vt* **IMPROVISE WHILE PERFORMING** to improvise or ad-lib a piece of music or lines in a play during a performance [Late 18C. < *feague,* 16C criminal slang for 'rob, tamper with' < ?] —**faker** *n* —**fakery** *n*

fake out *vt US* to deceive or surprise somebody, especially by bluffing (*informal*)

fake[2] /fayk/, **flake** *vt* (**fakes, faking, faked; flakes, flaking, flaked**) to coil or loop a rope so that it will not tangle when used ■ *n* a single coil or loop of a rope that has been faked [15C. < ?]

fakir /fáy keer, fə keér/, **fakeer, faqir** *n* 1 a religious Muslim, especially a Sufi, who lives by begging 2 a Hindu ascetic who lives by begging and whose religious practice often includes the performance of extraordinary feats of physical endurance [Early 17C. Directly or via French < Arabic, 'poor man'.]

fa-la /faa laá/, **fal la** *n* a refrain in 16th- and 17th-century English songs, using the meaningless syllables 'fa-la-la'

falafel /fə laáf'l/, **felafel** *n* a deep-fried ball of ground chickpeas seasoned with onions and spices [Mid-20C. Via Egyptian Arabic *falāfil* < Arabic *fulful* 'pepper'.]

Falange /fə lánj/ *n* a Spanish fascist movement founded in 1933 and dissolved in 1977. It was the official ruling party of Spain under Francisco Franco. [Mid-20C. < Spanish, 'phalanx'.] —**Falangist** *n*

Falasha /fə láshə/ (*plural* **-shas** *or* **-sha**) *n* a member of an Ethiopian Jewish religious group now largely living in Israel [Early 18C. < Amharic, 'exile'.]

falbala /fálbələ/ *n* a gathered trimming or ruffle used as decoration [Early 18C. < French.]

falcate /fál kayt/, **falcated** /fál kaytəd/ *adj* curved and tapering to a point like a sickle (*technical*) [Early 19C. < Latin *falcatus* < *falc-* 'sickle'.]

falchion /fáwlchən/ *n* a short sword with a broad slightly curved blade, used in medieval times [14C. Via Old French *fauchon* < Latin *falc-* 'sickle'.]

falciform /fálsi fawrm/ *adj* = **falcate** [Mid-18C. < Latin *falc-* 'sickle'.]

falcon /fáwlkən/ *n* 1 a fast powerful bird of prey related to the hawk that often catches birds as they fly. Family: Falconidae. 2 a female hawk that is trained to hunt small birds and animals [13C. Via Old French < late Latin *falcon-*.]

falconet /fáwlkə net/ *n* a small falcon. Native to: Asia. Genus: *Microhierax.*

falconine /fáwlkə nīn/ *adj* relating to, involving, or typical of a falcon

falconry /fáwlkənri/ *n* the breeding, training, and use of falcons or other hawks to hunt small prey and return from flight at a falconer's direction —**falconer** *n*

falderal /faáldə raal/, **folderol** /fóldə rol/ *n* 1 **TRINKET** an attractive but valueless object or trinket 2 silly nonsense (*dated*) 3 **SONG REFRAIN** a meaningless chorus or refrain in a song (*archaic*) [Early 19C. < *fol de rol,* nonsense refrain in songs.]

Faldo /fáldō/, **Nick** (*b.* 1957) British golfer. Full name **Nicholas Alexander Faldo**

faldstool /fáwld stool/ *n* 1 **FOLDING SEAT FOR BISHOP** a folding seat, especially one used by a bishop when officiating away from his throne or at another church 2 **FOLDING STOOL FOR WORSHIPPER** a small folding stool with a raised attachment like a desk at which a worshipper kneels to pray 3 **CORONATION STOOL FOR BRITISH SOVEREIGN** a stool on which the British sovereign kneels at his or her coronation [Old English *fældstōl* < FOLD[1] + STOOL; partly < medieval Latin *faldistolium* < Germanic]

Faliscan /fə lískən/ *n* an ancient language spoken in Italy, related to the Latin language that replaced it [Late 17C. < Latin *Faliscus* 'of Falerii', important city of Etruria.]

Falkirk /fáwl kurk/ 1 town in central Scotland. Population: 35,610 (1991). 2 council area in central Scotland. Area: 299 sq. km/115 sq. mi.

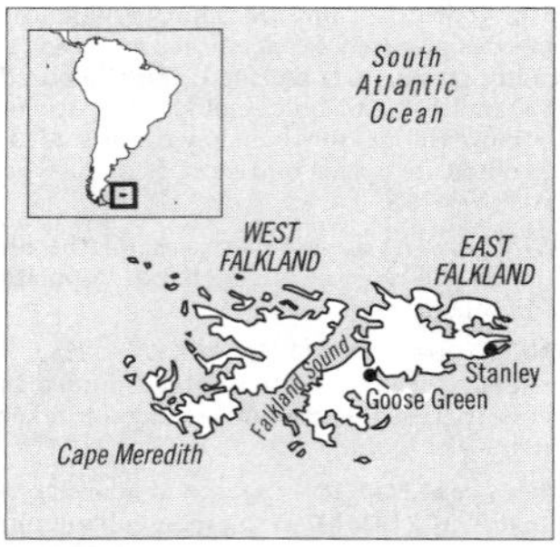

Falkland Islands

Falkland Islands /fáwklənd-/ group of islands and British dependency in the South Atlantic Ocean. Population: 2,100 (1993). Area: 12,173 sq. km/4,700 sq. mi.

fall /fawl/ *vi* (**falls, falling, fell** /fel/, **fallen** /fáwlən/) 1 **MOVE DOWNWARDS** to come down freely from a higher to a lower position, moved by the force of gravity ○ *The vase fell to the ground and shattered.* 2 **DROP OR BE LOWERED** to drop or be dropped or lowered ○ *The curtain fell at the end of the performance.* 3 **COME DOWN SUDDENLY FROM UPRIGHT POSITION** to drop or come down suddenly from an upright position, especially by accident ○ *The horse fell at the first fence.* 4 **BECOME LESS** to become lower or be reduced in amount, value, or quality 5 **BECOME LOWER IN PITCH** to become lower in pitch or volume 6 **BE TAKEN BY FORCE** to be conquered or captured by a military force 7 **DROP TO GROUND IN BATTLE** to drop to the ground in battle after being wounded or having died 8 **COLLAPSE POLITICALLY** to lose political power or be defeated ○ *The government fell after 18 months in office.* 9 **BE DRAPED** to hang down 10 **TAKE PLACE** to happen or occur as if falling on something and enveloping it ○ *Night fell suddenly.* 11 **DISPLAY DISAPPOINTMENT** to show an expression of disappointment ○ *Their faces fell when they heard the result.* 12 **GROW SAD** to become sad and gloomy or to lose hope ○ *Our hearts fell.* 13 **STOP TO LOOK** to settle or come to rest ○ *His gaze fell on an open book.* 14 **BE AVERTED** to look away or downwards ○ *Her eyes fell.* 15 **BEGIN TO BE IN SPECIFIED STATE** to begin to be in, or enter into, a specified state or condition ○ *The class eventually fell silent.* 16 **SIN** to sin or give in to temptation (*archaic*) ◊ **Fall** 17 **SLOPE** to slope downwards and away 18 **BE DUE** to become due ○ *When does the next payment fall?* 19 **BE LOST** to be lost to the bowling side in a cricket match ○ *The fourth wicket fell just after tea.* 20 **BECOME PREGNANT** to become pregnant (*regional*) ■ *n* 1 **ACT OF FALLING** the act of falling or moving down freely or suddenly 2 **SOMETHING FALLEN** something that falls or has fallen, or the amount that has fallen ○ *a heavy fall of snow* 3 **DISTANCE DOWN** the distance that something drops or could fall ○ *a ten-foot fall* 4 **LOWERING** a decrease in the amount, size, quantity, or quality of something ○ *Even a slight fall in prices is welcome.* 5 **SLOPE** a slope that heads downwards and away 6 **fall, Fall** *US, Can* = **autumn** *n.* 1 7 **WATERFALL** a waterfall or steep rapids (*often plural, often in placenames*) ○ *Niagara Falls* 8 **MILITARY LOSS** a military defeat or the loss of something to an enemy ○ *the fall of Leningrad* 9 **POLITICAL COLLAPSE** a loss of political power or control ○ *the fall of the government* 10 **SINNING** a giving in to temptation or the committing of a sin 11 **END OF HOISTING ROPE** the end of a rope or chain to which power is applied when hoisting something 12 **WRESTLING MOVE** a scoring move in wrestling in which one wrestler forces his or her opponent's shoulders to the floor for a specified period 13 **HAIRPIECE** a hairpiece of long hair, usually attached to the top of the head with the join covered over by the wearer's own hair 14 **DOWNWARD FACING PART OF IRIS BLOSSOM** the outer part of an iris flower, resembling a petal, that hangs down in front 15 in a cricket match, the loss of a wicket [Old English *feallan* < Germanic] ◇ **fall flat** to fail to have the intended effect ◇ **fall foul** *or* **afoul of** 1 to come into conflict with somebody or something 2 to collide with something ◇ **fall short** to be less than is needed ◇ **fall short of something** to fail to meet a desired standard

fall about *vi* to laugh noisily and uncontrollably (*informal*)

fall among *vt* to become associated unwittingly with somebody, something, or a group

fall apart *vi* 1 to collapse, fail, or break into pieces 2 to be in a state of great emotional distress (*informal*)

fall away *vi* 1 **DECREASE** to become smaller in number, quantity, or size ○ *Attendance fell away after the third week of the course.* 2 **SLOPE** to slope downwards 3 **STOP ASSOCIATING WITH** to withdraw friendship, devotion, or support

fall back *vi* 1 to retreat or move back, e.g. during a battle 2 to be overtaken by others in a race or contest

fall back on, fall back upon *vt* to resort to something, especially something familiar, if other plans do not work out

fall behind *v* 1 *vti* to fail to keep up with somebody or something 2 *vi* to be late in doing something, e.g. making a regular payment or completing a task ○ *He fell behind with the car payments.*

fall down *vi* 1 to collapse or drop to the ground 2 to be invalid or unsuccessful

fall down on *vt* to be unsuccessful or negligent in something

fall for *vt* 1 to become infatuated or in love with somebody or something 2 to be deceived by something

fall in *vi* 1 to join or form an organized rank ○ *The whistle blew and the soldiers fell in.* 2 to collapse inwards

fall in with *vt* 1 to meet and start associating with

somebody or a group **2** to agree or comply with something or somebody
fall off *v* **1** *vi* to decrease in size, number, or quality ○ *Share prices have fallen off in the last couple of days.* **2** *vti* to deviate from a course to sail downwind, or make a vessel sail downwind
fall on *vt* **1 fall on, fall upon** to attack somebody vigorously, especially by surprise (*literary*) **2 fall on, fall upon** to begin eating or doing something eagerly **3** = **fall to** *v.* 1
fall out *v* **1** *vi* **QUARREL** to have a quarrel with somebody, especially one that leads to strained relations **2** *vi* **OCCUR** to happen **3** *vti* **BREAK RANKS** to leave or break up an organized rank or position
fall over *vti* to drop accidentally to the ground, especially by tipping over or tumbling from an upright position ○ *I fell over a pile of books that had been left on the floor.* ○ *Be careful you don't fall over!* ◇ **fall over yourself** to be very eager or enthusiastic in doing something ○ *He was falling over himself to make everybody feel at home.*
fall through *vi* to fail to happen in the expected way
fall to *v* **1** *vt* **BE DUTY OF** to be the responsibility, obligation, or duty of somebody or a group ○ *It falls to the council to decide the matter.* **2** *vti* **START** to begin doing something **3** *vt* **BE GIVEN** to be given by right or inheritance to somebody
fall upon *vt* **1** = **fall on** *v.* 1, **fall on** *v.* 2 **2** = **fall to** *v.* 1

Fall *n* in Judaism and Christianity, the lapse of humankind into a sinful state as a result of Adam and Eve disobeying God

fal la *n* = **fa-la**

Falla /fī ə/, **Manuel de** (1876–1946) Spanish composer and pianist

fallacious /fə láyshəss/ *adj* **1** containing or involving a mistaken belief or idea **2** deceptive or liable to mislead people [Early 16C. Via Old French < Latin *fallaciosus* < *fallacia* (see FALLACY).] —**fallaciously** *adv* —**fallaciousness** *n*

fallacy /fálləssi/ (*plural* **-cies**) *n* **1 MISTAKEN BELIEF OR IDEA** something that is believed to be true but is erroneous **2 INVALID ARGUMENT** an argument or reasoning in which the conclusion does not follow from the premises **3 DECEPTIVENESS** the condition of being misleading or deceptive **4 LOGICAL ERROR IN ARGUMENT** a mistake made in a line of reasoning that invalidates it [15C. Via Old French < Latin *fallacia* 'deception' < *fallere* 'deceive'.]

fallback /fáwl bak/ *n* **1** something that can be used as a replacement or substitute if something else does not or would not work **2** a retreat or withdrawal —**fallback** *adj*

fallboard /fáwl bawrd/ *n US* the hinged cover that protects a piano keyboard when it is not being played

fallen past participle of **fall** ■ *adj* **1 KILLED** killed in battle **2 ON THE GROUND** on the ground after dropping down ○ *freshly fallen snow* ■ *npl* **PEOPLE WHO DIED IN WAR** those people killed in war, especially while fighting

fallen angel *n* in Christianity, any of the angels led by Satan who rebelled against God and were cast out of heaven

fallen arch *n* a flattening of the arch of the foot (*usually plural*)

fallen woman *n* a woman who is seen as sinful or dishonoured because she has had sexual relations outside marriage (*literary*)

faller /fáwlər/ *n* **1** a person, animal, or thing that falls **2** *US* somebody who cuts down trees

fallfish /fáwl fish/ (*plural* **-fish** *or* **-fishes**) *n* a large minnow known for its substantial nests, made by piling up small pebbles. Native to: E North America. *Semotilus corporalis.*

fall guy *n* (*informal*) **1** a person who is easily tricked or deceived **2** a person who takes the blame for another's mistake or wrongdoing

fallible /fálləb'l/ *adj* **1** liable to make mistakes **2** liable to be wrong or misleading [15C. < medieval Latin *fallibilis* < Latin *fallere* 'deceive'.] —**fallibility** /fállə bílləti/ *n* —**fallibleness** *n* —**fallibly** *adv*

falling-off *n* a decline in quality or quantity

falling-out (*plural* **fallings-out**) *n* a quarrel or disagreement, especially one that leads to strained relations with somebody

falling sickness *n* epilepsy (*archaic*)

falling star *n* ASTRON = **meteor** *n.* 2

fall line *n* **1 LINE ALONG TOP OF SLOPE** an imaginary line along the edge of higher land, marked by rapids and waterfalls, that indicates where rivers begin to descend more steeply from a highland region to a lowland one **2 NATURAL ROUTE OF DESCENT OF HILL** the natural route of descent on a hill between two given points **3 LINE CONNECTING HIGH AND LOW POINT** vertical line connecting a high and low point on a mountain or cliff

falloff /fáwl of/ *n* a decrease or decline, especially in the price of or demand for something

fallopian tube /fə lṓpi ən-/, **Fallopian tube** *n* either of two narrow tubes through which a female mammal's eggs pass from either of the ovaries to the womb [Early 18C. After Gabriele *Fallopio* (1523–62) Italian anatomist.]

fallout /fáwl owt/ *n* **1 RADIOACTIVE PARTICLES** a cloud of radioactive dust that is created by a nuclear explosion and settles back down to the earth **2 DESCENT OF RADIOACTIVE DUST** the descent to the earth of particles from a cloud of radioactive dust **3 INCIDENTAL CONSEQUENCES** consequences, especially undesirable ones, that result incidentally from a situation or event

fallout shelter *n* a place of refuge built to protect people from the effects of a nuclear weapon

fallow[1] /fállō/ *adj* **1 LEFT UNSEEDED AFTER PLOUGHING** left unseeded after ploughing for a period of time in order to recover natural fertility **2 CURRENTLY INACTIVE** currently inactive but with the possibility of activity or use in the future ■ *n* **FALLOW LAND** land that has been left fallow [13C. < Old English *fealh* < *fealgian* 'break up land by ploughing'.] —**fallowness** *n*

fallow[2] /fállō/ *adj* of a light yellowish-brown colour [Old English *fealu* < Indo-European] —**fallow** *n*

fallow deer *n* a deer, the male of which has broad flattened antlers and a brown coat spotted with white in summer. Native to: Europe, Asia. *Dama dama.*

Falmouth /fálməth/ seaside resort on the estuary of the River Fal in SE England. Population: 20,297 (1991).

false /fawlss, folss/ *adj* (**falser, falsest**) **1 INCORRECT** not conforming to facts or truth **2 MISTAKEN** resulting from a mistaken belief or misunderstanding **3 ARTIFICIAL** imitating, copying, or having the same function as the other thing named and replacing or used alongside it **4 DELIBERATELY DECEPTIVE** done with or having the intention of deceiving somebody **5 NOT GENUINE** intentionally made or adopted to deceive somebody **6 TREACHEROUS** disloyal and untrustworthy **7 CONFUSABLE WITH NAMED PLANT OR ANIMAL** superficially resembling and often mistaken for the plant or animal named ○ *false acacia* ■ *adv* (**falser, falsest**) **DISHONESTLY** in a dishonest and disloyal way (*literary*) [Pre-12C. Directly or via Old French < Latin *falsus* < *fallere* 'deceive'.] —**falsely** *adv* —**falseness** *n*

false acacia *n* a deciduous leguminous tree with spiny twigs, hanging clusters of fragrant flowers, and long seed pods. Native to: North America. Genus: *Robinia.* US term **locust** *n.* 4

false alarm *n* **1** a situation in which an alarm goes off unnecessarily **2** something that appears to be a problem but is not ○ *The company's impending bankruptcy proved to be a false alarm.*

false bedding *n* GEOL = **cross bedding**

false-card *vi* to play a card in bridge to mislead an opponent about the cards held in the suit led

false dawn *n* **1** light that appears in the east just before dawn **2** a sign that promises but does not deliver good results

false friend *n* **1** a word in a second language that closely resembles a word in somebody's first language but means something different **2** a friend proved to be disloyal and untrustworthy

false fruit *n* PLANT SCI = **pseudocarp**

falsehood /fáwlss hŏŏd, fólss-/ *n* **1 LIE** a lying or erroneous statement **2 UNTRUTH** something that is untrue **3 TELLING OF LIES** the telling of untruths

SYNONYMS See *lie.*

false imprisonment *n* the unlawful confinement of somebody

false keel *n* an extension to a boat's keel, added to protect the main keel or to increase stability

false memory syndrome *n* a situation in which examination, therapy or hypnosis has elicited apparent memories, especially of childhood abuse, that are disputed by family members and often traumatic to the patient

false move *n* an action showing an error of timing or judgment

false note *n* something that seems inappropriate, inconsistent, and badly timed

false position *n* a situation in which somebody is forced to act in an inconsistent or uncharacteristic way

false pregnancy *n* MED = **phantom pregnancy**

false pretences *npl* deception or misrepresentation in order to gain something from somebody ○ *He gained her trust under false pretences.*

false rib *n* any of the lower ribs, the bottom five pairs in humans, not connected directly to the sternum

false start *n* **1** a situation in which a competitor in a race breaks a regulation governing the starting procedure and the race has to be restarted **2** a failed attempt to begin something

false step *n* **1** an action showing an error of judgment **2** an act of stumbling

false topaz *n* CRYSTALS = **citrine** *n.* 1

falsetto /fawl séttō, fol-/ *n* (*plural* **-tos**) **1 HIGH SINGING METHOD** a method used by male singers to sing at a very high pitch by using more air and a combination of vocal chord vibration and head resonance **2 FALSETTO SINGER** a male singer who sings in a very high voice **3 FALSETTO VOICE** a very high voice used by a male singer ■ *adv* **IN FALSETTO VOICE** in an artificially or unusually high voice [Late 18C. < Italian, 'little false (one)' < *falso* 'false' < Latin *falsus* (see FALSE).]

falsework /fáwlss wurk, fólss-/ *n* a structure or frame that supports something that is being built

falsies /fáwlssiz, fólssiz/ *npl* two pads worn inside a bra to make the breasts look larger or more shapely (*informal*)

falsify /fáwlssi fī, fólss-/ (**-fies, -fying, -fied**) *vt* **1 ALTER FRAUDULENTLY** to alter something in order to deceive somebody **2 DISPROVE** to prove that something is incorrect **3 MISREPRESENT** to misrepresent the facts in order to mislead ○ *They falsified every detail of their story.* [15C. Directly or via French *falsifier* < medieval Latin *falsificare* 'act dishonestly' < Latin *falsus* (see FALSE) + *facere* 'do, make'.] —**falsifiability** /fáwlssi fī ə bílləti, fólss-/ *n* —**falsifiable** *adj* —**falsification** /fáwlssifi káysh'n, fólssi-/ *n* —**falsifier** *n*

falsity /fáwlssəti, fólss-/ (*plural* **-ties**) *n* **1** the fact or condition of being untrue **2** something that is incorrect or untrue [13C. Directly or via French < Latin *falsitas* < *falsus* (see FALSE).]

Falstaffian /fawl staáfi ən/ *adj* typical of the Shakespearean character Sir John Falstaff in being bawdy, pleasure-loving, given to outlandish bragging, and of great size

faltboat /fált bōt/ *n* a boat like a kayak consisting of waterproof fabric over a collapsible frame. US term **foldboat**

falter /fáwltər, fól-/ *v* **1** *vi* **LOSE CONFIDENCE** to become unsure and hesitant **2** *vi* **BEGIN TO FAIL** to lose strength, power, or vitality **3** *vi* **STUMBLE** to move unsteadily **4** *vti* **HESITATE IN SPEECH** to speak or say something hesitatingly ○ *Trembling with shame, she faltered an apology.* [14C. < ?] —**falterer** *n* —**falteringly** *adv* —**faltering** *adj*

SYNONYMS See *hesitate.*

fam. *abbr* **1** familiar **2** family

Famagusta /fámmə gŏŏstə/ seaport and resort in E Cyprus. Population: 20,516 (1989 estimate).

fame /faym/ *n* the condition of being very well known [12C. Via French < Latin *fama* 'talk, report, reputation'.]

USAGE fame or **notoriety**? In contemporary English ***notoriety*** is correctly used to mean only 'the condition of being well known for something disgraceful or otherwise undesirable', as in *a former politician whose notoriety stems from a society scandal.* ***Fame*** is simply 'the condition of being very well known', as in *a pilot whose fame* [not *notoriety*] *stems from his extraordinary recovery from terrible injuries.* The same distinction holds with the adjectives ***notorious*** ('infamous') and ***famous*** ('widely known').

famed /faymd/ *adj* very well known ○ *The restaurant was famed for its steaks.*

familial /fə mílli əl/ *adj* relating to or involving a family

familiar /fə mílli ər/ *adj* 1 OFTEN ENCOUNTERED well known, commonly seen or heard, and easily recognized 2 ACQUAINTED with a thorough knowledge and good understanding of something ○ *Are you familiar with the theory?* 3 FRIENDLY in or characteristic of a close personal relationship with somebody 4 IMPERTINENTLY INTIMATE unduly friendly or intimate in a way that is seen as presumptuous or impertinent (*dated*) ■ *n* 1 SPIRIT HELPING WITCH the supposed helper of a witch, usually a spirit with supernatural powers that takes the form of an animal, e.g. a cat 2 INTIMATE FRIEND a close friend and companion (*formal*) 3 LAY MEMBER OF MONASTERY a residential worker in a monastic community who has not taken a vow 4 HOUSEHOLD ATTENDANT OF POPE OR BISHOP a domestic servant in the household of a pope or Roman Catholic bishop [13C. Via French < Latin *familiaris* < *familia* (see FAMILY).] —**familiarly** *adv* —**familiarness** *n*

familiarise *vt* = **familiarize**

familiarity /fə mílli árrəti/ *n* 1 GOOD KNOWLEDGE thorough knowledge and understanding of something ○ *Familiarity with database systems would be an advantage.* 2 INTIMACY closeness and friendliness in a personal relationship 3 FAMILIAR QUALITY the quality of being familiar ○ *The place had a strange familiarity about it.* 4 UNWELCOME INTIMACY an intimacy that is improper and presumptuous (*dated*)

familiarize /fə mílli ə rīz/ (**-izes, -izing, -ized**), **familiarise** (**-ises, -ising, -ised**) *vt* to acquire or provide somebody with information or experience necessary for understanding or doing something ○ *You should familiarize yourself with the emergency procedure.* —**familiarization** /fə mílli ə rī záysh'n/ *n* —**familiarizer** *n*

familiar spirit *n* = **familiar** *n*. 1

~~**familier**~~ incorrect spelling of **familiar**

family /fámmli/ *n* (*plural* **-lies**) 1 GROUP OF RELATIVES a group of people who are closely related by birth, marriage, or adoption 2 PEOPLE LIVING TOGETHER a group of people living together and functioning as a single household, usually consisting of parents and their children 3 OTHERS IN SOMEBODY'S FAMILY the other members of the family to which somebody belongs ○ *He always spends Sunday afternoon with his family.* 4 OFFSPRING a child or set of children born to somebody ○ *They're not ready to start a family.* 5 LINEAGE all the people who are descended from a common ancestor 6 GROUP WITH SOMETHING IN COMMON a group whose members are related in origin, characteristics, or occupation 7 RELATED LANGUAGES a group of languages that have a common origin 8 SET OF RELATED ORGANISMS in taxonomic classification, a category of related organisms, comprising one or more genera 9 RELATED MATHEMATICAL SHAPES OR EXPRESSIONS a set of related mathematical curves, surfaces, or functions, usually expressed as a single equation containing one or more parameters or arbitrary constants ○ *a family of concentric circles* 10 RELATED ISOTOPES a group of radioactive isotopes that collectively constitute a decay series or chain 11 *US* BRANCH OF MAFIA a branch of the Mafia or of a similar large criminal group (*informal*) 12 *South Asia* WIFE somebody's wife ■ *adj* 1 USED BY FAMILY used, owned, or employed by a family, or suitable for one 2 APPROPRIATE FOR CHILDREN suitable to be experienced by families with children 3 SERVING FAMILIES serving families not just businesses or institutions [15C. < Latin *familia* 'servants of a household, household, family' < *famulus* 'servant'.] ◇ **in the family way** pregnant (*dated informal*)

family allowance *n UK, Can* an allowance formerly paid by the government in the United Kingdom and Canada to parents or guardians of children below a specified age. Now called **child benefit**. ◊ **child tax benefit**

family benefit *n* an allowance paid by a government to parents or guardians of dependent children, e.g. in New Zealand

family Bible *n* a large Bible handed down in a family from one generation to another

family circle *n* the members of a family who are closely related and usually who live together

family court *n* in the United States, Australia, and New Zealand, a court that rules on domestic disputes, especially those involving the care and custody of children

family credit *n* a regular payment formerly made by the UK government to families on a low income with at least one dependent child

Family Division *n* a branch of the High Court of Justice in England and Wales, handling divorce and cases concerning the custody of children

family doctor *n* a GP

family man *n* a married man who enjoys family life and spends a lot of time with his wife and children

family name *n* = **surname** *n*. 1

family planning *n* the use of birth control methods to choose the number and timing of children born into a family

family room *n* a room reserved for the use of people with children, especially in a pub

family tree *n* a chart that shows the relationships of members of a family over time, including dates of marriages, births, and deaths

famine /fámmin/ *n* 1 EXTREME FOOD SCARCITY a severe shortage of food resulting in widespread hunger 2 DEFICIENCY a severe shortage of something 3 EXTREME HUNGER extreme hunger and starvation [14C. < French, < *faim* 'hunger' < Latin *fames*.]

famine food *n* a crop or plant that is considered as an edible foodstuff only in times of severe food shortages

famish /fámmish/ *vti* to be extremely hungry, or make somebody extremely hungry (*often passive*) [14C. < obsolete *fame* < Old French *afamer* < Latin *fames* 'hunger'.] —**famishment** *n*

famous /fáyməss/ *adj* 1 known and recognized by many people 2 excellent and satisfying (*dated*) [14C. Via Old French < Latin *famosus* < *fama* 'talk, report, reputation'.] —**famously** *adv* —**famousness** *n*

famulus /fámmyōōləss/ (*plural* **-li** /-lī/) *n* a personal secretary or attendant, especially to a scholar or magician (*literary*) [Mid-19C. < Latin, 'servant'.]

fan[1] /fan/ *n* 1 DEVICE FOR MOVING AIR a device to cool or circulate currents of air, especially one with rotating blades 2 PERSONAL COOLING DEVICE a flat disc on a handle or a folding semicircular device for waving to and fro in order to cool the face 3 SOMETHING FAN-SHAPED something in the shape of an open hand-held fan, e.g. the tail of a peacock 4 WINNOWING MACHINE a series of revolving blades used to winnow or clean grain ■ *vt* (**fans, fanning, fanned**) 1 BLOW ON to blow a current of air steadily and lightly across or around something, either cooling or agitating it ○ *A cool breeze fanned the shore.* 2 MOVE AIR USING FAN to move air about using a fan 3 STIR UP to cause emotions to become more intense or a situation to become more volatile 4 SEPARATE GRAIN FROM CHAFF to winnow grain by blowing away the chaff 5 FIRE GUN WITH REPEATED CHOPPING MOVEMENT to fire a gun repeatedly by holding the trigger back and chopping at the hammer with the open hand [Pre-12C. < Latin *vannus* 'device for winnowing grain'.] —**fanner** *n*

fan out *vti* to spread or spread something out in the shape of an open hand-held fan

fan[2] /fan/ *n* 1 an enthusiastic admirer of a celebrity or public performer 2 = **fanatic** *n*. 2 [Late 19C. Shortening of FANATIC.]

Fanakalo /fánnəkəlō/, **Fanagalo** /-gəlō/ *n* a pidgin spoken in parts of South Africa, based on Zulu and English and developed mainly in mining communities of Namibia and Zimbabwe, and near Johannesburg [Mid-20C. Probably < Zulu (*kuluma*) *fana ka lo* '(speak) like this'.] —**Fanakalo** *adj*

fanatic /fə náttik/ *n* 1 a holder of extreme or irrational enthusiasms or beliefs, especially in religion or politics 2 an enthusiast about a pastime or hobby ■ *adj* = **fanatical** [Mid-16C. Directly or via French < Latin *fanaticus* 'inspired by a god, frenzied' < *fanum* 'temple'.] —**fanaticism** /fə náttisizəm/ *n*

fanatical /fə náttik'l/ *adj* excessively enthusiastic about a particular belief, cause, or activity —**fanatically** *adv* —**fanaticalness** *n*

fanaticise *vti* = **fanaticize**

fanaticize /fə nátti sīz/ (**-cizes, -cizing, -cized**), **fanaticise** (**-cises, -cising, -cised**) *vti* to make somebody fanatical about something, or become fanatical

fan belt *n* a continuous belt that turns a fan, especially one turning the cooling fan in the engine of a motor vehicle

fanciable /fánssi əb'l/ *adj* sexually desirable (*informal*)

fancier /fánssi ər/ *n* 1 somebody especially interested in or enthusiastic about something 2 somebody with a special interest in the breeding of a particular animal or plant

fanciful /fánssif'l/ *adj* 1 IMAGINARY based on imagination or dreams 2 IMAGINATIVE AND IMPRACTICAL led by imagination rather than realism and practicality 3 CURIOUSLY MADE strangely and imaginatively designed or made —**fancifully** *adv* —**fancifulness** *n*

fan club *n* an organization whose members are devoted to a celebrity or public performer, providing information and sometimes organizing special events

fancy /fánssi/ *adj* (**-cier, -ciest**) 1 NOT PLAIN elaborately and ornately decorated 2 INTRICATE intricately and skilfully performed 3 AIMING TO IMPRESS attempting or expected to impress 4 EXPENSIVE excessively priced or valued ○ *fancy prices* ○ *fancy restaurants charging high prices* 5 SELECTIVELY BRED describes animals that have been bred for specific features and qualities ■ *v* (**-cies, -cying, -cied**) 1 *vt* WISH FOR to want to do or have something ○ *I fancy a walk this afternoon.* ○ *Do you fancy a coffee?* 2 *vt* DESIRE to find somebody sexually desirable (*informal*) ○ *I'm sure he fancies you!* 3 *vr* FLATTER YOURSELF to have too high an opinion of yourself ○ *He rather fancies himself as a musician.* 4 *vt* SUPPOSE to be inclined to think that something is the case ○ *I fancy that it will be bright and sunny tomorrow.* 5 *vt* IMAGINE to form the idea of something in the imagination 6 *vt* IDENTIFY AS POTENTIAL WINNER to think that somebody will succeed ○ *Who do you fancy for the title?* ■ *interj* EXPRESSING SURPRISE used to express surprise (*informal*) ○ *Fancy! All that money!* ○ *Fancy that! I would never have believed it!* ○ *Fancy them splitting up after all these years!* ■ *n* (*plural* **-cies**) 1 SUDDEN LIKING an impulsive liking for somebody or desire for something ○ *The hat caught my fancy.* ○ *She seems to have taken quite a fancy to him.* 2 NOTION an unfounded belief about something 3 SOMETHING IMAGINARY something created by the imagination, especially something of a playful or superficial nature 4 LIKELY WINNER something or somebody thought likely to succeed or win 5 PLAYFUL IMAGINATIVENESS the faculty of using the imagination playfully or inventively 6 GOOD TASTE good critical taste and judgment (*formal*) 7 BOXING ENTHUSIASTS enthusiasts of a sport or pastime, especially boxing (*archaic*) [15C. Contraction of FANTASY.] —**fancily** *adv* —**fanciness** *n*

fancy dress *n* unusual clothing worn to a social gathering, often depicting a famous person, fictional character, or historical period [Because according to the wearer's fancy]

fancy-free *adj* free to go anywhere and do anything ○ *footloose and fancy-free*

fancy goods *npl* small items sold as gifts or novelties

fancy man *n* 1 the lover or boyfriend of a woman, especially a married woman (*dated informal*) 2 a pimp (*archaic*)

fancy woman *n* (*dated informal*) 1 the lover or girlfriend of a man, especially a married man 2 a prostitute

fancywork /fánssi wurk/ *n* embroidery and other decorative needlework

fan dance *n* an erotic dance in which large fans are used to mask and reveal parts of the dancer's nude body

fandangle /fan dáng g'l/ *n* a gaudy ornament or piece of jewellery of little value [Mid-19C. < ?]

fandango /fan dáng gō/ (*plural* **-gos**) *n* 1 a vigorous Spanish or Latin American dance in triple time, traditionally performed by a man and woman as a courtship ritual 2 the music for a fandango [Mid-18C. < Spanish.]

fanfare /fán fair/ *n* 1 a short dramatic series of notes played on trumpets or other brass instruments, especially to mark the arrival of somebody important 2 any dramatic and ostentatious event, especially an announcement or publicity stunt [Mid-18C. < French.]

fanfold /fán fōld/ *adj* folded into pleats by making alternate folds in opposite directions ○ *fanfold computer paper*

fang /fang/ *n* 1 CANINE TOOTH a long pointed tooth of a mammal on each side of the mouth towards the front 2 SNAKE'S TOOTH a tooth of a venomous snake, with a hollow or grooves through which venom is injected 3 SPIDER'S MOUTHPART either of the pair of mouthparts of a spider, from which poison is emitted ■ **fangs** *npl* TEETH the teeth (*informal*) [Pre-12C. < Old Norse, 'capture, grasp'.]

Fang /fang/ (*plural* **Fang** *or* **Fangs**) *n* 1 a member of a people who live mainly in the rain forests of Gabon, Equatorial Guinea, and Cameroon 2 the Bantu language spoken by the Fang people, belonging to the Benue-Congo branch of the Niger-Congo family of languages. Native speakers: 2 million. [Mid-19C. < French *Fan*, probably < Fang *Pangwe*.] —**Fang** *adj*

fan heater *n* an electric heater that blows out a current of warm air using a fan

fanjet /fán jet/ *n* AEROSP = **turbofan**

Fan Kuan /fán kwán/ (*fl.* 990–1030) Chinese artist

fan letter *n* a letter written to a celebrity by a fan

fanlight /fán līt/ *n* **1** a semicircular window above a door or another window, often with struts forming the shape of an open hand-held fan **2** a small rectangular window above a door. US term **transom** *n.* 3 **3** = **skylight**

fan mail *n* letters sent to celebrities by their fans

fanny /fánni/ (*plural* **-nies**) *n* **1** a highly offensive term for the female genitals (*taboo slang*) **2** *US, Can* the buttocks (*slang*) [Early 20C. < ?]

Fanny Adams /fánni áddəmz/ *n* tinned meat or stew, especially as fed to sailors (*archaic slang*) [Late 19C. After a young girl murdered and dismembered around 1867.]

fan palm *n* a palm tree with divided fan-shaped leaves

fantabulous /fan tábbyŏoləss/ *adj* extremely good (*humorous*) [Mid-20C. Blend of FANTASTIC + FABULOUS.]

fantail /fán tayl/ *n* **1 FAN-SHAPED TAIL OR END** a tail or the end of something shaped like an open handheld fan **2 PIGEON WITH FAN-SHAPED TAIL** a breed of domestic pigeon with a broad fan-shaped tail **3 BIRD WITH BROAD TAIL** a small flycatcher with a fan-shaped tail. Native to: Australia, New Zealand, Asia. Genus: *Rhipidura*. **4 GOLDFISH WITH BROAD TAIL** a goldfish with a broad double tail fin **5 WINDMILL SAIL** a secondary sail on a windmill that keeps the main sails facing into the wind **6** *US* **ROUNDED PART OF STERN** a rounded overhanging part of a ship's stern

fan-tan /fán tan/ *n* **1** a Chinese gambling game in which players bet on how many items that have been concealed under a bowl remain after being counted off in fours **2** a card game in which players seek to discard all their cards in a sequence based on the same suit as a seven that has been led [Late 19C. < Chinese, < *fān* 'turn, chance' + *tān* 'to spread out'.]

fantasia /fan táyzi ə, fántə zée ə/ *n* an instrumental composition in a free and improvisatory style, sometimes based on well-known melodies [Early 18C. < Italian, literally 'fantasy, imagination', via Latin < Greek *phantasia* (see FANTASY).]

fantasise *vti* = **fantasize**

fantasize /fántə sīz/ (**-sizes, -sizing, -sized**), **fantasise** (**-sises, -sising, -sised**) *vti* to form or indulge in fantasies of the imagination —**fantasist** /fántəssist/ *n*

fantast /fán tast/ *n* a person who has impractical daydreams [Late 16C. Via medieval Latin *phantasta* and German *Phantast* < Greek *phantastēs* 'boaster' < *phantazein* (see FANTASY).]

fantastic /fan tástik/, **fantastical** /fan tástik'l/ *adj* **1 EXCELLENT** extraordinarily good **2 BIZARRE** extremely strange or weird in appearance **3 INCREDIBLE** apparently impossible but real or true **4 UNLIKELY** unusual and unlikely to be successful **5 ENORMOUS** much larger than is usual, expected, or desirable **6 IMAGINARY** existing only in the imagination ■ *interj* **EXPRESSING PLEASURE** used to express amazement and approval (*informal*) ○ *You won the game? Fantastic!* [14C. Via French < Greek *phantastikos* < *phantazein* (see FANTASY).] —**fantasticality** /fan tásti kálləti/ *n* —**fantasticalness** *n*

fantastically /fan tástikli/ *adv* **1 VERY** extremely **2 VERY WELL** in a superb way **3 STRANGELY** in a weird and strange way

fantasy /fántəssi/ *n* (*plural* **-sies**) **1 MENTAL IMAGE OR DREAM** an image or dream created by the imagination **2 CREATION OF MENTAL IMAGES** in psychology, the creation of exaggerated mental images in response to an ungratified need **3 IMPRACTICAL IDEA** an unrealistic and impractical idea **4 IMAGINATIVE POWER** the creative power of the imagination **5 GENRE OF FICTION** a type of fiction featuring imaginary worlds and magical or supernatural events **6** MUSIC = **fantasia** ■ *vti* (**-sies, -sying, -sied**) = **fantasize** [14C. Via Old French < Greek *phantasia* 'appearance, imagination' < *phantazein* 'make visible' < *phainein* 'to show'.]

fantasy football *n* a competition in which participants create their own imaginary football team by choosing actual footballers from a number of different teams

Fanti /fánti/ (*plural* **-ti** *or* **-tis**), **Fante** (*plural* **-te** *or* **-tes**) *n* **1** a member of an African people living in the rain forests of Ghana and the Côte d'Ivoire **2** a dialect of Akan spoken in parts of Ghana and the Côte d'Ivoire [Early 19C. < Fanti.] —**Fanti** *adj*

Fantin-Latour /fóN taN la tŏor/, **Henri** (1836–1904) French painter and lithographer

fantod /fánt od/ *n* nervous anxiety (*informal*) ○ *He had a fit of the fantods.* [Mid-19C. < ?]

fan vaulting *n* a form of vaulting in which ribs fan out from the four corners of a bay, like a fan

fanworm /fán wurm/ *n* a marine worm that lives in a tube or burrows in the sea bed and has feathery tentacles resembling a fan, used for filtering food from the water. Families: Sabelidae and Serpulidae.

fanwort /fán wurt/ *n* an aquatic plant of the lily family with fan-shaped submerged and floating leaves. Genus: *Cabomba*.

fanzine /fán zeen/ *n* an amateur magazine produced for fans of a pastime or celebrity [Mid-20C. < FAN[2] + MAGAZINE.]

FAO *abbr* Food and Agriculture Organization (of the UN)

f.a.o. *abbr* for the attention of

FAQ /fak, éf ay kyŏo/ *abbr* **1 FAQ, FAQs** frequently asked questions **2** free alongside quay

faqir *n* ISLAM, RELIG = **fakir**

far /faar/ (**farther** /fáarthər/ *or* **further** /fúrthər/, **farthest** /fáarthist/ *or* **furthest** /fúrthist/) CORE MEANING: an adverb and adjective indicating that something is a long way away in distance or time ○ *These vessels had been venturing as far as Iceland for cod.* ○ *They were fishing in the area as far back as 1980.*

1 *adv* **A LONG WAY OFF** at, to, or from a great distance ○ *We saw the first outline of the shore far away.* **2** *adv* **A LONG TIME OFF** at or to a long time distant from the point of reference ○ *The well was contaminated as far back as 1986.* **3** *adv* **MUCH OR MANY** to or by a considerable degree ○ *There are far fewer factory jobs available these days.* **4** *adj* **DISTANT** remote in space or time ○ *He stood there, gazing into the far distance.* **5** *adj* **MORE DISTANT** more distant from somebody or something ○ *in a far corner of the room* **6** *adj* **EXTREME** having an extreme position in a particular direction ○ *His politics are far left of centre.* [Old English *feor(r)*, via Germanic, 'farther beyond' < Indo-European] —**farness** *n* ◇ **far and away** without a doubt and by a large margin ○ *She is far and away the best player that we have.* ◇ **far and near** everywhere ○ *Doctors from far and near flocked to his bedside.* ◇ **far and wide** covering a great distance ○ *The church bells will be heard far and wide.* ◇ **far from** indicates that something is not the case ○ *Such warm weather is far from typical of this time of year.* ◇ **far from it** on the contrary ○ *He was not the tallest boy in the class – far from it.* ◇ **far gone 1** in a state of deterioration and unable to function **2** very drunk (*informal*) ◇ **far out** used to express amazement and approval (*slang*) ◇ **go far 1** to be very successful **2** to last or be sufficient ○ *Three loaves of bread won't go far once my family gets going.* ◇ **go too far, take something too far** to do or say something that is unacceptable or that exceeds reasonable limits ○ *Harriet paused, and realized that she had gone too far.* ◇ **in so far as** to the extent that ◇ **so far 1** up to this moment **2** up to a certain point, extent, or degree ○ *Freedom of information can only go so far.* ◇ **so far so good** indicates satisfaction with progress made up to this point

Farabi /fə ráabi/, **al-** (873?–950?) Arabian philosopher

farad /fárrəd, fá rad/ *n* (*symbol* **F**) the SI unit of capacitance equal to that of a capacitor carrying one coulomb of charge when a potential difference of one volt is applied [Mid-19C. After Michael FARADAY.]

faradaic *adj* = **faradic**

faraday /fárrə day/ *n* (*symbol F*) a unit of electricity equal to that needed to deposit a unit amount of singly charged substance during electrolysis, equivalent to 96,485 coulombs [Early 20C. After Michael FARADAY.]

Faraday /fárrə day/, **Michael** (1791–1867) British physicist and chemist

faradic /fə ráddik/, **faradaic** /fárrə dáy ik/ *adj* relating to an intermittent alternating current produced in the secondary winding of an induction coil [Late 19C. < French *faradique*, after Michael FARADAY.]

faradise *vt* = **faradize**

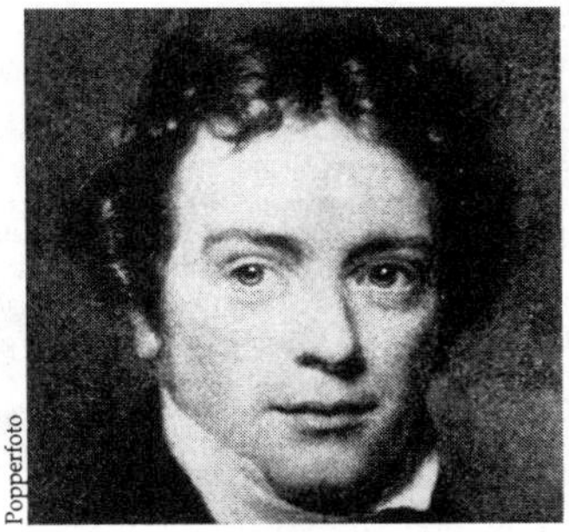

Popperfoto

Michael Faraday

faradism /fárrədizəm/ *n* the therapeutic application of an alternating electric current to stimulate nerve and muscle function [Late 19C. After Michael FARADAY.]

faradize /fárrə dīz/ (**-dizes, -dizing, -dized**), **faradise** (**-dises, -dising, -dised**) *vt* to use an alternating electric current to stimulate nerve and muscle function [Mid-19C. After Michael FARADAY.] —**faradization** /fárrə dī záysh'n/ *n* —**faradizer** *n*

farandole /fárrəndōl/ *n* **1** a lively dance from Provence in 6/8 or 4/4 time in which dancers link hands to form a weaving line following the leader **2** the music for a farandole [Mid-19C. Via French < modern Provençal *farandoulo*.]

faraway /fáarə wáy/ *adj* **1 REMOTE** a great distance away **2 SOUNDING DISTANT** heard from a distance **3 DREAMY** having a dreamy, absent-minded expression or appearance —**farawayness** *n*

farce /faarss/ *n* **1 COMIC PLAY** a comic play in which authority, order, and morality are at risk and ordinary people are caught up in extraordinary events **2 ABSURD SITUATION** a ridiculous situation in which everything goes wrong or becomes a sham **3 STYLE OF COMIC DRAMA** the style of comic drama in which authority, order, and morality are at risk and ordinary people are caught up in extraordinary events **4** FOOD = **forcemeat** [Early 16C. < French, 'stuffing' < Latin *farcire* 'to stuff'.]

farceur /faar súr/ *n* **1** an actor in or writer of farces **2** an intentionally comical person [Late 17C. < French, < *farce* (see FARCE).]

farcical /fáarssik'l/ *adj* **1** resembling a farce in being ridiculous and confused **2** performed or written in the style of a farce —**farcicality** /fáarssi kálləti/ *n* —**farcically** *adv*

far cry *n* a long way in distance or character

farcy /fáarssi/ *n* a form of the infectious horse disease glanders [14C. < French *farcin* < Latin *farcire* 'to stuff'.]

fardel /fáard'l/ *n* a bundle or pack of something tied up for carrying (*archaic*) [14C. < Old French, 'bundle, load' < *farde* 'bundle'.]

fare /fair/ *n* **1 COST OF TRAVEL** the amount charged for a journey **2 PASSENGER** a paying passenger in a taxi **3 FOOD** food that is provided, especially when simple and substantial **4 ENTERTAINMENT** the range of entertainment provided ■ *vi* (**fares, faring, fared**) **1 MANAGE IN DOING** to get on in a specified way in doing or experiencing something ○ *How did she fare in the exam?* **2 HAPPEN** to turn out in a specified way for somebody **3 TRAVEL** to go on a journey **4 EAT** to dine or be given food (*archaic*) [Old English *fær, faru* 'journey' < Germanic]

SPELLCHECK See *fair.*

Far East /faar éest/ a former term for the countries of East Asia, sometimes extended to include those of Southeast Asia (*dated*) —**Far-Eastern** *adj*

Fareham /fáirəm/ town in S England between Portsmouth and Southampton. Population: 55,563 (1991).

~~**Farenheit**~~ incorrect spelling of **Fahrenheit**

fare stage *n* **1** one of the divisions of a bus route, used for calculating the fare **2** a bus stop marking the boundary of a division in a bus route on which the fare is calculated

farewell /fair wél/ *n* **EXPRESSION OF PARTING GOOD WISHES** an expression of good wishes at parting ■ *adj* **SAYING GOODBYE** marking an end, conclusion, or leave-taking ■

interj GOODBYE used to express good wishes at parting (*literary*) ○ *Farewell, my friend!* [14C. < *Fare well*, said to somebody setting out on a journey.]

Farewell, Cape /fáir wel/ cape on the northern coast of the South Island, New Zealand

farfel /faárf'l/, **farfal** *n* pasta in the shape of small grains [Late 19C. < Yiddish *farfl* < Middle High German *varveln* 'noodles, noodle soup'.]

far-fetched *adj* exaggerated and unconvincing

far-flung *adj* **1** distributed over a wide area **2** at a great distance

Fargo /faárgō/ city in SE North Dakota. Population: 86,718 (1998 estimate).

Faridabad /fə reédə bad/, **Farīdābād** city in north-central India. Population: 617,717 (1991).

farina /fə reénə/ *n* **1** flour or meal made from wheat, nuts, or vegetables **2** starch, especially that made from potatoes [14C. < Latin, 'ground corn, flour, meal' < *far* 'spelt, grain'.]

farinaceous /fárri náyshəss/ *adj* containing or consisting of starch [Mid-17C. < late Latin *farinaceus* < Latin *farina* (see FARINA).]

farinose /fárrinōss, -nōz/ *adj* **1** consisting of or yielding starch **2** with a powdery or floury appearance, especially because of a covering of fine whitish hairs [Early 18C. < late Latin *farinosus* < Latin *farina* (see FARINA).]

farkleberry /faárk'lbəri/ (*plural* **-ries**) *n* a shrub of the heath family that has leathery leaves and hard black berries with stony seeds. Native to: SE United States. *Vaccinium arboreum*. [Mid-18C. < ?]

farl /faarl/ *n Scotland* a triangular oatcake, scone, or piece of shortbread, made by cutting a round cake into four sections [Late 17C. Contraction of *fardel* 'piece, quarter' < FOURTH + DEAL[1] (noun).]

farm /faarm/ *n* **1** AGRICULTURAL LAND AND BUILDINGS an area of land where crops are grown or animals are reared for commercial purposes, together with appropriate buildings **2** PLACE PRODUCING PARTICULAR ANIMALS OR CROPS an area of land or water where particular animals, birds, fish, or crops are raised for commercial purposes (*usually in combination*) ○ *a trout farm* **3** FARM BUILDINGS a farmhouse or group of farm buildings **4** LAND USED BY INDUSTRY a piece of land on which something is stored, produced, or processed, especially on an industrial scale (*usually in combination*) ○ *a sewage farm* ■ *v* **1** *vti* USE LAND FOR AGRICULTURE to use land for growing crops and rearing animals for sale **2** *vt* REAR SOMETHING COMMERCIALLY to rear animals, birds, or fish commercially **3** *vt* FIN, COMM = **farm out** *v.* 1 [14C. Via French, 'lease' < medieval Latin *firma* 'fixed payment' < Latin *firmare* 'fix, settle, confirm' < *firmus* 'firm'.] —**farmable** *adj* —**farming** *n*

LITERARY LINK ***Animal Farm***, a novel (1945) by George Orwell. A satirical allegory of Stalinist Russia, it describes how a group of farm animals, led by pigs, overthrow their human owner and try to run the farm on egalitarian principles. Corrupted by power, the pigs distort their ideology to support their increasingly brutal tyranny.

farm out *vt* **1** to send work out to be done by somebody else **2** to send children or animals to be looked after by somebody else

farmer /faármər/ *n* an owner or operator of a farm

farmer's lung *n* inflammation of the lungs marked by chronic shortness of breath and caused by an allergic reaction to fungal spores from mouldy hay

farmers' market *n* a market, usually held outdoors, where farmers sell fresh produce direct to the public

farm-fresh *adj* recently picked and delivered fresh from a producer to a seller ○ *farm-fresh vegetables*

farm hand *n* AGRIC = **farmworker**

farmhouse /faárm howss/ *n* (*plural* **-houses**) **1** a house on a farm, especially the main dwelling place of the farmer **2** = **farmhouse loaf** ■ *adj* produced on a farm or of a similar style or quality to that produced on a farm

farmhouse loaf *n* a large rectangular white loaf with a rounded top that is baked in a tin

farmland /faárm land/ *n* land that is suitable for farming or used by farmers

farmstay /faárm stay/ *n ANZ, Can* a stay on a farm as a paying guest, providing some experience of rural life

farmstead /faárm sted/ *n* a farm and all its buildings, regarded as a unit

farmworker /faárm wurkər/ *n* somebody hired to work on a farm. US term **farm hand**

farmyard /faárm yaard/ *n* an enclosed or surfaced area beside farm buildings

Farnborough /faárnbərə/ town in S England. Population: 52,535 (1991).

Farnham /faárnəm/, **John Peter** (*b.* 1949) British-born Australian recording artist

faro /fáirō/ *n* a card game in which players bet against the dealer on the order in which cards are turned up [Mid-18C. Probably alteration of PHARAOH, after Italian *faraone*.]

Faro /faárō/ seaport in S Portugal. Population: 31,966 (1991).

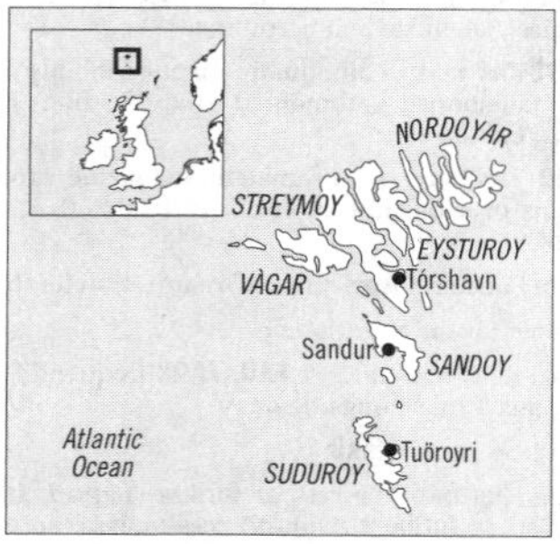

Faroe Islands

Faroe Islands /fáyrō ílandz/, **Faeroe Islands** group of islands that are a Danish territory in the North Atlantic Ocean, almost midway between Iceland and the Shetland Islands. Capital: Tórshavn. Population: 43,382 (1995). Area: 1,399 sq. km/540 sq. mi.

Faroese /fáirō eéz/ (*plural* **-ese**), **Faeroese** (*plural* **-ese**) *n* **1** the North Germanic language spoken on the Faroe Islands. Native speakers: 45,000. **2** somebody who comes from the Faroe Islands —**Faroese** *adj*

far-off *adj* distant in location or time

farouche /fə roósh/ *adj* **1** unsociable and lacking grace because of fierceness, sullenness, or shyness **2** menacing in appearance or behaviour [Mid-18C. Via French < medieval Latin *forasticus* < Latin *foras* 'out of doors, outside'.]

Farouk I /fə roók/ (1920–65) king of Egypt (1936–52)

far-out *adj* (*slang*) **1** strange and unconventional **2** extremely good or enjoyable —**far-outness** *n*

Farquhar /faárkər/, **George** (1678–1707) Irish dramatist

farrago /fə raágō/ (*plural* **-gos** *or* **-goes**) *n* a confused mixture of things [Mid-17C. < Latin, 'mixed fodder for cattle, medley' < *far* 'spelt, grain'.]

Farrakhan /fárrə kaán/, **Louis Abdul** (*b.* 1933) US religious leader. Born **Louis Eugene Walcott**

far-reaching *adj* with widespread implications, influences, or effects

Farrelly /fárrəli/, **Midget** (*b.* 1944) Australian surfer. Born **Bernard Farrelly**

Farrer /fárrər/, **William James** (1845–1906) British-born Australian agricultural scientist

farrier /fárri ər/ *n* a maker and fitter of horseshoes [Mid-16C. Via French < Latin *ferrarius* < *ferrum* 'horseshoe, iron'.] —**farriery** *n*

farrow[1] /fárrō/ *vi* to give birth to a litter of piglets ■ *n* a litter of young pigs [Old English *fearh* 'young pig' < Indo-European]

farrow[2] /fárrō/ *adj* not pregnant with a calf [15C. Probably < Flemish *verwe-*, *varwe-*, in *verwekoe*, *varwekoe* 'cow that has become barren'.]

farruca /fə roókə/ *n* a flamenco dance [Early 20C. < Spanish, 'Galician or Asturian' < *Farruco*, pet form of *Francisco* 'Francis'.]

farseeing *adj* = **farsighted** *adj.* 1, **farsighted** *adj.* 3

Farsi /faárssi/ *n* the official language of Iran, also spoken in Afghanistan, Bahrain, Tajikistan, and the United Arab Emirates, belonging to the Indo-Iranian branch of Indo-European. Native speakers: 30 million. Other speakers: 55 million. [Late 19C. Via Arabic, 'Persia', modern-day Iran < Persian *Pars*.] —**Farsi** *adj*

farsighted /faar sítid/ *adj* **1** **farsighted, farseeing** wise and able to anticipate the future **2** *US* OPHTHALMOL = **longsighted** *adj.* 1 **3** **farsighted, farseeing** able to see a long way —**farsightedly** *adv* —**farsightedness** *n*

fart /faart/ *vti* an offensive term meaning to release intestinal gases through the anus, usually with an accompanying sound (*slang*) ■ *n* **1** an offensive term for a release of intestinal gases through the anus (*slang*) **2** an offensive term for somebody who is considered to be unpleasant, boring, or irritating (*slang insult*) [Old English *feortan* < Indo-European]

fart about *vi* an offensive term meaning to waste time by behaving foolishly (*slang*)

farther /faárthər/ *adv* **1** TO GREATER DISTANCE to or at a point that is more distant in space or time **2** TO GREATER EXTENT to a greater degree or extent ■ *adj* **1** MORE DISTANT more distant in space or time **2** ADDITIONAL adding to the quantity or extent of something (*archaic*) [13C. Variant of FURTHER.] —**farthermost** *adj*

USAGE See ***further***.

farthest /faárthist/ *adv* **1** TO GREATEST DISTANCE to a more distant point in space or time than anything else **2** TO GREATEST EXTENT to a greater degree or extent than anything else ■ *adj* MOST DISTANT more distant in space or time than anything else

USAGE See ***further***.

farthing /faárthing/ *n* **1** a former British coin worth a quarter of an old penny **2** the lowest value or smallest amount [Old English *fēorthung* 'quarter of a penny' < *fēortha* 'fourth' + *-ing* 'fractional part'] ◇ **not have a brass farthing** to have no money or assets (*informal*)

farthingale /faárthing gayl/ *n* a structure worn under the skirt by women in the late 16th and early 17th centuries to give it the shape of a cone, bell, or drum [Early 16C. Via Old French *verdugale* < Spanish *verdugado* < *verdugo* 'rod, stick'.]

fartlek /faárt lek/ *n* SPORTS = **interval training** [Mid-20C. < Swedish, < *fart* 'speed' + *lek* 'play'.]

Far West *n US* the area of the continental United States west of the Great Plains

FAS *abbr* **1** foetal alcohol syndrome **2** free alongside ship

fasces /fáss eez/ *npl* a bundle of rods containing an axe with a projecting blade, carried in front of magistrates in ancient Rome [Late 16C. < Latin, plural of *fascis* 'bundle'.]

fascia /fáyshə, fáyshi ə, fáshə, fáyssi ə/ (*plural* **-ciae** /-shi ee/ *or* **-cias**) *n* **1** **fascia, facia** FLAT SURFACE ON BUILDING the flat horizontal surface immediately below the edge of a roof **2** **fascia, facia** NAMEPLATE OVER SHOP the flat surface that is above a shop window and usually carries the name of the shop **3** **fascia, facia** = **dashboard** *n.* 1 **4** CONNECTIVE TISSUE a sheet or band of connective tissue covering or binding together parts of the body, e.g. muscles or organs **5** **fascia, facia** BAND OF COLOUR a broad band of colour, e.g. on an insect [Mid-16C. < Latin, 'band, fillet, casing of a door'.] —**fascial** /fáysh'l/ *adj*

fasciate /fáshi ayt/, **fasciated** /-aytid/ *adj* describes plant stems or branches that have grown together and become abnormally flattened [Mid-17C. < Latin *fasciare* 'swathe' < *fascia* 'band, fillet'.] —**fasciately** *adv*

fascicle /fássik'l/ *n* **1** BUNDLE a small bunch or bundle of something **2** PLANT PARTS BUNCHED TOGETHER a cluster of plant parts such as branches, leaves, or stems **3** BUNDLE OF FIBRES a bundle of nerve, muscle, or tendon fibres **4** PART OF BOOK PUBLISHED AS INSTALMENT a section of a book published in instalments as a volume or pamphlet [15C. < Latin *fasciculus* 'small bundle' < *fascis* 'bundle'.] —**fascicled** *adj* —**fascicular** /fə skíkyoōlər/ *adj* —**fasciculate** /fə síkyoō layt, -lət/ *adj* —**fasciculately** *adv* —**fasciculation** /fə síkyoō láysh'n/ *n*

fascicule /fássi kyool/ *n* PUBL = **fascicle** *n.* 4 [Late 19C. < Latin *fasciculus* (see FASCICLE).]

fascinate /fássi nayt/ (**-nates, -nating, -nated**) *v* **1** *vti* to hold somebody's attention completely or irresistibly **2** *vt* to make somebody or something unable to move, especially out of fear [Late 16C. < Latin *fascinat-*, past participle of *fascinare* 'bewitch' < *fascinum* 'spell, witchcraft'.] —**fascinatedly** *adv* —**fascinator** *n*

fascinating /fássi nayting/ *adj* inspiring a great interest or attraction —**fascinatingly** *adv*

fascination /fássi náysh'n/ *n* **1 POWER TO CAPTURE ATTENTION** the power to hold somebody's attention completely or irresistibly **2 SOMETHING FASCINATING** something that inspires great interest **3 INTEREST** complete absorption in something interesting ○ *I can't understand his fascination with tarantulas.*

fascine /fə séen/ *n* a long piece or bundle of wood used for engineering purposes to line or fill a trench [Late 17C. Via French < Latin *fascina* < *fascis* 'bundle'.]

fascioliasis /fə sée ə lí əssiss, fássi ə-/ *n* a disease caused by an infestation of parasitic liver flukes [Late 19C. < modern Latin *Fasciola hepatica* 'liver fluke' < Latin *fasciola* 'small bandage' < *fascia* 'band, fillet'.]

fascism /fáshizəm/, **Fascism** *n* any movement, tendency, or ideology that favours dictatorial government, centralized control of private enterprise, repression of all opposition, and extreme nationalism —**fascist** /fáshist/ *n* —**fascistic** /fə shístik/ *adj*

QUICK FACTS ON... **FASCISM**

Key dates: 1920s–1940s
Key locations: Germany, Italy, Spain
Key elements: nationalism, anti-Semitism, totalitarianism, militarism
Key developments: rise of Nazism, Spanish Civil War, World War II
Key figures: Benito Mussolini, Adolf Hitler, Francisco Franco
Key works: *Mein Kampf* (My Struggle) (Adolf Hitler) 1925; translated 1939, *Triumph des Willens* (Triumph of the Will) 1934, *Olympiad* 1936 (Leni Riefenstahl)

fash[1] /fash/ *v Scotland, N England* **1** *vti* to annoy somebody, or be annoyed **2** *vi* to take the trouble to do something [Mid-16C. < French *fâcher* 'annoy' < assumed Vulgar Latin *fastidiare* 'to disgust' < Latin *fastidium* 'disgust'.]

fash[2] /fash/ *n US* fashion (*slang*) ■ *adj US* fashionable (*slang*) [Late 19C. Shortening.]

fashion /fásh'n/ *n* **1 CLOTHING STYLES** style in clothing, hair, and personal appearance generally, or the business of creating, promoting, or studying the latest styles **2 CURRENT STYLE** the style of dress, behaviour, way of living, or other expression that is popular at present ○ *a way of speaking that is no longer in fashion* **3 MANNER** a particular way of behaving or doing something **4 SHAPE** the form or shape of something **5 TYPE** a type or variety ■ *vt* **1 MAKE** to give shape or form to something ○ *fashion a chair from some leftover pieces of wood* **2 INFLUENCE** to change somebody's character or beliefs by influence or training ○ *attitudes fashioned by his grandparents* **3 ADAPT** to adapt something or make something suitable ○ *fashion it to fit over the bump in the middle* [14C. Via French *façon* 'shape' < Latin *faction-* (see FACTION[1]).] —**fashioner** *n* ◇ **after a fashion** in some way but not very well

-fashion *suffix* in the manner of

fashionable /fásh'nəb'l/ *adj* **1** following a style or fashion that is currently popular ○ *fashionable ideas* **2** popular with or frequented by rich, famous, or otherwise glamorous people ○ *a fashionable nightspot* —**fashionableness** *n* —**fashionably** *adv*

fashion-backward *adj* having little or no dress sense or awareness of fashion (*informal*)

fashion-forward *adj* having a highly developed dress sense and awareness of fashion (*informal*)

fashion house *n* a business that designs, makes, and sells fashionable clothes, typically associated with a named designer

fashionista /fásh'n ístə/ *n* (*informal*) **1** a devoted enthusiast of the fashion industry **2** a woman who is extremely fashion-conscious and knowledgeable about fashions [< FASHION + Latin *-ista* (see -IST]

fashion model *n* a professional model of clothes

fashion photography *n* the art or practice of taking photographs of models wearing clothes or clothing accessories, especially for fashion magazines

fashion plate *n* **1** an illustration showing a style of clothing, especially a current or new fashion **2** a wearer of the latest fashions

fashion ramp *n S Asia* the catwalk at a fashion show

fashion statement *n* an item of clothing or set of clothes that expresses something about the attitude, point of view, or lifestyle of the wearer

fashion victim *n* an overzealous or uncritical follower of fashion trends (*informal*)

~~**fashon**~~ incorrect spelling of **fashion**

Fassbinder /fáss bindər/, **Rainer Werner** (1946–82) German film director

fast[1] /faast/ *adj* **1 ACTING OR MOVING RAPIDLY** acting, functioning, or moving quickly, or capable of doing this **2 DONE QUICKLY** lasting or taking a relatively short time **3 RUNNING AHEAD OF TIME** indicating a time that is later than the correct time **4 CONDUCIVE TO RAPID SPEED** adapted to or allowing rapid movement **5 REQUIRING SPEEDY MOVEMENT** requiring agility and quickness of movement and reaction **6 WITH SHORT EXPOSURE** describes photographic equipment that requires or permits a relatively short exposure time **7 DEBAUCHED** energetically pursuing excitement and enjoyment (*informal*) **8 PROMISCUOUS** wanting or tending to start sexual relationships with people very soon after meeting them (*informal*) **9 TRICKY** using quick-wittedness to trick or cheat people (*informal*) **10 MADE EASILY** acquired very easily and sometimes dishonestly (*informal*) ○ *fast money* **11 UNFADING** not liable to fade or change colour **12 STRONG AND CLOSE** strong, close, and steadfast, e.g. in a relationship ○ *fast friends* **13 FASTENED** firmly attached, fastened, or fixed **14 SHUT** firmly closed ■ *adv* **1 RAPIDLY** at great speed **2 IMMEDIATELY** in quick succession **3 AT INCORRECT TIME** ahead of the correct time **4 SOUNDLY** deeply in a state of sleep **5 FIRMLY** allowing no movement or no chance of slipping or escaping ○ *held fast by ice* **6 RECKLESSLY** without regard to consequences (*informal*) ○ *live fast and die young* [Old English *fæst* 'firm' < Germanic] ◇ **pull a fast one** to trick or cheat somebody (*informal*)

fast[2] /faast/ *v* **1** *vi* **ABSTAIN FROM FOOD** to abstain from all or certain types of food, especially as an act of religious observance **2** *vt* **DEPRIVE OF FOOD** to deprive a person or animal of food ■ *n* **PERIOD OF FASTING** a period of time spent abstaining from food [Old English *fæstan* < Germanic, 'firm'] —**faster** *n*

fast-acting *adj* beginning to take effect soon after being used ○ *a fast-acting analgesic*

fastback /fáast bak/ *n* **1** a back of a car that forms a continuous curve downwards from the rear edge of the roof **2** a car with a fastback

fastball /fáast bawl/ *n* a baseball pitch at top speed

fast bowler *n* in cricket, a bowler who specializes in bowling the ball quickly —**fast bowling** *n*

fast break *n* in team sports, a swift counterattack made in an attempt to score before the opposing players have the chance to recover their defensive positions —**fast-break** *vi*

fast-breeder reactor *n* a nuclear reactor in which the chain reaction is maintained mainly by fast neutrons

fasten /fáass'n/ *v* **1** *vti* **SECURE** to attach something firmly, usually using parts or devices made to achieve this, or become firmly attached in this way **2** *vti* **SHUT TIGHTLY** to close something firmly or securely, or become firmly or securely closed **3** *vt* **HOLD FIRMLY** to use a tool, device, or body part to hold somebody or something firmly **4** *vti* **CONCENTRATE ATTENTION** to focus the mind or eyes concentratedly on something, or become focused in this way ○ *His suspicions fastened upon the woman sitting opposite him.* **5** *vi* **BECOME A NUISANCE** to become associated closely with somebody in a persistent and usually unwelcome manner ○ *just some bloke who fastened onto me in the street* [Old English *fæstnian* < Germanic, 'firm']

fastener /fáass'nər/ *n* a device, e.g. a button, hook, or zip, used to close something, especially a piece of clothing

fastening /fáass'ning/ *n* a device that fastens something, e.g. a clasp, hook, or lock

fast food *n* highly processed restaurant foods, e.g. burgers, that are prepared quickly or are available on demand (*hyphenated before nouns*) ○ *a fast-food diet*

fast-forward *n* **1 FUNCTION FOR WINDING TAPE FORWARDS** a function on an electronic recording device, e.g. a tape or video cassette recorder, that causes the tape to wind forwards quickly **2 BUTTON FOR FAST-FORWARD FUNCTION** a mechanism, e.g. a button or switch, used to control the fast-forward function on an electronic recording device ■ *vti* **1 ADVANCE TAPE RAPIDLY** to wind a tape forwards quickly on an electronic recording device **2 ADVANCE QUICKLY** to advance rapidly, or move something forwards rapidly, e.g. in time or in rate of progress (*informal*) ○ *decided to fast-forward negotiations so as to avoid a strike*

fastidious /fa stíddi əss/ *adj* **1** concerned that even the smallest details should be just right ○ *fastidious about his appearance* **2** easily disgusted by things that are not perfectly clean [15C. < Latin *fastidiosus* < *fastidium* 'disgust'.] —**fastidiously** *adv* —**fastidiousness** *n*

fastigia plural of **fastigium**

fastigiate /fa stíji ət, -ayt/, **fastigiated** /-aytid/ *adj* describes a tree or other plant with upright clustering branches that taper towards the top, e.g. a Lombardy poplar —**fastigiately** *adv*

fastigium /fa stíji əm/ (*plural* **-ums** *or* **-a** /-ə/) *n* a period during which an illness, often a fever, is at its most severe [Late 17C. < Latin.]

fasting /fáasting/ *n* abstention from all or certain types of food, especially as an act of religious observance

fast lane *n* **1** the lane of a motorway or dual carriageway that is used by vehicles travelling at high speed or overtaking slower traffic. US term **express lane 2** the kind of lifestyle that is busy, exciting, often highly stressful, and sometimes devoted to pleasure (*informal*) ○ *living life in the fast lane* —**fast-lane** *adj*

fast motion *n* filmed action that is faster than is naturally possible, achieved by shooting the film at a rate slower than that projected (*hyphenated before nouns*) ○ *a fast-motion sequence*

fastness /fáastnəss/ *n* **1 FIXEDNESS** the state or quality of being firm, fixed, or secure ○ *deceived about the fastness of their friendship* **2 UNFADING QUALITY** the ability of a dye to retain its colour and not to fade **3 FORTRESS** a fortress, stronghold, or other secure place (*archaic or literary*)

fast neutron *n* a neutron that has energy in excess of 1.5 MeV, sufficient to produce fission in uranium 238

fast stream *n* a group of employees selected for rapid promotion within an organization

fast-talk *vt* to influence or deceive somebody with false but appealing arguments (*informal*) ○ *fast-talked them into parting with the car keys* —**fast-talker** *n*

fast track *n* **1** a railway track for fast trains alongside one for slower trains **2** a rapid and sometimes highly competitive route to progress or advancement that exists alongside the slower conventional one (*informal*) ○ *a fast track to promotion for the brightest recruits*

fast-track *v* **1** *vti* **GO QUICKLY** to advance, develop, or process something rapidly, or be handled rapidly ○ *fast-tracking the best of the new recruits* **2** *vt* **DEAL WITH FIRST** to give priority to somebody or something ○ *fast-track an application* ■ *adj* **ADVANCING RAPIDLY** progressing rapidly or encouraging rapid progress —**fast-tracker** *n*

fat /fat/ *n* **1 NUTRITIONAL COMPONENT OF FOOD** any of a group of water-insoluble chemicals that are one of the main constituents of food **2 TISSUE CONTAINING FAT** animal or vegetable tissue made up of cells that contain fat **3 COOKING MEDIUM** a solid or liquid substance such as butter or sunflower oil that is derived from animals or plants and is used as a cooking medium or ingredient ○ *rub the fat into the flour* **4 EXCESS** amounts that are surplus to what is needed or wanted (*informal*) ○ *a budget with little fat* ■ *adj* (**fatter, fattest**) **1 OVERWEIGHT** having a body weight greater than is considered desirable or advisable **2 CONTAINING FAT** containing a lot of fat or too much fat ○ *pork that was rather fat* **3 THICK** very wide or large ○ *a fat book* **4 PROFITABLE** bringing large profits or financial rewards ○ *a fat defence contract* **5 REWARDING** providing good opportunities ○ *offered a fat part in a film* **6 RICH** owning great wealth **7 PLENTIFUL** with abundant contents, stocks, or supplies ○ *a fat savings account* **8 RICH IN CONTENT** with a high content of a particular material or substance, e.g. resin in wood or volatile hydrocarbons in coal **9 MINIMAL** very little (*informal*) ○ *A fat lot of help you are!* ■ *vti* (**fats, fatting, fatted**) **FATTEN AN ANIMAL** to fatten an animal, usually before slaughtering it [Old English *fæt(t)* < Indo-European] —**fatly** *adv* —**fatness** *n* ◇ **chew the fat** to have a leisurely conversation (*slang*) ◇ **the fat is in the fire** something irreversible has happened that will cause trouble

ϟ **FAT** /fat/ *n* in the MS-DOS disk-operating system, an internal store of information about the structure of files on a disk (*often before nouns*). Full form **file allocation table**

Fatah, Al /fáttə/ *n* a Palestinian political group that seeks to establish an independent Palestinian state. Formed in the 1950s, it became part of the Palestine Liberation Organization in 1968. [Late 20C. < Arabic *al* 'the' + acronym < *Ḥ(arakat) T(aḥrīr) F(ilastīn)* 'Movement for the Liberation of Palestine' (resembling *fataḥ* 'conquer').]

fatal /fáyt'l/ *adj* 1 LEADING TO DEATH causing or capable of causing death 2 RUINOUS causing destruction, disaster, or ruin ○ *a fatal mistake in calculations* 3 DECISIVE at which time important decisions or choices are made ○ *the fatal day of his first treasonous act* 4 PREDESTINED arranged or controlled by fate ■ *n US* INSTANCE OF DEATH an instance of death, especially one caused by a car, plane, train, or bus crash (*informal*) ○ *a fatal on the turnpike during rush hour* [14C. Directly or via French < Latin *fatalis* < *fatum* (see FATE).] —**fatally** *adv* —**fatalness** *n*

SYNONYMS See *deadly*.

fatalism /fáyt'lizəm/ *n* 1 the philosophical doctrine holding that all events are fated to happen and that human beings cannot therefore change their destinies 2 the belief that people are powerless against fate or the attitude of resignation and passivity that sometimes results from this belief —**fatalist** *n* —**fatalistic** /fáyt'l ístik/ *adj* —**fatalistically** *adv*

fatality /fə tálləti, fay-/ (*plural* **-ties**) *n* 1 UNEXPECTED DEATH a death resulting from accident or disaster ○ *The traffic accident resulted in three fatalities.* 2 DEADLINESS the ability to cause death, disaster, or destruction ○ *fatality associated with toxic waste exposure* 3 PREDETERMINATION BY FATE the quality or state of being predetermined by fate 4 EVENTS THOUGHT FATED an event or train of events thought to be determined by fate

fatality rate *n* SOC SCI = **death rate**

fata morgana /faàtə mawr gaánə/, **Fata Morgana** *n* a mirage or an illusion [< Italian, 'Morgan le Fay'; from the belief that a fairy caused the mirage frequently seen near the Strait of Messina]

fatback /fát bak/ *n US* fatty meat from the upper part of a side of pork, usually dried and cured by salt

fat body *n* 1 a fatty tissue in the bodies of insects, especially larvae, used as a source of energy during metamorphosis and hibernation 2 a fatty tissue found near the genital glands of certain amphibians and reptiles

fat camp *n US* a residential camp that helps children to lose undesired weight (*slang*)

fat cat *n* an extremely wealthy and privileged person, often somebody whose wealth is regarded as undeserved (*slang insult; hyphenated before nouns*)

fat cell *n* any cell that is specialized for the synthesis and storage of fat

fate /fayt/ *n* 1 FORCE PREDETERMINING EVENTS the force or principle believed to predetermine events 2 OUTCOME a consequence or final result ○ *What was the fate of the mission?* 3 DESTINY something consequential that inevitably happens to somebody or something 4 UNHAPPY CONSEQUENCE a disastrous or ruinous outcome ■ *vt* (**fates, fating, fated**) MAKE SOMETHING INEVITABLE to predetermine something, usually with negative results (*usually passive*) [14C. < Latin *fatum* 'something spoken (by the gods)' < past participle of *fari* 'speak'.] —**fated** *adj* ◇ **tempt fate** to do something risky that might end in misfortune or disaster, and depend too much on luck

fateful /fáytf'l/ *adj* 1 CRITICALLY IMPORTANT after which an important, often dire consequence seems to have been made inevitable ○ *a fateful decision* 2 DECIDED BY FATE predetermined or controlled by fate 3 OMINOUS prefiguring what is to come, especially when it is something disastrous ○ *a fateful sign* —**fatefully** *adv* —**fatefulness** *n*

Fates /fayts/ *npl* in Greek mythology, Clotho, Lachesis, and Atropos, often depicted as women of advanced years spinning a thread, who were believed to decree the events and duration of somebody's life. Roman equivalent **Parcae**

fat face *n* any typeface with wide main strokes and prominent serifs, producing a relatively heavy and dark image when set as text

fat farm *n* a health farm dedicated to helping people lose weight (*slang*)

fathead /fát hed/ *n* a person considered foolish or stupid (*slang insult*) —**fatheaded** /fát héddid/ *adj* —**fatheadedly** *adv* —**fatheadedness** *n*

fat hen *n* a common weed of the goosefoot family, with a mealy white covering over the whole plant. *Chenopodium album*. US term **pigweed** *n*. 2 [< ?]

father /faáthər/ *n* 1 MALE PARENT a male parent of a human being or animal 2 MAN ACTING AS PARENT a man who brings up and looks after a child as if he were its male parent 3 MALE ANCESTOR a man who is an ancestor, especially the founder of a family or people 4 FOUNDER a man who establishes, founds, or originates something ○ *the father of modern linguistics* 5 PRECURSOR a precursor, prototype, or early version of something 6 MALE LEADER a man who is a community or civic leader ○ *the town fathers* 7 OLDEST MEMBER the oldest or most senior member of an institution ■ *v* 1 *vt* HAVE OFFSPRING to beget offspring as a male parent 2 *vti* ACT AS FATHER to act as a father to somebody, especially giving advice, comfort, and protection 3 *vt* ORIGINATE to create, found, or establish something ○ *father a plan* [Old English *fæder* < Indo-European] —**fatherhood** *n*

LITERARY LINK ***Fathers and Sons***, a novel (1862) by Russian writer Ivan Turgenev. It deals with the conflicting attitudes towards social change (particularly the emancipation of serfs) among Russia's younger radical intelligentsia, represented by the novel's nihilistic protagonist, Bazarov, and the older liberal gentry, to which Turgenev himself belonged.

Father *n* 1 GOD in the Christian religion, God, especially when considered as the first person of the Trinity 2 CHR = **church father** 3 TITLE FOR CHRISTIAN CLERGYMAN a title and form of address used for Christian clergymen, especially in the Roman Catholic, Eastern Orthodox, and Episcopal churches 4 RESPECTFUL TITLE FOR MAN a respectful term of address for a man who is past middle age 5 PERSONIFICATION something personified as man of advanced years

Father Christmas *n* the patron saint of children, commonly identified with Saint Nicholas, usually depicted as a jolly old man with a white beard who brings presents at Christmas. US term **Santa Claus**

father confessor *n* 1 a Roman Catholic priest who hears confessions and gives advice 2 any man in whom somebody confides and whose advice is sought

father figure *n* a man whom other people look up to for advice, inspiration, or protection

father-in-law (*plural* **fathers-in-law**) *n* the father of somebody's husband or wife

fatherland /faáthər land/ *n* 1 somebody's native land or country 2 the native land of somebody's ancestors

father-lasher *n* a large sea scorpion with short spines. Native to: European and North Atlantic coastal waters. *Myoxocephalus scorpius* and *Myoxocephalus bubalis*.

fatherless /faáthərləss/ *adj* having no father or no one identified as father —**fatherlessness** *n*

fatherly /faáthərli/ *adj* having or showing the qualities associated with a father, usually love, support, and protection ○ *fatherly affection* —**fatherliness** *n*

father of the chapel *n* a shop steward representing members of a trade union in a printing office

Father's Day *n* a day observed as a celebration of fatherhood in Britain, the United States, Canada, Australia, and some other Commonwealth countries. Date: third Sunday in June.

Father Time *n* the personification of time as a bearded man of advanced years, usually wearing a robe and carrying a scythe and an hourglass

fathom /fáthəm/ *n* MEASURE OF WATER DEPTH a unit of length equal to 1.83 m/6 ft, used mainly in nautical contexts for measuring the depth of water ■ *vt* 1 MEASURE WATER DEPTH USING SOUNDING LINE to measure the depth of water, especially using a sounding line 2 COMPREHEND to understand something, usually something profound or mystifying ○ *couldn't fathom why he came back* [Old English *fæþm* < ?] —**fathomable** *adj* —**fathomer** *n*

fathomless /fáthəmləss/ *adj* 1 too deep to be measured 2 impossible to understand —**fathomlessly** *adv* —**fathomlessness** *n*

fatigue /fə teég/ *n* 1 MENTAL OR PHYSICAL EXHAUSTION extreme tiredness or weariness resulting from physical or mental activity 2 INABILITY TO RESPOND TO STIMULUS temporary inability of an organ or part such as a muscle or nerve cell to respond to a stimulus and function normally, following continuous activity or stimulation 3 INABILITY TO RESPOND TO SITUATION temporary inability of somebody to respond to a situation as a result of overexposure or excessive activity (*often in combination*) ○ *compassion fatigue* 4 WEAKENING OF MATERIAL UNDER STRESS the weakening or breakdown of a material subjected to prolonged or repeated stress 5 NONMILITARY WORK manual or menial work done by soldiers, often as a punishment (*often before nouns*) ■ **fatigues** *npl* BATTLEDRESS informal military uniforms worn day to day and in battle, as distinct from formal uniforms ■ *vti* 1 MAKE OR BECOME TIRED to tire somebody out, or become tired out, as a result of physical or mental activity 2 WEAKEN UNDER STRESS to weaken or break something, or become weakened or broken, when subjected to prolonged or repeated stress [Mid-17C. Via French, 'tire' < Latin *fatigare*.] —**fatigability** *n* —**fatigable** /fáttigəb'l/ *adj* —**fatigableness** /fáttigəb'lnəss/ *n* —**fatigued** *adj*

Fatima /fáttimə/ (606?–632 BC) youngest daughter of Muhammad

Fátima /fáttimə/ village in west-central Portugal, a place of pilgrimage for Roman Catholics. Population: 5,445 (1991).

Fatimid /fátti mid/, **Fatimite** /fátti mīt/ *n* 1 a member of a Muslim dynasty, descended from Muhammad's daughter Fatima and her husband Ali, that ruled North Africa and parts of Egypt and Syria from AD 909 to 1171 2 any descendant of Fatima and Ali [Mid-19C. < Arabic *Fāṭima* 'Fatima'.]

fat lip *n* a lip swollen from having been hit in a fist fight (*informal*) ○ *gave him a fat lip*

fat mouse *n* a nocturnal short-tailed mouse eaten as a delicacy because of its high stored fat content. Native to: dry regions of Africa. Genus: *Steatomys*.

fatshedera /fáts héddərə/ *n* a hybrid ornamental plant with glossy leaves. Flowers: pale green. *Fatsia japonica* × *Hedera helix*. [Mid-20C. < modern Latin *Fatsia* (genus of shrubs) + *Hedera* (genus of climbing plants < Latin, 'ivy').]

fatsia /fátsi ə/ *n* a shrub with deeply divided leaves, common as a houseplant. Flowers: white flowers, in clusters. *Fatsia japonica*. [< modern Latin]

fatso /fát sō/ (*plural* **-sos** or **-soes**) *n* an offensive term for somebody who is overweight (*slang insult*) [Mid-20C. Probably < *fats*, offensive term for an overweight person.]

fat stock *n* livestock that has been fattened and is ready for sale or slaughter

fatten /fátt'n/ *v* 1 *vti* MAKE OR BECOME FAT to become fat or fatter, or make somebody fat or fatter 2 *vti* FEED ANIMAL to make an animal fat by feeding it plentifully, usually for slaughter 3 *vt* ENLARGE to make something larger, richer, or fuller ○ *fatten your wallet* 4 *vt* FERTILIZE to make land or soil more fertile ○ *fatten the soil with manure* —**fattenable** *adj* —**fattener** *n*

fattening /fátt'ning/ *adj* 1 high in fat or calorie content, and so likely to make some people gain weight 2 becoming fat in readiness for slaughter —**fatteningly** *adv*

fatty /fátti/ *adj* (**-tier, -tiest**) 1 CONTAINING FAT containing fat or grease, especially in large or distasteful amounts 2 DERIVED FROM FAT derived from or chemically related to fat ○ *fatty alcohol* 3 WITH ACCUMULATED FAT containing accumulated fat, sometimes in undesirable amounts ○ *fatty tissue* ■ *n* (*plural* **-ties**) OFFENSIVE TERM an offensive term for somebody who is overweight (*informal insult*) —**fattiness** *n*

fatty acid *n* $C_nH_{n+1}COOH$ an organic acid belonging to a group that may occur naturally as waxes, fats, and essential oils and consisting of a straight chain of carbon atoms linked by single bonds and ending in a carboxyl group. Source: animal and plant materials.

fatty degeneration *n* deterioration in the function of an organ, e.g. the liver or heart, caused by the accumulation of unusually high levels of fats in its cells

fatty oil *n* CHEM = **fixed oil**

fatuity /fə tyoó əti/ (*plural* **-ties**) *n* (*formal*) 1 complacency combined with lack of intelligence or thought 2 an action or remark that is unintelligent or thoughtless —**fatuitous** *adj*

fatuous /fáttyoo əss/ *adj* showing lack of intelligence coupled with a lack of awareness ○ *a fatuous joke* [Early 17C. < Latin *fatuus*.] —**fatuously** *adv* —**fatuousness** *n*

fatwa /fát waa/, **fatwah** *n* a formal legal opinion or religious decree issued by an Islamic leader [Early 17C. < Arabic < *aftā* 'decide a point of law'.]

ϟ **fat wallet** *n* a digital wallet where credit card and digital certificate information are stored on a user's computer (*in e-commerce*)

ϟ **fatware** /fát wair/ *n* COMPUT = **bloatware**

faubourg /fō boorg/ *n* an inner suburb or quarter of a city, especially in France [15C. < French, alteration (after *faux* 'false') of Old French *forsborc* < Latin *foris* 'outside' + late Latin *burgus* 'fat' (< Germanic).]

fauces /fáw seez/ *npl* the passage between the back of the mouth and the pharynx [15C. < Latin, 'throat'.] —**faucal** /fáwk'l/ *adj* —**faucial** /fáwsh'l/ *adj*

faucet /fáwssit/ *n US* CONSTR = **tap**² *n.* 1 [14C. Via Old French *fausset* or Provençal *falset* < *falser* 'bore in' < late Latin *fausser, falsare* 'corrupt' < Latin *falsus* 'false'.]

Faulkner /fáwknər/, **William** (1897–1962) US writer —**Faulknerian** /fawk neéri ən/ *adj*

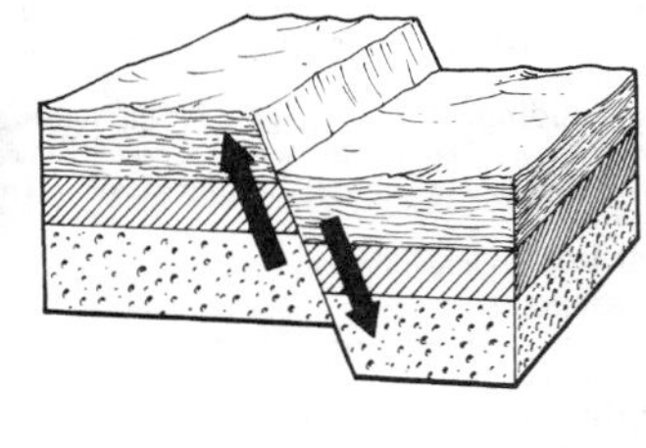

Fault: Displacement of rock layers in Earth's crust

fault /fawlt, folt/ *n* 1 **RESPONSIBILITY** responsibility for a mistake, failure, or act of wrongdoing 2 **PERSONAL SHORTCOMING** a failing or character weakness in somebody ○ *My main fault is laziness.* 3 **DEFECT** something that detracts from the integrity, functioning, or perfection of a thing 4 **MISTAKE** an error, especially in calculation 5 **MISDEMEANOUR** a wrongful action 6 **DISPLACEMENT IN EARTH'S CRUST** a displacement of rock layers in the Earth's crust in response to stress, accompanied by a break in the continuity of the rocks on each side of the fault line 7 **INVALID SERVE IN RACKET GAMES** a serve in certain racket games, e.g. tennis, that is invalid because it fails to land within a prescribed area 8 **PENALTY MARK IN SHOWJUMPING** a penalty mark awarded in showjumping for various errors such as a failure or refusal to clear a fence 9 **LOSING SCENT OF ANIMAL** an occasion on which the hounds in a hunt lose the scent of the animal they are chasing ■ *v* 1 *vt* **BLAME** to blame, criticize, or find a defect in somebody or something ○ *He gave an excellent performance that could not be faulted.* 2 *vi* **MAKE MISTAKE** to commit a fault or make a mistake (*archaic*) 3 *vi* **DISPLACE** to respond to stress by becoming displaced and developing as a geological fault (*refers to rock layers*) [13C. Via Old French *faut(e)* 'lack' < assumed Vulgar Latin *fallitum* 'failing' < Latin *fallere* 'fail'.] ◇ **find fault with somebody** *or* **something** to criticize somebody *or* something, often unfairly ○ *She's always finding fault with the children's work.* ◇ **to a fault** excessively ○ *She was rather naive, and generous to a fault.*

SYNONYMS See *flaw*.

faultfinding /fáwlt fìnding, fólt-/ *n* 1 constant and often petty complaining or criticism 2 the process of locating and diagnosing faults within an electrical, electronic, or mechanical system (*often before nouns*) ○ *faultfinding procedures* —**faultfinder** *n* —**fault-finding** *adj*

faultless /fáwltləss, fólt-/ *adj* having no faults or defects ○ *a faultless performance* —**faultlessly** *adv* —**faultlessness** *n*

fault line *n* a linear feature on the Earth's surface, occurring where displaced rock layers have broken through the Earth's surface

fault plane *n* the surface along which displacement of rock layers has taken place in a geological fault

⚡**fault tolerance** *n* the ability of a computer or network to preserve the integrity of data during a malfunction

faulty /fáwlti, fólti/ (**-ier, -iest**) *adj* containing defects, especially ones that cause malfunctions ○ *faulty wiring* —**faultily** *adv* —**faultiness** *n*

faun /fawn/ *n* in Roman mythology, a rural god, often depicted as a creature with the body of a man and the legs and horns of a goat. Greek equivalent **satyr** *n.* 1 [14C. Directly or via French < Latin *Faunus* 'Faunus'.]

SPELLCHECK See *fawn*.

fauna /fáwnə/ (*plural* **-nas** *or* **-nae** /-ee/) *n* 1 the animal life of a particular region or period, considered as a whole. ◊ **flora** *n.* 1 2 a catalogue or list describing the animals of a particular region or period [Late 18C. Via modern Latin < late Latin *Fauna* 'Fauna', an ancient Italian rural goddess, sister of FAUNUS.] —**faunal** *adj* —**faunally** *adv*

Faunus /fáwnəss/ *n* in Roman mythology, the god of nature, farming, and fertility. Greek equivalent **Pan**[1]

Fauré /fáwr ay/, **Gabriel** (1845–1924) French composer and organist

Faust /fowst/ (1480?–1540?) German fortune-teller and magician reputed to have sold his soul to the devil —**Faustian** *adj*

faute de mieux /fòt də myő/ *adv* in the absence of something better ○ *the feeling that she had married him faute de mieux* [< French, 'lack of better']

fauteuil /fō tő i/ *n* an upholstered armchair, usually with open sides (*technical*) [Mid-18C. Via French < Old French *faudestuel* 'folding chair' < Germanic.]

fauve /fōv/, **Fauve** *n* an artist belonging to a 20th-century movement in French painting (**fauvism**) characterized by the use of simple forms and bright colours (*often before nouns*) [Early 20C. < French, 'wild, wild animal', via Old French *falve* 'tawny' < Germanic.]

fauvette /fō vét/ *n* a small bird of the family of warblers, especially a garden warbler. Native to: Europe. [Late 18C. < French, < *fauve* 'wild, tawny' (see FAUVE).]

fauvism /fóvizəm/, **Fauvism** *n* an early 20th-century movement in painting, begun in about 1905 by a group of French artists, including Matisse, and characterized by the use of simple forms and vivid colours

QUICK FACTS ON... **FAUVISM**

Key dates: 1905–08
Key locations: France, especially Paris
Key elements: search for more expressive forms; rejection of naturalism; use of bright, contrasting colours, bold lines, simplified patterns; dynamism, vitality
Key figures: Henri Matisse, André Derain, Maurice de Vlaminck, Raoul Dufy, Albert Marquet, Kees van Dongen
Key works: *The Open Window, Collioure* (Matisse) 1905, *Woman with a Hat* (Matisse) 1905, *The Pool of London* (Derain) 1906, *Tugboat at Chatou* (Vlaminck) 1906
Key developments: expressionism, futurism, orphism

fauvist /fóvist/ *n* = **fauve** —**fauvist** *adj*

faux /fō/ *adj* made in imitation of a natural material, e.g. leather or fur [Late 20C. Via French < Latin *falsus* (see FALSE).]

faux ami /fóz a meé/ (*plural* **faux amis** /fó za meé/) *n* LING = **false friend** *n.* 1 [< French]

faux-naïf /fó nī eéf/ *adj* pretending to be simple or without sophistication (*literary*) [< French, 'falsely naive'] —**faux-naïf** *n*

faux pas /fó paá/ (*plural* **faux pas** /fó paáz/) *n* an embarrassing blunder that breaks a social convention of some kind [< French, 'false step']

SYNONYMS See *mistake*.

fava bean /faáva-/ *n US* PLANTS, FOOD = **broad bean** [Via Italian < Latin *faba*]

fave /fayv/ *n, adj* favourite (*slang*) [Mid-20C. Shortening.]

favela /fə véllə, faa-/ *n* a shantytown or slum area, especially in Brazil [Mid-20C. < Brazilian Portuguese.]

fave rave *n* a favourite person, thing, or experience, e.g. a favourite film, song, or food (*slang*)

favism /faávizəm/ *n* acute anaemia caused by an allergic reaction to broad beans or the plant's pollen, usually as a result of a hereditary enzyme deficiency [Early 20C. < Italian *favismo* < *fava* 'broad bean' (see FAVA BEAN).]

favonian /fə vőni ən/ *adj* (*literary*) 1 relating to the west or the west wind 2 benign or kind [Mid-17C. < Latin *favonianus* < *Favonius* 'west wind'.]

favor *n, v* US = **favour**

favour /fáyvər/ *n* 1 **KIND ACT** an act of kindness performed or granted out of good will ○ *lent me the car as a favour* 2 **APPROVING ATTITUDE** an approving, friendly, or supportive attitude ○ *They seem to be out of favour with the judges.* 3 **PREFERENCE** preferential treatment shown to somebody 4 **TOKEN OF LOYALTY** something given or worn as a token of love, allegiance, or good will 5 **SMALL GIFT** a small gift given to each guest at a party ■ **favours** *npl* **SEX** sexual intimacy, especially when consented to by a woman (*dated*) ■ *vt* 1 **PREFER** to show a preference for or to somebody or something ○ *He favoured loud suits and colourful ties.* 2 **TREAT WELL** to treat somebody or something with particular approval or kindness ○ *She has been favouring him since he got a new car.* 3 **SUPPORT** to express support for somebody or something ○ *voters who favoured reform* 4 **ASSIST** to be advantageous to somebody or something ○ *tax measures that favour the rich* 5 **SHOW SOMEBODY PREFERENTIAL TREATMENT** to distinguish somebody by giving him or her something valuable ○ *favoured him with a seat next to her* 6 **BE CAREFUL WITH** to treat or use something gently ○ *favouring a bad knee* 7 **RESEMBLE** to resemble somebody, usually a parent, in appearance ○ *favours his uncle* [14C. Via Old French, 'friendly regard' < Latin *favor* < *favere* 'be well disposed towards'.] —**favourer** *n*

favourable /fáyvərəb'l/ *adj* 1 **ADVANTAGEOUS** acting in a beneficial way ○ *favourable winds* 2 **PROMISING** suggesting future improvement or good results ○ *a favourable outlook* 3 **APPROVING** expressing approval or admiration ○ *a favourable reaction* 4 **GAINING APPROVAL** winning approval or favour 5 **CONSENTING** expressing agreement or consent ○ *a favourable response* —**favourableness** *n* —**favourably** *adv*

favoured /fáyvərd/ *adj* 1 **CHOSEN** preferred to any other ○ *The favoured plan is unfortunately the costliest.* 2 **DISTINGUISHED** enjoying the advantages of a particular thing ○ *a child favoured with his mother's looks and father's good nature* 3 **PRIVILEGED** enjoying advantages or privileges denied to others —**favouredness** *n*

favourite /fáyvərit/ *adj* **MOST LIKED** preferred or most liked ■ *n* 1 **MOST LIKED PERSON OR THING** somebody who or something that is liked or preferred above others ○ *Which author is your favourite?* 2 **SOMEBODY FAVOURED BY SUPERIOR** somebody who is treated with special favour by a superior 3 **ONE MOST LIKELY TO WIN** a competitor considered to be the most likely to win, especially in a horse race [Late 16C. Via obsolete French *favorit* < Italian *favorito*, past participle of *favorire* 'to favour' < *favore* 'favour' < Latin *favor* (see FAVOUR).]

favouritism /fáyvərətizəm/ *n* 1 the practice of giving special treatment or unfair advantages to a person or group ○ *The teacher was accused of showing favouritism towards certain pupils.* 2 the state of being a favourite person ○ *basking in your favouritism*

favus /fáyvəss/ *n* an infectious skin disease that affects people, especially on the scalp, and some domestic animals, causing the formation of dry yellowish incrustations. It is caused by a fungus, *Trichophyton schoenleinii*. [Mid-16C. < Latin, 'honeycomb'.]

Fawcett /fáwssit/, **Dame Millicent** (1847–1929) British suffragette. Born **Millicent Garrett**

Fawkes /fawks/, **Guy** (1570–1606) English conspirator

Fawkner /fáwknər/, **John Pascoe** (1792–1869) British-born Australian pioneer

fawn[1] /fawn/ *n* 1 **YOUNG DEER** a young deer, especially one that is unweaned or less than a year old 2 **YELLOWISH-BROWN COLOUR** a pale yellowish-brown colour ■ *vi* **HAVE YOUNG** to give birth to a fawn [14C. Via French *faon* 'young animal' < assumed Vulgar Latin *feton-* < Latin *fetus* 'offspring'.] —**fawn** *adj*

SPELLCHECK Do not confuse ***fawn*** with ***faun***, which has a similar sound. Beware: your spellchecker will not catch this error.

fawn[2] /fawn/ *vi* 1 to seek attention or curry favour by flattery and obsequious behaviour 2 to attempt to please somebody by showing enthusiastic affection [Old English *fagnian* 'rejoice' < *fægen* 'glad' < Germanic] —**fawner** *n* —**fawningly** *adv*

fax /faks/ *n* 1 **MESSAGE SENT ELECTRONICALLY** an image or document that is transmitted in digitized electronic form over telephone lines and reproduced in its original form on the receiving end 2 **SYSTEM FOR TRANSMITTING DOCUMENTS** a system of transmitting documents and images electronically over telephone lines (*often before nouns*) ○ *sent by fax* 3 **fax, fax machine TRANSMITTING MACHINE** a machine incorporating a telephone that sends and receives documents or images via fax ■ *vt* **SEND ELECTRONICALLY** to send a message or document electronically using a fax machine [Mid-20C. Shortening of FACSIMILE.]

⚡**fax-modem** *n* a modem that enables a computer to send and receive faxes

fax-on-demand *n* technology that sends a facsimile automatically to somebody who telephones a particular number for information

fay[1] /fay/ *n* a fairy, elf, or other small supernatural being from folklore (*literary*) ○ *'You are, upon the whole, a sort of fay, or sprite – not a woman!'* (Thomas Hardy, *Jude the Obscure*; 1895) [14C. Via Old French *fa(i)e* 'fairy' < Latin *Fata*, goddess of fate < *fatum* (see FATE).]

fay[2] /fay/ *vti* to join pieces of wood together tightly, or fit tightly inside another piece of wood [Old English *fēgan* < Indo-European, 'fasten']

fayre /fair/ a fair, especially one held to raise money for charity (*informal*) [Pseudo-archaic variant]

faze /fayz/ (**fazes, fazing, fazed**) *v* **1** *vt* to disconcert or disturb somebody ○ *News of the disaster didn't seem to faze her.* **2** *vi Ireland* to have a visible effect on somebody ○ *The cold didn't faze on him.* [Mid-19C. Variant of dialectal *feeze* 'frighten' < Old English *fēsian* 'drive away' < Germanic.]

SPELLCHECK Do not confuse ***faze*** with ***phase***, which has a similar sound. Beware: your spellchecker will not catch this error.

fazenda /fə zéndə/ *n* a large estate, farm, plantation, or cattle ranch, especially in Brazil or Portugal [Early 19C. Via Portuguese, originally 'place with things to be done' < Latin *facienda* 'things to be done' < *facere* 'do, make'.]

FBA *abbr* Fellow of the British Academy

FBI *n* a bureau of the US Department of Justice that deals with matters of national security, interstate crime, and crimes against the government. Full form **Federal Bureau of Investigation**

FC *abbr* **1** Football Club **2** Forestry Commission

FCA *abbr* Fellow of the Institute of Chartered Accountants (in England and Wales)

FCCA *abbr* Fellow of the Chartered Association of Certified Accountants

FCII *abbr* Fellow of the Chartered Insurance Institute

F clef *n* MUSIC = **bass clef**

FCO *abbr* Foreign and Commonwealth Office

FD[1] *abbr* Fidei Defensor

FD[2], **f/d, f.d.** *abbr* free delivery

FDA *n* the US federal agency that oversees trade in and the safety of food and drugs. Full form **Food and Drug Administration**

F distribution *n* a statistical measure of the spread or scattering of members of two observed random samples as a test of whether the samples have the same variability [Mid-20C. After Sir Ronald *Fisher* (d. 1962), British statistician.]

FDR *abbr* Franklin Delano Roosevelt

Fe *symbol* iron [< Latin *ferrum*]

fealty /fée əlti/ (*plural* **-ties**) *n* the loyalty sworn to a feudal lord by a vassal or tenant [13C. Via Old French *feau(l)te* < Latin *fidelitas* (see FIDELITY).]

fear /feer/ *n* **1 FEELING OF ANXIETY** an unpleasant feeling of apprehension or distress caused by the presence or anticipation of danger **2 FRIGHTENING THOUGHT** an idea, thought, or other entity that causes feelings of fear ○ *irrational fears* **3 REVERENCE** awe or reverence, especially towards God **4 WORRY** a concern about something that threatens to bring bad news or results (*often plural*) ○ *fears for their safe return* **5 CHANCE** chance or likelihood of an undesirable thing happening ○ *There's no fear that he'll misunderstand.* ■ *v* **1** *vti* **BE AFRAID** to be frightened of somebody or something or about taking action **2** *vt* **EXPRESS REGRETFULLY** to be sorry to say something (*formal*) ○ *I fear that you have not been successful on this occasion.* **3** *vt* **REVERE** to show respect for or be in awe of somebody or something [Old English *fǣr* 'calamity, danger', *fǣran* 'frighten' < Indo-European, 'to try']

fear for *vt* to be worried or apprehensive about somebody who or something that appears to be at risk or in danger

fearful /féerf'l/ *adj* **1 FRIGHTENING** causing or likely to cause fear ○ *a fearful storm* **2 WORRIED** feeling anxiety or apprehension ○ *fearful for the safety of her investment* **3 TIMID** nervous and easily frightened ○ *a fearful kitten* **4 SHOWING FEAR** arising from or expressing fear ○ *a fearful expression* **5 REVERENTIAL** feeling awe or reverence for somebody or something ○ *gazed in fearful wonder* **6 VERY BAD** extreme in degree, intensity, or badness (*informal*) ○ *had a fearful headache* —**fearfully** *adv* —**fearfulness** *n*

fearless /féerləss/ *adj* courageous in the face of dangers or challenges —**fearlessly** *adv* —**fearlessness** *n*

fearsome /féerssəm/ *adj* **1 FRIGHTENING** inspiring fear ○ *a fearsome howling* **2 IMPRESSIVE** evoking awe and respect **3 TIMID** easily frightened —**fearsomely** *adv* —**fearsomeness** *n*

feart /feert/ *adj Scotland* feeling or showing fear [Variant of AFRAID]

~~**feasable**~~ incorrect spelling of **feasible**

feasibility /féezə bíllәti/ (*plural* **-ties**) *n* **1** the degree to which something can be carried out or achieved (*often before nouns*) ○ *examining the feasibility of the proposed merger* **2** something that can be carried out or achieved ○ *That idea is not even a feasibility.*

feasibility study *n* a preliminary study undertaken to assess whether a planned project is likely to be practical and successful, and also estimating its cost

feasible /féezəb'l/ *adj* **1** capable of being accomplished or put into effect **2** reasonable enough to be believed or accepted ○ *a feasible plan* [15C. < French *faisable* < *fais-*, stem of *faire* 'do' < Latin *facere* 'do, make'.] —**feasibleness** *n* —**feasibly** *adv*

feast /feest/ *n* **1 CELEBRATORY MEAL** an elaborate meal for many people that celebrates an occasion **2 LARGE MEAL** any large and elaborate meal **3 SOMETHING VERY AGREEABLE** something that provides a great deal of pleasure ○ *a feast for the eyes* **4 RELIGIOUS CELEBRATION** a periodic religious celebration, often marked by a special meal ■ *v* **1** *vi* **ATTEND CELEBRATORY MEAL** to be present at a celebratory meal **2** *vi* **ENJOY EATING** to eat heartily or with enjoyment ○ *feasting on strawberries and cream* **3** *vt* **PROVIDE FEAST FOR** to entertain somebody with a feast **4** *vi* **TAKE DELIGHT** to derive great or prolonged pleasure from something ○ *feast on the magnificent scenery* [12C. Via Old French < Latin *festum*.] —**feaster** *n*

feast day *n* **1** a day on which a religious festival takes place **2** a day on which an elaborate celebratory meal is enjoyed

Feast of Dedication, Feast of Lights *n* JUDAISM = **Hanukkah**

Feast of Lots *n* JUDAISM = **Purim**

Feast of St Michael and All Angels *n* CHR = **Michaelmas**

Feast of Tabernacles *n* JUDAISM = **Sukkoth**

Feast of the Assumption *n* CHR = **Assumption** *n.* 2

Feast of the Holy Innocents *n* CHR = **Holy Innocents' Day**

Feast of Weeks *n* JUDAISM = **Shavuoth**

feat /feet/ *n* a remarkable act or achievement involving courage, skill, or strength ○ *She achieved the impressive feat of winning three gold medals.* [14C. Via Old French *fait* 'deed' < Latin *factum* (see FACT).]

feather /féthər/ *n* **1 PART OF BIRD'S PLUMAGE** an individual part of a bird's plumage, consisting of a hollow central shaft with numerous interlocking fine strands on either side **2 SOMETHING RESEMBLING FEATHER** something, e.g. the leaf of a plant, with light or wispy strands that give it a superficial resemblance to a feather **3 FLAW IN PRECIOUS STONE** a feather-shaped flaw in a precious stone **4 UNIMPORTANT THING** something small, trivial, or of minimal value **5 ARROW ATTACHMENT** a piece of a feather attached to the end of an arrow or dart to make it fly straight **6 BLUNT END OF ARROW** the end of an arrow that has a feather fitted on it, as distinct from its head **7 PART OF WOOD JOINT** a projecting strip of wood fitted into a groove in the edge of a board to form a joint **8 TRACK MADE BY PERISCOPE** the track made on the surface of the sea by a submarine's periscope **9 HORIZONTAL OAR POSITION** the horizontal position of an oar, after raising it from the water between strokes, that reduces wind resistance ■ **feathers** *npl* **1 LONG HAIR ON ANIMAL'S LEGS** fringes of hair on the legs or tail of certain dogs and horses **2 ATTIRE** the clothes that somebody is wearing (*dated*) ■ *v* **1** *vt* **FIT SOMETHING WITH FEATHERS** to fit something, e.g. an arrow, with a feather or feathers **2** *vt* **COVER SOMETHING WITH FEATHERS** to cover or decorate somebody or something with feathers **3** *vi* **GROW FEATHERS** to grow or form feathers (*refers to birds*) **4** *vti* **FRAY** to fray a surface or end by cutting it or wearing it away, or become frayed in this way **5** *vi* **SPREAD** to grow or move out at an angle from a central line, in a pattern resembling the structure of a feather **6** *vti* **TURN OAR BLADE HORIZONTAL** to turn an oar with the blade face parallel to the water, after raising it from the water between strokes, in order to reduce wind resistance **7** *vt* **ALTER PROPELLER BLADES** to change the angle of an aircraft's propeller so that the line of the blades is roughly parallel to the line of flight and air resistance is minimized **8** *vt* **CUT HAIR TO FORM LAYERS** to style hair by cutting and thinning, giving a layered texture **9** *vt* **CONNECT BOARDS WITH TONGUE-AND-GROOVE** to join two boards or pieces of wood by using a tongue-and-groove joint [Old English *feþer* < Indo-European, 'to fly'] —**feathered** *adj* —**feather-like** *adj* ◇ **a feather in somebody's cap** an act or achievement that gives somebody cause to be proud ○ *Being asked to give the after-dinner speech was a feather in my cap.*

featherbed /féthər bed/ (**-beds, -bedding, -bedded**) *vt* to pamper somebody or protect a person from unpleasantness

featherbedding /féthər bedding/ *n US* the practice of overstaffing or limiting production, especially in compliance with a union contract, in order to save or create jobs

feather boa *n* a long thin scarf made of feathers

featherbone /féthər bōn/ *n* a substitute for whalebone, originally made from the quills of domestic fowl, used as a corset bone

featherbrain /féthər brayn/ *n* a forgetful, thoughtless, or inattentive person (*informal insult*) —**featherbrained** *adj*

feather duster *n* a brush used for dusting, made of long feathers attached to a stick

featheredge /féthər ej/ *n* **1 TAPERED BOARD** a board or plank with a thin tapering edge **2 TAPERING EDGE OF BOARD** the thinner tapering edge of a wedge-shaped board or plank **3** PAPER = **deckle edge** ■ *vt* (**-edges, -edging, -edged**) **HONE TO AN EDGE** to taper a side or end of a board to a very thin edge

feather grass *n* a perennial grass plant that has feathery clusters of spikelets. Genus: *Stipa*.

featherhead /féthər hed/ *n* = **featherbrain** (*informal insult*) —**featherheaded** /féthər héddid/ *adj*

feathering /féthəring/ *n* **1 PLUMAGE** the feathers on a bird **2 FEATHERS ATTACHED TO ARROW** the feathers attached to an arrow or dart, or their arrangement **3 LONG HAIR ON ANIMAL'S LEGS** fringes of hair on the legs or tails of certain dogs and horses **4 PRINTING DEFECT** the spreading of ink in lines like veins through printed paper that is too absorbent

feather star *n* a free-swimming marine invertebrate animal with between five and ten feathery arms radiating from a central disc. Order: Comatulida.

featherstitch /féthər stich/ *n* ornamental embroidery stitching with a zigzag pattern ■ *vt* to sew or decorate something with featherstitch

featherweight /féthər wayt/ *n* **1 LIGHT BOXER** a professional boxer weighing not more than 57 kg/126 pounds, between bantamweight and lightweight **2 SPORTSPERSON** a competitor of light weight in other sports, e.g. wrestling **3 SOMETHING LIGHT** somebody or something that is very light, small, or insignificant

feathery /féthəri/ *adj* **1** similar to a feather or feathers, especially in lightness or softness **2** made of or covered in feathers —**featheriness** *n*

feature /féechər/ *n* **1 PART OF FACE** a part of a face that contributes to its distinct character, especially the eyes, nose, or mouth **2 DISTINCTIVE PART** a part of something that distinguishes it **3 FULL-LENGTH FILM** a full-length film or, formerly, the main film in a cinema programme **4 REGULAR ARTICLE** a regular item in a newspaper or magazine **5 MAIN STORY** a story or article that is given particular prominence in a newspaper or magazine **6 MAIN PROGRAMME** a television or radio programme that is considered highly important or popular **7 SPECIAL ATTRACTION** something offered as a special attraction, e.g. a particular aspect of something ○ *a refrigerator with several energy-saving features* **8 PROPERTY OF LINGUISTIC UNIT** a distinctive property of a linguistic unit ■ *v* (**-tures, -turing, -tured**) **1** *vt* **CONTAIN SOMETHING AS IMPORTANT ELEMENT** to have or present somebody or something as an important element of something ○ *This week's activities will feature pony-trekking and golf.* **2** *vti* **GIVE OR HAVE PROMINENCE IN PERFORMANCE** to give prominence to somebody taking part in a performance or to something performed or portrayed in a performance, or be given prominence in this way ○ *a movie featuring two of the most popular actors* **3** *vi* **FIGURE** to figure in or be a part of something ○ *Marriage doesn't feature in his plans.* **4** *vt* **RESEMBLE** to resemble somebody physically, especially facially (*regional*) ○ *She features her mother.* [14C. Via Old French faiture 'form' < Latin *factura* 'something made' < *fact-* (see FACT).] —**featured** *adj*

ϟ**feature creature** *n* somebody who adds excessive features to a design, software program, or website, often at the expense of coherence or utility (*slang*)

feature film *n* a full-length film for the cinema

feature-length *adj* being as long as a feature film ○ *a feature-length episode of a TV show*

featureless /feéchərləss/ *adj* lacking any characteristics or properties that can be considered distinctive

Feb. *abbr* February

febrific /fi bríffik/, **febriferous** /fi bríffərəss/ *adj* **1** capable of causing somebody to have a fever **2** affected by a fever [Early 18C. < obsolete French *fébrifique* < Latin *febris* 'fever'.]

febrifuge /fébbri fyooj/ *n* a drug that reduces fever [Late 17C. < French *fébrifuge* < Latin *febris* 'fever'.] —**febrifugal** /fi bríffyoog'l/ *adj* —**febrifuge** *adj*

febrile /feéb rīl/ *adj* relating to, involving, or typical of fever [Mid-17C. < French *fébrile* or medieval Latin *febrilis* < Latin *febris* 'fever'.]

February /fébbroo əri, fébbyoo-/ (*plural* **-ies**) *n* the second month of the year in the Gregorian calendar, usually made up of 28 days [14C. Via Old French *feverier* < Latin *februarius (mensis)* '(month) of purification'; from an annual Roman festival.]

~~**Febuary**~~ incorrect spelling of **February**

fec. *abbr* he or she made it [Latin *fecit*]

fecal *adj* US = **faecal**

feces *npl* US = **faeces**

feckless /fékləss/ *adj* **1** unable or unwilling to do anything useful **2** lacking the thought or organization necessary to succeed ○ *feckless attempts at starting a business* [Late 16C. < obsolete *feck* 'value, efficacy', shortening of EFFECT.] —**fecklessly** *adv* —**fecklessness** *n*

fecula /fékyŏolə/ (*plural* **-lae** /-lee/) *n* **1** a starch extracted as sediment from a mixture of water and crushed plants **2** a piece of excrement, especially an insect dropping [Late 17C. < Latin *faecula* 'crust of wine' < *faex* 'dregs, sediment'.]

feculent /fékyŏolənt/ *adj* very dirty or foul, especially polluted by excrement (*formal*) [15C. Directly or via French < Latin *faeculentus* < *faeces* (see FAECES).] —**feculence** *n*

fecund /fékənd, feék-/ *adj* **1** capable of producing much vegetation or many offspring (*formal*) **2** capable of producing many different works or works that are highly imaginative ○ *a fecund liar* [14C. Directly or via French < Latin *fecundus*.]

fecundate /fékən dayt, feék-/ (**-dates, -dating, -dated**) *vt* (*formal*) **1** to make somebody or something fruitful or productive **2** to fertilize something, or make somebody or something pregnant —**fecundation** /fékən dáysh'n, feék-/ *n*

fecundity /fi kúndəti/ *n* **1** the ability to produce offspring, especially in large numbers **2** the ability to produce many different and original ideas (*formal*)

fed past participle, past tense of **feed**

Fed /fed/, **fed** *n US* a Federal agent or official, especially an agent of one of the watchdog agencies such as the Federal Bureau of Investigation or the Environmental Protection Agency (*informal*)

Fed., **fed.** *abbr* **1** Federal **2** Federated **3** Federation

fedayee /fə daá yee/ (*plural* **-yeen** /-yeen/) *n* an Arab commando or guerrilla, especially one who fights against Israel [Mid-20C. < Arabic, Persian *fidā'ī* 'somebody who sacrifices himself or herself'.]

federal /féddərəl/ *adj* **1 MADE UP OF ALLIES** relating to a form of government in which several states or regions defer certain powers, e.g. in foreign affairs, to a central government while retaining some measure of self-government **2 CENTRAL** relating to a political unit established on a federal basis, especially its central government **3 ASSOCIATED** relating to or characteristic of a unified body with constituent elements that retain a measure of autonomy **4** *US* **OF A US ARCHITECTURAL STYLE** relating to, involving, or typical of a classical style of architecture, decoration, and furniture popular in the United States in the late 18th and early 19th centuries ■ *n* **SUPPORTER OF ALLIANCE** a supporter of joining an alliance [Mid-17C. < Latin *foeder-*, stem of *foedus* 'treaty'.]

Federal Bureau of Investigation *n* full form of **FBI**

Federal Court *n* in Australia, a national court that has jurisdiction in matters relating to corruption, bankruptcy, industrial relations, corporation law, taxation, and trade

federal district *n* an area in which the seat of the national government of a federation, e.g. the United States, is located

federal government *n* **1** the central government of a federation **2** in Australia, the national government based in Canberra

federalise *vt* POL = **federalize**

federalism /féddərəlizəm/ *n* **1** a political system in which several states or regions defer certain powers, e.g. in foreign affairs, to a central government while retaining a limited measure of self-government **2** the principle of a federal system of government, or support for such a system

Federalism *n* the political doctrine of the former Federalist Party of the United States

federalist /féddərəlist/ *n* a supporter of a federal system of government

Federalist *n* a supporter of the former Federalist Party of the United States

Federalist Party *n* a former political party of the United States advocating a strong centralized government within the federal system. Founded in 1787, it declined in influence after 1800.

federalize /féddərə līz/ (**-izes, -izing, -ized**), **federalise** /féddərə līz/ (**-ises, -ising, -ised**) *vt* **1** to bring various states together in a federal union **2** to place something under the control of a federal government —**federalization** /féddərə lī záysh'n/ *n*

Federal Reserve Bank *n* in the United States, any one of the 12 reserve banks responsible for regulating the affiliated banks in its own district

federate /féddə rayt/ (**-ates, -ating, -ated**) *vti* to join, or cause various bodies to join together, in a federation [Late 17C. < Latin *foederat-*, past participle of *foederare* < *foedus* 'treaty'.]

federation *n* **1 JOINING IN FEDERAL UNION** an act of joining in a federal union or a federal system of government **2 POLITICAL UNIT** a political unit formed from smaller units on a federal basis **3 ALLIANCE** a group of various bodies or parties that have united to achieve a common goal

Federation /féddə ráysh'n/ *n* **1** the uniting of the Australian colonies on the first day of 1901 to form the Commonwealth of Australia, ruled by a single federal government **2** an Australian architectural style, typical of the period during which Federation took place, that is characterized by redbrick walls, terracotta roof tiles, ornate window frames, and stained-glass windows

fedora /fi dáwrə/ *n* a soft felt hat with a brim and a crease along the length of its crown [Late 19C. < *Fédora*, drama by Victorien Sardou (1831–1908), French playwright.]

fed up *adj* having reached the limits of tolerance or patience with somebody or something (*informal*) ○ *I know she's fed up with working all the time.*

fee /fee/ *n* **1 PAYMENT FOR SERVICES** a payment for professional services **2 CHARGE MADE BY INSTITUTION** a charge made by an institution, e.g. for membership, entrance, or the administering of an examination **3 HERITABLE INTEREST IN LAND** a right to land that can be passed on by inheritance **4** HIST = **fief** *n.* 1 [14C. Via Anglo-Norman variant of Old French *feu* < medieval Latin *feudum* (see FEUD[2]).]

SYNONYMS See ***wage***.

---

feeble /feéb'l/ (**-bler, -blest**) *adj* **1** lacking physical or mental strength or health **2** unlikely to convince ○ *a feeble excuse* [12C. Via Old French *fe(i)ble* < Latin *flebilis* 'lamentable, weak' < *flere* 'weep'.] —**feebleness** *n* —**feebly** *adv*

SYNONYMS See ***weak***.

---

feeble-minded *adj* **1 OFFENSIVE TERM** an offensive term meaning below average in intelligence (*dated*) **2 UNINTELLIGENT** unintelligent or thoughtless (*insult*) **3 NOT WELL-THOUGHT-OUT** done without forethought or a well-conceived plan —**feeble-mindedly** *adv* —**feeble-mindedness** *n*

feed /feed/ *v* (**feeds, feeding, fed** /fed/) **1** *vt* **GIVE FOOD TO** to give food to a person or an animal **2** *vt* **GIVE AS FOOD** to give something as food to a person or an animal **3** *vt* **SERVE AS FOOD FOR** to serve as or be enough food for a person or an animal **4** *vi* **EAT** to eat food or take regular nourishment ○ *Most whales feed on plankton.* **5** *vt* **SUPPORT** to sustain or encourage a specific belief or behaviour ○ *Compliments merely feed vanity.* **6** *vt* **PROVIDE WITH NECESSARY MATERIAL** to provide the necessary materials for something to operate **7** *vti* **MOVE GRADUALLY** to move something gradually into, through, or out of something, or be moved in this way **8** *vt* **GIVE PERFORMER CUE** to deliver a line or cue to a fellow performer **9** *vti* **PASS BALL TO PLAYER** to pass a ball to a team-mate (*informal*) **10** *vt* **SUPPLY WITH POWER** to supply power or an electrical signal to a system, component, or station **11** *vt* **PUT BALL IN SCRUMMAGE ILLEGALLY** in rugby, to put the ball into the scrummage illegally by putting it at the feet of team-mates ■ *n* **1 ACT OF FEEDING** an act or occasion of feeding **2 FOOD** food, especially for animals or babies **3 LARGE MEAL** a meal, especially a large and satisfying one (*dated informal*) **4 MATERIAL PROVIDER** a device that supplies material to a machine, as does the paper tray on a printer **5 SOMEBODY WHO PROVIDES CUES** a person who delivers a line or cue to a performer [Old English *fēdan* < Germanic]

feed into *vt* **1** to add weight and impetus to something **2** to connect with and contribute to something larger, e.g. a road or river

feed up *vt* to give a person or an animal plenty of food to eat in order to build up that person's or animal's weight

feedback /feéd bak/ *n* **1 RETURN OF OUTPUT** the return of part of the output of a machine, system, or circuit to the input in a way that affects its performance **2 NOISE IN LOUDSPEAKER** the high whistling or howling noise caused by feedback in a loudspeaker **3 RESPONSE** comments in the form of opinions about and reactions to something, intended to provide useful information for future decisions and development

feedback circuit *n* a circuit in which a portion of the output signal is returned to the input, often in order to control or stabilize the circuit

feedback control loop *n* the connection or path that forms an electrical loop from the output to the input of a feedback circuit

feedback factor *n* a portion of an output signal that is returned to and combined with the input signal

feedback inhibition *n* an internal control on a hormone or enzyme that causes a reduction in activity once the end product reaches a certain concentration

feedback loop *n* a cycle in which two agents each act to reinforce the other's action

feedbag /feéd bag/ *n* **1** a bag or sack containing food for livestock **2** *US* = **nosebag**

feeder /feédər/ *n* **1 EATER** a consumer or giver of food **2 CONTAINER FOR ANIMAL'S FOOD** a device that supplies food for animals and birds ○ *a bird feeder in the garden* **3 BIB** a baby's bib or bottle (*dated*) **4 MACHINE PART** a part of a machine that accepts or controls the input of material to be processed ○ *a document feeder* **5 TRIBUTARY** a stream or river that joins the flow of a larger one **6 CONNECTING CARRIER** a road, railway, or airline that carries traffic from a relatively small place to a city in order to connect with a larger carrier **7 POWER LINE** a power line that carries power from a generating station to a substation or network **8 CONNECTION** a line that connects an aerial to a receiver or transmitter **9 PRIMARY SCHOOL** a primary school from which a secondary school receives an annual intake of pupils **10 PLANT REQUIRING FERTILIZER** a plant that requires a large amount of fertilizer to grow, and especially flower, well ○ *Fuchsias are gross feeders.*

feeding bottle *n* a bottle with a plastic or rubber teat used to give milk or other liquids to a baby or young animal

feeding frenzy *n* **1** an intense violent period of eating that occurs when a large number of animals of the same or related species, e.g. sharks or piranhas, converge on a food source **2** an instance of frantic activity centred on a person or organization that occurs when other people, especially journalists, sense an opportunity they can exploit (*informal*)

feeding ground *n* an area where animals, birds, or fish regularly come to feed

feedlot /feéd lot/ *n US* an area or building in which livestock are kept while being fattened for slaughter

feedstock /feéd stok/ *n* a raw material used in the industrial manufacture of a product

feedstuff /feéd stuf/ *n* feed for livestock, especially consisting of processed and balanced ingredients

feedthrough /feéd throo/ *n* an electrical conductor that connects two sides of a circuit board

feel /feel/ *v* (**feels, feeling, felt** /felt/) **1** *vt* **TOUCH** to perceive something using the sense of touch **2** *vt* **TOUCH SOMEBODY SEXUALLY** to touch somebody or a part of somebody's body for the purpose of sexual gratification **3** *vt* **EXAMINE** to test or examine something by touching it **4** *vt* **ADVANCE HESITANTLY** to make your way forward slowly, guided by the sense of touch or tentatively, because what is ahead is dark or uncertain **5** *vi* **USE TOUCH IN SEARCHING** to use the sense of touch to try to find something ○ *feel around for my keys* **6** *vt* **HAVE SENSATION IN BODY PART** to have physical sensation in a particular part of the body **7** *vt* **EXPERIENCE** to experience an emotion or physical sensation ○ *I feel no regret.* **8** *vi* **SEEM TO YOURSELF** to seem to yourself to be in a particular physical or emotional state ○ *Don't feel sad.* **9** *vi* **CAUSE PARTICULAR SENSATION** to cause a particular physical or emotional sensation ○ *The water feels cold.* **10** *vt* **BE AWARE OF** to be instinctively aware of something, usually an emotion, that is not visible or apparent **11** *vt* **BE AFFECTED BY** to be deeply affected emotionally by something painful **12** *vt* **THINK SOMETHING IS TRUE** to be convinced about something by instinct or intuition rather than concrete evidence ○ *I feel you're lying to me.* **13** *vt* **BELIEVE** to have the opinion or belief that something is the case ○ *She felt she could no longer carry on.* ■ *n* **1 ACT OF TOUCHING** an act of touching something **2 IMPRESSION GAINED FROM TOUCH** an impression of something gained through touching or being touched by it ○ *the feel of wool against the skin* **3 IMPRESSION SENSED** a particular impression, appearance, effect, or atmosphere sensed from something ○ *a hotel with a more traditional feel* **4 SENSE OF TOUCH** the sensation felt on touching something ○ *hot to the feel* **5 INSTINCT** an instinctive understanding of, or talent for, something ○ *He has a feel for these things.* **6 GROPE** an uninvited sexual touch (*informal*) [Old English *fēlan* < Indo-European] ◇ **feel like 1** to have an inclination or desire for something **2** to have or acknowledge a physical or emotional condition that is considered comparable to something else

feel for *vt* to experience sympathy or compassion for somebody

feel out *vt* to try to establish, often in an indirect way, the nature of a situation or somebody's attitude or opinion about something

feel up *vt* to touch somebody sexually, especially without permission (*informal*)

feel up to *vt* to consider yourself ready for something or able to do something

feeler /feélər/ *n* **1 SOMEBODY WHO FEELS** somebody who or something that feels something **2 TOUCHING ORGAN** an organ of touch in various animals, e.g. an insect's antenna **3 ATTEMPT TO TEST OTHERS' REACTION** something said or done to test the reaction of others to an idea, plan, or project

feeler gauge *n* a thin strip of metal of a specific size used to measure or set a gap between parts of a mechanism

feel-good *adj* causing, involving, or typical of a sense of wellbeing or satisfaction

feeling /feéling/ *n* **1 SENSE OF TOUCH** the sensation felt on touching something **2 ABILITY TO HAVE PHYSICAL SENSATION** the ability to perceive physical sensation in a part of the body ○ *Slowly the feeling returned to his fingers.* **3 SOMETHING EXPERIENCED PHYSICALLY OR MENTALLY** a perceived physical or mental sensation **4 SOMETHING FELT EMOTIONALLY** a perceived emotion **5 AFFECTION** the emotional response of love, sympathy, or tenderness towards somebody **6 ABILITY TO EXPRESS EMOTION** the capacity to experience strong emotions **7 IMPRESSION SENSED** a particular impression, appearance, effect, or atmosphere sensed from something ○ *There was a feeling of abandonment about the old house.* **8 INSTINCTIVE AWARENESS** an instinctive awareness or presentiment of something ○ *I have a feeling you're going to be disappointed.* **9 INSTINCTIVE UNDERSTANDING OR TALENT** an instinctive understanding of, or talent for, something ○ *has a real feeling for this kind of work* **10 EXPRESSIVE ABILITY** the ability to express strong emotion, especially in performance ○ *Play the piece again with more feeling.* ■ **feelings** *npl* **SENSIBILITIES** somebody's emotional susceptibilities ○ *I didn't want to hurt their feelings.* ■ *adj* **1 SENSITIVE TO TOUCH** able to experience the sensation of touch **2 EXPRESSIVE** expressing or full of strong emotion **3 HAVING STRONG EMOTIONS** easily or strongly affected by emotion —**feelingly** *adv*

fee simple (*plural* **fees simple**) *n* a form of property ownership in which the owner has outright and unconditional disposal rights. ◊ **fee tail**

feet plural of **foot**

fee tail (*plural* **fees tail**) *n* a form of property ownership in which the property may be inherited only by a particular line of heirs. ◊ **fee simple**

Fehling's solution /fáylingz-/ *n* a solution of copper sulphate, sodium potassium tartrate, and sodium hydroxide. Use: detection of aldehydes, including sugars. [Late 19C. After Hermann von *Fehling* (1812–85), German chemist.]

Fehling's test /fáylingz-/, **Fehlings test** *n* the use of Fehling's solution to detect the presence of aldehydes and sugars [See FEHLING'S SOLUTION]

feign /fayn/ *vt* **1 PRETEND** to make a show or pretence of something ○ *She feigned ignorance.* **2 INVENT** to make up or fabricate something **3 COPY** to imitate or copy somebody or something [13C. < French *feign-*, present stem of *feindre* 'pretend, shirk' < Latin *fingere* 'fabricate, form'.]

feijoa /fay yṓ ə/ *n* **1** a green fruit that tastes like pineapple and is eaten raw or cooked. Use: jams, preserves. **2** a tree that bears feijoas. Native to: South America. *Acca sellowiana*. [Late 19C. < modern Latin, after J. da Silva *Feijó* (1760–1824), Brazilian naturalist.]

feijoada /fáy zhoo aád aa/ *n* a Brazilian party dish of meat with rice, black beans, green vegetables, and hot pepper sauce [Mid-20C. < Portuguese, < *feijão*, any of various edible beans < Latin *phaseolus*.]

~~**feind**~~ incorrect spelling of **fiend**

feint[1] /faynt/ *n* **1 MOCK ATTACK** a mock attack by a military force, intended to draw the enemy's attention away from the true attack **2 DECEPTIVE MOVE** a deceptive move in a competitive sport **3 DECEPTIVE ACTION** a deceptive action made to disguise what is really intended ■ *vti* **MAKE FEINT** to carry out a feint [Late 17C. < French *feinte* 'sham, pretence' < past participle of *feindre* (see FEIGN).]

SPELLCHECK See ***faint***.

feint[2] /faynt/ *adj* describes paper with faint horizontal lines across it as a guide for writing [Late 17C. < French *feinte* < form of *feindre* (see FEIGN).]

feisty /fīsti/ (**-ier, -iest**) *adj* (*informal*) **1** characterized by spirited, sometimes aggressive, behaviour **2** *US, Can* likely to respond in an irritable or touchy way —**feistily** *adv* —**feistiness** *n*

felafel *n* COOK = **falafel**

feldspar /féld spaar/, **felspar** /fél-/ *n* an extremely common aluminosilicate mineral containing varying proportions of calcium, sodium, potassium, and other elements [Late 18C. Alteration of German *Feldspath*, literally 'field mineral'.] —**feldspathic** /feld spáthik/ *adj*

feldspathoid /féld spath oyd/ *n* a group of minerals similar to the feldspars but lower in silica [Late 19C. < German *Feldspath* 'feldspar'.]

felicitate /fə líssi tayt/ (**-tates, -tating, -tated**) *vt* to congratulate or wish somebody happiness (*formal*) [Early 17C. < late Latin *felicitat-*, past participle of *felicitare* 'make happy' < Latin *felix* 'happy'.] —**felicitator** *n*

felicitation /fə líssi táysh'n/ *n* an act of congratulating or wishing somebody happiness (*formal*) ■ **felicitations** *npl* used as a greeting or to wish somebody happiness (*formal*)

felicitous /fə líssitəss/ *adj* **1 APPROPRIATE** appropriate or highly suitable ○ *a felicitous choice of words* **2 PLEASANT** pleasing or agreeable **3 FORTUNATE** happy or fortunate [Mid-16C. < FELICITY.] —**felicitously** *adv* —**felicitousness** *n*

felicity /fə líssəti/ (*plural* **-ties**) *n* **1 HAPPINESS** happiness or contentment **2 SOMETHING PRODUCING HAPPINESS** something that creates happiness **3 APPROPRIATENESS** an appropriate or pleasing manner **4 SOMETHING APPROPRIATE** something appropriate or pleasing [14C. Via Old French < Latin *felicitas* < *felix* 'fruitful, happy'.]

felid /feélid/ (*plural* **-lids** *or* **-lid**) *n* an animal belonging to the cat family. Lions, tigers, and domestic cats are felids. Family: Felidae. (*technical*) [Late 19C. < modern Latin *Felidae* < Latin *feles* 'cat'.]

feline /feé līn/ *adj* **1 OF CAT FAMILY** belonging to or typical of animals of the cat family, including lions, tigers, and domestic cats **2 RESEMBLING CAT** similar to a cat, especially in graceful movement or stealthiness ○ *feline suppleness* ■ *n* **MEMBER OF CAT FAMILY** an animal belonging to the cat family. Domestic cats, lions, and tigers are felines. Family: Felidae. [Late 17C. < Latin *felinus* < *feles* 'cat'.] —**felinely** *adv* —**felineness** *n*

feline distemper *n* an infectious viral disease of cats that causes vomiting and diarrhoea and is often fatal

fell[1] /fel/ past tense of **fall**

fell[2] /fel/ *vt* **1 CHOP TREE DOWN** to cut down a tree **2 KNOCK SOMEBODY DOWN** to knock somebody down, or cause somebody to fall **3 SEW SEAM FLAT** to sew a seam by turning an edge over and sewing it down on the inside ■ *n* **1 NUMBER OF TREES CUT DOWN** an amount of timber cut down at one time or over one period **2 SEWN SEAM** a seam sewn by turning an edge over and sewing it down on the inside [Old English *fellan* 'cause to fall' < Germanic] —**fellable** *adj*

fell[3] /fel/ *adj* having an extremely cruel or vicious character (*archaic or literary*) [13C. < Old French *fel*, form of *felon* (see FELON[1]).]

fell[4] /fel/ *n* a hillside or mountainside without trees [13C. < Old Norse *fjall* 'hill' < Indo-European.]

fell[5] /fel/ *n* **1** the hide of an animal **2** the thin membrane between an animal's hide and its flesh [Old English, < Indo-European]

fella /féllə/ *n* a man or boy (*informal*) [Mid-19C. Representing nonstandard pronunciation of FELLOW.]

fellah /féllə/ (*plural* **-lahin** /féllə heén/ *or* **-laheen** *or* **-lahs**) *n* a member of the labouring class in an Arab country who lives off the land [Mid-18C. < Arabic *fallah* 'tiller of the soil' < *falahah* 'split, till the soil'.]

fellate /fe láyt/ (**-lates, -lating, -lated**) *vti* to perform oral sex for a man [Late 19C. < Latin *fellat-* (see FELLATIO).] —**fellation** *n* —**fellator** *n*

fellatio /fe láyshi ō/ *n* the sexual stimulation of a man's genitals using the tongue and lips [Late 19C. < modern Latin, < Latin *fellat-* past participle of *fellare* 'suck'.]

feller[1] /féllər/ *n* **1** a tree cutter **2** a person who or a machine attachment that fells seams

feller[2] /féllər/ *n* a man or boy (*informal*) [Early 19C. Representing nonstandard pronunciation of FELLOW.]

Fellini /fe leéni/, **Federico** (1920–93) Italian film director

fellmonger /fél mung gər/ *n* a preparer and seller of animal skins —**fellmongering** *n*

felloe /féllō/, **felly** /félli/ (*plural* **-lies**) *n* an outer rim of a wooden wheel, or a segment of this, with a metal tyre shrunk around it [Old English *felg* < Indo-European, 'turn']

fellow /féllō/ *n* **1 MAN OR BOY** a man or boy (*dated*) **2 BOYFRIEND** somebody's boyfriend (*dated informal*) **3 ONE OF PAIR** either one of a pair of objects **4 COMPANION** a companion or colleague (*dated*) **5 EQUAL** somebody or something of the same rank or quality **6 fellow, Fellow MEMBER OF UNIVERSITY STAFF** somebody on the governing board of a university or college, usually also a member of the teaching staff ○ *a Cambridge Fellow* **7 GRADUATE STUDENT** a graduate student who is supported by a university department to teach or do research ○ *a research fellow* ■ *adj* **BEING IN SAME GROUP** belonging to the same group, occupation, rank, or location [Old English *feolaga* 'partner' < Old Norse *félagi* < *fé* 'money']

LITERARY LINK ***Poor Fellow My Country***, a novel (1975) by Australian writer Xavier Herbert. Set in Northern Australia between 1936 and 1942, it depicts the disastrous effects of white settlement on Aboriginal peoples through the interwoven stories of pastoralists, government representatives, and local Aboriginals.

Fellow /féllō/ *n* a member of a learned or scientific society ○ *Fellow of the Royal College of Surgeons*

fellow feeling *n* an awareness of having interests in common with other people and feeling sympathy for them

fellow servant *n* an employee whose employer is not legally responsible for harm or injury done to him or her by another employee

fellowship /féllō ship/ *n* **1 COMMUNION** a sharing of common interests, goals, experiences, or views **2 SOCIETY** a group of people who share common interests, goals, experiences, or views **3 COMPANIONSHIP** companionship or friendly association **4 SIMILARITY** membership in a group, or the sharing of characteristics with others **5 MEMBERSHIP OF UNIVERSITY STAFF** membership of the governing board of a university or college, usually also involving teaching duties **6 GRADUATE POST** a university post awarded to a graduate student who is supported by a university department to teach or undertake research **7 FINANCIAL ENDOWMENT** a financial endowment set up to support graduate students

Fellowship *n* the fellows of a university or college considered as a body

fellow traveller *n* **1** a person who takes the same journey as another at the same time **2** a sympathizer with the cause of an organized group, especially the Communist Party, without joining it

fell-running /fél runing/ *n* the sport of competitive running over fells

fell-walking /fél wawking/ *n* the pastime of walking on fells

felly *n* = **felloe**

felo de se /feélō di seé/ (*plural* **felones de se** /fee lṓ neez di seé/ *or* **felos de se**) *n* **1** a person who commits suicide **2** an act of committing suicide [Early 17C. < Anglo-Latin, 'crime against yourself'.]

felon[1] /féllən/ *n* formerly in England and Wales, somebody guilty of a felony ■ *adj* characterized by evil or depravity (*archaic*) [13C. Via Old French < medieval Latin *fellon-* 'evildoer'.]

felon[2] /féllən/ *n* MED = **whitlow** [14C. < ?]

felonious /fə lṓni əss/ *adj* relating to felonies or a felony —**feloniously** *adv* —**feloniousness** *n*

felony /félləni/ (*plural* **-nies**) *n* formerly in England and Wales, and currently in the United States, a serious crime such as murder that is punished more severely than a misdemeanour [13C. < Old French *felonie* < *felon* (see FELON[1]).]

felsic /félssik/ *adj* describes igneous rocks or minerals that are light in colour, indicating relatively high levels of quartz and feldspars [Early 20C. < FELDSPAR + SILICA.]

felsite /fél sīt/ *n* a light-coloured igneous rock consisting chiefly of feldspar and quartz that can only be precisely classified by microscopic examination [Late 18C. < FELDSPAR.] —**felsitic** /fel síttik/ *adj*

felspar *n* MINERALS = **feldspar**

felt[1] /felt/ past tense, past participle of **feel**

felt[2] /felt/ *n* **1 WOOL OR ANIMAL-HAIR FABRIC** a fabric made from wool or animal hair by compressing, heating, or treating the fibres with chemicals **2 SYNTHETIC FABRIC** a synthetic fabric made by the process of matting, especially a heavy paper permeated with asphalt, used as a roof sealant ■ *v* **1** *vt* **MAKE INTO FELT** to make something into felt **2** *vt* **COVER WITH FELT** to cover something with felt ○ *felting the roof* **3** *vi* **BECOME MATTED** to become matted, or come to resemble felt [Old English, < Indo-European, 'strike, beat, pound'] —**felty** *adj*

felting /félting/ *n* **1** felt fabric **2** the process of making felt

felt pen *n* = **felt-tipped pen**

felt tip *n* **1** a pen point made from felt or a similar compressed fibre **2** = **felt-tipped pen**

felt-tipped pen *n* a pen with a point made from felt or a similar compressed fibre

felucca /fə lúkə/ *n* a small sailing boat with curving triangular sails (**lateen-rigged**), used in the Mediterranean and on the Nile [Early 17C. Via Italian < Mediterranean Arabic *fluka*.]

felwort /fél wurt/ *n* a plant of the gentian family. Flowers: purple. Native to: Europe, China. *Gentianella amarella*. [Old English *feldwyrt* 'field plant']

fem. *abbr* **1** female **2** feminine

FEMA /feémə/ *abbr US* Federal Emergency Management Agency

female /feé mayl/ *adj* **1 OF THE SEX THAT PRODUCES OFFSPRING** relating or belonging to the sex that produces sex sells (**gametes**) that fuse with male sex cells during sexual reproduction **2 RELATING TO WOMEN** relating to or belonging to women or girls **3 HAVING CARPELS** describes flowers that have carpels but no stamens **4 MADE WITH A RECESS** describes a component or part of a component, e.g. an electric socket, that has a recess designed to receive a corresponding projecting part ■ *n* **1 FEMALE PERSON OR ANIMAL** a female person or animal **2 OFFENSIVE TERM** an offensive term for a girl or woman **3 PLANT WITH FEMALE FLOWERS** a plant that has only female flowers [14C. Alteration (after MALE) of Old French *femelle* < Latin *femella* < *femina* (see FEMININE).] —**femaleness** *n*

female circumcision, female genital mutilation *n* the practice of circumcision of adolescent women in some cultures that generally involves the surgical removal of the clitoris or the sewing up of the vaginal opening

female impersonator *n* a man, often appearing as a solo theatrical performer, who dresses as and imitates a woman

feme /fem/ *n* in law, a woman or wife [Mid-16C. Via Anglo-Norman < Latin *femina* (see FEMININE).]

feme covert /-kúvərt/ (*plural* **femes covert**) *n* in law, a married woman [< Anglo-Norman 'covered woman']

feme sole /-sṓl/ (*plural* **femes sole**) *n* in law, a single woman, including women not married, widows, divorcées, and married women living independently and separately from their husbands [< Anglo-Norman]

femineity /fémmə neé i tee/ *n* the quality of looking and behaving in ways conventionally thought to be appropriate for a woman [Early 19C. < Latin *femineus* 'womanish' < *femina* (see FEMININE).]

feminine /fémmənin/ *adj* **1 CONVENTIONALLY CHARACTERISTIC OF WOMEN** conventionally believed to be appropriate for a woman or girl **2 ATTRIBUTED TO WOMEN** considered to be specific to women **3 EFFEMINATE** describes qualities, actions, or types of behaviour in a man or boy that are conventionally associated with women or girls **4 CLASSIFIED GRAMMATICALLY AS FEMALE IN GENDER** describes a class of words or forms in various languages that includes the majority of words referring to females ■ *n* **FEMININE WORD OR FORM** a word or form that in a particular language is classified grammatically as feminine [14C. Via Old French < Latin *femininus* < *femina* 'woman' < Indo-European, 'suck'.] —**femininely** *adv* —**feminineness** *n*

feminine caesura *n* a pause in a line of scanned verse that does not come immediately after a stressed syllable

feminine ending *n* **1** an inflectional morpheme attached to the end of a word that marks it as belonging to the feminine gender **2** an ending of a line of verse that ends with an extra unstressed syllable

feminine rhyme *n* a rhyme scheme in which the lines containing rhyming words end in unstressed syllables

~~**femininity**~~ incorrect spelling of **femininity**

femininity /fémmə nínnəti/ *n* **1 CONVENTIONALLY FEMININE QUALITY** the quality of looking and behaving in ways conventionally thought to be appropriate for a woman or girl **2 WOMEN** women as a group (*dated*) **3 CONVENTIONAL IDEA ABOUT WOMEN** a manner or feature commonly attributed to women **4 EFFEMINACY** the qualities, actions, or types of behaviour in a man or boy that are conventionally associated with women or girls

feminise *vt* SOC SCI = **feminize**

feminism /fémmənizəm/ *n* **1** belief in the need to secure, or a commitment to securing, rights and opportunities for women equal to those of men **2** the movement committed to securing and defending equal rights and opportunities for women equal to those of men [Mid-19C. < French *féminisme*.] —**feminist** *n, adj*

QUICK FACTS ON... **FEMINISM**

Key dates: mid-19th–early 20th centuries, 1960s–1970s
Key locations: United Kingdom, North America
Key elements: women's suffrage, reproductive rights, equal opportunity
Key developments: birth control, equal rights legislation, women's liberation movement
Key figures: Emmeline Pankhurst, Marie Stopes, Germaine Greer, Gloria Steinem, Betty Friedan
Key works: *A Vindication of the Rights of Women* (Mary Wollstonecraft) 1791, *The Feminine Mystique* (Betty Friedan) 1963, *The Second Sex* (Simone de Beauvoir) 1949, tr. 1953, *The Female Eunuch* (Germaine Greer) 1970, *Sexual Politics* (Kate Millett) 1970

feminize /fémmə nīz/ (**-nizes, -nizing, -nized**), **feminise** (**-nises, -nising, -nised**) *vt* **1 MAKE SOMETHING SUITABLE FOR WOMEN** to cause somebody or something to acquire characteristics considered suitable for women **2 MAKE SOMEBODY CONVENTIONALLY LIKE WOMAN** to make somebody behave in ways conventionally associated with women (*often passive*) **3 MAKE MALE DEVELOP FEMALE SEXUAL CHARACTERISTICS** to cause a man to develop secondary female sexual characteristics as a result of a hormone imbalance —**feminization** *n*

femme /fem/ *n* **1 WOMAN** a woman or girl (*dated informal*) **2 PERSON BEHAVING IN CONVENTIONALLY FEMININE WAY** a person who behaves in a conventionally feminine way (*slang*) ■ *adj* **BEHAVING IN FEMININE WAY** describes a person, originally usually a lesbian, who behaves in a conventionally feminine way (*slang*) [Early 19C. < French, < Latin *femina* (see FEMININE).]

femme fatale /fám fə taál/ (*plural* **femmes fatales** /fám fə taál/) *n* a woman who is considered to be highly attractive and to have a destructive effect on those who succumb to her charms (*disapproving*) [< French, 'deadly woman']

femora plural of **femur**

femoral /fémmərəl/ *adj* relating to, in, or involving the thigh or femur [Late 18C. < Latin *femor-*, stem of *femur* 'thigh'.]

femto- *prefix* (*symbol* **f**) a thousand million millionth (10^{-15}) ○ *femtometre* [< Danish or Norwegian *femten* 'fifteen']

femur /feémər/ (*plural* **femurs** *or* **femora** /fémmərə/) *n* **1 MAIN BONE IN HUMAN THIGH** the main bone in the human thigh, the strongest bone in the body **2 LARGE BONE IN VERTEBRATE LEG** a bone equivalent to the human thigh-bone in other vertebrates **3 INSECT LEG PART** the third and largest segment of an insect's leg, between the trochanter and the tibia [Mid-16C. < Latin, 'thigh'.]

fen /fen/ *n* a low-lying, inland marshy area, now often drained and cultivated because of its nutrient-rich soil. ◊ **Fens** [Old English *fen(n)* < Germanic]

fence /fenss/ *n* **1 ENCLOSING STRUCTURE** a structure erected to enclose an area and act as a barrier, especially one made of wood or with posts and wire **2 OBSTACLE** a specially constructed obstacle that horses must jump over in a race or as part of a showjumping circuit **3 BUYER OF STOLEN GOODS** a purchaser and reseller of stolen goods (*slang*) ■ *v* (**fences, fencing, fenced**) **1** *vt* **ENCLOSE AREA WITH FENCE** to enclose an area or bar a gap by erecting a fence **2** *vti* **DEAL IN STOLEN GOODS** to buy or sell stolen goods (*slang*) **3** *vi* **FIGHT WITH SWORD** to fight using a slender sword, formerly in combat, now as a competitive sport **4** *vi* **EVADE QUESTIONING** to avoid answering a question ○ *a candidate fencing with the press* **5** *vi* **ARGUE** to engage in repartee or witty argument with somebody [14C. Shortening of DEFENCE.] —**fenceless** *adj* —**fencer** *n* ◇ **mend fences** to restore good relations with a friend or neighbour after a dispute or quarrel ◇ **sit** *or* **be on the fence** to refuse to make a choice between sides in a dispute or contest

fence in *vt* **1** to enclose somebody or something inside a fence **2** to limit or restrain somebody's freedom of movement or action

fence off *vt* to enclose or separate something with a fence

fence-sitter *n* a person who is unwilling or unable to choose between sides

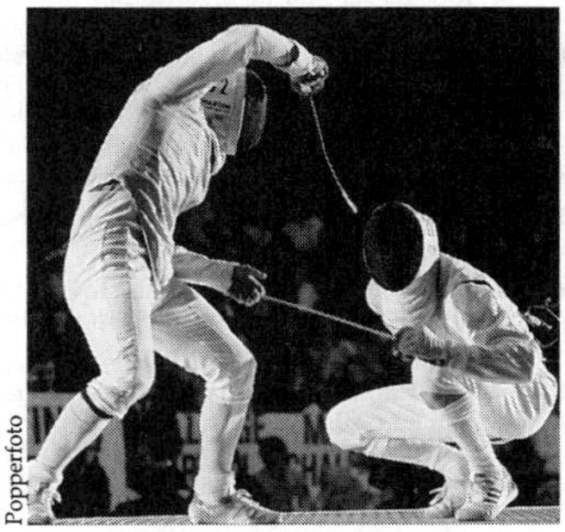

Fencing: As one fencer lunges forwards the other prepares to parry

fencing /fénssing/ *n* **1 SWORD FIGHTING** the art or practice of fighting with slender swords, formerly in combat, now as a competitive sport **2 FENCE MATERIALS** materials used in making fences, e.g. posts and wire **3 FENCES** fences considered collectively **4 EVASIVENESS** evasiveness in responding to questioning **5 REPARTEE** repartee or witty argument **6 DEALING IN STOLEN GOODS** the business of buying and selling stolen goods (*slang*)

fend /fend/ *vt* to defend somebody or something from harm (*archaic*) [13C. Shortening of DEFEND.]

fend for *vt* to support or provide for somebody, especially yourself ○ *He's used to fending for himself.*

fend off *vt* **1** to push somebody or something away or turn somebody or something aside **2** to push against an approaching vessel or object in order to prevent a collision

fender /féndər/ *n* **1 FIRE GUARD** a metal guard built onto the front of an open fire to prevent coals from falling out **2** *US* **METAL GUARD AT FRONT OF LOCOMOTIVE** a metal guard built onto the front of a locomotive to push away any obstruction and lessen injury to people or animals struck by the locomotive **3 PROTECTIVE CUSHION** an inflatable cylinder, rubber tyre, or something similar, hung over the side of the vessel to protect it from rubbing against a pier or another ship **4** *US* AUTOMOT = **wing** *n.* 12 **5** *US* CYCLING = **mudguard** *n.*

fender-bender *n* *US* a collision between vehicles in which only minor damage occurs (*informal*)

fender pile *n* a pile driven into the bottom of a body of water near a berth to protect the pier or wharf against damage by incoming vessels

Fenech /fénnək/, **Jeff** (*b.* 1964) Australian boxer

fenestella /fénnə stéllə/ (*plural* **-lae** /-lee/) *n* **1 PART OF ALTAR** a small opening for holding relics at the south side of an altar in a Roman Catholic church **2 NICHE IN CHANCEL WALL** a niche in the wall of a chancel that houses the piscina and credence table **3 WINDOW** a small window or similar opening in a wall [Late 18C. < Latin, diminutive of *fenestra* 'window'.]

fenestra /fi néstrə/ (*plural* **-trae** /-tree/) *n* **1 SMALL ANATOMICAL OPENING** a small anatomical opening covered by a membrane, e.g. either of two cavities (**fenestra rotunda, fenestra ovalis**) inside the ear **2 TRANSPARENT MARKING** a transparent marking on a moth's wing **3 WINDOW** a window or similar opening on the outer wall of a building [Early 19C. < Latin, 'window'.] —**fenestral** *adj*

fenestrated /fə néss traytid, fénnə-/, **fenestrate** /fə néss trayt, fénnə-/ *adj* **1 HAVING WINDOWS** made with windows or similar openings **2 WITH OPENINGS** with openings or perforations **3 WITH TRANSPARENT MARKINGS** describes a moth's wing that has transparent markings

fenestration /fénni stráysh'n/ *n* **1** the design and placing of windows in a building **2** the surgical cutting of an opening in the labyrinth of the inner ear to restore somebody's hearing

feng shui /fúng shwáy/ *n* a Chinese system that studies people's relationships to the environment in which they live, especially their dwelling or workspace, in order to achieve maximum harmony with the spiritual forces believed to influence all places [Late 18C. < Chinese, 'wind water'.]

Fenian /féeni ən/ *n* **1 IRISH REVOLUTIONARY** a member of an Irish revolutionary republican organization founded in the United States in 1857 to fight for Irish independence **2 LEGENDARY IRISH WARRIOR** a member of the legendary Irish warriors, the Fianna **3 OFFENSIVE TERM** an offensive term for an Irish Roman Catholic, especially one with nationalist tendencies (*regional*) [Early 19C. < Old Irish *féne*, the ancient population of Ireland.] —**Fenianism** *n*

fenland /fén land/ *n* a wide inland area of low-lying marshy land, especially in East Anglia

fennec /fén ek/ *n* a small large-eared desert fox with light tan fur. Native to: North Africa. *Vulpes zerda.* [Late 18C. Via Arabic *fanak* < Persian.]

fennel /fénn'l/ *n* **1** an aromatic plant, the seeds and feathery leaves of which have a light aniseed flavour. Use: cooking. Native to: Europe. Genus: *Foeniculum.* **2** a plant that produces a clump of short edible stalks resembling celery but with an aniseed flavour. *Foeniculum vulgare* var. *azoricum.* [Old English *finugle* < Latin *faeniculum*, diminutive of *faenum* 'hay']

Fens /fenz/ region of reclaimed marshland in E England. Area: 2,000 sq. km/772 sq. mi.

fentanyl /féntənil/ *n* a narcotic drug. Use: painkiller. [Alteration of the drug's chemical name]

fenugreek /fénnyoo greek/ *n* **1** the aromatic seeds of a leguminous plant. Use: in medicine, food flavouring. ○ *add a pinch of fenugreek* **2** the leguminous plant whose seeds are fenugreek. Native to: Europe, Asia. *Trigonella foenum-graecum.* [Old English *fenogrecum* and Old French *fenugrec* < Latin *faenugraecum* 'Greek hay', dried and used by the Romans for fodder]

fenuron /fénnyoo ron/ *n* $C_9H_{12}N_2O$ a white crystalline compound. Use: herbicide. [< alteration of PHEN- + UREA]

feoffee /fe fée/ *n* a vassal holding a fief granted by a feudal lord

FEP *abbr* front-end processor

-fer *suffix* a person or thing that bears ○ *conifer* [< Latin, < *ferre* 'carry']

feral /férrəl, féerəl/, **ferine** /fé rīn, féer īn/ *adj* **1** describes animals or plants that live or grow in the wild after having been domestically reared or cultivated **2** similar to or typical of a wild animal [Early 17C. < Latin *fera* 'wild animal'.]

fer-de-lance /fáir də laánss/ (*plural* **fer-de-lance** *or* **fer-de-lances** *or* **fers-de-lance** /fáir də laánss/) *n* a large, highly venomous snake of the pit viper family. Native to: tropical America. *Bothops atrox.* [Late 19C. < French, 'spearhead'.]

Ferdinand I /fúrdi nand/ (1005?–65) king of Castile (1035–65) and León (1037–65). Known as **Ferdinand the Great**

Ferdinand III (1608–57) king of Bohemia (1627–57) and Holy Roman Emperor (1637–57)

feretory /férrətəri/ (*plural* **-ries**) *n* a container or an area in a church where relics are kept [14C. < Old French *fiertre* < Greek *pheretron* 'bier' < *pherein* 'carry'.]

Fergana /fər gaánə/ city in E Uzbekistan. Population: 226,500 (1991).

feria /féeri ə/ (*plural* **-as** *or* **-ae** /féeri ee/) *n* in the Roman Catholic Church, any weekday that is not a feast day [14C. < Latin, 'holiday'.] —**ferial** *adj*

ferly /fúrli/, **ferlie** *n* (*plural* **-lies**) *Scotland* a curious object or occurrence ■ *adj* (**-lier, -liest**) *Scotland* not usually seen or experienced [Old English *færlić* 'dangerous, alarming, awesome' < *fǣr* (see FEAR)]

Fermanagh /fər mánnə/ former county in Ulster Province, NE Northern Ireland

Fermat /fər mát, fúr maa/, **Pierre de** (1601–65) French mathematician

fermata /fər maátə/ (*plural* **-matas** *or* **-mate** /-tay/) *n* **1** an act of holding a note, chord, or pause longer than the indicated time value **2** MUSIC = **pause** *n.* 4 [Late 19C. < Italian.]

ferment *vti* /fər mént/ **1 SUBJECT TO FERMENTATION** to subject something to fermentation, or be subjected to fermentation **2 STIR UP** to stir up somebody or something, or be stirred up **3 DEVELOP** to cause, develop or evolve something, or be developed or evolved ○ *Her brain was continually fermenting new schemes.* ■ *n* /fúr ment/ **1 COMMOTION** a state or situation of extreme agitation or commotion about something **2 SUBSTANCE CAUSING FERMENTATION** an agent, enzyme, or cell that causes fermentation [14C. < Old French *fermenter* < Latin *fermentum* 'yeast'.] —**fermentability** /fər méntə bílləti/ *n* —**fermentable** *adj* —**fermentative** *adj*

SPELLCHECK Do not confuse ***ferment*** with ***foment***, which has a similar sound. Beware: your spellchecker will not catch this error.

fermentation /fúr men táysh'n/ *n* the breakdown of carbohydrates by microorganisms

fermentation lock *n* a valve used in winemaking to seal a container of fermenting wine, allowing gas to escape but no air to enter

fermenter /fər méntər/ *n* **1** BIOCHEM = **ferment** *n.* 2 **2 fermenter, fermentor** an apparatus that maintains the ideal conditions for fermentation

fermi /fúrmi/ *n* a unit of length used mainly for nuclear distances, equivalent to 10^{-15} metre [Early 20C. After Enrico FERMI.]

Fermi /fúrmi/, **Enrico** (1901–54) Italian-born US physicist

Fermi-Dirac statistics *n* statistical mechanics used to find the energy distribution of particles that obey the Pauli exclusion principle (+ *singular or plural verb*) [After Enrico FERMI and Paul DIRAC]

fermion /fúrmi on/ *n* an elementary particle with a half-integral spin that obeys the Pauli exclusion principle. Electrons, protons, and neutrons are types of fermion. [After Enrico FERMI]

fermium /fúrmi əm/ *n* (*symbol* **Fm**) an artificially produced radioactive element. Source: bombardment of plutonium with neutrons. Use: tracer. [After Enrico FERMI]

fern /furn/ (*plural* **ferns** *or* **fern**) *n* a plant that has roots, stems, and fronds, but no flowers, and reproduces by means of spores. Order: Filicales. [Old English *fearn* < Indo-European] —**ferny** *adj*

Fernando de Noronha /fur nándō də no rónyə/ island group in the Atlantic Ocean off the coast of Brazil. Population: 1,266 (1980). Area: 26 sq. km/10 sq. mi.

Fernando Póo /fər nándo pō/ former name for **Bioko**

fern bar *n* a bar or restaurant with ferns for decoration

fernery /fúrnəri/ (*plural* **-ies**) *n* **1** a container or cultivated area in which ferns are grown **2** a collection of growing ferns

ferocious /fə rṓshəss/ *adj* **1** very fierce or savage **2** very intense [Mid-17C. < Latin *ferox* 'wild-looking'.] —**ferociously** *adv* —**ferociousness** *n* —**ferocity** /fə róssəti/ *n*

-ferous *suffix* bearing, containing, producing ○ *diamondiferous*

ferr- *prefix* = **ferro-**

Ferrara /fə raárə/ city in N Italy. Population: 351,856 (1997 estimate).

Ferrari /fə raári/, **Enzo** (1898–1988) Italian racing car driver and automobile manufacturer

ferredoxin /férrə dóksin/ *n* an iron-containing protein found in plants that is active in photosynthesis [Mid-20C. < Latin *ferrum* 'iron' + REDOX.]

ferret[1] /férrit/ *n* (*plural* **-rets** *or* **-ret**) a typically albino polecat bred for use in hunting rabbits or rats and kept as a pet. *Mustela eversmanni.* ■ *vti* to hunt rabbits or rats using a ferret [14C. Via Old French *furet* < assumed Vulgar Latin *furittus* 'little thief' < Latin *fur* 'thief'.] —**ferreter** *n* —**ferrety** *adj*

ferret about, ferret around *vi* to search in an area persistently ○ *ferreting about in a drawer*

ferret out *vt* **1** to force somebody or something out of a hiding place by persistent searching **2** to discover something hidden by persistent searching

ferret[2] /férrit/ *n* a narrow silk tape used for edging or binding fabric [Mid-17C. Probably alteration of Italian *fioretti* 'floss silk' < *fiore* 'flower'.]

ferret badger *n* a small tree-climbing badger. Native to: SE Asia. Genus: *Melogale.*

ferreting[1] /férriting/ *n* the practice of hunting rabbits or rats with ferrets

ferreting[2] /férriting/ *n* SEW = **ferret**[2] *n.*

ferri- *prefix* **1** = **ferro-** **2** ferric iron ○ *ferricyanide* [< Latin *ferrum* 'iron']

ferriage /férri ij/ *n* **1** the action or business of transporting passengers or cargo by ferry **2** the fee charged for carrying somebody or something by ferry

ferric /férrik/ *adj* containing iron, especially with a valency of three [Late 18C. < Latin *ferrum* 'iron'.]

ferric ammonium citrate *n* $Fe(NH_4)_3(C_6H_5O_7)_2$ a nontoxic iron salt. Use: treatment of anaemia.

ferric chloride *n* $FeCl_3$ a dark red iron-containing salt. Use: in medicine as an astringent, in industry as a coagulating agent.

ferric oxide *n* Fe_2O_3 a reddish-brown solid containing iron and oxygen. Source: rust, haematite. Use: pigment, in jeweller's rouge for polishing, on magnetic recording tape.

ferric sulphate *n* $Fe_2(SO_4)_3$ a pale yellow solid chemical containing iron, oxygen, and sulphur. Use: pigments, water purification, dyeing, medicine.

ferricyanide /férri sī́ ə nīd/ *n* any salt containing iron and six cyanide groups. Use: manufacture of pigments.

Ferrier /férri ər/, **Kathleen** (1912–53) British contralto

ferriferous /fe ríffərəss/ *adj* describes a rock or mineral deposit that contains iron, often at a level high enough to make extraction economically worthwhile [Early 19C. < Latin *ferrum* 'iron'.]

ferrimagnetism /férri mágnətizəm/ *n* a property of some substances, e.g. ferrites, in which two different types of iron having unequal magnetic moments occur aligned in antiparallel, giving an appreciable bulk magnetization —**ferrimagnet** *n* —**ferrimagnetic** /férri mag néttik/ *adj, n* —**ferrimagnetically** *adv*

Ferris wheel /férriss-/, **ferris wheel** *n* a fairground ride consisting of a giant revolving wheel with seats that hang down from its rim and stay horizontal as the wheel rotates [Late 19C. After G. W. G. *Ferris* (1859–96), US engineer.]

ferrite /férrīt/ *n* **1 MAGNETIC IRON OXIDE** a mixed oxide of iron and another metal such as cobalt or nickel. Use: in electronics, in magnets. **2 FORM OF IRON OCCURRING IN STEEL** a form of iron occurring in steel, cast iron, and pig iron **3 IRON MINERAL** a mineral containing iron oxide, e.g. magnetite. Source: as small grains in various rocks. [Mid-19C. < Latin *ferrum* 'iron'.]

ferritin /férritin/ *n* an iron-binding protein found in the liver that stores iron in the body [Mid-20C. < FERRI- + *-t-* + -IN.]

ferro- *prefix* **1** iron ○ *ferroalloy* **2** ferrous iron ○ *ferrocyanide* [< Latin *ferrum* 'iron']

ferroalloy /férrō álloy/ *n* an iron alloy, containing a large proportion of one or more other elements, that is added to molten metal during iron and steel production to give the required composition

ferrocene /férrō seen/ *n* $\mathbf{Fe(C_5H_5)_2}$ an orange-red crystalline solid in which an atom of iron is situated between two rings that are composed of five carbon and five hydrogen atoms [Mid-20C. < FERRO- + contraction of *cyclopentadiene*, a hydrocarbon.]

ferroconcrete /férrō kóng kreet/ *n* BUILDING = **reinforced concrete**

ferrocyanide /férrō sí ə nīd/ *n* any salt containing iron and six cyanide groups. Use: in blue pigments.

ferroelectric /férrō i léktrik/ *adj* describes a crystalline compound that has a natural spontaneous electric polarization that can be reversed by the application of an electric field ■ *n* a substance that is ferroelectric —**ferroelectrically** *adv* —**ferroelectricity** /férrō i lek tríssəti, -éllek-/ *n*

ferromagnesian /férrō mag néezh'n/ *adj* describes silicate minerals that contain high levels of iron and magnesium, e.g. olivines

ferromagnetic /férrō mag néttik/ *adj* with the property of ferromagnetism —**ferromagnetically** *adv*

ferromagnetism /férrō mágnətizəm/ *n* a property of some substances, including iron and some alloys, in which application of a weak magnetic field within a certain temperature range induces high magnetism —**ferromagnet** *n*

ferromanganese /férrō mang gə néez, férrō máng gə neez/ *n* an alloy of iron and manganese used to add manganese during the making of steel and cast iron

ferronneries /fe rónnəriz/ *n* a variety of ceramics that copies forms from metalwork, e.g. candlesticks (+ *singular verb*) [Early 20C. < French, 'iron work, wrought iron'.]

ferrosilicon /férrō síllikən/ *n* an alloy of iron and silicon. Use: in the production of steel and cast iron.

ferrotype /férrō tīp/ *n* a positive photograph made on a plate of sensitized iron

ferrous /férrəss/ *adj* containing iron with a valency of two [Mid-19C. < Latin *ferrum* 'iron'.]

ferrous oxide *n* **FeO** a black solid containing iron and oxygen. Use: manufacture of steel and enamels.

ferrous sulphate *n* $\mathbf{FeSO_4.7H_2O}$ a white or pale green iron salt. Use: in inks, tanning, treatment of iron-deficient anaemia.

ferrous sulphide *n* **FeS** a black solid containing iron and sulphur. Source: pyrites, marcasite. Use: making hydrogen sulphide.

ferruginous /fe ro͝ojinəss/ *adj* **1** containing or resembling iron **2** of a reddish-brown colour, like rust [Mid-17C. < Latin *ferrugin-* 'iron rust' < *ferrum* 'iron'.]

ferruginous duck *n* a common diving duck with reddish-brown plumage that lives in fresh or brackish water. Native to: Europe. *Aythya nyroca.*

ferrule /férrool, férrəl/, **ferule** *n* **1 PROTECTIVE CAP ON SHAFT** a usually metal cap or ring attached to the end of something long and thin, e.g. a walking stick, in order to strengthen it **2 CYLINDRICAL JOINT** a metal cylinder used to make a pipe joint **3 CONNECTION FOR FISHING ROD PIECES** a connection that joins the pieces of a fishing rod, consisting of male and female couplings that fit together ■ *vt* **FIT WITH FERRULE** to provide something with a ferrule [Early 17C. Alteration (after Latin *ferrum* 'iron') of *virolle* < Latin *viriae* 'bracelets'.]

ferry /férri/ *n* (*plural* **-ries**) **1 BOAT MAKING REGULAR SHORT CROSSING** a boat used to transport passengers, vehicles, or goods across water, especially one operating regularly across a river or narrow channel **2 COMMERCIAL TRANSPORT SERVICE** a commercial service transporting passengers, vehicles, or goods across water **3 PLACE WHERE FERRY BERTHS** a place where passengers, vehicles, or goods are transported across water by ferry **4 RIGHT TO OPERATE FERRY** a legal right to operate and charge for a ferry service ■ *v* (**-ries, -rying, -ried**) **1** *vt* **TRANSPORT BY FERRY** to transport somebody or something across water by ferry **2** *vi* **GO BY FERRY** to travel by ferry **3** *vt* **TRANSPORT PASSENGERS** to transport passengers or goods back and forth by any vehicle ○ *He had to ferry his children to school every morning.* **4** *vt* **DELIVER AIRCRAFT** to deliver an aircraft by flying it to its operator [14C. < Old Norse *ferja*, or stem of *ferjuskip* 'ferryboat', *ferjukarl* 'ferryman' < Germanic.]

ferryboat /férri bōt/ *n* TRANSP = **ferry** *n.* 1

ferryman /férri man, -mən/ (*plural* **-men** /-mən/) *n* an owner, operator, or worker of a ferry

fertile /fúr tīl/ *adj* **1 ABLE TO PRODUCE OFFSPRING** capable of breeding or reproducing **2 ABLE TO PRODUCE FRUITS OR SEEDS** able to produce sex cells, seeds, spores, or fruit **3 ABLE TO DEVELOP** describes an egg or seed that has the capacity to grow and develop **4 REPRODUCING OFTEN** producing many offspring **5 PRODUCING GOOD CROPS** describes an area that produces many plants, fruit, or crops **6 RICH IN PLANT NUTRIENTS** describes soil or land that is rich in the nutrients needed to sustain the growth of healthy plants **7 CREATIVE** readily able to produce new ideas ○ *a fertile imagination* **8 CAPABLE OF BECOMING FISSILE** capable of being converted into fissile or fissionable material, typically in a nuclear reactor [15C. Directly or via French < Latin *fertilis* < *ferre* 'bear, carry'.] —**fertilely** *adv* —**fertileness** *n*

Fertile Crescent /fúr tīl-/ *n* an area of fertile land in the Middle East reaching from Israel to the Persian Gulf and incorporating the Tigris and Euphrates rivers in Iraq

fertilisation *n* BIOL, AGRIC = **fertilization**

fertilise *vt* BIOL, AGRIC = **fertilize**

fertiliser *n* BIOL, AGRIC = **fertilizer**

fertility /fur tílləti/ *n* **1** the quality or condition of being fertile **2** the birthrate of a population [15C. Via French < Latin *fertilitas* < *fertilis* (see FERTILE).]

fertility cult *n* a form of religion using ceremonies meant to ensure the fertility of the people and agriculture of a community

fertility drug *n* a drug that stimulates ovulation. Use: in in vitro fertilization.

fertility factor *n* GENETICS = **sex factor**

fertilization /fúrti lī záysh'n/, **fertilisation** *n* **1 STARTING REPRODUCTION** the act or process of enabling reproduction by insemination or pollination **2 UNION OF MALE AND FEMALE GAMETES** the union of male and female reproductive cells (**gametes**) to produce a fertilized reproductive cell (**zygote**) **3 APPLYING FERTILIZER** the act or process of applying fertilizer to soil

fertilize /fúrti līz/ (**-lizes, -lizing, -lized**), **fertilise** (**-lises, -lising, -lised**) *vt* **1** to unite a female gamete with a male gamete, thus enabling the development of a new individual to take place **2** to apply fertilizer to soil or plants [Mid-17C. < FERTILE.] —**fertilizable** *adj*

fertilizer /fúrtilīzər/, **fertiliser** *n* **1** an organic or synthetic substance usually added to or spread onto soil to increase its ability to support plant growth **2** an agent that fertilizes plants or animals, e.g. an insect fertilizing a plant

ferule[1] /férrool, férrəl/ *n* a cane, rod, or flat piece of wood used to punish children by striking them, usually on the hand [15C. < Latin *ferula* 'fennel stalk, rod'.]

ferule[2] *n, vt* = **ferrule**

ferulic acid /fe ro͞olik-/ *n* an aromatic chemical found in some plants that is similar to vanillin [< Latin *ferula* 'fennel stalk, rod']

fervent /fúrvənt/ *adj* **1** showing ardent or extremely passionate enthusiasm **2** so hot as to glow (*archaic or literary*) [14C. Via Old French < Latin *fervent-*, present participle of *fervere* 'boil'.] —**fervency** *n* —**fervently** *adv* —**ferventness** *n*

fervid /fúrvid/ *adj* = **fervent** [Late 16C. < Latin *fervidus* < *fervere* 'to boil'.] —**fervidly** *adv* —**fervidness** *n*

fervor *n* US = **fervour**

fervour /fúrvər/ *n* **1** extreme intensity of emotion or belief **2** intense heat (*archaic or literary*) [14C. Via Old French < Latin *fervor* < *fervere* 'to boil'.]

Fès = **Fez**

fescue /fés kyoo/, **fescue grass** *n* a perennial grass that has narrow spiky leaves. Use: lawns, pasture. Genus: *Festuca*. [14C. Alteration of *festu* < Old French, 'straw' < Latin *festuca*.]

fesse /fess/, **fess** *n* a broad horizontal band crossing the middle section of a heraldic shield [15C. Via Old French *fesse* < Latin *fascia* 'band, sash'.]

fesse point *n* the central point of a heraldic shield

fess up /fess-/ *vi* US to admit to something (*informal*) ○ *Come on, fess up, was it you?* [Early 19C. Shortening of CONFESS.]

fest /fest/ *n* a gathering of people for a specific activity (*informal*) ○ *a music fest* [Mid-19C. Via German *Fest* < Latin *festum* 'feast, festival'.]

-fest *suffix* experience or event characterized by ○ *'Night of the Living Dead' is a real gore-fest.*

festal /fést'l/ *adj* festive (*archaic*) [15C. Via Old French < Latin *festum* 'feast, festival'.] —**festally** *adv*

fester /féstər/ *v* **1** *vi* **PRODUCE PUS** to produce pus because of an infection or ulceration, usually of the skin **2** *vi* **BECOME ROTTEN** to decay or rot **3** *vi* **DETERIORATE** to be in or enter a state of decline **4** *vti* **RANKLE** to become, or make somebody become, increasingly bitter, irritated, or resentful ■ *n* **SORE DISCHARGING PUS** a small sore or ulcer containing or discharging pus [14C. Via Old French *festre* 'pipe-like ulcer' < Latin *fistula*.]

festination /fésti náysh'n/ *n* a style of tottering walk that is characteristic of people with Parkinson's disease [Mid-16C. < Latin *festination-* < *festinare* 'to hurry'.]

festival /féstiv'l/ *n* **1 TIME OF CELEBRATION** a day or period of celebration, often one of religious significance **2 PROGRAMME OF CULTURAL EVENTS** a programme or series of performances or other cultural events, usually held at regular intervals, often in one place ■ *adj* **APPROPRIATE TO FESTIVAL** typical of or appropriate to a festival [14C. Via Old French < medieval Latin *festivalis* < Latin *festivus* (see FESTIVE).]

festivalgoer /féstiv'l gō ər/ *n* an attender of a festival

festive /féstiv/ *adj* **1** relating to, suitable for, or typical of a feast, festival, or holiday **2** marked by cheerfulness and joy [Mid-17C. < Latin *festivus* 'festive' < *festum* 'feast, festival'.] —**festively** *adv* —**festiveness** *n*

festive season *n* the period leading up to and including Christmas and the New Year

festivity /fe stívvəti/ *n* (*plural* **-ties**) **1 ENJOYMENT** the enjoyment or merrymaking typical of a celebration **2 CELEBRATION** a celebration, feast, or party ■ **festivities** *npl* **CELEBRATIONS** celebrations or merrymaking [14C. Directly or via French < Latin *festivitas* < *festivus* (see FESTIVE).]

festoon /fe sto͞on/ *n* **1 GARLAND** an ornamental chain of flowers, leaves, or ribbons hanging in a loop or curve between two points **2 ARTISTIC REPRESENTATION OF FESTOON** a carved or painted representation of a festoon, e.g. on a building, in a painting, or in pottery ■ *vt* **1 HANG FESTOONS ON** to decorate something with festoons **2 JOIN WITH FESTOONS** to join things together with festoons **3 SHAPE INTO FESTOONS** to make something into festoons [Mid-17C. Via French *feston* < Italian *festone* 'ornament for festivities' < assumed Vulgar Latin *festa* 'festivities' < Latin *festum* 'feast, festival'.] —**festooned** *adj*

festoon blind *n* a blind for a window, made of cloth gathered into rows that can be drawn up to hang in curves

festschrift /fést shrift/, **Festschrift** (*plural* **-schrifts** *or* **-schriften** /-shriftən/) *n* a volume of writings by various people collected in honour of somebody, e.g. a writer or scholar [Early 20C. < German, 'celebration-writing'.]

FET *abbr* field-effect transistor

feta /féttə/ *n* a firm crumbly salty cheese made from sheep's or goat's milk and preserved in brine, originally from Greece [Mid-20C. < modern Greek *pheta*.]

fetal *adj* = **foetal** (*technical*)

fetch[1] /fech/ *v* **1** *vt* **GO AND GET** to go after and bring back somebody or something ○ *She went upstairs to fetch her car keys.* **2** *vt* **CAUSE TO COME** to make somebody or something appear or come **3** *vt* **SELL FOR** to sell for a certain price ○ *The painting fetched £600 at an auction.* **4** *vti* **RETRIEVE** to retrieve animals that have been shot or something that has been thrown, e.g. a stick or ball ○ *The boy threw the ball and told the dog to fetch it.* **5** *vt* **UTTER** to utter a sigh or groan with a deep breath **6** *vt* **HIT SOMEBODY A BLOW** to hit somebody with a blow (*informal*) ○ *fetched the bully a slap on the face* **7** *vt* **DRAW IN BREATH** to draw in a breath **8** *vt* **PLEASE SOMEBODY** to attract or charm somebody (*often passive*) ○ *fetched by the notion of going to London* **9** *vt* **ARRIVE SOMEWHERE BY BOAT** to reach or arrive at a place by sailing ○ *fetched port at nightfall* **10** *vt* *Malaysia* **TAKE SOMEWHERE** to take somebody somewhere

○ *My neighbour fetches me to the office every morning.* ■ *n* 1 **ACT OF FETCHING** the act or an instance of fetching something or somebody 2 **STRATAGEM** a dodge, trick, or stratagem ○ *They used cunning fetches to swindle money out of the gullible.* 3 **DISTANCE WIND TRAVELS UNOBSTRUCTED** the distance wind or waves can travel without obstruction [Old English *feccean* < ?] —**fetcher** *n* ◇ **fetch and carry (for somebody)** to do menial tasks for somebody

fetch up *v* 1 *vi* **ARRIVE** to arrive or come to a halt somewhere (*informal*) ○ *After a week on the road, we fetched up at a small coastal town.* 2 *vi* **HALT SUDDENLY** to come to a sudden halt ○ *The boat fetched up on a sandbar.* 3 *vt* **CAUSE TO STOP** to make somebody or something come to a stop ○ *His abrupt tone fetched me up short.* 4 *vt* **VOMIT** to vomit something (*informal*)

fetch² /fech/ *n* a vision, apparition, or ghost appearing as the doppelgänger of a living person [Late 17C. < ?]

fetching /féching/ *adj* 1 pleasant, stylish, or becoming in appearance 2 having a charming or captivating quality —**fetchingly** *adv*

fête /fayt/, **fete** *n* 1 **BAZAAR** a bazaar, sale, or other event organized to raise money for a cause or for charity, especially if held outdoors ○ *a school fête* 2 **HOLIDAY** a holiday or day of celebration 3 **RELIGIOUS FESTIVAL** a religious festival such as a saint's day ■ *vt* (**fêtes, fêting, fêted; fetes, feting, feted**) **HONOUR SOMEBODY WITH FÊTE** to entertain or honour somebody with a fête, feast, or other lavish entertainment (*usually passive*) [Mid-18C. Via French, < Latin *festum* 'feast, festival'.]

SPELLCHECK See *fate*.

fête champêtre /fáyt shaaN péttrə/ (*plural* **fêtes champêtres** /fáyt shaaN péttrə/) *n* an outdoor party or festival [< French, 'rural festival']

fetich *n* RELIG, PSYCHIAT = **fetish**

feticide *n* = **foeticide** (*technical*)

fetid /féttid, féetid/, **foetid** *adj* with a rotten or offensive smell ○ *fetid odour of rotten meat* [15C. < Latin *fetidus* < *fetere* 'to stink'.] —**fetidly** *adv* —**fetidness** *n*

fetish /féttish/, **fetich** *n* 1 **OBJECT OF OBSESSION** an object, idea, or activity that somebody is irrationally obsessed with or attached to ○ *make a fetish of neatness* 2 **OBJECT AROUSING SEXUAL DESIRE** something, e.g. an inanimate object or nonsexual part of the body, that arouses sexual excitement in some people 3 **MAGICAL OBJECT** something, especially an inanimate object, that some people revere or worship because they believe it has magical powers or is animated by a spirit [Early 17C. Via French *fétiche* 'charm, sorcery' < Latin *factitius* 'made by art, artificial' (see FACTITIOUS).]

fetishise *vt* = **fetishize**

fetishism /féttishizəm/ *n* 1 **OBSESSION** excessive or obsessive attachment or devotion to something 2 **SEXUAL AROUSAL WITH FETISH** the use of a fetish to produce sexual arousal 3 **BELIEF IN FETISH** belief in, use of, or worship of a magical fetish —**fetishist** *n* —**fetishistic** /fétti shístik/ *adj* —**fetishistically** *adv*

fetishize /féttishīz/, **fetishise** *vt* to make a fetish of something

fetlock /fét lok/ *n* 1 **PROJECTION ON HORSE'S LEG** a part of the lower leg of a horse or related animal situated above and behind the hoof and projecting down from the associated joint 2 **HAIR ON FETLOCK** the tuft of hair growing on a fetlock 3 **fetlock, fetlock joint LEG JOINT** the joint at the fetlock [14C. Probably < form of FOOT + LOCK² 'hair'.]

fetor /féetər/, **foetor** *n* a strong offensive smell [15C. < Latin, < *fetere* 'to stink'.]

fetoscope *n* = **foetoscope** (*technical*)

fetter /féttər/ *n* (*often plural*) 1 **SHACKLE FOR ANKLES** a chain or shackle fastened to somebody's ankles or feet 2 **RESTRAINT** a means of confinement or restraint ○ *These harsh rules keep us in fetters.* ■ *vt* 1 **PUT FETTERS ON** to shackle somebody with fetters 2 **RESTRAIN** to confine, restrict, or restrain somebody or something ○ *fettered by her own inhibitions* [Old English *feter* < Germanic]

fettle /fétt'l/ *n* METALL = **fettling** ■ *vt* (**-tles, -tling, -tled**) 1 to remove moulding or excess material from a ceramic or metal casting 2 to line the hearth of a furnace with fettling, or repair the lining of a furnace [Old English *fetel* 'girdle, strap' < Germanic, 'hold'] —**fettler** *n* ◇ **in fine** *or* **good fettle** in good health, condition, or spirits

fettling /fétt'ling/ *n* loose refractory material, typically sand or ore, used to line the hearths of some types of furnace before adding the molten metal

fettuccine /féttə chéeni/, **fettuccini** *n* 1 pasta made in narrow flat strips, slightly narrower and thicker than tagliatelle (+ *singular or plural verb*) 2 a pasta dish made with fettuccine [Early 20C. < Italian, 'little ribbons'.]

fetus *n* = **foetus** (*technical*)

feu /fyoo/ *n* 1 **RIGHT OF USE** in Scotland, a right to use land or property in return for an annual payment (**feu duty**) 2 **FORMER TENURE FOR MONEY** a form of land tenure in feudal times in Scotland, based on paying rent in money or grain and not on military service 3 **LAND HELD BY FEU** in Scotland, a piece of land held by feu [15C. < Old French (see FEE).]

feuar /fyóo ər/ *n Scotland* a tenant of a feu

feud¹ /fyood/ *n* 1 **LONG VIOLENT DISPUTE** a bitter prolonged violent quarrel or state of hostility between families, clans, or other groups 2 **CONTINUOUS HOSTILITY** any prolonged dispute or quarrel ■ *vi* **PARTICIPATE IN FEUD** to take part in or perpetuate a feud [13C. < Old French *fe(i)de* 'vendetta, hostility' < Germanic.]

feud² /fyood/ *n* HIST = **fief** *n.* 1 [Early 17C. < medieval Latin *feudum* 'land or other property used as a reward for service' < Indo-European, 'wealth, cattle'.]

feud. *abbr* 1 feudal 2 feudalism

feudal /fyóod'l/ *adj* 1 relating to, typical of, or resembling feudalism 2 relating to a fief [Early 17C. < medieval Latin *feudalis* < *feudum* (see FEUD²).] —**feudally** *adv*

feudalise *vt* = **feudalize**

feudalism /fyóod'lizəm/ *n* 1 the legal and social system that existed in medieval Europe, in which vassals held land from lords in exchange for military service 2 a system of economic, political, or social organization resembling European feudalism, e.g. in medieval Japan —**feudalist** *n* —**feudalistic** /fyóod'l ístik/ *adj*

feudality /fyoo dálləti/ (*plural* **-ties**) *n* 1 the quality or condition of being feudal 2 a feudal holding or system

feudalize /fyóod'l īz/ (**-izes, -izing, -ized**), **feudalise** (**-ises, -ising, -ised**) *vt* to make something feudal in nature —**feudalization** /fyóod'l ī záysh'n/ *n*

feudatory /fyóodə tәri/ *n* (*plural* **-ries**) **TENANT OF FEUDAL LAND** somebody holding land by feudal tenure ■ *adj* 1 **INVOLVING FEUDAL RELATIONSHIP** relating to or typical of the relationship between a feudal lord and vassal 2 **SUBJECT TO OVERLORDSHIP** owing feudal allegiance to an overlord or another state [Late 16C. < medieval Latin *feudatorius* < past participle of *feudare* 'invest with feudal property' < *feudum* (see FEUD²).]

feuilleton /fóo i ton, fő i toN/ *n* 1 a section of a European newspaper containing reviews, serial fiction, and articles of general interest 2 an article, review, or other piece published in a feuilleton [Mid-19C. < French *feuillet* 'little leaf' < *feuille* 'leaf' < Latin *folium* 'leaf, page'.]

fever /féevər/ *n* 1 **ABNORMALLY HIGH BODY TEMPERATURE** a body temperature that is abnormally high, usually caused by bacterial or viral infections and commonly accompanied by shivering, headache, and an increased pulse rate. Technical name **pyrexia** 2 **DISEASE WITH FEVER** a disease in which people typically have an abnormally high body temperature, e.g. typhoid fever, yellow fever, and scarlet fever 3 **STATE OF EXCITEMENT** a state of intense agitation, excitement, or emotion (*often in combination*) ○ *On the morning of the wedding, everyone was in a fever of excitement.* 4 **CRAZE** an intense and often brief enthusiasm or craze ■ *vt* **AGITATE** to throw somebody into a state of agitation or excitement [Pre-12C. < Latin *febris*.]

fevered /féevərd/ *adj* 1 affected by fever 2 showing great activity, agitation, or excitement

feverfew /féevər fyoo/ *n* a perennial plant whose leaves are a popular remedy for headaches and migraine. Native to: Europe. *Tanacetum parthenium.* [Pre-12C. < Latin *febris* 'fever' + -FUGE.]

feverish /féevərish/ *adj* 1 **HAVING FEVER** affected by or having the symptoms of a fever 2 **RELATING TO FEVER** relating to, causing, or caused by fever ○ *a feverish cold* 3 **AGITATED** showing agitation, excitement, or restlessness —**feverishly** *adv* —**feverishness** *n*

fever pitch *n* a state of intense activity, agitation, or excitement

fever tree *n* a tree whose bark was used to treat malaria. Native to: SE United States. *Pinckneya pubens.*

few /fyoo/ CORE MEANING: a grammatical word used to indicate that there are not many or hardly any people or things ○ (det) *There were few books on the shelves.* ○ (det) *spending her few free hours relaxing in front of the television* ○ (pron) *Many people have entered the contest, but few will be successful.* ○ (pron) *Few of the gardens had been cared for.*

1 *npl, pron* a limited or exclusive number, e.g. an elite or minority of people ○ (n) *the fortunate few who managed to escape sickness this winter* ○ (n) *The needs of the many outweigh the needs of the few.* ○ (pron) *Few would have thought it.* 2 *det, pron* **a few** not very many people or things, but more than two, and sometimes more than might be expected ○ (det) *We had a few meetings before signing the contract.* ○ (pron) *Only a few ever achieve real artistic success.* ○ (pron) *A few of the kids wanted to watch a video.* [Old English *fēawa* < Indo-European] —**fewness** *n* ◇ **a good few** several, or a fairly large number (*informal*) ◇ **few and far between** scarce or infrequent (*informal*) ◇ **quite a few** a fairly large number (*informal*)

USAGE ***fewer*** or ***less***? ***Fewer*** is generally used with things you can count (*fewer meetings, fewer people*). ***Less*** is generally used with things you cannot count (*less time, less prestige*). The same rule applies to ***fewer than*** and ***less than***: *fewer than twenty people, less than a majority.* In an exception to the rule, ***less*** and ***less than*** are often used with nouns that indicate distance, weights and measurements, sums of money, and units of time, because they are regularly thought of as collective amounts instead of numbers. Thus, expressions like these are acceptable: *a house less than two kilometres down the road, used less than five gallons of petrol, gifts for fifty pounds or less,* and *arrived in less than four hours.* In addition, plural nouns can precede the set phrase OR LESS: *You may use the express checkout lane if you have eight items or less,* and *Explain your career goals in one hundred words or less.* Here, the plural nouns are regarded as collective amounts.

fey /fay/ *adj* 1 **OTHERWORLDLY** with a manner or appearance giving an impression of otherworldliness or unworldliness 2 **SUPERNATURAL** relating to or typical of magic or the supernatural 3 **CLAIRVOYANT** supposedly able to see into the future 4 *Scotland* **DOOMED TO DIE** believed to be doomed or destined to die, especially as indicated by peculiar, usually elated, behaviour [Old English *fǣge* 'fated to die' < Germanic] —**feyly** *adv* —**feyness** *n*

Feynman /fínmən/, **Richard** (1918–88) US physicist

Feynman diagram /fínmən-/ *n* a diagrammatic representation of interactions between elementary particles [After Richard FEYNMAN]

fez /fez/ (*plural* **fezzes**) *n* a brimless felt hat shaped like a cone with a flat top, usually red with a black tassel, worn by men in E Mediterranean and North African countries [Early 19C. Via French < Turkish *fes*.]

Fez /fez/, **Fès** /fess/ city in N Morocco. Population: 564,000 (1993).

Fezzan /fə zán/ desert region and former province in SW Libya

ff *abbr* fortissimo

ff. *abbr* 1 folios 2 following (*used of lines or pages*)

FHA *abbr US* 1 Federal Housing Administration 2 Future Homemakers of America

fhp *abbr* friction horsepower

FHSA *abbr* Family Health Services Authority

fiacre /fee áakrə/ *n* a small horse-drawn carriage with four wheels, formerly used for hire like a taxi [Late 17C. < French, after the Hôtel de St *Fiacre*.]

fiancé /fi ón say/ *n* the man to whom a woman is engaged to be married [Mid-19C. < French, past participle of *fiancer* 'betroth' < Old French *fiance* 'a promise'.]

fiancée /fi ón say/ *n* the woman to whom a man is engaged to be married [Mid-19C. < French, form of *fiancé* (see FIANCÉ).]

fianchetto /fi ən chéttō, -kéttō/ *n* (*plural* **-tos** *or* **-ti**) in chess, the development of a bishop by moving it from its original position to the second square of the adjacent knight's file ■ *vt* (**-tos, -toing, -toed**) to move a bishop using a fianchetto [Mid-19C. < Italian, 'little flank' < *fianco* 'flank'.]

Fianna /fée ənə/ *npl* in Irish mythology, a band of warriors celebrated for feats of heroism [Late 18C. < Irish, 'band of warriors and hunters'.]

Fianna Fáil /feē ənə fóyl, -faal/ *n* one of the two main Irish political parties, founded in 1926 [< Irish, 'warriors of Ireland']

fiasco /fi áskō/ (*plural* **-cos**) *n* a total failure, especially a humiliating or ludicrous one [Mid-19C. Via Italian, 'bottle' < medieval Latin *flasco* 'flask'; sense 'failure' from theatrical slang.]

fiat /feē at, fī at/ *n* **1** a formal or official authorization of something **2** an authoritative and often arbitrary command [14C. < Latin, 'let it be done'.]

fiat money *n* money that a government declares to be legal tender although it is not based on or convertible into coin and therefore depends on government decree to determine its value

fib /fib/ *n* an insignificant, harmless, or small lie (*informal*) ■ *vi* (**fibs, fibbing, fibbed**) to tell an insignificant, harmless, or small lie (*informal*) [Early 17C. < ?] —**fibber** *n*

SYNONYMS See *lie*.

fiber *n* US = **fibre**

Fibonacci number /feēbə naāchi-/ *n* a number in the unending Fibonacci sequence [See FIBONACCI SEQUENCE]

Fibonacci sequence *n* the unending series of numbers 0,1,1,2,3,5,8 ... in which each number except for the first two is the sum of the preceding two [After Leonardo *Fibonacci*, 13C Italian mathematician]

fibr- *prefix* = **fibro-** (*before vowels*)

fibre /fībər/ *n* **1 THIN THREAD** a long slender thread or filament **2 THREAD FOR YARN** a fine thread of a natural or synthetic material, e.g. cotton or nylon, that can be spun into yarn **3 CLOTH** cloth or material made of fibres **4 FIBROUS STRUCTURE** the texture or structure of a material made of fibres **5 ESSENTIAL CHARACTER** the fundamental character, quality, or makeup of something **6 STRENGTH OF CHARACTER** somebody's strength of character or sense of right and wrong ○ *the moral fibre of this nation* **7 COARSE FIBROUS SUBSTANCES IN FOOD** the coarse fibrous substances, largely composed of cellulose, that are found in grains, fruits, and vegetables, aid digestion, and clean out the intestines **8 LONG THICK-WALLED PLANT CELL** a long narrow plant cell with walls thickened with lignin that is a major component of the plant's supporting tissue **9 PLANT CELLS MAKING ROPE AND TEXTILES** strands of fibre cells removed from the stems or leaves of some plants, e.g. flax, that can be separated and woven **10 THIN ROOT** a thin narrow root of a plant **11 THREAD-SHAPED BODY STRUCTURE** a long thin structure of the body tissues, e.g. muscle cells and nerve cells [Mid-16C. Via French < Latin *fibra* 'filament'.] —**fibred** *adj*

fibreboard /fībər bawrd/ *n* building material made by compressing wood fibres into sheets

fibre bundle *n* a flexible group of parallel optical fibres held in a fixed arrangement

fibrefill /fībər fil/ *n* synthetic stuffing or insulating material. Use: cushions, duvets, clothing.

fibreglass /fībər glaass/ *n* **1** compressed glass fibres. Use: insulation. **2** a material made from fibreglass. Use: boat hulls, car bodies.

fibre media *n* the media that use paper, e.g. newspapers and magazines, as opposed to online publishing (*informal*)

fibre optics *n* the technology of transferring information, e.g. in communications or computer technology, through thin flexible glass or plastic tubes (**optical fibres**) using modulated light waves (+ *singular verb*) —**fibre-optic** *adj*

fibrescope /fībər skōp/ *n* an instrument that uses fibre optics to transmit images from inaccessible places such as the interior of the body. Use: microsurgery, diagnosis.

fibri- *prefix* = **fibro-**

fibriform /fíbbri fawrm, fībri-/ *adj* in the form of a fibre or fibres

fibril /fībrəl/, **fibrilla** /-lə/ (*plural* **-lae** /-lee, -/) *n* a small or delicate fibre or part of a fibre [Mid-17C. < modern Latin *fibrilla* 'little fibre' < Latin *fibra* 'fibre'.] —**fibrillar** /fī brillər, fi-/ *adj* —**fibrillary** *adj* —**fibrilliform** *adj* —**fibrillose** *adj* —**fibrillous** *adj*

fibrillate /fī bri layt, fíbbri-/ (**-lates, -lating, -lated**) *vti* to undergo, or make the heart or muscles undergo, rapid irregular beating or uncontrolled contraction (**fibrillation**) [Mid-19C. < modern Latin *fibrilla* (see FIBRIL).] —**fibrillative** *adj*

fibrillation /fībri láysh'n, fíbbri-/ *n* **1 RAPID IRREGULAR HEARTBEAT** rapid chaotic beating of the heart muscles such that the affected part of the heart may stop pumping blood **2 RAPID CONTRACTION OF MUSCLE FIBRE** rapid uncontrolled contraction of individual muscle fibres with little or no movement of the muscle as a whole **3 FORMATION OF FIBRES** the formation of fibres or fibrils

fibrin /fībrin, fíbb-/ *n* an insoluble fibrous protein that is produced in the liver from the soluble protein fibrinogen and helps in blood clotting [Early 19C. < FIBRE.] —**fibrinoid** /fībri noyd, fíbb-/ *adj* —**fibrinous** /fíbbrinəss/ *adj*

fibrinogen /fī brínnəjən, fi-/ *n* a soluble protein present in the blood that is activated by thrombin to form fibrin —**fibrinogenic** /fībrinō jénnik/ *adj* —**fibrinogenically** *adv* —**fibrinogenous** /fībri nójjənəss/ *adj*

fibrinolysin /fībrə nóllissin/ *n* any enzyme in blood that breaks down fibrin and blood clots

fibrinolysis /fībrə nóllississ/ *n* the destruction of fibrin and blood clots —**fibrinolytic** /fībrinō líttik/ *adj*

fibro /fībrō/ (*plural* **-bros**) *n Aus* **1** the material fibrocement (*informal*) **2** a house made of fibrocement [Mid-20C. Shortening.] —**fibro** *adj*

fibro- *prefix* **1** fibre ○ *fibroin* **2** fibrous tissue ○ *fibroma* [< Latin *fibra* 'fibre']

fibroblast /fībrō blast/ *n* a large flat cell in connective tissue that secretes collagen and elastic fibres

fibrocartilage /fībrō kaártilij, -tlij/ *n* strong, relatively inelastic cartilage containing bundles of collagen fibres

fibrocement /fībrō si mént/ *n Aus* a building material made of cement bound with asbestos fibres into sheets

fibrocystic /fībrō sístik/ *adj* describes an unusual growth of fibrous tissue that contains cystic spaces, occurring particularly in glandular tissue such as the breast

fibroid /fī broyd/ *adj* resembling or consisting of fibres or fibrous tissue ■ *n* a benign growth composed of fibrous and muscle tissue, especially one that develops in the wall of the womb

fibroin /fībrō in/ *n* a tough white protein secreted by spiders and silkworms that quickly solidifies into a strong thread

fibroma /fī brómə/ (*plural* **-mas** *or* **-mata** /-mətə/) *n* a nonmalignant tumour of fibrous connective tissue such as cartilage —**fibromatous** *adj*

fibromyalgia /fībrō mī ál jee ə/ *n* a disorder causing aching muscles, sleep disorders, and fatigue, associated with raised levels of the brain chemicals that transmit nerve signals (**neurotransmitters**)

fibrose[1] /fībrōss/ (**-broses, -brosing, -brosed**) *vi* to form tissue consisting of or resembling fibres [Late 19C. Back-formation < FIBROSIS.]

fibrose[2] /fībrōss/ *adj* containing or resembling fibres (*technical*)

fibrosis /fī brṓssiss/ *n* an abnormal thickening and scarring of connective tissue most often following injury, infection, lack of oxygen, or surgery —**fibrotic** /fī bróttik/ *adj*

fibrositis /fībrə sītiss/ *n* pain and stiffness, especially in the back muscles

fibrous /fībrəss/ *adj* **1** consisting of or resembling fibres **2** describes a mineral that crystallizes in thin elongated threads, e.g. asbestos —**fibrously** *adv* —**fibrousness** *n*

fibula /fíbbyoolə/ (*plural* **-lae** /-lee/ *or* **-las**) *n* **1 HUMAN LEG BONE** the outer and narrower of the two bones in the human lower leg between the knee and the ankle **2 ANIMAL LEG BONE** the thinner outermost bone of the two bones that form the lower leg or hind leg of terrestrial vertebrates between the knee and ankle **3 BROOCH** a brooch or clasp shaped like a modern safety pin, worn by the ancient Greeks and Romans to fasten cloaks [Late 16C. < Latin, 'brooch, clasp'.] —**fibular** *adj*

-fic *suffix* making, causing ○ *sudorific* [< Latin *-ficus* < *facere* 'make, do']

-fication *suffix* production, process ○ *versification* ○ *unification* [< Latin *-fication-* < *-ficatus*, past participle of verbs ending in *-ficare* 'make' < *facere* 'make, do']

fiche /feesh/ *n* (*informal*) **1** a microfiche **2** an ultrafiche [Mid-20C. Shortening.]

fichu /feē shoo/ *n* a woman's triangular scarf made of a lightweight material such as muslin or lace, worn around the neck and shoulders, especially in the 18th and early 19th centuries [Mid-18C. < French, 'knotted', past participle of *ficher* 'stick in' < Latin *figere* 'fix'.]

fickle /fík'l/ (**-ler, -lest**) *adj* likely to change, especially in affections, intentions, loyalties, or preferences [Old English *ficol* 'deceitful' < Indo-European, 'hostile'] —**fickleness** *n*

~~ficticious~~ incorrect spelling of **fictitious**

fictile /fík tīl/ *adj* **1 MALLEABLE** moulded or capable of being moulded, as clay can be for making pottery **2 MADE OF CLAY** moulded in earth or clay by a potter **3 RELATING TO POTTERY-MAKING** relating to the making of earthenware or pottery [Early 17C. < Latin *fictilis* < *fingere* 'make, shape'.]

fiction /fíksh'n/ *n* **1 LITERARY WORKS OF IMAGINATION** novels and stories that describe imaginary people and events **2 WORK OF FICTION** a novel, story, or other work of fiction **3 UNTRUE STATEMENT** something that is untrue and has been made up to deceive people ○ *The account she gave was pure fiction.* **4 ACT OF PRETENDING** the act of pretending or inventing something such as a story or explanation **5 SOMETHING ASSUMED TO BE TRUE** something that is assumed in law to be true regardless of whether or not it is really true [14C. Via Old French < Latin *fiction-* < *fingere* 'make, shape'.] —**fictional** *adj* —**fictionality** *n* —**fictionally** *adv*

fictionalize /fíksh'nə līz/ (**-izes, -izing, -ized**), **fictionalise** /fíkshənə līz/ (**-ises, -ising, -ised**) *vt* to make something into fiction ○ *a fictionalized life of Shakespeare* —**fictionalization** /fíksh'nə lī záysh'n/ *n*

fictitious /fik tíshəss/ *adj* **1 FALSE** not true or genuine, and intended to deceive ○ *He gave a fictitious name when confronted.* **2 FICTIONAL** invented by somebody's imagination, especially as part of a work of fiction **3 ASSUMED TO BE SO** assumed to be true for legal purposes, regardless of whether or not it really is [Early 17C. < Latin *ficticius* < *fingere* 'make, shape'.] —**fictitiously** *adv* —**fictitiousness** *n*

fictive /fíktiv/ *adj* **1** relating to fiction or imaginative invention **2** not genuine or true [Late 15C. Directly or via French < medieval Latin *fictivus* < *fingere* 'make, shape'.] —**fictively** *adv*

fid /fid/ *n* **1** a bar used to support a topmast on a ship **2** a tapered wooden implement used to separate the strands of a rope in splicing [Early 17C. < ?]

-fid *suffix* divided in parts ○ *multifid* [< Latin *-fidus* < *fid-*, stem of *findere* 'split']

FID DEF, Fid. Def. *abbr* Fidei Defensor

fiddle /fídd'l/ *n* **1 VIOLIN** a musical instrument of the viol or violin family, especially the violin **2 FRAUDULENT ACTIVITY** a fraudulent or illegal way of getting money (*informal*) **3 DELICATE OPERATION** a difficult activity or operation requiring intricate work with the hands (*informal*) ○ *It can be a bit of a fiddle trying to change the battery in this watch.* **4 TRIVIAL MATTERS** nonsensical or trivial matters or behaviour **5 GUARDRAIL ON SHIP'S TABLE** a small guardrail on top of a table or stove on a ship, used to prevent things from sliding off in rough weather ■ *v* (**-dles, -dling, -dled**) **1** *vi* **PLAY VIOLIN** to play the fiddle **2** *vi* **MOVE HANDS NERVOUSLY** to move the hands or fingers nervously or restlessly, or play with something in the hands in this way **3** *vi* **TAMPER** to interfere, meddle, or tamper with something (*informal*) ○ *Who's been fiddling with my computer?* **4** *vi* **TINKER WITH SOMETHING TO FIX IT** to manipulate or tinker with something to try to make it work properly ○ *She fiddled with the controls on the video recorder.* **5** *vt* **SWINDLE** to cheat or swindle somebody (*informal*) **6** *vt* **FALSIFY** to falsify something, e.g. financial accounts, especially for dishonest personal gain (*informal*) **7** *vt* **GET SOMETHING BY CHEATING** to get or achieve something by cheating or deceiving (*informal*) ○ *She fiddled her way into that job.* **8** *vti* **WASTE TIME** to waste time doing unimportant things ○ *fiddle the day away* [Pre-12C. < medieval Latin *vitula* 'instrument played at festivals' < Latin *vitulari* 'hold celebrations'.] ◇ **be on the fiddle** to be involved in making money by fraudulent or illegal means (*informal*)

fiddle about, fiddle around *vi* to waste time doing unimportant things (*informal*)

fiddleback /fídd'l bak/, **fiddleback chair** *n* a chair with a back shaped like the body of a violin

fiddle-de-dee /fídd'l dee deē/ *interj* used to express mild annoyance, disagreement, or impatience (*dated informal*) [Ending nonsensical]

fiddle-faddle /fídd'l fad'l/ *n* **NONSENSE** nonsense or trifling matters (*informal*) ■ *interj* **NONSENSE!** used to express the view that something is nonsense (*dated informal*) ■ *vi* (**fiddle-faddles, fiddle-faddling, fiddle-faddled**) **WASTE**

TIME to fuss, mess about, or waste time with unimportant matters (*informal*) [Late 16C. < FIDDLE + *faddle* 'nonsense'.] —**fiddle-faddler** *n*

fiddlehead /fídd'l hed/, **fiddleneck** /-nek/ *n* 1 an ornamental carving on a ship's bow, shaped like the scroll at the end of the fingerboard of a violin 2 US, Can the coiled frond of a young fern, often cooked and eaten as a delicacy

fiddle pattern *n* the design of a fork or spoon with a handle that has a tapering wide end —**fiddle-pattern** *adj*

fiddler /fídd'lər/ *n* 1 VIOLIN PLAYER a player of the violin, especially in folk music 2 SOMEBODY WHO TOYS WITH SOMETHING a person who aimlessly plays or fiddles with something 3 SWINDLER a cheat or swindler (*informal*) 4 MARINE BIOL = **fiddler crab**

Fiddler crab

fiddler crab *n* a small marine burrowing crab. Males have one enlarged claw that they move like a violinist's arm as a signal during courtship. Genus: *Uca*.

fiddlestick /fídd'l stik/ *n* (*informal*) 1 a bow for playing a violin 2 something that is unimportant or worthless ○ *I don't care a fiddlestick what you think.*

fiddlesticks /fídd'l stiks/ *interj* used to express mild annoyance, disagreement, or impatience [*dated informal*]

fiddlewood /fídd'l wŏod/ *n* 1 the hard wood of a tropical American tree 2 a tree that yields fiddlewood. Native to: tropical America. Genus: *Citharexylum*.

fiddling /fídd'ling/ *adj* petty or unimportant

fiddly /fíddli/ (-**dlier**, -**dliest**) *adj* difficult to do, handle, or use, usually because it involves small objects or intricate work with the hands (*informal*) ○ *Changing the battery in this type of watch can be quite a fiddly job.*

FIDE *abbr* World Chess Federation [French acronym < *Fédération Internationale des Échecs*]

Fidei Defensor /fi dáy ee da fén sawr, fídi T-/ *n* HIST, CHR = **Defender of the Faith** [< Latin]

fideism /fée day ìzəm, fídi-/ *n* the view that religious knowledge depends on faith and revelation [Late 19C. < Latin *fides* 'faith'.] —**fideist** *n* —**fideistic** /fée day ístik, fídi-/ *adj*

Fidelism /fée déllizəm/ *n* the practice or policies of Castroism [Mid-20C. After Fidel CASTRO.]

fidelity /fi délləti/ *n* 1 LOYALTY loyalty to an allegiance, promise, or vow 2 SEXUAL FAITHFULNESS faithfulness to a sexual partner, especially a husband or wife 3 FACTUAL ACCURACY accuracy in describing or reporting facts or details 4 PRECISION OF REPRODUCTION the extent to which an electronic device, e.g. a stereo system or television, accurately reproduces sound or images [15C. Directly or via French < Latin *fidelitas* 'faithfulness' < *fides* 'faith'.]

fidget /fíjjit/ *vi* 1 MOVE ABOUT NERVOUSLY to move about in a restless, absent-minded, or uneasy manner 2 FIDDLE NERVOUSLY to fiddle or play with something in a restless, absent-minded, or uneasy manner ○ *He kept fidgeting with his glasses as he spoke to her.* ■ *n* SOMEBODY WHO FIDGETS a person who behaves restlessly or absent-mindedly ■ **fidgets** *npl* UNEASINESS a state of restlessness or unease expressed by continual nervous movements [15C. < *fidge* 'twitch, fidget' < ?] —**fidgetingly** *adv*

fidgety /fíjjəti/ *adj* 1 tending to fidget 2 restless or ill at ease —**fidgetiness** *n*

fiducial /fi dyóoshi əl/ *adj* 1 FOUNDED ON TRUST founded on or relating to faith or trust (*formal*) 2 USED AS BASIS OF REFERENCE accepted or used as a standard of comparison,

measurement, or reference 3 RESEMBLING LEGAL TRUST resembling a legal trust [Late 16C. < late Latin *fiducialis* < Latin *fidere* 'to trust'.] —**fiducially** *adv*

fiduciary /fi dyóoshi əri/ *adj* 1 RELATING TO A TRUST RELATIONSHIP relating to the relationship between a trustee and the person or body for whom the trustee acts 2 RELATING TO A TRUST relating to or based on a trust ■ *n* (*plural* -**ies**) TRUSTEE a manager entrusted to control property or to act on behalf of and for the benefit of another [Late 16C. < Latin *fiduciarius* '(holding) in a trust' < *fidere* 'to trust'.] —**fiduciarily** *adv*

fie /fī/ *interj* used to express disapproval, annoyance, or disgust with somebody or something (*archaic*) [14C. Via French *fi* < Latin, expressing disgust at a stench.]

Fiedler /féedlər/, **Arthur** (1894–1979) US conductor

fief /feef/ *n* 1 a piece of land, rather than money, formerly granted by a feudal lord to somebody in return for service 2 = **fiefdom** [Early 17C. Via French < Old French *feu* < medieval Latin *feudum* (see FEUD[2]).]

fiefdom /féefdəm/ *n* 1 the lands controlled by a feudal lord 2 something such as territory or a sphere of activity that is controlled or dominated by a particular person or group

⚡ **field** /feeld/ *n* 1 AREA OF AGRICULTURAL LAND an area of open ground, especially an area used to grow crops or graze livestock 2 PLAYING AREA an open expanse of ground kept or marked out as a playing area for a particular sport 3 AREA RICH IN RESOURCES an area of land or seabed that is rich in an exploitable natural resource 4 BROAD AREA an expanse of something such as ice, snow, or lava 5 AREA OF ACTIVITY an activity or subject, especially one that is somebody's particular responsibility, speciality, or interest 6 PLACE OUTSIDE INSTITUTION the setting outside a workplace, office, school, or laboratory in which somebody has direct contact with clients, the public, or the phenomena being studied 7 AREA OF MILITARY OPERATIONS the scene or location of military operations or manoeuvres 8 BATTLEFIELD an area where a battle is fought 9 BATTLE a battle (*archaic literary*) 10 GROUP OF CONTESTANTS all the participants in a race or other competitive event 11 ALL PARTICIPANTS EXCEPT FAVOURITE all the participants in a race or competitive event except the favourite, winner, or leader ○ *five lengths ahead of the field* 12 ARRANGEMENT OF FIELDERS a particular arrangement of cricket fielders around the wicket 13 SET OF MATHEMATICAL ELEMENTS a set of mathematical elements having two properties that are like addition and multiplication for ordinary numbers 14 AREA OF FORCE an area or region within which a force exerts an influence at every point 15 OPTICS = **field of view** 16 STORAGE AREA FOR INFORMATION an area in a computer memory or program, or on a monitor screen, where information can be entered and manipulated 17 BACKGROUND FOR DESIGN the background surface or colour on which a design is displayed, e.g. on a flag, coin, or coat of arms ■ *v* 1 *vt* RETRIEVE BALL to retrieve, pick up, or catch a ball in play, usually after it has been struck by a batter in baseball or rounders or a batsman in cricket 2 *vi* BE A FIELDER to act as a fielder in cricket, baseball, or rounders 3 *vt* SELECT SOMEBODY FOR A COMPETITION to select a person, group, or team to participate in an event, especially a competitive event ○ *We did not have enough players to field a team* 4 *vt* DEPLOY A GROUP to send out a large number of people or things to accomplish a task, especially to deploy military forces for action 5 *vt* DEAL WITH QUESTION OR COMPLAINT to handle something such as a question or complaint [Old English *feld* < Indo-European, 'flat'] ○ **play the field** to avoid a romantic relationship with one person by dating many people

field ambulance *n* a team of medical workers who give first aid to wounded soldiers in the front line of a battle

field artillery *n* large guns mobile enough to be brought close to the front line of a battle

field battery *n* a small unit of field guns

field boot *n* a close-fitting boot that comes up to the knee

field coil *n* the coil of wire that, when carrying current, produces the magnetization inside an electrical motor or generator needed for it to operate

field cornet *n* a civilian invested with the authority of a military officer and empowered to act as a magistrate

fieldcraft /féeld kraaft/ *n* knowledge and experience of nature combined with the skills necessary for living outdoors or in the wild

field day *n* 1 TIME OF UNRESTRAINED ACTIVITY an opportunity for unrestrained or rewarding activity ○ *If the slightest hint of this gets out, the press will have a field day.* 2 US DAY FOR AMATEUR COMPETITIONS a day devoted to amateur outdoor sports and competitions, especially at a school 3 DAY FOR OUTDOOR ACTIVITIES a day spent in outdoor activities or study

field-effect transistor *n* a transistor, with three or more electrodes, in which the output current is controlled by a variable electric field

field emission *n* the liberation of electrons from the surface of a metallic conductor subjected to a strong electric field

fielder /féeldər/ *n* a player in cricket, baseball, or rounders who is positioned on the field of play to catch or retrieve the ball when it is struck by the batsman or batter

field event *n* an athletics event, e.g. the discus, javelin, long jump, or high jump, that takes place on an open area not on a track

fieldfare /féeld fair/ *n* (*plural* -**fares** *or* -**fare**) a migratory thrush with reddish-brown plumage, a grey head and rump, and a noisy call. Native to: Europe, Asia. *Turdus pilaris.* [Assumed Old English *feldefare* 'field dweller']

field glasses *npl* a pair of binoculars

field goal *n* 1 in American football, a score worth three points, made by kicking the ball over the crossbar from a point about ten yards behind the line of scrimmage 2 in basketball, a goal made during normal play by throwing the ball through the basket

field-grade officer *n* MIL = **field officer**

field guide *n* an illustrated manual that is used to identify plants, animals, or birds in their natural habitats

field hand *n* US a labourer on a farm

field hockey *n* US SPORTS = **hockey** *n*. 1

field hospital *n* a centre for medical treatment on a battlefield or in an isolated place

Fielding /féelding/, **Henry** (1707–54) British novelist and dramatist

field lens *n* the lens that is farthest from the eye in the compound eyepiece of an optical instrument

field magnet *n* an electromagnet or permanent magnet that supplies the magnetic field in an electric machine

field marshal *n* the highest ranking officer in the British Army and in some other armies

fieldmouse /féeld mowss/ *n* 1 a small mouse with large eyes and ears and a long tail that lives in fields and gardens. Native to: Europe, Asia. Genus: *Apodemus*. 2 US the most common North American vole. Genus: *Microtus*.

field mushroom *n* a common edible mushroom. *Agaricus campestris.*

field officer *n* a military officer of the middle rank, e.g. a major or colonel

field of fire *n* an area exposed to fire from a weapon or group of weapons

field of honour *n* a battlefield or the site of a duel

field of view *n* the area in the eyepiece of an optical instrument in which the image is visible

field of vision *n* the whole area that can be seen by the eyes when they are kept fixed in one direction

field poppy *n* PLANTS = **corn poppy**

Fields /feeldz/, **W. C.** (1880–1946) US actor and comedian. Born **William Claude Dukenfield**

fieldsman /féeldzmən/ *n* (*plural* -**men** /-mən/) a fielder in cricket

field sports *npl* outdoor country sports that involve killing or capturing animals, especially hunting, shooting, and fishing

fieldstone /féeld stōn/ *n* a stone found in fields and used, often in unfinished form, for building

field study *n* a piece of research undertaken outside the laboratory or place of learning, usually in a natural environment or among the general public

field test *n* a test carried out on a product under normal conditions of use —**field-test** *vt*

field trial *n* 1 INDUST = **field test** 2 a competition to determine how well hunting dogs perform

field trip *n* a trip made by students or researchers to study something firsthand

field winding *n* ELEC = **field coil**

fieldwork /féeld wurk/ *n* **1** work undertaken outside the school, office, or laboratory in order to gain knowledge through direct contact and observation **2** a temporary defensive earthwork or fortification —**fieldworker** *n*

fiend /feend/ *n* **1 DEVIL** an evil supernatural being, especially a devil from hell **2 SOMEBODY EVIL** a wicked or cruel person **3 PERSON WITH STRONG INTEREST** an enthusiast of a subject or activity [Old English *fēond* 'hated person, enemy' (hence 'the enemy of everyone', the devil) < *fēogan* 'to hate' < Germanic]

fiendish /féendish/ *adj* **1 DIABOLICAL** like a devil or demon **2 CUNNING AND MALICIOUS** characterized by devilish cunning, ingenuity, and malice **3 PERPLEXING** extremely difficult to solve or analyse **4 DISAGREEABLE** extremely bad or unpleasant (*informal*) —**fiendishly** *adv* —**fiendishness** *n*

~~**fient**~~ incorrect spelling of **feint**

fierce /feerss/ (**fiercer, fiercest**) *adj* **1 AGGRESSIVE** characterized by or showing aggression or anger ○ *a fierce guard dog* **2 VIOLENT OR INTENSE** characterized by the violence or intensity of the forces, activity, or participants involved ○ *It was a fierce battle.* ○ *a fierce storm* **3 PROFOUND** deeply and intensely felt and often aggressively expressed ○ *He felt a fierce loyalty to his family.* [13C. Via Anglo-Norman *fers* 'brave, proud, hostile' < Latin *ferus* 'wild, untamed'.] —**fiercely** *adv* —**fierceness** *n*

fieri facias /fí ə rī fáyshi ass/ *n* a legal document that authorizes a sheriff to sell enough of a debtor's property to settle the claim of a creditor [< Latin, 'you should cause to be done']

fiery /fíri/ (**-ier, -iest**) *adj* **1 GLOWING HOT** burning or full of fire **2 RED** bright red in colour **3 SHOWING INTENSE EMOTION** full of or prone to sudden extremes of emotions **4 SPICY** extremely hot or spicy to the taste —**fierily** *adv* —**fieriness** *n*

fiery cross *n* a burning wooden cross, originally carried by runners in the Scottish Highlands to call men to arms and later adopted by the Ku Klux Klan in the United States

fiesta /fi éstə/ *n* **1** a celebration or festival linked to a religious holiday, especially in Spanish-speaking countries **2** any festival or celebration [Mid-19C. Via Spanish < Latin *festum* 'feast, festival'.]

FIFA /féefə/ *n* the governing organization of international football [French acronym < *Fédération Internationale de Football Association*]

fife /fīf/ *n* a small high-pitched flute without keys, often used in military and marching bands [Mid-16C. Via German *Pfeife* or French *fifre* 'fife, fife player' < assumed Vulgar Latin *pipa* < Latin *pipare* 'peep, chirp'.] —**fifer** *n*

Fife /fīf/ council area in east-central Scotland. Area: 1,323 sq. km/511 sq. mi.

fife rail *n* a low rail round the lower part of the mast of a sailing ship, with belaying pins to which running rigging is attached [< ?]

FIFO /fīfō/ *abbr* first in, first out

fifteen /fif téen/ *n* **1** see table at **number** **2** a team of 15 players, especially a rugby union team [Old English *fīftēne* < *fīf* 'five' + *-tēne* (< Germanic, 'ten')] —**fifteen** *adj, pron*

fifteenth /fif téenth/ *n* see table at **number** —**fifteenth** *adj, adv*

fifth /fifth/ *n* **1** see table at **number** **2** in a diatonic scale, an interval stretching from one note to another five notes higher, or the sound made when both these notes are played simultaneously **3** MUSIC = **dominant** *n.* **1** **4** in some cars or motor vehicles, the fifth gear **5** BALLET = **fifth position** [Old English *fīfta* < *fīf* (see FIVE)] —**fifth** *adj, adv*

Fifth *n US* the Fifth Amendment (*informal*) ◇ **take the Fifth** *US* to refuse to answer an awkward or self-incriminating question (*informal*)

Fifth Amendment *n* an amendment to the US Constitution stating, among other things, that defendants or witnesses in criminal trials need not testify against or incriminate themselves and may not be retried for an offence a second time

fifth column *n* a secret or subversive group that seeks to undermine the efforts of others and promote its own ends [Originally supporters General Mola claimed to have inside Madrid during the Spanish Civil War, in addition to the four columns of his army besieging the city] —**fifth columnist** *n*

fifth-generation *adj* describes a highly advanced and as yet undeveloped level of computer technology, incorporating artificial intelligence

fifthly /fífthli/ *adv* used to introduce the fifth point in an argument or discussion

fifth position *n* a position in ballet in which the feet are turned outwards with the heel of the front foot level with and touching the base of the big toe of the back foot

fifth wheel *n* **1 SOMEBODY OR SOMETHING UNNECESSARY** somebody or something whose presence is superfluous or unwanted **2 SPARE WHEEL** a spare wheel for a four-wheeled vehicle **3 ARTICULATED BEARING OR COUPLING** a horizontal bearing that allows a vehicle's front axle to swivel left or right relative to its body, or that allows a trailer attached to a tractor vehicle to pivot

fiftieth /fífti əth/ *n* **1** see table at **number** **2** somebody's 50th birthday —**fiftieth** *adj, adv*

fifty /fífti/ *n* (*plural* **-ties**) **1** see table at **number** **2 £50 NOTE** a banknote worth 50 pounds ■ *npl* **1 NUMBERS 50 TO 59** the numbers 50 to 59, particularly as a range of Fahrenheit temperatures ○ *in the low fifties* **2 YEARS FROM 50 TO 59** the years from 50 to 59 in a century or somebody's life [Old English *fīftig* < *fīf* (see FIVE)] —**fifty** *adj, pron*

fifty-fifty *adj, adv* in two equally divided parts or shares ○ *We'll split the profits fifty-fifty.* ■ *adj* equally likely that either of two possibilities may come about ○ *a fifty-fifty chance*

fig[1] /fig/ *n* **1** a pear-shaped fruit with sweet flesh and many seeds, often preserved or dried **2** a tree that bears figs. Native to: tropical and subtropical regions. *Ficus carica.* [13C. Via Old French *figue* < Latin *ficus*.] ◇ **not give** *or* **care a fig for somebody** *or* **something** not to care about somebody or something at all

fig[2] /fig/ *n* the way somebody is dressed, usually in particularly grand or formal clothing (*archaic*) [Mid-19C. < variant of FEAGUE.]

fig. *abbr* **1** figurative **2** figure

fight /fīt/ *v* (**fights, fighting, fought** /fawt/, **fought**) **1** *vti* **USE VIOLENCE** to use violent physical means such as blows with fists or a weapon to try to overpower somebody **2** *vti* **GO TO WAR** to go to war, or engage in armed conflict with another country, force, or group **3** *vi* **TAKE PART IN WAR** to take part in a war or battle, e.g. as a member or unit of the armed forces involved in it **4** *vt* **CARRY ON BATTLE OR CONTEST** to enter into or carry on a battle or other contest such as an election or court case **5** *vi* **STRUGGLE DETERMINEDLY** to make a strenuous effort to do, obtain, achieve, or defend something **6** *vti* **OPPOSE** to make vigorous efforts to oppose, resist, or overcome something or somebody ○ *fight injustice* **7** *vi* **QUARREL** to argue or quarrel with somebody or with each other **8** *vti* **BOX AGAINST** to take part in a boxing match against somebody ■ *n* **1 VIOLENT ENCOUNTER** a conflict between individuals or groups in which each tries to do physical harm to, or defeat, the other **2 STRUGGLE** a determined effort to achieve or gain something or to resist or oppose something or somebody **3 VERBAL CONFRONTATION** a verbal dispute or quarrel **4 ABILITY OR WILLINGNESS TO FIGHT** the ability or willingness to continue a battle or struggle ○ *We've still got a lot of fight left in us.* **5 BOXING MATCH** a boxing match or similar contest [Old English *feohtan* 'to fight' < W Germanic] —**fightable** *adj* ◇ **fight it out** to fight or argue until a decisive result is obtained ◇ **fight shy of something** to try to avoid something

SYNONYMS ***fight, battle, war, conflict, engagement, skirmish, clash***

CORE MEANING: a struggle between opposing armed forces

fight a physical struggle between individuals or groups such as battalions or armies; **battle** a large-scale fight involving combat between opposing forces, warships, or aircraft as part of an ongoing war or campaign; **war** a state of hostilities between nations, states, or factions involving the use of arms and the occurrence of a series of battles; **conflict** warfare between opposing forces, especially a prolonged and bitter but sporadic struggle; **engagement** a hostile encounter involving military forces; **skirmish** a brief minor fight, usually one that is part of a larger conflict; **clash** a short fierce encounter, usually involving physical combat.

fight back *v* **1** *vi* **GET BACK AT SOMEBODY** to resist or retaliate when attacked **2** *vi* **COUNTERATTACK** to counterattack or make a determined effort to recover after initial defeat or difficulty **3** *vt* **RESTRAIN TEARS OR EMOTION** to suppress something such as tears or the outward expression of an emotion or impulse

fight off *vt* **1** to drive away or resist an attacker **2** to make an effort not to succumb to something such as an illness or an unpleasant feeling

fighter /fītər/ *n* **1 ATTACKING AIRCRAFT** a fast armed military aircraft designed principally to attack enemy aircraft **2 VERY DETERMINED PERSON** a determined person who struggles to achieve or resist something **3 SOLDIER** a person who fights, especially as a soldier **4 BOXER** a competitor in a boxing match

fighter-bomber *n* an aircraft designed to combine the roles of fighter and bomber

fighting chance *n* a possibility of success, but only with sustained effort

fighting cock *n* a male domestic fowl kept for fighting. US term **gamecock**

fighting fish *n* a small brightly coloured, highly aggressive freshwater fish with long flowing fins, often kept in aquariums. Native to: Southeast Asia. Genus: *Betta.*

fight-or-flight reaction *n* a set of physiological changes, including an increase in heart rate, blood pressure, and the flow of epinephrine, that constitutes the body's instinctive response to impending danger or other stress

fig leaf *n* **1** a stylized representation of a leaf of the fig tree, formerly used as a covering for the genitals in painting or sculpture **2** an unconvincing or inadequate attempt to conceal something considered shameful or wrong

figment /fígmənt/ *n* something produced by or only existing in somebody's imagination ○ *a figment of her imagination* [15C. < Latin *figmentum* 'formation, figure, creation' < *fingere* 'to form, shape'.]

figural /fíggərəl/ *adj* ARTS = **figurative** *adj.* **2**

figurant /fíggyŏŏrənt/ *n* a ballet dancer who does not perform solo [Late 18C. < French, present participle of *figurer* 'represent' < Latin *figura* (see FIGURE).]

figurante /fíggyŏŏ rónt/ *n* a female ballet dancer who does not perform solo [Late 18C. < French, form of *figurant* (see FIGURANT).]

figuration /fíggə ráysh'n/ *n* **1 USE OF MUSICAL FIGURES AS EMBELLISHMENT** the use of musical figures or other ornaments to embellish or vary a theme **2 GIVING SOMETHING FIGURATIVE FORM** the process of giving allegorical or emblematic form to something abstract, especially by representing it using human or animal figures **3 FIGURATIVE REPRESENTATION** a depiction of something in emblematic or allegorical form

figurative /fíggərətiv/ *adj* **1 NOT LITERAL** using or containing a nonliteral sense of a word or words **2 REPRESENTATIONAL** relating to or representing form in art by means of human or animal figures **3 REPRESENTING BY ALLEGORICAL FIGURES** using an allegorical or emblematic human or animal figure to represent an abstract idea or quality —**figuratively** *adv* —**figurativeness** *n*

LANGUAGE NOTE ***Figurative extension*** involves the use of a word in a nonliteral sense, usually in one of two ways:
1. The word is applied to someone or something new, with one or more characteristics of the original referent transferred to the new referent, e.g. calling a kind person an 'angel'.
2. The word is used to designate something else associated with its original referent, e.g. referring to wine as 'the grape'.

figure /fíggər/ *n* **1 SYMBOL REPRESENTING NUMBER** a symbol representing something other than a letter of the alphabet, especially a number **2 AMOUNT EXPRESSED NUMERICALLY** an amount or value expressed as a number **3 SOMEBODY'S BODY SHAPE** the shape of an individual human body, especially with regard to its slimness or attractiveness **4 REPRESENTATION** a representation of a human being in a picture or sculpture **5 HUMAN SHAPE SEEN INDISTINCTLY** a human shape seen in outline or indistinctly **6 SOMEBODY WITHIN PARTICULAR CONTEXT** an individual, especially with regard to status within a context, e.g. in history or in a community or profession ○ *She was a prominent figure in her community.* **7 SOMEBODY SERVING AS EXAMPLE** somebody regarded as having qualities that exemplify a specific role in life (*usually in combination*) ○ *father figure* **8 WAY SOMEBODY APPEARS TO OTHERS** the general impression somebody makes on other people **9 ILLUSTRATIVE DRAWING OR DIAGRAM** an illustrative drawing or diagram **10 SHAPE OR OUTLINE** something represented by a shape or outline **11 GEOMETRICAL FORM** any two- or three-dimensional geometrical form consisting of points, lines, curves, or planes **12 PATTERN OR DESIGN** a pattern or design, especially on cloth or wood **13 DANCE OR SKATING ROUTINE** a sequence of movements performed by dancers or ice skaters in a routine **14 GROUP OF MUSICAL NOTES** a short progression of musical notes that produces a single distinct impression **15 FORM OF SYLLOGISM** the form of a syllogism in Aristotelian logic as determined by the position of the middle term ■ **figures** *npl* **MATHEMATICAL CALCULATIONS** calculations involving numbers (*informal*) ■ *v* (**-ures, -uring, -ured**) **1** *vi* **BE INCLUDED** to appear, take part, or be included in something **2** *vt* **IMAGINE** to form an idea about or envision something **3** *vti* *US* **BE UNSURPRISING** to be or happen as expected ◇ *It just figures she'd show up late.* [13C. Via French < Latin *figura* 'form, shape, figure' < *fingere* 'make, shape'.] ◇ **cut a fine** *or* **sorry figure** to look impressive *or* unimpressive

figure on *vt US* to plan or assume that something should or will happen ◇ *We can figure on running at a loss this year.*

figure out *vt* **1** to find a solution or explanation for something **2** to reach a decision or conclusion about something

SYNONYMS See *deduce*.

figured /fíggərd/ *adj* decorated with a design or pattern

figured bass *n* a bass part of a musical composition, typically baroque or classical, in which the notes have numbers written above them to indicate which chords to play

figure eight *n US* = **figure of eight**

figurehead /fíggər hed/ *n* **1** a carving, usually of a full or half-length human figure, built into the bow of a sailing ship **2** the apparent head of an organization or institution who has no real responsibility or authority

figure-hugging /fíggər hugging/ *adj* fitting closely around the body and revealing its shape

figure of eight *n* an outline of the number eight formed with two loops and one continuous line, e.g. in figure skating or aerobatics. US term **figure eight**

figure of merit *n* a parameter or characteristic of a machine, component, or instrument that is used as a measure of its performance

figure of speech *n* an expression or use of language in a nonliteral sense in order to achieve a particular effect

figure skating *n* a form of competitive skating in which skaters trace patterns on the ice and perform spins, jumps, and other manoeuvres —**figure skater** *n*

figurine /fígga reen/ *n* a small ornamental figure, often of pottery or metal [Mid-19C. Via French < Italian *figurina* 'small figure' < Latin *figura* (see FIGURE).]

fig wasp *n* a wasp that breeds in caprifigs and pollinates the flowers of wild fig trees. Native to: Europe. Genus: *Blastophaga*.

figwort /fíg wurt/ *(plural* **-worts** *or* **-wort**) *n* a tall woodland plant of the snapdragon family. Flowers: small, greenish, in clusters. Genus: *Scrophularia*. [Mid-16C. < FIG[1] as dialect term for haemorrhoids, which it was used to treat.]

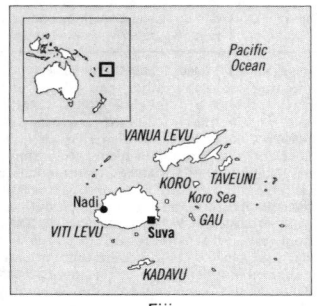

Fiji

Fiji /féeji/ island nation in the S Pacific Ocean north of New Zealand. Capital: Suva. Population: 792,441 (1997). Area: 18,376 sq. km/7,095 sq. mi.

FIGURES OF SPEECH

Figure of speech	Use	Example/Comment
alliteration	use of successive words that begin with the same or a similar sound	*'Judge jails japing juror'* (= headline)
antonomasia	use of a proper name as a common noun	*He's a regular Hitler.* (= dictatorial person)
assonance	use of similar sounds in successive words	*A stitch in time saves nine.*
chiasmus	repetition of a phrase with reversal of its elements	*One must eat to live, not live to eat.* (CICERO)
hendiadys	use of *and* to link equal words	*nice and soft*
hypallage *or* transferred meaning	use of an adjective to qualify a noun other than the one it literally refers to	*a sleepless night* (It is the would-be sleeper who is wakeful)
hyperbaton	reversal of usual word order	*These I like.*
hyperbole	deliberate use of exaggeration	*I've told you a million times not to do that.*
litotes	use of a double negative to state a positive	*a not uninteresting point*
meiosis	deliberate use of understatement	*not bad* (= good)
metaphor	use of a word in a non-literal sense, transferring attributes of the word to its new referent	*a lion of a man* (= a strong, fearless man)
metonymy	use of an attribute of something to stand for the thing itself	*olive branch* (= peace offering)
oxymoron	combining of two contradictory words in a single phrase	*a wise fool*
simile	explicit comparison between two things, using *like*	*Life is like a bowl of cherries.*
synecdoche	use of a word for part of a thing to designate the whole thing, or vice versa	*a fleet of one hundred sails* (= ships)
zeugma *or* syllepsis	use of a verb with two objects between which there is no relationship of meaning	*He took my money and his leave.* (= he took my money and he left)

Fijian /fee jée ən/ *n* **1** a language spoken on the islands of Fiji, belonging to the eastern branch of the Austronesian family of languages. Native speakers: 400,000. **2** somebody who comes from Fiji —**Fijian** *adj*

~~filagree~~ incorrect spelling of **filigree**

filament /fíllǝmǝnt/ *n* **1 SLENDER STRAND OR FIBRE** a slender strand or fibre of a material **2 WIRE CONDUCTOR IN LIGHT BULB** a thin wire that produces light in an incandescent bulb or emits electrons in a valve when electricity passes through it **3 FLOWER PART** the stalk that supports the pollen-bearing anther in the male reproductive organ (**stamen**) of a flower. ◊ **anther** *n*. **4 LONG STRAND OF CELLS** a long strand of similar cells joined end to end, as found in some bacteria and algae [Late 16C. < French, or modern Latin *filamentum* < Latin *filum* 'thread'.] —**filamentary** /fílla méntari/ *adj* —**filamentous** *adj*

filaria /fi láiri ǝ/ *(plural* **-ae** /fi láiri ee/ *or* **-a**) *n* a parasitic nematode worm that is carried as a larva by biting insects and lives as an adult in the blood or tissues of vertebrates, causing filariasis. Family: Filaridae. [Mid-19C. < modern Latin *Filaria* < Latin *filum* 'thread'.] —**filarial** *adj* —**filarian** *adj*

filariasis /fílla rí assiss/ *n* a disease caused by parasitic worms (**filaria**) that inflames and obstructs the lymphatic glands, sometimes resulting in elephantiasis

filature /fíllachar/ *n* **1 REELING OF SILK FROM COCOONS** the process of reeling silk fibres from cocoons **2 SILK REEL** a reel used in reeling silk fibres **3 SILK FACTORY** a factory for reeling silk fibres [Mid-18C. Via French < Italian *filatura* < Latin *filum* 'thread'.]

filbert /fílbərt/ *(plural* **-berts** *or* **-bert**) *n* **1 FOOD** = **hazelnut 2 TREES** = **hazel**. **1** [14C. < Anglo-Norman *philbert*, after St *Philibert*, whose feast day falls in August, when hazelnuts begin to ripen.]

filch /filch/ *vt* to steal something furtively, usually a small item or amount of little value (*informal*) [13C. < ?] —**filcher** *n*

SYNONYMS See *steal*.

⚡**file**[1] /fïl/ *n* **1 STORAGE FOR PAPERS** a folder, cabinet, or other container that holds papers for convenient storage and reference **2 ORDERED COLLECTION** a collection of related documents or papers arranged so they can be consulted easily **3 COMPUTER INFORMATION** a uniquely named collection of program instructions or data stored on a hard drive, disk, or other storage medium and treated as a single entity **4 LINE** a line of people or things standing or moving one behind the other ■ *v* (**files, filing, filed**) **1** *vt* **STORE IN ORDER** to arrange and store something in a file for future reference **2** *vt* **SUBMIT** to submit something such as a claim or complaint to the appropriate authority so that it can be put on record **3** *vi* **BRING A LAWSUIT** to make a formal application for something such as a divorce **4** *vt* **SEND IN A NEWS REPORT** to send in a report or story to a newspaper or news agency **5** *vi* **MOVE IN LINE** to move in line one behind the other [15C. < French *filer* 'thread on a string' < Latin *filum* 'thread'; because documents were hung on string for easy reference.] —**filer** *n*

file away *vt* **1** to store something in a file for future reference **2** to take careful note of something in order to remember it

file[2] /fïl/ *n* a metal tool, usually long and narrow and with sharpened ridges on one or more of its surfaces, that is used to smooth down or wear away wood or metal ■ *vti* (**files, filing, filed**) to smooth or wear away the surface of something using a file [Old English *feol* < Indo-European, 'cut, carve']

file cabinet *n US* COMM = **filing cabinet**

file clerk *n US* = **filing clerk**

⚡**file extension** *n* characters following the dot after the name of a DOS file, identifying the file type

filefish /fïl fish/ *(plural* **-fish** *or* **-fishes**) *n* a long bony tropical fish with rough-edged scales, a tiny mouth, and a sharp dorsal spine over the eye. Family: Balistidae.

⚡**file format** *n* the pattern and convention by which a program stores information in a file

⚡**file manager** *n* a computer program that arranges and manipulates files and directories

⚡**filename** /fíl naym/ *n* a set of characters, sometimes restricted in number, serving as an identifying title for a computer file and often including a file extension

⚡**file server** *n* a computer in a network that stores application programs and data files accessed by other computers

filet /fíllay/ *n* COOK = **fillet** *n.* 1 ■ *vt* COOK = **fillet** *v.* 1 [Mid-19C. < French (see FILLET).]

filet mignon /fíllay meen yon/ *n* a small round boneless piece of beef cut from the inside of the loin and usually grilled or fried [< French, 'dainty fillet']

filial /fílli əl/ *adj* **1** relating or appropriate to a child's relationship with, or feelings towards, his or her parents ○ *filial duty* **2** describes the first generation that results from crossing two parental lines [15C. Directly or via Old French < late Latin *filialis* 'of a son or daughter' < Latin *filius* 'son', *filia* 'daughter'.] —**filially** *adv* —**filialness** *n*

filiate /fílli ayt/ (**-ates, -ating, -ated**) *vt* **1** to determine the paternity of a child in a court of law, especially an illegitimate child **2** to affiliate somebody or something (*formal*) [Late 18C. < medieval Latin *filiat-*, past participle of *filiare* 'acknowledge as your child' < *filius* 'son', *filia* 'daughter'.]

filiation /fílli áysh'n/ *n* **1 PROCESS OF ESTABLISHING PATERNITY** the process of determining legally who is the father of a child whose paternity is in dispute **2 BEING SOMEBODY'S CHILD** the condition of being the child of particular parents (*formal*) **3 AFFILIATION** affiliation (*formal*) [15C. Via Old French < medieval Latin *filiation-* 'relationship as a child' < Latin *filuis* 'son', *filia* 'daughter'.]

filibeg /fílli beg/, **philibeg** *n Scotland* a kilt (*literary*) [Mid-18C. < Scottish Gaelic *feileadh-beag* 'little kilt'.]

filibuster /fílli bustər/ *n* a tactic such as a long irrelevant speech or several such speeches used to delay or prevent the passage of legislation ■ *vti* to try to stop legislation being passed by making long speeches [Mid-19C. Via Spanish *filibustero* < Dutch *vrijbuiter* 'pirate'.] —**filibusterer** *n* —**filibusterism** *n* —**filibusterous** *adj*

filicide /fílli sīd/ *n* (*formal*) **1** the killing by a parent of a son or daughter **2** a parent who kills his or her own son or daughter [Mid-17C. < Latin *filius* 'son', *filia* 'daughter'.] —**filicidal** /fílli sīd'l/ *adj*

filiform /fílli fawrm/ *adj* long, thin, and fine like a thread [Mid-18C. < Latin *filum* 'thread'.]

Filigree: Detail of decorative filigree and jewelled medieval book cover (1225–30)

filigree /fílli gree/ *n* **1 LACY METAL ORNAMENTATION** delicate decorative openwork made from thin twisted wire in silver, gold, or another metal **2 DELICATE WORK** a delicate ornamental tracery ■ *vt* (**-grees, -greeing, -greed**) **FORM SOMETHING INTO A DELICATE PATTERN** to form something into a delicate ornamental openwork design [Late 17C. Alteration of French *filigrane* < Italian *filigrana* < Latin *filum* 'thread' + *granum* 'grain'.] —**filigree** *adj*

filing[1] /fīəling, fīling/ *n* the activity of storing files in their proper place

filing[2] /fīling/ *n* a tiny particle or shaving of metal, such as might have been removed with a file (*often plural*) ○ *iron filings*

filing cabinet *n* a piece of office furniture containing drawers for storing files

filing clerk *n* an employee in an office who stores and retrieves documents and other records. US term **file clerk**

filing system *n* a method of organizing office files, especially one that identifies and organizes the major headings under which documents are to be filed

Filipino /fílli peenō/, **Pilipino** /pílla-/ *adj* **OF THE PHILIPPINES** relating to the Philippines, or their languages, peoples, or cultures ■ *n* **1 OFFICIAL LANGUAGE OF THE PHILIPPINES** the official language of the Philippines, an Austronesian language based on Tagalog. Native speakers: 15 million. **2 SOMEBODY FROM THE PHILIPPINES** somebody who comes from the Philippines [Late 19C. < Spanish, < (*las islas*) *Filipinas* 'the Philippines'.]

fill /fil/ *v* **1** *vti* **MAKE SOMETHING FULL OR BECOME FULL** to make a container full, or become full ○ *The bath filled rapidly.* **2** *vt* **TAKE UP ALL THE SPACE** to take up all or most of the space inside or cover the whole or most of the surface area of something ○ *the room was filled with light* **3** *vt* **COVER A BLANK AREA** to cover a page or a blank space on a page with writing or drawing **4** *vt* **BECOME ABUNDANT** to become present and very noticeable throughout something ○ *The scent of spring filled the air.* **5** *vt* **MAKE SOMEBODY FEEL SOMETHING POWERFULLY** to cause somebody to experience a strong emotion, usually to the exclusion of all others ○ *The news filled me with dread.* **6** *vt* **CLOSE UP A HOLE** to plug a hole, crack, or cavity in something **7** *vt* **MEET A NEED** to satisfy a need or requirement ○ *The retreat filled her need for solitude.* **8** *vt* **OCCUPY FREE TIME** to occupy a period of time with an activity ○ *They filled their days with DIY and gardening until she returned.* **9** *vt* **HOLD OFFICE** to hold a job or office and carry out the duties associated with it **10** *vt* **CHOOSE** to elect or appoint somebody to a job or position **11** *vt* **PUT A FILLING INTO** to put a type of food into something such as a cake or sandwich as its filling **12** *vt* **ADD TO RAISE A SURFACE LEVEL** to build up the surface of something with earth, stones, or other materials until it reaches a desired level **13** *vti* **POWER A SAIL WITH WIND** to stretch a sail and make it bulge out, or bulge out under the pressure of the wind ■ *n* **1 PLENTY** a sufficient or excessive quantity of something ○ *I've had my fill of his complaints.* **2 ENOUGH TO MAKE A CONTAINER FULL** enough of something to fill a container, or the act of filling a container **3 MATERIAL TO RAISE A SURFACE** material, e.g. earth or stones, used to build up the surface of something to a desired level **4 IMPROVISED MUSIC** music improvised to fill designated spaces in a jazz or other musical score [Old English *fyllan* < Germanic]

fill in *v* **1** *vt* **COMPLETE THE BLANK SPACES IN** to write information into the blank spaces on a form or document **2** *vt* **COLOUR A BLANK SPACE ON** to cover a blank space on something with colouring or shading **3** *vt* **PLUG A CAVITY AND MAKE THE SURFACE LEVEL** to put material into a cavity in a surface to make the surface level **4** *vt* **OCCUPY TIME** to spend a period of time that would otherwise be unoccupied in an activity **5** *vi* **BE A SUBSTITUTE** to act as a substitute for somebody **6** *vt* **GIVE SOMEBODY INFORMATION** to supply somebody with information about something **7** *vt* **BEAT SOMEBODY UP** to subject somebody to a beating (*slang*)

fill out *v* **1** *vt* to write information into the blank spaces on a form or document **2** *vti* to become or make something larger and more substantial

fill up *v* **1** *vti* **BECOME OR MAKE SOMETHING FULL** to become full, or make something full **2** *vt* **SATISFY SOMEBODY'S HUNGER** to give somebody the feeling of having eaten enough **3** *vi* **MAKE FUEL TANK FULL** to fill a vehicle's tank with fuel

fille de joie /fee də zhwaa/ (*plural* **filles de joie** /fee də zhwaa/) *n* a woman prostitute (*euphemistic*) [< French, 'girl of pleasure']

filled gold *n US* METALL = **rolled gold**

filler /fíllər/ *n* **1 SOMETHING THAT FILLS** somebody who or something that fills something **2 PLUGGING OR COATING SUBSTANCE** a substance used to plug a crack or cavity or smooth a surface before painting or varnishing **3 SUBSTANCE ADDED FOR BULK** a substance such as sizing that is used to fill spaces or add bulk or strength to a material **4 LESS IMPORTANT MATERIAL** something, often relatively unimportant, added to fill space, e.g. in a newspaper or between items in a broadcast or performance **5 TOBACCO FILLING** the tobacco inside a cigar or cigarette **6 PADDING** a material such as cotton or down that is used to stuff something such as a quilt or toy

fillér /fíllair/ *n* see table at **currency** [Early 20C. < Hungarian.]

filler cap *n* = **petrol cap**

fillet /fíllit/ *n* **1 BONELESS PORTION OF FISH OR MEAT** a boneless portion cut from a fish, a poultry breast, or the rib area of beef, lamb, or pork **2 RIBBON WORN AROUND THE HEAD** a ribbon worn across the forehead, as an ornament or to hold back the hair **3 FLAT NARROW MOULDING** a raised or sunken ornamental surface set between larger surfaces **4 DECORATIVE LINE ON THE COVER OF BOOK** a thin decorative line impressed onto the cover of a book, or the tool used to make it ■ *vt* **1 CUT A FILLET FROM** to cut and prepare boneless portions of fish, poultry, or meat **2 USE A FILLET AS BINDING OR DECORATION** to bind hair or decorate a surface with a fillet [14C. < Old French *filet* < Latin *filum* 'thread'.]

fill-in *n* a temporary replacement or substitute for somebody

filling /fílling/ *n* **1 PLUG FOR A DECAYED TOOTH** a plug made of metal or composite material used to fill a tooth cavity **2 GETTING SOMETHING FILLED** the process or an instance of having something such as a cavity in a tooth filled **3 SOMETHING USED TO FILL** a substance used to fill the space inside something, pad it, or add bulk to it **4 FOOD MIXTURE PUT INSIDE** a food mixture that is put inside something else such as a pie, pastry case, or sandwich **5 THREADS GOING ACROSS FABRIC** the horizontal threads or yarn in a woven fabric ■ *adj* **SATISFYING HUNGER** leaving somebody with the feeling of having eaten enough

filling station *n* TRANSP = **petrol station**

fillip /fíllip/ *n* **1 FEELING OF ENCOURAGEMENT** something that stimulates or encourages something or somebody **2 SNAPPING MOVEMENT OF THE FINGERS** a snapping of the tip of one of the fingers against the ball of the thumb in order to make a sound or to propel a small object ■ *vt* **1 PROPEL SOMETHING WITH A FILLIP** to strike or propel something by snapping the fingertip against the ball of the thumb **2 GIVE SOMEBODY OR SOMETHING AN INCENTIVE** to provide a stimulus or encouragement to somebody or something [15C. An imitation of the sound of flicking or snapping the fingers.]

fill light *n* in photography and film-making, a secondary source of light used to eliminate, reduce, or soften shadows

Fillmore /fíl mawr/, **Millard** (1800–74) US statesman and 13th president of the United States (1850–53)

fill-up *n* a filling of something, especially a vehicle's fuel tank

filly /fílli/ (*plural* **-lies**) *n* **1** a female horse under four years of age **2** an offensive term for a young woman or girl (*dated informal*) [15C. < Old Norse *fylja*.]

film /film/ *n* **1 SERIES OF MOVING PICTURES ON SCREEN** a series of real or fictional events recorded by a camera and projected onto a screen as a sequence of moving pictures, usually with an accompanying soundtrack. US term **movie** *n.* **2 FILMS COLLECTIVELY** films collectively, considered as a medium for recording events, a form of entertainment, or an art form **3 COATED STRIP FOR TAKING PICTURES** a thin translucent strip or sheet of cellulose coated with an emulsion sensitive to light, used in a camera to take still or moving pictures **4 VERY THIN SHEET** material, especially a plastic, in the form of a very thin, flexible, translucent or transparent sheet. Use: wrapping. **5 THIN LAYER** a thin coating of a substance such as dust, liquid, or ice covering the surface of something **6 SOMETHING MAKING A VIEW HAZY** a thin haze or mist or something similar that blurs somebody's view ■ **films** *npl* **FILM INDUSTRY** the film industry (*informal*) ■ *v* **1** *vt* **TAKE PICTURES OF** to record somebody or something on film **2** *vti* **MAKE A FILM** to make or be involved in the making of a film **3** *vt* **MAKE FILM OF** to make a film of a book, story, or event **4** *vi* **BE GOOD FOR FILMING** to be a suitable subject for cinematic treatment ○ *a story that would film well* **5** *vt* **COVER WITH THIN LAYER** to cover the surface of something with a thin coating of a substance [Old English *filmen* 'membrane, skin' < Indo-European]

film over *vi* to become covered with a thin or misty layer of something

film badge *n* a piece of photographic film incorporated into a badge and used to register the wearer's exposure to nuclear radiation

filmgoer /fílm gō ər/ *n* somebody who goes to a cinema to see films, especially on a regular basis. US term **moviegoer**

filmi /fílmi/ *adj S Asia* relating to the Indian film industry ■ *n* a star of the Indian film industry [Late 20C. < film.]

filmic /fílmi/ *adj* characteristic or reminiscent of a cinema film, especially in the techniques used to tell a story or describe a scene —**filmically** *adv*

film library *n* a large collection of cinema films or newsreels used as an archive or for hire

filmmaker /fílm maykər/ *n* a producer or director of cinema films —**filmmaking** *n*

KEY DATES IN THE HISTORY OF FILM

1894	Coin-operated kinetoscopes open in New York, London, and Paris
1895	First public screening of motion picture by French inventors Auguste and Louis Lumière, Paris
1902	*A Trip to the Moon*, by French film-maker Georges Méliès, pioneers narrative cinema and special effects
1908	US actor D. W. Griffith becomes director and develops many of film's story-telling conventions
1912	Canadian-born US director Mack Sennett opens Keystone Studios, introducing slapstick comedy and stars such as Chaplin
1922	*Toll of the Sea*, first Technicolor film
1922	*Nanook of the North*, by Robert Flaherty, first artistically notable documentary film
1923	*The Covered Wagon*, first major US Western
1925	Russian director Sergey Eisenstein pioneers use of montage in *Battleship Potemkin*
1927	*The Jazz Singer*, first feature-length talkie
1920s	Avant-garde artists such as Léger, Duchamp, Dali experiment with film as art form
1930	*Little Caesar* (producer Darryl F. Zanuck), first major US gangster film
1931	*Dracula, Frankenstein*, first US horror films

1931	*Alam Ara*, first Indian talkie, includes seven songs and heralds Bollywood film industry
1933	*42nd Street*, first major film musical
1935	*The 39 Steps*, first thriller by British director Alfred Hitchcock
1937	*Snow White and the Seven Dwarfs*, first animated feature by US producer Walt Disney
1939	*Gone With the Wind*, first Hollywood epic blockbuster
1941	US actor/director Orson Welles' innovative techniques in *Citizen Kane* achieve commercial success and artistic esteem
1943	Italian director Luchino Visconti makes *Ossessione*, first neorealist film
1953	Cinemascope wide-screen format introduced in *The Robe*
1959	*Breathless* and *The 400 Blows*, first French New Wave films
1962	*Dr No*, first James Bond film
1970	IMAX large-format projection system introduced at the Expo in Osaka, Japan
1971	*Shaft*, first US blaxploitation film
1970s	*Jaws, Star Wars*, first US special-effects blockbusters
1980s	Introduction of 70 mm photography, Dolby sound, and increasing use of computer graphics

film noir /film nwaàr/ (*plural* **films noirs** /film nwaàr/) *n* a cinematic genre popular in the 1940s and 1950s, often filmed in urban settings with extensive use of shadows, cynical in outlook, and featuring antiheroes [Mid-20C. < French, 'black film'.]

QUICK FACTS ON... **FILM NOIR**

Key dates: late 1930s–late 1950s
Key locations: France, United States
Key elements: intricate plot centred on a crime; gritty, urban setting; use of deep shadows, highlights, extreme close-ups, and long shots to create oppressive atmosphere; tone of cynicism
Key figures: Marcel Carné, Billy Wilder, Howard Hawks, Orson Welles (directors); Jean Gabin, Humphrey Bogart (actors)
Key works: *Quai des Brumes* (Carné) 1938, *Le Jour se Lève* (Carné) 1939, *Double Indemnity* (Wilder) 1944, *The Big Sleep* (Hawks) 1946, *The Killers* (Siodmak) 1946, *Touch of Evil* (Welles) 1958

filmography /film óggrǝfi/ (*plural* **-phies**) *n* a list of the films made by an actor or director or on a topic [Mid-20C. Blend of FILM + BIBLIOGRAPHY.]

filmsetting /film setting/ *n* a typesetting process that involves projecting the characters that are to be printed onto photographic film and then making printing plates from the film. US term **photocomposition** —**filmset** *vt* —**filmsetter** *n*

film star *n* a well-known film actor or actress. US term **movie star**

filmstrip /film strip/ *n* a length of developed photographic film containing a series of still images to be projected on a screen

filmy /filmi/ (**-ier, -iest**) *adj* **1** consisting or made of very thin translucent material **2** covered or misted over with a thin layer of something —**filmily** *adv* —**filminess** *n*

filmy fern *n* a small fern that grows in humid regions, has translucent leaves, and forms sheets on moist rocks. Genus: *Hymenophyllum*.

filo /feèlō/, **filo pastry** *n* very thin sheets of pastry dough used to make papery crisp small pastries or large dishes, used especially in Greek cooking. US term **phyllo** [Mid-20C. < Greek *phullo* 'leaf'.]

fils[1] /filss/ (*plural* **filses** *or* **fils**) *n* see table at **currency** [Late 19C. < Arabic *fals*, small copper coin.]

fils[2] /feess/ *n* in France and French-speaking countries, a word used after a man's or boy's surname to distinguish him from his father of the same name ○ *Henri Dupont fils*. ◊ **père** *n*. **2** [Late 19C. < French, 'son'.]

⚡ **filter** /filtǝr/ *n* **1 STRAINING DEVICE** a device made of or containing a porous material used to collect particles from a liquid or gas passing through it **2 POROUS MATERIAL USED FOR STRAINING** any porous layer or material such as sand, paper, or cloth, used in or as a filter **3 TINTED SCREEN** a tinted glass or dyed gelatine screen placed on a camera lens to reduce light intensity, exclude some types of light, control the rendering of colour, or distort an image **4 DEVICE RESTRICTING THE PASSAGE OF FREQUENCIES** an acoustic, electric, electronic, or optical device, instrument, or computer program that allows the passage of some frequencies or digital elements and blocks others **5** = **filter tip** *n*. **1 6 DIRECTIONAL TRAFFIC SIGNAL** an additional traffic signal at a junction, in the form of a green arrow, to indicate that vehicles may turn left or right while traffic going straight ahead is halted ■ *v* **1** *vt* **PASS SOMETHING THROUGH A FILTER** to put something such as a fluid, light, or electrical impulses through a filter to remove or recover something **2** *vi* **PASS THROUGH** to seep or pass through a filter or something that is intended to act as a barrier ○ *The sunlight filtered in through the shutters.* **3** *vi* **TRICKLE** to move or pass slowly and gradually ○ *People filtered into the auditorium.* **4** *vti* **TURN WHILE TRAFFIC AHEAD HALTED** to turn, or allow traffic to turn, right or left at a junction while the traffic going straight ahead is halted [14C. Via Old French *filtre* 'felt' (used for filtering liquids) < medieval Latin *filtrum* < Germanic.] —**filterability** /filtǝrǝ billǝtee/ *n* —**filterable** *adj* —**filterableness** *n* —**filterer** *n* —**filterless** *adj* —**filtrable** *adj*

filter bed *n* a thick layer of sand, gravel, clinker, or other filtering material in a tank, used to remove sewage or other impurities from liquids

filter cake *n* a deposit of semisolids or solids that are separated out and deposited between layers of filtering material after a fluid has been passed through them

filter coffee *n* **1** coffee made by passing hot water through finely ground coffee held in a filter made of paper, cloth, or wire mesh **2** coffee beans ground to the right consistency for making filter coffee

filter-feeder *n* an aquatic animal such as a clam, sponge, or baleen whale that feeds on particles or small organisms that it filters from the water —**filter-feeding** *n*

filter paper *n* porous paper used as or in a filter

filter tip *n* **1** a small cylindrical mouthpiece made of a dense porous material attached to the end of a cigarette to remove tar and other impurities from the smoke **2** a cigarette with a filter tip —**filter-tipped** *adj*

filth /filth/ *n* **1 FOUL DIRT** dirt or refuse that is disgusting or excessive **2 MORALLY OBJECTIONABLE MATERIAL** something considered morally objectionable or obscene, e.g. coarse language or explicit descriptions or depictions of sexual activity **3 OFFENSIVE TERM** an offensive term for the police (*slang*) [Old English *fylð* < Germanic]

filthy /filthi/ *adj* (**-ier, -iest**) **1 EXTREMELY DIRTY** extremely or disgustingly dirty ○ *Your hands are filthy!* **2 MORALLY OBJECTIONABLE** considered extremely morally objectionable or obscene **3 DESPICABLE** used to express contempt or strong disapproval (*informal*) ○ *a filthy liar* **4 UNPLEASANT** extremely unpleasant (*informal*) ■ *adv* **VERY** to an extreme degree (*informal*) ○ *filthy rich* —**filthily** *adv* —**filthiness** *n*

SYNONYMS See *dirty*.

filtrate /fil trayt/ *n* the material that emerges from a filtering process, usually a liquid or gas from which impurities have been removed ■ *vti* (**-trates, -trating, -trated**) to pass or put something through a filter [Early 17C. < modern Latin *filtrat-*, past participle of *filtrare* 'filter' < medieval Latin *filtrum* (see FILTER).]

filtration /fil tráysh'n/ *n* the process of passing or putting something through a filter

filum /fílǝm/ (*plural* **-la** /-lǝ/) *n* a fine part or structure of a living organism that is long and thin like a thread [Mid-19C. < Latin, 'thread, filament, fibre'.]

FIMBRA /fímbrǝ/ *abbr* Financial Intermediaries, Managers, and Brokers Regulatory Association

fimbria /fímbri ǝ/ (*plural* **-ae** /-ee/) *n* a fringed border or part in the body, e.g. that found at the entrance to the Fallopian tubes [Mid-18C. < Latin, 'border, fringe'.] —**fimbrial** *adj*

fimbriate /fímbri ǝt/, **fimbriated** /-aytid/ *adj* describes parts of organisms having a fringed border [15C. < Latin *fimbriatus* 'fringed' < *fimbria* 'border, fringe'.] —**fimbriation** /fímbri áysh'n/ *n*

fin /fin/ *n* **1 PART OF FISH USED FOR MOTION** a flexible organ, sometimes paddle-shaped or fan-shaped, extending from the body of a fish or aquatic animal and helping in balance and propulsion **2 PART ATTACHED TO HULL OF SUBMARINE** a wing-shaped often movable blade attached low on the hull of a vessel such as a submarine that helps to control and stabilize it **3 UPRIGHT PART OF AIRCRAFT'S TAIL** a fixed vertical surface at the tail of an aircraft giving stability and to which the rudder is attached **4 STABILIZING STRUCTURE ON ROCKET OR MISSILE** any small flat fixed structure extending from the body of a rocket, missile, or aircraft, often near the tail, to give stability in flight **5 RIB ON HEATING DEVICE** a flat metal part projecting from a heating mechanism such as a radiator that helps to increase the transfer of heat to the surrounding air **6 SWIMMING** = **flipper** *n*. **2 7 DECORATIVE EXTENSION ON CAR BODY** an ornamental extension on the body of a motor vehicle, especially on the rear wing ■ *vi* (**fins, finning, finned**) **SWIM USING FINS** to swim or beat the water with fins or show a fin above water [Old English *fin(n)* < Germanic] —**finned** *adj*

fin. *abbr* **1** finance **2** financial **3** finish

Fin. *abbr* **1** Finland **2** Finnish

finagle /fi náyg'l/ (**-gles, -gling, -gled**) *vti* to trick, cheat, or manipulate somebody in order to obtain or achieve something (*informal*) [Early 20C. < ?] —**finagler** *n*

final /fín'l/ *adj* **1 LAST** last of a number or series of similar things ○ *a final reminder* **2 ALLOWING NO CHANGE** conclusive and allowing no further discussion ○ *the editor's decision* *is final* 3 **ENDING** occurring at the end of something ○ *the final curtain* ■ *n* **END OF A SERIES** the last and most important in a series of sporting or other contests that decides the winner of a tournament or competition ■ **finals** *npl* 1 **LAST DECISIVE ROUNDS OF A TOURNAMENT** the last decisive rounds of a knockout tournament or competition during which the winners of previous rounds play each other 2 **LAST UNIVERSITY EXAMINATIONS** the examinations that take place at the end of a course of study at university or studies for a professional qualification [14C. Directly or via French < Latin *finalis* 'last' < *finis* 'final moment, end'.]

final accounts *npl* the set of accounts produced by a business at the end of its accounting year

final approach *n* the last stage of an aircraft's descent before landing, from its turning into line with the runway to the procedures immediately preceding touchdown

final cause *n* the ultimate goal towards which a process is directed

final cut *n* the approved and edited version of a film prior to its being released for viewing by the public

finale /fi naáli/ *n* 1 **FINAL THEATRICAL NUMBER** a scene or number that brings a stage performance or an act of a performance to an end 2 **FINAL MOVEMENT** a final movement or section of a musical composition 3 **FINAL EVENT IN A SERIES** an event that is the last or climactic event in a series [Mid-18C. Via Italian < Latin *finalis* (see FINAL).]

finalise *vt* = **finalize**

finalism /fīn'lizəm/ *n* the belief or proposition that all events are determined by their final causes —**finalistic** /fīnə lístik/ *adj*

finalist /fīn'list/ *n* a competitor who has qualified to take part in the finals of a contest

finality /fī nálləti/ (*plural* **-ties**) *n* 1 the quality, state, or condition of being concluded or decided, permitting no further progress or development ○ *He spoke with an air of finality.* 2 an act, belief, or statement that is final

finalize /fīnə līz/ (**-izes, -izing, -ized**), **finalise** (**-ises, -ising, -ised**) *v* 1 *vti* to bring something to a point at which everything has been agreed upon and arranged 2 *vt* to complete an agreement, sale, or other transaction —**finalization** /fīnə lī záysh'n/ *n* —**finalizer** *n*

finally /fīn'li/ *adv* 1 **AT LAST** after a long period of time or a long delay and often after previous unsuccessful attempts ○ *So you've finally decided to ask her out, have you?* 2 **DEFINITIVELY** in a way that rules out further continuance, change, or discussion ○ *The venue won't be finally decided until the next meeting.* 3 **AS LAST IN THE SERIES** as the last in a series of things or actions ○ *We visited Belgium, Holland, Germany, and finally Switzerland.* 4 **AS THE LAST WORD** used to introduce the last in a series of things said by somebody ○ *Finally, I'd like to thank all of you for coming here tonight.*

Final Solution, final solution *n* the plan to murder systematically all the Jews of Europe, conceived and put into action by the Nazis during World War II

finance /fī nanss, fi nánss/ *n* 1 **CONTROL OF MONEY** the business or art of managing the monetary resources of an organization, country, or individual ○ *high finance* 2 **MONEY REQUIRED** the money necessary to do something, especially to fund a project ■ **finances** *npl* **THE MONEY SOMEBODY HAS** the money at the disposal of a person, organization, or country ○ *It'll depend on the state of my finances at the end of the month.* ■ *vt* (**-nances, -nancing, -nanced**) **PROVIDE MONEY FOR** to raise or provide the money required for something or by somebody [14C. < French, < *finer* 'end, settle' < Latin *finis* 'end'.] —**financeable** *adj*

finance bill *n* an act passed by a legislature to raise or provide money for public expenditure

finance company, finance house *n* a business enterprise that loans money to individuals or companies against collateral, especially to buy items on hire purchase

financial /fī nánsh'l, fi-/ *adj* 1 relating to or involving money or finance 2 *ANZ* having enough or plenty of money to dispose of (*informal*) ○ *We're both working, so we're financial at the moment.* —**financially** *adv*

Financial Times Industrial Ordinary Share Index *n* an index of prices on the London Stock Exchange based on the average price of thirty shares. It is produced by the *Financial Times*.

Financial Times Stock Exchange 100 Index *n* full form of **FTSE 100 Index**

financial year *n* a 12-month period at the end of which all accounts are completed in order to furnish a statement of a company's, organization's, or government's financial condition. US term **fiscal year**

financier /fī nánssi ər, fi-/ *n* a wealthy investor who is skilled in financial matters [Early 17C. < French, < *finance* (see FINANCE).]

finback /fín bak/ *n* a large baleen whale that has a prominent dorsal fin. *Balaenoptera physalus.* ◊ **rorqual**

finch /finch/ *n* a small songbird with a short broad seed-eating bill and colourful plumage in males. Family: Fringillidae. [Old English *finc* < Germanic]

Finch /finch/, **Peter** (1916–77) British actor

find /fīnd/ *v* (**finds, finding, found** /fownd/, **found**) 1 *vt* **DISCOVER AFTER SEARCHING** to discover something or somebody after a search ○ *He was found wandering a mile from his home.* 2 *vt* **GET BACK** to recover something after losing it 3 *vt* **DISCOVER FOR FIRST TIME** to realize, understand, or locate something for the first time, especially by studying or observing ○ *We have to find answers to the problem of global warming.* 4 *vt* **DISCOVER ACCIDENTALLY** to notice or come across somebody or something by chance 5 *vt* **EXPERIENCE** to notice or experience something personally ○ *I think you'll find them easy to get along with.* 6 *vt* **MANAGE TO GET** to make a special effort to gather something together or summon something up ○ *I don't know where we'll find the money.* 7 *vt* **REACH GOAL** to succeed in reaching something aimed for ○ *He has finally found his true form as a world-class tennis player.* 8 *vt* **RECORD AS OCCURRING** to observe something such as a natural species as existing or occurring (*often passive*) 9 *vti* **REACH VERDICT** to decide about something or somebody at the end of a legal procedure, or announce the decision reached ○ *The jury found for the plaintiff.* 10 *vt* **SUPPLY NEED** to bring or provide something that is necessary for a process to occur ○ *You will need to find your own transport and equipment for the job.* 11 *vr* **BECOME CONSCIOUS OF YOUR OWN CONDITION** to become aware of being in a particular place or state ○ *He found himself in an empty street.* 12 *vr* **MAKE DECISIONS ABOUT YOUR OWN LIFE** to become more self-aware and self-motivated (*informal*) ○ *She finally found herself and became a successful artist.* ■ *n* **NEW DISCOVERY** something noteworthy or valuable that has been found, or somebody who is talented and is brought to public attention [Old English *findan* < Indo-European, 'tread, go'] —**findable** *adj*

find out *v* 1 *vti* to get to know something, especially by asking somebody or searching in an appropriate source, or just by chance ○ *I don't know how they found out about the proposed merger.* 2 *vt* to detect and expose an offence ○ *He was quickly found out and his lies exposed.*

finder /fīndər/ *n* 1 a locator of things 2 a small wide-angle telescope attached parallel to the optical axis of a larger telescope to help locate celestial objects

fin de siècle /fáN də syéklə/ *n* the final years of the 19th century, characterized as being a time of decadence and self-doubt (*hyphenated before a noun*) [< French, 'end of the century']

finding /fīnding/ *n* 1 **RESEARCH RESULT** a piece of information obtained from an investigation, especially scientific research 2 **VERDICT** a conclusion that is reached and recorded at the end of a judicial or other formal inquiry ■ **findings** *npl US* **MATERIALS FOR CRAFTWORK** small articles or tools used in making craftwork, e.g. metal clips used on earrings

fine[1] /fīn/ *adj* (**finer, finest**) 1 **QUITE WELL OR SATISFACTORY** in a good, acceptable, or comfortable condition (*informal*) 2 **NOT COARSE** made up of tiny particles 3 **SUNNY** with sunny and clear skies 4 **THIN** very thin, sharp, or delicate 5 **GOOD-LOOKING** very good to look at ○ *a fine view of the valley* 6 **OUTSTANDING** far better than the average ○ *a fine wine* 7 **UNPLEASANT** extremely unsuitable or undesirable (*informal; ironic*) ○ *This is a fine mess!* 8 **SPURIOUSLY IMPRESSIVE** sounding or looking good, but probably just for show (*ironic*) ○ *nothing but fine gestures* 9 **DELICATELY FORMED** showing special skill, detail, or intricacy, especially in artistic work 10 **SMALL AND DELICATE** set very closely and carefully together ○ *fine stitching* 11 **VERY SUBTLE** so particular or small that it may hardly be noticeable ○ *a fine distinction* 12 **EXTREMELY PURE** with any or most impurities removed, especially in a precious metal ■ *adv* 1 **WELL** very well (*informal*) ○ *It works just fine.* 2 **INTO SMALL PIECES** into tiny or delicate bits ○ *Chop the onions very fine.* ■ *v* (**fines, fining, fined**) 1 *vt* **SHARPEN** to make something thinner or sharper (*technical*) 2 *vti* **PURIFY** to purify beer or wine [13C. < French *fin* < Latin *finire* 'to finish' (see FINISH).] —**fineness** *n*

fine[2] /fīn/ *n* a sum of money that somebody is ordered to pay for breaking a law or rule ■ *vt* (**fines, fining, fined**) to take a fixed amount of money from somebody who has broken a rule or a law [13C. Via French *fin* < Latin *finis* 'end', in medieval Latin a sum to be paid on completion of legal proceedings.] —**finable** *adj*

fine[3] /feen/ *n* WINE = **fine champagne**

fine[4] /feé nay/ *n* the place on a music score that shows where the piece finishes after a repeated section, or the symbol that marks this place [Late 18C. < Italian, < Latin *finis* 'end'.]

fine art *n* 1 **CREATION OF BEAUTIFUL OBJECTS** artistic work that is meant to be appreciated for its own sake, rather than to serve some useful function 2 **COLLEGE COURSE IN ART** a course of study designed to teach students practical artistic skills as well as the theory and history of art 3 **PURE ART** any art form, e.g. painting, sculpture, architecture, drawing, or engraving, that is considered to have purely aesthetic value (*often plural*) 4 **IMPRESSIVELY DETAILED TECHNIQUE** something that requires great skill, talent, or precision (*informal*) ○ *the fine art of public speaking*

fine champagne /feén shaaN pánya/ *n* a liqueur brandy made in the Champagne region of France [Mid-19C. < French, 'fine (brandy from) Champagne'.]

fine chemical *n* a chemical product that is made in relatively small quantities and is typically high in cost, e.g. a flavouring or vitamin

fine-grained, fine-grain *adj* formed with a smooth, even, or closely-patterned grain

fine leg *n* 1 in cricket, a fielding position behind the batsman and close to the ball's line of flight, on the side opposite to the way the batsman's body is facing 2 a fielder in cricket who has been positioned at fine leg

finely /fīnli/ *adv* 1 into small, thin, or delicate pieces 2 in a careful, delicate, or sensitive way ○ *an actor finely tuned to her audience's reactions* ○ *finely wrought*

fine print *n* BUSINESS = **small print**

finery[1] /fīnəri/ *n* clothing, jewellery, or accessories that are especially dressy and smart, usually worn on special occasions [Late 17C. < FINE[1], after BRAVERY.]

finery[2] /fīnəri/ (*plural* **-ies**) *n* a furnace that converts cast iron into wrought iron [Late 16C. < French *finerie* < Old French *finer* 'refine'.]

fines herbes /feénz aírb/ *npl* a mixture of finely chopped herbs used to flavour a dish [< French, 'fine herbs']

finespun /fīn spún/ *adj* spun or stretched out thinly

finesse /fi néss/ *n* 1 **PHYSICAL SKILL** elegant ability and dexterity ○ *As a top-flight tennis star, she made up in finesse what she lacked in power.* 2 **TACTFUL TREATMENT** a delicate and skilful approach in dealing with a troublesome situation 3 **TACTIC IN BRIDGE** in bridge, an attempt to win a trick with a lower-value card while holding a higher card not in sequence, hoping that an opponent cannot play an intervening card ■ *vti* (**-nesses, -nessing, -nessed**) 1 **TRY WINNING TRICK WITH LOWER CARD** in bridge, to attempt to win a trick with a lower-value card while holding a higher card not in sequence, hoping that an opponent does not have an intervening card 2 **BE TACTFUL** to use, achieve, or handle something delicately and skilfully (*literary*) [Mid-16C. < French, 'fineness' < *fin* (see FINE[1]).]

fine structure *n* the separation of light of particular wavelengths produced by atoms or molecules into two or more very similar wavelengths, caused by the interaction of particular quantum mechanical properties

fine-tooth comb, fine-toothed comb *n* 1 a comb with very narrow tightly-set teeth 2 a thorough approach to an investigation or search, examining every detail ○ *went over the figures with a fine-tooth comb but failed to find the error*

fine-tune (**fine-tunes, fine-tuning, fine-tuned**) *v* 1 *vt* to adjust the engine of a motor vehicle to improve its performance 2 *vti* to make tiny adjustments to something in order to achieve the best possible performance or appearance —**fine-tuning** *n*

Fingal's Cave /fíng gəlz-/ cave on Staffa Island in the Inner Hebrides, off W Scotland. Height: 18 m/60 ft. Length: 70 m/228 ft.

ϟ**finger** /fíng gər/ *n* 1 **DIGIT OF THE HAND** any of the digits of the hand, sometimes excluding the thumb (*often before nouns*) 2 **PART OF GLOVE** any of the long narrow parts of a glove that fits the finger 3 **NARROW STRIP** something that resembles a finger in shape ○ *a finger of sand* 4 **LONG**

NARROW PORTION OF FOOD a small portion of food about as long and thick as a finger **5** APPROXIMATE QUANTITY OF ALCOHOL an approximate measure of alcoholic beverage in a glass, equal in depth to the width of a finger **6** APPROXIMATE UNIT OF LENGTH an approximate unit of measurement, equal to the width or length of a finger ■ *v* **1** *vt* TOUCH to feel or move the fingers across something, often in a gentle, affectionate, or thoughtful way **2** *vt* GIVE UP TO POLICE to tell the police about the whereabouts or illegal activities of somebody (*slang*) **3** *vti* PLAY INSTRUMENT USING THE FINGERS to handle the strings or keys of a musical instrument with the fingers **4** *vt* MARK WITH INSTRUCTIONS FOR FINGERING to show on a musical score which fingers the musician should use **5** *vt* LOCATE COMPUTER USERS to obtain and display information about other users of the same computer or on other computers connected through a network or the Internet [Old English, < Indo-European, 'five'] —**fingerer** *n* ◇ **cross your fingers** used to express a hope that things will turn out well ◇ **give (somebody) the finger** *US* to make an aggressively obscene gesture with the middle finger extended upwards and held towards somebody (*slang*) ◇ **have a finger in every pie** to be involved in many advantageous or lucrative projects ◇ **have a finger in the pie** to be involved in a particular project, especially in a way that other people find annoying ◇ **let something slip through your fingers** to fail to take advantage of something that would have been of benefit to you ◇ **put your finger on something** to identify something, especially something difficult or elusive ◇ **twist somebody round your little finger** to succeed in getting somebody to do exactly as you wish

fingerboard /fíng gər bawrd/ *n* a long strip of wood fixed on the neck of string instruments against which strings are pressed in order to vary the pitch

finger bowl *n* a small bowl of water set beside a place at a table so that fingers can be cleaned, e.g. after picking up food with the hands

finger buffet *n* a selection of food prepared for guests at a party to help themselves to and eat with their fingers, usually while standing

finger food *n* small items of food made to be eaten with the fingers

fingerfuck /fíng gər fuk/ *vt* a highly offensive term meaning to use the fingers to stimulate a woman's genitals (*taboo*)

finger hole *n* any one of a series of holes on a woodwind instrument that a player covers with the fingers in order to register a pitch

fingering /fíng gəring/ *n* **1** the use of the fingers to do something **2** the action or technique of using the fingers to play a musical instrument

Finger Lakes group of eleven glacial lakes in W New York

fingerling /fíng gərling/ *n* a small fish less than one year old, especially a salmon or trout

fingermark /fíng gər maark/ *n* a smear or greasy mark left after somebody has touched something

finger millet *n* a short-stemmed millet with an ear divided into five parts, cultivated widely in S India, Sri Lanka, and parts of Africa. *Eleusine coracana.* [Because its ears resemble the fingers of a hand]

fingernail /fíng gər nayl/ *n* a flat protective layer of keratin that covers the end part of a finger's upper surface

fingerpick /fíng gər pik/ *n* a musician's pick with a curved handle for attaching it to the finger. ◊ **flatpick** —**fingerpick** *vti*

finger post *n* a notice shaped like a pointing hand, indicating the direction, and usually the distance, to a particular place

fingerprint /fíng gər print/ *n* **1** PATTERN ON A FINGERTIP an impression of the curved lines of skin at the end of a finger that is left on a surface or made by pressing an inked finger on to paper **2** DISTINGUISHING CHARACTERISTIC a unique characteristic, mark, or pattern that can be used to identify somebody or something ■ *vt* RECORD THE FINGERPRINTS OF to press each of somebody's fingertips in ink and then on to paper to make a set of marks that can be used to identify the person

finger puppet *n* a very small puppet that is put over and operated by one finger

finger roll *n* a small narrow soft bread roll

fingerspelling /fíng gər spelling/ *n* a form of sign language communication using the fingers to gesture the spelling of words

fingerstall /fíng gər stawl/ *n* a sheath-shaped protective covering worn over an injured finger

fingertip /fíng gər tip/ *n* the tip of a finger ■ *adj* involving the use of the fingertips and so very sensitive or delicate ○ *fingertip controls* ◇ **have something at your fingertips** **1** to know all the details of something thoroughly **2** to have something available and nearby

fingertip search *n* a minute search of the area around the scene of a crime made by police officers on hands and knees looking for fragmentary evidence left on the ground

finger wave *n* a wave made by shaping damp hair with the fingers and a comb

finial /fíni əl, fínni əl/ *n* **1** ARCHITECTURAL DECORATION a carved decoration at the top of a gable, spire, or arched structure **2** FURNITURE DECORATION an ornamental feature, e.g. a carved knob, on the top or end of a part of a piece of furniture **3** CURVE IN A TYPEFACE a curve that ends a main stroke in some italic typefaces [15C. < assumed Anglo-Norman or Anglo-Latin word, 'final' < Latin *finis* 'end'.] —**finialled** *adj*

finicky /fínniki/ (**-ier, -iest**), **finicking, finical** /-k'l/ *adj* **1** concentrating too much on small unimportant details **2** complicated by trivial details [Late 16C. Probably altered < FINE[1] + *-ical*.] —**finickiness** *n*

SYNONYMS See ***careful***.

fining /fíning/ *n* **1** the process of clarifying a liquid, especially wine or beer **2** the process of removing undissolved gas from molten glass

finis /fínniss/ *interj* used to indicate that something has or must come to an end completely [14C. < Latin, 'end'.]

finish /fínnish/ *v* (**-ishes, -ishing, -ished**) **1** *vti* NO LONGER CONTINUE to come to an end, or bring something to an end **2** *vt* CONSUME to eat, drink, or use all of something **3** *vt* DESTROY to kill, ruin, or exhaust somebody or something (*informal*) ○ *His dishonesty finished him in business.* **4** *vt* COMPLETE THE SURFACE EFFECT OF to treat something, especially wood or metal, in order to achieve a desired surface effect **5** *vt* MAKE JUST RIGHT to give something or somebody the final touches, qualities, or skills that are required to create a desired effect ■ *n* **1** END PART the terminating part of something **2** SPECIAL TOP LAYER a surface texture or final coat applied to something, especially wood or metal ○ *a mirror with a gilt finish* **3** SPURT OF SPEED AT END a final part of a race, especially a sprint, acceleration, or challenge near the finishing line **4** QUALITY OF WORKMANSHIP the degree of care with which a product has been manufactured or a job of work has been carried out, judged by its final appearance [14C. < Old French *feniss-*, stem of *fenir* < Latin *finire* < *finis* 'end'.] —**finisher** *n*

finish off *vt* **1** COMPLETE to bring something to an end, e.g. by making it as complete as is wished or needed **2** USE UP to eat, drink, or use up all of something **3** DESTROY to kill, ruin, or exhaust somebody or something (*informal*)

finish up *v* **1** *vt* to eat, drink, or use up all of something **2** *vi* to be in a particular place or condition in the end, often not the planned one

finish up with *vt* to be left with something ○ *We finished up with nothing.*

finish with *vt* **1** to end a relationship or partnership with somebody (*informal*) **2** to stop using, wanting, or being interested in something

finished /fínnisht/ *adj* **1** produced and completed with skill and professionalism **2** with no further prospect of success or development

USAGE See ***done***.

finishing /fínnishing/ *n* the tasks that complete the production process of a garment, fabric, or material

finishing line *n* a real or imaginary line that marks the end of a race. US term **finish line**

finishing school *n* a fee-paying school for girls close to school-leaving age in which social skills, the arts, and academic courses are taught

finishing touch *n* a final small change or addition made to something

finish line *n US* = **finishing line**

Finisterre, Cape /fínni stáir/ promontory in NW Spain, forming the westernmost part of the mainland

finite /fí nīt/ *adj* **1** LIMITED with an end or limit ○ *We have only a finite amount of resources.* **2** COUNTABLE having a countable number of elements **3** MEASURABLE subject to measurable limitations **4** USING VERB appearing in a verb form that limits person, number, and tense [14C. < Latin *finitus*, past participle of *finire* (see FINISH).] —**finitely** *adv* —**finiteness** *n*

finitude /fínni tyood/ *n* the condition of being finite (*formal*)

fink /fingk/ *n US* **1** SOMEBODY STRONGLY DISLIKED a contemptible or unpleasant person (*dated slang insult*) **2** INFORMER an informant who gives an authority such as the police information that incriminates somebody (*dated slang disapproving*) **3** STRIKEBREAKER a worker who continues on the job while colleagues are on strike (*dated slang disapproving*) ■ *vi US* (*dated slang disapproving*) **1** INFORM ON OTHERS to give an authority information about another's criminal or bad behaviour ○ *He finked on his buddies after the police questioned him.* **2** BE A STRIKEBREAKER to continue to work in defiance of a strike [Late 19C. < ?]

fink out *vi US* to fail to do something after previously agreeing or volunteering to do it (*slang*)

fin keel *n* a fin-shaped part that extends downwards from the underside of a sailing boat to give extra stability

Finland

Finland /fínlənd/ republic in N Europe on the Baltic Sea. Capital: Helsinki. Population: 5,137,269 (1997). Area: 338,145 sq. km/130,559 sq. mi. Finnish **Suomi**

Finland, Gulf of arm of the Baltic Sea, between Finland and Estonia. Area: 30,044 sq. km/11,600 sq. mi.

Finlandize /fínnlən dīz/ (**-izes, -izing, -ized**), **Finlandise** (**-ises, -ising, -ised**) *vt* to make a small country or power act in an accommodating way towards a superpower rather than confronting it [Mid-20C. From the behaviour of Finland towards the Soviet Union after World War II.] —**Finlandization** /fínnlən dī záysh'n/ *n*

Finlay /fín lay/ river in north-central British Columbia, Canada. Length: 400 km/250 mi.

Finn /fin/ *n* **1** somebody who comes from Finland **2** somebody who speaks a Finnic language [Old English *Finnas* (plural)]

Finn /fin/, **Neil** (*b.* 1956) New Zealand singer and songwriter

finnan haddock /fínnən-/, **finnan haddie** *Scotland* /-háddi/ *n* haddock split and smoked on the bone over oak or peat, giving the flesh a pale yellow colour [< *Findon*, fishing village near Aberdeen]

Finnic /fínnik/ *n* a group of languages in NE Europe, belonging to the Finno-Ugric branch of Uralic. Native speakers: 7 million. ■ *adj* **1** relating to the Finnic group of languages or its speakers

~~**finnish**~~ incorrect spelling of **finish**

Finnish /fínnish/ *n* the official language of Finland, also spoken in Estonia and European Russia, belonging to the Finnic group of the Finno-Ugric branch of Uralic. Native speakers: 6 million. ■ *adj* relating to Finnish or the Finns

Finn MacCool /fín mə kóol/ *n* a legendary Irish hero, chief of the band of warriors known as the Fianna

Finno-Ugric /fínnō yóogrik/, **Finno-Ugrian** /-yóogri ən/ *n* a group of NE European languages that is one of two major branches of Uralic. Native speakers: 22 million. ◊ **Samoyed** *n.* 2 —**Finno-Ugric** *adj*

fino /feénō/ (*plural* **-nos**) *n* a very pale dry sherry [Mid-19C. < Spanish, 'fine' < Latin *finire* (see FINISH).]

finocchio /fi nóki ō/ (*plural* **-o** *or* **-os**) *n* PLANTS = **fennel** *n.* 2 [Early 18C. Via Italian < Latin *faeniculum* (see FENNEL).]

fin whale *n* ZOOL = **finback**

FIO *abbr* for information only

f.i.o. *abbr* for information only

fiord *n* = **fjord**

Fiordland National Park /fyáwrdlənd-/ national park on the southwestern coast of the South Island, New Zealand. Area: 12,116 sq. km/4,678 sq. mi.

Fiorentino /fyórrən teénō/, **Rosso** (1494–1540) Italian painter

fioritura /fi áwri tyóórə/ (*plural* **-re** /-ray/) *n* an embellished vocal figure in opera of the 17th and 18th centuries, similar to a cadenza and often improvised [Mid-19C. < Italian, < *fiorire* 'to flower' < Latin *florere* (see FLOURISH).]

fipple /fípp'l/ *n* a small wooden plug in a woodwind instrument or organ pipe that redirects air and creates vibrations [Early 17C. < ?]

fipple flute *n* an end-blown flute containing a fipple

fir /fur/ (*plural* **firs** *or* **fir**) *n* 1 an evergreen tree with needle-shaped leaves and erect female cones. Genus: *Abies.* 2 an evergreen tree that resembles a true fir, e.g. a Douglas fir [14C. < ?]

Firbank /fúr bangk/, **Ronald** (1886–1926) British novelist

Firdawsi /feer dówssi/ (940?–1020?) Persian poet

fire /fīr/ *n* 1 **PROCESS OF BURNING** the rapid production of light, heat, and flames from something that is burning, e.g. in the combustion of wood, coal, or petroleum 2 **BLAZE** the light, heat, and flames caused by something that is burning 3 **PILE OF BURNING FUEL** a collection of material such as logs or coal that is set alight and used as fuel for heating, cooking, or burning something 4 **HEATING DEVICE** an electric or gas-fuelled appliance that can be used to produce heat in a building 5 **DESTRUCTIVE BURNING** a situation in which something is destroyed or damaged by burning, e.g. a building or an area of land (*often before nouns*) ○ *fire damage* 6 **DISCHARGE FROM GUNS** a discharge of ammunition from one or more guns ○ *The troops advanced under heavy fire.* 7 **CONTINUOUS ATTACK** a series of things that follow each other quickly and relentlessly, especially if hostile or intimidating ○ *She took heavy fire from her political opponents.* 8 **LAUNCH OF PROJECTILE** the process or timing of sending off a missile or rocket 9 **GEM'S BRILLIANCE** the shine and sparkle of a gemstone 10 **PASSION** energy, spirit, or intensity of feeling ○ *the composer's creative fire* 11 **ONE OF ELEMENTS OF ANCIENTS** in ancient and medieval philosophy, one of the four elements, the active principle of fire, also considered important in astrology ■ *v* (**fires, firing, fired**) 1 *vti* **DISCHARGE BULLET** to discharge ammunition or a projectile 2 *vti* **LAUNCH SOMETHING FORCEFULLY** to launch something powerfully through the air 3 *vt* **DISMISS SOMEBODY FROM WORK** to dismiss somebody from employment (*informal*) 4 *vi* **START UP** to begin to burn fuel and start working ○ *The engine fired and the racing car took off.* 5 *vt* **STOKE OR FILL WITH FUEL** to keep supplying fuel to something, e.g. a furnace, engine, or oven 6 *vt* **BAKE IN A KILN** to put pottery into a kiln to be baked hard 7 *vt* **STRIKE WITH FORCE** to hit or throw something forcefully 8 *vt* **EXCITE** to arouse strong emotion in somebody (*often passive*) ○ *She was fired with enthusiasm.* 9 *vt* **DESTROY WITH FIRE** to cause something to burn, especially in order to destroy it (*formal or dated*) ○ *Crossing the border, the invaders fired the first town they encountered.* 10 *vt Malaysia, Singapore* **TELL OFF** to criticize or reprimand somebody (*informal*) ○ *The boss fired me twice last week.* ■ *interj* 1 **WARNING CRY** used to tell others that a dangerous fire has started 2 **COMMAND TO SHOOT** used to command the discharge of guns or other weapons, missiles, or projectiles ○ *Ready, aim, and fire!* [Old English *fȳr* < Indo-European] —**fired** *adj* —**firer** *n*
◇ **on fire** 1 in a condition of combustion in which flames, heat, and usually smoke are being produced 2 full of eagerness or passion ◇ **play with fire** to do something dangerous or risky ◇ **set fire to something** to make something start burning ◇ **set the world on fire** to do something remarkable or very successful ◇ **under fire** 1 shot at by weapons 2 subject to severe criticism

fire away *vi* 1 to begin or keep on shooting 2 to begin doing something, especially asking questions (*informal*)

fire off *vt* 1 to deliver a series of things, especially questions or demands 2 to discharge a bullet or some other projectile

fire up *v* 1 *vt* **GET GOING** to initiate the operation of something 2 *vti* **START TO BURN** to begin to burn, or set something burning 3 *vti* **MAKE ENTHUSIASTIC** to cause somebody to become enthusiastic

fire alarm *n* a bell or siren that is sounded if a fire starts

fire and brimstone *n* eternal punishment [See Genesis 19:24, Revelation 19:20]

fire ant *n* a predatory ant that inflicts a painful sting. Native to: tropical and temperate regions. Genus: *Solenopsis.* [< the burning sensation its sting causes]

firearm /fīr aarm/ *n* a portable weapon such as a pistol or rifle that fires ammunition

fireback /fīr bak/ *n* a metal lining placed behind a fireplace, or the area of wall where it is placed

fireball /fīr bawl/ *n* 1 **CENTRE OF A NUCLEAR EXPLOSION** the highly ionized spherical region of bright hot gas and dust at the centre of a nuclear explosion 2 **BRIGHT METEOR** an exceptionally bright meteor 3 **BALL LIGHTNING** a discharge of ball lightning 4 **DYNAMIC PERSON** an extremely energetic and dymanic person (*informal*)

fire blight *n* an infectious disease of apples, pears, and other fruit trees that blackens leaves and kills branches and is caused by the bacterium *Erwinia amylovora*

firebomb /fīr bom/ *n* a bomb designed to start a fire —**firebomb** *vti* —**firebomber** *n* —**firebombing** *n*

firebox /fīr boks/ *n* an enclosure for a fire in a stove, furnace, or the engine of a steam locomotive

firebrand /fīr brand/ *n* 1 a burning stick carried by somebody as a torch or a weapon 2 somebody with a strong or aggressive personality who encourages unrest

firebrat /fīr brat/ *n* a small wingless insect related to silverfish, found in warm moist places. *Thermobia domestica.*

firebreak /fīr brayk/ *n* a strip of land that has been cleared of trees, bushes, and any other combustible material in order to prevent a fire from spreading

firebrick /fīr brik/ *n* a brick that can withstand very high temperatures. Use: fireplaces, furnaces.

fire brigade *n* an organization of people trained to prevent, control, and extinguish fires and to rescue people from fires and other dangerous situations. US term **fire department**

firebug /fīr bug/ *n* a person who starts fires causing damage or destruction, especially repeatedly and for pleasure (*slang*)

fireclay /fīr klay/ *n* a durable clay that can withstand great heat. Use: firebricks, crucibles, furnace linings.

fire control *n* the control of naval or artillery fire directed at a target

firecracker /fīr krakər/ *n* a small paper or cardboard cylinder filled with an explosive that makes one or several loud bangs when it is lit

firecrest /fīr krest/ *n* a small bird of the warbler family, the top of the head of which is bright orange in the male and bright yellow in the female. Native to: Europe. *Regulus ignicapiullus.*

firedamp /fīr damp/ *n* a mixture of methane and other hydrocarbon gases that forms in coalmines and is explosive when mixed with air [< DAMP 'noxious gas']

fire department *n US* = **fire brigade**

firedog /fīr dog/ *n Southern US* HOUSEHOLD = **andiron**

fire door *n* 1 a fireproof door that is normally kept closed or locked, ensuring that any fire is confined to one area 2 an emergency exit opened from inside

fire drill *n* a rehearsal for evacuating a building quickly and safely in the event of a fire or other emergency

fire-eater *n* 1 an entertainer who appears to swallow flames from a burning stick 2 an aggressive, angry, or argumentative person (*informal*) —**fire-eating** *n*

fire engine *n* a large road vehicle equipped with ladders, hoses, and other equipment to fight fires and rescue people

fire escape *n* a specially designed means of getting clear of a building if it catches fire, especially an exterior metal stairway attached to the building

fire extinguisher *n* a cylindrical metal container holding a substance such as foam or vaporizing liquid that can be sprayed onto a fire

firefight /fīr fīt/ *n* a fierce battle involving a heavy exchange of gunfire

firefighter /fīr fītər/ *n* a person who attempts to control or extinguish fires, and to rescue people or things from danger —**firefighting** *n*

firefly /fīr flī/ (*plural* **-flies**) *n* a winged nocturnal beetle that, during courtship, produces an intermittent light from luminescent chemicals in its abdominal organs. Family: Lampyridae.

fireguard /fīr gaard/ *n* 1 a metal, usually meshed, screen that is put around the front of an open fire, mainly to stop sparks from flying out and to prevent people from going too close 2 = **firebreak**

firehouse /fīr howss/ *n US* EMERGENCIES = **fire station**

fire hydrant *n* an upright pipe, usually in a street, connected to a water main with a valve to which a hose can be attached, e.g. by firefighters

fire insurance *n* insurance that offers coverage against damage or loss due to fire

fire irons *npl* a collection of implements used for tending a fire in a fireplace, especially a shovel, tongs, poker, and brush

firelight /fīr līt/ *n* the flickering light given off by an open fire

firelighter /fīr lītər/ *n* a small piece of an inflammable substance that helps fuel to catch fire quickly

firelock /fīr lok/ *n* in early firearms, a mechanism that struck a spark from flint or steel and caused a charge to explode

fireman /fīrmən/ (*plural* **-men** /-mən/) *n* 1 **MAN WHO IS FIREFIGHTER** a man who is a firefighter, especially one who works for a fire brigade 2 **STOKER** a man who stokes a furnace, especially on a steam locomotive or steamboat 3 **DRIVER'S ASSISTANT** an assistant to the driver of an electric or diesel train

fire marshal *n US* 1 a state or local official whose job is to investigate suspicious fires and work in the areas of fire prevention and building inspection ○ *The fire marshal's office was called in to investigate the apartment house blaze.* 2 an employee of a plant or other industrial site who is responsible for firefighting equipment and fire safety procedures

fire opal *n* a translucent reddish opal

fireplace /fīr playss/ *n* a recess, usually with a mantelpiece above it, built into the wall of a room as a place to light an open fire

firepower /fīr powər/ *n* the capability of a military unit or weapon to direct effective fire at an enemy

fire practice *n* EMERGENCIES = **fire drill**

fireproof /fīr proof/ *adj* treated or manufactured so as to be impossible or very difficult to burn —**fireproof** *vt*

fire raiser *n* CRIME = **arsonist**

fire-resistant *adj* treated or made so that it is very slow to catch fire and burn

fire-retardant *adj* tending not to catch fire easily and therefore checking the spread of fire

fire sale *n* a sale of goods or property damaged in a fire

fire screen *n* 1 HOUSEHOLD = **fireguard** *n.* 1 2 a freestanding screen placed in front of a fireplace to act as a heat shield or as a decorative screen when a fire is not lit

fire ship *n* formerly, a ship loaded with explosives or combustibles that was set on fire and allowed to drift as a weapon among enemy ships

fireside /fīr sīd/ *n* the space around a fireplace or hearth ■ *adj* of a cosy, familiar, or homely nature

fire sign *n* one of the three signs of the zodiac, Aries, Leo, or Sagittarius, traditionally associated with a fiery, assertive, and dynamic temperament

fire station *n* a building where professional firefighters are stationed and their vehicles and equipment are kept

firestone /fīr stōn/ *n* a form of sandstone that can withstand great heat. Use: to line kilns and furnaces.

firestorm /fīr stawrm/ *n* 1 a large extremely intense fire sustained by strong inwardly rushing winds that feed a rising column of hot air 2 *US* a strong, sometimes violent, upheaval or outburst ○ *a firestorm of protest*

firethorn /fīr thawrn/ *n* PLANTS = **pyracantha**

fire trail *n Aus* a road through forest or bush land that enables firefighters to reach wildfires in remote areas

firetrap /fír trap/ *n* any building or structure regarded as a fire hazard, either because it is built of combustible materials or lacks adequate means of escape

firetruck /fír truk/ *n US* EMERGENCIES = **fire engine**

firewalking /fír wawking/ *n* the rite or practice of walking barefoot over hot coals, ashes, or stones —**firewalker** *n*

⚡**firewall** /fír wawl/ *n* **1** a fireproof wall put in place to ensure that if a fire occurs it is confined to one area **2** a piece of computer software intended to prevent unauthorized access to system software or data

fire watcher *n* a lookout for fires, especially a member of an air-raid patrol during World War II

firewater /fír wawtər/ *n* strong and harsh-tasting alcoholic spirits (*dated slang*)

fireweed /fír weed/ (*plural* **-weed** *or* **-weeds**) *n* PLANTS = **rosebay willowherb** [Because often the first to grow on land that has been burnt]

firewood /fír wood/ *n* wood that is burned as fuel

firework /fír wurk/ *n* **BRIGHT EXPLODING OBJECT** a package of manufactured chemicals designed to make a loud and brilliant explosion when lit (*often before nouns*) ○ *a firework party* ■ **fireworks** *npl* **1 SHOW USING FIREWORKS** a display of many brilliant fireworks **2 ANGRY OUTBURST** a display of violent temper (*informal*) **3 SPECTACULAR DISPLAY** any impressive display of talent (*informal*)

firing /fíring/ *n* the application of great heat to a ceramic object in a kiln, to harden it or to fix an applied substance such as a glaze

firing line *n* **1** an exposed position from which guns are fired at an enemy, or the troops who occupy it **2** the forefront of a movement, operation, or activity, especially one that is controversial

firing order *n* the sequence of ignition of the cylinders in an internal-combustion engine

firing party *n* = **firing squad**

firing pin *n* a pin behind the barrel of a firearm that strikes the container of explosive (**primer**) to make the cartridge fire

firing squad *n* a group of soldiers with the task of carrying out an execution by gunfire or delivering a ceremonial volley over a grave

firkin /fúrkin/ *n* **1** a British unit of capacity used especially in the brewing industry, equal to nine gallons **2** a small wooden tub formerly used for storing food or liquids [14C. Probably < assumed Middle Dutch *verdelkijn* 'small fourth' < *veerde* 'fourth'.]

firm[1] /furm/ *adj* **1 NOT YIELDING TO THE TOUCH** compact and solid when pressed ○ *a firm mattress* **2 SECURE** fixed securely and unlikely to give way ○ *a firm hold* **3 DETERMINED** showing certainty or determination ○ *You must be more firm with them.* **4 TRUSTWORTHY** reliable and able to be trusted **5 STEADY** showing no or few fluctuations ■ *adv* **UNYIELDINGLY** in a determined and unshakable way ○ *They stood firm despite a wave of criticism.* ■ *vti* **MAKE OR BECOME FIRM** to become firm or firmer, or make something firm or firmer [14C. Via Old French < Latin *firmus*.] —**firmly** *adv* —**firmness** *n*

firm up *v* **1** *vt* to make something more definite, clear, or less liable to change ○ *Let's firm up the date of the meeting.* **2** *vi* to become less liable to fluctuation

firm[2] /furm/ *n* a group of people who form a commercial organization selling goods or services [14C. < Italian *firma* < late Latin *firmare* 'confirm by signing' < Latin, 'strengthen' < *firmus* 'strong'.]

firmament /fúrmamənt/ *n* the sky, considered as an arch (*literary*) [13C. Via French < Latin *firmamentum* < *firmus* 'strong'.]

⚡**firmware** /fúrm wair/ *n* frequently used software stored on a memory chip in a computer rather than being part of a program [Because the instructions will not be lost when power is shut off]

firn /furn/ *n* GEOG = **névé** *n.* 1 [Mid-19C. Via German, 'of last year' < Old High German *firni* 'old'.]

firn wind *n* a summer wind that blows downhill off a glacier during the day

first /furst/ *adj* **1 BEFORE THE REST** preceding or ahead of any others in order **2 EARLIER THAN THE REST** occurring before any others in a series **3 MOST IMPORTANT** with a higher rank, significance, or authority than others in the same category **4 FUNDAMENTAL** forming a basis or foundation for something **5 BEST** best in quality or achievement ■ *n* **1 NEW THING** something that has not been done before or has not occurred before **2** see table at **number 3 FIRST GEAR** the lowest gear in a motor vehicle **4 HIGH ACADEMIC QUALIFICATION** an undergraduate university degree awarded for the highest level of academic achievement **5 FIRST GEAR** the lowest forward gear in a motor vehicle **6** BALLET = **first position** ■ *pron* **ONE AHEAD OF ANY OTHER** the one positioned before any other in achievement, rank, quality, or time ■ *adv* **1 BEFORE OTHERS** earlier than something or somebody else **2 ORIGINALLY** for the first time **3 INITIALLY** at the start **4 MORE WILLINGLY** used to indicate a preference [Old English *fyr(e)st* < Indo-European]

first aid *n* emergency medical treatment for somebody who is ill or injured, given before more thorough medical attention can be obtained

First Amendment *n US* an amendment to the US Constitution that forbids Congress from interfering with a citizen's freedom of religion, speech, assembly, or petition

first base *n* the initial base that a player attempts to reach in baseball ◇ **get to first base** *US* to succeed in the initial phase of an activity, especially in making advances to a prospective romantic or sexual partner (*informal*)

first-born *n* the first offspring to be born to a set of parents ■ *adj* born first of all

First Cause *n* in Christianity, God as the originator of everything

first class *n* **1** the highest rank, standard, or quality **2** the best accommodation offered on an aeroplane, ship, or train

first-class *adj* **1 BEST** of the highest standard of excellence **2 MOST LUXURIOUS** most exclusive and expensive **3 GIVEN PRIORITY IN THE POSTAL SERVICE** costing more to post and given priority in delivery —**first-class** *adv*

first cousin *n* ANTHROP = **cousin** *n.* 1

first-day cover *n* an envelope, often specially designed, that bears a newly issued stamp and a postmark for the day of issue

first-degree burn *n* a burn marked by pain and reddening of the skin but without blistering or charring of tissue

first-degree murder *n US* murder that is carried out with the planned and deliberate intention of killing somebody

first edition *n* **1 ORIGINAL COPY OF A BOOK** a copy of a book in its original printed and published format **2 ORIGINAL PRINTING OF A PUBLICATION** the total number of copies of a book issued by the original publisher in the first instance **3 FIRST NEWSPAPER OF DAY** the first batch or copy of a newspaper on a day of publication

first eleven *n* in football, cricket, and other team sports with eleven players per team, the best of several teams competing for the same club at different levels

first fifteen *n* in rugby, the best of several teams competing for the same club at different levels

first finger *n* ANAT = **index finger**

first-foot *n* **first-foot, first-footer** *Scotland* the first person to visit a household in the New Year ■ *vti Scotland* to be the first visitor to a household in the New Year

first-footing *n Scotland* the traditional practice of going to the house of a friend or neighbour soon after midnight on 31 December, with good wishes and gifts of food, drink, and fuel

first fruits *npl* **1** the first harvest of the season or year **2** the first results of an activity

⚡**first-generation** *adj* **1** relating to or being the children of parents who have left one country to settle in another **2** describes the earliest computers, which were based on vacuum tubes

firsthand /fúrst hánd/ *adj, adv* obtained directly from an original source rather than via somebody else

first lady *n* **1 first lady, First Lady** *US* **US LEADER'S SPOUSE OR WOMAN PARTNER** the wife of the President of the United States or of a US state governor, or the woman appointed by him to act as his official hostess **2 GOVERNMENT LEADER'S PARTNER** the wife or woman partner of a high government official, especially of a country's leader **3 WOMAN AT THE TOP** the most important or respected woman member of a profession or field of activity

first language *n* **1** the language that somebody learned in infancy **2** the principal language in a neighbourhood, district, region, or country

first lieutenant *n* **1** *US* a US Army, Marine, or Air Force commissioned officer of a rank above second lieutenant **2** a naval officer in charge of the upkeep and maintenance of a ship

first light *n* the earliest part or time of the day, when the sun begins to rise

firstling /fúrstling/ *n* the first of something, e.g. an offspring, product, or result (*archaic or literary*)

first love *n* **1** the experience of being in love for the first time **2** the first object of somebody's romantic love or affectionate admiration

firstly /fúrstli/ *adv* used to introduce the first point in an argument or discussion

first mate *n* an officer on a merchant ship or any non-naval vessel of a rank above second mate

First Minister *n* the title of the leader of the National Assembly of Northern Ireland, Scotland, or Wales

first name *n* a personal name that accompanies a family name to identify somebody fully

first night *n* the first public performance of a new production of a play or show, or the day on which this takes place (*hyphenated when used before a noun*) ○ *first-night nerves* —**first nighter** *n*

first offender *n* somebody with no previous criminal record who breaks the law and is convicted for the first time

first officer *n* **1** NAUT = **first mate 2** the aircraft commander, or captain, of a commercial aircraft

first-past-the-post *adj UK, Can* describes a voting system in which the winning candidate needs to receive more votes than any other candidate but does not need to get an absolute majority of the votes cast

first person *n* **1 VERB OR PRONOUN FORM** the form of a verb or pronoun referring to the speaker or writer, e.g. the pronoun 'I' in English **2 SET OF GRAMMATICAL FORMS** the grammatical set containing the forms indicating the first person **3 WRITING IN FIRST PERSON** a style of writing using first-person forms

first position *n* a position in ballet in which the feet are turned outwards with the heels touching

first post *n* the first of two bugle calls at the end of the day, signalling to military personnel that it is time to retire to barracks before lights out

first principle *n* a fundamental rule underlying a theory, faith, or procedure

first quarter *n* one of four phases of the Moon, during which one half of the Moon's visible surface is illuminated by the Sun

first-rate *adj* of the best quality or the highest standard

first reading *n* the introduction of a bill in a legislature prior to debate and a vote

first refusal *n* the right to decide whether or not to buy something before it is offered to other potential buyers

first school *n* in some localities, a school for pupils from five to eight years of age

first strike *n* the use of nuclear weapons against an enemy that is similarly armed, intended to destroy its military capacity and prevent it from attacking first (*hyphenated before nouns*) ○ *first-strike capability*

first thing *adv* **1** very early in the morning **2** before doing anything else

first water *n* the highest grade in gemstones

First World *n* the principal industrialized countries of the world, including the United States, the United Kingdom, the nations of W Europe, Japan, Canada, Australia, and New Zealand

First World War *n* HIST = **World War I**

firth /furth/ *n Scotland* a river estuary, or a wide inlet of the sea (*often in placenames*) [14C. < Old Norse *fjörðr*.]

fisc /fisk/ *n* **1** *US* a public treasury **2** royal funds, especially those belonging to a Roman emperor (*archaic*) [Late 16C. Directly or via French < Latin *fiscus* 'rush basket, purse, treasury'.]

fiscal /físk'l/ *adj* **1** relating to public revenues, especially the revenue from taxation ○ *fiscal prudence* **2** relating to financial matters in general ■ *n Scotland* = **procurator fiscal** [Mid-16C. Directly or via French < Latin *fiscalis* < *fiscus* 'rush basket, purse, treasury'.] —**fiscally** *adv*

fiscal year *n US* ACCT = **financial year**

Fischer /físhər/, **Bobby** (b. 1943) US chess player. Full name **Robert James Fischer**

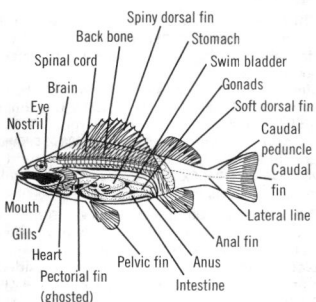

Spiny dorsal fin
Back bone
Stomach
Spinal cord
Swim bladder
Brain
Gonads
Eye
Soft dorsal fin
Nostril
Caudal peduncle
Caudal fin
Mouth
Lateral line
Gills
Anal fin
Heart
Anus
Pectoral fin (ghosted)
Pelvic fin
Intestine

Fish: Anatomy of a fish

Fisheye lens: View from a fisheye lens of Wall Street, New York City

Barnaby's

fish /fish/ n (plural **fish** or **fishes**) **1 AQUATIC VERTEBRATE WITH GILLS** any cold-blooded aquatic vertebrate animal that typically has jaws, fins, scales, a slender body, a two-chambered heart, and gills for providing oxygen to the blood (often before nouns) ○ a fish tank **2 FISH CONSUMED AS FOOD** the flesh of any edible fish eaten as food, either cooked or raw (often before nouns) ○ fish soup **3 SOMEBODY UNUSUAL** an odd or unusual person (informal) ○ an odd fish ■ v **1** vi **CATCH FISH** to use a rod, net, or some other method to bring fish out of the water **2** vt **CATCH FISH IN A PLACE** to try to get fish from a particular river, lake, or stream **3** vi **SEARCH** to feel around with the hands in order to find something (informal) [Old English fisc < Indo-European] ◇ **drink like a fish** to habitually drink a lot of alcoholic liquor (informal) ◇ **have other fish to fry** to have something else to do, usually something more interesting (informal) ◇ **like a fish out of water** ill at ease in a situation

fish for vt to search, especially in an indirect way or in difficult circumstances

fish out vt to find something or take something out, especially after searching with the hands (informal) ○ He fished out a coin from his pocket.

Fish n ZODIAC = **Pisces** n. **1**

fish and chips n a fillet of fish deep-fried in batter, served with chips (+ singular or plural verb)

fishbowl /fish bōl/ n **1** a round clear open-topped container of water in which a pet goldfish is kept **2** a place or condition of high public visibility and little or no personal privacy

fish cake n a round flat individual savoury cake made from cooked fish and potato, coated with breadcrumbs, and usually fried

fish duck n BIRDS = **merganser**

fish eagle n BIRDS = **osprey**

fisher /fishər/ n a species of marten, with dense dark brown fur. Native to: N North America. Martes pennanti.

Fisher /fishər/, **Andrew** (1862–1928) Scottish-born Australian statesman

fisherman /fishərmən/ n (plural **-men** /-mən/) n a man who fishes as a sport or occupation

fisherman's bend n a knot used to tie the end of a line to a ring or spar

fisherman's knot n a knot for joining the ends of two ropes, consisting of one or two overhand knots that tighten with tension on the line

fisherwoman /fishər woomən/ n (plural **-men** /-wimmin/) n a woman who catches fish as a sport or occupation

fishery /fishəri/ n (plural **-ies**) n **1 REGION OF WATER FOR FISHING** a region of water where industrial fishing is practised **2 FISHING INDUSTRY** the catching, processing, or selling of fish, including the industries and occupations involved in these activities **3 FISH BUSINESS** a business that harvests, processes, or sells fish **4 PLACE FOR REARING FISH** a region of water or a tank in which fish are reared **5 RIGHT TO FISH** the right to fish in an area

Fishes /fishiz/ n ZODIAC = **Pisces** n. **1**

fisheye lens /fish ī-/ n a wide-angle lens that gives an extremely wide field of vision, up to 180 degrees

fish farm n a place with facilities for rearing fish commercially —**fish farmer** n —**fish farming** n

fish finger n a rectangular stick of filleted or minced fish covered in breadcrumbs or batter, usually bought frozen in packs. US term **fish stick**

fish hawk n BIRDS = **osprey**

fishhook /fish hŏŏk/ n **1** a sharp metal hook used for catching fish **2** a symbol used in logic to represent a conditional such as 'if' or 'then'

fishing /fishing/ n the sport, industry, or occupation of catching fish

fishing ground n an area of sea where a country has the right to fish

fishing rod n a long flexible pole to which a line and usually a reel are attached for catching fish

fish joint n a connection in which two rails or beams are joined together by one or more fishplates

fish knife n a broad-bladed knife with blunt edges, used for eating fish

fish ladder n a series of pools on an incline separated by short increments so as to enable fish to swim up past a dam or other obstruction

fish louse n a small flat rounded crustacean with sucking mouth parts that lives as a parasite on fish. Class: Branchiura.

fishmeal /fish meel/ n a substance prepared from ground dried fish. Use: animal feed, fertilizer.

fishmonger /fish mungər/ n **1** a dealer in fish to eat **2 fishmonger, fishmonger's** a shop where fish is sold

fishnet /fish net/ n **1** open mesh fabric. Use: stockings, tights. **2** US, Can a net used to catch fish

fish owl n a large owl with sharp curved claws that lives in wooded country near water and feeds mainly on fish. Native to: S Asia. Genus: Ketupa.

fishplate /fish playt/ n a flat piece of metal bolted between two abutting rails or beams to join them, especially on a railway track [Mid-19C. < ?]

fishpond /fish pond/ n a pond where fish are found or kept

fishskin disease /fishskin-/ n ichthyosis (informal)

fish slice n a kitchen utensil with a flat slotted blade, used for turning over food during cooking

fish stick n US FOOD = **fish finger**

fishtail /fish tayl/ vi to move the tail of an aeroplane from side to side in order to reduce speed ■ adj describes the back of a skirt or dress that has a section that is closely gathered or pleated and then flares out

fishwife /fish wīf/ n **1** an offensive term for a woman who is regarded as loud-voiced and lacking in manners (insult) **2** a woman selling fish (archaic)

fishy /fishi/ (**-ier, -iest**) adj **1 LIKE FISH** like fish, especially in taste, smell, or coldness or sliminess to the touch **2 DUBIOUS** arousing suspicion (informal) **3 EXPRESSIONLESS** cold and expressionless, like the eye of a fish —**fishily** adv —**fishiness** n

Fisk /fisk/, **Sir Ernest Thomas** (1886–1965) British-born Australian telecommunications engineer

fissi- prefix **1** cleft, separated ○ fissipedal **2** biological fission ○ fissiparous [< Latin fiss-, past participle of findere 'split' < Indo-European]

fissile /fissīl/ adj **1** PHYS = **fissionable 2** describes a rock that can be split along a grain or a plane of cleavage, e.g. slate or schist [Mid-17C. < Latin fiss- (see FISSI-).] —**fissility** /fi síllati/ n

fission /fishən/ n **1 BREAKING UP** the act or process of separating into parts **2 SPLITTING OF ATOMIC NUCLEUS RELEASING ENERGY** the spontaneous or induced splitting of an atomic nucleus into smaller nuclei, usually accompanied by a significant release of energy **3 DIVISION OF AN ORGANISM** the division of a single-celled organism into two equal parts, each part growing into a complete organism [Early 17C. < Latin fission- < fiss- (see FISSI-).]

fissionable /fishʹnəb'l/ adj able to undergo nuclear fission —**fissionability** /fishʹnə billəti/ n

fission bomb n an atom bomb (technical)

fission-track dating n a way to determine the age of a mineral from tracks made by fission products of the uranium it contains

fissiparous /fi sippərəss/ adj describes an organism that reproduces by dividing into two equal parts, each of which grows into a complete organism —**fissiparously** adv

fissiped /fissə ped/ adj **fissiped, fissipedal** describes animals that have toes separated from each other, e.g. dogs and cats ■ n an animal with separate toes. Suborder: Fissipedia. [Mid-17C. < late Latin fissiped- < Latin fiss- (see FISSI-) + ped- 'foot'.]

fissure /fishər/ n **1 CRACK** a long narrow crack or opening, especially in rock **2 PROCESS OF SPLITTING** the process of dividing along a line **3 SPLIT IN BODY PART** a natural or pathological division in a body part **4 SCHISM IN GROUP** a division in a group or party ■ vti (**-sures, -suring, -sured**) **SPLIT OR CAUSE TO SPLIT** to split something along fairly regular lines, or undergo this process [14C. Directly or via French < Latin fissura < fiss- (see FISSI-).]

fist /fist/ n **1 CLENCHED HAND** a hand with the fingers closed in the palm **2 HAND** a hand (informal) **3 FISTFUL** a fistful (informal) **4 PRINTING** = **index** n. **7** ■ v **1** vt **HIT SOMEBODY WITH THE FIST** to hit somebody or something with a fist **2** vti = **fistfuck** (taboo offensive) [Old English fȳst < Germanic] —**fistful** n

fistfight /fist fīt/ n a fight in which bare fists are used

fistfuck /fist fuk/ vti a highly offensive term meaning to insert a fist into somebody's vagina or anus for sexual pleasure (taboo)

fistic /fistik/ adj relating to boxing (informal)

fisticuffs /fisti kufs/ npl fighting using the fists (archaic or humorous) [Early 17C. Probably < fisty 'with the fists' + CUFF[2] 'blow'.]

fistula /fistyoōlə/ (plural **-las** or **-lae** /-lee/) n an abnormal opening or passage between two organs or between an organ and the skin, caused by disease, injury, or congenital malformation [14C. Directly or via French < Latin fistula 'pipe, flute'.] —**fistular** adj —**fistulate** adj —**fistulous** adj

fit[1] /fit/ v (**fits, fitting, fitted**) **1** vti **BE THE RIGHT SIZE OR SHAPE** to be of a suitable size or shape for something or somebody **2** vti **BE APPROPRIATE** to be appropriate or suitable for something ○ make the punishment fit the crime **3** vti **BE COMPATIBLE** to agree or be in accordance with something ○ no one fitting that description **4** vt **TRY CLOTHING ON** to try clothing on somebody to determine if changes are necessary **5** vt **EQUIP** to provide somebody or something with equipment of a particular kind **6** vt **MAKE READY** to make somebody or something ready or suitable for a task, function, or purpose ○ an education that will fit her for a career in business **7** vt **INSTALL** to install something ■ adj (**fitter, fittest**) **1 APPROPRIATE** suitable, acceptable, or appropriate for a purpose **2 WORTHY** worthy or deserving of something ○ not fit to serve as an officer **3 WELL IN HEALTH** in good health **4 STRONG AND HEALTHY** physically strong and healthy, especially because of taking regular exercise ○ getting fit **5 APPEARING LIKELY TO DO SOMETHING** appearing likely to do something because of being in an extreme condition (informal) ○ looked fit to burst in a shirt too small for him ■ n **1 WAY THAT SOMETHING FITS** the way in which something conforms to standards of proper length, tightness, and shape **2 RELATIONSHIP FOR BEST FUNCTION** a relationship between corresponding parts or related things that enables proper functioning **3 CLOSENESS OF SURFACES** the closeness of contact between adjacent surfaces in a mechanical assembly [14C. < ?] ◇ **fit to be tied** very angry and exasperated (*informal*)

fit in *v* 1 *vi* to conform harmoniously to other members of a group or other things in a setting ○ *She's been able to fit in well at her new school.* 2 *vt* to find a time or place for somebody or something that does not disturb other arrangements ○ *The dentist can fit you in at three.*

fit out *vt* to equip or provide something or somebody with required items, e.g. supplies or clothes

fit up *vt* 1 to provide or equip somebody or something with something 2 to make somebody who is innocent appear guilty (*slang*)

fit[2] /fit/ *n* 1 a sudden occurrence of a physical activity or an emotional mood ○ *a fit of laughing* ○ *a coughing fit* 2 sudden violent convulsions, e.g. in a child with a high fever or somebody experiencing a seizure [14C. < ?] ◇ **by fits and starts** starting and stopping repeatedly ◇ **throw a fit** to show strong emotion, especially anger (*informal*)

fitch /fich/, **fitchet** /fíchit/ *n* ZOOL = **polecat** *n.* [15C. < Middle Dutch *fisse*.]

fitchet *n* ZOOL = **fitch**

fitful /fítf'l/ *adj* starting and stopping irregularly ○ *a fitful sleep* —**fitfully** *adv* —**fitfulness** *n*

fitment /fítmənt/ *n* something that can be detached or taken down

fitness /fítnəss/ *n* 1 **BEING PHYSICALLY FIT** the state of being physically fit 2 **SUITABILITY** suitability of somebody or something to a particular purpose 3 **ABILITY TO REPRODUCE SUCCESSFULLY** the ability of an individual to produce off-spring that survive and reproduce

fitness centre *n* a place with facilities such as exercise machines that people can use in order to improve or maintain their physical fitness

fitted /fíttid/ *adj* 1 **MADE TO FIT** tailored to fit closely to the body 2 **BUILT FOR A SPACE** built for and fixed into a designated space 3 **WITH FITTED FURNITURE** with fitted furniture 4 **CUT TO COVER FLOOR** cut to cover a floor area exactly

fitted sheet *n* a sheet with elastic at the corners that makes it fit snugly over a mattress

fitter /fíttər/ *n* 1 a maintainer, repairer, or assembler of mechanical equipment 2 a person who alters clothes to make them fit

fitting /fítting/ *adj* **SUITABLE** appropriate for the circumstances ○ *a fitting end to her career* ■ *n* 1 **DETACHABLE PART** a detachable part, especially for a device or machine 2 **TRYING ON OF CLOTHES** the trying on of a piece of clothing to see if it requires alteration 3 **FITTER'S WORK** the work performed by a fitter 4 **CLOTHES SIZE** a size of clothes or shoes ■ **fittings** *npl* **FURNITURE AND ACCESSORIES** furniture and accessories not permanently fixed to a building —**fittingly** *adv* —**fittingness** *n*

fitting room *n* a room for trying on or fitting clothes in a shop

fit-up *n* (*slang*) 1 = **frame-up** *n.* 1 2 a set and its props that are easily erected

Fitzgerald /fits jérrəld/, **Ella** (1917–96) US jazz singer

Fitzgerald, F. Scott (1890–1940) US writer. Full name **Francis Scott Key Fitzgerald**

Fitzgerald, G. F. (1851–1901) Irish physicist. Full name **George Francis Fitzgerald**

Fitzroy /fits roy/ river in N Western Australia. Length: 620 km/385 mi.

Fitzsimmons /fits símmənz/, **Bob** (1862–1917) British-born New Zealand boxer

five /fīv/ *n* see table at **number** [Old English *fīf* < Indo-European] —**five** *adj, pron*

five-and-dime, five-and-ten, five-and-ten-cent store *n* *US* a shop in the United States of a type, now obsolete, that sold household goods, toys, sweets, small pets, and other assorted items at reasonable prices

five-a-side *n* football with five players in each team, including the goalkeeper, usually played indoors

five-eighth *n* *ANZ* a rugby player positioned between the half-backs and three-quarters

five-finger *n* a plant, e.g. cinquefoil, that has leaves or flowers with five segments

fivefold /fīv fōld/ *adj* 1 **TIMES 5** with or equal to five times as much or as many 2 **WITH 5 PARTS** composed of five parts or sections ■ *adv* **BY FIVE TIMES AS MUCH** by five times as much or as many

five hundred *n* euchre or rummy in which the winner is the first to reach 500 points

five Ks *npl* the five distinctive features of dress worn by members of a Sikh order (**Khalsa**). ◊ **kesh, kangha, kirpan, kuccha, kara**

Five Nations *n* the original Iroquois Confederacy of five Native North American peoples, the Mohawk, Onondaga, Cayuga, Oneida, and Seneca, founded in the 16th century and lasting until 1722. ◊ **Six Nations**

five o'clock shadow *n* beard growth noticeable late in the day on a man who shaved in the morning

five of a kind *n* a poker hand consisting of four cards of the same denomination plus a wild card

fivepenny /fífpəni/ *adj* costing or worth five pence

Five Pillars of Islam *npl* ISLAM = **Pillars of Islam**

fivepins /fívpinz/ *n* a bowling game played in Canada in which five skittles are used (+ *singular verb*)

fiver /fívər/ *n* (*informal*) 1 a note worth five pounds 2 *US* a banknote worth five dollars

fives /fīvz/ *n* a game that resembles squash but in which the ball is hit with the hand or a bat (+ *singular verb*) [Mid-17C. Probably plural of FIVE.]

fivesome /fívsəm/ *n* a group of five people, usually taking part in some activity together

five-spice powder *n* a Chinese mixed spice consisting of star anise, anise or Szechuan pepper, cinnamon, fennel, and cloves

fivespot /fívspot/ *n* *US* a banknote worth five dollars (*slang*)

five-star *adj* having the highest quality

five-star general *n* a general of the highest rank, with an insignia of five stars

five stones *n* the game of jacks when five small stones are used as the throwing pieces (+ *singular verb*)

fix /fiks/ *v* 1 *vt* **MEND OR CORRECT** to repair, mend, or correct something 2 *vt* **AGREE** to agree, arrange, or settle something, especially a time or a price 3 *vt* **FASTEN** to fasten something in place 4 *vt* **ATTRIBUTE** to attribute something, especially blame 5 *vti* **MAKE OR BECOME SECURE** to make something stable, firm, or secure, or become so 6 *vt* **DIRECT** to direct or concentrate the eyes, attention, or mind 7 *vt* **HOLD SOMEBODY'S ATTENTION** to hold or capture the attention or interest of somebody ○ *fixed us with a baleful smile* 8 *vt* **INFLUENCE DISHONESTLY** to influence a person or outcome dishonestly (*informal*) ○ *The trial was fixed.* 9 *vt* **TAKE REVENGE ON** to take revenge on or punish somebody (*informal*) 10 *vt* *US* **PREPARE AS FOOD** to prepare something, especially a meal or a drink (*informal*) 11 *vt* *US* **ARRANGE OR ORDER** to arrange or put something in order (*informal*) 12 *vt* *US* **STERILIZE AN ANIMAL** to spay or castrate an animal (*informal*) 13 *vi* **INJECT A DRUG** to inject an illegal drug (*slang*) 14 *vt* **CONVERT NITROGEN TO A STABLE FORM** to convert atmospheric nitrogen to a stable or biologically available form, as soil bacteria do 15 *vti* **MAKE OR BECOME STABLE** to make a chemical or compound stable and nonvolatile, or undergo this process 16 *vt* **MAKE PERMANENT** to treat something such as a photographic film or plate with chemicals in order to make a permanent image 17 *vt* **PRESERVE FOR EXAMINATION** to preserve a specimen in a chemical solution for study under a microscope ■ *n* 1 **PREDICAMENT** a predicament or difficult situation (*informal*) ○ *in a fix* 2 **SUPERFICIAL SOLUTION** an immediate and often temporary solution (*informal*) ○ *a quick fix* 3 **CALCULATION OF POSITION** a calculation of the position of an object using radar or other forms of observation 4 **UNDERSTANDING** an understanding or identification of something (*informal*) ○ *Do you have a fix on what the problem is?* 5 **INFLUENCING DISHONESTLY** an instance of influencing an outcome or person dishonestly (*informal*) 6 **ILLEGAL DRUG INJECTION** an injection of an illegal drug (*slang*) 7 **STIMULATING DOSE** a dose of or exposure to something pleasurable and stimulating (*humorous*) ○ *a chocolate fix* [15C. < Latin *fix-*, past participle of *figere* 'to fix'.] —**fixable** *adj*

fix on *vt* to select something

fix up *vt* 1 **ARRANGE** to arrange something, e.g. a meeting or a date 2 **ARRANGE A CONTACT FOR** to arrange a business or social contact, or a romantic or sexual partner, for somebody 3 **REPAIR** to restore something to working order or proper order

fixate /fiks áyt/ (**-ates, -ating, -ated**) *v* 1 *vti* **FOCUS** to focus exclusively on something 2 *vt* **OBSESS** to obsess or preoccupy somebody or something totally 3 *vti* **FORM A FIXATION** to form or have a psychological fixation to a person or object 4 *vti* **BECOME OR MAKE FIXED** to make something stable or secure, or become so [Late 19C. < Latin *fix-* (see FIX).]

fixation /fik sáysh'n/ *n* 1 **OBSESSION** an obsession or preoccupation 2 **IMMATURE PSYCHOSEXUAL BEHAVIOUR** a theoretical abnormally strong libidinal attachment to a person or object, formed during early childhood, that results in neurotic or arrested psychosexual behaviour in adulthood 3 **CONVERSION OF NITROGEN** the conversion by soil bacteria of atmospheric nitrogen to a stable biologically available form 4 **STABILIZATION OF CHEMICAL** the process of stabilizing a chemical or compound 5 **PRESERVING FOR EXAMINATION** the preservation of biological specimens with chemicals

fixative /fíksətiv/ *n* 1 **LIQUID SPRAYED FOR PROTECTION** a liquid sprayed onto a drawing, photograph, or other surface to protect it 2 **GLUE** a substance used to hold something in place 3 **PERFUME ADDITIVE** a substance added to a perfume to make it evaporate less rapidly 4 **CHEMICAL PRESERVATIVE** a chemical solution that preserves a biological specimen for microscopic study 5 **FABRIC ADDITIVE** a substance applied to dyed fabrics to make the dye colourfast ■ *adj* **TENDING TO FIX** acting or tending to fix something

fixed /fikst/ *adj* 1 **SECURE** immovable or securely in position 2 **NOT SUBJECT TO CHANGE** not subject to change in amount or time 3 **NOT CHANGING** unchanging in expression 4 **AGREED ON** arranged or agreed upon 5 **HELD IN MIND** firmly or dogmatically held in the mind 6 **PROVIDED** in the position of having something at your disposal (*informal*) ○ *How are you fixed for money?* 7 **DISHONESTLY ARRANGED** unfairly or illegally arranged (*slang*) 8 **CHEMICALLY STABLE** combined in stable form ○ *fixed nitrogen* 9 **STABLE IN ZODIACAL TERMS** describes Taurus, Leo, Scorpio, and Aquarius, signs of the zodiac associated with stability —**fixedly** /fíksidli/ *adv* —**fixedness** /fíksidnəss/ *n*

fixed asset *n* an asset of a business that is central to its operation and is not traded (*usually plural*)

fixed cost *n* a business expense that does not vary according to the amount of business (*usually plural*)

fixed idea *n* PSYCHOL = **idée fixe**

fixed line *adj* describes a telephone that is connected to a network via underground or overground lines ○ *'The card is free and can be used from any mobile or fixed line phone'.* (*Marketing Week*; December 1998)

fixed oil *n* a nonvolatile oil composed of fatty acids, usually of animal or vegetable origin

fixed penalty *n* a fine for a specific amount given for a particular offence

fixed penalty notice *n* a ticket that the police can issue on the spot for minor motoring offences

fixed point *n* a temperature, e.g. boiling or freezing point, that has a fixed value under specific conditions and can be used to calibrate instruments

fixed-point *adj* describes numbers in which the decimal place is always in a fixed position

fixed-wing *adj* describes an aircraft that has stationary wings, especially as distinct from rotor blades

fixer /fíksər/ *n* 1 **SOMEBODY OR SOMETHING THAT FIXES** a person who or an object that fixes something 2 **SOMEBODY WHO ARRANGES SOMETHING DISHONEST** a person who arranges something, especially by dishonest or illegal means (*slang*) 3 **CHEMICAL IN PHOTOGRAPHY** a chemical that halts the development of a photographic image on film or paper

fixing /fíksing/ *n* a means for holding an item in place ■ **fixings** *npl* *US, Can* the ingredients required for a dish

fixity /fíksəti/ (*plural* **-ties**) *n* 1 the quality or state of being fixed and unchanging 2 something that is unchanging (*formal*)

fixture /fíkschər/ *n* 1 **OBJECT IN FIXED POSITION** an object with a fixed position and function 2 **ESTABLISHED PERSON** somebody considered to be permanently established in a place or position 3 **SPORTS EVENT** a sports event or its date 4 **SOCIAL EVENT** a select social event or its date [Late 16C. Probably alteration, after MIXTURE, of *fixure* < late Latin *fixura* < Latin *fix-* (see FIX).]

fizgig /fízgig/ *n* 1 a flippant or flirtatious girl (*dated*) 2 a firework that fizzes when in motion [Early 16C. Probably < FIZZ + *gig* 'giddy girl'.]

fizz /fiz/ *vi* (**fizzes, fizzing, fizzed**) 1 **PRODUCE GAS BUBBLES** to produce bubbles of gas 2 **HISS** to make a hissing or continuous soft crackling sound ■ *n* 1 **EFFERVESCENCE** the sparkling quality of a drink caused by bubbles of gas

2 **HISSING SOUND** a hissing or continuous soft crackling sound 3 **LIVELINESS** a quality of liveliness or excitement ○ *All the fizz has gone out of the election campaign.* 4 **SPARKLING DRINK** a sparkling drink, especially champagne [Mid-17C. An imitation of the sound.]

fizzer /fízzər/ *n Aus* an event that fails to live up to expectations (*informal*)

fizzle /fízz'l/ *vi* (**-zles, -zling, -zled**) 1 **MAKE HISSING SOUND** to make a gentle hissing sound 2 **FAIL AFTER GOOD START** to fail or peter out, especially after a good start ■ *n* 1 **HISSING SOUND** a gentle hissing sound 2 **FAILURE** a fiasco or total failure (*informal*) [Mid-16C. Probably < obsolete *fist* 'break wind' < Germanic.]

fizzy /fízzi/ (**-ier, -iest**) *adj* producing or containing gas bubbles —**fizzily** *adv* —**fizziness** *n*

fj *abbr* Fiji (*in Internet addresses*)

fjord /fee awrd/, **fiord** *n* a long narrow coastal inlet with steep sides, often formed by glacial action, especially along the western coast of Norway [Late 17C. Via Norwegian < Old Norse *fjörðr*.]

Fkr *abbr* Faroese krona

FL *abbr* 1 Florida 2 Liechtenstein (*international vehicle registration*) 3 Flight Lieutenant

fl. *abbr* 1 floor 2 florin 3 floruit 4 flute

Fl. *abbr* 1 Flanders 2 Flemish

Fla. *abbr* Florida

flab /flab/ *n* excess or unwanted fat on somebody's body (*informal*) [Early 20C. Back-formation < FLABBY.]

flabbergast /flábbər gaast/ *vt* to amaze or astonish somebody completely (*informal; usually passive*) [Late 18C. < ?]

flabby /flábbi/ (**-bier, -biest**) *adj* (*informal*) 1 having excess body fat or sagging flesh 2 done without vitality or force [Late 17C. Alteration of *flappy*.] —**flabbily** *adv* —**flabbiness** *n*

flabella plural of **flabellum**

flabellate /flə béllit/, **flabelliform** /flə bélli fawrm/ *adj* shaped like an open handheld fan [Late 18C. < Latin *flabellum* (see FLABELLUM).]

flabellum /flə béllәm/ (*plural* **-la** /-lə/) *n* 1 fan-shaped organ or body part 2 a fan with a long handle, formerly used in the Roman Catholic Church to keep away insects during the Mass [Mid-19C. < Latin, 'fan' < *flabrum* 'gust' < *flare* 'to blow'.]

flaccid /fláksid/ *adj* 1 soft, limp, or lacking firmness 2 lacking energy, enthusiasm, or competence [Early 17C. Directly or via French < Latin *flaccidus* < *flaccus* 'flabby'.] —**flaccidity** /flak síddəti, fla-/ *n* —**flaccidly** *adv*

~~**flacid**~~ incorrect spelling of **flaccid**

flack[1] /flak/ *n US, Can* a press agent or publicist (*slang*) ■ *vti US, Can* to act as a press agent or publicity agent for somebody (*slang*) [Mid-20C. < ?] —**flacker** *n* —**flackery** *n*

flack[2] *n* = **flak**

flacon /flákən/ *n* a small, often decorated, stoppered bottle used especially for perfume [Early 19C. < French (see FLAGON).]

flag[1] /flag/ *n* 1 **CLOTH FLOWN AS EMBLEM** a piece of cloth, often rectangular and flown from a pole, carrying a distinctive design and used as an emblem or for signalling 2 **DECORATION** a small ornament, emblem, or badge showing the colours and design of a flag 3 **NATIONAL IDENTITY SYMBOLIZED BY FLAG** national or group identity symbolized by a flag 4 **MARKING DEVICE** a marking device, e.g. a tab, attached to something to make it easier to identify or more conspicuous 5 MEDIA = **masthead** *n.* 2 6 NAVY = **flagship** *n.* 1 7 **HAIR FRINGE BENEATH DOG'S TAIL** a fringe of hair that grows on the lower part of the tail in some dog breeds, e.g. setters 8 **DEER'S TAIL** the tail of a deer 9 **PENALTY MARKER** a coloured cloth thrown to the ground by a football official in American football to indicate illegal play 10 **MARKER SHOWING A TAXI FOR HIRE** formerly, a small marker on a taximeter, raised to show a taxi's availability for hire 11 **COMPUTER PROGRAM MARKER** an indicator generated by a computer program to indicate a certain condition, e.g. an error 12 **NOTE MARKER** an angled line on the stem of a musical note, indicating its value ■ *vt* (**flags, flagging, flagged**) 1 **MARK** to mark something, e.g. a page or a place, in order to draw attention to it ○ *I've flagged the passages that need rewriting.* 2 **INDICATE** to draw somebody's attention to something ○ *'The...service is quick to flag up offers and discounts to new members'.* (*Internet Magazine*; November 1998) 3 **SEND INFORMATION BY FLAG** to send information using a flag or flags 4 **STOP VEHICLE BY WAVING AT DRIVER** to make a vehicle or its driver stop by making signs to the driver 5 **INDICATE PENALTY** to indicate a penalty in American football by throwing down a flag 6 **DECORATE SOMETHING WITH FLAGS** to decorate something with flags 7 **ATTRACT ANIMAL'S ATTENTION** to attract the attention or curiosity of wild game by waving something [Mid-16C. < ?] —**flagger** *n* ◇ **show the flag** to attend a gathering just to show loyalty or support towards a country, company, or family

flag[2] /flag/ (**flags, flagging, flagged**) *vi* 1 to become weak, tired, or less attentive 2 to hang down limply, or droop [Mid-16C. < ?]

flag[3] /flag/ *n* = **flagstone** *n.* 1 ■ *vt* (**flags, flagging, flagged**) to pave a surface with flagstones [15C. Probably < N Germanic.] —**flagged** *adj*

flag[4] /flag/ *n* 1 a plant of the iris family, usually one with large flowers and leaves 2 a long narrow leaf of a plant such as an iris [14C. < ?]

flag captain *n* the captain of the flagship of a fleet

flag day *n* a day on which people collect money for a charity, and those who contribute are given a small sticker. US term **tag day**

Flag Day *n* a holiday in the United States marking the official adoption of the design of the US flag in 1777. Date: 14 June.

flagella plural of **flagellum**

flagellant /flájjələnt/, **flagellator** /flájjə laytər/ *n* 1 a penitent who whips himself or herself as a means of repentance 2 a person who uses whipping to achieve pleasure [Late 16C. < Latin *flagellant-*, present participle of *flagellare* 'whip' < *flagellum* (see FLAGELLUM).] —**flagellantism** *n*

flagellar /flə jéllər/ *adj* relating to a flagellum

flagellate[1] /flájjə layt/ (**-lates, -lating, -lated**) *vt* to whip somebody, especially for sexual or religious purposes [Early 17C. < Latin *flagellat-*, past participle of *flagellare* 'to whip' < *flagellum* (see FLAGELLUM).]

flagellate[2] /flájjələt, -layt/ *n* **MICROORGANISM WITH FLAGELLA** a microorganism with tiny cellular appendages (**flagella**) ■ *adj* **flagellate, flagellated** 1 **RESEMBLING A LONG THREAD** similar to a long thin cellular appendage (**flagellum**) 2 **WITH APPENDAGES RESEMBLING THREADS** describes an organism or cell that has long thin cellular appendages (**flagella**) [Mid-19C. <FLAGELLUM.]

flagellation[1] /flájjəláysh'n/ *n* the act of whipping yourself or somebody else, especially for sexual or religious purposes

flagellation[2] /flájjə láysh'n/ *n* the formation or arrangement of flagella on an organism

flagellator /flájjə laytər/ *n* RELIG, PSYCHOL = **flagellant**

flagelliform /flə jéllə fawrm/ *adj* long, tapering, and very narrow [Early 19C. < FLAGELLUM.]

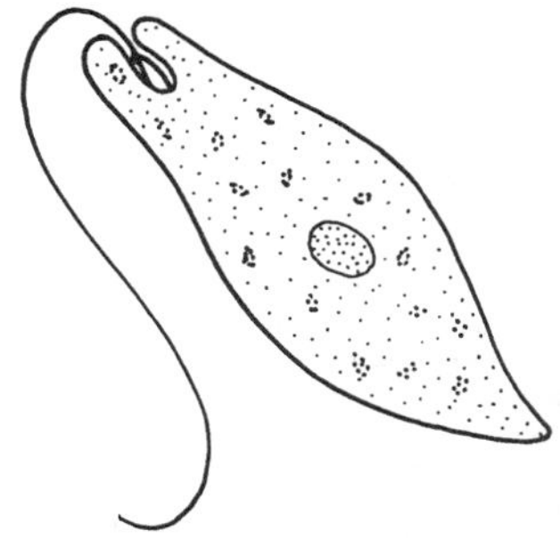

Flagellum

flagellum /flə jélləm/ (*plural* **flagella** /-lə/ *or* **flagellums**) *n* 1 a slender tapering narrow outgrowth of the cells of many microorganisms, e.g. protozoa, that is a means of locomotion 2 the very narrow terminal part of an insect's antenna [Early 19C. < Latin, 'little scourge' < *flagrum* 'scourge'.]

flageolet[1] /flájjə lét/ *n* a slender-podded variety of French bean that can be eaten either fresh or dried [Late 19C. Via French < Latin *phaseolus* 'bean'.]

flageolet[2] /flájjə lét/ *n* a musical instrument of the 16th and 17th centuries resembling the flute [Mid-17C. < French, 'little flute' < Old French *flageol* 'flute'.]

flag fall *n* the minimum amount charged for the hire of a taxi

flagging[1] /flágging/ *adj* decreasing in strength, power, or ability —**flaggingly** *adv*

flagging[2] /flágging/ *n* an area paved with flagstones

flagitious /flə jíshəss/ *adj* (*formal*) 1 extremely cruel, wicked, or vicious 2 notorious or infamous [14C. < Latin *flagitiosus* < *flagitium* 'shameful crime' < *flagitare* 'demand vehemently'.] —**flagitiously** *adv* —**flagitiousness** *n*

flagman /flágmən/ (*plural* **-men** /-mən/) *n* a holder of a flag, usually to make signals

flag of convenience *n* a flag of a country under which a ship is registered because of its favourable regulations, not for any real connection with the ship's owners or business

flag officer *n* a naval officer of a rank at or above rear admiral

flag of truce *n* a white flag flown to indicate surrender, a request or offer of conference, or other peaceful intent

flagon /flággən/ *n* 1 **JUG** a jug with a handle, narrow neck, spout, and sometimes a lid 2 **LARGE BOTTLE FOR ALCOHOLIC DRINK** a large bottle with a short or narrow neck for an alcoholic drink, especially cider 3 **FLAGON'S CONTENTS** the amount that a flagon will hold [14C. Via French *flacon* < late Latin *flascon-* 'flask'.]

flagpole /flág pōl/ *n* a pole on which a flag is flown

flag rank *n* a rank at admiral level that entitles the holder to fly a Royal Navy flag or pennant

flagrant /fláygrənt/ *adj* very obvious and contrary to standards of conduct or morality ○ *a flagrant violation of the suspect's civil rights* [15C. Directly or via French < Latin *flagrant-*, present participle of *flagrare* 'to burn'.] —**flagrance** *n* —**flagrancy** *n* —**flagrantly** *adv*

USAGE See ***blatant***.

flagship /flág ship/ *n* 1 **COMMANDING SHIP** the ship from which the admiral or unit commander controls the operation of a fleet 2 **MAIN COMMERCIAL SHIP** the main ship in a commercial fleet 3 **MOST IMPORTANT OF GROUP** the most important or prestigious among a group of similar and related things ○ *the flagship of the hotel chain*

flagstaff /flág staaf/ *n* = **flagpole**

flagstick /flág stik/ *n* the flagpole that marks the position of the hole on a putting green

flagstone /flág stōn/ *n* 1 a slab of stone or concrete used for making floors or paving 2 fine-textured rock that can be split into slabs suitable for use in paving

flag stop *n US* a station or place where a bus or train stops only when signalled by somebody waiting to board

flag-waving *n* an excessive and emotional display of patriotism —**flag-waver** *n*

Flaherty /flaáhərti/, **Robert Joseph** (1884–1951) US documentary filmmaker

flail /flayl/ *v* 1 *vti* **THRASH AROUND** to thrash or swing something around violently or uncontrollably, or move in this way 2 *vt* **HIT** to strike or hit something ■ *n* 1 **MANUAL THRESHING IMPLEMENT** a manual threshing implement consisting of a wooden handle attached to a free-swinging wooden or metal bar 2 **WEAPON SHAPED LIKE FLAIL** a weapon shaped like a threshing flail, used especially in the Middle Ages [Pre-12C. Probably via an assumed Old English word (influenced by Old French *flaiel*) < Latin *flagellum* (see FLAGELLUM).]

flair /flair/ *n* 1 a natural ability or aptitude 2 obvious elegance or stylishness [Late 19C. < French, 'sense of smell' < Old French *flairer* 'to smell' < late Latin *flagrare*, alteration of Latin *fragrare* 'emit an odour'.]

SPELLCHECK See ***flare***.

SYNONYMS See ***talent***.

flak /flak/, **flack** *n* 1 anti-aircraft fire directed from the ground 2 strong adverse criticism (*informal*) [Mid-20C. < German, acronym < *Flieger Abwehr Kanone* 'aeroplane defence canon'.]

flake[1] /flayk/ *n* 1 **SMALL FLAT PIECE** a small flat piece or small part of a layer broken or detached from a larger object 2 **SMALL MANUFACTURED ITEM** a small thin flat object that is manufactured, sold, and used or consumed in quantity **3** *US* **ODD PERSON** an eccentric or irrational person (*informal insult*) **4** *Aus* **FISH AS FOOD** the flesh of various types of shark and similar fish, sold as food and often used for fish and chips ■ *v* (**flakes, flaking, flaked**) **1** *vi* **FALL OFF IN FLAKES** to form into flakes and fall or peel off **2** *vt* **BREAK SOMETHING INTO FLAKES** to break something into flakes, or break flakes from something **3** *vt* **COVER SOMETHING WITH FLAKES** to cover or coat something with flakes [14C. Probably < N Germanic.] —**flaker** *n*

flake out *vi* to collapse or fall asleep because of exhaustion

flake^2 *n, vt* NAUT = **fake**^{2}

flake white *n* a pigment made from flakes of white lead

flak jacket *n* a reinforced vest or jacket for protection against gunfire or shrapnel

flaky /fláyki/ (**-ier, -iest**) *adj* **1 LIKE FLAKES** made of or similar to flakes **2 TENDING TO BREAK OFF IN FLAKES** forming or tending to break off in flakes **3** *US* **UNCONVENTIONAL** considered unconventional or irrational (*informal*) —**flakily** *adv* —**flakiness** *n*

flaky pastry *n* a pastry made from layers of pastry dough dotted with fat that puffs up and forms light layers when baked

flam /flam/ *n* a drumbeat of two nearly simultaneous strokes [Late 18C. Probably an imitation of the sound.]

flambé /flóm bay/, **flambée** *vt* (**-bées, -béeing, -béed**) to pour an alcoholic spirit over food and light it in order to burn off the alcohol and impart the flavour of the spirit to the food ■ *adj* served with an alcoholic spirit, usually brandy, that has been poured over the food and burnt off or left burning ○ *bananas flambé* [Late 19C. < French, past participle of *flamber* 'singe, pass through flame' < Latin *flamma* 'flame'.]

flambeau /flámbō/ (*plural* **-beaux** /-bōz/ *or* **-beaus**) *n* **1** a lighted torch made of wicks dipped in wax **2** a large decorative candlestick [Mid-17C. < French, 'torch, flame' < *flambe* (see FLAMBOYANT).]

Flamborough Head /flámbərə-/ headland in E Yorkshire, N England

flamboyant /flam bóyənt/ *adj* **1 SHOWY** showy and dashing in a self-satisfied way **2 BRIGHTLY-COLOURED** brightly-coloured and striking **3 HIGHLY DECORATED** elaborate or richly decorated **4 AUDACIOUS** unrestrained by prevailing standards of propriety **5 OF FRENCH GOTHIC ARCHITECTURE** used to refer to the final stage of French Gothic architecture from the 14th to the 16th centuries that is noted for its fine detailing and pointed decoration [Mid-19C. < French, present participle of *flamboyer* 'blaze' < *flambe* 'flame' < Latin *flamma* 'flame'.] —**flamboyance** *n* —**flamboyantly** *adv*

⚡**flame** /flaym/ *n* **1 HOT GLOWING BODY OF BURNING GAS** a hot glowing body of burning gas, often carrying fine incandescent particles **2 STRONG FEELING** an intense feeling or emotion **3 LOVER** a sweetheart or lover (*informal*) ○ *an old flame* **4 REDDISH-ORANGE COLOUR** a brilliant reddish-orange colour **5 ANGRY E-MAIL MESSAGE** a rude, abusive, or threatening e-mail message or newsgroup posting ■ *v* (**flames, flaming, flamed**) **1** *vi* **PRODUCE FLAME** to burn producing flame **2** *vi* **HAVE FIERY GLOW** to have or develop a fiery glow, especially suddenly ○ *Her cheeks flamed as she spoke.* **3** *vi* **FEEL STRONG EMOTION** to display or feel intense emotion **4** *vt* **SET FIRE TO SOMETHING** to set fire to something **5** *vt* **MAKE SOMETHING BURN** to make something burn (*archaic*) **6** *vti* **CRITICIZE SOMEBODY BY E-MAIL** to criticize somebody with offensive and disparaging e-mail [14C. Via Anglo-Norman and French < Latin *flamma* 'flame'.] —**flame** *adj* —**flamer** *n* —**flamy** *adj* ◇ **fan the flames** to make a tense or difficult situation worse ◇ **shoot somebody** *or* **something down in flames** to reject or refute an idea or suggestion emphatically

flame-arc lamp *n* a lamp that uses an electric arc maintained between carbon electrodes that are infused with metallic salts to provide colour to the flame

flame carbon *n* a carbon electrode containing metallic salts that, with other similar carbon electrodes, has the effect of colouring the arc produced between the electrodes

flame cell *n* a hollow excretory cell in certain invertebrates, e.g. flatworms, that has a tuft of projections (**cilia**) resembling hairs whose movement serves to force out waste products [Because the movement of the cilia suggests tongues of flame]

flame gun *n* a flame-thrower used to burn weeds

flamen /fláymən/ (*plural* **flamens** *or* **flamines** /flámmi neez/) *n* a priest in ancient Rome belonging to a group of 15, each of whom oversaw the rituals connected with a particular deity [14C. < Latin.]

flamenco /flə méngkō/ (*plural* **-cos**) *n* **1** a dance of Spanish origin with hand clapping and stamping of feet **2** the strongly rhythmic music that accompanies flamenco dancing [Late 19C. Via Spanish, 'Flemish person' < Middle Dutch *Vlaming*.]

flameout /fláym owt/ *n* the unintentional extinguishing of the flame of a jet engine in flight, e.g. through a failure of combustion or the fuel supply

flameproof /fláym proof/ *adj* **1 RESISTANT TO FIRE** resistant to catching fire (*often used of textiles and clothing*) **2 NOT EXPLOSIVE** describes electrical apparatus designed so that an explosion of inflammable gas inside will not ignite inflammable gas outside **3 FOR COOKING WITH DIRECT HEAT** describes containers that can be used when cooking on a hob or under a grill ■ *vt* **MAKE SOMETHING FLAME RESISTANT** to make something resistant to flames or combustion —**flameproofer** *n*

flame-retardant, flame-resistant *adj* made or chemically treated to resist catching fire

flame test *n* a test for the presence of various metals in a substance by noting the colours produced when a small amount is placed in a flame and vaporized

flame-thrower *n* a weapon that projects a stream of burning liquid

flame tree *n* **1** a tropical tree cultivated for its bright orange, yellow, or red flowers, e.g. royal poinciana **2** a tree with bright red flowers that bloom in spring before its leaves emerge. Native to: Australia. *Brachychiton acerifolius*.

⚡**flame war** *n* a period of repeated exchanges of abusive and insulting e-mail between individuals or groups

flamines plural of **flamen**

⚡**flaming** /fláyming/ *adj* **1 PRODUCING FLAMES** burning and producing flames **2 INTENSE** very angry, intense, or passionate ○ *flaming indignation* **3 GLOWING** brightly glowing ○ *flaming cheeks* **4 VIVID IN COLOUR** vivid in colour **5 USED TO EXPRESS ANGER** used to emphasize the following word or phrase and especially to express anger or annoyance (*informal*) ○ *I wish they wouldn't play their flaming music so loud!* ■ *n* **DELUGE OF CRITICAL E-MAIL** a large volume of abusive and insulting e-mail directed at somebody

flamingo /flə míng gō/ (*plural* **-gos** *or* **-goes** *or* **-go**) *n* **1** a large long-necked wading bird with a downward-curving bill, webbed feet, and pinkish-white feathers with black wing quills. Native to: tropical brackish waters. Family: Phoenicopteridae. **2** a deep pink colour tinged with orange [Mid-16C. Via Portuguese < obsolete Spanish *flamengo*.] —**flamingo** *adj*

flaming sword *n* a cultivated bromeliad, or subshrub. Flowers: yellow with reddish bract pigmentation. Native to: French Guiana. *Vriesea splendens*.

flammable /flámməb'l/ *adj* readily capable of catching fire —**flammability** /flámmə bílləti/ *n*

flan /flan/ *n* **1** an open, usually round, pastry or sponge case with a savoury or fruit filling **2** a circular metal blank ready to be stamped as a coin [Mid-19C. Via French < medieval Latin *fladon-* < Germanic.]

Flanders /flaándərz/ historical region of NW Europe comprising parts of present-day W Belgium, N France, and SW Netherlands

flâneur /flaa núr/ *n* an idler or loafer [Mid-19C. < French, < *flâner* 'stroll, lounge about'.]

flange /flanj/ *n* a projecting collar, rim, or rib on an object for fixing it to another object, holding it in place, or strengthening it [Late 17C. < ?] —**flanged** *adj*

flanged rail *n* an early form of rail with a raised edge (**flange**) on one side to stabilize wheels travelling on it

flank /flangk/ *n* **1 SIDE OF LOWER TORSO** either side of the body of a human being or an animal between the last rib and the hip **2 CUT OF MEAT FROM ANIMAL'S FLANK** a cut of meat, especially beef, from an animal's flank, that is typically tough and requires slow cooking in liquid **3 SIDE OF SOMETHING** the side of any object **4 SIDE OF MILITARY FORMATION** the left or right side of a military formation **5 SIDE OF SPORTS FIELD** either of the sides of a sports field ■ *vt* **BE BY SIDE OF** to be on or at the side of something or somebody ○ *He was flanked by secret service officers.* [Pre-12C. < French *flanc*.]

flanker /flángkər/ *n* **1** a soldier in a unit that protects the flank of a military column on the march **2** a wing forward who plays on either of the flanks **3** AMERICAN FOOTBALL = **flankerback** **4** AMERICAN FOOTBALL = **split end** *n.* 2

flankerback /flánkər bak/ *n* in American football, an offensive back positioned outside the play formation

flannel /flánn'l/ *n* **1 SOFT COTTON CLOTH** a soft cotton cloth with a nap on one side. Use: clothing, sleepwear, sheets. **2 SOFT WOOLLEN CLOTH** a soft closely woven woollen or wool-blend cloth. Use: clothing. **3** = **facecloth** **4 INSINCERE OR EVASIVE TALK** indirect, empty, deceptive, or flattering talk (*informal*) ■ **flannels** *npl* **1 TROUSERS MADE OF FLANNEL** clothing, especially trousers, made from flannel **2 WHITE TROUSERS WORN FOR CRICKET** white long trousers worn when playing particular sports, especially cricket ■ *v* (**flannels, flannelling, flanelled**) **1** *vt* **WRAP SOMEBODY IN FLANNEL** to wrap or clothe somebody in flannel or flannels **2** *vt* **CLEAN SOMETHING WITH FLANNEL** to wash, clean, or rub somebody or something with a flannel **3** *vti* **TALK IN EVASIVE OR INSINCERE WAY** to talk, or talk to somebody, in an evasive or flattering way, especially to deceive [14C. < ?] —**flannelly** *adj*

flannelboard /flánn'l bawrd/ *n* a board covered with flannel to which pictures and cloth cutouts will stick that is used in primary education

flannelette /flánnə lét/ *n* a light cotton cloth with a soft brushed surface on one side

flannelflower /flánn'l flowər/ *n* a wild plant with white flowers and soft white hairs. Native to: E Australia. *Actinotus helianthi*.

Flannery /flánnəri/, **Tim** (*b.* 1956) Australian biologist

flan ring *n* a round tin with a removable base, for cooking a flan or quiche

flap /flap/ *v* (**flaps, flapping, flapped**) **1** *vti* **MOVE WINGS UP AND DOWN** to move something up and down, especially wings or arms during or as if in flight, or be moved up and down in this way **2** *vi* **FLY BY MOVING WINGS** to fly by moving the wings repeatedly **3** *vti* **MOVE OR SWAY REPEATEDLY** to cause something to move or sway in one direction and then another repeatedly and often noisily, or move in this way ○ *flags flapping in the breeze* **4** *vi* **BE PANICKY** to be flustered or panicky (*informal*) **5** *vt* **HIT WITH BROAD OBJECT** to hit somebody or something with a broad flat object **6** *vt* **TOSS** to fling down or toss something (*informal*) ○ *flapped the report on the table* **7** *vt* **MAKE AN 'R' SOUND** to make an 'r' sound by briefly striking the roof of the mouth with the tongue, as in 'parrot' ■ *n* **1 FLAT THIN PIECE USED AS COVER** a flat thin piece attached along one edge, usually used as a cover for an opening **2 DUST JACKET PART** either of the two parts of a dust jacket that fold inside a book's cover and are usually printed with information about the book or author **3 ACT OR SOUND OF FLAPPING** an act of or the sound made by flapping ○ *The bird disappeared with a flap of its wings.* **4 A PANICKED STATE** a state of panic or upset (*informal*) ○ *Don't get into a flap about it.* **5 BLOW FROM BROAD OBJECT** a blow or slap from a broad object **6 AIRCRAFT WING CONTROL SURFACE** a narrow movable surface attached to the rear edge of an aircraft wing that is used to create lift or drag **7 MASS OF TISSUE FOR GRAFTING** a mass of tissue, used for surgical grafting, that remains partially attached and retains its blood supply **8 'R' SOUND** an 'r' sound made by briefly striking the roof of the mouth with the tongue, as in 'parrot' [14C. < ?] —**flappy** *adj*

flapdoodle /fláp dood'l/ *n* silly talk or nonsense (*slang*) [Mid-19C. < ?]

flapjack /fláp jak/ *n* **1** a cake made of oats, syrup, and butter and cut into squares before eating **2** *US* FOOD = **pancake** *n.* 1

flappable /fláppəb'l/ *adj* tending to get flustered or panicky (*informal*)

flapper /fláppər/ *n* **1 YOUNG UNCONVENTIONAL WOMAN OF THE 1920S** a young woman of the 1920s who disdained conventions of decorum and fashion **2 YOUNG BIRD** a bird that is learning to fly **3 SOMETHING FLAPPING AROUND** an object that flaps around **4 BROAD FLAT OBJECT** a broad flat object used for striking something

flare /flair/ *v* (**flares, flaring, flared**) **1** *vti* **BURN SUDDENLY AND BRIGHTLY** to burn, or cause something to burn, suddenly and brightly **2** *vi* **START UP AGAIN** to recur, worsen, or intensify suddenly **3** *vi* **BECOME ANGRY** to become suddenly angry **4** *vti* **WIDEN OUT** to widen out, or cause something to widen out ○ *Her nostrils flared.* **5** *vt* **SIGNAL SOMEBODY FOR HELP** to signal somebody for help by means of a device used to produce a light signal **6** *vt* **BURN OFF**

GAS to ignite and burn off unwanted waste gas in open air ■ *n* 1 SUDDEN BLAZE OF LIGHT a sudden blaze of light or fire, especially one used to signal distress or location or used for illumination ○ *the flare of naval signal lights* 2 DEVICE FOR PRODUCING FLARE a device used to produce a light signal calling for help ○ *a distress flare* 3 FLAME a sudden or unsteady flame ○ *the flare of distant oil wells* 4 WIDENING SHAPE a shape that widens out ○ *a long skirt with a flare* 5 OUTBURST OF EMOTION a sudden outburst, especially of a negative emotion ○ *a flare of anger* 6 SHORT AND WIDE PASS in American football, a pass to a back running laterally 7 UNWANTED LIGHT IN AN OPTICAL DEVICE unwanted light reaching a photographic image, especially when reflected from an internal lens 8 FLAME FOR BURNING OFF WASTE GAS a flame that burns off unwanted waste gas in the open air 9 INFLAMMATION an area of inflammation on the skin ■ **flares** *npl* TROUSERS WITH WIDE LEGS BELOW KNEE trousers with legs that widen significantly below the knee, first popular in the late 1960s [Mid-16C. < ?] —**flared** *adj*

SPELLCHECK Do not confuse ***flare*** with ***flair***, which has a similar sound. Beware: your spellchecker will not catch this error.

flareback /fláir bak/ *n* 1 a flame inside a gun's breech caused by the ignition of gases remaining after the weapon has been fired 2 a reaction or effect directed back towards a point of origin

flare stack *n* a large open-air burner used to dispose of excess flammable gas at an oil refinery, well, or platform

flare-up *n* 1 SUDDEN OUTBURST OF AGGRESSION a sudden occurrence of emotion or violence (*informal*) 2 RECURRENCE a recurrence of something, especially a disease 3 SUDDEN OCCURRENCE OF FIRE OR LIGHT a sudden occurrence or increase of fire or light

flaring /fláiring/ *adj* 1 BURNING DIMLY burning dimly or unsteadily 2 SHOWY bright and showy 3 BECOMING WIDER widening out —**flaringly** *adv*

flash /flash/ *v* 1 *vti* EMIT LIGHT SUDDENLY to cause light to appear suddenly or in brief bursts from something, or appear in this way 2 *vti* REFLECT LIGHT FROM ANOTHER SOURCE to reflect light suddenly or briefly, or make something such as a lamp reflect from a surface 3 *vti* CATCH FIRE SUDDENLY to burst into flame suddenly, or cause something to burst into flame 4 *vti* SIGNAL TO SOMEBODY WITH LIGHTS to signal to somebody or communicate something by quickly turning lights on and off 5 *vi* MOVE QUICKLY to move or pass very quickly in a particular direction 6 *vti* APPEAR MOMENTARILY to appear briefly, or cause something to appear briefly ○ *flash a message onto the screen* 7 *vi* EXPOSE BODY INDECENTLY IN PUBLIC to expose the genitals briefly and intentionally in public (*informal*) 8 *vt* DISPLAY OSTENTATIOUSLY to show off or display something in order to impress people (*informal*) ○ *She's always flashing her money around.* 9 *vt* FILL WITH RUSH OF WATER to fill something suddenly with a great flow of water 10 *vt* COAT FOR PROTECTION to cover the surface of an object with a thin coating, usually for protection or as a stage in processing 11 *vt* PROTECT ROOF FROM LEAKING to install flashing on a roof joint or window joint to make it waterproof ■ *n* 1 SUDDEN BURST OF LIGHT a sudden bright display of light, fire, or something bright ○ *flashes of lightning* 2 SUDDEN BURST OF MOOD OR THOUGHT a sudden occurrence of an emotional mood or intellectual activity ○ *a flash of inspiration* 3 LIGHT PATCH a patch of light or bright colour on a dark background, e.g. on an animal's coat 4 BRIGHT LIGHTING USED IN PHOTOGRAPHY the brief illumination of a subject for photographic purposes 5 DEVICE USED TO LIGHT PHOTOGRAPHIC SUBJECT a device used in flash photography to produce a short bright light (*informal*) 6 RUSH OF WATER a sudden rush of water down a watercourse, or a device that produces this 7 SHORT NEWS BROADCAST a sudden important news story requiring immediate broadcast (*informal*) 8 BADGE ON UNIFORM OR VEHICLE a badge or insignia on a uniform or vehicle 9 COLOURED STRIP WORN ON SOCKS in Highland dress, a short strip of coloured material folded over the garter and protruding below the folded-over top of the socks (*usually plural*) 10 LANGUAGE USED IN UNDERWORLD the language used by criminals, thieves, and their associates (*archaic slang*) ■ *adj* 1 SHOWY expensive or expensive-looking, especially in a showy and vulgar way (*informal*) ○ *with his big car and his flash clothes* 2 INSINCERE insincere, false, or counterfeit ○ *an outpouring of flash sentiment* 3 sudden and brief ○ *flash thunderstorms* [13C. Probably an imitation of the sound of splashing.] —**flashness** *n* ◇ **a flash in the pan** a sudden brief success that is not, or not likely to be, repeated ◇ **in a flash** 1 very rapidly 2 suddenly

flash back *vi* 1 to recall an intensely vivid memory of a traumatic experience 2 to go back to a scene at an earlier point in a narrative, out of chronological order, to fill in information or explain something in the present

flash forward *vi* to jump forward in time to a scene at a later point in a narrative, out of chronological order, usually for dramatic effect or irony

flashback /flásh bak/ *n* 1 PAINFUL MEMORY an intensely vivid memory of a traumatic experience that returns repeatedly 2 EARLIER EVENT OR SCENE a scene or event from the past that appears in a narrative out of chronological order, to fill in information or explain something in the present ○ *Much of the film's exposition is handled through flashbacks.* 3 DRUG AFTER EFFECT the later experiencing of the effects of a hallucinogenic drug such as LSD long after discontinuing use of the drug

flash blindness *n* temporary blindness after the flash of a gun discharge or other explosion, particularly at night

flashboard /flásh bawrd/ *n* a structure made of boards fitted at the top of a dam to add to its height and increase the amount of water that can be held back

flashbulb /flásh bulb/ *n* a small glass bulb filled with shredded metallic foil that produces a brief intense flash of light for taking photographs

flash burn *n* a burn caused by brief exposure to a source of intense heat

flashcard /flásh kaard/ *n* a card with words or numbers printed on it that is briefly displayed as a learning device

flasher /fláshər/ *n* 1 FLASHING LIGHT a light that flashes as a signal, especially one on a road vehicle used to indicate the direction in which the driver intends to turn 2 DEVICE MAKING LIGHT FLASH a device that switches a light on and off automatically to make it flash 3 SOMEBODY WHO EXPOSES PRIVATE PARTS a person, especially a man, who gains pleasure from publicly exposing the genitals (*informal*)

flash flood *n* a sudden and often destructive surge of water down a narrow channel or sloping ground, usually caused by heavy rainfall

flash-forward *n* a scene or event from the future that appears in a narrative out of chronological order, usually for dramatic effect or irony

flashgun /flásh gun/ *n* a device that holds a flashtube or flashbulb and automatically discharges it as the attached camera's shutter opens

flashing /fláshing/ *n* pieces of sheet metal attached around the joints and angles of a roof to protect against leakage

flashlight /flásh līt/ *n* 1 *US* = **torch** *n.* 1 2 a brief intense flash of light produced by a photographic lamp 3 any bright light that flashes, e.g. a beacon

⚡**flash memory** *n* a programmable read-only computer memory chip that can be erased and reprogrammed in blocks rather than single bytes

flashover /flásh ōvər/ *n* an unintended electric arc around or over the surface of an insulator

flash photography *n* photography that illuminates its subject with a brief flash of artificial light

flash photolysis *n* a method of studying photochemical reactions in gases in which the gas is exposed to very brief intense flashes of light and the results are analysed with a spectroscope

flashpoint /flásh poynt/ *n* 1 TEMPERATURE OF VAPOUR IGNITION the lowest temperature at which a flammable liquid will give off enough vapour to ignite briefly when exposed to a flame 2 CRITICAL STAGE the critical stage in some process, event, or situation at which action, change, or violence occurs 3 TROUBLE SPOT a place where violence is likely to break out suddenly, usually as a result of social or political tension

flashtube /flásh tyoob/ *n* a glass or quartz tube filled with xenon gas that emits a short intense burst of light for flash photography when electric current is passed through it

flash unit *n* a flashgun or a unit comprising a flashgun and reflector

flashy /fláshi/ (**-ier, -iest**) *adj* 1 smart and expensive-looking in an obvious or ostentatious way 2 showing momentary or superficial brilliance —**flashily** *adv* —**flashiness** *n*

flask /flaask/ *n* 1 SMALL BOTTLE a small glass bottle, often with a long neck, of the type used in laboratory work 2 HOUSEHOLD = **hip flask** 3 VACUUM FLASK a vacuum flask 4 ARMS, HIST = **powder flask** 5 MOULD USED IN FOUNDRY a frame packed full of sand, used in a foundry to make a mould 6 CONTAINER FOR SPENT NUCLEAR FUEL a very strong container in which irradiated nuclear fuel is transported [14C. < medieval Latin *flasca*, late Latin *flascon-*.]

flat[1] /flat/ *adj* (**flatter, flattest**) 1 LEVEL AND HORIZONTAL level and horizontal, without any slope 2 EVEN AND SMOOTH even and smooth, without any bumps or hollows 3 NOT CURVED not curved inwards or outwards ○ *a boat with a flat bottom* 4 WITH LITTLE CURVATURE with relatively little depth or curvature ○ *a vase with flat sides* 5 LYING HORIZONTAL in a horizontal position, parallel with or stretched out on the ground 6 TOUCHING SOMETHING ELSE with the whole extent touching another surface at all points ○ *Stand it flat against the wall.* 7 NO LONGER FIZZY having lost effervescence 8 WITHOUT ELECTRICAL CHARGE describes a battery that has lost its electrical charge 9 NOT FULL OF AIR no longer full of air ○ *a flat tyre* 10 BELOW CORRECT PITCH sounded or sounding a little lower than the intended pitch level 11 ONE SEMITONE BELOW NATURAL pitched one semitone below the specified note ○ *in the key of B flat* 12 LACKING EXCITEMENT without any interest or excitement ○ *Some days life just seems flat.* 13 FLAVOURLESS without flavour or seasoning ○ *This soup tastes rather flat.* 14 MONOTONOUS IN SOUND with no variation in pitch or intonation 15 COMMERCIALLY INACTIVE not commercially active ○ *The market is fairly flat at the moment.* 16 NOT VARYING not varying in amount or level ○ *They charge a flat fee of £50.* 17 EMPHATICALLY ABSOLUTE categorical and without any qualification ○ *a flat denial of the charges* 18 LOW-HEELED with low heels or no heels at all ○ *flat shoes* 19 NOT SHINY not shiny or glossy ○ *a flat white paint* 20 TIGHT stretched so as to be tight 21 WITH LOW ARCHES describes feet with arches so low that all the sole makes contact with the ground 22 INDICATING CESSATION OF PHYSIOLOGICAL ACTIVITY showing no variation on a monitoring machine, and thereby indicating that physiological activity has stopped ○ *a flat EKG* 23 RESEMBLING VOWEL SOUND IN 'FAT' describes the vowel 'a' as it is pronounced in 'fat' or 'badge' ■ *adv* (**flatter, flattest**) 1 BELOW PITCH below the intended pitch ○ *She tends to sing flat.* 2 VERY used to add emphasis (*informal*) ○ *flat broke* 3 EXACTLY no more and no less ○ *He ran the mile in four minutes flat.* 4 WITHOUT INTEREST not accruing any interest ○ *The bonds were trading flat.* ■ *n* 1 LEVEL SURFACE a flat part or surface ○ *the flat of a knife blade* 2 NOTE LOWERED BY SEMITONE a sign (♭) placed next to a note to show that it is to be lowered by a semitone, or a note that is lowered a semitone ○ *a key with four flats* 3 LARGE STRETCH OF LEVEL GROUND a large level stretch, e.g. of mud exposed at low tide or of salt deposits (*usually plural*) 4 DEFLATED TYRE a tyre that has become deflated (*informal*) 5 MOVABLE SCENERY theatrical scenery mounted on a movable wooden frame 6 SHIPPING = **flatboat** 7 BIG FLAT ENVELOPE a large flat piece of mail 8 HORSERACING OVER LEVEL GROUND horseracing over level ground with no fences to be jumped, or the season in which this takes place ■ **flats** *npl* LOW-HEELED SHOES shoes with low heels ■ *vt* (**flats, flatting, flatted**) *US* 1 = **flatten** *v.* 5 2 = **flatten** *v.* 6 [14C. < Old Norse *flatr* < Indo-European.] —**flatness** *n*

flat[2] /flat/ *n* 1 SET OF ROOMS ON ONE FLOOR living quarters in part of a building, usually on one floor. US term **apartment** *n.* 1 2 *NZ* SHARED HOUSE a house that is shared with people who are not relatives ■ *vi ANZ* SHARE A FLAT to share a flat with somebody (*informal*) [Early 19C. Alteration, after FLAT[1], of Scots *flet* 'interior of a house' < Old English *flet(t)* 'house, floor' < Germanic.]

flatbed /flát bed/ *n* 1 = **flatbed trailer** 2 = **flatbed truck**

flatbed lorry *n* TRANSP = **flatbed truck**

flatbed press *n* PRINTING = **cylinder press**

flatbed trailer *n* a trailer consisting of a completely open platform with no sides or railings

flatbed truck, flatbed lorry *n* a truck that has a completely open platform at the rear with no sides or railings

flatboat /flát bōt/ *n* a large boat with a flat bottom used for transporting goods on shallow waterways

flatbread /flát bred/ *n* bread baked in round flat loaves and usually made with unleavened dough, e.g. pitta, nan, chapatis, and tortillas

flat cap *n* 1 a cloth cap with a brim at the front and a flat soft top 2 a hat with a low crown and a narrow brim worn in the 16th and 17th centuries by men, especially Londoners

flatcar /flát kaar/ *n US* a railway freight wagon that has no roof or sides

flat-chested /-chéstid/ *adj* having small breasts

flatfish /flát fish/ (*plural* **-fish** *or* **-fishes**) *n* any fish with a flat body and both eyes on the upper side, including the flounder, sole, and halibut. Order: Pleuronectiformes.

flat food *n US* flat-packed food sold from vending machines, especially as eaten in offices during long uninterrupted sessions of work (*slang*)

flatfoot /flát fòot/ *n* **1** a condition of the feet in which the arches are so low that all of the sole makes contact with the ground. ◊ **splayfoot** *n.* 1 **2** (*plural* **-foots** *or* **-feet**) an offensive term for a police officer, typically one on foot patrol (*dated slang*)

flat-footed, flatfooted /flát fóotid/ *adj* **1 HAVING FLAT FEET** describes somebody with flatfoot **2 AWKWARD** awkward or clumsy (*informal*) **3 UNPREPARED** unable to react or respond quickly ○ *Her question caught me flat-footed.* ■ *adv* **UNEQUIVOCALLY** without beating about the bush (*informal*) ○ *'a good many come out flat-footed and said it was scandalous'* (Mark Twain, *The Adventures of Huckleberry Finn*; 1884) —**flat-footedly** *adv* —**flat-footedness** *n*

flathead /flát hed/ (*plural* **-heads** *or* **-head**) *n* **1** *ANZ* a flat-skulled fish. Native to: Indian and Pacific oceans. Family: Platycephalidae. **2** the flesh of a flathead used as food, especially in Australia and New Zealand

Flathead /flát hed/ (*plural* **-head** *or* **-heads**) *n* a member of a Native North American people who originally lived in W Montana and N Idaho

flatiron /flát ī ərn/ *n* an iron used to press clothes, especially one that has to be heated on a hearth or stove

flatland /flát land/ *n* an expanse of land that does not vary in height above sea level

flatlet /flátlət/ *n* a small flat that has only a few rooms

flatline /flát līn/ (**-lines, -lining, -lined**) *vi US* to show none of the electrical currents associated with heart activity on a cardiac monitor (*slang*) —**flatliner** *n*

flatly /flátli/ *adv* **1** firmly and without qualification ○ *They flatly rejected our offer.* **2** in a voice that shows no emotion

flatmate /flát mayt/ *n* somebody with whom a person shares a flat ○ *We're advertising for a new flatmate.*

flat out *adv* (*informal*) **1 AS QUICKLY AS POSSIBLE** as fast and energetically as possible ○ *The factory staff are working flat out to finish the order.* **2 FAST** at top speed **3 BLUNTLY** in a blunt manner ○ *told me flat out he didn't trust me*

flatpack /flát pak/ *n* an item of furniture that is sold as a set of pieces packed flat, for ease of storage and transportation, and assembled by the buyer

flatpick /flát pik/ *n* a flat thin piece of plastic or metal, usually triangular, used to pluck and strum a stringed instrument such as a guitar or banjo. ◊ **fingerpick**

flat race *n* **1** a horserace that is run over level ground, without fences to be jumped **2** in children's sports competitions, an ordinary race without obstacles or special features, e.g. sacks or eggs and spoons (*dated*) —**flat racing** *n*

flatten /flátt'n/ *v* **1** *vti* **MAKE OR BECOME FLAT** to make something flat or flatter, or become flat or flatter **2** *vr* **STAND FLAT** to press the body against a flat surface **3** *vt* **DEFEAT** to defeat somebody convincingly (*informal*) **4** *vt* **CRUSH OR HUMILIATE** to make somebody feel crushed or humiliated **5** *vt* **TAKE NOTE DOWN ONE SEMITONE** to lower a note one semitone. US term **flat**[1] *v.* 1 **6** *vt* **SING OR PLAY SOMETHING FLAT** to sing or play a note below the intended pitch. US term **flat**[1] *v.* 2 —**flattener** *n*

flatten out *v* **1** *vi* to become lower and relatively stable ○ *Stock prices have flattened out over the year.* **2** *vti* to spread out, or spread something out, over an area

flatter[1] /fláttər/ *v* **1** *vt* **COMPLIMENT SOMEBODY TO WIN FAVOUR** to compliment somebody too much, often without sincerity, especially in order to gain an advantage **2** *vt* **APPEAL TO SOMEBODY'S VANITY** to please somebody by paying him or her particular attention, especially with a request to take some prominent role ○ *I was flattered to be asked to judge the competition.* **3** *vt* **MAKE SOMEBODY OR SOMETHING LOOK GOOD** to show somebody or something to advantage, or make somebody or something seem better-looking than in reality ○ *a studio portrait that really flatters her* **4** *vr* **CONGRATULATE YOURSELF EXCESSIVELY** to feel satisfied with some aspect of yourself or with something you have done, especially when the perception is false ○ *He flatters himself on being a good judge of character.* [12C. < ?] —**flatterer** *n* —**flattering** *adj* —**flatteringly** *adv*

flatter[2] /fláttər/ *n* any tool used to make something flat, as used, e.g. by a blacksmith [< Old Norse *flatr* (see FLAT[1])]

flattery /fláttəri/ *n* **1** an act or instance of complimenting somebody, often excessively or insincerely, especially in order to gain an advantage **2** complimentary remarks, especially when excessive or insincere [14C. < Old French *flaterie* < *flater* 'flatter'.]

flatties /fláttiz/ *npl* shoes with a low heel or no heel at all (*informal*)

flattish /fláttish/ *adj* somewhat or relatively flat ○ *a flattish hairdo*

flattop /flát top/ *n* a hairstyle in which the hair is brushed up and then cut short and flat across the top

flat tuning *n* the tuning of a musical instrument, or of instruments playing together, such that the pitch of the notes is lower than normal

flatulent /fláttyòolənt/ *adj* **1 CAUSING WIND IN DIGESTIVE SYSTEM** causing excessive gas to be created in the stomach and intestines **2 FULL OF DIGESTIVE GAS** having excessive gas in the digestive system **3 POMPOUS OR SELF-IMPORTANT** having or showing excessive self-importance [Late 16C. Via French < modern Latin *flatulentus* < Latin *flatus* 'blowing, blast' < *flare* 'to blow'.] —**flatulence** *n* —**flatulency** *n* —**flatulently** *adv*

flatus /fláytəss/ (*plural* **-tus** *or* **-tuses**) *n* gas produced in the digestive system by bacterial fermentation and containing high amounts of hydrogen sulphide and methane, usually expelled from the body through the anus (*technical*) [Mid-17C. < Latin (see FLATULENT).]

flatware /flát wair/ *n US, Can* **1** DOMESTIC = **cutlery** *n.* 1 **2** dishes used for eating that are flat or relatively shallow, e.g. plates and saucers, as opposed to deeper pieces such as cups and bowls (**hollowware**)

flat-water *adj* done on a calm or slow-moving body of water

flatways /flát wīz/ *adv* with the flat side down or foremost

flatweave /flát weev/, **flat-woven** *adj* woven without a pile ○ *a flatweave carpet*

flatwise /flát wīz/ *adv* US = **flatways**

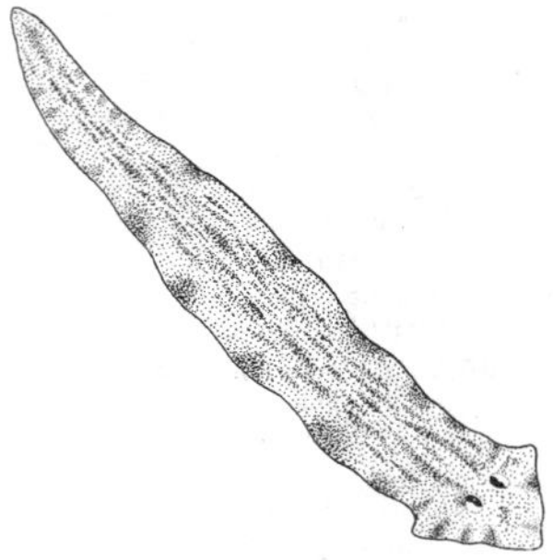

Flatworm

flatworm /flát wurm/ *n* a worm with a soft, flattened body. Phylum: Platyhelminthes.

flat-woven *adj* TEXTILES = **flatweave**

Flaubert /flṓ bair/, **Gustave** (1821–80) French novelist —**Flaubertian** /flō báirti ən/ *adj*

flaunching /fláwnching/ *n* a cement or mortar fillet that is designed to throw off water at the junction where a masonry chimney stack comes through a roof [Early 19C. < *flanch* 'to slope' < ?]

flaunt /flawnt/ *v* **1** *vt* **SHOW SOMETHING OFF** to display something ostentatiously ○ *She flaunts her wealth every chance she gets.* **2** *vr* **PARADE YOURSELF** to parade yourself without shame or modesty **3** *vti* **WAVE OR MAKE SOMETHING WAVE** to wave or flutter in the wind, or make something wave or flutter by moving it around (*dated*) ■ *n* **DISPLAY** an ostentatious display [Mid-16C. < ?] —**flaunter** *n* —**flauntingly** *adv*

USAGE Flaunt or **flout**? In terms of openly disobeying or defying a law or convention, only ***flout*** is the correct choice: *The driver flouted the law when he double-parked.* When expressing the idea of shameless or ostentatious display, the correct choice is ***flaunt***: *He flaunted his ill-gotten riches by purchasing a vulgar mansion and seven luxury cars.*

---

flautist /fláwtist/, **flutist** /flóotist/ *n* a player of a flute [Mid-19C. < Italian *flautisto* < *flauto* 'flute' < Provençal *flaüt*.]

flav- *prefix* = **flavo-** (*before vowels*)

flavanone /fláyvənōn/ *n* a substance derived from flavone [Mid-20C. < FLAVO- + -ANE + -ONE.]

flavin /fláyvin/ *n* any of a group of yellowish pigments present in plants and animals [Mid-19C. < Latin *flavus* 'yellow'.]

flavo- *prefix* **1** yellow **2** flavin ○ *flavoprotein* [< Latin *flavus* 'yellow' < Indo-European]

flavone /fláy vōn/ *n* one of a group of yellow plant pigments

flavonoid /fláyvə noyd/ *n* a naturally occurring phenolic compound belonging to a group that includes many plant pigments

flavoprotein /fláyvō prṓ teen/ *n* an enzyme that is involved in cell respiration

flavor *n, vt* US = **flavour**

flavour /fláyvər/ *n* **1 CHARACTERISTIC TASTE** an identifiable or distinctive quality of food or drink perceived with the combined senses of taste and smell ○ *The soup didn't have much flavour.* **2 SOMETHING ADDING FLAVOUR TO FOOD** a substance used to give food or drink an identifiable or distinctive taste **3 UNIQUE CHARACTERISTIC** the unique individual characteristic of an artistic work, especially a work of literature **4 TYPE** a type or kind of something (*informal*) ○ *'any flavor of mainframe you like'* (*The LOD/H Technical Journal, Issue 3*; 1988) **5 PROPERTY OF ELEMENTARY PARTICLES** a physical property that distinguishes types of quarks and some types of lepton ■ *vt* **1 GIVE FLAVOUR TO FOOD** to give food or drink an identifiable or distinctive taste, usually by adding something ○ *Flavour the stew with rosemary.* **2 GIVE SOMETHING UNIQUENESS** to give a unique characteristic to an artistic work, especially a work of literature ○ *A certain terseness flavours her prose.* [14C. Alteration, after SAVOUR, of Old French *flaor* 'aroma' < blend of Latin *flatus* 'blowing' + *foetor* 'stench'.] —**flavourer** *n* —**flavourful** *adj* —**flavourfully** *adv* —**flavourfulness** *n* —**flavourless** *adj* —**flavourlessly** *adv* —**flavourlessness** *n* —**flavoursome** *adj* —**flavoury** *adj*

flavour enhancer *n* a substance, especially monosodium glutamate, added to processed food or drink to improve or intensify its flavour

flavouring /fláyvəring/ *n* a natural or artificial substance added to food or drink to give it an identifiable taste

flaw[1] /flaw/ *n* **1 BLEMISH MAKING SOMETHING IMPERFECT** a defect in an object that makes it imperfect or less valuable **2 ABSTRACT IMPERFECTION** an imperfection, shortcoming, or weakness in something abstract ○ *There's a flaw in your argument.* **3 INVALIDATING DEFECT IN DOCUMENT** in a legal document, a defect that can make it invalid [14C. < ?] —**flawed** *adj*

SYNONYMS ***flaw, imperfection, fault, defect, failing, blemish***

CORE MEANING: something that detracts from perfection

flaw an unintended mark or crack that prevents something from being totally perfect and detracts from its value, or a weakness in somebody's character, or in a plan, theory, or system; **imperfection** a fault that makes a person or thing less than perfect; **fault** something that detracts from the integrity, functioning, or perfection of a thing, or a weakness in somebody's character, usually more serious than a flaw; **defect** a fault in a machine, system, or plan, especially one that prevents it from functioning correctly, or a personal weakness; **failing** something that mars somebody or something in some way, especially an unfortunate feature of somebody's character; **blemish** a mark of some kind that detracts from something's appearance, especially the complexion or skin, or a feature that detracts from somebody's otherwise undamaged reputation or record.

---

flaw[2] /flaw/ *n* **1** a brief gust of wind **2** a short storm or spell of bad weather [Early 16C. Probably < Middle Low German *vlāge*, or < N Germanic.] —**flawy** *adj*

flawless /fláwləss/ *adj* without any blemish or imperfection ○ *a flawless performance* —**flawlessly** *adv* —**flawlessness** *n*

flax /flaks/ *n* **1** a fine light-coloured plant fibre. Use: linen textiles. **2** a plant that yields oil from its seeds and flax from its stems. *Linum usitatissimum.* [Old English *flæx* < Indo-European, 'plait'] —**flaxy** *adj*

flaxen /fláks'n/ *adj* **1** of the pale greyish-yellow colour of flax **2** made from flax fibres

Flaxman /fláksman/, **John** (1755–1826) British sculptor and illustrator

flaxseed /fláks seed/ *n* = **linseed**

flaxseed oil *n* oil obtained from the seeds of the flax plant, especially as used in products to promote human and animal health. ◊ **linseed oil**

flay /flay/ *vt* 1 **LASH OR FLOG** to whip or beat a person or animal severely 2 **STRIP SKIN OFF** to remove the skin or outer covering from somebody or something 3 **CRITICIZE HARSHLY** to criticize somebody or something harshly and severely, and sometimes unfairly 4 **STRIP OF BELONGINGS** to take all the money or valuables from somebody, especially by the use of deceit, intimidation, or similar means (*dated*) [Old English *flēan* < Indo-European, 'to strike'] —**flayer** *n*

F layer *n* the transition zone between the solid inner core of the Earth and its more fluid outer layer, at a depth of approximately 5,100 km/3,200 mi

flea /flee/ *n* 1 a small wingless insect with legs adapted for jumping that sucks blood and lives as a parasite on warm-blooded animals. Order: Siphonaptera. 2 a small beetle or crustacean that resembles or jumps like a flea, e.g. a water flea, flea beetle, or sand flea [Old English *flēa(h)* < Indo-European] ◇ **send somebody away** *or* **off with a flea in his** *or* **her ear** to sharply reprimand somebody for something that he or she has done

SPELLCHECK Do not confuse ***flea*** with ***flee***, which has a similar sound. Beware: your spellchecker will not catch this error.

fleabag /flee bag/ *n* a dirty or scruffy living being, especially one that is infested with fleas (*informal*)

fleabane /flee bayn/ *n* a wild plant of the daisy family. Flowers: yellow. Genus: *Erigeron*. [Because of its supposed ability to repel fleas]

flea beetle *n* a very small beetle with large hind legs adapted for jumping. The beetle and its larvae are pests of vegetable crops. Subfamily: Halticinae.

fleabite /flee bīt/ *n* 1 the bite of a flea, or the small red mark caused by this 2 a small loss or petty annoyance (*informal*)

flea-bitten *adj* 1 **COVERED WITH FLEAS OR FLEABITES** covered with fleabites or infested with fleas 2 **CHEAP AND SHABBY** cheap, shabby, or run-down (*informal*) 3 **WITH PALE FLECKED COAT** describes a horse that has a pale coat with reddish-brown flecks

flea collar *n* a collar, usually for dogs or cats, containing a chemical that repels or kills fleas

flea-flicker *n* a play in American football in which the ball is quickly passed laterally from one player to another to confuse the defence

fleam /fleem/ *n* 1 a bevelled cutting edge on the teeth of a saw 2 a surgical knife formerly used to open a vein in bloodletting [15C. Via Old French *flieme* < Greek *phlebotomon* 'vein-cutter' < *phlebos* 'vein'.]

flea market *n* a market, usually outdoors, with individual stalls selling various kinds of merchandise, e.g. antiques, used household items, and cut-price goods

fleapit /flee pit/ *n* a cheap run-down cinema or theatre

fleawort /flee wurt/ (*plural* **-wort** *or* **-worts**) *n* a plant with furry leaves arranged in clusters. Flowers: yellow. Native to: Europe. Genus: *Senecio*. [Because of its supposed ability to repel fleas]

flèche /flaysh, flesh/, **fleche** *n* 1 **SLENDER CHURCH SPIRE** a slender spire, especially one that emerges from the roof of a church at the point where the ridges intersect 2 **BUTTRESS FEATURE** a joint at the top of a buttress, designed to add weight and assist in transferring load from roof to ground 3 **POINTED FORTIFICATION** a fortification with two faces that form a jutting angle [Early 18C. < French, 'arrow'.]

fléchette /flay shét/, **flechette** *n* a small arrow or dart used in various kinds of missiles or projectiles intended to kill or injure people [Early 20C. < French, 'little arrow' < *flèche* 'arrow'.]

fleck /flek/ *n* any one of a number of very small marks, streaks, or pieces scattered on a surface or throughout a block of something ○ *flecks of mica in granite* ■ *vt* to mark something with small streaks or spots ○ *Sunlight flecked the path ahead.* [14C. < ?]

Flecker /flékar/, **James Elroy** (1884–1915) British poet

flection *n* ANAT = **flexion**

fled past participle, past tense of **flee**

fledge /flej/ (**fledges, fledging, fledged**) *v* 1 *vt* **RAISE YOUNG BIRD** to raise a young bird until it can fly 2 *vi* **GROW FLIGHT FEATHERS** to grow the wing and tail feathers necessary for flying 3 *vt* **EQUIP ARROW WITH FEATHERS** to put feathers on an arrow 4 *vt* **PROVIDE WITH FEATHERS** to provide or cover something with feathers or something similar [Mid-16C. < obsolete *fledge* 'fledged, ready to fly' < Germanic.]

fledgling /fléjling/, **fledgeling** *n* 1 **YOUNG BIRD WITH NEW FLIGHT FEATHERS** a young bird that has recently grown the feathers necessary for flying 2 **SOMEBODY INEXPERIENCED** a young or inexperienced person ■ *adj* **INEXPERIENCED** inexperienced because still learning or just starting ○ *a fledgling business*

flee /flee/ (**flees, fleeing, fled** /fled/) *v* 1 *vti* to run away from something ○ *fled the burning building* 2 *vi* to pass or disappear quickly (*literary*) [Old English *flēon* < Indo-European] —**fleer** *n*

SPELLCHECK See ***flea***.

fleece /fleess/ *n* 1 **WOOLLY COAT OF SHEEP** the coat of wool on a sheep or similar animal 2 **WOOL SHORN FROM SHEEP** the wool shorn at one time from a sheep or similar animal 3 **SOFT COVERING** a soft woolly covering or mass ○ *rocks with a fleece of moss* 4 **SOFT FABRIC WITH NAP OR PILE** a soft warm fabric with a brushed nap or woolly pile. Use: outer garments, lining. 5 **WARM JACKET** a soft warm jacket ■ *vt* (**fleeces, fleecing, fleeced**) 1 **SWINDLE OUT OF MONEY** to take too much money from somebody by cheating or overcharging (*informal*) 2 **SHEAR SHEEP** to shear wool from a sheep 3 **COVER WITH SOMETHING RESEMBLING FLEECE** to cover something with something soft and woolly (*literary*) ○ *Clouds fleeced the summer sky.* [Old English *flēos* < W Germanic] —**fleecer** *n*

fleecy /fleessi/ (**-ier, -iest**) *adj* 1 consisting of fleece or something similar 2 soft and woolly in appearance or texture —**fleecily** *adv* —**fleeciness** *n*

fleet¹ /fleet/ *n* 1 a number of warships functioning as a single unit under one command, or all the ships of a nation's navy 2 a number of road vehicles, boats, or aircraft owned, working, or managed as a unit, usually by a commercial enterprise [Old English *flēot* 'ships' < *flēotan* 'to float, swim' < Germanic]

fleet² /fleet/ *adj* (*literary*) 1 moving quickly or nimbly 2 passing or fading quickly [Early 16C. Probably < Old Norse *fljótr* < Germanic.] —**fleetly** *adv* —**fleetness** *n*

fleet³ /fleet/ *n* a creek or inlet (*regional*) [Old English *flēot* < Germanic]

fleet admiral, Fleet Admiral *n* a US Navy officer of the highest rank, with an insignia of five stars

Fleet Air Arm *n* the branch of the Royal Navy concerned with air operations

fleet chief petty officer *n* a Royal Navy non-commissioned officer of a rank above petty officer

fleeting /fleeting/ *adj* passing or fading quickly [Old English, < *flēotan* (see FLEET¹)] —**fleetingly** *adv* —**fleetingness** *n*

SYNONYMS See ***temporary***.

Fleet Street *n* the people and practices involved in the British newspaper industry [After *Fleet Street* in central London, where most British national newspapers were formerly produced]

fleishig /fláyshik, flī-/, **fleishik** *adj* under Jewish dietary laws, relating to, containing, or used as meat or meat products. ◊ **pareve** [Mid-20C. < Yiddish *fleyshik* < *fleysh* 'meat'.]

Fleming /flémming/ *n* 1 somebody who comes from Flanders 2 a Belgian who speaks Flemish. ◊ **Walloon** *n.* 1 [Old English *Flæming*, directly and via Old Norse < Middle Dutch *Vlaminc*]

Fleming /flémming/, **Sir Alexander** (1881–1955) British microbiologist

Fleming, Ian (1908–64) British writer

Flemish /flémmish/ *adj* **OF FLANDERS** relating to Flanders, the Flemings, or their language or culture ■ *n* **BELGIAN LANGUAGE** one of the official languages of Belgium, belonging to the West Germanic group of the Germanic branch of Indo-European and closely related to Dutch. Native speakers: 5 million. ■ *npl* **PEOPLE OF FLANDERS** the people of Flanders, or Flemish-speaking people [14C. < Middle Dutch *Vlāmisch* < *Vlāmland* 'Flanders'.]

Flemish bond *n* a style of brickwork in which bricks laid with the end facing out (**headers**) alternate with those laid lengthwise (**stretchers**), horizontally and vertically

Flemish school *n* art and artists of the 15th and 16th centuries in The Netherlands

flense /flenss/ (**flenses, flensing, flensed**), **flench** /flench/ *vt* to strip the skin or blubber from a whale or seal [Early 19C. < Danish *flensa*.] —**flenser** *n*

flesh /flesh/ *n* 1 **SOFT TISSUE OF BODY** the soft tissues, primarily muscle and fat, that cover the bones of people and other animals 2 **HUMAN SKIN AS OUTER SURFACE** the outer surface of the human body 3 **UNWANTED WEIGHT** unwanted weight or fatty tissue (*informal*) ○ *could afford to lose some flesh* 4 **MEAT OF ANIMALS** the flesh of animals, including birds and fish, regarded as food 5 **PULP OF FRUITS AND VEGETABLES** the soft pulpy edible parts of fruits and vegetables, as opposed to the skin, core, stone, and other parts that are not usually eaten 6 **PEOPLE** people in general (*literary*) ○ *the way of all flesh* 7 **PHYSICAL ASPECT OF HUMANITY** the physical body along with its needs and limitations, as opposed to the soul, mind, or spirit 8 **SUBSTANCE** substance as distinct from form or style ○ *Actions give flesh to theory.* 9 COLOURS = **flesh colour** ■ *vt* 1 **INSTRUCT ANIMAL BY FEEDING** to teach a dog or bird to hunt by feeding it the meat of a freshly killed animal 2 **ACCUSTOM TO KILLING** to accustom somebody to bloodshed and the killing of other people (*literary*) 3 **GET BLOOD ON WEAPON** to thrust a pointed weapon into somebody's flesh, especially when using it for the first time (*literary*) 4 **CLEAN INSIDE OF ANIMAL SKIN** in tanning, to scrape away the soft tissue adhering to a hide [Old English *flǣsc* 'soft tissue, meat' < Germanic] ◇ **in the flesh** in person ◇ **press the flesh** to greet and shake the hands of many people in public, as a political or promotional exercise (*informal*)

flesh out *v* 1 *vt* to add substance and detail to something ○ *flesh out a business proposal* 2 *vi* to put on weight or become overweight (*informal*)

flesh and blood *n* 1 people, or a person, related to somebody by birth 2 = **flesh** *n.* 7 ■ *adj* **flesh-and-blood** representing life, people, and events in a way perceived as believable or realistic

flesh-colour *n* a pink colour with tinges of yellow or grey, like that of a white person's skin —**flesh-coloured** *adj*

flesher /fléshar/ *n* 1 in tanning, a person who or a device that removes any flesh adhering to the inside of an animal hide 2 *Scotland* a dealer in meat (*dated; still found on shop fronts*)

flesh fly *n* a fly whose larvae feed on the flesh of living or dead animals. Family: Sarcophagidae.

fleshings /fléshingz/ *npl* flesh scraped from an animal's hide

fleshly /fléshli/ (**-lier, -liest**) *adj* 1 **BODILY** relating to the human body ○ *the fleshly concerns of daily living* 2 **RELATING TO PHYSICAL PLEASURE** enjoying or concerned with the pleasures of the body 3 **NOT SPIRITUAL** not focused on spiritual matters —**fleshliness** *n*

fleshpot /flésh pots/ *n* a place known to provide sexual or sensual entertainment (*usually plural*) ○ *Police keep an eye on the local fleshpots.* [Mid-16C. See Exodus 16:3.]

flesh wound *n* a wound that penetrates the flesh but does not damage bones or vital organs

fleshy /fléshi/ (**-ier, -iest**) *adj* 1 **PLUMP** plump or fat 2 **WITH MORE FLESH** with thicker or softer flesh than other parts of the body ○ *the fleshy part of the hand at the base of the thumb* 3 **SOFT AND JUICY** with thick soft juicy pulp ○ *the fleshiest peaches of the season* —**fleshiness** *n*

fletch /flech/ *vt* ARCHERY = **fledge** *v.* 3 [Mid-17C. Alteration of FLEDGE, influenced by FLETCHER.]

fletcher /fléchar/ *n* a maker of arrows [13C. < Old French *flech(i)er* < *flèche* 'arrow'.]

Fletcher /fléchar/, **John** (1579–1625) English dramatist

fletchings /fléchingz/ *npl* the feathered part of an arrow

fleur-de-lis /flúr da leé/ (*plural* **fleurs-de-lis** /flúr da leéz/), **fleur-de-lys** (*plural* **fleurs-de-lys**) *n* 1 a heraldic symbol or design in the form of three tapering petals tied by a surrounding band, formerly used by the kings of France 2 PLANTS = **iris** *n.* 2 [< Old French *flour de lys* 'flower of the lily'] See illustration overleaf.

fleuret /flur rét, floor-/, **fleurette** *n* a decorative motif in the form of a small flower [Early 19C. < French, 'little flower' < *fleur* 'flower' < Old French *flour* (see FLOWER).]

Fleur-de-lis

flew past tense of **fly**[1]

flex[1] /fleks/ v 1 vt **BEND A BODY PART** to bend something, especially a joint of the body 2 vi **BEND** to bend or be able to be bent ○ *The board flexes as you step on it.* 3 vti **PRODUCE MUSCULAR CONTRACTION** to move or tense a muscle, or become tense or contracted ■ n **BENDING ABILITY** bending, or ability to bend [Early 16C. < Latin *flex*- (see FLEXIBLE).]

flex[2] /fleks/ n flexible insulated electric cable, especially that attached to an electrical appliance [Early 20C. Shortening of FLEXIBLE.]

~~flexable~~ incorrect spelling of **flexible**

flexatone /fléksə tōn/ n a percussion instrument consisting of a handle with a narrow metal sheet attached that is struck to produce a tunable sound

flexible /fléksəb'l/ adj 1 **ABLE TO BEND WITHOUT BREAKING** able to bend or be bent repeatedly without damage or injury 2 **ABLE TO ADAPT TO NEW SITUATION** able to change or be changed according to circumstances 3 **SUBJECT TO INFLUENCE** able to be persuaded or influenced [15C. Directly or via French < Latin *flexibilis* < *flex*-, past participle of *flectere* 'bend'.] —**flexibility** /fléksə bíllati/ n —**flexibleness** n —**flexibly** adv

flexile /fléksil, flék sīl/ adj = **flexible** adj. 1 [Mid-17C. < Latin *flexilis* < *flex*- (see FLEXIBLE).]

flexion /fléksh'n/, **flection** n 1 **BENDING OF LIMB** the bending of a limb or joint 2 **POSITION OF BENT PART** the position of a bent limb or joint 3 **BENDING** the bending of something, or its bent state [Early 17C. < Latin *flexion*- < *flex*- (see FLEXIBLE).] —**flexional** adj

flexitime /fléks tīm/ n a system that allows employees to set their own daily times of starting and finishing work, within certain limits [Late 20C. Blend of FLEXIBLE + TIME.]

flexography /flek sóggrəfi/ n a relief printing technique that uses a rotary press, a flexible plate, and a water-based ink [Mid-20C. < Latin *flex*- (see FLEXIBLE).] —**flexographer** n —**flexographic** /fléksə gráffik/ adj —**flexographically** adv

flexor /fléksər/ n a muscle that bends a joint or limb when it is contracted [Early 17C. < modern Latin, < Latin *flex*- (see FLEXIBLE).]

flextime /fléks tīm/ n US = **flexitime**

flexuous /fléksyoo əss/, **flexuose** /-ōss/ adj curving, winding, or turning (*formal*) [Early 17C. < Latin *flexuosus* < *flex*- (see FLEXIBLE).] —**flexuosity** /fléksyoō óssəti/ n —**flexuously** adv

flexure /flékshər/ n 1 a bending or being flexed 2 a bend or curve, e.g. in a body part or organ [Late 16C. < Latin *flexura* < *flex*- (see FLEXIBLE).] —**flexural** adj

flg. abbr 1 flagging[2] 2 flooring 3 following

flibbertigibbet /flíbbərti jíbbit, flíbbərti jibbit/ n a silly, irresponsible, or scatterbrained person, especially one who prattles or gossips (*dated*) [15C. Probably an imitation of the sound of meaningless prattle.]

flic /flik/ n a member of the French police (*slang*) [Late 19C. < French.]

flick[1] /flik/ n 1 **QUICK MOVEMENT** a quick jerking movement 2 **QUICK BLOW** a sharp light blow made with a quick jerking movement, usually of the finger 3 **SPLASH OF COLOUR** a light splash or streak ○ *flicks of paint left on the floor* 4 **PENALTY SHOT** in hockey, a penalty shot from the penalty spot ■ v 1 vti **HIT WITH QUICK BLOW** to hit something sharply or lightly with the end of something, usually in a quick jerking movement ○ *He flicked me*

with his towel. 2 vti **MOVE JERKILY** to move or make something move with a quick sharp jerk ○ *The cow's tail flicked back and forth.* 3 vt **MOVE WITH QUICK BLOW** to move, propel, or remove something with a sharp light blow or a quick movement of the finger or hand ○ *Would you flick that bug off me?* 4 vt **GUIDE THE BALL GENTLY** to guide the ball gently and deftly with your foot or head into the goal or to a team-mate 5 vti **TAKE PENALTY SHOT** to take a penalty flick [15C. An imitation of the sound of a light blow.]

flick through vt to turn the pages of a book or magazine quickly ○ *flicked through a couple of magazines while I waited*

flick[2] /flik/ n a film (*informal; in combination*) ■ **flicks** npl the cinema (*dated informal*) [Early 20C. Shortening of FLICKER; from the flickering of early films.]

flick[3] /flik/ n (*informal*) 1 *Wales, S England* animal fat found round kidneys and other offal 2 *N England* a side of bacon [Late 16C. Probably variant of FLITCH.]

flicker /flíkər/ vi 1 **SHINE UNSTEADILY** to burn or shine unsteadily 2 **FLUTTER OR MOVE JERKILY** to move with a fluttering or fast jerky motion 3 **APPEAR BRIEFLY** to appear or exist only briefly ○ *A smile flickered across her face.* ■ n 1 **FLUCTUATING LIGHT** an unsteady or wavering light ○ *the flicker of candles in the dark* 2 **QUICK MOVEMENT** a quick fluttering movement 3 **TRANSIENT FEELING OR EXPRESSION** a brief feeling that quickly passes, or an indication of this on somebody's face ○ *A flicker of joy briefly lit her eyes.* [Old English *flicorian* 'to flutter', suggestive of the movement] —**flickeringly** adv

flick knife n a pocketknife with a concealed blade that opens as soon as a button on the handle is pressed. US term **switchblade**

flier /flí ər/, **flyer** n 1 **AIRCRAFT PILOT** the pilot of an aircraft 2 **AIRCRAFT PASSENGER** a passenger on an aircraft ○ *frequent fliers* 3 **PRINTED SHEET WIDELY DISTRIBUTED** a short piece of printed matter, usually an advertisement, that is widely distributed 4 **STEP IN STRAIGHT STAIRCASE** a rectangular step in a straight flight of stairs 5 *US* **RISKY UNDERTAKING** a daring or risky financial undertaking (*informal*) 6 **FLYING START** a flying start (*informal*)

flight[1] /flīt/ n 1 **PROCESS OR ACT OF FLYING** the process or act of moving through the air or through space 2 **AIR JOURNEY** a journey through air or space in a form of transport ○ *daily flights of a thousand miles or more* 3 **SCHEDULED FLIGHT** a scheduled flight with a commercial airline, usually designated by letters and numbers ○ *flight TC546 to Vancouver* 4 **ABILITY TO FLY** the ability to travel through the air with wings 5 **SERIES OF STEPS BETWEEN FLOORS** a group of stairs that go from one level of a building to another ○ *We live three flights up.* 6 **GROUP FLYING TOGETHER** a group of aircraft or birds flying together, sometimes in a set pattern 7 **GROUP OF AIRCRAFT** a group of aircraft operating together as a separate unit ○ *the Queen's flight* 8 **RAPID MOVEMENT** swift passage, progress, or motion, especially through the air 9 **EXTRAORDINARY MENTAL FEAT** an act or the process of imagining extraordinary things ○ *flights of the imagination* 10 **TAIL OF ARROW OR DART** the feathers on an arrow or dart 11 **HURDLES ON RACETRACK** a line of hurdles across a racetrack ■ v 1 vi **FLY TOGETHER** to fly or migrate together 2 vt **SHOOT FLYING BIRD** in hunting, to shoot a bird as it flies 3 vt **PUT TAIL ON ARROW OR DART** to put feathers on an arrow or dart 4 vt **CAUSE TO FLOAT TOWARDS TARGET** to make a ball or dart seem to float inexorably towards its target [Old English *flyht* < Germanic]

flight[2] /flīt/ n the act of running away from something or somebody [12C. < assumed Old English, < Germanic.]

flight arrow n a light arrow used for long-distance shooting

flight attendant n somebody employed by an airline to attend to the needs, comfort, and safety of passengers during flights

flight bag n a soft suitcase of a size that can be carried on an aircraft

flight deck n 1 the upper deck of an aircraft carrier that is used as a runway 2 the compartment at the front of an aeroplane where the pilot, copilot, and flight engineer sit

flight engineer n the crew member of an aeroplane who monitors the performance of its systems, including the engines

flight envelope n a set of limits to performance, such as speed, altitude, range, payload, and manoeuverability, that exist in the design of an aircraft

KEY DATES IN THE HISTORY OF POWERED FLIGHT

1480–1510	Leonardo da Vinci sketches proposed flying machines in Italy
1903	Wright brothers achieve first powered controlled flight at Kitty Hawk, N Carolina
1909	Louis Blériot flies across English Channel
1910	First aircraft take off and land on US Navy ship
1914–18	Rapid development of biplanes for military purposes
1919	UK aviators J. Alcock and A. Whitten Brown fly nonstop across Atlantic
1924	US army pilots complete first round-the-world flight in 175 days
1927	Charles Lindbergh flies solo across Atlantic
1930	UK engineer Frank Whittle patents first jet engine
1936	First practical design for manoeuvrable helicopter by Heinrich Focke in Germany
1939	First successful jet aircraft, Heinkel He-178, is flown, in Germany
1941	Igor Sikorsky makes first US helicopter flight
1945	Development of legendary wartime aircraft, including the Hawker Hurricane and Supermarine Spitfire fighters and the Avro Lancaster and Boeing B-17 Flying Fortress bombers
1947	Charles E. Yeager, US Air Force pilot, breaks sound barrier
1952	De Havilland Comet is first passenger jet airliner (London to S Africa)
1957	Three Boeing B-52 bombers fly nonstop around the world
1970	Boeing 747 'jumbo jet' goes into service
1976	Concorde is first supersonic passenger jet airliner
2000	Development starts on first 'superjumbo' airliner, able to seat over 500

See also table at *space*

flight feather n any feather in a bird's wing or tail that is necessary for flight, usually a large one

flightless /flítləss/ adj describes birds that are incapable of flight

flight level n the height at which a particular aircraft is allowed to fly at a particular time

flight lieutenant *n* a Royal Air Force officer of a rank above flying officer

flight line *n* the area of an airfield, especially a military airfield, where aeroplanes are parked, serviced, and loaded or unloaded

flight of fancy *n* an idea or thought that is very imaginative but completely impractical or even ridiculous

flight path *n* the course taken by an aircraft, space vehicle, or projectile

flight plan *n* a record outlining the details of a proposed flight

flight recorder *n* an electronic instrument installed on an aircraft that records details of its performance in flight

flight sergeant *n* a Royal Air Force noncommissioned officer of a rank above sergeant

flight simulator *n* a computerized device that exactly reproduces the conditions that occur on the flight deck of an aircraft and that can be used to train pilots

flight surgeon *n* a medical officer in the US Air Force who practises aviation medicine and looks after the health of flight crews

flight-test *vt* to test the performance of an aircraft, spacecraft, missile, or component in flight —**flight test** *n*

flighty /flīti/ (**-ier, -iest**) *adj* unreliable, capricious, and constantly changing opinions, especially in the choice of sexual partners —**flightily** *adv* —**flightiness** *n*

flimflam /flím flam/ *n* (*slang*) **1 TRICK OR SWINDLE** a trick or attempt to cheat or swindle somebody **2 DECEPTIVE TALK** talk that confuses or deceives ■ *vt* (**-flams, -flamming, -flammed**) **CHEAT SOMEBODY** to swindle or cheat somebody (*slang*) [Mid-16C. < ?] —**flimflammer** *n* —**flimflammery** *n*

flimsy /flímzi/ *adj* (**-sier, -siest**) **1 FRAGILE** weak and easily broken **2 EASILY TORN** light, thin, and easily torn **3 UNCONVINCINGLY WEAK** unconvincing and difficult to believe ○ *The grounds for an appeal are flimsy at best.* ■ *n* (*plural* **-sies**) **CARBON COPY** a thin piece of carbon paper or a copy made with it [Early 18C. Probably < alteration of FILM after CLUMSY.] —**flimsily** *adv* —**flimsiness** *n*

SYNONYMS See ***fragile***.

flinch[1] /flinch/ *vi* **1** to make an involuntary small backward movement in response to pain or something frightening or shocking **2** to avoid thinking about something, confronting something, or doing something ○ *We will not flinch from danger.* [Mid-16C. < Old French *flenchir* 'turn aside' < Germanic, 'to bend'.] —**flincher** *n* —**flinchingly** *adv*

SYNONYMS See ***recoil***.

flinch[2] /flinch/ *vt* = **flense** *v.*

flinders /flíndərz/ *npl* tiny fragments [15C. < ?]

Flinders /flíndərz/ river in N Queensland, Australia. Length: 840 km/520 mi.

Flinders, Matthew (1774–1814) British explorer

Flinders bar /flíndərz-/ *n* a bar of soft iron mounted under a compass to compensate for local magnetism and prevent it affecting the reading of the compass [After Matthew FLINDERS]

Flinders Island island off NE Tasmania, Australia. Population: 924 (1996). Area: 2,089 sq. km/807 sq. mi.

Flinders Range mountain chain in E South Australia

fling /fling/ *v* (**flings, flinging, flung** /flung/) **1** *vt* **THROW VIOLENTLY** to throw something or somebody fast using a lot of force **2** *vr* **MOVE FORCEFULLY** to move forcefully in a way that seems impressive or dramatic ○ *She flung herself onto the chair and began to sob.* **3** *vt* **MOVE YOUR HEAD OR ARMS** to move your head or arms in a particular direction suddenly and dramatically **4** *vr* **WORK ENTHUSIASTICALLY AND ENERGETICALLY** to start doing something with great enthusiasm and energy ○ *She flings herself into every project she undertakes.* ■ *n* (*informal*) **1 SHORT AFFAIR** a brief sexual relationship **2 TIME FOR PLEASURE** a period of carefree enjoyment, especially before a more serious or worried period [13C. < N Germanic, < Indo-European, 'to strike'.] —**flinger** *n*

SYNONYMS See ***throw***.

fling off *vt* to take off a piece of clothing quickly, or remove forcefully something that is covering you

flint /flint/ *n* **1 VERY HARD QUARTZ THAT MAKES SPARKS** a very hard greyish-black fine-grained form of quartz that produces a spark when struck with steel occurring as nodules and bands in chalk **2 TOOL MADE OF FINE-GRAINED QUARTZ** a piece of fine-grained quartz shaped into a tool by prehistoric people **3 SPARK-MAKING ROCK** a piece of flint used to make a spark **4 PART OF CIGARETTE LIGHTER** the part of a cigarette lighter, consisting of a small iron alloy cylinder, that makes a spark [Old English, < Germanic, 'to split']

Flint /flint/, **F. S.** (1885–1960) British poet

flint corn *n* maize with kernels that contain hard starch, e.g. popcorn. *Zea mays.*

flint glass *n* high-quality glass containing lead oxide that has a high refractive index. Use: lenses, cut glass, costume jewellery.

flinthead /flínt hed/ *n* BIRDS = **wood stork**

flint-knapping *n* the activity, largely carried out by prehistoric people, of chipping and splitting flint to make tools —**flint-knapper** *n*

flintlock /flínt lok/ *n* **1** a firearm with a firing mechanism (**gunlock**) where a flint embedded in the hammer ignites a gunpowder charge **2** a firing mechanism (**gunlock**) that has a flint embedded in the hammer to produce the spark

Flintshire /flíntshər/ county in NE Wales. Population: 145,700 (1995). Area: 437 sq. km/169 sq. mi.

flinty /flínti/ (**-ier, -iest**) *adj* **1** hard, inflexible, and showing no emotion **2** containing or related to flint —**flintily** *adv* —**flintiness** *n*

flip /flip/ *v* (**flips, flipping, flipped**) **1** *vti* **TURN SOMETHING OVER** to turn something over from one side to the other with a quick movement of the wrist, hand, or fingers **2** *vt* **MOVE WITH QUICK LIGHT MOTION** to move or flick something with a small sharp quick motion ○ *She flipped the light on and walked in.* **3** *vt* **TOSS CARELESSLY** to throw or toss something carelessly and lightly ○ *flip a pen across the table* **4** *vti* **TURN PAGES OF READING MATERIAL** to turn the pages of a magazine or book quickly **5** *vti* **SPIN COIN** to flick the edge of a coin with your thumb so that it spins in the air before landing **6** *vi* **GET SUDDENLY ANGRY** to become very angry or upset suddenly (*slang*) ○ *When I told her I wouldn't help her, she just flipped.* **7** *vi* **GET EXCITED AT SOMETHING NICE** to become excited over something that is pleasurable or attractive (*slang*) ■ *adj* (**flipper, flippest**) **FLIPPANT** showing a lack of seriousness that is considered inappropriate (*informal*) ○ *a flip remark* ■ *n* **1 COIN'S SPIN** the spin of a coin or other object as it is tossed or thrown **2 TURNING OF BODY** a turning of the body through 360 degrees by springing from the ground or in diving **3 ALCOHOL AND EGG DRINK** an alcoholic drink containing beaten egg [Mid-16C. Probably an imitation of the sound.]

flipbook /flíp bo͝ok/ *n* a small book containing a series of images of the same thing in different positions that create the illusion of movement when the pages are turned quickly

flip chart *n* a visual aid consisting of a large pad of paper mounted on an easel, used to present information

flip-flop *n* **1 BACKLESS SANDAL** a backless foam-rubber sandal with a V-shaped strap secured between the toes and at the sides of the foot (*informal*) **2 BACKWARDS FLIP** a backwards flip of the body **3** *US* **CHANGE OF MIND** a change of opinion, especially by a politician (*informal*) **4 CIRCUIT WITH TWO STABLE STATES** an electronic circuit or mechanical device that has two stable states and can be switched between the two ■ *vi* (**flip-flops, flip-flopping, flip-flopped**) *US* **CHANGE OPINION** to change your opinion, especially when this leads to a change of policy (*informal*)

flippant /flíppənt/ *adj* showing a lack of seriousness that is thought inappropriate [Early 17C. < FLIP, after heraldic adjectives such as RAMPANT.] —**flippancy** *n* —**flippantly** *adv*

flipper /flíppər/ *n* **1 AQUATIC ANIMAL'S LIMB** a broad flat limb that an aquatic animal such as a penguin, seal, or whale uses for swimming **2 DIVER'S FOOTWEAR** a broad flat rubber extension worn on each of the feet to aid in swimming **3 PINBALL FEATURE** a small button-operated bat in a pinball machine that is used to keep the ball in play

flipping /flípping/ *adj, adv* used to emphasize annoyance or displeasure with something (*slang*) ○ *Will you turn that flipping music down?*

flip side *n* **1** the disadvantages involved in doing something as opposed to the advantages that have previously been mentioned (*slang*) **2** the song on a single record that the record company thinks will be less popular with record buyers, or the side of the record with that song on it (*dated*)

flirt /flurt/ *v* **1** *vi* **BEHAVE IN PLAYFUL AND ALLURING WAY** to behave in a playfully alluring way **2** *vt* **FLICK** to flick or jerk something ■ *n* **SOMEBODY BEHAVING WHO FLIRTS** a person who behaves in a playfully alluring way [Mid-16C. < ?] —**flirter** *n* —**flirtingly** *adv*

flirt with *vt* to consider an idea without doing anything serious about it or letting it have an effect ○ *flirted with the idea of going to college, but decided not to*

flirtation /flur táysh'n/ *n* **1** a short playful interaction based on lighthearted feeling or behaviour **2** a period of considering or participating in something in a superficial way ○ *a flirtation with vegetarianism*

flirtatious /flur táyshəss/ *adj* behaving playfully and in a way that gives the impression of sexual interest —**flirtatiously** *n* —**flirtatiousness** *adv*

flirty /flúrti/ (**-ier, -iest**) *adj* **1** flirtatious (*informal*) **2** suitable for a flirtatious person or a person in a flirtatious mood —**flirtily** *adv* —**flirtiness** *n*

flit /flit/ (**flits, flitting, flitted**) *vi* **1 MOVE FROM PLACE TO PLACE** to move quickly from one place to another without stopping for long **2 BE BRIEFLY PRESENT** to be briefly present or visible **3** *Scotland* **MOVE HOUSE** to move to a different residence [12C. < Old Norse *flytja* 'carry about' < Germanic, 'to float'.] —**flitter** *n*

flitch /flich/ *n* **1** a log cut lengthways from a tree, ready for further processing at a mill **2** a side of bacon or one side of a pork carcass without the leg or shoulder [Old English *flicce* < Germanic, 'to tear']

flitter /flíttər/ *vi* to move about in a restless or nervous way ■ *n* a rapid, repetitive, or back-and-forth movement in something small [14C. < FLIT.]

flittermouse /flíttər mowss/ (*plural* **-mice** /flíttər mīss/), **flitterbat** /flíttər bat/ *n* a bat (*regional*)

flitting /flítting/ *n* *Scotland* an act of moving house

float /flōt/ *v* **1** *vi* **REST ON SURFACE OF LIQUID** to move or rest on the surface of a liquid without sinking **2** *vt* **PLACE OR MOVE ON LIQUID** to place something or make something move on the surface of a liquid **3** *vi* **STAY UP IN AIR** to move slowly and lightly through the air **4** *vi* **BE HEARD OR SMELT FAINTLY** to carry across a distance, especially as a sound or smell ○ *The sound of laughter floated across the water.* **5** *vi* **MOVE GRACEFULLY** to move lightly and gracefully (*literary*) ○ *They floated across the dance floor.* **6** *vt* **PROPOSE PLAN** to propose a plan for consideration in order to see what response it receives (*informal*) **7** *vi* **LIVE AIMLESSLY** to live without a fixed purpose or plan **8** *vt* **SELL SHARES IN COMPANY** to finance a company by selling shares in it to the public on the stock exchange **9** *vt* **SELL SHARES OR BONDS** to offer shares or bonds for sale on a stock exchange **10** *vti* **ALLOW CURRENCY VALUE TO CHANGE** to allow the exchange rate value of a currency to fluctuate freely in an open market **11** *vt* **IRRIGATE LAND** to flood or irrigate land ■ *n* **1 FLOATING OBJECT** an object or device that floats or is used to keep another object buoyant **2 SWIMMING AID** a buoyant rectangular board that supports the arms and top of the body of a swimmer. US term **kickboard** **3 MONEY KEPT FOR CHANGE** a small amount of money in coins and notes that shopkeepers keep in the till so that they can give customers change **4 VEHICLE IN CARNIVAL PARADE** a truck or other large vehicle that has been elaborately decorated for a carnival parade **5** FISHING = **bobber** **6** *UK* **DELIVERY VEHICLE** a small, usually electrically-powered, delivery vehicle **7** *US* **CARBONATED DRINK WITH ICE CREAM** a carbonated drink with a scoop of ice cream floating in it **8 PADDLE WHEEL BLADE** a blade in a paddle wheel **9 PLASTERER'S TROWEL** a tool with a handle and flat rectangular blade for applying plaster to a wall **10 PERIOD BETWEEN DEPOSIT AND WITHDRAWAL** the period between the deposit of funds by a customer and the availability of the funds to the customer **11 BALL IN FLOW-REGULATING DEVICE** the hollow ball that rests on the water level in a tank as part of the device (**ballcock**) that regulates the flow of water into the tank **12** BIOL = **air bladder** [Old English *flotian* < Germanic] —**floatability** /flōtə bílləti/ *n* —**floatable** *adj*

float around *vi* to be the subject of frequent discussion or attention ○ *a rumour floating around about a pending engagement*

float chamber *n* a chamber in a carburettor that has a floating valve to control the entry and level of petrol

floater /flōtər/ *n* **1 SOMETHING FLOATING** somebody or something that is floating **2 WORKER SHIFTING TO VARIOUS TASKS** an employee who is switched from job to job as needed **3** *US* **CASUAL WORKER** a casual labourer who goes from job to job (*informal*) **4 DEAD BODY** a dead body found floating in water (*slang*) **5 SPOT INTERFERING WITH VISION** a shadow of opaque debris in the vitreous humour of the eye seen as a moving dark spot, or as a group of them, by the person affected. Technical name **muscae volitantes**

float glass *n* flat polished transparent glass made by solidifying molten glass as it floats on liquid of higher density, e.g. tin

floating /flṓting/ *adj* **1 NOT FIXED INTO POSITION** not fixed but moving around **2 OUT OF NORMAL POSITION** not in the normal place in the body, having moved out of position ○ *a floating kidney* **3 FLUCTUATING IN MONETARY VALUE** free to fluctuate in exchange rate value in relation to other currencies ○ *the floating euro*

floating assets *npl* BUSINESS = **current assets**

floating charge *n* an unsecured charge on the assets of a company that allows them to be commercially used until the company ceases operations or the creditor demands collateral

floating debt *n* short-term government borrowing

floating dock *n* **1** a large structure that can be submerged to let a ship enter and then raised with the ship inside to be used as a dry dock **2** a small dock supported by piles on which it can move up and down with the flow and ebb of the tide or changing water level caused by other means

floating island *n* a dessert consisting of custard on which are placed pieces of meringue that appear to float

⚡**floating-point** *adj* describes numbers in which the digits and the location of the decimal place are treated separately

floating policy *n* a marine insurance policy that covers loss of or damage to goods during transport, regardless of the ship carrying them

floating rib *n* a rib not attached to the breastbone. In humans the two lower ribs on each side are floating ribs.

floating voter *n* somebody who does not consistently vote for the same political party in elections. US term **swing voter**

floatplane /flṓt playn/ *n* a seaplane that has one or more floats that enable it to land on water

float tank *n* HEALTH = **flotation tank**

floaty /flṓti/ (**-ier, -iest**) *adj* **1** seeming to move slowly through the air **2** capable of floating easily

floc /flok/ *n* a woolly (**flocculent**) mass that forms in a liquid as a result of precipitation or the aggregation of suspended particles [Early 20C. Shortening of FLOCCULUS.]

floccillation /flóksə láysh'n/ *n* aimless plucking at bedclothes, a sign that a person is approaching death [Mid-19C. < modern Latin *floccillus* 'little tuft of wool' < Latin *floccus* 'tuft of wool'.]

floccose /flókōss/ *adj* describes plant parts that are covered with tufts of soft hair [Mid-18C. < late Latin *floccosus* < Latin *floccus* 'tuft of wool'.]

flocculate /flókyŏŏ layt/ (**-lates, -lating, -lated**) *vti* **1** to cause particles suspended in water to aggregate into clumps or masses that then sink or can be removed by filtering **2** to form, or cause clouds to form fluffy masses —**flocculation** /flókyŏŏ láysh'n/ *n*

floccule /flók yool/ *n* a small mass of woolly or cloudy particles [Mid-19C. < modern Latin *flocculus* (see FLOCCULUS).]

flocculent /flókyŏŏlənt/ *adj* **1 WITH FLUFFY APPEARANCE** having a fluffy or woolly appearance **2 WITH WOOLLY MASSES** describes the woolly mass of solids (**precipitate**) produced in a liquid by a chemical reaction **3 COVERED WITH TUFTS** covered with soft waxy tufts or flakes [Early 19C. < Latin *floccus* 'tuft of wool'.] —**flocculence** *n* —**flocculency** *n* —**flocculently** *adv*

flocculus /flókyŏŏləss/ (*plural* **-li** /-lī/) *n* a mass of gas that appears as either a dark or a bright spot on the surface of the Sun, often near to a sunspot [Late 18C. < modern Latin, 'small tuft of wool' < Latin *floccus* 'tuft of wool'.]

floccus /flókəss/ (*plural* **-ci** /flók sī/) *n* a tuft of woolly hair, or a fluffy or downy covering [Mid-19C. < Latin, 'tuft of wool'.]

flock /flok/ *n* **1 GROUP OF BIRDS OR SHEEP** a group of birds, sheep, or goats that travel, live, or feed together **2 CROWD OF PEOPLE** a large group of people of the same type **3 CONGREGATION** the members of a church congregation under the leadership of a priest or minister ■ *vi* **GO IN LARGE NUMBERS** to go to a place or event in large numbers [Old English *flocc* < ?]

flock paper *n* wallpaper with a raised pattern that is velvety to the touch [*Flock* 'powdered wool' (with which originally made) < Latin *floccus* 'tuft of wool']

Flodden Field /flódd'n-/ plain in N England, site of a battle in 1513 in which an English force heavily defeated the Scottish army

floe /flō/ *n* GEOG = **ice floe** [Early 19C. Probably < Norwegian *flo* 'layer'.]

SPELLCHECK Do not confuse ***floe*** with ***flow***, which has a similar sound. Beware: your spellchecker will not catch this error.

flog /flog/ (**flogs, flogging, flogged**) *vt* **1** to hit a person or animal very hard using something such as a whip, strap, or stick **2** to sell something (*informal*) [Late 17C. < ?] —**flogger** *n*

flokati /flə kaáti/ (*plural* **-tis**) *n* a handwoven woollen Greek rug with a shaggy pile [Mid-20C. < modern Greek *phlokatē* < Latin *floccus* 'tuft of wool'.]

flong /flong/ *n* a sheet of papier-mâché used to make a mould for a metal plate for printing a page of newspaper [Late 19C. < French *flan* 'mould' (see FLAN).]

flood /flud/ *n* **1 WATER COVERING PREVIOUSLY DRY AREA** a very large amount of water that has overflowed from a source such as a river or a broken pipe onto a previously dry area **2 HIGH TIDE** the flowing in to land of water, associated with a rising tide **3 HUGE NUMBER** a very large number of people or things ○ *a flood of complaints* **4** ELEC = **floodlight** *n*. 1 ■ *v* **1** *vti* **COVER AREA WITH WATER** to cover a previously dry area with large amounts of water, or be covered with large amounts of water **2** *vti* **OVERFLOW** to undergo conditions in which water overflows banks or barriers **3** *vi* **ARRIVE IN LARGE NUMBERS** to arrive somewhere in very large numbers ○ *Messages of support are still flooding in.* **4** *vt* **SEND MANY CALLS OR LETTERS TO** to send a very large number of calls, letters, or complaints to an organization (*usually passive*) ○ *We have been flooded with offers of help.* **5** *vi* **FEEL EMOTION SUDDENLY AND INTENSELY** to feel a particular emotion, sensation, or memory suddenly and intensely **6** *vt* **FILL MARKET TO EXCESS** to supply too much of a product to a market, pushing prices down and keeping them low **7** *vti* **SUPPLY TOO MUCH PETROL TO CARBURETTOR** to send too much petrol to a carburettor in a car engine, or be supplied with too much, so that the car fails to start **8** *vti* **FILL WITH LIGHT** to shine strongly so that a place becomes filled with a bright or glowing light (*literary*) **9** *vi* **BLEED A LOT FROM THE WOMB** to bleed profusely from the womb, e.g. after childbirth (*technical*) **10** *vi* **BLEED A LOT IN MENSTRUATION** to bleed profusely during a menstrual period (*technical*) [Old English *flōd* < Germanic] —**floodable** *adj* —**flooded** *adj* —**flooder** *n* ◇ **be in flood** to be very full of water, so that it overflows banks or barriers ◇ **be in floods of tears** to cry a lot

flood out *vt* to force somebody to leave a place or stop using something because flooding makes it impossible to stay or continue

Flood *n* in the Bible (Genesis 7–8), a devastating flood covering the earth, a sign of God's anger at humanity's wickedness

floodgate /flúd gayt/ *n* a gate in a sluice that is used to control the flow of water

floodlight /flúd līt/ *n* **1 POWERFUL LAMP USED AT NIGHT** a large powerful lamp that produces a strong broad beam of artificial light and is used to illuminate the outside of public buildings or sports events at night **2 POWERFUL BEAM OF LIGHT** a broad powerful beam of intense bright light produced artificially ■ *vti* (**-lights, -lighting, -lit, -lit** /flúd lit/) **LIGHT SOMETHING WITH FLOODLIGHTS** to illuminate something with floodlights

floodmark /flúd maark/ *n* the highest level reached by a tide or flood water, or a mark that indicates this level

flood meadow *n Wales, Ireland, SW England* low-lying land likely to be waterlogged in wet weather

floodplain /flúd playn/ *n* an area of low-lying land across which a river flows that is covered with sediment as a result of frequent flooding

flood tide *n* **1** the incoming tide, or the period of time between low water and the following high water **2** an irresistible or overwhelming force of feeling such as strong public outrage or enthusiasm

floodwall /flúd wawl/ *n* a wall built along the seashore or the bank of a river to prevent flooding of adjacent land

floodwater /flúd wawtər/ *n* the water of a flood that is carried over river and stream banks to inundate previously dry land

floor /flawr/ *n* **1 PART OF ROOM TO WALK ON** the flat horizontal part of a room on which people walk **2 STOREY** all the rooms on one level of a building ○ *an office on the fourth floor* **3 NATURAL GROUND LEVEL** the ground at the bottom of an ocean, lake, cave, valley, or forest **4 LEVEL AREA** a flat open space for an activity or seating ○ *Are your seats in the stands or on the floor?* **5 PART OF LEGISLATURE WHERE MEMBERS SIT** the part of the building housing a legislative body where the members sit and where official debates and discussions take place **6 PLACE WHERE SECURITIES ARE TRADED** the part of a stock exchange where securities, futures, or options contracts are traded **7 MANUFACTURING AREA OF FACTORY** the area of a factory where workers manufacture or assemble products **8 PART OF STORE FOR MERCHANDISE DISPLAY** the part of a shop where merchandise is displayed and sold **9 DANCE FLOOR** a dance floor (*informal*) **10 PEOPLE PRESENT AT MEETING** all the people present in the audience at a meeting, as opposed to the main speakers ○ *I'll take questions from the floor later.* **11 LOWEST LIMIT** a lower limit, e.g. on an interest rate or the value of an asset **12 PART OF CAR INTERIOR** the flat lower part of a motor vehicle's interior where the accelerator, clutch, and brake pedals are found and where the driver and passengers put their feet. US term **floorboard** *n*. 2 ■ *vt* **1 ASTONISH** to leave somebody astonished and unable to react ○ *He was floored by the announcement of the changes.* **2 KNOCK DOWN** to knock somebody down with a punch **3** *US* **PRESS ACCELERATOR DOWN HARD** to depress a motor vehicle's accelerator down as far as it will go in order to increase speed to the maximum (*slang*) [Old English *flōr* < Indo-European, 'flat'] —**floorer** *n* ◇ **have the floor** to address a meeting, or have the right to address a meeting ◇ **take the floor 1** to rise to speak to a group of people **2** to begin to dance, e.g. in a ballroom or nightclub ◇ **take to the floor** to begin to dance, e.g. in a ballroom or nightclub ◇ **wipe the floor with somebody** to defeat somebody completely and decisively (*informal*)

floorage /fláwrij/ *n* the floor area of a building

floorboard /fláwr bawrd/ *n* **1** one of the strips of wood that are used to make a wood floor **2** *US* CARS = **floor** *n*. 12

floorcovering /fláwr kuvvəring/ *n* **1** material such as carpeting for covering floor surfaces **2** a carpet, mat, or other piece of material for covering all or part of a floor surface

floor exercise *n* an event in a gymnastics competition that consists of a series of tumbling exercises in a timed routine performed on a mat

floor hockey *n US, Can* a version of hockey played using hockey sticks and a plastic puck or ball in a gymnasium

flooring /fláwring/ *n* the materials from which a floor is made

floor lamp *n US* = **standard lamp**

floor leader *n* a member of an American legislative body chosen by fellow party members to organize their activities and strategy on the floor of the legislature

floor-length *adj* describes a garment such as a dress that extends to the floor or the ankles

floor manager *n* **1** an employee of a department store or large shop who is in charge of one floor or department, supervising staff and dealing with customers' complaints **2** the stage manager of a television programme

floor plan *n* a plan of a room or floor of a building drawn to scale as if viewed from above

floorshow /fláwr shō/ *n* a series of shows featuring dancers, singers, comedians, or magicians at a nightclub

floorwalker /fláwr wawkər/ *n US* COMM = **shopwalker**

floozy /flóozi/ (*plural* **-zies**) *n* an offensive term that deliberately insults a woman as being vulgar and promiscuous (*informal*) [Early 20C. < ?]

flop /flop/ *vi* (**flops, flopping, flopped**) **1 SIT OR LIE DOWN HEAVILY** to sit or lie down heavily by relaxing the muscles and letting the body fall **2 MOVE LIMPLY** to move limply or heavily **3 FAIL COMPLETELY** to be completely unsuccessful (*informal*) ■ *n* **1 TOTAL FAILURE** a complete failure (*informal*)

2 HEAVY DULL SOUND the sound made by something falling heavily [Early 17C. Alteration of FLAP.] —**flopper** *n*

flophouse /flóp howss/ (*plural* **-houses** /flóp howziz/) *n US* = **dosshouse** (*informal*) [Early 20C. < FLOP 'lie down, sleep'.]

floppy /flóppi/ *adj* (**-pier, -piest**) soft and tending to hang down limply or loosely ■ *n* (*plural* **-pies**) COMPUT = **floppy disk** (*informal*) —**floppily** *adv* —**floppiness** *n*

floppy disk *n* a small flexible magnetically coated disk in a rigid plastic case on which data can be stored or retrieved by a computer [Late 20C. < its flexibility, as opposed to a HARD DISK.]

flops /flops/, **FLOPS** *abbr* floating-point operations per second (*indicates the speed of a computer*)

floptical /flóptik'l/ *adj* relating to a system for storing computer data on a disk that combines magnetic and optical technology [Late 20C. Blend of FLOPPY + OPTICAL.]

flor., fl. *abbr* floruit

flora /fláwrə/ (*plural* **-ras** *or* **-rae** /-ree/) *n* **1 PLANTS** plant life, especially all the plants found in a particular country, region, or time regarded as a group (*formal*) ○ *the flora of Australia.* ◊ **fauna** *n.* 1 **2 DESCRIPTION OF PLANTS** a systematic set of descriptions of all the plants of a particular place or time **3 BACTERIA THAT INHABIT BODY ORGANS** all the usually harmless bacteria inhabiting an area or part of the body, regarded as a group or population [Early 16C. < Latin *Flora*, Roman goddess of flowers < *flor-* 'flower'.]

floral /fláwrəl/ *adj* **1 CONSISTING OF FLOWERS** containing or made up of flowers **2 DECORATED WITH FLOWERS** ornamented or decorated with flowers or with representations of them **3 RELATING TO FLOWERS** relating to or being a part of a flower [Mid-17C. < Latin *Floralis* 'of Flora' or *flor-* (see FLORA).] —**florally** *adv*

Florence /flórrənss/ city in central Italy on the River Arno. Population: 379,681 (1997 estimate). Italian **Firenze**

Florentine /flórrən tīn/ *adj* **1 OF FLORENCE** relating to the Italian city of Florence, or its people or culture **2 TYPICAL OF ART OF RENAISSANCE FLORENCE** relating to the style of art or architecture in Florence during the Renaissance **3 WITH SPINACH** cooked or served with spinach ○ *eggs Florentine* ■ *n* **1 SOMEBODY FROM FLORENCE** somebody who comes from the Italian city of Florence **2 TYPE OF BISCUIT** a biscuit containing candied peel, fruit, and nuts and covered in a thick layer of chocolate [13C. < Latin *Florentinus* < *Florentia* 'Florence'.]

Florentine stitch *n* HANDICRAFT = **bargello**

Flores /flórress/ **1** one of the Lesser Sunda Islands in SE Indonesia. Population: 272,750 (1989). Area: 14,200 sq. km/5,480 sq. mi. **2** island in the NW Azores, in the N Atlantic Ocean. Population: 4,435 (1991). Area: 150 sq. km/58 sq. mi.

florescence /flaw réss'nss/ *n* flowering [Late 18C. < modern Latin *florescentia* < Latin *florescent-*, present participle of *florescere* 'begin to flower' < *florere* (see FLOURISH).] —**florescent** *adj*

Flores Sea sea between the eastern end of Java and the western end of the Banda Sea in Indonesia

floret /flórrət/ *n* **1** a small flower, especially one in a flower head consisting of many flowers **2** a small part into which the edible flower head of cauliflower or broccoli can be separated [Late 17C. < Latin *flor-* 'flower'.]

Florey /fláwri/, **Sir Howard Walter, Baron Florey of Adelaide and Marston** (1898–1968) Australian scientist

Florianópolis /flórri ə nóppəliss/ city in SE Brazil, on Santa Catarina Island. Population: 271,281 (1996).

floriated /fláwri aytid/ *adj* decorated with designs based on flowers and leaves [Mid-19C. < Latin *flor-* 'flower'.]

floribunda /flórri búndə/ *n* a hybrid cultivated rose. Flowers: small, in large sprays. [Late 19C. < modern Latin, form of *floribundus* 'flowering profusely' < Latin *flor-* 'flower'.]

floricane /fláwri kayn/ *n* a plant stem that flowers and bears fruit in its second year, e.g. in raspberries [< Latin *flor-* 'flower']

floriculture /fláwri kulchər/ *n* the growing of flowers as a crop [Early 19C. < Latin *flor-* 'flower', after HORTICULTURE.] —**floricultural** /fláwri kúlchərəl/ *adj* —**floriculturally** *adv* —**floriculturist** *n*

florid /flórrid/ *adj* **1** having an unhealthily glowing pink or red complexion **2** ornate and overly complicated in wording and general style [Mid-17C. Via French < Latin *floridus* 'flowery' < *flor-* 'flower'.] —**floridity** /flo ríddəti/ *n* —**floridly** *adv* —**floridness** *n*

Florida /flórridə/ state in the SE United States. Capital: Tallahassee. Population: 14,653,945 (1997). Area: 155,213 sq. km/59,928 sq. mi. —**Floridian** /flə ríddi ən/ *adj, n*

Florida Keys /-keez/ chain of islands and reefs in S Florida, extending into the Gulf of Mexico. Length: 309 km/192 mi.

floriferous /flaw ríffərəss/ *adj* bearing or able to bear many flowers [Mid-17C. < Latin *florifer* < *flor-* 'flower'.] —**floriferously** *adv* —**floriferousness** *n*

florilegium /fláwri leeji əm/ (*plural* **-a** /-ji ə/) *n* an anthology of literary extracts (*archaic*) [Early 17C. < modern Latin, 'gathering of flowers'.]

florin /flórrin/ *n* **1 OLD BRITISH COIN** a unit of currency used in Britain between 1849 and 1968, equivalent to two shillings **2 GOLD OR SILVER COIN** a gold or silver coin, especially a Dutch guilder **3 FLORENTINE COIN** a gold coin first minted in Florence in 1252, or any similar coin used elsewhere in Europe [14C. Via Old French < Italian *fiorino* < *fiore* 'flower' (because originally a coin bearing a lily) < Latin *flor-*.]

Florio /fláwri ō/, **John** (1553–1625) English lexicographer and translator

florist /flórrist/ *n* **1** a dealer in flowers and ornamental plants **2 florist, florist's** a shop that sells flowers and other ornamental plants [Early 17C. < Latin *flor-* 'flower'.]

floristics /flo rístiks/ *n* a branch of botany dealing with the types, numbers, distribution, and relationships of plant species in a particular area or particular areas (+ *singular verb*) [Late 19C. < FLORA.]

-florous *suffix* bearing flowers ○ *multiflorous* [< Latin *flor-* 'flower']

floruit /flórroo it/ *v* used, especially abbreviated as 'fl'., before the name or numeric designator of the period in the past when a specified person or movement was most active. (*formal*) [Mid-19C. < Latin, 'flourished'.]

flory /fláwri/ *adj* containing a fleur-de-lis [14C. < Old French *flo(u)ré* < *flour* (see FLOWER).]

Flory /fláwri/, **Paul John** (1910–85) US chemist

floss /floss/ *vti* **CLEAN BETWEEN TEETH** to clean between individual teeth using dental floss ■ *n* **1** DENT = **dental floss 2 SILKWORM FIBRES** short or waste fibres prepared from the outside of a silkworm's cocoon **3 PLANT FIBRES** the mass of fine silk fibres that covers the seeds of the ceiba tree or of a cotton plant **4 EMBROIDERY THREAD** an embroidery thread made up of six strands loosely twisted together that can be separated for fine work [Mid-18C. < ?] —**flosser** *n*

flossy /flóssi/ (**-ier, -iest**) *adj* **1** *US* ornate or showy in a flashy, often almost vulgar way **2** consisting of or looking like floss —**flossily** *adv* —**flossiness** *n*

flotage /flótij/ *n* **1** = **flotation** *n.* **2**, **flotation** *n.* **3 2** SHIPPING = **flotsam** *n.* 1

flotation /flō táysh'n/ *n* **1 SELLING OF SHARES IN COMPANY** the financing of a company by selling shares in it or a new debt issue or the offering of shares and bonds for sale on the stock exchange **2 FLOATING** the act, process, or condition of floating **3 CAPABILITY OF FLOATING** the ability to float on a liquid or remain on top of a soft surface (*technical*) **4 ADHERENCE OF TYRE TO SURFACE** the ability of a tyre tread to adhere to and remain on top of a soft surface such as wet ground or snow **5 SEPARATION PROCESS** a process for separating materials, e.g. a mixture of minerals in an ore, according to their different abilities to float in a given liquid [Early 19C. < FLOAT.]

flotation bags *npl* large bags that inflate when a helicopter or spacecraft lands in the sea and keep it afloat and upright

flotation tank *n* a sealed tank filled with salt water and minerals that somebody can float in to relieve stress

flotation therapy *n* a method of relieving stress that involves floating in salt water in a sealed tank while listening to music

flotel /flō tél/ *n* a moored boat or an oil rig that provides accommodation for workers on offshore oil rigs [Late 20C. Contraction of *floating hotel*.]

flotilla /flō tíllə/ *n* **1** a fleet of usually small vessels **2** a group of things operating or moving together [Early 18C. < Spanish, 'small fleet' < *flota* 'fleet', via Old French < Old Norse *floti*.]

flotsam /flótsəm/ *n* **1** wreckage, debris, or refuse from a ship, found floating in the water **2** people who live on the margins of society, such as vagrants, the homeless, or the destitute (*offensive in some contexts*) [Early 17C. < Anglo-Norman *floteson* < *floter* 'float' < Germanic.] ◇ **flotsam and jetsam** discarded objects or odds and ends

flounce[1] /flownss/ (**flounces, flouncing, flounced**) *vi* to move with exaggerated angry swaggering motions showing displeasure or indignation [Mid-16C. < ?] —**flounce** *n*

flounce[2] /flownss/ *n* a strip of cloth that has been gathered into pleats on one side and then stitched onto a garment or curtain as a decoration [Early 18C. Alteration of Old French *fronce* 'pleat' (probably after FLOUNCE[1]) < Germanic.]

flouncing /flównssing/ *n* material used to make flounces

flounder[1] /flówndər/ *vi* **1 MAKE UNCONTROLLED MOVEMENTS** to make clumsy uncontrolled movements while trying to regain balance or move forward **2 HESITATE IN CONFUSION** to act in a way that shows confusion or a lack of purpose **3 BE IN SERIOUS DIFFICULTY** to have serious problems and be close to failing [Late 16C. < ?]

flounder[2] /flówndər/ (*plural* **-der** *or* **-ders**) *n* **1 EDIBLE FLATFISH** an edible flatfish of shallow coastal waters. Families: Pleuronectidae and Bothidae. **2 EDIBLE EUROPEAN FLATFISH** an edible flatfish that has a greyish-brown mottled skin with orange spots and prickly scales. Native to: Europe. *Platichthys flesus.* **3 FLOUNDER AS FOOD** the flesh of a flounder used as food [15C. Via Anglo-Norman *floundre* < N Germanic.]

flour /flówər/ *n* **1 FINELY GROUND CEREAL GRAINS** a powder made by grinding the edible parts of cereal grains. Use: bread, cakes, pastry, sauce thickener. **2 GROUND FOODSTUFF** a finely ground powder made from any dried vegetable such as chickpea, banana, cassava, or potato ■ *vt* **COVER WITH FLOUR** to cover or coat food, food preparation utensils, or a work surface with flour [13C. Variant of FLOWER 'the best (ground meal)'.]

SPELLCHECK Do not confuse ***flour*** with ***flower***, which has a similar sound. Beware: your spellchecker will not catch this error.

~~flourescent~~ incorrect spelling of **fluorescent**

~~flouride~~ incorrect spelling of **fluoride**

~~flourine~~ incorrect spelling of **fluorine**

flourish /flúrrish/ *v* **1** *vi* **BE HEALTHY OR GROW WELL** to be strong and healthy or grow well, especially because conditions are right **2** *vi* **DO WELL** to sustain continuous steady strong growth **3** *vt* **WAVE** to wave something in a dramatic way that draws attention to it ■ *n* **1 HAND MOVEMENT** a dramatic body movement, such as a sweep of the hand, that attracts attention **2 LOOP OR CURL** an embellishment to something handwritten, such as a loop or curly line **3 ORNAMENTAL TRUMPET CALL** a fanfare heralding the arrival of an important person **4 SHORT PRELUDE OR POSTLUDE** a short, often improvised, passage at the beginning or end of a piece of music **5 SHOWY MUSICAL INTERLUDE** a brief, often showy, technical passage within a piece of music [13C. < Old French *floriss-*, stem of *florir* 'to bloom' < Latin *florere* < *flor-* 'flower'.] —**flourisher** *n*

floury /flów əri/ (**-ier, -iest**) *adj* **1** covered or coated with flour, or tasting of flour **2** easily crumbling when cooked ○ *floury potatoes*

flout /flowt/ *vt* to show contempt for a law or convention by openly disobeying or defying it [Mid-16C. < ?] —**flouter** *n* —**floutingly** *adv*

USAGE See ***flaunt***.

flow /flō/ *vi* **1 MOVE FREELY FROM PLACE TO PLACE** to move or be moved freely from one place to another in large numbers or amounts in a steady unbroken stream ○ *measures to allow traffic to flow freely* **2 CIRCULATE IN BODY** to move through the veins and arteries of the body (*refers especially to blood*) **3 BE SAID FLUENTLY** to be expressed uninhibitedly and eloquently ○ *The conversation began to flow.* **4 BE AVAILABLE IN QUANTITY** to be readily available and consumed in large amounts (*refers to alcoholic drinks*) **5 BE EXPERIENCED INTENSELY** to be experienced very intensely, often in a way that is visible to other people ○ *A wave of love flowed across her face.* **6 EMANATE AS RESULT** to derive from something as a result or series of results (*literary*) ○ *The consequences that flowed from the decision were worrying.* **7 HANG LOOSELY** to fall or hang loosely and gracefully ○ *Her long hair flowed over her shoulders.* **8 MOVE TOWARDS LAND** to move towards the land as the tide rises (*refers to the sea or tidal water*) **9 CHANGE**

SHAPE UNDER PRESSURE to change shape gradually in response to pressure without the development of cracks or fissures ■ *n* **1** **MOVEMENT OF FLUID OR ELECTRICAL CHARGE** the movement of liquid, gas, or electrical charge **2** **MASS OR QUANTITY FLOWING** a mass or quantity of material that is flowing or has flowed ○ *a giant lava flow pouring down into the valley* **3** **MENSTRUAL FLOW** the flow or quantity of blood during menstruation **4** **UNHINDERED STEADY MOVEMENT** a steady unbroken stream of people, goods, vehicles, money, or information from one place to another ○ *the unending flow of refugees* **5** **TIDAL MOVEMENT TOWARDS LAND** the movement of a rising tide towards the land **6** **ELOQUENT EXPRESSION OF THOUGHTS** the continuous eloquent expression of thoughts or ideas in speech or writing **7** *Scotland* **BOGGY EXPANSE** an expanse of wet peat bog ○ *the flow country* **8** *US* **EXPERIENCE OF HEIGHTENED AWARENESS** psychological and physical experience in which challenges presented are perfectly matched by the participants' skills, often resulting in heightened states of awareness, confidence, and performance [Old English *flōwan* < Indo-European] —**flowingly** *adv* ◇ **go with the flow** to follow the lead of other people and react to their opinions or actions rather passively

SPELLCHECK See *floe*.

flowage /flṓ ij/ *n* **1** **FLOWING** the act of flowing or overflowing **2** **OVERFLOWING WATER** the water resulting from overflow **3** **GRADUAL DEFORMATION** the gradual change in shape that occurs in certain solids, e.g. asphalt, that can flow without breaking when, e.g. heat is applied

flow chart *n* a diagram that represents the sequence of operations in a process

flow-charting *n* the designing of a flow chart or charts

flow cytometry *n* a diagnostic test revealing the arrangement and amount of DNA in a cell. Use: to distinguish benign cells from malignant ones, to monitor the effect of anticancer treatment.

flow diagram *n* BUSN = **flow chart**

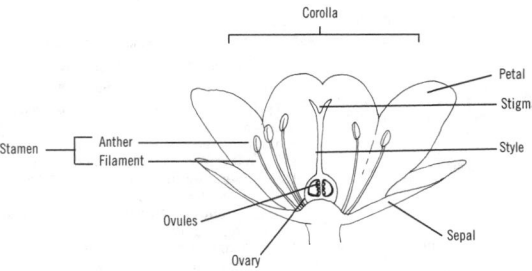

Flower: Cross-section of a flower

Corolla · Petal · Stigma · Style · Sepal · Ovary · Ovules · Anther · Filament · Stamen

flower /flṓw ər/ *n* **1** **COLOURED PART OF PLANT** a coloured, sometimes scented, part of a plant that contains its reproductive organs **2** **STEM WITH FLOWER** a plant stem with one or more flowers that has been picked from the plant on which it grew **3** **PLANT WITH FLOWERS** a small plant grown for the attractiveness of its flowers **4** **FLOWERING STATE** the state or period during which a plant has open blooms on it ○ *The roses are just coming into flower.* **5** **BEST** the best part of or most perfect example of something ○ *the flower of the nation's youth* **6** *N England* **USED TO ADDRESS SOMEBODY AFFECTIONATELY** used as a way of addressing somebody you like or love (*informal*) ■ **flowers** *npl* **FINE CHEMICAL POWDER** a fine powder produced by sublimation or condensation ■ *vi* **1** **PRODUCE BLOOMS** to begin to produce blooms **2** **DEVELOP TO MATURITY** to develop and reach maturity [12C. < Anglo-Norman *flur*, Old French *flour* < Latin *flor*- 'flower'.] —**flowered** /flṓw ard/ *adj*

SPELLCHECK See *flour*.

flowerbed /flṓwər bed/ *n* a clearly delineated area of a garden or park planted with flowering plants

flower child *n* a young person in the 1960s and 1970s who rejected materialism and war, especially the Vietnam War, and preached universal peace and love as the solution to the world's problems (*informal*) [< their custom of wearing or carrying flowers as a symbol of peace]

flower girl *n* **1** a young girl who carries flowers in the

procession at a wedding **2** a girl or woman who sells flowers in the street

flower head *n* **1** a cluster of small flowers on a single stem **2** a dense arrangement of flower buds, such as in cauliflower or broccoli

flowering /flṓwəring/ *adj* capable of producing noticeable flowers ■ *n* the moment in the development of an idea, style, or movement when it gains recognition and becomes successful

flowering currant *n* a deciduous shrub with dark green aromatic leaves. Flowers: small tubular red or pink. *Ribes sanguineum.*

flowering dogwood *n* a deciduous tree with inconspicuous flowers surrounded by showy white or pink bracts, and leaves that turn red or purple in autumn. *Cornus florida.*

flowering rush *n* a deciduous water plant similar to a rush that has narrow twisted leaves. Flowers: pink. *Butomus umbellatus.*

flower-of-an-hour (*plural* **flowers-of-an-hour**), **flower-of-the-hour** (*plural* **flowers-of-the-hour**) *n* a cultivated herbaceous annual plant that has oval serrated leaves. Flowers: creamy-white or pale yellow, trumpet-shaped. Native to: Europe. *Hibiscus trionum.* [Because its petals are short-lived]

flower-pecker *n* a small songbird with a long tongue that feeds on nectar, berries, and insects. Native to: Australia, SE Asia. Family: Dicaeidae.

flower people *npl* young 1960s-1970s peace activists, the flower children, regarded as a group (*informal*)

flowerpot /flṓwər pot/ *n* a clay or plastic container in which plants are grown

flower power *n* the idea advocated by some young people in the 1960s and 1970s that universal peace and love should replace the materialism and militarism of Western society [< its adherents' custom of wearing or carrying flowers as a symbol of peace and love]

flower pressing *n* the process of preserving cut flowers by laying them on a flat surface and pressing them with a heavy object

flowery /flṓwəri/ (-ier, -iest) *adj* **1** **POMPOUSLY LITERARY** full of ornate, overly elaborate expressions **2** **ORNAMENTED WITH FLOWERS** decorated or patterned with flowers **3** **LIKE FLOWERS** relating to flowers —**floweriness** *n*

flowmeter /flṓ meetər/ *n* an instrument for measuring the rate of flow of liquids or gases, especially in a pipe

flown past participle of **fly**[1]

flow-on *n* ANZ an increase in wages awarded to one union or group of workers as a result of a pay rise awarded to another union or group working in the same field, or the process by which this is done

flow sheet *n* **1** BUSN = **flow chart** **2** a schematic diagram showing the equipment and connecting pipes that make up a process plant and sometimes showing flow rates and quantities of material

flowstone /flṓ stōn/ *n* a layered deposit of calcium carbonate (**calcite**) on rock where water has flowed or dripped, e.g. on the walls or floor of a cave

flowy /flṓ i/ *adj* loose-fitting or free-hanging so as to complement the wearer's body movements attractively ○ *a flowy dress*

fl oz, fl. oz. *abbr* fluid ounces

FLQ *n* a terrorist organization seeking the secession of Quebec from Canada. Full form **Front de Libération du Québec**

Flt Lt, F/Lt, F. Lt *abbr* Flight Lieutenant

Flt Sgt *abbr* Flight Sergeant

flu /floo/ *n* a viral illness producing a high temperature, sore throat, running nose, headache, dry cough, and muscle pain [Mid-19C. Shortening of INFLUENZA.]

SPELLCHECK Do not confuse *flu* with *flue*, which has a similar sound. Beware: your spellchecker will not catch this error.

flucloxacillin *n* a penicillin drug. Use: treatment of streptococcal infections and pneumonia.

fluconazole *n* an antifungal drug

fluctuate /flúkchoo ayt/ (-ates, -ating, -ated) *vi* to change often from high to low levels or from one condition to another in an unpredictable way [Mid-17C. < Latin *fluctuat*-, past participle of *fluctuare* < *fluere* 'to flow'.] —**fluctuant** *adj* —**fluctuation** /flúkchoo áysh'n/ *n*

flue /floo/ *n* **1** **SMOKE OR HEAT OUTLET** a shaft, tube, or pipe used as an outlet to carry smoke, gas, or heat from a chimney or furnace **2** **flue, flue pipe** **ORGAN PIPE** an organ pipe in which the sound is produced by passing air across a lipped opening **3** **OPENING ON ORGAN PIPE** the lipped opening on an organ pipe that initiates vibrations and sound when air passes across it [15C. < ?]

SPELLCHECK See *flu*.

flue-cure (**flue-cures, flue-curing, flue-cured**) *vt* to cure tobacco with radiant heat supplied through flues from a furnace —**flue-cured** *adj*

flue gas *n* the smoke in the uptake of a boiler fire that consists mainly of carbon dioxide, carbon monoxide, and nitrogen

fluellin /floo éllən/, **fluellen** *n* an annual wild plant related to the toadflax, foxglove, and snapdragon. Genus: *Kickxia*. [Mid-16C. Alteration of Welsh (*llysiau*) *Llywelyn* 'Llewelyn's herbs', after LLEWELLYN AP GRUFFUDD or LLEWELYN AP IORWERTH.]

fluent /floo ənt/ *adj* **1** **ABLE TO SPEAK WITH EASE** able to speak a language effortlessly and correctly **2** **EFFORTLESSLY EXPRESSED** spoken or expressed effortlessly and correctly **3** **SMOOTHLY FLOWING** flowing in a smooth graceful way (*literary*) [Late 16C. < Latin *fluent*-, present participle of *fluere* 'flow'.] —**fluency** *n* —**fluently** *adv*

flue stop *n* an organ stop that controls a set of flue pipes

fluey /floo i/ (-ier, -iest) *adj* having the symptoms of flu

fluff /fluf/ *n* **1** **LIGHT BALLS OF THREAD** soft light balls of thread or fibre that collect together on material such as wool or cotton **2** **DOWNY FUZZ** the soft downy fuzz found on young birds or some seeds **3** **NONSENSE** something of no importance or consequence (*slang*) ■ *vt* **1** **DO BADLY** to do something badly because of loss of concentration or forgetfulness (*informal*) **2** **SHAKE SO AS TO INSERT AIR** to shake, pat, or brush something in order to get air into it **3** **RAISE FEATHERS** to raise the feathers in a way that makes the body appear bigger ■ *adj* US serving no useful purpose, especially purely decorative or eye-catching (*informal*) [Late 18C. < ?]

fluffy /flúffi/ (-ier, -iest) *adj* **1** **SOFT AND LIGHT** consisting of something soft and light to the touch such as wool or feathers **2** **DOWNY OR FEATHERY** covered in something soft and light to the touch such as down or feathers **3** **SOFT AND LIGHT IN TEXTURE** soft and light in texture because air has been beaten or whisked in —**fluffily** *adv* —**fluffiness** *n*

flügelhorn /floog'l hawrn/, **flugelhorn** *n* a brass instrument with valves, similar to a cornet but with a larger bell [Mid-19C. < German *Flügelhorn* 'wing horn'; from its use to signal to beaters on the flanks in a shoot.] —**flügelhornist** *n*

fluid /floo id/ *n* **1** **LIQUID** anything liquid (*not technical*) **2** **LIQUID OR GAS** a substance such as a liquid or gas whose molecules flow freely, so that it has no fixed shape and little resistance to outside stress ■ *adj* **1** **FLOWING** capable of flowing like a liquid or gas (*technical*) **2** **MOVING OR SMOOTHLY CARRIED OUT** smooth and graceful in a way that seems relaxed ○ *a series of fluid arm movements* **3** **UNSTABLE** likely to change ○ *The situation in the western sector is fluid.* [15C. Via Old French < Latin *fluidus* 'flowing' < *fluere* 'flow'.] —**fluidal** *adj* —**fluidally** *adv* —**fluidity** /floo íddati/ *n* —**fluidly** *adv* —**fluidness** *n*

fluid clutch *n* CARS = **fluid drive**

fluid dram *n* = **drachm** *n.* 1

fluid drive *n* a device for transmitting rotation between two shafts by means of the acceleration and deceleration of a hydraulic fluid by turbines with blades, used in automatic transmissions in motor vehicles

fluid dynamics *n* the scientific study of the forces acting on liquids and gases and the resulting movements of these fluids (*+ singular verb*)

fluidextract /flóo id éks trakt/ *n* a concentrated solution in alcohol of a plant-derived drug

fluidic /floo íddik/ *adj* **1** relating to fluids **2** relating to or operated by fluidics

fluidics /floo íddiks/ *n* the use of systems based on the movements and pressure of fluids to control operations, instruments, and industrial processes (*+ singular verb*)

fluidize /flóo i dīz/ (**-izes, -izing, -ized**), **fluidise** (**-ises, -ising, -ised**) *vt* **1** to make something fluid **2** to make a solid move as a fluid, e.g. by pulverizing it into fine powder and passing a gas through it to induce flow —**fluidization** /flóo i dī záysh'n/ *n* —**fluidizer** *n*

fluidized bed *n* a powder or other solid particulate material suspended in an upward flow of air or other gas that behaves like a fluid. It is an effective way to transfer heat or moisture between a gas and a solid.

fluid mechanics *n* the branch of mechanics that deals with the properties of gases and liquids and their application in practical engineering (*+ singular verb*)

fluid ounce *n* **1** a unit of liquid measurement in the imperial system equal to $\frac{1}{20}$ of an imperial pint or 28.41 ml **2** a unit of volume measurement in the US customary system equal to $\frac{1}{16}$ of a US pint or 29.57 ml

fluke[1] /flook/ *n* something surprising or unexpected that happens by accident (*informal*) ■ *vti* (**flukes, fluking, fluked**) to make a successful shot by accident, especially in pool, billiards, or snooker [Mid-19C. < ?]

fluke[2] /flook/ *n* **1** = **trematode** **2** a flatfish, especially a flounder (*regional*) [Old English *flōc* < Indo-European, 'be flat']

fluke[3] /flook/ *n* **1** PART OF ANCHOR either of the triangular blades at the end of each arm of an anchor **2** BARB ON HARPOON a barb on the head of a harpoon or an arrow, or the barbed head itself **3** PART OF WHALE'S TAIL either of the two horizontal lobes of the tail of a whale or similar sea animal, used in propelling the animal through the water [Mid-16C. < ?]

fluky /flóoki/ (**-ier, -iest**), **flukey** (**-ier, -iest**) *adj* accidentally and unexpectedly successful (*informal*) —**flukily** *adv* —**flukiness** *n*

flume /floom/ *n* **1** a narrow gorge with a stream running through it **2** an artificial water channel or chute used to transport logs, for studying water and sediment movement, or as part of a fairground ride [12C. Via Old French *flum* < Latin *flumen* 'river' < *fluere* 'flow'.]

flummery /flúmməri/ *n* **1** meaningless words, statements, or language, especially when intended as flattery (*literary*) **2** a cream, milk, or custard dessert set with gelatine [Early 17C. < Welsh *llymru*.]

flummox /flúmməks/ *vt* to leave somebody confused or perplexed and unable to react (*informal*) [Mid-19C. < ?]

flung past participle, past tense of **fling**

flunk /flungk/ *v* (*informal*) **1** *vti* to fail an exam or course **2** *vt US* to give a student a failing grade [Early 19C. < ?] —**flunker** *n*

flunk out *vi US* to be expelled from a school, college, or course because of poor academic performance (*informal*)

flunky /flúngki/ (*plural* **-kies**), **flunkey** (*plural* **-keys**) *n* **1** an assistant who carries out unimportant jobs for somebody and who behaves obsequiously to that person (*informal*) **2** a man who is a servant in livery, e.g. a footman [Mid-18C. < Scots, < ?] —**flunkyism** *n*

fluor /flóo awr/ *n* MINERALS = **fluorite** [Early 17C. < modern Latin (see FLUORIC).]

fluor- *prefix* = **fluoro-** (*before vowels*)

fluorapatite /flóor ráppə tīt/ *n* a common, fluorine-containing form of the mineral apatite

fluorene /flóor een/ *n* $C_{13}H_{10}$ a white insoluble crystalline solid. Source: coal tar. Use: manufacture of dyes. [Late 19C. < FLUORO- (because it fluoresces).]

fluoresce /floor réss/ (**-resces, -rescing, -resced**) *vi* to exhibit or undergo the phenomenon of fluorescence [Late 19C. Back-formation < FLUORESCENT.] —**fluorescer** *n*

fluorescein /floor réssi in, flóorə seen/, **fluoresceine** *n* an orange-red crystalline compound that fluoresces green in blue light. Use: to detect defects in the cornea. [Late 19C. < FLUORESCE + -EIN.]

fluorescence /floor réss'nss/ *n* **1** the emission of electromagnetic radiation, especially light, by an object exposed to radiation or bombarding particles **2** the radiation emitted as a result of fluorescence

fluorescent /floor réss'nt/ *adj* **1** CAPABLE OF FLUORESCING exhibiting or able to undergo fluorescence ○ *a fluorescent dye* **2** CONTAINING FLUORESCENT TUBES containing or produced by fluorescent tubes ○ *fluorescent lighting* **3** DAZZLING IN COLOUR very bright and dazzling in colour ○ *fluorescent pink* [Mid-19C. < FLUORSPAR (which has this property).]

fluorescent lamp, fluorescent light *n* an electric lamp containing a low pressure vapour, usually mercury, in a glass tube

fluorescent tube *n* the tube of a fluorescent lamp

fluoric /floo órrik/ *adj* relating to or produced from fluorine or fluorspar [Late 18C. < obsolete French *fluorique* < modern Latin *fluor* 'mineral used as a flux' < Latin *fluere* 'flow'.]

fluoridate /flóori dayt/ (**-dates, -dating, -dated**) *vt* to add small quantities of fluoride salts to a water supply —**fluoridation** /flóori dáysh'n/ *n*

fluoride /flóor īd/ *n* any chemical compound consisting of fluorine and another element or group [Early 19C. < FLUORINE.]

fluorimeter *n* PHYS = **fluorometer** —**fluorimetric** /flóori méttrik/ *adj* —**fluorimetry** *n*

fluorinate /flóori nayt/ (**-nates, -nating, -nated**) *vt* to treat something, or cause something to combine, with fluorine or a fluorine compound —**fluorination** /flóori náysh'n/ *n*

fluorine /flóor een/ *n* (*symbol* F) a toxic pale yellow gaseous element of the halogen group that is the most reactive and oxidizing agent known. Source: fluorspar, cryolite. Use: water treatment, making fluorides and fluorocarbons. [Early 19C. < modern Latin *fluor* (see FLUORIC).]

fluorite /flóor īt/, **fluorspar** *n* a variously coloured crystalline mineral consisting of calcium fluoride. Use: flux. [Mid-19C. < modern Latin *fluor* (see FLUORIC).]

fluoro- *prefix* **1** fluorine ○ *fluorocarbon* **2** fluorescence ○ *fluoroscope* [< FLUORINE, FLUOR]

fluorocarbon /flóorō kaárbən/ *n* a chemically inert compound containing carbon and fluorine. Use: nonstick coatings, lubricants, refrigerants, solvents.

fluorochemical /flóorō kémmik'l/ *n* any chemical compound containing fluorine

fluorochrome /flóorō krōm/ *n* a molecule or part of a molecule that exhibits fluorescence. Use: marker in biological specimens.

fluorography /floo róggrəfi/ *n* MED = **photofluorography**

fluorometer /floor rómmitər/ *n* an instrument used to detect and measure fluorescence —**fluorometric** /flóorō méttrik/ *adj* —**fluorometry** *n*

fluoroscope /flóorə skōp/ *n* an instrument with which X-ray images of the body can be viewed directly on a screen —**fluoroscopic** /flóorə sköppik/ *adj* —**fluoroscopically** *adv* —**fluoroscopist** *n* —**fluoroscopy** *n*

fluorosis /floor rṓssiss/ *n* a condition caused by excessive exposure to fluorine and marked by mottling of the teeth and damage to the bones —**fluorotic** /-róttik/ *adj*

fluorouracil /flóorō yóorəssil/ *n* a fluorine-containing drug. Use: treatment of some cancers.

fluorspar /flóor spaar/ *n* MINERALS = **fluorite** [Late 18C. < modern Latin *fluor* (see FLUORIC).]

fluphenazine /floo fénnə zeen/ *n* a tranquillizing antipsychotic drug. Use: treatment of schizophrenia. [Mid-20C. Contraction of *fluorophenothiazine*, its chemical name.]

flurry /flúrri/ *n* (*plural* **-ries**) **1** BURST OF ACTIVITY a short period when a lot of things happen **2** BURST OF WEATHER a short period of snowfall or rainfall, or a gust of wind ■ *v* (**-ries, -rying, -ried**) **1** *vt* MAKE UNCERTAIN to make somebody feel agitated and confused **2** *vi* SNOW LIGHTLY to snow lightly and intermittently ○ *It flurried for an hour or so, then it stopped.* [Late 17C. Probably blend of obsolete *flurr* 'flutter' + HURRY.]

flush[1] /flush/ *v* **1** *vti* GO RED to become or cause somebody to become red in the face or on the skin **2** *vti* HAVE ROSY COLOUR to glow or cause something to glow with a reddish colour **3** *vti* MAKE WATER FLOW THROUGH TOILET to clean a toilet by causing water to flow into the bowl, or undergo this process **4** *vt* DISPOSE OF IN TOILET to put something into the toilet and flush it **5** *vt* CLEAN WITH WATER to clean or clear something by liberally pouring water or another liquid into, on, or through it ■ *n* **1** SUDDEN FEELING a sudden intense feeling **2** BEGINNING OF GOOD TIME the beginning of an exciting or pleasurable period **3** SUDDEN RUSH OF THINGS a sudden increased number of things **4** REDDISHNESS an appearance of reddish colour **5** SURGE OF HEAT a sudden surge of heat **6** NEW GROWTH a burst of new growth appearing rapidly on a plant [13C. < ?] —**flushable** *adj* —**flusher** *n*

flush[2] /flush/ *adj* **1** LEVEL completely level so as to form an even surface **2** BESIDE OR AGAINST directly next to or closely against something ○ *The chairs were flush against the wall.* **3** TEMPORARILY RICH having plenty of money temporarily (*informal*) **4** ABUNDANT abundant or overflowing ○ *a party flush with celebrities* **5** WITH EVEN MARGIN with an even margin on a printed page, without any indentations ■ *adv* **1** COMPLETELY LEVEL so as to be completely level and form an even surface without sticking out **2** DIRECTLY directly or squarely ○ *was hit flush on the jaw* ■ *vt* FIT THINGS COMPLETELY LEVEL to fit two things so that they are completely level and form an even surface [Mid-16C. Probably < FLUSH[1].] —**flushness** *n*

flush[3] /flush/ *vt* to force a person or animal out of hiding ■ *n* a bird or birds frightened out of hiding [13C. < ?] —**flusher** *n*

flush[4] /flush/ *n* in poker and other games, a hand consisting of cards all in the same suit [Early 16C. Via obsolete French *flus* < Latin *fluxus* (see FLUX).]

flushed /flusht/ *adj* **1** red in the face **2** feeling excited or happy

fluster /flústər/ *vti* to make somebody nervous or agitated, or become so ■ *n* a nervous or agitated state [Early 17C. < ?] —**flustered** *adj*

flute /floot/ *n* **1** WIND INSTRUMENT WITH HIGH SOUND a woodwind instrument with a cylindrical narrow body usually held out to the right of the player, who blows across a hole in the mouthpiece to generate a high-pitched sound **2** INSTRUMENT WITHOUT A REED any wind instrument without a reed **3** ORGAN STOP an organ stop with a tone like a flute **4** GROOVE IN COLUMN a groove running down an architectural column **5** DECORATIVE GROOVE a decorative groove or pleat **6** TALL GLASS FOR SPARKLING WINE a tall narrow glass used for sparkling wines ■ *v* (**flutes, fluting, fluted**) **1** *vi* MAKE SOUND LIKE FLUTE to whistle, sing, or speak in a way that suggests the sound of a flute **2** *vt* MAKE FURROWS IN to make rounded grooves in something [14C. Via Old French *flaute*, Middle Dutch *flute* < Old Provençal *flaut*.] —**fluted** *adj*

fluter /flóotər/ *n* **1** a maker of fluting in something **2** a flautist

fluting /flóoting/ *n* **1** DECORATIVE FURROWS decoration with parallel grooves **2** MAKING DECORATIVE FURROWS the forming of decorative grooves **3** MAKING FLUTE SOUND playing the flute, or making sounds like those of the flute

flutist /flóotist/ *n* = **flautist**

flutter /flúttər/ *v* **1** *vi* WAVE GENTLY to move gently but with quick changes in direction or wavy motion **2** *vti* MOVE SOMETHING LIGHT to move something light or small in quick back-and-forth motions **3** *vti* FLAP WINGS to flap the wings rapidly **4** *vi* FLY to move by flapping the wings rapidly **5** *vi* BEAT RAPIDLY to beat rapidly, either as a disorder of the heart or because of nervousness or excitement **6** *vi* QUIVER to have a quivering feeling because of nervousness or excitement **7** *vt* MAKE NERVOUS to make somebody feel agitated or nervous (*usually passive*) **8** *vi* MOVE RESTLESSLY to move about in a restless or nervous way ■ *n* **1** QUICK MOVEMENT a rapid, repetitive, or back-and-forth movement in something small **2** AGITATION a state of nervous excitement or agitation **3** RAPID HEARTBEAT a condition marked by rapid, but regular, heartbeat **4** SOUND DISTORTION a high frequency distortion in the pitch of recorded sound **5** SMALL BET a small bet on something (*informal*) [Old English *floterian* < Germanic] —**flutterer** *n* —**flutteringly** *adv* —**fluttery** *adj*

flutter kick *n* a swimming technique that consists of moving the legs rapidly up and down in short strokes

flutter-tonguing *n* a technique in wind-instrument playing in which a fluttering tone is produced by making a rolled 'r' while blowing —**flutter-tongue** *vti*

fluty /floŏti/ (**-ier, -iest**) *adj* high-pitched and clear, like a flute

fluvial /floŏvi əl/ *adj* produced by or found in a river or stream [14C. < Latin *fluvialis* < *fluvius* 'river' < *fluere* 'to flow'.]

fluviomarine /floŏvi ō mə reèn/ *adj* **1** relating to water and sediment deposits of rivers in a marine environment **2** BIOL = **diadromous** [Mid-19C. < Latin *fluvius* 'river' (see FLUVIAL).]

flux /fluks/ *n* **1** CONSTANT CHANGE constant change and instability **2** SOLDERING AID a substance that promotes the fusion of two substances or surfaces, as in soldering or welding **3** RATE OF FLOW ACROSS AREA the rate of flow of something, such as energy, particles, or fluid volume, across or onto a given area **4** STRENGTH OF FIELD IN PARTICULAR AREA the strength of a field, e.g. a magnetic or electric field, acting on a particular area, equal to the area size multiplied by the component of the field acting at right angles to the area **5** ABNORMAL BODILY DISCHARGE an abnormal discharge or flow from the body, especially the bowels (*dated*) **6** SMELTING AID a substance added to molten ore that combines with impurities to form slag which can be extracted **7** GLAZE COMPONENT a substance added to a ceramic glaze to make it flow more readily **8** THEORY OF CHANGE the notion that change is the fundamental nature of reality, as described by Heraclitus **9** QUANTITY OF MOVEMENT the quantity of water or other material moved in a given direction during a given time period ■ *v* **1** *vti* MAKE OR BECOME FLUID to make something fluid, or become fluid **2** *vt* APPLY FLUX TO to apply flux to something, especially a joint being soldered [14C. Via Old French < Latin *fluxus*, < past participle of *fluere* 'flow'.]

flux density *n* the amount of flux per unit area

fluxion /flúksh'n/ *n* **1** a flow or discharge of liquid **2** a derivative representing the rate of change of a mathematical function in relation to an independent variable (*dated*) [Mid-16C. < French, or < Latin *flux-*, past participle of *fluere* 'flow'.] —**fluxional** *adj* —**fluxionally** *adv* —**fluxionary** *adj*

⚡**fly**[1] /flī/ *v* (**flies, flying, flew** /floō/, **flown** /flōn/) **1** *vi* MOVE THROUGH AIR to travel through the air using wings or an engine **2** *vi* TRAVEL IN AIRCRAFT to travel in an aircraft **3** *vt* TAKE OR SEND BY AIR to take or send goods or passengers in an aircraft **4** *vti* BE PILOT to pilot an aircraft or spacecraft **5** *vt* TRAVEL OVER AREA BY AIR to travel over a particular area in an aircraft **6** *vi* TRAVEL WITH AIRLINE OR IN CLASS to travel with a particular airline or in a particular class in an aircraft **7** *vti* FLOAT THROUGH AIR to make something such as a kite move through the air, or move through the air **8** *vti* DISPLAY FLAG ON POLE to display a flag by attaching it to a pole, building, or mast, or be displayed in this way **9** *vt* SHOW COUNTRY OF REGISTRATION to display a flag that indicates the country of registration **10** *vi* MOVE FREELY IN AIR to move freely because of the speed of the air ○ *She ran down the street, her hair flying.* **11** *vi* GO VERY FAST to go somewhere or leave somewhere at top speed **12** *vi* MOVE QUICKLY AND FORCEFULLY to move with speed and explosive force **13** *vi* PASS QUICKLY to pass very fast ○ *The weekend had simply flown.* **14** *vi* BE DISCUSSED INCREASINGLY to be passed on or gossiped about by a swiftly increasing number of people ○ *Bad news flies.* **15** *vi* BE QUICK TO DO SOMETHING to rush to do something quickly **16** *vi* US BE ACCEPTABLE to be acceptable, successful, or useful (*informal*) ○ *come up with a proposal that will fly* **17** *vi* DISAPPEAR to disappear or be used up quickly ○ *Money just flies out of her hands.* **18** *vt* HANG ABOVE STAGE to suspend lights or set components above a stage **19** *vt* USE HUNTING HAWK to cause a hawk to fly after prey ■ *n* (*plural* **flies**) **1** FRONT OPENING OF TROUSERS a covered zip or row of buttons at the front of a pair of trousers (*usually plural*) **2** ENTRANCE FLAP OF TENT a flap at the entrance of a tent **3** *US* CAMPING = **fly sheet 4** WIDTH OF FLAG the distance between the outer edge of a flag and the staff it is attached to **5** EDGE OF FLAG the outer edge of a flag **6** HORSE-DRAWN CARRIAGE in former times, a carriage for hire, drawn by one horse ■ **flies** *npl* AREA ABOVE STAGE the space above a stage in a theatre, where lights and scenery are hung [Old English *flēogan* < Indo-European] —**flyable** *adj* ◇ **fly high** to enjoy a period of great success or happiness ◇ **let fly (at somebody) 1** to speak angrily to somebody **2** to throw something ◇ **on the fly** while a computer program is running (*informal*) ◇ **send somebody** *or* **something flying** to cause somebody or something to go through the air by force of impact

fly at *vt* to attack somebody by rushing towards and hitting him or her, or with angry words. US term **fly into**

fly in *vi* to arrive by aircraft

fly into *vt* **1** to suddenly start feeling and expressing a strong emotion ○ *fly into a rage* **2** *US* = **fly at**

fly out *vi* to travel by plane to a particular destination or from a particular airport

fly[2] /flī/ (*plural* **flies**) *n* **1** SMALL TWO-WINGED INSECT a two-winged insect, many of which are of an order that includes pests. Order: Diptera. **2** FLYING INSECT any flying insect, e.g. a caddis fly or dragonfly (*usually in combination*) **3** FLY-FISHING LURE a fishhook with feathers or other attachments to make it resemble a flying insect, used in fly-fishing [Old English *flēoge* < Germanic] ◇ **a fly in the ointment** a problem that spoils a good situation ◇ **drink with the flies** *Aus* to drink alcohol by yourself (*informal*) ◇ **there are no flies on somebody** used to say that somebody is not lacking in intelligence or understanding

fly[3] /flī/ *adj* **1** smart and aware of everything that is happening (*informal*) **2** *US* stylish and fashionable (*slang*) [Early 19C. < ?]

fly agaric *n* a poisonous mushroom with a bright red or orange cap and white spots. *Amanita muscaria.* [< its former use as an insecticide]

fly ash *n* fine particles of ash resulting from the combustion of a solid fuel

flyaway /flī ə way/ *adj* easily made airborne or affected by a breeze ○ *flyaway hair*

flyback /flī bak/ *n* in a television tube, the rapid return of the electron beam in the direction opposite to scanning

flyblow /flī blō/ *n* the egg or larva of a blowfly or flesh fly, or an infestation with such eggs or larvae ■ *vt* (**-blows, -blowing, -blew** /-bloō/, **-blown** /-blōn/) to contaminate something with something such as the eggs or larvae of a blowfly

flyblown /flī blōn/ *adj* **1** WITH MAGGOTS containing maggots and therefore not fit to eat **2** DIRTY dirty and in bad condition **3** TAINTED contaminated with something undesirable

flyboat /flī bōt/ *n* a small fast boat [Late 16C. < Dutch *vlieboot* < *Vlie*, channel off the N coast of the Netherlands.]

fly bridge *n* NAUT = **flying bridge**

flyby /flī bī/ *n* a flight close to a particular position or object, especially a flight by a space vehicle close to a planet, usually for observation purposes

fly-by-night *adj* **1** UNSCRUPULOUS IN BUSINESS unscrupulous or not creditworthy in business or commerce **2** EPHEMERAL not lasting long ■ *n* **fly-by-night, fly-by-nighter 1** ABSCONDING DEBTOR a person who leaves without paying debts **2** DUBIOUS OR SHAKY BUSINESS a business with financial problems or a bad reputation

fly-by-wire *n* an aircraft flight control system that has electronic rather than mechanical controls

flycatcher /flī kachər/ *n* a songbird that has a slender bill and feeds on insects caught in flight. Families: Muscicapidae and Tyrannidae.

fly-drive *adj* describes a holiday or travel option that includes a flight and a hired car at the destination

flyer *n* = **flier**

fly-fish *vi* to fish using a rod, reel, line, and lure resembling a fly —**fly-fisher** *n* —**fly-fishing** *n*

flyfisherman (*plural* **-men**) *n* a fisherman who uses a rod, reel, line, and a lure resembling a fly

fly front *n* a covered zip or row of buttons at the front of a garment

fly gallery *n* a hidden platform above a stage from where objects suspended from the flies are controlled

fly half *n* RUGBY = **stand-off half**

flying /flī ing/ *adj* **1** ABLE TO FLY capable of flight **2** MOVING FAST moving very quickly **3** PASSING QUICKLY happening or passing very quickly **4** NOT HELD AT EDGE describes a sail held at the corners only, not the edge ■ *n* AIR TRAVEL travel by aircraft, or the piloting of aircraft

flying boat *n* a seaplane with a fuselage that acts like a boat's hull and provides buoyancy on water

flying bomb *n* any explosive robot plane, guided missile, or rocket bomb (*informal*)

flying bridge *n* an open deck of a boat or ship with a secondary set of navigational devices

Flying buttress

flying buttress *n* an exterior support for a wall (**buttress**) that sticks out from the wall and is typically arch-shaped, often used in Gothic cathedrals

flying doctor *n* ANZ a doctor who visits patients by aircraft

flying dragon *n* ZOOL = **flying lizard**

flying field *n* a small airfield from which aircraft, usually light aircraft, can operate

Flying fish

flying fish *n* a fish with fins that can be held out like wings, enabling it to glide short distances above the water. Native to: warm or tropical seas. Family: Exocoetidae.

flying fox *n* a large fruit bat with a wingspan up to 152 cm/5 ft. Native to: Australasia. Genus: *Pteropus*.

flying frog *n* a frog with webbed feet that it uses to glide between the trees in which it lives. Native to: Asia. *Racophorus reinwardii*.

flying gurnard *n* a marine fish that resembles the gurnard but has large fins enabling it to glide short distances above the water. Native to: tropics. Family: Dactylopteridae.

flying jib *n* on a boat or ship with more than one sail at the front, the foremost triangular sail projecting from the vessel

flying leap *n* a jump or leap taken while running

flying lemur *n* a mammal with a flap of skin between its front and back limbs that it uses to glide between the trees in which it lives. Native to: Southeast Asia. Family: Dermoptera.

flying lizard *n* a small lizard with a flap of skin between its front and back limbs that it uses to glide through the air. Native to: tropics. Genus: *Draco*.

flying machine *n* an aircraft, especially a very early one

flying mare *n* a wrestling manoeuvre in which the attacker grasps the opponent's arm and then turns to throw the opponent over the shoulder

⚡**flying mouse** *n* a computer mouse that can be lifted and used as a pointer in a three-dimensional environment

flying officer *n* a Royal Air Force officer of a rank above pilot officer

flying phalanger *n* a small marsupial that uses a flap of skin between its front and back limbs to glide between trees. Native to: Australasia. Family: Phalangeridae.

flying picket *n* a picketing striker who travels to various workplaces to support local strikes

flying saucer *n* a disc-shaped flying object believed to be an extraterrestrial spacecraft

flying squad *n* a group of police officers who can be quickly deployed

flying squirrel *n* a nocturnal squirrel that uses a flap of skin between its front and back limbs to glide between trees. Native to: N Europe, North America, Asia. Family: Petauristinae.

flying start *n* a start of a race in which competitors cross the starting line at racing speed ◇ **off to a flying start** begun or beginning very successfully

fly-kick *n* in certain martial arts, a kick executed in mid-air with one leg straight and the other flexed at the knee and hip

flyleaf /flī leef/ (*plural* **-leaves** /-leevz/) *n* the first page in a hardback book, which forms a continuous sheet with the page stuck inside the front cover [< FLY[1]]

flyman /flīmən/ (*plural* **-men** /-mən/) *n* somebody whose job is to operate scene elements from the flies in a theatre

Flynn /flin/, **Errol** (1909–59) Australian-born US actor. Born **Leslie Thomas Flynn**

Flynn, John (1880–1951) Australian missionary

fly-on-the-wall *adj* describes a TV documentary showing people in their daily lives

fly orchid *n* an orchid in which the lower part of the flower resembles an insect. Native to: Europe. *Ophrys insectifera.*

flyover /flī ōvər/ *n* **1** a bridge with a main road on it crossing another main road. ◊ **overpass 2** *US* AIR = **fly-past**

flypaper /flī paypər/ *n* paper coated with a sticky and poisonous substance that attracts and kills flies

fly-past *n* the flight of an aircraft or formation of aircraft over a place as a spectacle for people on the ground. US term **flyover** *n.* 2

flyposting /flī pōsting/ *n* putting up posters in places where they are not legally permitted

flysch /flish/, **Flysch** *n* a thick deposit of sedimentary rock formed in marine environments by erosion of adjacent steep mountains [Early 19C. < Swiss German.]

flyscreen /flī skreen/ *n* a screen made of wire mesh that fits over a window to exclude insects

flysheet /flī sheet/ *n* printed information or advertising on a sheet or pamphlet

fly sheet *n* a light tarpaulin secured over the top of a tent. US term **fly**[1] *n.* 3

flyspeck /flī spek/ *n* **1** FLY'S FAECES a tiny mark made by a fly's faeces **2** TINY MARK any tiny mark or stain ■ *vt* MARK WITH FLYSPECKS to mark something with the tiny spots of flies' faeces or similar stains (*usually passive*)

fly spray *n* a poisonous liquid that kills insects, sprayed from an aerosol

fly swatter *n* a tool used to strike and kill insects, consisting of a long flexible handle with a flat piece of plastic net attached

flyte /flīt/ (**flytes, flyting, flyted**), **flite** (**flites, fliting, flited**) *vti Scotland* to give somebody a severe but eloquent scolding [Old English *flītan*]

flyting /flīting/ *n Scotland* an angry but eloquent scolding or verbal exchange

fly-tipping *n* the illegal deposit of rubbish in unauthorized places —**fly-tipper** *n*

flytrap /flī trap/ *n* **1** PLANTS = **Venus flytrap 2** a device for catching flies

flyway /flī way/ *n* a route taken by migrating birds

flyweight /flī wayt/ *n* a boxer of the lightest weight in professional competition, up to 51 kg/112 lbs

flywheel /flī weel/ *n* a heavy wheel or disc that helps to maintain a constant speed of rotation in a machine or to store energy

flywhisk /flī wisk/ *n* a tool for brushing away flies, traditionally a bunch of horsehair attached to a handle

fm[1] *abbr* **1** fathom **2** from

ϟ **fm**[2] *abbr* Micronesia (*in Internet addresses*)

Fm *symbol* fermium

FM *abbr* **1** Federated States of Micronesia **2** field manual **3** figure of merit **4** frequency modulation

FMCG *abbr* fast-moving consumer goods

fml *abbr* formal

FMS *abbr* **1** false memory syndrome **2** flight management system

f-number *n* (*symbol* f) the ratio of the focal length to the effective diameter of a camera lens [Abbreviation of FOCAL]

ϟ **fo** *abbr* Faroe Isles (*in Internet addresses*)

FO *abbr* **1** field-grade officer **2** field order **3** finance officer **4** flight officer **5** flying officer **6** Foreign Office

fo. *abbr* folio

foal /fōl/ *n* an unweaned horse or related animal ■ *vti* to give birth to a foal [Old English *fola* < Indo-European, 'small']

foam /fōm/ *n* **1** MASS OF BUBBLES a mass of bubbles of gas or air on the surface of a liquid **2** THICK FROTHY SUBSTANCE a thick but light mixture that contains a lot of tiny bubbles ○ *Beat the egg whites into a foam.* **3** FIRE-EXTINGUISHING SUBSTANCE a thick chemical froth used to extinguish flames **4** MATERIAL CONTAINING BUBBLES rubber, plastic, or other material filled with many small bubbles of air to make it soft or light **5** FROTHY SALIVA frothy saliva produced as a result of exertion or disease **6** SEA the sea (*literary*) ■ *v* **1** *vi* PRODUCE BUBBLES to produce a mass of bubbles **2** *vi* PRODUCE FROTHY SALIVA to produce foam from the mouth **3** *vi* BE ANGRY to express great anger (*informal*) **4** *vt* FILL WITH BUBBLES to transform a material into foam by aerating it in liquid form and then solidifying it [Old English *fām* < Indo-European] —**foamily** *adv* —**foaminess** *n* —**foamy** *adj*

foamed slag *n* slag from a blast furnace that is aerated while it is still molten, used as a building or insulation material

foam rubber *n* rubber that has been aerated to form a spongy material. Use: mattresses, padding, insulation.

fob /fob/ *n* **1** CHAIN FOR POCKET WATCH a chain or ribbon used to attach a pocket watch to a waistcoat **2** ORNAMENT ON KEY RING an ornament attached to a key ring **3** ORNAMENT ON CHAIN a watch or ornament worn on the end of a chain or ribbon attached to clothing **4** POCKET FOR WATCH a small pocket for a watch on a waistcoat [Mid-17C. < ?]

fob off *vt* **1** MISLEAD SO AS TO STALL QUESTIONING to give false or inadequate information to somebody in order to stop further questions **2** GIVE SOMETHING INFERIOR TO to provide somebody with something different from and inferior to what the person wanted **3** GIVE SOMETHING UNWANTED TO to pass something unwanted to somebody else, using deceitful persuasion [Late 16C. < ?]

f.o.b., F.O.B., fob, FOB *abbr* free on board

focaccia /fə káchə, fō-/ *n* flat Italian bread, sprinkled with a topping before baking, and served hot or cold [Mid-20C. Via Italian < assumed Vulgar Latin *focacia* < Latin *focus* 'hearth, fireplace'.]

focal /fōk'l/ *adj* **1** PRINCIPAL main and most important **2** OF FOCUSING AN IMAGE relating to bringing an image into focus **3** AT OR FROM FOCAL POINT located at, passing through, or measured from, a focal point —**focally** *adv*

focal distance *n* OPTICS = **focal length**

focal infection *n* a bacterial infection in one part of the body that may cause symptoms elsewhere in the body

focalize /fōkə līz/ (**-izes, -izing, -ized**), **focalise** (**-ises, -ising, -ised**) *v* **1** *vti* to focus something, or bring something into focus **2** *vt* to limit something to a local area —**focalization** /fōkə lī záysh'n/ *n*

focal length *n* (*symbol* f) the distance from the centre of a lens or the surface of a mirror to the point at which light passing through the lens or reflected from the mirror is focused

focal-plane shutter *n* a camera shutter positioned just in front of the film, as opposed to one built into the lens

focal point *n* **1** the point at which parallel rays meeting a lens, curved mirror, or other optical system converge or appear to diverge **2** an object of concentrated or immediate attention

focal ratio *n* OPTICS = **f-number**

fo'c's'le *n* NAUT = **forecastle**

focus /fōkəss/ *n* (*plural* **-cuses** *or* **-ci** /fō sī/) **1** MAIN EMPHASIS concentrated effort or attention on a particular thing ○ *The committee's focus must be on finding solutions to the problem.* **2** AREA OF CONCERN an area of concern, responsibility, or investigation ○ *an inquiry with a narrow focus* **3** CONCENTRATED QUALITY a concentrated and unified quality ○ *to bring focus to the problem* **4** SHARPNESS OF IMAGE the quality of being sharply defined with clear edges and contrast **5** SEEING SHARPLY the condition of seeing sharply and clearly **6** (*plural* **-ci**) OPTICS = **focal point** *n.* 1 **7** (*plural* **-ci**) DISEASE ORIGIN the point from which a disease spreads or where it localizes **8** (*plural* **-ci**) EARTHQUAKE ORIGIN the point of origin within the earth of an earthquake or underground nuclear explosion **9** (*plural* **-ci**) POINT ON CONE a fixed point in a plane that in combination with a particular straight line specifies a conic section ■ *vti* (**-cuses** *or* **-cusses, -cusing** *or* **-cussing, -cused** *or* **-cussed**) **1** CONCENTRATE MAINLY ON to give your main attention to one thing or one aspect of a thing **2** ADJUST VISION TO SEE CLEARLY to adjust your vision so that you see clearly and sharply, or become adjusted for clear vision **3** ADJUST LENS to adjust a lens so that the image viewed is clear and sharp [Mid-17C. < Latin, 'hearth, fireplace'.] —**focusable** *adj* —**focuser** *n*

focused /fōkəst/, **focussed** *adj* **1** concentrated on a single thing **2** single-minded and determined

focus group *n* a small group of representative people who are questioned about their opinions as part of political or market research

focussed *adj* = **focused**

fodder /fóddər/ *n* **1** ANIMAL FOOD hay, straw, and similar food for livestock **2** MATERIAL FOR STIMULATING RESPONSE people, ideas, or images that are useful in stimulating a creative or critical response **3** EXPENDABLE PEOPLE OR THINGS people or things regarded as the necessary but expendable ingredient that makes a system or scheme work (*usually in combination*) ○ *case studies seized upon as thesis fodder* ■ *vt* FEED LIVESTOCK to give food to livestock [Old English *fōdor* < Indo-European, 'to feed'] —**fodderer** *n*

foe /fō/ *n* an enemy or opponent (*formal*) [Old English *gefā* < Indo-European, 'hostile']

FOE, FoE *abbr* Friends of the Earth

foehn /fōn/, **föhn** *n* a warm dry wind blowing down the lee slope of a mountain range, originally and especially the Alps [Mid-19C. Via German < Latin *favonius* 'west wind' < *favere* 'favour, be well disposed towards'.]

foetal /féet'l/, **fetal** *adj* relating to or characteristic of a foetus [Early 19C. < FOETUS.]

foetal alcohol syndrome *n* a condition affecting babies born to women who drank excessive amounts of alcohol during pregnancy, characterized by a range of effects including facial abnormalities and learning difficulties

foetal haemoglobin *n* a haemoglobin common in the foetus and newborn but normally present only in small amounts in adults except in certain forms of anaemia

foetal membrane *n* BIOL = **extraembryonic membrane**

foetal position *n* a body position in which the body lies curled up on one side with the head bowed and the legs and arms drawn in towards the chest

foeticide /féeti sīd/, **feticide** *n* **1** the act of destroying a foetus **2** an agent or drug used to destroy a foetus —**foeticidal** /féeti sīd'l/ *adj*

foetid *adj* = **fetid**

foetoprotein /féetō prō teen/, **fetoprotein** *n* a protein found in healthy foetuses that is also found in adults with some malignant conditions [Mid-20C. < FOETUS.]

foetor *n* = **fetor**

foetoscope /féetō skōp/, **fetoscope** *n* a fibre-optic device for viewing a foetus in the uterus [Late 20C. < FOETUS + *-scope.*] —**foetoscopy** /fee tóskəpi/ *n*

foetus /féetəss/, **fetus** *n* an unborn vertebrate at a stage when all the structural features of the adult are recognizable, especially an unborn human offspring after eight weeks of development [14C. < Latin, 'offspring'.]

USAGE In technical contexts, the spelling with **-fe-** is now the agreed international standard for **fetus** and all related words.

fog /fog/ *n* **1** THICK MIST condensed water vapour in the air at or near ground level **2** CLOUD a cloud of something in the air, e.g. smoke, that reduces visibility **3** HAZY MUDDLE a state of confusion or lack of clarity **4** OBSCURING AGENT something that serves to obscure or conceal ○ *a fog of excuses* **5** BLURRED AREA an area on a photograph that is unclear or obscured by stray light **6** SUSPENDED PARTICLES a cloud or suspension of liquid particles ■ *v* (**fogs, fogging, fogged**) 1 *vti* **MAKE OR BECOME OBSCURED** to cause condensation to form on a transparent surface, or become covered with condensation 2 *vt* **MAKE UNCLEAR** to make something unclear or confused 3 *vti* **EXPOSE SOMETHING TO LIGHT** to contaminate film or a developing image with light, usually accidentally, or undergo this process [Mid-16C. < ?] —**fogged** *adj*

fog bank *n* a mass of thick fog, especially at sea

fogbound /fóg bownd/ *adj* 1 unable to move or operate because of visibility diminished by fog 2 enveloped in fog

fogbow /fóg bō/ *n* a faint arc of light seen in fog opposite the sun

fogdog /fóg dog/ *n* a bright white spot seen in breaking fog near the horizon

fogey *n* = **fogy**

Foggia /fójji ə/ city of S Italy. Population: 155,674 (1992).

foggy /fóggi/ (**-gier, -giest**) *adj* 1 **CHARACTERIZED BY FOG** filled with or obscured by fog 2 **VAGUE** very unclear or hazy ○ *We only had a foggy idea of the visitor's name.* 3 **VISUALLY UNCLEAR** obscured or translucent because of a covering of condensation or something similar —**foggily** *adv* —**fogginess** *n*

Foggy Bottom *n* US the US Department of State in Washington, D.C., which is the US government department responsible for foreign policy and affairs (*informal*) [Mid-20C. Name for a low-lying area near the Potomac River in Washington, D.C.]

foghorn /fóg hawrn/ *n* a horn sounded on a ship or boat when fog reduces visibility, as a warning to other vessels

foglamp /fóg lamp/ *n* CARS = **fog light**

fog light *n* a front or rear light on a car with a beam designed to penetrate fog

fogy /fógi/ (*plural* **-gies**), **fogey** (*plural* **-geys**) *n* an old-fashioned person who resists change or novelty [Late 18C. < Scots, < ?] —**fogyish** *adj* —**fogyism** *n*

föhn *n* METEOROL = **foehn**

foible /fóyb'l/ *n* 1 an idiosyncrasy or small weakness (*usually plural*) 2 the weakest part of a sword blade from the middle to the point [Mid-17C. Via obsolete French < Old French *feble* (see FEEBLE).]

foie gras /fwaa graa/ *n* goose liver swollen by force-feeding the bird on maize, usually eaten as a pâté [Early 19C. < French, 'fatted liver'.]

foil[1] /foyl/ *n* 1 **METAL IN THIN SHEETS** metal in a very thin flexible sheet 2 **METAL COATING ON MIRROR** the thin reflective metal coating on the back of a mirror 3 **GOOD CONTRAST** a useful or interesting contrast to something 4 SHIPPING = **hydrofoil** *n.* 2 5 AIR = **aerofoil** 6 **ARC IN GOTHIC WINDOW** an arc at the top of a Gothic window ■ *vt* **COVER WITH FOIL** to cover or coat something with foil [14C. Via Old French < Latin *folium* 'leaf', *folia* 'leaves'.]

foil[2] /foyl/ *vt* 1 to prevent somebody from succeeding in something 2 to obscure the trail of prey in order to hinder pursuers [14C. < ?]

foil[3] /foyl/ *n* a long thin sword with a small disc on the end, used in fencing [Late 16C. < ?]

foils /foylz/ *n* the art or sport of fencing with foils (+ *singular verb*) —**foilsman** *n* —**foilswoman** *n*

foist /foyst/ *vt* 1 **IMPOSE** to force somebody to accept something undesirable 2 **INSERT SURREPTITIOUSLY** to introduce or insert something surreptitiously 3 **GIVE SOMEBODY SOMETHING INFERIOR** to give somebody something inferior on the pretence that it is genuine, valuable, or desirable [Mid-16C. Probably < Dutch dialect *vuisten* 'hold in your hand' (as when hiding dice) < Middle Dutch *vuist* 'fist'.]

Fokine /fo kéen/, **Michel** (1880–1942) Russian-born US dancer and choreographer. Born **Mikhail Mikhaylovich Fokine**

folacin /fólləssin/ *n* BIOCHEM = **folic acid** [Mid-20C. < FOLIC ACID.]

folate /fó layt/ *n* 1 BIOCHEM = **folic acid** 2 a salt or ester of folic acid [Mid-20C. < FOLIC ACID.]

fold[1] /fōld/ *v* 1 *vt* **BEND FLAT** to bend something thin and flat over on itself 2 *vt* **MAKE SMALLER BY FOLDING** to bend something over on itself more than once 3 *vti* **BEND TO MAKE COMPACT** to bend part of something so as to make it more streamlined or more compact ○ *a bicycle that folds to fit into the car* 4 *vt* **BEND LIMBS TOGETHER** to draw in the arms, legs, or hands towards the body, or place them together with the joints bent 5 *vt* **BRING WINGS TOGETHER** to bring the wings together or next to the body 6 *vt* **COVER** to wrap or cover something ○ *folded the note inside a magazine* 7 *vt* **PUT ARMS ROUND** to put your arms round somebody 8 *vi* **GO OUT OF BUSINESS** to fail and stop operating as a business 9 *vi* **GIVE UP HAND** in poker and other card games, to stop playing your hand in the belief that it cannot win 10 *vti* **BEND ROCK** to cause a layer of rock to bend, or undergo this process ■ *n* 1 **BENT PART** a part of something folded 2 **CREASE** a line, crease, or raised part made when something has been folded 3 **HANGING FOLDED PART** a part of something that hangs in a folded shape ○ *the folds of his cassock* 4 **COIL** a single coil in a rope, or a snake lying in coils 5 **BEND IN ROCK** a bend formed in a rock layer in response to forces in the rock 6 **SMALL VALLEY** a small valley in a hilly area [Old English *fealdan* < Indo-European, 'to fold'] —**foldable** *adj*

fold in *vt* to add a food ingredient to a mixture carefully and lightly

fold up *v* 1 *vti* to fold something completely, or become folded completely 2 *vi* to collapse from laughter, pain, or strong emotion

fold[2] /fōld/ *n* 1 **GROUP WITH THINGS IN COMMON** a group to which something or somebody naturally belongs because of shared interests or traits 2 **ENCLOSED AREA FOR SHEEP** an enclosed area where sheep or other livestock can be kept 3 **ENCLOSED ANIMALS** sheep or other livestock in a fold 4 **FLOCK** a flock of sheep ■ *vt* **ENCLOSE LIVESTOCK** to enclose livestock safely [Old English *fald* < ?]

-fold *suffix* 1 divided into parts ○ *manifold* 2 times ○ *tenfold* [Old English *-feald*; related to *fealdan* (see FOLD[1])]

foldaway /fōld ə way/ *adj* designed to be folded for compact storage

foldboat /fōld bōt/ *n* US NAUT = **faltboat** [< 'folding boat' < *falten* 'to fold' + *Boot* 'boat']

folder /fōldər/ *n* 1 **FOLDED CARD TO HOLD PAPERS** a piece of card folded to make a file in which papers can be held 2 **FILE CONTAINER** a conceptual container for computer files in some operating systems, corresponding to a directory or subdirectory 3 **FOLDED PAMPHLET** a circular printed on folded paper

folderol *n* = **falderal**

folding /fōlding/ *adj* designed to be folded for compact storage

folding door *n* a door consisting of hinged panels that fold against each other

folding money *n* money in the form of notes rather than coins (*informal*)

folding press *n* a wrestling manoeuvre in which the opponent is pressed into a foetal position and held down

foldout /fōld owt/ *n* PUBL = **gatefold** —**foldout** *adj*

foldup /fōld up/ *adj* designed to be folded for compact storage

foliaceous /fóli áyshəss/ *adj* 1 relating to or resembling a plant leaf or leaves 2 bearing leaves or similar structures [Mid-17C. < Latin *foliaceus* < *folium* 'leaf'.]

foliage /fóli ij/ *n* 1 **LEAVES** the leaves of a plant or tree 2 **LEAFY DECORATION** decoration consisting of or resembling plant leaves 3 **BUILDING ORNAMENTATION** architectural ornamentation based on leaves and stems [Mid-15C. Alteration (after Latin *folium*) of Old French *foillage* < *foille* 'leaf' < Latin *folium*.] —**foliaged** *adj*

foliage plant *n* a plant cultivated for its good-looking leaves

foliar /fóli ər/ *adj* relating to, producing, or being the leaves of a plant [Late 19C. < modern Latin *foliaris* < Latin *folium* 'leaf'.]

foliate *adj* /fóli ət, fóli ayt/ 1 **OF OR LIKE LEAVES** relating to or resembling leaves 2 **LEAF-SHAPED** in the shape of a leaf ■ *v* /fóli ayt/ (**-ates, -ating, -ated**) 1 *vt* **DECORATE WITH LEAVES** to decorate something with leaves or very thin layers 2 *vt* **MAKE METAL INTO FOIL** to form metal into a thin sheet or foil 3 *vt* **NUMBER A BOOK'S PAGES** to number the leaves of a book or manuscript 4 *vi* **DEVELOP FOLIAGE** to develop foliage 5 *vti* **LAYER** to separate something into very thin layers, or undergo this process [Early 17C. Adjective < Latin *foliatus* < *folium* 'leaf'; verb < Latin *folium*.]

-foliate *suffix* having leaves ○ *bifoliate* [< Latin *foliatus* (see FOLIATE)]

foliation /fóli áysh'n/ *n* 1 **LEAF FORMATION** the formation of leaves 2 **BEARING OF LEAVES** the state of being in leaf 3 **ORNAMENTATION** architectural ornamentation consisting of stylized foliage 4 **GOTHIC WINDOW DECORATION** architectural decoration consisting of carving between two arches (**cusps**) and arcs (**foils**) at the top of Gothic windows 5 **NUMBERING OF SHEETS** the numbering of consecutive leaves in a book or manuscript 6 **ROCK TEXTURE** a characteristic of metamorphosed rocks in which minerals are aligned in one direction so that the rock can readily be split into thin layers 7 **LEAF DECORATION** decoration with a design based on leaves

folic acid /fólik-, fóllik-/ *n* an important B complex vitamin, found in green vegetables and liver [< Latin *folium* 'leaf'; because found in leafy green vegetables]

folie à deux /fólli a dő/ (*plural* **folies à deux** /fólli a dő/) *n* a psychiatric disorder with symptoms common to two people who are very close [Late 19C. < French, 'dual delusion'.]

folio /fóli ō/ *n* (*plural* **-os**) 1 **LARGE BOOK OR MANUSCRIPT** a book or manuscript in the largest size usual for books 2 **LARGE SHEET FOR BOOK** a large sheet of paper that folds to give four pages 3 **PAGE NUMBERED ON FRONT** a paper or parchment page that is numbered on the front but not the back 4 **PAGE NUMBER** a page number (*technical*) 5 **MEASUREMENT FOR LEGAL DOCUMENTS** a unit for measuring the length of legal documents, usually 72 or 90 words in Britain and 100 in the United States 6 **LEDGER PAGE** a page, or two facing pages, of a ledger ■ *vt* (**-os, -oing, -oed**) **NUMBER PAGES** to number the pages in a book ■ *adj* **LARGE-FORMAT** printed in folio size [Mid-15C. < late Latin *folio* 'at the page' < Latin *folium* 'leaf, page'.]

folk /fōk/ *npl* **PEOPLE IN GENERAL** people, especially people of the same type (+ *plural verb*) ■ *n* MUSIC = **folk music** ■ *adj* 1 **TRADITIONAL IN COMMUNITY** traditional or passed down in a community or country 2 **RELATING TO IDEAS OF ORDINARY PEOPLE** coming from the traditional beliefs or ideas of ordinary people [Old English *folc* < Indo-European,'fill']

folk art *n* paintings and decorative objects made in a naive style

folk dance *n* 1 a dance that is traditional to a culture, community, or country 2 the music for a folk dance

Folkestone /fōkstən/ port and resort in SE England. Population: 45,587 (1991).

Folketing /fólkə ting/ *n* the parliament of Denmark [< Danish, 'people's assembly']

folk etymology *n* 1 the replacement of an unfamiliar word or form by a more familiar one 2 an idea about the origin of a word that is generally believed but is incorrect

folk hero *n* a person who is legendary to the public

folkie /fōki/ *n* (*informal*) 1 a folk singer or musician 2 a fan of folk music

folklore /fōk lawr/ *n* 1 **TRADITIONAL LOCAL STORIES** traditional stories and explanations passed down in a community or country 2 **LOCAL LEGENDS** stories and gossip that become traditional within a group of people 3 **STUDY OF TRADITIONS** the study of traditional stories, music, and customs —**folkloric** *adj*

folklorist /fōk lawrist/ *n* a student of the traditional stories, music, and customs of a culture or community —**folkloristic** /fōk law rístik/ *adj*

folk mass *n* a Christian mass in which folk music replaces some or all of the traditional music

folk medicine *n* medicine based on traditional customs and belief, often using herbal remedies

folk memory *n* a memory kept alive by a community and passed from one generation to the next

folk music *n* 1 traditional songs and music, passed from one generation to the next 2 modern music composed in imitation of traditional music

folk-rock *n* popular music that combines the melodies of folk music with the rhythms of rock music

folks /fōks/ *npl* 1 = **folk** *npl* 2 used to address a group of people (*informal*) ○ *Folks, we're ready to start now.* 3 parents or close family

folk song *n* 1 a traditional song that has been passed down orally 2 a modern song composed in the style of traditional folk music, often performed by a solo singer —**folk singer** *n* —**folk singing** *n*

folksy /fōksi/ (**-sier, -siest**) *adj* 1 **IN STYLE OF FOLK TRADITIONS** simple and unsophisticated in the tradition of folk crafts or folklore 2 US **FRIENDLY** friendly and informal 3 **AFFECTEDLY TRADITIONAL** artificially or affectedly traditional and homy —**folksily** *adv* —**folksiness** *n*

folk tale /fṓk tayl/, **folktale** *n* a story or legend that is passed down orally from one generation to the next and becomes part of a community's tradition

folkways /fṓk wayz/ *npl* the traditional customs and way of life pursued by a particular group of people

follicle /fóllik'l/ *n* **1** a small anatomical sac, cavity, or gland, involved in secretion or excretion **2** a dry case formed from a single fruit that splits along one side to release seeds [Early 15C. < Latin *folliculus* 'small sack' < *follis* 'bellows'.] —**follicular** /fo líkyǒolər/ *adj*

follicle-stimulating hormone *n* a hormone that stimulates the growth of egg follicles in the ovaries and the making of sperm in the testes

folliculitis /fo líkyǒo lítiss/ *n* inflammation of one or more follicles, especially of the hair, producing small boils

follies /fólliz/ *n* a somewhat old-fashioned theatrical revue with elaborate costumes, music, and dancing (+ *singular or plural verb*)

follow /fóllō/ *v* **1** *vti* COME AFTER to come after somebody or something in position, time, or sequence ○ *We had steak and chips followed by strawberries.* **2** *vt* ADD TO to add to something already done by doing something else, usually a related thing ○ *She followed her lecture with a demonstration.* **3** *vti* GO AFTER to go after or behind somebody or something, moving in the same direction, especially to find out where he, she, or it is going, or go to the same place ○ *The dog followed them home.* **4** *vt* KEEP UNDER SURVEILLANCE to have somebody's movements under constant surveillance ○ *We've had the suspect followed for the past week.* **5** *vt* WATCH CLOSELY to watch, observe, or pay close attention to somebody or something ○ *Her eyes followed me around the room.* **6** *vt* GO ALONG to go along something such as a road or path ○ *Follow the footpath to the edge of the forest.* **7** *vt* GO IN SAME DIRECTION AS to take the same course or go in the same direction as something else ○ *The road follows the river along the bottom of the valley.* **8** *vt* GO AS DIRECTED BY to go in the direction indicated by something such as a signpost **9** *vt* OBEY to act in accordance with something, especially with instructions or directions given by somebody else ○ *If you follow my instructions, nothing can go wrong.* **10** *vt* DEVELOP IN ACCORDANCE WITH to be or develop in accordance with something, usually something already known about or established ○ *The behaviour of such children usually follows the same pattern.* **11** *vt* BE INFLUENCED BY to be led, guided, or influenced by somebody or something ○ *They followed Plato in believing the material world to be essentially unreal.* **12** *vti* DO THE SAME AS to imitate or do the same as somebody or something ○ *She followed her father into medicine.* **13** *vti* UNDERSTAND to understand something such as an explanation or narrative ○ *He couldn't follow her explanation.* **14** *vt* ENGAGE IN ACTIVITY to engage in or practise something such as a career, occupation, or lifestyle ○ *I decided to follow a career in law.* **15** *vt* KEEP UP TO DATE WITH to keep yourself informed about or up to date with the progress of something you are interested in ○ *Are you following the television series about twins?* **16** *vt* BE ABOUT to be about somebody or something, especially to describe or depict what happens to somebody or something over a period of time ○ *The story follows a typical American family.* **17** *vti* RESULT FROM to happen after and as a result of something else ○ *Issue too many instructions and confusion invariably follows.* **18** *vti* BE LOGICAL RESULT to be a logical consequence of something ○ *That follows logically from their decision to cancel the project.* **19** *vt* READ MUSIC to read the words or music of something while listening to it **20** *vt Malaysia* ACCOMPANY to go with somebody ○ *Can I follow you to the market?* ■ *n* CUE GAMES = **follow shot** *n.* 1 [Old English *folgian, fylgan* < ?] —**followable** *adj* ◇ **as follows** as listed or described next

USAGE ***As follows*** is used when you introduce an enumeration, even when a plural noun comes before this phrase: *Our revised forecasts are as follows* [not *as follow*].

follow on *vi* **1** to continue or resume a course of action ○ *I'll follow on from where you left off.* **2** to begin a team's second innings immediately after finishing its first because its first-innings score is a specified number of runs less than that of the other team

follow out *vt* to carry something out in full or to the end

follow through *vti* **1** to take further action as a consequence or extension of a previous action, especially to continue something through to completion **2** to continue the movement of the arm or leg past the point of contact or release after hitting, throwing, or kicking a ball or other object in a sport

follow up *vt* **1** to act or make further investigations on the basis of information received ○ *Police are following up a new lead.* **2** to continue or add to something already done by doing some related thing ○ *I followed up my phone call with a letter of confirmation.*

follower /fóllō ər/ *n* **1** SOMEBODY LED a person who is led, guided, or influenced by somebody else **2** SUPPORTER a fan, supporter, or admirer of somebody or something, especially of a sports team **3** MEMBER OF ENTOURAGE a servant, attendant, or subordinate, usually one of a number of people accompanying an important person **4** IMITATOR somebody or something that copies or imitates something else **5** MOURNER a mourner (*regional*)

following /fóllō ing/ *adj* **1** NEXT coming after in time or sequence **2** ABOUT TO BE MENTIONED about to be mentioned or listed ○ *He has visited the following countries: Canada, France, and Australia.* **3** MOVING THE SAME WAY blowing or flowing in the same direction as somebody or something, especially a boat or aircraft, is travelling ○ *a following wind* ■ *n* **1** GROUP OF FOLLOWERS a group of people who admire or support somebody or something over a period of time ○ *The band has a large following in this country.* **2** SOMETHING TO BE SPECIFIED the people or things about to be mentioned or listed (+ *plural verb*) ○ *You will need the following: a piece of wood, a saw, a hammer, and some nails.* ■ *prep* AFTER after something ○ *Following the accident it was months before he felt safe in a car.*

follow-my-leader *n* a game in which the players, usually children, move along in a line, all copying the actions of the person at the front. US term **follow-the-leader**

follow-on *adj* CONTINUING OR RESULTING coming after as a continuation or consequence ■ *n* **1** CONTINUATION OR CONSEQUENCE OF PREVIOUS EVENT an action or event that is a continuation or consequence of a previous one **2** ACT OF FOLLOWING ON the immediate beginning of a second innings by a team that has been asked to follow on

follow shot *n* **1** in billiards and similar games, a shot that makes the cue ball continue to move in the same direction as the target ball after striking it **2** a camera shot in which the camera moves with the subject following alongside or behind

follow-the-leader *n US* = **follow-my-leader**

follow-through *n* **1** further action continuing or completing something previously done or begun ○ *Your follow-through on the project was less than satisfactory.* **2** the continuation of the movement of the arm or leg past the point of contact or release after hitting, throwing, or kicking a ball or other object in a sport

follow-up *n* **1** further action or investigation or a subsequent event that results from and is intended to supplement something done before ○ *The conference was intended as a follow-up to the summit meeting in Vienna.* **2** a book, film, article, or report that continues a story or provides further information —**follow-up** *adj*

folly /fólli/ (*plural* **-lies**) *n* **1** UNREASON thoughtlessness, recklessness, or thoughtless or reckless behaviour ○ *She realized, too late, the folly of her course of action.* ○ *It would be folly to continue.* **2** IRRATIONAL THING a thoughtless or reckless act or idea (*often plural*) **3** ECCENTRIC BUILDING a building of eccentric or overelaborate design, usually built for decorative rather than practical purposes **4** *US* MISGUIDED UNDERTAKING an undertaking that is excessively costly or extravagant, especially one that leads to financial loss or ruin [13C. < Old French *folie* < *fol* 'foolish' (see FOOL).]

Folsom /fṓlsəm/ *adj* relating to a prehistoric culture of the southern plains of North America that made leaf-shaped flint projectile points with a concave base [Early 20C. Village in NE New Mexico.]

foment /fō mént, fə mént/ *vt* to cause or stir up trouble or rebellion [14C. < late Latin *fomentare* < Latin *fomentum* 'warm soothing application' < *fovere* 'warm, keep warm'.] —**fomentation** /fṓ men táysh'n, fṓmən-/ *n*

SPELLCHECK See ***ferment.***

fomites /fṓmi teez/ *npl* inanimate objects capable of carrying germs from an infected person to another person, e.g. clothes or bedding [Mid-19C. < Latin, plural of *fomes* 'kindling wood'.]

fond[1] /fond/ *adj* **1** FEELING AFFECTION feeling love, affection, or a strong liking for somebody or something ○ *I've grown fond of this old house.* **2** LIKING liking or finding enjoyment in something ○ *She's too fond of the sound of her own voice.* ○ *His dog is fond of chasing rabbits.* **3** AFFECTIONATE showing or characterized by affection, love, or pleasant feelings ○ *fond memories of the time we spent there* **4** OVERLY DOTING feeling or showing excessive affection, often to the point of being overindulgent with somebody ○ *Her fond parents could deny her nothing.* **5** OVEROPTIMISTIC unrealistic, though often dearly wished for ○ *fond hopes* [14C. Probably < past participle of obsolete *fon* 'be foolish' < *fon* 'fool' < ?] —**fondly** *adv* —**fondness** *n*

fond[2] /fond, foN/ *n* a background, especially of a piece of decorated lace [Mid-17C. Via French < Latin *fundus* 'bottom'.]

Fonda /fóndə/, **Henry** (1905–82) US film and stage actor

Fonda, Jane (*b.* 1937) US film actor and political activist

Fonda, Peter (*b.* 1939) US film actor and director

fondant /fóndənt/ *n* **1** a smooth paste made from boiled sugar syrup, often coloured or flavoured. Use: filling for chocolates, coating for cakes, nuts, or fruit. **2** a sweet made from or filled with fondant [Late 19C. < French, present participle of *fondre* (see FONDUE).]

fondle /fónd'l/ (**-dles, -dling, -dled**) *v* **1** *vt* to stroke, handle, or touch something or somebody gently, in a loving or affectionate way ○ *idly fondling the cat's ears* **2** to touch or caress somebody in an aggressive or unwelcome way [Late 17C. Back-formation < obsolete *fondling* 'foolish person' < FOND[1].] —**fondler** *n*

fondue /fón dyoo, -doo/ *n* a dish eaten by dipping small pieces of food into the contents of a pot, usually melted cheese, hot oil, or a sauce, placed on the table [Late 19C. < French, form of past participle of *fondre* 'melt' < Latin *fundere*.]

font[1] /font/ *n* **1** RECEPTACLE FOR BAPTISMAL WATER a large container in a church for the water used in baptisms **2** RECEPTACLE FOR HOLY WATER a container for holy water, usually found at the entrance to a Roman Catholic church **3** HOLDER FOR LIQUID any holder for liquid, e.g. the part of an oil-burning lamp that contains the oil **4** ABUNDANT SOURCE somebody or something seen as a source or inexhaustible supply of something (*literary*) **5** FOUNTAIN a fountain, spring, or well (*literary*) [Pre-12C. < Latin *font-*, stem of *fons* 'spring'.] —**fontal** *adj*

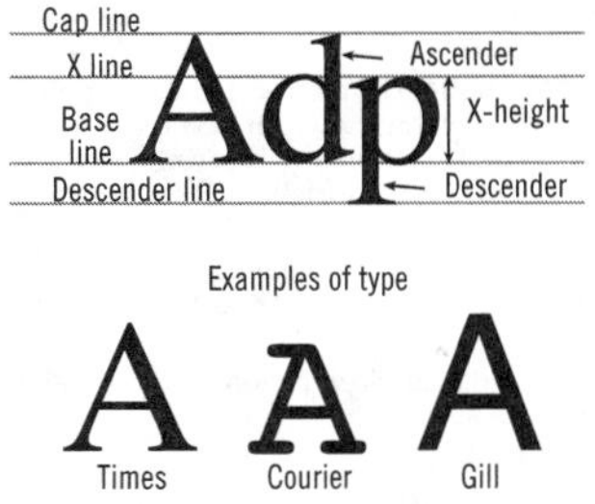
Cap line
X line
Base line
Descender line
Adp
Ascender
X-height
Descender
Examples of type
A A A
Times
Courier
Gill

Font

⚡**font**[2] /font/, **fount** /fownt, font/ *n* a full set of printing type or of printed or screen characters of the same design and size [Late 16C. < Old French *fonte* 'casting' < *fondre* (see FONDUE).]

Fontaine /fon táyn/, **Pierre F. L** (1762–1853) French architect

Fontainebleau /fóntinblō/ town in north-central France, site of a 16th-century chateau. Population: 18,037 (1990).

fontanel *n* US = **fontanelle**

fontanelle /fóntə nél/ *n* a soft, membrane-covered space between bones at the front and the back of a young baby's skull [15C. < Old French *fontenel* 'little spring' < *fontaine* (see FOUNTAIN).]

⚡**font cartridge** *n* a plug-in unit containing fonts of various sizes and styles

Fonteyn /fon táyn/, **Dame Margot** (1919–91) British ballet dancer. Born **Margaret Hookham.** See illustration overleaf.

fontina /fon téenə/ *n* a semihard mild Italian cheese [Mid-20C. < Italian dialect.]

food /food/ *n* **1** SOURCE OF NUTRIENTS material that provides living things with the nutrients they need for energy

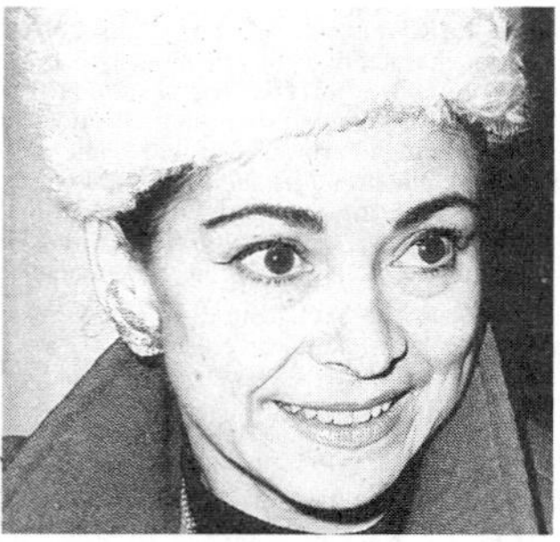
Barnaby's

Dame Margot Fonteyn

and growth 2 SOLID NOURISHMENT substances, or a particular substance, providing nourishment for people or animals, especially in solid as opposed to liquid form 3 MENTAL STIMULUS something that sustains or stimulates the mind or soul ○ *food for thought* [Old English *fōda* < Indo-European] —**foodless** *adj*

food additive *n* a natural or artificial substance that is added to food during processing to make it look or taste better or last longer

food bank *n US* a place where food is collected before being distributed to people who have no money

food chain *n* a hierarchy of different living things, each of which feeds on the one below

food court *n* the part of a shopping centre where snacks and light meals can be bought from a number of different outlets, often with a communal eating area

food fish *n* any fish that people eat

foodie /fo͞odi/, **foody** (*plural* **-ies**) *n* an enthusiast of cooking, eating, or shopping for good food (*informal*)

food mixer *n* an electrical kitchen appliance used to beat eggs or cream or to mix together the ingredients for cakes and batters

food poisoning *n* acute inflammation of the mucous membrane of the stomach and intestines caused by eating food contaminated with toxic substances or with microorganisms that generate toxins

food processor *n* an electrical kitchen appliance consisting of a container in which food is cut, sliced, shredded, grated, blended, beaten, or liquidized automatically by a variety of removable revolving blades

foodstuff /fo͞od stuf/ *n* something that can be eaten, especially one of the basic elements of the human diet (*usually plural*)

food web *n* the interlocking food chains within an ecological community

foody *n* = **foodie**

fool /fool/ *n* 1 UNINTELLIGENT PERSON a person considered to lack good sense or judgment ○ *Only a fool would invest in a scheme like this.* 2 RIDICULOUS PERSON a person considered to look or has been made to appear ridiculous ○ *I feel such a fool dressed like this.* 3 *US* ENTHUSIAST a person who is talented at, interested in, or fond of something specified ○ *an absolute fool for the finer things in life* 4 COURT ENTERTAINER formerly, somebody employed to amuse a monarch or noble, usually by telling jokes, singing comical songs, or performing tricks 5 CREAMY FRUIT DESSERT a cold dessert made from puréed fruit mixed with cream or custard ■ *adj US* UNINTELLIGENT AND NOT SENSIBLE showing a lack of good sense or judgment (*informal*) ○ *That fool salesman said it would fit.* ■ *v* 1 *vt* TRICK to trick or deceive somebody ○ *Don't be fooled by her promises.* 2 *vi* SPEAK IN JEST to say something jokingly or not seriously, or pretend, jokingly, that something false is true ○ *I was only fooling – of course you can come.* 3 *vi* BEHAVE COMICALLY to behave in a comical, playful, or silly way [13C. Via Old French *fol* 'fool, foolish' < Latin *follis* 'bellows, windbag'.] ◇ **be nobody's fool** to be wise enough not to be easily deceived ◇ **make a fool (out) of somebody** to deceive or trick somebody, or make somebody look ridiculous ◇ **make a fool of yourself** to act in a foolish, ridiculous, or embarrassing way

fool around, fool about *vi* 1 BEHAVE IRRESPONSIBLY to behave in a thoughtless or irresponsible way ○ *Don't fool around with those tools.* 2 CLOWN AROUND to behave in a silly or comical way 3 WASTE TIME to waste time by doing silly or unimportant things 4 *US* HAVE CASUAL SEX to participate in casual or illicit sexual relationships

fool with *vt* to treat or handle somebody or something without due care or respect ○ *Who's been fooling with the TV?*

foolery /fo͞oləri/ (*plural* **-ies**) *n* (*dated*) 1 irresponsible or playful behaviour 2 an irresponsible or playful act

foolhardy /fo͞ol haardi/ *adj* showing boldness or courage but not wisdom or good sense —**foolhardily** *adv* —**foolhardiness** *n*

foolish /fo͞olish/ *adj* 1 NOT SENSIBLE showing, or resulting from, a lack of good sense or judgment 2 SEEMING RIDICULOUS feeling or appearing ridiculous ○ *Wipe that foolish grin off your face!* 3 UNIMPORTANT lacking importance or substance ○ *a foolish little worry* —**foolishly** *adv* —**foolishness** *n*

foolproof /fo͞ol proof/ *adj* 1 designed to continue working properly in the face of any kind of human error, incompetence, or misuse 2 so well thought out that failure is thought to be impossible

foolscap /fo͞ol skap, fo͞olz kap/ *n* 1 a large size of paper, approximately 13.5 in by 17 in, mostly used for writing and printing 2 *US* = **fool's cap** [Late 17C. < the watermark of a fool's cap originally on the paper.]

fool's cap *n* a brightly coloured cap with points ending in bells or tassels, worn by court jesters

fool's errand *n* a task that is performed for no good reason or that fails to accomplish anything useful

fool's gold *n* a sulphide mineral with a golden lustre, especially pyrite

fool's mate *n* the quickest checkmate in chess, achieved on the second move by the player with the black pieces

fool's paradise *n* a state of happiness that is temporary and insubstantial because it is based on illusions or unrealistic hopes ○ *living in a fool's paradise*

fool's-parsley *n* a poisonous weed with finely divided leaves that resemble parsley. Flowers: white. Native to: Europe, naturalized in North America. *Aethusa cynapium.*

foosball /fo͞oz bawl/ *n US* = **table football**

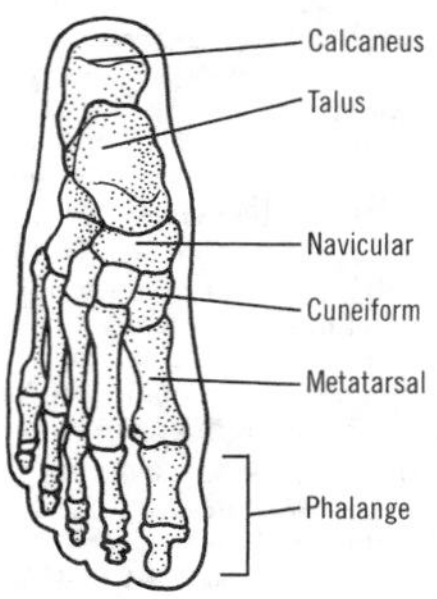
Calcaneus
Talus
Navicular
Cuneiform
Metatarsal
Phalange

Foot: Bone structure of a human foot

foot /fo͝ot/ *n* (*plural* **feet**) 1 PART AT END OF LEG the part of the leg of a vertebrate below the ankle joint that supports the rest of the body and maintains balance when standing and walking ○ *The wave knocked me off my feet.* 2 ORGAN OF ATTACHMENT an organ or muscle surface that an invertebrate, e.g. a mollusc, uses to grip or move itself along 3 UNIT OF LENGTH (*symbol* ') a unit of length in the imperial and US customary systems equal to .3048 m/12 in ○ *The aircraft is cruising at 30,000 feet* 4 LOWEST PART the bottom or lowest part of something ○ *a note scribbled at the foot of the page* 5 PART OF SOCK the part of a sock, stocking, or boot that is shaped to cover the foot 6 PART RESEMBLING FOOT something that is shaped like or acts like a human or animal foot, e.g. a shaped part at the end of the leg of a chair 7 LOWER PART OF PLANT the lower part of the stem of a plant, or the base of the spore-producing body (**sporophyte**) of mosses and liverworts 8 PART OF SEWING MACHINE the part of a sewing machine, close to the needle, that is lowered onto the material to hold it in position 9 WAY OF WALKING a particular way of walking 10 SOLDIERS WHO FIGHT ON FOOT soldiers who fight principally on foot, rather than on horses or in vehicles (+ *plural verb*) ○ *an officer commanding a company of foot* 11 UNIT OF POETIC METRE a basic unit of rhythm in poetry, made up of a fixed combination of stressed and unstressed or long and short syllables ■ **foots** *npl* 1 SEDIMENT the solid material that gradually falls to the bottom of various liquids, e.g. vegetable oil 2 FOOTLIGHTS footlights (*informal*) ■ *vt* 1 PAY FULL COST OF to pay the full amount of something ○ *We had to foot the bill for the party.* 2 ADD UP FIGURES to add up the figures in a column ○ *footed the columns of the budget* 3 MAKE FOOT OF SOCK in knitting or sewing, to add the part that will cover the foot to a sock or stocking [Old English *fōt* < Indo-European] —**footed** *adj* ◇ **a foot in the door** the first stage towards a goal, especially when this is difficult to achieve ◇ **drag your feet** to move or do something slowly and reluctantly on purpose (*informal*) ◇ **fall** *or* **land on your feet** to end up in a good position, especially after having been in a difficult situation ◇ **find your feet** 1 to become accustomed to a new situation and able to cope with it 2 to manage to stand up, especially after having fallen ◇ **foot it** 1 to walk rather than ride in a vehicle or on a horse ○ *We had to foot it all the way home.* 2 to dance (*dated*) ◇ **get off on the wrong foot** to begin something badly, e.g. a new relationship or job ◇ **get on** *or* **to your feet** 1 to rise from a reclining or sitting position 2 to return to a healthy or financially stable condition after a period of illness or financial difficulty ◇ **have somebody** *or* **something at your feet** to be the object of enormous admiration and devotion from somebody or something ◇ **have feet of clay** to have a weakness or flaw that is not obvious at first ◇ **have** *or* **keep both** *or* **your feet on the ground** to act and think sensibly and realistically ◇ **on foot** walking, as opposed to riding on horseback or in a vehicle ◇ **put your best foot forward** to try as hard as you can to impress or please somebody ◇ **put your feet up** to stop working and relax ◇ **put your foot down** 1 to be firm about something and make sure your wishes are obeyed or respected 2 to make a motor vehicle travel faster by pressing the accelerator ◇ **put your foot in it** to make an embarrassing mistake, especially by being tactless (*informal*) ◇ **set foot in** *or* **on something** to go to or into a place ○ *I'll never set foot in that place again.* ◇ **shoot yourself in the foot** to do something that unexpectedly turns out to be disadvantageous or harmful to your own interests ◇ **sweep somebody off his** *or* **her feet** to charm somebody completely or make him or her fall in love with you in a very short time

USAGE ***foot*** or ***feet***? When you combine ***foot*** with numbers above *one* in measuring distances, use the plural ***feet***: *Our property line is seven feet* [not *foot*] *from the school.* When ***foot*** is part of a hyphenated compound preceding a noun, use the singular ***foot*** even if the numeric part of the compound exceeds *one*: *a one-foot piece of timber*; *a ten-foot* [not *feet*] *piece of timber.* When ***foot*** is part of an unhyphenated numeric compound coming after the noun it refers to, use ***feet*** if the number exceeds *one*: *a piece of timber one foot long; a piece of timber ten feet* [not *foot*] *long.*

Foot /fo͝ot/, **Michael** (*b.* 1913) British politician and writer

footage /fo͝otij/ *n* 1 FILMED SEQUENCE SHOWING EVENT a shot or sequence of shots on film or video tape, usually of a particular scene or event, or the length of film or videotape that contains these shots ○ *They had some good footage of the president's visit to the island.* 2 SIZE IN FEET the size or amount of something measured in feet 3 LENGTH OF PIECE OF FILM the length of a piece of film in feet 4 PAYMENT BY SIZE payment by the foot for work 5 AMOUNT PAID the amount paid for work measured by the foot

foot-and-mouth disease *n* a highly contagious viral disease affecting animals with divided hooves, especially cattle, sheep, and pigs, in which the animal develops ulcers in the mouth and near the hooves

football /fo͝ot bawl/ *n* 1 GAME WITH ROUND BALL a game in which two teams of 11 players try to kick or head a round ball into the goal defended by the opposing team. US term **soccer** 2 *US* = **American football** 3 *Can* CANADIAN FOOTBALL a game that is similar to American football but takes place on a larger field, has 12 players on each team, and uses three rather than four moves to advance at least ten yards or score 4 BALL GAME any game in which two teams kick or carry a ball into a goal or over a line, e.g. rugby, Australian rules, or Gaelic football 5 BALL USED IN FOOTBALL the large round ball used in the game of football 6 PROBLEM PASSED AROUND a point or problem that is used as an excuse for argument by opposing groups, without any real attempt at finding a solution —**footballer** *n*

football pools *npl* 1 GAMBLING = **pools** 2 an organized form of gambling, mainly by post, that involves predicting the outcome of football matches

footbath /fo͝ot baath/ (*plural* **-baths** /-baath͟z/) *n* 1 a bowl used when bathing the feet, or a shallow pool where people can disinfect their feet before entering a swimming pool 2 the action of bathing the feet

footboard /fo͝ot bawrd/ *n* 1 a vertical part across the bottom end of a bedstead 2 a board or small platform used to support the feet in a vehicle

footboy /fo͝ot boy/ *n* a boy employed as a servant or page

foot brake *n* a brake operated by pressing a pedal with the foot, especially in a motor vehicle

footbridge /fo͝ot brij/ *n* a narrow bridge suitable for people walking and not for vehicles

foot-dragger *n* a person who is slow or reluctant to do what is required (*informal*) —**foot-dragging** *n*

⚡**footer**[1] /fo͝otər/ *n* 1 a piece of text, such as a title or date, below the main text on a page, especially one that is automatically inserted on each page by word-processing software 2 somebody or something of a specified height or length in feet (*usually in combination*) ○ *Both of her sons were six-footers.* 3 ARCHIT, BUILDING = **footing** *n.* 5

footer[2] /fo͝otər/, **fouter** *vi Scotland* **POTTER** to spend time doing trivial or useless things ○ *Can you not do something useful instead of footering about?* ■ *n Scotland* 1 **SOMEBODY DOING TRIVIAL THINGS** a person who does something trivial or useless, or who plays idly with something 2 **AWKWARD JOB** a job that is awkward or involves working with small parts ○ *It was a bit of a footer putting it back together again.* [Late 16C. < Old French *foutre* 'have sex with' < Latin *futuere.*]

footfall /fo͝ot fawl/ *n* the sound made by somebody's foot striking the ground as he or she walks

foot fault *n* a fault committed in tennis by a server whose foot touches any part of the baseline or court before the ball has been hit —**foot-fault** *vi*

footgear /fo͝ot geer/ *n* coverings worn on the feet, especially shoes and boots

foothill /fo͝ot hil/ *n* a hill at the bottom of a higher mountain or mountain range and forming part of the approaches to it (*often plural*)

foothold /fo͝ot hōld/ *n* 1 a place or thing that will support the foot of a climber, especially a crack, hollow, or ledge in a rock face 2 a secure starting position from which further advances can be made ○ *The company has gained a foothold in the multimedia industry.*

footie /fo͝otti/ *n* football (*informal*)

footing /fo͝oting/ *n* 1 **STABILITY OF FEET** a stable secure position for or placement of the feet when standing or walking ○ *He lost his footing on the icy slope.* 2 **BASE FOR PROGRESS** a foundation or basis for further advancement or development ○ *The project began on a firm financial footing.* 3 **STATUS** the status or condition of something, often in relation to something else ○ *The government moved swiftly to place the armed forces on a war footing.* 4 **RELATIONSHIP** the position or status of people in relation to one another ○ *I'm glad to be back on a friendly footing with her.* 5 **FOUNDATION** the foundation or base of a structure such as a wall or column

footle /fo͞ot'l/ (**-tles, -tling, -tled**) *vi* (*informal*) 1 **ACT AIMLESSLY** to waste time doing unnecessary or unimportant things 2 **ACT OR TALK POINTLESSLY** to talk nonsense, or behave in a pointless way ■ *n* **NONSENSE** silly nonsense [Late 19C. < ?] —**footler** *n*

footless /fo͝otləss/ *adj* lacking a foot or feet

footlights /fo͝ot līts/ *npl* 1 a row of lights along the front of the stage in a theatre, directed away from the audience and towards the performers 2 the theatre as a profession

footling /fo͞otling/ *adj* (*informal*) 1 having no importance or serious usefulness 2 lacking skill or competence

footloose /fo͝ot looss/ *adj* free to go anywhere and do anything because not limited by personal ties or responsibilities

footman /fo͝otmən/ (*plural* **-men**) *n* 1 **LIVERIED SERVANT** a man employed as a servant, especially a servant in uniform in a mansion or palace 2 **FIRESIDE STAND** a low metal stand, usually with four legs, for utensils in a fireplace 3 **SOLDIER** a soldier who fights on foot (*archaic*)

footmark /fo͝ot maark/ *n* = **footprint** *n.* 1

footnote /fo͝ot nōt/ *n* 1 **INFORMATION AT FOOT OF PAGE** a note at the bottom of a page, giving further information about something mentioned in the text above 2 **ADDITIONAL DETAIL** an extra comment or information added to what has just been said ○ *As a footnote, let me say that I only found this out yesterday.* 3 **MINOR DETAIL** a relatively unimportant part of a larger issue or event ○ *His career, considered glorious at the time, is now but a footnote in history.* ■ *vt* (**-notes, -noting, -noted**) **SUPPLY WITH FOOTNOTES** to provide a text with footnotes, or provide a footnote for a particular reference within the text

footpad[1] /fo͝ot pad/ *n* a robber or highwayman who operated on foot rather than on a horse (*archaic*) [Late 17C. < obsolete *pad* 'path, highwayman' < Dutch.]

footpad[2] /fo͝ot pad/ *n* a flat structure at the end of a leg of a spacecraft, designed to prevent the craft sinking into the surface it has landed on

foot passenger *n* a passenger on a car ferry who is not travelling with a motor vehicle

footpath /fo͝ot paath/ (*plural* **-paths** /-paath͟z/) *n* a narrow path for people on foot ○ *Please keep to the footpath.*

footplate /fo͝ot playt/ *n* the part of a railway locomotive from which the driver operates the controls

foot-pound *n* a unit of work equal to the work done by lifting a mass of one pound vertically against gravity through a distance of one foot

foot-pound-second *adj* relating or belonging to a system of measurements based on the foot, pound, and second as base units of length, mass, and time

foot-pound-second units, foot-pound-second system of units *n* MEASURE, PHYS = **fps units**

⚡**footprint** /fo͝ot print/ *n* 1 **OUTLINE OF FOOT** a mark made by the foot of a person or animal or a shoe, especially an indentation on something soft like snow or a dirty mark on a floor ○ *footprints in the ground below the window* 2 **SPACE OCCUPIED BY MACHINE** the area covered by something, especially the amount of space a piece of computer hardware occupies on a desk, floor, or other surface 3 **BROADCAST RANGE** the area over which something occurs or is effective, e.g. the area where a signal from a communications satellite can be received

footrace /fo͝ot rayss/, **foot race** *n* a race run by people on foot

footrest /fo͝ot rest/ *n* a support for both feet when sitting down, e.g. beneath a desk, or for one foot while standing, e.g. a low rail at a bar

footrope /fo͝ot rōp/ *n* 1 a rope to which the lower edge of a sail is stitched 2 a rope fixed beneath a ship's yard for sailors to stand on as they furl a sail

foot rot /fo͝ot rot/, **footrot** *n* 1 a bacterial infection of sheep and cattle that causes inflammation of the hooves 2 a fungal disease that causes the roots and base of a plant to rot

foot rule *n* a strip of wood, metal, or plastic, used for measuring and drawing straight lines, that is one foot long or is marked in feet

footsie /fo͝otsi/ *n* a form of flirtation in which people use their feet to touch the feet and legs of somebody else, especially done secretly while sitting at a table (*informal*) ◇ **play footsie** 1 to engage in footsie (*informal*) 2 *US* to collaborate with another person or organization, often in an underhand way (*informal*)

footslog /fo͝ot slog/ (**-slogs, -slogging, -slogged**) *vi* to march, tramp, or trudge on foot, especially over difficult ground such as thick mud —**footslogger** *n* —**footslogging** *n*

foot soldier *n* a soldier who fights principally on foot, not on horseback or in a vehicle

footsore /fo͝ot sawr/ *adj* with feet that are painful or tired, usually from too much walking —**footsoreness** *n*

footstall /fo͝ot stawl/ *n* 1 the pedestal or base of a structure, especially a pillar or statue 2 a stirrup on a sidesaddle

footstep /fo͝ot step/ *n* 1 **SOUND OF FEET** the sound made when somebody's foot hits the ground in walking ○ *I heard footsteps on the stairs.* 2 **MOVEMENT OF FOOT** the action of raising a foot and putting it down somewhere else while walking 3 **DISTANCE COVERED BY STEP** the distance covered by a single step in walking 4 **MARK MADE BY FOOT** a mark left by the sole of a foot or shoe 5 **STEP OR STAIR** a single step or stair on which to put a foot while moving up or down ◇ **follow in somebody's footsteps** to take the same course in life or work as another person in the past

footstone /fo͝ot stōn/ *n* a memorial stone at the foot of a grave

footstool /fo͝ot stool/ *n* a low stool, often with a padded top, on which to rest the feet while sitting down

footwall /fo͝ot wawl/ *n* the rock layer that lies immediately beneath a vein of ore or other mineral deposit or a fault plane

footway /fo͝ot way/ *n* a narrow path or walk for people on foot, e.g. beside a road or railway line

footwear /fo͝ot wair/ *n* coverings worn on the feet, especially shoes, boots, sandals, or slippers, but often including socks or stockings

footwell /fo͝ot wel/ *n* the hollow space below a motor vehicle's dashboard where people in the front seats can put their feet

footwork /fo͝ot wurk/ *n* 1 **MOTION OF FEET** the movement of the feet in sport or dancing, especially when skilfully done 2 **SKILFUL MANOEUVRING** skilful or devious manoeuvring in order to achieve or avoid something (*informal*) ○ *Their fancy footwork helped get them out of the problem.* 3 *US* **WORK THAT INVOLVES WALKING** work that involves a lot of moving around, especially on foot

footworn /fo͝ot wawrn/ *adj* 1 worn down or made thin by being walked on by many people for a long time 2 = **footsore**

foo yung /foo yúng, -yóng, -yo͝ong/, **foo young, fu yung** *n* a Chinese-style dish, similar to an omelette, in which the eggs are combined with beansprouts, onions, and meat or seafood. US term **egg foo yung** [Mid-20C. < Cantonese *fo͝o yung* 'hibiscus'.]

foozle /fo͞oz'l/ *vti* (**-zles, -zling, -zled**) to do something badly or clumsily, especially to bungle a shot in golf ■ *n* something done badly or clumsily, especially a bungled shot in golf [Mid-19C. < ?] —**foozler** *n*

fop /fop/ *n* a man who is so obsessed by fashion and vain about his own appearance that he becomes ridiculous [15C. < ?] —**foppery** *n* —**foppish** *adj* —**foppishly** *adv* —**foppishness** *n*

for (*stressed*) /fawr/; (*unstressed*) /fər/ CORE MEANING: a preposition indicating that something is directed at somebody, done to benefit somebody, or done on somebody's behalf ○ *Look – there's a letter for you.* ○ *I'd do anything for you.* ○ *The lawyer acted for some of the heirs.*
1 *prep* **AIMED AT** intended to be received or used by or aimed at somebody ○ *It's for you – it's a present.* ○ *advice for first-time buyers* 2 *prep* **TO THE BENEFIT OF** intending or intended to benefit somebody or something ○ *She would make any sacrifice for the cause.* 3 *prep* **ON BEHALF OF** on behalf of or instead of somebody or something ○ *Would you mind making my apologies for me?* 4 *prep* **IN THE SERVICE OF** in the service or employment of somebody or something ○ *She works for a large company.* 5 *prep* **TOWARDS** in the direction of ○ *The following day, we headed for Paris.* 6 *prep* **LASTING** indicating how long something lasts, continues, or extends ○ *The interview only lasted for a few minutes.* ○ *There was fog for the next mile or so.* 7 *prep* **BECAUSE OF** indicating a reason why something happens or is done ○ *I did it for love.* 8 *prep* **DESIGNED WITH A PURPOSE** indicating the purpose of an object, action, or activity ○ *That towel is for drying your hands on.* 9 *prep* **LINKS CONCEPTS** used to link two concepts, one of which is the object of the other ○ *a cause for concern* ○ *a passion for opera* 10 *prep* **IN EXCHANGE FOR** at a cost of or giving or receiving something in exchange ○ *I got this hat in the market for next to nothing* 11 *prep* **INSTEAD OF** instead of or in place of something, sometimes mistakenly ○ *You'll have to find a stand-in for him while he's away.* ○ *I took her for the boss.* 12 *prep* **GIVEN WHAT IS USUAL** with reference to the normal characteristics of something ○ *It's very warm for April.* 13 *prep* **INDICATING OCCASION** at, or planned to be at, a particular time, or on a particular occasion ○ *The meeting was scheduled for four o'clock.* ○ *Will you be home for Christmas?* 14 *prep* **INDICATES COMPARISON** indicating a comparison or equivalence between two things ○ *Pound for pound, the elephant's energy consumption is the lowest of all land animals.* 15 *prep* **IN ORDER TO GET** in order to get, achieve, have, keep, or become something ○ *Lee's hoping for promotion.* ○ *He was searching for a place to sit.* 16 *prep* **DESPITE** in spite of or notwithstanding something ○ *He enjoyed himself very much, for all his complaining.* 17 *prep* **INDICATES RESPONSIBILITY** indicating that somebody has the right or responsibility to do something ○ *I can't help you – it's for you to decide.* 18 *prep* **HAVING THE SAME MEANING** having the same meaning as another word or phrase

○ *The everyday term for rubella is German measles.* **19** *prep* **INDICATES CROSS-REFERENCE** indicating that information can be found elsewhere ○ *For further details, consult the owner's manual.* **20** *adv, prep* **IN SUPPORT OF** in favour of or in support of something ○ (prep) *Who's for the motion and who's against it?* ○ (adv) *Ten voted for, and eleven against.* **21** *conj* **BECAUSE** because, seeing that (*formal*) ○ *I left in haste, for I was already late for the appointment.* [Old English, < Indo-European, 'forward'] ◇ **be (in) for it** to be likely to be punished (*informal*)

USAGE See *because*.

for. *abbr* **1** foreign **2** forestry

f.o.r. *abbr* free on rail

for- *prefix* **1** away, down, falsely ○ *forfend* ○ *forswear* **2** completely, extremely ○ *forgather* [Old English; related to *for* 'before, in place of' (see FOR)]

fora plural of **forum**

forage /fórrij/ *n* **1 FOOD FOR ANIMALS** food for animals, especially crops grown to feed horses, cattle, and other livestock **2 SEARCH** a search or the process of searching for something, especially a search for food and supplies or a search among a varied collection of things **3 RAID BY SOLDIERS** a raid carried out by soldiers, especially to seize food or supplies ■ *v* (**-ages, -aging, -aged**) **1** *vi* **WANDER AROUND SEARCHING** to go from place to place looking for food and supplies **2** *vti* **RAID FOR FOOD** to raid a place, especially for food or supplies **3** *vi* **SEARCH** to search or try to find something ○ *He foraged around in the drawer and pulled out a faded photograph.* **4** *vt* **FIND BY SEARCHING** to obtain something, especially food, from a place by searching or rummaging ○ *She foraged a half-eaten cake from the bin.* **5** *vt* **FEED ANIMALS** to give fodder to horses, cattle, or other animals [14C. < Old French *fourrage* < *fuerre* 'fodder, straw' < Germanic.] —**forager** *n*

foram /fáwrəm/ *n* = **foraminifer** [Early 20C. Shortening.]

foramen /fə ráy men, fo-/ (*plural* **-ramina** /-rámminə/ *or* **-ramens**) *n* a natural opening or cavity in a human or animal body, usually one through which blood vessels and nerves pass through bone [Late 17C. < Latin, < *forare* 'bore a hole'.] —**foraminal** /-rámmin'l/ *adj* —**foraminous** *adj*

foramen magnum /-mágnəm/ *n* the opening at the base of the skull through which the spinal cord passes to become the medulla oblongata of the brain [Late 19C. < Latin, 'large opening'.]

foramen ovale /-ō vaáli/ *n* an opening in the wall between the two sides of the foetal heart that allows blood to pass from right to left [Mid-19C. < Latin, 'oval opening'.]

foramina plural of **foramen**

foraminifer /fórrə mínnifər/ (*plural* **-fera** /-ə/ *or* **-fers**) *n* a large, mainly marine protozoan that has a shell perforated with many small holes through which temporary cytoplasmic protrusions (**pseudopodia**) project. Order: Foraminfera. [Mid-19C. < modern Latin *Foraminifera* (plural) < Latin *foramen* (see FORAMEN) + *-fer* 'bearing'.] —**foraminiferal** /fo rámmi nífferəl, fórrəmi-/ *adj* —**foraminiferous** *adj*

forasmuch as /fərəz múch əz/ *conj* since or in view of the fact that (*archaic*)

foray /fóray/ *n* **1 SUDDEN RAID** a sudden attack or raid by a military force **2 EXPLORATION** an attempt at some new occupation or activity ○ *the ex-player's first foray into management* **3 BRIEF JOURNEY** a short trip or visit to a place, usually for a particular purpose ■ *v* **1** *vi* **MAKE INCURSION** to make a sudden attack or raid **2** *vt* **MAKE RAID ON** to raid or loot a place [14C. Back-formation < *forayer* < Old French *fourrier* < *fuerre* (see FORAGE).] —**forayer** *n*

forb /fawrb/ *n* any broad-leaved herbaceous plant that is not a grass, especially one that grows in a prairie or meadow [Early 20C. < Greek *phorbē* 'food' < *pherbein* 'to feed'.]

forbade, forbad past tense of **forbid**

forbear¹ /fawr báir/ (**-bears, -bearing, -bore** /-báwr/, **-borne** /-báwrn/) *v* (*formal*) **1** *vi* to not do or say something that you could do or say, especially when this shows self-control or consideration for the feelings of others ○ *I forbore to criticize their efforts, though criticism was well deserved.* **2** *vti* to tolerate something with patience or endurance ○ *patiently forbore their failures* [Old English *forberan*, literally 'bear against'] —**forbearer** *n* —**forbearing** *adj* —**forbearingly** *adv*

USAGE As a verb ***forbear*** is the only spelling. As a noun ***forebear*** is preferred.

forbear² *n* = **forebear**

forbearance /fawr báirənss/ *n* **1 PATIENCE** patience, tolerance, or self-control, especially in not responding to provocation (*formal*) **2 REFRAINING FROM ACTION** the fact of deliberately not doing or saying something when you could do or say it (*formal*) **3 REFRAINING FROM LEGAL RIGHT** the fact of not exercising a legal right, especially of not insisting on payment of a debt at the due date and giving the debtor more time to pay

Forbes /fawrbz/ town in central New South Wales, Australia. Population: 7,467 (1996).

Forbes, George William (1869–1947) New Zealand statesman

forbid /fər bíd/ (**-bids, -bidding, -bade** /-bád, -báyd/ *or* **-bad** /-bád/, **-bidden** /-bídd'n/ *or* **-bid**) *vt* **1 ORDER NOT TO DO** to tell somebody, especially forcefully, not to do or have something ○ *I forbid you to mention his name.* **2 NOT ALLOW** to state authoritatively that something must not be done ○ *The rules of the game strictly forbid the use of a dictionary.* **3 MAKE IMPOSSIBLE** to make something impossible or prevent it from happening (*formal*) ○ *Discretion forbids me to mention any names.* [Old English *forbēodan*, literally 'command against'] —**forbiddance** *n* —**forbidder** *n* ◇ **God** *or* **heaven(s)** *or* **Lord forbid** used to express the hope that something will not happen or be done

forbidden /fər bídd'n/ *adj* **1 NOT PERMITTED** not allowed by order of somebody or by law ○ *That's a forbidden subject in this company.* **2 OUT OF BOUNDS** to which entry is not allowed or allowed only to a certain person or group of people ○ *This part of the temple was forbidden to everybody except the high priest.* **3 IMPROBABLE OR DISALLOWED AS ENERGY LEVEL** describes an energy level or transition in a quantum mechanical system that is either highly improbable or disobeys selection rules and is therefore not allowed

Forbidden City *n* a walled complex of buildings (1421–1911) in Beijing, China, that includes the former Imperial Palace

forbidden fruit (*plural* **forbidden fruits** *or* **forbidden fruit**) *n* something desired or pleasurable that somebody is not allowed to have or do, especially some form of sexual indulgence that is illegal or considered immoral [< the fruit, forbidden to Adam and Eve, of the tree of knowledge of good and evil (Genesis 2:17)]

forbidding /fər bídding/ *adj* **1 HOSTILE** presenting an appearance that seems hostile or stern ○ *The mountains looked distant and forbidding.* **2 UNINVITING** appearing to involve a great deal of unpleasantness or difficulty ○ *the forbidding prospect of further difficulties ahead* **3 DANGEROUS OR THREATENING** appearing to present a danger or threat ○ *a rocky and forbidding shore* —**forbiddingly** *adv* —**forbiddingness** *n*

~~**forboding**~~ incorrect spelling of **foreboding**

forbore past tense of **forbear**¹

forborne past participle of **forbear**¹

force¹ /fawrss/ *n* **1 STRENGTH** the power, strength, or energy that somebody or something possesses ○ *Trees were blown down by the force of the storm.* **2 PHYSICAL POWER** physical power, effort, or violence used against somebody or something that resists ○ *The use of force should be a last resort.* **3 EFFECTIVENESS** the condition of being effective, valid, or applicable ○ *The new regulations come into force next week.* **4 NONPHYSICAL POWER** power or strength that is intellectual or moral rather than physical ○ *swayed by the force of your argument* **5 SOMEBODY OR SOMETHING WITH GREAT INFLUENCE** somebody or something that has great power or influence, especially in a particular field ○ *She remained a force in local politics until her death.* **6 GROUP ORGANIZED TO FIGHT** a body of military personnel, ships, or aircraft brought together to fight in a battle or a war ○ *A naval task force has been sent to the area.* **7 POLICE OFFICERS** a professional body of police officers ○ *He left the force in 1985.* **8 PEOPLE WORKING TOGETHER** a group of people who work together for a particular purpose **9 INFLUENCE THAT MOVES** (*symbol F*) a physical influence that tends to change the position of an object with mass, equal to the rate of change in momentum of the object **10 WIND STRENGTH** the strength of the wind, especially as measured on the Beaufort scale, from 0 to 12 (*often in combination*) ○ *a force nine gale* ■ **forces** *npl* **ORGANIZED MILITARY SERVICE** the professional military organizations belonging to a particular country ○ *Were you in the forces?* ■ *vt* (**forces, forcing, forced**) **1 COMPEL** to use superior strength, violence, or any kind of physical or mental power to make somebody or yourself do something against his, her, or your own will or inclination ○ *The weather forced us to turn back.* ○ *She forced herself to be polite to him.* **2 MOVE WITH STRENGTH** to use physical strength or violence to move something or somebody that puts up resistance ○ *If the key won't turn easily, don't force it.* ○ *I had to force the last bit of toothpaste out of the tube.* ○ *She forced the dog back into the house.* **3 CREATE BY STRENGTH** to create something, e.g. a way through something, using physical strength or another kind of power ○ *They forced a path through the jungle.* **4 OBTAIN BY PRESSURE** to obtain something or make something happen by using physical or mental pressure ○ *She's been trying to force a confrontation all week.* **5 BREAK OPEN** to open something that is locked or jammed by using power or effort, often breaking or damaging it in the process ○ *This door has been forced.* **6 STRAIN** to produce or use something in a strained or unnatural way ○ *Just agree with whatever she says and try to force a smile.* **7 MAKE PLANT MATURE** to cause a plant to flower or mature before its normal time **8 RAPE** to subject somebody to rape (*dated*) **9 MAKE PLAYER PLAY CERTAIN WAY** to give a player in a game no choice but to play a particular card or make a particular bid or move [13C. < Old French, < Latin *fortis* 'strong'.] —**forceable** *adj* —**forceless** *adj* —**forcer** *n* ◇ **in force 1** in a large or strong group **2** effective or valid ◇ **join forces** to combine together or combine with somebody else for a joint effort

force down *vt* **1** to eat or drink something very reluctantly, often because pressured to do so or to avoid offending somebody **2** to compel an aircraft to land, usually because of lack of fuel, damage, or bad weather

force on, force upon *vt* to make somebody or a group of people accept something unwillingly ○ *This method was forced upon us by head office.*

force² /fawrss/ *n N England* a waterfall [Early 17C. < Old Norse *fors* 'waterfall'.]

forced /fawrst/ *adj* **1 NOT NATURAL** not natural or spontaneous, but produced by an act of will ○ *The courtiers greeted the king's witticism with forced laughter.* **2 NECESSARY** not done voluntarily but out of necessity **3 COMPELLED** done because somebody who has power requires it —**forcedly** /fáwrssidli/ *adv* —**forcedness** /-sidnəss/ *n*

forced labour *n* work that somebody is made to do against his or her will, often as a punishment or to repay a debt

forced landing *n* an unscheduled landing that a pilot is compelled to make, usually because of an emergency

forced march *n* a march made as quickly as possible and without the normal amounts of rest

force-feed *vt* **1** to make people or animals swallow food, against their will, e.g. by putting it directly down their throat through a funnel or tube **2** to make people study or learn things, often without fully understanding or appreciating them, that they might reject if given the choice

force field *n* in science fiction, an invisible protective barrier around something

forceful /fáwrssf'l/ *adj* **1** possessing or characterized by strength and power **2** tending to make a powerful impression on people or to persuade people ○ *a forceful argument for merging our businesses* —**forcefully** *adv* —**forcefulness** *n*

force-land *vti* to land an aircraft before it gets to its destination because of an emergency ○ *The pilot had to force-land in a field.*

force majeure /fáwrss ma zhúr/ *n* **1** an unexpected event that crucially affects somebody's ability to do something and can be put forward in law as an excuse for not having carried out the terms of an agreement (*formal*) **2** a force that is superior in power or impossible to resist [Late 19C. < French, 'superior force'.]

force-march *vti* to make soldiers or prisoners march somewhere in the shortest possible time and without the normal amounts of rest ○ *The infantry escaped by force-marching back to the river crossing.* ○ *The captured personnel were force-marched north.*

forcemeat /fáwrss meet/ *n* finely chopped meat, fish, or vegetables mixed with other ingredients and used as a stuffing or garnish [Late 17C. < variant of FARCE.]

force of habit *n* the ability of a pattern of behaviour that has become habitual to reassert itself automatically even in situations where it is no longer appropriate ○ *Even after she retired, she woke at six every morning by force of habit.*

forceps /fáwr seps, -səps/ *npl* **1** a specialized surgical instrument resembling tongs or tweezers. Use: grasping or moving tissues or organs, for applying materials such as gauze pads during operations. **2** a body part that is shaped or works like pincers, e.g. the grasping parts of some insects [Mid-16C. < Latin, 'pincers'.]

force pump *n* a pump that uses pressure to move a liquid

forcible /fáwrssəb'l/ *adj* **1** using physical power against somebody or something that resists ○ *the forcible removal of the lock* **2** powerful or tending to persuade people ○ *It was a forcible reminder that we must be on our guard.* —**forcibility** /fáwrssə bílləti/ *n* —**forcibleness** *n* —**forcibly** *adv*

ford /fawrd/ *n* a shallow part of a river or stream where people, animals, or vehicles can cross it ■ *vt* to walk, ride, or drive across a river or stream at a place where the water is shallow [Old English, < Germanic] —**fordable** *adj*

Ford /fawrd/, **Ford Madox** (1873–1939) British novelist. Born **Ford Hermann Hueffer**

Gerald R. Ford

Ford, Gerald R. (*b.* 1913) US statesman and 38th president of the United States (1974–77)

Ford, Glenn (*b.* 1916) Canadian-born US film actor. Born **Gwyllyn Samuel Newton**

Ford, Harrison (*b.* 1942) US film actor

Henry Ford

Ford, Henry (1863–1947) US industrialist

Ford, John (1895–1973) US film director. Born **John Martin Feeney**

Forde /fawrd/, **Frank** (1890–1983) Australian statesman

fore /fawr/ *n* **FRONT** the front of something, or something at the front (*literary*) ■ *adj* **AT FRONT** having a position at or near the front of something, especially a ship, an aircraft, or an animal ■ *adv* **TOWARDS THE FRONT** at or towards the front, especially of a ship or aircraft ■ *interj* **WARNING ABOUT GOLF BALL** shouted to warn people that you are hitting a golf ball in their direction [Old English, 'before, previously' < Germanic] ○ **to the fore** to a position of prominence or importance

fore- *prefix* **1** before, earlier ○ *forejudge* **2** front, in front ○ *forebrain* [Old English, < *fore* (see FORE)]

fore-and-aft *adj* parallel to or running along the length of something, especially a ship

fore-and-after *n* a ship with a fore-and-aft rig

fore-and-aft rig *n* an arrangement of a ship's sails such that, when set, they are parallel to the length of the vessel

fore-and-aft sail *n* SAILING = **gaffsail**

forearm[1] /fáwr aarm/ *n* the part of the human arm between the elbow and the wrist, or the corresponding part of an animal's foreleg

forearm[2] /fawr aárm/ *vt* to prepare or arm somebody in advance

forearm smash *n* a blow struck with the forearm in wrestling

forebear /fáwr bair/, **forbear** *n* an ancestor, especially one who died a long time ago (*often plural*) [15C. < FORE- + variant of obsolete *beer* 'somebody who is' < BE.]

SPELLCHECK See **forbear**.

---

forebode /fawr bód/ (**-bodes, -boding, -boded**) *vti* (*formal*) **1** to be or give an advance warning of something that may happen, especially something undesirable ○ *The gathering clouds foreboded a terrible storm.* **2** to have a feeling that something bad is going to happen before it does —**foreboder** *n*

foreboding /fawr bóding/ *n* **1** PREMONITION a feeling that something bad is going to happen **2** BAD OMEN a sign or warning that something bad is going to happen ■ *adj* OMINOUS indicating, warning, or suggesting that something undesirable is likely to happen —**forebodingly** *adv* —**forebodingness** *n*

forebrain /fáwr brayn/ *n* the front section of the brain in adults or the frontmost of the three parts of the brain in an embryo

forecaddie /fáwr kadi/ *n* a caddie on a golf course who watches from the fairway to see where the balls land

forecast /fáwr kaast/ (**-casts, -casting, -casted, -cast** or **-casted**) *vt* **1** SUGGEST WHAT WILL HAPPEN to predict or work out something that is likely to happen, e.g. the weather conditions for the days ahead **2** BE EARLY SIGN OF to be an advance indication of something that is likely or certain to happen ■ *n* **1** WEATHER PREDICTION a prediction of weather conditions for the near future, usually broadcast on television or radio or printed in a newspaper ○ *Have you heard the forecast for tomorrow?* **2** PREDICTION OF FUTURE DEVELOPMENTS an estimation or calculation of what is likely to happen in the future, especially in business or finance —**forecastable** *adj* —**forecaster** *n*

forecastle /fóks'l/, **fo'c's'le** /fóks'l/ *n* **1** the space at the front end of a ship below the main deck, traditionally where the crew's quarters were located **2** a raised section of deck at the bow of a ship

fore-check *vi* to check a player of an opposing ice hockey team in the opposition's defensive zone —**fore-checker** *n*

foreclose /fawr klóz/ (**-closes, -closing, -closed**) *v* **1** *vti* END A MORTGAGE to take away a mortgagee's right to redeem a mortgage, usually because payments have not been made ○ *The bank foreclosed on the property.* **2** *vt* SHUT OUT to bar or exclude somebody or something (*formal*) **3** *vt* SETTLE BEFOREHAND to settle or resolve something in advance (*formal*) **4** *vt* PREVENT to prevent or hinder something (*formal*) **5** *vt* HOLD EXCLUSIVELY to have an exclusive right or claim to something (*formal*) [13C. < Old French *forclos*, past participle of *forclore* < Latin *foris* 'outside' + *claudere* 'shut, close'.] —**foreclosable** *adj*

foreclosure /fawr klózhər/ *n* a legal process by which a mortgagee's right to redeem a mortgage is taken away, usually because of failing to make payments

forecourse /fáwr kawrss/ *n* a foresail, especially the lowest of a ship's foresails

forecourt /fáwr kawrt/ *n* **1** an open area at the front of a building, especially one in front of a petrol station, hotel, or railway station **2** the part of the court nearest the net or front wall in games such as tennis, badminton, and handball

foredeck /fáwr dek/ *n* the part of a ship's deck between the bridge and the forecastle

foredoom /fawr doom/ *vt* to condemn something or somebody in advance to failure or destruction (*formal; usually passive*)

fore-edge *n* the outer edge of a printed page

forefather /fáwr faathər/ *n* (*often plural*) **1** a male ancestor, usually one who died long ago (*literary*) ○ *in the proud tradition of our forefathers* **2** a member of an earlier generation from whom traditions, values, or ideas have been inherited

forefend *vt* = **forfend**

forefinger /fáwr fing gər/ *n* ANAT = **index finger**

forefoot /fáwr foot/ (*plural* **-feet** /-feet/) *n* **1** either of the front feet of a four-legged animal **2** the front end of a ship's keel

forefront /fáwr frunt/ *n* **1** the most prominent, important, active, or responsible position in something **2** the part at or nearest the front of something

foregather *vi* = **forgather**

forego[1] /fawr gó/ (**-goes, -going, -went** /-wént/, **-gone** /-gón/) *vti* to go or come before something in position, time, or sequence (*archaic*) —**foregoer** *n*

forego[2] *vt* = **forgo**

foregoing /fawr gó ing, fáwr gō ing/ *adj* going or coming before something, especially in speech or writing ■ *n* in speech or writing, the thing that has just been mentioned ○ *As is evident from the foregoing, much remains to be done.*

foregone /fáwr gon/ *adj* **1** previously completed or determined **2** previous or former (*archaic*)

USAGE *foregone* If you use *foregone* by itself as a noun meaning 'foregone conclusion' or as an adjective meaning 'previously concluded or settled', you may incur criticism. Avoid sentences like these: *It's a foregone that the government will veto the treaty amendment. It is definitely not foregone that our team will make it to the final.* Substitute *a foregone conclusion* in these sentences.

---

foregone conclusion *n* something that will inevitably happen as a result of something else

⚡foreground /fáwr grownd/ *n* **1** PART THAT APPEARS NEAREST the part of a picture or scene that appears nearest the viewer **2** = **forefront** *n.* 1 ■ *adj* CURRENTLY RECEIVING COMMANDS currently receiving commands, usually through the keyboard, while other programs are operating independently ○ *foreground processing* ■ *vt* HIGHLIGHT to put something in an important position and so draw attention to it

foregut /fáwr gut/ *n* the front end of the embryonic gut in animals. In vertebrates it develops into the pharynx, oesophagus, stomach, and top part of the intestines.

forehand /fáwr hand/ *n* **1** STROKE IN RACKET GAMES in racket games, a basic stroke played with the palm of the racket hand facing forwards **2** FRONT PART OF HORSE the part of a horse in front of the rider and saddle ■ *adj* PLAYED AS FOREHAND in racket games, played with the palm of the racket hand facing forwards, or relating to a stroke played in this way ■ *adv* WITH FOREHAND STROKE in racket games, with a forehand stroke or action ■ *vt* PLAY WITH FOREHAND STROKE in racket games, to hit the ball with a forehand stroke —**forehanded** /fáwr hándid/ *adj, adv* —**forehandedly** *adv* —**forehandedness** *n*

forehead /fórrid, fáwr hed/ *n* the part of the face above the eyebrows, below the hairline and between the temples

forehock /fáwr hok/ *n* a cut of bacon taken from the front leg, including the hock and knuckle and the part up to the collar

forehoof /fáwr hoof/ (*plural* **-hooves** /-hoovz/ *or* **-hoofs**) *n* the hoof of either of the two front legs of a four-legged animal (**quadruped**)

foreign /fórrin/ *adj* **1** OF ANOTHER COUNTRY relating to, from, or located in a country or countries other than your own ○ *She speaks three foreign languages.* **2** DEALING WITH ANOTHER COUNTRY dealing with or involved with a country or countries other than your own ○ *foreign policy* **3** COMING FROM OUTSIDE introduced from outside into a place where it does not belong, often in the human body ○ *a foreign body in her eye* **4** UNCHARACTERISTIC not usually associated with a particular person or thing ○ *Such outbursts are quite foreign to her nature.* **5** IRRELEVANT not related or relevant (*formal*) ○ *observations that are foreign to the matter in hand* **6** BEYOND JURISDICTION being beyond the jurisdiction of a particular area or country [13C. From Old French *forein* < Latin *foras, foris* 'out of doors, abroad' < *fores* 'door'.] —**foreignly** *adv* —**foreignness** *n*

Foreign and Commonwealth Office *n* the official name of the Foreign Office in the United Kingdom

foreign bill *n* a bill of exchange that is issued in one country but payable in another

foreign correspondent *n* a journalist who sends news reports from other countries for broadcast or publication in his or her own country

foreign draft *n* = **foreign bill**

foreigner /fórrinər/ *n* **1** somebody who comes from a country other than your own **2** a person who does not feel or is not deemed to be part of a group

foreign exchange *n* **1** the currencies of countries other than your own or international currencies generally **2** the conversion of one currency into another or the buying and selling of different currencies

foreign legion *n* a section of an army consisting of foreign volunteers, especially that of the French army

foreign minister *n* a minister in a government who is responsible for relations with other countries

foreign ministry *n* in many countries, the department of government responsible for relations with other countries

foreign mission *n* **1** diplomatic personnel sent to represent their country abroad **2** missionaries who try to convert the inhabitants of another country to Christianity or another religion

foreign office *n* in the United Kingdom and some other countries, the department of the government that is responsible for relations with other countries. ◊ **Foreign and Commonwealth Office**

foreign secretary *n* the cabinet minister in the UK government responsible for relations with other countries and head of the Foreign and Commonwealth Office

foreign service *n* a country's diplomatic and consular staff, especially that of the United States

foreknowledge /fawr nóllij/ *n* knowledge or awareness that something is going to happen, either from information that has been acquired, or by paranormal means

forelady /fáwr laydi/ (*plural* **-dies**) *n US* HR = **forewoman** *n.* 1

foreland /fáwrlənd/ *n* **1** HEADLAND a stretch of land that juts out into the sea or an estuary **2** LAND IN FRONT land described in relation to what lies behind it, especially a plain in front of mountains **3** ROCK IN FRONT OF MOUNTAINS a stable undeformed mass of rock that juts out in front of a mountain belt

Foreland /fáwrlənd/ either of two headlands, North Foreland and South Foreland, in SE England

foreleg /fáwr leg/ *n* either of the two front legs of a four-legged animal (**quadruped**)

forelimb /fáwr lim/ *n* either of the two front limbs of a four-limbed vertebrate, e.g. a flipper, arm, wing, or fin

forelock[1] /fáwr lok/ *n* **1** a lock of hair that grows or falls over the forehead **2** the part of a horse's mane that falls forward between its ears ◇ **tug your forelock** to show too much respect or deference for somebody in authority (*dated*)

forelock[2] /fáwr lok/ *n* a pin or wedge inserted through the end of a bolt to stop it being removed

foreman /fáwrmən/ (*plural* **-men** /-mən/) *n* **1** a man who is in charge of a group of other workers, e.g. on a building site or in a factory **2** somebody chosen by the other members of a jury to be their leader —**foremanship** *n*

foremast /fáwr maast/; *nautical usage* /fáwrməst/ *n* the mast nearest the front or bow of a vessel with two or more masts

foremilk /fáwr milk/ *n* the relatively low-fat milk with a high sugar content that is produced by a woman's breast at the beginning of a breast feed

foremost /fáwr mōst/ *adj* **1** CHIEF most important or notable **2** FARTHEST FORWARD nearest to the front ○ *the foremost section of the aircraft* ■ *adv* **1** IN FIRST POSITION most importantly or in the most important position ○ *a partner who will put your interests foremost* **2** TO THE FRONT at or towards the front [Old English *formest* < *forma* 'first' + -EST, later interpreted as < FORE + -MOST]

foremother /fáwr muthər/ *n* a woman ancestor, usually one who died long ago

forename /fáwr naym/ *n* = **first name**

forenoon /fáwr noon/ *n* the period of time between dawn and noon or immediately before noon

forensic /fə rénssik, -rénzik/ *adj* **1** relating to the application of science to decide questions arising from crime or litigation ○ *forensic evidence* **2** relating to debate and formal argumentation ○ *forensic oratory* [Mid-17C. < Latin *forensis* 'of legal proceedings' < *forum* 'forum' (as a place for discussion).] —**forensicality** /fə rénssi kálləti, -rénzi-/ *n* —**forensically** *adv*

forensic medicine *n* the branch of medicine that has a specifically legal purpose, e.g. establishing the cause of a death

forensics /fə rénssiks, -rénziks/ *npl* the practice or study of formal debate (+ *singular or plural verb*)

foreordain /fáwr awr dáyn/ *vt* to arrange or determine an event in advance of its happening —**foreordainment** *n* —**foreordination** /fáwr awrdi náysh'n/ *n*

forepart /fáwr paart/ *n* **1** the front part of something or the part of something in front **2** the first or early part of a given period of time

forepaw /fáwr paw/ *n* either of the two front feet of a land mammal that does not have hooves

forepeak /fáwr peek/ *n* the interior part of a vessel nearest the bow

foreperson /fáwr purss'n/ (*plural* **-persons** *or* **-people** /-peep'l/) *n* **1** a skilled worker who is in charge of a group of other workers, e.g. on a building site or in a factory **2** somebody chosen by the other members of a jury to be their leader

fore plane *n* a plane used in carpentry or joinery for preliminary smoothing, intermediate in size between a jack plane and a jointer plane

foreplay /fáwr play/ *n* mutual sexual stimulation that takes place before intercourse

forequarter /fáwr kwawrtər/ *n* half of the front half of a pork, lamb, or beef carcass ■ **forequarters** *npl* the front legs, shoulders, and adjoining parts of a horse or similar animal

forereach /fawr reéch/ *v* **1** *vti* to gain on or pass another sailing vessel, especially when sailing into the wind **2** *vi* to continue moving in a ship after the sails have been taken down or the engine switched off

forerun /fawr rún/ (**-runs, -running, -ran** /-rán/, **-run**) *vt* **1** to serve as an indication of or anticipate something that is to happen (*formal*) **2** to go before something (*archaic*)

forerunner /fáwr runnər/ *n* **1** PREDECESSOR an earlier person or thing that had a role or function similar to somebody or something coming later ○ *the forerunner of the modern food processor* **2** SOMEBODY OR SOMETHING SHOWING FUTURE somebody or something that brings news of or is an indication of what is to happen ○ *a forerunner of unsettled weather* **3** ONE AHEAD OF OTHERS somebody or something that goes ahead of others, e.g. a skier who skis down a course just before the beginning of a race

foresail /fáwr sayl/; *nautical usage* /fáwrss'l/ *n* **1** the main square sail on the front mast of a square-rigged vessel **2** the main or lowest triangular sail on a fore-and-aft-rigged vessel

foresee /fawr seé/ (**-sees, -seeing, -saw** /-sáw/, **-seen** /-seén/) *vti* to know or expect that something is going to happen before it does ○ *He couldn't have foreseen the consequences of his actions.* —**foreseeable** *adj* —**foreseeably** *adv* —**foreseer** *n*

foreshadow /fawr sháddō/ *vt* to indicate or suggest something, usually something unpleasant, that is going to happen —**foreshadower** *n*

foreshank /fáwr shangk/ *n* **1** the upper part of either of the two front legs of a four-legged animal **2** a cut of meat taken from the foreshank of a lamb or sheep

foresheet /fáwr sheet/ *n* a rope used to keep a corner of a foresail in place ■ **foresheets** *npl* the part of an open boat that lies forward of the structural member used as the foremost rower's seat

foreshock /fáwr shok/ *n* a slight tremor or minor earthquake, often one of many and usually preceding a larger earthquake or volcanic eruption

foreshore /fáwr shawr/ *n* **1** the part of a shore that lies between the highest and lowest watermarks **2** the part of a shore between the high watermark and cultivated or economically exploited land

foreshorten /fawr sháwrt'n/ *vt* **1** in drawing, to make something appear shorter than it actually is in order to create a three-dimensional effect on the basis of the laws of perspective **2** to make a text shorter (*formal*)

foresight /fáwr sīt/ *n* **1** ABILITY TO THINK AHEAD the ability to envisage possible future problems or obstacles **2** PREMONITION an act or instance of knowing something beforehand **3** LOOKING FORWARDS the act of looking forwards **4** READING TAKEN IN SURVEYING in surveying, an observation or measurement made looking forwards **5** FRONT GUNSIGHT the front sight on a gun —**foresighted** /fawr sītid/ *adj*

foreskin /fáwr skin/ *n* a fold of skin that covers the end of the penis

forest /fórrist/ *n* **1** LARGE DENSE GROWTH OF TREES a large area of land covered in trees and other plants growing close together, or the trees growing on it **2** WOODLAND FOR HUNTING especially in former times, an area of woodland owned by a monarch and set aside for hunting **3** LARGE NUMBER OF UPRIGHT OBJECTS a collection of often tall upright objects, densely packed and so resembling a forest of trees ○ *a forest of microphones* ■ *vt* CREATE FOREST ON LAND to plant an area with a large number of trees [13C. Via Old French < late Latin *forestis (silva)* 'outside (woods)' < *foris* 'out of doors' (see FOREIGN).] —**forestal** *adj* —**forested** *adj* —**forestial** /fə résti əl/ *adj*

forestall /fawr stáwl/ *vt* **1** to prevent or hinder somebody from doing something or something from happening by acting in advance **2** to stop or slow down sales of a product at a one-off event or market by buying that product in large quantities beforehand [14C. < Old English *foresteall* 'ambush' < *steall* 'standing place' < Germanic.] —**forestaller** *n* —**forestalment** *n*

forestation /fórri stáysh'n/ *n* the planting or incidence of trees over a large area

forestay /fáwr stay/ *n* a rope or cable (**stay**) extending from the head of the foremast to the deck of a ship and used for supporting the mast

forester /fórristər/ *n* **1** MANAGER OF FOREST somebody engaged in forest management and conservation **2** FOREST DWELLER a person or animal living in a forest (*archaic*) **3** WOODLAND MOTH a woodland moth that flies by day. Family: Zyglaenidae.

forest floor *n* the layer of organic matter on the ground in a forest

forest green *adj* of a dark green colour, like the foliage on a pine tree ○ *forest-green uniforms* —**forest green** *n*

forestland /fórrist land/ *n* a piece of land covered with trees or set aside for the cultivation of trees

forest oriole *n* BIRDS = **oriole**

forest park *n* in New Zealand, a large forested area that is open to the public and has some recreational facilities

forestry /fórristri/ *n* **1** PLANTING AND GROWING TREES the science or skill of planting and growing trees or managing forests **2** FOREST MANAGEMENT the management of forests for profitable ends such as timber production **3** COMMERCIAL FORESTLAND forestland, especially that planted and commercially managed rather than growing naturally

foretaste /fáwr tayst/ *n* a sample or indication of what is to come ■ *vt* (**-tastes, -tasting, -tasted**) to have a sample or indication of what is to come

foretell /fawr tél/ (**-tells, -telling, -told** /-tṓld/) *vt* to predict what is going to happen, especially by means of supposed magic or supernatural powers (*literary*) —**foreteller** *n*

forethought /fáwr thawt/ *n* careful thought in order to be prepared for the future —**forethoughtful** /fawr tháwtf'l/ *adj* —**forethoughtfully** *adv* —**forethoughtfulness** *n*

foretoken *n* /fáwr tōk'n/ a warning sign of what is to come (*literary*) ■ *vt* /fawr tṓk'n/ to be or give a warning sign of what is to come (*literary*)

foretold past participle, past tense of **foretell**

foretop /fáwr top/; *nautical usage* /fáwrtəp/ *n* a platform at the top of a ship's foremast

fore-topgallant *adj* relating to the section of a mast directly above the foremast

fore-topmast *n* the mast above the platform at the top of a ship's foremast

fore-topsail *n* a sail attached to the mast above the platform at the top of a ship's foremast

forever /fər évvər/ *adv* **1 forever, for ever FOR ALL TIME** for all future time **2 forever, for ever FOR VERY LONG TIME** for a very long time or what seems so (*informal*) ○ *It's going to take me forever to finish this.* **3 CONSTANTLY** regularly or constantly, and often annoyingly (*informal*) **4 AT ALL TIMES** at all times or on every occasion (*literary*) ○ *From that moment on, she was forever careful.*

forevermore /fər èvvər máwr/, **for evermore** *adv* from now on and for all time (*literary*)

forewarn /fawr wáwrn/ *vt* to warn somebody about something that is going to happen (*often passive*) —**forewarner** *n* —**forewarningly** *adv*

forewing /fáwr wing/ *n* either of the pair of front wings on a four-winged insect

forewoman /fáwr wòomən/ (*plural* **-en** /-wimmən/) *n* **1** a woman who is in charge of a group of workers, e.g. on a building site or in a factory **2** a woman chosen by the other members of a jury to be their leader

foreword /fáwr wurd/ *n* an introductory note, essay, or chapter in a book, often written by somebody other than the author

foreyard /fáwr yaard/ *n* the lowest spar for supporting a sail on a foremast

Forfar /fáwrfər/ town in E Scotland. Population: 12,961 (1991).

forfeit /fáwrfit/ *n* **1 PENALTY FOR WRONGDOING** something that is taken away as a punishment or has to be given up to make up for a mistake or wrongdoing **2 PENALTY FOR BREAKING LAW** something that is taken away as a penalty for breaking a law or contract **3 GIVING SOMETHING UP** the act or an instance of giving something up or being deprived of something as a punishment **4 PENALTY IN GAME** an object that a player must give up or a task that a player must perform as a penalty in a game ■ *adj* **TAKEN AWAY AS PUNISHMENT** taken away or given up as a punishment for a mistake or wrongdoing ■ *vt* **1 LOSE** to lose something or have something taken away as punishment for a mistake or wrongdoing ○ *forfeit the right to your inheritance* **2 GIVE UP** to give something up willingly in order to pursue or obtain something else ○ *forfeited his peerage for a seat in the House of Commons* **3 TAKE AWAY AS PENALTY** to take something away as a penalty for breaking a law or contract [13C. < Old French *forfet*, past participle of *forfaire* 'commit a crime', literally 'do beyond' < *fors* 'beyond' < Latin *foris* (see FOREIGN).] —**forfeitable** *adj* —**forfeiter** *n*

forfeits /fáwrfits/ *n* a game in which a player must give something up or perform a task each time he or she commits a fault or loses a round (+ *singular verb*)

forfeiture /fáwrfichər/ *n* **1** something that has been taken away or has had to be given up as a penalty for breaking a law or contract **2** the act of forfeiting something

forfend /fawr fénd/, **forefend** *vti* to protect or secure against something happening (*archaic*) ○ *Heaven forfend that I should end up like that!*

~~**forfiet**~~ incorrect spelling of **forfeit**

forgather /fawr gáthər/, **foregather** *vi* (*formal*) **1 ASSEMBLE AS GROUP** to come together as a group **2 MEET BY CHANCE** to meet, usually by chance **3 ASSOCIATE** to spend time socially with somebody [15C. < Dutch *vorgaderen* 'meet, assemble', altered after GATHER.]

forgave past tense of **forgive**

forge[1] /fawrj/ *n* **1 METAL WORKSHOP** a workshop where metal is heated and shaped into objects by hammering **2 FURNACE FOR HEATING METAL** a furnace used to heat metal to a very high temperature **3 MACHINE FOR HAMMERING METAL** a machine with two tool faces that are brought together to hammer pieces of metal into specific shapes ■ *v* (**forges, forging, forged**) **1** *vti* **MAKE ILLEGAL COPY OF** to make or produce an illegal copy of something so that it looks genuine, usually for financial gain **2** *vt* **ESTABLISH WITH EFFORT** to establish and strive to develop something with great effort ○ *forge a durable relationship with the community* **3** *vt* **SHAPE METAL** to shape or form metal by heating and hammering it [13C. < French *forger* 'make' < Latin *fabricare* (see FABRICATE).] —**forgeability** /fáwrjə bíllәti/ *n* —**forgeable** *adj* —**forger** *n*

forge[2] /fawrj/ (**forges, forging, forged**) *vi* **1** to move forward with a sudden increase of speed ○ *forging past the runner on the inside* **2** to move slowly and steadily ○ *'We were forging through a narrow passage, rock-lined, and tube-like'.* (Edgar Rice Burroughs, *The Gods of Mars*; 1913) [Mid-18C. < ?]

forge ahead *vi* to move forward rapidly or steadily and persistently

forgery /fáwrjəri/ (*plural* **-ies**) *n* **1** the act of making or producing an illegal copy of something so that it looks genuine, usually for financial gain **2** an illegal copy of something, e.g. a document or painting, that has been made to look genuine

forget /fər gét/ (**-gets, -getting, -got** /-gót/, **-gotten** /-gótt'n/) *v* **1** *vti* **NOT REMEMBER** to fail or be unable to remember something ○ *I'll never forget my first day at school.* **2** *vt* **LEAVE BEHIND** to leave something behind accidentally ○ *I've forgotten my keys.* **3** *vti* **NEGLECT** to fail to give due attention to somebody or something ○ *Don't just disappear and forget about us all.* **4** *vt* **STOP WORRYING** to stop thinking or worrying about somebody or something ○ *I'd just forget about it if I were you.* **5** *vti* **NOT MENTION** to fail to mention somebody or something **6** *vr* **LOSE CONTROL** to lose control of your manners, emotions, or behaviour ○ *Oh dear, I'm forgetting myself! Let me take your coat.* [Old English *forgietan* 'miss your hold on' < Germanic] —**forgetter** *n* ◇ **forget it 1** used to let somebody know that something is not really very important and so not worth worrying about (*informal*) **2** used to tell somebody that you are definitely not going to do something that has been suggested, proposed, or asked of you (*informal*)

SYNONYMS See ***neglect***.

forgetful /fər gétf'l/ *adj* **1** tending to forget things **2** not giving due attention to somebody or something (*formal*) ○ *forgetful of his contractual obligations* —**forgetfully** *adv* —**forgetfulness** *n*

forget-me-not *n* a small herbaceous plant of the borage family. Flowers: small, delicate, pale blue. Genus: *Myosotis*. [Because worn by lovers]

forgettable /fər géttəb'l/ *adj* not easily remembered or not worthy of being remembered

forgive /fər gív/ (**-gives, -giving, -gave** /-gáyv/, **-given** /-gívv'n/) *v* **1** *vti* **STOP BEING ANGRY ABOUT** to stop being angry about or resenting somebody or somebody's behaviour **2** *vt* **PARDON** to excuse somebody for a mistake, misunderstanding, wrongdoing, or an inappropriateness **3** *vt* **CANCEL OBLIGATION** to cancel an obligation, e.g. a debt [Old English *forgiefan*, literally 'abstain from giving'] —**forgivable** *adj* —**forgivably** *adv* —**forgiver** *n*

forgiveness /fər gívnəss/ *n* **1** the act of pardoning somebody for a mistake or wrongdoing **2** the tendency to forgive offences readily and easily ○ *She had little forgiveness in her nature.* [Old English *forgiefenes*, literally 'forgiven-ness']

forgiving /fər gívving/ *adj* **1** willing to forgive, especially in most circumstances **2** allowing for or coping well with a degree of imprecision, lack of skill, or other imperfection ○ *You'll have to improve your technique or get a more forgiving fishing rod.* —**forgivingly** *adv* —**forgivingness** *n*

forgo /fawr gṓ/ (**-goes, -going, -went** /-wént/, **-gone** /-gón/), **forego** (**-goes, -going, -went, -gone**) *vt* to do without something, especially voluntarily ○ *forgo the comforts of home while travelling*

forgot past tense of **forget**

forgotten past participle of **forget**

~~**forhead**~~ incorrect spelling of **forehead**

~~**foriegn**~~ incorrect spelling of **foreign**

for instance *n* an example of something (*informal*) ○ *Give me a for instance.*

forint /fórrint/ *n* see table at **currency** [Mid-20C. < Hungarian, < Italian *fiorino* (see FLORIN).]

fork /fawrk/ *n* **1 UTENSIL FOR EATING** a small, usually metal utensil with a handle and two, three, or four prongs. Use: picking up food for eating, turning food in cooking. **2 GARDEN OR AGRICULTURAL TOOL** a garden or agricultural tool with a handle and usually three or four prongs **3 DIVIDING POINT** the point where a road or river divides into two or more parts **4 BRANCH** one of the branches that a road or river divides into **5 PART OF MACHINE** a part of a machine or device that has prongs or is fork-shaped **6 CHESS POSITION** a chess position in which two pieces are under attack from one of the opponent's pieces, usually the knight **7 FLASH OF LIGHTNING** a branch or flash of forked lightning ■ *v* **1** *vti* **MOVE WITH FORK** to carry, pick up, dig, or turn something over using a fork **2** *vi* **DIVIDE INTO TWO** to split into two or more branches (*refers to roads and rivers*) **3** *vi* **GO ALONG FORK** to take one of the branches that a road or river has divided into **4** *vt* **CAUSE TO BRANCH** to make something into a shape that branches in two **5** *vt* **MOVE PIECE IN CHESS** to position a chess piece so that it is threatening two of the opponent's pieces at the same time [Old English *forca*, via Germanic < Latin *furca* 'pitchfork'] —**forked** *adj* —**forkedly** *adv* —**forkedness** *n* —**forker** *n* —**forkful** *n*

fork out, fork up *vti* to pay the money required for something or spend a lot of money, often grudgingly (*informal*)

forkball /fáwrk bawl/ *n* in baseball, a pitch in which the ball is held between the spread index and middle finger —**forkballer** *n*

forked lightning *n* lightning that appears as a jagged line of light splitting into two or more branches near the ground. US term **chain lightning**

forked tongue *n* a tongue that speaks lies or words that are insincere or misleading (*literary or humorous*)

forklift /fáwrk lift/ *n* **1** a lifting device with two long rigid steel bars that can be raised and lowered, used especially to move pallets loaded with boxes or other goods **2** TECH = **forklift truck** ■ *vt* to lift or move heavy loads using a forklift

forklift truck *n* a small motor-driven vehicle equipped with a forklift, used especially in factories for moving goods on pallets

forlorn /fər láwrn, fawr-/ *adj* **1 LONELY AND MISERABLE** lonely and miserable, as though deserted or abandoned **2 DESOLATE** deserted or abandoned and showing signs of neglect **3 HOPELESS** desperate and doomed to failure (*literary*) [Old English *forloren*, past participle of *forlēosan* 'lose completely'] —**forlornly** *adv* —**forlornness** *n*

forlorn hope *n* **1 FUTILE HOPE** a desperate or futile hope **2 DESPERATE UNDERTAKING** a desperate or doomed undertaking **3 SOLDIERS ON DESPERATE MISSION** a group of soldiers sent on a very dangerous if not hopeless mission [By folk etymology < Dutch *forloren hoop* 'lost troop']

form /fawrm/ *n* **1 BASIC STRUCTURE** the nature, structure, or essence of a thing, considered apart from its content, colour, texture, or composition **2 MANIFESTATION** the particular way that something is or appears to be ○ *bonuses in the form of extra days off* **3 VARIETY** a type or kind of something that has various different types or kinds ○ *Friction is a form of energy.* **4 SHAPE** the shape or appearance of a thing that makes it identifiable ○ *a constellation in the form of a diamond* **5 INDISTINCT SHAPE** a shape like a person or other living thing that cannot be clearly made out ○ *a shadowy form in the distance* **6 DOCUMENT** a document, usually with blank spaces for answers or information to be supplied ○ *fill out the form* **7 CONDITION** the condition of an organization, team, performer, athlete, or animal, with regard to fitness, health, and ability to perform well ○ *a violinist at the top of her form* **8 TRACK RECORD** the previous record of a horse, athlete, or team **9 OUTLINE STRUCTURE** the structure, design, or arrangement of a work of art or piece of writing, as opposed to its content **10 MODE OF EXPRESSION** a fixed mode of literary or musical expression ○ *a strict adherence to sonata form* **11 MOULD OR FRAME** a mould, frame, or model within which or around which something can be shaped ○ *concrete forms* **12 SCHOOL CLASS** a class or year in a school **13 BEHAVIOUR** behaviour or manners with reference to propriety ○ *It's considered bad form to cheat at games.* **14 FORMULA** a fixed set of words or procedures, e.g. in a religious ceremony or a legal document **15 HUMAN SHAPE** a model of a human body or torso, used for fitting or displaying clothes **16 BENCH** a long low wooden seat or bench with no back rest **17** *US* PRINTING = **forme** **18 HARE'S LAIR** the lair or nest in which a hare lives **19 WORD IN RELATION TO ITS ROOT** a word considered in relation to its root or the word it is derived from **20 LOOK OR SOUND OF WORD** the way a word is written or how it sounds, as opposed to its meaning **21 SUBDIVISION OF VARIETY** a subdivision of a classification of organisms, usually indicating a minor difference among members, e.g. in colour **22 CRIMINAL RECORD** recorded past criminal activity (*slang*) ■ *v* **1** *vti* **GIVE SHAPE TO** to give a shape or arrangement to something, or take shape ○ *A circle of onlookers formed around the injured man.* **2** *vti* **START TO EXIST** to cause something to develop or exist, or begin to develop or exist, especially as part of a natural process ○ *Crystals began to form at the bottom of the jar.* **3** *vt* **MAKE** to make or construct something, often by arranging or combining component parts ○ *The plural is formed by adding an 's'.* **4** *vt* **CONCEIVE OF** to develop an opinion, impression, or idea in the mind ○ *not enough information to form an opinion* **5** *vt* **CAUSE TO DEVELOP** to influence somebody strongly through teaching, discipline, or example, and cause a particular personal development ○ *an early life in the country that formed his quiet nature* **6** *vt* **CREATE** to acquire or establish and develop something intangible, e.g. a habit or relationship ○ *considered forming an alliance* **7** *vt* **SERVE AS** to constitute or be a basic element or characteristic of something ○ *a mountain range forming a natural boundary between the two countries* **8** *vt* **SET UP** to establish something, e.g. a structure ○ *form a fan club* [13C. Via French < Latin *forma* 'mould, shape, beauty'.] —**formable** *adj* ◇ **take form** to become visible, distinct, or discernible ○ *A plan started to take form in his mind.* ◇ **true to form** as could be expected judging from somebody's past behaviour ○ *True to form, she was exactly twenty minutes late.*

-form *suffix* having a particular form ○ *fibriform* [< Latin *forma* 'mould, shape, beauty']

formal /fáwrm'l/ *adj* **1 CONVENTIONALLY CORRECT** characterized by or organized in accordance with conventions governing ceremony, behaviour, or dress ○ *He's terribly formal.* **2 OFFICIAL** done or carried out in accordance with established or prescribed rules ○ *We made a formal protest.* **3 METHODICAL** done in an organized and precise manner ○ *We don't have the skills in this lab to do formal research in artificial intelligence.* **4 NOT FAMILIAR IN STYLE** used in serious, official, or public communication but not appropriate in everyday contexts ○ *a formal word* **5 ELEGANT TO WEAR** suitable for wearing for an important occasion, e.g. a jacket and tie for men and a long dress or gown for women ○ *formal dress required* **6 ACQUIRED IN SCHOOL OR COLLEGE** undertaken or acquired by study in an educational institution, e.g. a school, college, or university ○ *no formal training as a journalist* **7 ORDERED** arranged or laid out in a regular, ordered, or symmetrical way ○ *a formal garden* **8 OF FORM** relating to the form of something **9 OFFICIALLY CONSTITUTED** officially constituted or organized as opposed to spontaneously developed ○ *a formal organization* **10 SYMBOLIC** relating to or using symbols and abstract structures rather than natural language **11 OF ESSENCE RATHER THAN CONTENT** relating to the structure or essence of something rather than its content ■ *n US* **CLOTHES** an outfit of clothing for an important social occasion, especially a woman's full-length dress ○ *a new formal for the ball* [14C. < Latin *formalis* < *forma* 'mould, shape, beauty'.] —**formally** *adv* —**formalness** *n*

formaldehyde /fawr máldi hīd/ *n* $HCHO$ a colourless gas with a distinctive smell. Use: in manufacture of resins and fertilizers, preservation of organic specimens. [Late 19C. < FORMIC.]

formalin /fáwrməlin/ *n* a solution of formaldehyde in water. Use: disinfectant, preservation of organic specimens. [Late 19C. < FORMALDEHYDE.]

formalise *vti* = **formalize**

formalism /fáwrm'lizəm/ *n* **1 EMPHASIS ON OUTWARD APPEARANCE** a strong or excessive emphasis on outward appearance or form instead of content or meaning **2 THEORY OF SYMBOLS** the view that mathematical symbols are meaningless, though mathematical concepts and structures can be valuable **3 STYLIZATION** stylization and emphasis on symbolism in theatrical productions —**formalist** *n* —**formalistic** /fáwrmə lístik/ *adj* —**formalistically** *adv*

formality /fawr mállәti/ (*plural* **-ties**) *n* **1 FORMALNESS** the quality or condition of being formal, or the degree to which something is formal ○ *dress to suit the formality of the occasion* **2 OFFICIAL PROCEDURE** an official procedure that must be followed as part of a longer procedure or event (*often plural*) ○ *several formalities to complete at customs* **3 NECESSARY BUT INSIGNIFICANT PROCEDURE** a procedure that must be followed because it is a rule or custom, but has little significance or effect in itself ○ *just a formality* **4 ATTENTION TO PROPRIETY** strict or excessive attention to propriety or ceremony

formalize /fáwrmə līz/ (**-izes, -izing, -ized**), **formalise** (**-ises, -ising, -ised**) *v* **1** *vt* **MAKE OFFICIAL** to make something official or valid, often by deciding on the details and then signing a document **2** *vt* **GIVE SHAPE TO** to give a particular shape or form to something **3** *vti* **MAKE SOMETHING FORMAL** to make something formal or more formal ○ *a formalized version of his earlier account* —**formalizable** *adj* —**formalization** /fáwrmə lī záysh'n/ *n* —**formalizer** *n*

formal logic *n* the branch of logic concerned with the formal methods of deducing conclusions from propositions

⚡**formal methods** *npl* methods of specifying and evaluating computer systems using techniques from mathematics and logic

formant /fáwrmənt/ *n* a frequency range where vowel sounds are at their most distinctive and characteristic pitch [Early 20C. Via German < Latin *formant-*, present participle of *formare* < *forma* 'mould, shape, beauty'.]

⚡**format** /fáwr mat/ *n* **1 STRUCTURE** the way in which something is presented, organized, or arranged ○ *change the format of the conference to accommodate more speakers* **2 LAYOUT** the layout and presentation of a publication, including its size, and the type of paper and type used ○ *a small-format reference work* **3 DATA ORGANIZATION** the structure or organization of digital data for storing, printing, or displaying ○ *files in ASCII format* ■ *vt* (**-mats, -matting, -matted**) **1 ARRANGE LAYOUT OF** to arrange the layout or organization of something **2 ORGANIZE DISK FOR DATA STORAGE** to organize a disk in such a way that data can be stored on it [Mid-19C. Via French and German < Latin *formatus (liber)* '(book) shaped (in a special way)' < *formare* (see FORMANT).]

formate /fáwr mayt/ *n* any salt or ester of formic acid [Early 19C. < FORMIC.]

formation /fawr máysh'n/ *n* **1 DEVELOPMENT** the process by which something develops or takes a particular shape ○ *a strong influence on the formation of her character* **2 CREATION** the process of creating something or coming into existence ○ *the formation of a bipartisan legislative committee* **3 SHAPE** the shape or structure that something develops into ○ *interesting cloud formations* **4 FORMAL PATTERN** the pattern into which a number of people or things are arranged ○ *Twelve planes flew past in formation.* **5 ROCK UNIT** a unit of rock consisting of a succession of strata or an igneous intrusion —**formational** *adj*

formation dance *n* a dance in which a line or circle of couples moves through a choreographed sequence of steps, often as a competition between teams —**formation dancing** *n*

formative /fáwrmətiv/ *adj* **1 INFLUENTIAL** important and influential, particularly in the shaping or development of character ○ *during their formative years* **2 USED TO FORM WORDS** relating to or used in the formation of derived words or inflected forms of words ■ *n* **WORD-FORMING ELEMENT** an element such as a suffix or prefix used in the formation of derived words or inflected forms of words —**formatively** *adv*

formative assessment *n* the assessment at regular intervals of a student's progress with accompanying feedback in order to help to improve the student's performance

form class *n* **1** GRAM = **part of speech 2** a group of words with one or more grammatical characteristics in common

form criticism *n* **1** textual criticism that examines the literary conventions used in order to discover the origin and history of a text or its creators **2** a method of analysing the Bible to determine the presumed original oral form of the written text by removing known historical conventions that emerged at a later period —**form critic** *n* —**form critical** *adj*

forme /fawrm/ *n* a body of typographic elements assembled in a metal frame (**chase**[4]) in preparation for printing. US term **form** *n.* 17 [15C. Variant of FORM.]

Formentera /fáwrmən táirə/ one of the Balearic Islands, in the W Mediterranean Sea. Population: 5,435 (1998). Area: 77 sq. km/30 sq. mi.

former[1] /fáwrmər/ *adj* **1 PREVIOUS** occurring at or existing in an earlier time or period ○ *met her on a former occasion* **2 HAVING BEEN** having had the name or status specified during an earlier period ○ *the former Soviet Union* **3 FIRST OF TWO** being the first of two things or people mentioned **4 PRECEDING** earlier or near the beginning of a text or list ○ *a conclusion inconsistent with the argument in the former part of the paper* ■ *n* **THE FIRST OF TWO** the first of two things or people mentioned ○ *Smith and Brown both work here, the former is an accountant and the latter is an engineer.* [12C. < Old English *forma* 'first' < Germanic + ER.]

USAGE former and **latter** The word ***former*** means the first of two, and ***latter*** means the second of two. To be clear, use these words in references to two and not more than two persons or things previously mentioned, as in *The symposium is for medical and nursing students, with the morning lectures directed to the former and the afternoon lectures directed to the latter.*

former[2] /fáwrmər/ *n* **1 SCHOOL STUDENT** a member of a form or class in a school, especially in Britain until the 1990s, when 'forms' were replaced by 'years' (*always used in combination*) ○ *a sixth former* **2 SHAPER** somebody or something that forms, creates, or shapes something **3 SHAPING TOOL** a tool used for giving the correct shape to an electrical coil or winding

formerly /fáwrmərli/ *adv* during or at an earlier period, but no longer

formestane /fawr méss tayn/ *n* an oestrogen-blocking drug. Use: treatment of some breast cancers.

formfitting /fáwrm fitting/ *adj* fitting tightly around the contours of the body ○ *formfitting sportswear*

formic /fáwrmik/ *adj* **1** relating to ants **2** relating to or containing formic acid [Late 18C. < Latin *formica* 'ant'.]

Formica /fawr míkə/ *tdmk* a trademark for a strong plastic laminate sheeting that is durable and easy to clean, and is often used to cover work surfaces, e.g. in kitchens

formic acid *n* $HCOOH$ a colourless corrosive liquid that occurs naturally in ants and some plants. Use: paper, textiles, insecticides, refrigerants.

formication /fáwrmi káysh'n/ *n* a neurologically based hallucination in which somebody feels as if insects are crawling on his or her skin [Early 18C. < Latin *formication-* < *formicare* 'crawl like an ant' < *formica* 'ant'.]

formidable /fáwrmidəb'l, fər míddəb'l/ *adj* **1 DIFFICULT TO DEAL WITH** difficult to deal with or overcome ○ *a formidable task* **2 AWE-INSPIRING** inspiring respect or wonder because of size, strength, or ability ○ *a formidable display of skill* **3 FRIGHTENING** causing fear, dread, or alarm [14C. Directly or via French < Latin *formidabilis* < *formidare* 'to fear' < *formido* 'terror'.] —**formidability** /fáwrmidə bíllәti, fər míddə-/ *n* —**formidableness** *n* —**formidably** *adv*

formless /fáwrmləss/ *adj* **1 SHAPELESS** lacking a clear shape or structure ○ *a formless figure in the mist* **2 DISORGANIZED** lacking apparent organization or structure **3 NOT MATERIAL** existing without a physical form ○ *formless beings* —**formlessly** *adv* —**formlessness** *n*

form letter *n* a printed letter that is sent out to a large number of people, e.g. one dealing with a frequently arising complaint, or one used in advertising

formula /fáwrmyōōlə/ (*plural* **-las** *or* **-lae** /-lee/) *n* **1 PLAN** a plan for or method of doing something ○ *draw up a peace formula between two countries* **2 METHOD** a prescribed and more or less invariable way of doing something to achieve a particular end **3 ESTABLISHED FORM OF WORDS** an established and recognized form of words, e.g. in a ceremony or legal document **4 SET OF SYMBOLS REPRESENTING CHEMICAL COMPOSITION** a representation of the chemical composition of a chemical compound using symbols to represent the types of atom involved **5 RULE EXPRESSED IN SYMBOLS** a rule or principle represented in symbols, numbers, or letters, often in the form of an equation ○ *a formula for calculating the distance between planets* **6 formula, Formula CATEGORY OF RACING CAR** a category of racing car according to technical specifications such as engine capacity, size, and weight, used as a basis for professional competition (*usually in combination*) ○ *formula one racing* **7 MILK FOR BABIES** a preparation used as an alternative to human breast milk [Early 17C. < Latin, 'little form' < *forma* 'mould, shape, beauty'.]

formulaic /fáwrmyōō láy ik/ *adj* **1** having the nature of or expressed in terms of a formula **2** unoriginal and reliant on previous models or ideas ○ *His writing is stilted and formulaic.* —**formulaically** *adv*

formularize /fáwrmyōōlə rīz/ (**-rizes, -rizing, -rized**), **formularise** (**-rises, -rising, -rised**) *vt* = **formulate** *v.* 3 —**formularization** /fáwrm yōōlə rī záysh'n/ *n* —**formularizer** *n*

formulary /fáwrmyōōləri/ *n* (*plural* **-ies**) **1 PHARMACEUTICAL REFERENCE BOOK** a reference book containing a list of pharmaceutical products **2 RELIGIOUS WRITINGS** a book or collection of writings or procedures, especially ones connected with a church ■ *adj* **OF FORMULA** relating to or having the nature of a formula

formulate /fáwrmyōō layt/ (**-lates, -lating, -lated**) *vt* **1 DEVISE** to draw something up carefully and in detail ○ *formulated his plan* **2 EXPRESS** to express or communicate something carefully or in specific words ○ *formulate an opinion* **3 EXPRESS IN FORMULA** to express something by means of or as a formula —**formulation** /fáwrmyōō láysh'n/ *n* —**formulator** *n*

formula weight *n* CHEM = **molecular weight**

formulise *vt* = **formulize**

formulism /fáwrmyōō lizəm/ *n* a belief in or reliance on formulas, especially inadequate or obsolete ones — **formulist** *n, adj* —**formulistic** /fáwrmyo͝o lístik/ *adj*

formulize /fáwrmyo͝o līz/ (**-lizes, -lizing, -lized**), **formulise** (**-lises, -lising, -lised**) *vt* = **formulate** *v.* 3 —**formulization** /fáwrmyo͝o lī záysh'n, fáwrmyə-/ *n*

form word *n* GRAM = **function word**

formwork /fáwrm wurk/ *n* a structure generally made of timber in which liquid concrete is placed, compacted, and allowed to harden

formyl /fáwr mīl/ *n* **HCO** a chemical group containing carbon, hydrogen, and oxygen [Mid-19C. < FORMIC.]

Fornax /fáwr naks/ *n* a small constellation of the southern hemisphere. See illustration at **constellation**

fornicate[1] /fáwrni kayt/ (**-cates, -cating, -cated**) *vi* to have sexual intercourse outside marriage [Mid-16C. < ecclesiastical Latin *fornicat-*, past participle of *fornicari* < Latin *fornic-* 'arch, brothel' (because prostitutes in Rome solicited under building arches).] —**fornicator** *n*

fornicate[2] /fáwrnikət/, **fornicated** /-kaytid/ *adj* with an arched, vaulted, or bending form [Early 19C. < Latin *fornicatus* < *fornic-* 'arch, vault'.]

fornication /fáwrni káysh'n/ *n* **1** sexual intercourse between two consenting adults, who are not married to each other **2** in the Bible, sexual intercourse between a man and woman who are not married, or any form of sexual behaviour considered to be immoral

fornix /fáwrniks/ (*plural* **-nices** /-ni seez/) *n* a structure or fold in the shape of an arch, especially either of two bands of white fibres that meet at the base of the brain [Late 17C. < Latin (stem *fornic-*), 'arch, vault'.]

Forrest /fórrist/, **Sir John, 1st Baron Forrest of Bunbury** (1847–1918) Australian explorer and politician

forsake /fər sáyk/ (**-sakes, -saking, -sook** /-so͝ok/, **-saken** /-sáykən/) *vt* **1** to withdraw companionship, protection, or support from somebody **2** to give up, renounce, or sacrifice something that gives pleasure [Old English *forsacan* 'abstain from disputing'] —**forsaken** *adj* —**forsakenly** *adv* —**forsakenness** *n* —**forsaker** *n*

~~**forseeable**~~ incorrect spelling of **foreseeable**

forsooth /fər so͞oth/ *adv* in truth (*archaic*) [Old English *forsoþ* 'for the truth']

Forster /fáwrstər/, **E. M.** (1879–1970) British novelist. Full name **Edward Morgan Forster**

forsterite /fáwrstə rīt/ *n* a magnesium silicate mineral of the olivine group [Early 19C. After J. R. *Forster* (1729–98), German naturalist.]

Forster-Tuncurry /fáwrstər tun kúrri/ port in N New South Wales, Australia, consisting of the twin towns of Forster and Tuncurry. Population: 15,943 (1996).

forswear /fawr swáir/ (**-swears, -swearing, -swore** /-swáwr/, **-sworn** /-swáwrn/) *v* (*archaic or literary*) **1** *vt* to vow to stop doing, having, or using something ○ *forswear political violence* **2** *vi* to be guilty of giving false evidence under oath [Old English *forswerian* 'renounce by swearing']

forsythia /fawr sīthi ə/ *n* a bush that flowers in early spring before its leaves emerge. Flowers: yellow. Genus: *Forsythia*. [Mid-19C. After William *Forsyth* (1737–1804), Scottish horticulturalist.]

fort /fawrt/ *n* **1** a building or group of buildings with strong defences, usually strategically located and guarded by troops **2** *US* a permanent military post consisting of several buildings ○ *Fort Bragg* [15C. Directly or via French < Italian *forte* 'strong (place)' < Latin *fortis* 'strong'.] ◇ **hold the fort** to take charge of something in the absence of the person usually responsible

fort. *abbr* fortification

Fortaleza /fórtə létsə/ port in NE Brazil, on the Atlantic Ocean. Population: 1,965,513 (1996 estimate).

fortalice /fáwrtəliss/ *n* a small fort or part of the fortifications of a larger fort [15C. < medieval Latin *fortalitia* < Latin *fortis* 'strong'.]

forte[1] /fáwr tay, fawrt/ *n* **1** something that somebody is particularly good at ○ *Cooking is not really my forte.* **2** the strongest section of a sword's blade, between the middle and the hilt [Mid-17C. Via French *fort* 'strong' < Latin *fortis*; later influenced by FORTE[2].]

forte[2] /fáwr tay, fáwrti/ *adv* to be played or sung loudly (*musical direction*) ■ *n* a note or passage of music played or sung, or to be played or sung, loudly [Early 18C. Via Italian, 'strong, loud' < Latin *fortis*.] —**forte** *adj*

fortepiano /fáwrti pi ánn ō/ (*plural* **-os**) *n* an early form of the piano, especially the piano of the 18th century [Mid-18C. < Italian, < *forte* 'loud' + *piano* 'soft'.]

forte-piano *adv* (*symbol* **fp**) starting loud and then becoming suddenly soft (*musical direction*) —**forte-piano** *adj*

forth /fawrth/ *adv* (*formal*) **1** forward in time, place, degree, or order ○ *from this day forth* **2** out into view ○ *brought forth the prisoner* [Old English *forþ* < Indo-European] ◇ **and so forth** used to indicate that there are more things of the kind just mentioned, without having to name them ○ *bottles, cans, jars, and so forth*

SPELLCHECK Do not confuse ***forth*** with ***fourth***, which has a similar sound. Beware: your spellchecker will not catch this error.

Forth /fawrth/ river in S Scotland that widens to form the Firth of Forth. Length: 188 km/117 mi.

Forth, Firth of estuary of the River Forth in SE Scotland. Length: 77 km/48 mi.

⚡**FORTH** *n* a high-level computer programming language used in scientific and industrial control applications

forthcoming /fawrth kúmming/ *adj* **1 FUTURE** about to appear or happen ○ *plans for the forthcoming celebration* **2 READY WHEN WANTED** available when required or requested ○ *We were assured that the money would be forthcoming.* **3 INFORMATIVE** willing to talk or give information ○ *not very forthcoming about his personal life*

forthright /fáwrth rīt/ *adj* **OUTSPOKEN** direct in speech or manner and very honest ■ *adv* **1 OUTSPOKENLY** in a direct and very honest way **2 IMMEDIATELY** at once (*archaic*) —**forthrightly** *adv* —**forthrightness** *n*

forthwith /fáwrth wíth, -wíth/ *adv* without delay

fortieth /fáwrti əth/ *n* **1** see table at **number 2** somebody's 40th birthday —**fortieth** *adj, adv*

fortification /fáwrtifi káysh'n/ *n* **1 STRUCTURE FOR DEFENCE** a structure or structures, e.g. a wall, ditch, or rampart, built in order to strengthen a place's defences (*often plural*) **2 BUILDING OF DEFENCES** the art or practice of strengthening or creating defences, e.g. by building walls or digging ditches **3 PLACE THAT CAN BE DEFENDED** a position or place that can be defended

fortified wine /fáwrti fīd-/ *n* a drink such as sherry, port, or Marsala that is made from wine to which a strong alcohol, such as grape brandy, has been added

fortify /fáwrti fī/ (**-fies, -fying, -fied**) *vt* **1 MAKE SAFER** to make a place less susceptible to attack by building or creating defensive structures such as walls, ditches, or ramparts **2 MAKE STRONGER** to strengthen or reinforce the structure of something ○ *fortify a sea wall* **3 ADD INGREDIENTS TO** to add further ingredients to food or drink in order to improve its flavour or add nutrients (*usually passive*) ○ *breakfast cereal fortified with vitamins* **4 ENCOURAGE** to give somebody physical, mental, or moral strength or encouragement **5 MAKE MORE POWERFUL** to make something more powerful or persuasive ○ *fortify an argument* [15C. Via French *fortifier* < late Latin *fortificare* 'make strong' < Latin *fortis* 'strong'.] —**fortifiable** *adj* —**fortifier** *n* —**fortifyingly** *adv*

fortis /fáwrtiss/ *adj* denoting a consonant, e.g. 'p' or 't', that is produced with great muscular tension and pressure of breath ■ *n* (*plural* **-tes**) a fortis consonant, such as 'p' or 't' [Early 20C. < Latin, 'strong'.]

fortissimo /fawr tíssimō/ *adv* extremely loudly (*musical direction*) ■ *n* (*plural* **-mos** *or* **-mi**) a passage of music, or an individual note or chord, played fortissimo [Early 18C. < Italian, 'loudest' < *forte* (see FORTE[2]).] —**fortissimo** *adj*

fortitude /fáwrti tyood/ *n* strength and endurance in a difficult or painful situation [14C. Via French < Latin *fortitudo* 'strength, courage' < *fortis* 'strong'.] —**fortitudinous** /fáwrti tyo͞odinəss/ *adj*

Fort Knox /fawrt nóks/ military post and reservation in central Kentucky, the site of the US Gold Depository since 1936. Area: 13,350 sq. km/5,154 sq. mi.

Fort Lauderdale /-láwdər dayl/ city in SE Florida, on the Atlantic Ocean. Population: 153,728 (1998 estimate).

fortnight /fáwrt nīt/ *n* a period of 14 days [Old English *feowertine niht* 'fourteen nights']

fortnightly /fáwrt nītli/ *adj, adv* occurring once every 14 days ■ *n* (*plural* **-lies**) a publication that appears once every two weeks

⚡**FORTRAN** /fáwr tran/ *n* the earliest high-level computer programming language [Mid-20C. Contraction of FORMULA + TRANSLATION.]

fortress /fáwrtrəss/ *n* **1** a fortified place with a long-term military presence, often including a town **2** something that is impenetrable or acts as protection [14C. < Old French *forteresse* 'strong place' < Latin *fortis* 'strong'.]

Fort Sumter National Monument /-súmtər-/ national monument in Charleston, South Carolina, on the site of a historic fort at the entrance to Charleston Harbor

fortuitous /fawr tyo͞o itəss/ *adj* **1** happening by chance, especially giving rise to a fortunate outcome **2** ⚠ bringing or indicating good fortune. [Mid-17C. < Latin *fortuitus* < *fors* 'chance, luck'.] —**fortuitously** *adv* —**fortuitousness** *n*

USAGE fortuitous or **fortunate**? The word ***fortuitous*** means 'accidental or unplanned', as in *a fortuitous encounter with my old roommate of 30 years ago, whom I hadn't seen since graduation*. Nowadays, it is frequently used in contexts where the chance event described has a fortunate outcome. An extended meaning, 'lucky', used in English at least since the 1920s, is controversial. Substitute ***fortunate*** for ***fortuitous*** when the meaning is *lucky*: *In a fortunate* [not *fortuitous*] *turn of events, we found a hatbox full of diamond jewellery on a park bench.*

fortuity /fawr tyo͞o əti/ (*plural* **-ties**) *n* **1** something that happens by chance or accident **2** lucky chance or accident

fortunate /fáwrchənət/ *adj* **1 LUCKY** enjoying good luck **2 RESULTING FROM LUCK** happening as a result of good luck **3 BRINGING LUCK** bringing good luck [14C. < Latin *fortunatus* < *fortuna* 'fate, luck'.] —**fortunateness** *n*

USAGE See ***fortuitous***.

fortunately /fáwrchənətli/ *adv* **1** by lucky chance **2** used to show that the speaker or writer is happy to be able to report something ○ *Fortunately, we've been given more time to finish the job.*

~~**fortunatly**~~ incorrect spelling of **fortunately**

fortune /fáwrchən/ *n* **1 GREAT WEALTH** a large amount of financial wealth or material possessions **2 LARGE SUM OF MONEY** an extremely large amount of money **3 fortune, Fortune FATE** chance, or the personification of chance, regarded as affecting human activities **4 LUCK** luck, especially good luck **5 DESTINY** an individual's destiny ■ **fortunes** *npl* **LIFE'S UPS AND DOWNS** chance happenings throughout life that may turn out well or badly [13C. Via French < Latin *fortuna* 'fate, (good) luck'.]

fortune cookie *n* a Chinese biscuit folded and baked around a piece of paper on which a saying or a prediction of somebody's fortune is written

fortune hunter *n* a person who seeks riches, especially by attempting to marry a wealthy partner —**fortune hunting** *n* —**fortune-hunting** *adj*

fortune teller *n* somebody who predicts the future, e.g. by reading palms or using tarot cards —**fortune-telling** *n, adj*

Fort William /-wíllyəm/ town in W Scotland, at the foot of Ben Nevis. Population: 10,391 (1991).

Fort Worth /-wúrth/ city in NE Texas. Population: 491,801 (1998 estimate).

forty /fáwrti/ *n* (*plural* **-ties**) **1** see table at **number 2 TENNIS POINT** in a game of tennis, the score awarded to a player with a score of thirty on winning a further point ■ **forties** *npl* **1 NUMBERS 40 TO 49** the numbers 40 to 49 **2 YEARS FROM 40 TO 49** the years from 40 to 49 in a century or somebody's life [Old English *feowertig* 'four tens' < *feower* 'four'] —**forty** *adj, pron*

forty-five *n* **1** a record smaller than an LP that is played at 45 revolutions per minute **2** *US, Can* a pistol with a .45 calibre.

Forty-Five *n* the Jacobite Rebellion of 1745 to 1746

fortyish /fáwrti ish/ *adj* **1** approximately 40 in number **2** about the age of 40

forty-niner /-nínər/ *n* a prospector in the gold rush of 1849 in California

fortysomething /fáwrti sumthing/ *n* somebody between 40 and 49 years of age (*informal*) ■ *adj* between 40 and 49 years of age

forty winks *n* a short sleep (*informal; takes a singular or plural verb*)

forum /fáwrəm/ (*plural* **forums** *or* **fora** /-rə/) *n* **1 PLACE TO EXPRESS YOURSELF** a medium, e.g. a magazine or newspaper, in which the public may debate an issue or express opinions **2 MEETING FOR DISCUSSION** a meeting to discuss matters of general interest **3 PUBLIC SQUARE IN ROMAN CITIES** a public square or marketplace in ancient Roman cities where business was conducted and the law courts were situated **4 LAW COURT** a law court or tribunal **5 INTERNET DISCUSSION GROUP** an Internet discussion group for participants with common interests [15C. < Latin, 'enclosed space around a house, marketplace' < *foris* 'out of doors'.]

forward /fáwrwərd/ CORE MEANING: to or towards a front position or direction ○ (adv) *Conover pushed his cup forward, but Johnny ignored it.* ○ (adj) *Most of the energy in petrol makes engines hot; less than half gets converted to forward motion.*

1 *adv* **AHEAD** to or towards what is ahead in space or time ○ (adv) *He sprang forward and embraced his grandmother.* **2** *adv* **PROGRESSING** towards a goal ○ *The company has taken a step forward in employee safety.* **3** *adv* **INDICATES IMPROVEMENT** indicates that something progresses or improves ○ *The EU is moving forward on monetary union.* **4** *adv* **TO FRONT OF VESSEL** towards the front of a boat or ship ○ *I was ordered forward to swab the deck.* **5** *adv* **TOWARDS THE FRONT** towards the front of something such as an aircraft or a building ○ *I'd like to be seated further forward.* **6** *adv* **TO PUBLIC ATTENTION** from obscurity into public view ○ *The unknown actor came forward and accepted the lead role.* **7** *adj* **AHEAD** directed towards what is ahead in space and time ○ *The magnetic field exerts a forward force on charged particles.* **8** *adj* **RELATING TO THE FUTURE** directed towards a future goal ○ *forward planning* **9** *adj* **AT FRONT OF VESSEL** situated at or near the front of a boat or ship ○ *the forward deck* **10** *adj* **AT THE FRONT** situated at or near the front of something such as an aircraft or a building ○ *The forward seats are the most popular.* **11** *adj* **UNRESTRAINED IN BEHAVIOUR** behaving boldly in defiance of moral or social restraints ○ *I'm not sure I approve of her behaviour – she's very forward.* **12** *adj NZ* **WELL** describes an animal in good condition **13** *n* **ATTACKING PLAYER** an attacking player in some team sports, e.g. football, rugby, hockey, or basketball **14** *vt* **REDIRECT MAIL** to send on mail from the address to which it was originally sent ○ *She was anxious to know if any letters might have come that had not been forwarded to her.* **15** *vt* **PROMOTE** to assist the progress of something ○ *I will do anything you like if it means we can forward your cause.* [Old English *forweard* 'in the direction of the front' < *fore* (see FORE)] —**forwardness** *n*

forward bias *n* a voltage applied to a semiconductor or a junction in such a device, in the direction that carries a higher current

forwarder /fáwrwərdər/ *n* an individual or company whose business is the collection, shipment, and delivery of goods

forwarding /fáwrwərding/ *n* the collection, shipment, and delivery of goods

forwarding address *n* a new address to which mail is to be redirected

forward-looking *adj* planning for or looking ahead to the future

forwardly /fáwrwərdli/ *adv* in a bold manner, defying moral or social restraints

forward market *n* a financial market in which contracts are entered for the purchase and sale of commodities and stocks that are to be delivered at a future date

forward pass *n* **1** in rugby, an illegal pass in which the ball goes forward **2** in American football, a pass thrown from a position behind the line of scrimmage in the direction of the opposing team's goal

forward roll *n* a movement in gymnastics in which the body is rolled over in a forward direction, placing the head on the ground and bringing the feet over the head

forwards /fáwrwərdz/ *adv* = **forward**

forward visibility *n* insight into future developments, or the ability to foresee them and plan for them

Fosbury flop /fózbəri-/ *n* a technique used in the high jump in which the contestant clears the bar with the back of the shoulders followed by the arched body [Mid-20C. After Richard (Dick) *Fosbury* (b. 1947), US athlete.]

foscarnet /foss kaar nət/ *n* an antiviral drug. Use: treatment of a type of herpes.

fossa[1] /fóssə/ (*plural* **-sae** /-see/) *n* a hollow, pit, or groove in a part of the body, e.g. a bone [Mid-17C. < Latin, 'ditch' (see FOSSE).]

fossa[2] (*plural* **-sas** *or* **-sa** /-see/) *n* a slender reddish-brown carnivorous mammal that resembles a cat, has sharp retractile claws, and feeds on small animals, birds, and insects. Native to: Madagascar. *Cryptoprocta ferox.* [Mid-19C. < Malagasy *fosa.*]

fosse /foss/ *n* a wide ditch, usually filled with water and used for defence [Pre-12C. Via French < Latin *fossa* < *fodere* 'dig'.]

Fosse /fóssi/, **Bob** (1927–87) US dancer, choreographer, and director. Full name **Robert Louis Fosse**

Fosse Way /fóss-/ Roman road in England that runs northeastwards from Axminster to Lincoln. Length: 300 km/200 mi.

fossick /fóssik/ *vi ANZ* **1** to rummage or look for something ○ *She fossicked around in the drawer for the key.* **2** to search for gold or gems in mines or streams that have already been worked [Mid-19C. < English dialect, 'ferret out, get by asking' < ?] —**fossicker** *n*

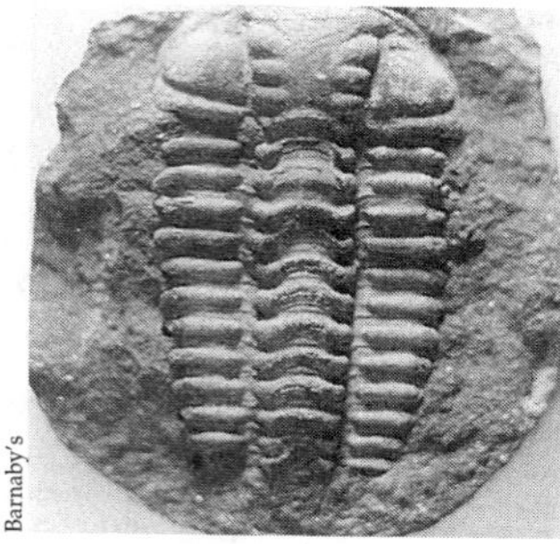

Barnaby's

Fossil: Trilobite

fossil /fóss'l/ *n* **1 PRESERVED REMAINS** the remains of an animal or plant preserved from an earlier era inside a rock or other geological deposit, often as an impression or in a petrified state **2 SOMEBODY WHO WILL NOT CHANGE** a person who is hopelessly out of date or unwilling to accept change (*informal insult*) **3 SOMETHING OUTDATED** something that has outlived its usefulness, e.g. a discredited theory **4 OLD WORD NOW USED SPECIFICALLY** a word or part of a word that was once used generally but now survives only in a few contexts, e.g. *couth* in *uncouth* [Mid-16C. Via French *fossile* < Latin *fossilis* 'dug up' < *fodere* 'dig'.]

fossil fuel *n* any carbon-containing fuel, e.g. coal, peat, petroleum, and natural gas, derived from the decomposed remains of prehistoric plants and animals

fossiliferous /fóssi líffərəss/ *adj* describes a rock or other geological deposit that has fossils within it

fossilize /fóssə līz/ (**-izes, -izing, -ized**), **fossilise** (**-ises, -ising, -ised**) *vti* **1** to convert something into a fossil, to preserve something as a fossil, or to become a fossil **2** to become outdated, fixed, or unchanging, or to make somebody or something incapable of change —**fossilizable** *adj* —**fossilization** /fóssə lī záysh'n/ *n* —**fossilized** *adj*

fossil water *n* water in underground strata that has accumulated over millions of years and is therefore not a renewable resource, unlike other ground water

fossorial /fo sáwri əl/ *adj* describes animals that have large forelimbs or other adaptations for digging and burrowing, or describes the parts of the body used for this purpose [Mid-19C. < medieval Latin *fossorius* < Latin *fossor* 'digger' < *fodere* 'dig'.]

foster /fóstər/ *v* **1** *vti* **REAR CHILD WHO IS NOT YOURS** to look after or bring up in your home a child who is not your own, often on a short-term basis and in exchange for payment by a local authority **2** *vt* **ARRANGE CARE FOR CHILD** to put a child temporarily in the care of adults who are not its parents **3** *vt* **NURTURE A CHILD** to provide a child with care and upbringing **4** *vt* **DEVELOP** to encourage the development of something **5** *vt* **KEEP ALIVE FEELING OR THOUGHT** to keep a feeling or thought alive ■ *adj* **PROVIDING OR RECEIVING PARENTAL CARE** giving or receiving a home and parental care and upbringing, usually on a short-term basis, although unrelated by blood or adoption ○ *a foster child* [Old English *fostrian* 'nourish, raise a child' < *foster* 'food' < Germanic] —**fosterer** *n*

Foster /fóstər/, **David** (*b.* 1944) Australian novelist

Foster, Norman, Baron Foster of Thames Bank (*b.* 1935) British architect

fosterage /fóstərij/ *n* **1 CARING FOR ANOTHER'S CHILD** the act of looking after or bringing up a child who is not one's own, often on a short-term basis and in exchange for payment by a local authority **2 BEING A FOSTER CHILD** the process of being looked after or brought up in a home by parents who are not one's own **3 ENCOURAGING DEVELOPMENT** the process of encouraging the development of something beneficial

fou /foo/ *adj Scotland* extremely drunk (*informal*) [Mid-16C. Alteration of FULL[1].]

Foucault /fóokō/, **Jean-Bernard Léon** (1819–68) French physicist

Foucault, Michel (1926–84) French philosopher

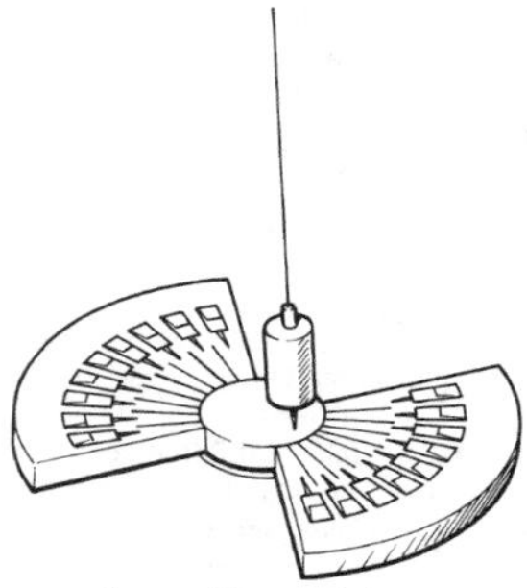

Foucault's pendulum

Foucault's pendulum /fóokōz-/ *n* a heavy free-swinging pendulum suspended by a long thin wire, whose plane of motion appears to change as the earth rotates [Mid-19C. After Jean-Bernard Léon FOUCAULT.]

fouetté /fwéttay, foo ə tay/ *n* a ballet step in which the dancer stands on one foot and moves the other leg quickly out and in again, often while doing a pirouette [Mid-19C. < French, past participle of *fouetter* 'whip'.]

fought past tense, past participle of **fight**

foul /fowl/ *adj* **1 DISGUSTING** disgusting to the senses ○ *They lowered themselves into the foul-smelling sewers.* ○ *brackish, foul-tasting water* **2 FILLED WITH DIRT** clogged with dirt or so obstructed as to be unusable **3 DIRTY** covered in dirt **4 CONTAMINATED** contaminated by impurities **5 UNPLEASANT** extremely unpleasant or disagreeable in nature (*informal*) **6 VULGAR** obscene or otherwise offensive in expression or behaviour **7 ILLEGAL IN SPORT** contrary to the rules of a sport **8 DISHONEST** behaving in an unfair and unacceptable way **9 INCLEMENT** describes weather that is stormy or wet and unpleasant **10 ROTTEN** decaying and rotten **11 EVIL** spiritually or morally vicious **12 ENSNARLED** entangled with something and unable to move **13 UNENJOYABLE** extremely low in quality ■ *n* **1 ILLEGAL ACTION IN SPORT** an illegal action against an opposing player, or an action that breaks the rules of a sport **2 ENTANGLEMENT PREVENTING MOVEMENT** in sailing, an entanglement or collision that prevents movement ■ *v* **1** *vti* **ACT ILLEGALLY IN SPORT** to act illegally against an opposing player, or violate a rule of a sport **2** *vti* **ENSNARL AND PREVENT MOVEMENT** to entangle or catch something so that it cannot move, or become entangled or caught and unable to move **3** *vti* **OBSTRUCT** to clog or block something, or to become clogged or blocked **4** *vt* **MAKE DIRTY** to make something dirty, especially by defecation **5** *vt* **BRING DISGRACE ON** to bring disgrace to a person or to somebody's reputation [Old English *ful* 'filthy, decaying' < Germanic] —**fouler** *n* —**foully** *adv* —**foulness** *n*

SPELLCHECK Do not confuse ***foul*** with ***fowl***, which has a similar sound. Beware: your spellchecker will not catch this error.

foul up *vti* **1** to do something badly or incompetently, or to be bungled or mismanaged (*informal*) **2** to choke, clog, or entangle something, or to become choked, clogged, or entangled

foulard /foo laar, -laard/ *n* **1** a soft silk or rayon fabric, usually patterned **2** something made of foulard, especially a scarf or handkerchief [Mid-19C. < French.]

foul ball *n* in baseball, a struck ball that lands outside a foul line

foul line *n* **1 LINE SHOWING FAIR OR FOUL BALL** in baseball, either of the lines extending from home plate through first and third bases to the end of the playing field **2 DESIGNATED LIMIT OF PLAY** in some sports, a boundary beyond which a ball or player is not permitted, e.g. the line in ten-pin bowling where the player must stop before releasing the ball **3 LINE FOR FREE THROWS** in basketball, either of two lines on a court from which players get unobstructed chances to make a basket after they have been fouled

foul-mouthed *adj* using obscene or otherwise offensive language, especially habitually

foul play *n* **1 UNFAIRNESS** unfair action or behaviour **2 CRIME** treachery or criminal violence **3 ACTION AGAINST RULES** action that is contrary to the rules of a sport

foul shot *n US, Can* = **free throw**

foul-up *n* a blunder or the confusion or failure that results from error (*informal*)

found[1] /fownd/ *vt* **1** to establish and organize something for the future, e.g. an institution or business **2** to support something, e.g. a conclusion, with evidence or reasoning [13C. Via French *fonder* < Latin *fundare* < *fundus* 'bottom, base'.]

found[2] /fownd/ *vt* **1** to cast something, especially metal or glass, by melting it and pouring it into a mould **2** to produce objects, e.g. machine parts, by melting metal or glass and pouring it into moulds [14C. Via French *fondre* 'dissolve and blend' < Latin *fundere* 'pour, melt'.]

found[3] past tense, past participle of **find**

foundation /fown dáysh'n/ *n* **1 SUPPORT FOR A BUILDING** a part of a building, usually below the ground, that transfers and distributes the weight of the building onto the ground (*often plural*) **2 SUPPORT FOR IDEA** the basis of something, e.g. a theory or an idea **3 BASE LAYER OF MAKE-UP** a cosmetic in liquid, cream, or cake form, usually coloured, that is applied as a base for make-up **4 ESTABLISHING OF INSTITUTION** the setting up of an institution or organization **5 CHARITABLE ORGANIZATION** an institution, e.g. a school, research establishment, charitable trust, or hospital, that has been formally set up with an endowment fund **6 FUND SUPPORTING INSTITUTION** an endowment fund that supports an institution **7 RULES OF AN INSTITUTION** the charter setting up an institution and the statutes and rules by which it is governed **8** CLOTHING = **foundation garment** —**foundational** *adj* —**foundationally** *adv*

foundation course *n* an introductory course, usually taken as a first level in more extended studies

foundation garment, foundation *n* a piece of women's underwear intended to control and shape the figure, e.g. a corset

foundation school *n* a state primary or secondary school that owns its own land and has responsibility for staffing and for admissions arrangements. ◊ **community school**

foundation stone *n* **1** a stone laid during a ceremony to mark the start of construction of a building or institution **2** the basis on which something is founded

foundation stop *n* an organ stop with a strong fundamental tone

foundation subject *n* any of ten subjects specified in the 1988 National Curriculum that must be studied in schools in England and Wales, three of which have priority as core subjects

founder[1] /fówndər/ *n* a person who establishes an institution, business, or organization

founder[2] /fówndər/ *v* **1** *vti* **SINK OR CAUSE TO SINK** to become filled with water and sink, or to make something sink **2** *vi* **BREAK DOWN** to collapse and fail ○ *Negotiations foundered on a single issue.* **3** *vi* **CRUMPLE** to give way and fall to the ground **4** *vi* **BE BOGGED DOWN** to become stuck in soft ground or snow **5** *vi* **STUMBLE** to stumble or injure a leg **6** *vti* **MAKE OR BECOME ILL BY OVERFEEDING** to make livestock ill by overfeeding or to become ill by overfeeding ■ *n* VET = **laminitis** [14C. < Old French *fondrer* 'send or sink to the bottom, fall in ruins' < Latin *fundus* 'bottom'.]

founder member *n* a member of an organization who also helped to found it

found-in *n US* somebody who is arrested during a police raid on an illegal business (*slang*)

founding father *n* a founder of an institution, movement, or organization

Founding Father *n* one of the members of the convention that drafted the US Constitution

foundling /fówndling/ *n* an abandoned baby of unknown parentage (*dated*) [13C. < past participle of FIND.]

found object *n* ARTS = **objet trouvé**

foundry /fówndri/ (*plural* **-ries**) *n* **1** a building equipped for the casting of metal or glass **2** the skill or practice of casting metal or glass

fount[1] /fownt/ *n* (*literary*) **1** a source of something **2** a fountain or spring of water [16C. Shortening of FOUNTAIN.]

fount[2] /fownt/ *n* = **font**[2]

fountain /fówntin/ *n* **1 ORNAMENTAL WATER FEATURE** an ornamental structure featuring a jet or jets of water, often emerging from a statue into a pool **2 NATURAL SPRING** a natural source of water **3 DRINKING FOUNTAIN** a small jet of drinking water, especially one in a public place that can be activated by a button or handle **4 SPRAY OF LIQUID** a jet of water or some other liquid **5 SPRAY OF SUBSTANCE** a sudden discharge of something into the air, e.g. sparks, lava, or steam **6 SOURCE** the source of something abstract **7 RESERVOIR OF LIQUID** a reservoir of liquid for use as needed, e.g. in an oil lamp or for printing ink [14C. < French *fontaine* < Latin *fontanus* 'of a spring' < *fons* 'spring'.]

fountainhead /fówntin hed/ *n* **1** a spring that is the source of a stream **2** the primary source of something abstract

fountain pen *n* a pen with a pointed metal tip (**nib**) that is supplied with ink from a refillable reservoir in the body of the pen or from an inserted cartridge

four /fawr/ *n* **1** see table at **number 2 CRICKET SHOT SCORING 4 RUNS** in cricket, a shot that hits the ground and then bounces out of bounds **3 4-OARED RACING BOAT** a light narrow racing boat with four oars **4 4-MEMBER ROWING CREW** a rowing crew with four members **5 BOWLING TEAM** a team of four bowls players ■ **fours** *npl* **BOAT RACES** races for boats with a crew of four [Old English *fēower* < Indo-European] —**four** *adj, pron*

four-ball *n* a match between two pairs of golfers in which the better score of each side at each hole is counted

four-by-four *n* a four-wheel-drive motor vehicle

four-by-two *n* a commonly used size of timber with a cross section measuring approximately 10 cm/4 in by approximately 5 cm/2 in. US term **two-by-four** *n.* 1

fourchette /foor shét/ *n* a small band that joins the folds of skin at the back of the opening to the vagina, sometimes torn in childbirth [Mid-18C. < French, 'small fork' < *fourche* < Latin *furca* 'pitchfork, forked stick'.]

four-colour *adj* describes a process by which full-colour printing is achieved by superimposing images in cyan, magenta, yellow, and black

four-cycle *adj US* AUTOMOT = **four-stroke**

four-dimensional *adj* having or determined by four dimensions, especially as in some formulations of relativity theory which use three spatial dimensions and a mathematically modified form of time as the fourth

Fourdrinier /foor drínni ər, -ni ay/ *n* a paper-making machine that produces a continuous web or roll of paper [Mid-19C. After Henry and Sealy *Fourdrinier*, British papermakers.]

four-eyes (*plural* **four-eyes**) *n* an offensive term for somebody who wears spectacles (*informal insult*)

four flush *n* a bad hand in poker, containing four cards of the same suit and one odd card

four-flush *vi* **1** to bet coolly and boldly in poker despite holding a bad hand, e.g. a four flush **2** *US* to try to mislead somebody in a bold way (*informal*) —**four-flusher** *n*

fourfold /fáwr fōld/ *adj, adv* **MULTIPLIED BY 4** four times as great in size or amount ■ *adj* **1 WITH 4 ELEMENTS** with four elements or members **2 CONSISTING OF 4 PARTS** consisting of four parts or made up of four parts

four-four-two *n* one of the most common outfield team formations in soccer, comprising four defenders, four midfielders, and two attackers

ϟ **4GL** *abbr* fourth-generation language

four-handed /fáwr handid/ *adj* **1** describes a game, especially a card game, played by four people **2** composed or arranged for two people to play at the piano

Fourier /fóorri ay/, **Charles** (1772–1837) French social scientist

Fourier analysis /fóori ər-, fóori ay-/ *n* the analysis of a periodic function using the terms of a Fourier series as an approximation [Early 20C. See FOURIER SERIES.]

Fourier series *n* an infinite trigonometric series of terms consisting of constants multiplied by sines or cosines, used in the approximation of periodic functions [Late 19C. After Jean Baptiste Joseph *Fourier* (1768–1830), French mathematician.]

four-in-hand *n* **1** a carriage drawn by four horses with one driver **2** a team of four horses drawing a carriage

four-leaf clover, four-leaved clover, four-leafed clover *n* a clover leaf divided into four leaflets instead of the usual three, believed to bring good luck to the person who finds it

four-letter word *n* a short English word relating to sex or excretion that is often used as a swearword and is generally regarded as offensive or taboo

four-o'clock (*plural* **four-o'clock** *or* **four-o'clocks**) *n* a plant with tubular red, white, or yellow flowers that open in the late afternoon. Native to: tropical America. *Mirabilis jalapa.*

404 /fáwr ō fáwr/ *n* a person who is considered ignorant or stupid (*slang insult*) [< an error message displayed on a Web browser when the page requested cannot be located]

fourpenny one /fáwrpəni-/ *n* a punch with the fist (*dated informal*) [< ?]

four-poster, four-poster bed *n* a bed with a tall post at each corner, from which a canopy and curtains are sometimes hung

fourragère /fóorə zhair/ *n* a braided cord awarded as a military decoration to a unit or individual, and usually worn on the left shoulder of a uniform [Early 20C. < French, < *fourrage* (see FORAGE).]

fourscore /fawr skáwr/ *adj* the number 80 or a quantity of 80 (*archaic*) ○ *fourscore years and ten*

foursome /fáwrsəm/ *n* **1** a group of four people, usually taking part in some activity together **2** a game of golf between two pairs of players, especially when each pair has one ball that the partners hit alternately

foursquare /fawr skwáir/ *adv, adj* showing certainty and determination ■ *adj* solidly built and strong

four-star *adj* describes petrol that has a high octane number ■ *n* high-octane petrol, once the most commonly used in vehicles with petrol engines

four-stroke *adj* having a piston that makes four strokes to complete a cycle (*refers to an internal-combustion engine*). US term **four-cycle**

fourteen /fawr téen/ *n* see table at **number** —**fourteen** *adj, pron*

fourteenth /fawr téenth/ *n* see table at **number** —**fourteenth** *adj*

fourth /fawrth/ *n* **1** see table at **number 2** in a standard musical scale, the interval between one note and another that lies three notes above or below it **3** in a standard musical scale, a note that is a fourth away from another note **4** BALLET = **fourth position** —**fourth** *adj, adv*

SPELLCHECK See *forth*.

fourth dimension *n* time in relativity theory modified mathematically and used in combination with the usual three spatial dimensions to specify the location in space and time of events —**fourth-dimensional** *adj*

fourth estate, Fourth Estate *n* journalists, the press, or the media in general [In addition to the three estates (the Lords Spiritual, the Lords Temporal, and the House of Commons)]

ϟ **fourth-generation language** *n* an advanced computer programming language that is more like human language than are the standard high-level programming languages

fourthly /fáwrthli/ *adv* used to introduce the fourth point in an argument or discussion

fourth position *n* a position in ballet in which the feet are turned outwards with the right leg extended so that the right foot is one step in front of the left foot

fourth-rate *adj* so bad that it is worse than second-rate and third-rate

Fourth World *n* the poorest or least developed countries in the Third World

~~fourty~~ incorrect spelling of **forty**

4WD *abbr* four-wheel drive

four-wheel drive *n* a system of transmitting power from the driving mechanism to all four wheels of a motor vehicle in order to provide better traction under difficult conditions

Fouta Djallon /fóottə yaá lon/, **Futa Djallon** plateau region in north-central Guinea. Highest peak: Massif du Tamgué 1,537 m/5,043 ft. Area: 77,700 sq. km/30,000 sq. mi.

fouter *n, v Scotland* = **footer**[2]

fovea /fóvi ə/ (*plural* **-ae** /-vi eə/) *n* **1** a small hollow in the surface of a part of the body **2** = **fovea centralis** [Late 17C. < Latin, 'small pit'.] —**foveal** *adj* —**foveate** /fóvi ayt, -ət/ *adj*

fovea centralis /-sen tráaliss/ *n* a shallow pit in the centre of the retina that is free of blood vessels and has the highest concentration of cells sensitive to colour and bright light (**cones**) [< Latin, 'central fovea']

Foveaux Strait /fóvō-/ stretch of the South Pacific Ocean between the South Island and Stewart Island, New Zealand. At its narrowest, it is 18 km/11 mi. wide.

foveola /fō veé ələ/ (*plural* **-lae** /-lee/) *n* a small fovea [Mid-19C. < Latin, < *fovea* 'small pit'.] —**foveolar** *adj* —**foveolate** /fóvi ə layt, -lət/ *adj* —**foveolated** *adj*

Fowey /foy/ seaport and resort in SW England. Population: 1,939 (1991).

fowl /fowl/ (*plural* **fowls** *or* **fowl**) *n* **1 CHICKEN** a common domesticated chicken **2 BIRD RELATED TO CHICKEN** a bird related to the chicken, e.g. a turkey, grouse, pheasant, or partridge. Order: Galliformes. **3 EDIBLE BIRD** any bird that is used as food or hunted for sport, e.g. a goose or duck **4 BIRD'S FLESH** the flesh of an edible bird, traditionally chicken, especially an old or male bird **5 BIRD** any bird at all (*archaic*) [Old English *fugol* 'bird' < Germanic]

SPELLCHECK See ***foul***.

fowler /fówlər/ *n* a shooter or trapper of wild birds

Fowles /fowlz/, **John** (*b.* 1926) British novelist

fowling /fówling/ *n* the shooting or trapping of wild birds as a livelihood or for sport

fowling piece *n* a light gun that fires small shot, used in hunting game birds

fox /foks/ *n* **1 WILD ANIMAL WITH BUSHY TAIL** a carnivorous mammal of the dog family that has a pointed muzzle, large ears, a long bushy tail, and usually reddish-brown or grey fur. Genus: *Vulpes*. **2 FOX FUR** the fur of the fox **3 TRICKSTER** a sly and cunning person (*informal*) **4** *US* **GOOD-LOOKING PERSON** a good-looking young person (*informal*) ■ *vt* **1 BAFFLE** to confuse or baffle somebody (*often passive*) **2 OUTWIT** to deceive or outwit somebody by means of sly trickery [Old English, < Indo-European] —**fox-like** *adj*

Fox /foks/ *n* **1 MEMBER OF NATIVE N AMERICAN PEOPLE** a member of a Native North American people who lived in Michigan, Wisconsin, Illinois, and Iowa, and now live mainly in Oklahoma and Iowa **2 ALGONQUIAN LANGUAGE** a language spoken in parts of Iowa and Oklahoma, belonging to the Algonquian group of Algonquian-Wakashan. Native speakers: 2,000. ■ *adj* **RELATING TO FOX** relating or belonging to the Fox people, or their language or culture

Fox /foks/, **Charles James** (1749–1806) British politician

Fox, George (1624–91) English religious leader

Fox, Vicente (*b.* 1942) Mexican political leader. Full name **Vicente Fox Quesada**

Fox, Sir William (1812–93) British-born New Zealand explorer, statesman, and painter

FOX /foks/ *abbr* Futures and Options Exchange

foxed /fokst/, **foxy** *adj* describes books or paper stained with yellowish-brown spots from having been kept in damp conditions

foxfire /fóks fīr/ *n* a luminescent glow produced by some fungi when in contact with rotting wood

Fox Glacier glacier on the SW coast of the South Island, New Zealand. Length: 14 km/9 mi.

foxglove /fóks gluv/ (*plural* **-glove** *or* **-gloves**) *n* a tall plant that is the source of the drug digitalis. Flowers: purple or white, thimble-shaped. *Digitalis purpurea*.

fox grape *n* a wild grape that has purplish fruit and is the source of many cultivated grape varieties. Native to: E United States. *Vitis labrusca*.

foxhole /fóks hōl/ *n* a small hole dug in the ground to protect a sniper or other soldier from enemy fire

foxhound /fóks hownd/ *n* a small short-haired dog that has great speed and stamina, belonging to either of two breeds that are used to hunt foxes

fox hunter *n* **1** a hunter of foxes for sport **2** a horse used for foxhunting

foxhunting /fóks hunting/ *n* a sport in which mounted hunters pursue a fox through open countryside with a pack of foxhounds

foxtail /fóks tayl/, **foxtail grass** *n* a grass with soft cylindrical spikes resembling the tail of a fox. Genera: *Alopecurus, Setaria* and *Hordeum*.

fox terrier *n* a small wire-haired or smooth-haired dog belonging to a breed that has a white coat with dark markings

foxtrot /fóks trot/ *n* **1 BALLROOM DANCE** a ballroom dance alternating longer slower walking steps and shorter quicker running steps, usually with four beats to the bar **2 MUSIC FOR FOXTROT** the music for a foxtrot **3 HORSE'S SLOW TROTTING PACE** a slowish pace for a horse, between a trot and a walk, in which it takes short steps in a broken rhythm [Early 20C. < the short steps of the fox.]

Foxtrot /fóks trot/ *n* a code word for the letter 'F', used in international radio communications

foxy /fóksi/ (**-ier, -iest**) *adj* **1 LIKE A FOX** like a fox, especially in appearance or through having a strong pungent smell **2 REDDISH-BROWN** of a reddish-brown colour, like fox fur **3 CRAFTY** clever in a cunning or deceitful way **4** *US* **ALLURING** sensually alluring (*informal*) **5** PUBL = **foxed** **6 SHARP OR MUSKY** having the rather sharp, pungent, or musky flavour of fox grapes —**foxiness** *n*

foyer /fóy ay, fwí ay/ *n* **1** the reception area in a public building such as a hotel or theatre **2** *US* the entrance hall or vestibule in a private house [Mid-19C. Via French < medieval Latin *focarius* < Latin *focus* 'fireplace, hearth'.]

fps *abbr* **1** feet per second **2 fps, f.p.s.** foot-pound-second **3** frames per second

fps units, fps system of units *n* a system of units based on the foot, second, and pound mass that is now almost wholly superseded by SI units

ϟ **fr** *abbr* France (*in Internet addresses*)

Fr *symbol* francium

FR *abbr* family room

fr. *abbr* **1** fragment **2** from

Fr. *abbr* **1** Father **2** France **3** French **4** Friday **5** Friar **6** Frau **7** franc

Fra /fraa/, **fra** *n* used as a title for an Italian monk or friar, the equivalent of the English title 'Brother' [Late 19C. < Italian, shortening of *frate* 'brother, friar' < Latin *frater*.]

fracas /frák aa/ (*plural* **-cas**) *n* a noisy quarrel or fight [Early 18C. < French, 'crash, roar' < Italian *fracassare* 'cause an uproar'.]

ϟ **fractal** /frákt'l/ *n* an irregular or fragmented geometrical shape that can be repeatedly subdivided into parts, each of which is a smaller copy of the whole. Fractals are used in computer modelling of natural structures that do not have simple geometric shapes, e.g. clouds, mountainous landscapes, and coastlines. [Late 20C. < French, < Latin *fract-* (see FRACTION).] —**fractal** *adj*

fraction /fráksh'n/ *n* **1 NUMBER THAT IS NOT A WHOLE** a number that is not a whole number, such as $\frac{1}{2}$ (**vulgar fraction**) or 0.5 (**decimal fraction**), formed by dividing one quantity into another **2 SMALL AMOUNT** a small part, amount, or proportion of something ○ *a fraction of the cost* **3 PART** a part or element of a larger whole or group **4 SEPARATED COMPONENT** an individual component or portion of a mixture, separated by differences in chemical or physical properties **5 BREAKING OF BREAD BY PRIEST** during Holy Communion in the Roman Catholic tradition, the breaking off of a piece of bread by the priest who places it in the chalice [14C. Via Old French < late Latin *fraction-* < Latin *fract-*, past participle of *frangere* 'break'.] ◇ **a fraction** by a very small amount or distance ○ *Move it just a fraction to the right*

fractional /frákshənəl/ *adj* **1 OF FRACTIONS** involving or relating to fractions **2 SLIGHT** very small or slight ○ *a fractional increase in temperature* **3 RELATING TO COMPONENT SEPARATION** relating to the process of separating individual components from a mixture on the basis of the chemical or physical properties that make them different from other components

fractional distillation *n* the process of separating components that have different boiling points from a volatile liquid, by first heating the liquid and then condensing and collecting the components as they vaporize

fractionalize /fráksh'nə līz/ (**-izes, -izing, -ized**), **fractionalise** (**-alises, -alising, -alised**) *vt* to divide something into parts or sections —**fractionalization** /fráksh'nə lī záysh'n/ *n*

fractionally /fráksh'nəli/ *adv* very slightly

fractionate /frákshə nayt/ (**-ates, -ating, -ated**) *v* **1** *vti* to divide or break, or to divide or break something, into parts (*formal*) **2** *vt* to separate a mixture into its components, e.g. by crystallization or distillation —**fractionation** /frákshə náysh'n/ *n* —**fractionator** *n*

fractious /frákshəss/ *adj* irritable and likely to complain or misbehave [Late 17C. < FRACTION.] —**fractiously** *adv* —**fractiousness** *n*

fracture /frákchər/ *n* **1 BREAK OF BONE** a break in a bone **2 ACT OF BREAKING** the act of breaking something, especially a bone **3 BREAK OR CRACK** a break, split, or crack in an object or a material **4 SPLIT IN SYSTEM OR ORGANIZATION** a split or division in something such as a system, organization, or agreement ○ *the fractures that are already starting to appear in the peace treaty* **5 ROCK BREAK** a break in a rock or mineral, across which there is a separation ■ *vti* (**-tures, -turing, -tured**) **1 BREAK** to break or crack something, especially a particular bone or a bone in a particular part of the body **2 CAUSE OR UNDERGO DAMAGE** to cause damage or disruption to something or destroy it, or to be damaged, disrupted, or destroyed [Mid-16C. Directly or via French < Latin *fractura* < *fract-* (see FRACTION).] —**fracturable** *adj*

frae /fray/ *prep Scotland* from [13C. Variant of FRO.]

fragile /frájj īl/ *adj* **1 EASILY BROKEN** easy to break, damage, or harm, usually because delicate or brittle ○ *The models were too fragile to be used as toys.* **2 EASILY DESTROYED** not strong, sound, or secure and unlikely to withstand any severe stresses and strains that may be put on it ○ *a fragile peace* **3 PHYSICALLY WEAK** in a weak or delicate bodily state, usually as a result of illness [15C. Directly or via French < Latin *fragilis* < source of *frangere* 'break'.] —**fragilely** *adv* —**fragileness** *n* —**fragility** /frə jílləti/ *n*

SYNONYMS ***fragile, delicate, frail, flimsy, frangible, friable***

CORE MEANING: easily broken or damaged

fragile not having a strong structure or not made of robust materials, and therefore easily broken or damaged; **delicate** similar to fragile, used especially of things that are beautiful or remarkable because of their fragility; **frail** easily broken or damaged, or physically weak and vulnerable to injury; **flimsy** too easily broken, torn, or damaged, especially used of badly or cheaply made goods, or of light and insubstantial clothing; **frangible** capable of being broken or easily damaged; **friable** easily reduced to tiny particles.

fragile-X syndrome *n* a genetic condition caused by an abnormal X chromosome with an apparently almost detached part near the end of the long arm, that causes learning difficulties in boys and men

fragment *n* /frágmənt/ **1 BROKEN PIECE** a piece, usually a small piece, broken off something or left when something is shattered **2 INCOMPLETE PIECE** an incomplete or isolated piece of something ○ *I noted down fragments of the conversation.* ■ *vti* /frag mént/ **1 BREAK INTO SMALL PIECES** to break, or break something, into small pieces ○ *The metal is designed to fragment on impact.* **2 BREAK UP** to lose, or cause something to lose, a sense of unity or cohesion, with the result that something splits into isolated and often conflicting elements ○ *Society is starting to fragment.* [Mid-16C. Directly or via French < Latin *fragmentum* < source of *frangere* 'break'.] —**fragmented** /frag méntid/ *adj*

fragmental /frag mént'l/ *adj* = **fragmentary**

fragmentary /frágməntəri/ *adj* consisting of the physical fragments or small disconnected items of something —**fragmentarily** *adv*

ϟ **fragmentation** /frágmən táysh'n, -men-/ *n* **1 BREAKING UP** the process of shattering or breaking up into fragments **2 LOSS OF UNITY** the loss of unity and cohesion and the breakup of something into isolated and often conflicting elements ○ *The result, inevitably, would be social fragmentation.* **3 SHATTERING OF EXPLOSIVE DEVICE** the scattering of the shattered parts of a grenade or other explosive device **4 BREAKING UP OF DATA PACKET** the breaking up of computer data into smaller nonconsecutive pieces for more efficient storage and transmission

fragmentation bomb *n* a bomb or shell with a thick casing that is designed to shatter on detonation into many destructive fragments in order to cause maximum damage or injury

fragmentation grenade *n* a grenade with a thick casing that is designed to shatter on detonation into many destructive fragments, causing maximum damage or injury

fragmentize /frágmən tīz/ (**-tizes, -tizing, -tized**) *vti US* = **fragment** *v.* 1, **fragment** *v.* 2

Fragonard /frágga naar/, **Jean Honoré** (1732–1806) French painter and engraver

fragrance /fráygrənss/ *n* **1 SWEET SMELL** a pleasant sweet odour ○ *a plant with an exotic heady fragrance* **2 SWEETNESS OF SMELL** the characteristic of being sweet-smelling **3 PERFUME** something such as a perfume or cologne, which has a distinctive smell ○ *a great new fragrance for men* ○ *fragrance-free cosmetics* —**fragranced** *adj*

SYNONYMS See *smell*.

fragrance strip *n* a sealed strip of card or paper included with something such as a magazine advertisement impregnated with a fragrance that is released when the cover is peeled off

fragrancy /fráygrənssi/ *n* = **fragrance** *n.* 2

fragrant /fráygrənt/ *adj* having a pleasant or sweet smell [15C. Directly or via French < Latin *fragrant-*, present participle of *fragrare* 'emit a (good or bad) odour'.] —**fragrantly** *adv*

fraidy-cat /fráydi-/ *n US* = **scaredy-cat** (*informal*) [< shortening of AFRAID]

frail /frayl/ (**frailer, frailest**) *adj* **1 WEAK** in a weakened state, or in bad health **2 EASY TO BREAK** made of weak or delicate materials and easy, or apparently easy, to break or damage **3 INSUBSTANTIAL** lacking any substantial foundation in fact or reality and unlikely to be realized or be successful ○ *frail hopes of success* **4 MORALLY WEAK** easily tempted and led into sin or wrongdoing [14C. Via Old French *fraile* < Latin *fragilis* (see FRAGILE).] —**frailly** *adv* —**frailness** *n*

SYNONYMS See *fragile*. See *weak*.

frailty /fráylti/ (*plural* **-ties**) *n* **1 WEAKNESS** physical weakness or weakness of materials and construction **2 MORAL WEAKNESS** inherent moral weakness in humanity or in an individual leading to difficulty in resisting temptation or avoiding wrongdoing **3 CHARACTER FLAW** a character flaw arising out of moral weakness (*often plural*) ○ *ordinary human frailties*

fraise /frayz/ *n* a cone-shaped grooved drill bit used for enlarging a previously drilled hole [Early 17C. < French, 'lining of a calf's abdomen'; from its numerous folds.]

Fraktur /frak toŏr/, **fraktur** *n* a thick ornate style of printed letter, the standard typeface for all printing in German until around the middle of the 20th century [Late 19C. Via German < Latin *fractura* (see FRACTURE).]

Fra Mauro /fraa máwrō/ *n* crater on the Moon north of Mare Nubium

framboesia /fram beèzi ə/ *n MED* = **yaws** [Early 19C. < modern Latin, < French *framboise* 'raspberry' (suggested by the sores produced by the disease).]

⚡**frame** /fraym/ *n* **1 SUPPORTING STRUCTURE** an underlying or supporting structure that consists of solid parts such as beams or struts between them and that has something built around or on top of it ○ *a bike with a steel frame* **2 SURROUNDING STRUCTURE** something that surrounds or encloses a particular space ○ *a picture frame* ○ *a door frame* **3 frame, frames LENS-HOLDING PART OF SPECTACLES** the part of a pair of spectacles that holds the lenses and fits around the wearer's face **4 PIECE OF EQUIPMENT** a piece of equipment made of bars fitted together with spaces between, e.g. for children to climb on or to help a person to walk ○ *a child's climbing frame* **5 HOLLOW SHAPE FOR NEEDLECRAFTS AND PAINTING** an open structure across which a piece of material can be stretched to be painted or embroidered or across which threads can be stretched for weaving **6 CONTEXT** the general background or context against or within which something takes place ○ *the story's historical frame* **7 HUMAN BODY** a person's body, especially with reference

to its size and shape ○ *He eased his enormous frame into the chair.* **8 SINGLE PICTURE ON STRIP OF FILM** any one of the individual pictures that make up a strip of cinema film or a single exposure on a strip of photographic negative or slide images **9 TV PICTURE** the picture that appears on a television screen **10 VISIBLE PART OF FILMED ACTION** in film, video, or TV, the particular area of action that is captured by the camera and forms the rectangular image that appears on the screen ○ *characters moving out of the frame to the left* **11 IMAGE BORDER** the border or set of borders of a projected image **12 SINGLE PICTURE IN COMIC STRIP** any one of the individual pictures that make up a comic strip **13** GARDENING = **cold frame 14** *US* **ROUND OF TEN-PIN BOWLING** any one of the 10 rounds in a ten-pin bowling game **15 GAME IN SNOOKER** any one of the individual games that make up a match in snooker, billiards, and pool. US term **rack**[1] *n.* 6 **16 TRIANGULAR TEMPLATE FOR SNOOKER BALLS** a wooden triangle used to arrange the target balls into their required positions at the beginning of a game of snooker or pool. US term **rack**[1] *n.* 6 **17 BALLS POSITIONED BY FRAME** the target balls when in position for the start of a game of snooker or pool. US term **rack**[1] *n.* 7 **18 SINGLE CYCLE OF PULSES** a single cycle of pulses in a string of repeated pulses **19** = **frame-up** *n.* 1 (*slang*) **20 DATA LINK LAYER** a data link layer with header and trailer information ■ *vt* (**frames, framing, framed**) **1 MOUNT IN A FRAME** to mount a picture in a frame **2 FORM SURROUNDING FRAMEWORK FOR** to form a surrounding border or a framework, especially a decorative or contrasting one, around something (*often passive*) ○ *a delicate face framed by abundant black hair* **3 CONSTRUCT IDEA OR STATEMENT** to construct or compose something that is to be written or spoken ○ *She framed her words carefully.* **4 EXPRESS IN PARTICULAR WAY** to express something in a particular type of language ○ *framed the argument in legal terms* **5 MOUTH WORDS** to mouth words silently **6 CAUSE TO APPEAR GUILTY** to make an innocent person appear guilty, e.g. by forging incriminating evidence (*slang*) **7 ARRANGE RESULT IN ADVANCE** to use dishonest or illegal methods to arrange the result of a contest in advance, e.g. by paying a player to lose deliberately (*slang*) ■ *adj* **WITH WOODEN FRAMEWORK** constructed on a framework of wooden beams, then covered with boards or shingles ○ *a white frame house with black shutters* [Old English *framian* 'make progress, be helpful, prepare, shape' < *fram* (see FROM).] —**frameable** *adj* —**framer** *n* ◇ **in the frame** among those who are involved in something or under consideration for something (*informal*)

Janet Frame

Frame /fraym/, **Janet** (*b.* 1924) New Zealand writer. Born **Janet Paterson Frame Clutha**

frame of mind *n* a person's psychological state, attitude, or mood at a particular time

frame of reference *n* **1** the set of norms, values, or ideas that affect the way somebody interacts with others, either in everyday life or in particular situations **2** a set of geometric axes used to determine the location of a point in space

frame story *n* a narrative that provides the framework within which a number of different stories, which may or may not be connected, can be told

frame-up *n* (*slang*) **1** a conspiracy to make an innocent person appear guilty, e.g. by forging incriminating evidence **2** a situation in which the result of a contest is dishonestly or illegally arranged in advance

framework /fráym wurk/ *n* **1 SYSTEM OF INTERCONNECTING BARS** a structure of connected horizontal and vertical bars with spaces between them, especially one that forms the skeleton of another structure **2 UNDERLYING SET OF**

IDEAS a set of ideas, principles, agreements, or rules that provides the basis for or the outline for something intended to be more fully developed at a later stage ○ *The purpose of this meeting is to provide a framework for the discussions at next week's conference.* **3 CONTEXT** the general background or context to a particular action or event ○ *within the framework of Jewish religious tradition* **4 ARTICLES WOVEN OR EMBROIDERED ON FRAME** articles produced by weaving or embroidering cloth on a frame

framing /fráyming/ *n* **1 FRAMES** frames or frameworks collectively **2 WAY SOMETHING IS FRAMED** the way that something is framed **3 COMPOSITION OF FILM SCENE** the composition of a scene within the visual field of the camera for shooting in a film **4 ADJUSTMENT OF FILM PROJECTOR SETTINGS** adjustment of the settings on a film projector so that the image is in the correct position on the screen

franc /frangk/ *n* see table at **currency** [14C. < French.]

France

France /fraanss/ republic and largest country in W Europe. Capital: Paris. Population: 58,609,285 (1997). Area: 543,965 sq. km/210,026 sq. mi.

France /fraaNss/, **Anatole** (1844–1924) French writer. Pseudonym of **Jacques Anatole François Thibault**

franchise /frán chīz/ *n* **1 LICENCE TO SELL COMPANY'S PRODUCTS** an agreement or licence to sell a company's products exclusively in a particular area or to operate a business that carries that company's name **2 RIGHT TO VOTE** the right to vote, especially to elect representatives to a national legislature or a parliament **3 PRIVILEGE GRANTED BY AUTHORITY** a right or privilege, or an exemption from a duty or obligation, granted by a government or other authority **4 AREA OF COMMERCIAL OPERATION** the area in which somebody has a commercial franchise **5** *US* **PROFESSIONAL TEAM** a professional sports team that is a member of an organized league **6 franchise, franchise player VALUABLE PLAYER** a player who is valuable and important to a team [14C. < French, < *franc* 'free' (see FRANK).] —**franchise** *vt* —**franchisee** /frán chī zeè/ *n* —**franchisement** *n* —**franchiser** *n*

Francis I /fraánssiss/ (1494–1547) king of France (1515–47)

Francis (of Assisi), St (1182–1226) Italian mystic and preacher. Born **Giovanni Francesco Bernardone**

Franciscan /fran sískən/ *n* a member of an order of friars and nuns, founded by St Francis of Assisi, that now has three separate branches and is largely devoted to missionary and charitable work [Late 16C. Via French < modern Latin *Franciscanus* < *Franciscus* 'Francis'.] —**Franciscan** *adj*

Francis of Sales, St (1567–1622) French churchman and writer

francium /fránss i əm/ *n* (*symbol* **Fr**) an unstable radioactive element of the alkali-metal group. Source: uranium ore, made artificially from actinium and thorium. [Mid-20C. After FRANCE, home of its discoverer.]

francize /frán sīz/ (**-cizes, -cizing, -cized**), **francise** (**-cises, -cising, -cised**) *vt Can* to make a person, business, or group adopt French as a working language, especially in Quebec [Late 20C. < French *franciser* < *français* 'French'.]

Franco /frángkō/, **Francisco** (1892–1975) Spanish general and authoritarian leader

Franco- *prefix* France, French ○ *Francophile* [< late Latin *Francus* 'Frank' < Germanic]

Franconian /frang kṓni ən/ *n* a group of medieval dialects of German spoken in an area extending from present-day Bavaria and Alsace, and up the Rhine valley — **Franconian** *adj*

Francophile /frángkō fīl/, **Francophil** /-fil/ *n* a person who likes France, the French people, and the French way of life ■ *adj* liking or admiring France, the French, or the French way of life —**Francophilia** /frángkə filli ə/ *n*

Francophobe /frángkō fōb/ *n* a person who dislikes France and the French people —**Francophobia** /frángkō fōbi ə/ *n*

Francophobic /frángkō fōbik/ *adj* having an intense dislike of France, French people, or the French way of life

francophone /frángkō fōn/ *n* **SPEAKER OF FRENCH** a person who speaks French, especially as his or her native language ■ *adj* **1 FRENCH-SPEAKING** having French as his or her native or main language **2 OF FRENCH-SPEAKING AREA** relating to a place where French is used as the main language, the official language, or a lingua franca ○ *Francophone Africa* —**Francophonic** /frángkō fónnik/ *adj*

frangible /fránjəb'l/ *adj* capable of being broken or damaged [15C. Directly or via Old French < medieval Latin *frangibilis* < *frangere* 'break'.] —**frangibility** /fránjə bílləti/ *n*

SYNONYMS See ***fragile***.

frangipane /fránji payn/ *n* an almond-flavoured cream or paste used in pastries, cakes, and other sweet foods [Mid-19C. < French, 'frangipani' (perfume made with bitter almonds).]

frangipani /fránji pánni, -paáni/ (*plural* **-is**) *n* **1 TREE WITH PERFUMED FLOWERS** a deciduous tree with strongly perfumed, white, yellow, or pink flowers. Native to: tropical America. Genus: *Plumeria*. **2 PERFUME** perfume derived from frangipani flowers, or imitating their scent **3** COOK = **frangipane 4 AUSTRALIAN EVERGREEN TREE** an evergreen tree with fragrant cream or yellow flowers. Native to: coastal E Australia. *Hymenosporum flavum*. [Mid-19C. After Muzio *Frangipani*, 16C Italian creator of a perfume for gloves.]

Franglais /fróng glay/, **franglais** *n* an informal form of French that includes many English loan words and phrases [Mid-20C. < French, blend of *français* 'French' + *anglais* 'English'.] —**Franglais** *adj*

frank /frangk/ *adj* **1 EXPRESSING TRUE OPINION** open, honest, and sometimes forceful in expressing true feelings and opinions **2 OPEN AND BLUNT** allowing people's true feelings and opinions to be openly and often bluntly stated **3 PLEASINGLY HONEST** having or showing an appealingly open and honest nature ○ *a frank manner that won her many friends* **4 UNDISGUISED** openly expressed, and so not concealed or disguised ○ *regarded him with frank loathing* ■ *vt* **1 PRINT MARK OVER STAMP** to print an official mark over the stamp on a letter or parcel to show that payment has been formally accepted **2 PRINT MARK TO SHOW POSTAGE PAID** to print a mark on a piece of mail, instead of using a postage stamp, to show that postage has been paid or that there is no postage charge ■ *n* **1 OFFICIAL MARK ON PIECE OF MAIL** an official mark printed on a piece of mail to show that postage has been paid or that postage is free of charge **2 RIGHT TO FREE MAIL DELIVERY** the right to have mailed items delivered free of charge [14C. Via French, 'free, generous, candid' < medieval Latin *francus* 'Frank, free'; from the granting of full political freedom in Gaul only to the Franks.] —**frankness** *n*

Frank /frangk/ *n* a member of a Germanic people who lived along the Rhine valley and spread westwards during the decline of the Roman Empire in the 4th century AD [Old English *Franca* < Germanic]

Frank /frangk/, **Anne** (1929–45) German-born Dutch diarist

Frankenstein /frángkən stīn/ *n* **1 CREATOR OF DESTRUCTIVE THING** a creator of something that causes ruin or destruction, or that brings about a personal downfall **2 Frankenstein, Frankenstein's monster OUT-OF-CONTROL INVENTION** a creation or invention that gets beyond its maker's control and threatens harm or destruction **3 MONSTER** a monster typically represented as a very large coarse-featured person, often with features such as bolts in the neck and a shambling walk [Early 19C. < novel by Mary Shelley (1818), in which the main character, Baron *Frankenstein*, creates a living man.]

Frankenstein food *n* food or a food product produced using genetic engineering (*slang disapproving*)

Frankfurt[1] /frángk furt/, **Frankfurt am Main** /-am mīn/ city in west-central Germany, on the River Main. Population: 656,200 (1994).

Frankfurt[2] /-an der ṓdər/, **Frankfurt an der Oder** city in NE Germany, on the River Oder. Population: 87,863 (1989).

frankfurter /frángk furtər/, **frankfurt** /-furt/ *n* a thin-skinned sausage, originally from Germany, made of finely minced smoked pork or beef and grilled, fried, or boiled [Late 19C. < German *Frankfurter Wurst*, smoked sausage first produced at Frankfurt am Main.]

Frankfurter /frángk furtər/, **Felix** (1882–1965) Austrian-born US jurist

frankincense /frángkin senss/ *n* an aromatic gum or resin from an African tree, used as incense, especially in religious ceremonies, and in perfumes [14C. < Old French *franc encens* 'superior-quality incense'.]

franking machine *n* a machine that prints an official mark on items to be posted, and records the cost of posting, as an alternative to the use of postage stamps. US term **postage meter**

Frankish /frángkish/ *n* **EXTINCT GERMANIC LANGUAGE** an extinct Germanic language spoken by the Franks ■ *adj* **1 OF FRANKS** relating to the Franks **2 OF FRANKISH** relating to Frankish

Franklin /frángklin/ river in SW Tasmania, Australia. Length: 120 km/75 mi.

Franklin, Aretha (*b.* 1942) US soul singer

Franklin, Benjamin (1706–90) American diplomat, printer, author, and scientist

Franklin, Sir John (1786–1847) British naval officer and explorer

franklinite /frángkli nīt/ *n* a black weakly magnetic mineral of the spinel group, containing iron, manganese, and zinc [Early 19C. After *Franklin*, New Jersey.]

frankly /frángkli/ *adv* **1** in an honest, sincere, and often blunt or forthright way ○ *a number of personal questions that he answered remarkably frankly* **2** used to indicate that you are expressing an honest personal opinion, often a negative one ○ *Most of what she said was, frankly, a pack of lies.*

frantic /frántik/ *adj* **1** in a state in which it is impossible to keep feelings or behaviour under control, usually through fear, worry, or frustration **2** characterized by great haste and excitement and great deal of usually disorganized activity [Early 16C. < French *frénétique* (see FRENETIC).] —**frantically** *adv* —**franticness** *n*

~~**franticly**~~ incorrect spelling of **frantically**

Franz-Josef Glacier /fránts jṓzəf-/ glacier on the W coast of the South Island, New Zealand. Length: 11 km/7 mi.

Franz Josef Land /fránts jṓzəf-/ archipelago of about 100 small ice-covered islands in the Arctic Ocean, in NW Russia. Area: 20,700 sq. km/8,000 sq. mi.

frap /frap/ (**fraps, frapping, frapped**) *vt* to tie something down, or tie things together, with ropes [Mid-16C. < Old French *fraper* 'hit'.]

frappé /fráppay/ *adj* **CHILLED** chilled or poured over crushed ice ■ *n* **1 ICED ALCOHOLIC DRINK** an alcoholic drink, especially a liqueur, served poured over crushed ice **2 COLD DESSERT** a dish consisting of fruit-flavoured water ice, served before a meal or as a dessert [Mid-19C. < French, past participle of *frapper* 'hit, chill'.]

Frappuccino /fráppoo cheénō/ *tdmk* a trademark for coffee blended with milk, crushed ice, and flavourings

Fraser /fráyzər/ river in south-central British Columbia, Canada. Length: 1,370 km/850 mi.

Fraser, Dawn (*b.* 1937) Australian swimmer

Fraser, Malcolm (*b.* 1930) Australian statesman

Fraser, Neale Andrew (*b.* 1933) Australian tennis player

Fraser, Peter (1884–1950) Scottish-born New Zealand statesman

Fraser Island island off the coast of S Queensland, Australia. Population: 100. Area: 1,662 sq. km/642 sq. mi.

frass /frass/ *n* insect excrement or debris left behind by an insect or insect larva [Mid-19C. < German, < *fressen* 'eat, devour'.]

frat /frat/ *n US* a fraternity at a college or university (*informal*) [Late 19C. Shortening.]

fraternal /frə túrn'l/ *adj* **1 OF BROTHERS** existing between brothers or felt by one brother for another **2 SHOWING FRIENDSHIP AND MUTUAL SUPPORT** showing friendship and mutual support between people or groups with the same interests or aims ○ *fraternal greetings* **3 OF FRATERNITIES** relating to or organized as a fraternity **4 FROM TWO SEPARATE OVA** describes twins that have developed from two separate ova, rather than a single ovum [15C. < medieval Latin *fraternalis* < Latin *frater* 'brother'.] —**fraternalism** *n* —**fraternally** *adv*

fraternise *vi* = **fraternize**

fraternity /frə túrnəti/ (*plural* **-ties**) *n* **1 PEOPLE WITH SOMETHING IN COMMON** a group of people with something in common, e.g. being in the same job or sharing the same pastime ○ *the banking fraternity* **2 BROTHERLY LOVE** feelings of friendship and mutual support between people ○ *liberty, equality, and fraternity* **3 SOCIETY FORMED FOR COMMON PURPOSE** a group or society formed by people who share the same interests **4** *US* **SOCIETY FOR COLLEGE MEN** a social society for men who are students at an American college or university, with a name consisting of individually pronounced Greek letters. ◊ **sorority** [14C. Via French < Latin *fraternitas* < *frater* 'brother'.]

fraternize /fráttər nīz/ (**-nizes, -nizing, -nized**), **fraternise** (**-nises, -nising, -nised**) *vi* to spend time with other people socially, especially people with whom you should not be friendly ○ *fraternizing with the enemy* [Early 17C. Via French < medieval Latin *fraternizare* < Latin *frater* 'brother'.] —**fraternization** /fráttər nī záysh'n/ *n* —**fraternizer** *n*

fratricide /fráttri sīd, fráytri-/ *n* **1** the crime in which somebody kills his or her own brother **2** a killer of his or her own brother [15C. Via French < Latin *fratricida* 'brother-killer'.] —**fratricidal** /fráttri sīd'l, fráytri-/ *adj*

Frau /frow/ (*plural* **Frauen** /frówən/ *or* **Fraus**) *n* used as a title, equivalent to English 'Mrs' or 'Ms', before the name or professional title of a married woman in German-speaking countries, and as a courtesy title for some unmarried women, especially of senior status ○ *Frau Koch* [Early 19C. < German, 'woman, wife'.]

fraud /frawd/ *n* **1 CRIME OF CHEATING PEOPLE** the crime of obtaining money or some other benefit by deliberate deception **2 SOMEBODY WHO DECEIVES** a deliberate deceiver of people, usually for financial gain **3 SOMETHING INTENDED TO DECEIVE** something that is intended to deceive people ○ *a story that was subsequently exposed as a fraud* [14C. Via Old French < Latin *fraud-* 'cheating, fraud'.]

fraud squad *n* the branches of the British police force that have special responsibility for investigating crimes of fraud

fraudster /fráwdstər/ *n* a criminal who obtains money or some other benefit by deliberate deception

fraudulent /fráwdyoolənt/ *adj* not honest, true, or fair, and intended to deceive people —**fraudulence** *n* —**fraudulently** *adv*

fraught /frawt/ *adj* **1** full of or accompanied by problems, dangers, or difficulties ○ *an evening fraught with embarrassment* **2** full of, or expressing, nervous tension and anxiety ○ *looking fraught and close to tears* [14C. < past participle of obsolete *fraught* 'load with cargo' < Middle Dutch or Middle Low German *vrachten*.]

Fräulein /fróy līn, frów-/ (*plural* **-lein** *or* **-leins**) *n* used as a title, equivalent to the English 'Miss', before the name or professional title of a girl or an unmarried woman in German-speaking countries, and also as a form of address ○ *Fräulein Bauer* [Late 17C. < German, 'little woman' < *Frau* 'woman, wife'.]

Fraunhofer lines /frównhṓfər-/ *npl* narrow dark lines in the Sun's spectrum, caused mainly by absorption in the cooler outer layers of the Sun's atmosphere [Mid-19C. After Joseph von *Fraunhofer* (1787–1826), German scientist.]

fraxinella /fráksi néllə/ *n* PLANTS = **gas plant** [Mid-17C. < modern Latin, < Latin *fraxinus* 'ash tree'; from the shape of the leaves.]

fray[1] /fray/ *vti* **1 HANG IN THREADS** to wear away the edge or surface of cloth or rope by friction, or be worn away, causing threads to hang loose ○ *The jacket had frayed at the cuffs.* **2 BECOME STRAINED** to become strained, causing irritability or anger, or cause somebody's nerves, temper, or patience to become strained ○ *Soon tempers would start to fray.* ■ *n* **WORN PART WITH LOOSE THREADS** a worn area on cloth or rope, with loose threads showing [15C. Via French *frayer* < Latin *fricare* 'rub'.]

fray[2] /fray/ *n* 1 an argument, quarrel, or fight ○ *Local newspapers were not slow to join the fray.* 2 an exciting, energetic, or stressful activity or situation ○ *back to the fray* [14C. Shortening of AFFRAY.]

Fray Bentos /fray bén toss/ port in W Uruguay, on the River Uruguay. Population: 20,135 (1985).

frazil /fráyzil, frázzil/ *n* ice that forms as small plates drifting in rapidly flowing water where it is too turbulent for pack ice to form [Late 19C. < Canadian French *frasil*.]

frazzle /frázz'l/ *n* 1 EXHAUSTED STATE a state of complete emotional and physical exhaustion 2 *US* FRAYED STATE a frayed or tattered condition ■ *vt* (**-zles, -zling, -zled**) EXHAUST to tire somebody out emotionally and physically [Early 19C. Probably blend of FRAY[1] + FRIZZLE[1] or obsolete *fazle* 'ravel'.] ◇ **to a frazzle** 1 into a state of complete emotional and physical exhaustion 2 completely, especially until something is thoroughly scorched, blackened, or charred

frazzled /frázz'ld/ *adj* exhausted and in a very confused or irritable state (*informal*)

freak[1] /freek/ *n* 1 STRIKINGLY UNUSUAL PERSON, ANIMAL, PLANT a person, animal, or plant that is strikingly unusual, and appears to be unique or occurs very rarely (*offensive in some contexts*) 2 UNUSUAL OCCURRENCE a highly unusual or unlikely occurrence, often brought about by a unique or very rare combination of circumstances 3 SOMEBODY UNCONVENTIONAL somebody who is thought to behave unusually or have unusual tastes or habits (*informal insult*) 4 FANATIC somebody who is fanatical about something (*informal*) ○ *a club for fitness freaks* 5 DRUG USER an addict or user of a particular drug (*slang*) 6 IMPULSE something somebody suddenly does or decides for no real reason ■ *adj* HIGHLY UNUSUAL OR UNLIKELY highly unusual or unlikely, and often brought about by a unique or very rare combination of circumstances ■ *vti* 1 BECOME OR MAKE OVEREMOTIONAL to become, or make somebody feel, very nervous, upset, or angry (*informal*) ○ *She'll freak when she hears what she missed by not going with us.* 2 BEHAVE STRANGELY ON DRUGS to experience or cause somebody to experience wild or irrational behaviour, sometimes accompanied by hallucinations or feelings of paranoia, often as a result of taking drugs (*slang*) [Mid-16C. < ?]

freak[2] /freek/ *vt* to streak or spot something with colour (*archaic*) [Mid-17C. < ?]

freaking /freéking/ *adj US* an offensive term expressing strong feelings by similarity in sound to other offensive terms (*slang*)

freakish /freékish/ *adj* 1 extremely, disconcertingly, or ridiculously unusual (*offensive in some contexts*) ○ *a freakish accident* 2 tending to change suddenly and unpredictably ○ *freakish weather* —**freakishly** *adv*

freak-out, freakout /freék owt/ *n* 1 an outburst of emotion or wild behaviour (*informal*) 2 a drug-induced bout of hallucination or paranoia, especially a frightening one (*slang*)

freaky /freéki/ (**-ier, -iest**) *adj* unusual, strange, or bizarre (*slang*) —**freakily** *adv* —**freakiness** *n*

freckle /frék'l/ *n* a harmless small brownish patch on somebody's skin, usually one of a cluster, that becomes larger and deeper in colour when the skin is exposed to the sun ■ *vti* (**-les, -ling, -led**) to become marked with, or mark something with, freckles [15C. Alteration of obsolete *frecken* 'freckle' < Old Norse *freknur* 'freckles'.] —**freckly** *adj*

Frederick II /frédrik/ (1712–86) king of Prussia (1740–86). Known as **Frederick the Great**

Fredericton /frédriktən/ capital of New Brunswick, Canada, in the south-central part of the province. Population: 46,507 (1996).

free /free/ *adj* (**freer, freest**) 1 NOT REGULATED not controlled, restricted, or regulated by any external thing ○ *You are free to choose.* 2 NOT A PRISONER not, or no longer, physically bound or restrained, e.g. as a prisoner or in slavery ○ *Once outside the prison walls he would be a free man.* ○ *They hoped to be set free within the week.* 3 NOT RESTRICTED IN RIGHTS not subject to censorship or control by a ruler, government, or other authority, and enjoying civil liberties ○ *It's a free country.* 4 SELF-RULING not ruled by a foreign country or power 5 DISREGARDING TRADITIONAL LIMITATIONS performed or written without being subjected to traditional conventions or restraints ○ *free verse* 6 NOT AFFECTED not subject to or affected by a particular thing, especially something undesirable (*often in combination*) ○ *drinking water that is free of contamination* ○ *a trouble-free trip* 7 NOT CONTAINING not containing something specified (*often in combination*) ○ *a salt-free diet* 8 COSTING NOTHING requiring no money to be paid ○ *Win a free meal for two.* 9 NOT BUSY not busy or working ○ *We've had virtually no free time since the kids were born.* ○ *She'll be free in a moment.* 10 NOT BEING USED not being used, reserved, or taken by somebody else ○ *no free seats left* 11 NOT ATTACHED not tied or attached to something ○ *grabbed the free end of the rope* 12 NOT BLOCKED not blocked or obstructed by anything ○ *allowing the free flow of electricity* 13 NOT PHYSICALLY RESTRICTED not restricted by something such as tight clothing, stiffness, or lack of space ○ *a layer of dirt interfering with the free movement of the mechanism* 14 GIVING SOMETHING READILY giving or expending something generously or too readily ○ *They're very free with their advice.* 15 NOT EXACT not following the original version of something word for word or very precisely ○ *a free translation* 16 OPEN AND HONEST spontaneous, open, and without awkwardness or reserve in speaking to or dealing with other people ○ *an appealingly free and open manner* 17 NOT CHEMICALLY COMBINED not chemically combined with another substance 18 NOT BOUND not permanently incorporated in a larger body such as an atom, molecule, or compound 19 FAVOURABLE favourable to sailing ○ *a free wind* 20 ABLE TO BE USED ALONE describes a unit of meaning (**morpheme**) that can be used on its own as a word, rather than needing to be part of another word. ◊ **bound**[5] *adj.* 1 ■ *adv* WITHOUT COST without paying any money ○ *They let you in free if you show your student card.* ■ *vt* (**frees, freeing, freed**) 1 RELEASE FROM CAPTIVITY to release somebody from physical bonds or restrictions, captivity, or slavery ○ *The defendants were freed after having been found not guilty.* 2 RID OF to remove a restriction, a burden, or an unwanted or undesirable thing from somebody or something ○ *freed from the responsibilities of high public office* 3 MAKE AVAILABLE to make somebody or something available for use or able to do something ○ *This should free you to do more of your own research.* 4 UNCLOG to clear something of an obstruction [Old English *freo* < Indo-European, 'dear, beloved'] —**freeness** *n* ◇ **for free** without paying ◇ **make free with somebody** to behave in too familiar and informal a way towards somebody ◇ **make free with something** to use something in an over-familiar or overindulgent way, without showing respect or restraint

USAGE See ***gift***.

free up *vt* 1 to make available for use something that is currently occupied, otherwise employed, or subject to a restriction ○ *I need to free up some space on my hard disk.* 2 to enable something that is tightly fastened, jammed, or blocked to move freely (*informal*)

free agent *n* 1 a person who does not depend on or is not answerable to or for somebody else 2 *US* a professional athlete who is in a position to sign a contract to play for any team

free alongside ship *adj, adv* with the cost of delivery to the quayside included, but not the cost of loading onto a ship

free association *n* 1 the spontaneous and uncensored expression of thoughts or ideas, allowing each one to lead to or suggest the next 2 in psychoanalysis, a technique for exploring a patient's unconscious by stimulating the spontaneous and uncensored expression of thoughts or feelings through the use of stimuli such as key words —**free-associate** *vi*

freebase /freé bayss/ *v* (**-basing, -based, -based**) 1 *vt* PREPARE COCAINE FOR SMOKING to prepare cocaine for smoking by heating it with water and a volatile liquid 2 *vti* SMOKE COCAINE to smoke freebased cocaine (*slang*) ■ *n* CONCENTRATED COCAINE cocaine that has been concentrated using water and a volatile liquid [< the 'freeing' of the concentrated cocaine base]

freebie /freébi/ *n* something given or obtained free of charge, especially a promotional gift (*informal*)

freeboard /freé bawrd/ *n* the distance between the deck of a ship and the level of the water

freebooter /freé bootər/ *n* a plunderer, especially a pirate [Late 16C. < Dutch *vrijbuiter* 'somebody who takes booty freely'.] —**freeboot** *vi*

freeborn /freé bawrn/ *adj* 1 born as a free citizen, rather than in slavery or serfdom 2 relating to or intended for people who are freeborn

Free Church *n* a Protestant church free from state control in running its affairs, having separated from the church established as the official church of the state

free climbing *n* mountain or rock climbing without aids such as spikes and ladders, though usually with ropes and other safety equipment

freedman /-mən, -men/ (*plural* **-men**) *n* a man who has been freed from slavery

freedom /freédəm/ *n* 1 ABILITY TO ACT FREELY a state in which somebody is able to act and live as he or she chooses, without being subject to any, or to any undue, restraints or restrictions ○ *live in freedom* 2 RELEASE FROM CAPTIVITY OR SLAVERY release or rescue from being physically bound, or from being confined, enslaved, captured, or imprisoned ○ *hostages enjoying their first taste of freedom for months* 3 COUNTRY'S RIGHT TO SELF-RULE a country's right to rule itself, without interference from or domination by another country or power 4 RIGHT TO ACT OR SPEAK FREELY the right to speak or act without restriction, interference, or fear ○ *were given the freedom to take photographs and interview workers* 5 ABSENCE OF SOMETHING UNPLEASANT the state of being unaffected by, or not subject to, something unpleasant or unwanted ○ *Freedom from want or fear is one of society's four principal freedoms.* 6 EASE OF MOVEMENT the ability to move easily without being limited by something such as tight clothing or lack of space ○ *Releasing the catch allows complete freedom of movement in all directions.* 7 RIGHT TO TREAT PLACE AS OWN the right to use or occupy a place and treat it as your own ○ *In the closed season, we had the freedom of the whole house and the beach.* 8 HONORARY CITIZENSHIP citizenship of a town or city, together with special privileges, formally awarded to somebody as an honour 9 FRANKNESS openness and friendliness in speech or behaviour 10 EXCESSIVE CONFIDENCE OR FAMILIARITY overconfidence, overfamiliarity, or a lack of proper restraint or decorum 11 FREE WILL the ability to exercise free will and make choices independently of any external determining force

Freedom Charter *n* a document setting out the basic rights of all South Africans, composed in 1955 in opposition to the Nationalist government and constituting the manifesto of the African National Congress

freedom fighter *n* a participant in an armed revolution against a government or political system regarded as unjust

free electron *n* an electron that is not bonded to an atom or molecule and so is free to move under external electric or magnetic fields

free energy *n* (*symbol G*) a measure of the capacity of a system to do work, or a measure of the likelihood of a particular chemical reaction to form products

free enterprise *n* the doctrine or practice of giving business the freedom to trade and make a profit without government control

free fall, free-fall *n* 1 DESCENT WITH UNOPENED PARACHUTE a descent through the air with an unopened parachute as the first part of a parachute jump 2 RAPID DECLINE a sudden, rapid, and uncontrollable decline or descent in a particular system ○ *The news sent the stock market into a free fall.* 3 UNRESTRICTED MOVEMENT IN GRAVITATIONAL FIELD an ideal state in which the only force to which something is subjected is the earth's gravitational attraction

free-fall (**free-falls, free-falling, free-fell, free-fallen**) *vi* 1 to descend towards the ground with an unopened parachute during the first part of a parachute jump 2 to undergo a sudden sharp drop in value, popularity, or credibility

free-fire zone *n* an area in a zone of conflict where troops may fire on targets at will without requesting permission from a higher command

free flight *n* the movement of a rocket or missile through the air after its engine has stopped

free-floating *adj* not committed or dedicated to one specific thing, especially a political party or cause

free-floating anxiety *n* a state of anxiety that is not associated with any specific event or external condition

Freefone /freé fōn/ *tdmk* a trademark for a phone system in which the holder of the phone number pays the cost of the call, rather than the caller

free-for-all *n* a disorganized argument, contest, or fight, usually with everybody present joining in (*informal*)

free form *n* a shape, especially a piece of sculpture, that is asymmetrical and irregular though usually with a flowing outline

freeform /frée fawrm/ *adj* **1** unconventional in shape or design, especially flowing and curving as opposed to regular or geometrical **2** spontaneously or individually created, rather than being produced in accordance with accepted or prescribed standards

free hand *n* complete freedom to take action or make decisions

freehand /frée hand/ *adj, adv* done by hand and without using drawing instruments such as rulers or compasses

freehanded /free hándid/ *adj* giving generously —**freehandedly** *adv* —**freehandedness** *n*

freehold /frée hōld/ *n* **1** legal ownership of a property giving the owner unconditional rights, including the right to grant leases and take out mortgages **2** a property that has freehold status —**freeholder** *n*

free house *n* a pub that is not owned by a particular brewery and so is free to sell whatever beers and other products it chooses

free jazz *n* a style of jazz, developed in the 1960s, that has no set harmonies or melodic patterns

free kick *n* in football, a kick of a stationary ball for an infringement by opponents, who must stand at least 10 yards from where the kick is taken

free labour *n* workers who do not belong to any trade union

freelance /frée laanss/ *n* **1 freelance, freelancer** SOMEBODY WORKING FOR DIFFERENT COMPANIES a self-employed person working, or available to work, for a number of employers, rather than being committed to one, and usually hired for a limited period **2** MAVERICK somebody, especially a politician, who is not committed to any group and takes action or forms alliances independently **3 freelance, free lance** MEDIEVAL MERCENARY a mercenary soldier in medieval Europe ■ *adj* WORKING AS A FREELANCE working or earning a living as a freelance ■ *adv* AS A FREELANCE independently, as a freelance ○ *worked freelance as a journalist* ■ *vi* (**-lances, -lancing, -lanced**) WORK AS A FREELANCE to work independently as a freelance [Early 19C. < the idea of a medieval knight with a lance offering his services to whoever was willing to pay.]

free-living *adj* able to live or move independently, rather than being parasitic, symbiotic, or sessile ○ *free-living organisms*

freeloader /fréelōdər/ *n* an exploiter of somebody else's generosity or hospitality (*informal*) —**freeload** /fréelōd, free lṓd/ *vi*

free love *n* sexual relationships without marriage or commitment to a single partner, especially as practised by the 19th- and early-20th-century avant-garde and in the 1960s

free lunch *n* something given free and with nothing expected in return (*informal*)

freely /fréeli/ *adv* **1** WITHOUT RESTRICTIONS without restrictions, controls, or limits ○ *able to move freely from country to country* **2** IN LARGE AMOUNTS in large or generous quantities ○ *Conversation flowed freely all night.* **3** OPENLY honestly and openly ○ *felt able to speak freely about his ordeal for the first time* **4** WITHOUT TIGHTNESS OR STIFFNESS without being restricted by something such as tight clothing, stiffness, or lack of space ○ *clothes that allowed him to move more freely* **5** USED TO EMPHASIZE HONESTY used to persuade others that you are being open and honest by accepting criticism ○ *I freely admit that mistakes were made.*

freeman /fréemən/ (*plural* **-men** /-mən/) *n* **1** a man who is not enslaved or not in serfdom **2** a man who has been formally given citizenship of a place, together with various special privileges, as an honour ○ *a freeman of the city*

Freeman /fréemən/, **Cathy** (*b.* 1973) Australian sprinter

free market *n* an economic system in which businesses operate without government control in matters such as pricing and wage levels —**free-market** *adj* —**free-marketeer** *n*

freemartin /frée maartin/ *n* a sterile female twin born with a male calf [Late 17C. < ?]

freemason /frée mayss'n/ *n* a member of an organization of skilled stonemasons travelling from place to place in medieval Europe [14C. < ?]

Freemason *n* a member of a worldwide society of men, the Free and Accepted Masons, that is known particularly for its charitable work and its secret rites

Freemasonry /frée mayss'nri/ *n* **1** the institutions, beliefs, and practices of the Freemasons **2 Freemasonry, freemasonry** an instinctive understanding and comradeship amongst people with something in common

⚡**freenet** /frée net/ *n* an online computer information network that charges no access fees, often run by volunteers as a public service

free on board *adj, adv* with the cost of delivery to a port and loading onto a ship included

free on rail *adj, adv* with the cost of delivery to a railway station and loading onto a train included

free port *n* **1** a port open to commercial ships from all countries on equal terms **2** a zone, connected to a port or airport, that allows the duty-free import of goods that are to be re-exported

free radical *n* a highly reactive atom or group of atoms with an unpaired electron

free-range *adj* **1** free to move about and feed at will, rather than being confined in a battery or pen ○ *free-range chickens* **2** produced by free-range poultry or livestock ○ *free-range eggs*

free rein *n* complete freedom to make decisions and take action without consulting anyone else

free ride *n* something obtained at no cost or with no effort

freesheet /frée sheet/ *n* a free newspaper or news sheet, especially one delivered to all the households in a particular area and funded by advertising

freesia /frée<u>zh</u>ə, fréezi ə/ *n* a plant grown from a corm, popular as a cut flower. Flowers: fragrant, tubular, brightly coloured. Native to: southern Africa. Genus: *Freesia*. [Late 19C. After Friedrich H. T. *Freese* (1795–1896), German physician.]

free skating *n* competitive ice skating in which the skater makes up his or her own programme from a list of approved moves

free space *n* a region in which there is no matter and no gravitational or electromagnetic fields

free speech *n* the right to express any opinion publicly

free spirit *n* a person who lives without regard to what convention dictates or what others expect —**free-spirited** *adj* —**free-spiritedness** *n*

free-spoken *adj* expressing opinions frankly, without worrying about embarrassing or offending others

freestanding /free stánding/ *adj* **1** standing alone, and not fixed to a wall, floor, or other structure for support **2** grammatically independent and able to function as a main clause

Free State[1] *n* US NONSLAVE STATE OF UNITED STATES any one of the US states that prohibited slavery before the American Civil War

Free State[2] province of South Africa, in the centre of the country, north of the Orange River

freestone /frée stōn/ *n* **1** a variety of masonry stone that has a uniform texture and can be chiselled without breaking or splitting, e.g. limestone or fine sandstone **2** a stone to which the flesh of a fruit does not cling, or any fruit that has such a stone

freestyle /frée stīl/ *adj* **1** WITH FREE CHOICE OF STYLE describes sporting events in which each competitor may use a style of his or her own choosing **2** USING FRONT CRAWL describes a swimming contest in which the competitors can use any swimming stroke, usually the front crawl stroke **3** NO-HOLDS-BARRED describes a wrestling style in which all legal holds and tactics are allowed ■ *n* FREESTYLE CONTEST a freestyle race or event —**freestyler** *n*

freestyle wrestling *n* = **all-in wrestling**

freet /freet/ *n Ireland* a superstition [Mid-16C. < Old Norse *frett* 'news, inquiry, augury'.]

freethinker /free thíngkər/ *n* an independent thinker who refuses to accept established views or teachings, especially on religion —**freethinking** *adj, n*

free thought *n* thinking that does not recognize the authority of, and is unrestricted by, established views or teachings, especially in religious matters

free throw *n* in basketball, an opportunity to shoot at the basket unhindered by the opposing players, awarded to a player who has been fouled

Freetown /frée town/ capital, largest city, and chief port of Sierra Leone, on the coast of W Africa. Population: 470,000 (1994 estimate).

free trade *n* international trade that is not subject to protective regulations or tariffs intended to restrict foreign imports —**free-trader** *n*

free verse *n* verse without a fixed metrical pattern, usually having unrhymed lines of varying length

free vote *n* a vote in the British parliament or any similar body in which members may vote according to their consciences and personal opinions rather than as instructed by their party leaders

⚡**freeware** /frée wair/ *n* any computer program or application that is available at no cost

freeway /frée way/ *n* **1** *US, Can, Aus* a limited-access road usually consisting of three lanes for vehicles moving in both directions, intended for travelling relatively fast over long distances **2** *US* a road that can be used without paying a toll

free-weight *n* a weight such as a dumbbell or barbell that is used for lifting exercises and is not attached to any other piece of apparatus

freewheel /free wéel/ *vi* **1** TRAVEL WITHOUT USING POWER to continue moving on a bicycle or in a vehicle without using power to drive the wheels ○ *Once you get to the top, you can freewheel all the way down the other side.* **2** LIVE IN CAREFREE WAY to live or act without conventional constraints, purpose, or regard for responsibilities ■ *n* **1** DEVICE ON BICYCLE a mechanism in the hub of the rear wheel of a bicycle that enables the rear wheel to continue to rotate when the rider stops pedalling **2** DEVICE IN MOTOR VEHICLE TRANSMISSION a mechanism in the transmission of a motor vehicle that disengages the drive shaft and allows it to rotate freely when revolving at a higher speed than the engine shaft

freewheeling /free wéeling/ *adj* **1** TRAVELLING WITHOUT POWER continuing to move without the use of power **2** *US, Can* CAREFREE without conventional constraints, purpose, or regard for responsibilities ○ *led a freewheeling life of travel and adventure* **3** *US, Can* UNSTRUCTURED not restricted by rules, formal structure, or established procedures ○ *a freewheeling discussion that touched on many topics* **4** WITH A FREEWHEEL relating to, having, or using a freewheel mechanism on a bicycle or vehicle

free will *n* the ability to act or make choices as a free and autonomous being and not solely as a result of compulsion or predestination ◇ **of your own free will** without being forced by somebody or something else

freewill /frée wil/ *adj* done willingly rather than by compulsion

free world *n* the countries of the world with democratic governments and capitalistic or moderately Socialistic economic systems, as opposed to those with totalitarian or Communist governments or economic systems

⚡**freeze** /freez/ *v* (**freezes, freezing, froze** /frōz/, **frozen** /frṓz'n/) **1** *vti* TURN TO SOLID THROUGH COLD to be changed, or cause liquid to change, into a solid by the loss of heat, especially to change water into ice or be changed into ice ○ *Salt water freezes at a lower temperature than fresh water.* **2** *vti* BECOME COVERED WITH ICE to become covered, or cause the surface of something to be covered, with ice ○ *The lake froze for only the second time in living memory.* **3** *vti* BECOME BLOCKED WITH ICE to become blocked, or cause something to become blocked, with ice ○ *Do you think it's cold enough to freeze the pipes in the attic?* **4** *vti* BECOME HARD THROUGH COLD to harden, or cause something to harden, through the effects of cold or frost ○ *We couldn't play because the ground was frozen solid.* **5** *vti* BECOME STUCK THROUGH COLD to become, or cause something to become, fixed or stuck to something else as a result of cold ○ *The wipers were frozen to the windscreen.* **6** *vt* PRESERVE WITH EXTREME COLD to preserve something, especially food, by subjecting it to and storing it at a temperature well below freezing point ○ *Store airtight up to two weeks or freeze.* **7** *vti* FEEL VERY COLD to feel, or cause somebody to feel, extremely cold ○ *They left us to freeze outside, while they went into the house.* **8** *vti* BE HARMED OR KILLED BY COLD to be harmed or killed, or harm or kill somebody or something, with cold or frost **9** *vi* DROP TO FREEZING POINT to be at or fall to a temperature at or below freezing point ○ *The forecast says it's likely to freeze again tonight.* **10** *vti* STOP MOVING to stop, or cause somebody to stop and remain still, e.g. as a result of fear or surprise or as part of a game ○ *A loose floorboard creaked in the passage; Jenny froze.* **11** *vi* COME TO A STANDSTILL THROUGH SHOCK to become unable to act, react, or speak in a normal way, usually through fear or shock ○ *I was OK in rehearsals, but in front of an audience, I simply froze.* **12** *vi* to stop responding (*refers to computers*) ○ *The screen freezes whenever I attempt to save a document.* **13** *vt* **TREAT ICILY** to discourage or intimidate somebody by behaving in an unfriendly or hostile way ○ *She froze him with an icy glare.* **14** *vt* **HALT BEFORE COMPLETION** to halt or limit the development or production of something ○ *The talks remain frozen at the procedural stage.* **15** *vt* **KEEP AT PRESENT LEVEL** to fix something such as prices, rents, or wages at a particular level, usually by government action to prevent an increase ○ *Interest rates were frozen at their 1996 level.* **16** *vt* **KEEP ASSET FROM DISAPPEARING** to prevent a financial asset from being sold or liquidated ○ *They froze her bank account.* **17** *vt* **PROHIBIT** to stop the manufacture, sale, or use of something **18** *vi* **BECOME UNFRIENDLY** to become suddenly unfriendly and uncommunicative ○ *When I asked him about campaign contributions, he simply froze.* **19** *vt* **ANAESTHETIZE** to anaesthetize part of somebody's body with a local anaesthetic (*informal*) **20** *vt* **STOP FILM AT PARTICULAR FRAME** to stop a moving film at a particular frame and show that frame as a still image **21** *vt* **CAPTURE INSTANT OF MOVEMENT** to produce a still photographic image of somebody or something in movement or action ○ *He pressed the Pause button, freezing her delighted expression.* ■ *n* **1 VERY COLD WEATHER** a period when the temperature drops and stays below freezing point, especially for a long time **2 RESTRICTION** a restrictive measure that prevents something such as prices, wages, or production from rising above a particular level ○ *a temporary freeze on imports* [Old English *frēosan* < Indo-European, 'freeze, burn']

SPELLCHECK Do not confuse ***freeze*** with ***frieze***, which has a similar sound. Beware: your spellchecker will not catch this error.

freeze out *vt* to exclude somebody from participation in something by cold or unfriendly treatment ○ *We feel we are being frozen out of the negotiations.*

freeze up *v* **1** *vi* to become blocked with ice **2** *vt* to hold something fast in ice so that it cannot move (*usually passive*) ○ *The ship was frozen up in the Arctic for three months.*

freeze-dry *vt* to preserve something, especially food, by first freezing it, then placing it in a vacuum to remove moisture before returning it to room temperature —**freeze-dried** *adj* —**freeze-drying** *n*

freeze-etching *n* the preparation of a specimen for examination by an electron microscope by freezing and fracturing it so that its internal structure can be seen and a replica made of it

freeze-frame *n* **1 FRAME OF FILM VIEWED SINGLY** a single frame of a film or video recording viewed as a static image **2 DEVICE ALLOWING VIEWING OF SINGLE FRAME** a device on a video recorder that enables a single static image to be viewed ■ *vt* **PRESENT AS STATIC IMAGE** to present something contained in a single frame from a film or video recording as a static image

freezer /fréezər/ *n* a storage cabinet, compartment, or room where food or other perishable goods can be frozen and preserved at a very low temperature

freezer burn *n* the pale dry spots that form when moisture evaporates from frozen food that is inadequately wrapped

freeze-up *n* a period of extremely cold weather

freezing /fréezing/ *adj* extremely cold ■ *n* the freezing point of water

freezing mixture *n* a mixture of substances, usually ice and salt, used in laboratories to produce a temperature below the freezing point of water

freezing point *n* the temperature at which a liquid solidifies, e.g. the temperature at which water turns to ice

free zone *n* an area at a port or in a city where goods may be received or stored without payment of customs duties

Frege /fráygə/, **Gottlob** (1848–1925) German mathematician and logician

F region *n* the highest part of the ionosphere that reflects high-frequency radio waves. It is divided into two layers, the F_1 that extends upwards from 180 km/112 mi. and is present only during the day, and the F_2 extending upwards from 300 km/186 mi.

Freiburg /frī burg/ city in SW Germany. Population: 197,800 (1994).

Freidel-Crafts reaction *n* a chemical reaction using metallic halides, e.g. aluminium chloride, or acids as catalysts. Use: chemical manufacture.

freight /frayt/ *n* **1 GOODS FOR TRANSPORT** goods or cargo carried by a commercial means of transport **2 COMMON CLASS OF TRANSPORT** the ordinary method or class of commercial transport for goods, slower and cheaper than express **3 CHARGE FOR CARRYING GOODS** a charge paid for the transport of goods **4** *US* RAIL = **freight train 5 BURDEN** a load or burden (*literary*) ■ *vt* **1 TRANSPORT GOODS** to send or transport goods or cargo by commercial carrier **2 LOAD WITH CARGO** to load a ship, train, aircraft, or vehicle with goods or cargo to be transported **3 HIRE SHIP** to hire or hire out a ship to transport goods and passengers **4 BURDEN** to load something or somebody with something such as feeling, significance, or emotion (*literary; usually passive*) [15C. < Middle Low German or Middle Dutch *vrecht*.]

freightage /fráytij/ *n* **1 TRANSPORT CHARGE** a charge paid for the transport of goods or cargo **2 COMMERCIAL CARRIAGE OF GOODS** the commercial transport of goods or cargo **3 GOODS CARRIED** the goods that are carried by a particular ship or vehicle

freight car *n* a railway wagon that carries freight, usually one that is enclosed

freighter /fráytər/ *n* **1** a ship or aircraft designed to carry freight **2** an employee who sends, forwards, or receives freight, or who charters something to carry freight

freight ton *n* a unit used in measuring and pricing freight in maritime shipping, varying according to the type of goods carried but usually corresponding to 1,000 kilograms or 40 cubic feet

freight train *n* a railway train that carries only freight

~~**freind**~~ incorrect spelling of **friend**

Frei Ruiz-Tagle /fráy roo éess taá glay/, **Eduardo** (*b.* 1942) Chilean government leader

~~**freize**~~ incorrect spelling of **frieze**

Fremantle /freé mant'l/ port in SW Western Australia. Population: 23,834 (1991).

fremitus /frémmitəss/ (*plural* **-tus**) *n* a vibration or tremor, resulting from a physical action such as speaking or coughing, felt by hand and used to assess whether the chest is affected by disease [Early 19C. < Latin, 'roaring' < *fremere* 'to roar'.]

frena plural of **frenum**

French /french/ *n* **1 LANGUAGE OF FRANCE** the official language of France and some other countries, belonging to the Romance group of Indo-European that developed from Latin. Native speakers: 70 million. Other speakers: 220 million. **2 FRENCH VERMOUTH** French vermouth ■ *npl* **FRENCH PEOPLE** the people of France [Old English *frencisc* < Germanic] —**French** *adj*

French bean *n* **1** a long slim green bean pod eaten whole as a vegetable. US term **string bean** *n.* 2 **2** a small bushy or tall climbing bean plant with slim green pods. Flowers: white or purplish. *Phaseolus vulgaris.* US = **string bean** *n.* 1

French bread *n* white bread in the form of a long slim cylindrical loaf with a crisp crust and soft inside

French Cameroons /-kámmə roónz/ former French-administered region in west-central Africa, now part of Cameroon

French Canada *n* the parts of Canada where French is spoken

French-Canadian *n* **1 French-Canadian, French Canadian** somebody who comes from a French-speaking part of Canada **2** the form of the French language spoken in Canada —**French-Canadian** *adj*

French chalk *n* a soft white variety of talc used by tailors to make marks on cloth and by dry cleaners to remove grease stains from clothes

French Creole *n* somebody of European and African descent whose ancestors were French immigrants to Trinidad

French cricket *n* an informal form of cricket that is played with bats and a soft ball, with the batter's legs acting as the wicket

French cuff *n* a wide cuff, usually for a shirtsleeve, designed to be folded back upon itself and fastened with a cuff link

French curve *n* a thin piece of plastic or other material with curved edges and a number of curved shapes cut out of it, designed to help designers and engineers draw curves

French door *n US* = **French window**

French dressing *n* **1** a salad dressing made of oil and vinegar with seasoning, whisked or shaken until emulsified or mixed **2** *US* a creamy salad dressing, usually made commercially, consisting of mayonnaise with tomato flavouring

French Equatorial Africa /-ekwə táwri əl-/ former French territory in west-central Africa, comprising the present-day countries of the Central African Republic, Chad, the Republic of Congo, and Gabon

French Foreign Legion *n* a section of the French army consisting of foreign volunteers

French fried potatoes *npl* thin strips of potato fried in deep fat

French fries *npl* thin strips of potato fried in deep fat

French Guiana /-gī ánnə, -gi aánə/ overseas region of France, on the NE coast of South America. Capital: Cayenne. Population: 114,808 (1990). Area: 91,000 sq. km/35,135 sq. mi. —**French Guianan** *adj, n* —**French Guianese** /-gī ə neéz, -gi-/ *adj, n*

French Guinea former name for **Guinea**

French heel *n* a curved heel of medium height for women's shoes

French horn *n* a brass musical instrument with a long looped pipe ending in a wide round bell, with other pipes and valves attached to it within the loop

Frenchify /frénchi fī/ (**-fies, -fying, -fied**) *vt* to give a French appearance or character to something or somebody, especially in a way considered overrefined and decadent —**Frenchification** /frénchifi káysh'n/ *n*

French India former territory comprising four French colonies on the coast of E India

French kiss *n* a kiss in which one partner's tongue is inserted in the other partner's mouth

French knickers *npl* women's wide-legged knickers

French knot *n* an embroidery stitch made by looping the thread around the needle before pushing it through the fabric

French leave *n* a quick departure or absence, without explanation or permission [< a supposed French custom of leaving a party without saying goodbye]

French letter *n* a condom (*dated informal*) [< ?]

Frenchman /frénchmən/ (*plural* **-men**) *n* a man who comes from France

Frenchmans Cap /frénchmənz-/ mountain in SW Tasmania, Australia. Height: 1,443 m/4,734 ft.

French marigold *n* a widely cultivated ornamental flower. Flowers: yellowish-orange heads with red petals. *Tagetes patula.*

French mustard *n* a mild-tasting mustard made with wine or unripe grape juice

French pleat *n* a woman's hairstyle in which the hair is formed into a vertical roll at the back of the head. US term **French roll**

French polish *n* shellac dissolved in alcohol, used as a varnish for wood

French-polish *vt* to varnish something with French polish

French press pot *n US* = **cafetière**

French Republican Calendar, French Revolutionary Calendar *n* the calendar adopted by the French during and briefly after the French Revolution. It had 12 months of 30 days, each made up of three ten-day weeks.

French roll *n* HAIR = **French pleat**

French roof *n* a mansard roof

French seam *n* a seam stitched twice, completely enclosing the raw edges of the fabric

French stick *n* a thin loaf of French bread

French Sudan former name for **Mali** (1898–1959)

French toast *n* sliced bread dipped in egg beaten with milk, lightly fried or grilled and served dusted with sugar, as a sweet, or as a savoury snack

French twist *n* HAIR = **French pleat**

French vermouth *n* unsweetened vermouth

French West Africa former French territory in W Africa, comprising the present-day countries of Benin,

Burkina Faso, Côte d'Ivoire, Guinea, Mali, Mauritania, Niger, and Senegal

French window *n* either of a pair of doors in an outside wall made of glass panels and opening in the middle (*usually plural*)

Frenchwoman /frénch wŏŏmən/ (*plural* **-en** /-wimin/) *n* a woman who comes from France

frenetic /frə néttik/ *adj* characterized by feverish activity, confusion, and hurry ○ *frenetic activity* [14C. Via French and Latin < Greek *phrenētikos* < *phrenitis* 'delirium' < *phrēn* 'mind'.] —**frenetically** *adv* —**freneticism** /-néttissizəm/ *n*

frenulum /frénnyŏŏləm/ (*plural* **-la** /-lə/) *n* **1** a small stiff bristle on the hind wing of moths that keeps the forewings and hind wings together during flight **2** a small fold of skin or membrane that limits the movement of an organ, typically smaller than a frenum [Early 18C. < modern Latin, 'small fraenum' < Latin *frenum* (see FRAENUM).]

frenum /freenəm/ (*plural* **-nums** *or* **-na**), **fraenum** (*plural* **-nums** *or* **-na** /-nə/) *n* a small fold of skin or membrane that limits the movement of an organ, especially the band of tissue connecting the tongue to the floor of the mouth [Mid-18C. < Latin *frenum* 'bridle' < *frendere* 'grind'.]

frenzied /frénzid/ *adj* characterized by uncontrolled activity, agitation, or emotion such as excitement or rage —**frenziedly** *adv* —**frenziedness** *n*

frenzy /frénzi/ *n* **1** a state of uncontrolled activity, agitation, or emotion such as excitement or rage **2** a burst of energetic activity [14C. Via Old French < medieval Latin *phrenesia* < Greek *phrenitis* (see FRENETIC).]

freq. *abbr* **1** frequency **2** frequentative **3** frequently

frequency /freekwənssi/ (*plural* **-cies**) *n* **1 frequency, frequence** FREQUENT OCCURRENCE the fact of happening often or regularly at short intervals ○ *quite good friends, judging by the frequency of his visits* **2** RATE OF OCCURRENCE the number of times that something happens during a particular period of time ○ *We're trying to establish the frequency of his visits. Did he come once a month?* **3** BROADCASTING WAVELENGTH a wavelength on which a radio or television signal is broadcast and to which a receiving set can be tuned **4** RATE OF RECURRENCE (*symbol* **ν** *or* **f**) the number of times that something such as an oscillation, a waveform, or a cycle is repeated within a particular length of time, usually one second **5** NUMBER OF OCCURRENCES OF STATISTICAL RESULT the number of times a particular result occurs in a statistical survey (**absolute frequency**), or the ratio of that number to the total results obtained in the survey (**relative frequency**)

frequency distribution *n* a way of classifying statistical data that allows comparisons of the results in each category

frequency modulation *n* a method of radio transmission in which the frequency of the wave carrying the signal is varied in accordance with the particularities of the sound being broadcast

frequent *adj* /freekwənt/ **1** OCCURRING OFTEN happening often or regularly at short intervals ○ *Her frequent appearances on television suggested she was moving up the party hierarchy.* **2** HABITUAL belonging to the class specified on a regular basis ○ *a frequent visitor to the museum* ■ *vt* /fri kwént/ GO OFTEN TO to go to or be in a place often [15C. Via French < Latin *frequent-* 'crowded, numerous'.] —**frequentation** /free kwen táysh'n/ *n* —**frequenter** *n* —**frequentness** *n*

frequentative /fri kwéntətiv/ *adj* describes a verb, verb form, or affix that expresses repeated action ■ *n* a frequentative verb, verb form, or affix

frequently /freekwəntli/ *adv* on many occasions with little time between them ○ *They change their address so frequently, it's difficult to know where to send the letter.*

fresco /fréskō/ *n* (*plural* **-coes** *or* **-cos**) **1** PAINTING DONE ON FRESH PLASTER a painting on a wall or ceiling done by rapidly brushing watercolours onto fresh damp or partly dry plaster **2** TECHNIQUE OF PAINTING ON FRESH PLASTER the technique or method of painting on fresh plaster ■ *vt* (**-coes, -coing, -coed**) PAINT WALL OR CEILING WITH FRESCO to paint a fresco on a wall or ceiling [Late 16C. < Italian, 'fresh' (referring to plaster).] —**frescoer** *n* —**frescoist** *n*

fresh /fresh/ *adj* **1** NOT STALE recently harvested or made and showing no sign of staleness or decay ○ *Peas fresh from the pod.* **2** NOT PRESERVED not having been preserved, matured, or processed, e.g. by canning or freezing ○ *You can't get fresh peas here, only canned or frozen.* **3** ADDITIONAL OR AS REPLACEMENT additional to or replacing something that existed, was used before, or is past its best ○ *I took out the old ink cartridge and put in a fresh one.* **4** NEW new or clean and showing no signs of previous use ○ *The hotel provides fresh towels.* **5** NOT AFFECTED BY TIME not changed, diminished, or spoiled by the passage of time ○ *Write it down while it's still fresh in your memory.* **6** WHOLESOME natural, pure, and wholesome, especially in smell ○ *the fresh smell of clean linen* **7** EXCITINGLY DIFFERENT excitingly or refreshingly different from what somebody is used to or what has been done previously ○ *fresh ideas.* **8** NOT TIRED alert and full of energy ○ *I'd better get this done while my mind is still fresh.* **9** NOT SALT describes water that is not salty **10** BLOWING STRONGLY describes a breeze or wind that is blowing quite strongly (*refers to a breeze or wind*) **11** COOL cool or colder than usual **12** BRIGHT pleasantly bright, light, and pure or clear **13** HEALTHY healthy-looking and clear in appearance ○ *a fresh complexion* **14** MAKING UNWANTED SEXUAL ADVANCES making inappropriate sexual overtures to somebody (*informal*) **15** OVERFAMILIAR bold and overfamiliar towards somebody, especially towards somebody considered a superior (*informal*) ○ *Don't you get fresh with me, young man.* **16** RECENTLY ARRIVED having recently come from a place, activity, or event ○ *Fresh from his trip to the Antarctic, Sir Ronald is in the studio to tell us about his experiences.* **17** WITHOUT EXPERIENCE lacking experience **18** HAVING RECENTLY CALVED having recently calved and able to give milk ■ *adv* RECENTLY quite recently ■ *n* COOL PERIOD the cool early part of the day [Old English *fersc* 'pure, not salty', and partly < Old French *freis* 'new, recent' < Germanic] —**freshness** *n*

SYNONYMS See ***new***.

fresh breeze *n* a force-five wind on the Beaufort scale, blowing at between 30 and 38 km/h/19 and 24 mph

freshen /frésh'n/ *v* **1** *vti* MAKE OR BECOME FRESH to make something fresh or fresher or to become fresh or fresher **2** *vi* INCREASE IN STRENGTH to blow more strongly (*refers to wind*) ○ *wind force three, freshening from the southwest* **3** *vt* REFILL A DRINK to refill somebody's glass or drink —**freshener** *n*

freshen up *v* **1** *vi* make yourself clean and neat by washing or changing clothes **2** *vt* = **freshen** *v.* 3

fresher /fréshər/ *n* a student in the first year at college or university (*informal*) US term **freshman** *n.* 1 [Late 19C. < shortening of FRESHMAN.]

freshet /fréshət/ *n* **1** a small sudden flood or rise in the level of a river, caused by heavy rainfall or a rapid thaw, especially after a period of dry weather **2** a stream of fresh water emptying into a body of salt water [Late 16C. Probably < Old French *freschete* < *freis* (see FRESH).]

fresh gale *n* a force-eight wind on the Beaufort scale, blowing at between 62 and 74 km/h/39 and 46 mph

freshly /fréshli/ *adv* done recently

freshman /fréshmən/ (*plural* **-men**) *n* **1** EDUC = **fresher 2** *US* a beginner, or a newcomer to a post or position

freshwater /frésh wawtər/ *adj* **1** relating to, consisting of, or living in fresh water **2** used on or accustomed to only inland waters, not the sea

Fresnel lens /fráy nel-/ *n* a thin lens of short focal length with a surface consisting of concentric rings, each having a curvature corresponding to a similar ring of a plain convex lens [Mid-19C. After Augustin-Jean *Fresnel* (1788–1827), French physicist.]

Fresno /fréznō/ city in central California. Population: 398,133 (1998 estimate).

fret[1] /fret/ *v* (**frets, fretting, fretted**) **1** *vti* WORRY to be or cause somebody to be worried, irritated, or agitated about something **2** *vti* WEAR AWAY to wear away or corrode the surface of something, or become worn away or corroded **3** *vt* MAKE BY CONSTANT RUBBING to create a hole or groove in something by constant wear or rubbing **4** *vti* FLOW IN RIPPLES to flow, or cause water to flow, with a constant busy rippling motion or with small choppy waves (*literary*) ○ *'I love the brooks that down their channels fret'* (Wordsworth, *Ode on Intimations of Immortality*; 1807) ■ *n* **1** FRETTING STATE a restless complaining state brought on by anxiety or irritation ○ *The baby's in a fret.* **2** HOLE MADE BY FRETTING a hole, groove, or mark made by constant wear or rubbing [Old English *fretan* 'devour' < Germanic, 'eat up']

fret[2] /fret/ *n* a small ridge across the fingerboard of a stringed instrument such as a guitar or sitar, indicating the position in which to place the fingers to produce a particular note [Early 16C. < ?] —**fretted** *adj*

fret[3] /fret/ *n* a pattern of repeated geometrical figures, usually consisting of straight lines, used as an ornament or in an ornamental border [14C. < Old French *frete* 'trellis'.] —**fret** *vt*

fretful /frétf'l/ *adj* easily worried, irritated, or agitated by something —**fretfully** *adv* —**fretfulness** *n*

fretman (*plural* **-men**) *n* a musician who plays guitar, especially in jazz or pop music (*slang*)

fretsaw /frét saw/ *n* a saw with a thin narrow fine-toothed blade usually mounted across a U-shaped frame, used for cutting curved shapes in wood [Mid-19C. < FRET³.]

fretwork /frét wurk/ *n* **1** ornamental woodwork made by cutting holes in a piece of wood with a fretsaw to create an intricate pattern of wood and spaces **2** decorative designs consisting of frets [Early 17C. < FRET³.]

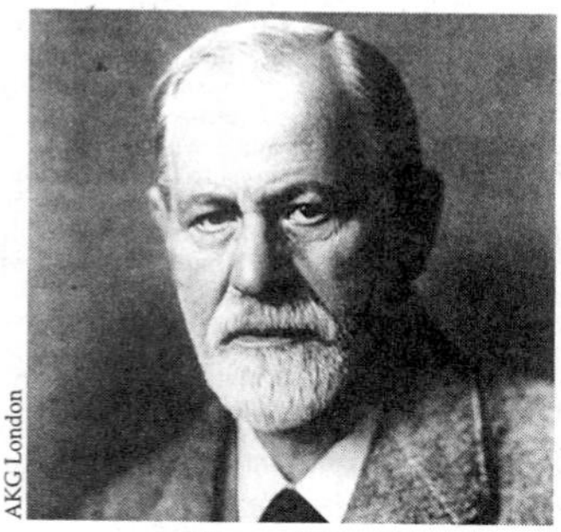

Sigmund Freud

Freud /froyd/, **Sigmund** (1856–1939) Austrian physician and founder of psychoanalysis

Freudian /fróydi ən/ *adj* **1** RELATING TO FREUD relating to Sigmund Freud, his writings, or his psychoanalytical theories and methods **2** CONCERNING ROLE OF SEXUALITY IN BEHAVIOUR demonstrating or understandable in terms of Freud's theories, especially with regard to sexuality and its role in human relations ■ *n* FOLLOWER OF FREUD somebody who follows Freud or is influenced by Freud's theories or methods of psychoanalysis

Freudianism /fróydi ənizəm/ *n* Freud's psychological theories and psychoanalytical methods, considered as a body of teaching, or adherence to these theories or methods

QUICK FACTS ON... **FREUDIANISM**

Key dates: 1890–1939
Key locations: Austria, United Kingdom, United States
Key elements: primacy of unconscious; influence of sexuality and childhood neuroses; interpretation of dreams; use of analysis to treat neuroses
Key figures: Sigmund Freud, Josef Breuer, Carl Jung, Alfred Adler, Ernest Jones, Erich Fromm
Key works: *Studies in Hysteria* (Breuer and Freud) 1895, *The Interpretation of Dreams* (Freud) 1900, *Beyond the Pleasure Principle* (Freud) 1920, *Hamlet and Oedipus* (Jones) 1949, *The Sane Society* (Fromm) 1955
Key developments: psychoanalysis, Jungian analytical psychology, use of dream imagery in art, psychotherapy

Freudian slip *n* an accidental mistake, usually the use of the wrong word in a sentence, thought to betray somebody's subconscious preoccupations

Freyberg /frī burg/, **Bernard Cyril, 1st Baron of Wellington and Munstead** (1889–1963) British-born New Zealand general and statesman

Freycinet Peninsula /fráyssinət-/ peninsula in E Tasmania, Australia. Length: 30 km/19 mi.

FRG *abbr* Federal Republic of Germany

Fri. *abbr* Friday

friable /frī əb'l/ *adj* easily reduced to tiny particles ○ *sand incorporated to make the soil more friable* [Mid-16C. Directly or via French < Latin *friabilis* < *friare* 'crumble'.] —**friability** /frī ə bílləti/ *n* —**friableness** *n*

SYNONYMS See ***fragile***.

friar /frī ər/ *n* a man belonging to any of several Roman Catholic religious orders [13C. Via French *frère* < Latin *frater* 'brother'.] —**friarly** *adj*

friar's balsam *n* a mixture containing benzoin. Use: as an inhalant, for colds and sore throats.

friar's lantern *n* SCI = **will-o'-the-wisp** *n.* 1

friary /frí əri/ (*plural* **-ies**) *n* a community of friars or the buildings in which they live

fricadel *n S Africa* = **frikkadel**

fricassee /fríkə say, -sáy, -see, -sée/ (*plural* **-sees**) *n* fish or meat such as chicken or veal cooked in white stock, or a wine and stock mixture, then thickened with cream [Mid-16C. < French *fricassée*, form of past participle of *fricasser* 'cut up and cook in sauce'.] —**fricassee** *vt*

fricative /fríkətiv/ *adj* describes a speech sound made by forcing the breath through a narrow opening [Mid-19C. < modern Latin *fricativus* < Latin *fricare* 'rub'.] —**fricative** *n*

friction /fríksh'n/ *n* 1 RUBBING the rubbing of two objects against each other when one or both are moving 2 DISAGREEMENT disagreement or conflict, stopping short of violence, between people, groups, or nations with differing aims or views 3 DELIBERATE RUBBING deliberate rubbing of a body part as a way of stimulating blood circulation, warming, or relieving pain 4 RESISTANCE ENCOUNTERED BY MOVING OBJECT the resistance encountered by an object moving relative to another object with which it is in contact [Mid-16C. Via French < Latin *friction-* < *fricare* 'rub'.] —**frictional** *adj*

friction clutch *n* a clutch in a vehicle or machine that transmits power through surface friction between two plates covered with a layer of a fibrous material, e.g. asbestos

friction match *n* a match that lights when rubbed against an abrasive surface

friction tape *n US* ELEC = **insulating tape**

Friday /frí day, -di/ *n* the fifth day of the week, coming after Thursday and before Saturday [Old English *Frīgedæg* 'day of the goddess Frigg']

Fridays /frídayz, -diz/ *adv* on every Friday

fridge /frij/ *n* a refrigerator [Early 20C. Shortening.]

fridge-freezer *n* a refrigerator and a freezer contained as two separate cabinets in a single upright unit

fried /frīd/ *adj* 1 COOKED BY FRYING having been cooked by frying 2 *US* INTOXICATED incapacitated by alcohol or drugs (*informal*) 3 *US* EXHAUSTED incoherent from fatigue (*slang*)

Friedan /free dán/, **Betty** (*b.* 1921) US feminist leader and author. Born **Betty Naomi Goldstein**

Friedman /freédmən/, **Milton** (*b.* 1912) US economist

Friedrich /freédrik/, **Caspar D.** (1774–1840) German painter

~~**frieght**~~ incorrect spelling of **freight**

friend /frend/ *n* 1 SOMEBODY EMOTIONALLY CLOSE a person who trusts and is fond of another ○ *I know her, in fact she's a friend of mine.* 2 ACQUAINTANCE a person who thinks well of or is on good terms with somebody else ○ *I've got a friend at the office who might be able to help out.* 3 ALLY an ally, or somebody who is not an enemy ○ *You can say what you like about the government, you're among friends here.* 4 ADVOCATE OF A CAUSE a defender or supporter of a cause, group, or principle ○ *She's no friend of tax-and-spend policies.* 5 PATRON a patron of a charity or institution ○ *a friend of the Bournemouth Symphony Orchestra* ■ *vt Malaysia, Singapore* BE SOMEBODY'S FRIEND to be friends with somebody (*informal*) ○ *I don't want to friend you any more!* [Old English *frēond* < Germanic, 'to love'] ◇ **be friends (with somebody)** to be a friend of or on friendly terms with somebody ◇ **make friends (with somebody)** to begin a friendship or get on friendly terms with somebody

Friend *n* a member of the Religious Society of Friends, called Quakers

Friend /frend/, **Donald Stuart Leslie** (1915–89) Australian artist

friendless /fréndləss/ *adj* without a friend —**friendlessness** *n*

friendly /fréndli/ *adj* (**-lier, -liest**) 1 AFFECTIONATE AND TRUSTING characteristic of or suitable to a relationship between friends ○ *She's been friendly to us since we moved in.* 2 HELPFUL tending to be beneficial or favourable towards somebody or something ○ *They're on quite friendly terms with one another, but I wouldn't say they were close.* 3 ON THE SAME SIDE not antagonistic towards or in conflict with another ○ *All the aircraft we saw were friendly.* 4 PLEASANT AND WELCOMING with a pleasant welcoming atmosphere 5 NOT FIERCELY COMPETITIVE not played or undertaken in a fiercely competitive mood 6 NOT PART OF A COMPETITION played mainly for practice or entertainment and not as a fixture in a competition or league 7 EASY TO USE safe or easy to use or operate, or easy to understand (*usually in combination*) ○ *made of child-friendly materials* 8 MAKING SEXUAL OVERTURES behaving in a way that reveals a sexual desire for somebody or a desire to start a sexual relationship with somebody (*used euphemistically*) ■ *n* (*plural* **-lies**) GAME NOT FORMING PART OF COMPETITION a game that is played mainly for practice or entertainment and not as a fixture in a competition or league ○ *a series of friendlies* —**friendlily** *adv* —**friendliness** *n* —**friendly** *adv* ◇ **be friendly with somebody** to be a friend of or on friendly terms with somebody

friendly fire *n* gunfire or artillery fire coming from your own or your allies' forces, not the enemy, and sometimes causing accidental death or injury

Friendly Islands /fréndli-/ = **Tonga**[2]

friendly society *n* an association of people who contribute regularly to a fund in order to provide themselves with sickness benefits, life assurance, and retirement pensions when required

friendship /frénd ship/ *n* 1 RELATIONSHIP BETWEEN FRIENDS a relationship between two or more people who are friends ○ *a friendship that has lasted more than 40 years* 2 MUTUALLY FRIENDLY FEELINGS the mutual feelings of trust and affection and the behaviour that typify relationships between friends ○ *Any feeling of friendship towards him had long since disappeared.* 3 FRIENDLY RELATIONS a relationship between individuals, organizations, or countries that is characterized by mutual assistance, approval, and support ○ *Anglo-American friendship*

Friends of the Earth *n* an international organization that lobbies and campaigns on environmental matters (+ *singular or plural verb*)

frier *n* COOK = **fryer**

fries *npl* = **French fries**

Friesian /freézh'n, freézi ən/ *n* an animal belonging to a breed of large black and white dairy cattle. US term **Holstein** ■ *n, adj* LANG, PEOPLES = **Frisian** [Early 20C. Variant of FRISIAN.]

Friesland /freézlənd/ province in N Netherlands that includes four of the West Frisian Islands. Capital: Leeuwarden. Population: 609,579 (1995). Area: 3,361 sq. km/1,298 sq. mi.

frieze[1] /freez/ *n* 1 a band of decoration running along the wall of a room, usually just below the ceiling 2 a horizontal band forming part of the entablature of a classical building, situated between the architrave and the cornice, and often decorated with sculpted ornaments or figures [Mid-16C. Via French *frise* < medieval Latin *frisium* < Latin *Phrygium (opus)* 'Phrygian (work)' (the Phrygians being famous for their crafts).]

SPELLCHECK See ***freeze***.

frieze[2] /freez/ *n* coarse shaggy woollen cloth [15C. Via French *frise* < medieval Latin *frisia* 'Frisian (cloth)'.]

frig /frig/ (**frigs, frigging, frigged**) *vti* (*taboo*) 1 a highly offensive term meaning to have sexual intercourse with somebody 2 a highly offensive term meaning to masturbate, or to masturbate somebody [Late 16C. < ?]
frig about, frig around *vi* an offensive term meaning to waste time or act in an aimless unproductive way (*slang*)

frigate /fríggət/ *n* 1 WARSHIP BETWEEN CORVETTE AND DESTROYER a British warship next in size below a destroyer and with a similar armament and function 2 *US* MEDIUM-SIZED WARSHIP a US warship of medium size, larger than a destroyer but smaller than a cruiser, and used mainly for escort duty 3 SAILING SHIP EQUIPPED FOR WAR a fast square-rigged fighting ship in the 18th and early 19th centuries, next in size below a ship of the line [Late 16C. Via French *frégate* < Italian *fregata.*]

frigate bird *n* a large tropical seabird with large powerful wings, dark-coloured plumage, a forked tail, and a down-turned beak. Family: Fregatidae. [Probably < its swift flight]

frigging /frígging/ *adj, adv* a highly offensive term expressing annoyance or disgust (*taboo*)

fright /frīt/ *n* 1 SUDDEN FEAR a sudden intense feeling of being threatened or in danger 2 BEING AFRAID an experience of fright 3 SOMETHING VERY UNPLEASANT LOOKING somebody or something that looks grotesque, ludicrous, or extremely unattractive (*informal*) ○ *My hair's a fright this morning.* [Old English *fryhto* < Germanic]

frighten /frīt'n/ *v* 1 *vti* to make somebody feel fear, or be made to feel fear 2 *vt* to force or drive somebody or something away through fear ○ *had frightened off all the competition* —**frightened** *adj*

frightener /frīt'nər/ *n* a person or thing that frightens somebody ◇ **put the frighteners on somebody** to frighten somebody into doing something or not doing something, especially for criminal purposes (*slang*)

frightening /frītning/ *adj* causing fear or alarm —**frighteningly** *adv*

frightful /frītf'l/ *adj* 1 VERY SERIOUS used to indicate the seriousness or severity of something ○ *now faced the frightful prospect of losing their farm* 2 FOUL extremely bad or unpleasant ○ *There is a frightful smell in the bedroom.* ○ *a frightful odour* 3 VERY GREAT used to indicate that somebody or something is an extreme example of something specified ○ *a frightful liar* ○ *The speaker turned out to be a frightful bore.* 4 TERRIFYING capable of causing fear, shock, or dread ○ *looked down from a frightful height* —**frightfulness** *n*

frightfully /frītfəli/ *adv* extremely or excessively ○ *I'm frightfully sorry, but you'll have to go.*

fright wig *n* a wig that is intended to be amusing, with long hair sticking out in all directions

frigid /fríjjid/ *adj* 1 SEXUALLY UNRESPONSIVE unable or unwilling to respond sexually, to enjoy sexual intercourse, or to have orgasm during intercourse 2 LACKING EMOTIONAL WARMTH without or behaving without warmth, friendliness, or enthusiasm 3 VERY COLD with a very cold temperature ○ *I was kept waiting in a frigid little room.* [15C. < Latin *frigidus* < *frigus* 'cold'.] —**frigidity** /fri jíddəti/ *n* —**frigidly** *adv* —**frigidness** *n*

Frigid Zone *n* either of two areas of the Earth's surface, one lying between the Arctic Circle and the North Pole, the other lying between the Antarctic Circle and the South Pole

frijol /fri hṓl/ (*plural* **-joles** /-hṓliz/), **frijole** /fri hṓli, -hṓ lay/; *or with Spanish pronunciation* /fri khṓl ay/ *n* in the cooking of Mexico and the SW United States, a bean such as the pinto, kidney, or black bean [Late 16C. Via Spanish, Catalan *fesol*, and Latin *phaseolus* < Greek *phasēlos* 'legume'.]

frikkadel /fríkə dél/, **fricadel** *n S Africa* a fried ball of minced meat [Late 19C. Via Afrikaans < French *fricadelle* < *fricasser* 'cut up and cook in sauce'.]

frill /fril/ *n* 1 DECORATIVE BAND WITH MANY FOLDS a decorative strip of material gathered into many tight folds and sewn along one edge 2 PAPER BAND WITH FRINGED EDGE a paper band with one edge cut into a decorative fringe, placed on bone ends as decoration 3 DECORATIVE PAPER BAND ROUND CAKE a decorative paper band with both edges cut into a fringe, wrapped around the side of a cake 4 RUFF OF FEATHERS, FUR, OR SKIN a ring of fur or feathers or a fold of skin around the neck of a bird or animal that looks like a frill 5 UNNECESSARY ADDITION an addition to something that is unnecessary, though it may enhance its appearance, interest, or value (*usually plural*) ○ *I just want a basic, simple, no-frills stereo.* ■ *vt* 1 MAKE INTO FRILL to make a strip of fabric or paper into a frill 2 ADD FRILL TO to decorate something with a frill [Late 16C. < ?] —**frilled** *adj* —**frilliness** *n* —**frilly** *adj*

frilled lizard *n* a large lizard, with a broad membrane of skin around its neck that it can spread out like a ruff. Native to: Australia. *Chlamydosaurus kingii.*

fringe /frinj/ *n* 1 DECORATIVE EDGING OF STRANDS a decorative border of short parallel strands or ravelled threads held closely together at one end by stitching and hanging loosely at the other end 2 HAIR HANGING OVER FOREHEAD a border of hair cut to fall over the forehead 3 ANY BORDER OR EDGING something that serves as or resembles a border 4 OUTER LIMIT the outer edge, or something considered to be on the outer edge and not central to an activity, interest, or issue (*often plural*) ○ *outposts on the fringes of civilization* 5 LESS IMPORTANT AREA an area of action that is far away from the centre of activity or interest in a particular field (*usually plural*) ○ *on the fringes of political life* 6 AREA BORDERING PUTTING GREEN the area surrounding a putting green on a golf course where the grass is allowed to grow slightly longer than it is on the green itself 7 FACTION members of a group or organization such as a political party who hold views not representative of the group and usually more extreme than those of the group 8 PART OF ARTS FESTIVAL part of an arts festival or similar event devoted to experimental or low-budget work 9 BAND PRODUCED BY DIFFRACTION OF LIGHT a light, dark, or coloured band of light produced by diffraction or interference **10** *US* **FRINGE BENEFIT** a fringe benefit (*informal*) ■ *adj* **1 OUTLYING** situated on the edge or away from the centre of something **2 MINOR** playing a minor role in a play or story **3 UNCONVENTIONAL** not part of the established or conventional mainstream of something such as the cinema, theatre, or medicine **4 NOT IN MAIN PART** not in the main part of something such as a conference or organization, especially if putting forward or discussing radical or unconventional ideas ■ *vt* (**fringes, fringing, fringed**) **1 FORM FRINGE AROUND** to form a fringe or border around something ○ *A thin moustache and beard fringed his lips.* **2 DECORATE WITH FRINGE** to decorate something with a fringe [14C. Via Old French < Latin *fimbriae* 'threads'.] —**fringed** *adj* —**fringy** *adj*

LITERARY LINK ***The Fringe Dwellers***, a novel (1961) by Australian writer Nene Gare. It tells the story of a mixed-race Aboriginal family, the Comeaways, who find themselves shunned and mistreated by white society and cut off from their Aboriginal traditions.

fringe area *n* an area at or just beyond the edge of a radio or television transmitter's range where signals are likely to be weak or distorted

fringe benefit *n* **1** an additional benefit provided to an employee, e.g. a company car or health insurance **2** any additional or incidental advantage derived from a particular activity

fringed orchis *n* an orchid with a fringed lip. Flowers: yellow, white, purple, greenish. Genus: *Habenaria*.

fringing reef *n* a coral reef that borders or is directly attached to the shore of an island or a continent

frippery /fríppəri/ (*plural* **-ies**) *n* **1 ARTICLE WORN FOR SHOW** a showy article of clothing or an adornment worn for display or effect **2 OSTENTATION** pretentious display or showiness **3 SOMETHING TRIFLING** something of little value or importance [Mid-16C. < French *friperie* < Old French *frepe* 'rag, old clothes'.] —**frippery** *adj*

frippet /fríppit/ *n* a frivolous or extrovert young woman (*informal dated*) [Early 20C. < ?]

Frisbee /frízbi/ *tdmk* a trademark for a plastic disc thrown from person to person in a game

Frisch /frish/, **Max** (1911–91) Swiss dramatist and novelist

frisé /freé zay/ *n* a fabric with long nap, usually of uncut loops. Use: upholstery, rugs. [Late 19C. < French, < past participle of *friser* 'curl'.]

Frisian /frízh'n, frízzi ən/, **Friesian** *n* **1** a West Germanic language spoken in the Netherlands and Germany **2** somebody who comes from Friesland or the Frisian Islands [Late 16C. < Latin *Frisii* 'the Frisians' < Old Frisian *Frīsa*.] —**Frisian** *adj*

Frisian Islands /freézi ən ílәndz/ group of islands in the North Sea off the coasts of the Netherlands, NW Germany, and SW Denmark

frisk /frisk/ *v* **1** *vi* to leap, skip, or dance around in a carefree way **2** *vt* to search somebody with a quick pass of the hands over clothes and into pockets [Early 16C. < Old French *frisque* 'lively'.] —**frisk** *n* —**frisker** *n* —**frisking** *n*

frisket /frískit/ *n* a thin frame that keeps a sheet of paper in position and masks any portions not to be printed while the sheet is being printed on a hand-operated press [Late 17C. < French *frisquette* < Old French *frisque* 'lively'.]

frisky /fríski/ (**-ier, -iest**) *adj* behaving or tending to behave in a lively, playful way —**friskily** *adv* —**friskiness** *n*

frisson /freésson, frísson, freesóN/ *n* a brief intense reaction, usually a feeling of excitement, recognition, or terror, accompanied by a physical shudder or thrill [Late 18C. Via French, 'shiver' < assumed Vulgar Latin *friction-* < Latin *frigere* 'be cold'.]

frit[1] /frit/ *n* **1 BASIC MATERIALS FOR GLASS** the basic materials from which glass, pottery glazes, or enamels are made, when they are in a partially bonded state at the beginning of the manufacturing process **2 GROUND FLUX** a flux that is stabilized by melting it with silica and regrinding it into a fine powder ■ *vt* (**frits, fritting, fritted**) **MAKE INTO FRIT** to fuse or partially fuse materials in order to make frit [Mid-17C. < Italian *fritta*, past participle of *friggere* 'fry' < Latin *frigere*.]

frit[2] /frit/ *adj* frightened (*regional*) [Early 19C. Past participle of obsolete *fright* 'frighten' < Old English *fryhtan* < Germanic.]

frit fly *n* a small black fly whose larvae are destructive to cereal crops. *Oscinella frit*. [< Latin *frit* 'speck on an ear of corn']

fritillary /fri tílləri/ (*plural* **-ies**) *n* **1** a plant of the lily family with long narrow leaves. Flowers: bell-shaped with spotted or chequered petals. Genus: *Fritillaria*. **2** a brownish butterfly with black spots or narrow bands on its wings and usually silver spots on the underside of its hind wings. Family: Nymphalidae. [Mid-17C. < modern Latin *Fritillaria* < Latin *fritillus* 'dice box'.]

fritter[1] /fríttər/ *n* a piece of meat, fish, vegetable, or fruit dipped in batter and fried [14C. < French *friture* < Latin *frict-*, past participle of *frigere* 'fry'.]

fritter[2] /fríttər/ *vt* to break, cut, or tear something into small pieces or shreds (*archaic*) [Early 18C. < obsolete *fritters* 'fragments, scraps' < ?]

fritter away *vt* to waste something by expending it in small quantities over a period of time on things that are not worthwhile

fritto misto /fríttō místō/ (*plural* **fritto mistos** *or* **fritti misti** /frítti místi/) *n* an Italian dish consisting of a mixture of bite-sized pieces of various foods such as seafood, meat, or vegetables, and sometimes sweet things such as cake, deep-fried in light batter [< Italian, 'mixed fry']

fritz /frits/ [Early 20C. < ?] ◇ **on the fritz** *US* out of order or not working properly (*informal*)

Friulian /fri óoli ən/, **Friulan** /-óolən/ *n* **1** a dialect of Rhaetian spoken in NW Italy **2** somebody who comes from the region of Friuli in SE Europe or who speaks Friulian [Late 19c. < *Friuli*, region of SE Europe in Slovenia and Italy.] —**Friulian** *adj*

frivol /frívv'l/ (**-ols, -olling, -olled**) *v* **1** *vi* to behave or spend time in a frivolous way **2** *vt* to spend or waste something such as time or money foolishly or frivolously [Mid-19C. Back-formation < FRIVOLOUS.] —**frivoller** *n*

frivolity /fri vóllәti/ (*plural* **-ties**) *n* **1 FRIVOLOUS BEHAVIOUR** silly and trivial behaviour or activities **2 SOMETHING FRIVOLOUS** a frivolous action or thing **3 TRIVIALITY** the state of being trivial and unimportant [Late 18C. < French *frivolité* < Latin *frivolus* 'silly, unimportant'.]

frivolous /frívvələss/ *adj* **1** lacking in intellectual substance and not worth serious consideration **2** silly and trivial [15C. < Latin *frivolus* 'silly, unimportant' < ?] —**frivolously** *adv* —**frivolousness** *n*

frizz /friz/ *vti* (**frizzes, frizzing, frizzed**) **FORM INTO TIGHT CURLS** to form, or cause the hair to form, a mass of tight curls or tufts ■ *n* **1 FRIZZED HAIR** a mass of tightly curled or tufted hair **2 FRIZZING** the frizzing of hair [Late 16C. < French *friser* 'to curl'.]

frizzle[1] /frízz'l/ (**-zles, -zling, -zled**) *vti* **1** to burn or shrivel, or to cause to burn or shrivel, especially while cooking **2** to sizzle while frying or cooking or to fry and cook something so that it sizzles [Mid-18C. Probably blend of FRY[1] + FIZZLE or SIZZLE.]

frizzle[2] /frízz'l/ *vti* (**-zles, -zling, -zled**) to frizz hair, or become frizzed ■ *n* a short tight curl [Mid-16C. Probably < FRIZZ.]

frizzy /frízzi/ (**-zier, -ziest**), **frizzly** /frízlee/ (**frizzlier, frizzliest**) *adj* forming or styled in tight curls —**frizzily** *adv* —**frizziness** *n* —**frizzliness** *n*

Frl. *abbr* Fräulein

fro /frō/ *adv* ◆ **to and fro** [13C. < Old Norse *frá* 'from'.]

Frobisher /frṓbishər/, **Sir Martin** (1535?–94) English navigator

frock /frok/ *n* **1 DRESS** a woman's or girl's dress (*dated*) ○ *I'll put on my posh frock if the mayor's going to be there.* **2 LOOSE OUTER GARMENT** a loose baggy outer garment with sleeves that covers the top half of the body to below the waist, traditionally worn by artists and farm workers **3 MONK'S GOWN** the loose full-length gown with wide sleeves worn by the monks, friars, or clerics of some religious orders **4 18C MAN'S COAT** an informal coat with narrow skirts and collar worn by men in the 18th century ■ *vt* **1 INDUCT AS MEMBER OF CLERGY** to invest somebody as a member of the clergy **2 ASSUME HIGHER RANK WITHOUT CORRESPONDING PAY** to assume the title, uniform, and authority, but not the salary, of the next highest military rank before being officially promoted to it [14C. < French *froc* < Germanic.]

frock coat *n* in the 19th century, a man's knee-length coat for formal day wear

froe /frō/, **frow** *n* a cutting tool with one end of its blade fastened at right angles to a short handle. Use: to split wood along the grain to make shingles or barrel staves. [Late 16C. < ?]

Froebelian /frə beéli ən/ *adj* relating to Friedrich Wilhelm August Froebel (1782–1852), the German educator who established the first kindergarten, or to the system of education through kindergartens (**the Froebel system**) that he advocated

frog[1] /frog/ *n* **1 SMALL WEB-FOOTED WATER ANIMAL** a small tailless amphibious animal with smooth moist skin, webbed feet, and long back legs used for jumping. Family: Ranidae. **2 NUT ON BOW** a nut used to secure and tighten the strings of a violin bow and hold them away from the bow stick **3 SUPPORT FOR FLOWERS IN ARRANGEMENT** an object, usually with spikes or perforations, used to support the stems of flowers when making a flower arrangement [Old English *frogga* < Germanic] ◇ **have a frog in your throat** to be hoarse and unable to speak clearly

frog[2] /frog/ *n* a decorative fastening for the front of a garment, consisting of a loop of braid or cord and a button, knot, or toggle that fits into the loop [Early 18C. < ?] —**frogged** *adj*

frog[3] /frog/ *n* a tough flexible pad in the middle of the sole of a horse's hoof [Early 17C. < ?]

frog[4] /frog/ *n* a steel plate used to guide the wheels of a train over a place where two rails cross one another [Mid-19C. < ?]

Frog /frog/, **frog** *n* an offensive term for a French person (*slang*) [Late 18C. < frogs' legs as a French dish.]

frogbit /fróg bit/ *n* a floating plant that grows in stagnant water and has heart-shaped leaves. Flowers: white. *Hydrocharis morsus-ranae*. [Late 16C. < *bit* in the obsolete sense 'something bitten, food'.]

frogeye /fróg ī/ *n* a fungal disease of plants that causes rounded spots to appear on the leaves

frogfish /fróg fish/ (*plural* **-fish** *or* **-fishes**) *n* a bottom-dwelling sea fish with a globe-shaped warty or prickly body and fins adapted for catching prey. Family: Antennariidae.

frogging /frógging/ *n* ornamental braid fastenings on the front of a jacket [Late 19C. < FROG[2].]

froghopper /fróg hopər/ *n* a jumping plant-sucking insect with larvae that produce cuckoo spit. US term **spittlebug** [Early 18C. < their shape and leap.]

frog kick *n* a kick used especially in swimming the breaststroke, in which the legs are first simultaneously bent, then straightened, to push the swimmer along

frogman /frógmən/ (*plural* **-men** /-mən/) *n* an underwater swimmer equipped with breathing apparatus, a wet suit, flippers, and other underwater gear, especially somebody engaged in military, police, or rescue work

frogmarch /fróg maarch/ *vt* to force somebody to walk with arms pinned behind the back ■ *n* the act or process of frogmarching somebody

frogmouth /fróg mowth/ *n* a nocturnal bird with grey or brown plumage and a wide mouth with a hooked bill. Native to: Australia, Asia. Family: Podargidae.

frogspawn /fróg spawn/ *n* a floating mass of fertilized frog's eggs in a transparent jelly

frog spit *n* **1** a foamy green mass of small aquatic plants or algae floating on the surface of a pond **2** INSECTS = **cuckoo spit**

frolic /fróllik/ *vi* (**-ics, -icking, -icked**) **PLAY LIGHTHEARTEDLY** to frisk about, behave, or play in a carefree, uninhibited way ○ *children frolicking on the sands* ■ *n* **1 SOMETHING LIVELY AND CAREFREE** a lively carefree game, action, or amusement **2 CAREFREE PLAY** lively carefree play or behaviour ○ *'As a result, Anne had the golden summer of her life as far as freedom and frolic went'.* (Lucy Maud Montgomery, *Anne of Green Gables*; 1908) [Early 16C. < Dutch *vrolijk* 'glad, joyous' < *vro* 'happy'.] —**frolicker** *n*

frolicsome /frólliksəm/ *adj* frisky and full of fun and high spirits

from (*stressed*) /from/; (*unstressed*) /frəm/ CORE MEANING: a preposition used to indicate the source or beginning of something, in terms of location, situation, or time ○ *The condition can manifest itself anytime from adolescence onward.* ○ *Most funding comes from government.* ○ *highlights from her latest novel* ○ *You can connect to our computer network from home.*

prep **1 RANGE** used to indicate a range, either of time, amount, or things ○ *We are open from 2 to 4:30.* ○ *They sell* *everything, from washing machines to magazines.* **2 DISTANCE** used to indicate the distance between two things or places ○ *The nearest town is not far from here.* **3 USING** indicating the materials or substances used in order to make something ○ *built from native pine* **4 CAUSE** used to indicate the cause of or reason for something ○ *low morale resulting from staff cuts* **5 RESTRAINT** used to indicate that an action does not happen or should not happen ○ *prevented from seeing her* [Old English *fram, from* < Indo-European, 'forward, towards']

USAGE from or **in**? ***From*** means, among other things, 'deriving from a source or beginning', as in *The condition can manifest itself at any time from adolescence onward.* Unlike ***in***, the word ***from*** does not have the meaning 'found, situated, or located somewhere', e.g. *In my essay I included 70 footnotes.* Avoid substituting ***from*** for ***in***, e.g. *From the very first sentence of his short story, he sets up a decidedly sombre mood.* Use *In the very first sentence. . . .*

fromage frais /frómmaazh fráy/ *n* a fresh cheese with a light creamy taste, a texture like thick cream or yoghurt, and a variable fat content [< French, 'fresh cheese']

Frome, Lake /frōm/ usually dry salt lake in NE South Australia. Area: 4700 sq. km/1800 sq. mi.

fromenty *n* BEVERAGES = **frumenty**

Fromm /from/, **Erich** (1900–80) German-born US psychoanalyst

frond /frond/ *n* **1** a large leaf divided into many thin sections that is found on many flowerless plants, especially ferns and palms **2** any growth that resembles the leaf of a fern or palm tree, especially a growth of seaweed that resembles leaves [Late 18C. < Latin *frond-*, stem of *frons* 'leaf'.] —**fronded** *adj*

front /frunt/ *n* **1 PART FACING FORWARD** the part or surface that faces forward, is intended to be seen first, has the main entrance, or is facing the direction of motion or the direction people face ○ *You can only see the front of the house from here.* **2 FORWARD AREA** the area, section, or position just ahead of, close to, or at the forward part of something ○ *You sit in the front and I'll ride in the back.* **3 FRONT DOOR** the front door or the area beyond it ○ *I'll go out the front, and you go out the back.* **4 FIRST PAGES** the beginning or first pages of a book or magazine **5 FAÇADE OF BUILDING** a façade of a building, especially the one that faces the street, or a part of it ○ *Bring the car around to the front.* **6 ADJOINING SIDE OF PROPERTY** the side of a property that borders something else, e.g. a street, lake, or river **7 FORWARD DIRECTION** the direction straight ahead ○ *Face the front.* **8 POSITION AHEAD** a place or position approximately ahead of somebody ○ *To our front was a clump of trees.* **9 LEADING POSITION** a prominent or leading position in any field of activity ○ *companies at the front of genetic research* **10 NOTICEABLE POSITION** a conspicuous position ○ *a disturbing aspect that came to the front* **11 ASPECT** a way of viewing a situation ○ *Things looked desperate on all fronts.* **12 SEASIDE PROMENADE** a street, area of land, or promenade running alongside the beach or shore at a seaside or lakeside resort **13 BATTLE ZONE** an area where armies are facing one another, or where fighting between armies is taking place ○ *soldiers returning from the front* **14 SPACE DEFENDED BY ARMY UNIT** the width of territory occupied or defended by an army or a military unit facing an enemy ○ *Each section was defending a front of some two miles.* **15 DIRECTION IN WHICH TROOPS ARE FACING** the direction in which troops are facing when formed up in line **16 AREA OF ACTIVITY** a stated area of activity or operations ○ *There have been a lot of changes on the domestic front.* **17 INTERFACE BETWEEN AIR MASSES** a line along which one mass of air meets another that is different in temperature or density **18 GROUP WITH COMMON PURPOSE** a group of people or organizations with a common purpose, especially a broad political coalition ○ *a national liberation front* **19 PART OF GARMENT** the part of a garment or the clothing that covers the front part of the body, especially the chest ○ *You've got gravy all down your front.* **20 DETACHABLE SHIRT FRONT** a detachable shirt front, especially part of a man's formal dress shirt **21 DELIBERATELY ASSUMED BEHAVIOUR** a manner or type of behaviour adopted by somebody in order to deal with a situation or disguise the person's true feelings ○ *put on a brave front* **22 COVER FOR ILLEGAL ACTIVITIES** an apparently respectable person, organization, or business acting as a cover for illegal or secret activities **23 FIGUREHEAD** a nominal leader or head who has no real authority **24 IMPERTINENCE** cheek or cockiness ○ *That took a bit of front!* **25 FACE** the face or forehead (*archaic*) ■ *adj* **1 AT THE FRONT** situated at, on, or near the front of something, or placed farther forward than others **2 PRODUCED WITH TONGUE FORWARD** produced with the back of the tongue close to the forward part of the roof of the mouth (*describes a vowel sound*) ■ *v* **1** *vti* **FACE TOWARDS** to have a front that faces towards something ○ *a hotel fronting the ocean* **2** *vt* **GIVE COVERING OR APPEARANCE TO** to give something a front or visible surface of a particular kind ○ *The building is fronted with red brick.* **3** *vt* **BE THE HEAD OF** to be the head, leader, or spokesperson of a group or organization such as a band ○ *a group fronted by a young lawyer from London* **4** *vt* **HOST A PROGRAMME** to act as the presenter or host of a television or radio programme **5** *vi* **ACT AS RESPECTABLE COVER FOR** to act as a respectable cover for something secret or illegal or for somebody doing something secret or illegal **6** *vt* **CONFRONT** to confront somebody or something (*archaic*) [13C. Via French < Latin *front-*, stem of *frons* 'forehead, front'.] ◇ **in front 1** leading or ahead of somebody or something else **2** close to or in the front of something, or further forward than somebody else **3** in the lead in a race or competition ○ *Polls show the current mayor far in front as the election nears.* ◇ **in front of 1** ahead of somebody or in the direction in which somebody is facing **2** close to the front of something **3** in the presence, sight, or hearing of somebody ◇ **out front 1** in front of the curtain or in the auditorium, as opposed to on the stage **2** at or to the front of a building ○ *I'll go out front and talk to them.* ◇ **up front 1** close or closer to the front of something **2** in advance, e.g. before any work is done or any goods are delivered

LITERARY LINK ***All Quiet on the Western Front***, a novel (1929) by German writer Erich Maria Remarque. This classic antiwar novel, which was based on the author's own experiences during World War I, is a grimly realistic account of trench warfare.

frontage /frúntij/ *n* **1 FRONT OF BUILDING** the front side of a building or piece of property **2 LAND BETWEEN BUILDING AND STREET** the land between a building and a street or road **3 LENGTH OF FRONT** the length of the front of a building or piece of land next to a street, river, or lake **4 PIECE OF LAND ADJOINING** a piece of land situated next to a street, river, or lake **5 OUTLOOK** the direction in which a building faces or its outlook

frontage road *n US* TRANSP = **service road**

frontal[1] /frúnt'l/ *adj* **1 AT OR IN THE FRONT** situated at or in the front of something **2 SHOWING THE FRONT OF** showing or depicting the front of somebody or of something, especially the full view of a naked body **3 TOWARDS ENEMY FRONT** directed against an enemy's front, usually across open ground ○ *a frontal attack* **4 DIRECT AND FORCEFUL** direct, forceful, and intended to be overwhelming **5 RELATING TO FOREHEAD** relating to the forehead or the front part of the skull **6 RELATING TO WEATHER FRONTS** involving or relating to weather fronts —**frontally** *adv*

frontal[2] /frúnt'l/ *n* **1** a cloth covering for the front of an altar **2** the façade of a building or tomb [14C. Via Old French *frontel* 'ornament for the forehead' < Latin *frontale* < *front-*(see FRONT).]

frontal bone *n* the bone forming the front part of the skull that shapes the forehead and part of the eye sockets and nasal cavity

frontal lobe *n* the front part of each hemisphere of the brain

frontal lobotomy *n* a prefrontal lobotomy

front bench *n* **1** in Parliament, the bench on each side nearest the floor of the House, reserved for Government ministers on one side and their Opposition counterparts on the other **2** the most important members of the Government or Opposition, who sit on the front bench in Parliament —**frontbencher** *n*

front burner *n* a position of importance or priority (*informal*) ○ *a scheme which seems to be no longer on the front burner* [< the part of a hob used for rapid cooking]

frontcourt /frúnt kawrt/ *n* **1** in basketball, the half of a court containing the basket in which a team attempts to score **2** the forwards and centre of a basketball team

front door *n* **1** the main entrance to a house or other building, closed by a door **2** the usual and unsuspicious way of achieving a position

⚡**front end** *n* **1** the user interface of a computer system **2** = **front-end processor**

⚡**front-end** *adj* **1** relating to the start of a process or project, especially a commercial or financial one ○ *heavy front-end costs* **2** relating to the user interface of a computer system

front-end load *n* an amount, making up a large part of the initial payments, paid by an investor in an insurance scheme or long-term investment, intended to cover commission and other expenses

front-end loading *n US* the practice of encouraging new recruits to a selling-from-home scheme to buy larger quantities of a product than they are likely to be able to sell (*slang*)

⚡**front-end processor, front end** *n* a computer that carries out preliminary processing on data before passing it to another computer for further processing

frontier /frun teér/ *n* **1 BORDERLAND** a border between two countries, or the land immediately adjacent to this ○ *cross the frontier into Spain* **2 EDGE OF SETTLEMENT** the part of a country with expanding settlement that is being opened up by hunters, herders, and other pioneers in advance of full urban settlement **3 LIMIT OF KNOWLEDGE** the furthest limit of knowledge in a particular field ○ *pushing back the frontiers of science* [14C. < Anglo-Norman *frounter*, French *frontière* 'front part (of an army)' < *front* (see FRONT).]

frontiersman /frún teerzmən, frun teérzmən/ (*plural* **-men** /-mən, -/) *n* a man living in a frontier area, especially an area newly opened up for settlement

frontierswoman /frún teerz wòomən, frun teérz wòomən/ (*plural* **-en** /-wimin, -/) *n* a woman living in a frontier area, especially an area newly opened up for settlement

frontispiece /frúntiss peess/ *n* **1 BOOK ILLUSTRATION** an illustration at the beginning of a book, usually facing the title page **2 BUILDING FAÇADE** the principal façade of a building, treated as a separate element **3 PEDIMENT** a pediment, usually ornamental, above a window or door [Late 16C. Via French *frontispice* (altered after PIECE) < late Latin *frontispicium* 'façade' < Latin *frons* 'forehead' + *specere* 'look at'.]

frontlet /frúntlət/ *n* **1 DECORATIVE BAND** a decorative band worn on the forehead **2 ANIMAL'S FOREHEAD** an animal's forehead, especially a bird's when it has a different colour from the rest of the head **3 ALTAR-CLOTH BORDER** a decorated border on the frontal of an altar [15C. < Old French *frontelet* 'little forehead band' < *frontel* (see FRONTAL[2]).]

front line, frontline /frúnt līn/ *n* **1** the forward line of a battle, position, or formation (*hyphenated when used before a noun*) **2** the most advanced, important, or conspicuous position in any situation **3** BASKETBALL = **frontcourt** *n.* 2

frontline /frúnt līn/ *adj* **frontline, front-line 1** that is the most advanced or important of its kind ○ *a frontline technological development* **2** relating to countries that border another country in which an armed conflict is taking place

front-load *vt* to assign the bulk of the costs of an insurance scheme or long-term investment to an early stage

front loader *n* a washing machine in which clothes are loaded through a door at the front rather than the top

front man *n* (*informal*) **1** an apparent leader of an organization or activity in which somebody else has the real power, secretly or illegally concealed **2** the lead singer of a band or other musical group

front matter *n* the material that appears in a book before the main text, e.g. the title page, the copyright information, the table of contents, and the preface

front office *n US* the management or executives of an organization

front of house *n* (*hyphenated before nouns*) **1** the parts of a theatre, cinema, concert hall, or other performance venue where members of the audience are usually admitted **2** the parts of a restaurant where customers sit and are served, as opposed to the kitchen

frontogenesis /fruntō jénnississ/ *n* the formation or development of a weather front

frontolysis /frun tóllississ/ *n* the weakening or disappearance of a weather front [Mid-20C. < FRONT + -LYSIS.]

fronton /frón ton, fron tón/ *n* a court used for the game of pelota or jai alai [Late 19C. < Spanish, 'gable, wall of a frontón' < *fronte* 'forehead' < Latin *front-* (see FRONT).]

front-page *adj* important or interesting enough to appear on the front page of a newspaper

front room *n* a sitting room in a house, often one reserved for more formal entertaining

front-run *vt US* to buy stocks before recommending them to other investors in order to benefit from any subsequent rise in their price

frontrunner /frunt rúnnər, frúnt runər/ *n* somebody in a leading position in a race or contest (*informal*) ○ *the new frontrunner in the party leadership contest*

frontwards /frúntwərd(z)/, **frontward** /-wərd/ *adv* towards or in the direction of the front

front-wheel drive *n* a system of powering motor vehicles that uses the engine to drive the front wheels only

frost /frost/ *n* **1 FROZEN WATER** crystals of frozen water deposited on a cold surface **2 FREEZING TEMPERATURE** an outdoor temperature below freezing point, resulting in the deposit of ice crystals ○ *had a hard frost as late as May* **3 CHILLY MANNER** a coldness of manner **4 FAILURE** something, e.g. an artistic performance or a new book, that meets with an unenthusiastic reception (*informal*) ○ *The opening night was a true frost.* **5 FREEZING** the act or process of freezing ■ *v* **1** *vti* **COVER WITH FROST** to cover something with frost, especially hoar frost, or become covered with frost **2** *vt* **MAKE OPAQUE** to make something, especially glass or a window, unable to be seen through by giving its surface a rough or fine-grained texture **3** *vt US* **PUT ICING ON** to cover a cake or other pastry with icing or frosting **4** *vt* **KILL BY FREEZING** to damage or kill crops or garden plants by frost [Old English *forst, frost* < Germanic]
frost up *vi* to become covered in frost or ice, especially in a way that hinders a function ○ *The freezer has frosted up so much that the door won't close.*

Frost /frost/, **Robert** (1874–1963) US poet

frostbite /fróst bīt/ *n* damage to body extremities caused by prolonged exposure to freezing conditions, characterized by numbness, tissue death, and gangrene ■ *vt* (**-bites, -biting, -bit, -bitten**) to damage something by prolonged exposure to freezing conditions (*usually passive*)

frostbound /fróst bownd/ *adj* confined to one place because of frost ○ *We were frostbound in our cabin for three days.*

frost-free *adj* describes an appliance such as a refrigerator or freezer that does not need to be defrosted

frost heave, frost heaving *n* the cracking of the surface of a road or piece of ground by the freezing and upward expansion of subsurface water, or a damaged surface resulting from this

frosting /fróstiŋ/ *n* **1 SOFT ICING** a variety of soft icing for cakes made by whisking egg whites and sugar over hot water or incorporating hot syrup into whisked egg whites **2** *US* **RICH ICING** icing that is typically thick and rich from the addition of milk, eggs, butter, or cream **3 ROUGH SURFACE** a roughened or dull surface produced on something, especially glass or metal

frost line *n* **1** the point below the surface of the ground beyond which frost will not penetrate **2** a line on a map joining places subject to the same number of frosts a year or to the same degree of frost

frost weathering *n* the shattering of rock caused by the freezing of water in surface cracks and hollows, and in the pore spaces

frostwork /fróst wurk/ *n* **1** the patterns made by frost on various surfaces, especially windows, that often resemble tracery or the fronds of ferns **2** decoration on metal or glass imitating the patterns made naturally by frost

frosty /frósti/ (**-ier, -iest**) *adj* **1 VERY COLD** cold enough for the formation of frost **2 COVERED IN FROST** covered in frost, especially hoarfrost **3 COLD IN MANNER** cold and unwelcoming in manner **4 WHITE LIKE FROST** looking like hoarfrost, especially in whiteness ○ *a shock of matted frosty hair* —**frostily** *adv* —**frostiness** *n*

froth /froth/ *n* **1 FOAM** a mass of bubbles in or on the surface of a liquid **2 FOAMY SALIVA** a foamy mixture of saliva and air bubbles produced at the mouth in some diseases or by exhaustion **3 TRIVIA** anything seen as being insubstantial or trivial ○ *The conversation at the party was mostly froth and posturing.* ■ *v* **1** *vt* **CAUSE TO FOAM** to make something produce foam, or cover something with foam **2** *vi* **CREATE FOAM** to produce foam or emerge as foam ○ *froth at the mouth* [14C. < Old Norse *froða* or *frauð*.]

froth flotation *n* MIN EXTRACT = **flotation** *n.* **5**

frothy /fróthi/ (**-ier, -iest**) *adj* **1** characterized by, covered in, or producing foam **2** with no serious content or purpose ○ *a frothy sitcom* —**frothily** *adv* —**frothiness** *n*

frottage /fróttaazh, fro táazh/ *n* **1** an art technique in which a rubbing is taken of a surface to create a design **2** the obtaining of sexual pleasure by rubbing the clothed body against that of others, usually strangers in crowded places [Mid-20C. < French, 'rubbing, friction' < *frotter* 'rub'.]

froufrou /froo froo/ *n* **1** the sound made by the rustling of silk, especially women's dresses **2** fancy trimmings or elaborate decoration, especially on women's clothes [Late 19C. < French, an imitation of the sound.]

frow *n* TECH = **froe**

froward /frṓ ərd/ *adj* stubbornly disobedient or contrary (*archaic*) [Old English *frāward* 'in a direction leading away from' < Old Norse *frá* 'from'] —**frowardly** *adv* —**frowardness** *n*

frown /frown/ *v* **1** *vi* to show a facial expression of displeasure or concentration by wrinkling the brow **2** *vt* to communicate something by frowning [14C. < Old French *froignier* 'to frown, snort' < *froigne* 'scowl'.] —**frown** *n* —**frowner** *n* —**frowningly** *adv*
frown on, frown upon *vt* to dislike or disapprove of something

SYNONYMS See ***disapprove***.

frowsty /frówsti/ (**-ier, -iest**) *adj* unpleasant to be in because of mustiness, staleness, or a bad smell ○ *a frowsty atmosphere in the room.* US term **frowzy** *adj.* **2** [Mid-19C. < ?] —**frowstiness** *n*

frowzy /frówzi/ (**-ier, -iest**), **frowsy** (**-ier, -iest**) *adj* **1** untidy or shabby in personal appearance or manner of dress ○ *a frowzy layabout* ○ *frowzy curtains at a tenement window* **2** = **frowsty** [Late 17C. < ?] —**frowziness** *n*

froze past tense of **freeze**

frozen /frṓz'n/ past participle of **freeze** ■ *adj* **1 WITH ICE** covered by or made into ice ○ *a frozen lake* **2 AFFECTED BY ICE** made inoperable, damaged, or obstructed by ice or freezing temperatures ○ *All trains are delayed because of frozen points.* ○ *no running water in the house because of frozen pipes* **3 EXTREMELY COLD** characterized by extreme cold ○ *the frozen north* **4 PRESERVED BY FREEZING** preserved by freezing for eating at a later time ○ *frozen pizza* **5 IMMOBILE** immobile or unable to move ○ *She stood there, frozen in terror.* **6 FIXED** deliberately fixed at a given level to avoid undesirable economic or social consequences **7 NOT TO BE SOLD** that cannot be sold or otherwise liquidated (*refers to assets*) ○ *the country's frozen assets* —**frozenly** *adv* —**frozenness** *n*

frozen shoulder *n* a condition in which a shoulder joint becomes stiff and painful, especially after having been kept in one position for a time

FRS *abbr* Fellow of the Royal Society

fructan /frúktən/ *n* a natural polymer, composed of units of fructose arranged in a chain, that is an important source of stored energy for some plants [Mid-20C. < FRUCTOSE.]

fructiferous /fruk tíffərəss, frŏŏk-/ *adj* describes a tree or other plant that bears fruit [Mid-17C. < Latin *fructifer* 'fruit-bearing' < *fructus* 'fruit' (see FRUIT).]

fructification /frúktifi káysh'n, frŏŏk-/ *n* **1 PRODUCTION OF FRUIT** the production of fruit or fruits by a tree or other plant **2 FRUIT OF SEED-BEARING PLANT** the fruit produced by a seed-bearing plant **3 SEED-BEARING PART** a seed-bearing or spore-bearing part of a plant, alga, or fungus

fructify /frúkti fī, frŏŏk-/ (**-fies, -fying, -fied**) *vti* to become, or cause to become, productive or fruitful [14C. Via French *fructifier* < Latin *fructificare* < *fructus* 'fruit' (see FRUIT).]

fructose /frúk tōz, -tōss, frŏŏk tōz, -tōss/, **fruit sugar** *n* a simple sugar found in fruits and honey [Mid-19C. < Latin *fructus* 'fruit' (see FRUIT).]

fructuous /frúk tyoo əss/ *adj* productive of much fruit, or full of fruit (*formal*) [14C. Directly or via Old French < Latin *fructuosus* < *fructus* 'fruit' (see FRUIT).]

frugal /frŏŏg'l/ *adj* **1** characterized by thriftiness and avoidance of waste **2** involving very little expense [Early 16C. Directly or via French < Latin *frugalis* < *frugi* 'economical, useful' < *frug*, stem of *frux* 'fruit, value'.] —**frugality** /froo gálləti/ *n* —**frugally** *adv* —**frugalness** *n*

frugivorous /froo jívvərəss/ *adj* describes an animal that eats mainly fruit [Early 18C. < Latin *frug-* 'fruit'.] —**frugivore** *n*

fruit /froot/ *n* **1 EDIBLE PART OF PLANT** an edible part of a plant, usually fleshy and containing seeds **2 OVARY OF PLANT** the ripened seed-bearing ovary of a plant **3 SPORE-PRODUCING PART** a spore-producing part of a plant **4 PRODUCE** the produce of any plant grown or harvested by humans ○ *the fruits of the field* **5 PRODUCT OF** the product or consequence of something done ○ *We are now seeing the fruits of our efforts.* **6 FRUITY TASTE** a fruity taste in wine ○ *a big red with lots of fruit* **7 OFFSPRING** the offspring of humans or animals (*dated*) **8** *US* **OFFENSIVE TERM** an offensive term for a homosexual man ■ *vti* **PRODUCE FRUIT** to bear fruit, or cause a plant or tree to bear fruit ○ *This variety fruits in August.* [12C. Via French < Latin *fructus* 'enjoyment, produce, fruit' < past participle of *frui* 'enjoy, have the use of').] ◇ **bear fruit** to be successful in the end, typically after planning and effort have been expended ◇ **old fruit** used as a term of address between men, especially between friends (*dated informal*)

fruitage /frŏŏtij/ *n* **1 FRUIT PRODUCTION** the production of fruit, the condition of a plant or tree when bearing fruit, or the time when this happens **2 FRUITS** fruits as a group **3 RESULT OR EFFECT** the results or cumulative set of effects deriving from a usually long-term process (*formal*)

fruitarian /froo táiri ən/ *n* a person who only eats fruit [Late 19C. After VEGETARIAN.]

fruit bat *n* a large bat of a kind, most of which eat fruit but some of which eat pollen or nectar. Native to: Europe, Asia, Africa. Suborder: Megachiroptera.

fruitcake /frŏŏt kayk/ *n* **1** a dense cake containing dried fruit **2** somebody considered to be irrational or out of touch with reality (*informal insult*)

fruit cocktail *n* a fruit salad made up of small or diced fruits such as pears, peaches, and pineapple, typically sold canned in syrup

fruit drop *n* **1** the falling from the tree of fruit that is not fully ripe **2** a fruit-flavoured boiled sweet

fruiterer /frŏŏtərər/ *n* a dealer in fruit [15C. < obsolete *fruiter* 'dealer in or handler of fruit' <French *fruitier* < *fruit* (see FRUIT).]

fruit fly *n* **1** a small insect that eats plant tissue. Order: Trypetidae. **2** a small insect that eats decaying fruit. Genus: *Drosophila*.

fruitful /frŏŏtf'l/ *adj* **1 BEARING MUCH FRUIT** bearing fruit, especially in abundance **2 PROLIFIC** producing many offspring ○ *a fruitful marriage* **3 CAUSING FERTILITY** causing or promoting fertility or productivity ○ *fruitful soil* **4 CREATIVE** highly productive or creative **5 SUCCESSFUL OR BENEFICIAL** producing useful results or benefits —**fruitfully** *adv* —**fruitfulness** *n*

fruiting body *n* a part of certain fungi from which spores are released

fruition /froo ísh'n/ *n* **1 COMPLETION** a state or point in which something has come to maturity or had a desired outcome ○ *Our plans have come to fruition.* **2 ENJOYMENT OF INTENDED OUTCOME** the enjoyment of a desired outcome when it happens **3 PLANT'S FRUIT PRODUCTION** the production of fruit by a tree or other plant [15C. Via French < late Latin *fruition-* < Latin *frui* 'enjoy, have the use of'.]

fruitless /frŏŏtləss/ *adj* **1** producing nothing or nothing worthwhile ○ *a fruitless discussion* **2** producing no fruit —**fruitlessly** *adv* —**fruitlessness** *n*

fruitlet /frŏŏtlət/ *n* **1** a fruit of smaller than normal size **2** any of the parts that make up a multiple fruit

fruit machine *n UK* a coin-operated gambling machine played by pushing a button or pulling a lever that makes pictures of fruit or other objects spin briefly

fruit salad *n* a mixture of pieces of fruit, usually in fruit juice or syrup, served as a dessert

fruit sugar *n* BIOCHEM = **fructose**

fruit tree *n* a tree cultivated for its fruit

fruitwood /frŏŏt wŏŏd/ *n* the wood of a fruit tree, especially when used in cabinet-making

fruity /frŏŏti/ (**-ier, -iest**) *adj* **1 OF FRUIT** relating to, resembling, or reminiscent of fruit **2 RICH IN TONE** rich and resonant in voice tone **3 SEXUALLY SUGGESTIVE** salacious or indecent in content (*informal*) —**fruitily** *adv* —**fruitiness** *n*

frumentaceous /frŏŏmən táyshəss/ *adj* made from, containing, or like wheat or any similar grain [Mid-17C. < late Latin *frumentaceus* < *frumentum* 'corn, grain'.]

frumenty /frŏŏmənti/, **fromenty** /frṓ-/, **furmenty** /fúr-/, **furmety** /fúrməti/, **furmity** *n* an old-fashioned pudding of wheat cooked to a porridge with added flavouring [14C. < Old French *frumentee, fourmentee* < *frument, fourment* 'grain' < Latin *frumentum*.]

frump /frump/ *n* a woman considered not to be good-looking or not to dress well (*informal insult*) [Mid-16C. Probably shortening of *frumple* 'wrinkle' < Middle Dutch *verrompelen* 'rumple completely'.] —**frumpily** *adv* —**frumpiness** *n* —**frumpish** *adj* —**frumpishly** *adv* —**frumpishness** *n* —**frumpy** *adj*

frusemide /frússə mīd/ *n* a diuretic drug. Use: treatment of hypertension and oedema. US term **furosemide** [Mid-20C. < Alteration of the first syllable of *furyl* 'chemical derived from furan' + *-sem-* < ?]

frustrate /fru stráyt/ *vt* (**-trates, -trating, -trated**) **1 THWART** to prevent somebody or something from succeeding or something from coming to fruition ○ *All attempts to put to sea were frustrated by high winds.* **2 DISCOURAGE** to make somebody feel discouraged, exasperated, or weary ■ *adj* **THWARTED** thwarted or blocked (*archaic*) [15C. < Latin *frustrat-*, past participle of *frustrari* 'deceive, frustrate, render useless' < *frustra* 'in vain, without effect'.] —**frustrater** *n* —**frustrating** *adj* —**frustratingly** *adv*

frustrated /fru stráytid/ *adj* feeling unfulfilled or unsatisfied

frustration /fru stráysh'n/ *n* **1 FRUSTRATING OF** an act or instance of causing somebody or something to be dissatisfied or unfulfilled **2 SOMETHING THAT THWARTS** something that blocks, thwarts, and upsets somebody all at the same time ○ *His lack of ambition was a frustration to his father.* **3 DISSATISFACTION** a feeling of disappointment, exasperation, or weariness caused by aims being thwarted or desires unsatisfied

frustule /frúss tyool/ *n* the hard cell wall of a microscopic organism (**diatom**) [Mid-19C. < Latin *frustulum* 'small piece' < *frustum* 'bit (cut off), piece (of a whole)'.]

frustum /frústəm/ *n* the part of a solid between its base and a plane that cuts it parallel to the base [Mid-17C. < Latin, 'bit (cut off), piece (of a whole)'.]

fry[1] /frī/ *v* (**fries, frying, fried**) **1** *vti* **COOK QUICKLY IN FAT** to cook something in fat over high heat, or be cooked in this way **2** *vi* **BECOME HOT OR OVERHEATED** to become extremely hot as a result of the surrounding environment or temperature (*informal*) ○ *We'll fry in this heat!* **3** *vti US* **EXECUTE OR BE EXECUTED** to execute somebody or be executed in an electric chair (*slang; offensive in some contexts*) ■ *n* (*plural* **fries**) **OFFAL** offal or a dish made from offal, especially as eaten fried [13C. Via French *frire* < Latin *frigere* 'roast, fry'.]

fry[2] /frī/ *npl* **1 YOUNG FISHES** the young of various fish **2 YOUNG ANIMALS** the young of various animals that breed or hatch in large numbers **3 CHILDREN** small offspring of human parents (*humorous*) [13C. Probably < Anglo-Norman *frei*, Old French *frai* 'spawn' < *froier* 'to spawn' < Latin *fricare* 'rub'.]

Fry /frī/, **Christopher** (*b.* 1907) British dramatist. Born **Christopher Harris**

Fry, Elizabeth (1780–1845) British prison reformer. Born **Elizabeth Gurney**

FRY *abbr* Federal Republic of Yugoslavia

Frye /frī/, **Northrop** (1912–91) Canadian literary critic

fryer /frī ər/, **frier** *n* **1** a vessel in which food is fried (*usually in combination*) **2** *US* a young chicken suitable for frying

frying pan *n* a shallow metal pan with a long handle, used for frying food ◇ **out of the frying pan (and) into the fire** from one difficult or dangerous situation to an even worse one

fry-up *n* (*informal*) **1** an act or occasion of frying several types of food together for a meal **2** a mixture of fried food

FSA *abbr* Fellow of the Society of Antiquaries

FSH *abbr* **1** follicle-stimulating hormone **2** full service history

f-stop *n* any setting for a lens aperture that corresponds with an f-number

ft *abbr* **1** foot *or* feet **2** fortification

FT *abbr* Financial Times

fth., fthm. *abbr* fathom

FT index *n* any share index compiled by the Financial Times

ϟ **FTP** *n* a standard procedure that allows one computer to transfer files to and from another over a network, e.g. the Internet. Full form **file-transfer protocol** ■ *vt* to transfer data using FTP

FTSE 100 Index /fŏŏtsi wun húndrəd-/ an average of the London stock exchange prices of the stocks of the 100 largest British companies, published daily. Full form **Financial Times Stock Exchange 100 Index**

fubsy /fúbsi/ (**-sier, -siest**) *adj* an offensive term meaning of short stature and wide girth (*slang*) [Late 18C. < obsolete *fub(s)* 'small plump person' < ?]

Fuchs /fŏŏks/, **Sir Vivian Ernest** (1908–99) British geologist and explorer

fuchsia /fyŏŏshə/ *n* **1** a widely-cultivated tropical plant or shrub. Flowers: purplish, reddish, or white, drooping. Genus: *Fuchsia.* **2** a brilliant deep purplish-pink colour [Late 18C. < modern Latin, after Leonhard *Fuchs.*] —**fuchsia** *adj*

fuchsin /fŏŏksin/, **fuchsine** /fŏŏk seen, -sin/ *n* $C_{20}H_{19}N_3.HCl$ a dark-green crystalline solid that when dissolved in water makes a bluish-red solution. Use: textile dye, bacteria stain, disinfectant. [Mid-19C. < French *fuchsine*, or directly < German *Fuchs* 'fox' (translation of French *Renard*, the company that first produced the dye).]

fuci plural of **fucus**

fuck /fuk/ *v* (*taboo*) **1** *vti* a highly offensive term meaning to have sexual intercourse **2** *vt* a highly offensive term used like a command, often followed by another word, to express anger, contempt, or rejection **3** *vt* a highly offensive term meaning to ruin, botch, or destroy something ■ *n* (*taboo*) **1** a highly offensive term for an act of sexual intercourse **2** a highly offensive term for somebody considered as a sexual partner of a particular quality **3** a highly offensive term for something of little or no value ■ *interj* a highly offensive term used without a following word to express exasperation, fear, or surprise or to add emphasis (*taboo*) [Early 16C. < ?]
fuck about, fuck around *vt* (*taboo*) **1** a highly offensive term meaning to behave stupidly or carelessly **2** a highly offensive term meaning to treat somebody in a careless, insincere, or inconsiderate way
fuck off *vi* (*taboo*) **1** a highly offensive term used as a command dismissing somebody in an angry or contemptuous way **2** a highly offensive term meaning to go away
fuck over *vt US* a highly offensive term meaning to treat people unjustly or take advantage of them (*taboo*)
fuck up *v* (*taboo*) **1** *vt* a highly offensive term meaning to damage or botch something **2** *vt* a highly offensive term meaning to make somebody confused or inflict emotional or mental damage on somebody **3** *vi* a highly offensive term meaning to make a bad mistake or bungle something
fuck with *vt US* a highly offensive term meaning to treat another person in a careless or disrespectful way (*taboo*)

fucker /fúkər/ *n* **1** a highly offensive term expressing extreme dislike for somebody (*taboo insult*) **2** a highly offensive term for any unnamed person (*taboo*)

fuckface /fúk fayss/ *n* a highly offensive term expressing extreme contempt for somebody (*taboo insult*)

fucking /fúking/ *adj* a highly offensive term intensifying or emphasizing a word or statement (*taboo*)

fuckup /fúk up/ *n* **1** a highly offensive term meaning a bad mistake or something bungled (*taboo*) **2** a highly offensive term meaning somebody regarded as an incompetent or bungling (*taboo insult*)

fuckwit /fúk wit/ *n* a highly offensive term for somebody thought to be unintelligent (*taboo*)

fucose /fyŏŏ kōz, -kōss/ *n* a five-carbon sugar found in plant polysaccharides [Early 20C. < FUCUS; from its presence in brown algae.]

fucoxanthin /fyŏŏ kō zánthin/ *n* a brown carotenoid pigment found in some algae [Late 19C. < FUCUS; from its presence in brown algae.]

fucus /fyŏŏkəss/ (*plural* **-ci** /fyŏŏssī/ *or* **-cuses**) *n* a green-ish-brown seaweed. Genus: *Fucus.* [Early 17C. Via modern Latin < Latin, 'rock lichen, red or purple colour' < Greek *phukos* 'seaweed'.] —**fucoid** /fyŏŏ koyd/ *adj*

fuddle /fúdd'l/ *v* (**-dles, -dling, -dled**) **1** *vt* **CONFUSE AS IF WITH DRINK** to make a person or mental faculty confused, often through intoxication **2** *vi* **DRINK TOO MUCH** to drink too much alcohol regularly (*archaic*) ■ *n* **FUDDLED STATE** a state of confusion or drunkenness [Late 16C. < ?]

fuddy-duddy /fúddi dudi/ (*plural* **fuddy-duddies**) *n* an old-fashioned or dull person, especially one past middle age (*informal; offensive in some contexts*) ○ *This is for kids, not fuddy-duddies like us.* [Early 20C. < ?]

fudge /fuj/ *n* **1 SWEET** soft toffee made by boiling milk and sugar and then beating the liquid until it crystallizes and becomes slightly grainy in texture **2 NONSENSE** nonsensical talk (*informal*) ■ *vti* (**fudges, fudging, fudged**) **ALTER TO DECEIVE** to fiddle with or otherwise alter something in order to deceive or remain noncommittal (*informal*) ○ *fudged the figures to make the bottom line look better* [Early 17C. < ?]

fuel /fyŏŏ əl/ *n* **1 SOURCE OF ENERGY** something that is burned to provide power or heat **2 SOURCE OF NUCLEAR ENERGY** the fissionable material used to create power in a nuclear generator **3 SOURCE OF STIMULATION** something that stimulates or maintains something else, especially an emotion ○ *Her refusal to answer questions added fuel to his curiosity.* ■ *v* (**-els, -elling, -elled**) **1** *vt* **SUPPLY WITH FUEL** to supply something with material to burn for power or heat **2** *vt* **STIMULATE** to stimulate or maintain something, especially an emotion **3** *vi* **OBTAIN FUEL** to take on supplies of fuel for running a vehicle [12C. Via Anglo-Norman *fuaille*, Old French *fouaille* < assumed Vulgar Latin *focalia* '(things) for the fire' < Latin *focus* 'fireplace, hearth'.] —**fueller** *n*

fuel cell *n* a device that generates electricity by converting the chemical energy of a fuel and an oxidant to electrical energy

fuel efficiency *n* the ability to make the best use of the fuel being used —**fuel-efficient** *adj*

fuel injection *n* a system for running an internal-combustion engine without using a carburettor, forcing vaporized fuel under pressure directly into the combustion chamber —**fuel-injected** *adj*

fuel oil *n* a product of liquid petroleum, burned chiefly to power ships and locomotives and to provide domestic heating

fuel rod *n* a metal tube containing nuclear fuel that is used in some types of nuclear reactor

Fuentes /fwént ayss/, **Carlos** (*b.* 1928) Mexican writer

fug /fug/ *n* a stale or airless atmosphere [Late 19C. Probably alteration of FOG.]

fugacious /fyoo gáyshəss/ *adj* **1** fleeting or passing away quickly (*formal*) **2** lasting only briefly before withering or dropping [Early 17C. < Latin *fugac-* 'fleeing swiftly' < *fugere* 'flee'.] —**fugaciously** *adv* —**fugaciousness** *n* —**fugacity** /-gássəti/ *n*

fugato /fyoo gaatō/ *adv, adj* in the style of a fugue ■ *n* (*plural* **-tos**) a piece of music in the style of a fugue [Mid-19C. < Italian, < past participle of *fugare* 'compose as a fugue' < *fuga* (see FUGUE).]

-fuge *suffix* something that drives out ○ *febrifuge* [Via French < Latin *fugere* 'flee', *fugare* 'drive out' < *fuga* 'flight']

fugitive /fyŏŏjitiv/ *n* **1 SOMEBODY WHO RUNS AWAY** a person who flees, e.g. from justice, enemies, or brutal treatment **2 SOMETHING ELUSIVE** an elusive or ephemeral thing ■ *adj* **1 RUNNING AWAY** fleeing, especially fleeing arrest or punishment **2 BRIEF** lasting only briefly ○ *the fugitive hours* **3 ITINERANT** moving around from place to place **4 FOR PARTICULAR OCCASION** written or composed for a particular occasion or on a subject of only passing interest ○ *a collection of essays, letters, and fugitive pieces* **5 HARD TO UNDERSTAND** difficult to understand or retain ○ *the fugitive nature of higher mathematics* [14C. Directly or via French < Latin *fugitivus* < *fugit-*, past participle of *fugere* 'flee'.] —**fugitively** *adv* —**fugitiveness** *n*

fugle /fyŏŏg'l/ (**-gles, -gling, -gled**) *vi* to act as or like a fugleman in training or leading others [Mid-19C. Back-formation < FUGLEMAN.]

fugleman /fyŏŏg'lmən/ *n* **1** formerly, a soldier used to teach drill movements by performing them in front of trainees **2** somebody acting as a leader or example to others [Early 19C. Alteration of German *Flügelmann* 'wing man, man on the flank'.]

fugue /fyoog/ *n* **1** a musical form in which a theme is first stated, then repeated and varied with accompanying contrapuntal lines **2 fugue, fugue state** a disordered state of mind, in which somebody typically wanders from home and experiences a loss of memory relating only to the previous, rejected, environment [Late 16C. Directly or via French < Italian *fuga* < Latin, 'flight'.] —**fugal** *adj* —**fugally** *adv*

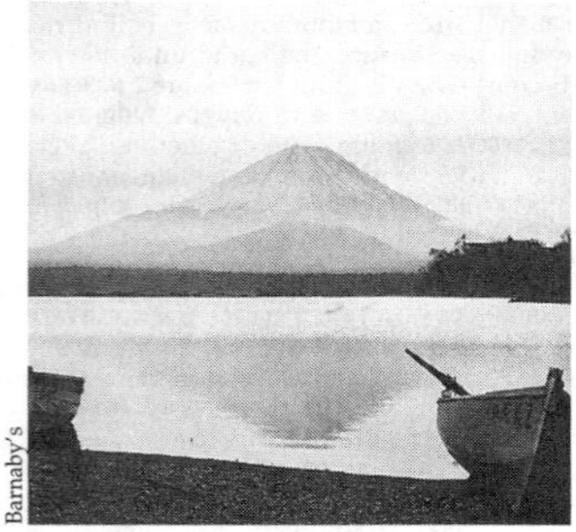
Barnaby's

Mount Fuji

Fuji, Mount /fo͝oji, -/, **Fujiyama** /fo͝oji aámə/ dormant volcano and the highest mountain in Japan, on central Honshu Island. Height: 3,776 m/12,387 ft.

Fujian /fo͞o jyén/, **Fukien** /fo͞o kyén/ province of SE China. Capital: Fuzhou. Population: 31,830,000 (1994). Area: 121,000 sq. km/46,720 sq. mi.

Fujimori /fo͝oji máwri/, **Alberto** (*b.* 1938) Peruvian politician and president (1999–2000)

Fujisawa /fo͝oji saáwə/ city on SE Honshu Island, Japan. Population: 350,370 (1990).

Fujita scale /fo͞o jeétə-/ *n* a scale used to rank tornadoes by the amount of damage they do to man-made structures and natural objects [Late 20C. After Tetsuya Theodore *Fujita* (1920–98), Japanese-born US chemist.]

Fujiyama /fo͝oji yaámə/ MOUNTAINS = **Fuji, Mount**

Fukien = **Fujian**

Fukui /foo ko͞o i/ city on west-central Honshu Island, Japan. Population: 252,743 (1990).

Fukuoka /fo͝oko͞o ṓkə/ port on N Kyushu Island, Japan. Population: 1,237,062 (1990).

Fukushima /fo͝oko͞o sheémə/ city on north-central Honshu Island, Japan. Population: 280,958 (1990).

Fukuyama /fo͝oko͞o yaámə/ city on SW Honshu Island, Japan, on the Inland Sea. Population: 365,612 (1990).

-ful *suffix* **1** full of ○ *hateful* **2** having the nature of ○ *rightful* **3** tending to ○ *forgetful* **4** an amount that fills ○ *capful* **5** full to ○ *brimful* [Old English, < *full* (see FULL)]

Fula /fo͞olə/ (*plural* **-la** *or* **-las**), **Fulah** (*plural* **-lah** *or* **-lahs**) *n* **1** a member of an ethnically diverse nomadic people living in western and central Africa **2** LANG = **Fulani** *n.* 1 [Late 18C. < Fulani *pulo* 'person'.] —**Fula** *adj*

Fulani /fo͞o laáni/ (*plural* **-ni** *or* **-nis**) *n* **1** a Niger-Congo language spoken over a large area of West Africa, especially in Nigeria, Guinea-Bissau, Burkina-Faso, Gambia, Benin, Guinea, and Senegal. Native speakers: 15 million. **2** PEOPLES = **Fula** *n.* 1 [Mid-19C. < Hausa.] —**Fulani** *adj*

Fulbright /fo͝ol brīt/, **J. William** (1905–95) US educator and statesman

fulcrum /fo͝olkrəm/ (*plural* **-crums** *or* **-cra** /-krə/) *n* **1** PIVOT the point or support about which a lever turns **2** PROP something that supports something else revolving about it or depending on it ○ *The fulcrum of the building plan is the major retail tenant.* **3** SUPPORT IN ANIMAL part of an animal that acts as a hinge or support, especially scales on the fins of some fish [Late 17C. < Latin, 'post or foot of a couch, bedpost' < *fulcire* 'prop up, support'.]

fulfil /fo͝ol fíl/ (**-fils, -filling, -filled**) *v* **1** *vt* ACHIEVE to do what is necessary to bring about or achieve something expected, desired, or promised ○ *went on to fulfil her early promise of greatness* **2** *vt* CARRY OUT to do what is necessary to carry out a request or command ○ *The instructions have been fulfilled to the letter.* **3** *vt* SATISFY to be good enough or of the type necessary to meet a standard or requirement **4** *vt* COMPLETE to do what is necessary to complete or bring something to an end **5** *vt* SUPPLY to supply the full amount of something ordered **6** *vr* REALIZE AMBITIONS to feel satisfied with what you are doing or realize your expectations or ambitions [Old English *fullfyllan* 'fill up, make full' < FULL¹ + FILL] —**fulfiller** *n* —**fulfilment** *n*

fulfill *vt* US = **fulfil**

fulfilling /fo͝ol fílling/ *adj* giving satisfaction to somebody as an activity or goal in life ○ *a fulfilling job opportunity*

fulgent /fúljənt/ *adj* shining or gleaming brilliantly (*literary*) [15C. < Latin *fulgent-*, present participle of *fulgere* 'flash, shine'.] —**fulgency** *n* —**fulgently** *adv*

fulgurate /fúlgyo͝o rayt/ (**-rates, -rating, -rated**) *v* **1** *vt* to destroy unwanted tissue, e.g. warts, using a high-frequency electric current **2** *vi* to flash with or like lightning (*formal*) [Mid-17C. < Latin *fulgurat-*, past participle of *fulgurare* 'lighten, flash' < *fulgere* 'flash, shine'.] —**fulgurant** *adj* —**fulguration** /fúlgyo͝o ráysh'n/ *n* —**fulgurous** *adj*

fulgurite /fúlgyo͝o rīt/ *n* a tube of hard, glassy material formed by lightning striking sand [Mid-19C. < Latin *fulgur* 'lightning'.]

fuliginous /fyoo líjjinəss/ *adj* (*formal*) **1** having the colour or consistency of soot or smoke **2** like soot in cloudiness or obscurity [Late 16C. Directly or via French *fuligineux* < late Latin *fuliginosus* < Latin *fuligin-*, stem of *fuligo* 'soot'.] —**fuliginously** *adv*

full¹ /fo͝ol/ *adj* **1** FILLED TO CAPACITY holding as much or as many as is possible **2** WITH MUCH OR MANY having a large amount or number of something ○ *full of mischief* **3** GREATEST IN EXTENT being at the highest degree or largest extent ○ *at full speed* ○ *an engine running at full revolutions* ○ *I like my coffee full strength.* **4** WITH NOTHING MISSING with nothing or nobody left out or missing ○ *the full complement of staff* **5** COMPLETELY DEVELOPED at the end or peak of development ○ *roses in full bloom* **6** COMPLETELY SO having reached or fulfilled all requirements for a position, rank, or description ○ *a full colonel* **7** HAVING EATEN ENOUGH satisfied by an amount eaten or drunk **8** BUSY filled with activity or achievement ○ *live a full life* **9** PLUMP fleshy and with a rounded shape **10** WITH SAME PARENTS sharing both natural parents ○ *my full brother* **11** CHARGED WITH EMOTION affected by strong deep emotion ○ *We left the place with full hearts and shining eyes.* **12** PREOCCUPIED deeply preoccupied with something ○ *She's always full of her latest schemes.* **13** SONOROUS with depth or power, e.g. of sound **14** RICHLY FLAVOURED with a rich strong flavour and substantial quality **15** WITH MUCH FABRIC made with a lot of fabric and not close-fitting **16** DRUNK drunk (*slang*) ■ *adv* **1** COMPLETELY to the greatest or complete extent ○ *turn full round* **2** EXACTLY in a precise or exact position ○ *He took a punch full on the mouth.* **3** VERY to a high degree ○ *What happened next we know full well.* ■ *n* FULLEST STATE the greatest extent or highest degree ○ *We enjoyed ourselves to the full.* ■ *v* **1** *vt* SEW GATHERS AND TUCKS to make a garment full by sewing gathers in it **2** *vi* BECOME FULL to wax and become full (*refers to the moon*) [Old English, < Indo-European] —**fullness** *n* ◇ **be full of yourself** to be very conceited and arrogant ◇ **full up** completely full ◇ **in full** to the complete amount or extent, omitting nothing ○ *The opera has never been performed in full.*

full² /fo͝ol/ *vti* to make cloth bulkier by dampening and beating it, or become bulkier by being dampened and beaten [14C. Probably back-formation < FULLER¹.]

fullback /fo͝ol bak/ *n* **1** DEFENDER a player in a defensive position in sports such as football, rugby, or hockey **2** ATTACKING PLAYER in American football, a player in the offensive backfield who lines up behind the quarterback and is used mainly for blocking **3** FULLBACK POSITION the position played by a fullback

full beam *n* the setting of a vehicle's headlights that sheds light far in front of the vehicle. US term **high beam**

full-blooded *adj* **1** healthily vigorous or forceful **2** of unmixed breed —**full-bloodedly** *adv*—**full-bloodedness** *n*

full-blown *adj* **1** in its most complete, extreme, strongest, or developed form ○ *full-blown malaria* **2** blooming and fully open

full board *n* board at a hotel or guest house that includes accommodation and all meals. US term **American plan**

full-bodied *adj* **1** with a rich strong flavour and substantial quality **2** rich in tone and strong in volume

full circle *adv* back to the starting point, usually after passing through various stages

full count *n* in baseball, the situation in which the batter has three balls and two strikes

full-court press *n* in basketball, the practice of putting pressure on opposing players in all parts of the court as opposed to merely defending the backcourt

full cousin *n* LAW = **cousin** *n.* 1

full dress *n* clothes suitable or prescribed for a ceremony or formal occasion (*hyphenated before nouns*)

full-dress *adj* of considerable importance and often complete or exhaustive ○ *a full-dress investigation*

full employment *n* the state of a country's economy in which everyone available for work has a job

fuller¹ /fo͝olər/ *n* somebody who makes cloth bulkier by dampening and beating it [Pre-12C. < Latin *fullo.*]

fuller² /fo͝olər/ *n* a hammer used by a blacksmith for forging grooves and spreading hot iron [Early 19C. < ?]

Fuller /fo͝olər/, **Buckminster** (1895–1983) US engineer, designer, architect, and writer

Fuller, Roy (1912–92) British poet and novelist

Fuller, Thomas (1608–61) English clergyman, author, and historian

fullerene /fo͝olla reen/ *n* a form of carbon made up of up to 500 carbon atoms arranged in a sphere or tube [Late 20C. Shortening of BUCKMINSTERFULLERENE.]

fuller's earth *n* an absorbent clay used in fulling cloth and in filtering liquids

full-faced *adj* with the whole of the face visible, facing the viewer ○ *a full-face portrait*

full-figured *adj* having a fleshy rounded body, or designed to be worn by somebody, especially a woman, with a fleshy rounded body

~~**fullfill**~~ incorrect spelling of **fulfil**

full-fledged *adj* US = **fully-fledged**

full-frontal *adj* **1** showing the whole front of the body including the genitals **2** whole-hearted and uninhibited (*informal*) ○ *She made a full-frontal attack on her opponents.*

full-grown *adj* US = **fully-grown**

full house *n* a poker hand containing three cards of the same value and a pair of a different value

full-length *adj* **1** REACHING TO THE ANKLES describes a garment such as a coat or skirt that extends to the ankles or floor **2** SHOWING WHOLE BODY describes a mirror or portrait showing the whole length of the body **3** NOT SHORTENED consisting of the whole or usual amount or duration of something

full marks *npl* **1** a perfect score in an assessment or examination **2** high praise or commendation (*informal*) ○ *Full marks to the driver for managing to find the place.*

full monty /-mónti/ *n* everything that is needed or appropriate or makes up a full set or the whole of something (*slang*)

full moon *n* **1** the phase of the Moon when its surface as seen from the Earth is fully illuminated by the Sun **2** the period of time during which the Moon appears fully illuminated as a circle

full-mouthed *adj* **1** having the complete set of adult teeth **2** said loudly or vigorously

full nelson *n* a wrestling hold in which one wrestler puts both arms beneath an opponent's arms from behind and then exerts pressure by clasping the hands at the back of the opponent's neck

full-on *adj* **1** ALL-OUT taken to the limits ○ *The wedding was a full-on display of pomp and ceremony.* **2** OUT-AND-OUT possessing a particular quality to the fullest extent ○ *he used to be a full-on computer nerd* **3** OVERPOWERING talkative and enthusiastic to an excessive degree ○ *She's a bit full-on, isn't she?*

full point *n* GRAM = **full stop**

full-rigged *adj* having at least three square-rigged masts

full-scale *adj* **1** having exactly the same dimensions and proportions as the original **2** done with total commitment of effort and resources ○ *a full-scale manhunt*

full-size, full-sized *adj* being the normal size for its kind

full stop *n* **1** the punctuation mark (.) that is used at the end of a sentence or in abbreviations. US term **period** *n.* 6 **2** a complete halt or an end ○ *This delay has brought production to a full stop.*

PUNCTUATION A ***full stop*** is used at the end of a sentence that is not a question or exclamation: *It rained last Saturday.* It is also used after some abbreviations: *at 11 a.m. on 7 Aug. 2000.* The full stop is increasingly omitted in abbreviations, especially in contractions (e.g. *Dr, St, Ltd*) and after capital letters (e.g. *BBC, USA, VCR*). Shortened forms used as words in their own right (e.g. *gym, disco, pub*) and acronyms pronounced as words (e.g. *Aids, laser, NATO*) should not be written with full stops. The same mark is used in decimal notation (*2.5 children*), where it is read as 'point'. It is also used in Internet addresses, where it is read as 'dot' (*.com*).

full time *n* the end of a match in football and other sports ■ *adv* during all of the time considered standard or appropriate for the activity in question

full-time *adj* 1 involving or using all of the time considered standard or appropriate for an activity, especially work ○ *a full-time student* 2 occurring at or indicating the end of a soccer or other match ○ *the full-time score* —**full-timer** *n*

full-wave rectifier *n* a circuit used in the design of electronic equipment such as radios, computers, and televisions that operates on both the positive and negative cycles of an alternating current

fully /fo͝olli/ *adv* 1 to the greatest extent possible or required ○ *The flight is fully booked.* 2 to the full extent of the time, quantity, or number specified ○ *We waited fully 40 minutes.*

⚡**fully featured** *adj* having the whole range of possible functions, capabilities, or options

fully-fledged *adj* 1 WITH ADULT FEATHERS having grown adult feathers and so being able to fly 2 COMPLETELY DEVELOPED at a point of complete development or maturity ○ *a fully-fledged microelectronics industry* 3 FULLY QUALIFIED with full status or rank ○ *a fully-fledged helicopter pilot*

fully-grown *adj* having developed to maturity or adulthood. US term **full-grown**

fulmar /fo͝olmər/ *n* a heavy short-tailed seabird. Native to: polar regions. Genus: *Fulmarus.* [Late 17C. < Old Norse *fúll* 'foul' (because it regurgitates its stomach's contents when disturbed) + *már* 'gull'.]

fulminant /fo͝olminənt/ *adj* 1 exploding violently 2 coming on suddenly and with severe symptoms of short duration [Early 17C. Directly or via French < Latin *fulminant-*, present participle of *fulminare* (see FULMINATE).]

fulminate /fo͝olmi nayt, fúl-/ *vti* (**-nates, -nating, -nated**) 1 SPEAK SCATHINGLY to express forcible criticism ○ *an article fulminating against the arms trade* 2 EXPLODE to detonate or explode violently, or cause something to detonate or explode violently ■ *n* EXPLOSIVE SALT OR ESTER any explosive salt or ester of fulminic acid, especially fulminate of mercury [15C. < Latin *fulminat-*, past participle of *fulminare* 'lighten, strike with lightning' < *fulmen* 'lightning'.] —**fulmination** /fo͝olmi náysh'n, fúl-/ *n* —**fulminator** *n* —**fulminatory** *adj*

fulminate of mercury *n* $HgC_2N_2O_2$ the mercury salt of fulminic acid. Use: in explosives and detonators.

fulminating /fo͝olmi nayting, fúl-/ *adj* 1 able or likely to explode or detonate 2 MED = **fulminant** *adj.* 2

fulminic acid /fo͝ol minnik-, ful-/ *n* HONC an unstable compound that smells of bitter almonds. Use: manufacture of explosives. [< Latin *fulmin-*, stem of *fulmen* 'lightning']

fulsome /fo͝olsəm/ *adj* 1 effusive or fawning to the point of being offensive ○ *embarrassed by their fulsome praise* 2 great in amount or intensity [13C. < FULL[1] + -SOME.] —**fulsomely** *adv* —**fulsomeness** *n*

USAGE ***Fulsome*** has several meanings that are quite different, and so when you use it, be sure that your surrounding context makes your intended meaning crystal clear. ***Fulsome*** is traditionally used to mean 'excessive' and 'offensively effusive or unctuous', as in *a fulsome display of marital love totally inappropriate in public* and *an interview laden with fulsome compliments for a notorious tyrant.* In the first example, you can substitute *excessive* and in the second you can substitute *effusive* or *unctuous.* Notice the extreme negativity of these uses. The meaning, 'abundant', which was once an original sense of ***fulsome*** in the 13th century, has been revived. It has been used so much in recent years that it has all but obscured the other meanings. This usage most commonly occurs in *fulsome praise* and *a fulsome apology*, as in *He is a true national hero, deserving of fulsome praise*, where *abundant* is the better, more precise choice. Instead of *a fulsome apology*, it is best to say *a full apology*, so that your readers will understand exactly what you mean.

fulvous /fo͝olvəss, fúl-/ *adj* of an orange-brown colour (*literary*) [Mid-17C. < Latin *fulvus* 'reddish-yellow'.]

Fu Manchu moustache /fo͞o manchoo-/ *n* a moustache with long drooping ends [After a character in the novels of Sax Rohmer]

fumaric acid /fyoo márrik-/ *n* $C_4H_4O_4$ a colourless crystalline solid. Source: some plants and moulds, or synthesized from benzene. Use: manufacture of resins. [Via modern Latin < late Latin *fumaria* 'fumitory' < Latin *fumus* 'smoke']

fumarole /fyo͞omərōl/ *n* a vent in a volcanic area from which steam and hot gases such as sulphur dioxide are emitted [Early 19C. Via Italian *fumaruolo* < late Latin *fumariolum* 'vent, smoke-hole' < Latin *fumus* 'smoke'.] —**fumarolic** /fyo͞omə róllik/ *adj*

fumatory /fyo͞omətəri/ *adj* relating to, involving, or typical of fumigation or smoking [Mid-19C. < assumed Latin *fumatorius* < *fumare* 'to smoke'.]

fumble /fúmb'l/ *v* (**-bles, -bling, -bled**) 1 *vti* GROPE CLUMSILY to grope clumsily in searching for something ○ *He fumbled in his pockets for his keys.* 2 *vi* HESITATE to act clumsily, hesitantly, or unsuccessfully ○ *She fumbled through the introductions.* 3 *vt* BUNGLE to do something clumsily or inefficiently ○ *This is your last chance, so don't fumble it.* 4 *vti* DROP OR MISHANDLE BALL in sports, to drop or fail to catch a ball ■ *n* FUMBLED ACTION an act or instance of fumbling [Mid-16C. < ?] —**fumbler** *n* —**fumblingly** *adv*

fume /fyoom/ *v* (**fumes, fuming, fumed**) 1 *vi* BE ANGRY to feel great anger, especially anger that is not fully expressed 2 *vi* EMIT GAS to emit gas, smoke, or vapour, or be emitted in this form 3 *vt* FUMIGATE to treat something with a gas, smoke, or other fumigant 4 *vt* DARKEN to expose wood, especially oak, to vapour or gas given off by ammonia in order to darken it (*usually passive*) ■ *n* 1 SMOKE smoke, gas, or vapour, especially when unpleasant or harmful (*often plural*) ○ *a chemical that emits noxious fumes when exposed to air* 2 ACRID SMELL an acrid or nauseating smell (*often plural*) 3 FIT OF ANGER a state of great anger [14C. Via Old French < Latin *fumus* 'smoke'.] —**fumingly** *adv* —**fumy** *adj*

fume cupboard *n* an enclosed ventilated chamber in which to conduct chemistry experiments involving harmful vapours

fumigant /fyo͞omigənt/ *n* a substance that gives off fumes, especially one used as a disinfectant or to kill pests [Late 19C. < Latin *fumigant-*, present participle of *fumigare* (see FUMIGATE).]

fumigate /fyo͞omi gayt/ (**-gates, -gating, -gated**) *vti* to treat something with fumes, especially to disinfect it or to kill pests [Mid-16C. < Latin *fumigat-*, past participle of *fumigare* 'to smoke' < *fumus* 'smoke'.] —**fumigation** /fyo͞omi gáysh'n/ *n* —**fumigator** *n*

fuming sulphuric acid *n* a very concentrated solution of sulphuric acid that gives off fumes

fumitory /fyo͞omitəri/ (*plural* **-ries**) *n* a sprawling herbaceous plant with deeply divided leaves and acrid-smelling roots. Flowers: pink or white, pouch-shaped. Native to: Europe. Genus: *Fumaria.* [14C. Via Old French *fumeterre* < medieval Latin *fumus terrae* 'smoke of the earth'; from its greyish foliage.]

fun /fun/ *n* 1 AMUSEMENT a time or feeling of enjoyment or amusement ○ *Just for fun, we wore silly hats.* 2 SOMETHING AMUSING something such as an activity that provides enjoyment or amusement ○ *Skiing is fun for the whole family.* 3 MOCKERY playful joking, often at the expense of another ○ *What's said in fun can still hurt.* ■ *adj* 1 AMUSING providing enjoyment or amusement (*informal*) ○ *We'll have a fun time tonight.* 2 CHEAP AND FLAMBOYANT flamboyant in style and often made of cheap synthetic materials, designed to be used or worn for fun ○ *fun jewellery* ■ *vi* (**funs, funning, funned**) BEHAVE PLAYFULLY to behave in a playful or joking way (*informal*) ○ *Don't pay any attention to him; he's just funning.* [Late 17C. < obsolete *fon* 'fool' < ?] ◇ **fun and games** activity, difficulty, or trouble (*informal; ironic*) ○ *A broken sprinkler in the stockroom overnight gave us some fun and games in the morning.* ◇ **like fun** 1 with great speed or effort (*informal*) ○ *We'll have to work like fun to finish this order on time.* 2 certainly not (*informal*) ○ *Like fun I am!* ◇ **make fun of somebody** *or* **something** to make somebody or something appear ridiculous ◇ **poke fun at somebody** *or* **something** to mock or ridicule somebody or something

Funabashi /fo͞onə báshi/ city on east-central Honshu Island, Japan, on Tokyo Bay. Population: 533,270 (1990).

Funafuti /fo͞onə fo͞oti/ atoll and capital of Tuvalu, in the W Pacific Ocean. Population: 3,432 (1991). Area: 2.6 sq. km/1 sq. mi.

funambulist /fyoo námbyo͝olist/ *n* an acrobat who walks while balancing on a suspended rope [Late 18C. < French *funambule* or Latin *funambulus* < *funis* 'rope' + *ambulare* 'to walk'.] —**funambulate** *vi* —**funambulism** *n*

Funchal /fo͞on shaál/ capital of the Madeira Islands, on the coast of S Madeira, in the North Atlantic Ocean. Population: 115,950 (1995 estimate).

⚡**function** /fúngksh'n/ *n* 1 PURPOSE an action or use for which something is suited or designed ○ *a watch with an alarm function* 2 ROLE an activity or role assigned to somebody or something 3 EVENT a social gathering or ceremony, especially a formal or official occasion ○ *a black-tie function* 4 VARIABLE QUANTITY DETERMINED BY OTHERS' VALUES a variable quantity whose value depends upon the varying values of other quantities 5 DEPENDENT FACTOR a quality or characteristic that depends upon and varies with another ○ *Success is a function of determination and ability.* 6 CORRESPONDENCE BETWEEN MEMBERS OF DIFFERENT SETS (*symbol* **f**) a relationship between two mathematical sets, in which each member of one set corresponds uniquely to a member of the other set 7 SINGLE COMPUTER OPERATION a named and stored basic operation of a computer yielding a single result when invoked 8 COMPUTER PROGRAM'S MAIN PURPOSE the purpose of a computer program or piece of computer equipment, e.g. database management or printing 9 ROLE OF WORD OR PHRASE a grammatical role performed by a word or phrase in a particular construction ○ *Noun phrases can fulfil many functions.* 10 UTILITY practical usefulness, as distinct from, e.g. aesthetic appeal ○ *the relationship between form and function* ■ *vi* 1 SERVE PURPOSE to serve a particular purpose or perform a particular role ○ *hats functioning both as fashion statements and as protection against the sun* 2 BE IN WORKING ORDER to operate normally, fulfilling a purpose or role ○ *When the heart ceases to function, the patient is clinically dead.* [Mid-16C. < Latin *function-* < *funct-*, past participle of *fungi* 'perform'.] —**functionless** *adj*

functional /fúngksh'nəl/ *adj* 1 PRACTICAL having a practical application or serving a useful purpose ○ *designs that are functional yet fun* 2 OPERATIONAL in good working order or working at the moment ○ *The lift will not be functional for several hours.* 3 HAVING NO ORGANIC CAUSE without apparent organic or structural cause ○ *a functional disorder* 4 RELATING TO LANGUAGE AS COMMUNICATION relating to the function of language as a communicating tool, rather than to its form ○ *functional linguistics* —**functionally** *adv*

⚡**functional acknowledgment** *n* a notification of receipt of an electronic data interchange transaction from the receiver to the sender (*in e-commerce*)

functional drink *n* a drink containing nutritional additives that is promoted as being beneficial to health and is sometimes substituted for an entire meal

functional food *n* food containing nutritional additives that is promoted as being beneficial to health ○ *'the first spread formulated to act against cholesterol in a market for so-called functional foods'* (*The Guardian*; April 1999)

functional genomics *n* the study of the relationships between gene structure and biological function in organisms

functional group *n* a group of atoms that reacts as a single unit and determines the properties and structure of a particular class of compounds, e.g. a hydroxyl group in alcohols

functional illiterate *n* somebody whose reading and writing abilities are inadequately developed to meet everyday needs —**functionally illiterate** *adj*

functionalism /fúngksh'nəlizəm/ *n* 1 BELIEF IN FUNCTION OVER FORM belief that the intended function of something should determine its design, construction, and choice of materials, or a 20th-century design movement based on this 2 PHILOSOPHY EMPHASIZING THE PRACTICAL any philosophy or system that gives practical and utilitarian concerns priority over aesthetic concerns 3 ASSESSMENT OF SOCIAL INSTITUTIONS BY ROLE the analysis and explanation of social institutions according to the function they perform in society, e.g. the family seen as an institution for social stability and cohesion —**functionalist** *n, adj*

⚡**functionality** /fúngkshə nállti/ the range of functions, capabilites, and options a computer offers

functional literacy *n* the level of skill in reading and writing that an individual needs to cope with everyday adult life

functional medicine *n* medical treatment that aims to blend traditional Western drug-based therapy with alternative forms of medicine

functional shift *n* a change in the grammatical function of a word, e.g. from noun to verb, as happens when the noun 'wallpaper' is used as the verb 'to wallpaper'

LANGUAGE NOTE ***Functional shift*** is a process in which a word shifts from one grammatical function to another. For example: 1. a noun can be used as a verb, e.g. *to access a computer file* 2. a verb as a noun, e.g. *having a laugh* 3. a noun as an adjective, e.g. *a prestige development* 4. an interjection as a verb, e.g. *Audiences were wowed by his new musical.* 5. an adverb as a noun, e.g. *the ins and outs*, or as a verb, e.g. *upping the limit*. Functional shift is sometimes controversial, but it has been a well-established phenomenon in English since the 16th century. Shakespeare used it enthusiastically: *'Be he ne'er so vile, this day shall gentle his condition'* (Henry V).

functionary /fúngksh'nəri/ (*plural* **-ies**) *n* an official, especially somebody with trivial duties

function change *n* LING = **functional shift**

⚡**function key** *n* a button on a computer keyboard or terminal that instructs the computer to perform a specific task

function shift *n* LING = **functional shift**

function word *n* a word that has little meaning on its own but serves a particular syntactic or semantic function in a phrase or sentence, e.g. a conjunction such as 'since' or 'but'

LANGUAGE NOTE Function words We are accustomed to think of a word as something that conveys a particular meaning, e.g. *pomegranate, red,* or *abdicate*. However, there is a group of words in English whose main role is not to convey meaning but to show grammatical relationships. Some have no meaning at all in the conventional sense, but they have a particular function to perform in a sentence. Thus, they are known as ***function words***. There are six categories: 1. conjunctions, introducing a clause: *and, but, that, where,* etc. 2. determiners (including articles): *a, some, the, this,* etc. 3. modal verbs: *can, must, will,* etc. 4. prepositions, signalling the beginning of a noun phrase: *at, below, in, of,* etc. 5. primary verbs: *be, do,* and *have* 6. pronouns: *anyone, I, this, which,* etc.

functor /fúngktər/ *n* **1** somebody or something that performs a function (*formal*) **2** LING = **function word** [Mid-20C. < FUNCTION.]

fund /fund/ *n* **1 SUPPLY** a source or stock of something **2 RESERVE OF MONEY** a sum of money saved or invested for a particular purpose **3 ORGANIZATION ADMINISTERING RESERVE OF MONEY** an organization that manages a sum of money for a particular purpose ■ **funds** *npl* **1 MONEY** money, especially money that is available to spend ○ *I'm a bit short of funds at the moment.* **2 UK GOVERNMENT SECURITIES** British government securities that finance the national debt and pay a fixed rate of interest ■ *vt* **1 PROVIDE MONEY FOR** to provide money needed to finance a project or keep it running (*often passive*) ○ *environmental projects funded by local government* **2 PROVIDE MONEY TO PAY DEBT** to provide a sum of money to pay off a debt or its interest **3 MAKE DEBT LONG-TERM** to convert a short-term debt into a long-term debt with a fixed rate of interest **4 PUT IN RESERVE** to store something up for future use ○ *a notebook in which snippets of overheard conversations are funded* [Mid-17C. < Latin *fundus* 'bottom'.] —**funder** *n*

fundament /fúndəmənt/ *n* **1** an underlying principle or theory on which something is founded (*formal; often plural*) **2** the buttocks or the anus (*archaic or humorous*) [13C. Via Old French < Latin *fundamentum* < *fundus* 'bottom'.]

fundamental /fúndə mént'l/ *adj* **1 BASIC** relating to or affecting the underlying principles or structure of something ○ *We need to make fundamental changes in our business.* **2 CENTRAL** serving as an essential part of something ○ *Free speech is one of the fundamental rights guaranteed by the US constitution.* **3 OF A CHORD'S LOWEST NOTE** relating to the lowest note of a chord in root position, the note that gives the chord its basic harmony **4 OF LOWEST FREQUENCY** relating to or produced by the lowest frequency component in a complex vibration ■ *n* **1 BASIC PRINCIPLE OR ELEMENT** a basic and necessary component of something, especially an underlying rule or principle (*often plural*) ○ *The class teaches the fundamentals of karate.* **2 PRINCIPAL TONE** the principal tone in a chord, from which other harmonics are generated **3 LOWEST FREQUENCY** the lowest frequency in a vibration or periodic wave —**fundamentally** *adv*

fundamental interaction *n* PHYS = **interaction** *n.* 3

fundamentalism /fúndə mént'lizəm/ *n* **1** a religious or political movement based on a literal interpretation of and strict adherence to doctrine, especially as a return to former principles **2** the belief that religious or political doctrine should be implemented literally, not interpreted or adapted —**fundamentalist** *n, adj* —**fundamentalistic** /fúndə ment'l ístik/ *adj*

fundamental law *n* the founding rules and principles or constitution on which a government is based, as distinct from its legislative acts

fundamental particle *n* PHYS = **elementary particle**

fundamental unit *n* MEASURE = **base unit**

-funded *suffix* with money provided by a particular institution or person

funded debt *n* that part of the national debt that has no deadline for repayment

~~**fundemental**~~ incorrect spelling of **fundamental**

fundholder /fúnd hōldər/ *n* a general medical practice that has opted to manage its own budget and contract directly with hospitals, rather than leave these administrative tasks to the local health authority

fundholding /fúnd hōlding/ *adj* having direct responsibility for budget management and liaison with hospitals for specialist treatment of patients, rather than dealing with administration via the local health authority

fundi[1] /fún di/ (*plural* **-dis**) *n S Africa* a learned person or an expert on a topic ○ *The political fundis got together to work out a compromise.* [Mid-20C. Probably < Ndebele, Xhosa, or Zulu *umfundi* 'disciple, learner'.]

fundi[2] plural of **fundus**

fundie /fúndi/, **fundy** (*plural* **-ies**) *n* a member of a fundamentalist political or religious group or a radical member of a generally moderate group (*informal; often considered offensive*) [Late 20C. < FUNDAMENTALIST.]

funding /fúnding/ *n* financial support

fundraiser /fúnd rayzər/ *n* **1** a solicitor of money for a nonprofitmaking organization, especially an organizer of campaigns to raise money **2** an activity or event that is intended to generate money to support a nonprofitmaking organization

fundraising /fúnd rayzing/ *n* the organized activity of soliciting and collecting funds for a nonprofitmaking organization

fundus /fúndəss/ (*plural* **-di** /-dī/) *n* the part of a hollow organ farthest from its opening, e.g. the part of the eye's retina opposite the pupil [Mid-18C. < Latin, 'bottom'.] —**fundic** *adj*

fundy *n* = **fundie**

Fundy, Bay of /fúndi/ inlet of the Atlantic Ocean in SE Canada, separating New Brunswick and Nova Scotia. Depth: 200 m/650 ft. Length: 275 km/171 mi.

funeral /fyoónərəl/ *n* **1 CEREMONY FOR SOMEBODY WHO HAS DIED** a rite held to mark the burial or cremation of a corpse, especially a ceremony held immediately before burial or cremation **2 END** an end to something's existence ○ *We have witnessed the funeral of the amateur game.* **3 FUNERAL PROCESSION** a procession of mourners following a body to its place of burial or cremation [14C. Via Old French *funerailles* 'funeral rites' < medieval Latin *funeralia* < late Latin *funeralis* 'of death rituals' < Latin *funer-*, stem of *funus* 'death ritual'.] ◇ **be somebody's funeral** to be somebody else's problem or worry (*informal*) ○ *If he wants to work extra hours, that's his funeral.*

funeral director *n* = **undertaker** *n.* 1

funeral home *n* US = **funeral parlour**

funeral parlour *n* a business establishment where corpses are prepared for burial or cremation and where a funeral service may also be performed and the body viewed by mourners. US term **funeral home**

funerary /fyoónərəri/ *adj* relating to or suitable for a burial or funeral [Late 17C. < late Latin *funerarius* < Latin *funer-* (see FUNERAL).]

funereal /fyoo neéri əl/ *adj* **1** relating to or suitable for a funeral **2** very slow, solemn, mournful, or dismal [Early 18C. < Latin *funereus* < *funer-* (see FUNERAL).] —**funereally** *adv*

funfair /fún fair/ *n* LEISURE = **fair**[2] *n.* 1

funfest /fún fest/ *n* US a party, especially one at which amusing activities are organized (*informal*)

fungi plural of **fungus**

fungible /fúnjib'l/ *adj* **1 PERISHABLE** perishable and traded or exchanged in measurable quantities or numbers **2 SUBSTITUTABLE** capable of being interchanged ■ *n* **SOMETHING TRADED OR SUBSTITUTED** a commodity that is fungible (*often plural*) [Late 17C. < medieval Latin *fungibilis* < Latin *fungi* 'perform'.] —**fungibility** /fúnjə bíllətee/ *n*

fungicide /fúnji sīd, fúng gi-/ *n* a substance used to destroy or inhibit the growth of fungi —**fungicidal** /fúnji sīd'l, fúng gi-/ *adj* —**fungicidally** *adv*

fungiform /fúnji fawrm, fúng gi-/ *adj* shaped like a mushroom

fungistat /fúnji stat, fúng gi-/ *n* a substance that inhibits the growth of fungi without killing them —**fungistatic** /fúnji státtik, fúng gi-/ *adj*

fungo /fúng gō/ (*plural* **-goes**) *n* in baseball, an act of hitting the ball high into the air using a special lightweight bat, usually to give fielders catching practice [Mid-19C. < ?]

fungoid /fúng goyd/ *adj* resembling, characteristic of, or caused by a fungus ○ *a fungoid growth* ■ *n* a fungus or a growth resembling a fungus

fungus /fúng gəss/ (*plural* **-gi** /-gī/ *or* **-guses**) *n* a single-celled or multicellular organism without chlorophyll that reproduces by spores and lives by absorbing nutrients from organic matter [Early 16C. < Latin.] —**fungal** *adj*

funicle /fyoónik'l/ *n* ANAT = **funiculus** [Mid-17C. Anglicization.]

funicular /fyoo níkyoōlər/ *adj* **1 OF ROPE'S TENSION** relating to a rope, especially its tension **2 ROPE-OPERATED** operated by a rope or cable, especially one wound or pulled by a machine **3 OF A FUNICULUS** relating to a funiculus ■ *n* **CABLE-OPERATED RAILWAY** a funicular railway or railway car [Mid-17C. < Latin *funiculus* (see FUNICULUS).]

funicular railway *n* a railway used on short steep inclines in which cars that counterbalance each other run on parallel tracks linked to a cable

funiculus /fyoo níkyoōləss/ (*plural* **-li** /-lī/) *n* **1** a cord-shaped part of the body such as the umbilical cord or a bundle of nerve fibres in the spinal cord **2** a stalk of a plant ovule that connects it or a seed to the placenta [Mid-17C. < Latin, 'little rope' < *funis* 'rope'.]

funk[1] /fungk/ *n* **1** a type of popular music that derives from jazz, blues, and soul and is characterized by a heavy rhythmic bass and backbeat **2** a rhythmic earthy quality in music (*slang*) [Mid-20C. Back-formation < FUNKY[1].]

funk[2] /fungk/ *n* (*dated informal*) **1 FEAR** a state of intense fear or panic ○ *in a funk about his exam tomorrow* **2 COWARD** an easily frightened or cowardly person ■ *vti* **NOT DO SOMETHING OUT OF FEAR** to fail to do something, to avoid doing it, because of fear (*dated informal*) ○ *I meant to tell her but funked at the last moment.* [Mid-18C. < ?]

funk[3] /fungk/ *n* US a strong unpleasant odour (*slang*) [Early 17C. < ?]

funked-up *adj* exhilarated by, fond of, or featuring funk music (*slang*)

funk hole *n* a place where somebody hides from danger

funky[1] /fúngki/ (**-ier, -iest**) *adj* **1 LIKE FUNK** with the backbeat and rhythmic bass typical of funk music **2 LIKE BLUES** resembling blues music (*slang*) **3 UNCONVENTIONAL** offbeat, creative, and novel (*informal*) ○ *a return to the funky styles of the 1970s* **4 US SMELLY** with a strong odour (*slang*) **5 US UNCOMFORTABLE** causing discomfort or unease (*slang*) ○ *Since we broke up, any conversation has been pretty funky.* [Mid-20C. < FUNK[3].] —**funkily** *adv* —**funkiness** *n*

funky[2] /fúngki/ (**-ier, -iest**) *adj* in a state of fear or panic (*informal*) [Mid-19C. < FUNK[2].] —**funkily** *adv* —**funkiness** *n*

funnel /fúnn'l/ *n* **1 UTENSIL USED IN POURING LIQUIDS** a cone-shaped utensil with a large opening at the top and a small opening or tube at the bottom, used to guide liquids and other substances into containers **2 CHIMNEY** a vertical pipe from which smoke and exhaust gases escape, especially one on a steamship or steam train ■ *v* (**-nels, -nelling, -nelled**) **1** *vti* **MOVE INTO NARROW SPACE** to move or direct something into and through a narrow space ○ *an efficient system for funnelling crowds through the turnstiles* **2** *vt* **CONCENTRATE RESOURCES SOMEWHERE** to direct or channel all of something from one place or use to another ○ *Funds were funnelled away from domestic projects.* **3** *vt* **MAKE FUNNEL-SHAPED** to form something into the shape of a funnel [15C. Via Provençal *fonilh* < Latin *infundibulum* < *infundere* 'pour in' < *fundere* 'pour'.]

funnel cloud *n* a funnel-shaped cloud that projects from the base of a thundercloud and often develops into a tornado

funnel-web spider, funnel-web *n* a large black highly venomous spider that makes funnel-shaped webs. Native to: Australia. Family: Dipluridae.

funnily /fúnnili/ *adv* **1 INTRODUCING COMMENT ON SOMETHING STRANGE** used to introduce a comment on something considered strange or odd ○ *Funnily enough, nobody seemed to notice.* **2 STRANGELY** in a way that seems strange or odd ○ *She has been acting funnily ever since the operation.* **3 COMICALLY** in an amusing or humorous way

funny /fúnni/ *adj* (**-nier, -niest**) **1 COMICAL** causing amusement, especially enough to provoke laughter **2 STRANGE** odd or perplexing ○ *That's funny, I can't find my keys.* **3 UNCONVENTIONAL** out of the ordinary in a quaint or comical way ○ *a funny little doorway through an arch* **4 UNWELL** slightly ill, e.g. nauseated or faint (*informal*) **5 TRICKY** sly, deceitful, or dishonest (*informal*) ○ *Don't try anything funny, or I'll call the police.* ■ *n* (*plural* **-nies**) **JOKE** an amusing remark or joke (*informal*) [Mid-18C. < FUN.] —**funniness** *n*

funny bone *n* **1** the point at the outside of the elbow where a nerve is so close to the longer arm bone that a blow often causes a tingling sensation (*informal*) **2** somebody's perception of what is amusing [< the tingling feeling when the nerve is hit]

funny business *n* dealings or goings-on that involve trickery, deceit, or dishonesty (*informal*)

funny farm *n* an offensive term, once considered humorous, for a psychiatric hospital (*slang*)

funny man /fúnni man/ *n* a man who is a comedian, clown, or humorist

funny money *n* (*informal*) **1 COUNTERFEIT MONEY** counterfeit or forged currency **2 ILLICITLY GAINED MONEY** money obtained from a legally or morally suspect source **3 CURRENCY WITH LITTLE VALUE** currency, especially an unfamiliar one, with an inflated value

fun park *n* an area with amusement facilities, especially water slides and rides

fun run *n* a noncompetitive run over a moderately long course, organized to promote health and fitness or to raise money for charity

funster /fúnstər/ *n* a person who likes to have fun or who enjoys telling or playing jokes (*informal*)

fur /fur/ *n* **1 MAMMAL'S COAT** the soft dense coat of hair on a hairy mammal **2 ANIMAL HAIR** hairs from an animal's coat **3 DRESSED PELT** a dressed pelt from an animal such as a mink or seal that includes the animal's soft coat of hair. Use: garments, decoration. **4 FUR COAT** a garment made from fur pelts, especially a coat, jacket, or stole **5 SOMETHING HAIRY** something with a fuzzy or hairy texture or appearance **6 COATING ON THE TONGUE** a whitish coating of dead cells on the tongue that sometimes accompanies an illness (*informal*) **7 LIME DEPOSIT** mineral deposits from hard water that cling to the insides of plumbing fixtures **8 PELT ON COAT OF ARMS** a representation of an animal skin on a coat of arms [14C. < obsolete *fur* 'to line' < Old French *forrer* < *forre* 'lining'.] —**furred** *adj* ◇ **make the fur fly** to cause trouble or a disturbance (*informal*)

fur up *vti* to coat the insides of plumbing fixtures and water containers with mineral deposits from hard water, or to become coated with these deposits

Fur /fur/ *n* a language spoken in parts of Chad and in W Sudan, belonging to the Nilo-Saharan family of African languages. Native speakers: 400,000. —**Fur** *adj*

fur. *abbr* furlong

furan /fyoo ran, fyoo rán/ *n* a colourless flammable liquid. Use: solvent, manufacture of polymers. [Late 19C. Contraction of FURFURAN.]

furanose /fyóorə nōz/ *n* a sugar made up of a ring of four carbon atoms and one oxygen atom

furbearer /fúr bairər/ *n* an animal with fur, especially fur with a high commercial value such as that of a fox or mink —**furbearing** *adj*

furbelow /fúrbelō/ *n* **1 RUFFLE** a gathered or pleated piece of material, especially as an ornament on a woman's garment **2 FLAMBOYANT BEHAVIOUR** a showy or pretentious way of behaving (*literary; often plural*) ■ *vt* **DECORATE WITH RUFFLE** to add a furbelow to a garment for ornamentation [Late 17C. < ?]

furbish /fúrbish/ *vt* **1** to brighten something by polishing ○ *stone steps scrubbed and brasses furbished* **2** to refurbish something (*literary*) [14C. < Old French *fourbiss-* < Germanic.] —**furbisher** *n*

furcate /fúr kayt/ *vi* (**-cates, -cating, -cated**) to divide into two separate strands or branches ■ *adj* divided into separate strands or branches ○ *furcate leaves* [Early 19C. < late Latin *furcatus* 'forked' < Latin *furca* 'fork'.] —**furcately** *adv* —**furcation** /fur káysh'n/ *n*

furcula /fúrkyóolə/ (*plural* **-lae** /-lee/) *n* the wishbone of a bird (*technical*) [Mid-19C. < Latin, 'small fork' < *furca* 'fork'.] —**furcular** *adj*

furfur /fúr fur/ (*plural* **-fures** /-fyóo reez, fúrfə-/) *n* a tiny piece of scaly or flaky skin, e.g. a particle of dandruff (*technical*) [< Latin, 'bran, scales']

furfuraceous /fúrfə ráyshəss/ *adj* **1** covered with or resembling particles of dandruff **2** relating to or resembling bran

furfural /fúrfəral/ *n* $C_5H_4O_2$ a colourless liquid with a distinctive smell. Source: plants. Use: manufacture of plastics, in oil refining, in agriculture.

furfuran /fúrfə ran/ *n* CHEM = **furan**

Furies /fyóoreez/, **furies** *npl* in Greek mythology, three terrifying snake-haired winged goddesses who mercilessly punished wrongdoing, especially when committed within families. ◊ **Eumenides**

furioso /fyóori ósső/ *adv* to be played with vigour and passion (*musical direction*) [Mid-17C. Via Italian < Latin *furiosus* (see FURIOUS).] —**furioso** *adj*

furious /fyóori əss/ *adj* **1** extremely or violently angry ○ *I was furious with him for spreading such lies.* **2** involving a great deal of energy, violence, or speed ○ *the pianist's furious assault on the keys* [14C. Via Old French < Latin *furiosus* < *furia* 'rage' (see FURY).] —**furiously** *adv* —**furiousness** *n*

furl /furl/ *vti* to roll up and secure something made of fabric, or be rolled up and secured ■ *n* a rolled-up section of something such as a flag or sail [Late 16C. < French *ferler* < *ferm* 'firm, firmly' + *lier* 'to tie'.]

furlong /fúr long/ *n* a measure of distance equal to 220 yards (approximately 201 metres), now used mainly on racecourses [Old English *furlang* < *furh* (see FURROW) + *lang* (see LONG[1])]

furlough /fúr lō/ *n* leave of absence from duty, especially military duty, or an official paper authorizing leave ■ *vt* to grant leave of absence to somebody, especially a member of the armed forces [Early 17C. < Dutch *verlo* 'leave'.]

furmenty *n* FOOD = **frumenty**

furmety *n* FOOD = **frumenty**

furmity *n* FOOD = **frumenty**

furn. *abbr* furnished

furnace /fúrniss/ *n* **1 ENCLOSURE PRODUCING GREAT HEAT** an enclosure in which heat is produced by burning fuel, e.g. to warm a building or smelt metal ○ *an oil furnace* **2 SOMEWHERE HOT** an intensely hot place (*informal*) ○ *This kitchen is a furnace!* **3 TERRIBLE EXPERIENCE** a testing or demanding experience [13C. Via Old French *fornais* < Latin *fornax*.]

Furneaux Group /fúrnō-/ group of islands off the coast of NE Tasmania, Australia. Population: 1,010. Area: 2,330 sq. km/900 sq. mi.

furnish /fúrnish/ *vt* **1** to provide and install furniture and other fittings, e.g. carpets and curtains, in a place ○ *The lobby is furnished in an Art Deco style.* **2** to supply something or provide somebody with something (*formal*) ○ *Could you furnish us with the names and addresses of clients?* [15C. < Old French *furniss-*, stem of *furnir* < Germanic.] —**furnisher** *n*

furnished /fúrnishd/ *adj* containing or supplied with furniture ○ *a furnished flat*

furnishings /fúrnishingz/ *npl* articles of furniture and other useful or decorative items for a room, such as carpets and curtains

furniture /fúrnichər/ *n* **1 TABLES AND CHAIRS** the movable items such as chairs, desks, or cabinets in an area such as a room or patio **2 TYPE SEPARATORS** strips of wood, metal, or plastic that are placed between type in order to make spaces and hold the type in place in the frame (**chase**) in which they are arranged **3 EQUIPMENT** the equipment or accessories used for an activity, e.g. a ship's tackle or a horse's saddle and harnesses (*archaic*) **4 FITTINGS ON WOODEN ARTICLES** the metal or plastic accessories fitted to an item of joinery or cabinetwork, e.g. door hinges and drawer handles [Early 16C. < Old French *fourniture* < *furnir* (see FURNISH).]

furniture beetle *n* a borer beetle with larvae that are destructive to furniture and other wood. *Anobium punctatum.*

furor /fyóorawr, fyóorə/ *n* US = **furore**

furore /fyoo ráwri/ *n* **1 UPROAR** an angry or indignant public reaction to something ○ *The verdict of not guilty created a furore in the courtroom.* **2 EXCITEMENT** a state of intense excitement or activity ○ *the furore surrounding the release of their latest album* **3 CRAZE** an enthusiastically embraced fad [Late 18C. Via Italian < Latin *furor* < *furere* 'to rage'.]

furosemide /fyoo róssə mīd/ *n* US PHARM = **frusemide** [Mid-20C. < first syllable of *furyl* 'chemical derived from furan' + *-sem-* < ?]

furphy /fúrfi/ (*plural* **-phies**) *n* Aus a rumour or piece of gossip, especially one that is not true (*slang*) [Early 20C. After the *Furphy* family, manufacturers of water carts (where troops swapped gossip) in Australia during World War I.]

Furphy /fúrfi/, **Joseph** (1843–1912) Australian writer

furrier /fúrri ər/ *n* **1** a dealer in furs **2** a person or establishment that makes or sells clothes and accessories of animal fur [14C. Alteration (after CLOTHIER) of *furrer* < Old French *forreor* < *forrer* (see FUR).]

furriery /fúrri əri/ *n* **1** fur accessories and articles of clothing considered collectively **2** the business or craft of a furrier

furring /fúring/ *n* **1 FUR PART OF CLOTHING** fur trim or lining for a garment **2 WHITE COVERING** a whitish coating, e.g. on the tongue of somebody who is ill **3 MAKING A SURFACE OF STRIPS** the placing of strips of wood, metal, or brick across the studs or joists in a building to create a firm and level foundation for plaster, plasterboard, flooring, or another surface **4 STRIPS USED UNDER SURFACE** strips used in a building for furring (*often before nouns*) ○ *furring strips*

furrow /fúrrō/ *n* **1 PLOUGH TRENCH** a narrow trench in soil made by a plough **2 GROOVE** a rut or groove in a surface **3 FOREHEAD WRINKLE** a wrinkle on the skin of the forehead **4** *S Africa* **IRRIGATION TRENCH** in South Africa, a narrow trench dug to deliver water to a field or garden ■ *vti* **MAKE FURROWS IN** to make furrows in something such as land or the forehead, or become marked with furrows ○ *He furrowed his brow.* [Old English *furh* < Indo-European] —**furrowed** *adj*

furry /fúri/ (**-rier, -riest**) *adj* **1 COVERED IN FUR** covered in or with a coat that is covered in fur ○ *furry animals* **2 LOOKING OR FEELING LIKE FUR** resembling fur in texture or appearance **3 COVERED IN WHITISH COATING** covered with a whitish coating of dead cells (*refers to the tongue or the inside of the mouth*)

fur seal *n* a seal with a double coat of fur, including a dense soft underfur that is highly valued for making garments. Genera: *Arctocephalus* and *Callorhinus*.

Fur Seal Islands /fúr seel-/ = **Pribilof Islands**

Fürth /fürt/ city in S Germany. Population: 108,000 (1993).

further /fúrthər/ *adj* **ADDITIONAL** that is more than or adds to the quantity or extent of something ○ *until further notice* ○ *Do you have anything further to add?* ■ *adv* **1 TO GREATER DISTANCE** to or at a point that is more distant in place or time ○ *We pushed further into the woods.* ○ *further into the future* **2 TO GREATER EXTENT** to a greater degree or extent ○ *Let's not pursue the matter any further.* **3 IN ADDITION** used to introduce an additional statement or point ○ *She said further that she would not accept any excuses.* ■ *vt* **ADVANCE** to help or give a boost to the progress of something ○ *All this media attention will further our cause.* [Old English *furþor, furþur* 'more forward' < Germanic] —**furtherer** *n* ◇ **further to** following on from something that has been written or discussed ○ *Further to our phone conversation, I would like to confirm the order.*

USAGE further or **farther**? Strictly speaking ***farther*** is the preferred spelling when referring to physical distance, as in *Have we much farther to go?* Now ***further*** is commonly used in this context, although its use is traditionally reserved for figurative contexts, as in *I have nothing further to add*, or *It took a further two phone calls before I got through.* ***Furthest*** and ***farthest*** behave similarly.

furtherance /fúrthərənss/ *n* the aiding or advancing of the progress of something ○ *In furtherance of our campaign, we ask that everyone make a contribution.*

further education *n* postschool education or training for adults that does not lead to a university degree

furthermore /fúrthər mawr, fúrthər máwr/ *adv* used to introduce an additional statement or point ○ *She claimed furthermore that he did not own the shop but only worked there.*

furthermost /fúrthər mōst/ *adj* most distant or remote ○ *the furthermost point on the pier*

furthest /fúrthist/ *adj* **MOST DISTANT** more distant in place or time than anything else ○ *In our solar system, Pluto is the furthest planet from the sun.* ■ *adv* **1 TO GREATEST DISTANCE** to or at a more distant point in space or time than anything else ○ *Whoever gets the furthest wins the prize.* **2 TO GREATEST EXTENT** to a greater degree or extent than anything else ○ *The dollar has fallen furthest against the pound for the last year.*

USAGE See ***further.***

furtive /fúrtiv/ *adj* **1** done in a way that is intended to escape notice ○ *conspirators exchanging furtive glances* **2** with the appearance, or giving the impression, of somebody who has something to hide [Early 17C. Via Old French < Latin *furtivus* 'hidden, stolen' < *furtum* 'theft' < *fur* 'thief' < Indo-European, 'carry'.] —**furtively** *adv* —**furtiveness** *n*

SYNONYMS See ***secret.***

furuncle /fyóor ungk'l/ *n* a boil on the skin (*technical*) [Late 17C. < Latin *furunculus* 'knob on a vine' < *fur* 'thief' (because it 'steals' the sap).] —**furuncular** /fyoo rúngkyoolər/ *adj* —**furunculous** /-kyooləss/ *adj*

furunculosis /fyoo rúngkyoo lóssiss/ *n* **1** a condition in which large areas of the skin are covered in persistent boils **2** a virulent bacterial disease that affects salmon and trout and can be devastating in densely populated waters, e.g. in fish farms

fury /fyóori/ (*plural* **-ries**) *n* **1 RAGE** violent anger ○ *She could not contain her fury any longer.* **2 BURST OF ANGER** a state or outburst of violent anger ○ *He stormed off in a fury.* **3 WILD FORCE** a state of excited or frenetic activity ○ *debris scattered in the wake of the tornado's fury* **4 OFFENSIVE TERM** an offensive term for a woman who is considered by the speaker to be malevolent and spiteful **5 fury, Fury** ♦ **Furies** [14C. Via Old French < Latin *furia* < *furere* 'to rage'.] ◇ **like fury** with great speed or energy

LITERARY LINK ***The Sound and the Fury***, a novel (1929) by US writer William Faulkner. Set in the American South, it recounts the financial and moral decline of a wealthy family and centres on the daughter Caddy.

SYNONYMS See ***anger.***

furze /furz/ (*plural* **furzes** *or* **furze**) *n* PLANTS = **gorse** [Old English *fyrs* < ?]

fusain /fyoo záyn, fyóo zayn/ *n* **1 CHARCOAL STICK** a fine stick of charcoal for drawing, made from wood from the spindle tree **2 CHARCOAL DRAWING** a drawing or sketch done with fusain charcoal **3 GREY COAL** dark grey bituminous carbon found in some kinds of coal [Late 19C. Via French, 'spindle tree, charcoal made from its wood' < Latin *fusus* 'spindle'.]

~~**fuschia**~~ incorrect spelling of **fuchsia**

fuscous /fúskəss/ *adj* of a dark greyish-brown colour [Mid-17C. < Latin *fuscus* 'dusky'.]

fuse[1] /fyooz/ *n* **ELECTRICAL CIRCUIT BREAKER** an electrical safety device containing a piece of a metal that melts if the current running through it exceeds a certain level, thereby breaking the circuit ■ *vti* (**fuses, fusing, fused**) **1 STOP WORKING BECAUSE OF DAMAGED FUSE** to stop functioning, or to cause an electrical circuit or appliance to stop functioning, because of a damaged electrical fuse ○ *In trying to find the fault, he managed to fuse all the other lights too.* **2 COMBINE** to unite or blend things, or become united or blended into a whole ○ *sensations and ideas fusing intimately together* **3 LIQUEFY** to melt something such as metal or plastic, or become melted at a very high temperature [Late 16C. < Latin *fus-*, past participle of *fundere* 'melt, pour'.] —**fused** *adj*

fuse[2] /fyooz/ *n* **1 EXPLOSIVE LEAD** a cord or trail of a combustible substance that is ignited at one end to carry a flame to an explosive device farther away **2 DETONATOR** a mechanical or electrical detonator that triggers an exploding device such as a bomb or grenade ■ *vt* (**fuses, fusing, fused**) **EQUIP DEVICE WITH DETONATOR** to equip an exploding device such as a bomb or grenade with a mechanical or electrical detonator [Mid-17C. Via Italian *fuso* 'spindle' < Latin *fusus*.]

fuse box *n* a box, often a cupboard fitted to a wall, that contains the fuses that protect all the electrical circuits in a building or part of a building

fused quartz, fused silica *n* INDUST = **quartz glass**

fusee /fyoo zée/, **fuzee** *n* **1** a large-headed match that is not easily extinguished in the wind **2** a conical pulley with a spiral groove, used in clock and watch mechanisms [Late 16C. Via French *fusée* 'spindle, fuse, flare' < Latin *fusus* 'spindle'.]

fuselage /fyóozə laazh, fyóozəlij/ *n* an aeroplane's body, containing the cockpit, passenger seating, and cargo hold but excluding the wings [Early 20C. < French, < Latin *fusus* 'spindle'.]

Fuseli /fyóoz'li/, **Henry** (1741–1825) Swiss painter and art critic. Born **Johann Heinrich Füssli**

fusel oil /fyóoz'l-/ *n* an oily liquid mixture. Source: insufficiently distilled alcoholic liquors. Use: solvent, in chemical manufacturing. [Mid-19C. < German, 'bad liquor'.]

Fushun /fóo shóon/ city in NE China. Population: 1,487,400 (1991).

fusible /fyóozəb'l/ *adj* easily melted or liquefied (*refers to metals and other materials*) ○ *fusible alloys* —**fusibility** /fyóozə bílləti/ *n*

fusiform /fyóozi fawrm/ *adj* tapering at both ends, like a spindle ○ *fusiform bacteria* [Mid-18C. < Latin *fusus* 'spindle'.]

fusil /fyóozil/ *n* a lightweight musket with a flintlock firing mechanism [Late 16C. < French, 'steel in a flintlock, musket' < late Latin *focus* 'fire'.]

fusilier /fyóozi léer/, **fusileer** *n* formerly, a soldier in a British army regiment that was armed with lightweight muskets (**fusils**) [Late 17C. < French, < *fusil* 'musket' (see FUSIL).]

fusillade /fyóozi layd, -laad/ *n* **1 BLAST OF GUNFIRE** a firing of several guns at once or in quick succession **2 ONSLAUGHT** a sustained attack or barrage, e.g. of missiles or words ■ *vt* (**-lades, -lading, -laded**) **FIRE AT ENEMY** to subject an enemy to a sustained burst of gunfire [Early 19C. < French, < *fusiller* 'shoot' < *fusil* 'musket' (see FUSIL).]

fusilli /fyoo zílli/ *npl* pasta in the form of short spiral shapes [Late 20C. < Italian, 'little spindles' < Latin *fusus* 'spindle'.]

fusion /fyóozh'n/ *n* **1 HEATING AND LIQUEFYING** the molten state of a substance, or the change it undergoes to become molten **2 BLENDING** the merging or blending of two or more things, e.g. materials or ideas ○ *a fusion of vegetarianism and pacifism* **3** INDUST = **nuclear fusion** **4 COMBINATION OF MUSICAL STYLES** the blending or resulting blend of musical styles or elements from more than one tradition, e.g. jazz and rock [Mid-16C. Directly or via French < Latin *fusion-* < *fundere* 'melt, pour'.]

fusion bomb *n* a nuclear bomb, especially a hydrogen bomb, whose explosion is caused by the energy released by a nuclear fusion reaction

fusion food, fusion cuisine *n* a style of cooking that uses ingredients and techniques from around the world, especially one that combines Eastern and Western influences

fusionism /fyóozh'nizəm/ *n* the formation of political coalitions, support for their formation, or belief in their effectiveness —**fusionist** *n, adj*

fuss /fuss/ *n* **1 COMMOTION** needlessly or excessively busy or excited activity **2 NEEDLESS WORRY** excessive concern over details or trivial matters **3 PROTEST** a complaint or protestation, often over something insignificant ○ *The kids made a fuss about going to bed early.* **4 ARGUMENT** a noisy disagreement or dispute ○ *There'll be a fuss if he gets home late again.* **5 DISPLAY OF AFFECTION OR CONCERN** an excited or abundant display of affection or affectionate concern ○ *irritated by the fuss they make of her little brother* **6 EXCESSIVE DECORATION** decoration or ornamentation regarded as excessive ○ *I want a dress without so much fuss around the neckline.* ■ *vi* **1 WORRY TOO MUCH** to be too concerned about details or trivial matters **2 FIDDLE WITH** to keep moving or touching something busily, nervously, or aimlessly ○ *He fussed with the dials, hoping he'd look like he knew what he was doing.* [Early 18C. < ?] —**fusser** *n* ◇ **not be fussed** to have no strong preference for something (*informal*) ○ *I'm not fussed where we sit.*

fussbudget /fúss bujit/ *n US* = **fusspot** (*informal*) [Early 20C. < BUDGET 'bundle'.]

fusspot /fúss pot/ *n* somebody who worries a lot about unimportant things (*informal*) US term **fussbudget**

fussy /fússi/ (**-ier, -iest**) *adj* **1 CONCERNED WITH MINOR THINGS** tending to worry over details or trivial things **2 CHOOSY** very dogmatic about likes and dislikes ○ *a very fussy eater* **3 ELABORATE** made or decorated with excessive detail ○ *a dress with a fussy lace collar*

SYNONYMS See ***careful.***

fustian /fústi ən/ *n* **1 COTTON-LINEN CLOTH** a coarse sturdy cotton-linen blend cloth **2 COTTON FABRIC WITH NAP** any hardwearing cotton fabric, e.g. corduroy or moleskin **3 BOMBAST** pompous or pretentious speech or writing [13C. Via Old French < medieval Latin *fustaneum*.] —**fustian** *adj*

fustic /fústik/ *n* **1 YELLOW DYE** a yellow dye obtained from the wood of certain trees **2 DYE-YIELDING AMERICAN TREE** a tree whose wood yields fustic. Native to: tropical America. *Chlorophora tinctoria.* **3 DYE-YIELDING EUROPEAN TREE** a sumac tree whose wood yields fustic. Native to: Europe. *Cotinus coggyria.* [15C. Via Old French *fustoc* < Arabic *fustuk* < Greek *pistakē* 'pistachio tree'.]

fustigate /fústi gayt/ (**-gates, -gating, -gated**) *vt* to criticize somebody or something severely (*literary*) [Mid-17C. < late Latin *fustigat-*, past participle of *fustigare* < Latin *fustis* 'wood, club' + *agere* 'do'.] —**fustigation** /fústi gáysh'n/ *n*

fusty /fústi/ (**-tier, -tiest**) *adj* **1** smelling of damp, dust, mildew, or age **2** old-fashioned and conservative in style, appearance, habits, or attitudes ○ *transform a rather fusty image* [Late 15C. < obsolete *fust* 'wine cask', via Old French < Latin *fustis* 'wood, club'.] —**fustily** *adv* —**fustiness** *n*

fut. *abbr* **1** future **2** futures

Futa Djallon = **Fouta Djallon**

futhark /fóo thaark/, **futhorc** /-thawrk/, **futhork** *n* the runic alphabet of 24 letters, used in NW Europe from the 3rd to 17th century [Mid-19C. < the first six letters: *f, u, þ, a* or *o, r,* and *k*.]

futile /fyoo tīl/ *adj* **1** with no practical effect or useful result **2** lacking serious value, substance, or a sense of responsibility [Mid-16C. < Latin *futilis* 'leaky, worthless'.] —**futilely** *adv* —**futileness** *n*

futilitarian /fyoo tílli táiri ən/ *n* a believer that human efforts are wasted and futile [Early 19C. < FUTILITY, after UTILITARIAN.] —**futilitarian** *adj* —**futilitarianism** *n*

futility /fyoo tílləti/ (*plural* **-ties**) *n* **1** lack of usefulness or effectiveness **2** an action that has no use, purpose, or effect

futon /fóo ton/ *n* **1** a firm Japanese-style cotton-covered mattress used as a seat or bed, either on the floor or on a wooden frame **2** a futon together with the wooden frame it sits on, especially a frame designed to convert from a sofa to a bed [Late 19C. < Japanese.]

futtock /fúttək/ *n* any curved middle timber forming the frame of a traditional wooden boat or ship [13C. < ?]

futtock plate *n* a circular metal plate fitted to the top of a ship's shorter masts

futtock shroud *n* a rope or rod stretching from the top of a taller mast to the top of a lower mast, to support the taller mast

future /fyóochər/ *n* **1 TIME TO COME** time that has yet to come ○ *saving money for the future* **2 HAPPENINGS TO COME** events that have not yet happened ○ *The future will be shaped by our advancing technology.* **3 FUTURE CONDITION** an expected or projected state ○ *Her future is bleak.* **4 TENSE REFERRING TO THINGS TO COME** the tense or form of a verb used to refer to events that are going to happen or have not yet happened ■ **futures** *npl* **COMMODITIES TRADED FOR LATER DELIVERY** goods or stocks sold for future delivery, or the contracts for them ■ *adj* **1 YET TO OCCUR** expected to be or happen at a time still to come ○ *my future sister-in-law* **2 OF OR IN TENSE EXPRESSING FUTURE** in or relating to the form of a verb that expresses actions or states that are going to happen or have not yet happened [14C. Via Old French < Latin *futurus* 'going to be'.]

futureless /fyóochərləss/ *adj* seeming to have no chance of developing or being successful ○ *ploughed money into futureless schemes* —**futurelessness** *n*

future perfect *n* the form of a verb expressing a completed action in the future, as 'will have finished' does in the sentence 'They will have finished by tomorrow'

future shock *n* difficulty in and stress from coping with rapid changes in society, especially technological changes

future tense *n* GRAM = future *n*. 4

futurism /fyóocherizem/ *n* 1 **futurism, Futurism** an early 20th-century artistic movement that attempted to express the dynamic nature of the modern age using technology as its subject 2 belief in the need to look to the future rather than reflect on the past, coupled with an optimism that personal and social fulfilment lies in the future —**futurist** *n, adj*

QUICK FACTS ON... **FUTURISM**

Key dates: 1909–15
Key locations: Europe, especially Italy
Key elements: rejection of artistic traditions; representation of vitality of modern life; glorification of speed, technology, and war; depiction of dynamic forces; primacy of intuition in creative processes
Key figures: Filippo Tommaso Marinetti (literature); Umberto Boccioni, Giacomo Balla, Gino Severini, Luigi Russolo, Carlo Carrà (painting); Antonio Sant'Elia (architecture)
Key events: publication of Futurist manifesto in *Le Figaro* 20 February 1909
Key works: *The City Rises* (Boccioni) 1910–11, *Dynamism of a Dog on a Leash* (Balla) 1912, *Dynamic Hieroglyphic of the Bal Tabarin* (Severini) 1912, *Unique Forms of Continuity in Space* (Boccioni) 1913, *Zang Tumb Tumb* (Marinetti) 1914
Key developments: expressionism, constructivism, vorticism, Dada; performance art; happenings

---

futuristic /fyóocha rístik/ *adj* 1 suggesting the future in something's design or technology 2 depicting life in some future time —**futuristically** *adv*

futurity /fyoo tyóorəti, -chóorəti/ (*plural* **-ties**) *n* 1 the future as a concept or state ○ *a grammatical construction expressing futurity* 2 an event that is going to happen or has not happened yet (*formal*) ○ *We'll have to await those futurities before we can make a decision.*

futurology /fyóochə rólləji/ *n* the study and forecasting of the future, with predictions based on the likely outcomes of current trends —**futurological** /fyóochərə lójjik'l/ *adj* —**futurologist** *n*

futz /futs/ *n US* an offensive term for a person despised by the speaker [Early 20C. Probably alteration of Yiddish *arumfartzen* 'fool around'.]

Fuxin /fóo shín/ city in NE China. Population: 635,473 (1990).

fu yung, fu yong *n* COOK = foo yung

fuzee *n* = fusee

Fuzhou /fóo zhó/ city in SE China, near the mouth of the Min River. Population: 1,652,228 (1991).

fuzz[1] /fuz/ *n* FLUFF a mass of short fine hairs or fibres ■ *vti* (**fuzzes, fuzzing, fuzzed**) 1 COVER SOMETHING WITH FUZZ to become covered or cover something with fuzz ○ *sweaters that fuzz after the first wash* 2 BLUR OR BECOME BLURRED to make something, e.g. an image or explanation, blurred or unclear, or become blurred or unclear ○ *All this talk has fuzzed my brain.* [Late 16C. Probably < Dutch or Low German.]

fuzz[2] /fuz/ *n* an offensive term for the police (*slang dated*) [Early 20C. < ?]

fuzzbox /fúz boks/ *n* an electrical device that distorts the sound that passes through it, especially a pedal-operated device wired to an electric guitar

fuzzy /fúzzi/ (**-ier, -iest**) *adj* 1 COVERED WITH FUZZ covered with a mass of short fine hairs or fibres 2 CONSISTING OF FUZZ in the form of a mass of short fine hairs or fibres 3 FRIZZY describes hair growing in a very tight curly mass 4 BLURRED not sharp enough to be seen or heard clearly ○ *a fuzzy picture* 5 INCOHERENT not clearly thought out or set out ○ *The initial plan was fairly fuzzy.* [Early 17C. < ?] —**fuzzily** *adv* —**fuzziness** *n*

fuzzyheaded /fúzzi héddid/ *adj* not thinking or communicating clearly (*informal*) ○ *a fuzzyheaded notion* —**fuzzyheadedness** *n*

⚡**fuzzy logic** *n* logic that allows for imprecise or ambiguous answers to questions, forming the basis of computer programming designed to mimic human intelligence

fuzzy-wuzzy /-wuzi/ (*plural* **fuzzy-wuzzies** or **fuzzy-wuzzy**) *n* 1 a highly offensive name that British soldiers gave to their Sudanese enemies during the North African campaigns of the late 19th century (*taboo offensive*) 2 a highly offensive term for a Black person (*dated taboo*)

fv *abbr* folio verso [Latin, 'on the reverse (left-hand) page']

fwd *abbr* forward

f.w.d. *abbr* 1 four-wheel drive 2 front-wheel drive

⚡**fx** *abbr* France, Metropolitan (*in Internet addresses*)

FX *abbr* 1 foreign exchange 2 (special) effects

FY *abbr* fiscal year

-fy *suffix* to make, cause to become ○ *gasify* ○ *ladify* [Via Old French *-fier* < Latin *facere* 'do, make']

⚡**FYI** *abbr* for your information (*in e-mails*)

fyke /fïk/, **fyke-net** *n* a bag-shaped fishing net, held open by hoops [Mid-19C. Via Dutch *fuik* < Middle Dutch *fuke*.]

fylfot /fíl fot/ *n* an old decorative or religious symbol in the form of a swastika [15C. < ?]

Fyn /fün/ second-largest island in Denmark, between S Jutland and Sjælland. Population: 470,528 (1996). Area: 2,978 sq. km/1,150 sq. mi.

fynbos /fáyn boss/ *n* the scrubland characteristic of the W Cape area of South Africa, consisting of bushes resembling heaths with hard leaves [Late 19C. < Afrikaans, literally 'fine bush'.]

FYROM *abbr* Former Yugoslav Republic of Macedonia

Fysh /fish/, **Sir Hudson** (1895–1974) Australian aviator and business executive

fz. *abbr* sforzando

Gg

g¹ /jee/ (*plural* **g's**), **G** (*plural* **G's** *or* **Gs**) *n* the seventh letter of the English alphabet, representing a consonant sound

g² used to refer to the seventh vertical row of squares from the left on a chessboard

g³ /jee/ *symbol* acceleration of free fall as a result of gravity

g⁴ *abbr* **1** gauge **2** gender **3** gram **4** guilder **5** guinea

G¹ /jee/ *n* (*plural* **G's** *or* **Gs**) **1** 'G'-SHAPED OBJECT something shaped like a letter 'G' **2** 5TH NOTE IN C MAJOR the fifth note of a scale in C major **3** SOMETHING THAT PRODUCES A G a string, key, or pipe tuned to produce the note G **4** SCALE BEGINNING ON G a scale or key that starts on the note G **5** WRITTEN SYMBOL OF G a graphic representation of the tone of G **6** GENERAL-AUDIENCE FILM RATING in the United States, Canada, Australia, and New Zealand, a cinema censorship classification meaning that a film or video is suitable for anyone to watch **7** gee *US* **$1000** one thousand dollars (*slang*) ■ *abbr* gay (*in personal ads*)

G² *symbol* **1** conductance **2** gravitational constant **3** guanine ■ *abbr* **4** guilder **5** guinea **6** Gulf (*in placenames*)

G³ *abbr* **1** giga- **2** good (*used in marking students' work*)

G. *abbr* Gulf (*in placenames*)

G8 /jee áyt/ *n* the group of the eight most industrialized nations in the world, comprising Canada, France, Germany, Italy, Japan, Russia, the United Kingdom, and the United States. Full form **Group of Eight**

⚡ga *abbr* Gabon (*in Internet addresses*)

Ga *symbol* gallium

⚡GA *abbr* **1** general agent **2** General Assembly (of the United Nations) **3** general average **4** Georgia **5** go ahead (*in e-mails*)

gab /gab/ (**gabs, gabbing, gabbed**) *vi* to talk at length about trivial matters (*informal*) ○ *We just sat there gabbing all afternoon.* [Early 18C. < ?] —**gab** *n* —**gabber** *n*

GABA *abbr* gamma-aminobutyric acid

gabardine /gábbər deen/ *n* **1** a smooth hard-wearing cotton, wool, or synthetic fabric woven with a pattern of parallel diagonal ridges (**twill**) ○ *a gabardine jacket* **2** a garment made of gabardine **3** CLOTHING = **gaberdine** *n*. **1** [Early 20C. Alteration of GABERDINE.]

gabble /gább'l/ (**-bles, -bling, -bled**) *v* **1** *vti* to speak or say something rapidly and incoherently **2** *vi* to make the high throaty sounds that geese and some other birds make [Late 16C. < ?] —**gabble** *n* —**gabbler** *n*

gabbro /gábbrō/ *n* a dark coarse-grained basic igneous rock containing calcium-rich plagioclase feldspar and pyroxene [Mid-19C. < Italian dialect, probably < Latin *glaber* 'smooth, bald'.] —**gabbroic** /gə brố ik/ *adj*

gabby /gábbi/ (**-bier, -biest**) *adj* talking or inclined to talk to an excessive, irritating degree (*informal*)

gabelle /gə bél/ *n* any tax, especially a tax imposed in a foreign country (*literary*) [15C. Via Old French *gabel* < Arabic *kabāla* 'tax, duty'.]

gaberdine /gábbər deen/ *n* **1** a long loose coat or smock made of coarse cloth, worn by men, especially Jewish men, during the Middle Ages **2** TEXTILES = **gabardine** *n*. **1 3** CLOTHING = **gabardine** *n*. **2** [Early 16C. < Old French *gauvardine*.]

Gabin /gábaN/, **Jean** (1904–76) French actor

gabion /gáybi ən/ *n* **1** a wickerwork basket filled with rocks, used as a temporary fortification **2** a cylindrical metal container filled with earth and stones, used in the construction and rerouting of waterways and in flood control [Mid-16C. Via French < Italian *gabbione* 'large cage' < *gabbia* 'cage' < Latin *cavea*.]

gable /gáyb'l/ *n* **1** the triangular top section of a side wall on a building with a pitched roof that fills the space beneath where the roof slopes meet **2** ARCHIT = **gable end 3** a triangular structure, e.g. a canopy over a door or window, added to a building for decoration [14C. Directly or via Old French < Old Norse *gafl*.] —**gabled** *adj*

LITERARY LINK *Anne of Green Gables*, a children's story (1908) by Canadian writer Lucy Maud Montgomery. Set on Prince Edward Island in Canada, it is the story of a vivacious 11-year-old orphan, Anne Shirley, who is sent to live with farmers Matthew and Marilla Cuthbert. Having expected a boy, the Cuthberts cannot hide their disappointment, but Anne's courage, spirit, and vivid imagination soon win them over.

Clark Gable

Gable /gáyb'l/, **Clark** (1901–60) US film actor

gable end *n* a side wall that comes to a peak where the slopes of a pitched roof meet

gable roof *n* a roof with two slopes and a gable at each end

Gabo /gaábō/, **Naum** (1890–1977) Russian-born US sculptor. Born **Neemia Pevsner**

Gabon /ga bón, gə bóN/ republic in west-central Africa on the Atlantic coast. Capital: Libreville. Population: 1,190,159 (1997). Area: 267,667 sq. km / 103,347 sq. mi. —**Gabonese** /gábbə neéz/ *n, adj*

Gaborone /gábbə rốni/ capital of Botswana, in the southeastern part of the country. Population: 133,468 (1991).

gad¹ /gad/ *vi* (**gads, gadding, gadded**) to go around having fun in a carefree and aimless manner (*humorous*) ○ *gadding about* ■ *n* carefree or aimless wandering (*archaic*) [15C. Probably back-formation < obsolete *gadling* 'wanderer' < Old English *gædeling* 'companion' < Germanic.] —**gadder** *n*

gad² /gad/ *n* **1** HEAVY TOOL a heavy steel or iron wedge with a pointed or chisel-shaped edge, used in mining to break coal, rock, or ore from the rock face **2** CATTLE PROD a sharp pointed tool used to drive cattle ■ *vt* (**gads, gadding, gadded**) SEPARATE MINERALS FROM ROCK to break up coal or ore using a gad [13C. < Old Norse *gaddr* 'goad, spike' < Germanic, 'pointed stick'.]

Gabon

gad³ /gad/ *interj* used to express surprise or to add emphasis (*archaic*) [15C. Alteration of GOD.]

gadabout /gádə bowt/ *n* a restless and aimless seeker of pleasure (*humorous*)

Gadaffi /gə dáffi/, **Qadaffi** /kə-/, **Muammar al-** (b. 1942) Libyan soldier and national leader (1969–)

gadarene /gáddə reèn/ *adj* rushing headlong en masse (*literary*) [Early 19C. Via Latin < Greek *Gadarēnos* 'inhabitant of Gadara', town in the Bible where a herd of swine rushed into the sea (Matthew 8:28).]

Gaddafi = Gadaffi

gaddi /gáddi/ *n S* Asia a seat of power [Mid-19C. < Panjabi *gaddī*, Marathi *gādī*, or Bengali *gādi* 'cushion'.]

gadfly /gád flī/ *n* (*plural* **-flies**) *n* **1** a fly that irritates livestock by biting them and sucking their blood. Family: Tabanidae. **2** a persistently annoying or irritating person [< GAD²]

gadget /gájjit/ *n* **1** a small device that performs or aids a simple task **2** a small object or device that appears useful but is often unnecessary or superfluous [Late 19C. < ?] —**gadgety** *adj*

gadgeteer /gájji teèr/ *n* an inventor or enthusiastic user of gadgets

gadgetry /gájjitri/ *n* gadgets collectively, especially when perceived as impressively complicated

gadid /gáydid/, **gadoid** /gáy doyd/ *n* a sea fish of the family that includes cod, haddock, and whiting. Family: Gadidae. ■ *adj* belonging to the family of sea fish that includes cod, haddock, and whiting [Mid-19C. < modern Latin *gadus* 'cod' < Greek *gados*.]

gadolinite /gáddəlinīt/ *n* a black or brown silicate mineral containing beryllium, iron, and yttrium. Source: pegmatites. [Early 19C. After Johan *Gadolin* (1760–1852), Finnish mineralogist.]

gadolinium /gáddə línni əm/ *n* (*symbol* **Gd**) a rare silvery-white metallic element. Source: monazite, bastnaesite. Use: high-temperature alloys, neutron absorber in nuclear reactors and fuels. [Late 19C. < GADOLINITE.]

gadroon /gə droón/, **godroon** *n* an ornamental feature that consists of a series of convex curves or inverted fluting. It is often applied as an edging to a curved surface, especially on silver. [Late 17C. < French *godron* 'pucker, crease'.] —**gadrooned** *adj* —**gadrooning** *n*

gadwall /gád wawl/ *n* a common freshwater duck with grey or brown plumage. Native to: Europe, North America. *Anas strepera*. [Mid-17C. < ?]

gadzooks /gad zóoks/ *interj* used to express surprise or as a mild oath (*archaic or humorous*) [Late 17C. < GAD[3] + *zooks* < ?]

Gael /gayl/ *n* **1** somebody from Scotland, Ireland, or the Isle of Man who speaks Gaelic **2** somebody from the Scottish Highlands [Mid-18C. < Scots Gaelic *Gael*, *Gàidheal* < Old Irish *Goídel*, plural of *Gáidil*.]

Gaelic /gáylik, gállik/ *n* **CELTIC LANGUAGE OF BRITISH ISLES** any of the forms of the Celtic language used in Ireland, Scotland, or the Isle of Man ■ *adj* **1 OF GAELIC** relating to any of the forms of the Celtic language of Ireland, Scotland, or the Isle of Man **2 OF GAELIC-SPEAKING PEOPLE** relating to Gaelic-speaking people or their culture

Gaelic coffee *n* = **Irish coffee**

Gaelic football *n* a game played in Ireland with 15 players on each side, the aim of which is to punch or kick a ball into or over a goal

Gaeltacht /gáyl ta*kh*t/ *n* the parts of Ireland or Scotland where Gaelic is spoken by a large proportion of the population [Early 20C. < Irish.]

gaff[1] /gaf/ *n* **1 HOOKED FISH POLE** a pole with a large hook on the end that is used to hold and land a large fish **2 POLE AT TOP OF SAIL** a pole attached at the back of a mast and used to support the upper edge of a gaffsail **3 METAL SPUR ON FIGHTING COCK** a metal spur that is fixed to the leg of a fighting cock **4 HOOK FOR SOMEBODY MAINTAINING OVERHEAD LINE** a climbing hook used by somebody erecting or repairing a telephone or power line ■ *vt* **1 CATCH FISH WITH HOOKED POLE** to catch and hold a fish with a gaff **2 ARM WITH A GAFF** to provide or arm something, e.g. a fighting cock, with a gaff [14C. < Old French *gaffe* 'boat hook' (see GAFFE).]

gaff[2] /gaf/ *n* worthless nonsense (*informal*) [Early 19C. < ?] ◇ **blow the gaff** to reveal a secret (*slang*)

gaff[3] *n* **1** the place where somebody lives (*dated slang*) ○ *Nice gaff you've got yourself here!* **2** a music hall or theatre (*dated informal*) [Early 19C. < ?]

gaffe /gaf/ *n* a clumsy social mistake or breach of etiquette, e.g. an undiplomatic remark [Early 20C. < French, originally 'boat hook', via Old French < Old Provençal *gaf*.]

gaffer /gáffər/ *n* **1** *UK* **BOSS** the boss, owner, or supervisor of a workplace (*informal*) **2 CHIEF LIGHTING ELECTRICIAN** the chief electrician in charge of lighting on a film or television set (*informal*) **3** *UK* **MAN** a man of advanced years, especially a man from the country (*informal*) **4 HUSBAND** somebody's husband (*regional*) [Late 16C. Probably contraction of GODFATHER.]

gaff-rig *n* a sailing vessel rigged with gaffsail —**gaff-rigged** *adj*

gaffsail /gáf sayl/ *n* a quadrilateral sail that extends behind the mast rather than across the boat. The upper edge is supported by a pole (**gaff**) attached to the mast. US term **fore-and-aft sail**

gaff-topsail *n* a small, usually triangular, sail set above a gaffsail

ϟ **GAFIA** *abbr* get away from it all (*in e-mails*)

gag /gag/ *n* **1 SOMETHING PUT OVER MOUTH** something such as a piece of cloth that is forcibly put over or into somebody's mouth to prevent the person from speaking or crying out **2 RESTRAINT OF SPEECH** a restraint on free speech ○ *put a gag on a newspaper* **3 COMIC WORDS OR ACTION** a comic story, action, or incident told or performed by an actor or comedian **4 TRICK** a trick, hoax, or practical joke (*informal*) **5 CLOSURE OF PARLIAMENTARY DEBATE** a procedure by which a parliamentary debate can be stopped and a vote taken immediately **6 MOUTH PROP** a device that is placed in a patient's mouth to keep it open during surgical work on the mouth or throat **7 CHOKING** an instance or the action of choking or retching (*informal*) ■ *v* (**gags, gagging, gagged**) **1** *vt* **PUT SOMETHING OVER SOMEBODY'S MOUTH** to put something over or into somebody's mouth to prevent the person from speaking or crying out **2** *vt* **RESTRAIN SPEECH** to prevent or restrain the free speech of somebody or something **3** *vti* **CHOKE OR RETCH** to make somebody nearly choke or retch, or to choke or retch **4** *vi* **TELL JOKES** to tell jokes or perform as a comedian (*informal*) **5** *vt* **PROP SOMEBODY'S MOUTH OPEN** to hold somebody's mouth open during surgery by means of a gag **6** *vt* **PUT STRONG BIT ON HORSE** to put a strong bit (**gag-bit**) on a horse **7** *vt* **OBSTRUCT PIPE OR VALVE** to stop up, block, or obstruct something such as a pipe or valve [15C. Probably an imitation of the sound of choking.]

gaga /gaá gaa/ *adj* (*informal*) **1** an offensive term that deliberately insults somebody's mental abilities, especially those of a person of advanced age **2** completely infatuated or very enthusiastic ○ *totally gaga about that boyfriend of hers* [Early 20C. < French, an imitation of the sound of mumbling.]

gagaku /gágga koo/ *n* an ancient form of Japanese classical music played at the imperial court and on ceremonial occasions [Early 20C. < Japanese.]

Gagarin /gə gaárin/, **Yuri** (1934–68) Soviet cosmonaut

Gagauz /gə gáwz/ (*plural* **-gauz** *or* **-gauzi** /-zi/) *n* **1** a Turkic language spoken in an area north of the Black Sea, especially in S Moldova, Ukraine, and Romania. Native speakers: 150,000. **2 Gagauz, Gagauzian** a member of a Turkic people who live in SW Moldova —**Gagauz** *adj*

gag-bit *n* a strong bit sometimes used to help control an unruly horse

gage[1] /gayj/ *n* (*archaic*) **1 PLEDGE** something that is given or left as security until a debt is paid or an obligation is fulfilled **2 TOKEN OF CHALLENGE** a glove or other object that is thrown down or offered as a challenge to fight **3 CHALLENGE** a challenge to fight ■ *vt* (**gages, gaging, gaged**) **OFFER AS PLEDGE** to offer something as security against a debt or other obligation (*archaic*) [13C. < Old French, < Germanic.]

gage[2] *n*, *vt* = **gauge**

gagger /gággər/ *n* a piece of metal used to wedge the core of a casting mould in position

gagging order *n* a court order that forbids any public commentary or media reporting on a case that is currently being heard in court

gaggle /gágg'l/ *n* **1** a flock of geese **2** a group of people, especially a noisy or disorderly group ○ *a gaggle of children* [14C. < ?]

gagman /gág man/ (*plural* **-men** /-men/) *n* ARTS = **gagster** *n.* 1 (*informal*)

gag order *n* US = **gagging order**

gagster /gágstər/ *n* (*informal*) **1** a writer or teller of jokes **2** *US* a trickster or practical joker

gahnite /gaá nīt/ *n* a dark green mineral consisting of zinc aluminium oxide [Early 19C. After J. G. *Gahn* (1745–1818), Swedish chemist.]

Gaia hypothesis /gī ə-/ *n* the theory put forward by James Lovelock that the Earth is a self-regulating organism with its own life cycle [Late 20C. < Greek *gaia* 'the Earth'.]

gaiety /gáy əti/ (*plural* **-ties**) *n* **1 JOYFULNESS** a lighthearted and lively feeling or way of behaving **2 SPIRITED ACTIVITY** joyful and lively activity or festivity **3 BRIGHT APPEARANCE** the showiness or bright colourful appearance of something such as clothing (*dated*) [Mid-17C. < Old French *gaieté* < *gai* 'happy'.]

gaijin /gī jin/ (*plural* **-jin**) *n* a foreigner in Japan or among Japanese people [Mid-20C. < Japanese.]

gaily /gáyli/ *adv* **1 JOYFULLY OR LIGHTHEARTEDLY** in a happy, cheerful, or carefree manner **2 SHOWING LACK OF CONCERN** showing a lack of concern or awareness **3 IN BRIGHT COLOURS** brightly or colourfully (*dated*)

gain[1] /gayn/ *v* **1** *vt* **ACQUIRE** to obtain something through effort, skill, or merit ○ *gain recognition as an actor* **2** *vt* **WIN BY COMPETING** to win something in competition or conflict ○ *gained second place in the dash* **3** *vt* **EARN** to earn or obtain something by work ○ *gain a living* **4** *vi* **PROFIT** to derive advantage from something ○ *No one stands to gain from the deal.* **5** *vti* **BECOME GREATER** to grow or increase or acquire more of something ○ *She was steadily gaining in confidence.* **6** *vt* **PERSUADE TO SUPPORT** to acquire the support of somebody through persuasion ○ *The movement quickly gained followers.* **7** *vt* **MAKE ARISE** to cause something to arise or become operative ○ *gain his confidence* **8** *vt* **ESTABLISH RELATIONSHIP** to begin to have or establish a particular relationship with somebody ○ *gain a mentor and a friend* **9** *vi* **GET BETTER** to improve or become better in some respect ○ *gaining in proficiency* **10** *vi* **GET CLOSER OR FARTHER AWAY** to come closer to somebody or something pursued, or increase the distance from a pursuer ○ *They are behind but they're gaining on us.* **11** *vti* **INCREASE IN OR BY** to come to have more of something or increase by a specified amount ○ *The pound had gained two points* **12** *vti* **RUN AHEAD OF CORRECT TIME** to run fast so as to record a time ahead, or a specified amount of time ahead, of the correct one ○ *My watch gains at least 10 minutes every day.* **13** *vt* **REACH** to arrive at a place that it was hoped to reach (*literary*) ○ *once we had finally gained the shore* ■ *n* **1 ACHIEVEMENT** an advantage or improvement that has been earned or acquired through effort ○ *despite the political gains of recent years* **2 AMOUNT INCREASED** an increase or profit of a specified amount ○ *a small weight gain* **3 BENEFIT** financial profit or personal advantage **4 MEASURE OF INCREASE IN SIGNAL STRENGTH** a ratio of the output power to the input power of an amplifier that is more than one and indicates an increase in signal strength ■ **gains** *npl* **ACQUISITIONS** something acquired, earned, or won, especially money [15C. < Old French *gaignier* < Germanic, 'graze, hunt'.] —**gainable** *adj*

SYNONYMS See ***get***.

gain[2] /gayn/ *n* **NOTCH TO FIT SOMETHING INTO** a notch or groove cut into a board so that another part can be fitted into it ■ *vt* **1 CUT NOTCH IN** to cut a notch or groove into a board so that another part can be fitted into it **2 FIT PART IN NOTCH** to fit a part into a gain or connect parts using a gain [Mid-19C. < ?]

gainer /gáynər/ *n* **1** somebody who or something that gains **2** a dive in which the diver jumps forwards, does a back somersault in the air, and enters the water feet first, facing away from the board

gainful /gáynf'l/ *adj* bringing profit or advantage —**gainfully** *adv* —**gainfulness** *n*

gainsay /gayn sáy/ (**-says, -saying, -said, -said** /gáyn séd/) *vt* (*formal*) **1** to say that something is false **2** to oppose or contradict somebody ○ *I won't gainsay you.* [14C. < Old English *gegn* 'against' < Germanic.] —**gainsayer** *n*

Gainsborough /gáynzbərə/, **Thomas** (1727–88) British painter

'gainst /genst, gaynst/, **gainst** *prep* against (*literary*) [Late 16C. Shortening.]

Gairdner, Lake /gáirdnər/ dry salt lake in south-central South Australia. Area: 4,800 sq. km/1,900 sq. mi.

gait /gayt/ *n* **1** a way of walking, running, or moving along on foot ○ *his familiar shambling gait* **2** any one of the four paces of a horse, walk, trot, canter, and gallop, each having a specific pattern of leg movements [15C. Variant of GATE 'way, street'.]

SPELLCHECK Do not confuse ***gait*** with ***gate***, which has a similar sound. Beware: your spellchecker will not catch this error.

-gaited *suffix* with a particular way of walking ○ *slow-gaited*

gaiter /gáytər/ *n* a strip of fabric, leather, or waterproof material covering the leg from the instep to either the ankle or the knee (*usually plural*) [Early 18C. < French *guêtre*.] —**gaitered** *adj*

Gaitskell /gáytskəl/, **Hugh** (1906–63) British politician

gal /gal/ *n* a girl or woman (*slang; sometimes offensive*) [Late 18C. Reproducing a pronunciation of GIRL.]

gal. *abbr* gallon

Gal. *abbr* Galatians

gala /gaálə/ *n* **1** a special festive occasion that typically includes entertainment **2** a sporting event, especially a swimming contest with a variety of different races and competitions [Early 17C. Via Old French *gale* 'merrymaking' < Arabic *khil'a* 'fine garment given as a present, festive attire, festive occasion'.]

galact- *prefix* = **galacto-**

galactagogue /gə lákta gog/ *adj* causing the production and secretion of milk ■ *n* an agent that stimulates the production and flow of breast milk [< GALACT- + Greek *agōgos* 'leading' < *agein* 'lead']

galactic /gə láktik/ *adj* relating or belonging to a galaxy, especially the Milky Way [Mid-19C. < Greek *galakt-* (see GALAXY).] —**galactically** *adv*

galactic cluster *n* ASTRON = **open cluster**

galactic equator, galactic circle *n* the imaginary circle on the sky formed by extending the plane that passes through the centre of the Galaxy. It is inclined at approximately 62° to the celestial equator.

galacto-, galact- *prefix* milk ○ *galactosaemia* [<Greek *galakt-* (see GALAXY)]

galactopoiesis /gə láktō poy éssiss/ *n* the production of milk by the cells of the glandular structure of the breast

galactopoietic /gə láktō poy éttik/ *adj* stimulating lactation ■ *n* a substance that stimulates lactation

galactorrhea *n* US = **galactorrhoea**

galactorrhoea /gə láktō reè ə/ *n* excessive milk flow during lactation, or spontaneous milk flow in the absence of childbirth and nursing

galactosaemia /gə láktō seèmi ə/ *n* a genetic disorder causing the absence of an enzyme necessary for the breakdown of galactose in milk to glucose

galactosamine /gə lák tōssə meen/ *n* an amino derivative of galactose, found in cartilage

galactose /gə láktōss/ *n* a six-carbon sugar that is a constituent of lactose

galactosemia *n* US = **galactosaemia**

galactosidase /gə láktō síd ayss, -dayz/ *n* an enzyme that breaks down lactose

galactoside /gə láktō síd/ *n* a compound made up of galactose combined with another sugar or a nonsugar

galago /gə laàgō/ (*plural* **-gos**) *n* ZOOL = **bushbaby** [Mid-19C. < modern Latin.]

galah /gə laà/ *n* 1 a common cockatoo with a grey back and wings, a pink breast and head, and a pale pink crest. Native to: Australia. *Eulophus roseicapillus*. 2 Aus a silly or thoughtless person (*informal insult*) [Mid-19C. < an Aboriginal language.]

Galahad /gállə had/ *n* 1 the purest knight of the Round Table in Arthurian legend, who succeeded in his quest for the Holy Grail 2 a man considered to be chivalrous, noble, or pure in actions or attitudes

galangal /gə láng g'l/ *n* 1 the pungent underground stem of a ginger plant, sold fresh or dried and ground. Use: cookery, medicine. 2 a plant of the ginger family grown for galangal. Native to: E Asia. *Alpinia officinarum*. 3 PLANTS = **galingale** [Pre-12C. Via Old French *galingal* < Arabic *kálanjān*.]

galantine /gállən teen/ *n* a dish of boned and cooked white meat, poultry, or fish, usually stuffed, moulded into shape, and served cold in its own jelly [14C. Via Old French < medieval Latin *galatina*.]

galanty show /gə lánti-/ *n* a play performed by manipulating paper figures and casting their shadows on a screen

Galapagos giant tortoise /gə láppəgəss-, -goss-/, **Galapagos tortoise** *n* a giant tortoise that is native to the Galápagos Islands. It grows up to 1.2 m/4 ft long and weighs up to 225 kg/500 lb. *Geochelone elephantopus*.

Galápagos Islands

Galápagos Islands /gə láppəgəss-/, **Galapagos Islands** group of islands in the Pacific Ocean off the coast of W Ecuador. Population: 9,785 (1990). Area: 7,844 sq. km/3,029 sq. mi.

Galapagos tortoise *n* ZOOL = **Galapagos giant tortoise**

galatea /gállə teè ə/ *n* a strong cotton fabric with a twill weave that is often striped. Use: clothes. [Late 19C. After HMS *Galatea*; originally used for children's sailor suits.]

Galatea /gállə teè ə/ *n* a small inner natural satellite of Neptune

Galaţi /ga látsi/ port in Romania, on the River Danube. Population: 641,647 (1997 estimate).

Galatians /gə láysh'nz/ *n* a book of the Bible believed to be a letter from St Paul to the people of Galatia (*+ singular verb*) [Early 17C. < *Galatia*, ancient country of central Asia Minor.]

galavant /gállə vant/ *vi* = **gallivant**

galaxy /gálləksi/ (*plural* **-ies**) *n* 1 a group of billions of stars and their planets, gas, and dust that extends over many thousands of light-years and forms a unit within the universe 2 a gathering of famous, brilliant, or distinguished people or things [14C. Via Old French < Greek *galaxias* (*kuklos*) 'milky (circle)' < *galakt-*, stem of *gala* 'milk'.]

Galaxy *n* ASTRON = **Milky Way**

galbanum /gálbənəm/ *n* a yellowish to green or brown aromatic bitter gum resin derived from several related Asian plants and used in incense or medicinally as a counterirritant. Genus: *Ferula*. [12C. Via Latin < Greek *khalbanē* < Semitic.]

Galbraith /gal bráyth/, **John Kenneth** (*b.* 1908) Canadian-born US economist

gale /gayl/ *n* 1 an extremely strong wind that measures 8 or 9 on the Beaufort scale and has a speed of between 63 km/39 mi. and 87 km/54 mi. per hour 2 a very strong wind [Mid-16C. < ?]

galea /gáy li ə/ (*plural* **-ae** /-ee/) *n* a part or organ shaped like a helmet, e.g. the upper petal of some flowers or one of the mouthparts of an insect [Mid-19C. < Latin, 'helmet'.] —**galeate** *adj*

Galen /gáylən/ (129–199?) Greek physician and scholar

galena /gə leènə/ *n* a lustrous blue-grey crystalline mineral consisting of lead sulphide. Use: source of lead and silver. [Late 17C. < Latin, 'lead at a certain stage of smelting'.]

galenical /gay lénnik'l/ *n* any medicinal preparation made from plant or animal tissue ■ *adj* made from plant or animal tissue rather than synthesized [Mid-17C. < GALEN.]

galenite /gáylə nīt/ *n* MINERALS = **galena**

galère /ga láir/ *n* 1 a group of people with a particular attribute or interest, especially something undesirable, in common 2 an unpleasant predicament [Mid-18C. Via French, 'galley' < Catalan *galera* < Middle Greek *galea*.]

Galibi /gaa leèbi/ (*plural* **-bi** *or* **-bis** /-biz/) *n* 1 a member of an indigenous South American people who live in French Guiana 2 a Carib language spoken in French Guiana [Late 19C. < Carib, 'strong man'.] —**Galibi** *adj*

Galilean[1] /gálli leè ən/ *n* 1 somebody who lives or was born or brought up in Galilee 2 a Christian (*archaic*) [Mid-16C. < Latin *Galilea* 'Galilee'.] —**Galilean** *adj*

Galilean[2] /gálli leè ən/ *adj* relating to the Italian scientist Galileo, his theories, or his inventions

Galilean satellite *n* any one of the four largest moons of Jupiter (Io, Europa, Callisto, and Ganymede), first observed telescopically by Galileo in 1610

Galilean telescope *n* an early telescope that has a convex lens for collecting light from the object and a concave lens as an eyepiece [After GALILEO]

galilee /gálli lee/ *n* a small porch or chapel found at the western end of some medieval churches or cathedrals [15C. Via Old French < medieval Latin *galilea*, after Latin *Galilea* 'Galilee'.]

Galilee /gálli lee/ region of ancient Palestine between the River Jordan and the Sea of Galilee

Galilee, Sea of freshwater lake on the River Jordan in NE Israel. Area: 166 sq. km/64 sq. mi.

Galileo /gálli láy ō/ (1564–1642) Italian physicist and astronomer. Born **Galileo Galilei**

galingale /gálling gayl/ *n* a plant of the sedge family with aromatic roots that were used medicinally in the past. Flowers: reddish, growing in a cluster directly from the stem. *Cyperus longus*. [Variant of GALANGAL.]

galiot /gálli ət/, **galliot** *n* 1 formerly, a light fast ship propelled by sails and oars used in the Mediterranean 2 formerly, a light shallow single-masted Dutch merchant ship [15C. < Old French, 'little galley' < medieval Latin *galea* 'galley'.]

galipot /gálli pot/ *n* crude turpentine in resin form that is obtained from several species of pine found in S Europe [Late 18C. Via French < Provençal *garapot* 'pine resin'.]

gall[1] /gawl/ *n* 1 AUDACITY impudent boldness ○ *And then he had the gall to tell us to leave!* 2 BITTER FEELING a feeling of bitterness or resentment (*literary*) ○ *Her betrayal turned his love to gall.* 3 BILE bile (*archaic*) [12C. < Old Norse *gall* 'bile' < Germanic, 'yellow'.]

gall[2] /gawl/ *n* 1 SORE CAUSED BY RUBBING a sore on the skin of an animal that is caused by friction 2 CAUSE OF ANGER something that angers or irritates somebody (*dated*) 3 ANGER a feeling of annoyance or anger (*dated*) ■ *vt* 1 MAKE ANGRY to make somebody extremely angry 2 BREAK THE SURFACE DUE TO FRICTION to break or damage a surface, especially the skin, by friction or rubbing [14C. < Middle Low German *galle* 'sore'.]

gall[3] /gawl/ *n* a swelling on a tree or plant caused by insects, fungi, bacteria, or external damage [14C. Via Old French < Latin *galla* 'oak apple'.]

gall. *abbr* gallon

Galla /gállə/ *n, adj* LANG, PEOPLES = **Oromo** [Late 19C. < ?]

gallamine /gállə meen/ *n* a short-acting but powerful muscle relaxant. Use: general anaesthesia. [Late 19C. < *Gallic* (< GALLIUM) + AMINE.]

gallant /gállənt, gə lánt/ *adj* 1 COURTEOUS courteous and thoughtful, especially towards women 2 BRAVE brave, spirited, and honourable (*literary*) 3 MAJESTIC grand and majestic (*archaic*) ■ *n* 1 MAN COURTEOUS TO WOMEN a man who is courteous and thoughtful in his behaviour towards women (*dated*) 2 MALE LOVER a man who is a woman's lover (*archaic*) 3 DANDY a fashionable young man (*archaic*) ■ *vti* WOO to court a woman (*archaic*) [14C. < Old French, present participle of *galer* 'make merry'.] —**gallantly** *adv*

Gallant /gə lánt/, **Mavis** (*b.* 1922) Canadian writer. Born **Mavis Young**

gallantry /gálləntri/ (*plural* **-ries**) *n* 1 COURAGE bravery, especially in war or in a situation of great danger 2 COURTESY courteous and thoughtful behaviour, especially towards women 3 SOMETHING GALLANT SAID OR DONE a courageous or chivalrous action or remark (*dated*)

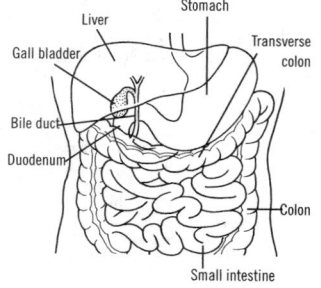

Gallbladder

gallbladder /gáwl bladər/ *n* a small muscular sac on the right underside of the liver, in which bile secreted by the liver is stored and concentrated until needed for the digestive process

Galle /gállə, gawl/ port on the southwestern coast of Sri Lanka. Population: 84,000 (1990 estimate).

galleass /gálli ass/, **galliass** *n* a large fast warship with three masts, used in the Mediterranean in the 16th and 17th centuries [Mid-16C. Via Old French < Old Italian *galeaza* 'large galley'.]

galleon /gálli ən/ *n* a large three-masted sailing ship used especially by the Spanish between the 15th and 18th centuries [Early 16C. Either via Middle Dutch *galjoen* < Old French *galion* 'large galley', or < Spanish *galeón*.]

galleria /gállə reè ə/ *n* a roofed court with shops or businesses opening onto it, usually at several levels [Late 19C. < Italian.]

gallery /gálləri/ (*plural* **-ies**) *n* 1 PLACE FOR ART EXHIBITIONS a place where artwork is exhibited and sometimes sold 2 COVERED WALKWAY a long covered passageway that is open on one or both sides 3 ENCLOSED WALKWAY a corridor, hall, or other enclosed passageway inside a building 4 LONG NARROW ROOM a long narrow space or room used for a particular purpose 5 BALCONY a balcony or passage running along the wall of a large building, often used for viewing an activity 6 UNDERGROUND PASSAGE an underground tunnel or passage, especially one made by an animal or one that is part of a mine or a military site 7 STUDIO a photographer's studio 8 PART OF THEATRE a seating area projecting from the back and sides out over the main floor of a theatre, especially the highest section of this area containing the cheapest seats 9 SEATS IN

THE GALLERY the seats located in the gallery of a theatre **10 AUDIENCE IN CHEAPEST SEATS** the people who sit in the gallery of a theatre **11 OFFENSIVE TERM** an offensive term applied to the general public, viewed as having no discrimination or sophistication **12 STAGE RIG** a narrow platform above a stage from which technicians can adjust lights, move props, or operate machinery **13 SPECTATORS** a group of spectators, especially at a tennis or golf match **14 ASSORTED COLLECTION** a varied collection of people or things ○ *a gallery of famous names* **15 SOUNDPROOF ROOM** a soundproof room with a glass front in a television studio, from which the director or technical staff can oversee the studio floor **16 SHIP'S BALCONY** a platform or balcony at the rear of a ship **17 DECORATIVE RAIL** a decorative metal or wooden rail on a table top, shelf, or tray [15C. Via Old French *galerie* 'portico' < medieval Latin *galeria*.] —**galleried** *adj* ◇ **play to the gallery** to do or say something that will appeal to those regarded as less educated, discriminating, or sophisticated

gallery forest *n* a strip of forest that grows along a river in an area where there are no other trees

galley /gálli/ (*plural* **-leys**) *n* **1 LARGE SHIP** a large ship propelled by oars or sails or both, that was used in ancient and medieval times, especially in the Mediterranean **2 ROWING BOAT** a long boat propelled by oars **3 KITCHEN** a kitchen on a boat, ship, train, or aircraft **4 PRINT TRAY** a long metal tray used for holding type that is ready for printing **5** PRINTING = **galley proof** [13C. Via Old French and medieval Latin < medieval Greek *galea*.]

galley proof *n* a first test copy of printed material, usually not divided into pages, on which corrections are marked

galley slave *n* **1** formerly, one of a team of convicts or enslaved men forced to row a galley **2** a person who is given menial tasks to do (*dated humorous*)

gallfly /gáwl flī/ (*plural* **-flies**) *n* an insect such as the gall midge or gall wasp that causes swellings (**galls**) on plants when it deposits its eggs on them

galliard /gálli aard/ *n* **1** a lively European dance in triple time popular in the 16th and 17th centuries **2** the music for a galliard [14C. < Old French.]

galliass *n* SHIPPING = **galleass**

Gallic /gállik/ *adj* **1** relating to France, or its language, people, or culture **2** relating to ancient Gaul or the Gauls [Late 17C. < Latin *Gallia* 'Gaul'.]

gallic acid /gállik-/ *n* $C_7H_6O_5$ a colourless crystalline solid. Source: plants, tannin. Use: tanning agent, manufacture of inks and paper, in photography. [< Latin *galla* 'oak apple' (used in making the acid)]

Gallicanism /gállikənizəm/ *n* a French movement in favour of giving more autonomy to the Roman Catholic Church in individual countries and reducing the authority of the pope —**Gallican** *adj, n*

Gallicise *vt* LANG = **Gallicize**

Gallicism /gállissizəm/ *n* a word or phrase of French origin used in another language

Gallicize /gálli sīz/ (**-cizes, -cizing, -cized**), **Gallicise** (**-cises, -cising, -cised**) *vti* to become French or like something French, or make something, e.g. a word, custom, or characteristic French —**Gallicization** /gálli sī záysh'n/ *n*

galligaskins /gálli gáskinz/ *npl* **1 BREECHES OR STOCKINGS** loose-fitting breeches or stockings that were worn by men in the 16th and 17th centuries **2 LOOSE TROUSERS** very loose-fitting trousers **3 LEATHER LEGGINGS** leather leggings worn in the 19th century [Late 16C. < ?]

gallimaufry /gálli máwfri/ (*plural* **-fries**) *n* a jumble of various things or people [Mid-16C. < French *galimafrée*.]

galling /gáwling/ *adj* with the effect of frustrating and annoying somebody —**gallingly** *adv*

gallinule /gálli nyool/ *n* an aquatic bird of swampy regions that both wades and swims and typically has dark plumage and a yellow-tipped red bill with a red shield above it. Family: Rallidae. [Late 18C. < modern Latin *gallinula* 'little hen'.]

galliot *n* SHIPPING = **galiot**

Gallipoli /gə líppəli/ peninsula in European Turkey, extending into the Dardanelles and including an important seaport of the same name

gallipot /gálli pot/ *n* a small pot used by chemists as a container for medicaments [15C. Probably < GALLEY, because galleys brought such goods from the Mediterranean.]

gallium /gálli əm/ *n* (*symbol* **Ga**) a rare metallic element, blue-grey when solid and silver when liquid. Source: coal, bauxite. Use: high-temperature thermometers, semiconductors, alloys. [Late 19C. < Latin *Gallia* 'France'.]

gallium arsenide *n* **GaAs** a dark-grey crystalline solid containing gallium and arsenic. Use: manufacture of semiconductors, solar cells, and lasers.

gallivant /gálli vant/, **galavant** *vi* (*informal*) **1** to travel around with no purpose except enjoyment **2** to flirt or play romantically [Early 19C. < ?]

galliwasp /gálli wosp/ *n* a lizard with a long body that is related to the slowworm. Native to: marshes of Central America and the Caribbean. Family: Anguidae. [Late 17C. < ?]

gall midge *n* a small fly resembling a mosquito whose larvae cause swellings (**galls**) on plants. Family: Cecidomyiidae.

gall mite *n* a mite that causes swellings (**galls**) on the fruits, leaves, or buds of plants. Family: Phytoptidae.

gallnut /gáwl nut/ *n* a small round swelling (**gall**) on a plant

galloglass /gállō glaass/, **gallowglass** *n* a medieval mercenary soldier or armed servant of a Celtic chieftain, especially in Ireland [15C. < Irish *gallóglach* 'young foreign servant, warrior'.]

gallon /gállən/ *n* **1 BRITISH UNIT OF VOLUME** a unit of capacity in the imperial system equal to eight imperial pints (approximately 4.55 litres) **2** *US* **US UNIT OF VOLUME** a unit of capacity in the US Customary system equal to eight US pints (approximately 3.79 litres) ■ *adj* **HOLDING A GALLON** with a capacity of one gallon ○ *a gallon jar* [13C. < Anglo-Norman *galon* < medieval Latin *galleta* 'jug'.]

gallonage /gállənij/ *n* **1** a capacity or amount measured in gallons **2** the rate at which a liquid is used, pumped, or transmitted, measured in gallons per second, minute, or hour

galloon /gə lóon/ *n* a narrow band of embroidery, lace, braid, or silver or gold thread, used as a trimming on clothes or upholstery [Early 17C. < French *galon* < *galonner* 'trim with braid'.] —**gallooned** *adj*

galloot *n* = **galoot**

gallop /gálləp/ *n* **1 FASTEST PACE OF HORSE** the fastest pace of a horse, in which all four feet are off the ground at the same time **2 FAST PACE OF FOUR-LEGGED ANIMAL** a fast movement similar to a horse's gallop made by any four-legged animal **3 FAST RIDE ON HORSE** a ride on a horse at a gallop ■ *v* **1** *vti* **RIDE HORSE FAST** to ride a horse at a gallop **2** *vt* **MOVE SOMETHING QUICKLY** to move or transport something at a gallop or at a very fast pace **3** *vi* **DO SOMETHING VERY FAST** to do something in a great hurry ○ *gallop through lunch* [Early 16C. < Old French *galoper*, variant of *waloper* < Germanic.] —**galloper** *n*

gallopade /gállə payd, -paad, gállə paád/ *n* DANCE, MUSIC = **galop** [Mid-18C. < French *galopade* < *galoper* (see GALLOP).]

galloping /gálləping/ *adj* **1** proceeding or developing at a very fast rate ○ *galloping pneumonia* **2** relating to or resembling a gallop, in speed or rhythm

Galloway[1] /gállə way/ region in SW Scotland —**Gallovidian** /gállə víddi ən/ *adj, n*

Galloway[2] /gállə way/ a cow of a hornless black breed of beef cattle [After GALLOWAY[1]]

gallowglass *n* HIST = **galloglass**

gallows /gállōz/ (*plural* **-lows**) *n* **1 FRAME FOR HANGING CRIMINALS** a wooden frame, usually made of two upright posts and a crossbeam with a noose attached, used to execute people by hanging **2 STRUCTURE RESEMBLING GALLOWS** a structure that resembles a gallows, e.g. one used to suspend slaughtered animals **3 EXECUTION BY HANGING** death by hanging as capital punishment for a criminal offence [13C. < Old Norse *gálgi* < Germanic, 'pole'.]

gallows bird *n* a person who deserves to be hanged (*archaic informal*)

gallows humour *n* macabre humour that finds irony or comedy in serious matters such as death

gallows tree *n* CRIME = **gallows** *n.* 1

gallstone /gáwl stōn/ *n* a small hard mass that forms in the gallbladder, sometimes as a result of infection or blockage

Gallup /gálləp/, **George** (1901–84) US public opinion analyst and statistician

Gallup poll /gálləp-/ *n* a survey in which a sample of people taken as a representative cross section of society are asked their opinions on a given subject

gallus /gálləs/ *adj Scotland* daring in a cocky or foolhardy way (*informal*) [Late 16C. Alteration of GALLOWS; originally 'fit to be hanged'.]

galluses /gálləssiz/ *npl US, Scotland* braces for trousers [Mid-19C. Plural of *gallus*, alteration of GALLOWS; from the two supports.]

gall wasp *n* a wasp that lays its eggs in plant tissue, causing swellings (**galls**). Family: Cynipidae.

galoot /gə lóot/, **galloot** *n* a person considered to be clumsy or thoughtless (*slang insult*) [Early 19C. < ?]

galop /gálləp, gə lóp/ *n* **1** a lively dance in double time popular in the 19th century **2** the music for a galop [Mid-19C. < French.]

galore /gə láwr/ *adj* in large quantities or numbers ○ *There'll be food galore at the party.* [Early 17C. < Irish *go leor* 'sufficiency'.]

galoshes /gə lóshiz/ *npl* a pair of waterproof shoes, often made of rubber, worn over other shoes as protection against rain or snow [14C. Via Old French *galoche* 'little sandal' < Latin *gallicula* < *gallica (solea)* 'sandal (from Gaul)'.]

Galtieri /gálti áiri/, **Leopoldo** (*b.* 1926) Argentinian general and national leader

galumph /gə lúmf/ *vi* (*informal*) **1** to walk or run in a boisterous or clumsy way **2** to stride or march in a prancing triumphant way [Late 19C. Blend of GALLOP + TRIUMPH.]

galuth /ga lóoth/ *n* the Jewish Diaspora [Late 20C. < Hebrew *gālūth* 'exile'.]

galv. *abbr* **1** galvanic **2** galvanized

galvanic /gal vánnik/ *adj* **1** relating to or involving the direct-current electricity that is chemically generated between dissimilar metals, e.g. in a battery **2** sudden, startling, or convulsive, like an electric shock or its effects [Late 18C. < French *galvanique*, after Luigi *Galvani* (see GALVANISM).] —**galvanically** *adv*

galvanic cell *n* ELEC ENG = **primary cell**

galvanic skin response *n* a change in the electrical conductivity of the skin caused by sweating and increased blood flow and linked to a strong emotion such as fear

galvanise *vt* = **galvanize**

galvanism /gálvənizəm/ *n* **1** the production of direct-current electricity from a chemical reaction, e.g. between dissimilar metals in a battery **2** the application of electricity to the human body to stimulate nerves and muscles as part of a medical treatment [Late 18C. < French *galvanisme*, after Luigi *Galvani* 1737–98, Italian anatomist.]

galvanize /gálvə nīz/ (**-nizes, -nizing, -nized**), **galvanise** (**-nises, -nising, -nised**) *vt* **1 STIMULATE TO ACT** to stimulate somebody or something into great activity **2 COAT METAL WITH ZINC** to coat a metal, usually iron or steel, with zinc to prevent corrosion **3 STIMULATE ELECTRICALLY** to stimulate the nerves or muscles of somebody's body using an electric current [Early 19C. < French *galvaniser*, after Luigi *Galvani* (see GALVANISM).] —**galvanization** /gálvə nī záysh'n/ *n* —**galvanizer** *n*

galvanometer /gálvə nómmitər/ *n* an instrument used to detect or measure the strength and direction of small electric currents by means of a coil in a magnetic field that moves a pointer or light —**galvanometric** /gálvənə méttrik/ *adj* —**galvanometry** *n*

Galway /gáwl way/ **1** seaport in W Republic of Ireland, on Galway Bay. Population: 57,000 (1996). **2** county in Connacht Province, W Republic of Ireland. Area: 5,939 sq. km/2,293 sq. mi. —**Galwegian** /gal wéejən/ *adj, n*

Galway Bay inlet of the Atlantic Ocean on the coast of W Republic of Ireland

gam[1] /gam/ *n* **1 MIGRATING WHALES** a group of migrating whales **2 SOCIAL VISIT BETWEEN WHALERS** a social visit between whalers or other sailors, especially while at sea (*informal*) **3** *New Zealand* **SEA BIRDS** a flock of sea birds ■ *vi* (**gams, gamming, gammed**) **MEET AT SEA** to meet socially, especially at sea (*informal*) [Mid-19C. < ?]

gam[2] /gam/ *n* somebody's leg, especially a woman's (*archaic slang or offensive*) [Late 18C. Probably alteration of *gamb* 'heraldic device resembling an animal's leg' < northern form of Old French *jambe* 'leg'.]

Gama /gáamə/, **Vasco da** (1469?–1524) Portuguese navigator and explorer

gama grass /gáamə-/ *n* a tall coarse grass that is grown in North America for fodder. *Tripsacum dactyloides.* [Mid-19C. < ?]

gamay /gámmay/ *n* a red grape used in making wine, especially Beaujolais [Mid-19C. After *Gamay,* village in Burgundy, France.]

gamba /gámbə/ *n* MUSIC = **viola da gamba**

gambade /gam báyd, -báad/ *n* RIDING = **gambado**[2] [Early 16C. < French, probably < Italian *gambata* < *gamba* 'leg'.]

gambado[1] /gam báydō/ (*plural* **-dos** *or* **-does**) *n* **1** either of a pair of protective leather holders for a rider's feet attached to a horse's saddle **2** either of a pair of rider's leggings [Mid-17C. < Italian *gamba* 'leg' + *-ado.*]

gambado[2] /gam báy dō/ (*plural* **-dos** *or* **-does**) *n* **1 LOW JUMP BY HORSE** in dressage, a low leap in which the horse has all four feet off the ground **2 LEAP** a leap or caper **3 PRANK** a prank or escapade [Early 19C. < Spanish *gambada* < *gamba* 'leg'.]

gambeer *n* INDUST = **gambier**

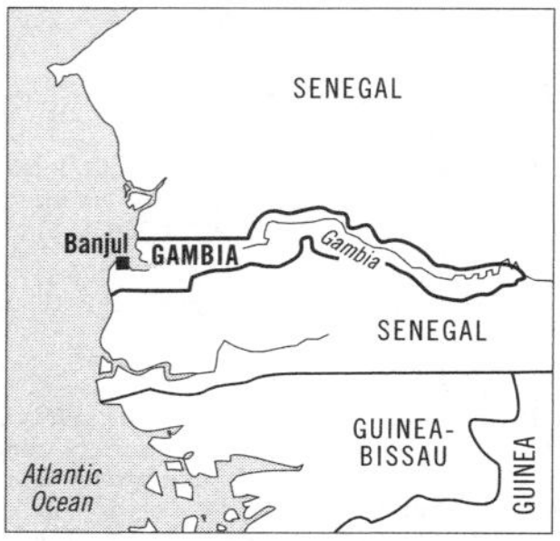

The Gambia

Gambia /gámbi ə/ **1 Gambia, the Gambia** republic on the coast of W Africa. Capital: Banjul. Population: 1,248,085 (1997). Area: 11,295 sq. km/4,361 sq. mi. **2** river in W Africa that rises in Guinea, flows westwards through the Gambia, and empties into the Atlantic Ocean near Banjul. Length: 1,100 km/700 mi. —**Gambian** *n, adj*

gambier /gám beer/, **gambir, gambeer** *n* a resinous astringent substance. Source: leaves of a tropical Asian woody vine. Use: medicinally as an astringent or tonic, in tanning and dyeing. [Early 19C. < Malay *gambir,* the plant.]

gambit /gámbit/ *n* **1 STRATAGEM** a manoeuvre or stratagem used to secure an advantage **2 CONVERSATIONAL OPENER** a remark used to open a conversation **3 OPENING MOVE IN CHESS** in chess, an opening move in which a player sacrifices a pawn or other minor piece in order to gain a strategic advantage [Mid-17C. < Italian *gambetto* 'act of tripping somebody up (in wrestling)' (after French *gambit*) < *gamba* 'leg'.]

gamble /gámb'l/ *v* (**-bles, -bling, -bled**) **1** *vi* **PLAY GAMES OF CHANCE** to play games such as poker or roulette that involve risking money, or bet on horse races or other events, in the hope of winning money **2** *vt* **BET MONEY** to bet a sum of money on the outcome of an event or competition **3** *vi* **TAKE A CHANCE ON** to take a risk in the hope and expectation of a desired result ○ *gambling on nice weather* **4** *vi* **ENDANGER** to behave in a way that risks harming somebody or something ○ *gambled with the success of the show* **5** *vt* **PUT SOMETHING DANGEROUSLY AT RISK** to lose or risk losing something, especially money, by betting or doing something dangerous or rash ○ *She gambled her inheritance away.* ■ *n* **1 BET** a bet made in the hope of winning money **2 SOMETHING DONE THAT IS RISKY** an action whose outcome is uncertain and very possibly undesirable ○ *I took a gamble on them being away from home.* [Early 18C. < GAME[1] + *-le,* literally 'keep on playing'.] —**gambler** *n*

gambling /gámbling/ *n* the practice of playing games of chance or betting in the hope of winning money

gamboge /gam bṓj, -bṓzh/ *n* **1 RESIN** a gum resin obtained from various Asian trees that produces a yellow pigment **2 YELLOW PIGMENT** a yellow pigment made from gamboge resin **3 YELLOW COLOUR** a strong yellow colour [Mid-17C. < modern Latin *gambaugium* < *Cambodia.*]

gambol /gámb'l/ *vi* (**-bols, -bolling, -bolled**) to leap or skip about playfully ■ *n* an instance of leaping about playfully [Mid-16C. Alteration of GAMBADE.]

gambrel /gámbrəl/ *n* **1** the joint of a leg of an animal, especially a horse, that corresponds to the human ankle **2** a frame in the shape of a horse's hind leg used by butchers for hanging animal carcasses **3** ARCHIT = **gambrel roof** [Mid-16C. < Old northern French *gamberel* < *gambier* 'forked stick' < *gambe,* variant of *jambe* 'leg'.]

gambrel roof *n* **1** a roof with sloping ends and sides and a small gable at both ends **2** *US, Can* a roof that has two slopes on each side, the lower slope being steeper than the upper

game[1] /gaym/ *n* **1 SOMETHING PLAYED FOR FUN** an activity that people participate in, together or on their own, for fun ○ *It's only a game!* **2 COMPETITIVE ACTIVITY WITH RULES** a sporting or other activity in which players compete against one another by following a fixed set of rules ○ *How many people do you need to play this game?* **3 MATCH** a particular occasion when a competitive game is played ○ *Saturday's game has been cancelled.* **4 PART OF MATCH** in sports such as tennis, a specific subsection of play that goes towards making up a set or match **5 ASPECT OF GAME** a particular aspect of a competition ○ *They lost because their attacking game was terrible.* **6 STYLE OF PLAYING** the style or level of skill with which somebody plays a particular sport ○ *raise your game* **7 NUMBER NEEDED TO WIN** the total number of points needed to win a contest **8 RULES GOVERNING SPORT** the rules governing a particular competition or sport **9 EQUIPMENT** an item or set of items such as a board, dice, counters, a pack of cards, or a piece of computer software that is needed to play a particular game ○ *a compendium of games* **10 ACTIVITY RESEMBLING GAME** any activity that resembles a game, e.g. one that involves intense interest and competitiveness and is carried out by its own specific and often unspoken rules **11 STRATAGEM** a way of behaving that is aimed at manipulating people or trying to deceive them ○ *So that's your game?* **12 ILLEGAL ACTIVITY** a strategy, activity, or behaviour that is questionable, and often illegal (*informal*) **13 OCCUPATION** a business or occupation (*informal*) ○ *the advertising game* **14 SOMETHING NOT TAKEN SERIOUSLY** an activity or situation that somebody does not treat seriously ○ *Life's a game as far as he's concerned.* **15 ANIMALS FOR HUNTING** wild animals, birds, or fish that are hunted for sport **16 MEAT OF HUNTED ANIMALS** the meat of wild animals, birds, or fish that have been killed for sport **17 RIDICULE** the act of ridiculing somebody for fun, or the target of ridicule, criticism, or trickery ○ *She's easy game for a trickster like him.* **18 MATHEMATICAL MODEL** a mathematical model describing a contest played under specified rules in which each participant has only partial control ■ **games** *npl* **EVENT WITH MANY SPORTING CONTESTS** an event that consists of many different sporting activities and usually lasts for several days ■ *adj* **1 READY AND WILLING** ready and willing to do something, especially something new or unusual **2 BRAVE** brave in spirit or character ■ *vi* (**games, gaming, gamed**) **GAMBLE** to play games of chance for money [Old English *gamen* < Germanic, 'people participating together'] —**gamely** *adv* —**gameness** *n* ◇ **a game of two halves** a game that might change later in the match, with the current loser starting to win ◇ **ahead of the game** anticipating and reacting more promptly than others to new developments ◇ **give the game away** to reveal a secret, usually without intending to ◇ **on the game** working as a prostitute (*informal*) ◇ **play the game** to follow the rules of a given situation, even if they are unspoken ◇ **the game's up** the plan or trick has failed or been discovered (*informal*)

game[2] /gaym/ *adj* an offensive term meaning injured or with impaired mobility (*dated*) [Late 18C. < ?]

game bird *n* a bird such as a pheasant or grouse that is hunted for sport

gamecock /gáym kok/ *n* BIRDS = **fighting cock**

game fish *n* **1** a freshwater fish that is highly prized for angling and eating, e.g. a trout or salmon. ◊ **coarse fish** **2** any fish, particularly any sea fish, that is caught for sport —**game fishing** *n*

game fowl *n* a domestic fowl bred and trained for fighting

gamekeeper /gáym keepər/ *n* somebody employed to look after birds or animals hunted for sport, e.g. on an estate or game reserve —**gamekeeping** *n*

gamelan /gámmə lan/ *n* an Indonesian orchestra that consists mainly of percussion instruments such as chimes, gongs, and wooden xylophones [Early 19C. < Javanese.]

game law *n* a law that controls the catching and killing of fish, birds, or other animals for sport, e.g. one that specifies the extent of a hunting or shooting season

game of chance *n* a game, usually played for money, in which the outcome depends to some degree on chance, e.g. on the throw of dice

game of skill *n* a game such as chess or bridge, in which the outcome depends entirely or principally on the skill of the players

game plan *n* **1** the strategy that a team or player devises beforehand to use during a game **2** a strategy that somebody devises to achieve a particular goal

game point *n* **1** in games such as tennis and badminton, a situation in which one player or side has only to win the next point to win the game **2** the point that will decide the final outcome of a game

game reserve, game preserve *n* a large area of land where birds or animals are kept in protected conditions in the wild, either for conservation purposes or to be hunted for sport

game room *n US* HOBBIES = **games room**

games /gaymz/ *n* gymnastics, athletics, team sports, and other forms of physical exercise taught to children at school (*+ singular verb*)

game show *n* a television programme in which people compete for money or prizes

gamesmanship /gáymzmənship/ *n* **1** the use of tactics or stratagems to gain an advantage in business, politics, or life ○ *political gamesmanship* **2** the use of unconventional but not strictly illegal tactics to gain an advantage in a competitive game —**gamesman** *n*

games room *n* a room in a house or public building that is set aside and equipped for games such as billiards or table tennis

gamet- *prefix* = **gameto-**

gametangium /gámmi tánji əm/ (*plural* **-a** /-ə/) *n* the part of a plant, especially an organ or cell in algae and fungi, where gametes are produced [Late 19C. < modern Latin *gameta* (see GAMETE) + Greek *aggeion* 'vessel'.] —**gametangial** *adj*

gamete /gámmeet/ *n* a specialized male or female cell with half the normal number of chromosomes that unites with another cell of the opposite sex in the process of sexual reproduction [Late 19C. < modern Latin *gameta* < Greek *gamos* 'marriage'.] —**gametic** /gə méttik/ *adj* —**gametically** *adv*

game theory *n* a mathematical theory primarily concerned with determining an optimal strategy for situations in which there is competition or conflict, such as in business activities or military operations —**game theoretic** *adj*

gameto-, gamet- *prefix* relating to a gamete [< GAMETE]

gametocyte /gə meétō sīt/ *n* **1** a cell that divides to produce two specialized male or female cells (**gametes**) **2** the malaria organism in the stage in its life cycle during which it reproduces in the blood of a mosquito

gametogenesis /gə meétō jénnəssis/ *n* the production of gametes from gametocytes by cell division (**meiosis**) —**gametogenic** *adj* —**gametogenous** /gámmi tójjənəss/ *adj*

gametophyte /gə meétō fīt/ *n* the phase in the life cycle of a plant in which sex organs and gametes are produced —**gametophytic** /gə meétō fíttik/ *adj*

game warden *n* somebody who looks after wild animals such as fish or birds, e.g. on a game reserve

gamey *adj* = **gamy**

gamin /gámm in/ *n* a young child, usually a boy, often homeless, who roams the streets (*archaic*) [Mid-19C. < French.]

gamine /gámmeen/ *n* **1 BOYISH GIRL** a girl or young woman who is boyish in appearance **2 GIRL STREET URCHIN** a young girl, often homeless, who roams the streets ■ *adj* **APPEALINGLY BOYISH** charmingly boyish in appearance [Late 19C. < French, form of *gamin* 'child on the streets'.]

gaming /gáyming/ *n* the practice of playing games such as poker or roulette for money ■ *adj* relating to or involving gambling games

gamma /gámmə/ *n* **1 3RD LETTER OF GREEK ALPHABET** the third letter of the Greek alphabet **2 SCHOOL MARK** the Greek letter gamma given as a mark to a student for a piece of academic work **3 THIRD ITEM** the third item in a list or classification system **4 MEASURE OF CONTRAST OF IMAGE** a measure of the degree of contrast in a developed photograph or a television image **5 3RD POSITION IN CARBON CHAIN** (symbol γ) the third position in a carbon chain or ring, starting from a particular group or atom ◼ *adj* **3RD NEAREST TO DESIGNATED ATOM** describes the third nearest atom to a designated atom or group of atoms in an organic molecule [15C. Via Latin < Greek.]

gamma-amino butyric acid *n* an inhibitory neurotransmitter

gamma camera *n* an instrument used in medicine to produce images of internal organs after the injection of a radioactive drug into the body, where the drug releases gamma rays

gamma decay *n* a radioactive decay process between two energy levels within a nucleus in which a gamma ray is emitted

gammadion /ga máydi ən/ *n* a pattern consisting of four capital Greek gammas, especially when joined at the centre to form a swastika [Mid-19C. < late Greek, < Greek *gamma* 'gamma'.]

gamma globulin *n* a protein component of blood serum that contains the antibodies, the body's main defence against infection

gammahydroxybutyrate /gámmə hī dróksi byóóti rayt/ *n* $C_4O_3H_8$ a colourless chemical compound that occurs naturally in animals, used for treating anxiety and as an anaesthetic

gamma radiation *n* electromagnetic waves of higher frequency and shorter wavelength than X-rays that are emitted by some radioactive isotopes or in some nuclear reactions

gamma ray *n* a high-energy photon emitted after nuclear reactions or spontaneously from the nucleus of a radioactive atom that lowers the energy level of the nucleus

gammon[1] /gámmən/ *n* **1** the lower part of a side of bacon, cooked whole or cut into slices **2** cured or smoked ham [15C. < Old N French *gambon* 'ham' < *gambe* 'leg'.]

gammon[2] /gámmən/ *n* a win in backgammon when the losing player has not succeeded in removing any pieces from the board [Mid-18C. < early form of GAME[1].] — **gammon** *vt*

gammon[3] /gámmən/ *n* false or meaningless talk that is intended to deceive somebody (*dated informal*) ◼ *vti* to trick or deceive somebody, especially by talking nonsense (*dated informal*) [Early 18C. < ?]

gammon[4] /gámmən/ *vt* to fasten a bowsprit to the front of a ship [Late 17C. < GAMMON[1], probably with reference to the tying up of a ham.]

gammy /gámmi/ (**-mier, -miest**) *adj* stiff or painful and unable to move as before, usually because of injury or some medical disorder (*informal*) ○ *a gammy leg* [Mid-19C. Variant of GAME[2].]

gamo- *prefix* **1** joined together ○ *gamophyllous* **2** sexual ○ *gamogenesis* [< Greek *gamos* 'marriage']

gamogenesis /gámmō jénnəssis/ *n* sexual reproduction (*technical*) — **gamogenetic** /-jə néttik/ *adj* — **gamogenetically** *adv*

Gamow /gám ov/, **George** (1904–68) Russian-born US theoretical physicist

gamut *n* **1 FULL RANGE** the entire range of something **2 COMPLETE RANGE OF MUSICAL NOTES** the whole series of recognized musical notes, from lowest to highest **3 LOWEST MEDIEVAL MUSICAL NOTE** the lowest note of medieval musical theory, two Gs below middle C **4 MEDIEVAL MUSICAL SCALE SYSTEM** the medieval scale system based around a repeated series of six notes (**hexachord**) [15C. Contraction of medieval Latin *gamma ut* < Greek *gamma*, letter representing the musical note one below the top note in the medieval scale, + *ut*, the lowest note.]

gamy /gáymi/ (**-ier, -iest**), **gamey** (**-ier, -iest**) *adj* **1 TASTING OF OR LIKE GAME** having a strong flavour like that of a wild bird or animal that is hunted for food **2 RANK-SMELLING** having a strong bad smell **3 LEWD** sexually suggestive or obscene —**gamily** *adv* —**gaminess** *n*

-gamy *suffix* **1** marriage ○ *polygamy* **2** reproductive union ○ *syngamy* **3** reproductive organs, method of fertilization ○ *karyogamy* [< Greek *gamos* 'marriage'] — **-gamic** *suffix* — **-gamous** *suffix*

Ganapati /gánnə pátti/ *n* RELIG = **Ganesha**

Ganda /gándə/ *n* a Bantu language spoken in Uganda. Native speakers: 4 million. [Mid-20C. < Bantu.] —**Ganda** *adj*

gander /gándər/ *n* **1 MALE GOOSE** an adult male goose. ◊ **goose** *n*. **2 2 OFFENSIVE TERM** an offensive term for somebody who is thought to be unserious and frivolous (*informal insult*) **3 LOOK** a look or glance at somebody or something (*informal*) [Old English *gandra* < Indo-European, 'goose']

Gander /gándər/ town in NE Newfoundland, Canada. Population: 10,364 (1996).

Gandhi /gándi/, **Indira** (1917–84) Indian stateswoman. Born **Indira Priyadarshini Nehru**

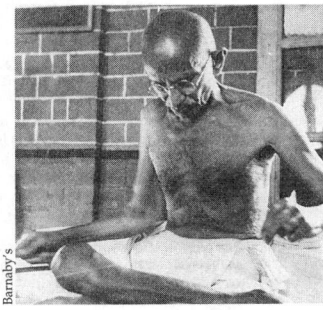
Mohandas Karamchand Gandhi

Gandhi, Mohandas Karamchand (1869–1948) Indian leader of the campaign for Indian independence. Known as **Mahatma Gandhi**

G & T, g and t *abbr* gin and tonic

gandy dancer /gándi-/ *n* US a labourer who lays or maintains railway tracks (*slang*) [< ?]

ganef /gaanəf/, **ganev** /gaanəv/, **ganof** /gónnəf/ *n* somebody regarded as unscrupulous, thieving, or cheating (*informal insult*) [Early 20C. Via Yiddish < Hebrew *gannāb*.]

Ganesha /gə neeshə/, **Ganesa** /-neessə/, **Ganesh** /-nésh/ *n* in Hinduism, the god of wisdom and problem-solving who is the son of Shiva and Parvati and is represented as a pot-bellied man with an elephant's head

ganev *n* CRIME = **ganef**

gang[1] /gang/ *n* **1 GROUP OF TROUBLE-MAKING YOUNG PEOPLE** a group of young people who spend time together for social reasons and may engage in delinquent behaviour **2 GROUP OF CRIMINALS** a group of people who work together for some criminal or antisocial purpose **3 GROUP OF WORKERS** a group of people working together, especially a group of labourers **4 PEOPLE WHO ENJOY EACH OTHER'S COMPANY** a group of people with similar interests who like to spend time together **5 SET OF TOOLS** a set of tools or devices arranged to be used or operated together ◼ *vt* **1 PUT OBJECTS IN GROUP** to group similar objects in a set **2 COMBINE SWITCHES** to combine several switches or devices on a single shaft so as to switch multiple connections at one time [12C. < Old Norse *gangr* 'journey'.]
gang up *vi* to join together in a group, especially in order to attack, intimidate, or oppose somebody
gang up on *vt* to join together in a group in order to attack, intimidate, or oppose somebody

gang[2] /gang/ *vi* Scotland to go (*nonstandard*) [Old English *gangan* < Germanic]

gang[3] /gang/ *n* MIN EXTRACT = **gangue**

Ganga /gáng gə/ *n* S Asia the River Ganges

gangbang /gáng bang/ *n* (*slang; considered offensive by some people*) **1 SERIAL INTERCOURSE WITH ONE PERSON** sexual intercourse between one consenting person and several others in succession **2 GANG RAPE** a multiple rape by a gang of people ◼ *v* (*slang; considered offensive by some people*) **1** *vti* **HAVE MULTIPLE INTERCOURSE WITH ONE PERSON** to participate in an occasion where several people in succession have intercourse with the same person **2** *vti* **GANG-RAPE** to gang-rape somebody **3** *vi* US **BE MEMBER OF VIOLENT GANG** to participate in the activities of a criminal or violent gang —**gangbanger** *n*

gangbusters /gáng bustərz/, **gangbuster** *adj* US unusually successful or effective (*slang*) ○ *It's a gangbusters promotion that brings the customers in.*

ganger /gángər/ *n* the foreman of a group of workers

Ganges

Ganges /gán jeez/ river in N India and Bangladesh, emptying into the Bay of Bengal. Length: 2,511 km/1,560 mi.

gangland /gáng land, -lənd/ *n* the world of organized crime —**gangland** *adj*

ganglia plural of **ganglion**

gangling /gáng gling/, **gangly** /gáng glee/ (**-glier, -gliest**) *adj* tall and thin, with a loose awkward gait [Early 19C. < ?]

ganglion /gáng gli ən/ (*plural* **-a** /-ə/ *or* **-ons**) *n* **1** a structure that contains a dense cluster of nerve cells **2** a harmless swelling similar to a cyst that forms on a joint or tendon [Late 17C. < Greek *gagglion* 'tumour, nerve bundle'.] —**ganglial** *adj* —**ganglionated** /gáng gli ə naytid/ *adj* —**ganglionic** /gáng gli ónnik/ *adj*

ganglioside /gáng gli ə sīd/ *n* a lipid occurring in the brain, nerves, and red blood cells [Mid-20C. < GANGLION + -OSE[1].]

gangly *adj* = **gangling**

gangplank /gáng plangk/ *n* a movable structure such as a bridge or plank used when boarding or disembarking from a ship

gang rape *n* a rape of one person by several people in succession —**gang-rape** *vti*

gangrene /gáng green/ *n* local death and decay of soft tissues of the body as a result of lack of blood to the area ◼ *vti* (**-grenes, -grening, -grened**) to affect body tissue with gangrene, or become affected, with gangrene [Mid-16C. Via French < Greek *gaggraina*.] —**gangrenous** /gáng grinəss/ *adj*

gangsta rap /gángstə-/ *n* rap music in which the lyrics tend to deal with gangs and killings [Alteration of GANGSTER]

gangster /gángstər/ *n* a member of an organized gang of criminals, especially a racketeer —**gangsterish** *adj* —**gangsterism** *n*

gangue /gang/, **gang** *n* worthless rock or other matter occurring in a vein or deposit within or alongside a valuable mineral. ◊ **matrix** *n*. **5** [Early 19C. Via French < German *Gang* 'way, lode'.]

gangway /gáng way/ *n* **1 NARROW WALKWAY** a narrow passageway, especially a temporary walkway **2 ENTRANCE IN SHIP'S SIDE** an opening in the side of a ship through which it is boarded by means of a gangplank **3** NAUT = **gangplank 4 AISLE BETWEEN SEATS** an aisle between seating, especially the one separating two blocks of seating in the House of Commons ◼ *interj* **MAKE WAY** used to indicate to people in a crowd that they should make way because somebody is coming through

ganja /gánjə, gaàn-/ *n* a potent form of marijuana used for smoking [Early 19C. < Hindi *gāja*.]

gannet /gánnit/ *n* **1** a large fish-eating seabird, typically white with black-tipped wings, that lives in offshore colonies in oceanic regions. Genus: *Morus*. **2** a gluttonous person (*informal*) [Old English *ganot* < Indo-European, 'goose'] See illustration overleaf.

Gannett Peak /gánnit-/ highest peak in Wyoming, in the western part of the state. Height: 4,207 m/13,804 ft.

ganof *n* CRIME = **ganef**

ganoid /gánnoyd/ *adj* describes a type of scale found on gars and other primitive fish, consisting of dentine-covered bone with a thick outer layer of a substance (**ganoine**) similar to enamel ◼ *n* a primitive fish that

Gannet

has ganoid scales [Mid-19C. < French *ganoïde* < Greek *ganos* 'brightness'.]

gansey /gánzi/ (*plural* **-seys**) *n* a heavy jumper, especially one worn by a fisherman (*regional*) [Late 19C. Alteration of GUERNSEY.]

Gansu /gán sòò/ province of N China. Capital: Lanzhou. Population: 23,780,000 (1994). Area: 454,000 sq. km/175,300 sq. mi.

gantline /gánt lìn, -lin/ *n* a rope run through a pulley on a mast and used to hoist people or things [Mid-18C. ?]

gantry /gántri/ (*plural* **-tries**) *n* 1 a frame spanning railway tracks and used to display signals 2 a spanning framework used to support machinery, e.g. the platform that supports a crane or the structure used to erect and service rockets [Late 16C. < ?]

Gantt chart /gánt-/ *n* a chart in which horizontal lines show the actual and projected amounts of time involved in completing a specific task or reaching specific levels of production [Early 20C. After the US engineer H. L. *Gantt* (1861–1919).]

Ganymede /gánni meed/ *n* 1 in Greek mythology, a beautiful young Trojan prince whom Zeus carried off to Mount Olympus to be cupbearer to the gods 2 the largest of Jupiter's moons

Gao /gaá ŏ, gow/ town and ancient trading centre in E Mali. Population: 54,874 (1987).

Gao Kegong /gów kə góng/ (1248–1310?) Chinese artist

gaol *n*, *vt* = **jail**

LITERARY LINK *The Ballad of Reading Gaol*, a poem (1898) by Oscar Wilde. Written while he was imprisoned for 'homosexual activities', it is the story of the trial and execution of murderer Charles Thomas Wooldridge, a fellow inmate at the jail. It deals with the harshness of prison conditions and the idea of forgiveness.

gaoler /jáylər/ *n* = **jailer**

gap /gap/ *n* 1 BREAK IN STRUCTURE a break or opening in a structure or arrangement, e.g. a fence or military defence line 2 SOMETHING MISSING an area where there is a complete or partial absence of something, such as data ○ *gaps in his employment record* 3 INTERVAL OF TIME an interval of time during which some action or event stops occurring ○ *a gap of three years* 4 DISPARITY a significant difference between two things, attitudes, or perceptions ○ *the gap between rich and poor* 5 PROBLEM CAUSED BY DISPARITY a problem caused by a difference between things, attitudes, or perceptions ○ *technology gap* ○ *generation gap* 6 OPENING BETWEEN MOUNTAINS a ravine or pass in a mountain range 7 ELEC ENG = **spark gap** ▪ *v* (**gaps, gapping, gapped**) 1 *vti* PRODUCE OR DEVELOP GAP to create a gap or opening in a barrier, or become open or separated by a gap 2 *vt* ADJUST SPARK PLUG GAP to adjust the gap between the electrodes of a spark plug 3 *vt N England* THIN OUT PLANTS to thin out plants to allow others more room to grow (*informal*) ○ *I hate having to gap the carrots.* [14C. < Old Norse, 'chasm'.] —**gappy** *adj*

gape /gayp/ *vi* (**gapes, gaping, gaped**) 1 STARE WITH MOUTH OPEN to stare in open-mouthed surprise or wonder 2 OPEN THE MOUTH to open the mouth wide 3 OPEN A GAP to open or split apart with a gap ▪ *n* 1 OPEN-MOUTHED STARE a stare of wonder or surprise in which the mouth is wide open 2 OPENING OF MOUTH an opening of the mouth, e.g. when surprised 3 YAWN an opening of the mouth to yawn 4 WIDTH OF OPEN MOUTH the width of the

open mouth of an animal 5 BIG GAP a wide opening in something [13C. < Old Norse *gapa* 'open the mouth'.]

SYNONYMS See *gaze*.

gaping /gáyping/ *adj* wide open and deep —**gapingly** *adv*

gap junction *n* a passage through the membranes of adjacent cells that allows the transfer of small molecules or ions between cells

gap-toothed *adj* with wide spaces between the teeth

gap year *n* a period of time taken off by a student after the completion of secondary education and before starting higher or further education

gar[1] /gaar/ (*plural* **gar** or **gars**) *n* a large primitive freshwater fish with a heavy armour of bony scales and a long toothy jaw. Native to: North and Central America. Family: Lepisosteidae. [Mid-18C. Shortening of GARFISH.]

gar[2] /gaar/ (**gars, garring, garred**) *vt Scotland* to make somebody do something (*nonstandard*) [13C. < Old Norse *gera* 'make'.]

garage /gárraazh, -rij/ *n* 1 BUILDING FOR MOTOR VEHICLES a building for parking or storing one or more motor vehicles 2 ESTABLISHMENT REPAIRING MOTOR VEHICLES an establishment that repairs and often sells motor vehicles, and that sometimes sells oil, diesel, and petrol 3 **garage, garage music** SOULFUL DANCE MUSIC a style of dance music inspired by disco and combining 4/4 rhythms with vocals, associated with soul music of the 1990s ▪ *vt* (**-rages, -raging, -raged**) PUT VEHICLE IN GARAGE to park or store a motor vehicle in a garage [Early 20C. < French, *garer* 'to shelter'.]

garage sale *n US, ANZ* a sale of used or unwanted household items that is held in the garage or driveway of the seller's home

Garagum Desert /gárra gum-/ desert occupying a large portion of Turkmenistan. Area: 285,000 sq. km/110,000 sq. mi.

garam masala /gaárəm mə saálə/ *n* a mixture of spices used in Indian cooking to impart a hot pungent flavour to a dish [Mid-20C. < Hindi *garam masālā* 'hot spices'.]

Garamond /gárrə mond/, **Garamond type** *n* a Roman typeface often used in books [Mid-19C. After Claude *Garamond* (1499–1561), French type founder.]

garantee incorrect spelling of **guarantee**

garb /gaarb/ *n* 1 TYPICAL OUTFIT a particular type of clothing, especially the uniform or typical outfit worn by a profession 2 APPEARANCE the outward appearance that somebody or something has ○ *The garb of compromise concealed their war plans.* ▪ *vt* DRESS to clothe somebody or yourself in a particular type of clothing [Late 16C. Via obsolete French *garbe* 'elegance' < Italian *garbo*.]

garbage /gaárbij/ *n* 1 NONSENSE talk or writing that is worthless nonsense or lies 2 SOMEBODY OR SOMETHING WORTHLESS somebody or something considered totally worthless 3 *US* DISCARDED WASTE discarded food waste or any other unwanted or useless material 4 WORTHLESS DATA inaccurate, useless, or meaningless data in a computer [15C. < Anglo-Norman.] —**garbagy** *adj*

garbage can *n US* = **dustbin**

garbage man *n US, Can, Aus* somebody employed to remove rubbish. ◊ **dustman**

garbage truck *n US, Can, Aus* a large motor vehicle used to collect and compact waste materials left bagged or in containers outside buildings. ◊ **dustcart**

garbanzo /gaar bánzŏ/ (*plural* **-zos**), **garbanzo bean** *n* FOOD = **chickpea** *n*. 1 [Mid-18C. < Spanish.]

garble /gaárb'l/ *vt* (**-bles, -bling, -bled**) 1 JUMBLE MEANING OF to confuse something unintentionally or through ignorance and thereby give the wrong impression 2 SCRAMBLE TRANSMISSION OF to cause the corruption of a transmitted message or signal ○ *The announcement was completely garbled.* ▪ *n* CONFUSING MESSAGE a confused or jumbled message, piece of information, or signal, or the confusing or jumbling of information [15C. Via Italian *garbellare* 'sift' and Arabic *garbala* < late Latin *cribellum* 'small sieve' < Latin *cribrum* 'sieve'.] —**garbled** *adj*

garbo /gaárbŏ/ (*plural* **-bos**) *n Aus* a garbage collector (*slang*) [Mid-20C. < GARBAGE.]

Garbo /gaárbŏ/, **Greta** (1905–90) Swedish-born US film actor. Born **Greta Gustaffson**

garboard /gaár bawrd/ *n* the continuous band of planking on a ship's hull next to its keel [Early 17C. < obsolete Dutch *gaarboord*.]

garbology /gaar bólləji/ *n US* the study of a cultural group by an examination of what it discards [Late 20C. < GARBAGE.] —**garbologist** *n*

García Márquez, Gabriel (*b.* 1928) Colombian writer

garçon /gaár son, -soN/ *n* a waiter in a French restaurant or café [Early 17C. < French.]

garda /gaárdə/ (*plural* **-daí** /gaar deé/) *n* a police officer in the Republic of Ireland and a member of the Garda [See GARDA.]

Garda /gaárdə/ *n* the police force of the Republic of Ireland [Early 20C. < Irish, shortening of *Garda Síochána* 'civic guard'.]

Garda, Lake /gaárdə/ lake in N Italy, the largest in the country. Area: 370 sq. km/143 sq. mi.

gardaí *plural* of **garda**

gardant *adj* HERALDRY = **guardant**

garden /gaárd'n/ *n* 1 CULTIVATED AREA AROUND HOUSE an area of cultivated land, often with a lawn, situated around, in front of, or behind a house (*often used in the plural in street names*) US term **yard**[2] *n*. 2 2 PLANTED AREA OF GROUND a plot of ground where plants such as fruits, vegetables, and flowers are grown 3 PARK a park or recreational area for the public, generally planted with flowers, shrubs, and trees (*often plural*) 4 FARMING REGION a fertile, well-cultivated region 5 OUTDOOR EATING AND DRINKING ESTABLISHMENT an eating or drinking establishment that serves its patrons outdoors ▪ *adj* 1 RELATING TO GARDENS produced in, frequenting, or used in a garden 2 COMMON of the common or ordinary kind. US term **garden-variety** ▪ *vi* LOOK AFTER GARDEN to plan or tend a garden [14C. Via Old N French *gardin* < Vulgar Latin (*hortus*) *gardinus* 'enclosed (garden)'.] —**gardener** *n* ◊ **everything in the garden is lovely** everything is fine

LITERARY LINK *The Secret Garden*, a children's story (1911) by Frances Hodgson Burnett. It is the tale of a lonely orphan, Mary Lennox, who is sent to live with her uncle Archibald, a widower whose wife died as a result of a fall from a tree in her beloved garden. In restoring the garden, Mary finds happiness and helps the family recover from its misfortune.

garden apartment *n US* 1 = **garden flat** 2 a block of flats that has a garden or lawn

garden centre *n* a retail establishment that sells plants and gardening equipment

garden city *n* a planned town with landscaped gardens and parks. ◊ **garden suburb**

garden flat *n* a flat on the ground floor or in the basement of a building with access to a lawn or garden. US term **garden apartment** *n*. 1

garden gnome *n* a small statue representing a gnome, used as an ornament in gardens

gardenia /gaar deéni ə/ *n* an evergreen tree or bush with shiny leaves. Flowers: white, fragrant. Native to: Africa, Asia. Genus: *Gardenia*. [Mid-18C. < modern Latin, after Alexander *Garden* (1730–91), Scottish-American naturalist.]

Garden of Eden *n* BIBLE = **Eden**

garden party *n* a large formal party held in a garden, especially in the grounds of a large house

garden suburb *n* a planned suburb with landscaped gardens and parks. ◊ **garden city**

garden-variety *adj US* ZOOL = **garden** *adj.* 2

garderobe /gaárd rŏb/ *n* 1 formerly, a wardrobe or room where clothes could be kept 2 formerly, a small toilet consisting of a bench with holes made above a pit, usually built into a wall or projecting from it [14C. < Old French, < *garder* 'keep' + *robe* 'robe'.]

gardian incorrect spelling of **guardian**

Gardner /gaárdnər/, **Erle Stanley** (1889–1970) US writer

Gardner, Wayne Michael (*b.* 1959) Australian motorcycle racer

Garfield /gaár feeld/, **James A.** (1831–81) US statesman and 20th president of the United States (1881)

garfish /gaár fish/ (*plural* **-fishes** or **-fish**) *n* 1 a fish that is greenish to dark blue with silvery sides and has elongated jaws with sharp teeth. Native to: temperate European seas. *Belone belone.* 2 ZOOL = **gar**[1] [15C. < Old English *gār* 'spear'; from the shape of its jaw.]

gargantuan /gaar gántyoo ən/ *adj* tremendously large in amount, number, or size [Late 16C. < *Gargantua*, giant hero of *Gargantua* by Rabelais.]

gargle /gaàrg'l/ v (-gles, -gling, -gled) 1 vti CLEANSE MOUTH AND THROAT to rinse or disinfect the mouth and throat by holding liquid in the back of the mouth and stirring it up with air breathed out from the lungs 2 vi MAKE GUTTURAL SOUND to make a sound like that made when rinsing the mouth with liquid ■ n 1 MOUTHWASH a liquid used to rinse the mouth 2 GUTTURAL SOUND a sound like that made when rinsing the mouth with liquid [Early 16C. < French gargouiller < Old French gargouille 'throat' < Latin gurgulio 'gullet'.]

Gargoyle

gargoyle /gaàr goyl/ n 1 GROTESQUE DRAINAGE SPOUT a spout in the form of a grotesque animal or human figure that projects from the gutter of a building and is designed to cast rainwater clear of the building 2 STATUE OF GROTESQUE FIGURE a grotesque carved figure 3 SOMEBODY LIKE CARVED FIGURE somebody thought to resemble a carved gargoyle (insult) [15C. < Old French gargouille (see GARGLE).]

garibaldi /gárri báwldi/, **garibaldi biscuit** n a flat square biscuit with a central layer of currants [Mid-19C. After GARIBALDI.]

Garibaldi /gárri báwldi/, **Giuseppe** (1807–82) French-born Italian patriot

garish /gáirish/ adj 1 GAUDY crudely showy ○ a garish outfit 2 OVERLY ORNAMENTED excessively ornate or elaborate ○ a garish balcony and staircase 3 DRESSED TOO BRIGHTLY wearing clothing or make-up that is extremely brightly coloured 4 TOO BRIGHT excessively bright ○ a hideous garish yellow [Mid-16C. < ?] —**garishly** adv —**garishness** n

garland /gaàrland/ n 1 FLOWER WREATH a wreath of intertwined flowers or leaves worn as an ornament or as a sign of honour 2 HANGING FLOWER DECORATION a festoon of flowers or paper hung as decoration 3 LITERARY COLLECTION a collection of short pieces of literature ■ vt DECORATE WITH GARLAND to decorate or adorn somebody or something with garlands [14C. < Old French garlande.]

Garland /gaàrland/, **Judy** (1922–69) US film actor and singer. Born **Frances Gumm**

garlic /gaàrlik/ n (plural -lic or -lics) 1 BULB a bulb or clove with a pungent odour and flavour that is commonly used in cooking 2 STRONG-TASTING PLANT a plant that is the source of garlic. Allium sativum. 3 PLANT SIMILAR TO GARLIC any plant related to or resembling true garlic [Old English gārlēac < gār 'spear' + LEEK] —**garlicky** adj

garlic bread n bread seasoned with butter and garlic and baked or toasted

garlic mustard n a hedgerow plant with heart-shaped leaves. Flowers: small, white, with a pungent garlicky smell. Native to: Europe, Asia. Alliaria petiolata.

garlic press n a small kitchen tool, usually metal or plastic, that minces a clove of garlic by squeezing it through small holes

garlic salt n a preparation of salt and powdered garlic used as a food seasoning

garlic sausage n a type of salami flavoured with garlic

garment /gaàrmənt/ n a piece of clothing ■ vt to put clothing on somebody (literary; often passive) [14C. < French garnement 'equipment' < garnir (see GARNISH).]

garment bag n a piece of soft-sided luggage specifically shaped for carrying dresses, suits, or other clothing on hangers

Garmo Peak /gaàrmō-/ former name for **Ismail Samani Peak**

garner /gaàrnər/ vt 1 GATHER IN to gather something into storage or into a granary 2 WIN OR GAIN to earn or acquire something by effort 3 GATHER INFORMATION to collect or accumulate something such as information or facts ■ n GRANARY a storage place for grain (archaic) [12C. Via Anglo-Norman gerner 'storehouse' < Latin granarium (see GRANARY).]

Garner /gaàrnər/, **Helen** (b. 1942) Australian writer

garnet /gaàrnit/ n 1 a variously coloured crystalline silicate mineral. Source: metamorphic and igneous rocks. Use: gems. 2 a dark red colour [13C. Probably via Middle Dutch garnate < Old French grenat 'dark red' < pome grenate 'pomegranate', because of its colour.] —**garnet** adj —**garnetiferous** /gaàrnə tíffərəss/ adj

garnierite /gaàrni ərīt/ n a soft green form of the mineral serpentine consisting of hydrated nickel magnesium silicate. Use: source of nickel. [Late 19C. After Jules Garnier (1839?–1904), French geologist.]

garnish /gaàrnish/ vt 1 ENHANCE FOOD OR DRINK to add something as an accompaniment to food or drink that enhances its flavour or appearance 2 EMBELLISH to decorate something with an ornament 3 LAW = **garnishee** v. 1, **garnishee** v. 2 ■ n 1 ENHANCEMENT FOR FOOD OR DRINK something added as an accompaniment to food or drink to enhance its flavour or appearance 2 SOMETHING DECORATIVE an ornament or decoration for something [14C. < French garniss-, stem of garnir 'equip, adorn, warn' < Germanic.] —**garnishing** n

garnishee /gaàrni shee/ (-ees, -eeing, -eed) vt 1 to take the money or property of a debtor by legal authority 2 to serve somebody with a legal summons concerning the taking of wages or property to satisfy a debt — **garnishee** n

garnishment /gaàrnishmənt/ n 1 a legal summons or warning concerning the taking of property or wages of a debtor to satisfy a debt 2 an ornamentation or embellishment on or of something

garniture /gaàrnichər/ n something that decorates or embellishes something [15C. < French, < garnir (see GARNISH).]

Garonne /ga rón/ river in SW France. Length: 575 km/357 mi.

garpike /gaàr pīk/ (plural -pikes or -pike) n 1 = **gar¹** n. 2 = **garfish** n. 1

garret /gárrət/ n a room at the top of a house, immediately below the roof [15C. < Old French garite 'watchtower' < garir 'defend' < Germanic, 'protect'.]

Garrett /gárrət/, **Peter** (b. 1953) Australian singer and political activist

Garrick /gárrik/, **David** (1717–79) British actor, theatrical manager, and playwright

garrison /gárrisən/ n 1 STATIONED TROOPS a body of troops stationed at a military post 2 PLACE FOR STATIONING TROOPS a military post where troops are stationed ■ vt 1 SUPPLY PLACE WITH TROOPS to provide a fort or town with a military post and troops 2 STATION TROOPS AT PLACE to station troops at a military post [13C. < Old French, 'fortification' < garir (see GARRET).]

garrotte /gə rót/, **garrote** n 1 EXECUTION BY STRANGULATION a method of execution in which an iron band is tightened around the neck of the condemned person until death occurs 2 METAL BAND USED IN EXECUTIONS a band of metal placed around the neck in order to execute somebody by strangulation 3 WEAPON FOR STRANGULATION a weapon consisting of a wire or cord with handles at either end, used in strangulation [Early 17C. < Spanish garrote 'cudgel, stick for tightening a cord'.]

garrulity /gə roòləti, ga-/ n excessive or pointless talkativeness

garrulous /gárrələss, gárr yoò-/ adj 1 excessively or pointlessly talkative 2 using many or too many words [Early 17C. < Latin garrulus < garrire 'to chatter'.] —**garrulously** adv —**garrulousness** n

SYNONYMS See talkative.

garter /gaàrtər/ n 1 an elastic band used to hold up a stocking, sock, or shirt sleeve 2 US CLOTHING = **suspender** n. 1 [14C. < Old French gartier < garet 'bend of the knee' < Celtic.] —**garter** vt

Garter n 1 = **Order of the Garter** 2 the badge that signifies membership of the Order of the Garter 3 membership in the Order of the Garter

garter belt n US CLOTHING = **suspender belt**

garter snake n a small nonpoisonous snake whose back is typically marked with yellow or red stripes running the length of the body. Native to: North and Central America. Genus: Thamnophis.

garter stitch n knitting done in the same stitch, whether knit or purl, for every row [< its use in making garters]

garth /gaàrth/ n a small courtyard or enclosed space [14C. < Old Norse garðr.]

Marcus Garvey

Popperfoto

Garvey /gaàrvi/, **Marcus** (1887–1940) Jamaican-born US civil rights advocate

Gary /gárri/ city in NW Indiana, on Lake Michigan. Population: 108,469 (1998 estimate).

gas /gass/ n (plural gases or gasses) 1 SUBSTANCE SUCH AS AIR a substance such as air that is neither a solid nor a liquid at ordinary temperatures and that has the ability to expand infinitely 2 FOSSIL FUEL a combustible gaseous substance such as natural gas or coal gas, used as a fuel 3 GAS FOR POISONING OR ASPHYXIATING a gaseous mixture used as a poison, irritant, or asphyxiating agent 4 ANAESTHETIC a gaseous substance used as an anaesthetic 5 US PETROL petrol for internal-combustion engines 6 US CAR ACCELERATOR the pedal used for accelerating a motor vehicle (informal) ○ step on the gas 7 US FLATULENCE gaseous product of digestion (informal) 8 METHANE AND AIR the highly explosive product of methane combined with air 9 SOMEBODY OR SOMETHING ENTERTAINING somebody or something such as an experience that is very thrilling or entertaining (informal) 10 NONSENSE meaningless empty talk (informal) ■ v (gases or gasses, gassing, gassed) 1 vt HARM WITH GAS to attack, injure, or kill a person or animal with a poisonous, irritating, or asphyxiating gas 2 vi RELEASE GAS to give off gas 3 vi TALK IDLY to talk too much, especially about unimportant matters (informal) [Mid-17C. < Dutch, alteration of Greek khaos 'empty space'.] —**gassing** n

gasbag /gáss bag/ n a garrulous talker, especially about trivial subjects (informal)

gas burner n the nozzle or opening from which gas issues and burns, e.g. on a cooker

gas chamber n a room in which people are killed by means of poisonous gas

gas chromatography n a method of separating the volatile constituents of a substance by means of gas, for the purpose of analysis —**gas chromatograph** n

gascon /gásskən/ n a boastful person [Late 18C. < Gascons' legendary boastfulness.]

Gascon /gásskən/ n 1 somebody who lives in or was born or brought up in Gascony, formerly a province in SW France 2 a dialect of French spoken in Gascony [14C. Via French < Latin Vascon-.] —**Gascon** adj

gas constant n (symbol R) the constant in an equation that describes the relation of the pressure and volume of a gas to its absolute temperature

gas-cooled reactor n a nuclear reactor that uses carbon dioxide or helium as a coolant

Gascoyne /gás koyn/ river in N Western Australia. Length: 760 km/470 mi.

gas-discharge tube n a tube containing gas from which light is emitted when an electric current is passed through the gas atoms and excites them

gaseous /gássi əss, gáyssi-/ adj 1 RESEMBLING GAS neither solid nor liquid and with a tendency to expand infinitely 2 VERBOSE having or using too many words, especially in a meaningless way (*informal*) 3 **CONTAINING GAS** full of or containing gas [Late 18C. After AQUEOUS.] —**gaseousness** *n*

gas exchange *n* the transfer of gases between an organism and its environment, e.g. the process by which oxygen enters the body and carbon dioxide is expelled from it via the lungs

gas fitter *n* a worker who fits and repairs gas pipes, fittings, and appliances

gas gangrene *n* a form of gangrene, caused by aerobic clostridia bacteria, in which gas forms in injured body tissue

gas-guzzler *n US* a motor vehicle that burns comparatively large amounts of fuel (*informal*)

gash /gash/ *n* a long deep narrow slash or cut [Mid-16C. Alteration of Old N French *garser* 'to cut', via late Latin *charaxare* 'sharpen' < Greek *kharassein*.] —**gash** *vt*

gasholder /gáss hōldər/ *n* a very large tank used to store gas that is used as combustible fuel

gasiform /gássi fawrm/ *adj* INDUST = **gaseous** *adj.* 1

gasify /gássi fī/ (**-fies, -fying, -fied**) *vti* to convert a solid or liquid into a gas, or become a gas —**gasification** /gássifi káysh'n/ *n*

gas jet *n* 1 UTIL = **gas burner** 2 a flame of burning gas

Gaskell /gásk'l/, **Elizabeth** (1810–65) British novelist

gasket /gáskit/ *n* 1 a piece of material such as rubber, used to render a joint impermeable to gas or liquid 2 a light line for securing a furled sail [Early 17C. < ?]

gaskin /gáskin/ *n* the part of the back leg of a four-legged hoofed animal, especially a horse, that is equivalent to the lower thigh in humans [Late 16C. < ?]

gas law *n* a law governing the physical behaviour of gases, e.g. Boyle's law or Charles's law

gaslight /gáss līt/ *n* 1 light produced by burning coal gas or natural gas 2 a lamp or fixture that produces light by burning gas

gas-liquid chromatography *n* SCI = **gas chromatography**

gaslit /gásslit/ *adj* illuminated by light from lamps or fixtures that burn gas

gasman /gáss man/ (*plural* **-men** /-men/) *n* a worker who checks gas meters in order to note the amount of gas used in a specific period

gas mark *n* a mark on the temperature regulator of the oven of a gas cooker, indicating a gradation of heat

gas mask *n* a mask provided with a filter and worn to protect the wearer's face and lungs from harmful gases

gas meter *n* a device installed inside or outside a residential or commercial building to measure the amount of gas consumed in a specific period

gasohol /gássəhol/ *n US* a fuel used in motor vehicles that consists of 90 per cent petrol blended with 10 per cent alcohol [Late 20C. Blend of GASOLINE + ALCOHOL.]

gas oil *n* a light petroleum distillate with a viscosity and boiling point between that of paraffin and lubricating oil

gasoline /gássəleen/ *n US* = **petrol**

gasometer /ga sómmitər/ *n* 1 an apparatus for measuring and storing gas in a laboratory 2 UTIL = **gasholder**

gasp /gaasp/ *n* 1 **SUDDEN BREATH** a sudden short audible intake of breath, e.g. in surprise or pain 2 **DIFFICULT BREATHING** a laborious effort to breathe ■ *v* 1 *vi* **LABOUR TO BREATHE** to breathe with difficulty 2 *vi* **BREATHE IN SHARPLY** draw in breath loudly and spasmodically 3 *vt* **SAY SOMETHING WITH GASP** to say something with a sudden intake of breath [14C. < Old Norse *geispa* 'yawn'.] ◇ **be gasping (for something)** to feel a desperate need for a drink or cigarette (*informal*) ◇ **the last gasp** somebody's final attempt or action, or the final phase of something

Gaspé Peninsula /ga spáy-/ peninsula in SE Quebec, Canada. Area: 29,500 sq. km/11,400 sq. mi.

gasper /gáaspər/ *n* a cigarette, especially a cheap one (*dated slang*)

gas plant *n* a perennial plant of the rue family with strong-smelling leaves that give off a flammable gas. Flowers: white. Native to: Europe, Asia. *Dictamnus albus*.

gasser /gássər/ *n* 1 a well that produces natural gas 2 = **gasbag** (*informal*)

gas station *n US* COMM = **petrol station**

gassy /gássi/ (**-sier, -siest**) *adj* 1 **FULL OF GAS** full of or containing gas such as carbon dioxide 2 **LIKE GAS** resembling gas 3 **VERBOSE** having or using too many words, especially in a meaningless way (*informal*) —**gassily** *adv* —**gassiness** *n*

gastarbeiter /gást aar bītər/ (*plural* **-ter** *or* **-ters**), **Gastarbeiter** (*plural* **-ter** *or* **-ters**) *n* an immigrant worker, especially one who came to the former West Germany in the 1960s and 1970s [Mid-20C. < German, 'guest worker'.]

gastight /gáss tīt/ *adj* preventing any gas from passing through

gastr- *prefix* = **gastro-**

gastrectomy /gass tréktəmi/ (*plural* **-mies**) *n* surgical removal of all or part of the stomach

gastric /gástrik/ *adj* relating to, involving, or near the stomach [Mid-17C. < modern Latin *gastricus* < Greek *gastēr* 'stomach'.]

gastric juice *n* the acidic digestive fluid secreted by glands in the stomach

gastric ulcer *n* an erosion in the stomach wall caused by gastric acid, digestive enzymes, and other factors that may include bacterial infection

gastrin /gástrin/ *n* a hormone produced in the stomach that increases the release of gastric juice

gastritis /gass trítiss/ *n* inflammation of the mucous membrane that lines the stomach

gastro- *prefix* stomach, belly ○ *gastrectomy* [< Greek *gastr-*, stem of *gastēr* 'belly' (see GASTRIC)]

gastrocnemius /gástrok néemi əss, -trək-/ (*plural* **-i** /-mī/) *n* the largest muscle in the calf of the leg, extending from the thigh bone to the Achilles tendon [Late 17C. Via modern Latin < Greek *gastroknēmia* 'calf of the leg' < *gastēr* 'stomach'; from its bulging form.]

gastroduodenostomy /gástrō dyoo ō dee nóstəmi/ (*plural* **-mies**) *n* a surgical operation in which the duodenum is joined to an opening made in the stomach wall

gastroenteritis /gástrō éntə rítiss/ *n* inflammation of the stomach and the intestines, with vomiting and diarrhoea, usually as a result of bacterial or viral infection

gastroenterology /gástrō éntə rólləji/ *n* the branch of medicine concerned with the study and treatment of diseases of the stomach and intestines and their associated organs —**gastroenterologic** /-éntərə lójjik/ *adj* —**gastroenterologist** *n*

gastrointestinal /gástrō in téstinəl/ *adj* relating to the stomach and intestines

gastrolith /gástrō lith/ *n* 1 a stone swallowed by an animal such as a bird or dinosaur, as an aid to the digestion of food 2 a stone that has formed in the stomach

gastronome /gástrənōm/, **gastronomist** /ga strónnəmist/ *n* a connoisseur of good food [Early 19C. < French, back-formation < *gastronomie* (see GASTRONOMY).]

gastronomy /ga strónnəmi/ (*plural* **-mies**) *n* 1 the art and appreciation of preparing and eating good food 2 a particular style of cooking or dining, e.g. one that is typical of a country or region [Early 19C. Via French *gastronomie* < Greek *gastronomia*, alteration of *gastrologia* 'study of the stomach'.] —**gastronomic** /gástrə nómmik/ *adj* —**gastronomically** *adv*

gastroplasty /gas tróppləsti/ (*plural* **-ties**) *n* a surgical operation to repair a malformation of the stomach

gastropod /gástrə pod/ *n* a mollusc that has a head with eyes, a large flattened foot, and often a single shell, e.g. a limpet, snail, or slug. Class: Gastropoda. [Early 19C. < modern Latin *Gastropoda* 'stomach-foot'.] —**gastropod** *adj* —**gastropodan** /ga stróppədən/ *adj* —**gastropodous** *adj*

gastroscope /gástrə skōp/ *n* an instrument passed through the mouth and used to examine the stomach, consisting of a flexible tube that contains optical fibres coupled to an eyepiece and light source —**gastroscopic** /-skóppik/ *adj* —**gastroscopy** /ga stróskəpi/ *n*

gastrostomy /gas tróstəmi/ (*plural* **-mies**) *n* a surgical operation in which an opening for a tube is made through the wall of the stomach and joined to an opening in the adjacent abdominal wall

gastrotomy /ga stróttəmi/ (*plural* **-mies**) *n* a surgical incision into the stomach, for examination of the cavity or to remove a foreign object

gastrula /gástroolə/ (*plural* **-las** *or* **-lae** /-lee/) *n* the stage in embryonic development after the blastula during which the embryo develops two layers [Late 19C. < modern Latin, 'little stomach' < Greek *gastēr* 'stomach'.] —**gastrular** *adj*

gastrulation /gástroo láysh'n/ *n* the process of cell movements by which a developing embryo forms distinct layers that later grow into particular organs —**gastrulate** *vi*

gas turbine *n* an internal-combustion engine in which a turbine is turned by hot gases consisting of compressed air and the products of the fuel's combustion

gasworks /gás wurks/ *n* a factory where gas for heating and illuminating is produced, especially from coal (+ *singular or plural verb*)

gat[1] /gat/ *n* a passage or channel of water that extends inland from a shore [Late 16C. Probably < Old Norse *gat* 'hole'.]

gat[2] /gat/ *n* a handgun (*dated slang*) [Early 20C. Shortening of GATLING GUN.]

gat[3] /gat/ past tense of **get**[1] (*archaic*)

ϟ **gate** /gayt/ *n* 1 **BARRIER ACROSS GAP** a movable barrier, usually on hinges, that closes a gap in a fence or wall 2 **OPENING IN WALL** an opening in a wall or fence 3 **OPENING IN DEFENSIVE STRUCTURE** an opening in a castle or city wall or other defensive structure 4 **POINT OF ACCESS** a means of access or entrance 5 **BARRIER AT TOLLBOOTH** a movable barrier restricting access, e.g. at a tollbooth 6 **STARTING GATE** a starting gate (*informal*) 7 **ARRIVAL OR DEPARTURE POINT** the area at an airport where passengers arrive and depart 8 **BARRIER FOR FLUID** a sliding barrier, valve, or other mechanism for regulating the passage of a fluid 9 **SPECTATORS** the total number of persons who pay for admission to an entertainment or sporting event 10 **MONEY FROM TICKETS** the total amount of money paid for tickets of admission to an entertainment or sports event 11 **PATH BETWEEN POLES** the space between two markers through which a skier passes in a slalom race 12 **LOGIC CIRCUIT** a logical device in a computer, with one output channel and one or more input channels, that emits a signal only when certain input conditions are met 13 **REGULATING SWITCH** an electronic switch that regulates the flow of current in a circuit 14 **FASTENING FOR OAR** a fastening with a hinge that serves to keep an oar in its rowlock 15 *N England, Scotland* **WAY** a path or road 16 *N England, Scotland* **HABIT** a habitual method or style of doing something ■ *vt* (**gates, gating, gated**) 1 **CONFINE TO SCHOOL GROUNDS** to punish a student by confining him or her to the school or college grounds 2 **CONTROL USING GATE** to control or regulate somebody or something with a gate 3 **PUT GATE IN** to install a gate in something, e.g. in a fence [Old English *geat* < Germanic, 'opening in a wall'. Partly < Old Norse *gata* 'path'.]

SPELLCHECK See *gait*.

gateau /gáttō/ (*plural* **-teaux** /-tōz/), **gâteau** (*plural* **-teaux**) *n* 1 a rich cake, usually consisting of several layers held together with a cream filling 2 savoury food baked and served in a form resembling a cake [Mid-19C. < French, 'cake'.]

gatecrasher /gáyt krashər/ *n* an attender of a party, entertainment, or sporting event without an invitation or ticket —**gatecrash** *vti*

gatefold /gáyt fōld/ *n* a page in a publication that is larger than the other pages and is folded to fit

gatehouse /gáyt howss/ (*plural* **-houses** /-howziz/) *n* a building or house above or beside a gate

gatekeeper /gáyt keepər/ *n* 1 a supervisor or guard who tends a gate 2 an individual or group that controls access to somebody or something

gateleg table /gáyt leg-/ *n* a drop-leaf table with movable legs that swing out to support the leaves

gate money *n* = **gate** *n.* 10

gatepost /gáyt pōst/ *n* one of the posts on either side of a gate

gater, 'gater *n US* ZOOL = **gator** (*informal*)

Gates /gayts/, **Bill** (*b.* 1955) US business executive. Full name **William Henry Gates III**

Gateshead /gáyts hed/ town in NE England. Population: 201,800 (1995).

Gates of the Arctic National Park and Preserve national park in N Alaska. Area: 30,448 sq. km/11,756 sq. mi.

ϟ **gateway** /gáyt way/ *n* 1 **OPENING WITH GATE** an opening that may be closed by a gate 2 **ACCESS POINT** a means of entrance or access to somebody or something 3 **COMPUTER-NETWORK CONNECTION** software or hardware that links two computer networks 4 **NETWORK ENTRY POINT** an entry point to a computer network

gateway drug *n* a drug that does not cause physical dependence but may lead to the use of addictive drugs

gather /gáthər/ *v* 1 *vti* **FORM INTO GROUP** to bring people or things together, or come together, to form a group 2 *vt* **HARVEST** to pick or harvest a crop 3 *vt* **COLLECT DATA** to compile something such as information or ideas from various sources 4 *vt* **ATTRACT FOLLOWING** to attract a group of people as supporters, followers, or an audience ○ *The street players have gathered quite a crowd.* 5 *vti* **ACCUMULATE** to accumulate a gradually increasing mass or quantity of something, or be accumulated gradually ○ *Clouds gathered on the horizon.* 6 *vt* **DRAW ON** to summon up energies, courage, or strength from within 7 *vt* **SURMISE** to conclude something from intuition or observation 8 *vt* **BRING CLOSE** to draw somebody or something close 9 *vt* **LIFT UP** to pick or scoop somebody or something up 10 *vti* **WRINKLE BROW** to draw the brow into wrinkles, or be drawn into wrinkles 11 *vt* **PULL FABRIC TOGETHER** to draw fabric together in a series of folds along a line of stitching 12 *vt* **PUT PAGES IN ORDER** to assemble the printed sections of a book in the correct order for binding 13 *vt* **PREPARE MOLTEN GLASS FOR BLOWING** to collect molten glass at the end of a tube for blowing and shaping 14 *vi* **FORM PUS-FILLED HEAD** to form and fill with pus ■ *n* 1 **FOLD IN FABRIC** one in a series of folds in fabric 2 **MOLTEN GLASS BALL** a ball of molten glass collected on a tube for blowing and shaping [Old English *gaderian* < Indo-European, 'bring together'] —**gatherer** *n*

SYNONYMS See ***collect***.

gathering /gáthəring/ *n* 1 **ASSEMBLY** a meeting or crowd of people 2 **CLUSTER OF THINGS** a collection of objects 3 **COLLECTING** the collecting of people or objects into a group 4 **BOIL** a pus-filled swelling 5 **FOLDS IN CLOTH** a series of folds in fabric

gathering stitch *n* a line of running stitches sewn with a single length of thread that can be pulled up to form gathers in the fabric

Gatling gun /gátling-/ *n* an early machine gun with multiple barrels firing in rotation [Mid-19C. After R. J. *Gatling* (1818–1903), US inventor.]

gator /gáytər/, **'gator, gater, 'gater** *n US* an alligator (*informal*) [Mid-19C. Shortening.]

GATT /gat/, **Gatt** *abbr* General Agreement on Tariffs and Trade

Gatún, Lake /ga tóon/ artificial lake in Panama, part of the Panama Canal system. Area: 430 sq. km/166 sq. mi.

Gatwick /gáttwik/ second largest airport serving London, to the south of the city

gauche /gōsh/ *adj* lacking grace or tact in social situations [Mid-18C. < French, 'left-handed'.] —**gauchely** *adv* —**gaucheness** *n*

gaucherie /gṓshəri, -rée/ *n* 1 a lack of grace or tact in social situations 2 an act that is graceless or tactless [Late 18C. < French, < *gauche* 'left-handed'.]

gaucho /gówchō/ (*plural* **-chos**) *n* a cowboy of the South American pampas or prairie [Early 19C. < American Spanish.]

gaud /gawd/ *n* a showy trinket or ornament [14C. < ?]

gaudery /gáwdəri/ (*plural* **-ies**) *n* showy and ostentatious clothing or jewellery, or its display

Gaudí /gowdi/, **Antoni** (1852–1926) Spanish architect

gaudy[1] /gáwdi/ (**-ier, -iest**) *adj* brightly coloured or showily decorated to an unpleasant or vulgar degree [15C. < GAUD.] —**gaudily** *adv* —**gaudiness** *n*

gaudy[2] /gáwdi/ (*plural* **-ies**) *n* an annual celebration or dinner held at certain universities and university colleges [Mid-16C. < Latin *gaudium* 'joy' < *gaudere* 'rejoice'.]

gauffer *vt, n* HAIR = **goffer**

gauge /gayj/, **gage** *vt* (**gauges, gauging, gauged; gages, gaging, gaged**) 1 **CALCULATE** to determine the amount, quantity, size, or extent of something ○ *It's quite difficult to gauge the distance accurately.* 2 **EVALUATE** to form a judgment of something uncertain or variable, especially somebody's behaviour, feelings, or abilities ○ *Try to gauge his mood before launching the proposal.* 3 **ENSURE CONFORMITY TO STANDARD** to ensure that something conforms to a standard of measurement ■ *n* 1 **MEASUREMENT** a standard measurement or scale of measurement 2 **MEASURING DEVICE** a device or instrument for measuring an amount or quantity or for testing accuracy 3 **CRITERION** a standard or system of measurement for assessing somebody or something ○ *a gauge of the applicant's ability* 4 **DISTANCE BETWEEN RAILS** the distance between the two rails of a railway track or tramway 5 **DISTANCE BETWEEN WHEELS** the distance between two wheels on an axle of a vehicle 6 **THICKNESS OF WIRE** the diameter of something, especially of wire or a needle 7 **THICKNESS OF A MATERIAL** the thickness of a thin material such as sheet metal or plastic film 8 **DIAMETER INSIDE GUN BARREL** the diameter of the inside of a gun barrel, especially a shotgun barrel 9 **RELATIVE POSITION** the position of a ship in relation to another vessel and the wind 10 **FINENESS OF A KNIT** the fineness of knitted fabric expressed in terms of the number of loops for each unit of width 11 **ADDED PROPORTION OF PLASTER OF PARIS** the proportion of plaster of Paris that is added to mortar to speed up the setting of the mixture [14C. < Old N French, variant of French *jauge*.] —**gaugeable** *adj*

gauger /gáyjər/ *n* 1 a customs officer whose job is to inspect bulk goods on which duty is supposed to be paid 2 a person who or instrument that gauges something

gauge theory *n* a theory describing the interactions between elementary particles by considering particles to be quantized fields

Gauguin /gṓ gaN/, **Paul** (1848–1903) French painter

Gauhati /gow haáti/ port in NE India, on the River Brahmaputra. Population: 584,342 (1991).

Gaul /gawl/ *n* 1 **ANCIENT FRANCE** an ancient region of W Europe that included large portions of France, Belgium, and neighbouring parts of Italy, the Netherlands, and Germany, first invaded by the Romans before 100 BC 2 **SOMEBODY FROM GAUL** somebody who came from ancient Gaul 3 **FRENCH PERSON** somebody who is French [15C. < Latin *Gallus*.]

gauleiter /gów lītər/, **Gauleiter** *n* 1 a political head of a district in Nazi Germany 2 a local official who behaves in a dictatorial manner [Mid-20C. < German, < *Gau* 'administrative district' + *Leiter* 'leader'.]

Gaulish /gáwlish/ *n* an extinct Celtic language spoken in Gaul before the Roman conquest ■ *adj* relating to ancient Gaul, or its people, language, or culture

Gaullism /gṓl izəm/ *n* 1 the nationalist and conservative principles and policies of General Charles de Gaulle, leader of France after World War II, and his followers 2 the political movement founded on the principles of Charles de Gaulle

Gaullist /gṓlist/ *n* a supporter of Gaullism or de Gaulle ■ *adj* relating to, typical of, or supporting Gaullism or de Gaulle

gault /gawlt/ *n* a heavy dense clay or soil high in clay content, especially that of a series of clay and marl beds in S England [Late 16C. < ?]

gaunt /gawnt/ *adj* 1 extremely thin and bony in appearance 2 stark in outline or appearance [15C. < ?] —**gauntly** *adv* —**gauntness** *n*

gauntlet[1] /gáwntlət/ *n* a glove with a long wide cuff that covers and protects part of the forearm [15C. < French *gantelet* 'little glove' < *gant* 'glove' < Germanic.] ◇ **throw down the gauntlet** to issue a challenge

gauntlet[2] /gáwntlət/ *n* a punishment formerly used in the military in which somebody was forced to run between two lines of men armed with weapons who beat him as he passed [Mid-17C. Alteration, influenced by GAUNTLET[1], of *gantlop* < Swedish *gatlopp* 'passageway'.] ◇ **run the gauntlet** to endure attack or criticism from all sides

gaur /gów ər/ *n* a large wild ox with a dark coat. Native to: mountains of SE Asia. *Bos gaurus*. [Early 19C. < Sanskrit *gaura* < Indo-European.]

~~**gaurd**~~ incorrect spelling of **guard**

Gause's principle /gáwziz-/, **Gause principle** /gáwz-/ *n* ECOL = **competitive exclusion** [After G. F. *Gause* (1910–), Russian biologist.]

gauss /gowss/ (*plural* **gauss**) *n* the cgs unit of magnetic flux density, equivalent to 10^{-4} tesla [Late 19C. After Karl Friedrich *Gauss* (1777–1855), German mathematician.]

Gaussian /gówssi ən/ *adj* with the characteristics or shape of a normal curve or normal statistical distribution [Late 19C. After Karl Friedrich *Gauss* (see GAUSS).]

Gaussian curve *n* STATS = **normal curve**

Gaussian distribution *n* STATS = **normal distribution**

Gauteng /khow téng/ province in N South Africa. Capital: Johannesburg. Population: 7,048,300 (1995). Area: 18,810 sq. km/7,260 sq. mi.

Gautier /gṓ tyay/, **Théophile** (1811–72) French writer

gauze /gawz/ *n* 1 **FINELY-WOVEN FABRIC** a thin, almost transparent, loosely-woven cotton or silk cloth. Use: curtains, clothes. 2 **SURGICAL DRESSING** a dressing for wounds made of loosely woven material such as cotton 3 **WIRE MESH** a thin mesh made of wire or other material 4 **PIECE OF WIRE GAUZE** a piece of wire gauze used as a screen or filter in something such as a smoker's pipe 5 **HAZE** a fine haze or mist [Mid-16C. < French *gaze*.] —**gauzily** *adv* —**gauzy** *adj*

gavage /gáv aazh/ *n* the feeding of an animal or a person through a tube passed into the stomach [Late 19C. < French, < *gaver* 'stuff down the throat'.]

gave past tense of **give**

gavel /gávv'l/ *n* a small hammer used by an auctioneer, a judge, or chair of a meeting to draw people's attention or to mark the conclusion of a transaction ■ *vti* (**-els, -elling, -elled**) to use a gavel to bring an end to something or to stop discussion [Early 19C. < ?]

gavial /gáyvi əl/ *n* ZOOL = **gharial** [Early 19C. Via French < Hindi *ghariyāl*.]

Gävle /yévvlə/ port in E Sweden. Population: 90,587 (1995).

gavotte /gə vót/ *n* 1 a French country dance in 4/4 time popular in the 18th century 2 the music for a gavotte [Late 19C. Via French < Provençal *Gavot* 'inhabitant of the Alps'.]

Gawain /gaáwayn/ *n* in Arthurian legend, a knight who was the enemy of Sir Lancelot and who fought a mysterious green knight

Gawd /gawd/, **gawd** *interj, n* God (*slang; used to suggest irony in oaths*)

gawk /gawk/ *vi* to stare stupidly (*informal*) ■ *n* an awkward or clumsy person (*dated insult*) [Late 17C. < ?]

SYNONYMS See ***gaze***.

gawky /gáwki/ (**-ier, -iest**) *adj* awkward and clumsy, often because of being tall and not well coordinated (*informal*) —**gawkily** *adv* —**gawkiness** *n*

Gawler /gáwlər/ town in S South Australia. Population: 15,484 (1996).

gawp /gawp/ *vi* to stare stupidly or rudely (*informal*) ○ *Don't just stand there gawping, help her!* [Late 17C. < ?]

SYNONYMS See ***gaze***.

gay /gay/ *adj* 1 **HOMOSEXUAL** homosexual in sexual orientation 2 **MERRY** full of light-heartedness and merriment (*dated*) 3 **BRIGHT IN COLOUR** brightly coloured (*dated*) 4 **CAREFREE** having or showing a carefree spirit (*dated*) 5 **DEBAUCHED** leading a debauched or dissolute life (*dated*) ■ *n* **HOMOSEXUAL PERSON** a homosexual, especially a homosexual man [13C. < Old French *gai* 'happy'.] —**gayness** *n*

Gay /gay/, **John** (1685–1732) English poet and dramatist

gayal /gə yál/ (*plural* **-yal** *or* **-yals**) *n* a wild or semi-domesticated ox with a dark coat and white leg markings. Native to: SE Asia. *Bos frontalis*. [Late 18C. < Bengali.]

gaydar /gáy daar/ *n* the supposed instinctive ability of gay people to identify others who are homosexual (*informal*) [Blend of GAY + RADAR]

Gaye /gay/, **Marvin** (1939–84) US singer and songwriter

Gay-Lussac's law /gay lóossaks-/ *n* the principle that when gases combine in a chemical reaction they do so in simple ratios of their volumes, and that any gaseous product is also produced in a simple ratio [Early 19C. After Joseph-Louis *Gay-Lussac* (1778–1850), French physicist.]

gay pride *n* a movement that encourages homosexual men and lesbians to be open and proud about their homosexuality (*informal*)

gaz. *abbr* 1 gazette 2 gazetteer

Gaza /gaázə/ seaport and principal city of the Gaza Strip, on the Mediterranean. Population: 294,000 (1992 estimate).

gazar /gə zaàr/ *n* a stiff loosely-woven silk [Mid-20C. < ?]

Gaza Strip region on the E Mediterranean coast bordering Egypt and Israel, under the control of the Palestinian National Authority. Population: 731,296 (1994). Area: 360 sq. km/139 sq. mi.

gaze /gayz/ *vi* (**gazes, gazing, gazed**) to look for a long time with a fixed stare ○ *He gazed longingly at the yacht.* ■ *n* a long steady look or stare [14C. < ?] —**gazer** *n*

SYNONYMS **gaze, gape, gawk, gawp, ogle, rubberneck, stare**
CORE MEANING: to look at somebody or something steadily or at length
gaze to look for a long time with unwavering attention; **gape** to look at somebody or something in surprise or wonder, usually with an open mouth; **gawk** or **gawp** (*informal*) to stare stupidly or rudely; **ogle** to look steadily at somebody for sexual enjoyment or to show sexual interest; **rubberneck** (*informal*) to stare at somebody or something in an over-inquisitive or insensitive way; **stare** to look at somebody or something directly and intently without moving the eyes away, as a result of curiosity or surprise, or to express rudeness or defiance.

gazebo /gə zeèb ō/ (*plural* **-bos** *or* **-boes** /-ōz/) *n* a small, usually open-sided and slightly elevated building, situated in a spot that commands a good view [Mid-18C. < ?]

gazelle /gə zél/ (*plural* **-zelles** *or* **-zelle**) *n* a small graceful swift antelope with long ringed horns and black face markings. Native to: plains of Africa and Asia. Genera: *Gazella* and *Procapra*. [Early 17C. < Old French *gazel*.]

gazette /gə zét/ *n* **1** NEWSPAPER a newspaper, especially the official paper of an organization ○ *the South London Gazette* **2** PUBLICATION WITH OFFICIAL NEWS an official publication in which government appointments, public notices, lists of bankruptcies, and other items appear ○ *the Court Gazette* ■ *vt* (**-zettes, -zetting, -zetted**) PUBLISH IN GAZETTE to publish or announce something or name somebody in a gazette (*often passive*) [Early 17C. Directly or via French < Italian *gazzetta* < Venetian dialect *gazeta de la novità* 'pennyworth of news'.]

gazetteer /gàzzə teér/ *n* a dictionary or index of places, usually with descriptive or statistical information

gazpacho /gaz pách ō, gəs paàch-/ (*plural* **-chos**) *n* a chilled Mexican or Spanish soup based on stock or tomato juice and containing chopped raw vegetables and seasoning [Early 19C. < Spanish.]

gazump /gə zúmp/ *vt* (*informal*) **1** to charge the buyer of a property more than the originally agreed price, usually after receiving a better offer for the property ○ *We've been gazumped!* **2** to subject somebody to a swindle [Early 20C. < ?] —**gazump** *n* —**gazumper** *n*

gazunder /gə zúndər/ *vt* to lower the amount of money that is being offered to the seller of a property after a price has already been agreed (*informal*) [Late 20C. Blend of GAZUMP + UNDER.] —**gazunderer** *n*

GB *abbr* **1** gilbert **2** Great Britain

GBE *abbr* Knight or Dame Grand Cross of the Order of the British Empire

GBH *abbr* grievous bodily harm

⚡**Gbyte** *abbr* gigabyte

Gc *abbr* gigacycle

GC *abbr* George Cross

GCB *abbr* Knight or Dame Grand Cross of the Order of the Bath

GCE *n* an examination for secondary-school pupils in England and Wales at Advanced level (**A level**) and formerly at Ordinary level (**O level**), set and marked by various independent examination boards. Full form **General Certificate of Education**

GCH *abbr* gas central heating

GCHQ *abbr* Government Communications Headquarters

G clef *n* MUSIC = **treble clef**

GCMG *abbr* Grand Cross of the Order of St Michael and St George

GCSE *n* an examination for 16-year-olds in England and Wales that includes coursework assessment by individual schools as well as examination by independent boards. Full form **General Certificate of Secondary Education**

GCVO *abbr* Grand Cross of the Victorian Order

⚡**gd** *abbr* Grenada (*in Internet addresses*)

Gd *symbol* gadolinium

Gdansk /gə dánsk/ city in N Poland, on the Gulf of Gdansk, an inlet of the Baltic Sea. Population: 462,800 (1995). German **Danzig**

g'day /gə dáy/ *interj* *Australian* hello or good day (*informal*) [Contraction]

Gdns *abbr* Gardens (*in addresses*)

GDP *abbr* gross domestic product

GDR *abbr* German Democratic Republic

Gdynia /gə dínnyə/ city in N Poland, on the Gulf of Gdansk. Population: 251,400 (1995).

⚡**ge** *abbr* Georgia (*in Internet addresses*)

Ge *symbol* germanium

ge- *prefix* = **geo-** (*before vowels*)

gean /geen/ *n* a tree from which the sweet cherry was developed. Native to: Europe, W Asia, North Africa. *Prunus avium*. [Mid-16C. < Old French *guine*.]

geanticline /jee ánti klĪn/ *n* a large region of rock raised up from the earth's surface [Late 19C. < Greek *gē* 'earth'.] —**geanticlinal** /jee ánti klĪn'l/ *adj*

gear /geer/ *n* **1** PART THAT TRANSMITS MOTION a toothed mechanical part, e.g. a wheel or cylinder, that engages with a similar toothed part to transmit motion from one rotating body to another **2** DEVICE TO TRANSMIT MOTION a mechanism that transmits motion from one part to another part for performing a specific function ○ *steering gear* **3** FIXED TRANSMISSION SETTING one of several fixed transmission settings in a vehicle that determine power or direction **4** LEVEL OF EFFICIENCY the particular speed or efficiency with which somebody works (*informal*) ○ *I feel as if I'm still in first gear.* **5** ENGAGED STATE the state of a vehicle when one of its gears is engaged ○ *The car won't start when it's in gear.* **6** MACHINERY a piece or system of machinery with a particular function **7** EQUIPMENT the equipment that is needed for a specific activity (*informal*) ○ *hiking gear* **8** CLOTHES clothes and accessories of a particular kind (*informal*) ○ *You've got to have the right gear.* **9** SAILING EQUIPMENT the equipment, rigging, and other objects that belong to a particular boat or sailor **10** ILLEGAL DRUGS illegal drugs (*slang*) **11** HARNESS a horse's harness ■ *vt* **1** PUT GEARS IN to equip something with gears **2** ENGAGE GEAR to put a vehicle into gear [13C. < Old Norse *gervi* 'make ready'.]

gear to, gear towards *vt* to adapt or adjust something so that it fits in or works effectively with something else (*usually passive*) ○ *We've tried to gear ourselves to the younger market.*

gear up *vti* to prepare somebody or take action in preparation for something or to do something (*usually passive or continuous*) ○ *We're all geared up for the next round of talks.*

gearbox /geer boks/ *n* **1** the protective casing surrounding a set of gears **2** a set of gears and the protective casing that covers it in a vehicle or engine ○ *A horrible clunking noise came from the gearbox.* US term **transmission** *n.* 5

gearing /geering/ *n* **1** SET OF GEARS a set of mechanical gears, or the power that it provides ○ *complaints about the gearing on the older model* **2** PROVIDING SOMETHING WITH GEARS the process or act of providing a system with gears **3** PROPORTION OF CAPITAL AS DEBT the ratio of a company's debt capital to the value of its ordinary shares. US term **leverage** *n.* 5

gear lever *n* a lever in a car or other vehicle or machine that is used to change or engage gears. US term **gearshift**

gearshift /geer shift/ *n* US, Can MECH ENG = **gear lever**

gear stick *n* MECH ENG = **gear lever**

gear train *n* a collection of gears used to transmit power

gearwheel /geer weel/ *n* MECH ENG = **gear** *n.* 1

gebel *n* GEOG = **jebel**

gecko /gék ō/ (*plural* **-os** *or* **-oes**) *n* a small tropical or subtropical nocturnal insect-eating lizard with hooked ridges on the pads of its feet that permit it to climb smooth vertical surfaces. Family: Gekkonidae. [Late 18C. < Malay dialect *geko(k).*]

gedanken experiment /gə dángkən-/ *n* a test of a hypothesis that can be performed only in the mind [Mid-20C. < German.]

geddit /géddit/ *interj* do you understand? (*slang*) ○ *We're goin' now, geddit.* [Late 20C. Fast speech pronunciation of *get it.*]

Gecko

gee[1] /jee/ *interj* **1** US EXPRESSING ENTHUSIASM used to express surprise or to register a reaction to something, especially an enthusiastic one **2** HURRY UP! used to urge a horse, cow, or similar animal to move faster, to go straight ahead, or to turn right ■ *vt* (**gees, geeing, geed**) **1** HURRY ANIMAL UP to urge a horse, cow, or similar animal to move faster, to go straight ahead, or to turn right **2** ENCOURAGE to encourage somebody to continue doing something or to do something faster (*informal*) [Mid-18C. < ?]

gee up *interj* used to urge a horse, cow, or similar animal to move faster, to go straight ahead, or to turn right ■ *vt* to urge a horse, cow, or similar animal to move faster, to go straight ahead, or to turn right

gee[2] *n* US MONEY = **G**[1] *n.* **7** (*informal*)

Gee /jee/, **Maurice Gough** (*b.* 1931) New Zealand novelist

gee-gee *n* a horse (*informal; usually by or to children*) [Mid-19C. Childish repetition of GEE[1].]

geek /geek/ *n* **1** SOMEBODY AWKWARD somebody considered unattractive and socially awkward (*insult*) **2** OUTRAGEOUS SIDESHOW PERFORMER a sideshow performer whose act consists of outrageous feats such as biting the heads off live animals **3** OBSESSIVE COMPUTER USER somebody who is a proud or enthusiastic user of computers or other technology, sometimes to an excessive degree (*informal*) [Late 19C. < ?] —**geeky** *adj*

Geelong /ji lóng/ seaport in Victoria, SE Australia. Population: 125,382 (1996).

geese plural of **goose**

gee whiz *interj* US = **gee**[1] *interj.* 1

gee-whiz *adj* US causing or characterized by wonderment (*informal*) ○ *a gee-whiz new electronic gadget*

Ge'ez /gée ez/ *n* an ancient language formerly spoken in Ethiopia and still the liturgical language in the Ethiopian Christian Church [Late 18C. < Ethiopic.] —**Ge'ez** *adj*

geezer /geézər/ *n* a man (*slang*) [Late 19C. Representing dialect pronunciation of GUISER.]

SPELLCHECK Do not confuse **geezer** with **geyser**, which has a similar sound. Beware: your spellchecker will not catch this error.

gefilte fish /gə fíltə-/ *n* a Jewish dish consisting of finely chopped fish mixed with crumbs, eggs, and seasoning and served as balls or cakes [Late 19C. < Yiddish, 'stuffed fish' (what the dish originally was).]

gegenschein /gáygən shīn/ *n* a faint elliptical glow in the night sky opposite the setting sun, caused by the reflection of sunlight by dust in space [Late 19C. < German, 'opposite glow'.]

Geiger counter /gígər-/, **Geiger-Müller counter** /-moollər-/ *n* an instrument used to detect and measure the intensity of ionizing radiation, e.g. particles from a radioactive substance [Early 20C. After Hans *Geiger* (1882–1945), German physicist.]

geisha /gáyshə/ (*plural* **-sha** *or* **-shas**), **geisha girl** *n* **1** a Japanese woman educated to accompany men as a hostess, with skills such as dancing, conversation, and music **2** a Japanese prostitute [Late 19C. < Japanese, 'entertainer'.]

Geissler tube /gísslər-/ *n* a discharge tube containing gas at low pressure that glows when an electrical current is passed through it [Mid-19C. After Heinrich *Geissler* (1814–79), German glass blower.]

gel[1] /jel/ *n* **1 SEMISOLID** a semisolid mixture of small particles of a solid in a liquid (**colloid**) **2 LIGHT FILTER** a sheet of coloured acetate used in theatre, television, and film lighting to create different lighting effects **3 HAIR STYLING PRODUCT** a substance with the consistency of jelly that is used for styling hair ■ *vi* (**gels, gelling, gelled**) **1 BECOME GEL** to become semisolid, having been in a liquid state **2 TAKE FORM** to take on a definite form (*informal*) ○ *The idea didn't begin to gel until I got home.* **3 GET ON** to get on well together (*informal*) [Late 19C. Shortening of GELATIN.] —**gelable** *adj*

gel[2] /gel/ *n* a girl (*dated; usually associated with the upper classes*) ○ *She's a fine gel!* [Representing a British upper-class pronunciation of GIRL]

gelada /jéllədə/ (*plural* **-das** *or* **-da**), **gelada baboon** *n* a large baboon with brown hair and a bare red patch on its chest. Native to: NE Africa. *Theropithecus gelada.* [Mid-19C. < Amharic *č'ällada.*]

gelate /jé láyt/ (**-ates, -ating, -ated**) *vi* to become or form a gel [Early 20C. Back-formation < GELATION[2].]

gelati plural of **gelato**

gelatin /jéllətin/, **gelatine** /-teen/ *n* **1 SEMISOLID PROTEIN** a transparent protein material made from boiling animal hides, bone, and cartilage that forms a firm gel when mixed with water. Use: foods, medicine, glue, photography. **2 SUBSTANCE WITH CONSISTENCY OF JELLY** a substance, e.g. agar, that resembles gelatin **3 JELLY-LIKE FOOD** a sweet food made of flavoured gelatin **4** THEATRE = **gel**[1] *n.* **2** [Early 19C. Via French *gélatine* < Italian *gelatina* < Latin *gelata* 'frozen'.]

gelatinize /ji látti nīz/ (**-nizes, -nizing, -nized**), **gelatinise** (**-nises, -nising, -nised**) *v* **1** *vti* to make something gelatinous, or become gelatinous **2** *vt* to coat a photographic medium with gelatin —**gelatinization** /ji látti nī záysh'n/ *n* —**gelatinizer** *n*

gelatinous /ji láttinəss/ *adj* **1** having a semisolid form resembling gelatin **2** relating to or containing gelatin —**gelatinously** *adv* —**gelatinousness** *n*

gelation[1] /jə láysh'n/ *n* the solidification of a liquid by freezing [Mid-19C. < Latin *gelation-* < *gelare* 'freeze'.]

gelation[2] /jə láysh'n/ *n* the process of becoming a gel [Early 20C. < GEL[1].]

gelato /jə laátō/ (*plural* **-ti** /-ti/ *or* **-tos**) *n* an Italian ice cream [Early 20C. < Italian, 'frozen' < Latin *gelare* 'freeze'.]

gelcap /jél kap/ *n* an oral medicine in which the drug is contained in a gelatin capsule

geld[1] /geld/ (**gelds, gelding, gelded** *or* **gelt, gelded** *or* **gelt** /gelt/) *vt* **1** to castrate an animal, especially a horse **2** to take away the strength or virility of somebody or something [13C. < Old Norse *gelda* < *geldr* 'barren'.]

geld[2] /geld/ *n* a land tax paid by landholders to the crown in late Anglo-Saxon and Norman times [15C. Via medieval Latin *geldum* < Old English *gield* 'payment'.]

gelding /gélding/ *n* a castrated horse or other animal. ◊ **stallion** *n.* **1** [14C. < GELD[1].]

Geldof /gél dof/, **Sir Bob** (*b.* 1954) Irish musician and philanthropist. Full name **Robert Frederick Xenon Geldof**

gelid /jéllid/ *adj* exceedingly cold (*literary*) [Early 17C. < Latin *gelidus* < *gelu* 'frost, intense cold'.] —**gelidity** /je líddəti/ *n* —**gelidly** *adv*

gelignite /jéllig nīt/ *n* dynamite consisting of gelled nitroglycerin, potassium nitrate, and wood pulp or guncotton [Late 19C. < GELATIN + Latin *ignis* 'fire'.]

Gellhorn /géll hawrn/, **Martha** (1908–98) US journalist and novelist

gelt past participle, past tense of **geld**[1]

gem /jem/ *n* **1 JEWEL** a precious stone that has been cut and polished for use as jewellery or decoration **2 SOMEBODY OR SOMETHING EXCELLENT** somebody or something considered to be valuable, useful, or beautiful (*informal*) ○ *Our babysitter is such a gem!* ■ *vt* (**gems, gemming, gemmed**) **DECORATE SOMETHING WITH GEMS** to decorate something with gems or with something resembling gems (*literary; usually passive*) [Pre-12C. < Latin *gemma* 'bud, jewel'.]

Gemara /gə maárə/ *n* the second part of the Talmud, forming a set of commentaries on the first part of the Talmud, the Mishnah [Early 17C. < Aramaic *gĕmārā* 'completion'.]

gemfish /jém fish/ (*plural* **-fishes** *or* **-fish**) *n* food fish prized for its delicate flesh. Native to: SE Australia. *Rexea solandri.*

geminate /jémmi nayt/ *adj* **geminate, geminated** growing or arranged in pairs ○ *a geminate leaf* ■ *vti* (**-nates, -nating, -nated**) to make something paired, or become paired or doubled [Late 16C. < Latin *geminat-*, past participle of *geminare* < *geminus* 'twin'.] —**gemination** /jémmi náysh'n/ *n*

Gemini /jémmi nī/ *n* **1 THE TWINS CONSTELLATION** a zodiacal constellation of the northern hemisphere containing the bright stars Castor and Pollux. See illustration at **constellation 2 THIRD ZODIAC SIGN** the third sign of the zodiac, represented by twins and lasting from approximately 21 May to 20 June **3 Gemini, Geminian SOMEBODY BORN UNDER GEMINI** somebody whose birthday falls between 21 May and 20 June [Pre-12C. < Latin, plural of *geminus* 'twin'.] —**Gemini** *adj*

Geminid /jémmi nid/ *n* a member of the major annual meteor shower that reaches its maximum on or about 13 December [Late 19C. < GEMINI, from where such meteors seem to radiate.]

gemma /jémmə/ (*plural* **-mae** /-m ee/) *n* an asexual bud-shaped structure that can detach from the parent plant and form a new individual [Late 18C. < Latin, 'bud, jewel'.] —**gemmaceous** /je máyshəss/ *adj*

gemmate /jémmayt/ *adj* forming gemmae or reproducing by means of gemmae ■ *vi* (**-mates, -mating, -mated**) to form gemmae or reproduce by means of gemmae [Early 17C. < Latin *gemmat-*, past participle of *gemmare* 'produce buds' < *gemma* 'bud, jewel'.] —**gemmation** /je máysh'n/ *n*

gemmiferous /je míffərəs/ *adj* **1** producing precious stones **2** bearing gemmae

gemmiparous /je míppərəs/ *adj* BIOL = **gemmate** *adj.*

gemmology /je mólləji/, **gemology** *n* the study of gems and gemstones —**gemmological** /jémmə lójjik'l/ *adj* —**gemmologist** /je mólləjist/ *n*

gemmulation /jémmyoo láysh'n/ *n* production of gemmules, or reproduction by means of gemmules

gemmule /jém yool/ *n* a reproductive structure produced by asexual reproduction in freshwater and marine sponges

gemology *n* GEOL = **gemmology**

gemsbok /gémz bok/ (*plural* **-boks** *or* **-bok**) *n* a large antelope with long straight horns and broad black markings on its head and upper legs. Native to: SW and E Africa. *Oryx gazella.* [Late 18C. Via Afrikaans < Dutch, 'wild antelope buck'.]

gemstone /jém stōn/ *n* a mineral or stone suitable for use in jewellery after cutting and polishing

gemütlich /gə mōōtlikh/ *adj* warm and friendly [Mid-19C. < German, < *Gemüt* 'heart, spirit'.]

gemütlichkeit /gə mōōtlikh kīt/ *n* warmth and friendliness [Mid-19C. < German, < *gemütlich* (see GEMÜTLICH).]

gen /jen/ *n* information (*informal*) [Mid-20C. < ?]
gen up /jén-/ (**gens up, genning up, genned up**) *v* (*informal*) **1** *vi* to find out all the information on a subject **2** *vt* to give somebody all the information on a subject (*usually passive*)

gen. *abbr* **1** gender **2** general **3** genitive **4** genus

Gen. *abbr* **1** General **2** Genesis

-gen *suffix* something that produces ○ *hallucinogen* [Via French *-gène* < Greek *-genēs* 'born' < Indo-European, 'beget'] —**-genic** *suffix* —**-geny** *suffix*

gendarme /zhónd aarm, zhaáNd-/ *n* **1** a police officer in France and French-speaking countries **2** a police officer (*slang*) [Mid-16C. < French, singular < *gens d'armes* 'men of arms'.]

gendarmerie /zhond aármәri, zhaaNd-/ *n* **1** gendarmes considered as a body **2** in France and French-speaking countries, a police station or police barracks [Mid-16C. < French, < *gendarme* (see GENDARME).]

gender /jéndər/ *n* **1** ⚠ **SOMEBODY'S SEX** the sex of a person or organism, or of a whole category of people or organisms (*often euphemistic to avoid the word 'sex'*) **2 FACT OF HAVING DIFFERENT GENDERS** the fact of people having or being aware of having different genders ○ *Gender is not an issue when we take on new staff.* **3 CATEGORIZATION OF NOUNS** the classification of nouns and pronouns in certain languages according to the forms taken by adjectives, modifiers, and other grammatical items associated syntactically with them **4 CATEGORY OF NOUN** any one of the categories, e.g. masculine, feminine, neuter, or common, into which nouns and pronouns are divided in languages that have gender [14C. < Old French *gendre* < Latin *gener-*, stem of *genus* 'birth, kind'.] —**genderless** *adj*

USAGE gender or **sex**? Traditionally, ***gender*** has referred to grammatical classifications in languages that have masculine, feminine, and neuter nouns, and ***sex*** has referred to the biological classifications to which gender is analogous. For some time, however, anthropologists have used ***gender*** to distinguish cultural categories from biological ones: *Gender roles are indistinct among the young of this society; the two sexes play together frequently.* Cultural and biological categories are interrelated, of course, and thus at times it can be difficult to decide which word is more appropriate. ***Gender*** has become the preferred form in the 21st century, as in *Gender is an important factor to consider when hiring new employees* and in idiomatic expressions such as *gender gap.*

gender bender *n* an offensive term for somebody who dresses or acts in a way that is intended to blur the traditional distinctions between men and women (*slang*) —**gender bending** *n*

gendered /jéndərd/ *adj* relating to or appropriate to one gender rather than the other ○ *gendered clothing*

gender gap *n* a noticeable difference in behaviour or attitudes between men and women or boys and girls

gender-neutral *adj* avoiding references to masculinity and femininity and their cultural associations

gene /jeen/ *n* the basic unit capable of transmitting characteristics from one generation to the next. It consists of a specific sequence of DNA or RNA that occupies a fixed position (**locus**) on a chromosome. [Early 20C. Via German *Gen* < Greek *genos* 'birth, race'.]

SPELLCHECK See ***jean.***

-gene *suffix* = **-gen**

genealogy /jeéni álləji/ (*plural* **-gies**) *n* **1 STUDY OF THE HISTORY OF FAMILIES** the study of the history of families and the line of descent from their ancestors **2 FAMILY HISTORY** a pedigree or line of descent that can be traced directly from an ancestor or earlier form, especially that of an individual or family **3 FAMILY TREE** a chart or table that shows the line of descent from an ancestor or earlier form, especially that of an individual or family **4 STUDY OF PLANT OR ANIMAL DEVELOPMENT** the study of the line of development of a plant or animal from earlier forms [14C. Via French *généalogie* < Greek *genealogia* < *genea* 'race, generation'.] —**genealogical** /jeéni ə lójjik'l/ *adj* —**genealogically** *adv* —**genealogist** *n*

gene amplification *n* the production of many copies of a section of DNA, naturally or by technological means

gene cloning *n* the process of producing any number of identical copies of a gene

gene expression *n* the process by which a gene's coded information is converted into the structures operating in a cell

gene flow *n* the natural transfer of genes from one population into the genetic make-up of another population through hybridization and interbreeding

gene frequency *n* the ratio of a specific variation of a gene (**allele**) to the total number of variations in a particular population

gene gun *n* a device that inserts DNA directly into cells

gene mutation *n* ◆ **point mutation**

~~**geneology**~~ incorrect spelling of **genealogy**

gene pool *n* **1** the total of all genes carried by all individuals in an interbreeding population **2** the total of all genes existing among all individuals of a species

gene probe *n* a fragment of DNA or RNA marked by a chemical or radioactive substance that will bind to a given gene, used as a tag in order to identify or isolate that gene

genera plural of **genus**

general /jénnərəl/ *adj* **1 OVERALL** relating to or including all or nearly all of the members of a category, group, or whole ○ *a general increase in demand* **2 USUAL** applying or happening in most cases ○ *as a general rule* **3 WIDESPREAD** shared or participated in by many ○ *a general sense that something ought to be done* **4 MISCELLANEOUS** having a varied content or wide scope ○ *a general store* **5 NOT SPECIALIZED** unspecialized or lacking specialized knowledge ○ *a book that was intended for the general reader* **6 NOT SPECIFIC** not specific, detailed, or clearly defined ○ *She spoke in the most general terms.* **7 HIGH-RANKING** with overall authority, or of superior rank ○ *a general manager* ■ *n* **1 general, General** HIGH RANKING OFFICER a British Army officer of a rank above lieutenant general **2** MIL = **general officer** **3** GENERAL ANAESTHETIC a general anaesthetic (*informal*) **4** GENERAL HOSPITAL a general hospital (*informal*) **5** THE PUBLIC the public as a whole (*archaic*) [12C. Via French < Latin *generalis* 'of the whole class' < *genus* 'race, kind'.] —**generalness** *n* ◇ **in general 1** as a whole **2** in most cases or circumstances

general anaesthetic *n* an anaesthetic that produces loss of sensation in the whole body together with unconsciousness

general assembly, General Assembly *n* **1** the highest governing body of various Presbyterian churches, especially the Church of Scotland, or the meeting of such a body **2** the assembly of the United Nations

general average *n* liability for loss or damage to an insured ship or its cargo that is shared among all those with an interest in the venture

General Certificate of Education *n* full form of **GCE**

General Certificate of Secondary Education *n* full form of **GCSE**

generalcy /jénnərəlsi, jénnrəlsi/ *n* the office of general, or the period during which this office is held

general delivery *n US* **1** = **poste restante** *n.* 1 **2** = **poste restante** *n.* 2

general election *n* an election in which the citizens of a country or state vote to elect representatives of all constituencies to a legislative body, e.g. the Houses of Parliament

General Headquarters *n* full form of **GHQ**

general hospital *n* a hospital that does not specialize in any one particular kind of medicine

generalisation *n* = **generalization**

generalise *vti* = **generalize**

generalissimo /jénnərə líssimō/ (*plural* **-mos**) *n* in some countries, the supreme commander of a combined military force consisting of the air force, navy, and army [Early 17C. < Italian, 'great general' < Latin *generalis* (see GENERAL).]

generalist /jénnərəlist/ *n* a person with knowledge, skills, or interests in many areas but with no speciality

generality /jénnə rálləti/ (*plural* **-ties**) *n* **1** STATE OF BEING GENERAL the quality or state of being general **2** GENERAL STATEMENT a statement or remark that concerns the main aspects of something rather than the details **3** GENERAL PRINCIPLE a statement or principle that is true or applies in most cases **4** UNIMPORTANT REMARK a remark about something that is not important in itself but is useful to open or keep up a conversation **5** MAJORITY the majority (*archaic*)

generalization /jénnərə lī záysh'n/, **generalisation** *n* **1** GENERAL STATEMENT a statement or conclusion that is derived from and applies equally to a number of cases ○ *not enough data to permit a generalization* **2** SWEEPING STATEMENT a statement presented as a general truth but based on limited or incomplete evidence **3** MAKING OF GENERALIZATIONS the making of general or sweeping statements **4** INFERENCE FROM INSTANCE the application of the rules of inference that go from an instance to a universal or to an existential statement **5** USE OF LEARNED RESPONSE the act of responding to a new stimulus in a similar way as to a conditioned stimulus

generalize /jénnərə līz/ (**-izes, -izing, -ized**), **generalise** (**-ises, -ising, -ised**) *v* **1** *vti* EXPRESS SOMETHING GENERAL to express something general on the basis of particulars **2** *vi* MAKE SWEEPING STATEMENT to state a supposed general truth about something on the basis of limited or incomplete evidence **3** *vti* GIVE WIDER USE TO to use something or be used in a wider or different range of circumstances **4** *vt* MAKE GENERALLY KNOWN to bring something into general use or to general knowledge (*usually passive*) **5** *vi* SPREAD to spread to other parts of the body **6** *vti* MAKE INFERENCE to infer a general conclusion from particulars or a universal statement from an instance —**generalizable** *adj*

generally /jénnərəli/ *adv* **1** USUALLY in most cases or circumstances **2** AS A WHOLE as a whole or without exception ○ *not meant for the public generally* **3** VAGUELY without being specific, detailed, or clearly defined ○ *spoke generally about his life* **4** WIDESPREAD so as to be widespread

general meeting *n* a meeting to which all members of a group or organization are invited

general officer *n* an officer of an army, navy, or air force of a rank above colonel

General of the Air Force *n* the highest-ranking officer in the US Air Force, above a general

General of the Armies *n* the highest-ranking officer in the US Army, above a General of the Army

General of the Army *n* the second-highest-ranking officer in the US Army, above a general and below the General of the Armies

general paralysis of the insane *n* full form of **GPI**

general practice *n* the work of a doctor who treats patients' general medical problems, referring them to hospitals for more specialized care

general practitioner *n* full form of **GP**[1] *n.*

general purpose *adj* useful for a wide variety of purposes

general relativity *n* PHYS = **relativity** *n.* 2

generalship /jénnərəl ship/ *n* **1** MILITARY COMMAND the art or practice of exercising military leadership **2** GENERAL'S RANK the rank or tenure of a general **3** LEADERSHIP skilful leadership or management of people or an organization

general staff *n* a group of military officers whose job is to assist senior officers in the planning and coordination of military operations

general studies *n* a course of study at school or university that covers a broad range of general topics rather than specializing in one specific area (+ *singular verb*)

general theory of relativity *n* PHYS = **relativity** *n.* 2

generate /jénnə rayt/ (**-ates, -ating, -ated**) *vt* **1** CREATE to bring something into existence or effect ○ *measures to generate more income* **2** PRODUCE ELECTRICITY to produce electricity from a power station or generator **3** PRODUCE ENERGY to produce or originate a form of energy through a chemical or physical process **4** PRODUCE SET to produce a set or sequence by the application of defined rules or the performance of defined operations **5** PRODUCE FORM to create a curve with a moving point or a surface with a moving curve [Early 16C. < Latin *generat-*, past participle of *generare* 'beget' < *genus* 'race, birth'.] —**generable** *adj*

generation /jénnə ráysh'n/ *n* **1** GROUP OF CONTEMPORARIES all of the people who were born at approximately the same time, considered as a group, and especially when considered as having shared interests and attitudes ○ *the younger generation* **2** STAGE IN DESCENT a single stage in the descent of a family or a group of people, animals, or plants, or the individuals belonging to the same stage ○ *three generations down the line* **3** TIME TAKEN TO PRODUCE NEW GENERATION the period of time that it takes for people, animals, or plants to grow up and produce their own offspring, in humans held to be between 30 and 35 years ○ *after three generations of war and conflict* **4** SPECIFIC GENERATION a particular numbered stage in the sequence of generations born or living in a country into which a family came as immigrants (*usually in combination*) ○ *first-generation immigrants* **5** NEW TYPE a particular stage in the development of a product or technology, especially one marking a significant advance ○ *one of the new generation of computers* **6** PHASE IN LIFE CYCLE one of the successive phases that make up the life cycle of certain organisms ○ *the gametophyte generation* **7** PRODUCTION OF POWER the production of electricity, heat, or some other form of energy **8** PRODUCTION OF YOUNG the act or process of bringing offspring into being **9** GENERATING OF GROUP OR SHAPE the act or process of generating a set, sequence, curve, or surface **10** NUCLEI IN CHAIN REACTION in a chain reaction, a group of nuclei that come from a previous group —**generational** *adj*

generation gap *n* the difference in attitudes, behaviour, and interests between people of different generations, especially between parents and their children

generation X, Generation X *n* the generation of people born roughly during the years 1965 to 1980 in Western countries, especially the United States, often regarded as disillusioned, cynical, or apathetic [< novel by Douglas Coupland, *Generation X: Tales for an Accelerated Culture*] —**generation Xer** *n*

generation Y, Generation Y *n US* the generation of people born approximately in or after 1980 in Western countries, especially the United States (*informal*) [After GENERATION X]

generative /jénnərətiv/ *adj* **1** relating to the production of young **2** involving the ability to produce or originate something ○ *generative linguistic theory* —**generatively** *adv* —**generativeness** *n*

generative cell *n* BIOL = **gamete**

generative grammar *n* the rules from which all the grammatical sentences, and only the grammatical sentences, of a language can be generated

generator /jénnə raytər/ *n* **1** DEVICE FOR PRODUCING ELECTRICITY a machine or device that is used to convert mechanical energy, e.g. that provided by the combustion of fuel, into electricity **2** DEVICE FOR PRODUCING GAS a device in which a gas is formed **3** ORIGINATOR somebody or something responsible for generating something such as an idea, plan, or strategy

generatrix /jénnə raytriks/ (*plural* **-trices** /-tri seez/) *n* an element such as a point or line that is used in the production of a geometric figure such as a curve or surface

generic /jə nérrik/ *adj* **1** SUITABLE FOR A BROAD RANGE usable or suitable in a variety of contexts ○ *generic software that can run on a variety of machines* **2** OF A GENUS relating to or characteristic of a genus **3** WITH GENERAL NAME describes a pharmaceutical product that does not have a brand name [Late 17C. < French *générique* < Latin *genus* 'race, kind'.] —**generically** *adv*

generosity /jénnə róssəti/ (*plural* **-ties**) *n* **1** KINDNESS willingness to give money, help, or time freely **2** NOBILITY nobility of character **3** SUBSTANTIAL SIZE pleasingly large size or quantity ○ *He ate everything, despite the generosity of the portions.* **4** GENEROUS ACT a generous, kind, or noble act [15C. < Latin *generositas* < *generosus* (see GENEROUS).]

generous /jénnərəss/ *adj* **1** KIND having or showing a willingness to give money, help, or time freely ○ *a very generous offer* **2** NOBLE having or showing nobility of character ○ *a generous gesture of forgiveness* **3** SUBSTANTIAL pleasingly large in size or quantity ○ *a generous slice of cake* **4** FULL-FLAVOURED describes wine that is rich and full-flavoured [Late 16C. Via French *généreux* < Latin *generosus* 'of noble birth' < *genus* 'race, birth'.] —**generously** *adv* —**generousness** *n*

SYNONYMS ***generous, magnanimous, munificent, bountiful, liberal***

CORE MEANING: giving readily to others

generous willing to give money, help, or time freely; **magnanimous** very generous, kind, or forgiving; **munificent** very generous, especially on a grand scale; **bountiful** (*literary*) generous, particularly to less fortunate people; **liberal** free with money, time, or other assets.

Genesee /jénnə seé/ river in Pennsylvania and New York, emptying into Lake Ontario. Length: 232 km/144 mi.

gene sequence *n* the order of nucleotides in a gene

gene sequencing, genetic sequencing *n* the process of determining the individual arrangement of nucleotides that compose a given gene

genesis /jénnəssiss/ (*plural* **-ses** /-seez/) *n* the time or circumstances of something's coming into being ○ *the genesis of this new project* [Early 17C. < GENESIS.]

Genesis *n* the first book of the Bible, in which the story of the creation of the world is told [Pre-12C. Via Latin < Greek.]

-genesis *suffix* production, origin ○ *sporogenesis* [Via Latin < Greek, 'birth']

gene splicing *n* a technique in which segments of DNA or RNA, often from different organisms, are combined, in order to be introduced into an organism

genet[1] /jénnit/ *n* **1** a small carnivorous mammal related to the civet that has a ringed tail, spotted sides, and retractable claws. Native to: wooded regions of S Europe and Africa. Genus: *Genetta*. **2** the fur of the genet [14C. < Old French *genette*.]

genet[2] *n* ZOOL = **jennet**

Genet /zhə náy/, **Jean** (1910–86) French writer

gene therapy *n* the treatment of a genetic disease through the insertion of normal or genetically altered genes into cells in order to replace or make up for the nonfunctional or missing genes

genetic /jə néttik/, **genetical** /-tik'l/ *adj* involving, resulting from, or relating to genes or genetics [Mid-19C. < GENESIS, after words such as *antithesis, antithetic*.] —**genetically** *adv*

genetically modified *adj* describes an organism that has received genetic material from another, resulting in a permanent change in one or more of its characteristics

genetically modified organism *n* a plant, animal, or microorganism produced by genetic engineering (*usually plural*) Full form of **GMO**

genetic code *n* the specific order of the nucleotide sequences in DNA or RNA that form the basis of heredity through their role in protein synthesis

genetic counselling *n* counselling that concerns the risks, treatments, and management of inherited genetic disorders for people with some likelihood of being affected by them, either personally or as parents — **genetic counsellor** *n*

genetic discrimination *n* discrimination against people, e.g. by insurance companies, on the grounds of some inherited disorder discovered in their genetic makeup

genetic drift *n* the random changes that occur in the gene frequency of small, isolated populations, resulting in the loss or preservation of certain genes over the generations

genetic engineering *n* GENETICS = **genetic modification** —**genetic engineer** *n*

genetic fingerprint *n* a DNA sequence taken from a region of a chromosome that is known to be highly variable, used as an accurate means of identifying an individual

genetic fingerprinting *n* GENETICS = **DNA fingerprinting**

geneticist /jə néttissist/ *n* a student of or specialist in genetics

genetic load *n* the average number of unfavourable recessive mutations per individual in a population

genetic manipulation *n* GENETICS = **genetic modification**

genetic map *n* a graphic representation of the specific arrangement of genes on a chromosome

genetic mapping *n* the technique or process of identifying genes on a chromosome

genetic marker *n* a known, usually dominant, gene that is used to identify specific genes, chromosomes, and traits known to be associated with that gene

genetic modification *n* the alteration and recombination of genetic material by technological means, resulting in transgenic organisms

QUICK FACTS ON... **GENETIC MODIFICATION (GM)**

Key elements: production of recombinant DNA molecules and their introduction into an organism; techniques include using a modified bacterium or bacteriophage that naturally inserts part of its DNA into the host organism, or direct gene transfer methods such as microinjection, electroporation, and particle bombardment

Key dates: 1953 DNA structure established (Watson & Crick); 1966 genetic code cracked (Nirenberg *et al.*); 1972 first recombinant DNA molecules produced (Berg); 1973 first microorganism with recombinant DNA (Cohen, Chang, and Boyer); 1982 first report of transgenic animals, mice (University of Ohio); 1983 first reports of genetically modified plant cells (Herrera-Estrella *et al.*); 2001 first genetically modified primate, a rhesus monkey called ANDi from the reverse initials of 'inserted DNA' (Shatten *et al.*)

Key technologies: recombinant DNA, transformation, cell and tissue culture, gene transfer

Key developments: potential medical benefits: production of human therapeutic proteins; progress in the study of genetic diseases using GM animals as models; progress in modifying animal organs for human transplants (xenotransplantation). Potential non-medical benefits: recombinant enzymes in food use; higher yields, disease resistance, and improved nutritional and processing quality in crop plants

genetic probe *n* GENETICS = **gene probe**

genetics /jə néttiks/ *n* **1** a branch of biology dealing with heredity and genetic variations (+ *singular verb*) **2** the genetic makeup of an organism or group of organisms (+ *singular or plural verb*)

gene transfer *n* the insertion of genetic material from one organism into another in a laboratory procedure, to produce a specific effect, e.g. resistance to disease

genetrix /jénnə triks/ (*plural* **-rices** /-tri seez/) *n* a biological mother (*technical*) ◊ **genitor** [15C. Directly or via Old French < Latin, < *gignere* 'beget'.]

geneva *n* BEVERAGES = **genever**

Geneva /jə neévə/ city in W Switzerland, at the western end of Lake Geneva. Population: 172,809 (1998). French **Genève** —**Genevan** *adj, n* —**Genevese** *adj, n*

Geneva, Lake largest lake in central Europe, straddling the border between Switzerland and SE France. Area: 583 sq. km/225 sq. mi.

genever /jə neévər/, **geneva** *literary* /-və/ *n* Dutch gin [Early 18C. Via Dutch < Old French *genevre* < Latin *juniperus* 'juniper'.]

Genghis Khan /géng giss kaán, jéng-/ (1167?–1227) Mongol conqueror. Born **Temujin**

genial /jeéni əl/ *adj* **1** having a kind and good-natured disposition or manner **2** pleasantly mild and warm so as to be conducive to life and growth ○ *a genial climate* [Mid-16C. < Latin *genialis* 'nuptial' < *genius* (see GENIUS).] —**geniality** /jeéni álləti/ *n* —**genially** *adv* —**genialness** *n*

genic /jénnik/ *adj* relating to or produced by a gene or genes —**genically** *adv*

geniculate /jə níkyoolət/ *adj* **1** bent at an angle like a knee ○ *geniculate antennae* **2** with a joint or joints that can be bent like a knee [Early 17C. < Latin *geniculatus* 'knotted' < *genu* 'knee'.] —**geniculately** *adv* —**geniculation** /jə níkyoo láysh'n/ *n*

genie /jeéni/ (*plural* **-nies** *or* **-nii** /-ni ī/) *n* a magical spirit in Arabian folklore that has supernatural powers and will obey the commands of the person who summons it. ◊ **jinni** [Mid-17C. Via French *génie* < Latin *genius* (see GENIUS).]

genii[1] plural of **genius** *n.* **4**, **genius** *n.* **5**, **genius** *n.* **6**

genii[2] plural of **genie**

genipap /jénni pap/ *n* **1** a reddish-brown fruit, resembling an orange. Use: preserves, drinks. **2** an evergreen tree that bears genipaps. Native to: tropical America. *Genipa americana*. [Early 17C. Via Portuguese *jenipapo* < Tupi *ianipaba*.]

genital /jénnit'l/ *adj* relating to the external sexual organs or to reproduction [14C. Directly or via French < Latin *genitalis* < *gignere* 'beget'.] —**genitally** *adv*

genital herpes *n* a sexually transmitted disease caused by the herpes simplex virus and affecting the genital and anal regions with painful blisters

genitals /jénnit'lz/, **genitalia** /-táyli ə/ *npl* the reproductive organs, especially the external sex organs

genital wart *n* a wart of the genital or anal area caused by a sexually transmitted virus

genitive /jénnətiv/ *n* **1** a grammatical form (**case**) in some inflected languages that affects nouns, pronouns, and adjectives and that usually indicates possession **2** a word or phrase in the genitive [14C. Directly or via French < Latin *genitivus* < *gignere* 'beget'.] —**genitive** *adj*

genitor /jénnitər/ *n* a natural or biological father (*technical*) ◊ **genetrix** [15C. Directly or via French < Latin, < *gignere* 'beget'.]

genitourinary /jénnitō yoórinəri/ *adj* relating to or affecting the genital and urinary organs

geniture /jénnichər/ *n* somebody's birth (*archaic*) [Mid-16C. Directly or via French < Latin *genitura* < *gignere* 'beget'.]

genius /jeéni əss/ *n* **1** SOMEBODY WITH OUTSTANDING TALENT somebody with exceptional ability, especially somebody whose intellectual or creative achievements gain worldwide recognition **2** OUTSTANDING TALENT exceptional talent of a particular kind **3** SOMEBODY WITH PARTICULAR SKILL a person with great specialized skill ○ *a genius with computers* **4** (*plural* **genii**) QUALITY a special quality that characterizes a place, period, or people **5** (*plural* **genii**) GUARDIAN SPIRIT in Roman mythology, a guardian spirit of a person, place, or institution **6** (*plural* **genii**) DEMON a supposed demon or supernatural being **7** INFLUENCE somebody or something that exerts a strong influence ○ *an evil genius* [14C. < Latin, 'guardian spirit' < *gignere* 'beget'.]

SYNONYMS See ***talent***.

genius loci /-lō sī/ *n* **1** the atmosphere that characterizes a place **2** the guardian spirit of a place [< Latin, 'spirit of the place']

genizah /ge neézə/ (*plural* **-zoth**) *n* a repository for Hebrew documents and sacred books that are no longer in use, e.g. because they are old and worn, but must not be destroyed [Late 19C. < Hebrew, 'hiding place' < *gānaz* 'hide'.]

genned-up /jénd-/ *adj* having acquired the necessary knowledge or information about somebody or something (*informal*)

genoa /jénnō ə, jə nó ə/, **genoa jib** *n* a particularly large triangular front sail on a sailing boat, especially a racing yacht [Mid-20C. After GENOA.]

Genoa /jénnō ə/ city in NW Italy, on the Gulf of Genoa, an inlet of the Ligurian Sea. Population: 659,754 (1993). —**Genoese** /jénnō eéz/ *n, adj*

genocide /jénnə sīd/ *n* the systematic killing of all the people from a national, ethnic, or religious group, or an attempt to do this [Mid-20C. < Greek *genos* 'race'.] —**genocidal** /jénnə sīd'l/ *adj* —**genocidally** *adv*

genome /jeé nōm/ *n* the full complement of genetic information that an individual organism inherits from its parents, especially the set of chromosomes and the genes they carry [Mid-20C. < Greek *genos* 'offspring, race' + CHROMOSOME.] —**genomic** /ji nómik/ *adj*

genomics /ji nómiks/ *n* the identification and study of gene sequences in the DNA of organisms (+ *singular verb*)

genotype /jénnə tīp/ *n* **1** the genetic makeup of an organism, as opposed to its physical characteristics (**phenotype**) **2** a group of organisms that share a similar genetic makeup [Early 20C. < German *Genotypus* < Greek *genos* 'offspring, race' + Latin *typus* (see TYPE).] —**genotypic** /jénnə típpik/ *adj* —**genotypically** *adv*

-genous *suffix* a suffix that forms adjectives from nouns ending in -gen and -geny

genre /zhónrə, zhóNrə/ *n* **1** one of the categories that artistic works of all kinds can be divided into on the basis of form, style, or subject matter **2** painting depicting household scenes [Early 19C. Via French, 'type' < Latin *genus* 'birth, kind'.]

SYNONYMS See ***type***.

genro /gén ró/ (*plural* **-ro**) *n* **1** in Japan in the 19th and early 20th centuries, a group of elder statesmen who advised the emperor (+ *singular or plural verb*) **2** a member of the genro advising the Japanese emperor [Late 19C. < Japanese, 'first elders'.]

gens /jenz/ (*plural* **gentes** /jén teez/) *n* **1** in ancient Rome, a group of aristocratic families with the same name, descended from a common ancestor on the male side (+ *singular or plural verb*) **2** a clan, especially one that traces its descent on the male side (*dated*) [Mid-19C. < Latin, 'race, clan'.]

gent /jent/ *n* a gentleman (*dated informal*)

gentamicin /jéntə míssin/ *n* a broad-spectrum antibiotic, usually administered by injection [Mid-20C. < *genta-* < ? + alteration of -MYCIN.]

genteel /jen teél/ *adj* **1** having or displaying refinement and good manners, especially manners that suggest, or are thought typical of, an upper-class background **2** overdoing the refinement, delicacy of behaviour, or snobbishness thought typical of the upper classes in order to create an impression of higher social status [Late 16C. < French *gentil* (see GENTLE).] —**genteelly** *adv* —**genteelness** *n*

genteelism /jen teélizəm/ *n* a word or phrase used in place of another one considered vulgar

gentes plural of **gens**

gentian /jénsh'n/ *n* **1** the dried roots and rhizome of a yellow-flowered plant. Use: digestive stimulant in herbal medicine. **2** a plant that belongs to either of two genera, one alpine and arctic, the other temperate. Flowers: bright blue, yellow, white, red, trumpet-shaped. Genera: *Gentiana* and *Gentianella*. [14C. < Latin *gentiana*, after *Gentius*, 2C BC king of Illyria.]

gentian blue *adj* of a purplish-blue colour —**gentian blue** *n*

gentian violet *n* a green dye derived from rosaniline that forms a violet solution in water. Use: as a biological stain, formerly, in antiseptic lotions.

gentile /jént īl/ *n* **1** NON-JEWISH PERSON a person who is not Jewish **2** SOMEBODY CHRISTIAN a Christian, as distinguished from a Jewish person **3** NON-MORMON in the Church of Jesus Christ of Latter-Day Saints, somebody who is not a member of this Church **4** HEATHEN a disbeliever in God (*disapproving*) ■ *adj* **1 NOT JEWISH** not belonging to the Jewish people or faith **2 CHRISTIAN** Christian, as distinguished from Jewish **3 DENOTING PLACE OR PEOPLE** describes a noun such as 'Welsh' or 'Texan' that gives the name of a place or a people [14C. < Latin *gentilis* 'of the same clan' (see GENTLE).]

Gentileschi /jénta léski/, **Artemisia** (1593?–1651) Italian painter

gentility /jen tíllati/ *n* **1 REFINEMENT** courteous and well-mannered behaviour, especially when it suggests an upper-class background **2 UPPER-CLASS STATUS** the status or way of life of somebody from the upper classes **3 PRETENTIOUSNESS** exaggeratedly refined, delicate, or snobbish behaviour, affected in order to create an impression of higher social status **4 MEMBERS OF THE UPPER CLASS** people from the upper classes (*+ singular or plural verb*) [14C. < French *gentilité* < *gentil* (see GENTLE).]

gentle /jént'l/ *adj* (**-tler, -tlest**) **1 KIND** having a mild and kind nature or manner **2 MILD** being moderate in force or degree so that the effects are not severe ○ *a gentle reprimand* **3 USING LITTLE FORCE** using little force or violence ○ *a gentle tap on the shoulder* **4 NOT STEEP** not very steep ○ *a gentle slope* **5 CHIVALROUS** having a gracious and honourable manner (*archaic*) **6 UPPER-CLASS** relating to or having a high social status or class ■ *vt* (**-tles, -tling, -tled**) **1 SOOTHE** to cause somebody to become less agitated by means of words or actions (*literary*) **2 TAME** to calm an animal and make it domesticated (*formal*) [Pre-12C. Via French *gentil* 'well-born' < Latin *gentilis* 'of the same clan' < *gens* 'race, clan'.] —**gentleness** *n* —**gently** *adv*

gentle breeze *n* a wind with a speed of between 13 and 19 km/8 and 12 mi. per hour

gentlefolk /jént'l fōk/, **gentlefolks** *npl* upper-class people (*archaic*)

gentleman /jént'lmən/ (*plural* **-men** /-mən/) *n* **1 POLITE AND CULTURED MAN** a cultured man who behaves with courtesy and thoughtfulness **2 MAN** used as a polite term to refer to a man, regardless of social position or behaviour ○ *Good morning, ladies and gentlemen.* **3 UPPER-CLASS MAN** a man from a high social class, especially a man with an independent income **4 MAN WITH A COAT OF ARMS** in

MAIN DIVISIONS OF GEOLOGICAL TIME

Million years ago	Division			Significant events
4,500+	pre-Archaean Aeon			formation of the Earth
3,800	Archaean Aeon			formation of land masses, oceans, atmosphere; first single-celled organisms, blue-green algae
2,500	Proterozoic Aeon			formation of mountains, glaciers, ozone layer; first invertebrates
570	Phanerozoic Aeon			
		Palaeozoic Era		
			Cambrian Period	formation of southern continent Gondwanaland; first shellfish, sponges
500			Ordovician Period	N America collides with Europe; primitive fish in shallow seas
435			Silurian Period	Europe separates from N America; first coral, land plants, insects
410			Devonian Period	Europe, Asia, Gondwanaland, America collide; first amphibians
360			Carboniferous Period	formation of coal, oil, gas deposits; first reptiles
290			Permian Period	continents combine to form Pangaea; first conifers, mass extinction of invertebrates
240		Mesozoic Era		
			Triassic Period	Pangaea breaks up; first dinosaurs, evergreen forests
205			Jurassic Period	N and S America move west; first mammals, birds
138			Cretaceous Period	Africa and India drift north; extinction of dinosaurs
65		Cenozoic Era		
			Tertiary Period	
			Paleocene Epoch	Antarctica and Australia split; first marsupials, hoofed mammals
55			Eocene Epoch	India joins Asia; first primates, bats, sea mammals
38			Oligocene Epoch	formation of Alps and Himalayas; first elephants, monkeys, great apes
24			Miocene Epoch	formation of Antarctic ice sheet, northern prairies; first humanlike apes
5			Pliocene Epoch	formation of Sierra Nevada range; primate ancestors of *Homo sapiens*
1.6		Quaternary Period		
			Pleistocene Epoch	ice ages; mammoths, sabre-toothed tigers, early humans
0.01			Holocene Epoch	melting ice sheets; extinctions caused by human activity, global warming

English history, a man who was not strictly of noble birth but was entitled to a coat of arms **—gentlemanliness** *n* **—gentlemanly** *adj*

gentleman-at-arms *n* a member of a troop of forty men who act as a ceremonial guard for the British sovereign on state occasions

gentleman-farmer *n* **1** a farmer with an independent source of income who farms for pleasure rather than for money **2** a man who owns a farm but employs a manager and staff to work it

gentleman's agreement, gentlemen's agreement *n* an agreement based on trust, not written down, and not enforceable by law

gentleman's gentleman *n* the manservant of an upper-class man (*dated*)

gentlemen's agreement = gentleman's agreement

gentlewoman /jént'l wŏŏmən/ (*plural* **-en** /-wimin/) *n* **1 POLITE AND CULTURED WOMAN** a polite and cultured woman who behaves with courtesy and thoughtfulness **2 UPPER-CLASS WOMAN** a woman from a high social class, especially a woman with an independent income **3 LADY'S PERSONAL ATTENDANT** a woman acting as a personal attendant to a lady of high social rank

gentoo /jén too/ (*plural* **-toos**) *n* a penguin with a distinctive white patch above each eye. Native to: Antarctic. *Pygoscelis papua.* [Mid-19C. < ?]

gentrify /jéntri fi/ (**-fies, -fying, -fied**) *vt* to transform a traditionally working-class area into a middle-class neighbourhood, usually at the expense of local character and with the result that property becomes unaffordable for local people **—gentrification** /jéntrifi káysh'n/ *n*

gentry /jéntri/ *n* **1 THE UPPER CLASSES** the group of people who make up the upper social classes (*takes a singular or plural verb*) **2 ENGLISH SOCIAL CLASS** the English social class that ranks just below the aristocracy and consists of families who are not of noble birth but are entitled to have a coat of arms (*takes a singular or plural verb*) **3 PEOPLE** people of a particular kind [14C. < Old French *genterie* 'nobility' < *gentil* (see GENTLE).]

gents /jents/ *n* a public toilet for men. US term **men's room**

genuflect /jénnyŏŏ flekt/ *vi* **1** to bend the right knee to the floor and rise again as a gesture of religious respect, particularly in a Roman Catholic or Anglican church **2** to show undeserved or unnecessarily deferential respect for somebody or something [Mid-19C. < ecclesiastical Latin *genuflectere* 'bend the knee' < Latin *genu* 'knee' + *flectere* 'bend'.] **—genuflection** /jénnyŏŏ fléksh'n/ *n* **—genuflector** *n*

genuine /jénnyoo in/ *adj* **1 REAL** having the qualities or value claimed ○ *a genuine Cézanne* **2 SINCERELY FELT** not affected or pretended ○ *a look of genuine surprise* **3 CANDID** honest and open in relationships with others ○ *a very genuine person* **4 OF UNMIXED BREEDING** being of unmixed breeding ○ *of genuine stock* [Late 16C. < Latin *genuinus*.] **—genuinely** *adv* **—genuineness** *n*

genus /jéenəs, jénn-/ (*plural* **genera** /jénnərə/) *n* **1 SET OF CLOSELY RELATED SPECIES** a category in the taxonomic classification of related organisms, comprising one or more species **2 BROADER TERM FOR** the more general class or kind in which something is included, e.g. the species 'dog' is included in the genus 'animal' **3 GROUP** a class or group of any kind [Mid-16C. < Latin, 'birth, race, kind'.]

geo- *prefix* **1** earth, soil ○ *geomagnetic* ○ *geophyte* **2** geography, global ○ *geostrategy* [< Greek *gē* 'Earth']

geobotany /jeè ō bóttəni/ *n* PLANT SCI = **phytogeography** **—geobotanical** /jeè ō bə tánnik'l/ *adj* **—geobotanist** *n*

geocentric /jeè ō séntrik/ *adj* **1 HAVING EARTH AT ITS CENTRE** describes the solar system when it is regarded as having the Earth as its centre **2 CONSIDERED FROM EARTH'S CENTRE** measured from, or considered as if viewed from, the centre of the Earth **3 WITH EARTH AS THE CENTRE OF FOCUS** having the Earth and its inhabitants as the centre of a theory or belief **—geocentrically** *adv*

geochemistry /jeè ō kémmistri/ *n* the study of the chemical composition of the Earth's solid matter, as well as the solid matter of other planets, meteors, and asteroids **—geochemical** *adj* **—geochemically** *adv* **—geochemist** *n*

geochronology /jeè ō krə nóllaji/ *n* the study of the ages and relative ages of geological events and rock formations **—geochronological** /jeè ō krónnə lójjik'l/ *adj* **—geochronologically** *adv* **—geochronologist** *n*

geochronometry /jeè ō krə nómmətri/ *n* the measurement of the age of a rock, mineral, or sequence of rocks, or of an event such as a volcanic eruption **—geochronometric** /jeè ō krónnə méttrik/ *adj*

geocorona /jeè ō kə rōnə/ *n* the outermost region of the Earth's atmosphere reaching to approximately 15 Earth radii in height and consisting mainly of hydrogen

geode /jeè ōd/ *n* **1** a roughly spherical rock mass containing a cavity lined or filled with crystals that have grown unimpeded and so are frequently perfectly formed **2** the crystal-lined cavity within a geode [Late 17C. Via Latin *geodes* < Greek *geōdēs* 'earthy' < *gē* 'Earth'.]

geodesic /jeè ō deéssik/ *adj* **1** relating to the geometry of curved surfaces **2** GEOG = **geodetic** ■ *n* the shortest line between two points on a curved or flat surface **—geodesist** *n*

geodesic dome *n* a dome that has many flat straight-sided faces formed by a framework of bars that intersect to form equilateral triangles or polygons

geodesic line *n* GEOM = **geodesic** *n.*

geodesy /jeè óddəssi/ *n* the branch of science that deals with the precise measurement of the size and shape of the Earth, the mapping of points on its surface, and the study of its gravitational field [Late 16C. Via modern Latin < Greek *geōdaisia* < *daiein* 'divide'.] **—geodesist** *n*

geodetic /jeè ō déttik/, **geodetical** /-déttik'l/ *adj* relating to the precise measurement of the Earth's surface or of points on its surface [Late 17C. < Greek *geōdaitēs* 'land surveyor' < *daiein* 'divide'.] **—geodetically** *adv*

geodetic survey *n* a survey of a very large area of land, with the curvature of the Earth's surface taken into account

geoduck /goò i duk/, **gweduc** *n* **1** a very large clam. Native to: NW Pacific coast of N America. *Panope generosa.* **2** the flesh of a geoduck used as food [Late 19C. < a Salishan language.]

geoeconomics /jeè ō eèkə nómmiks, -ékə-/ *n* the study of how the economies of the world's nations relate to and affect one another (*+ singular verb*) **—geoeconomic** *adj* **—geoeconomically** *adv* **—geoeconomist** /jeè ō i kónnəmist/ *n*

geog. *abbr* **1** geographic **2** geographical **3** geography

geographical /jeè əgráffik'l/, **geographic** /-gráffik/ *adj* relating to geography or to the geography of a specific region [Mid-16C. < French *géographique* or late Latin *geographicus* < Greek *geōgraphikos* < *geōgraphos* 'writer about the Earth'.] **—geographically** *adv*

geographical mile *n* MEASURE = **nautical mile** *n.* **2**

geography /ji óggrəfi/ (*plural* **-phies**) *n* **1 STUDY OF EARTH'S PHYSICAL FEATURES** the study of all the physical features of the Earth's surface, including its climate and the distribution of plant, animal, and human life **2 PHYSICAL FEATURES** the physical features of a place or region, e.g. mountains and rivers **3 LAYOUT OF A PLACE** the arrangement of the different parts of a building, city, or other place **4 ARRANGEMENT** the way that something is arranged and the relationships between its different parts ○ *the geography of the criminal mind* [15C. Via Latin < Greek *geōgraphia* 'writing about the Earth'.] **—geographer** *n*

geohazard /jeè ō hazərd/ *n* a natural phenomenon such as an earthquake, volcanic eruption, drought, or soil erosion that threatens human populations [GEO- + HAZARD]

geohydrology /jeè ō hī dróllaji/ *n* GEOL = **hydrogeology** **—geohydrologic** /jeè ō hīdrə lójjik/ *adj* **—geohydrologist** *n*

geoid /jeè oyd/ *n* **1** the slightly flattened sphere that is the shape of the Earth, used in calculating the precise measurements of points on the Earth's surface **2** a hypothetical surface of the Earth that would exist if a cross section were taken at sea level [Late 19C. < Greek *geoeidēs* (see GEODE).] **—geoidal** *adj*

geol. *abbr* **1** geologic **2** geological **3** geology

geological time *n* the period of time that extends from the beginning of the world to the present day

geology /ji óllaji/ *n* **1** the study of the structure of the Earth or another planet, in particular its rocks, soil, and minerals, and its history and origins **2** the rocks, minerals, and physical structure of a particular area [Mid-18C. < modern Latin *geologia* 'description of the Earth'.] **—geologic** /jeè ə lójjik/ *adj* **—geological** *adj* **—geologically** *adv* **—geologist** /jee óllajist/ *n*

geom. *abbr* **1** geometric **2** geometrical **3** geometry

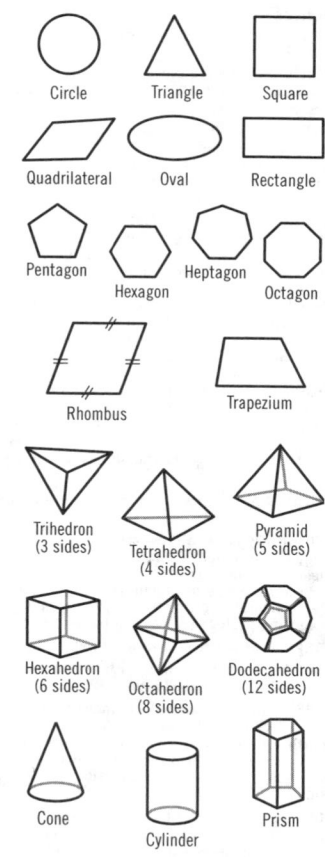

Circle   Triangle   Square

Quadrilateral   Oval   Rectangle

Pentagon   Heptagon
   Hexagon   Octagon

Rhombus   Trapezium

Trihedron (3 sides)   Tetrahedron (4 sides)   Pyramid (5 sides)

Hexahedron (6 sides)   Octahedron (8 sides)   Dodecahedron (12 sides)

Cone   Cylinder   Prism

Geometry: Shapes and solids

geomagnetic pole *n* GEOG = **magnetic pole** *n.* **2**

geomagnetic storm *n* METEOROL = **magnetic storm**

geomagnetism /jeè ō mágnətizəm/ *n* **1** the magnetic properties of the Earth **2** the study of the magnetic properties of the Earth **—geomagnetic** /jeè ō mag néttik/ *adj* **—geomagnetically** *adv*

geomancy /jeè ō manssi/ *n* the art or practice of making predictions based on patterns made by a handful of earth thrown on the ground or by lines connecting randomly placed dots [14C. Via medieval Latin < Greek *geōmanteia* 'divination from the Earth' < *manteia* 'divination'.] **—geomancer** *n* **—geomantic** *adj*

geometer /ji ómmitər/ *n* a student of or an expert in geometry [15C. Via late Latin < Greek *geōmetrēs* 'land measurer' < *gē* 'Earth' + *metrēs* 'measurer'.]

geometric /jeè ə métrik/, **geometrical** /-métrik'l/ *adj* **1 RELATING TO GEOMETRY** conforming to the laws and methods of geometry **2 USING SIMPLE LINES** using straight lines and simple shapes, e.g. circles or squares **3 INCREASING FAST** increasing or decreasing very rapidly ○ *geometric growth* [Mid-17C. Via French *géométrique* < Greek *geōmetrikos* < *geōmetrēs* (see GEOMETER).] **—geometrically** *adv*

Geometric *adj* relating to a period of ancient Greek culture, between 900 and 700 BC, noted for its decorative use of simple lines and shapes, especially on pottery

geometric mean *n* the average of a set of *n* values, described mathematically as the *n*th root of their product

geometric progression *n* a series of numbers in which each number is separated by the same numerical step

geometrics /jèe ə métriks/ *npl* straight lines and simple shapes, e.g. circles or squares, used in design and decoration (+ *singular verb*)

geometric series *n* a series of numbers (**geometric progression**) separated by a constant numerical step expressed as a sum, e.g. 1+4+16+64

geometrid /ji ómmətrid/ *n* a moth with a slender body and broad wings and larvae that crawl with a characteristic looping movement. Family: Geometridae. [Late 19C. < modern Latin *Geometridae* 'land measurers'.] —**geometrid** *adj*

geometrize /ji ómmə trīz/ (**-trizes, -trizing, -trized**), **geometrise** (**-trises, -trising, -trised**) *v* **1** *vt* to represent something in geometric form **2** *vti* to apply the principles of geometry to something —**geometrization** /ji ómmə trī záysh'n/ *n*

geometry /ji ómmətri/ *n* **1** MATHEMATICS OF SHAPES the branch of mathematics that is concerned with the properties and relationships of points, lines, angles, curves, surfaces, and solids **2** KIND OF GEOMETRY any subclass of geometry, e.g. a set of distinct theories or its application to a particular type of problem or object **3** ARRANGEMENT OF the way the different parts of something fit together in relation to each other [14C. Via French *géométrie* < Greek *geōmetria* 'measuring of the Earth' < *gē* 'Earth' + *metron* 'measure'.] —**geometrician** /jèe əme trísh'n, jee ómmə-/ *n*

geomorphic /jèe ō máwrfik/ *adj* relating to the surface features of the Earth or another planet

geomorphology /jèe ō mawr fólləji/ *n* the branch of geology that examines the formation and structure of the features of the surface of the Earth or of another planet's surface —**geomorphologic** /jèe ō mawrfə lójjik/ *adj* —**geomorphological** *adj* —**geomorphologically** *adv* —**geomorphologist** /jèe ō mawr fólləjist/ *n*

geophagy /ji óffəji/ *n* the eating of soil, clay, or chalk

geophone /jèe ə fōn/ *n* an electronic instrument that picks up vibrations in the Earth

geophysics /jèe ō fízziks/ *n* the branch of earth science that deals with the physics and physical processes of the Earth, especially using noninvasive techniques, e.g. acoustic surveys of the structure of rocks (+ *singular verb*) —**geophysical** *adj* —**geophysically** *adv* —**geophysicist** *n*

geopolitics /jèe ō póllətiks/ *n* the study of the relationship between a country's politics and its geography and population distribution, or of the effect that geography and population distribution have on political relations between countries (+ *singular verb*) ■ *npl* the relationships that exist between a country's politics and its geography or the influences that geography has on political relations between countries (+ *singular verb*) [Early 20C. Blend of GEOGRAPHY + POLITICS.] —**geopolitical** /jèe ō pə líttik'l/ *adj* —**geopolitically** *adv* —**geopolitician** /jèe ō póllə tísh'n/ *n*

geoponics /jèe ō pónniks/ *n* the scientific study of agriculture (+ *singular verb*) —**geoponic** *adj*

Geordie /jáwrdi/ *n* **1** somebody who comes from Tyneside, especially somebody who speaks the local dialect of English **2** the dialect of English spoken in Tyneside [Mid-19C. < local pronunciation of *Georgie*, diminutive of the name *George*.] —**Geordie** *adj*

George I /jawrj/ (1660–1727) king of Great Britain and Ireland (1714–27)

George II (1683–1760) king of Great Britain and Ireland (1727–60)

George III (1738–1820) king of the United Kingdom (1760–1820)

George IV (1762–1830) king of the United Kingdom (1820–30)

George V (1865–1936) king of the United Kingdom (1910–36)

George VI /jáwrj/ (1895–1952) king of the United Kingdom (1936–52)

George, Lake lake in E New York State, in the foothills of the Adirondack Mountains. Area: 114 sq. km/44 sq. mi.

George Cross *n* a British medal awarded, especially to civilians, for gallantry

Georgetown /jáwrj town/ district of NW Washington, D.C.

George Town /jáwrj town/ **1** capital of the Cayman Islands, Caribbean, on Grand Cayman Island. Population: 12,000 (1988). **2** town in N Tasmania, Australia. Population: 6,929 (1996). **3** city of W Malaysia, on Penang Island. Population: 219,380 (1991).

Georgia /jáwrjə/ **1** state in the SE United States. Capital: Atlanta. Population: 7,486,242 (1997). Area: 152,750 sq. km/58,977 sq. mi. **2** republic in S Caucasia, on the eastern coast of the Black Sea. Capital: Tbilisi. Population: 5,160,042 (1997). Area: 69,700 sq. km/26,900 sq. mi.

Georgian[1] /jáwrjən/ *adj* **1** OF 1714 TO 1830 IN BRITAIN relating to the time of the British kings George I, II, III, and IV, who reigned consecutively from 1714 to 1830 **2** OF 18C ARCHITECTURAL STYLE built in or imitating a style of architecture or furniture that flourished in Great Britain and the United States in the 18th and early 19th centuries **3** OF 20C LITERARY MOVEMENT relating to a movement in early 20th-century poetry that favoured traditional styles ■ *n* **1** SOMEBODY FROM GEORGIAN TIMES a person who lived during the Georgian period **2** GEORGIAN WRITER a writer whose works belong to the Georgian literary movement

Georgian[2] /jáwrjən/ *n* **1** LANGUAGE OF GEORGIA the official language of the Republic of Georgia, belonging to Kartvelian. Native speakers: 3.5 million. **2** SOMEBODY FROM GEORGIA somebody who comes from the Republic of Georgia **3** SOMEBODY FROM US STATE OF GEORGIA somebody who comes from the state of Georgia in the United States [15C. < *Georgia*, region (now republic) in the Caucasus or state of the United States.] —**Georgian** *adj*

Georgian Bay /jáwrjən-/ northeastern arm of Lake Huron, in SE Ontario, Canada. Area: 15,000 sq. km/5,800 sq. mi.

georgic /jáwrjik/ *adj* relating to or depicting rural life (*literary*) ■ *n* a poem about rural life [Early 16C. Via Latin < Greek *geōrgikos* < *geōrgos* 'farmer' < *gē* 'Earth'.]

geosphere /jèe ō sfeer/ *n* the solid matter of the Earth, as distinct from the seas, plants, animals, and surrounding atmosphere —**geospheric** /jèe ō sférrik/ *adj*

geostationary /jèe ō stáysh'nəri/ *adj* describes the orbit of satellite that circles the Earth above the equator at a speed matching the Earth's rotation, thus appearing to remain stationary, or the satellite itself

geostrategy /jèe ō stráttəji/ (*plural* **-gies**) *n* **1** the study of strategy in relation to the geopolitical situation of a country or region **2** the policy of a nation based on a combination of geographical and political factors —**geostrategic** /-strə tèejik/ *adj* —**geostrategist** *n*

geostrophic /jèe ō stróffik/ *adj* arising from the rotation of the Earth —**geostrophically** *adv*

geosynchronous /jèe ō síng krənəss/ *adj* AEROSP = **geostationary**

geosyncline /jèe ō síng klīn/ *n* a long broad depression in the Earth's crust where it has sunk over time as it has accumulated a thick layer of sedimentary deposits —**geosynclinal** /jèe ō sing klīn'l/ *adj*

geotaxis /jèe ō táksiss/ *n* movement by an organism or cell in response to the force of gravity —**geotactic** *adj* —**geotactically** *adv*

geotectonic /jèe ō tek tónnik/ *adj* relating to the large-scale structure of the Earth's crust —**geotectonically** *adv*

geothermal /jèe ō thúrm'l/, **geothermic** *adj* relating to or produced by the heat in the interior of the Earth —**geothermally** *adv*

geothermal energy *n* energy in the form of heat obtained from hot circulating ground water

geothermal gradient *n* the change in temperature encountered with depth within the Earth

geotropism /jee óttrəpizəm/ *n* plant growth or movement in response to gravity —**geotropic** /jèe ō tróppik/ *adj* —**geotropically** *adv*

Geraldton /jérrəldtən/ port in Western Australia, on Champion Bay. Population: 24,377 (1991).

geraniol /ji ráyni ol/ *n* $C_{10}H_{18}O$ a pale yellow or colourless alcohol that smells like geraniums. Source: essential oils. Use: in perfumes, flavourings. [Late 19C. < GERANIUM.]

geranium /jə ráyni əm/ *n* **1** PLANT WITH BRIGHTLY COLOURED FLOWERS a popular garden plant with large rounded leaves. Flowers: bright red, pink, white, on tall stalks. Genus: *Pelargonium*. (*not technical*) **2** PLANT WITH SAUCER-SHAPED FLOWERS a plant with divided leaves, e.g. cranesbill and herb Robert. Flowers: pink, blue, white, red, saucer-shaped. Genus: *Geranium*. **3** BRIGHT RED COLOUR a red colour tinged with orange, like that of a scarlet geranium [Mid-16C. Via Latin < Greek *geranion* < *geranos* 'crane'; from the resemblance of the spur on some species' fruit to a crane's bill.] —**geranium** *adj*

gerbil /júrb'l/ *n* a small rodent resembling a mouse with long back legs. Native to: hot dry parts of Africa and Asia. [Mid-19C. Via French *gerbille* < modern Latin *gerbillus*, diminutive of *gerboa* (see JERBOA).]

gerenuk /gérrinòok/ (*plural* **-nuks** *or* **-nuk**) *n* a slender East African antelope, the male of which has long horns that curve backwards. *Litocranius walleri*. [Late 19C. < Somali.]

gerfalcon /jur fáwlkən/ *n* BIRDS = **gyrfalcon**

geriatric /jérri áttrik/ *adj* **1** RELATING TO ELDERLY PEOPLE relating to the diagnosis, treatment, and prevention of illness in elderly people **2** OFFENSIVE TERM an offensive term meaning showing the effects of age ■ *n* ELDERLY PERSON an elderly person, in a medical context (*technical*) [Early 20C. < Greek *gēras* 'old age'.]

geriatrics /jérri áttriks/ *n* the branch of medicine that deals with the illnesses and medical care of elderly people (+ *singular verb*) ◊ **gerontology** —**geriatrician** /jérri ə trísh'n/ *n*

Géricault /zhaáyrikō/, **Théodore** (1791–1824) French painter

germ /jurm/ *n* **1** MICROORGANISM a microorganism, especially one that can cause disease **2** CELL the smallest element in an organism, e.g. a spore or a fertilized egg, that is capable of growing into a complete adult or part **3** BEGINNING the first sign of something that will develop ○ *the germ of an idea* [Mid-15C. Via French *germe* < Latin *germen* 'seed, sprout' < *gignere* 'beget'.]

german /júrmən/ *adj* having the same parents, or closely related ○ *brothers-german* [Via French *germain* < Latin *germanus* 'having the same parents' < *germen* (see GERM)]

German /júrmən/ *n* **1** SOMEBODY FROM GERMANY somebody who comes from Germany **2** LANGUAGE OF GERMANY the official language of Germany, Austria, and Liechtenstein and one of the official languages of Switzerland, also spoken elsewhere in the world, belonging to the Germanic branch of Indo-European. Native speakers: 100 million. Other speakers: 100 million. **3** SOMEBODY WHO SPEAKS GERMAN somebody whose first language is German [14C. < Latin *Germanus*, applied to a group of related peoples of northern and central Europe.] —**German** *adj*

germanate /júrmə nayt/ *n* a salt containing an anionic grouping of germanium and oxygen

German cockroach *n* a small brown cockroach that is a common pest throughout the world. *Blattella germanica*.

germander /jur mándər/ (*plural* **-ders** *or* **-der**) *n* a typically aromatic plant. Flowers: small, pink, white, or pale purple, with a small upper lip. Genus: *Teucrium*. [15C. Via medieval Latin *germandr(e)a* < Greek *khamaidrus* 'ground oak'.]

germane /jur máyn/ *adj* suitably related to something, especially something being discussed [Early 17C. Variant of GERMAN.] —**germanely** *adv* —**germaneness** *n*

German East Africa former German territory in East Africa, comprising present-day Burundi, Rwanda, and mainland Tanzania

Germanic /jur mánnik/ *n* EUROPEAN LANGUAGE GROUP a group of languages spoken across NW Europe that forms a branch of Indo-European. Native speakers: 500 million people. ■ *adj* **1** OF GERMANIC relating to the group of languages classified as Germanic **2** OF GERMANY relating to Germany, or its language, people, or culture [Mid-17C. < Latin *Germanicus* < *Germanus* (see GERMAN).]

germanise *vti* = **germanize**

Germanism /júrmənizəm/ *n* **1** GERMAN WORD a word or phrase borrowed or adapted from the German language **2** GERMAN QUALITY a custom or trait associated with German culture or people **3** LIKING FOR GERMANY fondness for Germany and all things German

Germanist /júrmənist/ *n* a student of or specialist in German language, literature, and culture

germanium /jur máyni əm/ *n* (*symbol* **Ge**) a brittle grey crystalline element that is a metalloid. Source: coal, zinc ore. Use: semiconductors, alloys. [Late 19C. < Latin *Germanus* (see GERMAN).]

germanize /júrmə nīz/ (**-izes, -izing, -ized**), **germanise** (**-ises, -ising, -ised**) *vti* to adopt German styles, tastes, institutions, or customs, or introduce them into something —**germanization** /júrmə nī záysh'n/ n

German measles n a highly contagious viral disease that causes swelling of the lymph glands and a reddish-pink rash on the skin. It affects children particularly. US term **rubella**

Germanophile /jur mánnə fīl/ n an admirer of Germany and the German people

Germanophobe /jur mánnə fōb/ n a hater of Germany or the German people

German shepherd n DOGS = **Alsatian** n. 1

German silver n METALL = **nickel silver**

Germany

Germany /júrməni/ federal republic in central Europe. Capital: Berlin. Population: 82,071,765 (1997). Area: 356,970 sq. km/137,827 sq. mi.

germ cell n BIOL = **germ** n. 2

germicide /júrmi sīd/ n a preparation that kills germs —**germicidal** /júrmi sīd'l/ adj

germinal /júrmin'l/ adj 1 relating to reproductive cells 2 relating to or belonging to the earliest stage in the development of something (formal) [Early 19C. < Latin germen (see GERM).] —**germinally** adv

germinal disc = **blastodisc**

germinal vesicle n the enlarged nucleus of an egg before it develops into an ovum

germinate /júrmi nayt/ (**-nates, -nating, -nated**) v 1 vti to start to grow from a seed or spore into a new individual 2 vi to be created and start to develop [Late 16C. < Latin germinat-, past participle of germinare < germen (see GERM).] —**germination** /júrmi náysh'n/ n —**germinative** adj —**germinator** n

Germiston /júrmistən/ city in NE South Africa. Population: 134,005 (1991).

germ layer n any of the three distinct layers of cells formed during an embryo's early stages of development (**gastrulation**)

germ line n a group of cells in a developing embryo from which reproductive cells (**gametes**) develop, regarded as the line of descent from one generation to another

germplasm n the hereditary material that is transmitted from one generation to another

germ theory n 1 the theory that all infectious and contagious diseases are caused by microorganisms 2 the theory that organisms develop from previous generations through the growth of germ cells

germ warfare n MIL = **biological warfare**

germy /júrmi/ (**-ier, -iest**) adj full of harmful microorganisms (informal) —**germiness** n

gerodontics /jérrō dóntiks/ n the branch of dentistry focusing on the needs of elderly people (+ singular verb) [Late 20C. < Greek gēras 'old age'.] —**gerodontic** adj

Gerona /jə rốnə/ city in NE Spain. Population: 71,858 (1998 estimate).

Geronimo

Geronimo /jə rónnimō/ (1829–1909) US Chiricahua Apache leader. Born **Goyathlay**

geront-, geronto- prefix ageing, old age ○ gerontology [Via French < Greek geront-, stem of gerōn 'old man']

gerontocracy /jérron tókrəssi/ (plural **-cies**) n 1 a system of government in which the elders are chosen as rulers 2 a group of elders who make up a government (+ singular or plural verb) —**gerontocrat** /jə róntə krat/ n —**gerontocratic** /jə róntə kráttik/ adj

gerontology /jérron tólləji/ n the scientific study of ageing and its effects. ◊ **geriatrics** —**gerontologic** /jə róntə lójjik/ adj —**gerontological** adj —**gerontologist** /jérron tólləjist/ n

Gerry /gérri/, **Elbridge** (1744–1814) US statesman and vice president of the United States (1813–14)

gerrymander /jérri mandər/ vti to manipulate an electoral area, usually by altering its boundaries, in order to gain an unfair political advantage in an election ■ n an unfair manipulation of an electoral area for political advantage [Early 19C. Blend of Elbridge GERRY + SALAMANDER, from the shape of an electoral district he created to favour his own party.]

Gershwin /gúrshwin/, **George** (1898–1937) US composer. Born **Jacob Gershvin**

Gershwin, **Ira** (1896–1983) US lyricist and dramatist. Born **Israel Gershvin**

gerund /jérrənd/ n 1 a noun formed from a verb, describing an action, state, or process. In English, it is formed from the verb's -ing form, as 'smoking' is in the phrase 'No smoking'. 2 a Latin noun ending in '-ndum', formed from a verb and describing an action, state, or process [Early 16C. < late Latin gerundium < Latin gerere 'carry on'.] —**gerundial** /jə rúndi əl/ adj

USAGE Gerunds or participles: possessives or not? Should you write *I was surprised to hear of him refusing* or *I was surprised to hear of his refusing*? If you use the first option, you regard the *-ing* word *refusing* as a participle (a part of an active verb construction that functions as an adjective modifying *him*). If you choose the second option, you regard the *-ing* word *refusing* as a gerund (a verbal noun). Here, *refusing*, if regarded as a gerund, is the equivalent and synonym of the noun *refusal*. When you regard such an *-ing* form as a noun, then you must use the possessive before it, whether the word in question is a pronoun like *his* or a noun. The second option is generally considered the correct choice, especially in formal writing. Nevertheless, the first option is overwhelmingly common in spoken English. The intent of the speaker or writer with respect to the choice of gerunds or participles is very apparent in the following examples as well. If you write *We were amused to watch the press secretary weaving and dodging during a contentious news conference*, what you mean is that you were amused to watch an evasive press secretary, where the adjective *evasive* can substitute for the participles *weaving/dodging*. If you write *We were amused to watch the press secretary's weaving and dodging during a contentious news conference*, you mean that you were amused by the press secretary's *evasions*-the noun equivalent of the gerunds *weaving/dodging*. If you substitute an adjective for a participle or a noun for a gerund to test the sense of your sentence, it will help you to decide what you really mean. Exceptions to this rule are these: When a plural noun like *visitors*, an abstract noun like *panic*, or a noun modified by other words like *member of Congress* is associated with a gerund as described here, the possessive is normally not used. Thus: *The guards will not put up with visitors roaming the corridors of the building. It was simply*

a case of panic overwhelming the speculators. There was something decidedly sleazy about a JP dealing with a convicted felon in such a friendly manner.

gerundive /jə rúndiv/ n a Latin adjective ending in '-ndus', formed from a verb and meaning 'that must or ought to be done' [15C. < late Latin gerundivus modus 'gerundive mood' < gerundium (see GERUND).] —**gerundival** /jérrən dīv'l/ adj

gesso /jéssō/ (plural **-soes**) n 1 a mixture of plaster and glue or size, used in sculpture and as a background for paintings 2 a painting done on gesso or a sculpture made from it [Late 16C. Via Italian < Latin gypsum (see GYPSUM).] —**gessoed** adj

Gestalt /gə shtált/ (plural **-stalts** or **-stalten**), **gestalt** n a set of things such as a person's thoughts and experiences considered as a whole and regarded as amounting to more than the sum of its parts [Early 20C. < German, 'shape'.] —**gestaltist** n

Gestalt psychology, **gestalt psychology** n a branch of psychology that treats behaviour and perception as an integrated whole and not simply the sum of individual stimuli and responses

Gestalt therapy, **gestalt therapy** n a form of psychotherapy in which emphasis is placed on feelings and on the influence on personality development of unresolved personal issues from the past

Gestapo /ge staápō/ n the secret state police under the Nazi regime in Germany, noted for its brutality [Mid-20C. German acronym < Geheime Staatspolizei 'Secret State Police'.]

gestate /jestáyt/ (**-tates, -tating, -tated**) vti 1 to carry offspring in the womb, or develop as offspring in the womb 2 to develop in the mind, or allow an idea or plan to develop in the mind [Mid-19C. < Latin gestat- (see GESTATION).]

gestation /je stáysh'n/ n 1 CARRYING OF OFFSPRING IN THE WOMB the process of carrying offspring in the womb during pregnancy 2 PERIOD OF DEVELOPMENT OF THE FOETUS the period of development of the offspring during pregnancy 3 DEVELOPMENT the development of an idea or plan in the mind, or the time it takes to develop [Mid-16C. < Latin gestation- < gestat- past participle of gestare 'carry in the womb' < gerere 'carry'.] —**gestational** adj —**gestatory** adj

gesticulate /je stíkyoo layt/ (**-lates, -lating, -lated**) vti to move the arms or hands when speaking [Early 17C. < Latin gesticulat-, past participle of gesticulari < gestus 'action, gesture' < gerere 'carry, act'.] —**gesticulation** /je stíkyoo láysh'n/ n —**gesticulative** /je stíkyōōlativ/ adj —**gesticulator** n —**gesticulatory** /-lətəri/ adj

gesture /jéschər/ n 1 BODY MOVEMENT a movement made with a part of the body in order to express meaning or emotion or to communicate an instruction 2 ACTION COMMUNICATING an action intended to communicate feelings or intentions 3 USE OF GESTURES the use of body movements to communicate ■ vti (**-tures, -turing, -tured**) MAKE A BODY MOVEMENT to make a movement with a part of the body in order to express meaning or emotion, or to communicate an instruction [15C. < medieval Latin gestura 'deportment' < Latin gerere 'carry, act'.] —**gestural** adj —**gesturally** adv

gesundheit /gə zoónt hīt/ interj used as an expression of good health to somebody who has just sneezed (humorous) [Early 20C. < German, 'health'.]

get¹ /get/ (**gets, getting, got** /got/, **got**) CORE MEANING: a verb indicating that somebody obtains, receives, earns, or is given something. It is often used instead of more formal terms such as 'obtain' or 'acquire'. ○ We're trying to ensure that our child gets a good education. ○ Where will they get the money to buy the land?
1 vi BECOME to become or begin to have a particular quality ○ When I get nervous, I get scared. 2 vt CAUSE TO BE DONE to cause something to happen or be done ○ I must get the car cleaned. 3 vt BRING to fetch or bring something ○ I'm going back to my apartment to get my watch. ○ I'll get your coat for you. 4 vt CATCH AN ILLNESS to be affected by an illness or medical condition ○ He got chicken-pox last year. 5 vi BE IN A PARTICULAR STATE to enter or leave a particular state or condition ○ Get ready to leave in five minutes. 6 vi MOVE SOMEWHERE to succeed in moving or arriving somewhere ○ It was already midnight when we got home. 7 vt BEGIN to begin doing something (informal) ○ Let's get going – we have to be there by eight. 8 v FORMS PASSIVES used instead of 'be' as an auxiliary verb to form passives ○ If you play with matches you will get burned.

9 *vt* ARREST to arrest or capture somebody (*informal*) ○ *They got him just as he was running out of the bank.* 10 *vt* MANAGE to manage or contrive something (*informal*) ○ *How did they get to be so successful?* 11 *vt* PREPARE FOOD to prepare a meal ○ *I'll get dinner tonight.* 12 *vt* PERSUADE to persuade somebody to do something ○ *Colleagues had tried to get her to take a vacation.* 13 *vt* UNDERSTAND to hear or understand something, e.g. a joke or somebody's point (*informal*) ○ *What's that? I didn't get what you said.* 14 *vt* USE A FORM OF TRANSPORTATION to take a particular form of transportation ○ *I don't want to drive – I'd rather get a plane.* 15 *vt* OBTAIN A RESULT to obtain a result, e.g. by experiment or calculation ○ *What's the answer? I get nine.* 16 *vt* RECEIVE A SIGNAL to receive a broadcast signal, e.g. a radio or television broadcast ○ *I can't get Channel 5 with that aerial.* 17 *vt* IRRITATE to annoy or irritate somebody (*informal*) ○ *That high whining noise really gets me.* 18 *vt* HAVE THE TIME to have the time or opportunity to do something ○ *I'll fix it as soon as I get the time.* 19 *vt* HAVE AN IDEA to have or receive an idea, impression, feeling, or benefit ○ *You've got the wrong impression – I'm not like that at all.* ○ *I get a lot of pleasure from his stories.* 20 *vt* MANAGE TO SEE to succeed in seeing something ○ *get a close-up look* 21 *vt* HIT to hit somebody (*informal*) ○ *The blow got him in the face.* 22 *vt* HAVE REVENGE ON to have revenge on somebody, especially by killing the person (*informal*) ○ *The heroes get Dracula in the end.* 23 *vi* GAIN ACCESS to gain access to somebody with intent to bribe him or her (*informal*) ○ *I thought he was incorruptible, but they finally got to him.* 24 *vi* LEAVE to leave (*informal; often in commands*) ○ *Now get!* [13C. < Old Norse *geta* < Indo-European, 'seize'.] —**getable** *adj* ◇ **get with it** become fashionable and responsive to new styles and ideas (*informal*)

SYNONYMS ***get, acquire, obtain, gain, procure, secure***

CORE MEANING: to come into possession of something

get to become the owner of something or to succeed in finding and possessing it; **acquire** to get possession of something, sometimes suggesting that time or effort was involved; **obtain** to get something, especially by making an effort or having the necessary qualifications; **gain** to get something through effort, skill, or merit; **procure** to get something, especially with effort or special care; **secure** to get something, especially after using considerable effort to persuade somebody to grant or allow it.

get about *vi* 1 MOVE ABOUT to be able to move with a medical condition 2 BECOME KNOWN to become known, especially contrary to somebody's wishes 3 TRAVEL to travel, especially contrary to expectations 4 = **get around** *v.* 1

get across *v* 1 *vti* to make something understood or to communicate clearly ○ *I don't seem to be getting across to you.* 2 *vt* to annoy or irritate somebody ○ *She's really managed to get across him, somehow.*

get after *vt* to keep telling somebody to do something in an annoying way (*informal*) ○ *You'll have to get after him if you want it finished by the weekend.*

get ahead *vi* to become successful, especially when compared to others ○ *He's a good worker, but he hasn't got what it takes to get ahead in this line of business.*

get along *vi* 1 *US* BE FRIENDLY WITH to be on good terms with somebody socially 2 MANAGE to make progress in a situation ○ *How's he getting along in the new job?* 3 LEAVE to leave a place (*often in commands*)

get around *v* 1 *vi* to be socially active and aware of what is happening ○ *I have the feeling you don't get around much.* 2 = **get round**

get at *vt* 1 REACH to succeed in reaching, finding, or making contact with somebody or something ○ *I'm determined to get at the truth if it takes all night.* 2 MEAN to imply, suggest, or be trying to say something ○ *What exactly are you getting at?* 3 CRITICIZE SOMEBODY REPEATEDLY to criticize somebody continually and unreasonably ○ *You're always getting at me, and I'm sick of it.* 4 BRIBE to bribe or influence somebody ○ *It was obvious that some of the committee had been got at by our rivals.*

get away *vi* 1 ESCAPE to escape from somebody or something ○ *They caught one man, but the rest got away.* 2 LEAVE A PLACE to succeed in leaving or spending time away from a place ○ *We hope to get away for a few days next month.* ■ *interj* EXPRESSING DISBELIEF used as an expression of disbelief ○ *Get away! He never said that – did he?*

get away with *vt* to manage to do something without being blamed or penalized or experiencing an expected bad result ○ *You could get away with a phone call, but it would be better to write.*

get back *vt* to recover something that has been given away, lent to somebody, or lost

get back at *vt* to take your revenge on somebody

get back to *v* 1 *vt* to return to a place, topic, or activity ○ *Let's get back to what Steve was saying earlier.* 2 *vi* to give somebody an answer or continue a discussion, especially by letter, e-mail, or telephone ○ *Leave it with me, and I'll get back to you as soon as possible.*

get behind *vt* to approve or support somebody or something ○ *I'd like to think we could all get behind the initiative for a new playground.*

get by *vi* to manage to survive or just make ends meet ○ *It's hard to get by on £50 a week.*

get down *v* 1 *vt* DEMORALIZE to make somebody demoralized or discouraged ○ *This job is beginning to get me down.* 2 *vt* WRITE to write something down, especially immediately 3 *vt* SWALLOW to swallow something, especially unwillingly or with difficulty ○ *The medicine smelled so bad I just couldn't get it down.* 4 *vi US* HAVE FUN to relax and enjoy yourself in an unrestrained way (*informal*) ○ *It's time to get down and party.* 5 *vi Malaysia* LEAVE VEHICLE to get out of a vehicle ○ *Where do you have to get down?*

get down to *vt* to start concentrating seriously on something or getting something done

get in *v* 1 *vi* TO ARRIVE to arrive somewhere, especially home ○ *When does your plane get in?* 2 *vi* BE CHOSEN to succeed in being admitted to a group or organization, e.g. by election or interview ○ *You know if they get in they'll change some of the old laws.* 3 *vti* GET INVOLVED WITH to become involved, or let somebody become involved, with a group or in an activity ○ *She got in with the golf club crowd.* 4 *vt* MANAGE TO DO to succeed in finding or making an opportunity to do something ○ *I don't think we can get four interviews in before lunch.*

get into *vt* 1 to begin to experience difficulties, or make somebody experience difficulties ○ *You got us into this mess, you sort it out.* ○ *You'll get into all kinds of trouble if you do that.* 2 to become involved or absorbed in something ○ *She's starting to get into programming.*

get off *v* 1 *vi* LEAVE to leave a place or position ○ *We have to get off at crack of dawn tomorrow.* 2 *vti* BE ABLE TO LEAVE WORK to be allowed to leave work, especially at the end of the working day ○ *What time do you get off this afternoon?* 3 *vt* SEND A COMMUNICATION OR PARCEL to send a written communication or parcel ○ *I need to get these letters off tonight.* 4 *vi* HAVE A LUCKY ESCAPE to experience only minor consequences of a mistake, misguided action, or accident ○ *Considering what might have happened, I think you got off very lightly.* 5 *vti* GAIN AN ACQUITTAL to be acquitted in a court of law, or successfully defend somebody in a court of law (*informal*) ○ *A good lawyer could get him off with no trouble.* 6 *vi US* BE SO BOLD to be bold enough to say or do something (*informal; usually disapproving*) ○ *Where does he get off thinking he can speak to me that way?* 7 *vi* BE AROUSED OR EXCITED to experience excitement, physical arousal, or the effects of a drug (*slang*)

get off with *vt* to start a flirtation or sexual relationship with somebody (*informal*)

get on *vi* 1 DEAL WITH A SITUATION to deal with a situation and make reasonable progress of a particular kind ○ *How's Ben getting on at school?* 2 BE FRIENDLY to have a reasonably friendly social relationship with somebody ○ *She gets on well with the neighbours.* 3 KEEP GOING to continue doing something ○ *I'd better get on – I've got a lot more to do.* 4 BECOME OLDER to become more advanced in years 5 BE ALMOST to be approaching a particular age, time, number, or amount ○ *We collected getting on for 200 signatures.*

get out *v* 1 *vti* LEAVE OR MAKE SOMEBODY LEAVE to leave a place or situation, or enable somebody to leave one 2 *vi* BECOME KNOWN to become widely known, especially contrary to somebody's wishes ○ *If this ever gets out, I'll be so embarrassed!* 3 *vt* PRODUCE OR PUBLISH to produce or publish something, especially a newspaper or magazine ■ *interj US* EXPRESSION OF DISBELIEF used as an expression of disbelief (*informal*) ○ *Get out! You actually said that?*

get out of *vt* to avoid doing or having to experience something, or enable somebody to avoid something ○ *He got out of paying for the meal.*

get over *vt* 1 RECOVER FROM to recover from an illness or bad experience ○ *He's upset, but he'll get over it.* 2 DEAL WITH A DIFFICULTY to overcome or cope with a difficulty ○ *Once she'd got over her lack of confidence, she enjoyed the meeting.* 3 MAKE PEOPLE UNDERSTAND OR ACCEPT to succeed in making something clear or persuasive ○ *He's very good at getting his ideas over to an audience.* 4 GET SOMETHING FINISHED to finish dealing with something boring, annoying, or unpleasant ○ *I just want to get the whole thing over with as soon as possible.*

get round, get around *v* 1 *vt* DEAL SUCCESSFULLY WITH OBSTRUCTION to manage to operate in spite of a regulation, prohibition, or difficulty ○ *There must be some way of getting round the regulations.* 2 *vt* PERSUADE SOMEBODY to talk or charm somebody into doing what you want ○ *could rely on Sheila to get round him* 3 *vi* SAY OR DO SOMETHING AT LAST finally to say or do something after delay, hesitation, or being involved with other things ○ *She somehow never gets round to cleaning the house.* 4 *vi* BECOME KNOWN to become widely known

get through *v* 1 *vt* SURVIVE DIFFICULT TIME to endure to the end of a difficult time or situation ○ *How I got through those weeks I just don't know.* 2 *vt* USE OR SPEND to use, eat, or spend something, especially a large amount in a short time ○ *We seem to be getting through the copier paper at an alarming rate.* 3 *vti* MAKE SOMEBODY UNDERSTAND to make somebody understand something that is being communicated ○ *How can I get it through to you that this is our only hope?* 4 *vi* SUCCEED IN CONTACTING to contact somebody, especially by telephone ○ *I finally got through to her.*

get to *vt* to start to annoy somebody ○ *His whining was beginning to get to me.*

get together *v* 1 *vi* MEET to meet for social or business purposes ○ *The project team needs to get together once a week or so.* 2 *vi* FORM AN ALLIANCE to form an alliance or relationship ○ *They may be getting together to corner the market.* 3 *vt* GATHER to bring together or accumulate something, especially money ○ *They managed to get together enough capital to start a business.* 4 *vt* GET SOMETHING ORGANIZED to organize your personal affairs or focus your approach on an activity (*informal*) ○ *took some time off to get her life together* ◇ **get it together** *vr* to become organized and calm so as to perform efficiently (*slang*) ○ *better get it together before his boss loses patience*

get up *v* 1 *vti* GET OUT OF BED to get out of bed, or make somebody get out of bed 2 *vi* STAND UP to rise to your feet from a seated position 3 *vt* ROUSE ENERGY to rouse your energy, strength, courage, or similar qualities ○ *I'm trying to get up the enthusiasm to go back to work.* 4 *vt* ORGANIZE to organize something by persuading other people to take part ○ *She got up a collection to help homeless people.* 5 *vt* DRESS to dress somebody in a particular way (*informal*) ○ *She was got up as Cleopatra.* 6 *vi* GET STRONGER to become stronger or more turbulent (*refers to wind or the sea*)

get up to *vt* to do something bad or annoying (*informal*) ○ *I have no idea what they've been getting up to while we've been away.*

get[2] /get/ *n* 1 *Scotland, N England* BRAT an unpleasant child (*often used as an insult, implying illegitimacy*) 2 MALE ANIMAL'S OFFSPRING the progeny sired by an animal, especially a racehorse 3 DIFFICULT TENNIS RETURN in tennis and some other racket games, a shot that makes a difficult return

geta /géttə/ (*plural* **-ta** *or* **-tas**) *n* a Japanese shoe with a wooden sole [Late 19C. < Japanese.]

getaway /géttə way/ *n* 1 an act of leaving a place, especially a quick exit made by somebody who has just committed a crime 2 an act of starting to move, e.g. in a race

get-go, getgo /gétgō/ *n US* the very beginning of something (*informal*) ○ *I knew from the get-go this thing wasn't going to work.*

Gethsemane, Garden of /geth sémməni/ in the Bible, the olive grove just outside Jerusalem where Jesus Christ was betrayed after the Last Supper (Matthew 26:36)

get-out *n* a means of avoiding or escaping from something such as an obligation or commitment (*often before nouns*) ○ *the contract had a get-out clause* ◇ **as...as all get-out** *US* to the greatest possible extent (*slang*) ○ *The ground was as flat as all get-out.*

getter /géttər/ *n* a substance added to absorb the unwanted product of a chemical process, e.g. the excess gas in a light bulb

get-together *n* a meeting or social gathering (*informal*)

get-tough *adj* taking a firm and decisive approach to social or political problems

Getty /gétti/, **J. Paul** (1892–1976) US oil executive

Gettysburg /géttiz burg/ borough in S Pennsylvania, site of a decisive Northern victory in 1863 during the American Civil War. Population: 7,025 (1990).

getup /gét up/, **get-up** *n* the costume or clothes that somebody is wearing (*informal*)

get-up-and-go *n* energy and enthusiasm (*informal*)

get-well *adj* expressing the hope that somebody will soon recover from an illness ○ *a get-well card*

geullah /gə óolla/ *n* a Jewish prayer of thanks to God for the deliverance of the Jews from Egypt

GeV *abbr* giga-electron volt

gewgaw /gyóo gaw/ *n* a showy but inexpensive object, especially an ornament [12C. < ?]

Gewürztraminer /gə vöorts tra meenər/ *n* 1 a white grape from which Gewürztraminer is made. Native to: Alsace, Germany. 2 a medium-dry, slightly spicy, white wine [Mid-20C. < *Gewürz* 'spice' + *Traminer*, type of grape < *Termeno*, village in N Italy.]

gey /gï/ *adv* Scotland 1 rather < 2 extremely (*nonstandard*) [Early 18C. Variant of GAY.]

geyser /geézə, gízə/ *n* 1 a spring that throws a jet of hot water or steam into the air at regular or irregular intervals 2 a boiler that heats water for use in the home, gas-fired and activated by turning on a tap [Late 18C. After *Geysir*, hot spring in Iceland < Old Norse *geysa* 'gush'.]

SPELLCHECK See *geezer*.

geyserite /gízə rīt/ *n* a grey or white mineral form of hydrated silica. Source: hot spring deposits.

⚡**gf** *abbr* French Guiana (*in Internet addresses*)

⚡**GFN** *abbr* gone for now (*in e-mails*)

G-force *n* the force of gravity

⚡**gg** *abbr* Guernsey (*in Internet addresses*)

GG *abbr* 1 Girl Guides 2 UK, Can, Aus, S Asia Governor General

gge *abbr* garage (*in advertisements*)

⚡**gh** *abbr* Ghana (*in Internet addresses*)

GH *abbr* 1 Ghana (*international vehicle registration*) 2 growth hormone

Ghana

Ghana /gáanə/ republic in West Africa, on the northern coast of the Gulf of Guinea. Capital: Accra. Population: 18,100,703 (1997). Area: 238,500 sq. km/92,090 sq. mi. —**Ghanaian** /gaa náy ən/ *n, adj*

Ghanaian English *n* a variety of English spoken in Ghana

~~Ghandi~~ incorrect spelling of **Gandhi**

gharial /gáiri əl, gárri-/ *n* a large Indian fish-eating crocodile. US term **gavial** [Early 19C. < Hindi *ghariyāl*.]

gharry /gárri/ (*plural* **-ries**) *n* S Asia a horse-drawn carriage in the Indian subcontinent, especially one for hire [Early 19C. < Hindi *gārī*.]

ghastly /gaástli/ *adj* (**-lier, -liest**) 1 HORRIFYING horrifying, shocking, or very upsetting ○ *She had a ghastly experience with the last dentist she went to.* 2 TERRIBLE very bad or unpleasant ○ *There's a ghastly smell coming from somewhere in this room.* 3 NOT WELL very unwell (*informal*) ○ *If I drink too much, I always wake up feeling ghastly in the morning.* 4 VERY PALE very pale or white, reminiscent of a ghost or a corpse (*literary*) ■ *adv* EXTREMELY used to emphasize paleness or whiteness ○ *'Her eyes grew large, her face ghastly pale.'* (Charlotte Gilman, *Herland*; 1915) [14C. < obsolete *gast* 'frighten' < Germanic.] —**ghastliness** *n*

ghat /gaat/ *n* in South Asia, a place on a river bank with steps down to the water, especially one where people bathe as a sacred rite or one near which the dead are cremated [Early 17C. < Hindi *ghāt*.]

Ghats /gaats/ ♦ Eastern Ghats, Western Ghats

ghazal /gáaz'l/ *n* 1 an Arabic, Persian, or Urdu lyric poem consisting of five or more couplets that may each have a different theme 2 a lyric poem in Urdu, set to music and sung in a distinctive style [Late 18C. Via Persian < Arabic *gazal*.]

Ghazali /ga zaáli/, **al-** (1058–1111) Muslim theologian and philosopher

ghazi /gaázi/ *n* a warrior who has fought for Islam against non-Muslims [Mid-18C. < Arabic *al-gāzī*, form of *gazā* 'invade'.]

GHB *abbr* gammahydroxybutyrate

ghee /gee/, **ghi** *n* clarified butter, especially as used in Indian cooking [Mid-17C. Via Hindi *ghī* < Sanskrit *ghrtam*.]

Ghent /gent/ city in W Belgium. Population: 226,464 (1996).

gherao /gə rówl/ *vt* S Asia to surround and virtually imprison an official, employer, or manager, typically at the workplace, as a form of political or industrial protest ■ *n* S Asia the surrounding and virtual imprisonment of an official, employer, or manager as a political or industrial protest [Mid-20C. < Hindi *ghernā* 'surround'.]

gherkin /gúrkin/ *n* 1 SMALL CUCUMBER a small cucumber. Use: pickling. 2 PRICKLY FRUIT a prickly hard-skinned fruit from a climbing plant. Native to: Caribbean. Use: pickling. 3 TROPICAL CLIMBING PLANT a climbing plant of the cucumber family that produces gherkins. Native to: Caribbean. *Cucumis anguria.* [Early 17C. < assumed obsolete Dutch *gurkkijn* 'small cucumber' < *gurk* 'cucumber'.]

ghetto /géttō/ (*plural* **-tos** or **-toes**) *n* 1 MINORITY'S AREA OF A CITY an area of a city lived in by a minority group, especially a run-down and densely populated area lived in by a group that experiences discrimination 2 JEWISH QUARTER in former times, an area in European towns in which the Jewish population was required to live 3 STATE OF SOCIAL EXCLUSION the social situation of any group of people who are segregated in some way from the mainstream of a society or culture, resulting in discrimination or restriction of opportunity [Early 17C. < Italian.]

ghetto blaster *n* a large radio and cassette or CD player with a built-in speaker at each end, carried by a handle at the top (*informal; often considered offensive*)

ghetto credibility *n* popularity and acceptability among black people, especially young urban black people (*slang; offensive in some contexts*)

ghettoize /géttō īz/ (**-izes, -izing, -ized**), **ghettoise** (**-ises, -ising, -ised**) *vt* 1 to restrict a minority group to a specific area of a city 2 to limit the opportunities of a group of people (*sometimes offensive*) —**ghettoization** /géttō T záysh'n/ *n*

ghi *n* COOK = ghee

ghillie *n* CLOTHING, FIELD SPORTS = gillie

ghost /gōst/ *n* 1 SUPPOSED SPIRIT REMAINING AFTER DEATH the spirit of somebody who has died, supposed to appear as a shadowy form or to cause sounds, the movement of objects, or a frightening atmosphere in a place 2 TRACE a faint, weak, or greatly reduced appearance, trace, or possibility of something ○ *The ghost of a smile hovered around her lips.* 3 SECONDARY IMAGE a faint duplicate image of something seen on a screen or through a telescope, and caused by the reception of a double signal or by a mechanical defect 4 NONEXISTENT PERSON OR THING an entity that seems to exist but does not, e.g. a name entered on a list by mistake 5 SOUL somebody's soul or spirit (*archaic*) 6 LITERAT = ghostwriter ■ *vt* to be the ghost writer of a work [Old English *gāst* < W Germanic] —**ghost-like** *adj* ◇ **give up the ghost** 1 to die (*literary*) 2 to stop working or functioning for good (*informal*)

LITERARY LINK *Ghosts*, a play (1881) by Norwegian dramatist Henrik Ibsen. Ibsen's penetrating study of hereditary determinism tells the story of Osvald Alving, who discovers that the girl he loves is actually his illegitimate half-sister and that he has inherited a degenerative sexually-transmitted disease from his father.

ghostbuster /gōst bustər/ *n* (*informal*) 1 a person supposedly able to drive away ghosts, poltergeists, and other apparitions 2 an employee of the Inland Revenue whose job is to track down people who have not declared their income for tax purposes

ghost crab *n* a white burrowing crab. Native to: sandy shorelines in many parts of the world. Genus: *Ocypoda.*

ghost dance *n* 1 a religious dance of Native North Americans, performed with the spirits of all the Native Americans murdered by the European immigrants 2 **ghost dance, Ghost Dance** a religious movement, widely spread among Plains Native American peoples in North America in the late 19th century, that promised the revival of traditional Native North American culture

ghosting /gōsting/ *n* the appearance of faint duplicate images on a screen or monitor or through a telescope

ghostly /gōstli/ (**-lier, -liest**) *adj* 1 like a ghost in being insubstantial, pale, or apparently not of this world 2 having an atmosphere or quality that suggests ghosts or the presence of ghosts ○ *the ghostly music that opens the symphony* —**ghostliness** *n*

ghost moth *n* a large pale moth, the male of which is white and the female pale yellow with orange markings. Native to: Europe. *Hepialis humuli.*

⚡**ghost site** *n* a website that is obsolete and no longer updated but that is still available for viewing

ghost story *n* a story about a ghost or ghosts, or a haunted place or person, intended to make the reader or hearer feel frightened or uneasy

ghost town *n* 1 a town with few or no inhabitants, especially one that was formerly a busy prosperous place, e.g. an abandoned mining town in the W United States 2 a normally or normally inhabited place that is deserted (*informal*) ○ *The business district is a ghost town on weekends.*

ghost train *n* a small open-topped train at a fairground that takes passengers through a dark space filled with amusingly frightening sights and sounds

ghost word *n* a word created through a mistake that may be copied afterwards into other texts and eventually enter a language

ghostwriter /gōst rītər/ *n* a writer of something for or with another person, the other person receiving sole credit as the author —**ghostwrite** *vti*

ghoul /gool/ *n* 1 SOMEBODY MORBIDLY INTERESTED IN REPULSIVE THINGS a person who is morbidly fascinated with death, disaster, or repulsive things 2 EVIL SPIRIT an evil and terrifying spirit 3 BODY-SNATCHING DEMON an evil demon in Islamic folklore that eats freshly buried bodies, and often abducts children or attacks unwary travellers [Late 18C. < Arabic *gūl*.]

ghoulish /góolish/ *adj* 1 showing an unpleasant or unhealthy fascination with death and destruction 2 terrifyingly hideous or cruel —**ghoulishly** *adv* —**ghoulishness** *n*

GHQ *n* the headquarters of an organization, especially a military headquarters commanded by a general. Full form **General Headquarters**

ghyll *n* GEOG = gill[3]

GHz *symbol* gigahertz

gi[1] /gee/, **gie** *n* an outfit worn for karate or judo [< Japanese]

⚡**gi**[2] *abbr* Gibraltar (*in Internet addresses*)

GI[1] /jee ï/ *n* US SOLDIER a soldier in the US armed forces ■ *adj* US 1 FOR SOLDIERS provided or issued by the armed forces for the use of its members ○ *a GI hat* 2 FOR VETERANS for veterans of the armed forces ○ *GI benefits* [Mid-20C. Abbreviation of *government issue*, reinterpretation of *GI* 'galvanized iron' on various items of US Army equipment.]

GI[2], **g.i.** *abbr* 1 galvanized iron 2 gastrointestinal

-gi /jee/ *suffix* S Asia a respectful form of address added to a name or title ○ *Michaelgi* ○ *doctorgi* [Variant of -JI]

giant /jī ənt/ *n* 1 VERY TALL CREATURE in fairy tales and legends, a being who is usually similar to a human in shape but is much taller, larger, and stronger 2 MYTHOLOGICAL BEING in Greek mythology, a being of immense size and strength who fought against Zeus and the other gods of Mount Olympus 3 SOMETHING LARGER THAN THE NORM a person, animal, plant, or organization that is much larger than the norm 4 SOMEBODY EXTRAORDINARILY ACCOMPLISHED somebody whose talents or achievements are particularly outstanding ○ *one of the giants of the silent-movie era* 5 MIN EXTRACT = **monitor**. n 10 6 ASTRON = **giant star** ■ *adj* 1 VERY BIG taller, larger, or more powerful than the norm ○ *a giant tidal wave* 2 LARGER THAN USUAL greater than the usual amount or number ○ *a giant saving* [13C. Via Old French *geant* < Greek *gigant-*.]

giant anteater *n* a large bushy-tailed anteater, now rare. Native to: pampas regions of South America. *Myrmecophaga tridactyla.*

giant clam *n* an extremely large clam, weighing as much as 230kg/500 lbs. Native to: Pacific and Indian oceans. *Tridacna gigas.*

giantess /jī an tess/ *n* in fairy tales, myths, and legends, a being who is similar to a woman in shape but is much taller, larger, and stronger

giantism /jī antizəm/ *n* MED = **gigantism**

giant-killer *n* a defeater of a superior or better known opponent, especially in sport, business, or politics —**giant-killing** *n*

giant panda *n* ZOOL = **panda** *n.* 1

giant peacock moth *n* a moth, mottled brown with an oval like an eye on each wing and a wingspan that can reach 15 cm/6 in. Native to: Europe. *Saturnia pyri.*

giant planet *n* any of the four largest planets in the solar system, Jupiter, Saturn, Uranus, and Neptune

giant redwood *n* TREES = **giant sequoia**

Giant's Causeway headland on the northern coast of Northern Ireland, consisting of thousands of polygonal columns of basalt, thought to be ancient lava formations

giant sequoia, giant redwood *n* a coniferous evergreen tree that grows up to 80 m/260 ft high. Native to: California. *Sequoiadendron giganteum.*

giant-sized *adj* much larger than others of the same type or class

giant star *n* a low-density star with a diameter up to 100 times greater than that of the Sun

giant tortoise *n* a very large tortoise with a shell that can grow to be 1.2 m/4 ft long. Native to: Galápagos and Seychelles islands. Genus: *Geochelone.*

giardia /jee aárdi a/ *n* 1 a single-celled protozoan, some forms of which live as parasites in the gut of humans and other vertebrates, causing an infection (**giardiasis**). Genus: *Giardia.* 2 MED = **giardiasis** [Early 20C. < modern Latin, after A. *Giard.*]

giardiasis /jee aar dí assis/ *n* infection of the gut by the water-borne microscopic protozoan giardia. It is usually caused by drinking contaminated water and results in severe diarrhoea and vomiting.

gib /gib/ *n* something such as a wedge, pin, bolt, or plate that is made of metal and holds another piece of metal or a machine part in place ■ *vt* (**gibs, gibbing, gibbed**) to hold something in place with a gib [Late 18C. < ?]

Gib /jib/ *n* Gibraltar (*informal*)

gibber /jíbbar/ *vi* to make sounds or speak words unintelligibly ○ *Stop gibbering and tell me what's gone wrong.* [Early 17C. Probably an imitation of the sound.] —**gibber** *n*

gibberellic acid /jíbbə réllik-/ *n* C₁₉H₂₂O₆ a plant growth hormone involved in stem elongation

$C_{19}H_{22}O_6$

gibberellin /jíbbə réllin/ *n* a plant hormone that promotes growth and seed germination [Mid-20C. < modern Latin *Gibbera,* genus of fungi < Latin *gibbus* 'hump'.]

gibberish /jíbbərish/ *n* spoken or written language perceived as incomprehensible, and probably not worth comprehending [Early 16C. Probably < GIBBER after SPANISH, POLISH, etc.]

gibbet /jíbbit/ *n* 1 HANGING POST an upright post with a beam projecting horizontally from its top, from which the bodies of executed criminals were hung on public display 2 CRIMINOL = **gallows** *n.* 1 ■ *vt* 1 HANG to execute somebody by hanging (*archaic*) 2 DISPLAY AFTER EXECUTION to display the body of a criminal on a gibbet after execution 3 ATTACK SOMEBODY'S REPUTATION to expose somebody to ridicule or contempt, especially in popular publications (*archaic*) [12C. < Old French *gibet* 'staff, gallows' < *gibe* 'staff'.]

gibbon /gíbbən/ *n* a small tree-dwelling ape with a slender body and long arms that allow it to swing rapidly and agilely from branch to branch. Native to: Southeast Asia. Genus: *Hylobates.* [Late 18C. < French.]

Gibbon /gíbbən/, **Edward** (1737–94) British historian

gibbous /gíbbəss/ *adj* 1 describes the moon or a planet before and after it is full, when it has more than half its disc illuminated 2 bulging outwards or swollen [14C. < late Latin *gibbosus* 'hunchbacked' < Latin *gibbus* 'hump'.] —**gibbosity** /gi bóssi ti/ *n* —**gibbously** *adv* —**gibbousness** *n*

Gibbs /gibz/, **J. Willard** (1839–1903) US physical chemist. Full name **Josiah Willard Gibbs**

Gibbs, May (1876–1969) British-born Australian writer and illustrator

Gibbs free energy *n* PHYS, CHEM = **free energy** [After J. Willard GIBBS.]

gibbsite /gíbzīt/ *n* a grey-white mineral consisting of hydrated aluminium oxide. Source: laterite, bauxite. Use: source of aluminium. [Early 19C. After George *Gibbs* (1776–1833), US mineralogist.]

gibe /jīb/, **jibe** *n* a comment that is intended to hurt or provoke somebody or to show derision or contempt ■ *vti* (**gibes, gibing, gibed; jibes, jibing, jibed**) to make deliberately provocative or mocking remarks about somebody or something [Mid-16C. < ?] —**gibingly** *adv*

giblets /jíbblats/ *n* the liver, heart, gizzard, and neck of a bird that has been prepared for cooking [14C. < Old French *gibelet* 'game stew'.]

Gibraltar

Gibraltar /ji bráwltar, -brólt-/ British dependency on a narrow promontory of the S Iberian Peninsula, at the western entrance to the Mediterranean Sea. Population: 27,170 (1995). Area: 5.8 sq. km/2.3 sq. mi. —**Gibraltarian** /ji brawl táiri ən, -brol-/ *n, adj*

Gibraltar, Rock of limestone and shale ridge near the tip of the S Iberian Peninsula. Height: 426 m/1,396 ft.

Gibraltar, Strait of channel connecting the Mediterranean Sea to the Atlantic Ocean and separating North Africa from the Rock of Gibraltar. Length: approximately 65 km/40 mi.

Gibran /ji bráan/, **Kahlil** (1883–1931) Lebanese-born US mystic, painter, and poet

Gibson /gíbs'n/, **Mel** (*b.* 1956) US-born Australian actor. Born **Columcille Gerard Gibson**

Gibson Desert /gíbs'n-/ desert in central Western Australia. Area: 156,000 sq. km/60,200 sq. mi.

gid /gid/ *n* a disease affecting livestock, especially sheep, that makes them walk and stand unsteadily, caused by a tapeworm larva [Early 17C. Back-formation < GIDDY.]

giddap /gi dáp/ *interj* = **giddyup**

giddy /gíddi/ (**-dier, -diest**) *adj* 1 DIZZY feeling unsteady and as if about to fall down 2 CAUSING DIZZINESS causing dizziness or a feeling of unsteadiness 3 NOT SENSIBLE not level-headed and sensible, and liable to act impulsively or behave foolishly (*dated*) [Old English *gidig* 'severely mentally ill' < Germanic] —**giddily** *adv* —**giddiness** *n*

giddyup /gíddi úp/ *interj* used to make horses go faster [Early 20C. Alteration of GET UP.]

Gide /zheed/, **André** (1869–1951) French writer

gie *n* MARTIAL ARTS = **gi**¹

Gielgud /géel gōod/, **Sir John** (1904–2000) British actor

GIF *abbr* graphic interchange format

gift /gift/ *n* 1 SOMETHING GIVEN something that is given to somebody, usually to give pleasure or to show gratitude ○ *a birthday gift* 2 SPECIAL TALENT a talent or skill that somebody appears to have been born with ○ *a gift for making people feel at ease* 3 SOMETHING EASILY GAINED something that is obtained or achieved easily, thus allowing an advantage (*informal*) ○ *The final goal was a gift from the Uruguay defence.* 4 ACT OF GIVING the act of giving something to somebody ○ *her gift of £500,000 to build a new school* ■ *vt* GIVE to give or concede something to somebody as a gift [13C. < Old Norse *gipt* < Germanic.]

◇ **be in the gift of somebody** to be something that somebody has the right or power to give

SYNONYMS See *talent.*

USAGE Marketing people are fond of the expression *free gift,* but because any *gift* worthy of its name is free using the two words together is unnecessary and should be avoided.

GIFT *n* a method designed to aid conception in which eggs are removed from a woman's ovary, mixed with sperm, and placed in one of her fallopian tubes. Full form **gamete intrafallopian transfer**

gift certificate *n US* = **gift token**

gifted /gíftid/ *adj* 1 TALENTED having great natural talent or intelligence 2 SHOWING TALENT showing that somebody has great natural talent ○ *a gifted performance* 3 EXCEPTIONAL requiring special education because of exceptional talent or intelligence ○ *a gifted student* —**giftedly** *adv* —**giftedness** *n*

SYNONYMS See *intelligent.*

gift of the gab *n* a natural ability to talk fluently, eloquently, or persuasively (*informal*)

gift of tongues *n* a form of speech produced in a state of religious ecstasy or trance, usually unintelligible and thought by some to manifest the influence of the Holy Spirit

gift shop *n* a shop selling small decorative or amusing items that are intended to be bought as gifts or souvenirs

gift token, gift voucher *n* a slip of paper issued by a shop that can be exchanged for goods worth its purchase price, usually given to somebody in an attractive card as a gift. US term **gift certificate**

giftware /gíft wair/ *n* goods such as china and crystal that are marketed for buying as gifts for other people

giftwrap /gíft rap/ *n* **giftwrap, giftwrapping** specially decorated paper used to wrap gifts ■ *vt* (**-wraps, -wrapping, -wrapped**) to wrap something in specially decorated paper

Gifu /gee foo/ city in central Honshu Island, Japan. Population: 410,324 (1990).

gig¹ /gig/ *n* 1 ONE-HORSE CARRIAGE a light open two-wheeled carriage pulled by a single horse 2 ROWING BOAT a small light rowing boat carried on board a sailing ship 3 RACING BOAT a light rowing boat used for racing [Late 18C. < ?]

gig² /gig/ *n* a performance by a musician or group of musicians at a venue where they are booked to play but do not regularly perform (*informal*) ■ *vi* (**gigs, gigging, gigged**) to give a musical performance to an audience in exchange for payment (*informal*) [Early 20C. < ?]

gig³ /gig/ *n* a gigabyte (*informal*) [Shortening]

giga- *prefix* 1 (*symbol* **G**) a thousand million (10⁹) ○ *gigaton* 2 a binary billion ○ *gigabyte* [< Greek *gigas* 'giant']

gigabit /gíggəbit/ *n* a unit of capacity of a computer local area network, equal to one megabyte of computer information, or 1,073,741,824 bits

gigabyte /gíggə bīt/ *n* a unit of computer data or storage space equivalent to 1,024 megabytes

gigacycle /gíggə sīk'l/ *n* a unit of electrical oscillation equal to 1000 million cycles

gigaflop /gíggə flop/ *n* a unit of computer processing speed equal to 1,000 million floating-point operations per second [Late 20C. < GIGA- + acronym < *floating-point operations per second.*]

gigahertz /gíggə hurts/ (*plural* **-hertz**) *n* (*symbol* **GHz**) a unit of frequency equal to 1000 million hertz, or cycles, per second

gigantic /jī gántik/ *adj* 1 very large, tall, or bulky 2 very great ○ *Clearing the site is a gigantic task in itself.* [Early 17C. < Latin *gigant-* 'giant' < Greek *gigas.*] —**gigantically** *adv*

gigantism /jī gántizəm, jī gan-/ *n* excessive growth due to overproduction of growth hormone by the pituitary gland before the end of adolescence

gigaton /gíggə tun, jíggə-/ *n* a unit of explosive force equal to 1000 million tons of TNT

gigawatt /gíggə wot, jíggə-/ *n* (*symbol* **GW**) a unit of electrical power equal to 1000 million watts

giggle /gígg'l/ *vti* (**-gles, -gling, -gled**) LAUGH LIGHTLY to laugh audibly but not loudly, sometimes without meaning to, in a way that is typical of children ■ *n* **1** NERVOUS LAUGH a quiet laugh that is often nervous or half-suppressed **2** SOMETHING FUN something that is fun or that makes somebody laugh (*informal*) ■ **giggles** *npl* FIT OF LAUGHTER an uncontrollable and recurring urge to laugh (*informal*) [Early 16C. An imitation of the sound.] —**giggler** *n* —**giggling** *adj* —**giggly** *adj*

GIGO /gígō/ *n* the principle that a computer program or process is only as good as the ideas and data put into it. Full form **garbage in, garbage out**

gigolo /jíggəlō/ (*plural* **-los**) *n* **1** a man who receives payments or gifts from a woman in exchange for being her sexual or social partner **2** a man whose job is to be a dancing partner or escort for a woman [Early 20C. < French, < *gigole* 'professional woman dance partner'.]

gigot /jíggət, zhígg-, zhiggō/ *n* **1** a French and Scottish cut of lamb or mutton taken from the leg **2** a leg of mutton [Early 16C. < French, 'small leg' < French dialect *gigue* 'leg' < *giguer* 'hop'.]

gigot sleeve *n* a sleeve that is close-fitting on the lower arm and full and loose on the upper arm [< its shape]

Gijón /gi hón/ seaport in NW Spain, on the Bay of Biscay. Population: 270,867 (1995).

Gila monster /heélə-, geélə-/ *n* a large brightly coloured venomous lizard that feeds on eggs and small mammals. Native to: desert areas of the SW United States and Mexico. *Heloderma suspectum*. [Late 19C. After the GILA RIVER.]

Gila River /heélə-, geélə-/ river in SW New Mexico and S Arizona. Length: 1,014 km/630 mi.

gilbert /gílbərt/ *n* a unit of magnetomotive force in the centimetre-gram-second system, equal to 0.7958 ampere-turns in the SI system [Late 19C. After William *Gilbert* (1544–1603), English physician and scientist.]

Gilbert /gílbərt/, **Sir W. S.** (1836–1911) British librettist and dramatist. Full name **Sir William Schwenck Gilbert**

Gilbert and Ellice Islands /-élliss-/ former British colony in the W Pacific Ocean, comprising present-day Tuvalu and part of Kiribati

Gilbert and George (*b.* 1942 and 1943) British performance artists and photographers

gild /gild/ *vt* **1** to cover something with a thin layer of gold leaf or of a substance that looks like gold **2** to give a golden colouring or tinge to something (*literary*) [Old English *gyldan* < Germanic] —**gilder** *n*

SPELLCHECK See ***guild***.

gilded /gíldid/ *adj* **1** ARTS = **gilt**[1] *adj.* **2** wealthy and privileged ○ *gilded youth*

gilding /gílding/ *n* **1** the process of applying a thin layer of gold leaf, or something that looks like gold, to a surface **2** ARTS = **gilt**[1] *n.* 1

Gilead, Mount /gílli ad/ mountain in NW Jordan that also gives its name to an area east of the River Jordan. Height: 1,096 m/3,597 ft.

Giles /jīlz/, **Ernest** (1835–97) British-born Australian explorer

gilet /zheé lay/ *n* **1** a bodice to a dress or a ballet-dancer's costume that is shaped like a waistcoat **2** a light sleeveless jacket, similar to a waistcoat but often longer, and sometimes made of padded or quilted material [Late 19C. < French.]

gill[1] /gil/ *n* **1** the organ that fish and some other aquatic animals use to breathe, consisting of a membrane containing many blood vessels through which oxygen passes **2** a thin radiating plate on the underside of the cap of a mushroom or other fungus where its spores are produced [14C. < Old Norse.] —**gilled** *adj* ◇ **green around the gills** looking on the point of being sick (*informal*) ◇ **to the gills** to the fullest possible extent

gill[2] /jil/ *n* a unit of liquid measure equal to a quarter of a pint (142 ml in the United Kingdom and 118 ml in the United States) [14C. Via Old French *gille* < late Latin *gillo* 'water pot'.]

gill[3] /gil/, **ghyll** *n* (*regional*) **1** a small fast-flowing stream, usually on a hill or mountain **2** a ravine with tree-covered sides [14C. < Old Norse *gil*.]

gill[4] /jil/, **jill** *n* a young woman (*archaic; sometimes offensive*) [15C. Shortening of the forename *Gillian*.]

Gilles de la Tourette syndrome /jeél-/ *n* full form of **Tourette syndrome**

Gillespie /gi léspi/, **Dizzy** (1917–93) US jazz musician. Full name **John Birks Gillespie**

gill fungus /gíl-/ *n* a fungus that produces its spores from gills underneath a cap

gillie /gílli/, **ghillie** *n* **1** *Scotland* somebody whose job is to assist or guide people who go angling or deer-stalking in Scotland **2** a low-cut tongueless shoe that laces across the foot and sometimes up the ankle [Late 17C. < Gaelic *gille*.]

Gillies /gílliss/, **Sir Harold** (1882–1960) New Zealand surgeon

Gillingham /jíllingəm/ town in SE England. Population: 95,800 (1995).

gill net /gíl-/ *n* a net that is suspended vertically in the water like a curtain in order to catch fish by their gills —**gillnetter** *n*

gill slit /gíl-/ *n* one of the openings on each side of the head of a fish or amphibian that contain its gills

gillyflower /jílli flowər/ *n* **1** a clove-scented pink or carnation **2** a scented flower such as a stock or wallflower (*archaic*) [14C. < Alteration (after FLOWER) of French *girofle*, via medieval Latin *caryophyllum* 'clove' < Greek *karuophullon* 'nut leaf'.]

Gilmore /gíl mawr/, **Dame Mary Jean** (1865–1962) Australian poet and journalist

gilt[1] /gilt/ *n* **1** a thin layer of gold, or a substance that looks like gold, applied to a surface **2** a bond issued by the government (*often plural*) [15C. < past participle of GILD.] —**gilt** *adj* ◇ **take the gilt off the gingerbread** to spoil something that somebody was enjoying or looking forward to having or doing

SPELLCHECK See ***guilt***.

gilt[2] /gilt/ *n* a young female pig, especially one that has not yet had a litter [14C. < Old Norse *gyltr*.]

gilt-edged *adj* **1** VERY SAFE FINANCIALLY very safe as an investment **2** WITH A GOLD EDGE having a gilded edge **3** EXCELLENT very good, especially because of being free of risk and advantageous (*informal*) ○ *This is a gilt-edged opportunity to recoup our losses.*

gimbal /jímb'l/ *n* **1** RING FOR HOLDING A COMPASS STEADY a pivoted ring mounted at right angles to one or two others to ensure that something such as a ship's compass always remains horizontal **2** CONNECTION OF REVOLVING PARTS an interconnection that allows one part of a mechanism such as a clock's works to revolve independently of another revolving part that contains it ■ *vt* (**-bals, -balling, -balled**) PUT ON GIMBALS to support something on gimbals [Late 16C. Variant of GIMMAL.]

gimcrack /jím krak/ *adj* showy or superficially appealing, but badly made and worthless [14C. < ?] —**gimcrack** *n* —**gimcrackery** *n*

gimel /gimm'l/ *n* the third letter of the Hebrew alphabet [< Hebrew *gīmel*]

gimlet /gímlət/ *n* **1** TOOL FOR BORING HOLES IN WOOD a small tool for boring holes in wood consisting of a slim metal rod with a sharp corkscrew end, fitted in a handle at a right angle **2** COCKTAIL WITH LIME JUICE a cocktail made of vodka or gin with lime juice ■ *adj* PIERCING seeming to penetrate or pierce somebody or something ○ *'to meet anew the gimlet glances'* (Thomas Hardy, *Jude the Obscure*; 1895) [14C. < Old French *guimbelet* 'small auger' < *guimble* 'auger' < Germanic.]

gimlet-eyed *adj* having eyes that seem to pierce and penetrate or to notice everything

gimmal /gímməl, jím-/ *n* MECH ENG = **gimbal** *n.* 1 ■ NAVIG = **gimbal** *n.* 2 [Late 16C. Alteration of obsolete *gemel* 'double ring', via Old French < Latin *gemellus* < *geminus* 'twin'.]

gimme /gímmi/ *contr* give me (*nonstandard*)

gimmick /gímmik/ *n* **1** DISHONEST TRICK a piece of trickery or manipulation intended to achieve a result dishonestly ○ *It's not a genuine offer, just a sales gimmick.* **2** US HIDDEN DISADVANTAGE a piece of concealed information that, if known, would make an offer or opportunity less attractive ○ *It sounds great, but what's the gimmick?* **3** SOMETHING ATTENTION-GRABBING something such as a new technique or device that attracts attention or publicity **4** GADGET an ingenious device, mechanism, or ploy, especially one that works in a concealed way [Early 20C. < ?] —**gimmicky** *adj*

gimmickry /gímmikri/ *n* **1** gimmicks in general **2** the use of a gimmick or gimmicks to deceive or attract attention

gimp /gimp/ *n* US **1** DIFFICULTY IN WALKING difficulty in walking, caused by injury or stiffness (*informal*) **2** OFFENSIVE TERM an offensive term for a person with a physical disability, especially somebody who has difficulty walking or who uses a wheelchair (*slang*) **3** CLUMSY PERSON a clumsy or ineffectual person (*slang insult; often considered offensive*) [Early 20C. < ?] —**gimpy** *adj*

gin[1] /jin/ *n* **1** a strong colourless alcoholic spirit distilled from grain and flavoured with juniper berries **2** gin rummy (*informal*) [Early 18C. Shortening of GENEVER.]

gin[2] /jin/ *n* **1** HOIST a simple hoist operated by hand **2** TRAP a snare or trap, usually one consisting of a noose made of wire for catching small animals ■ *vt* (**gins, ginning, ginned**) **1** CATCH SOMETHING IN GIN to trap an animal with a gin **2** CLEAN RAW COTTON to separate cotton from its seeds with a gin [13C. Shortening of Old French *engin* 'engine'.]

gin and it *n* a drink consisting of gin and Italian vermouth (*informal*) [< shortening of ITALIAN]

ginger /jínjər/ *n* **1** HOT-TASTING SPICE the hot-tasting edible underground stem (**rhizome**) of an Asian plant, used fresh in Asian cookery and as a spice in powdered form **2** PLANT a widely-cultivated plant that yields ginger. Native to: Asia. *Zingiber officinale*. **3** BROWNISH-YELLOW COLOUR a yellow colour with an orange or brownish tinge [Pre-12C. < Old French *gingi(m)bre*, via Latin and Greek < Pali *singivera*.] —**ginger** *adj* —**gingery** *adj*

ginger up *vt* to make something more lively, active, or interesting [< inserting a piece of ginger into the anus of a slothful horse]

ginger ale *n* an effervescent nonalcoholic drink flavoured with ginger

ginger beer *n* a mildly alcoholic cloudy effervescent drink made by fermenting a mixture of syrup and ginger

gingerbread /jínjər bred/ *n* **1** GINGER-FLAVOURED CAKE a moist dark cake made with syrup or treacle and flavoured with ginger **2** GINGER-FLAVOURED BISCUIT a ginger-flavoured biscuit, often cut into the stylized shape of a person, animal, or Christmas tree **3** ELABORATE DECORATION showy and elaborate decoration, especially on the outside of a building (*often before nouns*) ○ *a Victorian gingerbread style of cottage* [13C. By folk etymology (by association with BREAD) < Old French *gingembrat* 'preserved ginger' < medieval Latin *gingiber* 'ginger'.]

gingerbread man *n* a biscuit in the stylized shape of a person, made from gingerbread and often decorated with icing

ginger group *n* UK, Can a group, often within a party or association, whose aim is to stimulate debate and press for more radical or decisive action on something

gingerly /jínjərli/ *adv* in a very cautious, wary, or tentative way ○ *He gingerly unscrewed the radiator cap.* ■ *adj* very cautious, wary, or tentative ○ *Not for her the gingerly approach – she came straight out with the question.* [Early 16C. < ?] —**gingerliness** *n*

ginger nut, ginger snap *n* a small round crisp ginger-flavoured biscuit

ginger wine *n* wine made by fermenting bruised ginger with sugar and water

gingham /gíngəm/ *n* a light plain-weave cotton fabric with checks in white and another colour (*often before nouns*) ○ *a gingham dress* [Early 17C. Via Dutch *gingang* < Malay *genggang* 'striped'.]

gingiva /jin jīvə, jínjivə/ (*plural* **-vae** /-vee/) *n* gum around the roots of the teeth (*technical*) [Late 19C. < Latin.]

gingival /jin jīv'l, jínjiv'l/ *adj* relating to or affecting the gums (*technical*)

gingivectomy /jínji véktəmi/ (*plural* **-mies**) *n* a surgical operation to remove tissue from the gums

gingivitis /jínji vītiss/ *n* inflammation of the gums around the roots of the teeth

gingko *n* TREES = **ginkgo**

ginglymus /jíng glimәss/ (*plural* **-mi** /-mī/) *n* a hinge joint of the human body (*technical*)

gink /gink/ *n* somebody, especially a man, who is considered strange, unintelligent, or clumsy (*informal insult*) [Early 20C. < ?]

ginkgo /gíngkō/ (*plural* **-goes**), **gingko** (*plural* **-koes**) *n* a widely cultivated deciduous tree of primitive origin, with fan-shaped leaves. Native to: China. *Ginkgo biloba.* [Late 18C. Via Japanese < Chinese *yínxìng* 'silver apricot'.]

ginkgo biloba /-bi lōbə/ *n* a herbal preparation made from the pulverized leaves of the ginkgo tree. Use: to treat a variety of disorders. [< modern Latin genus name]

ginnel /gínn'l/ *n N England* a narrow alley or passageway between two walls or buildings [Early 17C. < ?]

ginormous /jī náwrməss/ *adj* extraordinarily large in size (*informal*) [Mid-20C. Blend of GIGANTIC + ENORMOUS.]

gin palace *n* a large bar or public house furnished or decorated in a gaudy and pretentious style (*dated*)

gin rummy *n* a card game similar to rummy in which two players collect sets and sequences of cards [< GIN1; pun on RUMMY1, as if < RUM1]

Ginsberg /gínzbərg/, **Allen** (1926–97) US poet

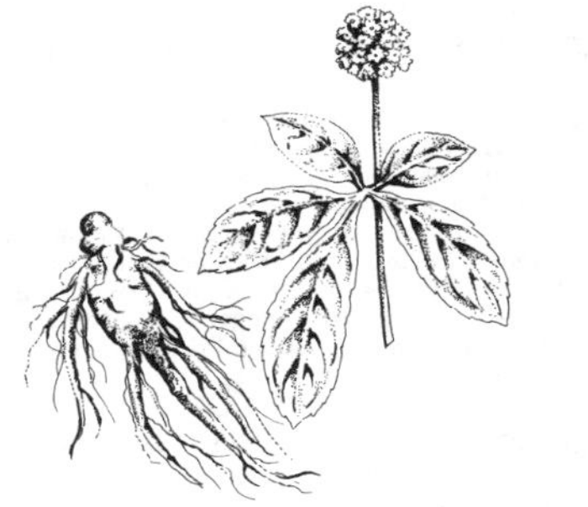

Ginseng

ginseng /jín seng/ (*plural* **-sengs** *or* **-seng**) *n* **1** a forked aromatic root used in traditional Chinese medicine and more widely used as a tonic **2** a plant that produces the ginseng root. Native to: Asia, North America. Genus: *Panax.* [Mid-17C. < Chinese *rénshēn* < *rén* 'man' + *shēn*, type of herb.]

gin sling *n* an iced drink consisting of gin, water, and lemon or lime juice

Giotto /jóttō/ (1266?–1337) Italian painter

gip *vt, n* = **gyp**2

gippo /jíppō/ (*plural* **gippos**) *n* = **gyppo** (*offensive regional*)

Gippsland /gíps land/ region in SE Victoria, Australia. Area: 31,000 sq. km/11,970 sq. mi.

gippy tummy /jíppi-/ *n* = **gyppy tummy** (*dated informal*)

Gipsy *n, adj* PEOPLES = **Gypsy**

giraffe /jə ráaf/ (*plural* **-raffes** *or* **-raffe**) *n* a ruminant mammal with an extremely long neck, long legs, and a yellowish coat mottled with brown patches that lives in open grassland. Native to: Africa. *Giraffa camelopardalis.* [Late 16C. Via French *girafe* or Italian *giraffa* < Arabic *zarāfa*.]

girandole /jírrəndōl/, **girandola** /ji rándələ/ *n* **1** WALL-MOUNTED CANDLEHOLDER a wall-mounted branched candleholder that often incorporates a mirror between the candlestick branches **2** STARBURST JEWELLERY an earring or pendant with a large central stone surrounded by several smaller ones **3** ROTATING FIREWORK an elaborate rotating firework **4** WATER JET a revolving water jet [Mid-17C. Via French < Italian *girandola* < late Latin *gyrare* 'gyrate'.]

Giraudoux /zhéerō doo/, **Jean** (1882–1944) French writer

gird1 /gurd/ (**girds, girding, girded** *or* **girt** /gurt/) *v* **1** *vr* GET READY to prepare yourself for conflict or vigorous activity **2** *vt* PUT BELT AROUND to put a girdle or belt around yourself or another person (*literary*) **3** *vt* FASTEN ON to secure something to yourself with a belt, straps, or a girdle (*literary*) **4** *vt* SURROUND to surround or encompass something (*literary*) ○ *a castle girded with a moat* **5** *vt* INVEST to provide somebody with or dress somebody in something that is a sign of rank or honour (*literary*) [Old English *gyrdan* < Germanic]

gird2 /gurd/ *vti N England* to jeer or gibe at somebody ■ *n N England* a gibe or taunt [12C. < ?]

girder /gúrdər/ *n* a large strong beam, often of steel, forming a main spanning and supporting part in a framework

girdle1 /gúrd'l/ *n* **1** WOMAN'S FOUNDATION GARMENT a woman's elasticated foundation garment or corset extending from the waist to the thigh **2** NARROW BELT a cord worn round the waist to hold in a large loose-fitting garment such as a kaftan or a monk's habit **3** SOMETHING THAT SURROUNDS anything that surrounds or encircles something (*literary*) **4** RING OF BONE a ring-shaped structure of bone, especially the pelvic girdle and pectoral girdle that support the upper and lower limbs **5** PART OF CUT GEMSTONE the outer edge of a gem, by which it is held in its setting **6** RING ROUND TREE TRUNK the ring round a tree trunk made by removing the bark and underlying tissue in order to kill the tree ■ *vt* (**-dles, -dling, -dled**) **1** SURROUND to surround or encircle something (*literary*) **2** CUT RING OF BARK FROM TREE to remove a ring of bark and underlying tissue from a tree trunk in order to kill the tree [Old English *gyrdel* < Germanic]

girdle2 /gúrd'l/ *n Scotland, N England* a griddle (*nonstandard*) [15C. Variant.]

girdler /gúrdlər/ *n* an insect that makes a groove round a branch or twig in which to lay its eggs, thereby killing the branch

giri /gírri/ *n* a social obligation or debt (*informal*) [< Japanese]

girl /gurl/ *n* **1** FEMALE CHILD a human female from birth until the age at which she is considered an adult **2** ⚠ YOUNG WOMAN a young woman (*often considered offensive*) **3** ⚠ ANY WOMAN a woman of any age, especially one who is a friend, a contemporary, or younger than the speaker (*informal; often considered offensive*) ○ *a night out with the girls* **4** DAUGHTER somebody's daughter, especially when a child (*informal*) **5** GIRLFRIEND a man's or boy's girlfriend **6** WAY OF ADDRESSING WOMAN used as a friendly, intimate, or patronizing form of address to a woman (*offensive in some contexts*) **7** OFFENSIVE TERM an offensive term for a young woman servant or employee (*dated*) **8** FEMALE CREATURE a female animal or other creature, especially a young one (*informal; often before nouns*) ○ *a girl kitten* [13C. < ?] —**girlhood** *n*

USAGE girl or **woman**? ***Girl*** is used more often as an alternative for ***woman***, especially in reference to a young woman, than *boy* is for *man*. (*Boy* in reference to an adult is normally found only in the plural or in meanings such as *boyfriend*.) However, the use of ***girl*** for a teenager or an adult is sometimes regarded as patronizing or disrespectful, especially when it comes from a man.

girl band *n* a pop group made up of personable young women who sing and dance to synthesized music but do not usually play instruments

girl Friday *n* a young woman whose job is to be somebody's personal assistant and to do general office work (*sometimes offensive*) [After *Man Friday*, all-round helper in *Robinson Crusoe* (1719) by Daniel DEFOE]

girlfriend /gúrl frend/ *n* **1** a girl or woman with whom somebody has a romantic or sexual relationship **2** a woman who is the friend of another woman

Girl Guide *n* a member of the Guides Association

girlie /gúrli/ *adj* **1** SHOWING NUDE WOMEN showing or involving naked or scantily dressed women (*often considered offensive*) **2** = **girly** ■ *n* **1** OFFENSIVE TERM an offensive term of address when used by a man to a woman **2** LITTLE GIRL a little girl (*dated informal*)

girlish /gúrlish/ *adj* **1** typical or characteristic of girls **2** more suitable for a girl than for an adult woman —**girlishly** *adv* —**girlishness** *n*

girl power *n* the ability of or opportunity for teenage girls and young women to make decisions for themselves and shape their own lives

Girl Scout *n* a member of the girls' branch of the worldwide Scout movement in the United States

girly /gúrli/ (**-ier, -iest**) *adj* extremely or deliberately feminine ○ *a girly lace collar*

girn /gurn/, **gurn** *vi* **1** *Scotland, N England* COMPLAIN to complain, whine, or grumble **2** *Scotland, N England* GRIMACE to make a bad-tempered or discontented face **3** PULL WEIRD FACES to use the facial muscles to pull and twist the face into an absurdly grotesque expression, especially in a competition [14C. Alteration of GRIN.]

giro /jīrō/ *n* (*plural* **-ros**) **1** BANK TRANSFER SYSTEM a system that enables money to be transferred quickly and cheaply between accounts or between the financial institutions of a country **2** BENEFIT CHEQUE a cheque, cashable at a post office, for the payment of a state benefit such as unemployment benefit (*informal*) ■ *vt* (**-ros, -roing, -roed**) PAY MONEY BY GIRO SYSTEM to pay or transfer money by the giro system [Late 19C. Via German < Italian, 'circulation (of money)'.]

giron *n* HERALDRY = **gyron**

Gironde /ji rónd, zhi róNd/ river estuary in SW France. Length: 72 km/45 mi.

girt past tense, past participle of **gird**1

girth /gurth/ *n* **1** DISTANCE ROUND the distance round something thick and cylindrical, e.g. a tree trunk or somebody's waist ○ *a man of ample girth* **2** SADDLE BAND a broad band fastened around the belly of a horse to keep a saddle in place ■ *vt* **1** SADDLE A HORSE to put or fasten a girth on a horse **2** SURROUND to surround or encircle something (*literary*) [14C. < Old Norse *gjǫrð* 'girdle'.]

gisarme /gi záarm/ *n* a medieval foot soldier's weapon that had a long shaft and a head with an axe blade on one side and a sharp point on the other [13C. < Old French *guisarme*.]

Gisborne /gízbərn/ administrative region on the North Island, New Zealand. Population: 46,089 (1996). Area: 13,703 sq. km/5,291 sq. mi.

Gish /gish/, **Lillian** (1893?–1993) US actor. Born **Lillian de Guiche**

gismo *n* = **gizmo**

gist /jist/ *n* **1** the essential point or meaning of something **2** the essential grounds for a legal action [Early 18C. < Old French *cest action gist* 'this action lies'.]

git /git/ *n* an offensive term for somebody regarded as annoying, troublesome, unpleasant, or thoughtless (*informal insult*) [Mid-20C. Variant of GET2.]

gite /zheet/ *n* a house, cottage, or apartment in France offering fairly simple accommodation that can be rented for a self-catering holiday [Late 18C. < French *gîte* 'stopping place'.]

gittern /gíttərn/ *n* a medieval stringed instrument that was a forerunner of the guitar [14C. Via Old French *guiterne* < Latin *cithara* (see CITHARA).]

~~**giutar**~~ incorrect spelling of **guitar**

give /giv/ (**gives, giving, gave** /gayv/, **given** /gívv'n/) CORE MEANING: a verb used to indicate that somebody presents or delivers something that he or she owns to another person to keep or use it ○ *He gave Brian £800 with the understanding he would pay the rest at a later date.* ○ *The programme would give education grants to people who do community service.* ○ *My mother gave me this cardigan for Christmas.* ○ *What will you give me for the car?* ○ *When we arrived they gave us badges with our names on.*

1 *vt* PASS SOMETHING TO SOMEBODY to place something that you are holding in the temporary possession of another person ○ *Could you give me the phone?* **2** *vt* GRANT SOMETHING TO SOMEBODY to allow somebody to have something such as power or a right ○ *Opponents of the bill claimed it gave too much power to the mine owners.* **3** *vt* COMMUNICATE to impart or convey something such as information, advice, or opinions **4** *vt* CONVEY to cause somebody to have an idea or impression ○ *Whatever gave you that idea?* **5** *vt* IMPART to make somebody experience a particular physical or emotional feeling ○ *She said the steady paycheque gave her a sense of security.* **6** *vt* PERFORM to carry out or perform something in public ○ *Not one of these actors gave a performance that was worthy of the prize.* **7** *vt* MAKE OR DO used with nouns referring to physical actions to indicate that the action is being made or done ○ *She gave Paul a quick, accusing glance.* **8** *vt* PROVIDE SERVICE to perform an action or service for somebody ○ *He gave her a foot massage to relax her.* ○ *The guide gave us a tour of the ruins.* **9** *vt* DEVOTE to devote or sacrifice something such as time or effort ○ *He gave his whole life to helping children in need.* **10** *vt* ORGANIZE to spend time organizing a social event ○ *They gave her a great send off when she retired last year.* **11** *vt* CAUSE TO BELIEVE to lead somebody to have a particular understanding about something ○ *I was given to understand that they would be coming to us for one weekend.* **12** *vt* VALUE to estimate something at a particular amount or value ○ *What do you give for his chances of getting her back?* **13** *vi* YIELD to collapse or break under pressure ○ *The wheel gave under the heavy load.* ○ *When people are under constant pressure from work and home, something has to give.* **14** *vt* CONCEDE to yield to somebody's opinion, or admit that somebody has an advantage or a specific characteristic or ability **15** *vt* TOAST to propose a toast to somebody ○ *I give you the* *bride and groom!* **16** *n* **RESILIENCE** the ability or tendency to yield under pressure [Old English *giefan* < Indo-European] —**giver** *n* ◇ **give me...** I'd rather do or have... (*informal*) ○ *Give me a quiet evening with a book any time.* ◇ **give or take** used to indicate that a figure given is fairly accurate, within the stated range ○ *worth about half a million, give or take a few thousand pounds*

SYNONYMS ***give, present, confer, bestow, donate, grant***

CORE MEANING: to hand over something to somebody

give to hand over a possession to somebody else to keep or use; **present** to give something in a formal or ceremonial way; **confer** (*formal*) to give somebody an honour, privilege, or award, often at a formal ceremony; **bestow** (*formal*) to present somebody with something, especially something unexpected or undeserved; **donate** to give a contribution to a charitable organization or another good cause, or, in a medical context, to give blood for blood transfusions or organs for transplant; **grant** to agree to allow a request, favour, or privilege, especially at the discretion of a person in authority, or formally or officially to give money.

give away *vt* **1 GIVE SOMETHING AS A PRESENT** to give or offer something without charging for it **2 DISCLOSE BY MISTAKE** to reveal information or a secret, often without meaning to **3 BETRAY** to betray somebody by providing information **4 PRESENT BRIDE TO HUSBAND AT WEDDING** to accompany a bride to her future husband's side and formally present her to him just before the words of the wedding ceremony are spoken **5 LET OPPONENT SCORE POINT** to allow an opponent to get an advantage, especially inadvertently, through poor or illegal play **6** *ANZ* **ABANDON** to abandon or give up on something

give back *vt* to return something, especially to its rightful or original owner

give in *v* **1** *vi* **LOSE** to admit defeat **2** *vi* **ACCEPT CONDITIONS** to accept demands or conditions **3** *vt* **HAND OVER** to hand over or deliver something, especially a piece of school work, to somebody who is expecting it ○ *He gave his essay in a week late.* **4** *vi US* **BREAK** to collapse or break under pressure

give of *vr* to devote or dedicate your time or energy to something

give off *v* **1** *vt* to send out or emit something **2** *vi N Ireland* to speak one's mind angrily (*informal*)

give on to *vt* to overlook or lead to something ○ *The French windows give on to a small paved area.*

give out *v* **1** *vt* **HAND OVER** to hand over or distribute something **2** *vt* **MAKE SOMETHING KNOWN** to declare something or make something known, especially publicly ○ *She gave out the exam marks in reverse order.* **3** *vt* **EMIT** to send out or emit something **4** *vi* **BE USED UP** to run out or be finished ○ *My courage gave out, and I couldn't face her after all.* **5** *vi* **STOP WORKING** to fail or stop working **6** *vt* **DISMISS A BATSMAN** in cricket, to declare that a batsman is dismissed

give over *vi* to stop doing something, especially something that is annoying to others (*informal; usually a command*)

give over to *v* **1** *vt* to dedicate or assign something to a particular purpose or use ○ *This area will be given over to a children's playground.* **2** *vr* to abandon yourself to an emotion or experience (*literary*) ○ *She gave herself over to despair.*

give up *v* **1** *vi* **SURRENDER** to surrender or admit defeat **2** *vt* **HAND OVER** to hand over or part with somebody or something ○ *She gave up her seat to the man with a baby.* **3** *vt* **STOP USING OR DOING** to stop or renounce using or doing something ○ *give up chocolate for a week* **4** *vt* **STOP TRYING** to abandon a pursuit that has a goal ○ *Darkness fell, but they didn't give up trying to finish the game or match.* **5** *vt* **LOSE HOPE FOR GOOD OUTCOME** to stop hoping for a good outcome with regard to somebody or something ○ *Where have you been? We'd given you up as lost.* **6** *vt* **DEVOTE YOURSELF TO** to devote or dedicate yourself to an emotion, experience, or activity, especially exclusively ○ *He gave himself up to working for the cause.* **7** *vt* **REVEAL INFORMATION** to reveal information or a secret ◇ **give it up for somebody** *or* **something** to applaud somebody or something enthusiastically (*informal*)

give up on *vt* **1** to abandon something, especially a plan **2** to lose hope about somebody or something

give way *vi* **1** to become useless, break, or otherwise fail, especially under weight or pressure or from age or wear **2** to slow down or stop in order to let another vehicle pass

give way to *vt* **1 HAND OVER** to allow somebody or something to have priority or to take precedence **2 BECOME** to be replaced or superseded by somebody or something ○ *The rain gave way to patchy sunshine.* **3 SHOW EMOTION** to allow something, especially an emotion, to be expressed

give-and-go (*plural* **give-and-gos**) *n US* in team games, an attacking move in which a player passes the ball or puck to another, runs or skates past an opponent, and receives it back immediately from the other player

give-and-take *n* (*informal*) **1** mutual cooperation and understanding between people or groups, often involving concessions on all sides **2** a useful exchange of ideas or information in which everyone involved benefits

giveaway /gív əway/ *n* **1 SOMETHING THAT REVEALS** something that serves to reveal, betray, or expose something ○ *Her accent's a dead giveaway.* **2 GIFT** something that is offered free of charge or at very little cost, often as a publicity gimmick or incentive to buy (*informal*) **3** MEDIA = **free-sheet 4** *US* **GAME SHOW** a radio or TV game show that offers contestants the chance to win prizes, especially cash prizes (*informal*) ■ *adj* (*informal*) **1 VERY INEXPENSIVE** extremely low in price **2 FREE** free of charge ○ *a giveaway sample of a new shampoo*

giveback /gív bak/ *n* something that is or has been returned (*informal*)

given /gívv'n/ past participle of **give** ■ *adj* **1 PARTICULAR** relating to a specific person, thing, or concept **2 ARRANGED EARLIER** previously arranged or specified **3 VALIDATED** validated or executed on the date mentioned (*formal*) ○ *this last will and testament given by my hand this 13th day of February 1898* ■ *prep* **1 GRANTED** assuming that somebody has the opportunity or ability to do or have something ○ *Given time, I'm sure we can find a solution.* **2 IN VIEW OF** taking into consideration ○ *given the uncertainty of the situation* ■ *n* **ACCEPTED FACT** a fact or event that is accepted as true or definite at the outset and that affects following or subsequent reasoning ◇ **given to** inclined to something or likely to do or be something

given name *n* the name or names that somebody is given at birth or baptism in addition to the family name

Giza /geézə/ city in N Egypt on the western bank of the River Nile. Population: 2,144,000 (1992).

gizmo /gízmō/ (*plural* **-mos**), **gismo** (*plural* **-mos**) *n* a gadget, especially a mechanical or electrical device considered to be more complicated than necessary or one whose name is not known or forgotten (*informal*) ○ *a new video recorder with all the latest gizmos* [Mid-20C. < ?]

gizzard /gízzərd/ *n* **1 PART OF BIRD'S DIGESTIVE TRACT** a thick-walled muscular sac in the alimentary tract of birds where food is broken down by muscular action and by small stones ingested for that purpose **2 DIGESTIVE STRUCTURE** a structure in invertebrates and fish where digestion takes place **3 STOMACH** the stomach or alimentary canal generally (*informal*) [14C. Via Old French *giser* < Latin *gigeria* 'cooked poultry entrails'.]

glabella /glə béllə/ (*plural* **-lae** /-lee/) *n* the part of the human forehead that lies just above the nose and between the eyebrows [Early 19C. < modern Latin, < Latin *glaber* 'hairless'.] —**glabellar** *adj*

glabrate /gláybrayt, -brət/ *adj* **1** BIOL = **glabrous** *adj.* **2** almost completely smooth and hairless [Mid-19C. < Latin *glabrare* 'make hairless' < *glaber* 'hairless'.]

glabrescent /glay bréssənt/ *adj* becoming hairless over time

glabrous /gláybrəss/ *adj* smooth and lacking hairs or bristles ○ *glabrous leaves* [Mid-17C. < Latin *glaber* 'hairless'.] —**glabrousness** *n*

glacé /glássay/ *adj* **1 GLAZED WITH SUGAR SOLUTION** coated with a sugar solution that results in a glazed finish ○ *glacé cherries* **2 MADE FROM ICING SUGAR AND LIQUID** made by mixing icing sugar and a liquid, usually water **3 SMOOTHLY GLOSSY** having a smooth glossy finish [Mid-19C. < French, past participle of *glacer* 'glaze' < *glace* (see GLACIER).]

Glace Bay /gláyss-/ town in NE Nova Scotia, Canada, on the Atlantic coast. Population: 23,038 (1996).

glacial /gláysh'l/ *adj* **1 RELATING TO GLACIER** relating to or caused by a glacier or glaciers ○ *glacial movements and deposits* **2 CONTAINING EXPANSES OF ICE** characterized by the presence of ice masses **3 ICE-AGE** describes any geological time when a large part of the Earth was covered in ice **4 FRIGID** icily cold ○ *a glacial wind* **5 COLDLY HOSTILE** unfriendly or hostile ○ *a glacial look* **6 DETACHED** characterized by detachment and an absence of emotion ○ *glacial determination* **7 SLOW** moving or advancing extremely slowly ○ *the glacial pace of the negotiations* ■ *n* **glacial, Glacial** GEOL = **glacial period** [Mid-17C. Via Old French < Latin *glacialis* 'icy' < *glacies* 'ice'.] —**glacially** *adv*

glacial acetic acid *n* acetic acid that is 99.8% or more pure [Because it forms crystals resembling ice]

glacial period, glacial epoch *n* any period of geological time when most of the Earth was covered in ice

glaciate /gláyssi ayt/ (**-ates, -ating, -ated**) *v* **1** *vti* to cover something, or become covered, with a glacier **2** *vt* to affect something by the action of a glacier, especially by erosion [Early 17C. < Latin *glaciat-*, past participle of *glaciare* 'freeze' < *glacies* 'ice'.] —**glaciation** /gláyssi áysh'n/ *n*

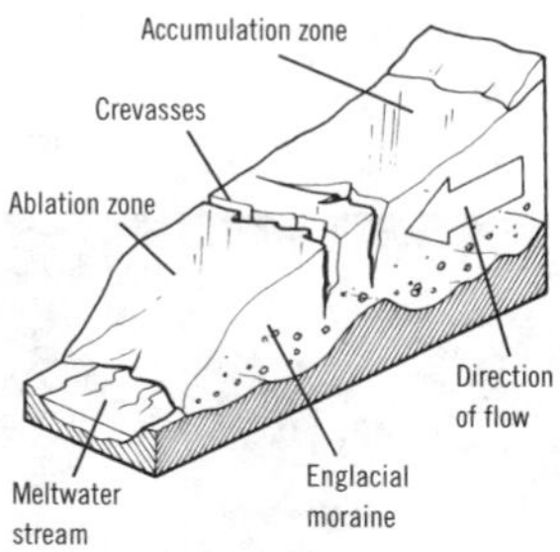
Accumulation zone
Crevasses
Ablation zone
Direction of flow
Englacial moraine
Meltwater stream

Glacier: Composition of a glacier

glacier /glássi ər/ *n* a large body of continuously accumulating ice and compacted snow, formed in mountain valleys or at the poles, that deforms under its own weight and slowly moves [Mid-18C. < French, < *glace* 'ice' < Latin *glacies*.] —**glaciered** *adj*

glacier cream *n* a sunblock designed to combat the effects of ultraviolet radiation that climbers experience above the snow line, where the sun reflects strongly off the snow

glacier meal *n* GEOL = **rock flour**

glaciology /gláyssi óllәji/ *n* the branch of scientific study concerned with the formation, movement, and effects of glaciers and ice in general —**glaciologic** /gláyssi ә lójjik/ *adj* —**glaciological** *adj* —**glaciologist** *n*

glacis /gláyssis/ (*plural* **-cises** /-si seez/ *or* **-cis** /-siz/) *n* **1 GENTLE INCLINE** a slope, especially one that is not very long or steep **2 DEFENSIVE SLOPE** a slope in front of a fortification designed to make it easier to fire on attacking forces **3 NEUTRAL TERRITORY** a stretch of neutral ground between two opposing or warring forces **4** MIL = **glacis plate** [Late 17C. < French, < Old French *glacier* (see GLANCE).]

glacis plate *n* the armoured plate at the front of a military tank [< its slant]

glad /glad/ *adj* (**gladder, gladdest**) **1 DELIGHTED** happy and pleased ○ *I'm so glad you came.* **2 CHEERFULLY WILLING** willing or ready to do something ○ *always glad to help* **3 GRATEFUL** appreciative of or grateful for something ○ *glad of the chance to relax* **4 PLEASING** giving pleasure, delight, or happiness ○ *on this glad occasion* **5 BRIGHT** bright and cheerful (*literary*) ○ *this glad June day* ■ *vti* (**glads, gladding, gladded**) **GLADDEN** to gladden somebody (*archaic*) [Old English *glæd* < Germanic] —**gladly** *adj* —**gladness** *n*

gladden /gládd'n/ *vti* to feel or cause somebody to feel cheerful and hopeful ○ *It gladdens my heart to hear that.*

glade /glayd/ *n* an area in a wood or forest without trees or bushes [Early 16C. < ?] —**glady** *adj*

glad hand *n* **1** a hand extended in welcome or greeting, especially one offered insincerely or for motives of self-advancement **2** a friendly welcome

glad-hand *vti* to offer somebody a friendly greeting or handshake, often insincerely or for motives of self-advancement —**glad-hander** *n*

gladiate /gláddi ət/ *adj* shaped like a sword ○ *the gladiate leaves of an iris* [Late 18C. < Latin *gladius* 'sword'.]

gladiator /gláddi aytər/ *n* **1 FIGHTER IN ROMAN ARENA** a professional fighter in ancient Rome who fought another combatant or a wild animal in public entertainments set in an arena **2 KEEN SUPPORTER OR CAMPAIGNER** a vigorous fighter or campaigner for or against a cause or person **3** *US* **BOXER** a professional boxer (*informal*) [Mid-16C. <

Latin, < *gladius* 'sword'.] —**gladiatorial** /gláddi ə táwri əl/ *adj*

gladiolus /gláddi ṓləss/ (*plural* **-lus** *or* **-li** /-lī/ *or* **-luses**), **gladiola** /-ṓlə/ (*plural* **-las** *or* **-la**) *n* **1** a widely grown plant with long sword-shaped leaves. Flowers: large, funnel-shaped, arranged in tall spikes. Native to: tropics, southern Africa. Genus: *Gladiolus.* **2** the large central part of the breastbone (**sternum**) [16C. < Latin, 'little sword' < *gladius* 'sword'.]

glad rags *npl* somebody's best clothes, reserved for special occasions (*informal*)

gladsome /gládssəm/ *adj* feeling, showing, or bringing happiness (*literary*) ○ *gladsome tidings* —**gladsomely** *adv* —**gladsomeness** *n*

Gladstone[1] /gládstən/ *n* a small four-wheeled horse-drawn carriage with a collapsible roof [Mid-19C. See GLADSTONE BAG.]

Gladstone[2] /gládstən/ coastal city in SE Queensland, Australia. Population: 35,055 (1991).

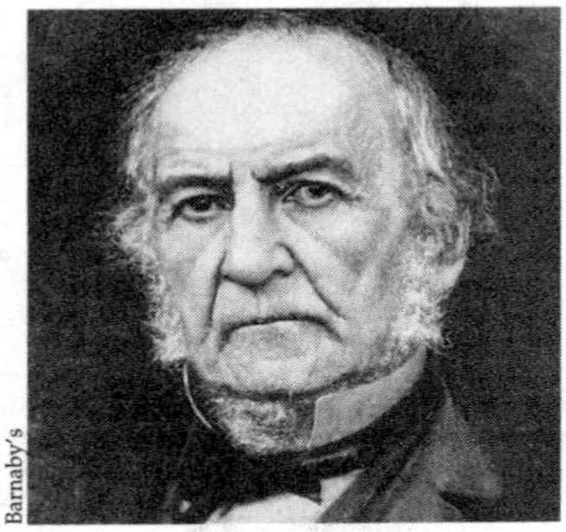
Barnaby's

W. E. Gladstone

Gladstone, W. E. (1809–98) British statesman. Full name **William Ewart Gladstone**

Gladstone bag *n* a small suitcase or portmanteau consisting of a rigid frame on which two compartments of the same size are hinged together [Late 19C. After W. E. GLADSTONE, noted for the amount of travelling he undertook in his public life.]

Glagolitic /glággō líttik/ *adj* **1** belonging or relating to an ancient Slavonic alphabet that was replaced by the Cyrillic alphabet **2** belonging or relating to a Roman Catholic community of SW Croatia, whose liturgical books are still written in the Glagolitic alphabet [Early 19C. < modern Latin *glagoliticus* < Serbo-Croatian *glagŏljica* < Old Church Slavonic *glagolŭ* 'word'.]

glair /glair/, **glaire** *n* **1 EGG WHITE** a sizing, glazing, or adhesive substance made from egg white and used especially in bookbinding **2 SUBSTANCE SIMILAR TO EGG-WHITE SIZING** a substance that resembles glair in appearance or function ■ *vt* **PUT GLAIR ON** to apply glair to something [14C. Via French < Latin *clarus* 'clear'.]

glam /glam/ *adj* **EXTREMELY GLAMOROUS** glamorous, especially in an overstated or ironic way (*slang*) ○ *a really glam dress* ■ *n* **1 EXTREME GLAMOUR** glamour, especially when it is overstated or ironic (*slang*) **2 GLAM ROCK** glam rock (*informal*) ■ *vt* (**glams, glamming, glammed**) **glam, glam up GLAMORIZE EXCESSIVELY** to make somebody or something glamorous, especially in an overstated or ironic way (*slang*) [Mid-20C. Shortening.]

Glamorgan /glə máwrgən/ former county in S Wales, comprising the present-day counties of Cardiff and Swansea

glamorize /glámmə rīz/ (**-izes, -izing, -ized**), **glamorise** (**-ises, -ising, -ised**) *vt* **1** to make somebody or something glamorous **2** to make something seem more interesting, romantic, or glamorous than it really is — **glamorization** /glámmə rī záysh'n/ *n* —**glamorizer** *n*

glamorous /glámmərəss/, **glamourous** *adj* **1** desirable, especially in an exciting, stylish, or opulent way ○ *a glamorous life-style* **2** dressed or made up to be good-looking, especially in a high-fashion manner ○ *glamorous models strutting along the catwalk* —**glamorously** *adv* —**glamorousness** *n*

glamour /glámmər/ *n* **1 EXCITING ALLURE** an irresistible alluring quality that somebody or something possesses by virtue of seeming much more exciting, romantic, or fashionable than ordinary people or things ○ *the glamour of a career in the movies* **2 EXPENSIVE GOOD LOOKS** striking physical good looks or sexual impact, especially when it is enhanced with highly fashionable clothes or makeup **3 SPELL** a magical spell or charm (*archaic*) [Early 18C. Alteration of GRAMMAR 'enchantment, spell'.] —**glamour** *adj*

glamourous *adj* = **glamorous**

glam rock *n* a style of pop music in the UK in the 1970s performed by singers and musicians wearing outrageous clothes, makeup, hairstyles, and platform-soled boots

glance /glaanss/ *v* (**glances, glancing, glanced**) **1** *vi* **LOOK QUICKLY** to look at something quickly, especially for only a second or two ○ *He glanced in our direction.* **2** *vi* **MAKE A CURSORY EXAMINATION** to look over or through something without really studying it **3** *vi* **TOUCH ON BRIEFLY** to make a brief or passing allusion to something ○ *an introductory course that merely glances at the wider historical issues* **4** *vi* **GLINT** to reflect or shine, especially intermittently or for only a short time ○ *green feathers glancing in the sunlight* **5** *vt* **STRIKE AT ANGLE** to strike something briefly or lightly at an angle ○ *The stone glanced his shoulder.* **6** *vt* **DEFLECT CRICKET BALL** in cricket, to hit a bowled ball with the bat held at an angle so that the ball is deflected to the leg side ■ *n* **1 QUICK LOOK** a quick look at somebody or something ○ *a glance in our direction* **2 PASSING MENTION** a brief mention of something ○ *The book takes only a brief glance at contemporary music.* **3 CURSORY EXAMINATION** a cursory quick examination of something ○ *I haven't even had a glance at the report yet.* **4 OBLIQUE STRIKE** an act or instance of something striking another thing briefly or lightly at an angle **5 GLINT OF LIGHT** a sudden or quick flash or gleam of light ○ *glances of sunlight through the trees* **6 DEFLECTION OF CRICKET BALL** in cricket, a stroke in which the bat is held at an angle so that the ball is deflected to the leg side [15C. Alteration (influenced by *glent* 'to shine') of *glace* < Old French *glacier* 'to slide' < *glace* (see GLACIER).] ◇ **at a glance** immediately and without having to make a close study ◇ **at first glance** initially or on first examination

glance off *vt* to come into quick light contact with something and then deflect at an angle ○ *The stone glanced off the windscreen.*

glancing /glaánssing/ *adj* **1 STRIKING OBLIQUELY** coming into contact with another object and then deflecting at an angle ○ *a glancing blow* **2 FLICKERING OR FLASHING** giving off light in a flickering or flashing manner **3 TEMPORARY** lasting only a short time —**glancingly** *adv*

gland[1] /gland/ *n* **1 SECRETING CELL MASS** a mass of cells or an organ that removes substances from the bloodstream and excretes them or secretes them back into the blood in concentrated or altered form with a specific physiological purpose **2 ORGANIC STRUCTURE RESEMBLING GLAND** an organ or other anatomical structure that resembles a gland, especially, in popular usage, a lymph node **3 PLANT ORGAN** a secreting organ or structure of a plant, e.g. a nectary gland [Late 17C. Via French < Latin *glandula* 'tonsil' < *glans* 'acorn'.] —**glandless** *adj*

gland[2] /gland/ *n* a metal sleeve fitted round a rotating shaft or rod to prevent leakage, e.g. round a shaft emerging from a ship's hull [Early 19C. Probably < Old Norse *glam* 'noise'.]

glanders /glándərz/ *n* an infectious, often fatal, disease of horses, characterized by ulcers of the skin, lungs, or upper respiratory tract and heavy discharge of mucus from the nose. It is caused by the bacterium *Pseudomonas mallei.* (+ *singular verb*) [15C. < Old French *glandres* 'swelling of the glands' < Latin *glandula* (see GLAND[1]).] —**glandered** *adj* —**glanderous** *adj*

glandes plural of **glans**

glandular /glándyŏŏlər/ *adj* **1 RELATING TO GLANDS** relating to, functioning as, or affecting a gland or glands **2 RESULTING FROM GLAND DYSFUNCTION** describes a condition caused by a malfunctioning gland or glands **3 HAVING GLAND** characterized by the presence of a gland or glands **4 BODILY** natural to the body, especially hormonally or sexually (*informal*) [Mid-18C. Via French *glandulaire* < Latin *glandula* (see GLAND[1]).]

glandular fever *n* an acute infectious disease caused by the Epstein-Barr virus and marked by fever, swelling of the lymph nodes, sore throat, and an increased amount of lymphocytes in the blood. Technical name **infectious mononucleosis**

glandule /glándyool/ *n* a small gland or a part resembling a small gland [14C. Directly or via French < Latin *glandula* (see GLAND[1]).]

glandulous /glándyŏŏləss/ *adj* ANAT, MED = **glandular** — **glandulously** *adv*

glans /glanz/ (*plural* **glandes** /glándeez/) *n* **1 glans, glans penis** the rounded tip of a penis **2 glans, glans clitoridis** the erectile tissue at the tip of a clitoris [Mid-17C. < Latin, 'acorn'.]

glare[1] /glair/ *vi* (**glares, glaring, glared**) **1 STARE STONILY** to stare intently and angrily **2 LOOK ANGRILY** to express or signal anger, disapproval, contempt, or another negative emotion by giving a steady stare **3 BE UNPLEASANTLY BRIGHT** to shine brightly and intensely, often dazzlingly **4 STAND OUT OBTRUSIVELY** to be very conspicuous, blatant, or obtrusive ○ *Mistakes glared from every page of the report.* **5 BE UNPLEASANTLY AND OVERLY ORNATE** to be overly decorated or garish ■ *n* **1 ANGRY LOOK** a prolonged stare, usually expressing anger, disapproval, contempt, or another negative emotion **2 EXCESSIVE BRIGHTNESS** dazzling or uncomfortable brightness ○ *a screen on the monitor to reduce glare* **3 MEDIA SPOTLIGHT** excessive attention from the media **4 GAUDY ORNAMENTATION** gaudy coloration or decoration [13C. < Middle Low German *glaren* 'gleam'.]

glare[2] /glair/ *n* **glare, glare ice** *US, Can* METEOROL = **black ice** ■ *adj US* having a smooth and slippery surface [Mid-16C. < ?]

glaring /gláiring/ *adj* **1 OBVIOUS** easily perceived or detected ○ *a report full of glaring mistakes* **2 ANGRY** expressing anger, disapproval, contempt, or another negative emotion ○ *a glaring look of sheer contempt* **3 UNPLEASANTLY BRIGHT** intensely or dazzlingly bright **4 GARISH** gaudy or brash, especially in a tasteless way ○ *painted in glaring oranges and greens* —**glaringly** *adv* —**glaringness** *n*

glary /gláiri/ (**-ier, -iest**) *adj* **1** staring steadily and often angrily ○ *glary eyes* **2** dazzlingly or uncomfortably bright ○ *a glary computer screen*

Glasgow /glaázgō, glázgō/ **1** city in SW Scotland on the River Clyde. Population: 616,430 (1996 estimate). **2** council area in west-central Scotland. Area: 175 sq. km/68 sq. mi.

glasnost /glássnost/ *n* a policy that commits a government or organization to greater accountability, openness, discussion, and freer disclosure of information than previously, especially that of Mikhail Gorbachev in the former Soviet Union. ◊ **perestroika** *n.* [Late 20C. < Russian, 'publicness'.]

glass /glaass/ *n* **1 TRANSPARENT SOLID SUBSTANCE** a hard, usually transparent, substance that shatters easily. Source: sand melted in combination with other oxides such as lime or soda without crystallizing them. Use: making such objects as windows, bottles, and lenses. **2 UNCRYSTALLIZED SUBSTANCE RESEMBLING GLASS** a solid substance similar to glass formed by melting and cooling without crystallizing **3 GLASS CONTAINER** a container without a handle made from glass, for drinking from **4 AMOUNT IN GLASS** the amount a drinking glass holds **5** HOUSEHOLD = **glassware 6 PROTECTING COVER** a cloche, greenhouse window, or insulating material used to protect germinating plants ○ *Keep the seedlings under glass for the first four weeks.* **7** HOUSEHOLD = **looking glass 8 BAROMETER** a barometer (*dated*) **9** OPTICS = **magnifying glass 10** GEOL = **volcanic glass** ■ *vt* **1 COVER WITH GLASS** to cover or fit something with glass ○ *glassed the porch* **2 INSERT INTO A GLASS CONTAINER** to put something into a glass container or one made of a material resembling glass ○ *glassed the specimens in formalin* **3 CUT USING GLASS** to injure somebody with a drinking glass or a broken part of a drinking glass, usually in the face (*slang*) [Old English *glæs* < Germanic] —**glass** *adj* —**glassful** *n* —**glasslike** *adj*

Glass /glaass/, **Philip** (*b.* 1937) US composer

glass blowing *n* the forming or shaping of a glass object by blowing air through a tube into a mass of semimolten glass —**glass blower** *n*

glass case *n* a display cabinet made mainly of glass and used to exhibit objects of interest or value

glass ceiling *n* an unofficial but real impediment to somebody's advancement into upper-level management positions because of discrimination based on the person's gender, age, race, ethnicity, or sexual preference

glass chin *n* BOXING = **glass jaw**

glass cloth *n* **1** a cloth, usually made of closely woven linen, used for drying glasses and dishes **2** a polishing cloth with fine particles of glass in it

glass cutter *n* **1** a tool used to cut glass or to etch designs into glass **2** somebody whose job is to cut glass or to make cut glass

glassed-in *adj* made using glass panes ○ *a glassed-in conservatory*

glass eel *n* a larval form of the American or European eel with a flattened transparent body. Native to: Atlantic Ocean.

glasses /gla̋assiz/ *npl* **1** a pair of sight-correcting or protective lenses set in frames that fit over the ears and sit on the bridge of the nose **2** a pair of binoculars

glass eye *n* an artificial eye made from glass, or material similar to glass, so as to resemble a natural eye

glass fibre *n* INDUST = **fibreglass** *n.* 2

glassfish /gla̋ass fish/ (*plural* **-fish** *or* **-fishes**) *n* **1 TROPICAL FISH POPULAR FOR AQUARIUMS** a small transparent tropical fish, often kept as an aquarium fish. Native to: coasts and rivers of Africa and the Indian and W Pacific Oceans. Genus: *Chanda.* **2 PACIFIC FISH** a slender, almost transparent, fish belonging to one of 14 species found in the NW Pacific Ocean. Family: Salangidae. **3 GLASSFISH AS FOOD** the flesh of a glassfish used as food

glass harmonica *n* a set of drinking glasses or glass bowls, filled to graduated levels with water, that produce sounds of different pitches when their rims are rubbed with a moist finger

glasshouse /gla̋ass howss/ (*plural* **-houses** /-howziz/) *n* **1** GARDENING = **greenhouse** *n.* **2** a military prison or detention centre (*slang*) **3** a public position that brings somebody a high level of media attention and scrutiny

glassine /gla se̋en/ *n* a transparent paper treated with a glaze to make it greaseproof and resistant to the passage of air. Use: book jackets, food packaging.

glass jaw *n* in boxing, a jaw that is highly vulnerable to an opponent's punches (*informal*)

glassmaker /gla̋ass maykər/ *n* somebody whose job is to make glass or glass objects —**glassmaking** *n*

glasspaper /gla̋ass paypər/ *n* a fine abrasive paper with one surface covered with powdered glass. Use: polishing, smoothing.

glass snake *n* a limbless lizard, or one with vestigial limbs, that can, as a defence mechanism, snap off its tail to confuse predators. Native to: Europe, Asia, North America. Genus: *Ophisaurus.* [< its brittle tail]

glassware /gla̋ass wair/ *n* objects made of glass considered as a group

glass wool *n* fine-spun glass fibres formed into a woolly mass. Use: insulation, as air filters, in the manufacture of fibreglass.

glasswork /gla̋ass wurk/ *n* **1** the technique or result of cutting and fitting glass, especially glass panes for windows, doors, and conservatories **2** the production or manufacture of glass or glass objects **3** HOUSEHOLD = **glassware** —**glassworker** *n*

glassworks /gla̋ass wurks/ (*plural* **-works**) *n* a factory for the manufacture of glass or glass objects

glasswort /gla̋ass wurt/ (*plural* **-wort** *or* **-worts**) *n* a plant with fleshy stems and small leaves that was formerly a source of the soda used in making glass. Native to: salt marshes. Genus: *Salicornia.*

glassy /gla̋assi/ (**-ier, -iest**) *adj* **1 SMOOTH AND SLIPPERY** having a highly smooth, slippery, often reflective, surface **2 LIKE GLASS** resembling glass in being smooth, reflective, or transparent **3 BLANKLY EXPRESSIONLESS** lacking expression or animation ○ *a blank glassy look* —**glassily** *adv* —**glassiness** *n*

glassy-eyed *adj* having a blank staring expression

Glastonbury /glástənbəri/ historic market town in SW England, site of a 10th-century abbey. Population: 8,100 (1993 estimate).

Glaswegian /glaaz we̋ejən/ *n* somebody who comes from Glasgow, Scotland [Early 19C. < GLASGOW, after NORWEGIAN.] —**Glaswegian** *adj*

Glauber's salt /glówbərz-/, **Glauber salt** *n* a colourless crystalline sodium sulphate. Use: in solar energy systems, manufacture of dyes, glass, and paper, laxative. [Mid-18C. After Johann Rudolf *Glauber* (1604–68), German chemist.]

glaucoma /glaw kṓmə/ *n* an eye disorder marked by abnormally high pressure within the eyeball that leads to damage of the optic disc [Mid-17C. Directly or via Latin < Greek *glaukōma* < *glaukos* 'blue-grey, green'.] —**glaucomatous** *adj*

glauconite /gláwkə nīt/ *n* a green clay mineral containing iron and potassium. Use: fertilizer. [Mid-19C. < German *Glaukonit* < Greek *glaukos* 'blue-grey, green'.] —**glauconitic** /gláwkə níttik/ *adj*

glaucous /gláwkəss/ *adj* **1** covered in a greyish, whitish, or bluish waxy or powdery substance that rubs off easily, e.g. the bloom on grapes **2** of a dull greyish-green or blue colour [Late 17C. < Latin *glaucus* 'blue-grey, green' < Greek *glaukos.*]

glaucous gull *n* a large gull with a white head and tail and a light-grey back and wings. Native to: northern regions. *Larus hyperboreus.*

glaur /glawr/ *n Scotland* soft or slimy mud [15C. < ?] —**glaury** *adj*

glaze /glayz/ *v* (**glazes, glazing, glazed**) **1** *vt* **COVER WITH FINISH LIKE GLASS** to put a clear or coloured coating on a ceramic object and fire it in a kiln, in order to fix the coloration, make it watertight, or give it a shiny appearance **2** *vt* **COAT WITH MILK OR EGG** to brush food with milk, egg, or sugar before baking in order to produce a shiny brown finish **3** *vt* **COAT OIL PAINTING** to give something, especially an oil painting, a transparent or semi-transparent coating in order to enhance or slightly alter the colour tones **4** *vt* **GIVE PROTECTIVE COVERING TO** to place a protective or decorative coating on something, especially a natural material such as leather, cotton, or paper **5** *vti* **MAKE OR BECOME GLASSY** to become, or cause the eyes to become, unfocused and expressionless as a result of loss of interest, distraction, or tiredness **6** *vt* **COVER WITH ICE** to put a thin layer of ice on something **7** *vt* **FIT WITH GLASS** to fit glass into or over something, especially a window, door, or picture ■ *n* **1 COVERING RESEMBLING GLASS** a shiny, smooth, transparent, or coloured glassy coating on a ceramic object, produced by firing the treated object in a kiln, or the substance or process employed to achieve this **2 COATING FOR FOOD** a shiny brown finish on food or the substance used for achieving this effect **3 COATING FOR OIL PAINTING** a transparent or semitransparent coating on something, especially an oil painting, used to enhance or slightly alter the colour tones, or the substance used to achieve this effect **4 PROTECTIVE COVERING** a protective or decorative coating on something, especially a natural material such as leather, cotton, or paper, or the substance used for making this kind of coating **5** *US* METEOROL = **glaze ice** [14C. < GLASS, after GRAZE[1], GRASS.] —**glazer** *n*

glaze over *vi* to become unfocused and expressionless as a result of loss of interest, distraction, or tiredness (*refers to eyes*) ○ *Her eyes glazed over as the sedative began to take effect.*

glaze ice, glazed frost *n* a thin coating of ice formed when rain or moisture in the air comes into contact with a surface that is cold enough to cause it to freeze. US term **glaze** *n.* 5

glazier /gláyzi ər/ *n* somebody whose job is to fit glass, especially in windows and doors

glazing /gláyzing/ *n* **1 HARD SHINY COATING** the glaze coating on an object **2 COVERING OF SOMETHING WITH GLAZE** an act or the process of putting a glaze on something **3 GLASS FOR WINDOW** glass in general, especially the type of glass used in doors or windows or glass that has been fitted in windows or doors **4 FITTING OF SOMETHING WITH GLASS** an act or the process of fitting glass into something

glazing bar *n* a wooden or metallic strip used to support or separate panes of glass in windows and doors

GLB *abbr* gay, lesbian, bisexual (*in personal ads*)

GLC *abbr* **1** gas-liquid chromatography **2** Greater London Council

gleam /gleem/ *vi* **1 SHINE BRIGHTLY** to shine brightly and continuously **2 FLASH FOR SHORT TIME** to flash, flicker, or appear briefly or indistinctly ■ *n* **1 BRIGHT SHINE** a steady bright shine **2 FLASH OF LIGHT** a beam of light, especially one that is reflected, dim, or coming from an indistinct source **3 BRIEF SHOW** a slight or momentary indication of something ○ *a gleam of interest* [Old English *glǣm* < Germanic] —**gleamer** *n* ◇ **a gleam in somebody's eye** something at the very earliest stage of planning or development

gleaming /gle̋eming/ *adj* shining, especially with health, cleanliness, or newness ○ *gleaming black hair* —**gleamingly** *adv*

glean /gleen/ *v* **1** *vt* to obtain information in small amounts over a period of time **2** *vti* to go over a field or area that has just been harvested and gather by hand any usable parts of the crop that remain [14C. Via Old French *glener* < late Latin *glennare* < Celtic.] —**gleaner** *n*

gleanings /gle̋eningz/ *npl* **1** objects or ideas that have been gathered or amassed over a period of time, especially when they form a collection or comprehensive whole **2** the usable parts of a crop that are left behind in a harvested field or area and can be gathered in by hand

gleba /gle̋ebə/ (*plural* **-bae** /-bee/) *n* the mass of tissue in which spores are formed in the fruiting bodies of certain fungi such as truffles and puffballs [Mid-19C. < Latin, 'clod'.]

glebe /gleeb/ *n* **1** land or soil, especially when considered as a source of abundant natural produce (*literary*) **2** a piece of land belonging to a church and given over temporarily to a member of the clergy to provide additional income [14C. < Latin *gleba* 'clod'.]

glee /glee/ *n* **1 GREAT DELIGHT** joyful or animated delight **2 GLOATINGLY JUBILANT FEELING** jubilant, often smug pleasure, especially as a result of somebody else's bad luck or failure **3 SONG FOR UNACCOMPANIED VOICES** a part song for three or more unaccompanied voices of a type that first became popular in England in the 18th century [Old English *glēo* < Germanic, 'merriment'] —**gleeful** *adj* —**gleefully** *adv* —**gleefulness** *n*

glee club *n US* a choral society that concentrates on singing short part songs

gleet /gleet/ *n* **1** inflammation of the urethra, accompanied by a discharge of pus and mucus, and characteristic of a late stage in the development of gonorrhoea **2** a discharge of pus and mucus in a late stage of gonorrhoea [14C. Via Old French *glette* 'slime' < Latin *glittus* 'sticky'.]

glei *n* GEOL = **gley**

Gleichschaltung /glīkh shaltōong/ *n* the forced standardization and complete suppression of all opposition in the political, social, and economic life and institutions of a country by an oppressive government or regime [Mid-20C. < German.]

Gleizes /glez/, **Albert** (1881–1953) French artist

glen /glen/ *n* a long narrow valley, especially in Scotland [15C. < Scottish Gaelic *gleann.*] ◇ **in the glens** in the heartland of Scotland

Glencoe /glén kṓ/ mountain pass in the Scottish Highlands. Length: 8 km/5 mi.

Gleneagles /glen e̋eg'lz/ picturesque valley in central Scotland

glengarry /glen gárri/ (*plural* **-ries**) *n* a small brimless hat with a crown creased from front to back and usually a pair of ribbons hanging from the back, worn especially as part of Scottish highland dress [Mid-19C. After *Glengarry* in the Highlands of Scotland.]

Glenn /glen/, **John** (*b.* 1921) US astronaut and senator

glenoid /gle̋en oyd/ *adj* **1** shaped like a small shallow cup or socket **2** relating to the cup-shaped socket in the shoulder that holds the head of the humerus [Early 18C. < French *glénoïde* < Greek *glēnē* 'eyeball, socket'.]

Glenrothes /glen róthiss/ town in east-central Scotland. Population: 38,650 (1991).

gley /glay/, **glei** *n* a sticky bluish-grey clay soil or soil layer that forms in heavily water-logged areas [Early 20C. < Ukrainian *glei̋.*]

glia /gle̋e ə/ *n* the network of supporting tissue and fibres that nourishes nerve cells within the brain and spinal cord. US term **neuroglia** [Late 19C. < Greek, 'glue'.] —**glial** *adj*

gliadin /glī́ ədin/, **gliadine** /-deen/ *n* a simple cereal protein, e.g. from wheat or rye [Mid-19C. < French *gliadine* < Greek *glia* 'glue'.]

glib /glib/ *adj* **1 SLICK** fluent in a superficial or insincere way ○ *a glib talker* **2 SUPERFICIAL** shallow and lacking thought or preparation ○ *a glib generalization* **3 CASUAL AND RELAXED** easy, unconcerned, and informal in attitude ○ *a glib smile* [Late 16C. < ?] —**glibly** *adv* —**glibness** *n*

glide /glīd/ *v* (**glides, gliding, glided**) **1** *vti* **MOVE SMOOTHLY** to move, or cause something to move, in a smooth, effortless, and often graceful way ○ *seals gliding through the water* **2** *vi* **CHANGE STATE SMOOTHLY** to pass smoothly, slowly, or gradually into a specified state ○ *gliding in and out of consciousness* **3** *vti* **LAND WITHOUT USING ENGINE** to bring an aircraft in to land without using the engine or by using a glider **4** *vi* **USE PORTAMENTO** to slide from one note to another in music **5** *vi* **MAKE INTERMEDIATE SPEECH SOUND** to produce an intrusive speech sound when moving from one point of articulation to the next **6** *vt* CRICKET = **glance** *v.* 6 ■ *n* **1 SMOOTH MOVEMENT** a smooth, effortless, and often graceful movement **2 SMOOTH FLOWING DANCE** a dance with a smooth flowing movement **3 DANCE STEP** a smoothly flowing dance step **4 LANDING WITHOUT USING ENGINE** a controlled aircraft descent using no engine power **5 SLOW-MOVING WATER** a stretch of calm, slowly flowing water in a river or large stream **6** MUSIC = **portamento 7 EXTENSION FOR TROMBONE** a piece of metal tubing used to extend the length of a trombone so that lower notes can be produced **8 INTERMEDIATE SPEECH SOUND** an intrusive speech sound produced when a speaker is moving from one point of articulation to the next, e.g. the /w/ sound in the middle of 'going' **9** PHON = **semivowel 10** CRICKET = **glance** *n.* 6 **11 METAL DISC ON FURNITURE** a metal or plastic disc fixed to the bottom of the leg of a piece of furniture, to facilitate moving it across the floor **12 METAL TRACK FOR DRAWER** a metal track along which a drawer can be slid in or out easily [Old English *glīdan* < Germanic]

glide path *n* the prescribed descent of an aircraft coming in to land that is shown to the pilot by means of a radio beam and acts as an aid to navigation

glider /glīdər/ *n* **1** an engineless aircraft that flies by riding air currents **2** ZOOL = **flying phalanger**

glide slope *n* AIR = **glide path** *n.*

glide time *n* NZ a system of working with flexitime

glim /glim/ *n* something such as a candle or lamp that is a source of light (*archaic slang*) [Late 17C. < ?]

glimmer /glímmər/ *vi* **1 EMIT DIM GLOW** to emit a faint or intermittent light **2 BE PRESENT TO SMALL EXTENT** to be present faintly or in only a small amount ○ *Hope still glimmered in their hearts.* ■ *n* **1 FAINT FLASHING LIGHT** a faint or intermittent glowing light ○ *a glimmer of campfires in the distance* **2 SMALL AMOUNT** a faint sign or small amount of something ○ *a glimmer of interest* [15C. Probably < N Germanic.]

glimmering /glímmərıng/ *n* = **glimmer** *n.* 2 ■ *adj* emitting a faint or intermittent light

glimpse /glimps/ *n* **1 BRIEF LOOK** a quick or incomplete look or sighting of somebody or something ○ *I just caught a glimpse of her face in the crowd.* **2 SMALL INDICATION** a small, brief, or indistinct indication or appearance of something ■ *v* (**glimpses, glimpsing, glimpsed**) **1** *vt* **CATCH BRIEF SIGHT OF** to see somebody or something briefly or incompletely **2** *vi* **TAKE BRIEF LOOK** to have a quick or incomplete look at or through something **3** *vi* **EMIT FAINT LIGHT** to give off a faint or intermittent light (*archaic*) [14C. Ultimately < Germanic.]

glint /glint/ *vi* **FLASH BRIEFLY** to gleam or flash, especially brightly or momentarily ○ *Anger glinted in her eyes.* ■ *n* **1 BRIEF FLASH** a slight or momentary gleam or flash ○ *a glint of daylight through the curtains* **2 SLIGHT INDICATION** a slight sign or indication of something ○ *a glint of humour in his eyes* **3 SHININESS** a shiny or glossy appearance [15C. Probably alteration of *glent* 'to gleam' < N Germanic.]

glioma /glī ṓmə/ (*plural* **-mata** /-mətə/ *or* **-mas**) *n* a tumour composed of connective tissue (**glial tissue**) of the nervous system and affecting the brain or spinal cord [Late 19C. < Greek *glia* 'glue'.] —**gliomatous** *adj*

glissade /gli saád/ *n* **1** a gliding ballet step in which one foot slides forwards, backwards, or to one side **2** a controlled slide down a snowy slope made without skis by somebody in a standing or crouching position [Mid-19C. < French, < Old French *glisser* 'to slide' < Old Dutch *glissen*.] —**glissade** *vi* —**glissader** *n*

glissando /gli sándō/ (*plural* **-di** /-dee/ *or* **-dos**) *n* **1** an act of sliding a finger or thumb up or down a keyboard or harp strings from one note to another **2** an act of sliding a finger along a stringed instrument's fingerboard or slowly moving a trombone's slide in and out to create a smooth change in pitch between two notes [Late 19C. < Italian, < Old French *glisser* (see GLISSADE).]

glisten /gliss'n/ *vi* **1** to shine brightly or reflect light from a wet surface ○ *leaves glistening after the rain* **2** to have a glossy sheen (*refers to hair or an animal's pelt*) [Old English *glisnian* < Germanic] —**glisten** *n*

glister /glístər/ *vi* to glitter brightly (*archaic*) [14C. Probably < Middle Low German *glistern*.]

glitch /glich/ *n* **1** a minor hitch or technical problem ○ *glitches in the software* **2** a sudden unwanted electronic signal such as results from a power surge or a temporary irregular supply of power [Mid-20C. Probably < Yiddish *glitsh* 'slip' < Old High German *glītan* 'to glide'.] —**glitchy** *adj*

glitter /glíttər/ *vi* **1 SPARKLE** to sparkle or shimmer brightly ○ *an evening gown glittering with sequins* **2 SHINE WITH EMOTION** to look bright or expressive with an emotion such as anger or love (*refers to eyes*) **3 BE VIVACIOUS** to exhibit liveliness and charm ○ *a radiant personality who glittered at every event she attended* **4 BE DAZZLING** to be characterized by the presence of somebody or something glamorous ○ *The event glittered with Hollywood stars.* ■ *n* **1 SPARKLY DECORATION** small pieces of reflective material, e.g. sequins **2 SPARKLING LIGHT** bright sparkling light **3 GLAMOUR** dazzling glamour ○ *the glitter of a command performance at the opera* [14C. < Old Norse *glitra*.] —**glitteringly** *adj* —**glittery** *adj*

glitterati /glíttə raáti/ *npl* famous, rich, or fashionable people thought of as a group, especially those who are frequently photographed by the press [Mid-20C. Blend of GLITTER + LITERATI.]

glitz /glits/ *n* **1** glamour, especially that associated with show business or celebrities **2** extravagant and often tasteless display, especially of wealth [Late 20C. Back-formation < GLITZY.]

glitzy /glítsi/ (**-ier, -iest**) *adj* **1** glamorous, especially in relation to show business or celebrities **2** extravagant and often tasteless, especially in the display of wealth [Mid-20C. Probably < German *glitzern* 'to glitter'.] —**glitzily** *adv* —**glitziness** *n*

Gliwice /gli vítsə/ city in S Poland. Population: 214,000 (1995).

gloaming /glṓmıng/ *n* the period of fading light after sunset but before dark (*literary*) [Old English *glōmung* < *glōm* 'twilight' < Germanic]

gloat /glōt/ *vi* to feel or express smug self-satisfaction about something such as an achievement, a possession, or somebody else's misfortune [Late 16C. < ?] —**gloat** *n* —**gloater** *n* —**gloatingly** *adv*

glob /glob/ *n* an amount of something soft or semiliquid (*informal*) [14C. < ?] —**globby** *adj*

ϟ **global** /glṓb'l/ *adj* **1 WORLDWIDE** relating to or happening throughout the whole world **2 OVERALL** taking all the different aspects of a situation into account **3 RELATING TO WHOLE OF SYSTEM** covering or affecting the whole of a computer system, program, or file **4 SPHERICAL** shaped like a globe or sphere —**globally** *adv*

globalise *vti* = **globalize**

globalism /glṓb'lizəm/ *n* the belief or advocacy that political policies should take worldwide issues into account before focusing on national or state concerns —**globalist** *n*

globalize /glṓbə līz/ (**-izes, -izing, -ized**), **globalise** (**-ises, -ising, -ised**) *vti* **1** to become or cause something, especially social institutions, to become adopted on a global scale **2** to become or cause something, especially a business or company, to become international or start operating at the international level —**globalization** /glṓbə lī záysh'n/ *n* —**globalizer** *n*

global village *n* the whole world considered as a single community served by electronic media and information technology

global warming *n* an increase in the world's temperatures, believed to be caused in part by the greenhouse effect

QUICK FACTS ON... **GLOBAL WARMING**

Key dates: 1827 'greenhouse effect' coined by French mathematician and physicist Jean-Baptiste Fourier; 1979 first World Climate Conference; 1988 United Nations creates Intergovernmental Panel on Climate Change (IPCC)
Key elements: release of gases by the burning of fossil fuels, industrialization, and deforestation, creating higher surface temperatures from heat trapped within the atmosphere (the greenhouse effect). Consequences: extremes of weather; melting of polar icecaps and rising of water levels threaten islands and low-lying coasts; potential severe disruption of agriculture and natural cycles of plants and animals.
Key developments: energy conservation; reforestation; reduction of fossil fuel emissions; use of alternative energy sources such as solar or wind power

globe /glōb/ *n* **1 MAP OF EARTH ON SPHERE** a hollow sphere representing the Earth and illustrated with the continents, seas, and islands, especially one showing and labelling the countries **2 EARTH** the planet Earth **3 HOLLOW SPHERICAL OBJECT** a rounded hollow object, especially one made of glass, e.g. a cover for a lamp, or a goldfish bowl **4 PART OF MONARCH'S REGALIA** a hollow sphere, usually made of gold or another precious metal, that forms part of a monarch's regalia and symbolizes the power or sovereignty of the ruler **5** *Scotland, Can, ANZ* **LIGHT BULB** a light bulb ■ *vti* (**globes, globing, globed**) **MAKE INTO OR BECOME GLOBE** to form, or cause something to form, a globe [Mid-16C. Directly or via Old French < Latin *globus* 'ball, sphere'.] —**globoid** *adj, n*

globe amaranth *n* an ornamental garden plant with colourful whorls of leaves and flower heads made up of several distinct blossoms. *Gomphrena globosa*.

globe artichoke *n* PLANTS, FOOD = **artichoke** *n.* 1, **artichoke** *n.* 2

globefish /glṓb fish/ (*plural* **-fish** *or* **-fishes**) *n* **1** = **puffer** *n.* 2 **2** = **porcupine fish** [< its shape when inflated]

globeflower /glṓb flowər/ *n* a poisonous plant with ball-shaped flowers, consisting of large white, pale-yellow, or orange sepals that almost entirely enclose the smaller petals. Genus: *Trollius*.

globetrot /glṓb trot/ (**-trots, -trotting, -trotted**) *vi* to travel frequently and to a great variety of distant destinations —**globetrotter** *n*

globigerina /glṓbijə reénə/ (*plural* **-nas** *or* **-nae** /-nee/) *n* a marine protozoan with a spiny rounded spiral shell. Genus: *Globigerina*. [Mid-19C. < modern Latin, < Latin *globus* 'ball, sphere' + *gerere* 'carry'.] —**globigerinal** *adj*

globigerina ooze *n* a deposit on the ocean floor that consists of globigerina shells and is found almost worldwide

globin /glṓbin/ *n* the protein component of haemoglobin [Late 19C. Shortening of HAEMOGLOBIN.]

globular /glóbbyōōlər/ *adj* **1** having the shape of a ball or globule **2** containing or consisting of globules [Mid-17C. < Latin *globolus* (see GLOBULE).] —**globularity** /glóbbyōō lárrəti/ *n* —**globularly** *adv*

globular cluster *n* an approximately spherical cluster of densely-packed stars, located within a spherical halo around the Milky Way galaxy

globule /glóbbyool/ *n* a small ball-shaped object, especially one that is liquid or semiliquid [Mid-17C. Via French < Latin *globulus* 'little globe' < *globus* 'ball, sphere'.]

globuliferous /glóbbyōō líffərəss/ *adj* composed of, containing, or producing globules

globulin /glóbbyōōlin/ *n* any of a group of globular proteins, some of which are involved in immunity

glochidium /glō kíddi əm/ (*plural* **-a** /-ə/) *n* **1 glochidium, glochid** a barbed hair or bristle that grows on plants such as the prickly pear or among the spores on ferns **2** the parasitic larva of certain mussels that has hooks or suckers used to attach itself to the fins or gills of fish. Family: Unionidae. [Late 19C. < modern Latin, < Greek *glōkhis* 'arrowhead'.] —**glochidial** *adj* —**glochidiate** /-ət/ *adj*

glockenspiel /glókən shpeel/ *n* a percussion instrument consisting of a set of tuned metallic bars, played by striking the individual bars with small light hammers [Early 19C. < German, 'bell-play'.]

glogg /glog/ *n* a hot punch consisting of brandy, red wine, and sherry, and flavoured with sugar, spices, fruit pieces, and blanched almonds [Early 20C. < Swedish *glögg*.]

glomerate /glómmərət/ *adj* **1** formed into a tight ball or cluster **2** tightly wound together, like a ball of string [Late 18C. < Latin *glomerat-*, past participle of *glomerare* 'make into a ball' < *glomus* 'ball of thread'.]

glomerule /glómmə rool/ *n* **1** a flat-topped flower head formed by a compact cluster of short-stalked flowers **2** a cluster of spores formed into a ball shape [Late 18C. Via French < modern Latin *glomerulus* (see GLOMERULUS).] —**glomerulate** /glo mérrələt/ *adj*

glomerulonephritis /glō mérrəlō nə frī́tiss/ *n* an inflammatory disease affecting the clusters of capillaries (**glomeruli**) in the cortex of a kidney

glomerulus /glō mérrələss/ (*plural* **-li** /-lī/) *n* **1** a tightly packed cluster of blood vessels, nerve fibres, or other cells **2** a round cluster of interconnected capillaries found in the cortex of a kidney, that remove body waste to be excreted as urine [Mid-19C. < modern Latin, 'little ball' < Latin *glomus* 'ball of thread'.]

gloom /gloom/ *n* **1 MURKY DARKNESS** a state of darkness or partial darkness, especially one where shadows or poor visibility create a cheerless or dispiriting atmosphere **2 DESPONDENCY** a feeling or atmosphere of despair, despondency, or misery ■ *v* **1** *vi* **BE DESPONDENT** to feel or look despondent or miserable **2** *vti* **MAKE OR BECOME DARK** to become, or cause something to become, dark [13C. < ?] ◇ **gloom and doom** a feeling or expression of despondency and a belief that disaster is about to strike

gloomy /glóomi/ (**-ier, -iest**) *adj* **1 MURKILY DARK** dark in a way that creates a cheerless or dispiriting atmosphere **2 SAD** sad and hopeless in offering little prospect that things will improve **3 DESPONDENT** feeling sad and without hope, often with a morbid or uninterested outlook on life —**gloomily** *adv* —**gloominess** *n*

gloop /gloop/ *n* semiliquid sticky or messy material (*informal*) US term **goop** *n.* 2 [Late 20C. An imitation of the sound it makes when poured or handled.] —**gloopy** *adj*

glop /glop/ *n US* (*informal*) **1** a soft lump or mixture of something, especially unappetizing food ○ *a glop of cold, greasy mashed potatoes* **2** something such as a piece of music or writing that is considered to be oversentimental or of little value [Early 20C. As GLOOP.] —**gloppy** *adj*

Gloria /gláwri ə/ *n* **1** a hymn or set of words in Latin that begins with the word 'Gloria' and is used in the Christian liturgy to praise God **2** the words of the Gloria set to music [15C. < Latin, 'glory'.]

Gloria in Excelsis /-ek sélsiss, -eks chélsiss/ *n* **1** a hymn or set of words in Latin that begins with the words 'Gloria in Excelsis' and is used in the Christian liturgy to praise God **2** the words of Gloria in Excelsis set to music [< Latin, 'Glory in the High Places']

Gloria Patri /-páatree/ *n* **1** a short hymn or set of words in Latin that begins with the words 'Gloria Patri' and is used in the Christian liturgy to praise God **2** the words of Gloria Patri set to music [< Latin, 'Glory to the Father']

glorified /gláwri fīd/ *adj* described in much more grandiose or fanciful terms than are warranted ○ *They call it an antique auction, but it's really just a glorified car-boot sale.*

glorify /gláwri fī/ (**-fies, -fying, -fied**) *vt* **1 MAKE APPEAR SUPERIOR** to cause something to seem more pleasant, important, or desirable than is actually the case **2 EXTOL** to praise somebody or something highly **3 PRAISE DEITY** to worship or offer praise to a deity —**glorification** /gláwrifi káysh'n/ *n* —**glorifier** *n*

gloriole /gláwri ōl/ *n* a halo around somebody's head [Mid-19C. Via French < Latin *gloriola* 'little glory' < *gloria* 'glory'.]

gloriosa /glawri óssə/ (*plural* **-sas** *or* **-sa**) *n* a tropical climbing plant of the lily family, popular as a greenhouse plant. Flowers: large, yellow, orange, red. Genus: *Gloriosa*. [< modern Latin, < Latin *gloriosus* (see GLORIOUS)]

glorious /gláwri əss/ *adj* **1 EXCEPTIONALLY LOVELY** beautiful in a way that inspires wonder or joy ○ *glorious summer weather* **2 OUTSTANDING** so good or distinguished as to merit praise and lasting fame ○ *a glorious career* **3 ENJOYABLE** highly enjoyable **4 INEBRIATED** uproariously drunk (*archaic informal*) [14C. Via Anglo-Norman, Old French < Latin *gloriosus* < *gloria* 'glory'.] —**gloriously** *adv* —**gloriousness** *n*

Glorious Revolution *n* the overthrow of King James II in 1688 that established the power of Parliament over the monarch

Glorious Twelfth *n* the first day of the grouse-shooting season on 12 August

glory /gláwri/ *n* (*plural* **-ries**) **1 EXALTATION** the fame, admiration, and honour that is given to somebody who does something important **2 ACHIEVEMENT** something that brings or confers admiration, praise, honour, or fame **3 PRAISE OF DEITY** praise and thanksgiving offered as an act of worship to a deity ○ *Glory to God in the highest.* **4 AWESOME SPLENDOUR** majesty or splendour **5 ASTOUNDING BEAUTY** beauty that inspires feelings of wonder or joy ○ *the glory of a bright spring morning* **6 HEAVEN** the idealized beauty and bliss of heaven **7 HALO** a halo around somebody's head ■ *interj* **EXPRESSING SURPRISE** used to express great surprise, shock, dismay, or pleasure (*dated*) [13C. Via Anglo-Norman, Old French < Latin *gloria*.] ◇ **glory be** used to express great surprise, shock, dismay, or pleasure (*dated*) ◇ **go to glory** to die (*dated*) ◇ **in your glory** in a state of great happiness, satisfaction, or triumph

glory in *vt* to derive great pride, pleasure, amusement, or satisfaction from something

glory-box *n ANZ* a collection of household goods that a woman collects to use when she is married (*dated*)

glory days *npl* a period of great success, achievement, or happiness, usually in the past ○ *They still remember the glory days when they were the acknowledged world leaders in their field.*

glory-of-the-snow (*plural* **glory-of-the-snow** *or* **glory-of-the-snows**) *n* a widely-cultivated, small bulbous plant of the lily family. Flowers: blue, early-blooming. Native to: E Mediterranean, W Asia. *Chionodoxa luciliae.*

Glos. *abbr* Gloucestershire

gloss[1] /gloss/ *n* **1 SHININESS** a shiny quality, especially on a smooth surface **2 DECEPTIVE AND SUPERFICIAL ATTRACTIVENESS** an attractive appearance that often conceals something unattractive or inferior **3** DIY = **gloss paint** **4 MAKEUP** a makeup or cosmetic designed to impart a shine ○ *lip gloss* ■ *vt* **1 MAKE SHINY** to apply a coating or gloss to a surface to make it shine **2 USE GLOSS PAINT ON** to apply gloss paint to something [Mid-16C. < ?]

gloss over *vt* to leave out negative information on purpose or address a subject superficially to make it appear more attractive or acceptable

gloss[2] /gloss/ *n* **1 EXPLANATORY PHRASE** a short definition, explanation, or translation of a word or phrase possibly unfamiliar to the reader, often located in a page margin or collected in an appendix or glossary **2 INTERPRETATION** an interpretation or explanation of something ○ *Her account provides an interesting gloss on the theme of widowhood.* ■ *vt* **1 EXPLAIN** to give a short definition, explanation, or translation of a word or phrase that may be unfamiliar to the reader **2 INSERT EXPLANATIONS IN** to add or enter the necessary glosses in a manuscript or piece of writing **3 GIVE MISLEADING EXPLANATION OF** to interpret or explain something in a deliberately misleading or negative way [Mid-16C. Via Old French < Latin *glossa* 'obscure word' < Greek *glōssa* 'tongue, language, obscure word'.]

glossa /glóssə/ (*plural* **-sae** /-see/ *or* **-sas**) *n* **1** a tongue (*technical*) **2** a structure resembling a tongue in the mouth of an insect [Late 19C. Via modern Latin < Greek *glōssa* 'tongue, language, obscure word'.] —**glossal** *adj*

glossary /glóssəri/ (*plural* **-ries**) *n* an alphabetical collection of specialist terms and their meanings, usually in the form of an appendix to a book [14C. < Latin *glossarium* < *glossa* (see GLOSS[2]).] —**glossarial** /glo sáiri əl/ *adj* —**glossarially** *adv* —**glossarist** *n*

glossectomy /glo séktəmi/ (*plural* **-mies**) *n* partial or total removal by surgery of the tongue

glossitis /glo sítiss/ *n* inflammation of the tongue [Early 19C. < Greek *glōssa* 'tongue'.] —**glossitic** /glo síttik/ *adj*

glossolalia /glóssō láyli ə/ *n* **1** RELIG = **speaking in tongues** **2** nonsensical or invented speech, especially resulting from a trance or schizophrenia [Late 19C. < Greek *glōssa* 'tongue, language, obscure word'.]

glossopharyngeal /glóssō farin jée əl/ *adj* relating to the tongue and pharynx [Early 19C. < Greek *glōssa* 'tongue'.]

glossopharyngeal nerve *n* either of the ninth pair of cranial nerves, which activate the muscles of the tongue, pharynx, and parotid gland

gloss paint *n* a paint that gives a smooth shiny durable surface, used especially as a final coat on wood

glossy /glóssi/ *adj* (**-ier, -iest**) **1 SHINY AND SMOOTH** having a smooth shiny surface or texture ○ *A glossy coat is the sign of a healthy animal.* **2 SUPERFICIALLY STYLISH** creating a superficial impression of wealth, beauty, or fashionable elegance (*informal*) ○ *a glossy lifestyle that conceals years of financial struggle* ■ *n* (*plural* **-ies**) **1 PHOTO WITH A SHINY FINISH** a photograph printed on shiny smooth paper ○ *Please provide an 8 x 10 glossy.* **2 GLOSSY MAGAZINE** a glossy magazine (*informal*) —**glossily** *adv* —**glossiness** *n*

glossy magazine *n* a magazine containing high-quality colour photographs, especially a fashion magazine. US term **slick** *n.* 2

glost firing /glóst-/ *n* the final high-temperature firing of ceramic ware once it has been coated with glaze, during which the glaze is melted and fused onto the pot [Probably < alteration of GLOSS[1]]

glottal /glótt'l/ *adj* **1** relating to the glottis **2** describes a speech sound that is produced by wholly or partially closing the glottis

glottal stop *n* a consonantal speech sound created by closing and then opening the glottis before a vowel, which produces a sudden audible release of air

glottis /glóttiss/ (*plural* **-tises** *or* **-tides** /-tti deez/) *n* **1** the elongated opening between the vocal cords at the upper part of a vertebrate's windpipe (**larynx**) **2** all of the anatomy of the larynx that is involved in producing the voice in a human or vertebrate animal [Late 16C. Via modern Latin < Greek, < *glōtta*, variant of *glōssa* 'tongue'.]

Gloucester /glóstər/ city in west-central England, noted for its cathedral. Population: 106,834 (1996 estimate).

Gloucestershire /glóstərshər/ county in west-central England, on the border with Wales. Area: 2,642 sq. km/1,024 sq. mi.

glove /gluv/ *n* **1 SHAPED COVERING FOR THE HAND** a shaped covering for the hand that includes five separated sections for the thumb and fingers, and extends to the wrist or the elbow **2** CLOTHING = **gauntlet**[1] **3 PROTECTIVE GLOVE** a padded glove worn to protect the hand in boxing, baseball, and cricket ■ *vt* (**gloves, gloving, gloved**) **PUT A GLOVE ON** to cover the hand with a glove or cover something with something that is like one ○ *Gloved and hatted, the electrician climbed the power pole.* [Old English *glōf* < Germanic, 'hand'] —**gloveless** *adj* ◇ **the gloves are off** used to indicate that a course of action is about to be pursued in a ruthless and uncompromisingly aggressive way ○ *The gloves are off in the political debate.*

glove box *n* **1** CARS = **glove compartment** **2** a sealed container that allows radioactive or toxic substances to be handled safely using a pair of gloves attached to openings in its sides

glove compartment *n* a small enclosed storage space in the dashboard of a vehicle

glove puppet *n* a puppet that fits over the hand like a glove and is operated by the user's thumb and fingers. US term **hand puppet**

Glover /glúvvər/, **Denis James Matthews** (1912–80) New Zealand writer

glow /glō/ *n* **1 LIGHT FROM SOMETHING HOT** a light produced by something that has been heated to a high temperature but is not in flame ○ *the glow of the embers in the grate* **2 SOFT STEADY LIGHT** a soft steady light, especially one without heat or flames ○ *the glow of the neon lights* **3 SOFT REFLECTED LIGHT** a soft warm reflected light ○ *the golden glow of the tapestries on the far wall* **4 ROSINESS OF COMPLEXION** a brightness or redness in somebody's complexion, e.g. because of exercise or good health ○ *the healthy glow that exercise gives you* **5 REDNESS OF EMBARRASSMENT** a redness of the face or complexion, especially one caused by embarrassment ○ *face suffused with a glow of shame* **6 HAPPY FEELING** a sense of happiness or wellbeing ○ *a warm glow of satisfaction* ■ *vi* **1 EMIT LIGHT AND HEAT** to emit light as a result of being extremely hot ○ *The embers of the fire still glowed in the grate.* **2 EMIT A SOFT STEADY LIGHT** to emit a soft steady light without heat or flames ○ *the neon signs glowing red and blue* **3 REFLECT LIGHT SOFTLY** to emit a soft warm reflected light ○ *the walls glowing orange and gold in the afternoon sun* **4 SHINE WITH HEALTH** to show the bright eyes and smooth skin that are a sign of good health, contentment, or high spirits **5 BE FLUSHED WITH EMBARRASSMENT** to have a blood rush to the face, especially because of embarrassment **6 FEEL WARM AND CONTENTED** to feel a pleasant warm sensation owing to happiness, satisfaction, or love ○ *The winning team glowed with pride.* [Old English *glōwan* < Germanic]

glower /glówər/ *vi* to stare or look at somebody or something with sullen anger or strong resentment ■ *n* a sullen or resentful stare or look [15C. < ?] —**gloweringly** *adv*

glowing /glṓ ing/ *adj* **1 SHINING SOFTLY AND STEADILY** emitting a soft steady light **2 REDDISH-GOLD** rich, strong, or bright in colour, especially when reddish or gold ○ *the glowing colours of autumn* **3 FULL OF PRAISE** praising somebody or something in very warm appreciative terms ○ *glowing reports of the performance* **4 ROSY** red or rosy as a result of excitement, wellbeing, or good health —**glowingly** *adv*

glow plug *n* a plug fitted to a diesel engine that makes it easier to start in cold weather by warming it up

glowworm /glṓ wurm/ *n* a larva of some types of firefly, or a beetle of a closely related family, that emits greenish light from organs in its abdomen. Families: Lampyridae and Phengodidae.

gloxinia /glok sínni ə/ *n* a tropical American plant popular as a house plant for its large colourful bell-shaped flowers. Genus: *Sinningia*. [Early 19C. After Benjamin *Gloxin*, 18C German botanist.]

gloze /glōz/ (**glozes, glozing, glozed**) *v* **1** *vt* to attempt to underplay or minimize something unpleasant or embarrassing ○ *tried to gloze over the scandalous story* **2** *vti* to use flattery on somebody (*archaic*) [13C. Via French *glose* < Latin *glossa* (see GLOSS2).]

gluc- *prefix* = **gluco-** (*before vowels*)

glucagon /glóokə gon/ *n* a pancreatic hormone that raises blood sugar by promoting conversion of glycogen to glucose in the liver [Early 20C. < GLUCO- + Greek *agōn*, present participle of *agein* 'lead'.]

glucan /glóo kan/ *n* a polymer derived from glucose that occurs naturally, e.g., in cellulose, starch, and glycogen

gluco- *prefix* glucose ○ *glucocorticoid* [< GLUCOSE]

glucocorticoid /glóokō cáwrti koyd/ *n* a steroid hormone (**corticoid**) that influences carbohydrate metabolism. Use: treatment of inflammatory conditions.

gluconeogenesis /glóokō neé ə jénnəsiss/ *n* the production of glucose by the liver from substances other than carbohydrates —**gluconeogenetic** /glóokō neé əjə néttik/ *adj*

glucose /glóokōz/ *n* **1** a six-carbon monosaccharide produced in plants by photosynthesis and in animals by the metabolism of carbohydrates **2** a syrup containing dextrose, maltose, dextrin, and water that is obtained from starch. Use: food manufacture, alcoholic fermentation. [Mid-19C. Via French < Greek *gleukos* 'sweet wine'.]

glucosidase /gloo kóssi dayz/ *n* an enzyme that splits glucose off glucosides

glucoside /glóokō sīd/ *n* a glycoside that yields glucose on hydrolysis —**glucosidal** *adj* —**glucosidic** /glóokō síddik/ *adj* —**glucosidically** *adv*

glucosuria /gloo kō sóori ə/ *n* MED = **glycosuria** —**glucosuric** *adj*

glucuronic acid /gloo kyoo ronik-/ *n* an acid derived from glucose that is present in cartilage and detoxifies poisons [Early 20C. < GLUCO- + Greek *ouron* 'urine'.]

glue /gloo/ *n* **1 ANIMAL-BASED ADHESIVE** an adhesive substance obtained by boiling animal parts such as bones, hides, horns, and hooves **2 ADHESIVE** a natural or synthetic substance used as an adhesive **3 SOMETHING THAT UNITES PEOPLE** a unifying factor or influence ○ *Mutual love and understanding is the glue that holds this family together.* ■ *vt* (**glues, gluing, glued**) **1 STICK THINGS TOGETHER** to stick things together or reconstitute something using an adhesive substance ○ *It took hours to glue the vase back together.* **2 KEEP SOMEBODY STILL** to cause somebody to remain still because of concentrating on something with full attention (*informal; often passive*) ○ *You've been glued to that computer all day!* [13C. Via French *glu* < Latin *gluten*.] —**glue-like** *adj* —**gluey** *adj* —**gluily** *adv* —**gluiness** *n*

glue ear *n* a condition affecting young children that results from poor drainage of the middle ear

glue-sniffing *n* the practice of inhaling the fumes from glues and volatile solvents in order to become intoxicated —**glue-sniffer** *n*

glug /glug/ *n* **1** a gurgling sound of a quantity of liquid being poured from a bottle or similar vessel **2** a quantity of liquid, especially of an alcoholic drink, drunk or poured from a bottle or similar vessel ○ *Here, have a glug of champagne.* [Late 17C. An imitation of the sound.] —**glug** *vti* —**gluggable** *adj*

gluhwein /glóo vīn/ *n* warmed red wine, flavoured with spices and added sugar [Late 19C. < German *Glühwein* < *glühen* 'to glow' + *Wein* 'wine'.]

glum /glum/ (**glummer, glummest**) *adj* quietly melancholic or miserable [Mid-16C. < variant of GLOOM 'feel or look despondent'.] —**glumly** *adv* —**glumness** *n*

glume /gloom/ *n* either of a pair of dry leaves at the base of the spikelet in an ear of grass [Late 18C. < Latin *gluma* 'husk'.] —**glumaceous** /gloo máyshəss/ *adj*

gluon /glóo on/ *n* a theoretical elementary particle without mass, thought to be involved in binding the subatomic particles (**quarks**) together [Late 20C. < GLUE.]

glut /glut/ *n* **EXCESS SUPPLY** a larger supply of something than is needed, especially of a crop or product ○ *There is usually a glut of fresh vegetables in August.* ■ *vt* (**gluts, glutting, glutted**) **1 SUPPLY MARKET WITH TOO MUCH** to supply a market with an excess of something, especially a product, leading to a fall in price ○ *Cheaper products from abroad glutted the market, lowering profits.* **2 GIVE SOMEBODY ENOUGH OR TOO MUCH** to feed or supply somebody with enough or more than enough of something [14C. Probably via Old French *gloutir* 'swallow' < Latin *gluttire* (see GLUTTON).]

glutaeus *n* ANAT = **gluteus**

glutamate /glóotə mayt/ *n* a salt or ester of glutamic acid, especially its sodium salt (**monosodium glutamate**)

glutamic acid /gloo támmik-/, **glutaminic acid** /glootə mínnik-/ *n* an amino acid found in plant and animal proteins that is an excitatory neurotransmitter [< GLUTEN + AMINE]

glutamine /glóotə meen/ *n* an amino acid found in proteins and synthesized by humans and animals [Late 19C. Blend of *glutamic* (see GLUTAMIC ACID) + AMINE.]

glutaminic acid *n* BIOCHEM = **glutamic acid**

glutaraldehyde /glóotə ráldi hīd/ *n* $C_5H_8O_2$ an oily water-soluble liquid. Use: disinfectant, tanning agent, biological fixative. [Mid-19C. < *glutaric* < GLUTEN.]

glutathione /glóotə thīōn/ *n* a peptide consisting of glutamic acid, cysteine, and glycine that is an important antioxidant [Early 20C. < *glutamic* (see GLUTAMIC ACID).]

glutei plural of **gluteus**

gluten /glóot'n/ *n* a mixture of two proteins found in some grains [Late 16C. Via French < Latin, 'glue'.]

gluteus /glóoti əss/ (*plural* **-i** /-ī/), **glutaeus** (*plural* **-i**) *n* any of the three large buttock muscles that move the thigh in humans, especially the gluteus maximus [Late 17C. Via Modern Latin < Greek *gloutos* 'buttock'.] —**gluteal** *adj*

gluteus maximus /-máksiməss/ (*plural* **glutei maximi** /-mī/) *n* the outermost of the three large gluteus muscles that form each buttock in humans [< modern Latin, 'largest gluteus']

glutinous /glóotinəss/ *adj* having a sticky consistency ○ *glutinous rice*

glutton /glútt'n/ *n* **1** an excessive eater or drinker **2** ZOOL = **wolverine** [13C. Via Old French < Latin *glutton-* < *gluttire* 'to swallow' < *gula* 'throat'.] —**gluttonous** *adj* —**gluttonously** *adv* ◇ **a glutton for punishment** a person who appears to need or enjoy difficulty, discomfort, or stress

gluttony /glútt'ni/ *n* the act or practice of eating and drinking to excess

glyc- *prefix* = **glyco-**

glyceride /glíssə rīd/ *n* an ester formed by the combination of glycerol with an acid. Source: animal and vegetable fats and oils. [Mid-19C. < GLYCERIN.]

glycerin /glíssərin/, **glycerine** *n* $C_3H_8O_3$ a thick, sweet, odourless, colourless, or pale yellow liquid. Source: fats and oils as a byproduct of soap manufacture. Use: solvent, antifreeze, plasticizer, manufacture of soaps, cosmetics, lubricants, and dynamite. [Mid-19C. < French, < Greek *glukeros*, alteration of *glukus* 'sweet'.]

glycerol /glíssə rol/ *n* glycerin (*technical*) [Late 19C. < GLYCERIN.]

glyceryl /glíssəril/ *n* a chemical group derived from glycerol [Mid-19C. < GLYCERIN.]

glyceryl trinitrate *n* CHEM = **nitroglycerine**

glycine /glīss een/ *n* an amino acid found in most proteins that is also an inhibitory neurotransmitter [Mid-19C. < Greek *glukus* 'sweet'.]

glyco-, **glyc-** *prefix* **1** sugar ○ *glycosuria* **2** glycogen ○ *glycolysis* [< Greek *glukus* 'sweet' < Indo-European]

glycogen /glīkəjən/ *n* a polysaccharide found in the liver and muscles that is easily converted to glucose for energy —**glycogenic** /glīkə jénnik/ *adj*

glycogenesis /glīkō jénnəsiss/ *n* the formation of glycogen from glucose —**glycogenetic** /-jə néttik/ *adj*

glycogenolysis /glī kōjə nóllississ/ *n* the breakdown of glycogen to glucose —**glycogenolytic** /-jénnə líttik/ *adj*

glycol /glī kol/ *n* **1** = **ethylene glycol** **2** = **diol** [Mid-19C. < GLYCERIN.] —**glycolic** *adj*

glycolic acid /glī kóllik-/ *n* a compound found in unripe fruit. Use: tanning, pesticides, pharmaceuticals, adhesives, plasticizers.

glycolipid /glī kō líppid/ *n* a sugar-containing lipid present in cell membranes

glycolysis /glī kólləssiss/ *n* the breakdown of glucose to pyruvate with release of usable energy —**glycolytic** /glīkō líttik/ *adj*

glycoprotein /glī kō prṓ teen/ *n* a protein that contains carbohydrate

glycoside /glīkō sīd/ *n* any of a group of compounds that hydrolyse to a sugar and a nonsugar [Mid-20C. < *glycose*, variant of GLUCOSE.] —**glycosidic** /glīko síddik/ *adj*

glycosuria /glīkōs syóori ə/ *n* the presence of sugar in the urine, usually a sign of diabetes [Mid-19C. < *glycose*, variant of GLUCOSE.] —**glycosuric** *adj*

glycosylation /glīkō sī láysh'n/ *n* the addition of a saccharide unit to a protein [Mid-20C. < *glycose*, variant of GLUCOSE.]

Glyndebourne /glīnd bawrn/ site of an annual international opera festival held in the village of Glynde in S England

⚡**glyph** /glif/ *n* **1 CARVED GROOVE IN ANCIENT GREEK ARCHITECTURE** an ornamental carved channel or groove, especially a vertical one like those on a Doric frieze **2 CARVED SYMBOL OR CHARACTER** a symbol or character, especially one that has been incised or carved out in a stone surface like the characters of the ancient Maya writing system **3 CHARACTER IN FONT** the symbol or symbols that form a single character in a font [Late 18C. Via French *glyphe* < Greek *gluphē* 'carving' < *gluphein* 'carve'.] —**glyphic** *adj*

glyptic /glíptik/ *adj* relating to the art of engraving or carving, especially on precious stones [Early 19C. Directly or via French *glyptique* < Greek *gluptikos* < *gluptēs* 'carver' < *gluphein* 'carve'.]

glyptics /glíptiks/ *n* CRAFT = **glyptography** (+ *singular verb*)

glyptography /glip tóggrəfi/ *n* the art or process of engraving or carving on precious stones —**glyptograph** /glíptə graaf, -graf/ *n* —**glyptographer** *n* —**glyptographic** /glíptō gráffik/ *adj* —**glyptographical** *adj*

gm[1] *abbr* gram

⚡**gm**[2] *abbr* Gambia (*in Internet addresses*)

GM *abbr* **1** general manager **2** genetic modification **3** genetically modified **4** George Medal **5** grand master **6** grant-maintained **7** guided missile

GMAT *abbr* Greenwich Mean Astronomical Time

GMO *n, abbr* genetically modified organism

GMS *abbr* grant-maintained status

GMT *abbr* Greenwich Mean Time

⚡**GMTA** *abbr* great minds think alike (*in e-mails*)

GMW *abbr* gram-molecular weight

⚡**gn** *abbr* Guinea (*in Internet addresses*)

gnarl /naarl/ *n* a hard lump, knot, or swelling on a tree trunk or branch [Early 19C. Back-formation < GNARLED.]

gnarled /naarld/ *adj* **1** twisted and full of knots ○ *an ancient gnarled tree* **2** twisted, misshapen, or weather-beaten because of age, hard work, or illness ○ *gnarled hands* [Early 17C. Alteration of *knurled*.]

gnash /nash/ *vt* to grind your teeth together, especially in pain, anger, or frustration ○ *almost gnashing his teeth at the sheer incompetence of the performance* [15C. < ?]

gnat /nat/ *n* a small two-winged biting fly such as a black fly or a midge [Old English *gnætt* < Indo-European]

gnatcatcher /nát kachər/ *n* a small songbird with a long tail and slender bill that feeds on insects. Native to: North America. Genus: *Polioptila*.

gnathic /náthik/, **gnathal** /náth'l/ *adj* relating to the jaw [Late 19C. < Greek *gnathos* 'jaw'.]

gnathion /náythi on/ *n* the lowest point on the midline of the lower jaw [Late 19C. < Greek *gnathos* 'jaw'.]

gnathostome /náythə stōm/ *n* a vertebrate that has a mouth with jaws, as do all vertebrates except agnathans. Superclass: Gnathostomata. [Early 20C. < Greek *gnathos* 'jaw' + *stoma* 'mouth'.]

-gnathous *suffix* having a particular kind of jaw ○ *prognathous* [< Greek *gnathos* 'jaw' < Indo-European]

gnaw /naw/ (**gnaws, gnawing, gnawed, gnawed** *or* **gnawn** *archaic* /nawn/) *v* **1** *vti* **CHEW** to chew or bite on something persistently, often reducing it gradually to a particular state ○ *a terrier gnawing away at a huge bone* **2** *vt* **MAKE BY CHEWING** to make something by grinding with the teeth and chewing ○ *The hamster escaped by gnawing a hole in its cage.* **3** *vt* **ERODE** to wear something away often until it reaches a particular shape or size ○ *The wind and waves had gnawed the rocks into fantastic shapes.* **4** *vi* **CAUSE WORRY** to cause somebody constant anxiety or distress ○ *That question still gnaws at me after all these years.* **5** *vi* **GRADUALLY REDUCE** to reduce the effectiveness or influence of something bit by bit ○ *a profound sense of unease that gnaws away at our sense of wellbeing* [Old English *gnagen* < Germanic] —**gnaw** *n* —**gnawable** *adj* —**gnawer** *n*

gnawing /náwing/ *adj* persistent and troubling or uncomfortable ○ *gnawing doubts* —**gnawingly** *adv*

gneiss /nīss/ *n* a coarse-grained high-grade metamorphic rock formed at high pressures and temperatures, in which light and dark mineral constituents are segregated into visible bands [Mid-18C. < German.] —**gneissic** *adj* —**gneissose** *adj*

gnocchi /nóki/ *npl* in Italian cookery, dumplings made of potato, semolina, or flour, usually boiled and served with soup or a sauce [Late 19C. < Italian.]

gnome[1] /nōm/ *n* **1** according to old folk tales, one of a race of small beings usually portrayed as hunchbacked men with long white beards who live in the earth guarding treasure **2** GARDENING = **garden gnome** **3** an offensive term deliberately insulting somebody thought of as small and, often, ugly [Mid-17C. Via French < modern Latin *gnomus*.] —**gnomelike** *adj* ◇ **the gnomes of Zurich** international bankers and financiers, especially those based in Switzerland (*dated humorous*)

gnome[2] /nōm/ *n* a short saying or proverb that expresses a general idea or principle [Late 16C. < Greek *gnōmē* 'opinion, judgment' < *gignōskein* 'know'.]

gnomic /nṓmik/ *adj* **1** resembling or containing proverbs or other short pithy sayings that express basic truths ○ *His gnomic utterances were widely quoted by journalists.* **2** opaque or difficult to understand —**gnomically** *adv*

gnomon /nṓ mon/ *n* **1** the arm of a sundial, used to show the time of day by the position of its shadow **2** the part of a parallelogram that is left when a smaller similar parallelogram has been taken from its corner [Mid-16C. Directly or via French or Latin < Greek *gnōmōn* 'indicator' < *gignōskein* 'know'.] —**gnomonic** /nō mónnik/ *adj* —**gnomonically** *adv*

gnosis /nṓssiss/ *n* knowledge of spiritual truths reputedly possessed by the ancient Gnostics, who believed them to be essential to salvation [Late 16C. < Greek *gnōsis* 'investigation, knowledge' < *gignōskein* 'know'.]

gnostic /nóstik/ *adj* relating to knowledge, especially knowledge of spiritual truths [Mid-17C. See GNOSTIC.]

Gnostic *n* a believer in Gnosticism [Late 16C. Via ecclesiastical Latin < Greek *gnōstikos* < *gignōskein* 'know'.] —**Gnostic** *adj*

Gnosticism /nóstissizəm/ *n* a pre-Christian and early Christian religious movement teaching that salvation comes by learning esoteric spiritual truths that free humanity from the material world, believed in this movement to be evil

gnotobiotics /nṓ tō bī óttiks/ *n* the scientific study of organisms living either in a germ-free or a controlled environment, as when a known contaminant has been introduced [Mid-20C. < Greek *gnōtos* 'known'.] —**gnotobiotic** *adj* —**gnotobiotically** *adv*

GNP *abbr* gross national product

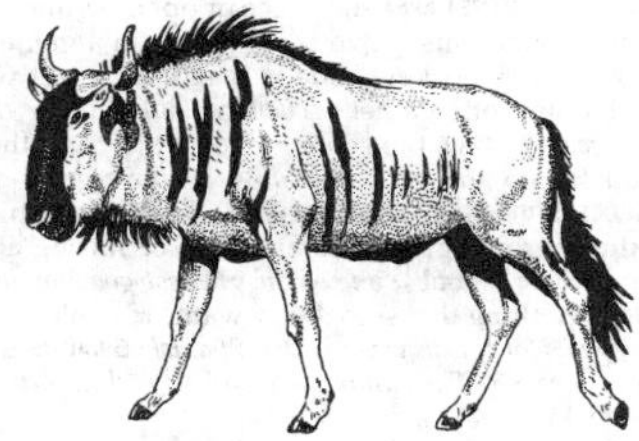

Gnu

gnu /noo/ (*plural* **gnu** *or* **gnus**) *n* a large African antelope with a head resembling that of an ox, short mane, beard, downward curving horns, and tufted tail. *Connochaetes gnou* and *Connochaetes taurinus*. [Late 18C. Probably via Dutch *gnoe* < Khoisan.]

GNVQ (*plural* **GNVQs**) *n* a post-16 qualification in the United Kingdom designed to provide vocationally orientated skills and knowledge for progression to employment or university. Full form **General National Vocational Qualification**

go[1] /gō/ (**goes, going, went** /went/, **gone** /gon/, *plural* **gos**) CORE MEANING: a basic intransitive verb of motion expressing movement from an unspecified point of departure or from a place that is already known or assumed ○ *Have you any idea where he went?* ○ *She never went anywhere without her spectacles.* ○ *Johnny went back inside for another coffee.* ○ *I've always wanted to go to Paris.* **1** *vi* **DEPART** to leave a place ○ *Please don't go.* ○ *He's going tomorrow.* **2** *vi* **MOVE TO ACT** to move towards a person or place with the intention of doing something specific ○ *We had to go and pick up our young son who was playing at a friend's house.* ○ *After the wedding they went to live in Spain.* **3** *vi* **PROCEED TO AN ACTIVITY** to leave a place and proceed towards an activity, often a recreational activity ○ *They go for a jog every morning.* **4** *vi* **ATTEND** to attend a place regularly ○ *She went to evening classes to get more qualifications.* **5** *vi* **TAKE PART** to take part in a television or radio programme ○ *The President went on television to defend his government's decision.* **6** *vi* **LEAD** to lead to, or begin or end at, a particular place (*refers to a route or travel service*) ○ *Take the road that goes into the city centre.* ○ *The new bus service will go from Edinburgh to London.* **7** *vi* **ELAPSE** to elapse or pass (*refers to time*) ○ *As time went on, he pursued lesser jobs.* **8** *vi* **BE ALLOTTED** to be allotted to a particular recipient or used for a particular purpose (*refers to money or other resources*) ○ *The house will go to his surviving children.* ○ *Much of her income went on household bills.* **9** *vi* **BE GIVEN** to be given to somebody as a quality or attribute ○ *The credit should go to the one who tries hardest.* **10** *vi* **BE DISCARDED** to be eliminated, given up, or got rid of ○ *Thousands of jobs will have to go* **11** *vi* **BE SPENT** to be spent or used up ○ *By the end of the evening all the food had gone.* **12** *vi* **LEAVE A JOB** to leave a job or organization ○ *He was costing the company thousands and had to go.* **13** *vi* **BLEND IN** to blend, harmonize, or be appropriate with something else ○ *They wanted to find a carpet that would go with the existing decor.* ○ *Those trousers just don't go.* **14** *vi* **FIT IN** to fit in a place because of being the right shape or size ○ *I tried to push the package through the letter box but it wouldn't go.* **15** *vi* **BELONG** to have somewhere as a usual or proper place ○ *The towels go in the cupboard in the bathroom.* **16** *vi* **BE PUT** to be put into something as one of the parts that form it ○ *all the elements that go into making a successful musical* **17** *vi* **FUNCTION** to function or operate ○ *Can you get my car going again?* ○ *Without capital to make it go, our business plan was merely hopes written out on paper.* **18** *vi* **FAIL** to get weaker and begin to fail or give way ○ *My eyesight is starting to go.* **19** *vi* **BREAK DOWN** to stop working properly and start to break down ○ *I think the battery may be going – the electrics are starting to play up.* **20** *vi* **DIE** to die (*euphemistic*) ○ *I'm afraid she has gone.* **21** *vi* **BECOME** to change so as to come to be in a particular state or condition ○ *Their pet's behaviour went out of control.* **22** *vi* **BE DRESSED OR EQUIPPED** to be in a particular state with regard to dress or equipment ○ *They went barefoot on the beach.* **23** *vi* **PROCEED** to proceed or happen in a particular way ○ *How did it go at work today?* ○ *We were trying to figure out what really went wrong.* ○ *The intruder went unchallenged.* **24** *vi* **MAKE A NOISE AS A SIGNAL** to make a noise such as a ring or a knock to attract attention ○ *She had just closed the front door when the phone went.* **25** *vi* **MAKE A NOISE** to make a particular noise ○ *The horn went beep.* ○ *Cows go 'moo'.* **26** *vi* **REACH A POINT** to proceed to or reach a particular position or level ○ *'The freedom she experienced, the indulgence with which she was treated, went beyond her expectations'.* (Thomas Hardy, *The Mayor of Casterbridge*; 1886) **27** *vi* **SERVE** to be of such a nature or quality as to do something ○ *It just goes to show how careful you have to be.* **28** *vi* **COMPARE** to compare with other people or things of the same kind ○ *As holidays abroad go, it was probably the best we've ever had.* **29** *vi* **SOUND** to proceed in terms of sound or words (*refers to a piece of music or writing*) ○ *How does that tune go again?* **30** *vi* **ACCOMPANY EACH OTHER** to occur with or be present at the same time as something else ○ *It's not necessarily the case that intelligence and common sense go together.* **31** *vi* **CIRCULATE** to circulate as information around a place or among people ○ *It soon went round the whole village that she had inherited a fortune.* **32** *vi* **HAVE RECOURSE** to turn to a procedure as a result of unresolved problems ○ *They couldn't agree, so they went to arbitration.* **33** *vi* **BE THE AUTHORITY** to be necessarily accepted as what will be the case in a given situation ○ *Whatever she says goes in our home.* **34** *vi* **ENDURE** to continue surviving or succeeding in a difficult situation ○ *Human beings can go for much longer without food than without water.* **35** *vt* **BET IN CARDS** to bet or bid a particular set of cards in a card game ○ *I go three clubs.* **36** *vt* **SAY** to say something quoted (*nonstandard*) ○ *So she goes, 'If you want it done then do it yourself'.* **37** *vi Carib* **WILL** will do something ○ *I go see you tomorrow.* **38** *vi* **EXPRESSING FUTURE ACTION** used to express future action or intent (*in progressive tenses*) ○ *What are we going to do?* **39** *n* **ATTEMPT MADE** an attempt or chance to do something ○ *She passed the exam on the second go.* **40** *n* **TURN TAKEN** a move or turn in a game ○ *It's your go.* **41** *n* **ENERGY** energy and vibrancy (*informal*) ○ *I've had so much more go since changing my diet.* **42** *adj* **FUNCTIONING** ready and operating properly (*informal*) ○ *All systems are go.* [Old English *gān* < Indo-European] ◇ **anything goes** used to indicate that anything is to be tolerated or accepted as the norm ○ *In this place almost anything goes!* ◇ **at one go** all at the same time ◇ **don't even go there** *US* don't mention that particular subject, or don't even think about it (*informal*) ◇ **have a go (at something)** to make an attempt at something (*informal*) ○ *He said that he had never skied before but he was willing to have a go at it.* ◇ **have a go at somebody** to attack somebody verbally (*informal*) ◇ **here we go!** used as a chant by football supporters either when their team is winning or to encourage their team to win ◇ **here we go (again)!** used to express displeasure or resignation that something, usually something bad, that has happened before is now happening again ○ *Here we go again! This old car simply won't start.* ◇ **it is all go** used to indicate that there is a lot of activity and hard work happening (*informal*) ○ *It's all go around here!* ◇ **make a go of something** to make a success of something ○ *They couldn't make a go of the relationship.* ◇ **on the go** very active and busy ○ *a two-career couple, always on the go* ◇ **there you go** *US* used to express general encouragement or approval to somebody else (*informal*) ◇ **there you go again** used to complain that somebody has done something bad or wrong yet again ○ *There you go again, misinterpreting and twisting what I'm saying.* ◇ **to go** to be taken home rather than consumed on the premises ○ *one pizza to go*

go about *v* **1** *vt* **TACKLE** to deal with a problem, assignment, or task **2** *vt* **CONSTANTLY BEHAVE IN SPECIFIED WAY** to spend a lot of time behaving in a specified way ○ *She's been going about causing trouble in the office.* **3** *vti* = **go around** *v.* 1 **4** *vti* = **go around** *v.* 2 **5** *vti* = **go around** *v.* 3 **6** *vi* **CHANGE TACK** to change tack in a sailing boat

go after *vt* to make a deliberate effort to get or find something seen as desirable or advantageous ○ *I decided to go after a teaching job I saw in the paper.*

go against *vt* **1** **OPPOSE** to be in opposition to something ○ *The government went against treasury advice and raised interest rates.* **2** **BE CONTRARY TO** to be the opposite of something ○ *This goes against everything I believe in.* **3** **BE UNFAVOURABLE TO** to be unfavourable to somebody ○ *He went to court wearing a confident smile but the verdict went against him.*

go ahead *vi* to start or continue with something, especially after a period of uncertainty or delay ○ *Let's go ahead and start our meal without her.*

go along *vi* **1** to accompany somebody on a journey ○ *I went along just to keep her company.* **2** to develop or progress in a manner specified, especially favourably (*informal*) ○ *Things were going along reasonably well until she lost her job again.*

go along with *vt* to accept something or obey somebody, especially reluctantly or to the surprise of others ○ *You can't go along with it – it's breaking the law.*

go around *v* **1** *vi* **KEEP COMPANY** to spend a lot of time with a particular person or as a member of a particular group ○ *We went around together all the time.* **2** *vi* **TRAVEL FROM PLACE TO PLACE** to travel from one place to another ○ *We tend to go around by taxi.* **3** *vti* **BE WIDELY KNOWN OR CURRENT** to be experienced or known by a lot of people, often in a particular place **4** *vti* **BE ENOUGH FOR EVERYONE** to be able to be distributed to everyone ○ *There aren't enough pens to go around, so you'll have to share.* ◇ **what goes around comes around** used to say that whatever happens now will have an effect in the future (*informal*)

go at *vt* to attempt something enthusiastically or energetically ○ *He went at the snow shovelling as if it were a race.*

go away *vi* **1** to leave the place where you live, especially in order to take a holiday (*informal*) ○ *Are you going away this summer?* **2** used to tell somebody to get away from you and leave the place where you are because he or she is annoying you ○ *Go away! I'm busy.*

go back *vi* **1** **ORIGINATE FROM A TIME** to originate from a particular date, period, or time ○ *a tradition that goes back hundreds of years to the time of Henry VIII* **2** **BE RESET AN HOUR EARLIER** to be required to be reset an hour earlier, to Greenwich Mean Time from British Summer Time **3** **RETURN TO WORK** to return to work after being absent, e.g. because of holidays, illness, or industrial action (*informal*) **4** *Malaysia* **GO HOME** to return to your home

go back on *vt* to change your mind about something you have agreed or promised to do ○ *You can't go back on what we originally agreed – a deal's a deal.*

go back over *vt* to subject something to careful further consideration ○ *Shall we go back over the evidence?*

go by *v* **1** *vi* PASS IN TIME to move onwards in terms of time ○ *As the years go by he gets more and more mellow.* **2** *vt* REGARD SOMETHING AS TRUE to treat advice or information as reliable or true **3** *vt* USE PARTICULAR SOURCE OF INFORMATION to use a particular way of doing something or finding something out ○ *All we had to go by was a soggy map.*

go down *vi* **1** SINK to sink beneath the surface of a body of water ○ *An oil tanker went down off the coast of Alaska.* **2** CRASH to fall from the air and crash ○ *The kite went down in the treetops.* **3** GO BELOW HORIZON to sink below the horizon ○ *The sun had already gone down by the time we got back.* **4** SUFFER DISGRACE to be disgraced or ruined (*informal*) ○ *If he goes down, he'll take the whole department with him.* **5** BE DEFEATED to be defeated in a vote or competition (*informal*) ○ *Manchester United went down 2–3 to Barnsley in the third round.* **6** BE RELEGATED in sports, to be relegated or demoted ○ *The local team only just managed to avoid going down this season.* **7** BE REMEMBERED to be remembered in a specified way ○ *She will surely go down as one of the greatest athletes of all time.* **8** BE RECEIVED to be received in a particular way ○ *an idea that didn't go down at all well with shareholders* **9** TAKE PLACE to happen or be happening (*slang*) ○ *Hey, what's going down?* ○ *When the robbery went down, the cops rushed to the scene.* **10** BE EATABLE OR DRINKABLE to be able to be eaten or drunk, especially easily or enjoyably (*informal*) ○ *With sick children, soup tends to go down more easily than solid foods.* **11** BECOME ILL to become ill with a specified illness (*informal*) ○ *Most of her class has gone down with the flu.* **12** MALFUNCTION to break down or stop working ○ *Since the airline's computers have gone down, we can't get flight information yet.* **13** BE SENT TO PRISON to be sent to prison, especially for a specified period (*informal*) **14** LEAVE UNIVERSITY AT THE END OF TERM to leave college or university at the end of term or the end of the academic year **15** FAIL TO ACHIEVE BRIDGE TRICKS in the game of bridge, to fail to attain the number of tricks that has been contracted for

go down on *vt* a highly offensive term meaning to perform oral sex on somebody (*taboo*)

go for *vt* **1** TRY TO OBTAIN SOMETHING YOU WANT to make an effort to obtain something because it is suitable for you or important to you (*informal*) ○ *I really think you should go for that sales job.* **2** LIKE A LOT to prefer, like, or be interested in a particular thing or person (*informal*) ○ *I don't really go for science fiction.* **3** CHOOSE to choose one particular thing rather than another (*informal*) ○ *I think I'll go for the chocolate cheesecake – how about you?* **4** ATTACK to attack somebody physically or verbally **5** COMMAND A PRICE to be worth or sold for a particular amount ○ *In the end the house went for far less than its market value.* **6** BE RELEVANT TO to apply or be relevant to somebody ○ *She needs to be more careful in her work – and that goes for you, too!* ◇ **go for it** not to stop or relax until you aggressively reach your goal (*slang; often as a command*) ○ *The coach told the team to get out there and go for it.* ◇ **have something going for you** to be in a situation where something is useful or helpful to you to a particular extent (*informal*) ○ *She has a lot going for her in the tennis championship, given her season's record.*

go forward *vi* to be required to be reset an hour later, to British Summer Time from Greenwich Mean Time ○ *The clocks go forward tonight.*

go in *vi* **1** BE OBSCURED to become hidden by clouds ○ *Once the sun went in, it got really cold sitting in the ski lift.* **2** BE LEARNT to be learnt, remembered, or understood (*informal*) ○ *However many times I read it nothing seems to go in.* **3** BEGIN AN ATTACK to launch an attack or begin another manoeuvre ○ *After the police went in, things rapidly got out of hand.* **4** BEGIN AN INNINGS in cricket, to begin an innings (*refers to a player or a team*)

go in for *vt* **1** ENTER A COMPETITION to enter a competition or sporting event **2** ENJOY DOING to enjoy a particular activity ○ *I don't really go in for team sports myself.* **3** CHOOSE A CAREER to choose a particular area of study or career ○ *decided to go in for the priesthood*

go into *vt* **1** BEGIN A CAREER to begin a job or career in a particular area of activity ○ *She went into advertising and made pots of money.* **2** LOOK INTO to examine or look into something in detail and with thoroughness **3** BE A FACTOR OF A NUMBER to be a factor of a particular number or amount ○ *15 won't go into 125.* **4** BE SPENT ON to be used or spent for a particular purpose ○ *Millions have gone into finding a cure.*

go in with *vt* to begin participating in a scheme or venture with other people ○ *I went in with four friends to start a restaurant.*

go off *v* **1** *vi* BECOME BAD to become bad, stale, or rancid ○ *Milk goes off very quickly in this weather.* **2** *vi* DETONATE to explode or be fired **3** *vi* BEGIN SOUNDING to start to ring, sound, or vibrate ○ *The smoke alarm goes off whenever we make toast.* **4** *vi* BE CARRIED OUT to be carried out or conducted in a particular manner ○ *I think the conference went off as well as could be expected.* **5** *vi* DEPART to set out or set out for a specific place ○ *There were endless TV images of soldiers going off to war.* **6** *vti* LEAVE PITCH OR STAGE to leave a sports pitch, stage, or other place ○ *The band went off early but came back to play three encores.* **7** *vi* START BEHAVING IN PARTICULAR WAY to change behaviour and start behaving in a particular way ○ *When I suggested a few changes he went off into hysterics.* **8** *vt* STOP LIKING to stop liking somebody or something previously liked ○ *I soon went off him once he started telling jokes.* ○ *went off the idea once he found out how much it cost* **9** *vi Aus* GO WELL to go exceptionally well (*slang*)

go off with *vt* to begin a relationship with somebody, especially abandoning a spouse or partner in order to do this

go on *v* **1** *vi* CARRY ON to continue in progress ○ *The dispute went on for another nine months before it was resolved.* **2** *vi* OCCUR to happen or take place ○ *I asked him what was going on.* **3** *vti* MAKE A PUBLIC ENTRANCE to make an entrance on a sports pitch, stage, or other public place ○ *She went on every night to rapturous applause.* ○ *The team went on the pitch feeling that they'd already won.* **4** *vi* TALK TOO MUCH to talk too much and much too long ○ *She's always going on about her yacht.* **5** *vi* CONTINUE SPEAKING to continue speaking, especially after a pause ○ *She then went on about the latest international incident.* **6** *vi* DO SOMETHING AFTERWARDS to do something after the time or period you are referring to ○ *She finished fourth, but went on to win the championship the following year.* **7** *vt* USE AS RELIABLE INFORMATION to use something as reliable information ○ *The police have very little to go on at this stage.* **8** *vt* ENJOY to like or enjoy something (*informal*) ○ *I don't go much on his new haircut.* **9** *vi* EXPRESSING ENCOURAGEMENT used to encourage somebody to do something, usually something the person is reluctant or afraid to try (*informal*) ○ *Go on, you'll have a great time skiing down that hill!* **10** *vi* EXPRESSING DISBELIEF used when you are pleading with somebody or when you are expressing pleading disbelief (*informal*) ○ *Oh, go on! I simply don't believe she could have done such a thing!* **11** *vt* APPROXIMATE to be close to a particular age, time, or number (*in progressives*) ○ *He must be going on 50.*

go on at *vt* to criticize or nag another person persistently or at length (*informal*) ○ *He's always going on at me about how scruffy I look.*

go out *vi* **1** SOCIALIZE to socialize and enjoy yourself away from home ○ *She loves going out, but he prefers to stay at home.* **2** FLOW OUTWARDS FROM SHORE to flow away from the shoreline ○ *The tide had gone out.* **3** GO OUT OF STYLE to stop being fashionable ○ *Muttonchops went out in the late 1800s.* **4** FINISH GAME to end your part in a game or competition by doing something you need to do ○ *You need to throw a six to go out.* **5** BE FORCED OUT OF GAME to be forced to quit a game or competition ○ *The two lowest scoring teams in each round go out.* **6** DATE to go on a date with somebody ○ *They've been going out for six months.* **7** BE BROADCAST to be broadcast on TV or the radio ○ *The programme went out last night.* **8** BE EXTINGUISHED to stop burning or functioning ○ *The fire has gone out.*

go out to *vt* **1** to be beaten by another team or contestant in a knock-out competition ○ *Liverpool went out to Newcastle in the semifinal.* **2** to be offered or extended to a person or group ○ *Our thoughts go out tonight to the friends and relatives of the victims.*

go over *v* **1** *vi* CHANGE TO NEW SYSTEM to change to a different system or way of doing things ○ *We went over from oil to gas when we got the central heating replaced.* **2** *vi* CHANGE ALLEGIANCE to change allegiance and start supporting somebody or something else ○ *In a surprise move, the MP went over to Labour.* **3** *vt* EXAMINE SOMETHING CAREFULLY to examine or check something carefully ○ *The police went over the car looking for fingerprints.* **4** *vt* REHEARSE AND MEMORIZE to practise or repeat something in order to learn it ○ *The actors were all busy going over their lines.*

go round *v* **1** *vti* = **go around 2** *vi* to go and visit another person ○ *Let's go round and see Dave.*

go through *v* **1** *vt* EXAMINE THOROUGHLY to examine or inspect something very carefully ○ *The police went through his luggage but found nothing suspicious.* **2** *vi* GAIN OFFICIAL APPROVAL to be accepted or approved officially, after having gone through channels or set procedural stages **3** *vt* UNDERGO UNPLEASANTNESS to undergo hardship or difficulties, usually in stages and over a period of time ○ *They're going through a series of business setbacks.* **4** *vt* CONSUME IN QUANTITY to use, eat, or spend something, especially a large amount in a short time ○ *They go through hundreds of pounds of groceries a week.* **5** *vi Aus* LEAVE to leave or depart (*informal*)

go through with *vt* to carry on with something until it has been completed or resolved, especially when this requires determination ○ *I'm determined to go through with this court case, come what may.*

go under *vi* **1** SINK IN WATER to sink below the surface of the water ○ *I managed to grab him as he went under for the third time.* **2** FAIL to close down or fail **3** LOSE CONSCIOUSNESS to lose consciousness, especially after being given an anaesthetic ○ *They began the operation as soon as she'd gone under.*

go up *vi* **1** BE BUILT to be constructed ○ *A new supermarket went up where the cinema used to be.* **2** BE DISPLAYED to be put on display ○ *A notice has gone up saying how we can be contacted.* **3** DETONATE OR IGNITE to explode or burst into flames ○ *The whole place went up in a matter of seconds.* **4** GO TO UNIVERSITY to go to or return to a college or university at the beginning of a term or academic year

go with *vt* **1** BE PART OF to be a normal or usual part of something ○ *The long hours go with the job.* **2** ADOPT OR FOLLOW AN IDEA to adopt or follow a particular approach or point of view ○ *Just go with the plan as it stands for the time being and we'll see what happens.* **3** DATE to spend time romantically and socially with somebody (*informal*) ○ *Anna's been going with Alex for a month now.* **4** HAVE SEX WITH to have sexual intercourse with somebody (*informal*)

go without *vt* to be deprived of something, e.g. money or food ○ *You'll have to go without breakfast if you want to catch the early train.* ○ *Sometimes the poor family just had to go without.*

go[2] /gō/ *n* a Japanese board game played with black and white stones on a surface marked with 19 lines intersecting each other to create 367 crossing points [Late 19C. < Japanese.]

goa /gṓ ə/ *n* a gazelle with a brownish-grey coat, the male of which has backward curving horns. Native to: Tibet. *Procapra picticaudata.* [Mid-19C. < Tibetan *dgoba.*]

Goa /gṓ ə/ state on the western coast of India. Capital: Panaji. Population: 1,235,000 (1994). Area: 3,813 sq. km/1,472 sq. mi.

goad /gōd/ *vt* **1** DRIVE TO ACT to provoke or incite somebody into action (*often passive*) **2** PROD WITH A STICK to prod an animal with a long pointed stick ■ *n* **1** POINTED ANIMAL PROD a long pointed stick used for prodding cattle and other animals **2** STIMULUS something used to motivate somebody or stir somebody into action [Old English *gād* < Germanic]

SYNONYMS See ***motive***.

go-ahead *n* permission or approval to proceed with something (*informal*) ○ *Once we get the go-ahead from the bank, we can get things moving.* ■ *adj* imaginative and ambitious ○ *a young go-ahead company at the forefront of information technology*

goal /gōl/ *n* **1** TARGET AREA the space or opening into which a ball or puck must go to score points in a game such as football or hockey, usually a pair of posts with a crossbar and often a net ○ *The kick landed just to the left of the goal.* **2** SCORE the score gained by getting the ball or puck into the goal ○ *leading by three goals to two* **3** SUCCESSFUL SHOT a successful attempt at hitting, kicking, throwing, or passing a ball or hitting a puck into or over a goal ○ *one of the greatest goals of all time* **4** AIM something that somebody wants to achieve ○ *One of my goals for this year is to learn Spanish.* **5** RACE'S END the end of a race ○ *The runners are still several minutes from the goal.* [14C. < ?]

goal area *n* in football, the rectangular area marked out in front of the goal within which goalkeepers may handle the ball

goal difference *n* in football and other sports, the difference between the number of goals scored for and against a team over a particular period

goal-directed *adj* strongly motivated and highly organized in achieving tasks that are specified in advance

goalie /gṓli/ *n* a goalkeeper (*informal*)

goalkeeper /gṓl keepər/ *n* in games such as football and hockey, a defensive player positioned in or near a goal whose main task is to keep the ball or puck from crossing the goal line into the goal

goal kick *n* **1** in football, a free kick taken from the six-yard-line by a defensive player when the ball has been driven out of play over the end line (**goal line**) by an opposing player **2** in rugby, a free kick by a member of the attacking team, aimed at clearing the defenders' crossbar and designed to convert a five-point try into a seven-point score

goalless /gṓl ləss/ *adj* **1** without any goals being scored ○ *A goalless semifinal left everyone feeling cheated.* **2** having no goals to aim for in life or work

goal line *n* in games such as football and hockey, the line where goalposts are positioned and over which the ball must pass or be carried to make a score

goalmouth /gṓl mowth/ (*plural* **-mouths** /-mowthz/) *n* in games such as football and hockey, the area directly in front of the goal

goal-oriented *adj* = **goal-directed**

goalpost /gṓl pōst/ *n* either of two posts, usually supporting a crossbar between them, that together mark the boundary of the goal in games such as football and hockey ◇ **move the goalposts** to change the rules or conditions after a project has started or a course of action has been embarked on ○ *We'll never finish the software if Marketing keeps moving the goalposts.*

goalscorer /gṓl skawrər/ *n* a player who scores or has just scored a goal

goaltender /gṓl tendər/ *n US* SPORTS = **goalkeeper**

goaltending /gṓl tending/ *n* **1** in basketball, illegal interference with a ball that is in its downward arc toward the basket or that is in or on the rim of the basket **2** *US* the act of trying to keep a puck or ball from entering a goal, especially in ice hockey

goanna /gō ánnə/ *n* a large monitor lizard of which there are several varieties. Native to: Australia. Genus: *Varanus*. [Mid-19C. Alteration of IGUANA.]

goat /gōt/ (*plural* **goats** *or* **goat**) *n* **1** an agile ruminant mammal that is related to sheep and has backward curving horns, straight hair, and a short tail. Kept for: wool, meat, milk. Genus: *Capra*. **2** a man who is regarded as lecherous (*insult*) **3** = **scapegoat** *n.* 1 [Old English *gāt* < Indo-European] —**goatish** *adj* ◇ **act** *or* **play the (giddy) goat** to behave in a silly way, often intentionally ◇ **get somebody's goat** to annoy or irritate somebody (*informal*) ○ *Their constant carping over trivia really gets my goat.*

Goat *n* ZODIAC = **Capricorn** *n.* 1

goat cheese, goat's cheese *n* cheese made from goat's milk

goatee /gō tée/ *n* a short pointed beard on the chin but not the cheeks [< its resemblance to a goat's beard]

goatfish /gṓt fish/ (*plural* **-fish** *or* **-fishes**) *n US* ZOOL = **red mullet** [< barbels beneath its mouth]

goatherd /gṓt hurd/ *n* a herder of goats

goatsbeard /gṓts beerd/ *n* **1** a plant with woolly stems. Flowers: large, yellow, resembling the dandelion. Native to: Europe, Asia, now also growing in the United States. *Tragopogon pratensis*. **2** a tall perennial plant. Flowers: small, white, in long spikes. Native to: E North America. *Aruncus dioicus*. [< the down on the seeds]

goat's cheese *n* FOOD = **goat cheese**

goatskin /gṓt skin/ *n* **1** SKIN OF A GOAT the skin or hide of a goat **2** LEATHER leather made from the skin of a goat **3** LEATHER WINE FLASK a wine container made from the skin of a goat

goat's milk *n* milk from a goat, used for drinking and for making cheese

goat's rue *n* a leguminous plant used for feeding livestock. Flowers: white, purple, or pink. Native to: Europe, Asia. *Galega officinalis*.

goatsucker /gṓt sukər/ *n* BIRDS = **nightjar** [< a belief that it sucked milk from goats]

gob[1] /gob/ *n* a lump of a soft or wet substance (*slang*) ○ *a huge gob of whipped cream* ■ *vi* (**gobs, gobbing, gobbed**) to spit or eject phlegm from the throat (*slang*) [14C. < Old French *gobe* 'mouthful' < *gober* 'swallow'.]

gob[2] /gob/ *n* the human mouth (*slang disapproving*) [Mid-16C. < ?]

gob[3] /gob/ *n* waste material from mining, e.g. clay or shale [Mid-19C. < ?]

gobbet /góbbit/ *n* **1** QUANTITY OF LIQUID a quantity of liquid, often in a sticky blotch ○ *Gobbets of grease covered the top of the stove.* **2** EXCERPT an extract from a text, especially one chosen for translation or comment in an examination **3** HUNK OF FOOD a piece or chunk of something, especially raw meat (*archaic*) [13C. < Old French *gobet* 'small mouthful' < *gobe* (see GOB[1]).]

gobble[1] /góbb'l/ (**-bles, -bling, -bled**) *vt* **1** to eat something quickly and greedily ○ *He gobbled up all the pizza.* **2** to use something up quickly or in large amounts (*informal humorous*) ○ *watching the payphone gobble her money* [Early 17C. Probably < GOB[1].]

gobble[2] /góbb'l/ *vi* (**-bles, -bling, -bled**) to make the characteristic gurgling sound of a male turkey or a sound resembling this ■ *n, interj* the gurgling sound made by a male turkey [Late 17C. An imitation of the sound.]

gobbledegook /góbb'ldigook/, **gobbledygook** *n* language that is difficult or impossible to understand, especially nonsense or prolix technical jargon (*informal*) ○ *This manual is full of gobbledegook.* [Mid-20C. An imitation of a turkey's gobble.]

gobbler /góbblər/ *n* a male turkey (*informal*)

Gobelin /gṓbəlin/ *n* a tapestry produced by the Gobelin factory in Paris, characterized by vivid pictorial scenes

go-between *n* a communicator or mediator between people during a negotiation, transaction, or secret operation

Gobi Desert /gṓbi-/ desert in N China and S Mongolia. Area: 1,300,000 sq. km/500,000 sq. mi.

goblet /góbblət/ *n* **1** a drinking vessel with a stem and base, especially one of metal or glass **2** a large bowl-shaped cup used formerly for drinking (*archaic*) [14C. < Old French *gobelet* 'small cup' < *gobel* 'cup'.]

goblet cell *n* a cell shaped like a goblet that secretes mucus

goblin /góblin/ *n* in folk tales, a creature resembling a small man of unpleasant appearance, usually evil or mischievous [14C. Probably via Anglo-Norman < medieval Latin *gobelinus*, a supposed spirit.]

gobo /gṓbō/ (*plural* **gobos** *or* **goboes**) *n* **1** a shield that is placed around a microphone to keep out unwanted sounds **2** a black screen placed around the lens of a camera or video camera to keep out unwanted light [Mid-20C. < ?]

gobshite /gób shīt/ *n Ireland, UK* an offensive term for a person who is regarded as contemptible, especially for being unintelligent or incompetent (*insult regional*) [Mid-20C. < GOB[2] + variant of SHIT.]

gobsmacked /gób smakt/ *adj* extremely surprised or shocked (*slang*)

gobstopper /gób stopər/ *n* a large hard sweet that changes colour as it is sucked. US term **jawbreaker** *n.* 3 [< GOB[2]]

gobstruck /gób struk/ *adj* = **gobsmacked** (*slang*)

goby /gṓbi/ (*plural* **-by** *or* **-bies**) *n* a small elongated spiny-finned freshwater or marine fish whose pelvic fins form a sucker. Family: Gobiidae. [Mid-18C. Via Latin *gobius* < Greek *kōbios*, a small fish.]

go-by *n* a slight or snub (*slang*) ○ *She tried to speak but he gave her the go-by.*

go-cart, go-kart *n* a light open-framed car large enough for a child or young teenager to sit in, containing a small engine and used for racing [Late 17C.< GO[1] 'walk'; originally a device for helping a baby to walk.]

god /god/ *n* **1** SUPERNATURAL BEING one of a group of supernatural male beings in some religions, each of which is worshipped as the personification or controller of some aspect of the universe ○ *Thor, the Norse god of thunder* **2** IMAGE a representation of a god, used as an object of worship ○ *the little bronze god standing in a niche above the altar* **3** SOMETHING THAT DOMINATES something that is so important that it takes over somebody's life (*informal*) ○ *worshipping the false god of fame* **4** SOMEBODY ADMIRED a man who is widely admired or imitated (*informal*) ○ *He was one of the rock music gods of the early Seventies.* ■ **gods** *npl* **1** FATE the entire group of supernatural beings viewed as deciding human fate **2** THEATRE GALLERY the highest tier of seats in a theatre (*informal*) [Old English, < Indo-European, 'that which is invoked']

God *n* **1** SUPREME BEING the being believed in monotheistic religions such as Judaism, Islam, and Christianity to be the all-powerful all-knowing creator of the universe, worshipped as the only god **2** THE TRINITY one supreme being worshipped by Christians in the form of three persons, Father, Son, and Holy Ghost ■ *interj* EXPRESSION OF STRONG FEELING used to express or emphasize feelings such as anger, helplessness, and frustration (*sometimes offensive*)

Godard /góddaar/, **Jean-Luc** (*b.* 1930) French film director

Godavari /gō daávəri/ river in central India, flowing from the Western Ghats to the Bay of Bengal. Length: 1,400 km/900 mi.

god-awful, God-awful *adj* extremely bad or unpleasant (*slang; sometimes offensive*)

godchild /gód chīld/ (*plural* **-children** /-childrən/) *n* somebody whose spiritual upbringing is made the responsibility of a godmother, godfather, or both

goddaughter /gód dawtər/ *n* a girl or woman who is somebody's godchild

goddess /gódd ess/ *n* **1** SUPERNATURAL BEING one of the group of supernatural female beings in some religions, worshipped as the personification or controller of some aspect of the universe **2** FIGURE OR IMAGE a representation of a goddess, used as an object of worship ○ *the statue of the goddess, standing in the temple's first niche* **3** SOMEBODY ADMIRED AND IMITATED a woman who is widely admired or imitated, especially for her beauty (*informal*) ○ *a screen goddess*

Gödel /gúrd'l/, **Kurt** (1906–78) Austrian-born US mathematician

godet /gō dét/ *n* a triangular piece of material inserted into a skirt or other garment to make it more flared or to widen it [Late 19C. < French.]

godfather /gód faathər/ *n* **1** a man who is somebody's godparent **2** a man who heads a criminal organization, especially a Mafia leader (*informal*)

God-fearing *adj* devout or deeply religious

godforsaken /gódfər sayk'n/ *adj* depressing, deserted, or empty ○ *The soldiers couldn't wait to get out of that godforsaken desert.*

God-given *adj* existing or applying as part of the natural order of the universe rather than arranged by humanity

godhead /gód hed/ *n* the nature or essence of being divine

Godhead /gód hed/ *n* the Christian God, especially when considered as the Holy Trinity

godhood /gód hood/ *n* RELIG = **godhead**

Godiva /gə dívə/, **Lady** (1040?–80?) English noblewoman said to have ridden naked to get taxes reduced

godless /gódləss/ *adj* **1** not believing in or worshipping God or any god (*disapproving*) **2** having an evil or immoral character or nature (*formal*) —**godlessly** *adv* —**godlessness** *n*

godlike /gód līk/ *adj* fit for God or a god, or having the qualities of a god or of God, e.g. superhuman power, beauty, or imagination

godly /gódli/ (**-lier, -liest**) *adj* **1** devoted to or worshipping God (*formal*) **2** fit for or having the divine qualities of God or a god —**godliness** *n*

godmother /gód muthər/ *n* a woman who is somebody's godparent

godown /gṓ down/ *n* a warehouse, especially in South and Southeast Asia [Late 16C. Via Portuguese *gudao* < Tamil *kitanku*, Kannada *gadangu* 'store'.]

godparent /gód pairənt/ *n* a sponsor of a baptized child who promises to take a personal interest in him or her

godroon /gə droón/ *n* CRAFT = **gadroon**

God's Acre *n* a churchyard or cemetery (*archaic*) [< German *Gottesacker*]

God's country *n* a nation or piece of land that is dearly loved

godsend /gód send/ *n* **1** something good that happens unexpectedly **2** something received that proves extremely useful, or somebody who arrives and gives much-needed help [Early 19C. < *God's send* < SEND[1] 'thing sent'.]

God's gift *n* an extremely admirable, valued, or talented person (*often ironic*) ○ *He thought he was God's gift to the film industry.*

God slot *n* a scheduled time for religious programmes on radio or television (*sometimes offensive*)

godson /gód sun/ *n* a man or boy who is somebody's godchild

God's own country *n* any country or piece of land seen as chosen and specially favoured

Godspeed /gód speed/ *interj* used to wish somebody a

safe journey or successful endeavour (*dated*) [15C. < *God speed you* 'may God speed you'.]

God squad *n* a Christian religious group, especially one that enthusiastically recruits new members (*informal humorous or disapproving; sometimes offensive*)

Godthåb /gód hawb/ former name for **Nuuk**

Godwin Austen, Mount /góddwin óstin/ = **K2**

godwit /gód wit/ *n* a large wading bird, found worldwide, that has a long, slightly upturned, bill and long legs and is related to curlews and sandpipers. Genus: *Limosa*. [Mid-16C. < ?]

Goebbels /góbl'z/, **Joseph** (1897–1945) German Nazi leader

goer /gó ar/ *n* **1** REGULAR ATTENDER a regular attender of something (*usually in combination*) ○ *festival-goers* **2** FAST MOVER a spirited or fast-moving person or animal (*informal*) **3** PROMISCUOUS PERSON a promiscuous or sexually uninhibited person (*slang; sometimes offensive*)

Goering /gúring, góring/, **Göring, Hermann** (1893–1946) German Nazi leader

Goethe /góta/, **Johann Wolfgang von** (1749–1832) German writer and scientist

goethite /gó thīt/ *n* an earthy, rust-coloured hydrated iron oxide mineral [Early 19C. After GOETHE.]

go-faster *adj* intended to make a motor vehicle look or sound sporty or fast (*informal*) ○ *a car with go-faster stripes*

gofer /gófar/ *n* a person who runs errands or performs other menial tasks (*informal*) [Mid-20C. < reduced pronunciation of *go for*.]

goffer /góffar/, **gauffer** *vt* **1** CRIMP HAIR to make hair wavy or crimped using a heated iron or similar device **2** PRESS FRILLS INTO FABRIC to press pleats into fabric to produce an ornamental frill using a heated iron or similar implement ■ *n* GOFFERING TOOL a tool used for goffering frills [Late 16C. < French *gaufrer* 'mark with a decorative tool' < *gaufre* 'honeycomb' < Middle Low German *wafel*.]

Gog and Magog /góg and máy gog/ *n* in parts of the Bible, the name given to the enemies of God's people

go-getter /gó géttar/ *n* an enterprising and forceful person (*informal*)

gogga /khókha/ *n* S Africa an insect or other small crawling or flying animal [Via Afrikaans < Khoikhoi *xoxon* 'organisms that slither or creep']

goggle /gógg'l/ *v* (**-gles**, **-gling**, **-gled**) **1** *vi* STARE WIDE-EYED to stare with eyes wide open, usually in astonishment **2** *vti* ROLL THE EYES to roll the eyes about, or roll about in the eye socket ■ *adj* BULGING bulging from the eye socket ○ *goggle eyes* [14C. Probably < a verb imitative of moving backwards and forwards.] —**goggle** *n* —**goggly** *adj*

goggle-box *n* a television set (*dated informal*)

goggle-eyed *adj* with staring eyes

goggles /gógg'lz/ *npl* protective glasses, usually made of plastic or glass and fitting tight to the face

go-go *adj US* **1** ENERGETIC characterized by energy and forcefulness **2** SPECULATIVE bringing or expected to bring quick or high returns on any investment ○ *These go-go stocks carry risk and are not for the timid investor.* **3** DISCO relating to or seen in discotheques or music clubs (*dated*) ■ *n* TYPE OF MUSIC a type of US popular music from the 1980s, an amalgamation of disco, funk, and Latin sounds [Doubling of GO¹, probably after French *à gogo* 'galore']

go-go dancer *n* an energetic, usually scantily dressed dancer, who entertains in a nightclub or pub (*dated*)

Goiânia /goy a̱ani a/ *city in south-central Brazil. Population: 972,766 (1996).

Goidelic /goy déllik/ *n* the northern branch of the Celtic family of languages, comprising Irish Gaelic, Scottish Gaelic, and Manx. Native speakers: 300,000. —**Goidelic** *adj*

going /gó ing/ *n* **1** ACT OF LEAVING an act of leaving somewhere **2** CONDITIONS UNDER FOOT the state of the ground as it affects ease and speed of movement, especially for horses in a race ○ *The going is good.* **3** CONDITIONS FOR PROGRESS conditions for making progress of any kind ○ *The going gets tough when you reach the rocky terrain.* ■ *adj* **1** SUCCESSFUL currently operating successfully **2** ACCEPTED AS STANDARD currently accepted as standard or valid ○ *the going rate for platinum* **3** EXISTING currently in existence or available ○ *the best going*

going-over (*plural* **goings-over**) *n* (*informal*) **1** THOROUGH EXAMINATION a thorough examination or check ○ *They*

gave the results a thorough going-over before making their report. **2** OVERHAUL an action by which something is thoroughly improved or restored to a previous condition, e.g. an act of cleaning, polishing, or dusting something ○ *The house got a complete going-over before the arrival of the in-laws.* **3** SCOLDING OR BEATING a verbal scolding or physical beating

goings-on /gō ingz-/ *npl* events or activities, especially of a noteworthy or suspicious nature (*informal*)

goiter *n US* = **goitre**

goitre /góytar/ *n* enlargement of the thyroid gland appearing as a swelling of the front of the neck [Early 17C. Via French < Latin *guttur* 'throat'.] —**goitrous** *adj*

go-kart *n* MOTOR SPORTS = **go-cart** *n*.

Golan Heights /gó lan-/ disputed upland region on the border between Israel and Syria, northeast of the Sea of Galilee. It was annexed by Israel in 1981. Area: 1,250 ft/485 sq. mi.

gold /góld/ *n* **1** YELLOW METALLIC ELEMENT (*symbol* Au) a soft, heavy, corrosion-resistant, yellow metallic element that is highly valued. Source: underground veins, alluvial deposits. Use: jewellery, alloys. **2** RICH YELLOW HUE a deep rich yellow colour that resembles that of the metal gold **3** THINGS MADE OF GOLD things made of gold, e.g. coins or pieces of jewellery **4** WEALTH much money or wealth **5** GOLD MEDAL a gold medal (*informal*) **6** BULL'S EYE the bull's eye of a target, which is usually gilt [Old English, < Indo-European] —**gold** *adj*

Goldberg /góldbarg/, **Whoopi** (b. 1949) US actor. Born Caryn Johnson

gold brick *n* a brick or other thing that appears to be made of gold but is not actually valuable

Gold Coast 1 city in SE Queensland, Australia, on the Pacific Coast. Population: 311,932 (1996). **2** former name for **Ghana**

goldcrest /góld krest/ *n* a small, common, very active, olive-green songbird with a yellow-and-black crown. Native to: Europe. *Regulus regulus*.

gold digger *n* **1** a person who seeks intimate relationships for material gain (*insult*) **2** a miner looking for gold deposits —**gold-digging** *n*

gold disc *n* **1** a golden replica of a recording that has achieved a specified exceptionally high number of sales. US term **gold record 2** the master disc from which a CD-ROM is made

gold dust *n* **1** small particles of gold occurring naturally **2** PLANTS = **alyssum** *n*. 2

golden /góld'n/ *adj* **1** COLOURED LIKE GOLD with the colour of gold ○ *golden hair* **2** MADE OF GOLD made largely or wholly of gold ○ *a golden crown* **3** EXCELLENT especially good ○ *a golden opportunity* **4** IDYLLIC describes a period when there is individual or general success, happiness, or prosperity ○ *the golden years of their lives* **5** FAVOURED popular or successful or likely to become so ○ *the golden boys and girls of the downhill ski circuit* **6** 50TH that is fiftieth in a series ○ *golden jubilee* —**goldenly** *adv* — **goldenness** *n*

golden age *n* **1** a period of great prosperity or achievement, especially in the arts **2** the first age of the world in classical mythology, characterized by idyllic happiness and innocence

golden ager /-áygar/ *n US* somebody over retirement age

golden anniversary *n* a fiftieth anniversary, e.g. of a wedding, or its celebration

Golden Bay inlet of the Tasman Sea, on the northern coast of the South Island, New Zealand

golden brown *n* a yellowish-brown colour —**golden-brown** *adj*

golden-brown alga *n* a freshwater or marine alga that is yellow to golden-brown in colour. Division: *Chrysophyta*. (*often plural*)

golden calf *n* an unworthy object that is esteemed or worshipped, especially money [< that worshipped by the Israelites (Exodus 32)]

golden chain *n* TREES = **laburnum** *n*.

Golden Delicious *n* a variety of eating apple with greenish or yellowish skin and a soft sweet flesh

golden eagle *n* a large dark-brown eagle with golden-brown feathers on its head and neck. Native to: mountainous regions of N hemisphere. *Aquila chrysaetos*.

goldeneye /góld'n ī/ *n* **1** a black-and-white diving duck with yellow eyes. Native to: northern regions. *Bucephala clangula* and *Bucephala islandica*. **2** an insect with yellow eyes and delicate lacy wings. Family: Chrysopidae.

Golden Fleece *n* in Greek mythology, the fleece of the winged ram Chrysomallus, kept in a sacred grove by King Aeëtes, from where it was stolen by Jason

Golden Gate Bridge

Golden Gate Bridge suspension bridge across the entrance to San Francisco Bay, California

golden hamster *n* a small mammal with tan fur, a short tail, and large cheek pouches for storing food, that is often kept as a pet or used as a laboratory animal. *Mesocricetus auratus*.

golden handcuffs *npl* generous benefits promised to an employee on joining a company to discourage him or her from leaving to work elsewhere (*informal*)

golden handshake *n* a large sum of money given to an employee to compensate for the loss of a job or compulsory early retirement (*informal*)

golden hello *n* a large sum of money given after an employment contract has been signed, offered as an inducement to somebody to take up a new job or join an organization (*informal*)

Golden Horde *n* the Mongol army that invaded and dominated large parts of E Europe in the 13th century

Golden Horn inlet of the Bosporus in European Turkey, forming the harbour of Istanbul. Length: 8 km/5 mi.

golden jubilee *n* a 50th anniversary, especially of a public event

golden lion tamarin *n* a small monkey with brilliant golden fur and mane. Native to: coastal forests of Brazil. *Leontopithecus rosalia*.

golden mean *n* **1** the middle course that avoids extremes in either direction **2** ARTS = **golden section**

golden nematode *n* a small worm that can infest potato fields, causing severe damage to crops and loss of productive farm land. *Heterodera rostochiensis*.

golden oldie *n* a song that was popular in the past and has remained popular or become popular again (*informal*)

golden parachute *n* an employment agreement that gives generous benefits to a senior executive who is forced to leave a company (*informal*)

golden pheasant *n* a brightly coloured long-tailed pheasant. Native to: mountainous regions of China and Tibet. *Chrysolophus pictus*.

golden plover *n* a migratory shore bird with brown and black plumage and gold spots on its head and back. Native to: N Europe. *Pluvialis apricaria*.

golden retriever *n* a medium-sized dog of a breed with soft cream to golden hair

golden robin *n* BIRDS = **Baltimore oriole**

goldenrod /góld'n rod/ (*plural* **-rods** *or* **-rod**) *n* a tall-stemmed, late summer-blooming plant. Flowers: small, yellow, in clusters. Native to: Europe, North America. Genus: *Solidago*.

golden rule *n* **1** any basic rule that must be followed **2** the rule of conduct that advises people to treat others in the same manner as they wish to be treated themselves

golden section *n* the proportion arising from the division of a straight line into two, so that the ratio of the whole line to the larger part is exactly the same as the ratio of the larger part to the smaller part [Because considered to be the most aesthetically pleasing proportion]

golden share *n* a controlling share retained by a government in a company that has been taken out of public ownership and privatized

golden syrup *n* a clear yellow syrup used in baking and for desserts

golden triangle *n* the part of Southeast Asia where Laos, Thailand, and Myanmar meet and where much opium is grown

golden wattle *n* a tree whose golden-yellow flowers are used as the floral emblem of Australia. Native to: Australia. *Acacia pycantha.*

goldfield /gṓld feeld/ *n* an area with gold mines

goldfinch /gṓld finch/ *n* a small finch with yellow and black markings. Native to: North America, Europe, Asia. Genus: *Carduelis.*

goldfish /gṓldfish/ (*plural* **-fish** *or* **-fishes**) *n* an orange-red freshwater aquarium and pond fish related to carps and minnows. Native to: E Asia. *Carassius auratus.*

goldfish bowl *n* **1** a clear glass or plastic bowl in which to raise and keep goldfish **2** a situation or place that is always open to public view or scrutiny

gold leaf *n* gold that is beaten out into very thin sheets and used for gilding and lettering

Goldman /gṓldmən/, **Emma** (1869–1940) Russian-born US anarchist

gold medal *n* a medal that is made of gold or something representing gold, given as a first prize for excellence or winning a competition —**gold medallist** *n*

gold mine *n* **1** a place where gold is mined **2** a rich source of something valuable, especially easily obtained wealth ○ *Some of the smaller shops are little gold mines.* —**gold-miner** *n* —**gold-mining** *n*

gold plate *n* **1** bowls, goblets, and other utensils made of gold **2** a thin coating of gold on another metal, usually produced by electroplating

gold-plated *adj* having a thin coating of gold, usually produced by electroplating —**gold-plate** *vt*

gold record *n US* MUSIC = **gold disc** *n.* 1

gold reserve *n* a fund of gold in coins or bullion held by a central bank and regarded as providing a foundation for a paper currency and security for borrowing

gold rush *n* **1** a sudden wave of migration to new territory because gold has been discovered there **2** a sudden rush to make money from a new source or by a new means

goldsmith /gṓld smith/ *n* a maker of or dealer in gold objects

Goldsmith /gṓld smith/, **Sir James** (1933–97) French-born British business executive

Goldsmith, Oliver (1730–74) Irish-born British writer

gold standard *n* **1** a system of defining monetary units in terms of their value in gold, usually accompanied by the free circulation of gold and free exchange of currency into it **2** the very best example of its kind

goldstone /gṓld stōn/ *n* MINERALS = **aventurine** *n.* 2

goldthread /gṓld thred/ *n* a low-growing evergreen plant. Native to: mossy woods or swamps in North America and Europe. Genus: *Coptis.*

Goldwyn /gṓldwin/, **Samuel** (1882–1974) Russian-born US film producer. Born **Schmuel Gelbfisz**

golem /gṓləm, góy-/ *n* in Jewish legend, a creature made of clay and brought to life by magical incantations [Late 19C. Via Yiddish < Hebrew *golem* 'shape, mass'.]

golf /golf/ *n* an outdoor game in which an array of special clubs with long shafts are used to hit a small ball from a prescribed starting point into a series of holes ■ *vi* to play the game of golf [15C. < ?] —**golfer** *n*

Golf *n* the NATO phonetic alphabet code word for the letter 'G', used in international radio communications

golf ball *n* a small hard ball used for playing golf

golf cart *n* a motorized vehicle used to drive around on a golf course during play

golf club *n* **1** STICK FOR HITTING GOLF BALLS a specially designed club with a long shaft and a metal or wooden head, used in golf to strike the ball **2** GOLFERS' ASSOCIATION an association of people who play golf, usually on the same course **3** PREMISES OF GOLFERS' ASSOCIATION the premises or facilities used by a golf club

golf course *n* an area of land designed for playing the game of golf

golfing /gólfing/ *n* the activity of playing golf (*often before nouns*) ○ *a golfing umbrella*

golf links *npl* a golf course situated beside the sea

golf widow *n* a woman whose husband or partner spends many hours playing golf (*informal*)

Golgi apparatus /gólji-/, **Golgi body, Golgi complex** *n* a membranous structure in the cytoplasm of cells consisting of layers of flattened sacs and functioning in the processing and transporting of proteins [Early 20C. After Camillo *Golgi* (1844–1926), Italian histologist.]

Golgotha /gólgəthə/ = **Calvary**

goliath /gə lī́ əth/, **Goliath** *n* a gigantic or overpowering opponent or competitor ○ *a corporation regarded as the goliath of the oil industry* [Late 16C. After GOLIATH.]

Goliath *n* in the Bible, a giant Philistine who was slain by David using a sling and a stone

Goliath beetle *n* a very large scarab beetle that can measure up to 15 cm/6 in in length and has bold black, white, and brown markings. Native to: tropical Africa. *Goliathus giganteus.*

Goliath frog *n* a very large frog that can measure up to 30 cm/12 in. Native to: central Africa. *Rana goliath.*

golliwog /gólli wog/, **golliwogg** *n* an offensively grotesque cloth doll with a black face and hair and brightly coloured clothes (*offensive*) [Late 19C. After a character in books by Florence Upton.]

golly[1] /gólli/ *interj* used to express surprise, amazement, or anxiety, or for emphasis (*dated informal*) ○ *Golly, we're in real trouble now!* [Late 18C. Alteration of GOD.]

golly[2] /gólli/ (*plural* **-lies**) *n* = **golliwog** (*offensive*) [Mid-20C. Shortening.]

gombeenism /góm beenizəm/, **gombeen** /góm been/ *n Ireland* money-lending at extortionate rates [Mid-19C. See GOMBEEN MAN.]

gombeen man *n Ireland* **1** a money-lender who charges exorbitant interest **2** a small-time entrepreneur [< Irish *gaimbín* 'usury']

gombroon /gómbroon/ *n* pottery made in Iran and elsewhere in imitation of white Chinese porcelain [Late 17C. After *Gombroon* (now Bandar Abbas), port in Iran.]

Gomorrah /gə mórrə/ *n* a place or society marked by evil, depravity, and promiscuousness (*disapproving*) [Early 20C. After an ancient city destroyed by God because of its wickedness (Genesis 19).]

gon- *prefix* = **gono-** (*before vowels*)

-gon *suffix* a figure having a particular number of angles ○ *undecagon* ○ *polygon* [< Greek *-gōnon* < *gōnia* 'angle, corner' < Indo-European, 'knee, bend']

gonad /gṓ nad, gónnad/ *n* an organ that produces reproductive cells (**gametes**), e.g. a testis or an ovary [Late 19C. < modern Latin *gonad-*, stem of *gonas* < Greek *gonos* 'seed, generation'.] —**gonadal** /gō náyd'l, go-/ *adj* —**gonadic** /gō náddik, go-/ *adj*

gonadotrophic /gónnədə trṓfik/, **gonadotropic** /-tróppik/ *adj* stimulating or acting on the gonads

gonadotrophin /gónnədə trṓfin/, **gonadotropin** /-trṓpin/ *n* a hormone secreted by the pituitary gland, and in some mammals by the placenta during pregnancy, that influences gonadal activity, including the onset of sexual maturity and regulation of reproductive activity

gonadotropic *adj* BIOCHEM = **gonadotrophic**

gonadotropin *n* BIOCHEM = **gonadotrophin**

Gonaïves /gō nī́v/ town in W Haiti. Population: 63,291 (1992).

Goncourt /góN koor/, **Edmond de** (1822–96) French novelist and diarist

gondola /góndələ/ *n* **1** VENETIAN CANAL BOAT a narrow flat-bottomed boat, used on the canals of Venice, that has a curved prow and stern and is moved along with a long pole **2** CAR BELOW A BALLOON a basket or cabin suspended from a balloon or airship, for carrying people or equipment **3** CABLE CAR a car or cabin suspended from cables, especially one attached to a ski lift **4** ISLAND OF SHELVES a free-standing shelving unit forming an island for displaying goods in a supermarket or other self-service shop [Mid-16C. Via Venetian Italian < Rhaeto-Romance *gondolà* 'to roll, rock'.]

gondolier /góndə léer/ *n* a person who guides a gondola through water, especially on the canals of Venice

Gondwanaland /gon dwáanə land/ ancient landmass, part of the supercontinent of Pangaea, comprising South America, Africa, peninsular India, Australia, and Antarctica. ◊ **Laurasia, Pangaea**

gone past participle of **go**[1] ■ *adj* **1** ABSENT absent after leaving somewhere ○ *She has been gone for hours.* **2** IRRECOVERABLE beyond hope of recovery ○ *All hopes for a truce are gone.* **3** USED UP having been completely used up **4** ADVANCED IN TIME more advanced than a particular time or age ○ *It's gone six and we'll be late.* **5** PREGNANT having been pregnant for a particular number of months ○ *She's eight months gone.* **6** DEAD no longer living (*informal*) **7** UNEASY giving a sensation of giddiness or sinking in the stomach **8** INFATUATED affected by a strong feeling of attraction towards somebody (*informal*) ○ *He's gone on your sister.* **9** EXHILARATED excited or exhilarated, e.g. while listening to music (*slang*)

goner /gónnər/ *n* somebody or something beyond hope of recovery, especially somebody who is dead or about to die (*slang*) ○ *It looks like he's a goner.*

gonfalon /gónfələn/ *n* a banner suspended from a crossbar, often with an edge cut like streamers, used as the standard of some medieval Italian republics or carried in church processions [Late 16C. Via Italian *gonfalone* < Old French *gonfanon* < Germanic, 'war banner'.]

gonfalonier /gónfələ néer/ *n* **1** a bearer of a gonfalon **2** the chief magistrate of some medieval Italian republics, who carried the republic's gonfalon

gong /gong/ *n* **1** RESONANT BRONZE PLATE a circular bronze plate that makes a resonant sound when struck with a mallet. Use: orchestral percussion instrument, to summon people to meals. **2** WARNING BELL a round metal bell that is struck by a mechanically operated hammer. Use: as an alarm. **3** MEDAL a medal or decoration (*slang*) ■ *v* **1** *vi* SOUND LIKE A GONG to sound resonantly like a gong **2** *vt* SUMMON to summon somebody with a gong [Early 17C. < Malay, an imitation of the sound made.]

Gongorism /góng gərizəm/ *n* a style in Spanish literature characterized by ornate devices, classical allusions, and deliberate obscurity [Early 19C. After *Góngora* y Argote (1561–1627), Spanish poet.] —**Gongoristic** /góng gə rístik/ *adj*

gonidium /gō níddi əm/ (*plural* **-a** /-ə/) *n* **1** an asexual reproductive cell in some algae, e.g. a zoospore **2** a chlorophyll-containing algal cell in the body (**thallus**) of a lichen [Mid-19C. < modern Latin, < Greek *gonos* 'offspring'.] —**gonidial** *adj*

goniometer /gṓni ómmitər/ *n* **1** an instrument for measuring angles, especially those between crystal faces **2** a device for establishing the bearing of an incoming radio signal [Mid-18C. < French *goniomètre* < Greek *gonia* 'angle'.] —**goniometric** /gṓni ə méttrik/ *adj* —**goniometrical** *adj* —**goniometry** *n*

gonion /gṓni on/ *n* the point on either side of the lower jaw where it turns upwards [Late 19C. < French, < Greek *gonia* 'angle'.]

goniotomy /gṓni óttəmi/ (*plural* **-mies**) *n* an operation to treat glaucoma by cutting into the narrow angle between the back of the cornea and the root of the iris to allow drainage of aqueous humour

⚡**gonk** /gongk/ *vti* to lie about something or embellish the truth, especially in an online conversation in a chat room (*slang*) ○ *Are you gonking me?* [Mid-20C. Invention.] —**gonk** *n*

gonna /gónnə, gúnnə/ *contr* going to (*nonstandard*)

gono- *prefix* sexual, generative, semen, seed ○ *gonophore* [< Greek *gonos* 'offspring, procreation' < Indo-European, 'beget']

gonococcus /gónnə kókəss/ (*plural* **-ci** /-kóksī/) *n* a spherical bacterium that causes gonorrhoea. *Neisseria gonorrhoeae.* [Late 19C. < GONORRHOEA.] —**gonococcal** /-kók'l/ *adj* —**gonococcic** /-kóksik/ *adj*

gonopore /gónnə pawr/ *n* an external reproductive pore in some insects and worms through which reproductive cells are secreted

gonorrhea *n* US = **gonorrhoea**

gonorrhoea /gónnə rée ə/, **gonorrhea** *n* a sexually transmitted bacterial disease that causes inflammation of the genital mucous membrane, burning pain when urinating, and a discharge [16C. Via modern Latin < Greek *gonorrhoia* 'flowing of semen' < *gonos* 'semen'.] —**gonorrhoeal** *adj*

-gony *suffix* **1** origin ○ *cosmogony* **2** method of reproduction ○ *schizogony* [< Greek *gonos* (see GONO-)]

Gonzales /gon zaáliz/, **Pancho** (1928–95) US tennis player. Full name **Richard Alonzo Gonzales**

gonzo /gónzō/ *adj* (*slang*) **1** US characterized by subjective interpretation and exaggeration ○ *Gonzo journalism is unlike the work of the impartial observer.* **2** unusual or strange [Late 20C. < ?]

goo /goo/ *n* (*informal*) **1** any sticky substance, typically something unpleasant **2** cloying emotionalism [Early 20C. < ?]

good /good/ (**better** /béttər/, **best** /best/) CORE MEANING: an adjective indicating that something is approved of or desirable ○ *It's a good idea to change your password now and again.* ○ *It's good to talk.*

1 *adj* **OF HIGH QUALITY** of a high quality or standard, either on an absolute scale or in relation to another or others ○ *The meal wasn't good.* ○ *He'll make a very good doctor.* ○ *I smashed one of my good plates.* **2** *adj* **SUITABLE** having the appropriate qualities to be something or to fit a particular purpose ○ *Futons make good chairs as well as beds.* ○ *The bicycle is good for short trips.* **3** *adj* **SKILLED** possessing the necessary skill or talent to do something ○ *I'm not a very good driver.* ○ *She's good at science.* **4** *adj* **VIRTUOUS** having or showing an upright and virtuous character ○ *You're a good man, Joe.* **5** *adj* **KIND** having or showing a kind and generous disposition ○ *She was always very good to me.* **6** *adj* **AFFORDING PLEASURE** affording pleasure or comfort ○ *He's a man who insists on the finer things in life: good food, good books, and the theatre.* **7** *adj* **UNDAMAGED** having undergone no deterioration or damage ○ *I smelled the meat and found it was still good.* **8** *adj* **AMPLE** sufficiently large ○ *Between them they have a good income.* **9** *adj* **HONOURABLE** worthy of honour or high esteem ○ *They come from a good family.* **10** *adj* **VALID** acceptable as true or genuine and sufficient for the purpose ○ *There had better be a good explanation for this mess.* ○ *Don't travel unless your insurance is good.* **11** *adj* **HELPFUL** helping somebody to organize thoughts or make decisions ○ *She gave me some good advice.* **12** *adj* **PLEASANT** pleasant to look at ○ *Don't let her good looks distract you from her intelligence.* **13** *adj* **BENEFICIAL** beneficial to health or wellbeing ○ *Eating lots of fruit is good for you.* **14** *adj* **FAVOURABLE** suitable and likely to produce the right results or conditions ○ *a good time to have a holiday* **15** *adj* **THOROUGH** that goes to the fullest extent of the action ○ *Take a good look round.* **16** *adj* **FINANCIALLY ADVANTAGEOUS** financially or commercially advantageous or reliable ○ *I made a few good investments last year.* **17** *adj* **GENUINE** that is what it appears to be ○ *a good ten pound note* **18** *adj* **OBEDIENT** well behaved and obedient ○ *The children are always good when we take them out.* **19** *adj* **WELL MANNERED** socially correct ○ *very good behaviour* **20** *adj* **ABLE TO DO MORE** remaining in operation or effect ○ *The car will be good for another 6,000 miles.* **21** *adj* **ABLE TO PAY** able to pay or contribute something or to allow a sum to be drawn ○ *He's good for at least £1,000.* **22** *adj* **THAT WILL BE PAID** that the debtor is expected to honour in full ○ *a good debt* **23** *adj* **PRODUCING A RESULT** able to produce a particular result ○ *John is always good for a laugh.* **24** *adj* **SIZABLE** considerable in extent or size ○ *a good selection of books on computers* **25** *adj* **FULL** at least a particular time or length ○ *It's a good 30 years since we met.* **26** *adj* **WITHIN BOUNDS** inside the required area for the shot to be allowed ○ *The umpire said that the ball was good.* **27** *adj* **USED IN EXCLAMATIONS** used in exclamations of surprise, dismay, or other strong feelings (*informal*) ○ *Good heavens! I've won first prize!* **28** *adj* **HEALTHY** well in health (*informal; in UK usually in negative statements*) ○ *I'm not feeling too good so I'll stay at home.* ○ *'How are you?' 'Good'.* **29** *interj* **EXPRESSING SATISFACTION** used to express satisfaction or pleasure in something that has just been said or to confirm it ○ *'They've just arrived'. 'Good'.* **30** *n* **BENEFICIAL EFFECT** something resulting in a beneficial effect or state ○ *the common good* ○ *What good will complaining do?* **31** *n* = **goodness** *n.* 1 **32** *n* **POSITIVE PART** the positive part or aspect of something ○ *You have to take the good with the bad in this agreement.* **33** *n* **SOMETHING WORTH HAVING** something worth having or achieving ○ *Let's work for the future good of the nation.* **34** *n* **ITEM OF MERCHANDISE** an article for sale or use, often one produced for later consumption. ◊ **goods 35** *npl* **VIRTUOUS PEOPLE** those who are virtuous and upright ○ *the great and the good* [Old English *gōd* < Germanic, 'unite'] ◇ **be (all) to the good** to be to somebody's benefit ◇ **be up to no good** to be in the process of doing or planning something wrong or illegal (*informal*) ◇ **for good** permanently from the time in question ○ *They've gone for good.* ◇ **give as good as you get** to contend as effectively as your opponent ◇ **good and** completely and entirely (*informal*) ○ *I'll get up in the morning when I'm good and ready, and not before.* ◇ **make good** to become successful, often after an unpromising start ◇ **make good something 1** to perform something successfully ○ *We must make good our attempt to win the trophy.* **2** to carry out something intended or promised ○ *She made good her promise to repay the money on time.* **3** to compensate for something, especially for damage or loss **4** to demonstrate the truth or correctness of something ○ *If you cannot make good these charges, the defendant will not stand trial.* ◇ **never had it so good** to have not possessed so many benefits before ◇ **to the good** richer by a particular amount of money ○ *By the end of the day, we were 50 pounds to the good.*

USAGE good or **well**? ***Good*** is the correct choice as an adjective after the linking verbs *be*, *appear*, and *seem*, and so-called sensory verbs such as *smell* and *taste*: *The jacket looks good. This steak tastes good.* ***Well*** is the correct choice as an adverb when it appears after other verbs that neither link nor designate sensory functions: *The jacket looks good and fits you well. Cook the steak well if you expect it to taste good.*

---

good afternoon *interj* used when people meet or part, or begin or end a telephone conversation, during the afternoon

Good Book *n* the Christian Bible

goodbye /good bī/ *interj* used when people part or end a telephone conversation ○ *Goodbye! I'll see you next year.* ■ *n* an act of making a farewell ○ *It's time to say our goodbyes and catch the plane.* [Late 16C. < *God be with you.*]

good cause *n* **1** something or somebody deserving help, especially a charity **2** a sufficient legal standard or reason

good day *interj* used when people meet or part, or begin or end a telephone conversation, during daylight hours (*formal*)

good evening *interj* used when people meet or part, or begin or end a telephone conversation, during the evening

good faith *n* honesty of intention ○ *an effort to fulfill the contract in good faith.*

good-for-nothing *n* a lazy and irresponsible person (*insult*) —**good-for-nothing** *adj*

Good Friday *n* a Christian holy day marking the death of Jesus Christ. Date: Friday before Easter Day.

Good Friday plant *n* PLANTS = **moschatel**

good guy *n* US a worthy or law-abiding person, especially in a novel or film (*informal*)

goodhearted /good haártid/ *adj* having or showing a kind and generous nature —**goodheartedly** *adv* —**goodheartedness** *n*

Good Hope, Cape of tip of the Cape Peninsula, SW South Africa

good-humoured *adj* disposed to be cheerful and friendly —**good-humouredly** *adv*

goodie *n* = **goody**

goodish /gooddish/ *adj* **1** moderately good in quality **2** moderately large in quantity or extent ○ *a goodish helping*

Good King Henry (*plural* **Good King Henrys** *or* **Good King Henry**) *n* a weed of the goosefoot family with arrow-shaped leaves. Flowers: small, green. *Chenopodium bonus-henricus.*

good life *n* a life of carefree comfort and luxury ○ *living the good life in Palm Springs*

good-looking *adj* having a pleasing appearance, especially a facial one —**good-looker** *n*

good looks *npl* a pleasant personal appearance, especially facial appearance

goodly /goodli/ (**-lier, -liest**) *adj* **1** **SOMEWHAT LARGE** moderately large in quantity or extent **2** **ATTRACTIVE** having a fine appearance (*archaic*) **3** **PLEASANT** of a pleasing quality (*archaic*) ○ *the goodly fellowship of the prophets* —**goodliness** *n*

goodman /goodmən/ (*plural* **-men** /-mən/) *n* the man in charge of a household or family, especially a married man (*archaic*)

Goodman /goodmən/, **Benny** (1909–86) US jazz musician. Full name **Benjamin David Goodman**

good morning *interj* used when people meet or part, or begin or end a telephone conversation, during the morning

good name *n* **1** somebody's reputation for honesty and integrity **2** South Asia somebody's last name or family name

good nature *n* a pleasant and obliging disposition

good-natured *adj* having or showing a pleasant and obliging disposition —**good-naturedly** *adv* —**good-naturedness** *n*

goodness /goodnəss/ *n* **1** **GOOD QUALITY** the quality of being good **2** **VIRTUOUSNESS** personal virtue or kindness **3** **GOOD PART** the nutrition or other benefit to be derived from something ○ *Vegetables lose a lot of their goodness if you overcook them.* ■ *interj* **EXPRESSING SURPRISE** used to express surprise or amazement or for emphasis ○ *Goodness! What was that?* ◇ **for goodness sake** used to express surprise, exasperation, or extreme anxiety, or for emphasis ◇ **goodness knows** used to indicate bafflement or lack of knowledge about something ○ *Goodness knows what they're doing out there at midnight.*

goodnight /good nīt/ *interj* used to convey good wishes when people part or end a telephone conversation at night, especially at bedtime

good-o *interj* = **good-oh**

good offices *npl* help or support, especially help in resolving a dispute

good-oh, good-o *interj* UK, Aus, US used to express approval or agreement (*informal*)

good old boy, good ol' boy, good ole boy *n* US a stereotype of a man who is part of a peer group and conforms to the behaviour characteristic of the group, especially a white man in parts of the rural S United States (*often offensive*)

goods /goodz/ *npl* **1** **MERCHANDISE** articles for sale or use, often those produced for later consumption, as opposed to services (+ *singular or plural verb*) **2** **PORTABLE PROPERTY** portable personal property **3** **MERCHANDISE MOVED BY RAIL** merchandise that is transported, especially by rail, as opposed to passengers (*often before nouns*) ○ *a goods train* **4** **SOMETHING PROMISED** something promised or expected (*informal*) ○ *You can rely on her to come up with the goods.* **5** **GENUINE ARTICLE** something that is genuinely what it should be (*slang;* + *singular or plural verb*) **6** **INCRIMINATING EVIDENCE** information or evidence that will incriminate somebody (*slang*)

Good Samaritan *n* a helper of those who are in trouble [< the parable of the Good Samaritan (Luke 10:30–37), who helps a man beaten by robbers]

goods and services tax *n* in Canada and New Zealand, a value-added tax charged on all goods and services

good-sized *adj* rather large in size ○ *The recipe called for a good-sized piece of chocolate.*

good-tempered *adj* having or showing a placid disposition —**good-temperedly** *adv* —**good-temperedness** *n*

good-time girl *n* a young woman whose chief aim is thought to be the pursuit of pleasure (*disapproving*)

good turn *n* a friendly act that helps or benefits somebody else ○ *One good turn deserves another.*

goodwife /good wīf/ (*plural* **-wives** /-wīvz/) *n* the woman in charge of a household or family, especially a married woman (*archaic*)

goodwill /good wil/ *n* **1** **FRIENDLY DISPOSITION** friendly disposition towards somebody or something (*often before nouns*) ○ *a goodwill gesture* **2** **WILLINGNESS** cheerful willingness to do something **3** **NONTANGIBLE VALUE OF BUSINESS** the value of a business over and above its tangible assets **4** **CHARITY SHOP** a shop that sells donated goods in order to raise money for charity

Goodwin Sands /goodwin-/ area of sandbanks at the entrance to the Strait of Dover, off the coast of SE England. Length: 16km/10 mi.

Goodwood /goodwood/ country estate and racecourse in S England

good word *n* a comment recommending somebody or made in favour or defence of somebody ○ *He promised to put in a good word for me.*

goody /gooddi/, **goodie** *n* (*plural* **-ies**) **1** **SOMETHING SWEET** something desirable, especially something sweet to eat (*often plural*) **2** **SOMEBODY GOOD** a good or law-abiding person, especially in a Western or a crime thriller ■ *interj* **INDICATES DELIGHT** expresses great pleasure (*informal*) ○ *Oh goody, ice cream!*

Goodyear /gŏŏd yeer/, **Charles** (1800–60) US inventor

goody-goody *n* (*plural* **goody-goodies**) = **goody two-shoes** ■ *adj* irritatingly well-behaved or smugly virtuous (*informal*) [Mid-19C. Reduplication of GOODY.]

goody two-shoes (*plural* **goody two-shoes**) *n* somebody smugly well-behaved, irritatingly virtuous, or sanctimonious (*informal*) [Mid-20C. < a character in a children's book.]

gooey /gŏŏ i/ (**-ier, -iest**) *adj* **1** sticky and soft ○ *gooey chocolate cake* **2** cloyingly sentimental (*informal*) ○ *a gooey romantic novel* —**gooeyness** *n*

goof /goof/ *n* (*informal*) **1** MISTAKE a mistake or blunder **2** UNINTELLIGENT PERSON an unintelligent or incompetent person (*insult*) ■ *v* (*informal*) **1** *vi* MAKE MISTAKE to make a thoughtless or unintelligent mistake **2** *vt* BOTCH to spoil something through incompetence or lack of intelligence [Early 20C. Probably < dialect *goff* 'somebody considered unintelligent', via French and Italian < medieval Latin *gufus* 'awkward, unintelligent'.]

goof around *vi US* to behave in a playful or silly way (*informal*) ○ *Once the pressure of exams was off, the students just goofed around.*

goof off *v US* to waste time instead of working (*informal*) ○ *The crew goofed off when the boss left early.*

goofball /gŏŏf bawl/ *n US* **1** somebody regarded as thoughtless or unintelligent (*slang insult*) **2** a barbiturate or other drug in the form of a pill (*slang*)

goofy /gŏŏfi/ (**-ier, -iest**) *adj* **1** silly or unintelligent (*informal insult*) **2** having or showing front teeth that protrude from the mouth (*informal*) ○ *a goofy grin* —**goofily** *adv* —**goofiness** *n*

googly /gŏŏgli/ (*plural* **-glies**) *n* in cricket, a ball that looks like a leg break on delivery and then moves unexpectedly in the opposite direction after it pitches [Early 20C. < ?]

googol /gŏŏ gol/ *n* the number equal to the numeral 1 followed by 100 zeros or 10^{100} [Mid-20C. Invention.]

googolplex /gŏŏ gol pleks/ *n* the number equal to the numeral 1 followed by 10^{100} zeros [Mid-20C. < GOOGOL + Latin *plexus* 'intricate, braided'.]

gook /gook/ *n US* an offensive term for an Asian person or somebody of Asian descent (*slang*) [Mid-20C. < ?]

gooly /gŏŏli/ (*plural* **-lies**), **goolie** *n* an offensive term for a testicle (*slang*) [Mid-20C. Probably < Hindi *goli* 'ball, bullet'.]

goon /goon/ *n* **1** CLUMSY PERSON a clumsy or uncouth person (*insult*) **2** SOMEBODY WHO ACTS SILLY a person who behaves foolishly or bizarrely as a joke (*informal*) **3** *US* THUG a professional gangster whose work is beating up or terrorizing people [Mid-19C. < ?]

goonda /gŏŏn daa/ *n S Asia* a ruffian or hooligan [Early 20C. < Hindi *gunḍā* 'rascal'.] —**goondaism** *n*

gooney /gŏŏni/ (*plural* **-neys**), **gooney bird** *n* an albatross, especially the black-footed albatross [Late 16C. < ?]

goop /goop/ *n* **1** somebody regarded as unintelligent or thoughtless (*slang insult*) **2** *US* = **gloop** (*informal*) [Early 20C. Alteration.] —**goopy** *adj*

goosander /goo sándər/ *n* a waterfowl with a narrow serrated bill and a dark head and white body in the male. Native to: Europe, North America. *Mergus merganser.* [Early 17C. Probably < GOOSE + Old Norse *andar-*, stem of *ond* 'duck'.]

goose /gooss/ *n* (*plural* **geese** /geess/) **1** LONG-NECKED WATER BIRD a large waterfowl with a long neck and webbed feet, noted for its seasonal migrations and distinctive honking sound. Subfamily: Anserinae. **2** FEMALE GOOSE a female goose. ◊ **gander** *n.* 1 **3** FLESH OF THE GOOSE the flesh of the goose, cooked and eaten as food **4** SILLY PERSON a silly person **5** TAILOR'S IRON an iron with a long curved handle, used by tailors for pressing and smoothing cloth **6** PROD IN THE BUTTOCKS a poke between or pinch on the buttocks (*slang*) ■ *vt* (**gooses, goosing, goosed**) (*slang*) **1** PROD IN THE BUTTOCKS to poke or pinch somebody on the buttocks **2** *US* SPUR TO ACTION to spur somebody on to action [Old English *gōs* < Indo-European] ◇ **kill the goose that lays the golden eggs** to destroy something that is or has been a regular, dependable source of profit or benefit

goose barnacle *n* a barnacle with a flattened shell, feathery appendages, and a fleshy stalk used to attach itself to surfaces, especially floating wood. Genus: *Lepas.*

gooseberry /gŏŏz bəri/ (*plural* **-ries**) *n* **1** ACID FRUIT an acid-tasting green or sometimes red fruit of a spiny plant, usually eaten cooked and sweetened (*often before nouns*) ○ *gooseberry pie* **2** SPINY FRUIT BUSH a spiny fruit bush that produces gooseberries. Native to: Europe, Asia. *Ribes uva-crispa.* **3** UNWANTED EXTRA PERSON an unwanted single person with a couple or a group otherwise made up of couples (*informal*) ○ *I don't want to play gooseberry.* [Mid-16C. < ?]

gooseberry stone *n* MINERALS = **grossularite**

goose bumps *npl* = **goose pimples**

gooseflesh /gŏŏss flesh/ *n* = **goose pimples**

goosefoot /gŏŏss fŏŏt/ *n* a weed with small greenish flowers and berries and leaves that resemble a goose's foot. Genus: *Chenopodium.*

goosegog /gŏŏz gog/ *n* a gooseberry (*informal*) [Early 19C. < variant of GOB[1].]

goosegrass /gŏŏss graass/ *n* an annual plant with slender sprawling stems, narrow leaves, tiny white flowers, and spiny round fruits that cling to animals and clothing. Native to: Europe, Asia. *Galium aparine.*

gooseneck /gŏŏss nek/ *n* something curved like a goose's neck or U-shaped, e.g. a pipe joint or a flexible neck on a lamp (*often before nouns*) ○ *a gooseneck lamp*

gooseneck barnacle *n* ZOOL = **goose barnacle**

goose pimples *npl* temporary pimples on the skin brought on by cold or fear, or by sudden excitement, and caused by contraction of connective tissues (**papillae**) at the base of hairs. US term **goose bumps** —**goose-pimply** *adj*

goose step *n* a military marching step performed with straight legs swung high in a forward movement —**goose-step** *vi*

goosy /gŏŏssi/ (**-ier, -iest**), **goosey** (**-ier, -iest**) *adj* **1** RESEMBLING A GOOSE similar to a goose **2** HAVING GOOSE PIMPLES affected by goose pimples or the nervousness or fear that can cause them (*informal*) **3** SILLY behaving in a silly or scatterbrained way

⚡**gopher** /gṓfər/ *n* **1** a small short-tailed rodent that has fur-lined cheek pouches and short legs and digs sizable burrows. Native to: North and Central America. Family: Geomyidae. **2** an Internet system that organizes files into menus containing links to text files, graphic images, databases, and additional menus (*often before nouns*) ○ *a gopher site* [Late 18C. < ?]

gopherwood /gṓfər wŏŏd/ *n* in the Bible, the wood from which Noah's ark was made, or the tree from which it came [Early 17C. < Hebrew *gōpher.*]

Gorakhpur /gáwrək poor/ city in north-central India. Population: 505,566 (1991).

goral /gáwrəl/ *n* a small short-horned antelope. Native to: Himalayas and adjacent Southeast Asia. Genus: *Nemorhaedus.* [Mid-19C. < a Himalayan language.]

gorb /gawrb/ *n Ireland* a glutton [Early 19C. < ?]

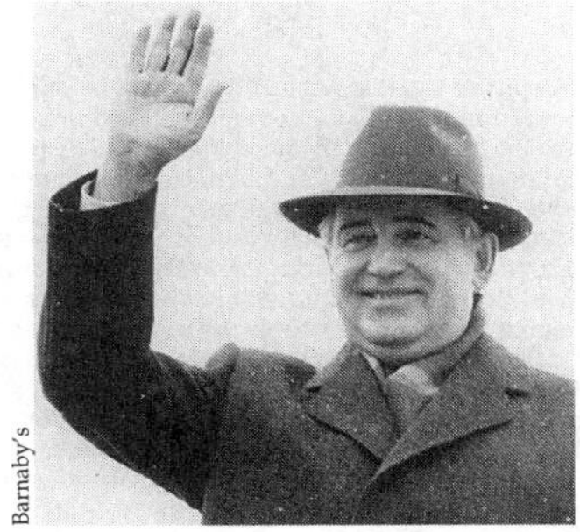

Mikhail Gorbachev

Gorbachev /gáwrbə chof/, **Mikhail** (*b.* 1931) Soviet statesman

Gorbals /gáwrb'lz/ district of Glasgow, Scotland

gorblimey *interj* = **cor blimey**

Gordian knot /gáwrdi ən-/ *n* a problem for which it is very difficult to find a solution [Late 16C. < the knot of *Gordius*, king of Gordium, which was to be loosed only by the future ruler of Asia: Alexander the Great sliced through it.]

Gordimer /gáwrdimər/, **Nadine** (*b.* 1923) South African novelist

Gordon /gáwrd'n/, **Adam Lindsay** (1833–70) Azores-born Australian poet

Gordon Bennett /gáwrd'n bénnit/ *interj* used to express surprise or annoyance (*informal*) [Late 20C. Alteration of GORBLIMEY, after James *Gordon* BENNETT.]

Gordon setter /gáwrd'n-/ *n* a gun dog with a long black-and-tan coat, belonging to a breed developed in Scotland [Mid-19C. After Alexander *Gordon*, 4th Duke of Gordon (1743–1827).]

gore[1] /gawr/ (**gores, goring, gored**) *vt* to pierce the flesh of a person or animal with horns or tusks [14C. < ?]

gore[2] /gawr/ *n* thick coagulating blood, especially blood shed as a result of violence [Old English *gor* 'dirt, dung' < Germanic]

gore[3] /gawr/ *n* a triangular piece of cloth used, e.g., in making a loose skirt [Old English *gāra* < ?] —**gored** *adj*

Gore /gawr/ town on the South Island, New Zealand. Population: 10,296 (1996).

Gore, Al (*b.* 1948) US statesman and vice president of the United States (1993–2001). Full name **Albert Arnold Gore, Jr.**

gorge /gawrj/ *n* **1** NARROW VALLEY a deep narrow, usually rocky, valley **2** CONTENTS OF STOMACH the contents of the stomach, especially when they are perceived as rising in the throat out of disgust or anger **3** ENTRANCE TO OUTWORK a narrow entrance at the rear of an outwork in a fortification **4** OBSTRUCTION IN PASSAGE a mass of something obstructing a passage, especially a mass of ice obstructing a river **5** HAWK'S CROP the crop of a hawk ■ *v* (**gorges, gorging, gorged**) **1** *vti* EAT GREEDILY to eat something greedily and to excess ○ *They gorged on chocolates.* ○ *They sat at the counter gorging meat and potatoes.* **2** *vt* = **engorge** *v.* 1 [14C. Via French, 'throat' < Latin *gurge* 'abyss, whirlpool'.] —**gorger** *n*

gorgeous /gáwrjəss/ *adj* **1** outstandingly beautiful or richly coloured ○ *dressed in gorgeous silks* **2** very pleasant (*informal*) ○ *a gorgeous spring morning* [15C. < Old French *gorgias* 'stylish, elegant'.] —**gorgeously** *adv* —**gorgeousness** *n*

gorget /gáwrjit/ *n* **1** ARMOUR FOR THROAT a crescent-shaped piece of armour for protecting the throat **2** PART OF NUN'S HEADDRESS the part of a nun's headdress that covers the neck and shoulders **3** NECKLACE a circular or crescent-shaped ornament worn round the neck **4** COLOURED BAND ON THROAT a band or patch of distinctive colour on the throat of a bird or other animal [15C. < Old French *gorgete* < *gorge* 'throat' (see GORGE).]

Gorgon /gáwrgən/ *n* **1** in Greek mythology, a monstrous woman with snakes for hair, who turned those who looked at her into stone **2** **gorgon, Gorgon** an offensive term for a woman regarded as very frightening or ugly (*insult*) [14C. < Latin *Gorgon-*, stem of *Gorgo* < Greek *Gorgō* < *gorgos* 'terrible'.] —**Gorgonian** /gawr gṓni ən/ *adj*

gorgonian /gawr gṓni ən/ *n* a coral with a flexible horny branched skeleton. Family: Gorgonacea. [Mid-19C. < modern Latin *Gorgonia* < Latin *Gorgon-* (see GORGON).] —**gorgonian** *adj*

Gorgonzola /gáwrgən zṓlə/, **gorgonzola** *n* a moist Italian blue cheese with a strong flavour [Late 19C. After a Milanese village.]

gorilla /gə rílla/ *n* **1** the largest ape, with a relatively short but very powerful body and coarse dark hair. Native to: central Africa. *Gorilla gorilla.* **2** a large or brutal person, especially a hired thug (*informal*) [Mid-19C. Via modern Latin < Greek *gorillas.*]

SPELLCHECK Do not confuse ***gorilla*** with ***guerrilla***, which has a similar sound. Beware: your spellchecker will not catch this error.

Göring = **Goering, Hermann**

Gorky /gáwrki/, **Gorki** former name for **Nizhniy Novgorod**

Gorky, Arshile (1904–48) Armenian-born US painter. Born **Vosdanig Manoog Adoian**

Gorky, Gorki, Maksim (1868–1936) Russian writer. Pseudonym of **Aleksei Maksimovich Peshkov**

Görlitz /gúrlits, gṓrlits/ city in east-central Germany, on the border with Poland. Population: 77,600 (1989).

gormandize /gáwrmən dīz/ (**-izes, -izing, -ized**), **gormandise** (**-ises, -ising, -ised**) *vti* to eat food gluttonously [Mid-16C. < GOURMANDISE 'gluttony'.] —**gormandizer** *n*

gormless /gáwrmləss/ adj lacking intelligence, common sense, or initiative (informal) [Mid-19C. Variant of gaumless < gaum 'understanding, heed' < Old Norse gaumr.]

~~gorrilla~~ incorrect spelling of **gorilla**

gorse /gawrss/ (plural **gorses** or **gorse**) n a spiny bush with yellow flowers and black pods. Genus: Ulex. [Old English gors < Indo-European, 'be prickly or rough']

Gorton /gáwrt'n/, **Sir John Grey** (b. 1911) Australian statesman

gory /gáwri/ (-rier, -riest) adj 1 BLOODY covered with blood or gore 2 ATTENDED BY BLOODSHED involving much bloodshed 3 HORRIBLE arousing horror or terror ○ the gory details —**gorily** adv —**goriness** n

Gosford /gósfərd/ coastal city in E New South Wales, Australia. Population: 162,447 (1991).

gosh /gosh/ interj used to express surprise, amazement, or pleasure (informal) [Mid-18C. Substitution for GOD.]

goshawk /góss hawk/ n a large hawk with broad rounded wings and a long tail. Native to: Europe, North America. Accipiter gentilis. [12C. < Old English goshafoc < forms of GOOSE + HAWK[1].]

gosling /gózling/ n a young goose [15C. < Old Norse gøslingr < gas 'goose'.]

go-slow n a protest by industrial workers in which they deliberately work slowly. US term **slowdown**

gospel /gósp'l/ n 1 a set of beliefs held strongly by a group or person 2 something believed to be absolutely and unquestionably true 3 MUSIC = **gospel music**

Gospel n 1 TEACHINGS OF JESUS CHRIST the teachings of Jesus Christ and the story of his life 2 BOOK OF BIBLE any of the biblical books Matthew, Mark, Luke, or John 3 BIBLE EXTRACT an extract from one of the Gospels read as part of a Christian religious service [Old English gōdspel 'good news' < forms of GOOD + SPELL[2]]

gospeller /góspələr/ n 1 a reader of the Gospel in a Christian religious service 2 a preacher of the Gospel (disapproving)

gospel music n highly emotional evangelical vocal music that originated among African American Christians in the S United States and was a strong influence in the development of soul music

gospel side n in a Christian church, the left side of the altar as faced by the congregation. ◊ **epistle side**

gospel truth n = **gospel** n. 2

Gosport /góss pawrt/ port in S England, on the English Channel. Population: 67,802 (1991).

goss /goss/ n gossip (slang) ○ all the latest goss [Shortening]

gossamer /góssəmər/ n 1 FINE COBWEBS a fine film of cobwebs, often seen floating in the air or covered with dew on the ground 2 DELICATE FABRIC a delicate, sheer fabric or gauze 3 SOMETHING SHEER AND DELICATE something delicate, sheer, and filmy [14C. Probably < GOOSE + SUMMER[1], period of mild autumn weather when goose was in season and such webs were often seen in the air.] —**gossamery** adj

gossan /góss'n, gózz'n/, **gozzan** /gózz'n/ n a yellow or red layer on the surface of minerals rich in iron oxide, produced by alteration and leaching of sulphide ores [Late 18C. Probably < Cornish, < gōs 'blood'.]

Gosse /goss/, **Sir Edmund William** (1849–1928) British writer

gossip /góssip/ n 1 CONVERSATION ABOUT PERSONAL MATTERS conversation about personal or intimate rumours or facts, especially when malicious 2 CASUAL CONVERSATION informal and chatty conversation or writing about recent and often personal events ○ They had a good gossip in the pub. 3 HABITUAL TALKER somebody given to spreading personal or intimate information about other people ■ vi SPREAD RUMOURS to tell people rumours or personal or intimate facts about other people, especially maliciously [Old English godsibb 'godparent, close friend' < GOD + SIB 'relative'] —**gossiper** n —**gossipry** n —**gossipy** adj

gossip column n a regular feature in a magazine or newspaper where rumours and personal or intimate facts about celebrities are exposed —**gossip columnist** n

gossipmonger /góssip mung gər/ n a spreader of gossip

gossoon /go sóon/ n Ireland a young boy (informal) [Late 17C. Via Irish < French garçon 'boy'.]

gossypol /góssi pol/ n a substance that inhibits sperm production. Source: cotton seeds. [Late 19C. < modern Latin Gossypium < Latin gossypion 'cotton tree'.]

got past participle, past tense of **get**[1]

Göta Canal /yőtə-/ waterway in SW Sweden, linking Gothenburg on the west coast with Stockholm on the east coast. Length: 558 km/347 mi.

gotcha /góchə/ interj used to indicate that somebody has been successfully tricked or caught out in some way or to indicate comprehension of something (informal) [Mid-20C. < a pronunciation of got you.]

Göteborg = **Gothenburg**

goth /goth/ n 1 SOMEBODY UNCIVILIZED an uncivilized or barbaric person 2 **goth, Goth** MUSICAL STYLE a style of popular music that combines elements of heavy metal with punk 3 **goth, Goth** FASHION OF DARK CLOTHES AND MAKEUP a style of fashion popular among men and women in the 1980s, characterized by black clothes, heavy silver jewellery, black eye makeup and lipstick, and often pale face makeup 4 **goth, Goth** SOMEBODY FOLLOWING GOTH MUSIC AND FASHION a fan of goth music and fashion

Goth /goth/ n a member of an ancient Germanic people who settled south of the Baltic and from the 3rd to the 5th centuries founded kingdoms in many parts of the Roman Empire [Old English gotan 'Goths'. < late Latin Gothi < Germanic.]

Gotham /góthəm/ n a nickname for New York City

Gothenburg /góth'n burg/ principal port in SW Sweden, on the River Göta estuary. Population: 449,189 (1995). Swedish **Göteborg**

gothic /góthik/ adj 1 UNCIVILIZED barbarous or uncivilized 2 LITERARY = **Gothic** adj. 4 ■ n 1 MUSIC = **goth** n. 2 2 FASHION = **goth** n. 3 3 SIMPLE TYPEFACE a simple sans serif typeface with strokes of uniform width 4 HEAVY ANGULAR TYPEFACE a heavy bold angular early typeface —**gothically** adv —**gothicness** n

Gothic: Interior of Cologne Cathedral, Germany (begun 1248)

Gothic /góthik/ adj 1 OF MEDIEVAL ARCHITECTURAL STYLE belonging to a style of architecture used in Western Europe from the 12th to the 15th centuries, and characterized by pointed arches, flying buttresses, and high curved ceilings 2 OF MEDIEVAL ARTISTIC STYLE belonging to a style of music, painting, or sculpture practised in parts of Europe from the 12th to the 15th centuries 3 OF MIDDLE AGES relating to the Middle Ages 4 **Gothic, gothic** OF EERIE FICTION STYLE belonging to a genre of fiction characterized by gloom and darkness, often with a grotesque or supernatural plot unfolding in an eerie or lonely location such as a ruined castle 5 OF THE GOTHS relating to the Goths, or their language or culture ■ n EXTINCT LANGUAGE OF ANCIENT GOTHS an extinct East Germanic language formerly spoken by the ancient Goths in parts of Scandinavia and around the Baltic Sea —**Gothically** adv —**Gothicize** vt —**Gothicizer** n —**Gothicness** n

QUICK FACTS ON... GOTHIC

Key dates: early 12th–early 16th centuries
Key locations: W Europe, especially France
Key elements: use of pointed arches, ribbed vaults, and flying buttresses to support high, curved ceilings; thin walls; wide façade with twin towers and massive doorway; incorporation of large stained-glass windows, detailed carvings, and monumental sculptures; rich decoration
Key figures: [early architects mostly unknown], Guy de Dammartin, Martin and Pierre Chambiges (architecture); Nicola and Giovanni Pisano, Claus Sluter (sculpture)
Key works: Church of St Denis, Paris (begun 1140?), Notre Dame cathedral, Paris (begun 1163), Chartres cathedral (begun 1194), Reims cathedral (begun 1210), Salisbury cathedral (begun 1220), Beauvais cathedral (begun 1225), Cologne cathedral (begun 1248)
Key developments: flamboyant styles in architecture; revival of statue as medium; increasing naturalism, expressionism, and illusionism in painting and sculpture; so-called International Gothic style of painting; improved building techniques enabling later architectural advances

Gothic arch n a pointed arch, as found in Gothic churches

gothicism /góthi sizəm/ n crudeness of style or manner, or an example of such crudeness

Gothicism n use of the Gothic style of architecture, art, or literature —**Gothicist** n

Gothic Revival n a style of architecture based on a reintroduction of the Gothic style, popular in the 18th and 19th centuries

Gotland /góttland/, **Gottland** island and county of Sweden, in the Baltic Sea. Population: 58,120 (1995). Area: 3,140 sq. km/1,212 sq. mi.

gotta /góttə/ vi got to (informal) [Representing a pronunciation]

gotten US past participle of **get**[1]

götterdämmerung /góttər dámməröóng/, **Götterdämmerung** n 1 in Germanic mythology, the destruction of the gods after battle with the forces of doom 2 the overthrow or violent ending of a regime or institution [Early 20C. < German, 'twilight of the gods'.]

Göttingen /góttingən/ university town in central Germany. Population: 127,900 (1994).

Gottland = **Gotland**

gouache /góo aàsh/ n 1 PAINTING TECHNIQUE a method of painting in which opaque watercolours are mixed with gum 2 PAINT USED IN GOUACHE the paint used in the gouache technique 3 A GOUACHE PAINTING a painting done with gouache [Late 19C. Via French < Italian guazzo 'puddle'.]

Gouda[1] /gówdə/ n a mild Dutch cheese, typically sold in a flattened sphere covered in wax [Mid-19C. After GOUDA[2].]

Gouda[2] /gówdə/ city in W Netherlands. Population: 69,916 (1994).

gouge /gowj/ vti (**gouges, gouging, gouged**) 1 CARVE OUT HOLE to cut or scoop a hole or groove in something, usually using a sharp tool 2 FORM ROUGHLY BY CUTTING to form something by roughly cutting it out of surrounding material 3 US OVERCHARGE to cheat somebody or act dishonestly by demanding an unreasonably high price for services or goods (informal) 4 INJURE SOMEBODY'S EYE to attack somebody's eye with the thumb ■ n 1 CHISEL WITH CONCAVE BLADE a chisel with a concave blade. Use: for cutting grooves and holes in wood. 2 SMALL HOLE a mark, groove, or hole, usually made with a pointed tool 3 US OVERCHARGING an instance of paying too much or being charged exorbitantly for goods or services (informal) [Late 15C. Via French < late Latin gubia, gulbia < Celtic.] —**gouger** n

goujon /góojan/ n a long strip of fish or chicken coated in egg and breadcrumbs and deep-fried [Mid-20C. < French (see GUDGEON[1]); from their shape.]

goulash /góol ash/ n 1 a stew of Hungarian origin, made with beef, veal, lamb, or pork and seasoned with paprika 2 a way of dealing cards that have already been arranged in a specific order, without shuffling them first [Mid-19C. < Hungarian gulyás, shortening of gulyás hús 'herdsman's meat'.]

Goulburn /góol burn/ city in E New South Wales, Australia. Population: 21,293 (1996).

Gould /goold/, **Shane** (b. 1956) Australian swimmer

gourami /góo raàmi/ (plural **-mi** or **-mis**) n a freshwater fish, many species of which are capable of breathing air and are often kept in aquariums. Native to: Southeast Asia. Family: Anabantidae. [Late 19C. Via Malay gurami 'freshwater carp' < Javanese grameh.]

Gourd

gourd /goord/ n 1 a hard-skinned fleshy fruit produced by several different plants related to cucumbers and marrows, eaten when ripe. Use: dried decorations, bowls, cups. 2 a plant that produces gourds [14C. Via Anglo-Norman *gurde* < Latin *cucurbita*.]

gourde /goord/ n see table at **currency** [Mid-19C. Via Haitian Creole < French *gourd* 'dull, heavy' < Latin *gurdus* 'unintelligent person'.]

gourmand /goormand/ n a lover of food who often eats excessively or greedily [15C. < French, 'glutton'.]

gourmandise /goorman deez/ n an appreciation of good food and drink [15C. < French, < *gourmand* 'glutton'.]

gourmet /goor may/ n a knowledgeable enjoyer of good food and drink ■ adj relating to high-quality food that is sophisticated, expensive, rare, or meticulously prepared [Early 19C. < French, alteration (influenced by *gourmand* 'glutton') of Middle French *groumet* 'servant, vintner's assistant' < English *groom*.]

gout /gowt/ n 1 a metabolic disorder mainly affecting men in which excess uric acid is produced and deposited in the joints, causing painful swelling, especially in the toes and feet 2 a large blob or clot of something, usually of blood [13C. Via Old French < Latin *gutta* 'drop of liquid'; from the belief that gout was caused by drops of a morbid fluid in the blood.]

goutweed /gowt weed/ n PLANTS = **ground elder** [< its use in treating gout]

gouty /gowti/ (**-ier, -iest**) adj 1 resulting from or causing gout 2 affected by or tending to contract gout —**goutiness** n

⚡ **gov** abbr government organization (in Internet addresses)

gov. /guv/ abbr 1 government 2 governor

~~govenor~~ incorrect spelling of **governor**

~~goverment~~ incorrect spelling of **government**

govern /gúvv'n/ v 1 vti HAVE POLITICAL AUTHORITY to be responsible officially for directing the affairs, policies, and economy of a state, country, or organization 2 vt CONTROL to control, regulate, or direct something 3 vt RESTRAIN to control something by restraint 4 vt HAVE INFLUENCE OVER to have or exercise an influence over something 5 vt CONTROL SPEED OF to maintain the speed of an engine or keep it from going above a specific level by controlling the fuel or steam supply 6 vt BE LAW FOR to be the defining rule for something 7 vt DETERMINE FORM OF WORD to dictate the inflection, mood, or case of another word [13C. Via Old French *governer* and Latin *gubernare* < Greek *kubernan* 'steer'.] —**governable** adj

governance /gúvv'nanss/ n 1 MANNER OF GOVERNMENT the system or manner of government 2 STATE OF GOVERNING A PLACE the act or state of governing a place 3 AUTHORITY control or authority (formal)

governess /gúvv'rnass/ n especially formerly, a woman employed to teach children in their own homes, and sometimes also to care for the children [15C. < Old French *governeresse*, form of *governeour* 'governor'.]

governessy /gúvv'rnassi/ adj like a strict or prim governess

governing body n a group of people appointed to supervise and regulate a field of activity or institution

government /gúvv'rnmant/ n 1 POLITICAL AUTHORITY a group of people who have the power to make and enforce laws for a country or area 2 STYLE OF GOVERNMENT a type of political system 3 THE STATE VIEWED AS RULER the state and its administration viewed as the ruling political

power 4 BRANCH OF GOVERNMENT a branch or agency of a government, taken as the whole (informal) 5 CONTROL the management or control of something 6 DETERMINATION OF INFLECTION the determination of the inflection, mood, or case of a word by another word 7 POLITICAL SCIENCE political science as a subject of study —**government** adj —**governmental** /gúvv'n mént'l/ adj —**governmentally** adv

USAGE Singular or plural? Like many collective nouns, **government** can be used with a singular or plural construction, depending on whether the emphasis is on the government as a body making joint decisions or on the individuals that constitute it.

governmentalize /gúvv'n mént'l īz/ (**-izes, -izing, -ized**), **governmentalise** (**-ises, -ising, -ised**) vt to put a sphere of activity under the power of the government

Government House n in Australia, the official residence of the Governor-General

governor /gúvv'nar/ n 1 GOVERNING BODY MEMBER a member of a governing body of an institution 2 GOVERNING OFFICIAL an appointed or elected official who governs a state, colony, or province for a specified term 3 PRINCIPAL PRISON OFFICER the principal officer in charge of a prison. US term **warden** n. 3 4 AUTHORITY FIGURE an authority figure such as an employer or boss (informal) 5 REGULATING DEVICE a device for regulating the speed of an engine 6 REPRESENTATIVE OF BRITISH CROWN IN AUSTRALIA the representative of the British crown in Australia at the level of state government —**governorship** n

governor general (plural **governors general** or **governor generals**) n 1 the representative of the British Crown in some countries of the Commonwealth of Nations 2 a governor who has authority over deputy governors —**governor-generalship** n

Governors Island island of SE New York State, in New York Bay south of Manhattan Island. Area: 70 hectares/175 acres.

govt abbr government

gowan /gów an/ n Scotland any yellow or white field flower, especially a daisy [Late 16C. Probably alteration of *golland* 'buttercup' < N Germanic.]

Gower Peninsula /gówar-/ rocky peninsula of S Wales. Length: 24 km/15 mi.

gowk /gowk/ n an offensive term for somebody considered unintelligent or awkward (insult regional) [14C. < Old Norse *gaukr* 'cuckoo'.]

gown /gown/ n 1 ELEGANT DRESS a woman's full-length elegant or formal dress for special occasions 2 LONG ROBE a long robe, often dark in colour, worn on official occasions by people such as judges, professors, university graduates, and barristers 3 LOOSE OUTER GARMENT a loose cloak or robe, e.g. the type worn by surgeons, that is worn to protect clothes 4 MEMBERS OF A UNIVERSITY the members of a university regarded as distinct from the rest of a town's population ■ vt DRESS IN GOWN to dress somebody in a loose robe [14C. Via Old French *goune* < late Latin *gunna* 'fur or leather garment'.]

gownsman /gównzman/ (plural **-men** /-man/) n a man, e.g. an academic, who wears a gown for professional reasons

goy /goy/ (plural **goyim** /góy im/ or **goys**) n 1 an offensive term for somebody who is not Jewish 2 a Jewish name for an unintelligent man or boy (insult) [Mid-19C. Via Yiddish < Hebrew *gōy* '(non-Jewish) nation or people'.] —**goyish** adj

Goya /góy a/, **Francisco de** (1746–1828) Spanish painter

goyim plural of **goy** (offensive)

gozzan n = **gossan**

⚡ **gp** abbr Guadeloupe (in Internet addresses)

GP[1] n a doctor who deals with patients' general medical problems, either at a surgery or, sometimes, at patients' homes. Full form **general practitioner**

GP[2] abbr 1 general pause 2 general practice 3 Grand Prix

GPI n a condition that occurs in the late stages of syphilis and is characterized by dementia, speech difficulty, and inability to move. Full form **general paralysis of the insane**

GPMU abbr Graphical, Paper, and Media Union

GPO abbr General Post Office

⚡ **GPRS** n a system that provides immediate and continuous access to the Internet from wireless devices

such as mobile phones. Full form **general packet radio service**

gps abbr gallons per second

GPS n a worldwide navigation system that uses information received from orbiting satellites. Full form **Global Positioning System**

GPU n the Soviet secret police, from 1922 to 1923 [< Russian *Gosudarstvennoe politicheskoe upravlenie* 'State Political Directorate']

⚡ **gq** abbr Equatorial Guinea (in Internet addresses)

⚡ **gr** abbr Greece (in Internet addresses)

gr. abbr 1 grade 2 grain 3 gram 4 gross

Gr. abbr 1 Greece 2 Greek

Graafian follicle /gra'afi an-/ n a small fluid-filled sac (**vesicle**) containing a maturing ovum [Mid-19C. After Regnier de *Graaf* (1641–73), Dutch anatomist.]

grab /grab/ v (**grabs, grabbing, grabbed**) 1 vt GRASP to grasp something quickly, suddenly, or forcefully ○ *Grab a pen and sit down.* 2 vti TRY TO GRASP to try to grasp something that is hard to reach or in short supply ○ *Stop grabbing or I won't give you any.* 3 vt SEIZE to take something violently or dishonestly ○ *grab the money and run* 4 vt HAVE EMOTIONAL IMPACT ON to appeal to, attract, impress, or affect somebody emotionally (informal) ○ *The film didn't really grab me.* 5 vt HURRIEDLY GET to obtain something quickly and without difficulty (informal) ○ *I'll just grab a bite to eat.* 6 vi US TAKE HOLD SUDDENLY to take hold suddenly or intermittently ○ *The brakes grabbed and the car went into a skid.* ■ n 1 GRABBING the act of grabbing something ○ *He made a grab at my arm.* 2 SOMETHING GRABBED something that is grabbed 3 DEVICE FOR GRABBING an apparatus or device used for grasping hold of something 4 GRABBING ABILITY the ability or capacity to hold something fast [Late 16C. Probably < Middle Dutch or Middle Low German *grabben*.] —**grabbable** adj —**grabber** n ◇ **up for grabs** available for the first comer to take or use (informal)

grab bag n 1 something composed of miscellaneous or mismatched components (informal) 2 US a box full of sealed bags containing unknown objects that can be purchased for a fixed price or are the prize of a party game

grab bar n a bar attached to a wall to provide a grip, e.g. near a bath or next to a toilet, for people who have difficulty in standing up

grabbing /grábbing/ adj with a character or way of behaving that attempts to obtain a large amount of something, especially money or something abstract like people's attention (usually in combination)

grabble /grább'l/ (**-bles, -bling, -bled**) vi 1 to scratch or search about with the hands 2 to tumble or fall to the ground on all fours [Late 16C. Probably < Dutch *grabbelen* < *grabben* 'grab'.] —**grabbler** n

grabby /grábbi/ (**-bier, -biest**) adj pushy and grasping (informal insult) —**grabbiness** n

graben /gra'aban/ n a broad valley, especially a rift valley [Late 19C. < German *Graben* 'ditch'.]

Grable /grayb'l/, **Betty** (1916–73) US actor, dancer, and singer. Full name **Elizabeth Ruth Grable**

grab rail n = **grab bar**

grace /grayss/ n 1 ELEGANCE elegance, beauty, and smoothness of form or movement 2 POLITENESS dignified, polite, and decent behaviour ○ *She fended off queries with her usual grace.* 3 GENEROSITY OF SPIRIT a capacity to tolerate, accommodate, or forgive people 4 PRAYER AT MEALTIMES a short prayer of thanks to God said before, or sometimes after, a meal 5 FIN = **grace period** 6 PLEASING QUALITY a pleasing and admirable quality or characteristic (usually plural) 7 GIFT OF GOD TO HUMANKIND in Christianity, the infinite love, mercy, favour, and goodwill shown to humankind by God 8 FREEDOM FROM SIN in Christianity, the condition of being free of sin, e.g. through repentance to God 9 MUSIC = **grace note** ■ vt (**graces, gracing, graced**) 1 CONTRIBUTE PLEASINGLY TO to make a pleasing contribution to an event, often by attending it (often ironic) ○ *So good of you to grace us with your presence.* 2 ADD ELEGANCE TO to add elegance, beauty, or charm to something 3 ORNAMENT to add ornamental or decorative notes to a piece of music [12C. Via Old French < Latin *gratia* < *gratus* 'pleasing'.] ◇ **fall from grace** to lose a favoured or privileged position ◇ **with (a) bad grace** in a rude and bad-tempered way ◇ **with (a) good grace** in a polite and willing way

Grace *n* used as a title when addressing a duke, duchess, or archbishop

Grace /grayss/, **Patricia** (*b.* 1937) New Zealand writer

Grace, W. G. (1848–1915) British cricketer. Full name **William Gilbert Grace**

grace-and-favour *n UK* a property, e.g. a flat, owned by the British monarch who allows somebody to live in it rent-free as a mark of special favour or gratitude

grace cup *n* a cup of wine or liquor passed round at the end of a meal for a final toast

graceful /gráyssf'l/ *adj* **1** showing elegance, beauty, and smoothness of form or movement **2** marked by poise, dignity, and politeness —**gracefully** *adv* —**gracefulness** *n*

graceless /gráyssləss/ *adj* **1** lacking elegance in form or movement **2** bad-mannered and undignified —**gracelessly** *adv* —**gracelessness** *n*

grace note *n* a note added to a piece of music as an embellishment, usually played quickly before a principal note and written smaller than a normal note on the page

grace period *n* the extra time allowed before having to pay a debt or complete a transaction

Graces *n* in Greek mythology, three sister goddesses, Aglaia, Euphrosyne, and Thalia, who have the power to grant charm, happiness, and beauty

gracile /gráss īl/ *adj* gracefully slender and slight (*literary*) [Early 17C. < Latin *gracilis*.] —**gracileness** *n* —**gracility** /gra síllәti/ *n*

gracious /gráyshəss/ *adj* **1 KIND AND POLITE** full of tact, kindness, and politeness ○ *a gracious refusal* **2 CONDESCENDINGLY POLITE** condescendingly indulgent and generous to perceived inferiors **3 ELEGANT** luxurious and elegant ○ *gracious living* **4 HAVING DIVINE GRACE** displaying divine grace, mercy, or compassion ■ *interj* **EXPRESSES SURPRISE** expresses surprise, dismay, or indignation [13C. Via Old French < Latin *gratiosus* 'agreeable' < *gratia* (see GRACE).] —**graciously** *adv* —**graciousness** *n*

grackle /grák'l/ *n* **1** a noisy blackbird with metallic black plumage and a long keel-shaped tail. Native to: North America. Genus: *Quiscalus.* **2** a starling with mostly black plumage. Native to: Europe, Asia. Genus: *Gracula.* [Late 18C. Via modern Latin *Gracula* < Latin *graculus* 'jackdaw'.]

grad /grad/ *n* a graduate (*informal*) [Shortening]

grad. *abbr* **1** gradient **2** graduated

gradable /gráydəb'l/ *adj* **1** capable of being graded **2** describes an adjective or adverb capable of having a comparative and superlative form —**gradability** /gráydə bílləti/ *n*

gradate /grə dáyt/ (**-dates, -dating, -dated**) *v* **1** *vti* to pass imperceptibly from one shade or degree of intensity to another, or cause something to do this **2** *vt* to arrange something in steps, grades, or ranks [Mid-18C. Back-formation < GRADATION.]

gradation /grə dáysh'n/ *n* **1 SERIES OF DEGREES** a series of gradual and progressive degrees, steps, or stages **2 SINGLE DEGREE** a degree, step, or stage in a gradual progression **3 DISCRETE ARRANGEMENT** the arrangement of something according to size, rank, or quality **4 COLOUR CHANGE** the gradual and progressive change from one colour or tone to another **5 VOWEL CHANGE** a change in the length or quality of a vowel within a word, signifying a change in function such as tense or number **6 LEVELLING OF LAND** the process of levelling land by erosion or deposition of sediment [Late 16C. Directly or via French < Latin *gradation-* 'making steps' < *gradus* 'step, stage'.] —**gradational** *adj* —**gradationally** *adv*

grade /grayd/ *n* **1 LEVEL IN A SCALE OF PROGRESSION** a level, step, or stage in a scale of progression, quality, or size (*often in combination*) ○ *low-grade ore* **2 MARK SHOWING A LEVEL** a mark to indicate a level, step, or stage in a process **3 MARK FOR QUALITY OF WORK** a mark or rating given for work in school or college, usually using the descending scale of A, B, C, D, E, and F ○ *She got a good grade for her essay.* **4 YEAR IN SCHOOL** a class or year in the US and Canadian school systems ○ *She'll be in the tenth grade this year.* **5 RANK** a rank or class **6 PEOPLE IN RANK** a group of people of the same rank **7 FOOD CLASSIFICATION** a category indicating the relative quality of food as determined by the US Department of Agriculture ○ *grade A eggs* **8** *US* **GRADIENT** a gradient or slope, especially on a road or railroad **9 UNIT OF ANGLE** a unit of angle equal to 0.9° **10 VOWEL FORM** a form of vowel morpheme when a vowel varies owing to gradation ■ *vt* (**grades, grading, graded**) **1 ARRANGE BY DEGREES** to arrange or classify things or people according to rank, quality, or level **2** *US* **ASSIGN A GRADE** to assign a mark or rating to something, e.g. a student's work **3 MAKE A ROAD LEVEL** to level a road or railway by adjusting its gradients [Early 16C. Via French < Latin *gradus* 'step, stage'.] ◇ **make the grade** to meet the required standard

grade crossing *n US* TRANSP = **level crossing**

graded sediment /gráydid-/ *n* a sediment deposited on land or the seabed in which there is an upward gradation of the grains from coarse to fine

gradely /gráydli/ *adj* decent, fine, and respectable (*regional*) ■ *adv* promptly and properly (*regional*) [13C. < Old Norse *greiðligr* < *greiðr* 'ready, prompt'.]

grade point average *n US, Can, Aus* the average of a student's marks over a fixed period, calculated by assigning a value of 4 to A, 3 to B, 2 to C, 1 to D, and 0 to F

grader /gráydər/ *n* **1 SOMEBODY WHO OR SOMETHING THAT GRADES** a person who or machine that grades something **2** *US* **STUDENT** a student in a particular grade in school ○ *first graders* **3 EARTH LEVELLER** a machine with a wide blade that levels earth, used in road construction

grade school *n US* an elementary or primary school

gradient /gráydi ənt/ *n* **1 STEEPNESS** the rate at which the steepness of a slope increases **2 SLOPE** an upward or downward slope, e.g. in a road or railway **3 MEASURE OF CHANGE** a measure of change in a physical quantity such as temperature or pressure over a specified distance **4 RATE OF GROWTH** any of a series of changes in the rate of growth or metabolism of an organism, cell, or organ **5 SLOPE ON A CURVE** the slope of a line or a tangent at any point on a curve ■ *adj* **SLOPING** sloping evenly and uniformly [Mid-17C. Partly < Latin *gradient-*, present participle of *gradi* 'walk' (< *gradus* 'step'), partly < GRADE after QUOTIENT.]

gradient post *n* a small post with arms to represent gradients that is used beside a railway line to indicate where the gradient changes

gradin /gráydin/, **gradine** *n* **1** a raised step above or behind an altar **2** one of a set of steps arranged on a slope [Mid-19C. Via French < Italian *gradino* 'small step' < *grado* 'step' < Latin *gradus*.]

gradual /grájjoo əl/ *adj* **1 HAPPENING SLOWLY** proceeding or developing slowly by steps or degrees ○ *a gradual improvement* **2 CHANGING SLOWLY** changing slowly ○ *a gradual incline* ■ *n* **1 SUNG VERSES** in some Christian services, a set of scriptural verses sung after the epistle at Communion **2 RELIGIOUS MUSIC BOOK** a book of music for the sung parts of the Communion service [15C. < medieval Latin *gradualis* < Latin *gradus* 'step, stage'.] —**gradually** *adv* —**gradualness** *n*

gradualism /grájjoo əlizəm/ *n* the principle, theory, or policy of allowing change, especially political change, to take place gradually rather than suddenly or drastically —**gradualist** *n, adj* —**gradualistic** /grájjoo ə lístik/ *adj*

graduand /grájjoo and/ *n* a student who is about to graduate from university [Late 19C. < medieval Latin *graduandus* 'somebody on whom a degree is being conferred' < *graduare* (see GRADUATE).]

graduate *n* /grájjoo ət/ **1 HOLDER OF A DEGREE** somebody who has obtained a first degree from a university or college **2** *US* **SOMEBODY WHO HAS COMPLETED A COURSE OF STUDIES** an obtainer of a diploma or degree, e.g. from a high school **3** *US* **CONTAINER WITH MARKINGS** a container such as a flask or tube with graduated markings that is used for measuring liquids ■ *v* /grájjoo ayt/ (**-ates, -ating, -ated**) **1** *vi* **RECEIVE DEGREE** to receive a degree from a university or college **2** *vi* **MOVE UP** to move upwards from one level or activity to another ○ *I've graduated from skiing to snowboarding.* **3** *vt* **MARK WITH DEGREES OR LEVELS** to mark something with units of measurement **4** *vt* **SORT BY DIFFERENCES** to sort something into groups according to quality, size, or type ■ *adj* /grájjoo ət/ EDUC = **postgraduate** *adj.* [15C. < medieval Latin *graduat-*, past participle of *graduare* 'confer a degree on' < Latin *gradus* 'step, stage'.] —**graduator** *n*

graduated /grájjoo aytid/ *adj* **1 IN STAGES** divided into regular steps or stages **2 MARKED WITH LINES** marked with lines to enable measurement **3 BASED ON INCOME** describes a system of taxation under which those with the greatest income or assets pay the highest percentage of tax

graduate school *n US* a university or university department for students who have obtained a first degree

graduation /grájjoo áysh'n/ *n* **1 COMPLETION OF STUDIES** the completion of a degree ○ *the number of credits required for graduation* **2 DEGREE CEREMONY** a ceremony in which degrees are awarded to students who have successfully completed their studies ○ *attended her grandson's graduation* **3 MARK ON AN INSTRUMENT** a unit of measurement or division marked on an instrument **4 DIVIDING PROCESS** the process of marking or dividing something according to quantity or quality

gradus /gráydəss/ *n* **1** a book of musical exercises arranged in order of difficulty **2** a dictionary designed to aid in writing Greek or Latin verse [Mid-18C. Shortening of *Gradus ad Parnassum* 'Steps to Parnassus', manual of Latin composition.]

Graecise *vt* = **Graecize**

Graecism /grée̍s izəm/, **Grecism** *n* **1** an idiom of the Greek language used in another language, often for stylistic effect **2** Greek style, spirit, or characteristics as related to Greek culture, arts, architecture, and philosophy [Late 16C. < medieval Latin *Græcismus* < Latin *Græcus* (see GREEK).]

Graecize /grée̍s īz/ (**-cizes, -cizing, -cized**), **Graecise** (**-cises, -cising, -cised**), **Grecize** (**-cizes, -cizing, -cized**), **Grecise** (**-cises, -cising, -cised**) *vt* to make something Greek or Hellenic in style or form so that it becomes characteristic of the culture, civilization, or language of the ancient Greeks

Graeco-, **Greco-** *prefix* Greece, Greek ○ *Graeco-Roman* [< Latin *Graecus* (see GREEK)]

Graeco-Roman, **Greco-Roman** *adj* **1** relating to, or typical of, both ancient Greece and ancient Rome or the influence of their civilizations **2** describes a style of wrestling allowing no hold below the waist and no use of the legs to obtain a fall

Graf /graaf/, **Steffi** (*b.* 1969) German tennis player

graffiti /grə fe̍eti/ *n* drawings or writing that is scratched, painted, or sprayed on walls or other surfaces in public places (+ *singular or plural verb*) [Mid-19C. < Italian, plural of *graffito* (see GRAFFITO).] —**graffitist** *n*

USAGE graffito or **graffiti**? ***Graffito*** is an Italian borrowing into English, and its plural in Italian is ***graffiti***. It is acceptable, however, to use ***graffiti*** as a singular when the meaning is 'inscriptions in general': *Graffiti has marred the walls on this block for far too long*, though *Graffiti have marred the walls...* is the more technically appropriate. ***Graffiti*** is also regularly used as a singular to mean 'an inscription': *It's just another gang-related graffiti*, though ***graffito*** is the more technically correct term.

---

graffito /grə fe̍et ō/ (*plural* **-ti** /-ti/) *n* **1** an instance of graffiti scratched, painted, or sprayed on a surface (*formal*) **2** an ancient drawing or inscription on a wall or rock surface [Mid-19C. < Italian, 'scribbling' < *graffio* 'scratching', via Latin *graphium* 'stylus' < Greek *grapheion* < *graphein* 'write'.]

~~**grafitti**~~ incorrect spelling of **graffiti**

graft[1] /graaft/ *n* **1 TRANSPLANTED TISSUE** a piece of living tissue or an organ that is transplanted to a part of a patient's body, either from a donor or another part of the patient's body **2 PLANT TISSUE JOINED TO ANOTHER PLANT** a piece of living tissue from the shoot of a plant that is joined to the stem and root system of another plant, resulting in the growth of a single plant **3 GRAFT LOCATION** the place where tissue is implanted by means of a graft **4 GRAFTED PLANT** a plant that is the product of a graft **5 JOINING PROCESS** the process of joining one thing to another ■ *vt* **1 TRANSPLANT TISSUE** to transplant a piece of living tissue or an organ to a part of a patient's body **2 UNITE PLANT TISSUE** to join a piece of tissue from a part of one plant to the stem and root system of another plant to produce desirable characteristics such as vigour or resistance to disease in the new plant **3 JOIN DISSIMILAR THINGS** to join two things that do not share a natural relationship or affinity for each other [15C. Via Old French *grafe* 'pencil' (from a similarity with the shoot of a plant) < late Latin *graphium* (see GRAFFITO).] —**grafter** *n*

graft[2] /graaft/ *n* **1 HARD WORK** hard work (*informal*) **2 CHEATING BY A CORRUPT INDIVIDUAL** the use of dishonest or illegal means to gain money or property by somebody in a position of power or in elected office **3 MONEY OBTAINED CORRUPTLY** something obtained illegally by taking advantage of high position or office ■ *v* (*informal*) **1** *vi* **WORK**

HARD to work hard **2** *vti* **GET BY DECEIT** to obtain money or property by deceit [Mid-19C. < ?] —**grafter** *n*

Grafton /gráaftən/ city in NE New South Wales, Australia. Population: 16,562 (1996).

Graham /gráy əm/, **Billy** (*b.* 1918) US evangelist. Full name **William Franklin Graham**

Graham, Katharine (*b.* 1917) US newspaper executive

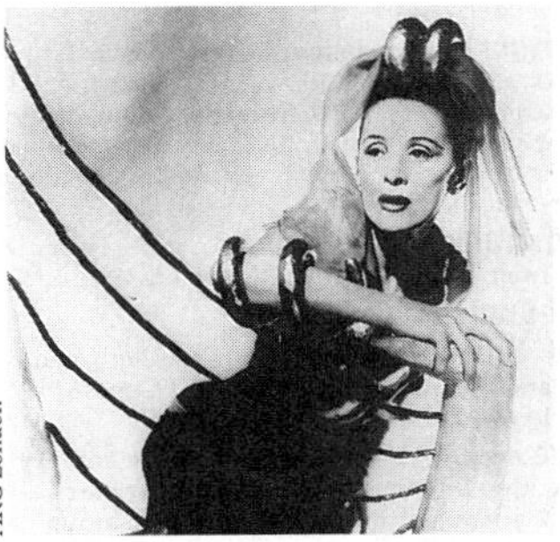

AKG London

Martha Graham: Performing in *Judith* (1957)

Graham, Martha (1893–1991) US dancer, choreographer, and teacher

graham cracker /gráy əm-/ *n US* a flat dry sweetened biscuit, light brown in colour and made from graham flour

Grahame /gráy əm/, **Kenneth** (1859–1932) British writer

graham flour *n US* unbolted whole-wheat flour [After Dr Sylvester *Graham* (1794–1851), American dietary reformer]

Graham Land /gráy əm-/ section of the N Antarctic Peninsula, part of the British Antarctic Territory

Graham's law /gráy əmz-/ *n* a law in chemistry relating the diffusion rate of a gas to the inverse square root of its density [After Thomas *Graham* (1805–69), Scottish chemist]

Grahamstown /gráy əmz town/ city in S South Africa. Population: 19,783 (1991).

grail /grayl/ *n* something that is eagerly sought after

Grail *n* according to medieval legend, the cup said to be used by Jesus Christ at the Last Supper, and by Joseph of Arimathea to collect his blood and sweat at the Crucifixion [14C. Via Old French *grael* < medieval Latin *gradalis* 'dish'.]

grain /grayn/ *n* **1 CEREALS** cereal crops **2 SMALL SEED** a small hard seed or fruit **3 TINY SINGLE PIECE** a tiny individual piece of something, e.g. sand or salt **4 SMALL AMOUNT** a tiny amount of something ○ *He doesn't have one grain of common sense!* **5 PATTERN IN MATERIAL** the arrangement, direction, or pattern of the fibres in wood, leather, stone, or paper ○ *When painting, follow the grain of the wood.* **6 UNIT OF WEIGHT** the smallest unit of weight in the avoirdupois (1/7000 pound) and apothecaries' systems (1/5760 pound), equal to approximately 0.065 grams **7 DIRECTION OF THREADS** the line of the threads in a fabric **8 SIDE OF LEATHER** the side of leather from which hair has been removed **9 SMALL CRYSTAL** a small crystal, especially one forming part of a crystalline solid **10 BASIC QUALITY** the basic quality or characteristic of something or somebody **11 PHOTOGRAPHIC PARTICLE** any of the small particles in a photographic emulsion that form an image, limiting the extent of possible enlargement **12 INTERFERENCE AFFECTING TELEVISION IMAGE** the granular effect on a television image caused by unwanted electrical signals **13 PROPELLANT FOR ROCKET** a mass of solid propellant for a rocket or missile **14 DYE** red or purple dye made from cochineal insects (*archaic*) ■ *v* **1** *vti* **GRANULATE** to break down into small particles or grains, or make something break down into small particles **2** *vt* **MIMIC PATTERN OF WOOD** to paint or stain a material with a pattern similar to wood or leather **3** *vt* **TREAT LEATHER** to soften or raise the pattern of leather **4** *vt* **REMOVE HAIR** to remove the hair from leather **5** *vt* **GIVE A GRAINY APPEARANCE** to give something a rough or granular appearance **6** *vt* **FEED GRAIN** to feed grain to an animal [13C. Via Old French < Latin *granum* 'seed'.] —**grained** *adj* —**grainer** *n* —**grainless** *adj* ◇ **go against the grain** to be contrary to somebody's natural inclinations, wishes, or feelings

grain alcohol *n* alcohol made from a fermented cereal

grainfield /gráyn feeld/ *n* a field in which grain is grown

Grainger /gráynjər/, **Percy** (1882–1961) Australian-born US pianist and composer

grains of paradise *npl* the peppery brown seeds of a W African plant. Use: to add piquancy to mulled wine and other drinks, formerly, in veterinary medicine.

grain weevil *n* a small beetle that feeds on and damages cereal grains. *Calendra granaria*.

grain whisky *n* whisky that is made from any fermented cereal other than malted barley

grainy /gráyni/ (**-ier, -iest**) *adj* **1 NOT CLEAR** describes a photograph that is unclear and poorly defined because of a large grain size or overenlargement **2 RESEMBLING GRAINS** resembling or composed of grains **3 NOT SMOOTH** having a granular rather than a smooth texture **4 LIKE WOOD GRAIN** resembling the grain of wood, leather, stone, or paper —**graininess** *n*

grallatorial /gráll ə táwri əl/ *adj* describes a bird with long legs adapted for wading [Mid-19C. < modern Latin *grallatorius* < Latin *grallator* 'stilt-walker' < *grallae* 'stilts'.]

gram[1] /gram/, **gramme** *n* (*symbol* g) a metric unit of mass, equal to 0.001 kg or equivalent to approximately 0.035 oz [Late 18C. Via French *gramme* and late Latin *gramma* < Greek *gramma* 'small weight'.]

gram[2] /gram/ *n* an edible bean, e.g. the chickpea, lentil, or mung bean, used as food [Early 18C. Via obsolete Portuguese < Latin *granum* 'seed'.]

gram. *abbr* **1** grammar **2** grammatical

-gram *suffix* **1** something written, drawn, or recorded ○ *trigram* ○ *oscillogram* **2** a message delivered by a third party ○ *telegram* ○ *kissagram* [< Greek *gramma* 'something written']

grama /gráamə/, **gramma** /grámmə/, **grama grass, gramma grass** *n* a pasture grass that grows in W North America and South America. Genus: *Bouteloua*. [Mid-19C. Via American Spanish < Latin *gramen* 'grass'.]

gram atom *n* a quantity of a chemical element whose mass in grams is the same as its atomic weight

gram calorie *n* MEASURE = **calorie** *n.* 1

gram equivalent *n* the quantity of a substance whose mass in grams is the same as its chemical equivalent weight

gramicidin /grámmi sídin/, **gramicidin D** *n* a toxic antibiotic applied externally in creams and drops [Mid-20C. < GRAM-POSITIVE + -CIDE.]

gramineous /grə mínni əss/, **graminaceous** /grámmi náyshəss/ *adj* **1** belonging to the grass family **2** resembling grass (*technical*) [Mid-17C. < Latin *gramineus* < *gramin-*, stem of *gramen* 'grass'.] —**gramineousness** *n*

graminivorous /grámmi nívvərəss/ *adj* that feeds on grass (*technical*) [Mid-18C. < Latin *gramin-* (see GRAMINEOUS).]

grammar /grámmər/ *n* **1 RULES FOR LANGUAGE** the system of rules by which words are formed and put together to make sentences **2 PARTICULAR SET OF LANGUAGE RULES** the rules for speaking or writing a particular language, or a specific analysis of the rules of language ○ *Spanish grammar* ○ *case grammar* **3 QUALITY OF LANGUAGE** the spoken or written form of language somebody uses, as related to accepted standards of correctness **4 GRAMMAR BOOK** a book dealing with the grammar of a language **5 ANALYTICAL SYSTEM** a systematic treatment of the elementary principles of a subject and their interrelationships [14C. Via Old French *gramaire* and Latin *grammatica* < Greek *grammatikos* 'relating to letters' < *grammat-*, stem of *gramma* 'written character, letter'.]

grammarian /grə máiri ən/ *n* **1** a person who is skilled in grammar **2** a writer on grammar, especially one who espouses prescriptive rules

grammar school *n* **1** in Britain and some Commonwealth countries, a state secondary school teaching children who are traditionally selected for high academic ability **2** *US* an elementary school

grammatical /grə máttik'l/ *adj* **1** in or relating to the rules of grammar **2** conforming to the accepted rules of grammar [Early 16C. < late Latin *grammaticalis* < Greek *grammatikos* (see GRAMMAR).] —**grammaticality** /grə mátti kálləti/ *n* —**grammatically** *adv* —**grammaticalness** *n*

gramme *n* MEASURE = **gram**[1]

~~**grammer**~~ incorrect spelling of **grammar**

gram molecule *n* a quantity of a molecular chemical compound whose mass in grams is the same as its molecular weight —**gram-molecular** *adj*

Grammy /grámmi/ *tdmk* a trademark for an award given annually for achievement in the recorded music industry

Gram-negative, gram-negative *adj* describes bacteria that lose the colour of a gentian violet stain, used in Gram's method of classifying bacteria

gramophone /grámmə fōn/ *n* a record player (*dated*) [Late 19C. Alteration of PHONOGRAM.]

grampa /grám paa/ *n* a grandfather (*informal; usually by or to children*) [Contraction of GRANDPAPA]

Grampian Mountains /grámpi ən-/ mountain range in central Scotland that forms a natural division between the Highlands and Lowlands. Highest peak: Ben Nevis 1,343 m/4,406 ft.

Grampian Region /grámpi ən-/ former region in NE Scotland, comprising the present-day council areas of Aberdeenshire and Moray

Grampians /grámpi ənz/ group of rugged red sandstone mountains in W Victoria, Australia. Highest peak: Mount William 1,168 m/3,832 ft.

Grampians National Park national park in W Victoria, Australia. Area: 1,670 sq. km/645 sq. mi.

Gram-positive, gram-positive *adj* describes bacteria that retain the colour of a gentian violet stain, used in Gram's method of classifying bacteria

gramps /gramps/ *n* a grandfather (*informal; usually by or to children*) [< contraction of GRANDPAPA]

grampus /grámpəss/ (*plural* **-pus** *or* **-puses**) *n* a large grey dolphin with a blunt snout, short flippers, and a tall dark grey fin. Native to: warm seas. *Grampus griseus*. [Early 16C. Alteration of Old French *graspeis* < medieval Latin *crassus piscis* 'fat fish'.]

Gram's method /grámz-/, **Gram's stain** *n* a technique used to classify bacteria according to their ability to lose or retain the colour of a gentian violet stain [Late 19C. After H. C. J. *Gram* (1853–1938), Danish physician.]

gran /gran/ *n* a grandmother (*informal; usually by or to children*) [Mid-19C. Shortening.]

grana plural of **granum**

Granada /grə náadə/ city of S Spain, site of the Alhambra. Population: 241,471 (1998 estimate).

granadilla /gránnə díllə/ *n* **1** a purple egg-shaped passion fruit **2** a tropical passionflower that produces granadillas. *Passiflora quadrangularis*. [Early 17C. < Spanish, 'little pomegranate' < *granada* 'pomegranate'.]

granary /gránnəri/ (*plural* **-ries**) *n* **1** a warehouse or storeroom for grain **2** a region where grain is abundant [Late 16C. < Latin *granarium* < *granum* 'seed'.]

Gran Chaco /gran chaákō/ region in south-central South America, extending from S Bolivia through Paraguay to N Argentina. Area: 647,500 sq. km/250,000 sq. mi.

grand /grand/ *adj* **1 OUTSTANDING** outstanding and impressive in appearance, extent, or style ○ *making a grand entrance* **2 IMPRESSIVE** impressive, ambitious, and far-reaching ○ *a grand plan* **3 WORTHY OF RESPECT** worthy of great respect by virtue of exceptional ability or high rank ○ *among the grandest orchestras of our time* **4 HAUGHTY** self-important or haughty ○ *His friends always act a bit grand around me.* **5 WONDERFUL** wonderful, enjoyable, and memorable ○ *We had a grand time.* **6 PRINCIPAL** main or principal ○ *And now we move into the Grand Banqueting Hall.* **7 TERRIFIC** respected and admirable (*informal*) ○ *She's a grand lass.* ■ *n* (*informal*) **1 1,000 POUNDS** a thousand pounds ○ *made ten grand on the deal* **2** MUSIC = **grand piano** [Early 16C. Via Old French < Latin *grandis* 'great, full grown'.] —**grandly** *adv* —**grandness** *n*

grand- *prefix* one generation further removed ○ *grandniece* [< GRAND]

grandad *n* = **granddad**

grandaddy *n* = **granddaddy**

grandam /grándəm/, **grandame** *n* a grandmother, or a woman who is no longer young (*archaic*) [13C. < Anglo-Norman *graund dame* 'grandmother'.]

~~**grandaughter**~~ incorrect spelling of **granddaughter**

grand-aunt *n* = **great-aunt**

grandbaby /gránd baybi/ *n* a grandchild who is still a baby

Grand Bahama /gránd bə haámə/ island of the W Bahamas, in the Atlantic Ocean off the coast of E Florida.

Population: 40,898 (1990). Area: 1,114 sq. km/430 sq. mi.

Grand Banks shallow section of the Atlantic Ocean, off SE Newfoundland, Canada. Area: 282,500 sq. km/109,000 sq. mi.

Grand Canal main waterway of Venice, Italy. Length: 3 km/2 mi.

Grand Canyon gorge in NW Arizona, carved by the Colorado River. Its width varies from 8 to 29 km/5 to 18 mi., and its depth can exceed 1.6 km/1 mi. Length: 443 km/227 mi.

Grand Canyon National Park national park in N Arizona, including the Grand Canyon. Area: 4,927 sq. km/1,902 sq. mi.

grandchild /gránd chīld/ (*plural* **-children** /-childrən/) *n* a child of your son or daughter

Grand Coulee Dam /-kóoli-/ concrete dam in north-central Washington State, on the Columbia River. Height: 168 m/550 ft.

granddad /grán dad/, **grandad** *n* (*informal*) **1** a grandfather **2** used as a rather disrespectful name for a man of advanced years (*sometimes offensive*)

granddaddy /grán dadi/ (*plural* **-dies**), **grandaddy** (*plural* **-dies**) *n* **1** a grandfather (*informal*) **2** something considered the oldest, first, or most important of its time

granddaughter /grán dawtər/ *n* a daughter of your son or daughter

grand duchess *n* **1 GRAND DUKE'S SPOUSE** the wife or widow of a grand duke **2 HIGH NOBLEWOMAN** a woman who holds a rank above that of duchess **3 RUSSIAN PRINCESS** in tsarist Russia, a daughter of a tsar, or a daughter of a tsar's descendants

grand duchy *n* a country, territory, or estate that has a grand duke or a grand duchess as its ruler

grand duke *n* **1** a nobleman who holds a rank above that of a duke **2** in tsarist Russia, a brother, son, uncle, or nephew of a tsar

grande dame /graáNd dám/ *n* a socially important, dignified, and usually older woman [< French, 'great lady']

Grande Dixence Dam /-díks'nss-/ concrete dam on the River Dixence, SW Switzerland. Height: 284 m/932 ft.

grandee /gran deé/ *n* **1** somebody highly influential and respected, especially a politician **2** a high-ranking Spanish or Portuguese nobleman [Late 16C. Via Spanish and Portuguese *grande* < Latin *grandis* 'great'.]

grandeur /gránjər/ *n* the quality of being great or grand and very impressive [Early 16C. < French, < *grand* (see GRAND).]

grandfather /gránd faathər/ *n* **1 FATHER OF YOUR PARENT** the father of your father or mother **2 ANCESTOR** a man who is somebody's ancestor **3 USED TO ADDRESS MAN** used as a name for a man considered to be advanced in years (*dated informal*) **4** *W Country* **WOODLOUSE** a woodlouse (*informal*) —**grandfatherly** *adj*

grandfather clause *n* **1** a clause in prohibitive legislation that makes exceptions for those already engaged in the activity that it bans or regulates **2** a clause in some Southern US states' constitutions, since declared unconstitutional, that waived electoral literacy requirements for descendants of those allowed to vote before 1867, effectively only white people

grandfather clock *n* a large clock in a tall case that stands on the floor

grand final *n* the last round in a series of contests, competitions, or sports matches

grand finale *n* the closing spectacular scene or section of a performance or other show

Grand Guignol /gaáN gee nyól/ *n* a sensational drama, often structured in short scenes with violent or horrific subject matter, that aims to horrify its audience [Early 20C. < *Le Grand Guignol*, theatre in Paris.] —**grand guignol** *adj*

grandiloquence /gran díllәkwәnss/ *n* a pompous or lofty manner of speaking or writing [Late 16C. < Latin *grandiloquus* 'speaking grandly' < *grandis* 'great' + *loqui* 'speak'.] —**grandiloquent** *adj* —**grandiloquently** *adv*

grandiose /grándi ōss/ *adj* **1 PRETENTIOUS AND POMPOUS** pretentious, pompous, and imposing **2 MAGNIFICENT** impressive and magnificent **3 OVERLY COMPLEX** too complicated and unrealistic ○ *a grandiose plan* [Mid-19C. Via French < Italian *grandioso* 'imposing' < *grande* 'great' < Latin *grandis*.] —**grandiosely** *adv* —**grandioseness** *n* —**grandiosity** /grándi óssəti/ *n*

grandioso /grándi óss ō/ *adj, adv* in a grand or imposing style (*musical direction*) [Late 19C. < Italian, 'grandly'.]

grand jury *n* in US and Canadian law, a panel of 12 to 23 jurors called to decide whether there are grounds for a criminal prosecution in a case —**grand juror** *n*

grandkid /grán kid/ *n* a grandchild (*informal*)

grand larceny *n* a robbery or theft of money or property with a value over the amount specified by law to constitute petty larceny

grandma /grán maa/ *n* a grandmother (*informal*) [Late 18C. Shortening.]

grand mal /graán mál/ *n* a serious form of epilepsy in which there is loss of consciousness and severe convulsions. ◊ **petit mal** [< French, 'great illness']

grandmama /grànmə maa/ *n* a grandmother (*dated*)

Grand Manan Island /-mə nán-/ island of SW New Brunswick, Canada, at the entrance to the Bay of Fundy. Population: 3,000. Area: 137 sq. km/53 sq. mi.

grand master, grandmaster /grán maastər/ *n* **1 TOP CHESS PLAYER** a champion chess player who plays at an international level **2 SOMEBODY OUTSTANDING** a person at the top of a particular field in ability or achievement **3 GROUP HEAD** a head of a brotherhood of knights or of a fraternal organization such as the Masons

grandmother /grán muthər/ *n* **1 PARENT'S MOTHER** the mother of your father or mother **2 ANCESTOR** a woman who is somebody's ancestor **3 USED TO ADDRESS WOMAN** used to address a woman of advanced years (*dated informal; sometimes offensive*) —**grandmotherly** *adj*

grandmother clock *n* a clock in a tall case that stands on the floor, smaller than a grandfather clock

Grand National *n* a famous British steeplechase, held annually at Aintree in Liverpool since 1839

grandnephew /grán nef yoo/ *n* = **great-nephew**

grandniece /grán neess/ *n* = **great-niece**

grand old man *n* a man, usually past middle age, who is respected for his contribution to some field of activity such as politics, music, or sport ○ *the grand old man of British jazz*

grand opera *n* an opera on a serious dramatic theme in which all the words are sung and there is no spoken dialogue

grandpa /grán paa/ *n* (*informal*) **1** a grandfather **2** a slightly disrespectful name for a man of advanced years (*sometimes offensive*)

grandpapa /grànpə paa/ *n* a grandfather (*dated*)

grandparent /gránd pairənt/ *n* the mother or father of your mother or father —**grandparental** /gránd pə rént'l/ *adj* —**grandparenthood** *n*

grand piano *n* a large piano in which the strings are fixed horizontally behind the keyboard in a long harp-shaped frame

Grand Pré /gron práy, graaN-/ village in central Nova Scotia, Canada

Grand Prix /grón preé/ (*plural* **Grand Prix** *or* **Grands Prix** /grón preé/) *n* **1** any one of a number of important international annual races for racing cars, held to decide the world motor-racing championship **2** any one of various competitions in a variety of sports that have the same importance and prestige as a Grand Prix in motor-racing [< French, 'big prize']

grandsire /gránd sīr/ *n* **1** a grandfather (*archaic*) **2** in bell-ringing, a method of change-ringing using an odd number of bells

grand slam *n* **1 WINNING OF ALL MAJOR COMPETITIONS** in some sports, e.g. tennis and golf, the winning of all of a specified group of major competitions by one player or team in one year **2 MAJOR COMPETITION** any one of a specified group of major competitions in a particular sport **3 WINNING OF ALL TRICKS** in bridge and similar card games, the winning of all 13 tricks in a game by one player or pair of players, or a contract to do so **4 4 RUNS** in baseball, a home run made when all the bases are loaded

grandson /grán sun/ *n* a son of your son or daughter

grandstand /gránd stand/ *n* **1 STRUCTURE FOR SPECTATORS' SEATS** an open building or platform, usually with a roof, containing rows of seats for spectators at a sports stadium or racecourse **2 SPECTATORS IN A GRANDSTAND** the spectators sitting in a grandstand ■ *adj* **UNOBSTRUCTED** clear, close, and unobstructed ○ *We had a grandstand view of the proceedings.* ■ *vi* **SEEK ATTENTION OR ADMIRATION** to show off in order to impress people, especially spectators —**grandstander** *n*

grandstand finish *n* a finish to a race or competition that is exciting because the outcome is unclear until the very end [Because the finish line is typically in front of the grandstand]

grand total *n* a final and complete total of all amounts to be added

grand tour *n* **1** a trip or tour that takes in visits to several places, or a visit that allows a complete inspection of all parts of one place **2** formerly, a tour of the main European cities and cultural centres undertaken by young upper-class Englishmen as a way of completing their education

Grand Trunk Canal canal linking the rivers Mersey and Trent in England. Length: 150 km/93 mi.

grand-uncle *n* = **great-uncle**

Grand Union Canal canal in southern and central England connecting the River Thames in central London with the Midlands

grange /graynj/ *n* **1** a large farmhouse or country house with other buildings such as stables or barns attached to it **2** a large farm building used for storing grain or hay (*archaic*) [13C. Via French < medieval Latin *granica villa* 'grain house' < Latin *granum* 'seed'.]

Grange *n* the Patrons of Husbandry, an association of US farmers founded in 1867 for their mutual support

grangerize /gráynjə rīz/ (**-izes, -izing, -ized**), **grangerise** (**-ises, -ising, -ised**) *vt* **1** formerly, to illustrate a book with pictures cut out of another book or books **2** formerly, to cut pictures out of a book or books in order to illustrate another one [Late 19C. After James *Granger* (1723–76), whose *Biographical History of England* had blank pages for illustrations.] —**grangerizer** *n*

grani- *prefix* grain, seed ○ *granivorous* [< Latin *granum*]

granita /grə neétə/ *n* a sweetened flavoured water ice with a grainy texture [Mid-19C. < Italian, form of *granito* (see GRANITE).]

granite /gránnit/ *n* **1 COARSE-GRAINED ROCK** a coarse-grained igneous rock made up of feldspar, mica, and at least 20 per cent quartz. Use: building. **2 TOUGHNESS** determination or toughness of character **3 STONE USED IN CURLING** the rounded stone used in the sport of curling [Mid-17C. < Italian *granito* 'grainy' < Latin *granum* 'seed'.] —**granitic** /grə níttik/ *adj* —**granitoid** /gránni toyd/ *adj*

graniteware /gránnit wair/ *n* **1** earthenware with a speckled glaze that gives it the appearance of granite **2** iron articles, e.g. pots and bowls, coated with a glaze that gives a finish with the appearance of granite

granivorous /gra nívvərəss/ *adj* that eats seeds

granny /gránni/ (*plural* **-nies**), **grannie** *n* **1 GRANDMOTHER** a grandmother (*informal*) **2 WOMAN OF ADVANCED YEARS** used as a slightly disrespectful name for a woman of advanced years **3 FUSSY PERSON** an annoyingly fastidious or fussy person (*insult*) **4 CHIMNEY COVERING** a revolving cap on a chimney pot **5** = **granny knot** [Mid-17C. Shortening of *grannam*, common pronunciation of GRANDAM.]

granny-bashing *n* violence against or an assault on a woman of advanced years, especially for the purpose of robbery (*informal*)

granny bond *n* a savings bond that is index-linked to inflation, originally offered only to people over retirement age (*informal*)

granny-dumping *n* the abandonment of a senior citizen who is in deteriorating mental or physical health by a family member or members in a public place (*disapproving*)

granny flat *n* a small self-contained flat that is in or attached to a house and is considered suitable for an elderly parent to live in independently of the rest of the family. US term **mother-in-law apartment**

granny gear *n* the lowest gear on a bicycle that makes it possible to pedal up steep inclines (*informal*)

granny glasses *npl* spectacles consisting of small lenses set in gold or steel frames

granny knot *n* a reef knot incorrectly tied and therefore likely to come apart

Granny Smith *n* an eating apple with green skin and crisp white flesh [Late 19C. After the nickname of Maria Ann *Smith* (1801–70), who first grew it in Sydney, Australia.]

granny specs *npl* = **granny glasses** (*informal*)

grano- *prefix* granite ○ *granolith* [Via German < Italian *granito* (see GRANITE)]

granodiorite /gránnō dī ə rīt/ *n* a coarse-grained igneous rock containing plagioclase and orthoclase, whose composition is intermediate between granite and diorite —**granodioritic** /gránnō dī ə ríttik/ *adj*

granola /grə nṓlə/ *n* a breakfast cereal consisting of rolled oats mixed with other ingredients such as dried fruit and nuts [Early 20C. Originally a trade name.]

granolith /gránnə lith/ *n* a paving material made from cement and granite chips —**granolithic** /gránnə líthik/ *adj*

granophyre /gránn ō fīr/ *n* a medium-grained light-coloured igneous rock consisting mainly of crystals of feldspar and quartz that have crystallized together [Late 19C. < German *Granophyr* < *Granit* 'granite' + *Porphyr* 'porphyry'.] —**granophyric** /gránn ō fírrik/ *adj*

Gran Paradiso /gram párrə de̍ezō/ mountain of N Italy, in the W Alps. Height: 4,061 m/13,323 ft.

grant /graant/ *vt* 1 **COMPLY WITH A REQUEST** to carry out or comply with a request for something 2 **ALLOW AS A FAVOUR** to give somebody something or allow somebody to have something, especially as a favour or privilege ○ *She refused to grant any interviews.* 3 **AGREE THE TRUTH OF** to acknowledge that what somebody else has said, or what a person thinks somebody else is thinking, is true ○ *He's a hard worker, I grant you, but hardly managerial material.* 4 **TRANSFER LEGALLY** to transfer property or rights in a legal transaction ■ *n* 1 **MONEY GIVEN FOR A PURPOSE** a sum of money given by the government, a local authority, or some other organization to fund such things as education, research, or home improvements 2 **GIFT** something that is given to somebody as a favour or privilege, or the giving of it ○ *a land grant* 3 **LEGAL TRANSACTION** something transferred from one person to another in a legal transaction, or the transaction itself 4 **TRANSFER DOCUMENT** a legal document recording a transaction in which something is transferred from one person to another 5 **AREA OF LAND** in the United States, a unit of territory in New Hampshire, Maine, or Vermont [13C. < Old French *granter*, variant of *creanter* 'guarantee', via assumed Vulgar Latin *credentare* < Latin *credere* 'believe'.] —**grantable** *adj* —**granter** *n* ◇ **take somebody for granted** to fail to realize or appreciate the value of somebody ◇ **take something for granted** 1 to assume that something is true without checking 2 to fail to appreciate or realize the value of something

SYNONYMS See ***give***.

Grant /graant/, **Cary** (1904–86) British-born US film actor. Born **Alexander Archibald Leach**

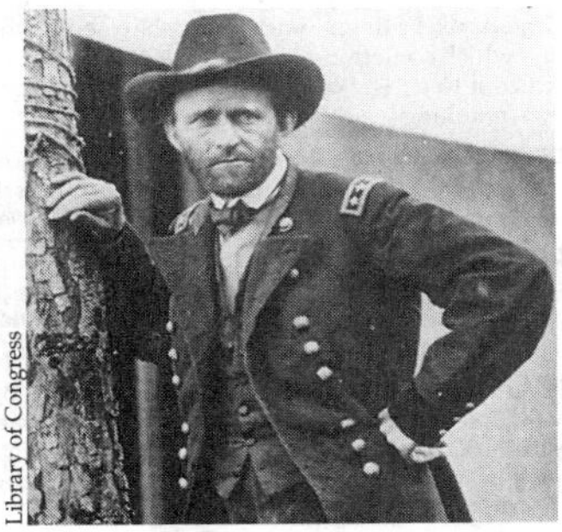

Ulysses S. Grant

Grant, Ulysses S. (1822–85) US statesman and 18th president of the United States (1869–77). Full name **Hiram Ulysses Simpson Grant**

grant aid *n* financial help provided to a school or other educational establishment by central government

grant-aid *vt* to give grant aid to somebody or something

grant-aided school *n* a school in which independent managers control the appointment of the teachers and the religious instruction given, and are required to pay part of the upkeep costs

granted /gra̍antid/ *adv, conj* used when acknowledging the truth of something that somebody has said or is thinking

grantee /graan te̍e/ *n* somebody to whom something is transferred in a legal transaction

Granth /grunt/ *n* RELIG = **Adi Granth** [Late 18C. Via Hindi < Sanskrit *granthaḥ* 'book, binding'.]

Grantham /gránthəm/ town in E England. Population: 33,243 (1991).

Granth Sahib *n* RELIG = **Adi Granth**

grant-in-aid (*plural* **grants-in-aid**) *n* a sum of money given as funding by a central government to a local government, or by central or local government to a department or institution

grant-maintained school *n* a self-governing school funded directly by central government rather than a local education authority

grantor /graan táwr, gra̍antər/ *n* somebody from whom something is transferred in a legal transaction

granular /grányoo̅lər/ *adj* 1 consisting of small grains or particles 2 appearing to consist of or be covered in small grains or particles [Late 18C. < late Latin *granulum* (see GRANULE).] —**granularity** /grányoo̅ lárrəti/ *n* —**granularly** *adv*

granulate /grányoo̅ layt/ (**-lates, -lating, -lated**) *v* 1 *vti* **MAKE INTO SMALL PARTICLES** to form or cause something to form into small grains or particles 2 *vti* **BECOME OR MAKE GRAINY IN TEXTURE** to become rough and grainy in texture or appearance, or give something a rough and grainy texture or appearance 3 *vi* **FORM HEALING WOUND TISSUE** to form the type of tissue that grows over healing wounds (**granulation tissue**) [Mid-17C. < late Latin *granulum* (see GRANULE).] —**granulative** *adj* —**granulator** *n*

granulated sugar /grányoo̅ laytid-/ *n* white sugar in the form of a coarse powder with large particles

granulation /grányoo̅ láysh'n/ *n* 1 **MAKING OF SMALL PARTICLES** the formation of small grains or particles 2 **GRAINY TEXTURE** a grainy texture or appearance 3 **SMALL LUMP** any one of the individual small lumps that, together, give something a rough grainy texture or appearance 4 **FORMATION OF TISSUE OVER HEALING WOUND** the formation of the type of tissue that grows over healing wounds (**granulation tissue**), or the tissue itself 5 **CELLULAR APPEARANCE OF SUN'S SURFACE** the cellular appearance of the Sun's disc when seen at high magnification [Early 17C. < late Latin *granulum* (see GRANULE).]

granulation tissue *n* connective tissue in the form of small grainy particles along with masses of tiny blood vessels that forms over healing wounds

granule /grán yool/ *n* 1 **SMALL PARTICLE** a small grain or particle 2 **SMALL ROCK FRAGMENT** a mineral or rock particle that is the size of a small grain 3 **TEMPORARY BRIGHT REGION ON SUN'S SURFACE** a temporary bright region on the Sun's surface, typically having an approximate diameter of 1,000 km/320 mi [Mid-17C. < late Latin *granulum* 'small seed' < Latin *granum* 'seed'.]

granulite /grányoo̅ līt/ *n* a coarse-grained metamorphic rock in which the minerals are of roughly equal size —**granulitic** /grányoo̅ líttik/ *adj*

granulocyte /grányoo̅lə sīt/ *n* a white blood cell that contains many granular particles in its cytoplasm —**granulocytic** /grányoo̅lə síttik/ *adj*

granuloma /grányoo̅ lṓmə/ (*plural* **-mas** *or* **-mata** /-mətə/) *n* a small mass of granulation tissue caused by chronic infection —**granulomatous** *adj*

granulose /grányoo̅ lōss/ *adj* 1 consisting of small grains or particles 2 appearing to consist of or be covered in small grains or particles

granum /gráynəm/ (*plural* **-na** /-nə/) *n* a stack of thin layers in a chloroplast in which the green pigment chlorophyll is contained [Late 19C. Via German < Latin, 'seed'.]

Granville-Barker /gránvil ba̍arkər/, **Harley** (1877–1946) British actor, producer, and dramatist

grape /grayp/ *n* 1 **EDIBLE FRUIT** a green or purple berry with sweet juicy flesh that grows in bunches on a vine, eaten fresh or used to make wine or grape juice 2 PLANTS = **grapevine** *n.* 1 3 **PLANT WITH FRUIT RESEMBLING GRAPES** a plant that produces fruit resembling grapes in some way ○ *Oregon grape* 4 **WINE** the drink wine (*humorous*) 5 ARMS = **grapeshot** 6 **DARK PURPLE COLOUR** a dark purple colour [13C. < Old French, 'bunch of grapes, hook (as used to harvest grapes)' < Germanic, 'hook'.] —**grape** *adj*

LITERARY LINK ***The Grapes of Wrath***, a novel (1939) by US writer John Steinbeck. A sympathetic portrayal of the plight of the rural poor during the Depression and an attack on capitalism, it tells of the tribulations suffered by the Joad family when they leave drought-stricken Oklahoma in search of work.

grape fern *n* any one of various ferns with fronds that bear clusters of spore capsules similar to grapes. Genus: *Botrychium.*

grapefruit /gráyp froot/ (*plural* **-fruits** *or* **-fruit**) *n* 1 a large round yellow or pinkish citrus fruit with very tart juicy flesh ○ *grapefruit juice* 2 an evergreen tree with large white flowers that produces grapefruits. *Citrus paradisi.* [Early 19C. Probably because the fruit grows in bunches, like grapes.]

grape hyacinth *n* a perennial plant belonging to the lily family. Flowers: usually blue, dense, cup-shaped, in clusters. Genus: *Muscari.*

grape ivy *n* an evergreen climbing plant commonly kept as a house plant. Native to: South America. *Rhoicissus rhomboidea.*

grapeshot /gráyp shot/ *n* a number of small iron balls fired simultaneously from a cannon in order to kill enemy soldiers [< the resemblance to a bunch of grapes]

grape sugar *n* a fruit sugar obtained from grapes

grapevine /gráyp vīn/ *n* 1 a vine on which grapes grow. Genus: *Vitis.* 2 the path of communication along which news, gossip, or rumour passes unofficially from person to person within a group, organization, or community (*informal*) ○ *I heard on the office grapevine that she was leaving.*

grapey /gráypi/ (**-ier, -iest**), **grapy** (**-ier, -iest**) *adj* looking or tasting like a grape or grapes —**grapiness** *n*

graph[1] /graaf, graf/ *n* a diagram used to indicate relationships between two or more variable quantities. The quantities are measured along two axes, usually at right angles. ■ *vt* to represent data by means of a graph, or add data to a graph [Late 19C. Shortening of *graphic formula.*]

graph[2] /graaf, graf/ *n* a symbol, letter, or combination of letters used in writing to represent the smallest discrete unit of speech [Mid-20C. < Greek *graphē* 'writing' < *graphein* 'write'.]

graph- *prefix* writing (*before vowels*) ○ *graphology* [< Greek *graphein* 'write']

-graph *suffix* 1 something written or drawn ○ *digraph* ○ *zincograph* 2 an instrument for writing, drawing, or recording ○ *pantograph* ○ *seismograph* [Via French or Latin < Greek *graphos* 'written, writing' < *graphein* 'write']

grapheme /grá feem/ *n* a written symbol, a letter, or a combination of letters that represents a single sound —**graphemic** /gra fe̍emik/ *adj* —**graphemically** *adv*

graphemics /gra fe̍emiks/ *n* LING = **graphology** *n.* 2 (+ *singular verb*)

-grapher *suffix* somebody who writes, draws, or records ○ *calligrapher* ○ *cinematographer* [< late Latin *-graphus* 'writer' < Greek *-graphos* < *graphein* 'write']

⚡**graphic** /gráffik/ *adj* 1 **VIVIDLY DETAILED** including a number of vivid descriptive details, especially exciting or unpleasant ones ○ *her graphic description of the accident* 2 **SHOWN IN WRITING** representing something such as a sound by means of letters or other written symbols 3 **SHOWN IN PICTURES** representing something in the form of pictures or images 4 **RELATING TO GRAPHS** given in or relating to the form of a graph or diagram 5 **OF GRAPHIC ARTS** relating to the graphic arts 6 **OF GRAPHICS** relating to graphics 7 **CONTAINING CRYSTALS LIKE LETTERS** containing crystal structures that resemble letters ■ *n* (*often plural*) 1 **PICTURE PRODUCED BY COMPUTER** a picture, design, or visual display of data produced by a computer program 2 **BOOK ILLUSTRATION** an illustration or diagram in a book or magazine 3 **DISPLAYED TEXT IN FILM** any part of a film that consists of illustration and text, e.g. titles, credits, or drawings [Mid-18C. Via Latin < Greek *graphikos* < *graphein* 'write'.] —**graphically** *adv* —**graphicness** *n*

graphicacy /gráffikəssi/ *n* the ability to use and understand such things as symbols, diagrams, plans, and maps [Mid-20C. < GRAPHIC, after *literacy.*]

graphical /gráffik'l/ *adj* MATH = **graphic** *adj.* 4

⚡**graphical user interface** *n* a user interface on a computer that relies on icons, menus, and a mouse rather than on typing in commands

graphic arts *npl* artistic processes such as drawing, calligraphy, engraving, and printmaking based on the use of lines rather than colour —**graphic artist** *n*

graphic design *n* the art of integrating text, typography, and illustrations in the production of books and magazines —**graphic designer** *n*

graphic equalizer *n* a device, e.g. on a radio or CD player, that allows adjustments to be made to the strength of sounds of different frequencies [Because the variable levels of the sounds are often displayed electronically in graphic format]

graphic novel *n* a fictional story for adults published in the form of a comic strip

⚡**graphics** /gráffiks/ *n* (+ *singular verb*) **1 DIAGRAMS AND ILLUSTRATIONS** the presentation of information in the form of diagrams and illustrations as opposed to words and numbers **2 DISPLAY OF COMPUTER DATA AS SYMBOLS** the art and science of storing, manipulating, and displaying computer data in the form of pictures, diagrams, graphs, or symbols **3 MATHEMATICAL DRAWING** the science of drawing something in accordance with mathematical principles, e.g. in architecture and engineering ■ *npl* ARTS = **graphic arts**

⚡**graphics card** *n* a circuit board that enables a computer to display screen information

⚡**graphics tablet** *n* a device consisting of an electronic pen and an electronically sensitive surface, used to enter designs into a computer by drawing them

graphite /gráf īt/ *n* a soft dark carbon that conducts electricity, occurs naturally as a mineral, and is also produced industrially. Use: batteries, lubricants, polishes, electric motors, nuclear reactors, carbon fibres, pencil lead. [Late 18C. < German *Graphit* < Greek *graphein* 'write'.] —**graphitic** /grə fíttik/ *adj*

graphitize /gráffi tīz/ (**-tizes, -tizing, -tized**), **graphitise** (**-tises, -tising, -tised**) *vt* **1** to convert something into graphite **2** to coat something with graphite, or mix graphite into it —**graphitizable** *adj* —**graphitization** /gráffi tī záysh'n/ *n*

grapho- *prefix* = **graph-**

graphology /gra fólləji/ *n* **1** the study of handwriting, especially in order to assess somebody's personality from patterns or features of his or her writing **2** the study of writing systems and their relationship to the sound systems of languages —**graphological** /gráffə lójjik'l/ *adj* —**graphologist** *n*

graph paper *n* paper on which a series of usually equally spaced vertical and horizontal intersecting lines has been imprinted to facilitate the drawing of graphs and diagrams

-graphy *suffix* **1** a method of writing or making an image by means of a particular process or technique ○ *chirography* ○ *radiography* **2** writing about or study of a particular subject ○ *biography* ○ *ethnography* [< Latin *-graphia* < Greek *graphein* 'write']

grapnel /grápn'l/ *n* **1** a device consisting of an iron shaft with several hooks at one end and a rope at the other by which it can be thrown to attach itself to something **2** an anchor with three or more arms, especially one for anchoring a small boat [14C. < Anglo-Norman, < Old French *grapon* < *grape* 'hook' (see GRAPE).]

grappa /gráppə/ (*plural* **-pas** *or* **-pa**) *n* an Italian brandy distilled from what remains of grapes after they have been pressed for wine-making [Late 19C. < Italian, 'grape stalk, brandy'.]

Grappelli /grə pélli/, **Stephane** (1908–97) French jazz musician

grapple /grápp'l/ *v* (**-ples, -pling, -pled**) **1** *vi* **STRUGGLE WITH SOMEBODY** to grab hold of somebody and struggle with him or her in a hand-to-hand fight **2** *vi* **STRUGGLE TO DEAL WITH SOMETHING** to struggle with something that is difficult to deal with, e.g. a problem that is difficult to solve or a concept or theory that is difficult to grasp **3** *vt* **GRAB** to grasp hold of somebody **4** *vt* **HOLD WITH A HOOKED DEVICE** to hook or hold something with a grapnel or other hooked device ■ *n* **1** = **grapnel** *n.* 1 **2 STRUGGLE** a close struggle **3 GRIP OR HOLD** in wrestling, a grip or hold on an opponent [14C. < Old French *grapil* 'small hook' < *grape* 'hook' (see GRAPE).] —**grappler** *n*

grappling /grápling/, **grappling iron, grappling hook** *n* = **grapnel** *n.* 1

graptolite /gráp tō līt/ *n* any one of various small floating sea animals that lived in colonies that existed between about 550 million and 325 million years ago and are now found as fossils. Orders: Graptoloidea and Dendroidea. [Mid-19C. < Greek *graptos*, past participle of *graphein* 'write'.]

grapy *adj* = **grapey**

Grasmere /graáss meer/ village in NW England, on Grasmere Lake. Population: 1,100 (1981).

grasp /graasp/ *v* **1** *vt* **TAKE HOLD OF** to take hold of somebody or something firmly, especially with the hand or hands ○ *He grasped her arm and led her out into the garden.* **2** *vi* **TRY TO TAKE HOLD OF** to attempt to take hold of somebody or something, especially with the hand or hands ○ *He grasped at the rope.* **3** *vt* **HOLD** to hold something, especially in the hand or hands ○ *She rushed into the room with a letter grasped in her hand.* **4** *vt* **TAKE AN OPPORTUNITY** to take the opportunity to do something when it arises **5** *vi* **TRY TO TAKE OPPORTUNITY** to attempt to take the opportunity to do something when it arises **6** *vt* **UNDERSTAND** to manage to understand something ○ *I just can't grasp what you're getting at.* ■ *n* **1 HAND GRIP** a hold or grip, especially in the hand or hands **2 UNDERSTANDING** somebody's understanding of or ability to understand something ○ *a poor grasp of the facts* **3 ABILITY TO ACHIEVE** ability to achieve or get something ○ *Success was within her grasp.* **4 CONTROL** power or control ○ *in the tyrant's grasp* [14C. < ?] —**graspable** *adj*

grasper /graáspər/ *n* **1** a person who is greedy for money **2** a person who grasps something

grasping /graásping/ *adj* greedy for money —**graspingly** *adv* —**graspingness** *n*

grass /graass/ *n* **1** (*plural* **grasses** *or* **grass**) **GREEN PLANT THAT FORMS LAWNS** a low green narrow-leaved plant that grows in fields and gardens, is eaten by animals such as cows and sheep, and is used to make lawns and playing fields **2 GRASS-COVERED AREA** an area of grass, e.g. a lawn or pasture **3 HOLLOW-STEMMED GREEN PLANT** a plant with hollow jointed stems and long narrow, usually green, leaves and tiny flowers arranged in spikes. Grasses include important food plants such as wheat, oats, barley, rice, rye, maize, millet, and sorghum as well as sugar cane and bamboo. Family: Gramineae. **4 PLANT RESEMBLING GRASS** a green plant such as goosegrass or knotgrass not related to the true grasses **5 MARIJUANA** the drug marijuana (*slang*) **6 INFORMER** an informer on somebody else, especially to the police (*slang*) ■ *v* **1** *vti* **COVER OR BECOME COVERED WITH GRASS** to become covered with grass, or cause ground to become covered with grass **2** *vi* **BE INFORMER** to inform on somebody, especially to the police (*slang*) **3** *vt* **FEED AN ANIMAL ON GRASS** to put an animal into a pasture to feed on grass **4** *vt* **BRING OPPONENT DOWN** to make an opponent fall to the ground [Old English *græs, gærs* < Indo-European] ◇ **not let the grass grow under your feet** to act without delay or wasting time ◇ **put somebody out to grass** to impose retirement on somebody, usually on grounds of age (*informal*)

LITERARY LINK ***Leaves of Grass***, a collection of verse (1855–92) by US poet Walt Whitman. Whitman constantly revised and expanded this collection to create a work that celebrates all aspects of human life from politics to the natural world and from procreation to mortality. Both its subject matter and its self-consciously modern style, based on long, loosely rhymed lines, were highly influential.

grass up *vt* to inform on somebody, especially to the police (*slang*)

Grass /grass/, **Günter** (*b.* 1927) German writer and political activist

grass box *n* the container attached to a lawn mower that catches the grass cuttings. US term **grass catcher**

grass carp *n* a plant-eating fish used for keeping water weeds under control. Native to: Russia, China. *Ctenopharyngodon idella.*

grass catcher *n US* GARDENING = **grass box**

grass cloth *n* cloth made from loosely woven plant fibres

grass court *n* a grass-covered tennis court

grass-green *adj* of the colour of green grass —**grass green** *n*

grasshopper /graás hopər/ *n* **1 JUMPING INSECT** a slender plant-eating flying and jumping insect that produces a buzzing or whirring sound by rubbing its back legs against its forewings. Order: Orthoptera. **2 CREAMY COCKTAIL** a cocktail consisting of crème de menthe, crème de cacao, and cream ■ *adj* **NOT ABLE TO FOCUS** unable to concentrate on one thing for very long ○ *have a grasshopper mind* [14C. < *grasshop* < Old English *gærshoppa.*]

grassland /graáss land/ *n* **1** land on which grass or low green plants are the main vegetation **2** land kept for pasture or for the production of forage crops

grass-of-Parnassus *n* a plant of the saxifrage family. Flowers: white. Native to: marshes, wet moorland. *Parnassia palustris.*

grass roots *npl* **1** the ordinary people in a community or the ordinary members of an organization, as opposed to the leadership **2** the origin, basis, fundamental aim, or basic meaning of something ○ *the grass roots of socialism*

grassroots /graáss roots/, **grass-roots** *adj* coming from, formed by, or involving the ordinary people in a community, or the ordinary members of an organization, as opposed to the leadership

grass snake *n* a common nonpoisonous dark green snake. Native to: Europe, North Africa, Asia. Genus: *Natrix.*

grass tree *n* a tree with an unbranching trunk topped by a tuft of leaves resembling grass. Native to: E Australia. Genus: *Xanthorrhoea.*

grass widow *n* a woman whose husband is frequently away from home or who has completely deserted her [Originally 'discarded mistress', thought of as having made love in a field]

grass widower *n* a man whose wife is frequently away from home or who has completely deserted him

grassy /graássi/ (**-ier, -iest**) *adj* **1** covered with grass **2** looking, tasting, or feeling like grass —**grassiness** *n*

grate[1] /grayt/ *n* **1 BARS IN FRONT OF FIRE** a framework of metal bars used to keep solid fuel such as coal or wood within a fireplace, stove, or furnace **2 FIREPLACE** a fireplace, stove, or furnace **3 BARS OVER OPENING** a framework of bars covering and blocking an opening **4 SIEVE FOR GRADING ORE** an iron plate with holes in it for grading crushed ore [14C. Via Old French < Latin *cratis* 'wickerwork'.]

grate[2] /grayt/ (**grates, grating, grated**) *v* **1** *vti* **MAKE INTO SMALL PIECES** to shred something by rubbing it against a rough surface or a tool with sharp-edged holes in it, or be shredded in this way ○ *He chose a cheese that grates easily.* **2** *vti* **MAKE NOISE OF RUBBING** to make a rough, vibrating, or creaking sound by being rubbed together, or cause things to make such a sound by rubbing them against each other ○ *Grasshoppers make their characteristic sound by grating their back legs against their wings.* **3** *vi* **IRRITATE** to be a source of irritation ○ *His constant sniggering really grates on me.* **4** *vt* **SAY SOMETHING IN HARSH VOICE** to say something in a harsh rasping voice [14C. < Old French *grater* 'scrape' < Germanic.] —**grated** *adj*

grateful /gráytf'l/ *adj* **1** having the desire or reason to thank somebody ○ *I'm very grateful to you for your help.* ○ *He received a grateful letter from them* **2** giving pleasure or comfort (*archaic or literary*) [Mid-16C. < obsolete *grate* 'pleasing, thankful' < Latin *gratus.*] —**gratefully** *adv* —**gratefulness** *n*

grater /gráytər/ *n* **1** a device with many sharp-edged holes against which something such as cheese can be rubbed to reduce it to shreds or fine particles **2** a person who grates something

graticule /grátti kyool/ *n* **1** OPTICS = **reticle** **2** the grid of latitudinal and longitudinal lines on a map [Late 19C. Via French < Latin *craticula* 'small grid' < *cratis* 'wickerwork'.]

gratification /gráttifi káysh'n/ *n* **1 SATISFACTION** pleasure or satisfaction **2 SOMETHING SATISFYING** something that gives pleasure or satisfaction **3 ACT OF PLEASING OR SATISFYING** the act of giving somebody pleasure or satisfaction

gratify /grátti fī/ (**-fies, -fying, -fied**) *vt* **1** to make somebody feel pleased or satisfied (*often passive*) **2** to satisfy a desire [15C. Directly or via French *gratifier* < Latin *gratificari* < *gratus* 'agreeable'.] —**gratifier** *n* —**gratifying** *adj* —**gratifyingly** *adv*

gratin /grátt aN/ (*plural* **-tins** *or* **-tin**) *n* **1** a crust of browned breadcrumbs or melted grated cheese on top of food. ◊ **au gratin** **2** a cooked dish with a breadcrumb or melted cheese crust [Mid-17C. < French, < Old French *grater* (see GRATE[2]).]

gratin dish *n* a shallow ovenproof container used for cooking or serving a gratin

gratinee /grátti náy/ *adj* cooked or served with browned breadcrumbs or melted grated cheese on top [Early 20C. < French *gratinée*, past participle of *gratiner* 'cook au gratin'.]

grating[1] /gráyting/ *n* **1** a framework of metal bars covering an opening **2** OPTICS = **diffraction grating** ■ **gratings** *npl* shreds or fine particles produced by grating something

grating[2] /gráyting/ *adj* **1** unpleasantly rough, harsh, or vibrating **2** irritating —**gratingly** *adv*

gratis /gráttiss, gráy-, gràa-/ *adj, adv* received or given without cost or payment [15C. < Latin, 'out of kindness' < *gratia* (see GRACE).]

gratitude /grátti tyood/ *n* a feeling of being thankful to somebody for doing something ○ *I'd like to find some way of expressing my gratitude to her for all she did.* [15C. Directly or via French < Latin *gratitudo* < *gratus* 'pleasing'.]

gratuitous /grə tyoō itəss/ *adj* **1 UNNECESSARY** unnecessary and unjustifiable ○ *gratuitous remarks* **2 FREE** received or given without payment or obligation **3 WITHOUT RETURN BENEFIT** not requiring any benefit or compensation in return [Mid-17C. Via French < Latin *gratuitus* 'freely given' < *gratus* 'pleasing'.] —**gratuitously** *adv* —**gratuitousness** *n*

gratuity /grə tyoō əti/ (*plural* **-ties**) *n* **1** a small gift, usually of money, given to somebody such as a waiter as thanks for service given **2** a sum of money given to somebody, especially a member of the armed forces, when he or she retires [15C. Via French *gratuité* < medieval Latin *gratuitas* 'gift' < Latin *gratus* 'pleasing'.]

graupel /grówp'l/ *n* small soft white ice particles that fall as hail or snow [Late 19C. < German, 'small hulled corn' < Slavic.]

grav /grav/ *n* (*symbol* **g**) a unit of acceleration that corresponds to the standard acceleration of free fall [Shortening of GRAVITY]

gravadlax *n* FOOD = **gravlax**

gravamen /grə váy men/ (*plural* **-vamens** *or* **-vamina** /-vámminə/) *n* **1** the most serious part of an accusation or charge made against an accused person **2** a grievance against somebody (*formal*) [Early 17C. < medieval Latin, 'grievance' < Latin *gravare* 'weigh upon' < *gravis* 'heavy'.]

grave[1] /grayv/ *n* **1 BURIAL PLACE** a hole dug in the ground for a dead person's body, or another place of interment **2 LAST RESTING PLACE** any final resting place ○ *the sunken ship's watery grave* **3 DEATH** the end of life ○ *health care from the cradle to the grave* ○ *went to an early grave* **4 END** the end or destruction of something ○ *the grave of his ambition* [Old English *græf* < Indo-European, 'scratch, dig'] —**graveless** *adj* ◇ **turn in his** *or* **her grave** used to emphasize how displeased or upset somebody who is dead would be if he *or* she knew what was happening

grave[2] /grayv/ (**graver, gravest**) *adj* **1 SERIOUS IN MANNER** solemn and serious in manner **2 HAVING SERIOUS EFFECT** very important and with serious consequences, and therefore needing to be thought about carefully **3 WITH POSSIBLE HARM OR DANGER** causing, involving, or arising from a threat of danger or harm or other bad consequences ○ *Things are looking pretty grave here as the air raid sirens wail.* [15C. Via French < Latin *gravis* 'heavy'.] —**gravely** *adv* —**graveness** *n*

grave[3] /graav/ *n* a mark used to indicate pronunciation, consisting of a little line sloping downwards to the right above a letter, as in ò and è ■ *adj* having a grave accent ○ *e grave* [Early 17C. < French, 'heavy' (see GRAVE[2]).]

grave[4] /grayv/ (**graves, graving, graved, graved** *or* **graven** /gráyv'n/) *vt* **1** to fix something firmly in the mind (*literary*) ○ *graved it in her mind* **2** to carve or engrave something (*archaic*) [Old English *grafan* 'dig, carve' < Germanic]

grave[5] /grayv/ (**graves, graving, graved**) *vt* to clean the bottom of a wooden ship and coat it with pitch [15C. Probably < French dialect *grave* 'sand, shore' < Old French (see GRAVEL), because the work was done while the ship was hauled up on a beach.]

grave[6] /graàv ay/ *adv* to be played seriously or solemnly (*musical direction*) [Late 16C. Via Italian < Latin *gravis* 'heavy'.] —**grave** *adj*

grave accent /graàv-/ *n* LING = **grave**[3]

graveclothes /gráyv klōthz/ *npl* the clothes or other wrappings that a dead body is buried in

gravedigger /gráyv diggər/ *n* somebody employed to dig graves

gravel /grávv'l/ *n* **1 SMALL STONES** small stones used for paths or for making concrete **2 ROCK FRAGMENTS** a deposit or stratum of loose fragmentary sedimentary material **3 SMALL PARTICLES IN KIDNEY OR BLADDER** hard particles in the kidney or bladder that are much smaller than kidney stones and can pass through the urinary tract without causing a blockage, although they may cause severe pain ■ *vt* (**-els, -elling, -elled**) **1 COVER WITH GRAVEL** to cover a surface with gravel **2 BEWILDER** to puzzle or confuse somebody [13C. < Old French, < *grave* 'pebbles, shore' < Celtic.]

gravel-blind *adj* almost totally sightless (*archaic; considered offensive in most contexts*) [After SAND-BLIND]

gravelly /grávv'li/ *adj* **1 GRATING** sounding rough or harsh ○ *a gravelly voice* **2 LIKE GRAVEL** like or covered with gravel **3 WITH GRAVEL** made or manufactured with gravel

gravel trap *n* an area of gravel beside a racetrack, intended to slow down and stop speeding vehicles that leave the track and enter it

graven past participle of **grave**[4]

graven image *n* a carving representing a god

graver /gráyvər/ *n* a tool used for carving or engraving

grave robber *n* a thief of objects from graves or tombs, usually valuable artefacts or corpses for dissection

Graves /graav/ *n* a white or red wine from the district of Graves in SW France

Graves /grayvz/, **Robert** (1895–1985) British poet and novelist

Graves' disease /gráyvz-/ *n* an inflammatory disorder of the thyroid gland commonly associated with protrusion of the eyes [Mid-19C. After Robert J. *Graves* (1796–1853), Irish physician.]

Gravesend /gráyvz énd/ port in SE England, on the River Thames. Population: 51,435 (1991).

graveside /gráyv sīd/ *n* the area surrounding a grave (*often before nouns*) ○ *a graveside service*

gravesite /gráyv sīt/ *n* the place where somebody's grave is

gravestone /gráyv stōn/ *n* an ornamental piece of stone put at the head of a grave, on which are written the name, birth date, and death date of the person buried there

graveyard /gráyv yaard/ *n* **1** a piece of ground, sometimes beside a church, set aside for people to be buried in **2** a place where old, unwanted, useless objects, especially old cars, are left

graveyard poetry *n* sad reflective poems about death, often set in graveyards and typically by 18th century British writers —**graveyard poet** *n*

graveyard shift *n* a shift of work running through the early hours of the morning, especially one running from midnight till eight o'clock the following morning, or the workers on such a shift

gravid /grávvid/ *adj* carrying young or eggs (*technical*) [Late 16C. < Latin *gravidus* < *gravis* 'heavy'.] —**gravidity** /gra víddəti/ *n* —**gravidly** *adv* —**gravidness** *n*

gravida /grávvidə/ (*plural* **-das** *or* **-dae** /-dee/) *n* a pregnant woman (*technical*) [Mid-20C. < Latin, form of *gravidus* (see GRAVID).]

gravimeter /grə vímmitər/ *n* **1** an instrument for measuring variations in the strength of the Earth's gravitational field from one place to another **2** an instrument used to measure the relative density of a substance [Late 18C. < French *gravimètre* < Latin *gravis* (see GRAVE[2]).]

gravimetric /grávvi métrik/ *adj* **1 RELATING TO MEASUREMENT OF WEIGHT** relating to or using the measurement of weight **2 OF CHEMICAL ANALYSIS AND WEIGHT** relating to chemical analysis involving the measurement of the weights of substances used in and produced by a chemical reaction. ◊ **volumetric 3 MEASURING GRAVITATIONAL VARIATIONS** relating to the measurement of variations in the strength of the Earth's gravitational field from one place to another —**gravimetrical** *adj* —**gravimetrically** *adv*

gravimetry /grə vímmətri/ *n* **1** the measurement of density or weight **2** the measurement of variations in the strength of the Earth's gravitational field from one place to another

graving dock *n* SHIPPING = **dry dock** [< GRAVE[5]]

gravitas /grávvi tass, -taas/ *n* a serious and solemn attitude or way of behaving [Early 20C. < Latin (see GRAVITY).]

gravitate /grávvi tayt/ (**-tates, -tating, -tated**) *v* **1** *vi* to move gradually and steadily to or towards somebody or something as if drawn by some force or attraction ○ *guests slowly gravitating to the kitchen* **2** *vti* to move or cause something to move under the influence of the force of gravity [Mid-17C. < modern Latin *gravitat-*, past participle of *gravitare* < Latin *gravitas* (see GRAVITY).] —**gravitater** *n* —**gravitative** *adj*

gravitation /grávvi táysh'n/ *n* **1** a gradual and steady movement to or towards somebody or something as if drawn by some force or attraction **2** the mutual force of attraction between all particles or bodies that have mass —**gravitational** *adj* —**gravitationally** *adv*

gravitational constant *n* the numerical factor relating force, mass, and distance in Newton's theory of gravitation

gravitational field *n* the region of space around an object that has mass, within which another object that has mass experiences the force of attraction

gravitational lens *n* a large astronomical object such as a galaxy whose gravitational field focuses or distorts the light from another object beyond it

gravitational redshift *n* the displacement of the spectrum of light emitted by an astronomical object towards longer wavelengths (**redshift**) because of the difference between the gravitational potential at the observer and source

gravitational wave *n* a hypothetical wave, predicted by relativity theory, that travels at the speed of light and propagates a gravitational field

graviton /grávvi ton/ *n* a hypothetical particle with zero charge and rest mass that is considered to be the quantum particle of the gravitational interaction [Mid-20C. < GRAVITATION.]

gravity /grávvəti/ *n* **1 GRAVITATIONAL FORCE** the attraction due to gravitation that the Earth or another astronomical object exerts on an object on or near its surface **2** PHYS = **gravitation** *n.* 2 **3 SERIOUSNESS** the serious nature of something because, e.g., of the worrying or significant consequences it has or could have **4 SERIOUS BEHAVIOUR** solemnity and seriousness in somebody's attitude or behaviour **5 HEAVINESS** the quality of being heavy **6 WEIGHT** the heaviness of something (*formal*) [15C. Via French < Latin *gravitas* 'heaviness' < *gravis* 'heavy'.]

gravity feed *n* a mechanism or process for supplying something such as fuel to a boiler or materials to a manufacturing process by their downward movement under the influence of gravity —**gravity-fed** *adj*

gravity wave *n* PHYS = **gravitational wave**

gravlax /gráv laks/, **gravadlax** /grávvəd-/ *n* a Scandinavian dish consisting of thin slices of dried salmon marinated in sugar, salt, pepper, and herbs [Mid-20C. < Swedish or Norwegian *gravlaks* 'buried salmon' (because originally marinated in a hole in the ground).]

gravure /grə vyoōr, -vyáwr/ *n* **1** PRINTING = **intaglio** *n.* 4 **2** a plate used in or a print produced by intaglio printing **3** PRINTING = **photogravure** [Late 19C. < French, < *graver* 'engrave'.]

gravy /gráyvi/ (*plural* **-vies**) *n* the juices produced by meat while it is being roasted, fried, or grilled, or a sauce made with these juices or another liquid and poured over cooked meat and vegetables [14C. < Old French *grave.*]

gravy boat *n* a small jug, usually long and narrow, in which gravy and other sauces are served

gravy ring *n* *Ireland* a doughnut

gravy train *n* a way of getting a large amount of money or other benefits for very little effort (*informal*) ○ *scrambling to get on the gravy train*

gray[1] *adj, n* US = **grey**

gray[2] /gray/ *n* (*symbol* **Gy**) the derived SI unit for the absorbed dose of ionizing radiation, equal to an absorption of 1 joule per kilogram [After L. H. *Gray* (1905–65), English radiobiologist.]

Gray /gray/, **Thomas** (1716–71) British poet

grayling /gráyling/ (*plural* **-lings** *or* **-ling**) *n* **1 FISH RESEMBLING TROUT** a freshwater fish with silvery scales and a large dorsal fin, valued as a game fish. Native to: Russia, China. Genus: *Thymallus.* **2 GRAYLING AS FOOD** the flesh of a grayling used as food **3 EUROPEAN BUTTERFLY** a common grey European butterfly. *Eumenis semele.*

graymail *n* US = **greymail**

gray scale *n* a printed scale for a range of shades of grey for text and graphics

Graz /graats/ city in SE Austria. Population: 237,810 (1991).

graze[1] /grayz/ (**grazes, grazing, grazed**) *v* **1** *vti* **EAT GRASS IN FIELDS** to eat grass and other green plants in a field or fields **2** *vt* **ALLOW ANIMALS TO EAT GRASS** to allow animals such as cows and sheep to eat grass in fields ○ *Her ranch now grazes 100,000 head of cattle.* **3** *vt* **USE LAND FOR FEEDING ANIMALS** to allow animals such as cows and sheep to eat the grass and green plants of a particular field or fields ○ *We usually graze those two fields over there.* **4** *vi* **EAT SNACKS** to eat snacks throughout the day instead of proper meals, especially while working (*slang*) **5** *vi* **EAT FOOD IN**

SUPERMARKET to eat food from the shelves of a supermarket while shopping without subsequently paying for it at the checkout (*slang*) **6** *vi* CHANGE TV CHANNELS to switch television channels frequently without watching much of any programme (*slang*) **7** *vi* KEEP STOPPING AND STARTING to perform an activity in a desultory manner, e.g. by picking up and putting down magazines without reading much of any one (*slang*) [Old English *grasian* < *græs* (see GRASS)] —**grazeable** *adj* —**grazer** *n*

graze[2] /grayz/ *v* (**grazes, grazing, grazed**) **1** *vti* TOUCH SOMETHING LIGHTLY to touch against the surface of something lightly in passing **2** *vt* BREAK THE SKIN SLIGHTLY to damage the surface of the skin of a part of the body slightly when it is rubbed against something rough and hard ■ *n* **1** SLIGHT BREAK IN SKIN slight and shallow damage to the skin caused by rubbing against something rough and hard **2** TOUCH the act of rubbing something or touching it lightly ○ *the graze of a bullet* [Late 16C. < ?]

grazier /gráyzi ər/ *n* **1** an owner of cattle that are raised and fattened for market **2** *Aus* a large-scale farmer who raises sheep or cattle

grazing /gráyzing/ *n* **1** FOOD FOR COWS AND SHEEP grass and green plants for animals such as cows and sheep to eat **2** LAND WITH GRASS land with grass suitable for animals such as cows and sheep to feed on **3** EATING OF SNACKS the eating of snacks throughout the day instead of proper meals, especially while working (*slang*) **4** EATING OF FOOD IN SUPERMARKET the eating of food from the shelves of a supermarket while shopping without subsequently paying for it at the checkout (*slang*) **5** CHANGING OF TV CHANNELS the switching of television channels frequently without watching much of any programme (*slang*) **6** FREQUENTLY STOPPING AND STARTING performing an activity in a desultory manner, e.g. by picking up and putting down magazines without reading much of any one (*slang*)

grazioso /grátsi ósső, graa-/ *adv* in a graceful way (*musical direction*) [Early 19C. < Italian.] —**grazioso** *adj*

grease *n* /greess/ **1** ANIMAL FAT thick soft animal fat, e.g. from cooked meat **2** THICK LUBRICANT a thick oily substance, especially one used to make machinery run smoothly **3** OIL FOR HAIR an oily substance used as a cosmetic for the hair **4** OILY WOOL untreated wool from sheep that still contains its natural oils, or the natural oils in this wool **5** BRIBERY bribes or bribery (*slang*) **6** LONG-HAIRED MOTORCYCLISTS long-haired motorcyclists considered collectively (*dated slang insult*) ■ *vt* /greess, greez/ (**greases, greasing, greased**) **1** PUT GREASE ON to put grease on something, e.g. in order to make it move smoothly or to stop something else sticking to it **2** MAKE EASIER OR QUICKER to make something such as progress or promotion easier or quicker (*informal*) ○ *His mother's money certainly greased his path to the boardroom.* [13C. Via Anglo-Norman *grece* < Latin *crassus* 'fat, thick'.] ◇ **grease somebody's palm** *or* **hand** to bribe somebody to do something (*informal*)

greaseball /gréess bawl/ *n* an offensive term for somebody habitually dirty or unkempt who has greasy hair (*slang insult*)

grease gun *n* a hand-held device for forcing grease into machinery to lubricate it

grease monkey *n* an offensive term for a mechanic, especially one who works on motor vehicles or aircraft (*slang insult*)

greasepaint /gréess paynt/ *n* a thick, greasy, or waxy form of coloured make-up used by actors

grease pencil *n* a pencil containing a core of a waxy coloured substance that can write on glossy surfaces

greaseproof /gréess proof/ *adj* not allowing oil or grease to soak into it or pass through it

greaseproof paper *n* paper that does not allow oil or grease to soak into it or pass through it. Use: in cooking, preparing, or wrapping food. US term **wax paper**

greaser /gréessər, greézər/ *n* **1** MECHANIC somebody whose job involves greasing machinery, especially a mechanic who works on motor vehicles or a ship's engineer (*slang*) **2** LONG-HAIRED MOTORCYCLIST a usually young, long-haired, leather-jacketed motorcyclist, especially a member of a motorcycle gang (*slang insult*) **3** SOMEBODY WHO TRIES TO GAIN FAVOUR a flatterer or groveller who tries to gain the favour or approval of a superior (*slang insult*)

greasewood /gréess wòod/ *n* **1** a spiny desert bush that yields an oil used as fuel. Native to: W North America. *Sarcobatus vermiculatus.* **2** a bush that is similar to or related to the greasewood, e.g. the creosote bush

greasy /gréessi, greézi/ (**-ier, -iest**) *adj* **1** MADE OF GREASE consisting of grease or something with the consistency of grease **2** THICK WITH GREASE covered with or containing grease, often a lot of grease or too much of it **3** HAVING EXCESSIVE NATURAL OILS producing or containing a lot of natural oils **4** PRODUCED BY GREASE caused by grease or something with the consistency of grease **5** SLIPPERY difficult to move, walk, or drive on because of wetness or iciness **6** SMARMY unpleasantly and insincerely flattering, friendly, or grovelling —**greasily** *adv* —**greasiness** *n*

greasy spoon *n* a small, cheap, and often dirty café, especially one that serves fried food (*informal*)

great /grayt/ *adj* **1** IMPRESSIVELY LARGE very large and impressive **2** LARGE IN NUMBER large in number or with many parts ○ *a great crowd of well-wishers* **3** BIGGER THAN OTHERS larger or more important than others of the same kind **4** MUCH extreme or more than usual ○ *It gives me great pleasure to introduce our speaker tonight.* **5** LASTING A LONG TIME lasting a long time, or covering a long distance **6** IMPORTANT very significant or important **7** EXCEPTIONALLY TALENTED with exceptional talents or achievements **8** POWERFUL powerful and influential **9** EXPERT able to do something very well (*informal*) ○ *Alice is great at spelling.* **10** VERY GOOD very good or pleasing (*informal*) ○ *It was great to hear your news.* **11** USEFUL very useful or suitable for a particular task (*informal*) ○ *This cast-iron pan is great for doing pancakes.* **12** BEING A GOOD EXAMPLE doing something often, enjoying something very much, or being a very good example of something ○ *Joe's a great one for the soaps – he never misses an episode.* **13** USED FOR EMPHASIS used to emphasize how much of a quality somebody or something has (*informal*) ○ *Their new house is a great big place out in the country.* ○ *I can't wear this – there's a dirty great hole in the front!* ■ *n* **1** SOMEBODY GREAT somebody whose fame or influence has proved to be long-lasting ○ *one of the all-time greats of blues music* **2** PART OF PIPE ORGAN the principal division of a pipe organ ■ *adv* VERY WELL very well (*informal*) ○ *That's it; you're doing great.* [Old English *grēat* 'thick, coarse' < Germanic] —**greatly** *adv* —**greatness** *n*

LITERARY LINK ***The Great Gatsby***, a novel (1925) by US writer F. Scott Fitzgerald. Set on Long Island, New York, it is the story of enigmatic businessman Jay Gatsby, a symbol of the American obsession with wealth and status whose attempts to revive a relationship with an old girlfriend lead to his downfall.

---

great- *prefix* **1** being a parent of somebody's grandparent **2** being a child of one of somebody's grandchildren

great ape *n* a large ape such as a gorilla, chimpanzee, or orang-utan

Great Attractor *n* a large aggregation of galaxies, approximately 150 to 350 million light-years away, whose gravitational pull might account for the unexpected motions of many galaxies including our own

great auk *n* a large flightless sea bird that was native to N Atlantic coasts until it was hunted to extinction in the middle of the 19th century. *Alca impennis.*

great-aunt *n* an aunt of somebody's father or mother

Great Australian Bight inlet of the Indian Ocean stretching 1,100 km/685 mi. from Cape Pasley in Western Australia to Cape Carnot in South Australia

Great Barrier Reef chain of coral reefs in the Coral Sea, off the coast of Queensland, Australia. Length: 2,010 km/1,250 mi. Area: 348,600 sq. km/134,600 sq. mi.

Great Basin drainage area covering most of Nevada and parts of Utah, Oregon, Idaho, and California. Area: 543,900 sq. km/210,000 sq. mi.

Great Bear *n* ASTRON = **Ursa Major**

Great Bear Lake freshwater lake in northwestern mainland Northwest Territories, Canada, lying astride the Arctic Circle. Area: 31,790 sq. km/12,270 sq. mi.

great blue heron *n* a large heron with greyish-blue plumage. Native to: North America. *Ardea herodias.*

Great Britain island of NW Europe, comprising England, Scotland, and Wales

great circle *n* a circle on the surface of a sphere such as the Earth that has a radius equal to the radius of the sphere, and whose centre is also the sphere's centre. ◊ **small circle**

greatcoat /gráyt kōt/ *n* a long thick heavy overcoat worn especially by soldiers

great crested grebe *n* a large diving waterfowl with no tail and a ruff on its head that is expanded during courtship rituals. Native to: Europe, Africa, Asia, Australia. *Podiceps cristatus.*

Great Dane *n* a very large dog with long legs, a square head and deep muzzle, and short hair, belonging to a breed originating in Germany [Because Germans were formerly called Danes]

Great Depression *n* a drastic decline in the world economy resulting in mass unemployment and widespread poverty that lasted from 1929 until 1939

great divide *n* **1** a major demarcation between two contrasting things, especially life and death **2** the boundary between life and death

Great Divide *n* GEOG = **Continental Divide**

Great Dividing Range system of mountain ranges and plateaus extending along the coast of E Australia. Highest peak: Mount Kosciusko 2,228 m/7,310 ft.

Greater Antilles /gráytər an tílleez/ island group in the Caribbean Sea, comprising Cuba, Jamaica, Hispaniola, and Puerto Rico, and forming the central island chain of the West Indies

Greater Bairam *n* an Islamic festival marking the end of the Islamic year. Date: seventy days after the end of Ramadan.

greater celandine *n* a plant of the poppy family that yields an orange-coloured latex used to treat eye and skin disorders. Flowers: yellow. *Chelidonium majus.* US term **celandine** *n.* **2**

Greater Sunda Islands /-súndə-/ ♦ **Sunda Islands**

greatest common divisor *n* MATH = **highest common factor**

~~**greatful**~~ incorrect spelling of **grateful**

Great Glen rift valley in Scotland, extending from the Moray Firth to Loch Linnhe. Length: 156 km/97 mi.

great-grandchild *n* a son or daughter of your grandchild

great-granddaughter *n* a daughter of your grandchild

great-grandfather *n* the father of your grandmother or grandfather

great-grandmother *n* the mother of your grandmother or grandfather

great-grandparent *n* the mother or father of your grandmother or grandfather

great-grandson *n* a son of your grandchild

great-hearted *adj* **1** with a generous and forgiving nature **2** not easily frightened or dispirited —**great-heartedly** *adv*

Great Indian Desert = **Thar Desert**

Great Karoo ♦ **Karoo**

Great Lake largest natural freshwater lake in Australia, on Tasmania. Area: 114 sq. km/44 sq. mi.

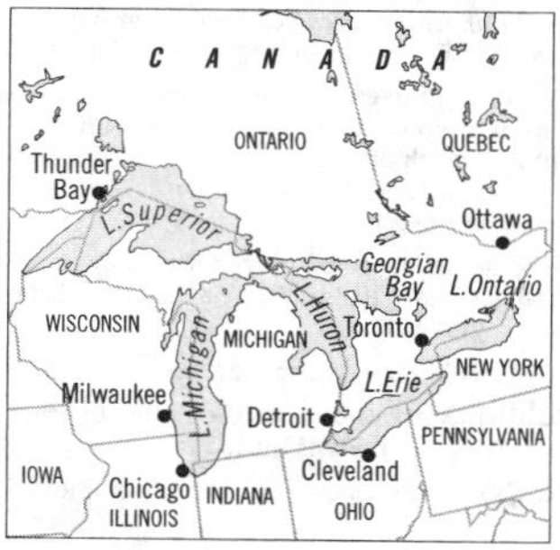

Great Lakes

Great Lakes group of five freshwater lakes in north-central North America, including Lakes Superior, Michigan, Huron, Erie, and Ontario. Area: 244,100 sq. km/94,250 sq. mi.

Great Leap Forward *n* the attempt by the People's Republic of China from 1958 to 1960 to modernize agriculture by labour-intensive methods

great-nephew *n* a son of somebody's nephew or niece

great-niece *n* a daughter of somebody's nephew or niece

great organ *n* the main keyboard of an organ, and the pipes and mechanism relating to it. ◊ **choir organ**

Great Plains vast grassland region in central North America, stretching from central Canada to S Texas. Area: 3,200,000 sq. km/1,200,000 sq. mi.

Great Power *n* a nation that has a far-reaching political, social, economic, and usually military influence internationally (*hyphenated before nouns*)

Great Rebellion *n* the Royalists' name for the English Civil War

Great Rift Valley depression extending more than 4,830 km/3,000 mi. from the valley of the River Jordan in Syria to Mozambique

Great Russian *n* (*dated*) 1 the Russian language 2 a member of the main Russian-speaking ethnic group in Russia —**Great Russian** *adj*

Great St Bernard Pass /-sənt búrnard-, -sán bər naárd-/ mountain pass in W Europe, on the border between Switzerland and Italy. Height: 2,468 m/8,090 ft.

Great Salt Lake shallow body of salt water in NW Utah. Area: 5,200 sq. km/2,000 sq. mi.

Great Sandy Desert desert in NW Australia. Area: 390,000 sq. km/150,000 sq. mi.

Great Schism *n* 1 the period between 1378 and 1415 when there were rival popes, one reigning in Rome and the other in Avignon 2 the separation of the Roman Catholic and Eastern Orthodox churches in 1054, as a result of theological disagreement

Great Seal *n* in the United Kingdom, the seal kept in the charge of the Lord Chancellor or, formerly, the Lord Keeper of the Seal, and used in sealing important state papers

great skua *n* a large brown predatory seabird that feeds on fish, eggs, and other adult birds. Native to: N Atlantic. *Catharacta skua.*

Great Slave Lake freshwater lake in the S Northwest Territories, Canada. Area: 28,570 sq. km/11,030 sq. mi.

Great Smoky Mountains National Park national park in SE United States, in W North Carolina and E Tennessee. Area: 2,106 sq. km/813 sq. mi.

great tit *n* a large great tit with a short bill and yellow, black, and white markings. Native to: Europe, Asia. *Parus major.*

Great Trek *n* a mass movement between 1836 and 1844 of Boer cattlemen in South Africa from the Cape to the north that eventually resulted in the establishment of the Transvaal and the Orange Free State

great-uncle *n* an uncle of your father or mother

Great Victoria Desert desert of Western Australia and South Australia. Area: 390,000 sq. km/150,000 sq. mi.

Great Wall *n* 1 a huge expanse of thousands of galaxies arranged in a supercluster that forms the largest system of astronomical objects observed in the universe 2 HIST = **Great Wall of China**

Great Wall of China *n* a vast Chinese defensive fortification begun in the 3rd century BC and running along the northern border of the country for 2400 km/1500 mi

Great War *n* HIST = **World War I**

great white shark *n* a large shark that is grey-brown with white underparts and preys on large fish, marine mammals, and carrion. Native to: warm and tropical waters. *Carcharodon carcharias.*

Great Yarmouth /-yaármath/ port in E England. Population: 56,190 (1991).

great year *n* a period of about 25,800 years, representing a complete cycle of the precession of the equinoxes

greave /greev/ *n* a piece of armour worn from the ankle to the knee (*usually plural*) [14C. < Old French *greve* 'calf, shin'.]

grebe /greeb/ (*plural* **grebes** *or* **grebe**) *n* a freshwater diving bird with lobed toes that is a strong swimmer. Family: Podicipedidae. [Mid-18C. < French *grebe*.]

Grecian /greésh'n/ *adj* 1 relating to the ancient Greek style of architecture or sculpture 2 PEOPLES = **Greek** *adj.* 1 ■ *n* 1 a Hellenist (*dated*) 2 LANG = **Greek** *n.* 1 — **Grecianize** *vt*

Grecism *n* = Graecism

Grecize *vt* = Graecize

Greco /grékô/, **El** (1541–1614) Greek-born Spanish painter. Born **Domenikos Theotokopoulos**

Greco- *prefix* = Graeco-

Greco-Roman *adj* HIST, ARTS, WRESTLING = **Graeco-Roman**

Greece

Greece /greess/ country in SE Europe, comprising the southernmost part of the Balkan Peninsula and numerous islands in the E Mediterranean. Capital: Athens. Population: 10,493,000 (1996). Area: 131,957 sq. km/50,949 sq. mi.

greed /greed/ *n* 1 the habit of eating to excess, or the desire to do so 2 an overwhelming desire to have more of something such as money than is actually needed [Late 16C. Back-formation < GREEDY.]

greedy /greédi/ (**-ier, -iest**) *adj* 1 eating to excess, or wanting to do so 2 having an overwhelming desire to have more of something such as money than is actually needed [Old English *grǣdig* < Germanic, 'hunger, greed'] — **greedily** *adv* —**greediness** *n*

greedyguts /greédi guts/ (*plural* **-guts**) *n* a greedy eater (*informal insult*)

greegree *n* ANTHROP = **grigri**

Greek /greek/ *n* 1 SOMEBODY FROM GREECE somebody who comes from Greece 2 LANGUAGE OF GREECE the official language of Greece and part of Cyprus. Native speakers: 12 million. 3 LANG = **Ancient Greek** ■ *adj* 1 OF GREECE OR GREEKS relating to Greece or its people, language, or culture 2 OF GREEK ORTHODOX CHURCH relating to the Greek Orthodox Church [Old English *grecas*, via Latin *Graecus* < Greek *Graikos* 'the Hellenic people'] ◊ **beware of Greeks bearing gifts** be careful of possible treachery from somebody who appears to be kind (*offensive in some contexts*) ◊ **it's (all) Greek to me** used to say that you cannot understand something

Greek Catholic *n* 1 a member of the Eastern Orthodox Church 2 a member of the Uniat Greek Church

Greek Church *n* CHR = **Greek Orthodox Church** *n.* 1

Greek cross *n* a cross consisting of four arms of the same length

Greek key *n* an ornate pattern for a cornice or border consisting of lines that change direction at right angles to form a continuous band

Greek Orthodox Church *n* 1 the national church of Greece, an independent section of the Eastern Orthodox Church 2 CHR = **Orthodox Church**

Greek salad *n* a salad of tomatoes, lettuce, cucumber, olives, oregano, and feta cheese

green /green/ *adj* 1 GRASS-COLOURED of a colour in the spectrum between yellow and blue, like the colour of grass 2 HAVING EDIBLE GREEN LEAVES consisting of or containing green leaves of vegetables ○ *a green salad* 3 GRASSY consisting of or containing grass, plants, or foliage 4 **green, Green** ADVOCATING PROTECTION OF THE ENVIRONMENT supporting or promoting the protection of the environment 5 MADE WITH LITTLE ENVIRONMENTAL HARM produced in an environmentally and ecologically friendly way, e.g. by using renewable resources 6 NOT RIPE unripe or not mature ○ *green bananas* 7 UNSMOKED still raw, not yet smoked 8 UNSEASONED describes newly cut and still unseasoned wood 9 UNTANNED describes leather that is not yet tanned 10 UNFIRED describes objects that are not yet fired 11 JEALOUS envious or jealous 12 SICKLY-LOOKING pale and sickly-looking, especially as a result of nausea

13 INNOCENT naive and lacking in experience, especially because of being new to something 14 NEW young, new, recent, or fresh ■ *n* 1 THE COLOUR OF GRASS a primary colour between yellow and blue in the spectrum, like the colour of grass 2 GREEN COLOURING a green pigment or dye 3 GREEN CLOTH green fabric or clothing 4 SOMETHING GREEN a green object 5 GRASSY AREA an area of ground that is covered with grass, especially a public or communal area 6 *Scotland* GRASSY AREA BELONGING TO HOUSE an area of grass belonging to a house or block of flats 7 GRASSY AREA FOR BOWLING an area of grass that is maintained for bowling and similar games 8 GRASSY AREA SURROUNDING A GOLF HOLE the closely mown area at the end of a fairway on a golf course on which the hole for the ball is located 9 FOLIAGE foliage used for decoration. US term **greens** *npl.* 2 10 **green, Green** ADVOCATE OF PROTECTION OF ENVIRONMENT a supporter or advocate of protecting the environment, especially a member of a political party concerned with environmental issues 11 US MONEY cash or paper money (*slang*) ■ *v* 1 *vti* BECOME GREEN to become green, or make something green 2 *vt* PLANT TREES IN to plant trees and develop parks in urban areas 3 *vti* BECOME AN ENVIRONMENTAL ADVOCATE to become, or make somebody become, aware of environmental issues [Old English *grene* < Germanic] —**greenish** *adj* —**greenly** *adv* —**greenness** *n* ◊ **go green** to become actively interested in environmental issues and support environmental causes

green alga *n* an alga found mostly in fresh water. Division: *Chlorophyta.*

greenback /green bak/ *n* US a US bank note of any denomination (*slang*)

Green Bay city in NE Wisconsin, on the southern shore of Lake Michigan. Population: 102,708 (1994).

green bean *n* a bean such as a French bean or runner bean that is eaten complete with its pod

green belt /green bélt/ *n* 1 a strip of undeveloped land around a city that cannot be built on because of government legislation preventing urban sprawl 2 an irrigated area of land on the edge of a desert, designed to prevent any further encroachment by the desert

Green Beret *n* (*informal*) 1 a British commando 2 a US Special Forces soldier [< the regulation green beret worn by members]

greenbottle /green bot'l/, **greenbottle fly** *n* a fly that is metallic green in colour and lays its eggs in rotting vegetation or flesh. Genus: *Lucilia.*

greenbrier /green brī ər/ *n* a trailing or climbing woody plant, often prickly, belonging to the lily family. Native to: tropical and temperate regions. Genus: *Smilax.*

green card *n* 1 US IDENTITY CARD in the United States, an identity card and work permit issued to nationals of other countries 2 DRIVING INSURANCE DOCUMENT an insurance document for motorists driving abroad 3 BRITISH DISABLED PERSON'S IDENTITY CARD in the United Kingdom, an identity card issued by the government to a disabled person —**green-carder** *n*

Greene /green/, **Graham** (1904–91) British writer

green earth *n* ART = **terre verte**

greenery /greénəri/ *n* 1 growing green foliage and plants 2 green leaves and small branches from trees and shrubs used for decoration

green-eyed monster *n* jealousy or envy

greenfield /green feeld/ *adj* 1 relating to or situated in a piece of open land that has not been built on 2 involving a completely fresh or radically new approach, not based on anything that has gone before

greenfinch /green finch/ (*plural* **-finches** *or* **-finch**) *n* a green-grey and yellow finch. Native to: Europe. *Carduelis chloris.*

green fingers *npl* a natural ability to make plants grow well. ◊ **green thumb** —**green-fingered** *adj*

greenfly /green flī/ (*plural* **-flies** *or* **-fly**) *n* a green winged aphid that is a pest of garden plants, houseplants, and crops

greengage /green gayj/ *n* 1 a sweet green plum 2 a tree that produces greengages. *Prunus domestica italica.* [Early 18C. After Sir William *Gage* (1657–1727), English botanist.]

greengrocer /green grōssər/ *n* 1 FRUIT AND VEGETABLE SELLER a dealer in fresh fruit and vegetables. ◊ **grocer** *n.* 1 2 **greengrocer, greengrocer's** (*plural* **-cer's**) FRUIT AND VEGETABLE SHOP a shop that sells fresh fruits and vegetables. ◊ **grocer** n. **2 3 AUSTRALIAN CICADA** a large bright-green Australian cicada. *Cyclochila australasiae*.

greengrocery /green grŏssəri/ n (*plural* **-ies**) **1** COMM = **greengrocer** n. **2 2** the trade or profession of a greengrocer ■ **greengroceries** npl fresh fruit and vegetables sold by a greengrocer

greenhead /green hed/ n a male mallard duck

greenheart /green haart/ (*plural* **-hearts** or **-heart**) n **1** an evergreen tree of the laurel family with dark greenish wood. Native to: tropical America. *Ocotea rodiaei*. **2** any tree similar to the greenheart

greenhorn /green hawrn/ n a naive and unsophisticated person

SYNONYMS See *beginner*.

greenhouse /green howss/ (*plural* **-houses** /-howziz/) n a glass or transparent plastic structure, often on a metal or wooden frame, in which plants that need heat, light, and protection from the elements are grown

greenhouse effect n warming of the Earth's surface as a result of atmospheric pollution by gases

greenhouse gas n a gas such as carbon dioxide, ozone, or water vapour that contributes to the warming of the Earth's atmosphere by reflecting radiation from the Earth's surface

greenie /green i/ n Aus a conservationist or environmentalist (*informal; often considered offensive*)

greening /green ing/ n **1 APPLE THAT IS GREEN WHEN RIPE** an apple that is green when ripe **2** the process of planting trees and other vegetation in an area **3** the process of becoming more aware, or increasing others' awareness, of the environment and environmental issues

green keeper n somebody who manages and maintains a golf course or bowling green. US term **greenskeeper**

Greenland

Greenland /green land/ island of Denmark, in the North Atlantic and Arctic oceans, off NE Canada. Population: 58,000 (1996). Area: 2,175,600 sq. km/840,000 sq. mi. — **Greenlander** n

Greenlandic /green lándik/ n a dialect of Inuit spoken in Greenland. Native speakers: 160,000. ■ adj relating to Greenland or its language, people, or culture

Greenland Sea section of the Atlantic Ocean off NE Greenland that is covered by pack ice for most of the year

green light n **1** a light that is green in colour and is used as a signal at intersections for vehicles or pedestrians to proceed **2** permission to start work on something, especially a project or plan

greenlight /green lĭt/ vt US to give approval or permission for something to proceed (*informal*)

greenling /green ling/ (*plural* **-lings** or **-ling**) n a fish with large pectoral fins, a large head, and a skin flap over each eye. Native to: N Pacific coastal waters. Family: Hexagrammidae.

greenmail /green mayl/ n the purchase of enough of a company's shares to threaten it with takeover, thereby forcing the company to buy back the stock at a higher price to avoid the takeover. ◊ **blackmail** n. **1**, **greymail** ■ vt to subject a company to greenmail [Late 20C. < GREEN 'money' + BLACKMAIL.] —**greenmailer** n

green man n an illuminated green symbol of a walking man at a pedestrian crossing that indicates that it is safe to cross

green manure n a growing crop that is ploughed directly back into the soil to act as a fertilizer

green monkey n a small olive green monkey that lives in large troops in woodlands or on the edge of savanna grasslands. Native to: Africa. *Cercopithecus aethiops sabaeus*.

green monkey disease n MED = **Marburg disease**

Green Mountains mountain range in the Appalachian system

Greenock /green ək/ seaport on the Firth of Clyde. Population: 50,013 (1991).

greenockite /green ə kīt/ n a yellowish crystalline mineral consisting of cadmium sulphide [Mid-18C. After Charles Murray Cathcart, Lord *Greenock* (1783–1859).]

green paper n in the United Kingdom or Canada, a document that contains the government's policy proposals that are to be discussed in Parliament. ◊ **white paper**

Green Party n a political party whose primary policy is the protection of the environment

Greenpeace /green peess/ n an international organization that advocates the protection of the environment and takes nonviolent action to achieve its aims

green pepper n an unripe sweet pepper eaten raw or cooked. *Capsicum annuum*. ◊ **red pepper**

green plover n BIRDS = **lapwing**

green pound n the British pound as a unit of exchange in trading farm produce from the European Union under the Common Agricultural Policy

green revolution n the introduction of modern farming techniques and higher-yielding, more pest-resistant varieties of crops in order to significantly increase crop production

greenroom /green room, -rŏŏm/ n a room in a studio, theatre, or concert hall where performers may relax before or after a performance or appearance

greens /greenz/ npl **1** vegetables with green leaves and stems, e.g. cabbage and spinach **2** US = **green** n. **9 3** US green clothing, e.g. US Army uniforms or operating room scrubs (*informal*)

greensand /green sand/ n sandstone flecked with the dark-green clay mineral glauconite

greenshank /green shangk/ (*plural* **-shanks** or **-shank**) n a large sandpiper with long greenish legs. Native to: Europe, Asia. *Tringa nebularia*.

greensickness /green siknəss/ n MED = **chlorosis** n. **2** — **greensick** adj

greenskeeper /greenz keepər/ n US SPORTS = **green keeper**

green snake n a snake that is yellow-green in colour and feeds on insects, especially grasshoppers. Native to: North America. Genus: *Opheodryas*.

greenstick fracture n a bone fracture usually occurring in children, in which one side of the bone is broken and the other side is bent [< GREEN 'immature' + STICK[1] because it resembles one]

greenstone /green stōn/ n **1** a green igneous rock containing the minerals feldspar and hornblende **2** a dark New Zealand jade. Use: Maori weapons, jewellery.

greenstrip /green strip/ n US a firebreak on open grassland, planted with vegetation that does not burn easily

greensward /green swawrd/ n a grass-covered area (*archaic or literary*)

greentailing /green tayling/ n environmentally responsible retailing that involves the sale of products with the least impact on the environment or that increases the ecological awareness of the consumer (*informal*) [< GREEN + *retailing*]

green tea n tea made from leaves that have been dried but not fermented, pale green in colour

green thumb n US, Can = **green fingers**

green turtle n a large marine turtle of warm waters, sometimes killed for food. *Chelonia mydas*. [< its green shell]

green vitriol n CHEM = **ferrous sulphate**

greenware /green wair/ n dry clay pieces before they have been fired

greenway /green way/ n US a stretch of undeveloped land close to an urban area that is kept for recreational use

Greenway /green way/, **Francis Howard** (1777–1837) British-born Australian architect

green-wellie adj relating to rich upper-class British people who enjoy country pursuits (*informal*) [< the stereotype of the clothing worn by such people]

Greenwich /grénnich, -ij/ borough of London, on the River Thames, site of the prime meridian, which passes through the Royal Greenwich Observatory. Population: 211,410 (1995).

Greenwich Mean Time n the time in a zone that includes the 0° meridian of Greenwich, London, used formerly as the main standard from which the time in other zones was calculated

Greenwich Village n a residential area in lower Manhattan, once popular with bohemians, artists, and writers and now a tourist attraction

greenwood /green wŏŏd/ n a forest or woods in the summer when the leaves are green (*archaic*)

green woodpecker n a large woodpecker with green feathers and a red crown that often feeds on the ground. Native to: Europe. *Picus viridis*.

Greer /greer/, **Germaine** (b. 1939) Australian writer and feminist

greet[1] /greet/ vt **1 WELCOME** to welcome somebody in a cordial and usually conventional way **2 ADDRESS COURTEOUSLY** to address somebody in a polite and usually conventional way on meeting **3 ADDRESS IN A LETTER** to address a person or group at the start of a letter using a set formula **4 REPLY TO** to receive or respond to something in a particular way ○ *The news was greeted with dismay*. **5 BECOME NOTICEABLE TO** to become perceptible to somebody, especially by way of the senses such as vision, hearing, or smell ○ *The smell of a cake baking greeted them*. [Old English *gretan* < W Germanic, 'resound']

greet[2] /greet/ vi Scotland (*nonstandard*) **1** to cry or weep **2** to complain whiningly [Old English *grētan* and *grēotan* 'cry' < Germanic] —**greet** n

greeter /greetər/ n somebody employed to greet customers in a restaurant or similar business

greeting /greeting/ n **1 FRIENDLY GESTURE** a cordial and often conventional gesture or expression used when welcoming, meeting, or addressing somebody **2 WELCOMING** an act of welcoming or addressing somebody with a greeting ■ **greetings** npl MESSAGE a friendly message or good wishes

greetings card n a folded piece of heavy paper with an image or design and a message to somebody to mark a special occasion

gregarine /gréggə reen/ n a protozoan that lives as a parasite in the digestive tracts of some insects, arthropods, annelids, and other invertebrates. Order: Gregarinida. ■ adj **gregarine, gregarinian** relating to or belonging to the order that comprises the gregarines [Mid-19C. < modern Latin *Gregarina* < Latin *gregarius* (see GREGARIOUS).]

gregarious /gri gáiri əss/ adj **1 FRIENDLY** very friendly and sociable **2 LIVING COMMUNALLY** describes organisms that live in groups **3 GROWING TOGETHER** describes plants that grow in clusters [Mid-17C. < Latin *gregarius* < *grex* 'flock'.] —**gregariously** adv —**gregariousness** n

Gregg /greg/, **Sir Norman McAlister** (1892–1966) Australian ophthalmologist

Gregorian calendar /gri gáwri ən-/ n the calendar introduced in 1582 by Pope Gregory XIII that is still in use and is a modification of the previous Roman calendar. ◊ **Julian calendar**

Gregorian chant n a liturgical chant of the Roman Catholic Church that is sung without accompaniment [< its supposed introduction by GREGORY I]

Gregorian telescope n an astronomical telescope that has a concave primary mirror with a central hole through which light is reflected from a smaller secondary concave mirror [After J. *Gregory* (1638–75), Scottish mathematician.]

Gregory I /gréggəri/, **St** (540?–604) pope (590–604). Known as **Gregory the Great**

greisen /gríz'n/ n a granite-derived rock consisting of mica and quartz [Late 19C. < German, probably < *greis* 'grey with age'.]

gremlin /grémlin/ n a tiny imaginary mischievous creature that is blamed for faults in tools, machinery, and electronic equipment (*informal*) [Early 20C. Probably after GOBLIN.]

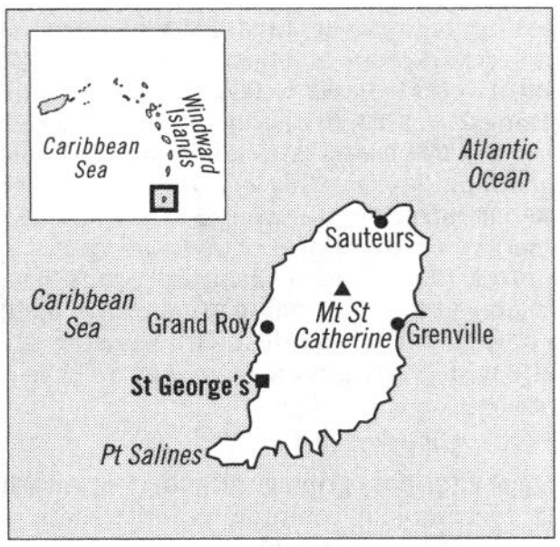

Grenada

Grenada /grə náydə/ state in the SE Caribbean Sea, comprising the island of Grenada and some of the S Grenadines. Capital: St George's. Population: 95,535 (1997). Area: 344 sq. km/133 sq. mi. —**Grenadian** *n, adj*

grenade /gri náyd/ *n* **1** a small bomb that is thrown by hand or shot from a rifle or other weapon **2** a sealed glass projectile that breaks on impact, releasing tear gas or chemicals to put out fires [Mid-16C. < French, alteration of *grenate* 'pomegranate' (shortening of *pome grenate*) after Spanish *granada*.]

grenadier /grénnə déer/ (*plural* **-diers** *or* **-dier**) *n* **1 GRENADE-CARRYING SOLDIER** formerly, a soldier armed with grenades **2 TALL STRONG SOLDIER** formerly, a soldier assigned to a special company of a regiment on the basis of exceptional height and ability **3 FISH** a bottom-dwelling sea fish with a tapering body and no tail fin. Family: Macrouridae. **4 FINCH** a finch with purple patches, a red beak, and a tapering tail. Native to: E Africa. *Uraeginthus ianthinogaster.* **5 WEAVERBIRD** a weaverbird with a black head and bright red plumage on its crown and back. Native to: Africa. *Euplectes orix.* [Late 17C. < French, < *grenade* (see GRENADE).]

Grenadier, Grenadier guard *n* a British soldier belonging to the first regiment of the Guards Division, the troops of the Royal Household ■ **Grenadiers** *npl* in the British army, the first regiment of the Guards Division, the troops of the Royal Household

grenadine[1] /grénnə deen/ *n* **1** a syrup made from pomegranates, used especially in cocktails **2** a reddish-orange colour [Late 19C. < French (*sirop de*) *grenadine* < *grenade* (see GRENADE).] —**grenadine** *adj*

grenadine[2] /grénnə deen/ *n* a gauzy silk or woollen dress fabric [Mid-19C. < French, 'silk with a texture like grain' < *grain* (see GRAIN).]

Grenoble /grə nṓb'l/ city in SE France. Population: 150,758 (1990).

grenz rays /grénz-/ *npl* low-energy X-rays produced by electrons accelerated through less than 25 kilovolts [< German *Grenze* 'boundary']

Gresham's law /gréshəmz-/, **Gresham's theorem** *n* the theory that bad money drives good money out of circulation because a currency of lower intrinsic value will be used whilst one of higher intrinsic value will be hoarded [Mid-19C. After Sir Thomas *Gresham* (1519?-79), founder of the Royal Exchange.]

Gretna Green /grétnə-/ village in SW Scotland, formerly the location of runaway marriages. Population: 3,149 (1991).

grevillea /grə vílli ə/ (*plural* **-leas** *or* **-lea**) *n* an ornamental evergreen tree or shrub. Native to: Australia, New Caledonia. Genus: *Grevillea.* [Mid-19C. < modern Latin, after Charles Francis *Greville* (1749–1809), Scottish horticulturist.]

grew past tense of **grow**

grey /gray/ *adj* **OF THE COLOUR OF ASH** of the colour of ash or lead ○ *a dull grey sky* ○ *city workers in grey suits* ■ *n* **1 COLOUR OF ASH** the colour of ash or lead **2 PIGMENT MADE FROM BLACK AND WHITE** a pigment or dye formed from a combination of black and white that is like the colour of ash or lead ○ *Use greys and blues to emphasize the mood.* **3 GREY CLOTHING** fabric or clothing that is grey in colour **4 grey, Grey CONFEDERATE SOLDIER** a soldier of the Confederacy in the American Civil War. ◊ **blue** *n.* **7 5 SOMETHING GREY** a grey object ■ *vi* **TURN GREY** to turn the colour grey ○ *His hair is greying.* [Old English *gr_æg* < Germanic] —**greyly** *adv* —**greyness** *n*

Grey /gray/, **Sir Edward, 1st Viscount Grey of Fallodon** (1862–1933) British statesman

Grey, Sir George Edward (1812–98) Portuguese-born British explorer and colonial administrator

Grey, Lady Jane (1537–54) queen of England (1553)

Grey, Zane (1872–1939) US writer of Westerns

grey area *n* **1 UNCLEAR SITUATION** a situation, subject, or category of something that is unclear or hard to define or classify **2 SOMETHING THAT CANNOT BE CLASSIFIED** a part of something that does not belong to any specific category but contains features of more than one **3 ECONOMICALLY DEPRESSED UK REGION** in the United Kingdom, a part of the country suffering from high unemployment

⚡**greybar land** /gráy baar-/ *n* the state of waiting for the grey bar graphic device on a computer screen slowly to fill up as a time-consuming computer process nears completion (*informal*)

greybeard /gráy beerd/ *n* **1** an elderly man (*dated*) **2** an earthenware container for alcohol —**greybearded** *adj*

grey eminence *n* = **éminence grise**

Grey Friar *n* a monk of the Franciscan order [< the colour of the order's habit]

greyhen /gráy hen/ (*plural* **-hens** *or* **-hen**) *n* a female black grouse

greyhound /gráy hownd/ *n* a tall slim fast-running dog with a smooth coat, narrow head, and long legs, widely used for racing [Old English *grīghund* < Germanic]

greyish /gráy ish/ *adj* slightly or somewhat grey in colour

grey jay *n* a bird of the crow family that is grey with black markings on the head and inhabits coniferous forests, especially spruce forests. Native to: North America. *Perisoreus canadensis.*

greylag /gráy lag/, **greylag goose** *n* a common wild goose that is light brownish-grey with a large orange or pink bill and is the ancestor of the domestic farm goose. Native to: Europe, Asia. *Anser anser.* [Early 18C. < GREY + dialect *lag* 'goose' < ?]

greymail /gráy mayl/ *n* a manoeuvre used by the defence in a spy trial whereby the government is threatened with the revelation of national secrets unless the case against the defendant is dropped [Late 20C. After BLACKMAIL.]

grey market *n* **1** trading in new shares before they have been officially issued on the stock exchange **2** clandestine but legal trading in goods either at excessively high prices or at prices well below the manufacturer's recommended price. ◊ **black market**

grey matter *n* **1** intelligence or brains (*informal*) **2** brownish-grey nerve tissue consisting mainly of nerve cell bodies within the brain and spinal cord. ◊ **white matter**

Greymouth /gráymәth/ town on the western coast of the South Island, New Zealand. Population: 10,250 (1998 estimate).

grey mullet *n* any fish of approximately 70 species worldwide, some of which are caught for food. Native to: tropical and temperate seas. Family: Mugilidae. US term **mullet** *n.* **2**

grey squirrel *n* a large tree squirrel that has grey fur with a reddish tinge in the legs and head. Native to: North America, Great Britain, Ireland, South Africa. *Sciurus carolinensis.* ◊ **red squirrel**

greywacke /gráy wakə/ *n* a conglomerate rock composed of well-rounded pebbles cemented by a sandy infill [Late 18C. < German *Grauwacke* 'grey sandstone'.]

grey water *n* waste water from sinks, baths, and kitchen appliances

greywether /gráy wethər/ *n* GEOL = **sarsen**

grey whale *n* a large baleen whale that has no dorsal fin but a line of bumps along part of its back. Native to: N Pacific coastal waters. *Eschrichtius gibbosus.*

grey wolf *n* a large intelligent highly social wild dog, varying in colour from white in the north of its range to black in the south. Native to: North America, Europe, Asia. *Canis lupus.*

gribble /gríbb'l/ *n* a small marine crustacean of the woodlouse family that burrows into submerged wooden structures. Genus: *Limnoria.* [Late 18C. < ?]

gricer /gríssər/ *n* a train spotter [Mid-20C. < ?]

grid /grid/ *n* **1 REFERENCE LINES ON A MAP** a network of evenly spaced horizontal and vertical lines on a map, used as a basis for finding specific points **2 ADJACENT SQUARES** a network of squares formed by horizontal and vertical lines **3 GRATING MADE OF BARS** a set of parallel or crisscrossing bars that form a grating **4 NETWORK** a network of cables, lines, or pipes for distributing electricity, gas, or water **5** UTIL = **national grid** *n.* **1 6 CONTROL ELECTRODE** the part of a electronic valve that controls the flow of current between the other electrodes, usually constructed as a metal screen or coil **7** MOTOR SPORTS = **starting grid 8** AMERICAN FOOTBALL = **gridiron** *n.* **3** [Mid-19C. Shortening of GRIDIRON.] —**gridded** *adj*

grid bias *n* a fixed voltage applied between the control electrode and the cathode in an electronic valve

gridder /gríddər/ *n US* an American football player (*informal*)

griddle /grídd'l/ *n* **1 HEATED COOKING SURFACE** a heavy flat metal plate heated and used for cooking food, especially batter mixtures **2 SIEVE USED BY MINERS** a sieve with a base formed from a wire mesh, used by miners ■ *vt* (**-dles, -dling, -dled**) **COOK ON A GRIDDLE** to cook something on a flat hot surface [Pre-12C. < Old French *gredil* 'gridiron' < Latin *cratis* 'crate'.]

griddlecake /grídd'l kayk/ *n* a cake similar to a scone, cooked on a griddle

gridiron /gríd ī ərn/ *n* **1** COOK = **grill**[1] *n.* **2 2 GRATING** a structure consisting of parallel bars **3 AMERICAN FOOTBALL FIELD** a field marked with parallel white lines, on which American football is played **4 AMERICAN FOOTBALL** the game of American football (*informal*) **5 STRUCTURE ABOVE A THEATRE STAGE** a structure of beams or bars above a theatre stage from which lighting and scenery are suspended [13C. Alteration of GRIDDLE, by association with IRON.]

gridlock /gríd lok/ *n* **1** a traffic jam in which congestion at one or two road junctions affects a wide area so that traffic is unable to move in any direction **2** a situation in which no progress can be made —**gridlocked** *adj*

grid reference *n* a reference, usually using numbers or letters, that specifies a position on a map or chart by referring to the superimposed grid

grief /greef/ *n* **1 INTENSE SORROW** great sadness, especially as a result of a death **2 CAUSE OF INTENSE SORROW** the cause of intense, deep, and profound sorrow, especially a specific event or situation **3 TROUBLE** annoyance or trouble (*informal*) [Pre-12C. Via Anglo-Norman *gref* < Old French *grief* 'grieved' < *grever* (see GRIEVE[1]).] ◇ **come to grief** to suffer misfortune or ruin ◇ **good grief** used to express surprise, exasperation, or dismay (*dated informal*)

grief-stricken *adj* deeply affected by sadness

Grieg /greeg/, **Edvard** (1843–1907) Norwegian composer

grievance /gréevənss/ *n* **1 SOMETHING THOUGHT REASON ENOUGH TO COMPLAIN** a cause for complaint or resentment that may or may not be well-founded **2 RESENTMENT** bitterness or anger at having received unfair treatment **3 FORMAL OBJECTION** a formal complaint made on the basis of something that somebody feels is unfair

grieve[1] /greev/ (**grieves, grieving, grieved**) *v* **1** *vti* to experience great sadness, e.g. at a death **2** *vt* to cause great sadness to somebody [Pre-12C. Via Old French *grever* 'to burden' < Latin *gravare* < *gravis* 'heavy, grave'.] —**griever** *n*

grieve[2] /greev/ *n Scotland* a farm supervisor or manager [Old English *grǣfa*, variant of *gerēfa* (see REEVE[1])]

grievous /gréevəss/ *adj* **1** extremely serious or significant **2** very bad or severe —**grievously** *adv* —**grievousness** *n*

grievous bodily harm *n* serious physical injury intentionally done to another person

griffin /gríffin/, **griffon** /gríffən/, **gryphon** *n* a mythical monster with the head and wings of an eagle and the body and tail of a lion [13C. Via Old French *grifoun* < Latin *gryphus* < Greek *grups.*] See illustration overleaf.

Griffin /gríffin/, **Walter Burley** (1876–1937) US-born Australian architect

Griffith /gríffith/, **D. W.** (1875–1948) US film director. Full name **David Lewelyn Wark Griffith**

Griffith Joyner /gríffith jóynər/, **Florence** (1959–98) US athlete. Born **Delorez Florence Griffith**. Known as **Flojo**

griffon /gríffən/ *n* **1** a small dog like a terrier belonging to a breed with wiry hair and a short muzzle **2** MYTHOL = **griffin** [Late 18C. Via French < Old French *grifoun* (see GRIFFIN).]

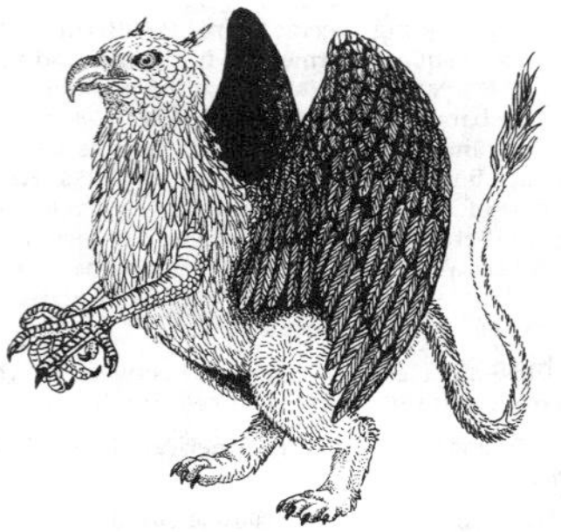

Griffin

griffon vulture *n* a large light-coloured vulture with dark wing and tail feathers. Native to: S Europe, North Africa, Middle East. Genus: *Gyps.*

grift /grift/ *n US* (*informal*) **1 FRAUD** a swindle or confidence trick **2 PROCEEDS FROM FRAUD** money made from a swindle or confidence trick ■ *vti US* **SWINDLE** to carry out a swindle, or obtain something by swindling (*informal*) [Early 20th. Probably alteration of GRAFT².] —**grifter** *n*

Grignard reagent /greén yaar-/ *n* any of a group of organometallic compounds whose molecules contain one magnesium and one halogen atom. Use: preparation of organic compounds. [Early 20C. After Victor *Grignard* (1871–1934), French chemist.]

grigri /greé gree/ (*plural* **-gris**), **greegree** (*plural* **-grees**), **gris-gris** (*plural* **gris-gris**) *n* an African talisman or fetish [Late 18C. Via American Spanish < Carib *grugru* 'palm'.]

grike /grīk/, **gryke** *n* a deep cleft in a bare limestone rock surface. ◊ **clint** [Late 18C. < ?]

grill¹ /gril/ *v* **1** *vti* **COOK UNDER OR OVER DIRECT HEAT** to cook food or be cooked by direct heat. US term **broil** *v.* 2 **2** *vt* **INTERROGATE** to interrogate or cross-examine somebody in a persistent manner (*informal*) **3** *vti* **SUBJECT TO GREAT HEAT** to subject somebody or something, or be subjected, to great heat, especially from the sun ■ *n* **1 PART OF COOKER RADIATING HEAT** a device in or on a cooker that radiates heat downwards. US term **broiler** *n.* 2 **2 PLATE FOR GRILLING** a flat plate made of parallel metal bars, used for grilling **3 GRIDIRON PATTERN** a pattern made on a surface by a grill or gridiron **4 FOOD COOKED ON GRILL** a dish or portion of food cooked on a grill **5 RESTAURANT SERVING GRILLED FOOD** an establishment that serves food cooked on a grill [Mid-17C. < French *griller* < *grille* (see GRILLE).] —**griller** *n*

SPELLCHECK Do not confuse ***grill*** with ***grille***, which has a similar sound. Beware: your spellchecker will not catch this error.

grill² *n* BUILDING, RACKET GAMES = **grille**

grillage /grillij/ *n* a framework of beams and crossbeams built as a foundation for a building on soft ground

grille /gril/, **grill** *n* **1 CRISSCROSSED BARS** a pattern or lattice of bars, especially in front of a window **2 PART OF COOLING SYSTEM** a metal grating that allows cooling air into the radiator of a vehicle's engine **3 REAL TENNIS WALL OPENING** in real tennis, the opening in one corner of an end wall of the court [Mid-17C. Via French < Old French *graille* < Latin *cratis* 'grating, hurdle'.] —**grilled** *adj*

SPELLCHECK See ***grill***.

grillroom /gril room, -rŏŏm/ *n* COMM = **grill¹** *n.* 5

grillwork /gril wurk/ *n* BUILDING = **grille** *n.* 1

grilse /grilss/ (*plural* **grilses** *or* **grilse**) *n* a salmon the first time it returns from the sea [15C. < ?]

grim /grim/ (**grimmer, grimmest**) *adj* **1 DEPRESSING** depressingly gloomy ○ *a grim economic forecast* **2 FORBIDDING** forbidding and unattractive in appearance ○ *a grim mining town* **3 STERNLY SERIOUS** stern in a frightening and unnerving way ○ *a grim, set look on his face* **4 UNPLEASANT** extremely unpleasant, distressing, or sinister ○ *a grim accident scene* **5 IRONIC** disquietingly ironic ○ *a grim reminder of humankind's penchant for folly* **6 ILL** unwell, especially as a result of overindulgence in alcohol (*informal*) **7 SHODDY** very low in quality (*informal*) ○ *put in a pretty grim performance* [Old English, < Germanic] —**grimly** *adv* —**grimness** *n*

grimace /grímməss, gri máyss/ *n* a contorted twisting of the face that expresses disgust or pain [Mid-17C. Via French *grimache* < Spanish *grimazo* 'caricature' < *grima* 'fright'.] —**grimace** *vi* —**grimacer** *n* —**grimacingly** *adv*

Grimaldi /gri máldi/ *n* a very large, dark-floored enclosure near the western edge of the moon

grimalkin /gri máwlkin, -málkin/ *n* an old female cat [Late 16C. < GREY + obsolete *malkin* 'cat'.]

grime /grīm/ *n* dirt or soot, usually accumulated in a black layer or ingrained into a surface ■ *vt* (**grimes, griming, grimed**) to coat something with dirt or soot [13C. < Middle Low German *greme.*]

Grimm /grim/, **Jakob** (1785–1863) German philologist and folklorist

Grim Reaper *n* a personification of death, shown as a cloaked man or skeleton holding a scythe

grimy /grīmi/ (**-ier, -iest**) *adj* heavily soiled, usually with dirt or soot —**grimily** *adv* —**griminess** *n*

SYNONYMS See ***dirty***.

grin /grin/ (**grins, grinning, grinned**) *vi* to smile broadly, usually showing the teeth [Old English *grennian* 'bare your teeth' < Indo-European, 'be open'] —**grin** *n* —**grinner** *n* ◇ **grin and bear it** to tolerate something unpleasant without complaining (*informal*)

grind /grīnd/ *v* (**grinds, grinding, ground** /grownd/, **ground**) **1** *vti* **PULVERIZE** to crush something into very small pieces by rubbing it between two hard surfaces, or be crushed in this way **2** *vti* **MAKE A RASPING NOISE** to rub two surfaces together with a grating noise, or make a grating noise by rubbing things together ○ *He ground the gears every time he shifted.* **3** *vt* **PUSH DOWN WITH TWISTING MOTION** to push something down firmly or crush something on a surface with a twisting or rotating motion **4** *vt US* COOK = **mince** *v.* 1 **5** *vt* **SMOOTH OR SHARPEN** to make something smooth or sharp by rubbing it against an abrasive surface **6** *vi* **MOVE NOISILY** to move with a grating noise **7** *vt* **TURN THE HANDLE OF** to operate something such as a barrel organ by turning its handle **8** *vi* **WORK HARD** to study or work hard, especially too hard (*informal*) **9** *vi* **DANCE EROTICALLY** to dance erotically with a circling of the hips (*informal*) ■ *n* **1 SOMETHING BORING AND REPETITIVE** something that is routine, dull, and tedious (*informal*) **2 GRINDING** an act of grinding **3 GRINDING NOISE** a grating noise like that of something grinding **4 TEXTURE** the texture of something that is ground **5** *US* **HARD WORKER** somebody who works or studies too hard (*informal*) **6 EROTIC DANCE MOVEMENT** an erotic circling and thrusting of the hips in dancing (*informal*) [Old English *grindan* < ?]

grind down *vt* to weaken somebody gradually by persistent oppression

grind on *vi* to continue in an unrelenting way

grind out *vt* **1 DO BY ROTE** to perform or produce something mechanically as a result of boredom or excessive familiarity with the process **2 SAY WITH ROUGH VOICE** to say something with a rough or grating voice **3 PUT OUT BY CRUSHING** to extinguish something by crushing it on a surface with a twisting motion

grinder /grīndər/ *n* **1** somebody or something that grinds something ○ *a coffee grinder* **2** a molar tooth

grinding /grīnding/ *adj* **1** oppressive and relentless ○ *grinding poverty* **2** characterized by a grating sound —**grindingly** *adv*

grindstone /grīnd stōn/ *n* **1** an abrasive wheel that sharpens or polishes something **2** any stone used for sharpening or polishing something **3** TECH = **millstone** *n.* 1

gringo /gríng gō/ (*plural* **-gos**) *n* in Spain and Latin America, a highly offensive term for an English-speaking foreigner (*insult*) [Mid-19C. < Spanish, 'foreigner'.]

griot /greé ō, gri ót/ *n* a member of a caste of professional oral historians in the Mali Empire [Early 19C. < French.]

grip¹ /grip/ *n* **1 HOLDING ACTION** an act of taking or keeping a firm hold of something **2 MANNER OF HOLDING** the way that somebody holds something ○ *a firm grip* **3 GRASP** a grasp or hold of something **4** = **handgrip** *n.* 2 **5** = **handgrip** *n.* 3 **6 HOLDING DEVICE** a device for holding something firmly **7 ABILITY NOT TO SLIP** the ability of something to adhere to a surface without slipping **8 CONTROL** power over somebody or something ○ *The dictator had millions of lives in his grip.* **9 COMPREHENSION** a proper understanding of something **10** HAIR = **hairgrip** **11 SMALL SUITCASE** a bag or small holdall **12 MEMBER OF FILM CREW** a member of a film or television crew who is responsible for moving equipment **13 STAGEHAND** a worker who moves sets and props in a theatre ■ *v* (**grips, gripping, gripped**) **1** *vt* **GRASP FIRMLY** to take or keep a firm hold of something **2** *vti* **STICK TO** to adhere to a surface without slipping **3** *vt* **TAKE CHARGE OF** to take control of somebody or something ○ *gripped by a sudden, awful realization* **4** *vt* **CAPTURE INTEREST OF** to capture somebody's interest, imagination, or attention ○ *a performance that gripped the audience* [Old English *gripe* 'grasp', *gripa* 'handful' < Germanic] —**gripper** *n* ◇ **get to grips with something** to begin to understand and deal with something ◇ **lose your grip** to stop being as effective or as much in control as formerly

grip² *n* MED = **grippe** (*dated*)

gripe /grīp/ *v* (**gripes, griping, griped**) **1** *vi* **GRUMBLE CONSTANTLY** to complain continually and irritatingly (*informal*) **2** *vti* **CAUSE STOMACH PAINS** to experience or cause somebody to suffer severe stomach pains (*informal*) **3** *vi* **SAIL INTO THE WIND** to sail into the wind against the action of the helm ■ *n* **MINOR COMPLAINT** a minor but irritating grievance (*informal*) ■ **gripes** *npl* **MOORING ROPES** ropes that hold a boat to a dock [Old English *grīpan* 'seize' < Germanic] —**griper** *n*

SYNONYMS See ***complain***.

gripe water *n* a medicine given to babies to relieve colic

griping /grīping/ *adj* describes stomach pains that are sudden, sharp, and intense

grippe /grip/, **grip** *n* influenza (*dated*) [Late 18C. < French, 'seizure'.] —**grippy** *adj*

gripping /gripping/ *adj* holding the interest and attention completely —**grippingly** *adv*

Griqua /greékwə/ (*plural* **-qua** *or* **-quas**), **Grikwa** (*plural* **-kwa** *or* **-kwas**) *n* **1** a member of a group of people of both African and European descent in South Africa **2** the Khoisan language spoken by the Griqua people [Mid-18C. < Nama.] —**Griqua** *adj*

Gris /greess/, **Juan** (1887–1927) Spanish-born French artist. Born **José Vittoriano González**

grisaille /gri záyl, -zī/ *n* **1** a method of painting that uses shades of grey **2** a work of art produced by the grisaille method [Mid-19C. < French, < *gris* 'grey'.]

griseofulvin /grízzi ō fŏŏlvin, gríss-, -fúlvin, gríssi ō fúlvin/ *n* an antibiotic obtained from a fungus. Use: treatment of fungal skin conditions. [Mid-20C. < modern Latin *Griseofulvum* < medieval Latin *griseus* 'grey' + Latin *fulvus* 'reddish-yellow'.]

grisette /gri zét/ *n* **1** formerly, a young working-class French woman **2** a species of edible fungus with a grey, orange, or brown cap. *Amanita fulva* and *Amanita vaginata.* [Early 18C. < French, < *gris* 'grey'.]

gris-gris *n* ANTHROP = **grigri**

Grisham /gríshəm/, **John** (*b.* 1955) US writer

griskin /grískin/ *n* lean meat from a loin of pork [Late 17C. < obsolete *grice* 'pig' < Old Norse *gríss.*]

grisly /grízzli/ (**-lier, -liest**) *adj* gruesomely unpleasant, or creating a sense of horror [12C. Ultimately < W Germanic, 'terror'.] —**grisliness** *n*

SPELLCHECK Do not confuse ***grisly*** with ***grizzly***, which has a similar sound. Beware: your spellchecker will not catch this error.

grison /grīss'n, gríz-/ (*plural* **-sons** *or* **-son**) *n* a weasel that has striking grey, white, and black markings, and is sometimes used to hunt chinchillas. Native to: South America. *Galictis vittata* and *Galictis cuja.* [Late 18C. < French, < *gris* 'grey'.]

grist /grist/ *n* **1 GRAIN GROUND INTO FLOUR** grain that is ground into flour **2 GRAIN PRODUCED AT ONE GRINDING** the quantity of grain that is ground in one batch **3 BREWING MALT** malt grain that is used for brewing [Old English, < Germanic] ◇ **grist to the** *or* **somebody's mill** a potential source of advantage or profit to somebody

gristle /gríss'l/ *n* tough cartilage, especially in meat prepared for eating [Old English, < ?] —**gristliness** *n* —**gristly** *adj*

gristmill /gríst mil/ *n* a mill where grain or corn is ground

grit /grit/ *n* **1 SAND OR STONE GRAINS** small pieces of sand or stone **2 SANDSTONE** sandstone, often used as a grindstone **3 TEXTURE OF GRAINS** the texture of stone used for grinding **4 PARTICLE SIZE** a measure of the size of particles ○ *coarse grit* **5 FIRMNESS OF CHARACTER** determination or strength of character ■ *vt* (**grits, gritting, gritted**) **1 CLENCH TEETH**

to clench the teeth, especially when under stress **2 COVER WITH GRIT** to cover something with grit, especially an icy road [Old English *grēot* < Germanic]

grits /grits/ *n US* coarsely ground hulled maize that is boiled and eaten hot with butter, especially at breakfast in the S United States (*+ singular or plural verb*) ■ *npl* grain that has had its husks removed or been coarsely ground [Late 16C. Plural of obsolete *grit* 'chaff' < Old English *grytta* 'coarse meal' < Germanic.]

gritstone /grít stōn/ *n* GEOL, INDUST = **grit** *n.* 2

gritter /gríttər/ *n* a vehicle that spreads grit or salt on icy roads

gritty /grítti/ (**-tier, -tiest**) *adj* **1 RESOLUTE** courageous, resolute, or persistent **2 REALISTIC** having a stark realism **3 LIKE OR WITH GRIT** resembling, containing, or covered with grit —**grittily** *adv* —**grittiness** *n*

grizzle[1] /grízz'l/ *vti* (**-zles, -zling, -zled**) **BECOME OR MAKE GREY** to make something grey, or become grey ■ *n* **1 GREY** a grey colour **2 GREY HAIR** hair that is grey or streaked with grey **3 GREY WIG** a grey-coloured wig [14C. < Old French *grisel* < *gris* 'grey'.]

grizzle[2] /grízz'l/ (**-zles, -zling, -zled**) *vi* (*informal*) **1** to cry and whine quietly and persistently (*refers to young children*) **2** to complain annoyingly and persistently [Mid-18C. < ?] —**grizzler** *n*

grizzled /grízz'ld/ *adj* **1** streaked with grey **2** with hair that is grey or streaked with grey

grizzly bear /grízzli-/, **grizzly** *n* a variety of brown bear that has brown fur tipped with white. Native to: NW North America. *Ursus arctos horribilis.*

groan /grōn/ *n* **1 MOURNFUL SOUND** a long low cry expressing pain or misery **2 LOUD CREAKING SOUND** a loud creaking sound of something affected by pressure **3 GRIEVANCE** an aggrieved complaint (*informal*) ■ *v* **1** *vi* **MOAN** to utter a moan **2** *vt* **EXPRESS WITH GROAN** to express something by means of a groan **3** *vi* **MAKE A LOUD CREAKING SOUND** to make a loud creaking sound as a result of pressure ○ *the ship's timbers groaned and creaked* **4** *vi* **COMPLAIN** to complain in an aggrieved way (*informal*) [Old English *grānian* < Indo-European, 'be open'] —**groaner** *n* —**groaningly** *adv*

groats /grōts/ *n* grain, especially oats, that has been crushed or has had the husks removed (*+ singular or plural verb*) [14C. < Old English *grotan* < Germanic.]

Gro-bag /grṓ bag/ *tdmk* a trademark for a plastic sack sold filled with compost and nutrients as a container for growing plants

grocer /grṓssər/ *n* **1** an owner or manager of a shop selling food and other household goods. ◊ **greengrocer** *n.* 1 **2 grocer, grocer's** (*plural* **-cer's**) a shop that sells food and other household goods. US term **grocery store**. ◊ **greengrocer** *n.* 2 [13C. Via Old French < medieval Latin *grossarius* 'wholesale dealer' < *grossus* 'large'.]

grocery /grṓssəri/ *n* (*plural* **-ies**) **1** COMM = **grocer** *n.* 2 **2** the trade or profession of a grocer ■ **groceries** *npl* goods, especially food, sold in a grocer's shop

grocery store *n US* COMM = **grocer** *n.* 2

grockle /grók'l/ *n SW England* a tourist, especially one from the Midlands or North of England (*insult*) [Mid-20C. Invention.]

grody /grṓdi/ (**-dier, -diest**) *adj US* disgusting or extremely unpleasant (*slang*) [Mid-20C. Alteration of GROTESQUE.]

Groening /grṓning/, **Matt** (*b.* 1954) US cartoonist

grog /grog/ *n* **1** a mixture of alcohol, especially rum, and water **2** *ANZ* a beverage that contains alcohol (*informal*) [Mid-18C. Shortening of *Old Grogram*, nickname of Admiral Edward Vernon (from his grogram cloak).]

groggy /gróggi/ (**-gier, -giest**) *adj* feeling weak or dizzy, especially because of illness or overindulgence —**groggily** *adv* —**grogginess** *n*

grogram /grógrəm/ *n* a stiff fabric of silk and wool or mohair. ◊ **grosgrain** [Mid-16C. < French *gros grain* 'coarse grain'.]

groin[1] /groyn/ *n* **1 AREA BETWEEN THIGHS AND ABDOMEN** the area between the tops of the thighs and the abdomen **2 GENITALS** the genitals, especially the testicles **3 EDGE BETWEEN VAULTS** a curved line forming the edge between two intersecting vaults [14C. < ?]

groin[2] *n* US = **groyne**

grommet /grómmit, grúm-/, **grummet** /grúm-/ *n* **1 PROTECTIVE EYELET** a protective eyelet in a material that prevents tearing either of the material or of a rope passed through it **2 REINFORCEMENT AROUND EYELET** a small ring of metal or plastic that reinforces an eyelet **3 RING TO FASTEN

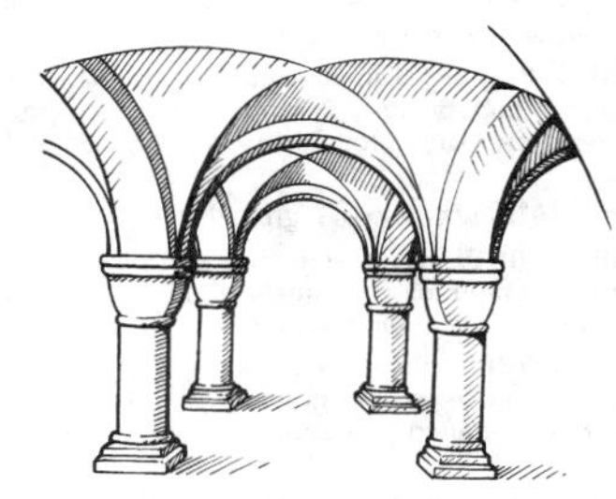

Groin

A SAIL** a ring used to fasten the edge of a sail to its stay **4 TUBE FOR DRAINING EAR** a small tube for draining the middle ear of somebody who has glue ear [Early 17C. < obsolete French *gromette* 'curb of a bridle' < *gourmer* 'curb'.]

gromwell /grómmwəl, -wel/ *n* a hairy flowering plant of the borage family that produces hard smooth white seeds. Genus: *Lithospermum.* [13C. < Old French *gromil.*]

Gromyko /grə méekō/, **Andrey** (1909–89) Soviet statesman

Groningen /grṓningən, grónn-/ city in NE Netherlands. Population: 172,701 (2000).

groom /groom, gro͝om/ *n* **1** = **bridegroom** **2 SOMEBODY WHO CARES FOR HORSES** somebody whose job is to look after horses by cleaning them and their stables **3 OFFICER IN ROYAL HOUSEHOLD** an officer in a royal household ■ *v* **1** *vt* **CARE FOR AN ANIMAL'S APPEARANCE** to clean and brush or comb an animal **2** *vti* **CLEAN ITS BODY** to clean the fur, skin, or feathers of another animal or of itself, often with the tongue (*refers to an animal, especially a dog or cat*) **3** *vt* **CARE FOR YOUR PERSONAL APPEARANCE** to keep somebody else's or your own personal appearance neat **4** *vt* **TRAIN** to train and prepare somebody for a particular position **5** *vt* **MAKE A PATH IN SNOW** to clear a path or track in snow by compacting the snow [12C. < ?] —**groomer** *n*

groomsman /gro͝omzmən, gro͝om-/ (*plural* **-men** /-mən/) *n* a man who is an attendant to a bridegroom

Groote Eylandt /gro͝ot ī́lənd/ island off NE Northern Territory, Australia, in the Gulf of Carpentaria. Population: 14,209 (1996). Area: 2,285 sq. km/882 sq. mi.

groove /groov/ *n* **1 NARROW PASSAGE** a narrow channel or path in a surface **2 TRACK CUT IN A RECORD** a spiral track cut into a vinyl record along which the needle of the record player passes **3 ROCK CLEFT** a cleft in rock **4 REGULARLY FOLLOWED PROCEDURE** a routine into which somebody has settled (*informal*) **5 SUITABLE ACTIVITY** an activity or situation suited to somebody's talents or tastes (*slang*) **6 MUSICAL BEAT** a strong beat or rhythm in music (*slang*) ■ *v* (**grooves, grooving, grooved**) **1** *vt* **MAKE A GROOVE** to cut a groove in a surface **2** *vti* **PLAY MUSIC RHYTHMICALLY** to play jazz or dance music with a strong beat (*slang*) [14C. < Dutch *groeve.*] —**groover** *n* ◇ **in the groove** playing or performing in a highly accomplished manner (*dated slang*)

groovy /gro͝ovi/ (**-ier, -iest**) *adj* **1** used, often as an exclamation, to describe somebody or something that is fashionable, excellent, or pleasing (*dated slang*) **2** used ironically of something that is unfashionable or out of touch with modern youth culture (*slang*) [Mid-20C. < *in the groove*, referring to a vinyl record.] —**groovily** *adv* —**grooviness** *n*

grope /grōp/ (**gropes, groping, groped**) *v* **1** *vi* **SEARCH BY FEELING** to search for something blindly or uncertainly by feeling with the hands **2** *vi* **BE WITHOUT GUIDANCE** to strive blindly or uncertainly for something ○ *groping for inspiration* **3** *vt* **EXPLORE UNCERTAINLY** to feel your way forward slowly and hesitantly, e.g. in the dark ○ *They groped their way back out of the tunnel.* **4** *vt* **FONDLE** to caress or touch somebody's body for sexual pleasure, often roughly, awkwardly, or without the person's consent (*informal*) ○ *A young couple were groping one another in the back row.* [Old English *grāpian* 'grasp at' < Germanic] —**grope** *n* —**groper** *n* —**gropingly** *adv*

groper /grṓpər/ *n* **1** *ANZ* a heavy-bodied large-jawed sea fish. Native to: tropical and temperate waters. Family: Serranidae. **2** the flesh of a groper used as food [Late 19C. Variant of GROUPER.]

Gropius /grṓpi əss/, **Walter** (1883–1969) German-born US architect and educator

grosbeak /grṓss beek/ *n* a finch with a large beak for crushing seeds. Native to: Europe, North America. Family: Fringillidae and Emberizidae. [Late 17C. < French *grosbec* 'large beak'.]

groschen /grósh'n, grṓ-/ (*plural* **-schen**) *n* **1** see table at **currency** **2** a German 10-pfennig coin (*informal*) **3** a former German silver coin [Early 17C. Via German < medieval Latin *(denarius) grossus* 'thick (penny)'.]

grosgrain /grṓ grayn/ *n* a heavy corded silk or rayon fabric. Use: trimmings, ribbons. [Mid-19C. < French, 'coarse grain'.]

gros point /grṓ-/ *n* **1** a large half cross-stitch used in embroidery. US term **raised point** *n.* 1 **2** embroidery done with gros point. US term **raised point** *n.* 2 [< French *gros point (de Venise)* 'large stitch (from Venice)']

gross /grōss/ *adj, adv* **WITHOUT DEDUCTIONS** before any usual deductions such as tax or expenses have been made ■ *adj* **1 OBVIOUSLY WRONG** flagrantly wrong or unmitigated ○ *a gross breach of the rules* **2 VULGAR** vulgar or coarse **3 WITHOUT GOOD TASTE** not sensitive to, or not able to appreciate, the finer things in life **4 EXTREMELY OVERWEIGHT** overweight to an unhealthy or repellent degree (*informal*) **5 LUXURIANT** growing thickly or densely **6 DISGUSTING** disgusting or highly unpleasant (*informal*) ■ *n* **1** (*plural* **gross**) **TWELVE DOZEN** a quantity of 144 or twelve dozen **2 SUM BEFORE DEDUCTIONS** a total, especially a total amount of money before any usual deductions are made ■ *vt* **EARN MONEY** to earn or make an amount of money as profit before any usual deductions are made [14C. Via French < late Latin *grossus* 'bulky, coarse'.] —**grossly** *adv* —**grossness** *n*

gross out *vt US* to be disgusting or repellent to somebody (*slang*) ○ *language that really grossed me out*

gross anatomy *n* a branch of anatomy dealing with body parts that are visible to the naked eye

gross domestic product *n* the total value of all goods and services produced within a country in a year, minus net income from investments in other countries

Grossglockner /grṓss glóknər/ highest peak in Austria, part of the Eastern Alps in S Austria. Height: 3,797 m/12,457 ft.

gross national product *n* the total value of all goods and services produced within a country in a year, including net income from investments in other countries

gross-out *n US* something considered disgusting or repellent (*slang*)

gross profit *n* the difference between sales revenue and the cost of goods sold

grossularite /gróssyo͝olə rīt/, **grossular** /gróssyo͝olər/ *n* a green garnet. Use: gems. [Early 19C. < German *Grossularit* < modern Latin *grossularia* 'gooseberry' (because the gem is green) < French *groseille.*]

grosz /grōsh/ (*plural* **groszy** /grṓshi/ *or* **grosze**) *n* see table at **currency** [Mid-20C. Via Polish *grosz*, Czech *groš* < medieval Latin *(denarius) grossus* 'thick (penny)'.]

Grosz /grōss/, **George** (1893–1959) German-born US artist. Born **Georg Grosz**

grot /grot/ *n* dirt, mess, or rubbish (*informal*) [Mid-20C. Back-formation < GROTTY.]

grotesque /grō tésk/ *adj* **1 DISTORTED** distorted, especially in a strange or disturbing way ○ *The flames cast grotesque shadows on the wall.* **2 INCONGRUOUS** seeming strange or ludicrous through being out of place or unexpected **3 BLENDING REALISTIC AND FANTASTIC** relating to or typical of a style of art that mixes the realistic and the fantastic ■ *n* **1 ART MIXING REALISTIC AND FANTASTIC** a style of art, especially in 16th-century Europe, in which representations of real and fantastic figures are mixed **2 GROTESQUE ARTISTIC PIECE** a piece of art in the grotesque style **3 SOMETHING GROTESQUE** somebody or something considered to be grotesque [Mid-16C. Via French < Italian *grottesca* 'like a grotto' < *grotta* (see GROTTO), from fanciful wall paintings found in excavated Roman ruins.] —**grotesquely** *adv* —**grotesqueness** *n*

grotesquerie /grō téskəri/, **grotesquery** (*plural* **-ries**) *n* **1** the grotesque quality of something **2** something grotesque, especially a piece of art in the grotesque style

grotto /gró tō/ (*plural* **-toes** *or* **-tos**) *n* **1** a cave, especially one with interesting natural features **2** an imitation cave, especially as an ornamental shelter in a formal garden [Early 17C. Via Italian *grotta* < Latin *crypta* (see CRYPT).]

grotty /grótti/ (**-tier, -tiest**) *adj* (*informal*) **1 DIRTY OR SHABBY** distastefully dirty, shabby, or in poor condition **2 GENERALLY UNPLEASANT** generally unpleasant or despicable **3 UNWELL** physically unwell [Mid-20C. < GROTESQUE.] —**grottily** *adv* —**grottiness** *n*

grouch /growch/ *vi* **COMPLAIN** to complain or grumble (*informal*) ■ *n* (*informal*) **1 COMPLAINT** an instance of complaining **2 COMPLAINER** a habitually bad-tempered or complaining person **3 BAD MOOD** a mood characterized by complaining or sulking ○ *a day-long grouch* [Late 19C. < ?] —**grouchily** *adv* —**grouchiness** *n* —**grouchy** *adj*

ground[1] /grownd/ *n* **1 LAND SURFACE** the surface of the land **2 EARTH** the earth or soil **3 LAND FOR A PURPOSE** an area of land used for a particular purpose (*often plural*) ○ *burial ground* **4 BATTLE AREA** the land held or fought over in battle ○ *The partisans retreated, yielding ground to the government troops.* **5 SUBJECT** an area of knowledge or debate ○ *Most of the ground had been covered in an earlier lecture.* **6 FOUNDATION** a reason or basis (*often plural*) ○ *There are grounds for believing his story.* **7 PAINTING SURFACE** an underlying surface or prepared area that paint is applied to **8 BACKGROUND** a background, e.g. the background of a painting or the background colour of a flag **9 FIRST COAT OF PAINT** a first coat of paint applied to a surface being decorated **10 SEA BOTTOM** the bottom of the sea, a river, or a lake **11 AREA BEFORE STUMPS IN CRICKET** the area that a batsman must stand in, measuring from the popping crease to the stumps ○ *He was run out before he could regain his ground.* **12** MUSIC = **ground bass 13** *US* ELEC ENG = **earth** *n.* 6 ■ **grounds** *npl* **1 SURROUNDING LAND** the land surrounding and belonging to a building (*sometimes singular*) **2 DREGS** the sediment or dregs of a drink, especially coffee ■ *adj* **ON THE GROUND** happening, living, or operating on the ground ○ *ground crews* ■ *v* **1** *vt* **GIVE SOMEBODY A FOUNDATION** to teach somebody the basics about something ○ *He had been well grounded in the techniques.* **2** *vt* **SUPPORT** to base ideas, arguments, or beliefs on something ○ *Her beliefs are grounded on an unshakable faith.* **3** *vt* **STOP A PILOT OR PLANE FLYING** to prevent or forbid an aircraft or aviator from flying ○ *Bad weather grounded all outgoing flights.* **4** *vt* **FORBID TO GO OUT** to restrict somebody to a place, especially a child to his or her home, as a punishment (*informal*) ○ *My dad grounded me for a week.* **5** *vti* **RUN VESSEL AGROUND** to become stranded in a vessel, or cause a vessel to become stranded by running aground ○ *The ferry grounded on a reef.* **6** *vi* **LAND ON THE GROUND** to land on the ground or hit the ground **7** *vt* **PUT ON THE GROUND** to put something on the ground ○ *ground your rifles* **8** *vt* **FIX** to fix something on or in something else as a foundation ○ *The fence posts are grounded in concrete.* **9** *vti* **HIT A BALL TO THE GROUND** to strike a ball so that it hits or rolls along the ground **10** *vt US* ELEC ENG = **earth** *n.* 7 **11** *vt* **PREPARE A PAINTING SURFACE** to apply a preparatory coat to a surface that is to be painted [Old English *grund* < Germanic] ◇ **break fresh** *or* **new ground** to do or discover something new ◇ **get (something) off the ground** to get something started or operating ◇ **hit the ground running** to begin to deal with a new situation with great energy and without delay, generally because of good prior preparation (*informal*) ◇ **hold** *or* **stand your ground** to stick resolutely to decisions, attitudes, or principles in the face of pressure to abandon them ◇ **run somebody** *or* **something to ground** to find somebody or something finally, after a long and determined search ◇ **suit somebody down to the ground** to be perfectly suited to or suitable for somebody ◇ **the moral high ground** a position of moral superiority in relation to other people ◇ **thin on the ground** few in number or rare

ground out *vi* to be put out in baseball after hitting a ground ball that is fielded and thrown to first base

ground[2] past participle, past tense of **grind**

groundbait /grównd bayt/ *n* bait thrown into water to attract fish

ground ball *n* in baseball, a ball that bounces on the ground or rolls along it after being hit

ground bass *n* a short bass part continually repeated as the basis for a changing melody

ground beetle *n* INSECTS = **carabid**

groundbreaking /grównd brayking/ *adj* new and pioneering or innovative [Early 20C. < *break ground* 'turn the first spade of earth for a new building'.] —**groundbreaker** *n*

groundburst /grównd burst/ *n* an explosion of a bomb or warhead on the ground rather than in the air

ground cherry *n* **1** a small round cherry-shaped fruit that has a papery husk **2** a plant on which ground cherries grow. Native to: North America. Genus: *Physalis.*

ground cloth *n US* CAMPING = **groundsheet**

ground control *n* the staff and equipment on the ground that monitor or guide the flight of an aircraft or spacecraft (+ *singular or plural verb*)

ground cover *n* plants that grow densely and close to the ground, especially growing wild in a forest or deliberately planted in a garden to prevent weeds or soil erosion

ground crew *n* people working in aviation, especially technicians or mechanics, who do not normally work in the air

grounded /grówndid/ *adj* having a secure feeling of being in touch with reality and personal feelings

ground elder *n* a perennial plant with underground creeping stems, regarded as a weed. Flowers: white. Native to: Europe, Asia. *Aegopodium podagraria.* US term **goutweed**

grounder /grówndər/ *n* BASEBALL = **ground ball**

ground floor *n* the floor of a building that is level with or nearest to street level ◇ **in** *or* **on the ground floor** involved in something, especially a business venture, at the earliest stage

ground fog *n* fog lying at or near ground level

ground frost *n* a temperature of 0°C or lower as registered on a thermometer touching the ground

ground game *n* hunted animals that cannot fly, e.g. hares and deer

ground glass *n* **1** glass with a roughened non-transparent surface produced by abrading or etching **2** glass that has been ground into fine particles. Use: abrasive, especially on glasspaper.

groundhog /grównd hog/ *n* ZOOL = **woodchuck**

Groundhog Day *n* in the United States and Canada, the day when groundhogs are said to emerge from hibernation to test the weather. Date: 2 February.

grounding /grównding/ *n* **1** training in or knowledge of the basics of something ○ *had a good grounding in maths* **2** an incident when a vehicle, especially a low-loading lorry with a long wheelbase, is stranded on a hump or hump-backed bridge in the road

ground ivy *n* an invasive evergreen ivy with scalloped leaves. Flowers: small, purple-blue. Native to: Europe, Asia, naturalized in North America. *Glechoma hederacea.*

groundkeeper *n US* OCCUPATIONS = **groundskeeper**

groundless /grówndləss/ *adj* not based on evidence or reason and not justified or true —**groundlessly** *adv* —**groundlessness** *n*

groundling /grówndling/ *n* **1 ANIMAL OR PLANT NEAR THE GROUND** an animal or plant that lives on or near the ground, or at the bottom of a river, lake, or the sea **2 STANDING SPECTATOR** in Elizabethan England, an audience member standing in front of the stage in the cheapest part of the theatre **3 AVIATION WORKER ON GROUND** a member of the ground crew at an airport or air force base (*slang*)

ground loop *n* a sharp involuntary turn made by an aircraft that is taxiing, taking off, or landing, caused by unbalanced drag

groundmass /grównd mass/ *n* in some kinds of rock, the fine-grained base rock in which larger crystals are embedded

groundnut /grównd nut/ *n* **1** FOOD = **peanut** *n.* 1 **2** PLANTS = **peanut** *n.* 2 **3** the edible tuber of a climbing vine **4** (*plural* **-nuts** *or* **-nut**) a climbing vine that bears groundnuts. Flowers: brownish, fragrant. Native to: North America. *Apios americana.*

groundnut oil *n* a mild cooking oil extracted from peanuts

groundout /grównd owt/ *n* in baseball, the dismissal of a batter as a result of hitting a ground ball that is fielded and thrown to first base

ground pine *n* **1** a variety of bugle plant. Flowers: two-lipped, yellow with red spots, pine-scented if crushed. Native to: Europe, North Africa. *Ajuga chamaepitys.* **2** a moss with spore-producing tissues grouped in cones. Native to: North America. Genus: *Lycopodium.*

ground plan *n* **1** a scale drawing of a floor of a building, especially the ground floor **2** a preliminary plan or general outline of something ○ *a ground plan for corporate expansion*

ground plum *n* **1** an edible green fruit that resembles a plum **2** a flowering plant that bears ground plums. Native to: central and W United States. Genus: *Astragalus.*

ground rent *n* rent paid by a person who leases land for a specified term, especially with a view to building on it

ground rule *n* (*often plural*) **1** a basic rule of procedure ○ *Let's establish a few ground rules before we go any further.* **2** a sports rule that is specific to a particular place of play

groundsel /grówndss'l/ *n* a yellow-flowered plant generally regarded as a weed. Native to: Europe, Asia. Genus: *Senecio.* [Old English *grundeswylige*, alteration of *gundeswilgie* 'pus-swallower', because of its use in poultices]

groundsheet /grównd sheet/ *n* a sheet of waterproof material placed on the ground to protect a sleeping bag or the floor of a tent from ground dampness. US term **ground cloth**

groundsill /grównd sil/ *n* the joist that is nearest to the ground in a timber structure

groundskeeper /grówndz keepər/, **groundkeeper** /grównd-/ *n US* SPORTS = **groundsman** —**groundskeeping** *n*

ground sloth *n* an extinct ground-dwelling sloth that is believed to be the ancestor of modern tree sloths. Native to: Americas. Family: Megalonychoidea.

groundsman /grówndzmən/ (*plural* **-men** /-mən/) *n* somebody who maintains a playing field or the grounds of a property. US term **groundskeeper**

ground speed *n* the speed of a flying aircraft measured in relation to the ground it is travelling over and used for calculating flight times

ground squirrel *n* a ground-dwelling burrowing rodent related to the tree squirrels. Native to: North America, Europe, Africa, Asia. Family: Sciuridae.

ground staff *n* workers who maintain a playing field (+ *singular or plural verb*)

ground state *n* the state of lowest energy for a particle, atom, molecule, or system

ground stroke *n* in tennis, a shot played from any part of the court after the ball has bounced

ground substance *n* the solid, semisolid, or liquid material that exists between the cells in connective tissue, cartilage, or bone

groundswell /grównd swel/ *n* **1** a deep wide up-and-down movement of the sea, often caused by a far-off storm or an earthquake **2** a strong growth of feeling or opinion that is evident but not always attributable to a specific source ○ *a groundswell of public opinion against the new measures*

ground water *n* water held underground in soil or permeable rock, often feeding springs and wells

ground wave *n* a radio wave transmitted directly from a transmitter to a receiver, without reflection from the ionosphere

groundwork /grównd wurk/ *n* basic preparatory tasks that form a foundation for something else

ground zero *n* **1 POINT OF NUCLEAR EXPLOSION** the point on the surface of land or water that is precisely the site of detonation of a nuclear weapon or the point immediately above or below it **2** the focal point or centre of activities for a particular event ○ *The war-torn country has been ground zero for an international terrorist network.* **3 BASIC LEVEL** the most basic level or starting point for an activity ○ *learning programming from ground zero*

group /groop/ *n* **1 SET OF PEOPLE OR THINGS** a number of people or things considered together or regarded as belonging together **2 PEOPLE WITH SOMETHING IN COMMON** a number of people sharing something in common such as an interest, belief, or political aim ○ *an unemployed workers' group* **3 BAND OF MUSICIANS** a small number of musicians, especially in pop music, who play together as a unit **4 COMPANIES UNDER COMMON CONTROL** a number of companies all controlled by a single company or common owner **5 SET OF FIGURES IN ARTISTIC WORK** a number of figures forming a distinct unit in a painting, sculpture, or other artistic composition **6 SET OF SEVERAL MILITARY UNITS** a military formation made up of several complementary units **7 AIR FORMATION BETWEEN SQUADRON AND WING** an air force formation made up of two or more squadrons, but smaller than a wing **8 COLLECTION OF ATOMS** a collection of atoms that is a distinct chemical unit, e.g. the hydroxy group **9 COLLECTION OF SIMILAR ELEMENTS** a set of chemical elements classified according to the vertical column they occupy in the periodic table ○ *the alkaline earth group of elements* **10 SET OF ROCK FORMATIONS** a collection of rock formations that date from the same geological era and are considered as a stratigraphic unit **11 MATHEMATICAL SET UNDER AN OPERATION** a set of mathematical entities that are related by a particular operation (*often before nouns*) ■ *vti* **FORM GROUP** to come together as a unit, or bring people or things together to form a unit ○ *onlookers grouped in ones and twos on the sidelines* ■ *adj* **OF GROUPS** relating to groups or forming a group ○ *group holidays* [Late 17C. Via French *groupe* < Italian *gruppo* 'group, knot'.] —**groupable** *adj*

USAGE When the members of a ***group*** are regarded as a unit or a whole, a singular verb is used: *The group has decided not to go on the afternoon tour,* i.e. everybody in the group has decided unanimously to skip that tour. When the members of a ***group*** are regarded as separate individuals or factions, a plural verb is used: *The group have been arguing all morning about going or not going,* i.e. some members want to go and others do not.

group captain, Group Captain *n* an officer in the Royal Air Force senior to a wing commander and junior to an air commodore

group dynamics *n* the interpersonal processes, conscious and unconscious, that take place in the course of interactions among a group of people (*+ singular verb*)

grouper /gróopər/ (*plural* **-pers** *or* **-per**) *n* **1** a heavy-bodied large-jawed sea fish. Native to: tropical and temperate waters. Family: Serranidae. **2** the flesh of a grouper used as food [Early 17C. < Portuguese *garupa*.]

groupie /gróopi/ *n* (*informal*) **1** an enthusiastic fan of a pop group, especially a female teenager seeking sexual intercourse with the object of her adulation **2** any enthusiastic fan or supporter

grouping /gróoping/ *n* a set of people or things gathered into a group

Group of Eight *n* full form of **G8**

group practice *n* a medical, dental, or veterinary practice operated by several doctors, dentists, or vets working together

group theory *n* the study of the formation and properties of mathematical groups

group therapy *n* the treatment of psychological problems by placing patients in groups and, under the guidance of a trained therapist, encouraging them to discuss their problems with each other —**group therapist** *n*

groupthink /gróop thingk/ *n* conformity in thought and behaviour among the members of a group, especially an unthinking acceptance of majority opinions

groupuscule /gróopə skyool/ *n* a small political group, especially a splinter group of extremists or activists regarded as marginal (*disapproving*) [Mid-20C. < French, 'very small group' < *groupe* 'group' after *corpuscule* 'corpuscle'.]

⚡**groupware** /gróop wair/ *n* software designed to be shared collaboratively by a number of users on a network

grouse[1] /growss/ (*plural* **grouse**) *n* a large game bird that nests on the ground on moors and in forests and is usually reddish-brown with feathered feet and legs. Family: Tetraonidae. [Early 16C. < ?]

grouse[2] /growss/ (**grouses, grousing, groused**) *vi* to complain in a grumbling, often self-serving way (*informal*) [Early 19C. < ?] —**grouse** *n* —**grouser** *n*

SYNONYMS See ***complain.***

grouse[3] /growss/ *adj ANZ* excellent or great (*slang*) [Early 20C. < ?]

grout /growt/ *n* **1 MORTAR FOR FILLING GAPS** thin mortar used to fill gaps, especially between tiles **2 PLASTER** fine plaster used to finish ceilings and walls ■ **grouts** *npl* **DREGS** the sediment that lies at the bottom of a liquid ■ *vt* **APPLY GROUT TO** to use grout to fill gaps, especially between tiles, or to finish a ceiling or wall [Old English *grūt* < Germanic] —**grouter** *n*

grove /grōv/ *n* **1** a small wood ○ *a hazel grove* **2** a plantation of trees grown for their produce [Old English *grāf* < ?]

grovel /gróvv'l/ (**-els, -elling, -elled**) *vi* **1 BEHAVE SERVILELY** to act in a servile way, showing exaggerated and false respect in order to please somebody or out of fear ○ *I've already apologized but now he wants me to grovel.* **2 CRAWL** to crawl or lie face down on the ground in humility or fear **3 WALLOW** to indulge in something unworthy (*literary*) [Late 19C. < obsolete *groof* 'with face downwards' < Old Norse *á grúfu* < *grúfa* 'proneness'.] —**groveller** *n* —**grovellingly** *adv*

grow /grō/ (**grows, growing, grew** /groo/, **grown** /grōn/) *v* **1** *vi* **GET BIGGER** to become larger in size through natural development **2** *vi* **BECOME LARGER** to expand or become larger in any way ○ *The number of members will grow rapidly.* **3** *vi* **INCREASE** to increase in degree ○ *Excitement is growing.* **4** *vi* **BE ABLE TO DEVELOP NATURALLY** to be capable of developing naturally and remaining in a naturally healthy state ○ *Flowers won't grow in this soil.* **5** *vi* **BE PRODUCT** to develop from something else ○ *Hatred grew out of mutual ignorance.* **6** *vi* **BECOME** to move from one condition to another, especially gradually ○ *The night grew cold.* **7** *vt* **CAUSE TO GROW** to make something, especially plants, grow and develop ○ *We grow tomatoes in the greenhouse.* **8** *vt* **DEVELOP NATURALLY** to produce something or allow it to be produced as part of a natural process ○ *He thought he might grow a moustache.* **9** ⚠ *vt* **EXPAND** to develop, expand, and stimulate something, especially a business, a line of business, or an economic market ○ *She was brought in to grow the firm's market share.* [Old English *grōwan* < Indo-European] —**grower** *n*

USAGE Metaphorical uses of ***grow*** as a transitive verb are sometimes considered unacceptable: *grow the economy* and *grow a stock portfolio.* There are no grounds for objecting to literal physical senses of the transitive verb: *grow a beard; grow corn.* Nor are there grounds for objecting to metaphorical uses of the intransitive verb: *The economy grew rapidly.*

grow into *vt* to develop in size, maturity, or capability to suit something

grow on *vt* **1** to become gradually more acceptable or pleasing to somebody **2** to become gradually more apparent or powerful to somebody

grow out of *vt* to become too mature or too big in size for something

grow up *vi* **1 BECOME ADULT** to develop into an adult **2 BEHAVE MORE MATURELY** to behave in a more mature and sensible way **3 COME INTO EXISTENCE** to come into existence and develop ○ *A town had grown up at the junction of the two rivers.*

growbag /grṓ bag/ *n* a plastic sack filled with compost and nutrients, sold as a container in which to grow plants

growing pains *npl* **1** pains in the limbs that adolescents are sometimes affected by, thought to be caused by rapid bodily growth **2** problems associated with the early stages of something such as a developing project

growing season *n* the time of year during which annual plants, especially farm crops, develop to maturity

growl /growl/ *v* **1** *vti* **MAKE HOSTILE SOUND** to make, or communicate something by means of, a low nonverbal sound in the throat that expresses hostility **2** *vti* **SPEAK IN HOSTILE WAY** to speak, or say something, in a deep voice that expresses impatience or hostility ○ *He was growling at the children.* **3** *vi* **MAKE RUMBLING NOISE** to make a low rumbling noise ■ *n* **1 ANIMAL'S HOSTILE NOISE** the low throaty noise made by a hostile animal, especially a dog **2 HOSTILE UTTERANCE** something said in a hostile throaty voice [Mid-17C. Probably < Old French *grouler* < Germanic, an imitation of the sound.] —**growling** *adj* —**growlingly** *adv* —**growly** *adj*

growler /grówlər/ *n* a person or animal that growls

grown past participle of **grow** ■ *adj* having developed and matured

grown-up *adj* **1 FULLY MATURE** fully developed and mature **2 FOR ADULTS** relating to or for adults ■ *n* (*plural* **grown-ups**) **ADULT** an adult person (*usually by or to children*) ○ *Ask a grown-up to put it in the oven for you.*

growth /grōth/ *n* **1 GROWING PROCESS** the process of becoming larger and more mature through natural development ○ *A child needs protein for healthy growth.* **2 INCREASE** an increase in numbers, size, power, or intensity **3 SOMETHING THAT GROWS** something that grows or has grown ○ *three days' growth of beard on his chin* **4 ABNORMAL TISSUE** an abnormal formation of tissue such as a tumour growing in or on an organ ■ *adj* **EXPANDING** in the process of expanding or developing, especially rapidly ○ *growth industries*

growth factor *n* a substance produced by cells that stimulates them to multiply

growth fund *n* **1** *US* a unit trust offering long-term appreciation of capital invested, rather than a high income **2** a unit trust that invests in stocks expected to appreciate significantly

growth hormone *n* a hormone, made and stored in the pituitary gland in the brain, that stimulates protein synthesis and the growth of the long bones of the limbs

growth regulator *n* a natural or synthetic preparation that promotes or inhibits plant growth

growth ring *n* a sheath of cells forming concentric rings in the cross-section of a woody stem or trunk, and representing the result of the yearly growth spurt that begins in the spring

growth substance *n* a chemical produced by a plant that regulates its growth and development, and is usually made in the shoot tip and transported to other regions

groyne /groyn/ *n* a structure resembling a wall built out into a river or the sea to protect the shore from erosion. US term **groin**[2] [Late 16C. < obsolete *groin* 'pig's snout', via Old French < late Latin *grunium* < Latin *grunnire* 'grunt'.]

grozer /grṓzər/ *n N England* a gooseberry (*informal*) [Early 16C. < French *groseille*.]

Grozny /grózni/, **Groznyy** capital of the Russian republic of Chechnya. Population: 372,742 (1995).

GRP *abbr* glass-reinforced plastic

grub /grub/ *v* (**grubs, grubbing, grubbed**) **1** *vt* **DIG UP** to dig or pull something out of the ground, especially without proper tools ○ *grubbing up potatoes* **2** *vt* **CLEAR GROUND** to remove roots and stumps from an area of ground **3** *vi* **SEARCH ON GROUND** to search on or in the ground for something **4** *vi* **SEARCH LABORIOUSLY** to search for something laboriously, usually by moving things and looking under things ○ *grubbing in the archives for evidence* **5** *vi* **TOIL** to work hard, especially at something dull or arduous ■ *n* **1 LARVA** the larva of various insects, especially beetles **2 FOOD** food, especially a meal (*informal*) [14C. < assumed Old English *grybban* < Indo-European, 'scratch, dig'.] —**grubber** *n*

grubby /grúbbi/ (**-bier, -biest**) *adj* **1 DIRTY** dirty or slovenly **2 HAVING GRUBS** infested with grubs **3 CONTEMPTIBLE** disliked or despised, especially for being sordid or dishonourable ○ *articles in his grubby little newsletter* —**grubbily** *adv* —**grubbiness** *n*

SYNONYMS See ***dirty.***

grub-kick *n* a kick in rugby that makes the ball travel along the ground

grub screw *n* a small screw with no head, used to fix a movable part in position

grubstake /grúb stayk/ *n* **1** *US, Can* **MONEY ADVANCED TO PROSPECTOR** supplies or money given to a prospector in return for a share in any profits **2 ADVANCE FOR STARTING UP BUSINESS** money or materials given to somebody starting a business in return for a share in any profits ■ *vt* (**-stakes, -staking, -staked**) *US, Can* **ADVANCE MONEY TO** to give money or supplies to somebody in business in return for a share of any profits [Mid-19C. < GRUB 'food' + STAKE[2].] —**grubstaker** *n*

Grub Street *n* the world of literary hackwork and those who work at it [After a former street in London]

grudge /gruj/ *n* **RESENTMENT** a feeling of resentment or ill will, especially one lasting for a long time ■ *vt* (**grudges, grudging, grudged**) **1 GIVE RELUCTANTLY** to allow or give something reluctantly ○ *He wouldn't grudge working late if he knew it was important.* **2 ENVY** to be envious or resentful of somebody for something [14C. < Old French *grouchier* 'grumble'.] —**grudger** *n*

grudge match *n* a match between players or teams who have a long-standing animosity between them or who have a particular score to settle

grudging /grújjing/ *adj* done or given reluctantly —**grudgingly** *adv* —**grudgingness** *n*

gruel /gróo əl/ *n* a thin porridge made by boiling meal, especially oatmeal, in water [14C. < Old French, < Germanic.]

gruelling /gróo əling/ *adj* extremely arduous or exhausting [< giving gruel as a punishment] —**gruellingly** *adv*

gruesome /gróossəm/ *adj* involving or depicting death or injury in a disturbing or sickening way [Late 16C. < obsolete *grue* 'shudder' < N Germanic.] —**gruesomely** *adv* —**gruesomeness** *n*

gruff /gruf/ *adj* **1** abrupt, angry, or impatient in manner or speech **2** harsh-sounding or throaty ○ *a gruff voice* [15C. < Flemish or Dutch *grof* 'rough, harsh'.] —**gruffly** *adv* —**gruffness** *n*

grumble /grúmb'l/ *v* (**-bles, -bling, -bled**) **1** *vi* **EXPRESS DISSATISFACTION** to complain or mutter in a discontented way **2** *vt* **SAY AS COMPLAINT** to say something as a complaint ○ *Some entrants grumbled that there wasn't enough time.* **3** *vi* **MAKE RUMBLING NOISES** to make rumbling or growling noises ○ *thunder grumbling in the distance* ■ *n* **1 COMPLAINT** a complaint or expression of discontent **2 RUMBLING NOISE** a rumbling or growling noise [Late 16C. Probably < Middle Dutch *grommelen* 'mumble, grunt'.] —**grumbler** *n* —**grumbly** *adj*

SYNONYMS See ***complain***.

grumbling /grúmbling/ *n* a muted complaint or protest ○ *grumblings of discontent* ■ *adj* with a tendency to complain —**grumblingly** *adv*

grummet *n* NAUT, MED = **grommet**

grump /grump/ *n* **SOMEBODY IN A BAD MOOD** a bad-tempered or sullen person (*informal*) ■ **grumps** *npl* **BAD-TEMPERED MOOD** a bad-tempered or sullen mood (*informal*) ○ *a fit of the grumps* ■ *vi* **COMPLAIN** to complain or be sullen (*informal*) [Early 18C. An imitation of somebody expressing displeasure.]

grumpy /grúmpi/ (**-ier, -iest**) *adj* bad-tempered or sullen —**grumpily** *adv* —**grumpiness** *n*

Grundyism /grúndi izəm/ *n* a prudish narrow-minded attitude towards other people (*disapproving*) [Mid-19C. < Mrs *Grundy*, character in Thomas Moreton's play *Speed the Plough* (1798).]

grunge /grunj/ *n* **1 FILTH** filth or rubbish (*informal*) **2 KIND OF ROCK MUSIC** a variety of rock music that emerged in the 1980s in the United States and owes much to punk and heavy metal (*often before nouns*) ○ *grunge rock* **3 UNKEMPT FASHION STYLE** a style of dress, popularized by fans of grunge music, typified by second-hand clothes worn in layers, heavy footwear, unkempt hair, and an overall scruffy appearance ○ *designer grunge* **4** *US* **SOMEBODY OBJECTIONABLE** an unattractive person, especially somebody who looks dirty or unkempt (*slang insult*) [Mid-20C. Back-formation < GRUNGY.]

grungy /grúnji/ (**-gier, -giest**) *adj* **1** dirty, shabby, inferior, or otherwise undesirable (*informal*) **2** relating to or typical of grunge music or grunge fashions [Mid-20C. < ?] —**grunginess** *n*

grunion /grúnyən/ *n* a small fish that spawns on beaches. Native to: coastal waters of California and Mexico. *Leuresthes tenuis.* [Early 20C. Probably < Spanish *gruñón* 'grunter' < Latin *grunnire* 'to grunt'.]

grunt[1] /grunt/ *v* **1** *vi* **MAKE NOISE OF A PIG** to make the half-nasal, half-throaty noise that a pig makes **2** *vti* **SAY SOMETHING IN THROATY BURST** to make a deep sound in the throat as an annoyed, half-hearted, or inattentive response to what somebody has said, or to indicate or say something in this way ○ *He grunted in acknowledgment of my greeting.* ■ *n* **1 NOISE OF PIG** a half-throaty, half-nasal noise that a pig makes, or a vocal sound that resembles it **2 MARINE FISH** a bony tropical marine fish that grunts when taken out of the water. Family: Pomadasyidae. [Old English *grunettan* < Indo-European] —**grunter** *n*

grunt[2] /grunt/ *n US* an infantryman in the US Army or Marine Corps, especially one serving in Vietnam [Mid-20C. Alteration of *ground* < *ground man* 'low-ranking railway worker'.]

gruntled /grúnt'ld/ *adj* pleased or happy (*informal humorous*) [Early 20C. Back-formation < *disgruntled*.]

gruntwork /grúnt wurk/ *n US* basic work that is necessary to the completion of a task but that is uninspiring or unrewarding (*informal*)

Grus /gróoss/ *n* a small constellation of the southern hemisphere. See illustration at **constellation** [Early 18C. < Latin *grus* 'crane (bird)'.]

Gruyère /gróo yair/ *n* a hard Swiss cheese with occasional holes in it that has a mild nutty slightly sweet flavour [Early 19C. After a town in Switzerland.]

gr wt *abbr* gross weight

gryke *n* GEOL = **grike**

gryphon /gríff'n/ *n* MYTHOL = **griffin**

⚡**gs** *abbr* South Georgia (*in Internet addresses*)

GS *abbr* **1** General Secretary **2** general staff

gsoh *abbr* good sense of humour (*in personal columns*)

G-spot *n* a highly sensitive small area in the vagina that, when stimulated, gives extreme sexual pleasure (*informal*) [Late 20C. After Ernst *Gräfenberg* (1881–1957), German gynaecologist.]

GSR *abbr* galvanic skin response

GST *abbr* goods and services tax

Gstaad /gə shtáat/ alpine ski resort in W Switzerland. Population: 2,500 (1980 estimate).

G-string *n* a piece of material covering only the pubic area, supported by a narrow cord between the buttocks and around the waist [Late 19C. < ?]

G-suit *n* a close-fitting garment worn by pilots and astronauts that counters the blackout effects of high acceleration by applying pressure to the legs and lower body, thereby reducing blood supply loss to the head [Mid-20C. Shortening of *gravity-suit*.]

⚡**gt** *abbr* Guatemala (*in Internet addresses*)

⚡**GTG** *abbr* got to go (*in e-mails*)

GTT *abbr* glucose tolerance test

⚡**gu** *abbr* Guam (*in Internet addresses*)

GU, g.u. *abbr* genitourinary

guacamole /gwàakə mṓli/ *n* avocado mashed or puréed with tomato and lightly spiced with chilli, served as a dip or in salads [Early 20C. Via American Spanish < Nahuatl *ahuacamolli* 'avocado paste'.]

guacharo /gwáachə rō/ (*plural* **-ros**) *n* BIRDS = **oilbird** [Early 19C. Via American Spanish *guácharo* < Quechua *wáhcha* 'orphan'.]

Guadalajara /gwàadələ háarə/ capital of Jalisco State, in west-central Mexico. Population: 1,633,216 (1995).

Guadalcanal /gwàadəlkə nál/ largest of the Solomon Islands, in the SW Pacific Ocean. Area: 6,475 sq. km/2,500 sq. mi.

Guadalquivir /gwàad'l kwi véer/ river in S Spain, emptying into the Gulf of Cádiz. Length: 657 km/408 mi.

Guadalupe /gwàadə lóop/ **1** river in SE Texas, emptying into the Gulf of Mexico. Length: 402 km/250 mi. **2** island off the Baja California coast of Mexico in the Pacific Ocean. Area: 207 sq. km/80 sq. mi. **3** city in NE Mexico. Population: 534,782 (1990).

Guadalupe Hidalgo /gwàadə loop hi dálgō/ former name for **Gustavo A. Madero**

Guadalupe Mountains mountain range extending from New Mexico to Texas. Highest peak: Guadalupe Peak 2,667 m/8,749 ft.

Guadeloupe /gwàadə lóop/ an overseas department of France consisting of a group of islands in the E Caribbean. Capital: Basse-Terre. Population: 418,000 (1993). Area: 1,780 sq. km/687 sq. mi.

Guadiana /gwa dyáanə/ river in S Spain, emptying into the Gulf of Cádiz. Length: 829 km/515 mi.

~~**guage**~~ incorrect spelling of **gauge**

guaiac /gwí ak, -ək/ *n* PHARM = **guaiacum** [Mid-16C. Anglicization.]

guaiacol /gwí ə kol/ *n* a yellowish oily liquid. Source: guaiacum resin, wood creosote. Use: expectorant, antiseptic, local anaesthetic. [Mid-19C. < GUAIACUM.]

guaiacum /gwí əkəm/ *n* an evergreen tree that has dark dense oily wood and yields a medicinal resin. Native to: tropical America. *Guaiacum officinale.* [Mid-16C. Via modern Latin < American Spanish *guayacán* < Taino.]

Guajiro /gwə héerō/ *n* a Native South American language of Venezuela and Colombia, belonging to the Arawakan group of languages. Native speakers: 300,000. [Mid-20C. After the *Guajira* peninsula in W Venezuela.] —**Guajiro** *adj*

Guam /gwaam/ largest of the Mariana Islands, in the NW Pacific Ocean, an unincorporated territory of the United States. Capital: Agana. Population: 156,974 (1996). Area: 549 sq. km/212 sq. mi. —**Guamanian** /gwaa máyni ən/ *n, adj*

guan /gwaan/ *n* a large tree-dwelling fruit-eating bird. Native to: Central and South America. Family: Cracidae. [Late 17C. Via American Spanish < Miskito *kwamu*.]

guanaco /gwə náa kō/ (*plural* **-cos**) *n* an animal similar and related to the domesticated llama and alpaca. Native to: dry regions of the Andes. *Lama guanaco.* [Early 17C. Via Spanish < Quechua *huanacu*.]

Guangdong /gwáng dóong/ province of S China, on the South China Sea. Capital: Guangzhou. Population: 66,890,000 (1994). Area: 197,100 sq. km/76,100 sq. mi.

Guangzhou /gwáng jṓ/ capital and chief port of Guangdong Province, China. Population: 3,560,000 (1993).

guanidine /gwáani deen/ *n* CH_5N_3 a strongly alkaline substance found in urine as a product of protein metabolism and in plant tissues. Use: manufacture of plastics and resins. [Mid-19C. < GUANO + -IDE + -INE.]

guanine /gwáa neen/ *n* (*symbol* **G**) a purine derivative that is one of the four bases in DNA and RNA [Mid-19C. < GUANO.]

guano /gwáa nō/ *n* **1** accumulated droppings of birds, bats, and seals, occurring where large established colonies of these animals are situated **2** fertilizer consisting of dried bird or bat droppings, and rich in nutrients, including urates, oxalates, and phosphates, or a synthetic fertilizer with properties similar to those of natural guano [Early 17C. Via American Spanish < Quechua *huanu* 'dung'.]

guanosine /gwáanō seen/ *n* a compound containing guanine and ribose [Early 20C. < GUANINE + RIBOSE.]

guanosine monophosphate *n* a constituent of the nucleic acids DNA and RNA that plays a part in various metabolic reactions and is composed of guanosine linked to a phosphate group

guanosine triphosphate *n* a nucleotide made of guanosine linked to three phosphate groups

Guantánamo Bay /gwan táanəmō-/ inlet of the Caribbean Sea in SE Cuba. It is the site of a major US naval base. Area: 78 sq. km/30 sq. mi.

Guanxiu /gwáan syóo/ (832–912) Chinese artist

guanylic acid /gwaa níllik-/ *n* BIOCHEM = **guanosine monophosphate** [Late 19C. < GUANOSINE.]

Guaporé /gwáppō ráy, gwáppə-/ river in W Brazil, flowing partly along the Brazil-Bolivia border. Length: 1,530 km/950 mi.

guar /góo aar/ *n* **1** a plant of dry regions widely grown as fodder and for its seeds, which are used to make gum. Native to: South Asia. *Cyamopsis tetragonolobus.* **2** INDUST = **guar gum** [Late 19C. < Hindi *guār*.]

guarani /gwáarə née/ (*plural* **-nies** *or* **-nis**) *n* see table at **currency** [Mid-20C. < GUARANI.]

Guarani /gwáarə née/ (*plural* **-ni** *or* **-nis**) *n* **1** a member of a Native South American people who live in parts of Paraguay, Uruguay, Bolivia, and Brazil **2** an official language of Paraguay, also spoken elsewhere in central South America, belonging to the Tupi-Guarani branch of Andean-Equatorial. Native speakers: 3 million. [Mid-18C. Via Spanish *Guaraní* < *Guarini*, a people of Paraguay.] —**Guarani** *adj*

guarantee /gárrən tée/ *n* **1 ASSURANCE** something that assures a particular outcome ○ *There's no guarantee that the plan will work.* **2 PROMISE OF QUALITY** a formal promise that a product will be repaired free of charge if it breaks or fails within a stated period or that substandard work will be redone ○ *a five-year guarantee.* **3 CERTIFICATE STATING PROMISE OF QUALITY** a document setting out a promise of quality made by a manufacturer or the provider of a service **4 PROMISE TO BE RESPONSIBLE** a formal promise by one person to take responsibility for the debts or obligations of another person if that person fails to meet them **5 SOMEBODY RECEIVING FORMAL ASSURANCE** a person or company given an assurance that somebody's debts or obligations will be dealt with **6** LAW, BUSINESS = **guarantor** ■ *vt* (**-tees, -teeing, -teed**) **1 ASSURE** to promise something, or make something certain ○ *We can't guarantee availability of seats on tomorrow's flight.* **2 PROMISE QUALITY OF GOODS** to give a formal, usually printed promise that a product will be repaired free of charge if it fails within a specified period, or that substandard work will be redone **3 ACCEPT RESPONSIBILITY FOR** to promise to fulfil another person's debts or obligations if that person fails to meet them [Late 17C. Probably alteration of GUARANTY.]

guarantor /gárrən táwr/ *n* a person who gives a guarantee, especially a formal promise to be responsible for somebody else's debts or obligations [Mid-19C. < GUARANTEE.]

SYNONYMS See ***backer***.

guaranty /gárrən tee/ *n* (*plural* **-ties**) **1** LAW, BUSINESS = **guarantee** *n.* 4 **2** something used as security for a formal promise **3** the giving of something as security for a promise **4** LAW, BUSINESS = **guarantor** ■ *vt* (**-ties, -tying, -tied**) LAW = **guarantee** *v.* 3 [Early 16C. < Anglo-Norman *guarantie* < Old French *garantir* 'to warrant' < *garant* 'warrant'.]

guard /gaard/ *vt* **1 PROTECT** to protect somebody or something against danger or loss **2 PREVENT ESCAPE OF** to watch over and prevent the escape of somebody held captive ○ *Two police officers were guarding the prisoner.* **3 CONTROL PASSAGE THROUGH** to watch over and control passage through an entrance or across a boundary ○ *All of the mountain passes are guarded by troops.* **4 PUT PROTECTIVE COVER ON** to equip a machine or device with a protective cover **5 CONTROL** to control or restrain something such as speech or behaviour ○ *guard your tongue* **6** *US* **HAMPER OPPONENT** in basketball, to prevent an opponent from scoring or playing effectively ■ *n* **1 PROTECTOR** a person or group that protects, watches over, restrains, or controls somebody or something ○ *The prisoner broke away from his guards.* **2 CEREMONIAL ESCORT** a usually mounted or motorized group forming a ceremonial escort **3 RAILWAY EMPLOYEE IN CHARGE OF PASSENGERS** a railway employee who is in charge of a train and whose job is to check tickets, announce stops, and attend to passengers' needs and safety. US term **conductor** *n.* 2 **4 ACT OF GUARDING** an act of guarding somebody or something, or the responsibility of guarding somebody or something **5 PROTECTIVE DEVICE** a device or part intended to protect the user against injury ○ *a guard on a lathe* **6 MEANS OF PROTECTION** any means of protection ○ *The pension is index-linked as a guard against inflation.* **7 DEFENCE** a defensive posture or state of mind ○ *Her guard was up.* **8 guard, Guard SOLDIER** in the British army and other armies, a soldier who belongs to any regiment originally formed to provide protection for the sovereign **9** *Ireland* **GARDA** a member of the Garda (*informal*) **10 BODY PROTECTION** a piece of tough material worn to protect a part of the body from injury **11 DEFENSIVE POSITION IN BASKETBALL** either of the two players in basketball who regularly defend the backcourt and initiate attacks **12 BATSMAN'S STANCE** in cricket, a position taken by a batsman when ready to receive a bowled ball [15C. < French *garde* (noun), *garder* (verb) < Germanic.] ◇ **off (your) guard** having relaxed the usual precautions against attack ◇ **on (your) guard** prepared against attack ◇ **mount** *or* **stand guard** to keep a watch or defensive posture

SYNONYMS See ***safeguard***.

guard against *vt* to be wary of something or take precautions against it

guardant /gaárdənt/, **gardant** *adj* describes an animal on a coat of arms having its face turned towards the observer ○ *a lion guardant* [Late 16C. < French *gardant*, present participle of *garder* 'guard'.]

guard cell *n* either of two specialized cells bordering pores in the epidermis of leaves that move to control the size of the aperture in response to changes in water levels

guard dog *n* a dog used for guarding property or people

guarded /gaárdid/ *adj* wary, cautious, or noncommittal — **guardedly** *adv* —**guardedness** *n*

SYNONYMS See ***cautious***.

guard hair *n* the long coarse outer hair on some mammals that forms a protective layer over softer underfur

guardhouse /gaárd howss/ (*plural* **-houses** /-howziz/) *n* a building used to house soldiers acting as guards and as a place for detaining military prisoners

Guardi /gwaárdi/, **Francesco** (1712–93) Italian painter

guardian /gaárdi ən/ *n* **1 PROTECTOR** somebody who or something that guards, protects, or preserves somebody or something **2 LEGALLY RESPONSIBLE INDIVIDUAL** a person who is legally entrusted to manage somebody else's affairs, especially those of a minor **3 SUPERIOR IN FRANCISCAN HIERARCHY** a superior in a Franciscan monastery [15C. < Anglo-Norman *gardein* < Old French *garder* 'to guard'.] —**guardianship** *n*

guardian angel *n* **1** somebody seen as the special protector of somebody's interests (*informal*) **2** an angel believed to look after a particular individual

Guardian Angel *n* a member of a vigilante group that patrols the streets of a city as a volunteer crime prevention squad

guard of honour *n* **1** a body of troops acting as a formal escort for somebody important during a ceremony **2** two racks of lamb joints arranged for roasting with bone ends curved inwards and interleaved

guardrail /gaárd rayl/ *n* **1** a rail acting as a safety barrier at the side of a staircase, road, or deck of a ship **2** an additional rail laid close inside the main running rail on tight curves and at points to help a train's wheels stay on the track

guard ring *n* a ring worn to stop another ring from slipping off the finger

guardroom /gaárd room, -ròòm/ *n* a room used by soldiers acting as guards and as a place for detaining military prisoners

guardsman /gaárdzmən/ (*plural* **-men** /-mən/) *n* a soldier who belongs to any of several regiments of the British army originally formed to provide protection for the sovereign

guard's van *n* a compartment, usually at the rear of a train, in which the guard travels

guar gum *n* gum extracted from the seeds of the guar plant. Use: to thicken and stabilize processed foods, in paper manufacture.

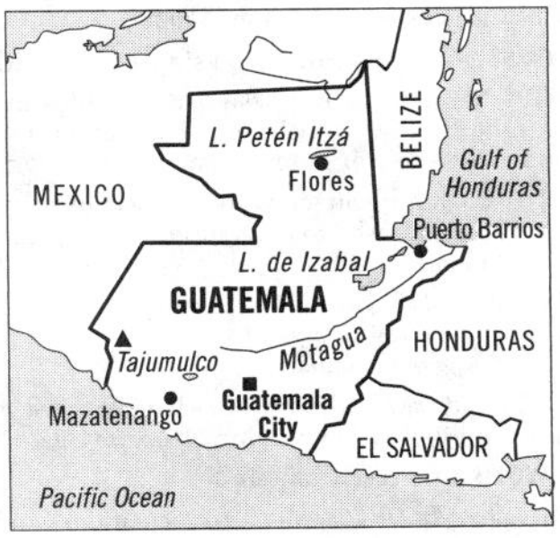

Guatemala

Guatemala /gwaàtə maálə/ country in Central America, on the Gulf of Honduras. Capital: Guatemala City. Population: 11,685,695 (1997). Area: 108,889 sq. km/ 42,042 sq. mi. —**Guatemalan** *adj, n*

Guatemala City capital of Guatemala, in the south-central part of the country. Population: 1,167,495 (1995 estimate).

guava /gwaávə/ *n* **1** a pear-shaped fruit with red or yellow-green skin and cream or pink flesh. Use: eaten raw, made into jam. **2** a tree that bears guavas. Native to: tropical America. Genus: *Psidium*. [Mid-16C. < Spanish *guayaba*, of Caribbean Native American origin.]

guayule /gwə yòòli/ *n* **1** rubber made from the sap of a bush **2** a bush whose sap is a source of guayule. Native to: SW United States, Mexico. *Parthenium argentatum*. [Early 20C. Via American Spanish < Nahuatl *cuauhuli* 'gum tree'.]

gubbins /gúbbinz/ *npl* bits and pieces (*informal*) ■ *n* **gubbins** (*plural* **-binses**) a gadget or device whose name somebody does not know or has forgotten (*informal*) [Mid-16C. < obsolete *gobbon* 'fragment' < Old French.]

gubernatorial /gòòbərnə táwri əl/ *adj* relating to, involving, belonging to, or typical of a governor, especially a United States governor [Mid-18C. < Latin *gubernator* 'governor' < *gubernare* (see GOVERN).]

guck /guk/ *n* a slimy, oily, gooey, or otherwise unpleasant substance (*informal*) [Mid-20C. < ?]

guddle /gúdd'l/ *n Scotland* a state of untidiness or confusion, or an untidy place (*informal*) ■ *vi* (**-dles, -dling, -dled**) *Scotland* to use the hands to catch fish by groping under the water from the banks of a river ○ *guddling for trout* [Mid-17C. < ?]

gudgeon[1] /gújjən/ *n* **1 SMALL FISH** a small freshwater fish that is often used as bait. Native to: Europe. *Gobio gobio*. **2 SOMEBODY SILLY** an easily duped person (*slang*) ■ *vt* **CHEAT** to dupe or cheat somebody (*slang*) [14C. Via Old French *goujon* < Latin *gobius* (see GOBY).]

gudgeon[2] /gújjən/ *n* a socket that a pin fits into, e.g. the pin of a hinge or the pivoting bolt of a ship's rudder [15C. < Old French *goujon* 'little gouge' < late Latin *gubia* (see GOUGE).]

gudgeon pin *n* a pin in a piston of an internal-combustion engine attaching to the little end of a connecting rod. US term **wrist pin**

guelder rose /géldər-/ *n* a bushy deciduous shrub with clusters of white flowers and red berries. Native to: Europe, Asia. *Viburnum opulus*. [Late 16C. After the Dutch province of *Gelderland*.]

Guelph[1] /gwelf/, **Guelf** *n* a member of a political party in medieval Italy that supported the authority of the pope and opposed the Ghibellines, who supported the Holy Roman Emperor's claim to rule Italy [Late 16C. Via Italian *Guelfo* < Middle High German *Welf*, leading dynasty of the Holy Roman Empire.] —**Guelphism** *n*

Guelph[2] /gwelf/ city in SE Ontario, Canada. Population: 95,821 (1996).

guenon /gwén nən, gə nón/ *n* a small long-tailed monkey that lives in trees. Native to: Africa. Genus: *Cercopithecus*. [Mid-19C. < French.]

guerdon /gúrd'n/ *n* a reward or recompense (*literary*) [14C. Via Old French < medieval Latin *widerdonum* 'repayment', partial translation of Old High German *widarlōn* 'giving back'.]

gueridon /gérri doN/ *n* a small round ornate table or stand with a central pedestal [Mid-19C. After French, < a character in French farce.]

guerilla *n* MIL = **guerrilla**

SPELLCHECK See ***gorilla***.

Guernica /gúrnikə, gur néekə/ town in N Spain, in the Basque Country, bombed in 1937 by German aircraft. Population: 16,400 (1989).

guernsey /gúrnzi/ (*plural* **-seys**) *n* **1 guernsey, Guernsey DAIRY COW** a light-brown and white dairy cow that produces rich milk, belonging to a breed originating on the island of Guernsey **2 SWEATER** a hand-knitted woollen sweater of a type that sailors and fishermen typically wear **3** *Aus* **SPORTS JERSEY** a sleeveless woollen shirt or jumper worn by a football player ◇ **get** *or* **be given a guernsey** *Aus* to be congratulated for something, or have your efforts acknowledged in some way

Guernsey /gúrnzi/ second largest of the Channel Islands, in the English Channel off France. Population: 58,867 (1991). Area: 64 sq. km/25 sq. mi.

guerrilla /gə ríllə, ge-/, **guerilla** *n* a member of an irregular paramilitary unit, usually with some political objective such as the overthrow of a government ○ *guerrilla warfare* [Early 19C. < Spanish, 'raiding party, skirmish' < *guerra* 'war'.]

SPELLCHECK See ***gorilla***.

guess /gess/ *v* **1** *vt* **PREDICT** to form an opinion about something without enough evidence to make a definite judgment ○ *She guessed the playing card he'd turn up.* **2** *vt* **CONCLUDE CORRECTLY** to arrive at a correct answer to or conjecture about something ○ *I guessed it would be you.* **3** *vi* **FORM OPINION** to form an opinion without knowing for sure **4** *vi* **FIND CORRECT ANSWER** to be correct in your thinking about what might be the case **5** *vt US, Can* **SUPPOSE** to think or suppose something ○ *I guess I'll have the steak.* ■ *n* **1 OPINION** an opinion or answer arrived at by guessing ○ *My guess is she'll head for home.* **2 ACT OF GUESSING** an act or the process of guessing ○ *Have another guess.* [13C. < N Germanic, < Germanic, 'try to get'.] —**guessable** *adj* —**guesser** *n* ◇ **anybody's guess** something that cannot be reliably predicted (*informal*)

guesstimate /géstimət/ *n* an estimate based largely on incomplete information or evidence (*informal*) ■ *vti* (**-mates, -mating, -mated**) to make an estimate of something based largely on incomplete evidence or information (*informal*) [Mid-20C. Blend of GUESS + ESTIMATE.]

guesswork /géss wurk/ *n* the process of making guesses, or the conclusions arrived at by guessing

guest /gest/ *n* **1 RECIPIENT OF HOSPITALITY** a recipient of hospitality **2 SOMEBODY ENTERTAINED AT ANOTHER'S EXPENSE** a recipient of a meal or entertainment that is paid for by somebody else ○ *Club members are allowed to sign two people in as guests.* **3 CUSTOMER** a person who pays to use the facilities of a hotel, restaurant, or other establishment **4 SOMEBODY ASKED TO JOIN OTHERS** a person who is invited by an organization or institution to receive hospitality ○ *We have a distinguished guest at the meeting* *tonight.* 5 **SOMEBODY MAKING SPECIAL APPEARANCE** a person who appears by invitation in a radio or television programme ○ *our special guest for tonight's show* 6 **ANIMAL USING ANOTHER'S NEST** an organism, especially an insect, that shares the shelter of another or lives alongside the other as a parasite ■ *vi* **MAKE SPECIAL APPEARANCE** to appear as a guest on a radio or television programme ■ *adj* 1 **APPEARING AS GUEST** appearing or invited as a guest 2 **FOR GUESTS** for guests to use [13C. < Old Norse *gestr.*] ◇ **be my guest** used to tell people that they are welcome to do as they please (*informal*)

guest beer *n* a beer kept on draught in a bar for a limited period only as an addition to the usual beers

guest book *n* a book or register that visitors or guests sign, e.g. at a bed-and-breakfast. ◊ **visitors' book**

guesthouse /gést howss/ (*plural* **-houses** /-howziz/) *n* 1 a small hotel or private home that offers accommodation to paying guests 2 *US* a small house used to accommodate visitors to a main house

guest night *n* an evening on which nonmembers are welcome to participate in the activities of a club or society

guest of honour *n* somebody invited to attend a gathering or event who is seen as highly important or the most important of the invited guests

guestroom /gést room, -ro͝om/ *n* a bedroom for visitors who stay for a short time

guest star *n* a well-known performer who makes a single or occasional appearance in a television or radio programme

guest-star *vti* to appear as a guest star, or feature somebody as a guest star

guest worker *n* a foreign national allowed to come and work, but not take up permanent residence, in another country

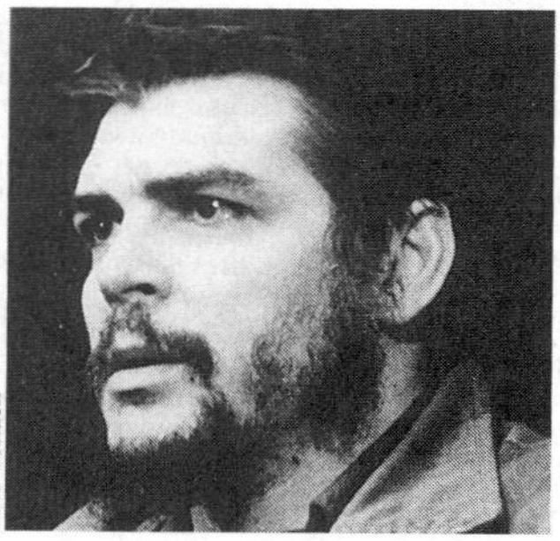

AKG London

Che Guevara

Guevara /gə vaárə/, **Che** (1928–67) Argentine-born South American revolutionary leader. Born **Ernesto Guevara de la Serna**

guff /guf/ *n* (*informal*) 1 nonsense or empty talk 2 *Scotland* a smell, especially a bad one [Early 19C. Probably suggesting a whiff of bad smelling air.]

guffaw /gə fáw/ *vi* to laugh loudly and raucously ■ *n* a loud and raucous laugh [Early 18C. An imitation of the sound.]

Guggenheim /gó͝oggən hīm/, **Peggy** (1898–1979) US art collector and philanthropist

GUI /go͞o i/ *abbr* graphical user interface

guidance /gīd'nss/ *n* 1 **LEADERSHIP** leadership or direction 2 **ADVICE** advice or counselling, especially counselling given to students on academic matters 3 **SYSTEMS THAT CONTROL FLIGHT** the systems and devices that control the flight of an aircraft, missile, or spacecraft ○ *onboard guidance*

guidance counsellor *n US* in a US high school, somebody who gives students personal, academic, and career counselling

guide /gīd/ *v* (**guides, guiding, guided**) 1 *vti* **SHOW THE WAY** to lead somebody in the right direction 2 *vt* **STEER** to steer a vehicle or animal 3 *vt* **HELP SOMEBODY LEARN** to teach somebody, or oversee training in something ○ *An instructor will be appointed to guide you through the course.* 4 *vt* **RUN ORGANIZATION** to control the affairs of an organization or body 5 *vt* **ADVISE** to advise or counsel somebody ○ *Be guided by your conscience.* ■ *n* 1 **SOMEBODY WHO SHOWS THE WAY** a person who leads and assists others in a place or towards a destination 2 **SOMEBODY WHO LEADS TOURISTS** a person who supervises a tour 3 **INFLUENCE ON DECISION** a strong influence on the decisions and behaviour of another ○ *Her grandmother's wisdom was her guide throughout life.* 4 PUBL, LEISURE = **guidebook** 5 **SOURCE OF INFORMATION** a publication or a section of a magazine or newspaper giving information on a subject ○ *a TV guide* 6 **CONTROLLING DEVICE** a device that controls the movement or operation of a machine 7 **guide, Guide MEMBER OF GIRLS' SCOUTING ORGANIZATION** a member of the Guides 8 **SOLDIER CONTROLLING MARCH** a soldier stationed at the side of a column of marching soldiers to control alignment and lead the way [14C. < Old French *guider* < Germanic.] —**guidable** *adj*

guidebook /gīd bo͝ok/ *n* a book containing information for tourists about a country, area, city, or institution

guided missile /gīdid-/ *n* a self-propelled missile that can be steered in flight by remote control or by an onboard homing device

guide dog *n* a dog trained to lead a sightless person

guideline /gīd līn/ *n* 1 an official recommendation indicating how something should be done or what sort of action should be taken in a particular circumstance 2 a line that shows a correct position, route, or alignment, e.g. a fine line printed as an aid to lining up text or illustrations on a page

~~**guidence**~~ incorrect spelling of **guidance**

guidepost /gīd pōst/ *n* a direction sign at a roadside

guiderail /gīd rayl/ *n* a rail designed to lead somebody in the right direction or help somebody move along, or to control the sideways movement of something

guide rope *n* a rope attached to an object or to another rope or cable and used to manoeuvre it into position or to steady a load

Guides /gīdz/ *npl* a worldwide scouting organization for girls ■ *n* a meeting of a group of Guides (+ *singular or plural verb*) ○ *going to Guides*

guideway /gīd way/ *n* a groove or channel that controls the direction in which a moving object travels

guide word *n US* PUBL = **catchword** *n.* 2

guiding /gīding/ *n UK, Can* the activities of the Guides

guiding light *n* a guide, example, or inspiration

Guido d'Arezzo /gweédō da rétsō/ (990?–1033?) Italian monk and music theorist

guidon /gīd'n/ *n* a regimental flag or pennant, or the soldier who carries it [Mid-16C. Via French < Italian *guidone* < *guida* 'guide'.]

guild /gild/, **gild** *n* 1 **ASSOCIATION OF PEOPLE WITH SIMILAR INTERESTS** a club, society, or other organization of people with common interests or goals 2 **MEDIEVAL TRADE ASSOCIATION** an association of merchants or craftspeople in medieval Europe, formed to give help and advice to its members and to make regulations and set standards for a particular trade 3 **GROUP OF ORGANISMS** a group of organisms that use the same environmental resources in a similar way [14C. Probably < Middle Low German, Middle Dutch *gilde* < Germanic.] —**guildship** *n* —**guildsman** *n* —**guildswoman** *n*

SPELLCHECK Do not confuse ***guild*** with ***gild***, which has a similar sound. Beware: your spellchecker will not catch this error.

guilder /gíldər/, **gulden** /go͝oldən/ (*plural* **-dens** *or* **-den**) *n* 1 see table at **currency** 2 a gold or silver coin formerly used in Germany, Austria, and the Netherlands [15C. Alteration of Dutch *gulden* 'golden'.]

Guildford /gílfərd/ city in SE England. Population: 65,998 (1991).

guildhall /gíld hawl/ *n* 1 the town hall in some towns 2 the meeting place of a modern or medieval guild

guild socialism *n* a socialist movement in Great Britain in the early 20th century advocating state ownership of industry but with each branch managed by guilds of workers —**guild socialist** *n*

guile /gīl/ *n* a cunning, deceitful, and treacherous quality or type of behaviour, or particular skill and cleverness in tricking or deceiving people [13C. Via Old French < Old Norse.] —**guileful** *adj* —**guilefully** *adv* —**guilefulness** *n*

guileless /gīl ləss/ *adj* having or showing no deceit or expectation of being deceived —**guilelessly** *adv* —**guilelessness** *n*

Guilin /gwáy lín/ city in SE China. Population: 376,362 (1991).

guillemot /gílli mot/ *n* a black-and-white or greyish narrow-billed diving sea bird of the auk family. Native to: N Atlantic, N Pacific. Genera: *Uria* and *Cepphus*. [Late 17C. < French, 'little William'.]

guilloche /gi lósh/ *n* an ornamental border formed by two or more interlaced bands round a series of interlocking circles [19C. < French.]

guillotine /gíllə teen/ *n* 1 **MACHINE FOR BEHEADING PEOPLE** a machine for executing people by beheading, consisting of a vertical wooden frame with grooves for a heavy sliding blade to be dropped from a height onto a person's neck 2 **EXECUTION BY GUILLOTINE** execution by means of the guillotine 3 **INSTRUMENT FOR CUTTING METAL OR PAPER** a cutting instrument, especially one for cutting sheet metal or paper, consisting of a platform with a blade attached to one side that is pulled down like a lever 4 **TIME LIMIT ON LEGISLATIVE DEBATE** a limit on the time available for debate on a piece of legislation, designed to speed up parliamentary proceedings and prevent opponents of the legislation obstructing its progress [Late 18C. After Joseph-Ignace *Guillotin* (1738–1814), French physician.] —**guillotine** *vt*

guilt /gilt/ *n* 1 **AWARENESS OF WRONGDOING** an awareness of having done wrong or committed a crime, accompanied by feelings of shame and regret ○ *feelings of guilt* 2 **FACT OF WRONGDOING** the fact of having committed a crime or done wrong ○ *an admission of guilt* 3 **RESPONSIBILITY FOR WRONGDOING** the responsibility for committing a crime or doing wrong ○ *Some of the guilt must attach to the parents.* 4 **LEGAL CULPABILITY** the responsibility, as determined by a court or other legal authority, for committing an offence that carries a legal penalty [Old English *gylt* < ?]

SPELLCHECK Do not confuse ***guilt*** with ***gilt***, which has a similar sound. Beware: your spellchecker will not catch this error.

guiltless /gíltləss/ *adj* not responsible for a crime or wrongdoing, or not deserving blame or criticism —**guiltlessly** *adv* —**guiltlessness** *n*

guilt trip *n* an exaggerated feeling or display of shame and regret, usually lasting some time (*informal*)

guilty /gílti/ (**-ier, -iest**) *adj* 1 **RESPONSIBLE FOR WRONGDOING** responsible for a crime, wrong action, or error and deserving punishment, blame, or criticism ○ *He was guilty of a serious error of judgment.* 2 **OFFICIALLY FOUND RESPONSIBLE FOR CRIME** found and declared responsible for committing an offence by a court or other legal authority 3 **ASHAMED OF WRONGDOING** aware of having done wrong or committed a crime and regretful and ashamed about it ○ *I still feel guilty about having forgotten your birthday.* 4 **SHOWING GUILT** indicating or suggesting that somebody feels guilt, has done wrong, or has something to hide ○ *a guilty look on his face* 5 **CAUSING GUILT** causing or likely to cause emotions of shame and regret ○ *a guilty secret* —**guiltily** *adv* —**guiltiness** *n*

guilty conscience *n* a feeling of shame at having done wrong

Guimard /gímaa/, **Hector** (1867–1942) French architect

guimpe /gimp, gamp/ *n* 1 a short blouse designed to be worn under a dress or pinafore 2 a starched cloth that covers the neck and shoulders, worn by some nuns as part of their habit [Mid-19C. < French, < Old French *guimple* 'wimple'.]

guinea /gínni/ *n* 1 a gold coin worth 21 shillings (£1.05p) that was a British unit of currency between 1663 and 1813 2 an amount equivalent to £1.05 or 21 shillings, the value of a guinea [Mid-16C. Because first made for trade with the *Guinea* coast of W Africa.]

Guinea /gínni/ republic in W Africa, on the Atlantic coast. Capital: Conakry. Population: 7,405,375 (1997). Area: 245,857 sq. km/94,926 sq. mi. —**Guinean** *adj, n*

Guinea-Bissau /gínni bi sów/ republic in W Africa, on the Atlantic coast. Capital: Bissau. Population: 1,096,000 (1996). Area: 36,125 sq. km/13,948 sq. mi.

guinea fowl *n* a bird related to pheasants, with a short tail and a bare head and neck, typically black with white speckles. Kept for: food. Native to: Africa. Subfamily: Numidinae. [Late 18C. After the *Guinea* coast of W Africa.]

guinea grass *n* a tall grass, grown in Central and South America and parts of the United States. Use: animal fodder. Native to: Africa. *Panicum maximum*. [Mid-18C. After the *Guinea* coast of W Africa.]

Guinea

Guinea-Bissau

guinea hen *n* a female guinea fowl

guinea pig *n* **1** a plump short-eared furry domesticated rodent, that is larger than a hamster and widely kept as a pet. Native to: South America. *Cavia porcellus.* **2** somebody or something used as the subject of an experiment, test, or trial [Mid-17C. After the *Guinea* coast of W Africa, probably from confusion with GUYANA.]

guinea worm *n* a long thin worm that lives as a parasite under the skin of people and animals and can grow to more that a metre in length. Native to: Africa, Asia. *Dracunculus medinensis.* [Late 17C. After the *Guinea* coast of W Africa.]

Guinevere /gwínni veer/ *n* in English legend, the wife of King Arthur and the lover of the knight Sir Lancelot

Guinness /gínniss/, **Sir Alec** (1914–2000) British actor

Guinness, Arthur (1725–1803) Irish brewer

guipure /gi pyóoə/ *n* a heavy large-patterned lace that is not made on a mesh base but is joined together by threads [Mid-19C. < French *guiper* 'cover with cloth or yarn' < Germanic, 'wind round'.]

guiro /gweérō/ (*plural* **-ros**) *n* a musical instrument of Central and South America, made from a gourd with grooves cut so that a rasping sound is created when a stick is scraped across it [Late 19C. < Spanish, 'gourd'.]

guise /gīz/ *n* **1** DECEPTIVE APPEARANCE a false outward appearance ○ *hiding her treacherous intentions under the guise of friendship* **2** FORM OR APPEARANCE a shape or form, especially a changed one, in which something presents itself or is presented ○ *old ideas in a new guise* **3** COSTUME a style of dress or personal appearance [14C. < French, < Germanic.]

guiser /gīzər/ *n Scotland* one of a group of children who go around their neighbourhood at Halloween offering to perform something, usually a song, in return for money or food [15C. < *guise* 'dress up' < GUISE.] —**guising** *n*

guitar /gi taár/ *n* a musical instrument with a long neck, a flat body shaped like a figure of eight, and usually six strings that are plucked or strummed [Early 17C. Via Spanish *guitarra* < Greek *kithara* 'cithara'.] —**guitarist** *n*

guitarfish /gi taár fish/ (*plural* **-fishes** or **-fish**) *n* a ray with long curving pectoral fins that give its body a guitar shape. Native to: tropical and subtropical waters. Family: Rhinobatidae.

Guitry /geé tree/, **Sacha** (1885–1957) Russian-born French dramatist and actor. Born **Alexandre Georges Guitry**

Guiyang /gwáy yáng/ capital of Guizhou Province, S China. Population: 1,279,002 (1991).

Guizhou /gwáy jṓ/ province in SW China. Capital: Guiyang. Population: 34,580,000 (1994). Area: 174,000 sq. km/67,200 sq. mi.

Gujarat /gōōjjə raát/ state in W India, on the Arabian Sea. Capital: Gandhinagar. Population: 44,235,000 (1994). Area: 196,024 sq. km/75,685 sq. mi.

Gujarati /gōōjjə raáti/ (*plural* **-ti**), **Gujerati** (*plural* **-ti**) *n* **1** an Indic language spoken in the Indian states of Gujarat and Maharashtra and in southern parts of Pakistan, belonging to the Indo-Iranian branch of Indo-European. Native speakers: 35 million. **2** a member of a people living mainly in the Indian state of Gujarat [Early 19C. < Hindi.] —**Gujarati** *adj*

Gujranwala /gōōjrən waálə/, **Gujrānwāla** city in NE Pakistan. Population: 658,753 (1981).

gulag /gōō lag/ *n* **1** POLITICAL PRISON IN FORMER USSR a prison or labour camp in the former Soviet Union, to which opponents of the government were sent **2** PRISON CAMP NETWORK the network of political prisons and labour camps in the former Soviet Union **3** DEPARTMENT ADMINISTERING PRISONS the department of the former Soviet security service that was responsible for running the network of political prisons **4** PRISON FOR DISSENTERS any place that dissenters are sent to, or the isolating or imprisoning of dissenters [Mid-20C. < Russian, acronym < *Glavnoe upravlenie ispravitelno-trudovykh lagerei* 'Chief Administration for Corrective Labour Camps'.]

gulch /gulch/ *n US, Can* a small rocky ravine, especially one with a fast-flowing stream running through it (*often in placenames*) [Mid-19C. < ?]

gulden *n* MONEY = guilder

gules /gyoolz/ *n* the colour red on a coat of arms [14C. < Old French *go(u)les* 'red fur neckpiece' < plural of *go(u)le* (see GULLET).]

gulf /gulf/ *n* **1** INLET OF SEA a large inlet of a sea similar to a bay but often larger and more enclosed by land (*often in placenames*) ○ *the Gulf of Mexico* **2** WIDE HOLE a deep wide hole in the ground **3** VAST DIFFERENCE a great difference, e.g. in points of view, regarded as dividing or separating people or groups [14C. Via French *golfe* < Greek *kolfos* 'bosom, bag, trough between waves, abyss'.]

Gulf States *n* **1** the countries that border the Persian Gulf, considered as an economic or geopolitical unit, especially in their role as oil producers **2** the states of the S United States that border the Gulf of Mexico, including Florida, Alabama, Mississippi, Louisiana, and Texas

Gulf Stream warm current of the Atlantic Ocean, flowing northeast from the Gulf of Mexico along the coast of North America then east to the coasts of the British Isles

Gulf War *n* **1** the war that took place during early 1991 in the Persian Gulf between United Nations forces and Iraq, following the invasion of Kuwait by Iraq in August 1990 **2** MIL, HIST = **Iran-Iraq War**

Gulf War syndrome *n* a group of medical symptoms, including fatigue, skin disorders, and muscle pains, experienced by some soldiers who fought in the Gulf War of 1991

gulfweed /gúlf weed/ *n* a brown seaweed that forms thick floating masses. Native to: tropical Atlantic. Genus: *Sargassum.*

gull[1] /gul/ *n* a common, fairly large, web-footed white-and-grey sea bird with a yellow beak. Native to: coastal North America and Europe. Genus: *Larus.* [15C. < Celtic.] —**gullery** *n*

gull[2] /gul/ *vt* to trick or deceive somebody (*archaic; often passive*) ■ *n* an easily deceived person (*archaic*) [Mid-16C. < ?]

Gullah /gúllə/ (*plural* **-lahs** or **-lah**) *n* **1** a member of a people of African descent who live along the coasts of South Carolina, Georgia, and N Florida, and on the neighbouring Sea Islands **2** the creole language of the Gullah people, a form of English that has been influenced by several West African languages. Native speakers: 300,000. [Mid-18C. < ?] —**Gullah** *adj*

gullet /gúllit/ *n* **1** the oesophagus or throat **2** a groove or indentation in the protoplasm of certain protozoans that has a function in the intake of food [14C. < Old French *goulet* 'little throat' < *go(u)le* 'throat' < Latin *gula.*]

gullible /gúlləb'l/ *adj* tending to trust and believe people, and therefore easily tricked or deceived [Early 19C. < GULL[2].] —**gullibility** /gúlə billəti/ *n* —**gullibly** *adv*

Gullit /hoóllit/, **Ruud** (b. 1962) Suriname-born Dutch footballer and manager

gullwing /gúll wing/ *adj* hinged at the top and opening upwards (*describes a type of car door*) ■ *n* an aircraft wing in which the section attached to the fuselage slants upwards and the outer section is horizontal, or an aircraft with such a wing

gully /gúlli/ *n* (*plural* **-lies**) **1** SMALL VALLEY a channel or small valley, especially one carved out by persistent heavy rainfall **2** NARROW MOUNTAIN PASSAGE a narrow passage between two rocky slopes on a mountain **3** CHANNEL MADE FOR WATER a gutter, open drain, or other artificial channel for water, especially one at a roadside **4** FIELDING POSITION a fielding position in cricket, between the last of the slips and point, or a fielder in this position ○ *standing at gully* **5** CHANNEL BY BOWLING LANE the channel on either side of a ten-pin bowling lane ■ *vti* (**-lies, -lying, -lied**) CUT OUT CHANNELS to wear away channels in land or soil, or to wash into channels, by heavy rainfall [Mid-17C. < French *goulet* (see GULLET).]

gulp /gulp/ *v* **1** *vt* SWALLOW FAST to swallow something greedily, hurriedly, or frantically, taking in large amounts at a time ○ *She gulped down her coffee and grabbed her coat.* **2** *vi* GASP to gasp or choke **3** *vi* MAKE SWALLOWING MOTION to make a swallowing movement with the throat, especially because of being frightened or nervous ○ *He gulped and looked around nervously for the exit.* **4** *vi* MAKE SWALLOWING SOUND to make a loud swallowing sound with the throat, especially because of drinking too fast ■ *n* **1** SWALLOWING MOTION OR SOUND a swallowing movement or noise made with the throat **2** AMOUNT SWALLOWED a quantity of something, especially a drink, consumed in one large swallow [15C. Probably < Middle Dutch *gulpen* 'swallow, guzzle'.] —**gulper** *n* —**gulpingly** *adv*

gulp back *vt* to attempt to stifle tears or sobs

gum[1] /gum/ *n* **1** STICKY PLANT SUBSTANCE THAT HARDENS a sticky substance found inside some plants, especially trees, that hardens when it is exposed to air and dissolves when put in water **2** ANY STICKY PLANT SUBSTANCE any sticky substance found inside plants, e.g. a resin **3** SOMETHING STICKY any sticky substance or deposit **4** ADHESIVE glue made from or containing a sticky plant substance or any soft synthetic glue used for sticking paper or other lightweight materials **5** TREE PRODUCING GUM any tree that produces gum. Genera: *Eucalyptus* and *Liquidambar* and *Nyssa.* **6** CHEWING GUM chewing gum (*informal*) **7** CHEWY SWEET a chewy fruit-flavoured sweet ■ *vt* (**gums, gumming, gummed**) STICK SOMETHING TO SOMETHING ELSE to stick something to something else, with or without gum or glue [14C. Via Old French *gomme* < Greek *kommi* < Egyptian *kemai.*]

gum up *vt* to block or immobilize something with a sticky substance that prevents parts from moving ○ *eyes all gummed up* ◇ **gum up the works** to bring everything to a halt, usually by being obstructive or incompetent (*informal*)

gum[2] /gum/ *n* the firm flesh that surrounds the roots of the teeth (*often plural*) [Old English *goma* < ?]

GUM *abbr* genitourinary medicine

gum acacia *n* INDUST = **gum arabic**

gum accroides /-ə króydeez/ *n* INDUST, MED = **acaroid resin**

gum ammoniac *n* INDUST = **ammoniac**

gum arabic *n* a sticky substance taken from some acacia trees. Use: in adhesives, confectionery, medicines. [Because the trees grow in the Middle East]

gumbo /gúmbō/ (*plural* **-bos**) *n* **1** PLANTS = okra *n.* 1, okra *n.* 2 **2** THICK STEW WITH OKRA a stew of fish, poultry, or meat that has been thickened with okra **3** US STICKY SOIL silty soil that turns very sticky and muddy when it becomes wet, found throughout the central United States **4** US MIXTURE a mixture or hotchpotch (*informal*) ○ *The band played a gumbo of Cajun, zydeco, and jazz music.* [Early 19C. < Louisiana French *gombo*, probably < Bantu.]

Gumbo /gúmbō/ *n* a French patois, incorporating aspects of African languages, that is spoken in Louisiana and the French West Indies —**Gumbo** *adj*

gumboil /gúm boyl/ *n* an abscess on the gum, especially near the root of a decayed tooth. Technical name **parulis**

gum boot *n* a waterproof boot made of rubber or plastic, especially one coming to just below the knee

gumdrop /gúm drop/ *n* a chewy fruit-flavoured sweet

gumma /gúmmə/ (*plural* **-mata** /-mətə/) *n* a rubbery tumour that can occur in the tertiary stage of syphilis [Early 18C. Via Modern Latin < Greek *kommi* (see GUM¹).] —**gummatous** *adj*

gummosis /gə mṓssiss/ *n* the production of too much gum by a tree, especially a fruit tree, as a result of infection, a wound, or adverse weather

gummous /gúmməss/ *adj* **1** sticky like the gum from a tree **2** containing gum

gummy¹ /gúmmi/ (**-mier, -miest**) *adj* **1** like gum, especially in being sticky or thick and slow-flowing **2** covered, clogged, or stuck together with a sticky substance of some kind —**gumminess** *n*

gummy² /gúmmi/ (**-mier, -miest**) *adj* with only the gums showing, but no teeth, usually because the person concerned has no teeth —**gummily** *adv*

gump /gump/ *vi* to muddle through difficult situations thanks to a series of lucky chances [Late 20C. < the 1994 film *Forrest Gump*.]

gumption /gúmpsh'n/ *n* (*informal*) **1** practical common sense and presence of mind ○ *Luckily, he had the gumption to call the police.* **2** the courage to take what action is needed ○ *He wouldn't have the gumption to say so, even if he disagreed.* [Early 18C. < ?]

gum resin *n* a naturally occurring mixture of gum and resin taken from some plants and trees, e.g. the yellow pigment gamboge

gumshield /gúm sheeld/ *n* a hard plastic cover that fits inside somebody's mouth over the teeth and gums, worn as protection from injury by people involved in contact sports such as boxing and rugby. US term **mouth guard**

gumshoe /gúm shoo/ *n US* a detective, especially a private investigator (*informal*) [< moving with stealth in rubber overshoes]

gum tree *n* any tree that produces gum. Genera: *Eucalyptus* and *Liquidambar* and *Nyssa*. ◇ **up a gum tree** in a difficult or impossible situation (*informal*)

gumwood /gúm wood/ *n* wood from any gum tree, especially a eucalyptus tree

gun /gun/ *n* **1 WEAPON THAT FIRES BULLETS** a weapon, anything from a small hand-held pistol to a large piece of artillery, with a metal tube through which bullets or missiles are fired by an explosive charge **2 DEVICE THAT FIRES** any tool or instrument that forces something out under pressure **3 SHOT FROM GUN** a shot fired from a gun, e.g. as a military salute or a signal for a race to begin, or the sound of the shot ○ *Wait for the gun.* **4 SOMEBODY WITH GUN** a person who is armed with a gun (*informal*) ○ *the fastest gun in the West* **5** *US* **ACCELERATOR** a vehicle's accelerator (*informal*) ○ *Give it the gun.* **6 HUNTER** a member of a party of hunters armed with shotguns ■ *vt* (**guns, gunning, gunned**) **PRESS THROTTLE** to rev up an engine (*informal*) [14C. Probably < Scandinavian name *Gunnhildr* < *gunnr* 'battle' + *hildr* 'war', from the custom of giving women's names to weapons.] ◇ **go great guns** to be working, operating, or doing something at great speed or very effectively and successfully ◇ **jump the gun 1** to start a race before the starting gun goes off **2** to act prematurely ◇ **stick to your guns** to refuse to change your plans or opinions even though you are under attack from other people

gun down *vt* to shoot and kill or severely injure somebody (*informal*)

gun for *vt* (*informal*) **1** to set out to attack or criticize somebody or bring about somebody's downfall **2** to plan or intend to get something for yourself ○ *She's gunning for a position in the Paris office.*

gunboat /gún bōt/ *n* a small fast ship with large guns mounted on it, used, e.g. by coastguards

gunboat diplomacy *n* negotiations between nations that involve threats to use military force

gun carriage *n* a platform with wheels on which a large military gun is mounted and transported or on which a coffin is laid during state funerals

gun control *n* legal measures to control, license, review, put conditions on, or restrict the ownership of firearms by members of the public

guncotton /gún kot'n/ *n* CHEM, INDUST = **nitrocellulose**

gun deck *n* the deck of a sailing warship, below the main deck, where the cannons were situated

gun dog *n* **1** a dog trained to find game and to bring back any game shot by a hunter or gamekeeper **2** a dog of a breed such as a pointer that is traditionally regarded as suitable for training as a hunter's or gamekeeper's dog

gunfight /gún fīt/ *n* a fight between two or more people armed with handguns, especially in the days of the Wild West —**gunfighter** *n*

gunfire /gún fīr/ *n* shots fired from a gun or guns, or the sound of shots

gunflint /gún flint/ *n* a small piece of flint that ignites the gunpowder in an old-fashioned flintlock gun

gunge /gunj/ *n* an unpleasantly sticky, slimy, or messy semiliquid substance (*informal*) [Mid-20C. < ?] —**gungy** *adj*

gung ho /gúng hṓ/ *adj* (*informal; hyphenated before nouns*) **1** eager to fight, especially in a military conflict **2** extremely or excessively enthusiastic or eager [Mid-20C. < Mandarin Chinese *gōnghé* 'work together', motto of US marines in Asia in World War II.]

gunite /gúnn īt/ *n* a concrete building material that is sprayed from a high-pressure gun onto a mould or over reinforced concrete or steel in light construction

gunk /gungk/ *n* a greasy messy near-solid mass (*informal*) [Mid-20C. Probably invented to suggest lumpy grease.] —**gunky** *adj*

gun lap *n* the last lap of an athletics race, signalled by the firing of a gun as the leading runner begins it

gun lobby *n* lobbyist groups who argue for the right of ordinary members of the public to buy and own guns, and who resist legislative attempts to put conditions on the ownership and availability of firearms and ammunition

gunlock /gún lok/ *n* the mechanism by which the gunpowder charge was exploded in early types of gun, e.g. flintlock, matchlock, or wheel lock

gunman /gúnmən/ (*plural* **-men** /-mən/) *n* **1** a man armed with a gun, especially a criminal or an assassin **2** a man skilled in firing guns

gunmetal /gún mett'l/ *n* **1 GREY BRONZE** a dark grey bronze. Use: formerly, to make cannons. **2 DARK GREY METAL** a dark grey alloy. Use: formerly, household and industrial items, children's toys. **3 gunmetal, gunmetal grey DARK GREY COLOUR** a dark bluish-grey colour —**gunmetal** *adj* —**gunmetal-grey** *adj*

Gunn /gun/, **Mrs Aeneas** (1870–1961) Australian writer. Born **Jeannie Taylor**

Gunn effect /gún-/ *n* in a semiconductor, the microwave oscillation produced by a steady electric field that is larger than the normal threshold value [Mid-20C. After J. B. *Gunn*, (1928-), Egyptian-born British physicist.]

gunnel¹ *n* NAUT = **gunwale**

gunnel² /gúnn'l/ (*plural* **-nels** *or* **-nel**) *n* a small fish that is similar to an eel. Native to: Atlantic and Pacific coastal waters. Family: Pholidae. [Late 17C. < ?]

Gunnell /gúnn'l/, **Sally** (*b.* 1966) British athlete

gunner /gúnnər/ *n* **1 SOLDIER WHO FIRES LARGE GUN** a soldier who operates a large gun **2 NCO WITH GUN-RELATED RESPONSIBILITIES** a warrant officer in the British navy or the US Marines who is responsible for training gun operators and running the ammunition stores **3 ARTILLERY SOLDIER** a soldier in an artillery regiment, especially a private

gunnera /gúnnərə/ (*plural* **-as**) *n* a tropical plant with huge leaves. Native to: South America. Genus: *Gunnera*. [Late 18C. < modern Latin, after J. E. *Gunnerus* (1718–73), Norwegian botanist.]

gunnery /gúnnəri/ *n* **1** the knowledge and techniques involved in the effective use of guns or in their design and construction **2** the use of guns, especially of large guns in battle

gunnery sergeant *n* a noncommissioned officer in the US Marines, equivalent to a sergeant first class in the US Army

gunny /gúnni/ (*plural* **-nies**) *n* **1** a sack made from coarse jute or hemp cloth. US term **gunnysack 2** coarse jute or hemp cloth. Use: sacks. [Early 18C. < Hindi *gonī*.]

gunplay /gún play/ *n* the shooting of guns, especially by armed criminals

gunpoint /gún poynt/ *n* the muzzle of a firearm ◇ **at gunpoint** under the threat of being shot and killed if orders are not obeyed

gunpowder /gún powdər/ *n* an explosive mixture of potassium nitrate, charcoal, and sulphur. Use: in fireworks and other explosives, e.g. in quarry blasting, formerly, as the charge in firearms.

Gunpowder Plot *n* a conspiracy by a group of Roman Catholics, including Guy Fawkes, to blow up Parliament in 1605

gunpowder tea *n* Chinese green tea with individual leaves rolled into small pellets

gunroom /gún room, -rŏŏm/ *n* **1** a room in a house where guns are kept, especially shotguns **2** the quarters of midshipmen and junior officers on a ship in the British navy

gunrunning /gún running/ *n* the smuggling of illegal arms into a country, usually in order to supply terrorist or insurrectionist organizations —**gunrunner** *n*

gunship /gún ship/ *n* a military aircraft, usually a helicopter, that is fitted with guns for intrinsic use against ground targets

gunshot /gún shot/ *n* **1 GUN'S NOISE** the sound of a gun being fired **2 BULLETS FIRED** bullets or shot fired from a gun **3 GUN'S RANGE** the maximum distance that a bullet fired from a gun can travel

gun-shy *adj* **1** extremely cautious, timid, or wary of taking risks **2** afraid of guns or the noise they make when fired

gunslinger /gún slingər/ *n* an armed fighter or criminal, especially in the frontier days of the Wild West (*informal*) —**gunslinging** *n*

gunsmith /gún smith/ *n* a maker, seller, or repairer of firearms

gunstock /gún stok/ *n* the shaped wooden or metal handle of a rifle that is pressed against the shoulder when the rifle is being fired

Guntur /gŏŏn tŏŏr/ city in SE India. Population: 471,051 (1991).

gunwale /gúnn'l/ *n* the top edge of a ship's sides that forms a ledge round the whole ship above the deck (*often plural*) [15C. Because used in the past to support guns.]

Guo Xi /gwṓ sheé/ (*fl.* 1060–75) Chinese artist

guppy /gúppi/ (*plural* **-pies**) *n* a small freshwater fish that has a brightly coloured tail, produces live young rather than eggs, and is popular in aquariums. Native to: Caribbean, South America. *Poecilia reticulata*. [Early 20C. After the Reverend R. J. Lechmere *Guppy* (1836–1916), who sent the first specimen from Trinidad to the British Museum.]

Gupta /gŏŏptə/ *n* an Indian dynasty of the 3rd to 6th centuries that established a loose empire in much of the subcontinent [Late 19C. After *Chandragupta*, the dynasty's founder.]

Gur /gŏŏ ər/ *n* a group of Niger-Congo languages spoken in W Central Africa. Native speakers: 10 million. —**Gur** *adj*

gurdwara /gúrd waarə/ *n* a Sikh temple or other place of worship where Sikh scriptures are kept [Early 20C. < Punjabi *gurduārā*.]

gurgle /gúrg'l/ (**-gles, -gling, -gled**) *v* **1** *vi* to make the deep bubbling noise that liquid makes when it is poured from a bottle **2** *vti* to make, or speak with a bubbling sound in the throat [Mid-16C. < assumed Vulgar Latin *gurguliare* < Latin *gurgulio* 'gullet'.] —**gurglingly** *adv*

Gurkha /gúrkə/ (*plural* **-kha** *or* **-khas**) *n* **1** a member of a Hindu people living mainly in Nepal **2** a Gurkha serving in the British or Indian army [Early 19C. < Nepalese *Gurkha*, placename.] —**Gurkha** *adj*

Gurkhali /gur kaáli/ *n* the form of Nepali that is the lingua franca of Gurkha soldiers, particularly those in the British army [Late 19C. < Nepalese *Gurkha*, placename.] —**Gurkhali** *adj*

Gurmukhi /gŏŏr mŏŏki/ *n* the script in which Punjabi is written [Late 19C. < Punjabi.]

gurn *vi* = **girn**

gurnard /gúrnərd/ (*plural* **-nards** *or* **-nard**) *n* **1** a widely distributed spiny-finned marine fish with an armoured head and sets of pectoral fins modified for crawling on the sea bottom. Family: Triglidae. **2** ZOOL = **flying gurnard** [14C. < Old French *gornart* < Latin *grunnire* 'grunt'; from the sound it makes when caught.]

gurney /gúrni/ (*plural* **-neys**) *n US* MED = **trolley** *n*. **2** [Late 19C. < ?]

guru /gŏŏ roo/ (*plural* **-rus**) *n* **1 HINDU OR SIKH RELIGIOUS TEACHER** in Hinduism and Sikhism, a religious leader or teacher 2 **LEADER OF RELIGIOUS GROUP** a spiritual leader of or intellectual guide for a religious group or movement, especially one being described as not mainstream 3 **SOMEBODY INFLUENTIAL** a prominent and influential leader or founder of something ○ *a meeting of the world's software gurus* 4 **REVERED TEACHER** a teacher or counsellor in spiritual or intellectual matters who is especially revered and followed by a particular person [Early 17C. < Sanskrit, 'elder, teacher'.]

Guru Nanak /go͝o roo naánək/ ➧ **Nanak**

Guru Nanak Jananti /-jə nánti/ *n* a Sikh festival marking the birthday of Guru Nanak. Date: November.

gush /gush/ *vti* 1 **FLOW OUT FAST** to flow out, or send a liquid out, rapidly and in large quantities 2 **SPEAK, BEHAVE, OR SAY EFFUSIVELY** to speak or behave in an extremely or exaggeratedly enthusiastic, affectionate, or sentimental way ○ *'Your children are simply delightful!' she gushed.* ■ *n* 1 **FLOW OF LIQUID** a fast or copious flow of liquid from somewhere 2 **EMOTIONAL OUTBURST** an outburst of over-enthusiastic or overemotional speech or behaviour [14C. Probably an imitation of the sound of liquid gushing.] —**gushing** *adj* —**gushingly** *adv*

gusher /gúshər/ *n* 1 an oil well from which oil flows freely and in large amounts, without having to be pumped 2 a person who speaks or behaves in an exaggeratedly emotional or enthusiastic way

gushy /gúshi/ (**-ier, -iest**) *adj* characterized by over enthusiastic or over emotional speech or behaviour —**gushily** *adv* —**gushiness** *n*

gusset /gússit/ *n* 1 **INSET PIECE OF FABRIC** a piece of fabric inserted in a garment where added strength or freedom of movement is needed 2 **FLAT PLATE REINFORCING A JOINT** a flat, often triangular plate, usually of steel or plywood, used to connect and reinforce a joint where several members meet at different angles, e.g. in a pitched roof 3 **CHAIN MAIL AT AN ARMOUR JOINT** a section of chain mail protecting the unarmoured joints of a suit of armour [14C. < French *gousset* 'little pod' < *gousse* 'pod, shell'.]

gussy up /gússi úp/ (**gussies up, gussying up, gussied up**) *vt US* to dress somebody in fancy clothes, or decorate something elaborately (*informal; often passive*) ○ *all gussied up in a frilly dress* ○ *The city was gussied up for the visit of the mayor.* [Mid-20C. < ?]

gust /gust/ *n* 1 **BURST OF WIND** a sudden violent rush of wind 2 **EMOTIONAL OUTBURST** an outburst of emotion such as anger ■ *vi* **BLOW IN BURSTS** to blow, or be blown by the wind, in sudden violent bursts [Late 16C. < Old Norse *gustr* < *gjósa* 'gush'.]

gustation /gu stáysh'n/ *n* the action of tasting, or the sense or faculty of taste (*formal*) [Late 16C. Directly or via French < Latin *gustation-* < *gustare* 'to taste'.] —**gustatorial** /gústə táwri əl/ *adj* —**gustatorily** /gústətərəli/ *adv* —**gustatory** /gústətəri/ *adj*

Gustav II Adolph /go͝ost aav áddolf/ (1594–1632) king of Sweden (1611–32). Known as **the Lion of the North**

Gustavo A. Madero /go͞o staávō aa mə dáirō/ city in south-central Mexico. Population: 1,268,068 (1990).

gusto /gústō/ *n* lively enthusiasm or enjoyment [Early 17C. Via Italian < Latin *gustus* 'taste'.]

gusty /gústi/ (**-ier, -iest**) *adj* 1 blowing or arising in gusts ○ *a gusty day* 2 exhibiting, or regularly suffering from, sudden outbursts of emotion, especially anger ○ *gusty waves of emotion* —**gustily** *adv* —**gustiness** *n*

gut /gut/ *n* 1 **ALIMENTARY CANAL** the whole of the alimentary canal in people and animals, from the mouth to the anus, or the lower part of it (**intestine**), from the stomach to the anus 2 **ABDOMEN** somebody's belly, especially if it is noticeably large (*slang disapproving*) ○ *I've got to work off this gut.* 3 **PLACE WHERE INSTINCTS ARE FELT** somebody's deepest instinctively felt emotions or responses, as distinct from rational or logical responses (*often before nouns*) ○ *What is your gut reaction to the proposal?* 4 INDUST = **catgut** 5 **FISHING CORD** cord made of fibrous material taken from silkworms. Use: fishing lines. ■ **guts** *npl* 1 **INTESTINES** the insides of a person or animal, especially the intestines 2 **STRENGTH OF CHARACTER** courage or boldness (*slang*) 3 **INNER OR CENTRAL PARTS** the inner or central parts of something, e.g. the working parts of a machine, or the basic principles that a theory is based on ■ *vt* (**guts, gutting, gutted**) 1 **REMOVE AN ANIMAL'S INSIDES** to remove the insides of a dead animal 2 **DESTROY A BUILDING'S INTERIOR** to destroy the internal parts of a building, leaving only the outer walls standing ○ *The factory was completely gutted in the fire.* 3 **EMPTY** to remove all the internal fixtures and furnishings from a room or building 4 **TAKE EXTRACTS FROM** to select extracts from a piece of writing for use elsewhere [Old English *guttas* < Indo-European, 'pour'] ◇ **bust a gut** to struggle or work exceptionally hard to get something done (*slang*) ◇ **hate somebody's guts** to dislike somebody very much (*informal*) ◇ **spill your guts** *US* to tell or confess everything (*informal*) ◇ **sweat your guts out** to work very hard (*informal*)

SYNONYMS See ***courage***.

GUT /gut/ *abbr* Grand Unified Theory

gutbucket /gút bukit/ *n* 1 a home-made instrument played like a double bass, made by fixing a stick to an upturned basin and stretching a string along its length 2 a simple but highly emotional style of jazz or blues

gut course *n US* a college or university unit that is very easy to pass (*informal*)

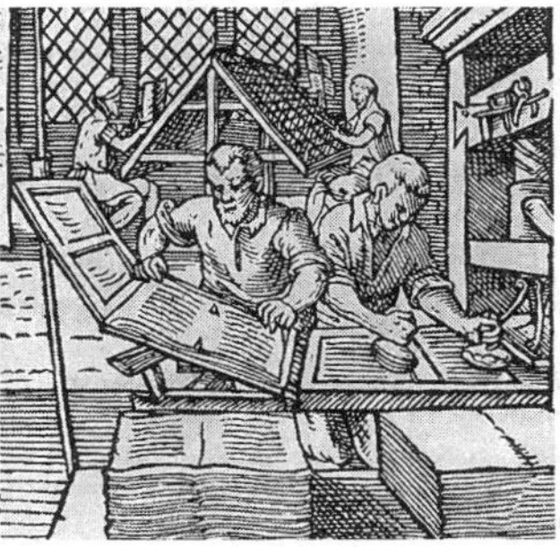

Popperfoto

Johannes Gutenberg: 15th-century engraving showing Gutenberg (left foreground) printing the Gutenberg Bible (1456?)

Gutenberg /go͝ot'n burg/, **Johannes** (1400?–68) German printer

Guthrie /gúthri/, **Sir Tyrone** (1900–71) British stage director

Guthrie, Woody (1912–67) US folk singer and composer. Full name **Woodrow Wilson Guthrie**

gut job *n US* the restoration or repair of a building that includes the removal and rebuilding of the interior (*informal*)

gutless /gútləss/ *adj* lacking in courage and determination —**gutlessness** *n*

SYNONYMS See ***cowardly***.

gut rehabilitation, gut renovation *n US* CONSTR = **gut job** (*informal*)

guts /guts/ *n* a very greedy person (*informal; + singular verb*)

gutsy /gútsi/ (**-ier, -iest**) *adj* (*informal*) 1 **COURAGEOUS** showing courage, boldness and determination 2 **DONE WITH EMOTION** done or performed with a great deal of vigour, passion, or emotion 3 **GREEDY** greedy or gluttonous —**gutsily** *adv* —**gutsiness** *n*

gutta /gúttə/ (*plural* **-tae** /-tee/) *n* 1 one of a series of ornaments shaped like drops that are attached to the underside of a Doric entablature 2 a drop of medicine (*dated; formerly used in the instructions on prescriptions to indicate dose to be taken*) [14C. < Latin, 'drop'.]

gutta-percha /gúttə púrchə/ *n* 1 a pliable substance made from a natural latex. Use: dental fillings, dressings, electrical insulation. 2 any tree whose latex is a source of gutta-percha. Native to: Southeast Asia. Genera: *Palaquium* and *Payena*. [Mid-19C. Alteration (influenced by Latin *gutta* 'drop') of Malay *getah perca* 'gum strips of cloth'.]

guttate /gútt ayt/, **guttated** /-aytid/ *adj* having or resembling drops or spots [Early 19C. < Latin *guttatus* < *gutta* 'drop'.]

guttation /gu táysh'n/ *n* the oozing out of water droplets from the uninjured surface of a plant leaf

gutted /gúttid/ *adj* 1 with the insides taken out, ready to be sold ○ *gutted haddock* 2 desperately disappointed or upset (*informal*) ○ *They were absolutely gutted when they lost the match.*

gutter /gúttər/ *n* 1 **RAINWATER CHANNEL ON A ROOF** a metal or plastic channel on a roof for carrying away rainwater 2 **RAINWATER CHANNEL ON A ROAD** a channel at the edge of a road that carries water into a drain 3 **POOR OR DEGRADED STATE** an impoverished and degraded existence or way of life ○ *She dragged me out of the gutter and made me respect myself.* 4 **CHANNEL ON TEN-PIN BOWLING LANE** the channel on either side of a ten-pin bowling lane 5 **INNER MARGINS OF BOOK** the blank space formed by the inner margins of two facing pages of a book 6 **SPACE BETWEEN STAMPS ON SHEET** the space between the printed design of one stamp and the next one on the sheet, where the perforations lie ■ *v* 1 *vi* **MELT QUICKLY** to burn down more quickly than usual because the melting wax has formed a channel on one side (*refers to a candle*) 2 *vi* **FLICKER** to flicker when on the point of being extinguished 3 *vt* **FORM CHANNELS IN** to wear away channels in the surface of something 4 *vi* **TRICKLE** to run in a narrow stream or trickle ○ *The overflow was guttering down the wall.* ■ *adj* **OF THE WORST KIND** of the most vulgar, corrupt, or morally degraded kind (*disapproving*) [13C. < Anglo-Norman *gotere* < Latin *gutta* 'drop'.]

gutter out *vi* 1 to go out after flickering for a while ○ *Most of the candles guttered out.* 2 to come to an end finally, after gradually declining ○ *The peace process had all but guttered out.*

~~gutteral~~ incorrect spelling of **guttural**

gutter ball *n* in ten-pin bowling, a ball that, when bowled, rolls into the gutter and does not knock over any pins

guttering /gúttəring/ *n* 1 the gutters on a roof 2 metal or plastic channels used as gutters

gutter press *n* low-quality newspapers and magazines that deal mostly with scandal and gossip rather than serious news

guttersnipe /gúttər snīp/ *n* (*insult*) 1 a child who wears dirty ragged clothes, has rough manners, and lives in the streets 2 somebody regarded as having a rough or vulgar manner, especially somebody with a lower-class background [Mid-19C. Via 'street cleaner' < 'common snipe' (a bird that likes wet muddy conditions).] —**guttersnipish** *adj*

guttural /gúttərəl/ *adj* 1 characterized by harsh and grating speech sounds made in the throat or towards the back of the mouth 2 PHON = **velar** *adj.* 1 ■ *n* a speech sound produced in the throat or at the back of the mouth [Late 16C. Directly or via French < medieval Latin *gutturalis* < Latin *guttur* 'throat'.] —**gutturalism** *n* —**gutturality** /gúttə rálləti/ *n* —**gutturally** *adv* —**gutturalness** *n*

gutturalize /gúttərə līz/ (**-izes, -izing, -ized**), **gutturalise** (**-ises, -ising, -ised**) *v* 1 *vt* to pronounce a speech sound in the throat or towards the back of the mouth 2 *vti* to speak or say something in a harsh rasping way —**gutturalization** /gúttərə lī záysh'n/ *n*

gutty /gútti/ (*plural* **-ties**) *n Scotland* a plimsoll (*informal; usually plural*) [Late 19C. < GUTTA-PERCHA.]

gut-wrenching *adj* having a very powerful effect on the feelings, especially in stirring up pity or sympathy

guv /guv/ *n* (*informal*) 1 used as a familiar term of address by one man to another, especially to one in a superior position 2 used by men and women as a term of address for their boss [Mid-19C. Shortening of GUVNOR.]

guvnor /gúvnər/ *n* 1 = **guv** *n.* 1, **guv** *n.* 2 2 used by upper-class young men to refer to or address their fathers (*dated informal*) ○ *The guvnor won't increase my allowance.* [Mid-19C. Representing a pronunciation of GOVERNOR.]

guy[1] /gī/ *n* 1 **MAN** a man (*informal*) 2 **MODEL BURNT ON BONFIRE** a home-made model of a man, like a scarecrow, originally intended as an effigy of Guy Fawkes, usually made by children and burnt on a fire on 5 November in Britain ○ *'Penny for the guy!'* 3 a scarecrow (*informal regional*) ■ **guys** *npl* **USED TO ADDRESS PEOPLE** used to address a group of people (*informal*) ○ *Hey, guys, where are you off to?* ■ *vt* **POKE FUN AT** to make fun of somebody or something, especially by a comical imitation [Early 19C. < *Guy* Fawkes (see GUY FAWKES NIGHT).]

guy[2] /gī/ *n* CONSTR, CAMPING = **guyrope** ■ *vt* to support or anchor something using ropes, cables, or chains [14C. Probably < Low German.]

Guyana

Guyana /gī aˈanə/ republic in South America, on the North Atlantic coast. Capital: Georgetown. Population: 711,759 (1997). Area: 214,969 sq. km/83,000 sq. mi. — **Guyanese** /gī ə neˈez/ adj, n

Guy Fawkes Night /gī fáwks-/ n CALENDAR = **Bonfire Night** [After *Guy Fawkes* (1570–1606), one of the conspirators in the Gunpowder Plot]

guyline /gī līn/ n CONSTR, CAMPING = **guyrope**

guyot /gee ō/ n a flat-topped underwater mountain, commonly found in the Pacific Ocean and considered to be an extinct volcano [Mid-20C. After Arnold Henri *Guyot*, (1807–84), Swiss-born US geologist and geographer.]

guyrope /gī rōp/, **guyline** /gī līn/ n a rope, wire, or chain tightened to hold something in position, e.g. any of the ropes pulled tight to keep a tent up

guywire /gī wīr/ n US = **guyrope**

Guzmán Blanco /gōoss mán blánkō/, **Antonio** (1829–99) Venezuelan statesman

guzzle /gúzz'l/ (**-zles, -zling, -zled**) vti to eat or drink something rapidly and in large quantities (*informal*) [Late 16C. < ?] —**guzzler** n

GVW abbr gross vehicle weight

✦**gw** abbr Guinea-Bissau (*in Internet addresses*)

GW symbol gigawatt

Gwalior /gwaˈali awr/ city in central India. Population: 692,982 (1991).

gweilo /gwī lō/ n Hong Kong a foreigner from the West (*informal*) [< Japanese]

Gwelo /gweˈelō/ former name for **Gweru**

Gwent /gwent/ former county in SE Wales

Gweru /gwáy roo/ city in central Zimbabwe. Population: 124,735 (1992).

Gwyn /gwin/, **Gwynn, Nell** (1650–87) English actor. Full name **Eleanor Gwyn**

Gwynedd /gwínnəth/ county in NW Wales. Area: 3,867 sq. km/1,494 sq. mi.

Gwynn ♦ **Gwyn, Nell**

✦**gy** abbr Guyana (*in Internet addresses*)

Gy symbol gray

gybe /jīb/, **jibe** vti (**gybes, gybing, gybed; jibes, jibing, jibed**) **1** SWING ACROSS BOAT to swing, or make a fore-and-aft sail swing, across from one side of the boat to the other when sailing before the wind **2** CHANGE DIRECTION IN SAILING SHIP to change direction, or cause a sailing ship to change direction, by turning away from the wind, as a result of a fore-and-aft-sail gybing ■ n ACTION OF GYBING a sudden shift of a sail back and forth or a change in direction [Late 17C. < obsolete Dutch *gyben*.]

gym /jim/ n **1** GYMNASIUM a gymnasium (*informal*) **2** PHYSICAL EDUCATION physical education, especially as a school subject (*informal*) **3** CHILD'S CLIMBING FRAME a sturdy metal or hard plastic frame designed for children's outdoor play and exercise (*often in combination*) [Late 19C. Shortening.]

gymkhana /jim kaˈana/ n **1** a community-based outdoor event with various activities relating to horse-riding **2** a place where a sporting event or contest is held (*dated*) [Mid-19C. Alteration (influenced by words such as GYMNAST) of Urdu *gendkānah* 'ball house'.]

gymnasium /jim náyzi əm/ (*plural* **-ums** *or* **-a** /-ə/) n a hall equipped for physical exercise or physical training of various kinds, e.g. in a school or a private club [Late

16C. Via Latin, 'school' < Greek *gumnasion* < *gumnazein* 'exercise naked, train' < *gumnos* 'naked'.]

gymnast /jim nast/ n an athlete who performs gymnastics, especially as a competitive sport [Late 16C. Directly or via French < Greek *gumnastēs* 'trainer of athletes' < *gumnazein* (see GYMNASIUM).]

gymnastic /jim nástik/ adj **1** relating to or involving gymnastics ○ *gymnastic equipment* **2** involving or demonstrating athleticism and agility ○ *a gymnastic dancing style* [Late 16C. Via Latin < Greek *gumnastikos* < *gumnazein* (see GYMNASIUM).] —**gymnastically** adv

gymnastics /jim nástiks/ n (+ singular verb) **1** PHYSICAL TRAINING USING GYMNASTIC EQUIPMENT physical training using equipment such as bars, rings, and vaulting horses, designed to develop agility and muscular strength **2** COMPETITIVE SPORT USING GYMNASTIC EQUIPMENT the competitive sport in which athletes perform a series of exercises on pieces of gymnastic equipment ■ npl **1** PHYSICAL EXERCISES movements, exercises, or activities that involve feats of physical strength and agility **2** ACTIONS DEMONSTRATING AGILITY AND SKILL the performance of a series of complex mental or physical operations of a particular kind, usually rapidly and with great agility and skill ○ *verbal gymnastics*

gymnosperm /jimnə spurm/ n a woody vascular plant such as a conifer, cycad, or ginkgo in which the ovules are carried naked on the scales of a cone [Mid-19C. Via modern Latin < Greek *gumnospermos* 'naked seed'.] —**gymnospermous** /jimnə spúrməss/ adj —**gymnospermy** /jimnə spurmi/ n

Gympie /gimpi/ town in SE Queensland, Australia. Population: 10,784 (1991).

gym rat n a person who spends much time exercising or playing a sport at a gymnasium (*informal*)

gym shoe n SPORTS, CLOTHES = **plimsoll**

gymslip /jím slip/ n a schoolgirl's sleeveless dress worn over a blouse as part of a school uniform

gyn- prefix = **gyno-** (*before vowels*)

gynae /gíni/ adj GYNAECOLOGICAL gynaecological (*informal*) ■ n (*informal*) **1** GYNAECOLOGIST a gynaecologist **2** GYNAECOLOGY gynaecology, or the department of a hospital that deals with this [Mid-20C. Shortening.]

gynaec-, gynaeco- prefix woman ○ *gynaecology* [< Greek *gunaik-*, stem of *gunē* 'woman']

gynaecocracy /jínni kókrəssi, gíni-/ (*plural* **-racies**) n political dominance by women, or a political system that gives supreme power to women

gynaecoid /jínni koyd, gíni-/ adj physically resembling or typical of a woman ○ *a gynaecoid pelvis*

gynaecol. abbr **1** gynaecological **2** gynaecologist **3** gynaecology

gynaecology /gíni kólləji/ n the branch of medicine that deals with women's health, especially with the health of women's reproductive organs —**gynaecological** /gínikə lójjik'l/ adj —**gynaecologist** n

gynaecomastia /jínni kō másti ə, gíni-/ n enlarged breasts on a man caused by hormonal imbalance or hormone therapy [Mid-19C. GYNAECO- + Greek *mastos* 'breast'.]

gynaecopathy /jínni kóppəthi, gíni-/ (*plural* **-pathies**) n a disease that affects only women

gynaephobia /jínnə fóbi ə, gínə-/ n an irrational and pathological fear of women

gynandromorph /ji nándrə mawrf/ n an organism, especially an insect, that has both male and female characteristics in a way abnormal for its species [Late 19C. < GYNANDROUS.] —**gynandromorphic** /ji nándrə máwrfik/ adj —**gynandromorphism** n —**gynandromorphous** adj —**gynandromorphy** n

gynandrous /jī nándrəss/ adj describes flowers such as orchids that have pistils and stamens united in a column [Mid-19C. < Greek *gunandros* 'of doubtful sex' < *gunē* 'woman' + *andr-* 'man'.]

gynarchy /jī naarki, gí-/ (*plural* **-chies**) n POL = **gynaecocracy** —**gynarchic** /jī naárkik, gī-/ adj

-gyne suffix **1** female ○ *androgyne* **2** female reproductive organ ○ *trichogyne* [< Greek *gunē* 'woman'] —**gynous** suffix —**gyny** suffix

gyneco- US = **gynaeco-**

gynecocracy n US = **gynaecocracy**

gynecol. US = **gynaecol.**

gynecology n US = **gynaecology**

gyno- prefix **1** female reproductive organ ○ *gynophore* **2** woman ○ *gynocracy* [< Greek *gunē* 'woman']

gynocracy /jī nókrəssi, gī-/ (*plural* **-cies**) n POL = **gynaecocracy**

gynoecium /jī neéssi əm, gī-/ (*plural* **-a** /-ə/) n the carpels of a plant considered together [Mid-19C. Alteration (influenced by Greek *oikos* 'house') of modern Latin *gynaeceum* 'women's apartments' < Greek *gunaikeios* 'of women' < *gunē* 'woman'.]

gynogenesis /jīnə jénnəssiss, gínə-/ n the development of an embryo without fusion of the egg and sperm nuclei, so that the embryo has only maternal chromosomes

Gyor /dyur, dyör/ port in NW Hungary, on the River Danube. Population: 127,000 (1995).

gyp[1] /jip/, **gip** vt (**gyps, gypping, gypped; gips, gipping, gipped**) CHEAT to cheat somebody, especially by overcharging (*informal*) ■ n **1** CHEATER a cheater or swindler (*insult*) **2** SCAM a scheme to trick or swindle people (*informal; sometimes offensive*) [Late 19C. < ?] —**gypper** n

gyp[2] /jip/, **gip** n pain, especially if sharp or severe (*informal*) ○ *His arthritis was giving him gyp.* [Late 19C. Contraction of GEE UP.]

gyppo /jíppō/ (*plural* **gyppos** *or* **gippos**) n **1** an offensive term for a Romany (*slang*) **2** an offensive term for an Egyptian, formerly used especially by British troops stationed in North Africa (*dated slang*) [Early 20C. Alteration of GYPSY and EGYPTIAN.]

gyppy tummy /jíppi-/, **gippy tummy** n a stomach upset with a bout of diarrhoea, especially one happening to a Western visitor in a hot Eastern country (*informal; sometimes offensive*) [< alteration of EGYPTIAN, because it was common in the Middle East]

gypsiferous /jip sífferəss/ adj containing gypsum

gypsophila /jip sóffilə/ n a plant of the carnation family popular in bouquets. Flowers: tiny, white or pink, on long branching stalks. Native to: Mediterranean. Genus: *Gypsophila*. [Late 18C. < modern Latin, 'chalk-loving' < Greek *gupsos* 'chalk', because it grows in chalky soil.]

gypsum /jípsəm/ n **1** a white or colourless mineral consisting of hydrated calcium sulphate. Use: cement, plaster, fertilizers. **2** plasterboard (*informal*) [14C. Via Latin < Greek *gupsos* 'chalk, gypsum'.]

gypsy /jípsi/ (*plural* **-sies**) n a person with a nomadic or unconventional lifestyle

Gypsy /jípsi/ (*plural* **-sies**), **Gipsy** (*plural* **-sies**) n an offensive term for a member of the Romany people [Mid-16C. Shortening of EGYPTIAN; because the Romany people were once thought to have come from Egypt.] —**Gypsy** adj

gypsy moth n a tussock moth with a spotted hairy caterpillar. Native to: Europe, but common in North America since the 19th century. *Lymantria dispar*.

gyral /jīrəl/ adj moving in a path that is spiral or circular —**gyrally** adv

gyrate /jī ráyt/ vi (**-rates, -rating, -rated**) to move with a circular or spiral motion, especially around a fixed central point ■ adj growing in a winding spiral or coil [Early 19C. < late Latin *gyrat-*, past participle of *gyrare* 'revolve' < Latin *gyrus* (see GYRUS).] —**gyrator** n —**gyratory** adj

gyration /jī ráysh'n/ n **1** movement in a circle around a fixed centre ○ *the gyration of the rotor* **2** a spiral or coil-shaped thing or part

gyre /jīr/ n a circle or spiral (*literary*) [Mid-16C. < Latin *gyrus* (see GYRUS).]

gyrene /jī reen, jī reén/ n a soldier in the US Marine Corps (*slang*) [Mid-20C. < ?]

gyrfalcon /júr fawlkən, -folkən/ n a large falcon varying in colour from white to dark brown. Native to: cold northern regions. *Falco rusticolus*. [14C. Alteration (by association with Latin *gyrare* 'revolve') of Old French *gerfaucon*.]

gyro /jírō/ (*plural* **-ros**) n US FOOD = **doner kebab** [Late 20C. < modern Greek *guros* 'turning'.]

gyro- prefix **1** spinning or rotating in a circle ○ *gyrostatics* **2** gyroscope, gyroscopic ○ *gyrostabilizer* [< Greek *guros* 'ring, circle']

gyrocompass /jírō kumpəss/ n a navigational compass fitted with a gyroscope instead of a magnet

gyromagnetic /jîrō mag néttik/ *adj* relating to or caused by the magnetism produced by the spinning motion of a charged particle ○ *gyromagnetic effect*

gyromagnetic ratio *n* the ratio of the magnetic moment to the angular momentum of a system

gyron /jîrən/, **giron** *n* in heraldry, a triangular form made by two blinds drawn from the edge of an escutcheon to meet at the fesse-point and occupying half of the quarter [Late 16C. < French, 'gusset' < Germanic.]

gyroplane /jîrō playn/ *n* an aircraft fitted with an un-powered rotor for producing lift. ◊ **autogiro**

gyroscope /jîrə skōp/ *n* a device consisting of a rotating heavy metal wheel pivoted inside a circular frame whose movement does not affect the wheel's orientation in space. Use: in compasses and other navigational aids, in stabilizing mechanisms on ships and aircraft. —**gyroscopic** /jîrə skóppik/ *adj* —**gyroscopically** *adv*

gyrostabilizer /jîrō stáybə līzər/ *n* a stabilizing system that uses gyroscopes to compensate and reduce the rolling or pitching motion of a ship or aircraft

gyrostat /jîrō stat/ *n* a gyroscope or gyrostabilizer in which the rotating wheel is pivoted within a rigid case [Late 19C. < GYRO- + Greek *statos* 'standing'.]

gyrostatics /jîrō státtiks/ *n* the science that deals with rotating bodies (+ *singular verb*) —**gyrostatic** *adj* —**gyrostatically** *adv*

gyrus /jîrəss/ (*plural* **-ri** /-rī/) *n* any rounded ridge on the outer layer of the brain [Mid-19C. Via Latin, 'circle' < Greek *guros* 'ring, circle'.]

Gy Sgt *abbr* gunnery sergeant

Gyumri /gyoŏmri/ city in NW Armenia. Population: 123,000 (1990).

gyve /jīv/ *n* a shackle or fetter, usually for the leg (*archaic; usally plural*) ■ *vt* (**gyves, gyving, gyved**) to shackle or fetter somebody, especially by the leg (*archaic*) [13C. < ?]

h[1] /aych/ (*plural* **h's**), **H** (*plural* **H's** *or* **Hs**) *n* the eighth letter of the English alphabet, representing a consonant sound

h[2] *symbol* **1** hecto- **2** Planck's constant

h[3] used to refer to the eighth vertical row of squares from the left on a chessboard

h[4] *abbr* **1** h, H harbour **2** h, H hard **3** h, H hardness **4** h, H height **5** h, H high **6** hit **7** horizontal **8** horn **9** hospital **10** hour **11** hundred **12** husband

H[1] /aych/ (*plural* **H's** *or* **Hs**) *n* something shaped like a letter 'H'

H[2] *symbol* **1** enthalpy **2** Hamiltonian function **3** henry **4** hydrogen **5** magnetic field strength

H1B visa /aych wun bee-/ *n* a special visa that allows people with high-level qualifications and skills to enter and work in the United States [< the form's reference number]

⚡ H2 *abbr* how to (*in e-mails*)

ha[1] /haa/, **hah** *interj* **1** expresses surprise, triumph, scorn, or happiness, depending on the way the speaker says it **2** a word repeated to represent in writing the sound of laughter [13C. Natural exclamation.]

ha[2] *symbol* hectare

Ha. *abbr* **1** Haiti **2** Haitian **3** Hawaii **4** Hawaiian

Haakon VII /háwk on/ (1872–1957) king of Norway (1905–57)

haar /haar/ *n* in E England and Scotland, a cold mist or fog off the North Sea coast, or rolling in from the North Sea (*regional*) [Late 17C. < ?]

Haarlem /haárləm/, **Harlem** city in W Netherlands. Population: 149,788 (1992).

Hab. *abbr* Habakkuk

Habakkuk /hábbəkək/, **Habacuc** *n* **1** in the Bible, a Hebrew priest who lived in the seventh century BC **2** one of the prophetic books of the Bible

habanera /hàbbə náirə/ *n* **1** a slow dance of Cuban origin in 2/4 time **2** the music for a habanera [Late 19C. < Spanish, 'of Havana'.]

habdabs /háb dabz/ *npl* a fit of extreme nervous anxiety or irritation (*informal*) [Mid-20C. < ?]

habdalah /hav daálə/, **havdalah** *n* a Jewish ceremony that marks the end of the Sabbath or another holy day, or a prayer said during the ceremony [Mid-18C. < Hebrew *habdālāh* 'separation, division'.]

habeas corpus /háybi əss káwrpəss/ *n* a writ issued in order to bring somebody who has been detained into court, usually for a decision on whether the detention is lawful [< Latin, 'you may have the body']

Haber-Bosch process /haàbər bósh-/ *n* CHEM = **Haber process** [After Fritz *Haber* (1868–1934) and Karl *Bosch* (1874–1940), German chemists]

haberdasher /hábbər dashər/ *n* **1** a dealer in small articles used in sewing, e.g. thread, ribbons, and buttons **2** US a dealer in men's clothing and accessories [14C. Probably < Anglo-Norman *hapertas* 'small items of merchandise'.]

haberdashery /hábbər dashəri/ (*plural* **-ies**) *n* **1** the items sold by a haberdasher **2** a shop, or a department in a larger store, that sells haberdashery

habergeon /hábbərjən/ *n* a sleeveless chain mail jacket worn under armour [14C. < French *haubergeon* < Old French *hauberc* (see HAUBERK).]

Haber process /haàbər-/ *n* a commercial process for catalytically producing ammonia from atmospheric nitrogen and hydrogen at high temperature and pressure [See HABER-BOSCH PROCESS]

~~**habeus corpus**~~ incorrect spelling of **habeas corpus**

habiliment /hə bíllimənt/ *n* GARMENT OR GARMENTS clothing (*formal; usually plural*) ■ **habiliments** *npl* **1** SPECIALIZED EQUIPMENT the equipment and gear needed for a task or activity **2** SPECIAL CLOTHES items of clothing associated with somebody's work or position or an occasion [Early 17C. < Old French *habillement* < *habiller* 'fit out' < *habile* (see HABILE).]

habilitate /hə bílli tayt/ (**-tates**, **-tating**, **-tated**) *v* **1** *vi* PREPARE FOR POSITION to qualify for employment or an office (*formal*) **2** *vt* US EQUIP A MINING OPERATION to provide a mine with the equipment and money needed for operation **3** *vt* CLOTHE to clothe somebody in a particular way (*literary*) [Early 17C. < medieval Latin *habilitat-*, past participle of *habilitare* < Latin *habilitas* (see ABILITY).] —**habilitation** /hə bílli táysh'n/ *n* —**habilitator** *n*

habit /hábbit/ *n* **1** SOMETHING DONE ALL THE TIME an action or behaviour pattern that is regular, repetitive, and often unconscious ○ *I really need to get into the habit of writing down what I spend.* ○ *He has a really annoying habit of finishing your sentences for you.* **2** ADDICTION an addiction to a drug (*slang*) **3** CLOTHES OF RELIGIOUS ORDER a long loose gown, usually black, brown, grey, or white, traditionally worn by nuns, friars, and monks **4** RIDING, CLOTHING = **riding habit 5** GROWTH PATTERN the characteristic appearance, behaviour, or growth pattern of a plant or animal **6** SHAPE OF A CRYSTAL the characteristic growth pattern or shape of a crystal **7** ATTITUDE somebody's attitude or general disposition ■ *vt* CLOTHE SOMEBODY SPECIALLY to dress somebody in clothing distinctive to a particular position or office (*literary*) [12C. Via Old French *abit* < Latin *habitus* < *habere* 'have, wear'.] ◇ **kick the habit** to become free of an addiction, or stop doing something that has been a long-standing practice

SYNONYMS *habit, custom, tradition, practice, routine, wont*

CORE MEANING: established pattern of behaviour

habit an action or behaviour pattern that is regular, repetitive, often unconscious, and sometimes compulsive; **custom** the way somebody normally or routinely behaves in a situation, or a traditional practice in a particular community or group of people; **tradition** a long-established action or pattern of behaviour in a particular community or group of people, especially one that has been handed down from generation to generation; **practice** an established way of doing something, especially one that has developed through experience and knowledge; **routine** a typical pattern of behaviour that is regularly followed on a day-to-day basis, sometimes with the suggestion that this is monotonous and tedious; **wont** (*formal*) something that somebody does regularly or habitually.

habitable /hábbitəb'l/ *adj* considered fit to be lived in ○ *A lot of structural work will be needed before the house is habitable.* [14C. Via Old French < Latin *habitabilis* < *habitare* (see HABITAT).] —**habitability** /hábbitə bíllati/ *n* —**habitableness** *n* —**habitably** *adv*

habitant /hábbitənt/ *n* **1** somebody living in a place **2** Can, US a farmer of French descent living in Canada or the United States [15C. < French, < Old French *habiter* 'dwell' < Latin *habitare* (see HABITAT).]

habitat /hábbi tat/ *n* **1** HOME ENVIRONMENT the natural conditions and environment, e.g. forest, desert, or wetlands, in which a plant or animal lives **2** TYPICAL LOCATION the place in which a person or group is usually found **3** ARTIFICIALLY CREATED ENVIRONMENT a sealed controlled environment in which people can live, e.g. to do research on the sea floor [Late 18C. < 3rd person present singular of Latin *habitare* 'possess, inhabit' < *habere* 'have'.]

habitation /hábbi táysh'n/ *n* **1** OCCUPANCY the occupancy of a place by people or animals **2** LIVING PLACE a place in which to live ○ *The squirrels found a new habitation in a hollow tree.* **3** DWELLINGS a group of dwellings and their inhabitants ○ *There is little evidence remaining of the ancient habitation.* [14C. Via Old French < Latin *habitation-* < *habitare* (see HABITAT).] —**habitational** *adj*

habit-forming *adj* capable of causing a physiological or psychological need in somebody

habitual /hə bíchoo əl/ *adj* **1** REGULAR done regularly and frequently **2** PERSISTING IN SOME BEHAVIOUR continuing in some practice as a result of an ingrained tendency **3** CHARACTERISTIC typical of somebody's character or behaviour ○ *She tackled the problem with her habitual single-mindedness.* —**habitually** *adv* —**habitualness** *n*

SYNONYMS See *usual*.

habituate /hə bíchoo ayt/ (**-ates**, **-ating**, **-ated**) *v* **1** *vt* MAKE SOMEBODY USED TO to accustom a person or animal to something through prolonged and regular exposure (*formal*) ○ *People living in cities become habituated to crowds.* **2** *vti* LEARN TO IGNORE to learn or teach a person or animal not to respond to a stimulus that is frequently repeated **3** *vi* BECOME ACCUSTOMED to become dependent on or less affected by a medical or illegal drug through frequent use [16C. < late Latin *habituat-*, past participle of *habituare* 'bring into a state' < Latin *habitus* (see HABIT).] —**habituation** /hə bíchoo áysh'n/ *n*

habitué /hə bítyoo ay/ (*plural* **-bitués**) *n* a regular visitor of a place [Early 19C. < French, < past participle of *habituer* < late Latin *habituare* (see HABITUATE).]

habitus /hábbitəss/ (*plural* **-tus**) *n* the general appearance, posture, or physical state of a patient, especially with regard to susceptibility to disease [Late 19C. < Latin (see HABIT).]

haboob /hə bòob/ *n* a violent sandstorm or dust storm that sweeps across the deserts of N Africa and Arabia and the plains of India [Late 19C. < Arabic *habub* 'violent storm'.]

Habsburg *n* HIST = **Hapsburg**

habu /haà boo/ (*plural* **-bus**) *n* a large poisonous snake. Native to: Okinawa and neighbouring Pacific islands. *Trimeresurus flavoviridis.* [Late 19C. < Japanese.]

háček /haà chek/ *n* a mark (˘) placed over a letter in some Slavic and other languages to indicate a change in pronunciation [Mid-20C. < Czech, 'small hook' < *hak* 'hook'.]

hachure /ha shyoor/ *n* any of the short parallel lines used for shading on a map to indicate the direction and steepness of a slope [Mid-19C. < French, < *hacher* 'mark with hatches, chop' (see HATCH[3]).]

hacienda /hássi éndə/ *n* **1** a large estate, farm, or ranch in Spain or Spanish-speaking parts of America **2** the main residence on a hacienda [Mid-18C. Via Spanish, 'domestic work, large estate' < Latin *facienda* 'things needing to be done' < *facere* 'do'.]

ϟ **hack**[1] /hak/ *v* **1** *vti* **CUT USING REPEATED BLOWS** to cut or chop something by striking it with short repeated blows using a sharp tool such as a knife or an axe **2** *vt* **CLEAR A WAY** to open a path by cutting through an obstruction ○ *I had to hack my way through the bureaucracy to get the job done.* **3** *vt* **CHOP OFF OR INTO PARTS** to cut, shape, or divide something roughly or carelessly (*informal*) ○ *He's hacked a whole chunk off that article I wrote for the magazine.* **4** *vi* **GET INTO A COMPUTER SYSTEM** to explore and manipulate the workings of a computer or other technological device or system, either for the purpose of understanding how it works or to gain unauthorized access **5** *vt* **COPE WITH** to succeed at or endure something (*informal*) ○ *I wonder if he can hack it.* **6** *vi* **MAKE A COUGHING NOISE** to cough persistently in short dry bursts with a rasping noise **7** *vt* **KICK FOOTBALL PLAYER'S SHINS** to commit a foul by kicking the shins of an opposing player in rugby or football **8** *vt* **HIT A BASKETBALL PLAYER'S ARM** to commit a foul in basketball by striking another player on the arm ■ *n* **1 QUICK CHOP** a short violent blow with a sharp tool **2 COUGHING NOISE** a short dry cough **3 CUT MADE BY HACKING** a rough cut made by a quick blow with a sharp tool, e.g. a notch in a tree made with an axe **4 TOOL FOR HACKING** a tool, e.g. a pickaxe, used for chopping something or breaking up hard ground **5 WOUND FROM A KICK** a wound from being kicked **6 DISABLING KICK IN FOOTBALL** a kick on the shins in rugby or football, meant to disable a player temporarily **7 SUCCESSFUL EFFORT** an extremely good, often very time-consuming, work effort that produces exactly what is needed (*informal*) [Old English *haccian* 'cut in pieces' < W Germanic]

hack[2] /hak/ *n* **1 HORSE FOR RIDING** a horse for riding or driving **2 OLD HORSE** a horse that is in bad condition through age or overwork **3 HORSE FOR HIRE** a horse that is hired out **4 HORSE RIDE** a ride on a horse, usually through the countryside **5 DRUDGE** a mediocre and unimaginative person, especially somebody engaged in dull or uninspired work **6 HIRED WRITER** a writer paid to produce routine often down-market writing, e.g. for newspapers or films (*disapproving*) **7 LOYAL PARTY WORKER** a political party member who serves the party unquestioningly (*disapproving*) **8** *US* **TAXI** a taxi (*informal*) ■ *v* **1** *vti* **TAKE HORSE RIDE** to ride a horse, or go on a horse ride, for pleasure, usually through the countryside **2** *vi US* **DRIVE A TAXI** to drive a taxi (*informal*) **3** *vi* **GO RIDING** to ride a horse for exercise at a normal pace ■ *adj* **TRITE** lacking quality and originality ○ *The film had a really hack plot.* [Early 18C. Shortening of HACKNEY.]

hack[3] /hak/ *n* **1 FEEDING RACK** a rack on which fodder for cattle is placed **2 FEEDING POST FOR HAWKS** in falconry, a board from which a hawk takes meat **3 PILE OF BRICKS** a pile or row of unfired bricks that have been laid out to dry [Late 16C. Variant of HATCH[1].]

hackamore /hákə mawr/ *n US* a bridle without a bit but with an adjustable band by which a rider can exert pressure on a horse's nose, used especially to break young horses [Mid-19C. Alteration (by association with HACK[2]) of Spanish *jaquima* < Arabic *shaqīmah* 'restraint, bit'.]

hackberry /hákbəri/ (*plural* **-ries**) *n* a tree of the elm family with soft yellowish wood and fruit resembling cherries. Native to: North America. *Celtis occidentalis.* [Mid-18C. < *hag* < N Germanic.]

ϟ **hacker** /hákər/ *n* **1 SOMEBODY ACCESSING ANOTHER'S COMPUTER** a computer user who gains unauthorized access to a computer system belonging to another **2 COMPUTER ENTHUSIAST** a person who is interested or skilled in computer technology and programming **3** *US* **AMATEUR PLAYER** a person who enjoys a sport but lacks skill in it **4 SOMEBODY WHO CHOPS** a cutter or chopper of something

hackie /háki/ *n US* a taxi driver (*informal*)

hacking cough *n* a repeated cough that is short, dry, and rasping

hacking jacket, hacking coat *n* a tweed or woollen jacket with side or back vents and a full skirt, worn especially for horse riding

hackle[1] /hák'l/ *n* **1 BIRD'S NECK FEATHER** any of the long slender feathers on the neck or lower back of a male bird, especially a fowl **2 FEATHERS USED IN A FISHING FLY** a tuft of feathers from the neck of a bird used in making an artificial fly for fishing **3 FISHING FLY MADE FROM FEATHERS** an artificial fly for fishing made from the neck feathers of a bird **4 FEATHERED ORNAMENT** an ornament made of feathers worn in the headdress of some Highland regiments **5 FLAX COMB** a steel comb with long teeth used to comb out flax, hemp, or jute fibres ■ **hackles** *npl* **HAIRS ON AN ANIMAL'S NECK** the hairs on the back of the neck and along the spine of an animal, especially a dog or cat, that stand up when it is threatened or angry ■ *vt* (**-les, -ling, -led**) **1 PUT FEATHERS ON A FISHING FLY** to trim an artificial fly with the neck feathers from a bird **2 COMB FLAX BEFORE SPINNING** to comb out flax, hemp, or jute fibres using a hackle [15C. Probably < assumed Old English *hacule* 'little hook' < Germanic.] —**hackler** *n* ◇ **make somebody's hackles rise, raise somebody's hackles** to produce anger or hostility in somebody

hackle[2] /hák'l/ (**-les, -ling, -led**) *vti* to mangle something by cutting it roughly [Late 16C. < HACK[1].]

hackly /hákli/ (**-lier, -liest**) *adj* having a rough jagged surface

Hackman /hákmən/, **Gene** (*b.* 1930) US film actor

hackmatack /hákmə tak/ *n* TREES = **tamarack** [Late 18C. < Algonquian *akemantek* 'snowshoe wood'.]

hackney /hákni/ *n* **1** a car, carriage, or similar vehicle providing a taxi service **2** a horse for riding or driving [13C. Probably after *Hackney*, NE London.] —**hackneyism** *n*

hackneyed /hák nid/ *adj* made commonplace and stale by overuse ○ *the same old hackneyed sales talk*

hacksaw /hák saw/ *n* a handsaw with a small-toothed steel blade stretched taut across a frame, used for cutting metal ■ *vt* (**-saws, -sawing, -sawed, -sawn** /hák sawn/ *or* **-sawed**) to cut something using a hacksaw

ϟ **hacktivism** /háktivizəm/ *n* the activity of breaking into and sabotaging a computer system via the Internet as a political protest ○ *'The apparent increase in hacktivism may be due in part to the growing importance of the Internet as a means of communication'.* (*Wired website*; April 1999) [Late 20C. Blend of HACKER + ACTIVISM.] —**hacktivist** *n*

hackwork /hák wurk/ *n* ordinary literary, artistic, or professional work that somebody is hired to do (*disapproving*)

had past tense, past participle of **have**

haddock /háddək/ (*plural* **-dock** *or* **-docks**) *n* **1** a fish that is related to but smaller than the cod. Native to: N Atlantic. *Melanogrammus aeglefinus.* **2** the flesh of a haddock used as food [14C. Via Anglo-Norman *hadoc* < Old French *(h)adot*.]

hade /hayd/ *n* the angle between the vertical plane and a plane containing a vein, fault, or lode ■ *vi* (**hades, hading, haded**) to be at an angle to the vertical [Late 17C. < ?]

Hadean aeon /háydi ən-/ *n* a unit of geological time, not confirmed by rock formation records, beginning approximately 4.6 billion years ago with the creation of the Earth [*Hadean* < HADES]

Hades /háy deez/ *n* **1 GREEK UNDERWORLD** in Greek mythology, the underworld kingdom inhabited by the souls of the dead. Roman equivalent **Dis** **2 GREEK GOD OF THE UNDERWORLD** in Greek mythology, the god of the underworld and husband of Persephone. Roman equivalent **Pluto** *n.* 1 **3 hades, Hades HELL** hell (*informal*) [Late 16C. < Greek *Haidēs*, god of the dead.] —**Hadean** *adj*

Hadhramaut /haádrə máwt/, **Hadramaut** coastal region of the S Arabian peninsula, in Yemen and Oman. Area: 155,400 sq. km/60,000 sq. mi.

Hadith /hádith/, **hadith** *n* the collected traditions, teachings, and stories of the prophet Muhammad, accepted as a source of Islamic doctrine and law second only to the Koran [Early 18C. < Arabic *ḥadīṯ* 'tradition'.]

hadj *n* = **hajj**

hadja *n* = **hajja**

hadji *n* = **hajji**

Hadlee /háddli/, **Sir Richard John** (*b.* 1948) New Zealand cricketer

hadn't /hádd'nt/ *contr* had not

Hadramaut = **Hadhramaut**

Hadrian /háydri ən/ (76–138) emperor of Rome (117–138)

Hadrian's Wall /háydri ənz-/ *n* a fortified wall built across N England in the early 2nd century on the orders of Roman emperor Hadrian, as a defence against the Picts

hadron /háddron/ *n* an elementary particle that is subject to the strong nuclear interaction [Mid-20C. < Greek *hadros* 'bulky'.] —**hadronic** /ha drónnik, hə-/ *adj*

hadrosaur /háddrə sawr/, **hadrosaurus** /-sáwrəss/ (*plural* **-uses**) *n* an amphibious plant-eating dinosaur with a snout resembling a duck's bill and strong hind legs for walking in swamps. Genus: *Anatosaurus.* [Late 19C. < modern Latin *hadrosaurus* < Greek *hadros* 'bulky' + *sauros* 'lizard'.]

hadst /hadst/ 2nd person present singular of **have** (*archaic*)

haecceity /hek sée əti, heek-, hīk-/ *n* the essential property that makes an individual uniquely that individual [Mid-17C. < medieval Latin *heicceitas* < Latin *haec* 'this'.]

Haeckel /hék'l/, **Ernst** (1834–1919) German zoologist and evolutionist

Haeckel's law /hék'lz, hée-/ *n* the theory proposing as a law that an embryo in each stage of development resembles an organism that its species descended from

haem /heem/ *n* the deep red, nonprotein portion of haemoglobin that contains iron [Early 20C. Back-formation < HAEMOGLOBIN.]

haem- *prefix* = **haemo-** (*before vowels*)

haema- /heémə/ *prefix* blood ○ *haemangioma* ○ *haemagglutinin* [< Greek *haima*]

haemagglutinate /heémə glóoti nayt/ (**-nates, -nating, -nated**) *vti* to cause red blood cells to clump together, or become clumped together —**haemagglutination** /heémə glóoti náysh'n/ *n*

haemagglutinin /heémə glóotinin/ *n* an agent such as a virus or an antibody that causes red blood cells to clump together

haemal /heém'l/ *adj* **1** found in or associated with the blood or blood vessels **2** located on or associated with the side of the body where the heart and major arteries and veins are found [Mid-19C. < Greek *haima* 'blood'.]

haemangioma /hi mánji ṓmə/ (*plural* **-mata** /-mətə/ *or* **-mas**) *n* a benign tumour or birthmark consisting of a dense, often raised cluster of blood vessels in the skin

haemat- *prefix* = **haemato-** (*before vowels*)

haematein /heémə teé in/ *n* a red-brown compound used to stain samples for microscope study

haematic /hee máttik/ *adj* relating to or acting on blood

haematin /heémətin/ *n* a breakdown product of haemoglobin

haematinic /heémə tínnik/ *adj* describes a drug or other agent that increases blood haemoglobin

haematite /heémə tīt/ *n* a black, brown, or red mineral consisting of iron oxide, often in very large deposits. Use: source of iron. [15C. Via Latin *hematites* < Greek *haimatitēs* 'blood-like (stone)'.] —**haematitic** /heémə títtik/ *adj*

haemato- *prefix* blood ○ *haematoblast* [< Greek *haimat-*, stem of *haima*]

haematoblast /hee máttō blast/ *n* an immature blood cell, especially a red blood cell

haematocrit /heémətō krit/ *n* **1** the percentage of a blood sample that consists of red blood cells, measured after the blood has been centrifuged and the cells compacted **2** a centrifuge used to compact the red blood cells in a blood sample in order to determine the percentage of the blood that consists of cells [Late 19C. < HAEMATO- + Greek *kritēs* 'judge' (see CRITIC).]

haematogenesis /heémətō jénnəsiss/ *n* PHYSIOL = **haematopoiesis** —**haematogenic** /heémətō jénnik/ *adj*

haematogenous /heémə tójjinəss/ *adj* **1 MAKING BLOOD** producing blood **2 OF BLOOD** originating in or derived from blood **3 SPREAD BY BLOOD** spread by means of blood

haematology /heémə tólləji/ *n* the branch of medicine devoted to the study of blood, blood-producing tissues, and diseases of the blood —**haematologic** /heémətə lójjik/ *adj* —**haematologically** /-lójjikli/ *adv* —**haematologist** /heémə tólləjist/ *n*

haematoma /heémə tṓmə/ (*plural* **-mas** *or* **-mata** /-mətə/) *n* a semisolid mass of blood in the tissues, caused by injury, disease, or a clotting disorder

haematophagous /heémə tóffəgəss/ *adj* feeding on blood [Mid-19C. < HAEMATO- + Greek *phagein* 'eat'.]

haematopoiesis /heémətō poy éessiss/, **haemopoiesis** /heémō-/ *n* the formation of red blood cells in the blood-forming tissues of the body —**haematopoietic** /-poy éttik/ *adj*

haematoxylin /heémə tóksilin/ *n* a dye used to stain microscope slides for study [Mid-19C. < modern Latin *Haematoxylum* < Greek *haimat-* 'blood' + *xulon* 'wood'.]

haematozoon /heémətō zṓ on/ (*plural* **-a** /-zṓ ə/) *n* a parasitic protozoan or other microorganism that lives in blood —**haematozoal** *adj*

haematuria /heéma tyoóri ə/ *n* the presence of blood in the urine, as a result of injury to or disease of the kidneys, ureters, bladder, or urethra —**haematuric** *adj*

-haemia *suffix* = **-aemia**

haemic /heémik/ *adj* relating to blood [Mid-19C. < Greek *haima* 'blood'.]

haemo- *prefix* blood ○ *haemolysis* [< Greek *haima*]

haemochromatosis /heémō krōmə tṓssiss/ *n* a genetic disorder in which there is excess accumulation of iron in the body leading to damage of many organs, especially the liver and pancreas [Late 19C. < HAEMO- + Greek *khroma* 'colour'.]

haemocoel /heémə seel/ *n* a body cavity in spiders, crustaceans, and other arthropods through which the blood or haemolymph circulates [Mid-19C. < HAEMO- + Greek *koilos* 'hollow'.]

haemocyanin /heémō sī́ ənin/ *n* a bluish pigment found in the blood or haemolymph of certain arthropods and molluscs that functions like haemoglobin, transporting oxygen to tissues [Late 19C. < HAEMO- + Greek *kuan(e)os* 'dark blue'.]

haemocyte /heémō sīt/ *n* a blood cell (*technical*)

haemodialysis /heémō dī álləsiss/ *n* dialysis of the blood (*technical*)

haemoflagellate /heémō flájjə layt/ *n* a flagellate protozoan that lives as a parasite in blood

haemoglobin /heémə glṓbin/ *n* an iron-containing protein in red blood cells that transports oxygen around the body

haemoglobinuria /heémə glṓbi nyoóri ə/ *n* the presence in the urine of haemoglobin that has been freed from red blood cells. ◊ **haematuria** —**haemoglobinuric** *adj*

haemolymph /heémōlimf/ *n* a fluid in certain invertebrates that functions like the blood in vertebrates [Late 19C. < HAEMO- + Latin *lympha* 'clear liquid'.] —**haemolymphatic** /heémō lim fáttik/ *adj*

haemolyse /heémə līz/ (**-lyses, -lysing, -lysed**) *vti* to destroy red blood cells [Early 20C. < HAEMO- + variant of -LYZE.]

haemolysin /heémō lī́ssin, hi móllissin/ *n* a bacterial toxin, antibody, or other agent that destroys red blood cells, releasing free haemoglobin

haemolysis /hi móllississ/ *n* the destruction of red blood cells —**haemolytic** /heémə líttik/ *adj*

haemolytic anaemia *n* anaemia that results from the destruction of red blood cells and may be caused by bacteria, genetic disorders, or toxic chemicals

haemophilia /heémə fílli ə/ *n* a disorder linked to a recessive gene on the X-chromosome and occurring almost exclusively in men and boys, in which the blood clots much more slowly than normally, resulting in extensive bleeding from even minor injuries —**haemophiliac** *n*

haemophilic /heémə fíllik/ *adj* **1** relating to, resembling, or affected with haemophilia **2** describes bacteria that are adapted to thrive in blood or a medium rich in blood

haemopoiesis *n* = **haematopoiesis**

haemoptysis /hi móptississ/ *n* the coughing up of blood or mucus containing blood (*technical*) [Mid-17C. < HAEMO- + Greek *ptysis* 'act of spitting'.]

~~**haemorrage**~~ incorrect spelling of **haemorrhage**

haemorrhage /hémmərij/ *n* **1 EXCESSIVE BLEEDING** the loss of blood from a ruptured blood vessel, either internally or externally **2 UNCONTROLLED LOSS** a large uncontrolled loss of something valuable ○ *a haemorrhage of cash that threatened the firm* ■ *v* (**-rhages, -rhaging, -rhaged**) **1** *vi* **BLEED HEAVILY** to bleed profusely and uncontrollably **2** *vti* **LOSE SOMETHING VALUABLE** to experience a sudden, uncontrolled, and massive loss of something valuable ○ *The failed business had been haemorrhaging money for months.* [15C. Via Old French or medieval Latin < Greek *haimorrhagia* < *haima* 'blood'+ *rhēgnunai* 'break, burst'.] —**haemorrhagic** /hémmə rájjik/ *adj*

haemorrhagic fever *n* a viral infection such as dengue or Ebola that results in fever, chills, and profuse internal bleeding from the capillaries

haemorrhoidectomy /hémməroy déktəmi/ (*plural* **-mies**) *n* a surgical procedure to remove haemorrhoids

haemorrhoids /hémmə roydz/ *npl* painful varicose veins in the canal of the anus —**haemorrhoidal** /hémmə róyd'l/ *adj*

haemosiderin /heémō síddərin/ *n* a protein that stores iron

haemostasis /heémō stáyssiss/, **haemostasia** /heémō stáyzi ə/ *n* **1** the stopping of bleeding or haemorrhaging in an organ or body part **2** the stopping of the blood flow through an organ or body part

haemostat /heémō stat/ *n* **1** a surgical instrument that stops bleeding by clamping a blood vessel **2** a chemical agent that stops bleeding

haemostatic /heémō státtik/ *adj* stopping or slowing down the flow of blood ■ *n* an agent that stops or slows down the flow of blood

hafiz /haáfiz/ *n* the title used to address somebody who has committed the Koran to memory [Mid-17C. Via Persian < Arabic *ḥāfiẓ* 'guardian'.]

hafnium /háfni əm/ *n* (*symbol* **Hf**) a bright silvery metallic element. Source: zirconium ores. Use: absorption of neutrons in nuclear reactor rods, manufacture of tungsten filaments. [Early 20C. < modern Latin, < *Hafnia*, Latin name for Copenhagen, Denmark.]

haft /haaft/ *n* the handle of a knife, axe, or other weapon or tool (*literary*) [Old English *hæft(e)* < Germanic] —**haft** *v* —**hafter** *n*

haftarah /haáftə raa/ (*plural* **-rahs** *or* **-roth** /-rōt/ *or* **-rot**), **haftorah** (*plural* **-rahs** *or* **-roth** *or* **-rot**), **haphtarah** (*plural* **-rahs** *or* **-roth** *or* **-rot**) *n* a reading from the Prophets following each lesson from the Torah in synagogue services on the Sabbath [Early 18C. < Hebrew *haphṭārāh* 'conclusion'.]

hag[1] /hag/ *n* **1** an offensive term that deliberately insults a woman's appearance, temperament, and age (*slang offensive insult*) **2** a witch, especially one late in life **3** ZOOL = **hagfish** [14C. < ?] —**haggish** *adj*

hag[2] /hag/ *n N England, Scotland* **1** a relatively firm spot in a bog **2** a boggy area on a moor [Mid-17C. < Old Norse *hǫgg* 'gap'.]

Hag. *abbr* Haggai

Hagar /háy gaar, -gər/ *n* in the Bible, an Egyptian servant of Sarah who bore Sarah's husband, Abraham, a son named Ishmael (Genesis 16, 21:1–21) [< Hebrew *Haghar*]

hagbut /hág but/ *n* = **harquebus** [Variant of HACKBUT] —**hagbuteer** /hág bu teér/ *n* —**hagbutter** *n*

hagfish /hág fish/ (*plural* **-fish** *or* **-fishes**) *n* a primitive jawless marine fish with an elongated body and a sucking mouth that it uses for feeding off other fishes. Family: Myxinidae.

Haggadah /hə gaádə/ (*plural* **-dahs** *or* **-doth** /-dōth/), **Haggada** (*plural* **-das** *or* **-doth**) *n* **1 RABBINIC LITERATURE ON BIBLICAL STORIES** those sections of the Talmud and other rabbinic literature that deal with biblical narrative and stories and legends on biblical themes rather than with religious law and regulations **2 BOOK CONTAINING THE PASSOVER SERVICE** the service for the ritual meal (**Seder**) celebrated by Jews at Passover, or the book containing this service **3 STORY OF ISRAELITES' EXODUS FROM EGYPT** the account of the Exodus of the Israelites from Egypt that is central to the Jewish Passover ritual [Mid-19C. < Hebrew *haggāḏāh* 'tale' < *higgīḏ* 'tell'.] —**haggadic** /hə gáddik/ *adj*

Haggai /hággī, hággay ī/ *n* **1** in the Bible, a Hebrew prophet who urged the Israelites to rebuild their temple in Jerusalem in prophecies believed to have been made in 520 BC **2** a book of the Bible that tells the story of the rebuilding of the Israelites' temple after their return to Jerusalem from exile in Babylon and records Haggai's prophecies [< Hebrew]

haggard /hággərd/ *adj* **1 TIRED-LOOKING** showing signs of tiredness, anxiety, or hunger on the face, e.g. dark rings around the eyes **2 WILD** wild and unruly in appearance **3 UNMANAGEABLE** in falconry, describes a hawk that has reached maturity before being captured and is therefore wild and unmanageable ■ *n* **HAWK** a captured wild adult hawk [Late 16C. < French *hagard* 'untamed' (used of hawks).] —**haggardly** *adv* —**haggardness** *n*

Haggard /hággərd/, **Sir H. Rider** (1856–1925) British novelist. Full name **Sir Henry Rider Haggard**

haggis /hággiss/ (*plural* **-gises**) *n* a Scottish dish made from offal mixed with suet, oats, onions, and seasonings and packed into a round sausage skin and usually boiled [15C. < ?]

haggle /hágg'l/ (**-gles, -gling** *or* **-gled, -gled**) *vi* to argue over something, e.g. a price or contract, in order to reach an agreement [Late 16C.< Variant of HACK[1].] —**haggle** *n* —**haggler** *n*

hagio- *prefix* saints, holy ○ *hagiolatry* ○ *hagioscope* [< Greek *hagios* 'holy']

hagiocracy /hággi ókrəssi/ (*plural* **-cies**) *n* **1** government by saints, prophets, or other holy people **2** a state or community governed by holy people

Hagiographa /hággi óggrəfə/ *n* the last of the three main parts into which the Hebrew Bible is divided [Late 16C. Via late Latin < Greek, < *hagios* 'holy' + *grapha* 'writings'.]

hagiographer /hággi óggrəfər/, **hagiographist** /-fist/ *n* **1 BIOGRAPHER OF SAINTS** a writer of biographies of the saints **2 REVERENTIAL BIOGRAPHER** a writer of biographies that treat their subjects with undue reverence **3 WRITER OF PART OF THE HEBREW BIBLE** any of the writers of the Hagiographa

hagiography /hággi óggrəfi/ (*plural* **-phies**) *n* **1** biography of a saint or the saints **2** biography that treats its subject with undue reverence —**hagiographic** /hággi ə gráffik/ *adj*

hagiolatry /hággi óllətri/ *n* the worship or idolizing of saints

hagiology /hággi óllәji/ (*plural* **-gies**) *n* **1 WRITINGS ABOUT SAINTS** literature about the lives of the saints **2 BIOGRAPHY OF A SAINT** a biography of a saint or a collection of such biographies **3 LIST OF SAINTS** an authoritative list of saints **4 COLLECTION OF SACRED WRITINGS** a collection or history of sacred writings —**hagiologic** /hággi ə lójjik/ *adj* —**hagiologist** *n*

hagioscope /hággi ə skōp/ *n* a narrow opening in an interior wall of a church that allows members of the congregation seated at the sides to see the altar —**hagioscopic** /hággi ə skóppik/ *adj*

hag-ridden *adj* **1** plagued by fear or mental anguish **2** an offensive term for a man thought to be troubled or dominated by women

Hague, The /thə háyg/ capital of South Holland Province, W Netherlands, seat of the Dutch government. Population: 444,661 (1993).

Hague /hayg/, **William** (*b.* 1961) British politician

hah *interj* = **ha**[1]

ha-ha[1] /haá haa/, **haw-haw** /háw haw/ *interj* **1** in writing indicates the sound of somebody laughing **2** teases or ridicules somebody (*informal*) ○ *'Where is it?' 'Ha-ha, wouldn't you like to know?'* [Old English. Natural exclamation.]

ha-ha[2] /haá haa/, **haw-haw** /háw haw/ *n* a deep ditch or steep change in level, sometimes supported by a wall, that marks the boundary of a large garden but is not visible from within it [Early 18C. < French; probably from a cry of surprise when finding one.]

Hahn /haan/, **Otto** (1879–1968) German physical chemist

hahnium /haáni əm/ *n* (*symbol* **Hn**) dubnium or hassium [Late 20C. After Otto HAHN.]

Haida /hī́də/ (*plural* **-da** *or* **-das**) *n* **1** a member of a Native North American people living along and off the coast of British Columbia and the adjoining Alaskan coast **2** the language of the Haida, now spoken by very few people [Early 20C. < Haida, 'people'.] —**Haida** *adj* —**Haidan** *adj*

Haidar Ali /hī́dər aáli/ (1722–82) Indian soldier and ruler

Haifa /hī́fə/ chief seaport of Israel, in the northern part of the country. Population: 252,300 (1996).

haik /hīk, hayk/, **haick** *n* a loose-fitting North African garment made from a rectangle of cloth, usually white, that is wrapped around the head and body [Early 18C. < Arabic *hā'ik*.]

Haikou /hī kṓ/ capital of Hainan Province in China, on the northern side of the island of Hainan. Population: 280,153 (1990).

haiku /hī́ koo/ (*plural* **-ku**) *n* a form of Japanese poetry with 17 syllables in three unrhymed lines of five, seven, and five syllables, often describing nature or a season [Late 19C. < Japanese, shortening of *haikai no ku* 'not serious verse'.]

hail[1] /hayl/ *n* **1** small balls of ice and hardened snow that fall like rain **2** a barrage of something, e.g. missiles or insults [Old English *hagol*, *hægl* < Indo-European] —**hail** *v*

hail[2] /hayl/ *vt* **1 GREET** to welcome or greet somebody upon meeting ○ *We hailed each other like long-lost buddies.* **2 ACCLAIM** to praise or approve a person, action, or accomplishment with enthusiasm ○ *The press hailed her as a child prodigy.* **3 SHOUT FOR ATTENTION** to attract the attention of somebody or something, e.g. a taxi or ship, by calling or signalling ■ *interj* **EXCLAMATION OF GREETING**

used to greet, welcome, or acclaim somebody (*archaic or literary*) [12C. Variant of HALE[1].] —**hail** *n* —**hailer** *n* ◇ **within hail** near enough to hear a shout or see a signal (*dated*)
hail from *vt* to live in or come from a particular place, especially as a birthplace or place of origin ◇ *Her husband hails from Manchester.*

Haile Selassie I /híli sə lássi/ (1892–1975) emperor of Ethiopia (1930–36, 1942–74). Born **Ras Tafari Makonnen**

hail-fellow-well-met *adj* very friendly, especially in a way that presumes an intimacy that does not exist ■ *n* an exuberantly friendly person [< the greeting *Hail, fellow! Well met!*]

Hail Mary (*plural* **Hail Marys**) *n* a Roman Catholic prayer to the Virgin Mary based on Gabriel's and Elizabeth's greetings to her as recorded in the Gospel of Luke in the Bible [Translation of medieval Latin *Ave, Maria*, opening words of the prayer]

Hailsham /háylshəm/, **Quintin Hogg, 2nd Viscount, Baron Hailsham of St Marylebone** (*b.* 1907) British politician

hailstone /háyl stōn/ *n* a pellet of ice and hardened snow that falls like rain

hailstorm /háyl stawrm/ *n* a storm that includes a downpour of hail

Hainan /hí nán/ province in SE China, comprising the island of Hainan in the South China Sea. Capital: Haikou. Population: 7,110,000 (1994). Area: 33,991 sq. km/13,124 sq. mi.

Haiphong /hí fóng/ port in N Vietnam, on the Red River delta. Population: 1,447,523 (1989).

hair /hair/ *n* **1 STRANDS GROWING ON THE HEAD OR BODY** the mass of fine flexible protein strands that grow from follicles on the skin of a person or animal, especially those on somebody's head **2 SINGLE STRAND** any of the fine strands that grow on the skin of a person or animal ◇ *The rug was covered with dog hairs.* **3 GROWTH ON A PLANT RESEMBLING HAIR** a thin flexible growth on a plant resembling a human or animal hair **4 FABRIC** fabric made from animal hair **5 TINY AMOUNT** a tiny amount or degree [Old English *hær* < Germanic] —**haired** /haird/ *adj* —**hairless** *adj* —**hairlessness** *n* ◇ **be tearing your hair out** to be very irritated or frustrated ◇ **have somebody by the short hairs** to have somebody in your control or power (*informal*) ◇ **let your hair down** to behave in a more relaxed way than usual (*informal*) ◇ **not turn a hair** to remain completely calm ◇ **split hairs** to argue about or give undue significance to fine distinctions and details ◇ **the hair of the dog (that bit you)** an alcoholic drink taken as a supposed cure for a hangover

SPELLCHECK Do not confuse **hair** with **hare**, which has a similar sound. Beware: your spellchecker will not catch this error.

hairball /háir bawl/ *n* a ball of hair that accumulates in the stomach of some animals, e.g. cats and cows, when they clean themselves

hairband /háir band/ *n* a strip of fabric worn on the head to keep the hair in place or out of the eyes

~~hair-brained~~ incorrect spelling of **harebrained**

hairbreadth *n* = hair's-breadth ■ *adj* exceedingly narrow

hairbrush /háir brush/ *n* a brush for smoothing and styling hair

hair cell *n* a sensory cell with fine projections resembling hairs, especially one in the inner ear that transmits information on sound or movement to the brain

haircloth /háir kloth/ *n* a thick, coarse fabric made from horse's or camel's hair. Use: upholstery.

haircut /háir kut/ *n* **1** a session in which somebody's hair is cut **2** the shape or style in which somebody's hair is cut ◇ *How do you like my new haircut?*

hairdo /háir doo/ (*plural* **-dos**) *n* the way in which somebody's hair has been cut or styled (*informal*)

hairdresser /háir dressər/ *n* **1** a professional cutter, stylist, or dresser of hair **2** a shop or salon where a hairdresser works

hairdressing /háir dressing/ *n* **1 CARE OF THE HAIR** the cutting, styling, colouring, or curling of hair **2 HAIRDRESSER'S PROFESSION** the occupation of a hairdresser **3 HAIR CARE PRODUCT** a preparation, e.g. an oil or gel, used to style or care for the hair

hair dryer *n* a device that uses heated air for drying hair, either hand-held or in the shape of a dome that fits over the head

hair follicle *n* a small tubular pit in the outer layer of skin (**epidermis**) enclosing the base of a growing hair

hairgrip /háir grip/ *n* a small metal or plastic pin bent double, used to grip the hair and keep it in place. ◇ **bobby pin**

hairline /háir līn/ *n* **1 WHERE HAIR BEGINS ON HEAD** the line across the top of the forehead behind which the hair grows **2 THIN LINE** a very narrow line that is barely visible **3 THIN STROKE** a very thin line on a typeface, or a typeface containing thin lines **4 FABRIC WITH FINE STRIPES** a textile pattern of very thin stripes or a fabric with such stripes

hairnet /háir net/ *n* a circular piece of fine netting with an elastic edge, worn to hold the hair in place, especially in bed

hairpiece /háir peess/ *n* a wig, toupee, or other piece of false hair, worn to conceal hair loss or to add bulk or length to somebody's natural hair

hairpin /háir pin/ *n* **1 BENT WIRE FOR HOLDING HAIR** a U-shaped piece of metal wire used to hold the hair in place **2 SOMETHING WITH A SHARP BEND** something with a U-shape resembling a hairpin, especially a sharp bend in a road **3 SYMBOL FOR CRESCENDO OR DIMINUENDO** a long V-shaped mark used in written music to indicate an increase or decrease in loudness (*informal*)

hair-raising *adj* causing intense fear or excitement ◇ *Landing on that makeshift runway was the most hair-raising experience of my life.* —**hair-raiser** *n* —**hair-raisingly** *adv*

hair's-breadth *n* a very small margin or distance

hair shirt *n* **1** a shirt made from a harsh scratchy haircloth that was once worn next to the skin by religious people as a form of self-imposed punishment **2** a self-imposed punishment in the form of private suffering

hair slide *n* a decorative clip with a hinged back used to hold hair in place

hair space *n* the thinnest space used to separate words and letters in typesetting

hairsplitting /háir splitting/ *n* overattention to unimportant details and fine distinctions, especially in an argument ◇ *Whether it was five past or ten past is just hairsplitting: you kept me waiting for over an hour.* —**hairsplitter** *n* —**hairsplitting** *adj*

hair spray *n* a substance sprayed onto the hair to hold it in place

hairspring /háir spring/ *n* a very fine coiled spring that controls the movement of the balance wheel in a watch or clock

hairstreak /háir streek/ *n* a brown or greyish tropical American butterfly with delicate streaks on the underside of its wings and fine tails resembling hairs on its hind wings. Subfamily: Theclinae.

hair stroke *n* a very fine line in writing or printing

hairstyle /háir stīl/ *n* the way in which somebody's hair is cut and arranged ◇ *How do you like my new hairstyle?* —**hairstyling** *n* —**hairstylist** *n*

hair trigger *n* **1** a gun trigger that needs very little pressure to activate it **2** a response or mechanism that reacts to the slightest provocation or impulse (*hyphenated before nouns*) [< the thin spring that it activates]

hair weave *n* false hair interwoven with somebody's own hair in order to conceal hair loss

hairweaving /háir weeving/ *n* the interweaving of a hairpiece with somebody's own hair, often done to disguise hair loss —**hairweave** *vt* —**hairweaver** *n*

hairworm /háir wurm/ *n* a long slender aquatic worm whose larva lives as a parasite on arthropods. Phylum: Nematomorpha.

hairy /háiri/ (**-ier, -iest**) *adj* **1 COVERED WITH HAIR** covered with hair or filaments resembling hair **2 MADE OF HAIR** made of hair, or similar in texture to something made of hair **3 FRIGHTENING** filled with dangers or difficulties (*informal*) —**hairiness** *n*

hairy woodpecker *n* a large woodpecker with black and white markings and a long bill. Native to: North America. *Picoides villosus.*

Haiti

Haiti /háyti/ republic in the N Caribbean, occupying the western third of the island of Hispaniola. Capital: Port-au-Prince. Population: 6,732,000 (1996). Area: 27,750 sq. km/10,714 sq. mi. —**Haitian** /háysh'n, haa éesh'n/ *n, adj*

Haitian Creole *n* the French-based creole spoken in Haiti. Native speakers: 4 million. —**Haitian Creole** *adj*

Haitink /hítingk/, **Bernard** (*b.* 1929) Dutch conductor

haj *n* = hajj

haja *n* = hajja

haji *n* = hajji

hajj /haj/ (*plural* **hajjes**), **hadj** (*plural* **hadjes**), **haj** (*plural* **hajes**) *n* the pilgrimage to Mecca, Saudi Arabia, that is a principal religious obligation of adult Muslims [Late 17C. < Arabic, 'pilgrimage'.]

hajja /hájjə/, **hadja, haja** *n* a Muslim woman who has made the pilgrimage to Mecca (*also as a title*) [< form of Turkish, Persian *hājī* (see HAJJI)]

hajji /hájji/ (*plural* **-jis**), **hadji** (*plural* **hadjis**), **haji** (*plural* **-is**) *n* a Muslim who has made the pilgrimage to Mecca (*also as a title*) [Early 17C. Directly or via Turkish < Persian *hājī* 'pilgrim' < Arabic *hajj* 'pilgrimage']

haka /haákə/ *n* **1** a traditional Maori war dance with vocal accompaniment by the dancers **2** a version of the traditional haka performed by sports teams, especially the New Zealand rugby team [Mid-19C. < Maori.]

hake /hayk/ (*plural* **hake** or **hakes**) *n* **1** a marine fish similar to the cod, with two dorsal fins and an elongated body. Genus: *Merluccius*. **2** the flesh of a hake used as food [15C. < ?]

hakea /haáki ə, háy-/ *n* a shrub or tree with hard woody fruit. Native to: Australia. Genus: *Hakea*. [Mid-19C. < modern Latin, after C. L. von *Hake* (1745–1818), German amateur botanist.]

hakim[1] /hə keém/, **hakeem** *n* a Muslim doctor who uses traditional remedies [< Arabic *hakīm* 'wise man']

hakim[2] /haákim/ *n* a Muslim judge, ruler, or administrator [Early 17C. < Arabic *hākim* 'ruler'.]

Hakluyt /hák loot/, **Richard** (1552?–1616) English geographer

Hakodate /haákō daá tay/ seaport on S Hokkaido Island, Japan, on Tsugaru Strait. Population: 289,806 (1999).

haku /haá koo/ *n* Hawaii a crown made of fresh flowers

hal- *prefix* = **halo-** (*before vowels*)

Halab /há lab/ = **Aleppo**

Halacha /hə laákə/, **Halakha, Halakhah** *n* the body of Jewish law beginning with the Pentateuch and developed by the rabbis [Mid-19C. < Hebrew *hā lākāh* 'law'.]

halal /hə laál, hállal/ *adj* **SUITABLE FOR MUSLIMS** describes meat from animals that have been slaughtered in the ritual way prescribed by Islamic law or relating to such meat ■ *n* **HALAL MEAT** halal meat ■ *vt* (**-lals, -lalling, -lalled**) **SLAUGHTER ANIMALS IN THE ISLAMIC WAY** to slaughter animals for meat in the ritual way prescribed by Islamic law [Mid-19C. < Arabic *halāl* 'lawful'.]

halala /hə laálə/ (*plural* **-la** or **-las**) *n* see table at **currency** [Mid-20C. < Arabic.]

halation /hə láysh'n/ *n* **1** a blurred bright patch around a light source on a photographic image **2** a patch or ring of glowing light round a bright object on a television screen [Mid-19C. < HALO.]

halberd /hálbərd/, **halbert** /-bərt/ *n* an axe blade and pick with a spearhead on top, mounted on a long handle and used as a weapon in the 15th and 16th centuries [15C. Via French < Middle High German *helmbarde* < *helm* 'handle' + *barde* 'hatchet'.] —**halberdier** /hálbər deér/ *n*

halcyon /hálssi ən/ *adj* **TRANQUIL** tranquil and free from disturbance or care (*literary*) ■ *n* **1 MYTHOLOGICAL BIRD** in Greek mythology, a bird resembling the kingfisher, believed to have had the power to calm the waves at the time of the winter solstice when it nested at sea **2 KINGFISHER** a kingfisher (*literary*) [14C. Via Latin < Greek *(h)alkuōn*, mythical bird.]

halcyon days *npl* **1** a time of happiness and tranquillity (*literary*) **2** two weeks of calm weather during the winter solstice

Haldane /háwl dayn/, **J. B. S.** (1892–1964) British geneticist. Full name **John Burdon Sanderson Haldane**

Haldane, Richard Burdon, Viscount Haldane of Cloan (1856–1928) British philosopher and politician

hale[1] /hayl/ (**haler, halest**) *adj* in robust good health ○ *hale and hearty* [Old English *hāl* (see WHOLE)] —**haleness** *n*

hale[2] /hayl/ (**hales, haling, haled**) *vt* **1** to pull or drag somebody or something with great effort (*archaic*) **2** to compel somebody to go somewhere, especially to court [13C. Via Old French *haler* < Old Norse *hala*.] —**haler** *n*

haler /haálər/ (*plural* **halers** *or* **haleru** /-lə roo/), **heller** /héllər/ (*plural* **-lers** *or* **-leru**) *n* see table at **currency** [Mid-20C. Via Czech < Middle High German *haller* 'silver coin', after *Hall*, Swabian town.]

Haley /háyli/, **Alex** (1921–92) US writer

Haley, Bill (1927–81) US musician. Full name **William John Haley**

half /haaf/ *n, adj, det, pron* **ONE OF TWO EQUAL PARTS** either of two equal or nearly equal parts into which a whole can be divided ○ *Arrange the apricot halves in a gratin dish.* ○ *The recession began in the second half of 1990.* ○ (adj) *You don't have to pay for the first half hour.* ○ (det) *I'll pay half the bill.* ○ (pron) *I invited 20, but only half showed up.* ■ *adj* **30 MINUTES AFTER** describes the time 30 minutes after a stated hour (*informal*) ○ *They're arriving for dinner at half six.* ■ *n* (*plural* **halves**) **1 PLAYING PERIOD** either of two periods of play into which some games are divided ○ *We started off well but failed to score in the second half.* **2 HALF FARE** a fare costing more or less half the ordinary amount, e.g. for a child or senior citizen, on public transport ○ *Two and two halves please.* **3 HALF A PINT** half a pint of beer or other alcoholic drink ■ *adj, adv* **PARTIAL** to some extent but not complete or completely ○ (adj) *She gave me a half-smile* ○ (adv) *She was half laughing, half crying* ■ *n* **SCHOOL TERM** either of two parts of an academic year ○ *We've got exams at the end of the half.* ■ *adj, adv* **EQUALLY** in equal parts ○ (adj) *We each have half ownership in the building.* ○ (adv) *He's half French, half Spanish.* [Old English *healf* < Germanic] ◇ **by half** to a too great extent ○ *I don't trust him – he's too friendly by half.* ◇ **go halves (with somebody)** to share something equally with somebody ○ *If we go halves on the petrol the journey shouldn't be too expensive.* ◇ **not do things by halves** to do things thoroughly and often on a large scale ◇ **not half 1** not at all ○ *Mmm! This cake's not half bad!* **2** much less than half ○ *She's not half as busy as you are.* ○ *This isn't half the fun I thought it would be.* **3** used as an understatement to indicate enthusiasm (*informal*) ○ *Just look at them – his new girlfriend can't half dance!*

USAGE Singular or plural? The noun ***half*** is singular, but the word is treated as plural when it is followed by a plural noun (with or without *of*) or when it refers back to a plural: *Half the people are late. The other half of them aren't coming at all. At least half are behaving inexcusably.* With many singular nouns, ***half*** can be used in the forms *half a share, half of a share,* and *a half share.*

---

half-and-half *adj* **WITH HALF OF EACH** containing half each of two things ■ *adv* **IN HALF** in two equal portions ■ *n* (*plural* **half-and-halfs**) **1 TWO THINGS MIXED EQUALLY** a mixture of two things in equal parts **2 MIXTURE OF ALCOHOLIC BEVERAGES** an alcoholic drink made up of equal parts of stout and beer or bitter and mild

half-arsed /-aarst/ *adj* (*slang*) **1** an offensive term meaning badly organized or carried out **2** an offensive term meaning lacking forcefulness or effectiveness

halfback /haáf bak/ *n* **1 PLAYER FORWARD OF THE LAST DEFENSIVE LINE** a player in a team sport who is positioned just in front of the last defensive line **2 SOCCER MIDFIELDER** a midfielder in soccer (*dated*) **3 POSITION OF A HALFBACK** the position of somebody playing as a halfback **4 PLAYER BEHIND THE SCRUM** either of the two players positioned immediately behind the scrum in rugby

half-baked *adj* (*informal*) **1** not well thought out and likely to fail **2** lacking the ability to act with reason and common sense ○ *That's about what you'd expect from a department run by a load of half-baked idealists.*

halfbeak /haáf beek/ *n* a small fish with a short upper jaw and long lower jaw. Native to: warm seas, lakes, and rivers. Family: Hemiramphidae.

half binding *n* bookbinding in which the back and sometimes the corners of a book are bound in one material and the sides in another

half-blood *n* **1 HALF-BROTHER OR HALF-SISTER** a person who is related to somebody else by having one parent in common **2 RELATIONSHIP SHARING ONE PARENT** the relationship between two people who have one parent in common **3** *US* **OFFENSIVE TERM** an offensive term for somebody of racially mixed parentage, especially Native American and white

half-blooded *adj* **1** having only one parent in common **2** an offensive term meaning with racially different parents

half-blue *adj* at the universities of Oxford and Cambridge, a player who is a substitute for a blue or who plays for the university in a minor sport

half board *n* the price of a room in a hotel for a night with breakfast and one main meal included (*hyphenated before nouns*)

half boot *n* a boot that reaches anywhere from the top of the ankle to mid-calf

half-bound *adj* describes a book that is bound on the back and sometimes the corners in one material and on the sides in another

half-breed *n* **1 OFFENSIVE TERM** an offensive term for a person of mixed racial parentage, especially Native American and white **2 OFFSPRING OF ONLY ONE PUREBRED PARENT** a domestic animal with only one parent of known pedigree **3 HYBRID ANIMAL OR PLANT** an animal or plant that is a hybrid product of two distinct types

half-brother *n* a son of one of your parents by a different partner

half-caste *n* an offensive term for somebody of mixed racial parentage —**half-caste** *adj*

half cock *n* a position on a single-action firearm in which the hammer is half-raised and locked so that the trigger cannot be pulled ◇ **go off at half cock 1** to fail because of poor planning, timing, or preparation **2** to do or say something before thinking about it

half-cocked *adj* **1** describes a single-action firearm with the hammer half-raised and locked so that the trigger cannot be pulled **2** lacking adequate planning, thought, or preparation

half-crown *n* a former British coin worth two shillings and sixpence

half-cut *adj* rather drunk (*informal*)

half-day *n* either the morning or the afternoon of a normal working day, especially when taken as a holiday

half-dead *adj* tired and worn-out (*informal*)

half-dollar *n* a US coin worth 50 cents

half gainer *n* a dive in which the diver jumps from the board facing forwards and then does a half backward somersault to enter the water headfirst, facing the board

half-hardy *adj* describes a plant that can survive outdoors in mild frosts

half-hearted *adj* with little enthusiasm and no real interest in the result —**half-heartedly** *adv* —**half-heartedness** *n*

half hitch *n* a knot made by looping a piece of rope round an object then passing the end of the rope round itself and through the loop

half-holiday *n* either the morning or afternoon of a working day taken as a holiday

half-hour *n* **1** a period of 30 minutes **2** the point in time 30 minutes after the start of an hour ○ *Isn't that clock supposed to chime on the half-hour?* —**half-hourly** *adv, adj*

half-inch *n* a measurement of length equal to half an inch or roughly 13 mm ■ *vt Cockney* to steal (*slang*)

half-length *adj* **1 SHOWN ABOVE THE WAIST** describes a portrait depicting the subject from the waist up but including the hands **2 REACHING TO THE KNEE** coming down to the knee rather than the ankles ■ *n* **PORTRAIT FROM WAIST UP** a portrait depicting the subject from the waist up but including the hands

half-life *n* **1** (*symbol* $T_{\frac{1}{2}}$) the time a radioactive substance takes to lose half its radioactivity through decay **2** the time it takes for half a given amount of a substance such as a drug to be removed from living tissue through natural biological activity

half-light *n* the soft dim light seen at dawn and dusk

half-line, half line *n* MATH = **ray**[1] *n.* **4**

half-marathon *n* a race on foot covering 21.243 km/13 mi. 352 yd

half-mast *n* the position, roughly halfway down a flagpole, to which a flag is lowered as a sign of respect when an important person dies ■ *vt* to position a flag roughly halfway down a flagpole as a mark of respect when an important person dies

half measure *n* an inadequate or ineffectual action

half-moon *n* **1 MOON SEEN AS A SEMICIRCLE** the moon when only half its face is illuminated during the first or last quarter **2 SOMETHING SEMICIRCULAR** anything with the shape of a semicircle or crescent **3 AREA OF THE FINGERNAIL** a pale semicircle at the base of the fingernail

half nelson *n* a hold in which a wrestler passes an arm under the opponent's arm from behind to the back of the neck and then levers the opponent's arm backwards [Because only one arm is held, not both, as in a full nelson]

half note *n US* MUSIC = **minim** *n.* **1**

halfpenny /háypni, -pəni/ *n* (*plural* **-ny** *or* **-nies**) a former British coin worth half an old or new penny, finally withdrawn in 1985

halfpennyworth /háypni wurth, háypərth/ *n* **1** an amount that could be bought for half a penny **2** a very small amount

half-pie *adj NZ* partly or poorly done (*informal*) [< ?]

half-pint *n* **1** half of a pint **2** an offensive term for a short person (*insult*)

halfpipe /haáf pīp/ *n* a structure in the shape of the bottom half of a pipe, built for freestyle snowboarding, in-line skating, and skateboarding

half-price *n* half the usual price ■ *adj, adv* at half the regular price

half relief *n* sculptural relief that projects roughly halfway from the background

half rhyme *n* an imperfect rhyme where there is a similarity in the sounds but not the identity of stressed vowels that is found in full rhymes

half seas over *adj* somewhat drunk (*dated informal*)

half-sister *n* a daughter of one of your parents by a different partner

half-size *n* a size that is halfway between two whole-numbered sizes ○ *Do you have half-sizes in this style?*

half-slip *n* a woman's undergarment that hangs from the waist and is worn as a lining for a skirt or dress

half sole *n* a sole on a shoe that covers the wide part at the front of the base

half-sole (**half-soles, half-soling, half-soled**) *vt* to put a new half sole on a shoe or boot

half step *n US* MUSIC = **semitone**

half term *n* a short holiday for schools halfway through an academic term (*hyphenated before nouns*)

half tide *n* the time during which the tide is halfway between its high and low levels

half-timbered *adj* built with a visible frame of wooden beams as well as plaster, stone, or brick —**half-timbering** *n*

half-time *n* a short break between the halves of a game during which players rest

half title *n* **1** the title of a book printed on the right-hand page before the main title page **2** a title printed on a separate page at the beginning of a section of a book

halftone /haáf tōn/ *n* **1** a shade or tone halfway between light and dark **2** a photoengraving process by which shading is produced by photographing an image through a screen, then etching a plate so that the shading is reproduced as dots

half-track *n* a military vehicle with wheels on the front axles and Caterpillar™ treads on the axles that supply motive power

half-truth *n* a statement that includes only some of the relevant facts or information and so is intended or likely to be misleading

half volley *n* a stroke or shot that makes contact with the ball immediately after it has bounced ■ *vti* **half-volley** (**half-volleys, half-volleying, half-volleyed**) to strike a ball immediately after it has bounced

halfway /ha͡af wáy/ *adv, adj* **1** at or to the middle point between two things in space or time ○ *reach the halfway point* **2** to only some extent, degree, or distance

halfway house *n* **1 COMPROMISE** a combination of the qualities of two things that may not be as good as either of them ○ *The style is a sort of halfway house between late romanticism and early modernism.* **2 REHABILITATION CENTRE** a hostel or centre designed to ease people back into society after their release from an institution, e.g. prison or a psychiatric hospital **3 HALFWAY TO THE END** the halfway point in progress towards a goal **4 STOPPING PLACE** a resting place for travellers halfway through a long journey

halfwit /ha͡af wit/ *n* an offensive term for somebody who is regarded as behaving in a thoughtless or unintelligent way —**half-witted** /haaf wíttid/ *adj* —**half-wittedly** *adv* —**half-wittedness** *n*

half-yearly *adv, adj* done or happening every six months or in the middle of the calendar or financial year

halibut /hállibət/ (*plural* **-buts** *or* **-but**) *n* **1** a large flatfish. Native to: N Atlantic, Pacific Oceans. Genus: *Hippoglossus.* **2** the flesh of a halibut used as food [15C. < form of HOLY + dialect *butt* 'flatfish' (< Middle Low German or Middle Dutch).]

Halicarnassus /hálli kaar nássəss/ ancient city in present-day SW Turkey. It was the site of the Mausoleum, the tomb of King Mausolus, which was one of the Seven Wonders of the World.

halide /háylīd, hállid/, **halid** /hállīd, -lid/ *n* a chemical compound of a halogen with another element or group of atoms [Late 19C. < HALOGEN.]

halier /hállyər/ *n* see table at **currency** [Mid-20C. Via Czech < Middle High German *haller* (see HALER).]

Halifax /hálli faks/ **1** town in N England. Population: 91,069 (1991). **2** capital of Nova Scotia, Canada, in the south-central part of the province, on the Atlantic Ocean. Population: 113,910 (1996).

haliplankton /hálli plangktən/ *n* plankton found in the sea

halite /háylīt, hállit/ *n* a colourless or white crystalline mineral consisting of sodium chloride. Source: dried up lake beds. Use: table salt, source of chlorine. [Mid-19C. < Greek *hals* 'salt'.]

halitosis /hálli tṓsiss/ *n* = **bad breath** [Late 19C. < Latin *halitus* 'health'.]

Halkomelem /hólkə máyləm/ (*plural* **-lem**) *n* **1** a member of a Native North American people whose traditional territory is in SW British Columbia **2** the Salish language spoken by the Halkomelem people —**Halkomelem** *adj*

hall /hawl/ *n* **1 ENTRANCE ROOM** an entrance room in a house, flat, or building, with doors leading to other rooms **2 CORRIDOR** a connecting passage or corridor with doors leading to other rooms **3 BUILDING WITH A LARGE PUBLIC ROOM** a building with a large room used for public events or activities such as meetings, entertainment, and exhibitions **4 LARGE ROOM** a large room in a building such as a school, university, or castle, used for such purposes as dining or receptions **5 LARGE HOUSE** the main house on a large estate **6** EDUC = **hall of residence 7 DINING ROOM** a large dining room in a university, college, or school [Old English, < Germanic, 'cover, conceal']

Hall /hawl/, **Ben** (1837–65) Australian bushranger. Full name **Benjamin Hall**

Hall, John (1824–1907) British-born New Zealand statesman

Hall, Ken (1901–44) Australian film director

Hall, Sir Peter (*b.* 1930) British theatre director

Hall, Rodney (*b.* 1935) Australian novelist and poet

Hall, Roger Leighton (*b.* 1939) British-born New Zealand playwright

hallah *n* JUDAISM = **challah**

Halle /hállə/ city in central Germany. Population: 311,400 (1990).

Hallé /hállay/, **Sir Charles** (1819–95) German-born British conductor and pianist

Hallel /ha͡a layl, hállel/, **hallel** *n* Psalms 113 to 118, recited during the Jewish morning service at festivals as an expression of joy [Early 18C. < Hebrew, 'praise'.]

hallelujah /hálli lóoyə/, **halleluiah, alleluia** /álli-/ *interj* **1 USED TO EXPRESS PRAISE TO GOD** used to express praise or thanks to God **2 USED TO EXPRESS RELIEF** used to express relief, welcome, or gratitude ○ *Hallelujah! The old car finally started.* ■ *n* **1 CRY OF 'HALLELUJAH!'** a thankful cry of 'hallelujah!' **2 HYMN OF PRAISE** a song or piece of religious music expressing praise to God [Old English, via Latin < Hebrew *hallĕlūyāh* 'praise ye the Lord']

Haller /hállər/, **Albrecht von** (1707–77) Swiss biologist

Halley /hálli, háwli/, **Edmond** (1656–1742) British astronomer

Halley's comet *n* a comet with an elliptical orbit around the Sun that passes through the inner solar system every 76 years, last observed in 1986

halliard *n* = **halyard**

Hall-Jones /háwl jṓnz/, **William** (1851–1936) British-born New Zealand statesman

hallmark /háwl maark/ *n* **1 MARK OF QUALITY** a mark showing that something is of high quality **2 DISTINGUISHING MARK** a feature of something that distinguishes it from others ○ *Discreet service is the hallmark of a fine restaurant.* **3 OFFICIAL MARK ON PRECIOUS METAL** a mark stamped on articles made of gold, silver, or platinum to show that the metal used meets the proper standards of purity ■ *vt* **STAMP WITH A MARK OF QUALITY** to stamp an article made of gold, silver, or platinum to show that the metal used meets the proper standards of purity [Early 18C. After *Goldsmiths' Hall* in London.]

hallo *interj, n* = **hello** ■ *interj, n, vti* = **halloo**

halloa *interj, n, vti* = **halloo**

hall of fame *n US* a museum where portraits, memorabilia, or belongings of people who have excelled in a particular sphere of activity such as baseball are displayed

hall of residence *n* a campus building where students live while attending a college or university. US term **dormitory** *n.* 2

halloo /hə lóo/, **halloa** /hə lṓ/, **hallo** *interj* **1 CALL TO ATTRACT ATTENTION** used to try to attract somebody's attention **2 CALL TO URGE ON HUNTING DOGS** used to spur on dogs in a hunt ■ *v* (**-loos, -looing, -looed; -loas, -loaing, -loaed; -los, -loing, -loed**) **1** *vi* **CALL OUT 'HALLOO!'** to utter a call of 'halloo!' **2** *vt* **SPUR ON WITH CALLS** to spur hunting dogs on by shouting halloos **3** *vt* **SHOUT** to shout out something to somebody [Late 17C. Alteration of *holla* < French *holà*.] —**halloo** *n*

hallow /hállō/ *vt* **1** to make somebody or something holy **2** to have great respect or reverence for somebody or something [Old English *hālgian* < Indo-European] —**hallower** *n*

Halloween /hállō éen/, **Hallowe'en** *n* the night of 31 October, the eve of All Saints' Day [Late 18C. Shortening of *All Hallow Even*, the eve of All Saints' Day (see ALLHALLOWS, EVEN[2]).]

Hallowmas /hállō mass/ *n* = **All Saints' Day** (*archaic*) [14C. Shortening of *Allhallowmas.*]

halls of ivy *npl US* institutions or an institution of higher learning, especially those regarded as particularly prestigious ○ *After four years in the halls of ivy, she had to adjust to a 9 to 5 job.* [< the traditional ivy-covered buildings]

hall stand *n* a piece of furniture, usually kept in the hall of a house, where people can hang their coats, hats, and umbrellas. US term **hall tree**

Hallstatt /hál stat/, **Hallstattian** /hal státti ən/ *adj* relating to or typical of a European culture of the late Bronze Age and early Iron Age [Mid-19C. After the town of *Hallstatt* in Austria, where a large burial site of the period was found.]

hall tree *n US* FURNITURE = **hall stand**

halluces plural of **hallux**

hallucinate /hə lóossi nayt/ (**-nates, -nating, -nated**) *vti* to imagine seeing, hearing, or otherwise sensing people, things, or events that are not present or actually occurring at the time [Early 19C. < Latin *hallucinat-*, past participle of *hallucinari* 'dream, be distracted'.] —**hallucinative** /-ətiv/ *adj* —**hallucinator** *n*

hallucination /hə lóossi náysh'n/ *n* **1** the perception of somebody or something that is not really there, often as a symptom of a psychiatric disorder or as a response to certain drugs **2** something that somebody imagines seeing, hearing, or otherwise sensing when it is not present or actually occurring at the time (*often plural*) —**hallucinational** *adj*

hallucinatory /hə lóossinətəri/ *adj* **1** relating to or involving the belief that something is being seen, heard, or otherwise sensed when it is not present or actually occurring **2** causing somebody to believe that he or she is seeing, hearing, or otherwise sensing things that are not present or actually occurring at the time

hallucinogen /hə lóossinə jen/ *n* a substance, especially a drug, that causes hallucinations, e.g. LSD —**hallucinogenic** /hə lóossinə jénnik/ *adj*

hallucinosis /hə lóossi nṓssiss/ *n* a psychiatric disorder that involves hallucinations

hallux /hálləks/ (*plural* **-luces** /hállyoo seez/) *n* the big toe on the human foot, or the first digit on the hind foot of some mammals, birds, reptiles, and amphibians (*technical*) [Mid-19C. Via modern Latin < Latin *hallus.*]

hallux valgus *n* a medical condition affecting the big toe in which its tip points towards the little toe and its base sticks out on the inner edge of the foot [*Valgus* < Latin, 'bowlegged']

hallway /háwl way/ *n* = **hall** *n.* 1, **hall** *n.* 2

halm *n* PLANT SCI = **haulm**

halma /hálmə/ *n* a board game similar to Chinese chequers [Late 19C. < Greek, 'leap'.]

Halmahera /hálmə heérə/ largest island of the Moluccas, Indonesia. Area: 17,800 sq. km/6,873 sq. mi.

halo /háylō/ *n* (*plural* **-loes** *or* **-los**) **1 CIRCLE OF LIGHT AROUND A SAINT'S HEAD** a ring or circle of light around the head of a saint in a religious painting **2 IMAGINED AURA OF GLORY** an aura of glory imagined to surround somebody or something famous or revered **3 SOMETHING RESEMBLING A RING OF LIGHT** something that resembles or suggests a ring of light **4 LIGHT CIRCLE AROUND MOON OR SUN** a circle of light around the Moon or Sun, caused by light refracting from ice crystals in the atmosphere **5 BODY OF STARS** a thinly populated spherical region of stars and other luminous objects surrounding a galaxy ■ *vt* (**-los, -loing, -loed**) **SURROUND WITH HALO** to surround somebody or something with a halo [Mid-16C. Via medieval Latin < Greek *halos* 'disc around the Sun or Moon'.]

halo- *prefix* **1** salt ○ *halobiont* **2** halogen ○ *halocarbon* [Via French < Greek *hals* < Indo-European]

halobiont /hállō bī ont/ *n* an organism that lives in a salty environment, especially the sea —**halobiontic** /hállō bī óntik/ *adj*

halocarbon /hállō kaárbən/ *n* a compound, e.g. fluorocarbon, containing carbon and a halogen

halocline /hállō klīn/ *n* a vertical gradient in the saltiness of the ocean

halo effect *n* the tendency to judge somebody as being totally good because one aspect of his or her character is good [< the halos of angels]

haloform /hállə fawrm/ *n* a chemical compound such as chloroform that is derived from methane and contains three halogen atoms

halogen /hálləjən/ *n* any of the five electronegative elements, fluorine, chlorine, iodine, bromine, or astatine ■ *adj* describes lamps or heat sources having a filament surrounded by halogen vapour ○ *a halogen bulb* [Mid-19C. Because they readily form salts when combined with metals.]

halogenate /hálləjə nayt/ (**-nates, -nating, -nated**) *vt* to treat something or combine it with a halogen —**halogenation** /hálləjə náysh'n/ *n*

halon /háy lon/ *n* a stable halocarbon used to put out fires

haloperidol /hállō pérri dol/ *n* a tranquillizing drug. Use: treatment of schizophrenia, mania, and psychoses. [Mid-20C. < HALO- + PIPERIDINE.]

halophile /hállō fīl/ *n* a plant that thrives in salty soil —**halophilic** /hállō fíllik/ *adj*

halophyte /hállō fīt/ *n* a plant capable of growing in salty soil —**halophytic** /hállō fíttik/ *adj* —**halophytism** *n*

halothane /hállō thayn/ *n* $C_2HBrClF_3$ a colourless liquid. Use: anaesthetic. [Mid-20C. < HALO- + ETHANE.]

haloumi /hə lóomi/ (*plural* **-mis**) *n* a salty white Greek cheese with a tough rubbery texture that is usually grilled until a crust has formed on both sides and eaten hot

Hals /halss/, **Frans** (1580?–1666) Flemish-born Dutch painter

halt[1] /hawlt, holt/ *n* **1 TEMPORARY STOP** an end or temporary stop ○ *The sudden rain brought the game to an abrupt halt.* **2 SMALL RAILWAY STATION** a small, often rural, station, especially one that has no ticket office or public toilets ■ *interj* **COMMAND USED TO MAKE SOMEBODY STOP** used to command somebody to stop ○ *Halt! Identify yourself!* ■ *vti* **STOP** to stop, or make somebody or something stop [Late 16C. < German *halten* 'stop, hold'.] ◇ **grind to a halt** to come gradually to a complete stop

halt[2] /hawlt, holt/ *vi* **1 ACT HESITANTLY** to act or behave without certainty or confidence **2 BE DEFECTIVE** to have defects or inconsistencies in logical development or in poetic rhythm **3 OFFENSIVE TERM** an offensive term meaning to have mild, moderate, or severe difficulty in walking (*archaic*) ■ *adj* **OFFENSIVE TERM** an offensive term meaning walking with difficulty (*archaic*) [Old English *healtian* 'walk with a limp' < Germanic]

halter /háwltər, hólt-/ *n* **1 ROPE DEVICE FOR A HORSE** an arrangement of ropes or leather straps put over the head of an animal, especially a horse, and used to lead it **2 BACKLESS GARMENT** a woman's garment, worn between the shoulders and waist, that fastens or passes behind the neck and leaves the arms, shoulders, and back bare **3 ROPE FOR HANGING** a rope with a noose, used to hang somebody **4 HANGING** death by hanging ○ *destined for the halter* [< Old English *hælftre* < Germanic, 'hold on to'] —**halter** *vt*

haltere /hál teer/ (*plural* **-teres** /-teér eez/) *n* either of a pair of projecting parts in insects of the fly family that are rudimentary hind wings and are used to maintain balance in flight [Mid-16C. < Greek.]

halter neck *n* **1** the upper part of a garment such as a dress or top that is tied behind the neck or back, leaving the shoulders bare **2** a garment such as a dress or top with a halter neck —**halter-neck** *adj*

haltertop /háwltər top, hólt-/ *n* CLOTHING = **halter** *n.* **2**

halting /háwlting, hólting/ *adj* hesitant or done with frequent irregular pauses ○ *halting speech* —**haltingly** *adv* —**haltingness** *n*

USAGE halting or **halted**? If you speak of something punctuated with hesitation or frequent interruptions, use the adjective ***halting***: *She answered the questions in a halting* [not *halted*] *manner.* ***Halted*** is the past tense and past participle of the verb *halt*, 'to stop'; it is not interchangeable with ***halting***.

halutz *n* = **chalutz**

halva /hálvə, hál vaa/, **halvah** *n* a Middle Eastern confection made from crushed sesame seeds and honey with various flavourings [Mid-17C. Via Turkish < Arabic *ḥalwā*.]

halve /haav/ (**halves, halving, halved**) *v* **1** *vt* **DIVIDE IN TWO** to divide something into two equal parts **2** *vt* **SPLIT EQUALLY** to divide something equally between two people **3** *vti* **REDUCE BY HALF** to reduce something by half, or be reduced by half **4** *vt* **SCORE EVENLY AT** in golf, to draw at a hole or match by playing the same number of strokes as an opponent [14C. < HALF.]

halves plural of **half**

halyard /hállyərd/, **halliard** *n* a rope used to raise or lower something, e.g. a sail or flag [14C. Alteration of *halier* < HALE[2].]

ham[1] /ham/ *n* **1 MEAT FROM A PIG'S THIGH** meat cut from the thigh of the hind leg of a pig after curing by salting or smoking ○ *a slice of ham* ○ *a ham sandwich* **2 PIG'S THIGH** the thigh of the hind leg of a pig **3 BACK OF THE LEG** the back of somebody's leg from the knee up to and including the buttock **4 HOLLOW AREA BEHIND THE KNEE** a hollow area behind somebody's knee [Old English *hamm* 'back of the knee' < Germanic, 'be crooked']

ham[2] /ham/ *n* somebody, especially an actor, who performs in an exaggerated showy style ■ *vti* (**hams, hamming, hammed**) to behave, overact, or perform a role in an exaggerated showy style [Late 19C. < ?] —**ham** *adj*

ham[3] /ham/ *n* a licensed amateur radio operator [Early 20C. < ?]

Ham / ham/ in the Bible, the second son of Noah, formerly considered to be the ancestor of the Hamite people (Genesis 10:1)

Hama /haám aa/, **Hamāh** city in west-central Syria. Population: 264,348 (1994).

hamadryad /hámmə drī əd, -ad/ *n* **1** in Greek and Roman mythology, a minor deity who lives in a tree and dies when the tree dies **2** ZOOL = **king cobra** [14C. Via Latin *Hamadryad-*, *Hamadryas* < Greek *Hamadruad-* < *hama* 'together' + *Druas* (see DRYAD).]

hamadryas baboon /hámmə drī əss-/ *n* a baboon, the adult male of which has a long silvery mane, that was sacred to the ancient Egyptians. Native to: NE Africa, Arabia. *Papio hamadryas*. [Late 19C. Via modern Latin < Latin *Hamadryas* (see HAMADRYAD).]

hamal /hə maál/, **hammal, hamaul** *n* a porter or servant in a Muslim country [Mid-18C. < Arabic *ḥammāl* < *ḥamala* 'carry'.]

Hamamatsu /hámmə mát soo/ coastal city on S Honshu Island, Japan. Population: 534,624 (1990).

hamantasch /haámən tash/ (*plural* **-taschen** /-tash'n/) *n* a triangular pastry filled with spiced dried fruit or poppy seeds and eaten during the Jewish feast of Purim [< Yiddish; < *Haman*, persecutor of the Jews in the Book of Esther + *tasch* < German *Tasche* 'bag, pocket']

hamartia /hə maárti ə/ *n* a defect in the character of the protagonist of a tragedy that brings about his or her downfall [Late 18C. < Greek, 'error, sin' < *hamartanein* 'miss the mark, make a mistake'.]

hamate /háy mayt/ *adj* shaped like a hook ■ *n* a small hook-shaped bone in the wrist, at the base of the third and little fingers [Early 18C. < Latin *hamatus* < *hamus* 'hook'.]

hamaul *n* = **hamal**

Hamburg /hám burg/ city in north-central Germany. Population: 1,705,872 (1997).

hamburger /hám burgər/ *n* **1 CAKE OF MINCED MEAT** a flat cake of minced meat, usually beef, that is grilled or fried and usually served in a bun **2 MINCED-BEEF SANDWICH** a sandwich containing a flat cake of grilled or fried minced beef or other meat in a bun, usually with other ingredients such as lettuce and condiments **3** *US* **MINCED BEEF** minced beef [Late 19C. < *Hamburg steak*, after HAMBURG, Germany.]

hame /haym/ *n* either of a pair of metal or wooden bars curved to fit over the neck of a draught animal and to which the traces are attached [14C. < Middle Dutch.]

Hamersley Range /hámmərzli ráynj/ range of mountains in NW Western Australia. Highest peak: Mount Meharry1,251 m/4,104 ft.

hametz /ha méts, kha-/ *n* JUDAISM = **chametz**

ham-fisted *adj* = **ham-handed** (*informal*) —**ham-fistedly** *adv* —**ham-fistedness** *n*

ham-handed *adj* **1** clumsy with the hands (*informal*) **2** having hands that are very large —**ham-handedly** *adv* —**ham-handedness** *n*

Hamhung /hám hŏong/, **Hamhŭng** city in east-central North Korea. Population: 701,000 (1987).

Hamilton /hámm'ltən/ **1** town in central Scotland. Population: 49,991 (1991). **2** capital of Bermuda, on Bermuda Island. Population: 1,000 (1990 estimate). **3** city in SE Ontario, Canada, at the western end of Lake Ontario. Population: 650,400 (1996). **4** city in the W North Island, New Zealand. Population: 117,000.

Hamilton, Emma, Lady (1765–1815) British courtier. Born **Emma Lyon**

Hamilton, James, 3rd Marquis and 1st Duke of Hamilton (1606–49) Scottish nobleman

Hamilton, Richard (*b.* 1922) British painter

Hamilton, Sir William (1788–1856) Scottish philosopher

Hamilton, Sir William Rowan (1805–65) Irish mathematician

Hamiltonian function /hámmil tṓni ən/ *n* (*symbol H*) a mathematical function used to describe the dynamics of a system, e.g. particles in motion, that uses momentum and spatial coordinates [Mid-19C. After Sir William Rowan HAMILTON.] —**Hamiltonianism** *n*

Hamilton Island island off the eastern coast of Queensland, Australia. Population: 1,500 (1996).

Hamite /hámm īt/ *n* a member of a group of peoples who live in North Africa [Mid-19C. After HAM.]

Hamitic /ha míttik, hə-/ *n* **GROUP OF AFRICAN LANGUAGES** a group of languages spoken in parts of NE Africa. Native speakers: 6 million. ■ *adj* **1 OF THE HAMITES** relating to the Hamites, or their language or culture **2 OF HAMITIC** relating to Hamitic

Hamito-Semitic /hámmitō-/ *n, adj* LANG = **Afro-Asiatic** (*no longer used technically*)

hamlet /hámmlət/ *n* **1** a small village or group of houses **2** a group of homesteads or households [14C. Via Old French *hamelet* 'small village' < *ham* 'village'.]

hammal *n* = **hamal**

Hammarskjöld /hámmər shōōld/, **Dag** (1905–61) Swedish diplomat

hammer /hámmər/ *n* **1 POUNDING TOOL** a hand tool consisting of a shaft with a metal head at right angles to it, used mainly for driving in nails and beating metal **2 MECHANICAL STRIKING TOOL** a powered mechanical striking tool used, e.g., in forging metal ○ *a steam hammer* **3 STRIKING PART** a part that strikes another in various devices, e.g. in a piano or striking clock **4 PART OF GUN** the part of the firing mechanism of a gun that delivers the impact that detonates the cartridge **5 OBJECT FOR THROWING** a heavy metal ball attached to a handle of flexible wire, thrown in an athletics field event **6** SPORTS = **hammer throw 7 AUCTIONEER'S GAVEL** a gavel used by an auctioneer **8** ANAT = **malleus** ■ *v* **1** *vti* **POUND IN** to force something such as a nail into something else by pounding it with a hammer **2** *vt* **BEAT INTO SHAPE** to beat something with a hammer, especially to shape it ○ *hammering tin into bowls* **3** *vt* **CAUSE TO BE REMEMBERED** to cause something to be remembered, realized, or understood by repeating it forcefully and frequently ○ *They had caution hammered into them by the driving instructor.* **4** *vti* **HIT HARD AND REPEATEDLY** to hit or strike something hard and repeatedly ○ *hammering at the door* **5** *vi* **PRODUCE A RHYTHMIC MOVEMENT** to produce fast, powerful, rhythmic movements or beats **6** *vt* **DAMAGE SEVERELY** to inflict serious damage on something **7** *vt* **GIVE A BEATING** to beat or batter somebody severely (*informal*) **8** *vt* **DEFEAT BY LARGE MARGIN** to inflict a convincing defeat on somebody, especially an opponent in a competitive sport (*informal*) ○ *Our team got hammered in last week's game.* **9** *vt* **CRITICIZE HEAVILY** to subject somebody or something to severe criticism (*informal*) ○ *The critics really hammered his last play.* **10** *vt* **FORMALLY DECLARE INSOLVENT** to announce the insolvency of a member of the Stock Exchange, who is then not allowed to trade **11** *vt* **CAUSE STOCK EXCHANGE MARKET TO DROP** to cause a Stock Exchange market to drop by suddenly selling a security or securities in large quantities [Old English *hamor* < Germanic, 'stone, stone tool'] —**hammerer** *n* ◇ **go** *or* **come under the hammer** to be up for auction or sale ◇ **go at it hammer and tongs 1** to do something with maximum energy and force **2** to fight or argue violently

hammer away at *vt* to work hard, determinedly, and steadily at something ○ *hammering away at the new novel*

hammer out *vt* **1 SHAPE WITH A HAMMER** to shape or reshape metal with a hammer **2 AGREE ON OR ESTABLISH** to agree on or establish something after prolonged discussion or argument ○ *hammer out a revised contract* **3 PLAY MUSIC ENERGETICALLY** to play a piece of music on a piano energetically and forcefully ○ *She can really hammer out a tune.*

Hammer /hámmər/, **Armand** (1898–1990) US industrialist, art collector, and philanthropist

hammer and sickle *n* a symbol of Soviet Communism representing industrial and agricultural workers, used on the flag of the former Soviet Union

hammer dulcimer *n* a large dulcimer played with light hammers and supported by a stand

Hammerfest /hámmər fest/ port in N Norway, the northernmost town in Europe. Population: 6,934 (1990).

hammerhead /hámmər hed/ (*plural* **-heads** *or* **-head**) *n* **1** a large brown wading bird with a prominent crest on the back of its head. Native to: tropical African wetlands, ponds, and lakes. *Scopus umbretta*. **2** ZOOL = **hammerhead shark 3** a fruit bat, the male of which has an enlarged square head and a muzzle shaped like the head of hammer. Native to: Africa. *Hypsignathus monstrosus*.

hammerheaded /hámmər héddid/ *adj* having a head shaped like a hammer

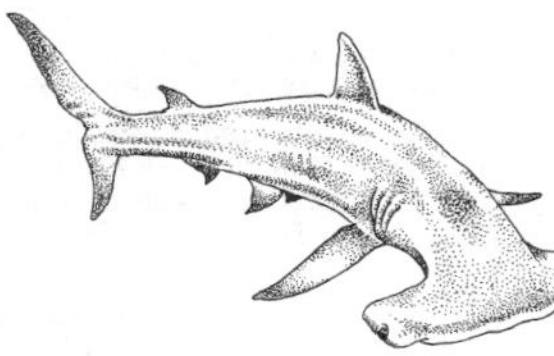

Hammerhead shark

hammerhead shark *n* a shark with a head that has a lateral extension on each side with an eye at the end. Genus: *Sphyrna.*

hammerkop /hámmər kop/ (*plural* **-kops** *or* **-kop**) *n* BIRDS = **hammerhead** *n.* 1 [Mid-19C. < Afrikaans *hamerkop* 'hammerhead'.]

hammerlock /hámmər lok/ *n* a wrestling hold in which an opponent's arm is twisted upwards behind the back [< ?]

Hammerstein /hámmər stīn/, **Oscar II** (1895–1960) US librettist

hammer throw *n* a field event in which competing athletes try to throw a heavy metal ball attached to a handle of flexible wire as far as they can

hammertoe /hámmər tō/ *n* **1** a medical condition of a toe in which the joint between the two small bones of the toe is permanently bent downwards in a claw shape **2** a toe affected by hammertoe

Hammett /hámmət/, **Dashiell** (1894–1961) US writer

hammock /hámmək/ *n* a hanging bed made of canvas or netting and suspended at both ends by ropes tied between two supports [Mid-16C. Via Spanish *hamaca* < Taino.]

Hammond /hámmənd/, **Dame Joan Hood** (1912–96) New Zealand-born Australian opera singer

Hampden /hámdən/, **John** (1594–1643) English political leader

hamper[1] /hámpər/ *vt* to prevent the free movement or action of somebody or something ■ *n* equipment on board a ship that is essential but likely to get in the way [14C. < ?] —**hamperer** *n*

SYNONYMS See *hinder.*

hamper[2] /hámpər/ *n* **1** a large basket with a cover that is used for carrying food, especially for picnics **2** *US* a large basket with a cover that is used for holding soiled laundry [14C. Via Anglo-Norman *hanaper* 'basket for holding goblets' < Old French *hanap* 'goblet' < Germanic.]

Hampshire[1] /hámpshər/ (*plural* **-shires** *or* **-shire**) *n* **1** a black-and-white pig of a breed developed in the United States from stock imported from Hampshire, England **2** a large English sheep of a breed with a black face and no horns

Hampshire[2] /hámpshər/ county in S England, bordering the English Channel. Area: 3,769 sq. km/1,455 sq. mi.

Hampshire Down *n* = **Hampshire**[1] *n.* 2

Hampton /hámptən/ city and port in SE Virginia. Population: 139,628 (1994).

Hampton Court royal palace in SW London, on the River Thames

hamster /hámstər/ *n* **1** a small rodent with a short tail and large cheek pouches for storing food, often kept as a pet. Native to: Europe, Asia. Family: Muridae. **2** a cordless computer mouse device that operates through an infrared connection [Early 17C. Via German < Old High German *hamustro.*]

hamstring /hám string/ *n* **1** LEG TENDON either of the two prominent common tendons of the three ham muscles behind the knee **2** ANAT = **hamstring muscle 3** TENDON IN AN ANIMAL'S LEG a large tendon at the back of the hock of an animal's hind leg ■ *vt* (**-strings, -stringing, -strung** /-strung/, **-strung** /hám strung/) **1** CUT THE HAMSTRING to cut the hamstring of a person or animal causing inability to use the leg normally (*often considered offensive*) **2** THWART to make somebody or something powerless or ineffective ○ *hamstrung by lack of funds*

hamstring muscle *n* any of three muscles at the back of the thigh that control certain leg movements, e.g. flexing the knee

hamstrung past tense, past participle of **hamstring**

Hamsun /hámsōōn/, **Knut** (1859–1952) Norwegian author. Pseudonym of **Knut Pedersen**

hamulus /hámmyōōləss/ (*plural* **-li** /-lī/) *n* a hook-shaped part at the end of a bone [Early 18C. < Latin, 'small hook' < *hamus* 'hook'.] —**hamular** *adj* —**hamulate** *adj* —**hamulose** *adj* —**hamulous** *adj*

hamza /hámzə/, **hamzah** *n* the sign (ʔ) used in Arabic script to represent a glottal stop [Early 19C. < Arabic.]

Han[1] /han/ (*plural* **Han** *or* **Hans**) *n* **1** a member of a Chinese dynasty that ruled from 206 BC to AD 220 and was responsible for systematizing Chinese bureaucracy, promoting Confucianism, and consolidating Chinese government and territory **2** = **Han Chinese** [Mid-18C. < Chinese *Hàn.*] —**Han** *adj*

Han[2] /han/ = **Han Jiang**

Hanabusa Itcho /hánnə bōōssə íchō/ (1652–1724) Japanese painter. Born **Shinko Tage**

Han Chinese *n* a member of the largest ethnic group in China —**Han Chinese** *adj*

Hancock /hán kok/, **Lang** (1909–92) Australian mineral prospector and industrialist

Hancock, Tony (1924–68) British comedian. Full name **Anthony John Hancock**

hand /hand/ *n* **1** END OF THE HUMAN ARM the part of the human arm below the wrist, consisting of a thumb, four fingers, and a palm and capable of holding and manipulating things **2** ANIMAL PART the part of an animal's limb that corresponds to a human hand in shape or function **3** POINTER ON A CLOCK a pointer on a clock, watch, dial, or gauge **4** PLAYER'S CARDS the cards dealt to a player in a card game ○ *a losing hand* **5** ROUND IN A CARD GAME a round in a card game **6** CARD PLAYER somebody who plays a particular card game **7** INFLUENCE the influence or directing action of somebody or something **8** PART a share in the performance of an action ○ *Who else had a hand in this?* **9** HELP help to do something ○ *Give me a hand moving this table.* **10** OFFER OF AGREEMENT a sign of agreement or acceptance, especially of an offer of marriage ○ *Here's my hand on it.* **11** SIDE side or direction ○ *surrounded by enemies at every hand* **12** CLAP a round of applause ○ *a big hand for our next contestant* **13** *US* TEXTILES = **handle** *n.* 4 **14** POSSESSION the possession, power, responsibility, or care of somebody ○ *Your future is in your own hands.* **15** DEGREE OF CLOSENESS a degree of closeness to actual involvement in something being talked about ○ *I heard about it at third hand.* **16** SAILOR a member of the crew of a vessel ○ *Attention, all hands!* **17** DOER a maker or doer of something, especially to a particular level of competence or experience ○ *I'm not much of a hand at hanging wallpaper.* ○ *an old hand at white-water rafting* **18** WORKER a worker, especially one doing manual work ○ *a farm hand* **19** HANDWRITING somebody's handwriting ○ *an admirably clear hand* **20** SKILL ability or skill ○ *She has a good hand for gardening.* **21** METHOD a distinctive way of doing something ○ *the bungling hand of an amateur* **22** MEASURE OF A HORSE'S HEIGHT a measure of the height of a horse, equal to 10.2 cm/4 in **23** PRINTING = **index** *n.* 7 **24** BUNCH a bunch of something, especially bananas **25** CUT OF PORK a cut of pork from the front leg of the animal ■ *v* **1** *vt* PASS BY HAND to pass something to somebody by hand ○ *She handed me a glass.* **2** *vt* LEAD BY THE HAND to help or lead somebody by the hand ○ *She handed her aunt into the taxi.* **3** *vti* FURL to furl a sail [Old English, < Germanic] —**handless** *adj* ◇ **at hand 1** nearby ○ *There was a bench close at hand, where they sat down.* **2** about to happen ◇ **be hand in glove (with somebody)** to cooperate with somebody, usually for some secret or illegal purpose ◇ **change hands** to pass to a different owner ◇ **force somebody's hand** to pressure somebody to do something against his or her will or earlier than planned ◇ **(from) hand to mouth** with barely enough to live on for your daily needs ◇ **hand in hand 1** in close cooperation **2** inseparably closely **3** holding hands ◇ **hold somebody's hand** to provide reassurance, guidance, and support to somebody ◇ **in hand 1** under control **2** remaining or unused ◇ **not turn a hand** *US* to make no attempt to help somebody ◇ **off somebody's hands** no longer somebody's responsibility or problem ◇ **on hand** near and available ◇ **on the one hand...on the other hand...** used to present two conflicting aspects of a situation ○ *On the one hand we have plenty of time, but on the other hand our resources are limited.* ◇ **out of hand** immediately and without consideration or explanation ◇ **overplay your hand** to make overconfident or heavy-handed use of an advantage or strong position and fail as a result ◇ **out of somebody's hands** unable to be influenced by somebody ◇ **take somebody** *or* **something in hand** to begin to bring somebody *or* something under control ◇ **throw in your hand 1** to admit defeat in a card game by laying your cards down **2** to admit or accept defeat ◇ **try your hand at something** to make an attempt at something, usually for the first time ◇ **turn your hand to something** to do something for the first time and be competent at it ◇ **wash your hands of somebody** *or* **something** to refuse to continue being responsible for somebody or something

hand down *vt* **1** BEQUEATH to pass something on to a later generation or time **2** PASS CLOTHES ON to pass clothes on from an older to a younger child **3** *US, Can* PRONOUNCE A VERDICT OR SENTENCE to decide on a verdict or sentence and announce it in court

hand in *vt* **1** to give or submit something to somebody ○ *She handed in her notice.* **2** to return or surrender something, especially something lost or illegal

hand off *vt* in rugby, to push or hold an opponent away or deflect a tackle with an open hand

hand on *vt* to pass something to the next person or generation

hand out *vt* **1** to distribute or give something by hand **2** to administer or award something

hand over *v* **1** *vt* to surrender somebody or give something away to somebody else ○ *Hand over the money and nobody gets hurt.* **2** *vti* to transfer control of a commentary during a broadcast to somebody else ○ *I'll now hand you over to our match commentator.*

hand axe *n* a chipped stone tool rounded at one end and pointed at the other, used for a variety of purposes during the Lower and Middle Palaeolithic periods

handbag /hánd bag/ *n* **1** WOMAN'S SMALL BAG a small bag, with or without a strap or handle, used by women to carry personal items such as keys, money, and cosmetics. US term **purse** *n.* 2 **2** TRAVELLING BAG a small light travelling bag that is easily carried by hand ■ *vt* (**-bags, -bagging, -bagged**) ATTACK VERBALLY to make a strong verbal attack on somebody or something (*informal; refers to a woman*)

handball /hánd bawl/ *n* **1** PROHIBITED HANDLING OF FOOTBALL in football, a rule infringement committed when a player other than a goalkeeper inside his or her penalty area uses a hand to control the ball **2** BALL GAME PLAYED AGAINST A WALL a game for two or four people in which players hit a small hard ball against a wall with their hands **3** BALL USED IN HANDBALL the small hard rubber or synthetic ball used in the game of handball **4** GOAL-SCORING BALL GAME a team game similar to basketball in which players dribble the ball and pass it, and goals are scored by hitting the ball into the goal with the hand —**handballer** *n*

handbarrow /hánd barrō/ *n* a flat rectangular board for transporting loads that has a pair of handles at either end and is carried by two people

handbell /hánd bel/ *n* a small bell held in the hand to be rung, often one of a tuned set used to play a musical piece or to practise ring-changing

handbill /hánd bil/ *n* a small sheet of paper with a notice or advertisement printed on it, distributed by hand

handblown /hánd blōn/ *adj* describes glassware blown using a hand-held tube ○ *a handblown vase*

handbook /hánd bōōk/ *n* **1** REFERENCE BOOK a reference book, especially one small enough to be carried in the hand, giving concise information on a particular subject **2** MANUAL a concise manual explaining how something works or how to use it **3** TRAVEL GUIDE a concise guide designed to help travellers and tourists find their way around a region, city, or other geographical location

handbrake /hánd brayk/ *n* **1** a brake operated manually by a lever, used to prevent a vehicle from rolling when stationary. US term **emergency brake** *n.* **2** either of two manual brakes on the handlebars of a bicycle or motorcycle, used to slow or stop the vehicle

handbreadth /hánd bredth, -bretth/, **hand's-breadth** /hándz-/ *n* the width of a hand, used as an approximate measure of length

h & c *abbr* hot and cold (water)

handcart /hánd kaart/ *n* a small cart with two or four wheels, pulled or pushed by hand

handclap /hánd klap/ *n* a clapping of the hands, done to gain attention, applaud, or keep a rhythm

handclasp /hánd klaasp/ *n* US = **handshake** *n.* 1

handcraft /hánd kraaft/ *n* = **handicraft** *n.* 3 ■ *vt* to make something using manual skill

handcuff /hánd kuf/ *npl* **handcuffs** DEVICE FOR RESTRAINING THE HANDS a pair of strong usually metal rings joined by a chain or bar, placed as a restraint around somebody's wrists and locked ■ *vt* 1 PUT IN HANDCUFFS to restrain somebody by using handcuffs 2 MAKE INEFFECTIVE to make somebody or something ineffective ○ *handcuffed by bureaucratic regulations*

handedness /hándidnəss/ *n* 1 the tendency to prefer the use of one hand over the other 2 the property of some objects whereby they cannot be superimposed on their mirror images

Handel /hánd'l/, **George Frederick** (1685–1759) German-born British composer

handfeed /hánd feed/ *vt* 1 to feed a person or an animal by hand 2 to feed material into a machine by hand rather than by means of an automatic or machine feed

handful /hánd fŏŏl/ *n* 1 AMOUNT CONTAINED BY THE HAND an amount that can be held in the hand 2 SMALL AMOUNT OR NUMBER a small amount or number of people or things ○ *Only a handful of students turned up for the lecture.* 3 SOMEBODY OR SOMETHING DIFFICULT a somebody or something that is difficult to cope with or control (*informal*) ○ *Together those two are a real handful!*

LITERARY LINK ***A Handful of Dust***, a novel (1934) by Evelyn Waugh. It tells the story of Tony Last, a haughty country gentleman whose wife leaves him for a young socialite. His response is to set off on an ill-advised expedition to South America, where he ends up the captive of an eccentric local.

---

hand glass *n* 1 a magnifying glass with a handle for holding in the hand 2 a small mirror for holding in the hand (*dated*)

hand grenade *n* a small bomb designed to be thrown by hand and detonated by a time fuse

handgrip /hánd grip/ *n* 1 = **grip** *n.* 2 2 HANDLE a handle or the part of something that can be held with the hand ○ *My motorbike needs a new handgrip.* 3 COVERING FOR A HANDLE a piece of material that covers a handle and makes it easier to keep hold of 4 TRAVELLING BAG a small light travelling bag that is easily carried by hand

handgun /hánd gun/ *n* a gun that can be held and fired in one hand

hand-held *adj* 1 made to be operated while held in the hand 2 filmed with a camera that is carried by the operator rather than mounted on a support ○ *black-and-white hand-held footage*

handhold /hánd hōld/ *n* 1 something for somebody climbing to grasp for support, e.g. a projecting piece of rock or a fissure in a cliff face 2 a firm grip with the hand or hands

handholding /hánd hōlding/ *n* the giving of reassurance and guidance to somebody

hand-hot *adj* describes hot water that is not too hot for putting the bare hands into

handicap /hándi kap/ *n* 1 HINDRANCE something that hinders or is a disadvantage to somebody or something 2 BALANCED CONTEST a contest in which individual competitors are given an advantage or disadvantage in an attempt to give every contestant an equal chance ○ *a handicap race* 3 ADDED ADVANTAGE OR DISADVANTAGE an advantage or disadvantage given to a competitor in a handicap 4 GOLFER'S COMPENSATION IN STROKES a compensation in strokes given to a golfer on the basis of skill in past performances 5 PHYSICAL OR MENTAL DISABILITY a particular way in which somebody is physically or mentally disabled (*often considered offensive*) ■ *vt* (**-caps, -capping, -capped**) 1 HINDER to hinder or be a disadvantage to somebody or something 2 GIVE SPORTS HANDICAPS to give an advantage or disadvantage to a competitor in a contest [Mid-17C. < *hand in cap* 'betting game in which contestants place their hands in a hat with their wagers'.]

handicapped /hándi kapt/ *adj* having a physical or mental disability (*often considered offensive*) ■ *npl* an offensive term for people who have a physical disability

handicapper /hándi kappər/ *n* 1 an assigner of handicaps to competitors in a contest 2 a forecaster of horse race results, especially somebody who provides published advice to betters

handicraft /hándi kraaft/ *n* 1 CRAFT a craft or occupation in which manual skill is needed, e.g. weaving 2 OBJECT MADE BY HAND something made using manual skill 3 MANUAL SKILL skill in making things with the hands [13C. Alteration of HANDCRAFT, after HANDIWORK.] —**handicrafter** *n*

handily /hándili/ *adv* 1 CONVENIENTLY in a convenient way ○ *handily close to the station* 2 SKILFULLY in a skilful way 3 US EASILY in an easy way ○ *She took the second set handily.*

handiwork /hándi wurk/ *n* 1 SOMEBODY'S ACTION the result of somebody's action ○ *The broken window was the handiwork of local vandals.* 2 WORK DONE BY HAND work done or produced by hand 3 SKILL the skill with which something is done, especially manual skill [Old English *handgeweorc* < *hand* 'hand' + *geweorc* 'body of work' < *weorc* 'work']

hand-jam *n* an act of wedging the hand into a rock crack to aid in climbing

handkerchief /hángkər chif, -cheef/ (*plural* **-chiefs** *or* **-chieves** /-cheevz/) *n* a square of cloth or absorbent paper used mainly to wipe areas of the face, especially the nose

hand-knit *vti* to knit something by hand, not on a machine

handle /hánd'l/ *n* 1 PART FOR HOLDING a part of a thing by which it is held, moved, or operated 2 NAME somebody's name (*slang*) ○ *What's your handle?* 3 MEANS an opportunity, pretext, or means of doing something 4 FEEL OF TEXTILE the feel of a fabric, used to determine its quality. US term **hand** *n.* 13 5 US TOTAL AMOUNT BET the total sum of money bet on a race, series of races, or other event ■ *v* (**-dles, -dling, -dled**) 1 *vt* TOUCH to touch, pick up, or move something with the hands ○ *Don't handle the merchandise.* 2 *vt* OPERATE to operate or make use of something with the hands 3 *vt* TAKE CHARGE OF to take care of or be responsible for something ○ *Who handles the import side of the business?* 4 *vt* DEAL WITH to deal with or cope with somebody or something ○ *She's good at handling difficult customers.* 5 *vt* BE MANAGER OF to manage or supervise somebody ○ *He handles a string of professional boxers.* 6 *vt* BE ABOUT to discuss or deal with a subject ○ *The novel handles the theme of unrequited love in an original way.* 7 *vt* TRADE IN to deal in particular goods 8 *vi* RESPOND TO CONTROL to respond to control or use, often in a particular way ○ *The little yacht handled like a dream.* [Old English *handle* (noun), *handlian* (verb) < HAND] —**handleability** /hánd'lə bílləti/ *n* —**handleable** *adj* —**handleless** *adj* ◇ **fly off the handle** to lose your temper, especially without justification (*informal*) ◇ **get a handle on something** to understand a situation fully or be able to control it fully ○ *It's a difficult problem to get a handle on.*

handlebar moustache /hánd'l baar-/ *n* a thick broad moustache that curls up at the ends like handlebars

handlebars /hánd'l baarz/ *npl* a bar with handles at each end, used to steer a vehicle such as a bicycle or motorcycle

handler /hándlər/ *n* 1 ANIMAL TRAINER somebody who trains or manages animals that perform in films, television programmes, or judged shows 2 SOMEBODY USING A TRAINED DOG somebody who uses a specially trained dog, e.g. in the police or armed forces 3 BOXER'S TRAINER a boxer's trainer or second 4 MANAGER somebody who manages the career of somebody or the running of something 5 DEALER OR OPERATOR somebody who works or deals with a particular thing ○ *a baggage handler for an airline*

handling /hándling/ *n* 1 WAY SOMEBODY HANDLES SOMETHING the way in which somebody handles or deals with something ○ *The report criticized his handling of the affair.* 2 TREATMENT the way in which a subject is treated or dealt with in a written work or other work of art 3 TRANSPORT AND PACKAGING the transport and packaging of goods ○ *The cost includes a charge for handling.* 4 RECEIVING STOLEN GOODS the receiving of goods known to be stolen

handmade /hánd máyd/ *adj* made by hand, not by machine ○ *handmade furniture*

handmaid /hánd mayd/, **handmaiden** /-mayd'n/ *n* 1 a woman or girl servant (*archaic*) 2 something that provides help or support in a subsidiary role (*literary*) ○ *Hard work and focus are the handmaids of genius.*

hand-me-down *n* 1 an item of clothing, usually outgrown, passed down from a family member or friend to another 2 something taken up or used by a person or group that has been used before and discarded

hand-off *n* in rugby, a pushing or holding away of an opponent or a deflection of a tackle with an open hand

handout /hánd owt/ *n* 1 something such as money or food given as charity to somebody in need 2 a document, such as a press release, an advertisement, or material accompanying a meeting or lecture that is distributed to a group

handover /hándōvər/ *n* 1 a surrendering of somebody or a giving away of something to somebody else ○ *the handover of power to the civilian authorities* 2 a transfer of the control of the commentary during a broadcast to somebody else

handpick /hánd pík/ *vt* 1 to choose somebody or something carefully and personally, e.g. members of a team 2 to pick or harvest something by hand, not by machine

hand plant *n* in skateboarding, a move in which the board is held to the feet with one hand while the skateboarder performs a handstand on a ramp or obstacle with the other

hand press *n* a printing press operated by hand

handprint /hánd print/ *n* a mark or impression made by the palm of the hand and fingers

hand puppet *n* US = **glove puppet**

handrail /hánd rayl/ *n* a rail to hold with the hand for support, e.g. at the side of stairs or a ramp

handsaw /hánd saw/ *n* a saw for use with one hand

hand's-breadth *n* = **handbreadth**

hands down *adv* 1 without encountering any problems, obstacles, or opposition 2 without any doubt whatsoever ○ *they won hands down*

hands-down *adj* accepted without any question [< a jockey not needing to ride hard to win]

handsel /hánss'l/, **hansel** *n* (*archaic*) 1 GOOD-LUCK GIFT a gift given for good luck at the beginning of something, especially a new year 2 FIRST PAYMENT a first payment for something, or the first money taken in by a new business ■ *vt* (**-sels, -selling, -selled**) (*archaic*) 1 GIVE GOOD-LUCK GIFT TO to give somebody a good-luck gift at the beginning of something, especially a new year 2 INAUGURATE to begin or launch something with ceremony 3 USE FOR FIRST TIME to use something or do something for the first time [14C. Blend of Old English *handselen* 'a handing over' + Old Norse *handsal* 'giving the hand'.]

handset /hánd set/ *n* the part of a telephone that is held in the hand and contains the parts used for speaking into and listening to

⚡**handshake** /hánd shayk/ *n* 1 a gesture of gripping and shaking another person's hand, used as a greeting or farewell and to seal an agreement 2 an exchange of signals between a computer and another computer or external device indicating that a link is established and communication is possible

⚡**handshaking** /hánd shayking/ *n* the exchanging of signals between a computer and another computer or external device indicating that a link is established and communication is possible

hands-off *adj* not wanting or needing to interfere in or control something ○ *The boss operates a hands-off policy with respect to the day-to-day running of the business.*

handsome /hánssəm/ *adj* 1 with good-looking facial features or a pleasing general appearance 2 amounting to a higher sum than expected —**handsomeness** *n*

handsomely /hánssəmli/ *adv* in an amount that is more than expected

hands-on *adj* 1 USING involving the actual use of something ○ *Learning computer skills is a hands-on process.* 2 INVOLVING PHYSICAL TOUCHING involving physical touching of something ○ *The children's science museum has many hands-on exhibits.* 3 PERSONALLY INVOLVED giving personal attention to or taking personal control of somebody or something ○ *She's very much a hands-on manager.*

handspike /hánd spīk/ *n* a metal bar used as a lever [Early 16C. Alteration of Dutch *handspaak* < *hand* 'hand' + *spaak* 'spoke'.]

handspring /hánd spring/ *n* a gymnastic movement in which somebody flips the body forwards or backwards and lands briefly on the hands before continuing the flip so as to land on the feet again

handstand /hánd stand/ *n* an act of balancing the body on the hands with the legs straight up in the air

hand-to-hand *adj* taking place at close quarters and involving bodily contact —**hand-to-hand** *adv*

hand-to-mouth *adj* having barely enough money or food for daily needs —**hand-to-mouth** *adv*

handwork /hánd wurk/ *n* work done by hand, not by a machine —**handworker** *n*

handwoven /hánd wṓv'n/ *adj* **1** woven on a hand-operated loom, not a mechanical one **2** woven using the hands

handwringing /hánd ringing/ *n* **1** the demonstration or expression of concern about something, often without any constructive action being taken **2** the repeated clasping and squeezing of the hands together as a result of anxiety or grief

handwrite /hánd rīt/ (**-writes, -writing, -wrote** /-rōt/, **-written** /-ritt'n/) *vt* to use a writing implement such as a pen or pencil to put words on paper

handwriting /hánd rīting/ *n* **1** writing done by hand using a pen or pencil **2** somebody's individual way of writing by hand ○ *I recognized my father's handwriting on the envelope.*

handwrought /hánd rāwt/ *adj* shaped by hand, especially by hammering

handy /hándi/ (**-ier, -iest**) *adj* **1** CONVENIENT located in a convenient place, especially nearby and easy to reach **2** USEFUL useful or easy to use **3** SKILFUL skilful at doing a number of different things —**handiness** *n*

handyman /hándi man/ (*plural* **-men** /-men/) *n* a person who earns pay by doing varied small jobs, or has the experience or skill to do them

⚡**hang** /hang/ *v* (**hangs, hanging, hung** /hung/) **1** *vti* SUSPEND to suspend or fasten something so that it is held up from above and not supported from below **2** *vt* FIX ON HINGES to fix something such as a door on hinges so that it can move freely **3** (*past and past participle* **hanged**) *vti* KILL WITH ROPE to kill somebody or yourself by fastening a rope round the neck and removing any other support for the body, or die in this way, especially as a form of legal execution **4** *vt* DECORATE to decorate or furnish a place or object with something ○ *hang the Christmas tree with lights and decorations* **5** *vt* PUT UP WALLPAPER to fix wallpaper onto walls, usually using a paste solution **6** *vti* DISPLAY A PAINTING to put pictures or paintings on display, or be put on display **7** *vt* LET DROOP to let something, especially the head, droop ○ *They should hang their heads in shame.* **8** *vt* SUSPEND A GUTTED ANIMAL to suspend meat or a recently killed game animal until the flesh begins to decompose slightly and becomes more tender and highly flavoured **9** *vt* PREVENT A JURY FROM DECIDING to prevent a jury from reaching a verdict (*usually passive*) **10** *vti* PITCH A BALL THAT FAILS TO BREAK in baseball, to pitch the ball in such a way that it fails to break, or be pitched in this way **11** (*past and past participle* **hanged**) *vt* EXCLAMATION INDICATING ANNOYANCE used as a euphemism for damn (*dated informal*) ○ *Hang it all!* ○ *I'll be hanged if I'll let them get away with this!* **12** *vt US* MAKE A TURN to make a particular turn, especially when driving a car (*informal*) ○ *Hang a right at the next street.* **13** *vi* BE UNRESOLVED to be unresolved or in doubt ○ *His academic future hangs in the balance.* **14** *vti* FOLD to fold or bend something over or across something, or be folded or bent over or across something **15** *vi* DRAPE to drape from a point of suspension in a particular way ○ *The jacket hung badly on her.* **16** *vi* ELAPSE SLOWLY to pass by or elapse slowly ○ *Time hung heavily when she was away.* **17** *vi* ALLOW NO INPUT OR OUTPUT to refuse additional input and be unable to generate output until rebooted (*refers to a computer*) ■ *n* **1** WAY OF HANGING the way that something hangs **2** SLOPE a downward slope **3** EXHIBITION OF ARTWORK an exhibition of artwork, especially paintings [Old English *hangian* (intransitive) < W Germanic] ◇ **get the hang of something** to learn a skill or activity thoroughly ◇ **not give** *or* **care a hang (for** *or* **about somebody** *or* **something)** to be completely unconcerned or indifferent about somebody or something (*dated informal*)

hang about *vi* = **hang around** ■ *interj* used to ask or command somebody to wait (*informal*)

hang around, hang about *vi* **1** to loiter or waste time **2** to spend time regularly with somebody ○ *He hangs around with the drama crowd.*

hang back *vi* to show reluctance to do something

hang in *vt* to endure or persevere in doing something (*informal*) ○ *She hung in as long as she could.*

hang on *v* **1** *vi* HOLD ON TIGHTLY to hold on tightly to something **2** *vi* KEEP GOING to persist in an endeavour in spite of obstacles or difficulties **3** *vt* DEPEND ON to depend on something **4** *vi* WAIT to wait or show patience for a short time **5** *vt* LISTEN CLOSELY TO to listen attentively to what somebody says

hang out *v* **1** *vt* SUSPEND OUTSIDE to put something outside, e.g. on a line, pole, or balcony, so that it will dry or so that it can be seen **2** *vi* BE AROUND SOMEWHERE to be regularly present somewhere (*informal*) **3** *vi US* SPEND TIME SOMEWHERE to spend time somewhere in a casual or relaxed way (*informal*) **4** *vi* ASSOCIATE to spend time regularly with somebody (*informal*)

hang over *v* **1** *vt* to be imminent or threatening for, or be unwelcomely associated with, somebody or something **2** *vi* to be put off to a later date ○ *Our holiday plans will hang over until next year.*

hang together *vi* to be consistent or cohesive

hang up *v* **1** *vt* to put something on a peg, hook, nail, or hanger **2** *vti* to end a telephone call by returning the receiver to its original position, often abruptly

hang upon *vt* = **hang on** *v.* **3**, **hang on** *v.* **5**

hangar /hángər/ *n* a large building in which aircraft are kept or repaired [Late 17C. Via French, 'shed' < Old French *hangard*.]

SPELLCHECK Do not confuse ***hangar*** with ***hanger***, which has a similar sound. Beware: your spellchecker will not catch this error.

hangdog /háng dog/ *adj* having an expression that indicates guilt or sadness [Late 17C. Originally referring to somebody who deserved to be hanged like a dog.]

hanger /hángər/ *n* **1** PEG OR HOOK a support from which something can be hung, e.g. a peg or hook **2** FRAME FOR GARMENT a triangular frame of metal, wood, or plastic over which clothes can be draped for storage or display **3** SOMEBODY WHO HANGS a hanger or suspender of something **4** SMALL WOOD a small wood on the side of a hill **5** SHORT SWORD a short sword worn on a belt

SPELLCHECK See ***hangar***.

hanger-on (*plural* **hangers-on**) *n* a person who latches on to a richer or more prominent person or group in the hope of gain

hang-glider *n* an aircraft without an engine that consists of a rigid frame in the shape of a wing, with the pilot usually suspended in a harness below the wing —**hang-gliding** *n*

hangi /húngi, hángi/ (*plural* **-i**) *n NZ* **1** a pit for cooking food outdoors using hot stones and damp cloths **2** a feast consisting of food cooked in a hangi [Mid-19C. < Maori.]

hanging /hánging/ *n* **1** METHOD OF KILLING the act of killing somebody by putting the neck in a noose and removing the support, especially as a form of legal execution **2** FABRIC HUNG ON A WALL a drapery, tapestry, or decorative fabric hung on a wall (*often plural*) ■ *adj* **1** PUNISHABLE BY DEATH punishable by death, or seen as deserving the death penalty ○ *a hanging offence* **2** SEVERE OR UNMERCIFUL tending to impose severe punishments, especially the death penalty ○ *a hanging judge* **3** AT THE TOP OF A SLOPE positioned at the top of a steep slope or height

hanging chad *n US* a rectangular chad still attached to a ballot paper but on one side only

hanging indent, hanging indentation *n* an indenting of all the lines of a paragraph of text except the first

hanging wall *n* the rocks that hang over a seam of coal or other mineral vein

hangman /hángmən/ (*plural* **-men** /-mən/) *n* **1** an official who carries out the death penalty of hanging **2** a game in which one player has to guess the letters of a word before the other player has drawn a stylized gallows, with one line for every wrong guess

hangnail /háng nayl/ *n* a small piece of skin partly detached from the side or base of a fingernail [Late 17C. By folk etymology < *agnail* 'corn on the foot' < Old English *angnægl* < *ang-* < Germanic 'tight', + NAIL.]

hangout /háng owt/ *n* a place frequented by a particular person or group of people, especially for relaxation (*informal*) ○ *the café was a favourite teen hangout*

hangover /háng ōvər/ *n* **1** the symptoms of headache, nausea, thirst, and sickness that result from drinking too much alcohol **2** something that remains from an earlier time

Hang Seng index /háng séng-/ *n* an index based on the relative prices of selected shares on the Hong Kong Stock Exchange

Hangul /háng gŏol/, **hangul** *n* the alphabet used for Korean writing [Mid-20C. < Korean *han kul* 'Korea alphabet'.]

hang-up *n* **1** a psychological or emotional problem or fixation about something (*informal*) **2** a persistent impediment or source of delay ○ *Bureaucratic inefficiency was the main hang-up.*

Hangzhou /háng jṓ/ capital of Zhejiang Province, SE China, at the head of Hangzhou Bay, an inlet of the East China Sea. Population: 2,305,741 (1991).

Han Jiang /hán jyáng/, **Han** river of central China. Length: 1,532 km/952 mi.

hank /hangk/ *n* **1** LOOSE BALL a piece of something such as hair, rope, or wool that has been wrapped round itself to form a loose ball **2** ATTACHMENT FOR A SAIL a ring-shaped fitting that can be opened to secure the leading edge of a sail **3** LENGTH OF YARN a length of yarn when reeled, e.g. a hank of cotton is 767 m/840 yd [14C. < Old Norse *hǫnk* < Germanic.]

hanker /hángkər/ *vi* to want something very badly and persistently ○ *hankering after something I can't have* [Early 17C. < ?] —**hankerer** *n*

~~**hankerchief**~~ incorrect spelling of **handkerchief**

hankie /hángki/, **hanky** (*plural* **-kies**) *n* a handkerchief (*informal*) [Late 19C. Shortening.]

Hanks /hangks/, **Tom** (*b.* 1956) US actor

hanky *n* = **hankie** (*informal*)

hanky-panky /-pángki/ *n* **1** frivolous and slightly indecent sexual activity **2** illicit or suspicious behaviour [Mid-19C. Alteration of HOCUS-POCUS.]

Hannibal /hánnib'l/ city E Missouri, on the Mississippi River. Population: 17,728 (1998 estimate).

Hannibal (247–183 BC) Carthaginian general

Hanoi /ha nóy/ capital of Vietnam, in the north of the country. Population: 3,056,146 (1989).

Hanover[1] /hánnōvər, ha nṓfər/ city in NW Germany. Population: 525,763 (1997).

Hanover[2] /hánnōvər, ha nṓfər/ *n* the royal house of Great Britain from 1714, when the elector of Hanover ascended the British throne as George I, until 1901, when Queen Victoria died

Hanoverian /hánnō véeri ən/ *adj* **1** OF HOUSE OF HANOVER relating to the British rulers from 1714 to 1901 **2** OF HANOVER relating to Hanover, Germany, or its people or culture ■ *n* HANOVERIAN MONARCH a supporter or monarch of the British Hanoverian line

Hansard /hán saard/ *n* the official published reports of proceedings in the British or Canadian parliaments or of similar legislative bodies in the Commonwealth [Late 19C. After Luke *Hansard* (1752–1828), British printer.]

Hanse /hánssə, hánzə, hanss/ *n* **1** = **Hanseatic League** **2** the fee paid by a new member of the Hanse [12C. < Old High German *hansa*, 'troop, company'.]

Hanseatic /hánssi áttik/ *adj* relating to the Hanseatic League or one of the towns in it [Early 17C. < medieval Latin *Hanseaticus* < *Hansa* 'the Hanseatic League'.]

Hanseatic League *n* an organized network of towns in N Europe from the 15th to the 17th centuries that protected each other and promoted trade with each other

hansel *n* = **handsel**

Hansen's disease /hánss'nz-/ *n* MED = **leprosy** [Early 20C. After Gerhard *Hansen* (1841–1921), Norwegian physician.]

hansom /hánssəm/, **hansom cab** *n* a covered two-wheeled vehicle drawn by one horse and carrying two passengers inside while the driver sits outside on a raised seat at the rear [Mid-19C. After Joseph Aloysius *Hansom* (1803–82), British architect.]

hantavirus /hántə vīrəss/ *n* a virus belonging to a group that affects small rodents and can be passed to humans, causing fever, headache, nausea, and vomiting

Hants. /hants/ *abbr* Hampshire

Hanukkah /hánnəkə, háan-, khaan-/, **Hanukah, Chanukah, Chanukkah** *n* a Jewish festival marking the rededication to Judaism of the Temple in Jerusalem in 165 BC. and celebrated by the kindling of eight lights. Date: from 25th day of Kislev, in December, for eight days. [Late 19C. < Hebrew *hanukkah* 'consecration'.]

Hanuman /húnnoō maán/ *n* **1 Hanuman, hanuman SACRED MONKEY** a slender long-tailed langur monkey of S Asia, considered sacred in India. *Presbytis entellus.* **2 MONKEY CHIEF** in Hinduism, a leader of monkeys who assists Rama **3 HINDU MONKEY GOD** a popular Hindu monkey god depicted in the epic Sanskrit poem Ramayana [Early 19C. < Sanskrit, 'large-jawed'.]

hao /how/ (*plural* **hao**) *n* see table at **currency** [Mid-20C. < Vietnamese.]

haole /hówli/ *n Hawaii* somebody, especially a white person, who lives in Hawaii but is not of Polynesian descent [Mid-19C. < Hawaiian.] —**haole** *adj*

hap[1] /hap/ *n* a happening or occurrence (*archaic*) ■ *vi* (**haps, happing, happed**) to happen or occur (*archaic*) [13C. < Old Norse *happ.*]

hap[2] /hap/ *n Scotland* something used to cover a person or bed, e.g. a cloak or quilt ■ *vt* (**haps, happing, happed**) *Scotland, US* to wrap up in warm clothes (*regional*) [13C. < ?]

hapax legomenon /háppaks lə gómmi non, -nən/ (*plural* **hapax legomena** /-nə/) *n* a word of which there is only one recorded use [Mid-17C. < Greek, 'said only once'.]

~~**hapen**~~ incorrect spelling of **happen**

ha'penny /háypni/ (*plural* **-nies**) *n* = **halfpenny** [Mid-16C. Contraction.]

haphazard /hap házzərd/ *adj* happening or done in a way that has not been planned [Late 16C. < HAP[1] + HAZARD, literally 'hazard of chance'.] —**haphazardly** *adv* —**haphazardness** *n*

haphtarah *n* JUDAISM = **haftarah**

hapl- *prefix* = **haplo-** (*before vowels*)

hapless /hápplәss/ *adj* unlucky or unfortunate —**haplessly** *adv* —**haplessness** *n*

haplite /háppllīt/ *n* GEOL = **aplite** —**haplitic** /hap líttik/ *adj*

haplo- *prefix* **1** single ○ *haplology* **2** haploid ○ *haplont* [< Greek *haplous* < Indo-European]

haplography /hap lóggrəfi/ *n* the accidental omission of a letter or syllable that should be repeated

haploid /háppIoyd/ *adj* having a single set of unpaired chromosomes —**haploid** *n* —**haploidic** *adj*

haplology /hap lólləji/ *n* the accidental omission of one or more repeated syllables or sounds when speaking —**haplologic** /háppla lójjik/ *adj*

haplont /há plont/ *n* an organism, especially an algal plant, that is haploid at one stage of its life cycle [Early 20C. < HAPLOID.] —**haplontic** /ha plóntik/ *adj*

haplosis /ha plṓssiss/ *n* the production of haploids during cell division (**meiosis**) [< HAPLOID]

ha'p'orth /háypərth/ (*plural* **ha'p'orth**) *n* = **halfpennyworth** [Late 17C. Contraction.]

happen /háppən/ *v* **1** *vi* **OCCUR** to take place ○ *How did it happen?* ○ *a go-getter who can really make things happen* **2** *vt* **DO SOMETHING BY CHANCE** to do something by chance and without a previous plan ○ *If you happen to see him, give him these keys.* **3** *vi* **AFFECT** to affect somebody or something, especially in an unpleasant way ○ *If anything happens to me, you'll regret it.* **4** *vi* **OCCUR BY CHANCE** to occur or exist by chance ■ *adv N England* **PERHAPS** used to suggest that something may occur or be the case ○ *Happen we'll go for a walk.* [14C. < HAP[1].]

happen along, happen by *vi US* to appear or pass by chance or unexpectedly (*informal*)

happen on *vt* to discover or encounter something or somebody by chance

happen upon *vt* = **happen on**

happenchance /háppən chaanss/ *n* = **happenstance** [Mid-20C. Alteration.]

happening /háppəning/ *n* **1 OCCURRENCE** something that occurs **2 ARTISTIC PERFORMANCE** an improvised or informal performance or demonstration, often dramatic in form and using audience participation (*informal*) ■ *adj* **FASHIONABLE** at the forefront of what is fashionable and exciting (*informal*)

happenstance /hápp'n stanss/ *n* a chance occurrence or event [Late 19C. Blend of HAPPENING + CIRCUMSTANCE.]

happi coat /háppi-/ *n* an open Japanese jacket that has wide loose sleeves and is usually tied with a sash, or a fashion garment resembling this [Late 19C. < Japanese.]

happily /háppili/ *adv* **1 FORTUNATELY** used to indicate that something that could have been difficult or disastrous is luckily the reverse ○ *Happily, no one was hurt.* **2 WILLINGLY** with willingness ○ *I'd happily contribute.* **3 IN A HAPPY WAY** in a pleased, contented, or joyful way

happy /háppi/ (**-pier, -piest**) *adj* **1 FEELING PLEASURE** feeling or showing pleasure, contentment, or joy ○ *happy smiling faces* **2 CAUSING PLEASURE** causing or characterized by pleasure, contentment, or joy ○ *a happy childhood* **3 SATISFIED** feeling satisfied that something is right or has been done right ○ *Are you happy with your performance?* **4 WILLING** willing to do something ○ *I'd be only too happy to help.* **5 FORTUNATE** resulting in something pleasant or welcome ○ *a happy coincidence* **6 TIPSY** slightly drunk (*informal*) **7 USED IN GREETINGS** used in formulae to express a hope that somebody will enjoy a special day or holiday ○ *Happy birthday!* **8 TOO READY** inclined to use a particular thing too readily or be too enthusiastic about a particular thing (*in combination*) ○ *trigger-happy* [14C. < HAP[1].] —**happiness** *n*

happy event *n* the birth of a baby (*informal*)

happy-go-lucky *adj* tending not to worry about the future

happy hard core *n* uplifting hard-core music, often achieving its emotional effect by the use of piano riffs over straightforward rhythms

happy hour *n* a period of time, usually in the late afternoon or early evening, during which a pub or bar serves alcoholic drinks at reduced prices

happy hunting ground *n* **1** among some Native American peoples, a place of peace and abundance to which people go after death **2** a place that provides plenty of something desired

happy medium *n* a satisfying compromise

~~**happyness**~~ incorrect spelling of **happiness**

Hapsburg /háps burg/, **Habsburg** /hábz-/ *n* a member of a German royal family, prominent between the 13th and 20th centuries in Europe, that included rulers of the Holy Roman Empire, Spain, and Austria-Hungary

hapten /háptən/, **haptene** /háp teen/ *n* an antigen that can only stimulate antibody production when combined with a specific protein [Early 20C. < Greek *haptein* 'fasten'.]

haptic /háptik/ *adj* relating to the sense of touch [Late 19C. < Greek *haptikos* < *haptesthai* 'grasp, touch' < *haptein* 'fasten'.]

haptoglobin /háptə glṓbin/ *n* any plasma protein that combines with free haemoglobin in the bloodstream [Mid-20C. < Greek *haptein* 'fasten'.]

haptotropism /háptō trṓpizəm/ *n* BIOL = **thigmotropism** [Late 19C. < Greek *haptein* 'fasten'.]

hapu /haá poo/ *n NZ* a principal social unit of Maori society, consisting of a group of extended families holding land in common that forms a division of a tribe [Mid-19C. < Maori.]

hara-kiri /hárrə kírri, -keér ri/ *n* a traditional form of suicide, sometimes ritually performed as a point of honour in Japan, involving disembowelment with a sword [Mid-19C. < Japanese, 'belly-cutting'.]

Harald I /hárrəld/ (850?–933?) king of Norway. Known as **Harald the Fairhaired**

harangue /hə ráng/ *vti* (**-rangues, -ranguing, -rangued**) to criticize or question somebody or try to persuade somebody to do something in a forceful angry way ■ *n* a loud, forceful, and angry speech criticizing somebody or trying to persuade somebody to do something [15C. Via French < medieval Latin *harenga.*] —**haranguer** *n*

Harar = **Harer**

Harare /hə raári/ capital of Zimbabwe, in the northeast of the country. Population: 1,478,810 (1992).

harass /hárrəss, hə ráss/ *vt* **1** to persistently annoy, attack, or bother somebody **2** to exhaust an enemy by repeatedly attacking [Early 17C. < French *harasser* < *harer* 'set a dog on (by crying "hare")'.] —**harasser** *n*

harassed /hárrəst, hə rást/ *adj* stressed and anxious because of having too much to do or worry about

harassment /hárrəssmənt, hə rássmənt/ *n* behaviour that threatens or torments somebody, especially persistently

Harbin /haár bín/ capital of Heilongjiang Province, NE China. Population: 3,433,629 (1991).

harbinger /haárbinjər/ *n* somebody or something that foreshadows or anticipates a future event [12C. < Old French *herberger* < *herbergier* 'provide shelter for an army' < Germanic.] —**harbinger** *v*

harbor *n, vti* US = **harbour**

harbour /haárbər/ *n* **1 PORT** part of a body of water near a coast in which ships can anchor safely (*often in placenames*) **2 PLACE OF REFUGE** any place that is safe and sheltered ■ *v* **1** *vt* **KEEP IN MIND** to continue to think privately about an emotion or thought for a long time ○ *had harboured a secret fear of the dark since childhood* **2** *vt* **SHELTER** to provide somebody with shelter or sanctuary **3** *vti* **KEEP A SHIP IN HARBOUR** to take shelter in a harbour, or shelter a ship in a harbour [Old English *herebeorg* 'lodging' < Germanic, 'army shelter'] —**harbourer** *n*

harbourage /haárbərij/ *n* = **harbour** *n.* 1, **harbour** *n.* 2

harbour master *n* an official who supervises and administers the general activities of a port or harbour

harbour seal *n* a small seal that is greyish-black with paler spots and lives on the northern coasts of North America, Europe, and Asia. *Phoca vitulina.*

hard /haard/ *adj* **1 NOT EASILY BENT** firm, stiff, or rigid and not easily cut, pierced, or bent ○ *a hard mattress* ○ *Do not move the object until the glue has gone hard.* **2 AWKWARD** difficult or awkward to do or achieve ○ *a hard decision* **3 DIFFICULT TO UNDERSTAND** difficult to understand or explain **4 INVOLVING EFFORT** involving a great deal of labour or effort ○ *a hard climb* **5 PERFORMING ENERGETICALLY** acting or producing something with energy or industriousness ○ *a hard worker* **6 MIGHTY** using a lot of force or violence **7 DEMANDING** making inflexible and heavy demands ○ *a hard taskmaster* **8 PROBLEMATIC** difficult and full of problems ○ *a hard life* **9 UNSYMPATHETIC** showing little or no sympathy, compassion, or gentleness ○ *She's as hard as nails.* **10 RESENTFUL** marked by resentment or bitterness ○ *no hard feelings* **11 REAL** demonstrably real, true, or certain ○ *cold, hard facts* **12 PENETRATING** seeming to penetrate and discover intentions or thoughts ○ *a hard stare* **13 TOUGH** tough, violent, and ruthless ○ *a hard man* **14 RADICAL** politically radical or extreme ○ *the hard left* **15 SEVERE** marked by weather conditions such as extreme cold or severe storms ○ *a hard winter* **16 VISUALLY HARSH** harsh and glaring to the sight **17 TOUGHENED** rough or leathery, and unyielding ○ *hard skin* **18 CONTAINING MINERAL SALTS** containing mineral salts and preventing soap from lathering well **19 CRISP** having a crisp, firm, or stale crust or texture **20 ERECT** stiff and erect (*informal*) **21** = **hardcore** *adj.* 2 **22 ABLE TO PENETRATE** describes radiation, especially high frequency X-rays, that has a high energy and is thus readily able to penetrate substances including metals, or relating to this ○ *hard vacuum* **23 STABLE** stable in value and in demand by currency traders **24 IN CASH** in the form of coins and paper money rather than, e.g., cheques **25 HIGH IN ALCOHOL** having a high alcoholic content, especially alcohol produced by distillation **26 ADDICTIVE** highly addictive and particularly dangerous to the health **27 PRONOUNCED LIKE 'K' OR 'G'** describes the consonants 'c' and 'g' when they are pronounced with a 'k' sound, as in 'come', and a 'g' sound, as in 'go' ■ *adv* **1 FORCEFULLY** with a lot of force ○ *hit the ball hard* **2 INTENSELY** to an extreme degree ○ *pulled the truck over hard* **3 ENERGETICALLY** with vigour and energy or industriousness ○ *worked hard* **4 WITH CONCENTRATION** with great mental concentration **5 WITH DIFFICULTY** with effort and great difficulty **6 COMPACTLY** into a solid or compact state ○ *set hard* **7 PAINFULLY** in a way that causes anguish or hardship ○ *hit hard by the recession* **8 SLOWLY** slowly and with difficulty ○ *hatred that dies hard* ■ *n* **1 BEACH WHERE BOAT CAN LAND** a beach or slope that is convenient for hauling vessels out of water **2 ROAD** a road across a foreshore [Old English *heard* < Indo-European, 'strength'] ◇ **be hard on somebody 1** to treat somebody severely **2** to be unfortunate for somebody ◇ **be hard put to do something** to find it difficult to do something ◇ **go hard with somebody** to cause difficulty or distress to somebody (*dated*) ◇ **hard by** close by

LITERARY LINK ***Hard Times***, a novel (1854) by Charles Dickens. This story of the loveless upbringing of Tom and Louisa Gradgrind contrasts the soullessness of utilitarianism, as personified by their father Thomas Gradgrind, with the natural warmth and generosity of the human spirit, symbolized by their adopted sister Sissy Jupe, a member of a travelling circus.

SYNONYMS ***hard, difficult, strenuous, tough, arduous, laborious***

CORE MEANING: requiring effort or exertion

hard requiring mental or physical effort or exertion to do or achieve; **difficult** requiring considerable planning or effort to accomplish; **strenuous** requiring physical effort, energy, stamina, or strength; **tough** needing great effort to deal with;

arduous requiring hard work or continuous physical effort; **laborious** requiring unwelcome, often tedious, effort and exertion.

hard-and-fast *adj* unable to be changed or adapted

Hardanger Fjord /haárd angər fyáwrd/ large fjord on the coast of SW Norway. Length: 183 km/114 mi.

hard-ass *n US* an offensive term for somebody who is perceived as inflexible and uncompromising (*slang insult*) —**hard-assed** *adj*

hardback /haárd bak/ *n* a book with a rigid cover

hardbake /haárd bayk/ *n* almond toffee (*archaic*)

hardball /haárd bawl/ *n* **1** *US* SPORTS = **baseball** *n.* 1 **2** *US, Can* tough or ruthless behaviour, especially in politics or business (*informal*) ○ *These guys play hardball.*

hard-bitten *adj* tough and experienced

hardboard /haárd bawrd/ *n* thin stiff sheets of compressed sawdust and wood chips

hard-boiled *adj* **1** describes an egg boiled until the yolk and white are firm **2** tough, realistic, and unsentimental (*informal*) —**hard-boil** *vt*

ϟ **hardboot** /haárd boot/ *vt* COMPUT = **coldboot**

hardbound /haárd bownd/ *adj* bound as a book in a stiff cover

hard case *n* a person who is rough, tough, and ruthless

hard cheese *interj* used to comment on, and express a lack of sympathy for, somebody's misfortune (*informal*)

hard coal *n* INDUST = **anthracite**

ϟ **hard copy** *n* data from a computer that is printed out, usually on paper, rather than read from the screen

hard core *n* **1 COMMITTED NUCLEUS** the most committed, faithful, and active members of a group or organization **2 FAST ROCK MUSIC** dance music with repetitive rhythmic synthesized sounds and a fast tempo **3 FOUNDATION** stones and other rubble used to form a foundation under roads or paving

hardcore, hard-core *adj* **1 UNCOMPROMISING** uncompromising and committed **2 SHOWING EXPLICIT SEX** depicting sexual acts in an explicit way **3 RELATING TO FAST ROCK MUSIC** having repetitive rhythmic synthesized sounds and a fast tempo

hardcover /haárd kuvvər/ *n* = **hardback**

ϟ **hard disk, hard drive** *n* a rigid disk inside a computer that holds a large quantity of data and programs

hard-edge *adj* describes a US style of abstract painting that arose in the 1960s and is marked by sharply outlined coloured forms

hard-edged *adj* realistic, direct, and uncompromising

harden /haárd'n/ *v* **1** *vti* **BECOME OR MAKE HARD** to become hard, firm, or solid, or make something become hard, firm, or solid ○ *The glue hardened overnight.* **2** *vti* **MAKE OR BECOME LESS SYMPATHETIC** to become or make somebody become more tough, callous, or unfeeling **3** *vti* **MAKE OR BECOME MORE DETERMINED** to become or make somebody become more determined and resolute **4** *vti* **MAKE OR BECOME STRONGER** to become or make somebody or something become stronger or more resistant **5** *vi* **STABILIZE** to become stable after fluctuation ○ *Prices are hardening.*
harden off *vti* to accustom a plant grown indoors to outdoor conditions by gradually exposing it to cold, wind, or sunlight before planting it out, or become accustomed to outdoor conditions in this way

hardened /haárd'nd/ *adj* **1 STRENGTHENED** having been made harder or stronger ○ *hardened steel* **2 SECURED AGAINST NUCLEAR ATTACK** strengthened in order to survive an attack by nuclear weapons **3 TOUGHENED BY EXPERIENCE** sufficiently experienced to have become blasé about something that most people would find unpleasant or difficult

hardener /haárd'nər/, **hardening** /haárd'ning/ *n* an ingredient or element that makes something hard, e.g. a substance added to paint to make it more durable

hardening of the arteries *n* the arterial disorder atherosclerosis (*no longer technical*)

hard-fisted *adj* not generous with money

hardhack /haárd hak/ (*plural* **-hacks** *or* **-hack**) *n* a shrub of the rose family with downy leaves and clusters of pink or white flowers. Native to: North America. *Spiraea tomentosa.* [Mid-19C. < ?]

hardhanded /haárd hándid/ *adj* showing little or no sympathy or pity —**hardhandedness** *n*

hard hat *n* **1 PROTECTIVE HELMET** a helmet made of metal or plastic worn for protection by workers in a factory or on a construction site **2** *US* **WORKER** a construction worker (*informal*) **3** *US* **CONSERVATIVE** a politically very conservative patriot (*informal*) —**hard-hat** *adj*

hardhead /haárd hed/ *n* a logical and unsentimental person

hardheaded /haárd héddid/ *adj* behaving in a shrewd, tough, and logical way that is not influenced by emotions —**hardheadedly** *adv* —**hardheadedness** *n*

hardheads /haárd hedz/ (*plural* **-heads**) *n* a plant of the daisy family with lance-shaped leaves. Flowers: reddish-purple, globular flowerheads. *Centaurea nigra.* (+ *singular verb*) US term **knapweed**

hardhearted /haárd haártid/ *adj* showing no sympathy for other people's feelings —**hardheartedly** *adv* —**hardheartedness** *n*

hard-hitting *adj* direct and uncompromising ○ *a hard-hitting documentary*

Hardie /haárdi/, **Keir** (1856–1915) British politician

Hardie Boys /haárdi bóyz/, **Sir Michael** (*b.* 1931) New Zealand lawyer and statesman

hardihood /haárdihòod/ *n* **1** the quality of being tough and able to withstand difficulty or hard work **2** bold audacity

Harding /haárding/, **Warren G.** (1865–1923) US statesman and 29th president of the United States (1921–23)

hard labour *n* a sentence of compulsory work imposed in addition to a term of imprisonment, not used as a sentence in the United Kingdom since 1948

hard landing *n* **1** an uncontrolled landing by an aircraft or spacecraft that results in its being damaged or destroyed **2** a downward trend in economic activity after a period of expansion

hardline /haárd līn/ *adj* inflexible and uncompromising —**hardliner** *n*

hard lines *interj* used to comment that somebody is or has been unfortunate (*dated; often used ironically*)

hardly /haárdli/ CORE MEANING: an adverb with negative meaning, used to indicate that something is true or exists to a very minimal extent ○ *She lived so privately, hardly anyone even spoke to her* ○ *Though we hardly knew him, we could sense his good humour.* ○ *I looked out of the window; it was hardly raining.*
adv **1 NOT** indicates that something is almost entirely untrue or impossible ○ *We are hardly going to give up with success in view.* ○ *It's hardly likely that I would tell you.* **2 ONLY WITH DIFFICULTY** only with great awkwardness, difficulty, or embarrassment ○ *I was so shocked I could hardly speak.* **3 SELDOM** indicates that something seldom occurs (*with a negative such as 'without'*) ○ *Hardly a day passes without acclaim for this exciting new invention.* **4 AS SOON AS** indicates that one event follows quickly after another ○ *Hardly had I rung the bell when the bolt was shot back.* **5 USED TO DISAGREE** used to indicate surprise, disagreement, or annoyance ○ *'I thought you were going at about sixty miles an hour'.'Well, hardly. Maybe forty'.*

USAGE ***Hardly,*** like *barely* and *scarcely,* has a negative force, rendering unnecessary the use of another negative in the clause or sentence: *I can* [not: *can't*] *hardly see you.* Note that *when* and not *than* is used in any continuation of the sentence: *Hardly* [or *barely* or *scarcely*] *had I begun to speak when* [not *than*] *she interrupted me.* (After *no sooner,* however, *than* is correct.) ***Hardly*** is limited to these special uses; the routine adverb from the adjective *hard* is *hard*: *They are all working hard to get ready for their exams.*

hard man *n* a man who is perceived as vicious and ruthless, probably with criminal tendencies

hard mouth *n* a horse's mouth that is insensitive to pressure from the bit, or a horse's ability to resist this pressure

hardmouthed /haard mówthd/ *adj* describes a horse that fails to respond when the rider pulls on the bit in the horse's mouth

hardness /haárdnəss/ *n* **1 FIRMNESS, SOLIDITY, AND COMPACTNESS** the state or quality of being firm, solid, and compact **2 UNYIELDING TOUGHNESS** the state or quality of being tough and unyielding **3 WATER QUALITY** the degree to which water contains mineral salts **4 DEGREE TO WHICH A METAL IS HARD** the degree to which a metal may be scratched, abraded, indented, or machined, measured according to any of several scales

hard news *n* news that concerns specific events and is strictly factual —**hard-news** *adj*

hard-nosed *adj* tough, realistic, and unsentimental (*informal*)

hard of hearing *adj* unable to hear as much as others do (*often considered offensive*)

hard-on *n* a highly offensive term for an erect penis (*slang taboo*)

hard palate *n* the bony front portion of the roof of the mouth

hardpan /haárd pan/ *n* a layer of hard matter, especially clay, that lies under soft soil and that plant roots cannot penetrate

hard-pressed *adj* **1** under a lot of pressure and without sufficient resources **2** finding something very difficult

hard put *adj* **hard put, hard put to it** not easily able to do something or, more generally, to cope

hard rock *n* a form of rock music that has simple lyrics and a strong insistent beat, and that is usually very loud

hard rubber *n* rubber treated with sulphur to make it hard and stiff

hard sauce *n US* FOOD = **brandy butter**

hard science *n* a science such as physics, chemistry, geology, and astronomy in which data can be precisely quantified and theories tested

hard sell *n* a direct, aggressive, and insistent way of selling or advertising. ◊ **soft sell**

hard-shell, hard-shelled *adj US* rigid and uncompromising in attitude

hardship /haárd ship/ *n* **1** difficulty or suffering caused by a lack of something, especially money **2** something that causes hardship

hard shoulder *n* an area at the side of a motorway where a vehicle can stop in an emergency. US term **shoulder** *n.* 6

hardstand /haárd stand/ *n US* TRANSP = **hard standing**

hard standing *n* a hard surface on which aircraft or heavy motor vehicles may be parked. US term **hardstand**

hard stuff *n* something that is intoxicating, addictive, and potentially very dangerous to the health (*informal*)

hardtack /haárd tak/ *n* a hard thin unsalted bread or biscuit formerly eaten aboard ships and as military rations

hardtop /haárd top/ *n* **1 CAR WITH DETACHABLE HARD ROOF** a car with no centre post between the side windows and a rigid metal or plastic detachable roof **2 DETACHABLE SOLID TOP FOR CAR** a detachable roof made of rigid metal or plastic for a car **3** *US* **CAR WITH METAL ROOF** a car with a non-detachable metal roof, as opposed to a convertible

hard up *adj* short of money (*informal*)

ϟ **hardware** /haárd wair/ *n* **1 IMPLEMENTS** tools and implements that are typically made of metal, e.g. hinges, hammers, and cutlery **2 COMPUTER EQUIPMENT** the equipment and devices that make up a computer system as opposed to the programs used on it **3 MILITARY WEAPONS** heavy military weapons and equipment **4 GUN** a gun or guns (*informal*)

hard-wearing *adj* not easily damaged or worn out through constant use

hard wheat *n* wheat with hard kernels and a high gluten content. Use: flour for bread.

ϟ **hardwire** /haárd wīr/ (**-wires, -wiring, -wired**) *vt* to build a function into a computer with hardware rather than programming

hardwood /haárd wòod/ *n* **1** wood from a broad-leaved tree as opposed to from a conifer **2** a tree that produces hardwood

hard word *n Ireland* (*informal*) **1** dismissal from employment **2** a reprimand or unfair criticism

hard-working *adj* tending to work industriously

hardy /haárdi/ (**-dier, -diest**) *adj* **1 ROBUST** sufficiently robust to withstand fatigue, hardship, or adverse physical conditions **2 NOT SENSITIVE TO COLD** describes plants that are able to live outdoors during the winter ○ *a hardy shrub* **3 COURAGEOUS** courageous and daring [13C. < French *hardi* < *hardir* 'become bold' < Germanic.] —**hardily** *adv* —**hardiness** *n*

Hardy /haàrdi/, **Oliver** (1892–1957) US actor

Hardy, Thomas (1840–1928) British novelist and poet

Hardy, Thomas Masterman (1769–1839) British sailor

Hardy-Weinberg law /haàrdi wín burg-/, **Hardy-Weinberg distribution** *n* a principle of genetics stating that gene frequencies remain constant from one generation to the next if mating is random and there are no outside influences such as mutation and immigration [Mid-20C. After G. H. *Hardy* (1877–1947), British mathematician, and Wilhelm *Weinberg* (1862–1937), German physician.]

hare /hair/ *n* (*plural* **hare** *or* **hares**) a fast-running animal that resembles a rabbit but is larger, has longer ears and legs, and does not burrow. Genus: *Lepus*. ▪ *vi* (**hares, haring, hared**) to run or move very fast [Old English *hara* < Germanic]

SPELLCHECK See *hair.*

Hare /hair/, **Sir David** (*b.* 1947) British playwright

hare and hounds, **hare and hounds race** *n* an outdoor game in which one group of players follows a trail of scraps of paper left by another group and tries to catch them up

harebell /hair bel/ *n* a low-growing delicate wild plant with slender stems. Flowers: blue, bell-shaped. Native to: northern temperate regions. *Campanula rotundiflora.*

harebrained /hair braynd/ *adj* regarded as impractical and likely to fail

Hare Krishna /hárri-/ *n* 1 a religious group that bases its practice on worship of the god Krishna 2 a member of Hare Krishna [Late 20C. < Sanskrit, 'O Lord Krishna', chant used by devotees.]

harelip /hair lip/ *n* an offensive term for a facial deformity, now rare, in which somebody born with the upper lip in two parts has had the separation incompletely rectified by surgery —**harelipped** *adj*

harem /haáiram, haà reem, haa reèm/ *n* 1 **WOMEN'S PART OF A HOUSE** the separate private quarters reserved for wives and concubines in a Muslim home 2 **GROUP OF WOMEN** the wives and concubines who live in a harem 3 **GROUP OF ANIMALS** a group of female animals of the same species associated for breeding purposes with one male 4 **WOMEN FOLLOWERS** any group of women admirers or followers (*humorous; sometimes offensive*) [Mid-17C. Via Turkish < Arabic *ḥaram* 'prohibited (place), women's quarters'.]

harem pants *npl* women's trousers made of soft thin cloth and having wide legs that are gathered at the ankle

Harer /haárar/, **Härer, Harar** city in E Ethiopia. Population: 77,202 (1989).

hare's-foot (*plural* **hare's-foot** *or* **hare's-foots**), **hare's-foot clover** *n* a clover that grows on sandy soil. Flowers: inconspicuous, white or pink. *Trefolium arvense.* [< the appearance of the soft hair about the flowers]

harestail /hairz tayl/ *n* a variety of cotton grass that grows on moors and has a single flower head [< its similarity to a hare's tail]

harewood /hair woòd/ *n* the greenish-coloured wood of the sycamore maple. Use: furniture. [Late 17C. < German dialect *Ehre* < Latin *acer* 'maple, sycamore'.]

Hargrave /haàr grayv/, **Lawrence** (1850–1915) British-born Australian aviator and explorer

Hargreaves /haàr greevz/, **James** (1720–78) British inventor

haricot /hárrikô/ *n* 1 a small white oval dried bean, cooked and eaten as a vegetable 2 a bean plant whose seeds are dried and stored as haricots. *Phaseolus vulgaris.* 3 = **French bean** [Mid-17C. < French.]

Harijan /húrrijan/ *n* a member of a class of people in South Asia whose touch was formerly considered to defile a Hindu of a higher caste [Mid-20C. < Sanskrit, 'God's people'.]

Haring /háiring/, **Keith** (1958–90) US painter

harissa /hǝ ríssa/ *n* a hot spicy oily paste used as an ingredient in N African and Middle Eastern cooking or as an accompaniment for dishes such as couscous

hark /haark/ *vi* to listen to something or somebody (*archaic*) [12C. Probably from assumed Old English *heorcnian* < Germanic.]

hark back *vi* 1 to think or speak again about something from the past 2 to be similar in some respects to something in the past

harken *vi* = **hearken**

harl /haarl/ *vt Scotland* to cover the exterior walls of a building with lime and gravel or sand ▪ *n Scotland* a mixture of lime and gravel or sand used for covering a building's exterior walls [13C. < ?]

Harlech /haàrlak/ village in NW Wales, dominated by the ruins of its castle. Population: 1,233 (1991).

Harlem[1] /haàrlam/ district of New York City, on Manhattan Island

Harlem[2] = **Haarlem**

Harlem Globetrotters /haàrlam glôb trottarz/ *npl* a US basketball team that tours widely to play exhibition matches during which the team displays skilled comic manoeuvres

harlequin /haàrlakwin/ *n* a clown or buffoon ▪ *adj* varied in colour and having a pattern of irregular shapes [Late 16C. Via obsolete French < *Hellequin*, legendary leader of night-raiding demon horsemen.]

Harlequin *n* a comic dramatic character featured in the Italian commedia dell'arte and the English harlequinade, usually shown wearing multicoloured diamond-patterned tights and a black mask

harlequinade /haàrlakwi náyd/ *n* 1 a pantomime, play, or other performance featuring a harlequin as a character 2 the action of clowning around or acting in a silly way

harlequin duck *n* a small diving duck that has blue and red plumage with black and white markings. Native to: North America, Iceland, E Siberia. *Histrionicus histrionicus.*

Harley Street /haàrli-/ *n* a street in central London famous for the number of eminent doctors who have private practices there

harling /haàrling/ *n Scotland* BUILDING = **harl** *n*.

harlot /haàrlat/ *n* a prostitute (*archaic or literary*) [13C. < Old French, 'vagabond, rogue, beggar'.]

Harlow /haàrlô/ town in SE England. Population: 74,629 (1991).

Harlow, Jean (1911–37) US actor. Born **Harlean Carpenter**

harm /haarm/ *n* physical or mental damage or injury ▪ *vt* to injure or damage somebody or something physically, mentally, or morally [Old English *hearm* < Germanic]

harmattan /haar mátt'n/ *n* an extremely dry dusty wind from the Sahara that blows towards the western coast of Africa, especially between November and March [Late 17C. < Twi *haramata*.]

harmful /haàrmf'l/ *adj* causing damage or injury ○ *The plant is harmful to humans.* —**harmfully** *adv* —**harmfulness** *n*

harmless /haàrmlass/ *adj* 1 not likely to cause offence or upset ○ *Don't worry; he's harmless enough.* 2 not likely to cause damage or injury —**harmlessly** *adv* —**harmlessness** *n*

harmonic /haar mónnik/ *adj* 1 **PRODUCED BY HARMONY** relating to, produced, or marked by harmony 2 **OF INTEGRAL MULTIPLE** describes a frequency that is an integral multiple of a fundamental frequency ▪ *n* 1 **MULTIPLE OF A FUNDAMENTAL FREQUENCY** a single oscillation having a frequency that is an integral multiple of a fundamental frequency, e.g. 220 Hz and 330 Hz are both harmonics of 110 Hz 2 **OVERTONE ON A STRINGED INSTRUMENT** an overtone produced on an instrument, e.g. by lightly touching a vibrating string at a point where the string to either side will continue to vibrate [Late 16C. Via Latin < Greek *harmonikos* < *harmonia* (see HARMONY).]

harmonica /haar mónnika/ *n* a small musical instrument whose narrow metal case houses a set of metal reeds that are made to sound by exhaling or inhaling air past them. ◊ **glass harmonica** [Mid-18C. Via Italian *armonica* < Latin *harmonicus* (see HARMONIC).]

harmonic analysis *n* the representation of a periodic function by a series of sines and cosines, especially by a Fourier series

harmonic distortion *n* the unwanted presence of distorted frequencies at the output of an electronic device, e.g. the output of an audio amplifier

harmonic mean *n* the reciprocal of the arithmetic mean of the reciprocals of a finite set of numbers

harmonic minor scale *n* a version of the minor scale in which the seventh note is raised by a semitone, both ascending and descending

harmonic motion *n* PHYS = **simple harmonic motion**

harmonic progression *n* any sequence of numbers whose reciprocals form an arithmetic progression, e.g. 1/2, 1/5, 1/8, 1/11

harmonics /haar mónniks/ *n* the branch of science that deals with the physical properties of musical sound (+ *singular verb*)

harmonic series *n* any infinite series of numbers constructed by adding the numbers in a harmonic progression to one another, e.g. 1/2+1/5+1/8+1/11

harmonious /haar môni ass/ *adj* 1 **RELATING TO HARMONY** relating to or sounding in harmony 2 **BLENDING PLEASANTLY** having a pleasing combination of parts or colours 3 **SHOWING ACCORD** characterized by friendly agreement or accord —**harmoniously** *adv* —**harmoniousness** *n*

harmonise *vti* = **harmonize**

harmonist /haàrmanist/ *n* 1 a skilled creator of musical harmony 2 a researcher of the similarities in parallel texts, especially the four Gospels —**harmonistic** /haàrma nístik/ *adj* —**harmonistically** *adv*

harmonium /haar môni am/ *n* an organ in which a pair of bellows operated by the player's feet blow air into the reeds to produce sound [Mid-19C. < French, < Latin *harmonia* 'harmony' or Greek *harmonios* (see HARMONY).]

harmonize /haàrma nīz/ (**-nizes, -nizing, -nized**), **harmonise** (**-nises, -nising, -nised**) *v* 1 *vti* **BLEND PLEASINGLY** to blend pleasingly, be in a pleasant combination, or make things combine pleasantly 2 *vt* **MAKE SYSTEMS SIMILAR** to make rules, regulations, or systems similar or in accord with each other 3 *vt* **ADD HARMONY TO** to provide a harmony for a melody 4 *vi* **PLAY IN HARMONY** to sing or play musical instruments in harmony —**harmonization** /haàrma nī záysh'n/ *n* —**harmonizer** *n*

harmonized sales tax *n* in the Canadian provinces of Nova Scotia, New Brunswick, and Newfoundland, a tax combining the goods and services tax and the provincial sales tax

harmony /haàrmani/ (*plural* **-nies**) *n* 1 **PLEASING COMBINATION OF SOUNDS** a pleasing combination of musical sounds 2 **HAPPY AGREEMENT** a situation in which there is agreement 3 **PLEASANTNESS IN ARRANGEMENT** a pleasing effect produced by an arrangement of things, parts, or colours 4 **STUDY OF CHORDS** the study of the way in which musical chords are constructed and function in relation to one another 5 **NOTES PLAYED TOGETHER** any combination of notes that are sung or played at the same time 6 **STUDY OF TEXTS** a study or collation of the similarities in parallel texts, particularly the four Gospels 7 **PARALLEL TEXT** a book or manuscript in which several versions of the same text, often a biblical text, are laid out in parallel columns ○ *a Gospel harmony* [14C. Via French and Latin < Greek *harmonia* 'agreement, concord' < *harmozein* 'fit together'.]

Harnack /haàrn ak/, **Adolf von** (1851–1930) German theologian

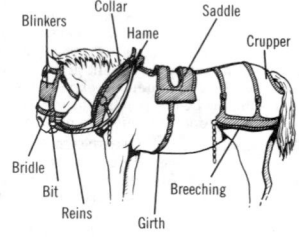

Harness

harness /haàrnass/ *n* 1 **LEATHER STRAPS FOR AN ANIMAL** a set of straps fixed together and fitted to an animal such as a horse so that it can be attached to a cart or carriage for pulling 2 **STRAPS FITTED TO A PERSON** an arrangement of straps fitted to somebody to fasten the person to something or to keep the person in position ▪ *vt* 1 **FIT AN ANIMAL WITH A HARNESS** to put a harness on an animal 2 **GET CONTROL OF AND USE** to gain control of something and use it for some purpose [13C. Via Old French *harneis* < assumed Old Norse *hernest* 'provisions for an army' < *herr* 'army'.] —**harnesser** *n* ◊ **in harness** 1 doing your usual work **2** working together cooperatively with a person or group

harness hitch *n* a knot with one loop and no free ends, used in tying harnesses

harness race *n* a horse race in which specially bred horses pull small carriages around a course wearing special harnesses to ensure that they move as required by rule

Harney Peak /haárni-/ highest peak in South Dakota, in the southwest of the state. Height: 2,207 m/7,242 ft.

Harold I /hárrald/ (*d.* 1040) king of the English (1037–40). Known as **Harold Harefoot**

Harold II (1020?–66) king of the English (1064–66)

haroseth /hə rṓseth/, **haroset** /hə rṓset/, **charoseth** /khə-/, **charoset** /khə-/ *n* a mixture of apples, nuts, spices, and wine, eaten as part of the Passover Seder meal [Late 19C. < Hebrew *harōset* < *heres* 'earthenware'.]

harp /haarp/ *n* **1 TRIANGULAR STRINGED INSTRUMENT** a triangular-shaped instrument that has a curved neck and strings stretched between the neck and the body, at an angle to the sound box **2 HARMONICA** a reed harmonica (*informal*) ■ *vi* **PLAY THE HARP** to play the harp [Old English *hearpe* < Germanic] —**harper** *n* —**harpist** *n*

harp on *vti* to repeat or stress something in a way that becomes tiresome

Harpers Ferry /haárpərz férri/ town in E West Virginia, at the confluence of the Potomac and Shenandoah rivers. Population: 308 (1990).

harpoon /haar poón/ *n* a long pointed piece of metal that is attached to a cord and thrown or fired from a gun in order to capture whales or other large sea animals ■ *vt* to catch a whale or other large sea animal using a harpoon [Early 17C. < Old French *harpon* 'clamp' < *harpe* 'dog's claw, clamp' < Greek *harpē* 'sickle'.] —**harpooneer** /haár poo néer/ *n* —**harpooner** *n*

harp seal *n* a brownish-grey earless seal that is whitish when very young, formerly hunted for its fur. Native to: coastal regions and ice floes of the North Atlantic Ocean. *Pagophilus groenlandicus.* [< the shape of its markings]

harpsichord /haárpsi kawrd/ *n* a keyboard instrument resembling a piano and having horizontal strings plucked by leather or quill points connected to the keys [Early 17C. < French *harpechorde* < Latin *harpa* 'harp' + *chorda* 'string'.] —**harpsichordist** *n*

Harpur /haárpər/, **Charles** (1813–68) Australian poet and playwright

harpy /haárpi/ (*plural* **-pies**) *n* an offensive term for a woman that deliberately insults her attitude towards others in the pursuit of personal goals (*insult*) [< HARPY]

Harpy /haárpi/ (*plural* **-pies**) *n* in Greek mythology, a monster that was half woman half bird of prey [14C. Directly or via French < Latin *harpyia* < Greek *harpuiai* (plural) 'snatchers' < *harpazein* 'seize'.]

harpy eagle *n* a huge eagle of lowland forests with a black back, white underparts, and a grey head with a double crest. Native to: S Mexico to N Argentina. *Harpia harpyja.*

harquebus /haárkwibəss/, **arquebus** /aár-/ *n* an early type of portable gun supported on a tripod by a hook or on a forked post [Mid-16C. Via French *(h)arquebuse* < Middle Dutch *hakebus* and related forms.] —**harquebusier** /haárkwibə séer/ *n*

~~**harrass**~~ incorrect spelling of **harass**

harridan /hárridən/ *n* an offensive term for a woman that deliberately insults her age and temperament (*insult*) [Late 17C. < ?]

harrier[1] /hárri ər/ (*plural* **-ers** *or* **-er**) *n* a slender hawk with long wings and tail that hunts by flying low over marshland and grassland to catch mice, snakes, frogs, and fish. Genus: *Circus.* [Mid-16C. < *harrow* 'rob', variant of HARRY; later influenced by HARRIER[3].]

harrier[2] /hárri ər/ *n* **1** a small hound, resembling a foxhound, used for hunting hares or rabbits **2** a cross-country runner (*often in the name of athletics clubs*) [15C. < ?]

harrier[3] /hárri ər/ *n* a repeated verbal or physical attacker, or a raider or pillager of a place

Harris /hárriss/ the southern part of the island of Lewis in the Outer Hebrides, Scotland. Area: 500 sq. km/193 sq. mi.

Harris, Sir Arthur Travers (1892–1984) British air marshal. Known as **Bomber Harris**

Harris, Frank (1856–1931) British journalist and writer

Harris, Max (*b.* 1921) Australian writer and publisher

Harris, Rolf (*b.* 1930) Australian artist and entertainer

Harrisburg /hárriss burg/ capital of Pennsylvania, in the south of the state. Population: 52,376 (1990).

Harrison /hárriss'n/, **Benjamin** (1726?–91) American patriot

Harrison, Benjamin (1833–1901) US statesman and 23rd president of the United States (1889–93)

Harrison, George (*b.* 1943) British musician

Harrison, Sir Rex (1908–90) British actor

Harrison, Tony (*b.* 1937) British poet

Harrison, William Henry (1773–1841) US statesman and 9th president of the United States (1840)

Harris tweed /hárriss-/ *n* a thick woven woollen cloth traditionally made in Harris in the Western Isles of Scotland

Harrogate /hárrəgət/ town in N England. Population: 147,635 (1996 estimate).

harrow[1] /hárrō/ *n* a piece of farm equipment with sharp teeth or discs that is used to break up soil and clods of dirt and to even up a ploughed field ■ *vti* to break up land by pulling a harrow over it, or be broken up with a harrow [12C. < Old Norse *herfi.*] —**harrower** *n*

harrow[2] /hárrō/ *vt* to harry somebody or something (*archaic*)

harrowing /hárrō ing/ *adj* evoking feelings of fear, horror, or disgust ○ *harrowing scenes of hurricane devastation* —**harrowingly** *adv*

Harrow School /hárrō-/ *n* a public school for boys in NW London —**Harrovian** /hə rṓvi ən/ *n*

harrumph /hə rúmf/ *vti* **1** to make comments of criticism and displeasure, often muttering so that listeners are aware of the tone but cannot hear the exact words **2** to clear the throat or make a noise that resembles the sound of clearing the throat [Mid-20C. An imitation of the sound.]

harry /hárri/ (**-ries, -rying, -ried**) *vt* **1** to cause somebody mental, emotional, or physical distress by repeated verbal or physical attacks ○ *The crows have harried the cat so badly that it no longer goes outside.* **2** to raid or pillage an area, or a town or village, especially during a war [Old English *hergian* 'ravage' < Germanic, 'army']

harsh /haarsh/ *adj* **1 DIFFICULT TO ENDURE** difficult to live in or endure because very uncomfortable or inhospitable ○ *a rugged and harsh environment* ○ *a harsh winter* ○ *harsh prison conditions* **2 SEVERELY CRITICAL** severely scrutinizing, critical, and rigid in manner **3 PUNITIVE** extremely exacting to the point of being punitive ○ *Harsh penalties will be imposed.* **4 JARRING** jarring or unpleasant to the senses [14C. < ?] —**harshen** *vti* —**harshly** *adv* —**harshness** *n*

Harsha /haárshə/ *n* a descendant of the Guptas in India, who created a loose empire in N India between 616 and 654

harslet *n* COOK = **haslet**

hart /haart/ (*plural* **harts** *or* **hart**) *n* a male deer, especially a male red deer over five years of age [Old English *heor(o)t* < Indo-European, 'horn, head']

Hart /haart/, **Lorenz** (1895–1943) US lyricist

Hart, Pro (*b.* 1928) Australian painter. Born **Kevin Charles Hart**

hartal /haar taál, hur taál, haár taal/ *n S Asia* a closing of shops and suspending of work, especially as an indication or means of political protest [Early 20C. < Hindi *haṛtāl* 'shop locking'.]

hartebeest /haárti beest/ (*plural* **-beests** *or* **-beest**) *n* a large social antelope that is fawn to dark brown in colour, with high shoulders, a sloping back, and a long head with large ringed horns. Native to: African sub-Saharan grasslands. Genus: *Alcelaphus.* [Late 18C. < obsolete Afrikaans.]

Hartford /haártfərd/ capital of Connecticut, in the north-central part of the state. Population: 124,195 (1994).

Hartlepool /haártli pool/ seaport in NE England. Population: 92,200 (1995).

Hartley /haártli/, **David** (1732–1813) British politician and inventor

Hartnell /haártnəl/, **Norman** (1901–79) British couturier

Hartog /haár tog/, **Dirk** (*fl.* 16th-17th centuries) Dutch navigator

hart's-tongue (*plural* **hart's-tongues** *or* **hart's-tongue**) *n* an evergreen fern that has narrow undivided fronds bearing rows of spore-producing organs. Native to: Europe, Asia. *Phyllitis scolopendrium.* [< the shape of its fronds]

harum-scarum /háirəm skáirəm/ *adj* exhibiting reckless disorganized abandon [Late 17C. Probably rhyming alteration of HARE (verb) + SCARE.] —**harum-scarum** *adv*

Harun ar-Rashid /ha roón al ra shéed/ (766–809) Abbasid caliph of Baghdad

haruspex /hə rú speks/ (*plural* **-pices** /-spi seez/), **aruspex** /ə-/ (*plural* **-pices**) *n* in ancient Rome, a priest who attempted to foretell the future, especially by examining the entrails of animals [15C. < Latin.]

Harvard system /haárvərd-/ *n* a bibliographic reference system in academic publishing, in which the author and date are given in the text, and the full reference is supplied in a general list of references [After *Harvard* University, Massachusetts.]

harvest /haárvist/ *n* **1 QUANTITY OF CROP** the quantity of a crop that is gathered or ripens during a particular season ○ *a record harvest of wheat* ○ *Variations in the world harvest can be tracked to 0.1 per cent.* **2 CROP THAT IS GATHERED** the crop that is gathered or ripens during a particular season ○ *A few days of rain can destroy an entire harvest of strawberries.* **3 SEASON IN WHICH CROPS ARE GATHERED** the season during which crop plants mature and crops are gathered **4 CONSEQUENCES** the results of past or prior actions or behaviour **5 REMOVAL OF ORGAN** the removal of an organ, fluid, or tissue for transplantation, testing, or research ■ *v* **1** *vti* **GATHER CROP** to gather a crop for use or sale ○ *The wood is harvested sustainably.* **2** *vt* **GATHER NONPLANT ITEMS** to collect or gather something other than a plant crop, e.g. fish raised commercially in a hatchery **3** *vt* **REAP RESULTS** to reap the results of past or prior actions or behaviour, whether good or bad ○ *In the aftermath of a violent civil war the beleaguered people harvested nothing but sorrow.* **4** *vt* **REMOVE ORGAN** to remove an organ, fluid, or tissue for transplantation, testing, or research [Old English *hærfest* 'autumn' < Indo-European, 'gather'] —**harvestable** *adj*

harvester /haárvist ər/ *n* **1** a machine that gathers crops from the fields, especially a combine harvester **2** a gatherer of crops, especially by hand ○ *Coffee harvesters are at risk from the bites of poisonous spiders.*

harvest festival *n* a Christian service of thanksgiving after a completed harvest

harvest home *n* **1** the gathering of the harvest, especially its safe completion **2** a celebration of the completion of the harvest (*hyphenated before nouns*) ○ *a harvest-home dance*

harvestman /haárvist mən/ (*plural* **-men** /-mən/) *n* **1** *US* INSECTS = **daddy longlegs** *n.* 2 **2** an agricultural labourer, especially, before agriculture became mechanized, one who left home to find work at harvest time

harvest mite *n* the bright-red parasitic larva of a free-living mite that feeds on the skin and other tissues of mammals, including humans, causing irritation and swelling. Genera: *Trombicula* and *Neotrombicula.* US term **chigger** *n.* 1 [Because common at harvest time]

harvest moon *n* the full moon nearest to the autumnal equinox

harvest mouse *n* a small reddish-brown mouse often found in grain fields. Native to: Europe, Asia. *Micromys minutus.*

Harvey /haárvi/, **William** (1578–1657) English physician

Harwich /hárrij, -ich/ seaport in E England. Population: 15,000.

Harwood /haár wood/, **Gwen** (1920–95) Australian poet. Born **Gwendoline Nessie Foster**

Harz Mountains /haárts-/ mountain range in central Germany. Highest peak: Brocken 1,141 m/3,743 ft.

has 3rd person present singular of **have**

has-been *n* a person who formerly was popular or important but is now largely forgotten (*informal*)

Hasegawa Tohaku /hássi gaáwə tō haákoo/ (1539–1610) Japanese artist

Hašek /hásh ek/, **Jaroslav** (1883–1923) Czech writer

hash[1] /hash/ *n* **1 hash, hash mark** SYMBOL **#** the symbol #, especially on a telephone keypad or a computer keyboard. US term **pound sign** *n.* 2 **2** FRIED DISH a dish made of cooked potatoes or other vegetables, usually combined with chopped-up pieces of cooked meat, and reheated, usually by frying ○ *corned-beef hash* ■ *vt* **1** APPLY ALGORITHM TO to apply an algorithm to a character string, especially in order to find an address of a record **2** *US* CUT INTO TINY PIECES to chop meat or vegetables into tiny pieces [Late 16C. < French *hacher* 'hack, cut into small pieces' < *hache* (see HATCHET).] ◇ **make a hash of something** to do something very badly (*informal*) ○ *I made a real hash of the exam – I couldn't answer any questions.* ◇ **settle somebody's hash** to assert yourself over somebody, especially somebody hostile or troublesome (*informal*)

hash out, hash over *vt US* = **thrash out** ○ *They hashed out their differences with an arbitrator.*

hash[2] /hash/ *n* hashish (*slang*) [Mid-20C. Shortening.]

hash browns *npl US* cooked potatoes chopped up, sometimes with onions, and fried until golden brown

hasheesh *n* DRUGS = **hashish**

HaShem /hásh em/ *n* in Judaism, a substitute word used when referring to God in contexts other than prayers or scriptural readings, because the name for God is too holy for such use [< Hebrew, 'the name']

Hashemite /háshə mīt/ *n* **1** a member of an ancient Arabian dynasty that included the prophet Muhammad and claimed to be directly descended from his great-grandfather, Hashim **2** a member of a modern Arabian dynasty that traces its lineage, via the prophet Muhammad's daughter Fatima, directly to the prophet Muhammad [Late 17C. After *Hashim*, Muhammad's great-grandfather.] —**Hashemite** *adj*

hashish /háshish, há sheesh, ha sheésh/, **hasheesh** /há sheesh, ha sheésh/ *n* a purified resin, prepared from the flowering tops of the female cannabis plant, that is smoked or chewed for its narcotic and intoxicating properties and is widely illegal [Late 16C. < Arabic *ḥašīš* 'dry herb, powdered hemp'.]

hash mark *n* **1** = **hash**[1] *n.* 1 **2** a line indicating how close to a sideline a football may be at the start of a play

Hasid /hássid/ (*plural* **-sidim** /-dim/), **Hassid** (*plural* **-sidim**), **Chassid** (*plural* **-sidim**), **Chasid** (*plural* **-sidim**) *n* a member of a Jewish movement of popular mysticism founded in Eastern Europe in the 18th century [Early 19C. < Hebrew *ḥāsīḏ* 'pious'.] —**Hasidic** /ha síddik/ *adj* —**Hasidism** /ha síddizəm/ *n*

Haskalah /háskə laá/, **Haskala** *n* the Jewish enlightenment movement, originating in 18th-century Germany and aiming to integrate Jews into W European society [< Hebrew *haśkālāh* 'enlightenment']

haslet /háyzlət, házlət/, **harslet** /haárzlət/ *n* meat loaf, well seasoned with herbs, made from the offal of pigs [14C. < Old French *hastelet* 'small piece of meat roasted on a spit' < *haste* 'spit'.]

hasn't /házz'nt/ *contr* has not

hasp /haasp/ *n* a hinged metal fastening that fits over a staple and is secured by a pin, bolt, or padlock [Old English *hæpse* 'fastening' < Germanic] —**hasp** *v*

Hassan II /hə saán/ (1929–99) king of Morocco (1961–99)

~~**hassel**~~ incorrect spelling of **hassle**

Hassid *n* JUDAISM = **Hasid**

hassium /hássi əm/ *n* (*symbol* **Hs**) an extremely rare, unstable element. Source: high-energy atomic collisions. [Late 20C. < modern Latin, < Latin *Hassias* 'Hesse'.]

hassle /háss'l/ *n* a source or the experience of aggravation or annoying difficulty (*informal*) ○ *It's just not worth the hassle.* ■ *vt* (**-sles, -sling, -sled**) to bother or annoy somebody, especially by continually asking that person to do something (*informal*) ○ *Stop hassling me about washing the car.* [Late 19C. < ?]

hassock /hássək/ *n* **1** a thick firm cushion used for kneeling on, especially in church **2** a thick clump of grass **3** *US* FURNITURE = **pouf**[1] *n.* 1 [Old English *hassuc* 'clump of grass' < ?]

hast /hast/ 2nd person present singular of **have** (*archaic*)

hastate /hás tayt/ *adj* describes a leaf that is shaped like an arrowhead, with a tip pointing forwards and two sideways-pointing lobes at the base [Late 18C. < Latin *hastatus* 'armed with a spear' < *hasta* 'spear'.]

haste /hayst/ *n* great speed, especially in situations where time is limited (*formal*) ○ *Make haste, or you will be very late!* ○ *The general proceeded with haste to his headquarters.* ■ *vti* (**hastes, hasting, hasted**) to hasten (*archaic literary*) [13C. < Old French, < Germanic.] ◇ **more haste less speed** a way of saying that it is not worth rushing something because too many mistakes will be made

hasten /háyss'n/ *v* **1** *vt* SPEED SOMETHING UP to make something happen more quickly ○ *A holiday would hasten his recovery.* **2** *vi* GO SOMEWHERE QUICKLY to go somewhere quickly or without delay **3** *vi* DO SOMETHING IMMEDIATELY to do or say something without delay, often in order to correct what might otherwise be a misleading impression ○ *'But she's perfectly right', he hastened to add.*

Hastings /háystingz/ town in S England, site of the Battle of Hastings in 1066. Population: 81,139 (1991).

Hastings, Warren (1732–1818) British colonial administrator

hasty /háysti/ (**-ier, -iest**) *adj* done, taking place, or acting in a hurry because of impetuosity or lack of time ○ *a hasty marriage* —**hastily** *adv* —**hastiness** *n*

hasty pudding *n* a sweet milk pudding made with flour, semolina, or tapioca [< ?]

hat /hat/ *n* **1** a covering for the head, worn for protection from the weather or as a fashion accessory ○ *The children hung their hats and coats up when they came in.* **2** a single area of interest, knowledge, or responsibility in an individual with many interests and responsibilities ○ *She put on her accountant's hat and gave the committee some suggestions for maximizing profits.* [Old English *hæt(t)*, via Germanic, 'hood, cowl', < Indo-European, 'to cover'] —**hatted** *adj* ◇ **hang up your hat 1** to retire from work **2** to settle down to a calmer, more stable lifestyle following an extended period of stress or activity ◇ **hats off to somebody** a way of saying that somebody has gained your respect or admiration ◇ **keep something under your hat** to keep something secret ◇ **my hat** used to express disbelief or disagreement (*dated*) ◇ **pass the hat round** to collect contributions for somebody or something ◇ **pull something out of the hat** to do, accomplish, make, or get something as if by a magic trick when the resources appear to be unavailable (*informal*) ◇ **take your hat off to somebody** to acknowledge admiration or respect for somebody ○ *You have to take your hat off to her – she's stuck by him for 25 years.* ◇ **talk through your hat** to talk nonsense (*informal*) ○ *You're talking through your hat, and I don't take a word of it seriously.* ◇ **throw your hat into the ring** to volunteer to take part in a particular contest ○ *I didn't think I'd get the job, but I decided to throw my hat into the ring anyway.*

hatband /hát band/ *n* a thin strip of leather, cloth, ribbon, or other material that is fixed round a hat just above the brim

hatbox /hát boks/ *n* a large hard box with a removable or liftable lid, used for storing, carrying, and protecting a hat or hats

hatch[1] /hach/ *n* **1** a door cut into the floor or ceiling of something, especially on a boat or an aircraft **2** a small connecting hole in a wall between two rooms, or the small doors that cover this hole ○ *an escape hatch* ○ *There's a serving hatch between the kitchen and the living room.* **3** CARS = **hatchback** [Old English *hæcc* 'lower half of a door, wicket' < Germanic]

hatch[2] /hach/ *v* **1** *vi* BREAK OPEN FOR RELEASE OF YOUNG to break open so that the young inside may be released **2** *vi* COME OUT OF EGG to emerge from an egg **3** *vt* CAUSE YOUNG TO EMERGE FROM EGG to cause a young organism, e.g. a chick, fish, or insect, to emerge from its egg ○ *Birds hatch their chicks by sitting on the nests.* **4** *vt* SECRETLY DEVISE A PLOT to secretly devise a plot, plan, or scheme, usually an illicit or illegal one, or one that is ill-advised in some way ■ *n* YOUNG ORGANISMS NEWLY HATCHED a group of young organisms, e.g. chicks, fish, or insects, that have just recently emerged from eggs ○ *This hatch contains more males than females.* [15C. < ?]

hatch[3] /hach/ *vti* in graphic art, to mark or cover something with parallel crossed lines to show shading, or be marked in this way [15C. < French *hacher* 'to chop' < *hache* (see HATCHET).] —**hatching** *n*

hatchback /hách bak/ *n* a car with a rear door that is hinged from the roof to allow easy access to storage space behind the rear seats

hatchery /háchəri/ (*plural* **-ies**) *n* a place where fish or poultry eggs are hatched commercially under artificial conditions ○ *a fish hatchery*

hatchet /háchit/ *n* a small axe that can be used with one hand ○ *wield a hatchet* [14C. < French *hachette* 'small axe' < *hache* 'axe' < medieval Latin *hapia* < Germanic.] ◇ **bury the hatchet** to make peace with somebody after a disagreement ○ *They fell out years ago, but it looks as if they've finally decided to bury the hatchet.* ◇ **do a hatchet job on somebody** *or* **something** criticize somebody or something severely, especially in print (*informal*) ○ *The reviewer did a hatchet job on the author of the novel.*

hatchet face *n* an unpleasantly long thin face with sharp or gaunt features —**hatchet-faced** *adj*

hatchet man *n* **1** a person who is employed to do something unpopular, especially to make cuts in staff or funding (*informal*) **2** *US, Can* a hired killer (*slang*)

hatchling /háchling/ *n* a bird, fish, insect, or other organism that has just hatched from an egg

hatchment /háchmənt/ *n* a diamond-shaped panel bearing the coat of arms of somebody who has died [Early 16C. Probably < obsolete French *hachement*, alteration of Old French *acesmement* 'adornment' < *acesmer* 'adorn'.]

hatchway /hách way/ *n* = **hatch**[1] *n.* 2

hate /hayt/ *v* (**hates, hating, hated**) **1** *vt* DISLIKE INTENSELY to dislike somebody or something intensely, often in a way that evokes feelings of anger, hostility, or animosity ○ *Love her or hate her, you have to admit she's got a great singing voice.* ○ *Having come to hate her husband, the defendant admits that she attempted to poison him.* **2** *vti* HAVE STRONG DISTASTE FOR to have strong distaste or aversion for something, somebody, or something that has to be done ○ *I hate this show; it's so boring.* ○ *They hate cleaning out the stable every day.* ○ *I hate to say it, but I know we're going to lose.* ■ *n* **1** FEELING OF INTENSE DISLIKE a feeling of intense dislike, anger, hostility, or animosity ○ *You could see the hate in his eyes.* **2** SOMETHING HATED something that is hated [Old English *hete* (noun), *hatian* (verb) < Indo-European] —**hateable** *adj* —**hated** *adj* —**hater** *n*

SYNONYMS See ***dislike***.

hate crime *n* a crime that is motivated by hate, prejudice, or intolerance of somebody's race, religion, ethnicity, or sexual orientation ○ *the target of a hate crime*

hateful /háyt f'l/ *adj* **1** characterized by malevolence or spite **2** eliciting feelings or reactions of hatred, detestation, or abhorrence —**hatefully** *adv* —**hatefulness** *n*

hate mail *n* mail that expresses the sender's anger about something, usually towards the recipient, in a threatening or offensive way

Hatfield /hát feeld/ town in SE England. Population: 31,104 (1991).

hatful /hát fōōl/ *n* a large quantity or number of something ○ *received a hatful of compliments on the performance*

hath /hath/ 3rd person present singular of **have** (*archaic*)

Hathaway /háthə way/, **Anne** (1556–1623) wife of William Shakespeare

hatha yoga /háthə-, hútta-/ *n* a low-impact yoga that helps to regulate breathing by exercises consisting of postures and stretches intended to sustain healthy bodily functioning and induce emotional calmness [< Sanskrit, 'force yoga']

hatpin /hát pin/ *n* a long thin pin, often with a decoration at the end, that is pushed through a hat and into the hair to keep the hat securely on the head

hatred /háytrid/ *n* a feeling of intense dislike, anger, hostility, or animosity [12C. < HATE + suffix < Old English *rǣden* 'state, condition'.]

SYNONYMS See ***dislike***.

Hatshepsut /hát shép soot/ (1520?–1483? BC) queen of Egypt (1503? –1483? BC)

hat stand *n* a tall free-standing piece of furniture consisting of a base with a pole fixed into it with hooks round the top on which hats, coats, and umbrellas can be hung

hatter /háttər/ *n* a maker or seller of hats

Hatteras, Cape /háttərəss/ promontory in E North Carolina, renowned for treacherous weather conditions

Hattersley /háttərzli/, **Roy, Lord** (*b.* 1932) British politician

hat trick *n* a series of three wins or successes, especially three goals scored by the same player in a game of football [Probably < the former cricketing practice of awarding a hat to a bowler who took three wickets with three consecutive balls]

hauberk /háw burk/ *n* a long, often sleeveless, tunic made of chain mail [13C. < Old French *hau(s)berc* < Germanic, 'neck-protector'.]

haugh /haw, haakh/ *n Scotland* a low-lying stretch of land in a river valley, often unproductive because of frequent flooding [Probably < Old English *healh* 'corner, nook, small hollow in a slope']

Haughey /háwhi/, **Charles** (*b.* 1925) Irish statesman

haughty /háwti/ (**-tier, -tiest**) *adj* behaving in a superior, condescending, or arrogant way ○ *She always took a haughty tone with the landlady.* [Mid-16C. < archaic *haught* < French *haut(e)* 'high'.] —**haughtily** *adv* —**haughtiness** *n*

haul /hawl/ *v* **1** *vt* **MOVE WITH EFFORT** to transport something that is heavy and bulky from one place to another **2** *vt* **DRAG** to pull or drag something with continuous and laborious movements **3** *vt* **CHANGE COURSE** to change a vessel's course so as to sail closer to the wind **4** *vi* **BLOW CLOSER TO BOW** to blow from a direction that is closer to a vessel's bow **5** *vt* **HOIST INTO DRY DOCK** to hoist a vessel from the water into a dry dock, e.g. to make repairs ■ *n* **1 STOLEN ITEMS** goods that have been stolen, or the value of these stolen goods ○ *The haul was mainly silver and paintings.* **2 CONFISCATED CONTRABAND** illegal goods that are confiscated by the authorities **3 SINGLE CATCH OF FISH** the amount of fish caught in a single catch **4 DISTANCE SOMETHING IS TRANSPORTED** a distance over which something is transported or pulled, or which somebody travels with difficulty [13C. Variant of HALE[2].]

SYNONYMS See *pull*.

haul off *vi* to manoeuvre a vessel in order to avoid something

haul up *vt* to force somebody to appear before a court or some other disciplinary body for judgment

haulage /háwlij/ *n* **1** the business or process of transporting goods, usually by road or rail **2** the cost of transporting goods, or the rate charged for transporting goods

hauler /háwlər/ *n US* TRANSP = **haulier**

haulier /háwli ər/ *n* a person or company whose business is transporting goods, especially by road. US term **hauler**

haulm /hawm/, **halm** *n* **1** the stems or stalks of grain, beans, peas, potatoes, or grasses, especially after harvesting. Use: thatching, litter. **2** a single stem of grain, beans, peas, potatoes, or grasses [Old English *h(e)alm* < Indo-European]

haunch /hawnch/ *n* **1 HIP, BUTTOCK, AND UPPER THIGH** the part of the body comprising the hip, buttock, and upper thigh ○ *She sat back on her haunches.* **2 ANIMAL LEG** one of the back legs of a four-legged animal, either when it is alive, or as a cut of meat **3 UPPER PART OF ARCH** the upper curving part of either side of an arch [12C. < French *hanche* < Germanic.]

haunt /hawnt/ *vt* **1 APPEAR TO SOMEBODY AS A GHOST** to frequent a place or appear to somebody in the form of a ghost or other supposed supernatural being **2 DISCOMFIT BY UNPLEASANT REMINDERS** to cause somebody unease, worry, or regret by continual presence or recurrence in his or her life ○ *haunted by doubt* **3 VISIT CONTINUALLY** to go often to a place ○ *She no longer haunts the late-night bars* ■ *n* **PLACE SOMEBODY OFTEN VISITS** a place that somebody likes and often visits ○ *a holiday away from the usual tourist haunts* [12C. < French *hanter* 'frequent a place' < Germanic, 'home'.] —**haunter** *n*

haunted /háwntid/ *adj* **1** inhabited by or visited regularly by a ghost or other supposed supernatural being **2** looking strangely frightened or worried

haunting /háwnting/ *adj* evoking strong emotion, especially a sense of sadness, that persists for a long time ○ *a haunting testament to war's destruction* —**hauntingly** *adv*

Hauraki Gulf /how raáki-/ inlet of Pacific Ocean in the NE of the North Island, New Zealand. Area: 2,290 sq. km/884 sq. mi.

Hausa /hówssə/ (*plural* **-sa** *or* **-sas**) *n* **1 MEMBER OF W AFRICAN PEOPLE** a member of a people living mainly in N Nigeria and S Niger **2 LANGUAGE OF W AFRICA** a language spoken in Nigeria, Niger, and other parts of E West Africa, belonging to the Chadic branch of Afro-Asiatic. Native speakers: 25 million. Other speakers: 40 million. **3 SPIRITUAL TRADITION OF NIGERIA** the tradition combining elements of Islam and of local religious beliefs associated with the Hausa [Early 19C. < Hausa.] —**Hausa** *adj*

hausfrau /hówss frow/ (*plural* **-fraus**) *n* a traditional housewife, conventionally believed to be interested mostly in her home and family (*offensive in some contexts*) ○ *She wanted a career, not a life as a hausfrau.* [Late 18C. < German, < *Haus* 'house' + *Frau* 'wife, woman'.]

Hausmann /hówssmən/, **Raoul** (1886–1970) Austrian poet and artist

Haussmann /óss man/, **George-Eugène, Baron** (1809–91) French town planner

haustellum /haw stélləm/ (*plural* **-la** /-lə/) *n* the tip of the proboscis, or elongated mouthpart, that is adapted for sucking food in many insects, e.g. flies [Early 19C. < modern Latin, 'small scoop' < Latin *haustrum* 'scoop' < *haurire* 'draw up'.]

haustorium /haw stáwri əm/ (*plural* **-a** /-i ə/) *n* a food-absorbing structure of a parasitic plant or fungus [Late 19C. < Latin *haustor* 'water-drawer, drinker' < *haurire* 'draw up'.]

hautboy /ó boy, hó-/ (*plural* **-boys**), **hautbois** (*plural* **-bois**) *n* **1** a strawberry with large fruit. Native to: Europe, Asia. *Fragaria moschata*. **2** an oboe (*archaic*) [Mid-16C. < French *hautbois* 'oboe' < *haut* 'high' (from its high pitch) + *bois* 'wood' < Germanic.]

haute couture /ót-/ *n* exclusive and expensive clothing made for an individual customer by a fashion designer, or the industry that produces such clothing [Early 20C. < French, 'high dressmaking'.]

haute cuisine /ót-/ *n* classic high-quality French cooking (*hyphenated before nouns*) [Early 20C. < French, 'high cooking'.]

haute école /ót ay kol/ *n* the skill and art of expert horsemanship [Mid-19C. < French, 'high school'.]

hauteur /ō túr/ *n* a haughty manner, feeling, or quality [Early 17C. < French, < *haute* 'high' < Latin *altus*.]

haut monde /ó mónd/ *n* the highest stratum of society, international or domestic, and those in it ○ *a denizen of the haut monde, invited to every international ball and gala* [Mid-19C. < French, 'high world'.]

Havana[1] /hə vánnə/ capital, port, and largest city of Cuba, on the northwestern coast of the country. Population: 2,241,000 (1995). —**Havanan** *adj, n*

Havana[2], **Havana cigar** *n* a high-quality cigar made in Cuba

Havant /hávvənt/ seaside town S England. Population: 46,510 (1991).

Havarti /hə vaárti/ *n* a moist pale semi-hard mild Danish cheese with tiny holes and a slightly rubbery texture [Mid-20C. After the farm of a 19C Danish cheese maker.]

havdalah *n* = **habdalah**

have (*stressed*) /hav/; (*unstressed*) /həv, əv/ (**has** (*stressed*) /haz/; (*unstressed*) /həz, əz/, **having, had** /had/, **had** (*stressed*) /had/; (*unstressed*) /həd, əd/) CORE MEANING: a verb indicating that somebody possesses something, either materially or as a characteristic or attribute ○ *She has a small cottage in the country.* ○ *He has beautiful eyes.*

1 *vt* **OWN** to be the owner or possessor of something ○ *I don't have a lot of money.* **2** *vt* **POSSESS A CHARACTERISTIC** to be the possessor of a quality or characteristic ○ *She had long blonde hair.* **3** *v* **FORMS PERFECT TENSES** used to form the following tenses or aspects: the present perfect, the past perfect, the future perfect, and the continuous forms of these (*before the past participle of a verb or at the beginning of a question, or with 'got' to indicate possession*) ○ *I have finished my dinner, thank you.* ○ *Have you finished yet?* ○ *I have got a new car.* **4** *v* **EXPRESSES COMPULSION** expresses compulsion, obligation, or necessity ○ *We have to do the economic analysis.* **5** *v* **EXPRESSES CERTAINTY** expresses conviction or certainty ○ *There just has to be a solution to the problem.* **6** *vt* **RECEIVE** to receive or obtain something ○ *I had a Christmas card from him.* **7** *vt* **EAT** to eat or drink something ○ *We have breakfast at eight.* **8** *vt* **THINK OF** to think of something, or hold something in the mind ○ *Listen! I have a good idea.* **9** *vt* **EXPERIENCE** to experience or undergo something ○ *He went to the carnival to have a good time.* ○ *I had a shock.* **10** *vt* **BE AFFECTED BY** to be affected by something, especially something of a medical nature ○ *I've had the flu for the last week.* **11** *vt* **ENGAGE IN** to engage or participate in something ○ *We had a long talk about cars.* **12** *vt* **ARRANGE** to organize or arrange something ○ *We had a party last week.* **13** *vt* **ARRANGE FOR SOMETHING TO BE DONE** to arrange for somebody to do something for you or on your behalf ○ *I've just had my hair cut.* **14** *vt* **TOLERATE** to tolerate or put up with something (*usually in negative statements*) ○ *I won't have such behaviour any longer!* **15** *vt* **RECEIVE** to receive somebody as a guest ○ *We had Mother to stay over Christmas.* **16** *vt* **BRING A CHILD INTO EXISTENCE** to be the parent of a child, or conceive, carry, or give birth to a child ○ *She's had three children and now she's having another one.* **17** *vt* **PUT SOMEWHERE** to put or place somebody or something in a particular place ○ *I'll have you two in the front row, please.* **18** *vt* **UNDERGO** to be the victim of an unpleasant action or experience ○ *I had my car stolen.* **19** *vt* **MAKE HAPPEN** to direct or cause somebody to do something, or cause something to happen ○ *If you see him tomorrow, have him call me.* **20** *vt* **CHEAT** to cheat or outwit somebody (*usually passive*) ○ *I think you've been had in this deal.* **21** *npl* **haves PRIVILEGED PEOPLE** people who are rich and privileged, especially compared with those who are not [Old English *habban* < Indo-European, 'grasp'] ◇ **have it** to declare or assert something ○ *Rumour has it that they are planning to get engaged.* ◇ **have had it 1** to have no prospect of success **2** to be too worn out, damaged, or exhausted to function properly (*informal*) ○ *I'm afraid this printer has just about had it.* ◇ **have had it with somebody** *or* **something** to have lost patience with somebody *or* something ◇ **have (got) it in for somebody** to dislike somebody and want to do that person harm ○ *Ever since I got the job the boss has had it in for me.* ◇ **have something on somebody** to have unfavourable information about somebody's activities ◇ **have it out (with somebody)** to engage in a spirited, aggressive argument over an issue with somebody ○ *OK, let's have it out now and get this settled once and for all.* ◇ **have to do with 1** to be relevant to ○ *Does your question have anything to do with the topic under discussion?* **2** to have a friendship or relationship with ○ *She will have nothing to do with him any more.* ◇ **have what it takes** to have the necessary skills, personality, or attitude to be successful at something ○ *He doesn't really have what it takes to be a professional actor.* ◇ **not having any (of something)** refusing to take part or become involved in something ○ *They tried to involve him in the conspiracy, but it soon became clear that he wasn't having any.*

USAGE See *do*.

have on *v* **1** *vt* to have an article of clothing on your body **2** *vt* to tell somebody something untrue as a joke or tease (*informal*)

have up *vt* to cause somebody to appear for trial (*informal*) ○ *He was had up for breaking and entering.*

Havel /haáv'l, hávv'l/, **Václav** (*b.* 1936) Czech statesman and dramatist

havelock /háv lok/ *n* a light-coloured cover for a soldier's cap, with a flap extending over the back of the neck to protect the head and neck from the sun [Mid-19C. After Sir Henry *Havelock* (1795–1857), British major-general.]

haven /háyv'n/ *n* **1** a place sought for rest, shelter, or protection ○ *a haven for wildlife* **2** a harbour or port facility where ships and boats come in and tie up (*literary*) [Pre-12C. < Old Norse *höfn* 'place that holds (ships)'.]

have-nots *npl* people who are not rich or privileged, especially compared with those who are ○ *a country with the highest income inequality between the haves and have-nots*

haven't /hávv'nt/ *contr* have not

haver /háyvər/ *n, interj* **haver, havers** *Scotland, N England* **NONSENSE** nonsense ■ *vi* **1 VACILLATE** to be unable to make a choice or come to a decision **2** *Scotland, N England* **TALK NONSENSE** to talk nonsense [Early 18C. < ?]

Haverfordwest /hávvərfərd wést, haárfərd-/ town in SW Wales. Population: 13,454 (1991).

haversack /hávvər sak/ *n* a strong bag carried on the back or the shoulder, used especially by travellers or hikers [Mid-18C. Via French *havresac* < obsolete German *Habersack* < *Haber* 'oats' + *Sack* 'bag'.]

Haversian canal /hə vúrsh'n-, hə vúrssi ən-/ *n* a tiny longitudinal channel in bone tissue [Mid-19C. After Clopton *Havers* (1650?-1702), English physician and anatomist.]

Haversian system *n* a Haversian canal along with the concentric layers of compact bone surrounding it

haversine /hávvər sīn/ *n* in mathematics, half the value of the versed sine [Late 19C. Contraction of *half versed sine*.]

havildar /hávv'l daar/ n S Asia an army or police officer of a rank equivalent to sergeant [Late 17C. Via Urdu hawildār < Persian hawāl(a)dār 'charge holder'.]

havoc /hávvak/ n **1 DEVASTATION** widespread damage, destruction, or devastation ○ the havoc wreaked by the storm **2 CHAOS** a condition or situation of disruptive chaos ■ adj Malaysia, Singapore **DIFFICULT TO CONTROL** difficult to control, manage, discipline, or govern (informal) ○ Her kids look really havoc! [15C. < Anglo-Norman (crier) havok '(to cry) havoc', signal to an army to seize plunder, alteration of Old French havo(t) 'pillage'.]

Havre de Grace /hávvar da gráss/ city in NE Maryland. Population: 10,092 (1996).

haw[1] /haw/ n **1 PLANTS** = **hawthorn 2** the round or oval fruit of the hawthorn, usually red or yellow and containing seeds [Old English haga < ?]

haw[2] /haw/ n a sound that people make when they are hesitating to speak ■ vi to make a sound indicative of hesitation while speaking [Mid-17C. An imitation of the sound.]

haw[3] /haw/ n VET = **nictitating membrane** [Early 16C. < ?]

haw[4] /haw/ interj used to command an animal or a team of animals to turn left [Late 17C. < ?]

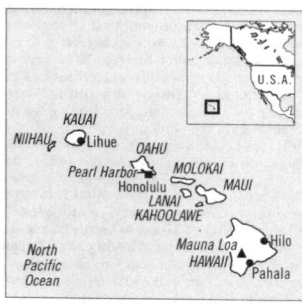
Hawaii

Hawaii /ha wí i/ **1** state of the United States in the N Pacific Ocean, consisting of eight main islands and over 100 others. Capital: Honolulu. Population: 1,183,723 (1997). Area: 16,729 sq. km/6,459 sq. mi. **2** largest island in the state of Hawaii. Population: 120,317 (1990). Area: 10,443 sq. km/4,028 sq. mi. —**Hawaiian** n, adj

Hawaii-Aleutian Standard Time n the standard time in the time zone centred on longitude 150° W, which covers an area of the Pacific Ocean that includes Hawaii and the W Aleutian Islands

Hawaiian appliqué n an appliqué in which a large central motif, from a design cut from folded paper, is applied to a foundation fabric and made into a quilt

Hawaiian English n a variety of English spoken in Hawaii

Hawaiian goose n BIRDS = **nene**

Hawaiian guitar n a small steel-strung guitar with a sliding glass or metal bar that fits across the strings in order to change the pitch of the whole instrument

Hawaii Standard Time, Hawaii Time n = **Hawaii-Aleutian Standard Time**

haway /ha wáy/ interj N England used as a greeting (informal)

Haweswater /háwz wawtar/ lake in NW England, now enlarged and used as a reservoir. Area: 3.8 sq. km/1.5 sq. mi.

hawfinch /háw finch/ (plural **-finches** or **-finch**) n a bird with a thick conical silvery beak, brown plumage, black-and-white wings, and a white-tipped tail. Native to: Europe, Asia. Coccothraustes coccothraustes. [< HAW[1]]

haw-haw[1] interj = **ha-ha**[1]
haw-haw[2] n = **ha-ha**[2]

Hawick /hoyk/ town in SE Scotland in the Scottish Borders district. Population: 15,812 (1991).

hawk[1] /hawk/ n **1 BIRD OF PREY** a diurnal bird of prey, typically having broad wings, a short hooked bill, strong talons, and a long tail. Subfamilies: Accipitridae and Buteoninae. **2 SOMEBODY FAVOURING FORCE** a person who favours the use of military force in implementing foreign policy. ◊ **dove**[1] n. **2 3 AGGRESSIVE COMPETITOR** a fiercely competitive, aggressive, predatory, or com-

bative person ○ a marketing hawk who wanted to put the competition out of business ■ v **1** vi **HUNT WITH HAWKS** to hunt for prey on the wing, or hunt for prey using hawks and similar birds of prey **2** vti **ATTACK ON THE WING** to pursue or attack while flying in a way similar to that of a hawk ○ big brown bats hawking at small prey ○ tiny birds hawking insects in the morning sky [Old English h(e)afoc < Indo-European, 'grasp'] —**hawker** n —**hawking** n —**hawkish** adj —**hawkishly** adv —**hawkishness** n

hawk[2] /hawk/ v **1** vi **CLEAR THE THROAT** to clear the throat noisily of phlegm **2** vt **COUGH UP PHLEGM** to clear the throat and noisily cough up phlegm ■ n **1 ATTEMPT AT CLEARING THROAT** a noisy attempt to clear the throat of phlegm **2 SALIVA OR PHLEGM** saliva or phlegm, especially when somebody spits it out [Late 16C. Probably an imitation of the sound.]

hawk[3] /hawk/ vti to engage in selling merchandise on the street or from door to door [14C. Probably back-formation < hawker, probably < Middle Low German höker < höken 'peddle'.] —**hawker** n

hawk[4] /hawk/ n a metal square with a wooden handle underneath, used by a plasterer to hold wet plaster or mortar before applying it to a surface [15C. < ?]

hawkbill n ZOOL = **hawksbill**

hawkbit /háwk bit/ (plural **-bits** or **-bit**) n a perennial plant with lobed leaves. Flowers: yellow. Native to: grasslands. Genus: Leontodon. [Early 18C. Blend of HAWKWEED + devil's bit.]

Hawke /hawk/, **Bob** (b. 1929) Australian politician. Full name **Robert James Lee Hawke**

Hawke Bay inlet of the South Pacific Ocean on the eastern coast of the North Island, New Zealand

Hawker /háwkar/, **Harry George** (1889–1921) Australian aviator

Hawke's Bay /háwks-/ administrative region of New Zealand. Population: 144,292 (1996). Area: 21,178 sq. km/8,177 sq. mi.

Hawkesbury /háwksbari/ river in E New South Wales, Australia. Length: 480 km/300 mi.

hawk-eyed adj quick to see things that are not obvious, often as a result of having very keen eyesight ○ The hawk-eyed appraiser spotted a tiny chip in the antique teapot.

Hawking /háwking/, **Stephen** (b. 1942) British physicist and mathematician

Hawkins /háwkinz/, **Coleman** (1904–69) US jazz musician

hawk moth n a moth with a thick body and long narrow wings that enable it to hover over flowers and feed on their nectar. Family: Sphingidae.

hawk owl n an owl with a long slender tail and brownish speckled plumage that resembles a hawk when in flight. Native to: North America, Europe, Asia. Surnia ulula.

Hawks /hawks/, **Howard** (1896–1977) US film director

hawk's beard (plural **hawk's beards** or **hawk's beard**) n a composite plant with milky juice. Flowers: small, yellow, resembling the dandelion. Genus: Crepis.

hawksbill /háwks bil/ (plural **-bills** or **-bill**), **hawksbill turtle, hawkbill** (plural **-bills** or **-bill**) n a tropical sea turtle, reaching 61 cm/2 ft in length that has a yellowish-brown shell of overlapping plates. Eretmochelys imbricata. [< the shape of its mouth]

hawk's-eye n a semiprecious stone that is a dark blue variety of crocidolite. Use: gems.

Hawksmoor /háwks moor, -mawr/, **Nicholas** (1661–1736) British architect

hawkweed /háwk weed/ (plural **-weed** or **-weeds**) n a composite, typically hairy, plant. Flowers: yellow or orange, rayed. Genus: Hieracium.

Haworth /hów arth/ village in N England. Population: 4,956 (1991).

Haworth, Sir Norman (1883–1950) British biochemist

haworthia /haw wáwrthi a/ (plural **-as** or **-a**) n a succulent herb with densely overlapping, often warty leaves, clustered in rosettes. Native to: southern Africa. Genus: Haworthia. [After Adrian Hardy Haworth (1768–1833), writer on succulent plants]

hawse /hawz/ n **1 LOCATION OF SHIP'S HAWSEHOLES** the area of a ship in which the hawseholes are to be found **2** = **hawsehole 3 SPACE BETWEEN BOW AND ANCHOR** the space between the bow and the anchors of a ship lying at anchor **4 ANCHOR DEPLOYMENT** the way in which a ship's anchor lines are deployed, starboard and port, when

both are deployed together at the same time ■ vi (**hawses, hawsing, hawsed**) **PITCH VIOLENTLY WHEN AT ANCHOR** to pitch violently when lying at anchor [13C < Old Norse hals, Old English h(e)als 'neck, ship's prow' < Indo-European, 'revolve']

hawsehole /háwz hōl/ n an opening in the bow of a ship through which a large heavy line is passed for towing or mooring the ship

hawsepipe /háwz pīp/ n a pipe on each side of a ship's bow for use in deploying and weighing anchor, with the anchor lines running through each pipe

hawser /háwzar/ n a large heavy cable that is used when mooring or towing a ship [13C. < Anglo-Norman haucer < Old French haucier 'to hoist' < Latin altus 'high'.]

hawser-laid adj describes rope composed of three strands made by being twisted in a left-handed direction that have then been twisted together in a right-handed direction

hawthorn /háw thawrn/ n a thorny shrub or tree of the rose family with white or pink flowers and reddish berries. Genus: Crataegus.

Nathaniel Hawthorne

Hawthorne /háw thawrn/, **Nathaniel** (1804–64) US writer. Born **Nathaniel Hathorne**

Hawthorne effect /háw thawrn-/ n social research findings attributable to the attention of researchers to the subjects of their research rather than to factors significant to the research topic [Mid-20C. After a plant of the Western Electric Company in Cicero (Chicago, Illinois).]

hay /hay/ n **CUT AND DRIED GRASS** grass or other plants that are cut, dried, and then often used as fodder ○ a bale of hay ■ v **1** vi **CUT AND STORE HAY** to mow hay and bale or roll it, and then store it ○ He's been haying all day. **2** vt **FEED WITH HAY** to feed animals with hay [Old English hēg 'something that can be cut down' < Indo-European, 'hew, strike'] ◇ **hit the hay** to go to bed (informal) ○ We hit the hay at nine, completely exhausted. ◇ **make hay while the sun shines** to take advantage of opportunities when they present themselves (informal)

haybox /háy boks/ n an insulated box, originally filled with hay, used to allow food that has been boiled to finish cooking without more fuel

haycock /háy kok/ n a cone-shaped pile of hay that is left in a field until it is dry enough to be stored

Hayden /háyd'n/, **Bill** (b. 1933) Australian statesman. Full name **William George Hayden**

Hay diet /háy-/ n a way of eating in which protein and carbohydrate foods are not eaten at the same time, claimed to be helpful for digestive complaints and weight loss [Mid-20C. After William Howard Hay (1866–1940), who devised it.]

Haydn /híd'n/, **Joseph** (1732–1809) Austrian composer

Hayek /hí ek/, **Friedrich A. von** (1899–1992) Austrian-born British economist

Hayes /hayz/, **Rutherford B.** (1822–93) US statesman and 19th president of the United States (1877–81)

hay fever n an allergic reaction to pollen that irritates the upper respiratory tract and the eyes, resulting in symptoms including a runny and itchy nose, itchy and watering eyes, and sneezing. Technical name **pollinosis**

hayfork /háy fawrk/ n **1** AGRIC = **pitchfork** n. **2** a machine-operated fork for moving hay

haylage /háy lij/ n silage made from partially dried grass [Mid-20C. Blend of HAY + SILAGE.]

hayloft /háy loft/ *n* a loft for storing hay over a stable or a barn

haymaker /háy maykər/ *n* **1 WORKER PROCESSING HAY** an agricultural worker whose job it is to cut, turn, toss, spread, or carry hay after it has been mown **2 MACHINE PROCESSING HAY** a machine for breaking down stems of hay to improve the drying process **3 POWERFUL SWINGING PUNCH** a powerful swinging punch, especially in a boxing match (*slang*) **4 SWEEPING STROKE WITH BAT** in cricket, a sweeping stroke with the bat

haymow /háy mō/ *n* **1** = **hayloft 2** a quantity of hay stored in a barn or loft

hayrack /háy rak/ *n* **1 RACK HOLDING FEED** a rack that holds hay and from which livestock feed **2 RACK ON CART** a rack attached to a cart to increase its capacity for carrying hay **3 CART WITH HAYRACK** a cart fitted with a hayrack

hayrick /háy rik/ *n* = **haystack**

hayride /háy rīd/ *n US* a ride taken for pleasure by a group of people in a wagon or other vehicle that is full of hay or straw

hayseed /háy seed/ *n* **1 GRASS SEED FROM HAY** grass seed that is shaken out of hay **2 PIECES OF GRASS** pieces of grass or straw that fall from hay **3** *US, Can* **OFFENSIVE TERM** an offensive term that deliberately insults somebody's rural base or background and his or her intelligence and level of sophistication (*informal insult*)

haystack /háy stak/ *n* a large pile of hay, especially one that is built in the open and covered with thatch for winter storage

Haywards Heath /háywərdz héeth/ town in S England. Population: 28,923 (1991).

haywire /háy wīr/ *adj* functioning erratically or not functioning at all (*informal*) ○ *A powerful magnet can make the television set go haywire.* [< the springy nature of wire used to tie up bundles of hay, and sometimes for makeshift repairs]

Hayworth /háywərth/, **Rita** (1918–87) US actor. Born **Margarita Carmen Cansino**

hazan *n* JUDAISM = **hazzan**

hazard /hάzzərd/ *n* **1 POTENTIAL DANGER** something that is potentially very dangerous **2 DANGEROUS OUTCOME** a dangerous or otherwise unwanted outcome, especially one resulting from the failure of an engineered system **3 DICE GAME** a dice game resembling craps **4 OBSTACLE ON GOLF COURSE** a natural or constructed obstacle on a golf course, e.g. a bunker or a lake **5 RECEIVER'S SIDE IN REAL TENNIS** in real tennis, the receiver's side of the court **6 SCORING STROKE IN BILLIARDS** a scoring stroke in billiards, made when a ball is pocketed, either a ball other than the striker's (**winning hazard**) or the striker's cue ball itself (**losing hazard**) ■ *vt* **1 SUGGEST TENTATIVELY** to offer a tentative explanation of something ○ *Would anyone like to hazard a guess as to what this could possibly mean?* **2 RISK LOSS OF** to chance or risk something, especially in order to gain something else [13C. Via Old French *hasard* 'game of chance played with dice' < Arabic *az-zahr* 'the dice, the chance'.]

hazard light *n* either of a pair of car lights, usually the indicators, that flash on and off to warn other drivers of potential danger

hazardous /hάzzərdəss/ *adj* potentially dangerous to beings or the environment —**hazardously** *adv* —**hazardousness** *n*

hazardous waste *n* a byproduct of manufacturing processes or nuclear processing that is toxic and presents a potential threat to people and the environment

hazard pay *n US* = **danger money**

hazard warning light *n* = **hazard light**

haze /hayz/ *n* **1 PARTICLES IN THE ATMOSPHERE** mist, cloud, or smoke suspended in the atmosphere and obscuring or obstructing the view **2 VAGUE OBSCURING FACTOR** something that is vague and serves to obscure something **3 DISORIENTED STATE** a mental or physical state or condition when feelings and perceptions are vague, disorienting, or obscured ■ *vi* (**hazes, hazing, hazed**) **BECOME SATURATED WITH PARTICLES** to become filled with suspended atmospheric particulate matter such as pollution ○ *It's going to be hot and muggy and in the afternoon it will begin to haze over.* [Early 18C. Probably back-formation < HAZY.]

hazel /háyz'l/ (*plural* **-zels** *or* **-zel**) *n* **1 SMALL TREE WITH EDIBLE NUTS** a shrub or small tree of the birch family with edible brown nuts. Genus: *Corylus.* **2 WOOD OF HAZEL** the wood of the hazel tree. Use: baskets, hurdles. **3** FOOD = **hazelnut 4 LIGHT BROWN COLOUR** a light-brown colour with a tinge of green or gold, like a ripe hazelnut [Old English *hæsel* < Indo-European] —**hazel** *adj*

hazelnut /háyz'l nut/ *n* an edible nut from a hazel tree

Hazlitt /hάzlit/, **William** (1778–1830) British essayist

HAZMAT /hάz mat/, **haz/mat** *abbr* hazardous material

hazy /háyzi/ (**-ier, -iest**) *adj* **1 VISUALLY OBSCURED** unclear, especially because partially obscured or obstructed by mist, cloud, or smoke **2 IMPRECISE** not specific or clearly remembered **3 NOT KNOWLEDGEABLE** showing a lack of understanding or knowledge [Early 17C. < ?] —**hazily** *adv* —**haziness** *n*

hazzan /haáz'n, khə zaán/ (*plural* **-zanim** /hə zaánim, khə-/ *or* **-zans**), **hazan** (*plural* **-zanim** /hə zaánim, khə-/ *or* **-zans**), **chazan** (*plural* **-zanim** /hə zaánim, khə-/ *or* **-zans**) *n* **1** a Jewish religious official who is the chief singer of the liturgy in a synagogue **2** a cantor in a synagogue [Mid-17C. < Hebrew *ḥazzān* 'cantor'.]

Hazzard /hάzzərd/, **Shirley** (*b.* 1931) Australian-born US writer

Hb *abbr* haemoglobin

HB *abbr* hard black (*of pencil lead*)

H-beam *n* a structural steel member shaped like an H in section

HBM *abbr* **1** Her Britannic Majesty **2** His Britannic Majesty

H-bomb *n* = **hydrogen bomb**

HC *abbr* House of Commons

HCF, hcf *abbr* highest common factor

HCG *abbr* human chorionic gonadotrophin

⚡**HCI** *abbr* human-computer interaction

hd *abbr* **1** hand **2** head

⚡**HD** *abbr* **1** hard disk **2** heavy-duty **3** high density **4** hard drive

HDL *abbr* high-density lipoprotein

HDT *abbr* Hawaii Daylight Time

HDTV *abbr* high-definition television

he[1] (*stressed*) /hee/; (*unstressed*) /hi, i/ *pron* used to refer to a male person or animal who has been previously mentioned or whose identity is known (*as the subject of a verb*) ■ *n* a male animal or boy, especially used of a new baby ○ *Is your puppy a he or a she?* [Old English; < Indo-European, 'this (here)']

he[2] /hay/ *n* the fifth letter of the Hebrew alphabet [Mid-17C. < Hebrew *hē*'.]

He *symbol* helium

HE *abbr* **1** His Eminence **2** His Excellency

head /hed/ *n* **1 TOP PART OF BODY** the topmost part of a vertebrate body, where the brain, eyes, nose, ears, mouth, and jaws are situated **2 MOST FORWARD SECTION OF BODY** the section of the body of an invertebrate that is forward of all other segments **3 CENTRE OF INTELLECT** the centre of a human being's faculties of intellect, emotion, and reasoning ○ *She worked out a solution in her head.* ○ *Use your head, and don't panic!* ○ *a good head for figures* **4 REPRESENTATION OF HUMAN HEAD** an artistic, photographic, or televised representation or image of a human being's face, hair, eyes, mouth, nose, and ears **5 LEADER OF OTHERS** the chief leader, supervisor, or manager **6** EDUC = **head teacher 7 CRISIS POINT** a critical juncture in a situation or series of events, at which time some action must be taken, however painful ○ *The dispute came to a head at the monthly meeting.* **8 MORE IMPORTANT END** the more important end of something ○ *Our guest sat at the head of the table.* **9 TOP OF LONG THIN OBJECT** the wider, often flattened, top of a long thin object ○ *He hit the nail on the head.* **10 HIGHEST PART** the highest or uppermost part of something ○ *the head of the valley* **11 FROTH ON BEER** the froth that forms on the top of beer when it is poured into a glass **12** (*plural* **head**) **COUNTABLE UNIT** a single unit in a number of people or animals, especially when they are being counted ○ *500 head of cattle* **13 MEASURE OF DISTANCE** the height or length of a head, used as a measure of distance between two individuals, especially racehorses at the winning post ○ *The favourite won by a head.* **14 TOP OF PLANT** the top part of a plant where a flower or a cluster of leaves grows **15 TOP OF PIMPLE** the visible pus-filled centre of a pimple or boil **16 DRUG USER** a habitual user of a drug (*slang; only in combination*) **17 HEADACHE** a headache (*informal*) ○ *I've got a terrible head.* **18 SOURCE OF RIVER** the source of a river or stream **19 PROMONTORY** a headland that juts out into the sea or other stretch of water (*often in placenames*) **20 OBVERSE OF COIN** the side of a coin that shows a leader's head or other main design **21 ELECTROMAGNETIC RECORDING DEVICE** the part of a machine such as a tape recorder that uses, e.g., magnetic tape to record, read, or erase sounds, images, or data (*often plural*) **22 SECTION IN TEXT** one of the main sections or topics of a written or spoken discourse **23 TITLE** a heading such as a newspaper headline or a title before a section in a text **24 SHIP'S TOILET** a lavatory on a ship (*slang*) **25 PART OF DRUM** the stretched membrane of a drum or tambourine **26 REQUIRED HEIGHT OF LIQUID** the height that the surface of a liquid has to be above a specified level to produce a stated pressure at the specified level **27 PRESSURE OF LIQUID** the pressure at the lower of two points in a column of liquid resulting from the difference in height **28 PRESSURE** the pressure exerted by a liquid or gas ○ *a head of steam* **29 PART OF COAL MINE** a passage where coal is mined underground **30 TERMINAL** the destination point of a transport route **31 DEVICE FOR HOLDING CUTTING TOOLS** a part of a boring or turning machine, e.g. a lathe, that holds cutting tools to the work in progress **32** ENG = **cylinder head 33** *Carib* **STATE OF MIND** somebody's specified state of mind at a given time, especially as perceived by others ○ *Wha' head you pushing?* **34 TABOO TERM** a highly offensive term for an act of performing oral sex on somebody (*taboo*) ■ *adj* **CHIEF** most important in rank ○ *the head gardener* ○ *I had a call from head office* ■ *v* **1** *vt* **CONTROL** to be in the first position of authority and exercise control over people or an organization **2** *vt* **BE AT FRONT OF** to be at the front or the top of something ○ *The mayor headed the procession as it entered the town.* ○ *The list was headed by some very well-known names.* **3** *vi* **GO IN CERTAIN DIRECTION** to move or go in a particular direction or to a particular position ○ *He headed towards the station.* ○ *I think we're heading for trouble here.* **4** *vt* **CAUSE TO GO SOMEWHERE** to make something move in a specified direction or to a certain place ○ *The pilot headed the plane in a northeasterly course.* **5** *vt* **BE OR GIVE A HEADING** to act as or supply a heading on a written page ○ *A short quotation heads each chapter of this book.* ○ *Let's head the letter with our logo.* **6** *vt* **HIT WITH HEAD** to use the head to hit a ball ○ *He headed the ball into the goal.* [Old English *hēafod* < Indo-European] —**headed** *adj* ◇ **above** *or* **over somebody's head** too difficult for somebody to understand ◇ **be head and shoulders above somebody** to be notably superior to somebody ◇ **be off your head** to be mentally disturbed ◇ **give somebody his** *or* **her head, let somebody have his** *or* **her head** to relax control or supervision of somebody ◇ **go off your head** to become completely irrational (*informal*) ◇ **go to somebody's head 1** to make somebody conceited or overconfident **2** to make somebody dizzy or light-headed ○ *The champagne went right to my head.* ◇ **have your head in the clouds** to be completely unrealistic, overoptimistic, or engaged in daydreaming ◇ **head over heels 1** rolling or turning so that the feet are in the air and the head below them so as to land on the back or the feet **2** completely ○ *They fell head over heels in love.* ◇ **keep your head** to remain calm or unexcited ◇ **knock something on the head** to put an end to something, or prevent it from developing any further (*informal*) ◇ **lose your head** to panic or lose self-control ◇ **over somebody's head** alternative for above somebody's head ◇ **rear its ugly head** used to say that something unpleasant appears or happens

head off *v* **1** *vt* **INTERCEPT** to stop a person or animal from proceeding in a particular direction by placing yourself between the person or animal and the goal sought ○ *Let's try and head the robbers off at the pass.* ○ *We took a short cut to head her off before she reached the station.* **2** *vt* **FORESTALL** to try in advance to prevent something from taking place, or to prevent somebody from doing something, that might prove difficult or unpleasant ○ *We need to head off any attempt to have the matter raised again in committee.* **3** *vi* **GO** to go, or leave a place and go, in a particular direction ○ *The others headed off down the hill while we stayed to enjoy the view a little longer.*

headache /héd ayk/ *n* **1** a pain in the head caused, e.g., by dilation of cerebral arteries or muscle tightness **2** something that causes worry or difficulty (*informal*) —**headachy** *adj*

headband /héd band/ *n* **1** a strip of fabric worn on the head to keep the hair in place or off the face **2** a band of usually absorbent material worn around the head across the forehead to absorb sweat and keep hair off the face

headbang /héd bang/ *vi* to dance to heavy metal music by moving the head violently backwards and forwards to the beat (*slang*)

headbanger /héd bangər/ *n* **1** somebody whose favourite music is heavy metal (*slang*) **2** an unintelligent or unreasonable person (*informal insult*)

head-bath *n S Asia* a bath that includes washing of the hair

headboard /héd bawrd/ *n* an upright board, often padded or covered in fabric, used to form the head of a bed

head boy *n* a boy in the senior years at a secondary school who has been elected to represent the school and to act as a role model for younger pupils

head-butt /héd but/ *vt* to hit somebody a deliberate hard blow with the forehead or the top of the head ■ *n* a deliberate blow with the forehead or the top of the head

headcase /héd kayss/ *n* an offensive term that deliberately shows contempt for or ridicules somebody's mental condition (*insult*)

headcheese /héd cheez/ (*plural* **-cheeses** *or* **-cheese**) *n US, Can* FOOD = **brawn** *n.* 3 [Because the ingredients are pressed together as in cheese-making]

head cold *n* a viral infection of the nose, throat, and bronchial tubes, characterized by coughing, sneezing, headaches, and nasal congestion

head collar *n* = **headpiece** *n.* 3

head count *n* the process of counting the people in a group one by one, or the number arrived at by this process ○ *After a head count, we found there were 265 people in the hall.*

headdress /héd dress/ *n* a decorative covering worn on the head, usually as a sign of rank, for ceremonial purposes, or as personal display

ϟ**header** /héddər/ *n* **1** SHOT WITH HEAD a deliberate use of the head to play, pass, or shoot the ball in football ○ *He scored with a flying header.* **2** HEADLONG FALL a headlong plunge or fall **3** HEADING FOR PAGE a heading for each page of a word-processed or faxed document, usually automatically inserted and consisting of text or a page number **4** PLACE FOR INFORMATION ABOUT MESSAGE a place at the top of an e-mail for information about the message, including subject, sender, and receiver **5** CROSSWISE BRICK a brick or stone positioned crosswise in a wall and level with its outer surface **6** MAKER, FITTER, OR REMOVER OF TOPS a person who, or a machine that, makes, fits, or removes the tops of something **7** ENG = **header tank**

header tank *n* a raised tank that ensures a constant pressure or supply of fluid to a system, especially water to a central heating system

headfast /héd faast/ *n* a mooring rope at the bow of a ship

headfirst /héd fúrst/ *adv, adj* in a movement or position where the head is in front of the rest of the body and is the first thing that reaches, enters, or strikes something ○ *He insisted on going down the slide headfirst.* ○ *taking a headfirst dive into the pool* ■ *adv* abruptly and without taking time to think about or prepare for something ○ *They rush into things headfirst and think about the consequences afterwards.*

headful /hédfo͝ol/ *n* **1** a large amount of something that has been learned, thought, or imagined (*informal*) ○ *a headful of facts* **2** a thick mass of hair ○ *a headful of curls*

head gate *n* **1** the gate that controls the flow of water into the upstream end of a canal lock **2** = **floodgate**

headgear /héd geer/ *n* **1** SOMETHING COVERING THE HEAD something worn on the head, especially a hat ○ *sporting some very natty headgear* **2** HOISTING MECHANISM AT MINESHAFT an apparatus at the top of a mineshaft for lifting things out of and lowering them into a mine **3** PART OF HARNESS the part of a harness that fits over a horse's head

head girl *n* a girl in the senior years at a secondary school who has been elected to represent the school and to act as a role model for younger pupils

headhunt /héd hunt/ *v* **1** *vt* to recruit, or attempt to recruit, an executive or highly valued employee from one company to fill a similar position in another enterprise ○ *The agency headhunted her to work for an American bank.* **2** *vi* to seek, collect, and preserve the heads of enemies as trophies or ceremonial objects —**headhunter** *n*

headhunting /héd hunting/ *n* **1** the business of recruiting people who already hold positions in companies to fill similar positions in other enterprises **2** the practice among some peoples of cutting off the heads of enemies killed in battle and preserving them as trophies or ceremonial objects

heading /hédding/ *n* **1** TITLE something that forms the head, top, edge, or front of something, especially as a title for a paragraph, section, chapter, or page ○ *The chapter headings are to be set in 24-point bold.* **2** CATEGORY OF SUBJECT MATTER any of the divisions into which the subject matter of a document, discourse, or discussion is divided ○ *That information definitely comes under the heading of matters not to be aired in public.* **3** COURSE the direction in which a ship or aircraft is travelling, often given as a compass bearing ○ *If we continue on our present heading we should sight land in one hour.* **4** MINE TUNNEL a horizontal tunnel in a mine, or the end of such a tunnel

headlamp /héd lamp/ *n* CARS = **headlight**

headland /héddlənd/ *n* **1** a narrow piece of land jutting out into water, usually with steep, high cliffs **2** a strip of land left unploughed at the edge of a field

headless /héddləss/ *adj* **1** without a head on the body **2** having no leader, guide, or director —**headlessness** *n*

headlight /héd līt/ *n* a powerful light attached to the front of a motor vehicle or a locomotive, or the beam of light cast by it ○ *He was driving without headlights.*

headline /héd līn/ *n* **1** TITLE OF NEWSPAPER ARTICLE a caption printed at the top of a page or article in a newspaper, usually in large heavy letters and often summarizing the content that follows it ○ *an article with the headline 'Sharp Fall in Share Prices'* **2** LINE AT TOP OF PAGE a line printed at the top of a page of a book or document giving the page number and sometimes other information such as the title or the author's name ■ **headlines** *npl* MAIN NEWS ITEMS the most important items of news covered by a newspaper or a news broadcast ○ *Her name has seldom been out of the headlines since she announced her intention to sue.* ○ *We bring you the headlines every hour on the hour.* ■ *vt* (**-lines, -lining, -lined**) **1** PROVIDE PROMINENT HEADING to give a prominent title or caption to something ○ *They headlined the story POP STAR ENTERS HOSPITAL.* **2** *US* PUBLICIZE AS STAR to present somebody as the leading attraction of a show **3** *US* APPEAR AS STAR to appear as the leading attraction of a show

headliner /héd līnər/ *n US* a performer who is advertised as a leading attraction in a show

headlock /héd lok/ *n* a hold in which a wrestler tightly grips an arm around an opponent's head

headlong /héd long/ *adv, adj* **1** WITH HEAD FOREMOST with the head in front of the rest of the body, especially in a rapid uncontrolled movement **2** MOVING FAST AND OUT OF CONTROL moving or travelling in a fast uncontrolled way **3** WITH TOO MUCH HASTE acting, happening, or done in an impetuous way with little or no thought for the consequences ○ *She had thrown herself headlong into an even worse situation.* [14C. < HEAD + -LING[2], altered by association with *-long* 'foremost'.]

head louse *n* a louse that lives on a human head among the hair, feeding by sucking blood and gluing its eggs to the hair shafts near the skin surface. *Pediculus humanus capitis.*

headman /hédmən, héd man/ (*plural* **-men** /-mən, -men/) *n* **1** the leader of a community or village in some small-scale societies **2** a leader or overseer

headmaster /hed maástər/ *n* a man who is in charge of a school —**headmasterly** *adj* —**headmastership** *n*

headmistress /hed místrəss/ *n* a woman who is in charge of a school —**headmistressy** *adj*

head money *n* a reward paid for the capture or killing of a fugitive or outlaw

headmost /héd mōst/ *adj* forward to the greatest extent

headnote /héd nōt/ *n* a brief note at the top of a chapter or a page that summarizes what follows, especially points of law or a legal decision

head of government *n* the person in charge of a country's or state's government

head of programming *n* an executive who is responsible for the selection of television or radio programmes. US term **program director**

head of state *n* the chief representative of a country or state, who may or may not also be the head of government

head of the river *n* **1** a regatta held on a river involving a series of races for rowing crews **2** the winner of a regatta held on a river

head-on *adv, adj* WITH FRONT FACING FORWARDS with the front facing towards something ○ *We were sailing head-on into the teeth of the gale.* ○ *a head-on collision* ■ *adv* WITHOUT EVASION OR COMPROMISE making no attempt to avoid the dangers or difficulties involved in something ■ *adj* UNCOMPROMISING involving direct, fundamental, and uncompromising opposition ○ *He tried to avoid a head-on clash with his business partner.*

headphones /héd fōnz/ *npl* a pair of listening devices joined by a band across the top of the head and worn in or over the ears

headpiece /héd peess/ *n* **1** DESIGN AT TOP OF PAGE an ornamental design printed at the beginning of a text **2** HEAD PROTECTOR a covering for the head, especially a protective one **3** BRIDLE PART the part of a horse's bridle that fits around the head

head pin *n* = **kingpin** *n.* 4

headquarter /hed kwáwrtər/ *v* **1** *vt* to provide somebody with a centre of operations ○ *They headquartered their office in a former barracks.* **2** *vi* to set up a headquarters ○ *She headquartered in Paris.*

headquarters /hed kwáwrtərz, héd kwawrtərz/ *n* (+ *singular or plural verb*) **1** the administrative centre from which the affairs of an organization are directed **2** a military commander's central office, from which operations are controlled and orders issued ○ *Napoleon's headquarters were in a disused windmill.* ○ *Headquarters is on the radio, wanting to know our precise position.*

headrace /héd rayss/ *n* a channel conveying water to a water wheel or turbine

headrail /héd rayl/ *n* **1** the end of the table from which a game of billiards is started, nearest the baulk line **2** a railing on a sailing vessel extending from the rear of the bow to the back of the figurehead

headreach /héd reech/ *n* the distance that a sailing boat makes to windward when tacking ■ *vt* to make a better distance than another boat when tacking

head register *n* the higher register or falsetto of men's and boys' singing voices in which tone production is concentrated in the head and assisted by sympathetic vibration of the nasal and skull cavities

headrest /héd rest/ *n* an often padded support for the head, usually on the back of a seat, especially in a motor vehicle

head restraint *n* an adjustable headrest fitted to the back of a seat of a motor vehicle, designed to prevent neck injuries in an accident

head rhyme *n* = **alliteration**

headroom /héd room, -ro͝om/ *n* the space or clearance overhead, e.g. in a room, doorway, the interior of a motor vehicle, or the underside of a bridge ○ *There's plenty of headroom in this car, even in the back seat.*

headsail /héd sayl/ *n* a sail attached to or set forward of the foremast

headscarf /héd skaarf/ (*plural* **-scarves** /-skaarvz/) *n* a woman's scarf in the form of a square of fabric, for wearing on the head or round the neck

head sea *n* waves or a current running in a direction opposite to the course of a ship

headset /héd set/ *n* a pair of earphones, often with a small mouthpiece attached to enable two-way communication

headshaking /héd shayking/ *n* a series of side-to-side movements of the head, communicating or suggesting something such as disagreement, doubt, or refusal ○ *I noticed a lot of headshaking in the audience as you made that claim.*

headship /hédship/ *n* **1** a position as the principal of a school **2** somebody's position or authority as a leader

headshot /héd shot/ *n* **1** a photograph or cinematic shot of a head, especially a person's head **2** a gunshot aimed to hit the head of a person or animal

headshrinker /héd shringkər/ *n US* a psychiatrist (*dated informal insult*)

headsman /hédzmən/ (*plural* **-men** /-mən/) *n* a public executioner who beheaded prisoners condemned to death

headsquare /héd skwair/ *n* = **headscarf**

headstand /héd stand/ *n* a position in gymnastics or yoga in which the body is balanced upside down on the head, usually using the hands for support

head start *n* an advantage in a competition or endeavour ○ *A good education gives you a head start when it comes to getting a job.*

headstock /héd stok/ *n* an assembly or part of a machine, especially in a lathe, that holds and supports a revolving part

headstone /héd stōn/ *n* 1 a slab of stone placed at the head of a grave as a memorial to the person or people buried there 2 ARCHIT = **keystone** *n.* 1

headstream /héd streem/ *n* a stream that is the source, or one of the sources, of a river

headstrong /héd strong/ *adj* self-willed and determined not to follow orders or advice —**headstrongly** *adv* —**headstrongness** *n*

heads up *interj US* a command to watch out, especially for danger from overhead, e.g. a falling object or a ball coming through the air

heads-up *n US* 1 **WARNING** an early warning to somebody that something, typically something undesirable, is soon to happen ○ *gave the law firm a heads-up on the impending subpoena* 2 **SOMETHING REQUIRING ATTENTION** something that requires alert attention ■ *adj US* **ALERT AND RESOURCEFUL** showing quick resourcefulness and alertness in doing or observing something

heads-up display *n US* TECH = **head-up display**

head teacher *n* a supervisor of teaching staff and overseer of a school's operation

head-to-head *adv, adj* **WITH A DIRECT ENCOUNTER** in or involving direct contact or confrontation ■ *adv* **WITH HEADS ADJACENT** placed or arranged with heads adjacent ○ *We put the beds head-to-head.* ■ *n* **DIRECT ENCOUNTER** a direct and immediate encounter

head trip *n US* (*dated slang*) 1 an experience that stimulates or excites somebody mentally 2 something done or a way of behaving that is intended mainly for personal gratification

head-up display *n* a display of instrument data projected onto a screen at eye level so that a pilot or driver does not have to look down to see it. US term **heads-up display**

head voice *n* MUSIC = **head register**

head waiter *n* the person in charge of a group of servers at a restaurant, often also responsible for taking reservations and seating customers

head wall *n* a cliff forming one end of a valley

headwaters /héd wawtəerz/ *npl* the streams that make up the beginnings of a river

headway /héd way/ *n* 1 **PROGRESS** progress towards achieving something ○ *We're unable to make much headway with the project.* 2 **FORWARD MOVEMENT** movement or rate of progress forwards 3 = **headroom** 4 **DIFFERENCE IN TIME OR DISTANCE** the interval or distance between two vehicles, trains, or ships travelling in the same direction along the same route ◇ **make headway** to make progress in doing something or going somewhere

headwind /héd wind/ *n* a wind blowing against the direction of travel

headword /héd wurd/ *n* a word or phrase that forms a heading at the start of a text and is usually printed in distinctive type, especially a main entry word in a dictionary

headwork /héd wurk/ *n* 1 mental activity or effort 2 decoration on the keystone of an arch

heady /héddi/ (**-ier, -iest**) *adj* 1 **EXHILARATING** causing or involving a feeling of energy, confidence, and elation 2 **INTOXICATING** causing a feeling of light-headedness or intoxication 3 **IMPETUOUS** impulsive and rash in behaviour —**headily** *adv* —**headiness** *n*

heal /heel/ *v* 1 *vt* **CURE FROM AILMENT** to make a person or injury healthy and whole 2 *vi* **REPAIR NATURALLY** to be repaired and restored naturally, e.g. by the formation of scar tissue ○ *The broken bone seems to be healing quite nicely.* 3 *vt* **RECTIFY** to repair or rectify something that causes discord and animosity ○ *Unless she can heal the rift within her party, she stands little chance in the election.* 4 *vti* **MORALLY PURIFY** to get rid of a wrong, evil, or spiritual affliction [Old English *hǣlan* < Germanic] —**healable** *adj*

SPELLCHECK Do not confuse ***heal*** with ***heel***, which has the same sound. Beware: your spellchecker will not catch this error.

heal-all *n* PLANTS = **selfheal**

healer /heélər/ *n* a curer or treater of illnesses or injuries

Healey /heéli/, **Denis, Baron Healey of Riddlesden** (*b.* 1917) British politician

healing /heéling/ *n* the process of curing somebody or something or of becoming well ○ *spiritual healing* ■ *adj* with the effect of curing or improving something ○ *healing lotions*

health /helth/ *n* 1 **PRESENCE OR ABSENCE OF WELLBEING** the general condition of the body or mind, especially in terms of the presence or absence of illnesses, injuries, or impairments 2 **OVERALL CONDITION** the general condition of something in terms of soundness, vitality, and proper functioning ○ *There is concern about the financial health of the company.* 3 **DRINKING TOAST** a toast drunk to wish for somebody's wellbeing and prosperity ○ *Here's a health to Her Majesty!* ■ *adj* 1 **DEVOTED TO GENERAL WELLBEING** with the function of maintaining physical and mental wellbeing among the general public and the administration of medical and related services 2 **GOOD FOR PEOPLE** promoting physical and mental wellbeing [Old English *hǣlþ* < Germanic]

health care *n* the provision of medical and related services aimed at maintaining good health in individuals or the public, especially through the prevention and treatment of disease

healthcare /hélth kair/ *adj* concerned with or involved in providing physical and mental services, preventive medicine, and treatment to individuals or the public

healthcare assistant /hélth kair-/ *n* somebody with no specialized training employed in a hospital or other healthcare facility to perform basic nursing-support tasks such as bedmaking or giving patients baths. US term **nurse's aide**

health centre *n* 1 a place, operated by a local authority, that houses a medical practice and other healthcare services 2 a place, operated by a school or university, that houses a medical practice and other healthcare services for students

health farm *n* a commercial establishment similar to a hotel, usually rural, that offers ways of improving health and fitness, e.g. a controlled diet, exercise, and massage. US term **health spa**

health food *n* food that is considered to be more beneficial to health than ordinary food, especially products that are organically grown or without chemical additives

healthful /hélthf'l/ *adj* beneficial to physical or mental health —**healthfully** *adv* —**healthfulness** *n*

USAGE See ***healthy***.

health hazard *n* something that poses a risk to people's health

health insurance *n* insurance to cover the costs or losses incurred if an insured person falls ill

health physics *n* the branch of physics that covers both the risk to health from ionizing radiation and protection measures to reduce such risk to an acceptable level (+ *singular verb*)

health salts *npl* mineral salts, e.g. magnesium sulphate, used as a mild laxative

Health Service Commissioner /hélth surviss kə míshənər/ *n* a senior British official who investigates complaints about services provided by healthcare authorities that have not been satisfactorily resolved at a lower level

health spa *n* = **health farm**

health tourism *n* the practice of visiting other countries specifically to benefit from the medical services available there, often because they are cheaper than at home —**health tourist** *n*

health visitor *n UK* a trained nurse who gives medical care and advice to people in their homes, especially to mothers of babies and young children, senior citizens, and to physically disabled people

healthy /hélthi/ (**-ier, -iest**) *adj* 1 **IN GOOD CONDITION** in good physical or mental condition 2 **BENEFICIAL TO HEALTH** helping to maintain or bring about good health ○ *a healthy diet* ○ *This is not a very healthy place to live.* 3 **SUGGESTIVE OF GOOD HEALTH** showing that somebody is in good health 4 **PSYCHOLOGICALLY SOUND** showing or encouraging moral or psychological soundness 5 **FUNCTIONING WELL** in a prosperous and efficient condition ○ *My bank balance isn't looking very healthy at the moment.* 6 **CONSIDERABLE** large, usually satisfyingly large, in size or quantity (*informal*) —**healthily** *adv* —**healthiness** *n*

USAGE healthy or **healthful**? It is sometimes argued that ***healthy*** should be used only to describe a living being that is in good health, and that ***healthful*** is the word for such things as habits or foods that promote good health. There is nothing wrong with observing this distinction, but there is also nothing wrong with using ***healthy*** as a synonym for ***healthful***, as reputable writers have been doing for centuries.

Heaney /heéni/, **Seamus** (*b.* 1939) Irish poet

heap /heep/ *n* 1 **ROUNDED PILE** a large number of things lying on top of one another, or a large quantity of material, forming a roughly rounded shape ○ *They'd left all their dirty clothes in a heap on the floor.* ○ *All that was left of the building was a heap of rubble.* 2 **SOMETHING OLD OR BATTERED** something that is old, dilapidated, or untidy-looking, especially an old building or car (*informal*) 3 **LARGE AMOUNT** a large quantity or amount (*informal; often plural*) ○ *Don't worry, we've got heaps of time.* ○ *I've got a heap of things to see to before I can go home.* ■ *vt* 1 **PUT IN A PILE** to collect or arrange something into a loose pile ○ *heaping the stuff all together in the middle of the yard* 2 **PILE UP** to load or put a lot of something into a shallow container, forming a roughly rounded mound 3 **GIVE IN ABUNDANCE** to give or supply something in large quantities or amounts ○ *They heaped scorn on my suggestion.* [Old English *hēap* < Germanic] ◇ **all of a heap** into a state of shock, surprise, or confusion (*informal*) ○ *The news was totally unexpected and it knocked me all of a heap.*

heap up *v* 1 *vti* to accumulate something, or be gathered, into a roughly rounded mound 2 *vt* to collect or acquire something in large amounts

heaped /heept/ *adj* containing something in an amount large enough to rise up in a small heap. US term **heaping**

heaping /heéping/ *adj US* = **heaped**

heaps /heeps/ *adv* very much or greatly (*informal*) ○ *I feel heaps better since I went to the doctor.*

hear /heer/ (**hears, hearing, heard** /hurd/) *v* 1 *vti* **PERCEIVE SOUNDS** to perceive or be able to perceive sound 2 *vti* **GET TO KNOW** to be informed of something, especially by being told about it 3 *vt* **LISTEN TO** to listen to somebody or something ○ *I've heard him on the radio.* 4 *vti* **UNDERSTAND** to understand fully by listening attentively ○ *Did you hear what I just said?* ○ *I won't stand for it, do you hear?* 5 *vt* **PRESIDE OVER** to consider something officially as a judge, commissioner, or member of a jury ○ *the judge who heard the case* 6 *vt* **ATTEND MASS** to attend Mass in a Roman Catholic church ○ *The congregation heard Mass at ten o'clock.* [Old English *hīeran* < Germanic] —**hearable** *adj* —**hearer** *n* ◇ **hear, hear** used as an exclamation to show great approval

SPELLCHECK Do not confuse ***hear*** with ***here***, which has a similar sound. Beware: your spellchecker will not catch this error.

hear from *vt* to receive a communication, e.g. a letter or telephone call, from a person, place, or organization

hear of *vt* to consider something as a possibility ○ *She wouldn't hear of their paying their own way.*

hear out *vt* to continue listening until somebody or something has finished

heard past tense, past participle of **hear**

SPELLCHECK Do not confuse ***heard*** with ***herd***, which has a similar sound. Beware: your spellchecker will not catch this error.

hearing /heéring/ *n* 1 **AWARENESS OF SOUND** the perception of sound, made possible by vibratory changes in air pressure on the ear drums ○ *My hearing's going, so you'll have to speak louder.* 2 **EARSHOT** the range within which something can be heard ○ *She moved out of hearing and I lost the end of the sentence.* 3 **CHANCE TO BE HEARD** an opportunity to be heard, especially a chance to state an opinion or fact ○ *All I want is for my views to get a fair hearing.* 4 **TRIAL** the trial of a case in a court of law 5 **PRELIMINARY EXAMINATION OF ACCUSED** a preliminary judicial examination of an accused person to decide whether the case should proceed to trial 6 **SESSION TO HEAR EVIDENCE** a session of an investigative or legislative body at which witnesses are heard

hearing aid *n* a small amplifying device to enable somebody to hear better, usually worn in or behind the ear

hearing dog *n* a dog trained to help a hearing-impaired person by indicating that it has heard a certain sound, e.g. the ringing of a telephone or doorbell

hearing-impaired *adj* with a reduced or deficient ability to hear

hearing loss *n* a measurable reduction of the ability to hear or distinguish sounds, especially of a specific frequency

hearken /haárkən/, **harken** *vi* to listen and pay attention (*archaic*) [Old English *he(o)rcnian* < HARK] —**hearkener** *n*

hearsay /heér say/ *n* information that is heard from other people —**hearsay** *adj*

hearsay evidence *n* evidence consisting of testimony about other people that is not based on direct or personal knowledge

hearse /hurss/ *n* a vehicle in which a coffin is carried to a funeral or a dead body is taken away [13C. Via French *herse* < Latin *hirpex* 'rake, harrow'.]

Hearst /hurst/, **William Randolph** (1863–1951) US publisher and politician

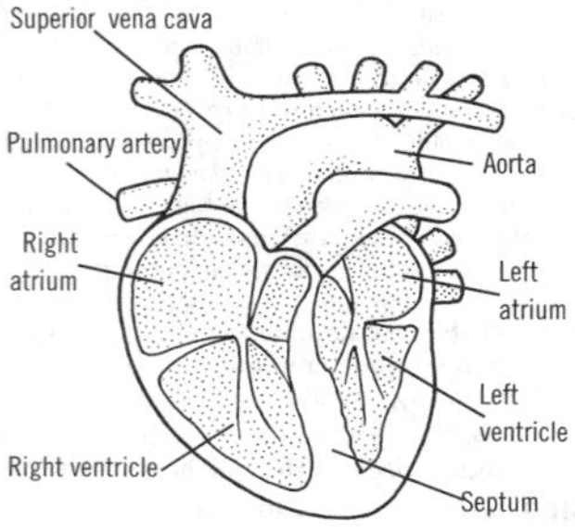

Heart: Human heart

heart /haart/ *n* **1 BLOOD-PUMPING ORGAN** a hollow muscular organ that pumps blood around the body, in humans situated in the centre of the chest with its apex directed to the left **2 POSITION OF CHEST ABOVE HEART** the area on the front of the human body that corresponds roughly to the position of the heart **3 BASIS OF EMOTIONAL LIFE** the human heart, considered as the source and centre of emotional life, where the deepest and sincerest feelings are located and an individual is most vulnerable to pain **4 CHARACTER** somebody's essential character ○ *He's an awkward cuss, but he's got a very good heart.* **5 COMPASSION** the ability to feel humane and altruistic feelings ○ *If she had any heart she would forgive him.* **6 AFFECTION** affection, love, or warm admiration ○ *The chorus's singing won the hearts of the audience.* **7 SPIRIT** the capacity for courage and determination ○ *The team played with a lot of heart.* ○ *They put their whole hearts into making a go of the business.* **8 DISPOSITION** a mood, mental state, or frame of mind **9 ESSENTIAL PART** the distinctive, significant, and characteristic centre of something ○ *the heart of rural England* **10 PART OF VEGETABLE AROUND CORE** the often tasty or succulent compact central part of a vegetable ○ *palm hearts* ○ *artichoke hearts* **11 ANIMAL HEART USED AS FOOD** the heart of an animal that is cleaned and trimmed, then cooked as food **12 DEPICTION OF HEART** a simplified and conventionalized picture of a heart as a rounded, roughly triangular shape, often used to signify love **13 PLAYING CARD** any one of a suit of cards marked with a symbolic depiction of one or more hearts. ◊ **hearts** *n.* 1 **14 BELOVED PERSON** a person who is intensely loved ○ *Come to me, dear heart.* [Old English *heorte* < Indo-European] ◇ **at heart** in essence or reality, and despite contrary appearances ◇ **break somebody's heart** to cause somebody intense unhappiness and suffering ◇ **do somebody's heart good** to make somebody feel happy or satisfied ◇ **eat your heart out 1** to brood about something that makes you feel unhappy (*informal*) **2** to be consumed with envy ◇ **have somebody's welfare** *or* **interests at heart** to have somebody's wellbeing or interests in mind ◇ **heart and soul** completely, or with the greatest devotion ◇ **in your heart of hearts** in your deepest inner feelings ◇ **learn** *or* **know something by heart** to memorize *or* have memorized something ◇ **lose heart** to become discouraged ◇ **not have the heart to do something** to be unable to bring yourself to do something that is liable to hurt somebody else ◇ **set your heart on something, have your heart set on something** to have something as your ambition or greatest wish ◇ **take heart** to become encouraged and more confident ◇ **take something to heart 1** to take something seriously **2** to be upset by something ◇ **wear your heart on your sleeve** to reveal your feelings openly ◇ **with all your heart** completely or very willingly

LITERARY LINK ***Heart of Midlothian***, a novel (1818) by Scottish writer Sir Walter Scott. It is set in the 1730s and tells the story of Effie Deans, who is wrongfully accused of the murder of a child. The title refers to the site of Effie's imprisonment: the Tolbooth jail in Edinburgh, in the county of Midlothian.

LITERARY LINK ***Heart of Darkness***, a novel (1902) by Joseph Conrad. It tells the story of Marlow, a young English steamboat captain who travels upriver deeper and deeper into the African jungle. He despises the European traders for their exploitation of Black Africans, who are themselves brutal, but when Marlow comes upon the mysterious Kurtz, an evil, charismatic white man ruling over an inland territory like a god, the young man is fascinated as well as repelled.

heartache /haárt ayk/ *n* a powerful feeling of sorrow, anguish, or regret

heart attack *n* **1** a sudden, serious, painful, and sometimes fatal interruption of the heart's normal functioning, especially due to a blockage in the coronary artery **2** a sudden severe shock (*informal*) ○ *I had a heart attack when I looked in the drawer and saw that the money was gone.*

heartbeat /haárt beet/ *n* **1 CONTRACTION OF HEART MUSCLE** a vigorous contraction of the lower chambers of the heart that drives blood through the body **2 CONTINUOUS PULSATION OF HEART** the continuous pulsating movement and sound made by a beating heart ○ *Her rapid heartbeat gradually slowed.* **3 DRIVING FORCE** the driving force behind something

heart block *n* a condition in which the nerve impulses that control the heartbeat are abnormal so that the ventricles and the atria no longer beat in time with one another

heartbreak /haárt brayk/ *n* intense unhappiness or grief

heartbreaker /haárt braykər/ *n* a creator of intense unhappiness, especially somebody with whom people fall in love and by whom they are later hurt

heartbreaking /haárt brayking/ *adj* causing intense sadness or distress —**heartbreakingly** *adv*

heartbroken /haárt brōkən/ *adj* feeling intensely unhappy or disappointed because of something that has happened ○ *The children were heartbroken when we had to cancel the trip.* —**heartbrokenly** *adv* —**heartbrokenness** *n*

heartburn /haárt burn/ *n* an uncomfortable burning sensation in the lower chest, usually caused by stomach acid flowing back into the lower end of the oesophagus [< HEART in the obsolete sense 'stomach']

heart disease *n* any medical condition of the heart or the blood vessels supplying it that impairs cardiac functioning

hearten /haárt'n/ *vt* to make somebody feel more cheerful and hopeful [< HEART in the obsolete sense 'encourage'] —**heartening** *adj* —**hearteningly** *adv*

heart failure *n* **1** cessation of the normal functioning of the heart, leading to death ○ *He died from heart failure at 92, while gardening.* **2** a condition in which the heart cannot pump blood in sufficient volume to meet the needs of the body, causing breathlessness, enlargement of the liver, swollen ankles, and other symptoms

heartfelt /haárt felt/ *adj* arising from strong and sincere emotion

Heartfield /haárt feeld/, **John** (1891–1968) German painter and graphic artist. Born **Helmut Herzfeld**

hearth /haarth/ *n* **1 FLOOR OF FIREPLACE** the floor of a fireplace, especially when it extends into the room **2 HOME LIFE** the fireplace of a home, thought of as a symbol of the home and the life of the family who live in it **3 PART OF FOUNDRY FURNACE** the lowest part of a foundry furnace where molten metal collects or ore is smelted [Old English *heorþ* < Germanic]

hearth rug *n* a rug for the floor in front of a fireplace

hearthside /haárth sīd/ *n* = **fireside** *n.*

hearthstone /haárth stōn/ *n* **1** a large stone used to form the hearth in a fireplace **2** a soft variety of stone or a compound of pipeclay and stone used to clean and whiten fireplaces and doorsteps

heartily /haártili/ *adv* **1 ENTHUSIASTICALLY** in a sincere and enthusiastic way **2 GOOD-NATUREDLY** in a loud, vigorous, good-natured way **3 COMPLETELY** in a full and complete way **4 HUNGRILY** with a good appetite

heartland /haárt land/ *n* **1** a central area of a country or region **2** an area of a country or region that has special economic, political, military, or sentimental significance (*often plural*)

heartless /haártləss/ *adj* having or showing no pity or kindness —**heartlessly** *adv* —**heartlessness** *n*

heart-lung machine /haárt lúng mə sheen/ *n* a machine that is used to take over the functions of the heart and lungs in pumping and oxygenating the blood, chiefly during heart surgery

heart massage *n* = **cardiac compression**

heart murmur *n* an unusual sound coming from the heart that can be detected by a stethoscope and may indicate the presence of a heart defect

heart rate *n* the number of heartbeats occurring within a specified length of time

heartrending /haárt rending/ *adj* causing intense sadness or distress, especially in sympathy with somebody else's unhappiness or hardship —**heartrendingly** *adv*

hearts /haarts/ *n* **1** a suit of cards marked with red heart symbols (+ *singular or plural verb*) **2** a card game in which players try to avoid winning cards of the suit hearts or the queen of spades or else to win all of these (+ *singular verb*)

heart-searching *n* a thorough and often painful examination of your own conscience, feelings, or motives

heartsease /haárts eez/ (*plural* **-eases** *or* **-ease**) *n* a pansy, especially a wild pansy, *Viola tricolor.*

heartsick /haárt sik/ *adj* deeply disappointed or sad ○ *I'm heartsick when I think of how things ought to have been.* —**heartsickness** *n*

heart-smart *adj* describes food that is low in fat and cholesterol and therefore reduces the risk of heart disease (*informal*)

heartsore /haárt sawr/ *adj* extremely sad or regretful (*archaic or literary*)

heartstrings /haártstringz/ *npl* somebody's feelings, especially tender emotions [< STRING 'tendon', from the earlier belief that tendons brace the heart]

heartthrob /haárt throb/ *n* an extraordinarily attractive person, especially a young film star or singer (*informal*)

heart-to-heart *adj* frank and intimate, often about personal matters ■ *n* a frank, intimate conversation

heartwarming /haárt wawrming/ *adj* inspiring warm or kindly feelings, usually by showing life and human nature in a positive and reassuring light —**heartwarmingly** *adv* —**heartwarmingness** *n*

heartwood /haárt wŏŏd/ *n* the wood at the centre of a tree trunk or branch that is older, darker, and harder than the wood surrounding it. Technical name **duramen**

heartworm /haárt wurm/ (*plural* **-worms** *or* **-worm**) *n* **1** a parasitic filarial worm that lives in the heart and associated blood vessels of members of the dog family, and occasionally in cats and seals **2** an infection of the heart in members of the dog family, and occasionally in cats and seals, that is caused by parasitic worms

hearty /haárti/ *adj* (**-ier, -iest**) **1 SINCERE AND ENTHUSIASTIC** sincere and expressed in a cheerful, enthusiastic way **2 LOUD AND ENTHUSIASTIC** done in an unrestrainedly loud, vigorous, but usually good-humoured way **3 HEALTHY** showing physical health, strength, and vigour **4 STRONGLY FELT** sincerely and strongly felt **5 SUBSTANTIAL AND NOURISHING** substantial or giving considerable satisfaction and nourishment ○ *I need a hearty breakfast to get my day started.* **6 OVERLOUD AND OVERENTHUSIASTIC** annoyingly or boorishly loud or boisterous, and usually overenthusiastic about sport or outdoor activities (*informal*) ■ *n* (*plural* **-ies**) **BOISTEROUS SPORTING TYPE** a loud boisterous person who usually is enthusiastic about sport or outdoor activities (*informal insult*) —**heartiness** *n* ◇ **my hearties** (*symbol* **Q**) comrades (*archaic; addressed especially to fellow sailors*)

heat /heet/ *n* **1 ENERGY PERCEIVED AS TEMPERATURE** a form of transferred energy that arises from the random motion of molecules and is felt as temperature, especially as warmth or hotness ○ *There was virtually no heat coming from the fire.* **2 DEGREE OF HOTNESS** the perceptible degree of hotness ○ *The heat in that kitchen is absolutely unbearable.* ○ *At what heat do I cook this?* **3 SOURCE OF HIGHER TEMPERATURE** a source of warmth, e.g. to cook something or to keep a building warm ○ *The heat turns off automatically when the room reaches a certain temperature.* **4 INTENSE EMOTION** emotional intensity, especially in the form of anger or excitement ○ *I replied with some heat that my conscience was perfectly clear.* ○ *in the heat of the moment* **5 TIME OF MOST ACTIVITY** the period or phase of something at which activity and excitement is at its most intense ○ *During the heat of the campaign, many rash promises were made.* **6 SPICY HOTNESS** the hot or burning sensation produced in the mouth by certain spicy foods **7 SEXUALLY RECEPTIVE STAGE** a time during a female mammal's reproductive cycle when she is fertile and ready to mate **8 PRELIMINARY ROUND** one of several preliminary rounds before a race or contest, especially one in which competitors are eliminated, or one that determines the main event's starting order **9 MENTAL PRESSURE** psychological pressure on a person or group, especially to produce or achieve something (*informal*) ○ *We're beginning to feel the heat as the deadline gets closer and closer.* **10** *US* **CRITICISM** harsh criticism or reproach (*slang*) ○ *What's your problem? Can't you take the heat?* **11 INTENSE POLICE ACTIVITY** intensive police activity carried out in order to catch criminal suspects (*slang*) **12** *US* **POLICE** the police (*slang*) ■ *vti* **RAISE TEMPERATURE** to become or make something warm or hot [Old English *hǣtu* < Germanic, 'hot'] —**heatless** *adj* ◇ **turn on** *or* **up the heat (on somebody)** to apply increased pressure on somebody (*slang*)

heat up *vti* **1** to make something hotter, or become hotter **2** to become or make something more intense, exciting, or excited

heat balance *n* INDUST = **energy balance**

heat barrier *n* SCI = **thermal barrier**

heat capacity *n* (*symbol C*) the quantity of heat required to raise the temperature of one mole or gram of a substance by one degree Celsius

heat death *n* a condition of a closed system in which energy is uniformly distributed throughout it, with none available for use

heated /héetid/ *adj* **1** made warm by artificially generated heat **2** showing emotional intensity or anger —**heatedness** *n*

heatedly /héetidli/ *adv* with anger or emotional intensity

heat engine *n* a machine that transforms heat into mechanical power, e.g. a steam or petrol engine

heater /héetər/ *n* **1 HEATING DEVICE** a device that uses fuel to produce heat in order to make something else warm or hot, especially a device to heat the air in a room or vehicle **2 HEATING ELEMENT IN VALVE** an element in a valve that carries the current for heating a cathode **3** *US* **HANDGUN** a revolver or other handgun (*dated slang*)

heat exchanger *n* a device, e.g. a car radiator, that transfers heat from one medium to another, usually by conduction through a solid barrier

heat exhaustion *n* a condition of physical weakness or collapse often accompanied by nausea, muscle cramps, and dizziness, that is caused by exposure to intense heat

heath /heeth/ (*plural* **heaths** *or* **heath**) *n* **1 SHRUBBY UNCULTIVATED LAND** a tract of uncultivated, open land with infertile, often sandy soil covered with rough grasses and small shrubs or heather **2 LOW SHRUB** a plant of a family that includes heather and some other low-growing evergreen shrubs, commonly found on heaths. Flowers: small, bell-shaped. Genera: *Erica* and *Calluna*. **3 BROWN BUTTERFLY** a butterfly with coppery-brown wings. Genus: *Coenonympha*. [Old English *hǣþ* < Germanic, 'unploughed land']

Heath /heeth/, **Ted** (*b.* 1916) British statesman. Full name **Sir Edward Richard George Heath**

heathen /héeth'n/ *n* **1** an offensive term that deliberately insults somebody who does not acknowledge the God of the Bible, Torah, or Koran **2** an offensive term that deliberately insults somebody's nonbelief in religion, way of life, or degree of knowledge [Old English *hǣþen* < Germanic, 'heath'] —**heathen** *adj* —**heathenish** *adj* —**heathenishly** *adv* —**heathenishness** *n* —**heathenize** *vti*

heather /héthər/ *n* **1** a low shrubby evergreen plant with spiky leaves that grows in clusters. Flowers: small purple, pink, or white, bell-shaped. Native to: heaths and mountainsides in Europe and Asia. *Calluna vulgaris.* **2** a purple colour tinged with pink and blue [14C. < ?] —**heather** *adj* —**heathery** *adj*

heather grass *n* a perennial grass with flat hairless leaves. Native to: Europe. *Sieglingia decumbens.* [Because it grows in the same places as heather]

heather mixture *n* a textile made of interwoven yarns of various colours, especially the colours of heather

heath grass *n* = **heather grass**

heath hen *n* **1** the female of the black grouse **2** *US* an extinct grouse related to the prairie chicken. Native to: New England. *Typanuchus cupido cupido.*

Heath Robinson /heeth róbbinss'n/ *adj* constructed or improvised in a way that looks ramshackle and wildly implausible, especially through being overelaborate or overingenious (*humorous*) ○ *It's a bit Heath Robinson, but it ought to stop the sausages rolling off the barbecue.* [Early 20C. After W. *Heath Robinson* (1872–1944), whose illustrations featured such devices.]

Heathrow /héeth ró/ largest and busiest airport serving London, to the west of the city

heating /héeting/ *n* **1** the operation of warming something, e.g. food, a room, or the interior of a building **2** the equipment that produces heat to warm something, e.g. a central heating system ○ *The heating doesn't come on again until six o'clock in the evening.*

heating element *n* an insulated or covered wire whose high resistance to an electrical current causes its temperature to rise, providing heat to surrounding materials, e.g. an electric blanket

heating pad *n* a fabric-covered pad that encloses an electric heating element and is used to apply heat to various parts of the body

heat island *n* an urban area where the air temperature is consistently higher than in the surrounding region because of the generation and retention of heat created by human activity and human-made structures

heat lightning *n* lightning seen near the horizon, especially on hot evenings, without the sound of thunder, thought to be a reflection on clouds

heat of combustion *n* the amount of heat produced when one mole of a substance is burned in oxygen

heat-proof *adj* not damaged or affected when exposed to heat, e.g. in an oven or over a flame

heat prostration *n* MED = **heat exhaustion**

heat pump *n* a mechanical or chemical device used to heat and air-condition buildings

heat rash *n* MED = **prickly heat**

heat-seal *vt* to make packaging material, usually a thin clear plastic film, airtight around something by applying heat and pressure

heat-seeking *adj* able to detect and follow infrared radiation from heat ○ *The aircraft was brought down by a heat-seeking missile.*

heat shield *n* a coating or structure designed to protect against the effects of very high temperatures, especially the coating that protects spacecraft during re-entry into the Earth's atmosphere

heat sink *n* a device, often a metal plate, that conducts and dissipates unwanted heat generated by an electronic component or power supply

heatstroke /héet strōk/ *n* a condition caused by prolonged exposure to high temperatures, in which people experience high fever, headaches, hot dry skin, physical exhaustion, and sometimes physical collapse and coma

heat-treat *vt* to bring metal to the desired hardness by alternately heating and cooling it —**heat treatment** *n*

heat wave *n* a period of unusually hot weather

heave /heev/ *v* (**heaves, heaving, heaved**) **1** *vt* **MOVE USING MUCH EFFORT** to pull, push, lift, or throw something heavy by exerting great physical effort, especially in a concentrated or concerted burst ○ *We picked up the sack between us and heaved it into the truck.* **2** *vi* **EXERT PHYSICAL EFFORT IN RHYTHMIC BURST** to exert great physical effort, especially in concentrated or concerted rhythmic bursts, when pulling on a rope or attempting to move something heavy ○ *All together now, heave!* ○ *We heaved and heaved, but the car remained firmly stuck in the mud.* **3** *vt* **DIRECT BY TOSSING** to throw something fairly heavy in a particular direction, often in a casual way (*informal*) ○ *Heave the empty boxes into that corner.* **4** *vi* **RISE AND FALL RHYTHMICALLY** to rise and fall in a rhythmic or spasmodic way ○ *After the long run his chest was heaving* **5** *vi* **MAKE A SUDDEN INVOLUNTARY MOVEMENT** to move suddenly in a violent involuntary motion, often associated with feelings of nausea ○ *The sight made my stomach heave.* ○ *The boat heaved to the port side.* **6** *vti* **VOMIT** to vomit something up or try to vomit (*informal*) **7** *vt* **LABORIOUSLY UTTER** to utter a sound, especially a sigh, with a long outflow of breath or with effort and pain ○ *We can heave a sigh of relief now that the waiting is over.* **8** (*past* **hove**) *vti* **MOVE A SHIP** to move or make a ship move in a particular direction **9** (*past* **hove**) *vi* **APPEAR** to become visible, like a ship appearing over the horizon ○ *Gradually, the end of summer hove into sight.* **10** *vt* **DISPLACE HORIZONTALLY** to displace rock strata or a mineral lode in a horizontal direction, usually by the intersection of other strata or another lode ■ *n* **1 EFFORTFUL BURST** a burst of physical effort to pull on something or move something heavy ○ *We gave one final heave and the tree began to topple over.* **2 THROW** an act of throwing something fairly heavy, or the distance something is thrown **3 UP-AND-DOWN MOVEMENT** a rhythmic or spasmodic movement that rises and falls **4 HORIZONTAL DISPLACEMENT** rock strata or a lode that is displaced horizontally **5 ACT OF VOMITING** an act of or attempt at vomiting (*informal*) ■ **heaves** *npl* **VOMITING ATTACK** an attack of vomiting or retching (*slang*) [Old English *hebban* 'lift' < Germanic] —**heaver** *n*

SYNONYMS See ***throw***.

heave down *vt* to turn a boat over for cleaning

heave to *vti* to bring a ship to a stop ○ *We hove to about a cable's length from her stern.*

heave-ho /heev hó/ *interj* used to command or encourage sailors to pull together on a rope ■ *n* dismissal from something or rejection by somebody (*informal*) ○ *He's just been given the heave-ho from his job.*

heaven /hévv'n/ *n* **1 Heaven, heaven PERFECT DWELLING PLACE AFTER DEATH** a place or condition of supreme happiness and peace where good people are believed to go after death, and, especially in Christianity, the dwelling place of God and the angels **2 BLISSFUL EXPERIENCE** an experience of blissful happiness ○ *It's heaven not to have get up early in the morning.* ○ *This place would be heaven, if it weren't for the people who live here.* **3 SKY OVERARCHING EARTH** the sky by day or at night as seen from Earth (*often plural*) ○ *After weeks of drought the heavens opened.* **4 Heaven, heaven POWER OF GOD** in Christian belief, the power of God to direct events on earth ○ *Heaven protect us!* ○ *a gift from heaven* ■ *interj* **heaven, heavens EXPRESSING ASTONISHMENT** used to express great surprise, annoyance, or gratitude (*informal*) ○ *Good heavens, is that the time?* [Old English *heofon* < ?] ◇ **for heaven's sake** used to express annoyance or exasperation ◇ **heaven knows** used to emphasize the truth of what somebody is saying ○ *Heaven knows, I've warned you about that already.* ◇ **heaven (only) knows** used to emphasize the fact that somebody is unable even to make a reasonable guess at something unknown or mysterious ○ *Heaven only knows what he's done with my keys.* ◇ **move heaven and earth** to do everything possible to make something happen

heavenly /hévv'nli/ (**-lier, -liest**) *adj* **1 OF GOD AND HEAVEN** belonging to the heaven and God of Christian belief ○ *A heavenly voice spoke to him out of the clouds.* **2 LOVELY** supremely delightful, delicious, or beautiful (*informal*) ○ *The chocolate mousse was heavenly.* ○ *a sweet little cottage with the most heavenly view* **3 IN THE SKY** in the sky or space as seen from Earth —**heavenliness** *n*

heavenly body *n* ASTRON = **celestial body**

heaven-sent *adj* happening or arriving at just the right time to help or benefit somebody greatly

heavenward /hévv'nwərd/, **heavenwards** /-wərdz/ *adv, adj* moving or directed upwards towards the sky or heaven ○ *He rolled his eyes heavenward.*

heaves /heevz/ *n* a chronic lung disorder in horses marked by difficulty in breathing and believed to be caused by dust, moulds, or other air pollutants (*informal; + singular or plural verb*)

heavier-than-air *adj* unable to float in air because it weighs more than the air it displaces, and thus only able to fly under power using aerodynamic lift

heavily /hévvili/ *adv* **1 WITH GREAT WEIGHT** with a great weight **2 LABORIOUSLY** in a slow, clumsy, or laborious way **3 SEVERELY** in a severe, onerous, or comprehensive way **4 IN LARGE NUMBERS** in large numbers or quantities **5 SADLY** in a sad and resigned way ○ *'It was my fault', he replied heavily.* **6 SERIOUSLY** in a serious or enthusiastic way (*informal*) ○ *I didn't know you were heavily into astrology.*

heaviness /hévvinəss/ *n* the condition of being heavy

Heaviside /hévvi sīd/, **Oliver** (1850–1925) British physicist

Heaviside layer /hévvi sīd-/ *n* = **E layer** [Early 20C. After Oliver HEAVISIDE.]

heavy /hévvi/ *adj* (**-ier, -iest**) **1 WEIGHING A LOT** weighing a relatively large amount and thus difficult to lift, carry, or move ○ *Daddy can't carry you any more, you're too heavy.* ○ *We put heavy stones on the corners of the rug to stop it blowing away.* **2 PRESENT IN LARGE AMOUNTS** occurring or produced in large amounts or in greater amounts than normal **3 FULL OR DENSE** involving or using a larger amount of material, or having a thicker, denser texture than usual **4 USING SOMETHING ABUNDANTLY** using or consuming something a great deal **5 NEEDING STRENGTH** needing much strength and effort ○ *heavy road work* **6 DEMANDING** difficult to fulfil or cope with, and often burdensome or oppressive **7 BUSY** filled with a large or larger than normal amount of activity, business, or commitments **8 POWERFUL** struck or striking with a great deal of weight or force **9 BROAD AND DARK** thick and dark-coloured or made with thick dark lines **10 EXPLICIT** intended to give emphasis to something and to make the meaning or intention obvious **11 UNSUBTLE** lacking subtlety or delicacy ○ *heavy sarcasm* **12 FLESHY** large and solidly fleshy ○ *a huge, heavy body* **13 CLUMSY** typical of somebody who is large and who moves slowly and deliberately or clumsily **14 AFFECTED BY TIREDNESS** tending to close or droop or feel weighed down by tiredness **15 SOUNDING LOUD AND DULL** loud and dull in sound, as if produced by something large hitting or falling onto something **16 INDUSTRIAL-SCALE** involved in large-scale industrial processes requiring large premises and a lot of equipment **17 RUGGED AND STRONG** specially adapted for rough work or for carrying large loads ○ *heavy excavating equipment* **18 LARGE-CALIBRE** firing large-calibre ammunition **19 WITH LARGE WEAPONS** carrying more or larger guns and armaments than is standard **20 SAD** sad or likely to make somebody feel sad **21 REQUIRING CONCENTRATION** requiring concentrated attention to be understood or appreciated ○ *a heavy novel* **22 TURGID** difficult and requiring effort rather than being pleasurable ○ *I'm trying to finish reading the novel, but it's heavy going.* **23 STRICT** strict or severe in behaviour **24 VIOLENT** using or prepared to use violence (*informal*) **25 POWERFUL AND LINGERING** strong and lingering in smell ○ *a heavy odour of leeks* **26 ROUGH** with large waves causing difficulties for boats **27 DARK AND OVERCAST** dark in colour and threatening rain or snow **28 SULTRY AND THREATENING** sultry and overcast, as if threatening a storm or thunder **29 HARD TO DIGEST** large in quantity and difficult to digest **30 WITH POWERFUL BEAT** describes rock music with a powerful, insistent beat **31 SERIOUS AND OPPRESSIVE** significant, oppressively serious, or emotionally demanding (*slang*) ○ *I had a heavy scene with my friend tonight.* **32 WITH HIGH ATOMIC WEIGHT** with a higher than normal atomic weight **33 WITH HIGH SPECIFIC GRAVITY** with a higher than normal specific gravity **34 MUDDY** wet, muddy, and not able to be travelled over at high speed ○ *Reports from the racecourse indicate that the going is heavy.* ■ *n* (*plural* **-ies**) **1 VILLAIN** a villain in a play, film, or other dramatic performance ○ *He played the heavy in a couple of westerns.* **2 SOMEBODY WHO IS VIOLENT** somebody hired to persuade people, by threats or violence, to do something (*slang; often plural*) ○ *He sent in a bunch of heavies to do his dirty work.* **3 BROADSHEET** a broadsheet newspaper (*informal; often plural*) ○ *None of the heavies ran the story.* **4** *US* **IMPORTANT PERSON** an important or influential person (*informal*) **5** *US* **HEAVYWEIGHT** a heavyweight, e.g., a heavyweight boxer (*informal*) **6** *Scotland* **STRONG BITTER BEER** a bitter brown beer ■ *adv* **HEAVILY** in a heavy way [Old English *hefig* < Germanic, 'lift']

heavy breather *n* **1** an anonymous maker of telephone calls who breathes loudly into the mouthpiece as a means of suggesting sexual excitement or a physical threat **2** a person who breathes noisily or with difficulty, usually because of a medical condition —**heavy breathing** *n*

heavy chain *n* either of the larger polypeptide chains in an antibody. ◊ **light chain**

heavy cream *n US* cream with a high fat content that can be whipped to make it thicker

heavy-duty *adj* **1** designed for hard wear or use in rough conditions **2** more serious, substantial, or intensive than usual (*informal*) ○ *a heavy-duty meeting*

heavy-footed *adj* slow, lumbering, or clumsy in walking

heavy goods vehicle *n* a road vehicle weighing more than 7.5 tonnes/16,500 lb, used for transporting goods

heavy-handed *adj* **1** lacking skill or delicacy in handling objects or dealing with people **2** relying on force or intimidation to exercise authority —**heavy-handedly** *adv* —**heavy-handedness** *n*

heavy-hearted *adj* feeling or showing sadness —**heavy-heartedly** *adv* —**heavy-heartedness** *n*

heavy hydrogen *n* an isotope of hydrogen with a mass number greater than 1, especially deuterium

heavy lifting *n* the lifting of heavy objects

heavy metal *n* **1** a style of loud rock music with a very strong beat (*hyphenated before nouns*) **2** a metal, often toxic to organisms, that has a relative density of 5.0 or higher, e.g. lead, mercury, copper, and cadmium

heavy oil *n* a mixture of hydrocarbons distilled from coal tar that is heavier than water

heavy particle *n* CHEM = **baryon**

heavyset /hévvi sét/ *adj* with a compact and powerful-looking build

heavy spar *n* the mineral form of barium sulphate

heavy water *n* D_2O water that has had its hydrogen atoms replaced with the hydrogen isotope deuterium. Use: nuclear reactors.

heavy-water reactor *n* a nuclear reactor in which heavy water is used as a moderator

heavyweight /hévvi wayt/ *n* **1 BOXER IN HIGHEST WEIGHT CATEGORY** a boxer of the heaviest weight class, in the professional ranks weighing more than 79.5 kg/175 lbs **2 CONTESTANT IN HEAVIEST WEIGHT CLASS** a contestant in the heaviest weight class of a sport **3 HEAVY PERSON OR THING** somebody or something whose weight is considerably above the average **4 SOMEBODY OR SOMETHING POWERFUL OR INFLUENTIAL** a person or organization with considerable power or influence, usually in a specified area (*informal*)

Heb. *abbr* **1** Hebrew **2** Hebrews

hebdomad /hébdə mad/ *n* (*formal*) **1** a group of seven people or things **2** a period of seven days [Mid-16C. Via late Latin < Greek *hebdomad-* 'the number seven, period of seven days' < *hepta* 'seven'.]

hebdomadal /heb dómmәd'l/ *adj* occurring on a weekly basis (*formal*)

Hebdomadal Council *n* the governing body of Oxford University

hebe /héebi/ *n* an evergreen shrub widely cultivated for its blue, mauve, or white flowers. Native to: S temperate regions. Genus: *Hebe.* [Mid-20C. After HEBE.]

Hebe /héebi/ *n* in Greek mythology, the goddess of youth and the daughter of Zeus and Hera [Early 17C. < Greek *Hēbē* 'youthful prime'.]

Hebei /hő báy/, **Hopeh** province in N China. Capital: Shijiazhuang. Population: 63,880,000 (1994). Area: 188,000 sq. km/72,600 sq. mi.

hebetude /hébbi tyood/ *n* mental lethargy (*literary*) [Early 17C. < late Latin *hebetudo* < Latin *hebet-* 'dull'.]

Hebr. *abbr* **1** Hebrew **2** Hebrews

Hebraic /hi bráy ik/, **Hebraical** /-ik'l/ *adj* relating to the Israelites, or their language or culture [14C. Via late Latin < Greek *Hebraikos* < *Hebraios* (see HEBREW).] —**Hebraically** *adv*

Hebraise *vti* = **Hebraize**

Hebraism /hée brayizəm/ *n* a feature of the Hebrew language, especially one borrowed by another language, or something frequently found among Hebrews or their culture [Late 16C. Via French or modern Latin < late Greek *Hebraismos* < *Hebraios* (see HEBREW).]

Hebraist /hée bray ist/ *n* a specialist in the study of Hebrew —**Hebraistically** /hée bray ístikli/ *adv*

Hebraize /hée bray īz/ (**-izes, -izing, -ized**), **Hebraise** (**-ises, -ising, -ised**) *v* **1** *vt* to give a language or culture Hebrew characteristics **2** *vi* to adopt Hebrew idioms or customs [Mid-17C. < late Greek *Hebraizein* < *Hebraios* (see HEBREW).] —**Hebraization** /hée bray ī záysh'n/ *n* —**Hebraizer** *n*

Hebrew /hée broo/ *n* **1** a Semitic official language of Israel, also spoken elsewhere in the world. Native speakers: 5 million. **2** PEOPLES, HIST = **Israelite** ■ *adj* **1** relating to Hebrew **2** LANG, HIST = **Hebraic** [13C. Via Old French *ebreu* < late Greek *Hebraios* < Aramaic *ibrāy*.]

Hebrew calendar *n* CALENDAR = **Jewish calendar**

Hebrews /hée brooz/ *n* in the Bible, an epistle that is thought to have been written towards the end of the first century AD (+ *singular verb*)

Hebrew Scriptures *npl* the Bible of Judaism, consisting of the Pentateuch, the Prophets, and the Hagiographa. ◊ **Torah**

Hebrides /hébbrə deez/ group of islands off W Scotland, including the Inner Hebrides, nearer the mainland, and the Outer Hebrides, farther to the northwest —**Hebridean** /hébbri dée ən/ *adj, n*

Hebron /hébbron/ town in the West Bank territory. Population: 70,400 (1994 estimate).

Hecate /hékəti/, **Hekate** *n* in Greek mythology, the goddess of darkness and the underworld [Late 16C. < Greek *Hekatē*, form of *hekatos* 'far-darting'.]

hecatomb /hékə tōm, hékə toom/ *n* **1** a public sacrifice and feast in ancient Greece or Rome, originally involving the slaughter of 100 oxen **2** any large-scale sacrifice (*literary*) [Late 16C. Via Latin < Greek *hekatombē* < *hekaton* 'hundred' + *bous* 'ox'.]

heck /hek/ *interj* used as a mild way of expressing annoyance, frustration, or of emphasizing a statement (*informal*) ○ *Oh heck, I suppose that means we can't go.* ■ *n* sometimes used as a less offensive alternative for the word 'hell' (*informal*) ○ *What the heck is going on?* [Late 19C. Euphemistic alteration of HELL.] ◇ **a** *or* **one heck of a** used to indicate that something is particularly large, intense, or impressive (*informal*) ○ *There's a heck of a lot still to do before closing time.*

heckelphone /hék'l fōn/ *n* a bass musical instrument of the oboe family, in pitch between the cor anglais and the bassoon [Early 20C. < German *Heckelphon*, after Wilhelm *Heckel* (1856–1909), German instrument-maker.]

heckle /hék'l/ *v* (**-les, -ling, -led**) **1** *vti* **INTERRUPT SOMEBODY WITH SHOUTING** to shout remarks, insults, or questions in order to disconcert somebody who is making a speech or giving a performance ○ *I don't mind being heckled, but when they start throwing things it does rather put me off.* **2** *vt* **DRESS FLAX OR HEMP** to comb flax or hemp ■ *n* **COMB FOR FLAX OR HEMP** a comb used for dressing flax or hemp [14C. Variant of HACKLE[1].] —**heckler** *n*

hect- *prefix* = **hecto-** (*before vowels*)

hectare /hék taar, -tair/ *n* a metric unit of area equal to 100 ares or 10,000 sq. m (2.471 acres) [Early 19C. < French, < Greek *hekaton* 'hundred' + French *are* 'unit of area' < Latin *area* 'open space'.]

hectic /héktik/ *adj* **1** characterized by continual activity and haste, the lack of any time to rest or relax, and a sense of things barely under control ○ *Things have been a bit hectic at work this week.* **2** symptomatic of or involving a recurrent afternoon fever, especially one accompanying tuberculosis ○ *hectic fever* ○ *a hectic flush* [14C. Via Old French < Greek *hektikos* 'habitual, consumptive' < *ekhein* 'have'.] —**hectically** *adv*

hecto- *prefix* (*symbol* **h**) one hundred ○ *hectogram* [Via French < Greek *hekaton* < Indo-European]

hectocotylus /héktō kóttiləss/ (*plural* **-li** /-lī/) *n* a tentacle with which male octopuses and related molluscs transfer sperm [Mid-19C. < modern Latin, < French *hecto-* (see HECTO-) + Greek *kotulē* 'cup, something hollow'.]

hectogram /héktō gram/, **hectogramme** *n* a metric unit of mass equal to 100 grams [Late 18C. < French *hectogramme* < *hecto-* (see HECTO-) + *-gramme* (see GRAM[1]).]

hectolitre /hékto leetər/ *n* a metric unit of capacity equal to 100 litres [Early 19C. < French, < *hecto-* (see HECTO-) + *litre* (see LITRE).]

hectometre /héktō meetər/ *n* a metric unit of length equal to 100 metres [Early 19C. < French *hectomètre* < *hecto-* (see HECTO-) + *mètre* (see METRE[1]).]

hector /héktər/ *vti* to speak to somebody in a loud, threatening, or domineering tone intended to intimidate [Mid-17C. < HECTOR.]

Hector *n* in Greek mythology, the main Trojan hero in the Trojan War and a son of King Priam and Queen Hecuba [14C. Via Latin < Greek *Hektōr* 'holding fast' < *ekhein* 'hold'.]

Hecuba /hékyoobə/ *n* in Greek mythology, the wife of King Priam of Troy and mother of 16 children, including Cassandra, Hector, and Paris [Via Latin < Greek *Hekabē*]

he'd (*stressed*) /heed/; (*unstressed*) /hid, id/ *contr* **1** he had **2** he would

heddle /hédd'l/ *n* one of the sets of vertical cords or wires in the frame on a loom that guides the warp threads [Early 16C. < ?]

hedge /hej/ *n* **1 ROW OF SHRUBS** a close-set row of bushes, usually with their branches intermingled, forming a barrier or boundary in a garden, park, or field **2 PROTECTIVE METHOD** a means of protection against something, especially a means of guarding against financial loss ○ *a hedge against inflation* **3 EVASIVE STATEMENT** an evasive or noncommittal statement ■ *v* (**hedges, hedging, hedged**) **1** *vt* **PUT BUSHES AROUND** to put a row of intermingled shrubs around an area of ground **2** *vi* **WORK ON HEDGES** to work at repairing, trimming, or planting a hedge, especially on a farm **3** *vt* **RESTRICT** to restrict the scope or applicability of something by means of something else, e.g. a set of regulations, conditions, or qualifications ○ *It was a promise, but hedged in with so many ifs and buts that I wouldn't rely on it.* **4** *vi* **BE EVASIVE** to avoid answering a question directly or definitely ○ *She could have given a straight answer, but instead she hedged.* **5** *vi* **TRY TO OFFSET POSSIBLE LOSSES** to take measures to offset any possible loss on a financial transaction, especially by investing in counterbalancing securities as a guard against price fluctuations [Old English *hegg* < Germanic, 'grasp'] —**hedger** *n* —**hedgy** *adj*

hedge fund *n* **1** *US* an investment company that is organized as a limited partnership and uses high-risk techniques in the hope of making large profits **2** a unit trust that invests in derivatives and other instruments that involve substantial risks and may yield extraordinary returns

hedge garlic *n* = **garlic mustard**

hedgehog /héj hog/ *n* **1** small mammal that has a small pointed head and a round body with stiff spines on the back and that can roll itself into a ball when attacked. Native to: Europe, Africa, Asia. Family: Erinaceidae. **2** an underwater obstacle designed to keep landing craft from reaching a beach by ripping holes in the hulls [15C. Because they make noises reminiscent of the squeals and grunts of pigs.]

hedgehop /héj hop/ (**-hops, -hopping, -hopped**) *vi* to fly very low above the ground, often so low that the aircraft must ascend to avoid obstacles on the ground —**hedgehopper** *n*

hedgerow /héj rō/ *n* a row of bushes or small trees forming a hedge, especially round a field or along a country road or path

hedge sparrow *n* = **dunnock**

hedonic /hee dónnik/ *adj* **1** concerned with pleasure **2** characteristic of or relating to hedonism or hedonists [Mid-17C. < Greek *hēdonikos* < *hēdonē* 'pleasure'.]

hedonism /heéd'nizəm, hédd'nizəm/ *n* **1** a devotion, especially a self-indulgent one, to pleasure and happiness as a way of life **2** a philosophical doctrine that holds that pleasure is the highest good or the source of moral values [Mid-19C. < Greek *hēdonē* 'pleasure'.] —**hedonist** *n* —**hedonistic** /heédə nístik, héddə-/ *adj* —**hedonistically** *adv*

-hedron *suffix* a figure or crystal having a particular number or kind of surfaces ○ *pentahedron* [Via modern Latin < Greek *hedra* 'seat, base'] —**-hedral** *suffix*

heebie-jeebies /heébi jeébiz/ *npl* uncomfortable nervous or anxious feelings (*slang*) ○ *There's something about thick fog that gives me the heebie-jeebies.* [Early 20C. Invention.]

heed /heed/ *vti* to give serious attention to a warning or advice and take it into account when acting ■ *n* serious attention paid to somebody or to something such as a warning, piece of advice, or request [Old English *hēdan* < Germanic] —**heeder** *n*

heedful /heédf'l/ *adj* paying attention to somebody or to something such as a warning, piece of advice, or danger —**heedfully** *adv* —**heedfulness** *n*

heedless /heédləss/ *adj* not paying attention to somebody or to something such as a warning, piece of advice, or danger —**heedlessly** *adv* —**heedlessness** *n*

heehaw /heé haw/ *n* **1 DONKEY'S BRAY** the natural sound made by a donkey **2 NOISY LAUGH** an unrefined noisy laugh (*informal*) ■ *vi* **1 BRAY LIKE DONKEY** to make a natural heehaw **2 LAUGH NOISILY** to laugh in an unrefined noisy way [Early 19C. An imitation of the sound.]

heel[1] /heel/ *n* **1 BACK OF FOOT** the back part of a person's foot immediately below the ankle, or the same part of an animal's foot or paw **2 BACK OF SHOE OR SOCK** the part of a sock, stocking, shoe, or boot that covers the back part of somebody's foot **3 BACK OF UNDERSIDE OF SHOE** the back, usually thicker, portion of the underside of a shoe or other footwear that raises the foot off the ground ○ *I'll need to get new heels on these boots.* **4 THICKER PART OF PALM** the thicker part of the palm of the hand, located next to the wrist **5 PART OF GLOVE** the part of a glove that covers the part of the palm located next to the wrist **6 BREAD CRUST** a crusty end of a loaf of bread **7 CHEESE RIND** the hard rind from a wedge of cheese **8 PART OF GOLF CLUB** the part of the head of a golf club where the shaft is attached **9 END OF VIOLIN BOW** the end of a violin bow that is held while playing the violin **10 PIECE ATTACHED TO CUTTING** a small piece of a plant stem or tuber left attached to a cutting to promote the growth of new roots **11 BOTTOM OF MAST** the bottom end of a ship's or boat's mast **12 STERN** the stern end of a ship's keel **13 OFFENSIVE TERM** an offensive term that deliberately insults somebody's, especially a man's, behaviour (*insult*) ■ **heels** *npl* **HIGH HEELS** high-heeled shoes ■ *v* **1** *vt* **FIT OR REPAIR SHOE'S HEEL** to fit, replace, or repair the heel of a shoe or boot **2** *vi* **FOLLOW BY SOMEBODY'S HEELS** to follow closely at somebody's heels when commanded (*refers to dogs*) **3** *vt* **DIG HEELS INTO** to hit or prod an animal being ridden with the heel **4** *vi* **MOVE HEELS** to move the heels to music or touch a surface with the heels when dancing **5** *vt* **MISHIT GOLF BALL** to mishit a golf ball with the heel of a club **6** *vt* **KICK** to kick a ball with the heel, especially in rugby to pass the ball out of the scrummage using the heel [Old English *hēla* < Germanic] —**heeled** *adj* —**heelless** *adj* ◇ **cool** *or* **kick your heels** to wait or be kept waiting for a long time (*informal*) ◇ **dig in your heels** to hold stubbornly to a position or attitude ◇ **(hard) on the heels of somebody** *or* **something 1** close behind somebody or something **2** soon after somebody or something ◇ **show (somebody) a clean pair of heels** to run away from somebody ◇ **take to your heels** to run off ◇ **to heel 1** directly behind the person with whom a dog is walking **2** under control or discipline ◇ **turn on your heel** to turn round suddenly

SPELLCHECK See ***heal***.

heel[2] /heel/ *vti* to lean over to one side so far as to be in danger of capsizing, or cause a ship or boat to lean in this way ○ *The ship heeled in the wind.* ■ *n* a leaning to one side, or the degree to which a ship or boat is leaning [Late 16C. Alteration of *hield* (taken as past participle) < Old English *hieldan* 'lean, bend' < W Germanic.]

heel-and-toe *adj* describes walking or racing that requires the heel of one foot to touch the ground before the toe of the other is lifted from the ground ■ *vi* (**heel-and-toes, heel-and-toeing, heel-and-toed**) to operate the brake and accelerator pedals at the same time with one foot, usually to keep the engine revolutions high when shifting to a lower gear while racing

heelball /heél bawl/ *n* a black waxy substance used by shoemakers to blacken the edges of the heels and soles of shoes and boots or a similar substance used for making brass-rubbings

heelbar /heél baar/ *n* a small shop or a counter in a large shop where repairs are made to shoe soles and heels, often while the customer waits

heel bone *n* the quadrangular bone that forms the heel of the foot. Technical name **calcaneus**

heeler /heélər/ *n* **1** a person or machine that fits, replaces, or repairs the heels of shoes or boots ○ *the quickest heeler in the shoe factory* **2** *Aus* an Australian sheep or cattle dog that herds by biting at the heels of the animals

heel in *vt* to place a bare-root plant at a sharp angle in a holding bed and cover the roots with soil until it can be planted properly [Old English *helian* 'conceal' < Germanic]

heelpiece /heél peess/ *n* the part of a sock, stocking, shoe, or boot that fits round the heel of the foot

heelpost /heél pōst/ *n* a post to which the hinges of a gate or door are attached

heeltap /heél tap/ *n* **1** a small quantity of an alcoholic drink remaining at the bottom of a glass after the rest has been swallowed **2** a layer of leather or other material in the heel of a shoe or boot

Hefei /hő fáy/, **Hofei** capital of Anhui Province, E China. Population: 1,000,000 (1991).

Hefner /héfnər/, **Hugh** (*b.* 1926) US publisher

heft /heft/ *vt* **1 LIFT** to lift up something heavy, especially with a burst of effort **2 ESTIMATE WEIGHT OF** to lift something in order to estimate its weight ■ *n* **GREAT WEIGHT** substantial heaviness or bulk [15C. Probably from HEAVE, after pairs such as *cleave, cleft.*] —**hefter** *n*

hefty /héfti/ (**-ier, -iest**) *adj* **1 POWERFULLY BUILT** big and strong in physique **2 HEAVY** large and heavy to lift **3 EXPENSIVE** involving a large sum of money **4 FORCEFUL** delivered with or characterized by great force and power **5 STRENUOUS** requiring a lot of effort to do **6 LARGER THAN USUAL** much larger than is usual or required —**heftily** *adv* —**heftiness** *n*

Hegel /háyg'l/, **G. W. F.** (1770–1831) German philosopher. Full name **Georg Wilhelm Friedrich Hegel** —**Hegelian** /hi gáyli ən/ *adj, n*

Hegelianism /hi gáyli ənizəm/ *n* the philosophy of G.W.F. Hegel, which proposes a unified solution to all philosophical problems through development of a reasoning process that ultimately interprets reality by way of the dialectic method

hegemony /hi gémməni, -jémməni/ *n* control or dominating influence by one person or group over others, especially by one political group over society or one nation over others [Mid-16C. < Greek *hēgemonia* 'leadership' < *hēgisthai* 'lead'.] —**hegemonic** /héggə mónnik, héjjə-/ *adj* —**hegemonism** /hi gémmənizəm, -jémmə-/ *n* —**hegemonist** *n*

hegira /héjjirə, hi jírə/, **hejira** *n* a flight or withdrawal from somewhere, especially to escape from danger [Late 16C. Via medieval Latin < Arabic *hijra* 'the leaving of home and friends'.]

Hegira /héjjirə, hi jírə/, **Hejira** *n* **1** the withdrawal of the Prophet Muhammad from Mecca to Medina to escape persecution **2** the Muslim era, dated from the first day of the lunar year in which Muhammad's withdrawal to Medina took place

heh /hay/ *interj* used to express surprise or to attract attention [14C. Natural exclamation.]

Heian /háyən/ *adj* characteristic of or relating to Japan from 794–1185, when Confucianism and other Chinese influences were at their height [Late 19C. < Japanese *Heian-kyo*, now Kyoto, former capital of Japan.]

Heidegger /hí degər/, **Martin** (1889–1976) German philosopher

Heidelberg /híd'l burg/ city in SW Germany, on the River Neckar. Population: 139,392 (1992).

Heidelberg man *n* an extinct early human of the Pleistocene epoch that is known mainly from a fossilized jawbone [Early 20C. After HEIDELBERG.]

heifer /héffər/ *n* a young cow, especially one that has never had a calf [Old English *heahfore* < ?]

Heifetz /hífits/, **Jascha** (1901–87) Lithuanian-born US violinist

heigh-ho /-hő/ *interj* used to express boredom, disappointment, or weary resignation ○ *Heigh-ho. Here we go again.*

height /hīt/ *n* **1 LENGTH UPWARDS** the distance between somebody or something's lowest point and highest point ○ *a steep cliff about 70 metres in height* **2 DISTANCE ABOVE A POINT** the distance that somebody or something is above the ground, sea, or another reference point **3 NOTICEABLE TALLNESS** the condition of being noticeably high or tall compared to others ○ *His height makes him stand out in a crowd.* **4 HIGH POSITION** a high place or position, especially one where somebody can see a view or how high up he or she is (*often plural*) **5 HIGHEST POINT** the top or highest point of something ○ *When you reach the height, you'll get a marvellous view.* **6 HIGH LEVEL** a high level of intensity or severity (*often plural*) ○ *Their arrogance is reaching new heights.* **7 HIGHEST LEVEL** the time of greatest intensity, activity, importance, or success ○ *She was at the height of her powers.* **8 EXTREME** the most extreme example of something ○ *It was the height of folly to have gone there on your own.* ■ **heights** *npl* **HILLS OR MOUNTAINS** an area of hilly or mountainous terrain, especially one that is noticeably elevated above the surrounding region (*often in placenames*) [Old English *hēhþu* 'highest part' < Germanic]

LITERARY LINK ***Wuthering Heights***, a novel (1847) by Emily Brontë. It is the story of a foundling, Heathcliff, whose mistreatment at the hands of his adoptive family leads him to seek revenge later in life. The novel is noted for its evocative descriptions of the Yorkshire moors, its complex morality, and its intensity of feeling.

heighten /hít'n/ *vti* **1 MAKE OR BECOME GREATER** to make something such as a feeling or emotion greater or more intense, or become greater or more intense ○ *His attempts to reassure them served only to heighten their fears.* **2 MAKE OR BECOME HIGHER** to make something higher, or become higher ○ *As protection, they heightened the city walls by a further three feet.* **3 APPEAR BRIGHTER OR MAKE SOMETHING BRIGHTER** to make something such as a colour appear brighter or stronger ○ *The sunlight heightened the flush on her cheeks.* —**heightened** *adj* —**heightener** *n*

~~heighth~~ incorrect spelling of **height**

Heilongjiang /háy lóong jī áng/ province in NE China, bordering Russia. Capital: Harbin. Population: 36,720,000 (1994). Area: 463,600 sq. km/179,000 sq. mi.

Heimdall /háym daal/, **Heimdal, Heimdallr** /-daalər/ *n* in Norse mythology, a giant warrior who was the god of light and dawn [< Old Norse *Heimdallr* < *heimr* 'home, world']

Heimlich manoeuvre /hīmlik-/ *n* an emergency method for treating choking that uses an upward thrust immediately below the breastbone to expel food or another blockage from the windpipe [Late 20C. After Henry J. *Heimlich* (born 1920).]

Heine /hīnə/, **Heinrich** (1797–1856) German poet

Heinkel /hīngk'l/, **Ernst** (1888–1958) German engineer

Heinlein /hīn līn/, **Robert** (1907–88) US writer

heinous /háynəss/ *adj* shockingly evil or wicked [14C. < Old French *haineus* < *hair* 'to hate' < Germanic.] —**heinously** *adv* —**heinousness** *n*

heir /air/ *n* **1** a holder of the right to receive a property, position, or title of somebody else when that person dies **2** an inheritor of something such as a tradition, problem, or characteristic ○ *Our generation is the unfortunate heir to decades of pollution.* [14C. Via Old French *(h)eir* < Latin *heres*.] —**heirless** *adj* —**heirship** *n*

SPELLCHECK See ***air***.

heir apparent (*plural* **heirs apparent**) *n* **1** an heir whose entitlement to receive an inheritance cannot be altered by the birth of another heir **2** the expected inheritor of somebody else's position, status, or influence

~~heirarchy~~ incorrect spelling of **hierarchy**

heir at law (*plural* **heirs at law**) *n* the heir of somebody's property under the law if that person dies without a valid will

heiress /áirəss/ *n* a woman or girl who receives or has by law the right to receive the property, position, or title of another when that person dies

heirloom /áir loom/ *n* **1** something valuable that has been in the possession of a family for a long time and has been passed on from one generation to the next **2** an item of personal property that is attached to the estate that the legal heir will inherit [< LOOM² in obsolete sense 'tool, utensil']

heir presumptive (*plural* **heirs presumptive**) *n* an heir whose entitlement to an inheritance will cease if another heir is born whose entitlement is greater

Heisenberg /hīz'n burg/, **Werner** (1901–76) German physicist

Heisenberg uncertainty principle *n* PHYS = **uncertainty principle**

heist /hīst/ *n US, Can* a theft or robbery, especially of money or valuables, usually involving the use of weapons (*slang*) ■ *vt US, Can* to steal or rob something, especially money or valuables, usually while carrying weapons (*slang*) [Mid-19C. Representing a local American pronunciation of HOIST.] —**heister** *n*

heitiki /hay téeki/ *n NZ* a Maori fertility symbol (**tiki**) carved from greenstone in the shape of a foetus, worn as a neck ornament [Mid-19C. < Maori, 'hanging image'.]

Hejaz /hee jáz/ province in W Saudi Arabia, on the Red Sea. Area: 348,600 sq. km/134,600 sq. mi.

hejira *n* = **hegira**

Hejira *n* ISLAM = **Hegira**

Hekate *n* = **Hecate**

Heke Pokai /hékay pōkī/, **Hone** (1810?–50) Maori leader

Hekla /héklə/ active volcano in SW Iceland. Height: 1,491 m/4,892 ft.

Hel /hel/, **Hela** /hé laa/ *n* **1** in Norse mythology, the goddess of the dead and the underworld **2** in Norse mythology, the underworld of the dead [< Old Norse]

HeLa cell /héelə-/, **Hela cell** *n* a cell from a strain of human cervical cancer cells that is used in medical and biological research [Mid-20C. Acronym < *Henrietta Lacks*, from whom the original cells were taken.]

held past tense, past participle of **hold**¹

Heldentenor /héldən tə nawr/ *n* a tenor or tenor voice with a robust dramatic quality that is suited especially for heroic roles in the operas of Richard Wagner [Early 20C. < German, 'hero tenor'.]

Helen /héllən/, **Helen of Troy** *n* in Greek mythology, the daughter of Zeus and Leda and the most beautiful woman in Greece. Her husband was Menelaus, the king of Sparta.

Helena /héllənə/ capital of Montana, in the W of the state. Population: 28,306 (1998 estimate).

Helena, St (248?–328?) Roman empress

Helene /hə léeni/ *n* a very small irregularly shaped natural satellite of Saturn, discovered in 1980

helenium /hi léeni əm/ (*plural* **-ums** *or* **-um**) *n* a plant of the daisy family that has yellow or dark reddish flowers or in cultivated varieties sometimes bicoloured flowers. Native to: North and South America. Genus: *Helenium*. [Early 17C. Via modern Latin < Greek *helenion*.]

Helen of Troy *n* = **Helen**

Helensvale /héllənz vayl/ town in SE Queensland, Australia. Population: 13,823 (1996).

heli /hélli/ (*plural* **-is**) *n* a rotary-wing aircraft (*informal*) [Shortening of HELICOPTER]

heli- *prefix* helicopter ○ *helipad* [< HELICOPTER]

heliacal /hi lī ək'l/ *adj* describes the rising or setting of a star that occurs at the same time as the rising or setting of the Sun, because of their near conjunction [Mid-16C. < late Latin *heliacus* < Greek *hēlios* 'sun'.] —**heliacally** *adv*

helianthemum /héeli ánthəməm/ *n* an evergreen perennial which forms a low mound. Flowers: white, yellow, pink, orange. Native to: United States, Europe, Asia Minor. Genus: *Helianthemum*. [Early 19C. < modern Latin, < Greek *hēlios* 'sun' + *anthemon* 'flower' (because the flower turns with the sun).]

helianthus /héeli ánthəss/ (*plural* **-thuses** *or* **-thus**) *n* a tall perennial plant related to sunflowers. Flowers: yellow, daisy-like. Genus: *Helianthus*. [Late 18C. < modern Latin, < Greek *hēlios* 'sun' + *anthos* 'flower' (because the flower turns with the sun).]

heliborne /hélli bawrn/ *adj* transported by helicopter

helic- *prefix* = **helico-** (*before vowels*)

helical /héllik'l/ *adj* in the shape of a helix or spiral [Late 16C. < Latin *helix* (see HELIX).] —**helically** *adv*

helical gear *n* a gear whose teeth are formed to curve along a spiral path on the surface of the gear on an axis oblique to the axis of the gear itself

helices plural of **helix**

helichrysum /hélli krīzəm/ (*plural* **-sums** *or* **-sum**) *n* an annual or perennial plant of the daisy family with flowers that retain their colour when dried. Genus: *Helichrysum*. [Mid-16C. < Latin, < Greek *helix* 'spiral' + *khrusos* 'gold'.]

helico- *prefix* helix, spiral ○ *helicograph* [< Greek *helik-*, stem of *helix*]

helicograph /hélliko graaf, -graf/ *n* an instrument for drawing spiral curves on a flat surface

helicoid /hélli koyd/ *adj* shaped or coiled like a spiral (*technical*) ○ *a helicoid shell* ■ *n* a spiral geometric surface that resembles a thread on a screw [Late 17C. < Greek *helicoidēs* < *helix* 'spiral'.] —**helicoidal** /hélli kóyd'l/ *adj* —**helicoidally** *adv*

helicon /héllikən, -kon/ *n* a large bass tuba that encircles the player's body, used in marching bands [Late 19C. < Mount *Helicon* in Greece, reputed home of the Muses; influenced by HELIX.]

helicopter /hélli koptər/ *n* an aircraft without wings that moves by means of large blades (**rotors**) that spin round above it ■ *vti* to travel or transport somebody or something in a helicopter ○ *The survivors were helicoptered to a hospital.* [Late 19C. < French *hélicoptère* < Greek *helix* 'spiral' + *pteron* 'wing'.]

helicopter gunship *n* a large heavily armed helicopter used to protect troops on the ground

heliculture /hélli kulchər/ *n* the science or profession of raising snails for food [< modern Latin *Helix*, genus of spiral-shelled molluscs < Greek *helix* 'spiral'] —**helicultural** *adj* —**heliculturalist** *n*

helideck /hélli dek/ *n* a deck on something such as a ship or offshore oil platform that is used as a landing site for helicopters

helio- *prefix* sun ○ *heliostat* [< Greek *hēlios* < Indo-European]

heliocentric /héeli ō séntrik/, **heliocentrical** /-séntrik'l/ *adj* **1** with the sun at the centre ○ *a heliocentric orbit* **2** measured from or considered as if viewed from the centre of the sun —**heliocentrically** *adv* —**heliocentricity** /-sen tríssəti/ *n*

heliodor /héeli ō dawr/ *n* a clear yellow variety of beryl from SW Africa. Use: gems. [Early 20C. < HELIO- + Greek *dōron* 'gift'.]

heliograph /héeli ə graaf, -graf/ *n* **1** an apparatus that is used to send messages in Morse code by flashes of reflected sunlight **2** an apparatus used to photograph the sun —**heliographer** /héeli óggrəfər/ *n* —**heliographic** /héeli ə gráffik/ *adj*

heliolatry /héeli óllətri/ *n* worship of the sun —**heliolater** *n* —**heliolatrous** *adj*

heliolithic /héeli ō líthik/ *adj* describes a culture or society characterized by worship of the sun and the construction of monuments or temples using huge stones (**megaliths**)

heliometer /héeli ómmitər/ *n* a refracting telescope with a divided objective that is used to measure small angular distances between celestial objects or points on the moon —**heliometric** /héeli ə méttrik/ *adj* —**heliometrical** *adj* —**heliometrically** *adv* —**heliometry** *n*

Heliopolis /héeli óppəliss/ city of ancient Egypt, in the Nile delta

Helios /héeli oss/ *n* in Greek mythology, the god of the sun. Roman equivalent **Sol** *n.* 2

helioseismology /héeli ō sīz mólləji/ *n* the scientific study of the sound waves in the sun's atmosphere

heliosphere /héeli ō sfeer/ *n* a spherical region round the sun, approximately 100 astronomical units in radius, outside which interstellar space begins

heliostat /héeli ō stat/ *n* an instrument with an automatically rotated mirror that reflects the sun's light in a constant direction, used to measure the sun's radiation [Mid-18C. < modern Latin *heliostata* or French *héliostat*, both < Greek *hēlios* 'sun' + *statos* 'standing'.] —**heliostatic** /héeli ō státtik/ *adj*

heliotaxis /héeli ō táksiss/ *n* movement towards or away from sunlight in an organism that is able to move about freely —**heliotactic** *adj*

heliotherapy /héeli ō thérrəpi/ *n* treatment of illness by exposure to direct sunlight

heliotrope /héeli ə trōp/ (*plural* **-tropes** *or* **-trope**) *n* **1 PLANT WITH PURPLE FLOWERS** a hairy plant of the borage family, especially a South American species cultivated for its small, very fragrant purple flowers. Genus: *Heliotropium*. **2 FLOWER THAT TURNS TOWARDS SUN** a plant with flowers that turn towards the sun **3 BLUISH COLOUR** a bluish-purple colour **4** MINERALS = **bloodstone 5 SURVEYING INSTRUMENT** an instrument used in geodesic surveying to reflect the Sun's rays over long distances [Pre-12C. Via Latin < Greek *heliotropion* < *helios* 'sun' + *tropos* 'turning'.] —**heliotrope** *adj*

heliotropism /héeli óttrəpizəm/ *n* growth towards sunlight by a plant. ◊ **phototropism** —**heliotropic** /héeli ə tróppik/ *adj* —**heliotropical** *adj* —**heliotropically** *adv*

heliozoan /héeli ō zṓ ən/ *n* a free-living, usually freshwater, protozoan that has a spherical shell and radiating projections (**pseudopodia**). Class: Heliozoa. [Late 19C. < modern Latin *Heliozoa* < Greek *hēlios* 'sun' + *zōion* 'animal'.] —**heliozoic** *adj*

helipad /hélli pad/ *n* an area where helicopters take off and land

heliport /hélli pawrt/ *n* an airport designed for helicopters

heliskiing *n* skiing in which skiers are taken to a usually remote ski slope by helicopter

helistop /hélli stop/ *n* a place where helicopters can take off and land, usually without the support facilities found at a heliport

helium /héeli əm/ *n* (*symbol* **He**) a nonflammable inert gaseous element that is colourless and odourless. Source: natural gas. Use: inert atmospheres, cryogenic research, lasers, inflating balloons. [Late 19C. < Greek *hēlios* 'sun' (because its existence was deduced from its emission line in the solar spectrum).]

helix /héeliks/ (*plural* **helices** /hélli seez/ *or* **helixes**) *n* **1 SPIRAL OR COIL** something in the form of a spiral or coil, e.g. a corkscrew or a coiled spring **2 SPIRAL CURVE** a mathematical curve that lies on a cylinder or cone and makes a constant angle with the straight lines lying in the cylinder or cone **3 RIM OF EAR** the rim of the external ear [Mid-16C. Via Latin < Greek.]

LITERARY LINK ***The Double Helix***, a memoir (1968) by US scientist James D. Watson. In this personal account of the landmark discovery of the structure of the DNA molecule in 1953, for which Watson later shared the Nobel Prize with Francis Crick and Maurice Wilkins, scientific research is shown to be a competitive race in which ego, politics, and luck play prominent roles.

hell /hel/ *n* **1 hell, Hell PLACE OF PUNISHMENT AFTER DEATH** according to many religions, the place where the souls of people who are damned suffer eternal punishment after death **2 hell, Hell DEVILISH POWER** according to some religions, Satan or the powers of evil that live in hell **3 UNDERWORLD** according to some religions, the place where the spirits of all people go after death **4 SUFFERING** a state or place of extreme pain or misery, or something or somebody that causes extreme pain or misery ○ *Finals are absolute hell.* ○ *She went through hell until she heard they were safe.* ■ *interj* **EXPRESSING ANNOYANCE** used to express annoyance or surprise (*sometimes offensive*) ○ *Hell! I've lost the key.* [Old English *hel(l)* < Indo-European, 'conceal'] ◇ **a** *or* **one hell of a** used as an intensifier (*informal*) ◇ **come hell or high water** whatever difficulties there may be ◇ **from hell** of the worst sort imaginable (*informal*) ○ *The bus ride in the snowstorm was a trip from hell.* ◇ **give somebody hell 1** to scold somebody severely (*informal*) **2** to cause somebody trouble or pain (*informal*) ◇ **hell for leather** extremely rapidly and often recklessly (*informal*) ◇ **hell to pay** serious trouble or punishment that is sure to result from something (*informal*) ◇ **(just) for the hell of it** just for amusement or excitement (*informal*) ◇ **like hell 1** very fast or very intensely (*informal*) **2** used to emphasize disagreement or denial (*informal*) ◇ **play (merry) hell with something** to cause harm, disruption, or damage to something (*informal*) ◇ **raise hell 1** to object to something strongly and loudly (*informal*) **2** to cause a noisy disturbance (*informal*) ◇ **the hell 1** used to emphasize annoyance (*informal*) ○ *Get the hell out of it. I'm trying to work.* **2** used to emphasize disagreement or denial (*informal*) ○ *Did he offer to help? The hell he did.*

he'll (*stressed*) /heel/; (*unstressed*) /eel, il/ *contr* **1** he will **2** he shall

Helladic /he láddik/ *adj* associated with or characteristic of the Bronze Age civilization that flourished in Greece from 3000 to 1100 BC [Early 19C. < Greek *Helladikos* < *Hellas* 'Greece'.]

Hellas /héllass/ **1** Greek name for Greece **2** extensive plain on the surface of Mars, in the southern hemisphere

hellbender /hél bendər/ *n* a large, dark grey salamander. Native to: rivers in eastern and central United States. *Cryptobranchus alleganiensis*.

hell-bent *adj* absolutely determined to do something, regardless of the consequences

hellcat /hél kat/ *n* an offensive term that deliberately insults a woman's temper and suggests that she is violent

hellebore /hélli bawr/ (*plural* **-bores** *or* **-bore**) *n* **1** an early-flowering, often poisonous perennial plant that has large divided leaves. Flowers: drooping white, pink, dark purple, sometimes green. Native to: Europe, Asia. Genus: *Helleborus*. **2** a poisonous plant with greenish flowers. Native to: North America. Genus: *Veratrum*. [Pre-12C. Via Old French < Greek *helleboros*.]

helleborine /héllibə rīn, -reen/ *n* an orchid often occurring in woodland. Native to: temperate regions. Genera: *Epipactis* and *Cephalanthera*. [Late 16C. Directly or via French < Latin *(h)elleborine* < Greek *helleborinē* 'plant like hellebore'.]

Hellen /héllən/ *n* in Greek mythology, a king of Thessaly and ancestor of the ancient Hellenic peoples

Hellene /hélleen/, **Hellenian** /he léeni ən/ *n* (*formal*) **1** an ancient Greek **2** somebody who comes from Greece [Mid-17C. < Greek *Hellēn* 'a Greek'.]

Hellenic /he léenik, -lénnik/ *adj* relating to ancient Greece, or its people, languages, or culture ■ *n* the branch of Indo-European consisting of the ancient and modern forms of Greek [Mid-17C. < Greek *Hellēnikos* < *Hellēn* 'a Greek'.] —**Hellenically** *adv*

Hellenise *vti* = **Hellenize**

Hellenism /héllənizəm/ *n* **1 ANCIENT GREEK CULTURE** the culture and civilization of ancient Greece, especially in the period after Alexander the Great when it spread to other parts of the Mediterranean and Middle East and North Africa **2 ADMIRATION FOR ANCIENT GREEK CULTURE** the enthusiasm for or adoption of ancient Greek culture or customs **3 GREEK CHARACTERISTIC** a Greek custom or idiom **4 GREEK NATIONAL CHARACTER** the supposed national character of the Greeks [Early 17C. < Greek *Hellēnismos* < *Hellēnizein* (see HELLENIZE).]

Hellenist /héllənist/ *n* **1** a specialist in the study of Greek language, literature, culture, or history, or an admirer of the Greeks and their culture **2** somebody, especially a Jew, who adopted Greek customs, language, and culture during the 4th to 1st centuries BC [Early 17C. < Greek *Hellēnistēs* < *Hellēnizein* (see HELLENIZE).]

Hellenistic /héllə nístik/ *adj* **1 OF ANCIENT GREEK CIVILIZATION** characteristic of or concerned with ancient Greek civilization from the late 4th to 1st centuries BC **2 OF GREEKS** characteristic of or associated with the Greeks **3 PREFERRING GREEK CULTURE** enthusiastic for or adopting ancient Greek culture or customs ○ *the Hellenistic Jews of Alexandria* —**Hellenistically** *adv*

Hellenize /héllə nīz/ (**-nizes, -nizing, -nized**), **Hellenise** (**-nises, -nising, -nised**) *vti* to adopt or make closer in character the language and culture of the ancient Greeks [Early 17C. < Greek *Hellēnizein* 'speak Greek, to make Greek' < *Hellēn* (see HELLENE).] —**Hellenization** /héllə nī záysh'n/ *n* —**Hellenizer** *n*

heller /héllər/ (*plural* **-ler**) *n* MONEY, COINS = **haler** [Late 16C. < German, after *Schwäbisch Hall*, town in Germany.]

Heller /héllər/, **Joseph** (1923–99) US writer

Hellespont /héllispont/ ♦ **Dardanelles**

hellfire /hél fīr/ *n* punishment in hell, often described as eternal torment in the flames of hell's fires ■ *adj* detailing the punishment sinners can expect in hell in a vigorous and emotional way

hellgrammite /hélgrə mīt/ *n* US the large aquatic carnivorous larva of the North American dobsonfly, often used as fish bait [Mid-19C. < ?]

hellhole /hél hōl/ *n* a terrifying, unbearable, or evil place

hellhound /hél hownd/ *n* **1** a fiend or fiendish, wicked person **2** a hound said to guard the gates of hell, especially in Greek mythology

hellish /héllish/ *adj* **1 VILE** so wicked or cruel that it seems characteristic of the devil **2 OF HELL** like, from, or typical of hell **3 DREADFUL** extremely unpleasant or difficult (*informal*) ○ *The exam was absolutely hellish.* ■ *adv* **EXTREMELY** used as an intensifier (*informal*) ○ *hellish difficult* —**hellishly** *adv* —**hellishness** *n*

Hellman /hélmən/, **Lillian** (1905–84) US playwright

hello /hə lṓ, he lṓ/, **hallo** /hə lṓ, ha lṓ/, **hullo** /hə lṓ, hu lṓ/ *interj, n* (*plural* **-los**) **1 WORD USED AS GREETING** a word used to greet somebody you meet, to answer a telephone call, or to begin a radio or television programme ○ *Hello. Nice to meet you.* ○ *After we had all said our hellos, we settled down to eat.* **2 WORD TO ATTRACT ATTENTION** a word used to attract attention ○ *Hello! Is there anyone in?* **3 WORD EXPRESSING SURPRISE** a word used to express surprise ○ *Hello! What's that doing here?* [Late 19C. Probably < French *holá* 'stop there!', used to attract attention.]

hell-raiser *n* somebody whose idea of having a good time involves behaving in ways that other people consider drunken, rowdy, and disruptive

Hell's Angel *n* a member of a Californian gang of motorcyclists, mostly men, typically dressing in denim and leather and originally noted for violent antisocial behaviour, or a member of any similar gang elsewhere

helluva /hélləvə/ *adj* used as an intensifier (*informal*) ○ *a helluva party* [Early 20C. Representing *hell of a*.]

helm[1] /helm/ *n* **1 SHIP'S STEERING APPARATUS** the apparatus used to steer a ship, especially the wheel or handle (**tiller**) by which the rudder is turned **2 POSITION OF CONTROL** a position of leadership or control within an organization, country, or enterprise ○ *The failing company needed a new chief at its helm.* ■ *vt* **1 STEER SHIP** to be at the helm of a ship steering it **2 DIRECT** to be at the head of an organization, country, or enterprise directing it [Old English *helma* < Germanic, 'handle'] —**helmless** *adj*

helm[2] /helm/ *n* an ancient or medieval helmet (*archaic or literary*) [Old English, < Germanic, 'conceal, cover']

helmet /hélmit/ *n* **1 HARD PROTECTIVE HEAD COVERING** a hat or other head covering made of a hard material and worn to protect the head from injury, often part of a uniform, suit of armour, or protective clothing **2 PROTECTIVE HAT** any protective hat, e.g. against cold weather or the heat of the sun **3 PART SHAPED LIKE HELMET** a part of an organism, e.g. a flower's sepal or corolla, resembling a helmet [15C. < Old French, diminutive of *helme* 'helmet' < Germanic.] —**helmeted** *adj*

helminth /hélminth/ *n* a parasitic worm, e.g. a fluke, nematode, or tapeworm [Mid-19C. < Greek *helminth-* 'intestinal worm'.] —**helminthoid** *adj*

helminthiasis /hélmin thī́ əsiss/ *n* infestation by parasitic worms, especially a disease caused by this

helminthic /hel mínthik/ *adj* **1** caused by or relating to flukes, nematodes, or other parasitic worms (**helminths**) **2** eradicating or expelling parasitic worms ■ *n* = **vermifuge**

helminthology /hélmin thólləji/ *n* the scientific study of parasitic worms —**helminthologist** *n*

Helmont /hél mont/, **Jan Baptista van** (1580–1644) Flemish chemist and physiologist

helmsman /hélmzmən/ (*plural* **-men** /-mən/) *n* **1** the steerer of a ship **2** a director of an organization, country, or enterprise ○ *the country's helmsman in the crisis* —**helmsmanship** *n*

helo /héllō/ (*plural* **-os**) *n* (*informal*) **1** a rotary-winged aircraft **2** an airport designed for helicopters [Mid-20C. Shortening and alteration of HELICOPTER.]

Héloïse /éllō eez/ (1098?–1164) French abbess and lover of Peter Abelard

helot /héllət/ *n* a serf or enslaved person [Early 19C. Via Latin *Helotes* < Greek *Heilōtes*, probably after *Helos*, town in Laconia whose inhabitants were enslaved.] —**helotage** *n*

Helot *n* in ancient Sparta, a member of a class of serfs claimed as property by the state but assigned to individual Spartans to work on their land [Late 16C. See HELOT.]

helotism /héllətizəm/ *n* **1** a political or social system in which one group, class, or nation is systematically oppressed by another **2** symbiosis found especially among ants, in which one species acts as workers for another, dominant species

help /help/ *v* **1** *vti* **ASSIST** to make it easier for somebody to do something, or possible for somebody to do something that one person cannot do alone, by providing assistance of some sort ○ *Let me help you with those packages.* ○ *Can you help me solve this problem?* **2** *vti* **ADVISE** to provide somebody with advice, directions, or other information ○ *I wonder if you could help me? I'm trying to find Belmont Road.* **3** *vti* **BE USEFUL** to make something easier or more likely ○ *It would help if you didn't keep shaking the ladder.* ○ *Would a degree help me get a better job?* **4** *vti* **MAKE THINGS BETTER** to bring about an improvement in something unpleasant, unbearable, or unfortunate ○ *I took a couple of aspirins, but they didn't help my headache.* ○ *You look ridiculous in that dress, and the hat doesn't help.* **5** *vti* **PROVIDE FOR SOMEBODY'S NEEDS** to provide somebody with something that he or she needs, especially money **6** *vti* **ADVANCE** to promote the advancement or improvement of something ○ *Opening a new sports centre won't cut out teenage crime, but it might help.* **7** *vt* **SERVE** to serve somebody in a shop, restaurant, or other establishment ○ *Can I help you, sir?* **8** *vt* **BRING FOOD** to give somebody or yourself a serving of food ○ *He helped himself to some cake.* **9** *vt* **KEEP FROM DOING** to keep somebody or yourself from doing something (*usually in negative statements*) ○ *We couldn't help overhearing your conversation.* ○ *I didn't want to laugh, but I couldn't help myself.* **10** *vt* **PREVENT** to prevent something from happening (*usually in negative statements*) ○ *The child couldn't have helped the accident.* ■ *n* **1 ASSISTANCE** something that is done for or given to somebody in order to make something easier, possible, or better ○ *I could do with some help in the kitchen.* **2 SOMEBODY OR SOMETHING THAT ASSISTS** a provider of aid or assistance to somebody ○ *The headaches are pretty bad, but the aspirins are a help.* **3 WAY OUT** a way of avoiding doing something or of undoing something (*often in negative statements*) ○ *Well, there's no help for it now but to start digging.* **4 SOMEBODY PAID TO CLEAN** a paid helper with the housework in somebody else's home **5 SERVANTS COLLECTIVELY** domestic servants as a group (+ *singular or plural verb*) ○ *told us that the help have to eat in the kitchen* ■ *interj* **CALLS FOR ASSISTANCE** used to call for assistance when somebody is in danger or difficulty [Old English *helpan* < Germanic] —**helper** *n* ◇ **help yourself** to take something for your own use, usually without permission

USAGE can't help but: Traditionally, speakers and writers had a choice between, for example, *can't help doing* and *can't* [or *cannot*] *but do*. The latter is now uncommon. *Can't help but do* is often seen, but it is a redundant mixture of the two forms, and should be avoided in favour of *can't help doing*.

help out *vti* to give somebody some help, e.g. by doing some work or giving money

⚡**help desk** *n* a service providing technical help and support for people using a computer package or network

helper T cell, **helper cell** *n* a white blood cell that is part of the body's immune response, recognizing foreign antigens and stimulating the production of cells to control them

helpful /hélpf'l/ *adj* providing or willing to provide assistance, information, or other aid ○ *You might find this book helpful.* —**helpfully** *adv* —**helpfulness** *n*

helping /hélping/ *n* an amount of food served to somebody at one time

helping hand *n* something done to assist somebody else

helpless /hélpləss/ *adj* 1 **NEEDING HELP** unable to manage without help 2 **DEFENCELESS** unprotected and unable to provide an adequate defence against an attack 3 **UNABLE TO ACT EFFECTIVELY** unable to do anything to prevent something happening ○ *He was helpless to stop the assault.* 4 **UNRESTRAINED** unable to exert control or restraint ○ *His jokes had us absolutely helpless.* —**helplessly** *adv* —**helplessness** *n*

helpline /hélp lῑn/ *n* a telephone service that provides advice or information to people who phone up with problems or inquiries

Helpmann /hélpmən/, **Sir Robert Murray** (1909–86) Australian ballet dancer and choreographer

helpmate /hélp mayt/ *n* a helpful companion or partner, especially a spouse

helpmeet /hélp meet/ *n* a helpmate, especially a wife (*archaic; sometimes offensive*) [Late 17C. < MEET² 'suitable', from 'an help meet for him' (Genesis 2:18, 20).]

Helsingborg /hélssing bawrg/ port in S Sweden, on the Öresund. Population: 111,853 (1993).

Helsingør /hélseng úr/ port in E Denmark, on the island of Zealand. Population: 43,302 (1992).

Helsinki /hel síngki/ capital and chief port of Finland, on the Gulf of Finland in the S of the country. Population: 546,317 (1999).

helter-skelter /héltər skéltər/ *adv, adj* 1 **HURRIEDLY** with hurry and confusion ○ *The rabbits rushed helter-skelter down their burrows.* 2 **HAPHAZARDLY** without order or organization ○ *The winds had knocked the huge trees helter-skelter all over the park.* ■ *n* 1 **SPIRAL SLIDE** a fairground amusement consisting of a high tower with a spiral slide round it 2 **CONFUSED STATE** a hurried or disorganized situation or state [Late 16C. Probably formed to suggest hurried action.]

helve /helv/ *n* the handle of a tool such as an axe, pick, or hammer [Old English *helfe* < Germanic]

Helvellyn /hel véllin/ mountain in NW England. Height: 950 m/3,118 ft.

Helvetia /hel vééshə/ Roman name for Switzerland

Helvetian /hel véesh'n/ *n* 1 somebody who was born in or is a citizen of Switzerland 2 a member of the Helvetii [Mid-16C. < Latin *Helvetia* 'Switzerland' < *Helvetius* 'of or with the Helvetii'.] —**Helvetian** *adj*

Helvetic /hel véttik/ *adj* relating to the religious teachings of Ulrich Zwingli and other Swiss Protestant reformers [Early 18C. < Latin *Helvetia* (see HELVETIAN).] —**Helvetic** *n*

Helvetii /hel véeshi ῑ/ *npl* a Celtic people who came from S Germany and migrated to Helvetia, where they settled during the second century BC [Late 19C. < Latin.]

Helvétius /hel véeshi əss/, **Claude Adrien** (1715–71) French philosopher

hem¹ /hem/ *n* 1 **FOLDED FABRIC EDGE** a neat nonfraying edge made by folding fabric over and stitching it down 2 HANDICRAFT = **hemline** *n*. 1 ■ *v* (**hems, hemming, hemmed**)

1 *vti* **MAKE HEM ON** to fold over and stitch down fabric to make a hem on something ○ *hem curtains* 2 *vt* **ENCLOSE** to surround and enclose somebody or something ○ *The small yard was hemmed about by a tall hedge.* [Old English, related to Old Frisian *hemme* 'enclosed land']

hem in *vt* to confine and restrict somebody or something

hem² /hem/ *interj* 1 a word used to represent the sound made by somebody clearing his or her throat or coughing quietly in order to attract attention, warn somebody else, or hide embarrassment or uncertainty ■ *vi* (**hems, hemming, hemmed**) to make the sound 'hem' or otherwise hesitate in speech [15C. An imitation of the sound.] ◇ **hem and haw** to hesitate while speaking or deciding about something

hem- *prefix* US = haem-

hema- *prefix* US = haema-

he-man (*plural* **he-men**) *n* a strong, muscular man (*informal*)

hemat- *prefix* US = haemat-

hemato- *prefix* US = haemato-

heme /heem/ *n* US = **haem**

Hemel Hempstead /hémm'l hémpstid/ town in Hertfordshire. Population: 79,235 (1991).

hemeralopia /hémmərə lốpi ə/ *n* impaired vision in daylight (*technical*) [Early 18C. < modern Latin, < Greek *hēmeralōps* 'day-blind eye'.] —**hemeralopic** /-lóppik/ *adj*

hemerocallis /hémmə rō kálliss/ *n* = **day lily** [Mid-17C. < Greek *hēmerokallis* 'lily that flowers for a day' < *hēmera* 'day' + *kallos* 'beauty'.]

hemi- *prefix* half, partial ○ *hemihydrate* ○ *hemimetabolous* [< Greek *hēmi-* < Indo-European]

-hemia = -aemia

hemicellulose /hémmi séllyoῦ lōss, -lōz/ *n* any polysaccharide found in plant cell walls [Because less complex than cellulose]

hemichordate /hémmi káwr dayt/ *n* a marine animal resembling a worm that has a rudimentary cartilaginous skeleton (**notochord**) and numerous gill slits. Phylum: Hemichordata. [Late 19C. < modern Latin *Hemichordata* < Greek *hēmi-* (see HEMI-) + Latin *chorda* (see CORD).] —**hemichordate** *adj*

hemicycle /hémmi sῑk'l/ *n* a structure or arrangement that has a semicircular shape [15C. Via French and Latin < Greek *hēmikuklion* 'semicircle'.] —**hemicyclic** /hémmi sῑklik, -síklik/ *adj*

hemidemisemiquaver /hémmi démmi sémmi kwáyvər/ *n* a note with a time value equal to half a demisemiquaver or one sixty-fourth of a semibreve. US term **sixty-fourth note**

hemihedral /hémmi heédrəl/ *adj* describes crystals that have only half the number of faces needed for complete symmetry

hemihydrate /hémmi hῑ drayt/ *n* a hydrate, e.g. plaster of Paris, that consists of two parts compound to one part water

hemimetabolous /hémmi mə tábbələss/, **hemimetabolic** /hémmi metə bóllik/ *adj* describes winged insects that lack complete metamorphosis, as do grasshoppers, whose increasingly larger nymphs approach adult form without going through a pupal stage

hemimorphic /hémmi máwrfik/ *adj* describes crystals that do not have a horizontal axis of symmetry, so that the top and bottom of the crystal display different forms [Mid-19C. < HEMI- + Greek *morphē* 'form'.]

Ernest Hemingway

Hemingway /hémming way/, **Ernest** (1899–1961) US writer

hemiola /hémmi ốlə/ *n* a rhythmic alternation of two notes in the place of three or three notes in place of two [14C. Via medieval Latin < Greek *hēmiolia* 'in the ratio of one and a half to one' < *holos* 'whole'.]

hemiplegia /hémmi pleéji ə/ *n* total or partial inability to move, experienced on one side of the body, and caused by brain disease or injury. ◊ **paraplegia, quadriplegia** [Early 17C. Via modern Latin < Greek *hēmiplēgia* < *plēgē* (see -PLEGIA).] —**hemiplegic** *adj, n*

hemipode /hémmi pōd/, **hemipod** /-pod/ *n* a small round-bodied ground-dwelling bird. Native to: grasslands of Africa, Australasia, S Europe, Asia. Family: Turnicidae. [Mid-19C. < HEMI- + Greek *podos* 'foot'.]

hemipteran /hi míptərən/ *n* an insect that has mouthparts adapted for piercing and sucking and two pairs of wings. Order: Hemiptera. [Late 19C. < modern Latin *Hemiptera* 'with half a wing' < Greek *pteron* 'wing'; from the partly hardened forewings of bugs.] —**hemipteran** *adj* —**hemipterous** *adj*

hemisphere /hémmi sfeer/ *n* 1 **HALF OF THE EARTH** one half of the Earth, especially a half north or south of the equator or west or east of the prime meridian 2 **HALF OF SPHERE** one half of a sphere or of anything spherical in shape 3 ANAT = **cerebral hemisphere** 4 **HALF OF CELESTIAL SPHERE** either half of the celestial sphere north or south of the celestial equator [14C. Via French or Latin < Greek *hēmisphairion* < *sphaira* 'ball'.] —**hemispheric** /hémmi sférrik/ *adj* —**hemispherical** *adj* —**hemispherically** *adv*

hemistich /hémmi stik/ *n* half of a line of poetry, usually separated from the rest by a caesura [Late 16C. Via late Latin < Greek *hēmistikhion* < *stikhos* 'line of verse'.]

hemizygous /hémmi zῑgəss/ *adj* having only one of a specified pair of genes, as, e.g., do the unpaired X chromosomes of male mammals

hemline /hém līn/ *n* 1 the bottom edge of a skirt, dress, or coat 2 the height of the hem of an item of women's clothing, especially the typical height of hems on fashionable women's clothing during a certain period ○ *Hemlines are up again.*

Hemlock

hemlock /hém lok/ (*plural* **-locks** *or* **-lock**) *n* 1 **POISONOUS PLANT** a very poisonous herbaceous plant of the carrot family that has small white flowers and finely cut leaves. *Conium maculatum.* 2 **POISON** a poison obtained from the fruit of the hemlock plant 3 **EVERGREEN TREE** an evergreen tree of the pine family with short blunt needles and small cones. Genus: *Tsuga*. ◊ **western hemlock** 4 **HEMLOCK WOOD** the wood of the hemlock tree. Use: construction, paper pulp. [Old English *hymlic(e), hemlic* < ?]

hemmer /hémmər/ *n* 1 a sewer of hems in clothes or other items 2 a sewing machine attachment for sewing hems

hemo- *prefix* US = haemo-

hemorrhoids *npl* US = haemorrhoids

hemp /hemp/ *n* 1 **TOUGH FIBRE FROM ASIAN PLANT** a tough fibre made from the stems of an Asian plant. Use: canvas, rope, paper, cloth. 2 **NARCOTIC DRUG** a narcotic drug smoked, chewed, eaten, or drunk to produce a mildly euphoric reaction 3 **PLANT** a plant that produces hemp. Native to: Asia. *Cannabis sativa.* 4 **TOUGH FIBRE LIKE HEMP** any strong fibre obtained from plant stems and used like hemp [Old English *henep* < Indo-European] —**hempen** *adj*

hemp agrimony *n* a tall composite plant with leaves like those of the hemp plant. Flowers: red, pink, or purple, in clusters. Native to: Europe, Asia, North Africa. *Eupatorium cannabinum.*

hemp nettle *n* **1** a bristly plant resembling the nettle with serrated leaves. Flowers: red, pink, purple, or white, two-lipped. Native to: Europe, Asia, naturalized in the United States. *Galeopsis tetrahit.* **2** any of several bristly plants that resemble the nettle. Native to: Europe, Asia. Genus: *Galeopsis.*

hemstitch /hém stich/ *n* **1 STITCH USED FOR HEMMING** a small overcast stitch used to secure a hem **2 DECORATIVE STITCH** a decorative stitch used to ornament the edge of a cloth, in which, after horizontal threads are removed, vertical threads are gathered in small regular bunches ■ *vti* **EDGE SOMETHING WITH HEMSTITCH** to hem or decorate an edge of cloth using hemstitch —**hemstitcher** *n*

hen /hen/ *n* **1 DOMESTIC FOWL** an adult female domestic fowl **2 FEMALE BIRD** any adult female bird **3 FEMALE AQUATIC ANIMAL** the female of some aquatic animals, e.g. the octopus, crab, and lobster **4 OFFENSIVE TERM** an offensive term that deliberately insults a woman's personality, activity, and age (*dated*) **5** *Scotland* **WAY OF ADDRESSING WOMAN OR GIRL** an affectionate or familiar term of address used to a woman or girl (*informal*) [Old English *henn* < Indo-European, 'sing'] —**hennish** *adj* —**hennishly** *adv* —**hennishness** *n* ◇ **rare** *or* **scarce as hen's teeth** extremely valuable and hard to find

Henan /hő nán/ province in E China. Capital: Zhengzhou. Population: 90,270,000 (1994). Area: 167,000 sq. km/64,500 sq. mi.

hen-and-chickens (*plural* **hen-and-chickens** *or* **hens-and-chickens**) *n* any of several plants, especially the houseleek, producing new plants as offsets that grow at the end of horizontal shoots or runners from the main plant [< the resemblance to young chicks surrounding the mother hen]

Henare /hénnəri/, **Sir James** (1911–89) New Zealand soldier

henbane /hén bayn/ *n* a poisonous plant of the nightshade family with hairy, sticky leaves and a strong unpleasant smell. Flowers: greenish. Use: source of the drugs hyoscyamine and scopolamine. Native to: Europe, Asia. *Hyoscyamus niger.*

henbit /hénbit/ *n* a plant of the mint family. Flowers: small, white or reddish-purple, lipped. Native to: Europe, Asia, now naturalized in the United States. *Lamium amplexicaule.* [< BIT[1] in the obsolete sense 'morsel of food']

hence /henss/ *adv* **1 BECAUSE OF THIS** from this cause or for this reason (*formal*) ○ *I lent him money before, and he never paid it back; hence my reluctance to lend him more.* ○ *Her grandfather was Polish, hence her interest in Polish culture.* **2 LATER THAN NOW** later than the present time (*formal*) ○ *I'm sure the company will be in a much better financial position a year hence.* **3 AWAY FROM HERE** away from this place (*archaic*) ○ *Get you hence.* [13C. < Old English *heonan* 'hence' + adverb suffix *-s* (as in *backwards, besides*).]

henceforth /hénss fáwrth/, **henceforward** /-fáwrwərd/, **henceforwards** *adv* from this time forwards

henchman /hénchmən/ (*plural* **-men**) *n* **1 SUPPORTER OF SOMEONE DUBIOUS** a supporter or associate of somebody in a dubious cause, e.g. a member of a criminal's entourage (*disapproving*) **2 LOYAL FOLLOWER** a loyal supporter or follower, especially of somebody who holds a high office or position **3 PAGE OR SQUIRE** a page or squire to somebody of high rank (*archaic*) [14C. < Old English *hengest* 'stallion'.]

hendeca- *prefix* forming words that signify eleven of something such as sides, facets, or units [< Greek *hendeka* 'eleven']

hendecasyllable /hén dekə silləb'l/ *n* a line of verse that consists of 11 syllables —**hendecasyllabic** /hén dekə si lábbik, hen dékə si lábbik/ *adj*

hendiadys /hen dī ədiss/ *n* a literary device expressing an idea by means of two words linked by 'and', instead of by a grammatically more complex form [Late 16C. < medieval Latin, < Greek *hen dia duoin* 'one through two'.]

Hendrix /héndriks/, **Jimi** (1942–70) US musician. Full name **James Marshall Hendrix**

henequen /hénnikin/, **henequin** *n* **1** a reddish fibre obtained from the leaves of a tropical American plant. Use: rope, twine, coarse fabric. ◊ **sisal 2** a plant that has large thick fibrous leaves shaped like swords that yield henequen. Native to: tropical America, chiefly the Yucatan peninsula of Mexico. *Agave fourcroydes.* [Early 17C. < Spanish.]

henge /henj/ *n* a prehistoric oval or circular area, often bounded by a mound or ditch, that contains standing stones or wooden pillars that were erected during the Neolithic or Bronze Age [Mid-18C. Back-formation < STONEHENGE.]

Hengist /héng gist/ (*d.* 488) Saxon leader

hen harrier *n* a slender, long-winged bird of prey that lives in open moorland and marshlands and preys on small animals. Native to: N Europe, North America. *Circus cyaneus.* US term **northern harrier**

henhouse /hén howss/ (*plural* **-houses** /-howziz/) *n* a shelter or small shed where hens or other domestic birds are housed

Henle's loop /hénliz-/ *n* ANAT = **loop of Henle**

henna /hénnə/ *n* **1 RED DYE** a deep red dye made made from plant leaves. Use: hair dye, cosmetics, fabric colourant. **2 SHRUB** a bush with leaves that yield the red dye henna. Native to: Asia, North Africa. *Lawsonia inermis.* **3 REDDISH-BROWN COLOUR** a rich reddish-brown colour [Early 17C. < Arabic *ḥinnā'*.] —**henna** *adj* —**henna** *vt*

hen night *n* a party or evening out for a woman who is about to be married, attended only by her women friends (*sometimes offensive*) ◊ **stag night**

henotheism /hénnə thi izəm/ *n* the worship of one god, e.g. as the special god of a social group or occupation, while acknowledging or believing in the existence of other gods [Mid-19C. < Greek *heno-* 'one' + *theos* 'god'.] —**henotheist** *n* —**henotheistic** /hénnə thi ístik/ *adj*

hen party *n* a celebration or night out that is exclusively for women (*sometimes offensive*)

henpeck /hén pek/ *vt* an offensive term meaning to annoy or torment a husband or partner through continual nagging and fault-finding [< hens' practice of plucking the cock] —**henpecked** *adj*

Henrietta Maria /hénri éttə mə reé ə/ (1609–69) French-born queen consort of Charles II of England

henry /hénri/ (*plural* **-ries**) *n* (*symbol* **H**) the SI unit of electrical inductance, equal to an electrical potential of one volt induced in a closed circuit by a current varying uniformly by one ampere per second [Late 19C. After Joseph *Henry* (1797–1878), US physicist.]

Henry /hénri/, **Prince** (*b.* 1984) British prince. Known as **Harry**

Henry I (1068–1135) king of the English (1100–35)

Henry II (1133–89) king of the English (1154–89)

Henry III (1207–72) king of England (1216–72)

Henry IV (1367–1413) king of England (1399–1413). Born **Henry Bolingbroke**

Henry V (1387–1422) king of England (1413–22)

Henry VI (1165–97) king of Germany and Holy Roman emperor (1169–97)

Henry VI (1421–71) king of England (1422–61, 1470–71)

Henry VII (1457–1509) king of England (1485–1509). Born **Henry Tudor**

Henry VIII (1491–1547) king of England and Ireland (1509–47)

Henry (the Lion) Duke of Saxony and Duke of Bavaria

Henry, Lenny (*b.* 1958) British comedian

Henry, O. (1862–1910) US writer. Pseudonym of **William Sydney Porter**

Henry's law *n* the principle that the amount of gas dissolved under equilibrium in a volume of liquid is in direct proportion to the pressure of the gas that contacts the liquid surface [Late 19C. After William *Henry* (1774–1836), British chemist.]

Henson /hénss'n/, **Jim** (1936–90) US puppeteer. Full name **James Maury Henson**

hep[1] /hep/ (**hepper, heppest**) *adj* hip (*dated slang*) [Early 20C. < ?]

hep[2] /hep/ *n* hepatitis (*informal*)

heparin /héppərin/ *n* an anti-clotting agent present in the body and also produced synthetically to treat thrombosis [Early 20C. < obsolete *hepar* 'sulphur compound', via late Latin < Greek *hēpar* 'liver'.] —**heparinoid** *adj*

hepat- *prefix* = **hepato-** (*before vowels*)

hepatectomy /héppə téktəmi/ (*plural* **-mies**) *n* surgical removal of all or part of the liver

hepatic /hi páttik/ *adj* **1 OF THE LIVER** relating to or affecting the liver **2 LIVER-COLOURED** of a brownish-red colour like that of liver **3 OF LIVERWORT FAMILY** relating to, belonging to, or resembling the members of the liverwort family of flowerless green plants ■ *n* **1 DRUG FOR TREATING LIVER DISEASE** any drug that treats liver disease **2** PLANTS = **liverwort** [14C. Via Latin < Greek *hēpatikos* < *hēpat-* 'liver'.]

hepatica /hi páttikə/ *n* woodland plant, related to the buttercup, that has three-lobed leaves. Flowers: white, lilac, purple. Native to: northern temperate regions. Genus: *Hepatica.* [15C. Via medieval Latin < Greek *hēpatikos* (see HEPATIC); from the shape of the leaves.]

hepatitis /héppə tītiss/ *n* inflammation of the liver, causing fever, jaundice, abdominal pain, and weakness

hepatitis A *n* a relatively mild form of hepatitis that is caused by a virus and transmitted through contaminated food and water. ◊ **hepatitis B**

hepatitis B *n* a sometimes chronic or fatal form of hepatitis that is caused by a virus and transmitted through contact with infected blood, blood products, and bodily fluids. ◊ **hepatitis A**

hepato- *prefix* liver ○ *hepatotoxic* [< Greek *hēpat-*, stem of *hēpar* < Indo-European]

hepatocellular /héppətō séllyōōlər, hi páttə séllyōōlər/ *adj* relating to liver cells

hepatocyte /hi páttə sīt, héppətə-/ *n* a cell of the liver

hepatogenous /héppə tójjənəss/ *adj* originating in the liver

hepatoma /héppə tṓmə/ (*plural* **-mas** *or* **-mata** /-mətə/) *n* a tumour of the liver

hepatomegaly /héppətō méggəli, hi páttə-/ *n* enlargement of the liver

hepatotoxic /héppətō tóksik, hi páttə-/ *adj* describes a condition in which the liver is damaged

hepatotoxicity /héppətō tok síssəti, hi páttə-/ (*plural* **-ties**) *n* **1** a condition in which the liver is damaged **2** the capacity or tendency of something to damage the liver

hepatotoxin /héppətō tóksin, hi páttə-/ *n* a substance that causes damage to the liver

Hepburn /hép burn/, **Audrey** (1929–93) Belgian-born US actor. Born **Edda van Heemstra Hepburn-Ruston**

Hepburn, Katharine (*b.* 1907?) US actor

hepcat /hép kat/ *n* a knowing and aware person, especially a jazz fan in the 1940s (*dated slang*)

Hephaestus /hi feéstəss/, **Hephaistos** /hi fístəss/ *n* in Greek mythology, the son of Hera and Zeus and the god of fire and fire-based arts such as metalwork. Roman equivalent **Vulcan**

Hepplewhite /hépp'l wīt/ *adj* in or relating to the style of furniture designed by George Hepplewhite, characterized by graceful curving lines, delicate inlays, and often floral or ribbon designs ■ *n* furniture or a piece of furniture made by or in the style of Hepplewhite

Hepplewhite /hépp'l wīt/, **George** (*d.* 1786) British furniture designer

hept- *prefix* = **hepta-** (*before vowels*)

hepta- *prefix* seven ○ *heptahedron* [< Greek *hepta* < Indo-European]

heptachlor /héptə klawr/ *n* a pesticide containing chlorine

heptad /hép tad/ *n* a set or series of seven [Mid-17C. < Greek *heptad-* 'the number seven' < *hepta* 'seven'.]

heptagon /héptəgən/ *n* a two-dimensional shape with seven angles and seven sides [Late 16C. Directly or via French < medieval Latin *heptagonum* < Greek *heptagōnos* 'having seven angles'.] —**heptagonal** /hep tággənəl/ *adj*

heptahedron /héptə heédrən/ (*plural* **-drons** *or* **-dra** /-heédrə/) *n* a solid figure with seven plane faces —**heptahedral** *adj*

heptamerous /hep támmərəss/ *adj* describes plant parts, e.g. petals or sepals, that grow or are arranged in groups of seven

heptameter /hep támmitər/ *n* a line of poetry or verse composed of seven metric feet [Late 19C. Via late Latin < Greek *heptametron* < *hepta* 'seven' + *metron* 'metre'.] —**heptametrical** /héptə méttrik'l/ *adj*

heptane /hép tayn/ *n* C_7H_{16} an isomeric form of an organic chemical, especially a colourless flammable liquid alkane hydrocarbon. Source: petroleum. Use: solvent, anaesthetic, determination of octane ratings.

heptarch /hép taark/ *n* one of the seven rulers in a heptarchy

heptarchy /hép taarki/ (*plural* **-chies**) *n* **1** government by seven rulers or leaders **2** a state governed by seven rulers or one divided into seven parts, each ruled by a different head —**heptarchic** /hep taárkik/ *adj* —**heptarchical** *adj*

Heptarchy /hép taarki/ *n* the association consisting of the seven English kingdoms of Kent, Sussex, Wessex, Essex, Northumbria, East Anglia, and Mercia during the period from the 5th to the 9th centuries

heptastich /héptəstik/ *n* a seven-line stanza or poem

Heptateuch /héptə tyook/ *n* the first seven books of the Bible, comprising Genesis, Exodus, Leviticus, Numbers, Deuteronomy, Joshua, and Judges. ◊ **Hexateuch, Pentateuch** [Late 17C. Via late Latin < Greek *heptateukhos* < *hepta* 'seven' + *teukhos* 'book'.]

heptathlon /hep táthlən, -lon/ *n* an athletic competition, often for women, in which each contestant must compete in seven events, which are typically the javelin, hurdles, high jump, long jump, shot put, sprint, and 800-metre race. ◊ **triathlon, pentathlon** *n.* **2, decathlon** [Late 20C. < HEPTA- + Greek *athlon* 'contest'.] —**heptathlete** /hep táth leet/ *n*

heptavalent /héptə váylənt/ *adj* describes a chemical element that has a valency of seven

heptose /héptōss, -ōz/ *n* a seven-carbon sugar

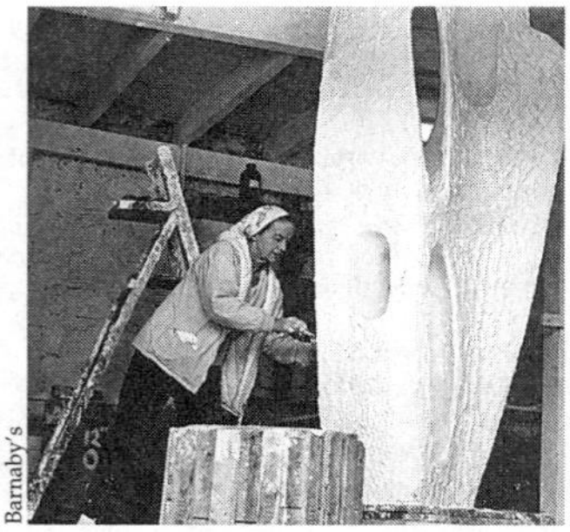

Dame Barbara Hepworth: Working on the plaster model for the bronze sculpture *Rock (Porthcurno)*

Hepworth /hép wurth/, **Dame Barbara** (1903–75) British sculptor

her *(stressed)* /hur/; *(unstressed)* /hər, ər/ *pron, det* **1** WOMAN OR GIRL NOT REFERRED TO BY NAME used to refer to a woman, girl, or female animal who has been previously mentioned or whose identity is known (*as the object or complement of a verb or preposition*) ○ (det) *Tell her I'll be there in ten minutes.* ○ (det) *We left the report with her.* ○ (det) *What is her name?* ○ (pron) *He handed her the car keys.* ○ (pron) *I know it's her.* **2** COUNTRY used to refer to a country or nation when it has been mentioned or its identity is known (*formal*) ○ (det) *Britain's dealings with her EU partners have often been complex.* **3** MACHINE used to refer to a car, machine, or ship ○ (pron) *Fill her up, will you?* ○ (det) *Sea water washed across her decks.* [Old English *hire* < Indo-European, 'this']

her. *abbr* **1** heraldic **2** heraldry

Hera /héerə/ *n* in Greek mythology, the wife of Zeus and goddess of marriage. Roman equivalent **Juno** *n.* **1**

Heracles /hérrə kleez/, **Herakles** *n* in Greek mythology, the son of Zeus and Alcmene, noted for his courage and great strength and the performing of 12 near-impossible labours. Roman equivalent **Hercules** *n.* **1** —**Heraclean** /hérrə klée ən/ *adj*

Heraclitus /hérrə klítəss/ (*fl.* 500? BC) Greek philosopher —**Heraclitean** /hérrə klíshi ən/ *adj*

Heraclius /he rákli əss/ (575?–641) emperor of the Byzantine Empire (610–641)

Herakles *n* MYTHOL = **Heracles**

Heraklion /hi raákli on/ port and largest city on Crete, in the E Mediterranean. Population: 117,167 (1991). Greek **Iráklion**

herald /hérrəld/ *n* **1** BRINGER OF NEWS a bringer or announcer of important news **2** SIGN OF WHAT WILL HAPPEN somebody or something that is a forerunner of something or gives an indication of something that is going to happen (*literary*) **3** OFFICIAL MESSENGER an official messenger and representative of a king or leader in former times **4** HERALDIC OFFICIAL an official who is concerned with heraldry and who is of a rank above the pursuivant **5** OFFICIAL AT MEDIEVAL TOURNAMENTS a performer of official duties at medieval tournaments and jousting contests ■ *vt* **1** SIGNAL to give or be a sign that something is going to happen **2** WELCOME to welcome or announce somebody or something with enthusiasm [14C. < Old French *herault* < Germanic, 'commander of the army'.]

heraldic /hə ráldik, he-/ *adj* belonging or relating to heraldry or heralds —**heraldically** *adv*

heraldry /hérrəldri/ (*plural* **-ries**) *n* **1** STUDY OF COATS OF ARMS the profession or study of the devising and granting of coats of arms and of determining who is entitled to bear them **2** COATS OF ARMS coats of arms and the symbols and conventions connected with them **3** POMP pomp and ceremony

heralds' college *n* HERALDRY = **College of Arms**

Herat /hə rát/ city in NW Afghanistan. Population: 177,300 (1988 estimate).

herb /hurb/ *n* **1** CULINARY AND MEDICINAL PLANT a low-growing aromatic plant used fresh or dried for seasoning in cooking, for its medicinal properties, or in perfumes (*often before nouns*) **2** PLANT WITHOUT WOODY STEMS a seed-producing flowering plant that does not produce woody stems and that forms new stems and leaves each season **3** MARIJUANA marijuana (*slang*) [13C. Via Old French < Latin *herba* 'grass, herb'.]

herbaceous /hər báyshəss/ *adj* **1** WITHOUT WOODY STEMS describes plants or plant parts that are fleshy and wither after each growing season, as opposed to plants such as trees that grow woody stems and are persistent **2** RESEMBLING LEAVES similar to leaves in colour and general appearance **3** OF AROMATIC PLANTS relating to aromatic herbs such as sage, dill, or thyme [Mid-17C. < Latin *herbaceus* < *herba* 'grass, herb'.] —**herbaceously** *adv*

herbaceous border *n* a flower bed that is mainly planted with perennial plants rather than with annuals

herbage /húrbij/ *n* **1** herbaceous plants, especially their leafy or succulent and edible parts **2** grass and other vegetation growing in fields, pasture land, and meadows [14C. Via Old French < medieval Latin *herbagium* < Latin *herba* 'grass, herb'.]

herbal /húrb'l/ *adj* characteristic of, consisting of, or made with aromatic herbs ■ *n* a book that lists individual herbs and describes their particular properties and possible uses [Early 16C. < medieval Latin *herbalis* < Latin *herba* 'grass, herb'.]

herbalist /húrbəlist/ *n* **1** SOMEBODY KNOWLEDGEABLE ABOUT HERBS a grower, collector, seller, or dispenser of aromatic herbs, especially those considered to have medicinal properties **2** *S Africa* TRADITIONAL DOCTOR a traditional doctor who uses herbs and other medicines to remedy illness and discomfort **3** BOTANIST a botanist, especially one concerned with the classification of plants (*archaic*)

herbal medicine *n* **1** a system of medical treatment based on the properties of medicinal herbs **2** a medication made from a herb or herbs

herbarium /hur báiri əm/ (*plural* **-ums** *or* **-a** /-ə/) *n* **1** a collection of dried plants, especially one in which the plants have been mounted, systematically classified, and labelled for use in scientific studies **2** a building, room, or other place where a herbarium is kept [Late 18C. < late Latin, < Latin *herbarius* 'herbalist' < *herba* 'grass, herb'.] —**herbarial** *adj*

herb bennet /-bénnit/ *n* a common wild plant that has long hairy stems and hooked seeds. Flowers: small yellow. Native to: Europe, Asia, North Africa. *Geum urbanum.*

herb Christopher (*plural* **herbs Christopher**) *n* PLANTS = **baneberry** *n.* **1** [After St CHRISTOPHER]

Herbert /húrbərt/, **George** (1593–1633) English poet and cleric

Herbert, Xavier (1901–84) Australian novelist

herb Gerard /-jérr aard/ (*plural* **herbs Gerard**) *n* PLANTS = **ground elder** [After St *Gerard* of Toul (935?–994)]

herbicide /húrbi sīd/ *n* a chemical preparation designed to kill plants, especially weeds, or to inhibit their growth —**herbicidal** /húrbi síd'l/ *adj* —**herbicidally** /-síd'li/ *adv*

herbivore /húrbi vawr/ *n* an animal that feeds only or mainly on grass and other plants. ◊ **carnivore** *n.* **1**, **omnivore** *n.* **1** [Mid-19C. < French, or back-formation < HERBIVOROUS.]

herbivorous /hur bívvərəss/ *adj* eating only or mainly grass or other plants [Mid-17C. < modern Latin *herbivorus* 'eating grass' < Latin *herba* 'grass, herb'.]

herbology /hur bólləji/ *n* the study of herbs and their use for medical purposes —**herbologist** *n*

herb Paris (*plural* **herbs Paris**) *n* a woodland plant having a whorl of four leaves at right angles to the stem and bearing a single black berry. Flowers: single greenish-yellow. Native to: Europe. *Paris quadrifolia.* [Partial translation of medieval Latin *herba paris* 'herb of a pair']

herb Robert /-róbbərt/ (*plural* **herbs Robert**) *n* a common plant of the cranesbill family having red-tinged leaves and stems with a strong and rather unpleasant odour. Flowers: small pink, purple. Native to: temperate N Europe, Asia. *Geranium robertianum.*

herby /húrbi/ (**-ier, -iest**) *adj* **1** WITH HERBAL TASTE OR SMELL tasting or smelling of herbs **2** OF AROMATIC HERBS associated with aromatic or medicinal herbs **3** FULL OF GROWING HERBS with a lot of growing herbs or grass

Herculaneum /húrkyŏŏ láyni əm/ ancient Roman town near modern Naples, destroyed with its neighbour Pompeii in the eruption of Vesuvius in AD 79

herculean /húrkyŏŏ lée ən, hur kyŏŏli ən/ *adj* requiring a great deal of strength, effort, stamina, or resources

Hercules /húrkyŏŏ leez/ *n* **1** ROMAN MYTHOLOGICAL HERO in Roman mythology, the son of Jupiter and Alcmena, noted for his courage and great strength and the performing of 12 near-impossible labours. Greek equivalent **Heracles** **2** (*plural* **-les** *or* **-leses**) VERY STRONG MAN a man with great or unusual strength **3** CONSTELLATION a constellation of the northern hemisphere. See illustration at **constellation** —**Herculean** /húrkyoo lée ən, hur kyŏŏli ən/ *adj*

hercules beetle *n* an exceptionally large South American beetle of the scarab family that can grow to over 15 cm/6 in in length. The male has two large projecting horns. *Dynastes hercules.*

Hercules' club *n* **1** a small tree or shrub of the ginseng family that has prickly leaves and bark that has medicinal properties. Native to: SE United States. *Aralia spinosa.* **2** a small spiny tree or shrub related to the citrus family with bark and berries that have medicinal properties. Native to: S United States. *Zanthoxylum clava-herculis.*

Hercynian /hur sínni ən/ *adj* relating to the period during the late Palaeozoic era when some of the major European mountain ranges were being formed [Late 16C. < Latin *Hercynia (silva)* < Greek *Herkunios (drumos)*, forested mountain region between the Carpathian Mountains and the River Rhine.]

herd /hurd/ *n* **1** LARGE GROUP OF DOMESTIC ANIMALS a large number of domestic animals, especially cattle, often of the same breed, that are kept, driven, or reared together **2** LARGE GROUP OF WILD ANIMALS a large number of wild animals of the same kind that live, feed, and travel as a group **3** LARGE GROUP OF PEOPLE a large group of people, often with a common interest, purpose, or bond ○ *herds of eager shoppers* **4** ORDINARY PEOPLE ACTING AS GROUP ordinary people, considered as acting or thinking as a group and lacking the ability to think as individuals (*disapproving*) ○ *She was never one to follow the herd.* ■ *v* **1** *vt* CONTROL GROUP OF ANIMALS to drive, keep, or look after domestic animals as a group **2** *vt* MOVE OR COLLECT A GROUP to move people or animals somewhere as a group or collect them into it ○ *We were herded onto buses.* **3** *vi* FORM OR MOVE IN A GROUP to gather together or go somewhere as a group [Old English *heord* < Indo-European, 'row, group'] ◇ **ride herd on somebody** *US* to supervise somebody strictly

SPELLCHECK See ***heard***.

herd-book /húrd bŏŏk/ *n* a book that gives details of the pedigrees of domestic animals, especially cattle or pigs

herder /húrdər/ *n US* AGRIC = **herdsman** *n.* **2**

Herder /húrdər, háirdər/, **Johann Gottfried von** (1744–1803) German philosopher and critic

herd instinct *n* the innate desire to belong to, be associated with, or imitate the behaviour of a group

herdsman /húrdzmən/ (*plural* **-men**) *n* **1** an owner or breeder of cattle or other livestock **2** somebody who tends or drives domestic animals in groups, especially on open pasture or land. US term **herder** *n.* [Alteration of Old English *heordman* 'herdsman', after such words as *craftsman*]

Herdwick /húrdwik/ *n* a hardy sheep with thick coarse wool belonging to a breed originating in the Lake District [Early 19C. < obsolete *herdwick* 'pasturage', literally 'herdsman's place'.]

here /heer/ CORE MEANING: an adverb used to refer to this place or this time ○ *How long have you been waiting here?* ○ *Winter is here.*

adv **1 THIS PLACE** in, at, or to the place where you are, or at a place near you ○ *Have you been here before?* ○ *Come and sit here, beside me.* **2 POINT OR STAGE** used to draw attention to a particular point or stage in a situation ○ *I want to say here, before I go further, that only part of the credit should be mine.* **3 NOW** indicates a situation or event that is happening at the present time ○ *The time for celebrations is here.* **4 INDICATES AN OFFER** indicates that somebody is offering something to somebody ○ *Here are some general guidelines.* ○ *Here's my card.* **5 INTRODUCES** used to introduce or draw attention to a topic ○ *Now, here is a question for everybody.* **6 LIFE ON EARTH** used to refer to people in general and their life on Earth ○ *Where did we come from? Why are we here?* [Old English *hēr* < Indo-European, 'this'] ◇ **(the) here and now** used to emphasize that you are talking about the present time ○ *I'm entitled to an explanation, and I want one here and now.* ○ *He outlined all sorts of schemes, but hadn't much practical advice about the here and now.* ◇ **here and there** in different places or at different points ◇ **here goes** used to indicate that somebody is about to perform an action ○ *This is my first move on the chessboard – here goes!* ◇ **here we go again** used to indicate that an event or situation is, tiresomely or irritatingly, about to repeat itself ○ *Here we go again – making a mountain out of a molehill.* ◇ **neither here nor there** not relevant and therefore not important

SPELLCHECK See *hear.*

hereabouts /héerə bówts/, **hereabout** /héerə bowt/ *adv* near here

hereafter /heer áaftər/ *adv* (*formal*) **1 AFTER THE PRESENT TIME** from now on or at a time in the future ○ *He believes this to be a universal law of nature; and we may hope hereafter to see the law proved true.* ○ *No one of us knows what may happen hereafter.* **2 IN ANY FOLLOWING PART** in any following part of an article or document ○ *Here is established a Commerce Technology Advisory Board (hereafter in this section referred to as the "Advisory Board").* ■ *adv, n* **LIFE AFTER DEATH** the life that is thought by some to exist after death (*formal*) ○ (adv) *Mercy and forgiveness will be ours hereafter.* ○ (n) *Your deeds will be judged in the hereafter.*

hereby /heer bī́, héer bī/ *adv* by means of this declaration, document, or ruling (*formal*) ○ *I hereby renounce all claim to the estate.*

hereditable /hi rédditəb'l/ *adj* capable of being inherited [15C. < obsolete French *héréditable* or medieval Latin *hereditabilis*, both < ecclesiastical Latin *hereditare* 'inherit' (see HEREDITAMENT).] —**hereditability** /hi rédditə bíllәti/ *n*

hereditament /hérri díttəmənt/ *n* **1** a piece of property that can be inherited **2** a piece of property that passes automatically to a legal heir unless a will specifies otherwise [15C. < medieval Latin *hereditamentum* < ecclesiastical Latin *hereditare* 'inherit' < Latin *hered-* 'heir'.]

hereditarian /hi réddi táiri ən/ *n* a believer that inherited characteristics are more important in determining people's character and behaviour than environmental and social factors —**hereditarian** *adj* —**hereditarianism** *n*

hereditary /hi rédditəri/ *adj* **1 PASSED ON GENETICALLY** passed genetically, or capable of being passed genetically, from one generation to the next **2 HANDED DOWN THROUGH GENERATIONS** handed down, or legally capable of being handed down, through generations by inheritance **3 HAVING INHERITED STATUS** holding a right, function, or property by right of inheritance **4 TRADITIONALLY HELD** possessed by or characteristic of both ancestors and descendants although not physically transmitted ○ *the family's hereditary fondness for city life* **5 RELATING TO INHERITANCE** relating to inheritance or heredity **6 SHARING A RELATIONSHIP OR PROPERTY** sharing or transmitting a particular relationship or property [15C. < Latin *hereditarius* < *hereditas* 'inheritance' (see HEREDITY).] —**hereditarily** *adv* —**hereditariness** *n*

heredity /hi rédditi/ (*plural* **-ties**) *n* **1** the transfer of genetically controlled characteristics, such as hair colour or flower colour, from one generation to the next in living organisms **2** the complete set of inherited characteristics of an organism [Mid-16C. Directly or via French < Latin *hereditas* 'inheritance' < *hered-* 'heir'.]

QUICK FACTS ON... **HEREDITY**

Key elements: transfer of physical or mental characteristics from one generation to another

Key dates: 1859 Darwin discusses inheritance of characters in selective breeding and evolution via natural selection; 1865 Mendel defines laws of heredity as a result of his study of pea plants; 1883 Weismann hypothesizes that males and females contribute equally to the heredity of offspring and that chromosomes are the bearers of heredity; 1902 Sutton hypothesizes that Mendel's 'factors' of inheritance are located on chromosomes and that chromosomes occur as pairs; 1909 Johannsen coins the term 'gene' to define the unit of heredity; 1910–11 Morgan shows that genes are carried on chromosomes and begins to map the chromosomal location of genes in the fruit fly; 1944 Avery *et al.* determine that genetic information is carried in DNA; 1953 Watson and Crick determine the structure of DNA, enabling the biochemical basis of inheritance to be understood

Key developments: molecular genetics; genetic modification

Key publications: *The Origin of Species* (Darwin) 1859; *Experiments in Plant Hybridization* (Mendel) 1865; *A Structure for Deoxyribose Nucleic Acid* (Watson and Crick) 1953, Nature 171: 737; *The Double Helix* (Watson) 1968

Hereford[1] /hérrifərd/ *n* a hardy cow that has a distinctive red coat with white markings, belonging to a breed originating in England and bred for beef [Early 19C. After the English county where first bred.]

Hereford[2] /hérrifərd/ city in W England. Population: 50,539 (1994 estimate).

Hereford and Worcester former county in W England

Herefordshire /hérrifərdshər/ county in W England. Area: 2,181 sq. km/842 sq. mi.

herein /heer ín/ *adv* (*formal*) **1** in this document, article, or proceeding ○ *Disclaimer: The views represented herein do not necessarily represent the views of the moderators.* **2** introduces a clause in which somebody states an opinion about the nature or cause of something or goes on to give further detail ○ *People are not always conscious of the effect their behaviour is having on others, and herein lies the main problem.*

hereinafter /héerin áaftər/ *adv* later in this document, article, or proceeding (*formal*) ○ *the European Monetary Institute (hereinafter referred to as EMI)*

hereinbefore /héerinbi fáwr/ *adv* earlier in this document, article, or proceeding (*formal*)

hereof /heer óv/ *adv* of or concerning this (*formal*)

Herero /hə ráirō, háirərō/ (*plural* **-ro** *or* **-ros**) *n* **1** a member of a people living mainly in Namibia and Botswana **2** a Bantu language spoken by the Herero. Native speakers: 25,000. [Mid-19C. < Bantu.] —**Herero** *adj*

heresiarch /hə réezi aark/ *n* a leader or founder of a heretical religious group or movement [Mid-16C. Via ecclesiastical Latin < ecclesiastical Greek *hairesiarkhēs* < Greek *hairesis* 'choice, group' (see HERESY) + *-arkhēs* 'ruler'.]

heresy /hérrəssi/ (*plural* **-sies**) *n* **1 UNORTHODOX RELIGIOUS OPINION** an opinion or belief that contradicts established religious teaching, especially one that is officially condemned by a religious authority **2 HOLDING OF UNORTHODOX RELIGIOUS BELIEF** the holding of, or adherence to, an opinion or belief that contradicts established religious teaching, especially one that is officially condemned by religious authorities **3 UNORTHODOX OPINION** an opinion or belief that does not coincide with established or traditional theory, especially in philosophy, science, or politics **4 HOLDING OF UNORTHODOX OPINION** the holding of an unorthodox opinion that is in conflict with established or traditional theory [12C. Via Old French < Greek *hairesis* 'choice, group' < *haireisthai* 'choose'.]

heretic /hérrətik/ *n* **1** a holder or adherent of an opinion or belief that contradicts established religious teaching **2** somebody whose opinions, beliefs, or theories in any field are considered by others in that field to be extremely unconventional or unorthodox [14C. Via Old French < Greek *hairetikos* 'able to choose' < *haireisthai* 'choose'.] —**heretical** /hə réttik'l/ *adj* —**heretically** *adv* —**hereticalness** *n*

hereto /heer tóo/ *adv* to this document, proceeding, or matter (*formal*)

heretofore /héertoo fáwr/ *adv* up until this time (*formal*) ○ *He had more liberty now than he had known heretofore.*

hereunder /heer úndər/ *adv* (*formal*) **1** after this introduction, heading, or sentence **2** by the terms of this instruction, agreement, or ruling

hereunto /heer ún too/ *adv* to this document, proceeding, or matter (*formal*)

hereupon /héerə pón/ *adv* **1** immediately after or in response to this ○ *Hereupon the entire delegation left.* **2** on this point, subject, or matter (*formal*) ○ *retired to deliberate before pronouncing hereupon*

Hereward the Wake /hérriwərd thə wáyk/ (*fl.* 1070) Anglo-Saxon rebel

herewith /heer wíth, heer wíth/ *adv* **1** with this letter or other written, typed, or printed message ○ *Herewith the documents you requested.* **2** by this statement, ruling, or document (*formal*) ○ *I herewith pronounce sentence of banishment.*

Herez /hə réz/, **Heriz** /-ríz/ *n* a high quality Persian rug woven with a pattern of flowers or trees [After *Heris*, Iranian town]

heriot /hérri ət/ *n* in feudal England, a tribute or gift, often a prized animal or a treasured possession, given by a tenant's or villein's family to his lord at the tenant's death [Old English *heregeatwa* 'army trappings'; originally referring to the return of weapons]

heritable /hérritəb'l/ *adj* **1** able to be passed on to an heir by the laws of inheritance **2** having the legal right or qualification to inherit something [14C. < French, < *hériter* 'inherit' < ecclesiastical Latin *hereditare* (see HEREDITAMENT).] —**heritability** /hérritə bíllәti/ *n* —**heritably** *adv*

heritage /hérritij/ *n* **1 SOMETHING SOMEBODY IS BORN TO** the status, conditions, or character acquired by being born into a particular family or social class ○ *the responsibilities that were his heritage* **2 RICHES OF PAST** a country's or area's history and historical buildings and sites that are considered to be of interest and value to present generations (*often before nouns*) ○ *the town's heritage trail* **3 SOMETHING PASSING FROM GENERATION TO GENERATION** something such as a way of life or traditional culture that passes from one generation to the next in a social group ○ *The celebration of Passover is part of the Jewish heritage.* **4 LEGAL INHERITANCE** property or land that is or can be passed on to an heir [13C. < Old French, < *hériter* (see HERITABLE).]

heritage industry *n* a branch of the the tourism industry responsible for preserving the art and artefacts of a place

heritor /hérritər/ *n* an inheritor of property by law (*archaic or technical*) [15C. < Anglo-Norman, < French *hériter* (see HERITABLE).]

Heriz *n* TEXTILES = **Herez**

herl /hurl/ *n* **1** the barb or barbs of a feather used for trimming an artificial fishing fly **2** a fishing fly trimmed with a barb or barbs of a feather [14C. Probably < Middle Low German *herle* 'fibre of hemp or flax'.]

herm /hurm/, **herma** /húrmə/ (*plural* **-mae** /-mee/ *or* **-mai** /-mī/) *n* a square pillar topped with a bust, usually of the god Hermes, used as a marker in ancient Greece and Rome, and as an ornament in classical architecture [Late 16C. Via Latin < Greek *Hermēs* 'Hermes'.]

Herman /húrmən/, **Sali** (1898–1993) Swiss-born Australian painter

hermaphrodite /hur máffrə dīt/ *n* **1 ORGANISM HAVING BOTH SEXES** a plant or animal having both male and female reproductive organs and secondary sexual characteristics **2 PERSON HAVING BOTH SEXES** a person who has both male and female sexual characteristics **3 SOMEBODY OR SOMETHING COMBINING CONTRADICTORY ELEMENTS** somebody or something that combines two very different elements or qualities or seems to belong to two different classifications at once [15C. Via Latin < Greek *Hermaphroditos* 'Hermaphroditus'.] —**hermaphrodite** *adj* —**hermaphrodism** *n* —**hermaphroditic** /hur máffrə díttik/ *adj* —**hermaphroditical** *adj* —**hermaphroditically** *adv* —**hermaphroditism** /-dītizəm/ *n*

hermaphrodite brig *n* a two-masted sailing vessel with a square-rigged foremast and a square-rigged topsail above a fore-and-aft rig on the mainmast

Hermaphroditus /hur máffrə dítəss/ *n* in Greek mythology, the son of Hermes and Aphrodite, whose body was merged with the body of the nymph Salmacis to become half male and half female

hermeneutic /húrmə nyoótik/, **hermeneutical** /-nyoótik'l/ *adj* **1** relating to or consisting in the interpretation of texts, especially the books of the Bible **2** serving to interpret or explain something (*formal*) [Late 17C. < Greek *hermēneutikos* 'of interpreting' < *hermēneuein* 'interpret' < *hermēneus* 'interpreter'.] —**hermeneutically** *adv* —**hermeneutist** *n*

hermeneutics /húrmə nyoótiks/ *n* (+ *singular verb*) **1 SCIENCE OF INTERPRETING TEXTS** the science and methodology of interpreting texts, especially the books of the Bible **2 THEOLOGY OF RELIGIOUS CONCEPTS** the branch of theology that is concerned with explaining or interpreting religious concepts, theories, and principles **3 PHILOSOPHY OF HUMAN BEHAVIOUR AND SOCIETY** the branch of philosophy that is concerned with the study and interpretation of human behaviour, structures of society, and how people function within these structures **4 DISCUSSION OF MEANING OF LIFE** in existentialism, deliberation on the meaning and purpose of life

Hermes /húr meez/ *n* in Greek mythology, the messenger of the gods and a son of Zeus. Roman equivalent **Mercury** *n*. 1

Hermes Trismegistus /-tríssmə jístəss, -gístəss/ *n* a name given to the Egyptian god Thoth by Greek neo-Platonists, who regarded him as a teacher of religion, magic, and alchemy

hermetic /hur méttik/, **hermetical** /-méttik'l/ *adj* **1 AIRTIGHT** so tightly or perfectly fitting as to exclude the passage of air **2 PROTECTED FROM OUTSIDE INFLUENCE** protected from or preventing any outside interference or influence ○ *lead a solitary, hermetic existence* **3 HARD TO UNDERSTAND** obscure and difficult for outsiders to understand **4 hermetic, Hermetic INVOLVING ALCHEMY OR MAGIC** associated with alchemy or magic [Mid-17C. < modern Latin *hermeticus* < HERMES TRISMEGISTUS.] —**hermetically** *adv*

hermit /húrmit/ *n* **1** a person who chooses to live alone and to have little or no social contact **2** somebody who, in early Christian times, chose to reject material things and to live apart from the rest of society, especially in order to be completely devoted to God [12C. Via Old French *hermite* or medieval Latin *heremita* < Greek *erēmitēs* < *erēmia* 'desert' < *erēmos* 'solitary'.] —**hermitic** /hur míttik/ *adj* —**hermitical** *adj* —**hermitically** *adv*

hermitage /húrmitij/ *n* **1** a building or shelter where a hermit lives or where a group of people live an isolated religious life **2** a place of isolation or solitude where somebody can live apart from society [13C. < Old French, < *hermite* 'hermit' (see HERMIT).]

Hermitage /húrmitij/ *n* a museum in St Petersburg, Russia, that contains one of the world's major collections of paintings

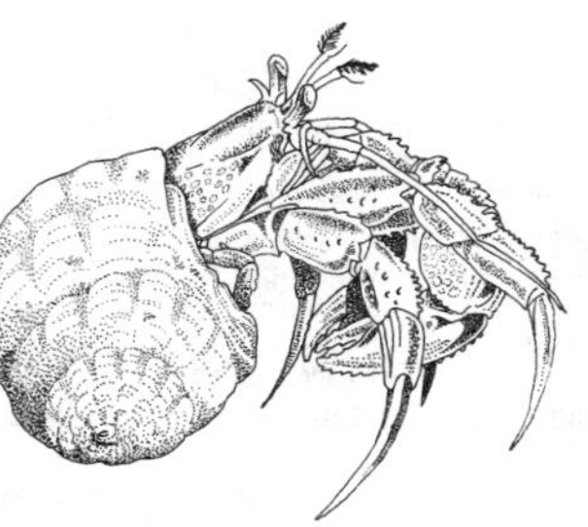

Hermit crab

hermit crab *n* a soft-bodied crab that takes over an empty mollusc shell, usually a whelk shell, and carries it around on its back for protection and to retire into. Order: Decapoda.

hermit thrush *n* a brownish songbird with a speckled breast, reddish tail, and a distinctive spiralling song reminiscent of the sound of a flute. Native to: North America. *Catharus guttatus.*

Hermon, Mount /-húrmən/ highest peak in the Anti-Lebanon Mountains, on the Syria-Lebanon border. Height: 2,814 m/9,232 ft.

hernia /húrni ə/ (*plural* **-as** *or* **-ae** /-ee/) *n* a condition in which part of an internal organ projects abnormally through the wall of the cavity that contains it, especially the projection of the intestine from the abdominal cavity. ◊ **diverticulum** [14C. < Latin.] —**hernial** *adj*

herniate /húrni ayt/ (**-ates, -ating, -ated**) *vi* to project through an abnormal opening in the wall of a body cavity or through a normal or potential opening that has become abnormally enlarged (*refers to an organ or body part*) —**herniated** *adj* —**herniation** /húrni áysh'n/ *n*

herniorrhaphy /húrni órrəfi/ (*plural* **-phies**) *n* the surgical repair of an abnormal opening in the wall of a body cavity

hero /heérō/ (*plural* **-roes**) *n* **1 REMARKABLY BRAVE PERSON** a performer of a brave action, or conspicuous possessor of other admirable qualities ○ *a war hero* **2 SOMEBODY ADMIRED** a person who is admired for outstanding qualities or achievements ○ *heroes of the war against poverty* **3 MAIN CHARACTER IN FICTIONAL PLOT** the principal man or boy character in a film, novel, or play, especially one who plays a vital role in plot development or around whom the plot is structured ○ *'Whether I shall turn out to be the hero of my own life, or whether that station will be held by anybody else, these pages must show'.* (Charles Dickens, *David Copperfield*; 1849–50) **4 MAN WITH SUPERHUMAN POWERS** in classical mythology, a man, especially the son of a god and a mortal, who is famous for possessing some extraordinary gift, e.g. superhuman strength ○ *the Greek heroes* **5** *US* **LONG SANDWICH** a sandwich made from a long roll or loaf of bread with a filling of meat and cheese with lettuce and tomato [Mid-16C. Via Latin < Greek *hērōs* 'hero, warrior'.]

Hero /heérō/ *n* in Greek mythology, a priestess of Aphrodite whose lover Leander swam the Hellespont to visit her every night, and who drowned herself after he drowned in the strait

Hero (of Alexandria) /heér ō əv állig zaándri ə/ (*b.* AD 20?) Greek mathematician and inventor

Herod (the Great) /hérrəd-/ (73–4 BC) king of Judea (37–4 BC)

Herod Agrippa I /hérrəd ə gríppə/ (10? BC–AD 44) king of Judea (41–44)

Herod Agrippa II /hérrəd rə gríppə/ (27–93?) Roman ruler in Palestine

Herod Antipas /hérrəd ánti pass/ (21 BC–AD 39) Galilean leader

Herodotus /hə róddətəss/ (484?–425? BC) Greek historian

heroic /hi rṓ ik/, **heroical** /-rṓ ik'l/ *adj* **1 COURAGEOUS** showing great bravery, courage, or determination ○ *a heroic fight against a disease* **2 SUITABLE FOR A HERO** characteristic of or suitable for a hero **3 LARGE OR EXTREME** large, extensive, or extreme, often daunting in aspect or done in response to a desperate situation ○ *heroic measures to save a person's life* **4 RELATING TO MYTHICAL HERO** characteristic of or involving the heroes of legend or mythology **5 IN OR OF HEROIC VERSE** written in or characteristic of heroic verse **6 LARGER THAN LIFE-SIZE** describes a piece of sculpture that is larger than life-size. ◊ **colossal** *adj.* 3 —**heroically** *adv* —**heroicalness** *n* —**heroicness** *n*

heroic age *n* a time in a culture's mythology when heroes were believed to exist, especially the time in ancient Greek legend up to and including the return from Troy

heroical *adj* = **heroic**

heroic couplet *n* two lines of verse in iambic pentameters that rhyme, usually part of a series of rhyming pairs

heroic drama *n* a play popular during the Restoration period, generally involving a warrior hero who must find a way to resolve a dilemma

heroic metre *n* LITERAT = **heroic verse**

heroic quatrain *n* a four-line unit of verse in which each line consists of five iambic feet and either alternate or adjacent lines rhyme

heroics /hi rṓ iks/ *npl* **1** rash, inappropriate, or extravagantly courageous behaviour or talk ○ *There is no room for heroics on this expedition.* **2** = **heroic verse**

heroic stanza *n* four lines of verse in which the first and third lines and the second and fourth lines rhyme

heroic tenor *n* MUSIC = **Heldentenor**

heroic verse *n* a verse form used in epic poetry or other narrative poetry on heroic subjects, especially the ancient Greek and Latin hexameter, the iambic pentameter, or the alexandrine

heroin /hérrō in/ *n* a white powder derived from morphine that is a highly addictive narcotic drug (*often before nouns*) [Late 19C. < German.]

SPELLCHECK Do not confuse ***heroin*** with ***heroine***, which has a similar sound. Beware: your spellchecker will not catch this error.

heroine /hérrō in/ *n* **1 REMARKABLY BRAVE WOMAN** a woman who commits an act of remarkable bravery or who has shown great courage, strength of character, or another admirable quality **2 ADMIRED WOMAN** a woman who is admired or looked up to for her qualities or achievements ○ *heroines of the women's suffrage movement* **3 MAIN WOMAN CHARACTER IN FICTIONAL PLOT** the principal woman or girl character in a film, novel, or play, especially one who plays a vital role in plot development or around whom the plot is structured

SPELLCHECK See ***heroin***.

heroism /hérrō izəm/ *n* remarkable physical or moral courage

heron /hérrən/ *n* a wading bird with a long neck, tapered beak, and often a crested head, that lives in freshwater habitats and feeds mainly on fish, frogs, and small mammals. Family: Ardeidae. [14C. < Old French, < Germanic.]

heronry /hérrənri/ (*plural* **-ries**) *n* an area where herons nest and raise their young

Herophilus /heer óffiləss/ (335?–280? BC) Greek anatomist

hero worship *n* **1** great admiration for somebody, especially if it borders on the excessive **2** the ancient Greek or Roman practice of worshipping a mythological hero or heroes

hero-worship *vt* to admire somebody, often to the extent of obsession —**hero-worshipper** *n*

herpes /húr peez/ *n* a viral infection causing small painful blisters and inflammation, most commonly at the junction of skin and mucous membrane in the mouth or nose or in the genitals [14C. Via Latin < Greek, < *herpein* 'creep'.]

herpes simplex /-sím pleks/ *n* either of two viral diseases marked by clusters of small watery blisters, one affecting the area of the mouth and lips and the other the genitals [< modern Latin, 'simple herpes']

herpesvirus /húr peez vīrəss/ *n* a DNA-containing animal virus that replicates in cell nuclei and causes such diseases as chickenpox, herpes, and shingles

herpes zoster /-zóstər/ *n* shingles (*technical*) [< modern Latin; *zoster* via Latin < Greek, 'girdle']

herpetic /-péttik/ *adj* relating to, affected by, or indicative of herpes ■ *n* a person affected by herpes (*technical*)

herpetology /húrpi tólləji/ *n* the scientific study of reptiles and amphibians [Early 19C. < Greek *herpeton* 'creeping thing, reptile' < *herpein* 'creep'.] —**herpetologic** /húrpitə lójjik/ *adj* —**herpetological** *adj* —**herpetologically** *adv* —**herpetologist** /húrpi tólləjist/ *n*

Herr /hair, hur/ (*plural* **Herren** /hérrən/) *n* the German equivalent of 'Mister', used as a title before a surname or profession [Mid-17C. < German.]

Herrenvolk /hérrən folk/ *n* in Nazi ideology the Germans as a master race (*often considered offensive*) [Mid-20C. < German, 'master people'.]

Herrera-Estrella /hə ráyrə estréllə/, **Luis** (*b.* 1956) Mexican geneticist

Herrick /hérrik/, **Robert** (1591–1674) English poet

herring /hérring/ (*plural* **-rings** *or* **-ring**) *n* **1 FISH OF N ATLANTIC** a small commercially important fish with silvery scales. Native to: N Atlantic. *Clupea harengus.* **2 FISH RELATED TO HERRING** any fish related to and resembling the herring. Family: Clupeidae. **3 HERRING AS FOOD** the flesh of a herring used as food [Old English *hǣring* < W Germanic]

herringbone /hérringbōn/ *n* **1 PATTERN OF V SHAPES** a regular geometric pattern made by placing two contrasting rows of slanting lines or blocks together so that they form rows of Vs, zigzags, or chevrons. Use: bricklaying, textiles, parquet flooring, weaving, embroidery. **2 FABRIC**

WITH HERRINGBONE PATTERN fabric woven in a herringbone pattern (*often before nouns*) ○ *a herringbone jacket* 3 METHOD FOR ASCENDING ON SKIS a method for climbing a slope on skis by facing the peak, with skis pointing out at an angle, and moving them upwards one step after the other ■ *v* (-bones, -boning, -boned) 1 *vti* DECORATE WITH HERRINGBONE to decorate or make something such as cloth with a herringbone pattern 2 *vi* GO UP SLOPE ON SKIS to ascend a slope on skis using the herringbone method

herringbone bond *n* decorative bricklaying in which the bricks are placed at an angle to one another to form a herringbone pattern

herringbone stitch *n* an embroidery stitch made with overlapping cross stitches that form a zigzag line, often used as a border stitch or hemming stitch

herring gull *n* a common gull with a body that is mainly white, a grey back, and grey wings with black tips. Native to: N hemisphere. *Larus argentatus*.

Herriot /hérri ət/, **Édouard** (1872–1957) French statesman

Herriot, James (1916–95) British author. Pseudonym of **James Alfred Wight**

hers /hurz/ *pron* 1 SOMETHING BELONGING TO HER indicates that something belongs or relates to a woman, girl, or female animal who has been previously mentioned or whose identity is known ○ *She drew my face to hers and kissed me.* ○ *I knew an uncle of hers.* 2 BELONGING TO A COUNTRY belonging to or associated with a country or nation when its identity is known (*formal*) 3 BELONGING TO A MACHINE belonging to or associated with a car, machine, or ship [14C. < HER + -'S.]

Herschel /húrsh'l/, **Caroline** (1750–1848) German-born British astronomer

Herschel, Sir John Frederick William (1792–1871) British astronomer

herself (*stressed*) /hər sélf/; (*unstressed*) /ər sélf/ CORE MEANING: the form of 'her' used in reflexive and emphatic contexts ○ *She did it herself.*

pron 1 REFERRING TO FEMALE SUBJECT OF VERB used to refer to the same woman, girl, or female animal as the subject of the verb ○ *She put her hand on the rail to support herself.* ○ *She decided to treat herself.* 2 USED FOR EMPHASIS used to emphasize or clarify which woman, girl, or female animal is being referred to, often introducing a note of surprise or awe ○ *I received a letter from the author herself.* 3 ALONE OR WITHOUT HELP used to show that a woman, girl or female animal is alone or unaided ○ *sitting by herself in the garden* ○ *wrote the song herself* 4 COUNTRY used to refer to a nation or country whose identity is known (*formal*) ○ *Britain is causing problems for herself with this policy.* 5 MACHINE used to refer to a car, machine, or ship 6 NORMAL SELF her normal self in terms of personality, health, or behaviour ○ *She's not herself today – I don't know what's the matter with her.*

herstory /húrstəri/ (*plural* -ries) *n* 1 history as it affects women or looked at from the point of view of women 2 the study or recording of the life experiences, achievements, or expectations of a particular woman or group of women [Late 20C. < HISTORY, as if *his-* were 'of him'.]

Hertford /haártfərd/ town in SE England. Population: 21,665 (1991).

Hertfordshire /haártfərdshər/ county in SE England. Area: 1,634 sq. km/632 sq. mi.

Herts. /haarts/ *abbr* Hertfordshire

hertz /hurts/ (*plural* **hertz**) *n* (*symbol* **Hz**) the SI unit of frequency equal to one cycle per second [Late 19C. After Heinrich HERTZ.]

Hertz /hurts/, **Heinrich** (1857–94) German physicist

Hertzian wave /húrtsi ən-, háirtsi ən-/ *n* a radio wave

Hertzog /húrts og/, **J. B. M.** (1866–1942) South African statesman. Full name **James Barry Munnik Hertzog**

Hertzsprung-Russell diagram *n* a graph that plots the brightness of stars against their spectral type or colour

Hervey Bay /haárvi-/ town in S Queensland, Australia. Population: 32,054 (1996).

Herzegovina /húrtsə gō veénə/ ◊ **Bosnia and Herzegovina**

Herzog /húrts og, háirs og/, **Werner** (*b.* 1942) German film director. Born **Werner Stipetic**

he's (*stressed*) /heez/; (*unstressed*) /eez/ *contr* 1 he is ○ *He's not the man I saw.* 2 he has ○ *He's finished his lunch.*

Heshvan /héshvən/, **Cheshvan** /khésh vaan, khéshvən/ *n* in the Jewish calendar, the second month of the civil year and the eighth month of the religious year

Hesione /hi sī́ əni/ *n* in Greek mythology, a princess whom Hercules rescued from a sea monster

hesitant /hézzitənt/ *adj* hesitating or reluctant to do or say something because of indecision or lack of confidence —**hesitance** *n* —**hesitancy** *n* —**hesitantly** *adv*

SYNONYMS See ***unwilling***.

hesitate /hézzi tayt/ (-tates, -tating, -tated) *vi* 1 to be slow in doing something, or pause while doing or saying something, often because of uncertainty or doubt 2 to be reluctant to do or say something ○ *If you're puzzled by anything, don't hesitate to ask.* [Early 17C. < Latin *haesitat-*, past participle of *haesitare* 'stick fast' < *haerere* 'stick'.] —**hesitater** *n* —**hesitatingly** *adv* —**hesitative** /hézzi taytiv/ *adj*

SYNONYMS ***hesitate, pause, falter, stumble, waver, vacillate***

CORE MEANING: to show uncertainty or indecision

hesitate to be slow in doing something, or take a short break in an activity, as a result of uncertainty or reluctance; **pause** to stop doing something briefly before carrying on, or to wait intentionally for a short period before doing something; **falter** to show a loss of confidence, especially to speak or say something with a series of short stoppages, for example because of nervousness, fear, awkwardness, or incompetence; **stumble** to speak or act hesitatingly, confusedly, or incompetently; **waver** to become unsure or begin to change from a previous opinion; **vacillate** to be indecisive or irresolute, changing between one opinion and another.

hesitation /hézzi táysh'n/ *n* 1 the act of hesitating or pausing 2 the state of being reluctant or undecided

Hesperian /he speéri ən/ *adj* 1 belonging to or connected with the west (*literary*) 2 relating to the Hesperides [Late 15C. < Latin *hesperius* 'western' < Greek *hesperios* < *hesperos* 'western, evening'.]

Hesperides /he spérri deez/ *npl* 1 in Greek mythology, the daughters of Atlas and Hesperus and the guards of a tree bearing golden apples 2 in Greek mythology, islands far to the west in which a tree with golden apples grew [Late 16C. < Greek, plural of *hesperis* 'western' < *hesperos* 'western, evening'.] —**Hesperidean** /héspə ríddi ən/ *adj*

hesperidin /he spérridin/ *n* a white or colourless crystalline glycoside. Source: citrus fruits. Use: treatment of capillary disease. [Mid-19C. < Greek *hesperid-*, stem of *hesperis* 'western' (see HESPERIDES).]

hesperidium /héspə ríddi əm/ *n* a fruit, e.g. a citrus fruit, made up of a thick leathery rind and soft segmented pulp [Mid-19C. < HESPERIDES, with reference to the golden apples.]

Hesperus /héspərəss/ *n* the planet Venus, especially just after sunset when it shines brightly (*literary*) [< Latin, < Greek *hesperos* 'western, evening']

Hess /hess/, **Rudolf** (1894–1987) German Nazi deputy leader

Hesse /hess, héssə/ state and historic duchy in west-central Germany. Capital: Wiesbaden. Population: 5,837,000 (1992). Area: 21,114 sq. km/8,152 sq. mi. —**Hessian** /héssi ən/ *adj, n*

Hesse, Hermann (1877–1962) German novelist and poet

hessian /héssi ən/ *n* a coarse strong jute or hemp fabric. Use: bags, upholstery. [Late 19C. After HESSE in Germany.]

Hessian fly *n* a small fly of the gallfly family that lays its eggs on the stems of grain plants, where the larvae bore into the stems and weaken them. *Mayetiola destructor.* [Because inadvertently brought to N America by Hessian troops]

hessite /héss īt/ *n* a grey metallic mineral composed of silver telluride. Use: source of silver. [Mid-19C. After G. H. *Hess* (1802–50), Russian chemist.]

hessonite /héssə nīt/ *n* = **essonite**

Hess's law /héssiz-/ *n* a law in chemistry stating that the heat absorbed or released during a reaction is the same whether the reaction occurs in one or several steps [After Germain Henri *Hess* (1802–50), Swiss-born Russian chemist]

Hester /héstər/, **Joy St Clair** (*b.* 1920) Australian artist

Hestia /hésti ə/ *n* in Greek mythology, the goddess of the hearth. Roman equivalent **Vesta** *n.* 1

Heston /hést'n/, **Charlton** (*b.* 1923) US actor. Born **John Charlton Carter**

Hesychast /héssi kast/ *n* a member of a school of meditative devotion developed by monks of the Greek Orthodox Church on Mount Athos —**Hesychastic** /héssi kástik/ *adj*

het /het/ *n* a heterosexual person (*slang disapproving*) ■ *adj* heterosexual (*slang disapproving*) [Shortening]

hetaera /hi teérə/ (*plural* -rae /-ree/ *or* -ras), **hetaira** /-tī́rə/ (*plural* -rai /-rī/ *or* -ras) *n* one of a special class of women who were used by the men of ancient Greece as prostitutes, and who were valued as highly cultured companions [Early 19C. < Greek, form of *hetairos* 'companion'.] —**hetaeric** *adj*

hetaerism /hi teérizəm/, **hetairism** /-tī́r-/ *n* 1 the social condition or institution of concubinage 2 the practice in some societies of sharing spouses or sexual partners —**hetaerist** *n* —**hetaeristic** /héttə rístik/ *adj*

hetaira *n* HIST = **hetaera**

hetairism *n* HIST = **hetaerism**

heter- *prefix* = **hetero-** (*before vowels*)

hetero /héttərō/ (*plural* -os) *n* a heterosexual person (*informal*) [Mid-20C. Shortening.] —**hetero** *adj*

hetero- *prefix* 1 different, other ○ *heterochromatic* 2 containing atoms of different kinds ○ *heterocyclic* [< Greek *heteros* 'other' < Indo-European, 'one of two']

heteroatom /héttərō atəm/ *n* a noncarbon atom in a heterocyclic compound

heterocercal /héttərō súrk'l/ *adj* describes a fish's tail in which the vertebral column bends upwards and extends into the upper and larger lobe of the tail-fin, as in some sharks [Mid-19C. < HETERO- + Greek *kerkos* 'tail'.]

heterochromatic /héttərō krə máttik/ *adj* containing many different colours —**heterochromatism** /-krṓmətizəm/ *n*

heterochromatin /héttərō krṓmətin/ *n* chromatic material that contains few genes but stains readily with basic dyes and appears as nodules between chromosomes. ◊ **euchromatin**

heterochromosome /héttərō krṓməssōm/ *n* a chromosome consisting mainly of heterochromatin, especially a sex chromosome

heteroclite /héttərə klīt/, **heteroclitic** /-klíttik/ *adj* describes a word that is formed in an unusual or irregular way [Late 15C. Via late Latin < Greek *heteroklitos* < *heteros* 'the other' + *klīnein* 'to lean'.] —**heteroclite** *n*

heterocyclic /héttərō sī́klik, -síklik/ *adj* describes or relating to a ring system composed of atoms in which at least one is not a carbon atom

heterodox /héttərə doks/ *adj* at variance with established or accepted beliefs or theories, especially in the field of religion [Early 17C. Via late Latin < Greek *heterodoxos* < *heteros* 'the other' + *doxa* 'opinion'.]

heterodoxy /héttərə doksi/ (*plural* -ies) *n* (*formal*) 1 the condition of being at variance with established or accepted beliefs or theories, especially in the field of religion 2 an opinion, belief, or theory that is at variance with established or accepted ones

heterodyne /héttərə dīn/ *vt* (-dynes, -dyning, -dyned) to combine a received radio-frequency wave with a wave of a different frequency to produce frequencies equal to the sum of and the difference between the original two signals ■ *adj* consisting of, produced by, or operated by heterodyning signals

heteroecious /héttə rō eéshəss/ *adj* describes a parasite such as a tapeworm that lives in two or more hosts in the course of its life cycle [Late 19C. < HETERO- + Greek *oikia* 'house'.] —**heteroecism** /-eéssizəm/ *n*

heterogamete /héttə rō gámmeet/ *n* 1 either of two reproductive cells (**gametes**) that differ in size, structure, and function, and that unite in the process of reproduction, e.g. the small sperm and large ova in humans 2 a reproductive cell produced by the sex that carries the chromosomes that determine the sex of the offspring

heterogametic /héttə rōgə méttik/ *adj* 1 describes the sex that produces reproductive cells (**gametes**) of two different types, one type producing males and the other females 2 relating to heterogametes

heterogamy /héttə róggəmi/ *n* 1 UNION OF DISSIMILAR REPRODUCTIVE CELLS in sexual reproduction, the union of two types of sex cell (**heterogamete**) that are dissimilar in size, structure, and function 2 ALTERNATING OF FORMS OF REPRODUCTION the alternation of sexual and asexual reproduction in certain species, e.g. aphids, in which every other generation is produced from the female with no need for a male **3 HAVING DIFFERENT FLOWERS ON ONE PLANT** the production on the same plant of two kinds of flower, one bearing both male and female organs and the other bearing only female organs or being asexual —**heterogamic** /héttərō gámmik/ *adj* —**heterogamous** *adj*

heterogeneity /héttərō jə neé əti, -náyəti/ *n* **1** the diverse nature of something **2** the state of being chemically heterogeneous

heterogeneous /héttərō jeéni əss/, **heterogenous** /héttə rójjenəss/ *adj* **1 CONSISTING OF DISSIMILAR PARTS** consisting of parts or individual elements that are unrelated or unlike each other **2 UNRELATED** not related or similar **3 WITH TWO OR MORE PHASES** describes a chemical substance that has two or more phases [Early 17C. < medieval Latin *heterogeneus* < Greek *heterogenēs* 'other kind' < *heteros* 'other' + *genos* 'kind'.] —**heterogeneously** *adv* —**heterogeneousness** *n*

heterogenesis /héttərō jénnəssiss/ *n* the appearance of a mutation in a population

heterogenetic /héttərō jə néttik/ *adj* **1 OF HETEROGENESIS** relating to heterogenesis **2 FROM DISPARATE ANCESTORS** derived from ancestors not closely related **3 MUTATING** reproducing by heterogenesis —**heterogenetically** *adv*

heterogenic /héttərō jeénik/ *adj* describes a reproductive cell (**gamete**), individual, or population that has more than one variant (**allele**) of a particular gene

heterogenous /héttə rójjənəss/ *adj* **1** = **heterogeneous** **2** originating outside the body, from another individual or species [Late 17C. Variant of HETEROGENEOUS.] —**heterogeny** *n*

heterogony /héttə róggəni/ *n* a life cycle involving alternating parasitic and free-living generations —**heterogonous** *adj* —**heterogonously** *adv*

heterograft /héttə rō graaft/ *n* a graft of living tissue from one animal to another of a different species

heterography /héttə róggrəfi/ (*plural* **-phies**) *n* **1** the use of different letters or groups of letters to represent the same sound or sounds **2** a writing system that uses different combinations of letters to represent the same sound or sounds [Late 18C. < HETERO-, after ORTHOGRAPHY.] —**heterographic** /héttərō gráffik/ *adj*

heterokaryon /héttərō kárri ən/ (*plural* **-a** /-ri ə/) *n* a cell that has two or more genetically different nuclei

heterokaryosis /héttərō kárri óssiss/ *n* the presence in a cell of two or more nuclei of different genetic origin —**heterokaryotic** /-óttik/ *adj*

heterologous /héttə rólləgəss/ *adj* **1 FROM DIFFERENT SPECIES** derived or taken from a different species **2 NOT CORRESPONDING** describes an antigen and an antibody that do not correspond to each other **3 IN UNUSUAL LOCATION** not normally found in the particular part of the body in which it has been found **4 DIFFERING IN STRUCTURE AND ORIGIN** describes organisms or parts that differ from each other in structure or origin [Mid-19C. < HETERO- + Greek *logos* 'relation, ratio'.] —**heterologously** *adv*

heterolysis /héttə rólləssiss/ *n* **1** the breaking of a chemical bond in a compound, producing particles or ions of opposite charge, e.g. the formation of sodium and chloride ions in a salt solution **2** the destruction of cells or proteins of one species by the action of enzymes or lysins from another, e.g. when the blood of one species causes the red blood cells of another species to rupture —**heterolytic** /héttərə líttik/ *adj*

heteromerous /héttə rómmərəss/ *adj* **1** with parts of different types **2** with flowers that do not have the same number of petals in each case or with other parts that are made up of different numbers of elements

heteromorphic /héttərō máwrfik/, **heteromorphous** /-máwrfəss/ *adj* **1 TAKING DIFFERENT FORMS DURING LIFE CYCLE** taking different forms at different stages of its life cycle **2 OF DIFFERENT SIZE OR SHAPE** differing in size or shape, as the X and Y sex chromosomes do **3 ABNORMAL** differing in shape, size, or structure from the normal form of an organism **4 INVOLVING ABNORMAL FORM** characterized by an abnormal form or forms —**heteromorphism** *n* —**heteromorphy** /héttərō mawrfi/ *n*

heteronomous /héttə rónnəməss/ *adj* **1** subject to other laws or rules or to laws and rules imposed by other people or institutions **2** describes parts of an organism that have different modes of development, growth, and different functions [Early 19C. < HETERO- + Greek *nomos* 'law'.] —**heteronomously** *adv* —**heteronomy** /héttə rónnəmi/ *n*

heteronym /héttərōnim/ *n* each of two or more words that are spelt the same, but differ in meaning and often in pronunciation, e.g. 'bow' (a ribbon) and 'bow' (of a ship) [Late 19C. < HETERO- + *-nym* as in SYNONYM.] —**heteronymous** /héttə rónnəməss/ *adj* —**heteronymy** *n*

heteroousian /héttərō oózi ən/, **heterousian** /héttə roózi ən/ *n* in Christian theology, somebody who believes that God the Father and God the Son are not formed of the same substance [Late 17C. < Greek *heter(o)ousios* 'other substance' < *heteros* 'other' + *ousia* 'substance'.] —**heteroousian** *adj*

heterophyllous /héttərō fílləss/ *adj* describes plants such as the sassafras tree that have different shapes of leaves on the same plant —**heterophylly** /héttə róffili/ *n*

heteroplasty /héttərō plasti/ (*plural* **-ties**) *n* **1** a surgical procedure to graft or transplant tissues or organs from one person or animal to another **2** SURG = **heterograft** —**heteroplastic** /héttərō plástik/ *adj*

heteroploid /héttərō ployd/ *adj* with a number of chromosomes that is, unusually, not an exact multiple of the basic chromosome number for that species ■ *n* a heteroploid cell or organism

heteropolar /héttərō pṓlər/ *adj* CHEM = **polar** *adj.* 7 —**heteropolarity** /-pō lárrəti/ *n*

heteropteran /héttə róptərən/ *n* an insect, e.g. a bedbug or another true bug, with mouthparts adapted for piercing and sucking, and partially hardened forewings with membranous tips. Order: Heteroptera. [Mid-19C. < HETERO- + Greek *pteron* 'wing'.] —**heteropteran** *adj*

heterosexism /héttərō séksizəm/ *n* discrimination against homosexual men and lesbians by heterosexuals —**heterosexist** *n, adj*

heterosexual /héttərō sékshoō əl/ *n* a person who is sexually attracted to members of the opposite sex —**heterosexual** *adj* —**heterosexually** *adv*

heterosexuality /héttərō sékshoō álləti/ *n* sexual desire or sexual relations between people of opposite sexes

heterosis /héttə rṓssiss/ *n* BIOL = **hybrid vigour** [Mid-19C. < Greek *heterōsis* 'making different' < *heteros* 'other'.]

heterostyly /héttərō stīli/ *n* the possession of styles of different lengths on different plants of the same species, which is an aid to cross-pollination by insects —**heterostyled** *adj* —**heterostylous** /héttərō stīləss/ *adj*

heterotrophic /héttərō tróffik/ *adj* obtaining nourishment by digesting plant or animal matter, as animals do, as opposed to photosynthesizing food, as plants do —**heterotroph** /héttərō trōf/ *n* —**heterotrophy** /-trōfi/ *n*

heterotropia /héttərō trṓpi ə/ *n* an alignment of the eyes that differs from the normal or usual

heterotypic /héttə rō típpik/, **heterotypical** /-típpik'l/ *adj* differing from the standard or normal type in an organism

heterousian *n, adj* CHR = **heteroousian**

heterozygote /héttə rō zī gōt/ *n* an animal or plant possessing two forms of a particular gene encoding some inheritable characteristic, which may therefore produce offspring differing from their parents and each other in that characteristic

heterozygous /héttə rō zīgəss/ *adj* describes a cell or organism that has two or more different versions (**alleles**) of at least one of its genes

heth /het, heth, k͟het, k͟heth/, **cheth** *n* the eighth letter of the Hebrew alphabet [Early 19C. < Hebrew *ḥēth*.]

hetman /hétmən/ (*plural* **-mans**) *n* MIL = **ataman** [Mid-18C. < Polish.]

het up *adj* extremely excited as a result of anticipation, anger, or anxiety (*informal*) [A past participle of HEAT]

heuchera /hyoōkərə, hóy-/ *n* a cultivated plant with low-growing heart-shaped leaves. Flowers: small, usually red, in sprays. Native to: North America. Genus: *Heuchera*. [Late 19C. < modern Latin, after J. H. *Heucher* (1677–1747), German botanist.]

heulandite /hyoōlən dīt/ *n* a variously coloured crystalline mineral of the zeolite family, containing calcium and sodium [Early 19C. After H. *Heuland* (1777–1856), English mineralogist.]

ϟ **heuristic** /hyoo rístik/ *adj* **1 ENCOURAGING DISCOVERY OF SOLUTIONS** relating to or using a method of teaching that encourages learners to discover solutions for themselves **2 INVOLVING TRIAL AND ERROR** using or arrived at by a process of trial and error rather than set rules **3 ABLE TO CHANGE** describes a computer program that modifies itself in response to the user, e.g. a spellchecker ■ *n* **PROCEDURE FOR GETTING SOLUTION** a helpful procedure for arriving at a solution but not necessarily a proof [Early 19C. < alteration of Greek *heuriskein* 'find'.] —**heuristically** *adv*

heuristics /hyoo rístiks/ *n* a method of solving a problem for which no formula exists, based on informal methods or experience, and employing a form of trial and error (**iteration**) (+ *singular verb*)

hevea /heévi ə/ *n* a tree whose bark contains a milky sap that provides rubber. Native to: Amazon jungle. Genus: *Hevea*. [Late 19C. Via modern Latin < Quechua *hyeve*.]

~~**heven**~~ incorrect spelling of **heaven**

Hevesy /hévvəshi/, **Georg von** (1885–1966) Hungarian chemist

hew /hyoo/ (**hews, hewing, hewed, hewn** /hyoon/ *or* **hewed**) *v* **1** *vti* **CUT DOWN OR UP** to cut, break, or destroy something, especially wood or stone, with a cutting implement, especially an axe **2** *vt* **MAKE BY CUTTING OR CARVING** to form or create something by cutting wood or stone ○ *hewed a path through the forest* **3** *vt* **SEVER FROM SOMETHING ELSE** to cut something off from a larger block or mass **4** *vti* **HIT WITH SWORD** to strike somebody with a sword or axe ○ *He hewed at his enemies with his claymore.* [Old English *hēawen* < Germanic] —**hewer** *n*

SPELLCHECK Do not confuse ***hew*** with ***hue***, which has a similar sound. Beware: your spellchecker will not catch this error.

hew to *vt US, Can* to conform closely to something, e.g. a code or procedure

Hewett /hyoō it/, **Dorothy** (*b.* 1923) Australian writer

Hewish /hyoō ish/, **Antony** (*b.* 1924) British astronomer

hex /heks/ *n* **1 CURSE** a curse or evil spell **2 BRINGER OF BAD LUCK** somebody believed to bring bad luck or misfortune ■ *vt* **1 CURSE OR BEWITCH** to put a curse or spell on somebody or something **2 HAVE BAD EFFECT ON** to appear to have a bad effect on something, as if it were cursed or bewitched ○ *A string of accidents hexed their first attempt to climb the mountain.* [Mid-19C. Via Pennsylvanian German < German *Hexe* 'witch'.] —**hexer** *n*

hex. *abbr* **1** hexagon **2** hexagonal

hex- *prefix* = **hexa-** (*before vowels*)

hexa- *prefix* six ○ *hexagon* [< Greek *hex* < Indo-European]

hexachlorophene /héksə kláwrə feen/ *n* $(C_6HCl_3OH)_2CH_2$ a white odourless organic compound that has antibacterial and antiseptic properties. Use: soaps, toothpaste, deodorants. [Late 20C. < HEXA- + CHLORO- + Greek *phaino-* 'shining'.]

hexachord /héksə kawrd/ *n* a series of six adjacent diatonic notes forming the basis of classical Greek and medieval music theory

hexadecanol /héksə dékə nol/ *n* CHEM, PHARM = **cetyl alcohol**

ϟ **hexadecimal** /héksə déssim'l/ *adj* using units of 16, in which the letters A to F are used as digits as well as the digits 0 to 9, as a basis for counting and ordering ■ *n* a number used to count or order in units of 16

hexagon /héksəgən/ *n* a two-dimensional figure that has six sides [Late 16C. < late Latin *hexagonum* < Greek *hexagōnos* 'six-cornered' < *hexa-* 'six'.] —**hexagonal** /hek sággən'l/ *adj* —**hexagonally** *adv*

hexagram /héksə gram/ *n* **1** a six-pointed star-shaped figure formed by extending the sides of a regular hexagon until they meet at six points **2** any of the 64 possible combinations of six broken or unbroken lines, used in divination, especially in the *I Ching*

hexahedron /héksə heédrən/ *n* a three-dimensional geometrical figure that has six plane faces, e.g. a cube [Late 16C. < Greek *hexaedron*, form of *hexaedros* 'six-sided' < *hexa-* 'six'.] —**hexahedral** *adj*

hexahydrate /héksə hī drayt/ *n* a crystalline compound, each molecule of which contains six loosely bound water molecules (**water of crystallization**) from which the water escapes when the compound is heated, leaving the compound unchanged

hexamerous /hek sámmərəss/, **hexameral** /-sámmərəl/ *adj* with parts, especially petals or stamens, arranged in sets of six —**hexamerism** *n*

hexameter /hek sámmitər/ *n* a line of verse that has six metrical feet, usually all in the same or a related metre [14C. < Latin, < Greek *hexametros* 'of six measures' < *hexa-* 'six' + *metron* 'measure'.] —**hexametric** /héksə méttrik/ *adj*

hexamine /héksə meen/ n a solid camping fuel sold in blocks [Mid-20C. Contraction of *hexamethylenetetramine*, an antibacterial agent.]

hexane /hék sayn/ n C_6H_{14} a volatile hydrocarbon. Source: petroleum. Use: ingredient of petrol, solvent.

Hexapla /héksəplə/ n an ancient version of the Hebrew Scriptures, compiled by the early Christian theologian, Origen, that contains six parallel versions of the text [Early 17C. < Greek *(ta) hexapla*, its title, form of *hexaplous* 'sixfold' < *hexa-* 'six'.]

hexapody /hek sáppədi/ (*plural* **-dies**) n a line of poetry consisting of six feet —**hexapodic** /héksə pódik/ adj

hexastich /héksə stik/, **hexastichon** /hek sásti kon/ (*plural* **-cha** /-kə/) n a unit of verse, e.g. a stanza or a short poem, that contains six lines [Late 16C. Via modern Latin *hexastichon* < Greek, 'of six rows' < *hexa-* 'six' + *stichos* 'row'.]

hexastyle /héksə stīl/ adj having six architectural columns or in the form of six columns ■ n a building, or a portico or other part, that has six columns

Hexateuch /héksə tyook/ n the first six books of the Bible, comprising Genesis, Exodus, Leviticus, Numbers, Deuteronomy, and Joshua. ◊ **Heptateuch, Pentateuch** [Late 19C. < Greek *teuchos* 'book', after *Pentateuch*.]

hexavalent /héksə váylənt/ adj having a chemical valency of six

hexcentric /héks séntrik/ n a six-sided metal chock used in rock climbing

hexokinase /héksō kī́ nayz, -nayss/ n an enzyme that catalyses the first stage of the production of lactic acid from glucose

hexosan /hék sō san/ n a polysaccharide made of linked hexose units

hexose /héksōz, -sōss/ n a simple sugar containing six carbon atoms

hex sign n a stylized sign incorporating a circle and other elements, used to ward off evil or bad luck

hexyl /héks'l/ n C_6H_{13} an organic group or radical derived from hexane and containing six carbon atoms

hey /hay/ interj 1 **DEMANDING ATTENTION** used to get somebody's attention (*informal*) 2 **EXPRESSION OF EMOTION** used to express surprise, irritation, or dismay 3 *US* **GREETING** used as a greeting (*informal*) [12C. Natural exclamation.]

heyday /háy day/ n the time of somebody's or something's greatest success, popularity, or power [Late 16C. < obsolete *heyda* 'hurrah' < ?, by association with DAY.]

Heyerdahl /háy ər daal, hī ər daal/, **Thor** (b. 1914) Norwegian anthropologist

Heysen /hī́z'n/, **Sir Hans** (1877–1968) German-born Australian painter

Heywood /háywŏŏd/, **Thomas** (1574?–1641) English dramatist

Hezekiah /hézzi kī́ ə/ (*fl.* 715 BC) king of Judah (715–687 BC)

h.f. abbr high frequency

HFC abbr hydrofluorocarbon

hg[1] abbr haemoglobin

hg[2] symbol hectogram

HGH abbr human growth hormone

HGV abbr heavy goods vehicle

hh abbr hands (*used as measure of a horse's height*)

HH abbr 1 double hard (*indicates hardness of lead on pencils*) 2 Her Highness 3 His Highness 4 Her Honour 5 His Honour 6 His Holiness

H-Hour n the appointed time for a military event such as a planned attack to take place [H *abbreviation of 'hour'*]

hi /hī/ interj 1 used as an informal greeting (*informal*) 2 used to attract somebody's attention (*archaic informal*) [12C. Natural exclamation.]

HI abbr 1 Hawaii 2 Hawaiian Islands 3 hearing-impaired

Hialeah /hī́ ə lee ə/ city in SE Florida. Population: 211,392 (1998 estimate).

hiatal /hī áyt'l/ adj relating to an opening, gap, or aperture in an organ of the body

hiatal hernia n MED = hiatus hernia

hiatus /hī áytəss, hi-/ (*plural* **-tuses** *or* **-tus**) n 1 **UNEXPECTED GAP** a break in something where there should be continuity 2 **OPENING** an opening or aperture in an organ, e.g. the opening in the diaphragm for the oesophagus

3 SEPARATION BETWEEN VOWELS a break in pronunciation between two vowels that are next to each other in consecutive syllables without an intervening consonant **4 OMISSION** a gap where something is missing, especially in manuscripts [Mid-16C. < Latin, 'gaping, opening' < *hiare* 'gape' < Indo-European.]

hiatus hernia n a hernia in which the part of the stomach around the oesophagus entrance is forced up into the chest cavity through the normal opening in the diaphragm for the oesophagus. US term **hiatal hernia**

Hiawatha /hī́ ə wóthə/ (*fl.* 1550) Native North American leader. Born **Heowenta**

hibachi /hi baáchi/ (*plural* **-chis**) n a portable barbecue of Japanese design, with a base for the fire with vents under it and one or more adjustable cooking racks [Mid-19C. < Japanese, 'fire bowl'.]

hibakusha /hi baákoŏshə, híbbə kooshə/ (*plural* **-sha** *or* **-shas**) n a survivor of the atomic bombing of Hiroshima or Nagasaki in 1945 [Mid-20C. < Japanese, 'somebody who suffers an explosion'.]

hibernaculum /híbər nákyoŏləm/ (*plural* **-la** /-lə/) n 1 the winter den of a hibernating animal or insect 2 the covering of a plant bud that protects it during its dormant phase [Late 17C. < Latin, < *hibernare* (see HIBERNATE).]

hibernal /hī búrn'l/ adj relating to winter as one of the six divisions of the year used to describe ecological communities [Early 17C. < late Latin *hibernalis* < *hibernus* 'wintry'.]

hibernate /híbər nayt/ (**-nates, -nating, -nated**) vi 1 to be in a sleep-like dormant state over the winter while living off reserves of body fat, with a decrease in body temperature and pulse rate and slower metabolism 2 to become less active, especially by staying at home rather than going out to socialize (*informal humorous*) [Early 19C. < Latin *hibernare* < *hiberna* 'winter quarters' < *hibernus* 'wintry'.] —**hibernation** /híbər náysh'n/ n —**hibernator** n

Hibernia /hī búrni ə/ n Ireland (*archaic or literary*) [< Latin, alteration of *Iverna*, via Greek *I(w)ernē* < Celtic] —**Hibernian** adj, n

Hibernicism /hī búrnissizəm/, **Hibernianism** /-búrni ənizəm/ n an Irish word, expression, or idiom in the English language. US term **Irishism**

Hiberno- prefix Irish [< medieval Latin *Hibernus* < Latin *Hibernia* (see HIBERNIA)]

Hiberno-English n the variety of English spoken in Ireland that has features from Irish Gaelic, including intonation and some Gaelic words and phrases —**Hiberno-English** adj

hibiscus /hi bískəss, hi-/ n a shrub or small tree of the mallow family. Flowers: large brightly coloured, prominent stamen tubes. Genus: *Hibiscus*. [Early 18C. Via Latin < Greek *hibiskos* 'marsh-mallow'.]

HIB vaccine /híb-/ n a vaccine that protects against the bacterium that causes meningitis, usually given in the first year of life [Late 20C. < *Haemophilus influenzae*, type B.]

hic /hik/ interj used to represent the sound of a hiccup [Late 19C. An imitation of the sound.]

hiccup /híkup/, **hiccough** n 1 **CONVULSIVE GASP** an abrupt involuntary contraction of the diaphragm that causes an intake of breath and closes the sound-producing folds at the top of the windpipe (vocal cords), resulting in a convulsive gasp 2 **GULPING SOUND** the gulping sound that accompanies a hiccup or a sound like this 3 **HITCH IN ARRANGEMENTS** a temporary setback to somebody's plans or arrangements (*informal*) ■ **hiccups, hiccoughs** npl **GULPING INTAKES OF BREATH** an attack of repeated involuntary spasms of the diaphragm, resulting in periodic noisy gulps of breath ■ v (**-cups, -cuping** *or* **-cupping, -cuped** *or* **-cupped**) 1 vi **PRODUCE A HICCUP** to have a spasm of the diaphragm resulting in a hiccup 2 vi **MAKE HICCUP NOISES** to make the sound of, or a sound like, a hiccup 3 vt **TALK WHILE HICCUPING** to say something while hiccuping [Late 16C. An imitation of the sound.]

hic jacet /hik jáysət, -yákət/ an inscription often found on gravestones, meaning 'here lies' [< Latin]

hick /hik/ n an offensive term that deliberately insults somebody's rural base or background and his or her intelligence and level of sophistication (*informal insult*) ■ adj remote from big cities and regarded as lacking in sophistication (*informal*) [Mid-16C. < *Hick*, old pet form of the first name *Richard*.]

Hick /hik/, **Graeme** (b. 1966) Rhodesian-born British cricketer

hickey /híki/ (*plural* **-eys** *or* **-ies**) n 1 *US, Can* = **doohickey** (*informal*) 2 *US, Can* **MARK ON SKIN** a mark on the skin caused especially by kissing, biting, or sucking and associated with physical intimacy (*informal*) 3 *US, Can* **PIMPLE** a pimple (*informal*) 4 **PRINTING ERROR** a printing error or imperfection [Early 20C. < ?]

US Signal Corps

Wild Bill Hickok

Hickok /híkok/, **Wild Bill** (1837–76) US law enforcer, gunfighter, and scout. Born **James Butler Hickock**

hickory /híkəri/ (*plural* **-ries**) n 1 **N AMERICAN NUT TREE** a deciduous tree of the walnut family with compound leaves and nuts that are edible in some species. Native to: North America. Genus: *Carya*. ◦ *a hickory nut* 2 **HICKORY WOOD** the hard light-coloured wood of a hickory tree. Use: tool handles, sports equipment, furniture. 3 **HICKORY STICK** a walking stick or switch made of hickory wood [Late 17C. < Algonquian, shortening of *pockerchicory, pohickery*, type of walnut.]

hid past tense, past participle of **hide**[1]

hidalgo /hi dálgō/ (*plural* **-gos**) n a Spanish nobleman of the lowest rank [Late 16C. < Spanish, contraction of *hijo de algo* 'son of something'.]

Hidalgo /hi dálgō/ state in east-central Mexico. Capital: Pachuca. Population: 2,100,000 (1995). Area: 20,987 sq. km/8,103 sq. mi.

Hidatsa /hi dátsə/ (*plural* **-sa** *or* **-sas**) n 1 a member of a Native North American people living along the Missouri valley in North Dakota 2 the Siouan language of the Hidatsa people [Late 19C. < Hidatsa *hiratsa* 'willow wood lodge'.] —**Hidatsa** adj

hidden[1] /hídd'n/ past participle of **hide**[1]

hidden[2] /hídd'n/ adj 1 made difficult to find or see ◦ *a hidden doorway* 2 not immediately obvious ◦ *The package included a number of hidden costs.* —**hiddenness** n

hidden agenda n a plan, motive, or aim underlying somebody's actions that is kept secret from others

hiddenite /hídd'n īt/ n a semiprecious stone that is a rare green variety of spodumene. Use: gems. [Late 19C. After W. E. *Hidden*, US mineralogist.]

hidden tax n = indirect tax

hide[1] /hīd/ v (**hides, hiding, hid** /hid/, **hidden** /hídd'n/ *or* **hid**) 1 vti **MOVE OUT OF SIGHT** to conceal yourself, or something or somebody else, from view 2 vt **KEEP SECRET** to prevent something from becoming known 3 vt **BLOCK VIEW OF** to obscure something by passing, or passing something, in front of it, or being temporarily or permanently in front of it ◦ *The clouds hid the sun for a while.* 4 vt **TURN AWAY** to turn away or cover the face or eyes with the hands, e.g., so that the expression cannot be seen or in order to avoid seeing something ■ n **WILDLIFE OBSERVATION POST** a place, often constructed to look like part of the natural environment, where somebody can hide in order to observe, or sometimes shoot, wild animals. US term **blind** n. 3 [Old English *hȳdan* < W Germanic]

hide out vi to be in, or go into, hiding

hide[2] /hīd/ n 1 the skin of some larger animals, e.g. deer, cow, or buffalo (*often in combination*) 2 a person's skin (*informal*) ◦ *'A vengeance on your crafty wither'd hide!'* (William Shakespeare, *The Taming of the Shrew*; 1593) [Old English *hȳd* < Indo-European] ◊ **neither hide nor hair of somebody** *or* **something** no trace of somebody or something ◊ **tan somebody's hide** to beat or whip somebody (*informal*)

hide[3] /hīd/ n in Old English law, a measure of land equal to 120 acres [Old English *hīd* 'measure of land for supporting a family' < Germanic]

hide-and-seek *n* a children's game in which one player lets the others hide, and then tries to find them

hideaway /hīdə way/ *n* a secluded place of retreat or concealment

hidebound /hīd bownd/ *adj* **1 NARROW-MINDED AND CONSERVATIVE** unwilling to countenance new ideas or new ways of doing things **2 WITH DRY, STIFF SKIN** with skin that is dry, stiff, and closely attached to the flesh, as a result of poor feeding ○ *hidebound cattle* **3 WITH TOO STIFF BARK** with bark too stiff for normal growth

hideous /híddi əss/ *adj* **1 HORRIBLE TO SEE** extremely unpleasant or horrible to see **2 HORRIBLE TO HEAR** frighteningly horrible to hear ○ *a hideous shriek* **3 MORALLY REPULSIVE** morally repulsive or disgusting **4 CAUSING SUFFERING** causing a great deal of suffering [14C. < Anglo-Norman *hidous*, Old French *hidos* < *hi(s)de* 'fear'.] —**hideously** *adv* —**hideousness** *n*

hideout /hīd owt/ *n* a place where somebody is hiding, especially somebody wanted by the police

hidey-hole /hídi hōl/, **hidy-hole** *n* a place of concealment for somebody or something (*informal*) [< variant of HIDING[1]]

hiding[1] /hīding/ *n* a place where somebody is hiding or can hide, or the state of being hidden [< HIDE[1]]

hiding[2] /hīding/ *n* the punishment of being beaten (*informal*) [< HIDE[2]] ◇ **on a hiding to nothing** in a situation in which there is no chance of success

hidrosis /hi drṓsiss, hī-/ *n* **1** the production or excretion of sweat (*technical*) **2** a skin disease that affects the sweat glands [Mid-19C. < Greek < *hidrōs* 'sweat'.] —**hidrotic** /-dróttik/ *adj*

hidy-hole *n* = **hidey-hole**

hie /hī/ (**hies, hieing** *or* **hying, hied**) *vi* to go somewhere in a hurry (*archaic*) [Old English, < ?]

~~**hiefer**~~ incorrect spelling of **heifer**

~~**hieght**~~ incorrect spelling of **height**

hier- *prefix* = **hiero-** (*before vowels*)

hierarch /hīr aark/ *n* somebody of high rank in a hierarchy, especially a priestly hierarchy [15C. Via medieval Latin *hierarcha* < Greek *hierarkhēs* 'ruling sacred person' < *hieros* 'sacred' + *arkhēs* 'ruling'.]

hierarchical /hīr áarkik'l/, **hierarchic** /hīr áarkik/ *adj* **1** relating to or arranged in a formally ranked order **2** administered by a hierarchy composed of members of the clergy —**hierarchically** *adv*

hierarchize /hīr aar kīz/ (**-chizes, -chizing, -chized**), **hierarchise** (**-chises, -chising, -chised**) *vt* to arrange something, e.g. an organization, in graduated ranks —**hierarchization** /hīr aar kī záysh'n/ *n*

hierarchy /hīr aarki/ (*plural* **-chies**) *n* **1 FORMALLY RANKED GROUP** an organization or group whose members are arranged in ranks, e.g. in ranks of power and seniority **2 FORMAL GRADING OF A GROUP** categorization of members of a group according to the importance of each **3 ANIMAL GROUP ORGANIZATION** a form of social organization in animals in which different members of a group possess different levels of status, affecting their feeding and mating behaviour **4 RANKED GROUP OF CLERGY** a body of clergy organized into ranks **5 SUBSET WITHIN A RANKED SYSTEM** a subset within a classification system, e.g. that for plants or animals **6 CONTROLLING GROUP IN FORMAL ORGANIZATION** those who are in charge of a formally organized group, especially the priests in control of the Roman Catholic Church or a local part of it

hieratic /hīr áttik/, **hieratical** /-áttik'l/ *adj* **1 OF PRIESTS** relating to priests **2 OF ANCIENT WRITING SYSTEM** relating to a cursive version of ancient Egyptian hieroglyphics **3 IN STYLIZED FORM** fixed, formal, and stylized in a traditional way, e.g. as ancient Egyptian art is ■ *n* **ANCIENT WRITING SYSTEM** a cursive version of ancient Egyptian hieroglyphics [Mid-17C. Via Latin < Greek *hieratikos* 'priestly' < *hiereus* 'sacred person' < *hieros* 'sacred'.] —**hieratically** *adv*

hiero- *prefix* holy, sacred ○ *hierocracy* [< Greek *hieros* < Indo-European]

hierocracy /hīr ókrəssi/ (*plural* **-cies**) *n* **1** government by clergy **2** a body of clergy that rules a place or country —**hierocratic** /hīrō kráttik/ *adj*

hieroglyph /hīrəglif/ *n* a symbol or picture used in a writing system to denote an object, concept, sound, or sequence of sounds, originally and especially in the writing system of the ancient Egyptians [Late 16C. Back-formation < HIEROGLYPHIC.]

hieroglyphic /hīrə glíffik/ *adj* **1 hieroglyphic, hieroglyphical** relating to or written in hieroglyphs **2** difficult to read (*informal*) ■ *n* = **hieroglyph** [Late 16C. Directly or via French < late Latin *hieroglyphicus* < Greek *hierogluphikos* 'sacred carving' < *hieros* 'sacred' + *gluphē* 'carving'.] —**hieroglyphically** *adv*

hieroglyphics /hīrə glíffiks/ *n* a writing system that uses symbols or pictures to denote objects, concepts, or sounds, originally and especially in the writing system of ancient Egypt (+ *singular verb*) ■ *npl* writing that is difficult to decipher or other indecipherable symbols (*informal*; + *plural verb*)

hierogram /hīrō gram/ *n* a symbol with religious significance

Hieronymian /hīrə nímmi ən/, **Hieronymic** /-nímmik/ *adj* relating to St Jerome [Mid-17C. < Latin *Hieronymus* 'Jerome'.]

hierophant /hīrō fant/ *n* **1 EXPLAINER OF MYSTERIES** an interpreter and explainer of obscure and mysterious matters, especially sacred doctrines or mysteries **2 INTERPRETER OF EVENTS** somebody who explains or comments on everyday matters (*formal*) **3 ANCIENT GREEK PRIEST** a priest who revealed the mysteries at the annual festival of Eleusis in ancient Greece [Late 17C. Via late Latin < Greek *hierophantēs* 'sacred person who reveals something' < *hieros* 'sacred' + *phen-*, stem of *phainein* 'reveal'.] —**hierophantic** /hīrə fántik/ *adj* —**hierophantically** *adv*

hifalutin *adj* = **highfalutin**

hi-fi /hī fī/ (*plural* **hi-fis**) *n* **1** a set of high-quality equipment for reproducing and usually recording sound, which may include a CD player, tape deck, turntable, tuner, amplifier, and speakers **2** = **high fidelity** [Mid-20C. Shortening of HIGH FIDELITY.]

higgledy-piggledy /hígg'ldi pígg'ldi/ *adj* disorganized and untidy ■ *adv* in a disorganized, untidy state ○ *'Jasper had already unpacked her young lady's things and laid them higgledy-piggledy in the spacious wardrobe'.* (L. T. Meade, *A Very Naughty Girl*; 1907) [Late 16C. Probably from the idea of pigs being messy, or being huddled together when herded.]

high /hī/ *adj* **1 OF GREAT HEIGHT** extending a long way from bottom to top, especially when viewed from the bottom **2 ABOVE** situated in a position above the onlooker or above somebody or something else referred to ○ *The window was too high for him to see in.* **3 IN HEIGHT ABOVE** above or stretching upwards from a known base level such as sea or ground level ○ *ten feet high* **4 ABOVE AVERAGE** greater than the normal or average, e.g. in quantity, number, quality, intensity, or cost, or well above a smaller or lower level or amount ○ *a high cost of living* **5 RAISED IN PITCH** raised in pitch towards the upper end of a range of sound ○ *can hit the high notes* **6 BLOWING STRONGLY** blowing with a great deal of force ○ *a high wind* **7 ADVANCED** advanced in development or complexity ○ *high finance* **8 BETTER** superior in quality, character, or morals ○ *sets a high example* **9 WITH ELEVATED RANK** important in status or rank ○ *a high official* **10 VERY FAVOURABLE** considering somebody or something to be particularly good ○ *held in high esteem* **11 AT A PEAK** at the busiest or most important stage ○ *high summer* **12 HAPPY** animated and cheerful ○ *in high spirits* **13 OVEREXCITED** overexcited or overstimulated **14 INTOXICATED** under the influence of alcohol or drugs (*slang*) **15 STRONG-SMELLING OR -TASTING** with a very strong smell or taste, either because it is pleasantly mature or because it has overmatured and begun to go bad **16 FAR FROM EQUATOR** at a considerable distance either north or south of the equator ○ *high latitude* **17 WITH TONGUE RAISED** formed with the back of the tongue close, or relatively close, to the roof of the mouth ○ *high vowel sounds* **18 high, High RITUALISTIC** favouring or involving formal and elaborate ritual and ceremonial **19 PRODUCING TOP SPEEDS** resulting in a relatively large number of revolutions of the driven part as compared with the driving part in a transmission gear, and giving the top speed of travel or rotation ■ *adv* **WAY UP** at, in, or into a high position ○ *The balloon rose high in the sky.* ■ *n* **1 TOP PLACE** a high level or position ○ *an all-time high* **2** METEOROL = **anticyclone** **3 TOP TEMPERATURE** the highest temperature reached or expected to be reached in a particular period ○ *Today's high will be in the nineties.* **4 ELATED STATE** a state of euphoria (*informal*) **5 INTOXICATED STATE** a state of intoxication by drugs or alcohol **6 high, High HIGH SCHOOL** a high school (*informal*) ○ *She goes to Kinross High.* **7** *US* AUTOMOT = **top**[1] *n.* 13 (*informal*) [Old English *hēah* < Germanic] ◇

high and dry 1 stranded and abandoned, and perhaps helpless **2** beyond the reach of water ◇ **high and low** in every conceivable place ◇ **high and mighty** arrogant and self-important ◇ **run high** to be at a level of great intensity

highball /hī bawl/ *n US* a long drink consisting of spirits mixed with ice and water or a carbonated drink ■ *vti* to travel, or drive a vehicle, at high speed (*slang*) [Earlier 'type of poker played with balls and a tall glass receptacle']

high beam *n US* TRANSP = **full beam**

high blood pressure *n* unusually high arterial blood pressure

highborn /hī bawrn/ *adj* born into an aristocratic family (*literary*)

highboy /hī boy/ *n US* FURNITURE = **tallboy**

high brass *n* brass consisting of 65 per cent copper and 35 per cent zinc

highbred /hī bred/ *adj* born of or descended from superior breeding stock

highbrow /hī brow/ *adj* dealing with serious subjects, especially cultural subjects, in an intellectual way ○ *'conceits which would be only highbrow wisecracks in inferior writing have fused into a form that can only be called inevitable, the way it should be'* (Northrop Frye, *The Bush Garden*; 1972) ■ *n* somebody with highbrow interests or tastes [< the idea that a high forehead signifies greater brain power] —**highbrowism** *n*

highchair /hī cháir/ *n* a small chair with long legs and often a detachable tray, for older babies and toddlers to use at mealtimes

High Church *n* a section of the Anglican Church that stresses the essential unity of Anglican Christianity with Roman Catholicism and Orthodoxy, holds traditional views about the sacraments, and favours ritual and ceremony

high-class *adj* **1** appealing to the rich or sophisticated, and therefore usually expensive **2** showing or having the kind of sophistication associated with wealth

high comedy *n* comedy with humour depending on witty dialogue and a clever plot rather than slapstick

high command *n* **1** the senior officers in a country's armed forces, who jointly take decisions on strategy and tactics **2** the main headquarters of a military force

High Commission *n* the embassy of one country of the Commonwealth of Nations in another Commonwealth country

High Commissioner *n* **1** the chief representative of a country of the Commonwealth of Nations in another Commonwealth country **2** the person leading an international commission

high-concept *adj* describes a film that contains features likely to attract a large audience, e.g. big stars, fast action, and glamour

high country *n* lands that are in a mountainous region, but not so high as to have no pastoral or agricultural use (*hyphenated before nouns*)

high court *n* in the United States, a superior court or a state's supreme court

High Court *n* **1 SUPREME COURT** the Supreme Court of the United States **2 MOST SENIOR COURT** a country's principal court, especially the High Court of Justice in England and Wales, or the High Court of Justiciary in Scotland **3 FEDERAL SUPREME COURT** in Australia, the federal supreme court and final court of appeal **4 MAIN CIVIL AND CRIMINAL COURT** in New Zealand, a civil and criminal court inferior to the Court of Appeal but superior to the District Courts **5 HIGHEST STATE COURT** in India, the highest court of a state

High Court of Justice *n* the principal court for civil cases in England and Wales

High Court of Justiciary *n* the principal criminal court in Scotland

high day *n* a day of religious celebration (*archaic*) ◇ **on high days and holidays** on special occasions

high-definition television *n* a television system with twice the scanning capacity of normal television systems, allowing for far greater definition and less flickering

high-density lipoprotein *n* an aggregate of fat and protein that transports cholesterol away from the arteries

high-end *adj* 1 sophisticated and discerning or likely to appeal to sophisticated and discerning people 2 having extensive and sophisticated capabilities and features ○ *high-end laptops*

high-energy *adj* 1 describes chemical reactions that take place with the release of substantial amounts of energy 2 especially in marketing, describes foods that can be broken down by the body to provide a ready supply of energy, e.g. glucose drinks or high-sugar items such as honey

high-energy physics *n* PHYS = **particle physics**

Higher /hī ər/ *n* 1 in Scotland, an examination in a single subject, usually taken after five or six years of secondary education (*often before nouns*) 2 in Scotland, a pass in a Higher examination

higher criticism *n* the establishment of the sources of biblical texts, using the techniques of textual criticism —**higher critic** *n*

higher education *n* education generally begun after Highers or A-levels, usually carried out at a university or college, and involving study for a degree, diploma, or similar advanced qualification

higher law *n* a moral law or ethical principle that is believed to be of greater validity than earthly law

higher mathematics *n* mathematics at an abstract and sophisticated level, including number theory and topology (+ *singular verb*)

higher-up *n* somebody in a position of authority or at a higher level in a hierarchy (*informal*)

highest common factor *n* the highest number that can be exactly divided into each member of a set of numbers. US term **greatest common divisor**

high explosive *n* a liquid or solid substance that undergoes explosive decomposition (**detonation**) without burning to produce a large release of energy. Use: rock blasting, military applications.

highfalutin /hīfə lo͞otin, -t'n/, **hifalutin, highfaluting** /-lo͞oting/ *adj* affecting a grand style in an unconvincing way (*informal*) [Mid-19C. < ?]

high fashion *n* = **haute couture**

high fidelity *n* extremely high-quality sound reproduction with minimal distortion, achieved with electronic equipment (*hyphenated before nouns*)

high-five *n* an informal greeting or gesture of elation or victory in which somebody slaps a raised palm against the raised palm of somebody else (*slang*) —**high-five** *vti*

high-flier, high-flyer *n* a highly successful person, or somebody who seems destined for great achievement

high-flown *adj* giving an unconvincing appearance of being elegant, refined, or exalted ○ *'a warning against high-flown pretensions'* (Henry James, *Roderick Hudson*; 1876)

high-flyer *n* = **high-flier**

high frequency *n* a radio frequency in the range 3–30 MHz or of wavelength 10–100 metres (*hyphenated before nouns*)

high gear *n* US AUTOMOT = **top gear**

High German *n* the form of German spoken originally in the southern part of the country that has become standard German —**High-German** *adj*

high-grade *adj* of a high quality, especially because of purity or concentration of contents

high ground *n* 1 an area of land higher than its surroundings 2 a position of superiority or advantage over others

high-handed *adj* overbearing and inconsiderate of other people's views or sensibilities —**high-handedly** *adv* —**high-handedness** *n*

high-hat *adj* SNOBBISH snobbish and arrogant (*archaic*) ■ *n* SNOB a snob (*archaic informal*) ■ *vti* (**high-hats, high-hatting, high-hatted**) *US, Can* BEHAVE SNOBBISHLY to treat somebody in a haughty, disdainful way (*dated*)

high-hat cymbals *npl* a pair of cymbals held horizontally on a stand, with the upper one made to rise and fall against the lower one by the drummer's foot

high heels *npl* women's shoes with tall, often slender, heels that raise the back of the foot off the ground

High Holidays, High Holy Days *npl* the period of Jewish festivals from Rosh Hashanah to Yom Kippur

high horse *n* an attitude of arrogance and haughty disregard for others (*informal*) ○ *is on her high horse this morning* ○ *told him to get off his high horse*

high hurdles *n* a track event for men, in which the athletes cover a distance of 110 m outdoors, jumping over hurdles 107 cm/42 in high (+ *singular or plural verb*)

highjack *v* = **hijack**

high jinks /hījingks/, **hijinks** *n* good-humoured boisterousness, frequently including mischievousness and pranks (*informal*; + *singular or plural verb*)

high jump *n* a sporting event in which the athletes run forward to gain momentum, and then jump over a horizontal pole —**high jumper** *n* —**high jumping** *n* ◇ **be for the high jump** to be about to be scolded, punished severely, or dismissed from a job (*informal*)

highland /hīlənd/ *n* HILLY LAND hilly ground, higher than its surroundings ■ **highlands** *npl* HILLY AREA an area or region that is largely hilly or mountainous. ◊ **Highlands** ■ *adj* RELATING TO HIGHLANDS relating to or coming from highlands —**highlander** *n*

Highland[1] *adj* relating to, found in, or originating from the Scottish Highlands —**Highlander** *n*

Highland[2] /hīlənd/ council area of N Scotland. Area: 25,784 sq. km/9,955 sq. mi.

Highland cattle *npl* cattle belonging to a hardy breed with long shaggy reddish-brown hair and long curved horns, originally bred in the Highlands of Scotland

Highland Clearances *npl* the forcible removal of tenants from their land by many 18th- and 19th-century landlords in the Scottish Highlands, usually to introduce sheep farming

Highland cow *n* a long-haired cow belonging to a breed originating in the Highlands of Scotland

Highland dress *n* a modern version of the traditional clothing of Highland men, comprising a tartan kilt, a sporran, knee-length socks, a tweed or plain wool jacket, and brogues

Highland fling *n* an energetic Scottish solo dance originally danced by men in Highland dress

Highland Games *n* an outdoor meeting at which there are competitions in various traditional Scottish sports, e.g. tossing the caber, in Scottish dancing, and in piping (+ *singular or plural verb*)

Highlands /hīləndz/ mountainous area of northern mainland Scotland

high-level *adj* involving participation by people at a high level in their organization or country, e.g. politicians, civil servants, or company directors

high-level language *n* a computer programming language with syntax and grammar crudely approximating a natural language

high-level waste *n* radioactive waste material retaining sufficient activity that it needs to be continuously cooled

high life *n* the luxurious lifestyle of fashionable society (*often used ironically*)

highlife /hī līf/ *n* a style of music that blends West African elements with jazz forms and is popular in West Africa

highlight /hī līt/ *n* 1 BEST PART the most memorable, important, or exciting part of an experience or event 2 REPRESENTATIVE PART an exemplary extract from a larger work that, along with others, is meant to represent it ○ *gave us highlights of the President's speech* 3 CONTRASTING PALE AREA an area in a very light tone in a painting or photograph that provides contrast, illumination, or the appearance of illumination 4 REFLECTION the reflection of a light source in a picture, e.g. the reflection of a studio light in shiny hair or the reflection of light in somebody's eye ■ **highlights** *npl* LIGHT STREAKS IN HAIR strands of hair that are deliberately made lighter than the rest of the hair ■ *vt* 1 EMPHASIZE to draw attention to something or make something particularly prominent or noticeable ○ *The report highlights the problems of inner-city areas.* 2 MARK WITH HIGHLIGHTER to mark something, e.g. parts of a text, with a highlighter pen 3 PUT STREAKS IN to put highlights in somebody's hair 4 ADD LIGHT AREAS IN to add highlights to parts of a picture to provide contrast, illumination, or the appearance of illumination

highlighter /hī lītər/ *n* 1 a broad-tipped felt pen, often with transparent, brightly coloured ink, for marking important passages of text 2 a cosmetic for the face that is used to emphasize features such as the eyes or cheekbones

high-low *n* 1 a variety of poker in which both high and low hands win 2 a signal to a bridge partner to lead a particular suit

highly /hīli/ *adv* 1 EXTREMELY very much ○ *highly likely to succeed* 2 FAVOURABLY very favourably ○ *highly regarded* 3 IN HIGH PLACE in a high position or rank ○ *highly placed officials who denied the story* 4 GREATLY to a great extent or in many ways ○ *highly improbable*

highly-strung *adj* by nature tense, nervous, or easily upset. US term **high-strung**

high-maintenance *adj* requiring an excessive amount of attention or effort to maintain ○ *a high-maintenance car* ○ *a high-maintenance relationship*

High Mass *n* an elaborate Roman Catholic Mass in which a choir sings much of the service

high-minded *adj* having or showing high moral principles —**high-mindedly** *adv* —**high-mindedness** *n*

high-muck-a-muck /hī múkə múk/, **high-muckety-muck** /-múkəti-/ *n US* somebody in a position of importance and authority who behaves in an overbearing way (*informal*) [Mid-19C. Probably < Chinook Jargon *hiyu muckamuck* 'ten portions of choice whalemeat', by association with HIGH.]

highness /hīnəss/ *n* the condition, state, or extent of being high

Highness *n* a title and style of address for members of a royal family other than a sovereign

high noon *n* 1 NOON EXACTLY the exact moment of noon 2 PEAK OF ACHIEVEMENT the high point or most creative part of somebody's career or achievements 3 **high noon, High Noon** CRUCIAL TIME a time of confronting a serious problem or making a hard decision

high-octane *adj* 1 describes fuel that has a high octane content 2 showing or demanding a high degree of commitment and effort in a drive for success (*informal*)

high-pitched *adj* 1 AT TOP OF SOUND RANGE towards the upper end of the range of audible sound 2 WITH STEEP SLOPE having a very steep slope 3 EMOTIONAL extremely emotional and intense 4 FORMAL AND ELABORATE in a formal and flowery style

high places *npl* positions of power, authority, or influence

high point *n* the most successful, enjoyable, or important part of a period of time, activity, or experience ○ *This new promotion marked the high point of his career.*

high-powered, high-power *adj* 1 DYNAMIC possessing great energy and impressive ability, especially as displayed in a professional environment ○ *a high-powered sales pitch* 2 INFLUENTIAL having a lot of power or influence 3 GREATLY ENLARGING giving a high magnification 4 VERY POWERFUL operating much more powerfully, or able to handle material of greater complexity and more quickly, than others of the same type

high-pressure *adj* 1 OPERATING AT GREATER THAN NORMAL PRESSURE using, or designed to withstand, forces exerted by liquid or gas at pressures higher than normal atmospheric pressure 2 STRESSFUL causing stress, e.g. from deadlines or excessive demands ○ *She's at her best in high-pressure situations.* 3 PERSISTENT aggressively persistent in seeking to bring about a result

high priest *n* 1 MAIN PROPONENT the leading figure propounding a doctrine or ideology 2 JEWISH CHIEF PRIEST a chief priest, especially the head of the priestly caste at the time of the Temple in Jerusalem 3 MORMON PRIEST a man who is a priest in the Church of Jesus Christ of Latter-Day Saints, belonging to the order of Melchizedek —**high priesthood** *n*

high priestess *n* 1 a woman who leads a religion or a religious group 2 the leading woman propounding a doctrine or ideology

high profile *n* a prominent position or presence in the public eye

high-profile *adj* in or intended to be in the public eye, e.g. to attract attention, support, or business

high relief *n* a version of relief sculpture in which the carving projects from the background to more than half its natural depth (*hyphenated before nouns*) ◊ **bas-relief**

High Renaissance *n* the period in European art between about 1490 and 1520, when the work of Leonardo da Vinci, Michelangelo, Raphael, and other great artists reached the highest point of Renaissance perfection

high resolution *n* the use in a video display or printed image of a large number of dots or lines to portray an image in great detail (*hyphenated before nouns*)

high-rise *adj* 1 **MULTISTOREY** consisting of several storeys, but usually fewer than for a skyscraper 2 **WITH HIGH HANDLEBARS** describes a child's bicycle that has small wheels, very high handlebars, and a long narrow seat ■ *n* 1 **TALL BUILDING** a multistorey building 2 **HIGH-RISE BICYCLE** a child's high-rise bicycle

high-risk recreation *n* a recreational activity that involves an element of danger, e.g. hang-gliding, skydiving, bungee jumping, and white-water rafting

high road *n* 1 a main road, usually in a town or village 2 the easiest or most direct way to somewhere

high roller *n US, Can* (*slang*) 1 a person or organization that spends money freely and extravagantly 2 a gambler who plays for high stakes —**high-rolling** *adj*

high school *n* 1 a secondary school, for pupils aged 11 to 16, 17, or 18 2 in the United States a school that includes grades 9 or 10 to 12

high seas *npl* the open ocean, not under any nation's jurisdiction

high season *n* the most popular time of year for holidays, when resorts are at their busiest. US term **peak season**

high sign *n US* a secret signal, often prearranged, given as a warning or to convey information

high society *n* the fashionable wealthy classes in society

high-sounding *adj* grandiose and pretentious but unlikely to come to anything

high-spirited *adj* lively and full of fun or mischief —**high-spiritedly** *adv* —**high-spiritedness** *n*

high spot *n* the most memorable, important, or exciting part of an experience or event

high-stakes *adj* in which somebody is likely to win or lose a great deal ○ *'Everyone is getting in the starting blocks for a high-stakes fight'. (The Washington Post*; November 1998)

high-sticking *n* in ice hockey, the offence of holding the hockey stick higher than is allowed by the rules

high street, High Street *n* 1 **MAIN STREET IN TOWN** a principal street where the main shops are located 2 **RETAIL TRADE** the ordinary retail sector of the national economy (*informal*) 3 **CONSUMERS GENERALLY** the public, when viewed as consumers (*informal*)

high-strung *adj US, Can* = **highly-strung**

high style *n* the most up-to-date and stylish fashion, especially in clothing (*hyphenated before nouns*)

high table *n* a table in a large dining hall in some schools and university colleges at which the staff, principal teachers, or fellows sit

hightail /hī tayl/ *vti* to rush away from a place (*slang*) [< the erect tail of a fleeing animal]

high tea *n* a meal served in the late afternoon or early evening, consisting of a cooked dish, usually hot, with bread and butter, cakes, and tea

high tech, hi-tech *n* 1 advanced technology and state-of-the-art techniques, especially in electronic engineering 2 a style of architecture and interior design that makes use of metal, glass, and plastic in a simple utilitarian way

high-tech /hī ték/, **hi-tech** *adj* 1 using or relating to advanced technological devices and methods 2 using metal, glass, and plastic in a simple utilitarian way in architecture and interior design

high technology *n* = **high tech** *n.* 1

high-tension *adj* designed for or operating at high voltage

high-test *adj* INDUST = **high-octane**

high tide *n* 1 **HIGHEST POINT OF TIDE** the tide at its highest level 2 **MOMENT OF HIGHEST TIDE** the time when the tide reaches its highest level 3 **PEAK** the culmination or high point of something

high-toned *adj* culturally, morally, or socially superior (*dated*)

high-top *n* a sports shoe that extends above the ankle to give it protection and support ■ *adj* having uppers that rise above the ankles and protect them

high treason *n* treason against somebody's own sovereign or country

high-up *n* = **higher-up** (*informal*)

highveld /hī velt/ *n* the high-altitude grassy plateau of Gauteng and neighbouring provinces in the northern part of South Africa

high-voltage *adj* involving a voltage higher than 650 volts

high water *n* 1 = **high tide** *n.* 1, **high tide** *n.* 2 2 the highest level reached by any stretch of water, e.g. during a flood (*hyphenated before nouns*) 3 the time when the water level of a river or other stretch of water is at its highest

high-water mark *n* 1 **HIGHEST WATER LEVEL** the highest level reached by any natural stretch of water, principally by the sea at high tide, but also, e.g., a river during a flood 2 **MARK SHOWING HIGHEST LEVEL** a mark drawn to indicate the highest level reached by any natural stretch of water 3 **PEAK** a high point in an enterprise ○ *Winning the book award was the high-water mark in her career.*

highway /hī way/ *n* 1 **PUBLIC ROAD** any public road (*formal; often before nouns*) 2 *US, Can* **MAIN ROAD** a principal road, especially one that connects towns or cities and is part of a numbered system (*often before nouns*) 3 **DIRECT WAY** a direct route or course ○ *the highway to fame*

Highway Code *n* a government-published booklet containing rules and information relating to the use of public roads in the United Kingdom

highwayman /hī wayman/ (*plural* **-men** /-mən/) *n* formerly, somebody who forced people travelling by road to stop, usually at gunpoint, and robbed them

highway patrol *n* the law enforcement agency that patrols the public highways in some states of the United States

highway robbery *n US* = **daylight robbery** (*informal*)

High Weald /hī wéeld/ region in SE England. Area: 1,460 sq. km/569 sq. mi.

high wire *n* a tightrope stretched high above the ground on which circus performers balance and perform acrobatics

high-wire *adj* holding the possibility of great risk, e.g. to life or reputation

High Wycombe /hī wíkəm/ town in south-central England. Population: 71,718 (1991).

HIH *abbr* 1 Her Imperial Highness 2 His Imperial Highness

hijack /hī jak/, **highjack** *vt* 1 **SEIZE AIRCRAFT, SHIP, OR TRAIN** to take control of a public transport vehicle, e.g. a passenger aircraft, while in transit, taking the people on board hostage, and diverting it to another destination 2 **STOP A VEHICLE TO ROB IT** to seize a motor vehicle, e.g. an armoured car carrying money, in order to rob it of its contents 3 **STEAL SOMETHING FROM A SEIZED VEHICLE** to steal merchandise, money, or any other items from a hijacked motor vehicle 4 **STEAL IDEA** to take somebody else's idea and use it, especially to the exclusion or detriment of the person from whom it was taken (*informal*) ■ *n* = **hijacking** [Early 20C. < ?] —**hijacker** *n*

hijacking /hī jaking/ *n* the forcible seizure of a public transport vehicle, e.g. a passenger aircraft, while in transit, taking those on board hostage, and compelling diversion of the vehicle to another destination

hijiki /hi jíki/ (*plural* **-kis** *or* **-ki**), **hiziki** /-zí-/ (*plural* **-kis** *or* **-ki**) *n* a Japanese seaweed that turns black when dried and is sold shredded to be used in cooking [Late 20C. < Japanese.]

hijinks *npl* = **high jinks**

hike /hīk/ *v* (**hikes, hiking, hiked**) 1 *vti* **TAKE A LONG WALK** to go for a long walk in the countryside, usually for pleasure 2 *vti* **GO ON A TRAINING MARCH** to march in a training exercise 3 *vt* **RAISE AMOUNT OF** to increase taxes, prices, or the level or quantity of something suddenly and by a large amount ○ *rumours that the banks plan to hike up interest rates* 4 *vt* **PULL SOMETHING UPWARDS** to pull or raise something with a sudden strong movement ■ *n* 1 **PLEASURABLE LONG WALK** a long walk, usually across country for pleasure 2 **SUDDEN LARGE INCREASE** a sudden large increase in prices, taxes, or the level or quantity of something ○ *an unexpected hike in interest rates* [Early 19C. < ?] —**hiker** *n* ◇ **take a hike** *US* to leave abruptly, or, more often, used to tell somebody who is unwelcome to leave (*informal*)

hike up *vti* to move up or become moved up from the proper position ○ *Her coat had hiked up at the back.*

Hilarion /hi lérri ən/, **St** (290?–371) Palestinian monk

hilarious /hi láiri əss/ *adj* causing great amusement [Early 19C. < Latin *hilaris* 'cheerful' < Greek *hilaros*.] —**hilariously** *adv* —**hilariousness** *n*

hilarity /hi lárrəti/ *n* amusement or merry laughter [15C. Via French *hilarité* < Latin *hilaritas* < *hilaris* (see HILARIOUS).]

Hilary term /híllәri-/ *n* the spring term at Oxford University and the Inns of Court [Late 16C. After *Hilarius* (300?–367), bishop of Poitiers, France.]

Hilbert /hílbərt/, **David** (1862–1943) German mathematician

Hildegard (of Bingen) /híldə gaard əv bíngən/, **St** (1098–1179) German writer and composer

hili plural of **hilus**

hill /hil/ *n* 1 **HIGH LAND** an area of land, usually rounded in shape, that is higher than the surrounding land but not as high as a mountain 2 **GRADIENT IN ROAD** a slope or gradient in a road ○ *You'll need to drop into second gear for this hill.* 3 **PILE OF EARTH** a pile of something such as earth ■ *vt* **MAKE EARTH INTO PILE** to pile up earth, especially around the base of plants [Old English *hyll* < Indo-European, 'be prominent'] —**hiller** *n* ◇ **over the hill** at an age considered too advanced in years for something, or supposedly past the prime of life

Hill *n* Capitol Hill (*informal*) ○ *has worked on the Hill for two years*

Hill /hil/, **Archibald** (1886–1977) British physiologist

Hill, Damon (*b.* 1960) British racing driver

Hill, David (1802–70) British photographer and painter

Hill, Ernestine (1899–1972) Australian author

Hill, Graham (1929–75) British racing driver

Hillary /hílləri/, **Sir Edmund** (*b.* 1919) New Zealand mountaineer and explorer

hillbilly /híl bili/ (*plural* **-lies**) *n US* a term used by people from the country to describe themselves with pride, but used by others as an insult to mean somebody ignorant and unsophisticated (*informal; offensive in some contexts*) [Early 20C. < pet form of the name *William*.]

hillbilly music *n* a variety of country music, especially the music of the Appalachian Mountains, that features fiddles, banjos, guitars, and hammer dulcimers

hill climb *n* a competition in which car or motorcycle drivers compete to set the fastest time in reaching the top of a steep slope

hillcrest /híl krest/ *n* the summit or the highest ridge of a hill

Hillel (the Elder) /híl el thi éldər/ (70? BC–AD 10?) Jewish rabbi and teacher

Hilliard /hílli ərd/, **Nicholas** (1547–1619) English painter and goldsmith

hill myna *n* a black bird of the starling family often kept as a cage bird because of its ability to mimic human words. Native to: S Asia. *Gracula religiosa*.

hillock /híllək/ *n* a small hill or mound —**hillocked** *adj* —**hillocky** *adj*

hillside /híl sīd/ *n* the slope or side of a hill

hill station *n* a village or government office in the northern hills or low mountain ranges of the Indian subcontinent, established by the British as respite from the summer heat for officials and their families

hilltop /híl top/ *n* the summit of a hill

hillwalking /híl wawking/ *n* the pastime of walking in hilly country —**hillwalker** *n*

hilly /hílli/ (**-ier, -iest**) *adj* 1 having many hills ○ *hilly countryside* 2 having a steep incline —**hilliness** *n*

hilt /hilt/ *n* the handle of a sword, knife, or dagger [Old English *hilt(e)* < Germanic] ◇ **(up) to the hilt** to the maximum

hilum /híləm/ (*plural* **-la** /hílə/) *n* 1 a scar on the seed of a plant indicating where it was attached to the ovule 2 ANAT = **hilus** [Mid-17C. < Latin, 'trifle'.]

hilus /híləss/ (*plural* **-li** /-lī/) *n* an opening through which blood vessels and nerves enter and leave an organ. US term **hilum** *n.* 2 [Mid-19C. < Modern Latin, alteration of HILUM.]

him (*stressed*) /him/; (*unstressed*) /im/ *pron* used to refer to a man, boy, or male animal who has been previously mentioned or whose identity is known (*used as the* *object or complement of a verb or preposition)* ○ *She handed him the phone without a word.* ○ *John closed the door behind him.* ○ *It's him, I know it's him.*

HIM *abbr* 1 Her Imperial Majesty 2 His Imperial Majesty

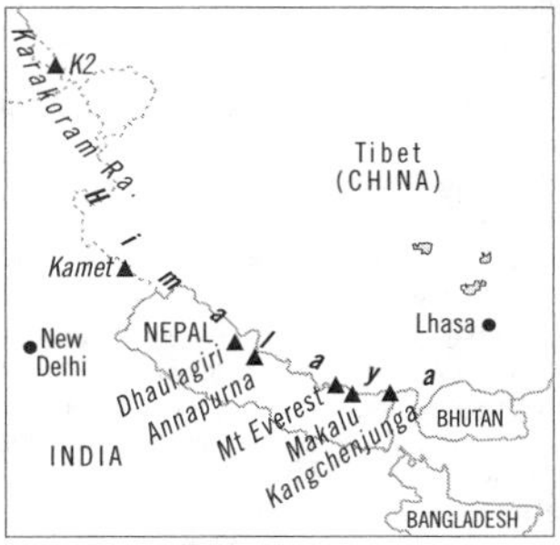

Himalaya

Himalaya /hímmə láy ə/, **Himalayas** /hímmə láy əz/ mountain system in Asia, forming the northern boundary of the Indian subcontinent. Highest peak: Mount Everest 8,848 m/29,028 ft. —**Himalayan** *adj*

Himalia /hi maáli ə/ *n* a small natural satellite of Jupiter, discovered in 1904 [Late 20C. Probably < Greek *himalis*, name for DEMETER < *himalios* 'abundant'.]

himation /hi mátti on/ *n* a loose outer garment worn by men and women in ancient Greece, consisting of a large rectangular piece of cloth draped over one shoulder and under the opposite arm [Mid-19C. < Greek, 'small garment' < *hima* 'garment' < *hennunai* 'clothe'.]

Himmler /hímmlər/, **Heinrich** (1900–45) German Nazi official

himself *(stressed)* /him sélf/; *(unstressed)* /im sélf/ CORE MEANING: the form of 'him' used in reflexive and emphatic contexts ○ *After a final struggle with himself, he handed the papers over.* ○ *If he himself doesn't know what he's doing, I don't see how I can help him.* ○ *He did it himself.*
pron 1 **REFERRING TO MALE SUBJECT OF VERB** used to refer to the same man, boy, or male animal as the subject of the verb ○ *He decided to treat himself.* ○ *his sense of pride in himself* 2 **USED FOR EMPHASIS** used to emphasize or clarify which man, boy, or male animal is being referred to, often introducing a note of surprise or awe ○ *a visit from the Prince himself* 3 **ALONE OR WITHOUT HELP** used to show that a man, boy, or male animal is alone or unaided ○ *sitting by himself in a corner* ○ *tied his shoelaces himself* 4 **NORMAL SELF** his normal self in terms of personality, health, or behaviour ○ *not feeling himself* 5 *Scotland, Ireland* **IMPORTANT MALE PERSON** an important, or often self-important, man or boy *(informal; often used ironically)* ○ *Himself is wanting a word.*

Himyarite /hímmyə rīt/ *n* (*plural* **-ites** *or* **-ite**) a member of an ancient people who lived in the S Arabian Peninsula ■ *adj* relating to the Himyarites, or their language or culture [Mid-19C. < *Himyar*, legendary king of Yemen.] —**Himyarite** *adj*

Hinayana /heénə yaánə/ *n* the form of Buddhism, mainly found in Sri Lanka and Southeast Asia, characterized by adherence to the early Pali scriptures and the nontheistic pursuit of purification through Nirvana [Mid-19C. < Sanskrit, 'lesser vehicle'.] —**Hinayanist** *n* —**Hinayanistic** /heénə yaa nístik/ *adj*

Hinchinbrook Island /hínchinbrŏŏk-/ island off the northeastern coast of Australia. Area: 394 sq. km/152 sq. mi.

Hinckley /híngkli/ town in central England. Population: 40,608 (1991).

Hincks /hingks/, **Sir Francis** (1807–85) Irish-born Canadian colonial administrator

hind[1] /hīnd/ *adj* at or forming the back part of an animal ○ *the hind legs of a donkey* [13C. Probably shortening of BEHIND.]

hind[2] /hīnd/ *n* 1 a female red deer 2 a spotted marine fish that is a type of groper. Native to: Atlantic Ocean. Genus: *Epinephelus*. [Old English, < Indo-European, 'hornless']

Hind. *abbr* 1 Hindi 2 Hindu 3 Hindustan 4 Hindustani

hindbrain /hīnd brayn/ *n* the rearmost part of the brain in a vertebrate embryo which develops into the cerebellum, pons, and medulla oblongata

Hindemith /híndə mit/, **Paul** (1895–1963) German composer and viola player

Hindenburg /híndən burg/, **Paul von** (1847–1934) Prussian-born German statesman

Hindenburg line *n* a strong defensive line of fortifications built by the German Army near the border between France and Belgium in 1916–17 and breached by an Allied offensive in 1918 [Early 20C. After Paul von HINDENBURG, who devised the plan.]

hinder[1] /híndər/ *vti* to delay or obstruct the development or progress of somebody or something ○ *A heavy snowfall has hindered rescuers' attempts to reach the stranded climbers.* ■ *n* in squash and handball, an opponent's accidental interference, preventing fair and unobstructed return of the ball [Old English *hindrian* < Germanic] —**hinderer** *n*

SYNONYMS ***hinder, block, hamper, hold back, impede, obstruct***

CORE MEANING: to put difficulties in the way of progress

hinder to delay or restrict the development or progress of something, either accidentally or by deliberate interference; **block** to prevent movement through, into, or out of something, or prevent something from taking place; **hamper** to restrict the free movement or action of somebody or something; **hold back** to keep something from happening or to restrain somebody from doing something; **impede** to interfere with the movement, progress, or development of somebody or something; **obstruct** to cause a serious delay in action or progress, or to cause a major physical blockage in a road or passageway.

---

hinder[2] /hīndər/ *adj* at or towards the rear of something [Old English, < ?]

~~**hinderance**~~ incorrect spelling of **hindrance**

Hindi /híndi/ *n* an Indic official language of India that developed from a literary form of Hindustani and is widely used as a lingua franca in many parts of the world. Native speakers: 200 million. Other speakers: 700 million. [Early 19C. < Urdu *hindī* < *Hind* 'India'.] —**Hindi** *adj*

hindmost /hīnd mōst/ *adj* farthest back or last *(literary)*

hindquarter /hīnd kwawrtər/ *n* either of the two back quarters of a carcass of beef, lamb, veal, or mutton consisting of one leg and one or two ribs ■ **hindquarters** *npl* the hind legs and adjoining parts of a four-legged animal

hindrance /híndrənss/ *n* 1 somebody or something that prevents or makes it difficult for somebody to do something 2 the act of obstructing progress

hindsight /hīnd sīt/ *n* the ability or opportunity to understand and judge an event or experience after it has occurred ○ *With hindsight we should have chosen a warmer colour for the dining room.* ○ *That's easy to say with the benefit of hindsight.*

Hindu /hin doó, hín doo/ *n* 1 **FOLLOWER OF HINDUISM** an adherent of Hinduism 2 **SOMEBODY FROM HINDUSTAN** somebody who comes from Hindustan ■ *adj* 1 **OF HINDUISM** relating to Hinduism 2 **OF HINDUS** relating to Hindus or their culture 3 **OF INDIA** relating to India, especially Hindustan, or its languages, peoples, or cultures [Mid-17C. Via Urdu < Persian *Hindū* < *Hind* 'India'.]

Hinduism /híndoo izəm/ *n* the religion of India and the oldest worldwide religion, characterized by a belief in reincarnation and a large pantheon of gods and goddesses

Hindu Kush /-kóosh/ mountain system in central Asia, mainly in Afghanistan but extending into Jammu and Kashmir. Highest peak: Tirich Mir 7,690 m/25,230 ft.

Hindustan /híndoo staán/ *n* the Hindi-speaking region of N India, stretching from the Himalayas to the Deccan and from Assam to Punjab, or the wider Hindi-speaking area of the Indian subcontinent

Hindustani /híndoo staáni/ *n* **GROUP OF INDIAN LANGUAGES** a group of Indian languages and dialects that includes all forms of Urdu and Hindi ■ *adj* 1 **RELATING TO HINDUSTAN** of Hindustan 2 **OF HINDUSTANI** relating to Hindustani [Early 17C. Via Urdu < Persian *Hindūstānī* 'of the Indian country'.]

Hindustani music *n South Asia* the classical music of N India

Hines /hīnz/, **Earl** (1905–83) US jazz musician. Full name **Earl Kenneth Hines**

hinge /hinj/ *n* 1 **JOINT** a movable joint of metal or plastic used to fasten two things, e.g. a box and its lid, together and allow one of them to pivot ○ *The hinges on the door need oiling.* 2 **LIGAMENT** a part in animals that operates like a hinge, as does the ligament that opens and closes the two halves of a clam or other bivalve mollusc 3 ANAT = **hinge joint** 4 **SOMETHING VITAL** something on which a subsequent action or an outcome depends 5 **STICKY PAPER STRIP** a thin gummed paper strip that is folded in half to affix postage stamps to the pages of an album [13C. Probably ultimately < Germanic.] —**hinged** *adj* —**hingeless** *adj*

hinge on *vt* to depend completely on something ○ *The success of the plan hinges on your full cooperation.*

hinge joint *n* a joint, e.g. a knee or elbow joint, that allows movement in only one plane. Technical name **ginglymus**

Hinkler /híngklər/, **Bert** (1892–1933) Australian aviator. Full name **Herbert John Louis Hinkler**

hinny /hínni/ (*plural* **-nies**) *n* the offspring of a stallion and a female ass [Early 17C. Via Latin *hinnus* < Greek *(g)innos*.]

Hinshelwood /hínsh'l wŏŏd/, **Sir Cyril Norman** (1897–1967) British chemist

hint /hint/ *vi* **SUGGEST SOMETHING INDIRECTLY** to convey an idea or information in a roundabout way ○ *The President hinted that he might not seek a second term.* ■ *n* 1 **INDIRECT SUGGESTION** an idea or information conveyed in a roundabout way ○ *Our daughter has been dropping hints that she'd like a guitar for her birthday.* 2 **PIECE OF ADVICE** a useful piece of advice ○ *The book had lots of useful hints on how to grow vegetables.* 3 **VERY SMALL AMOUNT** an amount or trace of something that is so small that it can only just be noticed ○ *The walls need a hint of yellow.* [Early 17C. Probably alteration of obsolete *hent* 'grasp' < Germanic.] —**hintingly** *adv* ◇ **take the hint** to understand what is being implied or suggested and to act accordingly

hinterland /híntər land/ *n* 1 **LAND ADJACENT TO WATER** the land that lies next to coastline or a river 2 **AREA SURROUNDING CITY** a region, including communities and rural areas, that surrounds a city and depends on it economically and culturally ○ *an analysis of Milan and its hinterland* 3 **REMOTE COUNTRY REGION** a region that is remote from cities or their cultural influence [Late 19C. < German, < *hinter* 'behind' + *Land* 'land'.]

hip[1] /hip/ *n* 1 **SIDE OF BODY BELOW WAIST** the region on either side of the body between the waist and the thigh 2 ANAT = **hip joint** 3 **ROOF ANGLE** the angle formed where two adjacent sides of a sloping roof meet 4 **POINTED END OF OBSTACLE** in skateboarding, the place where a ramp or obstacle comes to a point [Old English *hype* < Germanic] —**hipped** *adj*

hip[2] /hip/ *n* PLANT SCI = **rosehip** [Old English *hēope* < Indo-European, 'thorn']

hip[3] /hip/ (**hipper, hippest**) *adj* aware of and influenced by the latest fashions in clothes, music, or ideas *(slang)* ○ *He's one hip dude.* [Early 20C. Alteration of HEP[1].] —**hiply** *adv* —**hipness** *n* ◇ **be hip to something** *US* to be aware of something that is going on *(informal)*

hipbone /híp bōn/ *n* either of the two large bones forming the sides of the pelvis and made up of the ilium, ischium, and pubis, fused together in adults. Technical name **innominate bone**

hip boot *n* a boot reaching to the hip, usually worn by people who fish

hip flask *n* a small flat metal flask, usually containing an alcoholic beverage, that can be carried in a pocket. US term **flask** *n.* 2

hip hip hooray *interj* used as a cheer to express joy or approval of somebody or something [*Hip* < ?]

hip-hop *n* a form of popular culture that started in African American inner-city areas, characterized by rap music, graffiti art, and breakdancing [< HIP[3]]

hip-huggers /-huggərz/ *npl US* CLOTHING = **hipsters**

hip joint *n* the joint formed between the head of the thigh bone and the hipbone

Hipparchus /hi paárkəss/ (190?–120? BC) Greek astronomer and mathematician

hippeastrum /híppi ástrəm/ *n* a cultivated plant belonging to the daffodil family. Flowers: huge red or pink, funnel-shaped. Native to: Central and South

America. Genus: *Hippeastrum*. [Early 19C. < modern Latin, < Greek *hippeus* 'horseman' + *astron* 'star'.]

hipped roof *n* BUILDING = **hip roof**

hippie /híppi/, **hippy** (*plural* **-pies**) *n* a young person, especially in the 1960s, who rejected accepted social and political values and proclaimed a belief in universal peace and love (*informal*) [Mid-20C. < HIP[3].] —**hippiedom** *n* —**hippiehood** *n* —**hippieness** *n*

hippo /híppō/ (*plural* **-pos**) *n* a hippopotamus (*informal*) [Late 19C. Shortening.]

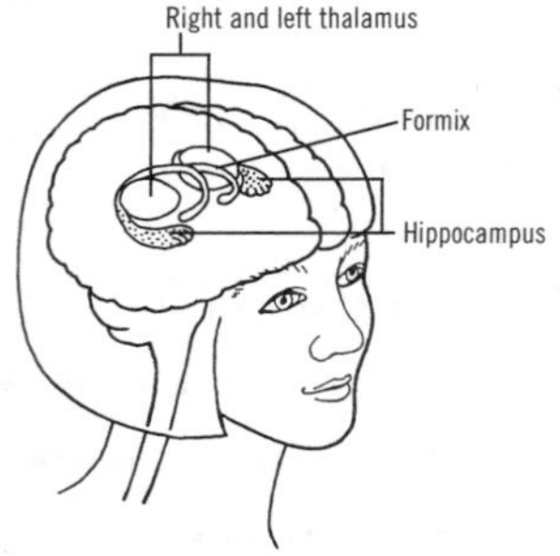

Hippocampus

hippocampus /híppō kámpəss/ (*plural* **-pi** /-pī/) *n* **1** a mythological sea creature with the head and forelegs of a horse and the tail of a fish **2** a curved ridge of tissue in each cerebral hemisphere of the brain, concerned with basic drives, emotions, and short-term memory and forming part of the limbic system [Late 16C. Via Latin < Greek *hippokampos* < *hippos* 'horse' + *kampos* 'sea monster'.] —**hippocampal** *adj*

hippocras /híppō krass/ *n* a medieval drink of spiced wine sweetened with honey [14C. Via Old French *hypocras* < medieval Latin *(vinum) Hippocraticum* '(wine of) Hippocrates'.]

Hippocrates /hi pókrə teez/ (460?–377? BC) Greek physician —**Hippocratic** /híppə kráttik/ *adj*

Hippocratic oath *n* an oath taken by newly qualified doctors to observe the ethical standards of their profession, specifically to seek to preserve life [Because Hippocrates was the supposed author of such an oath]

hippodrome /híppə drōm/ *n* **1** an open-air stadium in ancient Greece or Rome with an oval track that was used for horse or chariot racing **2** a variety theatre or circus (*dated*) [Late 16C. Via French and Latin < Greek *hippodromos* < *hippos* 'horse' + *dromos* 'racecourse'.]

hippogriff /híppə grif/ *n* a monster from Greek mythology with the body of a horse and the head, wings, and claws of a griffin [Mid-17C. Via French *hippogriffe* < Italian *ippogrifo* < Greek *hippos* 'horse' + Italian *grifo* 'griffin'.]

Hippolyta /hi póllitə/ *n* in Greek mythology, a queen of the Amazons, killed by Heracles

hippopotamus /híppə póttəməss/ (*plural* **-muses** *or* **-mi** /-mī/) *n* a large amphibious mammal of the rivers of eastern equatorial Africa that has a large head with a wide mouth, short legs, and a thick grey skin. *Hippopotamus amphibius*. [Mid-16C. Via Latin < Greek *hippopotamos* < *hippos* 'horse' + *potamos* 'river'.]

hippy[1] *n* = **hippie**

hippy[2] /híppi/ (**-pier, -piest**) *adj* having wide hips

hip roof *n* a roof with sloping ends as well as sides

hipster /hípstər/ *n* a person conversant with fashions in music, clothes, and social attitudes, especially an enthusiast of modern jazz (*slang*) [< HIP[3]]

hipsters /hípstərz/ *npl* trousers that end at the hips instead of the waist. US term **hip-huggers** [< HIP[1]]

hiragana /heérə gaánə/ *n* a cursive set of symbols or ideograms (**kana**) used by the Japanese for polite, informal, or casual writing, e.g. in newspapers and general literature. ◊ **kana** *n.* 1, **katakana** [Early 19C. < Japanese, 'plain syllabary'.]

hire /hīr/ *v* (**hires, hiring, hired**) **1** *vti* GIVE WORK to employ somebody to work for you **2** *vt* PAY FOR THE USE OF to rent something from somebody for a period of time ○ *hired the village hall for the wedding reception* ■ *n* ACT OF HIRING the activity of renting something to somebody or of making the services of somebody available to another for pay [Old English *hȳr* < Germanic] —**hirable** *adj*

hire out *vt* to rent something to somebody or make the services of somebody available to another for pay

hired gun *n US* = **hit man** (*slang*)

hired hand *n* a paid manual worker employed on a short-term basis, usually on a farm

hireling /hírling/ *n* a person who works only for money, especially at menial or unpleasant tasks (*disapproving*)

hire purchase *n* a financing arrangement enabling somebody to take possession of an expensive item while making regular payments on it, with legal ownership transferred only after it is paid for. ◊ **installment plan**

⚡**hi-res** /hī réz/ *adj* high-resolution and therefore showing a lot of detail (*informal*) ○ *a hi-res graphic* [Shortening]

Hiri Motu /heéri mṓ too/ *n* a pidginized form of Motu that is an official language of Papua New Guinea. Native speakers: 150,000. —**Hiri Motu** *adj*

Hirohito /heérō heétō/ (1901–89) emperor of Japan (1926–89)

Hiroshige /heérō sheé gay/ (1797–1858) Japanese artist

Hiroshima /hi róshimə, hírrə sheémə/ city on SW Honshu Island, Japan. It was devastated by the first atom bomb to be used in war, in August 1945. Population: 1,085,705 (1990).

hirple /húrp'l/ (**-les, -ling, -led**) *vi Scotland* to walk with a limp [15C. Probably < Old Norse *herpast* 'suffer from cramps'.]

Hirst /hurst/, **Damien** (*b.* 1965) British artist

hirsute /húr syoot/ *adj* **1** having a large amount of hair ○ *a hirsute young man* **2** describes a plant or plant part covered with long stiff hairs ○ *a hirsute leaf* [Early 17C. < Latin *hirsutus* 'shaggy'.] —**hirsuteness** *n*

hirsutism /húr syootizəm/ *n* excessive growth of hair, e.g. on a woman's face or body

hirudin /hi roódin/ *n* a substance produced by the salivary glands of leeches that prevents blood from clotting [Early 20C. < Latin *hirudo* 'leech'.]

his (*stressed*) /hiz/; (*unstressed*) /iz/ *det, pron* indicates something belonging or relating to a man, boy, or male animal who has been previously mentioned or whose identity is known ○ *He stood at the sink washing his hands.* ○ *The fault was all his.* ○ *I went to school with a cousin of his.*

Hispanic /hi spánnik/ *n* PEOPLES = **Hispanic American** ■ *adj* **1** OF SPAIN relating to Spain, or its language, people, or culture **2** OF SPANISH-SPEAKING PEOPLE relating to Spanish-speaking people or their culture **3** OF PEOPLE OF SPANISH DESCENT relating to people descended from Spanish or Latin-American people or their culture [Late 16C. < Latin *Hispanicus* < *Hispania* 'Spain'.]

Hispanic American *n* somebody who comes from the United States and is of Spanish or Latin American descent —**Hispanic-American** *adj*

Hispanicise *vt* = **Hispanicize**

Hispanicism /hi spánnisizəm/ *n* a Spanish word, expression, or other linguistic feature that has been adopted into another language [Mid-20C. < Latin *Hispania* 'Spain'.]

Hispanicist /hi spánnissist/ *n* a scholar of the languages and cultures of Spain and Spanish-speaking countries

Hispanicize /hi spánni sīz/ (**-cizes, -cizing, -cized**), **Hispanicise** (**-cises, -cising, -cised**) *vt* to make somebody or something Spanish in character, style, or culture —**Hispanicization** /hi spánni sī záysh'n/ *n*

Hispaniola /híspən yṓlə/ island of the West Indies southeast of Cuba, divided between Haiti and the Dominican Republic. Area: 78,460 sq. km/30,290 sq. mi.

Hispanism /híspənizəm/ *n* LING = **Hispanicism**

Hispanist /híspənist/ *n* = **Hispanicist**

Hispano /hi spánnō, hi spaán ō, híspə nō/ (*plural* **-nos**) *n* somebody of Spanish descent who lives in the SW United States [Mid-20C. < Latin *hispanus* 'Spanish'.]

hispid /híspid/ *adj* rough, especially covered with stiff hairs or bristles ○ *a hispid leaf* [Mid-17C. < Latin *hispidus*.] —**hispidity** /hi spíddəti/ *n*

hiss /hiss/ *v* **1** *vi* MAKE 'S' SOUND to make a sound like a loud continuous 's' ○ *the sound of car tyres hissing over a wet road* **2** *vti* SHOW NEGATIVE OPINION OF to show disapproval or dislike of somebody or something, e.g. a performance, by making a hissing sound **3** *vti* WHISPER LOUDLY to whisper loudly and angrily ○ *'Stop biting your nails', she hissed.* ■ *n* **1** SOUND LIKE 'S' a sound like a loud continuous 's' ○ *the hiss of escaping air* **2** SOUND EXPRESSING DISAPPROVAL a hissing sound used to express disapproval or dislike of something or somebody ○ *The news was greeted with a hiss.* [14C. An imitation of the sound.] —**hisser** *n*

Hiss /hiss/, **Alger** (1904–96) US lawyer and government official

hisself (*stressed*) /hiz sélf/; (*unstressed*) /iz sélf/ *pron* himself (*nonstandard*)

hist. *abbr* **1** histology **2** historic **3** historical **4** history

hist- *prefix* = **histo-** (*before vowels*)

histaminase /hi stámmi nayz, -nayss/ *n* an enzyme in the digestive system that inactivates histamine

histamine /hístə meen/ *n* an amine released by immune cells that produces allergic reactions [Early 20C. Blend of HISTIDINE + AMINE.] —**histaminic** /hístə mínnik/ *adj*

histidine /hístə deen/ *n* an amino acid involved in the repair of tissues that is also the precursor of histamine

histiocyte /hísti ə sīt/ *n* a large immobile scavenging cell (**macrophage**) found in connective tissue —**histiocytic** /hísti ə síttik/ *adj*

histo- *prefix* living tissue ○ *histochemistry* [< Greek *histos* 'web']

histochemistry /híst ō kémmistri/ *n* the biochemistry of cells and tissues —**histochemical** *adj* —**histochemically** *adv*

histocompatibility /hístōkəm páttə bílləti/ *n* the degree of similarity between certain antigens (**histocompatibility antigens**) that determines the degree of success of a tissue graft or blood transfusion —**histocompatible** /hístōkəm páttəb'l/ *adj*

histocompatibility antigen *n* an antigen occurring on the surface of tissue cells that is used in self-identification and determines the acceptance of a tissue graft or blood transfusion

histodialysis /hístō dī álləssiss/ *n* MED = **histolysis**

histogenesis /hístō jénnəssiss/ *n* the development of tissues —**histogenetic** /hístōjə néttik/ *adj* —**histogenetically** *adv* —**histogenic** /híst ō jénnik/ *adj* —**histogenically** *adv*

histogram /hístə gram/ *n* a statistical graph of a frequency distribution in which vertical rectangles of different heights are proportionate to corresponding frequencies

histology /hi stólləji/ *n* a branch of anatomy concerned with the study of the microscopic structures of animal and plant tissue —**histologic** /hístə lójjik/ *adj* —**histological** *adj* —**histologically** *adv* —**histologist** /hi stólləjist/ *n*

histolysis /hi stólləssiss/ *n* the breakdown and disintegration of bodily tissue —**histolytic** /hístə líttik/ *adj* —**histolytically** *adv*

histone /híst ōn/ *n* a simple protein bound to DNA, involved in the coiling of chromosomes [Late 19C. < German *Histon*.]

histopathology /hístōpə thólləji/ *n* a branch of pathology concerned with the study of the microscopic changes in diseased tissues —**histopathologic** /hístō páthə lójjik/ *adj* —**histopathological** *adj* —**histopathologically** *adv* —**histopathologist** /hístōpə thólləjist/ *n*

histophysiology /hístō fízzi ólləji/ *n* a branch of physiology concerned with the structure and function of tissues —**histophysiologic** /-fízzi ə lójjik/ *adj* —**histophysiological** *adj*

histoplasmosis /hístō plaz mṓssiss/ *n* a severe disease of the lungs with symptoms resembling flu, caused by the fungus *Histoplasma capsulatum* [Early 20C. < modern Latin *Histoplasma*, genus name.]

historian /hi stáwri ən/ *n* **1** a student of or expert in history **2** a writer of an account of historical events [15C. < French *historien* < Latin *historia* (see HISTORY).]

historiated /hi stáwri aytid/ *adj* describes decorative initials in books or maps and plans that are illustrated with symbolic flowers and animals [Late 19C. < French *historié* or directly < medieval Latin *historiare* 'adorn (with historical scenes), relate' < Latin *historia* (see HISTORY).]

historic /hi stórrik/ *adj* **1** important in or affecting the course of history ○ *Yalta, scene of the historic meeting between Roosevelt, Stalin, and Churchill* ○ *a historic decision affecting world peace* **2** = **historical** *adj.* 1

historical /hi stórrik'l/ *adj* 1 **EXISTING OR HAPPENING IN THE PAST** existing, happening, or relating to the past ○ *an important historical personage* 2 **USED IN THE PAST** worn or used by people in the past ○ *historical uniforms of the 18th century* 3 **SUPPORTED BY FACTS FROM HISTORY** based on or describing people who lived in the past or events that happened in the past ○ *historical fiction* ○ *a historical film* 4 **RELATING TO STUDY OF HISTORY** relating to or involving the study of history 5 **RELATING TO THE EVOLUTION OF PHENOMENA** relating to the gradual change and development of phenomena, e.g. languages or societies ○ *historical sociology* —**historicalness** *n*

historical geology *n* a branch of geology that deals with the geological history of the earth

historical linguistics *n* the study of language as it changes and develops through time

historically /hi stórrikli/ *adv* 1 according to or with reference to history or its course ○ *The law will prove to be historically significant.* 2 used to indicate that something has happened often in the past ○ *Historically, a rise in interest rates slows the rate of inflation.*

historical materialism *n* the part of Marx's theory of dialectical materialism that maintains that the development of social thought and institutions is based on material economic forces

historical novel *n* a novel set in the past that includes real events and people from that period

historical present *n* the present tense used to narrate actions that happened in the past to make them seem more vivid

historicise *vt* = **historicize**

historicism /hi stórrissizəm/ *n* 1 the belief that natural laws beyond human control determine historical events 2 the theory that each period of history has its own unique beliefs and values and can only be understood in its historical context —**historicist** *n*

historicity /hìstəríssəti/ *n* the state or fact of being historically authentic

historicize /hi stórri sīz/ (**-cizes, -cizing, -cized**), **historicise** (**-cises, -cising, -cised**) *vt* to give something the appearance of historical truth —**historicization** /hi stórri sī záysh'n/ *n*

Historic Places Trust *n* the statutory body in New Zealand whose duty it is to preserve historic sites, especially those of the Maori

historiography /hi stàwri óggrəfi/ *n* 1 **METHODS OF HISTORICAL RESEARCH** the principles, theories, or methods of historical research or writing 2 **THE WRITING OF HISTORY** the writing of history based on scholarly disciplines such as the analysis and evaluation of source materials 3 **AVAILABLE DATA ON HISTORICAL TOPIC** the existing findings and interpretations relating to a particular historical topic 4 **HISTORICAL LITERATURE** a body of historical literature [Mid-16C. Via medieval Latin < Greek *historiographia* < *historia* (see HISTORY) + *graphia* 'writing'.] —**historiographic** /hi stàwri ə gráffik/ *n* —**historiographical** *adj* —**historiographically** *adv*

history /hístəri/ (*plural* **-ries**) *n* 1 **WHAT HAS HAPPENED** the past events of a period in time or in the life or development of a people, an institution, or a place 2 **STUDY OF THE PAST** the branch of knowledge that records and analyses past events 3 **RECORD OF EVENTS** a chronological account of past events of a period or in the life or development of a people, an institution, or a place ○ *a history of Byzantium* 4 **PERSONAL BACKGROUND** the events and experiences of an individual's past ○ *We don't know very much about her personal history.* 5 **INTERESTING PAST** an interesting or colourful past ○ *The car has a bit of a history attached to it.* 6 **SOMETHING NO LONGER IMPORTANT** something that belongs to the past and is no longer important ○ *The scandal is history, as far as I'm concerned.* 7 **SOMEBODY NO LONGER IMPORTANT** a person who is no longer important or powerful (*slang*) ○ *If he's found guilty of bribery, he's history.* 8 **HISTORICAL PLAY** a play that deals with historical events [15C. Via Latin < Greek *historia* 'history, knowledge, narrative' < *histōr* 'learned man'.]

⚡**history list** *n* a record of the input of previous users of a computer available for reselection

histrionic /hìstri ónnik/, **histrionical** /-ónnik'l/ *adj* 1 overdramatic in reaction or behaviour ○ *Paul gave a histrionic sigh and slumped in his chair.* 2 relating to acting or actors (*formal*) [Mid-17C. < late Latin *histrionicus* < Latin *histrion-* 'actor'.] —**histrionically** *adv*

histrionics /hìstri ónniks/ *n* exaggerated emotional behaviour done for show or to get a reaction from somebody (+ *singular or plural verb*) ○ *Let's hope there won't be any histrionics when you tell them.* ■ *npl* performances of dramatic works (*formal;* + *plural verb*)

⚡**hit** /hit/ *v* (**hits, hitting, hit**) 1 *vti* **STRIKE DELIBERATELY** to strike somebody or something deliberately with the hand or something held in it ○ *He hit me on the jaw with a good solid punch.* 2 *vti* **COME INTO CONTACT** to come into violent contact with something ○ *His van skidded and hit a parked car.* 3 *vt* **MAKE BALL MOVE** to make something such as a ball move by striking it with a bat or racket ○ *She kept hitting the ball over the fence into the next garden.* 4 *vt* **STRIKE BUTTON OR KEY** to press or push a button or part of a machine (*informal*) ○ *Try to hit the keys smoothly.* 5 *vt* **MAKE A SCORE WITH BALL** to score points in a sport by striking a ball well or delivering it successfully to a target ○ *You'll need to hit a home run to win.* ○ *She hit the first goal in the second minute of the game.* 6 *vt* **STRIKE TARGET** to reach an intended target with a ball or missile 7 *vti* **COME TO MIND** to realize or become conscious of something ○ *It suddenly hit him that he was unlikely to see her again.* 8 *vt* **GIVE INFORMATION** to tell somebody something that may be of interest (*slang*) ○ *'Do you want to know what I think?' 'Okay, hit me'.* 9 *vt* **AFFECT BADLY** to have an adverse effect on somebody or something ○ *The rise in interest rates is going to hit exporters hard.* 10 *vt* **ARRIVE AT SPECIFIED LEVEL** to reach a particular level on a scale ○ *Unemployment has hit the 2 million mark.* 11 *vt* **PRODUCE ACCURATELY** to render or represent something accurately ○ *hit a high C* 12 *vt* **CONFORM TO** to conform to or agree with something ○ *Your comments hit a sympathetic note.* 13 *vt* **REACH A PLACE** to reach a particular place (*informal*) ○ *You'll hit a toll-free road about five miles farther on.* 14 *vi* **HAPPEN** to take place, usually with undesirable or adverse effects (*informal*) ○ *The storm hit before we could get home.* 15 *vt* **VIEW WEB PAGE** to visit or view a particular web page (*informal*) 16 *vt* **KILL USING HIRED HAND** to murder somebody, especially by employing a professional killer (*slang*) ○ *One of the croupiers got hit last night.* ■ *n* 1 **HARD BLOW** a hard blow delivered with the hand or something held in it ○ *She gave it a good hit.* 2 **COLLISION** a violent impact between things 3 **SOMETHING THAT HITS TARGET** a ball or missile that successfully strikes the target ○ *We've taken a couple of hits, but nothing serious.* 4 BASEBALL = **base hit** 5 **SUCCESS** a person who or thing that is popular or successful ○ *The band had a big hit with their last CD.* ○ *The clown was a hit with the kids.* 6 **EFFECT OF DRUG** a sense of a drug's effect (*slang*) 7 **SOMETHING GIVEN** a single item given or taken, e.g. a drink or a card at the game of pontoon (*slang*) 8 **PROFESSIONAL KILLING** a murder, especially one committed by a professional killer (*slang*) 9 **ACCESSING OF DATABASE OR INTERNET FILE** an instance of a user retrieving an item from a database or contacting a file, e.g. a home page, through the Internet ○ *Her home page has received 3,000 hits since she opened it last month.* [Pre-12C. < Old Norse *hitta* 'find'.] —**hittable** *adj* —**hitter** *n* ◇ **hit it off** to get on very well with somebody (*informal*)
hit back *vi* to retaliate against somebody or something for an attack
hit on, hit upon *vt* to think of a solution to a problem, especially by chance ○ *She then hit on the idea of painting the inside of the box black.*
hit out *vi* 1 to criticize somebody or something severely ○ *The bishop hit out at their human rights record.* 2 to try to strike somebody repeatedly ○ *When the baby is in a tantrum, she hits out at people trying to comfort her.*
hit up *v* 1 *vt* to ask somebody for something (*slang*) ○ *How come you're suddenly hitting me up for the cab fare?* 2 *vi ANZ* in racket games, to hit the ball back and forth without scoring points, in order to warm up before a game

Hitachi /hi taáchi/ coastal city on E Honshu Island, Japan. Population: 202,141 (1990).

hit-and-miss *adj* 1 *US* = **hit-or-miss** *adj.* 2 2 done in a careless haphazard way ○ *The survey was hit-and-miss, so we cannot trust the results.* US term **hit-or-miss** *adj.* 1

hit-and-run *adj* 1 **NOT STOPPING AFTER CAUSING AN ACCIDENT** describes or relating to a road accident in which the driver who has hit another person or motor vehicle leaves the scene without stopping ○ *a hit-and-run driver* 2 **FAST AND WITHOUT WARNING** relying on surprise and speed to overcome an enemy ○ *Three fighter planes launched a hit-and-run attack at dawn.* ■ *n* **HIT-AND-RUN ACCIDENT** a hit-and-run road accident

hitch /hich/ *v* 1 *vti* **HITCHHIKE** to hitchhike a ride (*informal*) ○ *We hitched down through Italy in three days.* 2 *vt* **JOIN SOMETHING POWERED TO SOMETHING ELSE** to connect two things so that one can move the other, e.g. a horse to a wagon or a trailer to a car 3 *vt* **FASTEN SOMETHING TO STOP IT** to fasten or tie something temporarily to keep it from moving away ○ *Hitch the boat to the dock before the current catches it.* ■ *n* 1 **OBSTACLE** an obstacle in the way of progress ○ *There's been a slight technical hitch.* 2 **MEANS OF CONNECTING TWO THINGS** a device used to connect two things, e.g. a ball on a vehicle for connecting a trailer 3 **KNOT THAT UNTIES EASILY** a knot that can be easily untied, used for temporarily securing a line to something 4 **TUG** a sudden pull on something [14C. < ?] —**hitcher** *n*
hitch up *vt* to pull up an article of clothing

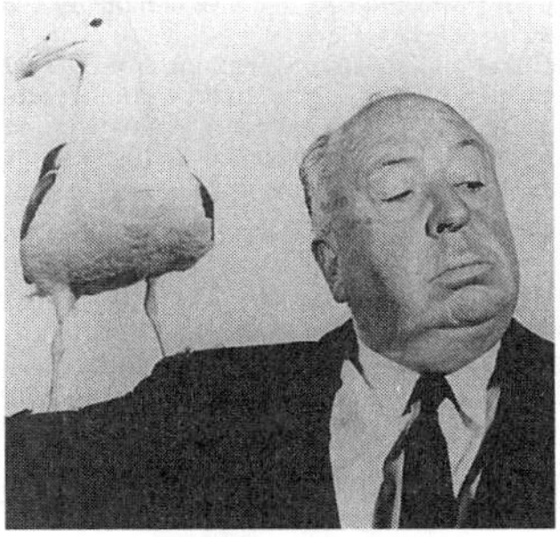

Sir Alfred Hitchcock

Hitchcock /hích kok/, **Sir Alfred** (1899–1980) British film director

hitched /hicht/ *adj* married (*informal*) ○ *They're getting hitched in a couple of weeks.*

hitchhike /hích hīk/ (**-hikes, -hiking, -hiked**) *vti* to get a ride from a passing vehicle, usually by standing at the side of the road and holding out the hand with the thumb raised —**hitchhiker** *n*

hitching post *n* a post or rail used to tie the reins of a horse to

⚡**hi-tech** /hī ték/ *n, adj* = **high tech, high-tech**

hither /híthər/ *adv* to this place (*archaic or humorous*) ○ *Come hither, child.* ■ *adj* on the near side of something (*archaic*) [Old English *hider* < Indo-European, 'here, this'] ◇ **hither and thither** in many directions in a disorderly way

hitherto /híthər tóo, híthər too/ *adv* up to the present time or the time in question ○ *Hitherto most people had paid cash.*

hit in (*plural* **hit ins** *or* **hits in**) *n* in hockey, a hit from the sideline awarded to the opposition when the team in possession of the ball fails to keep it on the pitch

Hitler /hítlər/, **Adolf** (1889–1945) Austrian-born German Nazi leader

Hitlerism /hítlərizəm/ *n* the extreme nationalistic ideology and fascistic policies developed by the Nazi Party under Adolf Hitler —**Hitlerist** *n* —**Hitlerite** *adj*

hit list *n* (*informal*) 1 a list of things or people who are considered problems to be dealt with in the near future 2 a list of potential murder victims

hit man *n* a hired assassin (*slang*) US term **hired gun**

hit-or-miss *adj* 1 = **hit-and-miss** *adj.* 2 2 sometimes successful and sometimes not. US term **hit-and-miss** *adj.* 1

hit out (*plural* **hit outs** *or* **hits out**) *n* in hockey, a hit taken from the 16-yard line that is awarded to the defence when the attacking team hit the ball over the goal line without scoring a goal

hit parade *n* a list of the best-selling pop records in the previous week (*dated*)

hit squad *n* (*slang*) 1 a team of hired assassins or other killers 2 a team of experts sent in to solve serious problems

Hittite /híttīt/ *n* 1 a member of an ancient Anatolian people whose empire was based in W Asia during the second millennium BC 2 an extinct Indo-European language spoken in Anatolia, parts of Syria, and surrounding areas during the second millennium BC [Mid-16C. < Hebrew *Ḥittīm* < Hittite *Hatti.*] —**Hittite** *adj*

hit-up *n ANZ* RACKET GAMES = **knock-up**

HIV *n* either of two strains of a retrovirus, HIV-1 or HIV-2, that destroys the immune system's helper T cells, the loss of which causes Aids. Full form **human immunodeficiency virus**

hive /hīv/ *n* 1 HOME FOR BEES a shelter in which a colony of social bees, especially honeybees, builds its nest 2 COLONY OF BEES a colony of honeybees ■ *v* (**hives, hiving, hived**) 1 *vti* PUT BEES INTO HIVE to gather in a hive, or cause bees to gather in a hive ○ *hive a swarm* 2 *vt* KEEP HONEY IN HIVE to store honey in a hive 3 *vt* KEEP TO USE LATER to store something for later use 4 *vi* LIVE CLOSELY TOGETHER to live closely in a group [Old English *hӯf* < Indo-European, 'round container'] —**hiveless** *adj* ◇ **a hive of industry** *or* **activity** a very busy, active place

hive off *vt* 1 to separate something from the whole or from a larger group, e.g. to divert work to a subsidiary company or to split a branch of knowledge into different areas 2 to transfer an industry from governmental to private ownership

hives /hīvz/ *n* MED = **urticaria** (+ *singular or plural verb*) [Early 16C. < ?]

HIV-negative *adj* having taken a test that revealed no antibodies to HIV in the bloodstream

HIV-positive *adj* shown by a test for antibodies to HIV in the bloodstream to be infected with the HIV virus

hiziki *n* FOOD = **hijiki**

⚡ **hk** *abbr* Hong Kong (*in Internet addresses*)

HK *abbr* House of Keys

hl *symbol* hectolitre

HL *abbr* House of Lords

HLA *n* the major antigen compatibility complex in humans that is genetically determined and is involved in cell self-identification and histocompatibility. Full form **human lymphocyte antigen**

⚡ **HLL** *abbr* high-level language

hm[1] *abbr* hectometre

h'm /m, hm/ *interj* used to represent a sound made while pausing during a conversation to consider something ○ *H'm, it'll take about two weeks.* [Mid-19C. Natural utterance.]

⚡ **hm**[2] *abbr* Heard & McDonald Islands (*in Internet addresses*)

HM *abbr* 1 headmaster 2 headmistress 3 heavy metal 4 Her Majesty 5 His Majesty

HMAS *abbr* 1 Her Majesty's Australian ship 2 His Majesty's Australian ship

HMCS *abbr* 1 Her Majesty's Canadian Ship 2 His Majesty's Canadian Ship

HMF *abbr* 1 Her Majesty's Forces 2 His Majesty's Forces

HMG *abbr* 1 Her Majesty's Government 2 His Majesty's Government

⚡ **HMI** *abbr* 1 Her Majesty's Inspector (of Schools) 2 human-machine interface

HMO *n US* a healthcare organization whose members pay fees and receive medical care from participating physicians, hospitals, and other providers. Full form **health maintenance organization**

Hmong /máwng, hə máwng/ (*plural* **Hmongs** *or* **Hmong**) *n* 1 a member of a people living in S China and mainly remote areas of N Laos, Thailand, and Vietnam 2 a language spoken in parts of S China and in Laos, Thailand, Vietnam, and the United States, forming a main branch of the Miao-Yao language family. Native speakers: 5 million. —**Hmong** *adj*

HMS, H.M.S. *abbr* 1 Her Majesty's Service 2 Her Majesty's Ship 3 His Majesty's Service 4 His Majesty's Ship

HMSO *abbr* 1 Her Majesty's Stationery Office 2 His Majesty's Stationery Office

⚡ **hn** *abbr* Honduras (*in Internet addresses*)

Hn *symbol* hahnium

HNC *n* a UK qualification in a technical subject that is recognized by many professional and technical establishments. Full form **Higher National Certificate**

HND *n* a UK post-school vocational award higher than the National Diploma. It requires the equivalent of two years' full-time study and is generally regarded as roughly equivalent to a university pass degree. Full form **Higher National Diploma**

ho[1] /hō/ (*plural* **hos** *or* **hoes**) *n* 1 an offensive term for a prostitute (*slang*) 2 an offensive term for a woman (*slang offensive insult*) [Late 20C. Pronunciation of WHORE.]

ho[2] /hō/ *interj* 1 EXPRESSING VARIOUS EMOTIONS used to express surprise, triumph, admiration or derision, depending on the way the speaker says it 2 CALL FOR ATTENTION used to attract somebody's attention 3 USED TO POINT OUT used to draw somebody's attention to something (*in combinations*) ○ *Land ho!*

Ho *symbol* holmium

Hoad /hōd/, **Lew** (1934–94) Australian tennis player. Full name **Lewis Alan Hoad**

hoar /hawr/ *adj* white or greyish white in colour, usually as a result of age or frost (*literary*) [Old English *hār* < Indo-European, 'shine']

hoard /hawrd/ *vti* to collect and store, often secretly, a large quantity of something such as food or money for use in the future [Old English *hord* < Indo-European] — **hoard** *n* —**hoarder** *n*

SPELLCHECK Do not confuse ***hoard*** with ***horde***, which has a similar sound. Beware: your spellchecker will not catch this error.

SYNONYMS See ***collect***.

hoarding /háwrding/ *n* 1 = **billboard**[1] *n.* ○ *an advertising hoarding* 2 a tall fence used to screen off a building site [Early 19C. < obsolete *hoard* 'hoarding' < ?]

hoar frost *n* the white frost that forms on grass or leaves in the morning when the dew freezes

hoarhound *n* PLANTS = **horehound**

hoarse /hawrss/ (**hoarser, hoarsest**) *adj* 1 sounding rough and grating 2 having a rough, harsh, grating voice [Old English *hās* < Germanic] —**hoarsely** *adv* —**hoarseness** *n*

SPELLCHECK Do not confuse ***hoarse*** with ***horse***, which has a similar sound. Beware: your spellchecker will not catch this error.

hoarsen /háwrss'n/ *vti* to become hoarse, or make the voice hoarse

hoary /háwri/ (**-ier, -iest**) *adj* 1 OVERUSED old and stale from overuse ○ *Not that hoary old chestnut about the chicken crossing the road?* 2 WHITE WITH AGE describes hair that has become white or grey with age 3 COVERED WITH PALE HAIRS covered with grey or white hairs ○ *a plant with hoary leaves* —**hoarily** *adv* —**hoariness** *n*

⚡ **HOAS** *abbr* hold on a second (*in e-mails*)

hoatching /hṓching/ *adj Scotland* full of people or things (*informal*) [< ?]

hoatzin /hō átsin, wa̋at seen/ *n* a bird with brownish plumage, a very small crested head, and a specialized digestive system for leaves. Native to: South America. *Opisthocomus hoazin.* [Mid-17C. Via American Spanish < Nahuatl *uatzin.*]

hoax /hōks/ *n* an act intended to trick people into believing something is real that is not ■ *vt* to trick people into believing something is real that is not [Late 18C. Probably alteration of HOCUS.] —**hoaxer** *n*

hob[1] /hob/ *n* 1 a flat surface containing cooking rings, hot plates, or burners 2 a small shelf or rack level with the top of the grate of a fireplace on which to set pans to keep them warm [Late 17C. Alteration of *hub* < ?]

hob[2] /hob/ *n* a hobgoblin or elf (*archaic*) [15C. < the name *Robert* or *Robin.*]

Hobart /hṓ baart/ capital of Tasmania, Australia, in the S of the island. Population: 126,118 (1996).

Hobbema /hóbbimə/, **Meindert** (1638–1709) Dutch painter

Hobbes /hobz/, **Thomas** (1588–1679) English philosopher and political theorist —**Hobbesian** *adj, n* —**Hobbism** *n* — **Hobbist** *adj, n*

hobbit /hóbbit/ *n* a member of an imaginary kind of good-natured little people who have brown furry legs and live underground [Mid-20C. Invention of J. R. R. TOLKIEN.]

hobble /hóbb'l/ *v* (**-bles, -bling, -bled**) 1 *vi* LIMP ALONG to walk haltingly and unsteadily, taking short steps 2 *vt* LIMIT HORSE'S MOVEMENT to tie the legs of a horse loosely together with a rope or strap to prevent it from moving away 3 *vt* RESTRICT SOMEBODY'S ACTIONS to put restrictions on somebody or something to slow or prevent progress ■ *n* 1 UNSTEADY WALK a halting unsteady walk 2 ROPE OR STRAP something such as a loop of rope or a strap used to tie the legs of a horse [13C. Probably < Low German.]

hobbledehoy /hóbb'ldi hóy/ *n* a clumsy or rude young man (*archaic*) [Mid-16C. < ?]

hobble skirt *n* a long skirt designed to be full at the hips but narrow at the ankles, first popular between 1910 and 1914

Hobbs /hobz/, **Jack** (1882–1963) British cricketer. Full name **Sir John Berry Hobbs**

hobby /hóbbi/ (*plural* **-bies**) *n* 1 an activity engaged in for pleasure and relaxation during spare time ○ *Our oldest boy's hobby is flying kites.* 2 a small grey falcon with chestnut legs, popular as a hunting bird. Native to: Europe, Asia, migrating to Africa. *Falco subbuteo.* [13C. Probably < *Hobin*, variant of the name *Robin.*]

hobbyhorse /hóbbi hawrss/ *n* 1 TOY HORSE FROM A STICK a toy consisting of a long stick with the shape of a horse's head at one end 2 HORSE FIGURE USED IN FOLK DANCES a representation of a horse that a Morris dancer or mummer wears around the waist so that it appears that the horse is being ridden 3 FAVOURITE TOPIC a favourite subject about which somebody will talk given the slightest opportunity

hobbyist /hóbbi ist/ *n* a person who has a hobby, especially a person who devotes a great deal of time to one

hobgoblin /hób góblin, hób goblin/ *n* 1 = **goblin** 2 a source of fear or worry [< HOB[2]]

hobnail /hób nayl/ *n* a short nail with a broad head that is used to protect the soles of boots —**hobnailed** *adj*

hobnob /hób nob/ (**-nobs, -nobbing, -nobbed**) *vi* to socialize in a familiar manner with somebody, especially somebody considered to be of a higher social class (*disapproving*) ○ *hobnobbing with the rich and famous* [Mid-18C. Probably < obsolete *hob or nob* 'have or not have'.]

hobo /hṓbō/ (*plural* **-boes**) *n* a poor and homeless person, especially somebody who travelled around the United States looking for work in the 1920s and 1930s [Late 19C. < ?]

hobson-jobson /hóbss'n jóbss'n/ *n* the assimilation of the sound of a word or words into the sound system of another language [Late 19C. < title of an Anglo-Indian glossary by Yule and Burnell < Arabic *Yā Ḥasan! Yā Ḥusayn!* 'O Hasan! O Husain!', cry used at Muslim ceremonies.]

Hobson's choice /hóbss'nz-/ *n* a choice between what is offered and nothing at all [Mid-17C. After the English liveryman Thomas *Hobson* (1554–1631), who would only let his customers take the horse nearest the door.]

Ho Chi Minh /hṓ chée mín/ (1890–1969) Vietnamese statesman. Born **Nguyen Tat Thanh**

Ho Chi Minh City the largest city of Vietnam, located in the south of the country. Population: 4,22,300 (1993).

hock[1] /hok/ *n* 1 ANIMAL'S LOWER LEG JOINT the joint in the hind leg of a four-legged animal such as a horse or cow, corresponding to the human ankle 2 FOWL'S ANKLE the ankle joint in the leg of a fowl 3 LEG OF MEAT a cut of cured meat, especially ham, taken from the lower joint of the leg immediately above the foot [Mid-16C. Shortening of obsolete *hockshin* < Old English *hōhsinu* 'heel-sinew' < *hōh* 'heel'.]

hock[2] /hok/ *n* German white wine, especially from the Rhineland [Early 17C. Shortening of obsolete *hockamore*, Anglicization of German *Hochheimer* < *Hochheim*, German town.]

hock[3] /hok/ *vt* to deposit something as security against money borrowed, with the risk of losing it if the money is not paid back by a certain time (*slang*) [Mid-19C. < Dutch *hok* 'prison, debt'.] ◇ **in hock** 1 left as security against money borrowed (*informal*) 2 in debt (*informal*) 3 in prison (*slang*)

hockey /hóki/ *n* 1 an outdoor sport played on grass between two teams of eleven, using wooden sticks with curved ends. The aim is to hit a small hard ball into the opposing goal. US term **field hockey** 2 *US* SPORTS = **ice hockey** [Early 16C. < ?]

Hockney /hókni/, **David** (*b.* 1937) British painter

Hocktide /hók tīd/ *n* a festival originally for the purpose of raising money. Date: formerly, second Monday and Tuesday after Easter. [15C. < *Hock-* 'beginning of the second week after Easter' < ?]

hocus /hṓkəss/ (**-cuses, -cusing** *or* **-cussing, -cused** *or* **-cussed**) *vt* (*archaic*) 1 DECEIVE to deceive or trick somebody 2 DOPE to incapacitate a person or animal with drugs 3 ADD DRUG TO ALCOHOLIC DRINK secretly to add a drug to an alcoholic drink [Late 17C. Shortening of HOCUS-POCUS.]

hocus-pocus /-pṓkəss/ *n* **1 CONJURER'S INCANTATION** a phrase or chant used by a magician or conjurer during a performance **2 MAGIC TRICK** a trick performed by a magician or conjurer **3 TRICKERY** a hoax or trickery ○ *The negotiations were ruined by the parties' hocus-pocus.* **4 CONJURER** a juggler or magician (*dated*) ■ *vti* **DECEIVE** to deceive or trick somebody [< pseudo-Latin *hax pax max Deus adimax*, used by conjurers]

hod /hod/ *n* **1** a V-shaped tray on the end of a long pole, usually carried on the shoulder. Use: carrying bricks, mortar, and other building materials. **2** = **coal scuttle** [Late 16C. < Old French *hotte* 'pannier, basket' < Germanic.]

hod carrier *n* somebody hired to carry bricks and mortar in a hod

hodden /hódd'n/ *n Scotland* a coarse, undyed, homespun woollen fabric produced in Scotland [Late 16C. < ?]

Hoddle /hódd'l/, **Glenn** (*b.* 1957) British footballer and manager

Hodge /hoj/ *n* a name for a typical agricultural labourer (*archaic*) [14C. Form of the first name *Roger.*]

hodgepodge /hój poj/ *n* = **hotchpotch** *n.* 1 [14C. Variant of HOTCHPOTCH.]

Hodgkin /hójkin/, **Alan** (1914–98) British physiologist

Hodgkin, Dorothy Mary (1910–94) Egyptian-born British chemist

Hodgkin, Thomas (1798–1866) British pathologist

Hodgkins /hójkinz/, **Frances Mary** (1869–1947) New Zealand painter

Hodgkin's disease /hójkinz-/ *n* a malignant form of lymphoma marked by progressive enlargement of the lymph nodes and spleen and sometimes of the liver [Mid-19C. After Thomas HODGKIN.]

hodman /hódmən/ (*plural* **-men** /-mən/) *n* = **hod carrier**

hoe /hō/ *n* a garden implement consisting of a long pole with a small flat metal blade set into one end at an angle. Use: weeding, turning over soil. [14C. < Old French *houe* < Germanic, 'cut down'.] —**hoe** *vti* —**hoer** *n*

hoedown /hṓ down/ *n Southern US, Can* **1** a noisy lively dance, especially a square dance, or a party for square dancing **2** the music for a hoedown [< the idea of stopping work]

⚡**HOF** *abbr* hall of fame (*in e-mails*)

Hofei /hṓ fáy/ = **Hefei**

Hoffman /hófmən/, **Dustin** (*b.* 1937) US actor

hog /hog/ *n* **1 PIG** a full-grown domestic pig, especially a castrated male pig **2** *US* **MEMBER OF THE PIG FAMILY** any mammal of the pig family, including both domesticated and wild species, e.g. the wild boar. Family: Suidae. **3 hog, hogg YOUNG SHEEP** a young sheep that is older than a lamb and that has not yet been sheared (*regional*) **4 SHIP'S BROOM** a broom used to clean the bottom of a ship while it is in the water ■ *v* (**hogs, hogging, hogged**) **1** *vt* **TAKE AN EXCESS OF** to take more of something or keep something for longer than is fair or polite (*informal*) ○ *He's been hogging the middle lane for the past two miles.* **2** *vt* **ARCH THE BACK** to arch the back upwards **3** *vt* **TRIM A HORSE'S MANE** to trim the mane of a horse very short, causing it to stand up like the bristles of a hog's back **4** *vti* **WARP** to cause the keel or plank of a ship to curve upwards in the middle, or curve in this way **5** *vt* **SCRUB WITH A BROOM** to clean a ship's bottom with a broom while the ship is in the water [Pre-12C. < ?] —**hog-like** *adj* ◇ **go the whole hog** to do something wholeheartedly or completely and without restraint (*slang*)

hogan /hṓgən/ *n* a traditional Navajo dwelling made of wood and mud, with a roof of earth [Late 19C. < Navajo.]

Hogan /hṓgən/, **Ben** (1912–97) US golfer. Full name **William Benjamin Hogan**

Hogan, Paul (*b.* 1940) Australian actor

Hogarth /hṓ gaarth/, **William** (1697–1764) British painter and engraver —**Hogarthian** /hō gaárthi ən/ *adj*

hogback /hóg bak/ *n* a steep and narrow low ridge produced by the erosion of the softer surrounding rock strata

hog badger *n* a nocturnal badger with an elongated snout with which it roots for insects and grubs. Native to: SE Asia. *Arctonyx collaris.* [< its cloven hooves]

hog cholera *n US* VET = **swine fever**

hogfish /hógfish/ (*plural* **-fish** *or* **-fishes**) *n* **1** a brightly coloured fish of the wrasse family, especially one with the first three spines of its dorsal fin thickened and elongated. Native to: tropical coral reefs. *Lachnolaimus maximus.* **2** = **pigfish** [< its grunting sound]

hogg *n* = **hog** *n.* 3 (*regional*)

Hogg /hog/, **James** (1770–1835) Scottish poet and novelist

hogget /hóggit/ *n* **1** *ANZ, UK, US* = **hog** *n.* 3 (*regional*) **2** the wool from a sheep 12 to 14 months old

hoggish /hóggish/ *adj* greedy, selfish, or slovenly —**hoggishly** *adv* —**hoggishness** *n*

Hogmanay /hógmə nay, hógmə náy/ *n Scotland* New Year's Eve as celebrated in Scotland and in parts of N England [Early 17C. Probably < Norman dialect *hoguinané*, said when exchanging New Year's gifts < Old French *aguillanneuf*, contraction of *accueillis l'an neuf* 'welcome the new year'.]

hognose snake /hógnōz-/, **hognosed snake** *n* a nonvenomous North American snake with a stout body and an upturned snout resembling a hog's that is used for burrowing. Genus: *Heterodon.* [*Hognose* from its upturned snout]

hognut /hóg nut/ *n* FOOD, TREES = **pignut, pignut**

hog's back *n* GEOG = **hogback**

Hog's Back /hógz bak/ ridge in SE England. Height: 154 m/505 ft.

hogshead /hógz hed/ *n* **1** a unit of capacity for liquids or dry goods, used especially for alcohol, having various values but typically 54 imperial gallons or 63 US gallons **2** a large cask or barrel, especially one having a capacity of one hogshead [14C. < ?]

hog-tie *vt US* **1** to tie the legs of an animal or the feet and hands of a person together **2** to hamper or impede somebody or something (*informal*)

hogwash /hóg wosh/ *n* **1** rubbish or nonsense (*informal*) ○ *What a pile of hogwash!* **2** leftovers of food that are given to pigs to eat

hogweed /hóg weed/ *n* any coarse weed such as sow thistle and knotweed

Hohhot /hṓ hót/ capital of Inner Mongolia, NE China. Population: 652,534 (1990).

ho hum /hṓ húm/ *interj* used to express boredom, disappointment, or resignation (*informal*) ○ *Ho hum, off we go, I suppose.* [Thought to suggest a yawn]

hoick /hoyk/ *vti* to pull or lift something or somebody violently or suddenly (*informal*) [Late 19C. < ?]

hoicks /hoyks/ *n* a shout in hunting, used to urge hounds to move along faster [Early 17C. < ?]

hoi polloi /hóypə lóy, hóy póllloy/ *n* ordinary people as opposed to the wealthy, well-educated, and cultivated elite [< Greek, 'the many']

hoist /hoyst/ *vt* **LIFT UP** to raise or lift somebody or something up, especially using a mechanical device such as a winch ■ *n* **1 DEVICE FOR LIFTING** a mechanical device or apparatus such as a winch or elevator designed for lifting people or heavy objects **2 LIFTING UP** an act of hoisting somebody or something **3 SIGNAL** a message or signal conveyed from ship to ship by flags hoisted up the mast **4 MEASURE OF A SAIL** the height of a sail or flag [15C. Alteration of *hoise* < ?] —**hoister** *n*

hoity-toity /hóyti tóyti/ *adj* arrogant and self-important (*informal*) [Alteration and repetition of obsolete *hoit* 'romp' < ?]

Hokan /hṓkən/ *n* a group of Native American languages of the SW United States, including Chumash, Yuman, and other languages and linguistic groups [Early 20C. < Hokan *hok* 'two'.] —**Hokan** *adj*

Hokan-Siouan *n* a family of Native North American languages including the Hokan, Siouan, and Muskogean languages —**Hokan-Siouan** *adj*

hoke /hōk/ (**hokes, hoking, hoked**) *vt* to introduce highly melodramatic or broadly comic elements into a story, play, or speech, in order to captivate an audience [Early 20C. Back-formation < HOKUM.]

hokey /hṓki/ (**-ier, -iest**) *adj* (*informal*) **1** *US, Can* obviously contrived or clearly not genuine **2** *US* corny, sentimental, or melodramatic [Mid-20C. < HOKE or HOKUM.] —**hokeyness** *n* —**hokily** *adv*

hokey cokey /hṓki kṓki/ (*plural* **hokey cokeys**) *n* a dance in which a circle of people, especially children, sing out instructions for movements that they perform at the same time. US term **hokey-pokey** *n.* 2 [< ?]

hokey-pokey /hṓki pṓki/ (*plural* **hokey-pokeys**) *n* **1** *NZ* a toffee, most often encountered as an ingredient in a flavour of ice cream **2** *US* DANCE = **hokey cokey** [< ?]

Hokkaido /ho kī́dō/ the second largest island of Japan, situated north of the main island of Honshu. Population: 5,643,647 (1990). Area: 78,460 sq. km/30,290 sq. mi.

Hokkien /hóki en/ *n* the form of the Chinese language that is most widely used in Singapore. Native speakers: 700,000. —**Hokkien** *adj*

hokku /hó koo/ (*plural* **-ku**) *n* = **haiku** [Late 19C. < Japanese, 'opening verse (of a sequence of comic verses)'.]

hokum /hṓkəm/ *n US* **1** something that on the surface appears to be true or credible but is in fact meaningless or untrue (*informal*) ○ *a load of hokum* **2** highly melodramatic or broadly comedic elements introduced into a story, play, or speech, in order to captivate an audience [Early 20C. < ?]

Hokusai /hṓkoo sī/, **Katsushika** (1760–1849) Japanese painter and book illustrator

hol- *prefix* = **holo-** (*before vowels*)

holandric /hō lándrik, ho-/ *adj* describes genetic traits carried on the Y chromosome and therefore carried and inherited only by males [Mid-20C. < HOLO- + ANDRO-.]

Holarctic /hō laárktik, ho-/ *adj* found in or typical of the regions of North America and Eurasia combined, which share many faunal characteristics

Holbein (the Elder) /hól bīn-/, **Hans** (1460?–1524) German painter

Holbein (the Younger), Hans (1497–1543) German painter

hold[1] /hōld/ *v* (**holds, holding, held** /held/) **1** *vt* **GRASP** to take something firmly and retain it in the hand or arms **2** *vt* **LIFT AND KEEP IN POSITION** to carry, lift, or support temporarily an object or part of the body in a particular position ○ *Hold the rope a bit higher.* **3** *vt* **FIX** to keep something fixed in a particular position ○ *The picture is held in place by two large hooks.* **4** *vt* **EMBRACE** to bring or have somebody within an embrace or supported by the arms **5** *vt* **CONTAIN** to be the place where something is or can be kept ○ *a basket to hold all your sewing equipment* **6** *vt* **KEEP IN CUSTODY** to keep somebody in a particular place or condition, especially in custody **7** *vt* **DELAY** to cause delay to somebody ○ *What held you so long?* **8** *vt* **RETAIN** to retain or reserve something for later use or collection by somebody else ○ *Ask if they can hold the tickets for us at the box office.* **9** *vt* **REFRAIN** to refrain from doing or saying something ○ *The captain told his soldiers to hold their fire.* **10** *vt* **STOP LEAVING** to stop something leaving or happening at the appointed time, usually for a particular purpose ○ *The guard held the train so that we could board.* **11** *vt* **KEEP BY FORCE** to keep possession of something by force, especially while under attack ○ *The insurgents held the town for some time before retreating.* **12** *vt* **HAVE CERTAIN CAPACITY** to contain or be able to contain a particular number or amount ○ *This cup holds eight ounces.* **13** *vt* **BE ABLE TO CONSUME** to consume something, especially alcohol, without ill effect **14** *vt* **ARRANGE** to arrange, take part in, or observe an activity or event ○ *They hold a party every Friday night.* **15** *vt* **POSSESS** to have the right to something as a possession or achievement ○ *The author holds the copyright to this book.* **16** *vt* **HAVE PARTICULAR POSITION** to fulfil the duties of a particular title, office, or position ○ *She has held the position of Director since 1994.* **17** *vti* **KEEP PROMISE** to keep a promise, or make sure that somebody keeps a promise or is true to a stated intention ○ *The lawyer held to his promise to bring them to justice.* **18** *vt* **BELIEVE OR FEEL** to have a particular belief, opinion, or feeling ○ *'We hold these truths to be self-evident'.* **19** *vt* **REGARD** to regard somebody or something in a particular way ○ *She holds her professor in very high esteem.* **20** *vt* **HAVE A PARTICULAR BEARING** to keep or carry the body or a part of it in a particular attitude or position ○ *The old general holds himself stiffly.* **21** *vt* **ENGROSS** to engage or captivate somebody or somebody's attention ○ *She held their attention with the dramatic tale of her rescue.* **22** *vt* **DECIDE LEGALLY** to decide or lay down something legally or authoritatively ○ *The appeals court held that the lower court acted properly.* **23** *vt* **SUSTAIN** to keep singing or playing a note or a chord without stopping ○ *The trumpeter held the note for at least a full minute.* **24** *vi* **PERSIST** to continue in a particular state or course ○ *I can't believe this run of bad luck will hold.* ○ *The snow still holds on the mountains.* **25** *vi* **REMAIN FIRM** to remain fast or firm and not break or give way ○ *The dam held throughout the flooding.* **26** *vi* **STAND FIRM** to maintain a position against attack or opposition ○ *Their defensive line held, despite heavy losses.* **27** *vi* **REMAIN VALID** to remain in force or continue to be valid ○ *Many old sayings still hold true.* **28** *vi* **STAY FINE** continue to be fine and, e.g., not rain, snow, or become cold (*refers to the weather*) ○ *We're meant to be going to a picnic on Saturday so I hope the weather holds.* **29** *vt* **LEASE** to maintain the right to use property by some kind of tenure, e.g. a lease or easement ○ *They held the farm under a very long lease.* **30** *vti* **WAIT ON TELEPHONE** to wait during a telephone call and not break the connection ○ *Could you hold, please, while I try to connect you?* ○ *Hold the line, please.* ■ *n* **1 GRASPING** the act or position of grasping or keeping possession of something ○ *no hold on reality* ○ *She grabbed hold of the rope and pulled herself aboard.* **2 WRESTLING TECHNIQUE** a position or manner of grasping an opponent in wrestling **3 SOMETHING GIVING SUPPORT** something that may be grasped or used as a support ○ *There were few holds on the sheer rock face.* **4 SOMETHING THAT RESTRAINS** a structure or receptacle used for keeping something in check, e.g. a lock on a canal **5 CONTROL** a controlling power or influence ○ *a firm hold on the public's imagination* **6 DELAYING** an act of delaying or restraining something, or an order to effect this ○ *Put a hold on their dinner order.* **7 MUSIC NOTATION** a symbol appearing above or below a note or rest, signalling that it can be prolonged beyond its prescribed time **8 PRISON** a prison cell or place of confinement **9 STRONGHOLD** a fortified place in a castle or other structure (*dated*) [Old English *haldan, healdan* < Germanic, 'guard, watch'] ◇ **get hold of somebody** *or* **something** to succeed in finding somebody or obtaining something ◇ **hold good** to apply to something, or be true or valid ◇ **hold it** used to tell somebody to stop or wait ◇ **hold something against somebody** to resent something that somebody has done and to bear a grudge because of it ◇ **on hold 1** waiting to be connected or reconnected to somebody during a telephone call **2** into or in a state of suspension or postponement ○ *We've had to put our holiday plans on hold.* ◇ **no holds barred** with no restrictions on what is allowed or included

hold back *v* **1** *vti* to keep back or restrain somebody from doing something ○ *His shyness holds him back from making friends.* **2** *vt* to withhold something or retain something within your own control ○ *accused of holding back vital information* ○ *holding back tears*

SYNONYMS See *hinder*.

hold down *vt* to do enough in a job or position to keep it (*informal*) ○ *He can't even manage to hold down one job, let alone two!*

hold forth *vi* to speak at length and sometimes tediously on a particular subject ○ *holding forth for hours about their flash new car*

hold in *vt* **1** to keep back or in check ○ *It was nearly impossible to hold in the hounds.* **2** to suppress something such as an emotion or feeling ○ *They held in their emotions throughout the crisis.*

hold off *v* **1** *vti* **REFRAIN** to refrain from doing something ○ *We decided to hold off until after the election.* ○ *It might be wise to hold off making any decisions until after the results come out.* **2** *vt* **RESIST** to keep somebody or something away or prevent somebody from approaching too close ○ *A handful of soldiers held off several enemy attacks.* **3** *vi* **NOT HAPPEN** to not produce bad weather conditions after threatening to do so ○ *The rain held off, and the barbecue went ahead as planned.*

hold on *vi* **1** to wait for a short while ○ *Hold on, and let's see if we can sort out this problem.* **2** to continue on a course of action or direction or maintain something such as a set of principles or a particular state of mind ○ *He held on until he knew all was lost.* ○ *The scientist held on to her theory and finally proved it correct.*

hold out *v* **1** *vt* **EXTEND** to stretch out or extend a part of the body, or offer something to somebody in doing this ○ *She held out her hand.* **2** *vi* **LAST** to keep up or continue to be in supply ○ *The water supply will hold out only until tomorrow night.* **3** *vi* **ENDURE** to continue to resist and not give in to something ○ *We managed to hold out for three days against the enemy.* **4** *vi* **RESIST** to refuse to settle something or accept something until all demands or conditions are met ○ *holding out for a 6% pay rise*

hold over *vt* **1** to postpone action on or consideration of something until a later date **2** to blackmail or shame somebody with information you possess (*informal*) ○ *You're not going to keep holding that over me, are you?*

hold together *vti* to remain united, or cause a group of people to remain united, often despite problems or disagreements ○ *He held the family together single-handed.* ○ *It was nothing more than a desire to earn money that held them together.*

hold up *v* **1** *vt* **CAUSE DELAY** to cause somebody or something to be late or take longer than intended ○ *Minor disagreements hold up any negotiation.* ○ *I was held up in traffic.* **2** *vt* **ROB** to rob a person or place using violence or threats, usually at gunpoint **3** *vt* **PRESENT** to show or display somebody or something for a specific reason ○ *The firefighter was held up as a good example of bravery.* **4** *vi* **ENDURE** to continue to function or survive ○ *How's the bike holding up?* ○ *You've been holding up well under the strain.* **5** *vi* **REMAIN SAME** to remain or be maintained at a particular level or in a particular state ○ *Prices have not held up well in this recession.* **6** *vi* **STAND UP TO SCRUTINY** to remain persuasive or convincing even after closer examination ○ *I don't think these ideas will hold up.* **7** *vi* **NOT PLAY HIGH CARD** to delay playing a high card in order to prevent a suit from being established

hold with *vt* to approve or agree with something ○ *She doesn't hold with that kind of thinking.*

hold[2] /hōld/ *n* the area below the deck of a ship or the area inside an aircraft in which cargo is carried [Late 16C. Alteration of HOLE, influenced by HOLD[1].]

holdall /hṓld awl/ *n* a capacious bag or case used for carrying miscellaneous items. US term **carryall** *n.* 1

holdback /hṓld bak/ *n* **1 SOMETHING THAT HINDERS** something that prevents somebody from doing or achieving something or that prevents an event or plan from going ahead **2 DEVICE ON A WAGON OR CARRIAGE** a device on the shaft of a wagon or carriage that attaches to the horse's harness, allowing the horse to hold back or back up the vehicle **3 SOMETHING HELD BACK** something withheld, usually wages or money

hold button *n* a button on a telephone that allows somebody to put a caller on hold

Holden /hṓldən/, **William** (1918–81) US actor

holder /hṓldər/ *n* **1 CONTAINER** something designed to hold another thing (*often in combination*) ○ *a candle holder* **2 OWNER** an owner or occupier of something, e.g. property or a title ○ *the current holder of the world title* **3 SOMEBODY WITH A PROMISE OF PAYMENT** somebody in possession of and legally entitled to receive payment on or negotiate a note, bill, or cheque

Hölderlin /húldərlin, hṓldər lin/, **Friedrich** (1770–1843) German poet

holdfast /hṓld faast/ *n* **1 CLAMP** a device such as a clamp or grip designed to hold something securely **2 PLANT'S MEANS OF ATTACHING ITSELF** an organ at the base of a seaweed, aquatic plant, or fungus that attaches the organism to a surface **3 FIRM GRASP** the action or fact of holding something fast or firmly

holding /hṓlding/ *n* **1 LEASED LAND** a piece of land that is leased from somebody else, especially when used for agricultural purposes **2 PROPERTY** legally owned property of any kind, but especially stocks or bonds (*often plural*) **3 ILLEGAL USE OF THE ARMS** use of the arms to hold or obstruct an opponent when such use is not allowed in the rules of a sport or game, e.g. in boxing **4 SENSE OF SECURITY** the ability of a therapist or parent to make a client or child feel contained and secure during times of growth or change

holding company *n* a company that has a controlling interest in one or more other companies through ownership of stocks or bonds

holding operation *n* a procedure or operation designed to maintain the present situation as it is

holding pattern *n* **1** a usually circular pattern held by an aircraft while awaiting permission to land **2** a state of suspended action or progress ○ *He's in a holding pattern until he knows whether he's been given the scholarship.*

holdover /hṓld ōvər/ *n* a performer or a presentation such as a play or series of concerts that continues beyond the term originally agreed

holdup /hṓld up/ *n* **1 ROBBERY** an act of robbing a person or place using violence or threats, usually at gunpoint **2 DELAY** an act of causing somebody or something to be late or take longer than planned ○ *Travel was slowed by holdups on the M40.* **3 WITHHOLDING OF CARD** the holding back of a card rather than playing it to take a trick early in the play of a hand

hole /hōl/ *n* **1 CAVITY** a hollow space in a solid object or area ○ *The hole had filled with water.* **2 APERTURE** a gap or opening in or through something ○ *a hole in my socks* **3 BURROW** a hollowed-out area in the earth where an animal such as a rabbit or mouse lives **4 UNPLEASANT PLACE** a dark or dirty place, especially a place where somebody lives (*informal*) **5 FLAW** a fault or flaw in something such as logic, an argument, or a position ○ *But there are so many holes in her theory.* **6 AWKWARD SITUATION** an awkward or embarrassing situation (*informal*) **7 PRISONER'S CELL** a prison cell or dungeon (*informal*) **8 MOBILE SPACE IN SEMICONDUCTOR** a space normally occupied by an electron in the lattice structure of a semiconductor material that is mobile and can act as a carrier of a positive charge **9 TARGET IN GOLF** a small round cavity or cup on a golf course into which the ball is hit **10 AREA OF GOLF COURSE** a part of a golf course that consists of a tee, a fairway, and a green with a hole and is a basic element in scoring ■ *v* (**holes, holing, holed**) **1** *vti* **PERFORATE** to make a hole or holes in something ○ *This new device holes a ream of paper perfectly.* **2** *vt* **PUT IN A HOLE** to hit or drive a ball into one of the holes of a golf course **3** *vi* **GO INTO A HOLE** to go or climb into a hole [Old English *hol* 'hollow', probably < Indo-European, 'hide, conceal'] —**holey** *adj* ◇ **make a hole in something** to use up a large part of something (*informal*) ○ *The monthly rent makes a considerable hole in my salary.* ◇ **pick holes in something** to find fault with something, often over minor imperfections

SPELLCHECK Do not confuse ***hole*** with ***whole***, which has a similar sound. Beware: your spellchecker will not catch this error.

hole out *vi* to hit a golf ball into a hole

hole up *vi* **1** to hide away somewhere (*slang*) **2** to go into a hole, cave, or other similar place to shelter or hibernate

hole-and-corner *adj* secret or secretive ○ *hole-and-corner activities*

hole in one (*plural* **holes in one**) *n* a shot in golf that enters the hole directly from the tee

hole-in-the-wall (*plural* **holes-in-the-wall**) *n* (*informal*) **1** a small unpretentious out-of-the-way place such as a little restaurant or other business **2** an automatic cash dispenser located in the outside wall of a bank or other building

Holi /hṓli/ *n* the Hindu festival of spring that honours the time when Krishna paid amorous attention to young women tending cows, during which people spray coloured water over each other [Late 17C. < Hindi *holī*.]

holiday /hólli day, -di/ *n* **1 DAY OF LEISURE** a day taken off or set aside for leisure and enjoyment, when somebody is exempt from work or normal activity **2 PERIOD OF LEISURE** a period of time free from work or normal activity and given over to leisure and recreation ○ *the summer holidays* ○ *on holiday in Spain* ○ *a holiday resort.* US term **vacation** *n.* 2 **3 LEGAL DAY OFF** a day set aside by law, statute, or custom as exempt from regular work or business activities, usually to celebrate or commemorate something that happened on or near that date **4 HOLY DAY** the day or days of a religious festival ■ *vi* **SPEND HOLIDAY** to go on or spend a holiday. US term **vacation** *v.* [Old English *hāligdæg* 'holy day']

Holiday /hólli day/, **Billie** (1915–59) US jazz singer. Born **Eleanora Fagan McKay Holiday**. Known as **Lady Day**

holiday camp *n* a purpose-built site, often by the sea, that provides accommodation, organized leisure activities, and facilities for people who go there for a holiday

holidaymaker /hólli day maykər, -di-/ *n UK, ANZ* somebody who is on holiday. US term **vacationer**

holier-than-thou /hṓli ər-/ *adj* aggressively or offensively pompous or self-righteous (*disapproving*) ○ *Her holier-than-thou attitude puts people off.* ■ *n* an aggressively or offensively pompous or self-righteous person or organization (*disapproving*) ○ *The chairman is regarded as one of the bigger holier-than-thous.*

holiness /hṓlinəss/ *n* the state or quality of being holy

Holiness *n* a title used in addressing or referring to the pope

holism /hólizəm/ *n* **1** the view that a whole system of beliefs must be analysed rather than simply its individual components **2** the theory of the importance of taking all of somebody's physical, mental, and social conditions into account in the treatment of illness [Early 20C. < Greek *holos* 'whole'.] —**holist** *n*

holistic /hō lístik/ *adj* including or involving all of something, especially all of somebody's physical, mental, and social conditions, not just physical symptoms, in the treatment of illness —**holistically** *adv*

holland /hólland/ *n* a strong smooth linen fabric. Use: upholstery. [14C. After HOLLAND.]

Holland /hóllənd/ **1** = **Netherlands 2** former administrative division of Lincolnshire, England, known as the Parts of Holland

Holland, Sir Sidney George (1893–1961) New Zealand statesman

hollandaise sauce /hóllən dáyz-/, **hollandaise** *n* a rich creamy piquant sauce made from butter, egg yolks, and vinegar or lemon juice [< French, form of *Hollandais* 'Dutch']

Hollands /hólləndz/ *n* Dutch gin (*archaic*) [Late 18C. < obsolete Dutch *Hollandsch genever* 'Dutch gin'.]

holler /hóllər/ *vti* **SHOUT** to call out or shout something (*informal*) ○ *If you need me, just holler!* ■ *n* (*informal*) **1 LOUD CRY** a loud cry or shout **2** *US* **WORK SONG** a work song originally sung by enslaved and labouring Black American people [Late 17C. Probably partly < Old French *halloer* 'pursue with shouting', an imitation of the sound, partly < French *holà* 'stop!' < *ho* 'ho' + *là* 'there'.]

hollow /hóllō/ *adj* **1 NOT SOLID** having empty space inside ○ *The tree trunk was hollow inside.* **2 CONCAVE** sunk deep into the surface of something **3 NOT FULL-TONED** resonating or echoing as if in an empty space ○ *It gave a huge, hollow, booming sound.* **4 INSINCERE** not sincere, genuine, or significant ○ *He gave a hollow laugh.* **5 HUNGRY** having the feeling of an empty stomach ■ *n* **1 CAVITY** a hollow or concave place or area, as in a tree trunk or somebody's back ○ *The child held the chick in the hollow of his hand.* **2 VALLEY** a sunken or low-lying area of the earth's surface ■ *v* **1** *vt* **MAKE A CAVITY IN** to form something by removing contents to leave a concave area or cavity **2** *vti* **MAKE OR BECOME HOLLOWED** to make something hollow, or become hollow ○ *eyes hollowed from lack of sleep* [Old English *holh* 'hollow place, hole, cave', related to HOLE] —**hollow** *adv* —**hollowly** *adv* —**hollowness** *n*

LITERARY LINK ***The Hollow Men***, a poem (1925) by T. S. Eliot. One of Eliot's most pessimistic works, it depicts a barren, ghostly land peopled by soulless beings. The oft-quoted words 'This is the way the world ends/ Not with a bang but a whimper' come from this poem.

SYNONYMS See ***vain***.

Hollows /hóllōz/, **Fred** (1930–93) New Zealand-born Australian ophthalmologist. Full name **Frederick Cossom Hollows**

hollowware /hóllō wair/ *n US* articles of tableware and kitchenware such as pots, bowls, cups, vases, and jugs that are hollow, as opposed to items such as plates and saucers

holly /hólli/ (*plural* **-lies**) *n* **1** an evergreen tree or shrub with glossy, prickly leaves and bright red berries. Genus: *Ilex*. **2** the leaves and berries of holly used especially as a Christmas decoration [12C. Shortening of Old English *hole(g)n* < Germanic.]

Holly /hólli/, **Buddy** (1938–59) US musician. Born **Charles Hardin Holley**

hollyhock /hólli hok/ *n* a very tall flowering plant of the mallow family with hairy stems. *Alcea rosea*. [13C. < alteration of HOLY + obsolete *hock* 'mallow' < ?]

holly oak *n* = **holm oak** [Because its foliage resembles holly]

Hollywood[1] /hólliwŏŏd/ *n* the US film industry as a whole

Hollywood[2] /hólliwŏŏd/ district of Los Angeles, California, a centre of the US film and television industry

holm[1] /hōm/, **holme** *n* **1** low-lying flat land next to a river or stream **2** a small island in a river, lake, or estuary, or near the coastal mainland [Pre-12C. < Old Norse *holmr* 'islet in a bay, meadow' < Indo-European, 'be prominent'.]

holm[2] /hōm/ *n* = **holm oak** [14C. Alteration of obsolete *hollin* < Old English *hole(g)n* (see HOLLY).]

holme *n* GEOG = **holm**[1]

Holmes /hōmz/, **Oliver Wendell** (1809–94) US physician and writer

Holmes, Oliver Wendell, Jr. (1841–1935) US jurist. Known as **the Great Dissenter**

Holmes à Court /hōmz ə kawrt/, **Robert** (1937–90) South-African-born Australian business executive

holmic /hōlmik/ *adj* resembling or containing the metallic element holmium

holmium /hōlmi əm/ *n* (*symbol* **Ho**) a silvery-white malleable metallic element of the rare-earth group. Source: gadolinite, monazite. [Late 19C. < *Holmia*, Latinized form of STOCKHOLM.]

holm oak *n* a broad-leaved evergreen tree grown widely for ornament. Native to: S Europe. *Quercus ilex*. [< HOLM[2]]

holo- *prefix* whole, complete ○ *hologynic* [< Greek *holos* 'whole, entire' < Indo-European]

holocaust /hóllə kawst/ *n* **1 COMPLETE DESTRUCTION BY FIRE** complete consumption by fire, especially of a large number of human beings or animals **2 TOTAL DESTRUCTION** wholesale or mass destruction of any kind **3 BURNT OFFERING** a sacrifice that is totally consumed by fire [13C. < Old French *holocauste* < Greek *holokaustos* 'burnt whole' < *kaiein* 'burn'.] —**holocaustal** /hóllə káwst'l/ *adj* —**holocaustic** *adj*

Holocaust /hóllə kawst/ *n* the systematic extermination of millions of European Jews, as well as Roma, Slavs, intellectuals, homosexual people, and political dissidents, by the Nazis and their allies during World War II ○ *Holocaust survivors*

Holocaust Day, Holocaust Memorial Day *n* an annual commemoration of the Holocaust, held in many countries on the 27th day of Nisan and in the United Kingdom on 27 January

Holocene /hóllō seen/ *n* the most recent epoch of the Quaternary period, extending to the present day [Late 19C. < French, < Greek *holos* 'whole' + *kainos* 'new, recent'.] —**Holocene** *adj*

holocrine /hóllō krin, -krīn/ *adj* relating to a gland such as a sebaceous gland whose secretions are derived from the substance of the gland itself

holoenzyme /hóllō én zīm/ *n* an active enzyme comprising a protein and coenzyme

hologram /hóllə gram/ *n* **1** a three-dimensional image of an object that is a photographic record of light interference patterns produced using a photographic plate and light from a laser **2** the image produced by a hologram

holograph /hóllə graaf, -graf/ *n* **1** a manuscript or other document entirely handwritten by its author **2** = **hologram** *n.* **1**, **hologram** *n.* **2** [Early 17C. Via late Latin < Greek *holographos* 'written whole'.] —**holograph** *adj*

holography /ho lóggrəfi/ *n* a method of recording and showing a three-dimensional image of an object using a photographic plate and light from a laser —**holographic** /hóllə gráffik/ *adj* —**holographically** *adv*

hologynic /hóllō jínnik, -gínik/ *adj* describes genetic traits that are inherited and passed on only by females [< HOLO- + Greek *gunē* 'woman']

holohedral /hóllō heédrəl/ *adj* describes crystals having all the faces required for complete symmetry

holomorphic /hóllō máwrfik/ *adj* CRYSTALS = **holohedral** —**holomorphism** *n*

holophrastic /hóllō frástik/ *adj* containing the idea of a sentence or phrase in one word, e.g. 'goodbye' [Mid-19C. < HOLO- + Greek *phrastikos* < *phrazein* 'tell'.]

holophytic /hóllə fíttik/ *adj* able to synthesize complex organic molecules by photosynthesis. ◊ **holozoic**

holoplankton /hóllō plángktən/ *n* organisms that remain free-swimming plankton throughout their life cycle

holothurian /hóllō thyŏŏri ən/ *n* a marine invertebrate animal (**echinoderm**) of the class that includes the sea cucumber. Class: Holothuroidea. [Mid-19C. < modern Latin *Holothuria* < Latin *holothurion*, a marine creature.] —**holothurian** *adj*

holozoic /hóllō zṓ ik/ *adj* obtaining nutrition from other organisms or organic matter, as most animals do. ◊ **holophytic**

hols /holz/ *n* holidays, especially school holidays or somebody's main annual holiday (*informal*) ○ *during the hols* [Early 20C. Contraction of *holidays*.]

Holst /hōlst/, **Gustav** (1874–1934) British composer

Holstein /hól stīn/, **Holstein-Friesian** *n* AGRIC = **Friesian** [Mid-19C. After a region, formerly of the Netherlands, now of N Germany.]

holster /hṓlstər/ *n* a holder for a pistol, usually worn on the hip or shoulder [Mid-17C. Probably < Dutch, < Indo-European, 'to cover'.] —**holster** *vt* —**holstered** *adj*

holt[1] /hōlt/ *n* a wood or copse (*archaic*) [Old English, < Germanic]

holt[2] /hōlt/ *n* the lair of an otter, or, sometimes, of some other burrowing animal [14C. Variant of HOLD[1] (noun).]

Holt /hōlt/, **Harold** (1908–67) Australian statesman

holus-bolus /hṓləss bṓləss/ *adv* all at once or all together (*archaic*) [Mid-19C. < ?]

holy /hṓli/ *adj* (**-lier, -liest**) **1 SACRED** relating to, belonging to, or coming from a divine being or power ○ *holy relics* **2 SAINTLY** devoted to the service of God, a god, or a goddess **3 PURE** morally and spiritually perfect and of a devoutly religious character ○ *a holy man* **4 CONSECRATED** dedicated or set apart for religious purposes ○ *these holy grounds* **5 AWE-INSPIRING** of a unique character, evoking reverence ○ *Gettysburg is a holy place for many Americans.* **6 USED IN EXPRESSIONS OF SURPRISE** used in various expressions to show surprise (*informal*) ○ *Holy smoke!* ■ *n* (*plural* **-lies**) **1 HOLY THING** something sanctified or venerated **2 HOLY PERSON** a devoutly religious, saintly person [Old English *hālig* < Germanic] —**holily** *adv*

Holy Alliance *n* an alliance between Russia, Prussia, and Austria in 1815 advocating government according to Christian principles

Holy Ark *n* = **ark** *n.* **4**

Holy City *n* **1** Jerusalem as a city of great religious significance **2** heaven in Christian tradition

Holy Communion *n* CHR = **Communion** *n.* **1**, **Communion** *n.* **3**

holy cow *interj US* used to express surprise or annoyance

Holy Cross *n* in Christianity, the cross that Jesus Christ died on

holy day *n* a day set aside for the celebration of a religious festival

holy day of obligation *n* a Roman Catholic festival on which Catholics are required to attend mass and abstain from certain types of work

Holy Family *n* in Christianity, the young Jesus Christ, his mother Mary, and Mary's husband, St Joseph, especially as represented in art

Holy Father *n* in the Roman Catholic Church, the pope

Holy Ghost *n* CHR = **Holy Spirit**

Holy Grail *n* CHR = **Grail**

Holyhead /hólli héd, hólli hed/ port in NW Wales, on the N of Holy Island. Population: 11,800 (1991).

Holyhead Island = **Holy Island 2**

Holy Innocents' Day *n* in the Christian church, 28 December, the day that commemorates the order given by Herod to massacre all baby boys in Bethlehem

Holy Island 1 = **Lindisfarne 2** island in NW Wales, off the coast of Anglesey. Area: 39 sq. km/16 sq. mi.

Holy Joe /-jṓ/ *n* (*dated slang*) **1** a clergyman **2** a sanctimonious or self-righteous person

Holy Land region on the E shore of the Mediterranean Sea, equivalent to the historic region of Palestine

Holy Loch inlet on the W shore of the Firth of Clyde, W Scotland

Holyoake /hṓli ōk/, **Sir Keith** (1904–83) New Zealand statesman

Holy Office *n* **1** a permanent committee of the Roman Catholic College of Cardinals that deals with doctrine and morals **2** HIST = **Inquisition**

holy of holies *n* **1** the inner chamber inside the Sanctuary in the Jewish Temple in Jerusalem, where the Ark of the Covenant was kept **2** any place considered to be especially sacred

holy orders *npl* **1 RITE OF ORDINATION** the rite or sacrament of ordination as a Christian minister or priest **2 MINISTER'S OR PRIEST'S RANK** the rank or position of a Christian minister or priest **3 ROMAN CATHOLIC OR ANGLICAN RANKS** in the Roman Catholic Church, the ranks of priest, deacon, and subdeacon, or in the Anglican Church, the ranks of bishop, priest, and deacon

Holy Roller *n* an offensive term for a member of a Christian group that worships in what is perceived to be an ecstatic or frenzied way, with shouting, bodily movements, and trances (*slang*) [< the movement of the body during worship]

Holy Roman Empire *n* an empire in Germany and N Italy (800–1806). ◊ **Roman Empire**

Holy Saturday *n* in Christianity, the Saturday preceding Easter Sunday

Holy Scripture *n* the Christian Bible or a specific part of it

Holy See *n* 1 in the Roman Catholic Church, the see of the pope as Bishop of Rome 2 in the Roman Catholic Church, the government departments, jurisdiction, and authority of the Vatican

Holy Sepulchre *n* in Christianity, the tomb in which the body of Jesus Christ was laid after the Crucifixion

holy smoke *interj US* used to express surprise or annoyance

Holy Spirit *n* in Christianity, the third person of the Trinity, understood as the spiritual force of God

holystone /hṓli stōn/ *n* a piece of soft sandstone used for scouring the decks of ships [< ?] —**holystone** *vt*

Holy Synod *n* the governing body of any of the Eastern Orthodox Christian churches

holy terror *n* a difficult or frightening person (*informal*) ○ *That child is a holy terror.*

Holy Thursday *n* 1 in the Anglican Church, Ascension Day 2 in the Roman Catholic Church, Maundy Thursday

Holy Trinity *n* CHR = **Trinity** *n.* 1

holy war *n* a war undertaken in the name of a particular religion

holy water *n* water that has been blessed by a priest and is used in a church for blessings, baptisms, and other holy rituals

Holy Week *n* in the Christian calendar, the final week of Lent, beginning on Palm Sunday and including Maundy Thursday, Good Friday, and Holy Saturday

Holy Writ *n* sacred Christian writings, especially the Bible

Holy Year *n* in the Roman Catholic Church, a period of remission from sin declared by the pope with certain conditions attached, usually at 25 year intervals

hom- *prefix* = **homo-** (*before vowels*)

homage /hómmij/ *n* 1 a show of reverence and respect towards somebody 2 a formal public acknowledgment of allegiance on the part of a vassal towards a feudal lord [13C. < Old French.]

hombre /ómbray/ *n US* a man (*informal*) [Mid-19C. Via Spanish < Latin *homo* 'human being'.]

homburg /hóm burg/ *n* a man's felt hat with an upturned brim and a lengthwise crease in the crown [Late 19C. After the town in W Germany where first worn.]

home /hōm/ *n* 1 RESIDENCE the place where a person, family, or household lives. 2 FAMILY GROUP a family or any other group that lives together ○ *Theirs was a happy home, full of love.* 3 BIRTHPLACE where somebody was born or brought up or feels he or she belongs ○ *Home is York.* 4 NATIVE HABITAT the place where something is most common or indigenous or where it originated 5 SAFE PLACE a place where a person or animal can find refuge and safety or live in security 6 PLACE OF ASSISTANCE an establishment where somebody who is in need of care, rest, or medical attention can stay or find help ○ *My grandmother moved into a home.* 7 GRAVE the place where somebody is imagined to dwell after death (*literary*) 8 GOAL the place or point that must be hit in order to score in many games or that must be reached in order to be safe from attack 9 BASEBALL = **home plate** ■ *adj* 1 DOMESTIC relating to somebody's own home or country 2 OF A HOUSEHOLD for or belonging to or produced in a dwelling or household ○ *She loved her son's home cooking.* 3 NATIVE happening in or coming from somebody's native territory or permanent base, especially a sports team's own ground ○ *The home team usually has the advantage* 4 EFFECTIVE to the point or central to achieving a goal ○ *She won the argument with that home thrust.* 5 PRINCIPAL belonging or relating to the headquarters of a business or enterprise ○ *She was promoted to the company's home office.* ■ *adv* 1 AT OR TO SOMEBODY'S HOME at or to the house, household, or country where somebody lives ○ *He desperately wanted to get home.* 2 EFFECTIVELY to the point or desired goal ○ *Her criticisms of his behaviour hit home.* 3 TO THE CENTRE to the centre or heart of something or as far as possible into a desired position ○ *In one stroke, she drove the nail home.* ■ *v* (**homes, homing, homed**) 1 *vi* GO HOME to go back to the house, household, or country where you live 2 *vi* RETURN HOME to return home, especially to fly home accurately (*refers to animals and birds*) 3 *vi* DWELL to have a home and live in it (*dated*) 4 *vt* TAKE OR SEND HOME to take or send somebody or something home (*dated*) 5 *vt* PROVIDE WITH A HOME to give a home to somebody or something (*dated*) [Old English *hām* < Germanic] —**home-like** *adj* ◇ **at home** 1 ready to receive visitors 2 at ease or in a familiar and friendly place 3 having knowledge of or familiarity with a subject or activity ◇ **come** *or* **be brought home to somebody** to be fully understood and appreciated by somebody ◇ **come home to roost** to result in undesirable or negative effects, usually after a fairly long period of time ◇ **home and dry** with something successfully completed ◇ **play away from home** to be sexually unfaithful to a spouse or partner (*informal*) ◇ **take home something** to earn a specific amount of money after all deductions, e.g. for tax, have been made

USAGE home or **house**? Many consider ***home*** an affectation when used anywhere that ***house*** would be appropriate: *Home for Sale.* ***Home*** is nonetheless useful to express the idea of dwelling places of various sorts, including flats and other dwellings that are not accurately described as houses. ***House***, in many contexts, suggests a single-family dwelling. For example, if *The tornado destroyed 17 homes* is meant to convey that 17 residential structures were demolished, the word should have been ***houses***. *Most homes in town lost electricity*, however, no doubt refers to households of all descriptions, so here ***homes*** is the better choice.

home in *vi* 1 to locate and proceed straight towards a target 2 to direct all attention or energy towards something ○ *She instinctively homed in on the weakest aspects of the production.*

Home (of the Hirsel) /hyoom ō thə húrsəl/, **Sir Alec Douglas-Home, Baron** (1903–95) British statesman and prime minister (1963–64)

home banking *n* an electronic banking system that allows a customer to carry out transactions at home

homebody /hṓm bodi/ (*plural* **-ies**) *n* a person who prefers home to other places (*informal*)

homebound /hṓm bownd/ *adj US* = **housebound**

homeboy /hṓm boy/ *n US* a man or boy from somebody's home town, state, or neighbourhood, especially somebody who shares that person's own culture and customs (*slang*)

homebred /hṓm bréd/ *adj* 1 bred or raised at home 2 without worldly experience

home-brew *n* an alcoholic beverage, especially beer, that has been brewed at home for personal consumption —**home-brewed** *adj*

homebuyer /hṓm bī ər/ *n* a buyer or prospective buyer if a house or flat

homecoming /hṓm kuming/ *n* the arrival home of somebody who has been away ○ *a party to celebrate his homecoming*

Home Counties counties nearest to London, usually including Kent, Surrey, Essex, Buckinghamshire, Berkshire, Hertfordshire, and East and West Sussex

home economics *n* the science or study of food, diet, cookery, childcare, and other subjects related to the running of a home, as taught in schools

home farm *n UK, S Africa* on an estate with a number of farms, the farm that produces food for the owner

home fries *npl US* boiled sliced potatoes fried in butter or oil

home from home *n* a place in which somebody feels as comfortable and relaxed as at home

home front *n* the civilian effort and activity at home in support of a war waged abroad ○ *On the home front valiant efforts are being made to get the harvest in on time.*

home furnishings *npl* articles such as furniture, bedding, lighting, wallpaper, and carpets that decorate a house and make it more comfortable

homegirl /hṓm gurl/ *n US* a girl or woman from somebody's home town, state, or neighbourhood, especially one who shares that person's own culture and customs (*slang*)

homegrown /hṓm grṓn/ *adj* 1 grown in somebody's own garden or on somebody's own land 2 produced by or coming from the area or region in question ○ *homegrown talent*

home guard *n* 1 a local volunteer force designed to defend an area while the regular army is fighting elsewhere 2 a member of a home guard

Home Guard *n* 1 an army of volunteer civilians formed in the UK during World War II to help protect and police the country 2 a member of a usually local or state military unit, especially an army unit (*dated*)

home help *n* 1 a paid helper for domestic tasks 2 a service provided by a local authority to help people in need with domestic tasks they cannot perform

homeland /hṓm land/ *n* 1 the country where somebody was born or where somebody lives and feels that he or she belongs 2 any partially self-governing region of South Africa created and set aside for the Black population under the former policy of racial apartheid

homeless /hṓmləss/ *adj* without a home of any kind ■ *npl* people without a home of any kind —**homelessness** *n*

homely /hṓmli/ (**-lier, -liest**) *adj* 1 COSY simple, comfortable, and unpretentious, as if it were somebody's home or part of one 2 UNPRETENTIOUS IN MANNER having a simple, unpretentious, and warm-hearted manner 3 *US* NOT GOOD-LOOKING plain or less than pleasing in appearance ○ *a rather homely face* —**homeliness** *n*

homemade /hṓm máyd/ *adj* 1 made at home using traditional methods rather than by a manufacturer ○ *Have you tried some of my homemade marmalade?* 2 roughly or crudely constructed to perform a specific function or purpose, usually by an individual in his or her home

homemaker /hṓm maykər/ *n* somebody who stays at home to manage a household

homeo- *prefix* similar, alike ○ *homeotherm* [< Greek *homoios* 'similar' < *homos* (see HOMO-)]

homeobox /hṓmi ō boks/ *n* a short section of nucleotides with a base sequence that is virtually identical in all genes that contain it

Home Office *n* in the United Kingdom, the department of the government that is responsible for domestic and internal affairs

homeomorphism /hṓmi ō máwrfizəm/ *n* a correspondence between the points of two geometrical shapes or two spaces in which each element can be paired with one from the other without any remaining —**homeomorphic** *adj*

homeopathy /hṓmi óppəthi/, **homoeopathy** *n* a complementary disease treatment system in which a patient is given minute doses of natural drugs that in larger doses would produce symptoms of the disease itself —**homeopath** /hṓmi ə path/ *n* —**homeopathic** /hṓmi ə páthik/ *adj* —**homeopathically** *adv* —**homeopathist** /hṓmi óppəthist/ *n*

homeostasis /hṓmi ō stáyssiss/, **homoeostasis** *n* a state of equilibrium or a tendency to reach equilibrium, either metabolically within a cell or organism or socially and psychologically within an individual or group —**homeostatic** /-státtik/ *adj*

homeotherm /hṓmi ō thurm/, **homoeotherm, homoiotherm** /hō móyə-/ *n* an organism whose stable body temperature is generally independent of the temperature of its surrounding environment [Late 19C. < HOMEO- + Greek *thermē* 'heat'.] —**homeothermic** /hṓmi ō thúrmik/ *adj* —**homeothermy** *n*

homeotic /hṓmi óttik/, **homoeotic** *adj* describes mutation in which one part or organ is transformed into another part associated with a different segment of the organism [Late 19C. < Greek *homoiōtikos* 'becoming like' < *homoios* (see HOMEO-).]

homeotic gene /hṓmi óttik-/ *n* a master gene that controls how different regions of an embryo develop their own distinct tissues and organs. Homeotic genes act by switching other genes on or off.

homeowner /hṓm ōnər/ *n* somebody who owns or holds a mortgage on a home, as opposed to renting it

⚡**homepage** /hṓm payj/ *n* 1 the opening page of an Internet website 2 somebody's personal website on the Internet

home plate *n* a flat slab marking the area over which a pitcher must throw the ball for a strike and on which a base runner must land in order to score

home port *n* the place of registry or regular base of a ship

homer /hṓmər/ *n* 1 HOMING PIGEON a homing pigeon (*informal*) 2 *US* HOME RUN a home run in baseball (*informal*) 3 HOMING DEVICE a device that provides signals for guiding missiles, ships, or aircraft to their destinations

Homer /hṓmər/ city in S Alaska. Population: 4,608 (1996).

Homer (*fl.* 8th century BC) Greek poet

home range *n* the specific geographical area to which an animal generally restricts its activities

Homeric /hŏ mérrik/ *adj* **1 OF HOMER** relating to Homer, his work, or his times ○ *'Thus vain and false are the mere human surmises and doubts which clash with Homeric writ!'* (Alexander William Kinglake, *Eothen*; 1844) **2 OF HOMER'S GREEK** relating to the early form of ancient Greek used in Homer's poetry **3 HEROIC** characteristic of a hero (*literary*) [Early 17C. Via Latin < Greek *Homērikos* < *Homēros* 'Homer'.] —**Homerically** *adv*

Homeric laughter *n* loud continuous laughter, like that of the gods in Homer's epic poems (*literary*)

Homeric simile *n* LITERAT. = **epic simile**

home rule *n* **1** the principle or practice of self-government by a part of a larger country or commonwealth such as a municipality, colony, territory, or principality **2** in the United States, the partial autonomy granted to cities and some counties, under which they manage their own affairs, in accordance with the Constitution

Home Rule *n* the political aim of the Irish nationalists between 1870 and 1920 in their struggle to secure self-government for Ireland

home run *n* in baseball, a hit that allows a player to make a circuit of all four bases and score a run, usually by hitting the ball out of the playing area

homeschool /hŏm skool/ *vti US* to teach children at home or be taught at home ■ *n* a school run typically by parents in the home for their children, using an approved curriculum

homeschooler /hŏm skoolar/ *n US* **1** a child who is undergoing or has undergone private education, typically by the parents at home **2** a parent who educates his or her child or children at home

Home Secretary *n* the head of the Home Office, in charge of internal and domestic affairs

home shopping *n* shopping done electronically from home either through an on-line retail service or a television shopping channel

homesick /hŏm sik/ *adj* feeling sadness and longing to be at home with family and friends when away from them —**homesickness** *n*

homespun /hŏm spun/ *adj* **1 PLAIN AND SIMPLE** simple and unpretentious **2 MADE BY HAND AT HOME** spun or woven by hand at home **3 MADE OF HOMESPUN FABRIC** made of fabric woven or spun by hand at home ■ *n* **1 ROUGH CLOTH** a coarse plain cloth woven from homespun thread **2 ROUGH CLOTH WOVEN ON POWER LOOM** a cloth similar to homespun, but woven on an automatic or electric loom

homestay /hŏm stay/ *n* **1** *US* a visit to somebody's home in a foreign country, often a stay by an exchange student in a family's home (*informal*) **2** *ANZ* bed-and-breakfast accommodation in a private home as opposed to a guesthouse

homestead /hŏm sted/ *n* **1 HOUSE, OUTBUILDINGS, AND LAND** a house, especially a farmhouse, with its dependent buildings and land, considered as a whole **2** *US* **RESIDENCE EXEMPT FROM FORCED SALE** in the United States, a house, adjoining land, and buildings declared as the owner's fixed residence and therefore exempt from seizure and forced sale for the recovery of debts **3** *ANZ* **MANAGER'S HOUSE** in Australia and New Zealand, the home of the manager or owner of a large farm **4** *US* **LAND CLAIMED BY SETTLER** in the United States or Canada, a piece of land occupied by a settler or squatter under the terms of the US Homestead Act or the Canadian Dominion Lands Act —**homesteader** *n*

home straight *n* **1** the part of a racecourse between the last turn and the finishing line. US term **home stretch** *n*. **1 2** the last part of a journey, task, or operation ○ *We're on the home straight now.* US term **home**. **stretch** *n*. **2**

home stretch *n US* HORSERACING = **home straight** *n*. **1 2** = **home straight** *n*. **2**

home-style *adj US* made or presented as it would be in somebody's home ○ *served a home-style meal in the hotel* ■ *adv US* in a way that resembles how something is prepared or served at home

home teacher *n* a teacher employed by the state system to teach in their own homes children with medical conditions that prevent them from going to school. US term **visiting teacher**

home town *n* the town or city where somebody was born, spent his or her childhood, or lives on a long-term basis

home truth *n* an unpleasant but true fact about somebody's character or behaviour that he or she is told by somebody else

hometz *n* JUDAISM = **chametz**

home unit *n ANZ* = **unit** *n*. **6**

home video *n* a video recording produced at home, often a recording of family celebrations and events

homeward /hŏmwərd/ *adv* **homeward, homewards** in the direction of home ○ *homeward bound* ■ *adj* going home or in the direction of home

homework /hŏm wurk/ *n* **1 SCHOOL WORK DONE AT HOME** school work that pupils do at home or outside lesson times **2 PREPARATORY WORK** facts that are found out about a particular subject, especially in preparation for writing or talking about it (*informal*) **3 PAID WORK DONE AT HOME** work done at home for money, especially piecework — **homeworker** *n* —**homeworking** *n* ◇ **do your homework** to do all the necessary research and preparation for something in a thorough manner

homey[1] /hŏmi/ (**-ier, -iest**), **homy** (**-ier, -iest**) *adj* feeling as comfortable and familiar as somebody's own home ○ *a homey little hotel* —**homeyness** *n*

homey[2] /hŏmi/, **homie** (*plural* **-ies**) *n US* = **homeboy**, **homegirl** (*slang*) [Late 20C. Shortening and alteration.]

homicidal /hŏmmi sīd'l/ *adj* capable of or intending to kill another human being unlawfully —**homicidally** *adv*

homicide /hŏmmi sīd/ *n* **1** the act or an instance of unlawfully killing another human being **2** a killer of another human being unlawfully [13C. Via French < Latin *homicidium, homicida* < *homo* 'human being' + *caedere* 'kill'.]

homiletic /hŏmmi léttik/, **homiletical** /-léttik'l/ *adj* **1** relating to the art of writing and preaching sermons **2** relating to, or in the style of, a sermon or homily [Mid-17C. Via late Latin < Greek *homilētikos* < *homilein* 'associate with, converse' < *homilos* 'crowd'.] —**homiletically** *adv*

homiletics /hŏmmi léttiks/ *n* the art of writing and preaching sermons (+ *singular verb*)

homily /hŏmmili/ (*plural* **-lies**) *n* **1 RELIGIOUS LECTURE** a sermon on a moral or religious topic **2 MORALIZING SPEECH** a speech or other piece of writing with a moralizing theme **3 TALK BASED ON BIBLICAL PASSAGE** in the Roman Catholic Church, an address based on the Scriptures of the day [14C. Via Old French < Greek *homilia* 'sermon' < *homilos* 'crowd'.] —**homilist** *n*

homing /hŏming/ *adj* **1** relating to or possessing the ability to find the way home after travelling a long distance **2** describes a missile or aircraft that has equipment that enables it to guide itself to its target

homing guidance *n* a system that enables a missile or aircraft to guide itself to its target

homing pigeon *n* a pigeon, used in racing and carrying messages, that is trained to return to its roost

hominid /hŏmminid/ *n* a primate belonging to a family of which the modern human being is the only species still in existence. Family: Hominidae. [Late 19C. < modern Latin *Hominidae* < Latin *homin-*, stem of Latin *homo* 'human being'.] —**hominid** *adj*

hominization /hŏmmi nī záysh'n/, **hominisation** *n* the theorized evolutionary development of human characteristics that set hominids apart from other primates [Mid-20C. < French *hominisation* < Latin *homin-* (see HOMINID).]

hominoid /hŏmmi noyd/ *adj* **1** resembling a human being **2** belonging or relating to the superfamily that includes human beings and apes. Superfamily: Hominoidea. [Early 20C. < Latin *homin-* (see HOMINID).]

hominy /hŏmmini/ (*plural* **-nies**) *n US* dried hulled kernels of maize that are eaten boiled [Early 17C. Contraction of Virginia Algonquian *uskatahomen*.]

hominy grits *npl US* grits

homo /hŏmo/ (*plural* **-mos**) *n* an offensive term for a homosexual man (*dated slang*) [Early 20C. Shortening.]

homo- *prefix* alike, same ○ *homograph* [< Greek *homos* < Indo-European, 'one']

homocentric /hŏmo séntrik, hŏmmo-/ *adj* describes circles and spheres that have the same centre

homocercal /hŏmo súrk'l, hŏmmo-/ *adj* describes a fish that has a tail with two symmetrical lobes that extend beyond the end of the vertebral column, or a tail of this kind

homochromatic /hŏmo krō máttik, hŏmmo-/ *adj* = **monochromatic** *adj*. **1**

homocyclic /hŏmo síklik, hŏmmo-, -síklik/ *adj* describes a

chemical compound in which molecules take the form of a ring in which all the atoms are the same

homoeo- *prefix* = **homeo-**

homoeopathy *n* = **homeopathy**

homoeostasis *n* = **homeostasis**

homoeotherm *n* = **homeotherm**

Homo erectus /hŏmo i réktəss/ *n* an extinct ancestor of the modern human being (**Homo sapiens**) living approximately 1.5 million years ago and known by fossils to have had an upright stature, a smallish brain, and a low forehead [< modern Latin, 'upright man']

homoerotic /hŏmo i róttik, hŏmmō-/ *adj* relating to or characterized by homosexual eroticism

homoeroticism /hŏmo i róttisizəm/, **homoerotism** /hŏmo érrətizəm/ *n* eroticism that is focused on or inspired by people of the same sex

homogametic /hŏmogə méttik/ *adj* producing gametes that have the same type of sex chromosome

homogamy /ho móggəmi/ *n* the condition of a flower in which male and female organs mature at the same time —**homogamous** *adj*

homogenate /ho mójjənət, -nayt/ *n* a substance produced by homogenizing

homogeneity /hŏmōjə nee əti, hómmō-, -náyəti/ *n* **1** the quality of being of the same or a similar nature **2** the quality of having a uniform appearance or composition [Early 17C. < medieval Latin *homogeneitas* < *homogeneus* (see HOMOGENEOUS).]

homogeneous /hŏmə jéeni əss, hómmə-/, **homogenous** /ho mójjənəss/ *adj* **1** having the same kind of constituent elements **2** having a uniform composition or structure [Mid-17C. < medieval Latin *homogeneus* < Greek *homogenēs* 'of the same kind'.] —**homogeneously** *adv* —**homogeneousness** *n*

homogenize /ho mójjə nīz/ (**-nizes, -nizing, -nized**), **homogenise** (**-nises, -nising, -nised**) *v* **1** *vt* to emulsify the fat particles in milk or cream so as to give it an even consistency **2** *vti* to become or cause something to become homogeneous [Late 19C. < HOMOGENEOUS.] —**homogenization** /ho mójjə nī záysh'n/ *n* —**homogenizer** *n*

homogenous *adj* = **homogeneous**

homogeny /ho mójjəni/ *n* a similarity in individuals, organs, or parts caused by a common ancestry

homograft /hŏmma graaft/ *n* a graft of tissue from one organism to another of the same species. ◊ **allograft**

homograph /hŏmma graaf, -graf/ *n* a word that is spelt in the same way as one or more other words but is different in meaning, e.g. the verb 'project' and the noun 'project' —**homographic** /hŏmma gráffik/ *adj*

Homo habilis /hŏmo hábbiliss/ *n* an extinct ancestor of the modern human being (**Homo sapiens**) living approximately 1.5 million years ago and characterized by its ability to make and use tools [< modern Latin, 'skilful man']

homoio- *prefix* = **homeo-**

homoiotherm *n* ZOOL = **homeotherm**

Homoiousian /hŏm moy óossi ən/ *n* a Christian who believes that Jesus Christ is of a similar, but not identical, substance to God. ◊ **Homoousian** ■ *adj* relating to the doctrine of the Homoiousians. ◊ **Homoousian** [Late 17C. < Greek *homoiousios* 'of similar substance' < *homoios* 'similar' + *ousia* 'substance'.] —**Homoiousianism** *n*

homologate /ho mólla gayt/ (**-gates, -gating, -gated**) *v* **1** *vti* to confirm or sanction the validity of something **2** *vt* to give official recognition to a prototype car or car component, thus allowing it to be used in a motor race [Early 16C. < medieval Latin *homologat-*, past participle of *homologare* 'agree' < Greek *homologos* 'agreeing' (see HOMOLOGOUS).] —**homologation** /ho mólla gáysh'n/ *n*

homological *adj* = **homologous** —**homologically** *adv*

homologize /ho mólla jīz/ (**-gizes, -gizing, -gized**), **homologise** (**-gises, -gising, -gised**) *vt* to make something have a similar or related structure, position, function, or value to something else —**homologizer** *n*

homologous /ho móllagəss/ *adj* **1 SIMILAR** sharing a similar or related structure, position, function, or value **2 HAVING SAME ORIGIN BUT DIFFERENT FUNCTION** sharing the same origin but having a different function, as do, e.g., the wing of a bird and the fin of a fish **3 OF RELATED CHEMICAL COMPOUNDS** relating to a series of organic chemical compounds such as a methylene group, each of which differs from the preceding by the addition of a constant component **4 HAVING IDENTICAL TISSUE** produced from identical tissue [Mid-17C. < medieval Latin *homologus* < Greek *homologos* 'agreeing' < *homos* 'same' + *legein* 'speak'.]

homolographic /ho móllə gráffik, hómmələ-/ *adj* MAPS = **equal-area** [Mid-19C. Alteration (after HOMO-) of *homalographic* < Greek *homalos* 'even, level'.]

homologue /hómmə log/ *n* **1** a part or organ that has the same evolutionary origin as another but differs in function, e.g. a bird's wing in relation to the fin of a fish **2** a homologous chemical compound [Mid-19C. < French, < Greek *homologos* 'agreeing' (see HOMOLOGOUS).]

homology /ho mólləji/ *n* **1** similar characteristics in two animals that are a product of descent from a common ancestor rather than a product of a similar environment **2** the correspondence between chemical compounds in a homologous series [Early 17C. Via late Latin < Greek *homologia* 'agreement' < *homologos* (see HOMOLOGOUS.]

homolosine projection /ho móllə sīn-, hō-/ *n* a map of the Earth's surface that distorts the oceans in order to represent the continents with a minimum of distortion [< HOMOLOGRAPHIC + SINE, because it is a homolographic projection based on sinusoidal curves]

homolysis /ho mólləssiss, hō-/ *n* the breakdown of a molecule into neutral atoms or radicals —**homolytic** /hómmə líttik, hṓmə-/ *adj*

homonym /hómmənim/ *n* **1 WORD WITH SAME SPELLING OR SOUND** a word that is spelt or pronounced in the same way as one or more other words but has a different meaning. ◊ **homograph, homophone** *n.* 1 **2 SOMEBODY WITH SAME NAME** somebody with the same name as somebody else **3 DUPLICATE TAXONOMIC NAME** a taxonomic name that is the same as one already designating a different species or genus and cannot therefore be used [Late 17C. < Latin *homonymum* < Greek *homōnumos* (see HOMONYMOUS).] —**homonymic** /hómmə nímmik/ *adj* —**homonymity** *n* —**homonymy** /ho mónnimi/ *n*

homonymous /hə mónniməss/ *adj* **1** relating to homonyms, or in the form of a homonym ○ *The words 'peace' and 'piece' are homonymous.* **2** having the same name as somebody or something else [Early 17C. < Latin *homonymus* < Greek *homōnumos* 'having the same name' < *onuma* 'name'.] —**homonymously** *adv*

Homoousian /hṓmō óossi ən/ *n* a Christian who believes that Jesus Christ is of the same substance as God, in accordance with the Council of Nicaea's definition of the Trinity. ◊ **Homoiousian** ■ *adj* relating to the doctrine of the Homoousians. ◊ **Homoiousian** [Mid-16C. < Greek *homoousios* 'of the same substance' < *homos* 'same' + *ousia* 'substance'.] —**Homoousianism** *n*

homophile /hṓmō fīl, hómmō-/ *adj* **1 ADVOCATING HOMOSEXUAL AND LESBIAN RIGHTS** supporting the rights of homosexual men and lesbians and appreciating their culture **2 HOMOSEXUAL OR LESBIAN** relating to or being homosexual or lesbian ■ *n* **HOMOSEXUAL PERSON** a homosexual man or lesbian, or somebody who is sympathetic to homosexuals and lesbians and supports their rights

homophobia /hṓmō fṓbi ə, hómmō-/ *n* an irrational hatred, disapproval, or fear of homosexuality, homosexual men and lesbians, and their culture [Mid-20C. < HOMOSEXUAL.]

homophobic /hṓmō fṓbik, hómmō-/ *adj* showing an irrational hatred, disapproval, or fear of homosexuality, homosexual men and lesbians, and their culture —**homophobe** /hṓmō fōb, hómmə-/ *n*

homophone /hómmə fōn/ *n* **1** a word that is pronounced in the same way as one or more other words but is different in meaning and sometimes spelling, as are 'hair' and 'hare' **2** a letter or diphthong that has the same sound as one or more other letters or diphthongs [Early 17C. < Greek *homophōnos* 'having the same sound'.]

homophonic /hómmə fónnik/ *adj* **1** relating to part music in which the parts move together in simple harmonization **2** LING = **homophonous** *adj.* 1 —**homophonically** *adv*

homophonous /ho móffənəss/ *adj* **1** being the same in sound or pronunciation although different in meaning or spelling, as, e.g. 'pale' and 'pail' **2** MUSIC = **homophonic** *adj.* 1

homophony /hə móffəni/ *n* **1** the quality of having the same pronunciation as one or more other words with a different origin and meaning **2** music of a largely chordal style in which there is no independence of voice parts, but rather a simple harmonization of a melody [Mid-18C. < Greek *homophōnia* 'unison' < *homophōnos* 'having the same sound'.]

homoplastic /hṓmō plástik, hómmō-/ *adj* describes a tissue graft that is obtained from a member of the same species as the recipient —**homoplastically** *adv*

homopolar /hṓmō pṓlər, hómmō-/ *adj* having uniform polarity —**homopolarity** /-pō lárrəti/ *n*

homopteran /ho móptərən, hō-/ *n* an insect that has the ability to suck plant juices through its mouthparts, e.g. a cicada, scale insect, or aphid. Order: Homoptera. [Mid-19C. < modern Latin *Homoptera* < Greek *homos* 'same' + *pteron* 'wing'.] —**homopteran** *adj*

Homo sapiens /-sáppi enz, -sáypi-/ *n* the species of modern human beings, the only extant species of the family that also included other species named Homo. Family: Hominidae. [< modern Latin, 'wise man']

homoscedastic /hṓmōski dástik, hómmō-/ *adj* characterized by equal statistical variances [Early 20C. < HOMO- + Greek *skedastos* 'able to be scattered' < *skedannunai* 'scatter'.] —**homoscedasticity** /-ski dass tíssəti/ *n*

homosexual /hṓmō sékshoo əl, hómmə-/ *n* **SOMEBODY ATTRACTED TO SAME SEX** a person who is sexually attracted to members of his or her own sex ■ *adj* **1 ATTRACTED TO SAME SEX** sexually attracted to members of the same sex **2 OF HOMOSEXUALITY** relating to sexual attraction or activity among members of the same sex

homosexuality /hṓmō sék shoo álləti, hómmə-/ *n* sexual attraction to, and sexual relations with, members of the same sex

homotaxis /hṓmō táksiss, hómmō-/ *n* a similarity of composition, arrangement, or fossil content among rock strata of different ages or locations —**homotaxial** *adj* —**homotaxially** *adv* —**homotaxic** *adj*

homozygote /hṓmō zígōt, hómmō-/ *n* an organism that has two identical genes at the same place on two corresponding chromosomes —**homozygotic** /-zī góttik/ *adj*

homozygous /hṓmō zígəss, hómmō-/ *adj* having two identical genes at the corresponding loci of homologous chromosomes —**homozygously** *adv*

Homs /homz/ city in W Syria, on the River Orontes. Population: 540,133 (1994).

homunculus /ho múng kyŏŏləss/ (*plural* **-li** /-lī/), **homuncule** /-kyool/ *n* **1** a diminutive human being without any deformity of physiology **2** in early biological theory, the fully formed human being that was thought to exist inside an egg or spermatozoon [Mid-17C. < Latin, 'little person' < *homo* 'human being'.] —**homuncular** *adj*

homy *adj* = **homey**[2]

hon /hun/ *n US* a term of affection or endearment used to address somebody (*informal*) [Early 20C. Shortening of HONEY.]

hon. *abbr* **1** honorary **2** honourable

Hon. *abbr* Honourable

honan /hṓ nán/ *n* a rough-woven raw silk fabric, originally from China [Early 20C. After *Honan*, province of N China.]

honcho /hónchō/ *n* (*plural* **-chos**) *US* a person who dominates a project, situation, or other people (*slang*) ■ *vt* (**-chos, -choing, -choed**) *US* to manage or organize people or events (*slang*) ○ *He's the one who honchoed their election campaign.* [Mid-20C. < Japanese *hanchō* 'group leader'.]

Honda /hóndə/, **Soichiro** (1906–92) Japanese engineer and business executive

Honduras /hon dyŏŏrəss/ republic in Central America, with coastlines on the Caribbean Sea and the Pacific Ocean. Capital: Tegucigalpa. Population: 5,666,000 (1996). Area: 112,492 sq. km/43,433 sq. mi. —**Honduran** *adj, n*

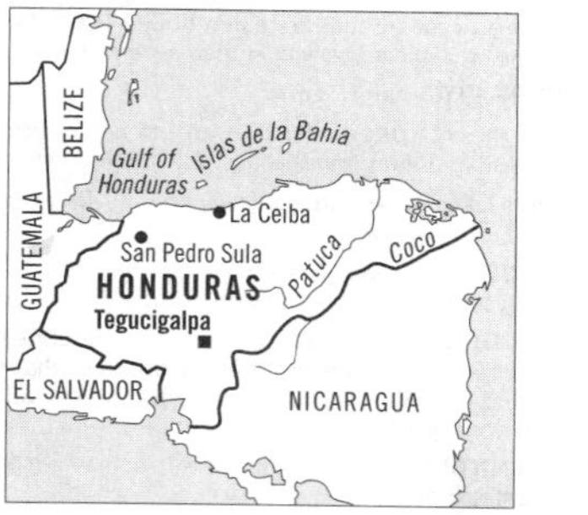

Honduras

Honduras, Gulf of inlet of the Caribbean Sea between S Belize, E Guatemala, and N Honduras

hone /hōn/ *vt* (**hones, honing, honed**) **1 IMPROVE WITH REFINEMENTS** to bring something to a state of increased intensity, excellence, or completion, especially over a period of time **2 SHARPEN ON WHETSTONE** to sharpen a blade on a fine whetstone ■ *n* **1 WHETSTONE** a fine-grained sedimentary rock used as a whetstone for sharpening razors and other cutting tools **2 MACHINE TOOL** a tool with a rotating abrasive head, used to bore holes [Old English *hān* 'whetstone' < Indo-European, 'sharpen'] —**honer** *n*

Honecker /hónnəkər/, **Erich** (1912–94) German statesman

Honegger /hónnigər/, **Arthur** (1892–1955) French composer

honest /ónnist/ *adj* **1 MORALLY UPRIGHT** never cheating, lying, or breaking the law **2 TRUTHFUL OR TRUE** expressing or embodying the truth **3 IMPARTIAL** presenting information in an impartial way **4 REASONABLE IN A PARTICULAR SITUATION** reasonable and acceptable, given the circumstances ○ *an honest mistake* **5 UNPRETENTIOUS** having simple manners and no pretensions ○ *honest country folk* **6 RESPECTABLE** respectable and virtuous (*dated*) [13C. Via Old French < Latin *honestus* 'honourable' < *honos* 'honour'.] —**honestness** *n* ◇ **honest to God** *or* **goodness 1** used to express surprise or shock **2** used to emphasize the truth of a statement

honest broker *n* a person, country, or organization that mediates in disputes [Translation of German *ehrlicher Makler*, describing Otto von BISMARCK]

honestly /ónnistli/ *adv* **1 FAIRLY OR JUSTLY** in a way that is fair, just, truthful, and morally upright **2 GENUINELY** really and truly ○ *Can you honestly say that you care?* ■ *interj* **USED TO EXPRESS SURPRISE** used to express surprise, annoyance, or disapproval

honest-to-God, honest-to-goodness *adj* completely real or authentic (*informal*) ○ *You made a real, honest-to-God mess of that.*

honesty /ónnisti/ (*plural* **-ties**) *n* **1 MORAL UPRIGHTNESS** the quality, condition, or characteristic of being fair, just, truthful, and morally upright **2 TRUTHFULNESS** truthfulness, candour, or sincerity ○ *In all honesty, I really didn't know.* **3 PLANT** a hardy plant with flat silvery seed pods that are often used for indoor decoration. Flowers: purplish or white. Native to: Europe. *Lunaria annua.*

honewort /hṓn wurt/ *n* a perennial plant. Flowers: small white, in clusters. Native to: Europe. *Trinia glauca.* [Mid-17C. *Hone* < ?]

honey /húnni/ *n* **1 SWEET SUBSTANCE MADE BY BEES** a sweet sticky golden-brown fluid produced by bees from the nectar of flowers. Use: in cooking, spread on bread. **2 SWEET SUBSTANCE MADE BY OTHER INSECTS** a sweet sticky substance produced from nectar by insects other than bees **3** *US, Can* **AFFECTIONATE TERM OF ADDRESS** a term of affection or endearment used to address somebody (*informal*) **4** *US* **SOMEBODY VERY NICE** an endearing or lovable person (*informal*) **5** *US* **SOMETHING EXTREMELY GOOD** an object, situation, or idea that is exceptionally good (*informal*) ○ *That's a honey of a motorboat!* **6 YELLOWISH-BROWN COLOUR** a yellowish-brown colour ■ *vt* (**-eys, -eying, -eyed** *or* **-ied**) *US* **TALK FLATTERINGLY TO** to talk to somebody in an affectionate and flattering way, especially insincerely and for selfish reasons (*informal*) [Old English *hunig* < Germanic] —**honey** *adj*

honey badger *n* = **ratel** [< its fondness for honey]

honey bear *n* = **kinkajou** [< its practice of sucking honey from the nests of bees]

honeybee /húnni bee/ *n* a honey-producing bee that lives in organized groups and has been domesticated for its honey and beeswax since ancient times. *Apis mellifera.*

honeybun /húnni bun/, **honeybunch** /-bunch/ *n US, Can* a term of affection or endearment used to address somebody (*informal*)

honey-buzzard *n* a bird of prey that feeds on honey from bees' nests. Native to: Europe. *Perno apivorus.*

honeycomb /húnni kōm/ *n* **1 STRUCTURE OF SIX-SIDED CELLS** a collection of hexagonal cells constructed of wax by bees inside a hive or nest in which honey is stored, eggs are laid, and larvae develop **2 CELLS CONTAINING HONEY EATEN**

AS FOOD a structure made up of waxy hexagonal cells containing honey that is extracted from a bees' hive or nest and eaten by animals and humans **3 SOMETHING RESEMBLING HONEYCOMB** an object resembling a honeycomb in pattern or structure, especially by consisting of a network of hexagons **4 HONEYCOMB-PATTERNED FABRIC** a soft fabric woven in a pattern of ridges and hollows like those in a honeycomb. Use: towels, bedcovers. ■ *vt* **1 PROVIDE WITH HOLES** to fill a wall, cliff, or structure with many cavities **2 INFILTRATE THOROUGHLY** to infiltrate a place or organization thoroughly ○ *an intelligence agency honeycombed by double agents* —**honeycombed** *adj*

honey creeper *n* **1** a small bird with brightly-coloured plumage and a long slender beak for sucking nectar from flowers. Native to: tropical America. Family: Coerebidae. **2** a bird that resembles the honey creeper of tropical America. Native to: Hawaii. Family: Drepanididae.

honeydew /húnni dyoo/ *n* **1** a sweet sticky substance deposited on leaves by aphids and certain other insects as a by-product of the juices they suck from plants **2** a sweet sticky substance produced by the leaves of some plants **3** FOOD = **honeydew melon** [< the belief that the substance was distilled from the air like dew] —**honeydewed** *adj*

honeydew melon *n* a melon with sweet green flesh and a smooth greenish-white rind. *Cucumis melo.*

honeyeater /húnni eetər/ *n* a slender bird, with a long beak and a long brush-tipped tongue for extracting nectar from flowers. Native to: Australia to Hawaii. Family: Meliphagidae.

honeyed /húnnid/, **honied** *adj* **1 INGRATIATING** intended to flatter or soothe **2 PLEASANT-SOUNDING** sweet and pleasant to hear **3 SWEETENED WITH HONEY** containing or sweetened with honey —**honeyedly** *adv*

honey fungus *n* a destructive fungus that grows at the base of trees, with a golden or brown cap and black spreading filaments (**hyphae**). *Armillaria mellea.* [< its colour]

honey guide *n* **1** a small bird that feeds on the wax and larvae remaining after people or animals have removed the honey from bees' nests. Native to: tropical African and Asian forests. Family: Indicatoridae. **2** dots or lines on the perianth of a flower that guide insects towards the nectar

honey locust *n* a thorny tree with compound leaves and pods containing a sweet pulp. Native to: E North America. Genus: *Gleditsia.*

honeymoon /húnni moon/ *n* **1** a holiday taken by a newly-married couple, usually immediately following the wedding or reception **2** a short period of harmony or goodwill at the beginning of a relationship, especially in politics or business [Originally 'waning affection', from the idea that although married love is at first as sweet as honey, it soon wanes like the moon] —**honeymoon** *vi* —**honeymooner** *n*

honey mouse *n* a small Australian marsupial with a very long snout adapted for feeding on pollen and honey, a long tail, and light brown fur with dark stripes. *Tarsipes spenserae.*

honey myrtle *n* a hardy shrub with pink or purple flowers in hairy spikes. Native to: Australia. Genus: *Melaleuca.*

honeysuckle /húnni suk'l/ *n* **1 CLIMBING SHRUB WITH FRAGRANT FLOWERS** a climbing shrub having twining stems. Flowers: fragrant, tubular with spreading twin-petal lobes. Genus: *Lonicera.* **2 AUSTRALIAN PLANT** a plant with large woody seed cones. Flowers: yellow, orange, red, grey, and green, spike-shaped clusters. Native to: Australia. Genus: *Banksia.* **3** *Ireland* **FUCHSIA** a fuchsia plant [< the belief that bees suck honey from it]

honeysuckle ornament *n* = **anthemion**

honey-sweet *adj* sounding or appearing sweet and attractive

hongi /hóng ee/ *n NZ* a Maori greeting in which two people rub noses [Mid-19C. < Maori.]

Hong Kong /hóng kóng/ special administrative region on the SE coast of China. It is a port and major commercial centre. Capital: Victoria. Population: 6,189,800 (1995). Area: 1,092 sq. km/422 sq. mi.

Hong Kong English *n* a variety of English spoken in Hong Kong

honied *adj* = **honeyed**

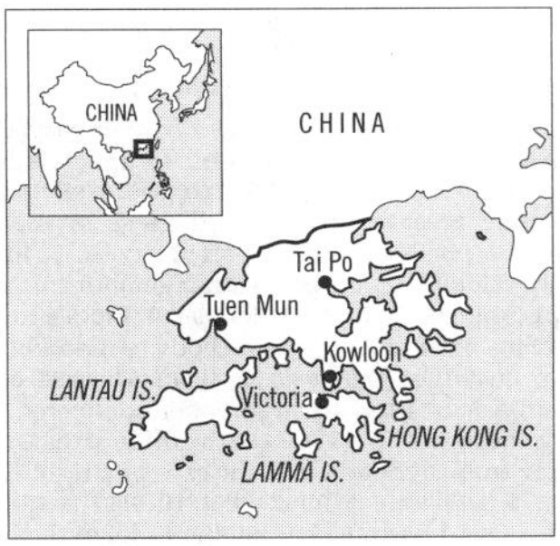

Hong Kong

honi soit qui mal y pense /ónni swaá kee mál ee pónss/ the French motto of the Order of the Garter, meaning 'shame upon him who thinks evil of it' [< French]

Honiton lace /hónnitən-, húnni-/, **Honiton** *n* lace with a pattern of sprigs of flowers [After *Honiton* in Devon]

honk /hongk/ *n* **1 CRY OF GOOSE** the raucous sound made by a goose **2 SOUND OF CAR HORN** the sound made by a car horn **3 SOUND RESEMBLING GOOSE OR CAR HORN** any sound, e.g. a laugh or a blowing of the nose, that resembles the sound made by a goose or a car horn ■ *v* **1** *vi* **PRODUCE HONK** to let out or give out a honk **2** *vti* **SOUND CAR HORN** to cause a car horn to make a honk [Mid-19C. An imitation of the sound.]

honker /hóngkər/ *n* **1** a person, animal, or object, e.g. a goose or a car horn, that makes a honking sound **2** a nose, especially a large one (*informal*)

honky /hóngki/ (*plural* **-kies**), **honkie** (*plural* **-kies**), **honkey** (*plural* **-keys**) *n US* an offensive term that deliberately insults a white person (*slang*) [Mid-20C. < ?]

honky-tonk /hóngki tongk/ *n* **1** *US* **CHEAP NIGHTCLUB** a cheap, noisy, and often disreputable bar or nightclub (*slang*) **2 RAGTIME PIANO-PLAYING** a style of ragtime with a heavy beat, usually played on an upright piano with a tinny sound **3 COUNTRY MUSIC** a style of country music associated with honky-tonks ○ *honky-tonk blues* ■ *vi US* **VISIT HONKY-TONKS** to frequent cheap noisy bars and nightclubs [Late 19C. < ?]

Honolulu /hónnə lóo loo/ capital of Hawaii, on the S coast of Oahu Island. Population: 395,789 (1998 estimate).

honor *n, vt* US = **honour**

honorarium /ónnə ráiri əm/ (*plural* **-ums** *or* **-a** /-ə/) *n* an amount of money paid to somebody, especially a professional person, for providing a service [Mid-17C. < Latin, 'gift made on being admitted to a post of honour' < *honor-* (see HONOUR).]

SYNONYMS See ***wage***.

honorary /ónnərəri/ *adj* **1 AWARDED AS HONOUR** given, elected, or awarded for outstanding service or distinguished achievements, rather than for the completion of formal educational or legal requirements **2 SYMBOLIZING HONOUR CONFERRED** representing the bestowal of an honour or distinction on somebody **3 UNPAID** holding an office awarded as an honour and receiving no payment for services provided in that office **4 NOT LEGALLY ENFORCEABLE** dependent on somebody's sense of honour and honesty for fulfilment, rather than on a legal agreement

honorific /ónnə ríffik/ *adj* **CONFERRING HONOUR** given as a mark of distinction, esteem, or respect ■ *n* **1 TITLE OF RESPECT** a title of respect, e.g. 'The Honourable', used in speech or writing **2 GRAMMATICAL FORM ACKNOWLEDGING INFERIORITY** a phrase or word, e.g. a pronoun or a verb inflection, that is used to show respect to somebody of a higher status

honoris causa /ho náwriss kówzə/ *adv* as a mark of honour ○ *a doctorate in humane letters conferred honoris causa* [< Latin, 'for the sake of honour']

honour /ónnər/ *n* **1 PERSONAL INTEGRITY** strong moral character or strength, and adherence to ethical principles ○ *It's a matter of honour.* **2 RESPECT** great respect and admiration **3 DIGNITY** personal dignity that sometimes leads to recognition and glory ○ *Although defeated, he accepted the loss with honour* **4 REPUTATION** somebody's good name or good reputation ○ *My honour is at stake.* **5 WOMAN'S REPUTATION** a woman's virginity or reputation for chastity (*dated*) **6 SOURCE OF PRIDE** somebody or something that brings respect or glory and is a source of pride to somebody or something else ○ *Your achievements are an honour to your parents and school.* **7 MARK OF DISTINCTION** something such as a gift, award, or gesture that signifies high achievement or respect **8 GREAT PRIVILEGE** a special privilege that is cherished, e.g. an opportunity to be introduced to somebody admired or respected or an opportunity to serve a worthy cause ○ *It is indeed an honour to have you here today.* **9 MEN'S CODE OF INTEGRITY** a code of integrity in some societies, e.g. in feudal Europe and medieval Japan, that men upheld by force of arms **10 RIGHT TO TEE OFF FIRST** the right to drive off first from the tee in golf ■ *npl* **1 honours, Honours ACADEMIC DISTINCTION** official recognition of academic excellence given to students by colleges and universities at graduation **2 honours HIGHEST CARDS** four or five of the highest cards, especially the ace, king, queen, jack, and ten of the trump suit ■ *vt* **1 ESTEEM** to have or show great respect and admiration for somebody or something **2 EXALT** to recognize somebody publicly or elevate somebody's status officially, usually by giving that person a title or an award **3 PAY TRIBUTE TO** to praise publicly and pay respect to somebody who has died **4 DIGNIFY** to give prestige to somebody or something such as an occasion by choosing to appear, accompany, or take part **5 TREAT SOMETHING AS MONEY** to accept a cheque or other financial instrument as money or as a substitute for money and pay it when it is due ○ *The bank won't honour a cheque without a signature.* **6 KEEP PROMISE** to keep a promise, or fulfil the terms of an agreement or contract **7 BOW TO PARTNER** to bow to another dancer in square dancing [12C. Via Old French < Latin *honor-*, stem of *honos.*] —**honoree** /ónnə rée/ *n* —**honourer** /ónnərər/ *n* —**honourless** *adj* ◇ **do somebody the honour of doing something** to make somebody feel proud and pleased by agreeing to do something for that person (*formal*) ○ *Will you do me the honour of dancing the last waltz with me?* ◇ **do the honours** to act as host or hostess by doing something for a group of guests, e.g. pouring wine, carving meat, or cutting a cake (*informal*) ◇ **honour bound** obliged by a promise or ethical principles to do something ◇ **in honour of somebody** *or* **something** in recognition of or for the glorification of somebody or something ○ *I'd like to propose a toast in honour of the bride and groom.* ◇ **on your honour 1** staking your reputation on something ○ *On my honour, I will tell the truth.* **2** being trusted to act in a particular way ○ *You are on your honour to behave well.*

Honour *n* used as a form of address to a judge ○ *Your Honour, may we approach the bench?*

honourable /ónnərəb'l/ *adj* **1 HAVING PERSONAL INTEGRITY** guided by, or with a reputation for having, strong moral and ethical principles **2 DESERVING OR GAINING HONOUR** worthy of or winning honour, respect, recognition, or glory **3 MORALLY UPRIGHT** upright and moral in intent (*formal*) ○ *I hope his intentions are honourable.* —**honourability** /ónnərə bílləti/ *n* —**honourableness** /ónnərəb'lnəss/ *n* —**honourably** *adv*

Honourable *adj* **1** used as a title of respect before somebody's name to indicate entitlement to respect because of an official position held or to address a parliamentary colleague ○ *My Honourable friend has spoken on this matter before.* **2** used as a courtesy title in the United Kingdom for the children of some members of the aristocracy

honourable discharge *n* an official dismissal from the armed forces, signifying that all duties have been honourably fulfilled

honourable mention *n* an official or public commendation, usually granted to somebody who has done well in a competition but not actually won an award

Honour Moderations *npl* at Oxford University, the first set of public examinations in some subjects according to which students are awarded first, second, or third class honours

Honours List *n* a list of individuals who have been or are to be awarded honours such as a peerage or membership of a chivalric order by the British monarch

honours of war *npl* **1** certain privileges that are accorded members of a defeated army **2** marks of respect paid by troops at the burial of another soldier

honour system *n* a system under which people are relied on to be honest without direct supervision

Hons *abbr* Honours

Hon. Sec. *abbr* Honorary Secretary

Honshu /hón shoo/ largest and most populous island of Japan. Population: 99,254,194 (1990). Area: 230,940 sq. km/89,166 sq. mi.

hooch[1] /hooch/, **hootch** *n US* cheap alcohol, especially illegally distilled spirits (*slang*) [Late 19C. Shortening of *hoochinoo*, after *Hoochinoo*, Tlingit village in Alaska.]

hooch[2] /hooch/ *interj Scotland* used to express exhilaration in traditional Scottish dancing

Hooch /hooch/, **Pieter de** (1629–84) Dutch painter

hood[1] /ho͝od/ *n* 1 **COVERING FOR HEAD** a loose covering for the head that is usually attached to the neck of a coat 2 **COVER FOR DEVICE** a cover for an appliance or machine, or a device such as a camera lens 3 *US* AUTOMOT = **bonnet** *n.* 2 4 **PART OF ACADEMIC ROBE** an ornamental piece of cloth, often trimmed with fur or luxurious fabric, that hangs from the shoulders of an academic robe to indicate the status of the wearer 5 **FOLDING ROOF** the folding roof of a carriage, pram, or convertible car 6 **COVER FOR CHIMNEY** a fixed or revolving cover fitted to the top of a chimney to prevent downdraught 7 **HEAD COVERING FOR FALCON** a bag placed over the head of a falcon to keep it calm when it is not hunting 8 **MARKING ON ANIMAL'S HEAD** a crest, marking, or other conspicuous part on the head of an animal ■ *vt* **COVER WITH HOOD** to cover the head of a person, animal, or bird with a hood [Old English *hōd* < Indo-European, 'to cover'] —**hoodless** *adj* —**hood-like** *adj*

hood[2] /ho͝od/ *n US* a hoodlum (*slang*) [Late 19C. Shortening.]

Hood /ho͝od/, **Samuel, 1st Viscount** (1724–1816) British admiral

-hood *suffix* 1 quality, state, condition ○ *knighthood* 2 a group of people ○ *brotherhood* 3 time, stage of life ○ *adulthood* [Old English *-hād* < Germanic]

hooded /ho͝oddid/ *adj* 1 **COVERED BY A HOOD** covered by or having a hood 2 **PARTLY HIDDEN** partly concealed or covered ○ *dark, hooded eyes* 3 **HAVING CREST** having a crest, markings, or a specialized structure on the head —**hoodedness** *n*

hooded crow *n* a crow that is a subspecies of the carrion crow with a black head, tail, and wings, and a grey body. Native to: Europe, Asia. *Corvus corone cornix.*

hooded seal *n* a large grey-spotted seal, the mature male of which has an inflatable sac near its nose. Native to: the North Atlantic and Arctic oceans. *Cystophora cristata.*

hoodie crow /ho͝odi-/, **hoodie** /ho͝odi/ *n Scotland* a hooded crow [Late 18C. < *hooded.*]

hoodlum /ho͝odləm/ *n* 1 a petty criminal or gangster, especially one prone to violence 2 a young person who is violent or prone to committing crimes [Late 19C. < ?] —**hoodlumish** *adj* —**hoodlumism** *n*

hood mould *n* CONSTR = **dripstone** *n.* 1

hoodoo /ho͞o doo/ *n* (*plural* **-doos**) 1 RELIG = **voodoo** *n.* 2 2 **BAD LUCK** bad luck or misfortune 3 **BRINGER OF BAD LUCK** somebody or something believed to bring bad luck ■ *vt* (**-doos, -dooing, -dooed**) **BE JINX TO** to appear to bring bad luck or misfortune to somebody or something [Late 19C. < ?] —**hoodooism** *n*

hoodwink /ho͝od wingk/ *vt* to deceive or dupe somebody, especially by being clever or cunning —**hoodwinker** *n*

hooey /ho͞o i/ *n* empty or nonsensical talk or ideas (*informal*) [Early 20C. < ?]

hoof /hoof, ho͝of/ *n* (*plural* **hooves** /hoovz, ho͝ovz/ *or* **hoofs**) 1 **FOOT OF HORNY MATERIAL** the foot of a horse, deer, cow, or similar animal, covered with horny material 2 **HORNY COVERING OF FOOT** the horny material covering the feet of animals such as horses, deer, and cattle 3 **ANIMAL WITH HOOVES** an animal such as a horse, deer, or cow that has hooves 4 **HUMAN FOOT** the foot of a human being (*slang humorous*) ■ *vt* 1 **TRAVEL DISTANCE ON FOOT** to walk a specified distance (*slang*) 2 **KICK** to kick or trample a person or animal [Old English *hōf* < Indo-European] —**hoofless** *adj* ◇ **hoof it** 1 to walk (*slang*) 2 to dance (*slang*) ◇ **on the hoof** 1 describes an animal that is alive and has not yet been butchered 2 without sufficient thought or attention (*informal*) 3 while moving around or doing something else (*informal*) ○ *eating lunch on the hoof*

hoofed /hooft, ho͝oft/, **hooved** /hoovd, ho͝ovd/ *adj* having hooves or with hooves of a specific size and type

hoofer /ho͞ofər, ho͝ofər/ *n US* a professional dancer, especially a tap dancer (*slang*)

hoofprint /ho͝of print, ho͝of-/ *n* an imprint of an animal's hoof

hoo-hah /ho͞o haa/, **hoo-ha** *n* a loud noisy fuss, controversy, or disturbance (*slang*) [Mid-20C. Probably < Yiddish *hu-ha*, an imitation of the sound.]

hook /ho͝ok/ *n* 1 **BENT PIECE OF METAL** a bent or curved piece of metal or other material, used to attach, suspend, fasten, or lift another object 2 **SOMETHING RESEMBLING HOOK** something resembling a curved piece of metal, especially a plant or animal part 3 FISHING = **fishhook** 4 AGRIC = **sickle** *n.* 1 5 **SNARE** a stratagem for trapping or snaring somebody 6 **SOMETHING THAT ATTRACTS** a means of attracting or interesting somebody, especially a potential customer (*informal*) 7 **SHORT SWINGING BLOW** in boxing, a short blow to an opponent delivered with a swing and a bent arm 8 **GOLF SHOT** a golf shot that swerves sharply from right to left in the case of a right-handed player 9 BASKETBALL = **hook shot** 10 **SHOT IN CRICKET** in cricket, a shot with the bat held parallel to the ground that sends the ball towards the leg side 11 **CREST OF WAVE** the crest of a wave that is about to break 12 **ACT OF RESTRAINING ICE HOCKEY PLAYER** the act of using an ice hockey stick to prevent another player from moving freely 13 **PART OF LETTER** in writing or printing, a short curve of a letter that extends above or below the line ○ *the hook of the 'g'* 14 **CATCHY REFRAIN** a pleasing and easily remembered refrain in a pop song ■ *v* 1 *vti* **FASTEN WITH HOOK** to fasten by means of hooks or hooks and eyes 2 *vt* **ATTACH ONE THING TO ANOTHER** to attach one thing to another by means of a specially designed mechanical device ○ *hook the trailer to the car* 3 *vti* **BEND LIKE HOOK** to curve or cause something to curve in the shape of a hook ○ *The road hooks sharply to the left.* 4 *vt* **ENSNARE** to catch or ensnare something using a hook 5 *vt* **CATCH ATTENTION** to attract and hold somebody's interest or attention 6 *vt* **MAKE ADDICTED** to cause somebody to become addicted or dependent on something, especially a drug (*slang*) 7 *vt* **HIT WITH CURVING BLOW** in boxing, to deliver a sharp curving blow to an opponent, using a curved or bent arm 8 *vt* **STRIKE SWERVING BALL** in golf, to strike the ball so that it swerves sharply from right to left in the case of a right-handed player 9 *vt* **SHOOT BASKETBALL** in basketball, to shoot the ball by sweeping the hand upwards and farther away from the basket while moving sideways towards the basket 10 *vt* **KICK BALL BACKWARDS** in rugby, to kick the ball backwards out of a scrum to the scrum half 11 *vt* **STRIKE CRICKET BALL** in cricket, to strike the ball towards the leg side with the bat held parallel to the ground 12 *vt* **RESTRAIN PLAYER WITH STICK** to use an ice hockey stick to prevent another player from moving freely 13 *vi* **BE PROSTITUTE** to work as a prostitute (*slang*) 14 *vt* **GORE** to gore a person or animal with the horns or tusks 15 *vt* **CUT WITH SICKLE** to cut grass or similar plants with a sickle 16 *vt* **MAKE RUG** to make a rug by pulling pieces of wool through holes in stiff canvas using a special hook 17 *vt* **STEAL** to seize and steal something (*slang*) [Old English *hōc* < Indo-European, 'hook, tooth'] —**hookless** *adj* ◇ **by hook or by crook** by some means or other ◇ **hook it** to run away (*dated slang*) ◇ **hook, line, and sinker** to a complete and total degree (*informal*) ○ *They fell for the story hook, line, and sinker.* ◇ **off the hook** 1 free of a difficult situation (*informal*) 2 with the receiver off its cradle so that no telephone calls can be received ◇ **sling your hook** to go away (*slang; usually a command*)

hook up *v* 1 *vt* to connect two or more electronic devices ○ *Is the microphone hooked up?* 2 *vti* to meet and become associated, or cause somebody to meet and become associated with somebody else (*informal*)

hookah /ho͝okə/ *n* an Asian pipe for smoking tobacco or marijuana, consisting of a flexible tube with a mouthpiece attached to a container of water through which smoke is drawn and cooled [Mid-18C. Via Urdu < Arabic *ḥuḳḳa* 'jar'.]

hook and eye (*plural* **hooks and eyes**) *n* 1 a fastening for clothes consisting of a small hook inserted into a metal or thread loop 2 *US* a latch for a gate or door consisting of a metal hook inserted into a screw eye

hookcheck *n* ICE HOCKEY = **hook** *n.* 12

Hooke /ho͝ok/, **Robert** (1635–1703) British scientist and architect

hooked /ho͝okt/ *adj* 1 **SHAPED LIKE HOOK** bent or shaped like a hook 2 **HAVING HOOK AT END** ending in a hook 3 **MADE USING YARN HOOK** made by hooking yarn through canvas 4 **ADDICTED** addicted to a drug (*slang*) 5 **OBSESSED WITH** in love with, compulsively attracted to, or obsessed with somebody or something (*slang*)

hooker[1] /ho͝okər/ *n* an offensive term for a prostitute (*slang*) [Mid-19C. < ?]

hooker[2] /ho͝okər/ *n* 1 a person, animal, or object that catches something by hooking it 2 a front row forward who hooks the ball out of the scrum

hooker[3] /ho͝okər/ *n* 1 a commercial fishing vessel that uses hooks and lines instead of nets 2 a large cargo boat with several sails, formerly used off the western coast of Ireland and now used as a pleasure craft [Mid-17C. < Dutch *hoeker*, shortening of Middle Dutch *hoeckboot* 'fishing boat' < *hoec* 'fish-hook'.]

Hooker /ho͝okər/, **Joseph** (1814–79) US general. Known as **Fighting Joe**

hookey *n* = **hooky**

hooknose /ho͝ok nōz/ *n* a nose with a noticeable curve, like an eagle's beak —**hooknosed** *adj*

Hook of Holland /ho͝ok əv hólland/ 1 cape of the SW Netherlands, on the North Sea. Dutch **Hoek van Holland** 2 port on the Hook of Holland

hook shot *n* in basketball, a shot that is made by sweeping the hand upwards and farther away from the basket while moving sideways towards the basket

hook-tip *n* a moth that has forewings ending in a hooked point. Genus: *Daepana.*

hookup /ho͝ok up/ *n* 1 **LINK BETWEEN SOURCE AND USER** a connection allowing a user access to a utility such as electricity, gas, or water ○ *a gas hookup* 2 **ELECTRONIC SYSTEM** a number of items of electronic equipment designed to operate together (*informal*) 3 **RELATIONSHIP** an alliance between people, groups, or things, especially an unlikely one (*informal*) ○ *a bizarre hookup between political enemies over an issue* 4 **CATCH IN OFFSHORE FISHING** in offshore big game fishing, an act of catching a fish on the end of the line

hookworm /ho͝ok wurm/ *n* 1 a blood-sucking, disease-causing nematode worm that bores through the skin, attaching itself to the intestinal walls with its hooked mouthparts. Family: Ancylostomatidae. 2 MED = **ancylostomiasis**

hookworm disease *n* MED = **ancylostomiasis**

hooky /ho͝oki/, **hookey** *n* absence, especially from school, without permission (*informal*) [Mid-19C. < ?] ◇ **play hooky** to be absent without permission, especially from school (*informal*)

hooley /ho͞oli/ (*plural* **-leys**) *n NZ, Ireland* a noisy merry party (*informal*) [Late 19C. < ?]

hooligan /ho͞oligən/ *n* an aggressive young man, especially one acting as part of a group, who commits acts of vandalism and violence in public places (*informal*) [Late 19C. < ?]

hooliganism /ho͞oligənizəm/ *n* acts of vandalism and violence in public places, committed especially by youths

hoop /hoop/ *n* 1 **RING HOLDING BARREL TOGETHER** the metal or wooden ring used to hold the staves of a barrel in place 2 **LARGE RING-SHAPED TOY** a large light ring of wood, metal, or plastic used as a toy or exercise aid 3 **PAPER-COVERED RING** a large light ring, often with paper stretched over it, through which circus animals or performers jump 4 **SUPPORT FOR SKIRT** a lightweight cane, wire, or whalebone ring, or a structure made of several such rings, used, especially formerly, to stiffen a woman's skirt or petticoat 5 **WIDE STIFF SKIRT** a petticoat or skirt stiffened by rings 6 **BAND FOR EMBROIDERY FABRIC** either of a pair of wooden or metal bands used to keep fabric taut when it is being embroidered 7 **EARRING** an earring formed from a continuous ring of metal 8 **PART OF FINGER RING** the part of a ring that the finger fits through 9 **RING HOLDING NET IN BASKETBALL** in basketball, the metal ring from which an open-bottomed net is suspended, through which the ball is thrown in order to score points 10 **CROQUET HOOP** in croquet, a metal arch through which the ball is driven ■ *vt* **PUT HOOP ROUND** to surround something with a hoop or band [Old English *hōp* < W Germanic] ◇ **jump** *or* **go through hoops (for somebody)** to go to extreme lengths to gain favour with somebody or to carry out somebody's wishes (*informal*)

hooper /ho͞opər/ *n* a maker or repairer of barrels

hoopla[1] /ho͞op laa/ *n* a fairground game in which a player tries to throw a small hoop over a prize in order to win it [Early 20C. < HOOP, influenced by HOOPLA[2].]

hoopla[2] /ho͞op laa/ *n US* 1 **LOUD CELEBRATION** noisy excited commotion or joyous celebrating (*informal*) 2 **GREAT PUBLIC UPROAR** a great amount of public fuss, commotion, or uproar with attendant publicity or media interest (*slang*) 3 **MISLEADING TALK** intentionally misleading talk or propaganda (*informal*) [Late 19C. < ?]

Hoopoe

hoopoe /hoö poo/ (*plural* **-poes** *or* **-poe**) *n* a bird with a pinkish-brown head and back, a very prominent crest, a downward-curving bill, and a loud cry. Native to: Europe, Asia. *Upupa epops.* [Mid-17C. Alteration of *hoop*, via Old French *huppe* < Latin *upupa*, an imitation of the bird's cry.]

hoop pine *n* a timber tree with rough bark. Native to: Australia. *Araucaria cunninghamii.*

hoop skirt *n* a long full skirt held out in the shape of a bell by a series of connected hoops, fashionable in the 18th and early 19th centuries

hoop snake *n* any harmless North American snake such as the mud snake that was once believed to be able to take its tail in its mouth and roll along like a hoop

hooray /hoö ráy/, **hurray** /hə ráy, hoö ráy/ *interj* used as a shout of happy excitement, victory, or jubilation ■ *n* a shout of happy excitement, victory, or jubilation [Late 17C. Alteration of HURRAH.]

Hooray Henry /hoö ray hénnri/ *n* a young upper-class man, generally educated at public school, who wears conservative clothes and behaves and speaks in a loud, extrovert manner (*informal*)

hoosegow /hoöss gow/ *n US* a jail (*slang*) [Early 20C. Via Mexican Spanish *juzgado* < Spanish *juzgado* 'courtroom' < past participle of *juzgar* 'judge' < Latin *judicare* (see JUDICATURE).]

hoot /hoot/ *n* **1** OWL'S CRY the long sad-sounding cry of some owls **2** SOUND LIKE OWL'S CRY a sound similar to an owl's cry, e.g. the sound made by a train whistle or car horn **3** LAUGHING SOUND a cry, especially of laughter, derision, or scorn **4** SOMEBODY OR SOMETHING HILARIOUS a highly amusing person, object, or situation (*slang*) ■ *v* **1** *vi* EMIT HOOT to emit or produce a hoot **2** *vi* MAKE LAUGHING SOUND to utter a sound of laughter, derision, or scorn **3** SOUND CAR HORN to cause a car horn to make a hoot **4** *vt* DRIVE PERFORMER OFF STAGE to drive a public performer or speaker off a stage by jeering **5** *vt* EXPRESS FEELING WITH JEERS to express a feeling such as contempt, derision, or scorn by jeering [12C. < ?] ◇ **not care** *or* **give a hoot** to show no interest or concern for something (*informal*)

hootch *n* = **hooch**[1]

hootenanny /hoöt'n anni/ (*plural* **-nies**) *n US* (*informal*) **1** an informal or impromptu performance by folk singers, in which the audience participates **2** an object or gadget for which the name is not known [Early 20C. < ?]

hooter /hoötər/ *n* **1** SOMEBODY OR SOMETHING THAT HOOTS a person, animal, or object that hoots, especially a horn **2** LARGE NOSE a nose, especially a large one (*slang humorous*) ■ **hooters** *npl US* OFFENSIVE TERM an offensive term for a woman's breasts, especially when large (*slang*)

hoot owl *n* an owl with a hooting call

hoots /hoots/ *interj Scotland* used to express impatience, disbelief, or annoyance (*informal*)

hooved *adj* = **hoofed**

Hoover /hoövər/ *tdmk* a trademark for a vacuum cleaner

Hoover /hoövər/, **Herbert** (1874–1964) US statesman and 31st president of the United States (1929–33)

Hoover /hoövər/, **J. Edgar** (1895–1972) US lawyer

Hoover Dam dam on the Colorado River, on the Arizona-Nevada border. Height: 221 m/726 ft.

hooves *plural* of **hoof**

hop[1] /hop/ *v* (**hops, hopping, hopped**) **1** *vi* JUMP LIGHTLY ON ONE FOOT to jump lightly or quickly, especially on one foot **2** *vi* JUMP LIGHTLY WITH ALL FEET to move in a series of small jumps using both or all feet **3** *vti* LEAP OVER to jump quickly or lightly over something **4** *vi* LIMP to walk with a limp **5** *vi* GET ON OR OFF to move quickly or lightly into, onto, out of, or off something, especially a vehicle (*informal*) **6** *vt US, Can* JUMP ABOARD to get on a plane, train, bus, or other vehicle, usually quickly or after a sudden decision to do so (*informal*) ○ *hop a plane to California* **7** *vt US* RIDE TRAIN WITHOUT TICKET to ride on a train secretly without paying (*informal*) **8** *vt* JOURNEY BY PLANE to make a journey by aeroplane across or over an area, especially a sea or ocean (*informal*) ■ *n* **1** SMALL QUICK JUMP a small jump on one, both, or all feet **2** FLIGHT a flight or leg of a flight in an aeroplane (*informal*) ○ *a short hop from New York to Chicago* **3** DANCE a social occasion at which people dance together, usually to popular music (*dated informal*) **4** *US* BOUNCE a bounce or rebound of a ball [Old English *hoppian* 'leap, limp' < Germanic] ◇ **catch somebody on the hop** to find somebody unprepared (*informal*) ◇ **keep somebody on the hop** to keep somebody busy and alert (*informal*)

hop[2] /hop/ *n* **1** CLIMBING VINE a climbing vine of the mulberry family with lobed leaves. Flowers: green, arranged in spikes that look like pine cones. *Humulus lupulus.* **2** *US* DRUG a narcotic drug such as opium (*dated slang*) ■ **hops** *npl* DRIED HOP FLOWERS the dried flowers of the hop plant. Use: in brewing, to add flavour to beer. [15C. < Middle Low German, Middle Dutch *hoppe*.] — **hoppy** *adj*

hop up *vt US* to make somebody excited, or intoxicated, especially with drugs (*slang; often passive*)

hop, skip, and jump *n* a short distance ○ *It's just a hop, skip, and jump to the station.*

hop, step, and jump *n* **1** ATHLETICS = **triple jump 2** = **hop, skip, and jump**

hope /hōp/ *vti* (**hopes, hoping, hoped**) WANT OR EXPECT to want to have or do something or for something to happen or be true, especially something that seems possible or likely ■ *n* **1** CONFIDENT DESIRE a feeling that something desirable is likely to happen ○ *The research offers hope to sufferers.* **2** LIKELIHOOD OF SUCCESS a chance that something desirable will happen or be possible ○ *There's not much hope that things will improve.* **3** WISH OR DESIRE something that somebody wants to have or do or wants to happen or be true ○ *My hope is that she will change her mind.* **4** SOURCE OF SUCCESS somebody or something that seems likely to bring success or relief ○ *We have to do this, it's our only hope.* **5** TRUST a feeling of trust (*archaic*) [Old English *hopian* (verb), *hopa* (noun) < ?] —**hoper** *n*

Hope /hōp/, **A. D.** (*b.* 1907) Australian poet and critic. Full name **Alec Derwent Hope**

Hope, **Bob** (*b.* 1903) British-born US comedian. Born **Leslie Townes Hope**

hope chest *n US* = **bottom drawer**

hopeful /hōpf'l/ *adj* **1** HAVING HOPE feeling fairly sure that something that is wanted will happen **2** GIVING HOPE making somebody feel confident that something desirable will happen ■ *n* SOMEBODY DESIRING SUCCESS a person who desires achievement, especially somebody who hopes to be successful in sport, the arts, politics, or something else —**hopefulness** *n*

Herbert Hoover

hopefully /hōpfəli/ *adv* **1** in a way that shows somebody's hope of having or receiving something **2** used to indicate that somebody hopes something will happen or will be the case

USAGE Sentence adverb: Many adverbs that express a wish or comment, for example *clearly, obviously,* and *thankfully,* are routinely used to qualify a whole sentence: *They clearly haven't understood the issue. Obviously, there is a problem. Thankfully, they didn't arrive too late.* Many people object when **hopefully** is used in this way — in, for example, *Hopefully, someone can resolve this* — typically on the grounds that there is no one present in the sentence who is meant to be doing the hoping. This argument would tell against a number of the well-established sentence adverbs as well. For example, in *They clearly haven't understood the issue,* 'they' are not finding anything clear. The grounds on which to object to **hopefully** as a sentence adverb may be illogical, therefore, but many people dislike it regardless. A recommendation often made is to replace the word with *it is to be hoped.* That, however, strikes many people as stilted and even worse than **hopefully.** Frequently the best choice is *let's hope,* or (in more formal contexts) *Let us hope that. . . .*

Hopeh /hō páy/ = **Hebei**

~~**hopeing**~~ incorrect spelling of **hoping**

hopeless /hōpləss/ *adj* **1** WITH NO HOPE OF SUCCESS unable to succeed or improve, or be resolved, helped, or cured **2** DESPAIRING feeling or showing no hope **3** VERY BAD showing a complete lack of ability, competence, or efficiency —**hopelessness** *n*

hopelessly /hōpləssli/ *adv* **1** in a way that shows somebody has no hope of success, relief, or of getting what he or she wants **2** actually or supposedly to too great a degree to be improved or of use

hophead /hóp hed/ *n* **1** *US* somebody addicted to a narcotic drug such as heroin (*slang*) **2** *ANZ* a drunkard (*informal*)

Hopi (*plural* **-pi** *or* **-pis**) *n* **1** a member of a Native North American people of NE Arizona **2** a Shoshonean language spoken in NE Arizona. Native speakers: 5,000. [Late 19C. < Hopi, 'peaceable'.] —**Hopi** *adj*

Hopkins /hópkinz/, **Sir Anthony** (*b.* 1937) Welsh actor

Hopkins, **Sir Frederick** (1861–1947) British biochemist

Hopkins, **Gerard Manley** (1844–89) British poet

hoplite /hóp līt/ *n* a heavily armed foot soldier in ancient Greece [Early 18C. < Greek *hoplites* < *hoplon* 'weapon' < *hepein* 'care for, work at'.] —**hoplitic** /hop líttik/ *adj*

hoplology /hop lólləji/ *n* the study of weapons and armour [Late 19C. < Greek *hoplon* (see HOPLITE).] —**hoplologist** *n*

hopper[1] /hóppər/ *n* **1** FUNNEL-SHAPED DISPENSER a large funnel-shaped container for storing and dispensing grain, fuel, or other materials **2** VEHICLE THAT DISCHARGES LOAD THROUGH FLOOR a wagon or railroad car with sloping floors designed to carry dry bulk goods such as grain or cement that are discharged through an opening in the bottom **3** SOMEBODY OR SOMETHING THAT HOPS somebody who or something that hops **4** JUMPING INSECT a jumping insect such as a leafhopper, treehopper, or froghopper. Order: Homoptera.

hopper[2] /hóppər/ *n* a machine used to harvest hops

Hopper /hóppər/, **Edward** (1882–1967) US artist

hop-picker *n* a person or machine that harvests hops

hopping /hópping/ *n* going from one place of a specified kind to another of the same kind (*usually in combination*) ○ *job-hopping*

hopping mad *adj* extremely angry (*informal*)

hopple *vt, n* = **hobble** v. 2, **hobble** n. 2 [Late 16C. Probably < Low German.] —**hoppler** *n*

hopsack /hóp sak/ *n* **1** a coarsely woven cotton or woollen fabric. Use: clothes. **2** a coarse hemp or jute fabric. Use: sacks, bags.

hopscotch /hóp skoch/ *n* a children's game in which players hop along squares marked in a pattern on the ground to pick up a small object thrown into one of the squares [Early 19C < SCOTCH[1] 'scratched line']

hop trefoil *n* a plant related to peas, beans, and clove. Flowers: yellow, resembling hops. Native to: N temperate grasslands. *Trifolium campestre.* US term **hop clover**

hor. *abbr* **1** horizon **2** horizontal **3** horology

hora /háwrə/, **horah** *n* 1 a traditional circle dance of Israel and Romania 2 the music for a hora [Late 19C. < Romanian *horă*, Hebrew *hōrāh*.]

Horace /hórrəss/ (65–8 BC) Roman poet. Full name **Quintus Horatius Flaccus** —**Horatian** /hə ráysh'n/ *adj*

Horae /háwr ee/ *npl* in ancient Greece, the goddesses of the seasons and the order of nature

horah *n* DANCE, MUSIC = **hora**

horal /háwrəl/ *adj* hourly (*formal*) [Early 18C. < late Latin *horalis* < Latin *hora* (see HOUR).]

horary /háwrəri/ *adj* (*formal*) 1 relating to an hour or hours 2 hourly [Early 17C. < medieval Latin *horarius* < Latin *hora* (see HOUR).]

Horatian ode *n* an ode that has several stanzas, each of which has the same rhythmic pattern

horde /hawrd/ *n* 1 THRONG a large group of people (*often plural*) 2 NOMADIC GROUP a group of nomads, especially of a people who live by hunting and foraging for food (**hunter-gatherers**) 3 SWARM OR PACK a large group of insects or other animals moving in a mass ■ *vi* (**hordes, hording, horded**) 1 FORM OR LIVE IN CROWD to gather together, move, or live in a large crowd or mass 2 LIVE IN GROUP to live together in a nomadic group [Mid-16C. Directly and via French and German < Polish *horda* < Turkish *ordu* 'camp, army'.]

SPELLCHECK See *hoard*.

Hordern /háwrdərn/, **Sir Michael** (1911–95) British actor

horehound /háwr hownd/, **hoarhound** *n* 1 a bitter perennial mint with downy leaves and square stems. Flowers: small white, yielding juice used as a flavouring and in cough remedies. Native to: Europe, Asia. *Marrubium vulgare*. 2 an extract of the horehound plant, or something flavoured with it, e.g. cough drops [Old English *hāre hūne* < *hār* 'hoar' + *hūne* 'horehound' < ?]

horizon /hə ríz'n/ *n* 1 PLACE WHERE EARTH MEETS SKY the line in the furthest distance where the land or sea seems to meet the sky 2 CIRCLE ON APPARENT SPHERE OF SKY a circle formed on the celestial sphere by a plane tangent to a point on the earth's surface 3 CIRCLE ON CELESTIAL SPHERE a circle formed on the celestial sphere by a plane through the centre of the earth and parallel to the tangent of a point on the earth's surface 4 DISTINCT LAYER OF SOIL a layer of soil having characteristics that distinguish it from other layers 5 GEOLOGICAL LAYER a distinct layer of rock or geological deposit within a stratum that can be dated, e.g. by its fossil content ■ **horizons** *npl* RANGE OF EXPERIENCE the range or limits of somebody's interests, knowledge, or experience [14C. Via Old French *orizon(te)* < Greek *horizōn (kuklos)* 'limiting (circle)', present participle of *horizein* 'limit' < *horos* 'limit'.] —**horizonal** *adj*

horizontal /hórri zónt'l/ *adj* 1 LEVEL parallel to the horizon 2 IN HORIZONTAL PLANE measured or operating in a plane parallel to the horizon 3 LYING DOWN lying down or in a reclining position (*informal*) 4 HAVING SAME STATUS being at or having the same level within a group of people ○ *a horizontal promotion* 5 APPLIED TO ALL applied equally to all members, parts, or aspects of something ○ *a horizontal bonus* 6 OF HORIZON relating to the horizon ■ *n* SOMETHING HORIZONTAL a horizontal line, surface, or position [Mid-16C. < French, or modern Latin *horizontalis* < late Latin *horizont-*, stem of *horizon* 'horizon' < Greek *horizōn* (see HORIZON).] —**horizontality** /hórri zon tálləti/ *n* —**horizontally** *adv* —**horizontalness** *n*

horizontal bar *n* 1 a metal bar fixed in a horizontal position and used for gymnastic exercises 2 a competitive gymnastics event involving feats of skill and strength on the horizontal bar

horizontal mobility *n* a change in social situation that does not involve a change in social status

hormogonium /háwrmə gṓni əm/ (*plural* **-a** /-ə/) *n* a section of a filament in some cyanobacteria that detaches and reproduces by cell division [Late 19C. < modern Latin, < Greek *hormos* 'chain' + *gonos* 'generation, seed'.]

hormone /háwr mōn/ *n* 1 CHEMICAL IN BODY a chemical produced in one tissue that produces a physiological response in another 2 CHEMICAL IN PLANTS a nonnutrient substance synthesized by plants that regulates growth and development 3 REGULATING CHEMICAL IN INSECTS a substance produced in the body of an insect that regulates various aspects of growth and development such as the change from larva to adult 4 REGULATING CHEMICAL a synthetic chemical that acts like a hormone [Early 20C. < Greek *hormōn*, present participle of *horman* 'set in motion' < *hormē* 'assault'.] —**hormonal** /hawr mṓn'l/ *adj* —**hormonally** *adv*

hormone replacement therapy *n* treatment to maintain previous levels of the hormone oestrogen in women during and after the menopause, e.g. to avoid bone weakness (**osteoporosis**) and protect against heart attacks

Hormuz, Strait of /hawr mo͞oz, háwrmo͞oz/ narrow waterway between Iran and the Arabian Peninsula, linking the Persian Gulf with the Arabian Sea

horn /hawrn/ *n* 1 NOISE-MAKING WARNING DEVICE a device, e.g. in a car, that produces a loud noise as a warning or signal (*often in combination*) 2 PROJECTION ON ANIMAL'S HEAD one of a permanent pair of pointed projections on the head of some mammals, e.g. the cow, sheep, or antelope, made of a sheath of hardened protein over bone 3 PROJECTION FROM NOSE OF RHINOCEROS a solid outgrowth of keratin and fused hair from the nasal bone of a rhinoceros 4 PROJECTION RESEMBLING HORN any hard, pointed, or horn-shaped projection on animals, birds, reptiles, fish, or insects 5 BRASS INSTRUMENT a wind instrument usually made of brass, with a long tube whose flared end produces a sound when the player's lips vibrate together into the mouthpiece 6 JAZZ INSTRUMENT a wind instrument played in a jazz band (*informal*) 7 SIMPLE WIND INSTRUMENT a simple or early musical instrument made from an animal's horn 8 HARD SUBSTANCE OF HORNS the hard substance that covers an animal's horns, consisting mainly of a tough protein (**keratin**) 9 SOMETHING MADE OF HORN something made with a piece of horn or from a synthetic substance resembling it 10 PROJECTION ON DEVIL'S HEAD either of a pair of parts resembling an animal's horns supposed to grow on the head of a cuckold or the devil 11 HORN-SHAPED THING something shaped like a horn, e.g. either of the tips of a crescent moon, the pommel of a saddle, or the pointed end of an anvil 12 SHARP PEAK a sharp pyramid-shaped mountain peak 13 HORN-SHAPED AREA a horn-shaped body of water or land 14 TABOO TERM a highly offensive term for an erection of the penis (*taboo*) 15 *US* TELEPHONE a telephone (*slang*) ■ *vt* 1 PROVIDE WITH HORNS to give something a horn or horns 2 ATTACK WITH HORNS to butt or gore somebody with the horns 3 *Carib, US* HAVE SEX WITH SOMEBODY ELSE'S PARTNER to make a cuckold of somebody by having a sexual relationship with the spouse or partner (*informal*) [Old English, < Indo-European, 'horn, head'] ◇ **draw in your horns** 1 to spend or invest less money than usual or before 2 to adopt a less active or less assertive position ◇ **lock horns (with somebody)** to engage in an argument or quarrel with somebody ◇ **on the horns of a dilemma** faced with making a decision between two things or two courses of action, each of which is problematic or unattractive

horn in *vi* to intrude, interfere, or get involved in something without invitation (*informal*)

Horn, Cape /hawrn/ cape at the southern extremity of South America. Height: 424 m/1,391 ft. Spanish **Cabo de Hornos**

hornbeam /háwrn beem/ *n* a tree with smooth greyish bark and hard white wood. Genus: *Carpinus*.

hornbill /háwrn bil/ *n* a noisy tropical bird that has a large curved bill with a horny protuberance. Family: Bucerotidae.

hornblende /háwrn blend/ *n* a dark green to black mineral of the amphibole group, containing calcium, iron, magnesium, and sodium [Late 18C. < German.] —**hornblendic** /hawrn bléndik/ *adj*

Horne /hawrn/, **Donald** (*b.* 1921) Australian writer and academic

horned /hawrnd/ *adj* having a horn or horns, or one or more projections that resemble horns

horned lizard *n* a small insect-eating lizard of the desert regions of the SW United States and Mexico that has a flattened body, a short tail, and spikes like horns on its head. Genus: *Phrynosoma*.

horned owl *n* a large owl with prominent ear tufts resembling horns. *Bubo virginianus*.

horned pout *n* ZOOL = **hornpout**

horned toad *n* ZOOL = **horned lizard**

horned viper *n* a poisonous snake of the desert regions of the Near East and Africa that has spines on its head that look like horns. *Cerastes cornutus*.

hornet /háwrnit/ *n* a large social stinging wasp that builds large group nests underground or hanging from a tree. Family: Vespidae. [Old English *hyrnet(u)* < Indo-European]

hornet's nest *n* a highly controversial issue or situation that is likely to lead to confrontation, opposition, or argument

hornfels /háwrn felz, -fels/ (*plural* **-fels**) *n* a fine-grained metamorphic rock composed of silicate minerals and formed through the action of heat and pressure on shale [Mid-19C. < German, 'horn rock'.]

hornist /háwrnist/ *n* a musician who plays a horn

horn of plenty *n* 1 ARTS = **cornucopia** *n.* 2 2 a funnel-shaped, black and brown edible fungus found in deciduous woodland in autumn. *Craterellus cornucopioides*.

hornpipe /háwrn pīp/ *n* 1 SAILORS' DANCE a lively British dance traditionally performed by sailors 2 MUSIC ACCOMPANYING HORNPIPE the music for a hornpipe 3 REED INSTRUMENT a musical instrument with a single reed and a mouthpiece made of horn, traditionally used to play the music for a hornpipe

hornpout /háwrn powt/ *n* a small fish with a large head and eight barbels. Native to: North America. *Ictalurus nebulosus*.

horn-rims, **horn-rimmed glasses** *npl* spectacles with frames made from dark-coloured horn or a synthetic substance made to resemble this —**horn-rimmed** *adj*

hornswoggle /háwrn swogg'l/ (**-gles, -gling, -gled**) *vt US* to cheat, trick, or deceive somebody (*informal*) [Early 19C. < ?]

horntail /háwrn tayl/ *n* an insect that resembles a wasp and whose larvae burrow in wood. Family: Siricidae.

hornworm /háwrn wurm/ *n* the caterpillar of certain hawk moths, with a projection on its tail that resembles a horn

hornwort /háwrn wurt/ *n* a rootless aquatic plant that grows in branching submerged masses and has finely dissected leaves and tiny flowers. Genus: *Ceratophylum*. [< its branching stem]

horny /háwrni/ (**-ier, -iest**) *adj* 1 AS TOUGH AS HORN hard or rough like horn 2 OF OR LIKE HORN made of or resembling horn 3 FEELING SEXY sexually excited, or easily aroused sexually (*informal*) 4 LOOKING SEXY sexually attractive (*informal*) 5 WITH HORNS having a horn or horns —**hornily** *adv* —**horniness** *n*

horol. *abbr* 1 horological 2 horology

Horologium /háwrə lṓji əm/ *n* a faint constellation of the southern hemisphere

horology /ho rólləji/ *n* 1 the study or science of measuring time 2 the art or skill of making clocks, watches, and other devices for telling the time [15C. < Greek *hōra* 'time, hour'.] —**horologic** /hórrə lójjik/ *adj* —**horological** *adj* —**horologically** *adv* —**horologist** /ho rólləjist/ *n*

horoscope /hórrə skōp/ *n* 1 the relative position of the stars or planets at a particular moment, especially somebody's time of birth, or a diagram showing this 2 an astrologer's description of an individual's personality and future based on the position of the planets in relation to the sign of the zodiac under which the person was born [Pre-12C. Via Latin < Greek *hōroskopos* 'time observer' < *hōra* 'time, hour' (of birth).] —**horoscopic** /hórrə skóppik/ *adj*

horoscopy /ho róskəpi/ *n* the making and interpretation of horoscopes

Horowitz /hórrə wits/, **Vladimir** (1904–89) Russian-born US pianist

horrendous /ho réndəss, hə-/ *adj* 1 sufficiently unpleasant, frightening, or shocking as to provoke horror 2 very large, great, or high, often unreasonably or excessively so (*informal*) ○ *horrendous prices* [Mid-17C. < Latin *horrendus* 'be shuddered at', a form of *horrere* (see HORRIBLE).] —**horrendously** *adj* —**horrendousness** *n*

horrible /hórrəb'l/ *adj* 1 VERY UNPLEASANT very bad, very unpleasant, or caused by anxiety or fear about something bad ○ *a horrible smell* 2 CAUSING HORROR sufficiently frightening, distressing, or shocking as to provoke horror ○ *a horrible crime* 3 NASTY unkind, rude, or badly-behaved (*informal*) [13C. Via Old French *(h)orrible* < Latin *horribilis* < *horrere* 'bristle, shudder with fear at'.] —**horribleness** *n*

horribly /hórrəbli/ *adv* 1 in an unpleasant, disagreeable, distressing, or shocking way 2 to a great or excessive extent ○ *horribly late*

horrid /hórrid/ *adj* 1 **NASTY** callously unkind or nasty (*informal*) ○ *a horrid thing to say* 2 **CAUSING DISGUST** provoking disgust or extreme displeasure ○ *a horrid taste* 3 **CAUSING HORROR** dreadful, shocking, or frightening enough to cause horror ○ *a horrid accident* 4 **BRISTLY** rough, shaggy, or bristly (*archaic*) [Late 16C. < Latin *horridus* 'bristly, rough, horrid' < *horrere* 'bristle, shudder with fear at'.] —**horridly** *adv* —**horridness** *n*

horrific /ho ríffik, hə-/ *adj* frightening or disturbing enough to cause horror [Mid-17C. Directly or via French *horrifique* < Latin *horrificus* < *horrere* 'bristle, shudder with fear at'.] —**horrifically** *adv*

horrify /hórri fī/ (**-fies, -fying, -fied**) *vt* 1 to make somebody feel horror, disgust, or fright 2 to make somebody shocked or dismayed [Late 18C. < Latin *horrificare* 'cause horror' < *horrere* 'bristle, shudder with fear at'.] —**horrification** /hórrifi káysh'n/ *n* —**horrified** *adj* —**horrifying** *adj* —**horrifyingly** *adv*

horripilation /ho ríppi láysh'n/ *n* the standing on end of somebody's hair, e.g. because of fear or cold [Mid-17C. < late Latin *horripilation-* < Latin *horripilare* 'become hairy' < *horrere* 'to bristle' + *pilus* 'hair'.]

horror /hórrər/ *n* 1 **INTENSE FEAR** a very strong, painful feeling of fear, shock, or disgust 2 **INTENSE DISLIKE** a feeling of distress or distaste ○ *He has a horror of spiders.* 3 **SOMETHING CAUSING HORROR** something, or an aspect of something, that causes a feeling of great fear or disgust ○ *the horrors of war* 4 **SOMETHING UNPLEASANT** a very unpleasant or unattractive thing (*informal*) ○ *The new building is an absolute horror.* 5 **SOMEBODY CAUSING DISLIKE** a disagreeable or ill-mannered person, especially a badly-behaved child (*informal*) ■ **horrors** *npl* (*informal*) 1 **FEELING OF TERROR** a feeling of great fear, anxiety, or hopelessness 2 HEALTH = **delirium tremens** ■ *adj* **GROTESQUE AND TERRIFYING** describes a genre of motion picture or literature intended to thrill viewers or readers by provoking fear or revulsion through the portrayal of grotesque, violent, or supernatural events [14C. Directly or via Old French < Latin, < *horrere* 'bristle, shudder with fear at'.]

horror story *n* 1 a story that is intended to frighten people, usually by describing gruesome or supernatural events 2 a true account of something very unpleasant or shocking

horror-struck, horror-stricken *adj* suddenly shocked, frightened, or dismayed

hors concours /awr koN ko͝or/ *adj* in the capacity or manner of somebody who is not competing [< French, 'out of the competition']

hors de combat /áwr də kóm baa/ *adj* out of action and often in a seriously wounded condition [< French, 'out of the fight']

hors d'oeuvre /awr dúrv/ (*plural* **hors d'oeuvre** *or* **hors d'oeuvres**) *n* a small portion of food served cold or hot before a meal to stimulate the appetite [< French, 'outside the work']

horse /hawrss/ *n* 1 **FOUR-LEGGED ANIMAL** a large four-legged animal with a mane, tail, hooves, and a long head. Kept for: riding, pulling vehicles, carrying loads. *Equus caballus.* 2 **STALLION OR GELDING** an adult male horse 3 **ANIMAL OF THE HORSE FAMILY** an animal, e.g. a donkey or zebra, that belongs to the family including the horse. Family: Equidae. 4 GYMNASTICS = **vaulting horse** 5 **FRAME OR SUPPORT** a frame or support, especially one mounted on four legs 6 **MOUNTED SOLDIERS** soldiers riding horses (+ *singular or plural verb*) 7 **MASS OF ROCK IN ORE** a mass of rock located in an ore vein 8 **HEROIN** heroin (*dated slang*) 9 **HORSEPOWER** horsepower (*informal; usually plural*) ■ **horses** *npl* **HORSE-RACING** horseracing, especially as a gambling activity (*informal*) ■ *v* (**horses, horsing, horsed**) 1 *vt* **GIVE SOMEBODY A HORSE** to provide somebody with a horse 2 *vti* **PUT OR GET ON A HORSE** to put a rider on a horse's back, or mount a horse 3 *vi* **BE IN HEAT** to be ready to mate with a male horse (*refers to a mare*) [Old English *hors* < Germanic] ◇ **flog a dead horse** to pursue a topic or course of action that is likely to be totally unproductive ◇ **from the horse's mouth** from a well-informed and reliable source ◇ **look a gift horse in the mouth** to criticize something that has been given to you

SPELLCHECK See *hoarse.*

horse around, horse about *vi* to play or fool around in a boisterous manner

horse-and-buggy *adj* adhering to things, fashions, or ideas that are old-fashioned and out of date

horseback /háwrss bak/ *adj, adv* on a horse's back ◇ **on horseback** sitting on or riding a horse

horse bean *n* a field bean with large seeds. Use: feeding animals. *Vicia faba.* [< its use as fodder for horses]

horsebox /háwrss boks/ *n* a vehicle, e.g. a lorry or railway car, used to transport horses. US term **horsecar**

horse brass *n* a flat, usually circular, polished brass ornament originally attached to a horse's harness and now sometimes hung on walls or beams in houses or bars for decoration

horsecar /háwrss kaar/ *n US* = **horsebox**

horse chestnut *n* 1 a large shiny brown inedible seed with a fleshy, sometimes spiny, husk 2 a large tree that has compound leaves, conical flower clusters, and sticky winter buds, and that bears horse chestnuts. Native to: northern hemisphere. Genus: *Aesculus.*

horsedrawn /háwrss drawn/ *adj* pulled by one or more horses

horsefeathers /háwrss fet͟hərz/ *n, interj US* nonsense (*humorous slang; + singular verb*) [Early 20C. Alteration of HORSESHIT.]

horseflesh /háwrss flesh/ *n* 1 horses collectively 2 the flesh of a horse, especially when sold or eaten as meat

horsefly /háwrss flī/ (*plural* **-flies**) *n* a large two-winged fly, the female of which sucks the blood of horses and other mammals. Genus: *Tabanus.*

Horse Guards *npl* a cavalry regiment that, with the Life Guards, forms the Household Cavalry responsible for guarding the sovereign, especially during public ceremonies ■ *n* the headquarters of the Horse Guards in Whitehall, London

horsehair /háwrss hair/ *n* 1 hair from a horse's mane and tail. Use: upholstery, mattress filling, cloth. 2 fabric woven from the hair of a horse's mane and tail

horsehair worm *n* ZOOL = **hairworm**

Horsehead nebula /háwrss hed-/ *n* a dark nebula in the constellation Orion, shaped like a horse's head

horsehide /háwrss hīd/ *n* the tough thick skin of a horse, or leather made from a horse's skin

horse latitudes *npl* either of two regions at sea near the latitudes 30° S and 30° N marked by high atmospheric pressure and light variable winds or calms [< ?]

horselaugh /háwrss laaf/ *n* a loud, coarse, and often scornful laugh

horseleech /háwrss leech/ *n* a large freshwater leech. Genus: *Haemopis.* [*Horse* because large or coarse]

horseless carriage *n* a motor car, at a time when horse-drawn vehicles were still the usual form of transport (*archaic*)

horse mackerel *n* a swift torpedo-shaped fish. Native to: Atlantic Ocean, Mediterranean Sea, Black Sea. *Trachurus trachurus.* [*Horse* because large or coarse]

horseman /háwrssmən/ (*plural* **-men** /-mən/) *n* a man who rides or is riding a horse, especially a man who does so with skill —**horsemanship** *n*

horsemint /háwrss mint/ *n* 1 a hairy wild mint. Flowers: small pinkish-purple, in elongated clusters. Native to: Europe, Asia. *Mentha longifolia.* 2 a coarse mint. Flowers: showy, yellow with purple spots. Native to: North America. *Monarda punctata.* [*Horse* because large or coarse]

horse mushroom *n* a large mushroom that smells of almonds. *Agaricus arvensis.* [*Horse* because large or coarse]

horse opera *n* in the cinema, a Western (*informal*)

horse pistol *n* a large pistol formerly used by horsemen and carried in a holster

horseplay /háwrss play/ *n* rough, boisterous, playful behaviour

horsepower /háwrss powər/ *n* a unit of power equal in the United Kingdom to 550 foot-pounds per second and in the United States to 745.7 watts [Supposedly equivalent to the work rate of a horse]

horse race /háwrss rayss/ *n* a race between horses ridden by jockeys on a flat circuit or over obstacles

horseracing /háwss rayssing/ *n* a sport in which horses ridden by jockeys race against each other, usually with spectators and others betting on the result

horseradish /háwrss radish/ *n* 1 a long slim pungent root. Use: in cookery, especially peeled and grated to make a hot, sharp-tasting sauce often served with beef. 2 a tall coarse plant that yields horseradishes. Flowers: white. *Amoracia lapathifolia.* [*Horse* because large or coarse]

horse sense *n* common sense (*informal*)

horseshit /háwrss shit/ *n* (*slang*) 1 *US* an offensive term for nonsense 2 an offensive term for the excrement of a horse

horseshoe /háwrss shoo/ *n* 1 **PROTECTION FOR A HORSE'S HOOF** a flat U-shaped piece of iron nailed to the bottom of a horse's hoof to protect it against hard surfaces 2 **GOOD-LUCK TOKEN** a representation of a horseshoe regarded as a symbol of good luck 3 **HORSESHOE-SHAPED THING** something that has the curved shape of a horseshoe ○ *'... every known superstition in the world is gathered into the horseshoe of the Carpathians ...'* (Bram Stoker, *Dracula*; 1897) ■ *vt* (**-shoes, -shoeing, -shoed**) RIDING = **shoe** *v.* 1 —**horseshoer** *n*

horseshoe arch *n* an arch that narrows slightly below the upper rounded part

horseshoe bat *n* a bat that has a horseshoe-shaped appendage that surrounds the nostrils. Native to: Europe, tropics. Family: Rhinolophidae.

horseshoe crab *n* a large marine arthropod that has a stiff pointed tail and rounded brown body resembling a horseshoe. Native to: E North America, Asia. Class: Merostomata.

Horseshoe Falls Canadian section of Niagara Falls, on the US-Canadian border. Height: 49 m/161 ft.

horseshoes /háwrss shooz/ *n US* a game in which players throw horseshoes at a post and score points based on how close they land to the post (+ *singular verb*)

horse show *n* a sporting event in which horses and usually riders are judged on their skills in a variety of competitions such as riding or jumping

horsetail /háwrss tayl/ *n* 1 a nonflowering plant that has a hollow jointed stem, tiny thin leaves, and spore-producing cones produced at the top of the stems. Genus: *Equisetum.* 2 a former emblem of rank of Turkish pashas in the Ottoman Empire

horse-trading *n* negotiation that involves bargaining and mutual compromise, often some shrewdness, and sometimes unscrupulous tactics such as secret or unofficial deals —**horse-trade** *vi* —**horse-trader** *n*

horsewhip /háwrss wip/ *n* a whip formerly used to keep a horse under control, e.g. when being driven, and usually made of a long strip of leather attached to a short handle ■ *vt* (**-whips, -whipping, -whipped**) to flog a person or animal with a horsewhip or with something similar, usually as a punishment —**horsewhipper** *n*

horsewoman /háwrss wo͝omən/ (*plural* **-en** /-wimin/) *n* a woman who rides or is riding a horse, especially one who does so with skill

horsey /háwrssi/ (**-ier, -iest**), **horsy** (**-ier, -iest**) *adj* 1 **RELATING TO HORSES** belonging to, relating to, or characteristic of a horse 2 **LOOKING LIKE A HORSE** heavy, awkward, and unattractive in appearance 3 **INTERESTED IN HORSES** very fond of horses and interested in activities involving horses such as riding, racing, show jumping, or hunting —**horsiness** *n*

Horsham /háwrshəm/ town in S England. Population: 39,894 (1991).

horst /hawrst/ *n* an elevated block of the Earth's crust forced upwards between faults [Late 19C. < German, 'heap, mass'.]

horsy *adj* = **horsey**

hort. *abbr* 1 horticulture 2 horticultural

Horta /háwtə/, **Baron Victor** (1861–1947) Belgian architect

hortative /háwrtətiv/ *adj* = **hortatory** (*formal*) [Early 17C. < Latin *hortativus* < *hortari* 'exhort'.] —**hortatively** *adv*

hortatory /háwrtətəri/ *adj* urging, encouraging, or strongly advising a course of action to somebody (*formal*) [Late 16C. < late Latin *hortatorius* < Latin *hortari* 'exhort'.] —**hortatorily** *adv*

horticulture /háwrti kulchər/ *n* 1 the science, skill, or occupation of cultivating plants, especially flowers, fruit, and vegetables, in gardens or greenhouses 2 a simple form of agriculture based on working small plots of land without using draught animals, ploughs, or irrigation [Late 17C. < Latin *hortus* 'garden'.] —**horticultural** /háwrti kúlchərəl/ *adj* —**horticulturally** *adv* —**horticulturist** *n*

Horus /háwrəss/ *n* in Egyptian mythology, the god of the sun, the sky, and goodness, usually depicted as having a falcon's head. Horus was the son of Isis and Osiris.

Hos. *abbr* Hosea

hosanna /hō zánnə/, **hosannah** *n, interj* a cry of praise to God [Pre-12C. Via late Latin < Greek *hōsanna* < Rabbinic Hebrew *hōša'nā*, shortening of Hebrew *hōšī'ā-nnā* 'save, (we) pray' (Psalm 118:25).]

Hosay /hō sáy/, **Hosein** /-sáyn/ *n* an Islamic religious festival marking the martyrdom of Imam Hosein. Date: 10th day of Moharram.

hose /hōz/ *n* **FLEXIBLE TUBE** a flexible tube or pipe, often made of rubber or plastic, through which fluids such as water or petrol can flow ■ *npl* **1** *US* **LEG COVERINGS** skintight leg covering such as stockings or socks **2 TIGHT-FITTING TROUSERS** a garment formerly worn by men, fitting closely to the legs and attaching to a doublet ■ *vt* (**hoses, hosing, hosed**) **1 DIRECT WATER ON** to spray, soak, wash, or rinse something or somebody with water from a hose **2** *US* **TRICK** to deceive or trick somebody (*slang*) [Old English *hosa* 'leg covering, husk' < Indo-European, 'to cover']

Hosea /hō zée ə/ *n* in the Bible, a short prophetic book

Hosein *n* = **Hosay**

hosel /hōz'l/ *n* the socket in the head of a golf club where the shaft is attached [Late 19C. < HOSE + *-el* 'small' < Latin *-ellus*.]

hosepipe /hōz pīp/ *n* a long hose for domestic use, e.g. for watering gardens or washing cars

hosiery /hōzi əri/ *n* socks, stockings, and tights, considered collectively

hospice /hóspiss/ *n* **1** a usually small residential institution for terminally ill patients where treatment focuses on the patient's wellbeing rather than a cure **2** in former times, a place where pilgrims, travellers, and the homeless or destitute were offered lodging, usually by a religious order [Early 19C. Via French < Latin *hospitium* 'guesthouse, hospitality' < *hospit-* 'host, guest'.]

hospitable /ho spíttəb'l, hóspitəb'l/ *adj* **1** friendly, welcoming, and generous to guests or strangers ○ *That's very hospitable of you.* **2** pleasant, agreeable, and providing what somebody needs to live comfortably ○ *a hospitable climate* [Late 16C. < French, < obsolete *hospiter* 'receive a guest' < Latin *hospit-* 'host, guest'.] —**hospitability** /hóspitə bíllati/ *n* —**hospitableness** /ho spíttəb'lnəss, hóspitəb'lnəss/ *n* —**hospitably** *adv*

hospital /hóspit'l/ *n* **1 BUILDING FOR MEDICAL CARE** an institution where people receive medical, surgical, or psychiatric treatment and nursing care **2 PLACE OF REPAIR** a place where something is mended **3 CHARITABLE HOME** a charitable institution providing shelter, care, or education for orphaned children, senior citizens, or the homeless or destitute (*archaic*) [13C. Via Old French, 'hostel' < medieval Latin *hospitale* 'guesthouse, inn' < Latin *hospit-* 'host, guest'.]

Hospital /hóspit'l/, **Janette Turner** (*b.* 1942) Australian novelist

hospital-acquired infection *n* a disease caught while being treated in hospital for something else ○ *'Each year, nearly 90,000 patients in the United States die of a hospital-acquired infection...'* (*New York Times Magazine*; February 1998)

hospital corner *n* each of the corners at the foot of a bed in which the bedclothes are tucked under the mattress in neat triangular folds

Hospitaler *n* US = **Hospitaller**

hospitalise *vt* = **hospitalize**

hospitalist /hóspit'list/ *n US* a doctor who specializes in the care of hospitalized patients, typically liaising with the patient's own doctor

hospitality /hóspi tálləti/ *n* a friendly welcome and kind or generous treatment offered to guests or strangers

hospitality suite *n* a room or suite of rooms where invited guests or clients of a company, delegates to a conference, or other official visitors are welcomed and provided with free refreshments

hospitalize /hóspitə līz/ (**-izes, -izing, -ized**), **hospitalise** (**-ises, -ising, -ised**) *vt* to admit somebody to hospital for treatment, diagnosis, or observation, usually as an inpatient —**hospitalization** /hóspitə lī záysh'n/ *n*

Hospitaller *n* **1** a member of a military religious order, the Knights of the Hospital of St John, founded in the late 11th century by European crusaders to care for sick pilgrims in Jerusalem **2 hospitaller, Hospitaller** a member of a religious order or charitable institution involved in the care of the sick, especially in hospital [14C. Via Old French *hospitalier* < medieval Latin *hospitalarius* < *hospitale* (see HOSPITAL).]

hospodar /hóspə daar/ *n* a prince or governor of Moldavia or Wallachia during the time of Ottoman rule [Late 16C. Via Romanian < Ukrainian.]

⚡**host**[1] /hōst/ *n* **1 SOMEBODY ENTERTAINING GUESTS** a person who invites and entertains guests **2 SOMEBODY INTRODUCING GUESTS ON A SHOW** somebody who presents a television or radio programme in which invited guests take part, e.g. a chat show or game show **3 PLACE WHERE AN EVENT IS HELD** a place or organization that provides the space and facilities for a special event, e.g. an international sporting competition **4 ORGANISM INFECTED BY A PARASITE** a human, animal, plant, or other organism in or on which another organism, especially a parasite, lives **5 GRAFT OR TRANSPLANT RECIPIENT** the recipient of a transplanted or grafted embryo, tissue, or organ **6 LANDLORD OF AN INN** an owner or manager of a pub or hotel (*dated*) **7 host, host computer MAIN COMPUTER IN A NETWORK** the main computer that controls certain functions or files in a network **8** *US* **RESTAURANT GREETER** somebody employed in a restaurant to greet and seat customers ■ *vt* **1 ACCOMMODATE AN EVENT** to provide the space and facilities for a special event, e.g. an international sporting competition **2 INTRODUCE GUESTS ON A SHOW** to act as the host of a television or radio programme **3 ENTERTAIN GUESTS** to be the host of a social or official gathering **4 CREATE A WEBSITE FOR** to create a website for somebody as a service [13C. Via Old French *(h)oste* 'host, guest' < Latin *hospit-*.]

host[2] /hōst/ *n* **1** a very large number of people or things **2** an army (*archaic*) [14C. Via Old French < Latin *hostis* 'stranger, enemy' (in medieval Latin, 'army').]

Host, host *n* the bread or wafer consecrated and eaten during the Christian ceremony of Communion [14C. Via Old French *(h)oiste* < Latin *hostia* 'sacrificial animal, victim'.]

hosta /hóstə/ *n* a perennial shade-loving plant with broad ribbed leaves. Flowers: white, blue, or lilac tubular, in clusters. Genus: *Hosta*. US term **plantain lily** [Early 19C. < modern Latin, after Nicolaus T. *Host* (1761–1834), Austrian botanist.]

hostage /hóstij/ *n* **1** somebody held prisoner by a person or group, e.g. a criminal or a terrorist organization, until certain demands are met or money is handed over **2** a person or group of people whose freedom of action is restricted or controlled by a more powerful organization by implied threats or other means [13C. < Old French *(h)ostage* < late Latin *obsidiatus* 'hostageship' < *sedere* 'sit'.] ◇ **a hostage to fortune** a remark or action that could potentially lead to trouble or difficulty and so is better avoided

host computer *n* = **host**[1] *n.* 7

hostel /hóst'l/ *n* **1** LEISURE = **youth hostel 2 SUPERVISED LODGING FOR WORKERS OR EX-OFFENDERS** a place where supervised lodging is provided to workers, juvenile offenders, or ex-offenders **3 ACCOMMODATION FOR HOMELESS** accommodation for people who are homeless **4 CHEAP INN** an inexpensive inn or place of lodging [13C. < Old French *(h)ostel* < medieval Latin *hospitale* (see HOSPITAL).]

hosteler *n* US = **hosteller**

hosteling *n* US = **hostelling**

hosteller /hóst'lər/ *n* a person who stays at hostels while travelling

hostelling /hóst'ling/ *n* staying at hostels, especially youth hostels, while travelling around for pleasure

hostelry /hóst'lri/ (*plural* **-ries**) *n* a hotel, pub, or inn (*archaic or humorous*)

hostess /hōstiss, hō stéss/ *n* **1 WOMAN ENTERTAINING GUESTS** a woman who invites, welcomes, and entertains guests, often providing them with food and drink **2 WOMAN INTRODUCING GUESTS ON SHOW** a woman who presents a television or radio programme in which invited guests take part, e.g. a chat show or game show **3 PAID DANCE PARTNER** a woman who is paid to be a man's dancing partner at a nightclub or dance hall **4** *US* **WOMAN GREETER IN A RESTAURANT** a woman who is employed in a restaurant to greet and seat customers **5** *US* **WOMAN ATTENDANT FOR PASSENGERS** a woman who is employed to provide for the safety and comfort of passengers on an aircraft, ship, train, or bus [12C. < Old French *(h)ostesse* < *(h)oste* (see HOST[1]).] —**hostess** *vti*

hostile /hós tīl/ *adj* **1 VERY UNFRIENDLY** showing or feeling hatred, enmity, antagonism, or anger towards somebody **2 AGAINST** strongly opposed to somebody or something ○ *hostile to the idea* **3 RELATING TO AN ENEMY** relating to, characteristic of, or belonging to an enemy, especially in warfare ○ *hostile fire* **4 ADVERSE** not favourable to life, health, development, or success ○ *a hostile environment* **5 AGAINST A MANAGEMENT'S WILL** opposed by the owner or management of a company ○ *a hostile takeover* [Late 16C. Directly or via French < Latin *hostilis* < *hostis* 'enemy, stranger'.] —**hostile** *n* —**hostilely** *adv*

hostile witness *n* a witness called by an opposing party who gives evidence against that party

hostility /ho stílləti/ *n* (*plural* **-ties**) **1 INTENSE AGGRESSION OR ANGER** a feeling or attitude of hatred, enmity, antagonism, or anger towards somebody **2 STRONG OPPOSITION** strong opposition to somebody or something **3 HOSTILE ACT** an aggressive act against somebody ■ **hostilities** *npl* **ATTACKS** open acts of warfare

⚡**hosting centre** *n* a business that provides Internet access and guarantees maintenance of Internet links to clients housing their own processors and software with it

hostler *n* = **ostler** (*archaic*)

hot /hot/ *adj* (**hotter, hottest**) **1 VERY WARM** at a high, relatively high, or very high temperature ○ *the hottest day of the year* **2 TOO WARM FOR COMFORT** feeling warmer than normal or desirable **3 VERY SPICY** spicy or peppery enough to cause a burning sensation in the mouth or throat **4 CAUSING CONTROVERSY** causing much discussion, disagreement, or controversy ○ *a hot topic* **5 DANGEROUS** unpleasant or uncomfortable because of antagonism, trouble, or danger (*informal*) ○ *It got too hot for him to handle.* **6 QUICKLY ANGERED** easily provoked or aroused ○ *a hot temper* **7 VIOLENT** felt, done, or expressed with forceful, intense energy ○ *hot competition* **8 INTENSE** bright and vivid ○ *hot pink* **9 CLOSE** following somebody or something very closely ○ *hot on the trail* **10 REQUIRING ATTENTION** requiring immediate attention and offering potential success or good fortune ○ *a hot tip* **11 TOPICAL** very recent or new and therefore of interest or importance ○ *hot off the press* **12 EXCITING** new, fresh, and exciting (*informal*) ○ *a hot new talent* **13 SUCCESSFUL** very popular or successful (*informal*) ○ *one of the hottest items in the range* **14 KNOWLEDGEABLE** having or showing great skill or knowledge (*informal*) ○ *not very hot at maths* **15** *US* **LUCKY** very lucky, e.g. in gambling (*informal*) **16 WISE** very good, wise, or sensible (*informal*) ○ *That idea's not so hot.* **17 WELL** well or good (*informal*) ○ *I don't feel too hot.* **18 NEAR THE ANSWER** very close to something to be found or discovered in a hunting or guessing game (*informal*) ○ *You're getting hotter.* **19 KEEN** enthusiastically eager (*informal*) ○ *She's really hot on jazz.* **20 STRICT** very strict about something (*informal*) ○ *He's hot on getting the paperwork right.* **21 PHYSICALLY ATTRACTED** physically attracted or aroused (*slang*) **22 PHYSICALLY ATTRACTIVE** physically attractive or exciting (*slang*) **23 STOLEN** obtained illegally, especially by stealing (*slang*) ○ *hot jewels* **24 ON THE RUN** wanted by the police (*slang*) ○ *a hot suspect* **25** *US* **EAGER** full of activity, energy, enthusiasm, or excitement **26 INVENTIVE AND EXCITING** with strong rhythms or exciting improvisation (*informal*) **27 POWERFUL** very fast and powerful (*slang*) **28 LIVE** electrically charged ○ *a hot wire* **29 RADIOACTIVE** dangerously radioactive **30 INFECTIOUS** extremely infectious or lethal **31** *US* **ANGRY** angry or agitated about something (*informal*) **32 IN AN ELEVATED ENERGY STATE** in an elevated energy state, usually caused by nuclear processes ○ *a hot atom* **33** *US* **ABSURD** funny, absurd, or unbelievable (*slang*) ■ **hots** *npl* **DESIRE** strong physical desire (*informal*) ■ *adv* **INTENSELY** in an eager, intense, or angry way ○ *They argued hot and long.* [Old English *hāt* < Germanic] —**hotness** *n* ◇ **blow** *or* **run hot and cold** to keep changing your mind, e.g. by being enthusiastic about something then unenthusiastic ◇ **hot to trot** eager and willing (*slang*)

hot up *vti* **1** to make something more intense, active, or exciting, or increase in intensity, activity, or excitement (*informal*) **2** to make something faster or more powerful, or increase in speed or energy

hot air *n* impressive or boastful talk about achievements or intentions that has no substance (*informal*)

hot-air balloon *n* a lighter-than-air craft in which a compartment for pilot and passengers is suspended from a large nylon balloon that holds heated air or helium

hotbed /hót bed/ *n* **1** an environment where something flourishes or happens frequently, especially something undesirable **2** a planting bed covered with glass and heated with electricity or by the action of fermenting manure to aid in quick germination of seeds and growth of plants

hot-blooded *adj* easily angered, excited, or physically aroused —**hot-bloodedness** *n*

hot button *n US* something that is known or likely to provoke a strong response, especially among voters or consumers ◇ **press somebody's hot button** *US* to provoke a strong immediate reaction, usually a predictable one

hot-button *adj US* arousing strong feelings (*informal*)

hotcake /hót kayk/ ◇ **sell like hotcakes** to sell very quickly

hotch /hoch/ *vi Scotland* to be surrounded by or full of a swarm of something [14C. < ?]

hotchpot /hóch pot/ *n* in law, the gathering together of property belonging to different people in order to divide it equally [14C. < Old French *hochepot* < *hocher* 'shake' + *pot* 'pot'.]

hotchpotch /hóch poch/ *n* **1** a mixture of several unrelated things. US term **hodgepodge 2** a stew consisting of a varied mixture of ingredients, usually mutton and vegetables [Late 16C. Rhyming alteration of HOTCHPOT.]

hot comb *n* a comb that can be heated, usually electrically, and used to style or straighten the hair

hot-comb *vt* to style or straighten the hair using a hot comb

hot cross bun *n* a sweet bun containing yeast, spices, and dried fruit and marked with a cross on the top, traditionally eaten hot on Good Friday

hot-desking *n* the practice of using whatever desk an employer has available rather than an assigned desk for each employee —**hot-desk** *vi*

hot dog *n* a long sausage typically served hot on a bread roll with toppings such as fried onions, mustard, or ketchup ■ *interj US* expresses strong approval, delight, or surprise (*informal*)

hot-dog (**hot-dogs, hot-dogging, hot-dogged**) *vi US* to perform difficult, dangerous, or acrobatic stunts in a showy or impressive manner in skiing, surfing, and similar sports (*slang*) —**hot-dogger** *n* —**hot-dogging** *n*

hotdrink /hót dringk/ *n W Africa* a drink with a high alcohol content, e.g. gin

hotel /hō tél/ *n* **1 PLACE FOR AN OVERNIGHT STAY** a building or commercial establishment where people pay for lodgings, meals, and sometimes other facilities or services **2** *Aus* **PUB** an establishment that sells alcoholic beverages **3** *S Asia* **RESTAURANT** a restaurant **4 CODE WORD FOR LETTER 'H'** a code word for the letter 'H', used in international radio communications [Mid-17C. Via French *hôtel* < Old French *hostel* (see HOSTEL).]

hotelier /hō télli ay, -télli ər/ *n* an owner or manager of a hotel [Early 20C. Via French *hôtelier* < Old French *hostelier* 'hosteler' < *hostel* (see HOSTEL).]

hotelkeeper /hō tél keepər/ *n* = **hotelier**

hotelling /hō télling/ *n* the practice of providing temporary desk space for an employee [Because a hotel is a temporary place to stay]

hot flash *n US* MED = **hot flush**

hot flush *n* a sudden hot feeling, sometimes accompanied by sweating and redness of the face, experienced by some women during the menopause and caused by an endocrine imbalance. US term **hot flash**

hotfoot /hót fòot, hót fòot/ *adv* with great haste ◇ **hotfoot it** to go with great haste and eagerness, usually on foot (*informal*)

hot-gospeller *n* a forceful or enthusiastic preacher or propagandist (*informal; offensive in some contexts*)

hothead /hót hed/ *n* an excitable or easily angered person

hotheaded /hót héddid/ *adj* too easily angered or excited and usually acting impetuously —**hotheadedly** *adv* —**hotheadedness** *n*

hothouse /hót howss/ *n* (*plural* **-houses** /-howziz/) **1 HEATED GREENHOUSE** a heated building, usually with glass walls and roof, in which tropical or delicate plants can grow at a stable warm temperature **2 CENTRE OF ACTIVITY** a place where a particular thing flourishes and develops, usually in an intensive way ○ *a hothouse of technological innovation* ■ *adj* **SENSITIVE** sensitive and delicate (*informal*) ○ *hothouse views on political strategy*

hothousing /hót howzing/ *n* a programme of providing children with intensive education

ϟ **hot key** *n* a computer key or combination of keys that provides a short cut for a particular function

hotline /hót līn/ *n* **1** a telephone number that enables members of the public to make direct contact with a special service offering information, advice, or help, usually on a serious or urgent matter **2** a telephone connection or similar link that allows direct communication between heads of government or other important people, especially in an emergency

ϟ **hotlink** /hót link/ *n* COMPUT = **hyperlink**

ϟ **hotlist** /hót list/ *n* a browser configuration file of a computer user's most recent hypertext link selections

hotly /hóttli/ *adv* **1** in an angry way **2** in an intense and committed way ○ *hotly contested*

hot-melt *n* a fast-drying adhesive applied in a molten state

hot metal *n* **1** printing type cast from molten metal in a crucible beside the printing machine **2** printing using hot metal type

hot money *n* funds transferred from one form of currency to another in order to take advantage of better exchange rates

hot pants *npl* **1** very brief close-fitting shorts for women, first fashionable in the early 1970s **2** very strong physical desire (*slang*)

hot plate *n* **1** a flat heated surface, usually part of a cooker, on which food can be cooked **2** a portable device with a flat heated surface on which cooked food can be heated or kept warm

hotpot /hót pot/ *n* a stew of meat and vegetables cooked slowly in the oven in a covered container

hot potato *n* a sensitive or controversial issue that is awkward or difficult to deal with

hot press *n* a machine used to apply heat and pressure to a material such as paper or cloth —**hot-press** *vt*

hot rod *n* a car that has been modified to make it go very fast (*slang*)

hot-rod (**hot-rods, hot-rodding, hot-rodded**) *v* (*slang*) **1** *vt* to modify a car or its engine to make it very fast or powerful **2** *vi* to drive a hot rod

hot-rodder *n* a driver of a hot rod (*slang*)

hot seat *n US* the electric chair (*slang*) ◇ **in the hot seat** facing or liable to face criticism or difficult questioning ○ *in the hot seat after the latest round of allegations*

hot shoe *n* a camera accessory used to connect the camera and an electric flash

hotshot /hót shot/ *n* a successful, important, or highly skilled person, especially one who is showily confident (*informal*)

hot spot *n* **1 PLACE OF POTENTIAL UNREST** an area where fighting or trouble is likely to break out **2 CENTRE OF ENTERTAINMENT** a place that is a centre of entertainment and social activity, e.g. a lively nightclub (*informal*) **3 SMALL AREA OF INTENSE HEAT** a small area of something, e.g. an engine, that is at a much higher temperature than the rest **4 AREA OF GEOTHERMAL ACTIVITY** a part of the Earth's surface subject to greater than usual geothermal activity

hot spring *n* a spring of water heated by geothermal energy. ◊ **geyser**

hotspur /hót spur/ *n* a rash or impetuous person [< *Hotspur*, nickname of Henry PERCY]

hot stuff *n* **1 VERY GOOD PERSON OR THING** an impressive, attractive, exciting, or important person or thing (*informal*) **2 ATTRACTIVE PERSON** a physically attractive person (*informal*) **3 SEXUALLY EXPLICIT THING** something, e.g. a book or photograph, that is particularly erotic or pornographic

Hottentot /hótt'n tot/ (*plural* **-tot** *or* **-tots**) *n* (*dated*) **1** an offensive term for a member of the Khoikhoi people **2** an offensive term for the languages of the Khoikhoi people [Late 17C. < Dutch, probably < a formula in a Nama song.]

Hottentot fig *n* a cultivated low-growing succulent plant with edible fruit. Flowers: purplish or yellowish, resembling daisies. Native to: southern Africa. *Carpobrotus edulis.*

hot ticket *n* a popular or fashionable person or thing

hotting /hótting/ *n* the performing of difficult or dangerous high-speed stunts and manoeuvres in a stolen car (*slang*)

hottish /hóttish/ *adj* fairly but not excessively hot

hot toddy *n* BEVERAGES = **toddy** *n.* 1

hot tub *n* a large round bathtub filled with hot water for one or more people to relax, bathe, or socialize in —**hot-tubbing** *n*

hotty /hótti/ (*plural* **-ties**) *n* somebody considered particularly attractive or sexy (*slang*)

hot war *n* armed conflict between groups or nations, as opposed to political hostility. ◊ **cold war**

hot-water bottle *n* a container, usually made of rubber, filled with hot water and used to warm a bed or part of the body

hot-wire (**hot-wires, hot-wiring, hot-wired**) *vt* to start a car by bringing the ignition wires into contact (*informal*)

Houdan /hòo dan/ *n* a domestic fowl belonging to a breed with black and white plumage and a characteristic full crest [Late 19C. After a village in the French department of Seine-et-Oise.]

Houdini /hoo deéni/, **Harry** (1874–1926) Hungarian-born US magician. Born **Ehrich Weiss**

hough /hok/ *n* **1** ZOOL = **hock**[1] *n.* 1 **2** *Scotland* a cut of beef from the leg, used in stewing ■ *vt* to hamstring an animal [Old English *hōh* 'heel' < Germanic]

hou high /hṓ-/ *n Hong Kong* a state of intoxication or excitement, e.g. from a drug (*slang*)

hoummos /hòommòoss/ *n* FOOD = **hummus**

hound /hownd/ *n* **1 DOG BRED FOR HUNTING** a dog originally bred for hunting, with floppy ears, short hair, and a deep bark (*often in combination*) **2 DOG** any domestic dog, especially one viewed with disapproval (*informal*) **3 UNPLEASANT PERSON** a contemptible or despicable person (*dated*) **4 ENTHUSIAST** an enthusiast of something (*informal*) ■ *vt* **1 PURSUE DOGGEDLY** to follow, chase, or pester somebody in a persistent or relentless manner **2 URGE OR NAG** to urge or force somebody to do something by nagging or harassment ○ *hounded out of office by a hostile press* [Old English *hund* 'dog' < Indo-European] —**hounder** *n*

houndfish /hównd fish/ (*plural* **-fish** *or* **-fishes**) *n* a small shark or dogfish

hounds /howndz/ *npl* the part of a ship's masthead that supports the topmast and the rigging [15C. Alteration of *hune* 'wooden projection below a masthead' < ?]

hound's-tongue *n* a coarse plant of the borage family with spiny clinging fruit. Flowers: small, reddish-purple. Native to: Europe, Asia. Genus: *Cynoglossum.* [< the shape and texture of its leaves]

houndstooth check /hówndz tooth-/, **hound's-tooth check** *n* a fabric design of small jagged checks

hour /owr/ *n* **1 60 MINUTES** 3,600 seconds or one of 24 equal parts of a day **2 60-MINUTE INTERVAL SHOWN ON A TIMEPIECE** one of the intervals of 60 minutes shown on a clock or watch ○ *There's a bus at 20 past the hour.* **3 TIME OF DAY** time of day, with emphasis on the general portion of day or night being referred to ○ *at this unearthly hour* **4 REGULAR TIME** a time at which something usually takes place or is done ○ *my lunch hour* **5 SIGNIFICANT PERIOD** a period during which something particularly significant happens ○ *Enjoy your hour of glory while it lasts.* **6 TIME OF SUCCESS** a time when somebody is powerful, successful, or famous ○ *This is your hour, so seize the opportunity!* **7 TIME OF DEATH** the time when somebody is going to die ○ *As he started falling, he thought his hour had surely come.* **8 MEASURE OF LONGITUDE** a measure of longitude equal to 15 degrees or one twenty-fourth of a great circle [12C. Via Old French *houre* < Latin *hora* < Greek *hōra* 'time period, season'.] ◇ **at any hour** at any time, day or night ◇ **of the hour** enjoying the highest degree of relevance, importance, or popularity at the current moment or particular time ○ *She is clearly the woman of the hour.*

SPELLCHECK Do not confuse ***hour*** with ***our***, which has a similar sound. Beware: your spellchecker will not catch this error.

hour angle *n* the angle, measured positively westwards, between the plane containing the observer and the Earth's poles and the plane containing a particular celestial body and the Earth's poles

hour circle *n* a great circle passing through the poles of the celestial sphere and intersecting the celestial equator at right angles, containing a point on the celestial sphere such as a star

hourglass /ówr glaass/ *n* a time-measurement device consisting of two transparent bulbs connected by a narrow tube and containing an amount of sand that takes a specified time to flow between the bulbs after inversion

hourglass figure *n* a woman's body shape, curving out above and below a narrow waist like the shape of an hourglass

hour hand *n* the shorter, wider hand of a nondigital clock or watch, which indicates the hour

houri /hóori/ *n* **1** in Islamic belief, one of the beautiful young women who attend Muslim men in paradise **2** an attractive woman (*dated; sometimes offensive*) [Mid-18C. Via French < Arabic *ḥawrāʼ* 'woman with dark eyes'.]

hourly /ówrli/ *adj* **1 EACH HOUR** happening at sixty-minute intervals ○ *hourly news* **2 OCCURRING A LOT** happening frequently or continually ○ *hourly changes* **3 CALCULATED BY THE HOUR** calculated as a particular amount for each hour worked ○ *hourly wages* **4 PAID BY THE HOUR** working for pay that is calculated as a particular amount for each hour worked ■ *adv* **1 SOON** at any time shortly from now ○ *Her arrival is expected hourly.* **2 OFTEN** frequently or continually ○ *The situation is changing hourly.* **3 BY THE HOUR** with a particular amount being paid for each hour worked

hours /owrz/ *npl* **1 LONG TIME** a long but unspecified amount of time (*informal*) **2 TIMES FOR DOING PARTICULAR THINGS** the times of day during which particular things are done ○ *during school hours* **3 TIME IN A 24-HOUR CLOCK** the time of day, when using a 24-hour clock ○ *The flight leaves at 1300 hours.* **4 CANONICAL HOURS** the canonical hours taken as a whole

Housatonic /hóossə tónnik/ river in NW Massachusetts and Connecticut. Length: 240 km/150 mi.

house *n* /howss/ (*plural* **houses** /hówziz/) **1 DWELLING** a building made for people to live in, especially one built for a single group of occupants **2 OCCUPANTS OF A HOUSE** all of the people who are in a house at one time, particularly the people who usually live there **3 COMMUNITY DWELLING** a building in which a community of people lives **4 BUILDING FOR ANIMALS** a building where animals are kept, especially in a zoo ○ *the monkey house* **5 PLACE WHERE PEOPLE PAY TO EAT** a place where members of the public pay for food, drink, or entertainment, e.g. a restaurant or club ○ *the speciality of the house* **6 THEATRE** a theatre, or the audience at a theatre ○ *The dancers performed to an appreciative house.* **7 BUSINESS OPERATION** a company or a corporation creating or selling a particular product ○ *a publishing house* **8 DIVISION OF SCHOOL** any of the groups into which the pupils of some schools are divided **9 house, House LEGISLATIVE GROUP** a legislative group in a government, or the place where it meets **10 house, House FAMILY LINE** a family line, including ancestors and descendants, especially a royal family ○ *the House of Windsor* **11 DIVISION OF THE ZODIAC** any one of the 12 divisions of the zodiac in astrology **12 ZODIAC SIGN** the sign of the zodiac in which a planet is found at a specific time **13 CURLING TARGET** an area of concentric circles at either end of an ice rink marked out for curling, with the target in its centre **14 FAST DANCE MUSIC** a style of dance music first developed by adding electronic beats to disco records, and later characterized by the addition of repetitive vocals, extracts from other recordings, or synthesized sounds ■ *interj* **USED TO CLAIM WIN AT BINGO** shouted by people playing bingo to claim that they have the full set of numbers needed to win a game (*informal*) ■ *vt* /howz/ (**houses, housing, housed**) **1 GIVE SOMEWHERE TO LIVE** to provide somebody with a place to live **2 CONTAIN** to contain, keep, or store something **3 PUT AWAY SAFELY** to put something away safely, e.g. oars or an anchor [Old English *hūs* < Germanic] ◇ **bring the house down** to provoke a great deal of laughter or applause ◇ **like a house on fire** very well, successfully, quickly, or strongly ○ *They got on like a house on fire.* ◇ **on the house** given free by somebody who would normally charge ◇ **play house** to take part in a children's game of pretending to be a family, with children playing the roles of both adults and children (*informal*) ◇ **put your house in order** to organize your life properly

USAGE See *home*.

house agent *n* COMM = **estate agent** *n.* 1

house arrest *n* a form of legal confinement in which people who have been arrested are not allowed to leave their own homes

houseboat /hówss bōt/ *n* a boat, especially a flat-bottomed river boat or barge, that is permanently moored and used as a house

housebound /hówss bownd/ *adj* unable to go out of doors because of illness or difficulty in travelling or because of severe weather. US term **homebound**

houseboy /hówss boy/ *n* a term referring to a man, especially in Africa or the Indian subcontinent, employed to perform various household tasks (*often considered offensive*)

housebreak /hówss brayk/ *vt* (**-breaks, -breaking, -broke** /-brōk/, **-broken** /-brōkən/) *US* = **housetrain** ■ *n US* = **break-in** *n.*

housebreaking /hówss brayking/ *n* the action of illegally forcing entry into a house or other building in order to commit a crime —**housebreaker** *n*

house call *n US* a visit made by a doctor or other professional to a patient or client at home

housecarl /hówss kaarl/ *n* any one of the household warriors of an early English or Danish nobleman or king [Old English *hūscarl* < Old Norse *húskarl* < *hús* 'house' + *karl* 'man']

housecoat /hówss kōt/ *n* a woman's outer garment, often loose and comfortable, worn at home

house cricket *n* a dark-brown cricket that can become a nuisance indoors. Native to: North America, Europe. *Acheta domesticus.*

housefather /hówss faat͟hər/ *n* a man who is responsible for a group of young people living in an institution such as a hostel

house finch *n* a small common finch, the male of which has a red forehead, throat, breast, and rump. Native to: United States, Mexico. *Carpodacus mexicanus.*

housefly /hówss flī/ (*plural* **-flies**) *n* a common fly that lives in and around human dwellings in most parts of the world and is responsible for spreading numerous diseases. *Musca domestica.*

house guest *n* a guest in somebody's home

household /hówss hōld/ *n* **PEOPLE WHO LIVE TOGETHER** the people who live together in a single home ■ *adj* **1 BELONGING TO A HOUSEHOLD** relating to, belonging to, or used in a household **2 FAMILIAR TO ALL** very widely known ○ *Thanks to the media, their personal problems are household knowledge.*

Household Cavalry *n* the cavalry regiments, the Horse Guards and the Life Guards, responsible for guarding the British sovereign, especially during public ceremonies

householder /hówss hōldər/ *n* an owner or renter of a house

household gods *npl* the deities believed to protect the home and its inhabitants, especially in the religion of ancient Rome. ◊ **lares and penates**

household goods *npl* **1** things that people use in a house, especially kitchen utensils and small electrical appliances. US term **housewares 2** *US* = **housewares**

household name *n* somebody or something that most people know about

household troops *npl* soldiers who accompany and guard a sovereign

household word *n* a popular saying, the name of a famous person, or an event that is very well known

househusband /hówss huzbənd/ *n* a man who does not go out to work but stays at home to manage a household [Mid-20C. After HOUSEWIFE.]

housekeeper /hówss keepər/ *n* **1** a person who looks after a house and its residents **2** somebody employed to carry out or manage the work of looking after somebody else's house and the people who live there

⚡**housekeeping** /hówss keeping/ *n* **1 HOUSEHOLD MAINTENANCE** the maintenance of a household, or the range of tasks involved in this **2 MONEY FOR RUNNING HOUSEHOLD** money used to pay for the things needed in maintaining a household ○ *Perhaps we could save a little extra from the housekeeping.* **3** *US* **MANAGEMENT OF PROPERTY AND EQUIPMENT** the management and upkeep of equipment and property for a business or other organization **4 MAINTENANCE OF COMPUTER SYSTEM** the performance of routine tasks needed to keep a computer system working efficiently

houseleek /hówss leek/ *n* a flowering succulent plant with rosettes of leaves at the base of the stems. Native to: Europe. Genus: *Sempervivum.* [Because formerly planted on walls and roofs to protect the house from lightning]

house lights *npl* the lights inside a theatre or auditorium that illuminate the area where the audience sits

housemaid /hówss mayd/ *n* a woman employed to do housework (*dated*)

housemaid's knee *n* a swelling of the fluid-filled sac in front of the kneecap, caused by kneeling too much

houseman /hówssmən/ (*plural* **-men** /-mən/) *n* a hospital intern (*dated*)

house martin *n* a small swallow with blue-black feathers, a white rump, and a forked tail. Native to: Europe, China, Africa. *Delichon urbica.* [< its habit of nesting under the eaves of houses]

housemaster /hówss maastər/ *n* a man who is in charge of the students living together in a house at a private boys' school

housemate /hówss mayt/ *n* a sharer of a house with one or more other people who are not relatives

housemistress /hówss mistrəss/ *n* a woman who is in charge of the students living together at some prep schools and colleges

housemother /hówss mut͟hər/ *n* a woman who is responsible for a group of young people living in an institution such as a boarding house or a private school

house mouse *n* a grey or brownish-grey mouse that is common worldwide and is a household pest. *Mus musculus.*

house music *n* MUSIC = **house** *n.* **14** [Probably after the *Warehouse*, nightclub in Chicago]

House of Assembly *n* **1** the law-making body or lower house of the legislature in some countries of the Commonwealth of Nations **2** the lower house of the state parliament in South Australia and Tasmania

house of cards *n* something that is unstable and likely to fall down, like a structure built of playing cards

House of Commons *n* the lower house of Parliament in the United Kingdom and Canada

house of correction *n* an institution where people convicted of minor offences were imprisoned in the past

house officer *n UK* a junior doctor at a hospital

house of God *n* = **house of worship**

House of Keys *n* the lower house of the legislature of the Isle of Man

House of Lords *n* the nonelected upper house of Parliament in the United Kingdom, made up of life peers, some hereditary peers, and some bishops

House of Representatives *n* **1 LOWER HOUSE OF CONGRESS** the lower house of Congress and of most state legislatures in the United States **2 AUSTRALIAN FEDERAL PARLIAMENT** the lower house of the federal parliament of Australia **3 PARLIAMENT OF NEW ZEALAND** the sole chamber of the New Zealand Parliament, formerly its lower chamber

House of the People *n* POL = **Lok Sabha**

house of worship, house of God *n* a church, temple, synagogue, or other building used for religious services

house organ *n* a magazine published by a business or other organization for its employees or customers, containing information about the company, its products, and its employees

housepainter /hówss payntər/ *n US* a professional painter of houses

houseparent /hówss pairənt/ *n* one of a married couple who is responsible for a group of young people living in an institution such as a children's home or boarding school. ◊ **housefather, housemother**

house party *n* **1** a party at somebody's home at which the guests stay overnight or for several days, especially at a wealthy person's country house **2** the group of guests attending a house party

houseplant /hówss plaant/ *n* a decorative plant grown indoors, especially one that would die if planted outdoors in a cold climate

house-proud *adj* taking pride in the appearance of your home and its state of cleanliness or repair, sometimes in an excessive or fussy way

house rule *n* a rule, usually not one of the regular rules in a game, that is observed in a casino or among a group of friends

house-sit *vti* to live in temporarily and take care of somebody else's house and property while that person is away

house sitter *n* an occupant of a house who takes care of it while its usual occupants are away [After BABYSITTER]

Houses of Parliament *npl* **1** the building in which the House of Commons and the House of Lords meet and work **2** the House of Commons and the House of Lords considered together ○ *The bill will go before the Houses of Parliament this year.*

house sparrow *n* a small hardy brown and grey bird with a black throat. Native to: Europe, Asia. *Passer domesticus.* [< its living in or near human settlements]

house-to-house *adj* going or done from one house to the next ○ *a house-to-house search*

housetop /hówss top/ *n* the very top or roof of a house

housetrain /hówss trayn/ *vt* to teach a domestic animal to excrete outdoors or in a particular place. US term **housebreak** *v.* —**housetrained** *adj*

housewares /hówss wairz/ *npl US* = **household goods**

housewarming /hówss wawrming/, **housewarming party** *n* a party that somebody gives to celebrate moving into a new house

housewife /hówss wīf/ (*plural* **-wives** /-wīvz/) *n* a woman who does not go out to work but stays at home to manage a household

housewifely /hówss wīfli/ *adj* **1** relating to, belonging to, done by, or thought appropriate for a housewife **2** showing the qualities traditionally thought appropriate for a housewife, e.g. tidiness and careful management of money

housework /hówss wurk/ *n* tasks such as dusting, vacuuming, washing clothes, and cooking that are regularly done in a house

housey-housey /hówssi hówssi/ *n* the game of bingo (*dated*) [Alteration of HOUSE]

housing[1] /hówzing/ *n* **1 ACCOMMODATION** houses and other buildings where people live, considered collectively ○ *Decent housing is often hard to find.* **2 PROVISION OF ACCOMMODATION** the provision of places to live ○ *Housing of the homeless is our first priority.* **3 MACHINE'S PROTECTIVE STRUCTURE** a frame or structure that protects part of a machine ○ *a wheel housing* **4 PLACE WHERE A PIECE FITS** a slot, groove, or hole in one piece of wood into which another piece is fitted **5 NICHE FOR A STATUE** a small recess or hollow in which a statue can be placed

housing[2] /hówzing/ *n* **1** a piece of cloth that covers the back of a horse, used for protection or decoration **2** the ornamental trappings for a horse (*often plural*) [Mid-17C. < Old French *houce* < medieval Latin *hultia* 'protective covering' < Germanic.]

housing association *n* a nonprofit-making organization that provides houses and flats at fair rents

housing estate *n* a planned area of houses or flats, usually built at the same time to a similar design, sometimes with a number of small shops

housing project *n US* a group of houses or flats built with public money for low-income families

housing scheme *n Scotland* a housing estate built by a local authority, originally made up of homes to be rented by council tenants

housing society *n UK, Can* an organization that owns or manages properties and lets them at moderate rents to its members

Housman /hówssmən/, **A. E.** (1859–1936) British poet and scholar. Full name **Alfred Edward Housman**

Houston /hyoóstən/ major port in SE Texas. Population: 1,786,691 (1998 estimate).

houting /hówting/ (*plural* **-ings** *or* **-ing**) *n* **1** a fish of the whitefish family that lives in salt water but produces its young in fresh water. Native to: Europe. *Coregonus oxyrhynchus.* **2** the flesh of a houting used as food [Late 19C. Via Dutch < Middle Dutch *houtic.*]

HOV *abbr* high occupancy vehicle

hove past participle of **heave** *v.* **8.** past tense of **heave** *v.* **9** (*formal*)

hovel /hóvv'l/ *n* a small, dirty, or poorly built house [14C. < ?]

hover /hóvvər/ (**-ers, -ering, -ered**) *vi* **1 FLOAT IN THE AIR** to float in the air without moving very far from the same spot **2 BE FLYING IN ONE SPOT** to stay in the air in the same position by rapidly beating the wings (*refers to birds*) **3 WAIT NEARBY** to wait near a person or place, usually in a nervous, inquisitive, or expectant way **4 BE UNDECIDED** to be unable to decide between alternatives **5 BE UNSTABLE** to be in a condition that is neither one of two alternatives nor the other ○ *He hovered between life and death.* **6 STAY AROUND THE SAME LEVEL** to stay near a particular point, changing only slightly ○ *Inflation has been hovering around the same level for several months.* [14C. < obsolete *hove* 'linger' < ?] —**hover** *n* —**hoverer** *n* —**hoveringly** *adv*

hovercraft /hóvvər kraaft/ (*plural* **-crafts** *or* **-craft**) *n* a vehicle that can travel over land and water supported by a cushion of air that it creates by blowing air downwards

hoverfly /hóvvər flī/ (*plural* **-flies**) *n* a fly that feeds on nectar and has a hovering style of flight. Many resemble wasps in colouring. Family: Syrphidae.

hover mower *n* a lawn mower with horizontally rotating blades that uses a cushion of downwards-directed air to lift itself slightly above the ground

hoverport /hóvvər pawrt/ *n* a place where hovercrafts load and unload [Mid-20C. < HOVERCRAFT + AIRPORT.]

how[1] /how/ *adv* **1 IN WHAT WAY** used to ask or report questions or to introduce statements about the manner in which something happens or is done ○ *How do I open the window here?* ○ *I don't know how you manage to sew so neatly.* **2 TO WHAT EXTENT** used to ask or report questions or to introduce statements about the quantity or degree of something ○ *How high is the roof?* ○ *Tell me honestly how serious the situation is.* **3 LIKE WHAT** used to ask or report questions or to introduce statements about the quality or success of something ○ *How was the film?* **4 USED IN EXCLAMATIONS** used in exclamations to emphasize a word or statement ○ *How beautiful she was!* ■ *rel adv* **IN WHATEVER WAY** used to indicate that it does not matter in what way somebody does something ○ *Fix it how you want – just as long as it gets fixed.* ■ *conj* **THAT** used to mention a fact or event ○ *Do you remember how we were ridiculed and derided?* [Old English *hū* < Indo-European] ◇ **how about 1** used to make a suggestion (*informal*) ○ *How about some lunch?* **2** used to change the subject of conversation (*informal*) ○ *That's enough of my ideas. How about your own policies?* ◇ **how are you (doing)?** used to ask about somebody's health, or simply as a greeting when you meet somebody, especially somebody already known ◇ **how do you do?** used when meeting somebody for the first time

how[2] *n* = **howe**[2]

Howard /hów ərd/, **Catherine** (1520?–42) queen of England (1540–42)

Howard, Sir Ebenezer (1850–1928) British town planner

Howard, John (1726–90) British penal reformer

Howard, John (*b.* 1939) Australian statesman

Howard, Leslie (1893–1943) British actor. Born **Leslie Howard Steiner**

Howard, Trevor (1916–88) British actor

howbeit /how beé it/ *adv* however or nevertheless (*formal*)

howdah /hówdə/ *n* a large seat for several people, often with a canopy, that rests on the back of an elephant [Late 18C. Via Urdu *haudah* < Arabic *hawdaj* 'litter carried by a camel'.]

how-do-you-do (*plural* **how-do-you-dos**) *n* **1** a greeting or welcome ○ *got to business as soon as the how-do-you-dos were finished* **2** a difficult or unsatisfactory situation (*informal*) ○ *a fine how-do-you-do* [< the greeting *how do you do?*]

howdy /hówdi/ *interj US* used as a greeting (*informal*) [Early 19C. < *how d'ye*, variant of *how do you do?*]

howe[1] /how/ *n Scotland* a hollow or valley (*often in placenames*) ○ *'We sat down, therefore, in a howe of the hillside'* (Robert Louis Stevenson, *Kidnapped*; 1886) [Pre-12C. Variant of HOLE.]

howe[2] /how/, **how** *n* a small prominent hill (*regional*) [14C. < Old Norse *haugr* 'mound' < Germanic.]

Howe /how/, **Sir Geoffrey, Baron of Aberavon** (*b.* 1926) British politician

Howe, William, 5th Viscount (1729–1814) British military commander

howe'er /how áir/ *contr* however (*literary*) [Contraction]

however /how évvər/ CORE MEANING: an adverb introducing some form of contrast ○ *I'm not sure how effective the campaign has been. I do, however, think that it has been distinctively different.*

1 *adv* **TO WHATEVER DEGREE** used to indicate that no matter what happens, a situation remains the same ○ *However objective it may believe itself to be, it is still only an opinion.* **2** *rel adv* **IN WHATEVER WAY** used to indicate that it does not matter in what way somebody does something ○ *Peel and prepare the potatoes however you like.* **3** *adv* **HOW** used as an emphatic form of 'how' ○ *What a surprise to see you! However did you find us?*

USAGE See ***although***.

USAGE When ***however*** appears within a sentence expressing ideas contrasting with what has been said in a previous sentence, put one comma before ***however*** and another after it: *The resort has closed for the season. Its staff members, however, are remaining on the property to service and repair the ski lifts.* ***However*** can also appear at the end of such a sentence, punctuated by a single comma just before it: *Its staff members are remaining on the property to service and repair the ski lifts, however.* Especially in American English, there is disagreement on whether ***however*** introducing a contrast should be used to start a sentence, but this is common in British English: *The chairman refused to resign. However, he soon changed his mind when further evidence came to light.* ***However*** has other meanings, and those meanings dictate whether or not you punctuate the word and how. If you use ***however*** to mean 'to whatever degree', 'in whatever way', or 'how' at the outset of an introductory main clause, put a comma after the clause, as in *However hard it snowed during the night, the road crews were able to clear the main arteries before the rush hour.* If ***however***, meaning 'in whatever way', modifies another adverb and the two appear as a pair in mid-sentence, put a comma before and after the two words: *The coaches have begun, however reluctantly, to admit major flaws in the team's defensive tactics.* It is redundant to pair *but* with ***however***. Use one word or the other, not both. Thus, this sentence is poor: *The flight was initially cancelled but it did manage to take off five hours late, however.* Keep *but* and drop ***however***.

howff /howf, hōf/, **howf** *n Scotland* a place where people often go to meet, especially a public house [Early 18C. < ?]

howitzer /hówitsər/ *n* a cannon with a bore diameter greater than 30 mm and a maximum elevation of 60 degrees that fires projectiles in a curved trajectory [Late 17C. Via Dutch *houwitser* < Czech *haufnice* 'catapult' < *hauf* 'heap' (of stones) < Germanic.]

howk /howk/ *vti Scotland* to dig or dig something up or out (*informal*) [14C. Originally *holk*, related to HOLE, HOLLOW.]

howl /howl/ *v* **1** *vi* **MAKE A WAVERING SOUND** to make a long wavering or whining sound ○ *a coyote howling* **2** *vi* **CRY OUT** to cry out in pain, anger, or distress **3** *vi* **ROAR WITH LAUGHTER** to laugh loudly and unrestrainedly (*slang*) **4** *vt* **CALL OUT** to call something out in a long wavering way ■ *n* **1 LONG MOANING CRY** a long sad wavering cry **2 LOUD CRY** a cry of pain, anger, or distress **3 DRAWN-OUT WAVERING SOUND** a long high loud wavering noise ○ *the howl of the wind* **4 SOMETHING OR SOMEBODY HILARIOUS** an extremely funny person or thing (*slang*) [13C. Probably an imitation of the sound.]

howl down *vt* to prevent somebody or something from being heard by making loud cries of protest or mockery

howler /hówlər/ *n* **1** a mistake that is so bad that it is funny (*informal*) **2** a person who or thing that makes a howling noise **3** ZOOL = **howler monkey**

howler monkey *n* any one of various tropical mainly leaf-eating monkeys of Central and South America that live in trees and have a very loud booming call. Genus: *Alouatta.*

howling /hówling/ *adj* **1 LOUD AND WAVERING** making a loud high wavering noise ○ *a howling gale* **2 DISMALLY DESOLATE** desolate or drearily empty of human beings (*literary*) ○ *alone in the howling desert* **3 VERY GREAT** extreme or great in degree (*informal*) ○ *Our presentation was a howling success!* ■ *n* **NOISE** a succession of long high wavering noises, e.g. animal cries or the sound of a strong wind ○ *the howling of the wind* —**howlingly** *adv*

Howlin' Wolf /hówlin woólf/ (1910–76) US musician. Born **Chester Arthur Burnett**

howsoever /hówssō évvər/ *adv* however (*formal or archaic*)

how-to *adj* giving practical information and instructions on the way to do something (*informal*) ○ *another how-to guide on home decorating*

howzat /hów zát/ *interj* an exclamation shouted at a cricket umpire by players claiming that a batsman is out (*informal*) [Late 20C. Alteration of *how's that?*]

Hoxha /hójjə/, **Enver** (1908–85) Albanian statesman

hoya /hóyə/ n = **waxplant** [Mid-19C. < modern Latin, after Thomas *Hoy* (d. 1821), British gardener.]

Hoy and West Mainland /hóy ənd wést-/ National Scenic Area in NE Scotland. The Old Man of Hoy is a pillar-shaped rock just off the coast of the island of Hoy. Area: 148 sq. km/57 sq. mi.

hoyden /hóyd'n/ n an offensive term that deliberately insults a young woman's self-control and thoughtfulness (*dated*) [Late 17C. Probably < Dutch *heiden* 'lout, heathen'.]

Hoyle /hoyl/, **Sir Fred** (*b.* 1915) British astronomer and writer

hp *abbr* horsepower

⚡**HP** *abbr* **1** hardy perennial **2** high pressure **3** hire purchase **4** home page (*in e-mails*) **5** Houses of Parliament

h.p. *abbr* **1** high pressure **2** hire purchase

HPV *abbr* human papilloma virus

HQ, h.q. *abbr* headquarters

hr[1] *abbr* hour

⚡**hr**[2] *abbr* Croatia (*in Internet addresses*)

HR *abbr* **1** Home Rule **2** human resources **3** *US* homeroom

H.R., HR *abbr* House of Representatives

HRE *abbr* **1** Holy Roman Emperor **2** Holy Roman Empire

HRH *abbr* **1** Her Royal Highness **2** His Royal Highness

hrs *abbr* hours

HRT *abbr* hormone replacement therapy

hryvnia /hrívni ə/ (*plural* **-a** *or* **-as**) n see table at **currency** [< Ukrainian]

Hs *symbol* hassium

HS *abbr* **1** High School **2** Home Secretary

HSC *abbr* Higher School Certificate

HSE *abbr* Health and Safety Executive

HSH *abbr* **1** Her Serene Highness **2** His Serene Highness

Hsien Nien /syén nyén/ n = **Chinese New Year**

HSRC *abbr* Human Sciences Research Council

HST *abbr* **1** harmonized sales tax **2** Hawaii Standard Time **3** high-speed train **4** hypersonic transport

ht[1] *abbr* **1** heat **2** height

⚡**ht**[2] *abbr* Haiti (*in Internet addresses*)

HT *abbr* **1** half-time **2** high tension **3** high tide

⚡**HTH** *abbr* hope this helps (*in e-mails*)

HTLV *abbr* human T-cell lymphotropic virus

HTLV-I n a virus associated with cancers of the lymphatic system. Full form **human T-cell lymphotropic virus I**

HTLV-II n a virus associated with leukaemia. Full form **human T-cell lymphotropic virus II**

⚡**HTML** *abbr* HyperText Markup Language

Hts *abbr* Heights

⚡**HTTP** *abbr* HyperText Transfer Protocol

⚡**hu** *abbr* Hungary (*in Internet addresses*)

Huainan /hwī nán/ city in E China. Population: 1,200,000 (1991).

Huang He /hwáng hő/ second longest river in China, flowing through the north-central part of the country. Length: 5,464 km/3,395 mi.

huarache /wə ráä chee/ n a sandal originally worn in Mexico, with the upper part made of woven leather straps [Late 19C. < Mexican Spanish, probably < Japanese *warachi* 'straw sandal'.]

hub /hub/ n **1** CENTRAL PART the central part of a wheel or a similar device that rotates, e.g. a propeller **2** CENTRE OF ACTIVITY a place that is a centre of activity or interest **3 hub, hub airport** CENTRAL AIRPORT a central airport that passengers can fly to from smaller local airports in order to catch an international or long-distance flight [Early 16C. < ?]

hubba-hubba /húbbə húbbə/ *interj* *US* used to express approval, enthusiasm, or pleasure (*dated slang*) [Mid-20C. < ?]

Hubble /húbb'l/, **Edwin** (1889–1953) US astronomer

hubble-bubble /húbb'l-l-/ n = **hookah** [Early 17C. Alteration of BUBBLE.]

Hubble constant /húbb'l-l-/, **Hubble's constant** n the ratio that expresses the rate of the universe's expansion, equal to the speed at which galaxies appear to be moving away from the Earth divided by their distance [Mid-20C. After Edwin HUBBLE.]

Hubble's law n the law holding that the speed at which distant galaxies are moving away from the Earth is proportional to their distance from the observer [Mid-20C. After Edwin HUBBLE.]

Hubble Telescope: A space shuttle astronaut repairs the Hubble Telescope

Hubble Telescope, Hubble Space Telescope n a telescope mounted on a satellite that orbits the Earth, used to observe distant parts of the universe and photograph them [Late 20C. After Edwin HUBBLE.]

hubbub /húbbub/ n **1** a confused din, especially a number of voices speaking at once **2** a fuss or period of excitement [Mid-16C. Probably < Celtic.]

hubby /húbbi/ (*plural* **-bies**) n a husband (*informal*) [Late 17C. Alteration of HUSBAND.]

hubcap /húb kap/ n a round cover that protects the outside of the central part of a vehicle's wheel

Hubei /hoõ báy/ province in central China. Capital: Wuhan. Population: 57,190,000 (1994). Area: 187,500 sq. km/72,394 sq. mi.

hubris /hyoõbriss, hoõ-/ n **1** excessive pride or arrogance **2** the excessive pride and ambition that usually leads to the downfall of a hero in classical tragedy [Late 19C. < Greek.] —**hubristic** /hyoo brístik, hoo-/ *adj* —**hubristically** *adv*

huckaback /húkə bak/, **huck** /huk/ n a coarse absorbent cotton or linen fabric. Use: towels. [Late 17C. < ?]

huckleberry /húk'lbəri/ (*plural* **-ries**) n **1** the edible, dark blue fruit of a shrub related to the blueberry **2** a shrub that bears huckleberries. Native to: North America. Genus: *Gaylussacia*. [Late 16C. Probably alteration of *hurtleberry* 'whortleberry'.]

huckster /húkstər/ n **1** AGGRESSIVE SALESPERSON an aggressive salesperson or promoter **2** RETAILER somebody who sells small articles, especially a street pedlar ■ v **1** *vt* PEDDLE MERCHANDISE to sell or peddle something **2** *vti* SELL AGGRESSIVELY to use aggressive methods to sell or promote something [12C. < ?]

⚡**HUD** /hud/ *abbr* head-up display

Huddersfield /húddərz feeld/ industrial town in N England. Population: 143,726 (1991).

huddle /húdd'l/ n **1** TIGHT GROUP a group of people or things gathered closely together **2** BRIEF TALK a quick private talk or gathering (*informal*) ■ v (**-dles, -dling, -dled**) **1** *vti* GATHER TIGHTLY TOGETHER to gather together in a tightly packed group, or make people or things do this ○ *The small crowd of spectators huddled together for warmth.* **2** *vi* CROUCH to draw your arms and legs tightly into your body, or move in close to something, often for shelter or comfort ○ *He huddled in a doorway to get out of the rain.* **3** *vi* TALK PRIVATELY to gather privately to confer, make plans, or gossip (*informal*) **4** *vt* DO SOMETHING HASTILY to make or put together something carelessly or hastily [Late 16C.]

Hudibrastic /hyoõdi brástik/, **hudibrastic** *adj* mock-heroic, especially written in the style or metre used by Samuel Butler in his poem *Hudibras*

Hudson /húdss'n/ river in E New York State, emptying into Upper New York Bay at New York City. Length: 492 km/306 mi.

Hudson, Henry (1565?–1611?) English navigator

Hudson, Rock (1925–85) US actor. Born **Roy Harold Scherer, Jr**

Hudson Bay almost landlocked inland sea of east-central Canada. Area: 730,000 sq. km/280,000 sq. mi. Depth: 258 m/846 ft.

Hudson's Bay Company /húdss'nz-/ n a fur-trading company chartered in England in 1670 to trade in North America and later much involved in fur trading, exploring, and claiming territory for the British crown [Because its original charter was to trade around Hudson Bay]

Hudson Strait body of water in NE Canada connecting Hudson Bay with the Atlantic Ocean and separating Baffin Island from N Quebec. Depth: 880 m/2,890 ft. Length: 720 km/450 mi.

hue /hyoo/ n **1** COLOUR a colour ○ *flowers of every hue* **2** SHADE OF COLOUR a specific shade of a colour ○ *a pleasing hue of green* **3** PROPERTY OF A COLOUR a property of a colour that enables it to be perceived, determined by its dominant wavelength **4** TYPE a type or kind in a particular range ○ *All hues of political opinion should be represented in the discussions.* **5** ASPECT the way that something looks ○ *This puts a completely different hue on the matter.* [Old English *hē(o)w* < Germanic]

SPELLCHECK See **hew**.

Hue /hway/ city in central Vietnam near the South China Sea. Population: 260,489 (1989).

hue and cry /hyoõ-/ n **1** a great uproar or commotion about something **2** formerly, a pursuit of somebody accused of a crime, with the pursuers calling on bystanders to join in the chase [< Anglo-Norman *hu e cri* 'outcry and cry']

-hued *suffix* of a particular colour or number of colours ○ *the many-hued rainbow* ○ *a rose-hued sunset*

huff /huf/ n **1** FIT OF THE SULKS a brief mood of anger or resentment at something somebody has done ■ v **1** *vti* ANGER SOMEBODY OR GET ANGRY to anger or offend somebody, or become angry or offended **2** *vi* BLOW OR PANT to blow, pant, or breathe laboriously **3** *vti* REMOVE OPPONENT'S PIECE to remove an opponent's draughtsman from the board as a penalty for failing to make an obligatory capture [Late 16C. An imitation of the sound of blowing.] ◇ **huff and puff 1** to blow or pant **2** to make noisy but empty threats or objections

huffy /húffi/ (**-ier, -iest**) *adj* easily offended or put into a huff —**huffily** *adv* —**huffiness** n

hug /hug/ v (**hugs, hugging, hugged**) **1** *vti* EMBRACE AFFECTIONATELY to put your arms round somebody's body and hold the person tight to show affection or pleasure **2** *vt* PUT YOUR ARMS ROUND to clasp your arms round a part of your own body ○ *hugging her knees to her chest* **3** *vr* PUT YOUR ARMS ROUND YOURSELF to put your arms round your own body, especially to keep warm **4** *vr* CONGRATULATE YOURSELF to congratulate yourself or show great delight **5** *vt* KEEP CLOSE to remain in close linear proximity to something while moving in a forward direction ○ *The boat hugged the coastline.* ■ n AFFECTIONATE EMBRACE an affectionate embrace [Mid-16C. Probably < N Germanic.] —**huggable** *adj* —**hugger** n

huge /hyooj/ (**huger, hugest**) *adj* **1** ENORMOUS very big in size or amount **2** LARGE IN SCOPE very large in scope or scale ○ *huge talent* **3** SIGNIFICANTLY SUCCESSFUL very important or successful (*informal*) ○ *This band are going to be huge.* [12C. Shortening of Old French *ahuge*.] —**hugeness** n

hugely /hyoõjli/ *adv* to a great degree ○ *hugely successful*

huggermugger /húggər mugər/ n MUDDLED MESS a disorderly mess or muddle ■ *adj* **1** DISORDERED confused or jumbled **2** SECRETIVE clandestine or secret [Early 16C. < ?] —**huggermugger** *adv*

Huggins, Sir William (1824–1910) British astronomer

Hughes /hyooz/, **Howard** (1905–76) US industrialist

Hughes, Langston (1902–67) US writer

Hughes, Richard (1900–76) British writer

Hughes, Robert (*b.* 1938) Australian art critic and writer

Hughes, Ted (1930–98) British poet. Full name **Edward James Hughes**

Hughes, Thomas (1822–96) British writer

Hughes, William Morris (1862–1952) British-born Australian statesman

Langston Hughes

Hugo /hyóogō/, **Victor** (1802–85) French poet, novelist, and dramatist

Huguenot /hyóogənō/ n a French Protestant, especially in the 16th and 17th centuries ■ adj relating to, belonging to, or typical of the French Protestant Church [Mid-16C. < French, alteration (based on the Besançon *Hugues*, leader of a Swiss political movement) of obsolete *eiguenot* < Swiss German *Eidgenosse* 'confederate', literally 'oath-companion'.] —**Huguenotism** /hyóogə notizəm/ n

huh /hu/ interj 1 shows surprise, inquiry, disdain, or lack of interest 2 invites comment, especially agreement, after an expressed opinion ○ Great shot, huh? [Early 17C. Natural exclamation.]

hui /hoo ee/ (plural **hui**) n NZ a social gathering in a Maori community [Mid-19C. < Maori and Hawaiian.]

huia /hoòyə/ (plural **-a**) n a New Zealand bird, now thought to be extinct, with tail feathers that were much prized by Maoris. *Heteralocha acutirostris*. [Mid-19C. < Hawaiian; an imitation of its whistle.]

hula /hoòlə/ n a Polynesian or Hawaiian dance involving swaying the hips and miming gestures with the hands [Early 19C. < Hawaiian.]

Hula-Hoop tdmk a trademark for a plastic ring that is placed around the waist and kept twirling by rhythmically moving the hips

hulk /hulk/ n 1 SOMEBODY BIG a big, powerful, and often clumsy person 2 EMPTY HULL the empty hull of a ship that has been wrecked or is too old to be sailed 3 UNWIELDY SHIP a heavy ship that is difficult to steer 4 SHELL OF A STRUCTURE the shell of any old, abandoned, or burnt-out structure or vehicle 5 OLD SHIP USED AS PRISON an old, permanently moored ship, used in the 19th century as a prison (often plural) ■ vi MOVE CLUMSILY to move in a clumsy or awkward way [Pre-12C. Probably via Anglo-Latin *hulcus* < Greek *holkas* 'merchant barge, ship that is towed' < *helkein* 'pull'.]

hulking /húlking/, **hulky** /-ki/ (**-ier, -iest**) adj large, bulky, and often clumsy

hull /hul/ n 1 BODY OF SHIP the body of a ship, excluding other parts, e.g. the masts and engines 2 BODY OF A VEHICLE the main body of a large vehicle such as a tank or aeroplane 3 ROCKET CASING the external casing of a rocket, missile, or spaceship 4 CALYX ON A STRAWBERRY the calyx on a strawberry that stays attached to the fruit when it is picked but is not eaten 5 OUTER COVERING the outer covering of a seed or fruit ■ vt 1 TAKE OFF A STRAWBERRY CALYX to remove the calyx from a strawberry 2 REMOVE THE OUTER RIND FROM FRUIT to remove the outer rind or shell from a fruit or vegetable [Old English *hulu* < Indo-European, 'cover, conceal']

Hull /hul/ port in NE England, on the Humber Estuary. Population: 268,600 (1995).

Hull, Bobby (b. 1939) Canadian ice-hockey player. Full name **Robert Marvin Hull**

Hull, Cordell (1871–1955) US statesman

hullabaloo /húllabə loõ/, **hullaballoo** n noisy excitement or fuss [Mid-18C. Alteration of *hollo-ballo* < *holla*, early variant of HELLO.]

hullo interj, n = hello

Hulme /hulm/, **Denny** (1936–94) New Zealand motor-racing driver. Full name **Dennis Clive Hulme**

Hulme /hyoom/, **Keri** (b. 1947) New Zealand writer

Hulme, T. E. (1883–1917) British poet, critic, and philosopher. Full name **Thomas Ernest Hulme**

hum /hum/ v (**hums, humming, hummed**) 1 vi MAKE A DRONING SOUND to make a steady prolonged droning sound ○ bees humming 2 vti SING WITH THE LIPS CLOSED to sing with lips closed and without words 3 vi GIVE OFF A LOW STEADY SOUND to be filled with a low, continuous, indistinct noise ○ a room that hummed with strange electronic equipment 4 vi BE EXTREMELY BUSY to be very busy or active (informal) ○ This place is really humming. 5 vi STINK to smell unpleasantly (informal) ■ n 1 DRONING NOISE a steady droning sound 2 BAD SMELL an unpleasant smell (informal) ■ interj EXPRESSION OF DISPLEASURE OR INDECISION a low sound made to express displeasure, doubt, surprise, or indecision [14C. An imitation of the sound.] —**hummable** adj ◇ **hum and haw** to hesitate while speaking or deciding about something

human /hyóomən/ adj 1 OF PEOPLE relating to, involving, or typical of human beings ○ human nature ○ human frailty 2 MADE UP OF PEOPLE composed of people ○ the human race ○ a human chain of protesters 3 COMPASSIONATELY KIND showing kindness, compassion, or approachability 4 IMPERFECT having the imperfections and weaknesses of a human being rather than a machine or divine being ○ Remember he's only human, so don't expect too much. ■ n PERSON a human being [14C. Via French *humain* < Latin *humanus*.] —**humanness** n

LITERARY LINK **The Human Comedy**, a collection of a hundred novels and stories (1833–50) by French writer Honoré de Balzac. By linking his novels and stories through the use of common themes and characters, Balzac planned an oeuvre that would portray the human species in all stages of its development and aspects of its behaviour.

human being n 1 a member of the species to which men and women belong. *Homo sapiens*. 2 a person, viewed especially as having imperfections and weaknesses ○ I'm a human being, not a machine.

humane /hyoo máyn/ adj 1 COMPASSIONATE showing the better aspects of the human character, especially kindness and compassion 2 INVOLVING MINIMAL PAIN without inflicting any more pain than is necessary 3 WITH AN EMPHASIS ON LIBERAL VALUES with an emphasis on respect for other people's views [15C. Variant of HUMAN.] —**humanely** adv —**humaneness** n

human ecology n a branch of sociology that studies the relationships between human beings and their natural and social environments

human engineering n COMM = ergonomics n.

humane society n any one of various organizations that promote compassionate treatment of animals

human ethology n the study of human behaviour, especially aggressive and submissive behaviour in social contexts

human factors engineering n COMM = ergonomics n.

human genome n the gene map of the entire chromosome set present in each nucleated human cell

Human Genome Project n a publicly funded international research initiative to sequence and identify human genes and record their positions on chromosomes

QUICK FACTS ON... **HUMAN GENOME PROJECT**

Key elements: sequencing and identifying genes of the human genome and recording their positions on the 46 individual chromosomes
Key dates: 1990 launch of publicly funded international reseach initiative; 1999 chromosome 22 fully mapped; 2000 chromosomes 5, 16, 19, and 21 mapped and draft genetic map completed; private company, Celera Genomics, also announces completion of a working draft; estimate of number of human genes is 30,000 to 40,000; 2003 expected completion date of project
Key technologies: bacterial artificial chromosomes; DNA sequencing, mapping; bioinformatics and computational biology; comparative and functional genomics
Key developments: medical benefits expected in: improved diagnosis of genetic and degenerative disease; earlier detection of genetic predisposition to disease; drug design and custom drugs; gene therapy. Nonmedical benefits expected in human evolutionary studies, anthropology, and forensic science
Key publications: *The DNA sequence of human chromosome 22* (Dunham et al.) 1999, Nature 402: 489–495; *Your Genes, Your Choices? Exploring the issues raised by Genetic Research* (Catherine Baker) 1999; *Cracking the Genome* (Kevin Davies) 2001

human immunodeficiency virus n full form of HIV

human interest n an element in something, especially a news report, that is about somebody's personal life or feelings and is expected to appeal to the public's sympathy or curiosity —**human-interest** adj

humanise vt = humanize

humanism /hyóomənizəm/ n 1 BELIEF IN A HUMAN-BASED MORALITY a system of thought that is based on the values, characteristics, and behaviour that are believed to be best in human beings, rather than on any supernatural authority 2 CONCERN FOR PEOPLE a concern with the needs, wellbeing, and interests of people 3 **humanism**, **Humanism** RENAISSANCE CULTURAL MOVEMENT the secular cultural and intellectual movement of the Renaissance that spread throughout Europe as a result of the rediscovery of the arts and philosophy of the ancient Greeks and Romans —**humanist** n, adj —**humanistic** /hyóomə nístik/ adj —**humanistically** adv

humanitarian /hyoo mánni táiri ən/ adj 1 CARING committed to improving the lives of other people ○ a humanitarian organization 2 HUMAN involving and affecting human beings, especially in a harmful way (informal) ○ a humanitarian disaster ■ n 1 CARING PERSON a person who seeks to improve the lives of other people 2 SOMEBODY BELIEVING IN HUMANITARIANISM a believer in the philosophical theory of humanitarianism [Mid-19C. < HUMAN, after UNITARIAN and EGALITARIAN.]

humanitarianism /hyoo mánni táiri ənizəm/ n a commitment to improving the lives of other people —**humanitarianist** n

humanities /hyoo mánnitiz/, **Humanities** npl 1 the liberal arts as subjects of study, as opposed to the sciences 2 the study of the language and literature of the ancient Greeks and Romans

humanity /hyoo mánnti/ n 1 HUMAN RACE the human race considered as a whole 2 QUALITIES OF A HUMAN BEING the qualities or characteristics considered as a whole to be typical of human beings 3 KINDNESS kindness or compassion for others

humanize /hyóomə nīz/ (**-izes, -izing, -ized**), **humanise** (**-ises, -ising, -ised**) vti 1 to make something human or like humans, or become human or like humans 2 to make or become humane in character, characteristics, or nature —**humanization** /hyóomə nī záysh'n/ n —**humanizer** n

humankind /hyóomən kínd/, **human kind** n all human beings considered as a whole ○ 'Human kind cannot bear very much reality'. (T. S. Eliot, Four Quartets, Burnt Norton; 1935)

humanly /hyóomənli/ adv 1 WITHIN THE LIMITS OF HUMAN ABILITY within the limits of human ability and knowledge ○ They did all that was humanly possible to save him. 2 IN A WAY TYPICAL OF HUMANS in a way generally considered to be typical of humans 3 ACCORDING TO HUMAN EXPERIENCE as far as human knowledge or experience can judge

humanmade /hyóomən mayd/ adj made by human beings and not occurring naturally ○ 'Humanmade materials gradually deteriorate even when exposed to unpolluted rain, but acid rain accelerates this process'. (United States Environmental Protection Agency website; April 1999)

human nature n the typical character that all human beings share, often seen as being imperfect

humanoid /hyóomə noyd/ adj describes a being from another planet that has the appearance or characteristics of a human —**humanoid** n

human papilloma virus n a virus that causes warts in the genital area of humans

human resources n the field of business concerned with recruiting and managing employees (+ singular verb) ○ a career in human resources ■ npl all the people who work in a business or organization, considered as a whole (+ plural verb)

human rights npl the rights that are considered by most societies to belong automatically to everyone, e.g. the rights to freedom, justice, and equality (sometimes singular)

Humber Estuary /húmbər-/ navigable estuary in NE England formed by the Trent and Ouse. Length: 64 km/39 mi.

Humberside /húmbər sīd/ former county of NE England

humble /húmb'l/ *adj* (**-bler, -blest**) **1 MODEST** modest and unassuming in attitude and behaviour **2 RESPECTFUL** feeling or showing respect and deference towards other people **3 LOWLY** relatively low in rank and without pretensions ○ *of humble origins* ■ *vt* (**-bles, -bling, -bled**) **1 MAKE FEEL LESS IMPORTANT** to make somebody feel less proud or convinced of his or her own importance **2 DEGRADE** to lower somebody in rank or importance [13C. Via Old French *(h)umble* < Latin *humilis* 'lowly' < *humus* 'earth'.] —**humbled** *adj* —**humbleness** *n* —**humbly** *adv*

humblebee /húmb'l bee/ *n* = **bumblebee** [15C. Probably alteration of Middle Low German *hummelbē* 'humming bee' < *hummel* 'hum, buzz' + *bē* 'bee'.]

humble pie *n* a pie formerly made using the entrails of a newly killed animal, especially a deer (*archaic*) [Mid-17C. Alteration of *umble pie* < *umbles* 'edible animal entrails', via French dialect *nombles* < Latin *lumbulus* 'small loin'.] ◇ **eat humble pie** to apologize or admit you have been wrong, especially in a way that makes you feel humiliated

humbling /húmbling/ *adj* making somebody lose confidence, self-importance, or pride —**humblingly** *adv*

Humboldt /húmbōlt/, **Friedrich Heinrich Alexander, Freiherr von** (1769–1859) German explorer and naturalist

Humboldt Current /húm bōlt-/ *n* a cold current of the South Pacific Ocean that flows north along the coastline of South America [After Baron Friedrich von HUMBOLDT]

humbug /húm bug/ *n* **1 NONSENSE** something that is silly or makes no sense **2 DECEPTION** something that is meant to deceive or cheat people **3 FRAUD** a deceiver of others who makes false claims **4 BOILED SWEET** a boiled mint-flavoured sweet, usually decorated with stripes ■ *vti* (**-bugs, -bugging, -bugged**) **DECEIVE** to take part in a deception or deceive somebody ■ *interj* **NONSENSE!** expresses the opinion that something is nonsense or deception (*archaic*) [Mid-18C. < ?]

humdinger /húmdingər/ *n* an exceptional or outstanding person or thing (*slang*) [Early 20C. Probably < HUM 'approving murmur' + *dinger* 'superlative thing'.]

humdrum /húm drum/ *adj* dull because of being too familiar and lacking variety [Mid-16C. Probably expressive alteration of HUM.]

Hume /hyoom/, **Basil, Cardinal** (1923–99) British Roman Catholic cardinal

Hume, David (1711–76) Scottish philosopher and historian

Hume, John (*b.* 1937) Northern Irish politician

humectant /hyoo méktənt/ *n* a substance such as a skin lotion that absorbs or helps retain moisture [Early 19C. < Latin *(h)umectare* 'moisten' < *(h)umectus* 'moist' < *(h)umere* 'be moist'.] —**humectant** *adj*

humeral veil *n* a silk shawl covering the shoulders and hands, worn by a Roman Catholic priest while holding sacred vessels

humerus /hyoòmərəss/ (*plural* **-i** /-rī/) *n* the long bone of the human upper arm or in a forelimb in other animals [14C. < Latin, 'upper arm'.] —**humeral** *adj*

humic /hyoòmik/ *adj* relating to, involving, containing, or typical of humus [Mid-19C. < HUMUS.]

humid /hyoòmid/ *adj* with a relatively high level of moisture in the air [14C. < Latin *(h)umidus* < *(h)umere* 'be moist'.] —**humidly** *adv* —**humidness** *n*

humidifier /hyoo míddi fī ər/ *n* a device or machine that keeps the air moist inside an enclosed space

humidify /hyoo míddi fī/ (**-fies, -fying, -fied**) *vt* to make something, especially the air, more moist or damp —**humidification** /hyoo míddifi káysh'n/ *n*

humidistat /hyoo míddi stat/ *n* an instrument that measures or controls the relative humidity of air [Early 20C. < HUMIDITY, after THERMOSTAT.]

humidity /hyoo míddəti/ *n* **1** the amount of moisture in the air **2** the condition of having a high amount of moisture in the air **3** = **relative humidity**

humidor /hyoòmi dawr/ *n* a container, often a box or jar, in which tobacco products, especially cigars, can be stored to prevent them from drying out [Early 20C. < HUMID, after CUSPIDOR.]

humify /hyoòmi fī/ (**-fies, -fying, -fied**) *vti* to turn a substance into humus, or turn into humus

humiliate /hyoo mílli ayt/ (**-ates, -ating, -ated**) *vt* to damage somebody's dignity or pride, especially publicly [Mid-16C. < late Latin *humiliare* < Latin *humilis* (see HUMBLE).] —**humiliating** *adj* —**humiliatingly** *adv* —**humiliator** *n*

humiliation /hyoo mílli áysh'n/ *n* **1 LOSS OF DIGNITY** the feeling or condition of being lessened in dignity or pride **2 LESSENING OF SOMEBODY'S DIGNITY** the act of damaging somebody's dignity or pride **3 SOMETHING THAT HUMILIATES** something that damages somebody's pride or dignity

humility /hyoo mílləti/ *n* the quality of being modest or respectful [13C. Via French *humilité* < Latin *humilitas* < *humilis* (see HUMBLE).]

~~**huminist**~~ incorrect spelling of **humanist**

Hummel /hoòmm'l/, **Johann Nepomuk** (1778–1837) German composer and pianist

hummingbird /húmming burd/ *n* a small brightly-coloured bird that can beat its wings rapidly, making a humming sound and allowing it to hover. Native to: Americas. Family: Trochilidae.

humming top *n* a child's spinning top that makes a humming sound as it spins

hummock /húmmək/ *n* **1** a small hill or mound **2** a ridge of ice in an ice field [Mid-16C. < ?] —**hummocky** *adj*

hummus /hoòmmooss/, **humus, hoummos** /hoòmməss/ *n* a Middle Eastern dip made with mashed chickpeas, tahini, oil, lemon juice, and garlic, combined into a thick paste [Mid-20C. < Arabic *ḥummus* 'chickpea'.]

humongous /hyoo múng gəss/, **humungous** *adj* extremely large in size or amount (*informal*) [Mid-20C. < ?] —**humongously** *adv*

humor *n, vt* US = **humour**

humoral /hyoòmərəl/ *adj* relating to, involving, or typical of body fluids, especially blood serum

humoresque /hyoòmə résk/ *n* a light or whimsical piece of music, especially in 19th-century music [Late 19C. Alteration of German *Humoreske* < *Humor* 'humour' < English.]

humorist /hyoòmərist/ *n* **1** a writer or performer of comic material **2** somebody known to be amusing and to have a quick wit

humorous /hyoòmərəss/ *adj* **1** amusing or intended to make people laugh **2** witty or able to make people laugh —**humorously** *adv* —**humorousness** *n*

humour /hyoòmər/ *n* **1 FUNNY QUALITY** the quality or content of something, e.g. a story, performance, or joke, that elicits amusement and laughter **2 ABILITY TO SEE SOMETHING IS FUNNY** the ability to see that something is funny or the enjoyment of things that are funny ○ *He has no sense of humour.* **3 FUNNY THINGS AS A GENRE** writings and other material created to make people laugh **4 SOMEBODY'S USUAL TEMPERAMENT** somebody's character or usual attitude ○ *a writer of melancholy humour* **5 MOOD** a temporary mood or state of mind **6 BODY FLUID** according to medieval science and medicine, any of the four main fluids of the human body, blood, yellow bile, black bile, or lymph, that determined a person's mood and temperament ■ *vt* **1 DO WHAT SOMEBODY WANTS** to do what somebody wants in order to keep him or her happy **2 COMPLY** to act in accordance with something (*archaic*) [14C. Via Anglo-Norman < Latin *humor* 'body fluid' < *humere* 'be moist'.]

humoured /hyoòmərd/ *adj* with a particular character or frame of mind (*usually in combination*) ○ *good-humoured*

humourless /hyoòmərləss/ *adj* **1** lacking a sense of humour **2** having no amusing aspect —**humourlessly** *adv* —**humourlessness** *n*

~~**humourous**~~ incorrect spelling of **humorous**

hump /hump/ *n* **1 BUMP ON AN ANIMAL'S BACK** a rounded protuberance on the back of some animals, e.g. camels and some cattle **2 CURVE OF THE BACK** a pronounced convex curvature of somebody's upper spine resulting from injury or disease, a congenital abnormality, or an accumulation of fat **3 BUMP IN A SURFACE** a rounded protruding mass such as a mound of earth ■ *v* **1** *vt* **MOVE WITH EFFORT** to carry something heavy with difficulty (*informal*) **2** *vti* **OFFENSIVE TERM** an offensive term meaning to have sexual intercourse with somebody (*slang*) **3** *vt* **MAKE INTO A HUMP** to form something into a hump [Mid-17C. Probably < Dutch *homp*, Low German *humpe*.] ◇ **over the hump** past the worst or most difficult part of something ◇ **the hump** a mood of annoyance, resentment, or unhappiness (*informal*)

humpback /húmp bak/ *n* **1** MED = **hunchback** **2** ZOOL = **humpback whale** **3** CIV ENG = **humpback bridge** **4** ZOOL = **pink salmon** *n.* 1

humpback bridge, hump-backed bridge *n* a small narrow bridge with a steep approach and descent

humpback whale *n* a large dark grey or black whale, up to 15.2 m/50 ft long, with a humped back and long white flippers, that feeds by sieving plankton and fish through baleen plates. *Megaptera novaeangliae.*

Humperdinck /hoòmpər dingk/, **Engelbert** (1854–1921) German composer

humph /humf/ *interj* used to expresses annoyance, doubt, or dissatisfaction [Mid-16C. Natural exclamation.]

Humphries /húmfriz/, **Barry** (*b.* 1934) Australian writer and performer

humpty-dumpty /húmpti dúmpti/ (*plural* **humpty-dumpties**) *n* an offensive term for somebody perceived as being short and overweight [Late 18C. < the nursery-rhyme character *Humpty-Dumpty*.]

humpy /húmpi/ (**-ier, -iest**) *adj* **1** having or full of humps **2** feeling irritable and easily annoyed (*informal*) —**humpiness** *n*

humungous *adj* = **humongous**

humus[1] /hyoòməss/ *n* a dark brown organic component of soil that is derived from decomposed plant and animal remains and animal excrement [Late 18C. < Latin, 'soil'.]

humus[2] *n* FOOD = **hummus**

Hun /hun/ *n* **1 MEMBER OF AN ASIAN NOMADIC PEOPLE** a member of a nomadic people, probably originating in north central Asia, who invaded China in the 3rd century BC and then spread westwards to Asia and Europe **2 DESTRUCTIVE PERSON** a barbaric and destructive person **3 OFFENSIVE TERM** an offensive term for a German person or the German people, used especially by their opponents during World Wars I and II (*dated slang*) [Old English *Hūne*, via Germanic < late Latin *Hunni* < Sogdian *xwn*]

Hunan /hoò nán/ province in central China. Capital: Changsha. Population: 63,550,000 (1994). Area: 210,500 sq. km/81,270 sq. mi.

hunch /hunch/ *n* **1 FEELING** an intuitive feeling about something **2 STOOP** a curved posture of the body with the head down and shoulders forwards **3** MED = **hump** *n.* **2** **4 PIECE** a large lump or slice of something (*dated*) ■ *vti* **BEND UPPER BODY FORWARDS** to bend the head down and the shoulders forwards, e.g. because of bad posture, illness, or the cold ○ *a typist hunching over the keyboard* ○ *hunched her shoulders against the wind* [15C. < ?]

hunchback /húnch bak/ *n* **1** a person with a hump on his or her back **2** a back that shows a pronounced curvature of the spine —**hunchbacked** *adj*

LITERARY LINK ***The Hunchback of Notre Dame***, a novel (1831) by French writer Victor Hugo. In this richly evocative medieval tragedy, Quasimodo, the hunchbacked bell-ringer at the Cathedral of Notre Dame in Paris, falls in love with a beautiful girl, Esmerelda. When corrupt priest Claude Frollo's harassment of Esmerelda results in her being executed for sorcery, Quasimodo murders Frollo by pushing him off the bell tower.

hundred /húndrəd/ *n* **1** see table at **number** **2 LARGE NUMBER** an unspecified large number (*usually plural*) ○ *attended by hundreds* **3 THIRD DIGIT TO LEFT OF DECIMAL** the number that is three places to the left of the decimal point in Arabic notation **4 100 RUNS** a score of 100 runs by a batsman in cricket **5 COUNTY SUBDIVISION** a historical subdivision of English, Irish, and some North American counties ■ **hundreds** *npl* **1 NUMBERS 100 TO 999** the numbers 100 to 999 **2 YEARS OF A CENTURY** the years of a specified century, regarded as those beginning with a particular number ○ *the seventeen-hundreds* [Old English, < Indo-European]

hundred per cent *adv* (*informal*) **1** in a complete or full way ○ *She is a hundred per cent in charge.* **2** completely fit and healthy ○ *I'm still not feeling a hundred per cent after the accident.*

hundreds-and-thousands *npl* tiny multicoloured sugar strands used for decorating cakes

hundredth /húndrədth/ *n* see table at **number**

hundredweight /húndrəd wayt/ *n* **1** a unit of mass in the British imperial system equal to 112 lb (50.80 kg) **2** *US* = **cental** **3** = **metric hundredweight** [Probably originally 100 pounds]

Hundred Years' War *n* a series of wars fought between England and France from 1337 to 1453 that resulted in the final expulsion of England from all French territories except Calais

hung[1] past participle, past tense of **hang**

hung[2] *adj* unable to form a majority and therefore make decisions or reach a verdict ○ *a hung jury* ○ *a hung parliament*

Hung. *abbr* 1 Hungarian 2 Hungary

Hungarian /hung gáiri ən/ *n* 1 somebody who comes from Hungary 2 the official language of Hungary, also spoken in parts of neighbouring countries, belonging to one of the Ugric subgroups of Finno-Ugric. Native speakers: 14 million. —**Hungarian** *adj*

Hungarian goulash *n* COOK = **goulash** *n*. 1

Hungary

Hungary /húng gəri/ republic in central Europe. Capital: Budapest. Population: 10,225,000 (1995). Area: 93,030 sq. km/35,919 sq. mi.

hunger /húng gər/ *n* 1 NEED TO EAT the need or desire for food 2 STARVATION lack of food leading to illness or death ○ *children dying of hunger* 3 CRAVING a great need or desire for something ○ *a hunger for knowledge* ■ *vi* CRAVE to feel a very strong need or desire for something [Old English *hungur* < Germanic]

hunger march *n* a march organized by unemployed people to draw attention to their plight

hunger strike *n* a refusal to eat over a period of time as a form of protest, especially by a prisoner —**hunger striker** *n*

hungover /hung óvər/, **hung over** *adj* suffering from the aftereffects of drinking too much alcohol

hungry /húng gri/ (**-grier, -griest**) *adj* 1 WANTING TO EAT wanting or needing food 2 AVID wanting or desiring something very much ○ *hungry for new experiences* 3 AMBITIOUS having great ambition or a powerful desire to win (*informal*) ○ *They won because they were hungrier than we were.* 4 CAUSING HUNGER using up a lot of energy and making somebody feel hungry ○ *hungry work* [Old English *hungrig*, related to *hunger*] —**hungrily** *adv* —**hungriness** *n* ◇ **go hungry** to go without food

hung up *adj* (*informal*) 1 obsessed with somebody or something ○ *He's completely hung up on her.* 2 in a state of worry or anxiety over something ○ *hung up over minor details*

hunk /hungk/ *n* 1 a large piece of something such as bread or cheese that is cut or torn off a larger portion 2 a man who is well-built and very physically impressive (*informal*) [Early 19C. < ?]

hunker /húngkər/ *vi* to squat down close to the ground [Early 18C. < ?]
hunker down *vi* US 1 to apply yourself seriously to something ○ *time to hunker down and start studying* 2 to hold your ground and refuse to change your mind (*informal*)

hunkers /húngkərz/ *npl* the hips, buttocks, and upper thighs of humans or animals (*dated informal*) [Mid-18C. Probably < HUNKER.]

hunky /húngki/ (**-ier, -iest**) *adj* masculine, well-built, and very physically attractive (*informal*)

hunky-dory /-dáwri/ *adj* absolutely fine or satisfactory (*informal*) [Probably alteration of *hunky* 'all right' < obsolete *hunk* 'place where a game player is safe from capture' < Dutch *honk* 'home']

Hunnish /húnnish/, **hunnish** *adj* destructive and barbarous

hunt /hunt/ *v* 1 *vt* SEEK PREY to pursue an animal with the aim of capturing or killing it for sport or food ○ *Cats hunt mice and small birds.* 2 *vt* SEEK OUT to search for and try to capture somebody 3 *vi* SEARCH to search persistently for something difficult to find ○ *hunting for his missing keys* 4 *vt* HOUND to seek out and harass or persecute somebody 5 *vi* CHASE ANIMALS WITH HOUNDS to engage in a sport involving the pursuit of an animal, usually a fox, on horseback and with the aid of hounds 6 *vt* USE ANIMAL IN BLOOD SPORT to use a horse or hounds for the purpose of chasing and killing game, typically a fox 7 *vt* HUNT IN A PARTICULAR PLACE to search a particular area for animals to capture or kill for sport or food 8 *vi* OSCILLATE ABOUT POSITION to oscillate about a fixed point ■ *n* 1 ACT OF SEARCHING the act of looking for somebody or something carefully, thoroughly, and persistently 2 SEEKING OF PREY a pursuit of animals to capture or kill them for sport or food ○ *a deer hunt* 3 HUNTING EXPEDITION an organized event in which riders and hounds, pursue a fox or deer with the aim of killing it for sport 4 hunt, Hunt ORGANIZED GROUP OF HUNTERS a group of people engaged in hunting as a sport ○ *She joined the local hunt.* [Old English *huntian* < Germanic] ◇ **hunt high and low for somebody** or **something** to search extremely thoroughly for somebody or something

Hunt /hunt/, **Geoff** (*b.* 1947) Australian squash player. Full name **Geoffrey Brian Hunt**

Hunt, Holman (1827–1910) British painter

Hunt, James (1947–93) British racing driver

Hunt, Leigh (1784–1859) British poet

Hunt, Sam (*b.* 1946) New Zealand poet

huntaway /húnta way/ *n* NZ a sheepdog that is trained to drive sheep forward from a position behind them

hunted /húntid/ *adj* startled and panic-stricken, as if being pursued or hunted ○ *a hunted look*

hunter /húntər/ *n* 1 PREDATOR a person or animal that hunts birds or animals for food or sport 2 HORSE a powerful fast horse that is bred for and used in hunting 3 DOG a dog that is specially bred for and used in hunting 4 SEEKER a seeker of somebody or something, especially as an occupation or hobby 5 WATCH a watch with a hinged metal cover to protect the watch face

Hunter /húntər/, **Bill** (*b.* 1941) Australian actor. Full name **William Hunter**

Hunter, John (1728–93) Scottish anatomist and surgeon

Hunter, William (1718–83) Scottish obstetrician

hunter-gatherer *n* a member of a society in which people live by hunting and gathering only, with no crops or livestock being raised for food

hunter-killer *adj* describes a naval force consisting of an antisubmarine warfare carrier and its associated elements

hunter's moon *n* the first full moon directly following the harvest moon

hunting /húnting/ *n* 1 the sport or practice of pursuing and killing or capturing wild animals 2 the process of searching for something, usually over a period of time ○ *job hunting*

hunting and gathering *n* seeking game and edible plants for subsistence, as practised by preagricultural and nomadic people, rather than raising livestock and crops for food

Huntingdon /húntingdən/ town in E England. Population: 18,000.

Huntingdonshire /húntingdənshər/ former county in E England, now part of Cambridgeshire

hunting ground *n* 1 a place where hunting takes place or that is suitable for hunting 2 a source of useful or desired objects or information ○ *The town is a great hunting ground for antiques.*

hunting horn *n* a horn used to give signals during hunting, especially foxhunting

hunting knife *n* a broad knife used for killing or gutting game

hunting spider *n* ZOOL = **wolf spider**

Huntington's chorea /húntingtənz ko rée ə/ *n* a hereditary disorder of the nervous system that manifests as jerky involuntary movements in early middle age, with behavioural changes and progressive dementia [Late 19C. After George *Huntington* (1851–1916), American neurologist.]

hunting watch *n* = **hunter** *n*. 5

huntress /húntrəss/ *n* a woman or goddess who hunts

hunt saboteur *n* an opponent of foxhunting who travels to hunts in order to try to prevent or disrupt their occurrence

huntsman /húntsmən/ (*plural* -**men** /-mən/) *n* 1 an official who is in charge of the hounds belonging to a hunt 2 a man who hunts, either for a living or for a pastime 3 ZOOL = **huntsman spider**

huntsman spider *n* a large spider with a light brown or grey hairy body that lives in hot and tropical regions. Family: Sparassidae.

Huon pine /hyóò on-/ *n* a large coniferous timber tree. Native to: South America, Australia, SE Asia. *Dacrydium franklinii.* [Early 19C. After the River *Huon* in S Tasmania.]

hup /hup/ *interj* used when lifting or raising something (*informal*) [Mid-20C. < ?]

huppah *n* JUDAISM = **chuppah**

Hurd /hurd/, **Douglas** (*b.* 1930) British politician

hurdies /húrdiz/ *npl* Scotland the buttocks or haunches [Mid-16C. < ?]

hurdle /húrd'l/ *n* 1 FRAME FOR RUNNER TO JUMP each of a number of light barriers over which runners have to jump in some athletics events 2 RACE OVER BARRIERS an athletics event in which runners have to race to clear a series of light barriers 3 OBSTACLE a difficulty or obstacle that has to be overcome 4 FENCE a light framework made of intertwined branches or wattle that is used as a temporary fence 5 FENCE USED IN HORSE RACE a fence of intertwined branches or wattle that horses race over, or a race over fences of this type 6 FRAME FOR CONVICTS a frame on which traitors were dragged and paraded before the public before being executed (*archaic*) ■ *v* (**-dles, -dling, -dled**) 1 *vi* RACE OVER HURDLES to run in an athletics event in which hurdles must be jumped 2 *vt* CLEAR RACING BARRIER to clear a barrier in a race 3 *vt* OVERCOME A DIFFICULTY to overcome an obstacle or difficulty 4 *vt* FENCE AREA to fence off an area with hurdles [Old English *hyrdel* < Indo-European, 'to turn'] —**hurdler** *n*

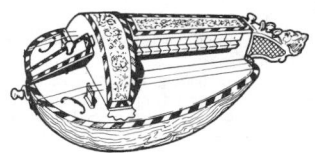

Hurdy-gurdy

hurdy-gurdy /húrdi gúrdi, húrdi gurdí/ (*plural* **hurdy-gurdies**) *n* 1 a mechanical musical instrument such as a barrel organ that is played by turning a handle 2 a medieval stringed instrument played by turning a crank attached to a rosined wheel that causes strings to vibrate while being controlled by a keyboard [Mid-18C. An imitation of the sound.]

hurl /hurl/ *v* 1 *vt* FLING to throw something with great force 2 *vt* YELL to utter something with great violence or vehemence ○ *hurling abuse* 3 *vti* PITCH to pitch a baseball 4 *vi* VOMIT to vomit, especially with considerable force (*slang*) ■ *n* 1 STRONG THROW a forceful throw, or the act of throwing something with great force 2 Scotland RIDE IN VEHICLE a ride in any vehicle with wheels 3 VOMIT vomit (*slang*) [12C. Probably suggests the action.] —**hurler** *n*

SYNONYMS See *throw.*

hurley /húrli/ *n* 1 Ireland the game of hurling 2 a long wooden stick with a curved end used in the game of hurling [Early 19C. < HURL.]

hurling /húrling/ *n* an Irish field sport resembling hockey and lacrosse that is played with broad sticks and a leather ball that is passed from player to player through the air

hurly-burly /húrli burli/ *n* noisy and bustling activity [Alteration of *hurling and burling*, playful formation based on HURL]

Huron /hyŏŏrən, -on/ (*plural* **-ron** *or* **-rons**) *n* a member of a confederacy of Iroquoian peoples who lived around the Great Lakes and now live in Quebec, Ontario, and Oklahoma [Mid-17C. Via French, 'boar' < Old French *hure* 'bristling hair'.] —**Huron** *adj*

Huron, Lake /hyŏŏrən/ second largest of the Great Lakes, in the United States and Canada. Area: 59,600 sq. km/23,000 sq. mi. Depth: 229 m/751 ft.

hurrah *interj, n* = **hooray** [Late 17C. Alteration of HUZZAH.]

hurray *interj, n* = **hooray**

Hurrian /hŏŏri ən/ *n* **1** a member of an ancient people who lived in Syria and Mesopotamia around 1500 BC **2** the unaffiliated language of the Hurrian people [Early 20C. < Hittite, Assyrian *Harri, Hurri.*] —**Hurrian** *adj*

hurricane /húrrikən, -kayn/ *n* **1 SEVERE STORM** a severe tropical storm with torrential rain and extremely strong winds **2 HIGH WIND** a wind with speeds above 119 km/74 mi. per hour and a force of 12 or above on the Beaufort scale **3 FAST FORCEFUL THING** somebody or something resembling a violent storm in force, speed, or effect [Mid-16C. Via Spanish *huracán* < Taino *hurakán* 'god of the storm'.]

hurricane deck *n* a deck on a ship with a cover from the sun

hurricane lamp *n* an oil or paraffin lamp with a glass cover to prevent the wick from being extinguished in wind or rain

hurried /húrrid/ *adj* done, made, or performed too quickly because of a real or perceived lack of time —**hurriedly** *adv* —**hurriedness** *n*

hurry /húrri/ *v* (**-ries, -rying, -ried**) **1** *vi* **RUSH** to move or do something with great or excessive speed because of a real or perceived lack of time **2** *vt* **SPEED UP** to make or encourage somebody or something to act with greater speed ○ *Hurry up and put your coat on!* ■ *n* **1 HASTE** a state in which somebody is doing something or moving at a great or excessive speed ○ *We were in such a hurry we left the tickets behind.* **2 URGENCY** the need to do something quickly ○ *What's the hurry?* [Early 17C. < ?] —**hurrying** *adj* —**hurryingly** *adv* ◇ **in a hurry** readily or willingly (*informal*)

hurry-scurry *n* an undue rush to do something [Mid-18C. Repetition of HURRY.]

hurst /hurst/ *n* a wood (*archaic*) [Old English *hyrst* < Germanic]

hurt /hurt/ *v* (**hurts, hurting, hurt**) **1** *vt* **INJURE** to cause physical pain in somebody or in yourself or part of the body ○ *hurt his back when he fell down* **2** *vti* **CAUSE PAIN** to experience physical pain, or cause somebody to experience physical pain ○ *Ouch! That hurts!* **3** *vti* **UPSET** to feel emotional pain, or make somebody feel emotional pain ○ *hurt by his unkind remarks* **4** *vti* **IMPAIR** to have a negative effect on something ○ *This could hurt her chances of re-election.* **5** *vi* **EXPERIENCE DIFFICULTIES** to undergo or experience difficulties or setbacks, e.g. in business or financial affairs (*informal*) ○ *too much competition, so the business is really hurting* ■ *n* **1 PAIN** emotional or mental pain or suffering ○ *after all the hurt he's caused* **2 INJURY** an injury or wound, whether emotional or physical ○ *old hurts* [12C. < Old French *hurter* 'ram, collide', probably < Germanic.] —**hurt** *adj* —**hurter** *n*

hurtful /húrtf'l/ *adj* causing emotional pain or suffering —**hurtfully** *adv* —**hurtfulness** *n*

hurtle /húrt'l/ (**-tles, -tling, -tled**) *vi* to move or travel at very high speed [13C. < HURT.]

husband /húzbənd/ *n* the man to whom a woman is married ■ *vt* to use and manage something economically, e.g. resources or money [Pre-12C. < Old Norse *húsbóndi* 'man in charge of the house, farmer' < *hús* 'house' + *bóndi* 'dweller', present participle of *búa* 'dwell'.] —**husbandage** *n* —**husbander** *n*

husbandman /húzbəndmən/ (*plural* **-men** /-mən/) *n* a farmer (*archaic*)

husbandry /húzbəndri/ *n* **1** the science, skill, or art of farming **2** the frugal and sensible management of resources

hush /hush/ *vti* **MAKE SOMEBODY BE QUIET** to become silent, or make somebody become quiet or silent ■ *interj* **BE QUIET** requests or demands for silence ■ *n* **SILENCE** a stillness or silence, especially after a period of noise or in expectation of something [Mid-16C. Probably back-formation < obsolete *husht* 'hush!', natural exclamation.]
hush up *vt* to prevent something, especially something dishonourable or discreditable, from becoming publicly known (*informal*)

hushaby /húshə bī/ *interj* used to lull a child to sleep [Mid-18C. < HUSH + *-aby* as in *lullaby.*]

hush-hush *adj* secret or confidential (*informal*)

hush money *n* money paid as a bribe not to disclose information (*informal*)

husk /husk/ *n* **1 OUTER PLANT COVERING** the outer membranous covering of some fruits, nuts, and grains **2 USELESS OUTER SHELL** an empty outer shell or covering that no longer serves any useful purpose ■ *vt* **REMOVE HUSKS FROM** to remove the husks from fruits, nuts or grains [14C. < ?] —**husker** *n*

husky[1] /húski/ *adj* (**-ier, -iest**) **1 THROATY** hoarse and dry, either naturally or as a result of illness or emotion ○ *a husky voice* **2** *US* **BURLY AND COMPACT IN PHYSIQUE** with a solid, burly, strong, and compact physique ○ *a husky boy* **3 RELATING TO HUSKS** containing or resembling husks ■ *n* **PADDED WAISTCOAT** a short padded or quilted waistcoat [Mid-16C. < HUSK.] —**huskily** *adv* —**huskiness** *n*

husky[2] /húski/ (*plural* **-kies**) *n* a large long-haired dog with a curled tail and pricked-up ears, originally bred in Arctic regions and trained to pull sleds [Mid-19C. Probably alteration of ESKIMO in *Eskimo dog.*]

huss /huss/ *n* the edible flesh of the European dogfish [15C. < ?]

Huss /huss/, **John** (1372?–1415) Bohemian nationalist and religious reformer

hussar /hŏŏ zaar/ *n* **1** a soldier in any European light cavalry unit in the 18th and 19th centuries that adopted an ornate uniform similar to that of the Hungarian cavalry in the 15th century **2** a member of the Hungarian cavalry in the 15th century [Mid-16C. Via Hungarian *huszár* 'light horseman' < Italian *corsaro* 'corsair'.]

Hussein I /hŏŏ sáyn/ (1935–99) king of Jordan (1952–99)

Hussein, Saddam (*b.* 1937) Iraqi national leader

Hussite /hússīt/ *n* a follower of the teachings of John Huss —**Hussitism** /hússitizəm/ *n*

hussy /hússi/ (*plural* **-sies**) *n* an offensive term that deliberately insults a woman's manner or behaviour (*dated or humorous*) [Mid-16C. Contraction of HOUSEWIFE (the original sense).]

hustings /hústingz/ *npl* **1** the political activities, e.g. speech-making and the organization of public rallies, that take place before an election **2** in Great Britain before 1872, a platform from which parliamentary candidates were nominated and addressed electors [Pre-12C. < Old Norse *húsþing* 'king's council' < *hús* 'house' + *þing* 'meeting'.]

hustle /húss'l/ *v* (**-tles, -tling, -tled**) **1** *vt* **PROPEL** to convey somebody roughly or hurriedly from a place ○ *hustled her into a waiting car* **2** *vi* **HURRY** to go somewhere or do something fast or hurriedly (*informal*) ○ *We'd better hustle, or we'll be late.* **3** *vt* **DEAL WITH SOMETHING FAST** to deal with something hurriedly ○ *Let's hustle this project along.* **4** *vti US* **SOLICIT CUSTOMERS IN SHADY DEALS** to solicit customers in shady or illegal deals, e.g. as a prostitute (*slang*) **5** *vt US* **SELL SOMETHING AGGRESSIVELY** to sell something aggressively, e.g. drinks in a bar **6** *vti US* **ENGAGE IN SMALL-TIME ILLEGAL DEALS** to engage in small-time crooked dealing, e.g. petty theft (*slang*) ■ *n* **NOISY ACTIVITY** lively, noisy, continual activity ○ *enjoyed the hustle and bustle of the big city* [Late 17C. < Dutch *hutselen* 'shake (repeatedly), toss', < *hotsen* 'shake'.]

hustler /hússlər/ *n* **1** somebody who engages in illegal activities, e.g. petty theft or illegal gambling, on a small scale (*informal*) **2** *US* a prostitute, especially a streetwalker or one who solicits in bars (*slang*)

Huston /hyŏŏstən/, **John** (1906–87) US film director and actor

hut /hut/ *n* a small single-storey building, often made of wood, that is used as a simple house or shelter, or for storage, temporary accommodation, or leisure or community activities ○ *a scout hut* ■ *vt* (**huts, hutting, hutted**) to provide huts for a place, especially for accommodation [Mid-16C. < ?]

hutch /huch/ *n* **1** a small shelter, usually constructed from wire and wood, for keeping small animals such as rabbits **2** *US* a cupboard with drawers and usually open shelves on top, often used for storing and displaying dishes and kitchen utensils [12C. Via French *huche* < medieval Latin *hutica.*]

Hutchinson-Gilford syndrome /húchins'n gílfərd-/ *n* MED = **progeria** [After Sir Jonathan *Hutchinson* (1828–1913) and Hastings *Gilford* (1861–1941), British physicians]

hutment /hútmənt/ *n* a group of huts forming a military encampment

Hutterite /húttərīt/ *n* a member of an Anabaptist religious group that immigrated from Moravia mainly to Alberta and Manitoba in Canada but also to areas of the NW United States where they formed farming communities [Late 19C. After Jacob *Hutter* (d. 1536), Moravian Anabaptist.]

Hutton /hútt'n/, **James** (1726–97) Scottish geologist

Hutt Valley /hút-/ urban area in the south of the North Island, New Zealand. Population: 131,000.

Hutu /hŏŏ too/ (*plural* **-tu** *or* **-tus**) *n* **1** a member of a people who are the most populous in Rwanda and Burundi **2** a Bantu language spoken in Rwanda and Burundi. Native speakers: 14 million. [Mid-20C. < Bantu.] —**Hutu** *adj*

hutzpah *n* = **chutzpah**

Huxley /húksli/, **Aldous** (1894–1963) British novelist and essayist

Huxley, Andrew (*b.* 1917) British physiologist

Huxley, Sir Julian (1887–1975) British biologist

Huxley, T. H. (1825–95) British biologist. Full name **Thomas Henry Huxley**

Huygens' eyepiece /hīgənz-/ *n* an eyepiece consisting of two planoconvex lenses with their flat sides towards the eye, fitted mainly on optical instruments that are used for observation rather than measurement [Mid-19C. After Christiaan *Huygens* (1629–95), Dutch physicist and astronomer.]

Huygens' principle *n* the proposition that every point on a wavefront acts as a source of secondary waves of light and that the wavefront at a later time is the envelope of these secondary waves [See HUYGENS' EYEPIECE]

Huysmans /hóys manss/, **Joris Karl** (1848–1907) French novelist

huzzah /hŏŏ zaa, hə-/ *interj* hooray (*archaic*) [Late 16C. < ?] —**huzzah** *n*

HV *abbr* **1** health visitor **2 HV, hv** high velocity **3** high voltage

HVAC *abbr* heating, ventilating, and air conditioning

⚡**HW** *abbr* **1** hazardous waste **2** high water **3** hot water **4** hit wicket **5** hardware (*in e-mails*)

Hwange National Park /hwáng gi-/ largest national park in Zimbabwe. Area: 14,651 sq. km/5,657 sq. mi.

Hwang Hai /wang hī/ ➧ **Yellow Sea**

HWM *abbr* high-water mark

hwy *abbr* highway

hwyl /hŏŏ il/ *n Wales* good spirit or enthusiasm (*informal*) ■ *interj Wales* used as a toast or to say goodbye (*informal*) [< Welsh]

hyacinth /hī ə sinth/ *n* a cultivated plant of the lily family. Flowers: fragrant pink, white, or blue, in spikes. Native to: NE Mediterranean. *Hyacinthus orientalis.* [Mid-16C. Via French and Latin < Greek *huakinthos* 'plant sprung from the blood of Hyacinthus'.] —**hyacinthine** /hī ə sín thīn/ *adj*

hyacinth bean *n* a deciduous woody-stemmed leguminous climbing plant. Flowers: pink, white. *Dolichos lablab.*

hyacinth orchid *n* a leafless orchid that usually grows near eucalyptus trees. Flowers: dark pink with white spots. Native to: Australia. *Dipodium punctatum.*

Hyacinthus /hī ə sínthəss/ *n* a young boy in Greek mythology who was loved and accidentally killed by the god Apollo, who made a flower grow on the spot where the boy died

Hyades /hī ə deez/ *n* a cluster of over 200 stars in the constellation Taurus, whose five brightest members form a V-shaped group

hyaena *n* ZOOL = **hyena**

hyal- *prefix* = **hyalo-** (*before vowels*)

hyalin /hī ə lin/ *n* a clear glassy material found in hyaline cartilage or formed as a product of some skin diseases

hyaline /hī ə lin, -leen, -līn/ *adj* clear, translucent, and containing no fibres or granular material

hyaline cartilage *n* the most common type of cartilage, consisting of a bluish-white elastic material containing fine collagen fibres that provides flexibility and support at the joints

hyaline membrane disease *n* = **respiratory distress syndrome**

hyalite /hī ə līt/ *n* a clear colourless variety of opal. Use: gems.

hyalitis /hī ə lītiss/ *n* inflammation of the transparent jelly (**vitreous humour**) that fills the chamber of the eye behind the lens

hyalo- *prefix* glass, glassy ○ *hyaloplasm* [< Greek *hualos* 'glass']

hyaloid /hī ə loyd/ *adj* clear and glassy in appearance

hyaloid membrane *n* a transparent insubstantial membrane surrounding the transparent jelly (**vitreous humour**) of the eye and separating it from the retina

hyaloplasm /hī ə lō plazəm/ *n* the clear component of cell cytoplasm, from which all specialized cell parts (**organelles**) and other granular constituents have been removed —**hyaloplasmic** /hī ə lō plázmik/ *adj*

hyaluronic acid /hī əlōō rónnik-/ *n* a complex viscous substance that lubricates joints and is present in connective tissue [< HYALOID (because first isolated in the vitreous humour) + *uronic* 'connected with urine']

hyaluronidase /hī əlōō rónnidayss, -dayz/ *n* an enzyme that breaks down hyaluronic acid

Hyannis /hī ánniss/ unincorporated settlement in SE Massachusetts, on the southern coast of Cape Cod. Population: 14,120 (1996 estimate).

hybrid /híbrid/ *n* **1 PLANT FROM CROSSING** a plant produced from a cross between two plants with different genetic constituents **2 ANIMAL FROM CROSS-SPECIES MATING** an animal that results from the mating of parents from two distinct species or subspecies **3 COMPOUND** something made up of a mixture of different elements **4 WORD FROM TWO LANGUAGES** a word that has derived from two different languages, e.g. 'appendicitis', in which 'appendic' is from Latin and 'itis' is from Greek **5 USING TWO FUELS** a vehicle with an engine that runs on electricity and petrol, which it can alternate between ■ *adj* **1 CROSSBRED** bred from two distinct species or subspecies **2 CONTAINING MIXED ELEMENTS** made up of different elements or components ○ *a hybrid literary form* **3 BEING A HYBRID** being or relating to a hybrid **4 UNUSUAL AS AN ELECTRONIC CIRCUIT** describes an electronic circuit that consists of two or more components not ordinarily combined with one another, e.g. a circuit that has integrated circuitry, transistors, and valves **5 WITH MULTIPLE INTEGRATED CIRCUITRY** describes an electronic circuit containing more than one integrated circuit, all of which are attached to the same ceramic substrate [Early 17C. < Latin *hybrida*.] —**hybridism** *n* —**hybridist** *n* —**hybridity** /hī bríddəti/ *n*

hybrid antibody *n* an artificial antibody synthesized to attach to two different antigens

hybrid bill *n* **1** a parliamentary bill with some provisions affecting the public domain and others affecting private interests **2** a bill encompassing a number of largely unrelated subject areas

⚡**hybrid computer** *n* a computer employing both analog and digital techniques

⚡**hybrid EDI** *n* a business exchange in which only one of the parties has electronic data interchange capabilities (*in e-commerce*)

hybridize /híbri dīz/ (**-izes, -izing, -ized**), **hybridise** (**-ises, -ising, -ised**) *vti* to generate a new form of plant or animal, either by human intervention or naturally, by combining the genes of two different species or subspecies —**hybridizable** *adj* —**hybridization** /híbri dī záysh'n/ *n* —**hybridizer** *n*

hybridoma /híbri dṓma/ *n* a hybrid cell produced by the fusion of a tumour cell with a normal antibody-producing cell, which then proliferates and yields large amounts of a monoclonal antibody

hybrid vigour *n* the increased growth, disease resistance, and fertility seen in hybrid species

hydathode /hída thōd/ *n* a pore in the outer layer of a leaf that secretes water when the rate of transpiration is low, e.g. in humid conditions [Late 19C. < Greek *hudat-*, stem of *hudōr* 'water' + *hodos* 'way'.]

hydatid /hídatid/, **hydatid cyst** *n* a cyst formed in human tissue that contains the larvae of a tapeworm [Late 17C. < modern Latin < Greek *hudatis* 'drop of water, watery vesicle' < *hudat-*, stem of *hudōr* 'water'.]

hydatid disease *n* a condition resulting from the presence of hydatid cysts in the liver, lungs, or brain, which can cause malignancies, blindness, epilepsy, and fever

Hyde Park /hīd-/ town in E New York State, on the Hudson River. Population: 21,230 (1990).

Hyderabad /hídərə bad/, **Hyderābād 1** former state in central India, now divided between the states of Andhra Pradesh, Karnataka, and Maharashtra **2** capital of Andhra Pradesh State, India. Population: 3,145,939 (1991). **3** city in SE Pakistan, on the River Indus. Population: 1,151,274 (1998).

hydnocarpate /hídnō kaʻar payt/ *n* a salt of hydnocarpic acid

hydnocarpic acid /hídnō kaʻarpik-/ *n* $C_{16}H_{28}O_2$ a fatty acid containing a carbon ring in its structure. Source: glycerides in chaulmoogra oil. [< *hydnocarpus*, plant yielding an oil containing this acid < Greek *hudnon* 'truffle' + *karpos* 'fruit', from the fruit's appearance]

hydr- *prefix* = **hydro-** (*before vowels*)

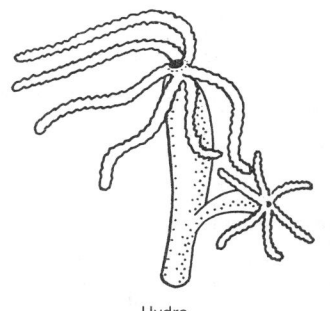

Hydra

hydra /hídrə/ (*plural* **-dras** *or* **-drae** /-drī/) *n* a freshwater polyp with a cylindrical body at one end and a mouth surrounded by tentacles at the other. Genus: *Hydra*. [Late 18C. Via modern Latin < Greek *hudra* 'water snake'.]

Hydra *n* **1** a constellation near the celestial equator. See illustration at **constellation 2** a monster in Greek mythology that had nine heads and was killed by Heracles

hydracid /hī drássid/ *n* an acid in which the hydrogen atoms are bound to an atom other than oxygen, e.g. hydrochloric acid

hydragogue /hídrə gog/ *n* a laxative that acts osmotically by drawing water into the intestinal canal from the blood, thereby softening the contents [Mid-17C. Via late Latin < Greek *hudragōgos* 'conveying water' < *hudr-* 'water'.]

hydra-headed *adj* with many heads or parts like heads

hydralazine /hī drállə zeen/ *n* a drug that lowers blood pressure [Mid-20C. < HYDRO- + PHTHALIC ACID + AZINE.]

hydrangea /hī dráynjə/ *n* an erect or climbing evergreen or deciduous shrub. Flowers: white, pink, or blue in large clusters in a variety of shapes. Native to: Asia. Genus: *Hydrangea*. [Mid-18C. < modern Latin, 'water pot'; from its cup-shaped seed pod.]

hydrant /hídrənt/ *n* an upright pipe, usually in a street, connected to a water main with a valve to which a hose can be attached, e.g. by the fire services [Early 19C. < HYDRO-.]

hydrarch /hī draark/ *adj* describes the development of a sequence of ecological stages that begins in a freshwater habitat such as a pond [Early 20C. < HYDRO- + Greek *arkhē* 'beginning'.]

hydrase /hī drayss, -drayz/ *n* an enzyme that catalyses the addition or removal of water

hydrastine /hī dráss teen, -tin/ *n* $C_{21}H_{21}NO_6$ a poisonous white substance. Source: roots of the goldenseal plant. Use: formerly, to stop haemorrhaging, shrink the uterus, reduce inflammation of mucous membranes. [Mid-19C. < modern Latin *hydrastis*, plant genus name < HYDRO-.]

hydrastinine /hī drásti neen, -nin/ *n* $C_{11}H_{13}NO_3$ an organic compound forming colourless crystals, soluble in water and resembling hydrastine in its medicinal properties

hydrate /hī drayt, hī dr-yt/ *vt* (**-drates, -drating, -drated**) **1 GIVE WATER TO** to provide water for somebody or something in order to re-establish or maintain a correct fluid balance **2 ADD WATER TO** to add water to a chemical compound so that different crystals are formed ■ *n* **COMPOUND CONTAINING WATER** a chemical compound containing water molecules that can usually be expelled by heating, without decomposition of the compound —**hydrator** *n*

hydrated /hī draytid, hī dráytid/ *adj* describes a compound that contains water

hydraulic /hī dróllik/ *adj* relating to or operated by a device in which pressure applied to a piston is transmitted by a fluid to a larger piston, giving rise to a larger force [Early 17C. Via Latin *hydraulicus* < Greek *hudraulikos* < *hudōr* 'water' + *aulos* 'pipe'.] —**hydraulically** *adv*

hydraulic brake *n* a brake in which force applied to a pedal is transmitted to the brake pads by an enclosed liquid, usually a glycol mixture

hydraulic coupling *n* an arrangement in which two pistons of different sizes are connected by an enclosed fluid that can transmit pressure from one piston to the other

hydraulic press *n* a device in which a relatively small force applied to a piston results in movement of a larger piston to which it is hydraulically coupled by an enclosed liquid

hydraulic ram *n* **1** the larger working piston of a hydraulic press **2** a device that uses the kinetic energy of a flow of water to raise water to a reservoir that is higher than the water source itself

hydraulics /hī drólliks/ *n* the study of water or other fluids at rest or in motion, especially with respect to engineering applications (+ *singular verb*)

hydrazide /hídrə zīd/ *n* a chemical compound formed when one of the hydrogen atoms in hydrazine is replaced by a radical containing the CO moiety [Late 19C. < HYDR- + AZO-.]

hydrazine /hídrə zeen/ *n* $H_2N.NH_2$ a highly reactive colourless liquid or white crystalline solid made from sodium hypochlorite and ammonia. Use: in rocket fuel. [Late 19C. < HYDR- + AZO-.]

hydrazoic acid /hídrə zṓ ik-/ *n* HN_3 a colourless liquid that is highly toxic and explosive in the presence of oxygen [< HYDR- + AZO-]

hydric /hídrik/ *adj* **1** containing or using considerable amounts of water **2** describes or relating to an environment that is extremely wet

hydride /hī drīd/ *n* a chemical compound formed between hydrogen and a more electropositive atom, e.g. sodium hydride, a transition metal, or via a covalent bond, e.g. boron hydride

hydrilla /hī drillə/ *n* (*plural* **-las** *or* **-la**) *n* a plant that grows underwater in large masses and oxygenates the water. Genus: *Hydrilla*. [Early 19C. < modern Latin, 'little hydra' < Latin *hydra* (see HYDRA).]

hydriodic acid /hídri óddik-/ *n* a colourless or pale yellow strong acid. Source: dissolving of hydrogen iodide gas in water. [< HYDR- + IODINE]

hydro[1] /hídrō/ (*plural* **-dros**) *n* **1 HYDROELECTRIC POWER PLANT** a power plant that generates electricity using water pressure **2 HYDROELECTRIC POWER** power generated using water pressure **3** *Can* **ELECTRIC POWER** electricity from an electric utility ○ *the hydro bill* [Early 20C. Shortening of HYDROELECTRIC.]

hydro[2] /hídrō/ (*plural* **-dros**) *n* a hotel, resort, or clinic offering hydropathic treatment [Late 19C. Shortening of *hydropathic treatment*.]

hydro- *prefix* **1** water, liquid, moisture ○ *hydrobiology* **2** hydrogen ○ *hydrocarbon* [< Greek *hudr-*, stem of *hudōr* 'water' < Indo-European]

hydroacoustics /hídrō ə kōōstiks/ *n* the branch of acoustics that studies how sound travels in water (+ *singular verb*)

hydrobiology /hídrō bī ólləji/ *n* the branch of biology that studies aquatic animals and plants —**hydrobiological** /hídrō bī ə lójjik'l/ *adj* —**hydrobiologist** *n*

hydrobromic acid /hīdrō brṓmik-/ *n* a colourless or pale yellow strong acid. Source: dissolving of hydrogen bromide gas in water.

hydrocarbon /hīdrō kaárbən/ *n* an organic chemical compound containing only hydrogen and carbon atoms, arranged in rows, rings, or both, and connected by single, double, or triple bonds —**hydrocarbonaceous** /-kaarbə náyshəss/ *adj* —**hydrocarbonic** /-kaar bónnik/ *adj* —**hydrocarbonous** /-kaárbənəss/ *adj*

hydrocele /hīdrō seel/ *n* an abnormal accumulation of watery liquid in a body cavity, especially in the sac round the testes

hydrocellulose /hīdrō séllyoolōss/ *n* a gelatinous substance formed when cellulose is mixed with water

hydrocephalus /hīdrō séffələss, -kéffələss/, **hydrocephaly** /hīdrō séffəli, -kéffəli/ *n* an abnormal increase of cerebrospinal fluid round the brain, resulting in infants in an enlargement of the head because the bones of the skull are still unfused [Late 17C. < modern Latin, < Greek *hudōr* 'water' + *kephalē* 'head'.] —**hydrocephalic** /hīdrō sə fállik, -kə-/ *adj* —**hydrocephaloid** /-séffə loyd, -kéffə-/ *adj* —**hydrocephalous** *adj*

hydrochloric acid /hīdrə klórrik-/ *n* **HCl** a strong colourless acid. Source: dissociation of hydrogen chloride gas in water. Use: industrial and laboratory processes.

hydrochloride /hīdrō kláwr īd/ *n* a salt formed when hydrochloric acid reacts with an organic base, e.g. aniline

hydrochlorofluorocarbon /hīdrō klawrō floorō kaárbən/ *n* a hydrocarbon in which some of the hydrogens are replaced by chlorine and fluorine, capable of damaging the ozone layer. Use: formerly, in refrigerants, aerosols, packing materials. [Late 20C. < HYDROCHLORIDE.]

hydrochlorothiazide /hīdrō kláwrō thī ə zīd/ *n* a drug used in the treatment of fluid retention and high blood pressure

hydrocolloid /hīdrō kólloyd/ *n* a substance that forms a gel when mixed with water —**hydrocolloidal** /hīdrōkə lóyd'l/ *adj*

hydrocoral /hīdrə kórrəl/ *n* a marine multicellular organism that lives in colonies and builds calcareous skeletons within which the animals live. Orders: Milleporina and Stylasterina.

hydrocortisone /hīdrə káwrtizōn/ *n* **1** a steroid hormone secreted by the adrenal cortex, involved in carbohydrate metabolism and the stress reaction **2** a synthetic form of hydrocortisone. Use: treatment of allergies, inflammation, and adrenal failure.

hydrocracking /hīdrō kraking/ *n* an industrial process in which the action of hydrogen under high pressure fragments long-chain hydrocarbons to produce more volatile compounds, e.g. petrol and paraffin

hydrocyanic acid /hīdrō sī ánnik-/ *n* a colourless weak acid that smells of almonds. Source: dissolving of hydrogen cyanide in water.

hydrodynamic /hīdrō dī námmik/, **hydrodynamical** /-námmik'l/ *adj* **1** relating to the mechanical properties of liquids **2** operated by a moving liquid —**hydrodynamically** *adv*

hydrodynamics /hīdrō dī námmiks/ *n* the area of fluid dynamics that is concerned with the study of liquids (+ *singular verb*) —**hydrodynamicist** /-námmissist/ *n*

hydroelectric /hīdrō i léktrik/ *adj* **1** generated by converting the pressure of falling or running water to electricity by means of a turbine coupled to a generator **2** relating to the generation of electricity by means of water pressure —**hydroelectrically** *adv* —**hydroelectricity** /hīdrō i lek trissəti/ *n*

hydrofluoric acid /hīdrō flóorrik-/ *n* an extremely poisonous corrosive colourless liquid. Source: dissolving of hydrogen fluoride in water. Use: etching glass, treatment of metal surfaces, cleaning masonry.

hydrofluorocarbon /hīdrō floorō kaárbən/ *n* a chemical compound composed of hydrogen, fluorine, and carbon. Use: preparation of plastics and pharmaceuticals.

hydrofoil /hīdrə foyl/ *n* **1** a boat with wing-shaped blades fixed to struts under the hull that lift the boat out of the water as speed increases **2** a wing-shaped blade that lifts a hydrofoil out of the water

hydroforming /hīdrō fawrming/ *n* **1** a high-temperature process in which hydrogen, with other catalysts, causes certain hydrocarbons to break down, lose hydrogen, and rearrange themselves into aromatic or cyclic forms **2** a process in which sheet metal is shaped by a punch forced against a flexible shaped block resting on a fluid-filled bag

hydrogel /hīdrə jel/ *n* a thick fluid like a jelly, formed by the addition of a substance to water

hydrogen /hīdrəjən/ *n* (*symbol* **H**) a highly reactive colourless gas, the lightest element and the most abundant in the universe. Source: water, most organic compounds. Use: industrial processes, production of ammonia, reduction of metal ores to metals. [Late 18C. < French *hydrogène* < Greek *hudōr* 'water' + French *-gène* (see -GEN).]

hydrogenase /hī drójjə nayss, -nayz/ *n* an enzyme that catalyses reduction reactions by hydrogen

hydrogenate /hī drójjə nayt/ (**-ates, -ating, -ated**) *vt* to add hydrogen to a compound in a chemical reaction —**hydrogenation** /hī drójjə náysh'n/ *n* —**hydrogenator** *n*

hydrogen bomb *n* an explosive weapon of mass destruction in which huge amounts of energy are released by the fusion of hydrogen nuclei

hydrogen bond *n* an electrostatic interaction between molecules of compounds in which hydrogen atoms are bound to electronegative atoms, e.g. oxygen and nitrogen

hydrogen bromide *n* **HBr** a colourless gas usually made by combination of hydrogen and bromine in the presence of a catalyst such as platinum

hydrogen carbonate *n* a salt of carbonic acid in which one hydrogen atom has been replaced, usually by a metal

hydrogen chloride *n* **HCl** a colourless fuming corrosive gas. Source: byproduct of organic chlorination reactions. Use: manufacture of PVC.

hydrogen cyanide *n* **HCN** an extremely poisonous colourless liquid or gas with a characteristic smell of almonds. Source: reaction between an acid and a metal cyanide.

hydrogen embrittlement *n* a process in which a metal is weakened by incorporation of hydrogen in or below its surface, e.g. during plating or etching

hydrogen fluoride *n* a colourless corrosive liquid. Source: action of sulphuric acid on a metal fluoride.

hydrogen iodide *n* **HI** a colourless poisonous gas. Source: reaction of hydrogen and iodine in the presence of a catalyst, usually platinum.

hydrogen ion *n* a positively charged ion of hydrogen that is formed by the removal of an electron from a hydrogen atom and is present in solutions of acids in water

hydrogenize /hī drójjə nīz/ (**-nizes, -nizing, -nized**), **hydrogenise** (**-nises, -nising, -nised**) *vt* CHEM = **hydrogenate** —**hydrogenization** /hī drójjə nī záysh'n/ *n*

hydrogenolysis /hīdrəjə nóllәssiss/ *n* the breaking of a bond in a molecule of an organic compound by the action of hydrogen, accompanied by the addition of a hydrogen atom to each of the fragments

hydrogenous /hī drójjənəss/ *adj* containing hydrogen

hydrogen peroxide *n* H_2O_2 a colourless viscous unstable liquid that readily decomposes in water and oxygen. Use: bleach, mild antiseptic, component in rocket fuel.

hydrogen sulphate *n* a salt containing the ion HSO_4O^-, formed when one hydrogen atom is removed from sulphuric acid by reaction with a metal, metal salt, or organic group

hydrogen sulphide *n* H_2S a colourless flammable poisonous gas with a characteristic smell of rotten eggs. Source: action of a mineral acid such as hydrochloric acid on a metal sulphide.

hydrogen sulphite *n* a salt containing the ion HSO_3^-

hydrogen tartrate *n* a salt or ester of tartaric acid, e.g. potassium hydrogen tartrate, that forms deposits in wine vats

hydrogeology /hīdrō ji ólləji/ *n* a branch of geology that studies the movement of subsurface water through rocks, and its effects —**hydrogeologic** /hīdrō ji ə lójjik/ *adj* —**hydrogeological** *adj* —**hydrogeologist** *n*

hydrography /hī dróggrəfi/ *n* the scientific study of seas, lakes, and rivers, especially the charting of tides and changes in coastal bathymetry or the measurement and recording of river flow —**hydrograph** /hīdrə graaf, -graf/ *n* —**hydrographer** *n* —**hydrographic** /hīdrə gráffik/ *adj* —**hydrographically** *adv*

hydroid /hī droyd/ *n* **1** a marine invertebrate animal with an internal body cavity that lives in colonies, forming growths like tufts. Order: Hydroida. **2** an asexual polyp that is part of the life cycle of hydrozoans [Mid-19C. < HYDRA.]

hydrolase /hīdrə layz, -layss/ *n* an enzyme that controls hydrolysis [Early 20C. < HYDROLYSIS.]

~~**hydrolic**~~ incorrect spelling of **hydraulic**

hydrologic cycle /hīdrə lójjik-/, **hydrological cycle** /-lójjik'l-/ *n* the water cycle (*technical*)

hydrology /hī drólləji/ *n* the scientific study of the properties, distribution, use, and circulation of the water of the earth and the atmosphere in all of its forms —**hydrologist** *n*

hydrolysate /hī dróllə sayt/ *n* a substance produced by hydrolysis

hydrolyse /hīdrə līz/ (**-lyses, -lysing, -lysed**) *vti* to undergo hydrolysis, or make a substance undergo hydrolysis [Late 19C. < HYDROLYSIS after ANALYSIS, ANALYSE.] —**hydrolysable** *adj* —**hydrolysation** /hīdrə lī záysh'n/ *n*

hydrolysis /hī dróllәssiss/ *n* a chemical reaction in which a compound reacts with water, causing decomposition and the production of two or more other compounds, e.g. the conversion of starch to glucose —**hydrolytic** /hīdrə líttik/ *adj* —**hydrolytically** *adv*

hydrolyze *vti* US = **hydrolyse**

hydromagnetics /hīdrō mag néttiks/ *n* MECH ENG = **magnetohydrodynamics** (+ *singular verb*) —**hydromagnetic** *adj*

hydromancy /hīdrō manssi/ *n* the attempt to find out about future events or unknown knowledge by studying the appearance or movement of water —**hydromancer** *n* —**hydromantic** /hīdrō mántik/ *adj*

hydromechanics /hīdrō mi kánniks/ *n* MECH ENG = **hydrodynamics** (+ *singular verb*) —**hydromechanical** *adj*

hydromel /hīdrō mel/ *n* a drink made of honey mixed in water [15C. Via Latin *hydromeli* < Greek *hudromeli* 'water honey' < *meli* 'honey'.]

hydrometallurgy /hīdrō me tállərji/ *n* the extraction of metals from ores by treating them with aqueous chemical solutions, including extraction by electrolysis and ion exchange —**hydrometallurgical** /hīdro metə lúrjik'l/ *adj*

hydrometeor /hīdrō meéti ər/ *n* a weather condition caused by condensation of water in the atmosphere, e.g. rain, snow, or fog —**hydrometeorological** /-meéti ərə lójjik'l/ *adj* —**hydrometeorologist** /-meéti ə róllәjist/ *n* —**hydrometeorology** *n*

hydrometer /hī drómmitər/ *n* a device, typically a sealed graduated tube containing a weighted bulb, used to determine the specific gravity, or density, of a liquid —**hydrometric** /hīdrō méttrik/ *adj* —**hydrometrically** *adv* —**hydrometry** *n*

hydronium ion *n* = **hydroxonium ion**

hydropathy /hī dróppəthi/ *n* the treatment of injuries or disease by applying water both internally and externally —**hydropath** /hīdrə path/ *n* —**hydropathic** /hīdrō páthik/ *adj* —**hydropathical** *adj* —**hydropathically** *adv*

hydroperoxide /hīdrōpə rók sīd/ *n* an intermediate compound formed during the oxidation of unsaturated organic substances and containing the group -OOH

hydrophane /hīdrə fayn/ *n* a translucent lustrous form of opal —**hydrophanous** /hī dróffənəss/ *adj*

hydrophilic /hīdrō fíllik/ *adj* dissolving in, absorbing, or mixing easily with water —**hydrophile** /hīdrə fīl/ *n* —**hydrophilicity** /hīdrōfi líssəti/ *n*

hydrophobia /hīdrō fṓbi ə/ *n* **1** MED = **rabies** **2** an extremely intense aversion to water, especially the fear of drinking water or other liquids

hydrophobic /hīdrō fṓbik/ *adj* **1** relating to or affected by an extreme fear of water **2** not dissolving in, absorbing, or mixing easily with water —**hydrophobe** /hīdrəfōb/ *n* —**hydrophobicity** /hīdrōfō bíssəti/ *n*

hydrophone /hīdrəfōn/ *n* an electronic receiver that can pick up sound travelling through water by converting acoustic energy into electromagnetic waves

hydrophyte /hīdrə fīt/ *n* a plant that will only grow in water or in a very damp environment —**hydrophytic** /hīdrə fíttik/ *adj*

hydroplane /hīdrō playn/ *n* **1 FAST BOAT** a motorboat designed so that it rises up out of the water at high speed and skims along the surface **2 VANE ON SUBMARINE** a horizontal vane on a submarine, used to control its vertical movement ■ *vi* (**-planes, -planing, -planed**) **1 SKIM THE SURFACE** to skim along on the surface of the water, especially in a hydroplane **2** = **aquaplane** *v.* 2

hydroponics /hīdrō pónniks/ *n* the growing of plants in a nutrient liquid with or without gravel or another supporting medium (+ *singular verb*) [Mid-20C. < HYDRO- + Greek *ponos* 'work'.] —**hydroponic** *adj* —**hydroponically** *adv* —**hydroponicist** /-pónnissist/ *n* —**hydroponist** /hī dróppənist/ *n*

hydropower /hīdrō powər/ *n* electric power generated using water power

hydroquinone /hīdrōkwi nṓn/, **hydroquinol** /-nṓl/ *n* $C_6H_4(OH)_2$ a white crystalline compound. Use: photographic developer, in paints, in motor oils, in medicines.

hydroscope /hīdrə skōp/ *n* an optical instrument constructed from a series of mirrors encased in a tube, used for observing objects deep beneath the surface of a body of water —**hydroscopic** /hīdrə skóppik/ *adj* —**hydroscopical** *adj* —**hydroscopically** *adv*

hydrosere /hīdrə seer/ *n* the sequence of plant communities that colonize the site when shallow open water becomes gradually silted up and transformed into forest or bog

hydroski /hīdrō skee/ *n* a hydrofoil on a seaplane, usually ski-shaped and retractable, used to give extra lift on takeoff

hydrosol /hīdrə sol/ *n* a colloidal solution in which the particles are suspended in water [Mid-19C. < HYDRO- + SOLUTION.] —**hydrosolic** /hīdrə sóllik/ *adj*

hydrosphere /hīdrə sfeer/ *n* the portion of the earth's surface that is water, including the seas and water in the atmosphere —**hydrospheric** /hīdrə sférrik/ *adj*

hydrostat /hīdrō stat/ *n* a device designed to regulate the height of fluid in a column or container

hydrostatic /hīdrō státtik/, **hydrostatical** /-státtik'l/ *adj* **1** relating to, involving, or typical of fluids that are at rest and the forces and pressures they exert **2** relating to, involving, or typical of hydrostatics [Mid-17C. Probably < modern Latin *hydrostaticus* or < its source Greek *hudrostatēs* 'hydrostatic balance' < *statikos* 'causing to stand'.] —**hydrostatically** *adv*

hydrostatics /hīdrō státtiks/ *n* the scientific study of the equilibrium of liquids at rest and the forces and pressures exerted by them (+ *singular verb*)

hydrostatic skeleton *n* the most primitive form of skeletal structure found in animals such as jellyfish and worms, consisting of layers of muscle around the fluid-filled body cavity

hydrotaxis /hīdrō táksiss/ *n* the response of an organism or cell to the presence of water or moisture, usually detected as movement —**hydrotactic** /-táktik/ *adj*

hydrotherapeutics /hīdrō thérrə pyoótiks/ *n* the scientific study and theory of the external use of water for healing (+ *singular verb*) —**hydrotherapeutic** *adj*

hydrotherapy /hīdrō thérrəpi/ *n* the treatment of disease by the external use of water, e.g. by exercising weakened limbs in a pool —**hydrotherapist** *n*

hydrothermal /hīdrō thúrm'l/ *adj* relating to or produced by extremely hot water, as are, e.g., rock formations —**hydrothermally** *adv*

hydrothorax /-tháw raks/ *n* an abnormal build-up of fluid in a pleural cavity, e.g. as a result of failing circulation caused by heart disease [Late 18C. < modern Latin, < Latin *thorax* 'chest'.] —**hydrothoracic** /hīdrō thaw rássik/ *adj*

hydrotropism /hī dróttrəpizəm/ *n* movement in a plant, e.g. by roots, towards or away from a source of water —**hydrotropic** /hīdrō tróppik/ *adj* —**hydrotropically** *adv*

hydrous /hīdrəss/ *adj* **1** containing water or moisture **2** containing or combined chemically with water molecules

hydroxide /hī drók sīd/ *n* OH^- a compound containing the hydroxyl group -OH, specifically an acid or base containing the hydroxyl ion

hydroxide ion *n* CHEM = **hydroxyl**

hydroxonium ion /hīdrók sṓni əm-/, **hydronium ion** *n* H_3O^+ the positive ion that is formed by the addition of a proton to a water molecule, usually in solutions of acids [Early 20C. < HYDRO- + *oxonium* < OXY-, after AMMONIUM.]

hydroxy /hī dróksi/ *adj* containing one or more hydroxyl groups

hydroxyapatite /hī dróksi áppə tīt/ *n* a hydrated calcium phosphate mineral

hydroxyl /hī dróksil/ *n* OH^- the negative ion formed by the attachment of an oxygen atom and a hydrogen atom [Mid-19C. < HYDRO- + OXY- + -YL.] —**hydroxylic** /hī drok síllik/ *adj*

hydroxylamine /hī dróksilə meén, hī dróksil ámmin/ *n* NH_2OH a colourless crystalline compound that decomposes at room temperature and explodes on heating. Use: reducing agent, in the synthesis of organic molecules.

hydroxylate /hī dróksi layt/ (**-ates, -ating, -ated**) *vt* to introduce hydroxyl into a compound —**hydroxylation** /hī dróksi láysh'n/ *n*

hydroxyl ion *n* = **hydroxyl**

hydroxyproline /hī dróksi prṓ leen/ *n* an amino acid derived from proline that is a component of collagen.

hydrozoan /hīdrō zṓ ən/ *n* a marine or freshwater invertebrate animal such as a polyp or jellyfish. Class: Hydrozoa. [Late 19C. < modern Latin *Hydrozoa* 'water animals' < Greek *zōia*, plural of *zōion* 'animal'.]

Hydrus /hīdrəss/ *n* a constellation of the southern hemisphere. See illustration at **constellation**

hyena /hī eénə/, **hyaena** *n* a carnivorous scavenging mammal resembling a dog, with a sloping back and loping gait. Native to: Africa, S Asia. Family: Hyaenidae. [14C. Directly or via Old French < Latin *hyaena* < Greek *huaina*, feminine of *hus* 'pig'.] —**hyenic** *adj*

hyetal /hī ət'l/ *adj* relating to rain or rainfall [Mid-19C. < Greek *huetos* 'rain'.]

hyeto- *prefix* rain ○ *hyetograph* [< Greek *huetos* < *huein* 'to rain']

hyetograph /hī ətō graaf, -graf/ *n* **1** a chart or graph showing the pattern of rainfall in an area **2** an instrument that automatically collects rain and measures its amount —**hyetographically** /hī ətō gráffikli/ *adv* —**hyetography** /hī ə tóggrəfi/ *n*

Hygeia /hī jeéə/ *n* in Greek mythology, the goddess of health

~~**hygeine**~~ incorrect spelling of **hygiene**

Hygiea /hī jeé ə/ *n* the fourth-largest asteroid, discovered in 1849

hygiene /hī jeen/ *n* **1** the science dealing with the preservation of health **2** the practice or principles of cleanliness [Late 17C. Directly or via French *hygiène* < modern Latin *(ars) hygieina* 'healthful art' < Greek *hugiēs* 'healthy'.]

hygienic /hī jeénik/ *adj* **1 OF CLEANLINESS** relating to the scientific study or principles of cleanliness **2 PROMOTING HEALTH** promoting health or cleanliness **3 GERM-FREE** clean or free from disease-causing microorganisms —**hygienically** *adv*

hygienics /hī jeéniks/ *n* = **hygiene** *n.* 1 (+ *singular verb*)

hygienist /hī jeenist/ *n* a student of or expert in the maintenance of hygiene

hygro- *prefix* moisture, humidity ○ *hygrometer* [< Greek *hugros* 'moist' < Indo-European]

hygrograph /hīgrə graf/ *n* an automatic hygrometer that records the humidity of the air

hygrometer /hī grómmitər/ *n* an instrument used to measure humidity —**hygrometric** /hīgrə méttrik/ *adj* —**hygrometrically** *adv*

hygrophilous /hī gróffələss/ *adj* adapted to growing in damp places

hygrophyte /hīgrə fīt/ *n* PLANT SCI = **hydrophyte** —**hygrophytic** /hīgrə fíttik/ *adj*

hygroscope /hīgrə skōp/ *n* an instrument that shows changes in the humidity of the air but does not measure the changes

hygroscopic /hīgrə skóppik/, **hygroscopical** /-skóppik'l/ *adj* capable of easily absorbing moisture, e.g. from the air —**hygroscopically** *adv* —**hygroscopicity** /hīgrəskō píssəti/ *n*

hygrostat /hīgrə stat/ *n* = **humidistat**

hying present participle of **hie**

Hyksos /híksoss/ (*plural* **-sos**) *n* a member of an ancient nomadic Asian group of people, probably of Semitic ancestry, who conquered and ruled Egypt between 1720 BC and 1560 BC [Early 17C. Via Greek *Huksōs* < Egyptian *heqa khoswe* 'foreign rulers'.] —**Hyksos** *adj*

hyla /hīlə/ *n* a tree frog of a genus found all over the world. Genus: *Hyla.* [Mid-19C. Via modern Latin < Greek *hulē* 'wood'.]

hylo- *prefix* matter ○ *hylotheism* [< Greek *hulē* 'wood, matter']

hylomorphism /hīlə máwrfizəm/ *n* the belief that all material objects are made up of matter, which is only potential, and form, which makes the object an actuality

hylotheism /hīlə theé izəm/ *n* the belief that God and the material world are the same

hylozoism /hīlə zṓ izəm/ *n* the belief that all matter is living [Late 17C. < HYLO- + Greek *zōē* 'life'.] —**hylozoic** *adj*

hymen /hī men/ *n* a thin mucous membrane that completely or partially covers the opening of the vagina [Mid-16C. Directly or via French < late Latin < Greek *humēn* 'membrane'.]

Hymen /hīmen/ *n* in Greek mythology, the god of marriage, often represented as a youth holding a torch

hymeneal /hī me neé əl/ *adj* relating to, involving, or typical of marriage (*literary*) ■ *n* a song or poem celebrating a wedding (*literary*) [Early 17C. < Latin *hymenaeus* 'wedding song, wedding' < Greek *humenaios* < *Humēn* 'Hymen'.] —**hymeneally** *adv*

hymenium /hī meéni əm/ (*plural* **-a** /-ni ə/ *or* **-ums**) *n* a layer of spore-bearing structures within or on the surface of the fruiting body of a fungus [Early 19C. Via modern Latin < Greek *humenion* 'small membrane' < *humēn* 'membrane'.] —**hymenial** *adj*

hymenopteran /hīmə nóptərən/, **hymenopteron** *n* an insect such as the wasp, ant, and sawfly that has two pairs of membranous wings and a very thin waist and that lives in socially complex colonies. Order: Hymenoptera. [Mid-19C. < modern Latin *Hymenoptera* < form of Greek *humenopteros* 'membrane-winged' < *humēn* 'membrane' + *pteron* 'wing'.] —**hymenopteran** *adj* —**hymenopterous** *adj*

hymn /him/ *n* **1 RELIGIOUS SONG** a song of praise to God, a god, or a saint **2 SONG OF PRAISE** a song of praise to somebody or something other than a deity ■ *v* **1** *vt* **SING IN PRAISE** to sing in praise of somebody or something **2** *vi* **SING HYMNS** to sing songs of praise [Pre-12C. Via Latin *hymnus* < Greek *humnos* 'song in praise of gods or heroes'.] —**hymnic** *adj*

hymnal /hímnəl/ *n* a book of church hymns

hymn book *n* a book that contains the words and sometimes the music of church hymns

hymnist /hímnist/ *n* a composer of hymns

hymnody /hímnədi/ (*plural* **-dies**) *n* **1** the composing or singing of hymns **2** hymns collectively, usually a group that share a specific characteristic such as time of composition or use in a particular church [Early 18C. Via medieval Latin *hymnodia* < Greek *humnōidia* 'singing of hymns' < *humnos* 'song in praise of gods or heroes'.]

hymnology /him nólləji/ (*plural* **-gies**) *n* **1** the study of religious hymns **2** CHR = **hymnody** —**hymnologic** /hímnə lójjik/ *adj* —**hymnological** *adj* —**hymnologist** *n*

hyoid /hī oyd/ *adj* relating to or involving the U-shaped hyoid bone ■ *n* = **hyoid bone** [Early 19C. Via French *hyoïde* < Greek *huoeidēs* 'shaped like the Greek letter upsilon' < *hu* 'upsilon'.]

hyoid bone *n* a U-shaped bone positioned at the base of the tongue and above the thyroid cartilage that supports the tongue and its muscles

hyoscine /hī ō seen/ *n* CHEM = **scopolamine** [Late 19C. < modern Latin *Hyoscyamus* (see HYOSCYAMINE).]

hyoscyamine /hī ō sī ə meen/ *n* a poisonous alkaloid, resembling atropine. Source: henbane, belladonna. Use: in medicine as a dilator and antispasmodic. [Mid-19C. < modern Latin *Hyoscyamus*, genus name of the henbane < Greek *huoskuamos* 'pig's bean' < genitive of *hus* 'pig' + *kuamos* 'bean'.]

hyp. *abbr* **1** hypotenuse **2** hypothesis **3** hypothetical

hyp- *prefix* = **hypo-** (*before vowels*)

hypabyssal /híppə bíss'l/ *adj* describes igneous rocks, especially in the form of dikes or sills, created when molten magma rose to the surface of the earth but solidified before reaching it —**hypabyssally** *adv*

hypaesthesia *n* an unusually reduced sensitivity to touch [Late 19C. < modern Latin, 'condition of sensation being below normal' < Greek *aisthēsis* 'sensation'.] —**hypaesthetic** /-théttik, -/ *adj*

hypaethral /hi peéthrəl, hī-/ *adj* with no roof or a roof that is partly open to the sky, in the style, e.g. of a classical temple [Late 18C. < Latin *hypaethrus* 'in the open air' < Greek *hupaithros* < *aithēr* 'air'.]

hypallage /hī pálləji/ *n* a figure of speech in which the usual relations of words or phrases are interchanged [Late 16C. Via late Latin < Greek *hupallagē* 'interchange' < *allag-*, stem of *allassein* 'to exchange' < *allos* 'other'.]

hypanthium /hī pánthi əm/ (*plural* **-a** /hī pánthi ə/) *n* the flat or cup-shaped area that bears the stamens, petals, and sepals of some plants, e.g. a rose or cherry [Mid-19C. < modern Latin, 'structure under the flower' < Greek *anthos* 'flower'.] —**hypanthial** *adj*

Hypatia /hī páyshə/ (375–415) Greek philosopher

hype[1] /hīp/ *n* **1 PUBLICITY** greatly exaggerated publicity intended to excite public interest in something such as a film or theatrical production **2 SOMEBODY OR SOMETHING OVERPUBLICIZED** a widely publicized person or thing **3 DECEPTION** a deception or dishonest scheme ■ *vt* (**hypes, hyping, hyped**) **1 PUBLICIZE** to promote somebody or something with intense publicity **2 ARTIFICIALLY BOOST SALES** to boost sales of a pop recording artificially by employing people to buy quantities of it at numerous outlets [Early 20C. Partly back-formation < HYPERBOLE, partly < slang *hyper* 'somebody giving short change' (< HYPER-).]

hype[2] /hīp/ *n* (*slang*) **1** a hypodermic needle or injection **2** a drug addict

hyped up *adj* highly stimulated or excited, especially by drugs (*slang*) [Mid-20C. < HYPE[2].]

hyper /hípər/ *adj* (*informal*) **1** behaving in an overexcited or hyperactive way **2** easily excited [Mid-20C. Shortening of HYPERACTIVE.]

hyper- *prefix* **1** over, above, beyond ○ *hyperextension* **2** excessive, unusually high ○ *hypertension* [< Greek *huper* 'above, beyond' < Indo-European]

hyperacidity /hípərə síddəti/ *n* a condition in which there is excessive production of stomach acid, usually associated with the formation of a peptic or duodenal ulcer

hyperactive /hípər áktiv/ *adj* unusually active, restless, and lacking the ability to concentrate for any length of time, especially as a result of attention deficit disorder —**hyperaction** *n* —**hyperactively** *adv* —**hyperactivity** /-ak tívvəti/ *n*

hyperaemia /hípər eémi ə/ *n* an unusually high level of blood in some part of the body —**hyperaemic** /hípər eémik/ *adj*

hyperaesthesia /hípər eess theézi ə/ *n* an unusually heightened sensitivity of some part of the body, e.g. the skin, or any of the senses [Mid-19C. < modern Latin, 'condition of extreme sensation' < Greek *aisthēsis* 'sensation'.] —**hyperaesthetic** /-théttik/ *adj*

hyperbaric /hípər bárrik/ *adj* relating to, involving, occurring at, or operating at pressures higher than normal [Mid-20C. < HYPER- + Greek *baros* 'weight'.] —**hyperbarically** *adv*

hyperbaton /hī púrbə ton/ *n* a figure of speech in which the expected word order is inverted for emphasis, e.g. in 'you I hate' [Mid-16C. Via Latin < Greek *huperbaton* 'overstepping' < *huperbainein* 'step over' < *bainein* 'step, walk'.]

hyperbola /hī púrbələ/ (*plural* **-las** *or* **-lae** /-lee/) *n* a conic section formed by a point that moves in a plane so that the difference in its distance from two fixed points in the plane remains constant [Mid-17C. Via modern Latin < Greek *huperbolē* 'excess' (see HYPERBOLE).]

hyperbole /hī púrbəli/ *n* deliberate and obvious exaggeration used for effect, e.g. 'I could eat a million of these' [15C. Via Latin < Greek *huperbolē* 'excess', literally 'overthrow' < *ballein* 'throw'.]

hyperbolic /hípər bóllik/, **hyperbolical** /-bóllik'l/ *adj* **1 OF HYPERBOLA** relating to, involving, or typical of a hyperbola **2 OF GEOMETRIC SYSTEM** produced by or relating to a geometric system in which two lines can pass through any point in a plane without intersecting a specific line in the same plane **3 OF HYPERBOLIC FUNCTION** connected with or relating to a hyperbolic function **4 OF HYPERBOLE** relating to, involving, or typical of hyperbole —**hyperbolically** *adv*

hyperbolic function *n* any of six functions analogous to trigonometric functions but related to a hyperbola rather than a circle

hyperbolize /hī púrbə līz/ (**-lizes, -lizing, -lized**), **hyperbolise** (**-lises, -lising, -lised**) *vti* to use deliberate and obvious exaggeration for effect

hyperboloid /hī púrbə loyd/ *n* a mathematical surface whose sections parallel to one coordinate plane form ellipses and those parallel to the other two coordinate planes form hyperbolas

hyperborean /hípər báwri ən/ *adj* **1** relating to the far northern regions **2** relating to peoples who live in the Arctic [Late 16C. < late Latin *hyperboreanus* < Latin *hyperboreus* < Greek *huperbore(i)os* < *boreios* 'northern' or *Boreas* 'north wind'.]

Hyperborean /hípər báwri ən/ *n* in Greek legend, a member of a people who lived beyond the north wind in a land that was always sunny and warm

hypercalcaemia /hípər kal seémi ə/ *n* an unusually high amount of calcium in the blood. US term **hypercalcemia** —**hypercalcaemic** *adj*

hypercapnia /hípər káppni ə/ *n* an unusually high level of carbon dioxide in the blood [Early 20C. < modern Latin, 'condition of excessive smoke' < Greek *kapnos* 'smoke'.] —**hypercapnic** *adj*

hypercharge /hípər chaarj/ *n* a property of elementary particles that is calculated by adding together a particle's baryon number and its quantum property of strangeness [Mid-20C. Contraction of *hyperonic charge* (< HYPERON).]

hypercholesterolaemia /hípərkə léstərə leémi ə/ *n* an unusually high level of cholesterol in the blood. US term **hypercholesterolemia** —**hypercholesterolaemic** *adj*

hypercomplex /hípər kómpleks/ *adj* **1** describes nerve cells found in the visual cortex area at the back of the brain that respond only to certain visual stimuli **2** describes a generalized complex number, e.g. a number with one real and three imaginary components

hypercorrect /hípərkə rékt/ *adj* **1** too greatly concerned about correctness **2** showing or being the result of hypercorrection —**hypercorrectly** *adv* —**hypercorrectness** *n*

hypercorrection /hípərkə réksh'n/ *n* a grammatical mistake or mispronunciation made by correcting something that is not actually wrong, e.g. saying 'between you and I' instead of 'between you and me'

hypercritical /hípər kríttik'l/ *adj* criticizing somebody or something too severely or too much —**hypercritically** *adv* —**hypercriticism** *n*

hypercube /hípər kyoob/ *n* a figure in four or more dimensions with sides that are all of the same length and angles that are all right angles

hyperemia *n* US = **hyperaemia**

hyperesthesia *n* US = **hyperaesthesia**

hypereutectic /hípər yoo téktik/, **hypereutectoid** /hípər yoo ték toyd/ *adj* describes a compound or alloy that contains a minor component in a higher proportion than in the mixture of the same elements that has the lowest melting point

hyperextension /hípərik sténsh'n/ *n* the movement of a limb beyond its normal range —**hyperextend** *vt* —**hyperextended** *adj*

hyperfine structure /hīər fīn-/ *n* the splitting of lines in a spectrum into two or more closely spaced fine lines, caused by magnetic interactions within atoms

hyperfocal distance /hípərfōk'l-/ *n* the distance between a camera lens and the closest object that is in focus when the lens is focused at infinity

hypergamy /hī púrgəmi/ *n* a custom in some societies that requires a woman to marry a man of a higher social class than the one to which she belongs

hyperglycaemia /hípər glī seémi ə/ *n* an unusually high level of sugar in the blood. US term **hyperglycemia** —**hyperglycaemic** *adj*

hypergolic /hípər góllik/ *adj* describes a rocket propellant that ignites on contact with an oxidizer [Mid-20C. < German *Hypergol* 'hypergolic fuel' < *hyper-* 'hyper-' + *erg-* 'work' (< Greek *ergon*).] —**hypergol** /hípər gol/ *n* —**hypergolically** *adv*

hyperhidrosis /hípər hi drōssiss, -hī-/ *n* excessive sweating, either generalized or localized to a particular part of the body

hypericum /hī pérrikəm/ *n* a herbaceous plant that grows in temperate regions with many cultivated forms, e.g. St John's wort. Genus: *Hypericum*. [15C. Via Latin < Greek *hupereikon* < *huper* 'over' + *ereikē* 'heath, heather'.]

hyperinflation /hípərin fláysh'n/ *n* very high and rapid monetary inflation that is so great as to threaten a nation's economic stability —**hyperinflationary** *adj*

hyperinsulinism /hípər ínsyŏŏlinizəm/ *n* an unusually high level of insulin in the blood, causing hypoglycaemia

Hyperion /hī peéri ən/ *n* **1** the seventh moon of Saturn, discovered in 1848 **2** in Greek mythology, one of the Titans, son of Gaea and Uranus

hyperirritability /hípər írritə bílləti/ *n* an unusually extreme response to stimuli —**hyperirritable** /-írritəb'l/ *adj*

hyperkeratosis /hípər kérrə tṓssiss/ *n* an excessive thickening of the outer layer of the skin —**hyperkeratotic** /-tóttik/ *adj*

hyperkinesia /hípər ki neézi ə, -kī neézhə/, **hyperkinesis** /-neéssiss/ *n* **1** excessively increased movement in a muscle, e.g. in a spasm **2** excessive activity in children, e.g. those affected by attention deficit disorder [Mid-19C. < HYPER- + Greek *kinēsis* (see KINESIS) + -IA.] —**hyperkinetic** /-néttik/ *adj*

⚡**hyperlink** *n* a word, symbol, image, or other element in a hypertext document that links to another element in the same document or in another hypertext document

hyperlipaemia /hípərli peémi ə/ *n* an excessive level of fats or lipids in the blood —**hyperlipaemic** *adj*

hyperlipidaemia /hípər líppi deémi ə/ *n* = **hyperlipaemia**

hypermarket /hípər maarkit/ *n* a very large self-service store that sells products usually sold in department stores as well as those sold in supermarkets, e.g. clothes, hardware, electrical goods, and food [Late 20C. Translation of French *hypermarché* < *marché* 'market' < Latin *mercatus* (see MARKET).]

⚡**hypermedia** /hípər meedi ə/ *n* a hypertext system that supports the linking of graphics, audio and video elements, and text

hypermeter /hī púrmitər/ *n* a line or metric foot of poetry that has one or more syllables in addition to those usually occurring in a metric foot or completed line of verse [Mid-17C. Via late Latin *hypermetrus* < Greek *hupermetros* (see HYPERMETROPIA).] —**hypermetric** /hípər méttrik/ *adj* —**hypermetrical** *adj*

hypermetropia /hípər mi trṓpi ə/, **hypermetropy** /-méttrəpi/ *n* MED = **hyperopia** (*technical*) [Mid-19C. < modern Latin, < Greek *hupermetros* 'beyond measure' < *metron* 'measure'.] —**hypermetropic** /-tróppik/ *adj* —**hypermetropical** *adj*

hypermnesia /hípərm neézi ə/ *n* an unusually powerful ability to remember exactly, sometimes a symptom of a psychiatric disorder [Mid-19C. < modern Latin, 'condition of extreme memory' < Greek *mnēsis* 'memory'.] —**hypermnesic** *adj*

hypernym /hípərnim/ *n* LING = **superordinate** *n.* 1

hyperon /hípə ron/ *n* a comparatively massive baryon that may be unstable or partially stable and is short-lived [Mid-20C. < HYPER- + -ON[1].]

hyperopia /hípər ṓpi ə/ *n* long-sightedness (*technical*) —**hyperopic** /-óppik/ *adj*

hyperostosis /hípər o stṓssiss/ *n* an unusual growth or thickening of bone [Mid-19C. < modern Latin, 'condition of excessive bone' < Greek *osteon* 'bone'.] —**hyperostotic** /-stóttik/ *adj*

hyperparasite /hípər párrə sīt/ *n* a parasite living on another parasite —**hyperparasitic** /hípər párrə síttik/ *adj* —**hyperparasitism** /-párrəsitizəm/ *n*

hyperparathyroidism /hípər parə thī roydizəm/ *n* an unusually high level of parathyroid hormone in the body, causing various disorders including kidney damage

hyperphagia /hípər fáyji ə/ *n* a condition in which somebody compulsively overeats over a long period —**hyperphagic** /-fájjik/ *adj*

hyperphysical /hípər fízzik'l/ *adj* not governed by the natural laws of physics —**hyperphysically** *adv*

hyperpituitarism /hípərpi tyŏŏ itərizəm/ *n* excessively high activity of the pituitary gland, sometimes causing unusual bodily growth —**hyperpituitary** *adj*

hyperplane /hípər playn/ *n* a figure in hyperspace that is the three-dimensional equivalent of a plane in ordinary space

hyperplasia /hípər pláyzi ə/ *n* unusual growth in a part of the body, caused by an excessive multiplication of cells —**hyperplastic** /-plástik/ *adj*

hyperploid /hípər ployd/ *adj* having an extra chromosome or section of a chromosome, e.g. in Down's syndrome, in which there is an extra copy or segment of chromosome 21 —**hyperploidy** *n*

hyperpnoea /hípərp neé ə, hípər-/ *n* unusually deep or fast breathing, e.g. after physical exertion. US term **hyperpnea** [Mid-19C. < modern Latin, 'extreme breathing' < Greek *pnoē* 'breathing'.] —**hyperpnoeic** *adj*

hyperpyrexia /hípər pī réksi ə/ *n* a very high fever [Late 19C. < modern Latin, 'extreme fever' < *pyrexia* (see PYREXIA).] —**hyperpyretic** /-réttik/ *adj* —**hyperpyrexial** *adj*

hyperrealism /hīpər reé əlizəm/ *n* a style in the visual arts that uses realism to achieve a striking effect rather than photographic representation of real life —**hyperrealist** /-reé əlist/ *adj, n* —**hyperrealistic** /-ree ə lístik/ *adj*

hypersensitive /hípər sénssətiv/ *adj* **1** very easily upset or offended **2** easily affected by a drug, allergen, or other agent —**hypersensitiveness** *n* —**hypersensitivity** /hípər sénssə tívvəti/ *n*

hypersexual /hípər sékshoo əl/ *adj* interested in or engaging in sexual activity to an abnormal extent —**hypersexuality** /-sekshoo álləti/ *n*

hypersonic /hípər sónnik/ *adj* relating to or moving at a speed of at least five times the speed of sound —**hypersonically** *adv*

hyperspace /hípər spayss/ *n* **1** space with more than three dimensions **2** in science fiction, a theoretical dimension in which things not physically possible in ordinary space such as intergalactic travel can happen —**hyperspatial** /hípər spáysh'l/ *adj*

hypersthene /hípərs theen/ *n* a green, brown, or black pyroxene mineral, containing iron and magnesium [Early 19C. < French *hypersthène* 'extremely strong (mineral)' < Greek *sthenos* 'strength'.] —**hypersthenic** /hípərs thénnik/ *adj*

hypersurface /hípər surfiss/ *n* a mathematical surface in hyperspace, analogous to a surface in three-dimensional space

hypertension /hípər ténsh'n/ *n* **1** unusually high blood pressure **2** arterial disease accompanied by high blood pressure

ϟ **hypertext** /hípər tekst/ *n* a system of storing images, text, and other computer files that allows direct links to related text, images, sound, and other data

ϟ **HyperText Markup Language** *n* the markup language used for creating documents on the World Wide Web

ϟ **HyperText Transfer Protocol** *n* the client/server protocol that defines how messages are formatted and transmitted on the World Wide Web

hyperthermia /hípər thúrmi ə/ *n* unusually high body temperature, especially when induced for therapeutic reasons [Late 19C. < modern Latin, 'condition of extreme heat' < Greek *thermē* 'heat'.] —**hyperthermal** *adj* —**hyperthermic** *adj*

hyperthyroidism /hípər thí roy dizəm/ *n* **1** the overproduction of thyroid hormones at dangerously high levels **2** the condition in which basal metabolism increases as a result of overactivity of the thyroid gland —**hyperthyroid** *adj*

hypertonic /hípər tónnik/ *adj* **1** having a higher osmotic pressure than another fluid **2** describes a body part, e.g. a muscle or artery, that is under unusually high tension —**hypertonia** /-tṓni ə/ *n* —**hypertonicity** /-tō níssəti/ *n*

hypertrophy /hī púrtrəfi/ *n* **1** ENLARGEMENT BY CELL GROWTH a growth in size of an organ through an increase in the size, rather than the number, of its cells **2** UNNECESSARY COMPLEXITY exaggerated or unnecessary growth or complexity ■ *vti* (**-phies, -phying, -phied**) GET BIGGER BY CELL GROWTH to grow larger through an increase in the size, rather than the number, of cells —**hypertrophic** /hípər trṓffik/ *adj*

hyperventilate /hípər vénti layt/ (**-lates, -lating, -lated**) *vi* to breathe unusually deeply or rapidly because of anxiety or organic disease and in excess of the body's requirements, causing too much loss of carbon dioxide

hyperventilation /hípər venti láysh'n/ *n* unusually deep or rapid breathing, caused by extreme anxiety or an organic disease, that leads to loss of carbon dioxide from the blood and often faintness

hypervitaminosis /hípər víttəmi nṓssiss/ *n* a condition in which unusual effects are caused by taking in too much of one or more vitamins

hypesthesia *n* US = **hypaesthesia**

hypha /hífə/ (*plural* **-phae** /hífee/) *n* a thread-like part of the vegetative portion of a fungus [Mid-19C. Via modern Latin < Greek *huphē* 'web'.] —**hyphal** *adj*

hyphen /híf'n/ *n* a punctuation mark (-) used at the end of a line when a word must be divided or to link elements in a compound word or phrase ■ *vt* = **hyphenate** [Early 17C. Via late Latin < late Greek *huphen* 'sign joining two syllables or words' < *hupo* 'under' + *hen*, neuter of *heis* 'one'.]

PUNCTUATION Use of **hyphen** A number of compound words and phrases are joined by hyphens: *thirty-seven; well-wisher; old-fashioned; mother-in-law.* For some the hyphens are optional, or inserted only when the word or phrase is used before a noun: *a coffee-table book; a well-timed attack* (but *the book on the coffee table; if the attack is well timed*). Most words with prefixes do not have a hyphen, exceptions being those where a capital letter follows the prefix (e.g. *pre-Christian*) and those where the word could be confused with another (e.g. *re-form* meaning 'form again' as distinct from *reform*). A hyphen is sometimes inserted when a prefix ending in a vowel is added to a word beginning with a vowel (e.g. *co-opt, de-ice*). In writing and printing a hyphen may also be used to show that a word has been broken at the end of a line. Note that the word must be divided between syllables (e.g. *stream-ing*, not *stre-aming*) and the hyphen is attached to the end of the first part, not the beginning of the second part. Ideally there should be at least two letters in each part of the divided word.

---

hyphenate /hífə nayt/ (**-ates, -ating, -ated**) *vt* to separate or join words or parts of words using a hyphen —**hyphenation** /hífə náysh'n/ *n*

hyphenated /hífə naytid/ *adj* **1** WITH HYPHEN split or joined by a hyphen **2** WITH HYPHEN IN SURNAME having a surname containing two or more family names connected by a hyphen **3** *US* BELONGING TO TWO CATEGORIES belonging to a group of people identified in two ways that may be joined as one term

hypn- *prefix* = **hypno-** (*before vowels*)

hypnagogic /hípnə gójjik/, **hypnogogic** *adj* in or relating to the state of drowsiness immediately before sleep [Late 19C. < French *hypnagogique* < Greek *hupno-* 'sleep' + *agōgos* 'leading' (see -AGOGUE).]

hypnagogic image *n* something of the nature of hallucination seen or imagined by somebody just before falling asleep

hypno- *prefix* **1** sleep ○ *hypnopompic* **2** hypnosis ○ *hypnoanalysis* [< Greek *hupnos*.< Indo-European.]

hypnoanalysis /hípnō ə nálləssiss/ (*plural* **-ses** /-seez/) *n* psychoanalysis carried out on people who are in a state of hypnosis —**hypnoanalytic** /-ánnə líttik/ *adj*

hypnogenesis /hípnō jénnəssiss/ *n* the process of inducing sleep or a state of hypnosis —**hypnogenetic** /-jə néttik/ *adj* —**hypnogenetically** *adv*

hypnogogic *adj* PSYCHOL = **hypnagogic**

hypnoid /híp noyd/, **hypnoidal** /hip nóyd'l/ *adj* relating to, involving, or resembling sleep or hypnosis

hypnology /hip nólləji/ *n* the scientific study of sleep or hypnosis —**hypnologic** /híppnə lójjik/ *adj* —**hypnologist** *n*

hypnopaedia /hípnə peédi ə/ *n* sleep-learning (*technical*) US term **hypnopedia** [Mid-20C. < HYPNO- + Greek *paideia* 'education'.]

hypnopompic /hípnə pómpik/ *adj* involving, typical of, or in the state between sleeping and waking [Early 20C. < HYPNO- + Greek *pompē* 'a sending away'.]

Hypnos /híp noss/ *n* in Greek mythology, the god of sleep, and the father of Morpheus, god of dreams [< Greek *Hupnos* 'sleep']

hypnosis /hip nṓssiss/ (*plural* **-ses** /-seez/) *n* **1** a sleep-like condition that can be artificially induced in people, in which they can respond to questions and are very susceptible to suggestions from the hypnotist **2** the technique or practice of inducing a state of hypnosis in people

hypnotherapy /híppnō thérrəpi/ *n* the use of hypnosis in treating illness, e.g. in dealing with physical pain or psychological problems —**hypnotherapist** *n*

hypnotic /hip nóttik/ *adj* **1** OF SLEEP OR HYPNOSIS producing sleep or hypnosis **2** SUSCEPTIBLE TO HYPNOSIS susceptible to being hypnotized **3** FASCINATING so fascinating that the attention of people watching or listening is absorbed completely (*informal*) ■ *n* **1** SOMETHING CAUSING SLEEP a drug or other agent that causes sleep or drowsiness **2** SOMEBODY EASILY HYPNOTIZED a person who can be hypnotized easily [Early 17C. Via French *hypnotique* < Greek *hupnōtikos* 'putting to sleep' < *hupnoun* 'put to sleep' < *hupnos* 'sleep'.] —**hypnotically** *adv*

hypnotise *vt* = **hypnotize**

hypnotism /hípnətizəm/ *n* **1** = **hypnosis** *n.* 2 **2** the theory and practice of hypnotizing people [Mid-19C. Shortening of *neuro-hypnotism* < HYPNOTIC.] —**hypnotist** *n*

hypnotize /hípnə tīz/ (**-tizes, -tizing, -tized**), **hypnotise** (**-tises, -tising, -tised**) *vt* **1** to put somebody into the sleep-like state of hypnosis **2** to fascinate or charm somebody utterly —**hypnotizability** /hípnə tīzə bílləti/ *n* —**hypnotizable** *adj* —**hypnotization** /híppnə tī záysh'n/ *n* —**hypnotizer** *n*

hypo[1] /hípō/ *n* (*plural* **-pos**) a hypodermic syringe or injection (*informal*) ■ *vt US* to stimulate somebody or something to action in order to achieve some purpose or goal (*dated informal*) [Early 20C. Shortening of HYPODERMIC.]

hypo[2] /hípō/ *n* sodium thiosulphate, used in photographic processing as a fixing agent (*informal*) [Mid-20C. Shortening of *hyposulphite*, another name for thiosulphate.]

hypo[3] /hípō/ *n* a hypoglycaemic episode (*informal*) ■ *adj* experiencing hypoglycaemia (*informal*)

hypo- *prefix* **1** under, below ○ *hypodermis* **2** unusually low ○ *hypotonia* **3** in a lower state of oxidation [< Greek *hupo* < Indo-European, 'under']

hypoacidity /hípō ə síddəti/ *n* an unusually low level of acidity, especially in the stomach

hypoallergenic /hípō állər jénnik/ *adj* not likely to cause an allergic reaction

hypoblast /hípə blast/ *n* **1** the inner germ layer of an embryo, which develops into the endoderm **2** BIOL = **endoderm** —**hypoblastic** /hípə blástik/ *adj*

hypocalcaemia /hípō kal seémi ə/ *n* an unusually low level of calcium in the blood. US term **hypocalcemia** —**hypocalcaemic** *adj*

hypocaust /hípō kawst/ *n* a system of central heating used by the ancient Romans, in which hot air from an underground furnace circulated beneath floors and between double walls [Late 17C. Via Latin *hypocaustum* < Greek *hupokauston* 'place heated from below' < *kaiein* 'burn'.]

hypocentre /hípō sentər/ *n* ARMS = **ground zero**

hypochlorite /hípə kláwrīt/ *n* a salt or ester of hypochlorous acid

hypochlorous acid /hípə kláwrəss-/ *n* HOCl a weak unstable greenish-yellow acid that occurs only in solution or in its salts. Source: dissolving of chlorine in water. Use: in bleach, disinfectants.

hypochondria /hípə kóndri ə/ *n* an excessive, usually long-term preoccupation with health and bodily sensations, accompanied by a deluded conviction of having a serious disease without objective evidence ■ plural of **hypochondrium** [Mid-16C. < late Latin (plural) 'upper abdomen' (formerly believed to be the seat of melancholy) < Greek *hupokhondrios* 'under the cartilage of the breastbone' < *khondros* 'cartilage'.]

hypochondriac /hípə kónndri ak/ *n* SOMEBODY WITH IMAGINARY ILLNESS a person who is unduly preoccupied with personal health and believes in the likelihood of becoming ill ■ *adj* **1** BELIEVING IN NONEXISTENT ILLNESS excessively preoccupied with health and persistently believing in a nonexistent illness **2** OF THE HYPOCHONDRIUM relating to, involving, or typical of the hypochondrium —**hypochondriacal** /hípə kon drí ək'l/ *adj* —**hypochondriacally** *adv*

hypochondriasis /hípə kon drí əssiss/ (*plural* **-ases** /-seez/) *n* PSYCHOL = **hypochondria** *n.*

hypochondrium /hípə kóndri əm/ (*plural* **-a** /-ə/) *n* the area of the upper abdomen on either side of the epigastrium below the lower ribs [Mid-17C. Back-formation < HYPOCHONDRIA (originally a plural form).]

hypocorism /hī pókərizəm/ *n* **1** a pet name, especially a diminutive or abbreviated form of somebody's full name (*formal*) **2** the use of a pet name to address somebody, instead of his or her full name [Early 16C. Via late Latin *hypocorisma* < Greek *hupokorisma* < *hupokorizesthai* 'play the child' < *korē* 'child'.] —**hypocoristic** /hī́pə kaw rístik/ *adj* —**hypocoristical** *adj* —**hypocoristically** *adv*

hypocotyl /hī́pə kóttil/ *n* the part of an embryo plant lying between its cotyledons and its radicle [Late 19C. < HYPO- + COTYLEDON.] —**hypocotylous** *adj*

hypocrisy /hi pókrəssi/ (*plural* **-sies**) *n* **1** the false claim to or pretence of having admirable principles, beliefs, or feelings ○ *It would be sheer hypocrisy for them to turn round and do what they criticise in others.* **2** an act or instance of hypocrisy ○ *the many hypocrisies of the party opposite* [12C. Via Old French *ypocrisie* < Greek *hupokrisis* 'acting a part' < *hupokrinesthai* 'act a part' < *krinein* 'to separate'.]

hypocrite /híppəkrit/ *n* a person who pretends to have admirable principles, beliefs, or feelings but behaves otherwise [12C. Via Old French *ypocrite* < Greek *hupokritēs* 'actor, pretender' < *hupokrinesthai* (see HYPOCRISY).]

hypocritical /híppə kríttik'l/ *adj* showing, originating from or of the nature of hypocrisy ○ *It would be hypocritical of me to congratulate you on defeating me.* —**hypocritically** *adv*

hypocycloid /híppə sī́ kloyd/ *n* a curve traced by a point on the circumference of a circle as it rolls along the inside circumference of another circle —**hypocycloidal** /-sī klóyd'l/ *adj*

hypoderm *n* PLANT SCI = hypodermis

hypodermic /híppə dúrmik/ *adj* relating to or involving the area of tissue lying beneath the skin ■ *n* a hypodermic injection, needle, or syringe (*informal*) [Mid-19C. < HYPO- + Greek *derma* 'skin'.] —**hypodermically** *adv*

hypodermic injection *n* an injection into tissue under the skin

hypodermic needle *n* **1** a thin hollow needle used with a syringe, suitable for administering hypodermic injections **2** a hypodermic syringe to which a needle has been fitted (*informal*)

hypodermic syringe *n* a plastic or glass syringe to which a thin hollow needle is attached, used to inject medicine under the skin or to withdraw fluids, especially blood, from under the skin

hypodermis /híppə dúrmiss/, **hypoderm** /híppə durm/ *n* **1 TISSUE UNDER SKIN** the layer of fatty tissue beneath the skin **2 SKIN BENEATH ANIMAL'S SHELL** the epidermis of some animals, e.g. arthropods, that secretes a shell or other outer covering **3 CELLS UNDER PLANT SURFACE** the usually supportive and protective layer of cells immediately under the outer covering of a plant [Mid-19C. < HYPO-, after EPIDERMIS.] —**hypodermal** *adj*

hypoesthesia /híppə ess theeẓhə, híppə ess theeẓi ə, híppə ess theeẓhi ə/ *n* US = hypaesthesia

hypoeutectic /híppō yoo téktik/, **hypoeutectoid** /-tékt oyd/ *adj* containing less of the minor component in a mixture or alloy than in the mixture of the same elements that has the lowest melting point

hypogastrium /híppə gástri əm/ (*plural* **-a** /-ə/) *n* the part of the front of the human abdomen that lies below the navel [Late 17C. Via modern Latin < Greek *hupogastrion* 'lower part of the belly' < *gastr-* 'belly'.] —**hypogastric** *adj*

hypogea plural of hypogeum

hypogeal /híppə jeé əl/, **hypogean** /-jeé ən/, **hypogeous** /-jeé əss/ *adj* **1** happening or living below ground **2** remaining below ground while the stem of the plant grows. ◊ **epigeal** *adj*. **1** [Late 17C. < late Latin *hypogeus* < Greek *hupogeios* 'underground' < *gē* 'ground, earth'.] —**hypogeally** *adv*

hypogene /híppə jeen/ *adj* describes rocks that are formed or lying beneath the earth's surface —**hypogenic** /híppə jénnik/ *adj*

hypogeous /híppə jeé əss/ *adj* PLANT SCI = hypogeal

hypogeum /híppə jeé əm/ (*plural* **-a** /-ə/) *n* an underground room or space in an ancient building, or an ancient underground burial chamber [Mid-17C. Via Latin < Greek *hupogeion*, form of *hupogeios* 'underground' (see HYPOGEAL).]

hypoglossal /híppə glóss'l/ *adj* **1** beneath or on the underside of the tongue **2** relating to or involving the hypoglossal nerve [Late 17C. < *hypoglossus* 'hypoglossal nerve' < HYPO- + Greek *glōssa* 'tongue'.]

hypoglossal nerve *n* either of the 12th pair of cranial nerves that serve the muscles of the tongue

hypoglycaemia /hī́pō glī́ seémi ə/ *n* the medical condition of having an unusually low level of sugar in the blood. US term **hypoglycemia** —**hypoglycaemic** *adj*

hypogynous /hī pójjinəss/ *adj* describes a flower such as a buttercup that has its petals, sepals, or other parts situated below and apart from its ovary [Early 19C. < modern Latin *hypogynus* < *hypo-* 'below' + Greek *gunē* 'woman', used to mean 'pistil'.] —**hypogyny** *n*

hypoid gear /hī́ poyd-/ *n* a gear often used in the transmission of motor vehicles, in which a hypocycloidal curve is used in arranging the meshing of the teeth [Early 20C. < ?]

hypolimnion /hī́pō límni ən/ (*plural* **-nia** /-ni ə/) *n* the lower and colder layer of water in a lake, largely stagnant and remaining at a constant temperature [Early 20C. < HYPO- + Greek *limnion* 'small lake' < *limnē* 'lake'.]

hypomania /hī́pō máyni ə/ *n* a condition of mild mania or excessive excitement, especially when part of a bipolar manic-depressive cycle —**hypomanic** /-mánnik/ *adj*

hyponasty /híppə nasti/ *n* greater than normal growth on the underside of a plant part, causing the part to bend upwards [Late 19C. < HYPO- + Greek *nastos* 'pressed close, compact'.] —**hyponastic** /híppə nástik/ *adj* —**hyponastically** *adv*

hyponym /híppənim/ *n* a word whose meaning is both narrower than and included in the meaning of a more general term. ◊ **superordinate** *n*. **1** —**hyponymy** /hī pónnimi/ *n*

hypophyge /hī póffiji/ *n* ARCHIT = apophyge [< Greek *hupophugē* 'evasion, flight from under' < *phugē* 'flight']

hypophysectomy /hī́pofi séktəmi/ (*plural* **-mies**) *n* surgical removal of the pituitary gland

hypophysis /hī póffississ/ (*plural* **-ses** /-seez/) *n* the pituitary gland (*technical*) [Late 17C. Via modern Latin < Greek *hupophusis* 'offshoot' < *phusis* 'growth'.] —**hypophyseal** /híppə fízzi əl/ *adj*

hypopituitarism /híppəpi tyoóitərizəm/ *n* failure of the pituitary gland to produce hormones, especially a deficiency in growth hormone, which can result in dwarfism —**hypopituitary** *adj*

hypoplasia /hī́pō pláyzi ə/, **hypoplasty** /hī́pō plasti/ *n* the failure of an organ or body part to grow or develop fully —**hypoplastic** /-plástik/ *adj*

hypoploid /híppə ployd/ *adj* having a chromosome number slightly less than the diploid number —**hypoploidy** *n*

hypopnea *n* = hypopnoea

hypopnoea /hī́ pópni ə/ *n* breathing that is unusually shallow and slow [Via modern Latin < Greek *hupopnoia* < *pnoia* 'breathing'.] —**hypopnoeic** /híppō neé ik/ *adj*

hyposensitivity /híppō sénssi tívvəti/ *n* an unusually low sensitivity to stimuli such as allergens —**hyposensitive** /híppō sénssitiv/ *adj*

hyposensitize /hī́pō sénsi tī́z/ (**-tizes, -tizing, -tized**), **hyposensitise** (**-tises, -tising, -tised**) *vt* to lower somebody's sensitivity to something, e.g. in the treatment of allergies —**hyposensitization** /hī́pō sénsi tī záysh'n/ *n*

hypostasis /hī́ póstəssiss/ (*plural* **-ses** /-seez/) *n* **1 SETTLING OF BODY FLUID** the settling of fluid in an organ or other part of the body, as a result of poor circulation, in patients kept in bed, and after death **2 ESSENCE** the essence or reality of something **3 ONE OF TRINITY** any of the three persons of the Christian Trinity **4 ESSENTIAL NATURE OF JESUS CHRIST** the essential nature of Jesus Christ, in which the divine and the human are believed to be combined [Early 16C. Via late Latin < Greek *hupostasis* 'sediment, foundation, essence' < *huphistasthai* 'stand under, support' < *histasthai* 'stand'.] —**hypostatic** /híppə státtik/ *adj* —**hypostatical** *adj* —**hypostatically** *adv*

hypostatize /hī́ póstə tī́z/ (**-tizes, -tizing, -tized**), **hypostatise** (**-tises, -tising, -tised**), **hypostasize** (**-sizes, -sizing, -sized**), **hypostasise** (**-sises, -sising, -sised**) *vt* **1** to treat something conceptual as if it is real **2** to personify or embody something —**hypostasization** *n* —**hypostatization** /hī́ póstə tī záysh'n/ *n*

hypostyle /híppə stī́l/ *adj* with a roof or ceiling that rests on many columns [Mid-19C. < Greek *hupostulos* 'resting upon pillars' < *stulos* 'pillar'.] —**hypostyle** *n*

hypotaxis /hī́pō táksiss/ *n* the subordinate status of one clause in relation to another separated from it by a subordinating conjunction [Late 19C. < Greek *hupotaxis* 'subjection' < *hupotassein* 'arrange under' < *tassein* 'arrange'.] —**hypotactic** *adj*

hypotension /hī́pō ténsh'n/ *n* unusually low blood pressure —**hypotensive** *adj, n*

hypotenuse /hī́ póttə nyooz/ *n* the longest side of a right-angled triangle, opposite the right angle [Late 16C. Via Latin *hypotenusa* < Greek *hupoteinousa* '(line) stretching under (the right angle)' < present participle of *hupoteinein* 'stretch under' < *teinein* 'stretch'.]

hypoth. *abbr* **1** hypothesis **2** hypothetical

hypothalamus /hī́pō thálləməss/ (*plural* **-mi** /-mī/) *n* a central area on the underside of the brain, controlling involuntary functions such as body temperature and the release of hormones —**hypothalamic** /hī́pōthə lámmik/ *adj*

hypothecate /hī póthə kayt/ (**-cates, -cating, -cated**) *vt* **1** to pledge property or goods as security for a debt without surrendering ownership **2** to designate money, especially public revenue, to be used for a specific purpose [Early 17C. < medieval Latin *hypothecare* < late Latin *hypotheca* 'deposit' < Greek *hupothēkē* < *hupotithenai* 'deposit as a pledge'.] —**hypothecation** /hī póthə káysh'n/ *n* —**hypothecator** *n*

hypothermal /hī́pō thúrm'l/ *adj* **1** relating to, involving, or typical of hypothermia **2** describes rocks and minerals formed deep underground at high temperatures

hypothermia /hī́pō thúrmi ə/ *n* **1** dangerously low body temperature caused by prolonged exposure to cold **2** lower-than-normal body temperature induced medically, e.g. to slow a patient's metabolism during heart surgery [Late 19C. < HYPO- + Greek *thermē* 'heat'.] —**hypothermic** *adj*

hypothesis /hī póthəsiss/ (*plural* **-ses** /-seez/) *n* **1 THEORY NEEDING INVESTIGATION** a tentative explanation for a phenomenon, used as a basis for further investigation **2 ASSUMPTION** a statement that is assumed to be true for the sake of argument **3 ANTECEDENT CLAUSE** the antecedent of a conditional statement [Late 16C. Via late Latin < Greek *hupothesis* 'foundation, base' < *thesis* 'placing'.] —**hypothesist** *n*

hypothesize /hī póthəsīz/ (**-sizes, -sizing, -sized**), **hypothesise** (**-sises, -sising, -sised**) *vti* to offer something as or form a hypothesis ○ *Let us, for the moment, hypothesize that the earth is flat.* —**hypothesizer** *n*

hypothetical /híppə théttik'l/, **hypothetic** /-théttik/ *adj* assumed or proposed for further investigation ○ *The question is purely hypothetical.* —**hypothetically** *adv*

hypothetical imperative *n* an imperative that depends on a condition, e.g. 'be kind to people if they are kind to you'. ◊ **categorical imperative**

hypothyroidism /hī́pō thī́ roydizəm/ *n* a deficiency in the production of thyroid hormones, or the resulting slowing of the metabolic rate —**hypothyroid** *adj*

hypotonia /híppə tṓnee ə/ *n* a condition in which the osmotic pressure in one fluid is lower than that in another, especially in the body [Late 19C. < HYPO- + Greek *tonos* 'tone'.]

hypotonic /híppə tónnik/ *adj* **1** with low or diminished muscle tone or tension **2** with low osmotic pressure than another fluid —**hypotonia** /-tóni ə/ *n* —**hypotonicity** /hī́pətə níssəti/ *n*

hypoventilate /hī́pō vénti layt/ (**-lates, -lating, -lated**) *vi* to breathe in an unusually slow and shallow way

hypoventilation /hī́pō vénti láysh'n/ *n* unusually slow and shallow breathing leading to a dangerous build-up of carbon dioxide in the blood

hypoxaemia /hī́ pok seémi ə/ *n* inadequate oxygen in the blood. US term **hypoxemia** [Late 19C. < HYP- + OXYGEN.] —**hypoxaemic** *adj*

hypoxemia *n* US = hypoxaemia

hypoxia /hī́ póksi ə/ *n* an inadequacy in the oxygen reaching the body's tissues [Mid-20C. < HYP- + OXYGEN.] —**hypoxic** *adj*

hypso- *prefix* height ○ *hypsometer* [< Greek *hupsos*]

hypsography /hip sóggrəfi/ (*plural* **-phies**) *n* GEOG = **hypsometry** —**hypsographic** /hípsə gráffik/ *adj* —**hypsographical** *adj*

hypsometer /hip sómmitər/ *n* **1** an instrument that uses the boiling point of water at different altitudes to measure the elevation of a given point on the earth's surface **2** an instrument for calculating the heights of trees by using the principles of geometric triangulation

hypsometry /hip sómmətri/ *n* the measurement of the elevation of land above sea level —**hypsometric** /hípsə méttrik/ *adj* —**hypsometrical** *adj* —**hypsometrically** *adv* —**hypsometrist** *n*

hyrax /hī́ raks/ (*plural* **-raxes** *or* **-races** /hī́rə seez/) *n* a small gregarious plant-eating mammal that resembles a rabbit with short ears and has toenails resembling hooves. Native to: the Mediterranean, SW Asia. Family: Procaviidae. [Mid-19C. Via modern Latin < Greek *hurax* 'shrew-mouse'.]

hyson /hī́ss'n/ *n* a Chinese green tea [Mid-18C. < Chinese *xīchūn* 'bright spring'.]

hyssop /híssəp/ *n* **1 AROMATIC HERB** a fragrant plant similar to mint, cultivated since medieval times as a medicinal herb. Flowers: fragrant, pink, white, or blue, in spikes. Native to: Europe, Asia. Use: in aromatherapy and alternative medicine. *Hyssopus officinalis.* **2 PLANT SIMILAR TO HYSSOP** a plant related to or similar to true hyssop **3 BIBLICAL PLANT** an unidentified plant whose twigs are described in the Bible as being used to sprinkle water during Hebrew religious ceremonies [Pre-12C. Via Latin *hyssopus* < Greek *hussōpos*.]

hyster- *prefix* = **hystero-** (*before vowels*)

hysterectomy /hístə réktəmi/ (*plural* **-mies**) *n* a surgical operation to remove a uterus —**hysterectomize** *vt*

hysteresis /hístə reèssiss/ *n* a delayed response by an object to changes in the forces acting on it, especially magnetic forces [Late 19C. < Greek *husterēsis* 'deficiency' < *husterein* 'be behind, come late' < *husteros* 'late'.] — **hysteretic** /-réttik/ *adj*

hysteria /hi steéri ə/ *n* **1 EMOTIONAL INSTABILITY CAUSED BY TRAUMA** an emotionally unstable state brought about by a traumatic experience **2 STATE OF EXTREME EMOTION** a state of extreme or exaggerated emotion such as excitement or panic, especially among large numbers of people ○ *press hysteria about ministerial sleaze* **3 LAUGHING OR CRYING** uncontrollable laughter or crying **4 CONVERSION DISORDER** conversion disorder (*dated*) [Early 19C. < Latin *hystericus* (see HYSTERIC).]

hysteric /hi stérrik/ *adj* = **hysterical** *adj.* 1, **hysterical** *adj.* 2, **hysterical** *adj.* 3 ■ *n* somebody affected by hysteria (*dated; sometimes offensive*) [Mid-17C. Via Latin *hystericus* < Greek *husterikos* 'affected in the womb' < *hustera* 'womb'.]

hysterical /hi stérrik'l/ *adj* **1 AFFECTED BY HYSTERIA** in a state of hysteria ○ *hysterical with grief* **2 RELATING TO HYSTERIA** relating to, caused by, or subject to hysteria **3 UNCONTROLLABLE** impossible to hold back or control ○ *hysterical sobbing coming from the next room* **4 EXTREMELY FUNNY**

causing uncontrollable laughter (*informal*) ○ *one hysterical sketch after another*

hysterics /hi stérriks/ *n* (+ *singular or plural verb*) **1** a state of uncontrollable laughter (*informal*) ○ *had them in hysterics with her stories* **2** a state of hysteria or an episode of hysterical behaviour

hystero- *prefix* **1** uterus ○ *hysterotomy* **2** hysteria ○ *hysterogenic* [< Greek *hustera* 'womb' < Indo-European]

hysterogenic /hístərə jénnik/ *adj* bringing about a state of emotional instability or hysteria

hysteron proteron /hístə ron próttə ron/ *n* a figure of speech in which the order of words or phrases is the reverse of what is usual, e.g. 'photographed in white and black' [Mid-16C. Via late Latin < Greek *husteron proteron* 'latter first'.]

hysterotomy /hístə róttəmi/ (*plural* **-mies**) *n* a surgical incision into a uterus, especially in order to carry out a caesarean section

Hz *symbol* hertz

i¹ /ī/ (*plural* **i's**), **I** (*plural* **I's** *or* **Is**) *n* **1** the ninth letter of the English alphabet, representing a vowel sound **2** the Roman numeral for 1 ◇ **dot the i's and cross the t's** to take care over the details of something ○ *We've drawn up the basis of the agreement but we have yet to dot the i's and cross the t's.*

i² *symbol* **1** the imaginary number $\sqrt{-1}$ **2** one **3** van't Hoff's factor

i³ *abbr* **1** incisor **2** indicate **3** interest **4** intransitive **5** island **6** isle

I¹ /ī/ *pron* a pronoun used by a speaker or writer to refer to himself or herself (*as the subject of a verb*) [Old English *ic* < Germanic, < Indo-European]

USAGE *I* or *me*? *I* is the subject form: *I agree.* **Me** is the object form, coming after verbs and prepositions: *She agrees with me.* That seems quite straightforward, but there are two areas where doubt creeps into people's minds:
1. Where *I* or *me*, or other personal pronouns, are linked to another pronoun or a noun by *and* or *or*. Is it *you and I* or *you and me*? If it is the subject of a sentence, the answer is easy: *you and I* (*You and I know better than that*). It is where the phrase is *not* the subject that confusion arises. Many people use *you and I* then too (*a present for you and I*). Technically this is grammatically defensible on the grounds that *you and I* is being treated as a single unit rather than three independent words, but in practice it is not accepted as Standard English, and *you and me* is to be preferred (*a present for you and me*). If in doubt, try leaving out the other part of the phrase: *a present for I* is clearly not grammatically correct.
2. Some people still get anxious about saying *It's me*, on the grounds that the traditionally correct formulation is *It's I*. In fact there are perfectly sound reasons for regarding *It's me* as grammatically acceptable, and anyway *It's I* now sounds so pompous that it scarcely qualifies for everyday discourse.

I² /ī/ (*plural* **I's** *or* **Is**) *n* something shaped like a letter 'I'

I³ *symbol* **1** electric current **2** iodine **3** ionization potential **4** isospin **5** moment of inertia **6** one **7** a particular affirmative categorical statement **8** unit matrix

I⁴ *abbr* **1** Imperial **2** (single column) inch (*of an advertisement*) **3** incumbent **4** independence **5** Independent **6** India **7** Indian **8** Inspector **9** Institute **10** Instructor **11** intelligence **12** International **13** interpreter **14** Ireland **15** Irish **16** Island **17** Isle **18** issue **19** Italian

-i- used as a connector to join word elements ○ *fossiliferous* [Via Old French < Latin]

Ia. *abbr* Iowa

-ia *suffix* **1** place names ○ *Australia* ○ *India* **2** a plural ○ *Saturnalia* **3** diseases or medical conditions ○ *dyslexia* **4** classes or genera ○ *mammalia* ○ *gardenia* **5** things belonging to or associated with something ○ *memorabilia* [Directly or via modern Latin < Latin, Greek]

IAA *abbr* **1** indoleacetic acid **2** International Advertising Association

IAAF *abbr* International Amateur Athletic Federation

IAB *abbr* **1** Industrial Advisory Board **2** Industrial Arbitration Board

⚡**IAC** *abbr* in any case (*in e-mails*)

Iacocca /ī ə kōkə/, **Lee** (*b*. 1924) US motor car executive. Full name **Lido Anthony Iacocca**

⚡**IAE** *abbr* in any event (*in e-mails*)

IAEA *abbr* International Atomic Energy Agency

IAF *abbr* Indian Air Force

-ial *suffix* connected with or belonging to something ○ *secretarial* ○ *imperial* [Directly or via French < Latin *-ialis*, *-iale*]

IAM *abbr* **1** Institute of Administrative Management **2** internal auditory meatus

iamb /ī am, ī amb/ *n* a unit of rhythm in poetry, consisting of one short or unstressed syllable followed by one long or stressed syllable [Mid-19C. Anglicization of IAMBUS.]

iambic /ī ámbik/ *adj* relating to or consisting of iambs ■ *n* **1** = **iamb 2** a poem or a line of poetry written in iambs (*often plural*)

iambic pentameter /ī ámbik-/ *n* the most common rhythm in English poetry, consisting of five iambs in each line. 'The quality of mercy is not strained' is an iambic pentameter.

iambus (*plural* **-buses** *or* **-bi**) *n* = **iamb** [Late 16C. Via Latin < Greek *iambos* 'iamb, lampoon' < *iaptein* 'attack in words'.]

-ian *suffix* belonging to, coming from, being involved in, or being like something ○ *Italian* ○ *Smithsonian* ○ *mathematician* [Directly or via French *-ien* < Latin *-ianus*]

Iapetus /ī áppitəss/ *n* a natural satellite of Saturn, discovered in 1671

IARC *abbr* International Agency for Research on Cancer

⚡**IAS** *abbr* **1** image analysis system **2** immediate access store **3** Indian Administrative Service **4** indicated air speed

Iaşi /yáshi/ city in E Romania. Population: 342,994 (1992).

-iasis *suffix* forms words for diseases characterized by or caused by something specified ○ *filariasis* [< *-i-* + Latin or Greek *-asis*, suffix of state or process]

IATA /ee aàtə, ī-/ *abbr* International Air Transport Association

-iatric *suffix* of a particular field of medicine ○ *psychiatric*

-iatrics *suffix* a particular field of medicine ○ *paediatrics*

iatrogenic /ī áttrō jénnik/ *adj* describes a symptom or illness brought on unintentionally by something that a doctor does or says [Early 20C. < Greek *iatros* 'doctor'.] — **iatrogenically** *adv*

-iatry *suffix* a particular field of medicine or medical treatment ○ *psychiatry* [< Greek *-iatreia* 'art of healing' < *iatros* 'doctor']

IAU *abbr* **1** International Association of Universities **2** International Astronomical Union

⚡**IAW** *abbr* in accordance with (*in e-mails*)

IB *abbr* **1** in bond **2** incendiary bomb **3** industrial business **4** International Baccalaureate **5** invoice book

ib. *abbr* ibidem

IBA *abbr* **1** Independent Broadcasting Authority **2** indolebutyric acid **3** International Bar Association **4** Investment Bankers' Association

Ibadan /i báddən/ capital of Oyo State, SW Nigeria. Population: 1,365,000 (1995 estimate).

IBD *abbr* **1** inflammatory bowel disease **2** ion-beam deposition

I-beam *n* a metal beam or girder that is shaped like a capital 'I' in cross section

Iberia /ī beèri ə/ **1** = **Iberian Peninsula 2** ancient region in the Caucasus, roughly equivalent to present-day E Georgia

Iberian /ī beèri ən/ *n* **1** a member of an ancient people who lived on the Iberian Peninsula or in the Caucasian state of Iberia **2** somebody who comes from Spain or Portugal —**Iberian** *adj*

Iberian Peninsula peninsula in SW Europe, divided into Spain, Portugal, and Gibraltar

iberis /ī beèriss/ *n* a cultivated low-growing plant. Flowers: white, pink, purple. Native to: Mediterranean. Genus: *Iberis*. [Mid-18C. < modern Latin.]

Ibero- *prefix* Iberia or Iberian

ibex /ī beks/ (*plural* **ibexes** *or* **ibex**) *n* a wild mountain goat with long knobbly backward-curving horns. Native to: Europe, Asia, North Africa. Genus: *Capra*. [Early 17C. < Latin.]

IBF *abbr* International Boxing Federation

⚡**IBG** *abbr* interblock gap

Ibibio /i bíbbi ō/ (*plural* **-o** *or* **-os**) *n* **1** a member of a people living in SW Nigeria, especially around the port of Calabar **2** the Benue-Congo language of the Ibibio. Native speakers: 2 million. [Early 19C. < Ibibio.] —**Ibibio** *adj*

ibid. /íbbid/ *abbr* ibidem

ibidem /íbbi dem/ *adv* used to cite the same book, publication, chapter, or page previously cited [Mid-18C. < Latin, 'in the same place' < *ibi* 'there' + *-dem* 'that'.]

Ibis

ibis /íbiss/ (*plural* **ibises** *or* **ibis**) *n* a gregarious wading bird with a downward-curving bill. Native to: warm and tropical climates. Family: Threskiornithidae. [14C. Via Latin < Egyptian *hbj*.]

Ibiza /i beétha/ **1** third largest of the Balearic Islands, in the W Mediterranean Sea. Area: 596 sq. km/230 sq. mi. **2** capital of the island of Ibiza, on the southeastern coast. Population: 29,447 (1996).

Ibizan hound /i beéthən-/ *n* a smooth-haired dog similar to, but smaller than, an Alsatian, with a light brown or reddish, sometimes spotted, coat, belonging to a breed originally developed in the Balearic Islands for hunting [Early 20C. After IBIZA.]

-ible *suffix* = **-able** [< Latin *-ibilis*] —**-ibility** *suffix*

Ibn Saud /íbbən sówd/, **Abdul Aziz** (1880?–1953) king of Saudi Arabia (1932–53)

Ibo /eebō/ (*plural* **Ibo** *or* **Ibos**), **Igbo** /igbō/ (*plural* **-bo** *or* **-bos**) *n* **1** a member of a people living in W Africa, especially in SE Nigeria **2** a language spoken in southern parts of Nigeria and in some areas of Niger, belonging to the Kwa group of Niger-Congo languages. Native speakers: 17 million. [Mid-18C. < Ibo.] —**Ibo** *adj*

IBRD *abbr* International Bank for Reconstruction and Development

IBS *abbr* irritable bowel syndrome

AKG London

Henrik Ibsen

Ibsen /íbss'n/, **Henrik** (1828–1906) Norwegian playwright

ibuprofen /ī byoo prṓ fen/ *n* a nonsteroidal anti-inflammatory drug. Use: relief of pain and inflammation, especially in arthritis and rheumatism. [Mid-20C. < ISO- + BUTYL + PROPIONIC + alteration of PHENYL.]

-ic *suffix* **1** of or relating to, having the nature of ○ *anarchic* ○ *Indic* **2** with a valency that is higher than that of a related compound or ion ending in *-ous* ○ *cobaltic* [Directly and via Old French *-ique* < Latin *-icus* < Greek *-ikos*]

i/c *abbr* **1** in charge (of) **2** in command

ICA *abbr* **1** ICA, ICAEW Institute of Chartered Accountants in England and Wales **2** Institute of Contemporary Arts **3** International Coffee Agreement **4** International Commodity Agreement **5** International Cooperation Administration

ICAO *abbr* **1** International Civil Aeronautics Organization **2** International Civil Aviation Organization

Icarus /íkərəs/ *n* **1** in Greek mythology, the son of Daedalus, who drowned in the sea while attempting to escape from Crete after the sun melted his wings of wax and feathers **2** an asteroid whose orbit is within 30 million km/19 million mi. of the Sun, closer than any other orbiting object —**Icarian** /ī kári ən/ *adj*

ICBM *abbr* intercontinental ballistic missile

ICC *abbr* International Chamber of Commerce

ice /īss/ *n* **1** FROZEN WATER water that has frozen into solid form ○ *puddles turning to ice* **2** EXPANSE OF FROZEN WATER an area, layer, or expanse of frozen water ○ *a polar bear far out on the ice* **3** SUBSTANCE LIKE ICE any substance resembling ice, e.g. the frozen form of carbon dioxide, known as dry ice **4** PIECES OF FROZEN WATER ice, either crushed or in cubes, used to cool drinks or food **5** ICE CREAM an ice cream (*often on signs*) ○ *hot dogs, burgers, and ices* **6** SKATING SURFACE a prepared frozen surface for ice skaters or ice-hockey players **7** COLDNESS animosity or excessive formality between people ○ *The room's atmosphere turned to ice when the two adversaries met.* **8** DIAMONDS diamonds, or jewellery in general, especially stolen merchandise (*slang*) **9** ILLEGAL DRUG a concentrated form of the drug methamphetamine (*slang*) ■ *adj* MADE OF ICE made of, containing, using, or for use on ice ○ *an ice cube* ○ *an ice sculpture* ○ *an ice axe* ■ *v* (**ices, icing, iced**) **1** *vi* FREEZE UP to sustain freezing and the development of a thin coating of ice on the surface ○ *The bridge iced, making it dangerous.* **2** *vt* PUT ICING ON CAKE to cover something such as a cake with icing **3** *vt* COOL A DRINK to chill a drink with ice [Old English *īs* < Germanic] —**iced** *adj* ◇ **break the ice** to overcome the initial restraint felt by people who have just met or who are meeting under awkward circumstances ◇ **cut no ice** to fail to impress or make a difference ◇ **on ice 1** in abeyance or in a state of being postponed ○ *We had so much work that we had to put the idea of a holiday on ice.* **2** being chilled in a

freezer, refrigerator, or among ice cubes ◇ **on thin ice** in an unsafe, difficult, or vulnerable situation (*informal*)

ice over *vi* to become covered with a layer of ice ○ *As soon as the loch iced over, people were out there with their skates.*

ice up *vi* to become coated with a layer of ice ○ *The car's windscreen will ice up if you don't put it in the garage.*

ICE *abbr* **1** ice, compress, elevation (*used as treatment for injuries and bruises*) **2** Institution of Civil Engineers **3** internal-combustion engine **4** International Cultural Exchange

Ice. *abbr* **1** Iceland **2** Icelandic

ice age *n* a period in the Earth's history when temperatures fell worldwide and large areas of the Earth's surface were covered with glaciers

Ice Age *n* the most recent ice age during which most of the northern hemisphere was covered with glaciers, occurring during the Pleistocene epoch

ice axe *n* a lightweight tool resembling an axe, used by mountaineers to cut handholds and footholds in ice and provide additional balance during a slide down a snow-covered slope

ice bag *n* a waterproof bag filled with ice and held against an injured part of the body to ease pain or reduce swelling

ice beer *n* beer brewed by a process that freezes the beer and removes some of the ice, thus increasing the beer's alcohol content

iceberg /íss burg/ *n* **1** a large mounded mass of ice that has broken away from a glacier and floats in the sea, with the greater part of its bulk under the water **2** US an unemotional or unfriendly person (*informal*) [Late 18C. < Dutch *ijsberg* 'ice mountain'.]

iceberg lettuce *n* a large round kind of lettuce with pale crisp juicy leaves, somewhat like cabbage leaves, that form a tight head when the lettuce is mature

iceblink /íss blingk/ *n* a yellowish glow in the sky, occurring when sunlight is reflected by a distant ice field

ice blue *adj* of a very pale blue colour —**ice blue** *n*

iceboat /íssbōt/ *n* = **icebreaker** *n*. 2

icebound /íss bownd/ *adj* unable to move because of being covered with or surrounded by ice

icebox /íss boks/ *n* **1** US, Can = **refrigerator** **2** a small freezer compartment inside a refrigerator **3** an insulated container or compartment filled with ice and used to keep food and drinks cool and fresh

icebreaker /íss braykər/ *n* **1** SOMETHING THAT RELAXES GROUP something such as a joke or game used to ease the initial tension, restraint, or awkwardness of a meeting or social gathering **2** SHIP FOR BREAKING ICE a ship with a reinforced bow used to break up ice and cut a passage through frozen navigable waters **3** TOOL FOR BREAKING ICE any tool designed to break up ice, e.g. a small hammer with a sharpened head

ice bucket *n* **1** a container in which ice cubes are kept cold, ready to be served in drinks **2** a container, sometimes on a stand, filled with ice cubes or a mixture of ice and water and used to keep a bottle of wine cool

icecap /íss kap/ *n* a thick permanent covering of ice and snow extending outwards in every direction, e.g. from the North and South Poles or from a mountain top

ice-cold *adj* extremely cold

ice cream *n* **1** a sweet frozen dessert or snack traditionally made with cream and egg yolks and flavoured with a variety of fruits or other extracts **2** a serving of ice cream, especially an ice-cream cone [Alteration of *iced cream*]

ice-cream cone, **ice-cream cornet** *n* **1** a hollow cone-shaped wafer designed to hold a serving of ice cream **2** an ice-cream cone containing a serving of ice cream

ice-cream soda *n* a refreshment consisting of ice cream in any kind of fizzy drink, sometimes with the addition of a flavoured syrup

ice dancing *n* figure skating in which a pair of skaters perform routines based on ballroom dancing, and in which lifts and separation are restricted in competition —**ice-dance** *vi* —**ice dancer** *n*

icefall /íss fawl/ *n* **1** a waterfall that has frozen solid **2** a face of a glacier on which the gradient is so steep that the ice breaks up into a jumble of blocks. ◊ **serac** [After WATERFALL]

ice fall *n* an avalanche or fall of isolated chunks of ice from a mountainside

ice field *n* a large, flat expanse of ice formed where the land surface is level, therefore making it easy for ice to accumulate

ice fish *n* a spiny-finned fish that has a semitransparent scaleless body and a low oxygen requirement, making it well suited to cold waters. Native to: Antarctic. Family: Chaenichthyidae.

ice floe *n* a sheet of floating ice smaller than an ice field

ice foot *n* a permanent band of ice along the coast of a polar region

ice hockey *n* a game played on ice by two teams of six skaters. Points are scored by hitting a rubber disc (**puck**) into the opposing team's goal with a long flat-bladed stick. US term **hockey** *n*. 2

icehouse /íss howss/, **ice house** *n* a building where ice is made, stored, and sometimes sold

Icel. *abbr* **1** Iceland **2** Icelandic

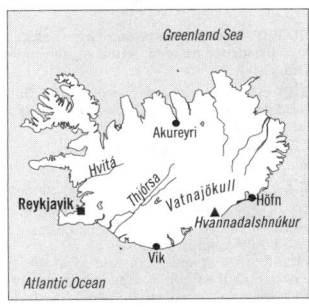

Iceland

Iceland /ísland/ island republic in the North Atlantic Ocean. Capital: Reykjavik. Population: 269,697 (1997). Area: 103,000 sq. km/39,800 sq. mi. —**Icelander** *n*

Icelandic /íss lándik/ *adj* relating to Iceland, or its people, language, or culture ■ *n* the North Germanic language of modern Iceland

Iceland moss *n* a greyish-brown lichen grown as a food and also used medicinally. Native to: the Arctic, northern Europe. *Cetraria islandica.*

Iceland poppy *n* a poppy with leafless stems. Flowers: white or yellow. Native to: Arctic regions. *Papaver nudicaule.*

Iceland spar *n* a transparent form of calcite. Use: optical instruments.

ice lolly *n* flavoured ice or ice cream frozen onto a stick

ice machine *n* a machine that produces ice cubes. US term **icemaker**

icemaker /íss maykər/ *n* US = **ice machine**

iceman /íss man/ (*plural* **-men** /-men/) *n* an explorer or mountaineer experienced in travelling on ice

ice milk *n* US a sweet frozen food like ice cream but made with skimmed milk

ice needle *n* a tiny needle-shaped ice crystal that forms in cold moist air and gathers with others into masses resembling clouds, often at high altitudes and in otherwise clear weather

Iceni /ī sée nī/ *npl* an ancient people of Britain who, under Queen Boudicca, attempted to overthrow the Romans in AD 61

ice pack *n* **1** an ice-filled cloth or bag held against an injured part of the body to ease pain or reduce swelling **2** an area of pack ice

ice pick *n* a lightweight hand-held pick for chipping away or breaking up ice

ice plant *n* **1** a clump-forming plant with thick pale-green leaves. Native to: Mediterranean. *Sedum spectabile.* **2** a low-growing plant with leaves that are covered with fine protruding sacs that glisten like ice crystals. Flowers: pink, white. Native to: southern Africa. *Mesembryanthemum crystallinum.*

ice point *n* the temperature, 0°C or 32°F, at which water freezes under a pressure of one atmosphere

ice rink *n* an area of frozen water used by ice-skaters, ice-hockey players, and curlers, especially an enclosed prepared surface

ice sheet *n* a thick covering of ice over a large area that remains for a long period of time

ice shelf *n* a thick mass of ice covering coastal land and extending out over the sea so that the extended portion floats

ice show *n* an entertainment performed by skaters on ice

ice skate *n* a boot with a metal blade fitted along the length of its sole, allowing the wearer to glide over an ice-covered surface

ice-skate (**ice-skates, ice-skating, ice-skated**) *vi* to glide over an ice-covered surface on ice skates —**ice-skater** *n*

ice skating *n* the sport or pastime of using ice skates to glide over an ice-covered surface

ice storm *n US* a rainstorm in conditions so cold that the rain freezes as it hits the ground, forming sheets of ice

ice volcano *n* a formation resembling a volcano, composed of plastic ice magma, found on the two moons of Uranus

ice water *n* 1 *US* very cold water or water chilled in a refrigerator or with ice cubes, served as a drink 2 water produced when ice melts

ICFTU *abbr* International Confederation of Free Trade Unions

I.Chem.E. *abbr* Institution of Chemical Engineers

I Ching /ee chíng/ *n* 1 an ancient Chinese system of divination, based on a book of Taoist philosophy and expressed in hexagrams chosen at random and interpreted to answer questions and give advice 2 the book containing the symbols used in I Ching divination and an accompanying text that the reader may consult for help in interpreting the symbols [Late 19C. < Chinese, literally 'Book of Changes'.]

ichneumon fly /ik nyóoman-/, **ichneumon wasp, ichneumon** *n* a slender insect related to and resembling a wasp that is a parasite of many insect pests, laying its eggs in insect larvae. Family: Ichneumonidae.

ichnite /ik nīt/, **ichnolite** /íknə līt/ *n* a fossilized footprint [Mid-19C. < Greek *ikhnos* 'footprint'.]

ichnography /ik nóggrəfi/ (*plural* **-phies**) *n* 1 the art or practice of drawing ground plans of the layout of buildings 2 a ground plan of the layout of a building [Late 16C. Directly or via French < Latin *ichnographia* < Greek *ikhnographia* 'track-drawing' < *ikhnos* 'track'.] —**ichnographic** /íknə gráffik/ *adj* —**ichnographical** *adj* —**ichnographically** *adv*

ichnolite *n* = **ichnite**

ichnology /ik nóllaji/ *n* the scientific study of fossilized footprints [Mid-19C. < Greek *ikhnos* 'footprint'.] —**ichnological** /íknə lójjik'l/ *adj*

ichor /í kawr/ *n* 1 a watery or slightly bloody discharge from a wound or an ulcer 2 the fluid said to run, instead of body fluid, through the veins of the gods in Greek mythology [Mid-17C. < Greek *ikhōr*.] —**ichorous** /íkərəss/ *adj*

ichthus /íkthəss/, **ichthys** /-thiss/ *n* a simple symbol that resembles a fish, consisting of two curves that bisect each other [< Greek *ikhthus* 'fish'.]

ichthy- *prefix* = **ichthyo-** (*before vowels*)

ichthyo- *prefix* fish ○ *ichthyology* [Via Latin < Greek *ikhthus* 'fish'.]

ichthyoid /íkthi oyd/ *n* a fish, or a vertebrate such as a lamprey or hagfish that is similar to a fish —**ichthyoid** *adj* —**ichthyoidal** /íkthi óyd'l/ *adj*

ichthyology /íkthi óllaji/ *n* the branch of zoology that deals with the scientific study of fish —**ichthyologic** /íkthi ə lójjik/ *adj* —**ichthyological** *adj* —**ichthyologically** *adv* —**ichthyologist** /íkthi óllajist/ *n*

ichthyornis /íkthi áwrniss/ *n* a prehistoric toothed bird, similar to a gull, that lived during the Cretaceous period. Genus: *Ichthyornis*. [Late 19C. < modern Latin, < Greek *ikhthus* 'fish' + *ornis* 'bird'.]

ichthyosaur /íkthi ə sawr/, **ichthyosaurus** /íkthi ə sáwrəss/ (*plural* **-ruses** *or* **-ri** /-sáwr ī/) *n* a prehistoric reptile with a long snout and paddle-shaped limbs that lived in the sea during the Mesozoic era. Order: Ichthyosauria. [Mid-19C. < modern Latin *Ichthyosauria* 'fish-lizards' < Greek *ikhthus* 'fish'.] —**ichthyosaurian** /íkthi ə sáwri an/ *adj*

ichthyosis /íkthi óssiss/ *n* a disease that causes the skin to become dry, thick, and scaly

ichthys *n* = **ichthus**

-ician *suffix* one who practises or specializes in ○ *musician* ○ *statistician* [< Old French *-icien* < *-ique* (see -IC)]

icicle /íssik'l/ *n* 1 a hanging tapered rod of ice, formed when dripping water freezes 2 an aloof or unemotional person (*informal*) [14C. < ICE + obsolete *ickle* 'icicle' < Old English *gicel* < Germanic.]

icily /íssili/ *adv* in a very aloof or unfriendly manner

icing /íssing/ *n* 1 **GLAZING FOR CAKES** a sugar-based decorative coating for cakes, either soft or hardened, made by mixing powdered sugar with water or another binding substance 2 **FORMATION OF ICE** the formation of ice on surfaces, e.g. on aircraft or ships ○ *Some roads will be liable to icing.* 3 **SHOOTING PUCK INTO OPPOSING TERRITORY** in ice hockey, the action of shooting the puck out of defensive territory and far into the opposing team's territory ◇ **the icing on the cake** something additional that makes something that was already good even better

icing sugar *n* powdered white sugar used to make icing, for sweetening, or for sprinkling. US term **confectioners' sugar**

ICJ *abbr* International Court of Justice

icky /íki/ (**-ier, -iest**) *adj* (*informal*) 1 **NASTY** generally nasty or unpleasant ○ *I had an icky feeling in their presence.* 2 **STICKY** disgustingly and messily sticky 3 **SENTIMENTAL** sentimental in a silly or childish way ○ *a script with some pretty icky lines* [Early 20C. < ?] —**ickiness** *n*

ICM *abbr* 1 Institute of Credit Management 2 Intergovernmental Committee for Migrations (*part of the UN*)

Icon: Eastern Orthodox icon of *Christus Acheiropoietus* in the Cathedral of the Assumption, Moscow

ᶠicon /í kon/ *n* 1 **icon, ikon** **IMAGE OF HOLY PERSON** a holy picture, carving, or statue of Jesus Christ, the Virgin Mary, or a saint, especially an oil painting on a wooden panel, used in worship in the Eastern Orthodox churches 2 **SOMEBODY FAMOUS** somebody or something widely and uncritically admired, especially somebody or something symbolizing a movement or field of activity ○ *the all-time rock 'n' roll icon.* 3 **PICTURE ON COMPUTER SCREEN** a small image on a computer screen that represents something, e.g. a program or device that is activated by a mouse click ○ *Open the program by clicking on its icon.* 4 **RECOGNIZABLE SYMBOL** a picture or symbol that is universally recognized to be representative of something ○ *The icon of a walking person is the international symbol to indicate that it's safe to cross the street.* [Mid-16C. Via Latin < Greek *eikōn* 'likeness, image'.]

icon- *prefix* = **icono-**

iconic /í kónnik/ *adj* 1 **CHARACTERIZED BY FAME** relating to or characteristic of somebody or something admired as an icon ○ *Their fame has grown to iconic proportions.* 2 **TYPICAL OF A RELIGIOUS ICON** relating to or characteristic of a religious icon ○ *iconic images* 3 **CONVENTIONAL** made in a conventional style or pose, especially that of ancient Greek statues of athletes —**iconically** *adv*

iconic memory *n* a form of memory in which objects are retained briefly but clearly as a visual image after the stimulus has been removed

icono- *prefix* icon, image ○ *iconolatry* ○ *iconoscope* [< Greek *eikōn*.]

iconoclasm /í kónnə klazəm/ *n* 1 a challenge to and overturning of traditional beliefs, customs, and values 2 the destruction of religious images used in worship or opposition to their use in worship

iconoclast /í kónnə klast/ *n* 1 **SOMEBODY CHALLENGING TRADITION** a challenger of traditional beliefs, customs, and values 2 **DESTROYER OF RELIGIOUS IMAGES** a destroyer or opponent of religious images used in worship 3 **HERETIC IN GREEK ORTHODOX CHURCH** a member of an 8th-century movement in the Greek Orthodox Church that tried to end the use of icons [Mid-17C. Via medieval Latin *iconoclastes* < medieval Greek *eikonoklastēs* 'image-breaker' < Greek *eikōn* 'image'.] —**iconoclastic** /í kónnə klástik/ *adj* —**iconoclastically** *adv*

iconography /íkə nóggrəfi/ *n* 1 **SET OF RECOGNIZED IMAGES** the set of symbols or images used in a particular field of activity, e.g. music or cinema, and recognized by people as having a particular meaning ○ *In the 1960s, peace signs and long hair were part of the iconography of rebellion.* 2 **SYMBOLS IN PAINTING** the symbols and images used conventionally in a genre of painting, or the study and interpretation of these symbols and images ○ *the iconography used in Renaissance paintings of the Virgin and Child* 3 **IMAGES OF SOMEBODY OR SOMETHING SPECIFIC** the collection, description, or study of images of somebody or something specific —**iconographer** *n* —**iconographic** /í kónə gráffik/ *adj* —**iconographical** *adj*

iconolatry /íkə nóllətri/ *n* the worshipping of religious images rather than of what they represent (*disapproving*) —**iconolater** *n*

iconology /íkə nóllaji/ *n* 1 the study of artistic images and their symbolism and interpretation 2 images or symbols or the images or symbols used in a specific field of activity —**iconological** /í kónnə lójjik'l/ *adj* —**iconologist** *n*

iconomatic /í kónnə máttik/ *adj* using images to represent the sounds of the names of things rather than the things themselves, e.g. in the transition from pictorial to phonetic representation, seen in the history of some languages [Late 19C. Contraction of *icononomatic* < Greek *eikōn* 'image' + *onomat-* 'name'.] —**iconomaticism** /-máttisizam/ *n*

iconoscope /í kónnə skōp/ *n* an early form of television camera tube in which an image is converted into electrical impulses

iconostasis /íkə nóstəssiss/ (*plural* **-ses** /-seez/), **iconostas** /í kónnə stass/ (*plural* **-tases**) *n* a screen on which icons are mounted, used in Eastern Orthodox churches to separate the area around the altar from the main part of the church [Mid-19C. < modern Greek *eikonostasis* 'place where images stand'.]

icosahedron /íkəssə heedrən/ (*plural* **-drons** *or* **-dra** /-heedrə/) *n* a solid geometric figure having 20 sides or faces [Late 16C. Via late Latin *icosahedrum* < Greek *eikosaedron* < *eikosi* 'twenty' + *hedra* 'base'.] —**icosahedral** *adj*

icositetrahedron /íkəssi téttrə heedrən/ (*plural* **-drons** *or* **-dra** /-drə/) *n* a solid geometric figure having 24 sides or faces [Mid-19C. < Greek *eikosi* 'twenty' + *tetra-* 'four'.]

ᶠICQ *n* a computer program that makes contact with a user who is chatting online

ᶠICR *abbr* 1 intelligent character recognition 2 Institute for Cancer Research

ICS *abbr* 1 instalment credit selling 2 Institute of Chartered Shipbrokers 3 International Chamber of Shipping 4 investors' compensation scheme

-ics *suffix* 1 a science, art, or knowledge ○ *physics* ○ *mathematics* 2 an activity or action ○ *callisthenics* [< -IC + -S; translation of Greek *-ika* (plural)]

icteric /ik térrik/ *adj* affected with, relating to, or resembling jaundice

icterus /íktərəss/ *n* jaundice (*technical*) [Early 18C. Via Latin < Greek *ikteros*.]

ictus /íktəss/ (*plural* **-tuses** *or* **-tus**) *n* 1 a seizure (*technical*) 2 the stress that falls on syllables in poetic rhythm [Early 18C. < Latin, 'stroke', past participle of *icere* 'to strike'.] —**ictal** *adj*

ICU *abbr* intensive care unit

icy /íssi/ (**-ier, -iest**) *adj* **1 ICE-COVERED** covered in or involving ice **2 VERY COLD** extremely cold, like ice ○ *Your hands are icy.* **3 UNFRIENDLY** very aloof or unfriendly ○ *his reserved manner and icy voice* —**iciness** *n*

id /id/ *n* in Freudian psychoanalytic theory, the part of the psyche that is unconscious and the source of primitive instinctive impulses and drives [Early 20C. < Latin, 'it'.]

Id 1 = **Eid-ul-Adha, Eid-ul-Fitr** 2 *South Asia* an Islamic holy festival

I'd /īd/ *contr* **1** I had ○ *I'd forgotten you were coming.* **2** I would or should

ID[1] *abbr* **1** identification **2** infectious disease(s) **3 ID, i.d.** inner diameter **4 ID, i.d.** inside diameter *or* internal diameter **5** Intelligence Department **6 ID, i.d.** intradermal **7** Idaho

ID[2] *vt* to identify somebody or check somebody's identity (*informal*) ○ *police to ID the suspect*

id. *abbr* idem

Id. *abbr* Idaho

-id *suffix* **1** objects, especially meteors, that appear to come from a specified constellation ○ *Perseids* **2** particular kinds of particle or body ○ *energid* **3** a member of a zoological family ○ *camelid* **4** a member of a dynasty ○ *Abbasid* [Directly or via French *-ide* < Latin *-ides* < Greek *-idēs* 'offspring of']

IDA *abbr* International Development Association

Ida. *abbr* Idaho

Idaho /ídə hō/ state in the NW United States. Capital: Boise. Population: 1,210,232 (1997). Area: 216,456 sq. km/83,574 sq. mi. —**Idahoan** /ídə hō ən, īdə hṓ ən/ *adj, n*

Ida Mountains /ídə-/ mountain range in NW Turkey. Highest peak: Mount Gargarus 1,767 m/5,797 ft.

IDB *abbr* **1** *S Africa* illicit diamond buyer **2** *S Africa* illicit diamond buying **3** Industrial Development Bank

ID card *n* a card identifying its carrier, having on it such information as name, age, and often an address and a physical description or photograph (*informal*)

IDD *abbr* **1** international direct dialling **2** insulin-dependent diabetes

-ide *suffix* **1** class of elements or compounds ○ *actinides* **2** organic compound derived from another compound ○ *anhydride* [< OXIDE]

idea /ī dée ə/ *n* **1 OPINION** a personal opinion or belief ○ *Do you have any ideas on how the problem should be tackled?* **2 SUGGESTION** a thought to be presented as a suggestion ○ *It was her idea to plant daisies.* **3 IMPRESSION** an impression or knowledge of something ○ *They saw us leaving together and got the wrong idea.* **4 PLAN** a realization of a possible way of doing something or of something to be done ○ *Watching the beaver building its dam gave me an idea.* **5 AIM** the aim or purpose of a project or plan ○ *The idea of the new scheme is to keep young people in school.* **6 GIST** the gist or précis of something such as a book, report, project, or plan ○ *give you only a broad idea now, with a detailed outline to follow* **7 THOUGHT** a thought about or mental picture of something such as a future or possible event ○ *Sometimes the idea of having to speak in public is worse than actually doing it.* **8 CONCEPT** a concept that exists in the mind only ○ *discussing the idea of morality* **9 MENTAL IMAGE** a mental image that reflects reality **10 MOTIF** a theme or motif that forms the basis of a piece of music throughout its development [14C. Via Latin < Greek, 'look' < *idein* 'to see'.] —**idealess** *adj* ◇ **get ideas** to become ambitious or begin thinking undesirable thoughts (*informal*) ◇ **have no idea** to know nothing at all, especially about a particular subject ◇ **what's the big idea?** used, often angrily, to ask about somebody's intention or about what is happening

USAGE idea or **ideal**? The word ***ideal*** is a noun and an adjective. As a noun it can mean 'a perfect example' (*the world's ideal* [not *idea*] *of a gallant warrior*), 'a principle' (*the ideal* [not *idea*] *of freedom of speech*), and 'a figment of the imagination only, especially one having no basis in reality' (*a child's ideal* [not *idea*] *of a fairy godmother*). As an adjective it means variously 'best' (*the ideal spot for a picnic*), 'perfect' (*in an ideal world*), and 'excellent' (*Postponing the meeting until tomorrow would be ideal*). Do not confuse this word with ***idea***, a noun only. It means variously 'an opinion, suggestion, impression, or plan', 'an aim or purpose', 'the gist of something', 'a rational mental image or concept', and 'a thought'. Thus, in terms of 'a mental image or rational concept', use *the inventor's great idea* [not *ideal*] *for an electric car.*

idea hamster *n US* somebody whose brain is constantly generating new ideas (*slang humorous*)

ideal /ī dée əl/ *n* **1 PERFECT EXAMPLE** an excellent or perfect example of something or somebody ○ *By her third film, she had become the world's ideal of beauty and grace.* **2 PRINCIPLE** a standard or principle to which people aspire ○ *political ideals* **3 IMAGINARY OBJECT OR CONCEPT** a concept that exists in the imagination only ■ *adj* **1 BEST** serving as the best or most perfect example **2 PERFECT** perfect but existing only in the imagination ○ *In an ideal world, such horrors wouldn't happen.* **3 EXCELLENT** excellent or perfectly suitable ○ *A later meeting would be ideal for me.* [15C. Directly or via French *idéal* < late Latin *idealis* < Latin *idea* (see IDEA).] —**idealless** *adj* —**idealness** *n*

USAGE See ***idea***.

ideal gas *n* a hypothetical gas that obeys the gas laws perfectly at all temperatures and pressures

idealise *vt* = **idealize**

idealised *adj* = **idealized**

idealism /ī dée əlizəm/ *n* **1 BELIEF IN PERFECTION** belief in and pursuit of perfection as an attainable goal ○ *youthful idealism* **2 LIVING BY HIGH IDEALS** aspiring to or living in accordance with high standards or principles **3 BELIEF THAT MATERIAL THINGS ARE IMAGINARY** the philosophical belief that material things do not exist independently but only as constructions in the mind

idealist /ī dée əlist/ *n* **1 SOMEBODY WITH HIGH IDEALS** somebody who aspires to or abides by high standards or principles **2 IMPRACTICAL PERSON** a perfectionist who rejects practical considerations ○ *too much of an idealist to compromise with her opponents* **3 BELIEVER IN PHILOSOPHICAL IDEALISM** a believer in a philosophy holding that material objects do not exist independently of the mind —**idealistic** /ī dée ə lístik/ *adj* —**idealistically** *adv*

ideality /īdi álləti/ *n* **1** the condition or quality of being ideal **2** existence as an idea only, rather than as a concrete object

idealize /ī dée ə līz/ (**-izes, -izing, -ized**), **idealise** (**-ises, -ising, -ised**) *vt* to think of or represent somebody or something as being perfect, ignoring any imperfections that exist or may exist in reality ○ *paintings that idealize feminine beauty* —**idealization** /ī dée ə lī záysh'n/ *n* —**idealized** *adj* —**idealizer** /ī dée ə līzər/ *n*

ideally /ī dée əli/ *adv* **1 IN AN IDEAL SITUATION** if everything were perfect or as desired ○ *Ideally, I'd like to finish the job by next week.* **2 PERFECTLY** in a perfect manner ○ *She is ideally suited to the post.* **3 THEORETICALLY** in theory or in the imagination

ideate /īdi ayt/ (**-ates, -ating, -ated**) *vti* to form an idea of something, or form ideas [Early 17C. < medieval Latin *ideat-*, past participle of *ideare* 'form an idea' < Latin *idea* (see IDEA).] —**ideation** /īdi áysh'n/ *n* —**ideational** *adj* —**ideationally** *adv* —**ideative** /īdi ətiv, -i aytiv/ *adj*

idée fixe /ée day feéks/ (*plural* **idées fixes** /ée day fíks/) *n* an idea that remains fixed and unchanging in the mind and often becomes an obsession [< French, 'fixed idea']

idée reçue /ée day rə syóo/ (*plural* **idées reçues** /-syóo/) *n* a conventional or commonplace idea [< French, 'received idea']

idem /íddem, ī-/ *pron* the same, especially a book, article, or chapter previously referred to [14C. < Latin (see IDENTITY).]

idempotent /ī dem pṓt'nt, ī démpətənt/ *adj* remaining unchanged when multiplied by itself [Late 19C. < Latin *idem* (see IDENTITY) + *potent-* 'powerful'.]

identic /ī déntik/ *adj* describes diplomatic notes sent, or diplomatic action taken, by two or more governments in exactly the same form [Mid-17C. < medieval Latin *identicus* 'identical' < *ident-*, combining form of Latin *idem* (see IDENTITY).]

identical /ī déntik'l/ *adj* **1** exactly the same as or equal to something else **2** being one single person or thing though appearing in different guises or disguises —**identically** *adv* —**identicalness** *n*

identical rhyme *n* perfect rhyme of a whole syllable, including consonants and vowels

identical twin *n* one of a pair of twins of the same sex and with the same genetic makeup who develop from a single fertilized egg

identification /ī déntifi káysh'n/ *n* **1 CONNECTION OF IDENTITY** the action or an act of recognizing and naming somebody or something or otherwise identifying him, her, or it **2 PROOF OF IDENTITY** something, especially a card or document, to prove that somebody is who he or she claims to be **3 STRONG FEELING OF AFFINITY** a powerful feeling of affinity with another person or group, which sometimes involves regarding somebody as a model and adopting his or her beliefs, values, or other characteristics

identification card *n* = **identity card**

identification parade *n* a group of people, including a suspect, shown by police to a witness to a crime in order to discover whether the witness can identify the person who committed it. US term **lineup** *n.* **3**

ϟ **identifier** /ī dénti fī ər/ *n* a symbol that identifies, indicates, or names a body of data

identify /ī dénti fī/ (**-fies, -fying, -fied**) *vt* **1** to recognize somebody or something and to be able to say who or what he, she, or it is **2** to consider two or more things as being entirely or essentially the same [Mid-17C. Directly or via French *identifier* < medieval Latin *identificare* 'make the same' < *ident-* (see IDENTITY).] —**identifiability** /ī dénti fī ə bílləti/ *n* —**identifiable** *adj* —**identifiably** *adv*

identify with *v* **1** *vt* to feel a strong sympathetic or imaginative bond with somebody or something and a sense of understanding and sharing his, her, or its nature or concerns **2** to consider somebody or something as closely linked with somebody or something, e.g. a school of thought or political movement (*often passive*)

Identikit /ī déntikit/ *tdmk* a trademark for a set of pictures showing varied facial features that can be combined to produce a human likeness, e.g. of a missing person or of a criminal suspect

identity /ī déntəti/ (*plural* **-ties**) *n* **1 WHAT IDENTIFIES SOMEBODY OR SOMETHING** who somebody is or what something is, especially the name by which somebody or something is known **2 ESSENTIAL SELF** the set of characteristics that somebody recognizes as belonging uniquely to himself or herself and constituting his or her individual personality for life **3 SAMENESS** the fact or condition of being the same or exactly alike **4** *ANZ* **CELEBRITY** a person who is well known for something (*informal*) **5 EQUATION TRUE FOR ALL ITS VARIABLES** a mathematical equation that remains valid whatever values are taken by its variables **6** MATH = **identity element** [Late 16C. < late Latin *identitas* < *ident-*, combining form of Latin *idem* 'same' < *id* 'that'.]

identity card *n* a card carrying the holder's name, address, date of birth, and other particulars, together with a photograph, that serves as proof of his or her identity for official purposes. US term **identification card**

identity crisis *n* **1** a period during which somebody feels great anxiety and uncertainty about his or her identity and role in life and society, typically experienced in adolescence or middle age **2** a period of anxiety or confusion about the nature, aims, and role of a group, organization, or business

identity element *n* an element of a set that leaves other elements unchanged when combined with them

identity matrix *n* a square matrix that has the numeral 1 in each position on the principal diagonal and 0 in all other positions

identity parade *n* CRIME = **identification parade**

ideo- *prefix* forms words whose meaning involves ideas ○ *ideomotor* [Via French < Greek *idea* (see IDEA)]

ideogram /íddi ə gram/, **ideograph** /íddi ə graaf, -graf/ *n* **1** a symbol used in some writing systems, e.g. those of Japan and China, that directly but abstractly represents a thing or concept itself rather than the word for it **2** a symbol or graphical character, e.g. '@' or '&', used to represent a word —**ideogrammatic** /íddi əgrə máttik/ *adj* —**ideogrammatically** *adv* —**ideographic** /íddi ə gráffik/ *adj* —**ideographically** *adv* —**ideography** /íddi óggrəfi/ *n*

ideologue /īdi ə log/ *n* an ideologist, especially a particularly zealous or doctrinaire supporter of an ideology

ideology /īdi ólləji/ (*plural* **-gies**) *n* **1** a closely organized system of beliefs, values, and ideas forming the basis of a social, economic, or political philosophy or programme **2** a set of beliefs, values, and opinions that shapes the way a person or a group such as a social class thinks, acts, and understands the world —**ideo-**

logical /ìdi ə lójjik'l/ *adj* —**ideologically** *adv* —**ideologist** *n*

ideomotor /ìdi ə mōtər/ *adj* describes body movements triggered by thoughts rather than by external stimuli

ides /īdz/, **Ides** *n* in the ancient Roman calendar, the name given to the 15th day of March, May, July, and October, or the 13th day of any other month (+ *singular or plural verb*) [12C. Directly or via French < Latin *idus* (plural).]

-idine *suffix* a chemical compound related to another compound ○ *histidine* [< -IDE + -INE]

idio- *prefix* private, individual, proper, or distinctive ○ *idiolect* ○ *idiomorphic* [< Greek *idios* 'one's own, private' < Indo-European, 'self']

idiocy /íddi əssi/ *n* **1** an offensive term for extreme lack of intelligence or foresight **2** an offensive term for an extremely unintelligent or thoughtless act **3** an offensive term in a now disused classification system for mental disability (*dated*) [Early 16C. < IDIOT.]

idioglossia /íddi ō glóssi ə/ *n* **1** a developmental speech defect in which a child substitutes different sounds for the correct ones, so that speech is intelligible only to parents or others familiar with it **2** the invention and use by a child or closely involved siblings of language that is unintelligible to anyone else [Late 19C. < Greek *idioglōssos* < *idios* 'distinct' + *glōssa* 'tongue'.]

idiogram /íddi ō gram/ *n* a photograph or diagram showing the chromosomes of a cell or organism arranged in their homologous pairs according to the standard numbering system for that particular organism

idiographic /íddi ō gráffik/ *adj* concentrating on particular cases and the unique traits or functioning of individuals, rather than on broad generalizations about human behaviour. ◊ **nomothetic** *adj.* 2

idiolect /íddi ə lekt/ *n* an individual person's vocabulary and particular and unique way of using language [Mid-20C. < IDIO- + DIALECT.] —**idiolectal** /íddi ə lékt'l/ *adj*

idiom /íddi əm/ *n* **1 FIXED EXPRESSION WITH NONLITERAL MEANING** a fixed, distinctive expression whose meaning cannot be deduced from the combined meanings of its actual words **2 NATURAL WAY OF USING A LANGUAGE** the way of using a language that comes naturally to its native speakers **3 STYLISTIC EXPRESSION OF PERSON OR GROUP** the style of expression of an individual or group **4 DISTINGUISHING ARTISTIC STYLE** the characteristic style of an artist or artistic group [Late 16C. Directly or via French *idiome* < late Latin *idioma* < Greek, 'property, peculiarity' < *idios* (see IDIO-).]

idiomatic /íddi ə máttik/, **idiomatical** /-máttik'l/ *adj* **1 CHARACTERISTIC OF NATIVE-SPEAKER USE** characteristic of, or in keeping with, the way a language is ordinarily and naturally used by its native speakers **2 OF THE NATURE OF AN IDIOM** having a meaning not deducible from the combined meanings of the words that make it up ○ *an idiomatic phrase* **3 CHARACTERISTIC OF PARTICULAR STYLE** characteristic of a particular style, or using a particular and distinctive style, especially in the arts —**idiomatically** *adv* —**idiomaticness** *n*

idiopathic /íddi ō páthik/ *adj* describes a disease or disorder that has no known cause —**idiopathically** *adv* —**idiopathy** /íddi óppəthi/ *n*

idiophone /íddi ō fōn/ *n* a percussion instrument, e.g. a gong or xylophone, that is made from resonating material that does not have to be tuned —**idiophonic** /íddi ō fónnik/ *adj*

~~**idiosyncracy**~~ incorrect spelling of **idiosyncrasy**

idiosyncrasy /íddi ō síngkrəssi/ (*plural* **-sies**) *n* **1** a way of behaving, thinking, or feeling that is peculiar to an individual or group, especially an odd or unusual one **2** an unusual or exaggerated reaction to a drug or food that is not caused by an allergy [Early 17C. Directly or via French *idiosyncrasie* < Greek *idiosugkrasia* 'personal mixing together' < *krasis* 'mixing'.] —**idiosyncratic** /íddi ō sing kráttik/ *adj* —**idiosyncratically** *adv*

idiot /íddi ət/ *n* **1** an offensive term that deliberately insults somebody's intelligence (*insult*) **2** an offensive term in a now disused classification system for somebody with an IQ of about 25 or under and a mental age of less than three years (*dated*) [14C. Via French < Greek *idiōtēs* 'private person, layperson' < *idios* (see IDIO-).]

idiot board *n* a placard, projector, or continuous roll of paper that prompts a television performer with lines to be spoken (*slang*)

idiot box *n* television or a television set (*slang*) [< the belief that watching too much television causes stupidity]

idiot card *n* MEDIA = **idiot board** (*slang*)

idiotic /íddi óttik/ *adj* an offensive term that deliberately insults somebody's behaviour as showing a lack of good sense or intelligence (*insult*) —**idiotically** *adv* —**idioticalness** *n*

idiot-proof *adj* constructed or designed so as not to fail or go wrong even if misused

idiot savant /éedi ō sa voN, íddi ət sávvənt/ (*plural* **idiot savants** /éedi ō sa voN, íddi ət sávvənt/ *or* **idiots savants** /éedi ō sa voN, íddi ət sávvənt/) *n* an offensive term for somebody who has a psychiatric disorder or a learning problem but who is exceptionally gifted in one particular area, e.g. rapid mental calculation, architectural drawing, or remembering facts [< French, 'learned idiot']

idiot tape *n* a tape for a typesetting machine that contains text but no formatting except markers for new paragraphs

ϟ **IDK** *abbr* I don't know (*in e-mails*)

idle /īd'l/ *adj* (**idler, idlest**) **1 LAZY** lazy and unwilling to work **2 NOT WORKING OR IN USE** not working, operating, producing, or in use **3 FRIVOLOUS** frivolous and a waste of time **4 NOT EARNING MONEY** not being used to yield a financial return ○ *idle funds* **5 UNFOUNDED** having no basis in fact ○ *idle gossip* **6 INEFFECTIVE** unlikely to be carried out or impossible to put into effect ○ *idle threats* ■ *n* **SPEED OF ENGINE WITH GEAR DISENGAGED** the state of a motor vehicle engine that is running but is not in gear ■ *v* (**idles, idling, idled**) **1** *vti* **PASS TIME AIMLESSLY** to be lazy and avoid work, or to pass the time lazily doing nothing in particular ○ *He idled away the morning.* **2** *vi* **MOVE SLOWLY AND AIMLESSLY** to move in a slow and lazy or aimless way **3** *vti* **RUN WITHOUT APPLYING POWER** to run gently with the gear disengaged, or to allow an engine to do this **4** *vt* *US, Can* **MAKE UNEMPLOYED** to make workers unemployed or inactive [Old English *īdel* 'worthless, empty' < Germanic] —**idleness** *n* —**idly** *adv*

SPELLCHECK Do not confuse ***idle*** with ***idol***, which has a similar sound. Beware: your spellchecker will not catch this error.

SYNONYMS See ***vain***.

idle pulley, idler pulley *n* a freely rotating pulley wheel that guides or takes up slack from a drive belt by pressing against it

idler /īdlər/ *n* **1** somebody who habitually avoids work or who is spending time in a lazy or relaxed way **2** MECH ENG = **idle wheel** *n.* 1

idler pulley *n* = **idle pulley**

idler wheel *n* = **idle wheel**

idle time *n* a period during which a device, machine, or employee is temporarily inactive

idle wheel, idler wheel *n* **1** a gear wheel or roller placed between two others to transmit motion between them without changing their speed or direction or to provide support **2** = **idle pulley**

idli /íddli/ *npl* *S Asia* steamed rice cakes eaten for breakfast, especially in S India [Mid-20C. < Malayalam and Kannada *iḍḍali*.]

idocrase /īdə krayz, -krayss/ *n* MINERALS = **vesuvianite** [Early 19C. < Greek *eidos* 'form' + *krasis* 'mixture'.]

idol /īd'l/ *n* **1 OBJECT OF ADORATION** somebody or something greatly and often fanatically admired and loved **2 OBJECT WORSHIPPED AS GOD** something such as a statue or carved image that is worshipped as a god **3 FORBIDDEN OBJECT OF WORSHIP** in monotheistic religions, any object of worship other than the one God [13C. Via French *idole* < Greek *eidōlon* 'image' < *eidos* 'form, shape'.]

SPELLCHECK See ***idle***.

idolater /ī dóllətər/ *n* **1** a worshipper of idols (*disapproving*) **2** a fanatical admirer of somebody or something [14C. < French *idolâtre* < Greek *eidōlolatrēs* 'image worshipper' < *eidōlon* (see IDOL).]

idolatry /ī dóllətri/ *n* **1** the worship of idols or false gods (*disapproving*) **2** extreme admiration or fanatical devotion to somebody or something [13C. Via French *idolâtrie* < Greek *eidōlolatreia* 'image-worship' < *eidōlon* (see IDOL).] —**idolatrous** *adj* —**idolatrously** *adv*

idolize /īdə līz/ (**-izes, -izing, -ized**), **idolise** (**-ises, -ising, -ised**) *vt* **1** to feel great admiration and respect for, or be fanatically devoted to, somebody or something **2** to worship something or somebody as an idol (*disapproving*) —**idolization** /īdə lī záysh'n/ *n* —**idolizer** *n*

ϟ **IDP** *abbr* integrated data processing

Idriess /éedrəss/, **Ion** (1890–1979) Australian novelist

ϟ **IDTS** *abbr* I don't think so (*in e-mails*)

idyll /ídd'l, íd'l/ *n* **1 EXPERIENCE OF SERENE HAPPINESS** an experience or period of serene and carefree happiness, usually in beautiful surroundings and often idealized **2 TRANQUIL CHARMING SCENE** a scene or event characterized by tranquillity, simple beauty, and innocent charm, usually in a rural setting **3 LITERARY PIECE ABOUT CHARMING RURAL LIFE** a short work in verse or prose, a painting, or a piece of music depicting simple pastoral or rural scenes and the life of country folk, often in idealized terms [Late 16C. Via Latin *idyllium* 'pastoral poem' < Greek *eidullion* 'small picture' < *eidos* 'form'.]

idyllic /i díllik, ī-/ *adj* **1** serenely beautiful, untroubled, and happy **2** like an idyll, especially in having a simple, unspoilt, and especially rural charm —**idyllically** *adv*

idyllist /ídd'list, íd'list/ *n* a writer, composer, or painter of idylls

ϟ **ie** *abbr* Ireland (*in Internet addresses*)

i.e. *abbr* that is to say [Latin *id est* 'that is']

USAGE See ***e.g.***

-ie *suffix* **1** one that is small or dear ○ *doggie* ○ *auntie* **2** one having a particular character ○ *sweetie* **3** one having to do with ○ *townie*

iechyd da /yáki daá/ *interj* *Wales* used as a drinking toast to wish somebody else good health [< Welsh, 'good health']

IEE *abbr* Institution of Electrical Engineers

-ier *suffix* = **er**

if /if/ CORE MEANING: a conjunction used to indicate the circumstances that would have to exist in order for an event to happen ○ *You can come with us if you want to.* ○ *Are you thinking of buying a new car? If so, talk to us first.* **1** *conj* **USED IN INDIRECT QUESTIONS** used in indirect speech to introduce a question that in direct speech requires the answer 'yes' or 'no' ○ *He asked the hotel receptionist if it was possible to hire a car.* **2** *conj* **MODIFYING A STATEMENT** used to indicate a modification to a statement, usually to add something negative or to indicate that there is less of something than originally expected ○ *The report will be with you at the end of the week, if not before.* ○ *a gallant, if misguided, attempt* **3** *conj* **INTRODUCING AN EXCLAMATION** used to introduce an exclamation expressing surprise or dismay ○ *If she isn't the most selfish person I've ever met!* **4** *n* **DOUBT** a doubt or uncertainty ○ *There is rather a large if about whether or not she'll finish her degree.* **5** *n* **CONDITION** a condition or qualification ○ *I'm not very happy about the ifs that have been put into the contract.* [Old English *gif* < Germanic] ◇ **ifs and buts** excuses or protests ◇ **ifs, ands, or buts** *US* excuses or protests ◇ **if only** used to introduce expression of a hopeless wish or regret ○ *If only you had told me sooner!*

LITERARY LINK ***If*** a poem (1910) by Rudyard Kipling. This poem is well known and loved by many for the message it contains, advocating such noble qualities as self-reliance, tolerance, modesty, and fortitude: 'If you can keep your head when all about you/ Are losing theirs and blaming it on you, . . . you'll be a man, my son!'.

USAGE Ambiguity of **if not**: In *We have hundreds, if not thousands, of items in stock*, the *if not* fairly plainly means 'or even'. In *It's a clever idea, if not a practical one*, it fairly plainly means 'although not'. But in *He's good-looking, if not really handsome*, it is unclear which of those meanings is intended — at least out of context. Often it is clear what *if not* means only because the context shows what the phrase must mean. Where it will not be clear, another wording is preferable.

USAGE When to use **if and when**: This expression is often used in cases where *if* or *when* alone would be enough, but there are occasions on which both are needed to convey a condition about both the likelihood and timing of an eventuality; in the sentence *Arrange repairs if and when necessary*, the omission of *if* could imply that repairs are always necessary at some point, and the omission of *when* could fail to make the point that repairs should be done promptly.

IF *abbr* intermediate frequency

IFC *abbr* International Finance Corporation (*of the UN*)

Ife /ee fay/ city in SW Nigeria. Population: 225,500 (1990).

iffy /íffi/ (**-fier, -fiest**) *adj* (*informal*) **1** of doubtful and probably low quality, not to be relied on, or arousing suspicion **2** doubtful and undecided about something —**iffiness** *n*

Ifni /éefni/ former overseas province of Spain, on the coast of SW Morocco

IFOR, Ifor *n* a NATO-led multinational force sent to maintain peace in the former Yugoslavia following the signing of the Dayton Accords. Full form **Implementation Force**

IFR *abbr* instrument flying regulations

IgA *n* a class of antibodies, found in respiratory and alimentary secretions as well as in saliva and tears, that help the body to neutralize harmful bacteria and viral antigens [Shortening of *immunoglobulin A*]

Igbo *n*, *adj* PEOPLES, LANG = **Ibo**

IgD *n* a class of antibodies, present on most cell surfaces and predominant in B cells, that help the body to resist antigens. ◊ **B cell** [Shortening of *immunoglobulin D*]

IgE *n* a class of antibodies, abundant in tissues, that help the body to expel intestinal parasites and cause allergic reactions in response to antigens [Shortening of *immunoglobulin E*]

IgG *n* a class of antibodies, predominant in serum, that pass through the placental wall into foetal circulation and help to prepare the immune system for the period of infancy [Shortening of *immunoglobulin G*]

igloo /íggloo/ *n* **1** an Inuit dwelling, usually dome-shaped and built from blocks of packed snow **2** any small dome-shaped shelter or structure [Mid-19C. < Inuit *iglu* 'house'.]

IgM *n* a class of antibodies, circulating in the blood and secretions, that help the body to resist viruses [Shortening of *immunoglobulin M*]

IGM *abbr* International Grandmaster

ign. *abbr* **1** ignites **2** ignition **3** unknown [Latin *ignotus*]

Ignatius (of Antioch) /ig náyshəss-/, **St** (35?–AD 107) bishop and martyr

Ignatius Loyola /ig náyshəss loy ólə, -lóyələ/, **St** (1491–1556) Spanish priest

igneous /ígni əss/ *adj* **1** describes rock formed under conditions of intense heat or produced by the solidification of volcanic magma on or below the Earth's surface **2** connected with or characteristic of fire (*formal*) [Mid-17C. < Latin *igneus* < *ignis* 'fire'.]

ignescent /ig néss'nt/ *adj* giving off sparks when struck, as a flint does [Early 19C. < Latin *ignescent-*, present participle of *ignescere* 'take fire'.]

ignes fatui plural of **ignis fatuus**

ignimbrite /ígnim brīt/ *n* a volcanic rock consisting of droplets of lava and glass that were welded together by intense heat [Mid-20C. < Latin *ignis* 'fire' + *imbr-* 'rain'.]

ignis fatuus /ígniss fáttyoo əss/ (*plural* **ignes fatui** /ig neez fáttyoo ī/) *n* **1** SCI = **will-o'-the-wisp** *n*. **2** something, e.g. a hope or an aim, that proves illusory or leads somebody astray (*literary*) [< Latin, 'foolish fire'; from its erratic movements]

ignite /ig nít/ (**-nites, -niting, -nited**) *v* **1** *vti* LIGHT FIRE OR BEGIN TO BURN to set fire to something, or catch fire **2** *vti* HEAT GAS UNTIL IT BURNS to heat a gas to the temperature at which it begins to burn **3** *vt* AROUSE EMOTION IN to cause a strong emotion to arise or show itself in somebody [Mid-17C. < past participle of *ignire* 'set on fire' < *ignis* 'fire'.] —**ignitability** /ig nítə bílləti/ *n* —**ignitable** *adj* —**igniter** *n*

ignition /ig níshʼn/ *n* **1** PROCESS OF IGNITING the process of setting something on fire **2** MEANS OF STARTING ENGINE a mechanism that determines when, where, and how a spark is delivered to an engine cylinder to ignite the fuel and start or run the engine **3** SPARK THAT IGNITES FUEL-AIR MIXTURE a spark in an internal-combustion engine that ignites and explodes a mixture of fuel and air

ignition point *n* the temperature at which a substance begins to burn and remain alight

ignoble /ig nóbl/ *adj* dishonourable, ungenerous, and contrary to the high standards of conduct expected of somebody (*formal*) [15C. Directly or via French < Latin *ignobilis* 'not noble' < (*g*)*nobilis* (see NOBLE).] —**ignobility** /ígnō bílləti/ *n* —**ignobly** *adv*

ignominious /ígnə mínni əss/ *adj* **1** involving a total loss of dignity and pride and making somebody or something appear shamefully weak and ineffective **2** deserving condemnation and contempt (*formal*) —**ignominiously** *adv* —**ignominiousness** *n*

ignominy /ígnəmini/ (*plural* **-ies**) *n* **1** a total loss of dignity and self-respect or an incurring of public disgrace **2** a disgraceful act (*formal*) [Mid-16C. Directly or via French *ignominie* < Latin *ignominia* 'lacking name' < *nomin-* 'name, reputation'.]

ignoramus /ígnə ráyməss/ *n* an offensive term that deliberately insults somebody's level of intelligence or education (*insult*) [Late 16C. < modern Latin, 'we do not know' < Latin, a form of *ignorare* (see IGNORE).]

ignorance /ígnərənss/ *n* **1** lack of knowledge or education **2** unawareness of something, often of something important

ignorant /ígnərənt/ *adj* **1** LACKING KNOWLEDGE lacking knowledge and education in general or in a specific subject **2** UNAWARE unaware of something ○ *ignorant of the danger* **3** RESULTING FROM LACK OF KNOWING caused by a lack of understanding or experience ○ *an ignorant mistake* **4** *Carib* QUARRELSOME quarrelsome and aggressive —**ignorantly** *adv* —**ignorantness** *n*

ignore /ig náwr/ (**-nores, -noring, -nored**) *vt* **1** to refuse to notice or pay attention to somebody or something **2** *Aus* to reject a bill of indictment on the grounds of insufficient evidence [Early 17C. Directly or via French *ignorer* < Latin *ignorare* 'not to know, to ignore' < (*g*)*noscere* 'know'.] —**ignorable** *adj* —**ignorer** *n*

Iguaçu /í gwaa sóo/ river in S Brazil and NE Argentina. Length: 1,200 km/745 mi.

Iguaçu Falls /í gwaa sóo-/ waterfall on the Iguaçu River, in S Brazil. Height: 80 m/260 ft.

Iguana

iguana /i gwaánə/ (*plural* **-nas** *or* **-na**) *n* a large plant-eating tropical lizard with a serrated fringe or crest running along its back from head to tail. Native to: South and Central America. Family: Iguanidae. [Mid-16C. Via Spanish < Arawak *iwana*.] —**iguanian** *adj*, *n*

iguanodon /i gwaánə don/ *n* a large long-tailed plant-eating dinosaur of the Jurassic and early Cretaceous periods. Genus: *Iguanodon*. [Early 19C. < IGUANA + *-odon* < Greek, variant of *odont-* 'tooth'; from the similarity of its teeth to those of an iguana.]

Ihimaera /íhi mírə/, **Witi** (*b*. 1944) New Zealand novelist

ihp *abbr* indicated horsepower

ihram /ee raám/ *n* **1** a white cotton robe worn by men when they are pilgrims to Mecca, formed from pieces of cloth wound around the waist and over the shoulder **2** the state of holiness conferred or symbolized by the wearing of the ihram [Early 18C. < Arabic *'iḥrām*.]

iid *abbr* independent identically distributed (*refers to two or more random variables*)

⚡**IINM** *abbr* if I'm not mistaken (*in e-mails*)

⚡**IIRC** *abbr* if I recall/remember correctly (*in e-mails*)

IJsselmeer /íss'l meer/ shallow freshwater lake in the N Netherlands

⚡**IJWTK** *abbr* I just want to know (*in e-mails*)

⚡**IJWTS** *abbr* I just want to say (*in e-mails*)

ikat /ée kaat, i kát/ *n* a technique for making patterned fabric by using tie-dyed yarn [Mid-20C. < Malay, 'tie, fasten'.]

⚡**IKBS** *abbr* intelligent knowledge-based system

ikebana /ík ay baánə, íki-/ *n* the Japanese art of arranging flowers in a formal balanced composition [Early 20C. < Japanese, 'living flowers'.]

Ike Taiga /í kay tígə/ (1723–76) Japanese painter

Ikhnaton = **Akhenaton**

ikon *n* RELIG = **icon** *n*. 1

⚡**IKWUM** *abbr* I know what you mean (*in e-mails*)

⚡**il** *abbr* Israel (*in Internet addresses*)

IL *abbr* Illinois

il- *prefix* = **in-**¹, **in-**² (*before l*)

-il *suffix* forming nouns and adjectives ○ *utensil* ○ *civil* [< Latin *-ilis*]

-ile¹ *suffix* of, relating to, capable of ○ *pulsatile* ○ *protrusile* [Via Old French < Latin *-ilis*]

-ile² *suffix* a portion of a particular size in a frequency distribution ○ *quartile* ○ *percentile* [< ?]

ilea plural of **ileum**

ileac /ílli ak/, **ileal** /ílli əl/ *adj* **1** relating to the ileum **2** relating to ileus [Early 19C. Alteration of ILIAC after ILEUM, ILEUS.]

~~**ilegal**~~ incorrect spelling of **illegal**

ileitis /ílli ítiss/ *n* inflammation of the ileum

ileostomy /ílli óstəmi/ (*plural* **-mies**) *n* **1** the surgical operation of making an opening through the abdominal wall into the ileum, so that waste can be discharged out of the body without passing through the colon **2** a surgical opening through the abdominal wall into the ileum

Ilesa /i láyshə/, **Ilesha** town in SW Nigeria. Population: 369,000 (1995 estimate).

ileum /ílli əm/ (*plural* **-a** /-ə/) *n* the third and lowest portion of the small intestine, extending from the jejunum to the pouch-shaped caecum at the beginning of the large intestine [Late 17C. < medieval Latin, variant of Latin *ilium* 'entrails'.]

ileus /ílli əss/ *n* inability of the contents of the intestines to pass through owing to physical obstruction or muscular inadequacy, often accompanied by extreme pain and vomiting [Late 17C. Via Latin < Greek *ileos* 'colic'.]

ilex /í leks/ *n* **1** any tree or shrub belonging to a genus whose best-known member is the holly tree. Genus: *Ilex*. **2** = **holm oak** [< Latin, 'holm oak']

Ilfracombe /ílfrə koom/ seaside resort in SW England. Population: 10,429 (1991).

ilia plural of **ilium**

iliac /ílli ak/ *adj* relating to the ilium and its surroundings [Early 16C. < late Latin *iliacus* 'relating to colic' < Latin *ilia* (see ILIUM).]

Iliad /ílli əd/ *n* an ancient Greek epic poem, describing the siege and capture of Troy, ascribed to Homer and probably composed by oral tradition over several centuries before 700 BC [Early 17C. < Latin *Iliad-* < Greek *Ilias* 'of Troy' < *Ilion* 'Troy'.] —**Iliadic** /ílli áddik/ *adj*

Iliamna /ílli ámnə/ volcanic peak in SW Alaska. Height: 3,053 m/10,016 ft.

Iliamna, Lake largest lake in Alaska, in the southwest of the state. Area: 2,647 sq. km/1,022 sq. mi.

ilium /ílli əm/ (*plural* **-a** /-ə/) *n* the wide flat upper portion of the pelvis that is connected to the base of the vertebral column [14C. < late Latin, 'flank, groin' < Latin *ilia* (plural) 'flanks'.]

ilk *n* kind or sort (*informal*) ○ *'save forlorn hopes and their ilk'* (Stephen Crane, *The Red Badge of Courage*; 1895) ■ *det Scotland* = **ilka** [Old English *ilca* 'same' < Indo-European, 'same' + Germanic, 'form'] ◊ **of that ilk 1** *Scotland* coming from or owning the place of the same name as your own **2** of that sort or type ○ *We don't like people of that ilk.*

ilka /ílkə/, **ilk** /ilk/ *det Scotland* each or every [12C. < *ilk* 'each' (< Old English *ylc*) + A-².]

Ilkeston /ílkstən/ town in central England. Population: 35,134 (1991).

ill /il/ *adj* (**worse** /wurss/, **worst**) **1** UNWELL not in good health, having a disease, or feeling unwell or nauseous **2** HARMFUL resulting in harm, pain, or trouble for somebody or something **3** UNKIND unkind and unfriendly ○ *ill feeling* **4** UNFAVOURABLE predicting a bad future or outcome ○ *an ill wind* **5** MORALLY BAD resulting from the actual or supposed moral badness of somebody or something ○ *of ill repute* **6 BAD** not up to the expected or required standard, e.g. of behaviour or competence ■ *adv* (**worse, worst**) **1 BADLY** badly, inadequately, or inappropriately ○ *prisoners who were ill treated* **2 UNFAVOURABLY** in an adverse or unfavourable way or so as to reflect badly on somebody or something ○ *It boded ill for the future.* **3 WITH DIFFICULTY** only with great difficulty and trouble ○ *She can ill afford the time at present.* ■ *n* **1 HARM** evil or harm, especially as a fate wished on somebody ○ *don't wish others ill* **2 UNFAVOURABLE OPINION** an unfavourable opinion of somebody or something ○ *spoke ill of them* **3 MISFORTUNE** trouble or misfortune, or a troublesome or distressing experience (*archaic*) [12C. < Old Norse *illr* 'evil, difficult', *illa* 'badly', *ilt* 'evil'.]

USAGE ill or **sick**? In general, somebody who feels ***ill*** is unwell in some way, often seriously, whereas somebody who feels ***sick*** may be less seriously ill or about to vomit. On the other hand, ***ill*** is less common in attributive position before a noun, and it is more natural to say *a sick child* than *an ill child*. So too there are set expressions in which ***sick*** is used but not ***ill***, for example *sick leave, sick note, to go sick*.

I'll /īl/ *contr* I will or shall

ill. *abbr* **1** illustrated **2** illustration **3** illustrator

Ill. *abbr* Illinois

ill-advised *adj* not wise, prudent, or sensible —**ill-advisedly** *adv*

ill-affected *adj* hostile or unfriendly towards somebody or something (*formal*)

ill-assorted, ill-sorted *adj* mismatched or incompatible

ill at ease *adj* uncomfortable and nervous

illation /i láysh'n/ *n* (*formal*) **1** an inference drawn from something **2** the act or process of making an inference [Mid-16C. < Latin *illation-* < *illat-* (see ILLATIVE).]

illative /i láytiv, íllə-/ *adj* **1 INFERENTIAL** involving or relating to the making of inferences (*formal*) **2 STATING INFERENCE** expressing or preceding an inference **3 OF CASE OF FINNISH NOUN** describes a noun case in Finnish and some other languages expressing motion towards something ■ *n* **1 SOMETHING THAT STATES INFERENCE** a word, phrase, or morpheme that expresses an inference **2 CASE OF FINNISH NOUN** the illative case in Finnish and similar languages [Late 16C. < Latin *illativus* < *illat-*, past participle of *inferre* (see INFER).] —**illatively** *adv*

Illawarra /íllə wórrə/ district in SE New South Wales, Australia. Population: 380,660 (1998).

ill-bred *adj* rude, impolite, or otherwise showing a lack of good manners or the results of a bad upbringing —**ill-breeding** *n*

ill-conceived *adj* not based on good planning, especially not having an aim or goal that is likely to be successfully achieved

ill-considered *adj* done or made unwisely or without sufficient thought about the consequences

ill-defined *adj* not clearly or sharply defined or thought out

ill-disguised *adj* apparent or visible, especially in somebody's expression, voice, or manner, because any attempt to conceal it is unsuccessful or perfunctory ○ *her ill-disguised contempt for them*

ill-disposed *adj* having an unfriendly or hostile attitude towards somebody or something

ill-dressed *adj* dressed in shabby, badly fitting, or unsuitable clothes

ϟ **illegal** /i leég'l/ *adj* **1 AGAINST THE LAW** forbidden by law **2 AGAINST THE RULES** not allowed by the rules of something such as a game **3 NOT PERMITTED BY COMPUTER** not permitted in a computer program ■ *n* **ILLEGAL IMMIGRANT** an illegal entrant of a country —**illegally** *adv*

SYNONYMS See ***unlawful***.

illegality /íllee gálləti/ (*plural* **-ties**) *n* **1** the fact of being forbidden by law or by the rules of something **2** an act that is against the law

illegalize /i leégə līz/ (**-izes, -izing, -ized**), **illegalise** (**-ises, -ising, -ised**) *vt* to declare officially and by law that something is illegal —**illegalization** /i leégə lī záysh'n/ *n*

illegible /i léjjəb'l/ *adj* impossible or very difficult to read —**illegibility** /i léjjə bílləti/ *n* —**illegibly** *adv*

illegitimate /íllə jíttəmət/ *adj* **1 AGAINST LAW OR RULES** not carried out, made, or constituted in accordance with the law, the rules governing a particular activity, or social norms and customs **2 BORN OUT OF WEDLOCK** born to parents who are not married to each other **3 NOT CORRECTLY REASONED** not correctly inferred or reasoned —**illegitimacy** *n* —**illegitimately** *adv*

ill-fated *adj* ending in, or doomed to, disaster

ill-favoured *adj* **1** unattractive in appearance, especially having an unattractive face **2** offensively objectionable (*literary*) —**ill-favouredly** *adv* —**ill-favouredness** *n*

ill feeling *n* animosity or resentment towards somebody, something, or each other

ill-founded *adj* with no sound basis in fact or logic

ill-gotten *adj* acquired dishonestly or illegally ○ *ill-gotten gains*

ill health *n* the state of being in poor physical or mental condition

ill humour *n* a bad mood or bad temper —**ill-humoured** *adj*

illiberal /i líbbərəl/ *adj* **1** narrow-minded and intolerant of ideas and behaviour that vary from an inflexibly conservative standard **2** ungenerous (*formal*) —**illiberalism** *n* —**illiberality** /i líbbə rálləti/ *n* —**illiberally** *adv*

illicit /i líssit/ *adj* **1** not allowed by the law **2** considered wrong or unacceptable by prevailing social customs or standards —**illicitly** *adv* —**illicitness** *n*

SPELLCHECK See ***elicit***.

SYNONYMS See ***unlawful***.

Illimani /éelyi mánni/ mountain in W Bolivia. Highest peak: Nevada Illimani 6,462 m/21,201 ft.

illimitable /i límmitəb'l/ *adj* with no limits or bounds (*formal*) —**illimitability** /i límmitə bílləti/ *n* —**illimitably** *adv*

Illinois[1] /ílli nóy/ (*plural* **-nois**) *n* a member of a confederacy of Algonquian peoples who lived in an area covering N Illinois, E Iowa, and S Wisconsin, and now live in NE Oklahoma —**Illinois** *adj*

Illinois[2] /íllə nóy/ **1** state in the north-central United States. Capital: Springfield. Population: 11,895,849 (1997). Area: 150,007 sq. km/57,918 sq. mi. **2** river in N Illinois. Length: 680 km/420 mi.

Illinoisan /-nóyən, -nóyz'n/, **Illinoisian** /-nóyzi ən/ *adj* relating to the state of Illinois —**Illinoisan** *n*

Illinois Waterway system of rivers and canals in Illinois that connects Lake Michigan with the Mississippi River. Length: 523 km/325 mi.

illiquid /i líkwid/ *adj* **1** not easily convertible into cash **2** without sufficient ready cash —**illiquidity** /ílli kwíddəti/ *n*

illite /íllīt/ *n* a clay mineral of the mica group containing potassium and aluminium. Source: shale, mudstone. [Mid-20C. After ILLINOIS[2].] —**illitic** /i líttik/ *adj*

illiterate /i líttərət/ *adj* **1 OFFENSIVE TERM** an offensive term for people who are not able to read and write **2 UNEDUCATED** having or showing little or no knowledge of a specific subject ○ *artistically illiterate* **3 MAKING MANY LANGUAGE MISTAKES** full of or making many basic errors in the use of language ○ *illiterate prose* ■ *n* **OFFENSIVE TERM** an offensive term for somebody who lacks education and knowledge, especially somebody who cannot read or write —**illiteracy** *n* —**illiterately** *adv* —**illiterateness** *n*

ill-judged *adj* showing a lack of good judgment or an incorrect assessment of a situation

ill-mannered *adj* rude or impolite —**ill-manneredly** *adv*

ill nature *n* a bad-tempered, unpleasant, or unkind disposition

ill-natured /-náychərd/ *adj* bad-tempered, unpleasant, or unkind —**ill-naturedly** *adv* —**ill-naturedness** *n*

illness /ílnəss/ *n* **1** a disease, sickness, or other such indisposition **2** a state of bad health

illocution /íllə kyoósh'n/ *n* an action such as naming, threatening, warning, or promising that is carried out simply by saying the appropriate words [Mid-20C. < IL- + LOCUTION.] —**illocutionary** *adj*

illogic /i lójjik/ *n* the quality or condition of having no basis in logic

illogical /i lójjik'l/ *adj* **1** not following the rules of logic, or not following logically from a previous premise, statement, or action **2** apparently unreasonable or perverse, especially in not being or not giving the expected response —**illogicality** /i lójji kálləti/ *n* —**illogically** *adv*

ill-omened /-ōmənd/ *adj* accompanied by signs suggesting disaster or failure

ill-sorted *adj* = **ill-assorted**

ill-starred *adj* doomed to end in failure or disaster [< the belief that an unpropitious arrangement of the astronomical objects at the start of an undertaking predetermined an unhappy outcome]

ill-tempered *adj* having or showing an irritable mood or disposition —**ill-temperedly** *adv*

ill-timed *adj* done or occurring at the wrong time and thus not having the desired effect

ill-treat *vt* **1** to behave cruelly or unkindly towards a person or animal **2** to misuse something or give something rough treatment —**ill-treatment** *n*

SYNONYMS See ***misuse***.

illume /i loóm, i lyoóm/ (**-lumes, -luming, -lumed**) *vt* to cast illumination on something (*archaic literary*) [Early 17C. Contraction of ILLUMINE.]

illuminance /i loóminənss/ *n* (*symbol* E_v) the amount of light, evaluated according to its capacity to produce visual stimulation, that reaches a unit of surface area during a unit of time

illuminant /i loóminənt/ *n* something that gives off or provides light [Mid-17C. < Latin *illuminant-*, present participle of *illuminare* (see ILLUMINATE).]

illuminate /i loómi nayt/ (**-nates, -nating, -nated**) *v* **1** *vti* **SHINE LIGHT ON** to make something visible or bright with light, or be lit up **2** *vt* **DECORATE WITH LIGHTS** to decorate something with lights for a celebration **3** *vt* **CLARIFY** to make something easier to understand and appreciate **4** *vti* **ENLIGHTEN** to provide somebody with knowledge or with intellectual or spiritual enlightenment (*literary; often passive*) **5** *vt* **ADD COLOURED ELEMENTS TO PAGE** to add coloured letters, illustrations, and designs to a manuscript or the borders of a page **6** *vt* **CAUSE TO LOOK HAPPY AND ANIMATED** to make something, especially somebody's face, look happy and animated [15C. < Latin *illuminat-*, past participle of *illuminare* 'light up' < *lumin-* 'light'.] —**illuminated** *adj* —**illuminative** *adj* —**illuminator** *n*

illuminati /i loómi naáti/, **Illuminati** *npl* any of various groups in history claiming to have received special religious or spiritual enlightenment, especially an 18th-century German secret society with deist and republican ideas [Late 16C. Via Italian < Latin, plural of *illuminatus*, past participle of *illuminare* (see ILLUMINATE).]

illuminating /i loómi nayting/ *adj* informative and enlightening, often by revealing or emphasizing facts that were previously obscure —**illuminatingly** *adv*

illumination /i loómi náysh'n/ *n* **1 ACT OF ILLUMINATING** the provision of light to make something visible or bright, or the fact of being lit up **2 USABLE LIGHT** the amount or strength of light available in a place or for a purpose **3 CLARIFICATION AND EXPLANATION** the process of clarifying or explaining something **4 ENLIGHTENMENT** intellectual or spiritual enlightenment **5 ORNAMENTATION OF PAGE** a coloured letter, design, or illustration decorating a manuscript or page, or the art or act of decorating written texts **6** PHYS = **illuminance 7 DECORATIVE STREET LIGHT** a group of coloured lights used to decorate streets and public buildings, especially at Christmas or other festive occasions —**illuminational** *adj*

illumine /i loómin/ (**-mines, -mining, -mined**) *vti* to illuminate somebody or something, or become illuminated (*formal*) [14C. Via French *illuminer* < Latin *illuminare* (see ILLUMINATE).] —**illuminable** *adj*

illuminism /i loóminizəm/ *n* the beliefs held by illuminati, especially their belief in or claim to special enlightenment

illus. *abbr* **1** illustrated **2** illustration **3** illustrator

ill-use *vt* = **ill-treat** *v.* 1 —**ill-usage** *n*

ill-used /il yoózd/ *adj* cruelly or harshly treated

illusion /i loózh'n/ *n* **1 SOMETHING WITH DECEPTIVE APPEARANCE** something that deceives the senses or mind, e.g. by appearing to exist when it does not or appearing to be one thing when it is in fact another **2 DECEPTIVE POWER OF APPEARANCES** the ability of appearances to deceive the mind and senses, or the capacity of the mind and senses to be deceived by appearances **3 FALSE IDEA** a false idea, conception, or belief **4 MISTAKEN SENSORY PERCEPTION** a misinterpretation of an experience of sensory perception, especially a visual one, where the stimuli are objectively present and the mistaken perception is due to physical rather than psychological causes **5 FINE GAUZE** a fine gauze. Use: trimming. [14C. Via French < Latin *illus-*, past participle of *illudere* 'play at' < *ludus* 'play, sport'.] —**illusionary** *adj* —**illusionless** *adj*

USAGE See ***allusion***.

illusionism /i lo͞ozh'nizəm/ *n* the use of pictorial techniques to create illusions

illusionist /i lo͞ozh'nist, i lyo͞o-/ *n* **1** a performer of magical tricks **2** an artist who creates pictorial illusions —**illusionistic** /i lo͞ozh'n ístik, i lyo͞o-/ *adj* —**illusionistically** *adv*

illusive /i lo͞ossiv, i lyo͞o-/ *adj* = **illusory** [Early 17C. < medieval Latin *illusivus* 'deceptive' < Latin *illus-* (see ILLUSION).] —**illusively** *adv* —**illusiveness** *n*

SPELLCHECK See ***elusive***.

illusory /i lo͞ozəri, i lo͞oss-/ *adj* produced by, based on, or consisting of an illusion [Late 16C. Directly or via French *illusoire* < ecclesiastical Latin *illusorius* 'ironical' < Latin *illus-* (see ILLUSION).] —**illusorily** *adv* —**illusoriness** *n*

illustrate /íllə strayt/ (**-trates, -trating, -trated**) *v* **1** *vt* **ACCOMPANY WITH PICTURES** to provide explanatory or decorative pictures to accompany a printed, spoken, or electronic text ○ *The book was illustrated with diagrams.* **2** *vti* **FULLY EXPLAIN** to clarify something by giving examples or making comparisons **3** *vt* **BE CHARACTERISTIC OF** to be a good example of something, or serve to demonstrate something and make it clear ○ *a case that illustrates the need for legislation* [Early 16C. < Latin *illustrat-*, past participle of *illustrare* 'light up' < *lustrare* (see LUSTRE).] —**illustratable** *adj* —**illustrator** *n*

illustration /íllə stráysh'n/ *n* **1 PICTURE THAT COMPLEMENTS TEXT** a drawing, photograph, or diagram that accompanies and complements a printed, spoken, or electronic text **2 PROVISION OF PICTURES ACCOMPANYING TEXT** the art or process of producing or providing pictures to accompany a text **3 SOMETHING THAT HELPS EXPLAIN** an example or comparison that helps to clarify or explain something —**illustrational** *adj*

illustrative /íllәstrətiv, i lús-, íllə straytiv/ *adj* serving to illustrate or explain something —**illustratively** *adv*

illustrious /i lústri əss/ *adj* extremely distinguished and deservedly famous [Mid-16C. < Latin *illustris* 'bright, famous' < *illustrare* (see ILLUSTRATE).] —**illustriously** *adv* —**illustriousness** *n*

illuviation /i lo͞ovi áysh'n/ *n* the process by which materials such as colloids and salts are washed from an upper layer of soil to a lower one [Early 20C. < IL- + *-luviation* (as in ELUVIATION).] —**illuviated** /i lo͞ovi aytid/ *adj*

ill will *n* a feeling or attitude of hostility, unfriendliness, or dislike towards somebody ○ *They bore us no ill will.*

ill-wisher *n* somebody who wishes misfortune or evil to come to another person

Illyria /i lírri ə/ ancient region along the Adriatic coast from Albania northwards

Illyrian /i lírri ən, i léeri ən/ *n* **1 HISTORICAL INHABITANT OF E ADRIATIC COAST** a member of a people who, from the late third century BC, occupied Illyria until they were conquered by the Romans around 33 BC **2 EXTINCT LANGUAGE OF ILLYRIANS** an extinct Indo-European language that was spoken in Illyria in ancient times, considered to be related to Albanian ■ *adj* **CHARACTERISTIC OF ILLYRIA** relating to Illyria, or its language, people, or culture

ilmenite /ílmə nīt/ *n* a mixed oxide mineral containing iron and titanium. Source: igneous and metamorphic rocks. [Early 19C. After the *Ilmen* Mountains in the S Urals, Russia.]

Iloilo /éelō éelō/ capital of Iloilo Province, in the central Philippines. Population: 363,778 (1999 estimate).

Ilorin /i lórrən/ capital of Kwara State, SW Nigeria. Population: 464,000 (1995 estimate).

ILS *abbr* instrument landing system

⚡**im** *abbr* Isle of Man (*in Internet addresses*)

I'm /īm/ *contr* I am

IM *abbr* **1** International Master **2** intramuscular

im- *prefix* = **in-**[1], **in-**[2] (*before b, m, and p*)

⚡**IMA** *abbr* I might add (*in e-mails*)

image /ímmij/ *n* **1 ACTUAL OR MENTAL PICTURE** a picture or likeness of somebody or something, produced either physically by a sculptor, painter, or photographer, or conjured in the mind ○ *concerned about his public image* **2 LIKENESS SEEN OR PRODUCED** the likeness of somebody or something that appears in a mirror, through a lens, or on the retina of the eye, or that is produced electronically on a screen **3 SOMEBODY CLOSELY RESEMBLING SOMEBODY ELSE** a person or thing bearing a close likeness to something or somebody else ○ *She's the image of her grandmother.* **4 CONSPICUOUS EXAMPLE** an extremely typical or extreme example of something ○ *behaviour that is the very image of greed* **5 EXAMPLE OF FIGURATIVE LANGUAGE** a figure of speech, especially a metaphor or simile **6 SET OF FUNCTION'S VALUES** the value of a mathematical function corresponding to a specific value of the function's variable ■ *vt* (**-ages, -aging, -aged**) **1 CREATE IMAGE OF** to produce a physical or mental image of something **2 MAKE VISUAL IMAGE OF BODY STRUCTURES** to produce a visual representation of bodily structures, using X-rays, ultrasound, radioactivity, heat, or magnetism and, usually, computerized scanning devices, as an aid to diagnosis and treatment **3 PICTURE IN MIND** to form a mental image of something **4 DESCRIBE SOMETHING IN VISUAL TERMS** to describe vividly or in visual terms **5 TYPIFY** to embody or typify something [12C. Via French < Latin *imago* 'likeness'.] —**imageable** *adj* —**imageless** *adj* —**imager** *n*

⚡**image compression** *n* a technique for reducing the amount of digitized information needed to store a visual image electronically

image converter *n* an optical-electronic device that reproduces an image formed by invisible radiation such as ultraviolet and infrared on a photoemissive surface as a visible-light image on a luminescent surface

image intensifier *n* an optical-electronic device that amplifies an image formed by visible radiation on a photoemissive surface to present an enhanced image on a luminescent surface

image-maker *n* somebody employed to create a favourable public image of a business, organization, product, or public figure

⚡**image map** *n* a graphic image with variable areas that computer users can click on to activate hypertext links

image orthicon /-áwrthi kon/ *n* a television camera tube in which an electron image on a photoemissive surface is focused onto a target for scanning

imagery /ímmijəri/ (*plural* **-ries**) *n* **1 METAPHORS AND SIMILES** the figurative language, especially metaphors and similes, used in poetry, plays, and other literary works **2 IMAGES IN THE MIND** a set of mental pictures produced by the memory or imagination or conjured up by a stimulus ○ *Her dreams were filled with surreal imagery.* **3 IMAGES IN ARTISTIC WORK** the pictorial images found in works of art such as paintings and sculptures **4 IMAGES COLLECTIVELY** a group or set of images considered together ○ *studying the CAT-scan imagery*

image tube *n* an optical-electronic device that converts invisible radiation into a visible image, as in an image converter, or amplifies visible radiation into an enhanced image, as in an image intensifier

imaginable /i májjinəb'l/ *adj* capable of being conceived or imagined ○ *the worst meal imaginable* —**imaginability** /i májjinə bíllәti/ *n* —**imaginably** *adv*

imaginary /i májjinəri/ *adj* **1** existing only in the mind, not in reality **2** relating to or containing imaginary numbers. ◊ **imaginary number, complex number** ■ *n* MATH = **imaginary number** [14C. < Latin *imaginarius* < *imagin-* 'likeness'.] —**imaginarily** /i màjji nárrili/ *adv*

imaginary number *n* a complex number in the form $a + ib$ where i is the square root of minus one, and b is not equal to zero. ◊ **real number**

imaginary part *n* the real number, b, in the complex number $a + ib$, where $i = \sqrt{-1}$

imaginary unit *n* the positive square root of –1

imagination /i májji náysh'n/ *n* **1 ABILITY TO VISUALIZE** the ability to form images and ideas in the mind, especially of things never seen or never experienced directly **2 CREATIVE PART OF THE MIND** the part of the mind where ideas, thoughts, and images are formed **3 RESOURCEFULNESS** the ability to think of ways of dealing with difficulties or problems —**imaginational** *adj*

imaginative /i májjinətiv/ *adj* **1 SKILLED AT VISUALIZING OR THINKING ORIGINALLY** good at thinking of new ideas or at visualizing things that have not been seen or experienced **2 ORIGINAL** new and original or not likely to have been easily thought up by somebody else ○ *an imaginative solution to a long-standing problem* **3 UNLIKELY** seeming untrue, implausible, or unlikely (*often used ironically*) **4 OF IMAGINATION** relating to the ability to form images and ideas in the mind —**imaginativeness** *n*

imaginatively /i májjinətivli/ *adv* in a new and original way that would not have occurred readily to most people

imagine /i májjin/ *v* (**-ines, -ining, -ined**) **1** *vti* **FORM AN IMAGE IN THE MIND** to form an image or idea of something in the mind ○ *I can just imagine his reaction!* **2** *vt* **SEE OR HEAR SOMETHING UNREAL** to see or hear something that is not there or to think something that is not true ○ *There's nothing there — you're imagining things!* **3** *vt* **ASSUME** to suppose or assume something ■ *interj* **imagine, imagine that EXPRESSION OF SURPRISE** expresses surprise or indignation [14C. Via French < Latin *imaginare* 'make an image of', *imaginari* 'picture to yourself' < *imagin-* 'likeness'.] —**imagined** *adj* —**imaginer** *n* —**imagining** *n*

~~**imaginery**~~ incorrect spelling of **imaginary**

imaging /ímmijing/ *n* **1** any technique, often computerized, used to obtain images of bodies or body parts for diagnosis, emergency rescue, or surveillance **2** the use of mental images to ease pain, alter the course of disease processes, or help in achieving a goal

imagism /ímmijizəm/ *n* a literary movement of early 20th-century US and English poets that sought to modernize poetic language by the use of ordinary language, free verse, and precise everyday imagery —**imagist** *n* —**imagistic** /ímmi jístik/ *adj* —**imagistically** *adv*

QUICK FACTS ON... **IMAGISM**

Key dates: 1909–17
Key locations: United States and England
Key elements: succinct verse; objectivism; precise visual images; colloquial language; free verse; wide-ranging subject matter
Key figures: Ezra Pound, Amy Lowell, Hilda Doolittle, Richard Aldington, F. S. Flint, D. H. Lawrence, T. E. Hulme
Key works: *Three Poems* (Doolittle) 1913, *Imagisme* (Flint) 1913, *Des Imagistes: An Anthology* 1914, *Men, Women, and Ghosts* (Lowell) 1916
Key developments: encouraged clarity and objectivism in poetry; modernism

imago /i máy gō, i maa gō/ (*plural* **-goes** *or* **-gines** /i májjə neez/) *n* **1** an insect in its sexually mature adult state **2** in psychoanalysis, an unconscious idealized mental picture, especially of a parent, that is formed early in life and retained in adulthood [Late 18C. < Latin 'likeness'.]

imam /i maam, i mám/ *n* **1 LEADER OF MOSQUE PRAYERS** a man who leads the prayers in a mosque **2 imam, Imam RELIGIOUS LEADER DESCENDED FROM MUHAMMAD** an Islamic religious leader regarded as a direct descendant of Muhammad or Ali and appointed by Allah **3 ISLAMIC COMMUNITY LEADER** a leader of an Islamic community **4 ISLAMIC SCHOLAR** a respected Islamic scholar, especially a founder of a school of theology or law [Early 17C. < Arabic *'imām* 'leader'.]

imamate /i maa mayt/ *n* **1** the title or position of an imam, or the period somebody spends as an imam **2** the area for which an imam is leader

IMarE *abbr* Institute of Marine Engineers

imaret /i maa ret/ *n* a place providing food and shelter for travellers and pilgrims in Turkey [Early 17C. Via Turkish < Arabic *'imāra* 'building'.]

Imari /i maari/ *n* a Japanese porcelain that is brightly decorated, especially with a floral design [Late 19C. After the port of *Imari* in Kyushu, Japan.]

IMAX /ī maks/ *tdmk* a trademark for a giant-screen, large-format film and motion-simulation entertainment complex, with a motion-picture screen that is ten times larger than a conventional screen and compatible with 3-D technology

imbalance /im bálləns/ *n* **1** an unevenness, inequality, or bias existing between two or more people or things, especially in their degree of emphasis, proportions, or function **2** a lack of harmony or an inability to function well or harmoniously, or something causing this state ○ *a hormonal imbalance* —**imbalanced** *adj*

imbecile /ímbə seel, ímbə sīl/ *n* **1** an offensive term that deliberately insults somebody's level of intellect (*insult*) **2** an offensive term in a now disused classification system for an IQ between 25 and 50 and a mental age of between three and seven years (*dated*) [15C. Via French < Latin *imbecillus* 'without support' < *baculum* 'stick, staff'.] —**imbecilic** /ímbə síllik/ *adj* —**imbecility** *n*

imbed /im béd/ *vt* = **embed**

imbibe /im bíb/ (**-bibes, -bibing, -bibed**) *v* **1** *vti* **DRINK** to drink something, especially alcohol (*formal or humorous*) **2** *vt* **TAKE IN MENTALLY** to take in and assimilate something such as an idea or experience (*literary*) **3** *vti* **ABSORB** to absorb moisture, gas, light, or heat (*formal*) [14C. < Latin *imbibere* 'drink in' < *bibere* 'to drink'.] —**imbiber** *n*

imbibition /ìm bi bísh'n/ *n* the absorption or adsorption of, e.g. liquid or heat, by a mixture (**colloid**) such as a gel [15C. < medieval Latin *imbibition-* 'absorption' < Latin *imbibere* (see IMBIBE).] —**imbibitional** *adj*

imbricate *adj* /ímbrikət, -kayt/ **1 CONSISTING OF OVERLAPPING TILES** consisting of overlapping tiles or slates **2 OVERLAPPING LIKE ROOF TILES** describes plant or animal parts that overlap in a regular pattern ■ *vti* /ímbrikayt/ (**-cates, -cating, -cated**) **OVERLAP OR BE OVERLAPPING** to lay things so that they overlap in layers, or to be overlapping in layers, in a similar way to roof tiles [Mid-17C. < Latin *imbricare* 'cover with pantiles' < *imbric-* 'roof-tile' < *imber* 'rain'.] —**imbricated** *adj* —**imbrication** /ìmbri káysh'n/ *n*

imbroglio /im bróli ō/ (*plural* **-glios**) *n* a confusing, messy, or complicated situation, especially one that involves disagreement or intrigue [Mid-18C. < Italian, < *brogliare* 'mix up', probably < Old French *brōoillier*.]

imbrue /im bróo/ (**-brues, -bruing, -brued**) *vt* to stain something, especially with blood (*archaic or literary*) [Early 16C. < Old French *embruer* 'to soil, spatter'.] —**imbruement** *n*

imbue /im byóo/ (**-bues, -buing, -bued**) *vt* **1** to make a thing or person rich with a particular quality (*usually passive*) ○ *a poem imbued with a strong sense of patriotism* **2** to saturate something with a substance, especially dye (*formal*) [Late 16C. < Latin *imbuere* 'moisten, stain'.]

IMCO *abbr* Intergovernmental Maritime Consultative Organization

ϟ **IME** *abbr* in my experience (*in e-mails*)

IMechE *abbr* Institution of Mechanical Engineers

~~**imediately**~~ incorrect spelling of **immediately**

IMF *abbr* International Monetary Fund

ϟ **IMHO** *abbr* in my humble opinion (*in e-mails*)

imidazole /ìmmi dázzōl, i míddəzōl/ *n* $C_3H_4N_2$ an organic white crystalline base that inhibits the action of histamine [Late 19C. < IMIDE + AZO- + -OLE.]

imide /ímmīd/ *n* any organic compound containing an NH group combined with an acid group and derived from ammonia [Mid-19C. < French, alteration of *amide* (see AMIDE).] —**imidic** /i míddik/ *adj*

imine /ímmeen, i méen/ *n* any organic compound containing an NH group combined with a nonacid group and derived from ammonia [Late 19C. Alteration of AMINE.]

IMinE *abbr* Institution of Mining Engineers

imipramine /i míppra meen/ *n* a tricyclic drug. Use: treatment of depression. [Mid-20C. Blend of IMINE, PROPYL, + AMINE.]

imit. *abbr* **1** imitation **2** imitative

imitate /ímmi tayt/ (**-tates, -tating, -tated**) *vt* **1 FOLLOW SOMEBODY'S EXAMPLE** to use somebody or something as a model, attempting to copy an existing method, style, or approach **2 MIMIC** to copy somebody else's behaviour, voice, or manner, often with humorous intent **3 BE OR LOOK LIKE** to be or look like something else ○ *a case of life imitating art* [Mid-16C. < Latin *imitari*.] —**imitability** /ìmmitə bílləti/ *n* —**imitable** *adj* —**imitator** *n*

SYNONYMS ***imitate, copy, emulate, mimic, take off, ape***

CORE MEANING: to adopt the behaviour of another person

imitate to copy another's behaviour, voice, or manner, sometimes in order to make fun of him or her; **copy** to do exactly what somebody else does; **emulate** to try to equal or surpass somebody else who is successful or admired; **mimic** to imitate somebody in a deliberate and exaggerated way, especially to amuse people; **take off** (*informal*) to imitate somebody to amuse people; **ape** to imitate somebody in an absurd or grotesque way.

imitation /ìmmi táysh'n/ *n* **1 ACT OF IMITATING** the act or an instance of imitating somebody or something **2 COPY OR FAKE** something made to be as much as possible like something else (*often before nouns*) ○ *imitation leather* **3 IMPRESSION OF SOMEBODY** the act of mimicking somebody, or an impression of somebody **4 REPETITION OF MUSICAL MOTIF** the repetition of a musical idea such as a melody or rhythmic figure in another part, often at another pitch and sometimes with variation ■ *adj* **NOT GENUINE** synthetic, intended as a copy of something, or not genuine —**imitational** *adj*

imitative /ímmitətiv/ *adj* **1** designed to be like something else, but usually inferior to the original **2** involving or practising imitation **3** = **onomatopoeic** —**imitatively** *adv* —**imitativeness** *n*

IMM *n, abbr* **1** International Mercantile Marine **2** International Monetary Market

immaculate /i mákyoolət/ *adj* **1** absolutely clean, tidy, and free from blemishes **2** showing faultless perfection [15C. < Latin *immaculatus* 'without stain' < *macula* 'blemish'.] —**immaculacy** *n* —**immaculately** *adv* —**immaculateness** *n*

Immaculate Conception *n* **1** the Roman Catholic doctrine that the Virgin Mary's soul was free from the stain of original sin from the moment of her soul's conception **2** the feast of the Immaculate Conception, celebrated in the Roman Catholic Church. Date: 8 December.

immanent /ímmənənt/ *adj* **1** existing within or inherent in something (*formal*) **2** existing in, and extending into, all parts of the created world [Mid-16C. < late Latin *immanere* 'dwell within' < Latin *manere* 'remain, dwell'.] —**immanence** *n* —**immanency** *n* —**immanently** *adv*

SPELLCHECK Do not confuse ***immanent*** with ***imminent***, which has a similar sound. Beware: your spellchecker will not catch this error.

immanentism /ímmənəntizəm/ *n* the belief that God exists in, and extends into all of, the created universe, including the individual —**immanentist** *adj, n* —**immanentistic** /ìmmənən tístik/ *adj*

Immanuel /i mánnyoo əl/, **Emmanuel** *n* the Messiah, referred to in Jewish and Christian scriptures, whom Christians believe to be Jesus Christ [15C. Via late Latin < Greek *Emmanouēl* < Hebrew *'immānū'ēl* 'with us is God'.]

immaterial /ìmmə téeri əl/ *adj* **1** lacking relevance or importance **2** not made of matter or not physically real —**immateriality** /ìmmə téeri álləti/ *n* —**immaterially** *adv* —**immaterialness** *n*

immaterialise *vt* = **immaterialize**

immaterialism /ìmmə téeri əlizzəm/ *n* a metaphysical doctrine holding that the material world does not exist except as ideas or perceptions in the mind, or that only spirits and nonphysical things exist

immaterialize /ìmmə téeri ə līz/ (**-izes, -izing, -ized**), **immaterialise** (**-ising, -ising, -ised**) *vt* to take away the physical substance of something and make it spiritual or intangible —**immaterialization** /ìmmə téeri ə lī záysh'n/ *n*

immature /ìmmə tyóor, ìmmə chóor/ *adj* **1 NOT FULLY DEVELOPED** young, and not fully grown or developed **2 CHILDISH** lacking the wisdom or emotional development normally associated with adults **3 STYLISTICALLY CRUDE AND IMPERFECT** not yet having attained the perfection of a later, or fully developed, style ○ *an example of the artist's immature period* —**immaturely** *adv* —**immatureness** *n* —**immaturity** *n*

immeasurable /i mézhərəb'l/ *adj* too large or too much to be measured —**immeasurability** /i mézhərə bílləti/ *n* —**immeasurableness** *n* —**immeasurably** *adv*

immediate /i méedi ət/ *adj* **1 WITHOUT PAUSE OR DELAY** happening or done at first, at once, or without delay ○ *the problem requires immediate attention* **2 NEAREST** nearest in time, space, or relationship ○ *only my immediate family were invited* **3 CURRENT** urgent or pressing, and so needing to be dealt with before anything else **4 HAVING DIRECT EFFECT** affecting something directly, without anything intervening **5 KNOWN FROM EXPERIENCE** relating to something that is known about from personal experience or by intuition **6 DERIVED FROM SINGLE PREMISE** describes an inference derived from a single premise, without any middle term, and often by conversion of a categorical statement [14C. Directly or via French < late Latin *immediatus* 'not separated' < Latin *mediatus*, past participle of *mediare* (see MEDIATE).] —**immediacy** *n* —**immediateness** *n*

immediate annuity *n* an annuity whose payments begin less than one year after it is bought

immediate constituent *n* the first level into which a linguistic unit is analysed, e.g. the subject and predicate as parts of a sentence

immediately /i méedi ətli/ *adv* **1 AT ONCE** without delay or without pausing beforehand **2 VERY CLOSELY** very closely in space or time **3 DIRECTLY** directly, and without anyone or anything in between ■ *conj* **AS SOON AS** as soon as or at the moment that

immemorial /ìmmi máwri əl/ *adj* so old that it seems always to have existed ○ *have known them since time immemorial* ○ *immemorial customs of the nation* —**immemorially** *adv*

immense /i ménss/ *adj* **1 HUGE** very large in extent or degree ○ *an immense desert* ○ *immense relief* **2 UNABLE TO BE MEASURED** too large to be measurable **3 EXCELLENT** very good or showing excellence (*informal*) [15C. Via French < Latin *immensus* 'not measured' < *mensus*, past participle of *metiri* (see MEASURE).] —**immenseness** *n* —**immensity** *n*

immensely /i ménsli/ *adv* to a very great extent or degree ○ *she was immensely rich*

immerse /i múrss/ (**-merses, -mersing, -mersed**) *v* **1 COMPLETELY COVER SOMETHING IN LIQUID** to put something into a liquid so that the liquid's surface covers it completely **2** *vr* **OCCUPY YOURSELF TOTALLY** to become completely occupied with something, giving all your time, energy, or concentration to it ○ *immersed herself in her work* **3** *vt* **BAPTIZE** to baptize somebody, especially in the Baptist Church, by lowering the person's head and upper body, or sometimes the whole body, into water [Early 17C. < Latin *immers-*, past participle of *immergere* 'plunge into' < *mergere* 'plunge'.]

immerser /i múrssər/ *n* an immersion heater (*informal*)

immersion /i múrsh'n/ *n* **1 COMPLETE INVOLVEMENT** involvement in something that completely occupies all the time, energy, or concentration available **2 INTENSIVE LANGUAGE TEACHING** an intensive method of teaching somebody a language, in which all teaching is carried out in the language that is being learned ○ *an immersion course in Gaelic* **3 PLACING OF SOMETHING UNDER LIQUID** the dipping of something into a liquid so that it is completely covered **4 BAPTISM BY DIPPING BODY IN WATER** the practice, especially in the Baptist Church, of baptism by lowering somebody's head and upper body, or sometimes the whole body, into water **5 DISAPPEARANCE OF AN ASTRONOMICAL OBJECT BEFORE AN ECLIPSE** the movement of an astronomical object, such as the Moon, into the shadow of another object, causing an eclipse

immersion heater *n* an electric water heater with the heating element completely submerged in the water, especially one that is part of a domestic hot-water tank

immersionism /i múrsh'nizəm/ *n* the belief that immersion is the only true method of baptism

immesh /i mésh/ *vt* = **enmesh**

immigrant /ímmigrənt/ *n* **1 SOMEBODY SETTLING IN COUNTRY** a newcomer to a country who has settled there **2 PLANT OR ANIMAL IN NEW PLACE** a plant or animal that establishes itself in a place where it was not found before ■ *adj* **SETTLING IN ANOTHER COUNTRY** relating to those who have come to settle in another country

immigrate /ímmi grayt/ (**-grates, -grating, -grated**) *vi* **1** to enter a new country for the purpose of settling there **2** to become established in a new environment —**immigrator** *n* —**immigratory** *adj*

immigration /ìmmi gráysh'n/ *n* **1 ARRIVAL OF SETTLERS IN A NEW COUNTRY** the act of people entering into a new country to settle permanently **2 PASSPORT CONTROL** the control point at an airport, seaport, or border crossing where people entering a country must stop to have their passports officially checked **3 Immigration** *US* **INS** the United States Immigration and Naturalization Service (**INS**) (*informal*) —**immigrational** *adj*

imminent /ímminənt/ *adj* about to happen or threatening to happen [Early 16C. < Latin *imminere* 'hang over' < *minere* 'to project'.] —**imminence** *n* —**imminently** *adv* —**imminentness** *n*

SPELLCHECK See ***immanent***.

immiscible /i míssəb'l/ *adj* describes two or more liquids that will not mix together to form a single homogeneous substance [Late 17C. < late Latin *immiscibilis* 'not subject to mixing' < Latin *miscere* 'to mix'.] —**immiscibility** /i míssə bíllati/ *n* —**immiscibly** /i míssə bíllati/ *adv*

immitigable /i míttigab'l/ *adj* incapable of being alleviated, weakened, or softened (*formal*) —**immitigability** /i míttigə bíllati/ *n* —**immitigableness** *n* —**immitigably** *adv*

immittance /i mítt'nss/ *n* the joint concept of electrical admittance and impedance [Mid-20C. Blend of IMPEDANCE + ADMITTANCE.]

immobile /i mố bĩl/ *adj* **1** without moving ○ *he stood perfectly immobile for a few seconds* **2** unable to move or be moved —**immobility** /immố bíllati/ *n*

immobilise *vt* = immobilize

immobiliser *n* AUTOMOT = immobilizer

immobilize /i mốbi līz/ (**-lizes, -lizing, -lized**), **immobilise** (**-lises, -lising, -lised**) *vt* **1** MAKE MOTIONLESS to make somebody or something completely still (*often passive*) **2** PUT MACHINE OUT OF ACTION to make a machine or device stop working or adjust or damage it so that it cannot be made to work **3** KEEP BROKEN LIMB STILL to rest a joint or keep the parts of a fractured limb fixed in place so that they are unable to move **4** TAKE OUT OF CIRCULATION to withdraw money or other capital from circulation to establish a reserve —**immobilization** /i mốbi līzáysh'n/ *n*

immobilizer /i mốbi līzar/, **immobiliser** *n* an electronic security device, fitted to a motor vehicle, that stops the engine from working and prevents the vehicle from being stolen

immoderate /i móddarat/ *adj* going beyond what is healthy, moral, appropriate, or socially acceptable —**immoderacy** *n* —**immoderately** *adv* —**immoderateness** *n* —**immoderation** /i móddə ráysh'n/ *n*

immodest /i móddist/ *adj* **1** boasting, or tending to boast **2** likely to embarrass, offend, or shock people, especially because of open references to sexual matters or exposure of parts of the body that are normally covered —**immodestly** *adv* —**immodesty** *n*

immolate /immə layt/ (**-lates, -lating, -lated**) *vt* (*literary*) **1** to kill a person or an animal, e.g. as a ritual sacrifice, or to commit suicide as a protest, especially by burning **2** to give up something that is highly valued [Mid-16C. < Latin *immolare* 'sprinkle with meal' < *mola* 'meal, millstone'; from the custom of sprinkling sacrificial victims with meal.] —**immolation** /immə láysh'n/ *n* —**immolator** *n*

immoral /i mórral/ *adj* contrary to accepted moral principles —**immorality** /ímmə rállati/ *n* —**immorally** *adv*

immoralist /i mórralist/ *n* a person who behaves immorally or who urges others to behave so

immortal /i máwrt'l/ *adj* **1** NEVER DYING able to have eternal life or existence **2** FAMOUS very famous and likely to be remembered for a long time ■ *n* **1** FAMOUS PERSON OR THING somebody or something so famous as to be recalled for a long time (*often plural*) **2** immortal, Immortal A GOD a god who lives forever, especially a god of ancient Greece or Rome —**immortality** /ímmawr tállati/ *n* —**immortally** *adv*

immortalise *vt* = immortalize

immortalize /i máwrt'l īz/ (**-izes, -izing, -ized**), **immortalise** (**-ises, -ising, -ised**) *vt* **1** MAKE SOMEBODY'S MEMORY LIVE ON to make somebody or something famous for a very long time, especially as the subject of a work of art such as a painting, novel, or film **2** GIVE ETERNAL LIFE TO to elevate a mortal person to the state of divinity or bestow eternal life on somebody **3** CAUSE TO REPRODUCE INDEFINITELY to cause something such as human cells to reproduce indefinitely —**immortalization** /i máwrt'l ĭ záysh'n/ *n*

immortelle /ímmawr tél/ *n* PLANTS = everlasting *n*. **2** [Mid-19C. < French, shortening of *fleur immortelle* 'undying flower'.]

immotile /i mố tĩl/ *adj* describes a plant or animal part that cannot move —**immotility** /immố tíllati/ *n*

immovable /i moóvəb'l/, **immoveable** *adj* **1** UNABLE TO BE MOVED fixed in a permanent position **2** OF FIXED OPINION sticking firmly to an opinion or decision **3** ALWAYS OCCURRING ON THE SAME DATE describes a religious festival that always falls on the same date each year, like, e.g., Christmas, but unlike Easter ■ *n* immovable, immoveable BUILDINGS OR LAND property that consists of land

or buildings (*often plural*) —**immovability** /i moóva bíllati/ *n* —**immovableness** *n* —**immovably** *adv*

immun. *abbr* **1** immunity **2** immunization **3** immunology

immune /i myoón/ *adj* **1** SAFE FROM PARTICULAR DISEASE protected from getting a particular disease because of natural resistance, resistance acquired after catching the disease, or resistance conferred by inoculation ○ *immune to smallpox* **2** RELATING TO DISEASE RESISTANCE relating to a body's resistance to disease or the creation of this resistance **3** NOT SUBJECT TO OR RESPONSIBLE FOR exempt from something that others are subject to or made to endure or perform ○ *immune from prosecution* **4** NOT AFFECTED not sensitive or susceptible to something ○ *immune to flattery* [Late 19C. < Latin *immunis* 'exempt from public service' < *munis* 'ready for service'.]

immune complex, **immunocomplex** /ímmyoónō kómpleks/ *n* a combination of a disease-causing agent (**antigen**) and its corresponding antibody that plays a role in some types of immune responses and may be associated with autoimmune disease

immune response *n* **1** the overall activity of the body's immune system following the arrival of a disease-causing agent (**antigen**) **2** the integrated defence mounted by an organism against a disease-causing agent (**antigen**), including the production of antibodies and white blood cells designed to destroy the antigen or render it harmless

immune system *n* the interacting combination of all the body's ways of recognizing cells, tissues, objects, and organisms that are not part of itself, and initiating the immune response to fight them

immunise *vt* = immunize

immunity /i myoónəti/ (*plural* **-ties**) *n* **1** a body's ability to resist a particular disease, whether existing naturally or as a result of inoculation or previous infection (**acquired immunity**) ○ *immunity to smallpox* **2** exemption or protection from something unpleasant, such as a duty or penalty, to which others are subject ○ *immunity from prosecution*

immunize /ímmyoó nīz/ (**-nizes, -nizing, -nized**), **immunise** (**-nises, -nising, -nised**) *vt* **1** to make somebody resistant to a particular disease, especially by inoculation ○ *immunized against tuberculosis* **2** give somebody exemption or protection from something to which others are subject, especially in a criminal matter under investigation —**immunization** /ímmyoó nī záysh'n/ *n* —**immunizer** *n*

immuno- *prefix* immune, immunity ○ *immunodeficiency* [< IMMUNE]

immunoassay /ímmyoónō ássay/ *n* a technique for measuring the amount of antigens and antibodies in tissue —**immunoassayist** *n*

immunochemistry /ímmyoónō kémmistri/ *n* the technique for revealing proteins in cells —**immunochemical** *adj*

immunocompetence /ímmyoónō kómpitənss/ *n* the ability of the body to develop an immune response in the presence of a disease-causing agent (**antigen**) —**immunocompetent** *adj*

immunocomplex /ímmyoónō/ IMMUNOL = immune complex

immunocompromised /ímmyoónō kómprə mīzd/ *adj* lacking an adequate immune response as a result of disease, exposure to radiation, or treatment with immunosuppressive drugs

immunodeficiency /ímmyoónō di físh'nssi/ (*plural* **-cies**) *n* the inability, either inborn or acquired, of the body to produce an adequate immune response to fight disease —**immunodeficient** *adj*

immunodepression /ímmyoónō di présh'n/ *n* = immunosuppression

immunodiagnosis /ímmyoónō dĩ ag nốssiss/ (*plural* **-noses** /-seez/) *n* the diagnosis of disease by studying the antibodies in a sample of blood serum —**immunodiagnostic** /-nóstik/ *adj*

immunoelectrophoresis /ímmyoónō i léktrō fə reёssiss/ *n* separation of mixtures of antigens and their measurement with specific antibodies —**immunoelectrophoretic** /-fə réttik/ *adj* —**immunoelectrophoretically** *adv*

immunofluorescence /ímmyoónō floor réss'nss/ *n* the labelling of antibodies or disease-causing agents (**antigens**) with a fluorescent dye in order to identify

or locate them in a tissue sample —**immunofluorescent** *adj*

immunogen /i myoónōjən/ *n* a substance that can prompt a response from the immune system

immunogenetics /ímmyoónō jə néttiks/ *n* the discipline that studies the genetic basis of the immune system (+ *singular verb*) —**immunogenetic** *adj* —**immunogeneticist** /-jə néttisist/ *n*

immunogenic /ímmyoónō jénnik/ *adj* creating immunity or an immune response —**immunogenically** *adv* —**immunogenicity** /-jə níssəti/ *n*

immunoglobulin /ímmyoónō glóbbyoólin/ *n* any of a group of antibodies formed by cells of the immune system and present in the blood

immunohaematology /ímmyoónō heёmə tólləji/ *n* the discipline concerned with all aspects of immunology relating to the blood, including blood groups and blood disorders —**immunohaematologic** /-heёmətə lójjik/ *adj* —**immunohaematological** *adj*

immunohematology /ímmyoónō heёmə tólləji/ *n* US = immunohaematology

immunology /ímmyoó nólləji/ *n* the scientific study of the way the immune system works in the body, including allergies, resistance to disease, and acceptance or rejection of foreign tissue —**immunologic** /ímmyoónə lójjik/ *adj* —**immunological** *adj* —**immunologically** *adv* —**immunologist** *n*

immunomodulation /ímmyoónō móddyoō láysh'n/ *n* the modification of some aspect of the immune system as part of a treatment, especially the suppression of the immune system in order to encourage the body to accept a transplanted organ —**immunomodulatory** /ímmyoónō móddyoōláţari, -móddyoō láytari/ *adj*

immunopathology /ímmyoónōpə thólləji/ *n* the study of disorders of the immune system and the resulting diseases or allergies —**immunopathologic** /-páthə lójjik/ *adj* —**immunopathological** *adj* —**immunopathologist** *n*

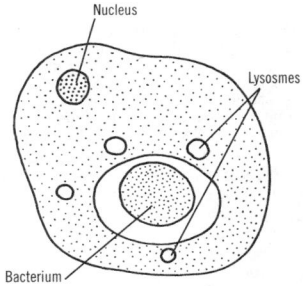

Immunoreaction: Section of immune cell ingesting and degrading disease-causing bacterium

immunoreaction /i myoónō ri áksh'n/ *n* the reaction between a disease-causing agent (**antigen**) and its specific antibody —**immunoreactive** *adj* —**immunoreactivity** /i myoónō ri ak tívvəti/ *n*

immunosuppression /ímmyoónō sə présh'n/ *n* the inhibition of the immune response, usually deliberately by administering drugs to prevent rejection of transplanted organs, but sometimes resulting from disease, as in the case of AIDS —**immunosuppressant** *adj, n* —**immunosuppressive** *adj, n*

immunotherapy /ímmyoónō thérrapi/ *n* treatment of disease or other disorders by strengthening the body's immune system, e.g. by administering antibodies —**immunotherapeutic** /-thérrə pyoótik/ *adj*

immure /i myoór/ (**-mures, -muring, -mured**) *vt* **1** to confine somebody in prison (*literary; usually passive*) **2** to shut away or seclude somebody (*formal; often passive*) [Late 16C. Directly or via French *emmurer* < Latin *immurare* 'wall in' < *murus* 'wall'.] —**immurement** *n*

immutable /i myoótəb'l/ *adj* not changing or not able to be changed —**immutability** /i myoótə bíllati/ *n* —**immutableness** *n* —**immutably** *adv*

✦**IMO** *abbr* **1** International Meteorological Organization

2 International Miners' Organization **3** in my opinion (*in e-mails*)

imp /imp/ *n* **1 NAUGHTY FAIRY** in children's stories, a small mischievous creature resembling a fairy **2 MISCHIEVOUS CHILD** a high-spirited or mischievous child **3 DEMON** a small demon or devil ■ *vt* **REPAIR A HAWK'S FEATHERS** to repair the broken wing of a hawk or falcon by grafting on new feathers [Old English *impa* 'young shoot, scion', *impian* 'to graft' < Greek *emphuein* 'implant' < *phuein* 'grow']

ϟ**IMP** *abbr* **1** interface message processor **2** International Match Point

imp. *abbr* **1** imperative **2** imperfect **3 imp., IMP.** imperial **4** impersonal **5** import **6** important **7** imported **8** importer **9** imprimatur

Imp. *abbr* **1** Imperator **2** Imperatrix

impact *n* /ím pakt/ **1 ACTION OF HITTING** the action of one object hitting another **2 FORCE OF COLLISION** the force with which one object hits another **3 STRONG EFFECT** the powerful or dramatic effect that something or somebody has. ■ *vti* /im pákt/ **1 STRIKE** to strike something with force **2** ⚠ **HAVE AN EFFECT ON** to have an immediate and strong effect on something or somebody. [Early 17C. < Latin *impactus*, past participle of *impingere* (see IMPINGE).] —**impaction** /im páksh'n/ *n*

USAGE Impact, noun and verb: The noun ***impact***, in its figurative meaning, should normally convey some sense of powerful or dramatic consequence, and should not just be an alternative word for *effect* or *impression*. To use it in a context like *He had an impact on everyone in the room* – except in highly unusual circumstances – is to devalue the word. Many careful users of the language dislike the verb ***impact*** in any figurative sense, regardless of whether the verb is followed by *on*: *This impacts the company favourably* and *This impacts on the company.* The verb is undeniably common in business communication, but you can avoid it by using *affect*, *change*, or the like.

impact adhesive *n* a powerful glue that begins to form a bond as soon as the two coated surfaces are brought together

impacted /im páktid/ *adj* **1 WEDGED SIDEWAYS UNDER THE GUM** describes an unerupted tooth wedged sideways against a barrier, usually the root of another tooth, and thus unable to break through the gum **2 WITH BROKEN ENDS JAMMED TOGETHER** describes a bone fracture with the broken ends jammed tightly together by the initial trauma **3 DIFFICULT TO MOVE** unable to be moved, usually because of being jammed in a narrow space

impact printer *n* a printing device in which ink is pressed onto the paper by the printing element

impact statement *n* a written statement outlining the effects of something on a particular person or place ○ *a consumer impact statement*

impact zone *n* in surfing, the best and at the same time most dangerous position on a wave, where the water is about to separate into droplets

impair /im páir/ *vt* to lessen the quality, strength, or effectiveness of something [14C. < Old French *empeirier*, literally 'make worse' < Latin *pejor* 'worse'.] —**impairable** *adj* —**impairer** *n* —**impairment** *n*

impaired /im páird/ *adj* with something specified that is absent or lessened, either temporarily or permanently (*usually in combination*) ○ *hearing-impaired*

impala /im paálə/ (*plural* **-las** *or* **-la**) *n* a large reddish-brown antelope with long curved horns that makes spectacular leaps when alarmed. Native to: Africa. *Aepyceros melampus.* [Late 19C. < Zulu.]

impale /im páyl/ (**-pales, -paling, -paled**), **empale** (**-pales, -paling, -paled**) *vt* **1** to pierce somebody or something with a pointed object (*often passive*) **2** to combine two coats of arms on a single shield, divided by a vertical stripe (**pale**) [Mid-16C. Directly or via French *empaler* < medieval Latin *impalare* 'put on a stake' < Latin *palus* 'stake'.] —**impalement** *n* —**impaler** *n*

impalpable /im pálpəb'l/ *adj* (*formal*) **1** not capable of being perceived by the senses **2** difficult to understand or grasp [Early 16C. Directly or via French < late Latin *impalpabilis* 'not touchable' < *palpare* 'touch gently'.] —**impalpability** /im pálpə bíllәti/ *n* —**impalpably** *adv*

impanation /impə náysh'n/ *n* according to some denominations of Christianity, the presence of the body and blood of Jesus Christ in bread and wine that has been consecrated for the service of Communion [Mid-16C. < medieval Latin *impanare* 'embody in bread' < Latin *panis* 'bread'.]

impanel /im pánn'l/ (**-els, -elling, -elled**), **empanel** /em-/ (**-els, -elling, -elled**) *vt* **1** to draw up a list of people to be selected for jury service **2** to select a jury from a list of eligible persons [15C. < Anglo-Norman *empaneller* 'put on a list' < Old French *panel* 'list, jury list' (see PANEL).]

impart /im paárt/ *vt* **1** to communicate information or knowledge **2** to give something a particular quality [Mid-16C. Via Old French *impartir* < Latin *impartire* 'give a share in' < *pars* 'part'.] —**impartation** /ím paar táysh'n/ *n*

impartial /im paársh'l/ *adj* having no direct involvement or interest and not favouring one person or side more than another —**impartiality** /im paárshi állәti/ *n* —**impartially** *adv* —**impartialness** *n*

impartible /im paártəb'l/ *adj* not to be divided up [Late 16C. < late Latin *impartibilis* 'not divisible' < *partire* (see PART).] —**impartibility** /im paártə bíllәti/ *n* —**impartibly** *adv*

impassable /im paássəb'l/ *adj* **1** impossible to travel on or through, e.g. because of being in bad condition or being blocked by snow **2** impossible to solve or overcome ○ *impassable obstacles to peace* —**impassability** /im paássə bíllәti/ *n* —**impassableness** *n* —**impassably** *adv*

impasse /am paáss, ám paass, im paáss, ím paass/ *n* a point at which no further progress can be made or agreement reached ○ *Talks have reached an impasse.* [Mid-19C. < French, < *im-* 'not' + *passer* (see PASS).]

impassible /im pássəb'l/ *adj* **1** not susceptible to or not capable of feeling physical pain or injury (*formal*) **2** not capable of feeling or expressing emotion (*formal or literary*) [14C. Via French < ecclesiastical Latin *impassibilis* 'not feeling' < Latin *pass-*, past participle of *pati* 'suffer'.] —**impassibility** /im pássə bíllәti/ *n* —**impassibleness** *n* —**impassibly** *adv*

impassion /im pásh'n/ *vt* to arouse strong feelings in somebody (*usually passive*) ○ *a crowd that was impassioned by his oratory* [Late 16C. < Italian *impassionare* < *passione* 'passion' < late Latin *passion-* (see PASSION).] —**impassioned** *adj* —**impassionedly** *adv*

impassive /im pássiv/ *adj* **1** showing no emotion, especially on the face **2** feeling no emotions at all, either positive or negative [Early 17C. Literally 'without suffering or passion'.] —**impassively** *adv* —**impassiveness** *n* —**impassivity** /ímpə sívvәti/ *n*

SYNONYMS ***impassive, apathetic, phlegmatic, stolid, stoic, unmoved***

CORE MEANING: showing no emotional response or interest

impassive showing no outward sign of emotion, especially on the face; **apathetic** not taking any interest in anything, or not bothering to do anything; **phlegmatic** generally unemotional and difficult to arouse; **stolid** solemn, unemotional, and not easily excited or upset; **stoic** showing admirable patience and endurance in the face of adversity without complaining or getting upset; **unmoved** showing no emotion, surprise, or excitement when this would normally have been expected.

impasto /im pástō/ *n* **1** the technique of applying paint so thickly that brush or knife strokes can be seen **2** paint applied so thickly that brush or knife strokes can be seen [Late 18C. < Italian, past participle of *impastare* 'paint thickly, encrust'.]

impatiens /im páyshi enz, -pátti-/ (*plural* **-tiens**) *n* PLANTS = **Busy Lizzie** [Late 18C. Via modern Latin < Latin, 'impatient'; because its capsules tend to burst open when touched.]

impatient /im páysh'nt/ *adj* **1 ANNOYED AT WAITING** annoyed or tending to be annoyed at being kept waiting or by being delayed **2 EAGER** eager to do something immediately, and unwilling to wait **3 EASILY ANNOYED** unable to tolerate a particular thing and easily annoyed by it ○ *He was impatient of formalities.* —**impatience** *n* —**impatiently** *adv*

impeach /im peéch/ *vt* **1** *US* **ACCUSE OFFICIAL OF OFFENCE** in the United States, to charge a serving government official with serious misconduct while in office **2** *US* **CAST OUT OF PUBLIC OFFICE** to remove somebody, especially a president, from public office because of having committed high crimes and misdemeanours (*formal*) **3 ACCUSE OF SERIOUS CRIME** to accuse somebody of a crime, especially treason or another crime against the state **4 BRING CHARGES AGAINST** to charge somebody with a crime or misdemeanour **5 DISPARAGE** to question a person's good character (*formal*) [14C. Via Old French *empecher* < late Latin *impedicare* 'entangle' < *pedica* 'snare'.] —**impeachability** /im peechə bíllәti/ *n* —**impeachable** *adj* —**impeacher** *n* —**impeachment** *n*

impeccable /im pékəb'l/ *adj* **1** so perfect or flawless as to be beyond criticism ○ *she had impeccable taste* **2** so perfect in character as to be incapable of sinning [Mid-16C. < Latin *impeccabilis* 'not liable to sin' < *peccare* 'sin'.] —**impeccability** /im pékə bíllәti/ *n* —**impeccably** *adv*

impecunious /ímpi kyoóni əss/ *adj* having little or no money, and so unable to lead a comfortable life [Late 16C. < obsolete *pecunious* 'wealthy' < Latin *pecunia* (see PECUNIARY).] —**impecuniosity** /ímpi kyoóni óssәti/ *n* —**impecuniously** *adv* —**impecuniousness** *n*

impedance /im peéd'nss/ *n* **1 PREVENTION OF PROGRESS** something that delays or prevents progress (*formal*) **2 OPPOSITION TO FLOW OF ALTERNATING CURRENT** (*symbol* Z) the opposition in a circuit to the flow of alternating current, consisting of resistance and reactance **3 RATIO OF SOUND PRESSURE TO VELOCITY** the ratio of the sound pressure in a medium to the velocity of the particles in the medium. ◊ **immittance**

impede /im peéd/ (**-pedes, -peding, -peded**) *vt* to interfere with the movement, progress, or development of something or somebody [Late 16C. < Latin *impedire* 'shackle the feet' < *ped-* 'foot'.] —**impeder** *n*

SYNONYMS See ***hinder.***

impediment /im péddimənt/ *n* **1 IMPAIRMENT** an impairment, especially one affecting speech **2 OBSTACLE** something that hinders progress in some way **3** (*plural* **-ments** *or* **-menta**) **LEGAL OBSTRUCTION** the reason a legal contract, e.g. a marriage, cannot be entered into [14C. < Latin *impedimentum* 'hindrance' < *impedire* (see IMPEDE).] —**impedimental** /im péddi mént'l/ *adj* —**impedimentary** /-méntәri/ *adj*

impedimenta /im péddi méntə/ *npl* **1** obstacles, hindrances, or obstructions to progress (*literary*) **2** equipment and baggage carried by soldiers (*formal*) **3** plural of **impediment** *n.* **3** [Early 17C. < Latin, plural of *impedimentum* (see IMPEDIMENT).]

impedor /im peédər/ *n* any circuit component that has impedance [< IMPEDANCE]

impel /im pél/ (**-pels, -pelling, -pelled**) *vt* **1** to force or make somebody feel the need to do something (*usually passive*) ○ *I felt impelled to protest* **2** to start or keep something or somebody moving in a particular direction (*formal*) [15C. < Latin *impellere* 'drive towards' < *pellere* 'to beat'.]

impeller /im péllər/ *n* the rotating part that transmits motion in a centrifugal pump, turbine, or blower

impend /im pénd/ *vi* **1** to be threateningly close to happening (*formal*) **2** to hover or hang above something, usually in a threatening way (*literary*) [Late 16C. < Latin *impendere* 'hang over' < *pendere* 'to hang'.] —**impendence** *n* —**impendency** *n* —**impendent** *adj*

impending /im pénding/ *adj* about to happen

impenetrable /im pénnitrəb'l/ *adj* **1 IMPOSSIBLE TO GET IN OR THROUGH** not able to be passed through or entered ○ *The woods formed an impenetrable barrier.* **2 INCOMPREHENSIBLE** impossible to understand or discern ○ *impenetrable legal jargon* **3 CLOSED TO INFLUENCE** not open to intellectual or moral influences, impressions, or ideas —**impenetrability** /im pénnitrə bíllәti/ *n* —**impenetrably** *adv*

impenitent /im pénnit'nt/ *adj* having or showing no regret or sorrow for sin or misbehaviour ■ *n* an unrepentant person —**impenitence** *n* —**impenitency** *n* —**impenitently** *adv*

imperative /im pérrətiv/ *adj* **1 NECESSARY** absolutely necessary or unavoidable ○ *It is imperative that justice is seen to be done.* **2 COMMANDING** forceful and demanding the obedience and respect of others (*formal*) **3 USED FOR GIVING ORDERS** describes the mood of a verb that expresses a command or request, e.g. the verb form 'come' in 'Come here!' ■ *n* **1 PRIORITY** something that must be done ○ *The general's imperative was to conquer or die.* **2 WAY OF COMMANDING** the form of a verb used to give an order **3 VERB EXPRESSING COMMAND OR REQUEST** a verb in the imperative mood, such as 'close' in 'Please close the door' [15C. < late Latin *imperativus* 'specially ordered' < Latin *imperare* 'to command' < *parare* 'prepare'.] —**imperatively** *adv* —**imperativeness** *n*

imperator /impə raá tawr/ *n* **1 ROMAN GENERAL** a victorious military commander during the time of the Roman Republic **2 ROMAN EMPEROR** the head of state of the Roman

Empire **3 ABSOLUTE RULER** an absolute ruler or commander [Mid-16C. < Latin, 'commander' < *imperare* (see IMPERATIVE).] —**imperatorial** /im pérrə táwri əl/ *adj*

imperceptible /ímpər séptəb'l/ *adj* very slight or gradual ○ *an imperceptible touch of the hand* —**imperceptibility** /ímpər séptə bílləti/ *n* —**imperceptibly** *adv*

imperceptive /ímpər séptiv/ *adj* lacking the ability to notice things or to understand somebody or something —**imperceptively** *adv* —**imperceptiveness** *n* —**imperceptivity** /ímpər sep tívvəti/ *n*

impercipience /ímpər síppi ənss/ *n* a lack of perception (*formal*) ○ *the impercipience of the egotist* —**impercipient** *adj*

imperf. *abbr* **1** imperfect **2** imperforate

imperfect /im púrfikt/ *adj* **1 FAULTY** having a fault or defect **2 NOT COMPLETE** lacking a part **3 NOT ABLE TO REPRODUCE** describes a flower that lacks either a stamen or a pistil and is therefore unable to reproduce **4 NOT PERFECT** describes a musical interval other than the fourth, fifth, or octave **5 ENDING ON 5TH NOTE OF SCALE** describes a cadence ending on the 5th note of the scale (**dominant**) rather than on the first note (**tonic**) **6 EXPRESSING INCOMPLETE ACTION** describes a verb or tense that expresses past action going on but not completed **7 UNENFORCEABLE** unable to be enforced ■ *n* **1 VERB TENSE** a grammatical tense used for expressing incomplete or habitual action in the past **2 VERB FORM** a form of a verb used to express the imperfect tense —**imperfectly** *adv* —**imperfectness** *n*

imperfect fungus *n* a fungus that forms only asexual spores (**conidia**). Order: Fungi Imperfecti.

imperfection /ímpər féksh'n/ *n* **1** something that makes a person or thing less than perfect **2** the possession of faults or defects

SYNONYMS See *flaw*.

imperfective /ímpər féktiv/ *adj* **INDICATING INCOMPLETE ACTION** describes a verb aspect expressing action that is not completed. ◊ **perfective** ■ *n* **1 VERB ASPECT** the imperfective aspect of the verb **2 VERB FORM** a verb form belonging to the imperfective aspect —**imperfectively** *adv*

imperforate /im púrfərit/ *adj* **1 WITHOUT AN OPENING** with no perforation or opening **2 PARTIALLY OR COMPLETELY CLOSED** lacking an opening of the normal size, especially because of abnormal development **3 WITH NO HOLES** produced without the perforations that allow easy tearing or division ■ *n* **STAMP WITHOUT PERFORATIONS** a stamp without perforations around it —**imperforation** /im púrfə ráysh'n/ *n*

imperia plural of **imperium**

imperial /im péeri əl/ *adj* **1 BELONGING TO EMPIRE OR EMPEROR** concerning or involving an empire or its ruler **2 INDICATING COUNTRY'S AUTHORITY** involving or relating to the authority of a country over colonies or other countries **3 SUPREMELY POWERFUL** holding supreme power ○ *All are subject to the imperial power of the state.* **4 GRAND** very grand or majestic **5 SUPERIOR** better in quality or larger in size **6 OF UK NONMETRIC MEASURES** belonging or conforming to the nonmetric system of weights and measures legally established in the United Kingdom that includes the foot, pound, and gallon ■ *n* **1 PAPER SIZE** the largest of the traditional US and UK paper sizes **2 RELATIVE OF EMPEROR OR EMPRESS** somebody belonging to an imperial family (*formal*) **3 SMALL BEARD** a tuft or point of hair grown on the chin or below the lower lip **4 TRUNK FOR LUGGAGE** a chest fitted into the top of a coach to store travellers' bags, or the part of a coach's roof where this chest fits **5 LARGE WINE BOTTLE** a wine bottle containing the equivalent of eight standard bottles, used for red Bordeaux [14C. Via French < Latin *imperialis* < *imperium* (see EMPIRE).] —**imperially** *adv*

imperial gallon *n* MEASURE = **gallon** *n.* 1

imperialism /im péeri əlizəm/ *n* **1 BELIEF IN EMPIRE-BUILDING** the policy of extending the rule or influence of a country over other countries or colonies **2 DOMINATION BY AN EMPIRE** the political, military, or economic domination of one country over another **3 TAKEOVER AND DOMINATION** the extension of power or authority over others in the interests of domination ○ *cultural imperialism* —**imperialist** *n, adj* —**imperialistic** /im péeri ə lístik/ *adj* —**imperialistically** *adv*

Imperial Valley /im péeri əl-/ valley in SE California. Length: 97 km/60 mi.

imperil /im pérrəl/ (**-ils, -illing, -illed**) *vt* to put something or somebody in danger —**imperilment** *n*

imperious /im péeri əss/ *adj* haughty and domineering [Mid-16C. < Latin *imperiosus* < *imperium* (see EMPIRE).] —**imperiously** *adv* —**imperiousness** *n*

imperishable /im pérrishəb'l/ *adj* **1** not liable to become spoilt, weak, or damaged through time and wear **2** not forgotten or ignored over time (*literary*) ○ *The imperishable quality of great literature distinguishes it from humbler writing.* —**imperishability** /im pérrishə bílləti/ *n* —**imperishableness** *n* —**imperishably** *adv*

imperium /im péeri əm/ (*plural* **-ria** /-ri ə/) *n* **1 SUPREME POWER** supreme or imperial power (*formal*) **2 LEGAL RIGHT TO COMMAND** the use of the power of the state to enforce the law **3 EMPIRE** an area controlled by a supreme power (*formal or literary*) [Mid-17C. < Latin (see EMPIRE).]

impermanent /im púrmənənt/ *adj* that will change, go away, disappear, or fade —**impermanence** *n* —**impermanency** *n* —**impermanently** *adv*

impermeable /im púrmi əb'l/ *adj* not permitting the passage of liquid, gas, or other fluid. ◊ **impervious** —**impermeability** /im púrmi ə bílləti/ *n* —**impermeableness** *n* —**impermeably** *adv*

impermissible /ímpər míssəb'l/ *adj* that cannot or will not be allowed —**impermissibility** /ímpər míssə bílləti/ *n* —**impermissibly** *adv*

impersonal /im púrs'nəl/ *adj* **1 NOT PERSONALIZED** not referring to individuals or reflecting personalities but focusing on events and facts ○ *an impersonal style of reporting* **2 ANONYMOUS** not considering people as individuals ○ *an impersonal bureaucracy* **3 COLD AND ALIENATING** making somebody feel insignificant and ignored as an individual ○ *The service in the restaurant was brisk and impersonal.* **4 WITHOUT HUMAN TRAITS** without any human characteristics or personality **5 NOT SPECIFIC** describes a clause or construction that includes a personal pronoun that does not refer to a specific person or thing, such as 'it is raining' or 'you shouldn't drink and drive' —**impersonality** /im púrssə nálləti/ *n* —**impersonally** *adv*

impersonalize /im púrs'nə līz/ (**-izes, -izing, -ized**), **impersonalise** (**-ises, -ising, -ised**) *vt* to make something neutral, lacking in human warmth, or without reference to individuals —**impersonalization** /im púrss'nə lī záysh'n/ *n*

impersonate /im púrssə nayt/ (**-ates, -ating, -ated**) *vt* **1** to mimic the voice, appearance, and manners of somebody else, especially in order to entertain **2** to pretend to be somebody else, especially in order to deceive [Early 17C. < Latin *persona* (see PERSON), after INCORPORATE.] —**impersonation** /im púrssə náysh'n/ *n* —**impersonator** *n*

impertinent /im púrtinənt/ *adj* (*formal*) **1** showing a bold or rude lack of respect, especially to a superior **2** not appropriate or relevant —**impertinence** *n* —**impertinency** *n* —**impertinently** *adv*

imperturbable /ímpər túrbəb'l/ *adj* not easily worried, distressed, or agitated ○ *The doctor's imperturbable manner soothed the distressed patient.* —**imperturbability** /ímpər túrbə bílləti/ *n* —**imperturbableness** *n* —**imperturbably** *adv*

impervious /im púrvi əss/ *adj* **1** remaining unmoved and unaffected by other people's opinions, arguments, or suggestions ○ *The directors were impervious to the growing resentment among the staff.* **2** not allowing passage into or through something [Mid-17C. < Latin *impervius* < *pervius* (see PERVIOUS).] —**imperviously** *adv* —**imperviousness** *n*

impetigo /ímpi tígō/ *n* a contagious infection of the skin caused by staphylococcal and streptococcal bacteria and characterized by blisters that form yellow-brown scabs [14C. < Latin, < *impetere* (see IMPETUS).] —**impetiginous** /-tíjjinəss/ *adj*

impetuosity /im péttyoo óssəti/ (*plural* **-ties**) *n* (*formal*) **1** a tendency to act rashly **2** an act performed on the spur of the moment after little or no consideration

impetuous /im péttyoo əss/ *adj* **1 ACTING IMPULSIVELY** acting on the spur of the moment, without considering the consequences **2 DONE ON IMPULSE** done without thought as a reaction to an emotion or impulse **3 VIOLENT** moving with great force and energy (*literary*) [14C. Via French *impétueux* < late Latin *impetuosus* < *impetus* (see IMPETUS).] —**impetuously** *adv* —**impetuousness** *n*

impetus /ímpitəss/ *n* **1** energy or motivation to accomplish or undertake something **2** a force that causes the motion of an object to overcome resistance and maintain its velocity [Mid-17C. < Latin, 'assault, force' < *impetere* 'assail' < *petere* 'seek'.]

impi /ímpi/ (*plural* **-i** *or* **-ies**) *n S Africa* a band of armed Zulu warriors or soldiers in precolonial times [Mid-19C. < Zulu.]

impiety /im pī əti/ (*plural* **-ties**) *n* **1 LACK OF RELIGIOUS RESPECT** a lack of due reverence for God or religion **2 UNGODLY ACT** an act that shows a lack of religious respect or devotion **3 LACK OF RESPECT** a lack of respect or dutifulness (*formal*)

impinge /im pínj/ (**-pinges, -pingeing, -pinged**) *vi* **1** to strike or hit something ○ *Loud noise can impinge on the eardrum, causing temporary hearing impairment.* **2** to affect the limits of something, especially a right or law, often causing some kind of restriction (*formal*) ○ *Members claimed that cancelling the ballot impinged on their voting rights.* [Mid-16C. < Latin *impingere* 'drive in forcibly' < *pangere* 'drive or fix in'.] —**impingement** *n* —**impinger** *n*

impious /ímpi əss, im pī əss/ *adj* **1** not showing due reverence for God or something holy **2** showing a lack of respect for somebody or something (*formal*) —**impiously** *adv* —**impiousness** *n*

impish /ímpish/ *adj* wicked in a playful way, without causing serious harm —**impishly** *adv* —**impishness** *n*

implacable /im plákəb'l/ *adj* impossible to pacify or to reduce in strength or force ○ *an implacable foe* ○ *an implacable ice storm* [15C. < Latin *implacabilis* < *placabilis* 'easily appeased' < *placare* (see PLACATE).] —**implacability** /im plákə bílləti/ *n* —**implacableness** *n* —**implacably** *adv*

implant *v* /im pla'ant/ **1** *vt* **ESTABLISH HABITS OR NOTIONS** to fix something deeply in somebody's mind or consciousness as a behaviour pattern, thought, or belief **2** *vt* **INSERT** to fit or fix something small into something larger, which then encases it ○ *Gold fillings, implanted in his front teeth, flashed when he smiled.* **3** *vt* **BURY** to fix something in the ground, especially so that it grows **4** *vt* **EMBED** to embed something such as a mechanical device in the body ○ *The hormone pellets are invisibly implanted just below the skin.* **5** *vi* **BECOME EMBEDDED** to become embedded in the lining of the womb ■ *n* /ím plaant/ **SOMETHING INSERTED DURING SURGERY** something inserted or embedded in the tissues or organs of the body during a surgical procedure, such as encapsulated drugs or fluid-filled sacs to replace or augment breast tissue —**implantable** *adj* —**implanter** *n*

implantation /ím plaan táysh'n/ *n* **1 BEING OR BECOMING IMPLANTED** the state of being or process of becoming fixed or embedded in something **2 SURGICALLY IMPLANTING IN THE BODY** the insertion or embedding of something into body tissues or organs during a surgical procedure **3 ATTACHMENT OF AN EMBRYO** the process by which or stage at which an embryo becomes embedded in the lining of the womb

implausible /im pláwzəb'l/ *adj* hardly likely to be true, acceptable, or possible —**implausibility** /im pláwzə bílləti/ *n* —**implausibleness** *n* —**implausibly** *adv*

implead /im pléed/ *vti* to bring a lawsuit against a person or an organization in court —**impleadable** *adj* —**impleader** *n*

implement *n* /ímplimənt/ **1 TOOL** a useful article of equipment, usually a specially shaped object designed to do a particular task ○ *writing implements* **2 REQUIREMENT** one thing needed in order to achieve something else (*formal*) ■ *vt* /ímpli ment/ **1 CARRY OUT OR FULFIL** to put something into effect or action ○ *The plan has yet to be fully implemented.* **2 GIVE TOOLS TO** to provide or equip somebody with the tools or other means to do something (*formal*) [15C. < late Latin *implementum* 'filling' < Latin *implere* 'fill in' < *plere* 'to fill'.] —**implemental** /ímpli mént'l/ *adj* —**implementation** /ímpli men táysh'n/ *n* —**implementer** *n*

implicate /ímpli kayt/ (**-cates, -cating, -cated**) *vt* **1 CONNECT WITH** to show that somebody or something played a part in or is connected to an activity, such as a crime **2 IMPLY** to imply or involve something as a consequence (*formal*) ○ *Do you not see that his words implicate an error on my part?* **3 ENTANGLE OR INTERWEAVE** to wreathe, twist, or knit things together (*literary*) [15C. < Latin *implicat-*, past participle of *implicare* 'entangle' < *plicare* 'to fold'.] —**implicative** /im plíkətiv, ímpli kaytiv/ *adj* —**implicatively** *adv*

implication /ímpli káysh'n/ *n* **1 INDIRECT SUGGESTION** something that is implied as a natural consequence of something else ○ *It is important to consider the wider implications of making such a decision.* **2 IMPLICIT UNDERSTANDING** the state of implying or being implied, without being plainly expressed **3 INVOLVEMENT** the involvement or entanglement of somebody in something ○ *his im-*

plication in the crime 4 **LOGICAL RELATION** in logic, a relationship between two propositions that holds when both propositions are true and fails when the first is true but the second is false —**implicational** *adj*

implicit /im plíssit/ *adj* 1 **IMPLIED** not stated, but understood in what is expressed ○ *Asking us when we would like to start was an implicit acceptance of our terms.* 2 **ABSOLUTE** not affected by any doubt or uncertainty ○ *implicit faith* 3 **CONTAINED** present as a necessary part of something ○ *Confidentiality is implicit in the relationship between doctor and patient.* [Late 16C. Directly or via French *implicite* < Latin *implicitus* 'entangled' < *implicare* (see IMPLICATE).] —**implicitly** *adv*

USAGE See ***explicit***.

implode /im plṓd/ (**-plodes, -ploding, -ploded**) *vti* to collapse inwardly with force as a result of the external pressure being greater than the internal pressure, or to cause something to collapse inwardly [Late 19C. < Latin *plodere* 'to clap', after EXPLODE.]

implore /im pláwr/ (**-plores, -ploring, -plored**) *vt* (*formal*) 1 to plead with somebody to do something ○ *The tenants implored their landlord not to sell the building.* 2 to beg or pray for something [Early 16C. Directly or via French *implorer* < Latin *implorare* 'call upon with tears' < *plorare* 'weep'.] —**imploration** /ímplə ráysh'n, ím plaw-/ *n* —**imploratory** *adj* —**implorer** *n*

imploring /im pláwring/ *adj* earnestly asking for something ○ *an imploring look* —**imploringly** *adv*

implosion /im plṓzh'n/ *n* the violent inward collapse of a vessel or structure resulting from the external pressure being greater than the internal pressure [Late 19C. < IMPLODE.]

implosive /im plṓssiv, -plṓziv/ *adj* indicating or relating to violent inward collapse —**implosively** *adv*

imply /im plī́/ (**-plies, -plying, -plied**) *vt* 1 to make something understood without expressing it directly 2 to involve something as a necessary part or condition ○ *Such impressive exam results imply good teaching and study methods.* [14C. Via Old French *emplier* < Latin *implicare* (see IMPLICATE).] —**implied** *adj*

USAGE See ***infer***.

impolite /ímpə lī́t/ *adj* not showing proper manners or respect —**impolitely** *adv* —**impoliteness** *n*

impolitic /im póllətik/ *adj* likely to be disadvantageous and therefore not advisable ○ *It would be impolitic to refuse.* —**impoliticly** *adv* —**impoliticness** *n*

imponderable /im póndərəb'l/ *adj* not quantifiable in terms of importance or effect ○ *Sheer inspiration remains an imponderable force in cultural and technological developments.* ■ *n* an event, factor, or other matter whose importance or effects cannot be calculated (*often plural*) ○ *just another of life's imponderables* —**imponderability** /im póndərə bílləti/ *n* —**imponderableness** *n* —**imponderably** *adv*

⚡ **import** *vt* /im páwrt/ 1 **BRING IN FROM ABROAD** to bring something or cause something to be brought in from another country, usually for commercial or industrial purposes 2 **BRING IN FROM OUTSIDE** to bring in something, e.g. knowledge or expertise, from an outside source 3 **TRANSFER DATA** to transfer data from one location to another in a computer or from one computer to another in a computer network, especially when a change of format is required 4 **IMPLY** to mean something, often in addition to what is actually expressed (*formal*) ○ *What does the legal motion really import here?* ■ *n* /ím pawrt/ 1 **SOMETHING BROUGHT FROM ABROAD** something that is brought into one country from another, usually for commercial or industrial purposes 2 **IDEA OR PERSON BROUGHT IN** an idea, practice, or person brought in from the outside ○ *The new accounting system is an import from the private sector.* 3 **IMPORTATION** the bringing in of something from abroad or an outside source ○ *Most governments forbid the import of such goods.* 4 **TRUE SIGNIFICANCE** meaning or significance ○ *a foreign-policy decision of great import* [15C. < Latin *importare* 'carry in' < *portare* 'carry'.] —**importability** /im páwrtə bílləti/ *n* —**importable** *adj* —**importation** /ím pawr táysh'n/ *n* —**importer** *n*

importance /im páwrt'nss/ *n* 1 considerable value, relevance, or interest ○ *It is difficult to overestimate the importance of this breakthrough to medical science.* 2 high position, rank, or reputation in society

important /im páwrt'nt/ *adj* 1 **HAVING VALUE OR SIGNIFICANCE** worthy of note or consideration, especially for its interest, value, or relevance ○ *an important scientific discovery* ○ *an important author* 2 **HIGH-RANKING** with high social position or influence among people 3 **POMPOUS** seeming to assume more status, significance, or value than is actually due ○ *strode into the room with an important air* [15C. < medieval Latin *important-*, present participle of *importare* (see IMPORT).] —**importantly** *adv*

~~**imporetent**~~ incorrect spelling of **important**

importunate /im páwrtyŏŏnət/ *adj* (*formal*) 1 continually asking for something, especially in a forceful, insistent, or troublesome manner ○ *importunate requests for a loan* 2 requiring immediate attention and action ○ *importunate requests for medical aid* [Early 16C. < Latin *importunus* (see IMPORTUNE).] —**importunately** *adv* —**importunateness** *n*

importune /im páwr tyoon, ím pawr tyŏŏn/ *vt* (**-tunes, -tuning, -tuned**) (*formal*) 1 **BOTHER INSISTENTLY** to ask somebody continually, repeatedly, or forcefully for something, especially in a troublesome way 2 **MAKE AN IMMORAL REQUEST** to ask somebody to have sexual relations in exchange for money ■ *adj* **IMPORTUNATE** persistent or pressing [Mid-16C. < French *importuner* or medieval Latin *importunari* < Latin *importunus* 'inconvenient, unseasonable' < *Portunus*, god of harbours.] —**importunacy** /im páwrtyŏŏnəssi/ *n* —**importunely** *adv* —**importuner** *n*

importunity /ím pawr tyŏŏnəti/ (*plural* **-ties**) *n* (*formal*) 1 the fact of being troublesomely demanding or insistent 2 a demand made repeatedly or insistently

impose /im pṓz/ (**-poses, -posing, -posed**) *v* 1 *vt* **LEVY OR ENFORCE** to lay down something compulsory, such as a tax or a punishment 2 *vt* **INSIST ON** to make people agree to something or comply with something by having superior strength or authority ○ *It broke his heart to see Western culture imposed on this dignified people.* 3 *vti* **INCONVENIENCE** to give people extra work or difficulties by forcing your company or your personal concerns on them 4 *vt* **ARRANGE PAGES** to order the pages of material such as a book or magazine for printing 5 *vt* **PASS OFF ON** to use deceit or fraud to give something to somebody or to persuade somebody to accept something 6 *vt* **LAY ON HANDS** to bless another, e.g. in confirmation or ordination, by laying hands on the person's head [15C. < French *imposer* (influenced by *poser* 'to put') < Latin *imponere* 'place into' < *ponere* 'to place'.] —**imposable** *adj* —**imposer** *n*

imposing /im pṓzing/ *adj* large and stately, thus creating an impression of grandeur —**imposingly** *adv* —**imposingness** *n*

imposition /ímpə zísh'n/ *n* 1 **EXTRA TROUBLE** a request or task, especially a time-consuming one, that is unreasonably expected of somebody 2 **ENFORCED DUTY** a tax, fee, or penalty that is imposed on people 3 **ESTABLISHING OR ENFORCING** the official or legal process of laying down something compulsory such as a tax, fee, or penalty 4 **ARRANGEMENT OF PAGES** the setting up and ordering of pages for printing 5 **DECEPTION** a deception or fraud (*literary*) 6 **BLESSING** the laying of hands on somebody's head in a religious sacrament such as ordination or confirmation

impossibility /im póssə bílləti/ (*plural* **-ties**) *n* 1 something that cannot exist or cannot be done ○ *Living without water is a physical impossibility.* 2 the likelihood that something will not happen or cannot be achieved ○ *the impossibility of finding another job close to home*

impossible /im póssəb'l/ *adj* 1 **NOT POSSIBLE** not able to exist or be done ○ *an impossible task* 2 **TOO DIFFICULT** very difficult to deal with and apparently without a solution ○ *The situation was impossible: I couldn't be honest without offending one of them.* 3 **UNENDURABLE** unbearably difficult or not possible to endure ○ *The humidity was impossible.* 4 **NOT BELIEVABLE** ridiculous or unreasonable, because it could not be true —**impossibleness** *n*

impossibly /im póssəbli/ *adv* 1 **INFURIATINGLY** to an infuriating or intolerable degree (*informal*) 2 **EXTREMELY** to an extent that is almost unbelievable ○ *impossibly thin slices* 3 **NOT BY ANY MEANS** in a way that could not be done or could not happen

impost[1] /ím pōst/ *n* 1 a tax or other payment levied on goods brought into a country 2 the weight a horse must carry, including that of the jockey, in a handicap race [15C. < Italian *imposta*, feminine past participle of *imporre* 'impose' < Latin *imponere* (see IMPOSE).]

impost[2] /ím pōst/ *n* the top part of a pillar, column, or wall, which may be decorated or moulded and on which a vault or arch rests [Mid-16C. < French, < Latin *impostus, impositus*, past participle of *imponere* (see IMPOSE).]

imposter *n* = **impostor**

imposthume *n* MED = **impostume**

impostor /im póstər/, **imposter** *n* a person who makes false claims of identity [Late 16C. Via French *imposteur* < Latin *impositor* < *imponere* (see IMPOSE).]

imposture /im póschər/ *n* the act of pretending to be somebody else in order to trick people, or an occasion on which this is done [Mid-16C. Via French < late Latin *impostura* 'a putting on' < Latin *imponere* (see IMPOSE).]

impotent /ímpətənt/ *adj* 1 unable to perform sexual intercourse, usually because erection of the penis cannot be achieved or sustained 2 without the strength or power to do anything effective or helpful —**impotence** *n* —**impotently** *adv*

impound /im pównd/ *vt* 1 **KEEP IN A CONFINED PLACE** to lock something such as an illegally parked car in an enclosure or compound 2 **TAKE INTO LEGAL CUSTODY** to take goods or possessions into official custody 3 **WITHHOLD LEGALLY** to withhold something by legal means 4 **HOLD A WATER SUPPLY** to save and collect water in a dam or reservoir [15C. 'Put into a pound' < POUND[3].] —**impoundable** *adj* —**impoundage** *n* —**impounder** *n* —**impoundment** *n*

impoverish /im póvvərish/ *vt* (*formal*) 1 **MAKE POOR** to cause somebody or something to be poor or poorer (*often passive*) 2 **SPOIL OR REDUCE IN QUALITY** to take away some part or quality belonging to something, leaving it in a worse or weaker condition than before ○ *a vocabulary impoverished by technical jargon* 3 **MAKE LESS RICH OR FERTILE** to take away the nutrients and richness from a substance such as soil [15C. < Old French *empoveriss-*, stem of *empov(e)rier* < *povre* (see POOR).] —**impoverisher** *n* —**impoverishment** *n*

impracticable /im práktikəb'l/ *adj* 1 that cannot be carried out effectively 2 not in a fit condition for use —**impracticability** /im práktikə bílləti/ *n* —**impracticableness** *n* —**impracticably** *adv*

impractical /im práktik'l/ *adj* 1 that will not work effectively or be without problems when put into practice 2 not able to perform practical tasks or deal easily with practical matters ○ *She is a brilliant academic, but completely impractical around the house.* —**impracticality** /im prákti kálləti/ *n* —**impractically** *adv* —**impracticalness** *n*

imprecate /ímpri kayt/ (**-cates, -cating, -cated**) *vti* to call down harm, especially a curse, on somebody (*formal*) [Early 17C. < Latin *imprecari* < *precari* (see PRAY).] —**imprecator** *n* —**imprecatory** /-kaytəri/ *adj*

imprecation /ímpri káysh'n/ *n* (*formal*) 1 **CURSE** an oath or curse 2 **CURSING** the calling down of harm on somebody 3 **SWEARING** swearing or blasphemy

imprecise /ímpri sī́ss/ *adj* not exact or accurate —**imprecisely** *adv* —**impreciseness** *n* —**imprecision** /-sízh'n/ *n*

impregnable /im prégnəb'l/ *adj* 1 too strong to be captured or opened by force ○ *an impregnable fortress* 2 unable to be shaken or destroyed by any outside influence ○ *impregnable faith* —**impregnability** /im prégnə bílləti/ *n* —**impregnableness** *n* —**impregnably** *adv*

impregnate *vt* /ím preg nayt/ (**-nates, -nating, -nated**) 1 **SATURATE** to incorporate a chemical into a porous material such as wood or cloth, especially by soaking it thoroughly with a liquid (*usually passive*) 2 **FILL** make something express or contain a particular quality or idea throughout (*literary*) 3 **MAKE PREGNANT** to make a woman or female animal pregnant ■ *adj* /im prégnət/ 1 **SATURATED** infused or saturated with something 2 **PREGNANT** pregnant or fertilized [Early 17C. < late Latin *impregnat-*, past participle of *impregnare* < Latin *praegnas* (see PREGNANT).] —**impregnation** /ím preg náysh'n/ *n* —**impregnator** *n*

impresario /ímprə saári ō/ (*plural* **-os**) *n* 1 **ENTERTAINMENT MANAGER** a producer or promoter of commercial entertainment ventures, especially in musical theatre 2 **BUSINESS HEAD OF OPERA OR BALLET COMPANY** somebody in charge of an opera or ballet company who is responsible for business affairs, contracting artists, and commissioning new works 3 **ENTERTAINER** a showman [Mid-18C. < Italian, 'somebody who undertakes' < *impresa*.]

imprescriptible /ìmpri skríptəb'l/ *adj* impossible to remove or violate ○ *the people's imprescriptible rights* [Late 16C. < medieval Latin *imprescriptibilis* < Latin *praescript-*, past participle of *praescribere* (see PRESCRIBE).] —**imprescriptibility** /ìmpri skríptə bíllәti/ *n* —**imprescriptibly** *adv*

impress[1] *v* /im préss/ **1** *vti* **AFFECT OR PLEASE GREATLY** to bring about a strong or lasting effect, usually favourable, on the mind or feelings of somebody (*often passive*) ○ *We were not impressed by the way we were treated.* **2** *vt* **MAKE CLEARLY UNDERSTOOD** to make sure that somebody has a clear and lasting understanding, memory, or mental image of something ○ *She impressed on every child her expectation of complete honesty.* **3** *vt* **PRESS SHAPE INTO** to make a pattern, design, or mark on something by pressing or stamping **4** *vt* **APPLY VOLTAGE** to apply a voltage to an electronic circuit or device ■ *n* /ím press/ **STAMP** a characteristic mark (*literary*) [14C. < French *empresser* < Latin *impressus*, past participle of *imprimere* 'press in' < *premere* 'to press'.] —**impresser** *n* —**impressibility** /im préssə bíllәti/ *n* —**impressible** /im préssəb'l/ *adj*

impress[2] /im préss/ *vt* **1** to seize by force for public use **2** to compel people to serve in a navy or army, especially by arbitrary means [Late 16C. < PRESS².] —**impressment** *n*

impression /im présh'n/ *n* **1 WHAT STAYS IN SOMEBODY'S MIND** a lasting effect, opinion, or mental image of somebody or something ○ *I made a bad impression by arriving late for the interview.* **2 GENERAL IDEA** a belief about or understanding of something ○ *I was under the impression that they were married.* **3 PRESSED-IN SHAPE** a pattern, design, or mark made by something hard being pressed onto something softer ○ *The intruder's boots had left an impression in the mud.* **4 IMITATING** entertainment in which a performer mimics the way a well-known person speaks and behaves, usually in a humorous or exaggerated way **5 MOULD TAKEN OF TEETH** a mould taken of the teeth and surrounding gums on which dentures, restorations, or dental appliances are constructed **6 COPIES OF A BOOK** all the copies of a book printed at one time, or the printing of these **7 COPY OF A BOOK** a printed copy of a book —**impressional** *adj* —**impressionally** *adv*

impressionable /im présh'nəb'l/ *adj* ready to accept or be impressed by the experiences, opinions, and personalities of other people —**impressionability** /im présh'nə bíllәti/ *n* —**impressionableness** *n* —**impressionably** *adv*

impressionism /im présh'nizəm/, **Impressionism** *n* **1** a style of painting that concentrates on the general tone and effect produced by a subject, without elaboration of details **2** a style of music, especially of late 19th-century France, characterized by the use of rich harmonies and tones rather than form to express scenes or emotions

QUICK FACTS ON... **IMPRESSIONISM**

Key dates: late 1860s–mid-1880s
Key locations: France
Key elements: rejection of academicism; naturalism, subjectivity, spontaneity; plein-air painting
Key figures: Édouard Manet, Claude Monet, Camille Pissarro, Pierre Auguste Renoir, Alfred Sisley, Berthe Morisot, Edgar Degas, Paul Cézanne
Key works: *The Balcony* (Manet) 1869, *Impression: Sunrise* (Monet) 1872, *Gare St-Lazare* (Monet) 1873, *The Moulin de la Galette* (Renoir) 1876, *The Absinthe Drinker* (Degas) 1876, *Waterlilies* (Monet) 1899
Key developments: neoimpressionism, postimpressionism, expressionism, modernism

impressionist /im présh'nist/ *n* **1 impressionist, Impressionist** an artist or composer who paints pictures or writes music in the style of impressionism, especially one active in France at the end of the 19th century **2** a performer who mimics the way well-known people speak and behave, usually in a humorous and exaggerated way

impressionistic /im préshə nístik/ *adj* **1** giving a broad picture or general idea rather than an exact description **2** concerning, involving, or in the style of impressionism or the impressionists in painting or music —**impressionistically** *adv*

impressive /im préssiv/ *adj* that makes a deep and usually favourable impression on the mind or senses —**impressively** *adv* —**impressiveness** *n*

imprest /ím prest/ *n* **1 ADVANCE OF MONEY** an advance payment of money, especially to somebody who is to carry out business for the state **2 LOAN TO DRAW ON** a loan, usually in the form of a petty cash account, that can be drawn on as needed **3 ADVANCE PAYMENT** a payment formerly made in advance to a British soldier or sailor on enlistment [Mid-16C. < obsolete *prest* 'loan' < Old French < *prester* 'lend' < Latin *praesto* 'at hand'.]

imprimatur /ìmpri maátər, -máytər/ *n* **1** authority to do, say, or especially print something (*formal*) **2** an authorization allowing a book or other work to be published, now usually confined to works sanctioned by the Roman Catholic Church [Mid-17C. < Latin, 'let it be printed'.]

imprint *n* /ímprint/ **1 PRESSED-IN SHAPE** a pattern, design, or mark that is made by pressing something down on or into something else **2 PRINTED PUBLICATION DETAILS** the name and address of the publisher and printer as shown at the front of a book **3 SPECIAL MARK** a printed or stamped sign on an object, e.g. to indicate its origin **4 LASTING EFFECT** an effect that remains and is recognizable for a long time ○ *The years of occupation left their imprint on all the inhabitants.* ■ *v* /im prínt/ **1** *vt* **MARK BY PRESSING** to put a shape or design on something, e.g. the surface of an object, using a stamp or printing device **2** *vt* **CAUSE TO REMAIN** to fix an image, memory, opinion, or idea in a vivid or lasting way ○ *The scene was imprinted on her memory.* **3** *vi* **ESTABLISH SOCIAL ATTACHMENTS** to learn an attraction to members of the same species or substitutes very early in life. ◊ **imprinting** —**imprinter** *n*

imprinting /im prínting/ *n* a form of rapid learning very early in an animal's social development that results in strong behavioural patterns of attraction to members of its own species, especially parents

imprison /im prízz'n/ *vt* to lock somebody up in prison —**imprisoner** *n* —**imprisonment** *n*

improbable /im próbbəb'l/ *adj* not likely to happen or to be true —**improbability** /im próbbə bíllәti/ *n* —**improbableness** *n* —**improbably** *adv*

improbity /im prṓbəti/ *n* lack of moral scruples or honesty

impromptu /im prómp tyoo/ *adj* **DONE OR SAID SPONTANEOUSLY** not prepared or planned in advance ○ *an impromptu speech* ■ *adv* **WITHOUT PRIOR THOUGHT OR PREPARATION** in an unrehearsed way ■ *n* **1 SHORT SOLO PIECE** a short instrumental piece whose style gives an impression of improvisation **2 SPONTANEOUS OR UNREHEARSED ACT** something done or said without planning [Mid-17C. Via French < Latin *in promptu* 'at hand' < *promptus* (see PROMPT).]

improper /im próppər/ *adj* **1 UNSUITABLE** not appropriate to the context, the nature of the case, or the purpose in view (*formal*) **2 RUDE** not in accordance with accepted good manners or decorum **3 IRREGULAR** not in accordance with the accepted standards of something such as a profession ○ *the improper handling of funds* —**improperly** *adv* —**improperness** *n*

improper fraction *n* a fraction in which the numerator is equal to or greater than the denominator, such as 6/4

impropriate *vt* /im prṓpri ayt/ (**-ates, -ating, -ated**) to put ecclesiastical property or tithes in lay hands ■ *adj* /im prṓpri ət/ in the hands of lay people (*refers to ecclesiastical property*) [Early 16C. < the past participle of Anglo-Latin *impropriare* 'to appropriate' < Latin *proprius* 'own'.] —**impropriation** /im prṓpri áysh'n/ *n* —**impropriator** *n*

impropriety /ìmprə prī́ əti/ (*plural* **-ties**) *n* conduct not considered correct, moral, or appropriate in a given context

improve /im próov/ (**-proves, -proving, -proved**) *v* **1** *vti* **MAKE OR BECOME BETTER** to make something better in quality or condition, or to become better ○ *His health is improving daily.* **2** *vt* **INCREASE THE VALUE OF** to make property, such as land or buildings, more valuable **3** *vt* **USE WELL** to make good use of or employ something to advantage [Early 16C. < Anglo-Norman *emprower* 'make a profit' < Old French *prou* 'profit' < late Latin *prode* 'profitable' < Latin *prodesse* (see PROUD).] —**improvability** /im próovə bíllәti/ *n* —**improvable** *adj* —**improvableness** *n* —**improvably** *adv* —**improver** *n*

improve on, improve upon *vt* to do better or be better than a particular thing, especially a previous standard or record ○ *improved on her previous time by four seconds*

improvement /im próovmənt/ *n* **1 GETTING OR MAKING BETTER** the process of making something better or of becoming better ○ *an improvement on her past performance* **2 CHANGE OR ADDITION** a change or addition that makes something better **3 ADVANCE IN VALUE** an increase in value, especially in the value of land or property **4 CHANGE THAT APPRECIATES VALUE** a change or addition, especially to property or land, that increases value ○ *home improvements*

improvident /im próvvidənt/ *adj* **1** failing to put money aside or give any thought to forward planning **2** not sensible, cautious, or wise (*formal*) [15C. Literally 'not foreseeing' < late Latin *provident-* (see PROVIDENT).] —**improvidence** *n* —**improvidently** *adv*

improvise /ímprə vīz/ (**-vises, -vising, -vised**) *vti* **1** to act or compose something, especially a sketch, play, song, or piece of music, without any preparation or set text to follow **2** to make a substitute for something out of the materials that happen to be available at the time ○ *If you haven't got a hammer, we'll have to improvise.* [Early 19C. Directly or via French < Italian *improvvisare* < Latin *improvisus* 'unforeseen' < *providere* (see PROVIDE).] —**improvisation** /ìmprə vī záysh'n/ *n* —**improvisational** *adj* —**improvisationally** *adv* —**improvisatorial** /ìmprə vīzə táwri əl/ *adj* —**improvisatory** /ìmprə vī záytəri/ *adj* —**improviser** *n*

imprudent /im próod'nt/ *adj* showing no care, forethought, or judgment —**imprudence** *n* —**imprudently** *adv*

impudent /ímpyoodənt/ *adj* showing a lack of respect and excessive boldness [14C. < Latin *impudent-* < *pudens* 'ashamed', present participle of *pudere* 'feel ashamed'.] —**impudence** *n* —**impudently** *adv* —**impudentness** *n*

impudicity /ìmpyoo díssəti/ *n* lack of modesty or shame (*formal*) [Early 16C. Directly or via French *impudicité* < Latin *impudicitas* < *pudere* 'feel ashamed'.]

impugn /im pyóon/ *vt* to suggest that something cannot be trusted, relied on, or respected ○ *Far be it from me to impugn his motives, but ...* [14C. < Latin *impugnare* 'fight against' < *pugnare* 'to fight' < *pugnus* 'fist'.] —**impugnable** *adj* —**impugner** *n* —**impugnment** *n*

impulse /ím puls/ *n* **1 FORCE DRIVING SOMETHING FORWARD** a driving force producing a forward motion **2 FORWARD MOTION** the motion produced by a driving force **3 SUDDEN URGE** a sudden desire, urge, or inclination (*often before nouns*) **4 INSTINCTIVE DRIVE** an instinctive drive or natural tendency **5 MOTIVE** a motivation or reason for a specific activity **6 FORCE ACTING OVER TIME** a measure of momentum arrived at by multiplying the average force acting on a body by the length of time it acts **7 NERVE OR MUSCLE SIGNAL** a progressive wave of biochemically generated energy that travels along a nerve fibre or muscle and stimulates or inhibits activity [Mid-17C. < Latin *impulsus*, past participle of *impellere* (see IMPEL).]

impulse buying *n* the purchase of goods that may be unnecessary, caused by the sudden urge or desire to have them

impulsion /im púlsh'n/ *n* **1 ACT OR INSTANCE OF URGING** the act of urging or forcing somebody into action, or an instance of this **2 MOVEMENT OR THRUSTING FORCE** a movement that comes from being pushed or thrust, or the force that creates this movement **3 SUDDEN DESIRE** a sudden desire, inclination, or urge

impulsive /im púlssiv/ *adj* **1 INCLINED TO ACT ON SUDDEN URGES** having a tendency to act on sudden urges or desires **2 SPONTANEOUS** based on or motivated by impulse **3 COMING IN BURSTS** acting or coming in short bursts **4 SHORT AND PERCUSSIVE** describes a sound that is of short duration and composed of a wide range of frequencies —**impulsively** *adv* —**impulsiveness** *n* —**impulsivity** /ìm pul sívvəti/ *n*

impunity /im pyóonəti/ *n* exemption from punishment, harm, or recrimination [Mid-16C. < Latin *impunitas* < *impunis* 'without punishment' < *poena* 'punishment'.]

impure /im pyóor/ *adj* **1 CONTAMINATED** unclean because containing something harmful **2 ADULTERATED** combined with something of inferior quality **3 SINFUL** tainted with sin **4 HAVING MIXED STYLES** combining a mixture of styles **5 MIXED WITH OTHER COLOURS** mixed with other colours —**impurely** *adv* —**impureness** *n*

impurity /im pyóorəti/ (*plural* **-ties**) *n* **1 LACK OF PURITY** the state or quality of being impure **2 CONTAMINANT** a substance that adulterates or contaminates something ○ *drinking water that was found to contain impurities* **3 SOMETHING ADDED TO A SEMICONDUCTOR** a small amount of a substance added to a pure semiconductor to control its electrical conductivity

impute /im pyóot/ (**-putes, -puting, -puted**) *vt* **1 ATTRIBUTE A BAD ACTION** to attribute a usually undesirable action or event to somebody ○ *'He had married her with that bad past life hidden behind him, and she had no faith left to* *protest his innocence of the worst that was imputed to him'.* (George Eliot, *Middlemarch*; 1872) **2 ATTRIBUTE A QUALITY** to attribute a quality to a person, cause, or source ○ *'it was charity to impute some of her unbecoming indifference to the languor of ill-health'* (Jane Austen, *Emma*; 1816) **3 CHARGE SOMEBODY RESPONSIBLE FOR ANOTHER'S CRIME** to bring legal charges against somebody because a person that he or she is responsible for has committed an offence **4 EXTEND A QUALITY TO SOMEBODY ELSE** to regard a quality such as righteousness that applies to somebody as also applying to another person associated with him or her [14C. Via French *imputer* < Latin *imputare* 'bring into the reckoning' < *putare* 'reckon'.] —**imputable** *adj* —**imputation** /ìmpyoo táysh'n/ *n* —**imputative** *adj* —**imputer** *n*

IMS *abbr* **1** *S Asia* Indian Medical Service **2** information management systems **3** Institute of Management Services

in[1] /in/ CORE MEANING: a grammatical word indicating that something or somebody is within or inside something ○ (prep) *The dinner's in the oven.* ○ (adv) *I called by, but you weren't in.*

1 *prep* **INDICATES A PLACE** indicates that something happens or is situated somewhere ○ *He spent a whole year in Russia.* **2** *prep* **INDICATES A STATE** indicates a state or condition that something or somebody is experiencing ○ *The banking industry is in a state of flux.* **3** *prep* **INDICATES AFTER** after a period of time that will pass before something happens ○ *She should be well enough to leave in a week or two.* **4** *prep* **DURING** indicates that something happens during a period of time ○ *He crossed the desert in 39 days.* **5** *prep* **INDICATES HOW SOMETHING IS EXPRESSED** indicates the means of communication used to express something ○ *I managed to write the whole speech in French.* **6** *prep* **INDICATES SUBJECT AREA** indicates a subject or field of activity ○ *She graduated with a degree in biology.* **7** *prep* **AS CONSEQUENCE OF** while doing something or as a consequence of something ○ *In reaching for a glass he knocked over the ashtray.* **8** *prep* **COVERED BY** indicates that something is wrapped or covered by something ○ *The floor was covered in balloons and toys.* **9** *prep* **INDICATES HOW SOMEBODY IS DRESSED** indicates that somebody is dressed in a particular way ○ *She was dressed in a smart suit.* **10** *prep* **PREGNANT WITH** pregnant with ○ *The cows were in calf.* **11** *adv* **ALIGHT** indicates that a fire is alight ○ *It was so cold that we had to keep the fire in all night.* **12** *adv* **HAVE INNINGS** indicates that a team or player in sports has an innings, e.g. in cricket ○ *Any volunteers to go in first?* **13** *adj* **FASHIONABLE** fashionable or popular ○ *In line skates are the in thing.* **14** *adj* **INTO OFFICE** indicates that a party or group has achieved or will achieve power or authority ○ *Everyone was very optimistic when the new party got in.* [Old English] ◇ **in between** between ○ *Normal light consists of a wave that vibrates up and down, side to side, and every direction in between.* ◇ **in for** indicates that somebody will experience something, e.g. a surprise or a shock ○ *Little did she know what she was in for.* ◇ **in on** having knowledge about or involvement in something ○ *The whole class was in on the plans for the surprise party.* ◇ **in that** introduces an explanation of a statement ○ *Action Park is unusual in that it fights lawsuits tenaciously and settles none.* ◇ **in with** associated with or friendly with ○ *a reporter perhaps too much in with the politicians to be objective* ○ *He's been getting in with a bad crowd.* ◇ **the ins and outs** all the detailed facts and points about something ○ *I don't know all the ins and outs of the matter, but she's leaving.*

USAGE See ***from***.

in[2] *abbr* India (*in Internet addresses*)

In *symbol* indium

in., in *abbr* inches

in-[1] *prefix* not ○ *insensitive* ○ *incomplete* [< Latin]

in-[2] *prefix* in, into, towards, within ○ *infighting* ○ *inbound* [< Latin]

-in *suffix* **1** a neutral chemical compound ○ *fibroin* ○ *digitalin* ○ *thrombin* **2** antibiotic ○ *streptothricin* **3** pharmaceutical ○ *warfarin* **4** toxic substance ○ *botulin* **5** antigen ○ *bacterin* **6** = **-ine** ○ *hyalin* [< Latin *in* 'in, into, on, during, against', or *in-* 'not']

inability /ìnnə bíllәti/ *n* a lack of the ability, means, or power to do something ○ *his inability to face the truth*

~~**inable**~~ incorrect spelling of **enable**

in absentia /ìn əb sénti ə/ *adv* in the absence of the person or persons concerned [< Latin, 'in absence']

inaccessible /ìnnək séssəb'l/ *adj* **1 DIFFICULT TO GET TO** difficult or impossible to gain access to or reach **2 DIFFICULT TO ACHIEVE** difficult or impossible to afford or attain **3 HARD TO UNDERSTAND** difficult or impossible to understand —**inaccessibility** /ìnnək séssə bíllәti/ *n* —**inaccessibly** *adv*

inaccuracy /in ákyoorəssi/ (*plural* **-cies**) *n* **1** lack of accuracy or correctness **2** an error or mistake

SYNONYMS See ***mistake***.

inaccurate /in ákyoorət/ *adj* not accurate or correct —**inaccurately** *adv* —**inaccurateness** *n*

inaction /in áksh'n/ *n* **1** failure to take action when action is necessary ○ *'But in a nation that demands action, Congress has become the master of inaction'.* (National Public Telecomputing Network, *Bush speeches in campaign '92*) **2** lack of activity, especially laziness or idleness

inactivate /in ákti vayt/ (**-vates, -vating, -vated**) *vt* to make something inactive or unable to function —**inactivation** /in ákti váysh'n/ *n*

inactive /in áktiv/ *adj* **1 NOT TAKING ACTION** taking no action or taking no part in an action that others are involved in **2 NOT BEING USED OR OPERATED** not in use, functioning, or operating **3 LAZY OR SEDENTARY** not involving or taking part in physical activity **4 DORMANT** describes a volcano that is not erupting but is not extinct **5 NOT IN ACTIVE SERVICE** not taking part in, or not being used for, active military service **6 INERT** having little or no chemical reactivity **7 HAVING LOW RADIOACTIVITY** having low or zero radioactivity **8 BIOLOGICALLY INERT** having little if any discernible effect on living things as a result of the loss of some property such as the ability to infect or create antigens **9 NOT DEVELOPING OR SHOWING SYMPTOMS** describes a disease that, though present in the body, is not developing or producing any symptoms —**inactively** *adv* —**inactiveness** *n* —**inactivity** /in ak tívvәti/ *n*

inadequate /in áddikwət/ *adj* failing to reach an expected or required level or standard ○ *inadequate supplies of food* —**inadequacy** *n* —**inadequately** *adv* —**inadequateness** *n*

inadmissible /ìnnəd míssəb'l/ *adj* not admissible or allowable, especially in a court of law —**inadmissibility** /ìnnəd missə bíllәti/ *n* —**inadmissibly** *adv*

inadvertent /ìnnəd vúrt'nt/ *adj* **1** done unintentionally or without thinking **2** failing to pay enough attention or take enough care [Mid-17C. < Latin *advertent-*, present participle of *advertere* (see ADVERT[1]).] —**inadvertence** *n*

inadvertently /ìnəd vúrt'ntli/ *adv* without intending to or without realizing

inadvisable /ìnnəd vízəb'l/ *adj* not to be advised or recommended —**inadvisability** /ìnnəd vízə bíllәti/ *n* —**inadvisably** *adv*

in aeternum /ín ee túrnəm/ *adv* eternally or forever (*formal*) [< Latin, 'in eternal']

inalienable /in áyli ənəb'l/ *adj* not able to be transferred or taken away, e.g. because of being protected by law —**inalienability** /in áyli ənə bíllәti/ *n* —**inalienably** *adv*

inalterable /in áwltərəb'l/ *adj* not able to be changed —**inalterability** /in áwltərə bíllәti/ *n* —**inalterably** *adv*

inamorata /in ámmə raátə/ (*plural* **-tas**) *n* a woman whom somebody loves or with whom somebody has a romantic relationship [Late 16C. < Italian, feminine of *inamorato* (see INAMORATO).]

inamorato /in ámmə raátō/ (*plural* **-tos**) *n* a man whom somebody loves or with whom somebody has a romantic relationship [Late 16C. < Italian, past participle of *inamorare* 'fall in love' < *amore* 'love' < Latin *amor*.]

inane /i náyn/ *adj* irritatingly silly or time-wasting [Mid-16C. < Latin *inanis* 'empty'.] —**inanely** *adv* —**inaneness** *n*

inanimate /in ánnimət/ *adj* **1 NOT LIVING** not alive **2 NOT LIVELY** not active, energetic, or lively ○ *'She had relapsed once more into the vacant inanimate creature who had opened the gate to us'.* (Wilkie Collins, *The Law and the Lady*; 1875) **3 RELATING TO NOUNS FOR NONLIVING THINGS** belonging to the category of nouns that refer to things and concepts considered to be without life [15C. < late Latin *inanimatus* 'lifeless' < Latin *animatus*, past participle of *animare* (see ANIMATE).] —**inanimately** *adv* —**inanimateness** *n*

inanition /ìnnə nísh'n/ *n* **1** exhaustion caused by lack of food or water or as a result of disease **2** lethargy or lack of vitality (*literary*) [14C. < late Latin *inanition-* < Latin *inanis* 'empty'.]

inanity /i nánnәti/ (*plural* **-ties**) *n* **1 MEANINGLESS QUALITY** meaninglessness or senselessness that suggests a lack of understanding or intelligence **2 SILLINESS** silliness or foolishness **3 SOMETHING INANE** something such as a silly remark that demonstrates or suggests inanity

inappetence /in áppitənss/, **inappetency** /-tənssi/ *n* lack of appetite (*formal*) —**inappetent** *adj*

inapplicable /ìnnə plíkəb'l/ *adj* not applicable, suitable, or relevant —**inapplicability** /ìnnə plikə bíllәti/ *n* —**inapplicably** *adv*

inapposite /in áppəzit/ *adj* unsuitable or out of place —**inappositely** *adv* —**inappositeness** *n*

inappreciable /ìnnə preéshəb'l/ *adj* too small to be noticed or significant —**inappreciably** *adv*

inappreciative /ìnnə preéshətiv/ *adj* feeling or showing no appreciation —**inappreciatively** *adv* —**inappreciativeness** *n*

inapproachable /ìnnə prṓchəb'l/ *adj* impossible to approach —**inapproachability** /ìnnə prōchə bíllәti/ *n* —**inapproachably** *adv*

inappropriate /ìnnə prṓpri ət/ *adj* not fitting, timely, or suitable —**inappropriately** *adv* —**inappropriateness** *n*

inapt /in ápt/ *adj* **1** not suitable or appropriate **2** lacking aptitude, capability, or skill —**inaptitude** *n* —**inaptly** *adv* —**inaptness** *n*

inarch /i naárch/, **enarch** *vt* to graft part of one plant onto another without separating it from its parent [Early 17C. < IN-[2] + ARCH[1], because the graft forms an arch between its parent and the new stock.]

inarguable /in aár gyoo əb'l/ *adj* impossible to deny or take an opposing view about —**inarguably** *adv*

inarticulate /ìn aar tíkyoolət/ *adj* **1 EXPRESSING YOURSELF POORLY** not good at choosing the right words or speaking fluently **2 NOT UNDERSTANDABLE** not understandable as speech or language **3 NOT EFFECTIVELY EXPRESSED** not clearly or effectively expressed **4 NOT SPOKEN ABOUT** not expressed, or not able to be expressed in words **5 UNABLE TO SPEAK** lacking the power to speak, especially because of feeling strong emotion **6 NOT JOINTED** describes certain body parts that have no joints or segments, e.g. the bones of the skull **7 HAVING SHELL WITHOUT HINGE** describes a class of brachiopods that have shells without a hinge and are held together only by muscles and the body wall —**inarticulacy** *n* —**inarticulately** *adv* —**inarticulateness** *n*

inartistic /ìn aar tístik/ *adj* **1 NOT CONFORMING TO THE RULES OF ART** not in accordance with the principles of art **2 NOT INTERESTED IN THE ARTS** having no appreciation of or sensitivity to the arts **3 LACKING ARTISTIC SKILL** possessing or demonstrating little or no artistic talent —**inartistically** *adv*

inasmuch as /ìnnəz múch əz/ *conj* **1** used to introduce an explanation or reason **2** used to introduce a comment that limits the extent of something [< IN + AS + MUCH, after French *en tant* 'in so much']

inattention /ìnnə ténsh'n/ *n* failure to take proper care or give enough attention to something

inattentive /ìnnə téntiv/ *adj* not paying attention or taking proper care —**inattentively** *adv* —**inattentiveness** *n*

inaudible /in áwdəb'l/ *adj* not loud enough to be heard —**inaudibility** /in áwdə bíllәti/ *n* —**inaudibly** *adv*

inaugural /i náwgyoorəl/ *adj* **1** relating to or marking an official beginning, e.g. of a newly elected president's term **2** being the first of a series, such as the first issue of a magazine [Late 17C. < French, < *inaugurer* 'inaugurate' < Latin *inaugurare* (see INAUGURATE).]

inaugurate /i náwgyoo rayt/ (**-rates, -rating, -rated**) *vt* **1 SWEAR FORMALLY INTO OFFICE** to install somebody in office with a formal ceremony **2 OPEN CEREMONIALLY** to open or mark the beginning of something with a formal ceremony or dedication **3 PUT INTO OPERATION** to initiate something or put it into operation, especially in a formal or official manner [Late 16C. < Latin *inaugurare* 'predict from birds' flight, install after observing the omens' < *augurari* 'to predict from omens' < *augur* 'augur'.] —**inaugurator** *n* —**inauguratory** /i náwgyoorətəri/ *adj*

inauguration /i náwg yoo ráysh'n/ *n* **1 INDUCTION INTO OFFICE** the formal placing of somebody in an official position, especially the President of the United States, or a ceremony held for this purpose **2 CEREMONIAL OPENING** a formal ceremony to open or mark the beginning of something such as a new building **3 PUTTING SOMETHING INTO OPERATION**

the act of bringing something into service or putting it into operation, or an occasion on which this is done

inauspicious /in aw spíshəss/ *adj* suggesting that the future is not very promising or that success is unlikely —**inauspiciously** *adv* —**inauspiciousness** *n*

inauthentic /ìn aw théntik/ *adj* not authentic or genuine —**inauthenticity** /ìn aw then tíssəti/ *n*

in-between *adj, adv* falling between others ○ *one of his in-between moods when you don't know what he'll say* ■ *n* somebody or something that falls between others ○ *the oldest, the youngest, and the in-betweens*

inboard /ín bawrd/ *adj* **1 LOCATED INSIDE A BOAT'S HULL** located inside the hull of a boat, not fitted to the outside **2 HAVING AN INBOARD ENGINE** having an inboard engine ■ *n* **BOAT WITH AN INBOARD MOTOR** a boat that has an inboard motor ■ *adv* **AWAY FROM THE SIDES** more towards the centre of an aircraft or boat than towards the sides or edges

inborn /ín bawrn/ *adj* inherited from parents or possessed from birth

inbound[1] /ín bownd/ *adj* arriving, incoming, or heading towards an airport, port, or station [Late 19C. < IN + BOUND[4].]

inbound[2] *vti* in basketball, to put the ball back into play by passing it from out of bounds to a player on the court [Late 20C. Back-formation < INBOUNDS.]

inbounds /ín bowndz/ *adj* involving returning the basketball into play ○ *on the ensuing inbounds play*

inbounds line *n* in American football, either of the two broken lines that run the length of the pitch

in-box *n US* = **in-tray**

inbreathe /ìn breeth/ (**-breathes, -breathing, -breathed**) *vt* to take something into the airways by breathing in

inbred /ín bred/ *adj* **1 INNATE** existing naturally, through being possessed from birth or inherited from parents **2 PRODUCED BY INBREEDING** produced by the mating of closely related individuals of a species ■ *n* **FORM RESULTING FROM INBREEDING** a person or an animal whose health and intelligence are affected because his, her, or its ancestors were too closely related to each other

inbreed /ìn bréed/ (**-breeds, -breeding, -bred** /-bréd/, **-bred**) *v* **1** *vti* to mate closely related individuals of a species with each other, especially over many generations **2** *vt* to cause something to develop in somebody —**inbreeder** *n*

inbreeding /ín breeding/ *n* the mating of closely related individuals of a species, especially over many generations

in-built *adj* **1** existing as part of somebody's character **2** fitted inside something or existing as a part of it

in-by *adv, adj Scotland* **1** further in, especially further inside a house **2** to or towards a house, especially the main or only house on a piece of land such as a farm [Early 18C. < IN + BY[1].]

inc. *abbr* **1** included **2** including **3** inclusive **4** income **5** incomplete **6 inc., Inc.** *US* incorporated **7** increase

Inca /íngkə/ (*plural* **-ca** *or* **-cas**) *n* **1** a member of a Native South American people whose empire, based in Peru and covering the Andean region, lasted from the 12th century until the mid-16th century **2** a king, noble, or ruler of the Inca empire [Late 16C. < Quechua, 'royal person'.] —**Inca** *adj* —**Incaic** /ing káyik/ *adj* —**Incan** *adj*

incalculable /in kálk yòoləb'l/ *adj* **1** too great or numerous to be measured **2** too uncertain to assess or plan for in advance —**incalculability** /in kàlkyòolə bílləti/ *n* —**incalculably** *adv*

incalescent /ìnkə léss'nt/ *adj* becoming warmer or hotter than before (*technical*) [Mid-17C. < Latin *incalescent-*, present participle of *incalescere* 'get hotter' < *calere* 'be hot'.] —**incalescence** *n*

in camera *adv, adj* **1 IN A COURT CLOSED TO THE PUBLIC** in a court from which the public is barred **2 IN A JUDGE'S CHAMBERS** in a judge's private chambers rather than in open court **3 IN PRIVATE** in private or in secret [< late Latin, 'in the chamber']

incandesce /ìn kan déss/ (**-desces, -descing, -desced**) *vti* to give off light as a result of being heated to a high temperature, or to cause something to give off light in this way [Late 19C. Back-formation < INCANDESCENT.]

incandescent /ìn kan déss'nt/ *adj* **1 GLOWING WITH HEAT** emitting light as a consequence of being heated to a high temperature **2 GLOWING BRIGHTLY** shining or glowing brightly **3 SHOWING INTENSE EMOTION** feeling or displaying intense emotion such as anger or romantic passion [Late 18C. Directly or via French < Latin *incandescere* 'to glow' < *candescere* 'become white' < *candidus* (see CANDID).] —**incandescence** *n* —**incandescently** *adv*

incandescent lamp *n* an electric lamp that produces light from an electrically heated filament

incantation /ìn kan táysh'n/ *n* **1** the ritual chanting or use of supposedly magic words **2** a set of words spoken or chanted as a supposedly magic spell [14C. Via French < Latin *incantare* 'to chant' < *cantare* 'sing'.] —**incantational** *adj*

incantatory /in kántətəri/ *adj* relating to or resembling the ritual chanting or use of supposedly magic words

incapable /in káypəb'l/ *adj* **1 LACKING NECESSARY ABILITY** lacking the ability, character, or strength required to do something **2 NOT GOOD ENOUGH** unable to function or perform adequately **3 UNABLE TO LOOK AFTER SELF** not able to look after yourself ○ *exhausted and incapable* **4 IMPOSSIBLE** too extreme for something to be possible ○ *damage incapable of repair* **5 LEGALLY INELIGIBLE** legally disqualified or ineligible —**incapability** /in kàypə bílləti/ *n* —**incapableness** *n* —**incapably** *adv*

incapacitant /ìnkə pássitənt/ *n* a substance such as tear gas that can temporarily incapacitate somebody, used especially in riot control and biological warfare

incapacitate /ìnkə pássi tayt/ (**-tates, -tating, -tated**) *vt* **1** to deprive somebody or something of power, force, or effectiveness **2** to disqualify somebody or make somebody legally ineligible —**incapacitation** /ìnkə passi táysh'n/ *n*

incapacity /ínkə pássəti/ (*plural* **-ties**) *n* **1 INABILITY OR INEFFECTIVENESS** lack of ability, force, or effectiveness **2 PHYSICAL OR MENTAL CHALLENGE** a physical or mental challenge **3 LEGAL DISQUALIFICATION** a legal or official disqualification

incapsulate *vti* = **encapsulate**

in-car *adj* fitted or provided inside a car

incarcerate /in káarssə rayt/ (**-ates, -ating, -ated**) *vt* (*formal*) **1** to put somebody in prison **2** to place somebody in a place or situation of confinement [Early 16C. < medieval Latin *incarcerat-*, past participle of *incarcerare* < *carcer* 'prison'.] —**incarceration** /in kàarssə ráysh'n/ *n* —**incarcerator** *n*

incardinate /in káardi nayt/ (**-nates, -nating, -nated**) *vt* **1 MOVE A PRIEST TO A NEW DISTRICT** to transfer a Roman Catholic priest to a new district under the authority of a different bishop **2 MAKE A PRIEST A CARDINAL** to promote a member of the Roman Catholic clergy to the position of cardinal **3 MAKE A PRIEST MOST SENIOR** to promote a Roman Catholic priest to the position of most senior member of the clergy within a particular church or area [Early 17C. < late Latin *incardinat-*, past participle of *incardinare* 'ordain as chief priest' < Latin *cardinalis* (see CARDINAL).] —**incardination** /in kàardi náysh'n/ *n*

incarnadine /in káarnə dīn/ *adj* **CRIMSON** of a crimson or blood-red colour (*literary*) ■ *n* **CRIMSON COLOUR** crimson or the colour of blood (*literary*) ■ *vt* (**-dines, -dining, -dined**) **MAKE CRIMSON** to tinge or stain something crimson or blood red (*literary*) [Late 16C. Via French < Italian *incarnatino* 'carnation', literally 'flesh-colour' < Latin *carn-* 'flesh'.]

incarnate *adj* /in káarnət/ **1 MADE HUMAN** having a bodily form, especially a human form **2 PERSONIFIED** being the epitome of something ○ *an adviser who is discretion incarnate* **3 PINK OR RED** describes plant parts that are pink or crimson ■ *vt* /in káar nayt/ (**-nates, -nating, -nated**) **1 SHOW IN HUMAN FORM** to give something a bodily form, especially a human form **2 PERSONIFY** to be the epitome or personification of something **3 CAUSE TO HAPPEN** to bring about or realize something that exists as an idea or theory only [14C. < ecclesiastical Latin *incarnatus*, past participle of *incarnari* 'be made flesh' < Latin *carn-* 'flesh' (see CARNAL).] —**incarnator** /in káar naytər/ *n*

incarnation /ìn kaar náysh'n/ *n* **1 PERSONIFICATION** somebody or something personifying, representing, or typifying a quality or idea **2 ONE LIFE IN A SERIES OF LIVES** one of a succession of lives or periods spent in the body of a particular animal or person **3 MANIFESTATION OF A GOD** a god's or spirit's appearance in human or animal form

Incarnation *n* in Christianity, God's taking human form as Jesus Christ

in case ◊ **case**[1]

incase *vt* = **encase**

incautious /in káwshəss/ *adj* rash or lacking in caution —**incaution** *n* —**incautiously** *adv* —**incautiousness** *n*

incendiarism /in séndi ərizəm/ *n* inflammatory talk or provocative behaviour designed or likely to cause civil unrest (*formal*)

incendiary /in séndi əri/ *adj* **1 CONTAINING CHEMICALS THAT CAUSE FIRE** containing highly flammable substances that will cause a fire on impact **2 LIKELY TO CATCH FIRE** able to catch fire spontaneously or cause a fire easily **3 INCITING CIVIL UNREST** designed or likely to cause civil unrest **4 RELATING TO ARSON** relating to or involving the illegal burning of property ■ *n* (*plural* **-ies**) **1 BOMB DESIGNED TO CAUSE FIRE** a bomb or missile containing a highly flammable substance such as napalm, designed to cause a fire on impact **2 SOMEBODY INCITING TROUBLE** an instigator of trouble or violence, especially for political motives (*formal*) **3 ARSONIST** somebody who illegally sets fire to property [15C. < Latin *incendiarius* < *incendium* 'conflagration' < *incendere* (see INCENSE[1]).]

incense[1] /ín senss/ *n* **1 SUBSTANCE BURNT FOR ITS FRAGRANT SMELL** a substance, usually fragrant gum or wood, that gives off a pleasant smell when burnt **2 SMOKE OR FRAGRANCE FROM INCENSE** the smoke or fragrant smell produced when incense is burnt **3 FRAGRANCE** a pleasant smell **4 PRAISE** praise or adulation ■ *v* (**-censes, -censing, -censed**) **1** *vti* **HONOUR A GOD WITH INCENSE** to honour a god by burning incense **2** *vt* **PERFUME WITH INCENSE** to perfume something with incense [13C. Via French *encens* < ecclesiastical Latin *incensum*, a form of *incensus*, past participle of Latin *incendere* 'set fire to' < the base of *candere* 'to glow'.] —**incensation** /ìn sen sáysh'n/ *n*

incense[2] /in sénss/ (**-censes, -censing, -censed**) *vt* to make somebody extremely angry [15C. Either < French *encenser* < *encens* 'incense', or < ecclesiastical Latin *incensare* < *incensum* (see INCENSE[1]).] —**incensement** *n*

incense cedar *n* **1** a coniferous evergreen tree of the cypress family, with scaly leaves and aromatic wood. Native to: North America, Asia, New Zealand. Genera: *Austrocedrus* and *Calocedrus* and *Libocedrus*. **2** the scented durable wood of the incense cedar. Use: household fragrance, moth repellent, decking, fence posts, pencils.

incensory /ín senssəri/ (*plural* **-ries**) *n* RELIG = **censer** [Early 17C. < medieval Latin *incensorium* < ecclesiastical Latin *incensum* (see INCENSE[1]).]

incentive /in séntiv/ *n* something that encourages or motivates somebody to do something ■ *adj* serving to encourage or motivate somebody [Early 17C. < Latin *incentivum* 'something that sets the tune' < *incinere* 'to sound' < *canere* 'sing'.] —**incentively** *adv*

SYNONYMS See ***motive***.

---

incentivise *vt* = **incentivize**

incentivize /in sénti vīz/ (**-izes, -izing, -ized**), **incentivise** (**-ises, -ising, -ised**) *vt* to motivate somebody by offering an incentive such as a higher rate of pay (*informal*)

inception /in sépsh'n/ *n* **1** the beginning of something (*formal*) **2** enrolment as a university student, especially one studying for a master's degree or doctorate (*dated formal*) [15C. Directly or via French < Latin *inception-* < *incipere* (see INCIPIENT).]

inceptive /in séptiv/ *adj* **1 INITIAL** representing or coming at the beginning of something (*formal*) **2 EXPRESSING THE IDEA OF STARTING** describes a verb or verb form that, in some languages, indicates the beginning of an action ■ *n* **1 INCEPTIVE ASPECT** the inceptive aspect of verbs **2 INCEPTIVE VERB** a verb in the inceptive aspect [Early 17C. < late Latin *inceptivus* < Latin *incipere* (see INCIPIENT).] —**inceptively** *adv*

incertitude /in súrti tyood/ *n* **1** doubt or uncertainty **2** lack of self-confidence

incessant /in séss'nt/ *adj* continuing for a long time without stopping [15C. Directly or via French < late Latin *incessant-* < *cessare* (see CEASE).] —**incessancy** *n* —**incessantly** *adv*

incest /ín sest/ *n* sexual activity between two people who are considered, for moral or genetic reasons, too closely related to have such a relationship [13C. < Latin *incestus* < *castus* 'pure'.]

incestuous /in sést yoo əss/ *adj* **1 RELATING TO OR INVOLVING INCEST** relating to or involving a sexual relationship between two people who are considered, for moral and genetic reasons, too closely related to have such a relationship **2 GUILTY OF INCEST** having had a sexual relationship with somebody considered to be too close a relative **3 UNHEALTHILY EXCLUSIVE OF OTHERS** unhealthily intimate or interconnected, especially so as to exclude the involvement or influence of others ○ *an incestuous friendship* —**incestuously** *adv* —**incestuousness** *n*

inch[1] /inch/ *n* 1 UNIT OF LENGTH (*symbol* ") a unit of length equal to 2.54 cm/$\frac{1}{12}$ of a foot 2 SMALL AMOUNT a very small amount, degree, or distance ○ *The committee won't budge an inch on this issue.* 3 AMOUNT OF RAIN OR SNOW a fall of enough rain or snow to cover a surface to a depth of one inch 4 UNIT OF ATMOSPHERIC PRESSURE a unit of atmospheric pressure equal to that needed to maintain a mercury column one inch high in a barometer ■ *vti* MOVE SLOWLY to move or cause somebody or something to move very slowly or by small degrees [Pre-12C. < Latin *uncia* 'one twelfth' < *unus* 'one'.]

inch[2] /inch/ *n* in Scotland and Ireland, a small island (*often in placenames*) [15C. < Scottish Gaelic *innis* 'island'.]

inchoate /in kō ət/ *adj* (*formal*) 1 JUST BEGINNING just beginning to develop 2 IMPERFECTLY FORMED only partly formed 3 CHAOTIC lacking structure, order, or organization [Mid-16C. < Latin *inchoatus*, past participle of *inchoare* 'begin'.] —**inchoately** *adv* —**inchoateness** *n* —**inchoation** /in kō áysh'n/ *n*

inchoative /in kṓ ətiv/ *adj*, *n* GRAM = **inceptive** *adj.* 2, **inceptive** *n.* 1, **inceptive** *n.* 2

Inchon /ín chón/, **Inch'ŏn** port in NW South Korea. Population: 2,307,618 (1995).

inchworm /inch wurm/ *n* INSECTS = **measuring worm**

incidence /ínssidənss/ *n* 1 RATE OF OCCURRENCE the frequency with which something occurs 2 INSTANCE OR MANNER OF SOMETHING HAPPENING an instance of something happening, or the manner in which it happens 3 IMPACT ON SURFACE the impact that something moving, e.g. a ray of light or a projectile, makes with a surface

USAGE incidents or **incidence**? Though pronounced similarly, these two words mean different things and so ought not to be confused. ***Incidents***, a plural noun, means 'events, occurrences', as in *Three incidents* [not *incidence*] *of speeding on campus have been reported. Five hundred incidents* [not *incidence*] *of Ebola virus were documented last year.* ***Incidence***, a singular noun, means variously 'the rate of occurrence of something happening' and 'an instance of something happening and how it happens', as in *studying the annual incidence* [not *incidents*] *of Ebola virus; increased incidence* [not *incidents*] *of poverty.*

incident /ínssidənt/ *n* 1 EVENT something that happens, especially a single event 2 VIOLENT OCCURRENCE a public occurrence, especially a violent one ○ *an incident outside a nightclub* 3 EVENT WITH POTENTIALLY SERIOUS CONSEQUENCES an event that may result in a crisis, especially one involving different countries ■ *adj* 1 RELATED accompanying something or occurring as a consequence of it (*formal*) 2 TOUCHING OR STRIKING coming into contact with a surface [15C. Directly or via French < Latin *incidere* 'fall upon' < *cadere* 'to fall'.]

USAGE See ***incidence***.

incidental /ínssi dént'l/ *adj* 1 RELATED OR ACCOMPANYING related to or accompanying something more important 2 OCCURRING BY CHANCE occurring by chance or without intention 3 OCCASIONAL unimportant or occasional 4 RESULTING occurring as a result of something (*formal*) ■ *n* MINOR ITEM something that is occasional or unimportant such as a minor expense

incidentally /ínssi dént'li/ *adv* 1 used to introduce additional information such as something that the speaker has just thought of 2 by chance or by accident

incidental music *n* music that accompanies the action of a film, play, or television programme, as distinct from theme music or songs that feature in a musical

~~**incidently**~~ incorrect spelling of **incidentally**

incinerate /in sínnə rayt/ (**-ates, -ating, -ated**) *vti* to burn to ashes, or cause something to burn to ashes, especially in an incinerator [15C. < medieval Latin *incinerare* < *ciner-* 'ashes'.] —**incineration** /in sínnə ráysh'n/ *n*

incinerator /in sínnə raytər/ *n* a furnace for destroying things by burning them, especially one used to burn rubbish

incipient /in síppi ənt/ *adj* beginning to appear or develop [Mid-17C. < Latin *incipient-*, present participle of *incipere* 'undertake' < *capere* 'to take'.] —**incipience** *n* —**incipiently** *adv*

incipit /ínssipit, ínki-/ *n* the opening word or words of a medieval manuscript or an early printed book, by which it is often known in the absence of a title [Late 19C. < Latin, 'it begins', a form of *incipere* (see INCIPIENT).]

incise /in síz/ (**-cises, -cising, -cised**) *vt* 1 to carve or engrave a pattern or design into something 2 to cut into something [Mid-16C. < French *inciser* < Latin *incis-*, past participle of *incidere* 'cut into' < *caedere* 'to cut'.]

incision /in sízh'n/ *n* 1 CUT OR ACT OF CUTTING a cut or the act of cutting, especially when performed by a surgeon 2 LEAF'S DEEPLY INDENTED EDGE a sharp indentation in the edge of a leaf 3 FACT OF BEING INCISIVE the fact or quality of being quick to understand or able to express something clearly

incisive /in síssiv/ *adj* 1 QUICK TO UNDERSTAND quick to understand, analyse, or act 2 EXPRESSING OR EXPRESSED CLEARLY characterized by clear and direct expression 3 HURTFUL designed to be cutting, unkind, or hurtful —**incisively** *adv* —**incisiveness** *n*

incisor /in sízər/ *n* one of the flat sharp-edged teeth in the front of the mouth, used for cutting and tearing food [Late 17C. < medieval Latin *dens incisor* 'cutter tooth' < Latin *incis-* (see INCISE).] —**incisal** *adj*

incite /in sít/ (**-cites, -citing, -cited**) *vt* to stir up feelings in or provoke action by somebody [15C. Via French *inciter* < Latin *incitare* 'urge on' < *citare* (see CITE).] —**incitation** /in sī táysh'n/ *n* —**incitement** *n* —**inciter** *n*

incivility /ínssi vílləti/ (*plural* **-ties**) *n* 1 rude or impolite behaviour or language 2 a rude or impolite act or remark

incl. *abbr* 1 including 2 inclusive

inclement /in klémmənt/ *adj* 1 unpleasant in being stormy, rainy, or snowy 2 showing little or no mercy (*formal*) [Mid-16C. Directly or via French *inclément* < Latin *inclement-* 'not clement' < *clement-* 'mild'.] —**inclemency** *n* —**inclemently** *adv*

inclination /ínkli náysh'n/ *n* 1 WAY SOMEBODY FEELS a feeling that pushes somebody to make a particular choice or take a particular decision 2 TENDENCY a tendency to do, prefer, or desire something 3 DEVIATION FROM LINE OR PLANE the tilting of something away from a line or surface, or the degree to which is it tilted 4 SLOPE a sloping surface 5 TILTING a bending of something, e.g. a bowing of the head 6 ANGLE ON GRAPH the angle between a line on a graph and the positive direction of the x-axis 7 SMALLER ANGLE the smaller angle between two lines or planes 8 ANGLE OF ORBIT the angle between a planet's orbit and the apparent orbit of the Sun in relation to the Earth 9 GEOG = **dip** *n.* 10 —**inclinational** *adj*

incline *vti* /in klín/ (**-clines, -clining, -clined**) 1 BE OR MAKE LIKELY TO ACT to tend, or make somebody tend, towards a particular belief or course of action 2 ANGLE OR BE ANGLED to lie at an angle or put something at an angle 3 BEND to bend something, especially the head or body when bowing or nodding ■ *n* /ín klīn/ 1 SLOPE a slope or sloping surface 2 RAIL = **inclined railway** [14C. Via Old French *encliner* < Latin *inclinare* 'lean towards' < *clinare* 'to lean'.] —**inclinable** *adj* —**incliner** *n*

inclined /in klínd/ *adj* 1 MOTIVATED moved or persuaded to do something ○ *I'm not inclined to listen to any more of this.* 2 TALENTED IN A PARTICULAR AREA naturally talented or interested in a particular field or area 3 SLANTED OR FORMING AN ANGLE sloping or forming an angle with something else

inclined railway *n* a railway system, used on particularly steep slopes, that uses a cable to pull trains upwards

inclinometer /ínkli nómmitər/ *n* 1 an instrument that measures angles or slopes such as the angle of an aircraft relative to the ground 2 an instrument used to determine the angle made by the Earth's magnetic field relative to the horizontal plane [Mid-19C. < Latin *inclinare* (see INCLINE).]

inclose *vt* = **enclose**

inclosure *n* = **enclosure** (*archaic*)

include /in klood/ (**-cludes, -cluding, -cluded**) *vt* 1 to have something as a constituent element 2 to make somebody or something part of a group [15C. < Latin *includere* 'enclose' < *claudere* 'to shut'.] —**includable** *adj*

included /in kloodid/ *adj* 1 CONTAINED WITHIN A GROUP forming part of a group or whole 2 NOT PROTRUDING describes the stamens or carpels of a flower that do not protrude beyond the edges of the petals 3 LOCATED BETWEEN INTERSECTING LINES formed by and contained in two intersecting lines —**includedness** *n*

including /in klooding/ *prep* used to introduce examples of people or things forming part of a particular group or whole ○ *It will cost you £39.95 including VAT.*

inclusion /in kloozh'n/ *n* 1 PRESENCE IN GROUP the addition of somebody or something to, or the presence of somebody or something in, a group or mixture 2 SOMEBODY OR SOMETHING INCLUDED somebody or something included in a group or mixture 3 SUBSTANCE TRAPPED INSIDE MINERAL a solid, liquid, or gas contained within a mineral or rock 4 FOREIGN PARTICLE IN METAL a particle of foreign material within a piece of metal 5 FOREIGN BODY IN CELL a non-living mass such as a starch grain or droplet of fat in the cytoplasm or nucleus of a cell 6 RELATION BETWEEN SETS the relation between two classes or sets when the second is a subset of the first [Early 17C. < Latin *inclus-*, past participle of *includere* (see INCLUDE).] —**inclusionary** *adj*

inclusion body *n* a mass of virus particles inside a cell, formerly used in the diagnosis of some viral infections

inclusive /in kloossiv/ *adj* 1 INCLUDING SPECIFIED LIMITS used to indicate that a span of time or a range within a series includes the dates, times, or other items stated at the beginning and end of the span ○ *the period from October 1 to July 31, inclusive* 2 INCLUDING MANY THINGS including many things or everything 3 INCLUDING SPEAKER AND PERSON ADDRESSED describes a pronoun such as 'we' that includes the speaker and the person or persons spoken to 4 BEING TYPE OF SENTENCE IN LOGIC describes a sentence in logic (**disjunction**) containing two propositions of which at least one and possibly both can be true. ◊ **exclusive** *adj.* 9 [Late 16C. < medieval Latin *inclusivus* < Latin *inclus-* (see INCLUDE).] —**inclusively** *adv* —**inclusiveness** *n*

incoercible /ínkō úrssəb'l/ *adj* not giving in to force or pressure from others

incognita /in kog neetə/ *adj*, *adv* with the identity disguised or hidden, e.g. under an assumed name (*describes a woman or girl*) [Late 17C. < Italian, feminine of *incognito* 'incognito'.] —**incognita** *n*

incognito /in kog neetō/ *adj*, *adv* IN DISGUISE with the identity disguised or hidden, e.g. under an assumed name ■ *n* (*plural* **-tos**) 1 SOMEBODY IN DISGUISE somebody who acts or travels in disguise so as to be unrecognizable 2 DISGUISE the character, disguise, or name assumed by somebody who is attempting to be unrecognizable [Mid-17C. Via Italian < Latin *incognitus* 'unknown' < *cognitus*, past participle of *cognoscere* 'learn' < *noscere* 'know'.]

incoherent /in kō heerənt/ *adj* 1 LACKING CLARITY OR ORGANIZATION not clearly expressed or well thought out, and consequently difficult to understand 2 UNABLE TO SPEAK OR EXPRESS CLEARLY unable to express thoughts or feelings clearly or logically 3 NOT COHESIVE not sticking together as a mass 4 OUT OF PHASE having the same frequency but not the same phase —**incoherence** *n* —**incoherently** *adv*

incombustible /ínkəm bústəb'l/ *adj* not capable of being burnt —**incombustibility** /ínkəm bústə bílləti/ *n* —**incombustible** *n* —**incombustibly** *adv*

income /ín kum/ *n* 1 the amount of money received over a period of time either as payment for work, goods, or services, or as profit on capital 2 a coming in or flowing in [14C. < Old Norse *innkoma* 'arrival'; later < IN + COME.]

income bond *n* a bond paying a rate of return in proportion to the issuer's income

income group *n* a section of the population grouped by income, e.g. for the purpose of market research

incomer /ín kummər/ *n* a new resident of a place

incomes policy *n* an economic policy that seeks to control inflation by controlling wage levels

income support *n* a social security payment made to unemployed people and people on low incomes

income tax *n* a tax paid on money made from employment, business, or capital (*hyphenated before nouns*)

incoming /ín kumming/ *adj* 1 ARRIVING arriving, coming in, or entering 2 TAKING UP NEW JOB about to take up a particular job or office 3 BEING RECEIVED being received or taken in ■ *n* ARRIVAL an arrival or entrance (*formal*) ■ **incomings** *npl* INCOME sums of money earned or received

incommensurable /ínkə ménshərəb'l/ *adj* 1 IMPOSSIBLE TO MEASURE not able to be compared or measured, especially because of lacking a common quality necessary for a comparison **2 HAVING NO COMMON FACTOR** having no common mathematical factor or measure other than 1 ■ *n* **SOMETHING INCOMMENSURABLE** something that cannot be compared or measured, especially a quality or a mathematical value —**incommensurability** /ìnkə ménshərə bíllәti/ *n* —**incommensurably** *adv*

incommensurate /ìnkə ménshərət/ *adj* **1** not proportionate to or up to the level of something **2** = **incommensurable** *adj.* 1 —**incommensurately** *adv* —**incommensurateness** *n*

incommode /ìnkə mṓd/ (**-modes, -moding, -moded**) *vt* to bother or inconvenience somebody (*formal*) [Late 16C. Directly or via French *incommoder* < Latin *incommodare* < *commodus* (see COMMODIOUS).]

incommodious /ìnkə mṓdi əss/ *adj* (*formal*) **1** uncomfortably lacking in space **2** causing trouble or inconvenience —**incommodiously** *adv* —**incommodiousness** *n*

incommunicable /ìnkə myóonikəb'l/ *adj* not able to be expressed or conveyed to others —**incommunicability** /ìnkə myóonikə bíllәti/ *n* —**incommunicably** *adv*

incommunicado /ìnkə myóoni kaádō/ *adj* prevented by circumstances or by force from communicating with other people [Mid-19C. < Spanish *incomunicado* < *incomunicar* 'deprive of communication' < Latin *communicare* (see COMMUNICATE).] —**incommunicado** *adv*

incommunicative /ìnkə myóonikətiv/ *adj* unwilling to communicate or provide information —**incommunicatively** *adv* —**incommunicativeness** *n*

incommutable /ìnkə myóotəb'l/ *adj* not able to be changed, exchanged for something else, or reduced in severity —**incommutability** /ìnkə myóotə bíllәti/ *n* —**incommutableness** *n* —**incommutably** *adv*

incomparable /in kómpərəb'l/ *adj* **1** so excellent, outstanding, or unique as to have no equal **2** impossible to compare with something else, because there is no basis for a comparison —**incomparability** /in kómpərə bíllәti/ *n* —**incomparableness** *n* —**incomparably** *adv*

incompatible /ìnkəm páttəb'l/ *adj* **1 UNABLE TO COOPERATE OR COEXIST** unable to exist, cooperate, function, or get along with somebody or something else because of basic differences **2 UNABLE TO BE HELD SIMULTANEOUSLY** unable to be held by one person simultaneously with another position or office **3 LIKELY TO BE REJECTED BY DONOR** describes a tissue transplant or blood that is rejected by a recipient's immune system **4 NOT SUITABLE FOR USE IN COMBINATION** describes two or more drugs that should not be used together **5 NOT ABLE TO BE POLLINATED OR GRAFTED** describes plants or varieties that cannot be successfully pollinated by or grafted onto each other **6 CONTRADICTORY** describes two propositions that cannot both be true at the same time **7 MATHEMATICALLY INCONSISTENT** not mathematically consistent —**incompatibility** /ìnkəm páttə bíllәti/ *n* —**incompatibleness** *n* —**incompatibly** *adv*

incompetent /in kómpitənt/ *adj* **1 BAD AT DOING SOMETHING** lacking the skills, qualities, or ability to do something properly **2 LACKING NECESSARY STATUS** not having the necessary legal status, validity, or powers for the purpose in question **3 DEFECTIVE** describes a body part such as a muscle that does not function properly ○ *an incompetent cervix* ■ *n* **SOMEBODY BAD AT DOING SOMETHING** somebody who cannot do something properly —**incompetence** *n* —**incompetently** *adv*

incomplete /ìnkəm pléet/ *adj* **1** lacking something such as a particular part that properly or desirably belongs with it **2** not yet finished or fully developed —**incompletely** *adv* —**incompleteness** *n* —**incompletion** /-pléesh'n/ *n*

incomplete fracture *n* a fracture that does not go all the way through a bone

incompliant /ìnkəm plī́ ənt/ *adj* unwilling to to be flexible and accommodating or to comply with something (*formal*) —**incompliance** *n* —**incompliantly** *adv*

incomprehensible /in kómpri hénssəb'l/ *adj* impossible or very difficult to understand —**incomprehensibility** /in kómpri hénssə bíllәti/ *n* —**incomprehensibleness** *n* —**incomprehensibly** *adv*

incomprehension /in kómpri hénsh'n/ *n* an inability or failure to understand

incompressible /ìnkəm préssəb'l/ *adj* difficult or impossible to compress —**incompressibility** /ìnkəm préssə bíllәti/ *n* —**incompressibleness** *n* —**incompressibly** *adv*

inconceivable /ìnkən séevəb'l/ *adj* **1** impossible to imagine or to grasp mentally and understand **2** so unlikely as to be beyond belief or thought impossible ○ *It's inconceivable that they should have made the same mistake twice.* —**inconceivability** /ìnkən séevə bíllәti/ *n* —**inconceivableness** *n* —**inconceivably** *adv*

inconclusive /ìnkən klóossiv/ *adj* not producing a clear-cut result, firm conclusion, or decisive proof of something —**inconclusively** *adv* —**inconclusiveness** *n*

incongruent /in kóng groo ənt/ *adj* not corresponding in structure or content —**incongruence** *n* —**incongruently** *adv*

incongruity /ìnkən gróo əti/ (*plural* **-ties**) *n* **1** the fact of being incongruous **2** something that does not seem to fit in with or be appropriate to its context

incongruous /in kóng groo əss/ *adj* **1** unsuitable, strange, or out of place in a particular setting or context **2** not in accord or consistent with something —**incongruously** *adv* —**incongruousness** *n*

inconsecutive /ìnkən sékyootiv/ *adj* not following in order one after another —**inconsecutively** *adv* —**inconsecutiveness** *n*

inconsequent /in kónsikwənt/ *adj* not following as a natural or logical result —**inconsequence** *n* —**inconsequently** *adv* —**inconsequentness** *n*

inconsequential /in kónssi kwénsh'l/ *adj* **1** of little or no importance **2** = **inconsequent** —**inconsequentiality** /in kónssi kwénshi állәti/ *n* —**inconsequentially** *adv* —**inconsequentialness** *n*

inconsiderable /ìnkən síddərəb'l/ *adj* **1** small in size, amount, or value (*often used with 'not'*) ○ *a not inconsiderable travel allowance that enabled me to choose the best hotels* **2** so unimportant as to be not worth considering (*formal*) —**inconsiderableness** *n* —**inconsiderably** *adv*

inconsiderate /ìnkən síddərət/ *adj* lacking thought or consideration for other people and their feelings —**inconsiderately** *adv* —**inconsiderateness** *n* —**inconsideration** /ìnkən síddə ráysh'n/ *n*

inconsistency /ìnkən sístənssi/ (*plural* **-cies**), **inconsistence** /ìnkən sístənss/ *n* **1** the fact of being inconsistent **2** something that contradicts something else or that is not in keeping with it

inconsistent /ìnkən sístənt/ *adj* **1 CONTAINING CONFLICTING OR CONTRADICTORY ELEMENTS** containing elements that conflict with or contradict each other **2 VARYING AND UNPREDICTABLE** unpredictable or unreliable in being likely to behave differently or achieve a different result if a particular situation is repeated **3 CONFLICTING OR INCOMPATIBLE** conflicting with or not corresponding to something such as a rule, principle, or expectation **4 LACKING COMMON VALUES IN AN EQUATION** not having a common set of values for the unknowns in an equation —**inconsistently** *adv*

inconsolable /ìnkən sṓləb'l/ *adj* so deeply distressed that nobody can offer any effective comfort —**inconsolability** /ìnkən sōlə bíllәti/ *n* —**inconsolableness** *n* —**inconsolably** *adv*

inconspicuous /ìnkən spíkyoo əss/ *adj* not easily seen or noticed —**inconspicuously** *adv* —**inconspicuousness** *n*

inconstant /in kónstənt/ *adj* **1** unfaithful in relationships (*literary*) **2** likely to change frequently and unpredictably ○ *an inconstant sea breeze* —**inconstancy** *n* —**inconstantly** *adv*

incontestable /ìnkən téstəb'l/ *adj* impossible to question or dispute —**incontestability** /ìnkən téstə bíllәti/ *n* —**incontestableness** *n* —**incontestably** *adv*

incontinent /in kóntinənt/ *adj* **1 UNABLE TO CONTROL BLADDER OR BOWELS** unable to control the bladder or bowels and liable to urinate or defecate involuntarily **2 LACKING SEXUAL CONTROL** lacking restraint in sexual matters **3 UNRESTRAINED** unrestrained and uncontrolled (*literary*) [14C. Directly or via French < Latin *incontinent-* 'not holding together' < *continere* (see CONTAIN).] —**incontinence** *n* —**incontinency** *n* —**incontinently** *adv*

incontrollable /ìnkən trṓləb'l/ *adj* **1** too strongly felt to be suppressed **2** too unruly or wild to discipline or control —**incontrollability** /ìnkən trōlə bíllәti/ *n* —**incontrollably** *adv*

incontrovertible /in kontrə vúrtəb'l/ *adj* certain, undeniable, and not open to question —**incontrovertibility** /in kontrə vúrtə bíllәti/ *n* —**incontrovertibleness** *n* —**incontrovertibly** *adv*

inconvenience /ìnkən véeni ənss/ *n* **1 LACK OF CONVENIENCE** the quality or fact of being inconvenient or causing discomfort, difficulty, or annoyance **2 ANNOYANCE** something that causes difficulties or annoyance ■ *vt* (**-iences, -iencing, -ienced**) **CAUSE DIFFICULTY TO** to cause somebody difficulties, especially relatively minor or unnecessary ones, or involving unwanted extra effort, work, or trouble

inconvenient /ìnkən véeni ənt/ *adj* causing or involving difficulties or unwanted extra effort, work, or trouble —**inconveniently** *adv*

inconvertible /ìnkən vúrtəb'l/ *adj* **1** not exchangeable for gold or silver **2** not exchangeable for the currency of another country —**inconvertibility** /ìnkən vúrtə bíllәti/ *n* —**inconvertibleness** *n* —**inconvertibly** *adv*

inconvincible /ìnkən vínssəb'l/ *adj* impossible or very difficult to convince —**inconvincibility** /ìnkən vínssə bíllәti/ *n* —**inconvincibleness** *n* —**inconvincibly** *adv*

incoordinate /ìnkō áwrdinət/ *adj* lacking coordination —**incoordinately** *adv*

incoordination /ìnkō áwrdi náysh'n/ *n* **1** an inability to control voluntary muscular movements **2** lack of organization or a consistent approach (*formal*)

incorporate *v* /in káwrpə rayt/ (**-rates, -rating, -rated**) **1** *vti* **JOIN WITH SOMETHING THAT EXISTS** to unite or combine something with, or include it within, something already formed **2** *vti* **MERGE THINGS** to merge, or to combine one thing with another, so as to form a united whole **3** *vti* **FORM OR BECOME CORPORATION** to form a corporation, or to give something the legal form of a corporation **4** *vt* **GIVE REAL FORM TO** to give material form to something (*formal*) ■ *adj* /in káwrpərət/ **1 UNITED** merged into a united whole (*formal*) **2 LEGALLY A CORPORATION** legally established as a corporation [14C. < late Latin *incorporare* 'make into a body' < *corpus* (see CORPUS).] —**incorporable** *adj* —**incorporated** *adj* —**incorporatedness** *n* —**incorporation** /in káwrpə ráysh'n/ *n* —**incorporative** *adj* —**incorporator** *n*

incorporeal /in kawr páwri əl/ *adj* **1** without a physical body or existing solely as a spirit (*formal*) **2** describes a legal entity that has no material existence of its own but is connected to an actual object such as a patent or copyright —**incorporeality** /-páwri állәti/ *n* —**incorporeally** *adv*

incorporeity /in káwrpə rée əti/ (*plural* **-ties**) *n* **1** the condition or quality of being incorporeal **2** something that is incorporeal

incorrect /ìnkə rékt/ *adj* **1** wrong, false, or inaccurate **2** not appropriate, suitable, or proper —**incorrectly** *adv* —**incorrectness** *n*

incorrigible /in kórrijəb'l/ *adj* **1 IMPOSSIBLE TO CHANGE** impossible to correct or reform ○ *incorrigible cynics* **2 UNRULY AND UNMANAGEABLE** very difficult to control or keep in order ■ *n* **SOMEBODY OR SOMETHING INCORRIGIBLE** somebody or something that is impossible or very difficult to change [14C. Directly or via French < Latin *incorrigibilis* 'not able to be corrected' < *corrigere* (see CORRECT).] —**incorrigibility** /in kórrijə bíllәti/ *n* —**incorrigibly** *adv*

incorrupt /ìnkə rúpt/ *adj* **1 UNSULLIED** morally pure and uncorrupted (*formal*) **2 NOT DECOMPOSED** unaffected by decay or spoiling (*archaic*) **3 FREE OF MISTAKES** without errors or alterations (*formal*) —**incorruption** *n* —**incorruptly** *adv*

incorruptible /ìnkə rúptəb'l/ *adj* **1** incapable of being morally corrupted, especially incapable of being bribed or motivated by selfish or base interests **2** incapable of being affected by decay or decomposition —**incorruptibility** /ìnkə rúptə bíllәti/ *n* —**incorruptibly** *adv*

incr. *abbr* **1** increase **2** increased **3** increasing **4** increment

increase *vti* /in kréess, íng kreess/ (**-creases, -creasing, -creased**) **MAKE OR BECOME LARGER OR GREATER** to make something larger in number, quantity, or degree, or become larger in number, quantity, or degree ■ *n* /íng kreess, in kréess/ **1 ENLARGEMENT** a rise to a greater number, quantity, or degree, or the amount by which something is increased **2 INCREASING IN SIZE** the process of becoming or of making something larger in number, quantity, or degree [14C. Via Old French *encreistre* < Latin *increscere* < *crescere* 'grow'.] —**increasable** *adj* —**increaser** /-ər/ *n*

SYNONYMS *increase, expand, enlarge, extend, augment, intensify, amplify*

CORE MEANING: to make larger or greater

increase to become or cause to become larger in number, quantity, degree, or scope; **expand** to become or cause to become larger or more extensive; **enlarge** to become or cause to become larger generally, or to broaden in scope and detail; **extend** to make larger in terms of length, area, period of time, or other existing limits; **augment** (*formal*) to add to something in order to make it larger or more substantial; **intensify** to become or cause to become greater in strength or degree; **amplify** to become or cause to become louder, or greater in intensity or scope.

---

increasingly /in kreéssingli/ *adv* ever increasing over time ○ *'As Election Day approaches, there is no front-runner, and the insults and accusations from both sides have been increasingly frequent and bellicose'.* (Susan K. Livio, *Election '96: Senate Race*; 1996)

~~**incredable**~~ incorrect spelling of **incredible**

incredible /in kréddəb'l/ *adj* **1 BEYOND BELIEF** impossible or very difficult to believe **2 MORE THAN THOUGHT POSSIBLE** unexpectedly or astonishingly large or great (*informal*) ○ *There's an incredible amount of food still left.* **3 AMAZING** very surprising ○ *It's incredible how many people have turned up.* **4 EXCELLENT** extraordinarily good, talented, or enjoyable (*informal*) —**incredibility** /in kréddə bílləti/ *n* —**incredibly** *adv*

incredulity /ínkrə dyoóləti/ *n* a state or feeling of disbelief

incredulous /in kréddyoóləss/ *adj* **1** unable or unwilling to believe something **2** showing or characterized by disbelief —**incredulously** *adv* —**incredulousness** *n*

increment /íngkrimənt/ *n* **1 INCREASE** an addition to or increase in the amount or size of something, especially one of a series of small, often regular or planned increases, e.g. to a salary **2 ACT OF INCREASING** the act or process of increasing **3 SMALL CHANGE IN MATHEMATICAL VALUE** a small positive or negative change in the value of a mathematical variable or function [15C. < Latin *incrementum* 'growth' < *increscere* (see INCREASE).] —**incremental** /íngkri mént'l/ *adj* —**incrementally** *adv*

incremental backup *n* backup in which only computer files modified since the last backup are copied

incrementalism /íngkri mént'lizəm/ *n* = **gradualism** *n*.

increscent /in kréss'nt/ *adj* showing a lighted surface area, especially that of the Moon, that is increasing in size [Late 16C. < Latin *increscere* (see INCREASE).]

incriminate /in krímmi nayt/ (**-nates, -nating, -nated**) *vt* **1** to provide evidence of somebody's guilt or make somebody appear guilty of a crime or mistake **2** to accuse somebody of a crime or error [Mid-18C. < late Latin *incriminat-*, past participle of *incriminare* 'make criminal' < *crimen* (see CRIME).] —**incriminating** *adj* —**incrimination** /in krímmi náysh'n/ *n* —**incriminator** *n* —**incriminatory** *adj*

incross /ín kross/ *n* an organism produced through inbreeding within the same strain or breed ■ *vti* to produce an organism by inbreeding or to be produced in this way

in-crowd *n* a small, fashionable, and exclusive or influential group, especially one that others want to be part of because of its prestige (*informal*)

incrust *vti* = **encrust**

incrustation *n* = **encrustation**

incubate /íngkyoo bayt/ (**-bates, -bating, -bated**) *v* **1** *vti* **SIT ON EGGS** to keep eggs warm by sitting on them so that the embryos inside can develop and hatch, or to be kept warm in this way **2** *vti* **KEEP BABY IN INCUBATOR** to keep a premature or unwell baby inside a controlled environment in order to keep it alive and assist its growth and development, or to be kept in such an environment **3** *vti* **GROW MICROORGANISMS IN CONTROLLED ENVIRONMENT** to keep cells or microorganisms at a controlled temperature in or on a medium so that they multiply, or to be kept in or on such a medium **4** *vi* **DEVELOP IN FAVOURABLE ENVIRONMENT** to be kept, or to develop while being kept, in a favourable environment, e.g. under a parent bird's body, in a incubator, or in a growth medium **5** *vti* **BUILD UP DISEASE-PRODUCING GERMS** to develop an infection, through the reproduction of germs, to the point at which the first signs of a disease appear, or to be developed in this way **6** *vti* **GRADUALLY BRING SOMETHING INTO BEING** to form or develop something, such as a plan or an idea, slowly and quietly over a period of time, or to be formed or developed in this way [Mid-17C. < Latin *incubare* 'lie down on' < *cubare* 'lie down'.] —**incubative** *adj* —**incubatory** *adj*

incubation /íngkyoo báysh'n/ *n* **1 PROCESS OF INCUBATING OR BEING INCUBATED** the process of incubating something such as an egg or an idea, the process of being incubated, or the period of time taken by either process **2 MAINTENANCE OF BABY IN CONTROLLED ENVIRONMENT** the keeping of a premature or unwell baby in an environment in which the temperature, humidity, and oxygen levels can be easily controlled **3 CONTROLLED GROWTH OF MICROORGANISMS** the maintenance of cells or microorganisms under a controlled temperature in or on a medium so that they can multiply **4 GROWTH OF DISEASE-CAUSING MICROORGANISMS** the development of an infection inside the body to the point at which the first signs of disease become apparent **5 GRADUAL DEVELOPMENT** the slow development of something, especially through thought and planning **6** = **incubation period** —**incubational** *adj*

incubation period *n* the period between the time somebody is infected with a disease and the appearance of its first symptoms

incubator /íngkyoo baytər/ *n* **1** a hospital apparatus, usually a transparent box, in which a premature or unwell baby is kept in a controlled environment to protect it from infection and assist its growth and development **2** an apparatus in which the temperature is kept at a constant level so that eggs can be artificially hatched or cells and microorganisms can multiply in or on a growth medium

incubus /íngkyoobəss/ (*plural* **-bi** /-bī/ *or* **-buses**) *n* **1** a male demon that was believed in medieval times to have sexual intercourse with women while they were asleep **2** a thing or factor that causes somebody much worry or anxiety, especially a nightmare or obsession (*literary*) [14C. < late Latin, 'nightmare' < Latin *incubare* 'lie down on'.]

incudes plural of **incus**

inculcate /in kul kayt/ (**-cates, -cating, -cated**) *vt* to fix something firmly in somebody's mind through frequent, forceful repetition [Mid-16C. < Latin *inculcat-*, past participle of *inculcare* 'stamp in' < *calcare* (see CAULK).] —**inculcation** /in kul káysh'n/ *n* —**inculcator** *n*

inculpate /in kul payt/ (**-pates, -pating, -pated**) *vt* to incriminate somebody or put the blame for something on somebody (*archaic*) [Late 18C. < late Latin *inculpat-*, past participle of *inculpare* 'put blame on' < Latin *culpa* 'blame, fault'.] —**inculpation** /ín kul páysh'n/ *n* —**inculpative** /in kúlpətiv/ *adj* —**inculpatory** /in kúlpətəri/ *adj*

incumbency /in kúmbənssi/ *n* (*formal*) **1 TENURE OF OFFICE** the period of time during which somebody occupies an official post **2 OFFICIAL POST** an official position, especially in a church or political organization **3 EXISTENCE AS A DUTY** the obligatory nature of something or the fact of its being a duty or obligation that must be performed **4 OBLIGATION** something such as a duty that is necessary or obligatory

incumbent /in kúmbənt/ *adj* **1 OBLIGATORY** necessary as a result of a duty, responsibility, or obligation (*formal*) ○ *It is incumbent on me to ensure that our generous hosts should not go unthanked.* **2 IN OFFICE** currently holding a position or office ■ *n* **SOMEBODY IN OFFICE** somebody currently holding an official post, especially in a church or political organization ○ *He took comfort in the fact that incumbents are often offered the chance of serving a second term of office.* [15C. < Latin *incumbent-*, present participle of *incumbere* 'lie in or on' < *-cumbere* 'lie down'.] —**incumbently** *adv*

incumber *vt* = **encumber**

incunable *n* PRINTING = **incunabulum**

incunabula /ínkyoo nábbyoolə/ *npl* the early stages or beginnings of something (*formal*) [Early 19C. < Latin, 'swaddling clothes, infancy' < *cunae* 'cradle'.]

incunabulum /ínkyoo nábbyooləm/ (*plural* **-la** /-lə/), **incunable** /in kyoonəb'l/ *n* a book printed from movable type before 1501 [Early 19C. < Latin, singular of *incunabula* (see INCUNABULA).]

incur /in kúr/ (**-curs, -curring, -curred**) *vt* **1** to become burdened with something such as a debt **2** to suffer something undesirable such as another person's anger or a financial loss as a result of an action ○ *incur their wrath* [15C. Via Old French *encourir* < Latin *incurrere* 'run into' < *currere* 'to run'.] —**incurrable** *adj* —**incurrence** *n*

incurable /in kyoórəb'l/ *adj* **1 IMPOSSIBLE TO CURE** not possible to cure **2 IMPOSSIBLE TO CHANGE** not possible to change ■ *n* **SOMEBODY OR SOMETHING IMPOSSIBLE TO CURE** a person or animal with an illness or condition that cannot be cured —**incurability** /in kyoórə bílləti/ *n* —**incurableness** *n* —**incurably** *adv*

incurious /in kyoóri əss/ *adj* showing no curiosity about or interest in something —**incuriosity** /in kyoóri óssəti/ *n* —**incuriously** *adv* —**incuriousness** *n*

incurrent /in kúrrənt/ *adj* flowing or running inwards into something [Late 16C. < Latin *incurrere* (see INCUR).]

incursion /in kúrsh'n/ *n* **1** a brief, hostile, and usually sudden invasion of somebody's territory **2** the act of flowing, running, or intruding into something, usually with unpleasant or damaging effects (*formal*) [15C. Directly or via Old French < Latin *incursion-* 'a running in' < *incurs-*, past participle of *incurrere* (see INCUR).] —**incursive** /in kúrssiv/ *adj*

incurvate *vti* /ínkur vayt/ (**-vates, -vating, -vated**) = **incurve** *v.* ■ *adj* /in kúr vayt/ curved or bending inwards [Late 16C. < Latin *incurvat-*, past participle of *incurvare* 'bend inwards' < *curvus* 'curved'.] —**incurvation** /ínkur váysh'n/ *n* —**incurvature** /in kúrvəchər/ *n*

incurve /in kúrv/ *vti* (**-curves, -curving, -curved**) to curve inwards, or to give something an inward curve ■ *n* a curve that bends inwards —**incurved** *adj*

incus /íngkəss/ (*plural* **-cudes** /in kyoód eez/) *n* a small bone, shaped like an anvil, found in the middle ear of mammals between the malleus and stapes bones. ◊ **malleus, stapes** [Mid-17C. < Latin *incus* 'anvil' < *incudere* (see INCUSE).] —**incudal** /íngkyood'l/ *adj* —**incudate** /íng kyoo dayt/ *adj*

incuse /in kyooz/ *adj* **STAMPED INTO COIN AS DESIGN** hammered, stamped, or impressed on a coin as a design ■ *n* **STAMPED-IN COIN DESIGN** a design stamped, hammered, or impressed on a coin ■ *vt* (**-cuses, -cusing, -cused**) **IMPRESS COIN DESIGN** to hammer or stamp a design on a coin [Early 19C. < Latin *incus-*, past participle of *incudere* 'hammer on' < *cudere* 'to beat' < Indo-European.]

IND *abbr* **1** India[1] (*international vehicle registration*) **2** in God's Name [Latin *in nomine Dei*]

ind., ind *abbr* **1** independence **2** independent **3** index **4** indicative **5** indirect **6** industrial **7** industry

Ind., Ind *abbr* **1** Independent **2** India[1] **3** Indian **4** Indiana **5** Indies

indaba /in daábə/ *n S Africa* **1** a long political meeting, conference, or consultation, originally held with or among indigenous peoples of South Africa **2** a problem or serious matter for somebody to think about or deal with (*informal*) [Early 19C. < Zulu, 'discussion'.]

indamine /índə meen/ *n* an organic base that forms blue or green salts. Use: manufacture of dyes.

indebted /in déttid/ *adj* **1** owing money to somebody **2** obliged or grateful to somebody for something such as assistance or a favour received [13C. Alteration of Old French *endetté*, past participle of *endetter* 'put in debt' < *dette* (see DEBT).]

indebtedness /in déttidnəss/ *n* **1** the condition of owing money to somebody or owing somebody thanks **2** the total amount somebody owes

indecency /in deéss'nsi/ (*plural* **-cies**) *n* **1** offensiveness according to accepted standards, especially in sexual matters **2** an act that offends against accepted standards of decency

indecent /in deéss'nt/ *adj* **1** unacceptable and offensive to accepted standards, especially in sexual matters **2** inappropriate under the circumstances and disapproved of by others ○ *The funeral was arranged with indecent haste.* —**indecently** *adv*

indecent assault *n* a sexual assault on somebody that does not involve rape

indecent exposure *n* the criminal offence of deliberately displaying part of the body, usually the genitals, to somebody else in public

indecipherable /índi sífərəb'l/ *adj* impossible or very difficult to read or understand —**indecipherability** /índi sífərə bílləti/ *n* —**indecipherableness** *n* —**indecipherably** *adv*

indecision /índi sízh'n/ *n* inability to reach a decision or uncertainty resulting from somebody's inability or refusal to reach a decision

indecisive /índi síssiv/ *adj* **1** unable or reluctant to make decisions generally or to come to a decision about something in particular **2** not producing a clear result, especially a clear victory for somebody —**indecisively** *adv* —**indecisiveness** *n*

indeclinable /índi klínəb'l/ *adj* existing in one form only and having no grammatical inflections, e.g. no plural form [15C. Via French < Latin *indeclinabilis* 'not declinable' < *declinare* (see DECLINE).] —**indeclinably** *adv*

indecorous /in dékərəss/ *adj* rather rude or shocking because of being considered socially unacceptable —**indecorously** *adv* —**indecorousness** *n*

indecorum /índi káwrəm/ *n* **1** behaviour that offends against what is socially acceptable and polite **2** an indecorous action

indeed /in deéd/ CORE MEANING: an adverb indicating agreement with or confirmation of something ○ *He is indeed an actor.* ○ *'Do you know that man?' 'Indeed I do'.*
adv **1 WHAT IS MORE** introduces a statement that strengthens or adds to a point just made ○ *I am willing, indeed eager, to speak on your behalf.* **2 FOR EMPHASIS** gives additional emphasis after a descriptive word or phrase ○ *The news, I learned, was grim indeed.* **3 INDICATES RESPONSE** expresses surprise, curiosity, or disbelief ○ *'He's applied for a job'. 'Has he indeed?'* [14C. < IN + DEED.]

indefatigable /índi fáttigəb'l/ *adj* never showing any sign of getting tired or of relaxing an effort [Early 17C. Directly or via obsolete French *indéfatigable* < Latin *defatigare* 'tire out' < *fatigare* (see FATIGUE).] —**indefatigability** /índi fáttigə bílləti/ *n* —**indefatigableness** *n* —**indefatigably** *adv*

indefeasible /índi feézəb'l/ *adj* impossible to annul, make void, or forfeit —**indefeasibility** /índi feézə bílləti/ *n* —**indefeasibleness** *n* —**indefeasibly** *adv*

indefectible /índi féktəb'l/ *adj* (*formal*) **1** not affected by decay or failure **2** without fault or imperfection [Mid-17C. < obsolete *defectible* 'liable to fail' < late Latin *defectibilis* < *defectus* (see DEFECT).] —**indefectibility** /índi féktə bílləti/ *n* —**indefectibly** *adv*

indefensible /índi fénssəb'l/ *adj* **1 PERMITTING NO EXCUSE** too bad or blameworthy to be in any way justified or excused ○ *indefensible conduct* **2 UNABLE TO BE PROTECTED** incapable of being defended from attack **3 INVALID** not based on fact, proof, or sound reasoning ○ *an indefensible argument* —**indefensibility** /índi fénssə bílləti/ *n* —**indefensibleness** *n* —**indefensibly** *adv*

indefinable /índi fínəb'l/ *adj* impossible or very difficult to describe, define, or analyze —**indefinability** /índi fínə bílləti/ *n* —**indefinableness** *n* —**indefinably** *adv*

indefinite /in déffənət/ *adj* **1 UNLIMITED** not fixed or limited in length, size, duration, or quantity **2 NOT CLEAR** not clear or not precisely defined or fixed **3 VAGUE AND UNCERTAIN** unable or unwilling to give a clear indication of thoughts or plans **4 TOO MANY TO COUNT** consisting of units that are too numerous to be counted precisely ○ *indefinite stamens* **5** PLANT SCI = **indeterminate** *adj.* **6** —**indefiniteness** *n*

indefinite article *n* a word such as 'a' or 'an' in English that designates a noun referring to something that has not been mentioned before and is simply any one of its kind ○ *Choose a book and write a review of it.*

indefinite integral *n* an integral that when differentiated equals a given function

indefinitely /in déffənətli/ *adv* **1** for a length of time that has no fixed or obvious end **2** in a general and unspecific or vague and imprecise way

indefinite pronoun *n* a pronoun, such as 'someone', 'nothing', or 'anything' in English, that does not refer to a particular person or thing

indehiscent /índi híss'nt/ *adj* not opening up to release seeds when ripe —**indehiscence** *n*

indelible /in délləb'l/ *adj* **1 IMPOSSIBLE TO REMOVE OR ALTER** physically impossible to rub, wash out, or alter **2 CONTAINING AN INDELIBLE SUBSTANCE** containing indelible ink or lead ○ *an indelible pencil* **3 PERMANENT** impossible to remove and therefore remaining forever [15C. Directly or via French *indélébile* < Latin *indelebilis* 'not defaceable' < *delere* 'blot out'.] —**indelibility** /in déllə bílləti/ *n* —**indelibleness** *n* —**indelibly** *adv*

indelicate /in déllikət/ *adj* **1** tactless, crude, or too frank, and therefore causing or likely to cause offence **2** crude, rough, or coarse in texture or appearance —**indelicacy** *n* —**indelicately** *adv* —**indelicateness** *n*

indemnify /in démni fī/ (**-fies, -fying, -fied**) *vt* **1** to provide somebody with protection, especially financial protection, against possible loss, damage, or liability **2** to pay compensation to somebody for damage, loss, or liability incurred [Early 17C. < Latin *indemnis* 'not injured' < *damnum* 'injury'.] —**indemnification** /in démnifi káysh'n/ *n* —**indemnifier** *n*

indemnity /in démnəti/ (*plural* **-ties**) *n* **1 INSURANCE** protection or insurance against possible loss or damage **2 EXEMPTION FROM PENALTIES** legal exemption from penalties or liabilities **3 COMPENSATION** a compensation paid for loss or damage [15C. Via French < late Latin *indemnitas* 'security for damage' < Latin *indemnis* (see INDEMNIFY).]

indemonstrable /índi mónstrəb'l/ *adj* impossible to prove or demonstrate (*formal*) —**indemonstrability** /índi mónstrə bílləti/ *n* —**indemonstrableness** *n* —**indemonstrably** *adv*

indene /ín deen/ *n* C_9H_8 a colourless toxic liquid. Source: coal tar, petroleum. Use: manufacture of synthetic resins. [Late 19C. < INDOLE + -ENE.]

indent[1] *v* /in dént/ **1** *vti* **BEGIN LINE IN FROM MARGIN** to start a line or row some distance in from the margin **2** *vt* **FORM RECESS IN** to form a deep recess in something (*often passive*) **3** *vt* **NOTCH** to make jagged, notched, or serrated edges in something **4** *vt* US **FIT NOTCHED EDGES** to join together two notched pieces of something **5** *vt* **TEAR COPIED DOCUMENT IN HALF** to tear a document, especially one containing two copies of the same text, in half along an irregular line **6** *vt* **DRAW UP IN DUPLICATE** to draw up a document in two or more exact copies **7** *vti* **ORDER USING OFFICIAL FORM** to place an order for supplies using an official form **8** *vt* **ORDER FOREIGN GOODS** to place an order for foreign goods, usually through an agent ■ *n* /ín dent, in dént/ **1 SPACE SET IN FROM MARGIN** a blank space left between the margin and the beginning of a line or row **2 INDENTURE** an indenture (*archaic*) **3 ORDER OF FOREIGN GOODS** an order for foreign goods, usually placed through an agent **4 OFFICIAL ORDER FOR SUPPLIES** a requisition or official order for supplies —**indented** *adj* —**indenter** *n*

indent[2] *vt* /in dént/ to press something inwards to form a dent ■ *n* /ín dent, in dént/ = **dent** *n.* **1** [14C. < IN-[2] + DENT.]

indentation /ín den táysh'n/ *n* **1 NOTCH OR RECESS** a notch, recess, or hollowed-out place in something such as an edge, a boundary line, or a coast **2 JAGGED EDGE** a series of notches or recesses, or the edge formed by this **3 LEAVING SPACE AT BEGINNING OF LINE** the leaving of space between the margin and the beginning of a line or row, or the blank space left **4 ACT OF INDENTING** the act of indenting something or the fact of being indented

indenture /in dénchər/ *n* **1 CONTRACT WITH APPRENTICE** a contract committing an apprentice or servant to serve a master for a specific period of time (*often plural*) **2 WRITTEN AGREEMENT** a written contract or agreement between two or more parties **3 DUPLICATE DOCUMENT WITH TORN EDGE** a document written in duplicate on a single sheet and torn in half so that the edges of the two resulting copies could be matched up to prove their authenticity **4 AUTHORIZED LIST** an official list or inventory that has been authenticated for use as a voucher ■ *vti* **CONTRACT SOMEBODY FOR SERVICES** to commit somebody to work as an apprentice or servant for a specified period of time by means of indentures —**indentureship** *n*

~~independant~~ incorrect spelling of **independent**

independence /índi péndənss/ *n* freedom from dependence on or control by another person, organization, or state

Independence Day *n* US a national holiday in the United States marking the signing of the Declaration of Independence in 1776. Date: 4 July.

independency /índi péndənssi/ (*plural* **-cies**) *n* **1** independence (*archaic*) **2** an independent state or territory

Independency *n* the principle or policy that each local Christian church or congregation should be free of external ecclesiastical control

independent /índi péndənt/ *adj* **1 NOT CONTROLLED BY ANOTHER** in politics, free from the authority, control, or domination of somebody or something else, especially not controlled by another state or organization and able to self-govern **2 ABLE TO FUNCTION BY ITSELF** able to operate or stand on its own because not dependent on another ○ *Each wheel has an independent suspension system.* **3 SELF-SUPPORTING** not forced to rely on another for money or support **4 SHOWING CONFIDENCE IN SELF** capable of thinking or acting without consultation with or guidance from others **5 DONE WITHOUT OBSTRUCTION** carried out or operating without interference or influence from interested parties ○ *an independent counsel* **6 SUFFICIENT TO LIVE ON** providing the means on which to live without having to work **7 independent, Independent NOT AFFILIATED TO POLITICAL PARTY** not a member, representative, or supporter of any political party **8 NOT SOLVABLE USING SOLUTION TO ANOTHER** describes a system of equations in which no single equation is necessarily solved using a solution to the others **9 NOT AFFECTING OTHER VARIABLES** in statistics, distributed in such a way that the value taken on by one variable leaves all others unaffected **10 NOT DEPENDENT ON AXIOM OR PROPOSITION** not proved from another logical axiom or proposition ■ *n* **1 SOMEBODY OR SOMETHING UNAFFECTED BY OTHERS** somebody or something that is free from control, dependence, or interference **2 independent, Independent NONPARTY POLITICIAN** somebody, especially a politician, who is not a member of, does not represent, or does not support any political party —**independently** *adv*

Independent *n* **1** a believer in the principle that each Christian church or congregation should be free of external ecclesiastical control **2** POL = **independent** *n.* **2**

independent clause *n* a clause that can stand on its own as a sentence, such as 'She'll go on holiday' in the sentence 'She'll go on holiday if she can raise the money'

independent invention *n* an invention arrived at independently, even though another group of people may have created the same invention in a different place at a different time

independent school *n* a school that is not financed or run by a local authority or the government

independent variable *n* **1** the variable in a mathematical statement whose value, when specified, determines the value of another variable or other variables **2** a variable that is manipulated in an experiment in order to observe the effect on another variable

in-depth *adj* giving careful consideration to all details and aspects of a subject —**in depth** *adv*

indescribable /índi skríbəb'l/ *adj* **1** impossible or very difficult to describe ○ *an indescribable sensation* **2** so intense or extreme as to defy description ○ *indescribable joy* —**indescribability** /índi skríbə bílləti/ *n* —**indescribableness** *n* —**indescribably** *adv*

~~indespensable~~ incorrect spelling of **indispensable**

~~indestructable~~ incorrect spelling of **indestructible**

indestructible /índi strúktəb'l/ *adj* impossible or very difficult to destroy —**indestructibility** /índi strúktə bílləti/ *n* —**indestructibleness** *n* —**indestructibly** *adv*

indeterminable /índi túrminəb'l/ *adj* **1** impossible to determine or ascertain exactly **2** impossible to resolve, answer, or settle —**indeterminableness** *n* —**indeterminably** *adv*

indeterminate /índi túrminət/ *adj* **1 NOT KNOWN EXACTLY** not known exactly **2 VAGUE** not definite, precise, or clear **3 UNPREDICTABLE** without a predictable result or outcome **4 HAVING NO NUMERICAL MEANING** having no numerical value or meaning, e.g. the expressions '0/0' or '0⁰' **5 WITH INFINITE NUMBER OF SOLUTIONS** having an infinite number of solutions **6 GROWING AT TIP** continuing to grow at the tip of the main stem instead of terminating in a flower bud. ◊ **determinate** *adj.* **3** —**indeterminacy** *n* —**indeterminately** *adv* —**indeterminateness** *n* —**indetermination** /índi túrmi náysh'n/ *n*

indeterminate sentence *n* a prison sentence that has a wide term, e.g. from one to five years, the date of release being determined by the prisoner's conduct and other factors

indeterminate vowel *n* = **schwa**

indeterminism /índi túrminizəm/ *n* the philosophical theory that human beings have free will and their actions are not always and completely determined by previous events. ◊ **determinism** —**indeterminist** *n* —**indeterministic** /índi túrmi nístik/ *adj*

ϟ **index** /ín deks/ *n* (*plural* **-dexes** *or* **-dices** /-di seez/) **1 ALPHABETICAL REFERENCE LIST** an alphabetical list of topics, peoples, or titles, giving the location of where they are mentioned in a text **2 CATALOGUE** a list of items in a set or collection, e.g. the books in a library, usually including details of where to find them **3 PUBLICATION LISTING ARTICLES** a periodical or book that lists published work alphabetically by subject, title, or author **4** PUBL = **thumb index** **5 INDICATOR** an indicator or sign of something ○ *One index of the gravity of the situation is the severance of diplomatic relations.* **6 POINTER** a pointer or needle, especially on a piece of scientific equipment **7 PRINTING CHARACTER** a character ☞ used by printers to draw attention to a paragraph, section, or note **8** MATH = **exponent** *n.* **4** **9 NUMBER GIVEN AS SUPERSCRIPT** a number or variable given as a superscript before a square-root sign showing which root is to be taken **10 SUBSCRIPT OR SUPERSCRIPT IDENTIFYING ELEMENT** a subscript or superscript numeral that identifies an element or range in a set or sequence **11 NUMBER EXPRESSING RELATIONSHIP** a scale, or a number on it, that expresses the price, value, or level of something compared to something else or to a base number **12 DATA STRUCTURE** a data structure that facilitates quick access to a specific part of a data store based on the value of key data within the store ■ *v* **1** *vt* **MAKE INDEX FOR** to compile an index for something such as a book or computer record **2** *vt* **PUT IN AN INDEX** to enter something such as a name, title, subject, or key word in an index **3** *vt* **INDICATE** to be a sign or indicator of something (*formal*) **4** *vt* **MAKE INDEX-LINKED** to make something index-linked [Late 16C. < Latin, 'forefinger', literally 'pointer'.] —**indexer** *n*

Index *n* = **Index Librorum Prohibitorum**

indexation /ín dek sáysh'n/ *n* the linking of wages, pensions, or other remuneration to an index representing the cost of living, so that they are automatically adjusted up or down as that rises or falls

index case *n* the first documented case of an illness in an epidemiological study

index finger *n* the finger next to the thumb

index fossil *n* the fossil of an organism that is specific to a particular geological age and is used for dating or identifying rocks or rock layers in which it is found

index fund *n* a mutual fund composed of companies listed in an important stock market index in order to match the market's overall performance

Index Librorum Prohibitorum /-IT bráwrəm prō híbbi táwrəm/ *n* a list formerly compiled by the Roman Catholic Church of books and publications that Church members were forbidden to read [< Latin, 'list of forbidden books']

index-linked *adj* adjusted up or down as the cost-of-living index rises or falls

index-linking *n* ECON = **indexation**

index number *n* a number used to indicate the change in a value or quantity, e.g. a price or unemployment, when compared to the level of that value or quantity at an earlier time

Index of Industrial Production *n* a report produced by the Central Statistical Office showing the performance of the main UK industries

index of refraction *n* PHYS = **refractive index**

India

India[1] /índi ə/ country in South Asia. Capital: New Delhi. Population: 966,783,171 (1997). Area: 3,165,596 sq. km/1,222,243 sq. mi.

India[2] /índi ə/ *n* a code word for the letter 'I', used in international radio communication

India ink *n* US = **Indian ink**

Indiaman /índi əmən/ (*plural* **-men** /-mən/) *n* a large merchant sailing ship formerly used to transport goods to and from India [Early 18C. < INDIA[1] + MAN 'ship', as in *man of war*.]

Indian /índi ən/ *n* **1** SOMEBODY FROM INDIA somebody who comes from India **2** △ NATIVE AMERICAN a Native North, South, or Central American (*sometimes considered offensive*) **3** OFFENSIVE TERM a language used by a Native North, South, or Central American people (*offensive*) ■ *adj* **1** RELATING TO INDIA relating to India, or its peoples, languages, or cultures **2** △ RELATING TO NATIVE AMERICANS relating to Native North, South, or Central Americans, or their languages or cultures (*sometimes considered offensive*)

Indiana /índi ánnə/ state in the north-central United States. Capital: Indianapolis. Population: 5,864,108 (1997). Area: 94,327 sq. km/36,420 sq. mi. —**Indianan** *n, adj*

Indian agent *n* an official in the United States or, formerly, in Canada, acting as a government representative to communities of Native North Americans

Indianapolis /índi ə náppəliss/ capital of Indiana, in the central part of the state. Population: 741,304 (1998 estimate).

Indian club *n* a club shaped like an elongated bottle, used in gymnastics and juggling

Indian English *n* a variety of English spoken in India

Indian file *n* an offensive term for single file (*dated; sometimes considered offensive*) [< a Native American custom of walking in single file]

Indian giver *n* US an offensive term for somebody who gives something and then asks for its return (*informal; sometimes considered offensive*)

Indian hemp *n* **1** PLANTS = **hemp 2** a perennial plant of the dogbane family whose roots can be used as a laxative and emetic. Native to: North America. *Apocynum cannabinum.*

Indian ink *n* US term **India ink 1** the black pigment, usually shaped into cakes or sticks, from which Indian ink is made **2** a liquid black ink made from a pigment that is a mixture of lampblack and a binding agent [From its originally being brought to Europe from China and Japan via India]

Indian meal *n* US = **cornmeal**

Indian Mutiny *n* a rebellion of Indian soldiers against British rule between 1857 and 1858

Indian Ocean ocean situated east of Africa. Depth: 7,725 m/25,344 ft. Area: 73,427,800 sq. km/28,350,500 sq. mi.

Indian Pacific *n* the train service in Australia that runs between Perth, on the shore of the Indian Ocean, and Sydney, on the shore of the Pacific Ocean

Indian paintbrush *n* a wild plant of the figwort family with brightly coloured bracts that look like flowers. Native to: North America. *Castileja linariaefolia.*

Indian pipe *n* a perennial woodland plant whose single white stem and nodding flower resembles a tobacco pipe. Native to: North America, Asia. *Monotropa uniflora.*

Indian red *n* **1** a red pigment made of iron oxide. Use: paint, cosmetics, polish. **2** a dark reddish-brown colour —**Indian red** *adj*

Indian rope-trick *n* the feat, performed by some magicians of the Indian subcontinent, of appearing to climb an erect unsupported length of rope

Indian Standard Time *n* the standard time in India, five-and-a-half hours later than Universal Coordinated Time

Indian subcontinent region comprising the countries of Bangladesh, India, and Pakistan

Indian summer *n* **1** a period of mild sunny weather occurring in autumn in the northern hemisphere **2** a calm or productive and enjoyable period towards the end of somebody's life or the end of a process, period, or activity [< ?]

Indian tobacco *n* a very poisonous annual plant of the bluebell family that has oval toothed leaves and swollen seed capsules. Flowers: small, purplish. Native to: North America. *Lobelia inflata.*

Indian-wrestle (**Indian-wrestles, Indian-wrestling, Indian-wrestled**) *vti* to attempt to force down an opponent's upraised arm or to throw a standing opponent off balance

Indian wrestling *n* a form of wrestling in which one opponent attempts to force down another's upraised arm or to throw a standing opponent off balance

India paper *n* a thin fine paper originally made in South Asia, used for prints and illustrations

India rubber *n* rubber (*dated*)

Indic /índik/ *n* a large group of languages of the Indian subcontinent, forming a major division of Indo-Iranian. Native speakers: 700 million. [Mid-19C. Via Latin *Indicus* < Greek *Indikos* < *Indos* 'the Indus river'.] —**Indic** *adj*

indic. *abbr* **1** indicating **2** indicative **3** indicator

indican /índikən/ *n* **1** a substance formed in the intestine by bacterial action and excreted in urine and sweat **2** an off-white crystalline sugar derivative found in plants. Use: original source of indigo dye. [Mid-19C. < Latin *indicum* 'indigo'.]

indicate /índi kayt/ (**-cates, -cating, -cated**) *v* **1** *vt* POINT TO to point something out or point to something **2** *vt* SHOW EXISTENCE OR TRUTH OF to be or provide a sign or symptom of something **3** *vt* REGISTER MEASUREMENT to register a measurement, e.g. of speed or temperature **4** *vt* SHOW WHAT SOMEBODY THINKS OR INTENDS to state or show an opinion, feeling, instruction, or intention, especially briefly or indirectly **5** *vt* SHOW WHAT SHOULD BE DONE to make somebody think that something should be done or used (*usually passive*) ○ *In a case like this, a firm approach is indicated.* **6** *vti* GIVE SIGNALS AS DRIVER to signal your intentions to other vehicles when driving, especially before turning or moving to the left or right **7** *vt* SHOW PRESENCE OF DISEASE to point out the presence of, or remedy for, a disease or syndrome [Early 17C. < Latin *indicare* 'point towards, show' < *dicare* 'proclaim'.] —**indicant** *n* —**indicatable** *adj* —**indicatory** /ín díkətəri/ *adj*

indicated horsepower *n* the theoretical power produced by a reciprocating engine such as a steam or internal-combustion engine, calculated as the power produced before reduction due to friction and mechanical movement

indication /índi káysh'n/ *n* **1** SIGN a sign, signal, or symptom that something exists or is true **2** ACT OF INDICATING an act of indicating or pointing to something **3** READING INSTRUMENT a reading shown on a measuring instrument **4** SOMETHING NECESSARY OR DESIRABLE something that is indicated as the right thing to do or use **5** MEDICAL SIGN a medical sign or symptom that shows the presence of a disease or a remedy for it —**indicational** *adj*

indicative /in díkətiv/ *adj* **1** INDICATING EXISTENCE OR TRUTH showing, suggesting, or pointing out that something exists or is true **2** RELATING TO BASIC MOOD OF VERBS relating to verbs in simple objective statements ■ *n* **1** BASIC MOOD OF A VERB the basic mood of a verb in languages such as English, used for ordinary objective statements **2** VERB IN BASIC MOOD a verb used in a simple statement of fact —**indicatively** *adv*

indicator /índi kaytər/ *n* **1** DRIVER'S SIGNAL a device on a motor vehicle, usually a flashing light, that indicates that the driver is turning or moving to the left or right **2** SOMETHING THAT SHOWS WHAT CONDITIONS ARE something observed or calculated that is used to show the presence or state of a condition or trend **3** MEASURING INSTRUMENT an instrument or gauge that measures something and registers the measurement **4** SOMETHING GIVING INFORMATION something such as a light, sign, or pointer that gives information, e.g. about which direction to take **5** CHEMICAL SHOWING SOMETHING a substance such as litmus that shows the presence or concentration of a particular material or chemical **6** ECOL = **indicator organism**

indicator diagram *n* a graph showing the variation of pressure and volume in a cylinder of a reciprocating engine

indicator organism *n* an organism whose presence or absence in an environment indicates particular conditions there, e.g. its oxygen level or the presence of a contaminating substance

indices plural of **index**

indicia plural of **indicium**

indicium /in díssi əm/ (*plural* **-a** /-ə/) *n* a sign indicating the presence or nature of something, e.g. a medical condition [Early 17C. < Latin, < *indic-*, stem of *index* (see INDEX).]

indicolite /índikə līt/ *n* a blue-coloured tourmaline. Use: gems. [Early 19C. < Latin *indicum* 'indigo'.]

indict /in dít/ *vt* **1** to charge somebody formally with commission of a crime **2** to accuse somebody of wrongdoing [14C. Via Anglo-Norman *enditer* < Latin *indicere* 'proclaim', literally 'say in' < *dicere* 'say'.] —**indictee** /indī tée/ *n* —**indicter** *n* —**indictor** *n*

indictable /in dītəb'l/ *adj* **1** liable to be charged with a criminal offence **2** making somebody liable to be charged with commission of a crime ○ *an indictable offence*

indiction /in díksh'n/ *n* a cyclic period of 15 years begun during the reign of Constantine the Great in the later Roman Empire at the end of which property was evaluated for taxation [14C. < Latin *indiction-* 'declaration' < *indictus*, past participle of *indicere* (see INDICT); from the declaration setting the valuation on which tax was assessed.] —**indictional** *adj*

indictment /in dītmənt/ *n* **1 STATEMENT OR FACT THAT ACCUSES** a statement or indication that something is wrong or somebody is to blame ○ *a stinging indictment of our prison system* **2 ACT OF INDICTING** the act of indicting somebody or the condition of being indicted **3 FORMAL CHARGE OF CRIMINAL WRONGDOING** a formal accusation of a serious crime **4 ACCUSATION OF CRIMINAL CONDUCT** a formal accusation of criminal conduct **5 ACCUSATION BY LORD ADVOCATE IN SCOTLAND** in Scotland, an accusation of crime brought by the Lord Advocate

indie /índi/ *n* a small independent business enterprise, especially one related to music (*slang*) ■ *adj* issued by small independent record companies, or playing the sort of music recorded by such companies (*slang*) [Early 20C. Shortening of INDEPENDENT.]

Indiennes /índi én/ *n* a fabric with small brightly-coloured French provincial patterns that are hand-printed using carved blocks [Late 19C. < French (*à l')indienne* '(in the) Indian (style)'.]

indifference /in dífrənss/ *n* **1 LACK OF INTEREST** lack of interest, care, or concern **2 UNIMPORTANCE** lack of importance or significance ○ *It's a matter of complete indifference to me whether you go or stay.* **3 LOW QUALITY** ordinariness or lack of quality

indifferent /in dífrənt/ *adj* **1 WITHOUT CARE OR INTEREST** showing no care or concern for, or interest in, somebody or something ○ *She was indifferent to their criticism.* **2 FAVOURING NEITHER SIDE** without bias or preference for one person, group, or thing rather than another **3 ONLY AVERAGE** average or low in quality **4 UNDIFFERENTIATED** not specialized or differentiated in cells or tissues **5 NEUTRAL** neutral and having no properties that are affected by a process or reaction [14C. Directly or via Old French < Latin *indifferent-* 'making no difference' < *different-*, present participle of *differre* 'differ'.]

indifferentism /in dífrəntizəm/ *n* the belief that variations in doctrine and practice within a religion are unimportant

indifferently /in díff rəntli/ *adv* **1 WITHOUT INTEREST** without showing interest or concern **2 NOT WELL** not very well **3 EQUALLY** without differences or exceptions (*formal*)

indigen *n* = **indigene**

indigence /índijənss/ *n* extreme poverty in which the basic necessities of life are lacking (*formal*)

indigene /índi jeen/, **indigen** /índijən/ *n* a native-born person or thing (*formal*) [Late 16C. Via French *indigène* < Latin *indigena* (see INDIGENOUS).]

indigenize /in díjji nīz/ (**-izes, -izing, -ized**), **indigenise** (**-ises, -ising, -ised**) *vti* to increase the use of local inhabitants for a task previously done by people from another country, usually the home country of an employing company —**indigenization** /in díjji nī záysh'n/ *n*

indigenous /in díjjinəss/ *adj* **1** originating in and typical of a region or country **2** natural or inborn (*formal*) [Mid-17C. < Latin *indigena* 'born in' < *gignere* 'beget'.] —**indigenity** /índi jénnəti/ *n* —**indigenously** *adv*

SYNONYMS See ***native***.

indigenous people *n* the people who occupy a region at the time of its contact with colonial powers or the outside world

indigent /índijənt/ *adj* lacking the necessities of life, such as food, clothing, and shelter (*formal*) ■ *n* an impoverished person (*formal*) [14C. Via Old French < Latin *indigent-*, present participle of *indigere* 'lack in' < *egere* 'to need'.] —**indigently** *adv*

indigestible /índi jéstəb'l/ *adj* **1** difficult or impossible to digest **2** hard to take in or understand (*informal*) —**indigestibility** /índi jéstə bílləti/ *n* —**indigestibly** *adv*

indigestion /índi jéschən/ *n* difficulty in digesting food, resulting in such symptoms as belching, heartburn, or stomach pains. Technical name **dyspepsia**

indigestive /índi jéstiv/ *adj* experiencing or resulting from indigestion

indignant /in dígnənt/ *adj* angry or annoyed at the apparent unfairness or unreasonableness of something [Late 16C. < Latin *indignant-*, present participle of *indignari* 'regard as unworthy' < *dignus* 'worthy'.] —**indignantly** *adv*

indignation /índig náysh'n/ *n* anger or annoyance because somebody or something seems unfair or unreasonable [14C. Directly or via Old French < Latin *indignation-* < *indignari* (see INDIGNANT).]

SYNONYMS See ***anger***.

indignity /indígnəti/ (*plural* **-ties**) *n* a situation that results in a humiliating loss of dignity or self-esteem

indigo /índigō/ (*plural* **-gos** *or* **-goes**) *n* **1 BLUE DYE** a blue dye. Source: formerly from plants, but now usually made synthetically. **2 PLANT YIELDING INDIGO DYE** a tropical plant of the pea family with fronds of pointed leaves and flowers, a source of indigo dye. Flowers: red or purple, in spikes. Genus: *Indigofera*. **3 DEEP PURPLISH-BLUE COLOUR** a deep purplish-blue colour that lies between blue and violet on the visible spectrum [Mid-16C. Via Portuguese < Greek *indikon* 'the Indian substance', a form of *Indikos* 'Indian' < *Indos* 'the River Indus'.] —**indigo** *adj*

indigo blue *n* = **indigo** *n.* **1**, **indigo** *n.* **3**, —**indigo-blue** *adj*

indigo bunting *n* a finch found in hedgerows and at the margins of woods, the male of which has brilliant indigo feathers. Native to: North America. *Passerina cyanea*.

indigo snake *n* a large harmless deep-blue snake that preys on small mammals. Native to: S United States, Central and South America. *Drymarchon corais*.

indigotin /in díggətin, índi gōtin/ *n* = **indigo** *n.* **1** [Mid-19C. < INDIGO + -IN.]

Indio /índi ō/ city in SE California. Population: 45,023 (1998 estimate).

indirect /índi rékt, índī-/ *adj* **1 NOT IN STRAIGHT LINE** not in a direct line, course, or path **2 NOT IMMEDIATE OR INTENDED** not occurring as an immediate or intended effect or consequence **3 DEVIOUS** not obvious or straightforward in approach **4 INVOLVING INTERMEDIATE STAGES** not obtained or proceeding from an immediate or straightforward relationship —**indirectly** *adv* —**indirectness** *n*

indirect cost *n* a business expense that is not directly connected with a particular product or operation

indirect discourse *n* = **indirect speech**

indirect free kick *n* a free kick in football from which a goal cannot be scored unless the ball touches another player before it passes over the goal line

indirection /índə réksh'n, índī réksh'n/ *n* **1 LACK OF DIRECTNESS** lack of directness in a path, course, or procedure **2 AIMLESSNESS** lack of a goal or goals **3 SOMETHING NOT HONEST AND STRAIGHTFORWARD** an approach or action that is devious or deceitful

indirect labour *n* work that is not considered in determining costs per unit in producing or manufacturing something, e.g. work done by clerical or maintenance staff

indirect lighting *n* reflected or diffused light used to avoid glare or shadows

indirect object *n* the recipient of the action shown by a verb and its direct object, e.g. 'the cat' in 'She gave the cat a meal'

indirect proof *n* proof of a conclusion by showing that assuming its negation will lead to a contradiction

indirect question *n* a question reported in indirect speech, e.g. 'He asked why you were not there'

indirect speech *n* a report of something said or written that conveys what was said, but not the exact words in their original form, as in 'She said she would join us later'

indirect tax *n* a tax levied on goods or services, instead of directly on companies and individuals

indiscernible /índi súrnəb'l/ *adj* impossible to see or to understand —**indiscernibility** /índi súrnə bílləti/ *n* —**indiscernibly** *adv*

indiscipline /in díssəplin/ *n* lack of control or discipline

indiscreet /índi skreét/ *adj* lacking tact or discretion —**indiscreetly** *adv* —**indiscreetness** *n*

SPELLCHECK Do not confuse ***indiscreet*** with ***indiscrete***, which has a similar sound. Beware: your spellchecker will not catch this error.

indiscrete /índi skreét/ *adj* not divided into parts or appearing not to consist of separate parts —**indiscretely** *adv* —**indiscreteness** *n*

SPELLCHECK See ***indiscreet***

indiscretion /índi skrésh'n/ *n* **1** lack of tact or good judgment **2** something said or done that is tactless or unwise ○ *apologizing for past indiscretions* —**indiscretionary** *adj*

indiscriminate /índi skrímminət/ *adj* **1** making no careful distinctions or choices **2** random, haphazard, or confused —**indiscriminately** *adv* —**indiscriminateness** *n* —**indiscrimination** /índi skrímmi náysh'n/ *n* —**indiscriminative** *adj*

indiscriminating /índi skrímmi nayting/ *adj* lacking discrimination or judgment —**indiscriminatingly** *adv* —**indiscriminative** /índi skrímminətiv/ *adj*

indispensable /índi spénssəb'l/ *adj* **1 NECESSARY** necessary, essential, or not to be dispensed with **2 HAVING TO BE FACED** unavoidable, especially as a duty ■ *n* **ESSENTIAL** something that is essential and cannot be dispensed with —**indispensability** /índi spénssə bílləti/ *n* —**indispensableness** *n* —**indispensably** *adv*

SYNONYMS See ***necessary***.

~~indispensible~~ incorrect spelling of **indispensable**

indispose /índi spṓz/ (**-poses, -posing, -posed**) *vt* **1 SICKEN** to make somebody ill (*archaic*) **2 MAKE UNFIT** to make somebody unfit for something (*formal*) **3 MAKE AVERSE TO** to make somebody dislike the prospect of something or be unwilling to do something (*formal*)

indisposed /índi spṓzd/ *adj* (*formal*) **1** too ill to do something **2** unwilling to say or do something, especially because of a feeling of annoyance

indisposition /índispə zísh'n/ *n* (*formal*) **1** an illness that is not serious **2** reluctance or unwillingness to do something

indisputable /índi spyóotəb'l/ *adj* impossible to doubt, question, or deny —**indisputability** /índi spyóotə bílləti/ *n* —**indisputableness** *n* —**indisputably** *adv*

indissociable /ín di sṓshəb'l/ *adj* unable to be separated, disconnected, or considered separately

indissoluble /índi sóllyóob'l/ *adj* incapable of being dissolved, broken, or undone —**indissolubility** /índi sóllyóo bílləti/ *n* —**indissolubly** *adv*

indistinct /índi stíngkt/ *adj* **1** giving an unclear impression to the sight or hearing **2** not clearly remembered, understood, or thought out —**indistinctly** *adv* —**indistinctness** *n*

indistinctive /índi stíngktiv/ *adj* without any distinguishing qualities or features —**indistinctively** *adv*

indistinguishable /índi stíng gwishəb'l/ *adj* **1** impossible to tell apart from somebody or something else ○ *His handwriting is indistinguishable from his father's.* **2** very hard to see, hear, or understand —**indistinguishability** /índi stíng gwishə bílləti/ *n* —**indistinguishably** *adv*

indite /in dīt/ (**-dites, -diting, -dited**) *vt* to write or compose something such as a poem, letter, or speech (*archaic or literary*) [14C. < Old French *enditer* 'compose in words in' < Latin *dictare* (see DICTATE).]

indium /índi əm/ *n* (*symbol* **In**) a soft silvery rare metallic element. Source: zinc and tin ores. Use: alloys, transistors, electroplating.

individual /índi víddyoo əl/ *n* **1 PARTICULAR PERSON** a particular person, distinct from others in a group. **2 SEPARATE THING** a separate entity or thing **3 SEPARATE ORGANISM** an independent organism separate from a group ■ *adj* **1 SEPARABLE FROM OTHERS** singular and separable from others in a group or class **2 OF OR FOR ONE PERSON** belonging to, relating to, or intended for one person only **3 VERY DISTINCTIVE** strikingly personal, unusual, or distinctive [15C. < medieval Latin *individualis* < Latin *individuus* 'not divisible' < *dividere* 'to divide'.]

individualise *vt* = **individualize**

individualism /índi víddyoo əlizəm/ *n* **1 PURSUIT OF PERSONAL GOALS** the pursuit of personal happiness and independence rather than collective goals or interests **2 PERSONAL TRAIT** a personal peculiarity or trait **3 POLITICAL BELIEF IN IMPORTANCE OF INDIVIDUAL** the belief that society exists for the benefit of the individual, who must not be constrained by government interventions or made subordinate to collective interests

individualist /índi víjjoo əlist/ *n* **1** a person of independent thought or behaviour **2** a believer in the philosophy of individualism —**individualistic** /índi vidyoo ə lístik/ *adj* —**individualistically** *adv*

individuality /índi vidyoo álləti/ (*plural* **-ties**) *n* **1** a specific personality, character, or characteristic that distinguishes one person or thing from another **2** the state or condition of being separate from others

individualize /índi víddyoo ə līz/ (**-izes, -izing, -ized**), **individualise** (**-ises, -ising, -ised**) *vt* **1 GIVE INDIVIDUAL CHARACTER TO** to give somebody or something a character that is separate and distinct from other people or things **2 TREAT INDIVIDUALLY** to consider or treat somebody or something specifically, as distinct from other people or things **3 ADAPT TO INDIVIDUAL REQUIREMENTS** to make, adapt, or modify something to suit a particular person —**individualization** /índi víddyoo ə lī záysh'n/ *n* —**individualizer** /índi víddyoo ə līzər/ *n*

individually /índi víddyoo əli/ *adv* as a separate person or entity, not as part of a group or class

individual medley *n* a swimming race divided into three or four equal parts, in each of which the swimmers must use a particular stroke such as backstroke, crawl, breaststroke, or butterfly

individuate /índi víddyoo ayt/ (**-ates, -ating, -ated**) *vt* to make somebody or something separate and distinct from others [Early 17C. < medieval Latin *individuat-*, past participle of *individuare* < Latin *individuus* (see INDIVIDUAL).] —**individuator** *n*

individuation /índi vidyoo áysh'n/ *n* **1** the act or process of making somebody or something separate and distinct from others **2** in Jungian psychology, the process of the development of the self, achieved by resolving the conflicts arising at life's transitional stages, in particular the transition from adolescence to adulthood

indivisible /índi vízzəb'l/ *adj* **1** not capable of being separated into parts **2** not capable of being divided by a given number without leaving a mathematical remainder —**indivisibility** /índi vizə bílləti/ *n* —**indivisibly** *adv*

indo- *prefix* a chemical compound derived from indigo ○ *indoxyl* [< INDIGO]

Indo- *prefix* **1** India ○ *Indo-Pacific* **2** Indic ○ *Indo-Iranian* [< INDIA¹, INDIC]

Indochina

Indochina /índō chínə/ peninsula of Southeast Asia that includes Myanmar, Thailand, Cambodia, Vietnam, Laos, and the Malay Peninsula —**Indochinese** /índō chī néez/ *adj, n*

indocile /in dō̆ stī̆l/ *adj* resisting discipline or instruction —**indocility** /índō sílləti/ *n*

indoctrinate /in dóktri nayt/ (**-nates, -nating, -nated**) *vt* to teach somebody a belief, doctrine, or ideology thoroughly and systematically, especially with the aim of discouraging independent thought or the acceptance of other opinions [Early 17C. < Old French *endoctriner* 'teach in' < medieval Latin *doctrinare* 'teach'.] —**indoctrination** /in dóktri náysh'n/ *n* —**indoctrinator** *n*

Indo-European *n* **1** a large family of languages spoken from South Asia to Western Europe, comprising the Balto-Slavonic, Germanic, Italic, Indo-Iranian, Celtic, Greek, Albanian, Armenian, Anatolian, and Tocharian branches **2** a speaker of an Indo-European language — **Indo-European** *adj*

Indo-Iranian *n* a group of languages spoken in the north of the Indian subcontinent and in parts of the Middle East, forming a branch of Indo-European and dividing into Indic and Iranian subgroups. Native speakers: 800 million. —**Indo-Iranian** *adj*

indole /índōl/, **indol** /-dol/ *n* C_8H_7N a crystalline compound. Source: plants, faeces, coal tar. Use: in perfumes, chemical reagent.

indoleacetic acid /índōlə seètik-, -ə séttik-/ *n* a plant hormone that stimulates growth and root formation in cuttings [< INDOLE + ACETIC]

indolebutyric acid /índōl byoo tírrik-/ *n* $C_{12}H_{13}O_2N$ a synthetic plant hormone that stimulates growth in stems [< INDOLE + BUTYRIC]

indolent /índələnt/ *adj* **1** lethargic and not showing any interest or making any effort **2** describes a disease or condition that is slow to develop or be healed, and causes no pain [Mid-17C. < late Latin *indolent-* 'insensitive to pain' < *dolent-*, present participle of *dolere* 'suffer pain'.] —**indolence** *n* —**indolently** *adv*

Indology /in dóllə ji/ *n* the study of the history, culture, or philosophy of the Indian subcontinent —**Indologist** *n*

indomethacin /índō méthassin/ *n* $C_{19}H_{16}ClNO_4$ a drug used to relieve pain, fever, and inflammation, especially from arthritis [Mid-20C. < INDOLE + METHYL + ACETIC + -IN.]

indomitable /in dómmitab'l/ *adj* brave, determined, and impossible to defeat or frighten [Mid-17C. < late Latin *indomitabilis* 'untamable' < *domitare* 'to tame'.] —**indomitability** /in dómmitə bílləti/ *n* —**indomitableness** *n* —**indomitably** *adv*

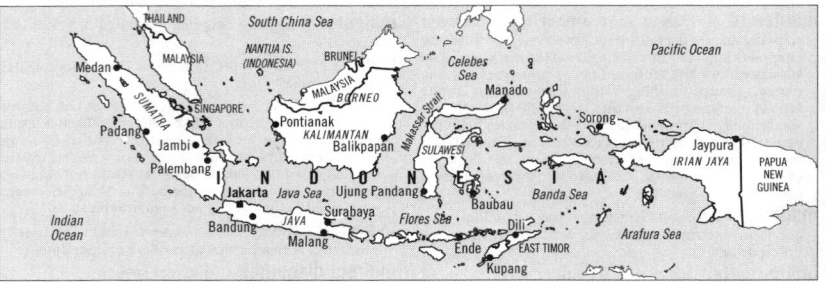

Indonesia

Indonesia /índə neèzi ə/ island republic of Southeast Asia. Capital: Jakarta. Population: 209,774,138 (1997). Area: 1,904,443 sq. km/735,310 sq. mi. —**Indonesian** *n, adj*

indoor /ín dáwr/ *adj* situated or done within a building [Early 18C. < IN + DOOR.]

indoor air quality *n* the condition of the air inside buildings, including the extent of pollution caused by smoking, dust, mites, mould spores, radon, and gases and chemicals from materials and appliances

indoor-outdoor *adj* designed to be used inside or outside a building

indoors /in dáwrz/ *adv* into or inside a building

Indo-Pacific /índō-/ *n* a large group of languages spoken in New Guinea and the surrounding islands. Native speakers: 3 million. —**Indo-Pacific** *adj*

Indore /in dáwr/ **1** former state, now part of Madhya Pradesh, central India **2** city in central India. Population: 1,091,674 (1991).

indorse *vt* = endorse

Indra /índrə/ *n* in Vedic mythology, a powerful warrior god and the ruler of the sky and weather

indraught /ín draaft/ *n* an inward flow or current of air

indrawn /ín dráwn/ *adj* **1** drawn in or pulled in **2** unresponsive or extremely reserved

indri /índri/, **indris** /índriss/ (*plural* **-dris**) *n* a large rare black-and-white lemur with large eyes, silky fur, and a rudimentary tail. Native to: Madagascar. *Indri indri.*

[Mid-19C. < Malagasy *indry!* 'look!' or *indry izy!* 'there he is!'.]

indubitable /in dyoobitab'l/ *adj* obvious or definitely true, and not to be doubted [Early 17C. Directly or via French < Latin *indubitabilis* 'not doubtful' < *dubitare* 'to doubt'.] —**indubitability** /in dyoobitə bílləti/ *n* —**indubitably** *adv*

induce /in dyoŏss/ (**-duces, -ducing, -duced**) *v* **1** *vt* **PERSUADE TO DO** to persuade or influence somebody to do or think something **2** *vt* **PRODUCE MENTAL OR PHYSICAL STATE** to cause or bring about a thought, feeling, or physical condition **3** *vti* **HASTEN BIRTH OF BABY** to make the process of labour or the birth of a baby start by a medical intervention, usually by administering a drug, before it happens naturally **4** *vt* **REASON FROM OBSERVATION** to make a statement based on the observation of facts **5** *vt* **PRODUCE BY INDUCTION** to produce an electric current or a magnetic field by induction [14C. < Latin *inducere* 'lead into, persuade' < *ducere* 'to lead'.]

induced drag *n* the drag force created by the lift of an aircraft

inducement /in dyoŏss mənt/ *n* **1** something that gives somebody a reason to do something, especially something that is offered as an incentive **2** the act of inducing something

SYNONYMS See *motive*.

inducer /in dyoŏssər/ *n* a substance that activates a structural gene within a cell

induct /in dúkt/ *vt* **1 FORMALLY ADMIT TO OFFICE** to install somebody formally in a position or office **2 INTRODUCE NEW IDEAS TO** to introduce somebody to new beliefs, knowledge, or ideas **3** *US* **ENLIST FOR MILITARY SERVICE** to enlist somebody formally for service in the military **4** *PHYS* = **induce** *v*. **5** [14C. < Latin *inductus*, past participle of *inducere* (see INDUCE).] —**inductee** /ín duk teè/ *n*

inductance /in dúktənss/ *n* **1** (*symbol* **L**) the property of an electric circuit or device whereby an electromotive force is created by a change of current in it or in a circuit near it **2** *PHYS* = **inductor** *n*. **2**

inductile /in dúktīl/ *adj* not pliable or yielding —**inductility** /ín duk tílləti/ *n*

induction /in dúksh'n/ *n* **1 PROCESS OF INDUCING** the process of inducing a state, feeling, or idea **2 PROCESS OF HASTENING BABY'S BIRTH** the act or the process of medically hastening, the birth of a baby **3 ACT OF INDUCTING** the act or process of inducting somebody into a position or an organization **4 CONCLUSION BASED ON EVIDENCE** a generalization based on observed instances, or the making of such generalizations, in the usual working method of scientists **5 CREATION OF ELECTRIC OR MAGNETIC FORCES** the process by which electric or magnetic forces are created in a circuit by being in proximity to an electric or magnetic field or a varying current without physical contact **6** *US* **ACT OF ENLISTING** the act of formally enlisting somebody into military service **7 PROCESS IN DEVELOPMENT OF EMBRYO** the process by which one part of an embryo affects the development of another, e.g. through the diffusion of hormones **8 SYNTHESIS OF ENZYME** the process by which the production of an enzyme is stimulated by the increased concentration of the substance it acts on **9 PROCESS OF MATHEMATICAL PROOF** a process for proving propositions with variables limited to positive integers by showing that the smallest instance is true and each following instance is derived from the one before — **inductional** *adj*

induction coil *n* a transformer that produces an intermittent high-voltage current from a low-voltage direct current by means of several wire windings and, often, a soft iron core

induction hardening *n* a process by which the outer surface of a metal is hardened by rapid heating and cooling

induction heating *n* a process for raising the temperature of a metal by inducing an electric current within it

induction motor *n* an alternating-current electric motor powered by the interaction of a varying magnetic field in its windings with the current induced in the rotor

inductive /in dúktiv/ *adj* 1 **OF ELECTRIC OR MAGNETIC INDUCTION** involving, operating by, or caused by electric or magnetic induction 2 **PRODUCING MENTAL OR PHYSICAL STATE** relating to the process of inducing a feeling, idea, or state 3 **REACHING A CONCLUSION BASED ON OBSERVATION** generalizing to produce a universal claim or principle from observed instances 4 **AFFECTING ANOTHER EMBRYONIC PART** producing an effect on another embryonic part by induction —**inductively** *adv* —**inductiveness** *n*

inductor /in dúktər/ *n* 1 **AGENT OF INDUCTION** somebody or something that inducts 2 **PART OF CIRCUIT GENERATING FORCE** a part of an electric circuit, usually a coil, in which an electromotive force is generated by inductance 3 **COMPONENT CAUSING INDUCTANCE** an electrical or electronic component designed to cause or work on inductance

indue *vt* = **endue**

indulge /in dúlj/ (**-dulges, -dulging, -dulged**) *v* 1 *vti* **HAVE OR PERMIT TREAT** to allow yourself or somebody else to experience something enjoyable 2 *vi* **DRINK ALCOHOL** to permit yourself to drink alcohol, especially to excess 3 *vt* **GIVE DEBTOR TIME TO PAY** to allow a debtor time to pay a bill [Early 17C. < Latin *indulgere* 'allow space for'.] —**indulger** *n*

indulged /in dúljd/ *adj* pampered, spoiled, or catered to

indulgence /in dúljənss/ *n* 1 **YIELDING TO SOMEBODY'S WISH** the gratification of or yielding to a wish 2 **SOMETHING ALLOWED AS LUXURY** something that somebody lets himself or herself or somebody else have, especially a luxury 3 **TOLERANT ATTITUDE** a kind or tolerant attitude towards somebody 4 **REMISSION OF PUNISHMENT FOR SIN** in Roman Catholicism, a grant by the pope of partial remission of time to be spent in purgatory or of some other consequence of a sin 5 **TIME FOR REPAYMENT** time given to a debtor to repay a bill

indulgent /in dúljənt/ *adj* permissive, tolerant, or humouring somebody's wishes —**indulgently** *adv*

induline /índyoŏ līn/, **indulin** /índyoŏ lin/ *n* one of a large group of blue dyes resembling indigo

indult /in dúlt/ *n* a dispensation from the pope that allows a special exception to Roman Catholic Church law [15C. Via French < late Latin *indultum* 'grant' < *indultus*, past participle of *indulgere* (see INDULGE).]

indumentum /índyoŏ méntəm/ (*plural* **-ta** /-tə/ *or* **-tums**), **indument** /índyoŏmənt/ *n* a covering of hairs on a plant, or of hair, fur, or feathers on an animal [Mid-19C. < Latin, 'garment' < *induere* 'put on'.]

induna /in dóonə/ *n S Africa* a Black advisor or overseer, such as a counsellor of a tribal chief or a supervisor in a mine, factory, or farm [Mid-19C. < Zulu.]

indurate *vti* /índyoŏ rayt/ (**-rates, -rating, -rated**) to make something hard or to become hard (*literary or technical*) ■ *adj* /índyoo rət/ unsympathetic or unfeeling (*literary*) [Mid-16C. < Latin *indurat-*, past participle of *indurare* 'make hard' < *durus* 'hard'.] —**indurative** /in dyóorətiv/ *adj*

induration /índyoŏ ráysh'n/ *n* 1 **HARDENING** the process of hardening something or of becoming hard (*literary or technical*) 2 **HARDENING OF GEOLOGICAL SEDIMENT** the process by which a soft geological sediment becomes hard 3 **HARDNESS IN BODY TISSUE** a hardness in body tissue, especially a tumour

Indus[1] /índəss/ river in W Tibet, Jammu and Kashmir, and Pakistan, flowing into the Arabian Sea. Length: 2,900 km/1,800 mi.

Indus[2] *n* a faint constellation of the southern hemisphere. See illustration at **constellation**

indus. *abbr* 1 industrial 2 industry

indusium /in dyóozi əm/ (*plural* **-a** /-zi ə/) *n* 1 a membrane on the underside of a fern leaf that protects developing spores 2 an enveloping protective membrane [Early 18C. < Latin, 'tunic' < *induere* 'put on'.] —**indusial** *adj*

industrial /in dústri əl/ *adj* 1 **OF INDUSTRY** relating to, used in, or created by industry 2 **WITH MANY DEVELOPED INDUSTRIES** having a large quantity of highly developed industries 3 **OF INDUSTRY'S WORKFORCE** relating to or involving workers in industry ■ **industrials** *npl* **SHARES IN INDUSTRIAL COMPANIES** the shares and interest-bearing securities of industrial companies —**industrially** *adv*

industrial accident *n* an accident, often causing serious injury, that is job-related in that it usually happens on a work site, e.g. a factory floor or a construction site

industrial action *n* any protest action, e.g. a strike, undertaken by employees against working conditions, layoffs, or other grievances. US term **job action**

industrial archaeology *n* the study of sites, buildings, and equipment used by industries in the past

industrial award *n Aus* a judgment made by an industrial commission or a similar body in settlement of a dispute between employees and employers

industrial commission *n* in Australia, a state government body that rules on disputes between employees and management

industrial democracy *n* the partial or complete management of an industrial workplace by those employed in it

industrial design *n* the art of designing the shape, size, or appearance of manufactured objects

industrial diamond *n* a small diamond that is not of gemstone quality and is often produced synthetically, used in the tips of drilling and cutting tools or in abrasives

industrial disease *n* a disease affecting people as a result of the work they do

industrial engineering *n* the study and practice of designing industrial operations

industrial espionage *n* the secret removal, copying, or recording of confidential or valuable information in a company for use by a competitor

industrial estate *n* a large area of land, usually on the edge of a town, where factories and businesses are concentrated in accordance with local planning regulations. ◊ **industrial park**

industrialisation *n* = **industrialization**

industrialise *vti* = **industrialize**

industrialism /in dústri əlizəm/ *n* the organization of an economy or a society around extensive manufacturing, rather than around agriculture, the production of handicrafts, or commerce

industrialist /in dústri əlist/ *n* an owner or controller of an industrial concern

industrialize /in dústri ə līz/ (**-izes, -izing, -ized**), **industrialise** (**-ises, -ising, -ised**) *vti* to adapt a country or group to industrial methods of production and manufacturing, across a wide area, with all the accompanying social changes, or to be adapted in this way —**industrialization** /in dústri ə lī záysh'n/ *n*

industrial medicine *n* a branch of medicine that specializes in the prevention or treatment of diseases, stresses, or hazards in the workplace

industrial melanism *n* the increase in the numbers of animals, especially moths, with dark coloration in places where industries create a lot of black smoke and predators more easily feed on lighter individuals

industrial misconduct *n* irregular or negligent conduct by an employee in a workplace, which may result in a penalty

industrial park *n US, ANZ* a large area of land where factories and businesses are concentrated in accordance with local zoning policy. ◊ **industrial estate**

industrial psychology *n* the study of human behaviour and attitudes in the workplace —**industrial psychologist** *n*

industrial relations *npl* 1 the relationship between management and employees in an industrial company 2 the relations and procedures between employers' organizations and trade unions that are institutionalized in an industrial society

Industrial Revolution *n* the social and economic changes in Great Britain, Europe, and the United States that began in the second half of the 18th century and involved widespread adoption of industrial methods of production

industrial sociology *n* the study of relationships and structures in industrial organizations

industrial-strength *adj* describes materials or chemicals that are strong or of a quality suitable for use in industry

industrial tribunal *n* a court that rules on disputes between employees and management

industrial union *n* a trade union made up of workers with different occupations who are all employed in one industry

Industrial Workers of the World *n* an international trade union with socialist aims that was founded in the United States in 1905 and lost influence after the 1920s

industrious /in dústri əss/ *adj* hard-working, conscientious, and energetic —**industriously** *adv* —**industriousness** *n*

industry /índəstri/ (*plural* **-tries**) *n* 1 **LARGE-SCALE PRODUCTION** organized economic activity connected with the production, manufacture, or construction of a particular product or range of products 2 **WIDESPREAD ACTIVITY** an activity that many people are involved in, especially one that has become commercialized or standardized ○ *the heritage industry* 3 **HARD WORK** diligent hard work (*formal or literary*) ○ *a hive of industry* [15C. Directly or via Old French *industrie* < Latin *industria* 'diligence' < *industrius* 'diligent', literally 'building in' < assumed *-struus* 'building'.]

industry-wide *adj* cutting across an entire field of commercial activity

Indus Valley Civilization *n* a Bronze-Age civilization that flourished in the lower Indus River Valley, mainly in present-day Pakistan and N India, from about 2500 to 1700 BC

indwell /in dwél/ (**-dwells, -dwelling, -dwelled** *or* **-dwelt, -dwelled** *or* **-dwelt** /in dwélt/) *vti* to inhabit, infuse, or abide within a person, community, or place (*formal*) —**indweller** *n*

Indy car /índi-/ *n* a single-seater car with a turbocharged rear engine, used in a form of motor racing that takes place at very high speeds around a banked oval circuit [Shortening of INDIANAPOLIS, site of the most famous Indy car race]

-ine *suffix* of, relating to, made of ○ *crystalline* ○ *murrhine* [Directly or via Old French < Latin *-inus*, Greek *-inos*]

inebriate /i née bri ayt/ *vt* (**-ates, -ating, -ated**) 1 **MAKE INTOXICATED** to cause somebody to become drunk or intoxicated 2 **EXCITE** to make somebody excited or exhilarated (*formal*) ■ *n* **INTOXICATED PERSON** a drunk or intoxicated person (*formal*) ■ *adj* **INTOXICATED** drunk or intoxicated (*formal*) [15C. < Latin *inebriatus*, past participle of *inebriare* 'make drunk in' < *ebriare* 'make drunk' < *ebrius* 'drunk'.] —**inebriated** *adj* —**inebriation** /i née bri áysh'n/ *n* —**inebriety** /ínni brī əti/ *n*

inedible /in éddəb'l/ *adj* unfit for consumption as food —**inedibility** /in éddə bílləti/ *n* —**inedibly** *adv*

inedited /in éddit id/ *adj* not having been edited or published

ineffable /in éffəb'l/ *adj* unable to be expressed in words [15C. Directly or via French < Latin *ineffabilis* 'unutterable' < *effari* 'speak out' < *fari* 'speak'.] —**ineffability** /in éffə bílləti/ *n* —**ineffableness** *n* —**ineffably** *adv*

ineffaceable /ínni fáyssəb'l/ *adj* incapable of being erased or removed (*formal*) —**ineffaceability** /ínni fáyssə bílləti/ *n* —**ineffaceably** *adv*

ineffective /ínni féktiv/ *adj* 1 not producing the desired result or effect 2 incompetent or inept —**ineffectively** *adv* —**ineffectiveness** *n*

ineffectual /ínni fékchoo əl/ *adj* 1 not competent, decisive, or authoritative enough to achieve desired aims 2 not able to produce a satisfactory outcome —**ineffectuality** /ínni fékchoo álləti/ *n* —**ineffectually** *adv* —**ineffectualness** *n*

inefficacious /ín efi káyshəss/ *adj* not having a positive or useful effect (*formal*) —**inefficaciously** *adv* —**inefficaciousness** *n* —**inefficacity** /-kássəti/ *n* —**inefficacy** /in éffikəssi/ *n*

inefficient /ínni físh'nt/ *adj* performing tasks in a way that is not organized or fails to make the best use of something, especially time —**inefficiency** *n*

inelastic /ínni lástik/ *adj* **1 NOT STRETCHY** unable to return quickly to its original shape and size after being bent, stretched, or squashed **2 NOT EASILY CHANGED** unable to incorporate changes or adapt to new circumstances easily **3 NOT AFFECTING TRANSLATIONAL KINETIC ENERGY** describes a collision that does not lead to an overall loss of translational kinetic energy **4 INSENSITIVE TO PRICE CHANGES** describes supply or demand that is not affected by fluctuations in price —**inelasticity** /ínni lass tíssəti/ *n*

inelegant /in élligənt/ *adj* **1** lacking grace, sophistication and good taste in appearance or behaviour **2** unnecessarily complicated or long —**inelegance** *n*

ineligible /in éllijəb'l/ *adj* not legally entitled or qualified to do, be, or get something —**ineligibility** *n*

ineluctable /ínni lúktəb'l/ *adj* inescapable and so unavoidable (*formal*) ○ *the ineluctable casualties of warfare* [Early 17C. < Latin *ineluctabilis* < *eluctari* 'struggle out of'.] —**ineluctability** /-lúktə bílləti/ *n* —**ineluctably** *adv*

inept /i népt/ *adj* **1** lacking the competence or skill for a particular task **2** not in keeping with what is right or proper for the circumstances [Mid-16C. < Latin *ineptus* 'not suitable' < *aptus* (see APT).] —**ineptitude** —**ineptly** *adv* —**ineptness** *n*

inequable /in ékwəb'l/ *adj* not fair or uniform

inequality /ínni kwóllati/ (*plural* **-ties**) *n* **1 DIFFERENCE IN STATUS** social or economic disparity between people or groups **2 LACK OF EQUAL TREATMENT** unequal opportunity or treatment based on social, ethnic, racial, or economic disparity **3 STATE OF BEING UNEQUAL** the condition or an instance of not being equal **4 UNEVENNESS ON SURFACE** variability or unevenness on the surface of something **5 STATEMENT INDICATING UNEQUAL QUANTITIES** a mathematical statement indicating that two quantities are not equal, represented by the symbols $<$, $>$, and $\neq$, meaning less than, greater than, and not equal to

inequitable /in ékwitəb'l/ *adj* showing bias or favouritism (*formal*) —**inequitableness** *n* —**inequitably** *adv*

inequity /in ékwəti/ (*plural* **-ties**) *n* **1** lack of fairness or justice (*formal*) **2** a situation or action that is not fair

inequivalve /in ékwi valv, -èekwi-/, **inequivalved** /in ékwi valvd, -èekwi-/ *adj* describes a bivalve mollusc whose valves are unequal in size or form

ineradicable /ínni ráddikəb'l/ *adj* impossible to get rid of —**ineradicability** /ínni ráddika bílləti/ *n* —**ineradicableness** *n* —**ineradicably** *adv*

inerrant /in érrənt/ *adj* **1** incapable of making a mistake (*formal*) **2** containing no mistakes —**inerrancy** *n*

inert /i núrt/ *adj* **1 MOTIONLESS** not moving or not able to move **2 NONREACTIVE** not readily changed by chemical or biological reaction **3 SLUGGISH OR UNMOTIVATED** lacking in energy or motivation [Mid-17C. < Latin *inert-* 'having no skill' < *ars* 'skill'.] —**inertly** *adv* —**inertness** *n*

inert gas *n* = noble gas

inertia /i núrshə/ *n* **1** inability or unwillingness to move or act **2** the property of a body by which it remains at rest or continues moving in a straight line unless acted upon by a directional force [Early 18C. < Latin, 'lack of skill, inactivity' < *inert-* (see INERT).] —**inertial** *adj* —**inertially** *adv*

inertial guidance, **inertial navigation** *n* navigation by conversion of the accelerations experienced into distances and directions

inertia-reel seat belt *n* a car seat belt that is able to unwind freely from a small metal drum at the side of the seat but locks if the car stops suddenly

inertia selling *n* the practice of sending unsolicited goods to people's homes and demanding payment if the goods are not returned

inescapable /ínni skáypəb'l/ *adj* impossible to avoid —**inescapability** /ínni skaypə bílləti/ *n* —**inescapably** *adv*

in esse /-éssi/ *adj* having actual existence as opposed to potential existence [< Latin, 'in existence']

inessential /ínni sénsh'l/ *adj* **1 NOT ESSENTIAL** not absolutely necessary **2 WITHOUT ESSENCE** without substance or being (*literary*) ■ *n* SOMETHING INESSENTIAL something that is unnecessary —**inessentiality** /ínni sénshi álləti/ *n* —**inessentially** *adv*

inessive /in éssiv/ *n* in the grammar of languages such as Finnish, a case of nouns and pronouns used to indicate the location of something [Late 19C. < Latin *inesse* 'be in or at' < *esse* 'be'.]

inestimable /in éstimǝb'l/ *adj* extremely useful or valuable —**inestimability** /in èstimǝ bílləti/ *n* —**inestimableness** *n* —**inestimably** *adv*

inevitable /in évvitǝb'l/ *adj* impossible to avoid or to prevent from happening ■ *n* something that is certain to happen [15C. < Latin *inevitabilis* 'not avoidable' < *evitare* 'shun'.] —**inevitability** /in èvvitǝ bílləti/ *n* —**inevitableness** *n* —**inevitably** /-bli/ *adv*

inexact /ínnig zákt/ *adj* **1** not entirely accurate **2** not thorough or careful —**inexactitude** /ínnig zákti tyood/ *n* —**inexactly** *adv* —**inexactness** *n*

inexcusable /ínnik skyoózǝb'l/ *adj* impossible to pardon or justify —**inexcusability** /ínnik skyoòzǝ bílləti/ *n* —**inexcusableness** *n* —**inexcusably** *adv*

inexhaustible /ínnig záwstǝb'l/ *adj* **1** impossible to use up **2** showing no sign of tiring —**inexhaustibility** /ínnig záwstǝ bílləti/ *n* —**inexhaustibleness** *n* —**inexhaustibly** *adv*

inexistent /ínnig zístənt/ *adj* not in existence

inexorable /in éksǝrǝb'l/ *adj* **1** impossible to stop (*formal*) **2** not moved by anyone's attempts to plead or persuade [Mid-16C. Via French < Latin *exorare* 'prevail upon' < *orare* 'pray'.] —**inexorability** /in èksǝrǝ bílləti/ *n* —**inexorableness** *n* —**inexorably** *adv*

inexpedient /ínnik speédi ǝnt/ *adj* not recommended or prudent (*formal*) —**inexpedience** *n* —**inexpediently** *adv*

inexpensive /ínnik spénssiv/ *adj* not costing much money —**inexpensively** *adv* —**inexpensiveness** *n*

inexperience /ínnik speéri ǝnss/ *n* **1** lack of expected or basic skills or knowledge **2** lack of sophistication —**inexperienced** *adj*

inexpert /in ékspurt/ *adj* lacking in skill or experience —**inexpertly** *adv* —**inexpertness** *n*

inexpiable /in ékspi ǝb'l/ *adj* so bad that it cannot be atoned for (*formal*) [15C. < Latin *inexpiabilis* < *expiare* (see EXPIATE).] —**inexpiableness** *n* —**inexpiably** *adv*

inexplicable /ínnik splíkǝb'l, in èksplikǝb'l/ *adj* unable to be explained or justified —**inexplicability** /ínnik splíkǝ bílləti, in èksplikǝ-/ *n* —**inexplicableness** *n* —**inexplicably** *adv*

inexplicit /ínnik splíssit/ *adj* not expressed or shown fully, openly, and unambiguously

inexpressible /ínnik spréssǝb'l/ *adj* impossible to put into words —**inexpressibility** /ínnik spréssǝ bílləti/ *n* —**inexpressibleness** *n* —**inexpressibly** *adv*

inexpressive /ínnik spréssiv/ *adj* conveying no feeling —**inexpressively** *adv* —**inexpressiveness** *n*

inexpugnable /ínnik spúgnǝb'l/ *adj* (*formal*) **1** impossible to take by force **2** impossible to overcome [15C. Via French < Latin *inexpugnabilis* < *expugnare* 'fight off' < *pugnare* 'to fight'.] —**inexpugnability** /ínnik spúgnǝ bílləti/ *n* —**inexpugnableness** *n* —**inexpugnably** *adv*

inexpungible /ínnik spúnjǝb'l/ *adj* impossible to remove or cancel out

inextensible /ínnik sténssǝb'l/ *adj* impossible to stretch to a greater length —**inextensibility** /ínnik sténssǝ bílləti/ *n*

in extenso /ín ik sténssō/ *adv* at its full length ○ *quote a passage in extenso* [< Latin, 'at a stretch']

inextinguishable /ínnik stíng gwishǝb'l/ *adj* impossible to extinguish or suppress —**inextinguishableness** *n* —**inextinguishably** *adv*

inextirpable /ínnik stúrpǝb'l/ *adj* impossible to remove or destroy (*formal*) [Early 17C. < Latin *inex(s)tirpabilis* < *ex(s)tirpare* (see EXTIRPATE).] —**inextirpableness** *n*

in extremis /ín ik streémiss/ *adv* in desperate circumstances, especially at the point of death ■ *adj* on the point of death [< Latin, 'in the extremes']

inextricable /ínnik stríkǝb'l, in èkstrikǝb'l/ *adj* **1 IMPOSSIBLE TO ESCAPE FROM** impossible to get free from **2 IMPOSSIBLE TO DISENTANGLE** impossible to disentangle or undo **3 HOPELESSLY COMPLEX** hopelessly involved or complex [Mid-16C. < Latin *inextricabilis* 'that cannot be disentangled' < *extricare* (see EXTRICATE).] —**inextricability** /ínnik stríkǝ bílləti, in èkstrikǝ-/ *n* —**inextricableness** *n* —**inextricably** *adv*

INF *abbr* intermediate-range nuclear forces

infallible /in fálb'l/ *adj* **1 NOT ERRING** incapable of making a mistake **2 INCAPABLE OF FAILING** certain not to fail **3 UNERRING IN DOCTRINE** incapable of being mistaken in matters of doctrine and dogma [15C. < medieval Latin *infallibilis* < Latin *fallere* 'deceive, disappoint'.] —**infallibility** /in fállǝ bílləti/ *n* —**infallibleness** *n* —**infallibly** *adv*

infamous /ínfǝmǝss/ *adj* **1** having an extremely bad reputation **2** so bad as to earn somebody an extremely bad reputation —**infamously** *adv*

infamy /ínfǝmi/ (*plural* **-mies**) *n* **1 NOTORIETY** the disgrace to somebody's reputation caused by an infamous act or behaviour **2 SHAMEFUL OR CRIMINAL CONDUCT** shameful or criminal conduct or character **3 EVIL DEED** a publicly known infamous act or event [15C. < French *infamie* < Latin *infamis* 'of ill repute', literally 'having no fame' < *fama* 'fame'.]

infancy /ínfǝnssi/ *n* **1 BABYHOOD** the condition or time of childhood before a baby walks or talks **2 BEGINNING** an early stage of development for an idea, project, or enterprise **3 TIME OF BEING MINOR** the condition or time in which a young person is not legally considered an adult

infant /ínfǝnt/ *n* **1 BABY** a very young child that can neither walk nor talk **2 YOUNG SCHOOLCHILD** a schoolchild between the ages of five and seven **3 LEGAL MINOR** a young person legally considered a minor ■ **infants** *npl* INFANT DEPARTMENT OF SCHOOL the infant department of a primary school (*informal*) ■ *adj* JUST BEGINNING in an early stage of development [14C. Via French *enfant* < Latin *infans* 'not speaking' < *fari* 'speak'.] —**infanthood** *n*

infanta /in fántǝ/ (*plural* **-tas**) *n* **1** the daughter of a Spanish or Portuguese king **2** the wife of an infante [Late 16C. < Spanish, Portuguese, feminine of *infante* (see INFANTE).]

infante /in fánti/ (*plural* **-tes**) *n* a son, other than the heir to the throne, of a Spanish or Portuguese king, especially the second son [Mid-16C. Via Spanish, Portuguese < Latin *infans* (see INFANT).]

infanticide /in fánti sīd/ *n* **1 MURDER OF INFANT** the killing of an infant **2 KILLING OF BABIES** the practice of killing newborn babies **3 KILLER OF INFANT** a killer of an infant —**infanticidal** /in fánti sīd'l/ *adj*

infantile /ínfǝn tīl/ *adj* **1 CHILDISH** showing a lack of maturity **2 RELATING TO INFANTS** relating to infants or infancy **3 IN FIRST STAGE OF EROSION** in the earliest stage of erosion —**infantility** /ínfǝn tílləti/ *n*

infantile paralysis *n* poliomyelitis (*dated*)

infantilise *vt* = infantilize

infantilism /in fántilizǝm/ *n* childish or immature behaviour

infantilize /in fánti līz/ (**-izes, -izing, -ized**), **infantilise** (**-ises, -ising, -ised**) *vt* **1** to make somebody infantile or to keep somebody in an infantile state **2** to treat somebody as or consider somebody to be infantile —**infantilization** /in fánti īl záysh'n/ *n*

infant mortality rate *n* the number of infant deaths during the first year of life per thousand live births

infantry /ínfǝntri/ (*plural* **-tries**) *n* the soldiers or a unit of soldiers who are trained to fight on foot [Late 16C. < French *infanterie* < Italian *infante* 'youth, foot soldier' < Latin *infans* (see INFANT).]

infantryman /ínfǝntrimǝn/ (*plural* **-men** /-mǝn/) *n* a soldier in the infantry

infant school *n* a school, or part of a school, for children between the ages of four or five and seven

infarct /in fàrkt/ *n* an area of tissue that has recently died as a result of the sudden loss of its blood supply, e.g. following blockage of an artery by a blood clot [Late 19C. < modern Latin *infarctus* < the past participle of Latin *infarcire* 'cram in' < *farcire* 'to stuff'.]

infarction /in faàrksh'n/ *n* **1** the formation of an infarct **2** = infarct

infatuate /in fáttyoo ayt/ (**-ates, -ating, -ated**) *vt* **1** to inspire a thoughtless or excessive passion in somebody for another person or thing **2** to make somebody behave irrationally as a result of a great, often temporary, passion for another person or thing [Mid-16C. < Latin *infatuat-*, past participle of *infatuare* 'make foolish' < *fatuus* 'foolish'.] —**infatuated** *adj* —**infatuatedly** *adv*

infatuation /in fáttyoo áysh'n/ *n* **1** a great, often temporary, and irrational passion for somebody or something **2** the person or object that somebody is infatuated with

SYNONYMS See *love*.

infauna /in fáwnǝ/ *npl* organisms that live in tubes or burrows beneath the surface of the sea floor [Early 20C. < IN-2 + FAUNA.] —**infaunal** *adj*

infeasible /ɪn feˈɪzəbˈl/ adj not practical or easily achieved —**infeasibility** /ɪn feɪzə bɪlləti/ n —**infeasibleness** n —**infeasibly** adv

⚡ **infect** /ɪn fékt/ vt 1 CAUSE INFECTION IN to contaminate or cause infection in a person or animal with a disease-producing agent 2 CAUSE COMMUNICABLE DISEASE IN to give a person or animal a communicable disease 3 ENTER PERSON OR ANIMAL to invade and live in the body of a person or animal (refers to microorganisms or endoparasites) 4 AFFECT to corrupt or adversely affect somebody or something 5 INFLUENCE SOMEBODY'S FEELINGS to communicate an emotion such as enthusiasm or fear to somebody 6 CONTAMINATE COMPUTER WITH VIRUS to copy to a computer system a computer virus that is capable of damaging the system's programs or data [14C. < Latin infect-, past participle of inficere 'to stain', literally 'dip in' < facere 'to do'.] —**infected** adj —**infector** n

infection /ɪn féksh'n/ n 1 STATE OF BEING INFECTED the reproduction and proliferation of microorganisms within the body 2 INFECTING OF OTHERS the transmission of infectious microorganisms from one person to another 3 INFECTING MICROORGANISM an infecting microorganism or agent 4 DISEASE a communicable disease 5 MORAL CORRUPTION something that corrupts somebody morally 6 TRANSMISSION OF FEELINGS the communication of emotions or attitudes between people

infectious /ɪn fékshəss/ adj 1 COMMUNICABLE describes a disease that is capable of being passed from one person to another 2 CAUSED BY BACTERIA caused by bacteria, viruses, or other microorganisms 3 CAUSING INFECTION bringing about infection 4 AFFECTING FEELINGS OF OTHERS capable of affecting the emotions and attitudes of others —**infectiously** adv —**infectiousness** n

infectious hepatitis n = hepatitis A

infectious mononucleosis n glandular fever (technical)

infective /ɪn féktiv/ adj 1 capable of producing an infection 2 capable of affecting the emotions and attitudes of others —**infectiveness** n —**infectivity** /ɪn fek tívvəti/ n

infelicity /ɪnfə líssəti/ (plural -ties) n 1 the inappropriateness of something, especially an expression, to a particular situation 2 something inappropriate to a situation or purpose, especially an expression [Early 17C. < Latin infelicitas 'unhappiness' < felix 'happy'.] —**infelicitous** adj —**infelicitously** adv

infer /ɪn fúr/ (-fers, -ferring, -ferred) v 1 vti CONCLUDE SOMETHING FROM REASONING to conclude something on the basis of evidence or reasoning 2 vt SUGGEST to suggest or lead to something as a conclusion 3 △ vt IMPLY to imply or suggest something. [Early 16C. < Latin inferre 'bring in' < ferre 'carry'.] —**inferable** adj —**inferably** adv —**inferrer** n

SYNONYMS See **deduce**.

USAGE infer or imply? Although infer is sometimes loosely used to mean imply, careful writers observe the distinction between the two words. Infer is to conclude something on the basis of reasoning or evidence: When the senator appeared enthusiastic at the environmental rally, we inferred that she would support stronger clean-air legislation. You may infer what you will, but when discussing the issues, I did not indicate any intention to support this legislation. Imply is to make something understood without expressing it directly: When the senator appeared enthusiastic at the environmental rally, her attitude implied that she would support stronger clean-air legislation.

inference /ɪnfərənss/ n 1 CONCLUSION a conclusion drawn from evidence or reasoning 2 REASONING PROCESS the process of reasoning from a premise to a conclusion 3 IMPLICATION something that is implied [Late 16C. < medieval Latin inferentia < Latin inferre (see INFER).] —**inferential** /ɪnfə rénsh'l/ adj —**inferentially** adv

inferior /ɪn feˈɪri ər/ adj 1 LOWER IN STANDING lower or low in rank, standing, or degree 2 NOT AS GOOD lower in quality or value 3 MEDIOCRE failing to meet a standard of quality, ability, or achievement 4 LOWER IN BODY describes a body part or organ situated beneath another similar part 5 BELOW CALYX describes a plant ovary located below a calyx 6 BETWEEN EARTH AND SUN orbiting or taking place between the Earth and the Sun 7 PRINTED BELOW THE LINE written or printed at a slightly lower level than the rest of the characters in a line, e.g. the '2' in 'CO₂' ■ n 1 LOWER RANKING PERSON somebody of lower status, rank, or quality 2 SUBSCRIPT CHARACTER a character printed or

written below the line [15C. < Latin, 'lower' < inferus 'below'.] —**inferiority** /ɪn feˈɪri órrəti/ n —**inferiorly** adv

inferiority complex n an overdeveloped sense of being inferior to other people

infernal /ɪn fúrn'l/ adj 1 RELATING TO UNDERWORLD relating to hell or the underworld 2 DIABOLICAL IN NATURE so extreme, wicked, or cruel as to be worthy of hell 3 VERY ANNOYING extremely annoying or unpleasant [14C. < Old French, < Latin infernus 'lower, the underworld'.] —**infernally** adv

inferno /ɪn fúrnō/ (plural -nos) n 1 a fire or a place that is burning fiercely 2 a place or situation that is reminiscent of hell [Mid-19C. Via Italian, 'hell' < late Latin infernus (see INFERNAL).]

LITERARY LINK The Inferno, a poem (1307?–20?) by Italian poet Dante Alighieri. The first part of the epic masterpiece The Divine Comedy, it describes the poet's journey through Hell with Virgil as his guide. The presence of certain historical figures among the damned, and the punishments they receive, reflect Dante's personal opinions and judgments on past issues and events.

infertile /ɪn fúr tíl/ adj 1 STERILE physically incapable of conceiving offspring 2 NOT PRODUCING CROPS incapable of producing crops 3 NOT FERTILIZED describes an egg that has not been fertilized —**infertilely** adv —**infertility** /ɪnfər tílləti/ n

infest /ɪn fést/ vt 1 to overrun a place or site in large numbers and become threatening, harmful, or unpleasant ○ clothing infested with lice 2 to live as a parasite on or in something [Mid-16C. Directly or via French infester < Latin infestare 'to attack' < infestus 'hostile'.] —**infestation** /ɪn fe stáysh'n/ n —**infested** adj —**infester** n

infibulate /ɪn fíbbyōo layt/ (-lates, -lating, -lated) vt to close the vagina partially by stitching it or closing it with a clasp. ♀ **female circumcision** [Early 17C. < Latin infibulat-, past participle of infibulare 'fasten with a pin' < fibula 'brooch'.] —**infibulation** /ɪn fíbbyōo láysh'n/ n

infidel /ínfid'l/ n (disapproving) 1 a person who does not believe in a particular religion, especially Christianity or Islam 2 a person who lacks religious beliefs [15C. Directly or via French infidèle < Latin infidelis 'unbelieving' < fidelis 'faithful' < fides (see FAITH).]

infidelity /ínfi délləti/ (plural -ties) n 1 UNFAITHFULNESS unfaithfulness or disloyalty, especially to a sexual partner 2 UNFAITHFUL ACT an act of unfaithfulness or disloyalty, especially to a sexual partner 3 DISBELIEF lack of religious faith (disapproving)

infield /ɪn feeld/ n 1 NEAR WICKET IN CRICKET area of a cricket field that is close to the wickets 2 BASEBALL DIAMOND the area of a baseball field bounded by home plate and the three bases 3 BASEBALL PLAYERS IN INFIELD the defensive baseball players in the infield considered together 4 AREA WITHIN RACETRACK the area bounded by a racetrack 5 FARMLAND CLOSE TO FARMHOUSE the farmland close to a farmhouse that is regularly manured and cropped

infielder /ɪn feeldər/ n a defensive baseball player in the infield

infighting /ɪn fíting/ n 1 conflict or rivalry between associates or members of the same organization 2 boxing or fighting at close range —**infighter** n

infill /ɪn fil/ n the filling of gaps, especially of vacant areas between existing buildings ■ vt to build new buildings in gaps between existing buildings —**infilling** n

infiltrate /ínfil trayt/ vti (-trates, -trating, -trated) 1 BREAK THROUGH SECRETLY to cross or send somebody into enemy territory without the enemy's knowledge ○ infiltrate troops behind enemy lines 2 GET IN POSITION TO DO HARM to establish somebody or become established within a place or organization with the intention of doing harm or gathering information ○ activists were infiltrated into local parties 3 PERMEATE FLUID THROUGH SUBSTANCE to pass through a substance by filtration, or make a liquid or gas pass through a substance by filtration ■ n ABNORMAL ACCUMULATION a substance such as fat that passes into tissues and cells and forms an abnormal accumulation —**infiltration** /ínfil tráysh'n/ n —**infiltrative** adj —**infiltrator** n

infimum /ínfiməm/ (plural -ma /-mə/) n a number less than or equal to all elements of a set, thus a lower bound, but greater than or equal to all other lower bounds of the set [Mid-20C. < Latin, 'lowest part'.]

infinite /ínfinət/ adj 1 NOT MEASURABLE without any finite or measurable limits 2 EXCEEDINGLY GREAT very great in size, number, or extent ○ He took infinite pains over it. 3 GREATER THAN ANY ASSIGNED VALUE greater in

number, size, or scope than any arbitrarily assigned value 4 WITH UNLIMITED SPATIAL EXTENT extending indefinitely or having unlimited spatial extent 5 WITH INDEFINITE ELEMENTS having an indefinitely extendable number of terms or elements 6 IN ONE-TO-ONE RELATIONSHIP able to be put into a one-to-one mathematical correspondence with a subset of itself ■ n SOMETHING INFINITE something that is infinite, e.g. space [14C. Via Old French < Latin infinitus 'not bounded' < finitus 'finite'.] —**infinitely** adv —**infiniteness** n

Infinite n used to refer to God

⚡ **infinite loop** n a series of instructions in a computer program containing errors that make it repeat endlessly

infinitesimal /ínfini téssim'l/ adj 1 TINY very small in number, amount, or degree 2 CLOSE TO ZERO able to assume values arbitrarily close to but greater than zero ■ n INFINITESIMAL NUMBER an infinitesimal number or function [Mid-17C. < modern Latin infinitesimus 'the number in a series corresponding to infinity' < Latin infinitus (see INFINITE).] —**infinitesimally** adv

infinitesimal calculus n MATH = calculus n. 1

infinitive /ɪn fínnitiv/ n a form of a verb with no reference to a particular tense, person, or subject. In English, an infinitive is usually preceded by the word 'to', as in 'to see'. [15C. < late Latin infinitivus, -ivus, + the infinitive (see INFINITE).] —**infinitival** /ɪn fínni tív'l/ adj —**infinitivally** adv

infinitude /ɪn fínni tyood/ n 1 the infinite nature of something 2 a very great number, degree, or extent [Mid-17C. < Latin infinitus (see INFINITE).]

infinity /ɪn fínnəti/ (plural -ties) n 1 SOMETHING WITHOUT LIMITS limitless time, space, or distance ○ beyond the Earth lay infinity 2 SOMETHING TOO GREAT TO COUNT an amount or number so great that it cannot be counted ○ an infinity of stars 3 STATE OF BEING INFINITE the state or quality of being infinite 4 CONCEPT OF BEING ALWAYS UNLIMITED the concept of being unlimited by always being larger than any imposed value or boundary 5 GEOMETRIC POINT AT INFINITE DISTANCE a part of a geometric figure situated an infinite distance from the observer, e.g. the hypothetical point at which parallel lines meet in Euclidean geometry 6 INFINITELY DISTANT POINT a point sufficiently far from a lens or mirror that the light emitted from it falls in parallel rays on the surface [14C. < French infinité < Latin infinitus (see INFINITE).]

infirm /ɪn fúrm/ adj 1 NOT STRONG lacking strength and vitality, e.g. because of sickness or age 2 IRRESOLUTE lacking firmness of character or a strong will 3 STRUCTURALLY UNSOUND having a structure that is not sound 4 LEGALLY UNSOUND invalid or not supported, e.g. a title to property or a claim ■ npl PEOPLE WHO ARE NOT STRONG people who lack strength and vitality, e.g. because of sickness or age (sometimes offensive) [14C. < Latin infirmus < firmus 'firm'.] —**infirmly** adv —**infirmness** n

SYNONYMS See **weak**.

infirmary /ɪn fúrməri/ (plural -ries) n a hospital or area within an institution where sick and injured people are cared for [15C. < medieval Latin infirmaria < Latin infirmus (see INFIRM).]

infirmity /ɪn fúrməti/ (plural -ties) n 1 LACK OF STRENGTH lack of strength and vitality 2 CHARACTER FLAW a weakness or failing in somebody's character 3 MINOR ILLNESS any medical condition that causes a lack of strength or vitality

infix /ɪn fiks/ vt 1 FIX SOMETHING FIRMLY IN SOMETHING ELSE to insert something into another thing in order to secure it 2 INSTIL to secure something firmly in the mind 3 PUT ELEMENT IN WORD to insert a linking element into a word. In the word 'acidophilus', the letter 'o' is an infix. ■ n AFFIX IN MIDDLE an affix inserted into the middle of a word —**infixation** /ínfik sáysh'n/ n —**infixion** n

infl. abbr 1 inflammable 2 inflorescence 3 influence 4 influenced

in flagrante delicto /ɪn flə gránti di líktō/, **in flagrante** adv 1 in the act of committing an offence 2 in the act of having sexual relations, especially illicit sexual relations [< Latin, 'in the heat of the crime']

inflame /ɪn fláym/ (-flames, -flaming, -flamed) v 1 vt PROVOKE A POWERFUL RESPONSE IN to excite somebody to an intense emotion such as anger or jealousy 2 vt MAKE SOMETHING STRONGER to make something, e.g. anger or jealousy, become more intense 3 vti SWELL AND TURN RED to become red and swollen, or to make bodily tissue become red and swollen, in response to injury or infection [14C. Via Old French *enflammer* < Latin *inflammare* < *flamma* 'flame'.] —**inflamed** *adj* —**inflamer** *n*

inflammable /in flámməb'l/ *adj* **1 EASILY SET ON FIRE** quickly and easily set on fire and burned **2 EASILY ROUSED** easily made angry or passionate ■ *n* **FLAMMABLE ITEM** something that is quickly and easily set on fire and burned [Early 17C. < medieval Latin *inflammabilis* 'liable to inflammation' < Latin *inflammare* (see INFLAME).] —**inflammability** /in flámmə bíllәti/ *n* —**inflammableness** *n* —**inflammably** *adv*

inflammation /ìnflə máysh'n/ *n* **1** swelling, redness, heat, and pain produced in an area of the body as a reaction to injury or infection **2** a heightening or stirring up of emotion

inflammatory /in flámmətəri/ *adj* **1** liable to arouse strong emotions, especially anger **2** caused or characterized by inflammation —**inflammatorily** *adv*

inflammatory bowel disease *n* a disease causing inflammation of the bowel, typically Crohn's disease or ulcerative colitis

inflatable /in fláytəb'l/ *adj* made of expandable material that can be filled with gas or air ■ *n* something, e.g. a ball, mattress, or boat, that can be filled with air or gas

inflate /in fláyt/ (**-flates, -flating, -flated**) *vti* **1 EXPAND WITH AIR** to fill something, e.g. a ball, mattress or boat, with air or gas, or to be filled with air or gas **2 MAKE SOMETHING APPEAR GREATER** to exaggerate the size or importance of something, or to become exaggerated in size or importance **3 INCREASE PRICES OR MONEY SUPPLY** to cause inflation in prices or the money supply, or to undergo inflation [15C. < Latin *inflat-*, past participle of *inflare* 'blow into' < *flare* 'to blow'.] —**inflator** *n*

inflated /in fláytid/ *adj* **1 UNDESERVEDLY GREAT** greater than is justified or normal ○ *an inflated sense of her own importance* **2 EXCESSIVELY HIGH** excessively or abnormally high **3 PRETENTIOUS** exaggerated or pompous in expression **4 BLOWN UP** expanded with air or gas —**inflatedly** *adv* —**inflatedness** *n*

inflation /in fláysh'n/ *n* **1 HIGHER PRICES** an increase in the supply of currency or credit relative to the availability of goods and services, resulting in higher prices **2 BEING INFLATED** the act of inflating something or the condition of being inflated **3 BEING PUFFED UP WITH PRIDE** being puffed up with pride

inflationary /in fláysh'nəri/ *adj* relating to or causing economic inflation ○ *inflationary policies*

inflationary spiral *n* a continuous economic cycle of higher prices causing higher wages, which in turn cause even higher prices

inflationism /in fláysh'nizəm/ *n* the advocacy or policy of deliberately causing economic inflation through an increase in the supply of available currency and credit —**inflationist** *adj, n*

inflect /in flékt/ *v* **1** *vt* **VARY PITCH OF VOICE** to change the pitch or tone of the voice **2** *vti* **CHANGE WORD FORM** to change the form of a word, e.g. to show a change in tense, mood, gender, or number, or to be changed in this way **3** *vt* **BEND** to make something turn from a direct line or course [15C. < Latin *inflectere* 'bend in' < *flectere* 'to bend'.] —**inflectable** *adj* —**inflected** *adj* —**inflective** *adj* —**inflector** *n*

inflection /in fléksh'n/, **inflexion** *n* **1 CHANGE IN PITCH** a change in the tone or pitch of the voice **2 WORD CHANGE** a change in the form of a word to show a grammatical change such as tense, mood, gender, or number **3 ALTERED FORM OF WORD** an altered form of a word, e.g. one showing a change in tense, mood, gender, or number, or the part of the word that changes in this way **4 BENDING** a turning from a straight line or course **5** MATH = **point of inflection** —**inflectional** *adj* —**inflectionally** *adv* —**inflectionless** *adj*

inflection point *n US* MATH = **point of inflection**

inflexed /in flékst/ *adj* describes a plant part that is bent inwards or downwards towards the stem [Mid-17C. < Latin *inflex-*, past participle of *inflectere* (see INFLECT).]

inflexible /in fléksəb'l/ *adj* **1 UNBENDING** adhering firmly to a viewpoint or principle **2 IMPOSSIBLE TO CHANGE** firmly established and impossible to change ○ *an inflexible rule* **3 RIGID** stiff and bendable only with difficulty —**inflexibility** /in fléksə bíllәti/ *n* —**inflexibleness** *n* —**inflexibly** *adv*

inflexion *n* = **inflection**

inflict /in flíkt/ *vt* **1** to cause damage, harm, or unpleasantness to somebody or something ○ *inflicted heavy casualties on the enemy forces* **2** to impose a burden on another [Mid-16C. < Latin *inflict-*, past participle of *infligere* 'strike upon' < *figere* 'to hit'.] —**inflictable** *adj* —**inflicter** *n* —**infliction** /in flíksh'n/ *n* —**inflictive** *adj*

USAGE See ***afflict***.

in-flight *adj* taking place or provided for passengers during an aircraft journey ○ *in-flight entertainment*

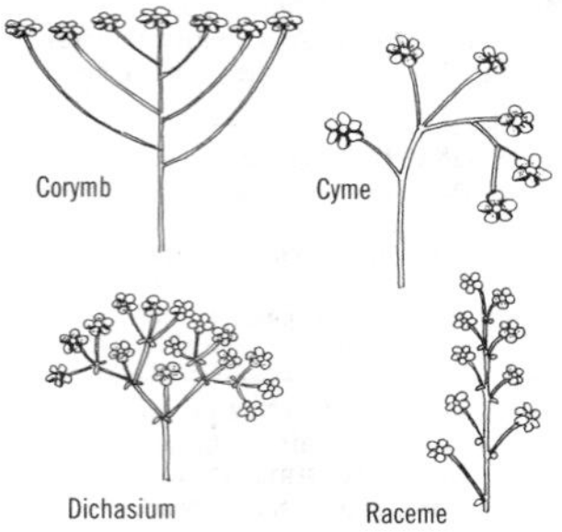
Corymb
Cyme
Dichasium
Raceme

Inflorescence

inflorescence /ìnflə réss'nss/ *n* **1 FLOWERING PART OF A PLANT** a flowering structure that consists of more than one flower and usually comprises distinct individual flowers **2 WAY FLOWERS GROW** the arrangement or manner in which flowers develop on a stalk **3 FLOWERING** the budding and flowering of a plant [Mid-18C. < modern Latin *inflorescentia* < Latin *inflorescere* 'come into flower' < *florescere* 'begin to flower'.]

inflow /in flō/ *n* **1 SOMETHING THAT FLOWS IN** something that flows in somewhere ○ *an inflow of fresh water into a lake* **2 INFLUX** an instance or process of something flowing in ○ *the inflow of visitors to the site* **3 PLACE WHERE AN INFLOW OCCURS** the point at which something flows in —**inflowing** *n*

influence /in floo ənss/ *n* **1 EFFECT** the effect of something on a person, thing, or event ○ *Picasso's influence on the course of 20th-century art* **2 POWER TO SWAY** the power that somebody has to affect other people's thinking or actions by means of argument, example, or force of personality ○ *She came under the influence of one of her teachers.* **3 SPECIAL ADVANTAGE** the power or authority that comes from wealth, social status, or position **4 SOMEBODY WHO CAN SWAY ANOTHER** somebody or something able to affect the course of events or somebody's thinking or action ○ *He's a bad influence on you.* **5 STARS' EFFECT ON PEOPLE** in astrology, an emanation that is believed to come from the stars and planets and to affect human characteristics, personality, and actions ■ *vt* (**-ences, -encing, -enced**) **1 SWAY** to persuade or sway somebody ○ *What influenced you in your choice of career?* **2 AFFECT** to have the power to affect something ○ *the factors that influence a nation's development* [14C. < medieval Latin *influentia* < Latin *influere* 'flow in' < *fluere* 'to flow'.] —**influenceable** *adj* —**influencer** *n* ◇ **under the influence** intoxicated by having drunk alcohol (*informal*)

~~**influencial**~~ incorrect spelling of **influential**

influential /ìn floo énsh'l/ *adj* having a great deal of power to sway people —**influentially** *adv*

influenza /ìn floo énzə/ *n* **1** a viral illness producing a high temperature, sore throat, runny nose, headache, dry cough, and muscle pain (*technical*) **2** a viral disease of domestic animals, usually characterized by fever and respiratory problems [Mid-18C. Via Italian < medieval Latin *influentia* (see INFLUENCE), referring to the influence of the stars.] —**influenzal** *adj*

influx /in fluks/ *n* **1** a sudden arrival of a large number of people or things ○ *dealing with the influx of tourists into the city* **2** a flowing in, especially of a stream or river [Late 16C. Via late Latin *influxus* < Latin, past participle of *influere* (see INFLUENCE).]

influx control *n* the control over the movement of black people into urban areas exerted by government under the system of rigid pass laws in South Africa during apartheid

info[1] /ínfō/ *n* information (*informal*) [Early 20C. Shortening.]

⚡ **info**[2] *abbr* general use (*in Internet addresses*)

infold *vt* = **enfold**

⚡ **infomediary** /ínfō méedi əri/ *n* a website providing specialist information for both producers of goods and customers

infomercial /ínfō múrsh'l/ *n* a commercial advertisement on television that is made to appear like a full-length interview or documentary programme [Late 20C. Blend of INFORMATION + COMMERCIAL.]

⚡ **infonesia** /ínfō néesi ə/ *n* inability to remember an item of information or its location, especially on the Internet (*informal*)

inform /in fáwrm/ *v* **1** *vt* **COMMUNICATE INFORMATION TO** to communicate information or knowledge to somebody ○ *The police informed us of the accident.* **2** *vr* **LEARN ABOUT** to familiarize yourself with a subject **3** *vi* **TELL POLICE** to give confidential or incriminating information about somebody else's activities, especially to the police **4** *vt* **UNDERLIE AND ANIMATE** to be an essential characteristic of something ○ *His religious beliefs inform his entire work.* **5** *vt* **GIVE STRUCTURE TO** to give structure or substance to something (*formal*) [14C. Via Old French *enformer* < Latin *informare* 'give form to' < *forma* 'shape'.]

informal /in fáwrm'l/ *adj* **1 FREE OF CEREMONY** relaxed and casual rather than ceremonious and stiff **2 UNOFFICIAL** not officially prepared, organized, or sanctioned ○ *The two sides in the conflict held informal talks.* **3 CASUAL AND EVERYDAY** suitable for casual or everyday situations ○ *informal dress* **4 COLLOQUIAL** more appropriate in spoken than written form —**informality** /ìn fawr mállәti/ *n* —**informally** *adv*

informal economy *n* economic activities organized without government approval, outside mainstream industry and commerce

informal vote *n ANZ* a spoiled ballot paper

informant /in fáwrmənt/ *n* **1** somebody who gives information to somebody else **2** somebody who gives confidential or incriminating information to the police about somebody else

informatics /ìnfər máttiks/ *n* INFO SCI = **information science** (+ *singular verb*) [Mid-20C. < INFORMATION, after Russian *informatika*.]

⚡ **information** /ìnfər máysh'n/ *n* **1 KNOWLEDGE** definite knowledge acquired or supplied about something or somebody ○ *a bulletin giving the latest information on the trial* **2 GATHERED FACTS** the collected facts and data about a particular subject **3** *US* TELECOM = **directory enquiries** **4 MAKING FACTS KNOWN** the communication of facts and knowledge **5 COMPUTER DATA** computer data that has been organized and presented in a systematic fashion to clarify the underlying meaning **6 FORMAL CRIMINAL ACCUSATION** a formal accusation of a crime brought before a court or magistrate —**informational** *adj* —**informationally** *adv*

⚡ **information age** *n* a period characterized by widespread electronic access to information through the use of computer technology

⚡ **information appliance** *n* a small portable digital information-processing machine compatible with an electronic network

⚡ **information processing** *n* the organization, manipulation, analysis, and distribution of data, nowadays typically carried out by computers

⚡ **information retrieval** *n* the process used to systematically store and retrieve computerized data

⚡ **information science** *n* the study of the collection, categorization, and distribution of data, particularly computer data

⚡ **information superhighway** *n* the worldwide computer network that includes the Internet, private networks, and proprietary online services

⚡ **information technology** *n* the use of technologies from computing, electronics, and telecommunications to process and distribute information

information theory *n* the mathematical study of the transmission, reception, storage, and retrieval of information based on the statistical analysis of communication between humans and machines

⚡ **information warfare** *n* an attack on a company's or country's essential computer systems, especially those controlling security, communications, and finance

informative /in fáwrmətiv/ *adj* providing useful information —**informatively** *adv* —**informativeness** *n*

informed /in fáwrmd/ *adj* **1** showing, having, or based on knowledge or understanding of a situation or subject ○ *informed criticism* **2** based on a proper knowledge and understanding of a situation or subject ○ *an informed decision* —**informedly** /in fáwrmidli/ *adv*

informed consent *n* agreement by a patient to undergo an operation or medical treatment or take part in a clinical trial after being informed of and having understood the risks involved

informer /in fáwrmər/ *n* **1** somebody who gives the police or authorities information about criminal activities **2** somebody or something that provides information about a subject or situation

infotainment /ínfō táynmənt/ *n* television programmes that deal with serious issues or current affairs in an entertaining way [Late 20C. Blend of INFORMATION + ENTERTAINMENT.] —**infotainer** *n*

⚡**infotech** /ínfō tek/ *n* information technology (*informal*) [Late 20C. Contraction.]

infra /ínfrə/ *adv* used in an explanatory note to refer a reader to a point later in a text, especially in the phrase 'vide infra' (*formal*) ◊ **supra** [Late 19C. < Latin.]

infra- *prefix* below, beneath, inferior ○ *infrasonic* ○ *infraclass* [< Latin *infra* 'below' < Indo-European]

infraclass /ínfrə klaass/ *n* a taxonomic category of organisms that is above an order and below a subclass

infracostal /ínfrə kóst'l/ *adj* lying below the ribs

infract /in frákt/ *vt* to fail to obey or fulfil a law, contract, or agreement [Late 18C. < Latin *infractus*, past participle of *infringere* 'destroy'.] —**infractor** *n*

infraction /in fráksh'n/ *n* a failure to obey or fulfil a law, contract, or agreement, or an instance of this [15C. Directly and via French < Latin *infraction-* < *infractus* (see INFRACT).]

infra dig /ínfrə díg/ *adj* below the standard of social behaviour that somebody usually maintains (*informal*) [Early 19C. Shortening of Latin *infra dignitatem* 'beneath dignity'.]

infrangible /in fránjəb'l/ *adj* (*formal*) **1** unable to be broken or separated into pieces **2** unable to be disregarded or violated —**infrangibility** /in fránjə bílləti/ *n* —**infrangibleness** *n* —**infrangibly** *adv*

infraorder /ínfrə awrdər/ *n* a category in the scientific classification of related organisms, comprising one or more families within an order —**infraordinal** /ínfrə áwrdin'l/ *adj*

infrared /ínfrə réd/ *n* the portion of the invisible electromagnetic spectrum consisting of radiation with wavelengths in the range 750 nm to 1 mm, between light and radio waves ○ *infrared radiation* ■ *adj* using, producing, or affected by infrared radiation [Late 19C. Because it lies below the red end of the visible spectrum.]

infrared astronomy *n* the study of astronomical objects by examining the wavelengths they emit in the infrared range

infrared photography *n* photography with film that is sensitive to infrared radiation, used, e.g., for taking pictures at night or in haze and in detecting camouflaged objects

infrasonic /ínfrə sónnik/ *adj* **1** relating to sound at frequencies below 20 Hz, which cannot be heard by human beings but can be felt as vibration **2** using or produced by infrasonic waves or vibrations —**infrasonically** *adv*

infrasound /ínfrə sownd/ *n* sound at frequencies below 20 Hz, which cannot be heard by humans but can be felt as vibration

infrastructure /ínfrə strukchər/ *n* **1** the system according to which a company, organization, or other body is organized at the most basic level **2** the large-scale public systems, services, and facilities of a country or region that are necessary for economic activity, including power and water supplies, public transport, telecommunications, roads, and schools

infrequent /in fréekwənt/ *adj* not appearing, happening, or encountered very often ○ *Her visits became more infrequent.* —**infrequence** *n* —**infrequency** *n* —**infrequently** *adv*

infringe /in frínj/ (**-fringes, -fringing, -fringed**) *v* **1** *vt* to fail to obey a law or regulation or observe the terms of an agreement **2** *vti* to take over land, rights, privileges, or activities that belong to somebody else, especially in a minor or gradual way ○ *infringing on our personal freedom* [Mid-16C. < Latin *infringere* 'to damage' < *frangere* 'to break'.] —**infringement** *n* —**infringer** *n*

infundibula plural of **infundibulum**

infundibulum /ín fun díbbyōōləm/ (*plural* **-la** /-lə/) *n* a funnel-shaped opening, passage, or structure in vertebrates such as the stalk connecting the pituitary gland to the brain or the opening of a fallopian tube into the ovary [Mid-16C. < Latin, 'funnel' < *infundere* 'pour in'.] —**infundibular** *adj* —**infundibulate** /ín fun díbbyōō layt, -lət/ *adj*

infuriate /in fyóori ayt/ (**-ates, -ating, -ated**) *vt* to make somebody extremely angry [Mid-17C. < medieval Latin *infuriare* < *furiare* 'to anger' < *furia* 'fury'.] —**infuriated** *adj* —**infuriatedly** *adv* —**infuriating** *adj* —**infuriatingly** *adv* —**infuriation** /in fyóori áysh'n/

infuse /in fyóoz/ (**-fuses, -fusing, -fused**) *v* **1** *vt* **PERVADE** to fill something with a strong emotion such as hatred, enthusiasm, or desire (*often passive*) **2** *vt* **INTRODUCE INTO SOMEBODY'S MIND** to fix an emotion, belief, or quality gradually but firmly in somebody else's mind **3** *vti* **STEEP IN LIQUID** to soak tea or herbs in liquid to extract the flavour or another property **4** *vt* **GIVE LIQUID USING DRIP** to introduce a solution such as saline, sucrose, or glucose using a drip into a vein, body cavity, or the intestinal tract in order to treat or feed somebody [15C. < Old French *infuser* < Latin *infundere* 'pour in' < *fundere* 'pour'.] —**infuser** *n* —**infusibility** /in fyóozə bílləti/ *n* —**infusible** *adj*

infusion /in fyóozh'n/ *n* **1** **ACT OF INFUSING** the act of of soaking something in a liquid in order to extract soluble matter **2** **ADMINISTERING OF LIQUID THROUGH DRIP** the introduction of a solution such as saline, sucrose, or glucose through a drip in order to treat or feed a patient **3** **LIQUID MADE BY INFUSING** a liquid such as tea that is made by infusing something **4** **LIQUID ADMINISTERED THROUGH DRIP** a solution introduced into the body by infusion **5** **INTRODUCTION OF SOMETHING NEEDED** the addition of a new or necessary quality or element to something ○ *an infusion of private capital into the project* [14C. Via Old French < Latin *infusion-* < the past participle of *infundere* (see INFUSE).]

infusorial earth /ínfyōō záwri əl-/ *n* MINERALS = **diatomaceous earth** *n.* 2

-ing[1] *suffix* **1** forming the present participle of verbs ○ *raining* **2** forming adjectives from words other than verbs ○ *swashbuckling* [Alteration of *-ende* < Old English]

-ing[2] *suffix* **1** action or process ○ *rowing* ○ *cooking* **2** result of ○ *building* [Old English *-ung, -ing*]

-ing[3] *suffix* somebody or something that has a particular character ○ *gelding* [Old English, 'belonging to']

ingather /in gáthər/ *v* **1** *vt* to gather in a harvest of something **2** *vi* to come together or assemble (*formal or literary*) —**ingatherer** *n*

ingenious /in jéeni əss/ *adj* **1** possessing cleverness and imagination **2** clever, original, and effective ○ *an ingenious solution* [15C. Via French *ingénieux* < Latin *ingeniosus* < *ingenium* 'mind'.] —**ingeniously** *adv* —**ingeniousness** *n*

USAGE ingenious or **ingenuous**? Though spelled similarly, these two words have different meanings and so should not be used interchangeably. ***Ingenious*** means 'inventive' and 'cleverly effective', as in *a famed researcher with an ingenious* [not *ingenuous*] *mind; an ingenious* [not *ingenuous*] *marketing strategy.* By contrast, ***ingenuous*** means 'innocently unworldly' and 'being or seeming to be honest, candid, and direct', as in *an ingenuous* [not *ingenious*] *young child; an ingenuous* [not *ingenious*] *answer to the reporter's hostile question.*

ingénue /ánzhə nyoo/ *n* a girl or young woman who is naive and lacks experience or understanding of life [Mid-19C. Via French < Latin *ingenuus* (see INGENUOUS).]

ingenuity /ínjə nyóo əti/ (*plural* **-ties**) *n* cleverness and originality [Late 16C. < Latin *ingenuitas* < *ingenuus* (see INGENUOUS).]

ingenuous /in jénnyoo əss/ *adj* **1** showing innocence and a lack of worldly experience **2** appearing honest and direct [Late 16C. < Latin *ingenuus* 'native, honest' < *gignere* 'beget'.] —**ingenuously** *adv* —**ingenuousness** *n*

USAGE See ***ingenious***.

ingest /in jést/ *vt* to take something such as food or liquid into the body by swallowing or absorbing it [Early 17C. < the past participle of Latin *ingerere* 'carry in' < *gerere* 'carry'.] —**ingestion** *n* —**ingestive** *adj*

Ingham /íngəm/ town in NE Queensland, Australia. Population: 5,012 (1996).

ingle /íng g'l/ *n* a fireplace, or an open fire burning in a fireplace (*archaic*) [Early 16C. < ?]

inglenook /íng g'l nōōk/ *n* **1** a recess for a seat or bench beside a large fireplace, sometimes covered by the chimney-breast **2** a seat built in an inglenook, especially one of two benches facing each other

inglorious /in gláwri əss/ *adj* **1** bringing shame or dishonour **2** not having received recognition, and so unknown or obscure (*archaic or literary*) [Mid-16C. < Latin *inglorius* < *gloria* 'glory'.] —**ingloriously** *adv* —**ingloriousness** *n*

ingoing /ín gō ing/ *adj* relating to entering a place or taking up a new position ■ *n* an amount paid by a new tenant for fixtures left by the previous tenant (*often plural*)

ingot /íng gət/ *n* **1** a metal casting that is shaped for easy working or for recasting, typically in an oblong **2** a mould used for the casting of ingots [14C. Probably < Old English *in* 'in' + *gotan*, past participle of *gēotan* 'pour'.]

ingot iron *n* very pure iron that is produced in the same way as steel but using methods that reduce the carbon, manganese, and silicon content

ingraft *vt* = **engraft** —**ingraftation** /in graaf táysh'n/ *n* —**ingraftment** *n*

ingrain /in gráyn/, **engrain** *vt* **IMPRESS SOMETHING ON SOMEBODY'S MIND** to impress a feeling, belief, or experience firmly and indelibly on somebody's mind (*usually passive*) ○ *The sight is still ingrained on my memory.* ■ *adj* **1** = **ingrained** *adj.* 1 **2** **PREDYED** dyed before being spun or woven ■ *n* **1** **PREDYED YARN OR FIBRE** yarn or fibre that is dyed before being spun or woven **2** **PREDYED RUG OR CARPET** a rug or carpet made of yarn or fibre that is dyed before being spun or woven [15C. < GRAIN 'kermes, cochineal, dye'.]

ingrained /in gráynd/ *adj* **1** **WORKED DEEP** worked into the surface, pores, or fibres of something and very difficult to remove ○ *ingrained dirt* **2** **IMPRESSED ON SOMEBODY'S MIND** firmly fixed in somebody's mind and only removed or challenged with difficulty **3** **HABITUAL** long-established or confirmed in a habit or practice —**ingrainedly** /in gráynidli/ *adv* —**ingrainedness** /-idnəss/ *n*

ingrate /ín grayt, in gráyt/ *n* an ungrateful person (*formal or literary*) ■ *adj* showing no gratitude (*formal or literary*) [15C. Via Old French < Latin *ingratus* 'ungrateful' < *gratus* 'grateful'.]

ingratiate /in gráyshi ayt/ (**-ates, -ating, -ated**) *vr* to try to enter somebody's favour, especially in order to gain an advantage ○ *It's no use trying to ingratiate yourself with me.* [Early 17C. < Italian *ingraziare* < *in grazia* 'into favour' < Latin *in gratiam* < *gratia* 'favour'.] —**ingratiation** /in gráyshi áysh'n/ *n* —**ingratiatory** *adj*

ingratiating /in gráyshi ayting/ *adj* designed to win somebody's approval, especially in order to gain an advantage —**ingratiatingly** *adv*

ingratitude /in grátti tyood/ *n* failure to show or express gratitude [14C. Directly or via Old French < Latin *ingratitudo* < *ingratus* 'ungrateful' < *gratus* 'grateful'.]

~~**ingrediant**~~ incorrect spelling of **ingredient**

ingredient /in gréedi ənt/ *n* **1** a component of a mixture, especially in cooking **2** an element required for a situation, relationship, or plan ○ *What are the ingredients for a happy marriage?* [15C. < Latin *ingredi* 'enter' < *gradi* 'to step'.]

Ingres /áng grə/, **Jean-Auguste-Dominique** (1780–1867) French artist

ingress /ín gress/ *n* **1** **ENTRY** entry into a place **2** **RIGHT OF ENTRY** the right to enter a place **3** **ENTRANCE** a way of entering a place [15C. < Latin, 'entrance' < *ingredi* 'enter' < *gradi* 'to walk'.]

ingressive /in gréssiv/ *adj* **1** **OF ENTRY** relating to entry into or the entrance to a place **2** **PRONOUNCED BY INHALING** describes a speech sound that is pronounced by inhaling rather than exhaling ■ *n* **1** GRAM = **inceptive** *n.* 1, **inceptive** *n.* 2 **2** **INGRESSIVE SPEECH SOUND** a speech sound pronounced by inhaling ■ *adj* GRAM = **inceptive** *adj.* 2 —**ingressiveness** *n*

Ingrian /ín gree ən/ *n* a Finno-Ugric language that is spoken in an area around the Russian-Estonian border. Native speakers: under 1,000. [Early 18C. < *Ingria*, region on the Gulf of Finland.] —**Ingrian** *adj*

in-ground *adj US* constructed or inserted into a hole in the ground ○ *in-ground swimming pools*

in-group *n* a group of people who show loyalty and preferential treatment to one another because they share common interests, beliefs, and attitudes

ingrowing /ín grṓ ing/ *adj* growing or appearing to grow inwards

ingrown /ín grṓn/ *adj* **1** GROWN INTO THE FLESH that has or appears to have grown into the flesh. ◊ **ingrowing 2** NATURAL having become a natural part of somebody's character over a long period of time **3** INWARD-LOOKING inward-looking and preoccupied with personal or local interests —**ingrownness** *n*

ingrowth /ín grōth/ *n* **1** growth or apparent growth into the flesh. ◊ **ingrowing 2** something that grows inwards, e.g. a hair

inguinal /íng gwin'l/ *adj* located in or affecting the groin [15C. < Latin *inguinalis* < *inguen* 'groin'.]

ingulf *vt* = **engulf** —**ingulfment** *n*

Ingush /íng gŏŏsh/ (*plural* **-gushes** *or* **-gush**) *n* a member of a people who live mainly in the Russian provinces of Ingushetia and Chechnya [Early 20C. < Russian *Ingúsh*, former autonomous area.]

inhabit /in hábbit/ *vt* **1** to live in or occupy a particular place **2** to be found in or pervade something ○ *the fears that inhabited each waking moment* [14C. Via Old French *enhabiter* < Latin *inhabitare* < *habitare* 'possess, dwell' < *habere* 'have'.] —**inhabitability** /in hábbitə bílləti/ *n* —**inhabitable** *adj* —**inhabitation** /in hábbi táysh'n/ *n* —**inhabited** *adj* —**inhabiter** *n*

inhabitant /in hábbitənt/ *n* a person or animal that lives in a particular place or area —**inhabitancy** *n*

inhalant /in háylənt/ *adj* breathed in through the nose or mouth as a medicine or for its soothing effect ■ *n* a substance in the form of a vapour or gas that is inhaled, especially as a medicine or for its soothing effect

inhalation /ínhə láysh'n/ *n* **1** an intake of breath through the nose or mouth into the lungs **2** a substance in the form of a vapour or gas that is inhaled, especially as a medicine or for its soothing effect [Early 17C. < medieval Latin, < Latin *inhalare* (see INHALE).] —**inhalational** *adj*

inhalator /ínhə laytər/ *n* **1** = **respirator** *n.* 1 **2** = **inhaler** *n.* 1

inhale /in háyl/ (**-hales, -haling, -haled**) *vti* to breathe in, or to draw a gas, liquid, or solid into the lungs through the nose or mouth [Early 18C. Either a back-formation < INHALATION, or < Latin *inhalare* 'breathe upon' < *halare* 'breathe'.]

inhaler /in háylər/ *n* **1** a small device used for inhaling medicine in the form of a vapour or gas in order to ease a respiratory condition such as asthma or to relieve nasal congestion **2** a person who inhales or who inhales something

inharmonious /ín haar mṓni əss/ *adj* **1** DISCORDANT lacking in harmony or sounding unpleasant **2** UNHAPPY characterized by disagreement and conflict **3** CLASHING clashing or not matching —**inharmoniously** *adv* —**inharmoniousness** *n*

inharmony /in háarməni/ *n* lack of harmony, accord, or agreement

inhaul /ín hawl/, **inhauler** /ín hawlər/ *n* a rope used to haul or hold in a sail

inhere /in héer/ (**-heres, -hering, -hered**) *vi* to be a natural and integral part of something (*formal*) [Mid-16C. < Latin *inhaerere* < *haerere* 'to stick'.]

inherent /in hérrənt, -héerənt/ *adj* unable to be considered separately from the nature of something because of being innate or characteristic ○ *the risks inherent in investing in the stock market* [Late 16C. < Latin *inhaerere* (see INHERE).] —**inherence** /in héerənss, -hérrənss/ *n* —**inherency** *n* —**inherently** *adv*

inherit /in hérrit/ *v* **1** *vti* RECEIVE SOMETHING WHEN SOMEBODY DIES to become the owner of something when somebody dies in accordance with legal succession or the terms of a will or as the result of a bequest or legacy **2** *vt* RECEIVE A CHARACTERISTIC OR QUALITY FROM A PARENT to receive a characteristic or quality as a result of its being passed on genetically **3** *vt* GET SOMETHING FROM A PREDECESSOR to take something over from the person or group who previously lived in a place or did a job [14C. Via Old French *enheriter* 'make an heir' < late Latin *inhereditare* 'inherit' < *hereditare* < Latin *heres* 'heir'.] —**inheritor** *n*

inheritable /in hérritəb'l/ *adj* **1** LAW = **heritable** *adj.* 1, **heritable** *adj.* 2 **2** describes a characteristic or quality that can be transmitted genetically from parent to offspring —**inheritability** /in hérritə bílləti/ *n* —**inheritableness** *n*

⚡**inheritance** /in hérritənss/ *n* **1** INHERITED WEALTH OR TITLE money, property, or a title that has been inherited or is to be inherited **2** OWNERSHIP OR SUCCESSION BY HEREDITY hereditary ownership of wealth or a title, or the succession to wealth or a title **3** RIGHT TO INHERIT the right of an heir to inherit wealth or a title when an ancestor dies **4** HERITAGE something that is inherited from the past **5** TRANSMISSION OF GENETICALLY CONTROLLED CHARACTERISTICS the transmission of genetically controlled characteristics or qualities from parent to offspring **6** CREATION OF OBJECT WITH SAME VARIABLES a feature of computer programming whereby a new object can be created from existing objects and, as a consequence of creation, possess the variables and methods of the parent object

inheritance tax *n* a tax levied on property received by inheritance or legal succession, calculated according to the value of the property received

inhibin /in híbbin/ *n* a hormone secreted by the gonads that inhibits production of follicle-stimulating hormone [Mid-20C. < Latin *inhibere* 'hinder'.]

inhibit /in híbbit/ *vt* **1** HOLD SOMETHING IN CHECK to stop something from continuing or developing ○ *changes in spending patterns that are likely to inhibit economic growth* **2** CONSTRAIN to prevent somebody from behaving or speaking freely or unself-consciously **3** STOP OR RESTRICT CHEMICAL REACTION to prevent or slow down a chemical reaction **4** INTERFERE WITH BODILY PROCESS OR ORGAN to slow down or adversely affect a bodily process or the action of an organ **5** PREVENT SIGNAL OR EVENT to prevent a specific signal or event from occurring **6** FORBID to forbid something (*archaic*) [15C. < the past participle of Latin *inhibere* 'hinder' < *habere* 'to hold'.] —**inhibitable** *adj* —**inhibitive** *adj*

inhibited /in híbbitid/ *adj* unable to behave spontaneously or express feelings openly —**inhibitedly** *adv* —**inhibitedness** *n*

inhibiter *n* = **inhibitor**

inhibition /ín hi bísh'n/ *n* **1** FEELING THAT INHIBITS a feeling or belief that prevents somebody from behaving spontaneously or speaking freely **2** SOMETHING THAT INHIBITS something that inhibits, or the act of inhibiting **3** INHIBITED MENTAL STATE a mental state in which somebody's activity or behaviour is stifled or obstructed **4** DIMINISHED RESPONSE TO STIMULUS in Pavlovian conditioning, the progressive weakening of a response to a stimulus after repeated presentations of the stimulus **5** IMPEDING CHEMICAL REACTION the slowing down or prevention of a chemical reaction **6** OBSTRUCTION OF BODILY PROCESS OR ORGAN the suppression or blocking of a bodily process or the action of an organ **7** SUSPENSION ORDER FROM BISHOP in the Church of England, an order from a bishop suspending a member of the clergy from his or her duties [14C. Via Old French < Latin *inhibition-* < *inhibere* (see INHIBIT).]

inhibitor /in híbbitər/, **inhibiter** *n* **1** SUBSTANCE SLOWING CHEMICAL REACTION a substance that stops or slows a chemical reaction ○ *a rust inhibitor* **2** SUBSTANCE HALTING BIOLOGICAL PROCESS a substance that prevents the action of an enzyme **3** SOMETHING THAT INHIBITS somebody or something that inhibits somebody or something else —**inhibitory** *adj*

in-home *adj* available in somebody's home

inhospitable /ín ho spíttəb'l, in hóspit-/ *adj* **1** not welcoming or friendly **2** harsh and difficult to live or work in ○ *an inhospitable climate* —**inhospitableness** *n* —**inhospitably** *adv* —**inhospitality** /in hospi tálləti/ *n*

in-house *adj* working, carried out, or existing within a company or organization ■ *adv* within a company or organization

inhuman /in hyóomən/ *adj* **1** VERY CRUEL showing great cruelty and a lack of humanity **2** UNFEELING giving an impression of being cold and unfeeling **3** NOT HUMAN not seeming to be human —**inhumanly** *adv* —**inhumanness** *n*

inhumane /ín hyoo máyn/ *adj* lacking compassion, and causing excessive suffering —**inhumanely** *adv* —**inhumaneness** *n*

inhumanity /ín hyoo mánnəti/ (*plural* **-ties**) *n* **1** great cruelty and lack of humanity **2** an act of great cruelty

inhume /in hyóom/ (**-humes, -huming, -humed**) *vt* to bury a dead body (*literary*) [Early 17C. < Latin *inhumare* < *humus* 'earth'.] —**inhumation** /ín hyoo máysh'n/ *n* —**inhumer** *n*

inimical /i nímmik'l/ *adj* (*formal*) **1** unfavourable to something ○ *activities inimical to the public good* **2** showing hostility [Early 16C. < late Latin *inimicalis* < Latin *inimicus* 'unfriendly' < *amicus* 'friend'.] —**inimicality** /i nímmi kálləti/ *n* —**inimically** *adv* —**inimicalness** *n*

inimitable /i nímmitəb'l/ *adj* impossible to imitate, especially because of being unique to a particular person or group ○ *She carried the speech off in her usual inimitable style.* —**inimitability** /i nímmitə bílləti/ *n* —**inimitableness** *n* —**inimitably** *adv*

inion /ínni ən/ *n* a projection of the occipital bone that forms a slight lump at the back of the skull just above the neck [Early 19C. < Greek, 'nape of the neck'.]

iniquitous /i níkwitəss/ *adj* immoral, especially in a way that results in great injustice or unfairness —**iniquitously** *adv* —**iniquitousness** *n*

iniquity /i níkwəti/ (*plural* **-ties**) *n* **1** great injustice or extreme immorality **2** a grossly immoral act [13C. Via Old French < Latin *iniquitas* < *iniquus* 'unjust' < *aequus* 'equal'.]

initial /i nísh'l/ *adj* **1** COMING AT START coming first ○ *My initial feeling was one of shock.* **2** COMING FIRST IN WORD relating to or used as the first letter or letters of a word ■ *n* **1** FIRST LETTER OF NAME the first letter of the name of a person, place, or organization **2** LARGE ORNATE FIRST LETTER the large and often highly decorative first letter of a verse, paragraph, or page, especially as seen in illuminated manuscripts **3** PLANT-TISSUE CELL a cell in the growing point (**meristem**) of a plant that gives rise to cells that will develop into different plant tissues ■ **initials** *npl* FIRST LETTERS OF SOMEBODY'S NAMES the first letter of each of the names of a person, place, or organization, used as an abbreviation or means of identification ■ *vt* (**-tials, -tialling, -tialled**) MARK SOMETHING WITH INITIALS to sign or mark a document with initials, especially in order to show approval or give authorization [Early 16C. < Latin *initialis* < *initium* 'beginning'.] —**initialer** *n*

⚡**initialise** *vti* = **initialize**

initialism /i nísh'lizəm/ *n* an abbreviation made up of initial letters that are all pronounced separately, e.g. UN for United Nations

⚡**initialize** /i níshə līz/ (**-izes, -izing, -ized**), **initialise** (**-ises, -ising, -ised**) *vti* to prepare a piece of computer hardware or software for use, often by resetting a memory location to its initial value —**initialization** /i níshə lī záysh'n/ *n* —**initializer** *n*

initially /i nísh'li/ *adv* at first or to begin with

initial public offering *n* a first-time sale of company securities on a stock exchange to public investors

Initial Teaching Alphabet *n* an alphabet of 44 symbols, each representing a single sound in English, used to teach children to read

initiate *vt* /i níshi ayt/ (**-ates, -ating, -ated**) **1** MAKE SOMETHING START to cause something, especially an important event or process, to begin ○ *to initiate talks* **2** TEACH SOMEBODY ABOUT SOMETHING NEW to introduce somebody to a new activity, interest, or area ○ *initiated me into the joys of snowboarding* **3** INTRODUCE SOMEBODY INTO GROUP to allow somebody take part in a ritual or ceremony in order to become a member of a group, organization, or religion ■ *n* /i níshi ət/ **1** SOMEBODY INITIATED INTO GROUP somebody who has been recently and ceremonially admitted to a group, organization, or religion **2** SOMEBODY NEWLY INTRODUCED somebody recently introduced to a new activity, interest, or area ■ *adj* /i níshi ət/ **1** RECENTLY INITIATED belonging or relating to those who have been recently introduced to a new activity, interest, or area **2** HAVING SECRET OR SPECIAL KNOWLEDGE knowing the secrets of a group, organization, or religion [Mid-16C. < the past participle of Latin *initiare* 'begin' < *initium* 'beginning'.] —**initiator** *n*

initiated /i níshi aytid/ *npl* those who know about something that seems difficult or complicated, or who know the secrets of a group, organization, or religion

initiation /i níshi áysh'n/ *n* **1** ACTION THAT MAKES SOMETHING START action that causes something, especially an important process or event, to begin ○ *the initiation of legal proceedings* **2** CEREMONY a usually secret or mysterious ceremony by which somebody is admitted to a group, organization, or religion (*sometimes used before a noun*) ○ *initiation rites* **3** INTRODUCTION TO SOMETHING NEW the introduction of somebody to a new activity, interest, or area [Late 16C. < Latin *initiation-* < the past participle of *initiare* 'begin'.]

initiative /i níshətiv, i níshi-/ *n* **1 ABILITY TO ACT ON YOUR OWN** the ability to act and make decisions without the help or advice of other people ○ *You'll just have to use your initiative.* **2 INTRODUCTORY STEP** the first step in a process that, once taken, determines subsequent events ○ *decided to take the initiative* **3 PLAN** a plan or strategy aimed at tackling a particular problem ○ *a peace initiative* **4 ADVANTAGEOUS POSITION** a favourable position that allows somebody to take pre-emptive action or control events ○ *lose the initiative* **5 RIGHT TO INTRODUCE NEW LEGISLATION** the right to bring a new law or measure before a legislative body **6 PROPOSAL OF LEGISLATION BY CITIZENS** a process valid in many US states and in Switzerland that allows citizens to propose legislation by petition ■ *adj* **OF INITIATION** used in or relating to initiation (*formal*) [Late 18C. < French, < the past participle of Latin *initiare* 'begin'.]

initiatory /i níshi ətəri, i níshətəri/ *adj* **1** occurring at or related to the beginning of something **2** used in or characteristic of an initiation

inj. *abbr* **1** injection **2** injury

inject /in jékt/ *v* **1** *vti* **PUT FLUID INTO THE BODY WITH SYRINGE** to introduce a drug, vaccine, or other fluid into part of the body using a syringe **2** *vt* **FORCE LIQUID OR GAS INTO** to force a liquid or gas through a small opening into a confined space ○ *They injected an insulating foam into the cavity between the walls.* **3** *vt* **ADD SOMETHING TO SITUATION** to introduce a particular quality or element into a situation ○ *an attempt to inject a little levity into the proceedings* **4** *vt* **PUT A ROCKET OR SATELLITE IN ORBIT** to put rocket or satellite in orbit or a spacecraft on a trajectory to its destination [Late 16C. < Latin *inicere* 'throw in' < *iacere* 'to throw'.] —**injectable** *adj*

injectant /in jéktənt/ *n* an injected substance

injection /in jéksh'n/ *n* **1 INJECTED DOSE OF DRUG** a dose of a particular drug in liquid form that is injected into the body with a syringe **2 INTRODUCTION OF FLUID WITH SYRINGE** the introduction of fluid into the body by means of a syringe **3 SPRAYING OF FUEL INTO ENGINE** the process of spraying fuel through a pump into the inlet manifold or cylinder of an internal-combustion engine, eliminating the need for a carburettor **4 ADDITION OF SOMETHING TO SITUATION** the introduction of a particular quality or element into a situation ○ *a cash injection* **5 PROVISION OF MONEY** a provision of money for a country, organization, project, or person in financial need **6 ONE-TO-ONE MAPPING OF SETS** a one-to-one mapping of two algebraic sets such that each element of each set corresponds to only one element of the other set **7 INTRODUCTION OF FLUID INTO CAVITY** a process for introducing a fluid such as a plastic under pressure into a cavity **8 SENDING OF SATELLITE INTO ORBIT** the placing of an artificial satellite into orbit or a space probe onto a trajectory **9 MOMENT OF SATELLITE INSERTION** the moment or place at which insertion of a satellite or space probe occurs —**injective** *adj*

injection moulding *n* a manufacturing process in which heated material (**thermoplastic**) is forced under pressure into a water-cooled mould —**injection-moulded** *adj*

injector /in jéktər/ *n* **1 PUMP THROUGH WHICH FUEL SPRAYS** a pump through which fuel is sprayed into the inlet manifold or cylinder of an internal-combustion engine **2 SYSTEM FOR FORCING WATER INTO BOILER** a system that forces water into a steam engine's boiler **3 PLAYER TAKING A PENALTY CORNER** in hockey, the player who takes a penalty corner

in-joke *n* a joke that is shared and understood only by a particular group of people

injudicious /ìnjoo díshəss/ *adj* lacking in judgment or discretion —**injudiciously** *adv* —**injudiciousness** *n*

Injun /ínjən/ *n* an offensive term for a Native North American (*dated*) [Late 17C. < a pronunciation of INDIAN.]

injunction /in júngksh'n/ *n* **1 COURT ORDER** a court order that requires somebody involved in a legal action to do something or refrain from doing something **2 COMMAND** a command or order, especially from somebody in a position of authority **3 ACT OF ORDERING** the act of ordering somebody to do or not to do something [15C. < late Latin *injunction-* < *injungere* 'enjoin' < *jungere* 'join'.]

injure /ínjər/ (**-jures, -juring, -jured**) *vt* **1 HURT** to cause physical hurt or damage to a person, animal, or body part **2 OFFEND** to cause somebody distress by an unkind action or words **3 DO LEGAL WRONG TO** to wrong somebody by word or deed in such a way that redress by legal means is available **4 DAMAGE SOMEBODY'S REPUTATION** to damage somebody's reputation, career, or chances of success [15C. Via Old French *injurier* < Latin *injuriare* < *injuria* (see INJURY).] —**injurable** *adj* —**injurer** *n*

injury /ínjəri/ (*plural* **-ries**) *n* **1 PHYSICAL DAMAGE** physical damage to the body or a body part ○ *They escaped without injury.* **2 WOUND** a specific instance of physical damage to a body part ○ *a serious back injury* **3 HARM TO REPUTATION** harm caused to somebody's career or reputation by scandal, rumour, or defamation **4 INFRINGEMENT OF RIGHTS** the violation of a person or group's rights, against which legal action can be taken [14C. Via Anglo-Norman < Latin *injuria* 'a wrong' < *injurius* 'unjust' < *jus* 'justice'.] —**injurious** /in jóori əss/ *adj* —**injuriously** *adv* —**injuriousness** *n*

injury benefit *n* a weekly payment made under the National Insurance system to somebody injured while at work, the amount of which is calculated according to the seriousness of the injury

injury time *n* extra time allowed at the end of some matches, especially football and rugby, to compensate for time spent attending to injured players during the game

~~**injust**~~ incorrect spelling of **unjust**

injustice /in jústiss/ *n* unfair or unjust treatment of somebody, or an instance of this [14C. Via Old French < Latin *injustitia* < *injustus* 'unjust' < *in-* 'not' + *justus* 'just'.]

ink /ingk/ *n* **1 LIQUID FOR WRITING, DRAWING, OR PRINTING** a coloured liquid or paste used for writing, printing, or drawing **2 LIQUID EJECTED BY OCTOPUS OR SQUID** a dark brown liquid (**sepia**) ejected from a gland (**ink sac**) near the anus by most cephalopods, including the octopus and the squid, to distract predators **3** *US* **PRINT PUBLICITY** publicity, especially in the print media (*slang*) ○ *The stunt got him all kinds of ink.* ■ *vt* **1 MARK SOMETHING WITH INK** to write or draw with ink on a piece of paper or other surface **2 ADD INK** to coat something with ink or apply ink to something, usually in preparation for printing **3** *US* **SIGN A CONTRACT** to put or obtain a signature on a contract or other document (*informal*) [13C. Via Old French *enque* < Greek *enkauston* 'purple ink' < *enkaiein* 'burn in'; from the process of encaustic painting.] —**inker** *n*

ink in *vt* **1** to go over the pencil lines of a drawing or design in ink **2** to spread ink on a surface in preparation for printing

Inkatha /in kaátə/ *n* a Zulu political party that was founded in South Africa in 1975 [Late 20C. Shortening of Zulu *Inkatha Yenkululeko Yesizwe* 'Coil of the Freedom of the Nation'.]

inkberry /íngk berri/ (*plural* **-ries**) *n* **1** an evergreen shrub that has leathery dark-green leaves and produces black berries. Native to: E North America. *Ilex glabra.* **2** PLANT SCI = **pokeweed** [Mid-18C. < the use of the berries for making ink.]

inkblot /íngk blot/ *n* **1** a stain or spot of spilled ink **2** any of the ten abstract patterns resembling an inkblot used in the Rorschach test

inkblot test *n* PSYCHOL = **Rorschach test**

ink-cap *n* a mushroom with a conical cap, on the underside of which are gills that dissolve into an inky black pulp after the spores mature. Genus: *Coprinus.* US term **inky cap**

inkhorn /íngk hawrn/ *n* a small portable ink container made from horn or a similar material and used in former times ■ *adj* excessively scholarly in style or language, especially in the use of terms derived from Latin and Greek

in-kind *adj US* **1** in the form of goods or services rather than in cash **2** giving something that is equivalent to what has been received

ϟ **ink-jet printer** *n* a printer that prints using particles or droplets of electrically charged ink from a matrix of tiny ink jets

inkle /íngk'l/ *n* a narrow linen tape. Use: trimmings. [Mid-16C. < ?]

inkling /íngkling/ *n* **1** a vague idea or suspicion about a fact, event, or person ○ *I had no inkling that he was unhappy.* **2** an indication of how to go about something ○ *Could you give me some inkling of where to look?* [Early 16C. < obsolete *inkle* 'utter in an undertone'.]

ink sac *n* a large gland with an opening close to the anus of most cephalopods, including the octopus and squid, from which ink (**sepia**) is ejected to distract predators

inkstand /íngk stand/ *n* **1** a rack or stand that is kept on a desk and contains pots of ink, pens, and other writing materials **2** = **inkwell**

inkwell /íngk wel/ *n* a small container for ink, especially one that fits into a hole in a desk

inky /íngki/ (**-ier, -iest**) *adj* **1** consisting of or covered in ink **2** black or dark blue in colour

inky cap *n US* FUNGI = **ink-cap**

INLA *abbr Ireland* Irish National Liberation Army

inlace *vt* = **enlace**

inlaid /ín láyd, ín layd/ *adj* **1** set into the surface of wood or another material, usually to provide decoration **2** decorated with an inlaid pattern

inland /ínlənd/ *adj* **1 NOT NEAR COAST OR BORDER** in or relating to the part of a country that is not near the coast or a border **2 WITHIN COUNTRY** occurring within a country, rather than between countries ■ *adv* **IN OR INTO INTERIOR OF COUNTRY** in or towards the interior of a country ■ *n* **INTERIOR OF A COUNTRY** the interior of a country

inland bill *n* a bill that is both drawn and payable in the United Kingdom

Inland Revenue *n* a government body responsible for the collection and administration of direct taxes such as income tax and corporation tax

Inland Sea /ínlənd-/ arm of the Pacific Ocean in Japan, between the islands of Honshu, Shikoku, and Kyushu. Length: 430 km/270 mi.

in-law /ín law/ *n* a relative by marriage (*informal*)

inlay *vt* /ín láy, ín lay/ (**-lays, -laying, -laid**) **1 SET SOMETHING INTO SURFACE** to set pieces of material such as wood, ivory, or stone into previously cut slots in a surface to form a decorative pattern **2 DECORATE SOMETHING WITH INLAID DESIGN** to decorate something such as a piece of furniture by setting pieces of wood, stone, ivory, or other material into its surface ■ *n* /ín lay/ **1 PIECES OF MATERIAL SET INTO SURFACE** pieces of material such as wood, ivory, or stone set into the surface of a piece of furniture to form a decorative pattern **2 DECORATIVE PATTERN** a decorative pattern formed by inlaying **3 GOLD OR PORCELAIN FILLING FOR TOOTH** a filling made of gold or porcelain that is inserted into a cavity in a tooth and cemented in position —**inlayer** *n*

inlet /ín let/ *n* **1 NARROW OPENING IN COASTLINE** a narrow stretch of water reaching inland from a sea or lake **2 STRETCH OF WATER BETWEEN TWO ISLANDS** a narrow stretch of water between two islands **3 PIECE OF EXTRA FABRIC** a piece of fabric put into the seam of a garment to make it bigger or for decoration **4 PASSAGE OR VALVE** an opening through which liquid or gas enters a machine or other device ■ *vt* (**-lets, -letting, -let**) = **inlay** *v.* 1, **inlay** *v.* 2 [13C. < IN + LET[1].]

inlier /ín lī ər/ *n* a rock formation in which older rocks are completely surrounded by younger rocks [Mid-19C. < IN-[2], after OUTLIER.]

in-line *adj* describes a device or machine in which similar parts are located together and in a straight line, e.g. the cylinders in an internal-combustion engine

in-line skates *npl* roller skates with each boot mounted on a single line of three or four narrow wheels

~~**inlist**~~ incorrect spelling of **enlist**

in loc. cit. *adv* = **loc. cit.**

in loco parentis /in lókō pə réntiss/ *adv* having or taking on the responsibilities of a parent when dealing with somebody else's child [< Latin, 'in the place of a parent']

inly /ínnli/ *adv* (*literary*) **1** in an inwards way **2** with deep or intimate understanding

inlying /ín lī ing/ *adj* situated within a country or region

inmate /ín mayt/ *n* a person who is confined to a prison or a psychiatric hospital [Late 16C. < IN + MATE[1] 'companion'.]

in medias res /in méedi ass ráyz/ *adv* straight in or into the middle of a sequence of events, especially in a literary narrative that has no introduction (*formal*) [< Latin, 'into the midst of things']

in memoriam /ín mi máwri əm/ *prep, adv* in memory of or in a person's memory (*in epitaphs and obituaries*) [< Latin]

inmesh *vt* = **enmesh**

inmigrant /ín mīgrənt/ *adj* coming from a different part of the same country ■ *n* somebody who travels from a different part of the same country

inmigrate /in mī grayt/ (**-grates, -grating, -grated**) *vi* to travel to a place from a different part of the same country —**inmigration** /ín mī gráysh'n/ *n*

inmost *adj* = **innermost** [Old English *innemest* < *inne* 'in' + *mest* 'most']

inn /in/ *n* **1 PUB** a small hotel or pub offering food and sometimes accommodation (*often used in pub names*) ○ *a country inn* **2 HOTEL** a place providing food and lodging for travellers (*dated*) **3 RESIDENCE FOR STUDENTS** formerly, a hall of residence for students, especially those studying law [Old English, < Indo-European, 'in']

innacurate incorrect spelling of **inaccurate**

innards /ínnərdz/ *npl* (*informal*) **1** the internal organs of the body, especially the intestines **2** the internal working parts of a machine or mechanical device [Early 19C. Alteration of INWARDS (plural noun).]

innate /i náyt/ *adj* **1 PRESENT FROM BIRTH** relating to qualities that a person or animal is born with **2 INTEGRAL** forming an integral part of something **3 COMING FROM THE MIND** coming directly from the mind rather than being acquired by experience or from external sources ○ *an innate sense of justice* **4 JOINED TO THE FILAMENT BY THE BASE** describes an anther that is joined to the filament by its base only **5 ORIGINATING WITHIN THE THALLUS** forming an integral part of the thallus [15C. < Latin *innatus*, past participle of *innasci* 'be born in' < *nasci* 'be born'.] —**innately** *adv* —**innateness** *n*

innate releasing mechanism *n* a process within the central nervous system of animals that, in response to certain stimuli, causes the animal to produce instinctive behaviour

inner /ínnər/ *adj* **1 NEAR OR CLOSER TO CENTRE** located near or closer to the centre of something ○ *the inner suburbs* **2 BEING OR OCCURRING INSIDE** located or happening on the inside of something ○ *an inner door* **3 OF THE MIND** relating to somebody's private feelings or happening in somebody's mind ○ *a quiet exterior that hid an inner confidence* **4 NOT OBVIOUS** needing to be examined closely or thought about in order to be seen or understood ○ *searching for the inner meaning of the text* **5 PRIVILEGED** most privileged or influential ○ *the inner circle* ■ *n* **1 PART OF TARGET** the part of a target, especially of a dartboard, surrounding the bull's-eye **2 HIT TARGET** a hit on the inner of a target [Old English *innera* < Indo-European, 'in'] —**innerly** *adv* —**innerness** *n*

inner bar *n* in England and Wales, all the barristers that comprise the King's or Queen's Counsel. ◊ **outer bar** [< Their precedence over ordinary barristers]

inner child *n* an adult's conception of himself or herself as a child, often used as a tool in therapeutic processes to explore feelings about the person's childhood

inner city *n* the central or innermost parts of a city, particularly when associated with social problems such as inadequate housing and high levels of crime and unemployment (*hyphenated when used before a noun*)

inner-directed *adj* guided by personal beliefs rather than by norms imposed by society

inner ear *n* the fluid-filled part of the ear, including the cochlea, which is responsible for hearing, and the semicircular canals, which control balance

Inner Light *n* in Quaker belief, the presence of God as a guiding force within the human soul

inner man *n* ◊ **inner woman** the soul or the spiritual or intellectual part of a man **2** the appetite of a man (*humorous*)

Inner Mongolia Autonomous Region autonomous region of N China. Capital: Hohhot. Population: 22,840,000 (1995). Area: 1,177,500 sq. km/454,600 sq. mi.

innermost /ínnər mōst/, **inmost** /ín mōst/ *adj* **1** most important, private, or personal ○ *innermost thoughts* **2** taking place or being situated farthest from the outside

inner planet *n* any of the four planets Mercury, Venus, Earth, or Mars whose orbits lie closest to the Sun and are within the asteroid belt. ◊ **outer planet**

inner product *n* MATH = **scalar product**

inner sole *n* a foot-shaped piece of leather, sheepskin, or synthetic material worn inside a shoe or boot to provide a better fit or added warmth

inner space *n* **1** the environment that exists beneath the surface of the sea **2** somebody's inner spiritual or psychological depths

---

innerspring /ínnər spring/ *adj* US FURNITURE = **interior-sprung**

Inner Temple *n* a law society that, together with Gray's Inn, Lincoln's Inn, and the Middle Temple, forms the Inns of Court

inner tube *n* a hollow rubber ring filled with compressed air that fits inside a pneumatic tyre

innervate /ínnur vayt/ (**-vates, -vating, -vated**) *vt* **1** to distribute nerves to an organ or body part **2** to cause a muscle, organ, or other part of the body to act —**innervation** /ínnur váysh'n/ *n* —**innervational** *adj*

innerve /i núrv/ (**-nerves, -nerving, -nerved**) *vt* to provide a person or object with nervous energy or something resembling such energy

innerwear /ínnər wair/ *n* clothing that is worn next to the skin, such as a vest or a slip

inner woman *n* ◊ **inner man** the soul or the spiritual or intellectual part of a woman **2** the appetite of a woman (*humorous*)

inning /ínning/ *n* one of the divisions of a game of baseball or softball during which each team bats until it makes three outs [Old English *innung* < *innian* 'put in' < IN]

innings /ínningz/ (*plural* **-nings**) *n* **1 TURN AT BATTING** the turn of a cricket player or team at batting **2 RUNS SCORED DURING AN INNINGS** the runs scored during the turn of a cricket player or team at batting **3 PERIOD OF SUCCESS** a period of opportunity or success, or a long active life or career ○ *He's had a good innings, and he's looking forward to retirement.*

Innisfail /ínnəss fayl/ coastal town in NE Queensland, Australia. Population: 8,987 (1996).

innit /ínnit/ *contr* **1** used as a tag question at the end of a statement (*nonstandard*) ○ *Nice weather, innit?* **2** Carib UK an all-purpose, question-forming word, corresponding not only to 'isn't it?' but to more or less all other similar phrases (*informal*) ○ *Spurs are playing Arsenal tomorrow, innit?* [Mid-19C. Contraction of *isn't it?*]

innkeeper /ín keepər/ *n* an owner or manager of an inn

innocence /ínnəss'nss/ *n* **1 ABSENCE OF GUILT** the state of not being guilty of a crime or offence **2 LAWFULNESS** the state of being permitted by law **3 HARMLESSNESS** harmlessness in intention **4 FREEDOM FROM SIN** freedom from sin or evil **5 LACK OF WORLDLY EXPERIENCE** a lack of experience of the world, especially when this results in a failure to recognize the harmful intentions of other people **6 IGNORANCE** ignorance of the serious consequences of something such as an act or remark [14C. Via Old French < Latin *innocentia* < *innocens* (see INNOCENT).] —**innocency** /ínnəss'nssi/ *n*

LITERARY LINK *The Age of Innocence*, a novel (1920) by US writer Edith Wharton. It tells the story of a young man's failure to rise above the repressive social conventions of fashionable New York society in the late 19th century. Newland Archer, a sensitive and intelligent lawyer, falls in love with his wife's cousin Ellen Olenska, a mysterious sophisticate who has returned from Europe bearing the social stigma of a marital separation. The novel reveals the subtle workings by which his elite tribe reaffirms its mores and thwarts his desire.

innocent /ínnəss'nt/ *adj* **1 NOT GUILTY** not guilty of a crime or offence **2 WITHIN THE LAW** permitted by or acting within the law ○ *innocent pastimes* **3 HARMLESS IN INTENTION** not intended to cause harm ○ *an innocent remark* **4 UNCORRUPTED** pure and uncorrupted by evil, sin, or experience of the world **5 NAIVE** more trusting or naive than most people through lack of experience of life or failure to recognize the motives of others **6 IGNORANT OF** having very little or no knowledge of something ○ *innocent of the finer points of etiquette* **7 LACKING** completely lacking in a particular quality ○ *innocent of any artistic skill* ■ *n* **1 BLAMELESS PERSON** a blameless vulnerable person, especially a very young child **2 NAIVE PERSON** a simple, naive, or inexperienced person [14C. Via Old French < Latin *innocent* < *in-* 'not' + present participle of *nocere* 'harm'.] —**innocently** *adv*

Innocent III /ínnəss'nt/ (1160?–1216) pope (1198–1216)

innoculation incorrect spelling of **inoculation**

innocuous /i nókyoo əss/ *adj* **1** not intended to cause offence or provoke a strong reaction and unlikely to do so ○ *an innocuous comment* **2** harmless in effect ○ *an innocuous-seeming white powder* [Late 16C. < Latin *innocuus* < *nocuus* 'hurtful' < *nocere* 'to harm'.] —**innocuously** *adv* —**innocuousness** *n*

---

innominate /i nómminət/ *adj* **1** without a name (*formal*) **2** anonymous (*literary*) [Mid-17C. < late Latin *innominatus* < *nominatus* 'named' < *nominat-* (see NOMINATE).]

innominate artery *n* a short artery rising from the arch of the aorta towards the right upper part of the body

innominate bone *n* a hipbone (*technical*) [Because early anatomists could not think of anything it resembled]

innominate vein *n* either of two large veins on opposite sides of the neck that join to form the superior vena cava, one of the two veins taking blood to the heart

innovate /ínnə vayt/ (**-vates, -vating, -vated**) *vti* to introduce a new way of doing something or a new device [Mid-16C. < Latin *innovat-* < *innovare* 'renew' < *novus* 'new'.] —**innovator** *n* —**innovatory** /ínnə váytəri, ínnə vaytəri/ *adj*

innovation /ínnə váysh'n/ *n* **1** the act or process of inventing or introducing something new **2** something newly invented or a new way of doing things ○ *suspicious of fax machines and other technological innovations* —**innovational** *adj*

innovative /ínnə vaytiv, ínnəvətiv/ *adj* new and original or taking a new and original approach —**innovatively** *adv* —**innovativeness** *n*

Innsbruck /ínz brook/ capital of the Tyrol Province, W Austria. Population: 118,112 (1991).

Innu /innoo/ (*plural* **-nu**) *n* the Algonquian language of the Innu people —**Innu** *adj*

innuendo /ínnyoo éndō/ (*plural* **-does** or **-dos**) *n* **1 HINT OF SOMETHING IMPROPER** an indirect remark or gesture that usually carries a suggestion of impropriety ○ *"I suppose Mary Garth admires Mr. Lydgate", said Rosamund, not without a touch of innuendo".* (George Eliot, *Middlemarch*; 1872) **2 INTERPRETATION OF POSSIBLY LIBELLOUS LANGUAGE** an interpretation of words that are claimed to be libellous where the meaning is not obvious, in a legal action for libel or slander **3 GLOSS FOR A TECHNICAL LEGAL WORD** an explanation of a technical legal word, usually given in brackets [Mid-16C. < Latin *innuendo* 'by intimation' < *innuere* 'nod to, signify'.]

Inuit *n* PEOPLES, LANG = **Inuit**

innumerable /i nyooměrəb'l/ *adj* too many to be counted [14thC. < Latin *innumerabilis* < *numerus* 'number'.] —**innumerability** /i nyooměra billəti/ *n* —**innumerableness** *n* —**innumerably** *adv*

innumerate /i nyooměrət/ *adj* lacking a basic knowledge of mathematics and unable to use numbers in calculation

inobservance /ínnəb zúrvənss/ *n* **1** lack of heed or attention **2** failure to comply with something, especially a rule, law, or custom —**inobservant** *adj* —**inobservantly** *adv*

inobtrusive /ínnəb troóssiv/ *adj* = **unobtrusive**

inoculant /i nókyoolənt/ *n* = **inoculum**

inoculate /i nókyoo layt/ (**-lates, -lating, -lated**) *vt* **1** to inject or introduce a serum, antigen, or a weakened form of a disease-producing pathogen into the body of a person or animal in order to create immunity to the disease ○ *inoculated every child against polio* **2** to introduce microorganisms into a culture medium [15C. < Latin *inoculare* 'to graft on a plant part' < *oculus* 'bud, eye'.] —**inoculability** /i nókyoolə billəti/ *n* —**inoculable** *adj* —**inoculation** /i nókyoo láysh'n/ *n* —**inoculative** *adj* —**inoculator** *n*

inoculum /i nókyooləm/ (*plural* **-la** /-lə/) *n* material injected into a person or animal to create resistance to a disease [Early 20C. < Latin *inoculare* (see INOCULATE).]

inodorous /in ódərəss/ *adj* having no smell

in-off *n* a shot in snooker in which the ball hits another ball before falling into a pocket

inoffensive /ínnə fénssiv/ *adj* not causing harm, annoyance, or offence ○ *the remark was inoffensive enough* —**inoffensively** *adv* —**inoffensiveness** *n*

inofficious /ínnə físhəss/ *adj* violating standards of morality or natural affection, especially failing to give an heir a just share of an inheritance ○ *an inofficious will* —**inofficiously** *adv* —**inofficiousness** *n*

İnönü /éen ö nöö/, **Ismet** (1884–1973) Turkish soldier and statesman

inoperable /in óppərəb'l/ *adj* **1** having advanced to a stage at which surgical intervention would serve no useful purpose **2** not practical or workable —**inoperability** /ín óppərə billəti/ *n* —**inoperableness** *n* —**inoperably** *adv*

inoperative /in óppərətiv/ *adj* **1** not functioning properly or as usual **2** not effective or no longer valid or able to be enforced —**inoperatively** *adv* —**inoperativeness** *n*

inopportune /in óppər tyoon/ *adj* happening at a bad moment or an inconvenient time —**inopportunely** *adv* —**inopportuneness** *n* —**inopportunity** /in óppə tyóonəti/ *n*

inordinate /in áwrdinət/ *adj* **1** beyond reasonable limits in amount or degree ○ *'capable of expressing an inordinate degree of unreason'* (Henry James, *Roderick Hudson*; 1876) **2** showing a lack of restraint or control (*archaic or literary*) [14C. < Latin *inordinatus* 'out of order' < *ordo* 'order'.] —**inordinacy** *n* —**inordinately** *adv* —**inordinateness** *n*

inorganic /ín awr gánnik/ *adj* **1** composed of minerals rather than living material **2** describes chemical compounds that contain no carbon, excluding the oxides of carbon, carbon disulphide, cyanides, and their associated acids and salts —**inorganically** *adv*

inorganic chemistry *n* the branch of chemistry relating to inorganic compounds

inosculate /in óskyoo layt/ (**-lates, -lating, -lated**) *v* **1** *vti* UNITE WITH to join and blend with something else **2** *vti* MERGE WITH to join or be joined by other blood vessels or nerve fibres by means of small openings **3** *vti* JOIN BY RUNNING TOGETHER to unite or join through a series of continuous small openings **4** TO CAUSE TO RUN TOGETHER to unite or join so as to become a continuous structure [Late 17C. < IN-[2] + Latin *osculare* 'provide with a mouth' < *osculum* 'little mouth' < *os* 'mouth'.] —**inosculation** /in óskyoo láysh'n/ *n*

inosine /ínnə seen, ín ō-/ *n* an organic compound (**nucleoside**) involved in the formation of purines and energy metabolism. Use: sports supplement, transplant management.

inositol /i nóssi tol/ *n* a cyclic alcohol that is a component of cell membranes and a precursor of various messenger molecules [Late 19C. < Greek *in-* 'sinew' + -OSE[2] + -ITE[1] + -OL.]

inotropic /ínnə tróppik, ínə-/ *adj* having an effect on the force of muscular contraction ○ *an inotropic drug* [Early 20C. < Greek *in-* 'sinew'.]

inpatient /in paysh'nt/, **in-patient** *n* somebody receiving medical treatment that requires a hospital stay ■ *adj* relating to, designed for, or used by inpatients

in perpetuum /ín pur péttyoo əm/ *adv* forever [< Latin]

in personam /ín pur sṓnəm/ *adj, adv* made about or directed at a person rather than at property. ◊ **in rem** [< Latin, 'against a person']

in petto /in péttō/ *adj* not disclosing publicly the name of a cardinal appointed by the pope [Late 17C. < Italian, 'in the breast'.]

inphase /ín fayz/ *adj* of the same electrical phase

INPO *abbr* in no particular order (*in e-mails*)

in posse /in póssi/ *adj* potentially rather than in reality [< Latin]

inpouring /ín pawring/ *n* a sudden flowing in of a large amount of something

in-process *adj* in the process of being manufactured

in propria persona /in prṓpri ə pur sṓnə/ *adv* in person, especially when unrepresented by a lawyer [< Latin, 'in your own person']

input /ín poot/ *n* **1** CONTRIBUTION a contribution to something, especially comments or suggestions made to a group **2** SOMETHING GOING IN something that enters a process or situation from the outside and is then acted upon or integrated ○ *sensory input* **3** ELECTRICITY DRIVING MACHINE power, electrical energy, or an electrical signal that enters a device and is usually recovered in the form of work or some other output effect **4** COMPUTER TERMINAL a terminal or connection where data enters a computer ■ *v* (**-puts, -putting, -putted** *or* **-put**) **1** *vti* CONTRIBUTE INFORMATION to provide information to help somebody make a decision (*informal*) **2** *vt* ENTER DATA to enter data into a computer —**inputter** *n*

input/output *n* hardware or software that controls the passage of information into and out of a computer or computer component

inquest /ín kwest/ *n* **1** an official inquiry held by a coroner into the facts of a case such as a sudden unexpected death or the discovery of something valuable that might be treasure trove **2** an investigation of the facts of a situation, particularly one that had an undesired outcome (*literary*) [14C. Via Old French *enqueste* < Latin *inquesta* < *inquirere* 'enquire'.]

inquietude /in kwī ə tyood/ *n* a worried or restless state of mind (*literary*) [15C. Via Late Latin *inquietudo* < Latin *quietus* 'quiet'.]

inquiline /íngkwi līn/ *n* an animal that lives in the nest or home of another species [Mid-17C. < Latin *inquilinus* 'tenant, lodger' < *incolere* 'inhabit' < *colere* 'dwell'.]

inquire /in kwír/ (**-quires, -quiring, -quired**), **enquire** (**-quires, -quiring, -quired**) *v* **1** *vti* to ask a question ○ *inquire about a job* ○ *The secretary inquired whether I intended to stay on another year.* **2** *vi* to try to discover the facts of a case [13C. Via Old French *enquerre* < Latin *inquirere* 'inquire into' < *quaerere* 'seek'.] —**inquirer** *n*

USAGE inquire or **enquire**? For many users, the two spellings are interchangeable, as with *enquiry* and *inquiry*. A useful distinction that some people maintain, however, is to use ***enquire*** and *enquiry* in contexts of casual requests for information, and to reserve ***inquire*** and *inquiry* for contexts of formal, official, or academic investigation: *He enquired after her health. Try directory enquiries. The police are inquiring into the circumstances that led up to his disappearance. There will have to be a public inquiry into the allegations.*

inquire after, enquire after *vt* to ask for news about another person's health or welfare

inquiring /in kwíring/, **enquiring** *adj* **1** eager to learn new things **2** appearing to want to know or learn something ○ *an inquiring glance from the attendant* —**inquiringly** *adv*

inquiry /in kwíri/ (*plural* **-ies**), **enquiry** (*plural* **-ies**) *n* **1** a formal investigation to determine the facts of a case **2** a request for information

inquisition /íngkwi zísh'n/ *n* **1** a succession of detailed and relentless questions **2** an inquiry or investigation that is harsh or unfair [14C. Via Old French *inquisicion* < Latin *inquirere* (see INQUIRE).] —**inquisitional** *adj* —**inquisitionist** *n*

Inquisition *n* a former organization in the Roman Catholic Church to find, question, and sentence those who did not hold orthodox religious beliefs

inquisitive /in kwízzətiv/ *adj* **1** eager for knowledge **2** too curious about other people's business [14C. Via Old French < late Latin *inquisitivus* < Latin *inquirere* (see INQUIRE).] —**inquisitively** *adv* —**inquisitiveness** *n*

inquisitor /in kwízzitər/ *n* **1** a relentless asker of searching or hostile questions **2 inquisitor, Inquisitor** an official working for the Inquisition [Early 16C. Via French < Latin < *inquirere* (see INQUIRE).]

inquisitorial /in kwízzə táwri əl/ *adj* **1** resembling a formal inquiry, especially in using rigorous or relentless questioning **2** describes a trial in which one person is both judge and prosecutor. ◊ **accusatorial** *adj.* 2 —**inquisitorially** *adv* —**inquisitorialness** *n*

inquorate /in kwáwrat, in kwáw rayt/ *adj* having too few people present to provide a quorum and therefore unable to make an official decision ○ *The meeting was declared inquorate.* [Late 20C. < QUORUM.]

in re /in rée, in ráy/ *prep* with regard to [< Latin, 'in the matter of']

in rem /in rém/ *adj* made about or directed at property rather than a person. ◊ **in personam** [< Latin, 'against a thing']

in rerum natura /in ráiroom na tóorə/ *adv* in the nature of things [< Latin]

in-residence *adj US* officially connected with a university or other institution, often as a teacher or lecturer, but allowed time for original creative work ○ *She completed her book while serving as poet-in-residence at a small college.*

INRI *abbr* Jesus of Nazareth, King of the Jews (*used as an inscription over the head of the crucified Jesus Christ*) [Latin *Iesus Nazarenus Rex Iudaeorum*]

inro /ínrō/ (*plural* **-ro**) *n* a small ornamented box worn hanging from the sash of a kimono with compartments for holding cosmetics, perfumes, and medicines [Early 17C. < Japanese *inrō* < *in* 'seal' + *rō* 'basket'.]

inroad /ínrōd/ *n* a sudden attack on an enemy camp (*archaic*) ■ **inroads** /ínrōdz/ *npl* a gradual encroachment on or of something ○ *young companies using electronic sales methods have made inroads into traditional markets* [Mid-16C. < IN + *road* 'a riding, raid'.]

inrush /ín rush/ *n* a sudden flooding or flowing in

ins. *abbr* **1** inscription **2 ins., Ins.** inspector **3** insulation **4** insurance

insalivate /in sálli vayt/ (**-vates, -vating, -vated**) *vt* to mix food with saliva in the process of chewing —**insalivation** /in sálli váysh'n/ *n*

insalubrious /ínssə lóo bri əss/ *adj* not pleasant, healthy, or wholesome —**insalubriously** *adv* —**insalubrity** *n*

insane /in sáyn/ *adj* **1** LEGALLY CONSIDERED AS PSYCHIATRICALLY DISORDERED legally incompetent or irresponsible because of a psychiatric disorder **2** LACKING REASONABLE THOUGHT showing a complete lack of reason or foresight (*informal*) ■ *npl* PEOPLE LEGALLY CONSIDERED AS PSYCHIATRICALLY DISORDERED persons who are legally incompetent or irresponsible because of a psychiatric disorder (*dated*) [Mid-16C. < Latin *insanus* < *sanus* 'healthy, sane'.] —**insanely** *adv* —**insaneness** *n*

insanitary /in sánnitəri/ *adj* dirty or unhygienic and thus likely to cause disease —**insanitariness** *n* —**insanitation** /in sánni táysh'n/ *n*

insanity /in sánnəti/ (*plural* **-ties**) *n* **1** extreme foolishness or an act that demonstrates it **2** legal incompetence or irresponsibility because of a psychiatric disorder

insatiable /in sáyshəb'l/ *adj* always needing more and impossible to satisfy [15thC. < Old French *insaciable* < Latin *satiare* (see SATIATE).] —**insatiability** /in sáyshə bílləti/ *n* —**insatiableness** *n* —**insatiably** *adv*

insatiate /in sáyshi ət/ *adj* insatiable (*literary*) [15C. < Latin *insatiatus* < *satiatus*, past participle of *satiare* (see SATIATE).] —**insatiately** *adv* —**insatiateness** *n*

inscape /ín skayp/ *n* the distinctive and essential inner quality of something, especially a natural object or a scene in nature [Mid-19C. Probably after LANDSCAPE.]

inscribe /in skríb/ (**-scribes, -scribing, -scribed**) *vt* **1** PUT WRITING ON to write, print, or engrave words or letters on a surface **2** WRITE SOMETHING ON A LIST to add a name to a list or book **3** WRITE A DEDICATION ON to write a signed message to somebody in a book or on a photograph, often when presenting it as a gift **4** DRAW A GEOMETRIC FIGURE WITHIN ANOTHER to draw a geometric figure within another so that all of the second figure lies within the first and touches it at as many points as possible ○ *inscribe a circle within a square* [15C. < Latin *inscribere* 'write on' < *scribere* 'write'.] —**inscribable** *adj* —**inscriber** *n*

inscription /in skrípsh'n/ *n* **1** words or letters written, printed, or engraved on a surface **2** a signed message written in a book or on a photograph, often when it is being presented as a gift [14C. < Latin *inscription-* < *inscribere* 'write on'.] —**inscriptional** *adj*

inscriptive /in skríptiv/ *adj* relating to or constituting an inscription —**inscriptively** *adv*

inscrutable /in skróotəb'l/ *adj* hard to interpret because not expressing anything obviously ○ *his inscrutable expression* [16C. Via Old French < ecclesiastical Latin *inscrutabilis* < Latin *scrutari* 'investigate'.] —**inscrutability** /in skróotə bílləti/ *n* —**inscrutableness** *n* —**inscrutably** *adv*

INSEAD /ínsi ad/, **Insead** *n* a leading European business school in Fontainebleau, France. Full form **Institut européen d'administration des affaires**

inseam /ín seem/ *n US* CLOTHING = **inside leg**

insect /ín sekt/ *n* **1** SMALL SIX-LEGGED ANIMAL an air-breathing invertebrate animal (**arthropod**) with a body that has well-defined segments, including a head, thorax, abdomen, two antennae, three pairs of legs, and usually two sets of wings. Class: Insecta. **2** SOMETHING LIKE INSECT a small animal that resembles an insect, e.g. a spider or centipede (*not used technically*) **3** CONTEMPTIBLE PERSON somebody viewed with contempt, especially somebody regarded as unimportant (*insult*) [Early 17C. < Latin *insectum* < *insecare* 'cut up' < *secare* 'to cut'.] —**insectan** /in séktən/ *adj*

insectarium /ínsek táiri əm/ (*plural* **-ums** *or* **-a** /-ə/), **insectary** (*plural* **-ries**) *n* a place for breeding or observing insects

insecticide /in sékti sīd/ *n* a chemical substance used to kill insects —**insecticidal** /in sékti síd'l/ *adj* —**insecticidally** *adv*

insectivore /in sékti vawr/ *n* **1** a small nocturnal mammal that feeds primarily on insects **2** any plant or animal that feeds primarily on insects [Mid-19C. < modern Latin *Insectivora* 'insect-eating', order name < *insecta* (see INSECT).] —**insectivorous** /ín sek tívvərəss/ *adj*

insecure /ínssi kyóor/ *adj* **1** NOT CONFIDENT anxious and lacking in self-confidence **2** NOT SAFE unsafe and unprotected ○ *insecure premises that are vulnerable to thieves* **3** LIKELY TO FALL liable to fall down or fall off ○ *an insecure walkway* —**insecurely** *adv* —**insecureness** *n*

insecurity (*plural* **-ties**) *n* **1** BEING INSECURE the state of being unsafe or insecure **2** UNSAFE FEELING a state of mind characterized by self-doubt and vulnerability **3** INSECURE PHENOMENON an instance or cause of being insecure

inselberg /ínz'l burg/ *n* an isolated hill or mountain, often heavily eroded on its lower slopes, rising abruptly from a plain [Early 20C. < German, 'island mountain'.]

inseminate /in sémmi nayt/ (**-nates, -nating, -nated**) *vt* to insert sperm into the reproductive tract of a female [Early 17C. < Latin *inseminare* 'to implant' < *semen* 'seed'.] —**insemination** /in sémmi náysh'n/ *n*

insensate /in sén sayt, -sət/ *adj* **1** WITHOUT FEELING inanimate and thus unable to feel anything **2** COLD AND HEARTLESS entirely lacking in sympathetic feeling or human kindness (*formal*) **3** THOUGHTLESS lacking in common sense or reasonable thought (*formal*) [15C. < ecclesiastical Latin *insensatus* < late Latin *sensatus* 'equipped with senses' < Latin *sensus* (see SENSE).] —**insensately** *adv* —**insensateness** *n*

insensible /in sénssəb'l/ *adj* **1** = **insensate** *adj.* 1 **2** NOT CONSCIOUS without feeling or consciousness **3** NOT AWARE OR RESPONSIVE unaware of or unresponsive to something **4** UNNOTICEABLE so small or gradual as to be almost imperceptible ○ *an insensible shift in emphasis* [14C. Via Old French < Latin *insensibilis* 'imperceptible' < *sensus* (see SENSE).] —**insensibility** /in sénssə bílləti/ *n* —**insensibleness** *n* —**insensibly** *adv*

insensitive /in sénssətiv/ *adj* **1** THOUGHTLESS insufficiently aware of other people's feelings and unable to respond to them appropriately **2** NOT REACTING PHYSICALLY not responsive to a physical stimulus such as touch or sound **3** INDIFFERENT AND UNRESPONSIVE indifferent to the importance of something and therefore not responding to it —**insensitively** *adv* —**insensitiveness** *n* —**insensitivity** /in sénssə tívvəti/ *n*

insentient /in sénshənt/ *adj* without life, consciousness, or perception —**insentience** *n*

inseparable /in séppərəb'l/ *adj* **1** sharing a close friendship and always seen or found together ○ *The two girls became inseparable.* **2** so closely linked as to be impossible to consider separately ○ *Reading and the ability to spell will seem inseparable.* —**inseparability** /in séppərə bílləti/ *n* —**inseparableness** *n* —**inseparably** *adv*

insert *vt* /in súrt/ **1** PLACE SOMETHING INSIDE to put something inside or into something else ○ *Insert the screws in the holes already drilled.* **2** ADD SOMETHING TO to add new material to the body of something, especially a text ■ *n* /ín surt/ **1** ADVERTISING SUPPLEMENT IN MAGAZINE a supplement in the form of a single sheet or booklet placed inside a magazine or newspaper, usually as advertising **2** ADDED PART a piece of fabric, usually contrasting, that is sewn into a main piece [15C. < Latin *serere* 'join'.] —**insertable** *adj* —**inserter** *n*

USAGE See ***assert***.

insertion /in súrsh'n/ *n* **1** ADDITION the act of putting something into something else **2** SOMETHING ADDED material that is inserted into a text **3** ATTACHMENT POINT the point of attachment of something, e.g. a leaf to its stem or a muscle to a bone it moves **4** INSERTED GENETIC MATERIAL a segment of DNA that is inserted into a gene sequence **5** AEROSP = **injection** *n.* 8, **injection** *n.* 9 —**insertional** *adj*

insertion stitch *n* an embroidery stitch that joins two pieces of fabric together and decorates the gap between them

in-service *adj* **1** taking place while somebody is employed full time ○ *an in-service training programme* **2** employed full time, especially in a particular job

insessorial /ín se sáwri əl/ *adj* describes birds that are adapted, or have feet that are adapted, for perching [Mid-19C. < modern Latin *Insessores*, former order name < *insidere* (see INSIDIOUS).]

inset *vt* /in sét/ (**-sets, -setting, -set**) PLACE A SMALLER THING IN A LARGER THING to insert something into a larger thing, e.g. a gem in a crown, or a small map in the corner of a larger map ■ *n* /ín set/ **1** SMALL THING PLACED IN SOMETHING LARGER something inserted into a larger thing ○ *a map of the state with city maps as insets* **2** CHANNEL a place where something flows in, especially the tide

INSET /ín set/, **Inset** *abbr* in-service education of teachers

inshallah /in shállə/, **insh'allah** *interj* an expression meaning 'if God wills', used to suggest that something in the future is uncertain [Mid-19C. < Arabic *in šā 'Allāh*.]

inshore /ín shawr/ *adj* near or towards the coast ○ *inshore waters* ■ *adv* towards the coast from the direction of the sea

inshrine *vt* = **enshrine**

inside /in síd, ín sīd/ CORE MEANING: a grammatical word indicating the interior part of something, the part that is enclosed by or surrounded with something, or the place or part within ○ (adv) *I opened the door and looked inside.* ○ (adj) *his inside jacket pocket* ○ (n) *I looked round the room, gnawing the inside of my cheek nervously.* ○ (pron) *The jewels are kept inside a locked box.*

1 *adj, prep* WITHIN ORGANIZATION happening or coming from within an organization ○ *They had inside knowledge about the takeover bid.* ○ *things that were going on inside the committee* **2** *adv, prep* RELATING TO INNER FEELINGS indicating emotions that are not expressed ○ *She doesn't like to look inside and face up to what she's really like.* ○ *Seeing her like that had snapped something inside him.* **3** ⚠ *prep* WITHIN SPECIFIED TIME done in a period of time less than the one stated (*informal*) ○ *We managed to completely redecorate the room inside seven hours.* **4** *adj* AT EDGE OF ROAD farthest from the centre of a road ○ *took the inside lane of the freeway* **5** *adv* IN PRISON serving time in prison (*informal*) ○ *He was inside for three years.* **6** *n* INNER EDGE the part of a road or path farthest from the centre ○ *was forced to overtake him on the inside* **7** *n* PRIVILEGED ACCESS a position that gives access to privileged information ○ *information from someone on the inside* **8** *npl* **insides** INTERNAL ORGANS the internal organs of the body, especially the stomach and bowels (*informal*) ◇ **inside of** ⚠ within a particular period of time (*informal*) ◇ **inside out** with the part that is normally inside facing outwards ◇ **know something inside out** to know something extremely well

USAGE inside, inside of or **within**? Though the idiomatic expressions ***inside*** and ***inside of*** in the sense 'within a given amount of time' are used in informal writing and conversation (*We'll be finished inside of a month*), the usage may be regarded as inappropriate to formal writing. Therefore, the safest choice is ***within***, as in *We'll be finished within a month.*

inside information *n* something secret or confidential known only to somebody who holds a position within a company or other organization

inside job *n* a crime carried out by or with the help of somebody who works for the individual or organization concerned (*informal*)

inside lane *n* the section of a multiple-lane road nearest to the left, used by vehicles being overtaken and those turning off the road

inside leg *n* US term **inseam** **1** the inner seam of a pair of trousers, from the crotch to the bottom of the trouser leg **2** the measurement of a trouser leg's inner seam

insider /in sídər/ *n* a member of a group who knows all about its inner workings

insider trading *n* profitable trading in securities that is done using access to privileged information

inside track *n* **1** the lane of an oval racetrack nearest the centre and thus shorter than the outer lanes **2** an advantageous position

insidious /in síddi əss/ *adj* slowly and subtly harmful or destructive [Mid-16C. < Latin *insidiosus* < *insidiae* 'ambush' < *insidere* 'sit on, lie in wait' < *sedere* 'sit'.] —**insidiously** *adv* —**insidiousness** *n*

USAGE insidious or **invidious**? Though both these words are spelled similarly and have negative meanings, they are not interchangeable. ***Insidious***, which comes from a Latin word meaning 'ambush', means 'slowly and subtly harmful': *Cancer can be an insidious illness. The candidate launched an insidious whispering campaign against his rival.* ***Invidious***, which comes from another Latin word meaning 'looking at with malice', means 'causing another to feel resentment because of unfair treatment', 'feeling envious; jealous', and 'slighting and discriminatory to another': *Their invidious accusations invite enmity. Her superior attitude has resulted in invidious scrutiny on the part of her competitors.*

insight /ín sīt/ *n* **1** PERCEPTIVENESS the ability to see clearly and intuitively into the nature of a complex person, situation, or subject **2** CLEAR PERCEPTION a clear perception of something ○ *thanked him for his remark and told him it was an interesting insight* **3** SELF-AWARENESS the ability of a person to understand and find solutions to his or her personal problems **4** PERCEPTION THAT HALLUCINATIONS ARE NOT REAL the perception, lacking in some psychiatric disorders such as schizophrenia, that symptoms such as delusions and hallucinations are not objective —**insightful** /ín sītf'l/ *adj* —**insightfully** *adv* —**insightfulness** *n*

insight meditation *n* = **vipassana**

insigne /in sígni/ *n* an insignia (*formal*)

insignia /in sígni ə/ (*plural* **-a** *or* **-as**) *n* **1** a badge of authority or membership of a group **2** an identifying mark or sign [Mid-17C. < Latin, < *insignis* 'marked' < *signum* 'sign'.]

insignificant /ínssig níffikənt/ *adj* **1** WITHOUT IMPORTANCE too small and unimportant to be relevant ○ *statistically insignificant* **2** WITHOUT MEANING having little or no meaning **3** POWERLESS lacking in power or status —**insignificance** *n* —**insignificantly** *adv*

insincere /ín sin séer/ *adj* not genuine and not reflecting true feelings —**insincerely** *adv* —**insincerity** /ín sin sérrəti/ *n*

insinuate /in sínnyoo ayt/ (**-ates, -ating, -ated**) *v* **1** *vti* to hint at something unpleasant or suggest it indirectly and gradually **2** *vr* to introduce yourself gradually and cunningly into a position, especially a place of confidence or favour [Early 16C. < Latin *insinuare* < *sinus* 'curve'.] —**insinuatingly** *adv* —**insinuative** /in sínnyoo ətiv/ *adj* —**insinuator** *n*

insinuation /in sínnyoo áysh'n/ *n* **1** something unpleasant artfully and indirectly suggested to another person **2** the act of hinting something unpleasant or suggesting it indirectly and gradually

insipid /in síppid/ *adj* **1** dull because lacking in character and lively qualities **2** bland and without flavour [Early 17C. Directly or via French < late Latin *insipidus* 'tasteless' < *sapidus* 'having a flavour'.] —**insipidity** /ínssi píddəti/ *n* —**insipidly** *adv* —**insipidness** *n*

insist /in síst/ *vti* **1** to state or demand something firmly in spite of disagreement or resistance from others ○ *She insisted that he was wrong.* ○ *Please, you must take it, I insist!* **2** to state something firmly and steadfastly ○ *They insist on punctuality.* ○ *He insisted there was nothing to worry about.* [Late 16C. < Latin *insistere* 'persist' < *sistere* 'to stand'.]

insistent /in sístənt/ *adj* **1** persistent in maintaining or demanding something ○ *She was most insistent.* **2** persistently calling for or compelling attention ○ *insistent pleas* —**insistence** *n* —**insistency** *n* —**insistently** *adv*

in situ /in síttyoo/ *adv, adj* in its natural or original place ○ *a useful tool for studying cell proliferation in situ under normal and pathological conditions* [< Latin]

insnare *vt* = **ensnare**

insobriety /ínssō brí əti/ *n* lack of moderation, especially in drinking

insofar as /ín sō fáar əz/ *conj* used to introduce a statement that explains or qualifies a previous statement

insolate /ínsō layt/ (**-lates, -lating, -lated**) *vt* to expose something to sunlight [Early 17C. < Latin *insolare* < *sol* 'sun'.]

insolation /ínssō láysh'n/ *n* **1** EXPOSURE TO SUNLIGHT exposure of something to sunlight **2** SUNSTROKE sunstroke (*technical*) **3** RATE OF SOLAR RADIATION the rate of solar radiation received per unit area

insole /ínssōl/ *n* **1** the inner lining of a shoe **2** a thin removable liner placed inside a shoe to make it warmer or more comfortable or to prevent the buildup of odour

insolent /ínssələnt/ *adj* showing an aggressive lack of respect in speech or behaviour [14C. < Latin *insolens* 'unusual, arrogant' < *solere* 'be accustomed'.] —**insolence** *n* —**insolently** *adv*

insolubilize /in sóllyōobə līz/ (**-lizes, -lizing, -lized**), **insolubilise** (**-lises, -lising, -lised**) *vt* to make something incapable of being dissolved in a liquid —**insolubilization** /in sóllyōobə lī záysh'n/ *n*

insoluble /in sóllyōob'l/ *adj* **1** incapable of being dissolved in a liquid **2** not able to be solved —**insolubility** /in sóllyōo bílləti/ *n* —**insolubleness** *n* —**insolubly** *adv*

insolvable *adj* = **insoluble** *adj.* 2 —**insolvability** /in sólvə bílləti/ *n*

insolvent /in sólvənt/ *adj* **1** BANKRUPT unable to pay debts **2** OF BANKRUPTCY relating to people or businesses that are bankrupt ■ *n* **BANKRUPT PERSON** somebody who is unable to pay any debts —**insolvency** *n*

insomnia /in sómni ə/ *n* inability to fall asleep or to remain asleep long enough to feel rested, especially as a problem continuing over time [Early 17C. < Latin *insomnis* 'sleepless' < *somnus* 'sleep'.] —**insomniac** *adj, n*

insomuch as /ínssō múch az/ *conj* used to introduce an explanation or reason

insomuch that *conj* used to indicate the extent to which something is true or is the case

insouciance /in sóossi ənss/ *n* cheerful lack of anxiety or concern [Early 19C. Via French < *soucier* 'to care' < Latin *sollicitare* 'to trouble'.] —**insouciant** *adj* —**insouciantly** *adv*

insoul *vt* = **ensoul**

insp. *abbr* **1** inspected **2 insp., Insp.** inspector

inspan /in spán/ (**-spans, -spanning, -spanned**) *vt S Africa* to harness an animal to a vehicle [Early 19C. Via Afrikaans < Dutch *inspannen.*]

inspect /in spékt/ *vt* **1** to examine something carefully in order to judge its quality or correctness ○ *She took the cheese out of the refrigerator and inspected it for mould.* **2** to examine or review something officially ○ *The barracks is inspected every day.* [Early 17C. < Latin *inspicere* < *specere* 'look at'.] —**inspectable** *adj* —**inspective** *adj*

inspection /in spéksh'n/ *n* **1** a critical examination of somebody or something aimed at forming a judgment or evaluation **2** an official authoritative examination ○ *a motor vehicle inspection*

inspection arms *n* a position in which a rifle is held diagonally in front of the body with the muzzle pointing upwards to the left and the rifle chamber open for inspection

inspector /in spéktər/ *n* **1** an official who examines something in order to judge its quality or compliance with rules or the law **2** a British police officer of a rank above sergeant —**inspectoral** *adj* —**inspectorial** /ín spek táwri əl/ *adj* —**inspectorship** *n*

inspectorate /in spéktərət/ *n* **1 GROUP OF INSPECTORS** a group or department of inspectors **2 INSPECTOR'S DISTRICT** an area supervised by an inspector **3 INSPECTOR'S DUTIES** the office or duties of an inspector

inspector general (*plural* **inspectors general**) *n* **1** an official who is the head of an inspectorate **2** a military officer who investigates and reports on organizational matters

insphere *vt* = **ensphere**

inspiration /ínspi ráysh'n/ *n* **1 STIMULUS TO DO CREATIVE WORK** something that stimulates the human mind to creative thought or to the making of art ○ *found inspiration in the landscape around her* **2 THING THAT INSPIRES** somebody or something that inspires others ○ *His book is an inspiration to all would-be travellers.* **3 CREATIVENESS** the quality of being stimulated to creative thought or activity, or the manifestation of this ○ *a moment of inspiration* **4 GOOD IDEA** a sudden brilliant idea **5 DIVINE INFLUENCE** divine guidance and influence on human beings **6 BREATHING IN** the drawing of air into the lungs [14C. Via Old French < Latin *inspiratio.*] —**inspirational** *adj* —**inspirationally** *adv*

inspirator /ínspi raytər/ *n* a device for drawing in a gas or vapour [Late 19C. < INSPIRE.]

inspiratory /in spírətəri/ *adj* relating to the process of breathing in [Late 18C. < INSPIRE.]

inspire /in spír/ (**-spires, -spiring, -spired**) *v* **1** *vti* **STIMULATE SOMEBODY TO DO** to encourage people into greater efforts or greater enthusiasm or creativity **2** *vt* **PROVOKE A FEELING** to arouse a particular feeling in somebody **3** *vt* **CAUSE CREATIVE ACTIVITY** to stimulate somebody to do something, especially creative work or the making of art **4** *vti* **BREATHE IN** to inhale air or a gas into the lungs [14C. Via Old French *enspirer* < Latin *inspirare* < *spirare* 'breathe'.] —**inspirable** *adj* —**inspirative** *adj* —**inspirer** *n*

inspired /in spírd/ *adj* **1** brilliant and creative ○ *an inspired rendition of a classic song* ○ *She was an inspired teacher.* **2** based on a particular motive or example (*usually in combination*) ○ *a Jesuit-inspired curriculum*

inspiring /in spíring/ *adj* making somebody feel more enthusiastic, confident, or stimulated —**inspiringly** *adv*

inspirit /in spírrit/ *vt* to give energy or courage to somebody (*archaic or literary*) —**inspiriter** *n* —**inspiriting** *adj* —**inspiritingly** *adv*

inspissate /in spíss ayt/ (**-sates, -sating, -sated**) *vti* to become thicker in consistency or to cause something to thicken, especially by boiling or evaporation [Early 17C. < Latin *inspissare* 'thicken' < *spissus* 'thick'.] —**inspissator** /ínspiss aytər/ *n*

inst. *abbr* **1** instant **2** instantaneous **3 inst., Inst.** institute **4 inst., Inst.** institution **5** institutional

instability /ínstə bílləti/ *n* **1** the quality of being unstable, erratic, or unpredictable **2** lack of steadiness or firmness

~~**instalation**~~ incorrect spelling of **installation**

⚡**install** /in stáwl/, **instal** *v* (**-stals, -stalling, -stalled**) **1** *vt* **FIT OR CONNECT** to put machinery or equipment into place and make it ready for use **2** *vt* **LOAD SOFTWARE** to load software onto a computer **3** *vt* **PLACE SOMEBODY IN OFFICE** to appoint somebody to a particular position or to induct somebody formally into office **4** *vr* **SETTLE IN** to settle yourself comfortably somewhere ■ *n* **ACT OF LOADING SOFTWARE** the act of loading software onto a computer ○ *'I opted for the full install, which can involve anything up to 72Mb of space'.* (*Internet Magazine*; November 1998) [15C. Directly or via Old French *installer* < medieval Latin *installare* 'place in office' < *stallum* 'stall'.] —**installer** *n*

installant /in stáwlənt/ *n* an appointer or formal inductor of somebody into office

installation /ínstə láysh'n/ *n* **1 ACT OF INSTALLING EQUIPMENT** the process of putting a piece of equipment or machinery in place and setting it up ready for use **2 PLACE WITH EQUIPMENT** a place housing equipment or machinery for a particular use ○ *a communications installation* **3 SOMETHING THAT HAS BEEN INSTALLED** a piece or system of equipment that has been put in place and made ready for use **4 MILITARY BASE** a military base or camp ○ *The artillery installation on the island is marked in red on the map.* **5 APPOINTING OF SOMEBODY TO POSITION** the act of appointing somebody to a particular position or of inducting somebody formally into office **6 ART EXHIBIT** an artwork assembled by the artist involving the arrangement of three-dimensional objects or the use of paint and other media directly on walls or floors ○ *an installation using video monitors and empty bottles*

⚡**installation program** *n* a computer program used in installing applications or hardware, usually with options for users to select

installment *n* US = **instalment**

installment plan *n US* a system for buying merchandise involving a series of payments at regular intervals instead of a single lump sum. ◊ **hire purchase**

instalment /in stáwlmənt/ *n* one of the parts of something that appears or is presented at intervals ○ *published in instalments* [Mid-18C. < Anglo-Norman *estallment* < Old French *estaler* 'to fix, place'.]

instance /ínstənss/ *n* **1 ILLUSTRATION** an example of a particular situation or event ○ *cited several instances of his being untruthful* **2 EVENT** an occurrence of something ○ *We can overlook it in this instance.* **3 LEGAL ACTION** a legal proceeding or lawsuit ■ *vt* (**-stances, -stancing, -stanced**) **GIVE AS EXAMPLE** to offer something as an example [14C. Via French *instance* < Latin *instantia* < *instant-* (see INSTANT).] ◇ **for instance** as an example ◇ **in the first instance** used to indicate something that is or happens first, before other events or stages (*formal*)

instant /ínstənt/ *adj* **1 IMMEDIATE** happening immediately, without delay ○ *She demanded instant service.* **2 QUICK TO PREPARE** quickly and easily prepared, often premixed, precooked, or powdered ○ *instant coffee* **3 SUDDEN** achieving a particular status very suddenly and effortlessly ○ *The play was an instant success.* **4 URGENT AND PRESSING** requiring immediate attention or an immediate response ○ *an instant need for help* **5 FROM THIS MONTH** happening in the current month (*archaic*) ○ *your letter of the 13th instant* **6 CURRENT** present or current (*archaic*) ■ *n* **1 SHORT TIME** an extremely brief period of time ○ *for an instant* **2 MOMENT IN TIME** a particular moment in time ○ *The instant I saw his face I knew that something was wrong.* **3 QUICKLY PREPARED PRODUCT** a quickly prepared item of food or drink ■ *adv* **INSTANTLY** instantly (*literary*) [15C. Via Old French < Latin *instant-*, present participle of *instare* 'be present' < *stare* 'to stand'.] —**instancy** *n* —**instantness** *n*

instantaneous /ínstən táyni əss/ *adj* **1** occurring immediately or almost immediately **2** indicating the value of something at a given moment in time, expressed as the average value of a varying quantity over an infinitesimally small time interval ○ *instantaneous velocity* [Mid-17C. < medieval Latin *instantaneus* < Latin *instant-* (see INSTANT).] —**instantaneity** /in stántə náy əti, -née əti/ *n* —**instantaneously** *adv* —**instantaneousness** *n*

instantiate /in stánshi ayt/ (**-ates, -ating, -ated**) *vt* to provide an example to support or explain something [Mid-20C. < INSTANCE.]

instantly /ínstəntli/ *adv* **1 IMMEDIATELY** immediately and without delay **2 URGENTLY** urgently or insistently (*archaic*) ■ *conj* **AS SOON AS** happening or done immediately after something else ○ *I phoned instantly I heard you were back.*

instant-on *adj* including a device that allows for a rapid start-up, eliminating the need for a warm-up period

instant replay *n US* SPORTS, MEDIA = **action replay**

instar /ín staar/ *n* in the life cycle of an arthropod such as an insect, a stage between two successive moults [Late 19C. < Latin, 'form, image'.]

instate /in stáyt/ (**-states, -stating, -stated**) *vt* to establish somebody in office —**instatement** *n*

in statu quo /in státtoo kwṓ/ *adv* in the same state [< Latin *in statu quo ante* 'in the (same) state as before']

instauration /ín staw ráysh'n/ *n* (*formal*) **1** the restoration of something that has lapsed or fallen into decay **2** the founding or establishment of something [Early 17C. < Latin *instaurare* 'renew'.] —**instaurator** /ín staw raytər/ *n*

instead /in stéd/ *adv* as a replacement or substitute for something [13C. < IN + *stede* 'place'.] ◇ **instead of** as an alternative to, or substitute for, something

instep /ín step/ *n* **1** the arched middle portion of the human foot between the ankle and toes, especially its upper surface **2** the part of a shoe that covers the middle portion of the foot [15C. < ?]

instigate /ínsti gayt/ (**-gates, -gating, -gated**) *vt* **1** to cause a process to start **2** to cause trouble, especially by urging somebody to do something destructive or wrong [Mid-16C. < Latin *instigare.*] —**instigation** *n* —**instigative** *adj* —**instigator** *n*

instil /in stíl/ *vt* **1** to impress ideas, principles, or teachings gradually on somebody's mind ○ *I tried to instil self-respect in my students.* **2** to pour medicine or another liquid into something drop by drop [15C. < Latin *instillare* < *stilla* 'drop'.] —**instillation** /ínsti láysh'n/ *n* —**instiller** *n* —**instilment** /-mənt/ *n*

instill *vt* US = **instil**

instinct /ín stingkt/ *n* **1 BIOLOGICAL DRIVE** an inborn pattern of behaviour characteristic of a species and shaped by biological necessities such as survival and reproduction **2 STRONG NATURAL IMPULSE** a powerful impulse that feels natural rather than reasoned ○ *followed his instincts and took to his heels* **3 KNACK** a natural gift or skill ○ *an instinct for putting people at ease* ■ *adj* **FILLED** completely filled or imbued with something (*formal*) ○ *a look instinct with compassion* [15C. < Latin *instinctus* 'impulse' < *instinguere* 'incite' < *stinguere* 'to sting'.] —**instinctual** /in stíngktyoo əl/ *adj* —**instinctually** *adv*

instinctive /in stíngktiv/ *adj* **1** relating to, prompted by, or based on a strong natural impulse ○ *an instinctive fear of water* **2** having a particular quality or skill spontaneously and without effort or instruction ○ *an artist with an instinctive feel for colour* ○ *an instinctive cook* —**instinctively** *adv* —**instinctiveness** *n*

institute /ínsti tyoot/ *vt* (**-tutes, -tuting, -tuted**) **1 START** to start or initiate something in an official or formal way ○ *institute legal proceedings* **2 APPOINT** to appoint somebody to an office, especially a religious one **3 SET SOMETHING UP** to set up or establish something ○ *institute a literary prize* ■ *n* **1 ORGANIZATION WITH SPECIALIZED GOAL** an organization for promoting something, such as art, science, or the well-being of a group **2 PLACE FOR ADVANCED STUDY** an educational institution, especially one concerned with technical subjects **3 PRINCIPLE** an established principle or rule ■ **institutes** *npl* **LAW SUMMARY** a summary of laws [14C. < Latin *instituere* 'establish' < *statuere* 'set up' < *stare* 'to stand'.] —**instituter** *n*

institution /ínsti tyoósh'n/ *n* **1 IMPORTANT ORGANIZATION** a large organization such as a college, hospital, or bank that is influential in the community **2 ESTABLISHED PRACTICE** an established law, custom, or practice ○ *the institution of marriage* **3 STARTING** the act of initiating or establishing something **4 LONG-ESTABLISHED PERSON OR THING** somebody or something that has been well-known and established in a place for many years (*informal*) **5 PLACE OF CARE OR CONFINEMENT** a place where people with mental or physical disabilities are cared for **6 LARGE AND POWERFUL INVESTOR** a large financial organization, e.g. a pension fund, that has considerable resources to make investments ○ *a mutual fund available only to institutions* — **institutional** *adj* —**institutionally** *adv* —**institutionary** *adj*

institutional bilingualism *n Can* the policy and practice of providing services in both English and French in Canadian public institutions, especially those of the federal government

institutionalise *vt* = **institutionalize**

institutionalism /ínsti tyōósh'nəlizəm/ *n* a belief in the merits of established customs and systems —**institutionalist** *n*

institutionalize /ínsti tyōósh'nə līz/ (**-izes, -izing, -ized**), **institutionalise** (**-ises, -ising, -ised**) *vt* **1** PUT SOMEBODY INTO AN INSTITUTION to put somebody into an institution such as a children's home, nursing home, or prison **2** ESTABLISH SOMETHING AS NORMAL to make something an established custom or an accepted part of the structure of a large organization or society **3** MAKE INTO OR LIKE INSTITUTION to convert something into an institution or make something resemble an institution —**institutionalization** /ínsti tyōósh'nə līˈzáysh'n/ *n*

institutionalized /ínsti tyōósh'nə līzd/ *adj* **1** having become an established custom or an accepted part of the structure of a large organization or society because it has existed for so long **2** lacking the will or ability to think and act independently because of having spent a long time in an institution such as a psychiatric hospital or prison

institutive /ínsti tyootiv/ *adj* serving to establish or being established —**institutively** *adv*

in-store *adj* happening, available, or situated within a large store, e.g. a supermarket or department store ○ *an in-store bakery*

instr. *abbr* **1** instruction **2** instructor **3** instrument **4** instrumental

instruct /in strúkt/ *v* **1** vti TRAIN to teach somebody a subject or how to do something **2** *vt* DIRECT to tell somebody to do something, especially with authority or as an order **3** *vt* OBTAIN LEGAL REPRESENTATION to ask or authorize a lawyer to act on your behalf and supply him or her with relevant information **4** *vt* GIVE SOMEBODY INFORMATION to inform somebody about something, especially in a formal or official manner ○ *We were instructed that the meeting had been postponed.* [15C. < Latin *instruct-*, past participle of *instruere* 'prepare, equip' < *struere* 'build'.] —**instructible** *adj*

SYNONYMS See *teach*.

⚡ **instruction** /in strúksh'n/ *n* **1** TEACHING OR THINGS TAUGHT teaching in a particular subject or skill, or the facts or skills taught ○ *driving instruction* **2** TEACHING PROFESSION OR PROCESS the profession of teaching or the teaching process **3** STATEMENT OF COMMAND a spoken or written statement of what must be done, especially delivered formally, with official authority, or as an order ○ *acting on instructions we received* **4** COMPUTER COMMAND a code that tells a computer to perform a specific operation ■ **instructions** *npl* **1** LIST OF THINGS TO DO printed information about how to do, make, assemble, use, or operate something ○ *The instructions are printed on the back of the packet.* **2** BRIEFING TO LAWYER the relevant information about a legal case given by a client to a solicitor or a solicitor to a barrister —**instructional** *adj* —**instructionally** *adv*

instructive /in strúktiv/ *adj* providing useful information or insight into something —**instructively** *adv* —**instructiveness** *n*

instructor /in strúktər/ *n* a teacher of something, often a sport or a practical skill ○ *a ski instructor* —**instructorship** *n*

instrument /ínstrōómənt/ *n* **1** TOOL a tool or mechanical device, especially one used for precision work in science, medicine, or technology **2** OBJECT THAT PRODUCES MUSIC an object used to produce music, e.g. by blowing through an opening, plucking or rubbing its strings, or striking it **3** MEASURING DEVICE a device that measures or controls something, such as a speedometer or voltmeter **4** MEANS OF DOING something or somebody used as a means of achieving a desired result or accomplishing a particular purpose (*usually singular*) ○ *The secret police were the state's instrument for controlling the populace.* **5** OBJECT USED FOR A PURPOSE an object that has been or could be used for a purpose ○ *hit on the head by a blunt instrument* **6** DOCUMENT a legal document (*formal*) ■ *vt* **1** ARRANGE MUSIC to write or arrange a piece of music for performance on musical instruments **2** SUPPLY WITH MEASURING DEVICES to equip something with instruments

for measurement or control [13C. Via Old French < Latin *instrumentum* < *instruere* 'prepare'.]

instrumental /ínstrōó mént'l/ *adj* **1** FOR INSTRUMENTS, NOT VOICES performed on a musical instrument, not with the voice **2** CONNECTED WITH INSTRUMENTS done with or produced by an instrument or instruments **3** MAKING SOMETHING HAPPEN playing an important part in achieving a result or accomplishing a purpose ○ *She was instrumental in getting the legislation passed.* **4** INDICATING THE MEANS OF DOING describing a noun case that indicates something is used for a purpose or is the means by which something is done **5** OF INSTRUMENTALISM relating to instrumentalism ■ *n* **1** MUSIC PLAYED BY INSTRUMENTS a piece of music that is performed on a musical instrument, not with the voice **2** NOUN FORM INDICATING MEANS the instrumental case, or a noun in the instrumental case —**instrumentally** *adv*

instrumentalism /ínstrōó mént'lizəm/ *n* the view that theories are useful tools for making predictions but cannot be literally true or false

instrumentalist /ínstrōó mént'list/ *n* **1** PLAYER OF INSTRUMENT somebody who plays a musical instrument **2** PROPONENT OF INSTRUMENTALISM a supporter or advocate of instrumentalism ■ *adj* FOR INSTRUMENTALISM supporting or advocating instrumentalism

instrumentality /ínstrōó men tálləti/ (*plural* **-ties**) *n* (*formal*) **1** somebody's interventionist action or thing ○ *'But for her instrumentality, the fatal knowledge would not have been imparted'.* (Elizabeth Gaskell, *Some Passages from the History of the Chomley Family*; 1865) **2** *US* in the United States, a subsidiary branch of a department or agency ○ *a department, agency, or instrumentality of the executive, legislative, and judicial branches of the federal government*

instrumental learning *n* a form of learning that takes place as a direct consequence of a reward or pleasant outcome for the learner

instrumentation /ínstrōó men táysh'n, ínstrəmən-/ *n* **1** ARRANGEMENT FOR MUSICAL INSTRUMENTS the composition, arrangement, or specified combination of music for instruments **2** MUSICAL INSTRUMENTS USED the instruments that are to perform a piece of music **3** EQUIPMENT FOR CONTROL OR OPERATION a set of instruments used for a particular purpose, e.g. operating a machine or controlling an aircraft **4** USE OF INSTRUMENTS the use of instruments as tools or for measurement or control **5** MAKING INSTRUMENTS the design, development, or manufacture of instruments for use in science, medicine, technology, or industry **6** MEANS the means or agency through which something is done (*formal*)

instrument board *n* = **instrument panel**

instrument flying *n* the flying of an aircraft using only information obtained from instruments rather than from what the pilot can see

instrument landing *n* landing an aircraft while relying on information from instruments rather than from looking out of the aircraft's window

instrument panel *n* a set of instruments mounted at the front of a machine or in front of somebody driving or steering a motor vehicle, aircraft, or ship

insubordinate /ín sə báwrdinət/ *adj* refusing to obey orders or submit to authority ■ *n* a person who refuses to obey orders or submit to authority —**insubordinately** *adv* —**insubordination** /ín sə báwrdə náysh'n/ *n*

insubstantial /ín səb stánsh'l/ *adj* **1** not very large, solid, or strong **2** not existing in reality ○ *an insubstantial apparition* —**insubstantiality** /ínssəb stanshi álləti/ *n* —**insubstantially** *adv*

insufferable /in súffərəb'l/ *adj* so annoying, unpleasant, or uncomfortable that it is unbearable —**insufferably** *adv* —**insufferableness** *n*

insufficiency /ínssə físh'nssi/ (*plural* **-cies**) *n* **1** NOT ENOUGH a smaller number or lesser amount than is needed ○ *an insufficiency of provisions for a long cruise* **2** UNFITNESS OR FAILURE inability or failure to perform competently, adequately, or normally ○ *cardiac insufficiency* **3** FAILURE TO MEASURE UP a failure to meet some standard or requirement ○ *the insufficiency of the causes presented to explain this phenomenon*

insufficient /ínssə físh'nt/ *adj* not enough in amount or quality to satisfy some purpose or standard ○ *We were given insufficient notice.* —**insufficiently** *adv*

insufflate /ínssə flayt, in súf layt/ (**-flates, -flating, -flated**) *vt* **1** BLOW INTO to blow or breathe into something (*formal*) **2** BLOW SOMETHING INTO A BODY CAVITY to blow something,

e.g. air, powder, or gas, into the lungs or some other body cavity in the course of medical treatment **3** BLOW ON to blow or breathe on something or somebody as part of a Christian religious sacrament or ritual such as baptism or exorcism, to symbolize the Holy Spirit [Late 17C. Latin *insufflat-* < *insufflare* < *sufflare* 'blow up'.] —**insufflation** /ínssə fláysh'n/ *n* —**insufflator** *n*

insular /ínssyōólər/ *adj* **1** LIMITED IN OUTLOOK concerned only with your own country, society, or way of life and not interested in new ideas or different cultures **2** NOT CLOSE TO OTHERS physically or emotionally removed from others **3** OF ISLANDS relating to or originating in an island **4** OF ISLANDS OF CELLS relating to a collection of cells or tissue reminiscent of an island [Mid-16C. Via French *insulaire* < late Latin *insularis* < Latin *insula* 'island'.] —**insularism** *n* —**insularity** /ínssyoo lárrəti/ *n* —**insularly** *adv*

insulate /ínssyoo layt/ (**-lates, -lating, -lated**) *vt* **1** to prevent or reduce the passage of heat, electricity, or sound into, from, or through something, especially by surrounding it with some material **2** to protect or isolate somebody from something, especially from something unpleasant or undesirable [Mid-16C. < Latin *insula* 'island'.] —**insulant** *n*

insulating tape *n* a thin strip of adhesive material that can be wrapped round bare wires or electrical connections to stop electricity from passing from them to somebody or something that touches them. US term **friction tape**

insulation /ínssyōó láysh'n/ *n* **1** MATERIAL THAT INSULATES material that prevents or reduces the passage of heat, electricity, or sound, e.g. a special fabric or a layer of air **2** PREVENTION OF CONDUCTION the act of covering or surrounding something to prevent or reduce the passage of heat, electricity, or sound **3** PROTECTION protection or isolation from something undesirable or unpleasant —**insulative** /ínssyōólətiv, -laytiv/ *adj*

insulator /ínssyōó laytər/ *n* a material or device that prevents or reduces the passage of heat, electricity, or sound

insulin /ínssyōólin/ *n* a pancreatic hormone that regulates the level of glucose in the blood [Early 20C. < Latin *insula* 'island', after the ISLETS OF LANGERHANS.]

insulin shock, insulin reaction *n* a severe drop in blood sugar resulting from an excess of insulin and marked by sweating, dizziness, trembling, and eventual coma

insult /in súlt/ *v* **1** vti BE OFFENSIVE to say or do something rude or insensitive that offends somebody else **2** *vt* SHOW CONTEMPT to say or do something suggesting a low opinion of somebody or something ○ *Don't insult me by offering me pity.* ■ *n* **1** OFFENSIVE WORDS OR ACTION a remark or action that offends somebody, usually because it is rude or insensitive **2** SOMETHING SHOWING CONTEMPT behaviour or words implying a low opinion of somebody, e.g. a payment that is much less than expected or deserved ○ *The article is an insult to the intelligence of the reader.* **3** INJURY OR AN INJURING AGENT an injury or trauma to the body or something that causes such harm [Mid-16C. Via French *insulter* < Latin *insultare* 'keep jumping on' < *salire* 'to jump'.] —**insulter** *n*

LANGUAGE NOTE Insults English has insult words for most races and cultures with which its speakers have come into extended contact, and for so-called minority groups within English-speaking society, even though such groups can and do constitute demographic majorities in many regions. When the people insulted are English speakers, the insulting words can and often do become part of their own vocabulary. Those insulted will generally avoid using these terms in interaction with their insulters, since to do so would be to endorse the insulters' view of them. However, amongst themselves they may well deliberately adopt an insult in order to subvert it or rob it of its power. For instance, Australian Aboriginals reportedly are not averse to using terms like *Abo* and *blackfella* when talking to each other, even though they are highly offensive when applied to them by non-Aboriginals. The best-known example of this is *nigger*. It began (in the 16th century) as a neutral term for a Black person, but in the latter part of the 18th century it started to be used by white people as an abusive term. In spite of this, there is ample evidence that Black Americans continued to use it in relation to themselves throughout the 19th century, and in the 20th century it became a positive term of solidarity and pride amongst Blacks (often defiantly spelled *nigga* or *nigguh* in this context). It remains, of course, strictly taboo for a white speaker. Similarly, other groups may defy their detractors by adopting the insults directed at them: gay people may refer to themselves, polemically, as *queer*, as in *Queer Nation*; and some feminists have struck back against ageist put-downs by reclaiming *crone* and making it their own.

insulting /in súlting/ *adj* causing offence because it is rude or insensitive or suggests a low opinion of somebody or something —**insultingly** *adv*

insuperable /in sóopərəb'l/ *adj* impossible to overcome, get rid of, or deal with successfully ○ *battling against insuperable odds* [14C. < Old French, < Latin *superare* 'overcome' < *super* 'above'.] —**insuperability** /in sóopərə bíllәti/ *n* —**insuperableness** *n* —**insuperably** *adv*

insupportable /ínssə páwrtəb'l/ *adj* **1** too great, unpleasant, or difficult to bear ○ *an insupportable claim* **2** impossible to justify or defend —**insupportableness** *n* —**insupportably** *adv*

insurable interest *n* a demonstrable interest in something covered by an insurance policy, the loss of which would cause deprivation or financial loss

insurance /in shóorənss, -sháwr-/ *n* **1 FINANCIAL PROTECTION AGAINST LOSS OR HARM** an arrangement by which a company gives customers financial protection against loss or harm, e.g. theft or illness, in return for payment (**premium**) **2 MONEY PAID BY AN INSURANCE COMPANY** the sum of money that an insurance company pays or agrees to pay if a specified undesirable event occurs **3 PREMIUM** the payment made to obtain insurance ○ *My car insurance has gone up again.* **4 INSURANCE BUSINESS** the commercial business of providing insurance **5 MEANS OF PROTECTION** an act, measure, or provision that gives protection against some undesirable event or risk ○ *provided a map as insurance against getting lost* [15C. < Old French *enseürance*.]

insurance policy *n* a written contract between an insurance company and a person or organization requiring insurance against loss or harm

insure /in shóor, -sháwr/ (**-sures, -suring, -sured**) *v* **1** *vti* to agree formally that, for a sum of money paid to a company, the company will pay compensation or costs if some specified harm or loss occurs to somebody or something ○ *The ring was insured for £5,000.* **2** *vi* to get protection from something undesirable that might happen, usually by making contingency plans or taking precautionary or preventive measures **3** *vt US* = **ensure** [15C. Variant of ENSURE.] —**insurability** /in shóorə bíllәti, -sháwrə-/ *n* —**insurable** *adj* —**insured** *adj, n*

USAGE See ***assure***.

insurer /in shóorər, -sháwr-/ *n* a company or individual providing insurance

insurgent /in súrjənt/ *n* a rebel against authority or leadership, especially a member of a group involved in an uprising ■ *adj* rebelling against authority or leadership, especially against a government or ruler of a country [Mid-18C. < Latin *insurgent-* < *insurgere* 'rise up' < *surgere* 'to rise'.] —**insurgence** *n* —**insurgency** *n* —**insurgently** *adv*

insurmountable /ín sər mówntəb'l/ *adj* impossible to overcome or deal with successfully —**insurmountability** /ín sər mowntə bíllәti/ *n* —**insurmountably** *adv*

insurrection /ínssə réksh'n/ *n* rebellion against the government or rulers of a country, often involving armed conflict [15C. < Latin *insurrection-* < *insurgere* 'rise up'.] —**insurrectional** *adj* —**insurrectionary** *n, adj* —**insurrectionism** *n* —**insurrectionist** *n, adj*

insusceptible /ín sə séptəb'l/ *adj* **1** not likely to be affected or influenced by something **2** not able to undergo some process —**insusceptibility** /ín sə séptə bíllәti/ *n* —**insusceptibly** *adv*

inswing /ín swing/ *n* in cricket, the curve of a bowl from the batter's off to leg side [Early 20C. Back-formation < INSWINGER.]

inswinger /ín swingər/ *n* **1** a ball that curves through the air from the batter's off to leg side **2** in football, a ball kicked, particularly from a corner, that curves through the air towards the goal

ϟ **int** *abbr* international organization (*in Internet addresses*)

int. *abbr* **1** (military) intelligence **2** intercept **3** interest **4** interim **5** interior **6** interjection **7** intermediate **8** internal **9 int., Int.** international **10** interpreter **11** intersection **12** interval **13** interview **14** intransitive

intact /in tákt/ *adj* **1 NOT DAMAGED** whole and undamaged ○ *Only two of the original plates remained intact.* **2 COMPLETE** without any missing parts or elements **3 WITHOUT ANY REMOVED PARTS** having all body parts in place and undamaged [15C. < Latin *intactus* 'untouched' < *tangere* 'to touch'.] —**intactly** *adv* —**intactness** *n*

intaglio /in táali ō, -tálli ō/ (*plural* **-glios** *or* **-gli** /in táal ee/) *n* **1 HOLLOWED-OUT DESIGN** a carving made by cutting a hollowed-out design into material such as stone **2 CARVING OF INTAGLIOS** the process or art of carving hollowed-out designs in material such as stone **3 CARVED GEM** a gem in which a hollowed-out design has been carved **4 PRINTING WITH INCISED PLATES** a printing technique in which the design is cut into the plate rather than protruding from it **5 INCISED PRINTING PLATE** a printing plate into which a design is cut or incised [Mid-17C. < Italian, < *intagliare* 'engrave' < *tagliare* 'to cut'.]

intake /ín tayk/ *n* **1 AMOUNT TAKEN IN** an amount taken in or consumed ○ *increase your intake of fluids* **2 PEOPLE TAKEN IN** the number of people admitted to a place or organization at a particular time or the people themselves ○ *The college has increased its intake of mature students.* **3 TAKING IN** the process of taking in some substance, especially by eating or drinking **4 OPENING THROUGH WHICH FLUID PASSES** an opening through which fluid enters a duct or contained area, e.g. that of a jet engine ○ *the fuel intake*

intangible /in tánjəb'l/ *adj* **1 NON-MATERIAL** without material qualities, and so not able to be touched or seen **2 HARD TO DESCRIBE** difficult to define or describe clearly, but nonetheless perceived ■ *n* **SOMETHING UNQUANTIFIABLE** an unquantifiable quality or asset ○ *such intangibles as duty* —**intangibility** /in tánjə bíllәti/ *n* —**intangibleness** *n* —**intangibly** *adv*

intangible asset *n* a business asset, e.g. a firm's customer goodwill, that is of value although it is not directly quantifiable in terms of goods produced or sold

intarsia /in táarssi ə/ *n* **1 WOOD INLAY** wood inlay using different colours of wood, common in the Italian Renaissance **2 MAKING OF INTARSIAS** the art or process of making intarsias, e.g. for wall panels **3 WAY OF KNITTING** knitting with two or more coloured yarns in which the new colour is introduced by twisting around the old, left hanging until it is needed again [Mid-19C. < German, alteration of Italian *intarsio* < Arabic *tarṣī*.]

integer /íntijər/ *n* **1** any positive or negative whole number or zero **2** a whole unit or entity (*technical*) [Early 16C. < Latin, 'complete, whole'.]

integral /íntigrəl, in téggrəl/ *adj* **1 NECESSARY OR CONSTITUENT** being an essential part of something or any of the parts that make up a whole ○ *Adequate funding is integral to the success of the venture.* ○ *Mealtimes are an integral part of family life.* **2 MADE UP OF PARTS** composed of parts that together make a whole **3 COMPLETE** without missing parts or elements **4 OF INTEGER** relating to an integer **5 RELATING TO INTEGRALS** relating to mathematical integrals or integration ■ *n* **1** = **definite integral 2** = **indefinite integral** [Mid-16C. < late Latin *integralis* < Latin *integer* 'whole'.] —**integrality** /ínti grállәti/ *n* —**integrally** *adv*

integral calculus *n* a branch of mathematics dealing with integrals and differential equations, used to determine areas, volumes, and lengths, and in many areas of applied mathematics

integrand /ínti grand/ *n* a mathematical function or equation to be integrated [Late 19C. < Latin *integrandus* 'to be integrated' < *integrare* 'integrate' < *integer* 'whole'.]

integrant /íntigrənt/ *adj* part of a whole (*formal*) ■ *n* an integral part of something (*formal*)

integrate /ínti grayt/ (**-grates, -grating, -grated**) *v* **1** *vti* **FIT IN WITH A GROUP** to become an accepted member of a group and its activities, or to help somebody do this **2** *vti* **MAKE INTO A WHOLE** to join two or more objects or make something part of a larger whole, or to become joined or combined in this way **3** *vt* **MAKE OPEN TO ALL** to make a group, community, place, or organization and its opportunities available to all, regardless of race, ethnic group, religion, gender, or social class **4** *vt* **FIND A MATHEMATICAL INTEGRAL** to find the definite or indefinite integral of a function or equation [Mid-17C. < Latin *integrat-* < *integrare* 'make whole' < *integer* 'whole'.] —**integrability** /íntigrə bíllәti/ *n* —**integrable** *adj* —**integrative** *adj*

integrated /ínti graytid/ *adj* **1 COMBINED OR COMPOSITE** made up of elements or parts that work well together ○ *an integrated transport system* **2 COMBINING DISSIMILAR THINGS** bringing together processes or functions that are normally separate **3 OPEN TO ALL PEOPLE** open to everyone, without restrictions based on race, ethnicity, religion, gender, or social class

ϟ **integrated circuit** *n* a tiny complex of electronic components contained on a thin chip or wafer of semiconducting material —**integrated circuitry** *n*

integration /ínti gráysh'n/ *n* **1 EQUAL ACCESS FOR ALL** the process of opening a group, community, place, or organization to all, regardless of race, ethnicity, religion, gender, or social class **2 ACCEPTANCE INTO A COMMUNITY** becoming an accepted member of a group or community **3 COMBINATION** a combination of parts or objects that work together well **4 MATHEMATICAL OPERATION** the mathematical process of finding the solution of a differential equation or a function whose differential equation is known **5 ORGANIZATION OF PERSONALITY TRAITS** the process of coordinating separate personality elements into a balanced whole or producing behaviour compatible with somebody's environment

integrationist /ínti gráysh'nist/ *n* a supporter or activist who works to promote and maintain integration ■ *adj* supporting or promoting racial integration

ϟ **integrator** /ínti graytər/ *n* **1** a computer component that performs numerical integration to solve differential equations **2** somebody or something that brings about integration

integrity /in téggrəti/ *n* **1 POSSESSION OF FIRM PRINCIPLES** the quality of possessing and steadfastly adhering to high moral principles or professional standards **2 COMPLETENESS** the state of being complete or undivided (*formal*) ○ *the territorial integrity of a nation.* **3 WHOLENESS** the state of being sound or undamaged (*formal*) ○ *Their refusal to participate in the experiment will undermine its integrity.* [15C. Via Old French < Latin *integritas* < *integer* 'whole'.]

integument /in téggyōōmənt/ *n* an outer protective layer or part of an animal or plant, e.g. a shell, rind, husk, or skin [Early 17C. < Latin *integumentum* < *integere* 'cover up' < *tegere* 'to cover'.] —**integumental** /in téggyōō mént'l/ *adj* —**integumentary** /in téggyōō méntəri/ *adj*

~~intelectual~~ incorrect spelling of **intellectual**

~~inteligence~~ incorrect spelling of **intelligence**

intellect /íntə lekt/ *n* **1** a person's ability to think, reason, and understand ○ *appeals to the intellect rather than the emotions* ○ *a highly developed intellect* **2** a very intelligent and knowledgeable person ○ *The commission called on some of our ablest intellects in its search for solutions.* [14C. Via Old French < Latin *intellect-* < *intellegere* (see INTELLIGENT).]

intellection /íntə léksh'n/ *n* (*formal*) **1** thinking, reasoning, or other mental activity **2** a thought or an idea —**intellective** *adj* —**intellectively** *adv*

intellectual /íntə lékchoo əl/ *adj* **1 RELATING TO THOUGHT PROCESS** relating to or involving the mental processes of abstract thinking and reasoning rather than the emotions **2 INTELLIGENT AND KNOWLEDGEABLE** having a highly developed ability to think, reason, and understand, especially in combination with wide knowledge **3 FOR INTELLIGENT PEOPLE** intended for, appealing to, or done by intelligent people ○ *intellectual pursuits* ■ *n* **INTELLIGENT PERSON** somebody with a highly developed ability to reason and understand, especially if also well educated and interested in the arts or sciences or enjoying activities involving serious mental effort [15C. Via Old French < late Latin *intellectualis* < *intellectus* 'intellect' < *intellegere* (see INTELLIGENT).] —**intellectuality** /íntə lekchoo állәti/ *n* —**intellectually** *adv* —**intellectualness** *n*

intellectualise *vti* = **intellectualize**

intellectualism /íntə lékchoo əlizəm/ *n* **1 EXERCISE OF POWER TO THINK** the development and use of the ability to think, reason, and understand **2 TOO MUCH ATTENTION TO THINKING** overemphasis on intellectual processes or pursuits **3 BELIEF THAT KNOWLEDGE COMES FROM REASONING** the doctrine that all that can truly be called knowledge is derived from reasoning —**intellectualist** *n* —**intellectualistic** /íntə lékchoo ə lístik/ *adj* —**intellectualistically** *adv*

intellectualize /íntə lékchoo ə līz/ (**-izes, -izing, -ized**), **intellectualise** (**-ises, -ising, -ised**) *v* **1** *vti* **CONSIDER SOMETHING RATIONALLY** to analyse, deal with, or explain something by thinking or reasoning exclusively **2** *vi* **THINK** to think or reason **3** *vti* **MAKE OR BECOME INTELLECTUAL** to make somebody or something intellectual or to become intellectual ○ *intellectualized poetry* **4** *vt* **REASON AWAY PROBLEMS** to protect yourself unconsciously from the emotional stress that would come from dealing with fears or problems by reasoning them away —**intellectualization** *n* —**intellectualizer** *n*

intellectual property *n* original creative work manifested in a tangible form that can be legally protected, e.g. by a patent, trademark, or copyright

intelligence /in téllijənss/ *n* **1 ABILITY TO THINK AND LEARN** the ability to learn facts and skills and apply them, especially when this ability is highly developed **2 SECRET INFORMATION** information about secret plans or activities, especially those of foreign governments, the armed forces, business enemies, or criminals **3 GATHERING OF SECRET INFORMATION** the collection of secret military or political information **4 PEOPLE GATHERING SECRET INFORMATION** an organization that gathers information about the secret plans or activities of an adversary or potential adversary and the people involved in gathering such information **5 INTELLIGENT SPIRIT** an entity capable of rational thought, especially one that does not have a physical form —**intelligential** /in télli jénsh'l/ *adj*

intelligence quotient *n* full form of **IQ**

intelligencer /in téllijənssər/ *n* a supplier or collector of information, especially about secret plans or activities (*archaic*)

⚡**intelligent** /in téllijənt/ *adj* **1 MENTALLY ABLE** having intelligence, especially to a highly developed degree **2 SENSIBLE OR RATIONAL** showing or resulting from an ability to think and understand things clearly and logically ○ *an intelligent solution* **3 ABLE TO STORE AND PROCESS DATA** with built-in electronic processing and data storage ability ○ *an intelligent terminal* **4 SELF-REGULATING** programmed to be able to adjust itself to changes in its environment and make deductions from information it processes [Early 16C. < Latin *intelligent-* < *intellegere* 'perceive, discern' < *inter-* 'between' + *legere* 'choose, read'.] —**intelligently** *adv*

SYNONYMS ***intelligent, bright, quick, smart, clever, able, gifted***

CORE MEANING: having the ability to learn and understand easily **intelligent** quick to learn and understand; **bright** showing an ability to think, learn, or respond quickly, especially used of younger people; **quick** alert, perceptive, and able to respond quickly; **smart** showing intelligence and mental alertness but sometimes suggesting insolent intelligence; **clever** having sharp mental abilities, sometimes suggesting showy or superficial cleverness; **able** capable or talented, also used in educational circles of children who are intelligent; **gifted** talented, especially artistically or creatively, also used in educational circles of children who are exceptionally intelligent.

intelligentsia /in télli jéntsi ə/ *n* the most intelligent, intellectual, or highly educated members of a society or community, especially those who are interested in the arts, literature, philosophy, and politics [Early 20C. Via Russian *intelligentsiya* < Latin *intelligentia* 'intelligence'.]

intelligible /in téllijəb'l/ *adj* **1** capable of being understood ○ *his ideas were barely intelligible* **2** perceptible only by the mind, not the senses [14C. Via Old French < Latin *intelligibilis* < *intellegere* (see INTELLIGENT).] —**intelligibility** /in téllijə bílləti/ *n* —**intelligibleness** *n* —**intelligibly** *adv*

Intelsat /ín tel sat/, **INTELSAT** *n* **1** an international organization whose membership includes the telecommunications agencies of most countries and that owns the communications satellites that orbit the Earth. Full form **International Telecommunication Satellite Organization 2** a telecommunications satellite launched by Intelsat

intemperate /in témpərət/ *adj* **1 DRINKING TO EXCESS** drinking too much alcohol, especially frequently **2 LACKING SELF-CONTROL** having or showing a lack of self-control, especially in expressing feelings or satisfying physical desires **3 TOO HOT OR COLD** extremely or unpleasantly hot or cold (*formal*) —**intemperance** *n* —**intemperately** *adv* —**intemperateness** *n*

intend /in ténd/ *v* **1** *vti* **MEAN TO DO** to have something in mind as a plan ○ *I really intended to write, but I didn't have time.* **2** *vt* **DO OR SAY FOR A PURPOSE** to do, say, or produce something with a particular purpose, use, target, or group of people in mind ○ *a dictionary intended for schoolchildren* **3** *vt* **MEAN** to signify or indicate something through speech or behaviour ○ *What impression did he intend to give us with such a remark?* [14C. Via Old French < Latin *intendere* < *in-* 'towards' + *tendere* 'to stretch'.]

intendant /in téndənt/ *n* an official or administrator in some countries, especially formerly in France, Spain, and Portugal, and currently in parts of Latin America [Mid-17C. Via Old French < Latin *intendent-* < *intendere* (see INTEND).] —**intendance** *n* —**intendancy** *n*

intended /in téndid/ *adj* **1 ENVISIONED** aimed at or designed for ○ *We were unable to reach our intended destination* **2 PLANNED** planned for the future **3 DELIBERATE** said or done deliberately ■ *n* **FUTURE HUSBAND OR WIFE** the person to whom somebody is engaged to be married (*dated or humorous*) ○ *He cherished the letter from his intended.* —**intendedly** *adv*

intending /in ténding/ *adj* planning to be or become something

intendment /in téndmənt/ *n* the meaning of something, especially a word or term, according to law

intens. *abbr* **1** intensifier **2** intensify **3** intensive

intense /in ténss/ *adj* **1 EXTREME** great, strong, or extreme in a way that can be felt ○ *intense heat* **2 EFFORTFUL OR ACTIVE** involving great effort or much activity ○ *showed intense dedication to the task* **3 CONCENTRATED** narrowly focused or concentrated ○ *an intense stare* **4 PASSIONATE** feeling or showing strong and deeply felt emotions in a serious way ○ *a very intense young student* [15C. Via Old French < Latin *intensus*, past participle of *intendere* (see INTEND).] —**intenseness** *n*

intensely /in ténssli/ *adv* **1 EXTREMELY** very much **2 STRONGLY** strongly or brightly ○ *intensely pink curtains* **3 PENETRATINGLY** in a fixed and penetrating way **4 PASSIONATELY** with great passion and enthusiasm

intensifier /in ténssi fī ər/ *n* **1** a word or phrase, e.g. 'definitely', 'quite', or 'hardly', that indicates the relative degree to which something applies, as in 'quite good' or 'hardly enough'. US term **intensive** *n.* **2** somebody or something that makes something larger, sharper, or stronger

intensify /in ténssi fī/ (**-fies, -fying, -fied**) *vti* **1** to make something greater or stronger, or to increase in strength or degree ○ *media interest intensified as the week progressed* **2** to do something with greater effort or more activity or to become more concentrated —**intensification** /in ténssifi káysh'n/ *n*

SYNONYMS See ***increase***.

intension /in ténsh'n/ *n* **1 MEANING OF EXPRESSION** the meaning of an expression as opposed to what it refers to **2 INTENSITY** intensity (*formal*) **3 INTENSIFICATION** intensification (*formal*) [Early 17C. < Latin *intension-* < *intendere* (see INTEND).] —**intensional** *adj* —**intensionally** *adv*

intensional object *n* a concept, property, or proposition as opposed to an individual, set, or truth value, which are the extensional counterparts of intensional objects

intensity /in ténssəti/ (*plural* **-ties**) *n* **1 QUALITY OF BEING INTENSE** the strength, power, force, or concentration of something ○ *The pain increased in intensity.* **2 INTENSE MANNER** a passionate and serious attitude or quality ○ *a rare emotional intensity in her work* **3 MAGNITUDE OF ENERGY** the strength of a source of energy, e.g. light, electricity, or sound, per unit area, mass, or time

intensive /in ténssiv/ *adj* **1 CONCENTRATED** involving concentrated effort, usually in order to achieve something in a comparatively short time ○ *an intensive course in German* **2 INCREASING PRODUCTION** relating to a form of agriculture in which scientific and technological methods, e.g. the use of chemicals that boost growth or crop yields, are used to increase productivity **3 MAKING HEAVY USE OF** requiring or using a great deal of a particular thing (*often in combination*) ○ *capital-intensive* **4 INDICATING HOW MUCH** describes a word or phrase, e.g. 'extremely', that emphasizes or intensifies the word that it modifies ■ *n* GRAM = **intensifier** *n.* 1 —**intensively** *adv* —**intensiveness** *n*

intensive care *n* the monitoring, care, and treatment of patients who are critically ill or critically injured, or the part of a hospital where this care takes place ○ *One of the survivors is still in intensive care.*

intensive care unit *n* a department of a hospital that is designed and equipped for the monitoring, care, and treatment of critically ill or critically injured patients

intent /in tént/ *n* **1 PLAN OR PURPOSE** something planned or the purpose that accompanies a plan ○ *'My intent is to use our attractive domestic market as the basis of a muscular free trade policy that will strengthen America's global economic reach...'* (National Public Telecomputing Network, *George H. W. Bush speeches in campaign '92*; 1992) **2 STATE OF MIND** somebody's state of mind when deliberately committing or planning to commit an illegal act **3 CONNOTATION** the meaning or significance of something, especially when not explicitly expressed ■ *adj* **1 WITH FIXED ATTENTION** with full attention or effort concentrated or focused on one thing ○ *Intent on her work, she lost track of the time.* **2 DETERMINED** showing great determination to do something ○ *They are intent on catching the early train.* [13C. < Old French *entent* < Latin *intendere* (see INTEND).] —**intently** *adv* —**intentness** *n* ◇ **to all intents and purposes** in effect the same, although not actually the same

intention /in ténsh'n/ *n* **1 AIM OR OBJECTIVE** something that somebody plans to do or achieve ○ *State your intentions.* **2 QUALITY OF PURPOSEFULNESS** the quality or state of having a purpose in mind ○ *She acted without intention.* ■ **intentions** *npl* **SOMEBODY'S MARRIAGE PLANS** somebody's plans with respect to marriage (*dated*) ○ *What are your intentions towards my daughter?* [14C. Via Old French < Latin *intention-* < *intendere* (see INTEND).]

intentional /in ténsh'nəl/ *adj* **1** done on purpose, not by accident **2** involving thoughts, e.g. beliefs or desires, about different kinds of objects, including those that have no actual existence —**intentionality** /in ténshə nálləti/ *n* —**intentionally** *adv*

inter /in túr/ (**-ters, -terring, -terred**) *vt* to bury the remains of a corpse in a grave or tomb [15C. < Old French *enterer* < IN + Latin *terra* 'earth'.]

inter- *prefix* **1** between, among ○ *interlinear* ○ *interstate* ○ *intercut* **2** mutual, reciprocal ○ *interchange* **3** involving two or more groups ○ *international* [Directly and via Old French *entre* < Latin *inter* 'between, among' < Indo-European, 'more in']

interabang *n* PRINTING = **interrobang**

interact /intər ákt/ *vi* **1** to have an effect on something else or one another **2** to be or become involved in communication, social activity, or work with somebody else or one another —**interactant** *n*

interaction /intər áksh'n/ *n* **1 COMMUNICATION OR COLLABORATION** communication between or joint activity involving two or more people **2 RECIPROCAL ACTION** the combined or reciprocal action of two or more things that have an effect on each other and work together **3 FORCE BETWEEN ELEMENTARY PARTICLES** any of the four fundamental forces acting between elementary particles, namely gravitational, electromagnetic, strong, and weak —**interactional** *adj*

interactionism /intər áksh'nizəm/ *n* in Western metaphysics, the theory that the mind and the body act on each other

⚡**interactive** /intər áktiv/ *adj* **1 COMMUNICATING OR COLLABORATING** involving the communication or collaboration of people or things **2 WITH USER-MACHINE COMMUNICATION** allowing or involving the exchange of information or instructions between a person and a machine such as a computer or a television **3 OPERATOR-CONTROLLED** operating on instructions entered by somebody at a keyboard or other input device —**interactively** *adv* —**interactivity** /intər aktívvitee/ *n*

interagency /intər áyjənssi/ *adj* involving two or more agencies, especially government agencies ○ *an interagency initiative*

inter alia /íntər áyli ə, -áali-, -álli-/ *adv* among other things ○ *budget funds for two new schools inter alia* [< Latin]

inter alios /íntər áyli ōss, -áali-, -álli-/ *adv* among other people [< Latin]

interallied /intər állīd/ *adj* involving the combined or mutual action of allies, especially in a war

interbank /intər bángk/ *adj* between, connecting, or involving two or more banks

interbreed /intər bréed/ (**-breeds, -breeding, -bred** /-bréd/, **-bred**) *vti* **1** to produce offspring by mating with a member of a different breed or species, or to mate an animal of one species or variety with one of another **2** to breed or make something breed within a closed population or narrow range of types

interbroker dealer /intər brṓkər-/ *n* a broker whose job is to make stock exchange dealings between other brokers easier

intercalary /in túrkələri/ *adj* **1 INSERTED INTO CALENDAR** added to the calendar year to keep calendar years concurrent with solar years **2 INDICATING YEAR WITH ADDITION** describes a year to which an intercalary day or month has been added **3 INSERTED OR INTRODUCED** inserted between other parts (*formal*) [Early 17C. < Latin *intercalarius* < *intercalare* (see INTERCALATE).]

intercalate /in túrkə layt/ (**-lates, -lating, -lated**) *v* **1** *vt* to insert an extra day or month into a calendar year to keep it consistent with the solar year **2** *vti* to place something into something else, inserting it between other elements, or to be placed between other elements (*formal*) [Early 17C. < Latin *intercalat-* < *intercalare* < *calare* 'proclaim'.] —**intercalation** /in túrkə láysh'n/ *n* —**intercalative** *adj*

intercaste /íntər kaást/ *adj S Asia* across caste boundaries

intercede /íntər seéd/ (**-cedes, -ceding, -ceded**) *vi* **1 PLEAD FOR** to plead with somebody in authority on behalf of somebody else, especially somebody who is to be punished **2 SPEAK FOR** to speak in support of somebody involved in a dispute **3 MEDIATE IN DISPUTE** to attempt to settle a dispute between other people [Late 16C. < Latin *intercedere* < *cedere* 'give way'.] —**interceder** *n*

intercellular /íntər séllyoòlər/ *adj* existing between cells ○ *an intercellular substance*

intercept /íntər sépt/ *v* **1** *vti* **INTERRUPT PROGRESS** to prevent people or objects from reaching their destination or target by stopping, diverting, or seizing them ○ *The contraband was intercepted by police at the dock.* **2** *vt* **GET THE BALL** in sports, to gain possession of a ball intended for an opponent **3** *vt* **MARK EXTENT** to include part of a curve, surface, or solid between two points or lines ■ *n* **1 DISTANCE BETWEEN THE ORIGIN AND AXIS CROSSING** the distance from the origin of a coordinate system to the point where a curve or surface crosses an axis **2 ACT OF INTERCEPTING** the intercepting of something, especially a radio transmission, a missile, or an aircraft **3 DIFFERENCE BETWEEN CALCULATED AND OBSERVED ALTITUDE** the difference between the calculated and observed altitude of a celestial object [15C. < Latin *intercept-* < *intercipere* < *capere* 'seize'.] —**interceptive** *adj*

intercepter *n* = interceptor

interception /íntər sépsh'n/ *n* **1** the act or an instance of intercepting somebody or something **2** something intercepted, especially a passed ball that is intercepted by an opponent while it is in the air

interceptor /íntər séptər/, **intercepter** *n* **1 FAST FIGHTER PLANE** a fast, very manoeuvrable fighter plane designed to intercept enemy aircraft **2 GUIDED MISSILE** a guided missile designed to intercept enemy missiles or spacecraft **3 ONE THAT INTERCEPTS** somebody or something that intercepts

intercession /íntər sésh'n/ *n* **1 INTERCEDING** the action of pleading on somebody's behalf **2 TRYING TO RESOLVE CONFLICT** the action of attempting to settle a dispute **3 PRAYER OR PETITION** prayer to God, a god, or a saint on behalf of somebody or something [15C. Via Old French < Latin *intercession-* < *intercedere* (see INTERCEDE).] —**intercessional** *adj* —**intercessor** /íntər séssər, -sessər/ *n* —**intercessorial** /íntərssə sáwri əl/ *adj* —**intercessory** *adj*

interchange *v* /íntər cháynj/ (**-changes, -changing, -changed**) **1** *vti* **SWITCH OR SWAP PLACES** to put each of two things in the place of the other or to change places with something else **2** *vti* **ALTERNATE OR FOLLOW EACH OTHER** to arrange things alternately in a series or to be arranged in this way **3** *vt* **EXCHANGE THINGS** to give something to somebody and receive a similar thing from them in return ■ *n* /íntər chaynj/ **1 EXCHANGE OF THINGS** an exchange of things, especially ideas, opinions, or information **2 ALTERNATION** the action of alternating or changing places **3 ROAD INTERSECTION** a major road junction where vehicles can, by means of slip roads, bridges, and underpasses, change from one road to another without stopping or crossing other traffic [14C. < Old French *entrechangier*.] —**interchanger** *n*

interchangeable /íntər cháynjəb'l/ *adj* capable of being switched, exchanged, or used in place of another or each other —**interchangeability** /íntər chaynjə bílləti/ *n* —**interchangeably** *adv*

⚡ **interchange control** *n* a function of electronic data interchange management software ensuring that all financial transactions sent are also received

interchange fee *n* a fee paid by an acquiring bank to an issuing bank as compensation for the time elapsed before the cardholder makes payment

intercity /íntər sítti/ *adj* involving, connecting, or occurring between two or more cities

intercoastal /íntər kóst'l/ *adj* connecting or occurring between ports on different coasts or two or more coastlines

intercollegiate /íntərkə leéjət/ *adj* involving or occurring between the members of two or more colleges or universities ○ *intercollegiate sports*

intercolumniation /íntərkə lúmni áysh'n/ *n* a system used to space columns in a colonnade, based on the use of their diameters as a measurement

intercom /íntər kom/ *n* a system or device for transmitting sound from one part of a building, aircraft, or ship to another [Mid-20C. Shortening of *intercommunication system*.]

intercommunal /íntərkə myoón'l/ *adj* existing or occurring between the members of two or more communities

intercommunicate /íntərkə myoóni kayt/ (**-cates, -cating, -cated**) *vi* **1** to communicate with each other **2** to be connected to something else or each other, especially to another room by means of a door in the dividing wall ○ *intercommunicating hotel rooms* —**intercommunication** /-myoóni káysh'n/ *n* —**intercommunicative** *adj* —**intercommunicator** *n*

intercommunion /íntərkə myoónyən/ *n* **1** an arrangement between different Christian denominations enabling members to receive the Communion at each other's services **2** a close association or relationship between people or groups, especially one that involves mutual participation or action

interconnect /íntərkə nékt/ *vti* **1** to be joined to something else or to a number of joined things, or to make something part of such a network (*often passive*) ○ *The rooms are interconnected to form a suite.* **2** to show a relationship between two or more things, or to be related —**interconnection** *n*

interconnective /íntərkə néktiv/ *adj* connecting or capable of connecting with something else or with each other —**interconnectivity** /íntərkə nék tívvəti/ *n*

intercontinental /íntər konti nént'l/ *adj* **1** involving or occurring between two or more continents **2** going from one continent to another —**intercontinentally** *adv*

intercontinental ballistic missile *n* a ballistic missile with a range of 3,000 to 8,000 nautical miles. ◊ **intermediate-range ballistic missile**

interconversion /íntərkən vúrsh'n/ *n* the conversion of two or more things, e.g. chemicals, into one another —**interconvert** *vt* —**interconvertibility** /íntərkən vurtə bílləti/ *n* —**interconvertible** *adj*

intercooler /íntər koolər/ *n* a heat exchanger that cools a fluid between successive stages of compression or chemical reaction

intercostal /íntər kóst'l/ *adj* situated or occurring between the ribs ○ *an intercostal nerve* [Late 16C. < Latin *costa* 'side, rib'.]

intercourse /íntər kawrss/ *n* **1** = sexual intercourse **2** communication or exchanges between people or groups, especially conversation or social activity [15C. Via Old French *entrecours* 'commerce' < Latin *intercursus* 'running between' < *currere* 'to run'.]

intercrop /íntər króp, -krop/ (**-crops, -cropping, -cropped**) *vti* to grow different crops in the same field, usually in alternate rows, or to plant a crop between the rows of another crop —**intercrop** /íntər krop/ *n*

intercultural /íntər kúlchərəl/ *adj* involving or occurring between different cultures or between people with different cultural backgrounds —**interculturally** *adv*

intercurrent /íntər kúrrənt/ *adj* **1** occurring during and changing the course of an already existing disease ○ *treating an intercurrent infection* **2** occurring at the same time as something else or during the period between two other events (*formal*) [Early 17C. < Latin *intercurrent-* < *intercurrere* 'run between' < *currere* 'to run'.] —**intercurrence** *n* —**intercurrently** *adv*

intercut /íntər kút/ (**-cuts, -cutting, -cut**) *vt* to alternate scenes or shots of a film or insert one scene into another during the editing process, usually to show different events taking place at the same time

interdenominational /íntər di nommi náysh'nəl/ *adj* involving, occurring between, or open to people from different religious groups

interdental /íntər dént'l/ *adj* **1 BETWEEN THE TEETH** existing between or designed for use between the teeth **2 WITH THE TONGUE BETWEEN THE TEETH** made by placing the tip of the tongue between the teeth ■ *n* **SOUND MADE WITH TONGUE BETWEEN TEETH** a sound made by putting the tip of the tongue between the teeth —**interdentally** *adv*

interdepartmental /íntər dee paart mént'l/ *adj* involving or occurring between different departments of the same organization or the people who work in them —**interdepartmentally** *adv*

interdependent /íntardi péndənt/ *adj* **1** unable to exist or survive without each other ○ *interdependent organisms* **2** relying on mutual assistance, support, cooperation, or interaction among constituent elements or members —**interdepend** *vi* —**interdependence** *n* —**interdependently** *adv*

interdict *n* /íntər dikt/ **1 PROHIBITIVE ORDER** a court order that prohibits something **2** *Scotland* **COURT ORDER BANNING SOMETHING TEMPORARILY** a court order that bans some action that has been complained of as being against the law until the matter is tried in the proper court **3 EXCLUSION FROM CHURCH SACRAMENTS** a ban imposed by a pope, church council, or bishop that excludes a person, group, or nation from the sacraments of the Roman Catholic Church ■ *vt* /íntər díkt/ **1 BAN BY LAW** to prohibit something or forbid somebody from doing something, especially in accordance with civil or ecclesiastical law **2** *US* **PREVENT ILLEGAL ENTRY** to prevent somebody or something entering a country illegally ○ *Patrols will be increased along the border to interdict smugglers.* **3 PREVENT ENEMY USE** to keep an enemy from using an area by troop movements or other means [13C. Via Old French *entredit* < Latin *interdictum* < *interdicere* 'prohibit' < *dicere* 'speak'.] —**interdiction** /íntər díksh'n/ *n* —**interdictor** *n* —**interdictory** *adj*

interdigital /íntər díjjit'l/ *adj* in the form of two series of parallel strips that fit together like the fingers of clasped hands —**interdigitally** *adv*

interdigitate /íntər díjji tayt/ (**-tates, -tating, -tated**) *vti* to fit together like the fingers of clasped hands or to place or hold objects together in such a pattern —**interdigitation** /íntər díjji táysh'n/ *n*

interdine /íntər dín/ *vi S Asia* to eat a meal with a person belonging to a different religion or caste

interdisciplinary /íntər díssiplinəri, -dissi plínnəri/ *adj* involving two or more academic subjects or fields of study

interest /íntrəst/ *n* **1 CURIOSITY OR CONCERN** a feeling of curiosity or concern about something that makes the attention turn towards it ○ *an interest in art* **2 QUALITY THAT ATTRACTS ATTENTION** a power, quality, or aspect of something that attracts attention, concern, or curiosity ○ *It's of no interest to me.* **3 ENJOYABLE THING** something that somebody enjoys doing (*often plural*) ○ *My leisure interests include sailing, music, reading, and walking.* **4 BENEFIT OR ADVANTAGE** the good, benefit, or advantage of somebody or something ○ *in the interests of peace* **5 INVOLVEMENT** somebody's involvement with something that makes its progress or success important to him or her ○ *took a personal interest in the progress of the project* **6 BORROWING CHARGE OR PAYMENT FOR MONEY USE** a charge made for a loan or credit facility, or a payment made by a bank or other financial institution for the use of money deposited in an account **7 SHARE** a legal right to claim a share in something, especially in a business or property, or the business or property itself **8 CONNECTION** a personal or commercial connection with something or somebody, especially when this prevents somebody from being objective or impartial ○ *had to declare a conflict of interest* ■ **interests** *npl* **INFLUENTIAL GROUP** a group of people in business or society who have the same aims or support the same cause, especially a powerful or influential group ■ *vt* **1 GET SOMEBODY'S ATTENTION** to attract or hold somebody's attention or arouse somebody's curiosity or concern ○ *It may interest you to know that the building used to be a mortuary.* **2 MAKE SOMEBODY WANT SOMETHING** to make somebody want to have or buy something, do something, or become involved with something ○ *I tried to interest him in helping with the preparations.* [15C. Via Old French < Latin, 'it matters' < *interesse* 'be in the middle' < *esse* 'be'.]

interested /íntrəstid/ *adj* **1 CURIOUS OR CONCERNED** paying attention to something or devoting time to something because of curiosity, concern, or enjoyment **2 WANTING** involved or wanting to be involved in something ○ *interested parties can call the free number* **3 AFFECTED OR INVOLVED** having a legal right or share in something or a personal or commercial connection with something —**interestedly** *adv* —**interestedness** *n*

interest group *n* **1** an occupational group such as a business organization, trade union, or professional association that is concerned mainly with the economic interests of its members **2** a group of people who share an interest in something such as a subject of study

interesting /íntrəsting/ *adj* **1** arousing curiosity, attracting or holding attention, or provoking thought **2** enjoyable because of being varied, challenging, stimulating, or exciting —**interestingly** /íntrəstingli/ *adv*

⚡**interface** /íntər fayss/ *n* **1 COMMON BOUNDARY** the surface, place, or point where two things touch each other or meet **2 BOUNDARY BETWEEN THINGS** a common boundary between objects or different phases of a substance ○ *an oil-water interface* **3 POINT OF INTERACTION** the place, situation, or way in which two things or people act together or affect each other or the point of connection between things **4 BOUNDARY ACROSS WHICH DATA PASSES** a common boundary shared by two devices, or by a person and a device, across which data or information flows, e.g. the screen of a computer **5 LINKING SOFTWARE** software that links a computer with another device, or the set of commands, messages, images, and other elements allowing communication between computer and operator **6 LINKING DEVICE** an electronic device or circuit or other point of contact between two pieces of equipment ■ *vti* (**-faces, -facing, -faced**) **1 HAVE OR GIVE COMMON BOUNDARY** to touch or meet at a surface, place, or point, or to make things join in this way **2 INTERACT** to act together or affect each other or to make things or people interact **3 SERVE AS INTERFACE** to connect or serve as an interface for two or more pieces of equipment —**interfacial** /íntər fáysh'l/ *adj* —**interfacially** *adv*

interfacing /íntər fayssing/ *n* a fabric that is used to stiffen or support collars, cuffs, or other parts of a garment

interfaith /íntər fáyth/ *adj* involving or occurring between people of different religious faiths

~~**interferance**~~ incorrect spelling of **interference**

interfere /íntər féer/ (**-feres, -fering, -fered**) *vi* **1 MEDDLE IN OTHERS' AFFAIRS** to participate in the affairs of others, especially by offering unwanted or unhelpful advice or by trying to resolve others' disputes ○ *It's not advisable to interfere in a private quarrel.* **2 HAVE UNDESIRABLE EFFECT** to delay, hinder, or obstruct the natural or desired course of something ○ *The weather interfered with our plans.* **3 CAUSE INTERFERENCE** to cause electronic interference **4 AFFECT DISPLACEMENT OR AMPLITUDE** to act together to increase, decrease, or cancel out displacement or amplitude **5 HIT HOOF AGAINST LEG** to hit one hoof against the opposite hoof or leg while walking (*refers to horses*) **6 TOUCH ILLICITLY** to touch somebody sexually in a way contrary to law or moral standards (*used euphemistically*) [15C. < Old French *s'entreferir* 'strike each other' < Latin *ferire* 'to strike'.] —**interferer** *n*

interference /íntər féeranss/ *n* **1 MEDDLING IN OTHERS' AFFAIRS** involvement in something without any invitation or justification ○ *He deeply resented any interference in his private life.* **2 HINDRANCE** hindrance or obstruction that prevents a natural or desired outcome **3 SIGNAL THAT INTERFERES** an unwanted signal that disrupts radio, telephone, or television reception **4 PROCESS OF WAVE INTERACTION** a process in light-wave transmission in which two or more waves are superimposed in such a way that they produce higher peaks, lower troughs, or a new wave pattern **5 LEGAL BLOCKING** in American football, the legal blocking of defensive players to protect and make way for the player carrying the ball —**interferential** /íntərfə rénsh'l/ *adj* ◇ **run interference 1** to carry out legal blocking of defensive players to protect and make way for the player carrying the ball **2** *US* to contribute help or support to somebody or something, especially by preventing others from acting as a hindrance (*informal*)

interfering /íntər féering/ *adj* deliberately becoming involved in other people's affairs in a way that is not needed and is unwelcome —**interferingly** *adv*

interferometer /íntərfə rómmitər/ *n* a device that uses an interference pattern to determine wave frequency, length, or velocity —**interferometric** /íntər feera méttrik/ *adj* —**interferometrically** *adv* —**interferometry** *n*

interferon /íntər féer on/ *n* a protein produced by cells in response to a virus that inhibits viral replication [Mid-20C. < INTERFERE + -ON.]

interfertile /íntər fúr tīl/ *adj* able to interbreed with other species or subspecies and produce viable offspring —**interfertility** /íntərfər tílləti/ *n*

interfile /íntər fíl/ (**-files, -filing, -filed**) *vt* to put an item or items among similar items in a file

interflow /íntər fló/ *vi* to merge into a single stream

interfluent /íntər flóo ənt/ *adj* **1** merging into a single stream **2** flowing between things or places [Mid-17C. < Latin *interfluent-*, present participle of *interfluere* 'flow together' < *fluere* 'to flow'.]

interfluve /íntər floov/ *n* **1** the ridge line separating two river catchments **2** a line joining points on one side of which water will flow to one river whilst on the other side water will flow to another river [Early 20C. Back-formation < *interfluvial*.] —**interfluvial** /íntər flóovi əl/ *adj*

interfold /íntər fóld/ *vt* to fold two or more things together

interfuse /íntər fyóoz/ (**-fuses, -fusing, -fused**) *vti* to mingle, blend, or fuse thoroughly, or to mix two or more things in this way [Late 16C. < Latin *interfus-* < *interfundere* 'pour together' < *fundere* 'pour'.] —**interfusion** *n*

intergalactic /íntərgə láktik/ *adj* situated, happening, or moving between galaxies, or involving two or more galaxies —**intergalactically** *adv*

intergenerational /íntər jennə ráysh'nəl/ *adj* occurring between, involving, or affecting people of two or more generations

interglacial /íntər gláysi əl, -gláysh'l/ *n* a period of warmer climate separating two periods of glaciation and displaying a characteristic sequence of changes in vegetation. —**interglacial** *adj*

intergovernmental /íntər guvvərn mént'l, -guvvər-/ *adj* involving representatives of or concerning relations between two or more governments —**intergovernmentally** *adv*

intergrade *vi* /íntər gráyd/ (**-grades, -grading, -graded**) **CHANGE BY STAGES** to be transformed from one form to another through a series of stages or forms that involve partial transitions ■ *n* /íntər grayd/ **1 TRANSITIONAL FORM** a transitional form or stage **2 TRANSITIONAL SOIL HORIZON** a transitional soil horizon between two distinctive soils —**intergradation** /íntər gray dáysh'n/ *n* —**intergradient** *adj*

intergroup /íntər gróop/ *adj* involving or concerned with relations between members of two or more racial or social groups

intergrowth /íntər grōth/ *n* growth of one thing into or within another thing, or among other things, or the result of such growth

interim /íntərim/ *adj* **1 HAVING TEMPORARY EFFECT** serving as a temporary measure until something more complete and permanent can be established **2 HOLDING TEMPORARY OFFICE** serving temporarily until a permanent replacement can be elected or appointed ■ *n* **INTERVENING TIME** a period of time between two occurrences or periods ○ *in the interim* [Mid-16C. < Latin, 'meanwhile'.]

interim dividend *n* a dividend paid by a company before the end of its financial year

interionic /íntər ī ónnik/ *adj* situated between or involving two or more ions

interior /in téeri ər/ *n* **1 INSIDE PART** the inside of something ○ *The interior of the church was dark.* **2 INSIDE OF BUILDING OR ROOM** the inside of a building or room considered especially with regard to its decoration and furnishing **3 PART FARTHEST IN FROM EDGE** the part of something that is far or farthest from its edge, boundary, or surface, especially the part of a country or continent that is remote or farthest from the coast **4 PICTURE OF INSIDE OF ROOM** a painting or photograph of the inside of a room **5 INSIDE SET OR SCENE** a setting or actual location that represents the inside of a building, or a scene filmed inside a building ■ *adj* **1 LOCATED INSIDE** located in, suitable for, or occurring inside something **2 CENTRAL** remote or farthest from the edge, boundary, or surface of something, especially from the coast of a country or continent **3 OCCURRING IN THE MIND** taking place within somebody's mind and usually not expressed out loud [15C. Directly or via French *intérieur* < Latin *interior* 'more in the midst of' < *inter* (see INTER-).] —**interiority** /in téeri órrəti/ *n* —**interiorly** *adv*

Interior *n* in the United States and some other countries, the internal affairs of the nation, especially as opposed to its foreign affairs ■ *adj* relating to the internal affairs of a country, especially as opposed to its foreign affairs

interior angle *n* **1** the angle formed between two adjacent sides of a polygon and lying in its interior **2** any of the four angles formed in the area between two lines by a third line that intersects them (**transversal**)

interior decoration *n* **1** = **interior design 2** the way that a room or building is decorated and furnished **3** the skill or trade of somebody who specializes in wallpapering and painting interiors —**interior decorator** *n*

interior design *n* the art or process of planning the decoration and furnishings of a room or building. US term **interior decoration** —**interior designer** *n*

interiorize /in téeri ə rīz/ (**-izes, -izing, -ized**), **interiorise** (**-ises, -ising, -ised**) *vt* PSYCHOL = **internalize** —**interiorization** /in téeri ə rī záysh'n/ *n*

interior monologue *n* an extended passage in a story or novel that expresses what a character is thinking and feeling. ◊ **stream of consciousness, soliloquy**

interior-sprung *adj* having many helical springs inside a thick padded cover. US term **innerspring**

inter-island /íntər-/ *adj* occurring between islands, or involving two or more islands

interj. *abbr* interjection

interject /íntər jékt/ *vti* to say or insert something in a way that interrupts what is being said or discussed [Late 16C. < Latin *interject-*, past participle of *interjicere* 'interpose', literally 'throw between' < *jacere* 'to throw'.] —**interjector** *n* —**interjectory** *adj*

interjection /íntər jéksh'n/ *n* **1** a sound, word, or phrase that expresses a strong emotion such as pain or surprise but otherwise has no meaning **2** something said loudly and abruptly or inserted in a text, especially something that interrupts what is being said or discussed —**interjectional** *adj* —**interjectionally** *adv*

interkinesis /íntərki néessis, -kī-/ *n* the period of rest between meiotic cell divisions, similar to the interphase stage in mitosis

interlace /íntər láyss/ (**-laces, -lacing, -laced**) *v* **1** *vti* to join together or interweave, often in an intricate pattern, by crossing over each other, or to cause two or more things to do this **2** *vt* to break up the flow or relieve the monotony of something by occasionally inserting something different such as jokes in a serious talk [14C. < Old French *entrelacier* 'lace together' < *lacier* 'to lace'.] —**interlacement** *n*

⚡**interlaced** /íntər láyst/ *adj* refreshing the image on a monitor screen by scanning first all odd and then all even numbered lines

⚡**interlaced scanning** *n* a technique used in television and computer monitors in which high vertical resolution is achieved by scanning all odd and then all even numbered lines

interlanguage /íntər lángwidj/ *n* a form of language produced by learners of a second language or foreign language, combining elements of two or more languages

interlard /íntər laárd/ *vt* to vary, punctuate, or interrupt speech or writing by interspersing other contrasting words or remarks [Mid-16C. < French *entrelarder* 'mix with layers of fat' < *larde* 'lard'.]

interlay /íntər láy/ *vt* (**-lays, -laying, -laid** /-láyd/, **-laid**) to lay or layer something between something else ■ *n* something laid between two surfaces

interleaf /íntər leef/ (*plural* **-leaves** /-leevz/) *n* an extra sheet or page, usually a blank one, inserted into a book

interleave /íntər léev/ (**-leaves, -leaving, -leaved**) *vt* to add extra sheets or pages, usually blank ones, between the pages of a book, e.g. to allow for notes or to protect illustrations [Mid-17C. < INTER- + LEAF.]

interleukin /íntər lóokin/ *n* a chemical found in white blood cells that stimulates them to fight infection [Late 20C. < INTER- + LEUCOCYTE + -IN.]

interleukin-1 /íntər lookin-/ *n* an interleukin that stimulates the production of other factors that activate the immune system

interleukin-2 /íntər lookin-/ *n* an interleukin that stimulates T-cells

interlibrary loan /íntər lībrəri-/ *n* **1 BOOK-BORROWING SYSTEM** a system by which libraries and library users can borrow books from other libraries **2 BORROWING OF A BOOK** a borrowing of a book through an interlibrary loan system **3 BOOK BORROWED** a book borrowed through an interlibrary loan system

interline[1] /íntər līn/ (**-lines, -lining, -lined**) *vt* to write or print words between the lines of writing or printing in a text or document [15C. < medieval Latin *interlineare* <

Latin *linea* (see LINE[1]).] —**interlineation** /íntər línni áysh'n/ *n*

interline[2] /íntər lín/ (**-lines, -lining, -lined**) *vt* to put an extra lining between the fabric and the lining of a curtain or piece of clothing [15C. < INTER- + LINE[2].]

interlinear /íntər línni ər/, **interlineal** /-línni əl/ *adj* **1** inserted between the lines of a text or document **2** written or printed with different versions of the same text on alternate or succeeding lines [14C. < medieval Latin *interlinearis* < Latin *linea* (see LINE[1]).] —**interlinearly** *adv*

interlining /íntər līning/ *n* an extra lining inserted between the fabric and lining of a curtain or piece of clothing to make it thicker or warmer, or the fabric used for this

interlink /íntər língk/ *vti* to connect something with something else in several ways, or to be connected together in several ways

interlock *vti* /íntər lók/ **1 FIT TOGETHER CLOSELY** to fit or fasten two or more things together closely and firmly, especially by means of parts that mesh, hook, or dovetail together, or to be fitted together in this way **2 OPERATE AS UNIT** to connect together as parts in such a way that all must move or operate if one does, or to be connected in this way ■ *n* /íntər lok/ **1 CONNECTING AND COORDINATING DEVICE** a device or mechanism that connects different parts or components of something such as a piece of machinery in order to coordinate and synchronize their action **2 CLOSE CONNECTION** a close connection by means of parts that fit or fasten together closely and firmly **3 TIGHTLY-KNITTED FABRIC** a fabric made with tightly-knitted stitches **4 CANVAS FOR NEEDLEPOINT** canvas used for needlepoint that has the warp and weft threads knotted together to prevent movement **5 COMPUTER SECURITY DEVICE** a security device such as a password system designed to prevent unauthorized use of a computer ■ *adj* **TIGHTLY-KNITTED** knitted with close, tight stitches

interlocking directorates *npl* boards of directors that have enough members in common to place the companies that they oversee under the same control

interlocution /íntərlō kyoōsh'n/ *n* a discussion or conversation involving two or more people (*formal*) [Mid-16C. < Latin *interlocution-* < *interlocut-*, past participle of *interloqui* 'interrupt', literally 'speak between' < *loqui* 'speak'.]

interlocutor /íntər lókyōōtər/ *n* **1** a participant in a discussion or conversation (*formal*) **2** a performer in a minstrel show who acted as the presenter and stood in the middle and bantered with the end men [Early 16C. < modern Latin, < Latin *interlocut-* (see INTERLOCUTION).]

interlocutory /íntər lókyōōtəri/ *adj* **1** involving or characteristic of conversation or discussion (*formal*) **2** issued provisionally during a lawsuit

interloper /íntər lōpər/ *n* **1** an intruder into a place, group, or gathering **2** an interferer in other people's affairs, especially a selfish one [Late 16C. After *landloper* 'vagabond' < Middle Dutch *landlooper* 'land-runner' < *loopen* 'to run'.] —**interlope** *vi*

interlude /íntər lood/ *n* **1** a relatively short period of time between two longer periods, during which something happens that is different from what has happened before and what follows **2** a short play, piece of music, or other entertainment performed during a break in the performance of a long work [14C. < medieval Latin *interludium* 'in-between-play' (because originally performed between the acts of a medieval mystery play) < Latin *ludus* 'play'.]

intermarriage /íntər márrij/ *n* **1** marriage between members of different religious, social, or racial groups, or an instance of this **2** marriage between people who belong to the same religious, social, or racial group, or an instance of this

intermarry /íntər márri/ (**-ries, -rying, -ried**) *vi* **1** to marry a member of a different religious, social, or racial group **2** to marry within a religious, social, or racial group

intermediary /íntər meédi əri/ *n* (*plural* **-ies**) **1 GO-BETWEEN** somebody who carries messages between persons or groups, or tries to help them reach an agreement **2 MEANS OR MEDIUM** something that functions as a means or medium for bringing something about ■ *adj* **1 MEDIATING** acting as a messenger or mediator between two or more people or groups **2 LYING IN BETWEEN** lying or occurring between two different forms, states, points, or extremes [Late 18C. < French *intermédiaire* < Latin *intermedius* (see INTERMEDIATE[1]).]

intermediate[1] /íntər meédi ət/ *adj* **1 BEING IN BETWEEN** lying or occurring between two different forms, states, points, or extremes ○ *an intermediate course* **2 CONTAINING BETWEEN 55% AND 66% SILICA** describes an igneous rock with a silica content of between 55 per cent and 66 per cent ■ *n* **1 SOMETHING BETWEEN TWO OTHER THINGS** something that lies or occurs between two different forms, states, points, or extremes **2 CHEMICAL FOR FURTHER REACTIONS** a chemical compound that is formed during a chemical reaction and is used in another reaction to obtain another compound **3 SHORT-LIVED CHEMICAL COMPONENT** a molecule, ion, or free radical that exists for a short time during a chemical reaction [15C. Directly or via French < medieval Latin *intermediatus* < Latin *intermedius* < *medius* 'middle'.] —**intermediately** *adv* —**intermediateness** *n*

intermediate[2] /íntər meédi ayt/ (**-ates, -ating, -ated**) *vi* to act as a go-between or mediator between two or more people or groups [Early 16C. < INTER- + MEDIATE.] —**intermediation** /íntər meédi áysh'n/ *n* —**intermediator** *n*

intermediate-acting *adj* having a period of therapeutic activity that is between that of long-acting and short-acting drugs

intermediate bulk container *n* a portable container for transporting liquids or solids that holds 500 to 1,000 litres/110 to 220 gallons or 500 to 1,500 kg/1,100 to 3,300 lb

intermediate court *n* a court at the middle level of the state court hierarchy in Australia, below the supreme courts but above the magistrates' courts

intermediate frequency *n* the frequency that an incoming signal is changed to in a heterodyne receiver prior to amplification

intermediate host *n* an animal that is the host for an immature parasite, which then moves on to a different host before reproducing

intermediate-level waste *n* radioactive waste from reactors and processing plants that is solidified, mixed with concrete, and stored in drums

intermediate-range ballistic missile *n* a ballistic missile that has a range of 1,200 to 1,600 km/750 to 1,000 mi. ◊ **intercontinental ballistic missile**

intermediate school *n* **1** *US* = **junior high, middle school** *n*. **2 2** in New Zealand, a school that takes children between the ages of 11 and 13

intermediate technology *n* simple technology that is environmentally sensitive and based on local resources

intermediate treatment *n* care for children affected by emotional or personality disorders or psychiatric conditions that do not require hospitalization but do require close monitoring

intermediate vector boson *n* an elementary particle that transmits weak interactions between other elementary particles

intermedin /íntər meédin/ *n* PHYSIOL = **melanocyte-stimulating hormone** [Mid-20C. < modern Latin *(pars) intermedia* 'intermediate (part) (of the pituitary)' < Latin *intermedius*.]

interment /in túrmənt/ *n* the burial of a corpse, usually accompanied by a funeral ceremony

intermesh /íntər mésh/ *vti* to engage or mesh with one another, or to cause something such as the teeth of cogwheels to do so

intermetallic /íntərmi tállik/ *adj* consisting of two or more metals in specific proportions

intermezzo /íntər métsō, -médzō/ (*plural* **-zos** *or* **-zi** /-métsi, -médzi/) *n* **1** a short piece of music that is performed between longer movements of an extended musical composition **2** a short musical composition, usually for solo piano **3** = **interlude** *n*. **2** [Late 18C. Via Italian < Latin *intermedius* 'intermediate' < *medius* 'middle'.]

interminable /in túrminəb'l/ *adj* so long and boring or frustrating as to seem endless ○ *interminable delays* [14C. Directly or via French < late Latin *interminabilis* 'unending' < Latin *terminare* (see TERMINATE).] —**interminability** /in túrminə bílləti/ *n* —**interminably** *adv*

intermingle /íntər míng g'l/ (**-gles, -gling, -gled**) *vti* to mix something together with something else, or to become mixed together ○ *The scents of jasmine and honeysuckle intermingled.*

intermission /íntər mísh'n/ *n* **1** *US* = **interval** *n*. **3 2** a pause in, or temporary discontinuation of, an activity [15C. Directly or via French < Latin *intermission-* < *intermiss-*, past participle of *intermittere* (see INTERMIT).]

intermit /íntər mít/ (**-mits, -mitting, -mitted**) *vti* (*formal*) **1** to discontinue doing something temporarily, or to be discontinued temporarily **2** to stop or cause something to stop for a short time or for short intervals [Mid-16C. < Latin *intermittere* 'interrupt', literally 'send between' < *mittere* 'send'.] —**intermittingly** *adv* —**intermittor** *n*

intermittent /íntər mítt'nt/ *adj* happening or coming from time to time [Mid-16C. < Latin *intermittere* (see INTERMIT).] —**intermittence** *n* —**intermittently** *adv*

SYNONYMS See *periodic*.

intermittent claudication *n* a cramping pain, induced by exercise and relieved by rest, that is caused by inadequate blood supply to the affected muscles, usually the calves

intermittent current *n* a unidirectional current that is interrupted periodically

intermittent fever *n* a fever that rises and falls and then returns, occurring in diseases such as malaria

intermix /íntər míks/ *vti* = **intermingle** —**intermixable** *adj*

intermodal /íntər mṓd'l/ *adj* describes containers designed to be transferred from one mode of transport to another while in transit, e.g. from a train to a ship to a lorry ■ *n* a container for goods that can be transferred from one means of transport to another during shipment without being unpacked

intermodulation /íntər moddyōō láysh'n/ *n* the undesired interaction of electronic signals or complex wave components to produce waves with frequencies equal to the sums and differences of integral multiples of the frequencies of the signals

intermolecular /íntərmə lékyōōlər/ *adj* occurring between or involving molecules —**intermolecularly** *adv*

intermontane /íntər mon táyn/ *adj* describes basins lying between two mountain ranges, and often filling up with sediment washed down from them

intermural /íntər myóorəl/ *adj* involving participants from two or more educational institutions, athletic clubs, or other groups

intern *v* /in túrn/ **1** *vt* **DETAIN** to detain somebody in confinement as being a security threat **2** *vi US* **WORK AS INTERN** to work as an intern, e.g. in a hospital ■ *n* /ín turn/ **intern, interne 1** *US, Can, Aus* **JUNIOR HOSPITAL DOCTOR** a junior doctor at a hospital **2** *US* **TRAINEE** an assistant or trainee who gains practical experience in an occupation [Mid-19C. Noun: < French *interne*; verb: < French *interner* < Latin *internus* (see INTERNAL).] —**internment** /in túrnmənt/ *n* —**internship** *n*

internal /in túrn'l/ *adj* **1 LOCATED INSIDE** located within or affecting the inside of something, especially the inside of the body ○ *internal organs* **2 INTENDED FOR USE INSIDE** effective when used or suitable for use inside something, especially the inside of the body **3 SELF-CONTAINED OR SELF-GENERATING** existing, evident in, or arising from the nature, structure, or qualities that somebody or something has ○ *internal cohesion* **4 OCCURRING WITHIN A COUNTRY** originating, operating, or located within a country's borders ○ *internal affairs* **5 MENTAL** involving or existing within the mind or spirit ○ *internal conflict* **6 OCCURRING WITHIN AN ORGANIZATION** working at or carried out within an organization or institution such as a school, college, or university ○ *internal e-mail* [15C. Directly or via Old French *internel* < medieval Latin *internalis* < Latin *internus* 'inwards, within' < *inter* (see INTER-).] —**internality** /íntər nálləti/ *n* —**internally** *adv* —**internalness** *n*

internal-combustion engine *n* an engine in which fuel is burnt in combustion chambers within the engine instead of in an external furnace and in which the energy released moves one or more pistons

internal ear *n* ANAT = **inner ear**

internal energy *n* (*symbol* ***U***) the total kinetic energy of the atoms and molecules of a system plus the potential energy of their mutual interaction

internalize /in túrnə līz/ (**-izes, -izing, -ized**), **internalise** (**-ises, -ising, -ised**) *vt* **1** to adopt the beliefs, values, and attitudes of others, either consciously or unconsciously **2** to deal with an emotion or conflict by thinking about it rather than expressing it openly —**internalization** /in túrnə lī záysh'n/ *n*

internal medicine *n* the branch of medicine concerned with the diagnosis and nonsurgical treatment of diseases affecting the internal organs, and with preventive medicine

internal resistance *n* the resistance within a source of electrical current such as a cell or generator

internal respiration *n* the metabolic use of oxygen by a cell to produce energy, resulting in the release of carbon dioxide

internal rhyme *n* a rhyme in which one of the rhyming words is within the line of poetry and the other is at the end of the same line or within the next line

internal secretion *n* a secretion, especially a hormone, that is absorbed into the blood directly after production

internal wave *n* a waveform that develops below the surface of a body of water where two water masses with different densities meet

international /íntər násh'nəl/ *adj* **1 INVOLVING SEVERAL COUNTRIES** involving two or more countries or their citizens **2 CROSSING NATIONAL BOUNDARIES** extending beyond or across national boundaries **3 OF RELATIONS AMONG NATIONS** concerned with relations between nations ■ *n* **1 CONTEST BETWEEN TEAMS FROM DIFFERENT COUNTRIES** a sports contest between teams or players from two or more countries, especially a football or rugby match between teams representing two countries **2 MEMBER OF AN INTERNATIONAL TEAM** a member of a team representing his or her country in an international event —**internationality** /íntər násh'n állәti/ *n* —**internationally** *adv*

International /íntər násh'nəl/ *n* any of four international Socialist, Communist, or Anarchist organizations formed in 1864, 1889, 1919, and 1938 respectively

International Atomic Time *n* a precisely determined system of measuring time in which a second is defined in terms of atomic events that are known to a high degree of accuracy

International Bank for Reconstruction and Development *n* = **World Bank**

International Brigade *n* any of seven mainly Communist and Socialist forces of volunteers from many different countries that fought on the Republican side during the Spanish Civil War

International Court of Justice *n* the chief judicial body of the United Nations, empowered to resolve international disputes between member nations who submit a case to the court

International Criminal Police Organization *n* full form of **Interpol**

International Date Line *n* an internationally agreed imaginary line running roughly along the 180° meridian of longitude, to the east of which the date is one day earlier than to the west

International Development Association *n* a specialized agency of the United Nations that provides credit to nations on easier terms than the World Bank

Internationale /íntər náshə náal/ *n* a revolutionary Socialist song written in France in 1871 and adopted as the anthem of the First, Second, and Third Internationals [Early 20C. < French *(chanson) internationale* 'international (song)'.]

International Finance Corporation *n* a specialized agency of the United Nations that is affiliated with the World Bank and promotes private enterprise in developing nations by providing risk capital

International Gothic *n* a style of painting and other visual art that emerged in Europe with the increasing exchange of ideas and techniques among European artists towards the end of the 14th century

International Grandmaster *n* a chess player of the highest rank awarded to a participant in international competitions

internationalise *vt* = **internationalize**

internationalism /íntər násh'nəlizəm/ *n* **1 COOPERATION BETWEEN COUNTRIES** a policy or spirit of cooperation and mutual understanding between countries **2 INTEREST IN OTHER COUNTRIES** a willingness and ability to understand and respect the concerns, attitudes, and ways of life of other countries **3 INTERNATIONAL CHARACTER OR QUALITY** the international character or quality of somebody or something

internationalist /íntər násh'nəlist/ *n* **1 ADVOCATE OF INTERNATIONAL COOPERATION** a supporter or advocate of greater cooperation and understanding between countries **2 SOMEBODY INTERESTED IN OTHER COUNTRIES** somebody who is interested in other countries and understands and respects their peoples and cultures ■ *adj* **FAVOURING INTERNATIONAL COOPERATION** favouring greater cooperation and understanding between countries

internationalize /íntər násh'nə līz/ (**-izes, -izing, -ized**), **internationalise** (**-ises, -ising, -ised**) *vt* **1** to make something international in character, structure, or outlook **2** to place something under the protection or control of several countries instead of one country —**internationalization** /íntər násh'nə lī záysh'n/ *n*

international law *n* the accepted rules that govern countries in their relations with other countries

International Master *n* a chess player of a rank in international competitions that is below International Grandmaster

International Modernism *n* ARCHIT = **International Style** *n.*

International Monetary Fund *n* a specialized agency of the United Nations that seeks to promote international monetary cooperation and the stabilization of national currencies and help nations resolve balance of payment problems

International Morse code *n* the form of Morse code used internationally

International Phonetic Alphabet *n* a system of letters and marks, mostly based on the letters of the Roman alphabet, used internationally to represent speech sounds

International Practical Temperature Scale *n* a scientific temperature scale, expressed in degrees Celsius, that has eleven fixed temperature reference points, including the boiling point of oxygen and the freezing point of gold

international relations *npl* political and other dealings between two or more countries ■ *n* the branch of political science that studies the relations between countries (+ *singular verb*)

International Standards Organization *n* an international organization established in 1947 to standardize such things as units of measurement and the meanings of technical terms

International Style *n* an early 20th-century architectural style in the United States and Europe that favoured the use of simple geometric lines, spacious interiors, and materials such as steel and reinforced concrete

International System (of Units) *n* an internationally accepted system of units of measurement used for scientific work. The basic units are the metre, kilogram, second, kelvin, mole, ampere, and candela, these being the basic quantities of length, mass, time, temperature, amount of substance, electric current, and luminous intensity.

International Telecommunication Union *n* a specialized agency of the United Nations that promotes international cooperation in telecommunications and allots radio frequencies for various purposes

international telegram *n* a message sent by telephone or telex from the United Kingdom to another country, where it is delivered in written or printed form

international unit *n* the amount of a hormone or vitamin required to produce a specific response

interne *n US* = **intern**

internecine /íntər née sīn/ *adj* **1** occurring within a group or organization **2** damaging or injuring participants on both sides of a conflict or struggle [Mid-17C. < Latin *internecinus* 'deadly' < *internecare* 'exterminate', literally 'kill completely' < *necare* 'kill' < *nex* 'death'.]

internee /íntər née/ *n* an inmate of a prison, prisoner-of-war camp, or other similar place, especially during a war

internesia /íntər néezhə/ *n US* an inability to remember either the location of or information contained in a Web site (*informal*) [Blend of INTERNET + AMNESIA]

Internet /íntər net/, **internet** *n* a network that links computer networks all over the world by satellite and telephone, connecting users with service networks such as e-mail and the World Wide Web

QUICK FACTS ON... **INTERNET**

Key elements: widespread use of personal computers; HTML (HyperText Markup Language), HTTP (HyperText Transfer Protocol), and URL (Uniform Resource Locator) standards; development of the World Wide Web

Key dates: 1960s Internet proposed by Ted Nelson; 1969 ARPAnet, conceived by the US Advanced Research Project Agency for national defence, becomes operational, connecting computer networks at four universities via the Internet Protocol; 1971 program for electronic messaging, or 'e-mail', written and a year later adapted to ARPAnet (Tomlinson); 1972 ARPAnet, now linking 50 networks, revealed to the public; 1990 text-only version of the World Wide Web made available (Berners-Lee); 1991 NSFnet, introduced by the National Science Foundation in 1985, replaces ARPAnet as the backbone of the Internet; 1993 graphical browser called Mosaic developed for the World Wide Web (Andreessen); 1995 commercial providers replace NSFnet as the backbone of the Internet

Key developments: e-mail, chat rooms, newsgroups, bulletin boards, Internet service providers, instant messaging; e-commerce

Key publications: *In-Line/On-Line: Fundamentals of the Internet and the World Wide Web* (Raymond Greenlaw and Ellen Hepp) 1999; *Weaving the Web: The Original Design and Ultimate Destiny of the World Wide Web by its Inventor* (Tim Berners-Lee and Mark Fischetti) 2000

Internet appliance *n* a portable or hand-held device used to access the Internet

Internet hotel *n* a place where a large number of computers are made available to businesses to handle outsourced Internet and server requirements

Internet payment system *n* a system for transferring funds electronically from customer to merchant and business to business

Internet protocol *n* the standard that controls the routing and structure of transmitted data

Internet service provider *n* a business that provides access to the Internet, usually for a monthly fee

interneuron /íntər nyóor on/ *n* a short nerve cell in the central nervous system that connects the nerve cells in a reflex arc, e.g. a sensory nerve to a motor nerve —**interneuronal** /-nyóorən'l/ *adj*

internist /ín turnist/ *n* a doctor who specializes in the diagnosis, prevention, and nonsurgical treatment of diseases affecting the internal organs [Early 20C. < INTERNAL + -IST.]

internode /íntər nōd/ *n* **1** the part of a plant stem between two nodes **2** the part of the axon of a nerve cell that lies between the nodes of Ranvier and is covered by the myelin sheath [Mid-17C. < Latin *internodium* < *nodus* 'knot'.] —**internodal** /íntər nṓd'l/ *adj*

inter nos /íntər nṓss/ *adv* between or among ourselves [< Latin]

internuncial /íntər núnsh'l/ *adj* **1** describes nerve cells that connect one nerve cell to another **2** acting as or connected with an internuncio of the Roman Catholic Church —**internuncially** *adv*

internuncio /íntər núnshi ō/ (*plural* **-os**) *n* **1** a diplomatic representative of the pope of a rank below a nuncio **2** a messenger or go-between (*formal*) [Mid-17C. Via Italian *internunzio* < Latin *internuntius* 'intermediate messenger' < *nuntius* 'messenger'.]

interoceanic /íntər ōshi ánnik/ *adj* occurring between or connecting two or more oceans

interoffice /íntər óffiss/ *adj* occurring between offices or involving two or more offices in the same organization ○ *an interoffice memo*

interpellate /in túrpə layt/ (**-lates, -lating, -lated**) *vt* in European legislatures, to interrupt a parliamentary debate by asking a question on an aspect of government policy [Late 19C. < Latin *interpellare* 'thrust yourself between' < *-pellare* 'thrust yourself', variant of *pellere* (see PULSE[1]).] —**interpellation** /in túrpə láysh'n/ *n* —**interpellator** *n*

interpenetrate /íntər pénni trayt/ (**-trates, -trating, -trated**) *vti* to spread, mix, or weave something in and throughout something else, or be spread, mixed, or woven in this way —**interpenetration** /íntər pénni tráysh'n/ *n*

interpersonal /íntər púrss'nəl/ *adj* concerning or involving relationships between people —**interpersonally** *adv*

interphalangeal /íntərfə lánji əl/ *adj* situated between the bones of the fingers or toes

interphase /íntər fayz/ *n* the period during which a cell is not actively dividing, when other activities such as DNA synthesis take place

interplanetary /íntər plánnitəri/ *adj* situated, happening, or moving between planets or involving two or more planets

interplay /íntər play/ *n* the way in which two or more people or things repeatedly act on and react to each other

interplead /íntər pleéd/ (**-pleads, -pleading, -pleaded** *or* **-pled, -pleaded** *or* **-pled** /íntər pléd/) *vi* to go to trial to resolve which of several claimants has the right to claim money or property held by a third party [Mid-16C. < Anglo-Norman *enterpleder* 'plead together' < *pleder* (see PLEAD).]

interpleader /íntər pleédər/ *n* a trial to resolve which of several claimants can sue for money or property held by a third party, instituted by the third party to avoid several proceedings

Interpol /íntər pol/ *n* an association of national police forces that promotes cooperation and mutual assistance in apprehending international criminals and criminals who flee abroad to avoid justice. Full form **International Criminal Police Organization**

interpolate /in túrpə layt/ (**-lates, -lating, -lated**) *v* **1** *vt* INSERT SOMETHING INTO SOMETHING ELSE to add one thing, often an unnecessary item, between the existing elements or items of something else **2** *vt* ADD WORDS TO TEXT to add a comment or extra words to a written text, often altering or falsifying the meaning **3** *vti* INTERRUPT BY SAYING to say something that interrupts what somebody else is saying **4** *vt* ESTIMATE VALUE OF MATHEMATICAL FUNCTION to estimate the value of a mathematical function that lies between known values, often by means of a graph [Early 17C. < Latin *interpolare* 'polish up'.] —**interpolation** /in túrpə láysh'n/ *n* —**interpolative** *adj* —**interpolator** *n*

interpose /íntər póz/ (**-poses, -posing, -posed**) *v* **1** *vti* INTERRUPT BY SAYING to say something that interrupts what somebody else is saying **2** *vt* PLACE BETWEEN PEOPLE OR THINGS to place yourself or something else between two people or things **3** *vti* INTERVENE WITH to intervene or interfere in a situation such as a dispute [Late 16C. < French *interposer*, alteration (influenced by *poser* 'to place') of Latin *interponere* 'place between' < *ponere* (see POSITION).] —**interposable** *adj* —**interposal** *n* —**interposer** *n* —**interposition** /íntərpə zísh'n/ *n*

~~**interpratation**~~ incorrect spelling of **interpretation**

ϟ **interpret** /in túrprit/ *v* **1** *vt* FIND MEANING OF to establish or explain the meaning or significance of something **2** *vt* PERFORM SOMETHING IN PARTICULAR WAY to perform something such as a play or piece of music in a way that conveys particular ideas or feelings about it **3** *vti* TRANSLATE to translate what is said in one language into another **4** *vt* EXECUTE COMPUTER PROGRAM to convert instructions in a computer program written in a high-level language into machine language and execute them, one instruction at a time [14C. Directly or via French *interpréter* < Latin *interpretari* 'explain' < *interpret-*, stem of *interpres* 'broker'.] —**interpretability** /in túrpritə bíllәti/ *n* —**interpretable** *adj* —**interpretably** *adv* —**interpretative** *adj* —**interpretatively** *adv* —**interpretive** *adj* —**interpretively** *adv*

interpretation /in túrpri táysh'n/ *n* **1** ESTABLISHMENT OF MEANING an explanation or establishment of the meaning or significance of something **2** ASCRIPTION OF PARTICULAR MEANING an ascription of a particular meaning or significance to something **3** PERFORMANCE the way in which an artistic work, e.g. a play or piece of music, is performed so as to convey a particular understanding of the work **4** TRANSLATION the oral translation of what is said in one language into another, so that speakers of different languages can communicate **5** *Scotland* COMPREHENSION a comprehension exercise **6** EXPLANATORY INFORMATION AT PLACE OF INTEREST explanatory information to help people understand what they are seeing or encountering at a place of interest —**interpretational** *adj*

interpretation centre *n* LEISURE = **visitor centre**

ϟ **interpreter** /in túrpritər/ *n* **1** TRANSLATOR an oral translator from one language to another **2** PERFORMER EXPRESSING PARTICULAR IDEAS someone who performs something, such as a play or piece of music, in a way that expresses ideas or feelings about it **3** PROGRAM EXECUTING INSTRUCTIONS a computer program that translates instructions in a program written in a high-level computer language into machine language and executes them —**interpretership** *n*

interpretive centre *n* LEISURE = **visitor centre**

interprovincial /íntərprə vínsh'l/ *adj* occurring between or involving provinces

interpupillary /íntər pyóopələri/ *adj* between the pupils of the eyes

interquartile range /íntər kwáwr tīl-/ *n* a measure of the spread of a group of values equal to the difference between the upper limit for the lower quarter and the lower limit for the upper quarter

interracial /íntər ráysh'l/ *adj* occurring between or involving different races —**interracially** *adv*

interregional /íntər reéj'nəl/ *adj* occurring between regions or involving two or more regions

interregnum /íntər régnəm/ (*plural* **-nums** *or* **-na** /-régnə/) *n* **1** TIME BETWEEN ONE REIGN AND THE NEXT the period of time between the end of one reign or regime and the beginning of the next **2** TIME WITHOUT GOVERNMENT OR CONTROL a period of time during which there is no government, control, or authority **3** INTERRUPTION a pause or gap in any continuous activity or series [Late 16C. < Latin, 'period between kingships' < *regnum* (see REIGN).] —**interregnal** *adj*

interrelate /íntərri láyt/ (**-lates, -lating, -lated**) *vti* to have a relationship in which each person or thing depends on or is affected by the others, or to cause people or things to have such a relationship —**interrelation** *n* —**interrelationship** *n*

interrenal /íntər reén'l/ *adj* situated between or connecting the kidneys

interrobang /in térrə bang/, **interabang** *n* a punctuation mark used at the end of, or sometimes in place of, an utterance that is both question and exclamation, especially to indicate disbelief [Mid-20C. Blend of INTERROGATION MARK + BANG[1] (printers' slang for an exclamation mark).]

interrog. *abbr* **1** interrogate **2** interrogation **3** interrogative

ϟ **interrogate** /in térrə gayt/ (**-gates, -gating, -gated**) *vt* **1** to question somebody thoroughly, often in an aggressive or threatening manner and especially as part of a formal inquiry, e.g. in a police station or courtroom **2** to transmit a request for information to a device or program with the expectation that an immediate response will trigger further interaction [15C. < Latin *interrogare* 'ask in the presence of' < *rogare* 'ask'.] —**interrogatee** /in térrə gəy teé/ *n* —**interrogator** *n* —**interrogee** *n*

ϟ **interrogation** /in térrə gáysh'n/ *n* **1** THOROUGH QUESTIONING the act or process of questioning somebody closely, often in an aggressive manner, especially as part of an official inquiry or trial **2** QUERY a question (*formal*) **3** TRANSMISSION OF A SIGNAL TO A COMPUTER the transmission of a signal to a device or program that triggers a response —**interrogational** *adj*

interrogation mark *n* = **question mark**

interrogative /íntə róggətiv/ *adj* **1** QUESTIONING questioning or seeming to question somebody or something **2** USED TO ASK A QUESTION consisting of or used in asking a question ■ *n* **1** WORD USED TO ASK A QUESTION a word or particle that is used to form a question, e.g. 'who', 'what', or 'where' **2** FORM OF QUESTION the form of a sentence that is used to ask a question —**interrogatively** *adv*

interrogatory /íntə róggətəri/ *adj* ASKING A QUESTION asking a question, used to ask a question, or in the form of a question (*formal*) ■ *n* (*plural* **-ries**) **1** QUESTION a question or series of questions **2** FORMAL WRITTEN QUESTION a formal written question asked during a legal proceeding and usually answered under oath —**interrogatorily** *adv*

ϟ **interrupt** /íntə rúpt/ *v* **1** *vti* HALT SPEAKER OR SPEAKER'S UTTERANCE to halt the flow of a speaker or of a speaker's utterance with a question or remark **2** *vti* DISTURB SOMEBODY OR SOMEBODY'S WORK to disturb somebody who is busy doing something, causing him or her to stop **3** *vt* CAUSE SOMETHING TO STOP to cause a break in the flow of something or put a temporary stop to something **4** *vt* TAKE BREAK FROM to discontinue doing something temporarily **5** *vt* OBSTRUCT VIEW to obstruct or block a view ■ *n* **1** SIGNAL TO SUSPEND OPERATION a signal to a computer processor to suspend the operation it is currently doing in favour of the operation that produced the interrupt signal **2** CIRCUIT INTERRUPT SIGNAL the circuit that conveys an interrupt signal [14C. < Latin *interrupt-*, past participle of *interrumpere* 'break apart' < *rumpere* 'to break'.] —**interrupter** *n* —**interruptible** *adj* —**interruptive** *adj* —**interruptively** *adv*

interrupted cadence *n* a cadence that does not end with the expected chord of the tonic but moves from the dominant to the submediant or subdominant

interrupted screw *n* a screw whose thread is broken in one or more places by a lengthways slot that enables a partial turn to lock or unlock the screw

interruption /íntə rúpsh'n/ *n* **1** the act of interrupting somebody, or something that interrupts somebody who is saying or doing something **2** a pause, break, or temporary halt in an ongoing activity or process

interscholastic /íntərskə lástik/ *adj* occurring between, involving, or representing two or more schools —**interscholastically** *adv*

inter se /íntər sáy, íntər seé/ *adv, adj* between or among themselves [< Latin]

intersect /íntər sékt/ *v* **1** *vti* CROSS to cross something, or to cross each other **2** *vt* GO THROUGH to follow a path across or through something **3** *vti* OVERLAP to overlap or have things in common with something or each other **4** *vti* HAVE POINTS IN COMMON to overlap geometrically so that a point or set of points is common to two or more figures [Early 17C. < Latin *intersect-*, past participle of *intersecare* 'cut between' < *secare* 'to cut'.]

intersection /íntər séksh'n/ *n* **1** ACT OF INTERSECTING the act or fact of intersecting **2** CROSSROADS a place where two roads or paths cross each other **3** CROSSING POINT the place or point where two things cross each other **4** OVERLAPPING an overlapping between two things such as different personal interests or political positions **5** COMMON POINT a point or set of points common to two or more intersecting geometric figures **6** SET OF COMMON ELEMENTS a set that consists of all of the elements common to two or more other sets, thus being the largest set contained in all of the others —**intersectional** *adj*

interservice /íntər súrviss/ *adj* occurring among the various branches of the armed forces

intersex /íntər seks/ *n* an organism with characteristics of both sexes

intersexual /íntər sékshoo əl/ *adj* **1** occurring between males and females or affecting their relations **2** having characteristics of both sexes —**intersexualism** *n* —**intersexuality** /-sekshoo állәti/ *n* —**intersexually** *adv*

interspace *n* /íntər spayss/ SPACE OR INTERVAL a space or interval of time between two things ■ *vt* /íntər spáyss/ (**-spaces, -spacing, -spaced**) **1** PUT SOMETHING BETWEEN TWO THINGS to put something in the spaces or gaps between things **2** INSERT SPACES BETWEEN to put spaces or breaks between things —**interspatial** /íntər spáysh'l/ *adj* —**interspatially** *adv*

interspecific /íntərspə síffik/ *adj* **1** created by crossing different species **2** occurring between or involving different species

intersperse /íntər spúrss/ (**-sperses, -spersing, -spersed**) *vt* **1** to break up the continuity or flow of something with something else **2** to put or insert something here and there among or in something else [Mid-16C. < Latin *interspers-*, past participle of *interspergere* 'scatter between' < *spargere* 'scatter'.] —**interspersedly** /íntər spúrssidli/ *adv* —**interspersion** *n*

interstadial /íntər stáydi əl/ *adj* relating to a short period of relatively warmer climate within an ice age [Early 20C. < INTER- + Latin *stadium* 'stage'.]

interstate *adj* /íntər stáyt/ OCCURRING BETWEEN STATES occurring between, connecting, or involving two or more states ■ *n* **interstate, interstate highway** MAJOR MOTORWAY BETWEEN US CITIES a limited-access road that forms part of the federally funded system of motorways connecting the major cities of the United States ■ *adv Aus* TO OR IN ANOTHER STATE to or in another state or states

interstation /íntər stáysh'n/ *adj* occurring between or connecting stations

interstellar /íntər stéllər/ *adj* situated, happening, or moving between stars, or involving two or more stars

intersterile /íntər stérrīl/ *adj* not capable of interbreeding —**intersterility** /íntərstə ríllәti/ *n*

interstice /in túrstiss/ *n* **1** SMALL SPACE a small opening, crack, or gap between two things **2** A SPACE IN A CRYSTAL LATTICE a gap between neighbouring atoms in the lattice of a crystal **3** SPACE IN BODY TISSUE a small space in a tissue or between parts of the body [15C. Via French < Latin *interstitium* < *intersistere* 'stand still in the middle' < *sistere* 'cause to stand' < *stare* (see STAND).]

ϟ **interstitial** /íntər stísh'l/ *adj* **1** RELATING TO GAPS forming, situated in, or relating to one or more small openings, gaps, or cracks **2** OCCURRING BETWEEN OTHER MINERALS located in the pores or between the crystals of a rock

3 OF COMPOUND CONTAINING METALS AND NONMETALS relating to a compound, e.g. a carbide, in which ions or atoms of a nonmetal occupy positions in a metal lattice **4 OCCURRING BETWEEN TISSUES** lying between parts of an organ or between groups of cells or tissues ■ *n* **UNSOLICITED ADVERTISEMENT ON INTERNET** an unsolicited advertisement on the World Wide Web that briefly precedes a selected page —**interstitially** *adv*

interstitial-cell-stimulating hormone *n* BIOCHEM = **luteinizing hormone**

interterritorial /intər terri táwri əl/ *adj* connecting or involving two or more territories

intertestamental /intər testə mént'l/ *adj* during, from, or relating to the period between the composition of the last books of the Hebrew Scriptures, called Old Testament by Christians, and the first books of the New Testament of the Bible

intertextuality /intər tekstyoo állәti/ *n* the relationship that exists between different texts, especially literary texts —**intertextual** /intər tékstyoo əl/ *adj* —**intertextually** *adv*

intertexture /intər tékschər/ *n* **1** an object or material that has been made by interweaving two or more things **2** an act of interweaving two or more things, or the fact of being interwoven

intertidal /intər tíd'l/ *adj* occurring within or forming the area between high and low tide levels in a coastal zone —**intertidally** *adv*

intertribal /intər tríb'l/ *adj* occurring between tribes or involving two or more tribes —**intertribally** *adv*

intertrigo /intər trígō/ *n* the inflammation of two skin surfaces that are in constant contact, caused by friction or sweat [Early 18C. < Latin, 'chafing of the skin' < assumed *interterere* 'rub together' < *terere* 'to rub'.]

intertropical /intər tróppik'l/ *adj* located or occurring between the Tropic of Cancer and Tropic of Capricorn

intertwine /intər twín/ (**-twines, -twining, -twined**) *vti* **1** to twist two or more things together, or to be or become twisted together or with something else **2** to link or involve something with something else, or to become linked or involved with each other ○ *Their lives had intertwined.* —**intertwinement** *n*

intertwist /intər twíst/ *vti* = **intertwine** *v.* 1

interunion /intər yóonyən/ *adj* occurring between or involving two or more unions, especially trade unions

~~interupt~~ incorrect spelling of **interrupt**

interurban /intər úrbən/ *adj* occurring between, connecting, or involving two or more towns or cities

interval /íntərv'l/ *n* **1 INTERVENING PERIOD OF TIME** a period of time between one event and the next **2 INTERVENING DISTANCE** the distance between one thing and another **3 BREAK IN PERFORMANCE** a break between parts of a musical or theatrical performance or cinema showing. US term **intermission** *n.* 1 **4 DIFFERENCE IN MUSICAL PITCH** the musical distance between the pitches of two notes **5 ALL NUMBERS BETWEEN TWO NUMBERS** a set containing all the real numbers or points between two specified real numbers or points, which are called the endpoints [14C. Via Old French *entreval(e)* < Latin *intervallum* 'space between ramparts' < *vallum* 'rampart'.] —**intervallic** /intər vállik/ *adj* ◇ **at intervals 1** at different points in time **2** at various locations

intervalometer /intərvə lómmitər/ *n* a device that is designed to activate a mechanism automatically and at regular intervals, especially one that operates a camera shutter [Mid-20C. < INTERVAL.]

interval signal *n* a particular piece of music or other sound that a radio station uses as its unique identifying signal, broadcasting it between and sometimes during programmes

interval training *n* a method of training, especially in athletics, that involves alternating between aerobic and nonaerobic exercise in the same session

intervene /intər véen/ (**-venes, -vening, -vened**) *vi* **1 ACT TO PRODUCE CHANGE** to take some action or get involved in something in order to change what is happening, especially to prevent something undesirable ○ *the referee had to intervene to stop the fight* **2 HAPPEN SO AS TO IMPEDE** to occur and as a result stop or delay something from happening **3 ELAPSE** to elapse between one point in time and another ○ *the intervening years* **4 BE SITUATED IN BETWEEN** to be located between two things **5 BREAK INTO A CONVERSATION** to break into a conversation or discussion **6 ENTER A LAWSUIT** to enter a lawsuit as a third party in order to protect your own interests **7 ACT TO MANIPULATE ECONOMIC MARKETS** to take economic action that is designed to counter a trend in a market, especially in order to stabilize a country's currency [Late 16C. < Latin *intervenire* 'come between' < *venire* (see VENUE).]

intervenor /intər véenər/, **intervener** *n* a party that enters a lawsuit as a third party in order to protect its interests

intervention /intər vénsh'n/ *n* **1 ACTION AFFECTING ANOTHER'S AFFAIRS** an action undertaken in order to change what is happening or might happen in another's affairs, especially in order to prevent something undesirable **2 MARKET MANIPULATION** economic action that is designed to counter a trend in a market, especially in order to stabilize a country's currency **3 BUYING OF SURPLUS BY EU** the purchase of agricultural produce by the European Union when the market price falls below a certain level (**intervention price**) because there is a surplus

interventionism /intər vénsh'nizəm/ *n* **1** political interference or military involvement by one country in the affairs of another **2** action by a government to influence and improve the country's economic situation or some aspect of it —**interventionist** *n, adj*

interventricular /intər ven tríkyóolər/ *adj* situated or occurring between the ventricles of the heart

intervertebral /intər vúrtibrəl/ *adj* situated or occurring between the vertebrae of the backbone —**intervertebrally** *adv*

intervertebral disc *n* one of the flexible plates of cartilage connecting adjacent vertebrae of the backbone that impart flexibility and act as shock absorbers to protect the spinal cord from impact, e.g. when running

interview /íntər vyoo/ *n* **1 MEETING FOR ASKING QUESTIONS** a meeting during which somebody is asked questions, e.g. by a prospective employer, a journalist, or a researcher **2 RECORD OF AN INTERVIEW** a transcript, report on, or recording of an interview ■ *v* **1** *vt* **ASK SOMEBODY QUESTIONS** to ask somebody a series of questions in an interview **2** *vi* **PERFORM IN AN INTERVIEW** to speak and answer in a particular way in an interview ○ *She always interviews well.* [Early 16C. < obsolete French *entrevue* < *entrevoir* 'see each other' < *voir* 'see' < Latin *videre*.] —**interviewable** *adj* —**interviewee** /intər vyoo ée/ *n* —**interviewer** *n*

inter vivos /intər vée voss/ *adv, adj* from one living person to another [< Latin, 'between the living']

intervocalic /intərvō kállik/ *adj* describes a speech sound occurring or inserted between vowels, e.g. between one word that ends with a vowel and another word that starts with a vowel —**intervocalically** *adv*

interwar /intər wáwr/ *adj* occurring between two wars, especially between World War I and World War II

interweave /intər wéev/ (**-weaves, -weaving, -wove** /-wṓv'n/, **-woven** /-wṓv/) *vti* **1** to weave something into or with something else, or to be woven together, into, or with something else **2** to combine something with something else, or to be combined with something —**interweavement** *n* —**interweaver** *n*

intestate /in tést ayt/ *adj* **1 LEAVING NO LEGALLY VALID WILL** not having made a legally valid will **2 NOT WILLED TO** not having been assigned to somebody in a legally valid will ■ *n* **SOMEBODY LEAVING NO LEGALLY VALID WILL** somebody who has died without having made a legally valid will [14C. Directly or via French *intestat* < Latin *intestatus* 'not having made a will' < *testari* 'make a will'.] —**intestacy** /in téstəssi/ *n*

intestinal /in téstin'l/ *adj* **1** found in or affecting the intestines **2** characteristic of, forming part of, or relating to the intestines —**intestinally** *adv*

intestinal flora *npl* bacteria present in a healthy intestine that complete digestion, synthesize vitamin K, and create an acid environment that prevents infection by harmful bacteria

intestine /in téstin/ *n* the part of the digestive system between the stomach and the anus or cloaca that digests and absorbs food (*often plural*) [15C. Via French < Latin *intestinus* 'internal' < *intus* 'within'.]

intifada /inti fáadə/ *n* the Palestinian uprising in the West Bank and Gaza Strip that started in 1987 in protest against the continued Israeli occupation [Late 20C. < Arabic *intifāḍa* 'a shaking off'.]

intimacy /íntiməssi/ (*plural* **-cies**) *n* **1 CLOSE RELATIONSHIP** a close personal relationship **2 QUIET ATMOSPHERE** a quiet and private atmosphere **3 DETAILED KNOWLEDGE** a detailed knowledge resulting from a close or long association or study **4 PRIVATE UTTERANCE OR ACTION** a private and personal utterance or action **5 SEXUAL ACT** a sexual act or sexual intercourse (*used euphemistically*)

intimate[1] /íntimət/ *adj* **1 CLOSE** having, involving, or resulting from a close personal relationship **2 COSY** quiet and private or secluded, enabling people to feel relaxed with each other **3 PRIVATE AND PERSONAL** so private and personal as to be kept secret or discussed only with a close friend or relative **4 SEXUAL** involving or having a sexual relationship (*used euphemistically*) **5 WORN NEXT TO THE SKIN** intended to be worn next to the skin or in a private setting **6 THOROUGH** very great and detailed as a result of extensive study or close experience ○ *an intimate knowledge of the workings of government* **7 CLOSELY CONNECTED** very close because of the influence of one thing on another ○ *the intimate connection between power and corruption* **8 INNERMOST** relating to or involving the innermost nature of something ■ *n* **CLOSE FRIEND** a close personal friend [Early 17C. < late Latin *intimatus*, past participle of *intimare* (see INTIMATE[2]).] —**intimately** *adv* —**intimateness** *n*

intimate[2] /ínti mayt/ (**-mates, -mating, -mated**) *vt* **1** to hint at something or let something be known in a quiet, indirect, or subtle way **2** to announce something formally [Early 16C. < late Latin *intimare* 'make known' < *intimus* 'innermost'.] —**intimater** *n* —**intimation** /ínti máysh'n/ *n*

intime /oN téem/ *adj* small, quiet, and private or secluded [Early 17C. Via French, 'intimate' < Latin *intimus* 'innermost'.]

intimidate /in tímmi dayt/ (**-dates, -dating, -dated**) *vt* **1** to frighten somebody into doing or not doing something, e.g. by means of violence or blackmail **2** to create a feeling of fear, awe, or inadequacy in another person [Mid-17C. < medieval Latin *intimidare* 'put in fear' < Latin *timidus* 'fearful'.] —**intimidatingly** *adv* —**intimidation** /in tímmi dáysh'n/ *n* —**intimidator** *n* —**intimidatory** /in tímmi dáytəri/ *adj*

intinction /in tíngksh'n/ *n* the act of dipping the Communion bread into the wine so that the person taking Communion receives both [Late 19C. < late Latin *intinction-* < Latin *intingere* 'dip in' < *tingere* 'moisten'.]

intitule /in títtyool/ (**-ules, -uling, -uled**) *vt* to give a title to an act of parliament [15C. Via French *intituler* < late Latin *intitulare* 'entitle' < Latin *titulus* 'inscription'.]

intl *abbr* international

into (*stressed*) /in too/; (*unstressed*) /íntə, íntŏŏ/ CORE MEANING: a preposition indicating that somebody or something is or moves inside something, either physically or figuratively ○ *I released the balloon into the air.* ○ *in case you get into difficulties* ○ *I decided to go into the army.* ○ *When did you go into partnership with them?*

prep **1 INDICATES MOVEMENT** moving or putting something from outside to the interior or inner part of something ○ *He stuck his hand into his pocket and pulled out a pencil.* **2 INDICATES MOVEMENT TO THE MIDST OF** indicates that something or somebody moves to the middle of something and becomes part of it or is surrounded by it ○ *He leapt into the water.* **3 INDICATES ENTRY** indicates entering a state, career, or period of time ○ *She decided to go into marketing.* ○ *He went on working until he was well into his seventies.* ○ *The fire department burst into action.* **4 INDICATES CONTACT WITH** indicates coming up against something accidentally ○ *I happened to bump into him last night quite by chance.* **5 INDICATES CHANGE** indicates becoming a new entity, shape, or form as a result of a change or transformation ○ *change water into wine* ○ *The caterpillar changes into a butterfly.* **6 INDICATES RESULT** indicates a situation resulting from somebody's persuasion ○ *My friends talked me into getting this haircut.* **7 INDICATES DIVIDEND** indicates the division of numbers ○ *9 into 63 equals 7.* **8 DIVIDED** indicates that something is divided so that it becomes several smaller parts ○ *She divided the cake into six, and gave each of us a slice.* **9 ENTHUSIASTIC ABOUT** indicates interest in or enthusiasm about something (*informal*) ○ *I was really into tennis that summer.* [Old English *in(n)tō* < IN + TO]

intolerable /in tóllərəb'l/ *adj* **1** so bad, difficult, or painful that it cannot be endured ○ *the pain was intolerable* **2** very unpleasant or annoying —**intolerability** /in tóllərə bílləti/ *n* —**intolerably** *adv*

intolerant /in tóllərənt/ *adj* **1 EASILY ANNOYED** easily angered or annoyed when things do not go as expected or desired **2 UNACCEPTING OF DIFFERENCES** refusing to accept people who are different or live differently, e.g. people of different races or religions **3 UNABLE TO TOLERATE** not able to endure or tolerate something —**intolerance** *n* —**intolerantly** *adv*

~~**intolerent**~~ incorrect spelling of **intolerant**

intonate /íntō nayt/ (**-nates, -nating, -nated**) *vt* **1 SAY IN PARTICULAR WAY** to say something in a particular tone of voice **2 SPEAK WITH VARYING PITCH** to speak with the rising and falling pitch that is typical of ordinary speech **3 PRONOUNCE CONSONANT WITH VOICING** to pronounce a consonant with a vibration of the vocal cords, as English speakers do when they pronounce the consonant 'v' as opposed to the consonant 'f' [Late 18C. < medieval Latin *intonat-*, past participle of *intonare* (see INTONE).]

intonation /íntō náysh'n/ *n* **1 PITCH OF THE VOICE** the rising or falling pitch of the voice when somebody says a word or syllable, or the rising and falling pattern of speech generally **2 INTONING** a saying or chanting of something in a solemn or serious way, or something said or chanted in this way **3 ACCURACY OF PITCH** accuracy of pitch in performing music **4 BEGINNING OF A PLAINSONG** the opening phrase of a piece of plainsong, sung by a soloist or just a few members of the choir —**intonational** *adj*

intonation contour, intonation pattern *n* the pattern of rising and falling pitch in speech that helps to distinguish between questions, statements, and other types of speech

intone /in tṓn/ (**-tones, -toning, -toned**) *v* **1** *vt* **SAY** to say something, especially in a slow and serious or solemn way (*formal*) **2** *vti* **CHANT PRAYER** to recite a prayer or other religious words in a chanting monotone **3** *vt* **START PLAINSONG** to sing the opening phrase of a piece of plainsong [14C. Directly or via Old French *entoner* < medieval Latin *intonare* '(to sing) in tone' < Latin *tonus* 'tone' < Greek *tonos* (see TONE).] —**intonement** *n* —**intoner** *n*

in toto /in tṓt ō/ *adv* in its entirety or as a whole ○ *The salary's nothing special, but in toto it's quite attractive when you consider compensation.* [< Latin]

intoxicant /in tóksikənt/ *n* something that causes physical or psychological intoxication, e.g. an alcoholic drink or great power ■ *adj* capable of making somebody intoxicated

intoxicate /in tóksi kayt/ (**-cates, -cating, -cated**) *v* **1** *vt* **MAKE DRUNK OR STUPEFIED** to make somebody drunk with alcohol or stupefied with drugs or other substances **2** *vt* **EXCITE** to make somebody intensely excited or overjoyed, often so much so that the person becomes irrational **3** *vti* **POISON** to poison somebody (*technical*) [15C. < medieval Latin *intoxicat-*, past participle of *intoxicare* 'to poison' < Latin *toxicum* 'poison' < Greek *toxicon* (see TOXIC).] —**intoxicable** *adj* —**intoxicated** *adj* —**intoxicatedly** *adv* —**intoxication** /-káysh'n/ *n* —**intoxicative** /-kaytiv/ *adj* —**intoxicator** *n*

intoxicating /in tóksi kayting/ *adj* **1** capable of making somebody drunk or stupefied (*formal*) **2** capable of making somebody intensely excited or overjoyed, often so much so that the person becomes irrational —**intoxicatingly** *adv*

intra- *prefix* within or inside ○ *intranasal* [Directly or via modern Latin, 'on the inside' < late Latin, < Latin *intra* < Indo-European]

intra-arterial *adj* within or introduced into an artery or arteries —**intra-arterially** *adv*

intra-articular *adj* within or introduced into a joint of the body

intra-atomic *adj* existing or occurring within an atom or atoms, rather than between atoms

intracardiac /íntrə kaárdi ak/ *adj* within or introduced into the heart —**intracardially** *adv*

intracellular /íntrə séllyōōlər/ *adj* within a cell or cells —**intracellularly** *adv*

intracerebral /íntrə sérrəbrəl/ *adj* existing or taking place inside the main part of the brain or cerebrum —**intracerebrally** *adv*

Intracoastal Waterway /íntrə kṓst'l-/ system of protected waterways in the E and SE United States, made up of the Atlantic Intracoastal Waterway and the Gulf Intracoastal Waterway. Length: 4,000 km/2,500 mi.

intracompany /íntrə kúmpəni/ *adj* within the same company or between employees or divisions of the same company

intracranial /íntrə kráyni əl/ *adj* within or introduced into the skull —**intracranially** *adv*

intractable /in tráktəb'l/ *adj* **1 STRONG-WILLED AND REBELLIOUS** resisting attempts to control, correct, or influence (*formal*) **2 DIFFICULT TO DEAL WITH** difficult to deal with or solve **3 DIFFICULT TO MANIPULATE** difficult to shape or manipulate —**intractability** /in tráktə bílləti/ *n* —**intractably** *adv*

SYNONYMS See ***unruly***.

intracutaneous /íntrə kyoo táyni əss/ *adj* = **intradermal** —**intracutaneously** *adv*

intradermal /íntrə dúrm'l/, **intradermic** /-mik/ *adj* within or introduced between the layers of the skin —**intradermally** *adv*

intradermal test *n* a test for immunity or allergic sensitivity involving the injection of small amounts of a test material into the skin through a fine needle

intradermic *adj* = **intradermal**

intrados /in tráy doss/ (*plural* **-dos** *or* **-doses**) *n* the inner curve of an architectural arch [Late 18C. < French, < Latin *intra* 'within' + French *dos* 'back' (< Latin *dorsum*).]

intragenic /íntrə jénnik/ *adj* located or occurring within the same gene

intralingual /íntrə líng gwəl/ *adj* occurring within a single language

intramolecular /íntrə mə lékyōōlər/ *adj* existing or occurring within a single molecule —**intramolecularly** *adv*

intramural /íntrə myóorəl/ *adj* **1** occurring within or involving members of a single college or university, instead of members of or teams from various colleges or universities **2** within the tissue of the wall of a blood vessel or other hollow body part

intramuscular /íntrə múskyōōlər/ *adj* within or into the substance of a muscle —**intramuscularly** *adv*

intranasal /íntrə náyz'l/ *adj* within or introduced into the nose —**intranasally** *adv*

intranational /íntrə násh'nəl/ *adj* existing or occurring within the boundaries of a single nation, rather than involving different nations

⚡**intranet** /íntrə net/ *n* a network of computers, especially one using World Wide Web conventions, accessible only to authorized users, e.g. those within a company

intransigent /in tránssijənt, -zijənt/, **intransigeant** *adj* firmly or unreasonably refusing even to consider changing a decision or attitude ■ *n* a person who refuses to compromise or change an attitude or decision, especially in politics [Late 19C. < French, < Spanish *los intransigentes*, a political party (literally 'the uncompromising ones') < *transigir* 'to compromise' < Latin *transigere* (see TRANSACTION).] —**intransigence** /in tránssijənss, -zi-/ *n* —**intransigently** *adv*

intransitive /in tránssitiv/ *adj* without a direct object, e.g. the verb 'die' in the sentence 'He was slowly dying' ■ *n* a verb that does not take a direct object —**intransitively** *adv* —**intransitiveness** *n*

intranuclear /íntrə nyóokli ər/ *adj* **1** existing or occurring within the nucleus of an atom **2** existing or occurring within the nucleus of a cell

intraocular /íntrə ókyōōlər/ *adj* within or introduced into the inside of the eyeball —**intraocularly** *adv*

intraperitoneal /íntrə pérritō neé əl/ *adj* within or introduced into the peritoneal cavity —**intraperitoneally** *adv*

intrapersonal /íntrə púrss'nəl/ *adj* relating to the internal aspects of a person, especially emotions —**intrapersonally** *adv*

intrapreneur /íntrəprə núr/ *n* an employee with a flair for innovation and risk-taking who is given unusual freedom to develop products or subsidiary businesses within a company [Late 20C. < INTRA- + ENTREPRENEUR.] —**intrapreneurial** *adj* —**intrapreneurialism** *n* —**intrapreneurially** *adv*

intraspecific /íntrəspə síffik/, **intraspecies** /-speésh eez, -speéss-/ *adj* existing within a single species or confined to members of one species

intrauterine /íntrə yóotə rīn/ *adj* existing, occurring, or designed to be used inside the womb

intrauterine device *n* a plastic or metal device that is inserted into the cavity of the womb in order to prevent pregnancy

intravascular /íntrə váskyōōlər/ *adj* within the blood vessels or a similar system in animals or plants —**intravascularly** *adv*

intravenous /íntrə veénəss/ *adj* **1** existing or occurring inside a vein, or administered into a vein **2** used in administering fluids or medicines into the veins —**intravenously** *adv*

intraventricular /íntrə ven tríkyōōlər/ *adj* within or introduced into a ventricle, such as one in the heart or brain —**intraventricularly** *adv*

intravital /íntrə vít'l/, **intravitam** /-veé tam/ *adj* occurring in or used on a living cell or organism [Late 19thC. < modern Latin *intra vitam* 'within life'.] —**intravitally** *adv*

in-tray *n* a tray on somebody's desk for papers that have not yet been dealt with

intrench *vti* = **entrench**

intrepid /in tréppid/ *adj* fearless and persistent in the pursuit of something (*literary or humorous*) [Late 17C. Directly or via French *intrépide* < Latin *intrepidus* 'not agitated' < *trepidus* 'agitated'.] —**intrepidity** /íntrə píddəti/ *n* —**intrepidly** *adv* —**intrepidness** *n*

~~**intrest**~~ incorrect spelling of **interest**

intricacy /íntrikəssi/ (*plural* **-cies**) *n* **1** the complex character of something that has many details, parts, or other elements **2** something that is complex and has many details, parts, or other elements (*often plural*)

intricate /íntrikət/ *adj* **1** containing many details or small parts that are skilfully made or assembled **2** with many interrelated elements, parts, or factors so as to be complex and difficult to understand or resolve [15C. < Latin *intricatus*, past participle of *intricare* 'entangle' < *tricae* 'impediments, tricks'.] —**intricately** *adv* —**intricateness** *n*

intrigant /íntrigənt/, **intriguant** *n* a deviser of secret plots or schemes (*archaic*)

intrigue *n* /in treeg, in treég/ **1 SECRET PLOTTING** secret scheming or plotting **2 SECRET PLOT** a secret scheme or plot **3 SECRET LOVE AFFAIR** a secret love affair (*archaic*) ■ *v* /in treég/ (**-trigues, -triguing, -trigued**) **1** *vt* **INTEREST** to make somebody greatly interested or curious **2** *vi* **SCHEME** to scheme or use underhand methods to achieve something [Early 17C. Via French < Italian *intrigo* < *intrigare* 'entangle' < Latin *intricare* (see INTRICATE).] —**intriguer** /in treégər/ *n* —**intriguingly** *adv*

intrinsic /in trínssik/, **intrinsical** /-trínssik'l/ *adj* **1 BASIC AND ESSENTIAL** belonging to something as one of the basic and essential elements that make it what it is **2 OF ITSELF** by or in itself, rather than because of its associations or consequences **3 FOUND IN BODY PART** occurring wholly within or belonging wholly to a part of the body, e.g. an organ [15C. Via French *intrinsèque* < late Latin *intrinsecus* 'inward' < assumed Latin *intrim* 'within'.] —**intrinsically** *adv*

intrinsic factor *n* a protein produced in the stomach that promotes the absorption of vitamin B_{12}

intrinsic semiconductor *n* a semiconductor of very high purity in which the density of charge carriers is that of the material itself and is not modified by the presence of impurities

intro /íntrō/ *n* an introduction, especially the opening few bars of a piece of pop music (*informal*) [Early 19C. Shortening.]

intro. *abbr* **1** introduction **2** introductory

intro- *prefix* **1** in, into ○ *intromission* **2** inward ○ *introvert* [< Latin *intro* 'to the inside']

introd. *abbr* **1** introduction **2** introductory

introduce /íntrə dyóoss/ (**-duces, -ducing, -duced**) *v* **1** *vt* **ACQUAINT WITH SOMEBODY ELSE** to present yourself or another person to somebody else and become acquainted with that person **2** *vt* **GIVE AUDIENCE FORETASTE** to tell an audience a little about what or whom they are going to see or hear **3** *vt* **BRING IN SOMETHING NEW** to bring something to a place, into existence, or into operation for the first time **4** *vt* **CAUSE TO EXPERIENCE SOMETHING NEW** to make somebody aware of something for the first time, or give a first experience of something **5** *vt* **PREFACE WITH SOMETHING ELSE** to begin an action with a preface of some sort, especially one designed to get people's attention **6** *vt* **TALK ABOUT SOMETHING NEW** to mention a matter for the first time **7** *vt* **PRESENT LEGISLATION FORMALLY** to present proposed legislation formally to an assembly, so that it can be debated and voted on **8** *vt* **INSERT** to insert one thing into another **9 BRING IN NEW SPECIES** to place or establish an individual or species of plant or animal in a new habitat or environment [15C. Either < Latin *introducere* 'lead in' < *ducere* 'to lead', or back-formation < INTRODUCTION.] —**introducer** *n* —**introducible** *adj*

introduction /íntrə dúksh'n/ *n* **1 EXPLANATORY SECTION AT BEGINNING** a section at the beginning of a book or of another piece of writing, e.g. one that summarizes what it is about or sets the scene **2 SOMETHING GIVING BASIC FACTS** a book or course of study that gives somebody basic facts or skills in a field **3 MAKING ACQUAINTANCE** the act of formally presenting somebody or yourself to somebody else and becoming acquainted **4 PRESENTATION** the act of presenting somebody or something to an audience, assembly, or other group **5 FIRST EXPERIENCE** somebody's first experience of something **6 BEGINNING OF PIECE OF MUSIC** the opening passage or movement of a piece of music **7 BRINGING IN SOMETHING NEW** the act of bringing something to a place, into existence, into operation, or into an activity for the first time **8 SOMETHING BROUGHT IN** something brought in from elsewhere or created **9 INSERTION** the insertion of something somewhere [14C. Directly or via French < Latin *introduction-* < *introduct-*, past participle of *introducere* (see INTRODUCE).]

introductory /íntrə dúktəri/ *adj* **1 GIVING FORETASTE** telling a little about what is to come **2 PROVIDING THE BASICS** providing the basic facts or skills **3 INITIAL** made or used when something begins or is first introduced [14C. Directly or via Old French *introductoire* < late Latin *introductorius* < *introduct-* (see INTRODUCTION).] —**introductorily** *adv* —**introductoriness** *n*

introgression /íntrə grésh'n/ *n* the incorporation of genes from one species into the gene pool of another as a result of hybridization [Mid-17C. < INTRO- + *-gression* 'going', as in PROGRESSION.] —**introgressant** *adj* —**introgressive** *adj*

introit /ín troyt/, **Introit** *n* **1** the part of the Roman Catholic Mass consisting of psalm verses and the Gloria Patri, said or sung when the priest first approaches the altar **2** a psalm or hymn sung as the minister enters the church at the beginning of the Anglican service of Holy Communion [15C. Via French < medieval Latin *introitus* < Latin, 'entrance', past participle of *introire* 'go in' < *ire* 'to go'.] —**introital** /in tróyt'l/ *adj*

introjection /íntrə jéksh'n/ *n* the unconscious adoption by somebody of the values or attitudes of somebody else, whom that person wants to impress or be accepted by [Mid-19C. < INTRO- + *-jection* as in PROJECTION.] —**introject** /íntrə jékt/ *vt*

intromission /íntrə mísh'n/ *n* the inserting or admitting of something into something else (*formal*) [Mid-16C. Directly or via French < medieval Latin *intromission-* < Latin *intromittere*.] —**intromissive** *adj*

intron /ín tron/ *n* a section of DNA that is not expressed in the gene product. ◊ **exon**[1] [Late 20C. < INTRAGENIC.]

introrse /in tráwrss/ *adj* pointing and opening inwards, as the anthers of some flowers do, releasing pollen towards the centre of the flower [Mid-19C. < Latin *introrsus*, contraction of *introversus* < *versus*, past participle of *vertere* 'to turn'.] —**introrsely** *adv*

introspect /íntrə spékt/ *vi* to undertake a detailed mental self-examination of feelings, thoughts, and motives [Late 17C. Directly or via Latin *introspectare* 'look into repeatedly' < *introspect-*, past participle of *introspicere* 'look into' < *specere* 'to look'.]

introspection /íntrə spéksh'n/ *n* the detailed mental self-examination of feelings, thoughts, and motives, especially when this is regarded as unhealthy or obsessive —**introspectional** *adj*

introspectionism /íntrə spéksh'nizəm/ *n* a school of psychology concentrating on the study of immediate subjective experience. US term **introspective psychology**. ◊ **behaviourism** —**introspectionistic** /íntrə spékshə nístik/ *adj*

introspective /íntrə spéktiv/ *adj* making a deep and candid examination of your own feelings, thoughts, and motives —**introspectively** *adv*

introspective psychology *n* PSYCHOL = **introspectionism**

introversion /íntrə vúrsh'n/ *n* **1** the tendency to be more interested in your own feelings and thoughts than in the people and world around you. ◊ **extroversion 2** a turning inwards of a hollow organ such as the womb into itself [Mid-17C. < INTROVERT.]

introvert *n* /íntrə vurt/ **1** a shy person who tends not to socialize much **2** a person whose feelings and thoughts are directed inward ■ *adj* = **introverted** [Mid-17C. < modern Latin *introvertere* 'turn in' < Latin *vertere* 'to turn'.]

introverted /íntrə vúrtid/ *adj* **1 SHY** tending to be shy and quiet or ill at ease in a group **2 INTERESTED IN OWN FEELINGS** interested more in your own feelings, thoughts, and motives than in other people and the world around you **3 TURNED INTO ITSELF** turned into itself or pulled back inside a larger part

intrude /in tróod/ (**-trudes, -truding, -truded**) *v* **1** *vi* **INVADE SOMEBODY'S PRIVACY** to disturb somebody's peace or privacy by going where you have not been invited or are not welcome **2** *vi* **HAVE UNPLEASANT EFFECT** to have an unpleasant or undesired effect on something **3** *vt* **ADD SOMETHING UNPLEASANT** to add or mention something inappropriate or unwanted (*formal*) **4** *vti* **MOVE INTO ROCK FORMATION** to move in a molten state into a pre-existing rock formation, or force molten rock into a pre-existing rock formation [15C. Partly < Latin *intrudere* 'thrust in' < *trudere* 'to thrust'; partly back-formation < INTRUSION.]

intruder /in tróodər/ *n* **1** an illegal entrant into a building or property, usually in order to commit a crime **2** a person who is present where he or she is not welcome

intrusion /in tróozh'n/ *n* **1 DISTURBANCE** a disturbing of somebody's peace or privacy by an unwelcome arrival or presence **2 SOMETHING UNWELCOME** an unwelcome presence or effect that disturbs or upsets something **3 UNLAWFUL ENTRY** an illegal entry into a place, often by force, in order to commit a crime (*formal*) **4 INTRUDED ROCK** a body of igneous rock, often massive with associated linear dykes and sills, that has moved while molten into older solid rocks with subsequent alteration of those rocks **5 MOVEMENT OF MOLTEN ROCK** the movement of molten rock (**magma**) into pre-existing rock [14C. Directly or via French < medieval Latin *intrusion-* < Latin *intrus-*, past participle of *intrudere* (see INTRUDE).] —**intrusional** *adj*

intrusive /in tróossiv/ *adj* **1 INTRUDING** causing a disturbance or having an unpleasant effect **2 FORMED BY INTRUSION** describes a rock formed by having moved while in a molten state into pre-existing rocks **3 OF CONNECTING SPEECH SOUND** describes a speech sound that is introduced between two words only to facilitate more fluent pronunciation —**intrusively** *adv* —**intrusiveness** *n*

intrust *vt* = **entrust**

intubate /íntyoo bayt/ (**-bates, -bating, -bated**) *v* **1** *vti* to insert a tube through the vocal cords and into the windpipe in order to provide a patient's lungs with oxygen, usually during surgery under anaesthesia **2** *vt* to treat a patient by inserting a tube into the windpipe so that oxygen can be supplied to the lungs [Late 19C. < IN-[2] + Latin *tuba* 'tube'.] —**intubation** /íntyoo báysh'n/ *n*

intuit /in tyóo it/ *vt* to be aware of or know something without having to think about it or learn it [Mid-19C. Back-formation < INTUITION.] —**intuitable** *adj*

intuition /íntyoo ísh'n/ *n* **1 INSTINCTIVE KNOWLEDGE** the state of being aware of or knowing something without having to discover or perceive it, or the ability to do this **2 INSTINCTIVE BELIEF** something known or believed instinctively, without actual evidence for it **3 IMMEDIATE KNOWLEDGE** immediate knowledge of something [15C. Directly or via French < late Latin *intuition-* 'consideration' < Latin *intueri* 'look upon' < *tueri* 'to look'.] —**intuitional** *adj* —**intuitionally** *adv*

intuitionism /íntyoo ísh'nizəm/ *n* **1 DOCTRINE OF INTUITIVE PERCEPTION** the doctrine that asserts that a perceived object is intuitively known to be real **2 ETHICAL PRINCIPLES UNDERSTOOD THROUGH INTUITION** the doctrine that knowledge of goodness or obligation and the principles governing them can be discerned through intuition **3 MATHEMATICAL THEORY** a theory in the foundation of mathematics that holds that only proofs constrained by certain restrictions are permitted. ◊ **formalism, logicism**

intuitive /in tyóo itiv/ *adj* **1** known directly and instinctively, without being discovered or consciously perceived **2** knowing things instinctively —**intuitively** *adv* —**intuitiveness** *n*

intumesce /íntyoo méss/ (**-mesces, -mescing, -mesced**) *vi* to become enlarged or swollen as a result of increased flow of blood or other fluids [Late 18C. < Latin *intumescere* 'swell up' < *tumescere* (see TUMESCENT).] —**intumescence** *n* —**intumescent** *adj*

intussuscept /íntəssə sépt/ *vti* to undergo, or cause part of a tubular structure to undergo, a partial sliding into itself, e.g. as part of the intestine sometimes does [Early 19C. Back-formation < INTUSSUSCEPTION.] —**intussusceptive** *adj*

intussusception /íntəssə sépsh'n/ *n* **1** a sliding of a portion of a tubular organ into another portion, especially a condition of the bowel in which this happens, creating swelling that leads to obstruction **2** the growth of the surface area of a cell wall by the incorporation of particles into the wall [Early 18C. Directly or via French < modern Latin *intussusception-* < Latin *intus* 'within' + *susception-* 'undertaking' < *suscept-*, past participle of *suscipere* (see SUSCEPTIBLE).]

intwine *vti* = **entwine**

intwist *vt* = **entwist**

~~**inuendo**~~ incorrect spelling of **innuendo**

Inuit /ínnoo it, -yoo-/ (*plural* **-it** *or* **-its**), **Innuit** (*plural* **-it** *or* **-its**) *n* **1** a member of an aboriginal people who live in the coastal Canadian Arctic and in Greenland **2** a language of the Inuit people, forming one branch of Eskimo-Aleut. Native speakers: 60,000. ◊ **Inuktitut** [Mid-18C. < Inuit, plural of *inuk* 'person'.] —**Inuit** *adj*

USAGE The Inuit Circumpolar Conference, held in 1977 in Barrow, Alaska, chose officially to replace the term *Eskimo* with ***Inuit*** (which means 'the real people'). *Eskimo* nonetheless remains in common use, appearing even in academic contexts. Because some may find it offensive, care should be exercised in using this word.

Inuktitut /i nóoktətoot/ *n* a language of the Inuit people, especially those in the E Arctic [Late 20C. < Inuit, 'the Inuit way'.]

inulase /ínnyoo layz, -layss/ *n* an enzyme that brings about the breakdown of inulin [Late 19C. < INULIN.]

inulin /ínnyoo lin/ *n* a fructose polysaccharide that is a food reserve found in the roots and tubers of various plants [Early 19C. < Latin *inula* 'elecampane'.]

inunction /in úngksh'n/ *n* **1** the rubbing in of oil or ointment **2** the anointing of somebody with oil as part of a religious ceremony (*formal*) [15C. < Latin *inunction-* <, *inunguere* 'anoint' (literally 'smear on') < *unguere* 'to smear'.]

inundate /ín un dayt, ínnən-/ (**-dates, -dating, -dated**) *vt* **1** to overwhelm somebody with a huge quantity of things that must be dealt with **2** to flood a place with water (*formal*) [Late 16C. Back-formation < INUNDATION.] —**inundator** *n* —**inundatory** /in úndətəri/ *adj*

inundation /ín un dáysh'n, ínnən-/ *n* **1** an accumulation of an overwhelming amount of things that somebody has to deal with **2** a flood of water [15C. Directly or via Old French *inondacion* < Latin *inundation-* < *inundare* 'flow onto' < *unda* (see UNDULATE).]

Inupiaq /i nóopi ak, i nyoo-/, **Inupik** /i nóo pik/ *n* a language of the Inuit people who live in N Alaska [Mid-20C. < Inuit, < *inuk* 'person' + *piaq* 'genuine'.]

Inupiat /i nóopi at, -nyoo-/ *npl* an Inuit people who live along the Beaufort Sea and Chukchi Coast of the Arctic Ocean [Late 20C. < Inuit (plural) < *inuk* 'person' + *piaq* 'genuine'.]

Inupik *n, adj* LANG = **Inupiaq**

inurbane /in ur báyn/ *adj* lacking good manners or sophistication —**inurbanely** *adv* —**inurbanity** /ín ur bánnəti/ *n*

inure /i nyóor/ (**-ures, -uring, -ured**), **enure** (**-ures, -uring, -ured**) *v* **1** *vt* to make somebody used to something unpleasant over a period of time, so that he or she no longer is bothered or upset by it **2** *vi* to come into operation or effect [15C. < assumed Anglo-Norman *eneurer* 'accustom by use' < assumed *eure* 'use' < Latin *opera* 'work'.] —**inurement** *n*

inurn /in úrn/ *vt* **1** to place a cremated body's ashes in an urn **2** to put a dead body in a grave (*formal*) —**inurnment** *n*

in utero /in yóotər ō/ *adv, adj* in or while still inside a woman's womb [< Latin]

inv. *abbr* **1** invariable **2** invented **3** invention **4** inventor **5** invoice

in vacuo /in vákyoo ō/ *adv* **1** in a vacuum **2** in isolation, without considering any evidence [< Latin]

invade /in váyd/ (**-vades, -vading, -vaded**) *v* **1** *vti* **ENTER COUNTRY BY MILITARY FORCE** to enter a country by force with or as an army, especially in order to conquer it **2** *vt* **ENTER AND SPREAD THROUGH** to enter and spread throughout something completely **3** *vt* **GO SOMEWHERE IN NUMBERS** to enter or be present in a place in great numbers **4** *vt* **SPOIL** to spoil something by interfering, interrupting, or reducing it **5** *vti* **CAUSE DISEASE** to enter and spread gradually throughout a part of the body, causing harm or damage **6** *vti* **GROW RAPIDLY AND HARMFULLY** to become established and spread rapidly in an area, crowding out the pre-existing plants [15C. Directly or via Old French *invader* < Latin *invadere* 'go in' < *vadere* 'to go'.] —**invadable** *adj* —**invader** *n*

invaginate /in vájji nayt/ (**-nates, -nating, -nated**) *vti* to push the wall of a cavity or hollow organ inwards or one section of a hollow organ into another, like a glove finger pushed into itself [Mid-17C. Back-formation < INVAGINATION.]

invagination /in vájji náysh'n/ *n* **1 PUSHING SOMETHING INSIDE ITSELF** the pushing of something into itself or partially inside out, like a glove finger pushed into itself, or the condition of something that results from this **2 INVAGINATED ORGAN** a hollow organ or body part that has been pushed back inside itself **3 INFOLDING OF CELL STRUCTURE** the process of folding a portion of a cell structure inwards, as when the cell membrane turns inwards during phagocytosis **4 FORMING OF HOLLOW GROWTH INSIDE** the pushing inwards of a layer of cells to produce a hollow ingrowth in something, as when the wall of the blastula forms the gastrula [Mid-17C. < medieval Latin *invaginare* 'sheathe' < Latin *vagina* 'sheath'.]

invalid[1] /in vállid/ *adj* **1** not legally binding or enforceable **2** not acceptable or correct because of being based on a mistake or employing flawed reasoning [Mid-16C. < Latin *invalidus* 'not strong' < *validus* (see VALID).] —**invalidly** *adv*

invalid[2] /ínvəlid, -leed/ *n* **1 SOMEBODY WITH PERSISTENT DISEASE** a patient who has been affected by a disease or medical disorder over a long period **2 OFFENSIVE TERM** an offensive term for somebody with disabilities (*dated*) ■ *adj* **1 AFFECTED BY PERSISTENT DISEASE** having a chronic disease or medical disorder **2 FOR SOMEBODY WITH PERSISTENT LONG-TERM DISEASE** intended for somebody who has a persistent long-term disease or medical disorder ■ *vt* **1 CAUSE TO BE AN INVALID** to cause somebody to have a persistent long-term disease or medical disorder **2 SEND HOME BECAUSE OF ILLNESS** to send somebody away or home for good, especially from the armed forces, because of long-term illness or severe injury [Mid-17C. < INVALID[1].]

invalidate /in vál li dayt/ (**-dates, -dating, -dated**) *vt* **1** to deprive something of its legal force or value **2** to prove that something is wrong or make something worthless —**invalidation** /in válli dáysh'n/ *n* —**invalidator** *n*

SYNONYMS See ***nullify***.

invalidism /ínvəlidizəm, -leed-/ *n* **1** chronic illness or medical disorder **2** an abnormal preoccupation with the state of personal health that causes somebody to live like an invalid. ◊ **hypochondriasis**

invalidity /invə líddəti/ *n* **1** a lack of soundness or accuracy that results from an error in reasoning **2** the condition of not being legally binding or enforceable

invalidity benefit *n* an allowance paid by the government to somebody whose long-term illness has prevented him or her from working for at least six months

invaluable /in vállyoo əb'l/ *adj* extremely useful or valuable —**invaluableness** *n* —**invaluably** *adv*

invariable /in váiri əb'l/ *adj* never changing or varying ■ *n* a mathematical quantity that is a constant —**invariability** /in váiri ə bílləti/ *n* —**invariableness** *n*

invariably /in váiri əbli/ *adv* always or almost always

invariant /in váiri ənt/ *adj* **1** = **invariable** *adj*. **2** describes a quantity or set of quantities that is not changed by a designated mathematical operation such as the transformation of coordinates ■ *n* a relationship that is not changed by a designated mathematical operation such as the transformation of coordinates —**invariance** *n* —**invariancy** *n*

invasion /in váyzh'n/ *n* **1 ATTEMPT TO CONQUER** a hostile entry of an armed force into a country's territory, especially with the intention of conquering it **2 ARRIVAL IN LARGE NUMBERS** the arrival of large numbers of people or things at one time ○ *an invasion of tourists* **3 SPOILING** a spoiling of something by interfering with it or taking some of it away **4 SPREAD OF SOMETHING HARMFUL** the arrival or spread of something that causes damage or harm **5 SPREAD OF DISEASE** the spread of disease-causing organisms or malignant cells in the body **6 AGGRESSIVE SPREAD OF PLANT** the aggressive spread of a plant species in an area, stifling the growth of pre-existing species [15C. Directly or via French < late Latin *invasion-* < Latin *invas-*, past participle of *invadere* (see INVADE).]

invasive /in váyssiv/ *adj* **1 ATTACKING** involving or mounting a military attack on a territory, especially with a view to conquering it **2 INTRUDING** involving an intrusion or infringement, e.g. of somebody's privacy or rights **3 ATTACKING ADJACENT TISSUE** having or showing a tendency to spread from the point of origin to adjacent tissue, as some cancers do **4 INTO PATIENT'S BODY** done by inserting something into or operating on the body through an incision or a natural orifice **5 GROWING AGGRESSIVELY** growing aggressively in an area and stifling the growth of pre-existing plants —**invasively** *adv* —**invasiveness** *n*

invective /in véktiv/ *n* an abusive expression, or language used to attack or blame somebody (*formal*) ■ *adj* using abusive language (*formal*) [15C. Directly or via French *invectif* < late Latin *invectivus* 'abusive' < Latin *invehere* 'carry in' < *vehere* 'carry'.] —**invectively** *adv* —**invectiveness** *n*

inveigh /in váy/ *vi* to speak angrily in criticism of or protest at something [15C. < Latin *invehere* (see INVECTIVE).] —**inveigher** *n*

inveigle /in váyg'l, -veég-/ (**-gles, -gling, -gled**) *vt* **1** to charm or entice somebody into doing something that he or she would not otherwise have done ○ *inveigled me into making the trip* **2** to obtain something by persuading somebody to give it [15C. < Anglo-Norman *envegler*, alteration of French *aveugler* 'deprive of sight' < assumed Vulgar Latin *aboculus* 'without eye' < Latin *oculus* 'eye'.] —**inveiglement** *n* —**inveigler** *n*

invent /in vént/ *vt* **1** to be the first to think of, make, or use something **2** to make up something false, e.g. a false excuse [15C. < Latin *invent-*, past participle of *invenire* 'come upon' < *venire* (see VENUE).] —**inventable** *adj* —**inventor** *n*

invention /in vénsh'n/ *n* **1 CREATED THING** a thing that somebody has created, especially a device or process **2 ACT OF CREATING** the creation of something new **3 LIE** a lie, or the telling of lies (*used euphemistically*) **4 CREATIVE ABILITY** the talent to create new things **5 SHORT INSTRUMENTAL WORK** a short instrumental work, usually for keyboard, that has two or three parts and employs the technique of counterpoint —**inventional** *adj* —**inventionless** *adj*

inventive /in véntiv/ *adj* **1 SKILLED AT INVENTING** good at creating new things **2 DISPLAYING CREATIVITY** displaying creativity or imagination in its design **3 INVOLVED IN INVENTION** involved in or concerned with invention —**inventively** *adv* —**inventiveness** *n*

inventory /ínvəntəri/ *n* (*plural* **-ries**) **1 LIST OF ITEMS** a list of things, especially items of property **2 RECORD OF ASSETS** a record of a business's current assets, including property owned as well as merchandise on hand and the value of work in progress and work completed but not sold **3 ASSETS** a company's assets as a whole, or the value of them **4 STOCK OF GOODS** the merchandise or stock that a store or company has on hand **5** *US* BUSINESS = **stocktaking** *n*. **2** ■ *vt* (**-ries, -rying, -ried**) **MAKE INVENTORY OF** to make an inventory of items or enter a specific item on an inventory [15C. < medieval Latin *inventorium*, alteration of late Latin *inventarium* 'list of what is found' < Latin *invenire* (see INVENT).] —**inventoriable** *adj* —**inventorial** *adj* —**inventorially** *adv*

inveracity /ínvə rássəti/ (*plural* **-ties**) *n* a lie, or the telling of lies (*humorous*)

Inverclyde /ínvər klíd/ council area in SW Scotland. Area: 162 sq. km/49 sq. mi.

inverness /ínvər néss/ *n* a long overcoat with a rounded collar and a detachable cape [Mid-19C. After INVERNESS.]

Inverness /ínvər néss/ city in N Scotland. Population: 62,647 (1991).

inverse /in vúrss, ín vurss/ *adj* **1 OPPOSITE OR REVERSING** opposite to or reversing something **2 INVOLVING OPPOSITELY AFFECTED VARIABLES** involving two variables that are in a mathematical relationship where, when one increases, the other decreases and vice versa ■ *n* **1 OPPOSITE** something that is a total opposite **2 ELEMENT OF SET** either of two elements of a set that when added together give 0, one being the negative of the other, e.g. 7 and –7 **3** MATH = **inverse function** **4 OPPOSITE LOGICAL PROPOSITION** a logical proposition in which both the subject and the predicate are the opposite of another proposition [15C. < Latin *inversus*, past participle of *invertere* 'turn upside down', literally 'turn in' < *vertere* 'to turn'.] —**inversely** *adv*

inverse function *n* a mathematical operation or function that exactly reverses another operation or function

inversely proportional *adj* **1** opposite in size, degree, or rate of development **2** involving a mathematical relationship in which an increase in one variable by a given factor brings about a decrease by the same factor in another

inverse square law *n* a law stating that the magnitude of a physical quantity varies inversely with the square of its distance from its source

inversion /in vúrsh'n/ *n* **1 REVERSAL** a reversing of the order, arrangement, or position of something **2 REVERSED STATE OR THING** a state in which the order, arrangement, or position of something is reversed, or something in such a state **3** GRAM = **anastrophe** **4 TEMPERATURE INCREASE WITH ALTITUDE** a stable atmospheric condition in which air temperature increases vertically upwards through a layer **5 INVERTING OF ORGAN** abnormal positioning of an organ, especially the abnormal turning inwards or inside out of an organ **6 INVERTED RATIO** the transformation of a mathematical proportion by inverting the ratio and order of its terms **7 CHANGING OF INTERVAL BY OCTAVE** a raising of the lower note of an interval, or a lowering of the upper note, by an octave **8 MOVING OF CHORD TONE** a moving of the root tone of a chord to a position other than the lowest **9 REVERSING OF MELODY INTERVALS** a converting of all the intervals in a melody from ascending to descending and vice versa **10 PRODUCTION OF OPPOSITE OPTICAL ACTIVITY** a chemical reaction in which an optically active compound gives a product with opposite optical configuration **11 CHROMOSOMAL MUTATION** a chromosomal mutation in which a block of genes in a segment is in reverse order —**inversive** *adj*

invert *vt* /in vúrt/ **1 REVERSE ARRANGEMENT** to reverse the order, position, or arrangement of something **2 MAKE OPPOSITE** to change something to its opposite or contrary **3 ALTER POSITION OF NOTES** to change the position or arrangement of the musical notes in an interval, chord, or melody to produce inversion **4 CHANGE OPTICAL CONFIGURATION** to convert an optically active isomer into an isomer with the opposite configuration **5 CONVERT LOGICAL PROPOSITION** to negate both the subject and predicate of a logical proposition ■ *n* /ín vurt/ **PRODUCT OF INVERSION** a substance obtained by optical inversion. ◊ **invert sugar** ■ *adj* /ín vurt/ **OPTICALLY INVERTED** subjected to optical inversion [Mid-16C. < Latin *invertere* (see INVERSE).] —**invertibility** /-bílləti/ *n* —**invertible** *adj*

invertase /in vúr tayz, -tayss/ *n* an enzyme that hydrolyzes sucrose

invertebrate /in vúrtibrət/ *n* **ANIMAL WITHOUT BACKBONE** an animal such as an insect or worm that does not have a backbone ■ *adj* **1 WITH NO BACKBONE** lacking a backbone or spinal column **2 OF INVERTEBRATES** relating to or consisting of animals that lack backbones **3 LACKING CHARACTER** lacking strength of character

inverted /in vúrtid/ *adj* **1 REVERSED** turned upside down, inside out, or back to front **2 WITH FUNDAMENTAL NOTE REPOSITIONED** modified so that the fundamental note of the chord is not the lowest note of the chord **3 WITH NOTES IN MIRROR IMAGE** with the musical notes so arranged that every ascending interval is made descending and vice versa

inverted comma *n* either of a pair of punctuation marks in double (" ") or single (' ') form, used around direct speech, quotations, and titles and to give special emphasis to particular words. US term **quotation mark**

PUNCTUATION ***Inverted commas*** are used to enclose direct speech and quotations: *'Where are you?' he called. Mae West said, 'A man in the house is worth two in the street'.* They are also used around some titles, e.g. those of poems, short stories, and articles: *Hilaire Belloc's poem 'On a Sundial'*, but titles of novels, plays, films, etc. are conventionally printed in italics instead. Inverted commas are often used to make a particular word or phrase stand out from the surrounding text, usually to draw attention to it or because the author is using it self-consciously or sceptically: *words such as 'toothbrush' and 'redcurrant'; in a more 'family-friendly' environment.* Either single (' ') or double (" ") inverted commas may be used in all these cases. Where one piece of direct speech occurs within another, or within a quotation, use inverted commas of the opposite type: *She said, 'I told him to leave and he asked "Why should I?"'*

inverted mordent *n* a musical ornament consisting of two notes of the same pitch separated by a third note one step above the others

inverted pleat *n* a flat symmetrical pleat formed by

folding the fabric to the front on either side of the section being pleated

inverted snob *n* a person who disapproves of his or her own or a higher social class —**inverted snobbery** *n*

inverter /in vúrtər/ *n* **1** somebody or something that inverts or causes an inversion **2** a device that changes direct current into alternating current and is commonly used on boats to operate devices such as radios from batteries

invert sugar *n* a mixture of glucose and fructose. Source: optical inversion of sucrose, fruits, honey. Use: in the food industry.

invest /in vést/ *v* **1** *vti* **BUY SHARES OR BONDS** to use money to buy or participate in a business enterprise that offers the possibility of profit, especially by buying shares or bonds **2** *vti* **DEPOSIT MONEY WITH BANK** to deposit money with a bank or other financial institution in an account that pays interest **3** *vti* **SPEND MONEY ON PROJECT** to spend money on something in the hope of a future return or benefit **4** *vt* **CONTRIBUTE EFFORT TO** to contribute time, energy, or effort to an activity, project, or undertaking in the expectation of a benefit **5** *vt* **GIVE SOMETHING A QUALITY** to provide somebody or something with a particular quality or characteristic **6** *vt* **CONFER SOMETHING ON** to confer something such as a power or right on a person or group ○ *The charter invests the directors with the right to spend money as they see fit.* **7** *vi* **MAKE PURCHASE** to use money to buy something, especially something that somebody should be able to use for a relatively long time (*informal*) ○ *It's time this family invested in a new car.* **8** *vt* **INSTALL IN OFFICIAL ROLE** to install somebody formally or ceremoniously in an official position (*formal*) ○ *The prince was invested in a ceremony held at the castle.* **9** *vt* **ADORN** to dress, clothe, or cover somebody or something with a garment or other covering (*literary*) **10** *vt* **BESIEGE** to lay siege to a place (*archaic*) [Mid-16C. Directly or via French *investir* < Latin *investire* 'clothe (in)' < *vestis* 'clothing'.] —**investable** *adj*

investigate /in vésti gayt/ (**-gates, -gating, -gated**) *v* **1** *vti* to carry out a detailed examination or enquiry, especially officially, in order to find out about something or somebody ○ *The local police are investigating a murder.* **2** *vi* to have a look or go and see what has happened ○ *We heard noises downstairs, so Fred went down to investigate.* [Early 16C. < Latin *investigare* 'look into for traces' < *vestigium* 'footprint'.] —**investigable** *adj* —**investigation** /in vésti gáysh'n/ *n* —**investigational** *adj*

investigative /in véstigətiv/, **investigatory** /-təri/ *adj* **1** responsible for or specializing in investigating **2** used in or relating to investigation ○ *investigative techniques*

investigator /in vésti gaytər/ *n* a professional seeker of facts about somebody or something, especially somebody who investigates crimes or prepares official or confidential reports. ◊ **private detective**

investigatory *adj* = **investigative**

investiture /in véstichər/ *n* **1** the formal installing of somebody in a position or role, especially an official one, or a ceremony held to mark this **2** the appointment of bishops in the Roman Catholic Church by a civil ruler instead of by the Church [14C. < medieval Latin *investitura* < Latin *investire* 'clothe' (see INVEST); because the person is clothed in the insignia of the position.]

investment /in véstmənt/ *n* **1** **USE OF MONEY FOR FUTURE PROFIT** the outlay of money, e.g. by depositing it in a bank or by buying shares in a company, with the object of making a profit **2** **MONEY INVESTED** an amount of money invested in something for the purpose of making a profit **3** **SOMETHING INVESTED** something such as a company, endeavour, or object that money is invested in with the goal of making a profit **4** **CONTRIBUTION TO ACTIVITY** a contribution of something such as time, energy, or effort to an activity, project, or undertaking, in the expectation of a benefit **5** **PURCHASE** a purchase, especially something that somebody should be able to use for a relatively long time (*informal*) **6** **INVESTITURE** the formal or ceremonial installing of somebody in a role or position, especially an official one (*formal*) **7** **SIEGE** a siege or besieging (*archaic*) **8** **MONEY IN COMPANY'S PROPERTY** the outlay of money that a company's existing buildings, equipment, and materials is equivalent to **9** **OUTER LAYERS OF ORGANISM** the outer layers of an animal or organ

investment analyst *n* a researcher employed by a brokerage firm to research investments

investment company *n* *US* a company that holds securities in other companies purely for investment

investment trust *n* a legal arrangement of investors that invests its capital in securities

investor /in véstər/ *n* a person, company, or other organization that has money invested in something, especially one that holds shares in publicly owned corporations

inveterate /in véttərət/ *adj* **1** fixed in a habit or practice, especially a bad one **2** firmly established and of long standing [14C. < Latin *inveteratus*, past participle of *inveterare* 'become old' < *veter-* 'old'.] —**inveteracy** *n* —**inveterately** *adv* —**inveterateness** *n*

inviable /in ví əb'l/ *adj* unable to survive, especially financially or biologically —**inviability** /in ví ə bíllәti/ *n* —**inviableness** *n* —**inviably** /in ví əbli/ *adv*

invidious /in víddi əss/ *adj* **1** making or implying an unfair distinction **2** unpleasant because producing or likely to produce jealousy, resentment, or hatred in other people [Early 17C. < Latin *invidiosus* < *invidia* 'ill will', literally 'looking at' < *videre* 'to look'.] —**invidiously** *adv* —**invidiousness** *n*

USAGE See *insidious*.

invigilate /in víjji layt/ (**-lates, -lating, -lated**) *vti* to supervise an examination, especially in order to prevent cheating. US term **proctor** *v.* [Mid-16C. < Latin *invigilare* 'to watch' < *vigil* 'awake'.] —**invigilation** /in víjji láysh'n/ *n*

invigilator /in víjji laytər/ *n* somebody who supervises students at an examination. US term **proctor** *n.* 2

invigorate /in víggə rayt/ (**-ates, -ating, -ated**) *vt* to fill somebody or something with energy or life [Mid-17C. Probably < *invigor* < Old French *envigourer* < Latin *vigor* 'vigour'.] —**invigoration** /in víggə ráysh'n/ *n* —**invigorative** *adj* —**invigoratively** *adv* —**invigorator** *n*

invigorating /in víggə rayting/ *adj* filling somebody or something with energy or life —**invigoratingly** *adv*

invincible /in vínssəb'l/ *adj* **1** **UNBEATABLE** incapable of being defeated or beaten as a result of great strength or skill **2** **TOO DIFFICULT TO OVERCOME** so great or difficult as to be impossible to overcome **3** **DEEP-ROOTED** too deep-rooted or ingrained to be altered [15C. Directly or via French < Latin *invincibilis* < *vincibilis* 'conquerable'.] —**invincibility** /in vínssə bíllәti/ *n* —**invincibleness** *n* —**invincibly** *adv*

inviolable /in ví ələb'l/ *adj* **1** secure from being infringed, breached, or broken **2** secure from violence or attack [15C. Directly or via French < Latin *inviolabilis* < *violabilis* 'that may be injured'.] —**inviolability** /in ví ələ bíllәti/ *n* —**inviolableness** *n* —**inviolably** *adv*

inviolate /in ví ələt/ *adj* **1** not subject to change, damage, or destruction **2** kept pure, untouched, or unblemished [15C. < Latin *inviolatus* < *violat-*, past participle of *violare* (see VIOLATE).] —**inviolacy** *n* —**inviolately** *adv* —**inviolateness** *n*

invisible /in vízzəb'l/ *adj* **1** **IMPOSSIBLE TO SEE** not able to be seen with the eyes **2** **HIDDEN** hidden from view **3** **MADE TRANSPARENT MAGICALLY** impossible to see as a result of magic or pseudo-scientific processes **4** **NOT EASILY NOTICED** not readily noticed or detected **5** **UNRECORDED STATISTICALLY** not reflected, recorded, or reported in economic statistics ■ *n* **1** **ITEM NOT IN FINANCIAL STATEMENT** an item not reported in a company's financial statement **2** **INVISIBLE PERSON OR THING** somebody or something that is invisible —**invisibility** /in vízzə bíllәti/ *n* —**invisibleness** *n* —**invisibly** *adv*

invisible ink *n* a liquid used to write something that cannot be seen until the paper is treated in some way, e.g. with heat

invitation /ínvi táysh'n/ *n* **1** **OFFER** an offer to come or go somewhere, especially one promising pleasure or hospitality, or the making of such an offer **2** **WRITTEN NOTE** a note or other message, especially a printed card, that contains an invitation **3** **ENCOURAGEMENT** encouragement to do something ■ *adj* **OPEN ONLY TO THOSE ASKED** open only to people who have been asked personally —**invitational** *adj, n*

invitation-only *adj* to which only people who have been sent a specific invitation will be admitted

invitatory /in vítətəri/ *adj* inviting or encouraging something

invite *vt* /in vít/ (**-vites, -viting, -vited**) **1** **ASK TO PARTICIPATE** to ask somebody in a polite or formal manner to come or go somewhere or to do something **2** **REQUEST** to ask for something or say that something would be welcome ○ *She invited questions from the audience.* **3** **PROVOKE** to encourage or provoke something that might not have happened otherwise ○ *an attitude that invites disaster* ■ *n* /ín vīt/ **INVITATION** an invitation (*informal*) [Mid-16C. Directly or via French *inviter* < Latin *invitare*.] —**invitee** /ín vī tée/ *n* —**inviter** *n*

inviting /in víting/ *adj* suggesting or offering pleasure or enjoyment ○ *Inviting smells were coming from the kitchen.* —**invitingly** *adv* —**invitingness** *n*

in vitro /in vée trō/ *adj, adv* in an artificial environment such as a test tube rather than inside a living organism [< Latin, 'in glass']

in vitro fertilization *n* fertilization of an ovum by sperm outside the body when normal conception is not achievable because of a woman's low fertility

in vivo /in vée vō/ *adj, adv* existing or carried out inside a living organism, as in a test or experiment [< Latin, 'in the living']

invocation /ínvə káysh'n/ *n* **1** **CALLING UPON HIGHER POWER** a calling upon a greater power such as God or a spirit for help **2** **PRAYER** a short prayer forming part of a religious service **3** **QUOTING OF SOMETHING AS A REASON** the act of calling upon or quoting something such as a law as a reason or justification **4** **INCANTATION SUPPOSEDLY SUMMONING DEMON** a casting of a spell in an attempt to make an evil spirit appear, or the spell itself —**invocational** *adj* —**invocatory** /in vókətəri/ *adj*

invoice /ín voyss/ *n* **1** **REQUEST FOR PAYMENT** a written record of goods or services provided and the amount charged for them, sent to a customer as a request for payment **2** **SHIPMENT OF GOODS** a shipment of goods that is recorded on an invoice ■ *vt* (**-voices, -voicing, -voiced**) **SEND INVOICE** to send somebody an invoice for payment [Mid-16C. Originally plural of obsolete *invoy* < obsolete French *envoy* < *envoyer* (see ENVOY).]

invoke /in vṓk/ (**-vokes, -voking, -voked**) *vt* **1** **CALL UPON GREATER POWER** to call upon a greater power such as God or a spirit for help **2** **USE IN SUPPORT** to quote, rely on, or use something such as a law in support of an argument or case **3** **ASK FOR** to ask or appeal for something **4** **ATTEMPT TO SUMMON DEMON** to call upon an evil spirit to appear, e.g. by casting a spell **5** **AROUSE** to create or arouse an idea, emotion, or image [15C. Via French *invoquer* < Latin *invocare* 'call upon' < *vocare* 'to call'.] —**invoker** *n*

involucre /ínvə lookər, -lòo-/ *n* a ring of modified leaves beneath a flower or flower cluster, e.g. in a dandelion or daisy flower [Late 16C. Directly or via French < Latin *involucrum* 'wrapper' < *involvere* 'roll into' < *volvere* 'to roll'.] —**involucral** /ínvə lòokrəl/ *adj* —**involucrate** /-lòokrət/ *adj*

involucrum /ínvə lòokrəm/ (*plural* **-cra** /-krə/) *n* **1** a growth of new bone that forms around a mass of dead or infected bone **2** PLANT SCI = **involucre** [Late 17C. < Latin (see INVOLUCRE).]

involuntarily /in vóllәntərәli/ *adv* without wanting or intending to

involuntary /in vóllәntəri/ *adj* **1** required or exacted against somebody's will or wishes **2** spontaneous or automatic, and not controlled or controllable by the mind —**involuntariness** *n*

involuntary manslaughter *n* the accidental and unlawful killing of one human being by another without planning of the killing in advance

involuntary muscle *n* a muscle that acts independently of the will, especially in reflex functions

involute /ínvə loot/ *adj* **1** **COMPLEX** complicated or intricate **2** **ROLLING INWARDS** having petals or leaves that roll inwards at the edges **3** **TIGHTLY WHORLED** describes a shell whose axis is hidden by tight whorls ■ *n* /ínvə loot/ **TYPE OF CURVE** a curve traced by the end of a taut thread that cannot be extended as it is wound upon or unwound from another curve ■ *vi* /ínvə lòot/ (**-lutes, -luting, -luted**) **BECOME INVOLUTE** to become complex or inwardly rolled, whorled, or curved [Mid-17C. < Latin *involutus* 'intricate', past participle of *involvere* (see INVOLVE).] —**involutely** *adv*

involuted /ínvə lòotid/ *adj* = **involute** *adj.* 1, **involute** *adj.* 2

involution /ínvə lòosh'n/ *n* **1** **COMPLICATION** an act of making something complicated or intricate, or the condition of being complicated or intricate **2** **SOMETHING COMPLEX** something complicated or intricate **3** **DECLINE IN FUNCTION** a decline or degeneration in the physiological function of an organ **4** **INVOLUTE PART** an involute part or structure **5** **DECREASE IN SIZE** a return to normal size of a body or body part after expansion **6** **RAISING OF QUANTITY TO POWER** the operation of raising a number, variable, or expression to a specified positive integral power, x^n. ◊ **evolution** *n.* 6 7 **COMPLEX GRAMMATICAL STRUCTURE** a complicated grammatical construction 8 **DEVELOPMENTAL PROCESS FORMING TUBE** the process by which certain cells grow inwards over the edge of an organ or part until they rejoin the structure to form a tube —**involutional** *adj*

involve /in vólv/ (**-volves, -volving, -volved**) *vt* 1 **CONTAIN** to contain or include as a necessary element of something 2 **CONCERN** to be a matter that concerns or affects somebody 3 **CAUSE TO PARTICIPATE** to make somebody part of, or make somebody take part in, an event or ongoing process 4 **IMPLICATE** to connect a person with something, especially something disreputable 5 **ENGROSS** to take up somebody's whole attention 6 **COMPLICATE** to make something complicated or difficult to follow (*often passive*) 7 **ENCLOSE** to envelop something (*literary; often passive*) [Late 14C. < Latin *involvere* 'enfold' < *volvere* 'to roll'.] —**involvement** *n* —**involver** *n* —**involving** *adj*

involved /in vólvd/ *adj* 1 **COMPLICATED** complicated or difficult to follow 2 **CONNECTED** connected with or participating in something 3 **IN RELATIONSHIP** participating in a romantic or sexual relationship —**involvedly** /in vólvdli, -vidli/ *adv*

invulnerable /in vúlnərəb'l/ *adj* 1 not capable of being wounded, damaged, hurt, or affected ○ *invulnerable to criticism* 2 not able to be successfully attacked — **invulnerability** /in vúlnərə bíllәti/ *n* —**invulnerableness** *n* —**invulnerably** *adv*

inward /ínwərd/ *adj* 1 **INSIDE** situated within something 2 **OF THE MIND OR SPIRIT** relating to or existing in the mind or spirit 3 **TOWARDS THE INSIDE** towards the inside or centre of something ■ *adv* 1 = **inwards** *adv.* 1 2 = **inwards** *adv.* 2 ■ *n* **THE INSIDE** the inner part (*literary archaic*) ○ *'To kiss the tender inward of thy hand'* (William Shakespeare, *Sonnets*; 1609) —**inwardness** *n*

Inward Light *n* = **Inner Light**

inwardly /ínnwərdli/ *adv* 1 to yourself, or without showing a feeling on the outside 2 on or to the inside

inwards /ínnwərdz/ *adv* **inwards, inward** 1 towards the inside or centre of something ○ *Several windows fell right inwards, through the weight of the snow against them.* 2 in, into, or towards the mind or spirit ○ *with thoughts turning inwards*

inweave /in wéev/ (**-weaves, -weaving, -wove** /-wṓv/, **-woven** /-wṓv'n/) *vt* to weave something into a fabric or design

inwrap *vt* = **enwrap**

inwreathe *vt* = **enwreathe**

in-your-face /-yər-/, **in-yer-face** *adj* (*slang*) 1 expressing opinions in a forceful, sometimes aggressive, way ○ *Her approach is a little too in-your-face for me.* 2 direct or provocative in a way that is designed to attract attention ○ *an in-your-face ad campaign*

⚡ **io** *abbr* British Indian Ocean Territory (*in Internet addresses*)

Io[1] *symbol* ionium (*archaic*)

Io[2] /ī ō/ *n* 1 in Greek mythology, the daughter of the river god Inachus, turned into a heifer by the god Zeus to protect her from the jealousy of his wife Hera 2 a large natural satellite of Jupiter, 3,640 km/2,260 m in diameter and remarkable for being volcanically active [Via Latin < Greek *Iō*]

⚡ **I/O** *abbr* input/output

IOC *n, abbr* International Olympic Committee

iod- *prefix* = **iodo-** (*before vowels*)

iodate /ī ə dayt/ *n* a salt of iodic acid such as sodium or potassium iodate. Use: in medicine. [Early 19C. < IODIC ACID.]

iodic /ī óddik/ *adj* relating to, containing, or caused by iodine, especially with a valency of five

iodic acid *n* HIO_3 a colourless or white crystalline solid that is soluble in water. Use: in analytical chemistry, disinfectant, deodorant, antiseptic.

iodide /ī ə dīd/ *n* a salt of hydriodic acid that contains the univalent anion ion I^-

iodinate /ī ədi nayt/ (**-nates, -nating, -nated**) *vt* to treat something with iodine or an iodine compound or add or substitute iodine atoms to or in an organic compound —**iodination** /ī ədi náysh'n/ *n*

iodine /ī ə deen/ *n* 1 (*symbol* **I**) a poisonous, dark grey to purple-black, lustrous, and nonmetallic crystalline element in the halogen family. Source: brine. Use: germicide, antiseptic, preparation of dyes, pharmaceuticals, tinctures, isotopes in medicine and industry. 2 a mixture of iodine and potassium iodide in alcohol. Use: topical antiseptic. [Early 19C. < French *iode* < Greek *iōdēs* 'violet-coloured' < *ion* 'violet'.] —**iodous** /ī óddəss/ *adj*

iodise *vt* = **iodize**

iodism /ī ədizəm/ *n* a form of poisoning caused by the ingestion of iodine or an iodine compound

iodize /ī ə dīz/ (**-dizes, -dizing, -dized**), **iodise** (**-dises, -dising, -dised**) *vt* to treat or combine something with iodine or an iodine compound —**iodization** /ī ə dī záysh'n/ *n* —**iodizer** *n*

iodo- *prefix* iodine ○ *iodophor* [< French *iode* (see IODINE)]

iodoform /ī óddə fawrm/ *n* CHI_3 a yellow volatile crystalline compound with a penetrating odour. Use: antiseptic, in ointments for minor skin diseases. [Mid-19C. < IODO- + FORMYL.]

iodophor /ī óddə fawr/ *n* a substance consisting of iodine and a surface-active agent in solution that slowly releases elemental iodine. Use: disinfectant. [Mid-20C. < IODO- + *-phor,* variant of -PHORE.]

iodopsin /ī ō dópsin/ *n* a photosensitive violet pigment in the retinal cones of the eye [Mid-20C. < Greek *iōdēs* (see IODINE) + OPSIN, after *rhodopsin*.]

iolite /ī ō līt/ *n* MINERALS = **cordierite** [Early 19C. < Greek *ion* 'violet'.]

IOM *abbr* Isle of Man

ion /ī ən, ī on/ *n* an atom or group of atoms that has acquired an electric charge by losing or gaining one or more electrons [Mid-19C. < Greek *ion* 'moving thing' < present participle of *ienai* 'go'; because an ion moves towards the electrode of opposite charge.]

-ion *suffix* 1 action or process ○ *eruption* ○ *erosion* 2 result of an action or process ○ *abrasion* 3 condition, state ○ *elation* [Via Old French < Latin *-ion-*]

Iona /ī ṓnə/ island in the Inner Hebrides, W Scotland. Population: 90. Area: 8.5 sq. km/3.28 sq. mi.

ion engine *n* a theoretical rocket engine that derives its thrust from the electrostatic acceleration of a stream of positive ions

Ionesco /ée ə nésk ō/, **Eugène** (1909–94) Romanian-born French dramatist

ion exchange *n* the interchange of ions of the same charge between a solution and a solid in contact with it —**ion exchanger** *n*

Ionia /ī ṓni ə/ region of ancient W Asia Minor, on the Aegean coast —**Ionian** *adj, n*

Ionian Islands /ī ṓni ən-/ group of seven Greek islands in the Ionian and Mediterranean seas. Population: 191,003 (1991). Area: 2,307 sq. km/891 sq. mi.

Ionian mode *n* the medieval musical mode corresponding to the modern C major scale

Ionian Sea arm of the Mediterranean Sea between the SE coast of Italy and W Greece

ionic /ī ónnik/ *adj* relating to or containing matter in the form of charged atoms or groups of atoms

Ionic *n* 1 **IONIAN DIALECT** an extinct dialect of Ancient Greek, that was spoken mainly in Ionia 2 **METRICAL FOOT** a metrical foot used in classical prosody, consisting of two long syllables followed by two short ones (**greater Ionic**) or two short syllables followed by two long ones (**lesser Ionic**) ■ *adj* 1 **OF ARCHITECTURAL ORDER** relating to or typical of the order of architecture characterized by fluted columns and capitals with spiral scroll-shaped ornaments 2 **IN IONIC METRE** relating to, typical of, or expressed in Ionic metre [Early 17C. < Greek *Iōnikos* 'of Ionia'.]

Ionic order *n* one of the five classical orders of architecture, characterized by fluted columns and capitals with spiral scroll-shaped ornaments

ionic propulsion *n* motion produced in reaction to the expulsion of a stream of accelerated ions

ion implantation *n* the use of a stream of electrically accelerated ions to implant impurities on or near the surface of the substrate during the manufacture of a semiconductor

ionisation *n* CHEM = **ionization**

ionise *vti* CHEM = **ionize**

ionization /ī ə nī záysh'n/, **ionisation** *n* a process in which an atom or molecule loses or gains electrons, acquiring an electric charge or changing an existing charge

ionization chamber *n* a device used to detect and measure ionizing radiation, consisting of a gas-filled tube with electrodes at each end between which a voltage is maintained

ionization potential *n* the energy needed to remove an electron from an atom or molecule and move it an infinite distance away

ionize /ī ə nīz/ (**-izes, -izing, -ized**), **ionise** (**-ises, -ising, -ised**) *vti* to undergo or cause something to undergo ionization —**ionizable** *adj*

ionone /ī ənōn/ *n* $C_{13}H_{20}O$ a yellow liquid smelling of violets. Source: plants. Use: manufacture of perfumes. [Late 19C. < Greek *ion* 'violet'.]

ionophore /ī ónnə fawr/ *n* a molecule found in lipid membranes that helps transport ions across the membrane [Mid-20C. < ION.]

ionosphere /ī ónnə sfeer/ *n* four layers of the Earth's upper atmosphere in which incoming ionizing radiation from space creates ions and free electrons that can reflect radio signals, enabling their transmission around the world [Early 20C. < ION.] —**ionospheric** /ī ónnə sférrik/ *adj* —**ionospherically** *adv*

ionospheric wave *n* MEDIA = **sky wave**

ion propulsion *n* AEROSP = **ionic propulsion**

ion rocket *n* a rocket powered by an ion engine

iontophoresis /ī óntəfə réessiss/ *n* the movement of ions through biological material under the influence of an electric current [Early 20C. < Greek *iont-*, present participle of *ienai* 'go'.] —**iontophoretic** /-fə réttik/ *adj* —**iontophoretically** *adv*

iota /ī ṓtə/ *n* 1 the ninth letter of the Greek alphabet 2 a very small amount of something ○ *anyone with an iota of sense* [Early 17C. Via Latin < Greek *iōta* < Semitic.]

iotacism /ī ṓtəsizəm/ *n* the tendency in speakers of modern Greek to use the sound of iota in place of the sound of other vowel characters such as eta or upsilon [Mid-17C. Via Latin < Greek *iōtakismos* < *iōta* (see IOTA).]

IOU /ī ō yóo/ *n* a written acknowledgment of a debt between the writer and somebody else [Representation of 'I owe you']

⚡ **IOW** *abbr* 1 Isle of Wight 2 in other words (*in e-mails*)

Iowa /ī əwə/ 1 state in the north-central United States. Capital: Des Moines. Population: 2,852,423 (1997). Area: 145,754 sq. km/56,276 sq. mi. 2 river in Iowa, emptying into the Mississippi River. Length: 530 km/330 mi. — **Iowan** /ī ō ən, ī ə wən/ *n, adj*

⚡ **IP** *abbr* 1 image processing 2 Internet protocol

IPA *abbr* 1 International Phonetic Alphabet 2 Institute of Practitioners in Advertising

ipecacuanha /íppi kakyoo ánnə/, **ipecac** /íppi kak/ *n* 1 an emetic made from dried roots 2 a shrub, the roots of which are a source of ipecacuanha. Native to: South America. *Cephaelis ipecacuanha*. [Early 17C. Via Portuguese < Tupi *ipe-kaá-guéne* 'low plant causing vomit'.]

Iphigenia /ífiji nī ə, i fíjji-/ *n* in Greek mythology, a daughter of Agamemnon, who was prepared to sacrifice her to Artemis in order to gain favourable winds for the Greek fleet to sail for Troy

⚡ **IPL** *abbr* initial program load

IPO *abbr* initial public offering

Ipoh /éepō/ capital of Perak State, W Malaysia. Population: 382,633 (1991).

ippon /i pón, íppon/ *n* a winning point awarded in judo or karate for perfect technique [Mid-20C. < Japanese.]

iproniazid /íprə nī əzid/ *n* a synthetic drug. Use: antidepressant, formerly, to treat tuberculosis. [Mid-20C. Blend of ISOPROPYL + ISONIAZID.]

ipse dixit /ípsi díksit/ *n* something asserted dogmatically and without proof [Late 16C. < Latin, 'he himself said it'.]

ipsilateral /ípsi láttərəl/ *adj* being on or affecting the same side of the body [Early 20C. Alteration of *ipselateral* < Latin *ipse* 'same' + LATERAL.] —**ipsilaterally** *adv*

ipsissima verba /ip síssimə vúrbə/ *npl* the precise words used in something that is quoted [< Latin, 'the very words']

ipso facto /ípsō fáktō/ *adv* as the result of a particular fact [< Latin, 'by the fact itself']

ipso jure /ípsō jóóri/ *adv* by reason of a particular law [< Latin, 'by the law itself']

Ipswich /ípswich/ **1** town in E England. Population: 113,642 (1996 estimate). **2** city in Queensland, E Australia. Population: 75,283 (1991).

⚡**iq** *abbr* Iraq (*in Internet addresses*)

IQ a measure of somebody's intelligence, obtained through a series of aptitude tests concentrating on different aspects of intellectual functioning. An IQ score of 100 represents 'average' intelligence. Full form **intelligence quotient**

Iqbal /ík bal/, **Sir Muhammad** (1875–1938) Indian philosopher, poet, and political leader

Iquique /ee keé kay/ capital of Tarapacá Region, N Chile. Population: 145,139 (1992).

Iquitos /ee keé toss/ port in NE Peru. Population: 266,175 (1993).

⚡**ir** *abbr* Iran (*in Internet addresses*)

Ir *symbol* iridium

⚡**IR** *abbr* **1** Inland Revenue **2** information retrieval **3** infrared (radiation)

Ir. *abbr* Ireland

ir- *prefix* = **in-¹, in-²** (*before r*)

IRA¹ *n* an organization of Irish nationalists originally set up to strive for an independent Ireland by force of arms and still dedicated to achieving the unity of the island of Ireland. Full form **Irish Republican Army**

IRA² /írə/ *n US* a plan in the United States that permits individuals to accumulate savings tax free until retirement. Full form **Individual Retirement Account**

irade /i raádi/ *n* a written decree of a Muslim ruler, especially, formerly, the sultan of Turkey [Late 19C. < Arabic *irādah* 'will, desire'.]

Iran

Iran /i raán, i rán/ republic in SW Asia. Capital: Tehran. Population: 67,540,002 (1997). Area: 1,648,000 sq. km/636,300 sq. mi.

Iranian /i ráyni ən/ *n* **1** a group of languages spoken in the region northeast of the Persian Gulf, a subgroup of the Indo-Iranian branch of Indo-European. Native speakers: 70 million. **2** somebody who comes from Iran —**Iranian** *adj*

Iran-Iraq War *n* the war fought between Iran and Iraq that lasted from 1980 to 1988, following the invasion of border territory in Iran by Iraq

Iraq /i raák, i rák/ republic in SW Asia. Capital: Baghdad.

Iraq

Population: 22,219,289 (1997). Area: 438,317 sq. km/169,235 sq. mi.

Iraqi /i raáki, i ráki/ *n* **1** somebody who comes from Iraq **2** the modern dialect of Arabic spoken in Iraq —**Iraqi** *adj*

irascible /i rássəb'l/ *adj* **1** easily provoked to anger or outbursts of temper **2** showing or typical of anger [Mid-16C. Via French < Latin *irascibilis* 'quick to anger' < *irasci* 'grow angry' < *ira* 'anger'.] —**irascibility** /i rássə bíllati/ *n* — **irascibleness** —**irascibly** *adv*

irate /ɪ ráyt/ *adj* **1** feeling great anger **2** showing or typical of great anger [Mid-19C. < Latin *iratus*, past participle of *irasci* 'grow angry'.] —**irately** *adv* —**irateness** *n*

~~irational~~ incorrect spelling of **irrational**

Irawadi GEOG = **Irrawaddy**

IRBM *abbr* intermediate-range ballistic missile

⚡**IRC** *abbr* Internet relay chat (*in e-mails*)

ire /ɪr/ *n* a feeling or display of deep anger or fury (*formal*) [13C. Via French < Latin *ira* 'anger'.] —**ireful** *adj*

SYNONYMS See *anger*.

Ireland

Ireland /írlənd/ **1** island of NW Europe, in the North Atlantic Ocean, comprising the Republic of Ireland and the British province of Northern Ireland. Area: 70,273 sq. km/27,133 sq. mi. **2** republic occupying most of the island of Ireland. Capital: Dublin. Population: 3,606,952 (1997). Area: 70,273 sq. km/27,133 sq. mi. Gaelic **Éire**

Ireland, Northern ◆ **Northern Ireland**

Ireland, David (*b.* 1927) Australian novelist

irenic /ɪ reénik, ɪ rénnik/, **irenical** /-ik'l/ *adj* promoting or intended to promote peace (*literary*) [Mid-19C. < Greek *eirēnikos* 'peaceable' < *eirēnē* 'peace'.] —**irenically** *adv*

irenicon /ɪ reénikon/ (*formal*)

irenics /ɪ reéniks, ɪ rénn-/ *n* a branch of theology that seeks to promote unity between different churches and religious groups (+ *singular verb*)

Irian Jaya /írri ən jíʹə/ province of Indonesia, consisting of the western half of New Guinea and a number of offshore islands. Capital: Jayapura. Population: 1,560,000 (1989). Area: 421,981 sq. km/162,928 sq. mi.

irid- *prefix* = **irido-** (*before vowels*)

iridaceous /írri dáyshəss/ *adj* relating or belonging to the family of flowering plants that includes the iris and crocus

iridectomy /írri déktəmi/ (*plural* **-mies**) *n* the surgical removal of part of the iris of the eye

iridescent /írri déss'nt/ *adj* **1** marked by or showing rainbow colours that appear to move and change as the angle at which they are seen changes **2** having a lustrous or brilliant appearance or quality —**iridescence** *n* —**iridescently** *adv*

iridic¹ /ɪ ríddik, ɪ-/ *adj* relating to, involving, or containing the element iridium [Mid-19C. < IRIDIUM.]

iridic² /ɪ ríddik, ɪ-/ *adj* relating to or typical of the iris of the eye [Late 19C. < Latin *irid-*, stem of *iris* 'iris (of the eye)'.]

iridium /ɪ ríddi əm, ɪ-/ *n* (*symbol* **Ir**) a brittle, corrosion-resistant, silver-white metallic element. Use: alloys for pen nibs, jewellery, watch and compass pivot bearings, surgical instruments, electrical contacts, chemical crucibles. [Early 19C. < Latin *irid-*, stem of *iris* 'rainbow'.]

irido- *prefix* **1** iris ○ *iridotomy* ○ *iridaceous* **2** rainbow ○ *iridescent* **3** iridium ○ *iridosmine* [Via Latin < Greek *irid-*, stem of *iris* (see IRIS).]

iridology /írri dólləji/ *n* a technique in alternative medicine by which diagnosis of various bodily disorders is claimed to be possible by examination of the fine structure of the iris of the eye —**iridologist** *n*

iridosmine /írri dóss mīn/, **iridosmium** /-dózmi əm/ *n* an ore and natural alloy of iridium and osmium in which the osmium content exceeds 35 per cent, with traces of platinum, rhodium, ruthenium, iron, and copper [Early 19C. Blend of IRIDIUM + OSMIUM.]

iridotomy (*plural* **-mies**) *n* a surgical operation in which the iris of the eye is cut into, nowadays using a laser

iris /íriss/ *n* **1** PART OF EYE the coloured part of the eye that consists of a muscular diaphragm surrounding the pupil and regulating the light entering the eye by expanding and contracting the pupil **2** FLOWERING PLANT a plant with long sword-shaped leaves and large. Flowers: many-coloured. Genus: *Iris*. **3** RAINBOW a rainbow (*literary*) **4** RAINBOW SHOW OF COLOURS a show of colours of various hues, like a rainbow **5** PHOTOGRAPHY = **iris diaphragm** [15C. Via Latin < Greek, 'rainbow, iris (of the eye)'.]

iris in *vi* to open up the iris diaphragm of a camera gradually in order to expand the picture area

iris out *vi* to close the iris diaphragm of a camera gradually in order to contract the picture area until the image darkens completely

iris diaphragm *n* a diaphragm consisting of adjustable thin plates that control the size of an aperture, especially one used in a camera to control the amount of light allowed to enter

Irish /írish/ *adj* **1** OF IRELAND relating to Ireland, or its language, people, or culture **2** OF IRISH GAELIC relating to the Irish Gaelic language **3** OF ENGLISH DIALECT OF IRELAND relating to the dialect of English spoken in Ireland ■ *npl* PEOPLE FROM IRELAND people who come from Ireland ■ *n* LANG = **Irish Gaelic** [13C. < Old English *Īr(as)* 'inhabitants of Ireland', probably < Old Irish *Ériu* 'Ireland'.] — **Irishness** *n*

Irish coffee *n* a hot drink of sweetened coffee containing Irish whiskey and topped with whipped cream

Irish elk *n* an extinct giant large-antlered deer of the Pleistocene epoch. Native to: Europe, Asia. Genus: *Megaloceros*.

Irish Gaelic *n* an official language of the Republic of Ireland, spoken mainly in the west of the country, belonging to the Celtic branch of Indo-European. Native speakers: 5,000. Other speakers: 1 million. — **Irish Gaelic** *adj*

Irish harp *n* a small diatonic harp constructed with a hollowed willow soundbox

Irishism /írishizəm/ *n* LANG = **Hibernicism**

Irishman /írishmən/ (*plural* **-men** /-mən/) *n* a man who was born in or who lives in Ireland, or who is of Irish descent

Irish moss *n* an edible red seaweed from which a complex carbohydrate food additive (**carrageenan**) is obtained. Native to: coasts of Europe and North America. *Chondrus crispus*.

Irish Republican Army *n* full form of **IRA**

Irish Sea body of water between Great Britain and Ireland. Area: 103,600 sq. km/40,000 sq. mi.

Irish setter *n* a setter with a silky reddish coat, originally bred in Ireland

Irish stew *n* a stew of lamb or mutton, potatoes, and onions

Irish terrier *n* a terrier with a wiry reddish coat, originally bred in Ireland

Irish whiskey *n* whiskey made in Ireland, principally of barley

Irish wolfhound *n* a large powerful hound with a rough shaggy coat, belonging to a breed developed in Ireland

Irishwoman /írish woˈomən/ (*plural* **-en** /-wimin/) *n* a woman who was born in or who lives in Ireland, or who is of Irish descent

iritis /ɪ rítiss/ *n* inflammation of the iris of the eye [Early 19C. < IRIS.] —**iritic** /ɪ ríttik/ *adj*

irk /urk/ *vt* to annoy somebody slightly, especially by being tedious [14C. Originally N English, 'grow weary or vexed'.]

SYNONYMS See *bother*.

irksome /úrksəm/ *adj* slightly annoying, especially by being tedious —**irksomely** *adv* —**irksomeness** *n*

Irkutsk /ur kŏŏtsk, eer-/ city in S Siberian Russia. Population: 639,000 (1992).

ϟ **IRL** *abbr* in real life (*in e-mails*)

IRO *abbr* **1** Inland Revenue Office **2** International Refugee Organization **3** international relief organization

iroko /ə rṓkō/ (*plural* **-kos**) *n* **1** a hard brown African wood often used instead of teak **2** a hardwood tree that produces iroko. Native to: tropical Africa. Genus: *Chlorophora*. [Late 19C. < Yoruba.]

ϟ **iron** /ī ərn/ *n* **1** METALLIC ELEMENT (*symbol* **Fe**) a heavy magnetic malleable ductile lustrous silvery-white metallic element that is present in very small quantities in the blood and is the fourth most abundant element in the earth's crust. Source: haematite, limonite, magnetite. Use: engineering and structural products. **2** HEATED TOOL a tool made of iron or steel, usually heated before and during use ○ *a soldering iron* **3** CLOTHES PRESSER a small electrical appliance with a flat metal base that is heated and used to press clothes **4** METAL-HEADED GOLF CLUB any golf club with a metal head, differentiated by numbers that indicate different angles of the face and lengths of the shaft **5** RIDING = **stirrup** *n*. 1 **6** *US* COMPUTER HARDWARE computer hardware, especially older and larger mainframes (*slang*) ○ *a company with some big iron* **7** HARSH CHARACTER a strong, unyielding, or hard aspect of somebody's nature ■ **irons** *npl* RESTRAINTS FOR ARMS OR LEGS manacles or fetters for restraining the arms or legs ■ *adj* **1** MADE OF IRON relating to or made of iron **2** VERY STRONG very strong or hard **3** TOUGH very robust or tough **4** UNYIELDING very determined, unyielding, or cruel ■ *v* **1** *vti* PRESS CLOTHES to press clothes or other fabrics with an iron to remove wrinkles **2** *vt* COVER WITH IRON to cover or clad something with iron [Old English *īren* < Germanic] ◇ **have several irons in the fire** to be involved in several different activities at the same time ◇ **pump iron** to do weightlifting exercises for body building or fitness (*slang*) ◇ **strike while the iron is hot** to act while circumstances are favourable to a successful outcome

iron out *vt* **1** to smooth away wrinkles in a garment or fabric using an iron **2** to settle a dispute or resolve a problem by removing difficulties

iron age *n* in Greek and Roman mythology, an era regarded as the third and last step in humankind's degeneration from the golden age

Iron Age *n* the period following the Bronze Age from 1500 BC onwards in the Middle East, during which iron was increasingly used in making tools and weapons

ironbark /ī ərn baark/ *n* a eucalyptus tree with hard rough bark

iron blue *n* $Fe_7C_{18}N_{18}\cdot 10H_2O$ an insoluble compound. Use: in fertilizers, as a blue pigment in paint, ink, and paper dyeing.

ironbound /ī ərn bownd/ *adj* **1** DECORATED WITH IRON wrapped or decorated with iron bands **2** HARSH stern or unyielding **3** RUGGED edged or enclosed with rocks (*literary*) ○ *an ironbound coast*

ironclad /ī ərn klad/ *adj* **1** COVERED OR PROTECTED WITH IRON covered with iron, especially as a protection or armour **2** STRONG strong, firm, or unyielding **3** IRREFUTABLE not capable of being attacked or refuted ○ *an ironclad alibi* ■ *n* ARMOURED SHIP a 19th-century wooden warship armoured with metal plates

Iron Cross *n* the highest German military decoration, instituted in Prussia in 1813 and awarded during World Wars I and II

iron curtain *n* an impenetrable barrier to understanding, awareness, or agreement

Iron Curtain *n* **1** the militarized border between the Communist bloc and W Europe during the Cold War, from the end of World War II until the fall of Communist governments between 1989 and 1991 ○ *'From Stettin in the Baltic to Trieste in the Adriatic, an iron curtain has descended across the continent'.* (Sir Winston Churchill *Fulton, Missouri, Speech*; 1946) **2** the policy of isolation that prevented W and E Europeans from travelling or communicating freely during the Cold War

iron grey *adj* of a dark greenish-grey colour —**iron grey** *n*

iron hand *n* strict, harsh, or despotic control —**iron-handed** /ī ərn hándid/ *adj* —**ironhandedness** *n*

iron horse *n* a steam-powered railway locomotive (*archaic*)

ironic /ī rónnik/, **ironical** /ī rónnik'l/ *adj* relating to, characterized by, using, or containing irony —**ironically** *adv*

USAGE Is it really *irony* or is it merely coincidence? When you use *irony, ironic*, and *ironically*, be sure that you use them in contexts associated with stark incongruity, inconsistency, or even folly, and not in contexts associated with things merely coincidental or improbable. This use of *ironically* is inappropriate, and *coincidentally* is the better choice: *Ironically, both the defence counsel and the prosecutor graduated from the same law school.* Appropriate use of **ironically** requires an incongruity between what is expected and what has happened in fact: *Ironically, because they lacked sophisticated computers they developed efficient algorithms that can now add to the power of supercomputers.*

ironing /ī ərning/ *n* **1** the act of pressing clothes or other fabrics to remove wrinkles **2** clothes that have been ironed or have to be ironed

ironing board *n* a covered, often padded board on legs on which clothes are ironed

ironize /ī ər nīz/ (**-izes, -izing, -ized**), **ironise** (**-ises, -ising, -ised**) *v* **1** *vi* to use irony or be ironic **2** *vt* to give something an ironic tone or make something ironic in nature

iron lung *n* an airtight metal cylinder encasing a patient up to the neck, formerly used to provide help in breathing by alternating air pressure within the cylinder

iron maiden *n* a medieval instrument of torture consisting of a hinged box shaped like a human body and lined with spikes that impale somebody placed inside as it is closed

iron man *n* **1** a man of great physical strength and endurance **2 iron man, Iron Man** *ANZ, US* an athletic competition for men held at a beach and including a variety of disciplines such as surfing, canoeing, swimming, and running

ironmonger /ī ərn mung gər/ *n UK* a dealer in tools and other articles made chiefly of metal —**ironmongery** *n*

iron oxide *n* any natural or synthetic compound of iron and oxygen

iron pan *n* a hard layer below the surface of sand or gravel in which iron salts from percolating water have precipitated, cementing the grains of the material together

iron pyrites *n* = **pyrite**

iron ration *n US* = **iron rations**

iron rations *npl* food designed to be used in an emergency, especially by military personnel. US term **iron ration**

ironside /ī ərn sīd/, **ironsides** *n* a man of great physical strength or endurance

Ironside /ī ərn sīd/ *n* a nickname given to King Edmund II of England

Ironsides /ī ərn sīdz/ *npl* the cavalry regiment led by Oliver Cromwell in the English Civil War

ironstone /ī ərn stōn/ *n* **1** any sedimentary rock that contains a large amount of iron ore **2** a hard and durable variety of white pottery

ironware /ī ərn wair/ *n* goods, especially kitchen utensils, made of iron

iron-willed *adj* extremely strong-willed

Iron Woman *n ANZ, US* an athletic competition for women held at a beach and including a variety of disciplines such as surfing, canoeing, swimming, and running

ironwood /ī ərnwŏŏd/ (*plural* **-woods** *or* **-wood**) *n* a tree with very hard timber, e.g. a hornbeam

ironwork /ī ərn wurk/ *n* something made of iron, e.g. a gate, especially when it is decorative

ironworker /ī ərn wurkər/ *n* **1** somebody employed in an ironworks **2** a maker of ironwork

ironworks /ī ərn wurks/ *n* a factory where iron is smelted or large metal goods are made (*+ singular verb*)

irony /īrəni/ (*plural* **-nies**) *n* **1** HUMOUR BASED ON OPPOSITES humour based on using words to suggest the opposite of their literal meaning **2** SOMETHING HUMOROUS BASED ON CONTRADICTION something said or written that uses sardonic humour **3** INCONGRUITY incongruity between what actually happens and what might be expected to happen, especially when this disparity seems absurd or laughable **4** INCONGRUOUS THING something that happens that is incongruous with what might be expected to happen, especially when this seems absurd or laughable **5** = **dramatic irony 6** = **Socratic irony** [Early 16C. Via Latin *ironia* < Greek *eirōneia* 'pretended ignorance' < *eirōn* 'dissembler'.]

USAGE See *ironic*.

Iroquoian /írrə kwóy ən/ *n* **1** a family of languages spoken by Iroquois peoples of E North America **2** a member of a Native North American people who speaks an Iroquoian language —**Iroquoian** *adj*

Iroquois /írrə kwoy/ (*plural* **-quois**) *n* a member of a former confederacy of six Native North American peoples, the Mohawk, Oneida, Seneca, Onondaga, Cayuga, and Tuscarora [Mid-17C. Via French < Algonquian.] —**Iroquois** *adj*

irradiant /i ráydi ənt/ *adj* radiating light or shining brightly [Early 16C. < Latin *irradiant-*, present participle of *irradiare* (see IRRADIATE).]

irradiate /i ráydi ayt/ (**-ates, -ating, -ated**) *v* **1** *vt* EXPOSE SOMETHING TO RADIATION to expose somebody or to or treat somebody or something with radiation or streams of particles **2** *vt* PRESERVE FOOD to treat food with electromagnetic radiation to kill microorganisms and slow down the process of ripening and gradual deterioration or rotting **3** *vt* LIGHT UP to make something brighter by shining light onto it **4** *vt* MAKE INTELLIGIBLE to make something intellectually clear **5** *vti* PHYS = **radiate** *v*. 1 [Early 17C. < Latin *irradiat-*, past participle of *irradiare* 'illumine' < *radius* 'ray'.] —**irradiative** *adj* —**irradiator** *n*

irradiation /i ráydi áysh'n/ *n* **1** IRRADIATING the act of irradiating somebody or something, or the state of being irradiated **2** LIGHTING EFFECT the visual effect by which a brightly lit thing appears larger against a dark background **3** MEDICAL RADIATION the medical use of radiation, e.g. X-rays, gamma rays, or neutrons

irradicable /i ráddikəb'l/ *adj* incapable of being eradicated [Early 18C. < medieval Latin *irradicabilis* < Latin *radicare* 'take root', wrongly understood as 'root out'.] —**irradicably** *adv*

irrational /i rásh'nəl/ *adj* **1** LACKING IN REASON contrary to or lacking in reason or logic **2** LACKING IN LOGIC unable to think logically **3** UNABLE TO THINK CLEARLY lacking the normal ability to think clearly, especially because of shock or injury to the brain **4** CONTAINING IRRATIONAL NUMBER describes an expression that contains an irrational number **5** CONTAINING METRIC IRREGULARITY describes an irregularity in the metre of a classical poem, usually where there is a long foot instead of a short one ■ *n* **1** IRRATIONAL PERSON an unclear or illogical thinker **2** MATH = **irrational number** [15C. < Latin *irrationalis* < *rationalis* (see RATIONAL).] —**irrationality** /i rásh'n állәti/ *n* —**irrationally** *adv* —**irrationalness** *n*

irrationalism /i rásh'nəlizəm/ *n* **1** the state of lacking reason or logic **2** the belief that feelings and intuition are more important than reason —**irrationalistic** /i rásh'nə lístik/ *adj*

irrational number *n* any real number that cannot be expressed as the exact ratio of two integers, e.g. $\sqrt{2}$ and π

Irrawaddy /írrə wóddi/, **Irawadi** principal river of Myanmar. Length: 2,100 km/1,300 mi.

irreal /i reél/ *adj* illusory or not actually existing — **irreality** /írri álləti/ *n*

irreclaimable /írri kláyməb'l/ *adj* not able to be reclaimed ○ *an irreclaimable desert* ○ *irreclaimable damages* —**irreclaimability** /írri kláymə bílləti/ *n* —**irreclaimableness** *n* —**irreclaimably** *adv*

irreconcilable /i rékən sīləb'l/ *adj* **1** INCOMPATIBLE not capable of being made to agree or coexist with something else **2** UNRESOLVABLE incapable of being resolved **3** IMPLACABLE determinedly hostile and unwilling to accept compromise —**irreconcilability** /i rékən sīlə bílləti/ *n* —**irreconcilable** /i rékən sīləb'l/ *n* —**irreconcilableness** *n* —**irreconcilably** *adv*

irrecoverable /írri kúvvərəb'l/ *adj* **1** impossible to get back or regain **2** impossible to repair or remedy — **irrecoverableness** *n* —**irrecoverably** *adv*

irredeemable /írri deéməb'l/ *adj* **1** UNABLE TO BE PAID OFF that cannot be ended by paying off the principal **2** NOT RECOVERABLE that cannot be made good once lost **3** NOT

REPAIRABLE impossible to repair **4 NOT CONVERTIBLE INTO COINS** that cannot be converted into coins **5 INCAPABLE OF REDEMPTION** refusing to reform and unable to be saved —**irredeemability** /ìrri deémə bíllәti/ *n* —**irredeemableness** *n* —**irredeemably** *adv*

irredenta /ìrri déntə/ *n* a territory that was once part of one country but is now ruled by another and is subject to claims that it should be returned to its former country [Early 20C. < Italian *(Italia) irredenta* (see IRREDENTIST).]

irredentist /ìrri déntist/ *n* a member of a group of people who support the return to their country of territories that used to belong to it but are now under foreign rule —**irredentism** *n*

Irredentist *n* a member of a former Italian organization that advocated the adding to Italy of Italian-speaking territories that were under foreign control [Late 19C. < Italian *irredentista* < *(Italia) irredenta* 'unrecovered (Italy)' < *redento* 'redeemed' < Latin *redemptus*, past participle of *redimere* (see REDEEM).]

irreducible /ìrri dyóossəb'l/ *adj* **1 INCAPABLE OF BEING DECREASED** not able to be made smaller **2 INCAPABLE OF SIMPLIFICATION** not able to be simplified or simplified further **3 IMPOSSIBLE TO FACTOR INTO LESSER POLYNOMIALS** describes a polynomial that cannot be factored into two polynomials of a lesser degree **4 IMPOSSIBLE TO REDUCE TO RATIONAL EXPRESSION** describes a radical that cannot be reduced to a rational expression —**irreducibility** /ìrri dyóossə bíllәti/ *n* —**irreducibleness** *n* —**irreducibly** *adv*

irreflexive /ìrri fléksiv/ *adj* describes a relation in which, if a has the relation to b, then b does not have the relation to a

irreformable /ìrri fáwrməb'l/ *adj* **1** incapable of being reformed **2** impossible to revise or alter —**irreformability** /ìrri fáwrmə bíllәti/ *n*

irrefrangible /ìrri fránjəb'l/ *adj* **1 INCAPABLE OF BEING DISOBEYED** impossible to disobey or violate (*formal*) **2 INCAPABLE OF BEING BROKEN** impossible to break or smash (*formal*) **3 INCAPABLE OF BEING REFRACTED** describes visible light or other radiation that cannot be refracted —**irrefrangibility** /ìrri fránjə bíllәti/ *n* —**irrefrangibleness** *n* —**irrefrangibly** *adv*

irrefutable /ìrri fyóotəb'l, i réffyòotəb'l/ *adj* impossible to refute or disprove [Early 17C. < late Latin *irrefutabilis* < Latin *refutare* 'refute'.] —**irrefutability** /ìrri fyóotə bíllәti, i réffyòotə-/ *n* —**irrefutableness** *n* —**irrefutably** *adv*

irregardless /ìrri gaárdləss/ *adv* = **regardless** (*nonstandard*) [Early 20C. Probably blend of IRRESPECTIVE + REGARDLESS.]

USAGE Since the prefix *ir-* means 'not' (as it does in *irrespective*), and the suffix *-less* means 'without', ***irregardless*** is a double negative and regarded as nonstandard. As such it is to be avoided, in favour of *irrespective* or *regardless*.

irregular /i réggyòolər/ *adj* **1 NOT OF UNIFORM APPEARANCE** not even, uniform, or symmetrical in appearance **2 OCCURRING AT ODD INTERVALS** not occurring at equally spaced intervals of time **3 NONCONFORMING** not conforming to common practices **4 BEHAVING UNACCEPTABLY** not conforming to accepted rules or standards of behaviour **5 UNOFFICIAL** not forming part of an official military body **6 NOT FORMED BY USUAL GRAMMATICAL RULES** not following the usual rules of word formation **7 CONSTIPATED** not having a regular daily bowel movement (*euphemistic*) **8 HAVING ASYMMETRICAL PARTS** not having symmetrical parts ■ *n* **SOLDIER NOT PART OF REGULAR FORCES** a soldier who is not part of an official military body [15C. Via Old French *irreguler* < medieval Latin *irregularis* 'breaking a rule' < *regularis* (see REGULAR).] —**irregularly** *adv*

irregularity /i réggyòo lárrəti/ (*plural* **-ties**) *n* **1 BEING IRREGULAR** the state of being irregular **2 IRREGULAR THING** something irregular, e.g. a bump in a road **3 UNAUTHORIZED THING** something unauthorized or unacceptable by usual standards

irrelative /i réllətiv/ *adj* **1** not related or connected **2** not relevant

irrelevant /i rélləvənt/ *adj* not relevant or important —**irrelevance** *n* —**irrelevancy** *n* —**irrelevantly** *adv*

~~**irrelevent**~~ incorrect spelling of **irrelevant**

irreligious /ìrri líjjəss/ *adj* **1** lacking in any religious faith **2** opposed to religion —**irreligiously** *adv* —**irreligiousness** *n*

irremediable /ìrri meédi əb'l/ *adj* impossible to remedy or put right [Mid-16C. < Latin *irremediabilis* < *remediare* 'to cure'.] —**irremediableness** *n* —**irremediably** *adv*

irremissible /ìrri míssəb'l/ *adj* **1** not able to be pardoned or excused **2** not able to be avoided or postponed [15C. Directly or via French < ecclesiastical Latin *irremissibilis* 'unpardonable' < Latin *remiss-*, past participle of *remittere* (see REMIT).] —**irremissibility** /ìrri míssə bíllәti/ *n* —**irremissibleness** *n* —**irremissibly** *adv*

irremovable /ìrri móovəb'l/ *adj* incapable of being removed —**irremovability** /ìrri móovə bíllәti/ *n* —**irremovableness** *n* —**irremovably** *adv*

irreparable /i réppərəb'l/ *adj* not able to be repaired or put right ○ *did irreparable damage to the computer* [15C. Directly or via Old French < Latin *irreparabilis* 'not to be recovered' < *reparare* 'recover'.] —**irreparability** /i réppərə bíllәti/ *n* —**irreparableness** *n* —**irreparably** *adv*

irrepealable /ìrri peéləb'l/ *adj* not able to be repealed —**irrepealability** /ìrri peélə bíllәti/ *n* —**irrepealableness** *n* —**irrepealably** *adv*

irreplaceable /ìrri pláyssəb'l/ *adj* not able to be replaced —**irreplaceability** /ìrri pláyssə bíllәti/ *n* —**irreplaceableness** *n* —**irreplaceably** *adv*

irrepressible /ìrri préssəb'l/ *adj* not able to be controlled ○ *irrepressible high spirits* —**irrepressibility** /ìrri préssə bíllәti/ *n* —**irrepressibleness** *n* —**irrepressibly** *adv*

irreproachable /ìrri próchəb'l/ *adj* not incurring any reproach or criticism [Mid-17C. < French *irréprochable* < *réprochable* 'reproachable'.] —**irreproachability** /ìrri próchə bíllәti/ *n* —**irreproachableness** *n* —**irreproachably** *adv*

irreproducible /i reépra dyóossəb'l/ *adj* impossible to reproduce —**irreproducibility** /i reéprə dyóossə bíllәti/ *n*

~~**irresistable**~~ incorrect spelling of **irresistible**

irresistible /ìrri zístəb'l/ *adj* **1** not able to be resisted or successfully opposed **2** so desirable as to be very difficult to resist [Late 16C. < medieval Latin *irresistibilis* < Latin *resistere* 'resist'.] —**irresistibility** /ìrri zístə bíllәti/ *n* —**irresistibleness** *n* —**irresistibly** *adv*

irresoluble /ìrri zóllyòob'l/ *adj* incapable of being solved, reconciled, or explained [Mid-17C. < Latin *irresolubilis* 'indissoluble' < *resolvere* 'melt'.] —**irresolubility** /ìrri zóllyòo bíllәti/ *n* —**irresolubly** *adv*

irresolute /i rézzə loot/ *adj* unsure and unable to take decisions —**irresolutely** *adv* —**irresoluteness** *n* —**irresolution** /i rézzə lóosh'n/ *n*

irresolvable /ìrri zólvəb'l/ *adj* **1** not able to be broken down into different parts **2** not able to be solved —**irresolvability** /ìrri zólvə bíllәti/ *n* —**irresolvableness** *n* —**irresolvably** *adv*

irrespective /ìrri spéktiv/ *adv* in spite of everything (*informal*) —**irrespectively** *adv* ◇ **irrespective of** without taking something into account

USAGE See ***irregardless***.

irresponsible /ìrri spónssəb'l/ *adj* **1** not having or showing any care for the consequences of personal actions **2** not capable of assuming responsibility —**irresponsibility** /ìrri spónssə bíllәti/ *n* —**irresponsibleness** *n* —**irresponsibly** *adv*

irresponsive /ìrri spónssiv/ *adj* not responding quickly or favourably —**irresponsively** *adv* —**irresponsiveness** *n*

irretrievable /ìrri treévəb'l/ *adj* **1** impossible to find or recover **2** impossible to repair or put right —**irretrievability** /ìrri treévə bíllәti/ *n* —**irretrievableness** *n* —**irretrievably** *adv*

~~**irrevelant**~~ incorrect spelling of **irrelevant**

irreverent /i révvərənt/ *adj* lacking in respect [Mid-16C. < Latin *irreverent-* < present participle of *revereri* (see REVERE).] —**irreverence** *n* —**irreverently** *adv*

irreversible /ìrri vúrssəb'l/ *adj* impossible to reverse or undo —**irreversibility** /ìrri vúrssə bíllәti/ *n* —**irreversibleness** *n* —**irreversibly** *adv*

irrevocable /i révvəkəb'l/ *adj* not able to be revoked, undone, or changed [14C. Directly or via French < Latin *irrevocabilis* 'that cannot be recalled' < *revocare* (see REVOKE).] —**irrevocability** /i révvəkə bíllәti/ *n* —**irrevocableness** *n* —**irrevocably** *adv*

irrigate /ìrri gayt/ (**-gates, -gating, -gated**) *vt* **1 SUPPLY WITH WATER** to bring a supply of water to a dry area, especially in order to help crops to grow **2 WASH OUT** to make water or liquid medication flow through or over a body part or wound **3 REFRESH** to make something fresh [Early 17C. < Latin *irrigat-*, past participle of *irrigare* 'to water in' < *rigare* 'to water'.] —**irrigable** *adj* —**irrigation** /ìrri gáysh'n/ *n* —**irrigational** *adj* —**irrigative** *adj* —**irrigator** *n*

irritable /ìrritəb'l/ *adj* **1 EASILY ANNOYED** easily annoyed or exasperated **2 SENSITIVE** extremely sensitive, especially to inflammation **3 RESPONSIVE TO STIMULI** describes an organism that is able to respond to stimuli [Mid-17C. < Latin *irritabilis* 'easily enraged' < *irritare* 'provoke'.] —**irritability** /ìrritə bíllәti/ *n* —**irritableness** *n* —**irritably** *adv*

irritable bowel syndrome *n* a condition of the bowel in which there is recurrent pain with constipation or diarrhoea or alternating attacks of these

irritant /ìrritənt/ *adj* causing irritation, especially physical irritation [Early 17C. < Latin *irritant-*, present participle of *irritare* 'provoke'.] —**irritancy** *n* —**irritant** *n*

irritate /ìrri tayt/ (**-tates, -tating, -tated**) *v* **1** *vti* **ANNOY** to cause somebody to feel annoyance or exasperation, or cause annoyance or exasperation **2** *vt* **INFLAME** to stimulate a body part excessively, causing a painful reaction, e.g. inflammation **3** *vt* **STIMULATE** to stimulate an organism so as to provoke a response [Mid-16C. < Latin *irritat-*, past participle of *irritare* 'provoke'.] —**irritating** *adj* —**irritatingly** *adv* —**irritative** *adj* —**irritator** *n*

irritation /ìrri táysh'n/ *n* **1 ANNOYANCE** a feeling of annoyance or exasperation **2 ACT OF ANNOYING** the act of causing annoyance or exasperation **3 SOMEBODY OR SOMETHING ANNOYING** something who or somebody that causes annoyance or exasperation **4 REACTION TO IRRITANT** a painful reaction, especially an inflammation, caused by an irritant **5 INFLAMING** the act of causing a painful reaction, especially an inflammation

irrupt /i rúpt/ *vi* **1** to enter suddenly or violently **2** to increase suddenly and rapidly, e.g. in number [Mid-19C. < Latin *irrupt-*, past participle of *irrumpere* 'break into a place' < *rumpere* 'to break'.] —**irruption** *n*

irruptive /i rúptiv/ *adj* entering or likely to enter suddenly —**irruptively** *adv*

IRS *abbr* Internal Revenue Service

Irtysh ♦ **Ob'-Irtysh**

Irving /úrving/, **Sir Henry** (1838–1905) British actor and theatrical manager. Born **John Henry Brodribb**

Irving, John (*b.* 1942) US novelist

Irving, Washington (1783–1859) US writer

is[1] 3rd person present singular of **be**

ϟ **is**[2] *abbr* Iceland (*in Internet addresses*)

ϟ **IS** *abbr* information services

is. *abbr* **1** island **2** isle

Is. *abbr* **1** Isaiah **2** Island (*in placenames*) **3** Isle (*in placenames*)

is- *prefix* = **iso-** (*before vowels*)

ISA /íssə/ *abbr* **1** individual savings account **2** International Standard Atmosphere

Isa. *abbr* Isaiah

Isaac *n* in the Bible, the son of Abraham and Sarah who was offered by his father as a sacrifice to God, but was saved at the last moment by divine intervention. He was the father of Jacob and Esau (Genesis 21–28).

Isabella I /ìzzə béllə/ (1451–1504) queen of Castile and León (1474–1504). Known as **Isabella the Catholic**

Isabella II (1830–1904) queen of Spain (1833–68)

isagogics /ìssə gójjiks/ *n* introductory studies, especially introducing the Bible in its literary and historical contexts (+ *singular verb*) —**isagoge** *n*

Isaiah /ī zí ə/ *n* **1** a Hebrew prophet who lived in the latter half of the 8th century BC **2** a book of the Bible that contains prophecies and apocalyptic material, traditionally attributed to Isaiah

isalobar /ī sállə baar/ *n* a contour line on a weather chart joining places where equal changes in atmospheric pressure occurred during a given time interval [Early 20C. < IS- + ALLO- + Greek *baros* 'weight', after ISOBAR.]

isatin /íssətin/ *n* $C_8H_5NO_2$ a water-soluble compound related to indigo and indole that crystallizes as orange needles. Use: manufacture of vat dyes. [Mid-19C. < Greek *isatis* 'woad'.] —**isatinic** /ìssə tínnik/ *adj*

ISBN *abbr* International Standard Book Number

ischaemia /i skeémi ə/, **ischemia** *n* an inadequate supply of blood to a part of the body, caused by partial or total blockage of an artery —**ischaemic** *adj*

Ischia /íski ə/ island off the coast of west-central Italy, in the Tyrrhenian Sea. Population: 17,600 (1990). Area: 47 sq. km/18 sq. mi.

ischium /íski əm/ (*plural* **-a** /-ə/) *n* the lowest and rearmost of the three bones that make up each half of the pelvis [Early 17C. Via Latin < Greek *iskhion* 'hip joint'.] —**ischial** *adj*

ISD *abbr* international subscriber dialling

⚡**ISDN** *n* a digital telephone network that can transmit both voice and data messages. Full form **Integrated Services Digital Network**

ISE *abbr* International Stock Exchange

-ise *suffix* = **-ize**

isentrope /íssentrōp/ *n* a line on a graph or chart linking points of equal entropy [Back-formation < ISENTROPIC]

isentropic /íssen tróppik/ *adj* **1** describes a reaction or process that takes place without a change in entropy **2** relating to an isentrope —**isentropically** *adv*

Iseult *n* ♦ **Tristan and Iseult**

-ish *suffix* **1** characteristic of, like, tending to ○ *churlish* ○ *babyish* ○ *bookish* **2** of or relating to, from ○ *Gaulish* **3** somewhat, approximately ○ *bluish* ○ *latish* [Old English *-isc* < Germanic]

Isherwood /íshərwŏŏd/, **Christopher** (1904–86) British writer

Ishiguro /íshi gŏŏrō/, **Kazuo** (*b.* 1954) Japanese-born British novelist

Ishmael /ísh mayl/ *n* **1** in the Bible, the son of Abraham (Genesis 16–21) **2** an outcast (*literary*)

Ishmaelite /íshmi ə līt/ *n* **1** a descendant of Abraham's son Ishmael **2** = **Ishmael** *n.* 2 (*literary*) —**Ishmaelitish** *adj* —**Ishmaelitism** *n*

Ishtar /ísh taar/ *n* in Babylonian and Assyrian mythology, the queen of heaven and goddess of fertility

Isidore (of Seville) /ízzə dawr əv sə víl/, **St** (560?–636) Spanish cleric, theologian, and encyclopedist

isinglass /ízing glaass/ *n* **1** a transparent or translucent gelatin made from the air bladders of various fish, especially the sturgeon. Use: clarifying agent, in adhesives and jellies. **2** MINERALS = **mica** [Mid-16C. < obsolete early Dutch *huysenblas* 'sturgeon's bladder' < *huysen* 'sturgeon' + *blas* 'bladder'.]

Isis[1] /íssiss/ *n* in Egyptian mythology, the goddess of fertility

Isis[2] /íssiss/ alternative name for the River Thames around Oxford, England

isiXhosa /íssi kóssa, -káwssa/ *n* LANG = **Xhosa** *n.* 2

isiZulu /íssi zŏŏloo/ *n* LANG = **Zulu** *n.* 2 [Mid-19C. < Zulu.]

Iskenderun /iss kéndə roon/, **Iskenderon** city in S Turkey, on the Gulf of Iskenderun. Population: 154,807 (1990).

isl. *abbr* **1** island **2** isle

Islam /íz laam, íss-/ *n* **1** the religion of Muslims, based upon the teachings of Muhammad **2** Muslim people, their culture, or their countries considered collectively [Early 17C. < Arabic *islām* 'submission (to God)' < base of *aslāma* 'he surrendered'.] —**Islamic** /iz lámmik, iss-/ *adj*

Islamabad /iz lámmabad/, **Islāmābād** capital of Pakistan, in the northeast of the country. Population: 204,364 (1981).

Islamise *vt* RELIG, LAW = **Islamize**

Islamism /ízz-, íssla-/ *n* RELIG = **Islam** *n.* 1

Islamize /ízzlə mīz, íssla-/ (**-izes, -izing, -ized**), **Islamise** (**-ises, -ising, -ised**) *vt* **1** to convert people or countries to Islam **2** to cause people, institutions, or countries to follow Islamic law —**Islamization** /ízzlə mī záysh'n, íssla-/ *n*

island /ílənd/ *n* **1** LAND SURROUNDED BY WATER an area of land, smaller than a continent, that is completely surrounded by water (*often in placenames*) **2** SOMETHING LIKE ISLAND something that is like an island because it is isolated or surrounded by something different ○ *'No man is an island, entire of itself'.* (John Donne, *Devotions upon Emergent Occasions*; 1624) **3** ISOLATED BODY PART a body part or group of cells that is different in construction from its surroundings ■ *vt* **1** MAKE INTO ISLAND to form something into an island **2** ISOLATE to cause somebody to feel isolated, e.g. from contact with peers or colleagues **3** SET WITH ISLANDS to provide a stretch of water with islands (*literary*) [Old English *īegland* < *īeg* 'island' (< Indo-European, 'water') + LAND] —**islander** *n*

island arc *n* an arc-shaped chain of islands, usually found in an area of volcanic or seismic activity

island-hop *vi* to travel from island to island within the same chain, especially as part of a holiday (*informal*)

Islands, Bay of bay on the NE coast of the North Island, New Zealand

islands of Langerhans *npl* ANAT = **islets of Langerhans**

Islands of the Blessed *npl* MYTHOL = **Hesperides** *npl.* 2

Islay /ílə, ī lay/ southernmost island of the Inner Hebrides, W Scotland. Population: 3,500. Area: 610 sq. km/236 sq. mi.

isle /īl/ *n* an island, often a small one (*literary*) [13C. Via Old French *ile, isle* < Latin *insula*.]

SPELLCHECK See ***aisle***.

Isle of Man ♦ **Man, Isle of**

Isle of Wight ♦ **Wight, Isle of**

islet /ílət/ *n* a small isle or island

islets of Langerhans /-lángər hanss/ *npl* clusters of endocrine cells found in the pancreas that secrete insulin and glucagon

Islip /ízlip/ **1** village in central England. Population: 600. **2** town in SE New York State, on Long Island. Population: 18,924 (1996 estimate).

ism /ízzəm/ (*plural* **isms**) *n* a movement, doctrine, or system of belief (*informal*) [Late 17C. < -ISM.]

-ism *suffix* **1** action, process ○ *mesmerism* ○ *volcanism* **2** characteristic behaviour or manner ○ *despotism* **3** state, condition ○ *conservatism* ○ *gangsterism* **4** unusual or unhealthy state ○ *caffeinism* **5** doctrine, system of beliefs ○ *defeatism* ○ *Calvinism* **6** prejudice ○ *sexism* **7** distinctive feature or trait ○ *Southernism* ○ *vulgarism* [Via Old French *-isme* < Latin *-ismus* < Greek *-ismos*]

Ismaili /íz maa éeli/ *n* a member of a branch of Shiite Muslims whose members believe that Ismail, son of the sixth imam, was the true seventh imam [Mid-19C. < Arabic, < the proper name *'Ismā'īl*.]

Ismailiyya /ízmə éeli ə/ city in NE Egypt. Population: 255,000 (1992).

Ismail Samani Peak /isma éel sə máani-/ highest peak in Tajikistan, in the centre of the country. Height: 7,495 m/24,590 ft.

isn't /ízz'nt/ *contr* is not ○ *It isn't ready yet.*

ISO *abbr* **1** Imperial Service Order **2** International Organization for Standardization

iso- *prefix* **1** equal, uniform ○ *isoelectric* ○ *isogloss* **2** isomeric ○ *isooctane* **3** of or for different members of the same species ○ *isoagglutination* [< Greek *isos* 'equal']

isoagglutination /íssō ə glooti náysh'n/ *n* the clumping together (**agglutination**) of red blood cells in one individual induced by antibodies in the serum of another individual of the same species —**isoagglutinative** /-ə glŏŏtinətiv/ *adj*

isoagglutinin /íssō ə glŏŏtinin/ *n* an antibody from one individual that causes the clumping together (**agglutination**) of red blood cells in another individual of the same species but of a different blood group

isobar /íssō baar/ *n* **1** a line drawn on a weather map that connects places with equal atmospheric pressure **2** one of two or more atoms or elements having the same mass number but different atomic numbers [Mid-19C. < Greek *isobaros* 'of equal weight'.] —**isobarism** *n*

isobaric /íssō bárrik/ *adj* **1** having constant or equal atmospheric pressure **2** relating to isobars

isobaric spin *n* PHYS = **isospin**

isobath /íssō bath/ *n* a line on a map of the sea that connects points that are at the same depth [Late 19C. < ISO- + Greek *bathos* 'depth'.] —**isobathic** /íssō báthik/ *adj*

isobutane /íssō byŏŏ tayn/ *n* C_4H_{10} a colourless gaseous hydrocarbon that is an isomer of butane. Use: fuel, refrigerant.

isocarboxazid /íssō kaar bóksəzid/ *n* an antidepressant drug [Mid-20C. < ISO- + contraction of CARBONYL + OX- + HYDRAZIDE.]

isocheim /íssō kīm/, **isochime** *n* a line on a weather map connecting places that have the same average temperature in winter [Mid-19C. < ISO- + Greek *kheima* 'winter weather'.] —**isocheimal** /íssō kīm'l/ *adj* —**isocheimenal** *adj*

isochromatic /íssōkrō máttik/ *adj* **1** = **orthochromatic** **2** having the same colour or wavelength of light

isochronous /ī sókrənəss/, **isochronal** /-krən'l/ *adj* **1** having the same frequency or periodicity **2** measured or occurring at the same time, or lasting for the same length of time —**isochronously** *adv*

isochroous /ī sókrō əss/ *adj* having the same colour throughout [Mid-19C. < ISO- + Greek *khrōs* 'colour'.]

isoclinal /íssō klīn'l/ *adj* **1** having the same inclination or slope **2** having the sides of a geological fold parallel to one another ■ *n* **1** GEOL = **isocline** *n.* 1 **2** MAPS = **isoclinic line**

isocline /íssō klīn/ *n* **1** a geological fold with rock beds that slope in the same direction **2** MAPS = **isoclinic line** [Late 19C. < Greek *isoklinēs* 'equally balanced' < *klinein* 'to lean'.]

isoclinic *adj* = **isoclinal**

isoclinic line *n* a line on a map connecting points on the Earth's surface that have the same magnetic dip

isocyanate /íssō sī ə nayt/ *n* a chemical compound containing the chemical group -NCO. Use: in resins, adhesives.

isocyanide /íssō sī ə nīd/ *n* a colourless liquid with a pungent odour that contains the chemical group -NC

isodiametric /íssō dī ə méttrik/ *adj* with diameters or axes of equal length

isodose /íssōdōss/ *n* a dose of radiation of equal intensity applied to more than one part of the body as a medical treatment

isodynamic /íssō dī námmik/ *adj* **1** having the same strength or intensity **2** connecting points on a map of the Earth's surface that have the same magnetic intensity

isoelectric /íssō i léktrik/ *adj* having exactly the same electric potential

isoelectric point *n* the pH value at which the electric force on a molecule in a solution is zero

isoelectronic /íssō i lek trónnik, -éelek-/ *adj* with the same number of electrons or the same outer atomic structure —**isoelectronically** *adv*

isoenzyme /íssō én zīm/ *n* BIOCHEM = **isozyme** —**isoenzymatic** /-én zī máttik/ *adj* —**isoenzymic** /-en zímmik/ *adj*

isogamete /íssō gámmeet/ *n* a gamete physically identical to another with which it unites to form a zygote —**isogametic** /-gə méttik/ *adj*

isogamy /ī sóggəmi/ *n* the fusion of isogametes in some algae and fungi during reproduction

isogeneic /íssōjə née ik/ *adj* IMMUNOL = **syngeneic** [Mid-20C. Alteration of ISOGENIC.]

isogenic /íssō jénnik/ *adj* having identical genes [Mid-20C. < ISO-+ Greek *genea* 'race'.]

isogenous /ī sójjənəss/ *adj* **1** describes bodily organs or parts that have the same or a similar origin **2** = **isogenic** —**isogeny** *n*

isogloss /íssō gloss/ *n* a line on a language map that surrounds an area within which a linguistic usage, e.g. a dialectal word, is found [Early 20C. < ISO- + Greek *glossa* 'language'.] —**isoglossal** /íssō glóss'l/ *adj* —**isoglossic** *adj* —**isoglottal** *adj* —**isoglottic** *adj*

isogonal *adj, n* MATH, PHYS = **isogonic**

isogonal line *n* = **isogonic line**

isogone /íssəgōn/ *n* = **isogonic line**

isogonic /íssō gónnik/, **isogonal** /ī sóggən'l/ *adj* having equal angles ■ *n* PHYS = **isogonic line** [Mid-19C. < Greek *isogōnios* 'equiangular'.]

isogonic line *n* a line on a map of the Earth's surface connecting points at which a compass would give the same deviation from true north

isograft /íssō graaft/ *n* a tissue graft taken from an individual genetically identical to the recipient of the graft, e.g. from an identical twin

isogram /íssō gram/ *n* MAPS, METEOROL = **isopleth**

isohel /íssō hel/ *n* a line on a map connecting places that receive the same number of hours of sunshine in the course of a year [Early 20C. < ISO- + Greek *hēlios* 'sun'.]

isohyet /íssō hī ət/ *n* a line on a map connecting places that receive the same amount of rainfall in the course of a year [Late 19C. < ISO- + Greek *huetos* 'rain'.] —**isohyetal** *adj*

isolate *vt* /íssə layt/ (**-lates, -lating, -lated**) **1 SEPARATE FROM OTHERS** to separate a person or a place from others of the same type **2 QUARANTINE** to keep somebody who is infected away from other people to prevent the spread of a contagious disease **3 CUT PLACE OFF** to make a place unreachable from the surrounding area ○ *Heavy snowfalls have temporarily isolated the town.* **4 FIND CAUSE OF** to discover which of a number of possible causes or factors is responsible for a particular phenomenon or problem ○ *He isolated a bug in the software as the cause of the failure.* **5 SEPARATE OUT** to separate out a chemical or biological material such as a virus or bacterium in order to identify and study it **6 INSULATE** to prevent a circuit or device from interacting with another or with an outside stimulus ■ *n* /íssələt/ **1 LONE PERSON OR GROUP** a person or a group separated or cut off from others **2 MICROORGANISM GROWN IN LABORATORY** a sample of biological material, especially a microorganism, that has been cultured for study **3 ONLY LANGUAGE OF FAMILY** a language that is the only known surviving member of its language family [Early 19C. Back-formation < ISOLATED < French *isolé* < late Latin *insulatus* 'made into an island' < Latin *insula* 'island'.] —**isolable** *adj* —**isolatable** *adj* —**isolator** *n*

isolated /íssə laytid/ *adj* **1 OFF BY ITSELF** far away from other inhabited areas or buildings **2 ALONE OR LONELY** without enough social contact, friends, or support **3 RARE** happening singly, rarely, or only once and unlikely to recur or prove a continuing problem ○ *an isolated incident*

isolated pawn *n* in chess, a pawn that is not supported by other pawns of the same colour round it

isolating /íssə layting/ *adj* LING = **analytic** *adj.* 5

isolation /íssə láysh'n/ *n* **1** the process of separating somebody or something from others, or the fact of being alone and separated from others **2** remoteness from other inhabited areas or buildings ◇ **in isolation 1** separate from other related factors or things ○ *we have to look at the problem in isolation* **2** alone and physically separated from other people

isolationism /íssə láysh'nizəm/ *n* **1** a government policy based on the belief that national interests are best served by avoiding economic and political alliances with other countries **2** electronic ambient music that is generally produced without beats, creating a soothing ambience with unusual sounds —**isolationist** *n, adj*

isolative /íssələtiv/ *adj* **1** relating to a sound change that occurs in all phonetic environments **2** causing somebody or something to be separated or cut off

Isolde *n* ◆ **Tristan and Iseult**

isolecithal /íssō léssith'l/ *adj* describes the eggs of mammals and some other vertebrates in which the yolk is evenly distributed throughout the egg

isoleucine /íssō lóo seen/ *n* an amino acid that is an isomer of leucine and is found in most proteins

isolex /íssō leks/ *n* a line on a language map that surrounds an area within which a particular word is used [Early 20C. < ISO- + Greek *lexis* 'word'.]

isoline /íssō līn/ *n* MAPS, METEOROL = **isopleth**

isologous /ī sólləgəss/ *adj* describes two organic compounds that have the same molecular structure but different atoms of the same valency [Mid-19C. < ISO- + Greek *logos* 'ratio'.]

isomagnetic /íssō mag néttik/, **isomagnetic line** *n* a line on a map connecting points of the same magnetic force —**isomagnetic** *adj*

isomer /íssəmər/ *n* **1** one of two or more molecules that have the same number of atoms but have different chemical structures and therefore different properties **2** one of two or more nuclides that have the same mass number and atomic number but different energy states and half-lives [Mid-19C. < Greek *isomerēs* 'sharing equally'.] —**isomeric** /íssō mérrik/ *adj*

isomerase /ī sómmə rayss, -rayz/ *n* an enzyme that converts one isomer into another

isomerise *vti* = **isomerize**

isomerism /ī sómmərizəm/ *n* **1** the existence of two or more molecules that are isomers **2** the existence of two or more nuclides that are isomers

isomerize /ī sómmə rīz/ (**-izes, -izing, -ized**), **isomerise** (**-ises, -ising, -ised**) *vti* to change something into an isomer or become an isomer —**isomerization** /ī sómmə rī záysh'n/ *n*

isomerous /ī sómmərəss/ *adj* with parts that are similar in number, markings, or other characteristics

isometric /íssō méttrik/, **isometrical** /-k'l/ *adj* **1 EQUAL** equal in dimension or measurement **2 INVOLVING PUSHING THE MUSCLES** describes exercises in which muscles are put under tension but not allowed to contract **3 WITH THREE EQUAL AXES** describes a crystalline system that has three equal axes at right angles to one another **4 WITH LINES IN SAME METRE** having the same number of metrical feet in each line of poetry **5 PROJECTED AT THE SAME ANGLE TO AXES** projected so that the plane of projection of a three-dimensional drawing is at an equal angle to each of the three axes of the object drawn [Mid-19C. < Greek *isometria* 'equality of measure'.] —**isometrically** *adv*

isometrics /íssō méttriks/ *n* a form of exercise in which the muscles are pushed against something fixed or against other muscles to strengthen them (+ *singular or plural verb*)

isometropia /íssōmə trópi ə/ *n* the condition of equal refraction of light by both eyes [< Greek *isometros* 'of equal measure' < *metron* 'measure']

isometry /ī sómmətri/ (*plural* **-tries**) *n* **1** equality of measure **2** a geometric transformation such as the rotation of a plane in which the distance between any two points is preserved

isomorph /íssō mawrf/ *n* a substance or organism that exhibits similarity in form or appearance to others (**isomorphism**)

isomorphic /íssō máwrfik/ *adj* **1** having the same form or appearance as another organism or the same organism at a different stage in its life cycle **2** describes mathematical sets with a one-to-one correspondence so that an operation such as addition or multiplication in one produces the same result as the analogous operation in the other **3** CHEM = **isomorphous** —**isomorphically** *adv*

isomorphism /íssō máwrfizəm/ *n* **1 SIMILARITY IN ORGANISMS** similarity in form or appearance between organisms of different ancestry or between different stages in the life cycle of the same organism **2 SIMILARITY BETWEEN CHEMICALS** similarity in crystalline form between chemicals **3 CORRESPONDENCE BETWEEN SETS** a one-to-one correspondence between sets such that an operation, e.g. addition or multiplication, in one produces the same result as the analogous operation in the other

isomorphous /íssō máwrfəss/ *adj* describes a chemical compound that is able to crystallize in a form similar to another chemical compound

isoniazid /íssō nī əzid/ *n* $C_6H_7N_3O$ a colourless crystalline compound. Use: to treat tuberculosis. [Mid-20C. < ISO- + contraction of *nicotinic* + HYDRAZIDE.]

isooctane /íssō ók tayn/ *n* $(CH_3)_3CCH_2$ a flammable isomer of octane. Use: determination of the octane number of fuel.

isopach /íssō pak/, **isopachyte** /íssō pák īt/ *n* a line on a map of the Earth's surface connecting points where a rock stratum has equal thickness [Early 20C. < ISO- + Greek *pakhus* 'thick'.]

isophone /íssō fōn/ *n* a line on a language map surrounding an area within which a particular pronunciation is used

isopiestic /íssō pī éstik/ *adj* METEOROL, PHYS = **isobaric** [< ISO- + Greek *piezein* 'to squeeze'] —**isopiestically** *adv*

isopleth /íssō pleth/ *n* a line on a map connecting points with the same value for variables such as temperature or air pressure. US term **isoline** [Early 20C. < Greek *isoplēthēs* 'equal in quantity'.] —**isoplethic** /íssō pléthik/ *adj*

isopod /íssō pod/ *n* a small invertebrate animal with a flattened body and seven pairs of legs. Order: Isopoda. [Mid-19C. < modern Latin *Isopoda* 'equal foot' < Greek *pod-* 'foot'.] —**isopodan** /ī sóppədən/ *adj* —**isopodous** *adj*

isoprenaline /íssō prénnə leen/ *n* PHARM = **isoproterenol** [Mid-20C. Contraction of *N-isopropylnoradrenaline*.]

isoprene /íssō preen/ *n* C_5H_8 a colourless flammable liquid hydrocarbon. Use: manufacture of synthetic rubber. [Mid-19C. < ISO- + contraction of *prophylene*.]

isopropanol /íssō prōpə nol/ *n* = **isopropyl alcohol**

isopropyl /íssō prōpil/ *n* C_3H_7 a chemical radical isomer of propyl

isopropyl alcohol *n* a colourless flammable alcohol. Use: antifreeze, rubbing alcohol, solvent.

isoproterenol /íssōprō térrə nol/ *n* a bronchodilator. Use: treatment of asthma. [Mid-20C. Contraction of *N-isopropylarterenol*.]

ISO rating *n* a measure of the sensitivity to light of a material such as photographic film or paper

isorhythm /íssō rithəm/ *n* a technique of musical composition of the 14th and 15th centuries that uses a repeated rhythmic pattern —**isorhythmic** /íssō ríthmik/ *adj*

isosceles /ī sóssə leez/ *adj* **1** describes a triangle in which two of the three sides are of equal length **2** describes a trapezium in which the two nonparallel sides are of equal length [Mid-16C. < late Latin, < Greek *isoskelēs* 'equally legged'.]

isoseismal /íssō sízm'l/, **isoseismic** /íssō sízmik/ *adj* relating to or showing equal strength of earthquake shock ■ *n* a line on a map connecting points of equal strength of earthquake shock

isosmotic /íss oz móttik/ *adj* CHEM = **isotonic** *adj.* 2 —**isosmotically** *adv*

isospin /íssō spin/ *n* (*symbol I*) a quantum characteristic of baryons and mesons that relates to the number of different values of electric charge they can have [Mid-20C. Contraction of ISOBARIC SPIN, ISOTOPIC SPIN.]

isostasy /ī sóstəssi/ *n* a state of equilibrium between forces such as accumulated ice pushing down on a section of the Earth's surface and those pushing up from below [Late 19C. < ISO- + Greek *stasis* 'stoppage'.] —**isostatic** /íssō státtik/ *adj* —**isostatically** *adv*

isostatic adjustment /íssō státtik-/ *n* a slow uplifting of the Earth's surface as a resulting of the removal of a load, e.g. the melting of a glacier

isotach /íssō tak/ *n* a line on a weather map connecting points where the wind speed is equal [Mid-20C. < ISO- + Greek *takhos* 'speed'.]

isotactic /íssō táktik/ *adj* describes a polymer having constituent molecules that give the polymer a repetitive spatial structure [Mid-20C. < ISO- + Greek *taktos* 'ordered'.]

isotherm /íssō thurm/, **isothermal** /íssō thúrm'l/, **isothermal line** *n* **1** a line drawn on a weather map that connects places with the same temperature **2** a line on a graph showing the relationship between variables, especially pressure and volume, at a constant temperature [Mid-19C. < French *isotherme* 'equal heat' < Greek *thermē* 'heat' or *thermos* 'hot'.] —**isothermal** *adj* —**isothermally** *adv*

isotone /íssətōn/ *n* either of two or more atoms with the same number of neutrons but different atomic numbers

isotonic /íssə tónnik/ *adj* **1 OF MUSCLE TENSION AND CONTRACTION** relating to the contraction and shortening of a muscle under relatively constant tension, e.g. in weightlifting **2 WITH EQUAL OSMOTIC PRESSURE** relating to or exerting equal osmotic pressure. US term **isosmotic 3 DESIGNED TO RESUPPLY THE BODY** specially formulated to supply the body's chemical needs in situations in which minerals and fluids are used up by the body, e.g. during vigorous exercise —**isotonically** *adv* —**isotonicity** /íssə to níssəti/ *n*

isotope /íssətōp/ *n* either of two or more forms of a chemical element with the same atomic number but different numbers of neutrons [Early 20C. < ISO- + Greek *topos* 'place'; because isotopes of the same name occupy the same place in the periodic table.] —**isotopic** /íssə tóppik/ *adj*

isotopic spin *n* PHYS = **isospin**

isotropic /íssō tróppik/, **isotropous** /ī sóttrəpəss/ *adj* having physical properties that do not vary with direction [Mid-19C. < ISO- + Greek *tropos* 'turn'.] —**isotropically** *adv* —**isotropism** /-trōpizəm/ *n* —**isotropy** /ī sóttrəpi/ *n*

isozyme /íssō zīm/ *n* one of two or more enzymes that are different chemically but function the same. US term **isoenzyme**

⚡**ISP** *abbr* Internet service provider

i-spin *n* QUANTUM PHYS = **isospin**

I-spy *n* a children's guessing game in which players try to guess which thing in visual range another player has in mind, having been given the first letter of the word

Israel /íz rayl/ republic in SW Asia, on the eastern shore of the Mediterranean Sea. Capital: Jerusalem. Population: 5,534,670 (1997). Area: 21,946 sq. km/8,473 sq. mi. —**Israeli** /iz ráyli/ *n, adj*

Israelite /ízzri ə līt, ízzrə-/ *n* **1** a member of the ancient Hebrew people descended from the patriarch Jacob **2** somebody who came from the ancient kingdom of Israel —**Israelitic** /ízzri ə líttik, ízzrə-/ *adj*

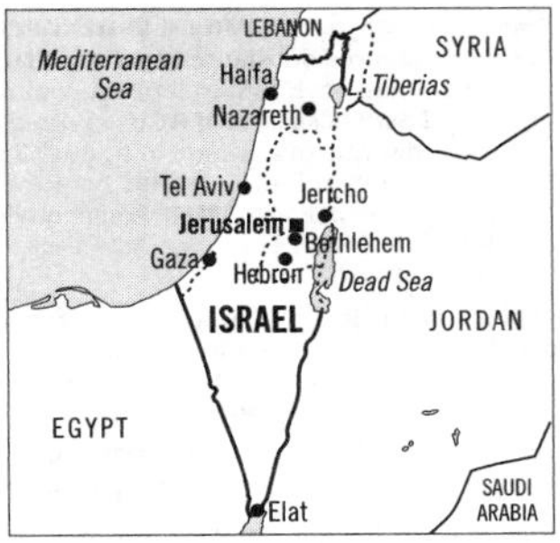

Israel

Israfil /ízzrə feel/, **Israfel** /-fel/, **Israfeel** /-feel/ *n* according to the Koran, the archangel who will herald the end of the world by sounding a trumpet on the Day of Judgment [< Hebrew, 'God heals']

~~**Isreal**~~ incorrect spelling of **Israel**

ISS *abbr* International Space Station

Issachar /íssə kaar/ *n* **1** in the Bible, a son of Jacob and Leah **2** one of the twelve tribes of Israel, descended from Issachar [Via late Latin < Greek < Hebrew *Yiśśākhār*]

Issigonis /íssi gṓniss/, **Sir Alec** (1906–88) Palestinian-born British car designer

ISSN *abbr* International Standard Serial Number

issuant /íssyoo-, íshyoo-/ *adj* in heraldry, displaying an animal rising up from something with only its upper body showing

issue /íssyoo, íshyoo/ *n* **1 SUBJECT OF CONCERN** a topic for discussion or of general concern ○ *I want to raise several issues at the meeting.* **2 MAIN SUBJECT** the central or most important topic in a discussion or debate ○ *The real issue is education.* **3 LEGAL MATTER IN DISPUTE** a legal matter in a dispute between two parties **4 COPY OF PUBLICATION** a copy of a magazine or newspaper published on a particular date **5 OFFICIAL RELEASE** a set of things such as new stamps or bonds that are made available for sale by an official body at a particular time **6 STOCK MADE AVAILABLE** a series of items such as shares in a company that becomes available at the same time **7 ALLOTTING** distribution of something by an official body ○ *the issue of parking permits* **8 OFFICIAL ALLOTMENT** something officially distributed or supplied ○ *government issue rations* **9 PROGENY** the offspring of a person ○ *died without issue* **10 FINAL OUTCOME** a final outcome or conclusion of a matter that is usually a solution to a problem or difficulty (*dated*) ○ *Let's bring our differences to an issue.* **11 WOUND PRODUCING DISCHARGE** an open wound or ulcer producing pus or blood **12 DISCHARGE FROM WOUND** pus or blood coming from an open wound or ulcer **13 PROFIT FROM PROPERTY** profits made from owning land or buildings **14 SOURCE OF FLOW** a place from which something flows **15 SYSTEM FOR TRACKING BOOK LOANS** the system in a library used for keeping track of current loans **16 ITEMS LOANED FROM LIBRARY** the number of items, e.g. books or CDs, borrowed from a library at one time ■ *v* (**-sues, -suing, -sued**) **1** *vt* **SUPPLY** to supply or distribute something officially **2** *vt* **ANNOUNCE PUBLICLY** to make public something such as a bulletin, statement, or warning, or deliver it officially to somebody ○ *The mayor's office issued a press release.* **3** *vt* **RELEASE FOR SALE** to make a set of things such as new stamps or bonds available for sale at a particular time **4** *vt* **PUBLISH** to publish something such as a newspaper, magazine, or book **5** *vi* **ORIGINATE** to emerge or come out from somewhere ○ *Smoke issued from the burning building.* **6** *vi* **ARISE FROM CONDITION** to result from or be produced by a particular thing or situation ○ *Our conclusions issue from analysis of the data.* **7** *vi* **ADD UP AS GAIN** to accrue in the form of interest or profit **8** *vi* **RESULT** to have as a result (*archaic*) [13C. < Old French, < Latin *exitus*, past participle of *exire* (see EXIT).] —**issuable** *adj* —**issuably** *adv* —**issuance** *n* —**issueless** *adj* —**issuer** *n* ◇ **at issue** under discussion or to be decided ◇ **take issue with somebody** *or* **something** to disagree with somebody about something

USAGE Avoid using *issue* as a vague substitute for more precise expressions such as *problem*, *difficulty*, or *point of disagreement*, as in *She has some issues with your presentation of the facts.* Say instead: *She has some problems...* The euphemistic use of *issues* to denote intentionally unstated problems, typically emotional or mental problems, should also be avoided, as in *He's one of those people who always has issues.*

issue price *n* the price of new securities when they are first offered to the public

issuing house *n* a financial institution that issues shares on behalf of a company that wants to become public

Issyk-Kul /i sík kóol/ lake in NE Kyrgyzstan. Area: 6,100 sq. km/2,360 sq. mi.

-ist *suffix* **1** practising a specific skill or profession ○ *psychologist* ○ *etymologist* **2** following a specific belief or school of thought ○ *idealist* ○ *Socialist* **3** somebody who plays a particular instrument ○ *oboist* **4** somebody who is prejudiced against a particular social grouping ○ *racist* ○ *sexist* [Directly or via Old French *-iste* < Latin *-ista* < Greek *-istēs*] —**-istic** *suffix*

Istanbul /ís tan bóol/, **İstanbul** largest city in Turkey, in the northwest of the country, on the Bosporus. Population: 7,615,000 (1994).

Isth., isth. *abbr* isthmus

isthmi plural of **isthmus**

Isthmian *adj* relating to the Isthmus of Panama or the Isthmus of Corinth

Isthmian Games *npl* a sports festival held in ancient Greece on the Isthmus of Corinth that included horse racing and chariot racing

isthmic /íssmik, ísth-/ *adj* relating to an isthmus in the body ○ *an isthmic constriction*

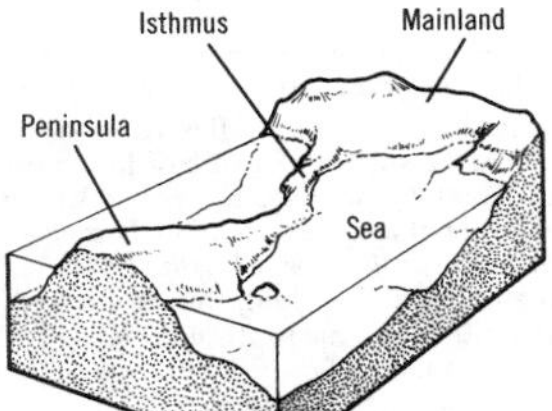

Isthmus

isthmus /íssməss, ísth-/ (*plural* **-muses** *or* **-mi** /-mī/) *n* **1** a narrow strip of land that joins two larger areas of land ○ *The isthmus connects North and South America.* **2** a narrow connection or passage between parts of the body [Mid-16C. Via Latin < Greek *isthmos* 'island'.] —**isthmian** *adj, n* —**isthmoid** *adj*

istle /ístli/, **ixtle** *n* a strong fibre from some tropical American plants such as agave or yucca. Use: rope, baskets, carpets. [Mid-19C. Via American Spanish *ixtle* < Nahuatl *ixtli*.]

Istria /ístri ə/ peninsula in NW Croatia and SW Slovenia. Area: 3,885 sq. km/1,500 sq. mi.

ISWIM *abbr* if (you) see what I mean (*in e-mails*)

it[1] /it/ CORE MEANING: a pronoun used to refer to an object or an animal ○ *It's a lovely baby.* ○ *They've had the dog a week, and they still haven't thought of a name for it.*

1 *pron* **INDICATING PARTICULAR SITUATION** used to refer to a situation just described, or to an unspecified or implied situation ○ *He's very upset, but he won't talk about it.* **2** *pron* **INDICATING POINT OF VIEW** used to indicate feelings or a viewpoint on a particular situation ○ *It's strange how things turn out.* **3** *pron* **INDICATING SOMETHING REPORTED** used in the formation of passive sentences reporting a situation ○ *It was reported that several people had been arrested.* **4** *pron* **INDICATING WEATHER** used as the subject of verbs such as 'be', 'get', 'seem', and 'feel' in order to describe something about the environment, e.g. the temperature or the weather ○ *It's cold and rainy.* **5** *pron* **INDICATING TIME** used to state the time, e.g. the time of day, the month, the year, or the season ○ *It's six o'clock.* **6** *pron* **INDICATING EXPERIENCE** used to refer to life or a particular experience ○ *What's it like being famous?* **7** *pron* **EMPHASIZING FOLLOWING CLAUSE** used to draw attention to the person, thing, or clause that immediately follows ○ *It's you who's always complaining!* ○ *It isn't that I don't care.* **8** *pron* **INDICATING CRISIS** the crucial or ultimate point, the perfect situation, person, or thing, or the death or end of somebody or something ○ *When the car turned over I really thought that was it.* **9** *pron* **ATTRACTIVE QUALITY** a quality considered by somebody to be the most important, e.g. talent, charm, sex appeal, or profitability (*informal*) ○ *You either have it or you don't.* **10** *pron* **SEX** sexual intercourse (*slang*) **11** *n* **PLAYER IN CHILDREN'S GAMES** in children's informal games, the player who must do something to the others, e.g. run after and touch them in the game of tag ○ *You're it!* [Old English *hit* < Germanic]

it[2] *abbr* Italy (*in Internet addresses*)

IT *abbr* information technology

ITA *abbr* **1** Independent Television Authority **2 ITA, i.t.a.** initial teaching alphabet

ital. *abbr* **1** italic **2** italics

Ital. *abbr* **1** Italian **2** Italy

Italian /i tállyən/ *n* **1** somebody who comes from Italy **2** the official language of Italy and an official language of Switzerland, a Romance language belonging to the Italic branch of Indo-European. Native speakers: 60 million. Other speakers: 60 million. [14C. < Italian *italiano* 'of Italy' < *Italia* 'Italy'.] —**Italian** *adj*

Italianate /i tállyə nayt/ *adj* expressed, done, or made in an Italian style or character

Italianesque /i tállyə nésk/ *adj* = **Italianate**

Italianise *vti* = **Italianize**

Italianism /i tállyənizəm/ *n* something that comes from or is typical of Italy, e.g. a word or phrase that is derived from Italian

Italianize /i tállyə nīz/ (**-izes, -izing, -ized**), **Italianise** (**-ises, -ising, -ised**) *vti* to make something Italian in character, or become Italian in character —**Italianization** /i tállyə nī záysh'n/ *n*

Italian sixth *n* a three-note chord consisting of an augmented sixth chord and a major third above the root of the chord, used for modulation and for providing colour

Italian sonnet *n* LITERAT = **Petrarchan sonnet**

Italian vermouth *n* a dark-coloured sweet vermouth made in Italy

italic /i tállik/ *adj* **1 HAVING PRINTED LETTERS SLOPING TO RIGHT** printed in or using letters that slope to the right **2 SLOPING TO RIGHT** handwritten in letters that slope to the right ■ *n* **ITALIC LETTER** a printed letter that slopes to the right, or a font that uses such letters (*often plural*) [Late 16C. < its introduction by an Italian printer in 1501.]

Italic *n* **BRANCH OF THE INDO-EUROPEAN LANGUAGE FAMILY** a branch of the Indo-European language family that includes many former languages of Italy, including Latin and Umbrian ■ *adj* **1 OF ITALIC** relating to the language family Italic **2 ANCIENT ITALIAN** dating from or used in ancient Italy

italicise *vt* PRINTING = **italicize**

Italicism /i tállissizəm/ *n* a word or phrase that is borrowed from Italian

italicize /i tálli sīz/ (**-cizes, -cizing, -cized**), **italicise** (**-cises, -cising, -cised**) *vt* to print a word, letter, or document in italics, or change words to an italic font —**italicization** /i tálli sī záysh'n/ *n* —**italicized** *adj*

Italo- *prefix* Italy or Italian ○ *Italo-American* [< ITALIAN]

Italophile /i tállō fīl/ *n* a person who loves Italy and Italians —**Italophilia** /i tállō fílli ə/ *n*

Italy /íttəli/ republic in S Europe. Capital: Rome. Population: 56,830,508 (1997). Area: 301,323 sq. km/116,341 sq. mi. See map overleaf.

Itar Tass /eé taar táss/, **ITAR-Tass** *n* a Russian news agency founded in 1992 to replace Tass, the news agency of the former Soviet Union [Late 20C. < Russian acronym < *Informatsionnoe telegrafnoe agentsvo Rossii* 'Information Telegraph Agency of Russia' + *Tass*.]

ITC *abbr* Independent Television Commission

itch /ich/ *v* **1** *vti* **WANT TO SCRATCH** to have, produce, or cause somebody to feel an irritating sensation on the body that provokes a desire to scratch the skin **2** *vi* **BE ANXIOUS TO DO** to be very eager or impatient to do something **3** *vt* **SCRATCH ITCHY SKIN** to scratch the skin where it itches (*nonstandard*) ■ *n* **1 FEELING OF WANTING TO SCRATCH** an irritating sensation in the body that provokes a desire to scratch the skin **2 LONGING** a restless or uneasy desire

Italy

for something **3 ITCHY SKIN DISORDER** a skin disorder such as scabies that causes the skin to itch [Old English *giccan* < Germanic] —**itchiness** *n* —**itching** *n* —**itchy** *adj*

itch mite *n* a tiny parasite that burrows into the skin and causes the disease scabies in humans. *Sarcoptes scabiei.*

it'd /ittəd/ *contr* **1** it would **2** it had

-ite[1] *suffix* **1** mineral, rock, ore, soil, fossil ○ *carnotite* ○ *nummulite* **2** descendant or follower of ○ *Hamite* ○ *Hussite* **3** native or resident of ○ *Israelite* ○ *urbanite* **4** organ, body part, cell, protozoan ○ *sporozoite* **5** commercial product ○ *cordite* **6** product of a chemical process ○ *evaporite* [Via Old French and Latin < Greek *-itēs*]

-ite[2] *suffix* salt or ester of an acid with a name ending in *-ous* ○ *phosphite* [Alteration of *-ATE*]

item /ítəm/ *n* **1 ONE IN A COLLECTION** a single thing in a group or collection of things **2 ONE IN A LIST** one in a list of things **3 BROADCAST OR PUBLISHED REPORT** a piece of information in a news report, e.g. in a newspaper or on television **4 BOOK-KEEPING ENTRY** one entry in a set of financial accounts **5 COUPLE IN A RELATIONSHIP** a couple who are linked in a romantic or sexual relationship (*informal*) ■ *adv* **INTRODUCING AN ITEM IN LIST** used to introduce an item in a list [Late 16C. < Latin *item* 'likewise' < *ita* 'thus, so'.]

itemize /ítə mīz/ (*-izes, -izing, -ized*), **itemise** (*-ises, -ising, -ised*) *vt* to list all of a set of related things ○ *an itemized bill* —**itemization** /ítə mī záysh'n/ *n* —**itemizer** *n*

iterance /íttərənss/ *n* = **iteration** *n*. **1** [Early 17C. < Latin *iterare* (see ITERATE).]

iterant /íttərənt/ *adj* marked by repetition or recurrence [Early 17C. < Latin *iterant-*, present participle of *iterare* (see ITERATE).]

iterate /íttə rayt/ (*-ates, -ating, -ated*) *vt* to say or do the same thing again [Mid-16C. < Latin *iterare* 'to repeat' < *iterum* 'again'.]

⚡iteration /íttə ráysh'n/ *n* **1 REPETITION** an instance or the act of doing something again **2 STEP-BY-STEP PROCESS** a process of achieving a desired result by repeating a sequence of steps and successively getting closer to that result **3 REPETITION OF STEPS** the repetition of a sequence of instructions in a computer program until a result is achieved **4 NEW VERSION** a different version of something, especially a new version of existing computer hardware or software

⚡iterative /íttərətiv/ *adj* **1** MATH, LOGIC = **recursive** *adj.* **2** **2** using repeated routines in a loop as part of a computer program **3** GRAM, LING = **frequentative** *adj.* **4** repeating again and again —**iteratively** *adv*

Ithaca /íthəkə/ **1** island off the coast of W Greece, in the Ionian Sea. Population: 3,646 (1981). Area: 96 sq. km/37 sq. mi. **2** city in south-central New York State. Population: 28,172 (1998 estimate).

ithyphallic /íthi fállik/ *adj* **1 OF HYMNS TO BACCHUS** relating to or composed in the metre used in hymns to the ancient Greek god Bacchus **2 SHOWING ERECT PENIS** in sculpture, painting, or other art, having or showing an

erect penis ■ *n* **HYMN** a hymn composed in ithyphallic metre [Early 17C. < late Latin *ithyphallicus* < Greek *ithuphallos* 'phallus carried in procession at festivals of Bacchus', literally 'straight phallus'.]

itinerant /ī tínnərənt/ *adj* travelling from place to place, especially to find work or as a part of work [Late 16C. < late Latin *itinerant-*, present participle of *itinerari* 'journey' < Latin *itiner-* 'way'.] —**itinerancy** *n* —**itinerant** — **itinerantly** *adv*

itinerary /ī tínnərəri/ *n* (*plural* **-ies**) **1 LIST OF PLACES TO BE VISITED** a plan for a journey listing different places in the order in which they are to be visited **2 RECORD OF JOURNEY** a written record of a journey to visit different places **3 GUIDEBOOK** a guidebook for travellers ■ *adj* **INTENDED FOR TRAVELLING** intended or used for the purpose of travelling [15C. < late Latin *itinerarius* < Latin *itiner-* 'journey'.]

itinerate /ī tínnə rayt/ (*-ates, -ating, -ated*) *vi* to move from place to place on a circuit (*refers to a judge or preacher*) [Early 17C. < late Latin *itinerari* (see ITINERANT).] —**itineration** /ī tínnə ráysh'n/ *n*

-itis *suffix* **1** inflammation, disease ○ *retinitis* **2** excessive interest in ○ *spectatoritis* [< Greek]

it'll /ítt'l/ *contr* it will ○ *It'll be so good to see you.*

⚡ITM *abbr* in the money (*in e-mails*)

Ito Jakuchu /ēetō ja koō choō/ (1716–1800) Japanese artist

-itol *suffix* polyhydric alcohol ○ *inositol* [< *-ITE*[1] + *-OL*[1]]

⚡ITRW *abbr* in the real world (*in e-mails*)

its /its/ *det* used to indicate that something belongs or relates to something ○ *The park changed its policy.* [Late 16C. < IT + *-'s* (possessive).]

> **USAGE** *its* or *it's*? The possessive form of the pronoun *it* is **its**, even though it does not have an apostrophe before the *s*. *The cat is licking its* [not *it's*] *paws.* **It's** is a contraction for *it is* or *it has. It's* [not *Its*] *going to rain tonight. It's* [not *Its*] *been rebuilt.*

it's /its/ *contr* **1** it is ○ *It's perfect.* **2** it has ○ *It's been rebuilt.*

itself /it sélf/ **CORE MEANING:** a reflexive pronoun used to refer back to the subject of a verb or for emphasis *pron* **1 USED TO REFER BACK** used to refer back to the subject of a verb when it is an object, animal, or abstract thing ○ *His ignorance finally revealed itself.* **2 USED TO EMPHASIZE** used to emphasize the thing that is referred to ○ *The house itself was cheap compared to the land.* **3 ITS NORMAL SELF** the way it usually feels or behaves ○ *The dog's not itself since we moved to the city.*

itsy-bitsy /ítsi bítsi/, **itty-bitty** /ítti bítti/ *adj* extremely small (*informal*) [Alteration of LITTLE + BIT[1]]

ITU *abbr* **1** intensive therapy unit **2** International Telecommunication Union

ITV *abbr* Independent Television

IU *abbr* **1** immunizing unit **2** international unit

IUCD *abbr* intrauterine contraceptive device

IUD *abbr* intrauterine device

-ium *suffix* chemical element, radical, or ion ○ *californium* [< modern Latin, alteration of *-um*]

IV[1] *abbr* **1** intravenous **2** intravenously

IV[2] (*plural* **IVs** or **IV's**) *n* US **1** the injection of quantities of a therapeutic fluid such as blood, plasma, saline, or glucose directly into somebody's vein at an adjustable rate **2** the equipment used to administer an IV [Mid-20C. Abbreviation of INTRAVENOUS.]

Ivan III /ī́van/ (1440–1505) grand prince of Muscovy (1462–1505). Known as **Ivan the Great**

Ivan IV (1530–84) tsar of Russia (1547–84). Known as **Ivan the Terrible**

Ivanovo /i vaanəvə/ city in central Russia. Population: 482,000 (1992).

I've /īv/ *contr* I have

-ive *suffix* tending to or performing ○ *illustrative* [Via Old French < Latin *-ivus*]

Ives /īvz/, **Charles** (1874–1954) US composer

IVF *abbr* in vitro fertilization

ivied halls *npl* US EDUC = **halls of ivy**

ivory /ī́vəri/ *n* (*plural* **-ries**) **1 MATERIAL OF ELEPHANT'S TUSKS** a hard cream-coloured substance (**dentine**) that forms the tusks of animals such as the elephant, walrus, and sperm whale **2 SOMETHING MADE OF IVORY** an object made of ivory, e.g. a figurine of a person or animal **3 CREAMY WHITE** a creamy-white colour ■ **ivories** *npl* **1 PIANO KEYS** the keys of a piano (*informal*) **2 TEETH** somebody's teeth (*slang*) **3 DICE** dice (*slang*) [13C. Via Old French *ivurie* < Latin *ebur*.] —**ivory** *adj*

ivory-billed woodpecker *n* a large, nearly extinct woodpecker with black-and-white plumage, a red crest in the male, and an ivory-coloured bill. Native to: S United States, Cuba. *Campephilus principalis.*

ivory black *n* a black pigment made from burnt ivory

Ivory Coast /ī́vəri-/ former name for **Côte d'Ivoire**

ivory gull *n* a small white gull that nests on rocky cliffs and winters on the edge of pack ice. Native to: Arctic. *Pagophila eburnea.*

ivory nut *n* the white nut of the ivory palm whose kernel is used to make buttons or other small items

ivory palm, **ivory-nut palm** *n* a low-growing palm tree that yields ivory nuts. Native to: Brazil, Peru. *Phytelephas macrocarpa.*

ivory tower *n* a state or situation in which somebody is sheltered from the practicalities or difficulties of ordinary life [Translation of French *tour d'ivoire*] —**ivory-towered** *adj*

ivy /ī́vi/ *n* (*plural* **ivies** or **ivy**) *n* **1** an evergreen climbing plant with woody stems and green, green-and-yellow, or green-and-white leaves that grows easily on walls or trees or along the ground. Genus: *Hedera.* **2** any climbing plant that resembles the true ivy, e.g. Boston ivy, Japanese ivy, poison ivy, or ground ivy [Old English *īfig* < Germanic] —**ivied** *adj*

Ivy League *n* a group of prestigious and respected universities in the NE United States consisting of Brown, Columbia, Cornell, Dartmouth, Harvard, Princeton, the University of Pennsylvania, and Yale [< the presumption that the universities' buildings were ivy-clad on account of their great age] —**Ivy League** *adj* —**Ivy Leaguer** *n*

iwi /ḗewi/ (*plural* **iwi**) *n* NZ a people or community [< Maori]

⚡IWIK *abbr* I wish I knew (*in e-mails*)

Iwo /ḗewō/ city in SW Nigeria. Population: 353,000 (1995 estimate).

Iwo Jima /ḗewə jēemə, ḗewō-/ largest of the Volcano Islands of Japan, in the W Pacific Ocean, east of Taiwan. Area: 36 sq. km/12 sq. mi.

⚡IWUTK *abbr* I want you to know (*in e-mails*)

IWW *abbr* Industrial Workers of the World

Ixion /ik sī́ən/ *n* in Greek mythology, a king of Thessaly who was bound to a perpetually turning wheel by Zeus as punishment for making sexual advances to Hera

ixtle *n* TEXTILES = **istle**

Iyar /ḗə yaar/ *n* in the Jewish calendar, the eighth month of the civil year and the second month of the religious year [Mid-18C. < Hebrew *iyyār.*]

⚡IYKWIM *abbr* if you know what I mean (*in e-mails*)

⚡IYSS *abbr* if you say so (*in e-mails*)

-ize *suffix* **1** to cause to be, make ○ *formalize* **2** to treat with or as ○ *chromize* ○ *lionize* **3** to become, become like ○ *crystallize* **4** to engage in ○ *extemporize* [Via Old French *-iser* < Latin *-izare* < Greek *-izein*] —**-ization** *suffix*

Izhevsk /i zhéfsk/ capital of Udmurtia, E Russia. Population: 787,340 (1995).

Izmir /ízmeer/, **İzmir** seaport in W Turkey. Population: 1,757,414 (1990).

Izmit /ízmit/, **İzmit** city in NW Turkey, on the Gulf of Izmit. Population: 208,748 (1996 estimate).

izzard /ízzərd/ *n* the letter 'z' (*archaic*) [Mid-18C. Alteration of ZED.]

j /jay/ (*plural* **j's**), **J** (*plural* **J's** or **Js**) *n* the tenth letter of the English alphabet, representing a consonant sound

j² *symbol* **1** electric current density **2** the imaginary number √−1

J¹ /jay/ (*plural* **J's** or **Js**) *n* something shaped like a letter 'J'

J² *symbol* joule

J³ *abbr* **1** jack **2** Journal **3** Judge **4** Justice

JA *abbr* Jamaica (*international vehicle registration*)

jab /jab/ *vti* (**jabs, jabbing, jabbed**) **1 PUSH SHARPLY** to make a short punching movement, or push something with a short punching movement **2 MAKE SHORT FAST PUNCH** to make a short fast punch at an opponent, e.g. in boxing ■ *n* **1 PUNCHING MOVEMENT** a short sharp punching movement **2 SHORT SHARP PUNCH** a short sharp punch, as used in boxing **3 INJECTION** an injection (*informal*) US term **shot¹** *n.* **14** [Early 19C. Variant of *job* 'pierce, thrust', an imitation of the sound of a brief forcible action.]

Jabalpur /júbb'l poŏr/ city in central India. Population: 739,961 (1991).

jabber /jábbər/ *vti* to talk or say something rapidly, so that it is incomprehensible ■ *n* rapid speech that is incomprehensible [15C. Probably an imitation of the sound.] —**jabberer** *n*

jabberwocky /jábbər woki/ (*plural* **-ies**) *n* speech or writing that is meaningless or often deliberately whimsical or humorous [Early 20C. < 'Jabberwocky', nonsense poem by Lewis Carroll.]

jabiru /jábə roŏ/ (*plural* **-rus** or **-ru**) *n* **1** a large tropical stork with white plumage and a naked head. Native to: Central and South America. *Jabiru mycteria*. **2** a large black-and-white stork. Native to: N and E Australia. *Xenorhynchus asiaticus*. [Late 18C. < Tupi-Guarani *jabirú* 'swollen-necked', from the large neck of the tropical storks.]

Jabiru /jábbə roŏ/ town in the Northern Territory, N Australia, inside Kakadu National Park. Population: 1,694 (1996).

jaborandi /jábbə rándi/ (*plural* **-dis** or **-di**) *n* **1** dried leaves that yield the drug pilocarpine **2** a bush of the rue family whose leaves yield pilocarpine. Native to: tropical America. Genus: *Pilocarpus*. [Early 17C. Via Portuguese < Tupi-Guarani *jaburandi* 'somebody who spits'; from the increased saliva of those who chew the leaves.]

jabot /zhábbō/ (*plural* **-bots**) *n* **1** an edging of ruffles at the upper front of a blouse or dress **2** formerly, a set of ruffles attached to the neckband and falling in tiers down the front of a man's shirt [Early 19C. < French, 'bird's crop, shirt frill'.]

jacamar /jákə maar/ (*plural* **-mars** or **-mar**) *n* a bird with a very long bill and bright blue or green feathers that lays its eggs in holes in the ground. Native to: South and Central America. Family: Galbulidae. [Early 19C. < French.]

jaçana /jássə naà, jə kaànə/ *n* a water bird with short rounded wings and tail and long toes that enable it to walk on floating plants. Native to: tropics, subtropics. Family: Jacanidae. [Mid-18C. Via Portuguese *jaçanã* < Tupi-Guarani *jasanã*.]

jacaranda /jákə rándə/ (*plural* **-das** or **-da**) *n* a widely cultivated tree or bush with ferny leaves, purple flowers, and fragrant wood. Native to: tropical America. Genus: *Jacaranda*. [Mid-18C. Via Portuguese < Tupi-Guarani *jakara'na*.]

jacinth /jássinth, jáyss-/ *n* a reddish variety of zircon. Use: gemstones. [13C. < Old French *iacinte* or medieval Latin *iacintus*, alteration of Latin *hyacinthus* 'blue stone'.]

jack¹ /jak/ *n* **1 LIFTING DEVICE** a portable device that uses a mechanical or hydraulic lifting system to raise heavy objects, especially cars, a short distance **2 PLAYING CARD** a playing card ranking between a ten and a queen, with a picture of a young man on it **3 ELECTRICAL SOCKET** a female socket designed to receive a male plug for completing a circuit **4 OBJECT USED IN JACKS** a small, usually metal object with six points that is used in the game of jacks **5 TARGET BALL USED IN LAWN BOWLING** a small, usually white ball that players aim at in bowling **6 MALE ANIMAL** the male of various animals, especially the donkey **7** *US* ZOOL = **jack rabbit 8 FLAG ON A SHIP** a small flag displayed to indicate the nationality of a ship **9 TROPICAL FISH** a warm-water marine fish that has a forked tail. Genus: *Caranx*. **10 BRACE ON MAST** either one of a pair of wooden braces (**crosstrees**) at the head of a topgallant mast used to hold the mast stays away from the mast **11 LABOURER** a labourer or somebody who does odd jobs (*usually in combination*) **12 DEVICE THAT TURNS SPIT** a device that mechanically turns a spit over an open fire **13** *US* **MONEY** money (*slang*) **14** *US* BEVERAGES = **applejack** ■ *vt* **1 RAISE SOMETHING WITH JACK** to raise a heavy object a short distance using a jack **2** *US* **ROB** to steal something, especially a car, from somebody (*slang*) **3 PRISE SOMETHING OPEN** to open something by prising it apart (*slang*) ◇ *Who jacked the door?* [14C. < the name *Jack*, nickname for *John*, often implying 'ordinary' or 'small'.] ◇ **every man jack** every single person

jack around *vi* to waste time, loaf, or act irresponsibly (*slang*) ◇ *Stop jacking around and get to work!*

jack in *vt* **1** to stop doing an activity or job (*informal*) **2 jack in, jack into** to connect somebody or something electronically to something (*slang*) ◇ *We're jacked into the Internet.*

jack off *vti* *US* a highly offensive term meaning to masturbate (*taboo*)

jack up *v* **1** *vt* **LIFT SOMETHING WITH JACK** to use a jack to lift a heavy object, especially a motor vehicle, off the ground **2** *vt* **INCREASE AMOUNT OF** to increase something, especially a price or salary, often to an unreasonably high level **3** *vti* **INJECT ILLEGAL DRUGS** to inject a drug, especially heroin, intravenously (*slang*) **4** *vi* *Aus* **REFUSE TO OBEY** to refuse to comply with instructions (*informal*)

jack² /jak/ *n* a short sleeveless coat of armour used in the Middle Ages made of canvas covered with metal plates [14C. Via Old French *jaque* < Spanish or Portuguese *jaco*.]

Jack /jak/ *n* NAVY = **Jack Tar** (*dated informal*)

jackal /ják awl, ják'l/ (*plural* **-als** or **-al**) *n* **1 WILD ANIMAL RESEMBLING DOG** a wild mammal resembling a dog, with long legs, large ears, and a bushy tail. Native to: Africa, South Asia. Genus: *Canis*. **2 MINION** a person who carries out menial, unpleasant, or questionable tasks **3 SWINDLER** a person who works with accomplices to deceive people, especially to swindle them [Early 17C. Via Turkish *çakal* < Persian *šagāl*.]

jackanapes /jákə nayps/ (*plural* **jackanapes**) *n* **1 IMPUDENT PERSON** an impudent, self-centred person (*dated*) **2 MISCHIEVOUS CHILD** a child who behaves mischievously or impertinently (*dated*) **3 MONKEY** a monkey (*archaic*) [Early 16C. Originally *Jack Napes* < ?]

jackass /ják ass/ *n* **1** a male donkey or ass (*slang*) **2** an offensive term that deliberately insults somebody's in-

telligence (*slang insult*) [Early 18C. < the name *Jack*.] —**jackassery** *n*

jack bean *n* a climbing plant of the pea family. Flowers: purple, in clusters. Use: forage. Native to: tropical America, S United States. *Canavalia ensiformis*.

jackboot /ják boot/ *n* **1 MILITARY BOOT** a sturdy long black leather boot that comes up to, or over, the knee, worn especially by the military in Nazi Germany **2 HARSH TREATMENT** military or other rule that is characterized by cruelty, oppression, or arbitrary aggression **3 RIDING BOOT** a heavy boot of hard leather worn for riding [Late 17C. < ?]

jack-by-the-hedge (*plural* **jack-by-the-hedges**) *n* PLANTS = **garlic mustard**

jack crevalle *n* **1** a spiny-finned, economically important fish. Native to: W Florida coast. *Caranx hippos*. **2** the flesh of a jack crevalle used as food

jackdaw /ják daw/ *n* a large noisy bird of the crow family known for stealing things, especially shiny objects. Native to: Europe, Asia. *Corvus monedula*. [Mid-16C. < the name *Jack*.]

Jackeen /ja keén/ *n* Ireland somebody from Dublin who is thought of as well-read, confident, and particularly proud of being from working- or lower-class origins, or sometimes by non-Dubliners as smugly clever (*offensive in some contexts*) [Mid-19C. Diminutive of the name *Jack*.]

jackeroo /jákə roŏ/ (*plural* **-roos**) *n* *Aus* a young male trainee worker on a sheep or cattle station (*informal*)

jacket /jákit/ *n* **1 SHORT COAT** a short, usually hip-length or waist-length coat, sometimes forming part of a suit **2 PROTECTIVE CLOTHING** something that is worn on the upper part of the body for protection or support **3 POTATO SKIN** the outer skin of an unpeeled cooked potato, especially a baked one **4** PUBL = **dust jacket 5** *US* RECORDING = **sleeve** *n.* **3 6 FLOPPY DISK CASING** the casing of a floppy disk **7** *US* **FOLDER** a strong envelope or folder for holding papers or documents **8 BOILER COVER** a cover or outer casing designed to insulate a boiler **9 OUTER CASING OF PIPE** an outer casing around a pipe that can be filled with steam or hot water to keep the contents of the pipe warm **10 OUTER CASING OF BULLET** an outer casing on certain bullets and other types of ammunition **11 COAT IDENTIFYING RACING DOG** a distinctive coloured coat for an animal, especially a racing greyhound ■ *vt* **PUT JACKET ON** to put a jacket on somebody or something, e.g. a book or record [15C. < French *jaquet*, diminutive of Old French *jacque* 'tunic' < *jacques* 'peasant' < the name *Jacques*.]

jacket potato *n* a potato that has been baked with the skin still on it and is served plain or with a filling

jackfish /ják fish/ (*plural* **-fish** or **-fishes**) *n* a pike, especially a young or small one [Late 16C. < JACK¹ implying 'small'.]

Jack Frost *n* a personification of frost, very cold wintry weather, or the effects that frost or cold weather can produce

jackfruit /ják froot/ (*plural* **-fruit** or **-fruits**) *n* **1** FOOD = **jak 2** a tree that bears jaks and produces fine-grained yellowish wood. Native to: tropical Asia. *Artocarpus heterophyllus*. [Mid-19C. < variant of JAK.]

Jack-go-to-bed-at-noon *n* PLANTS = **goatsbeard** *n*. **1** [Because the flowers close up at about noon]

jackhammer /ják hammər/ n a hand-held power tool, usually powered by compressed air and used for splitting or drilling rock, or for breaking up paved areas [< JACK¹ implying 'small']

Jackie-O /jáki ō/ adj describes a fashion style associated with Jacqueline Kennedy Onassis ○ *wearing a pair of Jackie-O sunglasses*

jack-in-office (plural **jacks-in-office**) n a self-important and inflexible petty official

jack-in-the-box (plural **jacks-in-the-box** or **jack-in-the-boxes**) n a child's toy consisting of a puppet on a spring inside a box

jack-in-the-pulpit n 1 a woodland plant with tiny flowers, in a thick spike surrounded by a sheath. Native to: E North America. *Arisaema triphyllum*. 2 = **cuckoo-pint**

jackknife /ják nīf/ n (plural **-knives**) 1 FOLDING KNIFE a knife that has a pivoted blade that fits inside the handle when it is not in use 2 DIVE a dive in which the diver jumps, bends the body at the waist while keeping the legs together and straight, then straightens out to enter the water headfirst ■ vi (**-knifes, -knifing, -knifed**) 1 LOSE CONTROL OF TRAILER to come to a halt with the trailer at an angle to the cab, as a result of sudden braking or swerving at speed (*refers to articulated lorries*) ○ *The lorry struck a patch of ice and jackknifed.* 2 DO JACKKNIFE DIVE to perform a jackknife dive [Early 18C. < ?]

jack ladder n = Jacob's ladder n. 1

Jacklin /jáklin/, **Tony** (b. 1944) British golfer

jack-of-all-trades (plural **jacks-of-all-trades**) n a versatile performer of varied tasks

jack-o'-lantern n a lantern made from a hollowed-out pumpkin that has facial features cut out of it, used as a part of Halloween decoration

jack pine n a pine tree with short needles arranged in pairs and curving cones, whose timber is used for paper pulp. Native to: N North America. *Pinus banksiana.*

jack plane n a large joinery plane used for rough planing of wood and other surfaces [< JACK¹ implying 'instrument']

jackpot /ják pot/ n 1 an amount of money won in a competition or lottery or as a payout from a fruit machine or other kind of gambling machine 2 an accumulated stake in poker games that can be competed for only by players holding a pair of jacks or a better hand [Late 19C. < a pair of jacks being the least required to compete for the pot in poker.] ◇ **hit the jackpot** to achieve great success, especially financially

jack rabbit n a large hare with long hind legs and extremely long ears. Native to: prairies of W North America. Genus: *Lepus.* [< JACKASS, because of its long ears]

jack rafter n any one of a set of sloping timber beams spanning between the eaves and the hip rafter of a roof [< JACK¹ implying 'small']

Jack Robinson [< ?] ◇ **before you can** or **could say Jack Robinson** without the slightest delay or hesitation (*informal*)

Jack Russell, Jack Russell terrier n a small terrier with short legs and a white coat with patchy markings in black, brown, or tan, or a combination of these colours [Early 20C. After John (Jack) Russell (1795–1883), who introduced the breed.]

jacks /jaks/ n a game involving picking up small metal or plastic pieces in a particular sequence between bouncing or throwing and catching a ball (+ singular verb) [Early 19C. Shortening of JACKSTONES.]

jackscrew /ják skroo/ n TECH = **screw jack**

jackshaft /ják shaaft/ n a short shaft that transmits power from a motor or engine to a machine

jacksie /jáksi/, **jacksy** (plural **-sies**), **jaxie, jaxy** (plural **-ies**) n an offensive term for the buttocks or anus [Late 19C. < JACK¹.]

jacksmelt /ják smelt/ n (plural **-smelts** or **-smelt**) n 1 a commercially important fish of the silverside family. Native to: N American Pacific coast. *Atherinopsis californiensis.* 2 the flesh of a jacksmelt used as food

jacksnipe /ják snīp/ (plural **-snipe** or **-snipes**) n a small wading bird with a short bill and legs and dark plumage. Native to: N Europe, Asia. *Limnocryptes minimus.* [< JACK¹ implying 'small']

Jackson /jáks'n/ capital of Mississippi State, in the central part of the state. Population: 188,419 (1998 estimate).

Jackson, Andrew (1767–1845) US statesman and 7th president of the United States (1829–37). Known as **Old Hickory**

Jackson, Glenda (b. 1936) British actor and politician

Jackson, Jesse (b. 1941) US civil rights leader, clergyman, and politician

Jackson, Mahalia (1911–72) US singer

Jackson, Marjorie (b. 1932) Australian sprinter

Jackson, Michael (b. 1958) US entertainer

Stonewall Jackson

Jackson, Stonewall (1824–63) US Confederate general. Born **Thomas Jonathan Jackson**

Jacksonville /jáks'n vil/ city in NE Florida. Population: 693,630 (1998 estimate).

jackstay /ják stay/ n 1 a rod attached to a horizontal beam (**yard**) on a mast, used for securing a sail 2 a support for the ring (**parrel**) that holds a boom to a mast

jackstone /ják stōn/ n a small piece of metal or plastic used in the game of jacks

jackstones /ják stōnz/ n GAME = **jacks** (+ singular verb) [Early 19C. < JACK¹ implying 'small'.]

jackstraw /ják straw/ n a small thin stick used in the game of jackstraws [Late 16C. < JACK¹ implying 'small'.]

jackstraws /ják strawz/ n a game that involves trying to remove small thin sticks from a pile one at a time without disturbing the rest of the pile (+ singular verb)

jacksy n = **jacksie** (offensive)

Jack Tar n a sailor (dated informal) [< the name Jack implying 'Everyman' + TAR² 'sailor']

Jack-the-lad n a cocky and flashy young man (informal) [< the nickname of Jack Sheppard, 18C thief]

Jack-the-rags (plural **Jack-the-rags**) n Wales a Jack-the-lad (informal)

Jack the Ripper /ják thə ríppər/ (fl. 1880s) nickname of a notorious, unidentified 19th century British serial murderer

jack-up, jack-up rig n an offshore oil rig with a floating hull and retractable legs that can be lowered to the seabed for support

Jacob¹ /jáykab/ n in the Bible, the second son of Isaac and Rebekah, and the grandson of Abraham

Jacob² /jáykab/, **Jacob sheep** n a sheep of a breed originally found in the Scottish Hebrides with two or four thick curved horns and a cream-coloured fleece with dark-brown patches on it [Mid-17C. After JACOB¹, who kept piebald sheep (Genesis 30:39).]

Jacobean /jákə bée ən/ adj 1 relating to King James I or to the period of his English reign (1603–25). 2 in the style of furniture, architecture, or drama fashionable during the reign of King James I. ■ n somebody, especially a prominent person, who lived during the reign of King James I of England [Late 18C. < ecclesiastical Latin Jacobus 'James'.]

Jacobean lily n a cultivated plant of the amaryllis family. Flowers: bright red. Native to: Mexico. *Sprekelia formosissima.* [After St James]

jacobin /jákəbin/ n a variety of pigeon with feathers over the neck and head that grow in the opposite direction to the others, giving it the appearance of having a

hood [Late 17C. < French jacobine, feminine of Jacobin (see JACOBIN).]

Jacobin /jákəbin/ n 1 FRENCH REVOLUTIONARY EXTREMIST a member of a group of left-wing extremists founded during the French Revolution 2 LEFT-WING EXTREMIST a political radical, especially one who holds extreme left-wing views 3 FRIAR a French Dominican friar ■ adj OF FRENCH JACOBINS relating to the Jacobins of the French Revolution or to their policies [14C. < Old French, < ecclesiastical Latin Jacobus; because the Jacobin friars were established at the church of St Jacques in Paris.] —**Jacobinic** /jákə bínnik/ adj —**Jacobinical** adj —**Jacobinically** adv —**Jacobinism** n

Jacobite /jákə bīt/ n 1 a supporter of King James II of England and his descendants in the Stuart claim to the British throne 2 a member of any of the Monophysite churches, especially of Syria [Late 17C. < ecclesiastical Latin Jacobus 'James'.] —**Jacobitic** /jákə bíttik/ adj —**Jacobitical** adj —**Jacobitism** n

Jacob sheep n = Jacob²

Jacob's ladder n 1 a ladder, used especially on ships, whose rungs are held together by ropes or chains, thus allowing it to be rolled up and stored in a small space 2 a wild or garden plant with leaves divided into several leaflets in an arrangement similar to a ladder. Flowers: blue, white. Native to: North America. Genus: *Polemonium.* [< Jacob's vision of a ladder reaching to heaven (Genesis 28:12)]

Jacob's staff n a medieval instrument for measuring distance [< the pilgrim's staff that is a symbol of St James (ecclesiastical Latin Jacobus), or the staff of Jacob (Genesis 30:10)]

jaconet /jákənit/ n a cotton fabric that is like muslin but slightly heavier. Use: clothing, bandages. [Mid-18C. Anglicization of Jagannāth(purī) in India.]

jacquard /ják aard/ n 1 WEAVING TECHNIQUE a technique for producing intricate patterns in material by means of punched cards that give instructions to use or withhold various colours of thread 2 LOOM ATTACHMENT a loom attachment with punched cards that makes jacquard patterns 3 INDUST = **jacquard loom** 4 PATTERNED MATERIAL a fabric that has been woven with a jacquard pattern [Mid-19C. After J. M. JACQUARD.]

Jacquard /ják aard/, **Joseph Marie** (1752–1834) French inventor

jacquard loom n a loom with an attachment for making jacquard patterns

Jacques-Cartier /zhák kaárti ay/ river in S Quebec, Canada. Length: 113 km/70 mi.

jactitation /jákti táysh'n/ n 1 UNCONTROLLED THRASHING AROUND violent and uncontrollable movements of the body and limbs, usually brought on by extremely high temperature, or occasionally by psychiatric disorders 2 HARMFUL LIE in law, a false boast or claim, especially one that is intended to harm another 3 BOASTING the act of boasting or exaggerating (literary) [Mid-17C. < medieval Latin jactitation- < Latin jactitare 'bring forward in public, boast' < jacere 'throw'.]

Jacuzzi /jə kōzi/ tdmk a trademark for a whirlpool bath with a system of underwater jets that deliver water under pressure in order to massage and invigorate the body

jade¹ /jayd/ n 1 a semiprecious stone made of either nephrite or jadeite, varying in colour from a deep green to yellow and brown to white. Use: ornaments, jewellery. 2 objects made of jade, collectively ○ *a collector of jade* 3 COLOURS = **jade green** [Late 16C. Via French l'ejade < Spanish piedra de ijada 'stone of the flanks' (because thought to cure pain in the renal areas) < Latin ilia 'flanks'.] —**jade** adj

jade² /jayd/ n (archaic) 1 TIRED OLD HORSE an old horse, especially one that is worn out through overwork 2 OFFENSIVE TERM an offensive term for a woman that deliberately insults her temperament or morality ■ vti (**jades, jading, jaded**) MAKE or BECOME EXHAUSTED to wear somebody out or become exhausted, especially through overwork (archaic) [14C. < ?]

jaded /jáydid/ adj 1 no longer interested in something, often because of having been overexposed to it 2 exhausted, especially through overwork —**jadedly** adv —**jadedness** n

jade green n a pale milky green colour, like that of some types of jade —**jade-green** adj

jadeite /jáyd īt/ n a usually greenish pyroxene mineral consisting of sodium aluminium silicate. Source: metamorphic rocks. Use: ornaments, jewellery. —**jaditic** /jay díttik/ adj

j'adoube /zha doób, zhə doób/ interj an expression used by a chess player who is about to adjust a piece on the board, to ensure that this will not be counted as an official move [Early 19C. < French, 'I dub' (touch on the shoulder).]

jaeger /jáygər/ n 1 a brownish or greyish predatory sea bird with narrow wings. Native to: N Pacific and Atlantic. Genus: *Stercorarius*. 2 a hunter, especially in Germany and Switzerland [Mid-19C. < German *Jäger* 'huntsman' < *jagen* 'hunt, pursue'.]

Jaén /haa én/ capital of Jaén Province, S Spain. Population: 101,938 (1991).

Jaffa /jáffə/, **Jaffa orange** n a variety of large thick-skinned juicy orange [Late 19C. After *Jaffa* (TEL-AVIV JAFFA).]

Jaffna /jáfnə/ port and capital of Northern Province, Sri Lanka. Population: 129,000 (1990 estimate).

jag[1] /jag/ n 1 JAGGED PROJECTION a sharp projection, especially of rock 2 *Scotland* INJECTION an injection (*informal*) ■ vt (**jags, jagging, jagged**) CUT SOMETHING UNEVENLY to cut notches in something, or cut something unevenly [14C. < ?]

jag[2] /jag/ n (*informal*) 1 PERIOD OF INTOXICATION a period of intoxication by drugs or alcohol 2 DRUNKEN STATE the state of being intoxicated from drugs or alcohol 3 BINGE a period of time spent doing something in an uncontrolled or excessive way [Late 16C. < ?]

Jagan /yaágən/, **Cheddi** (1918–97) Guyanan statesman

Jagannath /júggə naat, -nawt/, **Jagganath, Jagannatha** /júggə naathə/ n RELIG = **Juggernaut** [Mid-17C. See JUGGERNAUT.]

jagged /jággid/ adj 1 having sharp protruding parts or points ◇ *jagged peaks of the distant mountains* 2 having rough and uneven edges or surfaces ◇ *a hastily drawn, jagged portrait* —**jaggedly** adv —**jaggedness** n

Jagger /jággər/, **Mick** (b. 1943) British rock musician and songwriter. Full name **Michael Phillip Jagger**

jaggery /jággəri/ n unrefined brown sugar made in Southeast Asia from the sap of the date palm [Late 16C. Via Portuguese *xagara* < Sanskrit *śarkarā* 'sugar'.]

jaggy /jággi/ (**-gier, -giest**) adj (*informal*) 1 jagged 2 *Scotland* prickly and irritating to the skin

jaguar /jággyoo ər/ n a large cat related to the leopard but with a shorter tail and black spots inside black rings on its tawny coat. Native to: S North America, Central America, N South America. *Panthera onca*. [Early 17C. Via Portuguese < Tupi *jaguara*, Guarani *yaguará* 'carnivorous animal'.]

jaguarundi /jágwə rúndi/, **jaguarondi** /-róndi/ n a small slender cat that has a brownish, greyish, or reddish coat and small ears. Native to: Central and South America, occasionally SW United States. *Felis yagouaroundi*. ◊ **eyra** [Mid-19C. < Portuguese, < *jaguar* (see JAGUAR) + Tupi-Guarani *undi* 'dark'.]

Jah /jaa/ n God, especially in Rastafarianism [Mid-16C. < Hebrew *Yāh*, shortening of *Yahweh* 'Jehovah'.]

Jahveh, Jahweh n RELIG = **Yahweh**

jai alai /hī ə lī/ n a version of the game pelota, for two or four players. ◊ **pelota** n. 1 [Early 20C. < Spanish, < Basque *jai* 'festival' + *alai* 'merry'.]

Jai Hind /jī hínd/ interj S Asia an Indian slogan meaning 'victory to India', shouted especially at political rallies or used as a greeting [Mid-20C. < Hindi, < *jai* 'long live!' + *Hind* 'India'.]

jail /jayl/, **gaol** n 1 PLACE WHERE CRIMINALS ARE KEPT a secure place for keeping people found guilty of crimes or awaiting legal judgment ◇ *sentenced to three years jail* ■ vt 1 SEND SOMEBODY TO JAIL to sentence somebody to spend time in a jail ◇ *The judge jailed her for three months.* 2 LOCK SOMEBODY IN JAIL to keep somebody in a jail or other secure place ◇ *prisoners who were jailed in a dungeon* [13C. Via Old French *jaiole*, Old N French *gaiole* < Latin *caveola*, diminutive of *cavea* 'cage'.]

jailbait /jáyl bayt/ n an offensive term for a minor under the age of consent who is sexually desirable to somebody older (*slang*)

jailbird /jáyl burd/ n a current or former prisoner, especially somebody with more than one experience of prison (*slang*)

jailbreak /jáyl brayk/ n a forceful escape from jail or prison

jailer /jáylər/, **jailor, gaoler** n a supervisor or employee who is in charge of prisoners in a jail

jail fever n typhus (*dated*)

jailhouse /jáyl howss/ n US a jail (*informal*)

jailor n = jailer

Jain /jīn, jayn/, **Jaina** /jīnə, jáynə/ n a believer in or follower of Jainism [Late 18C. < Hindi, < Sanskrit *jaina* 'of a conqueror'.] —**Jain** adj

Jainism /jīnizəm, jáyn-/ n an ancient branch of Hinduism that rejects the notion of a supreme being and advocates a deep respect for all living things —**Jainist** adj

Jaipur /jī poór/ capital of Rajasthan State, N India. Population: 1,454,678 (1991).

jak /jak/, **jack** n a large greenish bulbous fruit produced by the jackfruit tree [Late 16C. Via Portuguese *jaca* < Malayalam *cakka*.]

Jakarta /jə kaártə/ capital and largest city of Indonesia, on the northwestern coast of the island of Java. Population: 9,160,5000 (1995).

jakes /jayks/ (*plural* **jakeses** or **jakes**) n 1 a lavatory, especially an outside one or one without running water 2 *W Country* human faeces, urine, or excrement generally (*informal*) [Mid-16C. < ?]

Jalalabad /jə laálə bad/, **Jalālābād** city in E Afghanistan. Population: 60,000 (1993).

Jalandhar /jállən daar/ = **Jullundur**

jalap /jálləp/ n a twining plant of the convolvulus family, the dried tubers of which have a purgative effect. Native to: Mexico. *Ipomoea purga*. [Mid-17C. Via French < abbreviation of Spanish *purga de Jalapa*, after the Mexican city of *Jalapa*.] —**jalapic** /jə láppik/ adj

jalapeño /hállə páy nyō/ (*plural* **-ños**), **jalapeño pepper** n a small hot pepper that is green or red when ripe and is used extensively in Mexican cooking. *Capsicum annuum*. [Mid-20C. < Mexican Spanish.]

jalopy /jə lóppi/ (*plural* **-ies**) n a rickety or battered old car (*dated informal*) [Early 20C. < ?]

jalouse /jə loóz/ (**-louses, -lousing, -loused**) vt *Scotland* to suspect that something is the case [Late 17C. < French *jalouser* 'envy, be jealous of'.]

jalousie /zhálloō zee/ n a shutter or window covering consisting of a set of angled parallel slats that can be opened to various degrees to control the amount of light or air passing through [Mid-18C. < French, literally 'jealousy'.]

jam[1] /jam/ v (**jams, jamming, jammed**) 1 vt PUSH SOMETHING IN FORCIBLY to push something into a tight space with force ◇ *jammed the clothes into the wardrobe* 2 vt FILL SOMETHING UP to fill a place with people or things pressed closely together ◇ *The fans jammed the streets to see their heroes.* ◇ *jammed the fridge with delicacies* 3 vti STOP WORKING to cause a piece of machinery or equipment to stick or stop working, or undergo such a stoppage ◇ *The photocopier jammed when I was in the middle of using it.* 4 vt BLOCK SOMETHING UP to block up something that functions as an exit, passage, or means of escape ◇ *Leaves had jammed the drains and gutters.* 5 vt PUT ON BRAKES HARD to apply the brakes of a car suddenly and hard 6 vt CRUSH PART OF BODY to injure a part of the body, especially by squeezing or squashing it ◇ *I jammed my finger in the door.* 7 vt INTERFERE WITH BROADCASTING SIGNALS to block a radio or TV signal, usually by broadcasting other signals on the same frequency 8 vt OVERWHELM SWITCHBOARD to overwhelm a switchboard with telephone calls 9 vt MAKE TAPE IMPOSSIBLE TO COPY to put a blocking device on something, especially a prerecorded video tape, in order to prevent it from being copied 10 vi IMPROVISE MUSIC TOGETHER to play music, especially jazz, rock, or pop, in an improvised way, often in a group ◇ *n* 1 TRANSP = **traffic jam** 2 DIFFICULT SITUATION a difficult, awkward, or embarrassing situation (*informal*) ◇ *a cash shortage that's got the company in a jam* 3 STOPPAGE an instance of something being blocked or prevented from functioning ◇ *a paper jam in the photocopier* 4 SIGNAL BLOCKAGE a blockage of radio or television signals 5 DEVICE TO PREVENT COPYING a device that prevents something, especially a prerecorded video tape, from being copied 6 MUSIC = **jam session** (*informal*) [Early 18C. < ?] —**jammable** adj —**jammer** n

jam[2] /jam/ n a spread made from fruit boiled with sugar ■ vt (**jams, jamming, jammed**) to make fruit into jam by boiling it with sugar [Mid-18C. < ?] —**jammy** adj

Jam. abbr 1 Jamaica 2 James

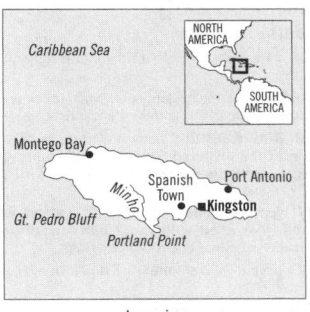

Jamaica

Jamaica /jə máykə/ island country in the N Caribbean Sea. Capital: Kingston. Population: 2,615,581 (1997). Area: 10,991 sq. km/4,244 sq. mi. —**Jamaican** n, adj

Jamaica pepper n FOOD = **allspice** n. 1

Jamaica rum n a slowly fermented rum that has a dark colour and a strong flavour

jamb /jam/, **jambe** n 1 either of the upright parts of a door or window frame or the sides of a fireplace 2 the inside vertical face of an opening [14C. Via Italian *gamba* or Old French *jambe* 'leg' < Greek *kampē* 'bend, joint'.]

jambalaya /jámbə lī ə, júmbə-/ n a Creole dish of rice with a mixture of fish and meat [Late 19C. Via Louisiana French < Provençal *jambalaia* 'stewed mixture of rice and fowl'.]

jambe n BUILDING = **jamb**

Jambi /jámbi/ port and capital of Jambi Province, W Indonesia, on the island of Sumatra. Population: 301,359 (1990).

jamboree /jámbə rèe/ n 1 a large-scale planned celebration with various events and entertainments 2 a large gathering of members of the Scout or Guide movement, often on an international scale [Mid-19C. < ?]

James[1] /jaymz/ n in the Bible, an epistle believed to have been written by James, a brother or relative of Jesus Christ

James[2] /jaymz/ river in W Virginia. Length: 547 km/340 mi.

James, St (fl. 1st century AD) one of the 12 apostles of Jesus Christ. Known as **St James the Great**

James, St (fl. 1st century AD) relative of Jesus Christ and a leader of the early Christian church in Jerusalem. Known as **St James the Just**

James, St (d. AD 62?). one of the 12 apostles of Jesus Christ. Known as **St James the Less**

James I (1208–76) king of Aragon (1213–76). Known as **James the Conqueror**

James I (1566–1625) king of England and Ireland (1603–25), also James VI of Scotland (1567–1625)

James II (1633–1701) king of England, Scotland, and Ireland (1685–88)

James, Henry (1843–1916) US-born British novelist

James, Jesse (1847–82) US outlaw

James, P. D., Baroness James of Holland Park (b. 1920) British novelist. Full name **Phyllis Dorothy James**

James, William (1842–1910) US philosopher and psychologist

James Bay southern extension of Hudson Bay, between W Quebec and NE Ontario, Canada. Area: 32,000 sq. km/12,355 sq. mi.

Jamesian /jáymzi ən/ adj relating to or characteristic of Henry James or his literary style, e.g. in containing long complex sentences, or describing emotional states and relationships in minute detail

Jameson /jáyms'n/, **Sir Leander** (1853–1917) British-born South African politician

Jamestown /jáymz town/ 1 city in SW New York State. Population: 33,154 (1996). 2 former village in SE Virginia, the first permanent English settlement in America

Jamestown Island /jáymz town-/ island in E Virginia, on the James River, the site of Jamestown village

James VI /jáymz/ ♦ **James I**

jamindari n = **zamindari**

jam jar n 1 a glass jar with a lid containing jam 2 a car (slang)

jammies /jámmiz/ npl pyjamas (informal; often used by or to children) [Late 20C. Shortening and alteration.]

Jammu and Kashmir /jámmoo-/ state in N India, a section of the disputed territory of Kashmir. Capital: Srinagar. Population: 7,720,000 (1991). Area: 101,387 sq. km/39,145 sq. mi.

jammy[1] /jámmi/ (**-mier, -miest**) adj 1 **STICKY WITH JAM** covered in or filled with jam 2 **LUCKY** lucky (informal) 3 **EXCELLENT** excellent or profitable (slang)

jammy[2] /jámmi/ (plural **-mies**) n S Africa an old car (slang humorous) [< ?]

jam-pack vt to fill a container or place extremely tightly or to capacity (informal)

jam session n a period of time spent making improvised music, especially jazz, rock, or pop music, as practice, for fun, or to experiment with new songs or techniques

Jamshedpur /júm shed poór/ city in E India. Population: 460,577 (1991).

Jan, Jan. abbr January

Janáček /yánna chek/, **Leoš** (1854–1928) Czech composer

Jane Doe /jáyn dő/ n US 1 a woman or girl, especially one who is involved in legal proceedings and whose identity is not known or is being protected 2 an average woman affected by everyday events [After JOHN DOE]

Janeite /jáyn īt/ n an expert on or admirer of the life and works of the English novelist Jane Austen

⚡**JANET** /jánnit/ n an Internet-linked computer network used by academics and researchers, especially those affiliated to universities and institutes of higher education [Acronym < Joint Academic Network]

jangle /jáng g'l/ vti (**-gles, -gling, -gled**) 1 **MAKE A METALLIC SOUND** to make a harsh metallic noise, or cause something made of metal to make such a noise ○ heard his keys jangling 2 **IRRITATE SOMEBODY'S NERVES** to put somebody's nerves on edge, or be tense and on edge ○ The shock jangled her nerves. ■ n 1 **METALLIC SOUND** a harsh metallic noise 2 **ARGUMENT** a disagreement or quarrel (dated) [13C. < Old French jangler 'to chatter'.] —**jangler** n —**jangly** adj

janissary /jánnissəri/ (plural **-ies**), **janizary** /-zəri/ (plural **-ies**) n 1 a member of the Turkish sultan's elite personal guard from the 14th century until 1826. Janissaries were recruited from Christians in the Balkans and disbanded as part of 19th-century reforms. 2 a loyal follower or supporter [Early 16C. Via French janissaire < Turkish yeniçeri 'new troops'.]

janitor /jánnitər/ n 1 US, Can, Scotland somebody whose job is to look after the cleaning and maintenance of a building, especially a school or an office block. ◊ **caretaker** n. 1 2 a doorkeeper (archaic) [Mid-16C. < Latin, 'door person' < janua 'door'.] —**janitorial** /jánni táwri əl/ adj

janizary n HIST = **janissary**

jankers /jángkərz/ n punishment for a serviceman or servicewoman who has committed a military offence (slang) [Early 20C. < ?]

Jan Mayen /yan mĭ' an/ uninhabited island of Norway, in the Arctic Ocean between Norway and Greenland. Area: 373 km/144 mi. Length: 63 km/39 mi.

Jansen /jánss'n/, **Cornelis** (1585–1638) Dutch theologian

Jansenism /jánss'nizəm/ n a religious movement of the 17th and 18th centuries based on the theological views of Cornelis Jansen, who maintained that there can be no good act without divine will or the grace of God —**Jansenist** n —**Jansenistic** /jánssə nístik/ adj —**Jansenistical** adj

jansky /jánski/ (plural **-skys**) n (symbol **Jy**) a unit used to indicate the strength of radio sources in astronomy, equal to 10^{-26} watts per square metre per hertz [Mid-20C. After Karl JANSKY.]

Jansky /jánski/, **Karl** (1905–50) US engineer

January /jánnyőő əri, jánnyŏŏri/ (plural **-ys**) n the first month of the year in the Gregorian calendar, made up

of 31 days [Pre-12C. < Latin Januarius (mensis) 'month of Janus'.]

Janus /jáynəss/ n 1 the Roman god of beginnings, of the past and the future, and of gates, doorways, and bridges, and of peace, traditionally depicted as having two faces 2 the tenth satellite of Saturn

Jap /jap/ n a highly offensive term for a Japanese person (taboo)

japan /jə pán/ n 1 **BLACK VARNISH** a lacquer that, when used to coat wood or metal, gives a glossy black finish 2 **VARNISHED OBJECTS** decorative work that has been coated with japan or a similar kind of varnish ■ vt (**-pans, -panning, -panned**) **APPLY JAPAN TO** to varnish an object with japan [Late 17C. After JAPAN.]

Japan

Japan /jə pán/ constitutional monarchy in East Asia, comprising four large islands and more than 1,000 lesser adjacent islands. Capital: Tokyo. Population: 125,688,711 (1997). Area: 377,837 sq. km/145,884 sq. mi.

Japan, Sea of body of water between Korea and Japan. Area: 1,012,945 sq. km/391,100 sq. mi.

Japan clover n an annual plant grown as a forage crop. Native to: China, Japan, now widely grown in the SE United States. Lespedeza striata.

Japan Current ♦ **Kuroshio**

Japanese /jáppə neéz/ (plural **-nese**) n 1 somebody who comes from Japan 2 the official language of Japan, also spoken in parts of Brazil and North America, whose linguistic affiliations are disputed. Native speakers: 126 million. —**Japanese** adj

Japanese beetle n a shiny green and brown scarab beetle that was accidentally introduced into the E United States where it is now a serious pest of cereal crops

Japanese garden n a garden designed according to formal Japanese rules, distinguished by its use of foliage plants, rocks, sand, and wooden garden paths, bridges, and pavilions

Japanese iris n a cultivated ornamental plant. Flowers: reddish-purple, large-petalled. Native to: Asia. Iris ensata.

Japanese knotweed n a tall fast-growing perennial plant with reddish-brown bamboo-like stems and clusters of creamy-white flowers. Originally an ornamental, it is now considered an invasive weed in many countries. Native to: E Asia. Fallopia japonica.

Japanese maple n a tree widely cultivated for its attractive deeply lobed leaves and purple flowers. Native to: Asia. Acer palmatum.

Japanese millet n a coarse annual grass that has edible seeds and is grown for fodder. Native to: Asia. Echinochloa frumentacea.

Japanese persimmon n 1 a red or orange fruit that is bitter when unripe 2 a tree that produces Japanese persimmons. Native to: Asia. Diospyros kaki.

Japanese plum n 1 a yellow or red fruit, often pickled or dried 2 a tree that bears Japanese plums. Native to: Asia. Prunus salicina.

Japanese umbrella pine n a coniferous tree widely grown for ornament, with needles arranged in whorls like the ribs of an umbrella. Native to: central Japan. Sciadopitys verticillata.

Japanize /jáppə nīz/ (**-nizes, -nizing, -nized**), **Japanise** (**-nises, -nising, -nised**) v 1 vti **SHOW JAPANESE INFLUENCE** to become, or make something become, Japanese in appearance, nature, or style 2 vt **INTRODUCE JAPANESE METHODS TO** to convert an area or industry to Japanese ways of working 3 vt **REPLACE WITH JAPANESE BUSINESS** to take a business over and replace it with a Japanese-based one —**Japanization** /jáppə nī záysh'n/ n

jape /jayp/ n a joke or an act of mischief (archaic or literary) ■ vti (**japes, japing, japed**) to joke, trick, or make fun of something (archaic or literary) [14C. < Old French japer 'yelp', influenced by gaber 'mock'.] —**japer** n —**japery** n

Japheth /jáy feth/ n in the Bible, the third son of Noah and brother of Shem and Ham

Japlish /jáplish/ n Japanese with many adoptions of English words, phrases, or idioms [Mid-20C. Blend of JAPANESE + ENGLISH.]

japonica /jə pónnikə/ n **PLANTS** = **camellia** n. 1 [Early 19C. < modern Latin, form of Japonicus 'of Japan'.]

Jaques-Dalcroze /zhák dal krốz/, **Emile** (1865–1950) Swiss music teacher and composer

jar[1] /jaar/ n 1 **STORAGE CONTAINER** a cylindrical container, usually one that has a wide mouth and a lid but no spout, typically made of glass, plastic, or earthenware ○ pickle jars 2 **JAR'S CONTENTS** the amount a jar holds, or the contents of a jar 3 **ALCOHOLIC DRINK** a glass of beer or other alcoholic drink (informal) ■ vt (**jars, jarring, jarred**) **PUT SOMETHING IN JAR** to put something into a jar, often sealing it in [Late 16C. Via French jarre < Arabic jarra.] —**jarful** n

jar[2] /jaar/ v (**jars, jarring, jarred**) 1 vti **IRRITATE** to have an irritating or upsetting effect on somebody's nerves or mind ○ Her constant moaning jars my nerves. 2 vt **DISTURB** to have a sudden unsettling effect on somebody ○ He needs something to jar him out of his reverie. 3 vi **CLASH** to look or seem bad or inappropriate in the context of something else ○ The ultramodern dormitories jar with the older, Gothic classroom buildings. 4 vti **GRATE** to make, or cause something to make, a harsh grating noise 5 vti **SHAKE** to start vibrating, or cause something to start vibrating ○ When the furnace comes on it jars the table. 6 vt **INJURE** to cause injury to a body part by jolting it ○ Sam jarred his neck in a car accident. ■ n 1 **PHYSICAL JOLT** an act of knocking against something with a sudden blow 2 **GRATING SOUND** a harsh grating noise [15C. Probably an imitation of a discordant sound.] —**jarring** adj —**jarringly** adv

jarbox /jaár boks/ n Ireland a kitchen sink (informal)

jardinière /zhaárdini áir, zhaárdin yáir/ n a large, usually decorative flower pot or other holder for plants [Mid-19C. < French, 'female gardener'.]

jargon[1] /jaárgən/ n 1 language that is used by a group, profession, or culture, especially when the words and phrases are not understood or used by other people ○ typesetters' jargon 2 pretentious or meaningless language (disapproving) ○ Cut the jargon and get to your point. 3 **LING** = **pidgin** ■ vi = **jargonize** v. 2 [14C. < Old French jargoun.] —**jargoneer** /jaárgə neér/ n —**jargonist** n —**jargonistic** /jaárgə nístik/ adj

jargon[2] /jaár gon/, **jargoon** /jaar gŏŏn/ n a colourless, pale, or smoky zircon [Mid-18C. Via French < Italian giargone < Persian zargūn 'gold-coloured'.]

jargonize /jaárgə nīz/ (**-izes, -izing, -ized**), **jargonise** (**-ises, -ising, -ised**) v 1 vt to convert ordinary language into jargon 2 vi to talk in jargon —**jargonization** /jaárgə nī záysh'n/ n

jargoon n MINERALS = **jargon**[2]

jari n CLOTHING = **zari**

jarl /yaarl/ n formerly, a chieftain or nobleman in Scandinavia [Early 19C. < Old Norse jarl 'earl'.] —**jarldom** n

Jarlsberg /yaárlz burg/ n a type of mild pale-yellow Norwegian cheese that has large holes in it [After Jarlesberg, Norway]

Jarman /jaármən/, **Derek** (1942–94) British film director and painter

jarosite /járrə sīt/ n a yellow to brown mineral consisting of hydrous iron potassium sulphate [Mid-19C. After the Jarosa ravine, S Spain.]

jarrah /járrə/ n 1 a dark reddish hard wood. Use: flooring, building. 2 a tree that yields jarrah. Native to: SW Australia. Eucalyptus marginata. [Mid-19C. < Aboriginal djarryl, jerrhyl.]

Jarrow /járrō/ town and port in NE England. Population: 29,325 (1991).

Jarry /zhárri/, **Alfred** (1873–1907) French dramatist and poet

Jaruzelski /yárrŏŏ zélski/, **Wojciech** (b. 1923) Polish statesman and general

Jas. abbr James

jasmine /jázmin, jássmin/ (plural **-mines** or **-mine**), **jessamine** /jéssəmin/ (plural **-mines** or **-mine**) n 1 a tropical or subtropical climbing plant often grown as a house or garden plant. Flowers: fragrant white, yellow, or red. Use: perfumes. Genus: Jasminum. 2 perfume made from the oil of a variety of jasmine [Mid-16C. Via French jasmin, jessemin < Persian yāsaman.]

jasmine tea n black tea flavoured with jasmine blossoms

Jason /jáyss'n/ n in Greek mythology, a prince who led a group of heroes on his ship, the Argo, on a quest to obtain the Golden Fleece and bring it back to Greece

jaspé /jás pay/ adj describes fabric that is streaked or veined with different colours like jasper [Mid-19C. < French, past participle of jasper 'to marble'.]

jasper /jáspər/ n 1 a red, iron-bearing chalcedony. Use: jewellery, ornaments. 2 CERAMICS = **jasperware** [13C. Via Anglo-Norman jaspre < Latin iaspidem < Greek iaspis 'jasper' < Semitic.]

jasperware /jáspər wair/ n an ornamental porcelain invented by Josiah Wedgwood in 1775. It usually has raised classical motifs in white on backgrounds of various colours.

Jat /jaat/ n a member of an Indo-European people living in the Punjab, NW India, and Pakistan [Early 17C. < Hindi Jāt.]

jato /jáytō/, **JATO** n an auxiliary jet or rocket designed to aid the combined thrust of aircraft jet engines during take-off. Full form **jet-assisted take-off**

jaundice /jáwndiss/ n 1 ILLNESS CAUSING YELLOW SKIN a condition in which there is yellowing of the whites of the eyes, skin, and mucous membranes, caused by bile pigments in the blood. Technical name **icterus** 2 CYNICAL STATE OF MIND an attitude that is characterized by cynical hostility, jealousy, or prejudice ■ vt (**-dices, -dicing, -diced**) 1 MAKE SOMEBODY CYNICAL to alter somebody's attitude for the worse, especially when it results in cynical hostility, jealousy, or prejudice 2 AFFECT SOMEBODY WITH JAUNDICE to affect somebody with jaundice, as a symptom of liver disease [14C. < Old French jaunice < jaune 'yellow'.] —**jaundiced** adj

jaunt /jawnt/ n a trip, especially a short one taken for fun or pleasure ■ vi to go on a short journey, usually for pleasure [Late 16C.]

jaunting car n in Ireland, a lightweight two-wheeled open vehicle pulled by a single horse and having lengthwise seats positioned so that passengers either face each other or sit back-to-back

jaunty /jáwnti/ (**-tier, -tiest**) adj 1 happy, carefree, and confident 2 fashionable and eye-catching in a casual way [Mid-17C. < French gentil 'polite, kind'.] —**jauntily** adv —**jauntiness** n

Jaurès /zhō réss/, **Jean** (1859–1914) French politician and newspaper editor

Jav. abbr 1 Javanese 2 Jav., jav. javelin

java /jáavə/ n US coffee, especially brewed coffee as opposed to instant coffee (informal) [Mid-19C. < JAVA².]

Java¹ /jáavə, jávə/ island in SE Asia, the most populous island in Indonesia. Population: 114,733,500 (1995). Area: 134,045 sq. km/51,755 sq. mi.

Java² /jáavə/ n a variety of rich coffee grown on Java and the surrounding islands

Java man n a fossil human found in Java and elsewhere in Indonesia, taken to be from the Palaeolithic Age

Javanese /jáavə neéz/ (plural **-nese**) n 1 somebody who comes from Java 2 a language spoken on Java, belonging to the Western branch of Austronesian. Native speakers: 70 million. —**Javanese** adj

Java Sea arm of the S Pacific Ocean between Borneo and Java. Area: 310,000 sq. km/120,000 sq. mi.

Java sparrow n a small weaverbird with grey and pink feathers and a stout red beak, popular as a cage and aviary bird. Native to: Indonesia. Padda oryzivora.

javelin /jávvəlin/ n 1 a long thin piece of wood, plastic, or metal with a pointed end, used as a weapon or thrown in field competitions 2 a field event in which competitors try to throw a javelin as far as possible [15C. < Middle French javeline, diminutive of Old French javelot.]

javelina /hávvə leénə/ n US ZOOL = **peccary** [Early 19C. < Spanish jabalina, feminine of jabalí 'wild boar' < Arabic jabalīy.]

Javelle water /jávv'l-, jə vél-/, **Javel water** n NaOCl a solution of sodium hypochlorite. Use: bleach, disinfectant. [Early 19C. After a village on the outskirts of Paris.]

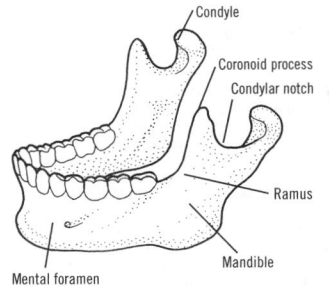

Jaw

jaw /jaw/ n 1 TOOTH-BEARING BONE either of the upper or lower bones that anchor the teeth and form the structural basis of the mouth in vertebrates 2 INVERTEBRATE BITING PART an invertebrate body part with a function or structure similar to a vertebrate jaw 3 GRIPPING PART either of two hinged parts of a tool or machine used to grip objects securely 4 FACE PART the lower, mobile part of the human face ◇ a strong square jaw 5 IMPUDENCE cheeky or impudent talk (slang) 6 LONG TALK a long conversation or discussion (slang) 7 MORALIZING TALK a moralizing talk or lecture (slang) ■ **jaws** npl 1 NATURAL ENTRANCE a narrow opening in something such as a cave, gorge, canyon, or other natural feature 2 DANGEROUS PLACE a situation that is dangerously close to something horrible or frightening ■ vi (slang) 1 TALK AT LENGTH to talk or gossip, usually at length 2 MORALIZE to give a moralizing talk or lecture [14C. < ?] —**jawed** adj —**jawless** adj

Jawara /jaáwərə/, **Sir Dawda** (b. 1924) Gambian statesman

jawbone /jáw bōn/ n a bone in the jaw, especially the lower jaw. ◇ **mandible, maxilla** ■ vt (**-bones, -boning, -boned**) US to coerce somebody to comply with something by using the authority of high office (informal) —**jawboner** n

jawbreaker /jáw braykər/ n 1 a long word that is difficult to pronounce (informal) 2 a machine that crushes rocks using powerful jaws 3 US FOOD = **gobstopper** (informal)

jaw-jaw n talking or conversation, especially when long-winded and pointless (informal) ■ vi to talk, especially in a long-winded way or without any obvious purpose (informal)

jawline /jáw līn/ n the shape of somebody's lower jaw

jay /jay/ n 1 a noisy, brightly coloured bird of the crow family. Family: Corvidae. 2 a heedless or chattering person (informal) [13C. Via Old French jay < Latin gaius.]

Jayawardene /jī ə waárdənə/, **J. R.** (1906–96) Sri Lankan statesman. Full name **Junius Richard Jayawardene**

Jaycee /jáy seé/ n in North America, Australia, and New Zealand, a member of a junior chamber of commerce, an organization for young people that promotes leadership and business skills [Mid-20C. < the initial letters of Junior Chamber.]

jaywalk /jáy wawk/ vi to cross a road or street anywhere other than at designated crossing places [Early 20C. <JAY 'heedless person'.] —**jaywalker** n —**jaywalking** n

jazz /jaz/ n 1 SYNCOPATED POPULAR MUSIC popular music that originated among Black people in New Orleans in the late 19th century and is characterized by syncopated rhythms and improvisation 2 STUFF unnamed related things or belongings (slang) ◇ Collect up the books and the rest of your jazz and let's get going. 3 LIVELINESS animated enthusiasm or vivacity (slang) 4 US NONSENSE information or ideas regarded as untrue, misconceived, or misleading (slang) ◇ Don't be fooled if she starts giving you that jazz about being broke. ■ vi PLAY OR DANCE TO JAZZ

to play or dance to jazz music [Early 20C. < ?] —**jazzer** n

jazz up vt 1 to make somebody or something more interesting or decorative (informal) ◇ jazzed up his wardrobe with some Hawaiian shirts 2 to make a piece of music more lively, especially by quickening the tempo or adding improvisations

jazz age n the era that immediately followed World War I and lasted until the beginning of the Depression in the United States, during which jazz increased in popularity

jazz band n a band that plays jazz, usually consisting of five or more instruments including one or more solo wind instruments and a rhythm section consisting of piano, double bass, and drums

jazzfest /jáz fest/ n a festival of jazz music

jazz-fusion n MUSIC = **jazz-rock**

jazzman /jáz man/ (plural **-men** /-men/) n a man who plays or writes jazz music

jazz-rock n jazz music that incorporates elements of rock music, especially its heavy repetitive beats and electronic amplification

jazzy /jázzi/ (**-ier, -iest**) adj 1 SHOWY showy, bright, and colourful (informal) 2 JAZZED UP TO APPEAL exaggerated and unrestrained, especially in an attempt to make something more appealing (informal) 3 LIKE JAZZ in the style of jazz music, especially with the syncopated rhythms of jazz —**jazzily** adv —**jazziness** n

JC abbr 1 jurisconsult 2 Justice Clerk

J.C. abbr 1 Jesus Christ 2 Julius Caesar

JCB tdmk a trademark for a machine with a large shovel at the front and a digging arm at the back, used in excavating and in moving earth and rubble

JCL n a powerful computer language for writing a script used to control the execution of programs in batch processing systems. Full form **job control language**

J-cloth tdmk a trademark for a disposable cloth used for cleaning, dusting, washing dishes, and other domestic jobs

JCR abbr junior common room

JCS abbr Joint Chiefs of Staff

JD abbr 1 juvenile delinquent 2 Diploma in Journalism

je abbr Jersey (in Internet addresses)

jealous /jéllass/ adj 1 ENVIOUS feeling bitter and unhappy because of another's advantages, possessions, or luck 2 SUSPICIOUS OF RIVALS feeling suspicious about a rival's or competitor's influence, especially in regard to a loved one 3 WATCHFUL possessively watchful of something ◇ keeps a jealous guard on his research 4 DEMANDING LOYALTY demanding exclusive loyalty or adherence (archaic) ◇ a jealous god. [13C. Via Old French gelos < Latin zelosus < Greek zelos 'jealousy, enthusiasm'.] —**jealously** adv —**jealousness** n

jealousy /jéllassi/ n 1 jealous feelings or behaviour 2 (plural **-ies**) an instance of feeling jealous ◇ a man of many jealousies

jean /jeen/ n a strong twill cotton. Use: work clothes, uniforms, overalls, jeans. ◇ a jean jacket [15C. Via Old French Janne < medieval Latin Janua 'Genoa'.]

SPELLCHECK Do not confuse **jean** with **gene**, which has a similar sound. Beware: your spellchecker will not catch this error.

jeans /jeenz/ npl casual trousers with raised seams, made from denim, jean, or some other strong fabric

jebel /jébb'l/, **djebel, gebel** n a hill or mountain in the Middle East or North Africa (often in placenames) [Mid-19C. < Arabic jabal 'mountain'.]

Jedda = Jiddah

jeelie /jeélí/, **jeely** n Scotland jam or jelly [Variant of JELLY¹]

jeep /jeep/ n a vehicle developed by the military in World War II with four-wheel drive, for use on poor roads or open terrain [Mid-20C. < GP, abbreviation of general purpose.]

Jeep /jeep/ tdmk a trademark for a four-wheel-drive vehicle suitable for rough terrain

jeepers /jeépərz/, **jeepers creepers** interj used to express surprise (informal) [Early 20C. Alteration of Jesus.]

jeepney /jeépni/ (plural **-neys**) n a jeep or similar vehicle that has been converted into a small bus, used in the

Philippines as a form of public transport [Mid-20C. Blend of JEEP + JITNEY.]

jeer /jeer/ *vti* to shout or laugh at somebody or something as an expression of disgust, scorn, or other displeasure ■ *n* a mocking or scornful laugh or shout [Mid-16C. < ?] —**jeerer** *n* —**jeeringly** *adv*

Jeeves /jeevz/ *n* a handy and reliable person known for providing ready solutions to problems (*informal*) [Mid-20C. < a character in the novels of P. G. WODEHOUSE.]

jeez /jeez/ *interj* used to express surprise, enthusiasm, or annoyance (*slang*) [Early 20C. Shortening of *Jesus*.]

Library of Congress

Thomas Jefferson

Jefferson /jéffərss'n/, **Thomas** (1743–1826) US statesman and 3rd president of the United States (1801–09)

Jefferson City /jéffərss'n-/ capital of Missouri, in the central part of the state. Population: 35,481 (1990).

Jeffrey /jéffri/, **Francis, Lord Jeffrey** (1773–1850) British critic and jurist

Jeffreys /jéffriz/, **Sir Alec J.** (b. 1950) British geneticist

jehad *n* ISLAM = **jihad**

Jehoshaphat /ji hóshə fat/ *n* in the Bible, a king of Judea who succeeded Asa and formed an alliance with Ahab of Israel against Syria. (1, 2 Kings; 2 Chronicles)

Jehovah /ji hóvə/ *n* a translation of the Hebrew name of God used in the Christian Bible [Mid-16C. < medieval Latin *Iehoua*, mistaken transliteration of *YHWH*, the name too sacred to pronounce, using the vowel points of Hebrew *ăḏōnāy* 'my lord'.]

Jehovah's Witness *n* a member of a religious group that believes in the imminence of Jesus Christ's personal reign on Earth and rejects secular law where it appears to conflict with the divine. Jehovah's Witnesses reject the doctrine of the Trinity.

Jehovist /ji hóvist/ *n* 1 BIBLE = **Yahwist** 2 a believer that the Hebrew word 'YHVH' in the Bible was pronounced like 'Jehovah' —**Jehovism** *n* —**Jehovistic** /jee hō vístik/ *adj*

Jehu /jée hyoo/ *n* a fast or reckless driver (*informal dated*) [Early 17C. After the King of Israel who drove 'furiously' (2 Kings 9:20).]

jejune /ji joon/ *adj* 1 BORING uninteresting and intellectually undemanding 2 CHILDISH lacking maturity or sophistication ○ *jejune chatter about concepts beyond their understanding* 3 WITHOUT PROPER NOURISHMENT lacking or not providing proper nourishment 4 BARREN not very fertile [Early 17C. < Latin *jejunus* 'fasting, meagre'.] —**jejunely** *adv* —**jejuneness** *n* —**jejunity** *n*

jejunostomy /ji joo nóstəmi/ *n* (*plural* -**mies**) *n* 1 a surgical operation that creates access from the outside of the body into the middle part of the small intestine (**jejunum**) so that nourishment can be directly introduced 2 the opening formed in a jejunostomy

jejunum /ji jóonəm/ *n* the section of the small intestine that is situated between the duodenum and the ileum and whose main function is the absorption of nutrients from digested food [Mid-16C. < modern Latin, < Latin *jejunus* 'fasting', because usually empty after death.] —**jejunal** *adj*

Jekyll /jéek'l/, **Gertrude** (1843–1932) British landscape gardener and writer

Jekyll and Hyde /jék'l ənd hīd/ (*plural* **Jekyll and Hydes**) *n* a person who has two distinct personalities, one good and the other evil [Late 19C. < *The Strange Case of Dr. Jekyll and Mr. Hyde* (1886), by R. L. Stevenson.]

jell /jel/ *v* 1 *vti* SOLIDIFY to become, or cause a substance to become, set or firm 2 *vti* TAKE SHAPE to become, or cause something to become, fixed or more definite in shape or form 3 *vi* GET ON WELL TOGETHER to bond in a way that gives rise to mutual cooperation ○ *'It's fun being with a bunch of guys who are fighting through adversity and jelling together'. (The Philadelphia Inquirer; 1997)* [Mid-18C. Back-formation < JELLY[1].]

jellaba /jélləbə, jə láábə/, **djellaba** *n* a long, loose, sleeved garment with a hood, of a type worn in Morocco and other parts of North Africa [Early 19C. < Moroccan Arabic *jellāb(a)*.]

jellify /jélli fī/ (-**fies**, -**fying**, -**fied**) *vti* to turn, or cause a substance to turn, into jelly —**jellification** /jéllifi káysh'n/ *n*

jelly[1] /jélli/ *n* (*plural* -**lies**) 1 WOBBLY DESSERT a transparent semi-solid fruit-flavoured dessert made from gelatin 2 FRUIT PRESERVE a fruit preserve that is made by boiling fruit juice, sugar, and sometimes pectin until it has a semisolid consistency 3 THICKENED MEAT STOCK a savoury semisolid food made from gelatin boiled with meat stock ○ *calf's foot jelly* 4 SUBSTANCE WITH JELLY CONSISTENCY any substance that has the consistency of jelly, especially a pharmaceutical preparation ○ *petroleum jelly* 5 SANDAL a sandal, especially a child's sandal, made from transparent flexible plastic (*often before nouns*) ■ *vti* (-**lies**, -**lying**, -**lied**) THICKEN to set, or cause something to set, into a jelly [14C. < Old French *gelee* 'frost, jelly' < Latin *gelare* 'freeze'.] —**jellied** *adj* —**jelly-like** *adj* ◇ **turn to jelly** to feel shaky because of extreme fear, nervousness, or exhaustion (*informal*)

jelly[2] /jélli/ *n* gelignite (*informal*) [Mid-20C. Shortening and alteration.]

jelly baby *n* a small fruit-flavoured jelly sweet in the shape of a baby

jelly bag *n* a bag used for straining the juice when making jelly or jam

jellybean /jélli been/ *n* a small bean-shaped fruit sweet with a hard coating and a soft jelly centre

jellyfish /jélli fish/ (*plural* -**fishes** *or* -**fish**) *n* 1 STINGING MARINE ANIMAL an invertebrate marine animal that, in its reproductive stage, has a nearly transparent body shaped like an umbrella with trailing tentacles bearing stinging cells. Phylum: Coelenterata. 2 MARINE ANIMAL LIKE JELLYFISH any invertebrate marine animal that looks similar to a true jellyfish 3 WEAK PERSON a weak or indecisive person (*informal*) ○ *I'm afraid I'm just a jellyfish when it comes to making decisions.*

jelly fungus *n* a fungus that grows on trees and has a gelatinous fruiting body. Order: Tremellales.

~~jelous~~ incorrect spelling of **jealous**

jemmy /jémmi/ *n* (*plural* -**mies**) a short crowbar used as a lever, usually for prising things open. US term **jimmy** *n*. ■ *vt* (-**mies**, -**mying**, -**mied**) to force something open with a jemmy. US term **jimmy** *v*. [Early 19C. < *Jemmy*, familiar form of the name *James*.]

je ne sais quoi /zhə nay say kwaá/ *n* an indefinable quality that makes somebody or something more attractive or interesting (*literary or humorous*) [Mid-17C. < French, 'I do not know what'.]

Jenkins /jéngkinz/, **Roy, Baron Jenkins of Hillhead** (b. 1920) British politician

Jenner /jénnər/, **Edward** (1749–1823) British physician

jennet /jénnit/, **genet** *n* 1 a female donkey 2 a small Spanish riding horse [15C. Via French *genet* < Spanish Arabic *Genēṭī* 'light horseman'.]

jenny /jénni/ (*plural* -**nies**) *n* 1 a female donkey 2 a female bird (*often before nouns*) ○ *a jenny wren* 3 MANUF = **spinning jenny** [Early 17C. < the name *Jenny*, diminutive of *Jane* or *Jennifer*.]

Jenolan Caves /jə nólən-/ cave system in SE New South Wales, Australia

jeopardize /jéppər dīz/ (-**izes**, -**izing**, -**ized**), **jeopardise** (-**ises**, -**ising**, -**ised**) *vt* to put somebody or something at risk of being harmed or lost ○ *jeopardizing the entire mission through their indiscretion*

jeopardy /jéppərdi/ *n* 1 the risk of loss, harm, or death ○ *The entire project is in jeopardy.* 2 the risk of being convicted when put on trial for a crime [14C. < Old French *jeu* (< Latin *jocus* 'pastime') + *parti* (past participle of *partir* 'divide'), literally 'even or divided game'.]

Jer. *abbr* 1 Jeremiah 2 Jersey 3 Jerusalem

Jerboa

jerboa /jur bṓ ə/ (*plural* -**as**) *n* 1 a small nocturnal rodent that has large ears, a long tufted tail, and long hind legs adapted for leaping. Native to: dry regions of Asia and Africa. Family: Dipodidae. 2 a small marsupial with long hind legs and a long bushy tail. Native to: central desert areas of Australia. Genus: *Antechinomys*. [Mid-17C. Via modern Latin *jerboa* < Arabic *yarbū'(a)*, *jarbū*.]

jeremiad /jérri mí ad/ *n* a long recitation of mournful complaints (*formal*) [Late 18C. < French *jérémiade* < *Jérémie* 'Jeremiah'.]

Jeremiah /jérri mí ə/ *n* 1 HEBREW PROPHET a Hebrew prophet who lived in Judah in the 7th and 6th centuries BC and was persecuted for prophesying the fall of Judah and Jerusalem and the Israelites' captivity in Babylon 2 BOOK OF THE BIBLE the book of the Bible that contains the prophecies of Jeremiah 3 NEGATIVE PERSON somebody with a gloomy outlook on the present and future

Jerez de la Frontera /he réss də la fron táirə/ city in SW Spain. Population: 182,939 (1991).

Jericho /jérrikō/ town in the West Bank. According to the Bible, it was destroyed by Joshua after he led the Israelites back from captivity in Egypt (Joshua 3–8). Population: 2,190 (1992 estimate).

jerid /jə reéd/ *n* a javelin used by Persian, Turkish, and Arabian horsemen, especially during the time of the Ottoman Empire [Mid-17C. < Arabic *jarīd* 'palm branch stripped of its leaves, javelin'.]

jerk[1] /jurk/ *v* 1 *vt* PULL SUDDENLY to pull somebody or something with a sudden strong movement ○ *He jerked her back from in front of the speeding car.* 2 *vti* MOVE JOLTINGLY to proceed, or cause something or somebody to proceed, with bumps and jolts ○ *The car jerked forwards.* 3 *vi* MOVE IN SPASM to move in response to muscular spasms (*refers to parts of the body*) 4 *vt* SAY SOMETHING ABRUPTLY to utter words or sounds suddenly and forcefully, e.g. from excitement ■ *n* 1 SUDDEN PULL a sudden and forceful pulling movement ○ *giving the door a jerk* 2 JOLTING MOTION an abrupt jolting or jarring motion ○ *moving in jerks* 3 TWITCH a spasmodic movement in a muscle 4 US, Can OFFENSIVE TERM an offensive term for somebody who is regarded as behaving foolishly (*slang insult*) 5 OVERHEAD LIFT IN WEIGHTLIFTING a lift in weightlifting in which a barbell is thrust from shoulder height to above the head ■ **jerks** *npl* 1 EXERCISES physical exercises, especially those such as press-ups that can be done without the use of special equipment (*dated informal*) 2 US SPASMODIC MOVEMENTS involuntary muscular movements often caused by nervousness or excitement [Mid-16C. < ?] —**jerker** *n*

jerk off *vi* a highly offensive term meaning to masturbate (*taboo*)

jerk[2] /jurk/ *vt* PRESERVE MEAT IN STRIPS to preserve meat by cutting it into long strips and drying it ■ *adj* 1 STRONGLY FLAVOURED AND SPICY made with strongly flavoured spices, including hot peppers and allspice, as a marinade or rub for grilled meats 2 SPICY AND GRILLED marinated in a jerk sauce and grilled [Early 18C. Via American Spanish *charquear* < Quechua *echarquini* 'prepare dried meat'.]

jerkin /júrkin/ *n* 1 a sleeveless coat or jacket worn by men or women 2 a man's close-fitting sleeveless tunic, often made of leather, worn in the 16th and 17th centuries [Early 16C. < ?]

jerky[1] /júrki/ (-**ier**, -**iest**) *adj* moving irregularly with sudden stops and starts —**jerkily** *adv* —**jerkiness** *n*

jerky[2] /júrki/ *n* meat cut into thin strips and dried [Mid-

19C. Via American Spanish *charqui* < Quechua *echarqui* 'dried flesh in long strips'.]

jeroboam /jérrə bṓ əm/ *n* a large wine or champagne bottle holding the equivalent of four standard wine bottles, 3 litres/108 fl. oz, or a Bordeaux wine bottle equivalent to six bottles, 4.5 litres/162 fl. oz [Early 19C. After *Jeroboam* 'a mighty man of valour' (I Kings 11:28).]

Jeroboam I /jérrə bṓ əm/ (*fl.* 10th century BC) king of Israel

Jeroboam II (*fl.* 8th century BC) king of Israel

Jerome /jə rṓm/, **St** (342?–420?) Croatian-born monk and scholar. Born **Eusebius Hieronymus**

Jerome, Jerome K. (1859–1927) British novelist

Jerry /jérri/ (*plural* **-ries**) *n* an offensive term for a German person, especially a German soldier in World War II (*dated slang insult*) [Early 20C. Alteration of GERMAN.]

jerry-build /jérri bild/ (**jerry-builds, jerry-building, jerry-built** /- bilt/) *vt* to build something as quickly and cheaply as possible, with little regard for quality [Mid-19C. < ?] —**jerry-builder** *n* —**jerry-building** *n* —**jerry-built** *adj*

jerry can *n* a flat-sided can with a capacity of approximately 20 litres/4.4 gal. of liquid, originally of German design and used in World War II [< alteration of GERMAN]

jersey /júrzi/ (*plural* **-seys**) *n* **1 CLOTHING MATERIAL** a knitted fabric, usually made with a plain or stocking stitch. Use: clothing. **2 SWEATER** a knitted woollen pullover **3 SHIRT FOR SPORTS** a long-sleeved shirt worn for playing sport, especially football and rugby [Late 16C. After JERSEY[1].]

Jersey[1] /júrzi/ largest and southernmost of the Channel Islands, in the English Channel. Population: 84,082 (1991). Area: 117 sq. km/45 sq. mi.

Jersey[2] /júrzi/ (*plural* **-seys**) *n* a pale brown dairy cow that produces particularly creamy milk, belonging to a breed originating on the island of Jersey

Jerusalem /jə róossələm/ historic city lying at the intersection of Israel and the West Bank. The whole of the city is claimed by Israel as its capital, but this is disputed internationally. Population: 602,100 (1997).

Jerusalem artichoke *n* **1** an edible tuber with reddish-brown knobbly skin and white flesh, eaten cooked as a vegetable **2** a perennial sunflower that produces Jerusalem artichokes. Native to: North America. *Helianthus tuberosus.* [< Italian *girasole* < *girare* 'turn' + *sole* 'sun']

Jerusalem cherry *n* a plant of the nightshade family with inedible orange or red berries, widely grown as a houseplant. Flowers: white. Native to: South America. *Solanum pseudocapsicum.*

Jerusalem oak *n* a strong-smelling plant of the goosefoot family that grows as a weed. Flowers: white. Native to: N United States, Canada. *Chenopodium botrys.*

Jerusalem thorn *n* a thorny leguminous bush with long clusters of yellow flowers. Native to: tropical America. *Parkinsonia aculeata.*

Jervis Bay /júrvəss-/ inlet of the Pacific Ocean, on the coast of E New South Wales, Australia. Area: 160 sq. km/60 sq. mi.

jess /jess/ *n* a short strap with a ring for attaching a leash, fastened round one of the legs of a falcon or other trained bird of prey ■ *vt* to put a jess on a bird [14C. Via Old French *ges*, form of *get* 'act of throwing' < Latin *jacere* 'to throw'.]

jessamine *n* PLANTS = **jasmine**

Jesselton /jéss'ltən/ former name for **Kota Kinabalu**

Jesse window /jéssi-/ *n* a window in a church depicting Jesus Christ's lineage from Jesse, the father of Kind David

jest /jest/ *n* **1 JOKE** something done or said in a playful joking manner (*literary*) ○ *Forgive my little jest.* **2 SOMETHING JOKED ABOUT** an object of scorn or derision (*archaic*) ■ *vti* **1 BE WITTY** to act, write, or speak cleverly or humorously about something (*literary*) **2 DERIDE** to treat somebody with derision or scorn (*archaic*) [13C. < Old French *geste* 'romantic exploit' < Latin *gerere* 'behave, perform'.] —**jestingly** *adv* ◇ **in jest** as a joke

jester /jéstər/ *n* **1** an entertainer employed at a medieval court to amuse the monarch and guests **2** a person who likes fun or making jokes

Jesuit /jézzyoo it/ *n* **1 MEMBER OF ROMAN CATHOLIC RELIGIOUS ORDER** a member of the Society of Jesus, a Roman Catholic religious order engaged in missionary and educational work worldwide **2 Jesuit, jesuit OFFENSIVE TERM** an offensive term for somebody regarded as crafty or scheming, especially somebody who uses deliberately ambiguous or confusing words to deceive others (*insult*) ■ *adj* **OF JESUITS** belonging or relating to the members of the Society of Jesus ○ *a Jesuit priest* [Mid-16C. < French *jésuite* or modern Latin *Jesuita* 'follower of Jesus' < *Jesus*.] —**Jesuitic** /jézzyoo íttik/ *adj* —**Jesuitical** *adj* —**Jesuitically** *adv* —**Jesuitism** /jézzyoo itizəm/ *n* —**Jesuitry** *n*

Jesus Christ /jéezəss-/, **Jesus** *n* **1 FOUNDER OF CHRISTIANITY** a Jewish religious teacher who lived from about 4 BC to AD 33. His life and teachings form the basis of Christianity. **2 HUMAN EMBODIMENT OF DIVINE** in Christian Science, the highest human embodiment of the divine idea ■ *interj* **OFFENSIVE TERM** an offensive term expressing frustration or dismay (*slang*)

Jesus freak *n* an offensive term for somebody who belongs to a youthful evangelical Christian group that is contemporary in tone (*slang*)

jet[1] /jet/ *n* **1 PRESSURIZED STREAM OF FLUID** a thin concentrated stream of liquid, air, or gas that is forced under pressure from a small nozzle or opening **2 HOLE THROUGH WHICH FLUID IS FORCED** a small opening or nozzle for letting out a stream of fluid **3** AIR = **jet engine** (*often before nouns*) ○ *using jet technology* **4 AIRCRAFT** an aircraft powered by jet engines (*often before nouns*) ○ *a jet landing strip* ■ *v* **1** *vi* **TRAVEL BY AIR** to travel by air, especially by modern passenger aircraft ○ *always jetting off to business meetings* **2** *vti* **FLOW FORCEFULLY IN THIN STREAM** to be emitted, or emit something, in a thin powerful stream ○ *Water jetted from the broken pipe.* [Late 16C. Via Old French *jeter* 'to throw' < Latin *jacere*.]

jet[2] /jet/ *n* **1** a dense black variety of the mineral lignite. Use: jewellery, ornaments. **2** COLOURS = **jet black** [14C. Via Old French *jaiet* < Latin *gagates* < Greek *Gagatēs*, after *Gagai*, town in Asia Minor.] —**jet** *adj* —**jettiness** *n* —**jetty** *adj*

JET /jet/ *abbr* **1** Joint European Torus **2** Joint European Transport

jet black *n* a very dark black colour —**jet-black** *adj*

jet boat *n* a boat powered by an engine that produces a pressurized stream of water directed backwards

jeté /zhə táy/ *n* a ballet leap from one leg to the other in which one leg is stretched forwards and the other backwards [Mid-19C. < French, past participle of *jeter* 'throw'.]

jet engine *n* an engine, especially one used to propel aircraft, that produces forward thrust by means of a rearward discharge of fluid, usually combustion gases

jet fighter *n* a fighter plane that is powered by a jet engine or engines

jetfoil /jét foyl/ *n* a passenger-carrying jet-powered hydrofoil

jet lag *n* an internal physical disturbance experienced by air travellers on flights across different time zones —**jet-lagged** *adj*

jetliner /jét līnər/ *n* a large passenger aeroplane powered by jet engines [Mid-20C. Blend of JET[1] + AIRLINER.]

jetpack /jét pak/ *n* a device fitted with pressurized metal containers that let out jets of gas, worn by astronauts on their back to enable them to move around in space outside a spacecraft

jet plane *n* an aeroplane powered by jet engines

jet propulsion *n* forward thrust that results from the rearward discharge of a jet of fluid, especially a jet engine's combustion gases —**jet-propelled** *adj*

jetsam /jétsəm/ *n* **1** cargo or equipment that either sinks or is washed ashore after being thrown overboard to lighten the load of a ship in distress. ◊ **flotsam 2** things that have been discarded as useless or unwanted [Late 16C. Contraction of JETTISON.]

jet set *n* wealthy people who travel internationally on a regular basis, especially in pursuit of pleasure (*informal*) —**jet-setter** *n* —**jet-setting** *n*

Jet Ski *tdmk* a trademark for a jet-propelled personal watercraft

jet stream *n* **1** a strong permanent high-altitude wind current that moves east in a meandering pattern, affecting the development and movement of weather systems **2** a flow of exhaust gases produced by a jet engine

jettison /jéttiss'n/ *vt* **1 THROW SOMETHING OVERBOARD** to throw something from a ship, aircraft, or vehicle **2 REJECT** to discard or abandon something, e.g. an idea or project ○ *plans that had to be jettisoned* ■ *n* **1 REJECTION** the discarding or rejecting of something **2 SHIP'S DISCARDED CARGO** the cargo and equipment thrown from a distressed ship to lighten it [15C. < Anglo-Norman *getteson* 'throwing cargo overboard' (to lighten a ship) < Latin *jectare* 'throw about'.] —**jettisonable** *adj*

jetty /jétti/ (*plural* **-ties**) *n* **1** a landing pier **2** a wall or other barrier built out into a body of water to shelter a harbour, protect a shoreline from erosion, or redirect water currents [15C. < Old French *jetee* 'something thrown (up as a breakwater)' < *jeter* (see JET[1]).]

jeu d'esprit /zhṓ de spree/ (*plural* **jeux d'esprit** /zhṓ-/) *n* a witticism, especially one that appears in a work of literature [Early 18C. < French, 'game of spirit or wit'.]

jeunesse dorée /zhṓ ness dáwray/ *n* young people who enjoy wealth and privilege (*literary*) [Mid-19C. < French, 'gilded youth'.]

Jevons /jévv'nz/, **William** (1835–82) British economist and mathematician

Jew /joo/ *n* **1 BELIEVER IN JUDAISM** somebody whose religion is Judaism **2 MEMBER OF SEMITIC PEOPLE** a member of a Semitic people descended from the ancient Hebrews, sharing cultural and religious ties based on Judaism **3 SOMEBODY FROM ANCIENT JUDAEA** somebody who lived or was born in ancient Judaea **4 Jew, jew OFFENSIVE TERM** an offensive term for somebody who is regarded as miserly (*dated slang*) ■ *adj* **OFFENSIVE TERM** an offensive term meaning belonging or relating to Jews or Judaism [Pre-12C. Via Old French *giu* < Latin *Judaeus*, Greek *Ioudaios* < Hebrew *yĕhūdī* < *yĕhūdāh* 'Judah', son of the patriarch Jacob, and the tribe descended from him.]

jewel /jóo əl/ *n* **1 PERSONAL ORNAMENT** an ornament, e.g. a ring, necklace, or bracelet, made of a gemstone placed in a setting of gold, silver, or other metal ○ *She wore her best jewels to the ball.* **2 GEMSTONE** a precious stone such as a diamond **3 WATCH BEARING** a small crystal or precious stone used as a bearing in a watch **4 PRIZED EXAMPLE** a fine example of a particular type of person or thing ○ *Her new teacher's such a jewel!* ■ *vt* (**-els, -elling, -elled**) **ADORN WITH JEWELS** to equip or decorate something with jewels [13C. < Anglo-Norman *juel* < *jeu* 'game' < Latin *jocus*.] ◇ **the jewel in the crown** the best or most outstanding example of something

jewel beetle *n* a beetle with an iridescent body that gives it a superficial resemblance to a gemstone. Native to: Australia. Family: Buprestidae.

jewel box, jewel case *n* a hinged plastic case in which a CD is sold and stored

jeweler *n* US = **jeweller**

jewelfish /jóo əl fish/ (*plural* **-fishes** *or* **-fish**) *n* a brightly coloured fish that is popular in aquariums. Native to: Africa. *Hemichromis bimaculatus.* [< its speckling of emerald green or sapphire]

jeweller /jóo ə lər/ *n* a maker, seller, or repairer of jewellery

jeweller's rouge *n* metal polish in the form of finely ground ferric oxide. US term **crocus** *n.* 3

jewellery /jóo əlri/ *n* articles worn on the body for decoration, e.g. necklaces, bracelets, earrings, and rings (*often before nouns*) ○ *a jewellery box*

Jewess /jóo iss/ *n* a highly offensive term for a Jewish woman or girl (*dated taboo*)

jewfish /jóo fish/ (*plural* **-fishes** *or* **-fish**) *n* a large dark spotted sea fish of the grouper family with rough scales. Native to: warm and tropical waters. *Epinephelus itajara.* [Probably because approved by Jewish dietary law]

Jewish /jóo ish/ *adj* **1** relating to or practising Judaism **2** belonging or relating to a people descended from the ancient Hebrews —**Jewishly** *adv* —**Jewishness** *n*

Jewish calendar *n* the lunar calendar of the Jewish religious year. It has 12 months, with 13 in leap years, and dates from 3761 BC, considered the year of Creation.

Jewry /jóori/ (*plural* **-ries**) *n* Jewish people in general or Judaism

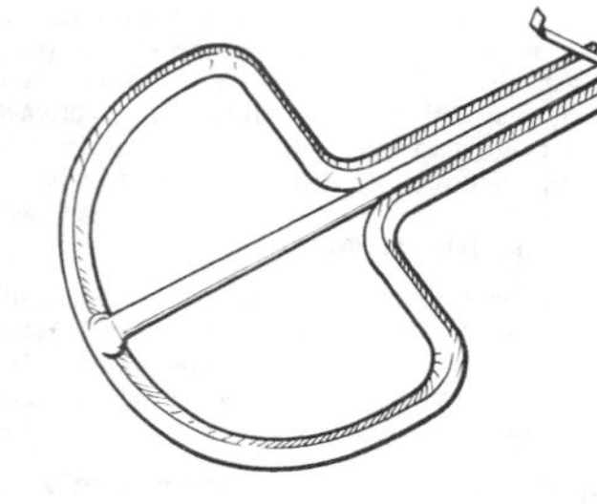

Jew's harp

jew's harp *n* a small musical instrument held between the teeth and played by plucking a protruding metal tongue [< ?]

Jezebel /jézzə bel/ *n* 1 a Phoenician princess and wife of King Ahab, who lived in the 9th century BC 2 **Jezebel, jezebel** an offensive term that deliberately insults a woman's sexual activity or interactions

⚡**JFF** *abbr* just for fun (*in e-mails*)

JFK *abbr* 1 John Fitzgerald Kennedy 2 John Fitzgerald Kennedy International Airport

Jhansi /jaanssi/, **Jhānsi** city in central India. Population: 300,850 (1991).

Jhelum /jeeləm/ river in NW India and NE Pakistan. Length: 772 km/480 mi.

JHVH, JHWH *n* BIBLE = **YHWH**

-ji /jee/ *suffix S Asia* a respectful form of address added to a name or title ○ *doctorji* ○ *Janeji* [Via Hindi < Sanskrit *jaya* 'conquering']

Jiang Qing /jyáng chíng/ (1914–91) Chinese political activist

Jiangsu /jyáng soó/ province in E China, on the Yellow Sea. Capital: Nanjing. Population: 70,210,000 (1994). Area: 102,600 sq. km/39,614 sq. mi.

Jiangxi /jyáng sheé/ inland province of SE China. Capital: Nanchang. Population: 40,150,000 (1994). Area: 164,800 sq. km/63,630 sq. mi.

Jiang Zemin /jyáng tsay mín/ (*b.* 1926) Chinese statesman

jiao /jow/ (*plural* **jiao**) *n* see table at **currency** [Mid-20C. < Chinese *jiǎo*.]

jib[1] /jib/ *n* a small triangular sail in front of the main or only mast on a sailing ship [Mid-17C. < ?]

jib[2] /jib/ *n* the projecting arm of a crane [Mid-18C. < ?]

jib[3] /jib/ (**jibs, jibbing, jibbed**) *vi* 1 to stop and refuse to move on (*refers to animals*) 2 to be reluctant to do something [Early 19C. < ?] —**jibber** *n*

jib boom *n* an extension of the spar that sticks out from the front of a sailing ship (**bowsprit**) and supports the jib

jibe[1] *n, vti* = **gibe**

jibe[2] *vti, n* SAILING = **gybe**

⚡**JIC** *abbr* just in case (*in e-mails*)

jicama /heékəmə/ *n* 1 a starchy tuberous root eaten raw in salads or cooked as a vegetable 2 the tropical plant of the pea family that produces the jicama root. *Pachyrhizus erosus*. [Early 17C. Via Mexican Spanish *jícama* < Nahuatl *xicama*.]

Jiddah /jíddə/, **Jedda** port in W Saudi Arabia, on the Red Sea. Population: 1,600,000 (1994 estimate).

jiffy /jíffi/, **jiff** /jif/ *n* the shortest possible length of time (*informal*) ○ *I'll be with you in a jiffy.* [Late 18C. < ?]

jig /jig/ *n* 1 **LIVELY DANCE** a folk dance in triple time, especially one with kicking or jumping steps ○ *an Irish jig* 2 **DANCING MUSIC** the music for a jig 3 **DEVICE FOR HOLDING PIECE OF WORK** the part of a woodworking or metalworking machine that holds the object to be worked on and guides the cutting or drilling tool 4 **WIGGLY FISHING LURE** a fishing lure made to attract a fish's attention through its motion as it is jerked around in the water 5 **MINERAL-WASHING DEVICE** a device that cleans and separates coal or other excavated minerals from waste material by shaking and washing ■ *v* (**jigs, jigging, jigged**) 1 *vti* **JERK AROUND QUICKLY** to move around, or cause something to move around, in a quick jerky way 2 *vi* **DANCE A JIG** to dance a jig 3 *vt* **CUT WITH A JIG** to cut or drill a piece of work using a jig as a guide 4 *vti* **FISH WITH A JIG** to fish, or catch a fish, using a jig 5 *vt* **CLEAN MINERALS WITH A JIG** to wash and separate coal or other excavated minerals with a jig [Mid-16C. < ?]

jigger[1] /jíggər/ *n* 1 **MEASURE FOR ALCOHOLIC SPIRITS** a measure used for alcoholic spirits, equal to approximately 1.5 fl. oz 2 **JIG OPERATOR** the operator of a mechanical jig 3 *US* **SOMETHING OR OTHER** an object whose name is not known or cannot be recalled (*informal*) 4 FISHING = **jig** *n.* 4 5 **SAIL AT STERN** a small sail near the stern of a small sailing boat 6 SAILING = **jiggermast** 7 **DEVICE WITH JERKING MOTION** a mechanical device, e.g. a drill, that operates with a jerking movement 8 **CUE REST** a cue rest in billiards (*informal*)

jigger[2] *n* INSECTS = **chigoe** *n.* 1 [Late 18C. Alteration of CHIGGER.]

jiggermast /jíggər maast/ *n* 1 the shorter mast near the stern of a small sailing boat 2 on a four-masted sailing ship, the mast nearest the stern

jiggery-pokery /jíggəri pókəri/ *n* devious, deceitful, or dishonest behaviour (*informal*) ○ *All this ridiculous jiggery-pokery going on behind my back!* [Late 19C. < ?]

jiggle /jígg'l/ *vti* (**-gles, -gling, -gled**) to move, or cause something to move, in small rapid movements in any direction ○ *He jiggled the ball before catching it* ■ *n* a rapid back-and-forth or up-and-down motion ○ *giving the key a quick jiggle in the lock* [Mid-19C. Blend of JIG + JOGGLE.] —**jiggly** *adj*

jigsaw /jíg saw/ *n* 1 **JIGSAW PUZZLE** a jigsaw puzzle 2 **POWER SAW FOR CURVES** a machine saw with a narrow blade, used for cutting curves and shapes ■ *vt* (**-saws, -sawing, -sawed, -sawed** *or* **-sawn** /-sawn/) **CUT SOMETHING USING JIGSAW** to cut or shape something using a jigsaw ■ *adj* **WITH COMPLEX STRUCTURE** with many interrelating parts forming a complex whole ○ *the jigsaw nature of politics*

jigsaw puzzle *n* 1 a puzzle in the form of interlocking irregularly shaped pieces that make a picture when fitted together 2 something that is made up of many interconnecting parts ○ *help the police to piece together this jigsaw puzzle of motives*

jihad /ji hád/, **jehad** *n* a campaign waged by Muslims in defence of the Islamic faith against individuals, organizations, or countries regarded as hostile to Islam [Mid-19C. < Arabic *jihād* 'effort'.]

Jilin /jeé lín/ province in NE China. Capital: Changchun. Population: 25,740,000 (1994). Area: 187,000 sq. km/72,200 sq. mi.

jill *n* = **gill**[4]

jillaroo /jíllə roó/ (*plural* **-roos**) *n Aus* a woman who is a trainee worker on a sheep or cattle station (*informal*) [Mid-20C. After *jackaroo*, variant of JACKEROO.]

jillion /jíllyən/ *n* a number or amount too great to specify (*informal*) [Mid-20C. After BILLION.]

jilt /jilt/ *vt* to break off a romantic relationship with somebody abruptly ■ *n* a person who abruptly breaks with a lover [Mid-17C. < ?]

Jim Crow /jím kró/, **jim crow** *n US* 1 **Jim Crow, jim crow, Jim Crowism, jim crowism** the practice of discriminating against Black people, especially by operating systems of public segregation (*informal*) 2 a highly offensive term for a Black person (*taboo*) [Mid-19C. After a Black character in a plantation song.]

jimjams /jím jamz/ *npl* (*informal*) 1 **DELIRIUM TREMENS** an attack of delirium tremens 2 **NERVOUSNESS** an attack of nervous anxiety 3 **PYJAMAS** a pair of pyjamas [Late 19C. Plural of obsolete *jimjam* 'trivial article, knick-knack'.]

jimmy /jímmi/ *n* (*plural* **jimmies**) *US* = **jemmy** *n.* ■ *vt* (**jimmies, jimmying, jimmied**) *US* = **jemmy** *v.* [Mid-19C. Alteration of JEMMY.]

Jimmy /jímmi/ *n Scotland* an informal way of addressing a man whose name is not known (*informal*) ○ *Hey, you, Jimmy!* [Mid-19C. Familiar form of the name *James*.]

Jimmy Woodser /-wóodzər/ *n ANZ* (*informal*) 1 somebody, usually a man, who drinks alone 2 a drink taken by somebody who is alone [Late 19C. < ?]

jimsonweed /jímss'n weed/ *n US* PLANTS = **thorn apple** [Late 17C. Alteration of *Jamestown*, Virginia.]

Jinan /jeé nán/, **Chi-nan** capital of Shandong Province, E China. Population: 2,450,931 (1991).

jingbang /jíng báng/ *n Scotland* a thing in its entirety (*informal*) ○ *the whole jingbang* [Mid-19C. < ?]

jingle /jíng g'l/ *n* 1 **METALLIC TINKLE** a light musical noise like that of small bells or pieces of metal being shaken together 2 **TUNE ASSOCIATED WITH SOMETHING ADVERTISED** a catchy tune or verse, usually one that is played repeatedly to advertise something ○ *the new jingle for the radio station* ■ *v* (**-gles, -gling, -gled**) 1 *vti* **MAKE A TINKLING SOUND** to make, or cause something to make, a light musical noise like that of small bells or pieces of metal being shaken together ○ *He jingled the coins in his pocket.* 2 *vi* **HAVE AN EASILY REMEMBERED SOUND** to have a sound or rhyme that is catchy or repetitious [14C. An imitation of the sound of small metallic objects shaken together.] —**jingly** *adj*

jingo /jíng gō/ (*plural* **-goes**) *n* a zealous patriot, especially somebody who advocates hostility towards other countries [Late 17C. < ?] —**jingoish** *adj* ◇ **by jingo** used to express surprise or annoyance (*dated informal*)

jingoism /jíng gō izəm/ *n* zealous patriotism expressing itself especially in hostility towards other countries —**jingoist** *adj, n* —**jingoistic** /jíng gō ístik/ *adj* —**jingoistically** *adv*

Jinja /jínjə/ city in SE Uganda. Population: 60,979 (1991).

jink /jingk/ *vi* to make quick sideways movements in order to evade somebody or something ■ *n* a quick evasive movement or manoeuvre [Late 17C. < ?]

Jinnah /jínnə/, **Muhammad Ali** (1876–1948) Indian and Pakistani statesman

jinni /jínni/ (*plural* **jinn** /jin/), **djinni** (*plural* **djinn**) *n* in Islamic mythology, a spirit that can take on various human and animal forms and makes mischievous use of its supernatural powers. ◊ **genie** [Early 19C. < Arabic *jinnī*.]

Jin Nong /jín nóng/ (1687–1764?) Chinese artist

jinriksha /jin ríkshə/, **jinricksha** *n* TRANSP = **rickshaw** *n.* 1 [Late 19C. < Japanese, < *jin* 'man' + *riki* 'strength' + *sha* 'vehicle'.]

jinx /jingks/ *n* an unseen force that is thought to bring bad luck, or somebody or something, e.g. a curse, that is thought to bring bad luck ○ *There must be a jinx on this expedition.* ■ *vt* to bring a supposed unseen force of misfortune to bear on something or somebody ○ *the feeling that they had been jinxed in some way* [Early 20C. Probably < *jynx* 'wryneck', from the bird's use in witchcraft.] —**jinxed** *adj*

JIT *abbr* just-in-time

jitney /jítni/ (*plural* **-neys**) *n US* a small bus that takes passengers on a regular route for a small fare [Early 20C. < ?]

jitter /jíttər/ *vi* **BEHAVE NERVOUSLY** to behave in a nervous or restless way (*informal*) ■ *n* 1 **RAPID SIGNAL FLUCTUATION** an undesired rapid movement of electrical signals or images, e.g. on a television or oscilloscope screen, because of circuit instability or faulty components 2 **DISTORTION IN DIGITIZED INFORMATION** a distortion in digitally transmitted or recorded sound or images, caused when two devices are not perfectly synchronized, e.g. the recording and playback devices of audio recordings ■ **jitters** *npl* **NERVOUS ATTACK** feelings of extreme nervousness and agitation (*informal*) ○ *He's got the jitters about his interview tomorrow.* [Early 20C. < ?]

jitterbug /jíttər bug/ *n* 1 an energetic 1940s jazz dance for couples 2 a jitterbug dancer [Mid-20C. < ?]

jittery /jíttəri/ *adj* 1 feeling nervous or agitated 2 making rapid jumpy movements —**jitteriness** *n*

jiujitsu *n* MARTIAL ARTS = **jujitsu**

Jivaro /heévə rō/ (*plural* **-ro** *or* **-ros**) *n* 1 a member of a Native South American people living in the tropical forests of Ecuador and NE Peru 2 a language spoken by the Jivaro people, belonging to the Equatorial branch of Andean-Equatorial. Native speakers: 20,000. [Mid-19C. < Spanish *jíbaro*.] —**Jivaro** *adj*

jive /jīv/ *n* 1 **JAZZ MUSIC** jazz or swing music, especially that of the 1930s and 1940s 2 **LIVELY DANCING STYLE** an uninhibited dance, often with a man swinging and throwing a woman, originally to jazz music and later to rock and roll 3 **JAZZ JARGON** the terminology and slang used by jazz musicians (*slang*) 4 *US* **INSINCERE TALK** smooth talk that is often deceptive or insincere (*slang*) ■ *v* (**jives, jiving, jived**) 1 *vi* **DANCE JIVE** to dance the jive 2 *vi* **TALK JIVE** to use the terminology and slang of jazz musicians (*slang*) 3 *vti US* **FLATTER** to flatter or deceive somebody with insincere talk (*slang*) ○ *I know when you're jiving me.* ■ *adj US* **INSINCERE** lacking sincerity or honesty (*slang*) ○ *His comments are so jive!* [Early 20C. < ?] —**jiver** *n*

JJ, JJ. *abbr* **1** Judges **2** Justices

Jl *abbr* **1** Joel **2** journal

⚡**jm** *abbr* Jamaica (*in Internet addresses*)

Jn *abbr* John

jnd *abbr* just noticeable difference

jnr, Jnr *abbr* junior

jo[1] /jō/ (*plural* **joes**) *n Scotland* somebody's boyfriend, girlfriend, or lover (*archaic or literary*) [Early 16C. Form of JOY.]

⚡**jo**[2] *abbr* Jordan (*in Internet addresses*)

Joan of Arc /jōn əv àark/, **St** (1412–31) French patriot and saint

João Pessoa /zhwów pe sō̃ ə/ capital of Paraíba State, NE Brazil. Population: 497,214 (1991).

⚡**job** /job/ *n* **1 PAID OCCUPATION** an activity such as a trade or profession that somebody does regularly for pay or a paid position doing this ○ *She's got a new job.* **2 TASK** something that remains to be done or dealt with ○ *I have several jobs to do this afternoon.* **3 ASSIGNMENT** an individual piece of work of a particular nature ○ *We managed to complete the job in under a week.* **4 FUNCTION** the role that somebody or something fulfils ○ *It's her job to look after the finances.* **5 DIFFICULTY** something that is difficult to accomplish ○ *I had quite a job getting it to start.* **6 QUALITY OF WORK DONE** a completed piece of work of a particular quality ○ *They did a very good job on the exterior.* **7 OBJECT** an object of some kind, especially a manufactured item (*informal*) ○ *one of those big four-wheel-drive jobs* **8 AFFAIR** something that happens or something that is done (*informal*) ○ *The party was one of those posh jobs.* **9 CRIME** a criminal act, especially a robbery (*informal*) ○ *he drove the getaway car for the job in Bermondsey* **10 PROGRAMMING TASK** a computer programming task run as a single application or unit ■ *v* (**jobs, jobbing, jobbed**) **1** *vi* **WORK OCCASIONALLY** to take occasional or casual work ○ *He jobs as a gardener from time to time.* **2** *vti* **DEAL IN WHOLESALE MERCHANDISE** to buy and sell merchandise as a wholesaler or agent **3** *vt* **DISTRIBUTE WORK TO OTHERS** to subcontract portions of contract work to others ○ *job out the plumbing work on the house* **4** *vi* **PROFIT FROM PUBLIC OFFICE** to make a private gain from working in a public position **5** *vi* **WORK AS STOCKJOBBER** to deal in stocks as a stockjobber (*dated*) [Mid-16C. < ?] ◇ **be a good job** to be a fortunate circumstance (*informal*) ○ *It's a good job you decided to stay in tonight.* ◇ **make the best of a bad job** to get the best result possible from an unfavourable situation ◇ **give something up as a bad job** to abandon something that seems unlikely to be going to change for the better ◇ **just the job** exactly what is needed ◇ **on the job 1** engaged in working **2** having sex (*slang*)

Job[1] /jōb/ *n* in the Bible, a righteous man whose faith withstood severe testing by God ○ *have the patience of Job*

Job[2] /jōb/ *n* the book of the Bible that describes Job's afflictions and eventual reward

job action *n US* = **industrial action**

jobber /jóbbər/ *n* **1** a person who does odd jobs or casual work **2** FIN, HIST = **stockjobber** *n.* 1

jobbery /jóbbəri/ *n* the corrupt practice of making private gains from public office, or an instance of this

jobbing /jóbbing/ *adj* working on a casual basis

Jobcentre /jób sentər/ *n* a local office, run by the government, where jobs are advertised and where people looking for work can receive help and advice

job club *n* a local association formed, under the auspices of a Jobcentre, to facilitate self-help in the search for work and to monitor progress in finding work

job description *n* an official written description of the responsibilities and requirements of a specific job, often one agreed between employer and employee

job-hunt *vi* to look for a job (*informal*) —**job hunter** *n*

jobless /jóbləss/ *adj* without a job ■ *npl* unemployed people considered collectively —**joblessness** *n*

job lot *n* a miscellaneous collection of articles, especially ones that are bought or sold together ○ *I bought it as a job lot.*

job-related illness *n* MED = **industrial disease**

Job's comforter *n* somebody who, though appearing or intending to comfort a distressed person, only succeeds in worsening the situation [< the friends who came to 'comfort' Job in his affliction (Job 5:17)]

job seeker *n* a person who is actively looking for employment

Jobseeker's Allowance /jób seekərz-/ *n* money that the government pays to unemployed people who are looking for jobs

job-sharing *n* the dividing up of the responsibilities of a single full-time job between two or more part-time workers —**job-share** *n, vi* —**job-sharer** *n*

Job's tears *n* (*plural* **Job's tears**) a grass plant with sword-shaped leaves and hard white spherical seeds that are used as beads. Native to: tropical Asia *Coix lacryma-jobi.* ■ *npl* the hard white seeds of Job's tears, used as beads, and as a cereal in East Asia [< its round shiny leaves]

jobsworth /jóbz wurth/ *n* a minor official who insists on following regulations to the letter, especially with the intention of being deliberately obstructive (*informal*) [Late 20C. < *It's more than my job's worth* (to do whatever is being requested).]

Jocasta /jə kástə/ *n* in Greek mythology, the wife of Laius and later of their son Oedipus

jock[1] /jok/ *n* a disc jockey (*informal*) [Late 18C. Shortening.]

jock[2] /jok/ *n* (*informal*) **1** *US* an athlete, especially a male athlete in college **2** a jockstrap [Mid-20C. Shortening of JOCKSTRAP.]

Jock /jok/ *n* used to refer to or address a Scottish person, especially a man (*informal; offensive in some contexts*) [Scottish form of *John*]

jockey /jóki/ *n* (*plural* **-eys**) **1 RIDER OF RACEHORSE** a rider of racehorses, especially professionally **2** *US* **OPERATOR** somebody whose work involves the use or operation of a particular device, vehicle, or object (*informal*) ○ *We desk jockeys need to get out and exercise more.* ■ *v* (**-eys, -eying, -eyed**) **1** *vti* **RIDE RACEHORSE** to ride a racehorse, especially as a professional jockey **2** *vi* **TRY TO GAIN ADVANTAGE** to manoeuvre in order to gain an advantage ○ *Watch them all jockeying for promotion.* **3** *vt* **MANIPULATE** to trick somebody, usually for personal gain ○ *She has been jockeyed into doing work for which he gets the credit.* [Late 16C. < familiar form of JOCK.]

jock itch *n US* MED = **dhobi itch**

jockstrap /jók strap/ *n* an elasticated belt with a pouch at the front, worn by sportsmen to support their genitals or to keep a protective cup in place [Late 19C. < slang *jock* 'genitals' < ?]

jocose /jə kóss, jō-/ *adj* (*literary*) **1** with a playful joking disposition **2** playfully humorous in style [Late 17C. < Latin *jocosus* 'full of joking' < *jocus* 'joke'.] —**jocosely** *adv* —**jocoseness** *n* —**jocosity** /jə kóssə ti, jō-/ *n*

jocular /jókyŏŏlər/ *adj* **1** with a playful joking disposition **2** intended to be funny [Early 17C. < Latin *jocularis* 'of a little joke' < *jocus* 'joke'.] —**jocularity** /jókyŏŏ lárrəti/ *n* —**jocularly** *adv*

jocund /jókənd/ *adj* cheerful and full of good humour (*literary*) [14C. Via Old French *jocond* (influenced by Latin *jocus* 'joke') < Latin *jucundus* < *juvare* 'please, help'.] —**jocundity** /jə kúndəti/ *n* —**jocundly** *adv*

Jodhpur /jód pŏŏr/ city in NW India. Population: 666,279 (1991).

jodhpurs /jód pərz/ *npl* riding breeches that are wide at the hip and narrow round the calves, often with reinforced patches at the knee and thigh where the rider's legs grip the horse [Late 19C. After JODHPUR.]

Jodrell Bank Experimental Station /jóddrəl-/ observatory in Cheshire

Joe /jō/, **joe** *n* an ordinary man (*informal*) [Late 18C. Familiar form of the name *Joseph*.]

Joe Bloggs /-blógz/ *n* the average man in the street (*informal*)

Joe Blow /jō bló/ *n US, Can, Aus* the average man in the street.

Joel /jō əl/ *n* **1** a Hebrew prophet who lived in the 6th century BC **2** the book of the Bible that contains the prophecies of Joel, dating from the years following the Israelites' Babylonian exile

joe-pye weed /jō pí-/ *n* a tall perennial plant with whorled leaves. Flowers: small, pink or purple, in clusters. Native to: North America. *Eupatorium maculatum* and *Eupatorium purpureum.* [Early 19C. After *Joe Pye*, Native American turned into this plant according to a traditional story.]

Joe Soap *n* used as a humorous way for somebody to refer to himself or herself, especially when feeling put upon (*informal*)

joey /jō i/ *n Aus* a young animal, especially a kangaroo still young enough to be carried in its mother's pouch [Mid-19C. < Aboriginal *joè*.]

Joffre /zhóffrə/, **Joseph** (1852–1931) French general

jog /jog/ *v* (**jogs, jogging, jogged**) **1** *vi* **TROT** to run at a slow steady pace ○ *He jogged across the road to the shop.* **2** *vi* **RUN FOR EXERCISE** to run at a slow steady pace as a fitness exercise ○ *She jogs round the park every morning.* **3** *vi* **GO SLOWLY BUT STEADILY** to move along at a slow steady pace ○ *The little steam train jogged along the track.* **4** *vi* **PLOD** to progress at a slow dull pace ○ *How are things? – Oh, you know: jogging along.* **5** *vt* **NUDGE** to give a light push or shake to something ○ *thought the photo might have jogged your memory* ■ *n* **1 NUDGE** a light push or shake **2 SLOW SPEED** a slow steady pace or motion ○ *moving along at a jog* **3 SPELL OF RUNNING** a spell of slow steady running for exercise ○ *I'm going for a quick jog.* [Mid-16C. < ?]

jogger /jóggər/ *n* somebody who runs at a moderate pace, often over long distances, for exercise ■ **joggers** *npl* loose-fitting trousers with an elasticated waist and ankles, used for jogging

jogging /jógging/ *n* a fitness or recreational activity that involves running at a moderate pace, often over long distances

joggle /jógg'l/ *n* **1 SHAKING ACTION** a gentle shaking motion or action **2 MASONRY JOINT** a joint between two pieces of masonry or concrete, in which a projection on one fits into a recess of the other ■ *v* (**-gles, -gling, -gled**) **1** *vti* **SHAKE** to shake something gently ○ *The table joggled and my drink spilt all over the place.* **2** *vt* **JOIN WITH JOGGLE** to join pieces of masonry or concrete with a joggle [Early 18C. < ?]

Jogjakarta /jóg jə kaártə/ city in SW Indonesia, on Java. Population: 412,400 (1990).

jog trot *n* **1** a slow steady running pace **2** a dull steady pace of life ○ *things going on at a jog trot*

Johannesburg /jō hánnəss burg/ capital of Gauteng Province, NE South Africa. Population: 712,507 (1991).

Johannine /jō hánnīn/ *adj* relating to the apostle John or to the books of the Bible attributed to him [Mid-19C. < late Latin *Joannes* 'John'.]

Johannsen /yō háns'n/, **Wilhelm** (1857–1927) Danish botanist

john /jon/ *n US* a toilet (*informal*) ○ *Where's the john?* [Early 20C. < the name *John*.]

John *n* **1** the fourth of the gospels of the Bible in which the life and teachings of Jesus Christ are described, traditionally thought to have been written by St John **2** a book of the Bible written in epistle form and traditionally attributed to St John

John /jon/, **St** (*d.* 101?) Judean apostle

John (1167–1216) king of England (1199–1216). Known as **John Lackland**

John II (1319–64) king of France (1350–64). Known as **John the Good**

John IV (1604–56) king of Portugal (1640–56)

John VI (1769–1826) king of Portugal (1816–26)

John (of Gaunt) /-gáwnt/, **Duke of Lancaster** (1340–99) English soldier and statesman

John (of Salisbury) /jón əv sáwlzbəri/ (1115?–80) English cleric, philosopher, and humanist

John (of the Cross) /jon/, **St** (1542–91) Spanish poet and mystic. Born **Juan de Yepes y Álvarez,**

John (the Baptist) /-thə báptist/, **St** (8? BC–AD 27?) Judean prophet

John /jon/, **Augustus** (1878–1961) British painter

John, Sir Elton (*b.* 1947) British rock singer and pianist. Born **Reginald Dwight**

John, Gwen (1876–1939) British painter

John Barleycorn /-baárli kawrn/ *n* (*literary or humorous*) **1** the personification of alcoholic drink **2** *Scotland* barley personified as the source of malt liquor

John Birch Society /-búrch-/ *n* a right-wing political organization formed in the United States to combat Communism

John Bull /-bŏŏl/ *n* **1** the personification of England and the English people **2** an individual Englishman, especially one regarded as embodying Englishness [Late

18C. After a character in *Law is a Bottomless Pit* (1712), by J. Arbuthnot.] —**John Bullish** *adj* —**John Bullishness** *n* —**John Bullism** *n*

John Chrysostom /-krissəstəm/ *St* (349–407) Syrian-born preacher

John Doe /-dō/ *n US* 1 an average man affected by everyday events (*informal*) 2 a man or boy in a legal proceeding whose identity is either not known or not revealed

John Dory /-dáwri/ *n* 1 a deep-sea fish with a large flat olive-yellow body, long dorsal spines, and large jaws. Native to: E Atlantic, Mediterranean. *Zeus faber.* 2 the flesh of a John Dory used as food

Johne's disease /yônəz-/ *n* a chronic disease of sheep, cattle, and other domestic animals, with symptoms of diarrhoea and loss of weight, caused by a bacterium that is related to the tuberculosis bacterium [Early 20C. After H. A. *Johne* (1839–1910), German veterinary surgeon.]

John Hancock /-hán kok/ *n US* somebody's signature (*informal*) [After the first person to sign the US Declaration of Independence]

John Henry /-hénri/ *n* 1 an African American hero in US folklore, renowned for his great strength 2 *US* somebody's signature (*informal*) [Partly after JOHN HANCOCK.]

johnny /jónni/ (*plural* **-nies**) *n* 1 **CONDOM** a condom (*slang*) 2 **MAN** a man or boy (*dated informal*) 3 *US* **HOSPITAL GOWN** a short gown that ties at the back, worn in hospitals by patients [Late 17C. Diminutive of *John*.]

Johnny-come-lately (*plural* **Johnny-come-latelies** or **Johnnies-come-lately**) *n* a recent arrival at a place, group, position, or point of view (*informal*) ○ *these Johnny-come-latelies and their 'new' ideas*

Johnny Reb /-réb/ *n US* a Confederate soldier in the American Civil War (*informal*) [Mid-19C. Shortening of *Johnny Rebel.*]

John o'Groats /jón ə gróts/ *n* village on the NE tip of Scotland

John Paul I /jón páwl/ (1912–78) pope (1978). Born **Albino Luciani**

John Paul II (*b.* 1920) pope (1978-). Born **Karol Wojtyła**

Johns /jonz/, **Jasper** (*b.* 1930) US artist

Amy Johnson

Johnson /jónss'n/, **Amy** (1903–41) British flyer

Johnson, Andrew (1808–75) US statesman and 17th president of the United States (1865–69)

Johnson, Jack (1878–1946) US boxer. Full name **Arthur John Johnson**

Johnson, Lyndon Baines (1908–73) US statesman and 36th president of the United States (1963–69)

Johnson, Magic (*b.* 1959) US basketball player. Born **Earvin Johnson, Jr.**

Johnson, Philip (*b.* 1906) US architect

Johnson, Samuel (1709–84) British critic, poet, and lexicographer —**Johnsonian** /jon sóni ən/ *adj*

Johnson grass *n* a coarse perennial variety of sorghum often grown as forage. Native to: Mediterranean. *Sorghum halepense.* [After William *Johnson*, an Alabama planter]

Johnston /jónstən/, **George** (1912–70) Australian writer

John Thomas *n* an offensive term for a penis (*slang*) [< ?]

Johor Strait /jə háwr-/ narrow body of water between Singapore and Malaysia

Lady Bird Johnson and Lyndon Baines Johnson

joie de vivre /zhwaʾà də veèvrə/ *n* energy and love of life [Late 19C. < French, 'joy of living'.]

join /joyn/ *v* 1 *vti* **BRING OR COME TOGETHER** to meet, or make two or more things meet, and become linked or united ○ *where the A4 joins the M4* 2 *vt* **FIX TOGETHER** to put or fix two or more things together ○ *Join the wing to the body with glue.* 3 *vt* **MAKE CONNECTION BETWEEN THINGS** to establish a connection between two or more things, e.g. by drawing a line between them ○ *Join the dots.* 4 *vti* **BECOME PART OF GROUP** to become a member of something such as a club, social group, company, team, or other organization ○ *I've joined the Mountaineering Club.* 5 *vt* **DO THE SAME AS** to agree to do the same as somebody ○ *I'm sure my colleagues will want to join me in thanking you for your visit today.* 6 *vt* **UNITE PEOPLE IN PARTNERSHIP** to bring two or more people into a partnership, e.g. a marriage 7 *vt* **MEET** to go to meet somebody ○ *I'll join you later.* 8 *vt* **SHARE SOMEBODY'S COMPANY** to enter into the company of another person ○ *Do you mind if I join you?* 9 *vti* **BE ADJACENT** to be next to something or to each other ○ *This room joins the bathroom.* ■ *n* **JOINT** a place where two or more things have been joined ○ *You can hardly see the join.* [13C. Via Old French *joign-*, present stem of *joindre* < Latin *jungere* 'join'.] —**joinable** *adj*

join in *vti* to take part in an activity along with other people ○ *Can I join in?*

join up *vi* 1 to enlist as a member of one of the armed forces, especially at the outbreak of hostilities 2 to meet somebody for a joint activity ○ *They join up with the same friends every year to go on holiday.*

joinder /jóyndər/ *n* 1 **ACT OF JOINING** a joining or bringing together of two things (*formal*) 2 **JOINING OF LEGAL PARTIES** a joining of two parties in a single lawsuit 3 **COMBINING OF LEGAL PROCEEDINGS** a joining of two causes of action or two defences in a single lawsuit 4 **ACCEPTANCE OF ISSUE** a formal acceptance of an issue offered in a lawsuit [Early 17C. < Anglo Norman, < Old French *joindre* 'to join'.]

joiner /jóynər/ *n* 1 a maker of wooden components for buildings, especially finished woodwork 2 somebody who readily joins clubs, societies, or organizations (*informal*)

joinery /jóynəri/ *n* 1 the visible finished woodwork in a building, e.g. door frames and window frames 2 the work of a joiner, or the techniques that a joiner uses

joint /joynt/ *adj* 1 **OWNED IN COMMON** owned in common by two or more people or concerns ○ *joint assets* 2 **COMBINED** existing and operating in combination ○ *the joint ravages of the weather and pollution* 3 **SHARING ROLE** sharing the same role or position with another person or body ○ *My brother and I were appointed joint executors of her will.* 4 **DONE TOGETHER** done or produced together with others ○ *A joint statement was issued by the three party leaders.* ■ *n* 1 **JUNCTION BETWEEN BONES** a part of the body, e.g. the knee, elbow, or skull, where bones are connected 2 **PLACE WHERE PARTS ARE JOINED** the place where parts or pieces of something are joined together 3 **PIECE OF MEAT** a large piece of meat prepared and cooked for several people, especially one that is roasted 4 **VENUE** a place of entertainment, e.g. a nightclub, especially one considered cheap or disreputable (*slang*) 5 **CANNABIS CIGARETTE** a cigarette containing cannabis (*slang*) 6 **JUNCTION BETWEEN SEGMENTS OF INVERTEBRATE** any of the points of connection between movable segments of the body in an insect, spider, crab, or other invertebrate 7 **DIVIDING POINT ON PLANT STEM** the place on a plant stem from which a leaf or branch grows 8 **CRACK IN ROCK** a crack or fissure in

rock, without any looseness or displacement of the surrounding mass 9 **HINGE OF BOOK COVER** either of the creases between the spine and the front and back covers of a book, especially a hardback 10 **A PLACE** a building or dwelling (*slang*) ■ *v* 1 *vt* **FIT TOGETHER** to fit or fix parts together by means of a joint 2 *vt* **DIVIDE INTO PIECES** to cut a carcass into pieces of meat for cooking 3 *vt* **PLANE EDGE OF BOARD** to plane and shape the edge of a board so that it fits with another edge to form a joint 4 *vi* **FORM JOINTS** to form joints in the stem during the growth process (*refers to cereal plants*) [13C. < French, past participle of *joindre* 'to join'.] —**jointed** *adj* —**jointing** *n* ◇ **out of joint** 1 dislocated or painfully displaced 2 disturbed or disrupted, usually as a result of some major change or upheaval

joint account *n* a bank account held in the names of more than one person, typically spouses or partners

Joint Chiefs of Staff *npl* the most important military advisory group to the president of the United States, consisting of the Chiefs of Staff of the Army and Air Force, the commandant of the Marine Corps, and the Chief of Naval Operations

joint defence *n* a defence strategy in which two or more defendants join and cooperate with one another so that their cases are heard together

jointer /jóyntər/ *n* 1 a tool for pointing the mortar in brickwork or stonework after it has been laid 2 a long plane used to shape the edges of planks into joints

jointly /jóyntli/ *adv* in conjunction with, or in cooperation with, a person or organization ○ *The copyright is jointly owned by the composer and the publisher.*

jointress /jóyntrəss/ *n* a woman on whom property has been settled by her husband at the time of their marriage

joint stock *n* stock held jointly, especially in a joint-stock company, a commercial enterprise whose capital is in shares that individual holders may transfer without the consent of the whole body

jointure /jóynchər/ *n* an estate or property settled by a husband on his wife at the time of their marriage, to take effect in the event of his death

joint venture *n* a business enterprise jointly undertaken by two or more companies, who share the outlay, risks, and profits (*hyphenated when used before a noun*)

jointworm /jóynt wurm/ *n* the larva of some wasps that forms a weakening swelling at the stem joint of a cereal plant. Family: Eurytomidae.

joist /joyst/ *n* a parallel beam of wood, metal, or concrete that supports a floor, roof, or ceiling [14C. < Old French *giste* 'beam supporting a bridge' < Latin *jacere* 'lie down'.]

jojoba /hō hṓbə/ (*plural* **-bas**) *n* 1 a waxy oil derived from the seeds of a desert tree. Use: shampoos, cosmetics. (*often before nouns*) 2 a desert bush or small tree whose seeds yield jojoba. Native to: SW North America. *Simmondsia chinensis.* [Early 20C. Via Mexican Spanish < Native American.]

joke /jōk/ *n* 1 **FUNNY STORY** a funny story, anecdote, or piece of wordplay that gets passed round and repeated 2 **CAUSE OF AMUSEMENT** anything said or done to make people laugh ○ *dressed up the dog in a hat and sunglasses as a joke* 3 **SOMETHING INADEQUATE** somebody or something that is laughably inadequate or absurd (*informal*) ○ *The surroundings were pleasant enough but the food was a joke.* ■ *v* (**jokes, joking, joked**) 1 *vti* **MAKE JOKES** to tell funny stories or say or do things to make somebody laugh 2 *vi* **NOT TO BE SERIOUS** to be trying to be amusing, rather than serious or in earnest ○ *We knew he was only joking.* 3 *vt* **TEASE** to make fun of somebody (*archaic*) [Late 17C. < Latin *jocus* 'jest, wordplay'.] ◇ **beyond a joke** having become a serious matter ◇ **be no joke** to be a serious or difficult matter (*informal*) ○ *It's no joke driving to work in the rush hour every day.*

joker /jṓkər/ *n* 1 **TELLER OF JOKES** a frequent teller or player of jokes 2 **CARD BEARING PICTURE OF JESTER** an extra playing card in a pack, bearing a picture of a jester, that in some games can be substituted for other cards 3 **ECCENTRIC PERSON** an amusing, entertaining, or entertainingly eccentric person (*informal*) 4 **INCONSIDERATE PERSON** somebody whose thoughtless or inconsiderate action is highly annoying (*informal*) ○ *I'm looking for the joker who double-parked outside my front door.* ◇ **the joker in the pack** an unpredictable element that makes planning or projections difficult (*informal*)

jokey /jṓki/ (**-ier, -iest**), **joky** *adj* good-humoured and amusing —**jokily** *adv* —**jokiness** *n*

jokingly /jṓkingli/ *adv* with the intention of making a joke rather than a serious comment or suggestion

joky *adj* = jokey

jolie laide /zhŏlli léd/ (*plural* **jolies laides** /zhŏlli léd/) *n* a woman whose facial features are not pretty in conventional terms, but nevertheless have a distinctive harmony or charm [< French, < *jolie* 'pretty' + *laide* 'ugly']

Joliot-Curie /zhŏlli ō kyoóri/, **Frédéric** (1900–58) French physicist. Born **Jean-Frédéric Joliot**

Joliot-Curie, Irène (1897–1956) French physicist. Born **Irène Curie**

Jolley /jŏlli/, **Elizabeth** (*b.* 1923) British-born Australian writer

jollification /jŏllifi káysh'n/ *n* the activities of people who are enthusiastically celebrating something in a happy, friendly way —**jollifications** *npl*

jollify /jŏlli fī/ (**-fies, -fying, -fied**) *v* **1** *vi* to indulge enthusiastically in happy celebrations (*dated*) **2** *vt* to make somebody cheerful or create a festive atmosphere in something

jollities /jŏllǝtiz/ *npl* events or festivities that celebrate something

jollity /jŏllǝti/ *n* cheerful, joking, or celebratory behaviour [13C. < Old French *jolite* < *joli* 'merry, pleasant'.]

jolly /jŏlli/ *adj* (**-lier, -liest**) **1** FRIENDLY AND CHEERFUL friendly and cheerful, especially in a hearty or exuberant way ○ *a jolly pink-cheeked woman* **2** HAPPY happily festive in tone or mood (*dated*) **3** ENJOYABLE bringing pleasure or enjoyment (*dated informal*) ○ *A picnic would be jolly.* ■ *adv* VERY used to emphasize the extent to which something is good or bad (*dated informal*) ○ *Jolly nice of you to come.* [13C. < Old French *joli* 'merry, pleasant'.] < ○ **get your jollies** *US* to get pleasure out of something (*slang*) ○ **jolly well** a phrase used in annoyance to add emphasis (*dated*) ○ *I'm not jolly well going to stand for it.*

jolly along *vt* to keep somebody happy or cooperative by using flattery or encouragement (*informal*) ○ *Try to jolly her along a little bit longer*

jolly up *vt* to make a person, place, or situation more lively or cheerful (*informal*) ○ *I thought some music might jolly things up a bit.*

jollyboat /jŏlli bŏt/ *n* a small boat carried on a larger ship, often one kept hoisted at the stern of the ship [Late 17C. < ?]

Jolly Roger /jŏlli rójjǝr/ *n* the flag traditionally flown by a pirate ship, depicting a white skull and crossbones against a black background [Late 18C. < ?]

Jolson /jṓlssǝn/, **Al** (1886–1950) Lithuanian-born US entertainer. Born **Asa Yoelson**

jolt /jōlt/ *v* **1** *vti* SHAKE OR JERK VIOLENTLY to shake or jerk suddenly and violently, or to make somebody or something shake or jerk suddenly and violently, especially as a result of a sudden movement **2** *vi* BUMP UP AND DOWN to bump up and down or shake from side to side while moving **3** *vt* SHAKE OR DISLODGE to knock or shake somebody or something violently enough to cause unsteadiness or loss of balance ○ *A major earthquake jolted the city.* **4** *vt* STARTLE INTO REALITY to startle somebody out of a daydream, fantasy, or other state of semiawareness ■ *n* **1** VIOLENT MOVEMENT a sudden violent movement or blow ○ *The train moved off again with a series of jolts.* **2** SHOCK OR REMINDER an emotional shock or a sharp reminder [Late 16C. < ?] —**joltingly** *adv* —**jolty** *adj*

Jon. *abbr* Jonah

Jonah[1] /jṓnǝ/ *n* **1** in the Bible, a Hebrew prophet of the 8th century BC who was swallowed by a great fish and vomited out three days later, unharmed **2** a book in the Bible that tells the story of Jonah, whose preaching caused the Assyrians to repent their wickedness

Jonah[2] /jṓnǝ/ *n* a bringer of bad luck —**Jonahesque** /jṓnǝ ésk/ *adj*

Jonathan /jŏnnǝthǝn/ *n* in the Bible, the eldest son of King Saul and close friend of David, who was killed in battle against the Philistines (1 Samuel 13–2 Samuel 21)

jones /jōnz/ *n* **1** *US* DRUG ADDICTION an addiction, especially a heroin addiction (*slang*) **2** *US* WITHDRAWAL drug withdrawal symptoms, especially from heroin (*slang*) **3** *US* HABITUAL CRAVING an all-consuming craving or desire for something (*slang*) **4** **jones, Jones** TABOO TERM a highly offensive term for a penis (*taboo*) [Late 20C. < ?]

Jones /jōnz/, **Alan** (*b.* 1947) Australian motor-racing driver

Jones, Ernest (1879–1958) British psychoanalyst

Jones, Inigo (1573–1652) English architect and stage designer

Jones, John Paul (1747–92) Scottish-born US naval commander

Joneses /jṓnziz/ *npl* neighbours, especially somebody's next-door neighbours ○ *keeping up with the Joneses* [Late 19C. < *Jones*, common British surname.]

jongleur /zhoN glúr/ *n* a wandering minstrel of medieval times who travelled about singing the compositions of troubadours or reciting epic poems in noble households or royal courts [Late 18C. Via French < Latin *joculator* 'jester' < *joculari* < *jocus* 'joke'.]

Jönköping /jȫn chöping/ *city* in S Sweden. Population: 113,557 (1993).

jonquil /jŏngkwil/ *n* **1** a variety of narcissus. Flowers: fragrant, yellow, short-tubed. Native to: S Europe. *Narcissus jonquilla.* **2** the golden-yellow colour of a jonquil [Early 17C. Via modern Latin *jonquilla* or French *jonquille* < Spanish *junquillo* 'little rush' < *junco* 'rush'.]

Jonson /jŏnss'n/, **Ben** (1573–1637) English playwright and poet

jootha /jṓothǝ/ *n* *S Asia* food that is considered polluted, usually because it has come in contact with somebody's saliva [< Hindi]

Scott Joplin

Joplin /jŏpplin/, **Scott** (1868–1917) US composer

joram *n* = jorum

Jordaens /yawr daánss/, **Jacob** (1593–1678) Flemish painter

Jordan

Jordan /jáwrd'n/ **1** kingdom in the Middle East. Capital: Amman. Population: 4,322,255 (1997). Area: 89,556 sq. km/34,578 sq. mi. **2** river in SW Asia, rising in Syria and flowing south through the Sea of Galilee to the Dead Sea. Length: 320 km/200 mi. —**Jordanian** /jawr dáyni ǝn/ *adj, n*

Jordan, Michael (*b.* 1963) US basketball player. Known as **Air Jordan**

Jordan curve *n* in mathematics, any simple closed curve, e.g. a circle or an ellipse [Early 20C. After M. E. C. *Jordan* (1838–1922), French mathematician.]

Jordan curve theorem *n* in geometry, a theorem holding that every simple closed curve divides a plane into two regions and serves as their boundary

jorum /jáwrǝm/, **joram** *n* a large drinking bowl or its contents [Mid-18C. < ?]

Joseph /jṓzif/ *n* in the Bible, the son of Jacob and Rachel, sold into slavery in Egypt by his jealous brothers

Joseph /jṓzif/, **St** (*fl.* 1st century BC) biblical figure

Joseph II (1741–90) Holy Roman Emperor (1765–90)

Joseph Bonaparte Gulf /jṓsǝf bŏnǝ paart-/ inlet of the Timor Sea in N Australia, between NE Western Australia and the NW Northern Territory

Joséphine /jṓzǝ feen/ (1763–1814) empress of the French (1804–09). Born **Marie Joséphine Rose Tascher de la Pagerie**

Joseph of Arimathea /-árrimǝ thee ǝ/, **St** (*fl.* 1st century AD) biblical figure who asked for the body of Jesus Christ, and buried it in his own tomb.

Josephson effect /jṓzifs'n-/ *n* the passage of an electric current through a thin insulating layer between two superconducting metals [Late 20C. After Brian David *Josephson* (1940–), British physicist.]

Josephson junction *n* in electrical or electronic circuits, a junction that utilizes the Josephson effect, consisting of two superconducting materials separated by a thin insulating layer

Josephus /jō seéfǝss/, **Flavius** (37?–AD 100?) Jewish historian and general. Born **Joseph Ben Matthias**

josh /jŏsh/ *v* (*informal*) **1** *vti* to make fun of somebody in a friendly, good-humoured way **2** *vi* to joke or indulge in banter with somebody [Mid-19C. < ?] —**josher** *n* —**joshingly** *adv*

Josh. *abbr* Joshua

Joshua /jŏshoo ǝ/ *n* **1** in the Bible, Moses' successor as leader of the Israelites **2** the book of the Bible that contains a narrative of the Hebrew invasion and partition of Canaan under Joshua's command

Joshua tree *n* a small tree-shaped yucca with sword-shaped leaves. Flowers: white, in clusters. Native to: deserts of SW United States. *Yucca brevifolia.* [Mid-19C. Probably after JOSHUA, because the tree's branching shape resembles somebody brandishing a spear (Joshua 8:18).]

Josiah /jō sī ǝ/ (648?–609 BC) king of Judah

joss /jŏss/ *n* an image or statue representing a Chinese deity [Early 18C. Via Javanese *dejos* < Portuguese *deus* 'god' < Latin.]

josser /jŏssǝr/ *n* an offensive term for a man, especially one considered unintelligent or objectionable (*slang insult*) [Late 19C. < JOSS.]

joss house *n* a Chinese shrine or temple containing images or statues of deities

joss stick *n* incense in the form of a stick of dried paste

jostle /jŏss'l/ (**-tles, -tling, -tled**) *vti* to knock or bump against somebody, or to push or elbow somebody deliberately, sometimes as an expression of aggression or hostility ○ *We managed to jostle our way to the front.* [Mid-16C. < JOUST.] —**jostler** *n*

jot /jŏt/ *vt* (**jots, jotting, jotted**) to write something down hastily for later reference ○ *jotted down the title in her notebook* ■ *n* a very small amount [15C. Via Latin < Greek *iōta* (see IOTA).]

jota /khō taa, hō-/ *n* a fast Spanish dance from Aragon, performed with castanets in 3/4 time, usually to voice and guitar accompaniment [Mid-19C. < Spanish.]

jotter /jŏttǝr/, **jotter pad** /jŏttǝr pàd/ *n* **1** a book or pad for making rough notes **2** *Scotland* a school exercise book

jotting /jŏtting/ *n* a hastily written note, comment, or observation

Jotun /yŏt'n, yō toōn/, **Jotunn** *n* a member of a race of giants with supernatural powers in Norse mythology

Jotunheim /yŏt'n haym, yō toōn-/ *n* the home of the giants in Norse mythology [< Old Norse *Jotunheimar*]

Jotunn *n* MYTHOL = Jotun

joule /jool/ *n* (*symbol* J) the SI unit of energy or work, equal to the work done when the application point of a one newton force moves one metre in the direction of application [Late 19C. After James JOULE.]

Joule /jool/, **James** (1818–89) British physicist

Joule effect *n* an increase in heat resulting from the passage of a current through a conductor

jounce /jownss/ *vti* (**jounces, jouncing, jounced**) to bounce up and down and rock from side to side while moving, or to make somebody or something move in this way ■ *n* a jolting, swaying, bouncing, or rocking movement [15C. < ?] —**jouncy** *adj*

jour. *abbr* 1 journal 2 journalist 3 journeyman

journal /júrn'l/ *n* 1 MAGAZINE OR PERIODICAL a magazine or periodical, especially one published by a specialist or professional body for its members, containing information and contributions relevant to their area of activity ○ *a medical journal* 2 DETAILED PERSONAL DIARY somebody's written daily record of personal experiences, rather more elaborate and detailed than a diary, 3 PRELIMINARY RECORD OF FINANCIAL TRANSACTIONS a book for recording daily transactions, especially in double entry book-keeping, using a formulaic style to ensure their correct entry in a ledger 4 OFFICIAL RECORD the official daily record of proceedings kept by an association or body, especially a legislative body or parliament 5 SECTION OF SHAFT a cylindrical section of a shaft designed to rotate inside a bearing [14C. Via French, 'daily' < late Latin *diurnalis* (see DIURNAL).]

journal box *n* the metal housing of a journal and its bearing

journalese /júrn'l éez/ *n* the style of writing supposedly associated with journalists, marked by the use of formulaic expressions (*disapproving*)

journalise *vti* = **journalize**

journalism /júrn'lizəm/ *n* 1 the profession of gathering, editing, and publishing news reports and related articles for newspapers, magazines, television, or radio 2 writing or reporting for the media as a literary genre or style

journalist /júrn'list/ *n* a writer or editor for a newspaper or magazine or for television or radio

journalistic /júrn'l ístik/ *adj* relating to journalism or similar in style to journalism —**journalistically** *adv*

journalize /júrn'l īz/ (-izes, -izing, -ized), **journalise** (-ises, -ising, -ised) *vti* to keep a journal or record something in a journal —**journalization** /júrn'l ī záysh'n/ *n* —**journalizer** *n*

~~**journel**~~ incorrect spelling of **journal**

journey /júrni/ *n* (*plural* **-neys**) 1 EXPEDITION SOMEWHERE a trip or expedition from one place to another 2 PROCESS OF DEVELOPMENT a gradual passing from one state to another regarded as more advanced, e.g. from innocence to mature awareness ○ *a spiritual journey* ■ *vi* (**-neys, -neying, -neyed**) TRAVEL to travel to a place or over a particular distance ○ *We are journeying into the unknown.* [12C. Via Old French *journee* 'day, day's work or travel' < Latin *diurnus* (see DIURNAL).] —**journeyer** *n*

journeyman /júrnimən/ (*plural* **-men** /-mən/) *n* (*often before nouns*) 1 an artisan who has completed an apprenticeship and is fully trained and qualified but still works for an employer ○ *a journeyman electrician* 2 a competent and reliable but unexceptional performer or exponent of something ○ *a good journeyman violinist* [15C. Literally, somebody qualified to work for a daily wage rather than as an apprentice.]

journo /júrnō/ (*plural* **-nos**) *n* a journalist (*informal*) [Mid-20C. Contraction.]

joust /jowst/ *n* MEDIEVAL TOURNAMENT a form of combat in medieval times held between two mounted knights in full armour who charged at, and tried to unseat each other with a lance ■ *vi* 1 ENGAGE IN A JOUST to take part in a joust 2 ENGAGE IN A CONTEST to take part in a contest against others ○ *candidates jousting for ninety minutes in a televised debate* [13C. < Old French *jouster* 'bring together' < Latin *juxta* 'close, beside'.] —**jouster** *n*

Jove /jōv/ *n* Jupiter [14C. Via Latin < Old Latin *Jovis.*] —**Jovian** /jōvi ən/ *adj* ◇ **by Jove** used to convey surprise, or to emphasize a conviction (*dated*)

jovial /jōvi əl/ *adj* cheerful in mood or disposition [Late 16C. Via French < Latin *jovialis* < *Jovis* 'Jove'.] —**joviality** /jōvi állati/ *n* —**jovially** *adv* —**jovialness** *n*

Jovian planet *n* any one of the four major planets, Jupiter, Uranus, Saturn, or Neptune

jowl[1] /jowl/ *n* 1 the jaw, especially the lower jaw 2 a cheek, especially a prominent one [Old English *ceafl* < Germanic]

jowl[2] /jowl/ *n* 1 a flaccid plump fold of flesh under somebody's chin 2 a dewlap under the neck of cattle or a wattle on the neck of a bird [Old English *ceole* < Germanic]

jowly /jówli/ (-ier, -iest) *adj* with a fold of flesh hanging under the neck —**jowliness** *n*

joy /joy/ *n* 1 GREAT HAPPINESS feelings of great happiness or pleasure, especially of an elevated or spiritual kind 2 SOMETHING THAT BRINGS HAPPINESS a pleasurable aspect of something or source of happiness ○ *His little granddaughter was a great joy to him.* ■ *vti* (**joys, joying, joyed**) REJOICE OR GLADDEN to derive joy from something, or to give somebody joy (*archaic or literary*) [12C. < French *joie* < Latin *gaudere* 'rejoice'.] ◇ **no joy** no success (*informal*)

Joyce /joyss/, **James** (1882–1941) Irish novelist

Joyce, William (1900–46) British traitor. Known as **Lord Haw-Haw**

joyful /jóyf'l/ *adj* 1 full of joy, or feeling, expressing, or showing joy 2 bringing or causing joy —**joyfully** *adv* —**joyfulness** *n*

joyless /jóyləss/ *adj* lacking in warmth or happiness —**joylessly** *adv* —**joylessness** *n*

joyous /jóyəss/ *adj* (*literary*) 1 full of joy, especially of a fervent and unrestrained nature 2 making people happy or joyful —**joyously** *adv* —**joyousness** *n*

joypop /jóy pop/ (**-pops, -popping, -popped**) *vi* to take illicit drugs occasionally rather than habitually (*slang*) —**joypopper** *n*

joyriding /jóy rīding/ *n* a crime involving stealing a car and driving it dangerously at high speed —**joyride** *n, vi* —**joyrider** *n*

⚡**joystick** /jóystik/ *n* 1 the control lever of an aircraft or of a small motor-powered vehicle 2 a hand-held control stick that allows a player to control the movements of a cursor on a VDU screen or a symbol in a video game

⚡**jp** *abbr* Japan (*in Internet addresses*)

JP *abbr* Justice of the Peace

J particle *n* PHYS = **J/psi particle**

⚡**JPEG** /jáy peg/ *n* a format for encoding high-resolution graphic images as computer files for storage and transmission. Full form **Joint Photographic Experts Group**

Jpn *abbr* 1 Japan 2 Japanese

J/psi particle *n* an unstable elementary particle of the meson group. It has a large mass, about 6,000 times that of an electron, and is thought to be formed from charmed quarks. [*J* + *psi* the 23rd letter of the Greek alphabet]

jr *abbr* junior

Jr *abbr* 1 Jeremiah 2 Junior

JSD *abbr* Doctor of Juristic Science [Latin *Juris Scientiae Doctor*]

⚡**JSYK** *abbr* just so you know (*in e-mails*)

⚡**JTLYK** *abbr* just to let you know (*in e-mails*)

Juan Carlos /wáan kaár loss/ (*b.* 1938) king of Spain (1975–)

Juan de Fuca, Strait of /jōō ən də fyōōkə/ body of water between S Vancouver Island, Canada, and NW Washington State. Length: 160 km/100 mi.

Juárez /waár ez/, **Benito Pablo** (1806–72) Mexican statesman and national hero

Juba /jōōbə/ city in S Sudan. Population: 114,980 (1993).

Jubbulpore /júbb'l poor/ former name for **Jabalpur**

jube /joob/ *n* ANZ a fruit-flavoured chewy sweet (*informal*) [Mid-20C. Shortening of JUJUBE.]

jubilant /jōōbilənt/ *adj* feeling or expressing great delight over a success, achievement, or victory [Mid-17C. < Latin *jubilant-*, present participle of *jubilare* 'call out, shout for joy'.] —**jubilantly** *adv*

Jubilate /jōōbi laáti, yōōbi laá tay/ *n* Psalm number 100, which is sung as a canticle in the Roman Catholic and Anglican churches

jubilation /jōōbi láysh'n/ *n* uninhibited rejoicing in the celebration of a victory or success [14C. < Latin *jubilation-* < *jubilare* 'call out, shout for joy'.]

jubilee /jōōbili, jōōbi lée/ *n* 1 SPECIAL ANNIVERSARY a significant anniversary of an important event such as a wedding or a monarch's succession 2 JOYFUL TIME a time or season of celebration 3 YEAR OF INDULGENCE SET BY THE POPE in the Roman Catholic Church, a period set by the Pope, traditionally every 25 years, in which forgiveness of sins is granted in return for acts of piety or repentance 4 YEAR OF RESTITUTION in Jewish history, a year of restoration or restitution that was proclaimed every 50 years by a countrywide blast of trumpets [14C. Via French *jubilé* < Latin *jubilaeus (annus)* '(year) of jubilee' < Hebrew *yōbēl* 'ram'; from the ram's horn with which the year of jubilee was proclaimed.]

Jubran /joo braán/ = **Gibran, Kahlil**

Jud. *abbr* 1 Judges 2 Judith

Judaea /joo dée ə/, **Judah** /jōōdə/ historic region in SW Asia, incorporating parts of present-day Israel and the West Bank

Judaeo- *prefix* Jewish, Judaism ○ *Judaeo-Christian* [Via Latin *Judaeus* (see JEW)]

Judaeo-Christian /joo dáyo/ *adj* in the shared tradition of Judaism and Christianity

Judah = **Judaea**

Judaic /joo dáy ik/, **Judaical** /-ik'l/ *adj* belonging to or relating to Judaism or Jews [15C. Via Latin *Judaicus* < Greek *Ioudaikos* < *Ioudaios* (see JEW).] —**Judaically** *adv*

Judaica /joo dáy ikə/ *npl* the Jewish religion, customs, and culture, or artefacts and historical and literary materials that relate to them [Early 20C. < Latin, form of *Judaicus* (see JUDAIC).]

Judaical *adj* JUDAISM = **Judaic**

Judaise *vti* = **Judaize**

Judaism /jōō day izəm/ *n* 1 the religion of the Jews that has its basis in the Bible and the Talmud 2 Jewish religious practices, customs, and culture as a way of life [14C. Via ecclesiastical Latin < Greek *Ioudaismos* < *Ioudaios* (see JEW).] —**Judaistic** /jōō day ístik/ *adj*

Judaize /jōō day īz/ (**-izes, -izing, -ized**), **Judaise** (**-ises, -ising, -ised**) *v* 1 *vi* to adopt the Jewish religion and Jewish cultural practices 2 *vt* to give something a Jewish character [Late 16C. Via ecclesiastical Latin *judizare* < Greek *ioudizein* < *Ioudaios* (see JEW).] —**Judaization** *n*

judas /jōōdəss/, **judas hole** *n* a peephole or very small window, e.g. in a door [Mid-19C. After JUDAS.]

Judas /jōōdəss/ *n* 1 one of Jesus Christ's disciples who betrayed him by identifying him with a kiss to the Jewish leaders in exchange for thirty pieces of silver (Luke 22) 2 a traitor, especially somebody who betrays a close friend or a cause or belief (*literary*)

Judas tree *n* a leguminous tree whose purplish-red flowers come out before the leaves. Native to: Europe, Asia. *Cercis siliquastrum.* [Mid-17C. After JUDAS, from the popular notion that he hanged himself from this tree.]

judder /júddər/ *vi* to shake or vibrate violently and rapidly or to move while shaking ○ *The car juddered along for a few more yards.* ■ *n* a violent, rapid vibration or shaking motion [Mid-20C. An imitation of the sound.]

Jude /jood/ *n* 1 one of the twelve apostles of Jesus Christ, the brother of James and author of the Book of Jude in the Bible 2 the last epistle of the Bible, probably written in the late 1st century AD

Judeo- *prefix US* = **Judaeo-**

Judezmo /jōō dézmō/ *n* LANGUAGE = **Ladino** *n.* 1 [< Ladino, 'Jewish']

Judg. *abbr* Judges

judge /juj/ *n* 1 SENIOR LAWYER a lawyer of high rank who supervises court trials, instructs juries, and pronounces sentence 2 ADJUDICATOR a person, sometimes one of several, appointed to assess entries or performances in a competition and decide on the winner or winners 3 SOMEBODY GIVING AN INFORMED OPINION an evaluator of quality, or somebody who can give an informed opinion on something ○ *a good judge of character* 4 JEWISH WARRIOR LEADER in Jewish history, any of a succession of warrior leaders who each temporarily held supreme power in Israel between Joshua's death and Saul's succession ■ *v* (**judges, judging, judged**) 1 *vt* ACT AS A LEGAL JUDGE to act as the judge of a legal case 2 *vt* BE JUDGE IN A CONTEST to act as a judge in a competition or, as an adjudicator, pronounce officially on the entries 3 *vti* ASSESS to assess the quality of something or estimate probabilities ○ *Each proposal has to be judged on its individual merits.* 4 *vt* CONSIDER to form an opinion of somebody or something, especially after thought or consideration ○ *She was judged to have the best qualifications.* 5 *vti* ESTIMATE to measure by guesswork, using the eye or some other sense as a rough guide ○ *You can't always judge people's ages by their voices.* 6 *vt* CONDEMN to criticize or condemn somebody on moral grounds [12C. Via Old French *juge* < Latin *judex* 'somebody who speaks the law' < *jus* 'law, right'.] —**judger** *n*

judge advocate *n* an officer appointed to oversee the proceedings and advise on points of law at a court martial

judgement *n* = **judgment**

Judges /júјiz/ *n* a book of the Bible that tells the story of the Israelites from Joshua's death in the 13th century BC to Samuel's birth in the 11th century BC (+ *singular verb*)

judgment /júјmənt/, **judgement** *n* **1 VERDICT** the decision arrived at and pronounced by a court of law **2 OBLIGATION RESULTING FROM A VERDICT** an obligation such as a debt that arises as a result of a court's verdict, or a document setting out an obligation of this kind (*often used before a noun*) **3 DECISION OF A JUDGE** the decision reached by one or more judges in a contest ○ *The judgment of the panel must be regarded as final.* **4 DECISION ON A DISPUTED MATTER** an opinion formed or decision reached in the case of a disputed, controversial, or doubtful matter **5 DISCERNMENT OR GOOD SENSE** the ability to form sound opinions and make sensible decisions or reliable guesses ○ *someone with shrewd commercial judgment* **6 OPINION** an opinion formed or given after consideration ○ *a snap judgment* **7 ESTIMATE BASED ON OBSERVATION** an estimate of something such as speed or distance, made with the help of the eye or some other sense **8 JUDGING OF** the judging of a case or a contest **9 DIVINE PUNISHMENT** a misfortune regarded as a divine punishment for folly or sin (*archaic or humorous*) ○ *The defeat was regarded as a judgment from God on the leader's pride.* **10 ACT OF MAKING A STATEMENT** the mental act of making or understanding a positive or negative proposition about something, e.g. in 'a chihuahua is a dog' or 'a lobster is not an insect' [13C. < Old French *jugement* < *jugier* 'to judge' < Latin *judicare* (see JUDICATURE).]

Judgment *n* **1** in Roman Catholic belief, God's decision at the instant of somebody's death on whether the soul is to be saved or damned **2** in Jewish, Islamic, and Christian traditions, God's final judgment of humankind (**the Last Judgment**), which is to take place at the end of the world

judgmental /juj mént'l/ *adj* tending to judge or criticize the conduct of other people —**judgmentally** *adv*

Judgment Day *n* in Jewish, Christian, and Islamic belief, the day at the end of the world when God delivers his final judgment on humankind

judicable /jóodikəb'l/ *adj* capable of being or liable to be tried in a court of law [Mid-17C. < late Latin *judicabilis* < *judicare* (see JUDICATURE).]

judicatory /jóodikətəri/ *adj* **judicatory, judicatorial RELATING TO A LEGAL SYSTEM** relating to a legal system or to judges or judgment ■ *n* (*plural* **-ries**) (*formal*) **1 LEGAL SYSTEM** a system of administering justice **2 LAW COURT** a court of law [Late 16C. < Latin *judicare* (see JUDICATURE).]

judicature /jóodikəchər, joo díkəchər/ *n* **1 ADMINISTERING OF JUSTICE** the administration or dispensation of justice **2 JUDGE'S OFFICE** the power or office of a judge, or a judge's tenure of office **3 JUDGE'S AREA OF AUTHORITY** the area of authority of a judge or a court of law **4 BODY OF JUDGES** a body of judges or of people holding judicial power **5 SYSTEM OF LAW COURTS** a law court or a system of law courts [Mid-16C. < medieval Latin *judicatura* < Latin *judicare* 'to judge' < *judex* (see JUDGE).]

judicial /joo dísh'l/ *adj* **1 RELATING TO JUDGES** relating or belonging to a body of judges or to the system that administers justice **2 RELATING TO COURT JUDGMENTS** relating to judges in performance of their duties or to judgment in a court of law **3 ENFORCED BY A LAW COURT** enforced or sanctioned by a court of law **4 APPROPRIATE TO JUDGES** appropriate to a judge or expected of a judge [14C. < Latin *judicialis* < *judicium* 'legal proceedings' < *judex* (see JUDGE).] —**judicially** *adv*

judicial review *n* **1** a reassessment or re-examination by judges of a decision or proceeding by a lower court or a government department **2** a constitutional right of the court system in some countries to review and cancel government legislation that is held to have been passed illegally

judicial separation *n* LAW = **legal separation**

judiciary /joo díshəri, -díshi əri/ *n* (*plural* **-ies**) **1 GOVERNMENT BRANCH DISPENSING JUSTICE** the branch of a country's central administration that is concerned with dispensing justice **2 COURT SYSTEM** a country's system of law courts **3 JUDGES IN GENERAL** a country's body of judges ■ *adj* **RELATING TO JUDGES** relating to courts, judges, and judgment [15C. < Latin *judiciarius* < *judicium* (see JUDICIAL).]

judicious /joo díshəss/ *adj* showing wisdom, good sense, or discretion, often with the underlying aim of avoiding trouble or waste ○ *a little judicious pruning* [Late 16C. < French *judicieux* < Latin *judicium* (see JUDICIAL).] —**judiciously** *adv* —**judiciousness** *n*

Judith /jóodith/ *n* **1** in the Bible, a Jewish woman who saved the city of Bethulia by beheading the general Holofernes **2** a book in the Roman Catholic version of the Bible and the Protestant Apocrypha that tells the story of Judith's heroism in saving her people

judo /jóodō/ *n* a Japanese martial art in which opponents use balance and body weight, with minimal physical effort, to throw or pin each other or hold each other in a lock [Late 19C. < Japanese, 'gentle way'.] —**judoist** *n*

judogi /joo dṓgi/ *n* the costume worn by participants in judo [Mid-20C. < Japanese.]

judoka /jóo dō kaa/ (*plural* **-kas** *or* **-ka**) *n* an expert or practitioner in the art of judo [Mid-20C. < Japanese.]

judy /jóodi/ (*plural* **-dies**), **Judy** (*plural* **-dies**) *n* a girl or woman (*dated slang; sometimes offensive*) [Early 19C. Pet form of the name *Judith*.]

Judy /jóodi/ *n* the wife of Punch in a traditional Punch-and-Judy puppet show

jug /jug/ *n* **1 POURING CONTAINER** a deep container for liquids that has a handle and has its rim shaped into a lip or spout for pouring **2** *US* **LARGE LIQUID-CONTAINER** a large container for liquids, typically of earthenware or glass, with a handle and a narrow mouth usually closed with a cork **3 LIQUID CONTAINED IN A JUG** the quantity of liquid held in a jug **4 GOOD HANDHOLD** a large, strong, and dependable handhold on a rock climb **5 PRISON** prison or jail (*humorous*) **6 OFFENSIVE TERM** an offensive term for a woman's breast (*slang*) ■ *vt* (**jugs, jugging, jugged**) **1 JAIL** to put somebody in jail (*humorous*) **2 STEW IN AN EARTHENWARE POT** to stew meat in a deep earthenware pot [15C. < ?]

jugate /jóo gayt, jóogət/ *adj* **1** describes leaves that consist of paired leaflets attached to a single leaf stalk **2** describes heads or busts on coins that are superimposed in profile one on another [Late 19C. < Latin *jugatus*, past participle of *jugare* 'join together'.]

jug band *n* a blues or jazz band featuring jugs as instruments, played by blowing across their rims

Jugendstil /yóogənd shteel/ *n* the equivalent in Germany and Austria of art nouveau, a style of design that influenced all the visual arts in Europe during the late 19th and early 20th centuries [Early 20C. < German, < *Jugend* 'youth' (title of a magazine) + *Stil* 'style'.]

jugged hare *n* a stew of hare meat, traditionally cooked in an earthenware pot or casserole dish

juggernaut /júggər nawt/ *n* **1** a very large long lorry for transporting goods in bulk **2** a force that is relentlessly destructive, crushing, and insensitive [Mid-19C. < JUGGERNAUT.]

Juggernaut *n* a form of the Hindu god Krishna [Mid-17C. < Sanskrit *Jagannātha* 'protector of the world'.]

juggins /júgginz/ *n* an offensive term for somebody regarded as easy to trick or naive (*dated*) [Late 19C. < ?]

juggle /júgg'l/ (**-gles, -gling, -gled**) *v* **1** *vti* **KEEP SEVERAL OBJECTS IN THE AIR** to keep several objects in motion in the air at the same time by throwing them and catching them in quick succession **2** *vt* **HAVE DIFFICULTY HOLDING** to keep adjusting your grip or stance in order to balance objects being held ○ *I was juggling coffee and a plate of sandwiches in one hand.* **3** *vt* **FIT INTO A SCHEDULE** to try to make something fit into a satisfactory pattern or schedule by careful arranging ○ *parents juggling careers and family life* **4** *vt* **REARRANGE DATA** to manipulate data in order to deceive ○ *juggling the company's books* [14C. Back-formation < JUGGLER.] —**jugglery** *n*

juggler /júgglər/ *n* a person who can juggle, especially a professional entertainer who juggles [Pre-12C. Via Old French *jogler* < Latin *joculator* 'jester' < *jocus* 'joke'.]

jugular /júggyoolər/ *adj* **1** relating to or situated close to the neck or throat **2** describes a fish that has pelvic fins in front of the pectoral fins ■ *n* ANAT = **jugular vein** [Late 16C. < late Latin *jugularis* < Latin *jugulum* 'collarbone, throat' < *jugum* 'yoke'.] ◇ **go for the jugular** to make an attack that is intended to be highly destructive and conclusive (*informal*)

jugular vein *n* any one of four pairs of veins in the neck that drain blood from the head

jugum /jóogəm/ *n* **1** a lobe that sticks out from the base of the forewing of some insects in order to couple it with the hind wing during flight **2** a pair of opposed leaflets in a compound leaf [Mid-19C. < Latin, 'yoke'.]

juice /jooss/ *n* **1 LIQUID FROM FRUIT OR VEGETABLES** the extractable liquid that is contained in fruit or vegetables, or a drink made from this liquid ○ *lemon juice* **2 BODILY FLUID** a natural fluid or secretion of the body **3 LIQUID FROM COOKING MEAT** the liquid that comes from a piece of meat when it is roasted or otherwise cooked **4 LIQUID EXTRACT** any liquid extract or essence, especially from biological material ○ *Pure penicillin was isolated from mould juice.* **5 FUEL OR POWER** fuel, especially petrol for a vehicle, or electricity (*informal*) **6 ALCOHOL** alcoholic drink (*slang*) **7** *US* **MONEY OR INFLUENCE** money or influence gained through or utilized in the service of corrupt or criminal activities (*slang*) **8** *US* **LOAN OR INTEREST** money lent at an extortionate rate of interest, or the interest extorted (*slang*) ■ *vt* (**juices, juicing, juiced**) **EXTRACT JUICE FROM** to extract the juice from a fruit or vegetable [13C. Via French *jus* < Latin, 'broth, sauce, vegetable juice'.] ◇ **stew in your own juice** to have to suffer the consequences of your actions without any help from others

juice up *vt* to make something or somebody more lively, exciting, or interesting (*slang*) ○ *juice the party up by bringing in a live band*

juice bar *n* a café serving freshly prepared fruit juices and other healthy food and drinks

juice box *n US* a small box of fruit juice for one person that is sold with a straw attached to it

juice extractor *n* HOUSEHOLD = **juicer**

juicehead /jóoss hed/ *n US* a heavy drinker or an alcoholic (*slang*)

juicer /jóossər/ *n* a kitchen appliance, usually electrically powered, for extracting the juice from fruit or vegetables

juicy /jóossi/ (**-ier, -iest**) *adj* **1 SUCCULENT** containing a lot of juice **2 PROVIDING INTEREST** repaying effort by providing plenty of stimulation and food for thought ○ *I like getting my teeth into a nice juicy problem.* **3 TITILLATING** containing scenes or details that evoke interest because of their sensational nature (*informal*) **4 LUCRATIVE** extremely profitable or productive (*informal*) **5 SEXUALLY DESIRABLE** desirable in a sexual way (*slang*) —**juicily** *adv* —**juiciness** *n*

jujitsu /joo jítsoo/, **jiujitsu** *n* a Japanese system of unarmed fighting devised by the samurai or the martial art based on it (*often used before a noun*) [Late 19C. < Japanese *jūjutsu* 'gentle skill'.]

juju /jóo joo/ *n* **1 OBJECT WITH SUPPOSED MAGICAL POWERS** an object revered among some West African peoples for the magical powers that it is thought to possess **2 SUPPOSED MAGIC POWER OF A JUJU** the magical or supernatural power associated with a juju **3 SPELL EFFECTED BY A JUJU** a spell put on something or somebody by means of a juju [Early 17C. < Hausa.] —**jujuism** *n*

jujube /jóo joob/ *n* **1 FRUIT** a plum-shaped dark-red fruit that is sometimes dried like a date **2 TREE** a tree that bears jujubes. Native to: Asia. *Ziziphus jujuba.* **3 CHEWY SWEET** a chewy, usually fruit-flavoured, sweet made of gum or gelatin [14C. Directly or via French < medieval Latin *jujuba* < Greek *ziziphos*.]

jukebox /jóok boks/ (*plural* **-boxes**) *n* a coin-operated machine that automatically plays selected records or compact discs

juke joint *n US* a roadside cafe where music is played on a jukebox for dancing (*informal*)

jukskei /yóok skay/ *n S Africa* an outdoor game in which skittle-shaped pegs are thrown at stakes set into the ground [Early 19C. < Afrikaans, 'yoke pin'.]

Jul. *abbr* July

julep /jóolip, jóo lep/ *n* BEVERAGES = **mint julep** [14C. Via Old French or medieval Latin < Persian *gulāb* 'rosewater'.]

Julian /jóoli ən/ *adj* **1** relating to or typical of Julius Caesar **2** relating to or reckoned according to the Julian calendar

Julian (of Norwich) /jóoli ən əv nórrich/ (1342–1416) English mystic

Juliana /jóoli áanə/ (*b.* 1909) queen of the Netherlands (1948–80)

Julian calendar /jóoli ən-/ *n* the twelve-month solar calendar introduced by Julius Caesar in 46 BC, consisting of 365 days, with an extra day every four years. ◊ **Gregorian calendar**

⚡**Julian date** *n* in computer programming, a date expressed as the number of days since 1 January of the current year

julienne /jòoli én, zhòoli-/ *adj* CUT THINLY cut into long thin matchstick strips ■ *n* CLEAR SOUP WITH VEGETABLE STRIPS a clear soup containing vegetables cut into thin matchstick strips ■ *vt* (-ennes, -enning, -enned) CUT INTO THIN STRIPS to cut vegetables into thin matchstick strips [Early 18C. < French, < the name *Jules* or *Julien*.]

Juliet /jòoli ət/ *n* 1 a small inner natural satellite of Uranus, discovered in 1986 2 a code word for the letter 'J', used in international radio communications

Juliet cap *n* a round close-fitting crocheted net cap for women, sometimes set with pearls [Early 20C. < the heroine of Shakespeare's *Romeo and Juliet*.]

Julius II /jòoli əss/ (1443–1513) pope (1503–13)

Jullundur /júlləndər/ city in NW India. Population: 519,530 (1991).

July /jòo lī/ (*plural* -lies) *n* the seventh month of the year in the Gregorian calendar, made up of 31 days [12C. Via Anglo-Norman *julie* < Latin *Julius* (referring to Julius CAESAR).]

Jumada /jòo máadə/ *n* in the Islamic calendar, either the fifth or the sixth month in the year, made up of 30 or 29 days [Late 18C. < Arabic *jumādā* < *jamada* 'freeze'.]

jumar /jòomər/ *n* **jumar clamp** a clip or clamp used in rock-climbing or ice-climbing that runs freely up a slack rope but tightens round the rope in response to weight applied from below ■ *vi* to climb using jumar clamps [Mid-20C. < ?]

jumbal /júmb'l/, **jumble** *n* a light sweet crisp biscuit or cake, traditionally made in the shape of a ring or an S [Early 17C. < ?]

jumbie /júmbi/ *n* *Carib* a spirit or ghost [Late 19C. < Kongo *zumbi* 'fetish'.]

jumble[1] /júmb'l/ *vti* (-bles, -bling, -bled) 1 PUT THINGS OUT OF ORDER to mix things together indiscriminately so that they are no longer neat or ordered 2 MUDDLE THINGS UP MENTALLY to muddle things up in the mind ■ *n* 1 MUDDLED MASS an untidy or disorganized mass of objects, images, or ideas ○ *His thoughts were all in a jumble.* 2 ARTICLES FOR JUMBLE SALE unwanted possessions that people hand over for selling at a jumble sale. US term **rummage** *n.* 2 [Early 16C. < ?]

jumble[2] *n* FOOD = **jumbal**

jumble sale *n* a sale of clothes and other goods, chiefly second-hand, usually to raise money for charity or for some specific purpose. US term **rummage sale**

jumbo /júmbō/ *n* 1 something or somebody that is extra large (*often before nouns*) ○ *a jumbo helping* 2 AIR = **jumbo jet** [Early 19C. < the name of a very large elephant at London Zoo, later sold to Barnum and Bailey's circus.]

jumboize /júmbō īz/ (-izes, -izing, -ized), **jumboise** (-ises, -ising, -ised) *vt* to increase the size of a ship, especially a tanker, by inserting a prefabricated central section

jumbo jet *n* a large wide-bodied commercial aircraft capable of carrying several hundred passengers

jumbuck /júm buk/ *n* *Aus* a sheep (*informal*) [Early 19C. < ?]

Jumna /júmnə/ river in N India flowing south into the River Ganges. Length: 153 km/95 mi.

jump /jump/ *v* 1 *vi* LEAVE A SURFACE WITH BOTH FEET to bend the knees and push the whole body quickly up off a surface or the ground 2 *vt* GET OVER to pass from one side of something to the other by jumping ○ *jump the fence* 3 *vti* JUMP AS A SPORTING SKILL in various sports such as horse-riding and skiing, to perform a movement in which the whole body leaves the ground ○ *Make sure you have your skis parallel before you attempt to jump.* 4 *vi* MOVE QUICKLY to move quickly in a particular direction ○ *Jump in and I'll give you a lift home.* 5 *vi* MAKE A MENTAL LEAP to make an illogical mental leap ○ *His mind keeps jumping from one thing to another.* 6 *vi* MOVE JERKILY to move jerkily, in contrast to progressing smoothly or keeping still ○ *Interference was making the picture jump.* 7 *vi* START IN SURPRISE to give a start of surprise or fright ○ *The noise made me jump.* 8 *vi* RISE SUDDENLY to rise or increase suddenly by a large amount ○ *The Nikkei Index jumped 35 points.* 9 *vti* LEAVE THE RAILS to come off the rails accidentally (*refers to trains*) 10 *vi* MAKE A PARACHUTE DESCENT to make a descent by parachute from an aircraft 11 *vt* AMBUSH to ambush somebody by attacking unexpectedly (*informal*) ○ *The guy jumped me.* 12 *vt* VIOLATE AN ENGAGEMENT BY LEAVING to abscond or desert in violation of an engagement, contract, or undertaking 13 *vti* OMIT to omit the intervening parts of something, especially passages of a text, sometimes inadvertently 14 *vi* OBEY IMMEDIATELY to carry out orders immediately (*informal*) ○ *When she speaks, you jump.* 15 *vt* OFFENSIVE TERM an offensive term meaning to have sexual intercourse with a woman (*slang*) 16 *vt* DRIVE THROUGH TRAFFIC LIGHTS to fail to stop at a set of traffic lights (*informal*) 17 *vt US* BOARD ILLEGALLY to board a train surreptitiously with the intention of travelling on it without paying (*informal*) 18 *vt* USURP OWNERSHIP to usurp ownership of a piece of land, especially a mining claim, on the grounds that the owner has abandoned it or not fulfilled the conditions of ownership 19 *vti* RAISE A BID to raise a partner's bid to indicate a strong hand 20 *vt* PASS A PIECE OVER AN OPPONENT'S PIECE in draughts, to capture an opponent's playing piece by passing a piece over it into an empty square ■ *n* 1 JUMPING MOVEMENT a jumping movement or the distance jumped ○ *a winning jump of 26 feet* 2 OBSTACLE OR APPARATUS USED IN JUMPING a specially constructed obstacle or other piece of apparatus for use in competitive jumping, e.g. a fence in steeplechasing or a platform from which skiers take off 3 LEAP OF A PARTICULAR DISTANCE IN SPORTS in field events, a leap of a particular distance or height, or the action of attempting or completing such a leap 4 SUDDEN RISE a sudden steep rise or increase in an amount ○ *a jump in property prices* 5 START OF SURPRISE an involuntary movement made when startled 6 SUDDEN TRANSITION a sudden transition or change of direction, representing a break in continuity or logical progression 7 PARACHUTE DESCENT a descent by parachute from an aircraft 8 CAPTURE OF AN OPPONENT'S PIECE in draughts, the move of jumping an opponent's piece and capturing it 9 DISCONTINUOUS NUMERIC INCREASE a point at which a function or a curve undergoes a sudden or major transition [Early 16C. < ?] —**jumpable** *adj* ◇ **jump to it** to hurry up and carry out orders or instructions (*informal*) ◇ **take a running jump** used dismissively as an instruction to go away (*informal*)

jump at *vt* to accept a chance or opportunity eagerly ○ *would jump at the chance*

jump on *vt* to make a sudden physical or verbal attack on somebody (*informal*) ○ *Pupils were jumped on for getting a question like that wrong.*

jump up *vi* to get to your feet immediately

jump ball *n* a restarting of play in a basketball game, in which the referee throws the ball up high between two opponents who each try to tip it towards a team member

jump bid *n* in bridge, a bid of one more than is necessary to raise the existing bid

jump cut *n* in film and television, a sudden abrupt change from one sequence to another

jumped-up *adj* having been promoted from a lower position and therefore not entitled to show arrogance or self-importance (*informal insult*)

jumper[1] /júmpər/ *n* 1 PERSON OR ANIMAL THAT JUMPS a person or animal that jumps or is trained to jump competitively 2 *Can* SLEDGE a sledge for use over rough terrain 3 BORING TOOL a heavy drill used in quarrying that, because of its repeated-impact action, has a jumping motion 4 WIRE FOR MAKING A CONNECTION a short length of wire for making an electrical connection or for cutting out part of a circuit

jumper[2] /júmpər/ *n* 1 a knitted garment for the top half of the body, usually with sleeves, that is pulled on over the head. US term **sweater** *n.* 1 2 *US* CLOTHING = **pinafore** *n.* 1 [Mid-17C. Probably < *jump* 'man's short coat', alteration of *jupe*, via Old French < Arabic *jubba*.]

jumper cables *npl US* ELEC ENG = **jump leads**

jumping bean *n* a seed of some Mexican bushes when it contains the larva of a small moth. The larva feeds on the seed pulp, making the seed move jerkily.

jumping gene *n* a genetic element that can move from place to place within the chromosomes of an organism

jumping jack *n* 1 a firework that has its gunpowder packed into a pleated tube, so that it jumps along the ground as each segment explodes 2 *US* a warm-up exercise in which the legs are flung apart while the hands are clapped or swung above the head

jumping mouse *n* a rodent that looks like a mouse but has long hind legs and a long tail. Native to: northern temperate regions. Family: Zapodidae.

jumping-off place *n* a very remote place, especially a point at the edge of civilization beyond which lies the wilderness

jumping-off point *n* 1 a place from which to begin a journey 2 a basis on which to begin an enterprise or a discussion 3 = **jumping-off place**

jumping plant louse *n* a small insect that is a weak flier but has enlarged hind legs for jumping. Family: Psyllidae.

jumping spider *n* a spider that fixes on its prey using an enlarged central pair of eyes, then pounces by rapidly extending its legs. Family: Salticidae.

jump jet *n* a jet aircraft that takes off and lands vertically

jump jockey *n* a jockey specially trained to jump horses over fences and ride in steeplechases, as distinct from a flat-racing jockey

jump leads *npl* a pair of electric cables used to start the engine of a vehicle that has a dead battery by connecting it to an external live battery. US term **jumper cables**

jump-off *n* 1 the start of something such as a race or a military attack 2 a final extra round of a showjumping competition, in which all the riders who have had clear rounds compete against the clock —**jump off** *vi*

jump pass *n* a pass that one basketball player makes to another while in mid-jump

jump rope *n US* = **skipping rope**

jump seat *n* a folding seat between the front and back seats of a taxicab or similarly large vehicle or a seat like this for temporary use in an aircraft or train

jump shot *n* a basketball shot made with one or both hands by a player who is at the highest point of a jump —**jump shooter** *n*

jump-start *vt* to start a motor vehicle by attaching it to an external battery using jump leads ■ *n* a jump-starting of a motor vehicle

jump suit *n* 1 a woman's casual one-piece suit combining top and trousers 2 a protective zip-up one-piece suit combining long trousers and jacket, worn by a parachutist when jumping

jumpy /júmpi/ (-ier, -iest) *adj* 1 very nervous or anxious 2 moving jerkily or erratically —**jumpily** *adv* —**jumpiness** *n*

jun. *abbr* junior

Jun. *abbr* June

Junagadh /joo náa gaad/, **Jūnāgadh** city in W India. Population: 130,484 (1991).

junco /júngkō/ (*plural* -cos) *n* a small finch with greyish plumage, a pink bill, and white outer tail feathers. Native to: North America. Genus: *Junco*. [Early 18C. Via Spanish < Latin *juncus* 'rush (plant)'.]

junction /júngksh'n/ *n* 1 PLACE WHERE THINGS JOIN a place where two or more objects, e.g. roads or railroad lines, join, meet, or cross 2 *UK* MOTORWAY EXIT a numbered point on a motorway at which traffic may join or leave 3 ELECTRICAL CONNECTION a connection between electrical wires or cables 4 LAYER BETWEEN METALS a layer of metal separating two metals with different properties and serving as a contact between them, especially in a thermocouple 5 SEMICONDUCTOR CONTACT a point in a semiconductor device at which regions with different electrical properties come into contact with each other 6 ACT OF JOINING the joining of things, or their joined state [Early 18C. < Latin *junction-* < *jungere* 'join'.] —**junctional** *adj*

junction box *n* an enclosed and protected box inside which electrical circuits are interconnected or branched for distribution

juncture /júngkchər/ *n* 1 POINT IN TIME a point in time, especially an important or critical one 2 JOINING PLACE a place where two or more things join (*formal*) 3 JOINING OF THINGS the joining of one thing with another, or their joined state (*formal*) 4 BREAK BETWEEN WORDS the break between one spoken word and another, or the pronunciation features that help a listener to recognize the break, distinguishing, e.g., between 'grey day' and 'grade A' [14C. < Latin *junctura* 'joint' < *jungere* 'join'.]

June /joon/ *n* the sixth month of the year in the Gregorian calendar, made up of 30 days [Pre-12C. Via French *juin* < Latin *(mensis) junius* '(month) of Juno'.]

Juneau /jòonō/ port and capital of Alaska, in the extreme south of the state. Population: 30,191 (1998 estimate).

Juneberry /jòon berri/ (*plural* -ries) *n* 1 TREES = **serviceberry** *n.* 1 2 FOOD = **serviceberry** *n.* 2 [Mid-19C. < the month when it blooms.]

June bug *n* a large brown flying beetle that is seen

in late spring and feeds on leaves. Native to: North America. Subfamily: Melolonthinae.

Juneteenth /jo͞on te͞enth/ *n US* a holiday commemorating the day on which enslaved labourers in Texas learned of the Emancipation Proclamation, which granted them freedom. Date: 19 June. [Blend of JUNE + NINETEENTH]

Jung /yo͝ong/, **Carl Gustav** (1875–1961) Swiss psychiatrist —**Jungian** *adj, n*

Jung Chang /jo͝ong cháng/ (*b.* 1952) Chinese-born US writer

Jungfrau /yo͝ong frow/ mountain in S Switzerland. Height: 4,158 m/13,642 ft.

Junggar Pendi /jo͝ong gáir péndi/, **Dzungaria** /dzo͝ong gáiri ə, zo͝ong-/ region in NW China, west of the Republic of Mongolia and east of Kazakhstan

jungle /júng g'l/ *n* 1 **TROPICAL FOREST** an area of tropical rainforest covered with vegetation so dense that it is largely impenetrable 2 **THICKLY COVERED AREA** any area covered with dense vegetation 3 **TANGLE** a tangled or confused mass 4 **COMPLEX MATTER** a frustratingly or impenetrably complex system 5 **HARSH PLACE** a harsh environment characterized by fierce competitiveness or struggle for survival 6 **SYNTHESIZED MUSIC GENRE** a rhythmically complex form of electronic dance music that is largely instrumental and shows the influence of jazz, dub, and techno. ◊ **drum and bass** [Late 18C. Via Hindi *jaṅgal* 'wasteland' < Sanskrit *jāṅgala* 'dry'.]

jungle fever *n* a severe form of malaria common in tropical regions, especially Southeast Asia

jungle fowl *n* a wild bird related to pheasants that is thought to be the ancestor of the modern domestic fowl. Native to: Asia. Genus: *Gallus.*

jungle gym *n US* LEISURE = **climbing frame**

jungle juice *n* alcohol, especially home-made, poor quality, or very strong alcohol (*informal*)

jungle telegraph *n* the communication and spreading of news, information, and rumours by word of mouth (*informal*)

junior /jo͞oni ər/ *adj* 1 **RELATING TO YOUTH** relating to youth, childhood, or children 2 **junior, Junior YOUNGER** younger in age, especially when referring to the younger of two family members, e.g. father and son, who share the same name 3 **LOW IN RANK** of relatively low rank or little experience ○ *a junior minister* 4 **SMALLER** smaller than the standard or expected size 5 **FOR CHILDREN BETWEEN 7 AND 11** relating to or involving schoolchildren between the ages of 7 and 11 ○ *junior school* 6 *US* **OF THIRD-YEAR STUDENTS** relating to or involving students in the third year of high school or college in the United States ■ *n* 1 **YOUNGER PERSON** a person younger than another being referred to ○ *My sister is three years my junior.* 2 **LOW-RANKING PERSON** somebody of relatively low rank or little experience 3 **STUDENT IN JUNIOR SCHOOL** a pupil in a junior school 4 **CHILD** a young person, especially somebody younger than a teenager 5 **junior, Junior** *US* **WAY OF ADDRESSING BOY** a form of address used for a boy or young man, affectionately to the son in a family or condescendingly to a stranger (*informal; offensive in some contexts*) 6 *US* **THIRD-YEAR STUDENT** a student in the third year of high school or college in the United States 7 **BARRISTER** in England and Australia, a barrister who has not yet qualified as a Queen's Counsel [13C. < Latin, 'younger' < *juvenis* 'young'.]

junior college *n US* a college offering students a two-year course of study that either terminates in an associate degree or corresponds to the first two years at a four-year college

junior common room *n* in some colleges and universities, a room provided for general use by students, as distinct from the senior common room, reserved for staff

junior high, junior high school *n US* a school that is intermediate between primary school and high school, embracing years six or seven to eight or nine

junior middleweight *n* 1 in professional boxing, a weight class that is lighter than middleweight and heavier than welterweight, for boxers weighing between 67 and 71 kg/147 and 154 lb 2 a boxer who fights at junior middleweight

junior miss *n US* a girl or young woman in her teenage years (*dated*)

junior school *n* a state-run school for children between the ages of 7 and 11

juniper /jo͞onipər/ *n* 1 an evergreen tree or shrub with small purple cones resembling berries that yield juniper oil. Genus: *Juniperus.* 2 the oil from juniper berries. Use: to flavour gin. [14C. < Latin *juniperus.*]

juniper tar, juniper tar oil *n* an oily brown substance. Source: wood of a species of juniper. Use: antiseptic soaps, pharmaceuticals.

junk[1] /jungk/ *n* 1 **RUBBISH** discarded things, or things regarded as worthless or causing clutter (*informal*) 2 **USED GOODS FOR SALE** second-hand goods offered for sale (*informal*) 3 **CHEAP STUFF** cheap and poorly made goods (*informal*) 4 **NONSENSE** meaningless or worthless talk (*informal*) 5 **HEROIN** narcotics, especially heroin (*slang*) ■ *vt* **DISCARD** to get rid of something as useless (*informal*) [14C. < ?]

junk[2] /jungk/ *n* a flat-bottomed sailing boat, popular in Chinese waters, that is high at the stern and has squarish sails, each supported on several battens [Mid-16C. Via Portuguese *junco* or Dutch *jonk* < Malay *jong.*]

junk bond *n* an investment bond that offers the possibility of a high return but at a high risk

Junker /yo͝ongkər/ *n* 1 an aristocratic landowner in Prussia, with great political power 2 an offensive term for a German army officer or official regarded as arrogant and dictatorial [Mid-16C. < German *Junker* 'young lord'.] —**Junkerdom** *n* —**Junkerism** *n*

Junkers /yo͝ongkərz/, **Hugo** (1859–1935) German aircraft engineer

junket /júngkit/ *n* 1 **EXPENSES-PAID TRIP** a trip taken at somebody else's expense, especially one taken by a politician at public expense 2 *US* **AMUSING OCCASION** an outing, excursion, or party of any kind 3 **SET MILK DESSERT** a dessert made from milk that has been set with rennet ■ *v* 1 *vi* **HAVE EXPENSES-PAID TRIP** to go on an expenses-paid trip, especially one paid for with public money 2 *vti US* **HOLD PARTY** to hold a party or entertain somebody with a party [14C. < French *jonquette* < *jonc* 'rush (plant)' < Latin *juncus.*] —**junketer** *n*

junk food *n* food that does not form part of a well-balanced diet, especially highly processed, high-fat savoury snack items eaten in place of or in addition to regular meals

junkie /júngki/, **junky** (*plural* **-ies**) *n* 1 a drug addict, especially somebody addicted to heroin (*slang*) 2 somebody whose interest in or liking for something resembles an addiction (*informal*) ○ *a football junkie*

junk mail *n* unsolicited mail, especially advertising material

junkman /júngk man/ *n US* = **rag-and-bone man** (*dated*)

junk shop *n* 1 a shop selling a variety of secondhand goods 2 a second-rate antique shop

junky /júngki/ *adj* (**-ier, -iest**) of very low quality or very little value ■ *n* = **junkie**

junkyard /júngk yaard/ *n* a place where junk is collected before being sold or processed

Juno /jo͞onō/ (*plural* **-nos**) *n* 1 in Roman mythology, the queen of the gods and wife of Jupiter. Greek equivalent **Hera** 2 a woman of queenly bearing and imposing beauty —**Junoesque** /jo͞onō ésk/ *adj*

junr, Junr *abbr* junior

junta /júntə, ho͝ontə, jo͝ontə/ (*plural* **-tas**) *n* 1 **NEW RULERS AFTER COUP** a group of military officers who have taken control of a country following a coup d'état (+ *singular or plural verb*) 2 **SECRET GROUP** a small group of people, especially one secretly assembled for a common goal (+ *singular or plural verb*) 3 **LATIN AMERICAN GOVERNMENT BODY** in some parts of Central and South America, a council or other legislative body within the government (*takes a singular or plural verb*) [Early 17C. < Spanish or Portuguese, < Latin *jungere* 'join'.]

junto /júntō, ho͝ontō, jo͝ontō/ *n* = **junta** *n.* 2 [Early 17C. Alteration.]

Jupiter /jo͞opitər/ *n* 1 in Roman mythology, the king of the gods. Greek equivalent **Zeus** 2 the largest planet in the solar system, fifth in order from the Sun. See table at **planet** [12C. < Latin, < *Jov-* 'Jove' + *pater* 'father'.]

Juppé /zho͞oppay/, **Alain** (*b.* 1945) French statesman

Jura /jo͞orə/ 1 island of the Inner Hebrides, W Scotland. Population: under 200 (1998). Area: 272 sq. km/105 sq. mi. 2 department of Franche-Comté, in east-central France. Area: 4,999 sq. km/1,930 sq. mi.

jural /jo͝orəl/ *adj* 1 relating to law or the administration of justice 2 relating to rights or obligations (*formal*) [Mid-17C. < Latin *jur-* 'law'.] —**jurally** *adv*

Jura Mountains mountain range between France and Switzerland. Highest peak: Crêt de la Neige 1,718 m/5,636 ft.

Jurassic /jo͞o rássik/ *n* the period of geological time during which dinosaurs flourished and birds and mammals first appeared, extending from 210 million years to 140 million years ago [Mid-19C. < French *Jurassique* < *Jura* 'Jura'.] —**Jurassic** *adj*

jurat /jo͝or at/ *n* 1 a closing statement on an affidavit, giving details of the parties to it, the witnesses, and the place and time of signing 2 a magistrate in France or the Channel Islands [15C. < medieval Latin *juratus* 'sworn man' < Latin *jurare* (see JURY).]

juridical /jo͞o ríddik'l/, **juridic** /-ríddik/ *adj* relating to judges, to the administration of the law, or to law in general —**juridically** *adv*

juridical days *npl* days on which law courts are in session

jurisconsult /jo͝oriss kón sult/ *n* an expert in law who gives advice on legal matters, especially in relation to civil or international law [Early 17C. < Latin *jurisconsultus* 'skilled in law'.]

jurisdiction /jo͝oriss díksh'n/ *n* 1 **LEGAL AUTHORITY** the authority to enforce laws or pronounce legal judgments 2 **RANGE OF LEGAL AUTHORITY** the area over which legal authority extends 3 **AUTHORITY** power or authority generally [13C. Via Old French < Latin *jurisdiction-* < *jus* 'law' + *diction-* 'saying'.] —**jurisdictional** *adj* —**jurisdictionally** *adv* —**jurisdictive** *adj*

jurisprudence /jo͝oriss pro͞od'nss/ *n* 1 **THEORY OF LAW** the philosophy or science of law 2 **LEGAL SYSTEM** a system of law, or the body of laws applied in a particular country or state 3 **BRANCH OF LAW** a branch of law, or the law as it applies to a particular area of life —**jurisprudent** *adj, n* —**jurisprudential** /jo͝orispro͞o dénsh'l/ *adj* —**jurisprudentially** *adv*

jurist /jo͝orist/ *n* 1 an expert in the science or philosophy of law, especially Roman or civil law 2 a student or graduate of law [15C. Directly or via French < medieval Latin *jurista* < Latin *jus* 'law'.] —**juristic** /joor ístik/ *adj* —**juristical** *adj* —**juristically** *adv*

juror /jo͝orər/ *n* 1 a member of a jury, especially in a court of law 2 a swearer of an oath, e.g. an oath of allegiance (*formal or literary*) [14C. Via Anglo-Norman *jurour* and Old French *jureor* < Latin *jurator* < *jurare* (see JURY).]

jury /jo͝ori/ (*plural* **-ries**) *n* 1 a group of people, usually twelve people, chosen to give a verdict on a legal case that is presented before them in a court of law 2 a group of people who judge a competition [14C. < Anglo-Norman, Old French *juree* 'oath, inquest' < Latin *jurare* 'swear' < *jus* 'law'.]

jury box *n* the part of a court where the jury sits

jury duty *n* LAW = **jury service**

juryman /jo͝orimən/ (*plural* **-men** /-mən/) *n* a man who is a member of a jury in a court of law

jury nullification *n* the decision that a jury is, for whatever reason, incapable of sitting

jury-rig (**jury-rigs, jury-rigging, jury-rigged**) *vt* to build something in a makeshift way or fit something out, especially a boat, with makeshift equipment

jury service *n* service as a member of a jury in a court of law. US term **jury duty**

jurywoman /jo͝ori wo͝omən/ (*plural* **-en** /-wimin/) *n* a woman who is a member of a jury in a court of law

jus gentium /júss jénti əm/ *n* international law [< Latin, 'law of nations']

jus sanguinis /júss sáng gwiniss/ *n* the principle in law according to which children's citizenship is determined by the citizenship of their parents [< Latin, 'right of blood']

jussive /júsiv/ *adj* GRAM = **imperative** *adj.* 3 [Mid-19C. < Latin *juss-*, past participle of *jubere* 'command'.]

jus soli /júss sōl ī/ *n* the principle in law according to which children's citizenship is determined by the place of their birth [< Latin, 'right of soil']

just /just/ *adv* 1 **IN THE IMMEDIATE PAST** a very short time ago ○ *The train has just left.* 2 **AT THIS MOMENT** indicating that somebody will begin doing something or something will start happening now (*used also with 'about to' and 'going to'*) ○ *I was just about to tell you.* 3 **ONLY** only or merely the thing, amount, or situation mentioned ○ *This is just a warning.* **4 BARELY** by only a small degree or margin ○ *I arrived just in time.* **5 USED FOR EMPHASIS** used to emphasize a statement, usually in order to express an emotion ○ *It's just plain wrong.* **6 EXACTLY** precisely the thing, amount, or situation mentioned ○ *It's just what you need.* **7 EXPRESSING AGREEMENT** used as a comment on a statement that has just been made, in order to express agreement ○ *It was exactly what we needed. Wasn't it just!* ■ *adj* **1 FAIR AND IMPARTIAL** acting with fairness and impartiality **2 MORALLY CORRECT** done, pursued, or given in accordance with what is morally right **3 REASONABLE** valid or reasonable [14C. Via French < Latin *justus* < *jus* 'law, right'.] —**justly** *adv* —**justness** *n* ◇ **just about** used to indicate that something is the case, but only by a very small degree or amount ◇ **just a moment** *or* **second** *or* **minute** used to ask someone to wait for a short time ◇ **just like that** without great effort, trouble, or inconvenience ○ *I can't move to another country just like that.* ◇ **just now 1** a very short time ago **2** at this very moment ◇ **just so 1** used to express agreement with or confirmation of a statement that has just been made **2** done or arranged precisely ○ *They wanted the room decorated just so.*

justice /jústiss/ *n* **1 FAIRNESS** fairness or reasonableness, especially in the way people are treated or decisions are made **2 APPLICATION OF LAW** the legal system, or the act of applying or upholding the law **3 VALIDITY** validity in law **4 GOOD REASON** sound or good reason **5** LAW = **justice of the peace** [12C. Via French < Latin *justitia* < *justus* (see JUST).] ◇ **bring somebody to justice** to arrest somebody to be tried in a court of law ◇ **do justice to somebody** *or* **something 1** to deal with somebody *or* something fairly **2** to convey the true qualities, especially the merits, of somebody *or* something ◇ **do yourself justice** to display your own abilities fully or perform to your full potential (*often in the negative*)

justice of the peace *n* somebody without legal training or qualifications who is appointed to judge minor criminal cases, perform marriages, administer oaths, and refer cases to higher courts

justiciable /ju stíshi əb'l/ *adj* **1** able or required to be tried in a court of law **2** able to be settled by applying the principles of law —**justiciability** /ju stíshi ə bílləti/ *n*

justiciary /ju stíshi əri/ *adj* relating to the administration of law ■ *n* (*plural* -**ies**) a judge or other officer who administers the law

justifiable /jústi fī əb'l/ *adj* capable of being shown as reasonable or merited according to accepted standards —**justifiability** /jústi fī ə bílləti/ *n* —**justifiableness** *n* —**justifiably** *adv*

justifiable homicide *n* killing that is deemed to be lawful, especially because it is carried out in self-defence or as the only way to prevent a crime

justification /jústifi káysh'n/ *n* **1 SOMETHING THAT JUSTIFIES** something, e.g. a reason or circumstance, that justifies an action or attitude **2 GIVING OF REASONS** the act of justifying something **3 ALIGNMENT OF MARGINS** adjustment of the lengths of spaces between and within words in text in order to make both left and right margins align **4 CHRISTIAN DOCTRINE** the Christian belief that people are absolved from all sin if they believe in Jesus Christ [14C. Directly or via French < late Latin *justification-* < *justificare* (see JUSTIFY).]

justificatory /jústifi kaytəri/, **justificative** /-kaytiv/ *adj* serving or acting to justify something [Late 16C. < medieval Latin *justificatorius* < late Latin *justificare* (see JUSTIFY).]

justify /jústi fī/ (-**fies**, -**fying**, -**fied**) *vt* **1 MAKE REASONABLE** to serve as an acceptable reason or excuse for something (*often passive*) **2 GIVE SOMEBODY REASON** to give somebody an acceptable reason for taking a particular action (*often passive*) **3 EXPLAIN** to give a reason or explanation why something was done **4 ALIGN MARGINS OF** to adjust the lengths of spaces between and within words in text in order to make both the left and right margins align **5 FREE FROM SIN** to free somebody from sinfulness through faith in Jesus Christ or by the grace of Jesus Christ **6 GIVE LEGAL REASON FOR** to provide a good reason in law for something, especially for committing the offence that is the subject of a criminal charge [14C. Via French *justifier* < late Latin *justificare* 'act justly, justify' < Latin *justus* (see JUST).]

Justinian I /ju stínni ən/ (482–565) emperor of Rome (527–65). Known as **Justinian the Great**

just-in-time *n* a manufacturing and stock-control system in which goods are produced and delivered as they are required

jut /jut/ *vti* (**juts**, **jutting**, **jutted**) to stick out, or make something stick out, especially beyond the surface or edge of something ■ *n* something that sticks out [Mid-16C. Alteration of JET¹.] —**jutting** *adj*

jute /joot/ *n* **1** coarse fibre from the bark of an Asian tree. Use: sacking, rope. **2** either of two plants of the linden family that provide jute. Native to: Asia. Genus: *Corchorus.* [Mid-18C. Via Bengali *jhuto* < Sanskrit *jūṭaḥ* 'matted hair'.]

Jute /joot/ *n* a member of a Germanic people from around the Rhine estuary who invaded SE England during the fifth century AD [Pre-12C. < Latin *Jutae* < Germanic.] —**Jutish** *adj*

Jutland /jútlənd/ peninsula in N Europe, comprising all of mainland Denmark and part of N Germany. Length: 338 km/210 mi.

Juvenal /joóvənəl/ (65?–AD 128?) Roman satirist

juvenescent /joóvə néssn't/ *adj* (*literary*) **1** youthful or young-looking **2** growing out of infancy and into childhood [Early 19C. < Latin *juvenescere* 'grow up'.] —**juvenescence** *n*

juvenile /joóvə nīl/ *adj* **1 YOUTHFUL** young or youthful **2 RELATING TO YOUNG PEOPLE** relating to, intended for, or suitable for young people ○ *a juvenile court* **3 IMMATURE** immature or childish ○ *juvenile behaviour* **4 NOT YET MATURE** describes a plant or animal that has not yet reached maturity **5 SEXUALLY IMMATURE** describes a bird that has developed contour feathers but is not yet sexually mature **6 FROM WITHIN THE EARTH** describes water or gas that has risen to the surface from within the earth for the first time ■ *n* **1 YOUNGSTER** a young person **2 IMMATURE ANIMAL OR PLANT** an animal or plant that has not yet reached maturity **3 ACTOR SUITED TO YOUTHFUL PARTS** an actor who plays youthful roles **4 BOOK FOR CHILDREN** a book intended to be read by young people [Early 17C. < Latin *juvenilis* < *juvenis* 'young'.] —**juvenilely** *adv* —**juvenileness** *n*

juvenile delinquent *n* a young person who habitually breaks the law, especially somebody repeatedly charged with vandalism or other antisocial behaviour —**juvenile delinquency** *n*

juvenile hormone *n* a hormone present in insect larvae that regulates the form of the larva after each moult

juvenilia /joóvə nílli ə/ *npl* works produced in a writer's, artist's, or composer's youth, especially before a mature style has developed

juvenility /joóvə nílləti/ *n* (*plural* -**ties**) **1 JUVENILE QUALITY** juvenile quality or state **2 IMMATURITY** foolishly immature behaviour **3 ACT OF IMMATURITY** an act of foolishly immature behaviour (*often plural*)

juxtapose /júkstə pōz/ (-**poses**, -**posing**, -**posed**) *vt* to place two or more things together, especially in order to suggest a link between them or emphasize the contrast between them [Mid-19C. < French *juxtaposer* < Latin *juxta* 'close' + French *poser* (see POSE).] —**juxtaposition** /júkstəpə zísh'n/ *n* —**juxtapositional** *adj*

Jy *symbol* jansky

Jyaistha /jī ástə/ *n* in the Hindu calendar, the third month of the year, made up of 29 or 30 days and falling in approximately May to June

K k

k[1] /kay/ (*plural* **k's**), **K** (*plural* **K's** *or* **Ks**) *n* the 11th letter of the English alphabet, representing a consonant sound

k[2] *abbr* **1** kilo- **2** knight **3** knit **4** knot

K[1] /kay/ (*plural* **K's** *or* **Ks**) *n* **1** something shaped like a letter 'K' **2** a kilometre (*informal*)

K[2] *symbol* **1** kaon **2** kelvin **3** kinetic energy **4** one thousand **5** one thousand pounds **6** potassium

⚡**K**[3] *abbr* **1** kilobyte **2** kilometre **3** king **4** knight **5** Köchel (*preceding a number in Köchel's catalogue of Mozart's works*) **6** kopeck **7** krona **8** krone **9** kwacha **10** kyat

K2 /kay tooˈ/ second-highest mountain in the world, in the Karakorum Range of the W Himalayas. Height: 8,611 m/28,251 ft.

ka /kaa/ *n* in ancient Egypt, the soul of a dead person, said to be able to reside in a statue of that person after death [Late 19C. < Egyptian.]

Kaaba /kaˈaba/ *n* a square building inside the great mosque in Mecca, containing a sacred stone (**Black Stone**) said to have been given by God. It is the most holy site in the Islamic religion. [Early 17C. < Arabic, 'the square house'.]

kabala *n* JUDAISM = **kabbalah**

Kabardian /kə baˈardi ən/ *n* a language spoken to the north of the Caucasus Mountains in S European Russia, belonging to the Abkhaz-Adyghean group of Caucasian languages. Native speakers: 300,000. [Late 19C. < Russian *Kabarda*, place name.] —**Kabardian** *adj*

kabbalah /kə baˈalə, kábbələ/, **kabbala, kabala, cabala, cabbala** *n* **1** a body of mystical Jewish teachings based on an interpretation of the Hebrew scriptures as containing hidden meanings **2** a set of secret or mystical beliefs [Early 16C. Via medieval Latin < rabbinical Hebrew *qabbalah* 'tradition' < *qibbel* 'receive'.] —**kabbalism** *n* — **kabbalist** *n*

kabbalistic /kábbə lístik/ *adj* **1** relating to the teachings of the kabbalah **2** mysterious or esoteric —**kabbalistically** *adv*

kabinett /kábbi nét/, **Kabinett** *n* the lowest grade of high-quality German table wine, typically dry to medium dry [Early 20C. < German *Kabinettwein* 'cabinet wine'; because it was kept in a special cellar.]

kabob *n* FOOD = **kebab**

kabuki /kə booˈki/ *n* traditional Japanese drama in which male actors play both male and female parts [Late 19C. < Japanese *ka* 'song' + *bu* 'dance' + *ki* 'art'.]

Kabul /kaˈabool/ capital of Afghanistan, in the centre of the country. Population: 700,000 (1993 estimate).

Kabyle /kə bílˈ/ (*plural* **-byles** *or* **-byle**) *n* **1** a member of a Berber people who live in NE Algeria **2** a Berber language spoken in NE Algeria. Native speakers: 3 million. [Mid-18C. Probably < Arabic *kabāˈil* 'tribes'.] — **Kabyle** *adj*

kaccha *n* = **kuccha**

kachina /kə cheeˈnə/ (*plural* **-nas**) *n* **1** any one of the spirits believed by the Native North American Hopi people to be the ancestors of human beings **2** a representation of a kachina, usually either a carved wooden doll or a costumed performer in a ceremonial dance [Late 19C. < Hopi *kacina* 'supernatural'.]

kadaitcha *n* ETHNOL = **kurdaitcha**

Kádár /kaˈad aar/, **János** (1912–89) Hungarian statesman. Born János Csermanck

Kaddish /káddish/ (*plural* **-dishim** /kə díshim/) *n* a prayer recited at the close of the sections of Jewish religious services, and by close relatives of a deceased person at times of mourning and anniversaries of the death [Early 17C. < Aramaic *qaddīs* 'holy'.]

Kaduna /kə dooˈnə/ capital of Kaduna State, north-central Nigeria. Population: 309,600 (1992).

kaffeeklatsch /káffay klachˈ/, **kaffee klatch** *n* US = **coffee klatsch** [Late 19C. < German, < *Kaffee* 'coffee' + *Klatsch* 'gossip'.]

Kaffir /káffər/, **Kafir** *n* **1** S Africa TABOO TERM a highly offensive term for a Black African person (*taboo*) **2 Kaffir, kaffir** OFFENSIVE TERM an offensive term referring to a person who is not a Muslim (*slang*) **3** XHOSA the Xhosa language (*dated*) [Mid-16C. < Arabic *kāfir* 'unbeliever, infidel'.]

kaffir corn *n* a variety of sorghum cultivated in southern Africa for its grain, used to make beer and as a fodder crop (*sometimes offensive*)

kaffiyeh *n* US = **keffiyeh**

Kafir *n* = **Kaffir**

Kafiri /káffəri/ *n* a language of NE Pakistan and Afghanistan, belonging to the Dardic branch of Indic [Early 20C. See KAFFIR.]

Kafka /káfkə/, **Franz** (1883–1924) Czech novelist

Kafkaesque /káfkə éskˈ/ *adj* **1** relating to or typical of the work of Franz Kafka **2** characterized by seemingly pointless, impersonal, and often disturbing over-complexity

kaftan /káf tan/, **caftan** *n* **1** a full-length tunic or robe for men, usually made of rich fabric, worn chiefly in E Mediterranean countries **2** a Western imitation of the kaftan, often brightly coloured and worn by men and women [Late 16C. Via Turkish *kaftan* < Persian *kaftān*.]

Kafue /kaa fooˈay/ river in central Zambia. Length: 1,570 km/980 mi.

Kagoshima /kággə sheeˈmə/ seaport on the coast of S Kyushu Island, Japan. Population: 536,752 (1990).

kagu /kaˈa goo/ *n* a large greyish flightless bird, now nearly extinct. Native to: New Caledonia. *Rhynochetos jubatus*. [Mid-19C. < Melanesian.]

kahikatea /kíˈka teˈe ə/ *n* a tall evergreen tree that is an important source of timber. Native to: New Zealand. *Podocarpus dacryioides*. [Early 19C. < Maori.]

kahki incorrect spelling of **khaki**

Kahlo /kaˈal ōˈ/, **Frida** (1907–54) Mexican painter

kahuna /kə hoònə/ *n* **1** US an important or influential person (*informal*) ○ *the big kahuna* **2** a Hawaiian priest or traditional healer [Late 19C. < Hawaiian.]

kai /kī/ *n* NZ food [Mid-19C. < Maori.]

kaiak *n* CANOEING, SHIPPING = **kayak**

Kaieteur Falls /kí ə toor-/ waterfalls in central Guyana, on the River Potaro. Height: 225 m/740 ft.

kaif *n* DRUGS = **kif**

Kaifeng /kíˈ fúng/ city in east-central China. Population: 507,763 (1990).

Kaikoura /kī koòrə/ town on the NE coast of the South Island, New Zealand. Population: 2,040 (1991).

Kaikoura Ranges twin mountain ranges near the coast of the NE of the South Island, New Zealand. Highest peak: Tapuaenuku 2,885 m/9,465 ft.

kail *n* FOOD = **kale**

kainite /kíˈ īt, káyn-/ *n* a variously coloured mixed sulphate and chloride mineral containing potassium and magnesium. Use: source of potassium, fertilizer. [Mid-19C. < German *Kainit* < Greek *kainos* 'new'.]

Kaipara Harbour /kī paˈa raa-/ wide inlet of the Pacific Ocean in the NW of the North Island, New Zealand. Area: 520 sq. km/201 sq. mi.

Kairouan /kī ər waˈan/ city in N Tunisia. Population: 102,600 (1994).

kaiser /kízər/ *n* any one of the former German, Austrian, or Austro-Hungarian emperors, especially the German emperor Wilhelm II, who ruled Germany during World War I [Old English *cāsare* < Greek *kaisar* < Latin *Caesar*, family name of Gaius Julius CAESAR] —**kaiserdom** *n* — **kaiserism** *n*

Kaiser /kízər/, **Georg** (1878–1945) German dramatist

kaiserin /kízərin/ *n* a German empress or the wife of a German emperor [Late 19C. < German, feminine of KAISER.]

kaizen /kíˈ zén/ *n* a Japanese business philosophy advocating the need for continuous improvement in a person's personal and professional life [Late 20C. < Japanese, 'improvement'.]

kaka /kaˈa kaa/ *n* a parrot with a long grey bill and greenish-brown plumage. Native to: New Zealand. *Nestor meridionalis*. [Late 18C. < Maori.]

kaka beak *n* an evergreen climbing plant. Flowers: bright red, shaped like a parrot's beak. Native to: New Zealand. *Clianthus puniceus*. [After the KAKA, because the leaves of the plant resemble its beak]

Kakadu National Park /kaaka dooˈ-/ national park in the Northern Territory, Australia. Area: 20,000 sq. km/7,722 sq. mi.

kakapo /kaaka pōˈ/ (*plural* **-pos**) *n* a large rare flightless nocturnal parrot with green plumage. Native to: New Zealand. *Strigops habroptilus*. [Mid-19C. < Maori.]

kakemono /káki mónˈō/ (*plural* **-nos**) *n* a Japanese wall hanging in the form of a tall narrow scroll, weighted at the base with a roller and decorated with a painting or with a text in ornamental handwriting [Late 19C. < Japanese, < *kake-* 'hang' + *mono* 'thing'.]

Kabuki

kakistocracy /káki stókrəssi/ (*plural* **-cies**) *n* government by the most unscrupulous or unsuitable people, or a state governed by such people [Early 19C. < Greek *kakistos* 'worst'.]

kala-azar /kállə ə zaàr/ *n* a severe, often fatal, tropical fever caused by a parasite that enters the body via a sandfly bite [Late 19C. < Assamese, < *kala* 'black' + *āzār* 'disease'.]

Kalachakra /kaàlə chukrə/ *n* a mandala, traditionally constructed out of grains of sand, depicting Buddhist deities in a portrayal of time

Kalahari Desert /kállə haàri-/ dry and semidry region in southern Africa, occupying much of Botswana and parts of Namibia and South Africa. Area: 260,000 sq. km/100,000 sq. mi.

Kalahari Gemsbok National Park /-gémz bok-/ national park in NW South Africa. Area: 9,591 sq. km/3,703 sq. mi.

kalanchoe /kállən kõ i/ *n* a cultivated succulent plant often grown as a pot plant for its shiny leaves. Flowers: small, bright red, pink, or white, in clusters. Native to: tropical Africa. Genus: *Kalanchoe*. [Mid-19C. Via modern Latin < French, < Chinese *gālàncài*.]

Kalashnikov /kə láshni kof/ *n* a Russian-manufactured semi-automatic assault rifle that is widely used as a weapon among terrorists and paramilitary organizations [Late 20C. < Russian, after M. T. *Kalashnikov* (1919–), its developer.]

Kalat /kə laàt/, **Kalāt** town in W Pakistan. Population: 11,000 (1981 estimate).

kale /kayl/, **kail** *n* **1** VARIETY OF CABBAGE a hardy heartless variety of cabbage with dark green curly leaves. *Brassica oleracea acephala*. **2** *Scotland* CABBAGE cabbage of any kind **3** *US* MONEY money (*slang*) [14C. Scottish variant of COLE.]

kaleidoscope /kə līdaskõp/ *n* **1** OPTICAL TOY an optical toy consisting of a cylinder with mirrors and coloured shapes inside that create shifting symmetrical patterns when the end is rotated **2** COMPLEX SCENE OR PATTERN a complex, colourful, and shifting pattern or scene **3** COMPLEX SET OF EVENTS a complex set of events or circumstances [Early 19C. < Greek *kalos* 'beautiful' + *eidos* 'form'.] —**kaleidoscopic** /kə līdə skóppik/ *adj* —**kaleidoscopically** *adv*

kalends *npl* CALENDAR = **calends**

Kalevala /kaàlə vaàlə/ *n* in Finnish legend, the land of the folk hero Kaleva, whose exploits are recorded in Finnish folk tales

Kaleyard School /káyl yaard-/ *n* a group of Scottish writers, active from the late 19th to the early 20th centuries, who wrote romantic portrayals of life in the Scottish Lowlands [*Kaleyard* 'kitchen garden' < KALE; from their portrayal of local town life]

Kalgoorlie-Boulder /kalgoòrli-/ city in S Western Australia. Population: 28,087 (1996).

Kali /kaàli/ *n* a terrifying Hindu goddess who is the devourer of time [< Sanskrit]

~~kaliedoscope~~ incorrect spelling of **kaleidoscope**

kalif *n* ISLAM = **caliph**

kalifate *n* ISLAM = **caliphate**

Kalimantan /kálli mántən/ region of Indonesia, occupying S Borneo. Population: 10,470,800 (1995). Area: 542,700 sq. km/209,500 sq. mi.

kalimba /kə límbə/ *n* an African instrument consisting of a soundboard with tuned metal or bamboo bars of varying lengths that are plucked to give sound [Mid-20C. < Bantu.]

Kalinin /kə leènin/ former name for **Tver**

Kaliningrad /kə leènin grad/ city in W Russia. Population: 512,508 (1995).

Kaliyuga /kaàli yoògə/ *n* in Hindu philosophy, the age of decadence [< Sanskrit]

kallikrein /kálli krèe in, kə líkri in/ *n* an enzyme present in blood, urine, and body tissue that, when activated, dilates blood vessels

Kalmar /kál maar/ port in S Sweden. Population: 56,863 (1994).

kalmia /kálmi ə/ *n* an evergreen bush that belongs to the heath family and has poisonous leaves. Native to: North America. Genus: *Kalmia*. [Mid-18C. < modern Latin, after Pehr *Kalm* (1716–79), Swedish botanist.]

Kalmyck /kál muk/ (*plural* **-mycks** or **-myck**), **Kalmuk** /kálmik/ (*plural* **-muks** or **-muk**) *n* **1** a member of a people who live in SW Russia **2** a language spoken by the Kalmyck people, belonging to the Mongolian branch of Altaic. Native speakers: 150,000. [Early 17C. < Russian *Kalmyk*.] —**Kalmyck** *adj*

kalpa /kálpə/ *n* in Hindu philosophy, an immeasurably long period of time [< Sanskrit]

Kaluza /kə loòzə/, **Theodor F. E.** (1885–1945) German mathematician

kama /kaàmə/ *n* sexual pleasure as the third of the four Hindu goals of life [< Sanskrit *kāma* 'love, desire']

kamacite /kámmə sīt/ *n* an alloy of nickel and iron. Source: meteorites. [Late 19C. < Greek *kamak-* 'vine pole'.]

Kamakura /kaàmə koòrə/ city on SE Honshu Island, Japan. Population: 174,307 (1993).

kamala /kə maàlə/ *n* **1** a powder obtained from the seeds of a spurge. Use: dye, formerly to treat worm infestations. **2** a tree belonging to the spurge family whose seeds yield kamala. Native to: South and Southeast Asia. *Mallotus philippinensis*. [Early 19C. < Sanskrit, probably < Dravidian.]

Kama Sutra /kaàmə soòtrə/ *n* an ancient Sanskrit text giving instruction on the art of lovemaking [Late 19C. < Sanskrit, < *kāma* 'love, desire' + *sūtra* 'precept'.]

Kamchatka Peninsula /kam chátkə-/ peninsula of E Russia that separates the Sea of Okhotsk from the Bering Sea and the Pacific Ocean. Area: 518,000 sq. km/200,000 sq. mi.

kame /kaym/ *n* a ridge of sand and gravel left by a melting glacier [Late 18C. < Scottish *kame* 'comb'.]

kameez /kə meèz/ (*plural* **-meez** or **-meezes**) *n* S Asia a long garment like a tunic, often worn by men and women over tight trousers (**churidars**) or loose pleated trousers (**salwar**) [Early 19C. < Arabic *kamīs*.]

Kamet, Mount /kaàmet, kə máyt/ mountain in the Himalayas, in N India. Height: 7,756 m/25,447 ft.

kami /kaàmi/ (*plural* **-mi**) *n* any one of the sacred powers that are worshipped in the Shinto religion of Japan [Early 17C. < Japanese.]

kamikaze /kámmi kaàzi/ *n* **1** JAPANESE SUICIDE PILOT a World War II Japanese pilot trained for the suicide mission of flying an aircraft packed with explosives into an enemy target, often a ship (*often before nouns*) ○ *a kamikaze pilot* **2** JAPANESE AIRCRAFT an aircraft used by a kamikaze, especially one designed specifically for suicide crashes (*often before nouns*) **3** RECKLESS PERSON a reckless person, often somebody whose actions seem self-defeating or self-destructive (*informal*) ■ *adj* RECKLESS reckless, especially seeming to invite failure or self-destruction (*informal*) [Late 20C. < Japanese, 'divine wind'.]

Kamilaroi /kámmələ roy/ (*plural* **-roi**) *n* **1** a member of a group of Australian Aboriginal peoples living in NE New South Wales **2** the language of the Kamilaroi people, now extinct [Mid-19C. < Kamilaroi.] —**Kamilaroi** *adj*

Kampala /kam paàlə/ capital of Uganda, in the south of the country. Population: 773,463 (1991 estimate).

Kampuchea /kámpoò chèe ə/ former name for **Cambodia** —**Kampuchean** *n*, *adj*

kamseen, **kamsin** *n* METEOROL = **khamsin**

Kamtok /kám tok/ *n* an English-based pidgin language used in Cameroon [Late 20C. < shortening of CAMEROON[1] + *tok*, alteration of TALK.]

Kan. *abbr* Kansas

kana /kaànə/ *n* **1** one of the syllabic writing systems used in Japanese. ◊ **hiragana, katakana 2** any one of the syllabic symbols used in kana [Early 18C. < Japanese.]

kanamycin /kánnə míssin/ *n* an antibiotic obtained from a soil bacterium. Use: treatment of infections resistant to other antibiotics. [Mid-20C. < modern Latin *kanamyceticus*.]

Kananga /kə náng gə/ capital of Kasai-Occidental Region in the S Democratic Republic of Congo. Population: 393,030 (1994).

Kanarese /kánnə reèz/ *n* (*plural* **-rese**) **1** a member of a people living in SW India, mainly in the Kanara region **2** LANG = **Kannada** *n*. ■ *adj* **1** relating to the region of Kanara in SW India **2** relating to Kannada

Kanawha /kə naà wə/ river in west-central West Virginia. Length: 160 km/97 mi.

Kanazawa /kánnə zaàwə/ seaport on N Honshu Island, Japan. Population: 442,868 (1990).

kanban /kán ban/ *n* **1** in the just-in-time manufacturing and stock-control system, a card bearing an order for goods, sent to a manufacturer or supplier **2** MANUF = **just-in-time** [Late 20C. < Japanese, 'sign'.]

Kanchenjunga /kúchən júng gə/ third-highest mountain in the world, in the Himalayas, on the border between Nepal and India. Height: 8,598 m/28,209 ft.

Kandahar /kándə haàr/ capital of Kandahar Province, S Afghanistan. Population: 225,500 (1988 estimate).

Kandinsky /kan dínski/, **Wassily** (1866–1944) Russian painter

Kandy /kándi/ capital of Central Province, in central Sri Lanka. Population: 104,000 (1990 estimate).

Kane /kayn/, **Paul** (1810–71) Irish-born Canadian artist

kanga /káng gə/, **khanga** *n* a brightly coloured and decorated piece of cotton cloth that women wrap around the body as a garment, originally and especially in East Africa [Mid-20C. < Kiswahili.]

kangaroo /káng gə roò/ *n* (*plural* **-roos**) **1** MARSUPIAL WITH POWERFUL HINDQUARTERS a large leaping marsupial with powerful hind legs, short forelegs, and a long tail. Native to: Australia, New Guinea. Family: Macropodidae. **2** **Kangaroo** AUSTRALIAN RUGBY PLAYER a member of the Australian national Rugby League team ■ *npl* **1 Kangaroos** AUSTRALIAN RUGBY LEAGUE TEAM the Australian national Rugby league team (*informal*) **2 kangaroos** AUSTRALIAN SHARES shares in Australian companies (*slang*) ■ *vi* (**-roos, -rooing, -rooed**) MOVE JERKILY to make jerky progress in a car as a result of improper use of the clutch or accelerator (*informal*) [Late 18C. < an Aboriginal name.]

kangaroo court *n* an unofficial or mock court set up spontaneously for the purpose of delivering a judgement arrived at in advance, usually one in which a disloyal cohort's fate is decided

kangaroo grass *n* a tall Australian species of grass used for fodder. *Themeda australis*.

Kangaroo Island /káng gə roò-/ island off the coast of South Australia. Population: 4,288 (1996). Area: 4,351 sq. km/1,680 sq. mi.

kangaroo paw *n* a tall hardy plant with downy green and red flowers. Native to: Australia. Genus: *Anigozanthos*.

Kangaroo rat

kangaroo rat *n* a small nocturnal jumping rodent with a long tail and long hind limbs. Native to: deserts of the United States and Mexico. Genus: *Dipodomys*.

kangaroo vine *n* a climbing vine with shiny green or mottled leaves. Native to: Australia. *Cissus antarctica*.

kangha /kánghə/ *n* a comb worn by baptized Sikhs as a symbol of religious loyalty [< Punjabi]

KaNgwane /kaàəng gwaàn ay/ former homeland in NE South Africa

kanji /kánji, kaànji/ (*plural* **-ji** or **-jis**) *n* **1** a Japanese writing system that uses pictorial characters based largely on Chinese ideograms **2** any one of the characters used in the kanji writing system [Early 20C. < Japanese, < *kan* 'Chinese' + *ji* 'letter, character'.]

Kannada /kaànədə, kán-/ *n* a Dravidian language spoken in some states of S India. Native speakers: 44 million. [Mid-19C. < Kannada *Kannaḍa*.] —**Kannada** *adj*

Kano /ka̅a̅no̅, ka̅yno̅/ capital of Kano State, N Nigeria. Population: 699,900 (1992).

Kano Masanobu /ka̅nno̅ ma̅ssa no̅boo/ (1453–90) Japanese artist

Kano Motonobu /ka̅nno̅ mo̅to̅ no̅boo/ (1476–1539) Japanese artist

Kanpur /ka̅an poo̅r/, **Kānpur** city in N India, on the River Ganges. Population: 1,874,409 (1991).

Kans. *abbr* Kansas

Kansas /ka̅nzass/ state in the central United States. Capital: Topeka. Population: 2,594,840 (1997). Area: 213,109 sq. km/82,282 sq. mi. —**Kansan** *n, adj*

Kansas City 1 largest city in Missouri, in the W of the state. Population: 441,574 (1998 estimate). 2 city in NE Kansas, directly across the state line from Kansas City, Missouri. Population: 149,767 (1990).

Kansas City jazz *n* a style of big band jazz music characterized by blues motifs and a relaxed beat

Kant /kant/, **Immanuel** (1724–1804) German philosopher —**Kantian** *adj* —**Kantianism** *n*

kanzu /ka̅n zoo/ (*plural* **-zus**) *n* a long garment resembling a robe, usually white and with long sleeves, worn by men in East Africa [Early 20C. < Kiswahili.]

Kaohsiung /ko̅w shyo̅o̅ng/ city in SW Taiwan, on the Taiwan Strait. Population: 309,062 (1997 estimate).

kaolin /ka̅y əlin/, **kaoline** *n* a fine white clay. Use: porcelain, ceramics, medicines. [Early 18C. < Chinese *gāolíng* 'high hill', hill in Jiangxi province.]

kaolinite /ka̅y əli nīt/ *n* $Al_2Si_2O_5(OH)_4$ a white or grey aluminosilicate clay mineral. Source: kaolin, altered feldspars. —**kaolinitic** /-lə nít tik/ *adj*

kaon /ka̅y on/ *n* (*symbol* **K**) an unstable elementary particle produced as a result of high-energy particle collision [Mid-20C. < *K-meson*.]

kapellmeister /kə pél mīstər/ *n* the director of a modern choir or, formerly, the director of the orchestra, choir, or opera in the household of a German prince [Mid-19C. < German, < *Kapelle* 'court orchestra' + *Meister* 'master'.]

kaph /kawf/ *n* the 11th letter of the Hebrew alphabet [Early 19C. < Hebrew, 'the palm of the hand'.]

Kapil Dev /ka̅ppil de̅v/ (*b.* 1959) Indian cricketer

Kapiti /ka̅ppiti/ urban area in the SW of the North Island, New Zealand. Population: 30,004 (1996).

kapok /ka̅y pok/ *n* silky fibre obtained from the seed covering of a tropical tree. Use: stuffing and padding material. [Mid-18C. < Malay.]

kapok bush *n* a small deciduous tree. Flowers: bright, yellow. Native to: Australia. Genus: *Cochlospermum*.

Kaposi's sarcoma /kə po̅ziz-/ *n* a cancer of connective tissue that causes purplish-red patches on the skin, most commonly found in equatorial Africa and in AIDS patients [Late 19C. After M. K. *Kaposi* (1837–1902), Hungarian dermatologist.]

kappa /ka̅ppə/ *n* the 10th letter in the Greek alphabet [< Greek]

Kaprow /ka̅ppro̅/, **Allen** (*b.* 1927) US artist

kaput /kə po̅ot, ka po̅ot/ *adj* broken, incapacitated, or not functioning (*informal*) [Late 19C. Via German *kaputt* < French (*être*) *capot* '(be) without tricks in the game of piquet'.]

kara /ka̅rrə/ *n* a steel bangle worn by baptized Sikhs as a symbol of religious loyalty. ◊ **five Ks** [< Punjabi]

karabiner /ka̅rrə be̅enər/, **carabiner** *n* a large oval or D-shaped metal ring with a spring clip that allows it to be attached to ropes, pitons, and other items of mountaineering equipment [Mid-20C. < German *Karabinerhaken* 'spring-hook'.]

Karachay-Cherkessia /kə̅ru chī chair ke̅ssi ə/ autonomous republic in SW European Russia. Capital: Cherkessk. Population: 434,100 (1994). Area: 14,100 sq. km/5,444 sq. mi.

Karachi /kə ra̅achi/ seaport and largest city of Pakistan, in the south of the country. Population: 5,180,562 (1981).

karahi /ku rī/ *n* a round frying pan with two handles used to prepare balti, a dish typical of Pakistan cuisine [Mid-20C. < Hindi.]

Karaism /ka̅irə izəm/ *n* the beliefs of a Jewish denomination (**Karaites**) founded in the 8th century. Its members accept the Bible as the sole source of religious law and reject rabbinical interpretations. [Late 19C. < Hebrew *qērāīm* 'Karaites' < *qārā* 'to read'.] —**Karaite** *n*

Hulton-Deutsch Collection/Corbis

Herbert von Karajan

Karajan /ka̅rrə yaan/, **Herbert von** (1908–89) Austrian conductor

Kara-Kalpak /kə ra̅a kəl pa̅ak/ (*plural* **Kara-Kalpaks** or **Kara-Kalpak**) *n* a Turkic language spoken by the Kara-Kalpak people. Native speakers: 300,000. [Early 18C. < Kirghiz, < *kara* 'black' + *kalpak* 'cap'.] —**Kara-Kalpak** *adj*

Karakoram Range /ka̅rrə ka̅wrəm-/ mountain range in the W Himalayas, in south-central Asia. Highest peak: K2 8,611 m/28,250 ft.

karakul /ka̅rrək'l/, **caracul** *n* 1 soft curly black wool from Central Asian lambs. Use: for coats. 2 a hardy sheep from Central Asia, the lambs of which provide karakul [Mid-19C. < Russian, after an oasis in Uzbekistan and two lakes in Tajikistan.]

Kara Kul /ka̅rrəkoo̅l/ dual lake system in E Tajikistan. Area: 363 sq. km/140 sq. mi.

Karamanlis /ka̅rrə ma̅nlis/, **Constantine** (1907–98) Greek statesman

Karamea Bight /ka̅rrəmi ə-/ large bay on the NW coast of the South Island, New Zealand

karaoke /ka̅rrə o̅ki, ka̅rro-/ *n* a form of entertainment in which amateur singers sing popular songs accompanied by prerecorded music from a machine that may also display the words on a video screen [Late 20C. < Japanese, < *kara* 'empty' + *oke*, shortening of *ōkesutora* 'orchestra'.]

Kara Sea /ka̅arə-/ arm of the Arctic Sea, off the coast of N Siberian Russia. Area: 777,000 sq. km/300,000 sq. mi.

karat *n US* METALL = **carat** *n*. 2

karate /kə ra̅ati/ *n* a traditional Japanese form of unarmed combat, now widely popular as a sport, in which fast blows or kicks are used [Mid-20C. < Japanese, < *kara* 'empty' + *te* 'hand'.]

karateka /kə ra̅ati ka/ *n* an expert or practitioner in karate [< Japanese, 'karate person']

Karbala /ka̅arbələ/, **Karbalā'** city in central Iraq. Population: 296,705 (1987).

Karelian /kə re̅eli ən/ *n* 1 a dialect of Finnish spoken in the NE European region of Karelia that formerly belonged to Finland but is now an autonomous republic. Native speakers: 120,000. 2 somebody who comes from Karelia —**Karelian** *adj*

Karen /kə ré n/ (*plural* **-rens** or **-ren**) *n* 1 a member of a people who live mainly in S and E Myanmar 2 a Tibeto-Burman language spoken in S and E Myanmar. Native speakers: 2 million. [Mid-18C. < Burmese *ka-reng* 'wild, unclean man'.] —**Karen** *adj*

Kariba, Lake /kə re̅ebə/ artificial lake on the border between Zambia and Zimbabwe, created by the Kariba Dam across the River Zambezi. Area: 5,180 sq. km/2,000 sq. mi.

Karl-Marx-Stadt /ka̅arl ma̅arks shtaat/ former name for **Chemnitz**

Karloff /ka̅ar lof/, **Boris** (1887–1969) British actor. Born **William Henry Pratt**

Karlovy Vary /ka̅ar lawvi va̅ari/ city in the NW Czech Republic. Population: 56,292 (1991).

Karlsruhe /ka̅arls roo̅ ə/ city in SW Germany. Population: 277,700 (1994).

karma /ka̅armə/ *n* 1 EASTERN PHILOSOPHY the Hindu and Buddhist philosophy according to which the quality of people's current and future lives is determined by their behaviour in this and in previous lives 2 ATMOSPHERE the atmosphere radiated by a place, situation, person, or object (*informal*) 3 DESTINY destiny or fate in general [Early 19C. < Sanskrit *karman* 'fate, action'.] —**karmic** *adj*

Karnak /ka̅ar nak/ village in E Egypt on the River Nile, on the site of ancient Thebes

Karnataka /kər na̅atəkə/, **Karnātaka** state in S India. Capital: Bangalore. Population: 48,150,000 (1994). Area: 191,791 sq. km/74,051 sq. mi.

Karnatak music /kər na̅atək-/, **Karnatic music** /kər na̅atik-/ *n* the classical music of S India, which often accompanies dance

karoo /kə ro̅o/ (*plural* **-roos**) *n* a dry plateau in southern Africa

Karoo /kə ro̅o/, **Karroo** semidesert plateau regions in W Cape Province, South Africa. Area: 259,000 km/100,000 sq. mi.

kaross /kə ro̅ss/ *n* a blanket made of animal skins, used in southern Africa as either a cloak or a mattress [Mid-18C. < Afrikaans *karos*.]

Karpov /ka̅ar pov/, **Anatoly** (*b.* 1951) Russian chess player

Karratha /kə ra̅athə/ town on the western coast of Western Australia. Population: 10,057 (1996).

karri /ka̅rri/ *n* 1 durable wood from a eucalyptus. Use: building. 2 a tree that yields karri. Native to: Australia. *Eucalyptus diversifolia*. [Late 19C. < Aboriginal.]

Karroo = **Karoo**

karsey *n* = **karzy**

karst /kaarst/ *n* a limestone landscape, characterized by caves, fissures, and underground streams [Late 19C. < German *der Karst*, plateau region in Slovenia.] —**karstic** *adj*

Karttika /ka̅artika/ *n* in the Hindu calendar, the eighth month of the year, made up of 29 or 30 days and occurring about the same time as October to November

Kartvelian /kaart ve̅eli ən/ *n* a family of languages including Georgian, spoken in the region south of the Caucasus. Native speakers: 4 million. —**Kartvelian** *adj*

Karumba /kərů̅mbə/ port in NW Queensland, Australia, on the Gulf of Carpentaria. Population: 1,043 (1996).

karyo- *prefix* cell nucleus ○ *karyoplasm* [Via modern Latin < Greek *karuon* 'kernel']

karyogamy /ka̅rri ó̅ggəmi/ *n* the fusion of cell nuclei that occurs during fertilization —**karyogamic** /ka̅rri ə ga̅mmik/ *adj*

karyogram /ka̅rri ə gram/ *n* a photograph or diagram of the chromosomes of a cell in sequence

karyokinesis /ka̅rri o̅ki ne̅essiss, -kī-/ *n* BIOL = **mitosis** —**karyokinetic** *adj*

karyology /ka̅rri ólləji/ *n* the study of cell nuclei, especially with reference to chromosomes —**karyologic** /ka̅rri ə lójjik/ *adj* —**karyological** *adj* —**karyologist** *n*

karyolymph /ka̅rri ō limf/ *n* BIOL = **nuclear sap**

karyoplasm /ka̅rri ō plazəm/ *n* BIOL = **nucleoplasm** —**karyoplasmic** /ka̅rri ō plázmik/ *adj*

karyosome /ka̅rri ō so̅m/ *n* a thickened mass of chromatin in a cell nucleus

karyotype /ka̅rri ō tīp/ *n* 1 CHARACTERISTICS OF CELL CHROMOSOMES the appearance and characteristics of the chromosomes of a cell, especially size, number, and form 2 PHOTOMICROGRAPH OF CELL CHROMOSOMES a photomicrograph in which a cell's chromosomes are arranged according to size and classification ■ *vt* (**-types, -typing, -typed**) DETERMINE CELL'S KARYOTYPE to determine the karyotype of a cell —**karyotypic** /ka̅rri ō típpik/ *adj* —**karyotypical** *adj* —**karyotypically** *adv*

karzy /ka̅arzi/ (*plural* **-zies**), **karsey, kazi** (*plural* **-zis**) *n* a toilet (*slang*) [Mid-20C. Alteration of Italian *casa* 'house'.]

Kasavubu /ka̅ssə voo̅ boo/, **Joseph** (1913?–69) Congolese statesman

kasbah /ka̅z baa/, **casbah** *n* 1 in North Africa, the older part of a city or town, often the market area 2 in North Africa, a fortress or palace

kasha /ka̅shə/ *n* a dish of cooked buckwheat resembling porridge, originally from E Europe [Early 19C. < Russian.]

Kashmir /kash me̅er/ disputed territory in the N of the Indian subcontinent. Area: 222,236 sq. km/85,806 sq. mi.

Kashmir, Azad /-àä zad/ section of Kashmir under Pakistani control. Area: 1,680 sq. km/650 sq. mi.

Kashmiri /kash meèri/ *n* 1 somebody who comes from Kashmir 2 the Dardic official state language of Kashmir, also spoken in neighbouring areas. Native speakers: 5 million. —**Kashmiri** *adj*

kashruth /káshrəth, kash root'/, **kashrut** *n* 1 the body of Jewish laws that relate to the preparation and fitness of foods and to items such as textiles and ritual scrolls to be used by Jewish people 2 the fitness of an item for use by Jewish people, as determined by reference to kashruth [Early 20C. < Hebrew, 'fitness'.]

Kasparov /káspə rof/, **Garry** (*b.* 1963) Armenian chess player. Born **Garri Weinstein**

Kassala /kə sàälə/, **Kassalā** city in NE Sudan. Population: 234,270 (1993).

Kassel /káss'l/, **Cassel** city in west-central Germany. Population: 201,900 (1994).

kata /káttə/ *n* 1 a sequence of movements in some martial arts such as karate, used either for training or to demonstrate technique [Mid-20C. < Japanese, 'model, pattern'.]

katabatic /káttə báttik/ *adj* describes a wind that moves down a slope, produced by the cooling of air at higher altitudes [Late 19C. < Greek *katabatikos* < *katabainein* 'go down'.]

katabolism *n* BIOCHEM = **catabolism**

Katahdin, Mount /kə táä dən/ mountain in N Maine, United States. Height: 1,605 m/5,267 ft.

katakana /káttə kaànə/ *n* a syllabic form of writing in Japanese that is used principally to transliterate loanwords. ◊ **kana** *n.* 1, **hiragana** [Early 18C. < Japanese, < *kata* 'side' + KANA.]

Kathak /kúttak/ *n* a classical dance from N India that tells a story [Mid-20C. < Sanskrit *kathaka* 'storyteller' < *kathā* 'story'.]

Kathakali /kaàthə kaàli/ *n* a form of drama from S India that interprets stories from Hindu classical literature by combining dance and mime [Early 20C. < Malayalam, < Sanskrit *kathā* 'story' + Malayalam *kali* 'play'.]

Katharevousa /káthə révvoòssə/ *n* a form of modern Greek, used in literature as opposed to everyday speech and writing, that employs some of the features of classical Greek. ◊ **Demotic** *n.* 1 [Early 20C. < Greek *kathareuousa* < *katharos* 'pure'.]

Katherine /káthrən/ town in north-central Northern Territory, Australia. Population: 7,979 (1996).

Katherine Gorge series of sandstone gorges in the Northern Territory, Australia, cut by the River Katherine

Kathmandu = **Katmandu**

Katmai, Mount /kát mī/ volcano in S Alaska, in Katmai National Park and Preserve. Height: 2,047 m/6,715 ft.

Katmai National Park and Preserve national park in SW Alaska, on the Alaska Peninsula. Area: 1,656,475 hectares/4,093,240 acres.

Katmandu /kát man doò/, **Kathmandu** capital of Nepal, in the central part of the country. Population: 419,073 (1991).

Katoomba /kə toòmbə/ town in SE New South Wales, Australia. Population: 17,700 (1996 estimate).

Katsina /kátsinə/ capital of Katsina State, N Nigeria. Population: 201,500 (1995 estimate).

Kattegat /káttə gat/ strait between SW Sweden and E Jutland, Denmark. Length: 225 km/140 mi.

katydid /káyti did/ *n* a large green grasshopper with very long antennae. Native to: North America. Genus: *Microcentrum*. [Late 18C. An imitation of the sound produced when the male rubs its front wings together.]

Katyn Forest /kə teèn/ forest near Smolensk, W European Russia

Katz /kats/, **Sir Bernard** (*b.* 1911) German-born British biophysicist

katzenjammer /káts'n jammər/ *n US* (*dated informal*) 1 DIN a loud and confused noise 2 HANGOVER a hangover 3 FEELING OF DEPRESSION a bewildered or discouraged state [Mid-19C. < German, < *Katze* 'cat' + *Jammer* 'distress'.]

Kauai /kaà wí/ fourth largest island in Hawaii. Population: 55,983 (1995). Area: 1,430 km/552 sq. mi.

Kauffman /kówfmən/, **Angelica** (1741–1807) Swiss painter

Kaufman, Mount /kówfmən/ former name for **Lenin Peak**

Kaufman, George S. (1889–1961) US playwright and director

kaumatua /kow maà too ə/ *n* a Maori elder or leader [< Maori *kaumātua* 'adult, elder']

Kaunas /kównəss/ city in central Lithuania. Population: 415,300 (1995).

Kaunda /kaa oòndə/, **Kenneth** (*b.* 1924) Zambian statesman

kauri /kówri/ *n* 1 an evergreen tree that yields strong light-coloured timber. Native to: New Zealand. *Agathis australis.* 2 INDUST = **kauri gum** [Early 19C. < Maori.]

kauri gum, **kauri resin** *n* the brittle resin of the kauri tree that is usually found in fossilized form. Use: varnishes.

kava /kaàvə/ *n* 1 a bush of the pepper family. Flowers: small, clustered in spikes. Native to: Polynesia. *Piper methysticum.* 2 a narcotic drink made from the roots of the kava plant [Late 18C. < Polynesian, 'bitter'.]

Kāveri = **Cauvery**

Kawabata /káwə báttə/, **Yasunari** (1899–1972) Japanese novelist

Kawaguchi /kaàwə goòchi/ city on SE Honshu Island, Japan. Population: 438,680 (1990).

Kawasaki /kaàwə saàki/ city on east-central Honshu Island, Japan, beside Tokyo Bay. Population: 1,173,603 (1990).

Kay /kay/, **John** (1704–64) British inventor

kayak /kí ak/, **kaiak** *n* 1 a lightweight fibreglass canoe used for leisure and in competitive sport 2 a traditional Inuit boat consisting of a light frame covered with skins and propelled by one or two people using double-bladed paddles [Mid-18C. < Inuit *qayaq*.] —**kayak** *vti* —**kayaker** *n*

kayo /káy ō/ *n* (*plural* **-os**) a knockout, especially in boxing (*slang*) ■ *vt* (**-os**, **-oing**, **-oed**) to knock somebody out, especially in boxing (*slang*) [Early 20C. < the pronunciation of KO.]

Kayseri /kíssəri/ capital of Kayseri Province, central Turkey. Population: 471,463 (1996 estimate).

kazachok /kaàzə chók/ *n* a Russian folk dance in which high kicks are made from a squatting position [Early 20C. < Russian, diminutive of *kazak* 'Cossack'.]

Kazakh /kə zák/, **Kazak** *n* 1 a member of a people of Central Asia living mainly in Kazakhstan 2 the Turkic official language of Kazakhstan, also spoken in Mongolia, China, and Afghanistan. Native speakers: 8 million. [Mid-19C. < Russian, < Kazakh *kazak*.] —**Kazakh** *adj*

Kazakhstan

Kazakhstan /kázzak staàn/ republic in Central Asia, on the Caspian Sea. Capital: Astana. Population: 16,881,793 (1997). Area: 2,717,300 sq. km/1,049,200 sq. mi.

Kazan /kə zán/, **Elia** (*b.* 1909) Turkish-born US stage and film director and novelist. Born **Elia Kazanjoglous**

Kazantzakis /kázzan zaàkiss/, **Nikos** (1883–1957) Greek writer

kazatsky /kə zátski/ (*plural* **-skies**), **kazatske** *n* DANCE = **kazachok**

Kazbek /kaaz bék/ peak on the border of Russia and Georgia, in the Caucasus Mountains. Height: 5,037 m/16,526 ft.

kazi *n* = **karzy**

kazoo /kə zoò/ (*plural* **-zoos**) *n* a toy instrument that makes a buzzing sound, consisting of a tube with a mouthpiece and a hole covered by a thin diaphragm [Late 19C. An imitation of its sound.]

✦**KB** *abbr* 1 kilobyte 2 King's Bench 3 king's bishop 4 Knight Bachelor

KBE *abbr* Knight (Commander of the Order) of the British Empire

KBP *abbr* king's bishop's pawn

✦**kbyte** *abbr* kilobyte

kc *abbr* kilocycle

KC *abbr* 1 Kennel Club 2 King's Counsel 3 Knight of Columbus

kcal /káy kal/ *abbr* kilocalorie

KCB *abbr* Knight Commander of the (Order of the) Bath

KCMG *abbr* Knight Commander of the Order of St Michael and St George

KCVO *abbr* Knight Commander of the Royal Victorian Order

✦**ke** *abbr* Kenya (*in Internet addresses*)

kea /keè ə/ *n* a large parrot with brownish-green feathers that lives in mountainous regions and feeds mainly on insects. Native to: New Zealand. *Nestor notabilis.* [Mid-19C. < Maori.]

Kean /keen/, **Edmund** (1787–1833) British actor

Keating /keèting/, **Paul** (*b.* 1944) Australian statesman

Keaton /keèt'n/, **Buster** (1895–1966) US silent film comedian. Born **Joseph Francis Keaton**

Keats /keets/, **John** (1795–1821) British poet —**Keatsian** *adj*

kebab /ki báb, kə baàb/, **kabob** *n* a selection of small pieces of tender food, e.g. poultry, meat, fish, or seafood, threaded onto a stick and grilled [Late 17C. < Arabic *kabāb*.]

Keble /keèb'l/, **John** (1792–1866) British cleric and poet

Kedah /kéddə/ state in NW Malaysia, on the Malay Peninsula. Capital: Alur Setar. Area: 9,426 sq. km/3,639 sq. mi.

keddah *n* = **Kheda**

kedge /kej/ *vti* (**kedges**, **kedging**, **kedged**) to move a vessel by pulling on a rope or cable attached to a light anchor, or to move in this way ■ *n* **kedge**, **kedge anchor** a light anchor, especially one that is lodged some distance from a vessel so that the vessel can be pulled towards it [15C. < ?]

kedgeree /kéjjə ree/ *n* 1 a dish of British origin based on an Indian dish, consisting of spiced rice with flaked smoked fish and hard-boiled eggs 2 a spicy dish of Indian origin, made from lentils, rice, and sometimes fish [Mid-17C. < Hindi *khicṛī*.]

keech /keech/ *n Scotland* an offensive term used as a swearword (*slang*) [Late 16C. < ?]

keek /keek/ *vi Scotland* to look at something, usually in a furtive way or through a narrow opening ■ *n Scotland* a brief, often furtive look at something [14C. < ?]

keel /keel/ *n* 1 SHIP'S STRUCTURAL ELEMENT the main structural element of a ship, stretching along the centre line of its bottom from the bow to the stern 2 AIRCRAFT'S STRUCTURAL ELEMENT any structure that looks or acts like a ship's keel, such as the main structural element of an aircraft's fuselage 3 PART LIKE A RIDGE a ridge-shaped part of an organism 4 SHIP a ship (*literary*) ■ *vti* CAPSIZE to capsize a vessel, or to capsize [14C. < Old Norse *kjölr.*] ◊ **on an even keel** in a stable, steady condition
 keel over *v* 1 *vi* to collapse or fall over, often through exhaustion or illness (*informal*) 2 *vti* NAUT = **keel** *v.*

keelage /keèlij/ *n* a docking fee for merchant ships, charged by a port

keelboat /keèl bōt/ *n* a covered river boat with a keel and shallow draught but no sail, propelled by rowing, poling, or towing, and used for transporting freight

keelhaul /keèl hawl/ *vt* 1 to drag somebody on a rope from one side of a vessel to the other under the keel as a form of punishment 2 to reprimand somebody severely (*informal*) [Mid-17C. < Dutch *kielhalen*.]

keelie /keèli/ *n Scotland* an offensive term for a lower-class man or boy from a town or city, especially a Glaswegian, regarded as being tough or rough [< Gaelic *gille*. Rare before the 19C.]

keelson /kélIss'n, kéelss'n/, **kelson** /kélss'n/ *n* a metal or wooden beam attached to the upper side of a boat's keel to reinforce it [13C. Probably < Old Norse *kjölsvīn* or < Low German *kielsvīn*.]

keen[1] /keen/ *adj* **1 ENTHUSIASTIC** very eager and willing ○ *not very keen on the idea* **2 ATTRACTED** attracted to or fond of somebody or something ○ *He's not very keen on tomatoes.* **3 ACUTE** quick to understand things ○ *a keen sense of humour* **4 SENSITIVE** finely tuned and able to sense minor differences, distinctions, or details ○ *a keen sense of smell* **5 INTENSE** intense and lively ○ *keen competition* **6 SHARP** with a sharp cutting edge (*literary*) ○ *a keen razor* **7 BITING** extremely cold and penetrating ○ *a keen wind* **8 COMPETITIVELY LOW** low and therefore competitive ○ *keen prices* **9** *US* **VERY GOOD** fine or very good (*dated slang*) ○ *a keen new bike* [Old English *cēne* 'brave, clever' < Germanic] —**keenly** *adv* —**keenness** *n*

keen[2] /keen/ *vi* to cry out or wail in grief, especially while lamenting the dead ■ *n* a lamentation for a dead person (*literary*) [Early 19C. < Irish *caoinin* 'I wail'.] —**keener** *n*

keep /keep/ *v* **1** *vti* **POSSESS** to hold or maintain something in your possession ○ *The sample is yours to keep.* **2** *vt* **MAINTAIN THE CONDITION OF** to maintain something or somebody in a particular place or condition ○ *Keep your arm up.* **3** *vt* **STORE** to store something in a place when it is not in use ○ *He keeps the keys in a drawer.* **4** *vti* **CONTINUE** to cause somebody or something to continue in a particular way or activity, or to continue in a particular way ○ *It keeps working even in a power failure.* **5** *vt* **SAFEGUARD INFORMATION** to refrain from telling a secret or other information ○ *keep a secret* **6** *vt* **SAVE** to save something for later use or withhold something from use ○ *Keep some in reserve.* **7** *vt* **BE TRUE TO** to fulfil a promise or other verbal commitment ○ *keep your word* **8** *vt* **FULFIL A RELIGIOUS DUTY** to observe a religious obligation ○ *keep kosher* ○ *keep the Sabbath* **9** *vt* **MAINTAIN A RECORD** to create or maintain something as a written record ○ *keep a diary* **10** *vi* **STAY** to remain in a particular condition ○ *The stove will keep warm for a while after the fire goes out.* **11** *vi* **MAINTAIN A COURSE** to follow a particular course or direction ○ *Keep straight ahead until the roundabout.* **12** *vi* **NOT SPOIL** to remain fresh or in a usable condition ○ *That fish won't keep in this hot weather.* **13** *vi* **CONTINUE** to do something repeatedly or continue to do something ○ *Keep smiling!* **14** *vi* **NOT REQUIRE ATTENTION** to be able to be postponed ○ *I think the dusting will keep till tomorrow.* **15** *vi* **BE IN PARTICULAR CONDITION** to be or remain in a particular condition, especially in terms of health ○ *How are you keeping?* **16** *vt* **HAVE SOMETHING FOR SALE** to have something in stock in order to sell it ○ *Do you keep chain-saw blades?* **17** *vt* **DETAIN** to make somebody wait or prevent somebody from going ○ *Could I keep you for a moment?* **18** *vt* **LOOK AFTER** to take care of a person or animal, providing what is required to live ○ *We've never kept pets.* **19** *vt* **HAVE AS LIVESTOCK** to breed an animal for profit ○ *keep cattle* **20** *vt* **EMPLOY** to employ somebody, especially in a household ○ *keep servants* **21** *vt* **RUN A BUSINESS OR HOUSEHOLD** to maintain a business, house, or other establishment ○ *He keeps house for the General.* **22** *vt* **SUPPORT FINANCIALLY** to provide financially for a spouse or lover (*archaic*) **23** *vt Malaysia* **PUT SOMETHING AWAY** to put something in the place where it is normally stored or kept ready for use ○ *I must just keep these papers in my desk before I leave.* ■ *n* **1 MAINTENANCE** food and lodging ○ *work for your keep* **2 CASTLE PART** a stronghold or the innermost fortified part of a castle [Old English *cēpan* 'take, observe'] ◇ **for keeps** permanently or forever (*informal*) ◇ **keep something to yourself** to refrain from revealing something ◇ **keep yourself to yourself** to avoid mixing or communicating with other people

keep at *vt* **1** to persevere with something, especially something difficult or strenuous **2** to persist in asking somebody to do something (*informal*) ○ *They kept at me to do more and more work in less and less time.*

keep away *v* **1** *vt* to prevent somebody or something from going near somebody or something **2** *vi* to avoid going near somebody or something

keep back *vt* **1 NOT TELL** to refrain from telling or revealing something **2 WITHHOLD SOMETHING FOR LATER USE** to hold something in reserve for later use or for another purpose **3 RESTRAIN** to restrain or confine something to a limit

keep down *v* **1** *vt* **OPPRESS** to maintain somebody or something in an inferior position or in a state of oppression **2** *vt* **MAINTAIN SOMETHING AT A LOW LEVEL** to maintain something at a low level, position, or number ○ *Keep the costs down.* **3** *vi* **STAY LOW** to stay in a place or position where you cannot be seen **4** *vt* **NOT VOMIT** to hold food or drink in your stomach without vomiting ○ *He hasn't been able to keep anything down since the operation.*

keep from *vt* **1 HIDE SOMETHING FROM** to refrain from disclosing something to somebody **2 RESTRAIN** to prevent somebody from doing something **3 SAFEGUARD** to protect somebody from something ○ *kept us from harm*

keep in *vt* **1 REPRESS A FEELING** to repress something that you feel ○ *keeps in her anger* **2 NOT LET SOMEBODY LEAVE** to make somebody stay in a place, e.g. a schoolchild after class, or a patient in hospital **3 PROVIDE SOMEBODY WITH** to provide somebody with a regular supply of something ○ *money to keep us in petrol*

keep in with *vt* to maintain a good relationship with somebody, often because this might be advantageous

keep off *v* **1** *vt* **PREVENT CONTACT** to prevent something or somebody from having direct contact with something or somebody else **2** *vti* **NOT TOUCH** to refrain from direct contact with something or somebody ○ *Keep off the grass!* **3** *vti* **NOT CONSUME** to prevent somebody from consuming something or to refrain from consuming something ○ *I was told to keep off caffeine.* **4** *vti* **NOT TALK ABOUT** to prevent somebody from discussing something or to refrain from discussing something ○ *We kept off the topic of money.* **5** *vi* **NOT BEGIN** to fail to start or appear ○ *Let's hope the rain keeps off until the games are over.*

keep on *v* **1** *vi* **CONTINUE** to continue ○ *They just kept on, even after we told them to stop.* **2** *vt* **NOT TAKE SOMETHING OFF** to continue wearing something **3** *vt* **NOT DISMISS** to continue to employ somebody **4** *vi* **PERSIST IN TALKING ABOUT** to talk repetitively or continuously about one thing in a way that makes others bored or annoyed (*informal*)

keep on at *vt* to pester or nag somebody about something (*informal*)

keep out *vti* to prevent somebody from entering or to refrain from entering a place

keep out of *vti* **1** to prevent somebody or something from exposure to something, or to avoid exposure to something ○ *keep it out of the rain* **2** to prevent somebody's involvement in something, or to avoid involvement in something ○ *Keep out of her way.*

keep to *vt* to adhere without deviation to a plan, course, or subject

keep up *v* **1** *vt* **MAINTAIN THE PRESENT LEVEL OF** to maintain something at its present level, not letting it fall or subside ○ *Keep up the good work.* ○ *That's excellent. Keep it up.* **2** *vi* **STAY EVEN WITH** to go as fast or make the same progress as somebody else **3** *vt* **MAINTAIN SOMETHING IN GOOD CONDITION** to make sure that something stays in good condition ○ *has a beautiful home but doesn't really keep it up* **4** *vt* **DELAY SOMEBODY'S SLEEP OR BEDTIME** to prevent somebody from sleeping or going to bed at night ○ *The music from the party kept us up till dawn.*

keep up with *vt* **1** to remain abreast of something that undergoes continuous change or progress **2** to stay in contact with somebody, especially by letter ○ *I still keep up with a few friends from school.* ◇ **keep up with the Joneses** to maintain a position of equal social status with your neighbours, especially in terms of possessions

keeper /kéepər/ *n* **1 MUSEUM GUARDIAN** a person who oversees a museum, gallery, or exhibition **2 WARDEN** somebody whose job is to look after or protect animals **3 CARETAKER** somebody in charge of a building (*usually in combination*) ○ *a lighthouse keeper* **4 PRISON GUARD** a guard of confined or restricted people, especially in a prison **5** OCCUPATIONS = **gamekeeper** **6 MAINTAINER** somebody who keeps or maintains something ○ *a good record keeper* **7 GOALKEEPER** a goalkeeper or wicketkeeper (*informal*) **8 HOLDING DEVICE** a device such as a clip used to keep something in place **9 BAR ACROSS A MAGNET'S POLES** an iron or steel bar placed across the poles of a permanent horseshoe magnet when it is not in use, to close the magnetic circuit and prevent demagnetization **10 PLAY IN AMERICAN FOOTBALL** in American football, a play in which the quarterback runs towards the goal with the ball —**keepership** *n*

Keeper of the Privy Purse *n* POL = **Privy Purse** *n.* 2

keeper ring *n* ACCESSORIES = **guard ring**

keep fit *n* a programme of physical exercises designed to keep the body in good condition

keeping /kéeping/ *n* **1** the act of looking after or caring for somebody or something **2** somebody's charge, custody, or possession ○ *It's in the bank's keeping.* ◇ **in keeping with** consistent with or suitable for something ◇ **out of keeping with** not consistent with or suitable for something

keepnet /kéep net/ *n* a long cylindrical net with wire hoops attached at regular intervals, placed in water and used to keep fish that have been caught alive

keepsake /kéep sayk/ *n* a small item or gift kept because it evokes memories of somebody or something [Late 18C. < KEEP + (for the) SAKE (of).]

keeshond /káyss hond/ (*plural* **-honds** *or* **-honden** /-hondən/) *n* a dog with a dense shaggy blackish-grey coat and a tightly curled tail, belonging to a breed developed in the Netherlands [Early 20C. < Dutch, 'Kees dog' < *Kees*, pet form of *Cornelis* 'Cornelius'.]

keester *n* ANAT = **keister**

kef *n* DRUGS = **kif**

keffiyeh /ka féeyə/ *n* a cotton headdress fastened by a band and worn by Arab men

Keflavik /kéffləvik/ town in SW Iceland. Population: 7,637 (1996).

keg /keg/ *n* **1 SMALL BARREL** a small barrel used for storing liquids **2 CONTENTS OF A KEG** the amount that a keg can hold **3 BEER BARREL** an aluminium barrel that is used for storing and transporting beer [Early 17C. Alteration of *cag* < Old Norse *kaggi*.]

keg beer *n* beer that is stored in and served from a pressurized aluminium barrel

keiretsu /kay rét soo/ (*plural* **-su**) *n* in Japan, a conglomerate headed by a major Japanese bank or one consisting of companies with a common supply chain linking wholesalers and retailers [< Japanese]

keister /kéestər, kīstər/, **keester** /kéestər/ *n US* the buttocks (*humorous slang*) [Late 19C. < ?]

Keitel /kīt'l/, **Wilhelm** (1882–1946) German field marshal

Kejimkujik National Park /kéjim kóojik-/ national park and wildlife preserve in S Nova Scotia, Canada. Area: 403 sq. km/156 sq. mi.

Kekulé formula /kékə lay-/ *n* the representation of a benzene molecule as a hexagonal ring with alternating single and double bonds linking six carbon atoms, each linked to one hydrogen atom at the vertices [Mid-20C. After Friedrich August *Kekulé* (1829–96), German physicist.]

Keller /kéllər/, **Helen** (1880–1968) US author and lecturer. Born **Helen Adams Keller**

Kelly /kélli/, **Gene** (1912–96) US film actor, dancer, and director. Full name **Eugene Curran Kelly**

Kelly, Grace (1929–82) US film actor

Kelly, Ned (1855–80) Australian bushranger and folk hero

kelly green /kélli-/ *adj US* of a bright green colour [Because green is associated with Ireland, where the surname *Kelly* is common] —**kelly green** *n*

keloid /kée loyd/ *n* an area of raised pink or red fibrous scar tissue at the edges of a wound or incision [Mid-19C. < French *kéloïde* < Greek *khēlē* 'crab claw'.] —**keloidal** /kee lóyd'l/ *adj*

kelp /kelp/ *n* **1** brown seaweed with thick broad fronds. Order: Laminariales. **2** the ash from kelp or other seaweeds. Use: a source of potash and iodine. [14C. < ?]

kelpie[1] /kélpi/, **kelpy** (*plural* **-pies**) *n* in Scottish folklore, a malicious water spirit that takes the form of a horse and lures people to death by drowning [Late 17C. < ?]

kelpie[2] /kélpi/ *n* a smooth-haired dog of an Australian breed of sheepdog [Early 20C. After *King's Kelpie*, the female dog that founded the breed.]

kelpy *n* MYTHOL = **kelpie**[1]

kelson *n* NAUT = **keelson**

kelt /kelt/ *n* a salmon that has returned to the river of its birth and recently spawned [14C. < ?]

kelvin /kélvin/ *n* (*symbol* **K**) the SI unit of absolute temperature, equal to 1/273.16 of the absolute temperature of the triple point of water, equivalent to one degree Celsius ■ *adj* relating to or measured on the Kelvin scale [Early 20C. After William Thomson, 1st Baron KELVIN.]

Kelvin /kélvin/, **William Thomson, 1st Baron** (1824–1907) British physicist

Kelvin scale *n* a temperature scale on which zero is the lowest possible temperature and the triple point of water is defined as 273.16K [Late 19C. After William Thomson, 1st Baron KELVIN.]

Kelvinside /kélvin sīd/ *n Scotland* an old-fashioned anglicized accent of Scottish English, considered affected. ◊ **Morningside** [After *Kelvinside*, Glasgow]

Kemerovo /kémmə rôvə/ city in S Siberian Russia. Population: 538,193 (1995).

kemp /kemp/ n a short coarse hair or fibre [14C. < Old Norse kampr 'beard, whisker'.] —**kempy** adj

Kempe /kemp/, **Margery** (1373?–1440?) English mystic

Kempe /kémpə/, **Rudolf** (1910–76) German conductor

Kempsey /kémpsi/ town in NE New South Wales, Australia. Population: 8,630 (1996).

kempt /kempt/ adj tidy and well looked after (archaic) [Old English cemd < the past participle of cemban 'comb' < Germanic]

ken /ken/ n somebody's knowledge or understanding ○ It's beyond my ken. ■ vti (**kens, kenning, kenned** or **kent** /kent/, **kenned** or **kent**) Scotland to know somebody or something [Old English cennan 'make known' < Indo-European]

Ken. abbr Kentucky

Kendal /kéndəl/ town in the Lake District, NW England. Population: 25,461 (1991).

Kendal green n a coarse thick green woollen cloth similar to tweed and formerly worn by foresters ■ adj of a light greyish-green colour [14C. After KENDAL.]

kendo /kéndō/ n a Japanese martial art in which people fence using bamboo sticks instead of swords [Early 20C. < Japanese, 'way of the sword'.]

Kendrew /kén droo/, **Sir John** (1917–97) British molecular biologist

Keneally /kə nèeli, kə nálli/, **Thomas** (b. 1935) Australian novelist

Kenilworth /kénn'l wurth/ town in central England, site of a ruined 12th-century castle. Population: 21,623 (1991).

Kennebec /kénnəbèk/ river in W and S Maine, United States, that flows south from Moosehead Lake to the Atlantic Ocean. Length: 264 km/164 mi.

Kennebunkport /kénnə búngk pawrt/ town in SE Maine, United States, on the Atlantic coast. Population: 3,356 (1990).

Kennedy, Cape /kénnədi/ former name for **Canaveral, Cape**

Kennedy, Mount mountain in the St Elias Range in SW Yukon Territory, Canada. Height: 4,238 m/13,905 ft.

Kennedy, Charles (b. 1959) British politician

Kennedy, Edmund (1818–48) Australian explorer

Kennedy, Edward M. (b. 1932) US politician. Known as **Ted Kennedy**

Kennedy, Jackie (1929–94) US first lady (1961–63). Born **Jacqueline Lee Bouvier**. Full name **Jacqueline Lee Kennedy-Onassis**

John F. Kennedy

Kennedy, John F. (1917–63) US statesman and 35th president of the United States (1961–63). Known as **Jack Kennedy**

Kennedy, Joseph P. (1888–1969) US businessman and government official

Kennedy, Nigel (b. 1956) British violinist

Kennedy, Robert F. (1925–68) US politician. Known as **Bobby Kennedy**

kennel /kénn'l/ n **1 HUT FOR DOG** a small outdoor structure like a hut, built for a dog to sleep in. US term **doghouse 2 ANIMAL'S LAIR** the lair of a wild animal such as a fox **3 PACK OF DOGS** a pack of hounds or dogs **4 HOVEL** a small house in bad condition (archaic) ■ npl **DOG BOARDING OR BREEDING PLACE** a place where dogs are bred and trained

and where people can leave their dogs while they are away (+ singular or plural verb) ■ vti (**-nels, -nelling, -nelled**) **PUT OR STAY IN A KENNELS** to put a dog into a kennels or to stay in a kennels [14C. < assumed Anglo-Norman kenil < Latin canis 'dog'.]

Kennelly-Heaviside layer /kénn'li hévvi sīd-/ n PHYS = **E layer** [Early 20C. After Arthur Edwin Kennelly (1861–1939), US electrical engineer, and Oliver Heaviside (1850–1925), British physicist.]

Kenneth I /kénnith/ (fl. mid-9th century), king of Scotland. Known as **Kenneth MacAlpin**

kenning /kénning/ n a metaphorical expression, often a phrase, used to denote another word in Old Norse and Old English poetry [Late 19C. < Old Norse, < kenna 'know'.]

Kenny /kénni/, **Elizabeth** (1886–1952) Australian nurse and physical therapist. Known as **Sister Kenny**

keno /kéenō/ n US, Aus a game of chance in which players wager on a set of numbers to be drawn at random [Early 19C. Via French quine 'set of five winning numbers' < Latin quini 'five each' < quinque 'five'.]

kenosis /ki nôssiss/ n according to Christian belief, Jesus Christ's act of partially giving up his divine status in order to become a man, as recorded in Philippians 2:6–7 [Late 19C. < Greek kenōsis 'an emptying' < heauton ekenōse 'emptied himself', phrase in Philippians 2:7.] —**kenotic** /ki nóttik/ adj

kenspeckle /kén spek'l/ adj Scotland easily seen or recognized [Mid-16C. Probably < Old Norse kennispeki < kenna 'know' + spak 'wise'.]

kent Scotland past participle, past tense of **ken**

Kent /kent/ county in SE England, and a former Anglo-Saxon kingdom. Area: 3,730 sq. km/1,440 sq. mi.

Kent, William (1686?–1748) English architect and landscape designer

kente /kénti/, **kente cloth** n a handwoven cloth from Ghana, usually very brightly coloured [Mid-20C. < Twi, 'cloth'.]

kentia /kénti ə/, **kentia palm** n a tall palm tree that is widely cultivated for its decorative foliage. Native to: Lord Howe Island. Howea forsterana. [Late 19C. < modern Latin, after William Kent.]

Kentish /kéntish/ adj **1 OF KENT** relating to the English county of Kent **2 OF OLD ENGLISH DIALECT** relating to the Kentish dialect ■ n **OLD ENGLISH DIALECT** a dialect of Old English spoken in the extreme southeast of England, probably from around the 5th century AD

kentledge /kéntlij/ n scrap iron or other heavy material used as permanent ballast on ships [Early 17C. < Old French quintelage 'ballast' < quintal (see QUINTAL).]

Kentucky¹ /ken túki/ state in the east-central United States. Capital: Frankfort. Population: 3,908,124 (1997). Area: 104,664 sq. km/40,411 sq. mi. —**Kentuckian** n, adj

Kentucky² river in central Kentucky. Length: 417 km/259 mi.

Kentucky bluegrass n a grass widely used for pastureland and lawns. Native to: Africa, Europe, Asia, naturalized in North America. Poa pratensis.

Kentucky Derby n a race for three-year-old horses that has been run annually since 1875 at Churchill Downs in Louisville, Kentucky

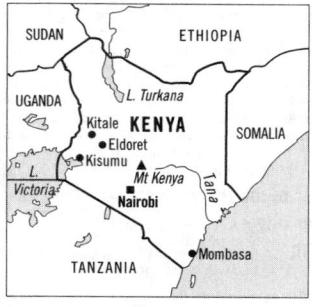

Kenya

Kenya /kényə, kèenyə/ republic in E Africa. Capital: Nairobi. Population: 27,838,597 (1997). Area: 582,646 sq. km/224,961 sq. mi. —**Kenyan** n, adj

Kenya, Mount extinct volcano in central Kenya. Height: 5,199 m/17,057 ft.

Kenyatta /ken yáttə/, **Jomo** (1897?–1978) Kenyan statesman. Born **Kamau wa Ngengi**

Kenyon /kényən/, **Dame Kathleen** (1906–78) British archaeologist

kephalin n BIOL = **cephalin**

kepi /káypi/ n a French military hat with a round flat top and a horizontal peak [Mid-19C. Via French képi < Swiss German Käppi 'little cap'.]

Kepler /képplər/ n a crater on the Moon in Oceanus Procellarum, 32 km/20 mi. in diameter

Kepler /képplər/, **Johannes** (1571–1630) German astronomer

Kepler's laws /képplərz-/ npl three mathematical statements that describe the movement of the planets in their orbits around the Sun [Late 18C. After Johannes KEPLER.]

kept past tense, past participle of **keep**

kept man n a man who is financially supported by a lover (often considered offensive)

kept woman n a woman who is financially supported, especially by a married man (often considered offensive)

Kerala /kérrələ/ state in SW India. Capital: Trivandrum. Population: 30,555,000 (1994). Area: 38,864 sq. km/15,005 sq. mi.

kerat- prefix = **kerato-** (before vowels)

keratectomy /kérrə téktəmi/ (plural **-mies**) n surgical removal of part of the cornea

keratin /kérrətin/, **ceratin** n a fibrous insoluble protein that is the main structural element in hair, nails, feathers, and hooves [Mid-19C. < Greek kerat- 'horn'.] —**keratinous** /kə ráttinəss/ adj

keratinization /kérrəti nī záysh'n, ke rátti nī-/, **keratinisation** n the deposition of keratin in skin cells, e.g. in hair and nails, giving them the texture of horn

keratinize /kérrəti nīz, ke rátti nīz/ (**-izes, -izing, -ized**), **keratinise** (**-ises, -ising, -ised**) vti to convert something into keratin, or become keratin

keratitis /kérrə tītiss/ n inflammation and swelling of the cornea

kerato- prefix **1** horny tissue ○ keratose **2** cornea ○ keratoplasty [< Greek kerat- 'horn' < Indo-European]

keratoid /kérrə toyd/ adj like horn in texture or appearance

keratopathy /kérrə tóppəthi/ n any noninflammatory disorder of the cornea

keratoplasty /kérrətō plasti/ (plural **-ties**) n plastic surgery on the cornea, especially corneal grafting — **keratoplastic** /kérrətō plástik/ adj

keratose /kérrə tôss, -tōz/ adj having a horny skeleton, as some sponges have

keratosis /kérrə tôssiss/ (plural **-ses** /-seez/) n **1** growth of hard horny tissue on the skin **2** a horny growth on the skin —**keratotic** /-tóttik/ adj

keratotomy /kérrə tóttəmi/ (plural **-mies**) n a surgical cutting of the cornea

kerb /kurb/ n a raised edge of stone or concrete separating the pavement from the road or street. US term **curb** n. **5** ■ vt to provide something with a kerb. US term **curb** v. **2** [Mid-17C. Variant of CURB 'enclosing framework'.]

kerb crawling n the act of driving slowly beside a pavement looking for a prostitute to pick up —**kerb crawler** n

kerb drill n a procedure for crossing a road safely on foot, especially one that is taught to children

kerb market n a stock market that is separate from the stock exchange, originally one operating in the street

kerbside /kúrb sīd/ n the edge of a street or a sidewalk bordered by a curb. US term **curbside**

kerbstone /kúrb stōn/ n any of the large stones used to make a kerb. US term **curbstone**

Kerch /kyurch/ seaport in S Ukraine, on the shore of the E Crimean Peninsula. Population: 176,000 (1990).

kerchief /kúrchif, kúr cheef/ n a square scarf for women, worn round the neck or as a headscarf [13C. < Anglo-Norman courchef or Old French cuevre-chef 'cover-head'.] —**kerchiefed** adj

Kerensky /kərénski/, **Aleksandr Fyodorovich** (1881–1970) Russian revolutionary leader

kerf /kurf/ *n* a cut or the width of a cut made by an axe, saw, or cutting tool [Old English *cerf* < W Germanic]

kerfuffle /kər fúff'l/, **carfuffle, kurfuffle** *n* a noisy disturbance or commotion (*informal*) [Early 19C. < ?]

Kerguelen Islands /kúrgilin-/ French island group in the S Indian Ocean. Area: 6,993 sq. km/2,700 sq. mi.

Kermadec Islands /kúrmə dek-/ island group in the S Pacific Ocean, a dependency of New Zealand. Area: 29 sq. km/11 sq. mi.

Kerman /kur maán/, **Kermān** capital of Kerman Province, SE Iran. Population: 311,643 (1991).

kermes /kúr miz/ (*plural* **-mes**) *n* **1** the dried bodies of female scale insects of the genus *Kermes*, or the purplish-red dye obtained from them. **2** TREES = **kermes oak** [Late 16C. Via French *kermès* < Arabic *ḳirmiz* 'kermes beetle'.]

kermes oak *n* a small evergreen oak tree that provides a habitat for the scale insects used to make kermes. Native to: Europe, Asia. *Quercus coccifera*.

kermis /kúr miss/, **kirmess, kermess** *n* an annual country fair that used to be held in the Netherlands and N Germany [Late 16C. < Dutch, 'mass on the anniversary of the church's dedication' < *kerk* 'church' + *misse* 'mass'.]

kern[1] /kurn/, **kerne** *n* **PART OF A CHARACTER** the part of a typographical character that projects beyond the body ■ *v* (**kernes, kerning, kerned**) **1** *vti* **BRING TYPE TOGETHER** to eliminate white space between adjacent letters that may appear too widely separated on a line **2** *vt* **OVERLAP ADJACENT CHARACTERS** to join adjacent printed characters or make them overlap [Late 17C. < French *carne* 'corner' < Latin *cardin-* 'hinge'.]

kern[2] /kurn/, **kerne** *n* a medieval Irish or Scottish light infantryman [14C. < Irish *ceithearn*.]

Kern /kurn/, **Jerome** (1885–1945) US composer

kerne *n* MIL, HIST = **kern**[2]

ϟ **kernel** /kúrn'l/ *n* **1 EDIBLE CORE** the edible content of a nut or fruit stone **2 CEREAL GRAIN** the grain of a cereal that contains a seed and husk **3 CENTRAL PART** the central or most important part of something ○ *a kernel of self-belief that never wavered* **4 ATOM STRIPPED OF ITS ELECTRONS** a positively charged atomic nucleus that has lost its valency electrons **5 KEY PORTION OF AN OPERATING SYSTEM** the core of a computer's operating system that resides in the memory and performs essential functions such as controlling memory and files and allocating system resources [Old English *cyrnel* 'little seed' < CORN[1]]

SPELLCHECK See ***colonel***.

kerning /kúrning/ *n* the addition or removal of space between individual characters in a piece of typeset text to improve its appearance or alter its fit

kernite /kúr nīt/ *n* a colourless or white crystalline mineral consisting of hydrated sodium borate. Use: source of borax and other boron compounds. [Early 20C. After *Kern* County, California.]

kernmantel rope /kúrn mant'l -/ *n* strong elastic rope made of sheathed nylon fibre [< German, 'core-casing']

kero /kérrō/ *n ANZ* kerosene (*informal*) [Mid-20C. Shortening.]

kerogen /kérrəjən/ *n* a fossilized insoluble organic material found in some sedimentary rocks, e.g. oil shales, yielding petroleum products when heated [Early 20C. < Greek *kēros* 'wax'.]

kerosene /kérrə seen/, **kerosine** *n US, Can, ANZ* a colourless flammable oil distilled from petroleum and used as a fuel for jet engines, heating, cooking, and lighting [Mid-19C. < Greek *kēros* 'wax'.]

Kerouac /kérrōō ak/, **Jack** (1922–69) US novelist. Full name **Jean Louis Kerouac**

kerplunk /kər plúngk/ *adv, interj* used to imitate the sound made by something heavy falling suddenly (*informal*) [An imitation of the sound]

Kerr /kur/, **Sir John** (1914–90) Australian statesman

Kerr effect /kúr-/ *n* **1** the property of some transparent substances that makes them refract doubly when placed in an electric field **2** the elliptical polarization of plane-polarized or unpolarized light when reflected from the polished pole of a magnetized material [Early 20C. After John *Kerr* (1824–1907), Scottish physicist.]

Kerry[1] /kérri/ (*plural* **-ries**) *n* a small black bull or dairy cow belonging to a breed that originated in Ireland [Mid-19C. After County KERRY[2].]

Kerry[2] /kérri/ county in Munster Province, SW Republic of Ireland. Area: 4,701 sq. km/1,815 sq. mi.

Kerry blue terrier, Kerry blue *n* a terrier with a dense but soft wavy bluish-grey coat, belonging to a breed that originated in Ireland [Early 20C. After County KERRY[2].]

kersey /kúrzi/ *n* a smooth woollen fabric. Use: coats. [14C. After *Kersey*, village in Suffolk.]

kerseymere /kérrzi meer/ *n* a fine soft woollen cloth with a fancy twill weave [Late 18C. Alteration of *cassimere*, suit fabric (<CASHMERE), after KERSEY.]

Kertész /kər tésh/, **André** (1894–1985) Hungarian-born US photographer

kerygma /kə rígmə/ *n* the proclamation of Jesus Christ's teachings, especially as taught in the Gospels [Late 19C. < Greek *kērugma* < *kērussein* 'proclaim'.] —**kerygmatic** /kérrig máttik/ *adj*

kesh /kaysh/ *n* the beard and uncut hair traditionally worn by baptized Sikh men as a symbol of religious loyalty. ◊ **five Ks** [< Punjabi *kes*]

Kesselring /késs'lring/, **Albert** (1885–1960) German field marshal

kestrel /késtrəl/ *n* a small falcon that hovers before diving on its prey. Genus: *Falco*. [14C. Probably < French dialect *casserelle* < French *crécerelle* 'rattle' < Latin *crepitacillum* 'small rattle' < *crepitare* 'to rattle'.]

ket- *prefix* = **keto-** (*before vowels*)

ketamine /kéttə meen/ *n* $C_{13}H_{16}ClNO$ a white crystalline powder. Use: general anaesthetic in human and veterinary medicine

ketch /kech/ *n* a small sailing ship with two masts [Mid-17C. Probably < CATCH.]

ketchup /kéchəp, kéch up/, **catchup** /káchəp, kách up/, **catsup** /kátsəp, káts up/ *n* a thick savoury sauce, usually made with tomatoes, that is served cold as a condiment [Late 17C. Probably via Malay *kĕchap* 'fish sauce' < Chinese (Cantonese) *k'ē chap* 'sauce'.]

ketene /keé teen/ *n* C_2H_2O a strong-smelling colourless highly reactive toxic gas. Use: as an agent to attach an acetyl group to an organic compound. [Early 20C. < KETONE.]

keto-, ket- *prefix* indicating a chemical compound containing a keto group, C=O ○ *ketosteroid* [< KETONE]

keto form /keétō-/ *n* one of two interconvertible forms of an organic compound, having a carbonyl group attached to two alkyl groups

ketogenesis /keétō jénnəssiss/ *n* the formation or stimulation of the production of ketone bodies, as happens in diabetes —**ketogenic** *adj*

ketone /keétōn/ *n* an organic compound, e.g. acetone, having a carbon atom doubly bonded to an oxygen atom and to two carbon atoms [Mid-19C. < German *Keton*, alteration of *Aketon* 'acetone'.] —**ketonic** /kee tónnik/ *adj*

ketone body *n* a mixture of ketones produced when body fat is broken down

ketone group *n* the carbonyl group, containing carbon atoms doubly bonded to an oxygen atom and linked to the carbon atoms of two other organic groups, a characteristic of all ketones

ketonuria /keétō nyóori ə/ *n* the presence of ketones in the urine, a dangerous feature of severe and uncontrolled diabetes

ketose /keé tōss, -tōz/ *n* a carbohydrate that contains a ketone group

ketosis /kee tóssiss, ki-/ *n* the condition resulting from overproduction of ketone bodies —**ketotic** /-tóttik/ *adj*

ketoxime /kee tók seem/ *n* an organic compound containing a nitrogen atom bonded to a hydroxyl group and a carbon atom, which is bonded to two ketones

Kettering /kéttəring/ town in central England. Population: 47,186 (1991).

kettle /kétt'l/ *n* **1 CONTAINER FOR BOILING WATER** a plastic or metal container with a handle, spout, and lid, used for boiling water **2 METAL POT** a metal pot used for cooking, usually one with a lid ○ *a fish kettle* **3 INDUSTRIAL CONTAINER** a large container with no lid that is used for refining metals with a low melting point **4 BASIN IN A GLACIAL DRIFT DEPOSIT** a steep-sided basin, often a lake or swamp, in a glacial drift deposit, caused by the melting of an ice mass left behind as the glacier retreated [Old English *cetel*, via Germanic < Latin *catillus* 'small cooking pot'] ◇ **a different kettle of fish** a different situation or person to be dealt with ◇ **a pretty** *or* **fine kettle of fish** an undesirable situation, usually one caused by somebody's negligence or incompetence

kettledrum /kétt'l drum/ *n* a percussion instrument consisting of a large copper or brass drum covered with a parchment skin that can be adjusted to alter the pitch —**kettledrummer** *n*

kettle hole *n* GEOL = **kettle** *n.* **4**

keV *abbr* kiloelectronvolt

kevel[1] /kévv'l/ *n* a sturdy bitt or bollard for securing the heavier cables on a ship [13C. Via Old Norman French *keville* 'pin, peg' < Latin *clavicula* 'small key'.]

kevel[2] /kévv'l/ *n* a two-headed hammer, one head with a sharp edge, the other with a point, used for breaking up or shaping stone [< ?]

Kew Gardens /kyoō-/ *n* an informal name for the Royal Botanic Gardens, Kew, located in W London. It holds the largest collection of plants in the world.

kewpie /kyoōpi/ *n* a plump doll with rosy cheeks and a curl of hair on its head [Originally a trademark]

kex /keks/ *n* the dried stems of a large hollow-stemmed plant such as cow parsnip or chervil [14C. < ?]

ϟ **key**[1] /kee/ *n* **1 INSTRUMENT FOR LOCKING** a metal bar with notches or grooves that, when inserted into a lock and turned, operates the lock's mechanism **2 DOOR OR LOCK OPENER** a device such as a plastic card with an encoded magnetic strip that operates a door or lock **3 INSTRUMENT FOR WINDING UP** a fitted tool that is turned repeatedly to wind up, set, or calibrate a mechanism **4 IMPORTANT ASPECT** the aspect of something that, once understood, provides a full understanding or explanation of the whole ○ *The key to this riddle lies in the subtle meanings of the words used.* **5 MEANS** a way or means of achieving something ○ *Continuity of effort is the key to success.* **6 STRATEGIC PLACE** a place that is strategically vital in gaining access to or controlling a larger area ○ *Istanbul is the key to the Bosporus.* **7 LIST OF ANSWERS** a list of the answers to a test or exercise **8 EXPLANATORY TEXT** a text that provides additional information on, or an explanation of, a work of literature, art, or music **9 TONAL CENTRE** the relationship between the notes of a scale and the scale's main note **10 MAIN NOTE OF A SCALE** the note on which a musical scale begins **11 INSTRUMENT FEATURE** the levers on a keyboard instrument that sound a note when pressed, or the metal buttons on a woodwind instrument that alter a note's pitch **12 MUSICAL SCALE** a system of related notes in a scale beginning on a particular note ○ *in the key of E* **13 KEYBOARD BUTTON** a button on a typewriter's or computer's keyboard or keypad that performs an operation when pressed **14 DATABASE FEATURE** a field in a database record that uniquely identifies that record **15 DEVICE FOR OPERATING CIRCUITS** a small manual device for opening, closing, or switching circuits ○ *a telegraph key* **16 METAL PIN** a metal wedge or pin used to lock together two structural or mechanical components, e.g. a shaft and a hub, to prevent movement relative to each other **17 CRYPTOGRAPHIC FEATURE** in cryptography, the sequence of symbols or characters that defines the makeup of an encoding mechanism **18 OUTLINE OF CHARACTERISTICS** an outline of the characteristics of an organism, used for taxonomic identification **19 IMAGE FEATURE** the tonal value of an image with regard to lightness, darkness, or colour intensity **20 SURFACE PREPARATION** the preparing of a surface, usually by making it rough or grooved, so that paint or some other finish will stick to it **21 PITCH OR QUALITY** the pitch or quality of an expressive sound, especially the voice ○ *answered in thoughtful key* **22 EXPLANATORY LIST** an explanatory list of the symbols or abbreviations used on a map or diagram **23 MOOD OF AN ART WORK** the general mood or style of a work of art, literature, or music **24** ARCHIT = **keystone** *n.* **1 25 WINGED FRUIT** a dry winged fruit like that of an ash or elm tree **26 BASKETBALL COURT AREA** the area at the ends of a basketball court between the base line and the foul line ■ *adj* **CRUCIAL** vital in achieving understanding or success ○ *the key points in the report* ■ *v* (**keys, keying, keyed**) **1** *vti* **TYPE** to use the keyboard of a computer ○ *a solid hour of keying* **2** *vt* **LOCK** to lock or adjust something with a key **3** *vt* **PREPARE A SURFACE** to prepare a surface, usually by making it rough or grooved, so that paint or another finish will stick to it **4** *vt* **PROVIDE WITH AN EXPLANATION** to provide something with an explanatory list or text **5** *vt* **REGULATE AN IN-**

STRUMENT'S PITCH to regulate the pitch of a musical instrument **6** *vt* ADAPT to bring something in line with or make something consistent with something else (*often passive*) **7** *vt* PUT A KEYSTONE IN to provide an arch with a keystone **8** *vt* MARK ARTWORK to mark artwork, or anything to be reproduced, with symbols that will allow different parts to be correctly aligned for reproduction **9** *vt* IDENTIFY to identify an organism or specimen [Old English *cǣg*]
key in *vt* to enter data, e.g. a password or PIN, by typing on a keyboard or keypad

key² /keé/ *n* a small low island of sand or coral, especially in the Gulf of Mexico or the Caribbean [Late 17C. < Old French *kay*, probably < Celtic.]

⚡**keyboard** /keé bawrd/ *n* **1** SET OF KEYS a set of keys laid out in a row or rows, e.g. for a computer or musical instrument **2** MUSICAL INSTRUMENT a musical instrument with a keyboard, especially an electronic instrument ■ *vti* INPUT DATA to enter information into a computer using a keyboard

⚡**keyboarder** /keé bawrdər/ *n* an operator of the keyboard of a computer or typesetting machine

keyboardist /keé bawrdist/ *n* a musician who plays a keyboard instrument

key card *n* a card, usually made of plastic with an encoded magnetic strip, giving access to a door or mechanism

⚡**key database** *n* a database that holds all keys used by a certificate authority

keyed up *adj* in a state of great excitement, tension, or nervousness (*informal*)

⚡**key escrow** *n* a system for encrypting computer data in which the decoding key is held by a third party

key grip *n* the chief grip in a film or stage crew

keyhole /keé hōl/ *n* the small hole in a lock into which a key fits

keyhole saw *n* = padsaw

keyhole surgery *n* surgery performed using instruments that can be introduced into the body through a very small hole and manipulated externally, thus avoiding the need for major incisions

Key Largo /-laàrgō/ one of the largest of the Florida Keys, off the tip of SE Florida. Length: 48 km/30 mi.

key light *n* the main studio or stage light that sets the overall level of light intensity for something that is being filmed, video-taped, or photographed

key money *n* a fee paid by a prospective tenant to a landlord or landlady in order to secure a tenancy

Keynes /kaynz/, **John Maynard, 1st Baron Keynes of Tilton** (1883–1946) British economist —**Keynesian** *n, adj*

Keynesianism /káynzi ən izəm/ *n* the theory that government spending must compensate for insufficient business investment in times of recession

---

QUICK FACTS ON... KEYNESIANISM

Key dates: mid-20th century
Key locations: England, United States
Key elements: increased money supply leads to greater employment and economic output; private investment affected by other influences besides interest rates; public spending needed in recessions to compensate for less business activity
Key figures: John Maynard Keynes; John Kenneth Galbraith
Key works: *The General Theory of Employment, Interest, and Money* (Keynes) 1936; *The Affluent Society* (Galbraith) 1958

---

keynote /keé nōt/ *n* **1** MAIN THEME the central or most important point or theme of something **2** MUSIC = tonic *n*. **4** ■ *adj* MOST IMPORTANT containing or outlining the most important themes or policies ■ *v* (-notes, -noting, -noted) **1** *vti* DELIVER A SPEECH to deliver an important speech to a conference or meeting **2** *vt* NOTE IMPORTANT POINTS to outline an important policy in a speech or report [Mid-18C. Originally 'first note of a scale'.]

keynote address *n* = keynote speech

keynoter /keé nōtər/, **keynote speaker** *n* a speaker who delivers the most important speech at a conference or political convention

keynote speech *n* the most important speech at a conference or political convention

---

⚡**keypad** /keé pad/ *n* **1** a small keyboard, e.g. on a calculator or television remote control, usually with numbers on the keys **2** the part of a computer keyboard in which the number and command keys are grouped

⚡**keypal** /keé pal/ *n* US somebody with whom regular e-mail is exchanged [After PEN PAL]

⚡**key-punch** *n* a machine, operated by keyboard, that punches holes in card or paper for use in a data-processing system ■ *vti* to use a key-punch to punch holes in a card or paper tape for data entry into a computer — **key-puncher** *n*

key ring *n* a metal ring used for keeping keys together, often with a decorative or identifying attachment

key signature *n* a group of sharps or flats printed on the staves at the beginning of a piece of music to show the key in which it is to be played

key stage *n* any of the four National Curriculum programmes of study that pupils are required to follow

keystone /keé stōn/ *n* **1** the wedge-shaped stone at the highest point of an arch that locks the others in place **2** something on which other interrelated things depend ○ *Alliances are the keystone of a country's security*

⚡**keystroke** /keé strōk/ *n* the pressing down of a computer or typewriter key on a keyboard, activating it

keyway /keé way/ *n* a longitudinal slot in two structural or mechanical components, e.g. in the hub or shaft of a wheel, into which a metal wedge or pin can be inserted

Key West city in S Florida, on Key West Island. Population: 24,832 (1990).

⚡**key word** *n* **1** REFERENCE POINT a word used as a reference point for further information or as an indication of the contents of a document **2** CODE WORD a word that is used as a key to a code **3** WORD WITH A SPECIAL MEANING TO A COMPUTER a sequence of letters and numbers, often in the form of a common word, with special significance to a computer database or programming or command language

kg¹ *symbol* kilogram

⚡**kg²** *abbr* Kyrgyzstan (*in Internet addresses*)

KG *abbr* Knight of the Order of the Garter

KGB *n* the secret police of the former Soviet Union [< Russian, < *Komitet Gosudarstvennoĭ Bezopasnosti* 'Committee of State Security']

kgf *symbol* kilogram-force

⚡**kh** *abbr* Cambodia (*in Internet addresses*)

Khabarovsk /kəba rófsk/ city in SE Russia, near the border of China. Population: 774,762 (1995).

khaddar /kaàdər/, **khadi** /kaàdi/ *n* a cotton cloth from South Asia that has a plain weave [Early 20C. < Punjabi *khaddar* or Hindi *khādar*.]

khaki /kaàki/ *n* **1** a dull brownish-yellow colour **2** a tough yellowish-brown fabric. Use: military uniforms. [Mid-19C. Via Urdu *kakī* 'dust-coloured' < Persian *kāk* 'dust'.] — **khaki** *adj*

khalif *n* ISLAM = caliph

khalifate *n* ISLAM = caliphate

Khalsa /kaàlssə/ *n* a strict Sikh religious order founded in 1699 by Guru Gobind Singh [Late 18C. Via Urdu < Arabic *kāliṣ* 'pure'.]

khamsin /kam seén, kámsin/, **kamseen, kamsin** *n* a dry dusty hot southerly wind that blows from the Sahara across Egypt and over the Red Sea from March to May [Late 17C. < Arabic *kamāsīn* < *kamsīn* 'fifty' (because it blows for about fifty days).]

khan¹ /kaan/ *n* **1** a medieval title formerly used by Mongol and Turkish rulers in various parts of Asia (*usually added to a name*) ○ *Genghis Khan* **2** a title of respect taken by various dignitaries in Central Asian countries ○ *the Aga Khan* [14C. Via Old French *chan* or medieval Latin *ca(a)nus* < Turkic *kān* 'lord, ruler'.]

khan² /kaan/ *n* an inn in Turkey and some other Central Asian countries [14C. < Persian *kān*.]

Imran Khan

Khan /kaan/, **Imran** (*b.* 1952) Pakistani cricketer

Khan, Jahangir (*b.* 1963) Pakistani squash player

khanate /kaà nayt/ *n* **1** the territory governed by a medieval Chinese emperor or a Mongolian or Turkish khan **2** the position or rank of a khan

khanga /kaànga/ CLOTHING = kanga

khapra beetle /kaàprə-/ *n* a beetle of Southeast Asia now common in other parts of the world, where it is a pest to grain farmers. *Trogoderma granarium*. [*Khapra* via Hindi < Sanskrit *khapara* 'thief']

Kharkov /kaàr kof/ city in E Ukraine. Population: 1,576,000 (1995).

Khartoum /kaar toòm/ capital of Sudan and of Khartoum Province, near the confluence of the Blue Nile and White Nile rivers. Population: 924,505 (1993).

khat /kaat/ *n* **1** fresh leaves and twigs that act as a stimulant when chewed or brewed as tea **2** an evergreen bush whose leaves and twigs are used as khat. Native to: Arabia, Africa. *Catha edulis*. [Mid-19C. < Arabic *kāt*.]

kheda /kéddə/, **khedah, keddah** *n* in India and Myanmar, an enclosure used to capture wild elephants [Late 18C. < Assamese, Bengali *khedā*.]

khedive /ki deèv/ *n* the title of the Turkish viceroys who governed Egypt from 1867 to 1914 while it was under Turkish rule [Mid-19C. Via French < Ottoman Turkish *kediv* < Persian *kadiw* 'prince' < *kudā* 'god'.] —**khedival** *adj* — **khedivate** /kə deèvət, -vayt/ *n*

khi /ki/ *n* (*plural* **khis**) = chi¹

Khmer /kmair, kə máir/ *n* (*plural* **Khmer** or **Khmers**) **1** MEMBER OF A CAMBODIAN PEOPLE a member of the most populous people in Cambodia **2** INHABITANT OF ANCIENT KINGDOM an inhabitant of an ancient kingdom that flourished in the Mekong valley between the 9th and 13th centuries AD **3** OFFICIAL LANGUAGE OF CAMBODIA the official language of Cambodia, belonging to Mon-Khmer. Native speakers: 5 million. [Late 19C. < Khmer.] — **Khmer** *adj*

Khmer Republic /kmair-/ former name for **Cambodia**

Khmer Rouge /-roòzh/ *n* the Cambodian Communist party that seized power in the civil war of 1975 and controlled the country until 1979 [< Khmer *Khmer* 'Cambodia' + French *rouge* 'red']

Khoikhoi /kóy koy/ (*plural* **-khoi** or **-khois**) *n* **1** a member of a formerly nomadic people now living mainly in Namibia **2 Khoikhoi, Khoi Khoi** a language spoken in Namibia and some parts of W South Africa, belonging to Khoisan and characterized by the use of click consonants. Native speakers: 55,000. [Late 18C. < Nama, 'men of men'.] —**Khoikhoi** *adj*

Khoisan /kóy saàn/, **Khoi-San** *n* a family of African languages spoken in parts of Namibia and Botswana and notable for the use of click consonants [Mid-20C. Blend of KHOIKHOI + SAN².] —**Khoisan** *adj*

Khomeini /kóm ay neè/, **Ruhollah, Ayatollah** (1900?–89) Iranian religious and political leader

khoum /koom/, **khum** *n* see table at **currency** [Late 20C. < Arabic *kums* 'one-fifth'.]

Khrushchev /kroòss chof/, **Nikita** (1894–1971) Soviet statesman

Khulna /koòlnə/ river port in SW Bangladesh. Population: 545,849 (1991).

khuskhus /kúskəss/, **khus-khus** PLANT SCI = vetiver [Early 19C. < Urdu, Persian *kaskas*.]

Popperfoto

Khyber Pass /kíbər-/ mountain pass in W Asia, the most important pass connecting Afghanistan and Pakistan

ϟ **KHYF** *abbr* know how you feel (*in e-mails*)

kHz *abbr* kilohertz

ϟ **ki** *abbr* Kiribati (*in Internet addresses*)

KIA *abbr US* know-it-all

Kiama /kī ámmə/ coastal town in SE New South Wales, Australia. Population: 10,647 (1991).

kiang /ki áng/ *n* a large wild ass. Native to: Tibetan plateau, Himalayas. *Equus hemionus kiang*. [Mid-19C. < Tibetan *kyang*.]

kia ora /kée ə áwrə/ *interj NZ* used as a greeting or to wish somebody good luck [Late 19C. < Maori, 'be well'.]

kibbe /kíbbə/ *n* a Middle Eastern dish made with minced lamb, pine nuts, and spices [Mid-20C. < Arabic *kubbah*.]

kibble[1] /kíbb'l/ *n* a large iron barrel used in wells or mines for lifting water, ore, or refuse to the surface [Via German *Kübel* < medieval Latin *cuppa* (see CUP)]

kibble[2] /kíbb'l/ (**-bles, -bling, -bled**) *vt* to grind something, e.g. grain, into small pieces [Late 18C. < ?]

kibbutz /ki bóots/ (*plural* **-butzim** /ki bóot seem/) *n* a communal farm or factory in Israel run collectively and dedicated to the principle that production work and domestic work are of equal value [Mid-20C. < modern Hebrew *qibbūs* 'gathering'.]

kibbutznik /ki bóotsnik/ *n* a person who lives and works on a kibbutz

kibe /kīb/ *n* a chapped or swollen area of skin, usually on the heel and often ulcerated, caused by exposure to cold [14C. < ?]

Kibei /kee báy/ (*plural* **-bei**) *n US* somebody born in the United States of Japanese parents and educated in Japan [< Japanese, 'go home']

kibitka /ki bítkə/ *n* **1 RUSSIAN SLEDGE** a covered sledge or wagon in Russia **2 TATAR TENT** a tent made of felt used by the Tatars of Central Asia **3 TATAR FAMILY** a family of Tatars [Late 18C. < Russian.]

kibitz /kíbbits/ *vi US* (*informal*) **1** to interfere or give unwanted advice, especially when watching a card game **2** to chat [Early 20C. Via Yiddish < German *kiebitsen*.] —**kibitzer** *n*

kiblah /kíbblə/, **kibla, qibla** *n* the direction of Mecca that Muslims must face when praying [Mid-17C. < Arabic *kibla* 'that which is opposite'.]

kibosh /kī bosh/ *vt* to put a stop to something [Mid-19C. < ?] ◇ **put the kibosh on something** to prevent something from happening or from being successful (*informal*)

kick /kik/ *v* **1** *vti* **STRIKE WITH THE FOOT** to strike something or somebody with the foot **2** *vti* **MOVE WITH THE FOOT** to make something move by striking it with the foot ○ *kick a ball around* **3** *vti* **MAKE A THRASHING MOVEMENT** to make a thrashing movement with the legs, e.g. when fighting or swimming ○ *Hold onto the side of the pool and kick your legs as hard as you can.* **4** *vti* **RAISE THE LEG HIGH** to raise the leg up high in a swift movement, e.g. in a dance ○ *an entire chorus line kicking in unison* **5** *vi* **RECOIL** to recoil when fired (*refers to firearms*) **6** *vti* **SCORE GOAL** in various football games, to score a goal by kicking ○ *He kicked a conversion to win the game.* **7** *vi* **BOUNCE HIGH** to bounce up high and quickly (*refers to a cricket ball*) ○ *On this wicket, a pace bowler should be able to make the ball really kick.* **8** *vi* **OBJECT** to show disapproval or object to something by not cooperating (*informal*) ○ *He kicked against the restrictions.* **9** *vr* **BLAME** to be irritated with yourself (*informal*) ○ *I'm kicking myself for missing the deadline.* **10** *vi US* **HAVE FUN** to have fun or spend time in an enjoyable way (*informal*) ■ *n* **1 BLOW WITH THE FOOT** a blow with the foot **2 LEG MOVEMENT** a thrashing movement with the leg ○ *a swimming kick* **3 RAISING OF THE LEG** a swift lift of the leg, e.g. in a dance ○ *a high kick* **4 KICKING OF A BALL** the striking of a ball with the foot ○ *opted for a kick instead of a pass* **5 PLEASURE** an exciting, pleasurable, or satisfying feeling (*informal*) ○ *She really gets a kick out of appearing on stage.* **6 STIMULANT EFFECT** a sudden stimulant effect, especially one produced by alcohol **7 POWER** power or strength ○ *That sauce has quite a kick to it.* **8 TEMPORARY INTEREST** a temporary interest, especially a strongly absorbing interest (*informal*) ○ *They're on a real health kick at the moment.* **9 RECOIL OF A GUN** the backward thrust of a gun when it is fired [14C. < ?] —**kickable** *adj* —**kicker** *n* ◇ **a kick in the pants** a reprimand given to somebody who is not showing enough enthusiasm or effort (*informal*) ◇ **kick somebody upstairs** to promote somebody to a seemingly higher position that is actually less important or influential (*informal*)

kick around *v* **1** *vt* **MISTREAT** to treat somebody badly and unfairly (*informal*) **2** *vt* **DISCUSS** to discuss a topic or range of topics in an informal way (*informal*) **3** *vti* **TRAVEL AIMLESSLY** to travel around a place without any fixed plans **4** *vi* **BE SOMEWHERE** to remain forgotten or neglected (*informal*)

kick back *v* **1** *vti* **PAY A BRIBE** to pay money illegally in order to buy concessions or favours (*informal*) **2** *vi* **REACT SUDDENLY** to react strongly and violently (*informal*) **3** *vi* **UNDERGO RECOIL** to recoil when fired (*refers to guns*) **4** *vt US* **RETURN SOMETHING STOLEN** to return stolen items or money to a shop or a person (*informal*) **5** *vi US* **RELAX** to relax comfortably (*informal*)

kick in *v* **1** *vi* **TAKE EFFECT** to start to take effect or come into operation (*informal*) ○ *I'll feel better once the antibiotics kick in.* **2** *vi US* **DIE** to die (*slang*) **3** *vti US, ANZ* **CONTRIBUTE** to contribute towards the cost of something (*informal*) ◊ **chip in** *v.* 1

kick off *v* **1** *vi* in football, to start play by kicking the ball off the centre spot **2** *vti* to start something or to begin (*informal*) ○ *Let's kick off tonight's show with our first guest.*

kick on *vi ANZ* to continue or persevere in doing something (*informal*)

kick out *vt* to throw somebody out or send somebody away (*informal*)

kick up *v* (*informal*) **1** *vt* **CAUSE** to cause or instigate something, usually something undesirable ○ *kick up a fuss* **2** *vi* **PROTEST** to protest or react in a way that causes trouble **3** *vi US* **GIVE TROUBLE** to misbehave or malfunction

kickabout /kíkə bowt/ *n* an informal game of football

Kickapoo /kíkə poo/ (*plural* **-poo** *or* **-poos**), **Kikapoo** (*plural* **-poo** *or* **-poos**) *n* **1** a member of a Native North American people who lived in SW Wisconsin and now live in Kansas, Oklahoma, and Texas **2** the Algonquian language of the Kickapoo. Native speakers: 4,000. [Late 17C. < Kickapoo *kiikaapoa*.] —**Kickapoo** *adj*

kickback /kík bak/ *n* (*informal*) **1** a sum of money paid illegally in order to gain concessions or favours **2** a strong or violent reaction

kickboard /kík bawrd/ *n* SWIMMING = **float** *n.* 2

kickboxing /kík boksing/ *n* a form of boxing that involves kicking as well as punching —**kickboxer** *n*

kickdown /kík down/ *n* a way of changing gear in a car with automatic transmission, that involves pressing hard on the accelerator pedal

kicking /kíking/ *n* a severe beating (*informal*) ■ *adj* excellent, exciting, or very enjoyable (*slang*)

kickoff /kík of/ *n* **1 START OF MATCH** in football, the place kick from the centre spot that begins the game **2 START** the start of something or the time when something starts (*informal*) **3 STARTING TIME** the time at which a game of football is due to start **4 START OF A GAME** in American football, the kicking of the ball at the beginning of a game, half, or after a touchdown or field goal ◇ **for a kickoff** to begin with, or as the first of several things (*informal*)

kick plate *n* a metal plate attached to a door at foot level to protect it

kick pleat *n* an inverted pleat at the lower back of a straight skirt to prevent the wearer from being hampered when walking

kickshaw /kík shaw/ *n* (*archaic*) **1** a trinket of little value **2** an exotic food delicacy [Late 16C. < French *quelque chose* 'something'.]

kicksin' /kíksin/ *n Carib* playing around and not acting seriously (*informal*)

kickstand /kík stand/ *n* a pivoting metal bar on a bicycle or motorcycle that can be pushed down into contact with the ground to keep the vehicle upright when it is stationary [Mid-20C. Because it is raised and lowered with the foot.]

kick-start *vt* **1 START A MOTORCYCLE** to start the engine on a motorcycle by stepping down hard on the kick-starter **2 START SOMETHING QUICKLY** to start or restart a process or activity quickly and forcefully ○ *policies designed to kick-start an ailing economy* ■ *n* **1** MOTORCYCLES = **kick-starter** **2 FORCEFUL START** a course of action that quickly and forcefully starts or restarts a process or activity (*informal*)

kick-starter *n* the pedal on a motorcycle that starts the engine when it is kicked downwards

kick turn *n* in skiing, a standing 180-degree turn made by swivelling each ski separately

kick wheel *n* a mechanical potter's wheel that is turned by a foot-operated treadle

kid[1] /kid/ *n* **1 CHILD** a young child (*informal*) **2 YOUNG GOAT** a young goat, antelope, or similar animal **3 YOUTH** a young person (*informal*) **4 SOFT LEATHER** soft leather made from the skin of a young goat **5** *US* **TERM OF ADDRESS** used as an informal term of address (*informal*) ○ *Here's looking at you, kid.* ■ *adj* **YOUNGER** younger, especially of two siblings (*informal*) ○ *his kid sister* ■ *vti* (**kids, kidding, kidded**) **BEAR YOUNG** to give birth to a young goat [12C. < Old Norse *kið*.] ◇ **our kid** *N England* my or our younger brother

SYNONYMS See *youth*.

kid[2] /kid/ (**kids, kidding, kidded**) *v* **1** *vti* to say something that is not true, especially as a joke or to tease somebody **2** *vt* to deceive or mislead somebody (*informal*) ○ *Don't kid yourself.* [Late 16C. < KID[1].] —**kidder** *n*

Kidd /kid/, **William** (1645?–1701) Scottish-born American pirate. Known as **Captain Kidd**

Kidderminster /kíddərminstər/, **Kidderminster carpet** *n* a type of ingrain carpet originally made in Kidderminster

kiddie *n* US = **kiddy**

kiddo /kíddō/ (*plural* **-dos** *or* **-does**) *n* **1** a child, young person, or friend (*slang*) **2** used as an informal term of address, especially to a young person (*informal*)

Kiddush /kíddəsh, kíddush/ (*plural* **-dushim**), **kiddush** (*plural* **-dushim**) *n* **1** in Judaism, a special blessing, usually for wine, said before a meal on the eve of the Sabbath or a holiday in order to consecrate the festival **2** a reception following the recitation of the Kiddush for the congregants, at which drinks and snacks are served [Mid-18C. < Hebrew *qiddūš* 'sanctification'.]

kiddy /kíddi/ (*plural* **-dies**), **kiddie** *n* a small child (*informal*)

kid glove *n* a glove of soft leather made from the skin of a young goat ◇ **handle somebody** *or* **something with kid gloves** to use great care or delicacy when dealing with somebody *or* something

kidglove /kid glúv/, **kid-glove** *adj* displaying tact and sensitivity

kidlit /kídlit/ *n US* literature for children (*informal*) [Late 20C. Shortening.]

Kidman /kídmən/, **Nicole** (*b.* 1967) Hawaiian-born Australian actor

Kidman, Sir Sidney (1857–1935) Australian landowner

kidnap /kíd nap/ *vti* (**-naps, -napping, -napped**) to take somebody away by force and hold him or her prisoner, usually for ransom ■ *n* = **kidnapping** [Mid-17C. < KID[1] + *nap* 'to steal'.] —**kidnapper** *n*

kidnapping /kíd naping/ *n* the action or crime of forcefully taking away and holding somebody prisoner, usually for ransom. Also called **kidnap**

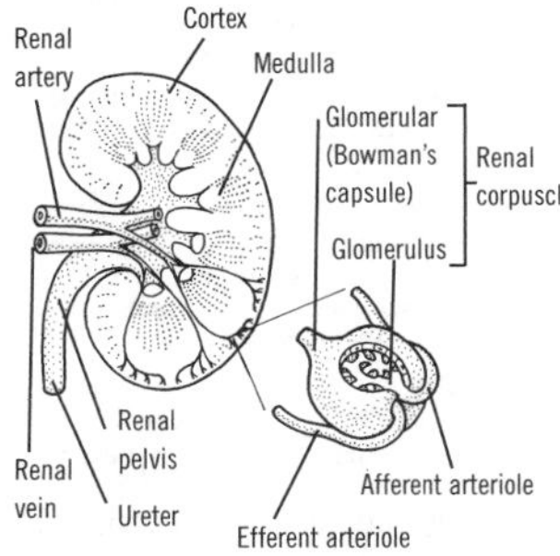

Kidney

kidney /kídni/ (*plural* **-neys**) *n* **1 WASTE-REMOVING VERTEBRATE ORGAN** either of a pair of organs in the abdomen of vertebrates that filter waste liquid resulting from metabolism of the blood, which is subsequently excreted as urine **2 INVERTEBRATE ORGAN** the organ in invertebrates that filters waste material for excretion **3 ANIMAL KIDNEY AS FOOD** the kidney of a pig, calf, ox, or lamb, eaten as meat **4 KIND** a kind, type, or disposition (*dated*) ○ *a person of a very different kidney* [14C. < ?]

kidney bean *n* **1** a small, usually dark red, edible bean shaped like a kidney **2** a widely cultivated annual plant that produces kidney beans. *Phaseolus vulgaris.*

kidney-shaped *adj* in the shape of an oval with a concavity in one side

kidney stone *n* a small hard mass that forms in the kidney, consisting mainly of phosphates, oxalates, and urates

kidney vetch *n* PLANTS = **okra** *n.* **1**

kidology /ki dólləji/ *n* the use of bluffing or deception (*informal*) [Mid-20C. < KID[2].]

kidskin /kíd skin/ *n* INDUST = **kid**[1] *n.* **4**

kids' stuff *n* (*informal*) **1** something considered suitable only for children or immature people **2** something that is very easy or very boring

kidult /kíddult/ *n* an adult who enjoys entertainment such as films or computer games intended mainly for children (*slang*) [Mid-20C. Blend of KID[1] + ADULT.]

kidvid /kíd vid/ *n* *US* a video for children (*informal*) [Late 20C. Shortening.]

Kiel /keel/ seaport and capital of Schleswig-Holstein State, in north-central Germany. Population: 246,586 (1997).

kielbasa /keel bássə/ *n* a spicy smoked Polish sausage [Mid-20C. Via Polish < Turkic *kūl bastī* 'roast pressed meat'.]

Kiel Canal canal in NW Germany connecting the North and Baltic seas. Length: 98 km/61 mi.

kier /keer/ *n* a vat in which yarn or cloth is bleached or dyed [Late 16C. < Old Norse *ker* 'tub'.]

Kierkegaard /keérkə gaard/, **Søren** (1813–55) Danish philosopher

kieserite /keézə rīt/ *n* a white to yellow crystalline hydrated magnesium sulphate mineral. Source: salt residues. [Mid-19C. After Dietrich *Kieser* (1779–1862), German physician.]

Kiev /keéyif/ capital and largest city of Ukraine, in the north-central part of the country. Population: 2,646,000 (1993).

kif /kif/, **kef** /kef/, **kaif** /kayf/ *n* marijuana, especially in North Africa [Early 19C. < Arabic *kayf, kef* 'pleasure'.]

Kigali /ki gaáli/ capital of Rwanda, in the centre of the country. Population: 232,733 (1991).

Kikapoo *n* PEOPLES, LANGUAGE = **Kickapoo** —**Kikapoo** *adj*

kike /kīk/ *n* *US* a highly offensive taboo term for a Jewish person (*taboo*) [Early 20C. < ?]

Kikongo /kee kóng gō/ *n* LANG = **Kongo**[1] *n.* **2** [Late 19C. < Kikongo.]

kikumon /kíkə mon, keékə mon/ *n* the emblem of the Japanese imperial family, in the form of a chrysanthemum [< Japanese]

Kikuyu /ki koó yoo/ (*plural* **-yu** *or* **-yus**) *n* **1** a member of a people living mainly in highland Kenya, especially around Mount Kenya **2** a Benue-Congo language spoken in parts of Kenya. Native speakers: 5 million. [Mid-19C. < Bantu.] —**Kikuyu** *adj*

Kilauea /keé low áy ə/ world's most active volcano, on central Hawaii Island. Height: 1,247 m/4,090 ft.

Kildare /kil dáir/ county in the province of Leinster, E Republic of Ireland. Area: 1,694 sq. km/654 sq. mi.

kilderkin /kílldər kin/ *n* **1** an obsolete British measurement for liquids, equivalent to about 18 gallons or 68 litres **2** a cask with a capacity of one kilderkin [14C. < Middle Dutch *kinderkin* 'small quintal'.]

kiley *n* *Aus* = **kylie**

kilim /ki leém, ki lím, keélim/ *n* a woven Middle Eastern rug with richly coloured geometric patterns [Late 19C. Via Turkish *Kilim* < Persian *gelīm*.]

Kilimanjaro, Mount /kílləmən jaárō/ highest mountain in Africa, in NE Tanzania. Height: 5,895 m/19,340 ft.

Kilkenny /kil kénni/ county in the province of Leinster, E Republic of Ireland. Area: 2,062 sq. km/796 sq. mi.

kill /kil/ *v* **1** *vti* **CAUSE SOMEBODY TO DIE** to cause the death of a person or an animal ○ *They were killed in a car crash.* **2** *vt* **RUIN** to cause something to end or be ruined ○ *The remark killed the conversation.* **3** *vt* **HURT PART OF SOMEBODY'S BODY** to cause severe physical pain or discomfort to somebody (*informal*) ○ *My feet are killing me!* **4** *vt* **OVERPOWER SOMETHING SUBTLE OR LESS STRONG** to destroy or severely damage an essential, often delicate quality in something by superimposing something stronger ○ *Her perfume killed the scent of the roses.* **5** *vt* **TIRE SOMEBODY OUT** to exhaust somebody completely (*informal*) ○ *These stairs kill me every time.* **6** *vr* **OVEREXERT YOURSELF** to push yourself too hard (*informal; often used ironically*) ○ *She was killing herself to get the job done on time.* **7** *vt* **SWITCH SOMETHING OFF** to disconnect the power to something electrical or mechanical so that it stops working (*informal*) ○ *Kill the engine.* **8** *vt* **MAKE TIME PASS** to use up spare time in some activity (*informal*) ○ *We had a couple of hours to kill before going to the airport.* **9** *vt* **CUT TEXT** to delete a piece of text from a publication or remove a particular amount from a text (*slang*) ○ *We had to kill half a column to make space for the ad.* **10** *vt* **BLOCK A PLAN** to prevent a proposal going through, e.g. the passing of a parliamentary bill **11** *vti* **BOWL SOMEBODY OVER** to have an overpowering effect on somebody, e.g. causing extreme admiration, helpless laughter, or utter amazement (*informal*) ○ *dressed to kill* **12** *vt* **DRINK ALL OF** to finish off a bottle of something, usually an alcoholic beverage (*slang*) **13** *vt* **CONTROL THE BALL** to bring a fast-moving ball under instant control **14** *vt* *US* **MAKE A BALL DEAD** in football, to stop the ball so that it is no longer in play (*informal*) **15** *vt* *US* **HIT A BALL HARD** to hit a ball very hard **16** *vt* **MAKE A BALL UNRETURNABLE** in racquet games, to hit the ball so hard, with such skill, or in such a direction that your opponent has no chance of returning it ■ *n* **1 KILLING** the moment or an act of killing something, especially prey or game, or the bull at the end of a bullfight **2 PREY** the prey killed by an animal or human being **3 DESTRUCTION OF ENEMY VEHICLE** the destroying of an enemy vehicle such as a plane, ship, or tank (*slang*) [13C. < assumed Old English *cyllan* < Germanic.] ◇ **be in at the kill** to be present at the end of something or the achievement of an aim, especially when you have worked to cause it

kill off *vt* **1** to destroy something utterly, especially the remaining members of a group of people or creatures ○ *The spray killed off all the aphids.* **2** to write in the death of a character, especially in a serial or soap opera

Killarney /ki laárni/ city in the SW Republic of Ireland. Population: 9,950 (1991).

killdeer /kíl deer/ *n* a large plover with brown and white plumage, two black breast bands, and a distinctive noisy cry. Native to: North America. *Charadrius vociferus.* [Mid-18C. An imitation of its call.]

killer /kíllər/ *n* **1 SOMEBODY OR SOMETHING THAT KILLS** somebody or something that kills other people or animals intentionally, especially one that does this more than once ○ *a killer crocodile* **2 SOMETHING VERY DIFFICULT** something that is very demanding or difficult (*informal*) ○ *This aerobics class is a killer.* **3 DESTRUCTIVE FORCE, PERSON, OR ORGANISM** somebody or something that destroys or is fatal **4 EXCEPTIONAL THING** something that is excellent or exceptional (*slang*) ○ *a killer performance*

⚡**killer app** *n* a highly popular computer application, seen as definitive (*slang*)

killer bee *n* an aggressive honeybee that was hybridized in Brazil from African and European strains and has spread north into Mexico and S Texas (*informal*)

killer cell *n* a T cell that is part of the body's immune system and attacks cells having specific antigens on their surface, e.g. cancer cells and those infected with a virus

killer instinct *n* **1** a tendency, capacity, or urge to kill **2** an overpowering drive to succeed, e.g. in business deals or sports, whatever the cost may be to other people

killer T cell *n* ANAT = **killer cell**

killer whale *n* a black-and-white toothed whale inhabiting colder seas. It grows up to 7.62 m/25 ft long, has a tall dorsal fin, and feeds mainly on fish and squid. *Orcinus orca.*

kill fee *n* *US* payment made to a writer, photographer, artist, or illustrator by a publisher who has decided not to publish the contracted work

killick /kíllik/, **killock** /kíllək/ *n* a small anchor, especially one made of a heavy stone [Early 17C. < ?]

Killiecrankie, Pass of /kílli krángki/ wooded pass in central Scotland

killifish /kíllifish/ *n* a freshwater fish about the size of a minnow, used in aquariums, as bait, and in mosquito control. Family: Cyprinodontidae. [Early 19C. < ?]

killing /kílling/ *n* **1 SLAYING** the act of causing the death of a human being or an animal **2 QUICK PROFIT** a large and quick profit (*informal*) ■ *adj* **1 EXHAUSTING** totally exhausting **2 FUNNY** hilariously funny **3 FATAL** causing or resulting in death —**killingly** *adv*

killing fields *npl* the site of mass slaughter, e.g. of civilians

killjoy /kíl joy/ *n* somebody whose behaviour prevents other people from having a good time

killock *n* SAILING = **killick**

kill shot *n* *US* in racket games, a shot that is hit so hard or accurately that it cannot be returned

Kilmarnock /kil maárnək/ town in central Scotland. Population: 44,307 (1991).

kiln /kiln, kil/ *n* a specialized oven or furnace used for industrial processes such as firing clay for pottery or bricks and for drying materials such as hops or timber ■ *vt* to dry, fire, or bake something in a kiln [Pre-12C. < Latin *culina* < *coquere* 'to cook'.]

kilo /keélō/ *n* **1** (*symbol* **k**) a kilogram **2** a code word for the letter 'K', used in international radio communications [Mid-19C. Shortening.]

kilo- *prefix* **1** (*symbol* **k**) a thousand (10^3) ○ *kilogram* **2** a binary thousand ○ *kilobyte* [Via French < Greek *khilioi* 'thousand']

⚡**kilobit** /kílləbit/ *n* 1,024 bits

⚡**kilobyte** /kíllə bīt/ *n* 1,024 bytes

kilocalorie /kíllō kalləri/ *n* PHYS, MEASURE = **calorie** *n.* **2**

kilocycle /kíllō sīk'l/ *n* a kilohertz

kilogram /kíllə gram/, **kilogramme** *n* (*symbol* **kg**) the basic unit of mass in the SI system, equal to 1,000 grams or 2.2046 lbs

kilohertz /kíllō hurts/ *n* 1,000 hertz

kilojoule /kíllə jool/ *n* one thousand joules

kilometre *n* 1,000 metres or 0.621 miles

kiloparsec /kíllō paar sek/ *n* 1,000 parsecs

kiloton /kíllō tun/ *n* **1** 1,000 tons **2** an explosive force equal to 1,000 tons of TNT

kilovolt /kíllə vōlt/ *n* 1,000 volts

kilowatt /kíllə wot/ *n* 1,000 watts

kilowatt-hour *n* a unit of energy equal to the work done by one kilowatt in one hour

kilt /kilt/ *n* **SCOTTISH GARMENT** a knee-length wrap-around tartan garment that is part of the traditional Scottish highland dress for men and is also worn by women and girls ■ *vt* **1 TUCK UP A SKIRT** to pull up a skirt and gather it into folds, so as to keep it out of water or mud or to allow more freedom of movement (*dated*) **2 PLEAT GARMENT** to form vertical pleats in the fabric of a garment, usually a skirt [Mid-18C. < dialect *kilt* 'tuck up, gird' < N Germanic.] —**kilted** *adj*

kilter /kíltər/ *n* good working order or condition ○ *The well pump is out of kilter.* [Mid-17C. Variant of *kelter* < ?]

kiltie /kílti/ *n* a person wearing a kilt, especially a kilted soldier from a highland regiment (*informal*)

Kimberleys /kímbərliz/ plateau region of NW Western Australia. Highest peak: Mount Hann 776 m/2,545 ft. Area: 360,000 sq. km/140,000 sq. mi.

kimberlite /kímbər līt/ *n* a form of igneous rock, found especially in South Africa, composed mainly of peridotite and often containing diamonds [Late 19C. After *Kimberley*, town in South Africa.]

kimchi /kímchi/ *n* a pickle made with vegetables such as cabbage and white radish seasoned with chilli, garlic, and ginger, regarded as the national dish of Korea [Late 19C. Via Korean *kimch'i* < Chinese.]

Kim Il Sung /kím il súng/ (1912–94) North Korean statesman. Born **Kim Song Ju**

kimono /ki mṓnō/ (*plural* **-nos**) *n* **1** a loose, floor-length, traditional Japanese garment that has wide sleeves, wraps in front, and is fastened with a sash **2** a Western garment, especially a dressing gown, similar to the Japanese kimono [Late 19C. < Japanese, < *ki* 'wear' + *mono* 'thing'.] —**kimonoed** *adj*

kin /kin/ *n* **1 FAMILY GROUP** somebody's relatives as a group (+ *plural verb*) **2 GROUP OR CLASS** a member of a group that shares characteristics with another group ○ *the starfish and its kin the sea urchin* **3 BLOOD RELATION** somebody related by blood ○ *He's not kin but we consider him one of the family.* ■ *adj* **RELATED** related to somebody [Old English *cyn(n)* < Indo-European]

-kin *suffix* little, dear ○ *limpkin* [Probably < Middle Dutch *-ki(j)n*]

kina /keénə/ *n* see table at **currency** [Late 20C. < Tok Pisin.]

Kinabalu, Mount /kínnəbə lóo/ mountain in E Malaysia, on the northern tip of Borneo. Height: 4,101 m/13,455 ft.

kinaesthesia /kín eess theézi ə, kīn eess-/, **kinaesthesis** /kín eess theéssiss, kīn eess-/ *n* the perception or sensing of the motion, weight, or position of the body as muscles, tendons, and joints move [Late 19C. < Greek *kinein* 'to move' + *aisthēsis* 'sensation'.] —**kinaesthetic** *adj* —**kinaesthetically** *adv*

kinase /kī nayss, -nayz/ *n* an enzyme that catalyses the transfer of a phosphate group from ATP [Early 20C. < KINETIC.]

Kincardineshire /kin kaárdinshər/ former county in E Scotland, now part of Aberdeenshire

kincob /kíng kob, -kəb/ *n* an Indian silk embroidered with gold or silver thread [Early 18C. < Urdu, Persian *kamkāb* 'gold or silver brocade', alteration of *kamkā* 'damask silk' < Chinese words, 'gold' and 'flower'.]

kind[1] /kīnd/ *adj* **1 COMPASSIONATE** having a generous, warm, compassionate nature **2 GENEROUS** showing generosity or compassion **3 AGREEABLE OR SAFE** not harsh, unpleasant, or likely to have destructive effects ○ *a detergent that is kind to the environment* **4 CARING** showing courtesy or caring about somebody (*formal*) ○ *my kindest regards to your family* **5 LOVING** full of love (*archaic*) [Old English *gecynde* 'innate, natural' < Germanic]

kind[2] /kīnd/ *n* **1 GROUP OF INDIVIDUALS THAT SHARE FEATURES** a group or class of individuals connected by shared characteristics ○ *What kind of fruit is this?* **2 SOMETHING INFERIOR** an example of something, especially if it is seen as inferior or doubtful ○ *Well, you could say it's a kind of tool, but how would you use it?* **3 ESSENCE** the primary character of something that determines the class to which it belongs ◇ **kind of** rather, to some extent, or in a way (*informal*) ○ *She seemed kind of upset when I talked to her.* ◇ **in kind 1** with goods or services and not money **2** with something of the same sort that was given ○ *If they attack us, they'll be paid back in kind.* ◇ **of a kind 1** like something else in some respects but not enough to be satisfactory **2** alike, or belonging to the same sort ○ *She's one of a kind, is Sarah.*

SYNONYMS See ***type***.

USAGE When *kind of* is followed by a plural word, there is a temptation to precede the whole phrase with a corresponding plural such as *these* or *those*, so that *this kind of thing* becomes *these kind of things*. However, such expressions (and ones on the same pattern employing *sort* or *type*) are widely regarded as ungrammatical. *These kinds of things* or *things of this kind* is to be preferred.

kinda /kīndə/ *contr* kind of (*nonstandard*) ○ *It's kinda strange.* [Early 20C. Alteration.]

kindergarten /kíndər gaart'n/ *n US* a school or class for young children, usually between the ages of four and six, immediately before they begin formal education [Mid-19C. < German, 'children's garden'.]

kind-hearted /-haártid/ *adj* **1** sympathetic and kind ○ *She's too kind-hearted to be angry with you for long.* **2** showing or arising from a sympathetic and generous nature ○ *a kind-hearted gesture* —**kind-heartedly** *adv* —**kind-heartedness** *n*

Kindi /kíndi/, **al-** (801?–873?) Arabian Islamic philosopher

kindle[1] /kínd'l/ (**-dles, -dling, -dled**) *vti* **1 START BURNING** to set something alight, or to begin to burn **2 BRIGHTEN OR GLOW** to make something glow, or to become bright **3 IGNITE EMOTION OR INTEREST** to become aroused, or to arouse feelings or interest ○ *The programme kindled his interest in antiquarian books.* [12C. < Old Norse *kynda*; influenced by Old Norse *kyndill* 'torch, candle'.] —**kindler** *n*

kindle[2] *n* a brood or a litter, e.g. of kittens ■ *vi* to give birth, especially to baby rabbits

kindling /kíndling/ *n* **1 FIRE-LIGHTING MATERIAL** something such as a bunch of small dry twigs used to start a fire because it burns easily **2 MAKING SOMETHING BURN** the act of making something start to burn **3 STIRRING UP OF EMOTION** the arousal of somebody's interest or feelings

kindly /kīndli/ *adj* (**-lier, -liest**) **1 FRIENDLY AND GENEROUS BY NATURE** sympathetic and kind **2 SHOWING SYMPATHY** arising from or showing a sympathetic and generous nature **3 PLEASANT** pleasant, mild, or comfortable ■ *adv* **1 PLEASE** used in polite requests ○ *Kindly take your seats.* **2 IN A KIND WAY** showing kindness and considerateness ○ *He kindly accompanied me home.* **3 TOLERANTLY** with tolerance and patience ○ *She kindly disregarded their lack of skill during the first few days.* —**kindliness** *n*

USAGE Misplaced modifier: ***Kindly*** is not restricted just to *kindness* as such but may also mean, approximately, '*please*'. In either case it should modify the action or thing wished for, not some other part of the sentence. The intention of, for example, *May we kindly request that patrons take their seats*, is to encourage patrons to be so kind as to sit down. Thus the sentence should be reworded as *May we request that patrons kindly take their seats.*

kindness /kīndnəss/ *n* **1** the practice of being or the capability to be sympathetic and compassionate **2** an act that shows consideration and caring ○ *How can we thank you for your many kindnesses?*

kindred /kíndrəd/ *adj* **1 SIMILAR** close to somebody or something else because of similar qualities or interests ○ *the kindred relationship between neuroscience and neurology* **2 RELATED BY BLOOD** related to somebody by blood (*formal*) ○ *the search for someone kindred to him* ■ *n* **1 AFFINITY** closeness to somebody not related to you by blood based, e.g. on similarity of character or interests ○ *a sense of kindred between the two candidates* **2 BLOOD RELATIONSHIP** relationship by blood or, less strictly, by marriage ○ *occasions that reinforce the ties of kindred* **3 SOMEBODY'S FAMILY** somebody's relatives as a group (+ *plural verb*) **4 CLAN** a family or group of closely related families, e.g. in the Celtic kin-based social system ○ *The Ui Neill were then the most powerful of the kindreds.* [12C. Originally *kinrede* < KIN + Old English *rǣden* 'condition'.] —**kindredness** *n* —**kindredship** *n*

kindred spirit *n* a person who resembles somebody else in character, interests, and temperament

kindy /kíndi/ (*plural* **-dies**) *n ANZ* a kindergarten (*informal*) [Mid-20C. Shortening and alteration.]

kine /kīn/ *npl* cows or cattle (*archaic*) [Old English *cȳna* 'of the cows', a plural of *cū* (see COW)]

kinematics /kínni máttiks/ *n* a branch of physics that deals with the motion of a body or system without reference to force and mass (+ *singular verb*) [Mid-19C. < Greek *kinēmat-* 'motion'.] —**kinematic** *adj* —**kinematically** *adv*

kinescope /kínnəskōp, kīnə-/ *n US* MEDIA = **television tube** [Mid-20C. Formerly a trademark.]

kinesics /ki neéssiks, kī-, -neéziks, -/ *n* the study of the ways in which people use body movements, e.g. shrugging, to communicate without speaking (+ *singular verb*) [Mid-20C. < Greek *kinēsis* (see KINESIS).]

kinesiology /ki neéssi óllәji, kī-, -neé zi-, -/ *n* **1** the study of the mechanics of motion with respect to human anatomy **2** a system of muscle testing that reveals and corrects musculoskeletal imbalances and identifies food sensitivities [Late 19C. < Greek *kinēsis* (see KINESIS).] —**kinesiologist** *n*

kinesis /ki neéssiss, kī-/ *n* the movement of a cell or organism in response to a stimulus such as light [Early 20C. < Greek *kinēsis* 'movement' < *kinein* 'to move'.]

-kinesis *suffix* **1** motion, activity ○ *psychokinesis* **2** cell division ○ *diakinesis* [< Greek *kinēsis* (see KINESIS)]

kinesthesia *n* US = **kinaesthesia**

kinetheodolite /kínnəth' óddə līt/ *n* an optical instrument that contains a cine camera and provides continuous footage of a moving target, e.g. a missile or satellite, along with its altitude and trajectory [Mid-20C. < KINESIS + THEODOLITE.]

kinetic /ki néttik, kī-/ *adj* relating to, caused by, or producing motion [Mid-19C. < Greek *kinētikos* 'for putting in motion' < *kinein* 'to move'.]

kinetic art *n* art, especially sculpture, with parts that move, e.g. when blown by the wind or activated by electricity —**kinetic artist** *n*

kinetic energy *n* (*symbol* T *or* E_k) the energy that a body or system has because of its motion

kinetics /ki néttiks, kī-/ *n* (+ *singular verb*) **1** PHYS = **dynamics** *n.* 4 **2** a branch of chemistry that studies rates of reactions

kinetic theory *n* a theory of the behaviour of gases that assumes heat is a process of energy transfer and the internal energy of a gas is the total energy of its particles

kineto- *prefix* motion, movement ○ *kinetosome* [< Greek *kinetos* 'moving' < *kinein* 'to move']

kinetoplast /ki néttə plast, kī-/ *n* a small cell body outside the nucleus and near the base of the flagellum in some protozoans

kinetosome /ki néttə sōm, kī-/ *n* BIOL = **basal body**

kinfolk /kínfōk/ *npl* somebody's relatives

king /king/ *n* **1 MAN OR BOY SOVEREIGN** a man or boy who rules as a monarch over an independent state **2 CHIEF** a ruler of a specific group ○ *Jupiter was king of the Roman gods* **3 BEST EXAMPLE** any animal considered as the best, strongest, or biggest of its kind ○ *The lion is variously called the king of beasts or the king of the jungle.* **4 PRE-EMINENT MAN** the principal man or pre-eminent male figure in a specific field ○ *king of the chat shows.* **5 HIGH COURT CARD** a card in each suit of a pack that carries the picture of a king **6 PRINCIPAL CHESS PIECE** the most important piece in chess, whose capture wins the game **7 CROWNED PIECE IN DRAUGHTS** a piece in the game of draughts that has reached the far side of the board and has been crowned, and may therefore move in any direction ■ *vt* **1 CROWN A PLAYING PIECE** to make a piece into a king **2 CROWN SOMEBODY KING** to make somebody a king [Old English *cyning* < Germanic] —**kingship** *n*

King /king/ *n* a title used to denote God or Jesus Christ

King /king/, **B. B.** (*b.* 1925) US blues musician. Born **Riley B. King**

King, Billie Jean (*b.* 1943) US tennis player. Born **Billie Jean Moffat**

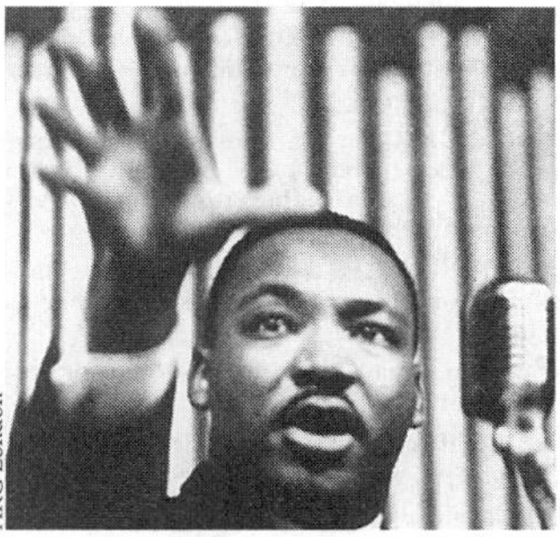

AKG London

Martin Luther King, Jr.

King, Martin Luther, Jr. (1929–68) US civil rights leader and clergyman

King, Stephen (*b.* 1947) US writer of horror stories

King, William Lyon Mackenzie (1874–1950) Canadian statesman

kingbird /kíng burd/ *n* a large songbird. Native to: America. Genus: *Tyrannus.*

kingbolt /kíng bōlt/ *n* a vertical bolt that joins the body of a carriage, wagon, or railway carriage to the front axle

King Charles spaniel *n* a small spaniel of a breed with a markedly domed head, snub nose, bulging eyes, floppy ears, and a tan or black coat with white patches [Late 19C. Named after CHARLES II, who was partial to the breed.]

king cobra *n* a very large poisonous cobra that eats other reptiles and can reach a length of 5.5 m/18 ft. Native to: Southeast Asia, Philippines *Ophiophagus hannah.*

King Country region in the west of the North Island, New Zealand

king crab *n* MARINE BIOL = **horseshoe crab**

kingcup /kíng kup/ *n* a plant of the buttercup family, especially a marsh marigold. Flowers: yellow.

kingdom /kíngdəm/ *n* **1 MONARCH'S TERRITORY** a state or people ruled over by a king or queen **2 SPHERE OF ACTIVITY** a realm or area of activity in which a particular thing is thought to dominate ○ *the kingdom of professional tennis* **3 HIGHEST CLASSIFICATION FOR NATURAL THINGS** any of the three groups, animal, vegetable, and mineral, into which natural organisms and objects are traditionally, as opposed to scientifically, divided

kingdom come *n* **1** the next world or the state after death **2** the point at which the world comes to an end (*informal*) [Late 18C. < *Thy kingdom come* (in the Our Father (Matt. 6:10)) 'May Thy kingdom come'.]

kingfish /kíng fish/ *n* **1** a large game fish. Native to: warm Atlantic coastal waters. Genus: *Menticirrhus*. **2** ZOOL = **king mackerel** **3** the flesh of a kingfish as food **4** ZOOL = **opah**

kingfisher /kíng fishər/ *n* a brightly coloured bird that usually has a short tail, a long stout bill, and sometimes a crest. Family: Alcidinidae. [15C. Originally *king's fisher*.]

King Island island off the coast of NW Tasmania, Australia. Population: 1,882 (1996). Area: 1,098 sq. km/424 sq. mi.

King James Bible, King James Version *n* = **Authorized Version**

kinglet /kínglət/ *n* **1** a small bird related to gnatcatchers and European warblers that has a black-edged yellow or reddish crown. Native to: North America. Genus: *Regulus*. **2** a minor king, e.g. of a contemptibly small or unimportant kingdom (*insult*)

kingly /kíngli/ (**-lier, -liest**) *adj* **1** stately and grand, as befits a king ○ *a kingly posture* **2** having or relating to the rank of king ○ *kingly duties* —**kingliness** *n*

king mackerel *n US* a mackerel often caught for sport. Native to: warm Atlantic waters. *Scomber cavalla*.

kingmaker /kíng maykər/ *n* somebody with the power and connections to influence who is appointed to important positions, usually within a government

king-of-arms (*plural* **kings-of-arms**) *n* a title given to principal heralds in the British colleges of arms

king of kings, King of Kings *n* **1** a title used for God or Jesus Christ **2** a male monarch who rules over other, subordinate kings

king of the castle *n* **1** the most important person in a group or place (*informal*) **2** a game in which a child stands on a piece of higher ground and keeps other children from taking it over

king of the hill *n US* a game in which a child stands on a piece of high ground and keeps other children from taking it over

King Peak mountain in the St Elias Range of SW Yukon Territory, Canada. Height: 5,173 m/16,972 ft.

king penguin *n* a large penguin. Native to: Antarctic. *Aptenodytes patagonica*.

kingpin /kíng pin/ *n* **1 LEADER** the most important person in a group or place (*informal*) **2 PART OF AXLE** a pivot pin that secures an axle to an axle beam and allows a vehicle to be steered **3 CRUX OF AN ARGUMENT** the most important point in an argument, upon which everything else depends **4 FRONT PIN IN A BOWLING ARRANGEMENT** the pin at the apex of a layout of the pins in tenpin bowling, which must be struck at a certain angle if all the pins are to be knocked down

king post *n* a vertical post that joins the apex of a triangular roof truss to the cross-beam. ◊ **queen post**

Kings /kingz/ *n* either of two books of the Bible, Kings I and II, that relate the histories of Israel and the kings of Judah (+ *singular verb*)

king salmon *n* ZOOL = **Chinook salmon**

King's Bench *n* the term used for the Queen's Bench Division when the reigning monarch is a man or boy. ◊ **Queen's Bench**

Kings Canyon /kingz-/ canyon in the south-central Northern Territory, Australia

King's Counsel *n* the term used for a Queen's Counsel when the reigning monarch is a man or boy

King's English *n* standard written or spoken British English, described as the most correct form of the language. It is called the Queen's English when the reigning monarch is a woman.

King's evidence *n* in English law, evidence for the prosecution given by somebody who took part in a crime, usually in exchange for leniency (*used when the reigning monarch is a man or boy*)

king's evil *n* scrofula (*archaic*) [< the belief that a king's touch could cure it]

Kingsford Smith /kíngzfərd smíth/, **Sir Charles Edward** (1897–1935) Australian aviator

King's highway *n* a public road, regarded as belonging ultimately to the monarch (*formal; used when the reigning monarch is a man or boy*)

king-size, king-sized *adj* **1 EXTRA BIG** larger, wider, or longer than the standard version of the same thing **2 FULL-SIZE** describes an extra-large size of bed, 1930 x 2032 mm/76 in x 80 in, or bedding made to fit this size of bed **3 VERY GREAT** very great in intensity, scope, or difficulty (*informal*) ○ *a king-size job to finish this weekend*

Kingsley /kíngzli/, **Charles** (1819–75) British writer and cleric

King's Lynn /kíngz lín/ historic town in E England. Population: 41,281 (1991).

king snake *n* a nonpoisonous constricting snake ranging from 0.6 metres/2 ft to 1.8 metres/6 ft in length and preying on small animals and other snakes. Native to: North America. Genus: *Lampropeltis*.

King's Proctor *n* in the United Kingdom, an official of the High Court of Justice who has the right to intervene in certain cases, including those involving divorces and wills, when there are charges of collusion among the people involved or suppression of facts (*used when the reigning monarch is a man or boy*)

king's ransom *n* an enormous sum of money

King's Regulations *npl* regulations that govern the armed forces of the UK and certain commonwealth countries (*used when the reigning monarch is a man or boy*)

king's shilling *n* in former times, a coin given to new military recruits as a symbol of enlistment into the British army (*used when the reigning monarch was a man or boy*) ◇ **take** *or* **earn the king's shilling** enlist in British army (*archaic*)

King's Speech *n* (*used when the reigning monarch is a man or boy*) **1** a speech given by the monarch at the opening of Parliament each year, setting out the government's proposed legislation **2** in the United Kingdom, a speech by the monarch to the nation and the Commonwealth broadcast on Christmas Day

Kingston /kíngstən/ **1** chief seaport and capital of Jamaica, on the SE coast of the island. Population: 538,100 (1995). **2** city in SE Ontario Province, Canada, on Lake Ontario at the mouth of the St Lawrence River. Population: 112,610 (1996). **3** city in E New York State. Population: 21,860 (1998 estimate).

Kingston upon Hull ♦ **Hull**

Kingston-upon-Thames historic town in SE England, on the River Thames. Population: 140,100 (1995).

kingwood /kíng wòod/ *n* **1** a hard fine-grained purplish wood. Use: cabinetwork. **2** the leguminous tree that yields kingwood. Native to: Brazil. *Dalbergia cearensis*.

kinin /kínin/ *n* **1** a polypeptide that causes dilation in blood vessels and contraction of smooth muscle **2** = **cytokinin** [Mid-20C. < ?]

kink /kingk/ *n* **1 TIGHT COIL** a tight twist or coil in an otherwise straight section of something such as rope, string, or wire **2 MUSCULAR SPASM** a sudden spasm in a muscle, especially a crick in the neck (*informal*) **3 MINOR DIFFICULTY IN** a slight difficulty or holdup in the progress of something (*informal*) **4 ECCENTRICITY** something that is eccentric or peculiar in somebody's personality or behaviour **5** *US* **ODD IDEA** a quirky, odd idea or impulse (*informal*) ○ *She got a kink in her head to swim across the Chesapeake Bay alone.* **6 SEXUAL ODDITY** an unusual sexual practice, especially one that might be considered deviant (*slang*) ■ **kinks** *npl Scotland* **LAUGHTER** convulsions of laughter (*nonstandard*) ○ *had us in kinks with his impressions* ■ *vti* **MAKE OR BECOME FULL OF TWISTS** to put a kink in something, or develop a kink [Late 17C. < Low German *kinke* 'twist in a rope'.]

kinkajou /kíngkə joo/ *n* a tree-dwelling fruit-eating mammal related to the raccoon that has a long prehensile tail, brownish fur, and large eyes. Native to: Central and South America. *Potos flavus*. [Late 18C. Via French *quincajou* < Algonquian, 'wolverine'.]

kinky /kíngki/ (**-ier, -iest**) *adj* **1 TIGHTLY COILED** full of tight coils ○ *kinky copper wire* **2 SEXUALLY DEVIANT** being or engaging in unusual sexual practices that may be considered deviant (*informal*) **3 ECCENTRIC** behaving in an unusual, idiosyncratic way (*informal*) **4 SEXUALLY PROVOCATIVE** intended to be provocative or sexually alluring, usually by being deliberately unusual or bizarre (*dated informal*) —**kinkily** *adv* —**kinkiness** *n*

kinky boot *n* a woman's leather boot extending to the knee or mid-thigh (*dated informal*)

kinnikinnick /kínnikə ník/ *n* **1** a mixture of dried leaves, bark, and sometimes tobacco, formerly smoked by some Native Americans **2** a plant such as sumac or dogwood used for making kinnikinnick [Late 18C. < Algonquian, 'mixture'.]

Kinnock /kínnək/, **Neil** (*b.* 1942) British politician

kino /kéenō/ (*plural* **-nos**) *n* a red astringent substance resembling resin, obtained by tapping any of several unrelated trees and used medicinally and for tanning in parts of Africa, India, Australia, and the West Indies [Early 19C. < a W African language, related to Mandingo *keno*, a kind of gum.]

Kinross /kin róss/ historic market town in central Scotland

kin selection *n* natural selection that favours self-sacrificing behaviour towards relatives because, even if the individual dies, those relatives that survive will carry some of its genes

Kinsey /kínzi/, **Alfred** (1894–1956) US biologist

kinsfolk /kínzfōk/ *npl* somebody's relatives

Kinshasa /kin shaássə/ capital of the Democratic Republic of the Congo, in the west of the country, on the River Congo. Population: 4,655,313 (1994).

kinship /kínship/ *n* **1** relationship by blood or marriage to another or others **2** relatedness through having characteristics in common, or through coming from the same origin ○ *kinship between Italic and Celtic languages*

Kinski /kínski/, **Klaus** (1926–91) Polish-born German actor

kinsman /kínzmən/ (*plural* **-men** /-mən/) *n* a man or boy who is somebody's relative [12C. < Old English *cynnes mann(um)*.]

kinswoman /-wòomən/ (*plural* **-en** /-wimin/) *n* a woman or girl who is somebody's relative [14C. After KINSMAN.]

Kintyre /kin tír/ peninsula of W Scotland, between the Firth of Clyde and the Atlantic Ocean. Length: 64 km/40 mi.

kiosk /kée osk/ *n* **1 SMALL ROOFED STREET STALL** a small permanent or temporary structure in the street from which items such as newspapers and sweets can be bought **2 SMALL STRUCTURE FOR ADVERTISING** a cylindrical structure that stands at a junction or on the street, used to post advertisements and announcements of events **3 TELEPHONE BOOTH** a small booth or shelter in which a public telephone is sited (*dated*) **4 MIDDLE EASTERN GAZEBO** a small open pavilion in the Middle East, especially in a garden [Early 17C. Via French *kiosque* < Turkish *köşk* 'villa' < Persian *kūšk* 'villa, palace'.]

Kiowa /kí ə waa/ (*plural* **-wa** *or* **-was**) *n* **1** a member of a Native North American people who lived in Montana and now live in Oklahoma **2** the language of the Kiowa people, related to Tanoan [Early 19C. < American Spanish *Caygua* < Kiowa *kygú* (plural).] —**Kiowa** *adj*

kip[1] /kip/ *n UK* **1 SLEEP** a sleep or a nap (*informal*) **2 BED** a bed or other place to sleep (*slang*) ○ *Is she still in her kip?* ■ *vi* (**kips, kipping, kipped**) *UK* **TAKE SLEEP OR NAP** to sleep or take a nap, often in a makeshift bed (*informal*) [Mid-18C. < Danish *kippe* 'cheap inn'.]

kip[2] /kip/ *n* a unit of weight equivalent to 455 kg/1,000 lb [Early 20C. < KILO- + POUND[1].]

kip[3] /kip/ (*plural* **kip**) *n* see table at **currency** [Mid-20C. < Thai.]

kip[4] /kip/, **kipskin** /kípskin/ *n* a hide taken from an immature animal, especially a calf or a lamb [14C. < Middle Dutch or Middle Low German, 'bundle (of hides)'.]

Kipling /kípling/, **Rudyard** (1865–1936) British writer and poet

kippa /ki paá/ (*plural* **-pot** /-pót/ *or* **-poth** /-pót/) *n* the skullcap worn by Jewish men and boys for prayer and by Orthodox Jewish men at all times [Mid-20C. < modern Hebrew *kippāh*.]

kipper /kíppər/ *n* **1 SMOKED HERRING** a fish, usually a herring, that has been cleaned, split open, and then salted and smoked **2 SALMON** a male salmon during the spawning season ■ *vt* **SMOKE FISH** to cure fresh fish, especially herring, by salting and smoking it (*usually passive*) [Old English *cypera* 'spawning salmon' < ?] —**kipperer** *n*

kippot plural of **kippa**

kippoth plural of **kippa**

kipskin *n* = **kip**[4]

kir /keer/ *n* an alcoholic drink made by adding cassis to dry white wine [Mid-20C. After Canon Félix *Kir* (1876–1968), mayor of Dijon, France.]

kirby grip /kúrbi-/ *n* a grip used to hold the hair in place. It consists of a piece of metal bent tightly over into two prongs, with the upper prong ridged. [Early 20C. < *Kirbigrip™*.]

Kirchhoff /kúrk of, kéerkh hof/, **Gustav** (1824–87) German physicist

Kirchner /kúrknər, kéerkhnər/, **Ernst Ludwig** (1880–1938) German artist

Kirghiz, Kirgiz *n, adj* LANG, PEOPLES = **Kyrgyz**

Kiribati /kírri báati/ independent state in the west-central Pacific Ocean, part of Micronesia. Capital: Tarawa. Population: 82,449 (1997). Area: 811 sq. km/313 sq. mi.

Kiritimati /kírri ti máati/ island forming part of Kiribati Republic. Population: 2,537 (1990). Area: 388 sq. km/150 sq. mi.

kirk /kurk/ *n Scotland* a church [12C. < Old Norse *kirkja* < Old English *cir(i)ce* (see CHURCH).]

Kirk *n Scotland* the Church of Scotland, the largest presbyterian church in Scotland

Kirk /kurk/, **Norman** (1923–74) New Zealand statesman

Kirkcudbright /kur kóobri/ town in SW Scotland. Population: 3,588 (1991).

Kirkcudbrightshire /kur kóobrishər/ former county in SW Scotland, now part of Dumfries and Galloway

Kirkwall /kúrk wawl/ capital of the Orkney Islands, NE Scotland, on the northern coast of Mainland Island. Population: 6,469 (1991).

Kirlian photography /kúr li ən-/ *n* a photographic process that records the radiation emitted by, or the aura surrounding an object in a high-frequency electric field [Late 20C. Named after Semyon D. and Valentina K. *Kirlian*, Russian technicians.]

Kirman /kər máan, keer-/ *n* a Persian carpet or rug [Late 19C. After *Kirman*, province in Iran.]

kirmess *n* LEISURE = **kermis**

Kirov /kée rof/ city in NE European Russia. Population: 487,000 (1990).

Kirovohrad /ki róvvə grad/ city in central Ukraine. Population: 278,000 (1995).

kirpan /keer páan/ *n* the short sword worn by baptized Sikh men as a symbol of religious loyalty. ◊ **five Ks** [Early 20C. Via Punjabi, Hindi < Sanskrit *kṛpāṇa* 'sword'.]

kirsch /keersh/, **kirschwasser** /kéersh vassər/ *n* a clear brandy distilled from black cherries, especially in Germany and France [Early 19C. < German, shortening of *Kirschwasser* 'cherry-water' < *Kirsche* 'cherry' < assumed Vulgar Latin *cerasia*.]

kirtle /kúrt'l/ *n* **1** a long gown or skirt worn by women from the Middle Ages to the 17th century **2** a long tunic or coat worn by men until the 16th century [Old English *cyrtel* 'short coat', via Germanic < Latin *curtus* 'short, cut short']

Kiruna /kéeroonə/ city in N Sweden. Population: 26,173 (1995).

Kisangani /kíssang gáani/ capital of Orientale Region, in N Democratic Republic of the Congo. Population: 417,517 (1994).

Kishinev /kíshi nyof/ former name for **Chişinău**

Kiska Island /kískə-/ largest and westernmost of the Rat Islands, SW Alaska. Area: 285 sq. km/110 sq. mi.

Kislev /kísslef, kiss lév/ *n* in the Jewish calendar, the third month of the civil year and the ninth month in the religious year [< Hebrew *Kislēw*]

kismet /kíz met, kízmət/ *n* **1** the will of Allah **2** fate or destiny [Mid-19C. Via Turkish < Persian *ḳismat* < Arabic *ḳisma(t)* 'lot, portion' < *ḳasama* 'he divided'.]

kiss /kiss/ *v* **1** *vti* **CARESS WITH THE LIPS** to touch somebody or something with the lips, either gently or passionately **2** *vti* **TOUCH GENTLY** in cue games, to come into very light contact while passing each other, or to touch another ball gently while passing it **3** *vt* **TOUCH GENTLY IN PASSING** to touch or brush against something lightly (*usually passive*) ○ *oranges kissed by the California sun* ■ *n* **1 CARESS DONE WITH THE LIPS** a gentle or passionate touch with the lips **2 GENTLE PASSING TOUCH** a very light, almost imperceptible touch in passing ○ *She felt the kiss of the evening breeze on her skin.* [Old English *cyssan* (verb) < *coss* (noun) < Germanic] —**kissable** *adj*

kiss off *v US, Can* (*slang*) **1** *vt* **REJECT** to reject somebody or something abruptly ○ *The boss kissed off that idea fast.* **2** *vt* **BE FORCED TO YIELD** to be compelled to give something up ○ *We had to kiss the trip off for lack of money.* **3** *vi* **GO AWAY** to leave immediately or leave somebody alone

kissagram /kíssə gram/ *n* a delivery service in which the messenger delivers a kiss instead of or as well as the message

kiss and tell *n* a book, article, or broadcast interview in which the author or interviewee publicly relates past sexual intimacy with somebody

kiss-and-tell *adj* revealing an earlier sexual experience with somebody else, especially when the information, considered to be confidential, is made public (*informal*)

kiss curl *n* a small flat curl of hair pressed on the forehead or in front of the ear. US term **spit curl**

kisser /kíssər/ *n* **1** a person who kisses ○ *not much of a kisser* **2** somebody's mouth (*slang*)

kissing ball *n US* mistletoe arranged in a ball shape, decorated with ribbons, and hung, e.g., in a hall or doorway during the Christmas season

kissing cousin *n* a person who is distantly related but can be kissed on meeting

kissing disease *n* glandular fever (*informal*)

Kissinger /kíssinjər/, **Henry** (*b.* 1923) German-born US statesman

kissing gate *n* a gate in a V- or U-shaped frame that allows only one person at a time to pass through

kiss of death *n* something or somebody whose presence will bring failure or disaster to something [< the Bible passage (Mark 14:44–46) in which Judas kissed Jesus Christ, thereby betraying him]

kiss of life *n* (*informal*) **1** mouth-to-mouth resuscitation **2** something that revives or restores an enterprise or, less commonly, somebody's spirits

kiss of peace *n* a gesture, usually either a kiss or handshake, used as a sign of Christian fellowship during Communion

kist[1] *n* ARCHAEOL = **cist**

kist[2] /kist/ *n Scotland, S Africa* a wooden storage chest variously used for blankets and linen, clothes, or a bride's trousseau [14C. < Old Norse *kista*, via Germanic < Latin *cista* (see CHEST).]

Kisumu /ki sóomoo/ port and capital of Nyanza Province, SW Kenya. Population: 185,100 (1989).

Kiswahili /kée swaa héeli/ *n* the Bantu national language of Tanzania and Kenya, widely used in Uganda, Congo, and neighbouring countries. Native speakers: 2 million. Other speakers: 20 million. [Mid-19C. < Bantu < *ki-*, a prefix, + *Swahili*.] —**Kiswahili** *adj*

kit /kit/ *n* **1 SET OF THINGS FOR USE TOGETHER** a set of articles, tools, or equipment used for a particular purpose **2 CONTAINER FOR SET** the container for a set of things ○ *a sewing kit* **3 SPECIAL CLOTHING AND EQUIPMENT** a special set of clothing and equipment assembled for a member of the armed forces or a sportsperson **4 SET OF PARTS FOR ASSEMBLING** a set of parts ready to be put together [14C. < Dutch *kitte* 'tankard, jug'.] ◇ **get your kit off** to take your clothes off (*slang*)

kit out *vt* to provide somebody with the clothes, and sometimes also equipment, needed to do something

Kitakyushu /kéetə kyóoshoo/, **Kitakyūshū** city in the north of Kyushu Island, Japan. Population: 1,026,455 (1990).

Kitasato Shibasaburo /kée taa sáato shée baasə bóoro/ (1852–1931) Japanese bacteriologist

kitbag /kít bag/ *n* a canvas bag, usually cylindrical, for holding military kit or a similar bag used by civilians, carried on the shoulder

kitchen /kíchin/ *n* a room or part of a room or building in which food is prepared and cooked [Pre-12C. < Latin *coquina* < *coquere* 'to cook'.]

kitchen cabinet *n* an informal unelected group of advisers to a head of government who are often believed to have more influence than the official cabinet

Kitchener /kíchənər/, **Horatio Herbert, 1st Baron Kitchener of Khartoum and 1st Earl of Broome** (1850–1916) British field marshal and politician. Known as **Lord Kitchener**

kitchenette /kíchi nét/ *n* a very small room, or part of another room, fitted out as a kitchen

kitchen garden *n* a garden in which vegetables, herbs, and sometimes fruit are grown for the use of a household —**kitchen gardener** *n*

kitchen midden *n* an area of an archaeological site that contains domestic refuse such as food waste, broken pottery, and pieces of other household artifacts, indicating long-term human occupation

kitchen tea *n ANZ* a women-only party held before a wedding, to which guests bring kitchen equipment as presents for the bride

kitchenware /kíchin wair/ *n* utensils used in the kitchen, including pots and pans, mixing bowls, chopping boards, knives, spoons, and gadgets

kite /kīt/ *n* **1 TOY FOR FLYING** a light framework covered in a thin light material, flown for fun in the wind at the end of a long string **2 SMALL SLIM HAWK** a small slim hawk with long pointed wings and a forked tail. Family: Accipitridae. **3 LIGHT SAIL** a light sail used in addition to a sailing ship's standard sails **4 AEROPLANE** an aeroplane (*archaic slang*) ○ *a rickety kite that could barely get off the runway* **5 FAKE FINANCIAL TRANSACTION** a negotiable bill, e.g. a cheque, that is fraudulently used to sustain credit by representing a fictitious monetary transaction (*slang*) ■ *v* **1** *vti* **PASS BAD CHEQUES** to write and pass bad cheques in order to sustain credit on a temporary basis, all the time using to advantage the period between writing them and their clearing (*slang*) **2** *vi* **GLIDE AS IF FLYING** to glide and soar like a kite [< Old English *cȳta* 'kite (bird)'] —**kiter** *n* ◇ **fly a kite 1** to do something or speak about something in order to test public opinion on it (*slang*) **2** to issue a fraudulent financial document such as a cheque without having enough funds to cover it (*slang*) ◇ **high as a kite 1** extremely excited or elated (*informal*) **2** extremely intoxicated or drug-affected (*informal*)

Kitemark /kīt maark/ *n* the official mark of approval of the British Standards Institution, shaped like a stylized kite, indicating that a manufactured item meets certain standards of quality and reliability

kit fox *n* a small slender fox that has large ears. Native to: W United States. *Vulpes macrotis*. [Early 19C. < ?]

kith /kith/ *n* somebody's friends and acquaintances (*dated*) [14C. < Old English *cȳþ(þ)* 'knowledge, friends' < Germanic.] ◇ **kith and kin** somebody's friends and relatives

kithara /kíthərə/ *n* MUSIC = **cithara**

kitsch /kich/ *n* **1** sentimentality, tastelessness, or ostentation in any of the arts ○ *The book jackets were pure kitsch.* **2** collectively, decorative items that are regarded as tasteless, sentimental, or ostentatious in style ○ *tourist shops full of kitsch* [Early 20C. < German, < *kitschen* 'throw together'.] —**kitschy** *adj*

kitten /kítt'n/ *n* the young of a cat ■ *vi* to give birth to young cats [14C. < Old French *chitoun*, diminutive of *chat* 'cat'.] ◇ **have kittens** to become angry, excited, or nervous about something (*informal*)

kitten heel *n* (*usually plural*) **1** a low heel on a woman's shoe **2** a woman's shoe with a low heel

kittenish /kítt'nish/ *adj* **1** behaving in a lively and playful way, as a kitten does **2** coyly flirtatious —**kittenishly** *adv* —**kittenishness** *n*

kittiwake /kítti wayk/ (*plural* **-wake** *or* **-wakes**) *n* a gull that nests on cliffs and winters on open oceans. Native to: northern regions. *Rissa tridactyla* and *Rissa brevirostris*. [Mid-17C. An imitation of its call.]

kittle /kítt'l/ *adj Scotland* difficult to deal with (*archaic*) [15C. < Old Norse *kitla* 'to tickle'.]

kitty[1] /kítti/ (*plural* **-ties**) *n* a kitten or cat (*informal*) [Early 18C. Shortening and alteration of KITTEN.]

kitty[2] /kítti/ (*plural* **kitties**) *n* **1 JOINT POOL OF MONEY** a fund of money contributed to by a group of people and used to buy something in common **2 PROPORTION OF THE OVERALL POT IN POKER** a portion of the total amount of money bet by all the players on each hand of poker **3 POOL OF BETS** the amount of money that has been bet by the players in a game **4 JACK** the jack in the game of bowls [Early 19C. Originally 'prison', < ?]

kitty-cornered, kitty-corner *adv, adj US* = **cater-cornered**

Kitty Hawk /kítti-/ town in NE North Carolina, on the Atlantic Ocean, site of the Wright brothers' successful glider and aeroplane experiments. Population: 2,336 (1998 estimate).

Kitwe /kít way/ town in north-central Zambia. Population: 338,207 (1990).

Kivu, Lake /kéevoo-/ freshwater lake between W Rwanda and the E Democratic Republic of the Congo. Area: 2,700 sq. km/1,040 sq. mi.

Kiwi

kiwi /keèwi/ n (plural **-wi** or **-wis**) **1** FLIGHTLESS BIRD a nocturnal flightless bird with a long slender beak and no tail. Native to: New Zealand. Genus: *Apteryx*. **2 kiwi, Kiwi** SOMEBODY FROM NEW ZEALAND somebody who comes from New Zealand (*informal*) **3** CHINESE VINE WITH EDIBLE FRUIT a vine that bears edible fruit with a greenish-brown fuzzy skin and sweet green pulp. Native to: China. *Actinidia chinensis*. **4** FOOD = **kiwi fruit** ■ *adj* RELATING TO NEW ZEALAND relating to New Zealand, its people, or culture (*informal*) [Mid-19C. < Maori, an imitation of its cry.]

kiwi fruit n the fruit of the kiwi plant, which has a greenish-brown fuzzy skin and sweet green pulp

KKK *abbr* Ku Klux Klan

KKt *abbr* king's knight

KKtP *abbr* king's knight's pawn

Klagenfurt /klàagən foort/ capital of Kärnten Province, S Austria. Population: 89,415 (1991).

Klaipeda /klípidə/ port in W Lithuania, on the Baltic Sea. Population: 202,800 (1995).

Klamath River /klámmath-/ river in Oregon and California, flowing into the Pacific Ocean. Length: 400 km/250 mi.

Klan /klan/ n the Ku Klux Klan (*informal*) —**Klanism** n

Klansman /klánzmən/ n (plural **-men** /-mən/) n a member of the Ku Klux Klan

klaxon /kláks'n/ n a loud electric horn [Early 20C]

Klee /klay/, **Paul** (1879–1940) Swiss painter

Kleenex /kleè neks/ *tdmk* a trademark for a soft facial tissue

Klein /klīn/, **Calvin** (b. 1942) US fashion designer

Klein, Melanie (1882–1960) Austrian psychoanalyst

Klein bottle /klīn/ n a one-sided surface formed by inserting the small open end of a tapered tube through the side of the tube and upward until it is contiguous with the larger end [Mid-20C. After Felix *Klein* (1849–1925), German mathematician.]

Klemperer /klémpərər/, **Otto** (1885–1973) German conductor

klepht /kleft/ n one of the Greeks who resisted Turkish rule in Greece from 1456 to 1832 and who lived in the mountains as outlaws and brigands [Early 19C. < modern Demotic Greek *klephtēs* 'thief' < Greek *kleptēs*.] —**klephtic** *adj*

kleptomania /kléptə máyni ə/ n an obsessive urge to steal, especially when there is no economic necessity

kleptomaniac /kléptə máyni ak/ n a compulsive thief —**kleptomaniacal** /-mə nī ək'l/ *adj*

kletterschuh /kléttər shoo/ n (plural **-schuhe** or **-schuhs** /-shoo ə/) n a lightweight climbing boot [Early 20C. < German, 'climbing shoe'.]

klick /klik/ n Can, US a kilometre (*informal*) [Mid-20C. < ?]

klieg light /kleèg-/ n a powerful carbon-arc light formerly used in making films [Early 20C. After John H. *Kliegl* (1869–1959) and Anton T. *Kliegl* (1872–1927), German-born US inventors.]

Klimt /klimt/, **Gustav** (1862–1918) Austrian painter

Kline /klīn/, **Franz** (1910–62) US artist

Klippel /klíppəl/, **Robert** (b. 1920) Australian sculptor

klipspringer /klíp springər/ n a small agile antelope with large ears. Native to: mountainous regions of Africa.

Oreotragus oreotragus. [Late 18C. < Afrikaans, 'cliff-springer'.]

Klondike /klón dīk/ region of NW Yukon Territory, Canada, named after the Klondike River, which traverses it

kloof /kloof/ n S Africa a gorge or mountain pass, usually wooded [Mid-18C. Via Afrikaans < Dutch *clove*.]

⚡**kludge** /klooj/, **kluge** n a makeshift combination of hardware and software put together to solve a computing problem that is effective but not suitable for manufacture (*slang*) ■ *vt* (**kludges, kludging, kludged; kluges, kluging, kluged**) to solve a computing problem using a kludge (*slang*) [Mid-20C. After BOTCH, FUDGE.] —**kludgy** *adj*

klutz /kluts/ n US, Can (*slang insult*) **1** an offensive term for somebody who is regarded as physically or socially clumsy **2** an offensive term for somebody who is regarded as unintelligent [Mid-20C. Via Yiddish *klots* 'wooden beam' < German *Klotz* 'clod'.] —**klutzy** *adj*

klystron /klí stron/ n an electron tube that uses an electric field to generate and amplify microwaves [Mid-20C. < Greek *klus*-, stem of *kluzein* 'wash over'.]

km[1] *abbr* kilometre

⚡**km**[2] *abbr* Comoros (*in Internet addresses*)

K-meson n = kaon

km/h *abbr* kilometres per hour

kn[1], **kn.** *abbr* **1** knot **2** krona **3** krone

⚡**kn**[2] *abbr* St Kitts and Nevis (*in Internet addresses*)

KN *abbr* king's knight

knack /nak/ n **1** an easy, clever way of doing something or handling a problem ○ *I can't get the knack of this software.* **2** a particular skill, especially one that might be innate or intuitive and therefore difficult to teach ○ *You certainly have a knack with children.* [14C. < ?]

SYNONYMS See *talent*.

knacker /nákər/ n **1** SOMEBODY WHO KILLS HORSES a buyer and slaughterer of old, worn-out, or injured horses for their body parts, e.g. their flesh and hide **2** DEMOLITION MERCHANT a buyer and demolisher of unwanted buildings who sells their materials for scrap ■ **knackers** npl TESTICLES testicles (*slang*) ■ *vt* TIRE OUT to exhaust somebody completely (*slang*) [Early19C. Originally 'saddler, harness maker' < ?] —**knackered** *adj*

knackwurst /nák wurst/, **knockwurst** /nók wurst/ n a spicy smoked Continental sausage similar to a frankfurter but shorter and thicker [Mid-20C. < German, 'crack-sausage' (because its skin cracks open when bitten) < *knacken* 'to crack'.]

knag /nag/ n **1** a knot in a piece of wood **2** a peg made of wood [15C. < Low German *knagge* 'knot, peg'.]

knap /nap/ (**knaps, knapping, knapped**) *vt* to chisel or hammer something such as a stone so that it breaks into flakes [15C. Probably < Low German or Dutch *knappen* 'to crack', an imitation of the sound.] —**knapper** n

knapping hammer n a mason's hammer used for splitting and roughly shaping stone

knapsack /náp sak/ n a cloth or leather bag with shoulder straps, designed for carrying personal items and supplies on a hiker's back [Early 17C. < Low German, < *knappen* 'bite, eat' + *Sack* 'sack'.]

knapweed /náp weed/ (plural **-weeds** or **-weed**) n PLANTS = hardheads [Early 16C. Alteration of Middle English *knopwed* 'knob-weed' < *knop* 'knob'; from the shape of its cluster of flowers.]

knar /naar/ n a knot on a tree or in wood [13C. < ?] —**knarred** *adj* —**knarry** *adj*

knave /nayv/ n **1** a man who is considered dishonest and deceitful (*archaic*) **2** CARDS = jack[1] n. **2** [Old English *cnafa* 'boy, male servant' < German /náyvəri/ n —**knavish** /-nayvi/ —**knavishly** *adv* —**knavishness** n

knawel /nawl, náw əl/ (plural **knawels** or **knawel**), **knawe** /naw/ (plural **knawes** or **knawe**) n a low-growing annual plant with narrow leaves, usually considered to be a weed. Flowers: small green. Native to: Europe, Asia. *Scleranthus annuus*. [Late 16C. < German *Knauel* 'knotgrass'.]

knead /need/ *v* **1** *vti* WORK DOUGH UNTIL SMOOTH to fold, press, and stretch a soft substance such as dough or clay, working it into a smooth uniform mass **2** *vt* MASSAGE MUSCLES to rub, squeeze, or press a part of the body with the hands, e.g. in order to relax the muscles **3** *vt* SHAPE

SOMETHING WITH THE HANDS to make or shape something out of a soft substance by kneading it [Old English *cnedan* < W Germanic] —**kneadable** *adj* —**kneader** n

SPELLCHECK See *need*.

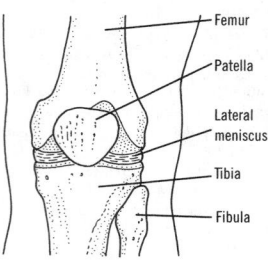

Knee

knee /nee/ n **1** MIDDLE JOINT OF THE HUMAN LEG the joint of the human leg between the thigh and the lower leg, where the femur and the tibia meet, covered in front by the kneecap (patella) **2** AREA AROUND THE KNEE JOINT the general area surrounding the knee joint **3** UPPER LEG the upper surface of the thigh of somebody sitting down ○ *Come and sit on my knee.* **4** PART OF TROUSERS the part of a piece of clothing, especially trousers, that fits around the knee **5** LEG JOINT IN ANIMALS the joint between the upper and lower parts of the hind legs in four-legged vertebrates and of the legs in birds **6** GROWTH ABOVE WATER FROM A ROOT a woody outgrowth from the roots of some trees that grow in saturated soils or standing water, which protrudes above the surface and enables them to breathe **7** OBJECT LIKE A KNEE something that resembles the human knee, e.g. a bent pipe ■ *vt* (**knees, kneeing, kneed**) HIT WITH THE KNEE to strike somebody with the knee [Old English *cnēow* < Indo-European, 'to bend'] ◇ **bring somebody to his** or **her knees** to reduce somebody to a state of abject weakness and vulnerability, or force somebody to admit defeat

knee action n front-wheel suspension in a car that allows each wheel to move independently in a vertical direction

knee breeches npl CLOTHING = breeches npl. **1**

kneecap /neè kap/ n **1** a flat triangular bone located at the front of the knee. Technical name **patella 2** SPORTS = kneepad ■ *vt* (**-caps, -capping, -capped**) to shoot somebody deliberately in the knees as a punishment in order to cause lasting difficulty in standing or walking (*informal*)

knee-deep *adj* **1** IN AS HIGH AS THE KNEES standing or sunk in something that reaches up to the knees ○ *be knee-deep in mud* **2** AS HIGH AS THE KNEES reaching up to the knees ○ *The river was only knee-deep.* **3** EXTREMELY INVOLVED IN completely occupied by or entangled in something ○ *knee-deep in work*

knee drop n in wrestling, a move in which an opponent is lifted into the air and then dropped over the bent knee of the lifter

knee-high *adj* reaching up to the knees ■ n a sock or stocking that comes up as high as the knee

kneehole /neè hōl/ n a hole made for the knees in a desk or other piece of furniture

knee jerk n an involuntary contraction of the thigh muscle that produces a sudden extension of the leg, usually in response to a light tap on the tendon below the kneecap

knee-jerk *adj* (*informal*) **1** given or occurring immediately and automatically, without thinking, and usually expressing habitual attitude or prejudice ○ *a knee-jerk opinion* **2** tending to respond in a predictable and often unthinking way to a situation ○ *a knee-jerk political hack*

kneel /neel/ (**kneels, kneeling, knelt** /nelt/ or **kneeled**, **knelt** or **kneeled**) *vi* to rest on, or get down on, one or both knees [Old English *cnēowlian* < *cnēow* (see KNEE)]

knee-length *adj* reaching up to or down to the knee or to just above or below the knee ○ *a knee-length skirt*

kneeler /neélər/ *n* = **hassock** *n.* 1

kneepad /neé pad/ *n* a covering that protects the knee from injury, especially during sports

kneepan /neé pan/ *n* ANAT = **kneecap** *n.* 1

knee sock *n* a sock that reaches to the knee

knees-up (*plural* **knees-ups**) *n UK* a lively noisy party, especially one with a lot of dancing (*informal*)

knee-trembler *n* an act of sexual intercourse performed standing up (*slang; offensive in some contexts*)

kneidel /knáyd'l, kníd'l/ *n* a small Eastern European dumpling made from potatoes or flour, served in soup or with stew, or filled with a savoury stuffing or fruit [Mid-20C. < Yiddish *kneydel*, alteration of Middle High German *knödel* 'dumpling'.]

knell /nel/ *n* 1 **SLOW BELL RING** the sound of a bell rung slowly, associated with solemnity or mourning, used to announce a death or funeral 2 **OMINOUS SIGNAL** something that signals death, disaster, or the end of something (*literary*) ■ *v* 1 *vti* **RING A BELL** to ring a bell slowly, or produce a slow ringing sound, especially as a sign of mourning or to announce a death or funeral 2 *vt* **SIGNAL SOMETHING OMINOUS** to announce or signal something such as a death, disaster, or the end of something (*literary*) [Old English *cnyll* < *cnyllan* 'to strike' < Indo-European]

Kneller /néllər/, **Sir Godfrey** (1646–1723) German-born English painter

knelt past participle, past tense of **kneel**

Knesset /knéss et, knéssit/, **Knesseth** *n* the parliamentary legislature of Israel [Mid-20C. < Hebrew, 'gathering'.]

knew past tense of **know**

Kngwarreye /kəng wúrray/, **Emily Kame** (1910?–96) Australian Aboriginal painter

Knickerbocker /níkər bokər/ *n US* 1 somebody descended from the early Dutch settlers of New York 2 somebody who comes from the state of New York (*informal*) [Early 19C. After Diedrich *Knickerbocker*, fictitious author of Washington Irving's *History of New York*.]

knickerbocker glory *n* a dessert consisting of layers of different flavours of ice cream, fruit, jelly, and cream, served in a tall conical glass dish

knickerbockers /níkər bokərz/ *npl* loose-fitting short breeches gathered at or just below the knee [Mid-19C. < ?]

knickers /níkərz/ *npl* 1 an undergarment worn by women and girls that covers the body from the waist to the tops of the legs or below and has separate legs or leg-holes 2 *US* CLOTHING = **knickerbockers** ■ *interj* used as a mild or self-consciously humorous swearword (*informal*) [Late 19C. Shortening.] ◇ **get your knickers in a twist** to become agitated, excited, or anxious (*informal*)

knick-knack, **nick-nack** *n* a small decorative ornament or object [Late 16C. < reduplication of KNACK.] —**knick-knackery** *n*

knickpoint /ník poynt/ *n* a point along a river's length at which it suddenly begins to flow in a steeper course [Early 20C. Partial translation of German *Knickpunkt* < *Knick* 'bend' + *Punkt* 'point'.]

knife /nīf/ *n* (*plural* **knives** /nīvz/) 1 **TOOL FOR CUTTING** a tool, usually with a sharp blade and a handle, used for cutting, slicing, or spreading 2 **STABBING WEAPON** a knife with a handle and a sharpened blade specifically made to be a weapon ■ *v* (**knifes, knifing, knifed**) 1 *vt* **STAB** to stab or cut somebody with a knife 2 *vt US* **BETRAY** to try to bring about somebody's downfall in a devious or dishonest way (*informal*) 3 *vi* **MOVE WITH A SWIFT SMOOTH MOTION** to move quickly, forcefully, and cleanly through something ○ *The hawk knifed through the air.* [Old English *cnīf* < Germanic] —**knife-like** *adj* —**knifer** *n* ◇ **have your knife in** *or* **into somebody** to feel hostility and malice towards somebody and wish to do him or her harm ◇ **the knives are out (for somebody)** there is general hostility towards somebody and a desire to cause that person difficulties or harm ◇ **twist** *or* **turn the knife (in the wound)** to try to make a difficult or painful situation even worse for somebody ◇ **under the knife** undergoing surgery (*informal*)

knife-edge *n* 1 **KNIFE'S CUTTING EDGE** the cutting edge of the blade of a knife 2 **OBJECT LIKE THE EDGE OF KNIFE** an object that is sharp, thin, and narrow 3 **CRITICAL TIME IN A SITUATION** a decisive and precarious point in a situation at which it is finely balanced between different possibilities or outcomes ○ *with the future of the project on a knife-edge* 4 **FULCRUM FOR A PRECISE INSTRUMENT** a metal wedge whose narrow edge is used as a fulcrum for a scale beam or a lever in a precision instrument

knife pleat *n* a narrow sharply-creased pleat, usually one of several folded in the same direction, especially in a skirt

knifepoint /nīf poynt/ *n* the sharp tip of a knife ◇ **at knifepoint** while being threatened with a knife

knife switch *n* an electric switch in which a hinged blade is placed between two contact clips

knight /nīt/ *n* 1 **MEDIEVAL SOLDIER OF HIGH RANK** in late medieval Europe, a noble in the military, promoted by the king after serving as a page and squire 2 **MEDIEVAL MOUNTED SOLDIER OF LOW RANK** in early medieval Europe, a tenant of a feudal lord who was required to serve as a soldier on horseback 3 **MAN WITH THE TITLE 'SIR'** a man who holds a nonhereditary title conferred by a ruler for personal achievement or public service 4 **HORSE'S HEAD CHESSPIECE** (*symbol* **N**) a chesspiece shaped like a horse's head that moves two squares horizontally and one vertically or two vertically and one horizontally 5 **MEMBER OF A BROTHERHOOD** a man who belongs to a special group or organization, especially a religious or secret brotherhood 6 **CHAMPION OF A CAUSE** a fervent supporter or defender of a cause or belief 7 **PROTECTOR OF A WOMAN** a man who is protective of and devoted to a woman ■ *vt* **MAKE A MAN A KNIGHT** to bestow a knighthood on a man [Old English *cniht* 'boy, male attendant' < Germanic] ◇ **knight in shining armour** a man who gallantly comes to the rescue of somebody in danger or difficulty

SPELLCHECK Do not confuse ***knight*** with ***night***, which has a similar sound. Beware: your spellchecker will not catch this error.

knight bachelor (*plural* **knights bachelors** *or* **knights bachelor**) *n* 1 a knight of the lowest rank who is not a member of any of the orders of knighthood 2 = **bachelor-at-arms**

knight-errant (*plural* **knights-errant**), **knight errant** (*plural* **knights errant**) *n* 1 a medieval knight who travelled around looking for adventure 2 a man preoccupied with ideas of adventure and romance —**knight-errantry** *n*

knighthead /nīt hed/ *n* either of two upright timbers supporting the inner end of the bowsprit of a sailing ship, to which mooring cables or ropes are sometimes attached [Early 18C. Because it often had a carving of a male head.]

knighthood /nīt hood/ *n* 1 **POSITION OF KNIGHT** the rank, title, or occupation of a knight 2 **CHIVALRY AND HONOUR** the qualities of chivalry, bravery, and honour, thought to be characteristic of a knight 3 **KNIGHTS** knights considered as a group

knightly /nītli/ (**-lier, -liest**) *adj* relating to knights, or characteristic of a knight, especially in being noble and chivalrous —**knightliness** *n*

knight marshal (*plural* **knights marshal**) *n* = **marshal** *n.* 4

Knight of Columbus *n* a member of a benevolent and fraternal organization of Roman Catholic men, founded in the United States in 1882 [Late 19C. After Christopher COLUMBUS.]

Knight of Pythias /píthi əss/ *n* a member of a benevolent and fraternal organization for men, founded in the United States in the 1860s

Knights Hospitallers, **Knights of St John of Jerusalem, Knights of the Hospital of St John of Jerusalem** *npl* a military and religious order founded by crusaders in the 12th century to protect a hospital in Jerusalem

Knights of the Round Table *npl* an order of knights said to have been created by King Arthur that figures prominently in Arthurian legends and chivalric poems [Because the knights sat at a round table, where no one could be seated in a position of superiority]

Knight Templar (*plural* **Knights Templar**) *n* a member of a Christian military order that was founded in Jerusalem in 1119 to protect pilgrims after the First Crusade and suppressed by the Pope in 1312

kniphofia /ni fōfi ə/ (*plural* **-as** *or* **-a**) *n* PLANTS = **red-hot poker** [Mid-19C. After Johann Hieronymus *Kniphof*.]

knish /kə nísh, knish/ *n* a piece of dough filled with meat, cheese, or potato and eaten as a snack or appetizer, especially in Jewish-American cooking [Mid-20C. Via Yiddish < Russian.]

knit /nit/ *v* (**knits, knitting, knitted** *or* **knit**) 1 *vti* **INTERLOCK WOOL LOOPS** to interlock loops of wool, using either long needles or a machine, or make a garment by this method 2 *vti* **USE A PLAIN STITCH** to use a basic plain stitch that forms a flat vertical loop on the front of a piece of knitting ○ *Knit one, purl one.* 3 *vti* **UNITE** to bring people or things together, or come together, in a close association 4 *vi* **BECOME HEALED** to grow together again after a fracture (*refers to a broken bone*) 5 *vti* **BRING THE BROWS CLOSER TOGETHER** to draw the brows together, or be drawn together, in a frown ■ *n* 1 **SOMETHING MADE BY KNITTING** a knitted garment or fabric 2 **WAY OF KNITTING** a method or style of knitting a garment or fabric 3 **PLAIN STITCH** a basic knitting stitch that forms a flat vertical loop on the face of something being knitted [Old English *cnyttan* 'tie in knots' < Germanic] —**knittable** *adj* —**knitter** *n*

SPELLCHECK Do not confuse ***knit*** with ***nit***, which has a similar sound. Beware: your spellchecker will not catch this error.

knitting /nítting/ *n* 1 the act or process of making knitted items or fabric by hand-held needles or by machine 2 an item that is in the process of being knitted

knitting needle *n* a long slim rod with a dull point, used in pairs in knitting

knitwear /nít wair/ *n* garments made from knitted fabric

knives plural of **knife**

knob /nob/ *n* 1 **ROUNDED HANDLE OR DIAL** a rounded projecting part attached to a door, drawer, appliance, or other object, used as a handle or a dial or switch 2 **ROUNDED PROJECTION** any rounded lump or part projecting from the surface of something 3 **RAISED ORNAMENTAL CARVING** a raised ornament in carved woodwork 4 **HILL** a rounded hill 5 **SMALL PIECE** a small piece of something ○ *a knob of butter* 6 **TABOO TERM** a highly offensive term for a penis (*taboo*) ■ *vti* (**knobs, knobbing, knobbed**) **TABOO TERM** a highly offensive term meaning to have sexual intercourse with somebody (*taboo; refers to a man*) [14C. < Middle Low German *knobbe* 'knot, knob, bud'.] ◇ **with knobs on** 1 used as a way of returning an insult and supposedly adding greater force to it (*informal; usually by or to children*) 2 to a great degree (*informal*)

knobbly /nóbbli/ (**-blier, -bliest**), **knobby** /nóbbi/ (**-bier, -biest**) *adj* having small hard rounded parts sticking out from the surface [Mid-17C. < *knobble* 'small knob' < KNOB.]

knobkerrie /nób kerri/, **knobstick** /nób stik/ *n* a short wooden stick with a knob at one end, used by some South African peoples as a weapon [Mid-19C. < KNOB + *kierie* 'club' (< Nama), after Afrikaans *knopkierie*.]

knock /nok/ *v* 1 *vi* **HIT REPEATEDLY** to strike loudly against something such as a door with the knuckles or an object in order to attract attention ○ *Someone's knocking at the door.* 2 *vi* **MAKE A LOUD NOISE BY COLLIDING** to produce a loud and usually repetitive noise by hitting something ○ *disturbed by a branch knocking against the window all night* 3 *vti* **DEAL BLOW** to strike somebody or something with a hard blow ○ *knock in a nail* 4 *vt* **PUT IN A PARTICULAR STATE WITH BLOW** to cause something or somebody to be in a particular state, e.g. unconscious or flat on the floor, with a blow ○ *He knocked me off balance.* 5 *vti* **COLLIDE OR CAUSE SOMETHING TO COLLIDE** to hit against something, especially accidentally, or cause something to hit against something else ○ *The glass broke when I knocked it against the table.* 6 *vt* **MAKE SOMETHING BY STRIKING** to produce something, especially a hole, by means of repeated blows 7 *vt* **CRITICIZE** to criticize or find fault with somebody or something (*informal*) ○ *Don't knock it until you've tried it.* 8 *vi* **PRODUCE REPEATED RAPPING SOUND** to make a regular rapping noise that is usually caused by faulty fuel combustion (*refers to a vehicle or its engine*) 9 *vt* **OFFENSIVE TERM** an offensive term meaning to have sexual intercourse with somebody (*slang*) ■ *n* 1 **BLOW OR COLLISION** a blow struck against somebody or something or a collision with somebody or something 2 **SOUND OF KNOCKING** the sound made by somebody or something hitting something, especially repeatedly 3 **REPEATED RAPPING SOUND IN ENGINE** a regular rapping noise made by an engine and usually caused by faulty fuel combustion 4 **CRITICISM** a disparaging or critical comment about somebody or something (*informal*) 5 **BAD EXPERIENCE** a painful, damaging, or distressing experience (*informal*) 6 **INNINGS** a batsman's innings (*informal*) [Old English *cnocian* < an imitation of the sound] ◇ **knock it off** used to demand that somebody stop doing or saying something (*informal*) ◇ **knock somebody dead** to amaze and delight somebody with the quality of a performance (*informal*)

knock about, knock around *v* (*informal*) **1** *vt* **BEAT** to abuse somebody physically **2** *vti* **TRAVEL AROUND** to travel to different places, or to different places within a specific area, especially without a specific itinerary **3** *vt* **HAVE A RELAXING TIME** to relax by doing nothing in particular **4** *vi* **SPEND TIME** to spend time habitually in the company of somebody **5** *vi* **BE IN SOME PLACE** to be somewhere in a place or area, though the exact whereabouts are uncertain ○ *I'm sure it's knocking around somewhere in this office.* **6** *vt* **DISCUSS SOMETHING SPECULATIVELY** to discuss something casually in order to hear different views **7** *vt* **KICK A BALL AROUND** to kick, hit, or throw a ball in an informal game

knock back *vt* (*informal*) **1 GULP A DRINK DOWN** to drink something, especially alcohol, very quickly **2 COST SOMEBODY MUCH MONEY** to cost somebody a large amount of money ○ *The repairs knocked me back £500.* **3 TAKE SOMEBODY ABACK** to come as an unwelcome surprise to somebody ○ *The news really knocked me back.* **4** *ANZ, Scotland* **REJECT** to dismiss or reject somebody or something

knock down *vt* **1 MAKE SOMEBODY OR SOMETHING FALL** to cause somebody or something to fall to the ground by striking or pushing **2 HIT SOMEBODY WITH VEHICLE** to hit and injure or kill somebody with a moving vehicle **3 DESTROY STRUCTURE** to demolish a building or part of a building **4 DISMANTLE** to take something apart for shipping or storage **5 PRONOUNCE SOMETHING SOLD** to show that something has been sold at an auction by striking a surface with a gavel **6 CUT PRICE OF** to reduce the price of something (*informal*) ○ *furniture knocked down by 50%* **7 MAKE SOMEBODY CUT PRICE** to persuade somebody to reduce the price of something

knock off *v* **1** *vti* **STOP WORKING** to finish work at the end of the day or to stop working or doing something in order to take a break (*informal*) **2** *vt* **CUT PRICE OF** to decrease the price of something by a particular amount **3** *vt* **DEDUCT** to deduct something from something, especially an amount from a price or a number of points from a score or total **4** *vt* **PRODUCE SOMETHING WITH EASE OR SPEED** to make or deal with something easily and quickly (*informal*) ○ *knocks off six or seven articles a month* **5** *vt* **KILL** to kill somebody, especially intentionally (*slang*) **6** *vt* **ROB OR STEAL** to rob a bank, shop, or other business, or to steal something (*slang*) **7** *vt US* **MAKE CHEAP COPY OF PRODUCT** to produce a cheap, sometimes illegal copy of a well-known product (*slang*) **8** *vt* **OFFENSIVE TERM** an offensive term meaning to have sexual intercourse with somebody (*slang*)

knock on *vti* in rugby, to make illegal use of the hand or arm to move the ball forwards

knock out *vt* **1 MAKE SOMEBODY UNCONSCIOUS BY HITTING** to cause somebody to lose consciousness by striking him or her **2 DEFEAT OPPOSING BOXER WITH PUNCH** in boxing, to knock an opponent down for a count of ten, thus winning the match **3 STUPEFY SOMEBODY WITH DRUGS OR ALCOHOL** to cause somebody to lose consciousness or fall asleep by means of drugs or alcohol **4 ELIMINATE OPPONENT FROM TOURNAMENT** to eliminate an opponent or team from a competition by winning a match or game **5 MAKE SOMETHING USELESS** to destroy something or make it inoperable ○ *The storm knocked out our electricity.* **6 TIRE SOMEBODY OUT** to exhaust somebody completely (*informal*) **7 PRODUCE SOMETHING WITH EASE OR SPEED** to make or do something easily or quickly **8 PLEASE OR IMPRESS SOMEBODY GREATLY** to overwhelm somebody with excitement or pleasure (*informal*) ○ *That music really knocks me out.* **9 SHOCK** to cause somebody to be greatly shocked (*informal*)

knock over *vt* **1 HIT WITH VEHICLE** to hit and injure or kill somebody with a moving vehicle. US term **run over** **2 MAKE SOMEBODY FALL** to cause somebody or something to fall by striking or pushing ○ *knocked my cup of coffee over* **3 ASTOUND** to overwhelm somebody with amazement or shock (*informal*) **4 ROB A PLACE** to rob a bank, shop, or other business (*informal*)

knock together *vt* to make something quickly, without much preparation, and often with little care (*informal*)

knock up *v* **1** *vt* **KNOCK ON DOOR TO WAKE** to wake somebody up by knocking on the door (*slang*) **2** *vt* = **knock together** (*informal*) **3** *vt* **TIRE SOMEBODY OUT** to make somebody very tired or ill (*slang*) **4** *vi* **HIT BALL IN PRACTICE** in racquet games, to hit the ball back and forth in practice with an opponent, especially before beginning a match **5** *vt* **SCORE RUNS** in cricket, to score a specific number of runs **6** *vt* **OFFENSIVE TERM** an offensive term meaning to make a woman pregnant (*slang*)

knockabout /nókə bowt/ *n* **1 COMIC PERFORMANCE** comedy characterized by boisterous physical activity, or an actor who specializes in this type of comedy **2 INFORMAL GAME** an informal ball game, especially an informal game of football (*informal*) ■ *adj* **1 USING SLAPSTICK** characterized by boisterous physical activity **2 STURDY AND INFORMAL** suitable for rough or casual activities

knock-back *n NZ, Scotland* a rejection (*informal*)

knockdown /nók down/ *n* **1 OVERWHELMING BLOW** a powerful emotional or physical blow **2 PRICE DROP** a reduction in the price of something **3** *ANZ* **INTRODUCTION** an introduction to somebody (*slang*) ■ *adj* **1 VERY POWERFUL** having an overwhelmingly powerful or very damaging effect **2 EASILY DISASSEMBLED** made to be taken apart easily **3 DISCOUNTED** reduced or very cheap ○ *a knockdown price*

knocker /nókər/ *n* **1 FIXTURE FOR KNOCKING ON DOOR** a metal fixture attached with hinges to the door of a house, used for knocking on the door **2 CRITIC** a carping or unfair critic (*informal*) ■ **knockers** *npl* **OFFENSIVE TERM** an offensive term for a woman's breasts (*slang*)

knock-for-knock *adj* describes an agreement between two insurance companies whereby each pays out for damage sustained by its policyholder in an accident involving a policyholder of the other company

knocking copy *n* advertising material aimed at persuading prospective customers of the inferiority of a rival product or service

knocking-shop *n* an offensive term for a brothel (*slang*) [< KNOCK 'have sexual intercourse with']

knock-knee *n* a condition in which the legs are permanently bent so that the knees are close together and the ankles are spread far apart ■ **knock-knees** *npl* the knees of somebody with knock-knee —**knock-kneed** *adj*

knockoff /nók of/ *n US* an inexpensive, sometimes illegal copy of a piece of well-known or popular merchandise (*informal*)

knock-on *adj* progressively affecting other people or things related directly or indirectly to whatever was first affected ○ *The knock-on effect will almost certainly cause further factory closures in the area.* ■ *n* in rugby, illegal use of the hand or arm to move the ball forwards

knockout /nók owt/ *n* **1 PUNCH WINNING A BOXING MATCH** in boxing, a punch that knocks an opponent down for a count of ten and so wins a contest **2 BOXING MATCH WON BY A KNOCKOUT** a victory in a boxing match by a knockout **3 BLOW CAUSING SOMEBODY TO BECOME UNCONSCIOUS** a blow that knocks somebody unconscious **4 ELIMINATION COMPETITION** a sports competition in which a person or team beaten in one game or match is eliminated from the entire competition **5 SOMEBODY OR SOMETHING STUNNING** somebody or something extremely attractive, good-looking, or enjoyable (*informal*)

knockout drops *npl* a solution, usually containing chloral hydrate, secretly put in a drink to render the drinker unconscious (*informal*)

knock-up *n* in racket games, a practice period with an opponent, especially before the beginning of a match

knockwurst *n* FOOD = **knackwurst**

knoll[1] /nōl/ *n* a small rounded hill or mound [Old English *cnoll* < Germanic] —**knolly** *adj*

knoll[2] /nōl/ *n, vti* knell (*archaic*) [14C. < Germanic.]

knop /nop/ *n* a small decorative knob [14C. < Middle Low German or Middle Dutch *knoppe* 'knob, knot'.] —**knopped** *adj*

Knossos /nósəss, knóssəss/ ruined city in N Crete, the centre of the Minoan civilization from about 3000 BC to 1100 BC

knot[1] /not/ *n* **1 OBJECT MADE BY TYING** a usually hard, lump-shaped object formed when a strand of something, e.g. string or rope, is interlaced with itself or another strand and pulled tight **2 WAY OF TYING** a way of joining or securing lengths of rope, thread, or other strands by tying the material together or around itself **3 A TANGLE** a tightly tangled mass of strands that are hard to separate **4 DECORATION** a piece of material such as ribbon or braid tied in a knot or bow and used as a decoration **5 HARD PATCH ON A TREE** a hard patch on a tree out of which a branch or stem grows **6 DARK WHORL IN TIMBER** a hard dark-coloured patch in cut wood at a point where a branch or stem formerly grew out of the tree **7 LUMP ON A TREE** a lump on a tree trunk or branch **8 LUMP IN THE BODY** a node, ganglion, lump, or swelling in the body **9 UNIT OF SPEED** (*symbol* **kn**) a unit of measurement for the speed at which a ship or aircraft travels, equivalent to one nautical mile per hour, approximately 1.85 km per hour/1.15 statute mph **10 INDICATOR MEASURING A SHIP'S SPEED** a division on a log line used for calculating the speed of a ship **11 TIGHT GROUP** a number of people or things grouped closely together **12 TENSE FEELING** a feeling of tightness or anxiety **13 PROBLEM** a difficult or complex problem ■ *v* (**knots, knotting, knotted**) **1** *vti* **MAKE A KNOT** to tie something in a knot, or be tied with a knot **2** *vti* **TO TANGLE** to tangle something, or become tangled **3** *vt* **MAKE WITH A PATTERN OF KNOTS** to produce something, e.g. a piece of macramé, that consists of a pattern of decorative knots **4** *vti* **BECOME TENSE** to become, or cause something to become, tight or tense with anxiety or fear ○ *My stomach knotted up.* [Old English *cnotta* < Germanic, 'round lump'] —**knotter** *n* ◇ **get knotted** an offensive term expressing disagreement or impatience with somebody (*slang*) ◇ **tie somebody (up) in knots** to make somebody completely confused, especially in trying to explain something ◇ **tie the knot** to get married (*informal*)

SPELLCHECK Do not confuse ***knot*** with ***not***, which has a similar sound. Beware: your spellchecker will not catch this error.

---

knot[2] /not/ *n* a small migratory sandpiper. Native to: the Arctic. *Calidris canutus* and *Calidris tenuirostris.* [15C. < ?]

knot garden *n* a herb or flower garden that has its plants arranged in an intricate pattern and sometimes also has trees and bushes trimmed in decorative designs

knotgrass /nót graass/ (*plural* **-grasses** *or* **-grass**) *n* a creeping plant with prominent nodes on its stems, considered a troublesome weed. Flowers: small, pink. *Polygonum aviculare.* [Early 16C. < its knotted stem.]

knothole /nót hōl/ *n* a hole in wood where a knot has fallen out or been removed

knotted /nóttid/ *adj* **1** tied in a knot, tangled up in knots, or made using decorative knots **2** WOODWORK = **knotty** *adj* **2** **3** describes a plant that has stems with swellings resembling knots

knotting /nótting/ *n* decorative weaving such as macramé or tatting, produced by interlacing and tying knots in the wool or thread

knotty /nótti/ (**-tier, -tiest**) *adj* **1 FULL OF KNOTS** full of tied or tangled knots **2 MARKED WITH KNOTS** containing or marked with many knots ○ *knotty pine* **3 PUZZLING OR COMPLEX** very difficult to understand or solve —**knottily** *adv* —**knottiness** *n*

knotty pine *n* pine wood that has many knots in it. Use: panelling, furniture.

knotweed /nót weed/ (*plural* **-weeds** *or* **-weed**) *n* PLANTS = **knotgrass.** ◊ **Japanese knotweed**

knotwork /nót wurk/ *n* decorative weaving produced by interlacing and tying knots in the cords

knout /nowt/ *n* a leather whip formerly used in imperial Russia for flogging ■ *vt* to flog somebody using a knout [Mid-17C. Via French < Russian *knut* < Old Norse *knútr* 'knot'.]

know /nō/ (**knows, knowing, knew** /nyoo/, **known** /nōn/) *v* **1** *vti* **HOLD INFORMATION IN THE MIND** to have information firmly in the mind or committed to memory ○ *They know the names of all the US presidents.* **2** *vti* **BE CERTAIN ABOUT** to believe firmly in the truth or certainty of something ○ *I know she wouldn't be late without a good reason.* **3** *vti* **REALIZE** to be or become aware of something ○ *I didn't know you cared.* **4** *vt* **COMPREHEND** to have a thorough understanding of something through experience or study ○ *know computers* **5** *vt* **HAVE ENCOUNTERED BEFORE** to be acquainted, associated, or familiar with somebody or something ○ *I have known John for years.* **6** *vt* **RECOGNIZE DIFFERENCES** to be able to perceive the differences or distinctions between things or people ○ *old enough to know right from wrong* **7** *vt* **IDENTIFY BY A CHARACTERISTIC** to recognize somebody or something by a distinguishing characteristic or attribute ○ *I'd know him anywhere by his peculiar laugh.* **8** *vt* **HAVE SEX WITH** to engage in sexual intercourse with somebody (*archaic*) [Old English *cnāwan* < Indo-European] —**knowable** *adj* —**knower** *n* ◇ **in the know** possessing information that is secret or known only to a small group of people ◇ **know something back to front** to be completely familiar with all the details of or facts about something ◇ **know something backward and forward** *US* to be completely familiar with all the details of or facts about something ◇ **know something backwards** to be completely familiar with all the details of or facts about something ◇ **not know**

where to put yourself to feel embarrassed (*informal*) ◇ **you know** used to fill a pause, add emphasis to a statement, or elicit a response from the listener (*informal*) ◇ **you never know** used to indicate that the outcome of events is uncertain and it is possible that something that seems unlikely could happen

SPELLCHECK Do not confuse **know** with **no**, which has a similar sound. Beware: your spellchecker will not catch this error.

know-all *n* somebody who professes to know more or better than anyone else about everything (*informal*) US term **know-it-all**

know-how *n* the practical ability and knowledge necessary to do something (*informal*)

knowing /nṓ ing/ *adj* **1 INDICATING PRIVATE KNOWLEDGE** suggesting that somebody knows a secret or something that others are unaware of ○ *a knowing smile* **2 ASTUTE** aware of things and able to act cleverly and judge shrewdly **3 INTENTIONAL** done on purpose —**knowingly** *adv* —**knowingness** *n*

know-it-all *n* US = **know-all**

knowledgable *adj* = **knowledgeable**

knowledge /nóllij/ *n* **1 INFORMATION IN MIND** general awareness or possession of information, facts, ideas, truths, or principles ○ *Her knowledge and interests are extensive.* **2 SPECIFIC INFORMATION** clear awareness or explicit information, e.g. of a situation or fact ○ *I believe they have knowledge of the circumstances.* **3 ALL THAT CAN BE KNOWN** all the information, facts, truths, and principles learned throughout time ○ *With all our knowledge, we still haven't found a cure for the common cold.* **4 INTERCOURSE** sexual intercourse (*archaic*) [14C. Probably < obsolete *knowlechen* 'acknowledge' < Old English *cnāwan* 'know' + -*lǣcan* < -*lāc* 'practice'.]

knowledgeable /nóllijəb'l/, **knowledgable** *adj* possessing or showing a great deal of knowledge, awareness, or intelligence —**knowledgeability** /nóllijə bíllэti/ *n* —**knowledgeableness** *n* —**knowledgeably** *adv*

⚡ **knowledge base** *n* **1** the computerized data in an expert system required for solving problems in a particular area **2** the facts required for solving a problem or problems

⚡ **knowledge industry** *n* businesses that specialize primarily in data processing or the development and use of information technology

knowledge worker *n* somebody working in an industry that produces information rather than goods, such as management consultancy or computer programming

known /nōn/ past participle of **know** ■ *adj* **1 ACKNOWLEDGED** generally recognized as or proven to be something ○ *a known criminal* **2 FAMILIAR** belonging to an established body of knowledge ○ *the limits of the known universe* ■ *n* **CERTAINTY** a fact or piece of information that is certain ○ *separate the knowns from the unknowns*

Knox /noks/, **John** (1513?–72) Scottish religious reformer

KNP *abbr* king's knight's pawn

Knt *abbr* knight

knuckle /núk'l/ *n* **1 FINGER JOINT** a joint of a finger, especially a joint connecting a finger to the hand **2 ROUNDED PROJECTION WHEN A FIST IS MADE** one of the rounded projections above a knuckle that appears on the back of a hand when a fist is made (*often plural*) **3 PIECE OF MEAT NEAR THE KNEE** a cut of meat consisting of the lower joint from the hind leg of a calf, pig, or lamb **4 HINGE PIVOT** the cylindrical part of a hinge through which the pin passes **5 MECH ENG** = **knuckle joint** *n.* **2** ■ *v* (**-les, -ling, -led**) **1** *vt* **APPLY KNUCKLES TO** to rub, hit, or press something with the knuckles ○ *knuckled her eyes in disbelief* **2** *vi* **HAVE KNUCKLES ON GROUND PLAYING MARBLES** to have the knuckles on the ground when shooting a marble with the thumb pressed into the bent forefinger [14C. < Middle Low German *knökel* 'small bone' < Germanic.] —**knuckly** *adj* ◇ **near the knuckle** rather indecent

knuckle down *vi* to work hard and conscientiously at something (*informal*)

knuckle under *vi* to give in to force or pressure used against you

knuckleball /núk'l bawl/ *n* in baseball, a slow pitch with little spin and an unpredictable flight, produced by releasing the ball from the knuckles and the thumb or the tips of two or three fingers —**knuckleballer** *n*

knucklebone /núk'l bōn/ *n* any knobbly bone forming part of a joint in the human finger (*informal*)

knucklebones /núk'l bōnz/ *n* GAME = **jacks** (+ *singular verb*)

knuckle-duster *n* a piece of metal worn over the knuckles and used to make a punch inflict greater injury. US term **brass knuckles**

knucklehead /núk'l hed/ *n* an offensive term for somebody who is regarded as unintelligent or thoughtless (*slang insult*) —**knuckleheaded** *adj*

knuckle joint *n* **1** a joint of the human finger **2** a hinge with a pin that fastens the ends of two rods together, allowing movement in one plane only

knuckler /núklər/ *n* BASEBALL = **knuckleball**

knuckle sandwich *n* a blow with the fist to the mouth (*slang*)

knur /nur/, **knurr** *n* a bump or knot on a tree trunk or in wood [15C. < ?]

knurl /nurl/ *n* **1 BUMP OR KNOB** a small hard knob or protuberance **2 RIDGE USED FOR GRIPPING** a ridge, especially one in a series that run along the edge of something, e.g. those on a thumbscrew that make it easier to grip ■ *vt* **PUT RIDGES ON** to give ridges to something, especially to make it easier to grip [Early 17C. Probably < KNUR.] —**knurly** *adj*

knurr *n* = **knur**

KO *n* (*plural* **KO's**) a knockout, especially in boxing (*informal*) ■ *vt* (**KO's, KO'ing, KO'd**) to knock somebody out, especially in boxing (*informal*) [Early 20C. < the initial letters of *knock out*.]

koa /kṓ ə/ (*plural* **koas** *or* **koa**) *n* a tree with grey bark that yields a valuable reddish- to yellowish-brown hardwood used in furniture-making. Native to: Hawaii. *Acacia koa*. [Early 19C. < Hawaiian.]

Koala

koala /kō áələ/, **koala bear** *n* a marsupial that resembles a small bear and has grey fur, a round face, and large ears. Native to: Australia. *Phascolarctos cinereus*. [Late 18C. < Dharuk *kūl(i)a*.]

koan /kṓ an/ (*plural* **-ans** *or* **-an**) *n* a Zen Buddhist riddle used to focus the mind during meditation and to develop intuitive thinking [Mid-20C. < Japanese *kōan* < Chinese *gōngàn* 'official business'.]

kob /kob/ (*plural* **kobs** *or* **kob**) *n* a large antelope of Central and West Africa with orange-brown fur. It lives in open grasslands near swamps or rivers. *Kobus kob*. [Late 18C. < Wolof *kooba*.]

Kobe /kṓbi/, **Kōbe** seaport on S Honshu Island, Japan, on Osaka Bay. Population: 1,477,410 (1990).

Koblenz /kṓ blénts/ city in west-central Germany. Population: 109,600 (1994).

kobo /kṓ bō/ (*plural* **-bo** *or* **-bos**) *n* see table at **currency** [Late 20C. < Nigerian English, alteration of COPPER[1].]

kobold /kóbbōld/ *n* in German folklore, a mischievous elf that lives in houses or a gnome that haunts underground places, especially mines [Mid-19C. < German, variant of *Kobalt* (see COBALT).]

Kobuk Valley National Park /kṓ búk-/ national park in NW Alaska. Area: 708,498 hectares/1,750,537 acres.

Koch /kokh/, **Robert** (1843–1910) German bacteriologist

Kodály /kṓd ī/, **Zoltán** (1882–1967) Hungarian composer

Kodiak[1] /kṓdi ak/ city in S Alaska, on NE Kodiak Island. Population: 7,677 (1996).

Kodiak[2] /kṓdi ak/ (*plural* **-aks** *or* **-ak**), **Kodiak bear** *n* a brown bear of the coastal areas and nearby islands of Alaska and British Columbia. *Ursus middendorffi*. [Late 19C. After KODIAK ISLAND.]

Kodiak Island island off SW Alaska, in the Gulf of Alaska. Area: 8,974 sq. km/3,465 sq. mi.

koeksister /kṓok sistər/ *n* S Africa a twisted or plaited doughnut, deep-fried in oil then dipped into cold sugar syrup and sometimes dried coconut [Early 20C. < Afrikaans.]

koel /kṓ əl/ (*plural* **koels** *or* **koel**) *n* a large long-tailed cuckoo. Native to: SE Australia. Genus: *Eudynamys*. [Early 19C. < Hindi *koē*.]

Koetsu Hon'Ami /ko áttsoo hōná ami/ (1558–1637) Japanese artist

kofta /kóftə/ (*plural* **kofta** *or* **koftas**) *n* S Asia an Indian dish consisting of minced meat, fish, or vegetables cooked in small balls [Late 19C. < Urdu, Persian *koftah* 'pounded meat'.]

kohen *n* JUDAISM = **cohen**

kohl /kōl/ *n* a chemical preparation used by women, especially in Asia and the Middle East, to darken the rims of their eyelids [Late 18C. < Arabic *kuḥl*.]

Kohl /kōl/, **Helmut** (*b*. 1930) German statesman

kohlrabi /kōl ráabi/ (*plural* **-bies**) *n* **1** a swollen turnip-shaped stem of a cabbage plant eaten as a vegetable **2** a cabbage producing kohlrabies. *Brassica oleracea* var. *gongylodes*. [Early 19C. Via German < the plural of Italian *cavolo rapa* < medieval Latin *caulorapa* < Latin *caulis* 'cabbage' + *rapa* 'turnip'.]

Kohoutek /kə hóot ek/ *n* a comet that passed around the sun in late 1973 and early 1974

koi /koy/ (*plural* **koi**), **koi carp** *n* a carp that is popular as an aquarium or ornamental pond fish because of its red-gold or white colouring. Native to: Japan, temperate regions of E Asia. *Cyprinus carpio*. [Early 18C. < Japanese.]

koine *n* **1** LANGUAGE = **lingua franca** *n.* **1 2** a dialect or regional variant of a language that becomes the standard language for a wider population of speakers [Late 19C. < Greek *koinē*, a form of *koinos* 'common'.]

Koine /kóy nee/ *n* the form of Greek, mostly derived from the Attic dialect, that became the standard language for Greek-speaking people during the Hellenistic period

kokanee /kō kánni/ (*plural* **-nees** *or* **-nee**), **kokanee salmon** *n* a small nonmigratory sockeye salmon. Native to: landlocked lakes from W North America to Siberia and Japan, but widely introduced to other areas. *Oncorhynchus nerka kennerlyi*. [Late 19C. < Shuswap *kəknǽxw*.]

Koko Nor /kṓkō nawr/ GEOG = **Qinghai Hu**

Kokoschka /kó kóshkə/, **Oskar** (1886–1980) Austrian-born painter and writer

kola /kṓlə/ *n* TREES = **cola**[1] *n.* 2

kola nut *n* TREES = **cola nut**

Kola Peninsula /kṓlə-/ peninsula in NW European Russia, between the Barents Sea and the White Sea. Area: 100,000 sq. km/40,000 sq. mi.

Kolar Gold Fields /kō láar-/ city in S Karnataka State, S India, near Bangalore. Population: 156,398 (1991).

Kolhapur /kṓl haa pōor/ city in SW India. Population: 406,370 (1991).

kolinsky /kə línski/ (*plural* **-skies**) *n* **1** the dark tawny fur of a weasel **2** a weasel that yields kolinsky. Native to: N Europe and Asia. *Mustela sibirica*. [Mid-19C. < Russian *kolinskiĭ* 'of Kola', after *Kola*, port in NW Russia.]

Kolkata ♦ **Calcutta**

kolkhoz /kōl kóz, -káwz, -háwz/ (*plural* **kolkhozes** *or* **kolkhoz** *or* **kolkhozy** /-zi/), **kolkoz** (*plural* **-kozes** *or* **-koz** *or* **-kozy**) *n* a collective farm in the former Soviet Union [Early 20C. < Russian, < *kol(lektivnoe) khoz(yaĭstvo)* 'collective farm'.]

kolkhoznik /kōl kóznik, -káwznik, -háwznik/ *n* a worker on a collective farm in the former Soviet Union

kolkoz *n* AGRIC = **kolkhoz**

Kol Nidre /kól níddray/ *n* **1** the prayer recited at the opening of the service on the eve of Yom Kippur **2** the service on the eve of Yom Kippur [Late 19C. < Aramaic *kol niḍrē* 'all the vows', its opening words.]

kolo /kṓlō/ (*plural* **-los**) *n* **1** a Serbian folk dance in which one or more dancers perform inside a circle of other dancers **2** the music for a kolo [Late 18C. < Serbo-Croat, 'wheel'.]

Kolonia /kə lṓni ə/ largest town in the Federated States of Micronesia, and capital of Pohnpei island state. Population: 6,600 (1994).

Kolyma Range /kə leémə-/ mountain range in NE Siberian Russia. Length: 2,100 km/1,300 mi.

komatik /kṓ matik/ *n* an Inuit sledge with wooden crossbars tied to the runners with rawhide [Early 19C. < Inuit *qamutik*.]

kombu /kóm boo/ *n* a kelp sold dried. Use: in Japanese cooking. [Late 19C. < Japanese.]

Komi /kṓmi/ (*plural* **-mi** *or* **-mis**) *n* **1** a member of a Uralic people who live in NE European Russia **2** the Finnic language of the Komi people, belonging to the Finno-Ugric branch of Uralic. Native speakers: 400,000. [Late 19C. < Komi.] —**Komi** *adj*

Komodo dragon /kə mṓdō-/, **Komodo lizard** *n* a large monitor lizard, growing to a length of 3 m/10 ft. Native to: island of Komodo, east of Java. *Varanus komodoensis*.

Komsomol /kómssə mol, kómssə mól/ *n* a Communist organization for young people in the former Soviet Union [Mid-20C. < Russian, < *Kommunisticheskiĭ Soyuz Molodëzhi* 'Communist Union of Youth'.]

Komsomolsk /kómssə molsk/ city in far SE Russia, on the River Amur. Population: 318,600 (1992).

Kongo[1] (*plural* **-gos** *or* **-go**) *n* **1** a member of a people who live along the lower River Congo in west-central Africa **2** the Bantu language spoken by the Kongo people in S Congo and N Angola. Native speakers: 7 million. Other speakers: 2 million. [Mid-19C. < Kongo.] —**Kongo** *adj*

Kongo[2] /kóng gō/ former kingdom in central Africa between present-day Gabon and N Angola

Königsberg /kōnigz burg/ former name for **Kaliningrad**

konimeter /kō nímmitər/ *n* an instrument for measuring the amount of dust in the air [Early 20C. < Greek *konis* 'dust' + METER.]

koniology /kṓni óllәji/ *n* the study of airborne dust and its effects on the environment [< Greek *konis* 'dust']

Konkani /kóngkə nee/ *n* a dialect of Marathi spoken in coastal Maharashtra in W India [Late 19C. < Marathi *kōkṇi*.]

kook /kook/ *n US* somebody whose behaviour is considered unpleasantly eccentric (*informal insult*) [Mid-20C. Probably shortening of CUCKOO.]

kookaburra /kóokə burrə/ (*plural* **-ras** *or* **-ra**) *n* a large kingfisher with a loud call that sounds like laughter. Native to: Australia and nearby islands. *Dacelo novaeguineae* and *Dacelo leachii*. [Mid-19C. < Wiradhuri *gugubarra*.]

kooky /kóoki/ (**-ier, -iest**) *adj US* considered to be unpleasantly eccentric (*informal insult*) —**kookily** *adv* —**kookiness** *n*

Kooning /kóoning/, **Willem de** (1904–97) Dutch-born US painter

Koons /koonz/, **Jeff** (*b.* 1955) US artist

Koori /kóori/ (*plural* **-ries**), **Koorie, koori** (*plural* **-ries**), **koorie** *n Aus* an Aboriginal of SE Australia (*informal*) [Mid-18C. < Awabakal *guri* 'man'.] —**Koori** *adj*

Kootenay[1] /kóotə nay/, **Kootenai** river of the NW United States and SW Canada. Length: 655 km/407 mi.

Kootenay[2], **Kootenai** *n, adj* LANG, PEOPLES = **Kutenai**

kop /kop/ *n S Africa* **1** a prominent crest of a hill **2** intelligence or common sense (*informal*) [Mid-19C. Via Afrikaans < Dutch, 'head'.]

kopek /kṓ pek/, **kopeck, copeck** *n* see table at **currency** [Early 17C. < Russian *kopeika* 'little lance'; from the figure of a tsar bearing a lance on the coin.]

kopiyka /kœ peékə/ *n* see table at **currency** [< Ukrainian]

kopje /kóppi/, **koppie** *n S Africa* a small hill [Mid-19C. Via Afrikaans < Dutch, 'small head' < *kop* 'head'.]

koppa /kóppə/ *n* the 17th letter of the ancient Greek alphabet, later adopted by the Romans as the letter 'q' [Late 19C. < Greek.]

koppie *n S Africa* = **kopje**

Kor. *abbr* Korea

kora /káwrə/ (*plural* **-ras**) *n* a West African 21-string lute that has a gourd resonator [Late 18C. < a W African language.]

Koran /kaw raán, kə-/, **Qur'an** *n* the sacred text of Islam, believed by Muslims to record the revelations of God to Muhammad [Early 17C. < Arabic *ḳur'ān* 'recitation' < *ḳara'a* 'recite'.] —**Koranic** /-ránnik/ *adj*

Kordofan /kawr dō faán/ former province in central Sudan

Kordofanian /káwrdō fáyni ən/ *n* a small group of languages spoken in S Sudan that may be distinct from other African languages or a branch of Niger-Congo —**Kordofanian** *adj*

kore /káw ray/ (*plural* **-rai** /-rī/) *n* a Greek sculpture of a clothed, standing young woman dating from the period 650 to 480 BC. ◊ **kouros** [Early 20C. < Greek *korē* 'maiden'.]

Korea, North /kə reé ə/ ♦ **North Korea**

Korea, South /kə reé ə/ ♦ **South Korea**

Korean /kə reé ən/ *n* **1** somebody who comes from North or South Korea **2** the Altaic official language of North and South Korea, also spoken in China, Japan, and Asiatic Russia. Native speakers: 60 million. Other speakers: 60 million. —**Korean** *adj*

Korean War *n* a war that lasted from 1950 to 1953 between North Korea, and its ally China, and South Korea, supported by United Nations troops, especially from the United States

korfball /káwrf bawl/ *n* a game similar to basketball that is played by two teams of twelve players, each team having six men or boys and six women or girls [Early 20C. < Dutch *korfbal* 'basket ball'.]

Kōrin /kṓrin/ (1658–1716) Japanese artist

korma /káwrmə/ (*plural* **-mas**), **qorma** (*plural* **-mas**) *n* a mildly spiced, creamy Indian dish of meat, seafood, or vegetables cooked in a cream or yogurt sauce [Late 19C. < Urdu *ḳormā*.]

Koror /kə ráwr/ capital and island of the Republic of Palau, in the W Pacific Ocean. Population: 11,552 (1997). Area: 21 sq. km/8 sq. mi.

Korsakoffian /káwrssə kóffi ən/ *adj* relating to the Wenicke-Korsakoff syndrome ■ *n* an offensive term for somebody who is affected by Wenicke-Korsakoff syndrome

koruna /ko róonə/ *n* see table at **currency** [Early 20C. < Czech, 'crown'.]

kos /kōss/ (*plural* **kos**) *n* in India, a unit of measurement used for land distances that varies in length from region to region, ranging from 1.6 to 4.8 km/1 to 3 mi [Early 17C. < Hindi, < Sanskrit *krośa* 'cry'.]

Kos ♦ **Cos**

Kosciuszko, Mount /kóssi úsk ō/ highest mountain in Australia, in the Snowy Mountains in SE New South Wales. Height: 2,228 m/7,310 ft.

Kościuszko /kóssi úsk ō/, **Tadeusz** (1746–1817) Polish national hero

kosher /kṓshər/ *adj* **1** RITUALLY PURE describes food that has been prepared so that it is fit and suitable under Jewish law **2** PREPARING OR SELLING KOSHER FOOD preparing or selling foods that are fit and suitable under Jewish law **3** REAL genuine, not false or fake (*informal*) **4** LAWFUL OR PROPER allowed by law or regarded as correct or proper (*informal*) ○ *Something's not kosher about his handling of the situation.* ■ *vt* PREPARE KOSHER FOOD to prepare food in a way that is fit and suitable under Jewish Law [Mid-19C. < Hebrew *kāšēr* 'fit, proper'.]

Kosovo /kóssəvə/ former autonomous province in SW Serbia. Population: 1,956,196 (1991). Area: 10,887 sq. km/4,203 sq. mi. Albanian **Kosova** —**Kosovan** *n, adj* —**Kosovar** /kóssə vaar/ *n, adj*

Kossuth /kóssooth, kósh oot/, **Lajos** (1802–94) Hungarian statesman

Kostunica /kosh tóonitsə/, **Vojislav** (*b.* 1944) Yugoslavian president of the Federal Republic of Yugoslavia (2000–)

Kosuth /kə sóoth/, **Joseph** (*b.* 1945) US conceptual artist

Kosygin /kə seégin/, **Aleksey** (1904–80) Soviet statesman

Kota Baharu /kṓtə baároo/ capital of Kelantan State, Malaysia, on the coast of the NE Malay Peninsula. Population: 220,000 (1991).

Kota Kinabalu /kṓtə kinəbə lóo/ capital of Sabah State, E Malaysia, on the South China Sea. Population: 55,997 (1993).

koto /kṓtō/ (*plural* **-tos**) *n* a Japanese musical instrument resembling a zither, with strings stretched over a convex wooden sounding board that are plucked [Late 18C. < Japanese.]

koulibiac /kóoli byák/, **koulibiaca** /-byákə/, **coulibiac** /kóoli byák/, **coulibiaca** /-byákə/ *n* a Russian-style fish pie, usually consisting of layers of cooked rice, fish, and eggs in pastry [Late 19C. < Russian *kulebyaka*.]

koumiss, koumis, koumyss *n* FOOD = **kumiss**

kouprey /kóo pray/ (*plural* **-preys** *or* **-prey**) *n* an endangered species of wild ox with a blackish-brown body and white markings on its back and feet. Native to: Cambodia, Vietnam. *Bos sauveli*. [Mid-20C. < Khmer.]

kouros /kóor oss/ (*plural* **-roi** /kóor oy/) *n* a Greek sculpture of a naked, standing young man from the period 650 to 480 BC. ◊ **kore** [Early 20C. < Greek, variant of *koros* 'boy'.]

Kowloon /kow lóon/ peninsula in SE China, forming part of Hong Kong. Population: 2,030,683 (1991).

kowtow /ków tów/ *vi* **1** KNEEL TO SHOW RESPECT formerly, in China, to kneel and touch the forehead to the ground in order to show respect, awe, or submission **2** BE SERVILE to behave in an extremely submissive way in order to please somebody in a position of authority ■ *n* **1** ACT OF KNEELING TO SHOW RESPECT a show of respect or worship made by kneeling and touching the forehead to the ground **2** SERVILE ACT an extremely submissive act aimed at pleasing somebody in a position of authority [Early 19C. < Chinese *kòutóu* 'strike (the) head'.] —**kowtower** *n*

ϟ **kp** *abbr* Korea, Democratic People's Republic of (*in Internet addresses*)

KP[1] *symbol* king's pawn

KP[2] *abbr* **1** Knight (of the Order) of St Patrick **2** *US* Knight of Pythias

kph *abbr* kilometres per hour

ϟ **kr** *abbr* Korea, Republic of (*in Internet addresses*)

Kr *symbol* **1** krona **2** krone **3** krypton

KR *symbol* king's rook

kr. *abbr* **1** krona **2** króna **3** krone

kraal /kraal/ *n S Africa* **1** a traditional rural village in Africa, usually consisting of a number of huts surrounded by a stockade (*sometimes offensive*) **2** a pen or other enclosure for livestock, especially cattle [Mid-18C. Via Afrikaans < Portuguese *curral* < Nama.]

Krafft-Ebing /kráft ébbing/, **Richard** (1840–1902) German neuropsychologist

kraft /kraaft/, **kraft paper** *n* tough, usually brown, paper made from chemically treated wood pulp. Use: bags, wrapping paper. [Early 20C. < shortening of Swedish *kraftpapper* 'strength paper'.]

krait /krīt/ *n* an extremely poisonous snake with brightly-coloured bands on its back. Native to: SE Asia. Genus: *Bungarus*. [Late 19C. < Hindi *karait*.]

Krakatau /krakə tów/, **Krakatoa** **1** small volcanic island in SW Indonesia, in the Sunda Strait between Java and Sumatra. Area: 15 sq. km/5.8 sq. mi. **2** volcano on the island of Krakatau, Indonesia. Height: 813 m/2,667 ft.

kraken /kraákən/ *n* in Norwegian folklore, a huge sea monster shaped like a giant squid [Mid-18C. < Norwegian.]

Kraków /kraákov/ city in S Poland. Population: 740,500 (1997 estimate).

krameria /krə meéri ə/ *n* a plant of a genus including some, e.g. rhatany, that have roots with medicinal uses and are used as dyes. Native to: South America. Genus: *Krameria*. [Mid-19C. After J. G. H. *Kramer* (d.1742), Austrian botanist.]

krans /kraanss/ (*plural* **kranses**), **krantz** /kraants/ (*plural* **krantzes**) *n S Africa* a sheer rock face, typically occurring in the form of a band of exposed rock around the summit of a mountain [Late 18C. Via Afrikaans < Dutch, 'coronet, chaplet'.]

Krasnodar /krassnə daár/ port in SW Russia. Population: 761,681 (1995).

Krasnoyarsk /krəsnə yaásk/ city in S Siberian Russia. Population: 1,122,874 (1995).

krater /kráytər/ *n US* ARCHAEOL = **crater** *n.* **4** [Mid-18C. Via Latin *crater* < Greek *kratēr* 'mixing bowl' < *kerannunai* 'to mix'.]

K ration *n* an emergency food ration consisting of one prepared meal, supplied to US soldiers fighting in World War II [Mid-20C. After Ancel Benjamin *Keyes* (b. 1904), American physiologist.]

kraut /krowt/ *n US* FOOD = **sauerkraut** [Mid-19C. < German, 'vegetable, cabbage'.]

Kraut /krowt/ *n* an offensive term for a German (*slang*) [Early 20C. See KRAUT.] —**Kraut** *adj*

Krebs /krebz/, **Sir Hans** (1900–81) German-born British biochemist

Krebs cycle *n* a sequence of biochemical reactions occurring in cells that is part of the metabolism of carbohydrates to produce energy [Mid-20C. After Sir Hans KREBS.]

Kreisler /kríssler/, **Fritz** (1875–1962) Austrian-born US violinist and composer

kremlin /krémlin/ *n* a fortress or citadel in any Russian city [Mid-17C. Via French < Russian *kreml* 'citadel'.]

Kremlin /krémlin/ *n* **1** the walled citadel in Moscow in which cathedrals, palaces, and the offices of the Russian government are located **2** the government of the former Soviet Union

Kremlinology /krémli nóllәji/ *n* the study of the government and policies of the former Soviet Union —**Kremlinological** /krémlinә lójjik'l/ *adj* —**Kremlinologist** *n*

kreplach /krép laak, -laakh/ *npl* a Jewish dish consisting of triangles or squares of pasta filled with liver or meat that are boiled and served in soup [Late 19C. < Yiddish *kreplech*, plural of *krepel* < German dialect *Kräppel* 'fried pastry'.]

krill /kril/ (*plural* **krill**) *n* a tiny marine crustacean resembling a shrimp that is the primary food of baleen whales and other animals that filter their food from seawater. Order: Euphausiacea. [Early 20C. < Norwegian *kril* 'small fry of fish'.]

krimmer /krímmәr/ *n* pale fur made from the soft curly wool of lambs from the Crimean Peninsula [Mid-19C. < German, < *Krim* 'Crimea'.]

Krio /kreé ō/ (*plural* **-os**) *n* **1** a creole language spoken in Sierra Leone, based on English and with a strong Yoruba influence. Native speakers: 50,000. Other speakers: 200,000. **2** somebody who speaks Krio [Mid-20C. Probably alteration of CREOLE.] —**Krio** *adj*

Kriol /kreé ol/ *n Aus* the English-based creole spoken by many Aboriginal people in N Australia [Mid-20C. < Kriol, alteration of CREOLE.]

kris /kreess, kriss/ *n* a Malay and Indonesian dagger with a wavy two-edged blade [Late 16C. < Malay *keris*.]

Krishna /kríshnә/ *n* in Hindu religion, the eighth incarnation of the god Vishnu, often depicted as a young cowherd [< Sanskrit *kṛṣṇa*] —**Krishnaism** *n*

Kristeva /kris teévә/, **Julia** (*b.* 1941) Bulgarian-born French psychoanalyst, linguist, and writer

Krivoy Rog /kri vóy rawk/, **Krivoi Rog** city in south-central Ukraine. Population: 724,000 (1991).

⚡**KRL** *abbr* knowledge representation language

kromesky /krә méski/ (*plural* **-kies**) *n* **1** in Polish or Russian cooking, a thin pancake containing a savoury or sweet filling **2** in Polish or Russian cooking, a small fritter or croquette of minced meat or fish wrapped in bacon [Mid-19C. < Polish *kromeczka* 'small slice'.]

krona /krṓnә/ (*plural* **-nor** /-nawr/) *n* see table at **currency** [Late 19C. < Swedish, 'crown'.]

króna /krṓnә/ (*plural* **-nur** /krṓnә/), **krona** (*plural* **-nur**) *n* see table at **currency** [Late 19C. < Icelandic, 'crown'.]

krone /krṓnә/ (*plural* **-ner** /krṓnә/) *n* see table at **currency** [Late 19C. < Danish, German, 'crown'.]

Kronecker delta /krónnikәr-/ *n* a mathematical function of two variables that takes on only two values: 0 when the variables are unequal, and 1 when the variables are equal [Early 20C. After Leopold *Kronecker* (1823–91), German mathematician.]

kroner plural of **krone**

kronor plural of **krona**

Kronos *n* MYTHOL = **Cronus**

Kronstadt /krṓnshtat/, **Kronshtadt** military port in NW European Russia, on Kotlin Island, in the Gulf of Finland. Population: 44,400 (1994).

krónur plural of **króna**

kroon /kroon/ (*plural* **kroons** *or* **krooni** /krooni/) *n* see table at **currency** [Early 20C. < Estonian, 'crown'.]

Kropotkin /krә pótkin/, **Pyotr Alekseyevich, Prince** (1842–1921) Russian revolutionary

Kroto /krṓtō/, **Sir Harold Walter** (*b.* 1939) British chemist

KRP *abbr* king's rook's pawn

Kruger /kroógәr/, **Paul** (1825–1904) South African statesman

Kruger National Park /kroógәr-/ national park in NE South Africa. Area: 19,485 sq. km/7,523 sq. mi.

Krugerrand /kroógәr rand/ *n* a South African gold coin weighing one ounce, intended mostly to be purchased as an investment [Mid-20C. < Paul KRUGER + RAND.]

Krugersdorp /kroógәrz dawrp/ city in NE South Africa. Population: 93,000 (1991 estimate).

kruller *n US* FOOD = **cruller**

krumhorn *n* MUSIC = **crumhorn**

krummholz /kroóm hōlts/ (*plural* **-holz**) *n* the stunted trees that grow just above the timberline on a mountain, or the high-altitude zone in which they grow [Early 20C. < German, 'crooked wood'.]

krummhorn *n* MUSIC = **crumhorn**

Krupp /kroop/, **Alfried** (1812–87) German industrialist and arms manufacturer

Krupp, Friedrich (1854–1902) German arms manufacturer

krypton /krípt on, kríptәn/ *n* (*symbol* **Kr**) a colourless inert gaseous element, constituting one millionth by volume of the atmosphere. Use: fluorescent lamps, lasers. [Late 19C. < Greek *krupton*, a form of *kruptos* 'hidden'.]

KS *abbr* Kansas

KStJ *abbr* Knight of the Order of St John

K selection *n* a process of natural selection that leads to a lowering of the birthrate when the population of a species approaches the maximum number that the environment can sustain [< *K*, the constant for carrying capacity in the population growth equation]

Kshatriya /kshátri ә/ *n* **1** the second of the four Hindu castes, originally a royal and warrior caste. In modern times, its members are professionals, administrators, or military personnel. **2** a member of the Kshatriya caste [Late 18C. < Sanskrit *kṣatriya* < *kṣatra* 'rule'.]

kt *abbr* kiloton

Kt *abbr* **Kt, kt** knight

KT *abbr* **1** Knight Templar **2** Knight (of the Order) of the Thistle

Kuala Lumpur /kwaálә loómpoor/ capital of Malaysia, on the S Malay Peninsula. Population: 1,145,075 (1991).

Kublai Khan /koóblә kaán/ (1215–94) Mongol leader and emperor of China

Kubrick /kyoóbrik/, **Stanley** (1928–99) US film director

kuccha /kúchә/, **kaccha** *n* a pair of short trousers worn by baptized Sikhs as a symbol of religious loyalty. ◊ **five Ks** [< Punjabi]

kuchen /koókhәn/ (*plural* **-chen**) *n* any cake that has been raised with yeast [Mid-19C. < German, 'cake'.]

Kuching /koó ching/ capital of Sarawak State, E Malaysia. Population: 147,729 (1991).

kudos /kyoó doss/ *n* praise, credit, or glory for an achievement (+ *singular verb*) ○ *Kudos is due to the president for the success of the negotiations.* [Late 18C. < Greek, 'praise, renown'.]

kudu /koó doo/ (*plural* **-dus** *or* **-du**), **koodoo** (*plural* **-doos** *or* **-doo**) *n* a large antelope, the male of which has long spiralling horns. Native to: Africa. *Tragelaphus strepsiceros* and *Tragelaphus imberbis*. [Late 18C. < Afrikaans *koedoe* < Xhosa *i-qudu*.]

kudzu /koód zoo/ *n* a hardy vine that has compound leaves and roots that contain a nourishing starch used medicinally. Flowers: purplish. Native to: E Asia. *Pueraria lobata*. [Late 19C. < Japanese *kuzu*.]

Kufic /koófik, kyoó-/, **Cufic** *adj* having an early angular style of Arabic writing used for Koranic manuscripts and inscriptions ■ *n* the Arabic alphabet written in Kufic script [Early 18C. After *Kufa*, ancient city south of Baghdad.]

kugel /koóg'l/ *n* a savoury pudding in Jewish cuisine, often of noodles or potatoes [Mid-19C. < Yiddish, 'ball' < Middle High German; probably from its traditional mound shape.]

Kuiper belt *n* a ring of small astronomical objects orbiting through the outer solar system, beyond the farthest planets, Neptune and Pluto

Ku Klux Klan /koó kluks klán/ *n* **1** a terrorist secret society organized in the S United States after the Civil War that used violence and murder to promote its white supremacist beliefs **2** a white supremacist organization founded in Georgia in 1915 [Mid-19C. < ?]

kukri /koókri/ (*plural* **-ris**) *n* a large knife with a sharp curved blade that gets broader towards the point, used by the Gurkhas in Nepal for hunting and fighting [Early 19C. < Nepali *khukuri*.]

kukui nut /koó koó i-/ *n Hawaii* the nut from the candlenut tree [< Hawaiian]

kulak /koó lak/ *n* a wealthy landowning peasant in Russia during the time between the emancipation of the serfs and the Stalinist era [Late 19C. Via Russian, 'fist, tight-fisted person' < Turkic *ḳol* 'hand'.]

kulfi /koólfi/ (*plural* **-fis**) *n S Asia* a rich Indian ice cream containing nuts

Kultur /koól toór/ *n* German culture, regarded as superior and used as a vehicle of German imperialism during the Hohenzollern and Nazi regimes [Early 20C. Via German < Latin *cultura* or French *culture* 'culture'.]

Kulturkampf /koól toór kampf/ *n* the struggle from 1871 to 1887 between the German government under Bismarck and the Roman Catholic Church over control of education, marriage, and Church appointments [Late 19C. < German, < *Kultur* 'culture' + *Kampf* 'struggle'.]

Kumamoto /koóma mṓtō/ city on W Kyushu Island, Japan. Population: 579,306 (1990).

kumara *n ANZ* = **kumera**

Kumasi /koo maássi/ capital of the Ashanti Region, central Ghana. Population: 399,300 (1990 estimate).

kumera /koómәrә/ (*plural* **-as**), **kumara** (*plural* **-as**) *n ANZ* a sweet potato [Late 18C. < Maori.]

kumiss /koómiss/, **koumiss, koumis, koumyss** *n* slightly alcoholic, fermented, and sour-tasting milk from a mare or camel, drunk by some of the peoples of Central and W Asia [Late 16C. < French *koumis*, German *Kumiss*, Polish and Russian *kumys* < Tartar *kumiz*.]

kumkum /koómkoom/ *n S Asia* a red round decorative mark worn on the forehead by Hindu women and girls, but traditionally not by widows [Mid-20C. < Sanskrit *kuṅkuma* 'saffron'.]

kümmel /kóomm'l/, **kummel** *n* a colourless liqueur or cordial that is flavoured with cumin and caraway seeds and is made primarily in the Baltic region [Mid-19C. < German, 'caraway seed' < Old High German *kumīn* 'cumin'.]

kumquat /kúm kwot/, **cumquat** *n* **1** a small oval orange fruit, related to citrus fruits, with sweet skin and tart flesh, eaten whole or preserved **2** an evergreen tree related to citrus species that produces kumquats. Native to: China. Genus: *Fortunella*. [Late 17C. < Chinese (Cantonese) *kam kwat* 'gold orange'.]

Kun /koon/, **Béla** (1886–1939?) Hungarian revolutionary

kuna /kṓnә/ (*plural* **-ne** /-ne/) *n* see table at **currency** [Late 20C. < Serbo-Croatian.]

Kuna *n* PEOPLES, LANG = **Cuna** —**Kuna** *adj*

kundalini /koóndә leéni/ *n* vital energy that Hindus believe lies dormant at the base of the spine until it is called into action, e.g. through yoga, to be used in seeking enlightenment [Late 19C. < Sanskrit *kundalinī* 'snake'; because it is likened to a coiled snake.]

Kundera /kúndәrә/, **Milan** (*b.* 1929) Czech writer

kune plural of **kuna**

kung fu /kúng foó, koóng-/ *n* a Chinese form of self-defence in which fluid, circular movements of the arms and legs are used to attack an opponent [Late 19C. < Chinese *gongfu* 'merit-master'.]

Kunlun Mountains /koón loón-/ mountain range in W China. Height: 7,723 m/25,338 ft. Length: 3,000 km/2,000 mi.

Kunming /koón míng/ capital of Yunnan Province, SW China. Population: 1,943,696 (1991).

Kununurra /kúnnә núrrә/ town in NE Western Australia. Population: 4,062 (1991).

kunzite /koónts īt/ *n* a semiprecious stone that is a reddish-purple variety of the mineral spodumene. Use: gems. [Early 20C. After George F. *Kunz*, US gem expert.]

Kuomintang /kwṓmin táng/ *n* the political party that established China as a republic in 1911, ruled China from 1928 to 1947 until defeated by the Communists, and then withdrew to rule in Taiwan [Early 20C. < Chinese *guómíndǎng* 'national people's party'.]

Kupffer cell /koópfәr-/ *n* a specialized cell (**macrophage**) that lines the minute blood-filled spaces in the liver and removes worn-out red blood cells, bacteria, and other debris from the bloodstream [Early 20C. After Karl Wilhelm von *Kupffer* (1829–1902), Bavarian anatomist.]

Kura /koó raá/ river in the Transcaucasia Region, flowing through Turkey, Georgia, and Azerbaijan, and emptying into the Caspian Sea. Length: 1,500 km/940 mi.

kurchatovium /kúrchә tṓvi әm/ *n* the name given to the element rutherfordium in the former Soviet Union [Mid-20C. After I. V. *Kurchatov* (1903–60), Russian nuclear physicist.]

Kurd /kurd/ n a member of a largely Muslim people who live in an area bordering Iraq, Turkey, and Iran [Early 17C. < Kurdish.]

kurdaitcha /kər dícha/, **kadaitcha** /kə dícha/ n among Aboriginal peoples of central Australia, a sorcerer who was responsible for avenging the death of a kinsman [Late 19C. < Aboriginal.]

Kurdish /kúrdish/ n an Iranian language spoken in Turkey, Iraq, Iran, Armenia, and Syria, belonging to the Indo-Iranian branch of Indo-European. Native speakers: 10 million. ■ adj relating to the Kurds, or their language or culture

Kurdistan

Kurdistan /kúrdi staàn/, **Kurdistān** region in SW Asia, encompassing parts of Turkey, Iraq, Iran, Armenia, and Syria, considered the homeland of the Kurdish people. Population: 26,000,000 (early 1990s).

kurfuffle /kər fúff'l/ n = **kerfuffle** (informal)

kurgan /koor gaàn, -gán/ n a burial mound built by a prehistoric culture of E Europe and N Iran [Late 19C. < Russian.]

kuri /koóri/ (plural **-ris**) n NZ **1 MONGREL** a mongrel dog **2 OFFENSIVE TERM** an offensive term for somebody who is regarded with dislike or hate [Mid-19C. < Maori.]

Kuril Islands /koóril/, **Kurile Islands** island chain extending from NE Hokkaido in Japan to S Kamchatka Peninsula in Russia. Population: 25,000 (1990). Area: 15,590 sq. km/6,020 sq. mi.

Kurosawa /koòrə saàwa/, **Akira** (1910–98) Japanese film director

Kuroshio /koo róshi ō/ warm current in the Pacific Ocean, flowing from the Philippines northeastwards along the coast of E Japan

kurrajong /kúrrə jong/ n a tree that has yellowish or red bell-shaped flowers and yields a tough fibre. Native to: E Australia. Brachychiton populneum. [Early 19C. < Aboriginal.]

Kurri Kurri-Weston /kúrri kuri wéstən/ urban area in SE New South Wales, Australia. Population: 12,555 (1996).

Kursk /koorsk/ city in west-central Russia. Population: 578,671 (1995).

kurta /koórta/ n a long loose collarless shirt worn by South Asian men [Early 20C. < Urdu, Persian kurtah.]

kurtosis /kər tóssiss/ (plural **-ses** /-seez/) n a measure of the extent to which a frequency distribution is concentrated about its mean [Early 20C. < Greek kurtōsis 'curvature' < kurtos 'bent'.]

kuru /koórroo/ n a fatal degenerative disease of the central nervous system similar to Creutzfeldt-Jakob disease that affects some peoples in New Guinea [Mid-20C. < a dialect of New Guinea, 'trembling'.]

Kush n BIBLE = **Cush**

Kuskokwim /kúskə kwim/ river in SW Alaska, flowing into the Bering Sea. Length: 1,170 km/724 mi.

Kutch, Rann of /kuch/ region of mud flats and salt marshes in W India and S Pakistan. Area: 21,000 sq. km/8,100 sq. mi.

Kutenai /koót'n ay, -ee/ (plural **-nai** or **-nais**), **Kootenai** (plural **-nai** or **-nais**), **Kootenay** (plural **-nay** or **-nays**) n **1** a member of a Native North American people living mainly in Montana, Idaho, and British Columbia **2** the language of the Kutenai people [Early 19C. < Blackfoot Kotonáai-.] —**Kutenai** adj

Kuwait

Kuwait /koo wáyt/ constitutional monarchy in SW Asia, at the NW tip of the Persian Gulf. Capital: Kuwait City. Population: 1,834,269 (1997). Area: 17,818 sq. km/6,880 sq. mi. —**Kuwaiti** n, adj

Kuwait City capital of Kuwait, in the E part of the country, on Kuwait Bay. Population: 31,241 (1993).

kV abbr kilovolt

kvass /kvaass, kvass/, **kvas, quass** n an alcoholic drink similar to beer, made in Russia and E European countries from rye or barley or from stale bread [Mid-16C. < Russian kvas.]

kvetch /kvech/ vi **COMPLAIN INCESSANTLY** to grumble and complain about things all the time (informal) ■ n (informal) **1 SOMEBODY INCESSANTLY COMPLAINING** a constant grumbler or complainer **2 COMPLAINT** a complaint about something [Mid-20C. < Yiddish kvetsh (noun), kvetshn (verb) < German Quetsche 'crusher', quetschen 'to crush'.]

kw abbr Kuwait (in Internet addresses)

kW abbr kilowatt

Kwa /kwaa/ n a group of languages in the Niger-Congo family that are spoken in West Africa, and include Yoruba and Ibo [Mid-19C. < Kwa.] —**Kwa** adj

kwacha /kwaàcha/ n see table at **currency** [Mid-20C. < Bantu, 'dawn'.]

Kwadi /kwaàdi/ n a Khoisan language spoken in SW Angola. Native speakers: 15,000. [Mid-20C. < Kwadi.] —**Kwadi** adj

Kwakiutl /kwaàki oòt'l/ (plural **-utl** or **-utls**) n **1** a member of a Native North American people who live on Vancouver Island and on the adjacent coast of British Columbia **2** the Wakashan language of the Kwakiutl people [Mid-19C. < Kwakiutl Kwáguł.] —**Kwakiutl** adj

Kwangju /kwung joò/ capital of South Chŏlla Province, SW South Korea. Population: 1,334,000 (1998 estimate).

kwanza /kwánzə/ (plural **-zas** or **-za**) n see table at **currency** [Late 20C. < Bantu]

Kwanzaa /kwaànzə/, **Kwanza** n a cultural and harvest festival celebrated by African Americans. Date: 26 December to 1 January. [Late 20C. < Kiswahili, 'first'.]

kwashiorkor /kwóshi áwr kawr, kwáshi-/ n malnutrition in children caused by inadequate intake of protein, common in African children weaned on to a traditional cornmeal diet [Mid-20C. < a name in Ghana, 'red boy' (from the symptomatic reddening of the hair).]

KwaZulu /kwaà zooloo/ former homeland in South Africa, now part of the province of KwaZulu-Natal

KwaZulu-Natal /kwaà zooloo nə taàl/ province in SE South Africa. Capital: Pietermaritzburg. Population: 8,713,100 (1995). Area: 91,548 sq. km/35,348 sq. mi.

kwela /kwáyla/ n a style of urban South African pop music [Mid-20C. < Afrikaans.]

kWh abbr kilowatt-hour

⚡**KWIC** /kwik/ abbr key word in context

⚡**KWIM** abbr know what I mean (in e-mails)

Kwinana /kwə naàna/ town in SW Western Australia. Population: 13,530 (1991).

⚡**KWOC** /kwok/ abbr key word out of context

⚡**ky** abbr Cayman Islands (in Internet addresses)

Ky., KY abbr Kentucky

kyanise vt = **kyanize**

kyanite /kí ə nīt/, **cyanite** /sí ə-/ n a bluish aluminosilicate mineral found as thin-bladed crystals or in masses. Source: metamorphic rocks. Use: gems, refractory. [Late 18C. < Greek kuan(e)os 'dark blue'.]

kyanize /kí ə nīz/ (**-nizes, -nizing, -nized**), **kyanise** (**-nises, -nising, -nised**) vt to preserve wood against decay by treating it with a corrosive sublimate [Mid-19C. After J. H. Kyan (1774–1850), Irish inventor of the process.]

kyat /ki aàt/ n see table at **currency** [Mid-20C. < Burmese.]

Kyd /kid/, **Thomas** (1558–94) English playwright

⚡**KYFC** abbr keep your fingers crossed (in e-mails)

kyle /kīl/ n Scotland a narrow passage of water between two areas of land [Mid-16C. < Gaelic caol < caol 'narrow'.]

Kyle of Tongue /kīl əf túng/ National Scenic Area on the northern coast of Scotland

Kyles of Bute /kīlz əv byoòt/ stretch of water in the Firth of Clyde, W Scotland. It is a National Scenic Area. Area: 119 sq. km/46 sq. mi.

kylie /kīli/, **kiley** (plural **-leys**) n Aus a boomerang that has one convex and one flat side [Mid-19C. < Aboriginal.]

kylix /kíliks, kílliks/ (plural **-lices** /-kees/) n a shallow two-handled cup, often with a footed stem, used in ancient Greece [Mid-19C. < Greek kulix.]

kymograph /kímō graaf, -graf/ n a device for recording variations in motion or pressure, e.g. of blood, consisting typically of a stylus and a rotating drum [Mid-19C. < Greek kumo- 'wave' < kuma.] —**kymographic** /kímō gráffik/ adj —**kymography** /kī móggrəfi/ n

Kyoto /ki ōtō/ city on S Honshu Island, Japan. Population: 1,461,000 (1990).

kyphosis /kī fóssiss/ n a permanent curving of the spine that makes somebody look hunched over [Mid-19C. < Greek kuphōsis < kuphos 'bent'.] —**kyphotic** /kī fóttik/ adj

Kyprianou /kípri aàn oo/, **Spyros** (b. 1932) Cypriot statesman

Kyrgyz /kúr giz/ (plural **-gyz**), **Kirghiz** (plural **-ghiz**), **Kirgiz** (plural **-giz**) n a member of a people living in Kyrgyzstan and Siberia —**Kyrgyz** adj

Kyrgyzstan

Kyrgyzstan /keèrgi staan/ republic in Central Asia. Capital: Bishkek. Population: 4,512,809 (1997). Area: 198,500 sq. km/76,640 sq. mi.

Kyrie /kirri ay, keèri-/, **Kyrie eleison** /-i láy son/ n **1** a form of prayer that begins with the words 'Lord, have mercy', used in the Roman Catholic, Greek Orthodox, and Anglican Churches **2** a musical setting for the Kyrie, often forming part of a sung Mass [< medieval Latin Kyrie eleison < Greek Kuriē eleēson 'Lord, have mercy']

Kyushu /kyoō shoo/, **Kyūshū** southernmost of the four major islands of Japan. Population: 13,269,000 (1990). Area: 36,554 sq. km/14,114 sq. mi.

⚡**kz** abbr Kazakhstan (in Internet addresses)

L¹ /el/, **L** (*plural* **L's** *or* **Ls**) *n* **1** the 12th letter of the English alphabet, representing a consonant sound **2** the Roman numeral for 50

l² *abbr* **1** latitude **2** law **3** left **4** length **5** lift **6** line **7** lira **8** live (*on plugs*)

L¹ /el/ (*plural* **L's** *or* **Ls**) *n* something shaped like a letter 'L'

L² *symbol* **1** angular momentum **2** inductance *n.* 1. **3** latent heat **4** luminance **5** luminosity **6** self-inductance

L³ *abbr* **1** Lake **2** large **3** Latin **4** League **5** learner **6** Liberal **7** Licentiate

L. *abbr* **1** Lake **2** League **3** Liberal **4** Licentiate

⚡**L8R** *abbr* later (*in e-mails*)

la¹ /laa, law/ *interj* US used to show surprise or to emphasize what is being said [Late 16C. Natural exclamation.]

la² /laa/ *n* MUSIC = **lah** [14C. < medieval Latin, originally a syllable sung to this note in a hymn to St John the Baptist.]

⚡**la³** *abbr* Laos (*in Internet addresses*)

La *symbol* lanthanum

LA *abbr* **1** legislative assembly **2** Library Association **3** local agent **4** Los Angeles **5** LA, **La.** Louisiana

laager /láàgər/, **lager** *n* a camp protected by a circle of wagons, formerly used by the Boers in South Africa ■ *vti* to form wagons into a circle to make a protected camp [Mid-19C. Alteration of obsolete Afrikaans *lager*.]

La Argentina /la aàrjən teèna/ (1888?–1936) Argentinean dancer. Born **Antonia Merce**

laari /laàri/ (*plural* **-ri** *or* **-ris**), **lari** (*plural* **-ri** *or* **-ris**) *n* see table at **currency** [Late 20C. Via Divehi < Persian *lārī*, after *Lār*, town north of the Persian Gulf.]

lab /lab/ *n* a laboratory (*informal*) [Late 19C. Shortening.]

Lab. *abbr* **1** Labour **2** Labrador

Laban /laàbən/, **Rudolf von** (1879–1958) Hungarian dancer and choreographer

labanotation /laàba nō táysh'n/ *n* a method of notating dance movements in detail, including the placement of the dancer's body, direction of movement, tempo, and dynamics [Blend of LABAN + NOTATION.]

labarum /lábbərəm/ (*plural* **-ra** /-rə/) *n* a military banner carried before Roman emperors, especially one with Christian symbols that was carried in front of Constantine the Great as a sign of his conversion to Christianity [Early 17C. < late Latin.]

labdanum /lábdənəm/, **ladanum** /láddənəm/ *n* a bitter resinous gum extracted from various rockroses. Use: flavourings, perfumes. [Early 16C. < medieval Latin, alteration of Latin *ladanum* < Greek *lēdanon* < *lēdon* 'mastic'.]

⚡**label** /láyb'l/ *n* **1** INFORMATIVE ATTACHMENT a piece of paper, fabric, or plastic attached to something to give instructions about it or identify it **2** DESCRIPTIVE WORD OR PHRASE a word or phrase used to describe a person or group **3** NAME OF A RECORD COMPANY the name of a record company, especially when displayed on a record, CD, or cassette **4** IDENTIFIER FOR PART OF COMPUTER PROGRAM a number or word that acts as a unique identifier for a part of a computer program **5** ARCHIT = **dripstone** *n.* **2** **6** HERALDIC DESIGN a figure on a heraldic shield consisting of a horizontal band with pendants and identifying the person to whom it belongs as an eldest son **7** CHEMICAL IDENTIFIER a substance, usually a radioactive isotope or dye, that can be traced to identify a compound as it

undergoes a chemical reaction or assimilation ■ *vt* (**-bels, -belling, -belled**) **1** ATTACH A LABEL TO to attach a label to something as identification or to give instructions **2** USE A DESCRIPTIVE WORD to describe somebody or something using a particular word or phrase ○ *resented being labelled as either liberal or progressive* **3** ATTACH A CHEMICAL LABEL to make a chemical substance identifiable with a marker such as a radioactive isotope or dye [13C. < Old French, 'ribbon, fillet'.] —**labeller** *n*

labellum /lə bélləm/ (*plural* **-la** /-lə/) *n* **1** the petal of an orchid that is its lowest and largest and forms a lip **2** the lobe at the end of an insect's proboscis that it uses for feeding on liquids [Early 19C. < Latin, 'small lip' < *labrum* 'lip'.]

labia plural of **labium**

labial /láybi əl/ *adj* **1** INVOLVING LIPS OR LABIA in, on, close to, or involving the lips or the labia **2** WITH LIPS CLOSED pronounced with the lips closed or nearly closed as, e.g. in the sounds 'b' and 'p' **3** MOVING AIR ACROSS AN EDGE describes an instrument or organ pipe that produces sound by the movement of air across a sharp edge ■ *n* **1** SOUND PRONOUNCED WITH LIPS CLOSED a speech sound pronounced with the lips closed or nearly closed as, e.g. in 'b' and 'p' **2** MUSICAL INSTRUMENT an instrument or organ pipe in which sound is produced by the movement of air across a sharp edge [Late 16C. < medieval Latin *labialis* < Latin *labia* 'lips'.] —**labially** *adv*

labialize /láybi ə līz/ (**-izes, -izing, -ized**), **labialise** (**-ises, -ising, -ised**) *vt* to pronounce a sound with the lips rounded —**labialization** /láybi ə lī záysh'n/ *n*

labia majora /-mə jáwrə/ *npl* the two thick outer folds of skin that surround the clitoris, the opening of the urethra, and the opening of the vagina of women and girls [< modern Latin, 'larger lips']

labia minora /-mi náwrə/ *npl* the two small folds of skin that lie immediately inside the labia majora of women and girls and join at the front to form the hood of the clitoris [< modern Latin, 'smaller lips']

labiate /láybi ət, -ayt/ *adj* **1** WITH A DIVIDED SET OF PETALS describes a flower such as a snapdragon that has its set of petals divided into two unequal and overlapping parts **2** OF THE MINT FAMILY belonging to the mint family ■ *n* PLANT OF THE MINT FAMILY any plant of the mint family. Family: Labiatae. [Early 18C. < modern Latin *labiatus* < Latin *labium* 'lip'.]

labile /láy bīl, láyb'l/ *adj* **1** liable to change **2** readily or frequently undergoing chemical or physical change ○ *a labile compound* [15C. < late Latin *labilis* 'prone to slip' < Latin *labi* 'to fall'.]

labio- *prefix* lips, labial ○ *labiodental* [< Latin *labium* 'lip']

labiodental /láybi ō dént'l/ *adj* pronounced with the upper teeth resting on the inside of the lower lip, as in the sounds 'f' and 'v' —**labiodental** *n*

labionasal /láybi ō náyz'l/ *adj* pronounced with the lips closed and the air being pushed through the nose, as in the sound 'm' —**labionasal** *n*

labiovelar /láybi ō veèlər/ *adj* pronounced by constricting the back of the mouth and closing the lips, as in the sound 'kw' —**labiovelar** *n*

labium /láybi əm/ (*plural* **-a** /-ə/) *n* **1** FOLD ROUND WOMEN'S GENITALIA any of the four folds, two inner (**labia minora**) and two outer (**labia majora**), that surround a woman's or girl's genital organs **2** INSECT MOUTHPART a mouthpart of some insects, formed from a fused pair of appendages **3** LIP OF A FLOWER the lower lip of the corolla of

a labiate flower **4** ANY LIP any part that looks or functions like a lip [Late 16C. < Latin, 'lip'.]

lablab /láb lab/ *n* PLANT SCI = **hyacinth bean** [Early 19C. < Arabic *lablāb*.]

labor *n*, *vti* US = **labour**

laboratory /lə bórrətəri/ (*plural* **-ries**) *n* **1** a place where research and testing is carried out **2** a room or place with appropriate equipment for teaching science or doing scientific work [Early 17C. < medieval Latin *laboratorium* 'place for work' < Latin *laborare* 'to work' < *labor* 'toil'.]

laborious /lə báwri əss/ *adj* **1** NEEDING EFFORT requiring a great deal of effort **2** NOT FLUENT showing signs of effort or difficulty rather than naturalness or fluency, especially in speech or writing **3** ENJOYING WORK happy or likely to work hard and long —**laboriously** *adv* —**laboriousness** *n*

SYNONYMS See *hard*.

Laborite /láybə rīt/ *n* a member or supporter of the Australian Labor Party

labor union *n* US POL = **trade union**

labour /láybər/ *n* **1** PHYSICAL WORK work done using the strength of the body ○ *sentenced to two years' hard labour* **2** WORKERS COLLECTIVELY the workers, especially manual workers, in a country, company, or industry considered as a group (*often before nouns*) **3** SUPPLY OF WORK the supply of work or workers for a particular job, industry, or employer **4** PARTICULAR PIECE OF WORK a particular piece of work, especially a difficult or long one (*often plural*) ○ *the labours of Hercules* **5** PROCESS OF CHILDBIRTH the process of giving birth to a baby from when the contractions start to the baby's delivery, or the time taken for this process (*often before nouns*) ○ *labour pains* ■ *v* **1** *vi* WORK HARD to work hard, especially at physical work ○ *laboured all day in the hot sun* **2** *vi* STRUGGLE to struggle to do something very difficult or very tiring ○ *laboured over the questions for several hours* **3** *vi* OPERATE WITH DIFFICULTY to have difficulty in running or functioning smoothly, e.g. because of being overloaded or defective (*refers to engines or machines*) **4** *vi* MOVE WITH DIFFICULTY to move with difficulty or great effort ○ *We laboured up to the summit.* **5** *vi* GIVE BIRTH to be in the process of giving birth to a baby **6** *vi* PITCH AND ROLL to pitch and roll heavily at sea (*refers to ships*) **7** *vt* OVEREMPHASIZE to continue trying to express or emphasize something when it is unnecessary ○ *There's no need to labour the point.* ◇ **a labour of love** something demanding or difficult that is done just for pleasure rather than for money

LITERARY LINK *Love's Labour's Lost*, a play by dramatist William Shakespeare (1594–95). Ferdinand, King of Navarre, and three of his lords agree to forgo the company of women in order to devote themselves to study. The arrival of the Princess of France and three of her ladies upsets their plans, giving rise to lively comedy and witty and poetic dialogue.

SYNONYMS See *work*.

labour under *vt* to be at a disadvantage because of believing something to be true that is not ○ *She had been labouring under the misconception that the problem was solved.*

Labour *n* = **Labour Party** (*+ singular or plural verb*) ■ *adj* supporting, belonging to, or associated with the Labour Party in the United Kingdom or New Zealand

labour camp *n* a prison where the prisoners have to do hard physical work under a harsh, typically cruel, regime

Labour Day *n* **1** a national holiday in the United States and Canada honouring working people. Date: 1st Monday in September. **2** CALENDAR = **May Day** *n.* 2

laboured /láybərd/ *adj* done with obvious effort or difficulty rather than naturally or gracefully

labourer /láybərər/ *n* somebody who works in a job that requires physical strength and stamina

labour exchange *n UK* a Jobcentre (*dated*)

labour force *n* INDUST = **workforce**

labour-intensive *adj* involving a relatively high number of workers or greater costs for labour than for other areas such as materials, machines, or design ○ *a labour-intensive industry*

labourism /láybərizəm/ *n* a political or social movement that upholds the rights of workers, or support for this movement

labourist /láybərist/ *n* a supporter of the rights of workers

Labourite /láybə rīt/ *n* a member or supporter of the Labour Party in the United Kingdom or New Zealand

Labour Party *n* **1** a British political party founded in 1900 to support the rights and interests of working people **2** a party with similar objectives in another country, e.g. New Zealand

labour-saving *adj* making it possible to do a task with greater ease ○ *labour-saving devices such as food processors and dishwashers*

labra plural of **labrum**

Labrador[1] /lábbrə dawr/ *n* a large dog with a short thick black, brown, or yellow coat, originally bred to fetch killed or injured game during a shoot [Early 20C. After LABRADOR[2].]

Labrador[2] /lábbrə dawr/ mainland portion of Newfoundland, E Canada, on the Labrador Sea. Area: 296,860 sq. km/114,618 sq. mi.

Labrador Current cold ocean current that flows south past Newfoundland, Canada, and W Greenland to join the Gulf Stream

labradorite /lábbrə dáwr īt/ *n* a variety of plagioclase feldspar, the colour of which shifts between blue and green depending on the angle it is seen from [After LABRADOR[2]]

Labrador Peninsula large peninsula in E Canada, including much of Quebec and the mainland portion of Newfoundland. Area: 1,619,000 sq. km/625,000 sq. mi.

Labrador retriever *n* ZOOL = **Labrador**[1]

Labrador Sea arm of the Atlantic Ocean that separates Labrador in E Canada from Greenland

Labrador tea *n* a low-growing evergreen shrub with bell-shaped flowers and leaves that are used in making a tea. Native to: N North America. *Ledum groenlandicum.*

labret /láy bret/ *n* an ornament made of bone, shell, or other materials that is worn pierced through the lip, especially by some peoples in East Africa and South America [Mid-19C. < Latin *labrum* 'lip'.]

labrum /láybrəm, láb-/ (*plural* **-bra** /-brə/) *n* a projecting upper mouthpart of some arthropods [Early 18C. < Latin, 'lip'.]

Labuan /lə bóo ən, lábyoo ən/ island in Malaysia, off the northern coast of Borneo. Population: 54,307 (1991). Area: 100 sq. km/40 sq. mi.

laburnum /lə búrnəm/ *n* a tree with poisonous leaves, bark, and seeds. Flowers: yellow, drooping. Native to: Europe, Asia. Genus: *Laburnum.* [Mid-16C. < Latin.]

labyrinth /lábbərinth/ *n* **1** CONFUSING NETWORK a place with a lot of crisscrossing or complicated passages, tunnels, or paths in which it would be easy to become lost **2** SOMETHING VERY COMPLICATED something that is made up of many different parts that is complicated and hard to understand ○ *You need legal advice to guide you through the labyrinth of regulations.* **3** INNER EAR a structure consisting of connected cavities or canals, especially the inside of the ear [14C. Directly or via French < Latin *labyrinthus* < Greek *laburinthos.*]

Labyrinth *n* in Greek mythology, the maze designed by Daedalus for King Minos of Crete to confine the Minotaur

labyrinth fish *n* a fish with a specialized labyrinthine breathing organ that allows it to breathe air out of water. Family: Anabantidae.

labyrinthine /lábbə rín thīn/, **labyrinthian** /-rínthi ən/ *adj* **1** consisting of or resembling a labyrinth of passages or paths ○ *a labyrinthine maze of backstreets* **2** extremely complicated and therefore difficult to understand

labyrinthitis /lábbərin thítiss/ *n* an illness in which the inner ear becomes inflamed, causing a loss of balance and nausea

labyrinthodont /lábbə rínthə dont/ *n* an extinct amphibian resembling the crocodile that lived in the Late Palaeozoic and Early Mesozoic eras. Order: Labyrinthodontia. [Mid-19C. < modern Latin *Labyrinthodontia* 'labyrinth-toothed' < Greek *laburinthos* 'labyrinth'.]

lac[1] /lak/ *n* a resinous substance secreted by some insects (**lac insect**). Use: formerly, source of shellac. [15C. < Portuguese *lac(c)a* < Persian *lāk*, Hindi *lākh* < Sanskrit *lākṣā* 'red dye'.]

lac[2] *n* MEASURE = **lakh**

LAC *abbr* leading aircraftman

Lacan /ləkaán/, **Jacques** (1901–81) French psychoanalyst

laccolith /lákəlith/ *n* a massive intrusion of igneous rock between beds of sedimentary rock, creating a dome-shaped structure [Late 19C. < Greek *lakkos* 'pond, pit'.] —**laccolithic** /lákə líthik/ *adj* —**laccolitic** /-líttik/ *adj*

lace /layss/ *n* **1** DELICATE FABRIC WITH PATTERNED HOLES a delicate fabric made by weaving cotton, silk, or a synthetic yarn in a pattern that leaves small holes between the threads (*often before nouns*) ○ *a lace shawl* **2** CORD USED TO TIE EDGES TOGETHER a long cord that is used to tie two parts of a garment, shoe, or boot together and is threaded through holes or around hooks **3** BRAID ON MILITARY UNIFORMS ornamental gold or silver braid used on military officers' uniforms and hats ■ *vt* (**laces, lacing, laced**) **1** FASTEN USING LACES to tie the edges of something with holes or hooks together by threading laces through the holes or round the hooks, pulling the edges close, and knotting the laces **2** THREAD A LACE THROUGH HOLES to thread a lace or cord through holes or round hooks **3** DECORATE WITH LACE to decorate or trim something with lace **4** ADD ALCOHOL TO A DRINK to add a small amount of alcohol or a drug to a drink or to food ○ *eggnog laced with rum* **5** ADD A SMALL AMOUNT TO to add an amount of something to something else to enhance it ○ *It was an intelligent article, laced with wit.* **6** STREAK WITH A DIFFERENT COLOUR to mark something with streaks of a different colour **7** BEAT to beat or thrash somebody (*informal*) **8** INTERTWINE to intertwine something with something else, e.g. fingers [12C. < Old French *laz* 'net, string' < Latin *laqueus* 'noose'.] —**lace like** *adj*

lace into *vt* **1** to fasten a corset or close-fitting garment around somebody by lacing it up **2** to attack somebody verbally or physically (*informal*)

lace up *vt* to fasten or tighten the laces of something such as a boot or corset

lacebark /láyss baark/ *n* TREES = **ribbonwood**

lace bug *n* a small bug with a delicate lacy vein pattern on its wings. Family: Tingitidae.

Lacedaemonian /lássədi mṓni ən/ *adj* relating to the ancient Greek city of Sparta [Mid-16C. < Latin *Lacedaemonius*, Greek *Lakedaimonios* 'of Lacedaemon (an ancient region)'.] —**Lacedaemonian** *n*

lace pillow *n* CRAFT, HANDICRAFT = **cushion** *n.* 7

lacerate *vt* /lássə rayt/ (**-ates, -ating, -ated**) **1** CUT JAGGEDLY to cut or gash the skin so that the wound is deep with irregular edges **2** DISTRESS DEEPLY to distress somebody deeply or agonizingly ■ *adj* /lássərət/ WITH JAGGED EDGES describes leaves or petals that have jagged or irregular edges [15C. < Latin *lacerat-*, past participle of *lacerare* 'tear to pieces' < *lacer* 'torn'.]

laceration /lássə ráysh'n/ *n* **1** a deep and jagged cut in the flesh **2** something that is deeply wounding to the feelings

Lacerta /lə súrtə/ *n* a small constellation of the northern hemisphere. See illustration at **constellation** [Late 18C. < Latin, 'lizard'.]

lacertid /lə súrtid/ *n* a lizard such as the common wall lizard or green lizard with rough irregular scales and bony plates on its skull. Family: Lacertidae. [Late 19C. < Latin *lacerta* 'lizard'.]

lace-up *n* a shoe or boot that fastens with laces —**lace-up** *adj*

lacewing /láyss wing/ *n* an insect with transparent wings and long antennae whose larvae feed on aphids and other insect pests. Superfamily: Hemerobioidea. [< the fine network of veins in its wings, likened to lace]

laches /láchiz, láy-/ *n* negligence or delay in doing something, especially in pursuing a legal claim [14C. < Anglo-Norman *laches(se)* 'negligence' < Old French *lasche* 'lazy' < Latin *laxus* 'loose'.]

Lachesis /lákississ/ *n* one of the three Fates in Greek mythology

Lachine /la sheén/ city in S Quebec Province, Canada, on Montreal Island in the St Lawrence River. Population: 40,077 (1999 estimate).

Lachlan /laák lən/ river in south-central New South Wales, Australia. Length: 1,480 km/920 mi.

lachrymal /lákrim'l/ *adj* **1** relating to tears or weeping (*literary*) **2** ANAT = **lacrimal** [Variant]

lachrymation *n* PHYSIOL = **lacrimation**

lachrymator *n* CHEM = **lacrimator**

lachrymatory /lákrimətəri, lákri máytəri/ *n* (*plural* **-ries**) a small bottle of a kind found in ancient tombs, thought in the past to have contained the tears of mourners ■ *adj* PHYSIOL = **lacrimatory**

lachrymose /lákri mōss, -mōz/ *adj* (*literary*) **1** crying or tending to cry easily and often **2** so sad as to make people cry [Early 18C. < Latin *lacrimosus* < *lacrima* 'tear'.] —**lachrymosely** *adv* —**lachrymosity** /lákri móssəti/ *n*

lacing /láyssing/ *n* a beating or thrashing (*informal*)

laciniate /lə sínni ət, -ayt/, **laciniated** /-aytid/ *adj* having a fringed, jagged, or lobed border [Mid-17C. < Latin *lacinia* 'fringe'.] —**laciniation** /lə sínni áysh'n/ *n*

lac insect *n* a South Asian insect, the female of which secretes a substance (**lac**) that was used in the past to make shellac. *Laccifer lacca.*

lack /lak/ *n* **1** SHORTAGE OR ABSENCE a shortage or complete absence of a particular thing ○ *Lack of sleep makes it difficult to concentrate.* **2** SOMETHING ABSENT something that is needed but is in short supply or missing ○ *Courage is a lack in him.* ■ *vt* **1** NOT HAVE not to have something that is needed ○ *the project lacked funding* **2** NOT HAVE ENOUGH to have too little of something ○ *What he lacks in patience, he makes up for in drive.* [13C. Probably < assumed Old English *lac* < Germanic.]

SYNONYMS ***lack, shortage, deficiency, deficit, want, dearth***

CORE MEANING: an insufficiency or absence of something

lack a complete absence of a particular thing; **shortage** a lack of something that is needed or required; **deficiency** a shortfall in the amount of something necessary, e.g. a particular nutrient in the human body, or an inadequacy in the supply or performance of something; **deficit** the amount by which something falls short of a target amount or level; **want** *or* **dearth** a scarcity or absence of something.

lackadaisical /lákə dáyzik'l/ *adj* without much enthusiasm, energy, or effort [Mid-18C. < *lackadaisy* 'alas', alteration of LACKADAY.] —**lackadaisically** *adv* —**lackadaisicalness** *n*

lackaday /lákə day/ *interj* used to express regret, disapproval, or dismay (*archaic*) [Late 17C. Shortening of *alack-a-day* < ALACK.]

lackey /láki/ *n* (*plural* **-eys**) **1** OBEDIENT FOLLOWER somebody excessively willing to obey another's orders **2** MAN SERVANT a man servant, especially a footman or valet who wears a uniform (*archaic*) ■ *vti* (**-eys, -eying, -eyed**) ACT AS LACKEY to act as a servant, especially a footman (*archaic*) [Early 16C. < French *laquais.*]

lackey moth *n* a moth whose caterpillars are striped and live in a web on a tree or shrub. Native to: England, Ireland. *Malacosoma neustria.* [< the caterpillar's striped markings, reminiscent of a footman's livery]

lacking /láking/ *adj* **1** without or with not enough of something that is needed ○ *The decor is decidedly lacking in good taste.* **2** not present or available ○ *A few of the pieces are lacking.*

lackluster *adj US* = **lacklustre**

lacklustre /lák lustər/ *adj* lacking energy, excitement, enthusiasm, or passion

Laconia /lə kǒni ə/ region in ancient Greece that occupied much of the Peloponnese

laconic /lə kónnik/, **laconical** /lə kónnik'l/ adj using very few words [Mid-16C. Via Latin < Greek *Lakōnikos* 'of Laconia, Spartan'; from the reputation of Spartans for terseness.] —**laconically** adv

laconism /lákənizəm/, **laconicism** /lə kónnissizem/ n 1 the use of very few words 2 something that is said in few words but is full of meaning [Late 16C. < Greek *lakōnismos* 'imitation of Spartan manners' < *Lakōn* 'Laconia'.]

La Coruña /la ko rúnya/ port and capital of La Coruña Province, in the autonomous region of Galicia, NW Spain. Population: 254,822 (1995).

lacquer /lákər/ n 1 **VARNISH** a varnish made from the sap of an E Asian tree. Use: protective coating, especially for wood. 2 **GLOSSY SYNTHETIC COATING** a hard, glossy, clear or coloured coating made up of resins or cellulose derivatives and a plasticizer in a volatile solvent 3 **HAIR SPRAY** hair spray (*dated*) 4 **ORNAMENTAL WOODEN OBJECTS** ornamental objects made of wood and coated with lacquer [Late 16C. < obsolete French *lacre* 'sealing wax', alteration of Portuguese *lac(c)a* (see LAC).] —**lacquer** n

lacquer tree n a poisonous sumach tree whose sap is used to make lacquer. Native to: Southeast Asia. *Rhus verniciflua*.

lacquerware /lákər wair/, **lacquerwork** /-wurk/ n ornamental objects, usually of wood, that have been coated with lacquer and sometimes inlaid

lacrimal /lákrim'l/ adj 1 relating to the glands that produce tears, or the ducts through which they drain 2 LITERAT = **lachrymal** adj. 1 [15C. < medieval Latin *lacrimalis* < Latin *lacrima* 'tear'.]

lacrimal duct n the passage carrying tears into the nose

lacrimal gland n a gland in the outer corner of the eye that produces tears

lacrimation /lákri máysh'n/, **lachrymation** n the production of tears in the eyes, especially excessive production as in crying or in reaction to a foreign body

lacrimator /lákri maytər/, **lachrymator** n a substance such as tear gas that makes tears form in the eyes

lacrimatory /lákrimətəri, -máytəri/, **lachrymatory** adj causing the eyes to produce tears

Lacrosse
Popperfoto

lacrosse /lə króss/ n a sport, originated by Native North Americans, in which two teams of ten players use sticks with a net pouch at one end (**crosse**) to throw and catch a small hard rubber ball (*often before nouns*) ○ *a lacrosse stick* [Early 18C. < Canadian French *(jeu de) la crosse* '(game of) the hooked stick' < Germanic.]

lact- prefix = **lacto-** (*before vowels*)

lactalbumin /lak tálbyōōmin/ n a milk protein that contains all the essential amino acids

lactase /lák tayss, -tayz/ n an intestinal enzyme that breaks down lactose into glucose and galactose [Late 19C. < LACTOSE.]

lactate[1] /lak táyt, lák tayt/ (**-tates, -tating, -tated**) vi to produce milk in the body (*refers to female mammals*) [Late 19C. Back-formation < LACTATION.]

lactate[2] /lák tayt/ n a chemical compound that is a salt or ester of lactic acid [Late 18C. < LACTIC.]

lactation /lak táysh'n/ n 1 the production of milk by the mammary glands 2 the period during which milk is produced by the mammary glands [Mid-17C. Directly or

via French < Latin *lactare* 'suckle' < *lact-* 'milk'.] —**lactational** adj

lacteal /lákti əl/ adj 1 **OF MILK** relating to milk or milk production 2 **CARRYING MILKY FLUID** carrying or containing a milky fluid (**chyle**) ○ *a lacteal vessel* ■ n **LYMPHATIC VESSEL** any lymphatic vessel that originates in the small intestine and carries a milky fluid (**chyle**) to the thoracic duct [Mid-17C. < Latin *lacteus* 'of milk' < *lact-* 'milk'.] —**lacteally** adv

lactescent /lak téss'nt/ adj 1 describes plants and insects that secrete a milky substance 2 looking like milk or becoming milky [Mid-17C. < Latin *lactescent-*, present participle of *lactescere* 'turn to milk' < *lactere* 'be milky' < *lact-* 'milk'.] —**lactescence** n

lactic /láktik/ adj relating to or derived from milk [Late 18C. < Latin *lact-* 'milk'.]

lactic acid n $C_3H_6O_3$ a colourless organic acid produced by muscles and found in sour milk. Use: preservative, in dyeing, manufacture of adhesives and pharmaceuticals.

lactiferous /lak tíffərəss/ adj 1 carrying or producing milk, or capable of producing milk ○ *a lactiferous duct* 2 describes a plant that produces a milky juice (**latex**) [Late 17C. < LACTO-.] —**lactiferousness** n

lacto- prefix 1 milk ○ *lactometer* 2 lactic acid 3 lactose [< Latin *lact-* 'milk']

lactobacillus /láktō bə sílləss/ (*plural* **-li** /-lī/) n a rod-shaped bacterium that produces lactic acid through fermentation. Genus: *Lactobacillus*.

lactoflavin /láktō fláyvin/ n BIOCHEM = **riboflavin**

lactogenic /láktō jénnik/ adj causing the mammary glands to produce milk

lactoglobulin /láktō glóbbyōōlin/ n any one of a group of globular proteins that occur in milk

lactometer /lak tómmitər/ n an instrument that is used to measure the density of milk

lactone /láktōn/ n a chemical compound belonging to a group derived from hydroxy acids, often occurring as the odour-bearing component of a plant product — **lactonic** /lak tónnik/ adj

lactoprotein /láktō prốt een/ n any protein that is present in milk

lactose /lák tōss, -tōz/ n 1 a sugar (**disaccharide**) composed of glucose and galactose. Source: milk. 2 a white crystalline form of lactose. Source: whey. Use: in food products and pharmaceuticals.

lactovegetarian /láktō véjjə táiri ən/ n a person who eats vegetables, grains, fruit, nuts, and milk products but not meat or eggs

lacuna /lə kyōōnə/ (*plural* **-nae** /-nee/ *or* **-nas**) n 1 a gap or place where something is missing, e.g. in a manuscript or a line of argument (*literary*) 2 a small pit or cavity, e.g. in bone or cartilage [Mid-17C. < Latin, 'hole' < *lacus* 'pond'.] —**lacunal** adj

lacunar /lə kyōōnər/ n 1 **CEILING WITH SUNKEN PANELS** a ceiling that has sunken panels in it 2 **SUNKEN PANEL IN A CEILING** a decorative sunken panel in a ceiling ■ adj **OF BODILY CAVITIES** relating to pits or cavities in tissue, e.g. in bone or cartilage, especially ones that are abnormal [Late 17C. < Latin, < *lacuna* (see LACUNA).]

lacustrine /lə kúss trīn/ adj 1 relating to lakes 2 growing, living, or formed in or at the edge of a lake [Early 19C. < Latin *lacus* 'lake'.]

LACW abbr leading aircraftwoman

lacy /láyssi/ (**-ier, -iest**) adj 1 made of or decorated with lace 2 having the appearance of lace ○ *The sky was patterned with lacy clouds.* —**lacily** adv —**laciness** n

lad /lad/ n 1 **YOUNG MAN** a boy or young man 2 **MAN** any man (*informal*) 3 **MAN WHO LOOKS AFTER HORSES** a man whose job is to look after horses in a stable ○ *The head lad accompanies the horses when they go racing.* ■ **lads** npl **MAN'S MALE FRIENDS** the group of male friends or colleagues that a man socializes with [13C. < ?] ◇ **a bit of a lad** used in an affectionate way to describe a man who has a lively, even irresponsible, lifestyle

LITERARY LINK *A Shropshire Lad*, a collection of verse (1896) by poet A. E. Housman. Although they express a pessimistic world-view, these short poems about life in rural England are much loved for their sensitive handling of universal themes (the passing of time, the fleeting nature of existence, the trials and disappointments of life).

Ladakh /lə daàk/ mountainous region of NW India, Pakistan, and China

Ladakhi /lə daàki/ n 1 a person who was born or brought up in Ladakh 2 the form of Tibetan spoken in Ladakh [Mid-19C. < Tibetan.] —**Ladakhi** adj

ladanum /láydənəm/ n INDUST = **labdanum**

ladder /láddər/ n 1 **DEVICE WITH RUNGS TO CLIMB ON** a portable piece of equipment with rungs fixed to sides made of metal, wood, or rope, used for climbing up or down 2 **PATH TO ADVANCEMENT** a series of hierarchical levels on which somebody moves up or down within an organization or society ○ *She joined the firm at a fairly low level but quickly moved up the ladder.* 3 **LINE OF MISSING STITCHES IN TIGHTS** a vertical line of stitches that have come undone in tights, a stocking, or a knitted garment, leaving only the horizontal stitches in place 4 **LIST OF RANKED PLAYERS** a list of contestants in an ongoing sports or games competition, arranged according to ability ■ vti **DAMAGE TIGHTS OR OTHER GARMENT** to damage tights, a stocking, or knitted garment so that a line of vertical stitches have come undone, leaving only the horizontal stitches, or develop a ladder in this way [Old English *hlæd(d)er* < Indo-European, 'to lean']

ladder-back n 1 a chair with a back formed by horizontal slats between the two vertical parts that form the sides 2 a chair back formed by horizontal slats between the two vertical parts that form the sides — **ladder-back** adj

ladder tournament n a tournament based on a list of ranked players in a game or sport, in which each player may challenge any other player who is one or two positions higher than him or her

laddie /láddi/ n a boy or young man (*informal*) ○ *How old are you, laddie?*

laddish /láddish/ adj relating to or traditionally associated with men whose behaviour conforms to a popular stereotype that features, e.g., an absorbing interest in sport and drinking alcohol and sexist attitudes towards women (*informal*) —**laddishly** adv —**laddishness** n

lade[1] /layd/ n (**lades, lading, laded, laden** /láyd'n/ *or* **laded**) v 1 vti **LOAD UP A SHIP WITH CARGO** to take on cargo or freight, or load up a ship with cargo or freight 2 vti **REMOVE LIQUID WITH A LADLE** to remove a measure of liquid using a ladle 3 vt **LOAD** to load something, or place a heavy burden on somebody (*dated*) [Old English *hladan* < Germanic]

lade[2] /layd/ n Scotland a stream, especially a millstream ○ *A wee boy was fishing in the lade.* [Early 18C. Probably variant of LEAD[1].]

la-de-da adj = **la-di-da**

~~ladel~~ incorrect spelling of **ladle**

laden past participle of **lade[1]** ■ adj 1 carrying a load, usually a heavy load (*often in combination*) ○ *He was laden down with shopping bags.* ○ *fruit-laden boughs* 2 weighed down by a problem or an unpleasant feeling such as doubt or unhappiness ○ *laden with guilt*

la-di-da /laà dee daà/, **lah-di-dah, la-de-da** adj speaking or behaving in a way that is affectedly upper-class (*informal*) [Late 19C. An imitation of affected pronunciation.]

ladies[1] /láydiz/ n a women's public toilet (*informal; + singular verb*) ○ *I think she went to the ladies.* = **ladies room**

ladies[2] plural of **lady**

ladies' fingers npl FOOD = **okra** n. 1

ladies' gallery n an area of the public gallery of the UK House of Commons that is restricted to women only

ladies' man, lady's man n a man who enjoys being with women and flirting with them

ladies room, ladies' room n = **ladies[1]** n.

ladies' tresses (*plural* **ladies' tresses**), **lady's tresses** (*plural* **lady's tresses**) n an orchid with slender spiral spikes of small white flowers. Genus: *Spiranthes*.

ladify vt = **ladyfy** (*offensive*)

Ladin /la deèn/ n a language spoken in some valleys in N Italy, belonging to the Rhaeto-Romance subgroup of Romance languages. Native speakers: 25,000. [Mid-19C. Via Rhaeto-Romance < Latin *Latinus* (see LATIN).] —**Ladin** adj

lading /láyding/ n freight or cargo being transported from one place to another

Ladino /lə deènō/ (*plural* **-nos**) n 1 a language based on Spanish with Hebrew elements, spoken by some

Sephardic Jews, usually written in a form of Hebrew script **2 Ladino, ladino** somebody of partially Spanish or indigenous ancestry in Central America who speaks Spanish [Late 19C. Via Spanish < Latin *Latinus* (see LATIN).] —**Ladino** *adj*

ladino clover *n* a large variety of white clover grown as forage. Native to: North America. [Via Italian < Latin *Latinus* (see LATIN)]

ladle /láyd'l/ *n* a spoon with a long handle and a deep bowl, used to serve soup and other liquids ■ *vt* (**-dles, -dling, -dled**) to serve food such as soup onto a plate using a ladle [Old English *hlædel* < *hladan* (see LADE[1])]
ladle out *vt* to give out generous or overgenerous amounts of something, especially something intangible (*informal*) ○ *ladled out praise*

Ladoga, Lake /laá dəgə/ largest lake in Europe, in NW Russia. Area: 18,390 sq. km/7,100 sq. mi.

lad's love *n* PLANTS = **southernwood**

lady /láydi/ (*plural* **-dies**) *n* **1 WOMAN** a woman, especially when addressed as part of a group ○ *Ladies and gentlemen, please take your seats.* **2 ARISTOCRATIC WOMAN** an upper-class woman **3 POLITE DIGNIFIED WOMAN** a woman who behaves very politely and with dignity **4 WIFE OR USUAL WOMAN COMPANION** a man's wife or usual woman companion (*informal*) **5 WOMAN FEUDAL SUPERIOR** a woman who, in medieval Europe, was a powerful land or property owner with authority over an area, castle, or community, e.g. a manor **6 COCAINE** the drug cocaine (*slang*) [Old English *hlǣfdīge* 'bread-kneader' < *hlāf* 'bread', earlier form of LOAF]

Lady *n* **1 TITLE FOR A WOMAN** used as an alternative title for a marchioness, countess, viscountess, or baroness **2 COURTESY TITLE FOR A WOMAN** used as a courtesy title for the daughter of an earl, marquess, or duke **3 FORM OF ADDRESS FOR A WOMAN** used as a form of address for the wife of a viscount, earl, marquess, baron, baronet, or knight, and the daughter of a duke, marquess, or earl

ladybird /láydi burd/ *n* a small round flying beetle that has red or orange outer wings with black spots. It eats aphids and other insects. Family: Coccinellidae. US term **ladybug**

lady bountiful *n* a woman who makes generous and well-publicized charitable donations

ladybug /láydi bug/ *n US* INSECTS = **ladybird**

Lady Chapel, lady chapel *n* a chapel dedicated to Mary, mother of Jesus Christ, that is inside a cathedral or church

Lady Day *n* the day in the Christian calendar on which the feast of the Annunciation is celebrated, used as a quarter day in England, Wales, and Ireland. Date: 25 March.

ladyfish /láydi fish/ (*plural* **-fish** *or* **-fishes**) *n* **1** a large silvery tropical sea fish, related to the tarpon and prized as a game fish. *Elops saurus.* **2** *US* ZOOL = **bonefish**

ladyfriend *n* a man's woman companion (*informal humorous; sometimes offensive*)

ladyfy /láydi fī/ (**-fies, -fying, -fied**), **ladify** (**-fies, -fying, -fied**) *vt* an offensive term meaning to cause a woman or girl to affect the manners of an upper-class woman —**ladyfied** *adj*

lady-in-waiting (*plural* **ladies-in-waiting**) *n* a woman who is an attendant for a queen or princess

lady-killer *n* a man who is extremely attractive to women

ladylike /láydi līk/ *adj* behaving or done in the polite dignified way expected of an upper-class woman —**ladylikeness** *n*

ladylove /láydi luv/ *n* a woman that a man is in love with (*dated*)

lady luck, Lady Luck *n* luck or good fortune personified as a woman (*literary; sometimes offensive*)

Lady Mayoress, lady mayoress *n* the wife of a Lord Mayor

Lady Muck *n* an offensive term for a woman who is thought to have an exaggerated sense of her own importance. ◊ **Lord Muck**

Lady of the Lake *n* a supernatural woman who plays various roles in Arthurian legend, sometimes considered to be the same person as Vivian, the lover of Merlin

lady's bedstraw *n* a wild plant with narrow leaves. Flowers: small, yellow, in clusters. Native to: Europe, Asia. *Gallium verum.*

ladyship /láydi ship/, **Ladyship** *n* a title used when addressing or referring to a woman with the title of 'Lady'

lady's maid *n* a woman who serves another woman, looking after her and her clothes and accessories

lady's man *n* = **ladies' man**

lady's mantle *n* a low-growing plant of the rose family. Flowers: small, yellow-green, in clusters. Genus: *Alchemilla.* [< the round shape of its leaves]

Ladysmith /láydi smith/ town in E South Africa. Population: 25,102 (1985).

lady's slipper, lady slipper *n* a wild orchid. Flowers: reddish, purple, yellow, resembling slippers. Native to: North America. Genus: *Cypripedium.*

lady's smock *n* PLANTS = **cuckooflower**

lady's tresses *n* PLANTS = **ladies' tresses**

Laënnec /la énnek/, **René** (1781–1826) French physician

Laertes /lay úr teez/ *n* in Greek mythology, the father of Odysseus

laetrile /láy ə trīl, -ətril, -trīl/ *n* a drug extracted from peach stones. Use: trial cancer treatment.

laev- *prefix* = **laevo-** (*before vowels*)

laevo- *prefix* **1** leftwards, anticlockwise ○ *laevorortation* **2** laevorotatory ○ *laevulose* [< French *lévo-* < Latin *laevus* 'left']

laevorotation /leévō rō táysh'n/ *n* a rotation to the left or anticlockwise, especially of the plane of polarized light

laevorotatory /leévō rō táytəri, -rṓtətəri/ *adj* **1** turning or circling in a anticlockwise direction or to the left **2** turning the plane of polarized light in an anticlockwise direction

laevulose /lévvyoo̅ lōss, -lōz/ *n* BIOCHEM = **fructose** [Late 19C. < LAEVO- + -ULE.]

Lafayette /lá fī ét/, **Marie Joseph Paul Yves Roch Gilbert du Motier, Marquis de** (1757–1834) French soldier and politician

La Fayette /lá fī ét/, **Marie Madeleine, Comtesse de** (1634–93) French novelist. Known as **Madame de La Fayette**

laff /laaf/ *n* a laugh (*nonstandard; often ironic*) ○ *a lot of tasteless laffs* [Late 20C. Representing a pronunciation of LAUGH.]

Laffer curve /láffər-/ *n* a graph summarizing the fact that tax revenues are low for very high and for very low tax rates, thus demonstrating that raising tax rates beyond an optimum point will discourage investment and decrease tax revenues [Late 20C. After Arthur B. Laffer (1942–), US economist.]

Laforgue /la fáwrg/, **Jules** (1860–87) French poet

lag[1] /lag/ *vi* (**lags, lagging, lagged**) **1 FALL BEHIND COMPARED WITH OTHERS** to go, develop, or progress more slowly than somebody or something similar so as to fall back or fall behind **2 SLACKEN** to decrease in strength or intensity ○ *Interest in the scandal has never lagged.* **3 DECIDE THE ORDER OF PLAY** to decide who is to play first in billiards by having each player rebound a ball from the top cushion as close as possible to the hand rail ■ *n* **1 PERIOD BETWEEN EVENTS** a period of time between one event and a related event **2 POSITION OF HAVING FALLEN BEHIND** the condition or an instance of having fallen behind **3 LAGGING IN BILLIARDS** an act or instance of lagging in billiards [Early 16C. < ?]

lag[2] /lag/ *vt* (**lags, lagging, lagged**) to insulate something such as a pipe or hot water tank with lagging to prevent freezing or heat escaping ■ *n* a strip of wood such as a stave of a barrel or a lath [Late 17C. Probably < N Germanic.]

lag[3] /lag/ *n* (*slang*) **1 PRISONER** a current or former prisoner **2 IMPRISONMENT** a period of imprisonment ■ *vt* (**lags, lagging, lagged**) **ARREST OR IMPRISON** to arrest somebody or put somebody in prison (*dated slang*) [Late 16C. < ?]

lagan /lággən/, **ligan** /lígən/ *n* cargo or wreckage lying on the sea bed, often with a buoy attached so that it can be recovered [Mid-16C. < Old French.]

Lagan Valley /ləgán-/ Area of Outstanding Natural Beauty in SE Northern Ireland

Lag b'Omer /lag bṓmər/ *n* a minor Jewish festival marking the day on which some of the restrictions on activities imposed during the Omer are lifted. Date: 18th day of Iyar, 33rd day of the Omer. [< Hebrew, < *lāg* 'thirty-third' (pronunciation of the letters LG that symbolize this number) + *bā* 'in the' + *ōmer* 'Omer']

lager[1] /laágər/ *n* **1** a light-coloured beer made with a low proportion of hops, usually stored for a period after brewing **2** a drink of lager [Mid-19C. Shortening of *lager beer*, partial translation of German *Lager-Bier* < *Lager* 'storehouse' + *Bier* 'beer'.]

lager[2] *n, vti* MIL = **laager**

Lagerkvist /laágər kvist/, **Pär Fabien** (1891–1974) Swedish novelist, poet, and playwright

Lagerlöf /laágər lőf/, **Selma Ottiliana Louisa** (1858–1940) Swedish novelist

lager lout *n* a young man who is perceived as behaving violently or disruptively, usually as a result of drinking alcohol (*informal insult*)

laggard /lággərd/ *n* a person who or thing that does not keep up with others ■ *adj* slow or reluctant to do something (*dated*) [Early 18C. < LAG[1].] —**laggardly** *adv, adj* —**laggardness** *n*

lagging /lágging/ *n* **1** insulating material used to keep heat from escaping, especially round a pipe or hot water tank **2** a wooden frame used in building, especially to support an arch while it is being built

lagniappe /lán yap, lan yáp/ *n* **1** *Southern US, Carib* a small present given by a shop to a customer who has just purchased something **2** *Southern US* an unexpected bonus or extra [Mid-19C. Via Louisiana French < American Spanish *la ñapa* 'the gift' < Quechua *yapay* 'to give more'.]

lagomorph /lággə mawrf/ *n* any plant-eating mammal with two pairs of incisors in the upper jaw specifically adapted for gnawing, e.g. the rabbit, hare, and pika. Order: Lagomorpha. [Late 19C. < modern Latin *Lagomorpha* < Greek *lagōs* 'hare' + *morphē* 'shape'.] —**lagomorphic** /lággə máwrfik/ *adj* —**lagomorphous** *adj*

lagoon /lə go̅on/ *n* **1** a coastal body of shallow water formed where low-lying rock, sand, or coral presents a partial barrier to the open sea **2** a small lake adjoining a larger one [Early 17C. Directly and via French < Italian, Spanish *laguna* < Latin *lacuna* (see LACUNA).] —**lagoonal** *adj*

Lagos /láygos/ largest city, chief port, and former capital of Nigeria, in the southwest of the country. Population: 1,484,000 (1995 estimate).

Lagrange /lə graáNzh/, **Joseph Louis, comte de l'Empire** (1736–1813) Italian-born French mathematician and astronomer

lah /laa/, **la** *n* the sixth note of a major scale in solfeggio. US term **la**[2] [Middle English < medieval Latin]

lahar /laá haar/ *n* a landslide or mudflow of volcanic debris, especially after a heavy rainfall [Early 20C. < Javanese.]

lah-di-dah *adj* = **la-di-da**

Lahnda /laándə/ *n* a language spoken in Pakistan, related to Punjabi [Early 20C. < Punjabi *lahandā* 'western'.] —**Lahnda** *adj*

Lahore /lə háwr/ capital of Punjab Province, NE Pakistan. Population: 5,063,499 (1998).

Lahti /látti/ city in S Finland. Population: 95,119 (1995).

laic /láy ik/, **laical** /láy ik'l/ *adj* relating to or involving followers of a religion who are not clergy [Mid-16C. Via late Latin *laicus* < Greek *laikos* 'of the people' < *laos* 'people'.] —**laically** *adv*

laicize /láy i sīz/ (**-cizes, -cizing, -cized**), **laicise** (**-cises, -cising, -cised**) *vt* to remove something from control or governance by the church or the clergy and give control of it to the lay community —**laicization** /láy i sī záysh'n/ *n*

laid past tense, past participle of **lay**[1]

laid-back *adj* very relaxed, easygoing, and unworried (*informal*) —**laid-backness** *n*

laid paper *n* a paper with a watermark of fine lines on it that are produced in the manufacturing process

laid work *n* embroidery based on a lattice of threads that is then decorated with filling stitches

laik /layk/ (**laiks, laiking, laiked**) *vti N England* to play, or play at something [14C. < Old Norse *leika* 'to play'.]

Lailat-ul-Qadr /láy lat o͝ol kaádər/ *n* an Islamic festival, the Night of Power, marking the sending down of the Koran to Muhammad. Date: 27th of Ramadan.

Laing /lang/, **R. D.** (1927–89) Scottish psychiatrist. Full name **Ronald David Laing**

lair /lair/ *n* **1 WILD ANIMAL'S DEN** a place where a wild animal rests or sleeps **2 PLACE TO BE ALONE IN** a retreat or hideaway

lairage (*informal*) **3 CATTLE ENCLOSURE** an enclosure for livestock **4** *Scotland* **GROUND FOR GRAVE** the ground for a single grave in a cemetery ■ *vti* **GO TO A LAIR** to go to a lair, or be taken or made to go to a lair (*refers to an animal*) [Old English *leger* 'act of lying, bed' < Indo-European]

lairage /láirij/ *n* a place where livestock are kept temporarily, e.g. at docks or a market

laird /laird/ *n Scotland* an owner of land, especially a large estate ○ *the laird of Shaws* [14C. Variant of LORD.]

laissez-faire /léssay fáir, láyssay-/, **laisser-faire** *n* **1** the principle that the economy works best if private industry is not regulated and markets are free **2** refusal to interfere in other people's affairs or the practice of letting people do as they please [< French, 'allow to do']

laissez-passer /léssay paá say, láyssay-/, **laisser-passer** *n* a document that permits the holder to travel freely, especially one given in lieu of a passport [< French, 'allow to pass']

laity /láy əti/ *npl* **1** the followers of a religion who are not clergy **2** all the people who are not members of a specific profession, as distinguished from those who are members [15C. < LAY².]

Laius /lí əss/ *n* a king of Thebes in Greek mythology, mistakenly killed by his son Oedipus

WORLD'S LARGEST LAKES

1	Caspian Sea	
Area	[143,000 sq. mi. / 370,000 sq. km]	
Location	*Europe/Asia*	
2	Lake Superior	
Area	[31,700 sq. mi. / 82,100 sq. km]	
Location	*North America*	
3	Lake Victoria	
Area	[26,830 sq. mi. / 69,490 sq. km]	
Location	*Africa*	
4	Lake Huron	
Area	[23,000 sq. mi. / 59,600 sq. km]	
Location	*North America*	
5	Lake Michigan	
Area	[22,300 sq. mi. / 57,800 sq. km]	
Location	*North America*	
6	Lake Tanganyika	
Area	[12,700 sq. mi. / 32,900 sq. km]	
Location	*Africa*	
7	Great Bear Lake	
Area	[12,270 sq. mi. / 31,790 sq. km]	
Location	*North America*	
8	Lake Baikal	
Area	[12,200 sq. mi. / 31,500 sq. km]	
Location	*Asia*	
9	Aral Sea	
Area	[12,050 sq. mi. / 31,220 sq. km]	
Location	*Asia*	
10	Lake Nyasa	
Area	[8,683 sq. mi. / 22,490 sq. km]	
Location	*Africa*	

lake¹ /layk/ *n* **1 INLAND BODY OF WATER** a large body of water surrounded by land **2 SURPLUS OF LIQUID PRODUCT** a large surplus of a liquid product, such as milk or wine, that is stored and not sold in order to prevent prices from becoming too low, especially in the European Union (*informal; usually in combination*) ◊ **mountain**. *n* **4 3 POOL OF LIQUID** a large pool of liquid that has collected or spilled somewhere ○ *A lake of hot grease covered the floor by the cooker.* [Pre-12C. Directly and via Old French *lac* < Latin *lacus* 'pond'.]

lake² /layk/ *n* **1** a bright translucent pigment of various colours, made by combining an organic dye with a metallic hydroxide or other inorganic substance **2** a red pigment made by combining cochineal with a metallic compound [Early 17C. Variant of LAC¹.]

Lake District region of mountains and lakes in NW England

Lake District National Park national park in NW England. Area: 2,243 sq. km/866 sq. mi.

lake dwelling *n* a home or settlement built on a platform supported by wooden posts over or by a shallow lake or river edge, especially in prehistoric times —**lake dweller** *n*

lakefront /láyk frunt/ *n* the land along the shores of a lake

lake herring *n* **1** a fish related to the whitefish. Native to: Great Lakes region of the United States. *Coregonus artedii.* **2** the flesh of a lake herring used as food

Lakeland terrier /láykland-/ *n* a wire-haired terrier with a black and tan coat, originally bred for fox-hunting [Early 20C. After *Lakeland* 'the Lake District', NW England.]

Lake Macquarie /-mə kwórri/ city in E New South Wales, Australia. Population: 162,026 (1991).

Lake of the Woods lake in central North America, in SW Ontario and SE Manitoba, Canada, and N Minnesota. Area: 4,390 sq. km/1,695 sq. mi.

Lake Poets *n* the poets Wordsworth, Coleridge, and Southey, who lived in the Lake District in the early 19th century

laker /láykər/ *n* **1** a boat or ship that is used on lakes rather than the sea **2** a fish living in a lake rather than the sea

lakeside /láyk sīd/ *n* the land at the edge of a lake

lake trout *n* ZOOL = **brown trout**

lakh /laak/ (*plural* **lakhs** *or* **lakh**), **lac** (*plural* **lacs** *or* **lac**) *n S Asia* the number 100,000, used especially for referring to sums of rupees [Early 17C. Via Hindi *lākh* < Sanskrit *laksam* 'mark, 100,000'.]

Lakota /lə kôtə/ (*plural* **-tas** *or* **-ta**) *n* **1** PEOPLES = **Teton¹** *n.* **1 2** LANG = **Teton¹** *n.* **2** [Mid-19C. < Teton *lakhóta*.]

Lakshmi /lákshmi/, **Laksmi** *n* the Hindu goddess of prosperity, wealth, and royalty, and wife of the god Vishnu

laky /láyki/ *adj* of a colour similar to a red form of the pigment lake

Lala /laá laa/ *n S Asia* a title equivalent to 'Mr', used in South Asia before men's names [< Hindi]

La-La *n US* used as a nickname for Los Angeles (*slang; often humorous*) ○ *moving to La-La*

lalang /laá laang/ *n* a tall coarse tropical grass. Native to: Malay Archipelago. *Imperata arundinacea.* [Late 18C. < Malay.]

-lalia *suffix* speech, speech disorder ○ *echolalia* [< Greek *lalia* 'talk' < *lalein* 'to talk']

Lalique glass /la leèk-/ *n* ornamental frosted glassware decorated with bas-relief figures, fruits, and flowers, designed by the French Art Nouveau craftsperson René Lalique (1860–1945)

Lallans /lállənz/, **Lallan** /lállən/ *n Scotland* the form of Lowland Scots used in revivals of Scots as a literary medium, especially in the 18th century and 20th century ■ *adj* relating to the Lowlands of Scotland or any dialect of Scots spoken there [Early 18C. < a pronunciation of LOWLAND.]

lallapalooza *n US* = **lollapalooza** (*slang*)

lallation /la láysh'n/ *n* a mispronunciation of 'r', especially one that sounds like 'l' [Mid-17C. < Latin *lallare* 'sing lullaby'.]

Lalor /láylər/, **Peter** (1827–89) Irish-born Australian civil engineer and politician

lam¹ /lam/ (**lams, lamming, lammed**) *v* (*informal*) **1** *vti* to hit somebody or something hard **2** *vi* to speak angrily to somebody [Late 16C. < ?]

lam² /lam/ *n US, Can* a hasty escape, especially to avoid arrest ■ *vi* (**lams, lamming, lammed**) *US, Can* to escape or run away, especially from the law (*informal*) [Late 19C. < LAM¹.] ◊ **on the lam** *US, Can* making a hasty escape, especially from the law (*informal*)

lama /laámə/ *n* **1** a Tibetan or Mongolian Buddhist monk **2** a title used for those individuals who are believed to

be the reincarnations of a Bodhisattva [Mid-17C. Alteration of Tibetan *bla-ma*.]

Lamaism /laámə izəm/ *n* a form of Mahayana Buddhism practised in Tibet and Mongolia that has non-Buddhist elements from India and from an older nature-worshipping religion —**Lamaist** *n*, *adj* —**Lamaistic** /laámə ístik/ *adj*

La Mancha /laa maánchə/ historic region occupying a high barren plateau in south-central Spain

Lamarck /lə maárk/, **Jean Baptiste, Chevalier de** (1744–1829) French naturalist and evolutionist —**Lamarckian** *adj*, *n*

Lamarckism /lə maárkizəm/ *n* the evolutionary theory of Jean Baptiste Lamarck that holds that evolution proceeds through the inheritance of characteristics acquired by individual organisms

Lamartine /la maar teèn/, **Alphonse Marie Louis Prat de** (1790–1869) French poet, historian, and statesman

lamasery /laámassəri/ (*plural* **-ies**) *n* a Tibetan or Mongolian monastery of lamas [Mid-19C. < French *lamaserie* 'lama dwelling' < *lama* (see LAMA).]

Lamaze /lə maáz/ *n US, Can* a method of natural childbirth by which a woman is physically and psychologically prepared through prenatal training [Mid-20C. After Fernand *Lamaze* (1890–1957), French physician.]

lamb /lam/ *n* **1 YOUNG SHEEP** an immature sheep, especially one under a year old and without permanent teeth **2 MEAT OF A LAMB** the meat of an immature sheep that is under a year old **3** CLOTHING = **lambskin** *n.* **1 4 SOMEBODY MEEK AND MILD** a gentle and innocent person, especially a baby or small child **5 SOMEBODY EASILY DECEIVED** a person who is easily cheated, especially financially ■ *vti* **GIVE BIRTH TO A LAMB** to give birth to a lamb [Old English, < Germanic] ◊ **like a lamb to the slaughter** calmly and without resistance going to face something unpleasant, difficult, or dangerous

Lamb *n* CHR = **Lamb of God**

Lamb /lam/, **Charles** (1775–1834) British essayist. Pseudonym **Elia**

Lamba /lámbə/ *n* a language spoken in Benin, belonging to the Gur branch of Niger-Congo. Native speakers: 29,000. [Early 20C. < Bantu.] —**Lamba** *adj*

lambada /lam baádə/ *n* **1** a fast rhythmic dance of Brazilian origin in which partners hold each other close and gyrate their hips **2** the music for a lambada [Late 20C. < Brazilian Portuguese, 'a beating'.]

Lambaréné /lámbə reèni, loNba ráynay/ capital of Moyen-Ogooué Region, W Gabon. Population: 42,316 (1993).

lambaste /lam báyst/ (**-bastes, -basting, -basted**), **lambast** /-bást/ *vt* to criticize somebody or something severely [Mid-17C. < LAM¹ + BASTE².]

lambda /lámdə/ *n* **1** the 11th letter of the Greek alphabet **2** the point of junction at the centre of the back of the cranium between the rear plate of the cranium (**occipital bone**) and the two upper plates (**parietal bones**) [Early 17C. < Greek.]

⚡**lambda calculus** *n* a descriptive theory of functions and the way they combine, used as the basis for certain high-level computer programming languages

lambdacism /lámdəssizəm/ *n* the erroneous substitution of 'l' for 'r' in speech [Mid-17C. Via late Latin < Greek *la(m)bdakismos* < *la(m)bda* 'lambda'.]

lambda hyperon *n* a short-lived elementary particle that has a mass approximately 1.1 times that of the proton and zero electric charge

lambdoid /lám doyd/, **lambdoidal** /lam dóyd'l/ *adj* describes the suture that joins bones at the back of the skull, shaped like the Greek capitalized lambda

lambent /lámbənt/ *adj* **1** GLEAMING softly gleaming or glowing (*literary*) **2 BRILLIANTLY LIGHT** having a light but brilliant touch **3 PLAYING OVER A SURFACE** flickering or playing as a flame over a surface without burning it (*literary*) [Mid-17C. < Latin *lambent-*, present participle of *lambere* 'lick'.] —**lambency** *n* —**lambently** *adv*

lambert /lámbərt/ *n* an SI unit of surface brightness (**luminance**) equivalent to one lumen per square centimetre [Late 19C. After Johann Heinrich *Lambert* (1728–77), German scientist.]

Lambeth walk /lámbəth-/, **Lambeth Walk** *n* a lively ballroom dance originating in England during the 1930s [Mid-19C. After a street in *Lambeth*, S London borough.]

Lambic /loN bík/ *n* a strong sour-tasting draught beer brewed in Belgium from aged hops [Late 19C. < French *alambic* 'still'.]

lambing /lámming/ *n* **1** the birth of lambs, or the season when they are born **2** the work of helping ewes give birth to lambs

lambkin /lámkin/ *n* an infant lamb, sometimes used as a term of endearment for a baby or small child

Lamb of God *n* Jesus Christ, seen as a sacrifice whose crucifixion and resurrection redeemed humankind

lambrequin /lámbrikin, lámbər-/ *n* **1 ORNAMENTAL HANGING** a decorative strip of drapery, hung along the top of a doorway, window, shelf, or mantelpiece **2 SCARF ATTACHED TO A KNIGHT'S HELMET** a veil, scarf, or piece of drapery attached to a knight's helmet to protect it from heat and rust **3** HERALDRY = **mantling 4 ORNAMENTAL BORDER ON A VASE** a decorative border near the top of a vase [Early 18C. Via French < assumed Dutch, 'small veil' < *lamper* 'veil'.]

Lambrusco /lam bróosk ō/ *n* a sweet sparkling red or white wine from N Italy [Mid-20C. Via Italian < Latin *labruscum* 'fruit of the wild grape Vitis labrusca' < *labrusca* 'wild vine'.]

lamb's ears (*plural* **lamb's ears**) *n* a perennial plant of the mint family that is often grown for its silvery woolly leaves. Flowers: small, purple. *Stachys byzantina.* [< the resemblance of the leaves to a lamb's ears]

lamb's fry *n* **1** lamb's testicles or internal organs, traditionally sold skinned and ready for cooking by frying **2** *ANZ* lamb's liver cooked for food [< English dialect *fry* 'internal part of an animal']

lambskin /lám skin/ *n* **1** the woolly pelt of a lamb, used for making or trimming winter clothing **2** the hide of a lamb, prepared as leather

lamb's lettuce *n* a lettuce with small rounded leaves and a slightly sweet, nutty flavour. US term **corn salad** [Translation of its old Latin name *lactuca agnina*]

lamb's tails *npl* the drooping catkins of the hazel tree

lambswool /lámz wŏol/, **lamb's wool** *n* fine soft wool sheared from a year-old lamb. Use: knitwear.

lame[1] /laym/ *adj* (**lamer, lamest**) **1 WALKING UNEVENLY** walking unevenly because of a leg injury or motion impairment (*offensive when used of people*) **2 INJURED** injured or with impaired strength or motion (*offensive when used of people*) **3 UNCONVINCING** inadequate, unconvincing, or unsatisfactory (*offensive in some contexts*) **4 INEFFECTIVE** ineffectual or inept (*offensive in some contexts*) ■ *vt* (**lames, laming, lamed**) **CAUSE INJURY** to cause a person or animal to be unable to walk evenly because of injury or impairment (*offensive when used of a person*) [Old English *lama* < Germanic, 'weak-limbed' < Indo-European, 'break by hitting'] —**lameness** *n*

lame[2] /laym/ *n* a thin plate of metal, especially one of the overlapping metal plates of which medieval armour was made from the mid-14th century [Late 16C. Via French < Latin *lamina* 'plate'.]

lamé /laá may/ *n* a fabric with gold or silver threads interwoven with silk, wool, or cotton [Early 20C. < French, 'worked with silver and gold thread' < Old French *lame* 'thin metal plate' < Latin *lamina* (see LAMINA).]

lamebrain /láym brayn/ *n US* an offensive term that deliberately insults somebody's intelligence (*slang insult*) —**lamebrained** *adj*

lamed /laámid/, **lamedh** /laá med/ *n* the 12th letter of the Hebrew alphabet [Mid-17C. < Hebrew *lāmēdh.*]

lame duck *n* **1 SOMEBODY OR SOMETHING WEAK** a person or thing considered as weak, inadequate, or unfortunate (*offensive when used of a person*) **2** *US* **OFFICE HOLDER UNABLE TO BE RE-ELECTED** an elected official who either will not or may not legally run for another term in office and has reduced power or effectiveness **3** *US* **OUTGOING OFFICE HOLDER WITH WEAKENED POWER** an elected official or group left seemingly powerless after a successor has been elected but has not yet taken over

lamella /lə méllə/ (*plural* **-lae** /-lee/) *n* **1 THIN PIECE OF BONE** any thin flat structure of bone or tissue **2 PART OF FUNGUS** a gill of a fungus **3 MEMBRANE LAYER** a membrane layer in a plant chloroplast **4 VAULT FRAMEWORK** a structural part of wood, metal, or reinforced concrete that is criss-crossed to form a vault [Late 17C. < Latin, 'small thin plate' < *lamina* 'plate'.] —**lamellar** *adj* —**lamellarly** *adv* —**lamellate** /lámmələt, lə méllət/ *adj* —**lamellated** /lámmə laytid/ *adj* —**lamellation** /lámmə láysh'n/ *n*

lamelli- *prefix* lamella ○ *lamelliform* [< LAMELLA]

lamellibranch /lə mélli brangk/ *n* ZOOL = **bivalve** [Mid-19C. < modern Latin *Lamellibranchia* < Latin *lamella* (see LAMELLA) + Greek *bragkhia* 'gills'.] —**lamellibranchiate** /lə mélli brángki ət/ *adj, n*

lamellicorn /lə mélli kawrn/ *adj* describes a beetle, e.g. a dung beetle, that has antennae composed of layered segments [Mid-19C. < modern Latin *Lamellicornia* < Latin *lamella* (see LAMELLA) + *cornu* 'horn'.] —**lamellicorn** *n*

lamelliform /lə mélli fawrm/ *adj* shaped like a thin plate or scale [Early 19C. < LAMELLA.]

lamely /láymli/ *adv* inadequately, unconvincingly, or ineptly

lament /lə mént/ *vti* **1 EXPRESS SORROW** to express sorrow about something **2 EXPRESS DISAPPOINTED REGRET** to express regret, annoyance, or disappointment ○ *She was lamenting the lack of funding for her project.* ■ *n* **1 EXPRESSION OF SADNESS** an expression of grief or sorrow **2 EXPRESSION OF REGRET** an expression of regret or disappointment **3 WORK LAMENTING A DEATH** a song or poem of mourning [Mid-16C. Directly or via French < Latin *lamentari* < *lamenta* 'laments'.] —**lamentation** /lámmən táysh'n/ *n* —**lamented** *adj* —**lamentedly** *adv* —**lamenter** *n* —**lamentingly** *adv*

lamentable /lámmәntəb'l/ *adj* **1** unsatisfactory, pitiful, or deplorable **2** sad and mournful (*literary*) —**lamentableness** *n* —**lamentably** *adv*

Lamentations /lámmən táysh'nz/ *n* a book of the Bible written in the form of elegies, according to tradition, by Jeremiah (*+ singular verb*)

lamia /láymi ə/ (*plural* **-as** *or* **-ae** /-ee/) *n* in Greek and Roman mythology, a blood-sucking witch who takes the form of a serpent, used as a bogey with which to threaten children [14C. Via Latin < Greek, 'mythical monster'.]

lamina /lámminə/ (*plural* **-nae** /-nee/ *or* **-nas**) *n* **1 THIN LAYER** a thin plate, layer, or flake **2 LEAF BLADE** the blade or flat part of a leaf **3 PROTECTIVE PLATE INSIDE A HOOF** in hoofed mammals, any of the parallel layers of sensitive tissue just inside the hard exterior of the hoof [Mid-17C. < Latin, 'plate, leaf'.]

laminal /lámmin'l/ *adj* describes speech sounds articulated using the blade or flat part of the tongue

laminar flow /lámminər-/ *n* a flow in a liquid or gas in which neighbouring layers do not mix but flow at different velocities

laminaria /lámmi náiri ə/ *n* a large brown seaweed (**kelp**) that has broad flat fronds. Genus: *Laminaria.* [Mid-19C. < modern Latin *Laminaria* < Latin *lamina* 'plate'; from the thin appendages.]

laminarin /lámmi naárrin/ *n* a carbohydrate occurring in brown algae [Mid-20C. < modern Latin *Laminaria* (see LAMINARIA).]

laminate *v* /lámmi nayt/ (**-nates, -nating, -nated**) **1** *vt* **COVER SOMETHING WITH A THIN LAYER** to cover something with a thin sheet of protective material, e.g. plastic or metal **2** *vt* **BOND LAYERS TOGETHER** to bond sheets or layers together so as to produce a strong and durable composite material **3** *vt* **FORM METAL INTO THIN LAYERS** to roll or beat metal into thin sheets **4** *vti* **SEPARATE INTO LAYERS** to split something, or be split, into thin layers ■ *n* /lámminət/ **MATERIAL MADE UP OF BONDED LAYERS** a product composed of layers or sheets bonded together —**laminable** *adj* —**laminated** *adj* —**laminator** *n*

lamination /lámmi náysh'n/ *n* **1 PROCESS OF BONDING LAYERS** the bonding together of thin layers of materials to form a composite material **2 FORMATION OF LAYERS** the formation of layers in something **3 THIN LAYER** a thin layer in something (*technical*) **4 THINLY LAYERED STRUCTURE** a structure composed of thin layers **5 THIN STEEL PLATE IN TRANSFORMER CORE** one of a number of thin steel or iron plates that are held together to form a transformer core

laminectomy /lámmi néktəmi/ (*plural* **-mies**) *n* a surgical operation to remove one or more sides of the rear arches of a spinal vertebra and gain access to the spinal cord or spinal nerve roots

lamington /lámmingtən/ *n ANZ* a small square sponge cake covered in chocolate icing and dried coconut [Early 20C. Originally 'Homburg hat', after Lord *Lamington*, governor of Queensland, Australia, 1895–1901.]

Lamington National Park /lámmingtən-/ national park in SE Queensland, Australia

Lamington Plateau high mountain plateau in the Macpherson Range, Queensland, Australia. Height: average 600 m/2,000 ft.

laminitis /lámmi nítiss/ *n* inflammation of the sensitive plates of tissue in a hoof, especially a horse's hoof, usually causing lameness

Lammas /lámməss/ *n* **1** a Christian religious feast marking St Peter's deliverance from prison. Date: 1 August. **2** a day formerly celebrated in England as a harvest festival. Date: 1 August. [Old English *hlāfmæsse* < earlier forms of LOAF[1] + MASS; by folk etymology by association with LAMB]

lammergeier /lámmər gī ər/, **lammergeyer** *n* a large rare vulture with dark wings and dark feathers that resemble a beard around its beak. Native to: mountains of S Europe, Africa, Asia. *Gypaetus barbatus.* [Early 19C. < German *Lämmergeier* 'lambs' vulture', because it can prey upon animals of that size.]

lamming /lámming/ *n* a thorough whipping or beating (*informal*)

Lamont /lə mónt/, **Norman** (*b.* 1942) British politician

lamp /lamp/ *n* **1 ELECTRIC LIGHT** a device that produces electric light **2 DEVICE PRODUCING LIGHT** a device that burns oil, gas, or wax to produce light **3 RADIATION SOURCE** a device that supplies ultraviolet light or infrared heat radiation, especially for medical or cosmetic treatment ○ *sun lamp* **4 SOURCE OF ENLIGHTENMENT** a source of enlightenment or inspiration (*literary*) [12C. < French *lampe* < Latin *lampas* < Greek, 'torch' < *lampein* 'to shine'.]

lampas[1] /lámpəss/ *n* an ornately patterned fabric resembling damask. Use: upholstery. [Mid-19C. < French.]

lampas[2] /lámpəss/ *n* the swelling of the mucous membrane covering the roof of the mouth in horses, often due to tooth eruption and therefore transient [Early 16C. < French, 'disease producing intense thirst'.]

lampblack /lámp blak/ *n* a fine powdery form of carbon that is deposited when oils containing carbon are burned. Use: pigment, printing ink, in electrodes.

lampbrush chromosome /lámp brush-/ *n* an enlarged chromosome covered with fine loops of chromatin, observed during the early part of meiosis [*Lampbrush*, loose translation of German *Lampencylinderputzer* 'lamp-glass cleaner'; because it resembles a brush for the inside of a lampshade]

lamp chimney *n* a glass cover that is placed over the wick of an oil or kerosene lamp to protect and control the flame

lampern /lámpərn/ (*plural* **-perns** *or* **-pern**) *n* a river fish of the lamprey family that resembles an eel. Native to: Europe. *Lampetra fluviatilis.* [14C. < Old French *lampreion* 'small lamprey' < *lampreie* (see LAMPREY).]

lamp glass *n* HOUSEHOLD = **lamp chimney**

lampion /lámpi ən/ *n* a small oil lamp, usually with a tinted glass chimney, formerly popular as a carriage light [Mid-19C. Via French < Italian *lampione* 'large lamp' < *lampa* 'lamp' < French *lampe* (see LAMP).]

lamplight /lámp līt/ *n* the light cast by a lamp —**lamplit** *adj*

lamplighter /lámp lītər/ *n* **1** formerly, an employee who lit gas streetlamps **2** *US, Can* a device used to light lamps

lamp oil *n* oil suitable as lamp fuel

lampoon /lam póon/ *n* a piece of satirical writing or verse ridiculing somebody or something ■ *vt* to use ridicule as a way of satirizing somebody or something in a piece of writing [Mid-17C. < French *lampon.*] —**lampooner** *n* —**lampoonery** *n* —**lampoonist** *n*

lamppost /lámp pōst/, **lamp post** *n* **1** a post or pillar that supports a streetlight **2** *Malaysia* an unwanted single person with a couple or a group otherwise made up of couples (*informal*) ○ *I don't want to play lamppost.*

lamprey /lámpri/ (*plural* **-preys**) *n* a freshwater jawless fish with a round sucking mouth for attaching itself to other fish and, in the case of adults, feeding parasitically on their blood. Family: Petromyzontidae. [13C. Via Old French *lampreie* < medieval Latin *lampreda.*]

lamprophyre /lámprə fīr/ *n* an igneous rock that occurs mainly as an intrusion or dyke containing large crystals, especially of biotite and mica [Late 19C. < German *lamprophyr*, 'shining purple' < Greek *(por)phureos* 'purple'.]

lampshade /lámp shayd/ *n* a cover, typically decorative, used to moderate and direct artificial light from a lamp

lamp shell n MARINE BIOL = **brachiopod** [< its resemblance to an ancient oil lamp and its wick]

lamp standard n TRANSP = **lamppost**

lampworking /lámp wurking/ n the process or technique of forming glass items made of rods and tubes by heating them with an oxygen-gas flame

⚡ **LAN** /lan/ abbr local area network

lanai /lə níl/ (plural **-nais**) n in Hawaii, an open roofed porch or verandah, often used as a living room [Early 19C. < Hawaiian.]

Lanark /lánnərk/ town in central Scotland. Population: 8,877 (1991).

Lanarkshire /lánnərkshər/ former county in S Scotland

lanate /láy nayt/ adj covered with or consisting of woolly hairs [Mid-18C. < Latin lanatus < lana 'wool'.]

Lancashire /lángkəshər/ coastal county in NW England. Area: 2,896 sq. km/1,183 sq. mi.

Lancaster[1] /láng kastər/ n the branch of the Plantagenet dynasty that ruled England from 1399 to 1461, founded by Henry duke of Lancaster (**Henry IV**)

Lancaster[2] /lángkəstər/ historic city in NW England. Population: 136,948 (1996 estimate).

Lancaster /láng kastər/, **Burt** (1913–94) US actor. Full name **Burton Stephen Lancaster**

Lancaster /lángkəstər/, **Sir Osbert** (1908–86) British cartoonist and writer

Lancastrian /lang kástri ən/ adj 1 relating to Lancashire or Lancaster 2 belonging to or supporting the royal house of Lancaster, especially during the 15th-century Wars of the Roses —**Lancastrian** n

lance /laanss/ n 1 CAVALRY SPEAR a long weapon with a metal point carried by cavalry in battle 2 HUNTING OR FISHING SPEAR a long pointed spear used in hunting or fishing 3 METAL-PIERCING DEVICE a thin metal tube or pipe through which a stream of oxygen is directed at a heated metal surface in order to pierce it ■ vt (**lances, lancing, lanced**) PIERCE WITH A SHARP INSTRUMENT to pierce flesh with a sharp instrument to let out pus [13C. Via French < Latin lancea.]

lance corporal n 1 an Army or Royal Marines non-commissioned officer of a rank above private 2 a marine in the US Marine Corps of a rank above private first class [< obsolete lancepesade 'officer of lowest rank', via Old French < Old Italian lancia spezzata 'broken lance']

lancelet /laansslət/ n a small slender translucent marine animal that is related to the ancestors of all vertebrates and lives buried in sand. Subphylum: Cephalochordata.

Lanceley /laanssli/, **Colin** (b. 1938) New Zealand-born Australian painter and sculptor

Lancelot /laansə lot/ n in Arthurian legend, the most famous of King Arthur's knights and the lover of Queen Guinevere

lanceolate /laanssi ə layt/ adj tapering to a point like the head of a lance [Mid-18C. < late Latin lanceolatus < Latin lanceola 'small lance' < lancea 'lance'.] —**lanceolately** adv

lancer /laanssər/, **Lancer** n a soldier on horseback armed with a lance

lance rest n a support for a lance attached to a medieval breastplate or saddle and used during a charge

lancers /laanssərz/ n (+ singular verb) 1 a square dance for 8 or 16 couples, originally a 19th-century quadrille 2 the music for a lancers

lance sergeant n a noncommissioned officer in some regiments of the British Army of a rank equivalent to corporal

lancet /laanssit/ n 1 a scalpel 2 ARCHIT = **lancet arch** 3 ARCHIT = **lancet window**

lancet arch n a narrow arch that comes steeply to a point, typical in Gothic architecture

lanceted /laanssitid/ adj 1 built with lancet arches or lancet windows, as in Gothic architecture 2 with an arched, steeply pointed top

lancet fish n a long-bodied carnivorous deep-sea fish with a long dorsal fin and sharp teeth. Alepisauridae. [< the sharpness of the fins]

Lancet window

lancet window n a window formed as one or more slender pointed arches

lancewood /laanss wŏŏd/ (plural **-woods** or **-wood**) n 1 tough flexible wood. Use: fishing rods, bows, cabinetmaking. 2 a tree that yields lancewood. Native to: tropical America, Caribbean. Oxandra lanceolata. [< the use of the wood in objects like fishing rods]

lanciform /laanssi fawrm/ adj shaped like a lance

Lancs /langks/ abbr Lancashire

land /land/ n 1 SOLID EARTH the solid part of the Earth's surface not covered by a body of water 2 EARTH FOR USE a part of the Earth's surface of a particular kind or that is used for a particular purpose ○ low-lying land ○ agricultural land 3 COUNTRYSIDE ground used for agriculture, or rural or agricultural areas as distinguished from villages, towns, or cities ○ He had worked on the land all his life. 4 OWNED GROUND an area of ground that somebody owns ○ publicly owned land ○ What are you doing on my land? 5 HOMELAND a territory, country, or nation inhabited by those who regard it as their home ○ her native land 6 AREA NOTABLE FOR an area, domain, or realm that is notable for something ○ She's living in the land of make-believe. 7 SMOOTH PARTS OF GROOVED AREA the unindented parts of a grooved surface, e.g. a ridge between grooves in the bore of a rifle 8 UNFURROWED SOIL the parts of the ground between furrows in a ploughed field 9 Scotland TENEMENT a tenement house ■ v 1 vi ARRIVE FROM PLANE to arrive by aircraft ○ We land at 8:43. 2 vti SET DOWN AIRCRAFT to come down, or bring an aircraft down, onto water or solid ground, especially at an airport ○ The Luton plane landed five minutes ago. 3 vti GO OR PUT SOMETHING ASHORE to arrive on shore from a ship, or put something ashore from a ship ○ We decided to land and explore the port. 4 vi COME DOWN THROUGH THE AIR to come down, or bring somebody or something down, from a height ○ The ball shot up and landed on the roof. 5 vt CATCH AND BRING A FISH IN to catch a fish and get it onto a boat or solid ground 6 vt OBTAIN to win, obtain, secure, or be awarded something desired ○ He finally landed the job he wanted. 7 vt HIT to succeed in hitting somebody or something ○ She landed a blow on his head. 8 vi APPEAR UNEXPECTEDLY to appear in an undesired and unexpected way ○ One problem after another landed in our lap. 9 vti END UP SOMEWHERE UNPLEASANT to end up or cause somebody or something to end up in an undesirable place or situation ○ It could land him in jail. [Old English, Germanic, 'particular (enclosed) area'] ◇ **be in the land of the living** to be alive or awake (humorous) ◇ **find out** or **see how the land lies** to assess a situation before taking action

land up vi UK, Can to finally get to a place or situation after a series of events or circumstances (informal) ○ land up on the streets

land with vt UK, Can to give somebody something to do or deal with, especially because no one else wants to do it (informal) ○ I was landed with the bill.

land agent n 1 the manager or administrator of a landed estate 2 an agent for the buying and selling of land — **land agency** n

Land art n an art form originating in the United States in the mid-1960s in which objects are created in natural settings, often in remote locations

landau /lán daw/ (plural **-daus**) n a four-wheeled horse-drawn carriage with a top that may be let down or folded back and a raised seat for the driver [Mid-18C. After Landau, town in Bavaria, Germany.]

landaulet /lán daw lét/, **landaulette** n 1 a small horse-drawn landau 2 a car that has a convertible top for the back seat, while the front seat is either roofed or open

land bank n a bank that issues loans using the borrower's property as security

land-based bookstore n US a bookshop that exists in a physical location, as opposed to one that exists as a website

land bridge n a tract of land that connects continents, permitting the passage of people and animals

land crab n any crab that lives mainly on land and breeds in the sea

landed /lándid/ adj 1 OWNING LAND possessing land, especially a large rural property 2 CONSISTING OF LAND consisting of a large area of land 3 Can OFFICIALLY A RESIDENT OF CANADA given official status as a resident in Canada prior to being granted citizenship

lander /lándər/ n a spacecraft designed to land on the surface of the Moon or a planet

landfall /lánd fawl/ n 1 an approach to, arrival on, or sighting of land, especially after a long journey by sea 2 the first land that somebody reaches after a long journey, especially by sea

landfill /lánd fil/ n 1 the disposal of waste material or refuse by burying it in natural or excavated holes or depressions 2 a site where waste material has been buried

land forces npl armed forces serving exclusively on land. ◊ **land army**

landform /lánd fawrm/ n a natural physical feature of the Earth's surface, e.g. a valley, mountain, or plain

land girl n a woman who did farm work as a member of the Land Army during World War I or II (offensive in some contexts)

landgrave /lánd grayv/ n 1 in Germany, from the 13th century to 1806, a count who had jurisdiction over a region 2 a title given to certain princes in central Germany after 1806 [Early 16C. < Middle Low German, < land 'land' + grave 'count'.]

landholder /lánd höldər/ n the owner or occupant of a piece of land —**landholding** n, adj

landing /lánding/ n 1 ACT OF COMING TO THE GROUND the act of reaching, touching, or alighting on the ground, e.g. after a jump or fall 2 ARRIVAL ON LAND an arrival on the ground after having been in the air or at sea 3 PLACE FOR LOADING OR UNLOADING a place for loading or unloading passengers or goods, especially from a ship ○ There is a good landing at most of the villages along the coast. 4 LEVEL AREA BETWEEN STAIRS a platform between flights of stairs or the floor at the top or foot of a flight of stairs

landing beacon n a radio transmitter at an airfield that sends a beam to guide aircraft on landing

landing beam n a radio beam emitted by a beacon at a landing field that enables incoming aircraft to make a landing

landing craft n a low open flat-bottomed boat designed for landing troops and equipment on shore from a ship

landing field n a place where aircraft can land and take off

landing gear n the wheels or floats and related mechanisms that are used by an aircraft or spacecraft when taking off and landing

landing net n a net like a bag fitted on a frame that is used by anglers to scoop up a hooked fish

landing speed n the minimum speed at which an aircraft has to be flying in order to land safely

landing stage n a floating or fixed wooden platform, used for loading or unloading passengers and goods from a boat

landing strip n AIR = **airstrip**

landlady /lánd laydi/ (plural **-dies**) n 1 WOMAN WHO RENTS OUT PROPERTY a woman who owns property that she rents to tenants 2 WOMAN WHO RENTS OUT LODGINGS a woman who owns or runs a place offering accommodation, e.g. a bed-and-breakfast, guesthouse, or lodging house 3 WOMAN RUNNING PUB a woman who manages a public house

landless /lándləss/ adj without having the ownership of land —**landlessness** n

landline /lánd līn/ n a telecommunications cable laid overland

landlocked /lánd lokt/ *adj* **1** closed in completely or almost completely by land **2** adapted to life in a freshwater environment, with no access to the sea, though being a species historically found in the ocean

landlord /lánd lawrd/ *n* **1 SOMEBODY WHO RENTS OUT PROPERTY** a person or organization that owns property that is rented to tenants **2 MAN WHO RENTS OUT LODGINGS** a man who owns or runs a place offering accommodation, e.g. a bed-and-breakfast, guesthouse, or lodging house **3 MAN RUNNING PUB** a man who manages a public house

landlubber /lánd lubbər/ *n* a person who is clumsy aboard a ship due to lack of experience at sea —**landlubberly** *adj*

landmark /lánd maark/ *n* **1 SOMETHING PROMINENT THAT IDENTIFIES A LOCATION** a prominent structure or geographical feature that identifies a location and serves as a guide to finding it **2 SOMETHING THAT REPRESENTS IMPORTANT NEW DEVELOPMENT** an event, idea, or item that represents a significant or historic development **3** *US* **SOMETHING PRESERVED FOR HISTORIC IMPORTANCE** a structure or site identified and preserved because of its historical significance **4 BOUNDARY MARKER** a conspicuous object, e.g. a tree or stone, that is recognized as marking the boundary of a piece of land ■ *adj* **HIGHLY SIGNIFICANT** marking a significant change or turning point in something, especially the law ○ *a landmark ruling*

landmass /lánd mass/ *n* a very large unbroken area of land, e.g. a continent or large island

landmine /lánd mīn/ *n* an explosive mine that is laid just under the surface of the ground and detonates if disturbed by pressure or the proximity of something such as metal

land office *n US, Can* a government office that administers and records sales and transfers of public land

land of milk and honey *n* **1** a land of prosperity and plenty promised by God to the Israelites **2** a rich and fertile area or region of plenty (*literary*)

land of Nod *n* an imaginary place where people who are sleeping are said to be (*informal humorous*) [Pun, after a place mentioned in *Genesis* 4:16]

landowner /lándōnər/ *n* an owner of land —**landownership** *n* —**landowning** *n, adj*

Landrace /lánd rayss/ (*plural* **-drace** *or* **-draces**) *n* a N European pig of a white lean long-bodied breed developed in Denmark [Mid-20C. < Danish, 'land breed'.]

landrail /lánd rayl/ *n* BIRDS = **corncrake** [< RAIL[3]]

land reform *n* the redistribution of agricultural land, especially by government measures, so that those owning none receive some of it

Land Registry *n* a government department in England and Wales at which land and its ownership are registered

land rights *npl ANZ* the claim of Aboriginal people to the ownership of an area of land, usually based on occupation before the arrival of immigrants

Land Rover *tdmk* a trademark for a four-wheel-drive vehicle

landscape /lánd skayp/ *n* **1 VISUALLY DISTINCT SCENERY** an expanse of scenery of a particular type, especially as much as can be seen by the eye **2 PAINTING OF VIEW** a painting, drawing, or photograph of scenery, especially rural scenery **3 THE PAINTING OR DRAWING OF SCENERY** the branch of art dealing with the painting, drawing, or photography of scenery **4 GENERAL SITUATION OF ACTIVITY** the general situation providing the background to a particular type of activity ○ *the economic landscape* **5 RANGE OF MENTAL CONCERNS** any characteristic group of intellectual or imaginative features (*literary*) ■ *adj* **PRINTED WITH LONG SIDES HORIZONTAL** photographed or printed so that the long sides of a picture or the lines of text are parallel to the long sides of a rectangular page. ◊ **portrait** ■ *vt* (**-scapes, -scaping, -scaped**) **MAKE LAND LOOK BETTER** to enhance the appearance of land by altering its contours and planting trees and shrubs for aesthetic effect (*often passive*) ○ *The property was beautifully landscaped.* [Late 16C. Anglicization of Dutch *landschap* 'condition of being land' < *land* 'land'.]

landscape architect *n* a planner and designer of environments, especially with the aim of making new buildings, roads, and other structures compatible with their natural surroundings —**landscape architecture** *n*

landscape gardener *n* a designer of grounds and gardens —**landscape gardening** *n*

landscaper /lánd skaypər/ *n US* a designer of grounds or gardens

landscapist /lánd skaypist/ *n* an artist who specializes in painting landscapes

Land's End cliff and promontory in Cornwall that forms the extreme southwestern tip of Great Britain

landshark /lánd shaark/ *n* an unethical dealer in land (*informal insult*)

landside /lánd sīd/ *n* **1** the part of an airport farthest from the aircraft **2** the flat part of a plough that faces unbroken land as it moves

landsknecht /lándz knekt/ *n* a mercenary foot soldier in Europe during the 16th century, especially a German pikeman [Early 17C. < German, 'servant of the country'.]

landsleit plural of **landsman**[2]

landslide /lánd slīd/ *n* **1 SUDDEN COLLAPSE OF LAND** the collapse of part of a mountainside or cliff so that it descends in a disintegrating mass of rocks and earth **2 MASS OF LOOSENED ROCK AND EARTH** a disintegrating mass of rock and earth that suddenly descends from a mountainside or cliff **3 CONSPICUOUS TRIUMPH** an overwhelming victory, especially in an election

landslip /lánd slip/ *n* GEOG = **landslide** *n.* 1

landsman[1] /lándzmən/ (*plural* **-men** /-mən/) *n* somebody who lives and works on land rather than at sea

landsman[2] /lándzmən/ (*plural* **-leit** /-līt/) *n* a fellow Jew from the same district or area, originally in Eastern Europe [Mid-20C. Via Yiddish < Middle High German *lantsman* 'man from the (same) country'.]

Landsturm /laánt shtoorm/ *n* **1** in some European countries, a general draft of people for conscription into the armed forces **2** in some European countries, a military force of people drafted from the general population [Early 19C. < German, 'land storm'.]

Landtag /laánt taak/ *n* the legislative assembly of a German or Austrian state [Late 16C. Via German < Middle High German *lanttac* 'land day'.]

land tax *n* an annual tax levied on landed property in the United Kingdom, abolished in 1963

landward /lándwərd/ *adj* facing towards the land

landwards /lándwərdz/ *adv* in the direction of land

Landwehr /laánt vair/ *n* in German-speaking countries, a reserve military force [Early 19C. < German, 'national defence'.]

Landy /lándi/, **Michael John** (*b.* 1930) Australian athlete

land yacht *n* a wind-driven vehicle resembling a boat with a mast, sails, and three wheels, for use on beaches or other hard surfaces

lane /layn/ *n* **1 NARROW STREET** a narrow path, road or street, typically in older town areas or in the countryside, often enclosed by walls or hedges **2 TRACK INTO WHICH ROAD IS DIVIDED** a division of a road, street, or motorway wide enough for a single line of motor vehicles **3 TRACK ASSIGNED TO RACER** a track assigned to a competitive runner on a racing track or a swimmer in a swimming pool **4 SHIPPING ROUTE** a route assigned to a ship on a journey, especially through a congested area of sea **5** AIR = **air lane** **6 STRIP OF FLOOR IN BOWLING ALLEY** the long strip of polished wooden flooring along which bowls are rolled in a bowling alley **7 DIVISION OF BASKETBALL COURT** an area of a basketball court extending from the free-throw line to just below the basket [Old English] ◇ **in the fast lane** at a fast, hectic, or stressful pace associated with success and achievement

Lane /layn/, **William** (1861–1917) British-born Australian journalist and political activist

lane discipline *n* the degree of care and restraint exercised by drivers when using busy multilane roads, avoiding constant lane changing, cutting-in, driving too closely to vehicles in front, and risk-taking

lang /lang/, **k.d.** (*b.* 1961) Canadian-born US singer. Full name **Kathryn Dawn Lang**

Lang /lang/, **Fritz** (1890–1976) German-born US film director

Lange /lóngi/, **David Russell** (*b.* 1942) New Zealand statesman

langlauf /laáng lowf/ *n* **1** SKIING = **cross-country skiing** **2** a contest in cross-country skiing [Early 20C. < German, < *lang* 'long' + *Lauf* 'a run' (< Germanic).] —**langlaufer** *n*

langley /lángli/ (*plural* **-leys**) *n* a unit of solar radiation equivalent to one calorie per square centimetre [Mid-20C. After Samuel P. *Langley* (1834–1906), US aviation pioneer.]

langouste /long gόost/ *n* ZOOL = **spiny lobster** [Mid-20C. Via French < Old Provençal *lagosta* < Latin *locusta* 'locust, crustacean'.]

langoustine /lóng gōo steén/ *n* **1** a large prawn or small lobster. Native to: N Atlantic. **2** the flesh of a langoustine used as food [Mid-20C. Via French < Latin *locusta* 'locust, crustacean'.]

langrage /láng grij/, **langridge** *n* shot consisting of a case filled with fragments of iron, formerly used for tearing the sails and rigging of enemy ships [Mid-18C. < ?]

Langrenus /láng grinəss/ *n* crater visible in the SE quadrant of the Moon, 132 km/82 mi. in diameter

langridge *n* = **langrage**

langsyne /láng sīn/, **lang syne** *adv Scotland* long ago (*literary*) ○ *It all happened langsyne.* ■ *n Scotland* a time long past (*literary or humorous*) ◊ **auld lang syne**

Langtry /lángtri/, **Lillie** (1853–1929) British actor. Born **Emilie Charlotte Le Breton**

ϟ **language** /láng gwij/ *n* **1 SPEECH OF GROUP** the speech of a country, region, or group of people, including its diction, syntax, and grammar **2 COMMUNICATION WITH WORDS** the human use of spoken or written words as a communication system **3 SYSTEM OF COMMUNICATION** a system of communication with its own set of conventions or special words **4 NONVERBAL COMMUNICATION BETWEEN ANIMALS** a nonverbal form of communication used by birds and animals **5 NONVERBAL COMMUNICATION BETWEEN HUMANS** the use of signs, gestures, or inarticulate sounds to communicate something **6 SPECIALIST VOCABULARY** the forms of expression used by those in a specified group or sphere of activity **7 STYLE OF VERBAL EXPRESSION** the verbal style by which people express themselves ○ *the language of diplomacy* **8** COMPUT = **programming language** [13C. < French *langage* < *langue* 'tongue' < Latin *lingua*.] ◇ **speak the same language** to have values and interests in common with somebody so that it is possible to communicate effectively

SYNONYMS ***language, vocabulary, idiolect, tongue, dialect, slang, jargon, parlance, lingo, -speak, -ese***

CORE MEANING: communication by words

language the human use of spoken or written words as a communication system, or the particular system of communication prevailing in a specific country, nation, or community; **vocabulary** the body of words that make up a particular language; **idiolect** an individual person's speech habits or vocabulary; **tongue** a particular language used by a specific country, nation, or community; **dialect** a regional variety of a language, or a form of a language spoken by members of a particular social class or profession; **slang** words, expressions, and turns of phrase used instead of standard terms in casual speech or writing, or by a particular group of people; **jargon** terms associated with a particular specialized activity, profession, or culture, especially terms that are not generally understood by outsiders; **parlance** the style of speech or writing used by people in a particular context or profession; **lingo** (*informal*) the way of speaking associated with a particular, usually specialized, group of people; **-speak** a suffix added to nouns to describe the language used by a particular group of people or in a particular context, suggesting that this way of speaking or writing is obscure or difficult to follow; **-ese** a suffix added to nouns to describe the language associated with a group of people, especially when it is like jargon.

language laboratory *n* a room equipped with audio or multimedia equipment for use in learning languages

langue /longg/ *n* language regarded as a communication system and the common property of a speech community (*technical*) ◊ **parole** *n.* 5 [14C. Via French < Latin *lingua* 'tongue'.]

langue de chat /lóng də shaá/ (*plural* **langues de chat** /lóng də shaá/) *n* a small narrow flat biscuit often coated with chocolate [< French, 'cat's tongue']

langue d'oc /lóngg dók/ *n* the group of French dialects, usually considered to include Provençal, spoken in southern parts of medieval France [< French, 'language of "oc"'; from the use of *oc* (< Latin *hoc*) for 'yes']

Languedoc /lóngg dók/ historical region and former province in S France, stretching from the Pyrenees to the River Rhône

langue d'oïl /lóngg dóy/ *n* the group of French dialects spoken in the northern part of medieval France [<

French, 'language of 'oïl''; from the use of *oïl* (< Latin *hoc ille*) for 'yes']

languet /láng gwet/ *n* something, e.g. a part in a machine or instrument, that is shaped like a tongue [14C. < Old French *languete* 'small tongue' < *langue* 'tongue' < Latin *lingua*.]

languid /láng gwid/ *adj* **1 WITHOUT ENERGY** lacking vigour and energy **2 SLUGGISH** sluggish or slow-moving **3 LISTLESS** listless and indifferent [Late 16C. Directly or via French < Latin *languidus* < *languere* 'be weak'.] —**languidly** *adv* —**languidness** *n*

languish /láng gwish/ *vi* **1 BE NEGLECTED OR DEPRIVED** to undergo hardship as a result of being deprived of something, typically independence, freedom, or attention **2 BECOME LESS SUCCESSFUL** to decline steadily, becoming less vital, strong, or successful **3 PINE** to long for something that is being denied [14C. < Old French *languiss-*, stem of *languir* < Latin *languere* 'be weak or faint'.] —**languisher** *n* —**languishing** *n, adj* —**languishingly** *adv* —**languishment** *n*

languor /láng gər/ *n* **1 TIREDNESS** a pleasant feeling of weariness or weakness **2 LISTLESSNESS IN SPEECH OR BEHAVIOUR** listlessness and indifference in speech or behaviour **3 HEAVINESS IN ATMOSPHERE** an oppressive heaviness or sultriness in the air [13C. Via Old French < Latin, < *languere* 'be weak'.]

languorous /láng gərəss/ *adj* **1 WEAK AND RELAXED** lazily or pleasantly lacking vigour and vitality **2 LISTLESS** listless and indifferent **3 SLUGGISH** slow-moving or sluggish —**languorously** *adv* —**languorousness** *n*

langur /láng gər, lang go͝or/ *n* a slender, leaf-eating monkey with a long tail, bushy eyebrows, and a chin tuft. Native to: Southeast Asia. Genus: *Presbytis*. ◊ **leaf monkey** [Early 19C. < Hindi *langūr* < Sanskrit *lāṅgūla* 'having a tail'.]

laniard *n* = **lanyard**

laniary /lánni əri/ *adj* describes a tooth adapted for tearing food [Early 19C. < Latin *laniarius* 'of a butcher' < *lanius* 'butcher' < *laniare* 'to tear'.] —**laniary** *n*

laniferous /lə níffərəss/, **lanigerous** /lə níjjərəss/ *adj* wool-bearing or wool-covered [Mid-17C. < Latin *lanifer* < *lana* 'wool'.]

lank /langk/ *adj* **1** limp and straight ○ *lank hair* **2** long and slender [Old English *hlanc* 'lean' < Germanic, 'flexible'] —**lankly** *adv* —**lankness** *n*

lanky /lángki/ (**-ier, -iest**) *adj* tall and thin in a bony, ungracefully angular way —**lankily** *adv* —**lankiness** *n*

lanner /lánnər/ (*plural* **-ners** *or* **-ner**) *n* a large falcon, the female of which is used especially in falconry. Native to: Africa, Southeast Asia, Mediterranean. *Falco biarmicus*. [13C. < French *lanier*.]

lanneret /lánnə ret/ (*plural* **-ets** *or* **-et**) *n* a male lanner, smaller than the female and used in falconry

lanolin /lánnəlin/, **lanoline** /lánnə leen/ *n* a fat extracted from sheep's wool. Use: in skin ointments. [Late 19C. < Latin *lana* 'wool' < Indo-European.]

Lansing /lánsing/ **1** capital of Michigan, in the south-central part of the state. Population: 127,812 (1994). **2** village in NE Illinois. Population: 28,512 (1998 estimate).

lantana /lan táynə, -taánə/ (*plural* **-nas** *or* **-na**) *n* an ornamental evergreen shrub of the vervain family. Native to: tropical America. Genus: *Lantana*. [Late 18C. Via modern Latin < Italian dialect, 'wayfaring tree', which it resembles.]

lantern /lántərn/ *n* **1 PORTABLE LAMP** a portable case with transparent or translucent sides that protects and holds a lamp **2 LIGHTHOUSE ROOM** a room containing the large lamp at the top of a lighthouse **3 STRUCTURE WITH WINDOWS** a structure with windows on all sides, resembling a lantern, e.g. one at the top of a dome **4 STAGE LIGHT** a light for illuminating a stage or part of a stage [13C. Via French < Greek *lamptēr* 'torch, lamp' < *lampein* 'to shine'.]

lantern-eyed fish *n* a sea fish with luminous organs under each eye that it can turn on and off at will. Family: Anomalopidae.

lantern fish *n* a small bony deep-sea fish with rows of luminous spots along its body. Family: Myctophidae.

lantern fly *n* a tropical insect with an elongated head that resembles a lantern and was formerly thought to emit light. Family: Fulgoridae.

lantern jaw *n* a long bony lower jaw, typically projecting beyond the upper jaw —**lantern-jawed** *adj*

lantern pinion *n* a gearwheel used in clocks and watches that has two circular discs connected by cylindrical pins

lantern slide *n* a transparent slide, typically made of glass, for projection onto a screen by a slide projector or magic lantern

lantern wheel *n* TECH = **lantern pinion**

lanthanide /lánthə nīd/ *n* an element of the lanthanide series of rare earths [Early 20C. < LANTHANUM.]

lanthanide series *n* a group of the rare earths that range from lanthanum at atomic number 57 to lutetium at atomic number 71

lanthanum /lánthənəm/ *n* (*symbol* **La**) a silvery ductile metallic element resembling aluminium that belongs to the rare-earth group. Source: monazite, bastnaesite. Use: glass manufacture. [Mid-19C. < Greek *lanthanein* 'lie hidden' (because it was discovered hidden in cerium oxide).]

lanugo /lə nyo͞ogō/ (*plural* **-gos** *or* **-go**) *n* a covering of soft downy hairs, especially those on a developing human foetus or newborn infant [15C. < Latin, < *lana* 'wool'.] —**lanuginous** /lə no͞ojinəss/ *adj* —**lanuginousness** *n*

Lanús /la no͞oss/ city in E Argentina. Population: 468,561 (1991).

lanyard /lányərd/, **laniard** *n* **1 CORD WORN ROUND THE NECK** a cord worn round the neck by military and naval personnel or by Scouts and Guides for carrying something such as a whistle or penknife **2 SHORT ROPE ABOARD SHIP** a short rope or cord used to hold or fasten something on a ship **3 CORD FOR FIRING A CANNON** a cord tied to the breech mechanism of a cannon and used to fire it [14C. Anglicization (influenced by YARD[1] 'spar') of French *lanière* 'strap' < *lasne*.]

Lanzarote /lanzə ráwti/ easternmost of the Canary Islands, Spain. Population: 76,413 (1995). Area: 805 sq. km/311 sq. mi.

Laocoön /lay ókō on/, **Laocoon** *n* a Trojan priest of Apollo who warned the Trojans about the Wooden Horse and was killed along with his two sons by sea serpents after he gave his warning

laodicean /láy ōdi seé ən/, **Laodicean** *adj* lacking in religious or political commitment [Early 17C. < Latin *Laodicea*, city in modern-day Turkey, whose Christians were rebuked for indifference (*Rev.* 3:16).] —**laodicean** *n*

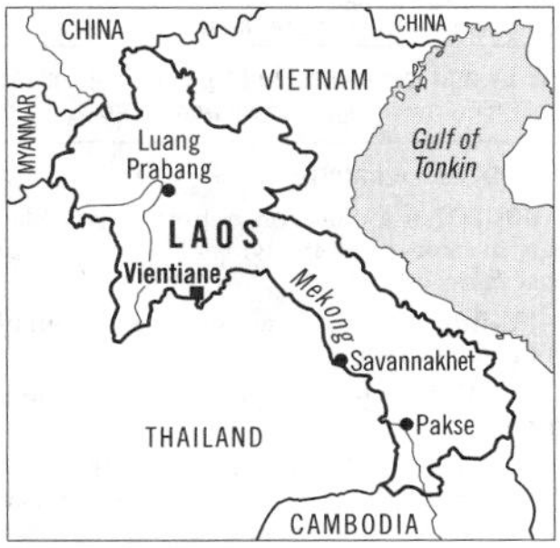

Laos

Laos /lowss/ independent state of Southeast Asia. Capital: Vientiane. Population: 5,116,959 (1997). Area: 236,800 sq. km/91,430 sq. mi. —**Laotian** /lówsh'n, lay ōsh'n/ *n, adj*

Lao-tzu /lów tso͞o/ (570?–490? BC) Chinese philosopher. Known as **Master Lao**

lap[1] /lap/ *n* **1 TOP OF SOMEBODY'S THIGHS WHEN SITTING** the level area provided by the upper surface of the thighs of somebody who is seated **2 PART OF CLOTHING RESTING ON THE THIGHS** the part of a garment that hangs loosely across the thighs of somebody seated **3 VALLEY** a hollow in the contours of land, especially the gap between hills [Old English *læppa* 'flap of a garment, lobe' < Germanic] —**lapful** *n* ◇ **drop in** *or* **into your lap** to be given as something welcome and unexpected ◇ **drop something in somebody's lap** to become or make something somebody's responsibility ◇ **in the lap of luxury** in great luxury and comfort ◇ **in the lap of the gods** beyond human control or influence

lap[2] /lap/ *n* **1 ONE CIRCUIT OF A TRACK** a single circuit of a racetrack or running track or one length of a swimming pool **2 STAGE** a phase in an extended project, enterprise, or journey **3 OVERLAPPING PART** an overlapping part of something **4 LENGTH GOING ONCE ROUND A REEL** a length of fabric, thread, or rope that goes once round a roller, drum, or reel **5 POLISHING DISC** a rotating disc for cutting or polishing something such as glass or gemstones ■ *v* (**laps, lapping, lapped**) **1** *vt* **PASS COMPETITORS BY A COMPLETE CIRCUIT** to overtake a competitor on a racetrack or running track after having completed at least one circuit more than he or she has **2** *vi* **COMPLETE ONE TRACK CIRCUIT** to run one complete circuit around a track **3** *vt* **WRAP IN** to enfold or enwrap somebody in something (*literary; often passive*) **4** *vti* **OVERLAP** to overlap something (*literary*) **5** *vt* **POLISH OR CUT HARD SURFACES** to polish or cut something hard such as glass, metal, or gemstones **6** *vt* **FORM FIBRES INTO A BAND** to arrange fibres so that they lie one against the other and form a band [14C. < LAP[1].] —**lapper** *n*

lap[3] /lap/ *vti* (**laps, lapping, lapped**) **1 DRINK WITH THE TONGUE** to drink a liquid by scooping it into the mouth with the tongue **2 WASH GENTLY AGAINST A SURFACE** to flow or splash gently against a surface ■ *n* **1 DRINKING WITH TONGUE** the action of drinking liquid by scooping small amounts of it into the mouth with the tongue **2 SOUND OF MOVING LIQUID** the sound of a liquid gently flowing or splashing against something **3** *S Africa* **RAG** a rag or small piece of cloth [Old English *lapian* < Germanic] —**lapper** *n*

lap up *v* **1** *vti* = **lap**[3] *v.* 1 **2** *vt* to drink or eat something enthusiastically **3** *vt* to enjoy something eagerly and uncritically

La Palma /la paálmə/ one of the Canary Islands, Spain. Population: 82,183 (1995). Area: 725 sq. km/280 sq. mi.

laparoscope /láppərə skōp/ *n* an instrument in the shape of a tube that is inserted through the abdominal wall to give an examining doctor a view of the internal organs

laparoscopy /láppə róskəpi/ (*plural* **-pies**) *n* examination of the internal organs of the abdomen using a laparoscope [Mid-19C. < Greek *lapara* 'flank'.] —**laparoscopic** /láppərə skóppik/ *adj* —**laparoscopist** *n*

laparotomy /láppə róttəmi/ (*plural* **-mies**) *n* a surgical incision through the abdominal wall made to allow investigation of an abdominal organ or diagnosis of an abdominal disorder [Mid-19C. < Greek *lapara* 'flank'.]

La Paz /la páz/ capital of Bolivia, in the western part of the country. Population: 711,036 (1992).

lap belt *n* a safety belt that is fitted to the seat of a motor vehicle and fastens across the lap

lapboard /láp bawrd/ *n* a thin flat board that is laid across the knees to serve as a table or writing surface

lap-chart *n* a record of each lap made by a motor vehicle in a race, showing each vehicle's exact position

lap dancer *n* a striptease artist who dances erotically close to or in the lap of a customer —**lap dancing** *n*

lapdog /láp dog/ *n* **1** a small gentle-natured dog **2** a person who unthinkingly obeys somebody else's command, especially in an organization or institution

lapel /lə pél/ *n* either of the two folded-back front edges of a jacket that are continuous with the collar [Mid-17C. Diminutive of LAP[1] 'part of a garment that projects'.] —**lapelled** *adj*

lapidary /láppidəri/ *adj* **1 ENGRAVED ON STONE** engraved in stone or on a gemstone **2 OF ENGRAVING GEMSTONES** relating to the art of engraving gemstones **3 DIGNIFIED AND ELEGANT** careful, elegant, and dignified in style (*formal*) ■ *n* (*plural* **-ies**) **CUTTER OF PRECIOUS STONES** an expert cutter, polisher, or engraver of gemstones [14C. < Latin *lapidarius* 'of stone' < *lapid-* 'stone'.]

lapidate /láppi dayt/ (**-dates, -dating, -dated**) *vt* (*literary*) **1** to throw stones at somebody **2** to stone somebody to death, especially as a punishment for wrongdoing [Early 17C. < Latin *lapidare* < *lapid-* 'stone'.] —**lapidation** /láppi dáysh'n/ *n*

lapis lazuli /láppiss lázzyo͞o lī, -li/ *n* a deep blue semi-precious stone containing lazurite. Use: jewellery. ■ *adj* of the same deep brilliant blue as lapis lazuli [< Latin *lapis* 'stone' + medieval Latin *lazuli* 'of lapis lazuli' < Persian *lāžward* 'lapis lazuli']

lap joint *n* a joint made by overlapping the ends of two parts or pieces and fastening them together —**lap-jointed** *adj*

Laplace /laa pláss/, **Pierre Simon** (1749–1827) French astronomer and mathematician

Lapland /láplənd/ Arctic region extending across the

northern parts of Norway, Sweden, Finland, and the Kola Peninsula of Russia —**Laplander** *n*

La Plata /laa plaá tə/ capital of Buenos Aires Province, E Argentina. Population: 676,128 (1991).

lap of honour *n* an extra lap round a racetrack or running track run by the winner of a race or game to acknowledge the presence and applause of spectators

Lapp /lap/ *n* **1** an offensive term for a member of the Sami people **2** an offensive term for the language of the Sami people [Late 16C. < Swedish.] —**Lapp** *adj*

lapped joint *n* CONSTR = **lap joint**

lappet /láppit/ *n* **1** a loose fold or flap of fabric on a garment **2** a lobe or hanging flap of flesh such as a cow's dewlap or the wattle on a bird's head [15C. < LAP[1] + -ET.]

lappet moth *n* a large purplish-brown moth whose furry larvae have flaps along their sides. *Gastropacha quercifolia*.

lap pool *n* a pool designed for swimming laps, sometimes with a pump to create a current against which to swim

lap robe *n US, Can* a small rug that wraps round the knees

lapsang souchong /láp sang-/ *n* a large-leafed type of black Chinese tea with a smoky flavour [Late 19C. *Lapsang* an invention.]

lapse /laps/ *n* **1 ERROR** a momentary fault or failure in behaviour or morality **2 GAP IN CONTINUITY** a break in the continuity of something **3 PERIOD** a passage of time **4 FAILURE TO ACT IN TIME** a failure to exercise a right within a specified period of time, e.g. the failure to buy a property before the termination of an option to buy ■ *vi* (**lapses, lapsing, lapsed**) **1 GRADUALLY COME TO A STOP** to gradually come to an end or stop doing something **2 DECLINE** to decline in value, quality, or conduct ○ *Their standards have lapsed.* **3 LOSE SIGNIFICANCE** to decline gradually, becoming less important **4 BECOME VOID** to become null and void through disuse, negligence, or death **5** = **elapse** *v.* [14C. < Latin *lapsus* 'falling, failure' < the past participle of *labi* 'fall'.] —**lapsable** *adj* —**lapser** *n* ◇ **a lapse from grace** a failure in moral conduct or religious belief

lapse into *vi* **1** to revert to a previous state, especially of quiet or inactivity **2** to revert to a previous habit or way of life, often an undesirable one

lapsed /lapst/ *adj* **1** no longer committed to something, especially religious faith or observance **2** expired or terminated

lapse rate *n* the rate at which the temperature of the atmosphere falls as altitude increases

lapstrake /láp strayk/ *adj* SHIPPING = **clinker-built** ■ *n* a boat built with overlapping planks [Late 18C. < LAP[2] + STRAKE.]

Laptev Sea /láptef-/ arm of the Arctic Ocean off N Siberian Russia. Area: 714,000 sq. km/276,000 sq. mi.

⚡**laptop** /láp top/ *n* a small portable personal computer, often battery operated, usually consisting of a case that opens to reveal a screen in the upper part and a keyboard in the lower part

Laputan /lə pyoót'n/ *adj* concentrating on absurdly impractical ideas or projects, often to the exclusion of things that need to be done [Mid-19C. < *Laputa* (in Jonathan Swift's *Gulliver's Travels*), whose inhabitants were given to unrealistic hopes.]

⚡**lapware** /láp wair/ *n* software for children that includes simple text and animation for telling stories

lapwing /láp wing/ (*plural* **-wings** *or* **-wing**) *n* a bird of the plover family that has a long crest and spurs and is noted for its shrill cry and erratic flight. Genus: *Vanellus*. [Old English *hleapewince* (altered by folk etymology) 'leaping from side to side' < LEAP + assumed ancestor of WINK]

~~**laquer**~~ incorrect spelling of **lacquer**

Lara /laárə/, **Brian** (*b.* 1969) Trinidadian cricketer

larboard /laárbərd/ *n* the port or left side of a vessel (*archaic*) [Late 16C. Alteration of *laddeborde* 'loading side'.]

~~**larcency**~~ incorrect spelling of **larceny**

larceny /laárss'ni/ *n* the unlawful taking and removal of another person's property (*dated*) [15C. < Anglo-Norman, < Latin *latrocinium* 'theft' < *latro* 'thief' < Greek *latron* 'pay, wages'.] —**larcener** *n* —**larcenist** *n* —**larcenous** *adj* —**larcenously** *adv*

larch /laarch/ (*plural* **larches** *or* **larch**) *n* **1** a deciduous tree of the pine family with clusters of needle-shaped leaves and erect cones. Genus: *Larix*. **2** the durable wood of the larch tree [Mid-16C. < Middle High German *larche* < Latin *larix*.]

lard /laard/ *n* **WHITE COOKING FAT** white, slightly soft, pork fat. Use: cooking, in ointments and perfumes. ■ *v* **1** *vti* **ADD LARD TO MEAT BEFORE COOKING** to thread strips of fat or fatty bacon through holes made in a lean cut of meat to keep the meat moist while cooking **2** *vt* **INCLUDE EXTRA WORDS** to include an unnecessary or undesirable amount of additional material in a speech or piece of writing [14C. < French *lard* 'bacon' < Latin *lar(i)dum*.] —**lardy** *adj*

larder /laárdər/ *n* a cool place, especially a small room or large cupboard, used for storing food [13C. < Anglo-Norman, < Latin *lar(i)dum* 'lard'.]

larding-needle *n* a long thick metal needle that grips one end of a strip of fat to allow it to be threaded through lean meat to keep it moist while cooking

Lardner /laárdnər/, **Ring** (1885–1933) US humorist and writer. Full name **Ringgold Wilmer Lardner**

lardy cake *n* a small, sweet, usually square or oblong cake made with yeast dough folded and rolled with lard, fruit, and sugar

Laredo /lə reédō/ city in S Texas, on the border with Mexico. Population: 175,783 (1998 estimate).

lares and penates *npl* **1** the household deities of the ancient Romans. The lares were believed to protect the household from danger, while the penates were believed to bring wealth. **2** a family's treasured or valuable possessions (*dated*) [Late 16C. < Latin.]

large /laarj/ (**larger, largest**) *adj* **1 VERY BIG** comparatively big in size, number, or quantity, or bigger in size, number, or quantity than is usual or expected **2 OF TALL HEAVY BUILD** tall and well-built, heavy set, broad, or overweight **3 SPACIOUS** occupying a comparatively big space or a bigger space than is usual or expected ○ *a large house* **4 IMPORTANT** significant or general in scope, extent, or effect ○ *a large view of the subject* **5 GENEROUS** generous in spirit or attitude **6 FAVOURABLE** blowing in a favourable direction ○ *a large wind* [12C. Via Old French < Latin *larga*, feminine of *largus* 'abundant'.] —**largeness** *n* ◇ **at large 1** as a widely based and general group of people **2** escaped or free and possibly dangerous ◇ **by and large** speaking generally ◇ **large it, live large** to live or celebrate in an extravagant way (*informal*)

USAGE by and large or **by in large**? Do not substitute the incorrect form *'by in large'* for ***by and large***.

large calorie *n* = **calorie**

large copper *n* a common butterfly with black and orange markings on its wings. Native to: Europe. *Lycaena dispar*.

large-handed *adj* very generous or magnanimous —**large-handedness** *n*

large-hearted *adj* generous, kind, or understanding —**large-heartedness** *n*

large intestine *n* the end section of the alimentary canal reaching from ileum to anus, and consisting of the caecum, colon, and rectum. Its function is to extract water and form faeces.

largely /laárjli/ *adv* **1** for the most part or mainly **2** on a big or grand scale

large-minded *adj* characterized by a liberal attitude —**large-mindedly** *adv* —**large-mindedness** *n*

large-print *adj* set in type that is bigger than normal for the benefit of partially sighted readers ○ *a large-print book*

larger-than-life *adj* very confident, impressive, flamboyant, and likely to attract attention (*not hyphenated after verbs*)

large-scale *adj* **1** comparatively big in size and showing a lot of detail **2** extensive in scope or scale

⚡**large-scale integration** *n* the process of integrating a large number of circuits, often several thousand, on a silicon chip

largesse /laar jéss/, **largess** *n* **1 GENEROSITY** the generous giving of gifts, money, or favours **2 GIFTS** the gifts, money, or favours given as a result of somebody's largesse **3 LIBERALITY** generosity or liberality, especially in spirit or attitude [13C. Via French < Latin *largus* 'abundant'.]

Large White *n* a large white pig of a UK breed raised for its meat

larghetto /laar géttō/ *adv* at a fairly slow tempo, but slightly faster than largo (*musical direction*) ■ *n* (*plural* **-tos**) a larghetto movement or musical piece [Early 18C. < Italian, 'little largo' < *largo* 'broad'.] —**larghetto** *adj*

largish /laárjish/ *adj* quite big, rather than enormous

largo /laárgō/ *adv* at a fairly slow and broad tempo, more slowly than lento but faster than grave (*musical direction*) ■ *n* (*plural* **-gos**) a largo movement or musical piece [Late 17C. < Italian, 'broad'.] —**largo** *adj*

lari[1] /laári/ (*plural* **-ri** *or* **-ris**) *n* see table at **currency** [Late 20C. < Georgian.]

lari[2] /laári/ *n* MONEY = **laari**

lariat /lárri ət/ *n US, Can* **1** = **lasso** *n.* **2** a tethering rope, especially one used to hold a grazing animal in one place [Mid-19C. < Spanish *la reata* 'the rope' < *reatar* 'tie again' < Latin *aptare* 'adjust'.]

Larissa /lə ríssə/ *n* a small inner natural satellite of Neptune, of an irregular shape and discovered in 1989 by Voyager 2

lark[1] /laark/ *n* a small songbird with brownish plumage, found worldwide and noted for its song. Family: Alaudidae. [Old English *lāferce*, earlier *lǣwerce*] ◇ **get up** *or* **rise** *or* **be up with the lark** to get up from bed very early

lark[2] /laark/ *n* **1 MISCHIEVOUS ADVENTURE** adventurous or risky fun **2 INNOCENT FUN** a carefree or harmless piece of fun **3 AREA OF ACTIVITY** an activity, pastime, or job referred to as though it is not being taken very seriously (*informal*) ■ *vi* **1 HAVE FUN** to have fun, especially in a boisterous or good-humoured way **2 ACT MISCHIEVOUSLY** to behave in a mischievous, annoying, or irresponsible manner [Early 19C. < ?] —**larker** *n* —**larkiness** *n* —**larkish** *adj* —**larkishness** *n* —**larky** *adj*

lark about, lark around *vi* to have fun in a playful, childish, or irresponsible way

Larkin /laárkin/, **Philip** (1922–85) British poet and jazz critic

larkspur /laárk spur/ *n* a delphinium plant. Flowers: pink, white, or blue, in spikes. Genus: *Delphinium*. [Late 16C. < the resemblance of the spurred flowers to the lark's long hind claws.]

Larne /laarn/ town in E Northern Ireland. Population: 30,000 (1995).

La Rochelle /la ro shél/ seaport in W France, on the Bay of Biscay. Population: 76,584 (1999).

Larousse /la roóss/, **Pierre** (1817–75) French lexicographer

larrigan /lárrigən/ *n* a knee-high boot with the leg part made of oiled leather, worn especially by lumberjacks, trappers, and woodsmen [Late 19C. < ?]

larrikin /lárrikin/ *n ANZ* **1 UNCONVENTIONAL PERSON** an unconventional or nonconformist person, especially in public life **2 SOMEBODY MISCHIEVOUS** a mischievous or playful person (*informal*) **3 LOUT** somebody regarded as behaving in an unruly or disruptive manner (*dated insult*) [Mid-19C. < ?]

larrup /lárrəp/ *vt* to beat or flog a person or animal ■ *n* a blow, especially one delivered with a lot of force [Early 19C. < ?] —**larruper** *n*

Larson /laárss'n/, **Gary** (*b.* 1950) US cartoonist

larva /laárvə/ (*plural* **-vae** /-vee/) *n* **1** the wingless immature worm-shaped form of many insects that develops into a pupa or chrysalis before becoming an adult insect **2** the immature, early-stage form of frogs and other animals that undergo marked changes during metamorphosis [Mid-17C. < Latin, 'ghost'.] —**larval** *adj*

larvicide /laárvi sīd/ *n* a chemical used to kill larvae —**larvicidal** /laárvi sīd'l/ *adj*

Larwood /laár wŏod/, **Harold** (1904–95) British cricketer

laryng- *prefix* = **laryngo-** (*before vowels*)

laryngeal /lə rínjəl, -rínji əl, lárrin jeé əl/ *adj* **1** belonging to, relating to, situated in, or affecting the larynx **2** describes a speech sound produced in the region of the larynx [Late 18C. < modern Latin *laryngeus* < *laryng-* 'larynx' < Greek *larugg-*.] —**laryngeally** *adv*

laryngectomy /lárrin jéktəmi/ (*plural* **-mies**) *n* the surgical removal of all or part of the larynx

larynges plural of **larynx**

laryngitis /lárrin jítiss/ *n* inflammation of the larynx, usually accompanied by hoarseness and coughing —**laryngitic** /-jíttik/ *adj*

laryngo- *prefix* larynx ○ *laryngotomy* [Via modern Latin < Greek *larugg-*, stem of *larugx*]

laryngology /lárring góllәji/ *n* a branch of medicine dealing with diseases and conditions of the larynx and vocal cords —**laryngologic** /lә ríng gә lójjik/ *adj* —**laryngologically** *adv* —**laryngologist** *n*

laryngopharynx /lә ríng gō fárringks/ (*plural* **-pharynges** /-fә rín jeez/ *or* **-pharynxes**) *n* the part of the throat immediately behind the voice box or larynx, and extending downwards to the top of the gullet or oesophagus

laryngoscope /lә ríng gә skōp/ *n* a medical instrument consisting of a short metal or plastic tube fitted with a tiny light bulb, used when examining the larynx

laryngoscopy /lárring góskәpi/ (*plural* **-pies**) *n* an examination of the entrance to, or interior of, the larynx, for the purpose of diagnosis or to facilitate the passage of a tube through the larynx —**laryngoscopic** /lә ríng gә skóppik/ *adj*—**laryngoscopically** *adv*—**laryngoscopist** *n*

laryngotomy /lárring góttәmi/ (*plural* **-mies**) *n* a surgical procedure in which an incision is made in the larynx

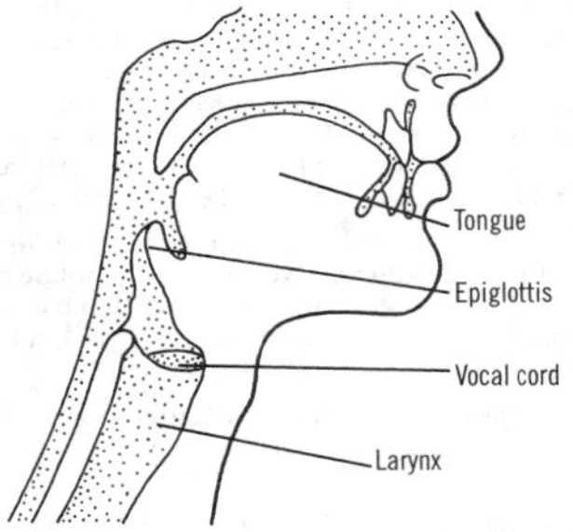

Larynx

larynx /lárringks/ (*plural* **larynges** /lә rín jeez/ *or* **larynxes**) *n* the cartilaginous box-shaped part of the respiratory tract between the level of the root of the tongue and the top of the trachea [Late 16C. Via modern Latin < Greek *larugx*.]

lasagne /lә zánnyә, -sánn-, -zaán-/ (*plural* **-gnes** *or* **-gne**), **lasagna** (*plural* **-gnas** *or* **-gne**) *n* **1** thin flat sheets of fresh or dried pasta **2** a dish of Italian origin consisting of alternate layers of lasagne and filling [Mid-19C. < Italian, plural of *lasagna* < Latin *lasanum* 'cooking vessel'.]

La Salle /lә sál/ city in north-central Illinois. Population: 9,717 (1990).

lascar /láskәr/, **Lascar** *n* a South Asian or Southeast Asian sailor, army servant, or artilleryman (*dated*) [Early 17C. < Persian, Urdu *laškarī* 'soldier' < *laškar* 'army, camp'.]

Lascaux /láskō/ site of an underground cave in SW France that contains outstanding examples of Stone Age art

lascivious /lә sívvi әss/ *adj* **1** showing a desire for, or unseemly interest in, sex **2** provoking or exciting lust [15C. < late Latin *lasciviosus* < Latin *lascivus* 'lustful'.] —**lasciviously** *adv* —**lasciviousness** *n*

Lasdun /lázdәn/, **Sir Denys** (1914–2001) British architect

lase /layz/ (**lases, lasing, lased**) *vi* to emit the type of single-wavelength radiation produced by a laser [Mid-20C. Back-formation < LASER.]

laser /láyzәr/ *n* a device that utilizes the ability of certain substances to absorb electromagnetic energy and re-radiate it as a highly focused beam of synchronized single-wavelength radiation [Mid-20C. Acronym < *Light Amplification by Stimulated Emission of Radiation*.]

⚡**laser card** *n* COMPUT = **smart card**

⚡**laser disk** *n* COMPUT = **optical disk**

⚡**laser printer** *n* a computer printer using a focused laser beam to place an image on a photosensitive drum, which uses electrostatic charge to print the image

laser ring gyro *n* a navigation system for aircraft that uses measurement of laser light in a closed circuit

laser welding *n* the process of using a laser to join tissues together in order to seal up wounds

lash[1] /lash/ *n* **1 STROKE WITH A WHIP** a stroke with a whip or some other long flexible object, often one of several given as a punishment **2 EYELASH** an eyelash **3 MOVEMENT LIKE A WHIP** a movement like that of a whip being cracked ○ *The lion gave a lash of its tail.* **4 END OF A WHIP** the flexible end of a whip **5 SEVERE SCOLDING** a severe reproof or verbal attack ○ *He felt the full lash of his father's tongue.* **6 IMPACT** a strong or powerful, often continuous, impact of something, especially a natural element, against a surface ○ *the lash of waves onto the beach* ■ *v* **1** *vti* **SMASH ONTO** to have a strong or powerful, often continuous, impact on a surface ○ *Heavy seas lashed the shore.* **2** *vti* **CRITICIZE** to criticize somebody or something severely ○ *She lashed into her critics.* **3** *vt* **WHIP** to hit somebody or something with a whip or an object like a whip, often repeatedly as a form of punishment ○ *Prisoners were lashed severely.* **4** *vti* **FLICK TO AND FRO** to flick something from side to side sharply so that it moves like a whip, or move in this way ○ *The cat lashed its tail angrily.* **5** *vt* **INCITE PEOPLE** to encourage strong emotion such as anger in others, especially in a crowd ○ *The fans had lashed themselves into a fever of enthusiasm.* —**lasher** *n*

lash out *vi* **1 SUDDENLY ATTACK VERBALLY** to attack somebody or something verbally and suddenly **2 SUDDENLY ATTACK PHYSICALLY** to start suddenly to attack somebody or something with uncontrolled movements **3 SPEND A LOT OF MONEY** to spend money extravagantly on something (*informal*)

lash[2] /lash/ *vt* to tie something tightly or securely to another object [15C. < ?] —**lasher** *n*

lashing[1] /láshing/ *n* **1** a beating with a whip or something resembling a whip **2** a severe rebuke or critical attack

lashing[2] /láshing/ *n* rope, string, or cord used for securing things

lashings /láshingz/ *npl* generous or plentiful amounts of something

lash-up *n* an object hastily made or put together, especially in order to meet emergency needs

lasket /láskit/ *n* a loop on a sail for fastening an extra sail [Early 18C. < ?]

Las Palmas /las pálmәss/ seaport and capital of Las Palmas Province, NE Grand Canary Island, Spain. Population: 342,030 (1991).

La Spezia /la spétsi ә/ naval base and capital of La Spezia Province, Liguria Region, NW Italy. Population: 103,008 (1990).

lass /lass/ *n* **1 YOUNG WOMAN** a girl or young woman (*sometimes offensive*) **2 GIRLFRIEND** a girlfriend or sweetheart **3** *N England, Scotland* **WOMAN** a woman of any age [14C. Probably related to Old Norse *laskura* 'unmarried'.]

Lassa fever /lássә-/ *n* an infectious, often fatal, viral disease of West Africa marked by high fever, muscle pain, ulcers of the mucous membranes, headaches, haemorrhaging, and heart and kidney failure [Late 20C. After *Lassa*, village in Nigeria.]

Lassalle /la sál/, **Ferdinand** (1825–64) German politician

Lassen Volcanic National Park /lássәn-/ national park in NE California. Its main feature is the volcanic Lassen Peak, 3,187 m/10,457 ft high. Area: 430 sq. km/166 sq. mi.

Lasseter /lássәtәr/, **Harold Bell** (1880–1931) Australian prospector. Born **Lewis Hubert Lasseter**

lassie /lássi/ *n N England, Scotland* (*informal*) **1 WOMAN** a girl or young woman (*sometimes offensive*) **2 GIRLFRIEND** a girlfriend or sweetheart **3 DAUGHTER** a daughter

lassitude /lássi tyood/ *n* a state of weariness accompanied by listlessness or apathy [15C. Via French < Latin *lassitudo* < *lassus* 'weary'.]

lasso /lә sóo, la-, lássō/ *n* (*plural* **-sos**) a long stiff piece of rope or cord with a sliding noose at one end, used especially for catching horses and cattle ■ *vt* (**-sos, -soing, -soed**) to use a lasso or other length of rope to catch a horse, cow, or other animal [Mid-18C. < American English pronunciation of Spanish *lazo* < Latin *laqueus* 'noose'.] —**lassoer** *n*

last[1] /laast/ CORE MEANING: a grammatical word indicating that something is the most recent or final of all ○ (adj) *She was married last April.* ○ (adj) *John turned and took a last look at the band.* ○ (adv) *Allow me to apologize for the uncomfortable circumstances under which we last met.* ○ (adv) *He got to the meeting last.* ○ (pron) *Her new album's even better than the last.*

1 *adj, pron* **MOST RECENT** occurring most recently ○ (adj) *I saw him last Tuesday.* ○ (pron) *This flood may turn out to be even worse than the last.* **2** *adj, pron* **AFTER ALL THE OTHERS** being or occurring after all the others ○ (adj) *He is believed to be the last person to see her before she left.* ○ (pron) *Your first complaint may well be your last.* **3** *adj, pron* **ONLY REMAINING** the final or only person, thing, or part remaining ○ (adj) *This machine just ate my last pound coin!* ○ (pron) *Here – finish up the last of the cake.* **4** *adj, pron* **LEAST SUITABLE** least suitable, appropriate, or likely ○ (adj) *She's the last person we want on this project.* ○ (pron) *I am the last to criticize you in any way.* **5** *adj* **RELATING TO THE END** relating to the end of somebody's life **6** *adv* **MOST RECENTLY** on the most recent occasion ○ *When I last spoke to them they sounded fine.* **7** *adv* **AFTER ALL THE OTHERS** after all the others in a series or order **8** *adv* **FINALLY** as the final point ○ *Last, I'd like to mention all the people who helped to make this evening a success.* **9** *n* **FINAL MOMENT** the final moment, especially of life ○ *She remained cheerful to the last.* [Old English *latost* (adv.) 'after all the others' < Germanic] ◇ **at last** finally or in the end ○ *I've found you at last – I've been looking everywhere.* ◇ **at long last** eventually, after a long delay or many difficulties ○ *They fought the case for years and at long last got some compensation.* ◇ **breathe your last** to die (*literary*) ○ *I was by her side when she breathed her last.* ◇ **every last** everything without exception ○ *They ate it up, every last piece of it.* ◇ **last but not least** the final thing to be mentioned but important nevertheless ○ *And of course, last but not least, we thank the staff of customer relations.* ◇ **the last of somebody** *or* **something** **1** the last remaining person, thing, or part of something, or the last in a sequence ○ *That's the last of the bread – I'll get some more tomorrow.* **2** somebody's final contact with or news of somebody or something ○ *You haven't heard the last of this – I'm going to complain.*

last[2] /laast/ *vti* **1** to continue to exist or happen for a period of time ○ *The festival lasted for three hours.* ○ *The voyage lasted eight days.* **2** to continue to be used or available for a period of time ○ *The provisions lasted for ten days.* ○ *The fruit lasted us a week.* [Old English *læstan* 'last, follow' < Germanic]

last out *vt* **1** to be an adequate supply for a particular length of time ○ *I think we've got enough food to last out the week.* **2** to survive for a particular length of time ○ *The vet said she didn't think Prince would last out the night.*

last[3] /laast/ *n* a wooden or metal block shaped like a human foot that a shoemaker or cobbler uses for making and repairing footwear [Old English *læste* < *lāst* 'sole of the foot, footprint' < Germanic, 'follow']

last[4] /laast/ *n* a unit of measurement that has different values in different contexts including the values of 80 bushels and two tons [Old English *hlæst* 'load' < Germanic]

last-born *adj* youngest in a particular family

last call *n US* a bartender's request for last drink orders before closing time (*informal*) ◊ **last orders**

last-ditch *adj* done or taken when all other options have been exhausted

last-gasp *adj* done as a last measure when all other options have failed

last-in, first-out *n* **1** a method of accounting in which it is assumed that the most recently purchased items in an inventory are the first to be sold **2** the dismissal of staff beginning with those who were employed most recently, used as a way of reducing personnel (*informal*)

lasting /laásting/ *adj* continuing for a very long time or indefinitely ■ *n* a strong durable twill fabric. Use: shoe uppers. —**lastingly** *adv* —**lastingness** *n*

Last Judgment *n* RELIG = **Judgment Day**

lastly /laástli/ *adv* as the final thing at the end of a series

last minute *n* the latest time that it is possible to do something and still be in time —**last-minute** *adj*

last name *n* = **surname**

last orders *npl, interj* the final opportunity to buy drinks before a pub, bar, or other place selling alcohol closes. ◊ **last call**

last post *n* **1** a bugle call given to signal the end of the day at a UK military establishment and the lowering of the flag at last light **2** a bugle call that is given at a UK military funeral

last resort *n* something tried or done when everything else has failed

last rites *npl* 1 in the Roman Catholic Church, religious rites performed for somebody who is close to death 2 in Christianity, religious rites accompanying a burial or funeral

last spike *n US* the final section completing a rail line, symbolized by the final spike driven to secure the rails

last straw *n* a minor annoyance that, because it comes at the end of a series of other misfortunes, makes a situation unbearable [< the fable of the camel whose back was broken by the last straw added to its load]

Last Supper *n* the last meal that Jesus Christ ate with his disciples before his crucifixion, commemorated by Christians in the Communion ceremony

last thing *adv* immediately before going to bed for the night

last time *adv Malaysia, Singapore* during or at an earlier period, but no longer ○ *Last time I lived in Ipoh.* [Probably translation < Chinese]

last word *n* 1 FINAL REMARK IN A DISCUSSION the final thing to be said, especially at the end of an argument, disagreement, or discussion 2 ULTIMATE DECISION the final decision on something 3 BEST the best of its kind ○ *the last word in convenience*

Las Vegas /laas váygəss/ city in S Nevada. Population: 404,288 (1998 estimate).

lat[1] /laat/ (*plural* **lati** /látti/ *or* **lats**) *n* see table at **currency** [Late 20C. < Latvian, shortening of *Latvija* 'Latvia'.]

lat[2] /lat/ *n* a latissimus dorsi (*informal*) [Shortening]

lat. *abbr* latitude

Lat. *abbr* 1 Latin 2 Latvia

Latakia /la táki ə/ seaport and capital of Latakia Governorate, NW Syria. Population: 311,784 (1994).

latch /lach/ *n* 1 DEVICE FOR KEEPING DOORS SHUT a device for holding a door, gate, or other opening closed consisting of a movable or liftable bar that drops into a hole or notch 2 DOOR LOCK a door lock that needs a key to be opened from the outside but not the inside ■ *vt* LOCK SOMETHING WITH A LATCH to close or lock something with a latch [Old English *læccan* 'to grasp' < Indo-European]

latch on *vi* to finally grasp something or understand (*informal*)

latch onto *vt* 1 to remain constantly in somebody's company even if the person would prefer other company or solitude 2 to become particularly interested in something

latchkey /lách kee/ (*plural* **-keys**) *n* a key for lifting a latch, especially one on an outside door or gate

latchkey child *n* a child who returns from school to an empty home because the adults in the family are still at work

latchstring /lách string/ *n* a string attached to a latch and passed through a hole in a door to allow somebody to open it from the other side

late /layt/ *adj* (**later, latest**) 1 AFTER AN EXPECTED TIME happening or arriving after an expected or arranged time ○ *Hurry up or we'll be late!* 2 AFTER THE USUAL TIME happening or done after the normal or usual time ○ *a late lunch* 3 NEAR THE END OF A PERIOD near the end of a particular period of time ○ *The meeting is scheduled for late morning.* 4 INTO THE NIGHT well into the evening or night ○ *It's late – time for bed.* 5 ⚠ DEAD having died, especially fairly recently ○ *my late grandfather.* 6 UP UNTIL RECENTLY having recently, but no longer, done something, lived somewhere, or belonged to a group or organization ○ *That reporter, late of the European bureau, is now moving to Southeast Asia.* 7 DONE TOWARDS THE END OF A CAREER produced near the end of somebody's career or life ○ *a late Degas* ■ *adv* (**later, latest**) 1 NOT ON TIME after an expected or arranged time ○ *He arrived late.* 2 BEYOND THE USUAL TIME after the usual or normal time ○ *She had to work late.* 3 NEAR THE END OF A PERIOD towards the end of a period of time ○ *These birds tend to nest late in the year.* 4 WELL INTO EVENING at or until a point well into the evening or night ○ *Their flight is due late on Friday.* 5 RECENTLY relatively recently ○ *She didn't pack her bags until as late as yesterday.* [Old English *læt* < Indo-European, 'to let go'] —**lateness** *n* ◇ **of late** recently

SYNONYMS See *dead.*

USAGE When to use **late** for 'the deceased': In obituaries or death announcements the person in question is hardly ever described as *the late...* . Nor is it usual for somebody who died centuries ago to be described that way. The word's purpose is to serve as a reminder that the person in question is no longer living. In an obituary, that much is obvious, so *late* is not needed. Nor is it needed in historical contexts, except to indicate that somebody was dead by a given time: *In 1553 Mary Tudor was entitled to the crown by her late father's testament.*

late blight *n* a disease of potatoes, caused by a fungus, in which both tubers and foliage decay

latecomer /láyt kummər/ *n* 1 a person who arrives late for an event 2 a recent participant or valuer of something ○ *a latecomer to Bach*

late developer *n* a child whose potential in some or all aspects of school work develops later than is the case for the majority of his or her contemporaries

lateen /lə teén/ *adj* describes a triangular sail hung on a yard attached to a small mast, or a ship with such a sail [Mid-16C. < French *(voile) latine* 'Latin (sail)' < Latin *Latinus* (see LATIN); because it was used in the Mediterranean.]

lateen-rigged *adj* using a lateen sail

late Greek *n* the form of Greek used from around the 3rd to the 9th centuries AD

late Hebrew *n* the form of Hebrew used from around the 12th to the 18th centuries AD

late Latin *n* the written form of Latin used from around the 3rd to the 7th centuries AD

lately /láytli/ *adv* within the last few days or weeks, or not too long ago

laten /láyt'n/ *vti* to grow late, or make something late

latency period *n* PSYCHOANAL = **latent period**

La Tène /la tén/ *adj* relating to an Iron-Age culture that flourished in Europe from the fifth to the first centuries BC [Late 19C. After *La Tène*, district in Switzerland.]

latent /láyt'nt/ *adj* 1 HIDDEN present or existing, but in an underdeveloped or unexpressed form 2 DORMANT dormant or undeveloped but able to develop normally under suitable conditions 3 PRESENT BUT UNEXPRESSED present in the unconscious but not consciously expressed [Early 17C. < Latin *latent-*, present participle of *latere* 'be hidden'.] —**latency** *n*

latent content *n* in psychoanalysis, the content of a dream that is hidden or repressed, and is represented in symbols

latent heat *n* (*symbol L*) the heat that is absorbed or emitted when a substance undergoes a physical phase change but that does not make the substance change temperature

latent image *n* the invisible image recorded on light-sensitive materials such as photographic film or paper but not yet developed

latent learning *n* learning that is not apparent when it occurs, but that can be inferred later from improved performance

latent period *n* 1 TIME BETWEEN STIMULUS AND RESPONSE the interval between the application of a stimulus and the start of a response 2 DISEASE INCUBATION PERIOD the incubation period of a disease 3 THEORETICAL CHILDHOOD DEVELOPMENTAL STAGE in Freudian theory, a period between five or six years of age and adolescence when sexual interest is suppressed

latent print *n* a fingerprint that is left at a crime scene and remains invisible until chemically treated

latent time *n* PHYSIOL = **latent period** *n.* 1

later /láytər/ comparative of **late** ■ *adv* after a particular period of time, the present time, or the time being discussed ■ *interj* used to say goodbye for now (*informal*)

lateral /láttərəl/ *adj* 1 AT THE SIDE belonging to, relating to, located at, or affecting the side 2 SIDEWAYS IN A CAREER involving transfer to a different position in an organization or career, but without greater status or advancement 3 RELATING TO LATERAL THINKING involving or relating to the use of lateral thinking 4 WITH AN INCOMPLETE OBSTRUCTION OF AIR describes a speech sound produced with the tip of the tongue touching the alveolar ridge so that air moves around the outside of one or both sides of the tongue. The only lateral sound in English is /l/. ■ *n* 1 PART AT THE SIDE a part, appendage, movement, or object at the side of something 2 LATERAL SPEECH SOUND a lateral speech sound such as /l/ in English [15C. < Latin *lateralis* < *later-* 'side'.] —**laterally** *adv*

lateralization /láttərə lī záysh'n/, **lateralisation** *n* the localization of the control centre for a particular function, e.g. speech, on the right or left side of the brain

lateral line *n* a line of sensory pores along the head and sides of fish and some amphibians that detect pressure, current variations, and vibrations

lateral thinking *n* a way of solving problems by unconventional or apparently illogical means rather than using a traditionally logical approach

laterite /láttə rīt/ *n* a reddish mixture of clayey iron and aluminium oxides and hydroxides formed by the weathering of basalt under humid, tropical conditions [Early 19C. < Latin *later* 'brick'.] —**lateritic** /láttə ríttik/ *adj*

latest /láytist/ superlative of **late** ■ *adj* newest, most recent, or most up-to-date ■ *n* the newest, most recent, or most up-to-date news, fashion, or version of something (*informal*)

late tackle *n* in a game such as football, a foul resulting from an attempt to tackle an opposing player after the ball has been passed

latex /láy teks/ (*plural* **-texes** *or* **-tices** /-ti seez/) *n* 1 a milky white liquid produced by some plants such as the rubber tree 2 a suspension of rubber or plastic (**polymer**) particles in water. Use: manufacture of emulsion paints, adhesives, other products. [Mid-17C. < Latin, 'liquid'.]

lath /laath, lath/ *n* 1 STRIP USED IN A FRAMEWORK one of the thin strips of wood used to form a framework to support plaster, tiles, or slates 2 SUPPORT FOR PLASTERING a sheet of metal or a framework of wire mesh used as a support for plasterwork 3 THIN STRIP OF WOOD a thin strip of wood, especially one used in the building trades ■ *vt* ATTACH LATHS TO to attach or nail laths to a surface before plastering, tiling, or fixing slates [Old English *lætt* < Germanic]

lathe[1] /layth/ *n* a machine for working wood or metal, in which the piece being worked is held and rotated while a cutting tool is applied to it ■ *vt* (**lathes, lathing, lathed**) to shape wood or metal using a lathe [14C. Probably < Old Danish *lad* 'stand, framework'.]

lathe[2] /layth/ *n* a former administrative division of the English county of Kent [Old English *læþ* < Germanic, 'land']

lather /laáthər, láthər/ *n* 1 SOAPY FROTH foam that is produced by soap or detergent used with water 2 SWEATY FROTH white foam produced during periods of extremely heavy sweating, especially by horses 3 AGITATED STATE a state of agitation or nervous anxiety (*informal*) ■ *v* 1 *vti* PRODUCE LATHER to produce a lather using a soap or detergent 2 *vt* COAT WITH LATHER to coat something with lather [Old English *læþor* < Indo-European, 'to wash'] —**lathery** *adj*

lathyrism /láthirizəm/ *n* a neurological disease of humans and domestic animals, caused by eating certain legumes and characterized by lack of strength in or inability to move the legs [Late 19C. < modern Latin *Lathyrus* < Greek *lathuros*, species of vetch.]

latices plural of **latex**

laticifer /la tíssifər/ *n* a duct that produces latex in some plants [Early 20C. < Latin *latici-* 'liquid'.] —**laticiferous** /látti síffərəss/ *adj*

latifundium /látti fúndi əm/ (*plural* **-a** /-ə/) *n* in ancient Rome, an agricultural estate, especially one that was worked by enslaved labourers [Mid-17C. < Latin, < *latus* 'broad' + *fundus* 'landed estate'.]

Latin /láttin/ *n* 1 ANCIENT ROMAN LANGUAGE the extinct Indo-European language of ancient Rome and its empire, adopted in medieval Europe as the language of education, culture, religion, and government 2 SOMEBODY FROM ANCIENT LATIUM somebody who came from ancient Latium in west central Italy 3 SOMEBODY SPEAKING A ROMANCE LANGUAGE somebody who speaks a language derived from Latin, especially somebody living in Latin America or S Europe ■ *adj* 1 OF LATIN relating to Latin 2 OF PEOPLE SPEAKING ROMANCE LANGUAGES relating to a people using a language derived from Latin, especially a people living in Latin America or in S Europe 3 OF THE ROMAN CATHOLIC CHURCH belonging or relating to the Roman Catholic Church 4 WRITTEN IN THE ROMAN ALPHABET written in or relating to the Roman alphabet [Pre-12C. < Latin *Latinus* 'of the people of Latium, Roman' < *Latium*, ancient region in Italy.]

Latina /la teénə/ *n US* a woman or girl of Latin American descent who comes from the United States [Mid-20C. < American Spanish, feminine of *Latino* (see LATINO).]

Latin alphabet *n* LING = **Roman alphabet**

Latin America 1 the entire western hemisphere south of the United States 2 those countries of the Americas that developed from the colonies of Spain, Portugal, and France —**Latin American** *adj, n*

Latinate /látti nayt/ *adj* derived from, relating to, or characteristic of Latin

Latin Church *n* CHR = **Roman Catholic Church**

Latin cross *n* an upright cross in which the lowest limb is longer than the other three, often associated with Christianity

Latinian /la tínni ən/ *n* a group of ancient Italic languages that included Latin —**Latinian** *adj*

Latinise *vt* = **Latinize**

Latinism /láttinizəm/ *n* a word or phrase borrowed from Latin

Latinist /láttinist/ *n* an expert in or student of Latin

Latinity /la tínnəti/ *n* a style or level of expertise in using Latin

Latinize /látti nīz/ (**-izes, -izing, -ized**), **Latinise** (**-ise, -ising, -ised**) *vt* 1 TRANSLATE INTO LATIN to translate something into Latin, or give a Latin form to something such as a name 2 TRANSCRIBE SOMETHING INTO THE ROMAN ALPHABET to transcribe words into the Roman alphabet from another alphabet 3 MAKE LIKE THE ROMAN CATHOLIC CHURCH to cause something to resemble the practices of the Roman Catholic Church 4 MAKE MORE ROMAN to make people adapt to Roman customs and styles —**Latinization** /látti nī záysh'n/ *n* —**Latinizer** *n*

Latin-Jazz *n* a form of jazz music that is a mixture of both Afro-Cuban music and Fusion

Latino /la teènō/ (*plural* **-nos**) *n* US 1 somebody who comes from a country of Latin America 2 somebody of Latin American descent who comes from the United States [Mid-20C. < American Spanish, < Spanish, 'Latin' < Latin *Latinus* (see LATIN).]

Latin Quarter area in central Paris, on the Left Bank of the River Seine

latish /láytish/ *adj* fairly late, or later than is desirable or expected ○ *a latish supper* ■ *adv* at a fairly late time, or later than is desirable or expected ○ *They arrived latish.*

latissimus dorsi /la tíssiməss dáwr sī/ (*plural* **latissimi dorsi** /- líssimee-/) *n* either of the two broad triangular muscles along the sides of the back [Shortening of modern Latin *musculus latissimus dorsi* 'broadest muscle of the back']

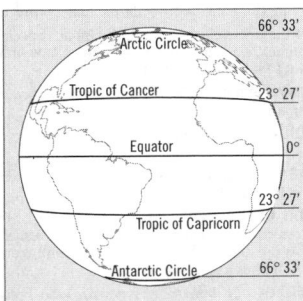
Latitude

latitude /látti tyood/ *n* 1 IMAGINARY LINE AROUND THE EARTH an imaginary line joining points on the Earth's surface that are all of equal distance north or south of the equator 2 AREA OF THE EARTH'S SURFACE a region of the Earth's surface near a particular latitude (*often plural*) ○ *snow showers in the northerly latitudes* 3 ROOM TO MANOEUVRE enough scope or leeway for some freedom of choice, action, or thinking ○ *It's a very creative job, allowing me a great deal of latitude.* 4 DEGREE OF TOLERANCE OF EXPOSURE ERROR the degree of over- or underexposure that light-sensitive material can accommodate and still provide an acceptable image [14C. < Latin *latitudo* 'breadth' < *latus* 'broad'.] —**latitudinal** /látti tyoódin'l/ *adj* —**latitudinally** *adv*

latitudinarian /látti tyoodi náiri ən/ *adj* 1 allowing some freedom in attitude, beliefs, behaviour, or interpretation, especially in religious matters 2 relating to a movement in the Church of England in the 17th century that accepted the authority of bishops but denied that

this was divine in origin [Mid-17C. < Latin *latitudin-*, stem of *latitudo* (see LATITUDE).] —**latitudinarian** *n*

latke /látkə/ *n* a fried flat cake of grated potato with beaten egg [Early 20C. < Yiddish, < Russian *latka* 'earthenware cooking vessel'.]

Latona /la tōnə/ *n* in Roman mythology, the mother of Apollo and Diana by Jupiter. Greek equivalent **Leto**

latosol /látta sol/ *n* a soil variety that is common in tropical or subtropical regions and is rich in iron and aluminium [Mid-20C. < LATERITE + Latin *solum* 'ground'.]

latrine /la treèn/ *n* a toilet, especially a communal one on a military base [13C. < Latin *latrina*, contraction of *lavatrina* < *lavare* 'wash'.]

-latry *suffix* worship ○ *iconolatry* [< Greek *latreia*]

latte /láttay/ *n* an espresso coffee with frothy steamed milk [< Italian, 'milk']

latter /láttər/ *n* SECOND OF TWO the second of two people or things ○ *She went out with Joe and Sam, eventually marrying the latter.* ■ *adj* 1 CLOSING near or relatively near the end of something ○ *spent the latter part of the day relaxing by the pool* 2 LATER more recent or more advanced in time ○ *In his latter years he became very forgetful.* [Old English *lætra* (adjective), *lator* (adverb), comparatives of *læt*, earlier form of LATE]

latter-day *adj* resembling a particular person or type of person from the past ○ *thought of himself as a latter-day Roosevelt*

Latter-Day Saint *n* a member of the Church of Jesus Christ of Latter-Day Saints, founded by Joseph Smith in 1830 in the United States and centred in Salt Lake City, Utah

latterly /láttərli/ *adv* recently or in the most recent period ○ *He was quite ill for a while, but latterly seems to have returned to normal.*

lattice /láttiss/ *n* 1 CRISSCROSS FRAMEWORK an interwoven open-mesh frame made by criss-crossing strips of wood, metal, or plastic to form a pattern 2 SOMETHING MADE FROM LATTICE something such as a door, gate, or fence that is made from or consists of a lattice 3 INTERWOVEN FORM a representation of a lattice framework, especially a heraldic one 4 ARRANGEMENT OF POINTS a regular geometrical arrangement of points or objects, e.g. the atoms in a crystal ■ *vti* PROVIDE A LATTICE to make, decorate something with, or provide a lattice [14C. < Old French *lattis* < *latte* 'lath' < Germanic.]

latticework /láttiss wurk/ *n* = **lattice** *n.* 1

Latvia

Latvia /látvi ə/ republic in NE Europe, bordering the Baltic Sea. Capital: Riga. Population: 2,421,163 (1997). Area: 63,700 sq. km/24,600 sq. mi.

Latvian /látvi ən/ *n* 1 somebody who comes from Latvia 2 the official language of Latvia, also spoken in W European Russia, belonging to the Balto-Slavonic branch of Indo-European. Native speakers: 3 million. —**Latvian** *adj*

laud /lawd/ *vt* PRAISE to glorify somebody or praise somebody highly ■ *n* 1 GREAT PRAISE high praise, acclaim, or glorification (*formal*) 2 SONG OF PRAISE a hymn of praise or glorification 3 MORNING PRAYER the first prayer of the day in some Christian churches, especially the Roman Catholic Church (*often plural*) [14C. < Old French *laude* < Latin *laud-* 'praise'.] —**laudatory** /láwdətəri/ *adj* —**lauder** *n*

SPELLCHECK Do not confuse **laud** with **lord**, which has a similar sound. Beware: your spellchecker will not catch this error.

Laud /lawd/, **William, Archbishop of Canterbury** (1573–1645) English cleric

Lauda /lówdə/, **Niki** (*b.* 1949) Austrian racing car driver

laudable /láwdəb'l/ *adj* admirable and worthy of praise —**laudability** /láwdə billəti/ *n* —**laudableness** *n* —**laudably** *adv*

laudanum /láwd'nəm/ *n* a solution of opium in alcohol. Use: formerly, for pain relief. [Mid-16C. < ?]

laugh /laaf/ *v* 1 *vti* MAKE SOUNDS EXPRESSING AMUSEMENT to make sounds from the throat while breathing out in short bursts or gasps as a way of expressing amusement 2 *vt* BRING TO PARTICULAR STATE BY LAUGHING to cause somebody or yourself to be in a particular state by laughing long and hard ○ *We both laughed ourselves silly.* 3 *vi* MOCK to mock somebody or something 4 *vi* SHOW CONTEMPT to express amusement, contempt, or disrespect for something ○ *laugh in the face of adversity* 5 *vi* MAKE A NOISE LIKE LAUGHTER to make a noise that sounds like somebody laughing (*refers to some birds and mammals*) ■ *n* 1 SOUND MADE WHEN LAUGHING a series of sounds made when somebody laughs 2 SOMETHING FUNNY OR ENJOYABLE a time of great fun and enjoyment, or something that gives fun and enjoyment (*informal*) ○ *had a real laugh with Bob and Patty* 3 SOMEBODY FUNNY a funny or entertaining person ○ *You'll like him; he's a good laugh.* [Old English *hlæhhan*] —**laugher** *n* ◇ **have the last laugh** to be proved right or successful after being treated with disbelief, lack of confidence, or scorn

laugh down *vt* to reject something with contemptuous laughter ○ *The entire committee laughed down the new design.*

laugh off *vt* to trivialize or treat as amusing something serious or important ○ *Later we laughed the incident off as just a silly mistake.*

laughable /láafəb'l/ *adj* so inadequate as to cause laughter or ridicule —**laughableness** *n* —**laughably** *adv*

laughing gas *n* CHEM = **nitrous oxide** (*informal*)

laughing jackass *n* a kookaburra (*dated*)

laughingly /láafingli/ *adv* 1 with laughter that shows amusement or contempt at something or somebody funny or ridiculous ○ *She laughingly dismissed this idea and changed the subject.* 2 in a form of words that is amusingly or contemptibly inappropriate ○ *what the brochure laughingly calls 'spacious accommodation'*

laughing stock *n* somebody whose behaviour has made him or her an object of ridicule or fun

laughter /láaftər/ *n* 1 the sound or an act of laughing 2 happiness or fun expressed by laughing [Old English *hleahtor*]

Laughton /láwt'n/, **Charles** (1899–1962) British-born US actor

laugh track *n* recorded laughter added to the soundtrack of a radio or television programme

Launceston /láwn stən/ 1 historic town in SW England. Population: 6,800 (1994). 2 port in N Tasmania, Australia. Population: 67,701 (1996).

launch¹ /lawnch/ *vt* 1 FIRE INTO THE AIR to send a rocket, missile, or spacecraft into the air or the upper atmosphere 2 PUT TO SEA to push or put a vessel into the water so that it is ready to sail 3 LAUNCH FOR THE FIRST TIME to send a newly built vessel into the water for the first time, usually with a special ceremony 4 BEGIN to begin an attack, campaign, investigation, or other carefully planned activity ○ *The police have launched an investigation.* 5 PUT ON SALE to put a new product on sale to the public and begin promoting it 6 THROW WITH GREAT FORCE to throw or propel something, especially forcefully ■ *n* 1 START FOR A NEW PRODUCT an occasion such as a party at which a new product is launched ○ *the launch of her new book* 2 TIME WHEN A ROCKET IS LAUNCHED the occasion when a rocket, missile, or spacecraft is launched 3 TIME WHEN A SHIP IS LAUNCHED the occasion when a boat or ship is launched, especially for the first time 4 START OF A CAMPAIGN the start of something, especially a carefully planned activity such as a military offensive, an investigation, or a campaign [14C. < Anglo-Norman *launcher*, variant of Old French *lancier* 'pierce' < *lance* (see LANCE).]

launch into *vt* to begin a particular activity suddenly and enthusiastically ○ *The professor launched into yet another of his theories about how dinosaurs became extinct.*

launch out *vi* to start doing something new or untried ■ to spend money extravagantly (*informal*)

launch² /lawnch/ *n* 1 **LARGE MOTORBOAT** a large powerful motorboat 2 **SMALL MOTORBOAT ON A LARGE SHIP** a small motorboat carried on a large ship 3 **LARGEST BOAT ON AN OLD WARSHIP** the largest boat formerly carried by a man-of-war [Late 17C. < Spanish *lancha* 'pinnace'.]

launch complex *n* a site containing the people and equipment needed for a rocket, missile, or spacecraft launch

launcher /láwnchər/ *n* a device or platform for firing something such as a rocket or missile

launch pad, launching pad *n* 1 a platform, usually in a launch complex, from which a rocket, missile, or spacecraft is launched 2 a starting point from which great or successful progress is made, e.g. in somebody's career

launch party *n* a party held to celebrate and to introduce a new book, author, book publisher, or retailer

launch shoe *n* a device on an aircraft used for launching a missile

launch vehicle *n* a rocket that is used to launch a spacecraft or satellite into space

launch window *n* the restricted period during which a rocket or other projectile can be successfully launched

launder /láwndər/ *v* 1 *vt* **WASH AND IRON** to wash dirty clothes or linen and, often, iron them as well 2 *vi* **BE WASHABLE** to be able to be washed ○ *It's a beautiful fabric, but I doubt that it would launder well.* 3 *vt* **MAKE MONEY APPEAR LEGAL** to pass illegally acquired money through a legitimate business or bank account in order to disguise its illegal origins ■ *n* **TROUGH FOR WASHING ORE** a trough for washing ore [Late 16C. < *launder* 'somebody who washes linen', contraction of *lavender* < Latin *lavare* 'wash'.] —**launderable** *adj* —**launderer** *n*

launderette /láwndə rét, -drét/, **laundrette** *n* a laundry, usually self-service, containing coin-operated washing and drying machines

laundress /láwndrəss/ *n* a woman who does washing and ironing, especially one who does other people's washing and ironing as a way of earning a living (*dated*) [Mid-16C. < *launder* (see LAUNDER).]

laundrette *n* = **launderette**

Laundromat /láwndrə mat/ *US, Can, Aus* a service mark for a self-service coin-operated commercial laundry

laundry /láwndri/ (*plural* **-dries**) *n* 1 **DIRTY WASHING** dirty clothes or linen put aside to be washed and ironed 2 **CLEAN WASHING** freshly washed clothes or linen 3 **WASHING AND IRONING PLACE** a place, especially a commercial establishment or a communal room in a building, where clothes and linen can be washed and ironed [Early 16C. Shortening of obsolete *lavendry* < Latin *lavare* 'wash'.]

laundry detergent *n US* = **washing powder**

laundry list *n* a lengthy list of items, usually things wanted or needed

laundryman /láwndrimən/ (*plural* **-men** /-mən/) *n* 1 somebody whose job involves working in a laundry or cleaners 2 a man whose job involves collecting dirty washing and delivering it back after it has been washed and ironed or cleaned (*dated*)

laundrywoman /láwndri wŏŏmən/ (*plural* **-women** /-wimmin/) *n* a woman whose job involves working in a laundry or cleaners

Launfal /láwnfəl/ *n* in the legend of King Arthur, one of the knights at the court

Laurasia /law ráyzi ə, -ráyshə/ northern part of the ancient supercontinent of Pangaea

laureate /láwri ət, lórr-/ *n* 1 **AWARD WINNER** a recipient of a prize or honour for outstanding achievement in the arts or sciences 2 **POET LAUREATE** a poet laureate ■ *adj* 1 **CROWNED WITH LAUREL** crowned with laurel as a sign of honour (*literary*) 2 **MADE OF LAUREL** made of laurel leaves or branches [14C. < Latin *laureatus* < *laurea* 'laurel tree' < *laurus*.] —**laureateship** *n*

laurel /lórrəl/ *n* 1 PLANTS = **bay**³ *n.* 1 2 **TREE OR BUSH RESEMBLING LAUREL** any tree or bush whose leaves, aroma, or berries are similar to those of the laurel, e.g. the mountain laurel and cherry laurel 3 **WREATH OF LEAVES** the leaves of the bay woven into a wreath and used as a mark of honour or victory in ancient times, e.g. to crown the winners of athletic events ■ **laurels** *npl* **HONOUR FOR ACHIEVEMENT** honour won for an achievement ■ *vt* (**-rels, -relling, -relled**) 1 **CROWN WITH LAUREL** to crown somebody with laurel as a sign of honour (*literary*) 2 **GIVE SOMEBODY AWARD** to honour somebody with an award or prize [14C. Via Old French *lorier* < Latin *laureola* 'small bay branch' < *laurus* 'bay tree'.] ◇ **look to your laurels** to be careful not lose a successful or winning position because of a better performance by somebody else ◇ **rest on your laurels** to be satisfied with your success and do nothing to improve on it

Laurel /lórrəl/, **Stan** (1890–1965) British-born US comedian. Born **Arthur Stanley Laurel Jefferson**

Laurentian Mountains /lo r-nsh'n-/ mountain range in S Quebec, Canada, that runs north of the St Lawrence River. Height: 1,190 m/3,905 ft.

Laurentian Plateau = **Canadian Shield**

lauric acid /láwrik-, lórrik-/ *n* $C_{12}H_{34}O_2$ a crystalline fatty acid. Source: coconut and laurel oils. Use: manufacture of soaps, insecticides, cosmetics, lauryl alcohol. [Late 19C. *Lauric* < modern Latin *laurus* < Latin, 'laurel'.]

Laurier /lórri ər/, **Sir Wilfrid** (1841–1919) Canadian lawyer, journalist, and statesman

lauryl alcohol /láwrəl-, lórrəl-/ *n* $C_{12}H_{27}O$ a crystalline solid that is insoluble in water. Use: manufacture of detergents. [Early 20C. < shortening of *lauric* (see LAURIC ACID).]

Lausanne /low zán/ city of W Switzerland, on Lake Geneva. Population: 114,161 (1998).

lav /lav/ *n* a toilet (*informal*) [Early 20C. Shortening of LAVATORY.]

lava /laávə/ *n* 1 molten rock that originates in the Earth's mantle and flows from a volcano or a fissure on land or the ocean floor 2 rock formed from solidified lava, typically full of small air holes caused by escaping volcanic gases [Mid-18C. Via Italian < Neapolitan dialect.]

lavabo /lə vaábō, lə váy-/ (*plural* **-boes**) *n* 1 **lavabo, Lavabo RELIGIOUS RITUAL** a priest's ritual washing of the hands and reciting from the Psalms during the Communion service in some Christian churches 2 **BASIN ATTACHED TO A WALL** a basin with a water tank above attached to a wall, often used as a planter 3 **WASHBASIN** a washbasin or washstand 4 **PLACE FOR WASHING IN A MONASTERY** a place for washing in a monastery [Mid-18C. < Latin, 'I will wash', a form of *lavare* 'wash'.]

lavage /lávvij, la vaázh/ *n* the washing out of a hollow body organ, e.g. the stomach, using a flow of water [Late 18C. < French *laver* 'wash'.]

Laval /lə vál/ 1 city in S Quebec Province, Canada, on Île-Jésus in the St Lawrence River. Population: 330,393 (1996). 2 city in W France. Population: 50,473 (1990).

Laval, Pierre (1883–1945) French statesman

lava-lava /laávə laávə/ *n* a rectangular piece of printed cotton worn wrapped around the waist by the people of Samoa and other parts of Polynesia [Late 19C. < Samoan.]

lavaliere /lə vállì áir/ *n* a pendant on a chain worn around the neck [Late 19C. After Louise de *la Valière*.]

lavatera /lávvə teérə, lə váttərə/ (*plural* **-ras** *or* **-ra**) *n* a plant or bush such as the tree mallow. Flowers: pink, white, purple. Native to: Europe, but naturalized in California. Genus: *Lavatera*. [Mid-18C. < modern Latin, after the brothers *Lavater*, 17C and 18C Swiss doctors and naturalists.]

lavatorial /lávvə táwri əl/ *adj* 1 containing childish references to faeces or urine (*disapproving*) 2 relating to or suitable for a public lavatory

lavatory /lávvətri/ (*plural* **-ries**) *n* 1 a toilet or a small room or cubicle containing a toilet 2 a room or building with washing and toilet facilities [14C. < late Latin *lavatorium* < Latin *lavare* 'wash'.]

lave /layv/ *n Scotland* remainder [Old English *lāf* < Germanic]

lavender /lávvəndər/ *n* 1 **FRAGRANT PLANT** a low-growing aromatic bush with fine needle-like leaves that produces a fragrant oil. Flowers: fragrant bluish-purple, in clusters. *Lavendula officinalis*. 2 **FLOWERS AND LEAVES** the dried flowers and leaves of the lavender plant. Use: essential oil, perfume for clothes, linen, toiletries. 3 **PALE PURPLE COLOUR** a pale bluish-purple colour [14C. < Anglo-Norman *lavendre* < medieval Latin *lavendula*.] —**lavender** *adj*

lavender water *n* perfume or toilet water made from the flowers of the lavender plant

laver¹ /láyvər/ *n* 1 a large basin in the temple in Jerusalem and in modern synagogues used for ritual washing 2 a basin to wash in (*archaic*) [14C. Via Old French *laveor* < late Latin *lavatorium* (see LAVATORY).]

laver² /laávər/ *n* a dried edible seaweed of the red algae family. Genus: *Porphyra*. [12C. < Latin.]

Laver /láyvər/, **Rod** (*b.* 1938) Australian tennis player

laver bread /laávər-/ *n* a Welsh dish made from boiled seaweed mixed with oatmeal, formed into cakes, and fried, traditionally in bacon fat

laverock /lávvərək/ *n Scotland, N England* a skylark (*archaic*) [Old English *lāferce* (see LARK¹)]

lavish /lávvish/ *adj* 1 **ABUNDANT** given or produced in abundance or to excess 2 **GENEROUS** giving or spending generously or to excess ■ *vt* **BE EXTRAVAGANT WITH** to give or spend something generously or to excess [15C. < Old French *lavasse* 'torrential rain' < *laver* 'wash, pour'.] —**lavisher** *n* —**lavishly** *adv* —**lavishness** *n*

Lavoisier /lə vwaázi ay/, **Antoine Laurent** (1743–94) French chemist

law /law/ *n* 1 **BINDING OR ENFORCEABLE RULE** a rule of conduct or procedure recognized by a community as binding or enforceable by authority 2 **PIECE OF LEGISLATION** an act passed by a parliament or similar body 3 **LEGAL SYSTEM** the body or system of rules recognized by a community that are enforceable by established process ○ *You are forbidden by law from entering the premises.* 4 **CONTROL OR AUTHORITY** the control or authority resulting from the observance and enforcement of a community's system of rules ○ *Nobody is above the law.* 5 **BRANCH OF KNOWLEDGE** the branch of knowledge or study concerned with the rules of a community and their enforcement ○ *went to university to study law* 6 **AREA OF LAW** the body of law relating to a particular subject or area 7 = **common law** 8 **LAWYERS** the legal profession 9 **LEGAL ACTION** legal action or proceedings 10 **LAW ENFORCEMENT AGENT OR AGENCY** a person or organization responsible for enforcing the law, especially the police 11 **STATEMENT OF SCIENTIFIC TRUTH** a statement of a scientific fact or phenomenon that is invariable under given conditions ○ *the laws of physics* 12 **MATHEMATICAL PRINCIPLE** a general relationship that is assumed or proved to exist between expressions 13 **GENERAL RULE OR PRINCIPLE** a general rule or principle that is thought to be true or held to be binding [Pre-12C. < Old Norse *lǫg* 'laws' < *lag* 'something set down' < Germanic, 'put'.] ◇ **be a law unto yourself** to refuse to obey the rules, conventions, or suggestions made or upheld by others ◇ **lay down the law** to express an opinion in an overbearing or dogmatic way ◇ **take the law into your own hands** to try to obtain revenge or justice without involving the police, courts, or usual legal procedures

Law *n* 1 the principles set out in the Bible, especially the Pentateuch, said to be the divine will. ◊ **Law of Moses, Mosaic Law** 2 JUDAISM = **Pentateuch**

Law /law/, **Bonar** (1858–1923) Canadian-born British statesman

law-abiding *adj* voluntarily and habitually obeying the law

law agent *n* in Scotland, a solicitor qualified to represent a client in a sheriff court

law and order *n* 1 the strict enforcement of the law (*hyphenated before nouns*) ○ *law-and-order issues* 2 the stability created by the observance and enforcement of the law within a community

lawbreaker /láw braykər/ *n* a person who breaks the law —**lawbreaking** *n, adj*

law centre *n* a place where citizens can obtain legal advice free of charge, paid for out of public funds

law court *n* a court where legal cases are heard

lawful /láwf'l/ *adj* 1 **PERMITTED BY LAW** not forbidden by the law 2 **AUTHORIZED BY LAW** authorized or recognized by the law 3 **OBEYING THE LAW** obeying or conforming to the law —**lawfully** *adv* —**lawfulness** *n*

lawgiver /láw givər/ *n* 1 a giver of a code of laws to a people 2 LAW = **lawmaker** —**lawgiving** *n*

lawks /lawks/ *interj* used to express surprise or concern (*dated or regional regional*) [Mid-18C. Variant of *lawk*, alteration of LORD.]

Lawler /láwlər/, **Ray** (*b.* 1921) Australian playwright

lawless /láwləss/ *adj* 1 **UNREGULATED** uncontrolled or unregulated 2 **AGAINST THE LAW** contrary to the law 3 **WITHOUT LAW** having no laws —**lawlessly** *adv* —**lawlessness** *n*

Law Lords *npl* those members of the House of Lords qualified to take part in judicial business

lawmaker /láw maykər/ *n* a drafter and enactor of laws —**lawmaking** *n, adj*

lawman /láw man, -mən/ (*plural* **-men** /-mən/) *n US* an officer responsible for enforcing the law, e.g. a sheriff

law merchant *n* the principles and rules governing commercial transactions, which originated in English common law and are codified in US law

lawn[1] /lawn/ *n* an area of closely mown grass, often part of a garden [Mid-16C. Alteration of *laund* < Old French *launde* 'wooded district, heath' < Celtic.]

lawn[2] /lawn/ *n* a fine light cotton or cotton-and-polyester fabric. Use: clothing, household linen. [15C. After *Laon*, France.] —**lawny** *adj*

lawn bowling *n US* = **bowls**

lawn mower *n* a machine, often power-operated, that cuts grass with rotating blades

lawn tennis *n* a game for two or four players played on a hard or grass court of standard dimensions in which the players hit balls with rackets across a central net

law of averages *n* **1** the principle that over the long term laws of probability will influence all events that are subject to them **2** the unscientific but reasonable assumption that things are bound to change some time ○ *We have had bad weather for our holiday for the past six years, so by the law of averages we should get some sunshine this year.*

law of diminishing returns *n* the principle that a continual increase in effort or investment does not lead to a continual increase in output or results

law of effect *n* the theory that behaviour that is rewarded is more likely to be repeated than behaviour that is not rewarded

law of large numbers *n* the principle that a large sample is more likely than a smaller sample to have the characteristics of the whole

Law of Moses *n* RELIG = **Mosaic Law**

law of nations *n* LAW = **international law**

law of nature *n* a broadly applicable principle relating to natural phenomena

law of parsimony *n* SCI = **Occam's razor**

law of supply and demand *n* the economic principle that the price charged for a product is determined by the level of demand and the quantity available

law of the jungle *n* aggressive or competitive behaviour based on the principle that self-interest and survival are of prime importance

law of the sea *n* the international rules that govern the use of the oceans, derived from custom, treaties, and judicial decisions

law of war *n* a rule or body of rules that governs the rights and duties of those engaged in international war

Lawrence /lórrənss/, **Bruno** (1949–95) British-born New Zealand actor

Lawrence, D. H. (1885–1930) British writer

Lawrence, Gertrude (1898–1952) British actor. Born **Gertrud Alexandra Dagmar Lawrence Klasen**

Lawrence, Marjorie Florence (1908–79) Australian opera singer

lawrencium /lə rénssi əm/ *n* (*symbol* **Lr**) a short-lived radioactive metallic element. Source: produced artificially from californium and other elements. [Mid-20C. After Ernest O. *Lawrence* (1901–58), US physicist.]

Lawson /láwss'n/, **Henry Hertzberg** (1867–1922) Australian writer

Lawson, Louisa (1848–1920) Australian writer, publisher, and feminist. Born **Louisa Albury**

Lawson, Nigel, Baron Lawson of Blaby (*b.* 1932) British politician

Lawson, William (1774–1850) British-born Australian explorer

lawsuit /láw soot, -syoot/ *n* a legal action brought between two private parties in a court of law

lawyer /láwyər, lóyər/ *n* a qualified professional adviser on legal matters who can represent clients in court

lax /laks/ *adj* **1** NOT STRICT not strict or careful enough **2** NOT TENSE not tight or tense **3** WITH TENDENCY TO DIARRHOEA not easily controlled and producing loose faeces **4** PRONOUNCED WITH RELAXED MUSCLES pronounced with the muscles of the jaw relaxed rather than tense, as, e.g., is the 'a' in 'hat' [14C. < Latin *laxus* 'loose'.] —**laxly** *adv* —**laxness** *n*

laxation /lak sáysh'n/ *n* the action of making something loose, or the process of becoming loose

laxative /láksətiv/ *n* a drug or other substance that promotes bowel movements [14C. < Old French *laxatif* < medieval Latin *laxativus* 'loosening' < Latin *laxare* 'loosen' < *laxus* 'loose'.] —**laxative** *adj*

laxity /láksəti/ *n* the condition or fact of being not strict or careful enough

Laxness /laáks ness/, **Halldór** (1902–98) Icelandic novelist and playwright

lay[1] /lay/ *v* (**lays, laying, laid**) **1** *vt* SET SOMETHING DOWN to put something down, often carefully, in a horizontal position ○ *I laid the files on my desk.* **2** *vt* PUT IN RESTING POSITION to place somebody or something in a position of rest ○ *It was time to lay the baby down for a nap.* **3** *vt* BURY to bury somebody or something in the ground ○ *They laid him in the family plot.* **4** *vt* PLACE SOMETHING ON SURFACE to arrange, place, or spread something on, over, or along a surface ○ *They are laying the carpet tomorrow.* **5** *vt* PRESS SOMETHING DOWN FLAT to smooth something down or make something lie flat ○ *The cat laid back its ears.* **6** *vt* ARRANGE THINGS ON TABLE to prepare a table for a meal by setting out the required items **7** *vt* ARRANGE FUEL FOR FIRE to prepare a fire by arranging fuel, usually in a grate **8** *vti* PRODUCE EGGS to produce or deposit eggs ○ *All the hens are laying.* **9** *vti* BET to place a bet with somebody **10** *vt* IMPOSE to impose something as a burden, duty, or penalty ○ *lay a tariff on imported products* **11** *vt* ATTRIBUTE to impute or attribute something ○ *He laid the blame on me.* **12** *vt* BRING TO BEAR to bring something to bear ○ *laid emphasis on the fact that we must study to excel* **13** *vt* CAUSE DECREASE to cause something to decrease or subside ○ *Our discussion laid everyone's fears.* **14** *vt* DEVISE to devise, organize, or prepare something **15** *vt* MAKE PREPARATIONS to prepare something as a basis **16** *vt* OFFENSIVE TERM an offensive term meaning to have sexual intercourse with somebody (*slang*) **17** *vt* ARRANGE STRANDS OF ROPE to twist strands together to make a rope or cable **18** *vt* PUT CANNON IN POSITION to establish the direction and elevation of a cannon or a battery of cannon **19** *vt* TREAT HEDGE TO KEEP IT THICK to partially cut through some of the branches of a hedge, bending them over horizontally and pegging them to the ground to keep the hedge thick and dense ○ *hedge laying* **20** *vi* LIE DOWN to be in or adopt a lying position (*nonstandard*) ○ *Lay down on the sofa and have a rest.* **21** *vi* PUT EFFORT INTO to apply effort vigorously to a task ○ *The rowing team laid to their oars.* **22** *vi* BE IN OR GO TO POSITION to put a boat in a specified position, or move in a specified direction ■ *n* **1** WAY SOMETHING LIES the way or position in which something lies ○ *wanted to inspect the lay of the property* **2** OFFENSIVE TERM an offensive term for a partner in sexual intercourse (*slang*) **3** OFFENSIVE TERM an offensive term for sexual intercourse (*slang*) **4** TWIST OF ROPE OR CABLE STRANDS the arrangement of strands in a rope or cable, determined by the number, length, angle, and direction of twist **5** SHARE OF PROCEEDS a share in the proceeds of a whaling expedition [Old English *lecgan* < Germanic, 'put'] ◇ **be laid low** to become ill or incapacitated ◇ **lay it on (thick)** to exaggerate greatly, especially in order to flatter somebody ◇ **lay yourself open to something** to put yourself in a position that will make you liable to be blamed, criticized, or attacked

lay about *vti* to strike blows in all directions

lay aside *vt* **1** to give up on or abandon something ○ *'Be not the first by whom the new are tried, nor the last to lay the old aside'.* (Alexander Pope, *An Essay on Criticism*; 1711) **2** to put something away for the future

lay away *vt* **1** to put something away for the future **2** to set merchandise aside for future delivery

lay before *vt* to present something for consideration by somebody

lay by *vt* **1** to set something aside for the future **2** *ANZ* to purchase goods from a shop by placing a deposit then paying off the remainder in instalments, without interest

lay down *v* **1** *vt* SURRENDER to put down, surrender, or sacrifice something **2** *vt* DECIDE ON RULE to formulate a rule or principle **3** *vt* STORE FOR FUTURE to acquire and store something for future use **4** *vt* PLACE BET to place a bet **5** *vt* DELIVER MILITARY FIRE to deliver a concentration of military fire **6** *vi* LIE DOWN to lie down in a horizontal position (*nonstandard*)

lay in *vt* to acquire and store something for future use

lay into *vt* **1** to attack somebody forcefully in words (*informal*) **2** to attack somebody forcefully with blows

lay off *v* **1** *vt* TERMINATE THE EMPLOYMENT OF to stop employing somebody, often temporarily, when there is insufficient work to be done **2** *vti* STOP DOING to stop doing or using something (*informal*) **3** *vti* STOP IRRITATING to stop bothering somebody (*informal*) **4** *vt* MEASURE OR MARK SOMETHING OFF to measure off a distance or mark out the boundaries of something **5** *vt* REDUCE RISK ON BET to reduce risk as a bookmaker by placing all or part of a bet with another bookmaker

lay on *vt* **1** APPLY to apply something by spreading it **2** APPLY OR USE TO EXCESS to apply, administer, or use something in an exaggerated manner **3** PROVIDE SOMETHING SPECIAL to provide or arrange something, often in an elaborate or extravagant manner **4** INSTALL AN AMENITY to provide or install a supply of something such as gas or electricity

lay out *v* **1** *vt* SPREAD SOMETHING OUT FOR DISPLAY to arrange things or spread things out for display **2** *vt* PLAN OR DESIGN to plan or design something in detail **3** *vt* PREPARE SOMEBODY FOR BURIAL to prepare a body for burial **4** *vt* KNOCK UNCONSCIOUS to knock somebody unconscious (*informal*) **5** *vt* SPEND MONEY to spend money, especially in large quantities **6** *vr* MAKE AN EFFORT to make a considerable personal effort

lay over *vi US, Can* to make a brief stop during a journey

lay to *vi* to make a ship or boat stop, e.g. by turning a sailing vessel into the wind

lay up *vt* **1** STORE FOR FUTURE to store something for future use **2** CONFINE SOMEBODY WITH INJURY OR ILLNESS to prevent somebody from leading a normal active life, usually temporarily because of injury or illness (*usually passive*) ○ *He was laid up with a bad back.* **3** STOP USING SHIP OR BOAT to take a ship or boat out of service, usually temporarily, e.g. by moving it to a dry dock for maintenance or repairs

lay[2] /lay/ *adj* **1** belonging to or involving the people of a church who are not members of the clergy **2** without expertise or professional training in a particular field [14C. Directly or via Old French *lai* < late Latin *laicus* (see LAIC).]

lay[3] /lay/ *n* **1** a short narrative poem that is sung **2** a medieval lyric or narrative song [13C. < Old French *lai*.]

lay[4] /lay/ past tense of **lie**[1]

layabout /láy ə bowt/ *n* a lazy person who loafs around and does no work

lay attendant *n* in Buddhist monasteries, somebody who is responsible for taking care of tasks that the monks are forbidden to undertake

layaway /láy ə way/ *n* a method of purchasing something in which the purchaser pays a deposit and the seller keeps the goods until full payment is made

layback /láy bak/ *n* a way of climbing a vertical crack in a rock by leaning back and pulling on one side of the crack and pushing against the other side with the feet

lay brother *n* in a Christian religious order, a man who has taken vows, but does not take part in the full liturgical programme and serves as an ancillary or manual worker

lay-by (*plural* **lay-bys**) *n* **1** *UK* a short strip of ground alongside a main road where vehicles can stop for a short time **2** *ANZ* a method of purchasing goods by placing a deposit and then paying off the full price in instalments, without interest, delivery of goods being made when full payment is received

lay days *npl* the time allowed in port for a ship to load or unload its cargo without extra payment

lay-down *n US* an easy target or victim (*slang*) ○ *I robbed ten lay-downs before being caught.*

layer /láyər/ *n* **1** FLAT COVERING OR SHEET-LIKE THICKNESS a single thickness of something that lies over or under something or between other similar thicknesses **2** SOMEBODY WHO LAYS somebody whose work is laying something such as tile or brick (*usually in combination*) **3** LAYING HEN a hen that lays eggs **4** ROOTED PLANT SHOOT a branch or shoot that has been bent over and covered with soil to make it take root and grow into a new plant ■ *v* **1** *vti* MAKE LAYERS OF to apply or arrange things as separate thicknesses, or form into separate thicknesses **2** *vt* CUT HAIR IN DIFFERENT LENGTHS to cut somebody's hair in overlapping sections of different lengths, usually in order to give shape to a hairstyle **3** *vt* PROPAGATE PLANT BY ROOTING SHOOTS to bend a shoot over and cover it with soil to make it take root as a new plant, or take root as a result of this procedure

layer cake *n* a sponge cake that consists of two or more layers sandwiched together with cream, jam, or other filling

layering /láyəring/ *n* a method of propagating plants by covering a branch or shoot with soil so that it takes root while still attached to the parent plant

layette /lay ét/ *n* a complete set of clothing and accessories for a newborn baby [Mid-19C. < French, 'small drawer' < Old French *laie* 'drawer, box' < Middle Dutch *laege* < Germanic, 'load'.]

lay figure *n* **1** a jointed model of the human body used by artists **2** a submissive or insignificant person

laying on of hands *n* placing the hands on somebody's head in certain religious ceremonies or rituals, e.g. ordination and faith healing

Laylat al-Miraj /láylat al mi r-j/ *n* an Islamic festival, the Night of Ascent, marking the ascent of Muhammad to heaven. Date: 27th of Rajab. [< Arabic, 'night of the ascent']

layman /láymən/ (*plural* **-men** /-mən/) *n* **1** a person who is not trained in a profession ○ *a law book for the layman* **2** a person who does not belong to the clergy

layoff /láy of/ *n* **1** a dismissal of employees, usually temporary **2** the time during which employees are out of work

lay of the land *n* = **lie of the land** (*informal*)

layout /láy owt/ *n* **1 WAY THINGS ARE ARRANGED** the way component parts or individual items are arranged **2 DESIGN SHOWING RELATIVE POSITIONS** a design or plan showing the way things are arranged **3 DESIGN OF PRINTED MATTER** the design or arrangement of all the elements of printed material, e.g. an advertisement or the pages of a book **4 PAGE SHOWING DESIGN** a page or pages showing the design for printed material **5 DESIGNING OF PRINTED MATERIAL** the art of designing printed material

layover /láyōvər/ *n US, Can* a brief stop during a journey

layperson /láy purss'n/ (*plural* **-people** /-peep'l/) *n* **1** a person who is not trained in a profession **2** a person who does not belong to the clergy

lay reader *n* a lay member of a church, especially an Anglican church or the Roman Catholic Church, who is authorized to read some parts of the service

lay-up *n* a basketball shot made close to the basket, usually made one-handed and by bouncing the ball off the backboard

laywoman /láy wòomən/ (*plural* **-en** /-wimin/) *n* **1** a woman who is not trained or expert in a particular area **2** a woman who does not belong to the clergy

lazar /lázzər, láyzər/ *n* a poor and sick person, especially somebody affected by leprosy (*archaic*) [13C. Via medieval Latin *lazarus* < Latin *Lazarus*, a beggar (Luke 16:20).]

lazaretto /lázzə réttō/ (*plural* **-tos**), **lazaret** /lázzə rét/, **lazarette** *n* **1 QUARANTINE FACILITY** a building or ship used to hold people during a period of quarantine **2 SHIP'S STORAGE SPACE** a storage space below deck near the stern of a ship **3 HOSPITAL FOR CONTAGIOUS DISEASES** a hospital for the treatment of contagious diseases such as leprosy, especially in former times [Mid-16C. < Italian *lazzaretto*, blend of *lazzaro* 'leper' (< medieval Latin *lazarus*; see LAZAR) + Venetian dialect *nazareto*, hospital in Venice after Santa Maria di *Nazaret* 'St Mary of Nazareth'.]

laze /layz/ (**lazes, lazing, lazed**) *v* **1** *vi* to relax and do no work ○ *I just lazed in the shade with a book.* **2** *vt* to pass time idly ○ *laze the day away* [Late 16C. Back-formation < LAZY.]

laze around, laze about *vti* to relax, doing nothing that requires effort

lazulite /lázzyòo līt/ *n* a blue, glassy, rare phosphate mineral containing aluminium, iron, and magnesium. Use: gems. [Early 19C. < *(lapis) lazuli*.]

lazurite /lázzyòo rīt/ *n* a deep violet-blue or greenish-blue rare aluminosilicate mineral that contains sodium and is the main constituent of lapis lazuli [Late 19C. Via medieval Latin *lazur* < Arabic *lāzaward* 'lapis lazuli'.]

lazy /láyzi/ (**-zier, -ziest**) *adj* **1 NOT WANTING TO WORK** unwilling to do any work or make an effort **2 CONDUCIVE TO IDLENESS** contributing to an unwillingness to work or make an effort ○ *a lazy spring day* **3 SLOW** moving slowly ○ *a lazy river* **4 SLOPING** shown as a brand on livestock as a letter or number rotated through 90 degrees from an upright position ○ *a lazy H* [Mid-16C. < ?] —**lazily** *adv* —**laziness** *n*

lazy bed *n Scotland, Ireland* a bed about 2 m/6 ft wide where seed potatoes for cultivation are laid on the surface and covered with soil

lazybones /láyzi bōnz/ (*plural* **-bones**) *n* somebody who is lazy or without ambition (*informal*)

lazy daisy stitch *n* a single unattached chain stitch in embroidery, often worked in a circle to resemble the petals of a flower

lazy eye *n* **1** an eye disorder in which vision is impaired for no apparent reason, or an eye affected by this disorder (*not used technically*) ◆ **amblyopia 2** a disorder in which the eyes appear to be looking in different directions, or an eye affected by this disorder

lazy Susan /-sóoz'n/ *n* a revolving tray holding a selection of items such as cheeses or sauces, usually placed in the middle of a dining table

lazy tongs *npl* tongs that can be used to grasp objects at a distance, usually by bringing together the handles to extend the jointed arms

⚡**lb** *abbr* Lebanon (*in Internet addresses*)

L-band *n* the range of frequencies of electromagnetic waves from 390 megahertz to 1550 megahertz used for radar

LBO *abbr* leveraged buyout

LBV *abbr* Late Bottled Vintage (*refers to port that is six years old*)

lbw *abbr* leg before wicket

⚡**lc** *abbr* **1** left centre (*of a stage*) **2** letter of credit **3** loco citato **4** lower case **5** St Lucia (*in Internet addresses*)

LC *abbr* **1** Lance Corporal **2** landing craft **3** Library of Congress

L/C, l/c, lc *abbr* letter of credit

lcd *abbr* least common denominator

LCD *abbr* **1** liquid-crystal display **2 lcd** lowest common denominator

l'chaim /lə khàa yim/, **lechayim** *interj* a word used to express good wishes just before drinking an alcoholic drink ■ *n* a small drink of alcohol used to toast somebody or something [Mid-20C. < Hebrew *lĕḥayyīm* 'to life']

lcm *abbr* least common multiple

LCM *abbr* landing craft, mechanized ■ *n*, *abbr* **lcm** lowest common multiple

L/Cpl *abbr* lance corporal

ld *abbr* **1** lead **2** load

Ld *abbr* **1** Limited (company) **2** Lord

LD *abbr* **1** learning disability **2** learning-disabled **3** lethal dose

LD50 *n* a toxicological test in which the dose that kills 50 per cent of a group of test animals is calculated

LDC *abbr* less-developed country

ldg *abbr* **1** landing **2** loading

Ldg *abbr* Leading

LDL *abbr* low-density lipoprotein

L-dopa *n* a natural substance that stimulates the production of dopamine in the brain. Use: treatment of Parkinson's disease. [Mid-20C. < the initial letters of *laevorotatory*, and of DI-[1] + OXY- + PHENYL + ALANINE.]

⚡**LDR** *abbr* long-distance relationship (*in e-mails*)

L-driver *n* somebody who is learning to drive

LDS *abbr* **1** Latter-day Saints **2** praise be to God forever **3** Licentiate in Dental Surgery

lea /lee/ *n* **1** a grassy field or meadow (*literary*) **2** a field sown with grass [Old English *lēah* 'meadow, clearing']

LEA *abbr* Local Education Authority

lea. *abbr* **1** league **2** leather

leach /leech/ *v* **1** *vti* **DEPRIVE OR BE DEPRIVED OF** to take something away slowly, or be slowly taken away ○ *have the joy leached from life* **2** *vt* **REMOVE SOMETHING BY DISSOLUTION** to remove soluble components from a solid mixture by the use of a solvent **3** *vi* **LOSE SOLUBLE MATERIAL** to lose soluble material by dissolution ■ *n* **1 CONTAINER USED IN LEACHING** a porous container used to hold a solid mixture through which a solvent is run in order to remove soluble components **2 MIXTURE USED IN LEACHING** a solid mixture through which a solvent is run in order to remove soluble components **3 LIQUID CONTAINING LEACHED SUBSTANCE** a solution containing a substance leached from a solid mixture [Old English *leccan* < Germanic] —**leachability** /leècha bílləti/ *n* —**leacher** *n*

Leach /leech/, **Bernard** (1887–1979) British potter

leachate /leè chayt/ *n* **1** a liquid containing soluble material removed from a solid mixture through which the liquid has passed **2** the liquid produced in a landfill from the decomposition of waste within the landfill

Leacock /leè kok/, **Stephen** (1869–1944) British-born Canadian writer

lead[1] /leed/ *v* (**leads, leading, led, led** /led/) **1** *vti* **GUIDE** to show the way to others, usually by going ahead of them ○ *He led us down the mountain.* **2** *vti* **BE THE WAY SOMEWHERE** to be the route or direction that goes to a particular place or in a particular direction ○ *That street leads to the school.* **3** *vt* **BRING** to bring a person or animal along with physical guidance, e.g. by holding the person's hand or pulling a horse's reins **4** *vt* **COMMAND OTHERS** to control, direct, or command others ○ *He led an infantry division in Burma during the war.* **5** *vt* **BE IN CHARGE OF** to have a principal part or guiding role in something **6** *vt* **BE PRINCIPAL MUSICIAN** to be the principal performer of an orchestra or of a section of an orchestra **7** *vt* **INFLUENCE SOMEBODY TO DO** to cause somebody to think or act in a particular way ○ *I was led to believe the house had been sold.* **8** *vi* **RESULT IN** to bring about a particular outcome ○ *Her hard work ultimately led to widespread recognition.* **9** *vt* **LIVE LIFE** to go through life or spend time in a particular way ○ *We all lead very busy lives.* **10** *vt* **BE AT THE START** to be at the beginning or front of something ○ *Your name leads the waiting list.* **11** *vti* **BE AHEAD OF OTHERS** to be ahead in a race or competition ○ *is leading in the election* **12** *vt* **BE MOST SUCCESSFUL** to be the most successful at something and set an example to others ○ *They lead the world technologically.* **13** *vti* **GUIDE DANCE PARTNER** to guide a partner in a ballroom dance **14** *vt* **ASK WITNESS LEADING QUESTION** to suggest to a witness an answer to a question by phrasing the question in a way that will elicit the desired response **15** *vt* **CHANNEL OR CONVEY** to guide something through a passage such as a conduit or channel **16** *vti* **PUT DOWN FIRST CARD** to play the first card in a trick in a card game, often obliging others to play a card of the same suit if they can **17** *vi* **AIM THE FIRST BLOW** to direct the first of a series of punches **18** *vi* **LEAVE BASE EARLY** to leave a base as a runner before a pitch in baseball **19** *vt* **AIM AHEAD OF** to aim something such as a missile or ball at a point in front of a moving target to allow for the time of flight ■ *n* **1 FRONT POSITION OR PRINCIPAL ROLE** the front position, first place, or principal role ○ *The Prime Minister took the lead in condemning the attacks.* **2 FORWARD POSITION** a position ahead of all competitors ○ *Which party has the lead in the opinion polls?* **3 FRONTRUNNER** somebody or something ahead of all competitors **4 DISTANCE BETWEEN FIRST AND SECOND** the margin by which somebody or something is ahead of all competitors ○ *She had a narrow lead as the runners entered the last lap.* **5 STAR ROLE IN PERFORMANCE** a principal role in a play, film, or show ○ *He will play the male lead in the film version.* **6 SOMEBODY WITH STARRING ROLE** somebody who has a principal role in a play, film, or show **7 ROLE OF SOMEBODY IN COMMAND** the role of somebody who directs or guides others ○ *take the lead in a discussion* **8 PRECEDENT** an example or precedent ○ *follow his lead* **9 TIP OR CLUE** a piece of helpful or useful information ○ *The police are following up a number of leads.* **10 INTRODUCTION TO NEWS ITEM** an introduction to a news story **11 HEADLINE ITEM** the most important story in a newspaper or news broadcast ○ *The conflict should make the lead in all tomorrow's papers.* **12 LINE USED TO CONTROL ANIMAL** a strap, chain, or rope used to control the animal it is attached to, especially one used when walking a dog ○ *Dogs must be kept on a lead at all times.* US term **leash** *n.* 1 **13 WIRE CONDUCTING ELECTRICITY** an insulated electrical conductor used to connect two points in a circuit, e.g. a cable connecting an appliance to a source of electricity **14 WATER CHANNEL THROUGH ICE** a water channel through an ice field **15 DIRECTION OF ROPE** the direction in which a rope runs **16 FIRST CARD PLAYED** the first card played in a trick in a game **17 RIGHT TO PUT DOWN FIRST CARD** the right to play a card first in a trick in a game **18 POSITION OF BASE RUNNER** a position taken by a runner off one base of a baseball diamond towards another **19 PUNCH** an attacking punch **20 DISTANCE AHEAD OF MOVING TARGET** the distance a missile, ball, or other projectile is aimed in front of a moving target to allow for the time of flight **21** GEOL = **lode** *n.* 1 [Old English *lǣdan* < Germanic]

USAGE lead or **led**? ***Led***, the past tense and past participle of the verb ***lead***, 'to guide, command, be in charge', etc. is the correct choice in sentences like this: *The captain led* [not *lead*] *the troops through the jungle.* There is also a noun spelled ***lead***, pronounced like ***led***, and meaning 'a heavy metallic element': *found a high degree of lead* [not *led*] *in the paint.*

lead off *v* 1 *vi* to begin doing something 2 *vt* to be the first batter in a baseball or softball lineup or innings
lead on *vt* 1 to lure somebody with an offer or promise that is later withdrawn 2 to persuade somebody to do something foolish or wrong ○ *She doesn't let the older kids lead her on.*
lead up to *vt* 1 to prepare the way for something 2 to approach a subject gradually or indirectly

lead[2] /led/ *n* 1 **CHEMICAL ELEMENT** (*symbol* **Pb**) a heavy bluish-grey metallic element that bends easily. Source: galena, cerussite. Use: car batteries, pipes, solder, radiation shields. 2 **DEVICE FOR MEASURING DEPTH** a weight on the end of a line used to measure the depth of water 3 **WEIGHT FOR FISHING LINE** a lead weight used on a fishing line 4 **AMMUNITION FOR GUNS** bullets or shot for firearms 5 **GRAPHITE IN A PENCIL** a long thin stick of graphite used in a pencil for writing or drawing 6 **STRIP BETWEEN LINES OF TYPE** in traditional hot-metal printing, a thin strip of metal between lines of type that creates the space between lines on the printed page ■ **leads** *npl* 1 **LEAD STRIPS BETWEEN GLASS PANES** strips of lead used to hold the small glass panes in place in a decorative window or art object 2 **SHEETS OF LEAD** sheets of lead used to cover a roof 3 **ROOF COVERED WITH LEADS** a roof covered with lead sheets ■ *vt* 1 **COVER SOMETHING WITH LEAD** to cover, fill, or weight something with lead 2 **INSERT STRIP BETWEEN LINES OF TYPE** to put a thin strip of metal between lines of type to create a space on the printed page 3 **SECURE GLASS USING LEADS** to hold small panes of glass together with strips of lead [Pre-12C. < Germanic.] —**leady** *adj* ◇ **swing the lead** to avoid work, often by feigning illness

lead acetate /léd-/ *n* $Pb(C_2H_3O_2)_2{\cdot}3H_2O$ a poisonous crystalline compound. Use: manufacture of paints, varnishes, mordant in dyeing and printing cottons.

lead arsenate /léd-/ *n* $Pb_3(AsO_4)_2$ a poisonous crystalline compound. Use: insecticide.

lead azide /léd-/ *n* $Pb(N_3)_2$ a colourless crystalline compound. Use: detonator in explosives.

lead balloon /léd-/ *n* a total failure ○ *went down like a lead balloon*

Leadbelly /léd beli/ (1885?–1949) US singer and guitarist. Born **Huddie William Ledbetter**

lead carbonate /léd-/ *n* $PbCO_3$ a poisonous white solid. Use: pigment in paints.

lead chromate /léd-/ *n* $PbCrO_4$ a poisonous yellow crystalline substance. Use: pigment.

lead crystal /léd-/ *n* glass containing a high proportion of lead, used to make decorative items, especially tableware

lead dioxide /léd-/ *n* PbO_2 a poisonous brown crystalline compound. Use: batteries, explosives, textile dyeing.

leaded /léddid/ *adj* 1 containing or treated with lead or a compound of lead 2 containing many small panes of glass held together with strips of lead

leaden /léd'n/ *adj* 1 **OF LEAD** made of lead 2 **DULL AND GREY** of a dull grey colour, like lead ○ *leaden skies* 3 **TIRED AND HEAVY** tired, heavy, and hard to move ○ *My legs felt stiff and leaden from miles of walking.* 4 **SLOW** sluggish or laboured ○ *a leaden pace* 5 **LIFELESS** lacking spirit or vitality —**leadenly** *adv* —**leadenness** *n*

leader /léedər/ *n* 1 **SOMEBODY WHOM PEOPLE FOLLOW** a guide or director of others 2 **SOMEBODY OR SOMETHING IN THE LEAD** somebody or something in front of all others, e.g. in a race or procession 3 **SOMEBODY IN CHARGE OF OTHERS** the head of a nation, political party, legislative body, or military unit 4 **PRINCIPAL MUSICIAN** the principal performer of an orchestra or of a section of an orchestra 5 **MUSICAL CONDUCTOR** a conductor of a band or group 6 **NEWSPAPER ARTICLE EXPRESSING EDITOR'S OPINION** a newspaper article expressing the opinion of the editor 7 *US* MARKETING = **loss leader** 8 **MAIN STEM** the main growing shoot of a tree or bush 9 **BLANK END OF TAPE** a short strip of blank film or recording tape at the beginning or end of a reel, used for threading 10 **LINE CONNECTING HOOK** a short length of nylon or other material attached to a fishing line and used to connect a lure or hook 11 **LINE AT END OF FISHING LINE** a short length of heavy fishing line or wire tied to the end of the main line to prevent sharp-toothed fish from breaking off the hook ■ **leaders** *npl* **GUIDE IN PRINTED MATTER** dots or dashes in printed material used to guide the eye across a page

leadership /léedər ship/ *n* 1 **OFFICE OR POSITION OF LEADER** the office or position of the head of a political party or other body of people 2 **ABILITY TO LEAD** the ability to guide, direct, or influence people 3 **GUIDANCE** guidance or direction 4 **LEADERS** a group of leaders (+ *singular or plural verb*)

lead glass /léd-/ *n* glass that contains a high proportion of lead oxide. Use: decorative objects, optical components.

lead-in /léed-/ *n* 1 an introduction to something such as an item on television or a topic for discussion 2 a wire that connects an outside aerial with a transmitter or receiver

leading[1] /léeding/ *adj* 1 most important or well known 2 ahead of all others, e.g. in a race or procession

leading[2] /lédding/ *n* 1 lead strips around small panes in windows or art objects ○ *The leading in the stained-glass window needs repair.* 2 the spacing between lines of type in traditional hot-metal printing

leading aircraftman /léeding-/ *n* a man in the Royal Air Force, of a rank above aircraftman

leading aircraftwoman /léeding-/ *n* a woman in the Royal Air Force, of a rank above aircraftwoman

leading article /léeding-/ *n* MEDIA = **leader** *n.* 6

leading dog /léeding-/ *n NZ* a dog in New Zealand trained to run ahead of a flock of sheep and control them

leading economic indicator /léeding-/ *n* an economic variable that tends to show the direction of future economic activity

leading edge /léeding-/ *n* 1 **MOST ADVANCED POSITION** the forefront of development in technology, science, or some other field (*hyphenated before nouns*) 2 **FRONT EDGE** the forward edge of an aircraft wing, propeller, or aerofoil 3 **INNER EDGE OF CURTAIN** the vertical edge of a curtain that faces the middle of the window

leading lady /léeding-/ *n* the actor who has the principal female role in a play or film

leading light /léeding-/ *n* an influential or exemplary person

leading man /léeding-/ *n* the actor who has the principal male role in a play or film

leading note /léeding-/ *n* the seventh note of the diatonic scale. US term **leading tone**

leading question /léeding-/ *n* a question asked in a way that prompts the desired answer, e.g. 'Do you think the government should be wasting taxpayers' money on such a venture?'

leading rating /léeding-/ *n* a Royal Navy non-commissioned officer of a rank above a rating

leading tone /léeding-/ *n US* = **leading note**

lead line /léd-/ *n* a line, weighted at one end, used to measure the depth of water

lead monoxide /léd-/ *n* **PbO** a poisonous yellow or reddish-yellow lead compound. Use: manufacture of storage batteries, pottery, glass, rubber, pigment in paints.

lead oxide /léd-/ *n* any of several oxides of lead, e.g. litharge and red lead

lead poisoning /léd-/ *n* poisoning from the absorption of lead into the body, the chronic form of which can cause damage to the nervous system, brain, liver, and gastrointestinal tract

lead replacement petrol /léd-/ *n* lead-free petrol for compulsory use in vehicles that were designed to be used with leaded petrol, introduced as a way of improving air quality and protecting the environment

lead screw /léed-/ *n* a threaded shaft that controls the movement of a machine part, e.g. the tool carriage of a lathe

leadsman /lédzmən/ (*plural* **-men** /-mən/) *n* a user of a lead line to measure the depth of water

lead tetraethyl /léd-/ *n* = **tetraethyl lead**

lead time /léed-/ *n* 1 the length of time in advance of a deadline that somebody must know or have something 2 the time needed to do something measured from start to finish, e.g. from design to production or from placing an order to delivery of the goods ○ *How much lead time do you need?*

Leadville /léd vil/ city in central Colorado. Population: 2,638 (1998 estimate).

leadwort /léd wurt, -wawrt/ *n* a tropical garden plant. Flowers: blue, white, red, in spikes. Genus: *Plumbago.*

leaf /leef/ *n* (*plural* **leaves** /leevz/) 1 **PLANT PART FOR PHOTOSYNTHESIS** a flat green part that grows in various shapes from the stems or branches of a plant or tree and whose main function is photosynthesis 2 **FOLIAGE** the foliage of a plant or tree, or the time when a plant or tree has leaves 3 **PAPER IN BOOK** a sheet of paper in a book 4 **VERY THIN METAL FOIL** a very thin sheet of metal such as gold or silver used, e.g. to decorate an art object 5 **PART OF TABLE TOP** a hinged or removable section of a table top 6 **PART OF DOOR** a hinged or sliding section of a door, shutter, or gate 7 **PART OF SPRING IN VEHICLE** one of the metal strips that form a spring in a vehicle suspension system (**leaf spring**) ■ *vi* **GROW LEAVES** to put out new leaves [Old English *lēaf* < Germanic] —**leafless** *adj* ◇ **take a leaf out of somebody's book** to follow somebody else's usually good example ◇ **turn over a new leaf** to start to behave in a more acceptable way
leaf through *vt* to turn the pages of a book or magazine quickly and casually

leafage /léefij/ *n* leaves or foliage

leaf beetle *n* a beetle, e.g. the Colorado beetle or the flea beetle, that feeds on the leaves of plants and can be destructive to cultivated crops. Family: Chrysomelidae.

leaf curl *n* a disease of plants that causes the leaves to curl

leafcutter ant /léef kuttər-/ *n* a tropical American ant that cuts leaves into pieces to use as fertilizer for the fungi it grows in its nest for food. Genus: *Atta.*

leafcutter bee *n* a common solitary bee that usually nests in the ground or in a natural cavity and lines its nest with pieces of leaves. Family: Megachilidae.

leaf fat *n* the dense layers of fat surrounding the kidneys, especially a pig's kidneys, often used for making lard

leaf fish *n* a tropical freshwater fish that is laterally flat so that it appears like a floating dead leaf. Family: Nandidae.

leafhopper /léef hoppər/ *n* a slender spindle-shaped leaping insect found worldwide that sucks the sap from plants and spreads plant diseases. Family: Cicadellidae.

leaf insect *n* an insect with a flat body that resembles a leaf in shape and colour. Native to: S Asia. Family: Phyllidae.

leaf lard *n* a high-quality lard made from the fat surrounding the kidneys of pigs (**leaf fat**)

leaflet /léeflət/ *n* 1 **FREE PRINTED MATERIAL** a sheet of printed paper, usually folded, that is distributed free as part of an advertising or information campaign 2 **SMALL LEAF** a small or young leaf 3 **PART OF LEAF** a division of a compound leaf ■ *vti* **DISTRIBUTE LEAFLETS** to hand out or distribute leaflets in a particular place or to a particular group of people

leafleteer /léeflə téer/, **leafleter** /léeflətər/ *n* a writer or distributor of leaflets

leaf miner *n* any insect whose larvae tunnel into and feed on leaf tissue, including several species of very small moths and a particular species of fly. Family: Agromyzidae.

leaf monkey *n* a leaf-eating Asian monkey related to the langurs. Genus: *Presbytis.* ◊ **langur**

leaf mould *n* 1 nitrogen-rich compost or soil that consists mainly of decomposed leaves 2 a fungal growth on leaves

leaf roll *n* a viral disease of potatoes that is transmitted by aphids and causes the leaves to curl upwards

leaf roller *n* a small moth whose larvae roll leaves to protect themselves while they eat them

leaf scar *n* the mark left on a stem when a leaf falls

leaf sheath *n* the part at the bottom of the leaf that surrounds the stem in grasses

leaf spot *n* a fungal or bacterial plant disease that causes discoloured spots to develop on leaves

leaf spring *n* a spring made of several curved metal strips of different lengths (**leaves**) bracketed together, used in motor vehicle suspension systems

leafstalk /léef stawk/ *n* a stalk by which a leaf is attached to a stem. Technical name **petiole**

leaf trace *n* the structure that carries fluid between the main stem and the base of the leaf in plants

leafy /léefi/ (**-ier, -iest**) *adj* 1 **WITH MANY LEAVES** covered with or having many leaves 2 **WITH MANY TREES THAT HAVE**

LEAVES with many trees and therefore a lot of foliage **3** PRODUCING LEAVES producing broad leaves as distinct from blades or needles **4** WITH EDIBLE LEAVES having edible leaves ○ *leafy vegetables* —**leafiness** *n*

league[1] /leeg/ *n* **1** GROUP WITH COMMON GOALS an association of nations, states, organizations, or businesses with common interests or goals **2** GROUP OF SPORTS CLUBS an association of sports clubs or teams that compete with each other **3** LEVEL OF SKILL a level of performance or skill ○ *Her painting is not in the same league with yours.* **4** *Aus* RUGBY LEAGUE rugby league (*informal*) ■ *vti* (**leagues, leaguing, leagued**) FORM INTO LEAGUE to join with others for a common interest or goal, or bring people together for such a purpose [15C. Via French *ligue* 'pact' < Italian *liga* < Latin *ligare* 'bind'.] ◇ **in league (with somebody)** collaborating with somebody, usually for a questionable purpose

league[2] /leeg/ *n* a measure of distance of variable length, usually about 5 km/3 mi., no longer in general use [14C. < late Latin *leuga* < Gaulish.]

league football *n Aus* rugby league (*informal*)

League of Nations *n* an alliance of nations established in 1920 to promote world peace and cooperation that was replaced by the United Nations in 1946

leaguer /leégər/ *n US, Can* a member of a sports league

league table *n* **1** LIST OF SPORTS TEAMS OR PLAYERS a list of the members of a sports league arranged in order of rank **2** LIST OF RANKING ORDER a comparison of performance in any area involving competition ■ *npl* WRITTEN REPORT OF UK SCHOOLS' EXAM RESULTS a comparison of UK schools' performance in National Curriculum tests and other public examinations (*informal*)

leak /leek/ *n* **1** HOLE OR CRACK an unintentional hole or crack that permits something such as liquid, gas, or light to escape or enter **2** ACCIDENTAL ESCAPE OR ENTRY the accidental escape or unwanted entry of something, usually by way of an unintentional hole or crack **3** ESCAPING LIQUID OR GAS something that escapes through an unintentional hole or crack **4** ACCIDENTAL ESCAPE OF ELECTRICITY a place through which an electric current escapes accidentally, or the resulting loss of electricity **5** MEANS OF ESCAPE a means of escape, or the resulting loss by means of it ○ *We need to plug the leak in our finances.* **6** DISCLOSURE OF SECRETS an unofficial release of confidential information, usually to the media **7** ACT OF URINATION an act of urination (*slang*) ■ *vti* **1** LET SOMETHING IN OR OUT to let something escape or enter accidentally, or escape or enter in this way **2** DISCLOSE SECRETS OR BE DISCLOSED to release confidential information unofficially or covertly, usually to the media, or become publicly known in such a way ○ *She leaked the details of the deal to the press.* [15C. < ?] —**leaker** *n*

SPELLCHECK Do not confuse ***leak*** with ***leek***, which has a similar sound. Beware: your spellchecker will not catch this error.

leak out *vi* to become known unintentionally or be disclosed unofficially

leakage /leékij/ *n* **1** ESCAPE OR ENTRANCE OF LIQUID, GAS, ETC a gradual escape or entrance of something such as oil, gas, or electric current by a leak **2** SOMETHING THAT ESCAPES OR ENTERS an amount of something that escapes or enters by leaking **3** DISCLOSURE OF SECRETS the unofficial release of confidential information, usually to the media

Leakey /leéki/, **Louis** (1903–72) British archaeologist and paleontologist

Leakey, Mary (1913–96) British archaeologist and paleontologist. Born **Mary Douglas Nicol**

Leakey, Richard (*b.* 1944) Kenyan-born British archaeologist and paleontologist

leakproof /leék proof/ *adj* **1** designed to prevent any of the contents from escaping or anything unwanted from entering **2** not allowing breaches in secrecy or confidentiality (*informal*)

leaky /leéki/ (**-ier, -iest**) *adj* **1** letting liquid or gas in or out accidentally through holes or cracks **2** allowing breaches in secrecy or confidentiality (*informal*) —**leakily** *adv* —**leakiness** *n*

leal /leel/ *adj Scotland* loyal and true (*archaic*) [14C. Via Anglo Norman *leal* < Old French *leel* (see LOYAL).]

Leamington Spa /lémmingtən spaá/ town in central England. Population: 55,396 (1991).

lean[1] /leen/ *v* (**leans, leaning, leant** /lent/ *or* **leaned**) **1** *vi* BEND OR INCLINE to be in or move to a position that is at an angle to the vertical **2** *vti* REST SOMETHING OR BE SUPPORTED to rest against something for support, or rest something against something else **3** *vi* TEND TOWARDS to have a preference or inclination for a particular thing or course of action ■ *n* TILTED POSITION a position that is at an angle to the vertical [Old English *hleonian* < Indo-European, 'slope']

lean on *vt* **1** DEPEND ON to be dependent on somebody **2** GET SUPPORT FROM to gain moral support from somebody ○ *You can always lean on me.* **3** INTIMIDATE SOMEBODY INTO DOING to put pressure on somebody to do something (*informal*)

lean[2] /leen/ *adj* **1** WITHOUT EXCESS FAT having no excess fat ○ *a tall, lean physique* **2** NOT FATTY having little or no fat ○ *lean meat* **3** NOT PRODUCTIVE not productive or profitable ○ *lean harvest* **4** ECONOMICAL AND EFFICIENT not using any more resources than necessary ○ *runs a lean business* **5** WITH FEW MINERALS low in mineral content ○ *lean ore* **6** LOW IN COMBUSTIBLE MATERIAL describes a mixture of fuel and air that is low in combustible material ○ *a lean fuel mixture* ■ *n* MEAT WITHOUT FAT meat with little or no fat [Old English *hlǣne* < Germanic] —**leanly** *adv* —**leanness** *n*

SYNONYMS See ***thin***.

Lean /leen/, **Sir David** (1908–91) British film director

lean-burn *adj* designed to run on a mixture that has a high proportion of air to fuel in order to reduce air pollution ○ *a lean-burn engine*

leaning /leéning/ *n* an inclination or tendency towards something such as a particular set of opinions

Barnaby's

Leaning Tower of Pisa

Leaning Tower of Pisa bell tower of the cathedral in Pisa, Italy, built between 1173 and 1350 and well known for its tilt

leant past tense, past participle of **lean**[1]

lean-to (*plural* **lean-tos**) *n* **1** an outbuilding with a slanted roof that rests against the wall of a larger building **2** a shed or shack with a roof that slopes in one direction

leap /leep/ *v* (**leaps, leaping, leapt** /lept/ *or* **leaped**) **1** *vi* JUMP FORCEFULLY to make a jump with a long or high arc ○ *She leapt over the stream with ease.* **2** *vi* MOVE AS IF BY JUMPING to move abruptly, as if by jumping up or across something ○ *The dog leapt into her arms.* **3** *vi* ABRUPTLY SWITCH TO to move abruptly to a new thought or action ○ *The reporters leapt to the conclusion that wrongdoing had occurred.* **4** *vi* GO UP SUBSTANTIALLY to increase suddenly and sizably ○ *Stock prices leaped to new highs.* **5** *vt* JUMP to jump over an obstacle ○ *didn't think he could leap the stream* **6** *vt* MAKE ANIMAL JUMP to cause an animal to jump over something ■ *n* **1** ARCHING JUMP a long high jump **2** DISTANCE OF JUMP the distance covered by a leap ○ *a leap of almost three metres* **3** PLACE TO JUMP a place over or from which to leap **4** LARGE INCREASE a sudden and sizable increase ○ *The market has made many leaps this quarter.* **5** MUSICAL INTERVAL a large interval in music [Old English *hlēapan* < Germanic, 'run'] —**leaper** *n* ◇ **a leap in the dark** an action taken without knowing what the outcome or consequences will be ◇ **in** *or* **by leaps and bounds** extremely rapidly

leap at *vt* to be quick to accept or take advantage of something ○ *He leapt at the chance to play the lead in the film.*

leap out at *vt* to be suddenly or immediately obvious to somebody ○ *The answer just leaps out at you.*

leapfrog /leép frog/ *n* VAULTING GAME a game in which players take turns bending over so that another player can vault over them with the legs wide apart and the hands placed on their backs ■ *v* (**-frogs, -frogging, -frogged**) **1** *vti* PLAY LEAPFROG to vault over somebody in the game of leapfrog **2** *vt* VAULT OVER to vault over a person or obstacle in a style similar to that used in the game of leapfrog **3** *vti* PASS EACH OTHER ALTERNATELY to take turns overtaking each other ○ *The two drivers were leapfrogging down the racetrack.* **4** *vi* ADVANCE QUICKLY to advance quickly in status or position, usually bypassing competitors or colleagues ○ *She started the day in seventh place but soon leapfrogged into first.* **5** *vt* CIRCUMVENT to evade something by passing around it

leap second *n* a second added at the end of June or December to a timekeeping system in order to keep measured time synchronized with the movement of the Earth around the Sun [After LEAP YEAR]

leapt past tense, past participle of **leap**

leap year *n* a year with an extra day, 29 February, added to make up the difference between the 365-day calendar and the actual duration of the Earth's orbit of the Sun. Leap years usually occur every four years. [Probably because any given date falls two days later than in the preceding year, instead of one]

Lear /leer/, **Edward** (1812–88) British writer and artist

learn /lurn/ (**learns, learning, learned** *or* **learnt** /lurnt/) *v* **1** *vti* COME TO KNOW to acquire knowledge of a subject or skill through education or experience ○ *I'm learning to play the piano.* **2** *vti* FIND OUT to gain information about somebody or something ○ *I just learned that Jim is arriving tomorrow.* **3** *vt* MEMORIZE to memorize something, e.g. facts, a poem, a piece of music, or a dance ○ *I have to learn the periodic table for my exam.* **4** *vt* TEACH SOMEBODY to teach a topic or skill to somebody (*nonstandard*) [Old English *leornian* < Indo-European, 'track'] —**learnable** *adj*

learned /lúrnid/ *adj* **1** HIGHLY EDUCATED well-educated and very knowledgeable ○ *a learned professor* **2** SCHOLARLY showing or requiring much education and knowledge **3** HONOURABLE used in addressing or referring to a lawyer in court ○ *my learned friend* **4** ACQUIRED, NOT INSTINCTUAL describes behaviour or knowledge that is acquired through training or experience rather than being instinctual [14C. Originally the past participle of LEARN 'teach'.] —**learnedly** *adv* —**learnedness** *n*

learned helplessness *n* somebody's failure to take action to make his or her life better, arising from a sense of not being in control

learner /lúrnər/ *n* **1** a person who studies or learns to do something **2** **learner, learner driver** a person who is learning to drive a motor vehicle

learner's permit *n US* = **provisional licence**

learning /lúrning/ *n* **1** ACQUIRING OF KNOWLEDGE the acquisition of knowledge or skill **2** ACQUIRED KNOWLEDGE knowledge or skill gained through education ○ *a man of great learning* **3** CHANGE IN KNOWLEDGE a relatively permanent change in, or acquisition of, knowledge, understanding, or behaviour

learning curve *n* **1** the rate at which a new subject or skill is learned ○ *the steep learning curve expected by the syllabus* **2** a graph that shows the relation between the rate at which knowledge or a skill is learned and the time spent acquiring it

learning disability, learning difficulty *n* a condition that either prevents or significantly hinders somebody from learning basic skills or information at the same rate as most people of the same age

learning-disabled *adj* prevented or hindered by a learning disability from learning basic skills or information at the same rate as most people of the same age (*not hyphenated after verbs*) ○ *materials aimed specifically at learning-disabled children*

learning theory *n* the theory that behaviour can be explained in terms of how people and animals learn to respond to a stimulus, e.g., learning by rewards and punishments (**operant conditioning**) and learning by association (**classical conditioning**)

learnt past tense, past participle of **learn**

leary /leéri/ *adj* = **leery**

lease /leess/ *n* **1** RENTAL CONTRACT a legal contract allowing somebody exclusive possession of another's property for a particular time in return for rent **2** LENGTH OF LEASE the period of time covered by a lease ○ *Our lease is six months.* ■ *vt* (**leases, leasing, leased**) **1** RENT SOMETHING TO to rent property to somebody under the terms of a lease **2** RENT SOMETHING FROM to rent property from somebody under the terms of a lease ○ *We've leased a* *cottage for the summer.* [14C. < Anglo-Norman *les* < *lesser* 'to lease', variant of Old French *laissier* (see LEASH).] —**leasable** *adj* —**leaser** *n* ◇ **a new lease of life** renewed freshness or vigour, usually resulting from some minor change

leaseback /leéss bak/ *n* an arrangement in which a property is sold and then leased to its former owner by its new owner

leasehold /leéss hōld/ *n* **1** the holding of a property through a lease **2** a property that is leased —**leaseholder** *n*

leash /leesh/ *n* **1** = **lead**[1] *n.* 12 **2 RESTRAINT** something that controls or restrains somebody ○ *Our supervisor keeps us on a short leash.* **3 THREE ANIMALS TOGETHER** a set of three animals of one type, especially hounds ■ *vt* **RESTRAIN** to restrain your emotions or impulses or the emotions or impulses of somebody under your control [13C. < Old French *laisse* < *laissier* 'let go' < Latin *laxare* 'loosen' < *laxus* 'loose'.]

least /leest/ CORE MEANING: the smallest or lowest quantity or degree

1 *adj, adv, pron* **SMALLEST AMOUNT POSSIBLE** a smaller amount than anything or anyone else ○ *He went up the steps without showing the least anxiety.* ○ *what I liked the least of all* ○ *The least said the soonest mended.* **2** *adv* **LESS OF A QUALITY THAN OTHERS** having less of a particular quality than most other people or things ○ *one of the least appealing films of the year* **3** *adj* **EXTREMELY SMALL** used to emphasize that something is so small as to be virtually nonexistent ○ *She had not the least idea of what was going on with me.* **4** *adv* **TO A SMALLER DEGREE** indicates that something happens or is true to a smaller degree than at any other time ○ *I had been appointed to take charge while I least expected anything of the sort.* **5** *pron* **THE MINIMUM** used to indicate the minimum that should be done in a situation ○ *The least you can do is to make yourself thoroughly acquainted with the procedure.* [Old English *lǣst*, contraction of *lǣsest* < *lǣs* 'less'] ◇ **at least 1** not less than a particular amount ○ *It'll take at least two days to finish.* ○ *We travelled at least forty-five miles without a rest.* **2** in any case and despite anything else ○ *At least you've got a job, which is more than I have.* **3** indicates a correction or change ○ *The answer seemed right, or at least close enough.* ◇ **least of all** emphasizes that a negative applies to one case in particular ○ *No one must know of our discovery – least of all our competitors.* ◇ **not (in) the least** not in the slightest ○ *The only noteworthy point about him was of the negative sort – he was not in the least like his sister.* ○ *I'm not the least bit tired.* ◇ **not least** emphasizes something particularly important ○ *It is too early to be sure, not least because the weather may change.* ◇ **to say the least** without exaggerating or overstating the case ○ *We were, to say the least, surprised at her rudeness.*

least common denominator *n* MATH = **lowest common denominator** *n.* 1

least common multiple *n* MATH = **lowest common multiple**

least squares *n* a method of finding the best curve to fit a set of statistical data points by squaring the distance that each point is from a given curve, summing the squares, and choosing the curve for which the sum has the minimum value

leastways /leést wayz/ *adv* in any case and despite anything else (*informal*)

leastwise /leést wīz/ *adv* leastways (*regional*)

leat /leet/ *n* a trench that brings water to a mill or factory [Old English *(wæter) gelæt* '(water) channel' < an earlier form of LET]

leather /léthər/ *n* **1 TANNED AND DRESSED HIDE** the processed hide of animals with the fur or feathers removed **2 POLISHING CLOTH** a piece of leather used for polishing something **3 MATERIAL LIKE LEATHER** something that is like leather in appearance or texture ○ *fruit leather* **4 SOMETHING MADE OF LEATHER** an item or part of an item that is made of leather **5 DOG'S EARFLAP** the flap of a dog's ear ■ **leathers** *npl* **MOTORCYCLISTS' LEATHER CLOTHING** the protective leather jacket, trousers, boots, and gloves worn by motorcyclists ■ *adj* **1 MADE OF LEATHER** made of leather or a material that looks like leather **2 INVOLVING SADOMASOCHISM OR FETISHISM** wearing, or for people who wear, leather clothing as a symbol of interest in sadomasochism or as a fetish ■ *vt* **1 COVER SOMETHING IN LEATHER** to give something a covering of leather **2 PUNISH SOMEBODY PHYSICALLY** to beat a person or animal severely, especially by using a leather strap (*dated informal*) [Old English *lether-* < Indo-European]

leatherback /léthər bak/ *n* the largest of the living sea turtles, which has a flexible shell ridged with bone and covered with leathery skin. *Dermochelys coriacea.*

Leatherhead /léthər hed/ town in S England. Population: 42,903 (1991).

leatherjacket /léthər jakit/ *n* the tough-skinned larva of some crane flies that is considered to be a pest because it destroys grass roots

leatherneck /léthər nek/ *n US* a member of the United States Marine Corps (*slang*) [< the leather collar that was part of the uniform]

leatherwear /léthər wair/ *n* clothing and accessories made of leather [After *sportswear* or *footwear*]

leatherwood /léthər wòod/ *n* **1** a deciduous tree with pliable branches and bark. Native to: E North America. *Dirca palustris.* **2** PLANTS = **titi**[2] *n.* 2

leatherwork /léthər wurk/ *n* **1** the craft of sculpting, cutting, or burning designs into leather **2** items made from leather, especially decorated leather —**leatherworker** *n* —**leatherworking** *n*

leathery /léthəri/ *adj* looking or feeling like leather, especially having a grainy surface or a tough unyielding consistency —**leatheriness** *n*

leave[1] /leev/ (**leaves, leaving, left** /left/) *v* **1** *vti* **DEPART** to go away from a person or place ○ *I leave the office at five o'clock daily.* **2** *vt* **LET SOMEBODY CONTINUE DOING** to go away from somebody in order to allow that person to do something ○ *You run along and leave me to my paperwork.* **3** *vt* **CAUSE SOMETHING TO REMAIN** to give something to somebody or put something in a place before departing ○ *I left my number with Dan.* **4** *vt* **LET SOMETHING REMAIN BEHIND ACCIDENTALLY** to forget to bring something away from a place ○ *I must have left my keys at the office.* **5** *vt* **GIVE SOMETHING IN WILL** to bequeath something as a legacy ○ *He plans to leave all his money to charity.* **6** *vt* **PRODUCE SOMETHING THAT REMAINS** to cause a residue, trace, or mark to remain ○ *The snails left trails on the path.* **7** *vt* **NOT CHANGE CONDITION OF** to allow something or somebody to remain unchanged in a certain state ○ *I left my coat on.* ○ *Leave your sister alone.* **8** *vt* **HAVE SOMETHING REMAINING** to cause an amount to remain by removing some amount or part ○ *Six minus four leaves two.* **9** *vt* **SET SOMETHING ASIDE** to save or keep something for somebody's use ○ *I left some cake for you.* **10** *vt* **DESERT** to abandon a person or place ○ *She has left the city to live in the country.* **11** *vt* **HAVE SOMEBODY AS SURVIVOR** to be survived by somebody after death ○ *He leaves a wife and two young sons.* **12** *vti* **GIVE UP POSITION IN** to end participation in a group or activity ○ *She left that job for a better one.* **13** *vt* **GIVE JOB TO ANOTHER** to transfer control of or responsibility for something to somebody ○ *Leave the typing to me.* **14** *vt* **REJECT** to reject something offered ○ *That's the best I can offer, take it or leave it.* [Old English *lǣfan* < Indo-European, 'to stick'] ◇ **leave go** *or* **hold of somebody** *or* **something 1** to stop holding somebody or something (*nonstandard*) ○ *Leave go of my arm!* **2** to stop bothering somebody, or stop interfering in a situation ◇ **leave it at that** to do or say no more about something ◇ **leave much to be desired** to be highly unsatisfactory ◇ **leave somebody to himself** *or* **herself** to go away and allow somebody to be alone (*often passive*) ◇ **leave well (enough) alone** to leave a situation as it is rather than risk making it worse

USAGE leave or **let**? Either ***leave*** or ***let*** is correct if you mean 'to avoid bothering someone or to stop bothering somebody in order to allow that person to continue to do something': *Leave/let your sisters alone. Leave me to get on with my work. Let me get on with my work.* The only choice is ***let*** if you mean 'to allow or permit somebody to do something': *Let me finish this first. Let* [not *leave*] *us be.*

leave behind *vt* **1** to move ahead of somebody or something proceeding at a slower pace (*often passive*) **2** to dismiss something from the mind ○ *She left her worries behind as she headed for the Bahamas.*

leave off *v* **1** *vi* to stop doing something ○ *Leave off chatting and listen for a change!* **2** *vt* to stop doing or making use of something ○ *You can leave your coats off since it's so warm.*

leave out *vt* to fail to include somebody or something, whether by choice or accident ○ *I felt left out of the party.* ◇ **leave it out!** used to tell somebody to stop saying or doing something annoying (*informal*)

leave[2] /leev/ *n* **1 PERIOD OF PERMITTED ABSENCE** time off from work or duty, with official permission ○ *He'll get a month's paternity leave.* **2 PERMISSION** permission to do something (*formal*) ○ *He was given leave to present his proposal.* **3 FAREWELL** the act of saying goodbye to somebody ○ *We took our leave of the host and went on to the next party.* [Old English *lēaf* 'pleasure, approval' < Indo-European, 'desire'] ◇ **take leave of your senses** to become entirely irrational or lose all sense of reality

leave[3] /leev/ (**leaves, leaving, leaved**) *vi* to grow foliage ○ *The oak has started to leave.* [13C. < LEAF.]

leaven /lévv'n/ *n* **leaven, leavening 1 RAISING AGENT** a substance used to make dough rise, especially yeast or other fermenting agents **2 SOMETHING THAT ENLIVENS** something that lightens the weight or mood of something (*literary*) ○ *with a leaven of wit* ■ *vt* **1 MIX YEAST IN** to add leaven to dough **2 MAKE FOOD RISE** to cause bread or cake to rise using leaven **3 ENLIVEN** to lighten the atmosphere or mood of something (*literary*) ○ *His story leavened the mood of the gathering.* [14C. < Old French *levain* < Latin *levare* 'to raise'.]

Leavenworth /lévv'n wurth/ city in NE Kansas, site of Fort Leavenworth, a military post, and Leavenworth Federal Penitentiary. Population: 39,431 (1996).

leave of absence *n* **1** permission to have time off from work or another duty for a particular period ○ *I requested a leave of absence so that I could take a finance course.* **2** the time spent away from work or another duty with leave of absence ○ *His leave of absence included the holidays.*

leaves plural of **leaf**

leave-taking *n* a saying of goodbye before leaving somebody (*literary*) ○ *After a tearful leave-taking, we set off.*

leavings /leévingz/ *npl* something that somebody has left behind or that is left over from something, usually of little value

Leavis /leéviss/, **F. R.** (1895–1978) British literary critic. Full name **Frank Raymond Leavis**

Lebanon

Lebanon /lébbənən/ republic in SW Asia, on the east of the Mediterranean Sea. Capital: Beirut. Population: 3,111,828 (1997). Area: 10,452 sq. km/4,036 sq. mi. —**Lebanese** /lébbə neéz/ *n, adj*

lebensraum /láybənz rowm/ *n* **1** additional land in Eastern Europe that the Nazi government claimed was necessary for the continued political and economic development of Germany **2** adequate room for life or development [Early 20C. < German, 'living space'.]

lebkuchen /láyb kookən/ (*plural* **-chen**) *n* a rich decorated German gingerbread, traditionally baked in a wide variety of shapes and sizes for Christmas and other celebrations [Early 20C. Via German < Middle High German *lebekuoche* < *lebe* 'loaf' + *kuoche* 'cake'.]

Lebowa /lə bṓ ə/ former homeland in N South Africa

Lebrun /lə brúN, lə brṓN/, **Albert** (1871–1950) French statesman

Le Carré /lə kárray/, **John** (*b.* 1931) British novelist. Born **David John Moore Cornwell**

lech /lech/, **letch** *n* (*informal*) **1 LECHER** a lecher **2 INTENSE DESIRE** a lustful desire for somebody **3 INSTANCE OF LECHERY** an act or instance of lechery ■ *vi* **BEHAVE LEWDLY** to behave lewdly towards somebody (*informal*) [Late 18C. Probably back-formation < LECHER.]

Le Chatelier's principle /lə sha tél yayz-/ *n* the principle that a change affecting a chemical equilibrium is offset by compensatory changes in other components of the equilibrium, thus producing little overall effect [Early 20C. After Henri Louis *Le Chatelier*.]

lechayim *interj*, in BEVERAGES = **l'chaim**

lecher /léchər/ *n* a man who behaves lewdly and lustfully in a way regarded as distasteful (*disapproving*) [12C. < Old French *lecheor* < *lechier* 'to lick' < Germanic.]

lecherous /léchərəss/ *adj* expressing or displaying lewdness in a way regarded as distasteful —**lecherously** *adv* —**lecherousness** *n*

lechery /léchəri/ *n* lustful behaviour, especially by a man, that is regarded as distasteful

lechwe /láychwi/ *n* 1 an antelope with long narrow hooves and long backward-pointing horns. Native to: marshes, riverbanks in Botswana and Zambia. *Kobus leche*. 2 an antelope with a white shoulder patch. Native to: wetlands of the upper Nile valley. *Kobus megaceros*. [Mid-19C. Probably < Sesotho *lets'a*.]

lecithin /léssithin/ *n* a phospholipid found in cell membranes that also plays a role in fat metabolism [Mid-19C. < French *lécithine* < Greek *lekithos* 'egg yolk'.]

lecithinase /lə síthi nayss, -nayz/ *n* BIOCHEM = **phospholipase**

Leclanché cell /lə klaàn shay-/ *n* a primary cell, the common dry cell, having a carbon anode, zinc cathode, and sal ammoniac as the electrolyte [Late 19C. After Georges *Leclanché* (1839–82), French chemist.]

Le Corbusier
AKG London

Le Corbusier /lə káwr boòzi ay/ (1887–1965) Swiss-born French architect and designer. Pseudonym of **Charles-Édouard Jeanneret**

lect /lekt/ *n* a variety within a language, having its own rules [Late 20C. Back-formation < DIALECT.]

lect. *abbr* 1 lecture 2 lecturer

lectern /léktərn/ *n* 1 a tall slender table with a slanted top on which an open book can rest, used in churches and synagogues for reading scriptures to the congregation 2 a stand with a slanted top on which a book or lecture notes can rest before a standing speaker [14C. Via Old French *letrun* < late Latin *lectrum* < Latin *lect-*, past participle of *legere* 'to read'.]

lectin /léktin/ *n* any of a group of plant proteins [Mid-20C. < Latin *lect-*, past participle of *legere* 'to read'.]

lection /léksh'n/ *n* 1 a variant reading of a text in a particular edition or translation 2 a passage from Scripture that is set to be read on a particular day as part of the liturgy of a Christian service [Early 17C. < Latin *lection-* 'reading' < *legere* 'to read'.]

lectionary /léksh'nari/ (*plural* **-ies**) *n* a schedule of scriptural readings to be read at church services over the course of the year

lector /lék tawr/ *n* 1 a public university teacher, especially a man who is a foreign language instructor in his own language at a European university. ◊ **lectrice** 2 a public reader of scriptural passages to a congregation or a religious community [14C. < Latin, 'reader' < *lect-*, past participle of *legere* 'to read'.]

lectrice /lek treèss/ *n* 1 a woman who is a university teacher, especially a woman who is a foreign language instructor in her own language at a university. ◊ **lector** *n*. 1 [Late 19C. < French, feminine of *lecteur* < Latin *lector* (see LECTOR).]

lecture /lékchər/ *n* 1 INSTRUCTIONAL SPEECH an educational speech on a particular subject made before an audience ○ *I missed the lecture on Shakespeare's use of irony.* 2 TEACHING SESSION a class meeting at which a lecture is

given ○ *The course involves two lectures and two lab sessions per week.* 3 REPRIMAND a speech intended as a reprimand ■ *v* (**-tures, -turing, -tured**) 1 *vti* GIVE EDUCATIONAL SPEECH to deliver a speech before a group of people as a method of instruction ○ *He lectures on stress management all over the country.* 2 *vi* BE UNIVERSITY LECTURER to be employed as a lecturer at a university ○ *She lectures at the University.* 3 *vt* REPRIMAND to reprimand somebody by making a speech about how a person should behave ○ *lecturing the congregation about church attendance* [13C. Via French < medieval Latin *lectura* 'reading' < Latin *lect-*, past participle of *legere* 'to read'.]

lecture hall, lecture theatre *n* US = **lecture theatre**

lecturer /lékchərər/ *n* 1 a teacher at a university who ranks lower than a professor 2 an informative speaker on a specific topic, especially as a professional ○ *a lecturer's tour*

lectureship /lékchər ship/ *n* a post at the rank of lecturer in a British institution of higher education ○ *The University has three lectureships open.*

lecture theatre *n* a large room with a stage for a speaker and desks and chairs for an audience, arranged so that the whole audience can see the speaker. US term **lecture hall**

led past tense, past participle of **lead**[1] (*often used in combination*) ○ *The concern for safety is consumer-led rather than industry-led*

USAGE See **lead**[1].

LED *n* a semiconductor that emits light when a current passes through it. Use: indicator lights on electronic equipment. Full form **light-emitting diode**

Leda /leèdə/ *n* 1 in Greek mythology, a queen of Sparta. She was the mother of Helen of Troy, Clytemnestra, and Castor and Pollux. 2 a very small natural satellite of Jupiter discovered in 1974

lederhosen /láydər höz'n/ *npl* a pair of Bavarian leather shorts, usually with braces, worn by men and boys [Mid-20C. < German, 'leather trousers'.]

ledge /lej/ *n* 1 NARROW SHELF AGAINST WALL a narrow shelf or moulding fixed to a wall that serves a decorative or protective purpose 2 FLAT SURFACE PROJECTING FROM ROCK FACE a narrow flat projecting rock shelf, e.g. on the vertical surface of a cliff 3 UNDERWATER RAISED SURFACE a raised surface underwater such as a reef or ridge, especially one found near a shore 4 ROCK LAYER a layer of ore-bearing rock [Mid-16C. < ?] —**ledged** *adj* —**ledgy** *adj*

ledger /léjjər/ *n* 1 FINANCIAL RECORD BOOK a book or page with columns for debits and credits, on which to transcribe financial records 2 HORIZONTAL GRAVESTONE a gravestone that lies flat on the ground 3 SCAFFOLDING BEAM a horizontal beam in a scaffolding that is attached to the uprights and supports the beams (**putlogs**) 4 FISHING = **ledger-tackle** ■ *vi* FISH WITH LEDGER-TACKLE to fish using ledger-tackle [Early 16C. Probably < *leggen*, earlier form of LAY[1].]

ledger board *n* 1 a horizontal board, especially the top rail of a fence 2 a narrow horizontal board attached to a row of studs to support joist ends

ledger line, leger line *n* a short line added above or below a musical staff to accommodate notes that are higher or lower than those on the staff

ledger-tackle *n* a fishing line with a weight attached near its end, used to anchor the line so that the bait floats near the bottom of the water

Leduc /lədoòk/ *town* in central Alberta, Canada. Population: 13,970 (1991).

lee /lee/ *n* 1 SHIP SIDE AWAY FROM WIND the side of a ship away from the source of the wind 2 PROTECTIVE COVER shelter from the elements when the wind is blowing ○ *in the lee of the wall* ■ *adj* AWAY FROM WIND on or towards the side of a ship, natural feature, or object that is away from the wind [Old English *hléo* 'shelter' < Indo-European, 'warm'.]

Lee /lee/, **Gypsy Rose** (1914–70) US entertainer and novelist. Born **Louise Rose Hovick**

Lee, John A. (1891–1982) New Zealand politician and writer

Robert E. Lee
Library of Congress

Lee, Robert E. (1807–70) US Confederate general. Full name **Robert Edward Lee**

Lee, Spike (*b.* 1957) US film writer and director. Born **Shelton Jackson Lee**

leeboard /leè bawrd/ *n* either of two movable wooden or metal shelves on the outside of a ship's hull that prevent sideways movement caused by the wind [Because it prevents making leeway]

leech[1] /leech/ *n* 1 BLOOD-SUCKING WORM a freshwater worm that sucks blood or eats flesh. Class: Hirudinea. 2 EXPLOITER OF OTHERS a person who clings to or exploits somebody else, e.g. for financial support 3 DOCTOR a physician (*archaic informal*) ■ *v* 1 *vt* BLEED SOMEBODY USING LEECHES to bleed a patient using leeches 2 *vi* EXPLOIT to cling to or take advantage of somebody, e.g. for financial support (*informal*) [Old English *lǽce*] —**leech-like** *adj*

leech[2] /leech/, **leach** *n* 1 a vertical edge of a square sail 2 the edge of a fore-and-aft sail that is farthest from the mast or stay [15C. < ?]

Leeds /leedz/ *city* in N England. Population: 725,000 (1995).

leek /leek/ *n* an edible plant with dark green coiled leaves rising from a close-set white base, related to the onion. *Allium porrum*. [Old English *léac* < Germanic]

SPELLCHECK See **leak**.

Leek /leek/ *town* in central England. Population: 18,167 (1991).

Lee Kuan Yew /leè kwaàn yoò/ (*b.* 1923) Singaporean statesman

leer /leer/ *vi* to look or smile in a way that suggests unpleasantly lustful or malicious intent ■ *n* an unpleasantly lustful or malicious look or smile [Mid-16C. Probably < obsolete *leer* 'cheek' < Old English *hléor*.]

leery /leèri/ (**-ier, -iest**), **leary** (**-ier, -iest**) *adj* regarding somebody or something with suspicion (*informal*) ○ *I'm leery of anyone who approaches me on the street.* [Early 18C. < ?] —**leeriness** *n*

lees /leez/ *npl* sediment that settles in wine or other alcoholic beverages during fermentation [14C. Plural of obsolete *lee* < Old French *lie* < medieval Latin *lia* < Celtic.]

lee shore *n* a shore that is in the direction away from the wind, relative to a ship

leet[1] /leet/ *n* a court formerly held at regular intervals by the lords of English manors [13C. < Anglo-Norman *lete*.]

leet[2] /leet/ *n* Scotland a list of applicants or candidates for a post or office [15C. < ?]

Leeuwin, Cape /loò ən/ *promontory* in SW Western Australia

leeward /leèwərd/; *nautical* /loò ərd/ *adj* AWAY FROM WIND on or towards a location, especially the side of a ship, that is away or sheltered from the wind ■ *adv* AWAY FROM WIND away from where the wind is coming from ■ *n* PLACE AWAY FROM WIND a place or direction away or sheltered from the wind

Leeward Islands /leèward-/ chain of islands in the West Indies, between the Atlantic Ocean and the Caribbean Sea. The principal islands include Antigua, Guadeloupe, Montserrat, and St Kitts. Area: 3,297 sq. km/1,237 sq. mi.

leeway /leè way/ *n* 1 LATITUDE FOR VARIATION the permissible margin for variation or deviation from something

2 FALLING BEHIND falling behind in progress or performance ◦ *He's got a lot of leeway to make up at work after his holiday.* **3 DEVIATION FROM COURSE** the sideways movement of a ship or aircraft from its course, caused by strong winds

Le Fanu /léffə nyoo/, **Sheridan** (1814–73) Irish novelist and journalist

left[1] /left/ *adj* **1 WEST WHEN FACING NORTH** on or towards the west when somebody or something is facing north ◦ *Her left leg is broken.* **2 left, Left ADVOCATING POLITICAL AND SOCIAL CHANGE** supporting liberal, socialist, or communist political and social changes or reform **3 ON LEFT WHEN LOOKING DOWNSTREAM** on the river bank to the left of somebody facing downstream **4 TO RIGHT OF AUDIENCE** on or relating to that part of a stage that is to the left of somebody standing on it and facing the audience ◦ *Exit stage left.* ■ *adv* **ON LEFT SIDE** on or towards the left side of somebody or something ◦ *The pole is leaning left a bit.* ■ *n* **1 LEFT SIDE** the left side of somebody or something ◦ *The house is on your left.* **2 left, Left LIBERALS, SOCIALISTS, AND COMMUNISTS** people who support liberal, socialist, or communist political and social changes or reform **3 LEFT-HANDED PUNCH** a blow delivered with the left hand ◦ *took a hard left to the jaw* **4 LEFT-HANDED PUNCHING ABILITY** a boxer's left hand with respect to its ability to deliver a punch ◦ *He's got a good left.* [13C. < Old English *lyft-* 'weak'.]

left[2] past tense, past participle of **leave**[1]

left atrioventricular valve *n* ANAT = **mitral valve**

Left Bank area in central Paris, south of the River Seine

left-brain *adj* relating to or involving skills or knowledge such as analytical or linguistic ability that are believed to be associated with the left half of the cerebrum —**left brain** *n*

⚡ **left-click** *vti* to press and release the left button on a computer mouse

~~leftenant~~ incorrect spelling of **lieutenant**

left face *vi* (**left faces, left facing, left faced**) *US* to turn 90° to the left (*usually a command*) ■ *n US* a turn 90° to the left

left field *n* **1** *US* **VERY UNUSUAL POSITION** a position that is so different from mainstream beliefs that it is not generally taken seriously (*informal*) **2 SECTION OF OUTFIELD** the part of the outfield in baseball that is to the batter's left **3 OUTFIELDER'S POSITION** the position held by the baseball player who is responsible for fielding balls that are hit to left field ◊ **left field** *adj* **UNCONVENTIONAL** going beyond the bounds of a genre, especially in modern popular music ◊ **out in left field** *US* in an erroneous or very unconventional position or state (*informal*) ◊ the position held by a player who is responsible for catching balls that are hit to left field

left fielder *n* a baseball player who is responsible for fielding balls hit to left field

left-footed *adj* **1** having a natural tendency to lead with or use the left foot, especially in playing sports such as football **2** performed using the left foot ◦ *a left-footed shot on goal*

left-footer *n* an offensive term for a Roman Catholic

left-hand *adj* **1** on or towards the left **2** intended for or done by the left hand

left-handed *adj, adv* **1 USING LEFT HAND** using the left hand, rather than the right, for tasks such as writing and reaching for and manipulating objects **2 STARTING SWING FROM LEFT** swinging from the left to the right ■ *adj* **1 DONE WITH LEFT HAND** done using the left hand **2 NOT SINCERE** ironic and insincere ◦ *a left-handed compliment* **3 CLUMSY** lacking skill or grace **4 TURNING RIGHT TO LEFT** spiralling towards the left **5** LAW = **morganatic**

left-hander /-hándər/ *n* a person who uses chiefly the left hand for ordinary tasks

leftie *n* = **lefty**

leftish /léftish/ *adj* tending to be relatively left-wing in politics

leftism /léftizəm/ *n* the advocating of liberal, socialist, or communist political and social change or reform — **leftist** *adj, n*

left-luggage office *n* a room in a railway or bus station where luggage can be temporarily deposited

leftmost /léftmóst/ *adj* in the position farthest to the left

leftover /léftövər/ *adj* REMAINING UNUSED remaining after the rest of something has been used or eaten ■ *n* SOMETHING REMAINING something that remains from a previous period of time while everything else associated with

that period has disappeared ■ **leftovers** *npl* SAVED FOOD food remaining from a previous meal or meals, saved and served again or made into a new dish ◦ *I made this soup from leftovers.*

leftward /léftwərd/ *adj* moving towards or located on the left ■ *adv* = **leftwards**

leftwards /léftwərdz/, **leftward** /léftwərd/ *adv* towards the left

left wing *n* **1 MEMBERS OF ORGANIZATION MOST FAVOURING CHANGE** a subgroup of a larger organization that advocates greater political and social change or reform than the rest of the organization **2 FIELD LEFT OF OPPONENT'S GOAL** the side of a playing field that is to the left of a player facing the opponent's goal **3 SOMEBODY PLAYING ON LEFT WING** a player whose position in a team is on the left wing — **left-wing** *adj* —**left-winger** *n*

lefty /léfti/ *n* (*plural* -**ies**), **leftie** *n* (*informal*) **1** somebody with left-wing beliefs **2** *US, Can* a person who is left-handed ◦ *How many lefties are on the team?*

leg /leg/ *n* **1 LOWER LIMB** a limb that animals and people use for standing, walking, running, or jumping, either including or excluding the foot **2 SUPPORTING POLE** a part of an object that looks like a human or animal lower limb and is used for support ◦ *a table leg* **3 MEAT FROM ANIMAL'S OR FOWL'S LEG** the meat, including the bone, from the back hindquarter of a four-legged mammal, or from the leg of a bird, that is cooked and eaten as food **4 BRANCH OF OBJECT** one of the extensions of a branched object **5 CLOTHING FOR LEG** the portion of a piece of clothing that covers all or part of the human leg ◦ *trouser leg* **6 RIGHT-ANGLE SIDE OF TRIANGLE** either of the two sides of a right-angled triangle that extends from the right angle **7 SECTION OF JOURNEY** a part of a journey that is separated from other parts by a period of rest or by a change in direction or the manner of travel **8 SAILING COMPLETED ON ONE TACK** the distance travelled by a boat on a single tack **9 RELAY RACE PORTION** one of the parts of a relay race that a single athlete completes **10 PORTION OF SPORTS COMPETITION** one of several stages, events, or games that is part of a larger competition but is treated independently of the other parts and has its own winner **11 ONE OF TWO FOOTBALL GAMES** either of two games in a competition played between two football teams, one game being played at home, the other away **12 LEFT-HAND PART OF CRICKET FIELD** in cricket, the part of the field that lies on the left of and behind a right-handed batsman as he or she stands in position to hit the ball [13C. < Old Norse *leggr*.] ◊ **get your leg over** to have sex (*slang*) ◊ **have legs** *US* to be likely to enjoy a sustained period of popularity or success (*informal*) ◊ **leg it 1** to run away, especially in order to escape from somebody or something (*informal*) **2** to walk or run (*informal*) ◊ **not have a leg to stand on** to have nothing to justify or support an attitude or position (*informal*) ◊ **on your last legs** on the verge of collapse or breakdown ◊ **pull somebody's leg** to tell somebody something untrue as a tease or for fun (*informal*) ◊ **shake a leg 1** to hurry up (*usually in commands*) **2** to dance (*dated informal*) ◊ **show a leg** to get out of bed in the morning (*dated informal; usually in commands*) ◊ **stretch your legs** to go for a walk after a period of being seated or stationary ◊ **talk the hind legs off a donkey** to talk a great deal (*informal*)

leg. *abbr* **1** legal **2** legate **3** legato **4** legislation **5** legislative **6** legislature

legacy /léggəsi/ *n* (*plural* -**cies**) **1 BEQUEST MADE IN WILL** money or property that is left to somebody in a will **2 SOMETHING FROM PAST** something that is handed down or remains from a previous generation or time ■ *adj* **OUTDATED OR DISCONTINUED** associated with something that is outdated or discontinued [14C. Via Old French *legacie* 'office of a delegate' < medieval Latin *legatia* < Latin *legatus* (see LEGATE).]

legal /léeg'l/ *adj* **1 LAW-RELATED** relating to the law or to courts of law ◦ *took legal action* **2 OF OR FOR LAWYERS** relating to lawyers or to law as a profession **3 UNDER THE LAW** established under the law ◦ *the legal age of consent* **4 PERMITTED BY LAW** allowed under the law ◦ *Parking on the grass isn't legal.* **5 ESTABLISHED BY LAW COURT** recognized or established by a court of law, rather than a court of equity [15C. Via French < Latin *legalis* < *leg-* 'law'.] — **legally** *adv*

SYNONYMS *legal, lawful, decriminalized, legalized, legitimate, licit*

CORE MEANING: describes something that is permitted, recognized, or required by law

legal permitted, recognized, or required by law; **lawful** a

less common word meaning legal; **decriminalized** no longer categorized as a criminal offence; **legalized** previously categorized as illegal and now declared legal; **legitimate** complying with the law, or under the law; **licit** (*formal*) a rarely used word meaning legal.

legal age *n* the age established by law after which somebody is considered to be an adult

legal aid *n* **1** legal advice or representation that is provided by an organization at low or no cost to people who cannot afford to pay for legal services **2** public funds used for legal advice and representation for people who cannot afford private lawyers ◦ *Legal aid paid for his defence.*

legal cap *n* *US* ruled white writing paper used by lawyers that is 216 mm/8½ in by 350 mm/14 in to 406 mm/16 in, with the fold at the top

legal eagle *n* a lawyer, especially a skilful or successful one (*slang*)

legalese /léegə léez/ *n* language that is typically used in legal documents and is generally considered by lay people to be difficult to understand

legal holiday *n* *US* a day established as a holiday by law, when government offices, schools, and post offices are typically closed

legalise *vt* = **legalize**

legalism /léegəlizəm/ *n* **1** strict adherence to a literal interpretation of a law, rule, or religious or moral code **2** a word or phrase in legal jargon —**legalist** *n* —**legalistic** /léegə lístik/ *adj* —**legalistically** *adv*

legality /li gálliti/ *n* (*plural* -**ties**) **1** the state of being in accordance with the law ◦ *the legality of the corporation's activities* **2** something required by law, especially when a technical detail (*often plural*) ◦ *We have to take care of certain legalities before opening the business.*

legalize /léegə līz/ (-**izes**, -**izing**, -**ized**), **legalise** (-**ises**, -**ising**, -**ised**) *vt* to make an activity legal by making or changing a law —**legalization** /léegə lī záysh'n/ *n*

legal medicine *n* LAW = **forensic medicine**

legal reserve *n* *US* an amount of money that a financial organization such as a bank or insurer is required to keep as security against debts (*often plural*)

legal separation *n* separation of a married couple that is recognized by a court of law, or the court decree establishing such a separation

legal tender *n* the currency that is valid for the payment of a debt and must be accepted by a creditor

Legaspi /lə gásspi/, **Legazpi** capital of Albay Province, Philippines. Population: 121,120 (1990).

legate /léggət/ *n* **1** an emissary of the pope, especially one who represents the Vatican in other countries **2** an official representative of a government, especially a diplomat [12C. Via French < Latin *legatus* < the past participle of *legare* 'send as an envoy, bequeath'.] —**legateship** *n* —**legatine** /léggə tīn/ *adj*

legatee /léggi teé/ *n* a recipient of a bequest made in a will

legation /li gáysh'n/ *n* **1 DIPLOMAT'S RESIDENCE** the official local residence of a senior diplomat assigned to a country **2 DIPLOMATIC STAFF** the staff of a legation **3 DIPLOMATS ON MISSION** a group of representatives sent on a mission, especially a diplomatic mission **4 SENDING OF DIPLOMATIC REPRESENTATIVE** the sending of a representative on a diplomatic mission **5 DIPLOMATIC MISSION** a mission performed by a diplomatic representative **6 LEGATE'S POSITION** the status or office of a legate [14C. Directly or via French < Latin *legare* 'send as an envoy'.]

legato /li gáatō/ *adv* in a smooth, even manner, often indicated in a musical score by a curved line (**slur**) connecting the notes to be so played (*musical direction*) ■ *n* (*plural* -**tos**) a piece of music, or a section of a piece, played legato [Mid-18C. < Italian, 'tied together'.] — **legato** *adj*

legator /li gáytər/ *n* a person who has made a will to bequeath something

Legazpi = **Legaspi**

leg before wicket *adj* forced to end a cricket innings as a result of being hit on the leg by a ball that would otherwise have hit the wicket ■ *n* in cricket, the dismissal of a batsman as a result of the leg obstructing a ball that would otherwise have hit the wicket

leg-break *n* in cricket, a ball with a bounce that spins from the leg side to the off side

leg bye *n* in cricket, a run scored after the ball hits some part of the batsman's body other than the hand, without touching the bat

legend /léjjənd/ *n* 1 **OLD STORY** a story that has been passed down for generations, especially one that is presented as history but is unlikely to be true 2 **OLD STORIES** a group of stories presented as history but unlikely to be true 3 **MODERN MYTH** a popular myth that has arisen in modern times 4 **CELEBRITY** somebody famous admired for a particular skill or talent 5 **INSCRIPTION** an inscription, especially a title or motto, on an object 6 **CAPTION** a caption for an illustration 7 **MAP KEY** an explanation of the symbols used on a map [14C. Via French *légende* < medieval Latin *legenda* 'things to be read' < Latin *legere* 'to read'.]

legendary /léjjəndəri/ *adj* 1 **BELONGING TO LEGEND** described or commemorated in a legend ○ *the legendary figure of Hercules* 2 **CONTAINING LEGENDS** retold for generations as history but unlikely to be completely or even partially true ○ *the legendary tales of ancient warriors* 3 **LIKE SOMETHING IN LEGEND** appropriate for a legend ○ *an organization of legendary proportions* 4 **FAMOUS** very famous in contemporary society —**legendarily** *adv*

legendry /léjjəndri/ (*plural* **-ries**) *n* a collection or group of legends

Léger /láy zhay/, **Fernand** (1881–1955) French painter

legerdemain /léjjərdə máyn/ *n* 1 sleight of hand (*dated*) 2 a display of skill or cleverness, especially for deceitful purposes ○ *a dazzling display of political legerdemain* [15C. < French *léger de main* 'light of hand'.]

leger line *n* = **ledger line**

leges /lée jeez/ plural of **lex**

-legged *suffix* with a particular number of legs ○ *four-legged*

legging /légging/ *n* **PROTECTIVE COVERING FOR LOWER LEG** a protective covering made of a strong material that is wrapped around the lower leg by labourers and players in certain sports ■ **leggings** *npl* 1 **CLOSE-FITTING TROUSERS** women's trousers or footless tights made of stretchy material that fit very closely to the legs and hips 2 **PROTECTIVE OUTER TROUSERS** waterproof or insulated outer trousers that are worn for protection from snow, rain, and cold

leggy /léggi/ (**-gier, -giest**) *adj* 1 **WITH LONG LEGS** having very long legs in relation to the rest of the body 2 **WITH SHAPELY LEGS** having long good-looking legs ○ *a leggy supermodel* 3 **SPINDLY IN GROWTH** with long thin stems that have few and widely spaced leaves

leghorn /lég hawrn/ *n* 1 **BLEACHED STRAW** fine bleached straw made from a type of Italian wheat 2 **STRAW FABRIC** a fabric made from plaited leghorn straw 3 **STRAW HAT** a hat made from leghorn straw [Mid-18C. After *Leghorn* (Livorno), Italy.]

Leghorn[1] *n* a small domestic fowl that produces white eggs [Mid-18C. After *Leghorn* (Livorno), Italy.]

Leghorn[2] /lég hawrn/ ♦ **Livorno**

legible /léjjəb'l/ *adj* clear enough to be read [15C. < late Latin *legibilis* < *legere* 'to read'.] —**legibility** /léjjə bíllәti/ *n* —**legibleness** *n* —**legibly** *adv*

legion /léejən/ *n* 1 **ROMAN ARMY DIVISION** in ancient Rome, an army division of 3,000 to 6,000 soldiers, including cavalry 2 **LARGE BODY OF SOLDIERS** a large military unit, especially an army ○ *the French Foreign Legion* 3 **ORGANIZATION OF EX-MILITARY PERSONNEL** an association of ex-servicemen and ex-servicewomen ○ *the Royal British Legion* 4 **MULTITUDE** a large number of people or things (*often used in the plural*) ○ *Their complicated affairs are managed by a legion of accountants.* ■ *adj* **MANY** very numerous (*literary*) ○ *dissatisfied customers and their legion complaints* [12C. Via Old French < Latin *legion-* < *legere* 'choose'.]

legionary /léejənəri/ *adj* belonging to, typical of, or forming a legion ■ *n* (*plural* **-ies**) a member of a legion, especially a Roman legion

legionnaire /léejə náir/, **Legionnaire** *n* 1 **SOMEBODY IN LEGION** a soldier in a legion, especially the French Foreign Legion 2 **SOMEBODY IN ROYAL BRITISH LEGION** a member of the Royal British Legion 3 **SOMEBODY IN AMERICAN LEGION** a member of the American Legion [Early 19C. < French *légionnaire* < *légion* (see LEGION).]

Legionnaires' disease *n* a virulent and sometimes fatal form of pneumonia caused by a bacterium and spread mainly by the water droplets in air conditioning systems [< its first recognized occurrence at an American Legion convention in Philadelphia in 1976]

Legion of Honour *n* a French order of merit awarded for illustrious military or civil service

Legion of Merit *n US* a US military decoration awarded to military personnel from any country for exceptional and outstanding service

legis. *abbr* 1 legislation 2 legislative 3 legislature

legislate /léjji slayt/ (**-lates, -lating, -lated**) *v* 1 *vi* to write and pass laws 2 *vt* to make laws or rules designed to bring about some action or condition ○ *Parliament can't legislate good manners.* [Early 18C. Back-formation < LEGISLATOR.]

legislation /léjji sláysh'n/ *n* 1 the process of writing and passing laws 2 a law or laws passed by an official body

legislative /léjjislətiv/ *adj* 1 **RELATING TO LAW-MAKING** involved in the writing and passing of laws 2 **RELATING TO LAW-MAKING BODY** relating to or part of a legislature 3 **ENACTED BY LAW** created by governmental legislation ○ *There is no legislative solution to this problem.* —**legislatively** *adv*

legislative assembly, Legislative Assembly *n* 1 **US LAW-MAKING BODY** the two-chamber legislature of some US states 2 **LOWER HOUSE OF COMMONWEALTH LEGISLATURE** the lower house of a two-chamber state legislature in some Commonwealth countries, especially that of some Australian states 3 **SINGLE-CHAMBER COMMONWEALTH LEGISLATURE** a single-chamber legislature, especially the legislature of most Canadian provinces and some Australian states 4 **GROUP WITH POWER TO PASS LAWS** any official body with law- or rule-making powers

legislative council, Legislative Council *n* 1 **COMMITTEE OF STATE SENATORS AND REPRESENTATIVES** a permanent committee consisting of members of both houses of a two-chamber state legislature who discuss issues of common concern and plan a legislative programme for the next session 2 **UPPER HOUSE IN TWO-CHAMBER LEGISLATURE** the upper house of the two-chamber legislature in some Commonwealth countries, e.g. in most Indian and Australian states 3 **LEGISLATURE IN FORMER BRITISH COLONY** the single-chamber legislature of some former British colonies

legislator /léjji slaytər/ *n* a writer of or voter on laws, especially as a member of a legislature [15C. < Latin *legis lator* 'proposer of a law' < *lex* 'law' + *latus*, past participle of *ferre* 'bring'.] —**legislatorial** /léjjislə táwri əl/ *adj* —**legislatorship** *n*

legislature /léjjisləchər/ *n* an official body, usually chosen by election, with the power to make, change, and repeal laws [Late 17C. < LEGISLATOR.]

legist /léejist/ *n* a specialist in law, especially classical law [15C. < French *légiste* < Latin *leg-* 'law'.]

legit /lə jít/ *adj* 1 **LEGAL** complying with the law (*slang*) 2 **HONEST AND TRUTHFUL** telling the truth and not trying to deceive (*slang*) ○ *Is his story legit?* 3 **PRESENTING SERIOUS DRAMAS** performing professionally produced dramatic theatre that is considered to be serious art, in contrast to such forms as revues and musical comedy (*informal*) [Late 19C. Shortening of LEGITIMATE.]

legitimate *adj* /lə jíttimət/ 1 **LEGAL** complying with or under the law ○ *legitimate tax deductions* 2 **CONFORMING TO ACKNOWLEDGED STANDARDS** complying with recognized rules, standards, or traditions ○ *not a legitimate excuse for missing school* 3 **NOT SPURIOUS** well-reasoned and sincere ○ *We have legitimate reasons for worrying about the quality of our water.* 4 **BORN IN WEDLOCK** born of legally married parents 5 **WITH RIGHT OF INHERITANCE** having the right to inherit something, such as the throne in a monarchy 6 **RELATING TO SERIOUS PROFESSIONAL DRAMA** performing or involving professionally produced dramatic works that are considered to be serious art, in contrast to such forms as revues and musical comedy ■ *vt* /lə jítti mayt/ 1 LAW = **legitimize** *v.* 1 2 = **legitimize** *v.* 2 [15C. < medieval Latin *legitimatus*, past participle of *legitimare* 'make legal' < Latin *legitimus* 'lawful' < *lex* 'law'.] —**legitimacy** *n* — **legitimately** *adv* —**legitimateness** *n* —**legitimation** /lə jítti máysh'n/ *n* —**legitimator** *n*

legitimatize /lə jíttimə tīz/, **legitimatise, legitimise** *vt* = **legitimize** —**legitimatization** /lə jíttimə tī záysh'n/ *n*

legitimist /lə jíttimist/ *n* 1 a believer in monarchy through inheritance or in a specific person's claim to inherit a throne 2 in the 19th century, a supporter of the Bourbon claimants to the French throne [Mid-19C. < French *légitimiste* < *légitime* 'legitimate' < Latin *legitimus* (see LEGITIMATE).] —**legitimism** *n* —**legitimist** *adj*

legitimize /lə jítti mīz/ (**-mizes, -mizing, -mized**), **legitimise** (**-mises, -mising, -mised**), **legitimate** (**-mates, -mating, -mated**), **legitimatize** (**-tizes, -tizing, -tized**) *vt* 1 to make something lawful, by making, changing, or repealing laws or by decree 2 to argue or prove that a claim or action is lawful or reasonable [Mid-19C. < Latin *legitimus* (see LEGITIMATE).] —**legitimization** /lə jítti mī záysh'n/ *n* —**legitimizer** *n*

legless /légglәss/ *adj* 1 having no legs 2 extremely drunk, especially too drunk to stand (*informal*)

legman /lég man/ (*plural* **-men** /-mən/) *n US* 1 somebody employed in an office to run errands and gather information 2 a reporter who gathers information for a story, especially from firsthand sources

Lego /léggō/ *tdmk* a trademark for a toy consisting of plastic building blocks and other components

leg-of-mutton /lég ə mút'n/, **leg-o'-mutton** *adj* shaped like a sharply tapered triangle

leg-pull *n* an amusing deception or practical joke (*informal*) [< *pull somebody's leg*] —**leg-puller** *n* —**leg-pulling** *n*

legroom /lég ro͝om, -ro͞om/ *n* space in front of a seat for somebody's legs, especially enough space to stretch out and move the legs

Le Guin /lə gwín/, **Ursula** (*b.* 1929) US writer. Born **Ursula Kroeber**

legume /léggyoom/ *n* 1 a plant that has pods as fruits and roots that bear nodules containing nitrogen-fixing bacteria 2 a seed, pod, or other part of a legume, used as food [Mid-17C. Via French *légume* < Latin *legumen* 'bean'.]

leguminous /li gyo͝ominəss/ *adj* 1 belonging to or typical of the family of plants that has pods as fruits and roots that bear nodules containing nitrogen-fixing bacteria 2 resembling a leguminous plant or its seed pods [Mid-17C. < Latin *leguminosus* < *legumin-* 'bean'.]

leg up *n* (*informal*) 1 **UPWARDS BOOST** help for somebody to get up onto something, e.g. a horse or a wall, by lifting the person's leg upwards or using your linked hands as a support 2 **CAREER HELP** help for somebody to move up in a hierarchy or a field of activity 3 *US* **POSITION OF SUPERIORITY** an advantage that other people do not have in an activity

legwarmer /lég wawrmər/ *n* a knitted tube that covers the calf and sometimes also the top of the foot, and is typically worn by a dancer during practice (*usually plural*)

legwork /lég wurk/ *n* preparatory research for a project that is usually physically demanding or involves a lot of walking (*informal*)

Le Havre /lə haávrə/ seaport in N France, on the English Channel. Population: 190,905 (1999).

Lehrer /lairər/, **Tom** (*b.* 1928) US teacher and songwriter

lei[1] /lay/ (*plural* **leis**) *n* a garland of flowers, especially one worn around the neck in Hawaii and other parts of Polynesia [Mid-19C. < Hawaiian.]

lei[2] plural of **leu**

Leibniz /līb nits/, **Leibnitz, Gottfried Wilhelm von, Baron** (1646–1716) German philosopher and mathematician —**Leibnizian** /līb nítsi ən/ *adj, n*

Leicester /léstər/ city in central England. Population: 270,600 (1991).

Leicester, Robert Dudley, 1st Earl of (1532–88) English courtier

Leicestershire /léstərshər/ county in central England. Area: 2,553 sq. km/986 sq. mi.

Leichhardt /līk haart/, **Ludwig** (1813–48?) Prussian-born Australian naturalist and explorer

Leics *abbr* Leicestershire

Leiden /láydən/, **Leyden** city in W Netherlands. Population: 117,196 (2000).

Leif Ericson /leéf érrikss'n/ (975–1020) Icelandic explorer

Leigh /lee/, **Mike** (*b.* 1943) British playwright and film director

Leigh, Vivien (1913–67) British actor

Leighton Buzzard /láyt'n búzzərd/ town in central England. Population: 32,610 (1991).

Leinster /línstər/ historic province in E Ireland

Leipzig /lípsig/ city in east-central Germany. Population: 487,700 (1994).

leishmaniasis /leeshmə nî əssiss/ *n* an infection such as kala-azar and some other skin diseases that are caused by a protozoan that is a parasite in the tissue of vertebrates [Early 20C. < modern Latin *Leishmania*, after Sir William Boog *Leishman* (1865–1926), Scottish pathologist.]

leister /leestər/ *n* a stick with three prongs, used for spearing fish ■ *vt* to catch fish using a three-pronged spear [Mid-16C. < Old Norse *ljóstr* < *ljósta* 'to strike'.]

leisure /lézhər/ *n* time during which somebody has no obligations or work responsibilities, and therefore is free to engage in enjoyable activities [13C. < Anglo-Norman *leisour* < Old French *leisir* 'be permitted' < Latin *licere*.] ◇ **at your leisure** at the time and pace that suits you ◇ **gentleman** *or* **lady of leisure** describes a man or woman who does not have to work for a living (*humorous*)

leisure centre *n* a public establishment that provides the space and equipment for recreational activities such as sports, games, and hobbies

leisured /lézhərd/ *adj* 1 having a lot of free time, especially because of having enough money not to have to work for a living 2 = **leisurely** *adj*.

leisurely /lézhərli/ *adj* leisurely, leisured relaxed, unhurried, and enjoyable, usually because done during free time ○ *a leisurely stroll in the park* ■ *adv* in a slow and relaxed manner —**leisureliness** *n*

leisure society *n* a society in which a greater proportion of people's time is spent at leisure than at work

leisurewear /lézhər wair/ *n* comfortable informal clothing such as a tracksuit, appropriate for relaxation or play

Leith /leeth/ port of Edinburgh, Scotland, on the Firth of Forth

leitmotif /lîtmō teef/, **leitmotiv** *n* 1 a musical theme that recurs in the course of a work to evoke a particular character or situation, especially typical of the operas of Richard Wagner 2 a recurring theme, e.g. in literature or history [Late 19C. < German, < *leiten* 'to lead' + *Motiv* 'motif'.]

Leitrim /leetrim/ county in Connacht Province, N Republic of Ireland. Area: 1,525 sq. km/589 sq. mi.

Leizhou Peninsula /láy jō-/ peninsula in SE China, separating the Gulf of Tonkin from the South China Sea

lek[1] /lek/ *n* see table at **currency** [Early 20C. < Albanian, after *Lek* Dukagjin, Albanian lawyer.]

lek[2] /lek/ *n* an area of ground that some birds such as the black grouse use as a stage for communal breeding displays and courtship during the mating season [Late 19C. < ?]

lekker /lékər/ *adj* S Africa enjoyable and pleasing (*informal*) ■ *adv* S Africa used to express pleasure or approval (*informal*) ○ *The team is playing lekker!* [Early 20C. Via Afrikaans < Middle Dutch.]

LEM /lem/ *abbr* lunar excursion module

Lemaître /lə méttrə/, **Georges-Henri** (1894–1966) Belgian astrophysicist and priest

leman /lémmən, leemən/ (*plural* **-mans**) *n* somebody loved, e.g. a sweetheart or lover (*archaic*) [12C. Variant of *leofman* 'beloved person' < LIEF + MAN.]

Le Mans /lə maàN, lə maánz/ city in NW France. Population: 146,105 (1999).

lemma[1] /lémmə/ (*plural* **-mas** *or* **-mata** /-mətə/) *n* 1 ASSUMPTION FOR THE SAKE OF ARGUMENT a proposition that is assumed to be true in order to test the validity of another proposition 2 SUBJECT HEADING a heading that indicates the topic of a work or passage 3 DICTIONARY HEADWORD the headword of a dictionary entry [Late 16C. Via Latin < Greek *lēmma* 'something taken (for granted)'.]

lemma[2] /lémmə/ *n* the lower of two bracts surrounding the flower of a grass [Mid-18C. < Greek, 'husk' < the past participle of *lepein* 'peel'.]

lemmata plural of **lemma**[1]

lemming /lémming/ *n* 1 a rodent with a small thick furry body and furry feet that lives in subarctic regions. Genus: *Lemmus* and *Dicrostonyx*. 2 a member of a large group of people who blindly follow one another on a course of action that will lead to destruction for all of them [Early 18C. < Norwegian.]

Lemmon /lémmən/, **Jack** (*b.* 1925) US actor

lemniscus /lem nískəss/ (*plural* **-ci** /-si, -kee/) *n* a bundle of fibres, especially a bundle of nerve fibres [Mid-19C. Via Latin < Greek *lēmniskos* 'ribbon'.]

Lemming

Lemnos /lémnoss/ island in E Greece, in the N Aegean Sea. Population: 15,721 (1981).

lemon /lémmən/ *n* 1 YELLOW OR GREEN CITRUS FRUIT a yellow or, in some climates, green oval citrus fruit with a thick fragrant rind and sour juicy flesh 2 TREE THAT BEARS LEMONS a tree with glossy leaves and spiky branches that is widely cultivated to produce lemons. *Citrus limon.* 3 PALE YELLOW COLOUR a pale yellow colour typical of the rind of a lemon 4 LEMON DRINK a drink made from lemon juice 5 DEFECTIVE PRODUCT something that is defective or disappointing, especially a car that does not run properly (*informal*) 6 SILLY PERSON somebody regarded as unintelligent or thoughtless (*informal*) ○ *I feel a lemon now.* ■ *adj* OF A PALE YELLOW COLOUR having the pale yellow colour typical of the rind of a ripe lemon [14C. Via French *limon* < Arabic *līmūn*.]

lemonade /lémmə nayd/ *n* 1 FIZZY DRINK a sweet, fizzy, clear soft drink 2 DRINK MADE FROM LEMONS a still soft drink made from fresh lemons, sugar, and water 3 DRINK OF LEMONADE a drink of lemonade ○ *ordered a lemonade and two coffees*

lemon balm *n* a widely-cultivated plant of the mint family that has lemon-scented leaves. Flowers: small, white or pinkish. Native to: S Europe.

lemon curd, **lemon cheese** *n* a thick sweet creamy-yellow spread made from lemons, sugar, eggs, and butter and usually eaten on bread

lemon drop *n* a small lemon-flavoured boiled sweet

lemon grass *n* a grass native to S India that is cultivated in the tropics for a lemon-scented oil distilled from its leaves, and for use as a flavouring in cooking. *Cymbopogon citratus.*

lemon sole *n* 1 a common flatfish, prized as a food fish. Native to: NE Atlantic, North Sea. *Microstomus kitt.* 2 the flesh of a lemon sole used as food

lemon-squeezer *n* a device for extracting juice from lemons, usually consisting of a raised fluted cone onto which a halved lemon is pressed, set in a shallow bowl where juice collects. US term **reamer** *n.* 2

lemon verbena, **lemon vervain** *n* a widely cultivated shrub with leaves that produce a lemony fragrance when crushed. Flowers: small, lavender. Native to: South America. *Lippia triphylla.*

lemon yellow *n* COLOURS = **lemon** *n.* 3 —**lemon-yellow** *adj*

lempira /lem peerə/ *n* see table at **currency** [Mid-20C. After *Lempira*, 16C chieftain who fought against the Spanish conquerors of Honduras.]

lemur /leemər/ *n* a primate with a long snout, large ears, and a long tail. Native to: Madagascar and nearby islands. Family: Lemuridae. ◇ **ring-tailed lemur** [Late 18C. Via modern Latin < Latin *lemures* (see LEMURES), because it is nocturnal.]

Lena /leenə/ river in Siberian Russia, emptying into the Laptev Sea. Length: 4,313 km/2,680 mi.

lend /lend/ (**lends**, **lending**, **lent** /lent/) *v* 1 LET SOMEBODY BORROW to allow somebody to take or use something on the understanding that it will be returned later 2 *vti* GIVE SOMEBODY MONEY FOR LIMITED TIME to allow a person or business to use a sum of money for a particular period of time, usually on condition that a charge (**interest**) is paid in return ○ *The bank lent us money at a good interest rate.* 3 *vt* ADD to give a certain quality or character to something ○ *The candles lend an air of intimacy to the room.* [Old English *lænan* < Germanic] —**lendable** *adj* ○

lender *n* ○ **lend itself to something** to be suitable for a particular purpose or occasion

lending library *n* a library or department of a library where the public can borrow books, and often audio tapes, videotapes, and CDs

Lendl /lénd'l/, **Ivan** (*b.* 1960) Czechoslovakian-born US tennis player

lenes plural of **lenis**

Lenglen /laaN glaàN/, **Suzanne** (1899–1938) French tennis player

length /length/ *n* 1 DISTANCE FROM END TO END the distance along something from end to end, or a measurement taken of this distance ○ *The length of the garden is 25 yards.* 2 QUALITY OF LONGNESS the condition or state of being long ○ *The garden is designed to give a sense of length and openness.* 3 HOW LONG SOMETHING TAKES the time something lasts or takes from beginning to end ○ *The length of the second act is about 75 minutes.* 4 HOW LONG SOMETHING IS how long something is when measured from beginning to end ○ *The second volume is a massive 400 pages in length.* 5 LONG PIECE a piece of something long and narrow ○ *a length of copper piping* 6 UNIT OF MEASUREMENT a piece of something such as cloth that is measured or bought in units of a standard size ○ *bought three lengths of fabric* 7 END TO END IN SWIMMING POOL the distance from one end of a swimming pool to the other 8 SET DISTANCE a particular distance, e.g. between two points 9 HOW LONG GARMENT IS how high the hem of a coat, skirt, or dress is above the ground or below the wearer's waist, or how much of the wearer's legs it shows 10 WINNING DISTANCE in something such as a boat race or horse race, the distance between two competitors, measured according to how long a single boat or horse is ○ *two lengths ahead with only 100m to go* 11 HOW LONG SOUND TAKES TO MAKE the amount of time required to articulate a vowel or syllable 12 DISTANCE BALL BOUNCES FROM BATSMAN in cricket, the distance from the batsman at which the ball bounces [Old English *lengþ* < Germanic] ◇ **at length 1** in great detail and for a long time (*formal*) **2** after some time or following a delay

-length *suffix* extending all the way to a particular part of something ○ *shoulder-length hair*

lengthen /léngth'n/ *vti* to make something longer, or become longer ○ *The weeks lengthened into months and still no news came.* —**lengthener** *n*

lengthways /léngth wayz/, **lengthwise** /-wīz/ *adv, adj* in relation to something's length from end to end ○ *attempting to force the suitcase into the boot lengthways*

lengthy /léngthi/ (**-ier, -iest**) *adj* lasting for a long time, especially excessively long —**lengthily** *adv* —**lengthiness** *n*

lenient /leeni ənt/ *adj* showing tolerance or mercy in dealing with crime or misbehaviour [Mid-17C. < Latin *lenient-*, present participle of *lenire* 'soothe' < *lenis* 'smooth'.] —**lenience** *n* —**leniency** *n* —**leniently** *adv*

Vladimir Ilyich Lenin

Lenin /lénnin/, **Vladimir Ilyich** (1870–1924) Russian revolutionary leader. Born **Vladimir Ilyich Ulyanov**

Leninakhan /lénninə kaàn/ former name for **Gyumri** (1924–90)

Leningrad /lénnin grad/ former name for **St Petersburg** (1924–90)

Leninism /lénninizəm/ *n* the political, social, and economic theories of Lenin, which he developed from Marxist theory —**Leninist** *n, adj*

Lenin Peak /lénnin-/ mountain on the border between Tajikistan and Kyrgyzstan, in the Trans-Alai Range of the Pamirs. Height: 7,134 m/23,406 ft.

lenis /léeniss/ *adj* describes a consonant produced using little breath and muscle power ∎ *n* (*plural* **-nes** /-neez/) a consonant that is produced using little breath and muscle power [Early 20C. < Latin, 'smooth'.]

lenition /li nísh'n/ *n* the use of little breath and muscle power when articulating consonants [Early 20C. < Latin *lenis* 'smooth'.]

Lennon /lénnən/, **John** (1940–80) British singer, songwriter, and musician

leno /léenō/ (*plural* **-nos**) *n* **1** an open weave created in textiles by twisting together pairs of warp threads to lock the weft threads in place **2** a fabric made using a leno weave [Late 18C. < French *linon* < *lin* 'flax' < Latin *linum*.]

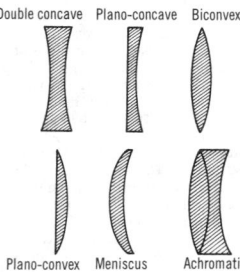
Double concave Plano-concave Biconvex

Plano-convex Meniscus Achromatic

Lens: Cross-sections of different lenses

lens /lenz/ *n* **1** TRANSPARENT PIECE OF GLASS FOR FOCUSING a piece of curved and polished glass or other transparent material that forms an image by refracting and focusing light passing through it **2** SYSTEM OF LENSES a system of two or more lenses that is used in an optical instrument such as a telescope or camera **3** OPHTHALMOL = **contact lens 4** LIGHT-FOCUSING PART OF THE EYE the part of the eye that focuses light to produce an image on the light-sensitive cells of the retina. It is nearly spherical and convex on both sides, and sits behind the pupil. **5** BEAM-FOCUSING DEVICE a device that focuses a beam of electrons or radiation other than light [Late 17C. < Latin, 'lentil'; from its shape.]

lent past participle, past tense of **lend**

Lent /lent/ *n* the period of 40 weekdays before Easter observed in some Christian churches as a period of prayer, penance, fasting, and self-denial. It commemorates the 40 days that Jesus Christ spent fasting in the wilderness. [13C. Shortening of LENTEN.]

Lenten /léntən/, **lenten** *adj* happening in or suitable for Lent, especially in being meagre [Old English *lencten* 'spring' < Germanic]

~~lenth~~ incorrect spelling of **length**

lentic /léntik/ *adj* relating to or inhabiting still or slow-moving water [Mid-20C. < Latin *lentus* 'slow'.]

lenticel /lénti sel/ *n* a pore in the outer layer of a woody plant stem, through which gases pass from inside the stem to the atmosphere, or vice versa [Mid-19C. < modern Latin *lenticella* 'little lentil' < Latin *lens* 'lentil'.] —**lenticellate** /lénti séllət/ *adj*

lenticular /len tíkyoŏlər/ *adj* **1** shaped like a biconvex lens in having two convex faces **2** relating to a lens or lenses [15C. < Latin *lenticularis* < *lenticula* (see LENTIL).]

lentil /lént'l/ *n* **1** a seed that is lens-shaped, brown, grey, green, or black on the outside and yellow or orange inside, and rich in protein **2** a plant of the pea family grown to produce lentils. Native to: Mediterranean, W Asia. *Lens culinaris*. [14C. Via French *lentille* < Latin *lenticula* 'little lentil' < *lens* 'lentil'.]

lentisk /léntisk/ *n* TREES = **mastic tree** [14C. < Latin *lentiscus*.]

lentissimo /len tíssimō/ *adv* very slowly (*musical direction*) [Early 20C. < Italian, superlative of *lento* 'slow'.] —**lentissimo** *adj*

lentivirus /lénti vīrəss/ *n* a retrovirus causing illness that characteristically does not produce symptoms until some time after infection [Late 20C. < Latin *lentus* 'slow' + -I- + VIRUS.]

lent lily *n* a daffodil (*literary or dated*) [Because it often blooms during Lent]

lento /léntō/ *adv* at a slow tempo (*musical direction*) ∎ *n* (*plural* **-tos**) a piece of music, or a section of a piece, to be played lento [Early 18C. Via Italian < Latin *lentus* 'slow'.] —**lento** *adj*

Lenya /lénnyə/, **Lotte** (1900–81) Austrian actor and cabaret singer. Real name **Karoline Wilhelmine Blamauer**

Lenz's law /léntsiz-/ *n* the principle that a current induced by a changing magnetic field will itself produce a magnetic field that opposes the original [Mid-19C. After German physicist Heinrich Friedrich Emil Lenz (1804–65).]

Leo /léeō/ (*plural* **-os**) *n* **1** CONSTELLATION IN NORTHERN HEMISPHERE a constellation of the northern hemisphere. See illustration at **constellation 2** FIFTH SIGN OF THE ZODIAC the fifth sign of the zodiac, represented by the lion and lasting from approximately 23 July to 22 August **3** SOMEBODY BORN UNDER LEO somebody whose birthday falls between 23 July and 22 August [Pre-12C. < Latin, 'lion'.] —**Leo** *adj* —**Leonian** /lee ốni ən/ *n*

Leo I /lée ō/, **St** (400?–461) pope (440–461). Known as **Leo the Great**

Leo III (680?–741) Byzantine emperor (717–741)

Leo IX, St (1002–54) pope (1049–54). Born **Bruno of Egisheim**

Leo X (1475–1521) pope (1513–21). Born **Giovanni de Medici**

Leo XIII (1810–1903) pope (1878–1903). Born **Vincenzo Gioacchino Pecci**

Leo Minor *n* a small inconspicuous constellation of the northern hemisphere. See illustration at **constellation**

Leominster /lémstər/ **1** town in W England. Population: 9,543 (1991). **2** city in central Massachusetts. Population: 39,263 (1996).

León /lay ốn/ **1** capital of León Province, in the Castile-León autonomous region, NW Spain. Population: 147,780 (1995). **2** city in central Mexico. Population: 758,279 (1990).

Leonard /lénnərd/, **Sugar Ray** (b. 1956) US boxer. Born **Ray Charles Leonard**

Leonardo da Vinci /lée ō naárd ō də vínchi/ (1452–1519) Italian painter, sculptor, architect, engineer, and scientist

Leoncavallo /láy ong ka vállō/, **Ruggero** (1858–1919) Italian composer

leone /lee ốn/ *n* see table at **currency** [Mid-20C. < Sierra Leone.]

Leonid /lée ənid/ *n* a member of an annual meteor shower that reaches its maximum on or about 17 November [Late 19C. After LEO *n*. 1, from where such meteors seem to radiate.]

Leonidas /li ốnni dass/ (d. 480 BC) king of Sparta (490?–480 BC)

leonine /lée ə nīn/ *adj* relating to or characteristic of a lion, e.g. in strength or appearance [14C. Directly or via French < Latin *leoninus* < *leo* 'lion'.]

leopard /léppərd/ *n* **1** a large slender member of the cat family with a fawn to orange-red coat spotted with black rosettes. Native to: Africa, Asia. *Panthera pardus*. **2** in heraldry, an image of a lion viewed from the side facing left, with its head turned towards the viewer and one front leg raised [13C. Via Old French < late Greek *leopardos* < *leōn* (see LION) + *pardos* (see PARD[1]).]

leopard cat *n* a small wild cat with spots like those of a leopard. Native to: S and E Asia. *Felis bengalensis*.

leopardess /léppərd ess/ *n* a female leopard, usually an adult one

leopard frog *n* a common frog whose colour ranges from grey to brown, with light-edged dark spots and paler lengthwise ridges. Native to: North America. *Rana pipiens*.

leopard lily *n* an ornamental flowering plant. Flowers: orange-red with black-speckled petals. Native to: SW United States. *Lilium pardalinum*.

leopard moth *n* a large white moth with black spots whose caterpillar bores into trees, causing damage, and may be considered a pest. Native to: Europe, Asia, North Africa, North America. *Zeuzera pyrina*.

leopard's bane *n* a plant with clusters of yellow flowers resembling daisies on long stalks. Native to: Europe, Asia. Genus: *Doronicum*.

leopard seal *n* a seal with a spotted dark grey back and paler belly that lives as a solitary hunter, feeding mainly on penguins. Native to: Antarctic waters. *Hydrurga leptonyx*.

Leopold I /lée ə pōld/ (1640–1705) Holy Roman Emperor (1658–1705), king of Bohemia (1656–1705), and king of Hungary (1655–87)

Leopold II (1747–92) Grand Duke of Tuscany and Holy Roman Emperor (1790–92)

Leopold II (1835–1909) king of Belgium (1865–1909)

Leopold III (1901–83) king of Belgium (1934–51)

Léopoldville /lée ə pōld víl/ former name for **Kinshasa**

leotard /lée ə taard/ *n* a tight-fitting one-piece elastic garment that covers the torso and is worn especially by dancers, gymnasts, and acrobats [Late 19C. After French trapeze artist Jules Léotard (1830–70).]

lep /lep/ *vi* (**leps**, **lepping**, **lept** /lept/) *Ireland* to leap (*informal*) ∎ *n N Ireland* an act of leaping (*informal*) [Variant of LEAP]

Lepautre /lə pốtr/, **Pierre** (1648–1716) French interior designer

Lepcha /lépchə/ (*plural* **-chas** or **-cha**) *n* **1** a member of a people who live in the NE Indian state of Sikkim **2** a Tibeto-Burman language spoken in the NE Indian state of Sikkim. Native speakers: 65,000. [Early 19C. < Nepali *lāpche*.] —**Lepcha** *adj*

Le Pen /lə pén/, **Jean-Marie** (b. 1928) French politician

leper /léppər/ *n* **1** somebody affected with leprosy **2** a person who is shunned by the rest of society [14C. Via French *lèpre* < late Latin *lepra* 'leprosy' < Greek *lepros* (see LEPROUS).]

lepido- *prefix* flake, scale ○ *lepidolite* [< Greek *lepid-*]

lepidolite /li píddə līt, léppidə-/ *n* a mica ranging in colour from pinkish-purple to grey. Use: an ore of lithium.

lepidopteran /léppi dóptərən/ *n* a butterfly or moth. Lepidopterans have four wings covered in tiny overlapping scales, and sucking mouthparts. Their larvae are caterpillars. Order: Lepidoptera. [Mid-19C. < modern Latin Lepidoptera < Greek *lepis* 'scale' + *pteron* 'wing'.]

lepidopterist /léppi dóptərist/ *n* an expert in or student of butterflies and moths

leprechaun /léppri kawn/ *n* in Irish folklore, a small man with magical powers, often dressed in green, who works as a shoemaker and is believed to know where treasure is hidden [Early 17C. < Irish *leipreachán* 'small body'.]

leprosarium /lépprə sáiri əm/ (*plural* **-a** /-ri ə/) *n* a hospital for the treatment of patients with leprosy [Mid-19C. < late Latin *leprosus* (see LEPROUS).]

leprose /léppröss/ *adj* = **leprous** *adj.* **2** [Mid-19C. < late Latin *leprosus* or its source *lepra* (see LEPER).]

leprosy /lépprəssi/ (*plural* **-sies**) *n* a curable tropical disease mainly affecting the skin and nerves that can cause tissue change and, in severe cases, loss of sensation and disfigurement [Mid-16C. < LEPROUS.] —**leprotic** /le próttik/ *adj*

leprous /lépprəss/ *adj* **1** having or relating to leprosy **2** resembling the physical symptoms of leprosy, especially in being pale or scaly ○ *a leprous white deposit spreading across the cellar walls* [12C. Via Old French < late Latin *leprosus* < Greek *lepros* 'scaly' < *lepos* 'scale'; from the white scales that form on the skin.]

-lepsy *suffix* seizure ○ *narcolepsy* [Via modern Latin *-lepsia* < Greek *lēpsis* < *lēp-*, stem of *lambanein* 'seize']

lept past tense, past participle of **lep**

lept- *prefix* = **lepto-** (*before vowels*)

lepta plural of **lepton**[1]

lepto- *prefix* thin, slender ○ *leptosome* [< Greek *leptos*, past participle of *lepein* 'peel']

leptomeningeal /léptō mə nínji əl/ *adj* relating to the two soft inner layers of the three membranes (**meninges**) that surround the brain

lepton[1] /lép ton/ (*plural* **-ta** /-tə/) *n* a subunit of Greek currency, used only in calculations [Early 18C. < Greek *leptos* 'small'.]

lepton[2] /lép ton/ *n* a fundamental subatomic particle such as the electron, muon, neutrino, and their antiparticles that interacts only weakly with other particles [Mid-20C. < Greek *leptos* 'small'.] —**leptonic** /lep tónnik/ *adj*

leptosome /léptō sōm/ *adj* belonging to a physiological type that is tall with long lean limbs

leptospirosis /léptō spī róssiss/ *n* an infectious disease occurring in human beings and domestic animals and affecting the kidneys and liver, caused by spiral-shaped bacteria (**spirochaetes**) of the genus *Leptospira*. ◊ **Weil's disease** [Early 20C. < modern Latin *Leptospira* 'small coil'.]

leptotene /léptō teen/ *n* the initial part of the first phase of reproductive cell division (**meiosis**), when the chromosomes start to appear as thin threads [Early 20C. < Greek *leptos* 'thin' + *tainia* 'band, ribbon'.]

Lepus /léppəss, léepəss/ *n* a small constellation of the southern hemisphere. See illustration at **constellation**

Lérida /lay réedə/ capital of Lérida Province, in the autonomous region of Catalonia, NE Spain. Population: 114,367 (1995).

Lermontov /lyérməntəf/, **Mikhail Yuryevich** (1814–41) Russian poet and novelist

Lerner /lúrnər/, **Alan Jay** (1918–86) US playwright and lyricist

Lerwick /lúr wik/ largest town of the Shetland Islands, NE Scotland, on Mainland Island. Population: 7,336 (1991).

lesbian /lézbi ən/ *n* a woman who is sexually attracted to other women ■ *adj* involving or relating to lesbians [< the poems of SAPPHO of *Lesbos*]

lesbianism /lézbi ənizəm/ *n* sexual attraction and sexual relations between women

Lesbos /léz boss/ island in E Greece, in the Aegean Sea. Population: 104,620 (1981). Area: 1,637 sq. km/632 sq. mi. —**Lesbian** *adj, n*

Les Cayes /lay káy/ town and seaport in SW Haiti. Population: 36,000 (1994 estimate).

lese majesty /léez májjəsti/, **lèse majesté** *n* **1** disrespect towards the authority or dignity of somebody or something **2** a criminal offence against a ruler or head of state [15C. Via French < Latin *laesa majestas* 'violated majesty'.]

lesion /léezh'n/ *n* **1** a physical change in a body part that is the result of illness or injury **2** a wound, especially an area of skin that is broken or infected [15C. Via French < Latin *laesion-* < the past participle of *laedere* 'injure'.]

SOUTH AFRICA
Caledon
Leribe
Mont aux Sources
Maseru
LESOTHO
Orange
Mafeteng
Orange
Quthing
SOUTH AFRICA

Lesotho

Lesotho /lə sṓtō/ kingdom in southern Africa, bordered on all sides by South Africa. Capital: Maseru. Population: 2,049,275 (1997). Area: 30,355 sq. km/11,720 sq. mi.

lespedeza /léspə déezə/ (*plural* **-zas** *or* **-za**) *n* a plant of the pea family with leaves that have three leaflets, grown for forage and to control erosion. Genus: *Lespedeza*. [Late 19C. < modern Latin, (erroneously) after Vincente Manuel de *Céspedes*, 18C Spanish governor of E Florida.]

less /less/ CORE MEANING: a grammatical word used to indicate a smaller amount of something

1 *det, pron* **SMALLER AMOUNT** a smaller amount or proportion of something ○ *New cars tend to emit less air pollution.* ○ *Last month less of her salary was taken up with household expenses.* **2** *adv* **TO A SMALLER DEGREE** to a smaller extent or degree ○ *Demanding? I've never known a less demanding patient!* ○ *I see her much less than I used to.* **3** *prep* **MINUS** indicating that a number or amount is subtracted from a previously mentioned number or amount ○ *Total: £500, less £50 expenses.* ○ *I earned £45,000 last year, less tax and insurance.* [Old English *lǣssa* < Germanic] ◇ **less than** not having a particular quality ○ *Her whole attitude towards me has been less than pleasant.* ◇ **no less** expressing surprise or admiration at the importance of somebody or something ○ *He had borrowed money at Homburg from no less a person than Lord Montbarry.* ○ *The author says our whole universe, no less, is only one of many.* ◇ **much** *or* **still** *or* **even less** emphasizing that something is done or happens to a smaller extent than something mentioned in the previous statement (*after a negative statement*) ○ *She could not fix her attention on any object or feel sensations, much less have conscious thoughts.*

-less *suffix* **1** without, lacking ○ *headless* ○ *restless* **2** unable to be ○ *fathomless* [Old English *-lēas* < *lēas* 'without' < Germanic]

lessee /le sée/ *n* a person who leases a property from another [15C. < Anglo-Norman, past participle of *lesser* (see LEASE).]

lessen /léss'n/ *vti* to make something less, or become less

Lesseps /léssəps/, **Ferdinand Marie, Vicomte de** (1805–94) French diplomat and engineer

lesser /léssər/ *adj, adv* less significant or smaller in size or amount

Lesser Antilles /lésser an tílleez/ island group in the Caribbean, stretching from Puerto Rico southeastwards to the coast of Venezuela and comprising the Virgin Islands, Leeward Islands, and Windward Islands

Lesser Bairam *n* an Islamic festival held each year at the end of Ramadan

lesser celandine *n* PLANTS = **celandine** *n.* 1

lesser omentum *n* ◊ **omentum**

Lesser Slave Lake /léssər slayv-/ lake in central Alberta, Canada. Area: 1,168 sq. km/451 sq. mi.

Lesser Sunda Islands ◊ **Sunda Islands**

Express Newspapers

Doris Lessing

Lessing /léssing/, **Doris** (*b.* 1919) British novelist. Born **Doris May Tayler**

Lessing, Gotthold Ephraim (1729–81) German dramatist and critic

lesson /léss'n/ *n* **1** **INSTRUCTION PERIOD** a period of time spent teaching or learning a subject ○ *I'm old enough to start taking driving lessons.* **2** **MATERIAL TAUGHT** material to be taught or studied **3** **USEFUL EXPERIENCE** something that acts as an example, punishment, or warning by teaching something not previously understood or accepted **4** **NEW OR BETTER KNOWLEDGE** some useful knowledge or sense that results from direct experience ○ *I think there's a lesson there for all of us – think ahead.* **5** **lesson, Lesson BIBLE PASSAGE** a passage from the Bible that is read out to the congregation during a church service ○ *Today's lesson is from the book of Matthew.* **6** **REBUKE** a strong criticism or telling-off, usually instructing or reminding somebody how to behave correctly ○ *I need to give him a lesson in how to behave properly.* ■ *vt* (*archaic*) **1** **INSTRUCT** to teach somebody **2** **CRITICIZE FOR WRONGDOING** to scold somebody for doing something wrong [12C. Via French *leçon* < Latin *lection-* 'reading' < *legere* 'to read'.]

lessor /le sáwr, léssawr/ *n* a person or organization that leases a property to another [14C. < Anglo-Norman *lessour* < *lesser* (see LEASE).]

lest /lest/ *conj* in order to prevent something happening, especially something causing fear ○ *must stay out of sight lest we be discovered* [Old English *þȳ lǣs þe* 'by which less that']

let[1] /let/ *vt* (**lets, letting, let**) **1** **NOT PREVENT** to allow something to happen or somebody to do something ○ *You should let him explain what happened.* ○ *I won't let anything get in the way of us living a happy life together.* ○ *I never let myself worry about the future.* **2** **PERMIT** to give somebody permission to do something ○ *I want to go to the disco but Dad won't let me.* **3** **EXPRESSING A SUGGESTION** used to express a suggestion, an offer, or an order ○ *Let's eat – I'm starving.* ○ *Let me take that bag for you – you must be exhausted.* ○ *Let the show go on!* **4** **MAKE SOMETHING PASS SOMEWHERE** to allow or make something pass from one place to another ○ *You need to let some air out of those tyres.* ○ *Open the window and let some fresh air in.* **5** **EXPRESSING RESIGNATION** used to indicate indifference to what happens or what somebody does, even though it may be unpleasant ○ *Let them do their worst.* ○ *If he wants to leave then let him – see if I care!* **6** **MAKE AS A MATHEMATICAL ASSUMPTION** used to introduce an assumption or hypothesis ○ *Let the point P be on a line L.* **7** **RENT OUT PROPERTY** to allow people to use land, rooms, or a building in return for rent **8** *Ireland* **UTTER** to utter something (*informal*) ■ *n* **1** **GRANT OF LEASE** the granting of a lease **2** **RIGHT TO RENT** permission to lease a building or piece of property [Old English *lǣtan* 'leave behind, allow' < Indo-European, 'let go'] ◇ **let alone** used to introduce something that is even less likely or probable than what has just been mentioned ◇ **let go (of something)** to stop holding something ○ *She let go of her mother's hand and ran onto the playground.* ◇ **let yourself go** **1** to start acting in a much more relaxed or less inhibited way than usual **2** to stop caring about your appearance ◇ **let somebody have it** to deliver a physical or verbal attack on somebody

USAGE See ***leave***.

let down *vt* **1** **LOWER** to move something, or allow something to move, to a lower position ○ *It was getting dark, so she let down the curtains.* **2** **DISAPPOINT** to disappoint somebody by not meeting expectations ○ *Sorry to let you down, but I won't be able to make it tonight.* **3** **MAKE AIR COME OUT OF** to make the air come out of an inflated object until it goes flat **4** **LENGTHEN GARMENT** to lengthen clothing or part of a piece of clothing by shortening the hem ○ *let down the sleeves of the coat* **5** **ALLOW HAIR TO HANG DOWN** to undo long hair so that it falls to its full length

let in *vt* **1** to allow somebody to enter somewhere such as a building or a room ○ *They refused to let her in the house.* **2** to allow water or air into something that is meant to be sealed ○ *Their boat had hit a rock and was letting in water.*

let in for *vt* to become involved in something that turns out to be more difficult or complicated than expected (*informal*) ○ *didn't realize quite what I was letting myself in for*

let in on *vt* to allow somebody to know about something

let into *vt* **1** **SHARE INFORMATION WITH** to allow somebody to know about something **2** **ALLOW TO ENTER** to allow somebody to enter somewhere **3** **ALLOW TO JOIN A CLUB** to allow somebody to join an organization or club

let off *v* **1** *vt* **EXCUSE SOMEBODY FROM PUNISHMENT** to allow somebody to avoid something such as an unpleasant task or a punishment ○ *I'll let you off this time, but you'd better behave from now on.* **2** *vt* **MAKE SOMETHING EXPLODE** to fire shots from a gun or make a firework or explosive blow up **3** *vt* **LET A PASSENGER GET OUT** to allow somebody to get off a vehicle such as a bus or train **4** *vti* **BREAK WIND** to break wind (*informal*)

let on *v* **1** *vi* **SHARE A SECRET** to share a secret with somebody (*informal*) ○ *He didn't let on that he was very rich.* **2** *vi* **PRETEND** to make somebody believe something that is not true ○ *She let on that she was upset, but she wasn't really that bothered.* **3** *vt* **LET A PASSENGER GET ON** to allow somebody to board a vehicle such as a bus or train

let out *vt* **1** **MAKE A LOUD YELL** to make a loud or piercing sound using the voice ○ *let out a scream* **2** **RELEASE** to set a person or animal free from being confined or trapped **3** **RELEASE SOMEBODY FROM PRISON** to release somebody from prison early or temporarily **4** **ALLOW SOMEBODY TO LEAVE** to allow somebody to leave a place such as a building or room **5** **ENLARGE A GARMENT** to make a piece of clothing, or a specific part of it, wider than it was before **6** **SPREAD INFORMATION** to allow previously secret information to become more widely known **7** **RENT OUT PROPERTY** to make a place available for letting ○ *They have recently let out a suite of rooms on the third floor.*

let through *vt* to allow somebody or something to pass

through a crowd ○ *Cars were pulling over to let an ambulance through.*
let up *vi* 1 to become slower, calmer, or quieter ○ *Once the rain lets up a bit we'll have a look outside.* 2 to stop working hard or being angry ○ *He never lets up, does he.*
let up on *vt* to treat somebody or something in a more relaxed, gentle, or kind way

let[2] /let/ *n* 1 REPLAYED SERVICE SHOT in games such as tennis and squash, a service in which the ball is obstructed and the service has to be played again 2 REPLAYED POINT the point that is replayed because of a let 3 DIFFICULTY OR OBSTACLE something that prevents somebody doing something or makes it more difficult (*formal*) ○ *without let or hindrance* [12C. < Old English *lettan* 'hinder'.]

-let *suffix* 1 small one ○ *wavelet* 2 something worn on ○ *anklet* [< Old French *-elet* < *-el* 'small one' (< Latin *-ellus*) + *-et* (see -ET)]

letch *n, vi* = **lech**

Letchworth /léch wurth/ town in SE England. Population: 31,418 (1991).

letdown /lét down/ *n* 1 an occasion when somebody or something disappoints expectations, or the feeling of disappointment that results ○ *After all the hype the concert was a bit of a letdown.* 2 the descent of an aircraft in preparation for landing, before the actual landing approach

lethal /leéth'l/ *adj* 1 causing or able to cause death 2 causing disaster or destruction ○ *a move that was lethal to his career* [Late 16C. < Latin *lethalis* < *lethum*, alteration of *letum* 'death', by association with Greek *lēthē* 'forgetfulness'.] —**lethality** /lee thálləti/ *n* —**lethally** *adv* —**lethalness** *n*

SYNONYMS See ***deadly***.

lethal dose *n* the amount of a drug or other substance that will cause death when administered. ◊ **median lethal dose**

lethargic /lə thaárjik/ *adj* 1 physically slow and mentally dull as a result of tiredness, disease, or drugs 2 causing a state of physical slowness and mental dullness —**lethargically** *adv*

lethargy /léthərji/ *n* 1 a state of physical slowness and mental dullness as a result of tiredness, disease, or drugs 2 lack of energy, activity, or enthusiasm [14C. Via Old French *litargia* < Greek *lēthargia* < *lēthargos* 'forgetful' < *lēthē* 'forgetfulness'.]

Lethbridge /léth brij/ city in S Alberta, Canada. Population: 63,053 (1996).

Lethe /leéthi/ *n* in Greek and Roman mythology, a river in Hades whose water made those who drank it forget their past [Mid-16C. Via Latin < Greek *lēthē* 'forgetfulness'.] —**Lethean** *adj*

Leto /leétō/ *n* in Greek mythology, the mother of Apollo and Artemis by Zeus. Roman equivalent **Latona**

let-out *n* a way of freeing yourself from or avoiding something you have committed yourself to

let's *contr* let us ○ *Let's just wait and see what happens.*

Lett /let/ *n* PEOPLES = **Latvian** *n.* 1 [Late 16C. Via German *Lette* < Latvian *Latvi.*]

letter /léttər/ *n* 1 MESSAGE SENT BY MAIL a piece of handwritten or printed text addressed to a recipient and typically sent by post 2 SYMBOL USED TO SPELL WORDS a written or printed symbol representing a sound or set of sounds in a language and used to spell words 3 PRINTING FONT a typeface or font ■ *vt* WRITE ON to write letters or words on something [13C. Via French *lettre* < Latin *littera* 'letter of the alphabet, (plural) document'.]

⚡**letter bomb** *n* 1 an envelope with an explosive device inside it, addressed and sent through the post and designed to blow up when it is opened 2 an e-mail message with a destructive code attached to it

letterbox /léttər boks/ *n* 1 a narrow opening in a door, through which letters and packages can be posted. US term **mail slot** 2 MAIL = **postbox** 3 a private box or other place to which mail for a specific person or organization is delivered

letter card *n* 1 a card that is folded over and sealed before being posted, usually with perforations for tearing the sealed edges when opening it 2 a long folding letter with postcard scenes printed down the back that can be folded, sealed, and then posted like a postcard

letter carrier *n* somebody employed to deliver letters or other mail (*formal*)

lettered /léttərd/ *adj* 1 WITH LETTERS WRITTEN ON IT marked with letters of the alphabet 2 EDUCATED knowledgeable and cultured, especially in literary matters 3 LITERATE able to read and write

letterform /léttər fawrm/ *n* the shape of a letter of the alphabet

letterhead /léttər hed/ *n* 1 a printed heading for official stationery, usually containing a company's name, address, telephone and fax numbers, and often including a logo and other details 2 a piece of writing paper with a printed letterhead ○ *Send in a letterhead along with your invoice details.*

lettering /léttəring/ *n* 1 letters of the alphabet written, printed, inscribed, or painted on something 2 the physical process of forming letters, or the way they are formed

Letterman /léttərmən/, **David** (*b.* 1947) US television presenter

letter of credit *n* a letter from a bank, usually for presentation to another branch or bank, authorizing it to issue credit or money to the person named

letter of intent *n* a signed statement outlining an intention to form an agreement or arrangement

letter of introduction *n* a letter written by somebody to introduce one person to another

letter-perfect *adj US* 1 = **word-perfect** *adj.* 1 2 = **word-perfect** *adj.* 2

letterpress /léttər press/ *n* 1 PRINTING BY USE OF PRESSURE a printing technique that transfers ink by pressing raised type onto paper 2 PRINTED MATERIAL material that is printed using the letterpress technique 3 TEXT text as opposed to illustrations

⚡**letter-quality** *adj* of a quality high enough to be compared to conventional printing

letters /léttərz/ *n* (+ *singular or plural verb*) 1 literature or literary culture 2 knowledge and education

letters credential *npl* LAW = **letters of credence**

letters of administration *npl* an official court order appointing somebody as the administrator of a deceased person's estate when no valid will exists

letters of credence *npl* an official document presented to a government in order to authenticate the official status of a diplomatic representative of another country

letters of marque *npl* 1 a formal document issued by one country authorizing one of its private citizens to take possession of goods, or sometimes citizens, belonging to another country 2 an official document issued by one country authorizing one of its citizens to fit a ship with weapons in order to attack or seize another country's ships and cargo

letters patent *npl* an official document stating that somebody has been granted the exclusive right to make and sell a new product

letters testamentary *npl* an official document authorizing somebody to assume the responsibilities and duties of executor of the will of a deceased person

letting /létting/ *n* a property that is being let

lettuce /léttiss/ *n* a common plant that is widely grown for its edible leaves, which are usually eaten in salads. Genus: *Lactuca.* [13C. < Old French *letuës* < Latin *lactuca* < *lac* 'milk'; from the milky sap of its stalk.]

let-up *n* a pause, especially in something unpleasant (*informal*) ○ *I can take criticism, but with her there's no let-up.*

leu /láy oo/ (*plural* **lei** /lay/) *n* see table at **currency** [Late 19C. < Romanian, 'lion'.]

leucine /lóo seen/, **leucin** /lóossin/ *n* an essential amino acid [Early 19C. < Greek *leukos* 'white'.]

Leucippus /loo síppəss/ (450?–370 BC) Greek philosopher

leucite /lóo sīt/ *n* a white or grey aluminosilicate mineral containing potassium. Source: igneous rocks. Use: source of aluminium and potash for fertilizers. [Late 18C. < Greek *leukos* 'white'.]

leuco- *prefix* 1 white, pale, colourless ○ *leucoplakia* 2 leucocyte ○ *leucopenia* 3 white matter of the brain ○ *leucodystrophy* [< Greek *leukos* 'white, clear'. Ultimately < Indo-European 'lightness'.]

leucoblast /lóokō blaast/, **leukoblast** *n* an immature white blood cell (**leucocyte**)

leucocyte /lóokə sīt/, **leukocyte** *n* a white blood cell (*technical*) —**leucocytic** /lóokə síttik/ *adj* —**leucocytoid** /-sī toyd/ *adj*

leucocytosis /lóokə sī tóssiss/, **leukocytosis** *n* a marked increase in the number of white blood cells (**leucocytes**), usually because of infection or disease —**leucocytotic** /-tóttik/ *adj*

leucoderma /lóokə dúrmə/, **leukoderma** *n* MED = **vitiligo** [Late 19C. < LEUCO- + Greek *derma* 'skin'.]

leucodystrophy /lóokō dístrəfi/, **leukodystrophy** *n* a degenerative disease of nerve fibres or white matter that impairs brain function, sight, and motion, leading to death, often at an early age

leucoma /loo kṓmə/, **leukoma** *n* a dense white scar on the cornea of the eye, caused by disease or injury [Early 18C. Via modern Latin < Greek *leukōma* 'white tumour' < *leukos* 'white'.]

leucopenia /lóokō peéni ə/, **leukopenia** *n* an abnormal reduction in the number of white blood cells (**leucocytes**) —**leucopenic** *adj*

leucoplakia /lóokō pláyki ə, -plák-/, **leukoplakia** *n* a precancerous condition that is seen as small thickened white patches, usually inside the mouth or vulva [Late 19C. < LEUCO- + Greek *plax* 'flat surface'.]

leucoplast /lóokə plast/, **leucoplastid** /lóokə plastid, lóokə plástid/ *n* a common minute colourless body (**plastid**) found inside plant cells and used for storing food

leucorrhoea /lóokə reé ə/ *n* thick whitish or yellowish discharge from the vagina —**leucorrhoeal** *adj*

leucosis *n* = **leukosis**

leucotomy /loo kóttəmi/ (*plural* **-mies**) *n* a surgical operation that involves cutting nerve fibres, especially in the frontal lobes of the brain

leucotriene /lóokə treen/, **leukotriene** *n* a short-range chemical messenger in various tissues that plays a role in inflammation [Late 20C. < LEUCO- + *triene* 'chemical compound containing three double bonds'.]

leukaemia /loo keémi ə/ *n* an often fatal cancer in which white blood cells displace normal blood, leading to infection, shortage of red blood cells (**anaemia**), bleeding, and other disorders [Mid-19C. < LEUCO-.] —**leukaemic** *adj*

leukemia *n* US = **leukaemia**

leuko- *prefix* MED = **leuco-**

leukoblast *n* ANAT = **leucoblast**

leukocyte *n* ANAT = **leucocyte**

leukocytosis *n* MED = **leucocytosis**

leukoderma *n* MED = **leucoderma**

leukodystrophy *n* MED = **leucodystrophy**

leukoma *n* MED = **leucoma**

leukopenia *n* MED = **leucopenia**

leukoplakia *n* MED = **leucoplakia**

leukorrhea *n* US = **leucorrhoea**

leukosis /loo kṓssiss/, **leucosis** *n* any animal disease in which the blood contains an abnormally high number of white blood cells (**leucocytes**) [Early 18C. < Greek *leukōsis* < *leukon* 'make white' < *leukos* 'white'.]

leukotomy *n* US = **leucotomy**

leukotriene *n* = **leucotriene**

Leunig /lóonig/, **Michael** (*b.* 1945) Australian cartoonist

lev /lev/ (*plural* **leva** /lévvə/) *n* see table at **currency** [Late 19C. < Bulgarian, variant of *lăv* 'lion', probably < Greek *leōn*.]

LEV *abbr* low emission vehicle

Lev. *abbr* Leviticus

Levant /li vánt/ former name for the region in the E Mediterranean comprising modern-day Lebanon, Israel, and parts of Syria and Turkey [15C. < French, 'rising'; because the sun appears to rise there.] —**Levantine** /lévv'n tīn/ *n, adj*

levanter /li vántər/ *n* a strong easterly wind that blows in the W Mediterranean area, especially in the late summer

levator /lə váytər/ *n* 1 a muscle that helps to lift the body part to which it is attached 2 a surgical instrument used to lift up a body part, especially a bone or a tooth [Early 17C. < Latin, 'lifter' < *levare* (see LEVER).]

levee[1] /lévvi, lévvay/ *n* 1 NATURAL EMBANKMENT BESIDE A RIVER a natural embankment alongside a river, formed by sediment during times of flooding 2 ARTIFICIAL EMBANKMENT BESIDE A RIVER an artificial embankment alongside a river, built to prevent flooding of the surrounding land ■ *vt* (-ees, -eeing, -eed) BUILD A LEVEE to provide a river with an embankment to prevent flooding [Early 18C. < French *levée*, feminine past participle of *lever* (see LEVER).]

levee[2] /lévvi, lə váy/ *n* 1 an occasion when a noble or royal receives visitors informally soon after getting up in the morning 2 a court reception at which a prince or sovereign receives men visitors [Late 17C. < French *levé*, variant of *lever* 'rising' < *lever* (see LEVER).]

level /lévv'l/ *n* 1 HEIGHT FOR MEASUREMENT a position, line, or flat surface according to which height is measured ○ *10,000 feet above sea level* 2 HEIGHT OF A SURFACE FROM BOTTOM the height of a surface from the ground or from the bottom of its container ○ *The level of the river had fallen alarmingly during the summer.* 3 STATED HEIGHT a particular height ○ *flying below the level of the tree tops* 4 RANK OR SCALE a particular position in a range of relative scales or values ○ *playing tennis at the professional level* 5 AMOUNT the amount or concentration of something ○ *My job has a low stress level but few prospects.* 6 ASPECT a quality or aspect of something ○ *It's a film that works well on a number of different levels.* 7 POSITION OF A PARTICULAR FLOOR the relative position of a particular floor or other plane in a structure, e.g. a building or bridge ○ *The storeroom is down on the second level.* 8 HORIZONTAL SURFACE a horizontal surface or area of land 9 SURVEYING INSTRUMENT an instrument used in surveying to measure the relative heights of different points in the landscape 10 MEASUREMENT OF HEIGHT in surveying, a measurement taken of the relative heights of different points in a landscape 11 *US* CONSTR = **spirit level** 12 HORIZONTAL MINE TUNNEL a horizontal tunnel in a mine ■ *adj* 1 NOT SLOPING flat and horizontal, with an even surface or top 2 EVEN smooth or even ○ *We wanted a house with a completely level lawn.* 3 EQUAL equal to or even with another individual or group in rank, ability, or condition ○ *The two teams have drawn level after six games.* 4 ALONGSIDE next to or alongside somebody or something else ○ *His car drew level as we approached the bend.* 5 STEADY steady, consistent, or unchanging 6 = **level-headed** 7 OF A PARTICULAR LEVEL relating to or characteristic of a particular rank or condition (*usually in combination*) ■ *v* (-els, -elling, -elled) 1 *vt* FLATTEN SOMETHING EVENLY to make something even, flat, and horizontal ○ *We spent days levelling the ground before we could start building.* 2 *vt* DEMOLISH AND FLATTEN to completely destroy a building, place, or area and leave it flattened ○ *The village had been levelled by the hurricane.* 3 *vt* KNOCK SOMEBODY DOWN to knock somebody to the ground, especially with a punch or blow (*informal*) ○ *levelled him with one punch* 4 *vi* BE HONEST WITH to speak frankly and honestly to somebody (*informal*) ○ *I'd better level with you right now – I'm leaving the company and going it alone.* 5 *vti* MEASURE THE ELEVATION OF LAND in surveying, to measure the elevation of an area of land 6 *vti* MAKE OR BECOME EQUAL to make two things or people equal in position or of the same standard or value, or become equal in position, standard, or value ○ *Another goal in the final few minutes levelled the scores again.* 7 *vti* AIM A GUN to aim or point a weapon ○ *He levelled his pistol at the target.* 8 *vt* DIRECT ATTENTION AT to direct criticism or an attack towards somebody in a purposeful way ○ *Criticism has been levelled at a number of prominent politicians.* [14C. < Old French *livel* 'tool for determining levelness' < Latin *libra* 'balance, scales'.] —**levelly** *adv* —**levelness** *n* ◇ **on the level** honest and trustworthy (*informal*)

level off *vti* 1 **level off, level out** to make an aircraft fly level with the ground, especially after climbing or descending ○ *We passed through the clouds and eventually levelled off at about 10,000 feet.* 2 to reach a level and become stable and unchanging ○ *Stock prices seem to have levelled off.*

level crossing *n* a place where a road crosses a railway line, usually with a system of warning signals and barriers that close automatically when a train is approaching. US term **grade crossing**

leveler *n* US = **leveller**

level-headed *adj* remaining rational and fully in control in difficult situations or emergencies —**level-headedly** *adv* —**level-headedness** *n*

leveller /lévvələr/ *n* 1 a factor that makes situations or people more equal, especially by removing distinctions based on status or privilege ○ *Time is a great leveller; we all end up the same way in the end.* 2 a person who advocates equality in society for everyone

Leveller /lévvələr/ *n* a member or supporter of a radical Parliamentarian movement during the Civil War, calling for religious tolerance, legal equality, a universal male vote, and the abolition of the monarchy

levelling screw *n* one of usually several screws on the bottom of something such as a scientific instrument or a washing machine that can be adjusted to make the piece of equipment stand level

level of attainment *n* the level that a child has reached on the eight-point scale by which the National Curriculum assesses pupils between the ages of 5 and 14 in the United Kingdom

level pegging *n* in a game or competition, the same position, score, or level of achievement as somebody else ○ *After four rounds we were both on level pegging.* ○ *It's level pegging at the moment, though anything could happen in the next round.* [< the use of pegs in parallel rows in a board to show card players' scores]

Leven, Loch /leévən/ lake in east-central Scotland. Area: 26 sq. km/10 sq. mi.

lever /leévər/ *n* 1 RIGID BAR USED FOR LEVERAGE a rigid bar that pivots about a point (**fulcrum**) and is used to move or lift a load at one end by applying force to the other end 2 DEVICE OR MACHINE a mechanical device or machine that operates using leverage 3 WAY OF ACHIEVING a device, tactic, or situation that can be used to advantage ■ *vt* MOVE WITH A LEVER to move something using a lever [13C. < Anglo-Norman, 'something that raises' < Old French, 'to raise' < Latin *levare* < *levis* 'light'.]

Lever /leévər/, **William Hesketh, 1st Viscount Leverhulme** (1851–1925) British industrialist and philanthropist

leverage /leévərij/ *n* 1 ACTION OF A LEVER the action of a lever pivoting about a point 2 MECHANICAL ADVANTAGE the mechanical advantage gained by using a lever 3 POWER TO GET THINGS DONE power over other people, especially something that gives an advantage but is not referred to openly ○ *He uses the leverage of seniority with the more junior employees.* 4 BORROWING OF MONEY TO PURCHASE COMPANY the borrowing of money to purchase a company, in the hope that it will make enough profit to cover the interest payable on the loan 5 FIN = **gearing** *n.* 3 ■ *v* (-ages, -aging, -aged) 1 *vti* BORROW MONEY HOPING TO MAKE MORE to borrow money in order to buy a company, relying on it making enough profit to cover the interest payable on the loan 2 *vt US* OPTIMIZE to increase, enhance, or optimize something ○ *a guide on how to leverage revenues from your website*

leveraged buyout *n* a takeover strategy in which a controlling proportion of a company's shares is bought using borrowed money, the collateral for which is assets belonging to the purchased company

leveret /lévvərət/ *n* a young hare, especially one less than a year old [14C. < Anglo-Norman, 'little hare' < *levre* 'hare' < Latin *lepus*.]

Leverrier /lə vérri ay/, **Urbain Jean Joseph** (1811–77) French astronomer

Levi /leév ī/ *n* in the Bible, the third son of Jacob and patriarch of the house of Levi (Genesis 29:34)

Levi /lévvi/, **Primo** (1919–87) Italian novelist, poet, and scientist

leviathan /lə vī́ əth'n/ *n* 1 **leviathan, Leviathan** MONSTER in the Bible, a large beast or sea monster 2 SOMETHING HUGE something extremely large and powerful in comparison with others of its kind 3 WHALE a whale or other large sea animal (*literary*) [14C. Via late Latin < Hebrew *liwyātān*.]

levigate /lévvi gayt/ (-gates, -gating, -gated) *v* 1 *vt* GRIND MINERAL INTO POWDER to grind a mineral into a fine powder with water, forming a smooth paste or slurry 2 *vt* SEPARATE PARTICLES IN LIQUID to separate fine particles from coarser ones by suspending them in a liquid 3 *vti* FORM A MIXTURE to form a smooth uniform liquid mixture, e.g. a paste or gel [15C. < Latin *levigat-*, past participle of *levigare* 'make smooth'.] —**levigation** /lévvi gáysh'n/ *n*

levirate /leévirət, lévvi-/ *n* the practice by which a man may be required to marry his brother's widow [Early 18C. < Latin *levir* 'husband's brother'.] —**leviratic** /leévi ráttik, lévvi-/ *adj*

Levi-Strauss /lévvi strówss/, **Claude Gustave** (*b.* 1908) French social anthropologist

levitate /lévvi tayt/ (-tates, -tating, -tated) *v* 1 *vti* to rise and float in the air, or make something rise and float in the air, seemingly in defiance of gravity 2 *vt* to support a patient on a cushion of air during treatment for severe burns [Late 17C. < Latin *levis* 'light'.] —**levitation** /lévvi táysh'n/ *n* —**levitational** *adj* —**levitator** *n*

Levite /leé vīt/ *n* a member of the Hebrew tribe of Levi, chosen to assist the priests of the Jewish Temple. The Levites were descended from Jacob's son Levi and constituted one of the twelve tribes of Israel. [14C. < ecclesiastical Latin *levita* < Greek *levitēs*, after *Levi* 'Levi'.]

Levitical /lə víttik'l/ *adj* 1 belonging or relating to the Levites 2 relating to the book of Leviticus, especially those portions containing laws relating to ritual or moral precepts

Leviticus /lə víttikəss/ *n* a book of the Bible, the third book of the Pentateuch, containing the priestly tradition of the Levites [14C. < late Latin, 'of the Levites' < Greek *levitēs* (see LEVITE).]

levity /lévvəti/ *n* remarks or behaviour intended to be amusing, especially when they are out of keeping with a serious occasion [Mid-16C. < Latin *levitas* < *levis* 'light'.]

levo- *n* US = **laevo-**

levodopa /leévō dṓpə/ *n* full form of **L-dopa**

levorotation[1] *n* US = **laevorotation**

levorotation[2] *adj* US = **laevorotatory**

levulose *n* US = **laevulose**

levy /lévvi/ *v* (-ies, -ying, -ied) 1 *vt* OFFICIALLY DEMAND TAX PAYMENTS to use government authority to impose or collect a tax 2 *vt* RAISE AN ARMY to enlist troops for military service, often by force 3 *vt* DECLARE WAR to declare war on somebody 4 *vi* SEIZE PROPERTY TO FULFIL A JUDGMENT to seize property in accordance with a legal ruling ■ *n* (*plural* -ies) 1 TAX money raised under government authority 2 THE RAISING OF TAX the act of collecting taxes under government authority 3 ARMY a group of soldiers drafted under government authority 4 CONSCRIPTION the act of drafting soldiers under government authority [15C. < French *levée* (see LEVEE[1]).] —**leviable** *adj* —**levier** *n*

lewd /lood, lyood/ *adj* sexual in an offensive way [Old English *lǣw(e)de* 'lay, not in holy orders'] —**lewdly** *adv* —**lewdness** *n*

Lewes /lóo əss/ town in SE England. Population: 15,376 (1991).

lewis /lóo iss/ *n* an iron attachment consisting of linked pieces that fit into a dovetailed opening in a stone, used to grip heavy stones before lifting them [Mid-18C. Probably < French *lous*, plural of *lou(p)* 'kind of siege engine', literally 'wolf' < Latin *lupus*.]

Lewis /lóo iss/, **Carl** (*b.* 1961) US athlete

Lewis, C. S. (1898–1963) Irish-born British critic, scholar, and novelist. Full name **Clive Staples Lewis**

Lewis, Essington (1881–1961) Australian engineer and company director

Lewis, Gilbert Newton (1875–1946) US chemist

Lewis, Jerry (*b.* 1926) US actor, screenwriter, film director, and film producer. Born **Joseph Levitch**

Lewis, Sinclair (1885–1951) US novelist

Lewis, Wally (*b.* 1959) Australian rugby league player

Lewis, Wyndham (1882–1957) British painter, novelist, and critic

Lewis acid *n* a substance that can accept a pair of electrons from a base to form a covalent bond [Mid-20C. After Gilbert Newton LEWIS.]

Lewis base *n* 1 a substance that can donate a pair of electrons to an acid to form a covalent bond 2 a substance that donates an electron pair to an acid during the formation of a covalent bond [Mid-20C. After Gilbert Newton LEWIS.]

Lewis gun *n* a gas-powered machine gun with a circular magazine, first used in World War I [Early 20C. After US soldier Colonel Isaac Newton *Lewis* (1858–1931).]

lewisite /lóo i sīt/ *n* $C_2H_2AsCl_3$ a colourless or brownish oily poisonous liquid. Use: in gaseous form in chemical warfare during World War I. [Early 20C. After Winford Lee *Lewis* (1878–1943), US chemist.]

Lewis rule of eight *n* the observation that chemical elements react together by losing, gaining, or sharing electrons so that they attain eight electrons in their outer shells [Mid-20C. After Gilbert Newton *Lewis* (1875–1946), US chemist.]

lewisson /loǒ iss'n/ *n* = **lewis**

Lewis with Harris /loǒ iss wit͟h hárriss/ largest and northernmost island of the Outer Hebrides, W Scotland. Population: 21,737 (1991). Area: 2,134 sq. km/824 sq. mi.

LeWitt /lə wít/, **Sol** (*b.* 1928) US artist

lex /leks/ (*plural* **leges** /lée jeez/) *n* a named law or set of laws [Late 18C. < Latin, 'law'.]

lexeme /léks eem/ *n* a fundamental unit of the vocabulary of a language that may exist in a number of different forms, e.g. 'make' existing as 'makes, making, maker, made' [Mid-20C. < LEXICON.]

lexica plural of **lexicon**

lexical /léksik'l/ *adj* **1** relating to the individual words that make up the vocabulary of a language **2** relating to a lexicon or lexicography [Mid-19C. < Greek *lexikos* (see LEXICON).] —**lexicality** /léksi kálləti/ *n* —**lexically** *adv*

lexicalize /léksikə līz/ (**-izes, -izing, -ized**), **lexicalise** (**-ises, -ising, -ised**) *vti* to form a single word from existing words, or be formed in this way, in order to express something previously conveyed by several words or a phrase, e.g. 'shoplifting' —**lexicalization** /léksikə lī záysh'n/ *n*

lexical meaning *n* the meaning of the base word in the set of inflected forms (**paradigm**). In the paradigm 'throw, throws, throwing, threw, thrown', the lexical meaning is 'throw'.

lexicog. *abbr* **1** lexicography **2** lexicographic

lexicography /léksi kóggrəfi/ *n* the writing and editing of dictionaries [Mid-17C. < Greek *lexikos* (see LEXICON).] —**lexicographer** *n* —**lexicographic** /léksikə gráffik/ *adj* —**lexicographically** *adv*

lexicology /léksi kólləji/ *n* the branch of linguistics dealing with the use and meanings of words and the relationships between items of vocabulary [Early 19C. < Greek *lexikos* (see LEXICON).] —**lexicological** /léksikə lójjik'l/ *adj* —**lexicologically** *adv* —**lexicologist** *n*

lexicon /léksikən, -kon/ (*plural* **-cons** *or* **-ca** /-kə/) *n* **1** a reference book that alphabetically lists words and their meanings, e.g. of an ancient language **2** the entire stock of words belonging to a branch of knowledge or known by somebody [Early 17C. Via modern Latin < Greek *lexikon*, a form of *lexikos* 'of words' < *lexis* 'word' < *legein* 'speak'.]

lexigraphy /lek síggrəfi/ *n* a system of writing in which each character stands for a word [Early 19C. < Greek *lexis* (see LEXICON).]

Lexington /léksingtən/ town in NE Massachusetts. Population: 28,974 (1996 estimate).

lexis /léksiss/ *n* the entire stock of words in a language [Mid-20C. < Greek (see LEXICON).]

lex talionis /-talli ṓniss/ *n* the legal principle that prescribes retaliating in kind for crimes committed [< Latin, 'law of retaliation']

ley[1] /lay, lee/ (*plural* **leys**) *n* any ancient path in Britain that led from hilltop to hilltop and touched on water sources and places of worship [Variant of LEA]

ley[2] /lay, lee/ (*plural* **leys**) *n* an area of arable land temporarily put down to grass [Old English *lǣge* < Germanic]

Leyden = **Leiden**

Leyden jar *n* an early device for condensing static electricity consisting of a glass jar coated inside and outside with metal foil and with a conducting rod passing through an insulated stopper [Mid-18C. After *Leyden*, former spelling of LEIDEN.]

ley farming *n* the practice of growing grass in fields normally planted with grain or other tilled crops in order to prevent the soil from becoming exhausted [< assumed Old English *lǣge* 'fallow', related to LIE[1]]

ley line *n* a straight line linking ancient landmarks and places of worship, believed to follow the course of former routes and popularly associated with mystical phenomena

L-form *n* a bacterium that lacks cell walls [After the *Lister* Institute in London]

lh *abbr* left hand

LH *abbr* **1** luteinizing hormone **2** left hand

Lhasa /laássə/ city and capital of the autonomous region of Tibet, SW China. Population: 161,788 (1991).

Lhasa apso /laássə ápsō/ (*plural* **Lhasa apsos**) *n* a small dog of a Tibetan breed with a long straight coat, hair that falls heavily over the eyes, and a fluffy tail that curls over the back [Early 20C. *apso* < Tibetan, 'sentinel'.]

lherzolite /lúrzə līt/ *n* a coarse-grained rock containing minerals high in iron and magnesium that is believed to originate in the Earth's mantle

LH-RH *abbr* luteinizing hormone-releasing hormone

li[1] /lee/ (*plural* **li**) *n* a traditional Chinese unit of distance, now standardized at 500 m/547 yd [Late 16C. < Chinese *lǐ*.]

li[2] *abbr* Liechtenstein (*in Internet addresses*)

Li *symbol* lithium

liability /lī ə bílləti/ *n* (*plural* **-ties**) **1 OBLIGATION UNDER THE LAW** legal responsibility for something, especially costs or damages **2 DEBT** anything for which somebody is responsible, especially a debt **3 DISADVANTAGE** something that holds somebody back or causes trouble **4 SOMEBODY WHO IS A BURDEN** a person who prevents a successful outcome or causes social embarrassment **5 LIKELIHOOD** likelihood or probability of something happening ■ **liabilities** *npl* **MONEY OWED** all debts and other financial obligations that appear on a balance sheet

liable /lī əb'l/ *adj* **1** having legal responsibility for something, especially costs or damages **2** likely to experience or do something, often something unpleasant or hazardous [15C. Probably < French *lier* (see LIAISON).]

liaise /li áyz/ (**-aises, -aising, -aised**) *vi* to establish or maintain close cooperation with somebody [Early 20C. Back-formation < LIAISON.]

liaison /li áyz'n, -zon/ *n* **1 COORDINATION** the exchange of information or the planning of joint efforts by two or more people or groups, often of military personnel **2 COORDINATOR** a person who coordinates communication between two or more people or groups **3 UNMARRIED LOVE AFFAIR** a romantic and sexual relationship between people who are not married to each other, especially when secret **4 PRONOUNCED CONSONANT LINKING TWO WORDS** in spoken French, the pronunciation of the usually silent final consonant of a word when it is followed by another word beginning with a vowel **5 SOMETHING USED TO THICKEN A LIQUID** a thickening agent such as egg yolks or flour used in soups and sauces [Mid-17C. < French, < *lier* 'bind' < Latin *ligare*.]

liana /li aánə/, **liane** *n* a woody climbing tropical vine [Late 18C. < French *liane*.] —**lianoid** *adj*

Liao /lée ow/ river in NE China. Length: 1,125 km/700 mi.

Liaoning /lyów níng/ province in NE China. Capital: Shenyang. Population: 40,670,000 (1994). Area: 151,000 sq. km/58,300 sq. mi.

Liaoyang /lée ow júng/, **Liao-yang** city in NE China. Population: 559,719 (1991).

Liaquat Ali Khan /lée ə kwaat aáli kaán/ (1895–1951) Pakistani statesman

liar /lī ər/ *n* a teller of untruths

Liard /lée ərd/ river in W Canada, rising in the S Yukon Territory and flowing through N British Columbia and the SW Northwest Territories to the Mackenzie River. Length: 1,115 km/700 mi.

~~liase~~ incorrect spelling of **liaise**

~~liason~~ incorrect spelling of **liaison**

Liassic /lī ássik/ *adj* belonging to or dating from the oldest division of the European Jurassic period, noted for its fossils of dinosaurs [Mid-19C. < French *liassique* < *Lias* 'division of the European Jurassic period' < Old French *liais* 'hard limestone'.]

lib /lib/ *n* liberation of an oppressed group (*dated informal; used in names of political campaigns in combination*) ○ *gay lib* [Mid-20C. Shortening of LIBERATION.] —**libber** *n*

lib. *abbr* **1** librarian **2** library

Lib. *abbr* Liberal

~~libary~~ incorrect spelling of **library**

libation /lī báysh'n/ *n* **1 POURING OF LIQUID AS A RELIGIOUS OFFERING** the pouring out of a liquid such as wine or oil as a sacrifice to a god or in honour of a dead person **2 SOMETHING POURED OUT AS A SACRIFICE** a liquid such as wine or oil poured out as a religious offering **3 ALCOHOLIC DRINK** an alcoholic drink (*humorous*) [14C. < Latin *libation-* < *libare* 'pour out'.] —**libational** *adj*

Lib Dem *abbr* Liberal Democrat

libel /līb'l/ *n* **1 DEFAMATION** a false and malicious published statement that damages somebody's reputation **2 ATTACKING SOMEBODY'S REPUTATION** the making of false and damaging statements about somebody **3 WRITTEN STATEMENT** the plaintiff's written statement in a case under Admiralty law or in an ecclesiastical court ■ *vt* (**-bels, -belling, -belled**) **1 DEFAME** to publish false and malicious statements that damage somebody's reputation **2 ATTACK** to give a false and damaging account of somebody **3 BRING A SUIT FOR LIBEL** to bring a suit for libel against somebody under Admiralty law or in an ecclesiastical court [14C. Via Old French < Latin *libellus* 'little book' < *liber* (see LIBRARY).] —**libeller** *n* —**libellist** *n* —**libellous** *adj* —**libellously** *adv*

SYNONYMS See ***malign***.

Liberace /líbbər aáchi/ (1919–87) US pianist. Born **Wladziu Valentino Liberace**

liberal /líbbərəl/ *adj* **1 BROAD-MINDED** tolerant of different views and standards of behaviour in others **2 PROGRESSIVE POLITICALLY OR SOCIALLY** favouring gradual reform, especially political reforms that extend democracy, distribute wealth more evenly, and protect the personal freedom of the individual **3 GENEROUS** generous with money, time, or some other asset ○ *My great-aunt was liberal in her bequests.* **4 GENEROUS IN QUANTITY** large in size or amount ○ *a liberal helping* **5 NOT LITERAL** not limited to the literal meaning in translation or interpretation **6 CULTURALLY ORIENTED** concerned with general cultural matters and broadening of the mind rather than professional or technical study ○ *a liberal education* **7 OF BRANCH OF PROGRESSIVE JUDAISM** relating or belonging to a branch of Progressive Judaism, characterized by radical revision of the liturgy and an emphasis on ethical teaching **8 OF POLITICAL LIBERALISM** relating to a political ideology of liberalism ■ *n* **LIBERAL PERSON** a person who favours tolerance or open-mindedness [14C. Via French < Latin *liberalis* < *liber* 'free'.]

SYNONYMS See ***generous***.

Liberal *adj* supporting, belonging to, or associated with a Liberal Party, e.g. in the United Kingdom, Canada, or Australia ■ *n* a member or supporter of a Liberal Party, e.g. in the United Kingdom, Canada, or Australia

liberal arts *npl* **1** college and university subjects that are intended to provide students with general cultural knowledge, e.g. languages, literature, history, and philosophy **2** the medieval studies known as the trivium and quadrivium

liberal democracy *n* a political system that has free elections, a multiplicity of political parties, political decision made through an independent legislature, and an independent judiciary, with a state monopoly on law enforcement

Liberal Democrat *n* a member of the British Liberal and Social Democratic Party

liberalise *vti* = **liberalize**

liberalism /líbbərəlizəm/ *n* **1 PROGRESSIVE VIEWS** a belief in tolerance and gradual reform in moral, religious, or political matters **2 POLITICAL THEORY STRESSING INDIVIDUALISM** a political ideology with its beginnings in W Europe that rejects authoritarian government and defends freedom of speech, association, and religion, and the right to own property **3 FREE-MARKET ECONOMICS** an economic theory in favour of free competition and minimal government regulation **4 CHRISTIAN THEOLOGICAL MOVEMENT** a movement in modern Protestantism stressing intellectual freedom and the moral content of Christianity over the doctrines of traditional theology —**liberalist** *n* —**liberalistic** /líbbərə lístik/ *adj*

liberality /líbbə rálləti/, **liberalness** /líbbərəlnəss/ *n* **1 GENEROSITY** generous provision of money, time, or some other asset **2 LARGENESS** largeness in size or amount **3 BROAD-MINDEDNESS** tolerance of different views and standards of behaviour in others

liberalize /líbbərə līz/ (**-izes, -izing, -ized**), **liberalise** (**-ises, -ising, -ised**) *vti* to reform and become less strict, or reform something and make it less strict —**liberalization** /líbbərə lī záysh'n/ *n* —**liberalizer** *n*

liberally /líbbərəli/ *adv* **1** giving money, time, or some other asset with generosity **2** in large quantities or amounts

liberalness *n* = **liberality**

Liberal Party *n* **1** one of the main British political parties that evolved from the Whigs and eventually merged with the Social Democratic Party in 1988 to form the Social and Liberal Democratic Party, later known as the Liberal Democrats **2** a major Canadian political party at both the national and provincial levels that first came to power nationally in 1873

Liberal Party of Australia *n* a conservative Australian political party founded in 1944 as an antisocialist organization that, except for 1972 to 1974, has always been in coalition with the National Party

liberal studies *n* a combined arts subject intended to provide students with general cultural knowledge, provided as an element of a more specialized, technical, or vocational course at school or college (+ *singular verb*)

Liberal Unionist *n* a member of the former British Liberal Party who disagreed with Gladstone's policy on Irish Home Rule from 1886 onwards

liberate /líbbə rayt/ (**-ates, -ating, -ated**) *vt* **1 SET SOMEBODY FREE PHYSICALLY** to release an individual, group, population, or country from political or military control or from any severe physical constraint **2 RELEASE SOMEBODY FROM SOCIAL STEREOTYPING** to set somebody free from traditional socially imposed constraints such as those arising from stereotyping by sex or age **3 STEAL** to steal something (*informal*) **4 RELEASE GAS DURING A CHEMICAL RE-ACTION** to free something such as a gas from combination in a chemical compound during a chemical reaction [Late 16C. < Latin *liberare* < *liber* 'free'.] —**liberatingly** *adv* —**liberation** /líbbə ráysh'n/ *n* —**liberationist** *n* —**liberator** *n*

liberation theology *n* a movement in Roman Catholic religious teaching that argues that the Church should work actively to combat social, political, and economic oppression —**liberation theologian** *n*

Liberia

Liberia /lī beéri ə/ republic in W Africa, on the North Atlantic Ocean. Capital: Monrovia. Population: 2,602,068 (1997). Area: 99,067 sq. km/38,250 sq. mi. —**Liberian** *adj, n*

libero /leébərō/ (*plural* **-ros**) *n* in football, a sweeper (*informal*) [Mid-20C. < Italian, 'free' < Latin *liber*.]

libertarian /líbbər táiri ən/ *n* **1** a believer in the doctrine of free will **2** a believer in the principle that people should have complete freedom of thought and action [Late 18C. < LIBERTY.] —**libertarianism** *n*

libertine /líbbar teen, -tīn/ *n* somebody, usually a man, who indulges in pleasures that are considered immoral and who has sexual relationships with many people [14C. < Latin *libertinus* < *libertus* 'somebody freed from slavery' < *liber* 'free'.] —**libertinage** *n* —**libertinism** *n*

liberty /líbbərti/ (*plural* **-ties**) *n* **1 RIGHT TO CHOOSE** the freedom to think or act without being constrained by necessity or force **2 FREEDOM** freedom from captivity or slavery **3 BASIC RIGHT** a political, social, and economic right that belongs to the citizens of a state or to all people (*often plural*) **4 BREACH OF ETIQUETTE** an action or remark that violates the polite distance usually left between people and that may strike the person at whom it is directed as insultingly familiar [14C. Via French *liberté* < Latin *libertas* < *liber* 'free'.] ◇ **at liberty 1** free or freed after a period of imprisonment or other constraint **2** free or allowed to do something ◇ **take liberties with 1** behave inappropriately towards somebody, especially by way of excessive familiarity or sometimes sexual harassment **2** to be deliberately inaccurate when dealing with facts (*disapproving*) ◇ **take the liberty** be bold enough to do something, sometimes without permission

liberty bodice *n* a close-fitting sleeveless undergarment for the upper body made of thick soft cotton

and worn by children, especially young girls [Because it was less restrictive than a corset]

liberty hall, Liberty Hall *n* a place where people are free to do whatever they want (*informal*)

liberty horse *n* a horse that performs tricks in the circus in a group and without a rider

Liberty Island /líbbárti -/ island in New York Bay, SE New York State, the site of the Statue of Liberty. Area: 5 hectares/12 acres.

liberty ship *n* a cargo ship mass-produced in the United States during World War II

libidinous /li bíddinəss/ *adj* having or expressing strong sexual desires [15C. < Latin *libidinosus* < *libido* 'desire'.] —**libidinously** *adv* —**libidinousness** *n*

libido /li beédō/ (*plural* **-dos**) *n* **1** sexual drive **2** in some theories, the psychic and emotional energy in people's psychological make-up that is related to the basic human instincts, especially the sex drive [Early 20C. < Latin, 'desire'.] —**libidinal** /li bíddin'l/ *adj* —**libidinally** *adv*

Li Bo /leè bố/ (701–762) Chinese poet

LIBOR /líˈ bawr/ *abbr* London Inter-Bank Offered Rate

Libra /leébrə/ *n* **1 CONSTELLATION IN THE SOUTHERN HEMISPHERE** a small constellation of the southern hemisphere. See illustration at **constellation 2 SEVENTH SIGN OF THE ZODIAC** the seventh sign of the zodiac represented by a pair of scales and lasting from approximately 23 September to 22 October **3 SOMEBODY BORN UNDER LIBRA** somebody whose birthday falls between 23 September and 22 October [Pre-12C. < Latin, 'balance, scales'.] —**Libra** *adj*—**Libran** *n*

librarian /lī bráiri ən/ *n* a worker in or manager of a library [Late 17C. < Latin *librarius* (see LIBRARY).] —**librarianship** *n*

⚡**library** /líbrəri, líbri/ (*plural* **-ies**) *n* **1 PLACE WHERE BOOKS ARE KEPT** the room, building, or institution where a collection of books or other research materials is kept **2 COLLECTION OF THINGS** a collection of books, newspapers, records, tapes, or other materials that are valuable for research **3 COLLECTION OF SOFTWARE** a collection of things for use on a computer, e.g. programs or diskettes, or a collection of routines or instructions used by a computer program [14C. < French *librairie* < Latin *libraria* 'bookshop', a form of *librarius* of books' < *liber* 'book, bark of a tree'.]

library edition *n* a set of books, published in a series, that are either by a single author or on the same subject and are alike in size and format

Library of Congress *n* the national library of the United States, located in Washington, D.C. and founded by an Act of Congress in 1800. It contains more than 28 million books and pamphlets as well as presidential papers, music, photographs, and recordings.

library science *n* LIBRARIES = librarianship

libration /lī bráysh'n/ *n* a real or apparent oscillation in the orbit of one astronomical object as seen from the one around which it orbits, especially as seen in the Moon from the Earth [Early 17C. < Latin *libration-* < *librare* 'balance' < *libra* 'balance, scales'.] —**librate** *vi* —**librational** *adj*

~~**libray**~~ incorrect spelling of **library**

libretti plural of **libretto**

librettist /li bréttist/ *n* a writer of the words for a dramatic musical work such as an opera or musical

libretto /li bréttō/ (*plural* **-tos** *or* **-ti**) *n* the words of a dramatic musical work such as an opera, including both the spoken and the sung parts [Mid-18C. < Italian, 'little book' < *libro* 'book' < Latin *liber*.]

Libreville /leebrə veèl/ chief port and capital of Gabon, on the Gulf of Guinea. Population: 365,650 (1993 estimate).

Libya /líbbi ə/ country in North Africa, on the Mediterranean Sea. Capital: Tripoli. Population: 5,484,202 (1997). Area: 1,757,000 sq. km/678,400 sq. mi. —**Libyan** /líbbi ən/ *n, adj*

Libyan Desert /líbbi ən-/ arid region in NE Africa, in Libya, Egypt, and Sudan, the northeastern part of the Sahara Desert

lice plural of **louse**

licence /líss'nss/ *n* **1 PERMIT** a printed document that gives official permission to a specific person or group to own something or do something. US term **license** *n.* **1 2 LEGAL AUTHORIZATION** official permission to do something, either

Libya

from a government or under a law or regulation. US term **license** *n.* **2 3 CHANCE TO DO SOMETHING** the opportunity to do something, especially when this goes beyond normal limits ◇ *a licence to print money.* US term **license** *n.* **3 4 PERMISSION TO BEND THE TRUTH** the freedom of a writer or artist to rearrange the facts of ordinary life in order to make a more striking effect ◇ *artistic licence.* US term **license** *n.* **4 5 LACK OF RESTRAINT** excessive freedom in behaviour or speech that gives a bad name to liberty. US term **license** *n.* **5 6** *Scotland* **AUTHORITY TO PREACH** a permission to enter the ministry of a Presbyterian church following a period of probation [14C. Via French < Latin *licentia* 'freedom' < *licere* 'be allowed'.]

licence plate *n* Can a number plate on a vehicle

license /líss'nss/ *n* US **1** = licence *n.* **1 2** LAW = licence *n.* **2 3** = licence *n.* **3 4** = licence *n.* **4 5** = licence *n.* **5** ■ *vt* (**-censes, -censing, -censed**) to give official permission for somebody to do something or for an activity to take place (*often passive*) ◇ *He was licensed to practise medicine in the United States.* [Variant of LICENCE] —**licensor** *n*

licensed premises *npl* an establishment that is legally permitted to sell alcoholic drinks

licensee /líss'n seé/ *n* a person or company that is officially permitted to do something, especially to sell alcohol

license plate *n* US = number plate

licentiate /lī sénshi ət/ *n* **1 SOMEBODY AUTHORIZED IN A PRO-FESSION** a person who has been granted a licence to practise something, such as a profession or skill **2 ACADEMIC DEGREE** a degree awarded by some European universities that ranks one step below that of a doctorate **3 SOMEBODY WITH A LICENTIATE DEGREE** somebody holding the degree of licentiate **4 PRESBYTERIAN PREACHER** somebody licensed to preach but not perform the sacraments in a Presbyterian church, usually a trainee minister who has not yet been ordained [15C. < medieval Latin *licentiatus*, past participle of *licentiare* 'permit' < Latin *licentia* (see LICENCE).]

licentious /lī sénshəss/ *adj* pursuing desires aggressively and selfishly, unchecked by morality, especially in sexual matters [15C. < Latin *licentiosus* < *licentia* (see LICENCE).] —**licentiously** *adv* —**licentiousness** *n*

lichee *n* FOOD = **lychee**

lichen /líkən, líchən/ (*plural* **-chen** *or* **-chens**) *n* a grey, green, or yellow plant appearing in often flat patches on rocks and other surfaces that is a complex organism consisting of fungi and algae growing together in symbiosis [Early 17C. Via Latin < Greek *leikhēn*.] —**lichened** *adj* —**licheniform** /lī kénni fawrm/ *adj* —**lichenoid** *adj* —**lichenous** *adj*

Lichfield /lích feeld/ city in central England. Population: 28,666 (1991).

lich-gate *n* = **lych-gate**

Lichtenstein /líktən stīn/, **Roy** (1923–97) US painter, graphic artist, and sculptor

licit /líssit/ *adj* allowed by law [15C. < Latin *licitus*, past participle of *licere* 'be allowed'.] —**licitly** *adv* —**licitness** *n*

SYNONYMS See *legal*.

---

lick /lik/ *v* **1** *vt* **PASS THE TONGUE OVER** to move the tongue across the surface of something, either to wet or clean it or as a way to move something into the mouth **2** *vti* **BRUSH AGAINST** to touch or lightly move against something **3** *vt* **BEAT** to give somebody a physical beating (*informal*) 4 *vt* **DEFEAT A COMPETITOR** to defeat somebody easily or thoroughly (*informal*) ■ *n* 1 **MOVEMENT OF THE TONGUE OVER** a movement of the tongue across the surface of something 2 **QUICKLY APPLIED COATING** a quick coat of something, especially paint ○ *a lick of paint* 3 **PUNCH** a punch or blow (*informal*) 4 **BRIEF IMPROVISATION** a distinctive few notes or short phrase in pop music or jazz, often improvised (*informal*) 5 GEOG = **salt lick** *n.* 1 6 **MEDICINAL BLOCK FOR ANIMALS** a block of salt or chemical material to be licked by domestic animals as medicine [Old English *liccian* < Germanic] —**licker** *n*

lickerish /líkərish/, **liquorish** *adj* (*archaic*) 1 taking an excessive or unfair amount, without concern for the needs of others 2 continually thinking about sex or trying to make sexual contact with others [15C. Alteration of *lickerous* < Anglo-Norman, < French *lecheros* 'lecherous' < *lecheor* (see LECHER).]

lickety-split /líkəti splít/ *adv US, Can* very quickly (*informal*) [*Lickety* < LICK]

licking /líking/ *n* (*informal*) 1 a beating or spanking 2 a severe defeat or setback

lickspittle /lík spitt'l/ *n* a person who shows undue deference towards social superiors or powerful people (*literary*)

licorice *n* US = **liquorice**

lictor /líktər/ *n* one of a group of minor officials in ancient Rome whose duties included carrying the fasces as a symbol of authority and clearing the way for the chief magistrates [14C. < Latin.]

lid /lid/ *n* 1 **TOP FOR A CONTAINER** a cover of a container that can be removed or raised on a hinge to open the container 2 ANAT = **eyelid** 3 **RESTRAINT** a restraint or control on something that keeps it within acceptable bounds (*informal*) ○ *He promised to keep a lid on manufacturing costs.* 4 BIOL = **operculum** *n.* 3 5 *US* **OUNCE OF MARIJUANA** a quantity of marijuana, usually an ounce (*slang*) [Old English *hlid* < Indo-European, 'cover, something that bends over'] ◇ **flip your lid** to react to something or somebody in the strongest, most emotionally uncontrolled manner possible (*slang*)

lidar /lí daar/ *n* a device, similar in operation to radar, that uses pulses of laser light to analyse atmospheric phenomena [Mid-20C. Blend of LIGHT[1], DETECTION + *ranging*.]

Liddell Hart /lídd'l haárt/, **Basil Henry** (1895–1970) British journalist and military strategist

Lidice /líddichi, líddissi/ village in W Czechoslovakia, now the Czech Republic, the scene of a massacre of villagers by Nazi German forces during World War II

lido /leédō, lídō/ (*plural* **-dos**) *n* an outdoor swimming pool, or a section of beach, that is open to the public [Late 17C. After Italian *Lido*, bathing beach near Venice.]

Lido /leédō/ island reef in NE Italy, separating the Venice Lagoon from the Adriatic Sea. Population: 20,950 (1980).

lidocaine /lídə kayn/ *n* PHARM = **lignocaine** [Mid-20C. < ACETANILIDE.]

lie[1] /lī/ *vi* (**lies, lying** /lī ing/, **lay** /lay/, **lain** /layn/) 1 **RECLINE** to stretch out on a surface that is slanted or horizontal ○ *She was lying on the sofa.* 2 **BE PLACED FLAT ON A SURFACE** to be positioned on and supported by a horizontal surface ○ *A book lay open on his bedside table.* 3 **BE LOCATED SOMEWHERE** to be located in a particular place ○ *Mexico lies south of the United States.* 4 **BE BURIED** to be buried in a particular place ○ *Here lies Martha, beloved daughter of John and Mary.* 5 **BE IN A SPECIFIED POSITION IN A COMPETITION** to be in a specified position in a race or a competition ○ *She's lying third in the overall ratings.* 6 **BE IN A PARTICULAR STATE** to be or continue to be in a particular condition or state ○ *It lay hidden for years.* 7 **BE IN A PARTICULAR DIRECTION** to extend or be in a particular direction ○ *The city lies beneath us, glittering with a thousand lights.* 8 **BE IN STORE** to be still to come ○ *A great deal of hard work lies ahead of us.* 9 **STAY UNDISTURBED** to remain undiscussed or undisturbed ○ *Let sleeping dogs lie.* 10 **BE ACCEPTABLE IN LAW** to be acceptable as an assertion or as evidence in court ■ *n* 1 **ANIMAL'S RESTING PLACE** a place where an animal returns to rest or hide 2 **POSITION OF A GOLF BALL** the position of a golf ball after it comes to rest on a golf course or putting green ○ *The ball has quite a good lie, in spite of being in the rough.* [Old English *licgan* < Indo-European]

lie around, lie about *vti* 1 to sit around doing nothing in particular (*informal*) 2 to be left lying and not cleared away

lie back *vi* to relax by stretching out flat on the back or reclining in a chair, especially one that tilts backwards

lie down *vi* 1 **LIE ON A SURFACE** to stretch out flat 2 **REST IN BED** to rest, especially in bed ○ *I need to lie down for an hour or two.* 3 **REMAIN PASSIVE** to do nothing or make no response ○ *I'm not going to take this lying down.*

lie in *vi* to sleep or stay in bed past the time you usually get up (*informal*)

lie off *vti* to stay close to the shore or to another ship

lie to *vi* to remain motionless, facing the wind

lie with *v* 1 *vt* to be the responsibility of a particular person or persons 2 *vi* to have sexual intercourse with somebody (*archaic*)

lie[2] /lī/ *vi* (**lies, lying** /lī ing/, **lied**) 1 **DELIBERATELY SAY SOMETHING UNTRUE** to say something that is not true in a conscious effort to deceive somebody ○ *He lied about his age in order to get into the army.* 2 **BE DECEPTIVE** to give a false impression ○ *Don't forget that appearances can lie.* ■ *n* 1 **FALSEHOOD** a false statement made deliberately ○ *She told me she wasn't seeing anyone else, but that was a lie.* 2 **WRONG IMPRESSION** a false impression created deliberately ○ *I'm beginning to feel that my whole life is a lie.* [Old English *lēogan* 'lie', *lyge* 'lie' < Germanic]

SYNONYMS ***lie, untruth, falsehood, fabrication, fib, white lie***

CORE MEANING: something that is not true

lie a false statement made deliberately; **untruth** something that is presented as being true but is actually false; **falsehood** a lie or an untruth; **fabrication** an invented statement, story, or account devised with intent to deceive; **fib** (*informal*) an insignificant harmless lie; **white lie** a minor harmless lie, usually told to avoid hurting somebody's feelings.

Liebfraumilch /leéb frow milk, -milch/ *n* a slightly sweet German white wine from the Rhine region [Mid-19C. < German, < *lieb* 'dear' + *Frau* 'lady' (after the Virgin Mary, patroness of the convent where it was produced) + *Milch* 'milk'.]

Liebig /leébig/, **Justus, Baron von** (1803–73) German chemist

Liechtenstein

Liechtenstein /líkhtən shtīn/ independent principality in central Europe. Capital: Vaduz. Population: 31,389 (1997). Area: 160 sq. km/62 sq. mi.

lied /leet/ (*plural* **lieder** /leédər/) *n* a German folk or art song, especially an art song of the 19th century with a solo voice part and interwoven piano accompaniment of equal importance (*usually plural*) [Mid-19C. < German, 'song'.]

lie detector *n* a device for finding out whether somebody is telling the truth during questioning

lie-down *n* a short rest, especially in bed (*informal*)

lief /leef/ *adv* readily or without reluctance (*archaic*) [Old English *lēof* < Germanic]

liege /leej/ *n* 1 **FEUDAL LORD** a lord or sovereign who deserves loyalty and service under feudal law 2 **VASSAL** a vassal or subject who owes loyalty and service to a lord or sovereign under feudal law ■ *adj* **LOYAL** faithful or loyal (*archaic*) [13C. Via French *lige* < medieval Latin *leticus* < *letus* 'colonist with limited freedom', probably < Germanic, 'free'.] —**liegedom** *n*

Liège /li ézh/ capital of Liège Province, E Belgium. Population: 190,525 (1996).

liegeman /leéj man/ (*plural* **-men** /-mən/) *n* 1 HIST = **liege** *n.* 2 2 a faithful or loyal follower

lie-in *n* a sleep or rest in bed until later than your usual time for getting up (*informal*)

lien /leen, leé ən/ *n* the legal right to keep or sell somebody else's property as security for a debt [Mid-16C. Via French < Latin *ligamen* 'bond' < *ligare* 'bind'.]

lie of the land *n* the general appearance or state of an area or situation presenting itself to somebody (*informal*) US term **lay of the land**

lierne /li úrn/ *n* a reinforcing rib in the vaulting of a Gothic cathedral or other roofed structure [Mid-19C. < French, < *lier* 'bind' < Latin *ligare*.]

~~**liesure**~~ incorrect spelling of **leisure**

lieu /lyoo, loo/ *n* place or stead (*archaic*) [Mid-16C. Via French < Latin *locus* 'place'.] ◇ **in lieu** instead of something else already mentioned or that is usual in the current situation

Lieut *abbr* Lieutenant

lieutenant /lef ténnənt/ *n* 1 **DEPUTY** an assistant to or substitute for somebody else 2 **ARMY OFFICER** in the British and Canadian Army and in many other armed forces, a commissioned officer of a rank above second lieutenant 3 **NAVY OFFICER** a US Navy officer of a rank above lieutenant junior grade, or a British or Canadian navy officer of a rank above sub lieutenant 4 **POLICE OFFICER OR FIREFIGHTER** a US police or fire department officer of a rank above sergeant [14C. < French, 'somebody who holds a place' < *lieu* (see LIEU) + *tenant* (see TENANT).] —**lieutenancy** *n*

lieutenant colonel *n* in the US, British, and Canadian armies, the US and Canadian air forces, and the US Marine Corps, an officer of a rank above major

lieutenant commander *n* an officer in the US, British, or Canadian navies, or in the US Coast Guard, of a rank above lieutenant

lieutenant general *n* in the US, British, and Canadian armies, the US and Canadian air forces, and the US Marine Corps, an officer of a rank above major general

lieutenant governor *n* 1 an elected official in a United States state government of a rank below governor 2 an official appointed by the Canadian federal government who acts for the Crown as the representative of the British monarch in a province —**lieutenant governorship** *n*

Lifar /li faár/, **Serge** (1905–86) Russian-born French dancer and choreographer

life /līf/ (*plural* **lives** /līvz/) *n* 1 **EXISTENCE IN THE PHYSICAL WORLD** the quality that makes living animals and plants different from dead organisms and inorganic matter 2 **LIVING INDIVIDUAL** a living being, especially a person, often used when referring to the number of people killed in an accident or a war (*usually plural*) ○ *Two hundred lives were lost in the crash.* 3 **LIVING THINGS CONSIDERED TOGETHER** a group of living things, usually of a particular kind ○ *She was an expert on plant life in the Amazon.* 4 **WHOLE TIME SOMEBODY IS ALIVE** the entire period during which somebody is, has been, or will yet be alive ○ *All my life I've wanted to learn to fly.* 5 **TIME WHEN SOMETHING FUNCTIONS** the period during which something continues to function ○ *Cheap batteries usually have short lives.* 6 **SOME PART OF SOMEBODY'S LIFE** a particular aspect of somebody's life ○ *social life* 7 **HUMAN ACTIVITY** human existence or activity in general ○ *real life* 8 **LIFE IMPRISONMENT** life imprisonment (*informal*) 9 **WAY IN WHICH SOMEBODY LIVES** the character or conditions of an individual's existence ○ *Most people in this city lead hard lives.* 10 **CHARACTERISTIC WAY OF LIVING** a way of living that is characteristic of a particular place or group ○ *country life* 11 **BIOGRAPHY** an account of somebody's life, usually in writing, but sometimes in other media such as film, video, or radio ○ *He was the author of 'The Life of Galileo'.* 12 **VITALITY** animation and vitality, or something that produces animation or vitality ○ *We liked him because he was so full of life.* 13 **ARTIST'S SUBJECT** something real used as a subject by an artist, especially human models, who are often nude ○ *She always insisted on painting from life.* [Old English *līf* < Germanic] ◇ **get a life** to do something to improve your situation or change your lifestyle for the better (*informal*)

life-and-death, life-or-death *adj* extremely important or serious, especially when somebody's life is at stake ○ *a life-and-death struggle*

life assurance *n* a plan under which regular payments are made to a company during somebody's lifetime, and in return the company pays a specified sum to the person's beneficiaries after the person's death. US term **life insurance**

life belt *n* a belt or ring made of material that floats, worn to keep somebody from sinking or drowning

lifeblood /līf blud/ *n* **1** blood when considered as necessary in maintaining life (*literary*) **2** something that is vitally important to the welfare of a larger entity ○ *Donations are the lifeblood of this organization.*

lifeboat /līf bōt/ *n* **1** a small boat kept on the deck or railings of a larger ship, for use if the ship has to be abandoned **2** a boat used for rescuing people from ships in trouble at sea

life buoy *n* a float used in an emergency to keep somebody's head and shoulders above water until help arrives

life-challenging *adj US* **1** describes a medical condition likely to cause the death or severe disablement of a person affected with it ○ *a life-challenging illness* **2** capable of changing people's way of life or outlook on life ○ *a life-challenging invention*

life crisis *n* a major disruptive event that happens in somebody's lifetime, e.g. bereavement or divorce

life cycle *n* **1** the series of changes of form and activity that a living organism undergoes from its beginning through its development to sexual maturity ○ *the life cycle of the snail* **2** the complete process of change and development during somebody's lifetime or the useful life of something such as an organization

life estate *n* property that belongs to a particular person but that cannot be sold or passed on to anyone else until after the death of that person

life expectancy *n* the number of years that somebody can be expected to live, according to statistics ○ *The rise in life expectancy can be traced to advances in nutrition and medical care.*

life force *n* PHILOS = **élan vital**

life form *n* **1** the characteristic form of an organism at maturity **2** any living organism ○ *They scanned the surface of the planet for life forms.*

lifeguard /līf gaard/ *n* somebody trained in rescue techniques whose job is to watch over swimmers at a beach or swimming pool and save those in danger of drowning

Life Guards *n* a cavalry regiment that together with the Horse Guards forms the Household Cavalry responsible for guarding the sovereign, especially during public ceremonies

life history *n* **1** ENTIRE STAGES OF LIFE all the changes experienced by a living organism, from its conception to its death **2** SOMEBODY'S LIFE STORY the story of somebody's life **3** SOMEBODY'S LIFE STORY USED FOR RESEARCH an account of the life of an individual derived from oral or documentary evidence and used in social research

life imprisonment *n* a punishment in which somebody convicted of a crime must remain in prison for the rest of his or her life

life insurance *n US* = **life assurance**

life jacket *n* a sleeveless jacket made of light material or filled with air, used to keep somebody afloat in water

lifeless /līfləss/ *adj* **1** DEAD dead, or seeming to be dead **2** WITHOUT LIFE not capable of supporting life **3** DULL lacking excitement or animation —**lifelessly** *adv* —**lifelessness** *n*

SYNONYMS See ***dead***.

lifelike /līf līk/ *adj* looking alive or representing real life accurately

lifeline /līf līn/ *n* **1** a rope or cable used for safety in dangerous manoeuvres, especially at sea, e.g. attached to a diver's helmet or stretched along the deck of a boat **2** a means of communication or support that is extremely important to the survival of an isolated person or group

life list *n* a birdwatcher's record of all the species of birds sighted in a lifetime

lifelong /līf long/ *adj* lasting the whole of a lifetime

life mask *n* a cast made of a living person's face, using plaster or another soft substance that hardens when it dries

life-or-death *adj* = **life-and-death**

life partner *n* the person with whom somebody has decided to spend the rest of his or her life in a sexual and romantic relationship ○ '*... makes people believe that somewhere there really is the life partner who will provide the ecstatic happiness depicted in opera...*' (*The New York Times*; April 1999)

life peer *n* a person who is granted a title and seat in the House of Lords only for a lifetime —**life peerage** *n*

life preserver *n US* a life belt or life jacket

lifer /līfər/ *n* somebody sentenced to life imprisonment (*informal*)

life raft *n* a raft usually made of inflatable plastic designed for use during an emergency at sea

lifesaver /līf sayvər/ *n* **1** *ANZ* a lifeguard **2** a provider or source of greatly needed help

lifesaving /līf sayving/ *adj* RESCUING OR REVIVING used to rescue people or keep them alive ■ *n* **1** RESCUING OF PEOPLE techniques or efforts to rescue people from danger, especially from drowning **2** *Aus* MULTI-ACTIVITY AUSTRALIAN WATER-BASED SPORT in Australia, the activities of a lifesaver or a team of lifesavers formalized as a multi-activity sport

life science *n* a principal branch of science concerned with plants, animals, and other living organisms and including biology, botany, and zoology (*often plural*)

life sentence *n* a court verdict that condemns a convicted criminal to life in prison for the rest of his or her life

life-size *adj* being the size of the original in life

life span *n* **1** the length of time that a member of a particular species can be expected to remain alive **2** the length of time that something can be expected to last or function

life span psychology /līf span-/ *n* a field of psychology that studies human development from birth to death

lifestyle /līf stīl/ *n* the way of life that is typical of a person, group, or culture

lifestyle vehicle *n* a vehicle that combines features of a saloon and an off-road vehicle

life-support *adj* designed to keep somebody alive in an environment such as space that does not support life or to maintain breathing, heartbeat, and other vital functions in somebody who is seriously ill

life-support system *n* **1** a piece of technical equipment that temporarily performs a vital body function, e.g., respiration, when somebody's own organ cannot because of injury or disease **2** a piece of technical equipment that is designed to provide normal living conditions when these are not available, especially in space

life's work *n* something that is the product, result, or culmination of somebody's working life. US term **lifework**

life table *n* INSUR = **mortality table**

life-threatening *adj* very dangerous or serious with the possibility of death as an outcome

lifetime /līf tīm/ *n* **1** TIME REMAINING ALIVE the length of time that somebody or something remains alive **2** TIME THAT SOMETHING REMAINS USEFUL the length of time that something remains useful or in working order **3** LONG TIME an extremely long time (*informal*)

lifework /līf wúrk/, **life's work** *n US* = **life's work**

LIFFE /liffi/ *abbr* London International Financial Futures and Options Exchange

Liffey /liffi/ river in the E Republic of Ireland. Length: 80 km/50 mi.

LIFO /līfō/ *abbr* last in, first out

lift[1] /lift/ *v* **1** *vt* RAISE to carry or raise something from one position to another, higher position **2** *vi* MOVE HIGHER to move to a higher level than before **3** *vt* MOVE SOMETHING UPWARDS to direct something upwards ○ *lifting her eyes from the book* **4** *vi* GO UPWARD to move, especially mechanically, in an upward direction ○ *Just press the button, and the boot will lift automatically.* **5** *vt* TAKE SOMETHING FROM A PLACE to take hold of something and move it somewhere else ○ *She lifted the CD from the rack.* **6** *vt* CARRY IN AN AIRCRAFT to transport somebody or something in an aircraft ○ *The rescue helicopter lifted the stranded climbers to safety.* **7** *vt* MAKE SOMETHING INVALID to revoke something or make something no longer apply ○ *The government has decided to lift the trading restrictions.* **8** *vti* CHEER SOMEBODY OR BECOME CHEERED to make somebody happier or more cheerful, or become happier or more cheerful ○ *A cup of hot tea will lift your spirits.* ○ *His low spirits lifted after a few songs.* **9** *vi* DIMINISH to clear, disappear, or become less severe ○ *I think we should wait until this fog lifts.* **10** *vt* RAISE SOMEBODY OR SOMETHING'S STATUS to have the effect of raising somebody or something in terms of status, respect, or public or official estimation ○ *Her latest novel has lifted her into the league of best-selling authors.* **11** *vt* IMPROVE to raise the level of a performance or enhance a skill **12** *vt* MAKE SOMETHING BE HEARD to make something be heard or be heard more easily or clearly ○ *The choir lifted their voices in song.* **13** *vt* HARVEST to dig up a plant for its edible underground tubers ○ *lift potatoes* **14** *vt* DIG UP A PLANT FOR TRANSPLANTING to dig up a plant in order to transplant it **15** *vt* REMOVE WRINKLES SURGICALLY to perform cosmetic surgery on a face to tighten the skin and so reduce wrinkling or on a woman's breasts to reduce or eliminate sagging. ➧ **lift**[2] **16** *vt* STEAL to steal something or take something away without the owner's permission or knowledge (*informal*) ○ *OK! Who's lifted my pen this time?* **17** *vt* PLAGIARIZE SOMEBODY'S WORK to take and use somebody else's work without attributing it to its creator (*informal*) ○ *She was accused of lifting her first two paragraphs from a report on a Web page.* **18** *vt* ARREST to arrest somebody (*informal*) ○ *Max got lifted for causing a disturbance.* **19** *vt* HIT BALL HIGH INTO THE AIR to hit a cricket or golf ball high into the air **20** *vt* STOP A MILITARY ASSAULT to cease the firing of artillery or naval guns during a combat operation or assault so as to allow ground personnel to move forwards ■ *n* **1** CAGE MOVING BETWEEN FLOORS OF A BUILDING a mechanically or electrically operated cage or platform, housed inside a shaft that runs vertically between the floors of a building or other construction, used for transporting people or things. US term **elevator** *n.* 1 **2** RIDE IN A VEHICLE a free ride as a passenger in somebody else's motor vehicle (*informal*) ○ *Do you want a lift to the airport?* **3** RISE IN SPIRITS a rise in spirits, mood, or emotions that can often be attributed to a specific cause ○ *audiences turning to feel-good movies to give themselves a lift* **4** RAISING OF SOMEBODY OR SOMETHING a placing of somebody or something in a higher position **5** FORCE NEEDED TO RAISE the power or force available, necessary, or used for raising something **6** WEIGHT RAISED a weight or an amount of something that is or can be raised **7** DEGREE OF RISE the degree or distance by which something rises ○ *a moderate lift in temperature* **8** UPWARD FORCE ACTING ON AN AIRCRAFT the combination of forces that act to cause an aircraft to leave the ground and stay in the air **9** FORCE MAKING A HOT-AIR BALLOON RISE the force, usually provided by heated air, that makes a hot-air balloon or airship rise into the sky **10** RAISING A PARTNER IN THE AIR an act of raising a partner in pairs skating or ice dancing as part of a choreographed sequence **11** CLOTHING = **heeltap** *n.* 2 **12** SOMETHING ADDED TO A SHOE a layer of material that is put inside a shoe or added to the heel of a shoe to make the wearer appear taller **13** WATER PUMPS USED IN MINING a set of pumps used to pump water out of a mineshaft to the surface **14** AMOUNT OF EXTRACTED ORE the amount of ore extracted from a seam [12C. < Old Norse *lypta* < Germanic.] —**liftable** *adj* —**lifter** *n*

lift off *vi* to leave a launching pad and head upwards into the atmosphere (*refers to spacecraft*)

lift[2] /lift/ *n US* a surgical operation to alter a part of the body for cosmetic effect (*informal*) ○ *Who did your lift?* [Shortening of FACELIFT]

liftoff /lift of/ *n* **1** the time when a rocket or spacecraft leaves the launching pad **2** the initial thrust that sends a rocket or spacecraft upwards from the launching pad into the atmosphere

lig /lig/ (**ligs, ligging, ligged**) *vi* (*informal*) **1** to do nothing habitually, often abusing the generosity of others **2** to associate with powerful people, especially in the entertainment world, in order to benefit materially from the association, e.g. in the form of invitations to parties [Mid-20C. Originally dialect, 'lie about', variant of LIE[1].]

ligament /liggəmənt/ *n* **1** a sheet or band of tough fibrous tissue that connects bones or cartilages at a joint or supports an organ, muscle, or other body part **2** something that forms a connection or bond [14C. < Latin *ligamentum* < *ligare* 'bind'.] —**ligamental** /liggə mént'l/ *adj* —**ligamentary** *adj* —**ligamentous** *adj*

ligan *n* NAUT = **lagan**

ligand /liggənd, līgənd/ *n* an atom, molecule, group, or ion that is bound to a central atom of a molecule, forming a complex [Mid-20C. < Latin *ligandus* < *ligare* 'bind'.]

ligase /lī gayz, -gayss/ *n* an enzyme that joins two molecules, especially in living organisms [Mid-20C. < Latin *ligare* 'bind'.]

ligate /lī gayt, li gáyt/ (**-gates, -gating, -gated**) *vt* to bind something or tie something up (*technical*) [Late 16C. < Latin *ligare* 'bind'.] —**ligative** /lĭggətiv/ *adj*

ligation /lī gáysh'n/ *n* **1** the tying of something with a surgical ligature **2** something that is used for binding things or tying things up (*formal*)

ligature /lĭggəchər/ *n* **1 SOMETHING USED FOR TYING** something that is used for binding things or tying things up **2 TYING PROCESS** the process of binding something or tying something up **3 BOND** a unifying link or bond (*formal*) **4 SURGICAL THREAD FOR TYING OFF A DUCT** a piece of surgical thread used to tie off a duct or blood vessel in order to cut off the supply of body fluid normally running through it **5 CHARACTER CONSISTING OF JOINED LETTERS** a character or piece of type, e.g. 'æ', that consists of two or more letters joined together **6** MUSIC = **tie** *n.* 8 **7 SYMBOL IN MEDIEVAL MUSIC** a symbol indicating a group of notes to be sung to one syllable in the notation of medieval music **8 REED-HOLDER ON WOODWIND INSTRUMENT** on a woodwind instrument, a band, usually made of metal, that holds the reed to the mouthpiece [14C. < French, < Latin *ligare* 'bind'.]

liger /lígər/ *n* the offspring that results from breeding a male lion with a female tiger. ◊ **tigon** [Mid-20C. Blend of LION + TIGER.]

Ligeti /lígəti, li gétti/, **György** (*b.* 1923) Hungarian composer

ligger /líggər/ *n* (*informal*) **1** a lazy person who abuses the generosity of others **2** a person who consorts with influential people in the hope of a benefit, e.g. invitations to parties

light[1] /līt/ *n* **1 ENERGY PRODUCING BRIGHTNESS** the energy producing a sensation of brightness that makes seeing possible **2 QUALITY OF LIGHT** a particular kind or quality of brightness ○ *We won't get good photographs in this fading light.* **3 ARTIFICIAL SOURCE OF LIGHT** an artificial source of illumination, e.g. an electric lamp or a candle ○ *switch the light on* **4 VISIBLE ELECTROMAGNETIC RADIATION** electromagnetic radiation in the range visible to the human eye, between approximately 4,000 and 7,700 angstroms **5 ELECTROMAGNETIC RADIATION** electromagnetic radiation that has wavelengths of any length **6 PATH THAT LIGHT TAKES** the path that light takes or somebody's share or access to light ○ *asked her to move out of my light* **7 DAYLIGHT** the condition of brightness created by the rays of the sun during the day ○ *keep filming while there's still some light left* **8 DAWN** the arrival of the sun's brightness at the beginning of the day ○ *get up before light to go running* **9 REPRESENTATION OF LIGHT IN ART** the representation of light or the effect it has in a work of art **10 TRAFFIC SIGNAL** a signal that controls the movement of traffic ○ *Turn right at the first set of lights.* **11 GENERAL NOTICE** general or public notice, attention, or knowledge ○ *facts that only recently came to light* **12 WAY SOMETHING IS VIEWED** the manner in which somebody or something is regarded, especially by the public ○ *These actions have shown the committee in a particularly bad light.* **13 SOMETHING THAT IGNITES** a source of fire, especially a match ○ *Have you got a light?* **14 GLEAM IN SOMEBODY'S EYE** a glint in somebody's eye that is taken to indicate a particular mood or expression ○ *had a mischievous light in her eye* **15 WINDOW** a window or other opening in a building, designed to let sunlight in ■ *adj* **1 FULL OF BRIGHTNESS** full of illumination or relatively well lit ○ *a light airy room* **2 PALE** of a relatively pale shade ○ *decorated in light green* ■ *v* (**lights, lighting, lit** /lit/ *or* **lighted**) **1** *vti* **START BURNING** to begin to burn, or cause something to begin to burn ○ *still trying to light the barbecue?* **2** *vt* **ILLUMINATE** to illuminate, brighten, or shine on something ○ *Hundreds of stars lit the night sky.* **3** *vt* **GIVE SOMETHING AN ANIMATED LOOK** to give somebody's eyes or face a happy or animated look ○ *A playful smile lit his face.* **4** *vt* **LEAD SOMEBODY WITH A LIGHT** to lead or direct somebody with a source of illumination such as a torch ○ *The usherette lit the way to our seats.* [Old English *lēoht* < Indo-European] ◇ **bring something to light** to reveal something ◇ **come to light** to be revealed ◇ **go out like a light** to fall asleep very quickly and deeply (*informal*) ◇ **in the cold light of day** when things are seen for what they really are rather than being seen in an unrealistically favourable light ◇ **in (the) light of something** taking into consideration what is known or what has just been said or found out ◇ **the light of somebody's life** the person somebody cherishes the most ◇ **punch** *or* **put somebody's lights out** to give somebody a severe beating ◇ **see the light 1** to have a sudden understanding or appreciation of something **2** to be converted to a faith, belief, or point of view ◇ **see the light of day** to be published or made publicly known ◇ **shed** *or* **throw** *or* **cast light on something** make it possible or easier to understand something ◇ **strike a light** used to express surprise, shock, or disbelief (*dated informal*)

light into *vt* to attack somebody or something either verbally or physically (*informal*)

light out *vi US* to leave a place in a hurry (*informal*)

light up *v* **1** *vti* **LIGHT A CIGARETTE OR PIPE** to light something such as a cigarette, cigar, or pipe and begin smoking it **2** *vt* **ILLUMINATE** to cast light on somebody or something **3** *vi* **BEGIN SHINING** to start to shine **4** *vti* **MAKE OR BECOME CHEERFUL** to become, or cause something or somebody to become, animated or cheerful

light[2] /līt/ *adj* **1 NOT HEAVY** weighing comparatively little **2 WEIGHING TOO LITTLE** weighing less than is correct or less than would be expected ○ *This sack is a couple of ounces light.* **3 LIGHTWEIGHT** made of thin fabric ○ *light summer apparel* **4 NOT DENSE** low in density or intensity ○ *only a light shower* **5 NOT FORCEFUL** performed with little physical force ○ *She felt a light tap on her shoulder.* **6 EASY TO DO** involving relatively little effort or exertion ○ *a little light weeding* **7 CONSUMING LITTLE OF** consuming something in small quantities only ○ *a light eater* **8 LESS SEVERE THAN POSSIBLE** considered less severe or harsh than might have been the case ○ *a light sentence* **9 UNIMPORTANT** of relatively little importance or seriousness ○ *a light, throwaway remark* **10 NOT INTELLECTUALLY DEMANDING** not meant for serious study or contemplation ○ *some light holiday reading* **11 SHORT OF** lacking the usual or expected quantity of something ○ *a nice flavour but a bit light on salt* **12 UNWORRIED** not burdened by worries or troubled ○ *a light heart* **13 DIZZY** slightly dizzy or not quite thinking clearly, e.g. because of fatigue, alcohol, or drugs ○ *a light head* **14 NIMBLE** moving with grace, nimbleness, and agility ○ *She's very light on her feet.* **15 EASILY DIGESTED** easily digested or not very filling ○ *a light snack* **16 light, lite LOW IN CALORIES** low in calories, especially containing less than the usual amount of sugar or fat **17 light, lite LOW IN ALCOHOL** having a very low alcohol content **18 FLUFFY AND WELL RISEN** of a light, flaky, fluffy, and well-risen consistency ○ *a very light pastry* **19 DELICATELY FLAVOURED** having a fresh delicate flavour ○ *a light rosé* **20 EASILY WOKEN** easily woken or disturbed when asleep ○ *a light sleeper* **21 EASILY WORKED** loose, well aerated, and therefore easily worked ○ *light soil* **22 CARRYING SMALL WEIGHTS** designed to carry something that is relatively low in weight or relatively small in bulk ○ *a light delivery van* **23 NOT LOADED** not containing or carrying a full load **24 MANUFACTURING SMALL PRODUCTS** involved in the manufacture of comparatively small products, especially consumer goods made without the use of heavy machinery **25 WITH A LOW BOILING POINT** having a relatively low boiling point **26 NOT HEAVILY ARMED** carrying only hand-held weapons ○ *a light infantry brigade* **27 UNSTRESSED** describes a syllable that is not stressed or accented **28 OF LOW VALUE** describes a bid in bridge that is made on a lower-than-normal number of points **29 WITH TOO FEW TRICKS** describes a bridge player who has taken too few tricks to make a contract **30 IMMORAL** with low moral standards, especially relating to sexual behaviour (*archaic*) ■ *adv* **1 LENIENTLY** in a casual or lenient way **2 WITH LITTLE LUGGAGE** with only a small amount of luggage ○ *to travel light* ■ *vi* (**lights, lighting, lighted** *or* **lit** /lit/, **lighted** *or* **lit**) **1 COME TO REST** to come to rest on a branch after flight (*refers to birds*) **2 GET DOWN FROM A VEHICLE** to get down from a horse, vehicle, or other form of transport (*dated*) [Old English *lēocht* < Indo-European] ◇ **make light of something** to treat something as unimportant

Light *n* **1** God as a source of spiritual illumination and strength **2** CHR = **Inner Light**

Light /līt/, **William** (1786–1839) British-born Australian soldier and surveyor

light adaptation, light adaption *n* the rapid changes that occur in the eye to permit vision when moving from darkness to light —**light-adapted** *adj*

light air *n* a wind of between 1.6 and 4.8 km/1 and 3 miles per hour, classified as force one on the Beaufort scale

light aircraft *n* an aircraft that has a takeoff weight that does not exceed 5,670 kg/12,500 lbs. US term **light plane**

light breeze *n* a wind of between 6.4 and 11 km/4 and 7 mi. per hour, classified as force two on the Beaufort scale

light bulb *n* a source of artificial light in the form of a near-spherical glass case containing a filament that emits light when an electric current is passed through it

light chain *n* the shorter of the two main polypeptides that make up an antibody molecule. ◊ **heavy chain**

light-coloured *adj* of a pale shade or hue

light-emitting diode *n* full form of **LED**

lighten[1] /līt'n/ *vti* **1 MAKE OR BECOME LESS HEAVY** to become less heavy, or make something less heavy **2 BECOME OR MAKE SOMETHING LESS BURDENSOME** to become, or cause something to become, less of a burden or chore **3 BECOME OR MAKE SOMETHING MORE CHEERFUL** to become, or make somebody or something become, more relaxed or lively ○ *The mood of the gathering lightened a little.*

lighten up *vi* to become less gloomy, serious, or angry (*informal*)

lighten[2] /līt'n/ *v* **1** *vti* **MAKE OR BECOME PALE** to become, or cause something to become, pale or paler in colour **2** *vi* **GLOW** to give off shining or glowing illumination **3** *vi* **FLASH** to flash across the sky (*refers to lightning*)

lightening /līt'ning/ *n* the process or time during late pregnancy when the foetal head begins to descend into the mother's pelvis, resulting in a lessening of pressure on the diaphragm

SPELLCHECK Do not confuse ***lightening*** with ***lightning***, which has a similar sound. Beware: your spellchecker will not catch this error.

lighter[1] /lītər/ *n* **1** a small typically gas-filled container with a flint or other spark-producer that produces a flame used for lighting something that is smoked such as a cigarette, cigar, or pipe **2** a person or device that lights, illuminates, or ignites something (*usually in combination*) ○ *a firelighter*

lighter[2] /lītər/ *n* a flat-bottomed open cargo boat or barge, used especially for taking goods to or from a larger vessel when it is being loaded or unloaded [14C. < ?]

lighter-than-air *adj* describes aircraft such as hot-air balloons and dirigibles that weigh less than the air they displace ■ *n* an aircraft, e.g. a hot-air balloon or a dirigible, that weighs less than the air it displaces

lightface /līt fayss/ *adj* **lightface, light-faced** having characters formed from relatively narrow lines (*refers to printed type*) ■ *n* printed type that is lightface

lightfast /līt faast/ *adj* describes a dye or dyed fabric whose shade or colour is unchanged by exposure to light, especially sunlight [Early 20C. After COLOURFAST.] —**lightfastness** *n*

light-fingered *adj* **1** skilled at and likely to try shoplifting, pickpocketing, or petty stealing **2** able to move the fingers quickly and nimbly, and therefore good at doing intricate jobs —**light-fingeredness** *n*

light flyweight *n* **1** a weight category in amateur boxing for competitors whose weight does not exceed 48 kg/106 lbs **2** an amateur boxer who competes at light flyweight level

light-footed *adj* able to walk or run with light agile easy-flowing steps —**light-footedly** *adv* —**light-footedness** *n*

lightheaded /līt héddid/ *adj* **1** slightly dizzy or euphoric, e.g. as an effect of caffeine, alcohol, or fatigue **2** having a tendency to behave in a frivolous or immature way —**lightheadedly** *adv* —**lightheadedness** *n*

lighthearted /līt haártid/ *adj* **1** not weighed down with worries or troubles **2** entertaining in an amusing carefree way —**lightheartedly** *adv* —**lightheartedness** *n*

light heavyweight *n* **1 WEIGHT CATEGORY IN PROFESSIONAL BOXING** a weight category in professional boxing for competitors who weigh between 72.5 and 79.5 kg/160 and 175 lbs **2 WEIGHT CATEGORY IN AMATEUR BOXING** a weight category in amateur boxing for competitors who weigh between 75 and 81 kg/165 and 179 lbs **3 WEIGHT CATEGORY IN WRESTLING** a weight category in wrestling for competitors who weigh between 87 and 97 kg/192 and 214 lbs. ◊ **heavyweight, middleweight 4 BOXER COMPETING AT LIGHT HEAVYWEIGHT** a professional or amateur boxer who competes at light heavyweight level **5 WRESTLER COMPETING AT LIGHT HEAVYWEIGHT** a wrestler who competes at light heavyweight level. ◊ **heavyweight, middleweight**

lighthouse /līt howss/ (*plural* **-houses** /līt howziz/) *n* a strategically placed coastal building, often a tall round tower, with a powerful flashing light, designed to guide sailors or warn them of dangers such as rocks

LITERARY LINK ***To the Lighthouse***, a novel (1927) by Virginia Woolf. Set at the holiday home of the Ramsay family on a Scottish island, it explores the changing roles and attitudes of contemporary women, using stream-of-consciousness narrative.

lighting /líting/ *n* **1 TYPE OF LIGHT** light of a particular quality or type, or the equipment that produces it ○ *subdued lighting* **2 EQUIPMENT FOR PROVIDING ARTIFICIAL LIGHT** the equipment used for providing artificial light and light effects on a theatre stage or a television or film set **3 EFFECT PRODUCED BY LIGHTS** the overall effect produced by the lights used on a theatre stage or a television or film set **4 QUALITY OF LIGHT IN ARTWORK** the amount or type of light in a photograph, painting, or other artwork

lighting cameraman *n* somebody responsible for the lighting and camerawork for a film

lighting-up time *n* the time, at night or in the late afternoon, when drivers of road vehicles are legally required to put their headlights on

lightly /lítli/ *adv* **1 WITH LITTLE FORCE** without exerting much pressure, force, or weight **2 WITH LEVITY** without seriousness **3 GRACEFULLY** in an easy graceful way **4 SPARINGLY** in small or sparing amounts

light meter *n* PHOTOGRAPHY = **exposure meter**

light middleweight *n* ◊ **junior middleweight 1** a weight category in amateur boxing for competitors who weigh between 67 and 71 kg/148 and 157 lbs **2** an amateur boxer who competes at light middleweight level

light-minded *adj* not capable of thinking seriously —**light-mindedly** *adv* —**light-mindedness** *n*

lightness[1] /lítnəss/ *n* **1** the illumination of something relative to its surroundings **2** the attribute of an object or a colour that enables an observer to quantify the amount of light it appears to reflect

lightness[2] /lítnəss/ *n* **1 RELATIVE SLIGHTNESS OF WEIGHT** the condition of something that weighs relatively little **2 RELATIVE SLIGHTNESS OF FORCE** the condition of something that has relatively little force ○ *lightness of touch* **3 EASE OR DELICACY** the ease or delicacy with which something is done **4 NIMBLENESS** ease and rapidity of movement **5 UNTROUBLED STATE** total freedom from worry and trouble **6 LEVITY** lack of the seriousness that is required or expected

lightning /lítning/ *n* flashes of light seen in the sky when there is a discharge of atmospheric electricity in the clouds or between clouds and the earth, usually occurring during a thunderstorm ■ *adj* very fast and often very sudden [14C. Variant of *lightening* < LIGHTEN[2].]

SPELLCHECK See ***lightening***.

lightning arrester *n* a device, often an aerial, that protects a piece of electrical equipment from damage by lightning or some other electrical surge by diverting the electricity to the ground

lightning bug *n Can, US* = **firefly**

lightning chess *n* a fast form of chess in which players either have a limited time to make each move or have to complete all their moves within a set time

lightning conductor *n* a metal rod attached to the highest point of a building or other structure to protect it from lightning by conducting the lightning to the ground. US term **lightning rod** *n.*

lightning rod *n US* = **lightning conductor**

lightning strike *n* **1** an industrial strike that happens at short notice and often without union support **2** an attack carried out suddenly and without warning

light opera *n* MUSIC = **operetta**

⚡**light pen** *n* a pen-shaped light-sensitive device used to manipulate information on a computer screen by touching the screen directly

light plane *n* AVIAT = **light aircraft**

light pollution *n* excessive artificial light, especially street lighting in towns and cities that prevents the night sky from being seen clearly

lightproof /lít proof/ *adj* designed so as not to be penetrated or affected by light

light railway *n* a railway designed for light traffic, often with a narrower gauge or subject to lower-than-standard speed and weight limits

light reaction *n* the first stage of photosynthesis when light energy is absorbed by chlorophyll and converted into chemical energy that is stored as ATP

light reflex *n* the normal contracting of the pupil of the eye in response to increased light

lights[1] /líts/ *npl* the lungs of domestic animals, especially those of pigs, sheep, or cattle when they are used in making pet food or, occasionally, food for people [Pre-12C. < LIGHT[2], because the lungs are full of air.]

lights[2] /líts/ *npl* the ideas, theories, or principles peculiar to a particular person ○ *You must, in the end, act according to your lights.* [Early 16C. < LIGHT[1].]

light-sensitive *adj* affected in some way by the presence of light, as are some materials such as photographic film or silicon sheets

lightshade /lít shayd/ *n* HOUSEHOLD = **lampshade**

lightship /lít ship/ *n* a ship with a bright flashing light that functions as a lighthouse, especially one that is anchored in a place where a permanent structure would be impracticable

light show *n* **1** a spectacle in the form of a display of colourful moving lights, often a feature of a live pop or rock concert **2** a form of entertainment in which moving coloured lights are synchronized with recorded music, usually synthesized instrumental music. ◊ **son et lumière**

lightsome /lítsəm/ *adj* (*archaic or literary*) **1** feeling and displaying happiness and freedom from worry **2** with a graceful lightness of movement [15C. < LIGHT[2].] —**lightsomely** *adv* —**lightsomeness** *n*

lights out *n* **1** the time at night when people, especially those in the armed forces, prison, boarding schools, and other institutions, are supposed to go to sleep **2** a bugle call, gong, or other signal sounded at lights out

⚡**light stylus** *n* COMPUT = **light pen** *n.*

light water *n* ordinary water, as opposed to heavy water

lightweight /lít wayt/ *adj* **1 NOT HEAVY IN WEIGHT OR TEXTURE** relatively light in weight and in texture **2 LACKING INTELLECTUAL DEPTH** fairly frivolous or trivial and requiring little or no intellectual effort ■ *n* **1 INSIGNIFICANT PERSON OR THING** somebody or something regarded as insignificant or without influence, often in a particular area ○ *a political lightweight* **2 WEIGHT CATEGORY IN PROFESSIONAL BOXING** a weight category in professional boxing for competitors who weigh between 59 and 61 kg/130 and 135 lbs **3 WEIGHT CATEGORY IN AMATEUR BOXING** a weight category in amateur boxing for competitors who weigh between 57 and 60 kg/126 and 132 lbs **4 BOXER COMPETING AT LIGHTWEIGHT** a boxer who competes at lightweight level **5 WEIGHT CATEGORY IN WRESTLING** a weight category in wrestling for competitors who weigh between 52 and 57 kg/115 and 126 lbs **6 WRESTLER WHO COMPETES AT LIGHTWEIGHT** a wrestler who competes at lightweight level

light welterweight *n* **1** a weight category in amateur boxing for competitors who weigh between 60 and 63.5 kg/132 and 140 lbs **2** an amateur boxer who competes at light welterweight level

light-year *n* a unit of distance in astronomy equal to the distance that light travels in a vacuum in one mean solar year, approximately 9.46 billion km/5.88 billion mi ■ **light-years** *npl* a very long way in time, distance, or some other quantity or quality (*informal*)

lign- *prefix* = **ligni-** (*before vowels*)

ligneous /lígni əss/ *adj* consisting of or with the appearance or texture of wood [Early 17C. < Latin *ligneus* < *lignum* (see LIGNI-).]

ligni- *prefix* wood ○ *lignicole* [< Latin *lignum* 'wood, firewood' < Indo-European, 'to collect']

lignicole /lígni kōl/, **lignicolous** /lig níkələss/ *adj* living or growing in or on wood [Mid-19C. < LIGNI- + Latin *colere* 'inhabit'.]

lignify /lígni fī/ (**-fies, -fying, -fied**) *vti* to become woody and relatively rigid as lignin is deposited in cell walls, or to make plant parts woody in this way [Early 19C. < Latin *lignum* (see LIGNI-).] —**lignification** /lígnifi káysh'n/ *n*

lignin /lígnin/ *n* the complex polymer in plant cell walls that gives the plant rigidity [Early 19C. < Latin *lignum* 'wood'.]

lignite /líg nīt/ *n* GEOL = **brown coal** —**lignitic** /lig níttik/ *adj*

ligno- *prefix* wood ○ *lignocellulose* [< Latin *lignum* (see LIGNI-)]

lignocaine /lígnō kayn/ *n* a strong local anaesthetic applied externally to the gums or given by injection. Use: in dentistry. US term **lidocaine**

lignocellulose /lígnō séllyoō lōss, -lōz/ *n* a strengthening substance composed of lignin and cellulose, found in woody tissues of plants

lignum vitae /lígnəm víti/ *n* TREES = **guaiacum** [Late 16C. < Latin, 'wood of life'; from the medicinal uses of the wood and its resin.]

ligroin /líggrō in/ *n* a solvent in the form of a flammable liquid mixture of hydrocarbons. Source: distillation of petroleum. [Late 19C. < ?]

ligula /líggyoōlə/ (*plural* **-lae** /líggyoō lee/ *or* **-las**) *n* **1** the tip of the lower lip (**labium**) of an insect, which typically has four lobes **2** PLANT SCI = **ligule** *n.* **1** [Mid-18C. < Latin, 'strap', variant of *lingula* 'little tongue' < *lingua* 'tongue'.] —**ligular** *adj*

ligule /líggyool/ *n* **1 ligule, ligula** an outgrowth at the junction of the leaf sheath and leaf blade in a grass, typically a membranous or scaly flap but in some grasses a ring of hairs **2** the strap-shaped extension of florets found in the flower heads of some members of the daisy family and in some grasses [Early 19C. < Latin *ligula* (see LIGULA).] —**ligulate** *adj*

Ligurian Sea /li gōori ən-/ arm of the Mediterranean Sea between NW Italy and Corsica and Elba

likable /líkəb'l/, **likeable** *adj* pleasant and friendly and therefore easy to like —**likability** /líkə bílləti/ *n* —**likableness** *n* —**likably** *adv*

Likasi /li kaássi/ city in the SE Democratic Republic of the Congo. Population: 299,118 (1994).

like[1] /līk/ CORE MEANING: a preposition indicating that two things or people are similar or share some of the same features ○ *Vivid red phone booths, looking like London imports, stood nearby.*

1 *prep* **RESEMBLING** having a resemblance to somebody or something ○ *She wrapped the towel like a turban on her head.* ○ *He looks like the hero type to me!* **2 SUCH AS** as a typical instance or example of ○ *She won't go to loud places like bars.* ○ *I bought things like fishing tackle and waders.* **3 INDICATES CHARACTERISTICS** indicates qualities, characteristics, or features (*often in questions*) ○ *What's it like, being a mother?* ○ *When you go on like this, do you know what you sound like?* **4 TYPICAL OF** in a manner typical or characteristic of somebody or something (*often negative*) ○ *It's just like her to say catty things.* **5 INCLINED TOWARDS** having a tendency or desire for something ○ *I felt like screaming when I found the kitchen floor flooded.* **6 WITH A SUGGESTION OF** as though something might happen ○ *It looks like rain this morning.* **7** ⚠ *conj* **AS** in the same way or manner as something ○ *To ski like she does requires great athletic ability.* **8** ⚠ **AS IF** as though or as if (*nonstandard*) ○ *Butch hops out of the car like it was on fire.* ○ *Like I'd tell you a secret!* **9** *adv* **IN A PARTICULAR WAY** in a particular way or manner (*informal*) ○ *He fixed the chair like new.* **10** ⚠ **USED AS FILLER OR FOR EMPHASIS** used especially in conversation as a filler or for emphasis (*nonstandard*) ○ *You're, like, feeling stressed today, aren't you?* ○ *There were, like, hundreds of people there.* **11 USED AS FINAL EMPHASIZER** used in conversation, tacked on to the end of an adjective, adverb, phrase, or clause, to modify its force or as a filler (*regional*) ○ *Can you lend me a fiver? Just till tomorrow, like.* **12** ⚠ **INTRODUCES DIRECT SPEECH** used informally to introduce what somebody says (*nonstandard*) ○ *Susan is like 'It's not for me' and Brandon is like, 'You had me worried' and Susan is like, 'Don't worry, I'm not going anywhere'.* **13** *n* **SOMETHING SIMILAR** a thing or set of things similar to another ○ *window boxes, planters, flower pots, and the like* **14 COUNTERPART** one person or thing that is regarded as similar or almost identical to another ○ *We won't see his like again in this decade.* **15** *adj* **ALIKE** having exactly the same or almost identical qualities or characteristics ○ *These two cats are as like as though they were of the same litter.* [12C. < Old Norse *líkr*, shortening of *glíkr* < Germanic.] ◇ **like as not** to a probable or likely extent ○ *Like as not he'll show up very late.* ◇ **like so** in the manner demonstrated ○ *Spread the fabric out like so.* ◇ **the likes of** people or things of the particular sort ○ *Such luxuries aren't for the likes of us.*

USAGE like as a conjunction and a filler: You will be criticized if you use the conjunction ***like*** to mean 'as', 'as if' or 'as though' when introducing a fully developed clause (i.e. one with a subject and a verb). Avoid constructions like these:

It sounds like she may resign. This pizza smells and tastes like a good pizza should. Recast the sentences: *It sounds as if she may resign. This pizza smells and tastes good, just the way it should.* It is acceptable to use ***like*** in a comparison as long as you do not include a verb in the matter following ***like***: *She ran the company just like a tyrant.* Avoid using ***like*** as a meaningless filler, or to introduce speech: *'What were the main characters doing in Chapter One?' 'They were, like, trying to understand the reasons men make war'. She was like, 'Don't worry, I'll do it'.* Such usage is nonstandard in oral and written communications on any level except in fictional dialogue.

like[2] /līk/ *v* (**likes, liking, liked**) **1** *vt* **ENJOY** to regard something as enjoyable ○ *I like cross-country skiing.* ○ *Do you like prunes?* **2** *vt* **CONSIDER PLEASANT** to regard somebody as pleasant and enjoy that person's company ○ *I like a man with a sense of humour.* ○ *Do you like your new teacher?* **3** *vt* **WANT** to want to have or do something ○ *Would you like some coffee?* ○ *I'd like to meet your brother.* **4** *vt* **REGARD IN A POSITIVE WAY** to have a positive opinion about something or somebody ○ *How do you like her prose style?* **5** *vi* **HAVE A PREFERENCE** to have a specified or unspecified preference or inclination ○ *We can leave later than seven if you like.* ○ *If you like, I'll show you round the house.* ■ *n* **PREFERENCE** something that is preferred over others ○ *a full litany of her likes and dislikes* [Old English *līcian* 'please', related to Old Norse *līkr* (see LIKE[1])]

LITERARY LINK ***As You Like It***, a play (1599?) by William Shakespeare. Its complex plot revolves around Rosalind, daughter of Duke Ferdinand, and her love for a young knight, Orlando, which results in her being banished to the forest, where she is eventually reunited with her lover.

like[3] /līk/, **liked** /līkt/ *vi Southern US* to be on the verge or point of doing or almost doing a particular thing (*informal*) ○ *I like to have died when I saw her in that getup.* [15C. < LIKE[1].]

-like *suffix* resembling or characteristic of ○ *workmanlike* [< LIKE[1]]

likeable *adj* = **likable**

liked *vi Southern US* = **like**[3]

likelihood /līkli hòòd/ *n* **1** the chance of something happening **2** something that is likely to happen ◇ **in all likelihood** very probably

likely /līkli/ *adj* (**-lier, -liest**) **1 PROBABLE** that will probably happen **2 PLAUSIBLE** fit to be believed (*often used ironically*) **3 SUITABLE** appropriate for a specified activity or purpose **4 PROMISING** with a good chance of success or victory ■ *adv* **PROBABLY** to a probable degree or extent ○ *It will very likely snow tomorrow.* [14C. < Old Norse *(g)līkligr* < *līkr* (see LIKE[1]).] ◇ **(as) likely as not** very probably

~~**likelyhood**~~ incorrect spelling of **likelihood**

like-minded *adj* sharing the same or similar views, opinions, tastes, values, or outlook —**like-mindedness** *n*

liken /līkən/ *vt* to compare something or somebody to another, especially in order to point out the similarities

likeness /līknəss/ *n* **1** similarity of appearance among or between people or things **2** a representation of somebody or something, e.g. a painting or statue, often considered in terms of how accurately it represents the person or thing [Old English *(ge)līknes* < *gelīc* 'alike' < Germanic, 'body']

Likert scale /līkert-/ *n* a scale measuring the degree to which people agree or disagree with a statement, usually on a 3-, 5-, or 7-point scale [Mid-20C. After Rensis *Likert* (1903–81), US psychologist.]

likewise /līk wīz/ *adv* **1** in the same or a similar way **2** used to state that the same applies in a second or subsequent case ○ *She works as a teacher; her brother likewise.* [15C. Contraction of *in like wise* 'in similar manner'.]

liking /līking/ *n* **1** a feeling of enjoying something or finding it pleasant **2** personal taste or choice [14C. < LIKE[2].]

SYNONYMS See ***love***.

lilac /līlək/ (*plural* **-lacs** *or* **-lac**) *n* **1** an ornamental bush or small tree. Flowers: fragrant, white, mauve, or purple in sprays. Native to: Europe, Asia. Genus: *Syringa*. **2** a pale pinkish-purple colour tinged with blue [Early 17C. Via French < Persian *līlak* 'blueish'.] —**lilac** *adj*

lilangeni /leé lang gáyni/ (*plural* **emalangeni** /émmə lang gáyni/) *n* see table at **currency** [Late 20C. < Bantu.]

Lilburn /líl burn/, **Douglas Gordon** (*b.* 1915) New Zealand composer

Lilburne /líl burn/, **John** (c. 1614–57) English political agitator and pamphleteer

liliaceous /lílli áyshəss/ *adj* describes plants that belong to the lily family [Mid-18C. < late Latin *liliaceus* < Latin *lilium* 'lily'.]

Lilienthal /leéli ən taal/, **Otto** (1848–96) German inventor and aeronautical engineer

Lilith /líllith/ *n* **1** in Hebrew Scripture, the first woman, believed to have been created before Eve **2** in Jewish folklore, an evil spirit of a woman, believed to lurk in deserted places and attack children

Liliuokalani /lee leé òò ō kaa laáni/ (1838–1917) queen of Hawaii (1891–93)

Lille /leel/ city in N France. Population: 184,657 (1999).

Lillee /lílli/, **Dennis Keith** (*b.* 1949) Australian cricketer

Lilliputian /lílli pyóosh'n/, **lilliputian** *n* **SMALL PERSON OR THING** a person or thing that is unusually small in height ■ *adj* **1 TINY** unusually small **2 TRIVIAL OR PETTY** of little or no importance or significance [Mid-18C. After *Lilliput* in *Gulliver's Travels* (1726) by Jonathan Swift, country whose people were only 15 cm/6 in. tall.]

Lilo /līlō/ *tdmk* a trademark for an inflatable bed for use in swimming-pools or on the sea

⚡**LILO** *n* a data storage method in which data stored last is retrieved last. Full form **last in, last out**

Lilongwe /li lóng wi/ capital and second largest city of Malawi, in the central part of the country. Population: 1,000,000 (1998 estimate).

lilt /lilt/ *n* **1 VARIATION IN VOICE PITCH** a pleasant rising and falling variation in the pitch of a person's voice **2 CHEERFUL PIECE OF MUSIC** a cheerful song or piece of music, especially one that is easy to sing along with (*archaic*) **3 BOUNCY STEP** a light bouncy way of walking, often taken as an indication of a cheerful disposition ■ *v* **1** *vti* **SAY OR SING SOMETHING CHEERFULLY** to say, sing, or play something in a cheerful way, often with pleasant variations in pitch **2** *vi* **WALK BOUNCILY** to walk or move in a bouncy cheerful way [14C. < ?] —**lilting** *adj*

lily /lílli/ *n* (*plural* **-ies**) **1 PERENNIAL PLANT** a perennial plant with blade-shaped leaves that grows from a bulb. Flowers: single, large, sometimes trumpet-shaped. Genus: *Lilium*. **2 PLANT RESEMBLING A LILY** a plant that resembles a lily **3** HERALDRY = **fleur-de-lis** *n.* 1 **4 WHITE OR PURE THING** somebody or something that is particularly white or pure (*dated*) ■ *adj* **PALE** unusually pale in colour or shade [Pre-12C. < Latin *lilium*.] ◇ **gild the lily** to try to improve something that is already good or beautiful enough

lily-livered *adj* lacking in courage (*dated*) [< the idea that a cowardly person's liver is pale through lack of bile, thought to engender courage]

lily of the valley (*plural* **lilies of the valley** *or* **lily of the valley**) *n* a small poisonous ornamental plant with two long, oval, dark green leaves. Flowers: small, white or pale pink, sweet-scented, bell-shaped, drooping and growing from a single spike. Native to: North America, Europe, Asia. Genus: *Convallaria*. [Translation of Latin *lilium convallium*, unidentified plant]

lily pad *n* a floating leaf of a water lily

lily-white *adj* **1** unusually pale in tone and unblemished **2** without any admixture

Lima[1] /leémə/ *n* a code word for the letter 'L', used in international radio communications

Lima[2] /leémə/ capital of Peru, in the west-central part of the country, on the Pacific Ocean. Population: 6,464,693 (1998 estimate).

lima bean /līmə-, leémə-/ *n* a pale green edible seed produced by a cultivated plant of the bean family. *Phaseolus limensis* and *Phaseolus lunatus*. [Mid-18C. After LIMA[1].]

limacine /límmə sīn, -sin, līmə-, -/ *adj* **1** belonging or relating to the slug family of invertebrate terrestrial molluscs **2** resembling a slug in appearance or movement [Late 19C. < Latin *limac-* 'slug, snail'.]

limaçon /límmə son/ *n* a heart-shaped mathematical curve that is generated by a point on a line that intersects with a circle and rotates about a point on the circle [Late 19C. < French, 'snail shell' < Latin *limac-* 'slug, snail'.]

Limassol /límasol/ port in S Cyprus. Population: 152,900 (1997 estimate).

Limavady /límmə váddi/ town in NW Northern Ireland. Population: 10,764 (1991).

limb[1] /lim/ *n* **1 BODY PART** an arm, leg, or similar appendage, e.g. a wing or flipper **2 LARGE BRANCH** a major branch of a tree **3 ASSOCIATED PERSON OR ORGANIZATION** somebody or something affiliated with a larger group or organization **4 PART STICKING OUT** a part that sticks out, e.g. on a building or a mountain range [Old English *lim*] —**limbed** *adj* —**limbless** *adj* ◇ **be out on a limb** to be in an isolated position, without support ◇ **go out on a limb** to express a viewpoint that risks being controversial

limb[2] /lim/ *n* **1 RIM OF A PLANET** the illuminated edge of the Sun, the Moon, or a planet **2 ARC-SHAPED SCALE ON A MEASURING DEVICE** an arc-shaped scale on an instrument such as a sextant that measures angles **3 END OF A PLANT PART** the expanded end of a plant part, especially of a sepal, petal, or leaf **4 RIM OF A FLOWER** the flared outer rim of a bell- or trumpet-shaped flower **5 PART OF A BOW** either of the two halves of a bow used in archery [14C. Directly or via French *limbe* < Latin *limbus* 'edge'.]

limbate /lím bayt/ *adj* describes flowers that are a different colour at the edges ○ *limbate carnations* [Early 19C. < late Latin *limbatus* < Latin *limbus* 'edge'.]

limber[1] /límbər/ *adj* **1 SUPPLE AND AGILE** able to move with elastic ease and nimble quickness **2 FLEXIBLE** able to be bent easily ■ *vti* **MAKE OR BECOME FLEXIBLE** to become, or cause something to become, flexible or supple [Mid-16C. Probably < LIMBER[2], from its ease of movement.] —**limberness** *n*

limber up *vi* to do gentle physical exercises to loosen and warm the muscles prior to taking part in more strenuous physical activity

limber[2] /límbər/ *n* a two-wheeled vehicle that forms the detachable front part of a gun carriage ■ *vt* to attach a gun or other piece of field equipment to a limber [Early 17C. < ?]

limbi plural of **limbus**

limbic /límbik/ *adj* **1** belonging to a limbus or situated in or near a limbus **2** belonging to or situated in the limbic system [Late 19C. < French *limbique* < Latin *limbus* 'edge'.]

limbic system *n* an interconnected system of brain nuclei associated with basic needs and emotions, e.g. hunger, pain, pleasure, satisfaction, sex, and instinctive motivation

limbo[1] /límbō/ *n* **1 limbo, Limbo** in Roman Catholic theology, the place that is believed to be home to the souls of children who have died before baptism, and the souls of the righteous who died before Jesus Christ **2** a state in which somebody or something is neglected or is simply left in oblivion [14C. < Latin, 'on the border (of hell)', form of *limbus* 'border'.] ◇ **in limbo** in a state of uncertainty or of being kept waiting

limbo[2] /límbō/ (*plural* **-bos**) *n* a West Indian dance in which the body is bent backwards from the knees and moved under a horizontal boundary that is placed progressively lower [Mid-20C. Alteration of LIMBER[1].]

Limbourg Brothers /lím burg-/, **Pol, Herman, and Jehanequin** (*fl.* 1400–16) Flemish illuminators

Limburger /lím burgər/, **Limburger cheese, Limburg cheese** /lím burg-/ *n* a soft white Belgian cheese with a strong smell and taste [Mid-19C. < Dutch or German, after *Limburg*, province of NW Belgium.]

limbus /límbəss/ (*plural* **-bi** /-bī/) *n* the edge of various organs or body parts, e.g. the area in the eyeball where the cornea and sclera meet [15C. < Latin, 'edge, border'.]

lime[1] /līm/ *n* **1 CALCIUM OXIDE** the chemical calcium oxide **2 CALCIUM USED FOR IMPROVING SOIL** any of several forms of calcium, especially calcium hydroxide, used for improving soil that has a low calcium content **3 BIRDLIME** the substance birdlime ■ *vt* (**limes, liming, limed**) **1 SPREAD CALCIUM ON** to spread calcium, often in the form of ground limestone, on soil in order to reduce its acidity **2 PAINT WITH WHITEWASH** to cover a surface with whitewash **3 SMEAR WITH BIRDLIME** to smear twigs or branches with birdlime in order to catch small birds **4 BLEACH WOOD** to treat wood with lime so that it has a pale bleached appearance ○ *kitchen cabinets of limed ash* **5 CATCH BIRDS OR ANIMALS USING BIRDLIME** to catch small birds or animals using birdlime or some other sticky substance [Old English *līm* < Germanic]

lime[2] /līm/ *n* **1 SMALL GREEN FRUIT** a small acid-tasting citrus fruit with a thin green rind and green flesh **2 EVERGREEN TREE** a small evergreen citrus tree that bears limes.

Native to: Asia. *Citrus aurantifolia.* **3 NON-ALCOHOLIC DRINK** a non-alcoholic drink made from or tasting of the juice of limes ■ *adj* COLOURS = **lime-green** [Mid-17C. Via French < Arabic *līma* 'citrus fruit'.]

lime[3] /līm/ *n* **1 lime, lime tree** a deciduous hardwood tree with heart-shaped leaves and clusters of white, yellowish, or green flowers, often planted for shade or ornament, or grown for timber. Native to: N hemisphere. Genus: *Tilia.* US term **linden 2** the wood of the lime tree [Early 17C. Alteration of *line* < Old English *lind* (see LINDEN).]

limeade /līm áyd/ *n* a non-alcoholic, usually carbonated drink made from or tasting of lime juice

lime-green *adj* of the pale green colour of a lime

limekiln /līm kiln/ *n* an oven that is used for heating limestone to produce quicklime

limelight /līm līt/ *n* **1 FOCUS OF ATTENTION** the focus of attention or public interest **2 LAMP IN WHICH QUICKLIME IS HEATED** a lamp used as an early form of stage lighting in which quicklime is heated to produce a brilliant light **3 LIGHT PRODUCED BY LIMELIGHT** the light that a limelight lamp produces

limerick /límmərik/ *n* a five-line humorous poem with regular metre and rhyme patterns, often dealing with a risqué subject and typically opening with a line such as 'There was a young lady called Jenny' [Early 19C. Probably < nonsense songs with this rhyme scheme, with the refrain 'will you come up to LIMERICK'.]

Limerick /límmərik/ **1** chief city in the SW Republic of Ireland. Population: 79,000 (1996). **2** county in Munster Province, SW Republic of Ireland. Area: 2,686 sq. km/1,039 sq. mi.

limescale /līm skayl/ *n* a white deposit that forms on a surface such as the inside of a kettle or boiler because of the evaporation of water containing lime

limestone /līm stōn/ *n* sedimentary rock formed from the skeletons and shells of marine organisms that consists chiefly of calcium carbonate and is used widely in construction and in making lime and cement

limewater /līm wawtər/ *n* a clear alkaline solution of calcium hydroxide in water, used in skin lotions and as an antacid

limey /līmi/ *n US, Can, ANZ* (*slang*) **1** an offensive term for a British person **2** an offensive term for a British commercial or naval vessel ■ *adj US, Can, ANZ* an offensive term meaning belonging or relating to the United Kingdom (*slang*) [Late 19C. Shortening of *lime-juicer*, because sailors in the British Navy drank lime juice to prevent scurvy.]

liminal /límmin'l/ *adj* belonging to the point of conscious awareness below which something cannot be experienced or felt [Late 19C. < Latin *limin-* 'threshold'.]

limit /límmit/ *n* **1 FURTHEST POINT, DEGREE, OR AMOUNT** the furthest point, degree, amount, or boundary, especially one that cannot or should not be passed or exceeded ○ *impose a spending limit* **2 MAXIMUM OR MINIMUM AMOUNT ALLOWED** the maximum or minimum amount, or the largest or lowest quantity, that is available or allowed ○ *an upper age limit of 12 years* **3 BOUNDARY OF AN AREA** the boundary or edge of an area, or something that marks a boundary or edge (*often plural*) ○ *the city limits* **4 RESTRICTION** a feature or circumstance that restricts what can be done ○ *a time limit* **5 MAXIMUM MONEY ALLOWED IN BETTING** the maximum amount of money that can be staked at any one time in various games of chance **6 MAXIMUM OF A MATHEMATICAL FUNCTION** a numerical value approached by a mathematical function as the independent variable of the function approaches infinity or some specified value **7 VALUE SPECIFYING AN INTEGRAL'S RANGE** one of the two given values specifying the range over which a definite integral is evaluated ■ *vt* **1 RESTRICT** to restrict something or somebody in number or quantity, or restrict something to a specified group ○ *had to limit the number of guests because of space problems* **2 BE BOUNDARY TO** to be or act as a boundary to a specified area [14C. < Latin *limit-* 'boundary'.] —**limitable** *adj* ◇ **be the limit** to be so bad as to be almost beyond what somebody is able or prepared to tolerate ◇ **over the limit** with more alcohol in the bloodstream than the driver of a vehicle is legally permitted to have

limitary /límmitəri/ *adj* (*archaic*) **1** on which limits are imposed **2** imposing limits of some kind

limitation /límmi táysh'n/ *n* **1 RESTRICTION** an imposed restriction that cannot be exceeded or sidestepped ○ *limitations on the height of vehicles* **2 RESTRICTING FLAW** a disadvantage or weakness in a person or thing (*often plural*) ○ *One of the limitations of the program is the amount of memory it requires.* **3 SETTING OF A LIMIT** the act of limiting something ○ *damage limitation* **4 MAXIMUM DELAY ALLOWED** a stated period of time within which a legal action must start **5 LEGAL RESTRICTION** a legal restriction on the powers that somebody has

limit down *n* under futures exchange rules, the point reached by a commodity price that has fallen by the maximum amount allowed in a single day's trading

limited /límmitid/ *adj* **1 WITH A LIMIT IMPOSED** on which some form of limit or restriction is imposed ○ *We have limited space available.* **2 LACKING FULL SCOPE** existing at or below the full degree or extent, usually far below ○ *limited powers* **3 OF RELATIVELY LITTLE TALENT** with talents or skills that fall short of what is expected or required **4 LACKING FULL AUTHORITY** lacking a full range of powers, especially because of constitutional or legal limitations **5 limited, Limited WITH RESTRICTED SHAREHOLDER LIABILITY** describes a company or other business enterprise whose shareholders' liability for any debts or losses is restricted —**limitedly** *adv* —**limitedness** *n*

limited company *n* a company in which the shareholders' liability for any debts or losses is restricted

limited edition *n* an edition, especially of a book or an art print, of which only a set number of copies have been made (*hyphenated before nouns*) ○ *limited-edition prints*

limited liability *n* an investor's liability for no greater a proportion of a company's debt than is represented by the value of his or her financial stake in the business

limited partner *n* a business partner who has no management responsibility and whose liability for company debts is limited to his or her financial stake —**limited partnership** *n*

limited war *n* a war in which it is not the aim of the participants to defeat or destroy the enemy totally, especially a war in which nuclear weapons are available but are not used

limiter /límmitər/ *n* **1** an electronic circuit that limits the amplitude of an output wave to a specified value **2** somebody or something that has a restricting effect

limiting /límmiting/ *adj* **1** imposing limits of some kind, especially limits on the scope for development, progress, or improvement ○ *a limiting factor* **2** identifying rather than describing the referent of a noun, as the possessive adjective 'your' does in the phrase 'your house'

limitless /límmitləss/ *adj* very great in amount, extent, or degree ○ *limitless resources* —**limitlessly** *adv* —**limitlessness** *n*

limit order *n* an order instructing an investment broker to buy or sell something at a specified price or better within a certain period of time

limit point *n* a point in a set of mathematical points, such that for every neighbourhood around the point at least one other point in the set is contained in the neighbourhood

limit up *n* under futures exchange rules, the point reached by a commodity price that has risen by the maximum amount allowed in a single day's trading

limn /lim/ *vt* (*literary*) **1** to draw or paint a picture of somebody or something, especially in outline **2** to describe something in words [15C. Alteration of *lumine* 'illustrate a manuscript' < Old French *luminer* < Latin *luminare* 'illumine' < *lumin-* 'light'.] —**limner** *n*

limnetic /lim néttik/ *adj* relating to or living in the deep open water of a freshwater pond or lake [Late 19C. < Greek *limnētēs* 'living in marshes' < *limnē* 'marshy lake'.]

limnology /lim nólləji/ *n* the scientific study of lakes and other bodies of fresh water, including their physical and biological features [Late 19C. < Greek *limnē* 'marshy lake'.] —**limnological** /límnə lójjik'l/ *adj* —**limnologically** *adv* —**limnologist** *n*

limo /límmō/ (*plural* **-os**) *n* a limousine (*informal*) [Mid-20C. Shortening.]

Limoges[1] /li mṓzh/ *n* a fine porcelain made in the town of Limoges, France, since the 19th century

Limoges[2] /li mṓzh/ town in central France. Population: 133,968 (1999).

limonene /límmə neen/ *n* $C_{10}H_{16}$ a liquid unsaturated hydrocarbon that smells like lemon and is found in the essential oils of citrus fruits and peppermint. Use: a wetting agent and in making resins. [Mid-19C. < German *Limonen* < *Limone* 'lemon'.]

limonite /līmə nīt/ *n* a hydrated iron oxide ore that varies in colour from dark brown to yellow [Early 19C. < German *Limonit* (replacing *Wiesenerz* 'meadow ore') < Greek *leimōn* 'meadow'.] —**limonitic** /līmə níttik/ *adj*

Limousin /límmoo zan, -záN/ *n* a breed of large hardy beef cattle that originated in Limousin, a former province of central France

limousine /límmə zeén, -zeen/ *n* **1** a large luxurious car, usually chauffeur-driven, with a partition between the chauffeur and passengers **2** *US* a vehicle used to transport passengers to and from an airport, usually between a hotel and airport [Early 20C. < French, feminine of *Limousin* 'caped cloak', after *Limousin*, France.]

limp[1] /limp/ *vi* **1 WALK UNEVENLY** to walk with an uneven step, usually because of having an injured leg **2 PROCEED WITH DIFFICULTY** to move or continue with great difficulty ○ *The business limped through the recession.* ■ *n* **IMPAIRED GAIT** a way of walking or running that involves a motion impairment, either slight or more extensive (*offensive in some contexts*) [Late 16C. Probably back-formation < obsolete *limphalt* 'lame' < Old English *lemphealt* < *lemp-* + HALT[2].] —**limper** *n*

limp[2] /limp/ *adj* **1 FLEXIBLE** without stiffness or rigidity **2 WEAK** without strength, power, or firmness ○ *a limp handshake* **3 LACKING FORCE** without energy, vitality, or enthusiasm **4 LACKING VOLUME OR SUBSTANCE** without a firm or substantial feel or texture **5 NOT STIFFENED BY BOARDS** describes a book cover that is not stiffened by boards but is made of more durable material than a paperback **6 UNCONVINCING** not very convincing [Early 18C. < ?] —**limply** *adv* —**limpness** *n*

limpet /límpit/ (*plural* **-pets** *or* **-pet**) *n* a marine gastropod mollusc that has a low rough conical shell and clings to rocks [Pre-12C. Via medieval Latin *lampreda* < late Latin *lampetra*.]

limpet mine *n* an explosive device that can be attached to the hull of a ship

limpid /límpid/ *adj* **1 CLEAR** clear and transparent **2 LUCID** expressing something in a way that is clear and easy to understand ○ *limpid prose* **3 UNWORRIED** emotionally calm and composed [Early 17C. Directly or via French *limpide* < Latin *limpidus* 'clear'.] —**limpidity** /lim píddəti/ *n* —**limpidly** *adv* —**limpidness** *n*

limpkin /límpkin/ (*plural* **-kins** *or* **-kin**) *n* a wading bird with a long neck, a long curved bill, long legs, and short rounded wings. Native to: South America, SE North America. *Aramus guarauna.* [Late 19C. < LIMP[1]; from its limping walk.]

Limpopo /lim pṓpō/ river in SE Africa, rising in N South Africa and flowing through S Mozambique to the Indian Ocean. Length: 1,800 km/1,100 mi.

limp-wristed *adj* an offensive term meaning effeminate (*insult*) [< the attitude offensively associated with effeminate men]

limulus /límmyŏŏləss/ (*plural* **-li** /-lī/ *or* **-lus**) *n* a member of a group of arthropods that includes the horseshoe crab. Genus: *Limulus.* [Mid-19C. Via modern Latin < Latin, 'somewhat sidelong' < *limus* 'oblique'; from the crab's motion.]

limy /līmi/ (**-ier, -iest**) *adj* **1** smeared with birdlime **2** consisting of, containing, or similar to lime

lin. *abbr* **1** lineal **2** linear

linac /línnak/ *n* PHYS = **linear accelerator** [Mid-20C. Shortening.]

Linacre /línnəkər/, **Thomas** (c. 1460–1524) English humanist and physician

linage /līnij/, **lineage** *n* **1** the number of lines in a printed text **2** a fixed payment per line of printed text made to the author

linalool /li nállō ol/, **linalol** /línnə lol/ *n* a colourless liquid with a pleasant smell. Source: essential plant oils. Use: manufacture of perfumes. [Late 19C. < Mexican Spanish *linaloē* 'lignaloes'.]

Lin Biao /lín byów/ (1907?–71) Chinese military and political leader

linchpin /línch pin/, **lynchpin** *n* **1** a pin placed crosswise through an axle to prevent a wheel from coming off **2** somebody or something that is an essential element in the success of something such as a team or a plan [14C. < obsolete *linch* 'linchpin' < Old English *lynis*, + PIN.]

Lincoln[1] /língkən/ *n* a heavy-fleeced sheep of a breed originally developed in Lincolnshire and raised mainly for its meat

Lincoln[2] /língkən/ **1** city in E England, noted for its cathedral. Population: 84,300 (1995). **2** capital of Nebraska, in the southeastern part of the state. Population: 213,088 (1998 estimate).

Library of Congress

Abraham Lincoln

Lincoln, Abraham (1809–65) US statesman and 16th president of the United States (1861–65)

Lincoln green *adj* of a bright green colour [Early 16C. After LINCOLN[2] 1.] —**Lincoln green** *n*

Lincolnshire /língkənshər/ county in E England, bordering the North Sea. Area: 5,885 sq. km/2,272 sq. mi.

Lincolnshire Wolds /-wṓldz/ region of chalk hills in E England

Lincs. *abbr* Lincolnshire

linctus /língktəss/ (*plural* **-tuses**) *n* a medicinal syrup given to relieve coughs and soothe sore throats [Late 17C. < medieval Latin, '(medicine) for licking' < Latin *lingere* 'to lick'.]

Lind /lind/, **Jenny** (1820–87) Swedish soprano. Known as **the Swedish Nightingale**

lindane /lín dayn/ *n* $C_6H_6Cl_6$ a white poisonous crystalline powder that biodegrades very slowly. Use: insecticide, weedkiller. [Mid-20C. After Teunis van der *Linden*, Dutch chemist.]

Lindbergh /línd burg/, **Charles Augustus** (1902–74) US aviator and engineer. Known as **Lucky Lindy**

linden /líndən/ (*plural* **-dens** *or* **-den**) *n* TREES = **lime**[3] *n.* 1 [Late 16C. <*linden* 'made of linden wood' < Old English *lind* 'linden' < Germanic.]

Lindisfarne /líndiss faarn/ island off the coast of NE England. Area: 5 sq. km/1.93 sq. mi.

Lindrum /líndrəm/, **Walter Albert** (1898–1960) Australian billiards player

Lindsay /líndzi/, **Jack** (1900–90) Australian writer and historian

Lindsay, Norman Alfred William (1879–1969) Australian artist and writer

Lindsay, Vachel (1879–1931) US poet

lindy /líndi/, **lindy hop** *n* a lively dance for couples that is similar to the jitterbug [Early 20C. < *Lindy*, nickname of Charles LINDBERGH.]

line[1] /līn/ *n* **1 LONG NARROW MARK** a long narrow mark or stroke made on or in a surface **2 FACIAL MARK** a wrinkle or crease in the skin of the face (*often plural*) **3 TRACED PATH OF POINT** an imaginary path that has length but not width, traced by a moving point **4 ONE-DIMENSIONAL ELEMENT** a straight geometrical element that has length but not width or thickness and whose identity is determined by two points **5 BORDER** a boundary or division between two properties, jurisdictions, or political units **6 CONFINING BOUNDARY** a long narrow mark that shows the boundary of any of the divisions of a playing area or race track **7 ROUTE** a rail, sea, or air route served by a transport organization **8 TRACK** the track on which a railway train runs **9 FIXED RAILWAY ROUTE** a particular part of a railway network **10 TRANSPORT COMPANY** a company that runs a regular service of buses, ships, or aircraft on a route **11 THIN ROPE** a length of rope or wire **12 ELECTRIC CABLE** a cable used for transmitting electric power or electronic messages **13 CONNECTION** a telephone connection **14 PART OF STAVE** any of the five horizontal marks that make up a stave **15 MELODY** the notes that make up a melody **16 SERIES** a series of people, usually in the same family, who follow one another in the same job or role ○ *the last in a long line of musicians* **17 TYPE OF MERCHANDISE** a particular type of product or merchandise **18 ROW OF PRINT** a row of words or numbers on a page or other surface ○ *a few lines of doggerel* **19 POSITIONED FORMATION** a formation of troops, ships, weapons, or fortifications positioned in a place (*often plural*) ○ *behind enemy lines* **20 FIGHTING FORCE** the military or naval units of a country that actually go into battle **21 NARROW BAND OF FREQUENCIES** a narrow band of frequencies in an electromagnetic spectrum **22 AMERICAN FOOTBALL PLAYERS** either of the two rows of opposing players facing each other on either side of the line of scrimmage in American football **23 LIMIT** any limit or division ○ *a thin line between happiness and misery* **24** *US* **ODDS** odds for wagering **25 SHAPE** the characteristic shape or contour of something (*often plural*) **26 DIRECTION** a path or direction of movement **27 APPROACH** a course or approach followed in doing something ○ *must decide what line to take before the meeting* **28 POLICY** a policy, a way of thinking, or a version of something ○ *What's the government line on this?* **29 SPECIALIZED FIELD** a particular area of interest, work, activity, or expertise **30 ACTOR'S WORDS** the words spoken that make up an actor's part (*often plural*) **31 USEFUL INFORMATION** useful information or an insight into something **32 BRIEF MESSAGE** a short written message ○ *Why not drop me a line?* **33 EQUATOR** the equator (*dated*) **34 ROW** a row of people or things **35** *US* = **queue** *n.* 1 **36 PART OF TELEVISION PICTURE** any of the horizontal scans that make up the picture on a television screen **37 DECEIVING TALK** something said to deceive, impress, or attract somebody (*informal*) ○ *gave me that old line about the dog eating his report card* **38 AMOUNT OF A DRUG** a portion of a drug, such as cocaine, scraped into a long thin row to be inhaled (*slang*) **39** *Ireland* **ROAD** a road, especially a new road **40** *Scotland* **NOTE OF AUTHORIZATION** a note of authorization, especially a medical certificate issued by a doctor (*informal*) ■ **lines** *npl* **1 CERTIFICATE** a certificate, especially a marriage certificate **2 SCHOOL PUNISHMENT** a phrase or sentence that a school pupil is made to write out a specified number of times as a punishment, or the material that is actually written out ■ *vt* (**lines, lining, lined**) **1 MARK A LINE ON** to mark something with lines **2 ARRANGE ALONG AN EDGE** to arrange or be arranged along the edge or length of something [Pre-12C. Directly or via Old French *ligne* < Latin *linea* 'linen string, line', a form of *lineus* 'made of linen' < *linum* 'flax, linen'.] —**linable** *adj* ◇ **all along the line** throughout or at every stage in something ◇ **draw the line** to restrict or set limits at a particular point ◇ **hold the line 1** to keep a telephone connection open while waiting to speak to somebody **2** to resist a military attack without giving ground or allowing a formation to be broken ◇ **in line 1** arranged in an orderly row **2** in keeping with a policy or obedient to a set of rules ◇ **in line for** likely to receive something such as a promotion or position ◇ **in line with** in agreement or conformity with something ◇ **lay it on the line** to speak about something frankly (*informal*) ◇ **lay** *or* **put something on the line** to risk by some action the loss of something valuable (*informal*) ◇ **off line** temporarily not connected in an electronic communications system ◇ **on line** connected in an electronic communications or other system ◇ **out of line 1** *US* rude and disrespectful (*informal*) **2** *US* unruly or out of control (*informal*) ◇ **read between the lines** to deduce something that is not made explicit (*informal*) ◇ **toe the line** to comply with what is expected

line up *v* **1** *vti* **FORM A ROW** to form a row or form people or things into a row **2** *vi* **FORM A QUEUE** to form a queue to wait for a turn **3** *vt* **PROVIDE** to organize, provide, or make something available to somebody ○ *had lined up a programme of entertainments for us* **4** *vti* **ALIGN THINGS** to align two or more things or be in alignment

line[2] /līn/ (**lines, lining, lined**) *vt* **1 REINFORCE** to cover or reinforce the inside or unexposed surface of something ○ *a jacket lined with silk* **2 COVER** to completely cover something with something else ○ *The walls were lined with books.* **3 FILL** to fill or supply something with something else ○ *a good hot meal to line your stomach* [14C. < obsolete *line* 'spun flax' < Old English *līn*, probably < Latin *linum* 'flax'; from the use of linen to line garments.]

lineage[1] /línni ij/ *n* **1** the line of descent from an ancestor to a person or family **2** a group of people related by descent from a common ancestor [14C. < French *lignage* < *ligne* (see LINE[1]).]

lineage[2] /línij/ *n* MEDIA = **linage**

lineal /línni əl/ *adj* in or from a direct line from an ancestor —**lineally** *adv*

lineament /línni əmənt/ *n* **1 FACIAL FEATURE** a feature or contour of a face (*literary*) **2 CHARACTERISTIC FEATURE** a characteristic feature, especially of something immaterial (*literary*) **3 FEATURE OF LAND** a major topographical feature, such as a long fault plane, that reveals something about its subsurface [15C. < Latin *lineamentum* 'line' < *lineare* 'make straight' < *linea* 'line'.]

linear /línni ər/ *adj* **1 RELATING TO LINES** relating to, consisting of, or using lines **2 RELATING TO A STRAIGHT LINE** relating to a straight line or capable of being represented by a straight line **3 CHANGING PROPORTIONALLY** changing proportionally and representable on a graph as a straight line (*refers to variables*) ○ *There's no linear relation between mortality and size.* **4 WITH CLEARLY DEFINED LINES** dominated by clearly defined lines rather than relying on the effects of colour **5 OF THE FIRST DEGREE** about or in the first degree relative to a mathematical variable **6 WITH OUTPUT VARYING AS INPUT DOES** with an output that varies directly with the input **7 LONG AND NARROW** describes a leaf that is long and narrow —**linearity** /línni árrəti/ *n* —**linearly** *adv*

Linear A /línni ər-/ *n* an undeciphered writing system, dating from about 1500 BC and found on clay remains in Crete

linear accelerator *n* a device that propels charged particles in straight paths by using alternating high-frequency voltages

linear algebra *n* a branch of algebra dealing with linear transformations, vector spaces, matrices, and determinants

Linear B *n* an early form of Greek that dates from about 1400 BC, found on clay remains in Crete and the Greek mainland, and deciphered about 1952

linear equation *n* an equation with no variable raised to a power

linear function *n* MATH = **linear transformation**

linear induction motor *n* = **linear motor**

linearize /línni ə rīz/ (**-izes, -izing, -ized**), **linearise** (**-ises, -ising, -ised**) *vt* to form or project something into a line —**linearization** /línni ə rī záysh'n/ *n*

linear measure *n* any system or unit used to measure length

linear momentum *n* PHYS = **momentum** *n.* 3

linear motor *n* an electric motor in which the motion between the rotor and stator is linear so that thrust is produced along a straight line

linear perspective *n* a form of perspective in which drawings or paintings are given apparent depth by showing parallel lines as converging on the horizon

linear programming *n* a method of finding the maximum and minimum values of a linear transformation using variables that are subject to constraints

linear transformation *n* a mathematical transformation in which the resulting variables are neither multiplied together nor raised to any power

lineation /línni áysh'n/ *n* **1** division into or arrangement of lines **2** the outline of an image

linebacker /lín bakər/ *n* a player in American football who takes a position near and behind the defensive line —**linebacking** *n*

line breeding *n* the deliberate mating of closely related individuals in order to retain characteristics of a common ancestor

line cut *n* a photoengraving made from a line drawing

line dancing *n* a style of dancing to country-and-western music in which dancers perform in rows —**line dance** *n, vi* —**line dancer** *n*

line drawing *n* a drawing done entirely in lines, with tones shown by the thickness or closeness of the lines

line engraving *n* an engraving in which lines are cut by hand into a metal plate from which the print is made

line item *n* an item of important financial data presented on a separate line, such as in a ledger or an annual report

line judge *n* = **linesman** *n.* 2

Lineker /línnəkər/, **Gary** (*b.* 1960) British footballer

lineman /línmən/ (*plural* **-men** /-mən/) *n* **1** *US* COMMUNICATION = **linesman** *n.* 3 **2** in American football, a player on the forward line, especially a centre, guard, tackle, or tight end **3** a surveyor's assistant who marks points or positions

line management *n* the managers in a company who are involved in production or the central part of the business, as opposed to managers of service sectors

line manager *n* a manager in a company who is involved in production or the central part of the business and to whom a non-management-level employee is directly answerable

linen /línnin/ (*plural* **-en** *or* **-ens**) *n* **1** a thread or durable fabric made from the spun fibres of flax **2** clothes, table coverings, undergarments, or bedclothes made from linen or cotton (*often plural*) [Old English *līnen* 'made of flax' < *līn* 'flax' < Indo-European]

linen paper *n* fine paper that is made from flax fibres or given a finish to resemble linen

line of credit *n* the amount of credit that a customer is allowed to draw on. US term **credit line**

line officer *n* an officer who serves in combat

line of fire *n* **1** the path taken by a bullet or missile fired from a weapon **2** a position exposed to a threat, attack, or criticism

line of force *n* an imaginary curve whose tangent at any point is that of the electric or magnetic field that is operating there

line of sight *n* **1** an imaginary line from an observer to a distant object **2** a straight path, unobstructed by the horizon, between a transmitting and receiving aerial

line-out *n* a restart of play in rugby union

⚡**line printer** *n* a printing device that prints a line at a time rather than one character at a time

liner[1] /línər/ *n* **1** a passenger ship or aeroplane run by a shipping line or airline **2** COSMETICS = **eyeliner**

liner[2] /línər/ *n* **1** something used as a lining or padding **2** a protective sleeve, usually made of metal, fitted inside or outside a cylindrical component

liner notes *npl US* RECORDING = **sleeve notes**

linesman /línzmən/ (*plural* **-men** /-mən/) *n* **1 REFEREE'S ASSISTANT** in sports such as tennis, football, and American football, an official who assists the referee or umpire, e.g. by signalling that the ball is out of play **2 AMERICAN FOOTBALL OFFICIAL** an official in American football who watches for infringements, marks the downs, and places the ball in position **3 SOMEBODY MAINTAINING PHONE OR POWER LINES** somebody who installs or repairs telephone or power lines. US term **lineman** *n.* 1

line spectrum *n* a spectrum, produced by a gas emitting light or a gas selectively absorbing light emitted by another source, that consists of a series of distinct parallel lines

linesperson /línz purss'n/ (*plural* **-sons**) *n* in sports such as tennis, football, and American football, an official who assists the referee or umpire, e.g. by signalling that a ball is out of play

line squall *n* a strong storm advancing along a weather front

lineswoman /línz wŏŏmən/ (*plural* **-en** /-wimmin/) *n* in sports such as tennis, football, and American football, a woman official who assists the referee or umpire, e.g. by signalling that a ball is out of play

lineup /lín up/, **line-up** *n* **1 LIST OF PLAYERS** a list of players in a team together with the positions they play in **2 TELEVISION SCHEDULE** a programming schedule of a television network **3** *US* CRIME = **identification parade** **4 GROUP UNITED IN A PURPOSE** a group of people or organizations recruited for a cause or common purpose such as raising funds for a charity

ling[1] /ling/ (*plural* **ling** *or* **lings**) *n* a fish related to the cod, whose flesh is used as food. Native to: coastal waters of Greenland and N Europe. Genus: *Molva*. [13C. < ?]

ling[2] /ling/ *n* PLANTS = **heather** *n.* 1 [Old English *lyng*]

-ling[1] *suffix* **1** one connected with or resembling ○ *hatchling* **2** small one ○ *princeling* ○ *spiderling* [Old English]

-ling[2] *suffix* in a particular manner or condition ○ *darkling* [Old English]

Lingala /ling gaálə/ *n* a language belonging to the Bantu group of Benue-Congo and used as a lingua franca in the Democratic Republic of Congo. Native speakers: 10 million. [Early 20C. < Bantu.] —**Lingala** *adj*

lingam /líng gəm/ *n* **1 PHALLIC SYMBOL** a stylized phallus, used to represent the Hindu god Shiva **2 PENIS** a penis **3 SANSKRIT MASCULINE GENDER** the masculine gender in Sanskrit grammar [Early 18C. < Sanskrit *liṅga* 'mark, phallus'.]

lingcod /líng kod/ (*plural* **-cod** *or* **-cods**) *n* a spiny-finned large-mouthed game fish whose flesh is used as food. Native to: North Pacific Ocean. *Ophidion elongatus*. [Mid-20C. < LING[1] + COD[1].]

linger /líng gər/ *vi* **1 DELAY LEAVING** to put off leaving a place because you are reluctant to go **2 WAIT AROUND** to wait around or move about a place slowly and idly **3 BE BARELY ALIVE** to remain alive, although very weak, while gradually dying **4 TAKE TIME TO DO** to take longer than is usual to do something, e.g. to complete a task or look at somebody or something, usually because you are enjoying yourself ○ *Her eyes lingered on the letter.* **5 PERSIST** to remain fixed in the mind or noticed by the senses for a long time [13C. < obsolete *lengen* 'to delay' < Old Norse *lengja* 'lengthen'.] —**lingerer** *n*

lingerie /lánzhəri, lónzhəri, láNzhəri/ *n* women's underwear and nightdresses [Early 19C. < French, 'things made of linen' < *linge* 'linen' < Latin *lineus* 'made of flax'.]

lingering /líng gəring/ *adj* **1 DRAWN-OUT** long and drawn-out, especially with pain **2 SLOW** done slowly in order to prolong something as long as possible **3 PERSISTING IN THE MIND** remaining for some time in the thoughts or mind —**lingeringly** *adv*

lingo /líng gō/ (*plural* **-goes**) *n* a language that is not the speaker's native language, or a specialized set of terms requiring to be learned like a language (*informal*) [Mid-17C. < ?]

lingua /líng gwə/ (*plural* **-guae** /-gwee/) *n* the tongue or a part resembling one [Late 17C. < Latin, 'tongue'.]

lingua franca /líng gwə frángkə/ (*plural* **lingua francas** *or* **linguae francae** /-gwee-kee/) *n* **1** a language or mixture of languages used for communication by people who speak different first languages **2** the mixed language used chiefly by merchants throughout Mediterranean ports until the 18th century, consisting mainly of Italian with elements of French, Spanish, Greek, Arabic, and Turkish [Late 17C. < Italian, 'Frankish tongue'.]

lingual /líng gwəl/ *adj* relating to, using, or similar to the tongue [Mid-17C. < medieval Latin *lingualis* < Latin *lingua* 'tongue'.] —**lingually** *adv*

linguine /ling gwéeni/, **linguini** *n* pasta made in long narrow flat strips [Mid-20C. < Italian *linguine*, plural of *linguina* 'little tongue' < *lingua* 'tongue' < Latin.]

linguist /líng gwist/ *n* **1** a speaker or adept learner of several languages **2** an expert in or student of linguistics [Late 16C. < Latin *lingua* 'tongue'.]

linguistic /ling gwístik/ *adj* **1** relating to language or languages **2** relating to linguistics —**linguistically** *adv*

linguistic atlas *n* a collection of maps showing the distribution of varying language features in a region

linguistic form *n* an identifiable unit of speech such as a word, prefix, phrase, or sentence

linguistic geography *n* the study of regional variation in speech —**linguistic geographer** *n*

linguistic philosophy *n* a form of philosophy prevalent during the 20th century, asserting that the function of philosophy is to clarify philosophical expressions by analysing and explaining them

linguistics /ling gwístiks/ *n* the systematic study of language (+ *singular verb*)

lingulate /líng gyŏŏlət, -layt/, **lingulated** /-layted/ *adj* shaped like a tongue [Mid-19C. < Latin *lingulatus* < *lingula* 'little tongue' < *lingua* 'tongue'.]

liniment /línnəmənt/ *n* a liquid such as one containing alcohol and camphor, rubbed into the skin to relieve aches or pain [15C. < late Latin *linimentum* < Latin *linire* 'to smear'.]

linin /línin/ *n* a connective material in a cell nucleus [Mid-19C. < Greek *linon* 'thread'.]

lining /líning/ *n* a layer or a material used to cover, protect, or insulate the inner or unexposed surface of something [14C. < LINE[2].]

link[1] /lingk/ *n* **1 PART OF A CHAIN** any of the connected rings or loops that make up a chain, or something resembling a loop in a chain **2 CONNECTION** something that ties, connects, or relates two or more things **3 ROUTE** any part of a transport system, especially a connection between major routes **4 UNIT FOR COMMUNICATING BROADCASTS** a broadcasting unit or system used to relay radio or television signals, e.g. a transmitter, receiver, or relay station **5 SURVEYOR'S UNIT OF LENGTH** a unit of length used in surveying equal to 20.12 cm/7.92 in, and one hundredth of a chain ■ *vti* **CONNECT** to connect, join, or associate somebody or something with another or to become joined with another [14C. < Old Norse *hlekkr* 'link' < Germanic, 'bending'.] —**linker** *n*

link up *v* **1** *vti* to join, connect, or unite somebody or something with another or to become joined with another **2** *vi* to meet and join with somebody or something else

link[2] /lingk/ *n* a burning torch used in the past to give light [Mid-16C. < ?]

linkage /língkij/ *n* **1 LINK** a link or connection or the fact of being connected **2 DIPLOMATIC PROCEDURE** a procedure in diplomacy that requires progress towards an overall objective to depend on concessions made by the various parties on other related issues **3 SYSTEM OF INTERCONNECTED PARTS** a system of interconnected rods, springs, or levers that transmit motion in a mechanism **4 ASSOCIATED GENES** the proximity of two or more genes on a chromosome, which tends to cause them to be inherited together

linkage group *n* two or more genes on a chromosome that tend to be inherited as a group

Linklater /língk laytər/, **Eric Robert Russell** (1899–1974) British writer, journalist, and broadcaster

linkman /língk man, -mən/ (*plural* **-men** /-men/) *n* BROADCAST = **anchorman** *n.* 2

Linköping /líng chúrping/ city in SE Sweden. Population: 131,370 (1995).

links /lingks/ *n* (+ *singular or plural verb*) **1** a golf course, especially one near the sea **2** *Scotland* an area of gently undulating sandy ground near a seashore [Old English *hlincas*, plural of *hlinc* 'ridge']

linkup /língk up/ *n* a connection or association between two or more things or people

Linlithgow /lin líthgō/ town in E Scotland. Population: 11,866 (1991).

linn /lin/ *n* a waterfall or a pool at the foot of a waterfall (*regional*) [Old English *hlynn* 'torrent']

Linnaeus /li née əss, -náy-/, **Carolus** (1707–78) Swedish naturalist. Born **Carl von Linné** —**Linnaean** /li née ən, -náy-/ *adj*

linnet /línnit/ (*plural* **-nets** *or* **-net**) *n* a small brownish songbird of the finch family, the male of which has a red breast and forehead. Native to: Europe, Africa, Asia. *Carduelis cannabina*. [Early 16C. < Old French *linette* < *lin* 'flax' < Latin *linum*; from its diet of flaxseed.]

Linnhe, Loch /línni/ inlet of the Atlantic Ocean in W Scotland. Length: 50 km/31 mi.

lino /línō/ *n* linoleum (*informal*) [Early 20C. Shortening.]

linocut /línō kut/ *n* a print made from a design that has been cut in relief into a piece of linoleum and mounted on a block of wood, or the design itself

linoleate /li nṓli ayt/ *n* any salt or ester of linoleic acid [Mid-19C. < *linoleic* (see LINOLEIC ACID).]

linoleic acid /línnō lée ik-/ *n* $C_{18}H_{32}O_2$ an essential fatty acid, found in grains and seeds [< Latin *linum* 'flax' + OLEIC]

linolenic acid /línnō léenik-/ *n* $C_{18}H_{30}O_2$ a colourless liquid, essential to human nutrition. Source: linseed and other natural oils. Use: manufacture of paints and synthetic resins. [Translation of German *Linolensäure* < *Linolsäure* 'linoleic acid', with insertion of *-en* '-ene']

linoleum /li nṓli əm/ *n* a tough washable floor covering, made from canvas or other material coated under heat and pressure with powdered cork, rosin, and linseed oil [Late 19C. < Latin *linum* 'flax' + *oleum* 'oil'.]

linsang /lín sang/ (*plural* **-sangs** *or* **-sang**) *n* **1** a carnivorous mammal related to and resembling the civet and genet that has spotted or banded fur and a long tail. Native to: forests of S Asia. Genus: *Prionodon*. **2** an animal similar to the Asian linsang. Native to: forests of West Africa. Genus: *Poiana*. [Early 19C. < Javanese *lingsang*.]

linseed /lín seed/ *n* the seed of the flax plant, from which linseed oil and various medicinal preparations are derived [Old English *līnsǣd* 'flax seed' < *līn* (see LINEN)]

linseed oil *n* oil obtained from the seeds of flax plants, used in making linoleum and in paints and inks to help them dry more quickly. ◊ **flaxseed oil**

linsey-woolsey /línzi woŏlzi/ n a coarse cloth made from linen interwoven with wool or cotton [15C. < linsey (probably after Lindsey, Suffolk) + WOOL -sey for rhyme.]

linstock /lín stok/ n a long staff with a forked end designed to hold a lighted match, used in the past to fire cannons [Mid-16C. < Dutch lontstok < lont 'match' + stok 'stick'.]

lint /lint/ n 1 MATERIAL FOR MEDICAL DRESSINGS a soft absorbent material made from cotton or linen. Use: wound dressing. 2 THREAD OR FLUFF little pieces of thread or fluff 3 COTTON FIBRES the fibres that surround unprocessed cotton seeds [14C. < ?] —**linty** adj

lintel /línt'l/ n a horizontal beam that supports the weight of the wall above a window or door [14C. < Old French, < Latin limit- 'boundary'; influenced by Latin limin- 'threshold'.]

lintie /línti/ n Scotland a linnet [Late 18C. < Scots lintwhite 'linnet' < Old English, < lín (see LINEN) + -twige 'plucker'.]

⚡LINUX /línəks/ tdmk a trademark for a computer operating system that is a free implementation of the UNIX operating system

Linz /lints/ capital of Upper Austria Province, N Austria. Population: 203,044 (1991).

lion /lí ən/ n 1 BIG WILD PREDATORY CAT a large wild member of the cat family that lives in extended family groups and hunts cooperatively for prey. It has a tawny yellow coat and the males have a shaggy mane. Native to: Africa, India. Panthera leo. 2 HERALDIC SYMBOL the lion used as a symbol in heraldry, e.g. as the national emblems of Great Britain and of Scotland 3 SOMEBODY BRAVE AND STRONG a brave, strong, or fierce person 4 CELEBRITY an admired and celebrated person [13C. Via Anglo-Norman liun < Latin leon < Greek leōn.]

Lion n 1 ZODIAC = Leo n. 1 2 a member of a Lions Club

Lion, Gulf of /lí ən/ wide inlet of the Mediterranean Sea in S France

lion dance n a traditional Chinese ritual performed to bring good luck, especially at Chinese New Year, in which two men dance costumed in a large ornamental lion head and body

lioness /lí ə ness/ n a female lion

Lionfish

lionfish /lí ən fish/ n (plural -fish or -fishes) n a scorpion fish with a striped body, long spiny fins, and venomous dorsal spines. Native to: tropical Pacific Ocean. Genus: Pterois.

lionhearted /lí ən haártid/, **lion-hearted** adj very brave —**lionheartedness** n

lionize /lí ə nīz/ (-izes, -izing, -ized), **lionise** (-ises, -ising, -ised) vt to make somebody into a celebrity or treat somebody like a celebrity —**lionization** /lí ə nī záysh'n/ n —**lionizer** n

Lion Rampant n 1 a heraldic image of a red lion standing up on its hind legs, one of the national emblems of Scotland 2 a flag of Scotland with a red lion rampant on a yellow background

Lions Club n any club belonging to the International Association of Lions Clubs, an organization founded in the United States in 1917 to promote fellowship and service in local communities

lion's share n the largest part or share of something [Late 18C. < Aesop's story in which a lion manages to get the whole kill in a hunt for himself.]

lip /lip/ n 1 PART OF MOUTH either of two fleshy folds around the mouth that help control eating, drinking, and the production of sounds by the mouth 2 SOMETHING LIKE A LIP something like a lip, especially an edge or rim of something hollow 3 IMPERTINENCE impudent or disrespectful talk (slang) 4 PART OF VULVA any of the two sets of folds of skin (labia) at the opening of the vulva ■ vt (lips, lipping, lipped) 1 TOUCH WITH LIPS to touch something with the lips 2 FORM LIP OF to form or be a lip of something [Old English lippa < Indo-European, 'lip'] ◇ **bite your lip** to stop yourself from saying something you want to say (informal) ◇ **button your lip** to stop speaking, not begin speaking, or to keep a secret (slang) ◇ **a stiff upper lip** a brave and composed bearing, with no giving way to emotion (informal)

lipa /léepa/ (plural -pa or -pas) n see table at currency [< Croatian]

lipaemia /li peémi a/ n the presence of excessive fat in the blood

Lipari Islands /líppəri-/ group of volcanic islands off the coast of N Sicily, in the Tyrrhenian Sea. Area: 44 sq. km/114 sq. mi.

lipase /lí payss, líppayss, lí payz, líppayz/ n a pancreatic enzyme that breaks down fats

lip balm n = lip salve

lipectomy /li péktəmi, lī-/ (plural -mies) n the surgical removal of fatty tissue from beneath the skin

Li Peng /lí peng/ (b. 1928) Chinese statesman

lip gloss n a cosmetic used on the lips to make them look shiny

lipid /líppid/, **lipide** n a biological compound that is not soluble in water [Early 20C. < French lipide < Greek lipos (see LIPO-) + French -ide '-id'.] —**lipidic** /li píddik/ adj

Lipizzaner /líppit saànər/, **Lippizaner** n a compact, usually white or grey horse, belonging to a breed often used in equestrian displays [Early 20C. < German, after Lipizza, near Trieste, Italy.]

lip liner n a cosmetic, usually in soft pencil form, used to outline the lips before lipstick is applied

lip microphone n a microphone designed to be held close to the user's mouth to reduce background noise

Li Po /lee pô/ = Li Bo

lipo- prefix fat, fatty tissue ○ lipolysis [< Greek lipos 'fat' < Indo-European, 'to stick']

lipogenesis /líppō jénnəsiss, līpō-/ n the formation of fatty acids and other lipids in the body

lipoic acid /li pô ik-/ n a sulphur-containing fatty acid that plays a role in carbohydrate metabolism

lipoid /lípp oyd, lī poyd/ adj containing or resembling fat ■ n a substance resembling fat —**lipoidal** adj

lipolysis /li pólləsiss, lī-/ n the breakdown of fats into fatty acids and glycerol —**lipolytic** /líppō líttik, līpō-/ adj

lipoma /li pô̂ma, lī-/ (plural -mas or -mata /-mətə/) n a benign tumour made up of fatty tissue —**lipomatous** /-pómmətəss, -pô̂mətəss/ adj

lipophilic /líppō fíllik, līpō-/ adj with a chemical affinity for lipids

lipopolysaccharide /líppō pólli sákə rīd, līpō-/ n a complex of lipid and polysaccharide that forms the outer layer of some bacteria

lipoprotein /líppō prô teen, līpō-/ n a complex of lipids and proteins that carries lipids around the body

liposome /líppō sōm, līpō-/ n a tiny artificial sac with a double layer of lipids, used to carry a drug to targeted cells in the body

liposuction /líppō suksh'n, līpō-/ n cosmetic surgery in which fat is removed from under the skin by vacuum suction

lipotropic /líppō trôpik, līpō-, -tróppik/ adj preventing or reducing the accumulation of fat in the liver

lipotropin /líppō trôpin, līpō-/ n either of two pituitary hormones that trigger the breakdown of fats in the body

-lipped suffix having a particular kind of lip or lips

lippie n COSMETICS = lippy n.

Lippizaner n = Lipizzaner

lippy /líppi/ adj (-pier, -piest) tending to say impudent things (informal) ■ n lippy, lippie lipstick (informal)

lip-read (lip-reads, lip-reading, lip-read /-red/) vti to

understand what is said by watching how somebody's lips move rather than by listening —**lip-reader** n

lip-reading n understanding spoken words by watching lip movements, rather than by listening

lip salve n an ointment used on the lips, often in stick form, especially to relieve chapping or dryness. US term **lip balm**

Lipscomb /lípskəm/, **William Nunn, Jr.** (b. 1919) US chemist

lip service n support or agreement that does not appear to be sincere because the words spoken are not followed up by appropriate action or behaviour

lipstick /lip stik/ n an oily cosmetic in stick form, in a plastic or metal tube, used to colour the lips

lip-synch /-singk/, **lip-sync** vti to pretend to sing or speak by moving lips in synchronization with a recorded song or speech, or to perform a song or speech in this way

lipuria /li pyoŏri a/ n the presence of fat in the urine [Late 19C. < modern Latin, < Greek lipos 'fat' + ouron 'urine'.]

liq. abbr 1 liquid 2 liquor

liquate /li kwáyt/ (-quates, -quating, -quated) vt to heat an alloy or ore to a temperature high enough to separate the constituents with the lowest melting point from the rest [Mid-17C. < Latin liquat-, past participle of liquare 'liquefy'.] —**liquation** /li kwáysh'n/ n

liquefacient /líkwi fáysh'nt/ n something that liquefies or helps to liquefy something else ■ adj capable of liquefying or helping to liquefy something [Mid-19C. < Latin liquefacient-, present participle of liquefacere (see LIQUEFY).]

liquefaction /líkwi fáksh'n/ n the process of liquefying something or the state of having been liquefied [14C. < late Latin liquefaction- < Latin liquefacere (see LIQUEFY).]

liquefied natural gas n 1 a gas, liquefied under pressure. Source: byproduct of petroleum or natural gas. Use: fuel for heating, cooking, and transportation. 2 natural gas in liquid form. Use: replacement for diesel fuel to power vehicles.

liquefied petroleum gas n a mixture of petroleum gases liquefied under pressure. Use: as heating or engine fuel

liquefy /líkwi fī/ (-fies, -fying, -fied) vti to become or cause something to become liquid [14C. Via French liquéfier < Latin liquefacere < liquere 'be liquid' + facere 'make'.] —**liquefiable** adj —**liquefier** n

liquer incorrect spelling of liqueur

liquescent /li kwéss'nt/ adj becoming or tending to become liquid [Early 18C. < Latin liquescent-, present participle of liquescere 'become liquid' < liquere 'be liquid'.] —**liquesce** vi —**liquescence** n —**liquescency** n

liqueur /li kyoŏr/ n a sweet flavoured alcoholic drink usually considered an after-meal beverage [Mid-18C. Via French < Latin liquor 'fluid'.]

liquid /líkwid/ n 1 FLOWING SUBSTANCE a substance in a condition in which it flows, that is a fluid at room temperature and atmospheric pressure, and whose shape but not volume can be changed 2 FRICTIONLESS CONSONANT a consonant that is pronounced without friction and is capable of being prolonged like a vowel. In modern English, 'l' and 'r' are liquids. ■ adj 1 CONSISTING OF A LIQUID relating to, characteristic of, or consisting of a liquid or liquids 2 SMOOTH AND FLUENT moving or produced in a smooth and fluent way 3 CONVERTIBLE TO CASH easily converted into cash 4 CLEAR clear and shining 5 ARTICULATED WITHOUT FRICTION describes a consonant that is articulated without friction and capable of being prolonged like a vowel [14C. Via Old French liquide < Latin liquidus 'fluid' < liquere 'be fluid'.] —**liquidly** adv —**liquidness** n

liquid air n a pale blue mixture of gases, mainly oxygen and nitrogen, that has been cooled and liquefied to be used in manufacturing pure gases and as a refrigerant

liquidambar /líkwid ámbər/ (plural -bars or -bar) n a tree that exudes a yellowish aromatic balsam. Native to: North and Central America, Asia. Genus: Liquidambar. [Late 16C. < modern Latin, < Latin liquidus (see LIQUID) + medieval Latin ambar 'amber'.]

liquidate /líkwi dayt/ (-dates, -dating, -dated) v 1 vti PAY DEBT to pay a debt or other financial obligation 2 vti WIND UP A BUSINESS to wind up a business, paying off its liabilities from its assets, or to cease trading as a business in this way 3 vt CASH ASSETS to turn assets into cash

4 *vt* **KILL** to kill or dispose of somebody [Mid-16C. < late Latin *liquidat-*, past participle of *liquidare* 'melt' < Latin *liquere* 'be liquid'.] —**liquidation** /líkwi dáysh'n/ *n*

liquidator /líkwi daytər/ *n* somebody appointed to oversee the liquidation of a business

liquid crystal *n* a liquid that changes between being clear and cloudy depending on variations in temperature or applied voltage. Use: visual display units.

liquid-crystal display *n* a display of numbers or letters in a calculator, watch, or other electronic device, created by applying electricity to cells made of liquid crystal to make some of them look darker

liquid glass *n* CHEM = **water glass** *n.* 2

liquidise *vti* = **liquidize**

liquidiser *n* = **liquidizer**

liquidity /li kwíddəti/ *n* 1 the state or quality of being liquid 2 assets that can easily be converted into cash

liquidize /líkwi dīz/ (**-izes, -izing, -ized**), **liquidise** (**-uidises, -uidising, -uidised**) *v* 1 *vti* to become liquid or cause something to become liquid 2 *vt* to make something solid into a liquid using a liquidizer

liquidizer /líkwi dīzər/, **liquidiser** *n* HOUSEHOLD = **blender** *n.* 1

liquid measure *n* any unit or system of units for measuring liquid volume or capacity

liquid paraffin *n* a clear oil distilled from petroleum and used as a laxative and skin softener. US term **mineral oil**

liquor /líkər/ *n* 1 **ALCOHOLIC BEVERAGE** an alcoholic drink, especially of the type produced by distillation, e.g. whisky, rather than of the type produced by fermentation, e.g. wine or beer 2 **COOKING LIQUID** a reduced liquid or juice left after cooking food, used as a sauce or as a basis for sauces 3 **SOLUTION OF DRUG** a concentrated solution of a drug 4 **WATER IN WHICH MALT IS STEEPED** warm water added to malt in order to produce wort in the brewing process ■ *vti* **STEEP MALT IN WATER** to steep malt in warm water in order to form wort in the brewing of beer [13C. Via Old French < Latin.]

liquored up *adj US* drunk (*informal*)

liquorice /líkərish, -iss/ (*plural* **-rice**) *n* 1 **DRIED BLACK PLANT ROOT** the dried black root of a perennial plant or an extract made from it. Use: laxative, confectionery, brewing. 2 **KIND OF SWEET** a dense rubbery sweet that is usually made in black or red strips and flavoured with liquorice 3 **PLANT WITH A SWEET ROOT** a perennial plant with spiked blue feathery leaves and a root with a sweet flavour. Native to: Mediterranean. *Glycyrrhiza glabra*. [12C. Via Anglo-Norman *lycorys* < Greek *glukurrhiza* < *glukus* 'sweet' + *rhiza* 'root'.]

liquorish *adj* = **lickerish** (*archaic*)

liquor store *n US* a store that sells alcoholic beverages for consumption off the premises

lira /léerə/ (*plural* **-re** /léerə, -r ay/) *n* see table at **currency** [Early 17C. Via Italian < Latin *libra*, a measure of weight.]

Lisbon /lízbən/ capital of Portugal, in the west-central part of the country. Population: 601,180 (1995 estimate).

Lisburn /líz burn/ town in E Northern Ireland. Population: 42,110 (1991).

lisle /līl/ *n* a strong smooth fine cotton thread or fabric. Use: gloves, stockings. [Mid-16C. After *Lisle* (Lille), N France.]

Lismore /líz mawr/ city in NE New South Wales, Australia. Population: 27,245 (1991).

lisp /lisp/ *n* 1 **SPEECH DEFECT** a minor speech defect in which the sounds 's' and 'z' are pronounced like the soft 'th' sound in 'third' or 'thick' 2 **SPEECH SOUND** the sound produced when 's' and 'z' are pronounced like the soft 'th' sound in 'third' or 'thick' ■ *vti* 1 **PRONOUNCE 'S' LIKE 'TH'** to pronounce something or speak so that 's' and 'z' are pronounced like the soft 'th' sound in 'third' or 'thick' 2 **SPEAK LIKE A CHILD** to speak in a childish or halting way [Old English *wlyspian* < Germanic, < an imitation of the sound] —**lisper** *n* —**lisping** *adj, n* —**lispingly** *adv*

⚡**LISP** /lisp/ *n* a high-level computer programming language, used in artificial intelligence, that converts data into lists [Mid-20C. Contraction of *List Processing (language)*.]

Lissajous figure /léessə zhoo-/ *n* the mathematical curve formed by combining two repeating vibrations that are at right angles to each other [Late 19C. After French physicist Jules Antoine *Lissajous* (1822–80).]

Lissitzky /li síttski/, **El** (1890–1941) Russian artist

lissom /líssəm/, **lissome** *adj* 1 slender and able to bend easily and gracefully 2 quick, light, and graceful in movement [Late 18C. Alteration of LITHESOME.] —**lissomly** *adv* —**lissomness** *n*

⚡**list**[1] /list/ *n* 1 **ORDERED SERIES** a series of related words, names, numbers, or other items that are arranged in order, one after the other ○ *a list of people to call* 2 **SET OF DATA** an ordered set of data ■ *v* 1 *vt* **ARRANGE ITEMS AS ORDERED SERIES** to arrange a series of related words, names, numbers, or other items one after the other ○ *She listed the things she intended to get done that afternoon.* 2 *vt* **INCLUDE IN ORDERED SERIES** to include somebody or something in a series of words, numbers, or other items arranged one after the other ○ *He's listed among the founding members in the club brochure.* 3 *vt* **CATEGORIZE** to place somebody in a category or classification ○ *She lists herself as a club member but never attends meetings.* 4 *vt* **ADMIT SECURITY TO EXCHANGE** to admit a security for trading on an exchange 5 *vt* **OFFICIALLY PROTECT BUILDING** to state officially that a building is one of a specified group that cannot be demolished or altered without government permission because they are of special architectural or historical importance 6 *vti* **ENLIST** to enlist or enlist somebody (*archaic*) [Late 16C. < French *liste* < Germanic.]

list[2] /list/ *n* 1 ARCHIT = **fillet** *n.* 3 2 **FURROWS FORMING RIDGE** a ridge of earth formed by two furrows ploughed side by side 3 **SELVAGE** a selvage (*archaic*) ■ **lists** *npl* **FENCED AREA IN TOURNAMENT** an area of combat in a medieval tournament enclosed by a fence of high stakes ■ *vt* 1 **COVER SOMETHING WITH STRIP OF MATERIAL** to cover or border something with a band of cloth or other material 2 **CUT STRIP OF WOOD** to cut a narrow strip of wood, especially sapwood, from a board or plank (*archaic*) 3 **FORM RIDGE FROM FURROWS** to plough together two furrows of earth to form a ridge [Old English *līste* < Germanic, 'band, strip'] ◇ **enter the lists** to begin to take part in a fight or argument (*formal*)

list[3] /list/ *vti* to lean or make a ship lean to one side ■ *n* an inclination to one side, especially one developed by a ship [Mid-17C. < ?]

list[4] /list/ *vt* (*archaic*) 1 **WISH** to choose, wish, or like something 2 **PLEASE** to give pleasure to somebody ■ *n* **DESIRE** a choice, wish, or liking (*archaic*) [Old English *lystan* < Indo-European, 'be eager']

list[5] /list/ *vti* to listen (*archaic*) [Old English *hlystan*]

listed /lístid/ *adj* 1 **INCLUDED IN LIST** included in a list, catalogue, or directory ○ *a listed phone number* 2 **OFFICIALLY PROTECTED** placed on an official list of buildings that cannot be demolished or altered without government permission because they are of special architectural or historical importance 3 **TRADABLE ON EXCHANGE** placed on a list of securities that may be traded on an exchange [< LIST[1]]

listed building *n* a building on an official list of structures that cannot be demolished or altered without government permission because they are of special architectural or historical importance

listed company *n* a business whose securities may be traded on an exchange

listed security *n* a security that may be traded on an exchange

listel /líst'l/ *n* ARCHIT = **fillet** *n.* 3 [Late 16C. < Italian *listello* 'small border' < *lista* 'border' < Germanic.]

listen /líss'n/ *vi* 1 **MAKE CONSCIOUS EFFORT TO HEAR** to concentrate on hearing somebody or something ○ *We listened for the sound of the geese overhead.* 2 **PAY ATTENTION** to pay attention to something and and take it into account ○ *She wouldn't listen to my advice.* ■ *n* **ACT OF HEARING** an act of making an effort to hear something (*informal*) ○ *Why not give their new CD a listen?* [Old English *hlysnan* (influenced by LIST[5]) < Indo-European, 'to hear']
listen in *vi* 1 **EAVESDROP** to listen to other people, sometimes without their knowing it 2 **LISTEN TO RADIO** to listen to a radio broadcast 3 **MONITOR TELECOMMUNICATIONS** to monitor radio or telephone communications
listen up *vi* to pay attention or listen carefully (*informal*)

listenable /líss'nəb'l/ *adj* pleasant to listen to or suitable for listening to —**listenability** /líss'nə bílləti/ *n*

listener /líss'nər/ *n* a person who listens, especially to a radio broadcast

listenership /líss'nər ship/ *n* the number or kind of people who listen to a radio broadcast, programme, or station (*takes a singular or plural verb*)

listening post *n* 1 an advanced position near enemy lines from which troops can detect the enemy's movements 2 a post or area where information or intelligence is gathered

lister /lístər/ *n US, Can* a plough that heaps earth on both sides of a furrow [Late 17C. < LIST[2].]

Lister /lístər/, **Joseph, 1st Baron** (1827–1912) British surgeon

listeria /li stéeri ə/ *n* a rod-shaped aerobic parasitic bacterium that causes disease, especially listeriosis. Genus: *Listeria*. [Mid-20C. < modern Latin, after Joseph LISTER.]

listeriosis /li stéeri ṓssiss/ *n* a disease of the nervous system of mammals, birds, and occasionally humans that can cause fever, meningitis, miscarriage, or premature birth and is spread by eating food contaminated with listeria [Mid-20C. < LISTERIA.]

⚡**listing** /lísting/ *n* 1 **SOMETHING ENTERED IN LIST** an entry in a list, catalogue, or directory 2 **LIST** a list, catalogue, or directory 3 **PRINTOUT** a printout of a computer file or program 4 **PLACE ON OFFICIAL LIST OF SECURITIES** a place on an official list of securities that can be traded on an exchange ■ **listings** *npl* **LISTS OF EVENTS** published lists of films, plays, or other cultural events, containing information such as times, locations, and ticket prices [Mid-17C. < LIST[1].]

listless /lístləss/ *adj* lacking energy, interest, or the willingness to make an effort [15C. 'Without pleasure' < LIST[4].] —**listlessly** *adv* —**listlessness** *n*

Liston /lístən/, **Sonny** (1917?–70) US boxer. Born **Charles Liston**

list price *n* a published or advertised retail price of something that can often be discounted by the seller

⚡**listserv** *n* a free Internet service that functions as a forum, allowing users to take part in e-mail discussions

Liszt /list/, **Franz** (1811–86) Hungarian pianist, composer, and conductor

lit 1 past participle, past tense of **light**[1] 2 past participle, past tense of **light**[2]

lit. *abbr* 1 litre 2 literal 3 literally 4 literary 5 literature

litany /líttəni/ (*plural* **-nies**) *n* 1 a series of sung or spoken liturgical prayers or requests for the blessing of God, including invocations from a priest or minister and responses from a congregation 2 a long and repetitious list of things such as complaints or problems ○ *recited a litany of complaints about the system* [13C. Via Old French *letanie* < Greek *litaneia* 'prayer' < *litanos* 'entreating' < *litē* 'supplication'.]

litas /lée taass/ (*plural* **-tas**) *n* see table at **currency** [Late 20C. < Lithuanian.]

LitB = **LittB**

litchi *n* FOOD = **lychee**

lit. crit. *abbr* literary criticism

LitD, **LittD** EDUC = **LittD** [Shortening of Latin *Litterarum Doctor*]

lite /līt/ *adj* low in alcohol, calories, sugar, or fat (*in labelling or advertising foods and beverages*) [Mid-20C. Variant of LIGHT[2].]

-lite *suffix* mineral, rock, fossil ○ *halite* ○ *coprolite* [Via French < Greek *lithos* 'stone']

liter *n* US = **litre**

literacy /líttərəssi/ *n* 1 the ability to read and write at a conventionally accepted level 2 knowledge of or competence in a subject or area of activity ○ *computer literacy* ○ *emotional literacy*

literal /líttərəl/ *adj* 1 **FOLLOWING BASIC MEANING** adhering strictly and concisely to the basic meaning of an original word or text ○ *a literal reading of the story of Noah* 2 **WORD FOR WORD** exactly following the order or meaning of an original word or text 3 **USED TO EMPHASIZE TRUTH OF STATEMENT** used to emphasize that something is true ○ *That's the literal truth.* 4 **TAKING THINGS AT FACE VALUE** understanding words, behaviour, and situations in a simple way that ignores context or implications 5 **FACTUAL AND UNIMAGINATIVE** simple in an unimaginative way that sticks solely to the facts ○ *a literal account of the incident for the court* 6 **USING ALPHABETICAL LETTERS** involving or expressed by letters of the alphabet ■ *n* **PRINTING ERROR** a misprint, especially involving a single alphabetical letter [14C. Via Old French < Latin *literalis* < *littera* 'letter'.] —**literalness** *n*

literalism /líttərə lizəm/ *n* **1** strict adherence to the basic or primary meaning of a word or text **2** the realistic representation of something in art or literature —**literalist** *n* —**literalistic** /líttərə lístik/ *adj* —**literalistically** *adv*

literally /líttərəli/ *adv* **1** in a way based on the explicit meaning of a word or text **2** ⚠ used to emphasize another word or a phrase (*informal*) ○ *I was literally freezing.*

USAGE literally used for emphasis: In formal contexts, avoid using ***literally*** for emphasis in the sense *actually* or *really*, especially when combined with a colourful figure of speech: *The President is literally breathing fire.* Say instead *The President is breathing fire* or *The President is really livid.*

literary /líttərəri/ *adj* **1 RELATING TO LITERATURE** relating to literature, writing, or the study of literature **2 FORMALLY EXPRESSED** typical of literature rather than everyday speech **3 PROFESSIONALLY INVOLVED WITH LITERATURE** involved with literature or writing as a profession **4 KNOWLEDGEABLE ABOUT LITERATURE** well-read or knowledgeable about literature [Mid-17C. < Latin *literarius* < *littera* 'letter'.] —**literarily** *adv* —**literariness** *n*

literary agent *n* somebody whose job is to negotiate business contracts on behalf of an author

literary executor *n* a manager of literary property on behalf of an author's estate

literate /líttərət/ *adj* **1 ABLE TO READ AND WRITE** having the ability to read and write **2 KNOWLEDGEABLE** having a good understanding of a particular subject **3 WELL-EDUCATED AND WELL-READ** well-educated and cultured, especially with respect to literature or writing **4 SKILFULLY WRITTEN** showing skill in the techniques of writing ○ *a literate account of the voyage* ■ *n* **1 SOMEBODY CAPABLE OF READING AND WRITING** somebody who is able to read and write **2 SOMEBODY WITH EXTENSIVE EDUCATION** a well-educated, learned, or cultured person [15C. < Latin *litteratus* < *littera* 'letter'.] —**literately** *adv* —**literateness** *n*

literati /líttə ráa tee/ *npl* (*formal*) **1** intellectuals or the educated class **2** authors and other people closely or professionally involved with literature and the arts [Early 17C. Directly or via Italian < Latin *litterati* 'lettered people' < *littera* 'letter'.]

literation /líttə ráysh'n/ *n* the representation of sounds or words by means of alphabetical letters [Early 20C. < Latin *littera* 'letter'.]

literature /líttərəchər/ *n* **1 WRITTEN WORKS WITH ARTISTIC VALUE** written works such as fiction, poetry, drama, and criticism that are recognized as having important or permanent artistic value **2 BODY OF WRITTEN WORKS** the body of written works of a culture, language, people, or period of time ○ *Russian literature* **3 WRITINGS ON SPECIFIC SUBJECT** the body of published work concerned with a particular subject ○ *scientific literature* **4 PRINTED INFORMATION** printed matter that gives information, in the form of, e.g., brochures or leaflets **5 PRODUCTION OF LITERARY WORKS** the creation of literary work, especially as an art or occupation [14C. Via Old French < Latin *litteratura* < *litteratus* (see LITERATE).]

lith. *abbr* **1** lithograph **2** lithography

Lith. *abbr* **1** Lithuania **2** Lithuanian

lith- *prefix* = **litho-** (*before vowels*)

-lith *suffix* **1** mineral, rock, stone ○ *batholith* **2** stone structure or implement ○ *megalith* ○ *microlith* **3** calculus, concretion ○ *otolith* [Via modern Latin *-lithus* < Greek *lithos* 'stone' < ?]

litharge /líth aarj/ *n* CHEM = **lead monoxide** [14C. Via Old French *litarge* < Greek *litharguros* < *lithos* 'stone' + *arguros* 'silver'.]

lithe /līth/ (**lither, lithest**) *adj* able to move or bend the body lightly and gracefully ○ *a lithe gymnast* [Old English *līþe* 'gentle' < Indo-European, 'flexible'] —**lithely** *adv* —**litheness** *n*

Lithgow /líthgō/ town in SE New South Wales, Australia. Population: 11,441 (1996).

lithia /líthi ə/ *n* CHEM = **lithium oxide** [Early 19C. Alteration of *lithion* < Greek *lithos* 'stone'.]

lithiasis /li thī əssiss/ *n* the formation or presence of stones formed by mineral concretions in the body, e.g. in the kidney, gall bladder, pancreas, or salivary glands [Mid-17C. Via modern Latin < Greek, < *lithos* 'stone'.]

lithic[1] /líthik/ *adj* **1** consisting of stone **2** relating to undesirable mineral concretions in the body, e.g. kidney stones [Late 18C. < Greek *lithikos* < *lithos* 'stone'.]

lithic[2] /líthik/ *adj* relating to lithium [Early 19C. < LITHIUM.]

-lithic *suffix* of a particular stage in human beings' use of stone implements ○ *Neolithic* [< Greek *lithos* 'stone']

lithium /líthi əm/ *n* (*symbol* **Li**) a soft silver-white element that is the lightest metal known. Source: spodumene, lepidolite. Use: alloys, ceramics, batteries, in compounds as a medical treatment for bipolar disorder. [Early 19C. < LITHIA.]

lithium carbonate *n* Li_2CO_3 a white crystalline salt. Use: in ceramics and glass, treatment of bipolar disorder.

lithium fluoride *n* **LiF** a white, slightly water-soluble powder. Use: manufacture of ceramics.

lithium hydride *n* a white translucent powder or crystal. Use: organic synthesis, production of hydrogen.

lithium oxide *n* Li_2O a white alkaline solid that absorbs carbon dioxide and water vapour. Use: manufacture of ceramics and glass.

litho., lithog. *abbr* **1** lithograph **2** lithography

litho- *prefix* **1** stone ○ *lithosphere* **2** calculus, concretion ○ *lithotomy* [< Greek *lithos* 'stone' < ?]

lithography /li thóggrəfi/ *n* a printing process using a plate on which only the image to be printed takes up ink [Early 19C. < German *Lithographie* < Greek *lithos* 'stone' + *graphein* 'write'; because the plate was originally a porous stone.] —**lithograph** /líth ō graaf, -graf/ *n, vti* —**lithographer** *n* —**lithographic** /líthə gráffik/ *adj* —**lithographically** *adv*

lithoid /líth oyd/, **lithoidal** /li thóyd'l/ *adj* consisting of or resembling stone [Mid-19C. < Greek *lithoeidēs* < *lithos* 'stone'.]

lithology /li thólləji/ *n* **1** the scientific study of rocks **2** the physical characteristics of a rock or a rock formation —**lithological** /líthə lójjik'l/ *adj* —**lithologically** *adv* —**lithologist** *n*

lithophane /líthə fayn/ *n* a piece of thin translucent porcelain or china with an intaglio design

lithophyte /líthə fīt/ *n* **1** a plant that grows on rock and absorbs nutrients from the atmosphere **2** an organism such as a coral that is composed in part of stony material —**lithophytic** /líthə fíttik/ *adj*

lithopone /líthə pōn/ *n* a white pigment that is a mixture of barium sulphate and zinc sulphide and is used in making paints and linoleum [Late 19C. < Greek *litho-* 'stone' + *ponos* 'product'.]

lithosphere /líthə sfeer/ *n* the solid outer layer of the Earth above the asthenosphere, consisting of the crust and upper mantle —**lithospheric** /líthə sférrik/ *adj*

lithotomy /li thóttəmi/ (*plural* **-mies**) *n* the surgical removal of a stone from an organ or duct of the body, especially the urinary tract or bladder —**lithotomic** /líthə tómmik/ *adj* —**lithotomist** *n*

lithotripsy /líthō tripsi/ *n* the fragmentation of a stone in the urinary system or gall bladder, e.g. with ultrasound shock waves, so that the gravel can be passed naturally [Mid-19C. < LITHO- + Greek *tripsis* 'rubbing'.]

lithotripter /líthə triptər/ *n* a device that breaks up kidney stones using ultrasound shock waves [Early 19C. Alteration of *litho(n)triptor* < Greek *lithōn thruptika* 'capable of pulverizing stones' < *lithos* 'stone' + *thruptein* 'to crush'.]

Lithuania /líthyoo áyni ə/ republic in NE Europe, bordering the Baltic Sea. Capital: Vilnius. Population: 3,617,104 (1997). Area: 65,300 sq. km/25,200 sq. mi.

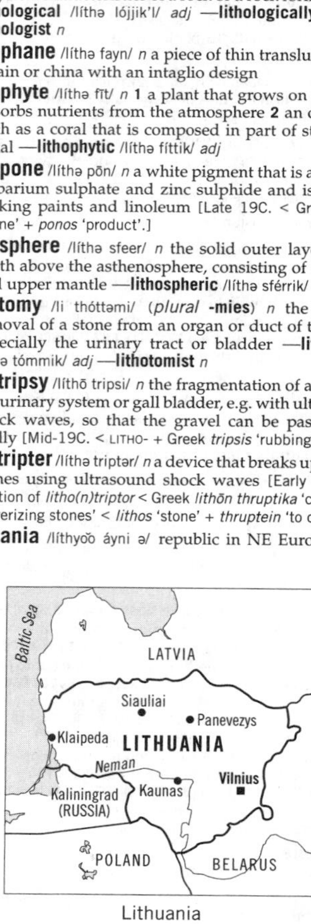

Lithuania

Lithuanian /líthyoo áyni ən/ *n* **1** somebody who comes from Lithuania **2** the official language of Lithuania, also spoken in W European Russia, belonging to the Balto-Slavonic branch of Indo-European. Native speakers: 4 million. —**Lithuanian** *adj*

litigant /líttigənt/ *n* somebody engaged in a lawsuit —**litigant** *adj*

litigate /lítti gayt/ (**-gates, -gating, -gated**) *vti* to contest or be involved in a lawsuit [Early 17C. < Latin *litigat-*, past participle of *litigare* < *lit-* 'lawsuit' + *agere* 'to drive'.] —**litigable** *adj* —**litigator** *n*

litigation /lítti gáysh'n/ *n* **1** the act or process of bringing or contesting a lawsuit ○ *The matter is in litigation.* **2** a lawsuit (*technical*)

litigious /li tíjjəss/ *adj* **1 INCLINED TO GO TO LAW** tending or wanting to take legal action ○ *a litigious person* **2 RELATING TO LEGAL ACTION** relating to litigation **3 QUARRELSOME** inclined to quarrel or argue (*formal*) [14C. < French *litigieux* < Latin *litigium* 'litigation' < *litigare* (see LITIGATE).] —**litigiously** *adv* —**litigiousness** *n*

litmus /lítməss/ *n* a powdery substance obtained from lichens. Use: indicator for acids or bases, turning red in acids and blue in bases. [14C. < Old Norse *litmosi* < *litr* 'dye' + *mosi* 'moss'.]

litmus paper *n* a strip of paper treated with litmus, used to find out if something is an acid or a base

litmus test *n* **1** a test in which litmus is used to find out if something is an acid or a base **2** a test in which a single factor determines the outcome ○ *The candidate's stance on free trade was a litmus test for the nomination.*

litotes /lítō teez, lī tōt eez/ (*plural* **-tes**) *n* a deliberate understatement, often expressed negatively, as in 'I am not unmindful of your devotion' [Late 16C. Via late Latin < Greek *litotēs* < *litos* 'simple'.]

~~**litrature**~~ incorrect spelling of **literature**

litre /leétər/ *n* a unit of volume equal to 1 cubic decimetre or 1.056 liquid quarts [Late 18C. Via French *litre* < Greek *litra*, unit of measure.]

LittB, LitB *abbr* **1** Bachelor of Letters **2** Bachelor of Literature [< Latin *Litterarum Baccalaureus*]

LittD, LitD *abbr* **1** Doctor of Letters **2** Doctor of Literature [< Latin *Litterarum Doctor*]

litter /líttər/ *n* **1 SCATTERED RUBBISH** pieces of rubbish that have been carelessly left on the ground, especially in a public place or outdoors **2 MESSY STATE OR PLACE** a large number of objects that have been scattered around untidily or a place that is in an untidy state ○ *I found her working away in the litter of her study.* **3 ANIMAL OFFSPRING** a group of young animals born at the same time from the same mother **4 BEDDING FOR ANIMALS** material such as hay or straw that is used as bedding for animals **5 MATERIAL FOR PET'S TOILET TRAY** a dry absorbent substance, often in the form of granules, that is spread in a shallow container where a pet, especially a cat, can urinate or defecate when indoors **6 GROUND SURFACE OF FOREST** the surface layer of a forest floor, consisting of partly decomposed leaves and twigs **7 STRETCHER WITH LONG SHAFTS** a piece of cloth stretched between two long poles on either side that is used to carry a sick person or a dead body (*dated*) **8 COUCH FOR CARRYING PASSENGER** a couch with poles on either side, used to transport a single passenger on people's shoulders or on animals ■ *v* **1** *vti* **MAKE PLACE UNTIDY** to make a place, especially a public place or the outdoors, untidy by leaving or scattering rubbish **2** *vt* **COVER PLACE WITH SCATTERED OBJECTS** to put a place in disorder by leaving scattered objects in it ○ *Toys littered the playroom floor.* **3** *vt* **FILL WITH THINGS** to fill something with or contain many examples of a particular thing ○ *an essay littered with spelling mistakes* **4** *vti* **HAVE YOUNG** to give birth to young (*refers to animals*) **5** *vt* **SUPPLY ANIMAL WITH BEDDING** to provide an animal with hay or straw for bedding [14C. Via Anglo-Norman *litere* < medieval Latin *lectaria* < Latin *lectus* 'bed'.] —**litterer** *n*

~~**litterature**~~ incorrect spelling of **literature**

litterbug /líttər bug/ *n* = **litter lout** (*informal disapproving*)

litter lout *n* somebody who leaves litter in public places or outdoors (*informal disapproving*) US term **litterbug**

littermate /líttər mayt/ *n* one of several animal young born or reared in the same litter

little /lítt'l/ (**-tler, -tlest**) CORE MEANING: an adjective meaning 'small' or 'young', or a grammatical word indicating that something exists in small quantities ○ (adj) *It was* *only a very little mistake!* ○ (adj) *He was helping the little boy put on his boots.* ○ (det) *There was a little food left.* ○ (det) *There was little chance of winning.*

1 *adj* **SMALL** small or of less than average size ○ *He gave her a little Christmas tree ornament.* **2** *adj* **YOUNG** young ○ *I met her when she was just a little girl.* **3** *adj* **YOUNGER** refers to a younger sister or brother ○ *My little sister is always causing problems.* **4** *adj* **SMALL AND PLEASANT** small in a pleasant or good-looking way ○ *a cute little button nose* ○ *one of his sweet little habits* **5** *adj* **SHORT** short or quick ○ *Wait a little while.* ○ *He turned and gave them a little nod.* **6** *adj* **TRIVIAL** of no importance ○ *It's the little things that count when you're sharing a house.* **7** *det, pron* **A SMALL AMOUNT** a small amount of something (*after 'a'*) ○ *We paid only a little for it.* ○ *A little of what you fancy does you good.* **8** *det, pron* **NOT MUCH** only a very small amount ○ *The cleanups had little or no effect on the environment.* ○ *She would eat very little.* ○ *Little of what was said meant much to me.* **9** *adv* **HARDLY** hardly or not at all ○ *Little did he know what was in store for him.* **10** *adv* **NOT OFTEN** on rare occasions ○ *We visit him very little these days.* [Old English *lȳtel* < Germanic, 'small'] —**littleness** *n* ◇ **little by little** gradually; by small degrees ○ *Little by little I grew too drowsy to think.* ◇ **no little** considerable ○ *They commenced eating with no little appetite.* ◇ **not a little** a lot ○ *I was shocked and not a little embarrassed.*

little auk *n* a small squat northern seabird of the auk family with a strong bill. Its dark-coloured throat and breast change to white in winter. *Alle alle.* US term **dovekie**

Little Barrier Island /lítt'l bárri ər-/ uninhabited island off the northeastern coast of the North Island, New Zealand. Area: 28 sq. km/11 sq. mi.

Little Bear *n* ASTRON = **Ursa Minor**

Little Bighorn /-bíg hawrn/ river in S Montana. Length: 145 km/90 mi.

Little Dipper *n US, Can* ASTRON = **Ursa Minor**

little end *n* the part of a connecting rod that attaches to the gudgeon pin in an internal-combustion engine or reciprocal pump

Little Englander *n* somebody who emphasizes the interests of the United Kingdom rather than taking an international perspective (*disapproving*)

little finger *n* the smallest finger of the human hand, located furthest from the thumb

little folk *npl* MYTHOL = **little people** *npl.*

little grebe *n* a small diving bird with brown plumage, the smallest European grebe. *Tachybaptus ruficollis.*

little green man *n* an imaginary person from outer space (*humorous*)

little hours, Little Hours *npl* the hours of prime, terce, sext, and nones in the divine office to be recited every day by members of Roman Catholic orders

Little Ice Age *n* a period of cold weather marked by growth in alpine glaciers that began 5,000 years ago and extended to as late as the 19th century in certain parts of the world

Little John *n* in English legend, a particularly tall and strong member of Robin Hood's band of men

Little League *n* a baseball league for boys and girls from 8 to 12 years old, divided into administrative bodies for the United States, Canada, South America, East Asia, and Europe —**Little Leaguer** *n*

little magazine *n* a literary magazine primarily made up of work by writers who have yet to become established, usually having a limited circulation and a small format

little man *n* **1** an average person, as opposed to an important or wealthy one **2** somebody who operates a small business or invests on a small scale

little office, Little Office *n* a Roman Catholic office similar to but shorter than a divine office, especially a liturgical service of psalms and prayers to the Virgin Mary

little owl *n* a small owl that eats insects and small rodents and has speckled brown feathers, a broad head, and a low forehead. Native to: Europe, Africa, Asia. Genus: *Athene noctua.*

little people *npl* tiny imaginary or mythological beings such as fairies, elves, and leprechauns

Little Richard /lítt'l ríchərd/ (*b.* 1935) US pianist and singer. Born **Richard Wayne Penniman**

Little Rock /-rók/ capital of Arkansas, in the central part of the state. Population: 175,303 (1998 estimate).

Little Russia former region that included Carpathian Ruthenia, E Poland, Ukraine, and the western shores of the Black Sea

little slam *n* the winning of 12 out of the 13 tricks in a deal in the game of bridge

little theater *n* **1** *US, Can* a small, usually noncommercial theatre that produces experimental drama **2** *US* a form of noncommercial drama emphasizing experimental work

little toe *n* the fifth and smallest toe of the human foot, located furthest from the big toe

little woman *n* an offensive term for a wife (*dated*)

Littlewood /lítt'l wòod/, **Joan** (*b.* 1914) British theatre director

littoral /líttərəl/ *adj* **1 ON OR NEAR A SHORE** on or near a shore, especially the zone between the high and low tide marks **2 SHORE-LIVING** living on or near a shore ■ *n* **SHORE** a shore or coastal region [Mid-17C. < Latin *littoralis* < *litor-* 'shore'.]

lit up *adj* drunk (*slang*)

liturgical /li túrjik'l/, **liturgic** /-jik/ *adj* **1** relating to liturgy **2** relating to religious worship or to a service of worship, especially Communion —**liturgically** *adv*

liturgics /li túrjiks/ *n* the study of public worship or liturgies (*+ singular verb*)

liturgiology /li túrji óllәji/ *n* = **liturgics** —**liturgiologist** *n*

liturgist /líttərjist/ *n* **1 STUDENT OF LITURGIES** somebody who studies or compiles liturgies **2 PRACTITIONER OF LITURGY** a person who performs the liturgy **3 SUPPORTER OF LITURGIES** a person who favours using liturgies —**liturgism** *n* —**liturgistic** /líttər jístik/ *adj*

liturgy /líttərji/ (*plural* **-gies**) *n* a form and arrangement of public worship laid down by a church or religion [Mid-16C. Via Old French *liturgie* < Greek *leitourgia* 'service, worship' < *leitourgos* 'public servant' < *leitos* 'public'.]

Liturgy /líttərji/ (*plural* **-gies**), **liturgy** (*plural* **-gies**) *n* the form of service used to celebrate Communion in a Christian denomination, especially the Eucharist in Eastern churches

Litvinov /lit véen of/, **Maksim** (1876–1951) Russian revolutionary and diplomat. Born **Meier Wallach**

Liu Shaoqi /lyóo shów chée/, **Liu Shao-ch'i** (1898–1969) Chinese political leader

livable /lívvəb'l/, **liveable** *adj* **1 COMFORTABLE** comfortable or suitable for living in ○ *a very livable flat* **2 WORTH LIVING** endurable and worthwhile ○ *It's very tense at home, but still livable.* **3 ENJOYABLE AS LIVING COMPANION** enjoyable to live with —**livability** /lívvə bílləti/ *n* —**livableness** *n*

live[1] /liv/ (**lives, living, lived**) *v* **1** *vi* **BE ALIVE** to be alive or have life **2** *vi* **STAY ALIVE** to remain alive or to continue living ○ *lived through a serious illness last year* **3** *vi* **MAKE A HOME** to reside in a particular place or way ○ *He lived in Bangkok for two years.* ○ *She lives alone.* **4** *vti* **LEAD CERTAIN TYPE OF EXISTENCE** to have a particular kind of life ○ *live comfortably* **5** *vi* **MAKE A LIVING** to earn or make a living ○ *She wants to be an actor but lives by waiting on tables.* **6** *vti* **FULLY ENJOY LIFE** to enjoy life to the fullest ○ *He really knows how to live.* **7** *vi* **CONTINUE** to persist or continue ○ *Her fame lives on.* **8** *vt* **EXPERIENCE** to experience or go through something ○ *earthquake survivors living a nightmare* **9** *vti* **MAKE LIFE CONFORM** to make your life conform to something such as a philosophy or religion ○ *lived her faith* ○ *lived by strict rules* **10** *vi* **BE KEPT SOMEWHERE** to be found or kept in a particular place (*informal*) ○ *The spare car keys live in this drawer.* [Old English *libban, lifian* < Indo-European, 'to stick'] ◇ **live and let live** to be tolerant of others ◇ **live it up** to live or celebrate in an extravagant way (*informal*)

live down *vt* to live in a blameless or commendable way long enough for something shameful to be forgotten

live in *vi* to live at your place of work

live off, live on *vt* to depend on somebody or something as a source of financial support or for a livelihood ○ *He lived off his parents.* ○ *They live on a small private income.*

live on *vt* **1** = **live off 2** to eat a certain type of food in order to survive or thrive ○ *The koala lives on eucalyptus leaves.*

live out *v* **1** *vt* **DO SOMETHING PREVIOUSLY IMAGINED** to do in reality what had previously only been imagined or fantasized about ○ *live out a dream* **2** *vt* **LIVE UNTIL END OF PERIOD** to spend the rest of your life or a period of time in a certain manner or place **3** *vi* **LIVE SOMEWHERE OTHER THAN WORKPLACE** to live away from the place where you work

live through *vt* to experience and survive something difficult or dangerous

live together *vi* to share the same home and have a sexual relationship without being married

live up to *vt* to meet somebody's expectations or desires or match somebody's good example

live with *vt* **1** to accept or tolerate something difficult or unpleasant ○ *The house is tiny, but we'll just have to live with it.* **2** to cope with or match somebody or something (*slang*)

live[2] /līv/ *adj* **1 LIVING** alive or living **2 BROADCAST AS IT HAPPENS** broadcast while an event is happening ○ *Tonight's show is live from Paris.* **3 IN PERSON** appearing or performing in front of an audience or in person, rather than recorded or filmed ○ *I'd rather dance to live music.* **4 RECORDED DURING PERFORMANCE** recorded while a performance is happening ○ *live footage of the concert* **5 RELEVANT TO CURRENT CONCERNS** relevant to current interests or concerns ○ *a live topic* **6 CONNECTED TO POWER SOURCE** connected to an electrical power source ○ *a live wire* **7 CHARGED WITH EXPLOSIVE** containing an explosive and able to be used ○ *live ammunition* **8 BURNING** burning or glowing ○ *live coals* **9 WITH LIVING BACTERIA** made using living bacteria ○ *live yoghurt cultures* **10 BRIGHT OR VIVID** bright or brilliant, especially in terms of colour **11 ACTIVE** describes a volcano that is still active **12 HIGHLY RESONANT** with highly resonant or reverberant acoustics **13 IN PLAY** in play (*informal*) **14 FOUND AS ORIGINAL ROCK** describes a rock or mineral that is found free and not mined or quarried ■ *adv* **1 IN PERSON** in front of an audience or in person ○ *performing live here tomorrow night* **2 BROADCAST WHILE EVENT HAPPENS** broadcast at exactly the same time as a performance or event happens ○ *a live transmission* [Mid-16C. Shortening of ALIVE.]

liveable *adj* = **livable**

live-bearer /līv-/ *n* a fish that gives birth to living young, rather than producing eggs —**live-bearing** *adj*

live birth /līv-/ *n* the birth of a living infant —**live-born** *adj*

lived-in /lívd-/ *adj* **1** with a comfortable but slightly worn or untidy look that it is consistent with actual or current occupation **2** showing the effects of life's experiences

livedo /li véedō/ (*plural* **-dos**) *n* a bluish-black patch of discoloured skin caused by the settling of blood, especially after death [< modern Latin, < Latin *livere* 'be bluish in color']

live-forever /lív-/ *n* **1** = **houseleek 2** = **orpine** [So called because it lives for a long time]

live-in /lív-/ *adj* **1** living in your place of employment ○ *a live-in nanny* **2** sharing a home with a sexual partner

livelihood /līvlihòod/ *n* work done to earn a living, or whatever provides a source of income [13C. Alteration of Old English *līflād* 'way of living' < *līf* 'life'.]

live load *n* the variable load or weight borne by a structure such as a bridge, in addition to its own weight

livelong[1] /lív long/ *adj* used to emphasize how long a period of time seems to last or how tedious it feels (*literary*) [14C. < LIEF; influenced by LIVE[1].]

livelong[2] /lív long/ *n* PLANTS = **orpine** [Late 16C. < LIVE[1] + LONG; from its longevity.]

lively /līvli/ (**-lier, -liest**) *adj* **1 FULL OF ENERGY** full of life and energy ○ *two lively children* **2 ANIMATED** animated, exciting, or intellectually stimulating ○ *A lively discussion ensued.* **3 ENTHUSIASTIC** active and enthusiastic ○ *Pat takes a lively interest in local politics.* **4 FULL OF MOVEMENT** full of activity or movement ○ *a lively dance* **5 VIVID** clear, distinct, and vivid ○ *possessed a lively recollection of the events of that summer* **6 BRILLIANT IN COLOUR** bright and colourful in a good-looking way **7 REFRESHING** stimulating or refreshing ○ *a lively little breeze* **8 SPRINGY** bouncy or springy ○ *a lively ball* **9 RESPONSIVE** very responsive to the helm (*refers to boats*) [Old English *līflīc* 'lifelike'] —**livelily** *adv* —**liveliness** *n* ◇ **look** *or* **step lively** to hurry up and get going

~~**livelyhood**~~ incorrect spelling of **livelihood**

liven /līv'n/ *vti* to become, or make somebody or something, lively or cheerful ○ *What can we do to liven up the party?* ○ *At the sound of its trainer's voice, the sick horse livened considerably.* [Early 18C. < LIFE.] —**livener** *n*

live oak *n* an evergreen oak with a short broad trunk, leathery leaves, and hard timber, often grown for shade.

Native to: SW North America, N South America. *Quercus virginianus*. [< LIVE²; from its being evergreen]

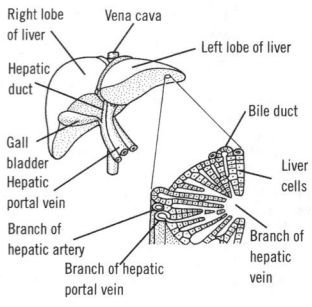

Liver

liver¹ /lívvər/ *n* **1 LARGE VITAL ORGAN** a glandular vascular organ in vertebrates that secretes bile, stores and filters blood, and takes part in many metabolic functions, e.g. the conversion of sugars into glycogen **2 INVERTEBRATE ORGAN** a glandular organ of invertebrates involved with digestion and metabolism **3 LIVER CONSIDERED AS FOOD** the liver of a mammal, fowl, or fish eaten as food or taken as medicine **4 DARK BROWN COLOUR** a dark brown colour tinged with red or grey [Old English *lifer* < Indo-European, 'to stick', later 'life'; once believed to make blood] —**liver** *adj*

liver² /lívvər/ *n* somebody who lives in a specified way ○ *a fast liver* [14C. < LIVE¹.]

liver-coloured *adj* of a reddish-brown colour resembling liver

liver fluke *n* a parasitic worm that infests the liver of mammals, including humans. *Fasciola hepatica*.

liverish /lívvərish/, **livery** /lívvəri/ *adj* **1 WITH LIVER DISORDER** affected by a liver disorder **2 IRRITABLE** bad-tempered or irritable **3 LIKE LIVER** resembling liver, especially in colour (*informal*) —**liverishness** *n*

Liverpool /lívvər pool/ *n* port in NW England, on the River Mersey. Population: 467,995 (1996 estimate).

Liverpool Plains rich agricultural region of E New South Wales, Australia

Liverpool Range mountain range in E New South Wales, Australia. Highest peak: Oxleys Peak 1,372 m/4,500 ft.

Liverpudlian /lívvər púddli ən/ *n* somebody who comes from Liverpool [Mid-19C. < alteration of LIVERPOOL, substituting *puddle* for *pool*.] —**Liverpudlian** *adj*

liver salts *n* a solution of mineral salts. Use: to relieve indigestion. (+ *singular or plural verb*)

liver sausage *n* a sausage containing cooked minced liver, usually eaten cold as a spread. US term **liverwurst**

liver spot *n* a usually dark brown patch of pigmentation on the skin, usually occurring later in life [< its colour]

liverwort /lívvər wurt/ *n* a small dense green plant that grows on moist surfaces and resembles moss. Class: Hepaticae. [Old English *liferwyrt*, translation of medieval Latin *hepatica*; from its lobed shape]

liverwurst /lívvər wurst/ *n* US ◊ **liver sausage** [Mid-19C. Partial translation of German *Leberwurst* 'liver sausage'.]

livery¹ /lívvəri/ (*plural* **-ies**) *n* **1 UNIFORM** an identifying uniform worn by members of a group or trade, especially men and boys who are servants of a household or feudal retainers **2 EMBLEM OR DESIGN** a distinctive colour scheme or design used by a company to make its property and vehicles easily identifiable **3 CHARACTERISTIC APPEARANCE** a distinctive colouring, marking, dress, or outward appearance (*literary*) **4 PROFESSIONAL CARE OF HORSES** the care, feeding, and stabling of horses for money **5 HIRING OF HORSES** the business of hiring out horses [14C. < Old French *livree* 'delivery' < Latin *liberare* 'liberate' < *liber* 'free'.] —**liveried** *adj*

livery² *adj* = liverish (*informal*)

livery company *n* any one of several chartered companies of the City of London entitled to wear an identifying uniform

liveryman /lívvəriman/ (*plural* **-men** /-mən/) *n* **1** a member of a livery company **2** somebody who owns or works in a livery stable

livery stable *n* **1** a stable where horses and carriages are kept for hire **2** a stable that accommodates and looks after horses for their owners

livestock /lív stok/ *n* animals raised for food or other products, or kept for use, especially farm animals such as meat and dairy cattle, pigs, and poultry

live trap /lív-/ *n* a trap designed to catch a wild animal without injuring it

live wire /lív-/ *n* **1** a wire connected to a source of voltage **2** an enthusiastic and energetic person (*informal*)

livid /lívvid/ *adj* **1 FURIOUS** very angry **2 WITH BLUISH BRUISED COLOUR** bluish or discoloured as a result of bruising **3 ASHEN** very pale, especially unnaturally **4 GREYISH** tinged with grey [15C. Directly or via Old French < Latin *lividus* < *livere* 'be bluish in colour'.] —**lividity** /li víddəti/ *n* —**lividly** *adv*

living /lívving/ *adj* **1 ALIVE** alive, not dead ○ *every living thing* **2 LIKE THE REAL THING** realistic or true to life ○ *a living likeness* **3 INTERESTING AND RELEVANT** interesting in a way that is relevant and useful ○ *make history a living subject* **4 SUITABLE FOR DOMESTIC LIFE** designed for living in, especially for social and recreational activities ○ *lots of living space in the home* **5 STILL USED** still used or in existence ○ *a living language* **6 NATURAL** in a natural condition or place ○ *living water* ■ *n* **1 MONEY OR MEANS OF EARNING** a means of earning money to live on, or the money somebody earns to live on ○ *What do you do for a living?* **2 MAINTENANCE OF WAY OF LIFE** a means of sustaining or maintaining a way of life ○ *improve your standard of living* **3 MANNER OF LIFE** quality of life or a particular way of life ○ *likes country living* ■ *npl* **THOSE WHO ARE ALIVE** people who are alive ■ *n CHR* = **benefice** *n*. 1

SYNONYMS *living, alive, animate, extant*

CORE MEANING: having life or existence

living not dead, or, of inanimate things, still in existence; **alive** not dead; **animate** physically alive, used especially to distinguish animals and plants from inanimate objects such as rocks, water, or buildings; **extant** still in existence.

---

living death *n* a life or period of time that is full of misery or pain

living fossil *n* an organism that is virtually unchanged from early geological time and belongs to a group whose other members are extinct. Gingko trees and coelacanths are living fossils.

living picture *n* = tableau vivant

living room *n* a room in a house where people usually relax or entertain guests. ◊ **sitting room**

living standard *n* = standard of living

Livingston /lívvingstən/ *town* in central Scotland. Population: 41,647 (1991).

Livingstone /lívvingstən/ *city* in S Zambia. Population: 82,218 (1990).

Livingstone, David (1813–73) British physician, missionary, and explorer

Livingstone daisy *n* a cultivated mesembryanthemum. Flowers: brightly coloured, like large daisies. *Mesembryanthemum criniflorum*. [Mid-20C. < ?]

living wage *n* a wage that will allow a worker to support a family in reasonable comfort

living will *n* a document, typically signed in advance while in good health, in which somebody declines to be kept alive artificially by life-support systems in the event of a terminal illness

Livonia /li vốni ə/ *ancient Baltic region*, comprising most of present-day Estonia and Latvia —**Livonian** *adj, n*

Livorno /li váwrnō/ *port* in NW Italy, on the Ligurian Sea. Population: 166,394 (1992). English **Leghorn**

Livy /lívvi/ (59 BC–AD 17) Roman historian

lixiviate /lik sívvi ayt/ (**-ates, -ating, -ated**) *vti* to leach (*archaic*) [Mid-17C. < late Latin *lixiviare* < *lixivium* (see LIXIVIUM).] —**lixivial** *adj* —**lixiviation** /lik sívvi áysh'n/ *n*

lixivium /lik sívvi əm/ (*plural* **-ums** or **-a** /-ivvi ə/) *n* a solution, e.g. lye, obtained by leaching [Mid-17C. < late Latin, < Latin *lixivius* 'made into ashes or lye' < *lix* 'lye'.]

lizard /lízzərd/ *n* **1 FOUR-LEGGED REPTILE** a reptile with a long scaly body, movable eyelids, a long tapering tail, and four legs, typically living in hot dry regions. Suborder: Sauria. **2 LARGE REPTILE RESEMBLING LIZARD** any large reptile with four legs and a tapering tail that resembles the lizard, e.g. the alligator, crocodile, or certain dinosaurs

3 LEATHER MADE FROM LIZARD SKIN leather made from the skin of a lizard [14C. Via Old French *lesard* < Latin *lacertus* 'lizard'.]

Lizard, The /lízzərd/ *peninsula* in SW England. Its tip, Lizard Head or Lizard Point, is the southernmost point in England.

lizard fish *n* a slender, large-mouthed, predatory sea fish with a head shaped like that of a lizard. Family: Synodontidae.

Lizard Island *island* off the coast of Queensland, Australia

LJ *abbr* Lord Justice

Ljubljana /lyoõ bli áänə/ *capital* of Slovenia, in the central part of the country. Population: 269,972 (1995 estimate).

⚡lk *abbr* Sri Lanka (*in Internet addresses*)

'll *after a pronoun* /l/; *after a vowel* /əl/; *after a consonant* /'l/ *contr* **1** will **2** shall

LL *abbr* **1** late Latin **2** Lord Lieutenant **3** Low Latin

ll. *abbr* lines

llama /láämə/ *n* **1** a domesticated long-haired South American mammal related to camels. Kept for: load-carrying, wool. *Llama glama*. **2** llama wool or cloth [Early 17C. Via Spanish < Quechua.]

Llandaff /lándəf, hlan dáf/ *suburb* of Cardiff, SE Wales

Llandrindod Wells /hlan drín dod wélz/ *town* in E Wales, known for its mineral springs. Population: 4,362 (1991).

Llandudno /hlan dúdnō/ *town* in N Wales. Population: 14,576 (1991).

Llanelli /hla néthli/ *port* in S Wales. Population: 44,953 (1991).

Llanfair /hlan vír/ *village* on Anglesey Island, NW Wales. Population: 3,101 (1991).

Llangefni /hlan gévni/ *town* on Anglesey Island, NW Wales. Population: 4,643 (1991).

Llangollen /hlan góthlən/ *town* in N Wales. Population: 3,267 (1991).

llano /láänō/ (*plural* **-nos**) *n* a large open grassy plain, especially in Latin America and the SW United States [Early 17C. Via Spanish < Latin *planus* 'flat'.]

LLB *abbr* Bachelor of Laws [Shortening of Latin *Legum Baccalaureus*]

LLD *abbr* Doctor of Laws [Shortening of Latin *Legum Doctor*]

Llewellyn /lə wéllin, hlə-/, **Richard** (1907–83) British author. Pseudonym of **Richard Doyle Vivian Llewellyn Lloyd**

Llewelyn ap Gruffudd /-ap gríffith, hlə-/ (*d.* 1282) prince of Gwynedd (1258–82)

Llewelyn ap Iorwerth /-ap yáwr wurth, hlə-/ (*d.* 1240) prince of Gwynedd. Known as **Llewelyn the Great**

Lleyn Peninsula /hlīn-/ *peninsula* in W Wales, between Cardigan Bay and Caernarvon Bay. Length: 45 km/28 mi.

LLM *abbr* Master of Laws [Shortening of Latin *Legum Magister*]

Lloyd /loyd/, **Clive** (*b.* 1944) West Indian cricketer

Lloyd, Harold (1893–1971) US comedian

Lloyd, Marie (1870–1922) British music-hall entertainer. Born **Matilda Alice Victoria Wood**

Lloyd George /lóyd jáwrj/, **David, 1st Earl of Dwyfor** (1863–1945) British statesman

Lloyd Webber /-wébbər/, **Andrew, Lord Lloyd Webber of Sydmonton** (*b.* 1948) British composer

lm *symbol* lumen

⚡LMC *abbr* lost my connection (*in e-mails*)

⚡LMK *abbr* let me know (*in e-mails*)

⚡LMKOWOTO *abbr* let me know one way or the other (*in e-mails*)

ln *symbol* natural logarithm

LNG *abbr* liquefied natural gas

lo /lō/ *interj* used to draw attention to something (*archaic or literary*) [Old English *lā*]

loach /lōch/ *n* a freshwater fish related to the carp, with a long slender body and barbels around its mouth. Native to: Europe, Asia. Family: Cobitidae. [14C. < Old French *loche*.]

⚡load /lōd/ *n* **1 SOMETHING CARRIED OR TRANSPORTED** something that is carried by an animal, person, or vehicle, especially something heavy or bulky **2 AMOUNT CARRIED IN**

ONE TRIP the amount of material, goods, or people that are carried in one journey (*often in combination*) ○ *delivered a boatload of passengers to the island* **3 WORK DEMANDED OF PERSON** the amount of work that a person or machine is required to do ○ *unhappy about his teaching load this term* **4 MENTAL BURDEN** something that makes somebody feel mentally weighed down, e.g. responsibility, worry, or guilt ○ *carrying around a load of guilt* **5 QUANTITY THAT MACHINE CAN COPE WITH** the amount that can be handled by a machine at one time, especially the amount of clothes that can be handled by a washing machine **6 SINGLE CHARGE FOR GUN** a single charge of ammunition for a firearm **7 AMOUNT OF DRAWN ELECTRICAL POWER** the amount of electrical power that is drawn from a line or source **8 DEVICE DRAWING ELECTRICAL POWER** any device to which electrical power is delivered **9 FORCE AND WEIGHT ON STRUCTURE** the total force and weight that a structure, e.g. a bridge, is designed to withstand **10 WORK REQUIRED OF MECHANICAL DEVICE** the work required of or placed on an engine or machine, measured in kilowatts or horsepower ■ **loads** *npl* **LARGE AMOUNT OR NUMBER** a large amount or a lot of (*informal*) ○ *We had loads of guests at the party.* ■ *adv* **loads VERY MUCH** very much or a great deal (*informal*) ○ *feeling loads better* ■ *v* **1** *vti* **PUT SOMETHING ON VEHICLE** to put cargo or passengers on a vehicle, ship, or aircraft or to have cargo or passengers put on ○ *The aircraft is now loading.* **2** *vt* **PUT SOMETHING ON PERSON OR ANIMAL** to put a load on an animal or give a load to a person so that it can be carried **3** *vt* **PUT DISK IN DRIVE ON COMPUTER** to put a disk or tape in a drive on a computer **4** *vti* **PUT ROUNDS IN GUN** to put ammunition into a firearm ○ *loaded the rifle* **5** *vt* **PUT PROGRAM IN COMPUTER** to transfer data or a program to the main memory of a computer **6** *vt* **PUT SOMETHING IN MACHINE** to put into a machine the items that it will work on, e.g. clothes for washing **7** *vti* **PUT SOMETHING IN CAMERA** to put a film, plate, or tape in a camera or to take in a film, plate, or tape **8** *vt* **WEIGHT ONE SIDE OF DICE** to weight one side of a dice or roulette wheel so that it has a bias towards certain numbers **9** *vt* **ADD EXTRA CHARGE TO INSURANCE PREMIUM** to add an extra charge to an insurance premium, e.g. because of an increased risk **10** *vt* **INCREASE ELECTRIC OUTPUT OF GENERATOR** to increase the output produced by or drawn from a circuit or generator **11** *vt* **INCREASE WORK REQUIRED OF ENGINE** to increase the work required from an engine or motor [Old English *lād* 'course, way' < Indo-European, 'go ahead'] ◇ **a load of** used to say emphatically that something is ridiculous or nonsensical (*informal*) ○ *a load of nonsense* ◇ **get a load of** to look at or listen to something or somebody (*informal*)

loaded /lṓdid/ *adj* **1 WITH FULL LOAD** carrying a full load **2 CONTAINING AMMUNITION** containing bullets or other ammunition and ready to fire **3 WITH HIDDEN IMPLICATION** with a hidden or secondary implication designed to trick somebody into making an admission or commitment ○ *That is a loaded question.* **4 RICH** extremely rich (*slang*) ○ *Her parents are loaded.* **5** *US* **DRUNK** very drunk (*slang*) **6** *US* **INTOXICATED BY DRUGS** under the influence of drugs (*slang*) **7 WEIGHTED UNFAIRLY** with one side weighted to prevent dice or a roulette wheel from operating randomly

Loader /lṓdər/, **Danyon Joseph** (*b.* 1975) New Zealand swimmer

load factor *n* **1** the payload of an aircraft for a particular flight, expressed as a percentage of the maximum allowable payload **2** an external load divided by the weight of an aircraft

loading /lṓding/ *n* **1 WEIGHT CARRIED** a load or weight carried **2 FILLER** material added to something to improve certain properties or add weight **3 ADDITIONAL INSURANCE PREMIUM** an additional insurance premium or higher rating incurred by items that are more valuable or at greater risk **4 ADDITION OF INDUCTANCE** the addition of inductance to a transmission line to improve its performance over a given frequency band **5** *Aus* **ADDITIONAL WAGE** a payment made to workers over and above the basic wage in recognition of special skills or unfavourable conditions such as overtime or weekend work

loading gauge *n* the height and width limits that apply to trains, including external loads, on particular railways

load line *n* NAUT = **Plimsoll line**

loadmaster /lṓd maastər/ *n* somebody who oversees the loading of cargo on a military or commercial transport aircraft

load shedding *n* a temporary reduction in a supply of electricity as a method of reducing the demand on the generator

loadstar *n* ASTRON = **lodestar**

loadstone *n* GEOL = **lodestone**

loaf[1] /lōf/ (*plural* **loaves** /lōvz/) *n* **1 QUANTITY OF BREAD** a quantity of bread, shaped and baked as a whole, to be cut into slices for eating **2 BLOCK OF FOOD SHAPED LIKE LOAF** a quantity of food baked in a loaf tin or shaped to form a rectangular block and baked (*in combination*) **3 BRAIN** common sense or intelligence (*slang*) ○ *Use your loaf!* [Old English *hlāf*]

loaf[2] /lōf/ *vi* to do very little and spend time in a lazy, rather wasteful way [Mid-19C. Probably back-formation < LOAFER.]

loafer /lṓfər/ *n* **1** a casual leather slip-on shoe **2** a lazy person who avoids work and wastes time [Mid-19C. < ?]

loaf sugar *n* sugar in the shape of a large solid cone, formed using 19th-century methods of processing and purifying using large clay moulds

loam /lōm/ *n* **1 FERTILE WORKABLE SOIL** an easily-worked fertile soil consisting of a mixture of clay, sand, and silt and sometimes also organic matter **2 CLAY AND SAND MIXED FOR BUILDING** a mixture of moist clay and sand used for making bricks and in plastering ■ *vt* **USE LOAM IN BUILDING JOB** to use loam in the process of covering, filling, or coating something [Old English *lām* 'clay, earth' < Indo-European, 'slippery'] —**loamy** *adj*

loan[1] /lōn/ *n* **1 MONEY LENT** an amount of money given to somebody on the condition that it will be paid back later **2 LENDING** the act of letting somebody use something temporarily **3** LING = **loanword** ■ *vt* ⚠ **LEND** to allow somebody to borrow something on the condition that it is returned ○ *Loan me five pounds, will you?* [12C. < Old Norse *lán*.] ◇ **on loan 1** being lent or borrowed **2** working at a temporary location because additional help or expertise is needed there

---

USAGE loan or **lend**? If you are letting somebody else temporarily use physical property or money of yours, it is quite acceptable to use the verb ***loan***, as in *I loaned him some lunch money.* This verb, however, can be used only with reference to the temporary lending of physical property or assets in a physical, nonfigurative transaction. If the context is not literal or physical, ***lend*** is the only choice: *The evidence lends credence to the witness's prior testimony. The subtle use of strings lends fluidity to the composition.*

---

loan[2] /lōn/ *n* **1** *Scotland* a rural pathway or grassy cattletrack **2** an open area used for milking cows [14C. Variant of LANE.]

loanback /lṓn bak/ *n* the opportunity for a person to borrow from his or her own pension fund

Loan Council *n* a federal body set up in Australia in 1924 to monitor borrowing by state governments

loan shark *n* a lender of money at unduly high rates of interest (*disapproving*)

loansharking /lṓn shaarking/ *n* the activity or business of lending money at excessively high rates of interest

loan translation *n* a word or expression that enters a language as a direct translation from another

loanword /lṓn wurd/, **loan word** *n* a word from one language that has become part of everyday usage in another, often with slight modification

loath /lōth/, **loth** *adj* unwilling or reluctant to do something [Old English *lāþ* 'loathsome']

SYNONYMS See ***unwilling***.

---

loathe /lōth/ (**loathes, loathing, loathed**) *vti* to dislike somebody or something intensely [Old English *lāþian* < Indo-European, 'despise'] —**loather** *n*

~~**loathesome**~~ incorrect spelling of **loathsome**

loathing /lṓthing/ *n* intense dislike of somebody or something —**loathingly** *adv*

SYNONYMS See ***dislike***.

---

loathsome /lṓthsəm/ *adj* arousing intense dislike and disgust —**loathsomely** *adv* —**loathsomeness** *n*

loaves plural of **loaf**[1]

lob /lob/ *v* (**lobs, lobbing, lobbed**) **1** *vti* **HIT BALL IN HIGH ARC** to hit or throw a ball in a high curving trajectory **2** *vt* **THROW CASUALLY** to throw something in a casual careless way **3** *vi* **MOVE SLOWLY** to move slowly or heavily ■ *n* **1 HIGH ARCHING SHOT** a ball hit or thrown in a high curving path **2 BALL OVER TENNIS PLAYER'S HEAD** a ball that travels over the head of a tennis player [Late 16C. Probably < Low German.] —**lobber** *n*

Lobachevsky /lóbbə chéfski/, **Nikolay Ivanovich** (1793–1856) Russian mathematician

lobar /lṓbər/ *adj* relating to or affecting a lobe, e.g. in the lungs

lobate /lṓ bayt/, **lobated** /lō báytid/ *adj* **1** having toes with rounded flaps on either side, as grebes have **2** having or resembling a lobe or lobes —**lobately** *adv*

lobby /lóbbi/ *n* (*plural* **-bies**) **1 ENTRANCE AREA IN PUBLIC BUILDING** a large entrance hall or foyer immediately inside the door of a hotel, theatre, or other public building **2 PUBLIC AREA IN LEGISLATIVE BUILDING** a public area in or near a legislative building where people can meet and petition their political representatives **3 VOTING CORRIDOR** either of the two rooms in Parliament where members of both houses of Parliament vote for or against bills and proposals **4 GROUP TRYING TO INFLUENCE POLICY** a group of campaigners and representatives of particular interests who try to influence political policy on a particular issue (+ *singular or plural verb*) ○ *the environmental lobby* ○ *a lobby group* **5 ATTEMPT TO INFLUENCE POLICY** a visit to a legislative building to petition political representatives, organized by a campaign group as a protest or in an attempt to influence policy ■ *v* (**-bies, -bying, -bied**) **1** *vti* **PETITION POLITICIANS OR INFLUENTIAL PEOPLE** to attempt to persuade a political representative or influential person to support or fight a particular cause **2** *vt* **CAMPAIGN ABOUT LEGISLATION** to campaign for or against a particular piece of legislation by attempting to influence politicians [Mid-16C. < medieval Latin *lobia* 'cloister, covered walk' < Germanic.] —**lobbyer** *n*

lobbyist /lóbbi ist/ *n* a person who is paid to lobby political representatives on an issue —**lobbyism** *n*

lobby system *n* the system of employing professional lobbyists to attempt to influence political policy

lobe /lōb/ *n* **1 EARLOBE** an earlobe **2 ROUNDED BODY PART** a rounded division or projection of an organ or part in the body, especially in the lungs, brain, or liver **3 ROUNDED PROJECTING PART** a rounded part that projects from the main body of something **4 ROUNDED PLANT PART** a rounded segment on a leaf that is not divided all the way to the midrib [15C. Via late Latin *lobus* < Greek *lobos*.] —**lobed** *adj*

lobectomy /lō béktəmi/ (*plural* **-mies**) *n* the surgical removal of a lobe, e.g. of the lungs, liver, or thyroid

lobefin /lṓbfin/ *n* ZOOL = **crossopterygian** —**lobefinned** *adj*

lobelia /lō beéli ə/ *n* a low-growing or trailing summer-flowering plant. Flowers: white to purple. Genus: *Lobelia*. [Mid-18C. After Matthias de *Lobel* (1538–1616), Flemish botanist.]

Lobito /loo beétoo/ city and port in W Angola. Population: 150,000 (1983).

Lobito Bay arm of the Atlantic Ocean off W Angola

loblolly boy /lób loli-/, **loblolly man** *n* in former times, a junior sailor acting as a medical assistant on board ship [< *loblolly* 'thick gruel', a shipboard remedy]

lobola /lō bṓlə/, **lobolo** /lō bṓlō/ *n* a payment, often in cattle, made by a groom's family to his bride's family before their wedding in some parts of S and E Africa [Mid-19C. < Bantu.]

lobopod /lṓbə pod/ *n* a soft-bodied invertebrate with legs, especially a tardigrade or onychophoran, regarded as a distant relative of modern arthropods. Subphylum: Lobopodia. [Mid-20C. < modern Latin *lobosus* 'having many lobes' + PODIUM.]

lobotomize /lə bóttə mīz/ (**-mizes, -mizing, -mized**), **lobotomise** (**-mises, -mising, -mised**) *vt* **1** to carry out a surgical operation in which nerves to the prefrontal lobe of the brain are severed **2** to make somebody feel sluggish, mentally numb, or lacking in energy or vitality (*informal*)

lobotomy /lə bóttəmi/ (*plural* **-mies**) *n* a prefrontal lobotomy [Mid-20C. < LOBE.]

lobscouse /lób skowss/ *n* a stew of meat and vegetables thickened with ship's biscuits, traditionally eaten by sailors [Early 18C. < ?]

lobster /lóbstər/ *n* **1 HARD-SHELLED SEA CREATURE** a hard-shelled sea crustacean with a pair of large pincers, five pairs of limbs, eyes on stalks, and long antennae. Family: Homaridae. **2 SPINY LOBSTER** a crustacean similar in appearance to the true lobster but without the two large pincers, especially the spiny lobster. Family: Palinuridae. 3 **LOBSTER'S FLESH AS FOOD** the flesh of a lobster used as food ■ *vi* **CATCH LOBSTERS** to catch lobsters using a boat and pot [Old English *loppestre* from ?]

lobsterman /lóbstərmən/ (*plural* **-men** /-mən/) *n* 1 a professional fisher of lobsters 2 a boat designed for catching lobsters

lobster pot *n* a trap in the form of a basket, used for catching lobsters

lobule /lóbbyool/ *n* 1 a small lobe 2 a section or division of a lobe [Late 17C. < LOBE.] —**lobular** *adj* —**lobularly** *adv* —**lobulate** *adj* —**lobulation** /lóbbyoo láysh'n/ *n* —**lobulose** *adj*

lobworm /lób wurm/ *n* 1 ZOOL = **lugworm** *n.* 1 2 a large earthworm used by anglers as bait [Mid-17C. < LOB 'something hanging'.]

local /lṓk'l/ *adj* 1 **IN NEARBY AREA** relating to, situated in, or providing a service for a particular area, especially the area near home or work ○ *the local school* 2 **TYPICAL OF PARTICULAR AREA** typical of, or only found in, a particular area ○ *the local dialect* 3 **NOT WIDESPREAD** not covering a wide area or the whole country ○ *There have been local outbreaks of the disease.* 4 **RELATING TO GOVERNMENTAL REGION** relating to a comparatively small region that controls some aspects of practical government such as housing or education ○ *local elections* 5 **AFFECTING SMALL PART** affecting only a specific part of a human's or animal's body ○ *local infection* 6 **STOPPING EVERYWHERE** stopping at all the stations or bus stops on a route ○ *local trains and buses* 7 **TO A PHONE NUMBER NEARBY** made to a phone number within a fairly small radius and therefore charged at a lower rate than long-distance calls ○ *a phone for local calls only* ■ *n* 1 **SOMEBODY WHO COMES FROM PARTICULAR AREA** a native or long-term resident of a place 2 **NEIGHBOURHOOD PUB** a pub close to where somebody lives that the person visits regularly (*informal*) ○ *I stopped at the local on the way home from work.* 3 **STOPPING TRAIN OR BUS** a train or bus that stops at all the stations or stops on the route 4 **LOCAL ANAESTHETIC** a local anaesthetic (*informal*) 5 *US, Can* **BRANCH OF ORGANIZATION** a branch or office, especially of a labour union, situated in and serving members or clients only in one locale [14C. Via French < late Latin *localis* < Latin *locus* 'place'.] —**locally** *adv* —**localness** *n*

local anaesthetic *n* a drug, usually given by injection, that eliminates pain, though not necessarily all sensation, in a particular area of the body without affecting consciousness

⚡**local area network** *n* a network of personal computers and peripheral devices linked by cable and able to share resources

local authority *n* the body that has political and administrative powers to control a particular city or region. US term **local government** *n.* 2

local colour *n* unusual or traditional features of a particular place that make it interesting

locale /lō kaál/ *n* the place in which something happens or in which the action in a book or film takes place [Late 18C. Alteration of French *local* 'local'.]

local examination *n* a UK examination, e.g. the GCSE, set by a national examination board but held at local schools and colleges around the country

local government *n* 1 the government of a town, city, or region at a local level by locally elected politicians ○ *worked in local government all his life* 2 *US* = **local authority**

localise *vti* = **localize**

localism /lṓkəlizəm/ *n* 1 a phrase, expression, or custom peculiar to the people in a particular area 2 interest in local matters and customs rather than in national or global issues, sometimes resulting in a limited perspective —**localist** *n*

locality /lō kálləti/ (*plural* **-ties**) *n* 1 **PARTICULAR PLACE** a particular place, district, or neighbourhood 2 **SETTING FOR EVENT** the place or setting where something happens 3 **SITUATION IN SPACE OR TIME** the fact of being situated at a particular point in space or time

localize /lṓkə līz/ (**-izes, -izing, -ized**), **localise** (**-ises, -ising, -ised**) *v* 1 *vti* **CONFINE OR BE CONFINED TO PLACE** to become confined to or restrict something to a particular area 2 *vt* **FIND LOCATION OF** to find the source or location of something 3 *vt* **DECENTRALIZE CONTROL OF** to transfer power or control from a central authority to local bodies —**localizable** *adj* —**localization** /lṓkə lī záysh'n/ *n*

local option *n* the power granted to a local government to decide whether to implement a particular policy, especially with regard to the sale of alcohol

Locarno /lo kaárnō/ town in S Switzerland. Population: 14,312 (1998).

locate /lō káyt/ (**-cates, -cating, -cated**) *v* 1 *vt* **FIND** to discover where something is 2 *vi* **ESTABLISH BUSINESS IN PLACE** to establish a residence or business in a particular place ○ *conveniently located for the airport* 3 *vt* **POSITION** to put something in a particular place [Early 16C. < Latin *locat-*, past participle of *locare* < *locus* 'place'.] —**locatable** *adj* —**locater** *n*

location /lō káysh'n/ *n* 1 **POSITION** the site or position of something 2 **FILM SETTING** a place away from a studio where scenes for a film are shot ○ *The film was shot on location in Scotland.* 3 **DISCOVERY** the discovery of something ○ *A metal detector is an essential aid in the location of buried treasure.* 4 **POSITIONING OF** the positioning or siting of something or somebody in a particular place 5 *Scotland* **HIRING SOMETHING OUT** a contractual state under Scots law in which somebody has agreed to hire out either an object or his or her services —**locational** *adj*

locative /lókətiv/ *adj* **INDICATING PLACE OR DIRECTION** with the grammatical ending or form that indicates place or direction ■ *n* 1 **GRAMMATICAL CASE** the grammatical case indicating place or direction 2 **WORD IN LOCATIVE CASE** a word or expression in the locative case [Early 19C. < LOCATE.]

locator /lō káytər/ *n US* 1 an establisher of the boundaries of a piece of land or a mining claim 2 a device that helps somebody locate something, such as a table or index

loc. cit., **in loc. cit.** *adv* in the place cited. Full form **loco citato**

loch /lokh, lok/ *n Scotland* 1 a lake 2 a narrow arm of the sea stretching inland [14C. < Scottish Gaelic.]

lochan /lókhən, lókən/ *n Scotland* a small lake or pool [Late 17C. < Scottish Gaelic, 'small loch'.]

Lochgilphead /lokh gílp hed/ town in west-central Scotland. Population: 2,521 (1991).

lochia /lóki ə/ *n* the normal vaginal discharge of cell debris and blood after childbirth [Late 17C. < Greek *lokhia* < *lokhos* 'childbirth'.] —**lochial** *adj*

Loch na Keal /lókh na keél/ sea loch on the island of Mull, Scotland, designated a National Scenic Area

Loch Rannoch and Glen Lyon /lokh ránnəkh ənd glen lī ən/ National Scenic Area in central Scotland

loci plural of **locus**

⚡**lock**[1] /lok/ *n* 1 **FASTENING MECHANISM** a mechanism used to fasten or secure a door, window, or lid, especially one operated by a key 2 **GATED SECTION OF CANAL** a short section of a canal or river with gates at each end and a mechanism for letting water in and out. Boats enter the lock and are raised or lowered as the water level is altered and then exit to a higher or lower section of the waterway. 3 **DEGREE OF WHEEL TURN** the degree to which the wheels of a vehicle pivot as the car turns 4 **WRESTLING HOLD** a wrestling hold in which a wrestler twists or puts pressure on part of the other wrestler's body 5 **GUN PART** the part of a gun that makes the charge explode 6 **BLOCKING DEVICE** a device, e.g. one operated by a password, that prevents an unauthorized person from using something 7 **PLAYER IN A RUGBY SCRUM** either of the two players in the second row in a rugby scrum 8 **AIRLOCK** an airlock ■ *v* 1 *vti* **FASTEN USING LOCK** to fasten something or become fastened using a lock 2 *vt* **PUT IN A SECURE PLACE** to put something into a safe place or container that can be locked ○ *Her diamonds are locked in a safe deposit box.* 3 *vt* **SECURE PLACE** to make a building or vehicle secure by locking the doors and windows 4 *vt* **PREVENT UNAUTHORIZED USE OF** to prevent something from being used by an unauthorized person, e.g. via software 5 *vti* **FIX OR BE FIXED IN PLACE** to become fixed in one position, or fix something in one position, so that it cannot move normally 6 *vt* **HOLD FIRMLY** to hold somebody tightly ○ *locked in a passionate embrace* 7 *vt* **TRAP IN A DIFFICULT SITUATION** to put somebody in a situation or conflict from which it is difficult to escape ○ *locked into a lengthy argument* 8 *vt* **PUT LOCKS ON WATERWAY** to put locks on a stretch of canal or river 9 *vi* **GO THROUGH CANAL LOCKS** to go through a series of locks on a boat, or take a boat through a series of locks 10 *vt* **SECURE TYPE IN PRESS** to secure metal type in a press 11 *vt* FIN = **lock up** *v.* 4 [Old English *loc*] —**lockable** *adj* ◇ **lock, stock, and barrel** completely

lock away *vt* = **lock up** *v.* 1, **lock up** *v.* 2

lock in *vt* to prevent somebody from leaving a room or building by locking the door

lock on *vti* to find a target and track it automatically, or to make a radar or missile find and track a target

lock out *vt* 1 to prevent somebody from entering a place by locking the door 2 to prevent workers from entering their workplace, usually as a strategy in an industrial dispute

lock up *v* 1 *vt* **IMPRISON** to put somebody into prison, a secure hospital, or other institution that deprives him or her of freedom 2 *vt* **STORE IN A SECURE PLACE** to put valuables in a secure locked place 3 *vti* **SECURE BUILDING** to make a building secure by locking all the doors and windows 4 *vt* **INVEST IN LONG-TERM PLAN** to put money into a form of savings or investment that does not allow easy access to the funds

lock[2] /lok/ *n* 1 **PIECE OF HAIR** a group of hairs that hang together, on somebody's head or cut off 2 **WISP OF FIBRE** a small bunch of wool, cotton, or other fibre ■ **locks** *npl* **HAIR** somebody's hair (*literary*) [Old English *locc*]

lockage /lókij/ *n* 1 **PASSAGE THROUGH LOCK** the passage of a boat through a canal or river lock 2 **FEE** a fee paid by a boat to pass through a lock 3 **LOCKS** a number of locks on a canal or river

Locke /lok/, **John** (1632–1704) English philosopher

locker /lókər/ *n* 1 **LOCKABLE COMPARTMENT** a small lockable cupboard or compartment where personal belongings can be left, e.g. at a swimming pool, gym, school, or workplace 2 **TRUNK** a trunk or low chest, used for storage 3 **SOMEBODY OR SOMETHING THAT LOCKS** a person who or device that locks something

Lockerbie /lókərbi/ town in SW Scotland. Population: 3,982 (1991).

locker room *n* a room containing lockers, where people change their clothes for sports or swimming

locker-room *adj* typical of or suitable only for a men's locker room ○ *telling locker-room jokes*

locket /lókit/ *n* a small decorative metal case with a hinged cover containing a picture or memento, worn on a neck chain or bracelet [14C. < Old French *locquet* 'small latch' < *loc* 'latch' < Germanic.]

lockfast /lók faast/ *adj Scotland* fastened with a lock and consequently attracting a harsher penalty if broken into

lock forward *n* RUGBY = **lock**[1] *n.* 7

lock-in *n* a session of after-hours drinking inside a pub (*informal*)

lockjaw /lók jaw/ *n* 1 = **trismus** 2 = **tetanus** *n.* 1

lockkeeper /lók keepər/ *n* somebody employed to look after or control a lock on a waterway and collect any fees payable

locknut /lók nut/ *n* 1 a second nut tightened on a first to prevent it from loosening 2 a nut designed to lock itself in place once tightened

lock-on *n* the point at which a radar or missile locates and starts to track a target

lockout /lók owt/ *n* the preventing of workers from entering their workplace, a tactic sometimes used by management in an industrial dispute

lockram /lókrəm/ *n* a coarse linen fabric [15C. < French *locrenan*, alteration of *Locronan*, village in Brittany.]

locksmith /lók smith/ *n* a maker, seller, installer, and repairer of locks and keys —**locksmithing** *n*

lockstep /lók step/ *n* 1 a form of military marching with soldiers close together and all moving forward with the same foot at the same time 2 *US* a process or routine that is standardized and inflexible ○ *'It's a lockstep process, and if at any point the virus makes a mistake, the host will almost certainly kill it'.* (Virginia Morell, *The Killer Cat Virus that Doesn't Kill Cats*, (*Discover Magazine*; *July 1995*)

lock stitch *n* the usual stitch made by a sewing machine, formed by the thread above the fabric interlocking with the bobbin thread

lockup /lók up/ *n* 1 **PLACE WITH PRISON CELLS** a small prison, a block of cells at a police station, or a similar place where prisoners are kept for a short time 2 **GARAGE** a garage, usually one of several grouped together, that can be rented (*often before nouns*) ○ *a lockup garage* 3 **SHOP** a small shop with no accommodation attached to it (*often before nouns*) ○ *a lockup shop* 4 **SECURING OF BUILDING** the securing of a building by locking it 5 **TIME FOR LOCKING BUILDING** the time at which a building is locked

loco[1] /lṓkō/ *n* a railway locomotive (*informal*) [Mid-19C. Shortening.]

loco[2] /lṓkō/ *adj* wildly irrational (*informal*) ■ *vt* to poison an animal with locoweed [Late 19C. < Spanish, 'irrational'.]

loco[3] /lṓkō/ *adj* indicating that the performer should return to playing notes in the original register, negating a previous direction that they should be played an octave higher [Early 19C. < Italian, 'at the place'.] —**loco** *adv*

loco citato /lṓkō si taátō/ *adv* full form of **loc. cit.** [< Latin, 'in the place cited']

loco disease *n* a disease of cattle, sheep, and horses in the W United States and Canada, caused by eating locoweed. It affects the animals' nervous systems, with symptoms of weakness, trembling, and inability to move.

locoman /lṓkōmən/ (*plural* **-men** /-mən/) *n* a train's engine driver or other engine crew (*informal*)

locomotion /lṓkə mṓsh'n/ *n* movement or the power to move from one place to another [Mid-17C. < Latin *loco* 'from a place' + MOTION.]

locomotive /lṓkə mṓtiv/ *n* **RAIL ENGINE** a railway engine ■ *adj* **1 MOVABLE** able to move about freely **2 RELATING TO LOCOMOTION** relating to, allowing, or aiding in the ability to move ○ *locomotive organs* [Early 17C. < modern Latin *locomotivus* < Latin *loco* 'from a place' + late Latin *motivus* 'moving' (< Latin *mot-*, past participle of *movere* 'to move').]

locomotor /lṓkə mṓtər/ *adj* relating to or aiding in locomotion ○ *locomotor hyperactivity* [Late 19C. < Latin *loco* 'from a place' + MOTOR.]

locomotor ataxia *n* MED = **tabes dorsalis**

locomotory /lṓkə mṓtəri/ *adj* able to move independently

locoweed /lṓkō weed/ *n* a perennial plant of the pea family, found in W North America. Animals that eat it can contract loco disease. Genera: *Oxytropis* and *Astragalus*. [Late 19C. < LOCO[2].]

locule /lókyool/, **loculus** /lókyŏŏləss/ (*plural* **-li** /-lī/) *n* a small cavity, chamber, or cell in a plant or animal [Late 19C. Via French < Latin *loculus* 'small place' < *locus* 'place'.] —**locular** *adj* —**loculate** *adj* —**loculation** /lókyŏŏ láysh'n/ *n*

locum /lṓkəm/, **locum tenens** /-ténnenz/ (*plural* **locum tenentes** /-te nén teez/) *n* somebody, especially a doctor or a member of the clergy, who stands in to do the job of another who is away or unwell [Mid-17C. < medieval Latin *locum tenens* 'somebody holding the place' < Latin *locus* 'place' + *tenere* 'to hold'.]

locus /lṓkəss/ (*plural* **-ci** /lṓ sī/) *n* **1 PLACE** a place where something happens **2 SET OF POINTS** a set of points, the positions of which satisfy a set of algebraic conditions **3 GENE POSITION** the position of a gene in a chromosome [Early 18C. < Latin, 'place' < ?]

locus classicus /-klássikəss/ (*plural* **loci classici** /lṓ sī klássi sī/) *n* a much-quoted passage from an authoritative or standard text [< Latin, 'classical place']

locust /lṓkəst/ *n* **1 SWARMING GRASSHOPPER** a grasshopper found in warm regions that often swarms and devours crops and vegetation. Family: Acrididae. **2 POD-BEARING TREE** a leguminous pod-bearing tree, such as the honey locust, swamp locust, and carob **3** TREES = **false acacia** **4 HARD WOOD** the hard yellowish wood of a locust tree [14C. Via French < Latin *locusta*.]

locution /lə kyṓosh'n/ *n* **1** a phrase or expression typically used by a group of people **2** the way in which somebody speaks [15C. Directly or via French < Latin *locut-*, past participle of *loqui* 'speak'.]

Lod /lod/ city in central Israel. Population: 45,500 (1992).

lode /lōd/ *n* **1** a deposit or vein of ore **2** a waterway that acts as a drain off the land in an area of fenland [Old English *lād* (see LOAD)]

loden /lṓd'n/ *n* **1** a thick waterproof woollen cloth. Use: coats, jackets. **2** the dark-green colour of loden cloth [Early 20C. < German.] —**loden** *adj*

lodestar /lṓd staar/, **loadstar** *n* **1** the North Star (**Polaris**), used for navigation or as a reference position in astronomy **2** something that somebody uses as a model or principle to guide behaviour (*literary*) [14C. < LODE 'course' + STAR.]

lodestone /lṓd stōn/, **loadstone** *n* **1** magnetite or a piece of magnetite with magnetic properties **2** somebody or something that attracts others like a magnet [Early 16C. < LODE 'leading'.]

lodge /loj/ *n* **1 SMALL GATEKEEPER'S HOUSE** a small house in the grounds of a large country house, usually near the main gate, traditionally occupied by a gatekeeper, gardener, or estate worker **2 COUNTRY BUILDING** a cabin or other building in the country providing temporary accommodation, e.g. as a holiday home or a temporary shelter for campers, walkers, skiers, or hunters **3 INN OR HOTEL** a large house or hotel **4 PORTER'S ROOM** a room or set of rooms at the entrance to a university college for use by the college porter or caretaker **5 BRANCH OF UNION OR SOCIETY** a local branch or chapter of a society such as the Freemasons, or an organization such as a trade union **6 MEETING HALL** a hall or other meeting place used by a branch of a society **7 NATIVE N AMERICAN DWELLING** a dwelling traditionally used by Native North American people, e.g. a wigwam, hogan, or longhouse **8 BEAVER'S DEN** the den of certain animals, especially the dome-shaped structure built by a beaver ■ *v* (**lodges, lodging, lodged**) **1** *vt* **REGISTER COMPLAINT OR APPEAL** to make a formal complaint, accusation, or appeal by handing the documents to the appropriate authority **2** *vt* **DEPOSIT SOMETHING IN SAFE PLACE** to put something somewhere or give it to somebody for safekeeping **3** *vti* **STICK OR GET STUCK** to become jammed or embedded somewhere, or to jam or embed something somewhere ○ *His head was lodged between the railings.* **4** *vi* **LIVE IN SOMEBODY'S HOUSE** to live in somebody's house, free or as a paying guest (*dated*) ○ *She is lodging with her sister.* **5** *vt* **PUT IN ACCOMMODATION** to place somebody in temporary accommodation ○ *They were evacuated and lodged in a nearby school overnight.* **6** *vt* **GIVE SOMEBODY POWER TO ACT** to invest somebody with the power or authority to do something ○ *powers that are lodged with the cabinet* **7** *vti* **BEAT CROPS FLAT** to flatten crops, or be flattened by the wind and rain [13C. < Old French *loge* 'hut' < Germanic, 'roof made of bark'.]

Lodge /loj/, **David John** (*b.* 1935) British novelist, critic, and scholar

Lodge, Henry Cabot (1850–1924) US politician

lodgement *n* = **lodgment**

lodgepole pine /lój pōl-/ *n* a pine with two types of cones, one of which releases seeds only after a forest fire. Native to: W North America. Genus: *Pinus contorta*. [< Native North Americans' use of the trunks as supports for lodges]

lodger /lójjər/ *n* a renter of a room in somebody else's house ○ *'...the small kitchen in which she cooked the food for her lodgers'* (Jack London, *The People of the Abyss*; 1905)

lodging /lójjing/ *n* somewhere to stay temporarily ○ *We asked where we could find lodging for the night.* ■ **lodgings** *npl* a room or rooms in a boarding house or private home available for rent (*dated*)

lodging house *n* a private home or boarding house offering accommodation for rent (*dated*)

lodgment /lójmənt/, **lodgement** *n* **1 PLACING OF SOMEBODY IN ACCOMMODATION** the accommodation of somebody in a particular place (*formal*) **2 PLACE TO STAY** a temporary place to stay (*formal*) **3 ACCUMULATION OR BLOCKAGE** a build-up of something, especially when this causes a blockage **4 FOOTHOLD IN ENEMY TERRITORY** a small area of land that has been captured and held on the edge of enemy territory

lodicule /lóddi kyool/ *n* any of the tiny scales at the base of the ovary of the flower of certain grasses [Mid-19C. < Latin *lodicula* 'small coverlet' < *lodix* 'blanket'.]

Lodz /wooch/, **Łódź** /wooj/ city in central Poland. Population: 825,600 (1995).

Loeb /lōb/, **Jacques** (1859–1924) German-born US physiologist

loess /lṓ ess, löss/ *n* a fine-grained yellowish-brown deposit of soil left by the wind [Mid-19C. < German *Löss* < Swiss German *lösch* 'loose'.]

Loewe /lō/, **Frederick** (1904–88) US composer

Loewi /lṓ i/, **Otto** (1873–1961) German pharmacologist

Lofoten Islands /lō fṓtən-/ group of rock islands off NW Norway, in the Norwegian Sea. Population: 26,241 (1970). Area: 4,044 sq. km/1,600 sq. mi.

loft /loft/ *n* **1 ROOF SPACE** the area between the ceiling of the top floor of a building and the roof (*often before nouns*) ○ *We've got so much junk in the loft!* ○ *loft conversions* ○ *loft ladder* **2 UPPER FLOOR OF BARN** the upper floor of a barn or stable, used for storing hay ○ *a hay loft* **3 GALLERY** a gallery or balcony, especially the gallery where the organ is situated in a church ○ *the organ loft* **4** *US* **UPPER FLOOR OF WAREHOUSE OR FACTORY** an upper floor of a commercial building such as a factory or warehouse, typically converted to residential or studio use **5 PIGEON COOP** a shelter in which domesticated pigeons are kept ○ *a pigeon loft* **6 SLANTING ANGLE ON GOLF CLUB** the angle of the face of a golf club designed to drive the ball high into the air **7 THICKNESS OF FABRIC** the thickness and fluffiness of fabric, especially as an indication of its warmth ■ *vt* **1 HIT BALL HIGH** to hit a ball in a high arching path in golf or cricket **2 KEEP IN LOFT** to store something in a loft [Pre-12C. < Old Norse *lopt* 'air, upstairs room'.]

lofty /lófti/ (**-ier, -iest**) *adj* **1 HAUGHTY** behaving in a falsely superior or haughty manner **2 EXALTED** exalted and refined **3 HIGH-RANKING** of the highest rank or status **4 VERY HIGH** very high or tall ○ *lofty peaks*

log[1] /log/ *n* **1 PIECE CUT FROM TREE** a section of the trunk or a thick branch of a tree that has been cut for fuel or building material **2 RECORD OF JOURNEY** a record of a journey made by a ship or aircraft, detailing all events, or the book in which it is kept **3 RECORD OF EVENTS** any detailed record of events **4 DEVICE FOR MEASURING SPEED** a float attached to a ship by a line, formerly used for measuring the ship's speed ■ *v* (**logs, logging, logged**) **1** *vt* **RECORD EVENT IN LOG** to record information or an event in a log ○ *The computer will log all these transactions automatically.* **2** *vti* **FELL TREES** to cut down the trees growing on a particular area of land **3** *vti* **CUT UP TREE FOR LOGS** to cut up a tree to produce logs for fuel or building **4** *vt* **TRAVEL PARTICULAR DISTANCE OR SPEED** to travel a particular distance, time, or speed that is then recorded in a log ○ *These checks are made routinely once the aircraft has logged 100,000 miles.* [14C. < ?] ◇ **sleep like a log** to sleep very soundly

ϟ **log in** *vti* COMPUT = **log on**

ϟ **log off, log out** *vi* to end a session on a computer by typing in the appropriate command

ϟ **log on, log in** *vti* to gain access to a computer system by entering a name and password or other appropriate commands

ϟ **log out** *vi* = **log off**

log[2] /log/ *n* a logarithm (*informal*) [Mid-17C. Shortening.]

Logan, Mount /lṓgən/ highest peak in Canada, in the St Elias Range in SW Yukon Territory. Height: 5,959 m/19,551 ft.

loganberry /lṓgənbəri/ (*plural* **-ries**) *n* **1** a prickly trailing hybrid plant that bears loganberries. Native to: W United States, NW Mexico. *Rubus ursinus loganobaccus*. **2** a purplish-red fruit similar to a large raspberry [Late 19C. After James H. *Logan* (1841–1928), US horticulturalist.]

logaoedic /lóggə éedik/ *adj* describes a poem or line of verse in which different metrical feet are mixed to give an effect like speech or prose [Mid-19C. Via late Latin < Greek *logaoidikos* < *logos* 'speech' + *aoidē* 'song'.]

logarithm /lóggə rithəm/ *n* the power to which a base must be raised to equal a given number. For example, the logarithm of 8 to the base 2 is 3, since $2^3 = 8$. [Early 17C. < modern Latin *logarithmus* < Greek *logos* (see LOGOS) + *arithmos* 'number'.] —**logarithmic** /lóggə ríthmik/ *adj* —**logarithmically** *adv*

logbook /lóg bŏŏk/ *n* **1** a book containing a record of a journey made by a ship or aircraft **2** a document issued formerly in the UK giving details of a vehicle and its owners [Late 17C. Because it recorded all *loggings*, measurements of the ship's speed.]

log cabin *n* **1** a simple house made with logs **2** a patchwork design formed from strips of fabric attached round each side of a central square

loge /lōzh/ *n* **1** *US* the area in a theatre at the front of the upper level **2** a small private enclosure or box in a theatre [Mid-18C. Via French < Old French (see LODGE).]

logger /lóggər/ *n US* a person or company in the business of harvesting trees for wood

loggerhead /lóggər hed/ *n* **1** ZOOL = **loggerhead turtle** **2** BIRDS = **loggerhead shrike** **3** a tool consisting of a ball or bulb on a long handle that can be heated and used to melt pitch **4** somebody perceived as unintelligent (*archaic*) [Late 16C. Probably < *logger* 'block for hobbling a horse' < LOG[1].] ◇ **at loggerheads** involved in a quarrel or feud

loggerhead shrike *n* a shrike with grey plumage, black and white wings and tail, a black facial mask, and a hooked beak. Native to: North America. *Lanius ludovicianus*.

loggerhead turtle *n* a large flesh-eating sea turtle that has a large head and rounded shell. *Caretta caretta*.

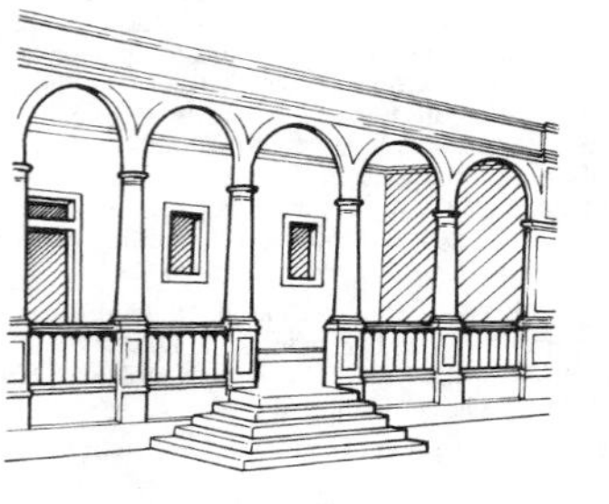

Loggia

loggia /lójji ə, lṓ-/ (*plural* **-gias** *or* **-gie** /-jay/) *n* **1** a covered open-sided walkway, often with arches, along one side of a building **2** a balcony in a theatre [Mid-18C. Via Italian < Old French *loge* (see LODGE).]

logging /lógging/ *n* the job of felling, trimming, and transporting trees

logia plural of **logion**

⚡**logic** /lójjik/ *n* **1 THEORY OF REASONING** the branch of philosophy that deals with the theory of deductive and inductive arguments and aims to distinguish good from bad reasoning **2 SYSTEM OF REASONING** any system of or an instance of reasoning and inference **3 SENSIBLE ARGUMENT AND THOUGHT** sensible rational thought and argument rather than ideas that are influenced by emotion or whim **4 REASONING OF PARTICULAR FIELD** the principles of reasoning relevant to a particular field **5 INESCAPABLE RELATIONSHIP AND PATTERN OF EVENTS** the relationship between certain events, situations, or objects, and the inevitable consequences of their interaction **6 CIRCUIT DESIGN** the circuit design and principles used by a computer in its operation [14C. Via French *logique* < Greek *logikē (tekhnē)* '(art) of reason' < *logos* 'word'.]

logical /lójjik'l/ *adj* **1 SENSIBLE AND BASED ON FACTS** based on facts, clear rational thought, and sensible reasoning **2 ABLE TO THINK RATIONALLY** able to think sensibly and come to a rational conclusion based on facts rather than emotion **3 OF PHILOSOPHICAL LOGIC** relating to philosophical logic —**logicality** /lójji kálləti/ *n* —**logicalness** *n*

logical atomism *n* the philosophical theories of Bertrand Russell and Ludwig Wittgenstein's early period that analyse a proposition in terms of its relation to certain philosophically basic propositions

logical consequence *n* a proposition that is implied by valid reasoning from true propositions

logical constant *n* a connective expression such as 'not', 'or', 'if ... then' or 'if and only if' that is used in formal logic

logically /lójjikli/ *adv* **1** in a rational well-reasoned way ○ *consider something logically* **2** using good or rational reasoning ○ *Your conclusion follows logically.*

logical positivism *n* a theory in linguistic philosophy that holds that in order for a sentence to be cognitively meaningful, it has to be verifiable

logical truth *n* a proposition that is necessarily true

⚡**logic bomb** *n* a piece of software that interferes with the proper working of the computer's operating system

⚡**logic circuit** *n* a computer switching circuit that performs operations on input signals

logician /lə jísh'n/ *n* somebody whose special training is in philosophical logic

logicism /lójjisizəm/ *n* the theory at the base of mathematics that mathematics is reducible to logic broadly construed to include set theory

⚡**login** *n* COMPUT = **logon**

logion /lóggi on/ (*plural* **-a** /-gi ə/) *n* a saying attributed to Jesus Christ that is not in the New Testament [Late 19C. < Greek, 'oracle' < *logos* 'word'.]

logistic[1] /lə jístik/ *adj* relating to an uninterpreted calculus or system of symbolic logic [Early 17C. < medieval Latin *logisticus* < Greek *logos* 'word, reckoning'.] —**logistician** /lójji stísh'n/ *n*

logistic[2] /lə jístik/, **logistical** /-tik'l/ *adj* **1** involving the planning and management of how things are moved, especially military forces or industrial goods **2** involving the planning and management of any complex task [Mid-20C. < French *logistique* (see LOGISTICS).] —**logistically** *adv*

logistics /lə jístiks/ *n* (+ *singular or plural verb*) **1 ORGANIZATION OF COMPLEX TASK** the planning and implementation of a complex task **2 MOVEMENT MANAGEMENT** the planning and control of the flow of goods and materials through an organization or manufacturing process **3 ORGANIZATION OF TROOP MOVEMENTS** the planning and organization of the movement of troops, their equipment, and supplies [Late 19C. < French *logistique* < *loger* 'to lodge' < Old French *loge* (see LODGE).]

logjam /lóg jam/ *n* **1** a situation where something is blocked or at a standstill and is unable to progress **2** *US, Can* a blockage caused by floating logs in a river

log line *n* a line from a ship trailing a floating log to determine the ship's speed

logo /lṓgō/ (*plural* **-gos**) *n* a design used by an organization on its letterhead, advertising material, and signs as an emblem by which the organization can easily be recognized [Mid-20C. Shortening of LOGOGRAM, LOGOTYPE.]

logo- *prefix* word, thought, speech ○ *logotype* [< Greek *logos* (see LOGOS)]

logogram /lóggə gram/, **logograph** /lóggə graf, -graf/ *n* a symbol that represents the meaning of a whole word or phrase —**logogrammatic** /lóggəgrə máttik/ *adj* —**logogrammatically** *adv*

logogriph /lóggō grif/ *n* a word puzzle, especially an anagram [Late 16C. < French *logogriphe* < Greek *logos* 'word' + *griphos* 'fishing-basket'.]

logomachy /lo gómməki/ (*plural* **-chies**) *n* an argument about the use or meaning of words [Mid-16C. < Greek *logomakhia* < *logomakhein* 'to fight with words' < *logos* 'word'.]

⚡**logon** /lóggon/, **login** /lóggin/ *n* **1** the act of logging on to a computer **2** a name and password or other appropriate commands used for logging on to a computer

logorrhoea /lóggə rée ə/ *n* excessive talkativeness, especially when the words are uncontrolled or incoherent, as is seen in certain psychiatric conditions —**logorrhoeic** *adj*

Logos /lóggoss/ *n* **1** Jesus Christ, so named in St John's Gospel, as the word of God, the personification of the wisdom of God and divine wisdom as the means for human salvation **2** the divine wisdom of the word of God [Late 16C. < Greek, 'word, reason'.]

logotype /lóggō tīp/ *n* **1** a single piece of type that has different unconnected characters on it **2** a logo

logroll /lóg rōl/ *vti US* to trade votes with political colleagues to support one another's interests [Mid-19C. Back-formation < LOGROLLING.]

logrolling /lóg rōling/ *n US* the striking of a deal between colleagues in a legislature whereby support is given to a piece of legislation on the understanding that the favour will be returned at a later date ○ *'The national interest will lose out to the logrolling trade-offs of Congressional business'.* (*Bush speeches in campaign '92*; 1992) [Early 19C. < the US custom of neighbours helping each other to clear land by rolling logs to burn them.]

-logue *suffix* speech ○ *monologue* [Via French < Greek *-logos* 'speaking' < *logos* 'word']

logwood /lóg wòod/ *n* a spiny leguminous tree whose wood yields a purplish-red dye. Native to: West Indies, Central America. *Haematoxylon campechianum*. [Late 16C. Because the tree's wood was imported in log form.]

-logy *suffix* **1** speech, expression ○ *haplology* **2** science, study ○ *musicology* [Directly and via French < Greek *-logia* < *logos* 'word, reason' and < *-logos* 'speaking' (see LOGOS)]

loin /loyn/ *n* **1 BACK BETWEEN RIBS AND HIPS** the area on each side of the backbone of a human or animal between the ribs and hips **2 MEAT CUT FROM LOIN OF ANIMAL** a prime cut of tender meat taken from the backbone and rib area of a pig, lamb, or calf and sold either as joints or cut into chops ■ **loins** *npl* **AREA BELOW WAIST** the hips and the front of the body below the waist, considered as the part of the body that should be covered and as the site of the sexual organs (*literary*) [14C. Via Old French *loigne* < Latin *lumbus*.] ◇ **gird (up) your loins** to prepare yourself to do something difficult and challenging

loincloth /lóyn kloth/ *n* a cloth covering the hips and the genital area

Loire /lwaar/ longest river in France, rising in the southeast and flowing to the Bay of Biscay in the northwest. Length: 1,020 km/634 mi.

loiter /lóytər/ *vi* **1** to stand around without any obvious purpose **2** to do something in a slow lazy way, often stopping to rest [15C. < ?] —**loiterer** *n*

Loki /lṓki/ *n* in Norse mythology, a handsome giant god who was the embodiment of evil

Lok Sabha /lṓk súbbə/ *n* the lower chamber of the Indian Parliament. ◊ **Rajya Sabha** [< Hindi, 'people's assembly']

⚡**LOL** *abbr* laughing out loud (*in e-mails*)

Lolita /lo léetə/ *n* a young teenage girl regarded or depicted as the object of sexual desire [Mid-20C. After the main character in *Lolita* (1958), novel by Vladimir Nabokov.]

loll /lol/ *vi* **1** to relax in a reclining or leaning position **2** to droop or hang down in a loose floppy way [14C. < ?]

Lolland /lólland/ island of SE Denmark, in the Baltic Sea. Population: 72,026 (1994). Area: 1,241 sq. km/479 sq. mi.

lollapalooza /lólləpə lóozə/, **lalapalooza** /lálləpə lóozə/, **lallapalooza** *n US* somebody or something that is wonderful or a particularly remarkable example of its kind (*informal*) [Early 20C. < ?]

lollipop /lólli pop/ *n* a large boiled sweet fixed onto a stick [Late 18C. < ?]

lollipop lady *n* a woman employed to stop traffic to allow schoolchildren to cross a road (*informal*) ◊ **school crossing patrol** [< the shape of the sign used]

lollipop man *n* a man employed to stop traffic to allow schoolchildren to cross a road (*informal*) ◊ **school crossing patrol** [< the shape of the sign used]

lollop /lólləp/ *vi* **1** to move along in a bouncy relaxed clumsy way **2** to loll or lounge about [Mid-18C. < LOLL, influenced by GALLOP.] —**lollopy** *adj*

lollo rosso /lóllō róssō/ *n* a variety of lettuce with curly red-tipped leaves

lolly /lólli/ (*plural* **-lies**) *n* **1 LOLLIPOP** a lollipop (*informal*) **2** *UK* **ICE LOLLY** an ice lolly (*informal*) **3 MONEY** money (*informal*) **4** *Aus* **SWEET** a sweet made from boiled sugar [Mid-19C. Shortening of LOLLIPOP.]

lollygag /lólli gag/ (**-gags, -gagging, -gagged**), **lallygag** /lálli gag/ *vi US* to have fun by wasting time in an idle way (*dated*) [Mid-19C. < ?] —**lollygagger** *n*

Loma /lṓmə/ *n* either of two languages belonging to the Niger-Congo family spoken in NW Liberia and Côte d'Ivoire. Native speakers: 100,000. [Mid-20C. < Loma.] —**Loma** *adj*

Lomax /lṓm aks/, **Alan** (*b.* 1915) US ethnomusicologist

Lomax, John (1867–1948) US ethnomusicologist

Lombard /lómbərd, -baard/ *n* **1** somebody who comes from Lombardy in Italy **2** a member of an ancient Germanic people who settled in N Italy during the 6th century AD

Lombardy /lómbərdi/ autonomous region in north-central Italy. Capital: Milan. Area: 23,859 sq. km/9,211 sq. mi. Population: 8,940,594 (1991). —**Lombardic** /lom báardik/ *adj*

Lombardy poplar *n* a variety of poplar that has upright branches and a tall narrow shape. *Populus nigra italica*.

Lombok /lómbok/ island of the Lesser Sunda Islands, S Indonesia. Population: 2,403,399 (1990). Area: 5,180 sq. km/2,000 sq. mi.

Lomé /lṓ may/ capital of Togo, on the Bight of Benin. Population: 450,000 (1990).

loment /lṓ ment/, **lomentum** /lō méntəm/ (*plural* **-menta**) *n* a pod or fruit of certain plants that splits and separates at maturity into one-seeded segments [Mid-19C. < Latin *lomentum* 'cosmetic made of bean-meal' < *lavare* 'to wash'.]

Lomond, Loch /lṓmənd/ largest lake in Scotland, in the west-central part of the country. Area: 70 sq. km/27 sq. mi.

London /lúndən/ **1** capital of the United Kingdom of Great Britain and Northern Ireland, in SE England. Population: 7,007,100 (1995). **2** city in SW Ontario, Canada. Population: 325,646 (1996). —**Londoner** *n*

London, Jack (1876–1916) US writer. Full name **John Griffith London**

Londonderry /lúndən deri/ **1** city in NW Northern Ireland. Population: 72,334 (1991). **2** former county of Northern Ireland

London pride *n* a variety of saxifrage with rosettes of fleshy leaves. Flowers: pale pink in clusters on long stems. *Saxifraga urbium.*

lone /lōn/ *adj* **1 SOLITARY** having no one else around **2 ONLY** only or sole **3 ISOLATED** situated in an isolated position **4 SINGLE** without a husband, wife, or partner **5 LONELY** lonely and having no companions (*literary*) [14C. Shortening of ALONE.]

lone hand *n* **1** a hand played in some card games without help from a partner, or a player without a partner **2** a person who lives or works alone

lonely /lṓnli/ (**-lier, -liest**) *adj* **1 FEELING ALONE** having or causing a feeling of being alone and sad **2 ISOLATED** isolated and rarely visited **3 LACKING SUPPORT** lacking companionship, aid, or encouragement **4 SOLITARY** having no one or nothing else around (*literary*) —**loneliness** *n*

lonely hearts *adj* relating to people who are looking for a partner for a romantic relationship

~~lonelyness~~ incorrect spelling of **loneliness**

lone pair *n* a pair of unshared electrons in a molecule that are not involved in bonding in that molecule

loner /lṓnər/ *n* a person who prefers to work or be alone

lonesome /lṓnssəm/ *adj US* **1 SAD FROM BEING ALONE** feeling sad, or causing a feeling of sadness, because of being alone **2 DESOLATE** isolated from human habitation **3 ALONE** having no one or nothing else around —**lonesomely** *adv* —**lonesomeness** *n*

lone wolf *n* a person who prefers to work or be alone

long[1] /long/ *adj* **1 EXTENDING CONSIDERABLE DISTANCE** extending a relatively great length or height **2 GOING ON FOR LENGTHY PERIOD** lasting for an extended period of time **3 HAVING MANY ITEMS** containing a relatively large number of parts or individual items **4 OF SPECIFIED LENGTH** of a specified length, height, total, number, or duration ○ *a book 300 pages long* **5 LONGER THAN IT IS WIDE** with a greater length than width ○ *Look in the long box, not the square one.* **6 BEYOND WHAT IS WANTED** extending in time or space beyond what is considered normal, reasonable, or desirable **7 MORE DISTANT OR LENGTHY** the more or most distant or lengthy of two or more things ○ *the long way home* **8 ABLE TO REACH CONSIDERABLE DISTANCE** capable of reaching or travelling far ○ *to have a long reach* **9 SEEMING TO LAST FOREVER** appearing to be or take more time than is really the case ○ *a long hour waiting* **10 GOING FAR BACK IN TIME** extending back in time ○ *a long memory* **11 CONTAINING MUCH LIQUID** containing a large quantity of liquid to drink, especially of a thirst-quenching kind ○ *a long cold drink on a hot day* **12 EXTENSIVE** exhaustive and critical ○ *Take a good long look at yourself.* **13 RISKY** with an uncertain outcome **14 HAVING PLENTY OF** possessing enough or more than enough of something (*informal*) ○ *a politician who is long on rhetoric* **15 HOLDING STOCK IN ANTICIPATION OF RISE** describes shares and other securities or commodities that are held with the expectation that prices will rise **16 DRAWN OUT IN PRONUNCIATION** describes a speech sound that is relatively drawn out **17 DESCENDED FROM LONG VOWEL** describes an English vowel sound that is historically descended from vowels that were drawn out in pronunciation, e.g. the ones in English 'beet' and 'bite' **18 ACCENTED** describes a syllable in accentual verse that is stressed **19 OF GREATER METRICAL DURATION** describes a syllable in quantitative verse that is the one of the two types that is of greater duration ■ *adv* **1 FOR LONG TIME** for or during a lengthy period of time ○ *Have you been here long?* **2 FAR** at or to a great distance ○ *hit the ball long* **3 FOR CERTAIN TIME** for or during a particular length of time ○ *work all day long* **4 AT ANOTHER TIME** at a time much later or earlier than the time specified ○ *long after he left* **5 IN LONG STOCK POSITION** in a long position in securities or commodities ■ *n* **1 A LONG TIME** a lengthy period of time ○ *Will you be visiting for long?* **2 LONG SOUND** a long syllable or sound **3 SIZE FOR TALL PEOPLE** a garment or garment size designed for somebody tall ■ **longs** *npl* **1 LONG TROUSERS** trousers with full-length legs (*informal*) **2 LONG-DATED GILT-EDGED SECURITIES** gilt-edged securities with more than 15 years to run before redemption **3 SECURITIES HELD UNTIL PRICES RISE** securities or commodities that are held with the expectation that prices will rise [Old English, < Germanic] —**longness** *n* ◇ **as** *or* **so long as 1** during the time that **2** because of the fact that **3** on the condition that ◇ **before long** before much time passes ◇ **long since** a long time ago ◇ **no longer** until the present but not for any further time ◇ **not long for** something with little time remaining for something ◇ **so long** good-bye (*informal*) ◇ **the long and the short of it** the basic idea or facts

long[2] /long/ *vi* to have a strong desire or yearning for somebody or something, especially somebody or something unattainable or not within immediate reach ○ *She longed for a bit of excitement in her life.* [Old English *langian* < Germanic]

SYNONYMS See ***want.***

Long /long/, **Richard** (*b.* 1945) British artist

long. *abbr* longitude

long-ago *adj* relating to or in the distant past ○ *long-ago civilizations*

longan /lóngən/, **lungan** /lúngən/ *n* **1** an evergreen tree that produces longans. Flowers: small, yellowish-white. Native to: tropical and subtropical Asia. *Euphoria longan.* **2** a small juicy fruit with a yellowish-brown exterior, white juicy flesh, and a large black seed. Use: Chinese health food, cooked with herbal medicine. [Mid-18C. < Chinese *lóngyan* 'dragon's eye'.]

long-awaited *adj* hoped for and expected for a considerable time

Long Beach 1 city in SW California. Population: 430,905 (1998 estimate). **2** city in SE New York State, on an island off S Long Island. Population: 34,244 (1998 estimate).

longboat /lóng bōt/ *n* **1** the longest boat, usually a seaworthy rowing boat, carried on board a sailing ship, especially a merchant ship **2** = **longship**

long bone *n* any long cylindrical limb bone in vertebrates that contains marrow and ends in an enlarged head that unites to form a joint with another bone

longbow /lóngbō/ *n* a large powerful hand-drawn bow made from a long piece of slightly curved wood and a bowstring, used, especially in medieval England, for hunting and in warfare —**longbowman** *n*

longcase clock /lóng kayss-/ *n* FURNITURE = **grandfather clock**

long-chain *adj* describes a molecule or substance that has a relatively long chain of atoms, especially carbon atoms

long-dated *adj* describes a gilt-edged security that has more than 15 years to run before redemption

long-day *adj* requiring long periods of daylight, usually more than 12 hours, followed by short nights in order to mature and flower

long-distance *adj* **1 FOR LONG WAY** travelling or extending a relatively long way **2 BETWEEN DISTANT PHONES** relating to or providing telephone service between places that are far apart **3 BETWEEN DISTANT PLACES** occurring between places that are far apart ○ *a long-distance romance* ■ *adv* **USING LONG-DISTANCE LINE** using a long-distance telephone line

long division *n* a method or instance of dividing one number by another in which each step is written out in full

long dozen *n* a set of 13 items

long-drawn-out *adj* going on for an undesirably long period of time

longe *n, vt* = **lunge**[2]

long-eared owl *n* a medium-sized owl with distinctive pointed ear tufts that lives in coniferous forests. Native to: Europe, Asia, North America. *Asio otus.*

Long Eaton /-éet'n/ town in central England. Population: 44,826 (1991).

longeron /lónjərən/ *n* a main structural component of an aeroplane's fuselage that runs from one end of the aeroplane to the other [Early 20C. < French, 'beam' < Latin *longus* 'long'.]

long-established *adj* having been in existence for a long time in a position of general respect or widespread success

longevity /lon jévvəti/ (*plural* **-ties**) *n* **1 LONG LIFE** long duration of life **2 DURATION OF LIFE** the length of a person's or animal's life **3 CAREER SPAN** the length of somebody's employment or career [Early 17C. < late Latin *longaevitas* < Latin *longaevus* 'of a long age' < *aevum* 'age'.] —**longevous** *adj*

long face *n* a facial expression showing unhappiness, disappointment, or seriousness —**long-faced** *adj*

Longfellow /lóng fel ō/, **Henry Wadsworth** (1807–82) US poet

long finger *n Ireland* a state of being postponed for a long time (*informal*)

Longford /lóngfərd/ county in Leinster Province, central Republic of Ireland. Area: 1,044 sq. km/403 sq. mi.

Longford, Francis Aungier Pakenham, 7th Earl (*b.* 1908) British politician

Longford, Raymond Hollis (1878–1959) Australian actor and director

longhair /lóng hair/ *n* **1** *US* **SOMEBODY DEDICATED TO ARTS AND MUSIC** somebody dedicated to the arts and especially to classical music (*informal*) **2 CAT WITH LONG FUR** a domestic cat with long fur **3** *US* **LONGHAIRED MAN** somebody with long hair, especially a hippie man (*dated informal disapproving*) —**longhaired** *adj*

longhand /lóng hand/ *n* words and letters written by hand in full, rather than in shorthand

long haul *n* (*informal*) **1** *US* **LENGTHY PERIOD** a long period of time **2 LOT OF WORK** a long-lasting job or ordeal **3 LONG DISTANCE** an extensive distance

long-haul *adj* relating to travel or transportation over long distances

long-headed /-héddid/ *adj* perceptive and wise (*archaic or literary*) [< the belief that a long head indicated wisdom]

long hop *n* a short delivery in cricket that is very easy to hit

longhorn /lóng hawrn/ (*plural* **-horns** *or* **-horn**) *n* **1** a red or variegated cow with long horns, belonging to a breed of beef cattle of Spanish origin that was once very common in the SW United States **2** a cow belonging to a breed that has long horns

long-horned beetle *n US* INSECTS = **longicorn**

long house *n* **1** *US, Can* a long bark-covered communal dwelling place built by some Native North American peoples, especially the Iroquois **2** a communal dwelling housing entire extended families and found, e.g. in Borneo or Sarawak

long hundredweight *n* MEASURE = **hundredweight** *n.* **1**

longicorn /lónji kawrn/ *n* a beetle with long antennae, long legs, and a narrow, often brightly coloured body. The larvae of many species are wood borers. Family: Cerambycidae. US term **long-horned beetle** ■ *adj* having long antennae [Mid-19C. < modern Latin *Longicornia* 'long-horned ones' < Latin *cornu* 'horn'.]

longing /lónging/ *n* a persistent and strong desire, usually for somebody or something unattainable or not within immediate reach ■ *adj* expressing yearning or desire —**longingly** *adv*

Long Island island in SE New York State. Queens and Brooklyn, two boroughs of New York City, are situated at its western end. Population: 6,861,474 (1990). Area: 4,463 sq. km/1,723 sq. mi.

Long Island Sound inlet of the Atlantic Ocean between N Long Island, New York, and S Connecticut. Area: 3,364 sq. km/1,299 sq. mi.

longitude /lónji tyood, lónggi-/ *n* **1** the angular distance east or west of the prime meridian that stretches from the North Pole to the South Pole and passes through Greenwich, England. Longitude is measured in degrees, minutes, and seconds. **2** a region near a particular longitude [14C. < Latin *longitudo* 'length' < *longus* 'long'.]

longitudinal /lónji tyóodin'l, lónggi-/ *adj* **1 GOING FROM TOP TO BOTTOM** extending from the top to the bottom of something **2 OVER TIME** relating to development over a period of time **3 OF LONGITUDE** relating to longitude or length —**longitudinally** *adv*

longitudinal wave *n* a wave, e.g. a sound wave, that is propagated in the same direction in which the particles of the medium vibrate

long jenny *n* a shot in billiards in which the ball goes into a far pocket after striking another ball [< JENNY 'losing hazard with the object ball near a cushion']

long johns /-jonz/ *npl* underpants with full-length legs, or one-piece underwear covering the torso, arms, and legs [< the name *John*]

long jump *n* a field event in which competitors jump for distance, usually from a running start into a sand pit

long-lasting *adj* continuing for a long time

longleaf pine /lóng leef-/ *n* a pine tree with long needles, orange-brown bark, and dense resinous wood. Native to: SE United States. *Pinus palustris.*

long lease *n* in England and Wales, a lease for a period of more than 21 years on a house that is the occupants' main residence

long leg *n* a position in cricket on the leg side behind the batsman's wicket and close to the boundary, or a fielder occupying this position

long-legged /-legd, -léggid/ *adj* **1** with long legs **2** capable of running quickly

long-life *adj* specially treated to last for a long time ○ *long-life milk*

long-lived *adj* living, lasting, or enduring for a long time

long-lost *adj* not seen for a long period of time (*humorous*)

long measure *n* **1** MEASURE = **linear measure** **2** LITERAT = **long metre**

long metre *n* a four-line stanza in which the second and fourth lines always rhyme and the first and third sometimes rhyme

Longo /lóng ō/, **Robert** (*b.* 1953) US painter, sculptor, filmmaker, and performance artist

long-off *n* a position in cricket on the off side, behind the bowler and close to the boundary, or a fielder occupying this position

long-on *n* a position in cricket on the leg side, behind the bowler and close to the boundary, or a fielder occupying this position

long pig *n* human flesh as eaten by cannibals [Translation of a Polynesian name]

long-playing record *n* full form of **LP**

long-range *adj* **1 EXTENDING WELL INTO THE FUTURE** extending a long time into the future **2 TRAVELLING LONG DISTANCES** able to travel long distances **3 ABLE TO HIT DISTANT TARGET** relating to weapons that are capable of hitting a target a considerable distance away

Longreach /lòng réech/ town in central Queensland, Australia. Population: 3,766 (1996).

longship /lóng ship/ *n* a narrow wooden ship with oars and a large square sail used by the Vikings

longshore /lóng shawr/ *adj* living, working, or situated on the coast [Early 19C. Shortening of ALONGSHORE.]

longshoreman /lóng shawrmən/ (*plural* **-men** /-mən/) *n US* SHIPPING = **docker**

long shot *n* **1 SOMEBODY OR SOMETHING UNLIKELY TO WIN** somebody or something that is unlikely to win a race or competition **2 BET UNLIKELY TO WIN** a bet on somebody or something that is unlikely to win a race or competition **3 VENTURE UNLIKELY TO SUCCEED** a venture, guess, or possibility that has little chance of success, although, if successful, it would be very profitable or rewarding **4 CAMERA SHOT OF DISTANT OBJECT** a camera shot taken some distance from the object or scene [Originally 'shot fired at a distance'] ◇ **(not) by a long shot** (not) in any way at all (*informal*)

long-sighted *adj* **1** able to see distant objects more easily than near objects, which can be seen clearly only by strongly focusing the eyes. US term **farsighted** *adj.* **2** **2** taking future problems or needs into consideration —**long-sightedly** *adv* —**long-sightedness** *n*

Longs Peak /lóngz-/ mountain in N Colorado. Height: 4,345 m/14,255 ft.

longspur /lóng spur/ (*plural* **-spurs** *or* **-spur**) *n* a bunting with brownish plumage and long-clawed hind toes. Native to: N United States, Canada, the Arctic. Genera: *Calcarius* and *Rhyncophanes.*

long-standing *adj* having existed or been going on for a long period of time

long-suffering *adj* patient and enduring in the face of suffering or difficulty ■ *n* patience and endurance in the face of suffering or difficulty —**long-sufferingly** *adv*

long suit *n* **1** the suit to which the majority of cards in a player's hand belong **2** somebody's strongest quality or talent (*informal*)

long-tailed duck *n* a long-tailed duck with a black back and wings, a white breast, and a brown-and-white head. Native to: Arctic seas. *Clangula hyemalis.* US term **oldsquaw**

long-tailed tit *n* a small black, white, and pink tit with a distinctive call. Native to: Europe, Asia. *Aegithalos caudatus.*

long term *n* the period of time continuing from now long into the future

long-term *adj* **1 IN FUTURE** relating to or affecting a time long into the future **2 WITH LONGER ACCOUNTING PERIOD** with or relating to an accounting period of longer than one year **3 MATURING IN NUMBER OF YEARS** maturing only after a long time, usually a number of years **4 LONG-LASTING** continuing for a long period of time

longtime /lóng tīm/ *adj* having continued in existence for a long period of time

long tom *n* **1 LONG-BARRELLED CANNON USED BY NAVY** a swivelling cannon with a long barrel, used in the past by the navy **2 LONG-RANGE CANNON USED BY ARMY** a long-range cannon used by the army **3 AUTOMATIC ANTIAIRCRAFT GUN** a large-calibre automatic antiaircraft gun (*slang*)

long ton *n* MEASURE = **ton**[1] *n.* **2**

Longueuil /lóng gayl, loN göyi/ city in S Quebec Province, Canada, on the St Lawrence River. Population: 127,977 (1996).

longueur /long gúr/ *n* a period of boredom, e.g. a boring passage in a book or a boring scene in a dramatic work [Late 18C. < French, 'length' < *long* 'long' < Latin *longus.*]

long vacation, long vac *n* a period of roughly three months in the summer when law courts and universities are closed

long view *n* the consideration of how events or circumstances are likely to develop in the long term

long wave *n* **1** a radio wave with a wavelength of 1,000m or more (*hyphenated when used before a noun*) **2** the broadcasting or receiving of radio waves of 1,000 metres or more in length (*hyphenated before nouns*)

longways /lóng wayz/ *adj, adv* = **lengthways**

long-winded /-wíndid/ *adj* **1** tediously wordy in speech or writing **2** capable of doing physical exercise for a relatively long period of time without getting short of breath —**long-windedly** *adv* —**long-windedness** *n*

SYNONYMS See ***wordy.***

longwise /lóng wīz/ *adj, adv US, Can* = **lengthways**

Longyearbyen /lóng yeer byen/ town on Spitsbergen Island, N Norway

loo[1] /loo/ (*plural* **loos**) *n* a lavatory or toilet (*informal*) [Mid-20C. < ?]

loo[2] /loo/ (*plural* **loos**) *n* **1** a gambling card game in which players place the money they are betting in a pool **2** a bet placed in the pool in a game of loo [Late 17C. < French *lantur(e)lu*, refrain of a song.]

loofah /lóofə/ *n* **1** a sponge made from the dried fibrous interior of an oblong fruit of a tropical gourd **2** a tropical vine of the gourd family that bears the large oblong fruits from which loofah sponges are made. Genus: *Luffa.* [Late 19C. < Arabic *lūfa.*]

look /lŏŏk/ *v* **1** *vti* **DIRECT EYES** to turn the eyes towards or on something **2** *vi* **USE EYES TO SEARCH** to use the eyes to examine, watch, or find somebody or something ○ *We looked everywhere.* **3** *vi* **SEEM AS SPECIFIED** to appear in a specified way ○ *He looks tired.* **4** ⚠ *vi* **CONSIDER** to direct the attention towards something in order to consider it ○ *Let's look at the entire situation.* **5** *vt* **FIT SOMETHING BY APPEARANCE** to have an appearance that is in accordance with something ○ *He looks his age.* **6** *vi* **USE EYES IN SPECIFIED WAY** to use the eyes in a specified way ○ *He looked intently at the ball.* **7** *vi* **FACE SPECIFIED WAY** to face a specified direction or have a specified view ○ *The room looks over the lake* **8** *vt* **EXPRESS** to communicate something by an expression ○ *She looked her anger at all of us.* **9** *vi* **PAY ATTENTION** used to tell somebody to pay attention or see something ○ *Look, why don't we split the difference?* ○ *Look! There he goes!* ■ *n* **1 ACT OR INSTANCE OF LOOKING** an act or instance of looking, e.g. to examine, watch, or find something ○ *Take a look at this.* **2 WAY SOMEBODY OR SOMETHING APPEARS** an impression conveyed by a manner or quality ○ *He has the look of someone enjoying himself.* **3 EXPRESSION** a facial expression that communicates something ○ *a meaningful look* **4 FASHION** an appearance, style, or fashion, especially of dress or hairstyle ■ **looks** *npl* **OUTWARD APPEARANCE** somebody's outward physical appearance, especially if it is pleasing ○ *good looks* [Old English *lōcian* < Germanic]

USAGE look at: Though often used orally and in informal writing, as in *Informed sources tell us that the High Court is going to look at the case*, some people object to this wording as vague and unacceptably casual when used in formal settings. Choose a more precise word such as *examine, study, investigate, analyse*, or *scrutinize*, depending on your intended meaning.

look after *vt* to care for or be responsible for somebody or something

look ahead *vi* to think about or plan for the future

look back *vi* **1** to think about the past or past experiences **2** to visit again later on (*informal*)

look down on, look down upon *vt* to regard or treat somebody or something as inferior or with contempt

look for *vt* **1** to try to find somebody or something **2** to hope for or anticipate something ○ *We're looking for a successful year.*

look forward to *vt* to anticipate a future event with excitement or pleasure

look in *vi* to pay a short visit (*informal*)

look into *vt* to carry out a careful investigation of something such as a possibility, problem, or crime

look on *v* **1** *vi* to be a spectator or witness **2** **look on, look upon** *vt* to regard somebody or something in a particular way

look out *v* **1** *vi* to take care to avoid danger **2** *vt* to search for and find something among a number of things, especially personal belongings

look out for *vt* **1** to watch for somebody or something to appear (*informal*) **2** to take particular care of somebody or something

look over *vt* **1** to inspect a property by visiting it and walking round it **2** to inspect or examine somebody or something either quickly or carefully

look through *vt* to fail to acknowledge somebody's presence, either intentionally or unintentionally

look to *vt* **1** to hope or expect that somebody or something will do or provide something **2** to want or hope to do something (*informal*) ○ *if you're looking to upgrade your computer*

look up *v* **1** *vt* **SEARCH FOR IN REFERENCE BOOK** to search for information, e.g. by consulting a reference book **2** *vi* **IMPROVE** to become better **3** *vt* **VISIT** to locate somebody, especially for a visit

look upon *vt* = **look on** *v.* **2**

look up to *vt* to have respect and admiration for somebody

lookalike /lóokə līk/ *n* somebody or something that looks like somebody or something else (*informal*)

looker /lóokər/ *n* **1** a watcher, observer, or spectator **2** a good-looking person, especially a girl or woman (*informal; sometimes offensive*)

looker-on (*plural* **lookers-on**) *n* = **onlooker**

look-in *n* (*informal*) **1** an opportunity to participate in something or be considered for something **2** a visit of short duration

looking glass *n* a mirror (*archaic*)

looking-glass *adj* characterized by the complete reversal of everything normal (*dated*) [< *Through the Looking Glass* (1871) by Lewis Carroll]

lookout /lóok owt/ *n* **1 CAREFUL WATCH** an act of watching carefully for somebody or something **2 SOMEBODY WATCHING FOR DANGER** a person who watches carefully for signs of attack or danger **3 PLACE GIVING GOOD VIEW** a place or structure that affords a good view for observation **4 PROBLEM** a problem or concern (*informal*) ○ *That's your lookout.* **5 PROSPECT** a prospect or outlook (*informal*)

lookover /lóokōvər/ *n* a quick inspection or examination of something

look-see *n* a brief look or inspection (*informal*)

ϟ **look-up** *n* a computer procedure in which a term or value is matched against a table of stored information

loom[1] /loom/ *vi* **1 BE SEEN AS LARGE SHAPE** to appear as a large or indistinct, and sometimes menacing, shape **2 BE ABOUT TO HAPPEN** to be imminent, often in a threatening way ■ *n* **APPEARANCE OF SOMETHING LARGE** an appearance of something, usually something large and threatening (*literary*) [Mid-16C. < ?]

loom[2] /loom/ *n* **1** a hand-operated or machine-operated device for weaving thread or yarn into cloth **2** the middle part of an oar between the blade and the handle [Old English *gelōma* 'tool']

loon[1] /loon/ *n US* BIRDS = **diver** *n.* **2** [Mid-17C. < ?]

loon^{2} /loon/ *n* **1** an offensive term that deliberately insults somebody's mental condition or intelligence (*slang insult*) **2** *Scotland* a boy or young man [15C. < ?]

looney *adj, n* = **loony**

loony /lóoni/, **looney, luny** *adj* (**-ier, -iest**) **1 OFFENSIVE TERM** an offensive term meaning irrational **2 SILLY** silly, thoughtless, or strange (*informal*) ○ *loony ideas* ■ *n* (*plural* **-ies;** *plural* **-eys**) **1 OFFENSIVE TERM** an offensive term that deliberately insults somebody's intelligence and ability to act rationally (*slang insult*) **2 SOMEBODY SILLY** a person who behaves eccentrically or thoughtlessly (*informal; often considered offensive*) [Mid-19C. Shortening and alteration of LUNATIC.] —**loonily** *adv* —**looniness** *n*

loony bin *n* an offensive term for a hospital for people who have psychiatric disorders (*informal*)

loop^{1} /loop/ *n* **1 CIRCLE OR OVAL MADE WITH STRING** a circular or oval shape formed by a line or something such as a piece of string that curves back over itself **2 CIRCLE OR OVAL FOR FASTENING OR HOLDING** something that has a closed or nearly closed circular or oval shape and is often used to carry or fasten something **3 CONTRACEPTIVE DEVICE** a contraceptive device in the shape of a loop of plastic or metal that is placed in a woman's womb **4 CLOSED CIRCUIT** a closed electric circuit **5 SET OF COMMANDS IN COMPUTER PROGRAM** a set of instructions in a computer program that is repeated a certain number of times or until a certain objective has been achieved **6 FLIGHT MANOEUVRE** a flight manoeuvre in which a plane flies vertically in a circle ○ *to loop the loop* **7 RAILWAY BRANCH LINE** a railway branch line that leaves the main line and then joins it again later on **8 PIECE OF FILM OR TAPE** a piece of film or tape joined at both ends to allow repeated use of images or sound, especially in dubbing procedures **9** ELEC = **loop aerial 10 COMMON FINGERPRINT PATTERN** the commonest pattern of a human fingerprint formed by U-shaped ridges **11 SKATING JUMP AND TURN** a jump in which a skater takes off from the outer back edge of a blade, turns in the air, and lands again on the same blade's outer back edge ■ *v* **1** *vti* **MAKE LOOP** to form or make something form the shape of a loop **2** *vt* to fasten, join, or arrange something using a loop **3** *vi* **CURVE** to move in a curved path [14C. < ?] ◇ **in** *or* **out of the loop** *US* belonging *or* not belonging to the people who are decision-makers or are fully informed (*informal*) ◇ **knock** *or* **throw somebody for a loop** *US* to surprise, shock, or upset somebody (*informal*)

loop^{2} /loop/ *n* a loophole in a wall (*archaic*) [14C. < ?]

loop aerial *n* an aerial consisting of a coil of wire wound around a frame

looped /loopt/ *adj* **1** formed into a circular or oval shape **2** *US* drunk (*dated slang*)

looper /lóopər/ *n* **1** a maker or cause of loops **2** INSECTS = **measuring worm**

loophole /lóop hōl/ *n* **1 GAP IN LAW** a small mistake or omission in a rule or law that allows it to be circumvented **2 SLIT IN WALL** a small slit or hole in a wall, especially one in a fortified wall for firing guns or other weapons through ■ *vt* (**-holes, -holing, -holed**) **MAKE LOOPHOLES IN WALL** to provide a wall with loopholes [< LOOP^{2}]

loop knot *n* a square knot that leaves a single loop hanging free

loop line *n* RAIL = **loop**^{1} *n.* 7

loop of Henle /-hénli/ *n* the part of the kidney tubule in birds and mammals that forms a loop between the cortex and medulla [Mid-19C. After Friedrich Gustav *Henle* (1801–85), German anatomist and pathologist.]

loopy /lóopi/ (**-ier, -iest**) *adj* **1** having or consisting of loops **2** an offensive term meaning considered to be irrational

Loos /looss/, **Adolf** (1870–1933) Austrian architect

loose /looss/ *adj* (**looser, loosest**) **1 NOT FIRMLY FIXED** not firmly fastened or fixed in place ○ *a loose floorboard* **2 SLACK** not fastened or pulled tight ○ *a loose knot* **3 NOT TIGHT-FITTING** not fitting closely and thus baggy **4 FREE** allowed to move around freely without any restraint **5 NOT PACKAGED** not enclosed in a container or bound together ○ *loose tea* **6 NOT FIRMLY PACKED** not compact or dense in texture or arrangement ○ *loose soil* **7 IMPRECISE** not exact, literal, or precise ○ *a loose translation* **8 FLEXIBLE** not strictly controlled or organized ○ *a loose arrangement* **9 AVAILABLE** not earmarked for a particular purpose ○ *loose funds* **10 RELAXED** relaxed or free from tension (*informal*) **11 IRRESPONSIBLE** lacking restraint or a sense of propriety ○ *loose talk* **12 PROMISCUOUS** having many sexual partners **13 TOO FLUID** too fluid in consistency ○ *loose stools* **14 ACCOMPANIED BY PHLEGM** accompanied by the production of phlegm or mucus ○ *a loose cough* ■ *adv* (**looser, loosest**) **FREELY** freely or without restraint ■ *v* (**looses, loosing, loosed**) **1** *vt* **SET FREE** to release a person or animal from restraint or confinement **2** *vt* **UNTIE KNOT** to undo, untie, or unfasten something **3** *vti* **MAKE SOMETHING LESS TIGHT** to make something less tight, or be made less tight **4** *vt* **RELEASE FROM OBLIGATION** to release somebody from an obligation or pressure **5** *vti* **FIRE MISSILE** to fire an arrow, bullet, or other missile ■ *n* **RUGBY PLAY** any part of the play in rugby other than scrums, line-outs, or set kicks [12C. < Old Norse *lauss* < Germanic.] —**loosely** *adv* —**looseness** *n* ◇ **be on the loose 1** to be free from confinement, e.g. a prison **2** to be free from responsibilities and having a good time (*informal*) ◇ **let loose** *US* to obtain relief from tension or worry (*informal*)

USAGE loose or **lose**? ***Lose*** is a verb only, meaning variously 'to mislay', 'fail to win', etc. as in *Don't lose* [not *loose*] *possession of the ball, or you'll lose the game.* ***Loose*** is an adjective, adverb, and verb. As an adjective it means variously 'not firmly fixed', 'not restrained', etc. as in *loose* [not *lose*] *floorboards; loose* [not *lose*] *dogs running through the alley.* As an adverb it means 'freely', as in *dogs running loose* [not *lose*]. As a verb it means variously 'to untie', 'to make less tight', and 'to fire a projectile', as in *loosed her grip; loosed the taut anchor line; loosed a volley of arrows.*

loosebox /lóoss boks/ *n* an enclosed compartment forming part of a stable in which the horse is not tied up but can move around. US term **box stall**

loose cannon *n* an unpredictable or indiscreet person, often causing trouble for colleagues or associates (*slang*)

loose cover *n* a fitted cover for a sofa or an armchair that can be easily removed. US term **slipcover**

loose end *n* a small part of something, e.g. a project or a story, that has not been completed or fully explained (*informal; often plural*) [Referring to the end of a string left hanging] ◇ **at a loose end** restless and a little bored because of having nothing to do (*informal*)

loose-fitting *adj* large, baggy, and not fitting closely to the body ○ *loose-fitting trousers*

loose head *n* the rugby prop forward occupying the position to the left of the hooker in the front row of a scrum

loose-jointed *adj* **1** agile and supple in movement **2** having joints that fit loosely or that are very mobile —**loose-jointedness** *n*

loose-leaf *adj* with pages that can be removed and replaced easily

loose-limbed /-límd/ *adj* having supple legs and arms

loosen /lóoss'n/ *v* **1** *vti* **BECOME OR MAKE LESS TIGHT** to become or make something become less tight or fixed **2** *vt* **UNTIE HAIR OR KNOT** to untie something such as hair or a knot **3** *vt* **RELAX CONTROL OVER** to lessen control, pressure, or strictness **4** *vt* **MAKE BOWELS MORE REGULAR** to make somebody's bowel movements more fluid or regular

loosen up *v* **1** *vti* to do exercises or exercise muscles or joints in order to become more limber, e.g. prior to strenuous activity **2** *vi* to become less tense, strict, or serious

loose smut *n* a disease of cereal grasses in which powdery spore masses replace the grain head

loosestrife /lóoss strīf/ (*plural* **-strifes** *or* **-strife**) *n* **1** a plant of the primrose family with clusters of yellow flowers. Genus: *Lysimachia.* **2** a plant with spikes of purple flowers. Genus: *Lythrum.* [Mid-16C. Translation (as if < Greek *lusimakhos* 'loosening strife') of Latin *lysimachia*, after *Lysimachus*, Greek physician.]

loose-tongued *adj* liable to gossip or reveal information that should not be told (*informal*)

loot /loot/ *n* **1 SPOILS OF WAR OR RIOT** money or goods that have been pillaged during wartime or a riot **2 STOLEN GOODS** money or goods that have been stolen or obtained illegally **3 MONEY** money (*informal*) **4 LOT OF PRESENTS OR PURCHASES** a large amount of goods that have been bought or given on one occasion (*informal*) ■ *vti* **STEAL LOOT FROM** to steal valuables from a place during wartime or a riot [Mid-19C. < Hindi *lūṭ*.] —**looter** *n*

lop^{1} /lop/ *vt* (**lops, lopping, lopped**) **1 CUT BRANCH OFF TREE** to cut a branch off a tree cleanly **2 CUT OFF** to cut off something, e.g. hair or a limb, with one stroke **3 GET RID OF** to eliminate somebody or something as superfluous **4 TAKE AMOUNT OFF PRICE** to deduct an amount from a price ■ *n* **CUT-OFF BRANCH** a branch that has been cut off [Early 16C. Originally 'small branches'.] —**lopper** *n*

lop^{2} /lop/ (**lops, lopping, lopped**) *v* **1** *vti* to hang or allow something to hang loosely **2** *vi* to move with an awkward slouching posture [Late 16C. Thought to suggest the action of flopping about.]

lope /lōp/ *v* (**lopes, loping, loped**) **1** *vi* **RUN IN LONG EASY STRIDES** to run in a relaxed and easy way, taking long strides **2** *vti* **CANTER** to canter or to make a horse canter with a long easy stride ■ *n* **LONG-STRIDING GAIT** a relaxed and easy gait with long strides [13C. < Old Norse *hlaupa* 'to leap'.] —**loper** *n*

lop-eared /-éerd/ *adj* describes domestic rabbits, dogs, and goats that have loosely hanging ears

lophophorate /lófə fáw rayt/ *n* an animal such as a bryozoan or brachiopod that has a circular or horseshoe-shaped array of ciliated tentacles (**lophophores**) surrounding the mouth, used for feeding —**lophophorate** *adj*

lophophore /lóffō fawr/ *n* a circular or horseshoe-shaped structure of tentacles round the mouth of a bryozoan or brachiopod that is used for capturing food [Mid-19C. < Greek *lophos* 'crest'.]

lopolith /lóppō lith/ *n* a basin-shaped body of igneous rock formed by the penetration of magma between existing layers of rock [Early 20C. < Greek *lopas* 'basin'.]

lopsided /lop sídid/ *adj* **1** leaning or drooping to one side **2** unevenly balanced because one side is larger, stronger, or heavier than the other [Early 18C. < LOP^{2}.]

loquacious /lo kwáyshəss/ *adj* tending to talk a great deal [Mid-17C. < Latin *loquaci-* < *loqui* 'speak'.] —**loquaciously** *adv* —**loquaciousness** *n* —**loquacity** /lo kwássəti/ *n*

SYNONYMS See ***talkative***.

loquat /lṓ kwot, -kwət/ (*plural* **-quats** *or* **-quat**) *n* a small pear-shaped orange-yellow sweet but slightly tangy fruit, eaten raw or cooked [Early 19C. < Chinese *luh kwat* 'rush orange'.]

loran /láwrən/ *n* a long-distance radio navigation system by which a ship or aircraft determines its position using radio signals sent out by two ground stations [Mid-20C. Acronym < *long-range navigation*.]

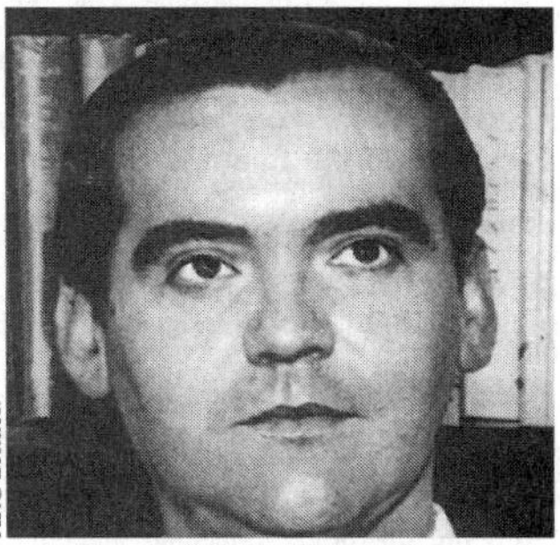

Federico García Lorca

AKG London

Lorca /láwrkə/, **Federico García** (1898–1936) Spanish poet and playwright

lord /lawrd/ *n* **1 ARISTOCRAT** a man who is a member of the nobility, especially in Great Britain **2 FEUDAL SUPERIOR** in medieval Europe, a powerful land- or property-owner, with authority over an area, castle, or community, e.g. the lord of a manor **3 POWERFUL MAN** a man who has considerable power, authority, or influence over others, e.g. a business tycoon ■ *vti* **ACT IN A SUPERIOR WAY** to act in a superior, masterful, or bullying way towards others [Old English *hlāford*, contraction of *hlāfweard* 'loaf-guardian' < *hlāf*, earlier form of LOAF^{1}] ◇ **lord it (over somebody)** to act in a superior, masterful, or bullying way towards somebody (*disapproving*)

SPELLCHECK See ***laud***.

Lord *n* **1 CHRISTIAN GOD** a title Christians give to God or specifically to Jesus Christ **2 JEWISH GOD** a title that Jews give to God **3 TITLE FOR A MAN** used as an alternative title for a marquess, earl, viscount, or baron **4 COURTESY TITLE FOR A MAN** used as a courtesy title for the younger son or sons of a marquess or duke **5 FORM OF ADDRESS FOR A MAN**

used as a form of address for an earl, viscount, or baron, and for the younger son of a duke or marquess **6 TITLE OF HIGH-RANKING OFFICIAL** a title given to some high-ranking British officials ■ *interj* **EXPRESSING SURPRISE** used to express surprise, concern, or annoyance about something (*informal*) ■ **Lords** *npl* **HOUSE OF LORDS** the House of Lords [Old English]

Lord Advocate *n* the chief law officer in Scotland, responsible for the public prosecution service and the administration of the criminal justice system

Lord Chamberlain *n* the official in charge of the British royal household

Lord Chancellor *n* the cabinet minister in the British government who is the Speaker in the House of Lords and the official in charge of the judiciary in England and Wales

Lord Chief Justice *n* in England, a judge who is the Lord Chancellor's deputy and president of the Queen's Bench Division of the High Court of Justice

Lord High Chancellor *n* POL, LAW = **Lord Chancellor**

Lord Howe Island /-hów-/ island off E New South Wales, Australia, in the south Pacific Ocean. Population: 369 (1996). Area: 145 sq. km/56 sq. mi.

Lord Justice of Appeal (*plural* **Lord Justices of Appeal**) *n* in England, a judge in the Court of Appeal

Lord Lieutenant *n* the representative of the sovereign in a UK county

lordling /láwrdling/ *n* a young lord

lordly /láwrdli/ (**-lier, -liest**) *adj* **1** arrogant, aloof, and behaving in a superior way **2** very grand, magnificent, and suitable for a lord —**lordliness** *n*

Lord Mayor *n* the mayor of the City of London and some other large British boroughs and cities, e.g. York

Lord Muck *n* an offensive term for a man who is thought to have an exaggerated sense of his own importance. ◊ **Lady Muck**

Lord of Appeal *n* a judge who assists the House of Lords in hearing appeals

Lord of Hosts *n* the Christian God

Lord of the Flies *n* MYTHOL = **Beelzebub**

lordosis /lawr dṓssiss/ (*plural* **-doses** /-seez/) *n* **1** an unusual inward curving of the spine in the lower part of the back, which may be medically significant **2** an inward arching of the back of female mammals during sexual stimulation [Early 18C. Via modern Latin < Greek *lordōsis* < *lordos* 'bent backwards'.] —**lordotic** /-dóttik/ *adj*

Lord President of the Council (*plural* **Lord Presidents of the Council**) *n* the cabinet minister in the UK government who presides over meetings of the Privy Council

Lord Privy Seal (*plural* **Lords Privy Seal**) *n* a senior cabinet minister in the UK government with no specific portfolio

Lord Protector *n* POL = **Protector**

Lord Provost *n* the chairman and head of the local authority in one of the five major Scottish cities, Edinburgh, Glasgow, Aberdeen, Perth, and Dundee

lords-and-ladies (*plural* **lords-and-ladies**) *n* PLANTS = **cuckoopint** [Said to be because some plants have dark spadices ('lords') and some light ('ladies')]

Lord's Day *n* the Christian Sabbath

lordship /láwrd ship/ *n* the position held by, land owned by, or period of tenure of, a lord

Lordship /láwrd ship/ *n* a respectful way to refer to or address a judge, bishop, or some nobles

Lord's Prayer *n* the most important prayer in Christianity, which Jesus Christ taught to his disciples according to the Gospels of Luke and Matthew

Lords Spiritual *npl* the Anglican Archbishops of Canterbury and York and the 24 most senior bishops of England and Wales, who are entitled to sit in the House of Lords

Lord's Supper *n* RELIG = **Holy Communion**

Lord's Table *n* **1** Holy Communion in the Protestant Church **2** the altar or communion table in a Protestant church

Lords Temporal *npl* the UK peers sitting in the House of Lords who are not archbishops or bishops

lordy /láwrdi/ *interj US* used to express surprise, shock, or disappointment (*dated informal*)

lore[1] /lawr/ *n* **1** acquired knowledge or wisdom on a particular subject, e.g. local traditions, handed down by word of mouth and usually in the form of stories or historical anecdotes **2** knowledge that has been acquired through teaching or experience [Old English *lār* 'teaching, learning' < Germanic]

lore[2] /lawr/ *n* **1** the part on either side of a bird's head between its eyes and the base of the bill **2** the area on a snake's or a fish's face between its eyes and its mouth [Early 17C. < Latin *lorum* 'strap, thong'.]

Lorelei[1] /lórrə lī, láwrə-/ *n* a legendary beautiful woman said to live on a rock near the Rhine and lure sailors onto the rocks with enchanting songs

Lorelei[2] /lórrə lī, láwrə-/ cliff overlooking the River Rhine between Mainz and Koblenz, west-central Germany. Height: 120 m/390 ft.

Loren /láwr en, law rén/, **Sophia** (*b.* 1934) Italian actor. Born **Sofia Scicolone**

Lorentz /lórrənts/, **Hendrik Antoon** (1853–1928) Dutch theoretical physicist

Lorentz-Fitzgerald contraction /lórrənts fits jérrəld-/ *n* the consequence of relativity that causes a reduction in length of an object travelling at a speed approaching that of light [Early 20C. After Hendrik Antoon LORENTZ and George F. FITZGERALD.]

Lorentz transformation *n* one of the equations relating space and time that holds between two observers of an event who are moving with uniform velocity relative to each other [Early 20C. After Hendrik Antoon LORENTZ.]

Lorenz /láw rents/, **Konrad** (1903–89) Austrian zoologist and ethnologist

lorgnette /lawr nyét/ *n* a pair of glasses or opera glasses with a short handle at the side [Early 19C. < French, < *lorgner* 'to squint, peer at' < Germanic.]

lorica /lórrikə/ (*plural* **-cae** /-kee/) *n* **1** a lightweight loose-fitting external shell that protects ciliated or flagellated protozoans **2** a protective metal or leather garment covering the chest and back, worn by the ancient Romans [Early 18C. < Latin, 'breastplate' < *lorum* 'strap'.]

loriciferan /lórri síffərən/ *n* a microscopic bottom-dwelling sea animal that has an ovoid body covered in protective spiny plates and a flexible retractable mouth tube. Phylum: Loricifera. [Mid-19C. < modern Latin *Loricifera* < Latin *lorica* 'breastplate'.]

lorikeet /lórri keet, lórri kéet/ (*plural* **-keets** *or* **-keet**) *n* a small brightly coloured long-necked parrot with a bristle-tipped tongue for extracting nectar and pollen from flowers. Native to: Australia, Pacific Islands. Genera: *Trichoglosus* and *Glossopsitta*. [Late 18C. < LORY, after PARAKEET.]

lorimer /lórrimər/, **loriner** /lórrinər/ *n* formerly, a craftworker who made small metal accessories for horses, e.g. bits and spurs [13C. < Old French *lorenier* < *lorain* 'harness strap' < Latin *lorum* 'strap'.]

loris /láwriss/ (*plural* **-ris**) *n* a small slow-moving tree-dwelling nocturnal primate with large eyes, dense woolly fur, a vestigial index finger, and no tail. Native to: tropical S Asia. [Late 18C. < French.]

Lorrain /lə ráyn/, **Claude** (1600–82) French painter. Born **Claude Gellée**

Lorraine /lə ráyn/ region in E France. Capital: Metz. Population: 2.3 million. Area: 23,540 sq. km/9,100 sq. mi.

lorry /lórri/ (*plural* **-ries**) *n* a large vehicle for transporting goods by road [Mid-19C. < ?]

lory /láwri/ (*plural* **-ries** *or* **-ry**) *n* a small brightly coloured parrot with a bristle-tipped tongue for extracting nectar and pollen from flowers. Native to: Australia, Indonesia. Subfamily: Loriidae. [Late 17C. < Malay *lori*.]

Los Alamos /los állə moss/ city in central New Mexico, site of a major nuclear weapons research facility. Population: 11,420 (1996 estimate).

Los Angeles /los ánjələss, -leez/ city in SW California, the second most populous city in the United States. Population: 3,597,556 (1998 estimate).

lose /looz/ (**loses, losing, lost**) *v* **1** *vti* **FAIL TO WIN** to fail to win a victory, e.g. in a contest, argument, war, game, or in court **2** *vt* **MISLAY** to be unable to find something, often only temporarily **3** *vt* **HAVE SOMETHING TAKEN AWAY** to cease to possess or have something, e.g. a job or home **4** *vt* **CEASE HAVING QUALITY** to cease having a quality, belief, attitude, or characteristic ○ *He's lost the will to live.* **5** *vt* **CEASE HAVING ABILITY OR SENSE** to cease having a particular ability or sense, e.g. through illness or an accident ○ *He lost his sight in the war.* **6** *vt* **EXPERIENCE REDUCTION IN** to experience a reduction in something, e.g. weight or heat **7** *vt* **BE UNABLE TO FIND WAY** to be unable to find the way ○ *lost his way* **8** *vt* **MAKE SOMEBODY FAIL TO WIN** to be the cause of somebody's failure to win something ○ *The goalie's inexperience lost us the match.* **9** *vt* **NOT USE TO ADVANTAGE** to waste or fail to take advantage of something, e.g. time or an opportunity **10** *vt* **BE UNABLE TO CONTROL** to be unable to control or maintain something ○ *He loses his composure easily.* **11** *vt* **HAVE LOVED ONE DIE** to suffer the loss of somebody through death, e.g. a loved one, a patient, or a baby **12** *vt* **LEAVE SOMEBODY FOLLOWING BEHIND** to escape from or leave behind somebody who is in pursuit **13** *vt* **CONFUSE** to fail to make somebody understand something ○ *You've lost me there.* **14** *vt* **NO LONGER SEE OR HEAR** to be unable to see or hear somebody or something any longer **15** *vti* **RUN SLOW** to be or become slow by an amount of time (*refers to a timepiece*) [Old English *losian* 'perish, destroy, lose' < *los* (see LOSS)] —**losable** *adj* —**losableness** *n* ◇ **lose it 1** to become removed from reality (*informal*) **2** to be unable to maintain emotional control or composure (*informal*)

USAGE See ***loose***.

lose out *vi* to fail to win or obtain something in a competition or rivalry (*informal*)

loser /loózər/ *n* **1** a person or team that has failed to win a particular contest **2** an unsuccessful or unlucky person who seems destined to fail repeatedly (*insult*)

Losey /lṓzi/, **Joseph** (1909–84) US film director

losings /loózingz/ *npl* money or possessions that are lost, especially through gambling

loss /loss/ *n* **1 FACT OF NO LONGER HAVING** the fact of no longer having something or of having less of something **2 DEATH** the death of somebody **3 SOMEBODY OR SOMETHING LOST** somebody or something that has been lost **4 MONEY SPENT IN EXCESS OF INCOME** the amount of money by which a company's expenses exceed income (*often plural*) **5 SAD FEELING** a feeling of sadness, loneliness, or emptiness at the absence of somebody or something **6 REDUCTION** a reduction in the level of something, especially in the body ○ *weight loss* **7 INSTANCE OF LOSING CONTEST** an instance of losing a competition, race, or contest **8 DROP IN POWER CAUSED BY RESISTANCE** a drop in power caused by resistance in an electric circuit **9 INSTANCE OR AMOUNT OF CLAIM** an instance or the amount of a claim made by an insurance policyholder [Old English *los* 'ruin, destruction' < Germanic] ◇ **at a loss** uncertain what to say or do ◇ **cut your losses** to withdraw from a situation in which there is no possibility of winning

loss adjuster *n* somebody employed by an insurance company to assess the financial losses incurred through, e.g. accident, theft, fire, or natural disaster, and determine the amount of compensation. US term **adjuster**

⚡**lossage** /lóssij/ *n* a failure caused by a bug or a malfunction during a computer operation

loss leader *n* an item sold at a price below its cost in the hope that customers who buy it will also buy other things

lossmaker /lóss maykər/ *n* a business, organization, or industry that does not make a profit —**lossmaking** *adj*

loss ratio *n* the ratio of the losses paid out in a year by an insurance company against the income from premiums

lost /lost/ *v* past tense, past participle of **lose** ■ *adj* **1 MISLAID** unable to be found for the moment **2 UNABLE TO FIND THE WAY** unable to find the way to a place **3 NOT USED PROPERLY** wasted or not taken advantage of **4 UNAPPRECIATED** not understood or appreciated by somebody **5 LACKING CONFIDENCE** unable to cope with a job or situation, usually because of inexperience or lack of confidence **6 GONE** no longer in existence or use **7 PREOCCUPIED** completely absorbed or involved in something ○ *lost in thought* **8 CONFUSED BY SOMETHING COMPLICATED** confused or bewildered by something complicated or poorly explained **9 DESTROYED** destroyed or killed **10 LACKING MORALS** morally or spiritually past hoping for (*formal*) ◇ **get lost** used to tell somebody in a blunt and rude way to go away (*informal*)

lost and found *n US* = **lost property** *n.* 2

lost cause *n* a person who cannot be made to change, or something that cannot succeed

Lost Generation, lost generation *n* **1** the large numbers of young men who were killed in World War I **2** the group of authors, including Ernest Hemingway and F. Scott Fitzgerald, who came to prominence shortly after World War I.

lost property *n* US term **lost and found 1** personal possessions that have been accidentally left in a public place, e.g. in a cinema or on a train **2 lost property, lost property office** a place in a public building, e.g. a theatre or railway station, where personal possessions that have accidentally been left behind are kept for reclaiming by their owners

lost tribes *n* the ten Hebrew tribes that separated from the other two to create a kingdom in N Israel after Solomon's death. They were defeated by the Assyrians in 721 BC and may have become assimilated, but legend predicts their return.

lost wax *n* a method of casting metal in which a wax model is coated with a material with a high melting point

lot /lot/ *pron* **MANY** a large number of people or things ■ *n* **1 A SET** a set or group of things or people **2 ITEMS IN AUCTION** an item or group of items on sale at an auction ○ *I bought the silver as one lot.* **3 GROUP** a particular group of people (*informal*) ○ *Don't expect any help from that lot.* **4 DESTINY** the things somebody has or experiences in life ○ *our lot in life* **5** *US* **PIECE OF LAND** a small area of land that has fixed boundaries ○ *a vacant lot* **6 FILM STUDIO** a film studio together with the land that belongs to it ■ **lots** *npl* **LARGE NUMBERS OR LARGE AMOUNT** large numbers of people or things or a large amount ○ *Lots of us went.* ○ *I've got lots left.* ■ *adv* **lots MUCH** a great deal (*informal*) ○ *I'm feeling lots better, thanks.* [Old English *hlot* 'object used to make decisions by chance; portion; destiny'] ◇ **a lot 1** to a great extent or degree (*informal*) ○ *Fishing has changed a lot in the last century.* **2** often or much of the time (*informal*) ○ *We went out to restaurants a lot.* ◇ **a whole lot** very much or a great deal (*informal*) ◇ **draw** *or* **cast lots** to choose something at random, e.g. a straw or piece of paper, to determine an outcome ○ *We cast lots to decide who should go first.* ◇ **the lot** everything, or everything considered as one ○ *Personality, looks, brains... she's got the lot.*

USAGE a lot or **alot**? The superficial similarity of ***a lot*** to adjectives and adverbs like *alone* and *aloud* gives rise to a temptation to treat the expression as one word, but this is nonstandard usage. In formal writing, *much, many, a great deal of*, etc. can be substituted for **a lot**.

Lot /lot/ in the biblical Book of Genesis, the son of Haran, brother of Abraham.

Lot /lō/ **1** department in Midi-Pyrénées Region, SW France. Area: 5,217 sq. km/2,014 sq. mi. **2** river in SW France. Length: 483 km/300 mi.

lota /lṓtə/, **lotah** *n* a small round water container, usually made of brass or copper, used in South Asia [Early 19C. < Hindi *loṭā*.]

loth /lōth/ *adj* = **loath**

Lothair II /lō tháir/ (1075–1137) king of Germany and Holy Roman Emperor (1125–37)

Lothario /lō thaári ō, -thaíri ō/ (*plural* **-os**), **lothario** *n* a man who attempts to persuade women to enter sexual affairs with him [Mid-18C. After a character in *The Fair Penitent* (1703), tragedy by Nicholas Rowe.]

Lothian /lṓth̲i ən/ former region of SE Scotland, approximately equivalent to the present-day council areas of East Lothian, Midlothian, West Lothian, and the City of Edinburgh

loti /lṓti/ (*plural* **maloti** /maa lṓti/) *n* see table at **currency** [Late 20C. < Sesotho, after the *Maloti* Mountains in Lesotho.]

lotic /lṓtik/ *adj* describes ecological communities that live in swift-flowing water [Early 20C. < Latin *lotus*, past participle of *lavare* 'wash'.]

lotion /lṓsh'n/ *n* a thick liquid preparation that is applied to the skin for cosmetic or medical reasons [14C. Directly or via French < Latin *lotion-* < *lot-*, past participle of *lavare* 'wash'.]

lottery /lóttəri/ (*plural* **-ies**) *n* **1** a large-scale gambling game, usually organized to raise money for a public cause, in which numbered tickets are sold and a draw is held to select the winning numbers **2** an activity, situation, or enterprise with an outcome dependent on chance [Mid-16C. Probably < Dutch *loterij* < *lot* 'lot'.]

lotto /lóttō/ (*plural* **-tos**) *n* **1** a game resembling bingo, in which numbers are called at random and players try to be the first to cover all the corresponding numbers on their cards **2 lotto, Lotto** a state-run lottery in Australia and some other countries, and in some US states, in which players buy tickets bearing combinations of numbers [Late 18C. Directly or via French *loto* < Italian *lotto* < assumed Frankish *lot* 'lot'.]

lotus /lṓtəss/ (*plural* **-tuses** *or* **-tus**) *n* **1 MYTHOLOGICAL FRUIT CAUSING DROWSINESS** a fruit in Greek mythology that made people who ate it feel a pleasant drowsiness **2 MYTHOLOGICAL PLANT BEARING LOTUS FRUIT** a plant in Greek mythology that bore the lotus fruit, thought to be the date or jujube **3 SACRED WHITE WATER LILY** a water lily sacred to the ancient Egyptians. Flowers: white. Native to: tropical Africa and Asia. *Nymphaea lotus.* **4 SACRED PINK WATER LILY** a water lily with large leaves, regarded as sacred in S Asia, China, and Tibet. Flowers: fragrant, pink. Native to: Asia, Australia. *Nelumbo nucifera.* **5 PLANT OF PEA FAMILY** a plant of the pea family. Flowers: yellow, pink, or white. Genus: *Lotus.* **6 LOTUS FLOWER IN SACRED ART** a representation of the flower of either of the sacred lotus plants, common in ancient Egyptian, Hindu, and Buddhist sacred art [15C. Via Latin < Greek *lōtos*, applied to a variety of plants.]

lotus-eater *n* **1** a lazy, self-indulgent person **2** somebody who, in the *Odyssey*, lived in a state of idle stupor after feeding on the legendary lotus

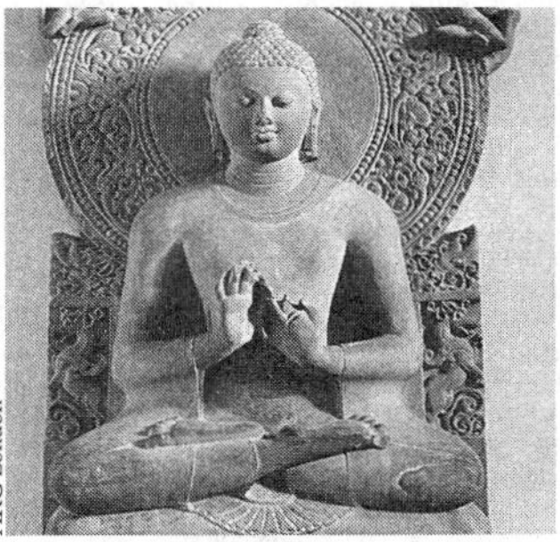
AKG London

Lotus position: Seated *Buddha*, Uttar Pradesh, northern India

lotus position *n* a sitting position, used especially in yoga and meditation, in which the legs are crossed in such a way that each foot rests on top of the other leg's thigh [< its supposed resemblance to a lotus blossom]

Louangphrabang /loo áng prə báng/ city in N Laos, on the Mekong River. Population: 68,000 (1995 estimate).

louche /loosh/ *adj* disreputable or of doubtful morality [Early 19C. Via French, 'cross-eyed, shady' < Latin *luscus* 'one-eyed'.]

loud /lowd/ *adj* **1 HIGH IN VOLUME** high in volume of sound **2 EXPRESSING SOMETHING NOISILY** expressing something forcefully and frequently ○ *loud protests* **3 VISUALLY SHOCKING** shockingly bright in colour or bold in design ○ *a loud shirt* **4 OFFENSIVE** noisy, coarse, and offensive ■ *adv* **LOUDLY** in a loud way [Old English *hlūd* < Indo-European, 'hear'] —**loudly** *adv*

louden /lówd'n/ *vti* to become louder, or to make a sound louder

loudhailer /lówd háylər/ *n* a portable device for amplifying the voice consisting of a loudspeaker with an integrated amplifier and microphone. US term **bullhorn**

loudmouth /lówd mowth/ (*plural* **-mouths** /-mowt̲h̲z, -mowt̲h̲s/) *n* a loud and talkative person, especially a gossip or braggart (*informal*) —**loudmouthed** /lówd mowt̲h̲d, -mowtht/ *adj*

loudness /lówdnəss/ *n* **1** the degree of volume of sound **2** the magnitude of the physiological effect produced when a sound stimulates the ear

loud pedal *n* MUSIC = **sustaining pedal**

loudspeaker /lówd spéekər/ *n* an electronic or electromagnetic device used to convert electrical energy into sound energy, providing the audible sound in equipment such as televisions, radios, CD players, and public-address systems

loudspeaker van *n* a van or other vehicle provided with a loudspeaker so that political or other messages can be delivered to people in the streets and adjacent houses. US term **sound truck**

Lou Gehrig's disease /loŏ gérrigz-/ *n* MED = **amyotrophic lateral sclerosis** [Mid-20C. After Henry *Louis Gehrig* (1903–41), US baseball player who died from the disease.]

lough /lok̲h̲, lok/ *n Ireland* **1** a lake **2** a long inlet of the sea [13C. Probably < Old Irish *loch* 'lake'.]

Loughborough /lúfbərə/ town in central England. Population: 46,867 (1991).

louis *n* MONEY = **louis d'or**

Louis XIV /loŏ i/ (1638–1715) king of France (1642–1715). Known as **the Sun King**

Louis XV (1710–74) king of France (1715–74)

Louis XVI (1754–93) king of France (1774–93)

Louis, Joe (1914–81) US boxer. Known as **the Brown Bomber**

louis d'or /loŏ i dáwr/ (*plural* **louis d'or**), **louis** (*plural* **-is**) *n* **1** a former gold coin of France used from the 17th century to the Revolution **2** a former gold coin worth 20 francs used in France after the Revolution [Mid-17C. < French, 'louis of gold', after *Louis* XIII of France.]

Louisiana /loo èezi áanna/ state in the S United States, on the Gulf of Mexico. Capital: Baton Rouge. Population: 4,351,769 (1997). Area: 128,595 sq. km/49,651 sq. mi. —**Louisianan** *n, adj*

Louisiana Purchase territory of the W United States purchased from France in 1803. It extended from the Gulf of Mexico northwards to the Canadian border and from the Mississippi River westwards to the Rocky Mountains. Area: 2,100,000 sq. km/800,000 sq. mi.

Louis Philippe /loŏ i fee léep/ (1773–1850) king of the French (1830–50). Known as **the Citizen King**

Louisville /loŏ i vil/ largest city in Kentucky, in the north of the state. Population: 255,045 (1998 estimate).

lounge /lownj/ *n* **1 SITTING ROOM IN HOUSE** a sitting or living room in a house **2 PUBLIC ROOM FOR RELAXING** a room in a public building or vehicle, e.g. a hotel, airport, or ship, in which people may relax or wait **3** LEISURE = **lounge bar 4 BACKLESS COUCH WITH HEADREST** a couch without a back but with a headrest at one end **5 PERIOD OF LOUNGING** a period of relaxation, laziness, or inactivity ○ *having a lounge on the sofa after lunch* ■ *v* (**lounges, lounging, lounged**) **1** *vi* **LIE OR SIT LAZILY** to sit or act in a casual, relaxed way **2** *vti* **PASS TIME LAZILY** to pass time in a relaxed or lazy way ○ *lounged the afternoon away* [Early 16C. < ?]

lounge bar *n* an area in a pub or hotel with more comfortable or elegant furnishings than the public bar, and sometimes selling more expensive drinks

lounge lizard *n* **1** a man who goes to places or events attended by the rich and famous, especially in order to approach wealthy women (*slang insult*) **2** *US* a frequent patron of cocktail lounges (*slang*) [Probably < the negative associations of reptiles]

lounger /lównjər/ *n* **1** an extendable chair or a lightweight, usually adjustable, couch designed to be comfortable for the user **2** a sitter or walker in a casual relaxed way

lounge suit *n* a man's suit consisting of a jacket and trousers, occasionally also including a waistcoat, all made from the same cloth, worn as formal daywear

lounge suite *n Aus* a three-piece set of furniture, usually consisting of a couch and two armchairs

loup /lowp/, **lowp** *vti Scotland* to leap or jump ■ *n Scotland* a leap or a jump [14C. < Old Norse *hlaupa* 'to leap' < Germanic.]

loupe /loop/ *n* a magnifying glass used especially by jewellers and watchmakers [Late 19C. < French, 'flawed gem'.]

loup-garou /loŏ ga roŏ/ (*plural* **loups-garous**) *n US* a werewolf (*dated*) [Late 16C. < French, < Old French *leu* 'wolf' (< Latin *lupus*) + *garoul* 'werewolf' (< Germanic, 'man-wolf').]

louping ill /lówping-/ *n* a serious viral disease spread by ticks that damages the central nervous system, causing tremors and difficulty in mobility. It affects many animals, including sheep, cattle, goats, and pigs.

lour *vi, n* = **lower**[2]

Lourdes /loordz/ town in SW France, famous for its Roman Catholic shrine. Population: 16,301 (1990).

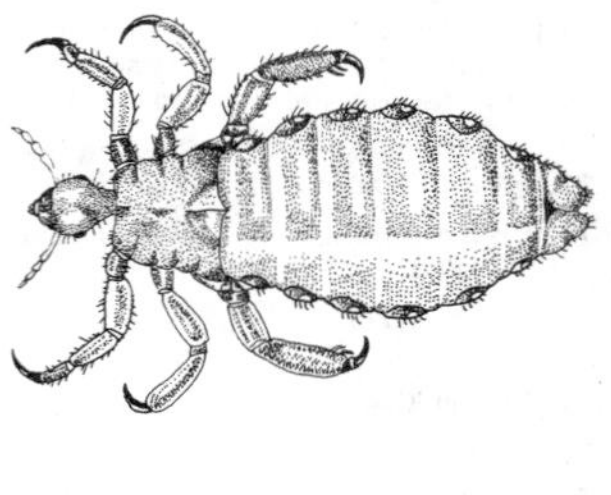

Louse

louse /lowss/ *n* (*plural* **lice** /līss/) **1 PARASITIC INSECT** a small wingless insect that lives as a parasite on humans and other animals. There are sucking lice, e.g. head and body lice, and biting lice, e.g. bird lice. **2 SMALL INVERTEBRATE ANIMAL** a small invertebrate animal, e.g. a wood louse (*often in combination*) **3** (*plural* **louses**) **OFFENSIVE TERM** an offensive term that deliberately insults somebody's behaviour and attitude towards others (*insult*) ■ *vt* (**louses, lousing, loused**) MED = **delouse** [Old English *lūs* < Indo-European]

louse up *vti* to mishandle a situation or task so that it is ruined (*informal*)

louse fly *n* a parasitic fly that clings to birds and mammals with strong bristly legs and is typically wingless. Family: Hippoboscidae.

lousewort /lówss wurt/ *n* a plant of the snapdragon family with feathery leaves. Flowers: white, yellow, or pinkish-purple, in spikes. Native to: northern regions. Genus: *Pedicularis*. [< the belief that sheep feeding on it became infested with lice]

lousy /lówzi/ (**-ier, -iest**) *adj* **1 INFERIOR** inferior or second-rate (*informal*) **2 UNPLEASANT** unpleasant or unacceptable (*informal*) ○ *a lousy way to treat somebody* **3 ILL** painful or in bad health (*informal*) **4** *US* **HAVING A LOT OF** having a large amount of something (*informal*) ○ *His parents are lousy with money.* **5 LOUSE-INFESTED** infested with lice —**lousily** *adv* —**lousiness** *n*

lout /lowt/ *n* an offensive term that deliberately insults the behaviour and attitude of somebody, especially a young man (*insult*) [Mid-16C. < ?]

Louth[1] /lowth/ county in Leinster Province, E Republic of Ireland. Area: 821 sq. km/317 sq. mi.

Louth[2] /lowth/ town in E England. Population: 14,248 (1991).

loutish /lówtish/ *adj* marked by crude and unpleasant behaviour —**loutishly** *adv* —**loutishness** *n*

Louvain /loo váN/ town in central Belgium. Population: 87,132 (1996).

louvar /lóo vaar/ (*plural* **-vars** *or* **-var**) *n* a large deep-sea tropical fish with a blunt head, silvery-pink body, and bright red fins. *Luvarus imperialis*. [Late 20C. Probably < modern Latin *luvarus* < Italian dialect (Sicilian) *luvaru*.]

louvre /lóovər/, **louver** *n* **1 FRAME WITH HORIZONTAL SLATS** a frame on a door or window supporting spaced horizontal slats angled to admit air and light but not rain ○ *a set of louvre doors* **2 SLAT IN LOUVRE** an individual slat in a louvre **3 ANY SLATTED OPENING** any slatted opening, generally for ventilation or cooling **4 ROOF STRUCTURE RELEASING SMOKE** a structure such as a lantern or turret on the roof of a building, especially a medieval building, that allows smoke to escape [14C. < Old French *lover* 'skylight'.] —**louvred** *adj*

Louvre /lóovrə/ *n* a museum in Paris that contains the national art collection, including such famous works as the *Mona Lisa* and *Venus de Milo*

lovable /lúvvəb'l/, **loveable** *adj* attracting or worthy of love or affection —**lovability** /lúvvə bíllәti/ *n* —**lovableness** *n* —**lovably** *adv*

lovage /lúvvij/ *n* a perennial herb cultivated for its small aromatic fruit used in seasoning. Flowers: greenish. Native to: Mediterranean. *Levisticum officinale*. [14C. Alteration of Old French *levesche* < late Latin *levisticum*, alteration of *ligusticum*, 'of Liguria', region in Italy.]

lovat /lúvvət/ *n* a muted dusty yellowish or bluish-green colour [Early 20C. Probably after Lord *Lovat* (1802–75), Scottish nobleman who popularized tweeds in muted colours as hunters' dress.]

love /luv/ *v* (**loves, loving, loved**) **1** *vti* **FEEL TENDER AFFECTION FOR** to feel tender affection for somebody, e.g. a close relative or friend, or for something such as a place, an ideal, or an animal **2** *vti* **FEEL DESIRE FOR** to feel romantic and sexual desire and longing for somebody **3** *vt* **LIKE VERY MUCH** to like something or like doing something very much ○ *I love watching old movies on TV.* **4** *vt* **SHOW KINDNESS TO** to feel and show kindness and charity to somebody ○ *love one another and love your neighbour* **5** *vt* **VENERATE** to worship and venerate God **6** *vt* **HAVE SEXUAL INTERCOURSE WITH** to have sexual intercourse with somebody (*dated*) ■ *n* **1 VERY STRONG AFFECTION** an intense feeling of tender affection and compassion ○ *Young children need unconditional love.* **2 PASSIONATE ATTRACTION AND DESIRE** a passionate feeling of romantic desire and sexual attraction **3 KIND PERSON** a kind or pleasant person (*informal*) ○ *Be a love and pour me a cup of tea.* **4 SOMEBODY MUCH LOVED** a person who is loved romantically ○ *He was her first real love.* **5 ROMANTIC AFFAIR** a romantic affair, possibly sexual **6 STRONG LIKING** strong liking for or pleasure gained from something ○ *his love of music* **7 SOMETHING ELICITING ENTHUSIASM** something that elicits deep interest and enthusiasm in somebody ○ *Music was his greatest love but he also liked ballet.* **8 BELOVED** used as an affectionate word to somebody loved **9 TERM OF FRIENDLY ADDRESS** used as a friendly term of address, usually to a woman (*informal*) ○ *Here's your change, love.* **10 SCORE OF ZERO** a score of zero in sports and games, e.g. tennis, squash, and whist **11 GOD'S LOVE FOR HUMANITY** the mercy, grace, and charity shown by God to humanity **12 WORSHIP OF GOD** the worship and adoration of God [Old English *lufian* < *lufu* 'love' < Indo-European, 'to love']

SYNONYMS ***love, liking, affection, fondness, passion, infatuation, crush***

CORE MEANING: a strong positive feeling towards somebody or something

love an intense feeling of tender affection and compassion, especially strong romantic or sexual feelings between people; **liking** a feeling of enjoying something or or finding it pleasant, or personal taste or choice; **affection** fond or tender feelings towards somebody or something; **fondness** a feeling of affection or preference; **passion** intense or overpowering emotion, either love for somebody, usually of a strong sexual nature, or strong liking or enthusiasm for something; **infatuation** an intense but short-lived, often unrealistic love for somebody, usually of a romantic or sexual nature; **crush** (*informal*) a temporary romantic *infatuation*, especially in teenagers and young people.

---

loveable *adj* = **lovable**

love affair *n* **1** a sexual or romantic relationship between people who are not married to one another or who do not live together in a permanent relationship **2** an intense liking or enthusiasm for something ○ *his love affair with the cinema*

love apple *n* PLANTS = **tomato** *n.* **1** [Translation of French *pomme d'amour*, German *Liebesapfel*]

love beads *npl* a necklace of coloured beads, first popular with hippies in the 1960s

lovebird /lúv burd/ *n* **1** a small greenish short-tailed parrot, noted for close bonding and mutual preening between mates and popular as a cage bird. Native to: Africa. Genus: *Agapornis*. **2** a lover, especially one who is publicly affectionate (*usually plural*)

lovebite /lúv bīt/ *n* a small patch of bruised skin, often on the neck, caused by a partner's sucking kiss

love child *n* the child of parents who are not married to each other

loved one *n* a spouse, partner, or close family member

love feast *n* **1** a symbolic meal shared among Christians as a symbol of love and charity **2** a meal held with the intention of stimulating goodwill

love game *n* a game in tennis and some other sports in which the loser scores no points [< LOVE, 'zero']

love handles *npl* two regions of fat located at either side of the back just above the pelvis (*humorous informal*)

love-in *n* a relatively large gathering in which participants experience feelings of love and mutual support (*dated*)

love-in-a-mist *n* an annual flowering plant. Flowers: white or pale blue, surrounded by very fine bracts. *Nigella damascena*. [*Mist* < the mass of threadlike bracts that surrounds the flower]

~~**loveing**~~ incorrect spelling of **loving**

love knot *n* a knot or bow of ribbon used to symbolize love

Lovelace /lúv làyss/, **Richard** (1618–57) English poet

loveless /lúvləss/ *adj* **1 EMPTY OF LOVE** devoid of love ○ *a loveless marriage* **2 NOT SHOWING LOVE** not exhibiting or giving love ○ *a loveless glance* **3 UNLOVED** not receiving love ○ *a loveless child*

love-lies-bleeding *n* a tropical plant. Flowers: small, red, in drooping clusters. Native to: S Asia. *Amaranthus caudatus*. [< the resemblance of the flowers to a flow of blood]

love life *n* the romantic or sexual relationships in somebody's life

Lovell /lúvv'l/, **Sir Bernard** (*b.* 1913) British astronomer

lovelock /lúv lok/ *n* a long lock of hair separated from the rest by a ribbon, worn forward over the shoulder in the 16th century, or worn on the forehead in later periods

Lovelock /lúv lok/, **Jack** (1910–49) New Zealand athlete

lovelorn /lúv lawrn/ *adj* terribly unhappy because of unrequited love or difficulties with love —**lovelornness** *n*

lovely /lúvli/ *adj* (**-lier, -liest**) **1 BEAUTIFUL AND PLEASING** beautiful and pleasing, especially in a harmonious way ○ *a lovely view* **2 DELIGHTFUL** very enjoyable or pleasant ○ *we had a lovely time* **3 CARING** loving or friendly and caring ○ *she's a lovely person* **4 ATTRACTING LOVE** attracting or inspiring love in others ■ *n* (*plural* **-lies**) **SOMEBODY OR SOMETHING GOOD-LOOKING** an attractive thing or person, especially a woman (*often in the plural; sometimes considered offensive*) ○ *Farewell, my lovely!* [Old English *luflic*] —**loveliness** *n*

lovemaking /lúv mayking/ *n* **1** sexual activity between lovers, especially sexual intercourse **2** courtship or wooing (*dated*)

love nest *n* a place, such as a small flat or secluded house, where lovers can be together

love potion *n* a magical drink intended to stimulate sexual desire in the person who consumes it for the person who gives it

lover /lúvvər/ *n* **1 SEXUAL PARTNER** somebody's sexual partner, especially if the two are not married to each other **2 SOMEBODY HAVING LOVE AFFAIR** either of two people involved in a love affair (*often plural*) **3 SOMEBODY DEVOTED TO PARTICULAR THING** a person who is devoted to or adores something (*often in combination*) ○ *opera-lovers*

LITERARY LINK ***Lady Chatterley's Lover***, a novel (1928) by D. H. Lawrence. Lawrence's last novel, it describes an aristocratic woman's search for love and sexual satisfaction after her husband is crippled in war. The novel's notoriety has obscured its many qualities, including its insightful analysis of contemporary social and political values.

---

lover's knot *n* = **love knot**

love seat *n* a small sofa that seats two people

lovesick /lúv sik/ *adj* listless or distracted because of love —**lovesickness** *n*

lovey /lúvvi/ (*plural* **-eys**) *n* used as an affectionate form of address, especially to a woman (*informal*)

lovey-dovey /-dúvvi/ *adj* showing affection in an excessive or excessively sentimental way (*informal*) [< pet-forms of LOVE, DOVE[1]]

loving /lúvving/ *adj* **1** showing or feeling affection **2** done with enjoyment and careful attention —**lovingly** *adv* —**lovingness** *n*

loving cup *n* **1** a large drinking vessel with two or more handles, sometimes passed between people at a banquet **2** an ornamental vessel with two handles awarded to the winner of a sports contest [< its use at banquets]

loving kindness *n* tender compassion for other people

low[1] /lō/ *adj* **1 WITHOUT GREAT HEIGHT** relatively little in height between the top and bottom ○ *a low fence* **2 CLOSE TO THE GROUND** located close or closer than usual to the ground or the base of something ○ *The sinking sun was low in the sky.* **3 BELOW AVERAGE** below the average or expected degree, amount, or intensity ○ *The lowest rainfall in fourteen years.* **4 CONTAINING SMALL AMOUNT** having or containing a relatively small amount ○ *low in calories* 5 WITH LITTLE MONETARY VALUE small in monetary value ○ *low prices* 6 LACKING MONEY lacking resources, especially money (*informal*) ○ *Can you lend me some cash, I'm a bit low.* 7 OF BAD QUALITY bad in quality or having little value ○ *low standards* 8 OF LITTLE IMPORTANCE having little importance or urgency ○ *low priority* 9 NEAR DEPLETION approaching or near depletion ○ *We're low on supplies.* 10 TURNED DOWN OR DIMMED adjusted so that there is less of something ○ *low lighting* 11 QUIET at a quiet, soft, or hushed level ○ *a low murmur* 12 DEEP IN PITCH with a relative pitch that is closer to bass than soprano sounds ○ *Her singing voice was a low soprano* 13 SMALL small or relatively small ○ *a low risk* 14 NEAR BOTTOM OF SCALE near the beginning or bottom of something measured on a scale ○ *The temperature was in the low 80s.* 15 DISPIRITED melancholy, hopeless, or dispirited ○ *in low spirits* 16 LACKING PHYSICAL STRENGTH lacking in physical strength or vitality ○ *feeling low after a dose of flu* 17 SHOWING NECK AND CHEST cut to show more than usual of the wearer's neck and bosom ○ *a low neckline* 18 PROVIDING SLOW SPEED providing a relatively slow speed ○ *a low gear* 19 LACKING STATUS lacking status or rank 20 UNCOMPLIMENTARY unfavourable or uncomplimentary ○ *a low opinion of someone* 21 UNPRINCIPLED without principles or morals 22 VULGAR full of vulgarity or coarseness 23 NEAR EQUATOR near to the equator 24 NOT COMPLEX simple in organic structure 25 PRONOUNCED WITH LOW TONGUE pronounced with the tongue lying low on the bottom of the mouth ○ *a low vowel* ■ *adv* 1 IN LOW POSITION in or to a low position, state, degree, or level ○ *Turn the gas down low.* 2 NEAR GROUND near or nearer to the ground ○ *flew low over the trees* 3 WITH A DEEP PITCH with a low or deep pitch ○ *Play it a semitone lower.* 4 QUIETLY in a soft or quiet way 5 AT SMALL PRICE at a low or small price ■ *n* 1 SOMETHING LOW something such as a position or degree that is low ○ *Sales dropped to an all-time low.* 2 BAD WEATHER REGION a region of low barometric pressure that results in bad weather 3 UNHAPPY PERIOD an unhappy or unfortunate experience or period of somebody's life [12C. < Old Norse *lágr*.] —**lowness** *n* ◇ **lay somebody low** to cause somebody to feel overcome or helpless, e.g. with illness or exhaustion (*usually passive*) ○ *laid low with influenza*

low[2] /lō/ *n* a characteristic mooing sound made by a cow or similar animal ■ *vti* to make a mooing sound [Old English *hlōwan* 'bellow' < Indo-European, 'shout']

lowball /lṓ bawl/ *vti US* to deliberately quote a price or estimate that is lower than the eventual cost [< *lowball*, game of draw poker in which the player with the lowest-ranking hand wins the pot]

low blow *n* an unfair comment or blow (*informal*) [< boxing]

lowborn /lṓ báwrn/ *adj* being of common rather than aristocratic parentage

lowbred /lṓ bréd/ *adj* 1 with a rude and vulgar manner (*insult*) 2 = **lowborn**

lowbrow /lṓ brow/ *adj* unsophisticated or trivial and not requiring intellectual effort to be understood or appreciated (*disapproving*) ■ *n* somebody who has unsophisticated or unintellectual tastes [Early 20C. After HIGHBROW.]

low-cal /-kál/ *adj* with few calories or fewer calories than usual

Low Church *n* a branch of the Church of England that favours less ritual and ceremony and prefers an evangelical approach to services

low comedy *n* comedy based on slapstick and coarse actions rather than more sophisticated forms of humour

Low Countries region in NW Europe, made up of Belgium, the Netherlands, and Luxembourg. Population: 26,016,000 (1995). Area: 73,943 sq. km/28,550 sq. mi.

low-density *adj* having a low concentration of something in an area

low-density lipoprotein *n* the type of lipoprotein that carries cholesterol to cells and tissue

lowdown /lṓ down/ *n* significant information about somebody or something, especially information that is not widely known (*informal*) ○ *waiting for someone to give us the lowdown* [Early 20C. < *low down* 'very low' or *low-down* 'contemptible'.]

low-down *adj* mean and contemptible (*informal*)

low earth orbit *n* an orbit that is nearer to the Earth than a geostationary orbit

Lowell /lṓ əl/, **Amy Lawrence** (1874–1925) US poet and critic

Lowell, Robert (1917–77) US poet

low-end *adj* inexpensive compared to a group of similar products

lower[1] /lṓ ər/ *adj* 1 BELOW physically below another thing, especially one of the same type ○ *the lower lip* 2 REDUCED OR LESS reduced or less in amount ○ *agreed to work for lower wages* 3 CLOSER TO BOTTOM closer to the bottom or base of something ○ *camped on the lower slopes of the mountain* 4 OF LESS IMPORTANCE of less importance or inferior status ○ *lower rank* 5 EARLIER IN GEOLOGICAL PERIOD relating to the earlier part of a geological period or system 6 LESS ADVANCED less advanced in terms of development or complexity 7 FARTHER FROM SOURCE indicating that part of a river that is farthest away from the source ○ *the lower Rio Grande* ■ *v* 1 *vt* BRING TO LOWER LEVEL to move something down to a lower level or to move something downwards ○ *lower the flag* 2 *vti* REDUCE OR FALL to reduce something or fall in quantity, quality, or value ○ *Interest rates have been lowered by the Bank of England.* 3 *vt* REDUCE IN DEGREE to reduce something in degree 4 *vt* LOOK DOWNWARDS to move the head or eyes downwards ○ *She lowered her eyes.* 5 *vr* HUMILIATE YOURSELF to reduce your dignity or the respect in which you are held ○ *I wouldn't lower myself to discuss it.* 6 *vt* REDUCE VOLUME OF SOUND to reduce the volume of sound that something produces ○ *lower your voice* 7 *vt* REDUCE SOUND PITCH to bring a sound to a lower pitch 8 *vt* MODIFY VOWEL SOUND to change the sound of a vowel by pushing the tongue to the bottom of the mouth ■ *n* SOMETHING LOWER something that is the lower of two or more things [12C. Comparative of LOW[1].]

lower[2] /lów ər/, **lour** /lowr/ *vi* 1 BE OVERCAST to be overcast and threatening storms or heavy rain 2 LOOK ANGRY to look angry or sullen ■ *n* SCOWL a scowl or miserable look [13C. < ?] —**lowering** *adj* —**loweringly** *adv*

lower bound *n* a number that is less than or equal to all the members of a set

Lower California /lṓ ər-/ = **Baja California**

Lower Canada southern portion of Quebec Province, Canada, from 1791 to 1840

Lower Carboniferous *n* GEOL = **Mississippian** *n.* 2

lower case *adj* written in small rather than capital form (*hyphenated when used before a noun*) ○ *written with a lower-case 'p'* ■ *n* the small rather than capital form of letters ○ *printed in lower case* [Late 17C. Because types for small letters were kept in the lower of two type cases.]

lower chamber *n* POL = **lower house**

lower class *n* the social group considered to occupy the lowest position in a hierarchical society, typically composed of manual workers and their families (*often plural*) —**lower-class** *adj*

lower deck *n* 1 the next deck in a ship above the hold 2 a ship's ordinary seamen and petty officers considered as a group (*informal*)

lower house, lower chamber *n* one of two legislative houses, generally more directly representative and larger than the other house

Lower Hutt /lṓ ər hút/ city in the S North Island, New Zealand. Population: 98,000 (1998 estimate).

lowermost /lṓ ər mōst/ *adj* very lowest

lower school *n* the younger pupils in a secondary school, usually those in the first three or four years

lower world *n* the dwelling place of the dead, often considered to be beneath the ground

lowest common denominator *n* 1 the lowest multiple shared by all the denominators in a set of fractions. US term **least common denominator** 2 the mass of ordinary people, particularly when considered to have low critical standards and to lack taste

lowest common multiple *n* the lowest whole number that is divisible without a remainder by all of the members of a set of numbers. US term **least common multiple**

Lowestoft /lṓ iss toft, lṓ stoft/ port in E England. Population: 55,200 (1994 estimate).

low-fat *adj* prepared with a reduced amount of fat

low frequency *n* a radio frequency ranging from 30 to 300 kilohertz

Low German *n* the German dialects that are spoken in N Germany. ◊ **Middle Low German** [Because it is spoken in the low-lying part of Germany]

low-grade *adj* 1 bad or inferior in quality or grade 2 describes a medical condition, especially a fever, that is mild and not serious

low-hanging fruit *n* a target that is easy to accomplish, or a problem that is easy to solve ○ *Pick the low-hanging fruit first*

low-impact *adj US* 1 not requiring a lot of energy or effort 2 causing little or no damage to the surrounding environment

low-income *adj* having a relatively small income or used by people on a relatively small income ○ *low-income families* ○ *low-income housing*

low-key, low-keyed *adj* 1 RESTRAINED restrained and understated in character ○ *a relatively low-key campaign* 2 SUBDUED IN COLOUR subdued or of low intensity, particularly in colour 3 DARK-TONED describes a photograph or painting made up of dark tones and containing few highlights

lowland /lṓlənd/ *n* land that is relatively flatter or lower than adjacent land —**lowland** *adj*

Lowlands /lṓləndz/ region of Scotland lying south of the Highlands —**Lowlander** *n*

low-level *adj* 1 situated or done at a low or lower than usual level 2 relatively low in terms of importance, status, expertise, or intensity

ϟ**low-level language** *n* computer-oriented programming language such as assembly language in which instructions are in a code closer to machine code than to human language

lowlife /lṓ līf/ *n* 1 CRIMINAL OR ASSOCIATE a criminal or somebody who associates with criminals (*informal*) 2 SOMEBODY IMMORAL a disreputable and immoral person (*informal insult*) 3 CRIMINAL OR IMMORAL PEOPLE people who are thought to have criminal tendencies or extremely low morals, regarded as a group (*informal insult*) —**lowlife** *adj*

lowlights /lṓ līts/ *npl* strands of hair that are dyed a shade darker than the natural hair colour. ◊ **highlight** *npl.*

low-loader *n* a truck or railway carriage built with a low platform so as to make it easier to load and unload heavy goods

lowly /lṓli/ *adj* (**-lier, -liest**) 1 LOW IN STATUS low in rank, status, or importance 2 MEEK with a meek and humble way of behaving 3 SIMPLE AND MODEST simple, plain, and modest in character ■ *adv* (**-lier, -liest**) 1 IN MEEK WAY in a humble or meek way 2 AT LOW VOLUME at a subdued pitch or volume —**lowliness** *n*

low-lying *adj* at a lower level or closer to sea level than neighbouring ground

low-maintenance *adj* 1 requiring only a little attention or effort to maintain (*informal*) ○ *As clients go, they're pretty low-maintenance.* 2 needing little effort or expense to keep in a good condition ○ *a low-maintenance garden*

Low Mass, low mass *n* a plain Mass celebrated in a Roman Catholic or Anglican church that is recited, not sung

low-minded *adj* thinking or behaving in a coarse vulgar way —**low-mindedly** *adv* —**low-mindedness** *n*

low-necked *adj* cut to have a low neckline

lowp *vti, n* = **loup**

low-pass filter *n* an electronic filter that blocks signals above a specified cut-off frequency but allows those below it to pass through unchanged

low-pitched *adj* 1 low in pitch or tonal range ○ *a low-pitched hum* 2 with a shallow slope ○ *a low-pitched roof*

low point *n* the least successful, enjoyable, or important part of a period of time, activity, or experience ○ *the low point of the evening*

low-pressure *adj* 1 having, exerting, or working under little pressure 2 relaxed, easygoing, or presenting little stress

low profile *n* a way of behaving in which somebody deliberately seeks to avoid attention or publicity ○ *keep a low profile*

low-profile *adj* 1 deliberately avoiding attention or publicity 2 having a wide tread relative to its radial height ○ *low-profile tyres*

low relief *n* SCULPTURE = **bas-relief** [Translation of French *bas-relief*]

⚡**low-res** /lṓ rez/ *adj* low-resolution [Shortening]

⚡**low-resolution** *adj* relating to a device such as a computer screen or printer in which the text or pictures are not sharply defined

low rise *n* a building consisting of only a few storeys [After HIGH-RISE] —**low-rise** *adj*

Lowry /lṓwri/, **L. S.** (1887–1976) British painter. Full name **Laurence Stephen Lowry**

low-slung *adj* closer to the ground or the floor than usual

low spirits *npl* a state of unhappiness, hopelessness, or despondency ◇ *The search party was in low spirits after three days.* —**low-spirited** *adj* —**low-spiritedly** *adv* —**low-spiritedness** *n*

Low Sunday *n* the Sunday after Easter [Probably in contrast to the 'high' feast of Easter Sunday]

low tech *n* low technology [Shortening] —**low-tech** *adj*

low technology *n* simple technology, especially that used to make basic items or perform basic tasks. ◊ **high technology**

low-tension *adj* capable of carrying low voltage or operating under low-voltage conditions

low tide *n* 1 a tide at its lowest level, or the time of day when this occurs 2 a lowest or worst point

low water *n* 1 OCEANOG = **low tide** *n.* 1 2 a very difficult situation or point

low-water mark *n* 1 LOWEST LEVEL OF WATER the lowest level reached by a body of tidal or fresh water 2 LINE MARKING LOW-WATER MARK a natural or artificial line marking a low-water mark 3 LOWEST POINT a lowest or most difficult point

lox[1] /loks/ *n* smoked salmon [Mid-20C. Via Yiddish *laks* < German *Lachs* 'salmon'.]

lox[2] /loks/ *n* liquid oxygen, especially when used as an oxidizer for rocket fuel [Early 20C. < *l(iquid) o(xygen) (e)x(plosive)*; later misinterpreted by folk etymology as < *l(iquid) ox(ygen)*.]

loxodrome /lóksə drōm/ *n* MAPS = **rhumb line** *n.* 1 [Late 19C. Back-formation < LOXODROMIC.]

loxodromic /lóksə drómmik/, **loxodromical** /lóksə drómmik'l/ *adj* relating to a map in which the rhumb lines appear straight, or to the rhumb lines on such a map [Late 17C. < French *loxodromique* < Greek *loxos* 'oblique' + *dromos* 'course'.] —**loxodromically** *adv*

loxodromic curve *n* MAPS = **rhumb line** *n.* 1

loyal /lóyəl/ *adj* 1 remaining faithful to a country, person, ruler, government, or ideal 2 expressing or relating to loyalty [Mid-16C. Via French < Old French *loial*, variant of *leial* < Latin *legalis* (see LEGAL).] —**loyally** *adv* —**loyalness** *n*

loyalist /lóy əlist/ *n* a firm supporter of a country, ruler, or government —**loyalism** *n*

Loyalist /lóyəlist/ *n* 1 SUPPORTER OF ULSTER UNION WITH BRITAIN a Northern Ireland Protestant who wishes to continue Northern Ireland's political union with Britain 2 AMERICAN WHO SUPPORTED BRITISH an American who supported the British during the War of American Independence 3 SPANISH CIVIL WAR SUPPORTER OF GOVERNMENT a supporter of the republican government during the Spanish Civil War

loyalty /lóyəlti/ (*plural* -**ties**) *n* 1 the quality or state of being loyal 2 a feeling of devotion, duty, or attachment to somebody or something (*often plural*) [14C. < Old French *loialté* < LOYAL (see LOYAL).]

loyalty card *n* a card issued to customers by a supermarket or chain store allowing them to qualify for rewards or discounts if they continue to shop there

lozenge /lózzinj/ *n* 1 MEDICATED TABLET a medicated tablet that soothes the throat 2 DIAMOND SHAPE a diamond-shaped figure 3 DIAMOND-SHAPED IMAGE a diamond-shaped design or device on heraldic arms [14C. < Old French *losenge* 'windowpane, small square cake'.] —**lozenged** *adj*

Lozi /lṓzi/ (*plural* -**zis** *or* -**zi**) *n* a language of W Zambia, related to Sotho. Native speakers: 450,000. [Mid-20C. < Bantu.] —**Lozi** *adj*

LP[1] *n* a long-playing gramophone record that turns at 33⅓ revolutions per minute

LP[2] *abbr* 1 Lord Provost 2 low pressure

LPG *abbr* liquefied petroleum gas

L-plate *n* a small square sign consisting of a red letter 'L' on a white background to indicate that a driver has not yet passed the driving test [L shortening of *learner*]

⚡**LPM**, **lpm** *abbr* lines per minute (*refers to a computer printer*)

LPS *abbr* 1 lipopolysaccharide 2 Lord Privy Seal

⚡**lr** *abbr* Liberia (*in Internet addresses*)

Lr *symbol* lawrencium

LR *abbr* 1 living room (*in advertisements*) 2 Lloyd's Register (of Shipping)

LRP *abbr* UK lead replacement petrol

⚡**ls** *abbr* Lesotho (*in Internet addresses*)

LSD *n* a hallucinogenic drug made from lysergic acid that was used experimentally as a medicine and is taken as an illegal drug [< German *L(yserg)s(äure)-D(iäthylamid)* 'lysergic acid diethylamide']

L.S.D, **l.s.d.** *abbr* pounds, shillings, pence [Latin *librae, solidi, denarii*]

LSE *abbr* London School of Economics

LSO *abbr* London Symphony Orchestra

⚡**lt** *abbr* Lithuania (*in Internet addresses*)

LTA *abbr* Lawn Tennis Association

Lt Cdr *abbr* Lieutenant Commander

Lt Col *abbr* Lieutenant Colonel

Ltd, **ltd** *abbr* limited (liability) (*after the name of a British company*)

Lt Gen *abbr* Lieutenant General

⚡**LTR** *abbr* long-term relationship (*in e-mails*)

⚡**lu** *abbr* Luxembourg (*in Internet addresses*)

Lu *symbol* 1 lutetium ■ *abbr* 2 Luxembourg

Lualaba /loo ə laábə/ headstream of the River Congo in the SE Democratic Republic of the Congo. Length: 1,800 km/1,100 mi.

Luanda /loo ándə/ capital of Angola, in the northwestern part of the country, on the Atlantic Ocean. Population: 1,200,000 (1988 estimate).

luau /lóo ow/ *n* a Hawaiian feast, usually with music and entertainment [Mid-19C. < Hawaiian *lū'au*.]

Luba /lóobə/ a group of Bantu languages or dialects of the S Congo, around Kinshasa. Native speakers: 8 million. [Late 19C. < Bantu.] —**Luba** *adj*

lubber /lúbbər/ *n* 1 a big person who is regarded as clumsy or unintelligent (*insult*) 2 a landlubber [14C. < ?] —**lubberly** *adj, adv*

lubber line, **lubber's line** *n* a mark on a ship's compass that indicates the vessel's heading

lubber's hole *n* a space in a platform around a mast, allowing a sailor to climb through the space and stand on the platform

lubber's line *n* NAUT = **lubber line**

lube /loob/ *n* US, Aus a lubricant (*informal*) ■ *vt* (**lubes**, **lubing**, **lubed**) US, Aus to apply lubricant to something (*informal*)

Lübeck /lṓo bek/ city in north-central Germany. Population: 217,300 (1994).

Lubitsch /lóobich/, **Ernst** (1892–1947) German-born US actor and film director

Lublin /lṓoblin/ city in SE Poland. Population: 353,300 (1995).

lubricant /lóobrikənt/ *n* 1 a substance, typically oil or grease, applied to a surface to reduce friction between moving parts 2 somebody or something that eases or facilitates a solution to a potentially difficult or awkward situation —**lubricant** *adj*

lubricate /lóobri kayt/ (-**cates**, -**cating**, -**cated**) *v* 1 *vti* APPLY LUBRICANT to apply an oily or greasy substance to something in order to reduce friction for moving parts 2 *vt* MAKE SLIPPERY to make something slippery 3 *vt* MAKE SOMETHING RUN SMOOTHLY to make something run smoothly and without problems [Early 17C. < Latin *lubricare* < *lubricus* 'slippery'.] —**lubrication** /lóobri káysh'n/ *n* —**lubricational** *adj* —**lubricative** *adj* —**lubricator** *n*

lubricious /loo bríshəss/, **lubricous** /lóobrikəss/ *adj* (*literary*) 1 lewd, obscene, or intended to be sexually exciting 2 slippery or oily [Late 16C. < Latin *lubricus* 'slippery'.] —**lubriciously** *adv*

lubricity /loo bríssəti/ *n* behaviour that is obscene or unchaste (*formal*) [15C. Directly or via French < late Latin *lubricitas* < Latin *lubricus* 'slippery'.]

lubricous *adj* = **lubricious**

Lubumbashi /lóoboom báshi/ capital of Shaba Administrative Region, SE Democratic Republic of the Congo. Population: 851,381 (1994).

Lucania, Mount /loo káyni ə/ mountain in the St Elias Range, SW Yukon Territory, Canada. Height: 5,226 m/17,147 ft.

lucarne /loo kaàrn/ *n* a dormer window [Mid-16C. Via French < Provençal *lucana*.]

Lucas /lóokəss/, **George** (*b.* 1944) US film director and producer

Lucas van Leyden /lóokəss van līd'n/ (1494–1533) Dutch painter and engraver

Lucca /lóokə/ capital of Lucca Province, Tuscany Region, north-central Italy. Population: 100,508 (1992).

Luce /looss/, **Maximilien** (1858–1941) French artist

lucent /lóoss'nt/ *adj* 1 shining with a glowing light 2 translucent or clear [15C. < Latin, present participle of *lucere* (see LUCID).] —**lucency** *n* —**lucently** *adv*

lucerne /loo súrn/ *n* PLANT SCI = **alfalfa** [Mid-17C. Via French < modern Provençal *luzerno*, originally 'glowworm' < Latin *lucerna* 'lamp' < *lucere* (see LUCID).]

Lucerne /loo súrn/ city in central Switzerland. Population: 61,656 (1994).

Lucerne, Lake of lake in central Switzerland. Area: 114 sq. km/44 sq. mi.

lucid /lóossid/ *adj* 1 EASILY UNDERSTOOD clear and easily understood ◇ *a lucid explanation* 2 RATIONAL rational, and mentally clear, especially only for a period between episodes of delirium or psychosis 3 SHINING emitting light [Late 16C. < Latin *lucidus* < *lucere* 'to shine' < *luc-*'light'.] —**lucidity** /loo síddəti/ *n* —**lucidly** *adv* —**lucidness** *n*

lucifer /lóossifər/ *n* a friction match (*archaic*) [Mid-19C. < *lucifer match*, originally a trade name.]

Lucifer /lóossifər/ *n* 1 a rebellious archangel who is held to be the same as Satan 2 the planet Venus appearing before sunrise as the morning star [Pre-12C. < Latin, 'the planet Venus', literally 'light-bearing' < *luc-* 'light'.]

luciferase /lóossifər ayz, -ayss/ *n* an enzyme that stimulates the oxidation of luciferin

luciferin /loo síffərin/ *n* a substance in the cells of bioluminescent organisms that emits light on enzymatic oxidation

luciferous /loo síffərəss/ *adj* bringing or emitting light

Lucina /loo sínə/ *n* in Roman mythology, Juno in her capacity as goddess of childbirth

~~lucious~~ incorrect spelling of **luscious**

luck /luk/ *n* 1 GOOD FORTUNE good fortune ◇ *a stroke of luck* 2 CHANCE the arbitrary distribution of events or outcomes ◇ *a game of luck* 3 FORTUNATE OR UNFORTUNATE EVENT something fortunate or unfortunate that happens to somebody, or a series of such events ◇ *Just my luck!* 4 SOMETHING BEARING LUCK an event, action, or object regarded as bringing good or bad luck ◇ *It's said to be bad luck to walk under ladders.* [15C. Probably < Low German *luk*.]

luck into *vt* US to obtain something desirable or experience something pleasurable by chance

luck out *vi* US to be lucky enough to succeed by chance (*informal*)

luckenbooth /lúkən booth/ *n* a Scottish brooch design in the shape of a silver heart, given in the past as a token of love or betrothal [15C. 'Booth that can be locked' (where such brooches were sold); *lucken*, past participle of obsolete *louk* 'lock' < Old English *lūcan*.]

luckily /lúkili/ *adv* as a result of or the occasion for good luck

luckless /lúkləss/ *adj* without success or fortune —**lucklessly** *adv* —**lucklessness** *n*

Lucknow /lúk now/ capital of Uttar Pradesh State, N India. Population: 1,619,115 (1991).

luckpenny /lúk peni/ (*plural* -**nies**) *n* a coin kept or given to bring good fortune

lucky /lúki/ (-**ier**, -**iest**) *adj* 1 FORTUNATE having good fortune ◇ *You were lucky not to be seriously injured.* 2 BRINGING GOOD FORTUNE producing or bringing good fortune ○ *lucky charm* 3 **RESULTING FROM GOOD LUCK** as a result of good luck ○ *lucky escape* —**luckiness** *n*

LITERARY LINK ***Lucky Jim***, a novel (1954) by Kingsley Amis. The protagonist of this satire on academic life, Jim Dixon, is a junior lecturer at a provincial university and the plot revolves around his problematic relationships with his employers, colleagues, and girlfriend.

lucky dip *n* 1 a game in which somebody takes a prize out of a container which is filled with soft material such as sawdust or shredded paper and within which prizes are hidden 2 a situation or venture with a large element of chance (*informal*)

lucrative /lóokrətiv/ *adj* producing profit or wealth [15C. < Latin *lucrativus* < *lucrari* 'to gain' < *lucrum* 'gain'.] —**lucratively** *adv* —**lucrativeness** *n*

lucre /lóokər/ *n* money, wealth, or profit (*dated or humorous*) ○ *filthy lucre* [14C. Directly or via French < Latin *lucrum* 'gain'.]

Lucretia /loo kréeshə/ (*fl.* 6th century BC) Roman matron

Lucretius /loo kréeshəss/ (94?–55 BC) Roman poet and philosopher

lucubration /lóokyoo bráysh'n/ *n* 1 a written work resulting from prolonged study, often having a scholarly or pedantic style (*usually plural*) 2 long hard study, especially at night [Late 16C. < Latin *lucubration-* < *lucubrare* 'compose at night' < *luc-* 'light'.] —**lucubrate** /lóokyoo brayt/ *vi*

luculent /lóokyoolənt/ *adj* 1 easy to understand 2 shining or glowing [15C. < Latin *luculentus* < *luc-* 'light'.]

Lucullan /loo kúllən/ *adj* lavish or overindulgent, especially with regard to food [Mid-19C. < Latin *Lucullanus* < Licinius *Lucullus*, 1C BC Roman general.]

Lucullus /loo kúlləss/, **Lucius Licinus** (110?–56 BC) Roman general

lud /lud/ *n* used to address a judge in court, either as 'm'lud' or 'my lud' [Early 18C. Hurried form of LORD.]

Luddite /lúddīt/ *n* 1 an opponent of technological or industrial change 2 a worker who was involved in protests in the United Kingdom in the 1810s against new factory methods of production and who favoured traditional methods of work [Early 19C. < ?] —**Luddism** *n* —**Luddite** *adj*

Lüderitz /lóodərits/ town in SW Namibia, on the Atlantic Ocean. Population: 6,000 (1990).

ludic /lóodik/ *adj* playful in a way that is spontaneous and without any particular purpose (*literary*) [Mid-20C. < French *ludique* < Latin *ludere* 'to play' < *ludus* 'game'.]

ludicrous /lóodikrəss/ *adj* utterly ridiculous because of being absurd, incongruous, impractical, or unsuitable [Early 17C. < Latin *ludicrus* < *ludus* 'play'.] —**ludicrously** *adv* —**ludicrousness** *n*

Ludlow /lúdlō/ town in W England

ludo /lóodō/ *n* a board game in which counters progress according to a player's dice throw [Late 19C. < Latin, 'I play', a form of *ludere* 'to play' < *ludus* 'game'.]

Ludwigshafen /lóodvigs hafən/ port in SW Germany, on the western bank of the River Rhine. Population: 168,100 (1994).

lues /lóo eez/ *n* syphilis [Mid-17C. < Latin, 'plague'.]

luff /luf/ *v* 1 *vt* **SAIL TOO CLOSE TO WIND** to bring a boat closer in to the wind, or to sail too close to the wind, so that the sails flap 2 *vi* **FLAP** to flap when a boat is in a position too close to the wind (*refers to a sail*) ■ *n* **FRONT EDGE OF SAIL** the front edge of a sail [12C. < Old French *lof*.]

Luftwaffe /lóoft vaffə/ *n* the German Air Force [Mid-20C. < German, 'air weapon'.]

lug[1] /lug/ *n* 1 **PROJECTING PART** a projecting part, especially one by which something can be moved, rotated, or supported 2 **PROJECTION FOR ELECTRICAL CONTACT** a small metal projection to which an electrical conductor or wire may be attached, usually by soldering or using mechanical pressure 3 **SMALL PROJECTION IMPROVING TRACTION** a small projection on a tyre or boot that helps provide traction 4 **FRUIT OR VEGETABLE BOX** a box for vegetables or fruit 5 **EAR** an ear, especially the external ear (*informal*) 6 **CLUMSY MAN** a man, especially one who is regarded as unintelligent or clumsy (*informal insult*) [14C. Probably < N Germanic.]

lug[2] /lug/ *vt* (**lugs, lugging, lugged**) 1 **PULL SOMETHING WITH EFFORT** to carry or pull something that is heavy or bulky, using great effort 2 **INTRODUCE IRRELEVANTLY INTO DISCUSSION** to introduce irrelevant material into a discussion or conversation ■ *n* **ACT OF PULLING A LOAD** the effort or action of pulling something very heavy [15C. Probably < N Germanic, related to Swedish *lugg*.]

lug[3] /lug/ *n* NAUT = **lugsail** [Mid-19C. Shortening.]

lug[4] /lug/ *n* ZOOL = **lugworm** *n.* 1 [Early 17C. < ?]

Luganda /loo gándə/ *n* LANG = **Ganda** [Late 19C. < Bantu.]

Lugano /loo gáanō/ town in S Switzerland. Population: 25,771 (1998).

Lugano, Lake lake in S Switzerland and N Italy. Area: 49 sq. km/19 sq. mi.

luge /loozh/ *n* a racing toboggan on which the riders lie on their backs with their feet pointing forwards ■ *vi* (**luges, luging, luged**) to race on a luge [Late 19C. Via Swiss French < medieval Latin *sludia*.] —**luger** *n*

luggage /lúggij/ *n* suitcases, bags, and other items for carrying personal belongings during a journey (*often before nouns*) ○ *the luggage compartment* [Late 16C. < LUG[2].]

luggage rack *n* 1 *US* = **roof rack** 2 an overhead frame in a train or bus for passengers to keep small items of luggage on

luggage van *n* a railway carriage for storing rail users' luggage and bicycles

lugger /lúggər/ *n* a small boat for fishing or pleasure sailing that is rigged with a lugsail [Mid-18C. < ?]

lughole /lúg hōl/ *n* an ear, especially the hole of the ear (*informal*)

lug nut *n* a large nut that screws onto a heavy bolt, especially one used to attach a wheel to a motor vehicle

Lugosi /loo gṓssi/, **Bela** (1884–1956) Hungarian-born US actor. Born **Bela Ferenc Denzso Blasko**

lugsail /lúg sayl, lúgss'l/ *n* a four-sided sail bent on a yard that crosses the mast at an angle [Late 17C. Probably < LUG[1].]

lugubrious /lə góobri əss/ *adj* extremely mournful, sad, or gloomy [Early 17C. < Latin *lugubris* < *lugere* 'mourn'.] —**lugubriously** *adv* —**lugubriousness** *n*

lugworm /lúg wurm/ *n* 1 a segmented sea worm that burrows in sandy shores, has rows of tufted gills, and is often used as angling bait. Genus: *Arenicola.* 2 MARINE BIOL = **fanworm** [Early 19C. < LUG[4].]

Luhansk /loo hánsk/, **Luhans'k** city in E Ukraine. Population: 504,000 (1991).

Luhrmann /lúrmən/, **Baz** (*b.* 1962) Australian film and theatre director

Lukács /lóo kach/, **György** (1885–1971) Hungarian philosopher, critic, and politician

Luke /look/ *n* the third of the gospels of the Bible in which the life and teachings of Jesus Christ are described. It is thought to have been written by St Luke.

Luke /look/, **St** (*fl.* AD 1st century) evangelist

lukewarm /look wáwrm/ *adj* 1 just slightly warm, especially when expected to be hot 2 showing or having little enthusiasm, interest, support, or conviction [14C. < obsolete *luke* 'lukewarm' < ?] —**lukewarmly** *adv* —**lukewarmness** *n*

Luleå /lóolə ō, lóoli-/ seaport in N Sweden, at the head of the Gulf of Bothnia. Population: 71,106 (1995).

lull /lul/ *v* 1 *vt* **SOOTHE OR CALM** to soothe or calm a person or animal, especially by using gentle sounds or motions 2 *vt* **MAKE SOMEBODY FEEL SAFE** to give somebody a false sense of security so that an unpleasant situation takes the person by surprise ○ *They lulled us into thinking we still had time.* 3 *vi* **BECOME CALM** to become calm or calmer ■ *n* **PERIOD OF CALM** a brief interval of calm or decreased activity [14C. Probably an imitation of the sound of soothing a child.]

lullaby /lúllə bī/ *n* (*plural* **-bies**) 1 **GENTLE SONG** a gentle song for soothing a child, especially into sleep 2 **MUSIC FOR LULLABY** instrumental music in the style of a lullaby ■ *vt* (**-bies, -bying, -bied**) **SOOTHE CHILD WITH LULLABY** to soothe a child with a lullaby [Mid-16C. < obsolete *lulla* 'lullaby', imitation of the sound of soothing a child + *-by*, as in BYE-BYE.]

Lully /lóolli/, **Jean-Baptiste** (1633–87) Italian-born French composer

lulu /lóo loo/ *n* a remarkable or outstanding person, object, or idea (*slang*) [Late 19C. Alteration of *looly* in *looliest looly of the loolies*.]

Luluabourg /loo lóo ə boorg/ former name for **Kananga**

lum /lum/ *n Scotland* a chimney or chimney stack (*informal*)

lumbago /lum báygō/ *n* pain in the lower or lumbar region of the back [Late 17C. < Latin, < *lumbus* 'loin'.]

lumbar /lúmbər/ *adj* relating to or situated in the loins or the small of the back [Mid-17C. < medieval Latin *lumbaris* < Latin *lumbus* 'loin'.]

SPELLCHECK Do not confuse ***lumbar*** with ***lumber***, which has a similar sound. Beware: your spellchecker will not catch this error.

lumbar puncture *n* the insertion of a needle between two lumbar vertebrae into the spinal cord in order to obtain a sample of cerebrospinal fluid for diagnosis or to introduce medication

lumber[1] /lúmbər/ *n* 1 *US* = **timber** *n.* 1 2 **UNWANTED OBJECTS** large objects that are not being used and are stored out of sight ■ *v* 1 *vt* **BURDEN SOMEBODY WITH TASK** to burden somebody with something unpleasant or unwanted, especially a responsibility or a task (*informal*) 2 *vti US, Can* **TURN TREES INTO TIMBER** to cut down the trees in a region and convert them into saleable timber 3 *vt* **PILE THINGS TOGETHER** to pile things together haphazardly [Mid-16C. Originally 'disused articles of furniture'.] —**lumberer** *n*

SPELLCHECK See ***lumbar***.

lumber[2] /lúmbər/ *vi* to move clumsily or heavily [14C. < ?]

lumberjack /lúmbər jak/ *n* 1 *US, Can* a cutter and transporter of trees for timber 2 *US* CLOTHING = **lumberjacket** [Mid-19C. < JACK[1].]

lumberjacket /lúmbər jakit/ *n* a work jacket made from thick, warm material, usually brightly coloured with a checked pattern [Mid-20C. < its being of a type worn by lumberjacks.]

lumberyard /lúmbər yaard/ *n US* = **timberyard**

lumen /lóomin/ (*plural* **-mens** *or* **-mina** /-minə/) *n* 1 **UNIT OF LUMINOUS FLUX** (*symbol* **lm**) the SI unit of luminous flux, equal to the amount of light crossing a unit area at a unit distance from a light source of luminous intensity of one candela 2 **SPACE WITHIN TUBE** the space inside any tubular structure in the body, e.g. an intestine, artery, or vein 3 **CAVITY IN PLANT** the cavity within a plant cell wall [Late 19C. < Latin, 'light, opening'.]

Lumet /loo mét/, **Sidney** (*b.* 1924) US actor, director, and screenwriter

Lumière /lóomi air/, **Auguste** (1864–1948) French inventor

Lumière, Louis (1862–1954) French inventor

luminaire /lóomi náir/ *n* a tungsten or fluorescent light fitting [Early 20C. < French, < Old French *luminarie* (see LUMINARY).]

luminance /lóominənss/ *n* 1 (*symbol L*) the condition or quality of emitting or reflecting light 2 a measure of the brightness of a surface equal to the amount of luminous flux arriving at, passing through, or leaving a unit area of surface [Late 19C. < *luminant* 'luminous' < Latin *luminant-*, present participle of *luminare* 'illuminate' < *lumin-* 'light' (see LUMINOUS).]

luminaria /lóomi náiri ə/ *n Southwest US* a small candle set inside a paper bag that has been weighted with sand, usually placed outdoors with others as a Christmas decoration [Mid-20C. < Mexican Spanish, < Spanish, 'decorative light' < late Latin, 'lamp', plural of *luminarium* (see LUMINARY).]

luminary /lóominəri/ *n* (*plural* **-ies**) 1 **EMINENT PERSON** an eminent or famous person 2 **SUN, MOON, OR STAR** an object, especially an astronomical one, that emits light (*literary*) ■ *adj* **CHARACTERIZED BY LIGHT** relating to or characterized by light [15C. Directly or via Old French *luminarie* < late Latin *luminarium* < Latin *lumin-* 'light'.]

luminesce /lóomi néss/ (**-nesces, -nescing, -nesced**) *vi* to emit light by phosphorescence, fluorescence, or bioluminescence [Late 19C. Back-formation < *luminescent* (see LUMINESCENCE).]

luminescence /lóomi néss'nss/ *n* 1 the emission of light produced by means other than heat (**incandescence**), e.g. phosphorescence, fluorescence, or bioluminescence 2 the light emitted by luminescence [Late 19C. < *luminescent*, < Latin *lumin-* 'light'.] —**luminescent** *adj*

luminiferous /lóomi níffərəss/ *adj* generating or giving off light [Early 19C. < Latin *lumin-* 'light'.]

luminol /lo͝omi nol/ *n* $C_8H_7N_3O_2$ a white crystalline compound. Use: chemical testing. [Mid-20C. < Latin *lumin-* 'light'.]

luminosity /lo͝omi nóssəti/ (*plural* **luminosities**) *n* **1 STATE OF BEING LUMINOUS** the state or quality of being luminous **2 ENERGY RADIATED BY ASTRONOMICAL OBJECT** (*symbol L*) the energy radiated per second by a astronomical body **3 STRENGTH OF LIGHT EMITTED** the visual perception of the extent to which an object emits light **4 SOMETHING LUMINOUS** something that emits light

luminous /lo͝ominəss/ *adj* **1 LIGHT-EMITTING** emitting or reflecting light **2 BRIGHT** startlingly bright ○ *luminous orange* **3 ILLUMINATED** brightly illuminated **4 UNDERSTANDABLE** clear and easy to understand **5 INSPIRING** enlightened and inspiring **6 RELATING TO LIGHT** evaluated on the basis of the visual sensation produced in an observer rather than energy measurements [15C. Directly or via French < Latin *luminosus* < *lumin-* 'light, opening'.] —**luminously** *adv* —**luminousness** *n*

luminous energy *n* (*symbol* Q_V) the total amount of light emitted by a source

luminous flux *n* (*symbol* Φ_V) the rate of emission of light evaluated by the visual sensation it produces

luminous intensity *n* (*symbol* I_V) the amount of light emitted by a source in a particular direction

lumme /lúmmi/, **lummy** *interj* used to express surprise or shock (*dated informal*) [Late 19C. < *(Lord) love me.*]

lummox /lúmməks/ *n* somebody considered clumsy or unintelligent (*informal insult*) [Early 19C. < ?]

lummy *interj* = **lumme** (*archaic*)

lump[1] /lump/ *n* **1 SOLID CHUNK** a small irregularly shaped solid mass or piece **2 TUMOUR** a tumour or other swelling in the body **3 SUGAR CUBE** a small cube of solid sugar **4 LARGE AND CLUMSY PERSON** a large and unintelligent or clumsy person (*informal insult*) **5 CASUAL CONSTRUCTION WORKERS** a collective term for workers in the building trade who are casual and do not belong to a union (*informal*) **6** *Scotland* a big, fleshy, slow-moving person (*informal*) ■ *v* **1** *vt* **GROUP THINGS TOGETHER CARELESSLY** to consider people, ideas, or objects as a single group, often without good reason ○ *All the students were lumped together as lazy.* **2** *vi* **MOVE HEAVILY** to move in a heavy and clumsy manner ○ *He lumped along.* ■ *adj* **IN LUMPS** in small cubes or lumps ○ *lump sugar* [14C. < ?]

lump[2] /lump/ *vt* to endure something unpleasant that cannot be changed (*informal*) ○ *like it or lump it* [Late 16C. < ?]

lumpectomy /lum péktəmi/ (*plural* **-mies**) *n* a surgical operation for breast cancer in which the surgery is limited to the removal of the visible and palpable tumour only [Late 20C. < LUMP[1].]

lumpen /lúmpən, lo͝om-/ *adj* (*disapproving*) **1 MARGINALIZED** living, or regarded as living, on the margins of society **2 NOT EDUCATED OR ENLIGHTENED** stupidly content with a life regarded as intellectually empty and socially inferior ■ *npl* **LUMPEN PEOPLE** people regarded by others as lumpen (*disapproving; + plural verb*) [Mid-20C. Back-formation < LUMPENPROLETARIAT.]

lumpenproletariat /lúmpən prōlə táiri ət, lo͝om-/ *n* (*+ singular or plural verb*) **1** in Marxist analysis, people regarded as living on the margins of society, particularly criminals, homeless people, and the long-term unemployed **2** people from the lowest social class who are regarded as too content with a life supposedly intellectually empty and socially inferior (*disapproving*) [Early 20C. < German, < *Lumpen*, plural of *Lump* 'ragamuffin' + French *prolétariat* (see PROLETARIAT).]

lumpfish /lúmpfish/ (*plural* **-fishes** *or* **-fish**) *n* **1** the eggs of a northern sea fish used as food **2** a northern sea fish with a short scaleless body covered with rows of thorny lumps. Family: Cyclopteridae. [Early 17C. < Middle Dutch *lumpe* 'cod'.]

lumpish /lúmpish/ *adj* **1** tending to move awkwardly or slowly and heavily **2** regarded as having no intelligence, energy, or enthusiasm (*insult*) —**lumpishly** *adv* —**lumpishness** *n*

lumpsucker /lúmp sukər/ *n* ZOOL = **lumpfish** [Mid-18C. < obsolete *lump* 'lumpfish'.]

lump sum *n* an amount of money that is given in a single payment, rather than being divided into smaller periodic payments

lumpy /lúmpi/ (**-ier, -iest**) *adj* **1 WITH LUMPS** having or filled with lumps, especially when lumps are unwanted, e.g. in the upholstery of a chair or the mattress of a bed **2 LACKING SMOOTHNESS OF TEXTURE** describes semiliquid foods, e.g. sauces and soups, that lack the normal appetizing smoothness of texture **3 CUMBERSOME** with a cumbersome quality or appearance **4 CHOPPY** having or exhibiting short choppy waves —**lumpily** *adv* —**lumpiness** *n*

Lumumba /lo͞o mo͝ombə/, **Patrice** (1925–61) Congolese statesman

Luna /lo͞onə/ *n* the goddess of the Moon in Roman mythology. Greek equivalent **Selene** [14C. < Latin, 'moon'.]

lunacy /lo͞onəssi/ (*plural* **lunacies**) *n* **1** behaviour that is regarded as unintelligent, inconsiderate, or misguided, or an example of it **2** an offensive former term for any psychiatric disorder that rendered patients legally incompetent and required them to be taken into care (*archaic offensive*) [Mid-16C. < LUNATIC.]

luna moth /lo͞onə-/ *n* a large moth that has spotted light-green wings with long thin extensions at the back that look like tails. Native to: North America. *Actias luna*. [< Latin, 'moon'; from the crescent-shaped spots on its wings]

lunar /lo͞onər/ *adj* **1 RELATING TO MOON** relating to a moon or its movement around a planet, especially the Moon in relation to the Earth **2 USED FOR TRAVEL TO THE MOON** for use in space travel to or on the Moon **3 CRESCENT-SHAPED** in the shape of a crescent moon **4 PALE** pale and cold-looking, as the Moon is compared to the Sun [15C. < Latin *lunaris* < *luna* 'moon'.]

lunar caustic *n* silver nitrate, especially when formed into small sticks (*archaic*)

lunar cycle *n* a principal means of establishing a calendar, based on the cycles of the moon. The Muslim calendar is based on the lunar cycle.

lunar eclipse *n* an eclipse of the Moon caused by the Earth passing between the Sun and the Moon and casting its shadow on the Moon

lunar excursion module *n* AEROSP = **lunar module**

lunarian /loo náiri ən/ *n* in mythology and science fiction, an inhabitant of the Moon [Early 18C. < Latin *lunaris* (see LUNAR).]

lunar module *n* a small spacecraft used to travel from an orbiting command module to the surface of the Moon and back

lunar month *n* **1** the time between one new moon and the next, a period of about 29.5 days. It is the time the Moon takes to make one complete orbit of the Earth. **2** a period of four weeks

Lunar New Year *n* the Chinese New Year, which usually occurs at a point between late January and mid-February

lunarscape /lo͞onər skayp/ *n* a rugged barren landscape of strange rock formations, similar to the surface of the Moon

lunar year *n* a period of 12 lunar months

lunate /lo͞on ayt/ *adj* **lunate, lunated** shaped like a crescent moon ■ *n* ANAT = **lunate bone** [Late 18C. < Latin *lunatus* < *luna* 'moon'.]

lunate bone *n* a bone of the wrist that articulates with the bones of the forearm [< its shape]

lunatic /lo͞onətik/ *adj* **1 THOUGHTLESS** thoughtless, ridiculous, or reckless **2 OFFENSIVE TERM** an offensive term formerly meaning affected by a psychiatric disorder (*archaic*) ■ *n* **1 OFFENSIVE TERM** an offensive former term for somebody who has a psychiatric disorder (*archaic offensive*) **2 IRRESPONSIBLE PERSON** somebody considered wildly reckless (*informal insult*) [13C. Via French *lunatique* < late Latin *lunaticus* 'moonstruck' < Latin *luna* 'moon'.]

lunatic fringe *n* people whose views are regarded as eccentrically radical (*insult*)

lunation /loo náysh'n/ *n* TIME = **lunar month** *n.* 1 [14C. < medieval Latin *lunation-* < Latin *luna* 'moon'.]

lunch /lunch/ *n* **1 MIDDAY MEAL** a meal eaten in the middle of the day, especially a light meal that is not the main meal of the day (*often before nouns*) **2 FOOD EATEN AT MIDDAY** the food prepared and eaten at the midday meal ○ *Our lunch was soup and salad.* ■ *vi* **EAT LUNCH** to eat lunch, especially a specified kind of lunch eaten somewhere other than at home [Early 19C. Shortening of LUNCHEON.] ◇ **out to lunch** an offensive term that means displaying thoughtlessness or unusual behaviour in a way that suggests a loss of touch with reality (*insult*)

LITERARY LINK ***The Naked Lunch***, a novel (1959) by US writer William Burroughs. This controversial portrayal of drug abuse consists of a series of surreal episodes linked by themes and characters and described in language that is by turns clinical, hallucinatory, poetic, and scatological.

lunchbox /lúnch boks/ *n* a container for sandwiches or other foods carried somewhere, e.g. to work, to eat for lunch

luncheon /lúnchən/ *n* (*formal*) **1** lunch **2** an organized gathering in the middle of the day, with invited guests being served a meal and often offered some form of entertainment [Mid-17C. Probably alteration of *nuncheon* 'snack' < NOON + obsolete *schench* 'drink'.]

luncheonette /lúnchə nét/ *n* US a small fairly simple restaurant

luncheon meat *n* processed meat, e.g. ham mixed with cereal, sold in a tin or sliced, and usually eaten cold

luncheon voucher *n* a voucher that can be exchanged for food in participating restaurants, sandwich bars, and other food establishments at lunchtime

lunchroom /lúnch room, -ro͞om/ *n* US a room in a school or office where people can buy lunch or eat a packed lunch

lunchtime /lúnch tīm/ *n* the time, around the middle of the day, when lunch is usually eaten (*often before nouns*)

Lund /lo͝ond/ city in S Sweden. Population: 96,557 (1995).

Lunda /lo͝ondə/ *n* a Bantu language spoken in western central Africa, especially in Zaïre. Native speakers: 82,000. [Late 19C. < Bantu.] —**Lunda** *adj*

Lundy /lúndi/ island in SW England, in the Bristol Channel. Area: 4.24 sq. km/1.64 sq. mi.

lune /loon/ *n* **1** a crescent-shaped area on the surface of a plane or sphere defined by two semicircles whose common end points are diametrically opposed **2** CHR = **lunette** *n.* 6 [Early 18C. Via French < Latin *luna* 'moon'.]

Lüneburg /lo͞onə burg/ town in north-central Germany. Population: 60,100 (1989).

lunette /loo nét/ *n* **1 CRESCENT-SHAPED OBJECT** any object that has a crescent shape **2 WINDOW IN DOMED CEILING** an arch-shaped window at the height of a domed ceiling **3 SEMICIRCULAR PANEL** a semicircular panel on a wall, containing a window, painting, or frieze **4 VEHICLE'S TOWING RING** a metal ring on a vehicle to which a rope can be attached for towing **5 CRESCENT-SHAPED MOUND OF SILT** a crescent-shaped mound of fine silt or clay similar in form to a sand dune, found especially near the edge of a temporary lake **6 CONTAINER USED IN ROMAN CATHOLIC MASS** in the Roman Catholic Church, a crescent-shaped container in which the consecrated bread is placed during a Mass [Late 16C. Via French, 'little moon' < Latin *luna* (see LUNAR).]

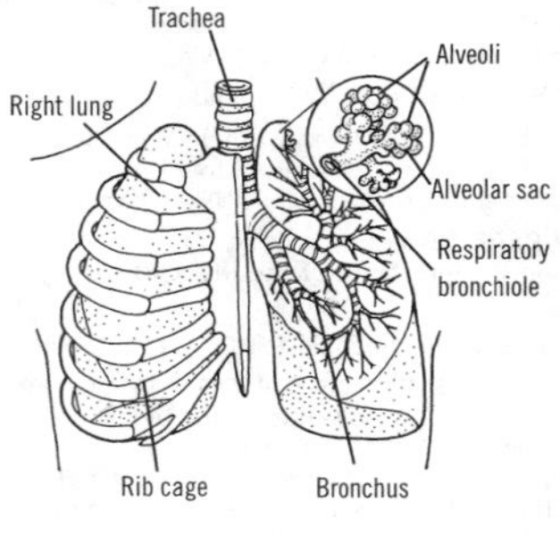
Trachea
Alveoli
Right lung
Alveolar sac
Respiratory bronchiole
Rib cage
Bronchus

Lung

lung /lung/ *n* **1** in air-breathing vertebrate animals, either of the paired spongy respiratory organs, situated inside the rib cage, that transfer oxygen into the blood and remove carbon dioxide from it (*often before nouns*) **2** a respiratory organ found in invertebrate animals, especially the highly vascular region of the mantle cavity in some terrestrial snails [Old English, < Indo-European, 'light'] —**lungful** *n* ◇ **at the top of your lungs** extremely loudly (*informal*)

lunge[1] /lunj/ *n* **1 SUDDEN FORWARD MOVEMENT** a sudden strong attacking movement forwards **2 QUICK THRUST** a sudden thrust made at an opponent ■ *vi* (**lunges, lunging, lunged**) **1 MOVE SUDDENLY FORWARDS THREATENINGLY** to make a sudden attacking movement, thrusting forwards **2 MAKE A QUICK THRUST** to execute a sudden thrust at an opponent, especially with the sword or épée extended parallel to the floor [Mid-18C. Alteration of French *allonger* < Old French *alongier* 'lengthen' < Latin *longus* 'long'.]

lunge[2] /lunj/, **longe** /lunj, lonj/ *n* **1 HORSE-TRAINING ROPE** a long rope used to hold a horse while it is being trained **2 HORSE-TRAINING AREA** an enclosed circular area where young horses are trained ■ *vt* (**lunges, lunging, lunged; longes, longing, longed**) **TRAIN USING LUNGE** to train a horse using a lunge [Early 18C. < French *longe* 'cord' < Old French *alongier* (see LUNGE[1]).]

lungfish /lúng fish/ (*plural* **-fishes** *or* **-fish**) *n* a bony freshwater fish with one or two lungs for breathing air as well as gills that often becomes inactive during the dry season. Native to: swamps and pools in Australia, Africa, and South America. Order: Dipneusti.

lungi /lóong gi/, **lungyi** *n* a long piece of cloth, often brightly coloured, traditionally worn by men as a loincloth in the Indian subcontinent and like a skirt by men and women in Myanmar [Early 17C. Via Hindi *lungī* < Persian.]

lungworm /lúng wurm/ *n* a parasitic nematode worm that inhabits the lungs of mammals and birds, sometimes causing coughs or respiratory distress

lungwort /lúng wurt/ *n* **1 WOODLAND PLANT** a perennial woodland plant once used to treat respiratory disorders. Flowers: tubular, purple or blue, often pink as buds. Native to: Europe, Asia. Genus: *Pulmonaria*. **2 PLANT OF BORAGE FAMILY** a plant of the borage family. Flowers: blue, in dangling clusters. Native to: northern temperate regions. Genus: *Mertensia*. **3 LICHEN RESEMBLING LUNG TISSUE** a lichen having a superficial resemblance to lung tissue, dark green when wet and pale greenish-brown when dry. *Lobaria pulmonaria*. [Old English *lungenwyrt*]

lungyi *n* CLOTHING = **lungi**

lunisolar /lóoni sṓlər/ *adj* relating to both the Sun and the Moon, especially to the gravitational pull of both the Sun and the Moon

lunitidal interval /lóoni tíd'l-/ *n* the time between the moon's passing a given point and the next high tide at that point

lunula /lóonyòolə/ (*plural* **-lae** /-lee/), **lunule** /lóo nyool/ *n* a semicircular mark, especially the white crescent-shaped area at the base of the fingernail (*technical*) [Late 16C. < Latin, 'small moon' < *luna* 'moon'.] —**lunular** *adj* — **lunulate** *adj*

luny *adj, n* = **loony**

Luo /lóo ō/ (*plural* **-o** *or* **-os**) *n* **1** a member of an African people who migrated from the Upper Nile Valley, founding a dynasty among Bantu-speaking people in the lake region of E Africa **2** a Nilotic language spoken in parts of Kenya and Tanzania. Native speakers: 6 million. [Early 20C. < Luo.] —**Luo** *adj*

Luoyang /lṓ yáng/ city in east-central China. Population: 1,246,076 (1991).

lupin /lóopin/ *n* an annual or perennial plant with seeds in pods. Flowers: various colours, in tall spikes. Native to: N hemisphere. Genus: *Lupinus*. [14C. < Latin *lupinus* (see LUPIN).]

lupine[1] /lóo pīn/ *adj* **1** relating to a wolf or wolves **2** wildly hungry or greedy in behaviour or character [Mid-17C. < Latin *lupinus* < *lupus* 'wolf'.]

lupine[2] *n* US = **lupin**

lupulin /lóopyòolin/ *n* a sticky yellow powder found in hop cones and containing the resins and essential oils that give beer its bitter taste [Early 19C. < modern Latin *lupulus* < Latin, 'hop plant', literally 'little wolf' < *lupus* 'wolf'.]

lupus /lóopəss/ *n* **1** = **lupus erythematosus 2** = **lupus vulgaris** [Late 16C. < Latin, 'wolf'.]

Lupus /lóopəss/ *n* a constellation of the southern hemisphere. See illustration at **constellation**

lupus erythematosus /-érri theemə tṓssəss/ *n* either of two inflammatory diseases affecting connective tissue, one largely confined to the skin, the other affecting the joints and internal organs [*Erythematosus* < modern Latin, < Greek *eruthēma* (see ERYTHEMA)]

lupus vulgaris /-vul gáiriss/ *n* tuberculosis of the skin in which reddish-brown patches develop on the face, leading to tissue destruction and scarring [< modern Latin, 'common lupus']

lurch[1] /lurch/ *vi* **1 MOVE VIOLENTLY** to lean or pitch suddenly to one side **2 MOVE UNSTEADILY** to move along unsteadily, swaying from side to side ■ *n* **SUDDEN SIDEWAYS MOVEMENT** a sudden unbalanced movement to the side [Late 17C. < ?] —**lurchingly** *adv*

lurch[2] /lurch/ *n* in the card game cribbage, the state of being left with less than 30 points or half the winner's score at the end of a game [14C. < ?] ◇ **leave somebody in the lurch** to leave somebody in a difficult or embarrassing situation and offer no help

lurcher /lúrchər/ *n* a long-limbed crossbred dog that has predominant greyhound features [Early 16C. < *lurch* 'to lurk', probably variant of LURK.]

lure /lyoor, loor/ *vt* (**lures, luring, lured**) **1 ENTICE** to persuade somebody to go somewhere or do something by offering something tempting **2 RECALL FALCON** to persuade a falcon to return by swinging a device in the air to attract its attention ■ *n* **1 SOMETHING THAT ENTICES** something that attracts or entices somebody to do something or go somewhere **2 ATTRACTION** the attractive or tempting quality that something has **3 DEVICE ATTRACTING FISH** a device attached to a fishing line to attract fish **4 DEVICE FOR RECALLING FALCON** a device swung through the air to attract or recall a falcon, usually a leather bag attached to the end of a line [13C. < Old French *luere* < Germanic.] — **lurer** *n*

lurgy /lúrgi/ *n* any illness or infection (*informal*) [Mid-20C. < ?]

Luria /lóori ə/, **Isaac ben Solomon** (1534–72) Palestinian mystic and scholar. Known as **The Lion**

lurid /lyóorid, lóor-/ *adj* **1 HORRIFYING OR SHOCKING** sensational and shocking, with graphic details of horror, devastation, or violence **2 UNATTRACTIVELY BRIGHT** of a sickeningly intense brightness or boldness of colour ○ *a lurid green* **3 GLOWING UNNATURALLY** glowing with an unnaturally vivid brightness **4 PALLID** with a pale sickly complexion [Mid-17C. < Latin *luridus* 'pale yellow, ghastly'.] —**luridly** *adv* —**luridness** *n*

Lurie /lóori/, **Alison** (*b.* 1926) US novelist and scholar

⚡**lurk** /lurk/ *vi* **1 MOVE OR WAIT FURTIVELY** to move about furtively, or wait in a concealed position or a shadowy corner, especially with the intention of doing something wrong ○ *a figure lurking in the bushes* **2 EXIST UNSUSPECTED** to exist as an unsuspected threat or danger **3 READ BUT NOT SEND MESSAGES** to read messages sent to an online discussion forum without contributing (*slang*) ■ *n ANZ* **SCAM** a sly or underhanded scheme (*informal*) [13C. Probably < Low German or N Germanic.] —**lurker** *n* —**lurking** *adj*

Lusaka /loo sáakə, -zaákə/ capital of Zambia, in the south-central part of the country. Population: 982,362 (1990).

luscious /lúshəss/ *adj* **1 SWEET AND JUICY** with a rich, sweet, and juicy taste **2 ROMANTIC AND EMOTIONAL** written in a dramatic and romantic style with a strong appeal to the emotions and senses **3 DESIRABLE** very desirable physically, especially with a strong and direct sexual presence (*informal*) [14C. Alteration of *licious* < ?] —**lusciously** *adv* —**lusciousness** *n*

lush[1] /lush/ *adj* **1 GROWING VIGOROUSLY** producing a lot of vigorous rich young growth **2 WITH RICH TASTE** tasting rich, sweet, and juicy **3 LUXURIOUS** with luxurious decoration and furnishings **4 IN A DRAMATIC STYLE** written in a dramatic style that is intended to produce an emotional response **5 SEXY** voluptuously sensual in appearance or behaviour (*informal*) [15C. Probably alteration of *lache* 'loose, weak', via Old French, 'soft' < Latin *laxus* 'loose'.] — **lushly** *adv* —**lushness** *n*

lush[2] /lush/ *n US* (*slang*) **1 HEAVY DRINKER** a drunkard **2 ALCOHOL** alcoholic drink ■ *vi US* **DRINK HEAVILY** to drink too much alcohol regularly (*slang*) [Late 18C. < ?]

Lushun /lóo shóon/, **Lü-shun** town and seaport in NE China, opposite the coast of N Shandong Peninsula

Lusitania /lóossi táyni ə/ ancient region and Roman province, corresponding approximately to present-day Portugal and W Spain —**Lusitanian** *adj, n*

lust /lust/ *n* **1 SEXUAL DESIRE** the strong physical desire to have sex with somebody, usually without associated feelings of love or affection **2 EAGERNESS** great eagerness or enthusiasm for something ○ *a lust for power* ■ *vi* **1 DESIRE SEXUALLY** to feel a strong desire to have sex with somebody **2 BE EAGER FOR** to have a very strong desire to obtain something [Old English, 'pleasure, desire' < Indo-European, 'be eager'] —**lustful** *adj* —**lustfully** *adv* — **lustfulness** *n*

luster *n, vt* US = **lustre**

lustra plural of **lustrum**

lustral /lústrəl/ *adj* **1** serving to purify the spirit or relating to ceremonies of religious purification **2** taking place once every five years [Mid-16C. < Latin *lustralis* < *lustrum* 'purification'.]

lustrate /lu stráyt, lús trayt/ (**-trates, -trating, -trated**) *vt* to make somebody or something spiritually pure by means of a special religious ceremony [Early 17C. < Latin *lustrare* 'to purify by lustral rites' < *lustrum* 'purification'.] — **lustration** /lu stráysh'n/ *n* —**lustrative** /lústrətiv/ *adj*

lustre /lústər/ *n* **1 SOFT SHEEN** a soft sheen of reflected light, especially from metal that has been polished gently **2 SHININESS** a bright and shiny condition or tone **3 SPLENDOUR** the glory and magnificence of a great achievement **4 POLISH** polish or wax used to give something a shiny finish **5 CHANDELIER** a chandelier or candelabrum made of cut glass, designed to reflect the light **6 GLASS PENDANT ON CHANDELIER** any decorative piece of cut glass hanging from a chandelier **7 GLAZE ON POTTERY** an opalescent metallic glaze on pottery, especially porcelain **8 LIGHT REFLECTED BY A MINERAL** the quality and amount of light reflected from the surface of a mineral **9 GLOSSY FABRIC** fabric with a sheen or glossy surface **10** TIME = **lustrum** *n.* 1 ■ *vt* (**-tres, -tring, -tred**) **1 IMPART GLOSSY FINISH TO** to impart a glossy finish or coating to something **2 GLORIFY** to give something a glorious or magnificent quality [Early 16C. < French, < Latin *lustrare* 'to brighten' < *lustrum* 'purification'.]

lustrous /lústrəss/ *adj* with a soft shine or gloss —**lustrously** *adv* —**lustrousness** *n*

lustrum /lústrəm/ (*plural* **-trums** *or* **-tra** /-trə/) *n* (*formal*) **1** a period of five years **2** purification of the entire ancient Roman people, taking place every five years after the census [Late 16C. < Latin, 'purification'.]

lusty /lústi/ (**-ier, -iest**) *adj* **1 STRONG AND HEALTHY** in extremely good physical health, especially possessing great stamina and strength **2 ENERGETIC** full of energy, vitality, and enthusiasm **3 LUSTFUL** strongly desiring sex —**lustily** *adv* —**lustiness** *n*

lusus naturae /lóossəss nə tyóor ee/ (*plural* **lusus naturae** *or* **lususes naturae**) *n* something that has developed abnormally (*formal*) [< Latin, 'sport of nature']

lute[1] /loot/ *n* a plucked musical instrument of the 14th to the 17th centuries resembling the guitar but with a flat, pear-shaped body [13C. < Old French *lut* < Arabic *al-'ūd* 'wood'.]

lute[2] /loot/ *n* **1 SEALANT USED IN THE BUILDING TRADE** any substance, e.g. clay or cement, used for sealing apertures, joints, or porous surfaces in the building trade **2 FLOUR AND WATER PASTE** a paste of flour and water used in cooking as a seal, e.g. to keep a casserole lid on tight **3 PASTE USED IN DENTISTRY** a paste used in dentistry to attach a crown or cap onto a tooth ■ *vt* **SEAL WITH LUTE** to seal, pack, or coat something using lute [14C. Directly or via French < medieval Latin *lutum* < Latin, 'mud, potter's clay'.]

luteal /lóoti əl/ *adj* relating to the stage of the menstrual cycle between the formation of a yellow mass of tissue (**corpus luteum**) after the release of an ovum and the start of the next period [Early 20C. < Latin *luteus* 'yellow'.]

lutein /lóoti in/ *n* **1** the yellow carotenoid pigment found in many plants and egg yolks **2** a powdered preparation of the tissue (**corpus luteum**) formed following the release of an ovum [Mid-19C. < Latin *luteus* 'yellow'.]

luteinising hormone *n* = **luteinizing hormone**

luteinising hormone-releasing hormone, luteinising hormone-releasing factor *n* = **luteinizing hormone-releasing hormone**

luteinizing hormone /lóoti inīzing-/, **luteinising hormone** *n* a pituitary hormone that causes the ovary to produce one or more eggs, to secrete progesterone, and to form the corpus luteum, and causes the testes to secrete male sex hormones

luteinizing hormone-releasing hormone, luteinising hormone-releasing hormone, luteinizing hormone-releasing factor, luteinising hormone-releasing factor *n* a hormone released by the hypothalamus that triggers the secretion of luteinizing hormone by the pituitary

lutenist /lóotənist/ *n* a player of a lute [Early 17C. < medieval Latin *lutanista* < *lutana* 'lute'.]

luteolin /lóoti ōlin/ *n* a yellow pigment found in some plants [Mid-19C. Via French < modern Latin *luteola* < Latin *luteolus* 'yellowish' < *luteus* 'yellow'.]

lutetium /loo teésham, -shi əm/ n (*symbol* **Lu**) a silvery-white metallic element that belongs to the rare-earth group. Source: monazite. Use: catalyst in the nuclear industries. [Early 20C. < Latin *Lutetia* 'Paris', native city of its discoverer, chemist Georges Urbains.]

Luther /loóthər/, **Martin** (1483–1546) German theologian and religious reformer

Lutheran /loótharən/ n a Christian who is a member of the Protestant church established by Martin Luther (**Lutheran Church**) ▪ adj relating or belonging to Lutheranism

Lutheranism /loótharənizəm/ n the first form of Protestantism, founded by Martin Luther in 16th-century Germany. It focuses on the teachings of Jesus Christ and stresses individual faith over collective church authority.

luthier /loóti ər/ n a maker and repairer of violins and other stringed instruments [Late 19C. < French, < *luth* 'lute' < Old French *lut* (see LUTE[1]).]

Luthuli /loo toóli/, **Albert** (1899–1967) South African political leader

lutist /loótist/ n US MUSIC = lutenist

Luton /loót'n/ town in central England. Population: 167,300 (1991).

Lutosławski /loótə slaávski/, **Witold** (1913–94) Polish composer and conductor

Lutyens /lúttyənz/, **Sir Edwin Landseer** (1869–1944) British architect

lutz /loöts/ n a figure-skating jump from the back edge of one skate, landing on the back edge of the other, with one or more full rotations [Mid-20C. Probably after the Swiss figure skater Gustave *Lussi*.]

Lützen /loöts'n/ town in east-central Germany

luv /luv/ n used as an informal spelling of 'love', especially when somebody is being addressed (*informal*)

luvvie /lúvvi/, **luvvy** (*plural* **-vies**) n an actor or somebody whose behaviour conforms to a stereotype of actors (*informal humorous or disapproving*) [Late 20C. Variant of *lovey*, stereotypically used by actors.] —**luvviedom** n —**luvviness** n

Luwian /loö i ən/ n an extinct Anatolian language belonging to Indo-European [Early 20C. Translation of German *Luwisch* < *Luwia* 'Luwia', region in Asia Minor.] —**Luwian** adj

lux /luks/ (*plural* **lux** or **luces** /loö seez/) n (*symbol* **lx**) the SI unit of illumination, equal to one lumen per square metre [Late 19C. < Latin *lux* 'light'.]

luxate /luk sáyt, lúk sayt/ (**-ates, -ating, -ated**) vt to displace the bones of a joint (*technical*) [Early 17C. < Latin *luxare* < *luxus* 'dislocated'.] —**luxation** /luk sáysh'n/ n

Luxembourg

Luxembourg /lúksəm burg/ **1** grand duchy in W Europe. Capital: Luxembourg (City). Population: 420,415 (1997). Area: 2,586 sq. km/998 sq. mi. **2** largest and southernmost province of Belgium. Capital: Arlon. Population:241,339 (1996). Area: 4,440 sq. km/1,714 sq. mi. —**Luxembourger** n

Luxembourg City capital of Luxembourg, in the south-central part of the country. Population: 76,446 (1995).

Luxembourgish /lúksəm burg ish/ n the official language of Luxembourg, a form of German with many French elements —**Luxembourgish** adj

Luxemburg /lúksəm burg/, **Rosa** (1871–1919) Polish-born German political activist

Luxor /loök sawr, lúk-/ town in east-central Egypt, on the River Nile. Population: 146,000 (1992).

luxulyanite /luk soölyə nīt/ n a rare granite that contains needles of tourmaline in quartz and feldspar [Late 19C. After *Luxullian*, village in Cornwall.]

luxuriant /lug zyoóri ənt, luk syoóri-, lug zhoóri-/ adj **1** LUSH with a lot of young rich healthy growth ○ *luxuriant ground cover* **2** GROWING PROFUSELY growing thickly and profusely ○ *a luxuriant mane of dark curly hair* **3** ELABORATE written in an elaborate, showy, and dramatic style **4** PRODUCTIVE producing vast quantities of something [Mid-16C. < Latin *luxuriant*, present participle of *luxuriare* (see LUXURIATE).] —**luxuriance** n —**luxuriantly** adv

luxuriate /lug zyoóri ayt, luk syoóri-, lug zhoóri-/ (**-ates, -ating, -ated**) vi **1** to enjoy something in a self-indulgent way, taking great pleasure from the luxury and comfort that it offers **2** to grow vigorously and successfully [Early 17C. < Latin *luxuriat-*, past participle of *luxuriare* < *luxuria* 'profusion'.]

luxurious /lug zyoóri əss, luk syoóri-, lug zhoóri-/ adj **1** very comfortable, with high-quality expensive fittings or fabrics **2** with a liking for luxury or used to living in it —**luxuriously** adv —**luxuriousness** n

luxury /lúkshəri/ (*plural* **luxuries**) n **1** PLEASURABLE SELF-INDULGENT ACTIVITY an activity that gives great pleasure, especially one only rarely indulged in **2** NONESSENTIAL ITEM an item that is desirable but not essential, and often expensive or hard to get (*often before nouns*) **3** GREAT COMFORT expensive high-quality surroundings, and the great comfort that they provide (*often before nouns*) [14C. Via Old French *luxurie* < Latin *luxuria* 'profusion, excess' < *luxus* 'dislocated'.]

Luzon /loo zón/ largest island in the Philippines, in the northern part of the country. Population: 30,759,000 (1990). Area: 104,690 sq. km/40,421 sq. mi.

✦ **lv** abbr Latvia (*in Internet addresses*)

Lviv /lə víf/, **L'viv, Lvov** /lə vóf/ city in W Ukraine. Population: 806,000 (1995).

Lvov = Lviv

LW abbr **1** long wave **2** low water

lwei /lə wáy/ (*plural* **lweis** or **lwei**) n see table at **currency** [Late 20C. < Bantu.]

LWM, lwm abbr low water mark

lx symbol lux

✦ **ly** abbr Libya (*in Internet addresses*)

✦ **LY** abbr love you (*in e-mails*)

-ly suffix **1** like, having the characteristics of ○ *brotherly* ○ *kindly* **2** in a particular manner ○ *briefly* **3** recurring at a particular interval of time ○ *monthly* [The adjective is < Old English *-līc*; the adverb < Old English *-līce*. Both ultimately < Indo-European 'body, form', which is also the ancestor of English *like* and *alike*.]

lyase /lī ayz, -ayss/ n an enzyme that catalyses either the formation of a double bond, or the addition of a chemical group at a double bond [Mid-20C. < Greek *luein* 'to loosen'.]

lycanthrope /líkənthrōp, lī kán-/ n a werewolf (*literary*) [Early 17C. Via modern Latin < Greek *lukanthrōpos* < *lukos* 'wolf' + *anthrōpos* 'human being'.]

lycanthropy /lī kánthrəpi/ n in horror stories and legends, the transformation of a person into a wolf

lyceum /lī seé əm/ n **1** a building where concerts, lectures, and other public events take place (*usually in names of buildings*) **2** US an organization that arranges or sponsors public events and entertainment [Late 16C. Via Latin < Greek *Lukeion* (*gymnasion*), school near Athens, a form of *Lukeios*, epithet of Apollo.]

lychee /lī chee, lī cheé/, **litchi, lichee** n **1** a small round fruit with a reddish skin, sweet whitish translucent pulp eaten fresh or dried, and a smooth hard seed **2** a tree of the soapberry family that produces lychees. *Litchi chinensis*. [Late 16C. < Mandarin Chinese *lìzhī*.]

lych-gate /lích-/, **lich-gate** n a covered gateway into a churchyard. Traditionally, coffin-bearers would rest the coffin there before carrying it into the church. [15C. < Old English *līc* 'body, corpse' + GATE.]

Lycian /líssi ən/ n **1** somebody who came from the ancient region of Lycia, on the coast of SW Asia Minor **2** an extinct Anatolian language spoken by the ancient Lycians —**Lycian** adj

lycopene /líkə peen/ n a powerful antioxidant of the carotenoid group, found in tomatoes and used in many antioxidant dietary supplements [Mid-20C. < modern Latin *Lycopersicon* < Greek *lukos* 'wolf' + *persikos* 'peach'.]

lycopodium /líkə pódi əm/ n **1** a plant that is a kind of club moss, with long branching stems covered in small leaves. It has small spore-carrying cones. Genus: *Lycopodium*. **2** a flammable powder, composed of spores of lycopodium and other club mosses. Use: formerly for coating for pills and suppositories, in fireworks, in foundry work. [Early 18C. < modern Latin, < Greek *lukos* 'wolf' + *pod-* 'foot'; from its claw-like root.]

lycopsid /lī kópsid/ n a nonflowering plant with small, simple leaves that reproduces by spores. Living examples such as club mosses do not resemble their tree-sized Carboniferous ancestors. Class: Lycopodiatae. [Mid-20C. < modern Latin *Lycopsida* < Greek *lukos* 'wolf'.]

Lycra /líkrə/ tdmk a trademark for a lightweight stretchy polyurethane fabric. Use: clothing, particularly sportswear, swimwear.

lyddite /líddīt/ n a powerful explosive consisting mainly of picric acid mixed with 10 per cent nitrobenzene and 3 per cent petroleum jelly [Late 19C. After *Lydd*, Kent, England, where first tested.]

Lydgate /líd gayt/, **John** (1370?–1450?) English monk and poet

Lydia /líddi ə/ ancient country in present-day NW Turkey, on the Aegean Sea —**Lydian** adj, n

lye /lī/ n a strong solution of sodium hydroxide or potassium hydroxide in water. Use: industrial drain and oven cleaners. [Old English *lēag* < Indo-European, 'to wash']

Lye /lī/, **Len** (1901–80) New Zealand artist

Lyell /lī əl/, **Sir Charles** (1797–1875) British geologist

lygus bug /lígəss-/ n a plant-eating insect that is especially common in North America, where it is a pest of cotton and other crops. Genus: *Lygus*. [*Lygus* < modern Latin, < Greek *lugos* 'chaste-tree, withy']

lying present participle of lie[1], lie[2]

lying-in (*plural* **lyings-in**) n the period of time leading up to and immediately following childbirth, during which women used to be confined to bed (*archaic; often before nouns*)

lyke-wake /lík-/ n a vigil held over the body of somebody who has died, often accompanied by festivities (*archaic*) [14C. < Old English *līc* 'body, corpse' + WAKE[1].]

Lyme disease /līm-/ n an infectious bacterial disease transmitted by ticks, in which skin rash, fever, and headache precede arthritis and nervous disorder [Late 20C. After *Lyme*, Connecticut, USA.]

Lyme Regis /līm reéjiss/ seaside resort in S England. Population: 3,851 (1991).

Lymington /límmingtən/ town and seaport in SW England. Population: 13,508 (1991).

lymph /limf/ n a fluid containing white cells, chiefly lymphocytes, that is drained from tissue spaces by the vessels of the lymphatic system. It can transport bacteria, viruses, and cancer cells. [Late 17C. Directly or via French < Latin *lympha* 'water'.]

lymph- prefix = lympho- (*before vowels*)

lymphadenopathy /lim fáddi nóppəthi, lím fadi-/ (*plural* **-thies**) n any disease, disorder, or enlargement of the lymph nodes

lymphatic /lim fáttik/ adj **1** RELATING TO THE LYMPH SYSTEM relating to lymph or the lymphatic system **2** SLUGGISH without any energy or enthusiasm ▪ n VESSEL TRANSPORTING LYMPH a vessel that transports or contains lymph

lymphatic system n a network of vessels that transport fluid, fats, proteins, and lymphocytes to the bloodstream as lymph, and remove microorganisms and other debris from tissues

lymph gland n a popular but inaccurate term for a lymph node

lymph node n any oval body in the lymphatic system that produces and houses lymphocytes and filters microorganisms and other particles from lymph, thus reducing the risk of infection

lympho- prefix lymph, lymphocyte, lymphatic system ○ *lymphocytosis* [< LYMPH]

lymphoblast /límfō blast/ n an immature cell that develops into a lymphocyte

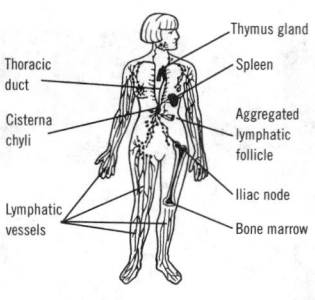

Lymphatic system

lymphoblastic /límfō blástik/ *adj* relating to the production of lymphocytes

lymphoblastic leukaemia *n* a disease in which there is great overproduction of immature lymphocytes

lymphocyte /límfō sīt/ *n* an important cell class in the immune system that produces antibodies to attack infected and cancerous cells, and is responsible for rejecting foreign tissue

lymphocytosis /límfō sī tóssiss/ *n* an increase in the number of lymphocytes in the bloodstream, occurring, e.g. in some persistent infections and forms of leukaemia

lymphogranuloma venereum /límfō gránnyŏō lŏ́mə və neéri əm/ *n* a sexually transmitted disease caused by a bacterial infection, in which there is swelling of the genital lymph nodes and, especially in men, a genital ulcer [< modern Latin, 'venereal granuloma of the lymph nodes']

lymphoid /límf oyd/ *adj* relating to lymph, lymphatic tissue, or the lymphatic system

lymphokine /límfō kīn/ *n* any soluble substance released by lymphocytes that influences other immune cells [Mid-20C. < LYMPHO- + Greek *kinein* 'to move'.]

lymphoma /lim fṓmə/ (*plural* **-mas** *or* **-mata** /-mətə/) *n* a malignant tumour originating in a lymph node, e.g. Hodgkin's disease or any of the range of cancers known as non-Hodgkin's lymphomas

lymphopoiesis /límfō poy eéssiss/ *n* the production of lymphocytes, which occurs mainly in the bone marrow, thymus, lymph nodes, spleen, and tonsils —**lymphopoietic** /-poy éttik/ *adj*

Lynbrook /lín brŏok/ village in SE New York State, on the shore of S Long Island. Population: 19,341 (1998 estimate).

lynch /linch/ *vt* to seize somebody believed to have committed a crime and put him or her to death immediately and without trial, usually by hanging [Early 19C. < LYNCH LAW.] —**lyncher** *n* —**lynching** *n*

Lynch /linch/, **David** (*b.* 1946) US film director

Lynch, Jack (1917–99) Irish statesman. Born **John Lynch**

lynch law *n* the condemnation and punishment of somebody by a mob or self-appointed group without a legal trial [Early 19C. After Capt. William *Lynch* (1724–1820), Virginian planter and justice of the peace.]

lynch mob *n* a group of people who capture and hang somebody without legal arrest and trial, because they think the person has committed a crime

lynchpin *n* ENG = linchpin

Lynn /lin/, **Dame Vera** (*b.* 1917) British singer. Known as **the Forces' Sweetheart**

lynx /lingks/ (*plural* **lynx** *or* **lynxes**) *n* a short-tailed cat with a lightly mottled yellowish- to reddish-brown coat and tufted ears. Native to: northern coniferous forests. Genus: *Lynx*. [14C. Via Latin < Greek *lugx*.]

Lynx /links/ *n* a faint constellation of the northern hemisphere. See illustration at **constellation**

lynx-eyed *adj* with very good eyesight

lyo- *prefix* dissolution, dispersion ○ *lyophobic* [< Greek *luein* 'loosen, dissolve' (see LYSIS)]

lyolysis /lī ólləssiss/ *n* the reaction of a salt with a solvent to form an acid and a base

Lyon = Lyons

Lyonnais /lee əN áy/ historic region of SE France, equivalent to the present-day Loire and Rhône departments

lyonnaise /leé ə náyz/ *adj* cooked with onions [Early 19C. < French (*à la*) *lyonnaise* 'in the manner of Lyons'.]

Lyons /lee óN/, **Lyon** /lī́/ city in east-central France. Population: 422,444 (1990).

Lyons /lī́ ənz/, **Dame Enid Muriel** (1897–1981) Australian politician. Born **Enid Muriel Burnell**

Lyons, Sir Joseph (1848–1917) British business executive

Lyons, Joseph Aloysius (1879–1939) Australian statesman

lyophilic /lī ō fíllik/ *adj* describes a finely dispersed solid (**colloid**) that forms a stable dispersion

lyophilize /lī óffi līz/ (**-lizes, -lizing, -lized**), **lyophilise** (**lyophilises, lyophilising, lyophilised**) *vt* to freeze-dry something (*technical*) —**lyophilization** /lī óffi lī záysh'n/ *n* —**lyophilizer** *n*

lyophobic /lī ō fṓbik/ *adj* describes a finely dispersed solid (**colloid**) that forms an unstable dispersion

Lyra /lī́rə/ *n* a small prominent constellation of the northern hemisphere. See illustration at **constellation**

lyrate /lī́rət, -ayt/ *adj* **1** in the shape of a lyre **2** describes a leaf that has a broad rounded apex and small lateral lobes at the base [Mid-18C. < Latin *lyra* < Greek *lura*.]

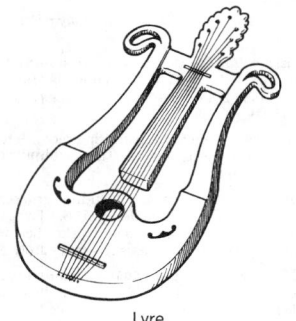

Lyre

lyre /līr/ *n* a plucked string instrument associated with ancient Greece and consisting of a U-shaped frame with a crossbar from which the strings stretch down to the soundbox [12C. Via Old French < Greek *lura*.]

lyrebird /līr burd/ *n* a ground-dwelling bird, the male of which has long tail feathers that form into a lyre shape during courtship. Native to: mountain forests of SE Australia. Family: Menuridae.

lyric /lírrik/ *adj* **1** EXPRESSING PERSONAL FEELINGS relating to poetry that often has a musical quality and expresses personal emotions or thoughts ○ *a lyric poet* **2** WITH LIGHTNESS OF VOICE singing with a voice that has a light quality and a vocally undramatic delivery **3** WITH LIGHTNESS OF MUSICAL QUALITY having or played with a light smooth nondramatic quality that suggests singing **4** RELATING TO THE LYRE relating to or written for the lyre ■ *n* **1** SONG WORDS the words of a song, especially a popular song (*often plural*) **2** SHORT PERSONAL POEM a short poem expressing personal feelings or thoughts [Late 16C. Via French < Greek *lurikos* 'singing to the lyre' < *lura* 'lyre'.]

lyrical /lírrik'l/ *adj* **1** LITERAT, MUSIC = lyric *adj.* **1**, lyric *adj.* **2**, lyric *adj.* **3 2** wildly enthusiastic and emotional about something ○ *critics waxing lyrical about the new exhibition* —**lyrically** *adv* —**lyricalness** *n*

lyricism /lírrissizəm/ *n* **1** a lyric style in poetry or music **2** emotional and enthusiastic expressions of feelings or opinions

lyricist /lírrissist/ *n* **1** a writer of words for songs, especially popular songs **2** a writer of lyric poems

lyrist /lī́rist/ *n* **1** a player of a lyre **2** MUSIC = lyricist. **1** [Mid-17C. Via Latin *lyrista* < Greek *luristēs* < *lura* 'lyre'.]

lys- *prefix* = lyso- (before vowels)

lyse /līss, līz/ (**lyses, lysing, lysed**) *vti* to undergo, or cause cells to undergo, destruction by disruption of the bounding membrane (**lysis**) [Early 20C. Back-formation < LYSIS, after *analyse*.]

Lysenko /li séngk ṓ/, **Trofim Denisovich** (1898–1976) Russian geneticist and agronomist

Lysenkoism /lī séngkō izəm/ *n* a biological doctrine, presented by T. D. Lysenko in the 1930s, maintaining that environmental characteristics acquired by an organism during its lifetime can be inherited by its offspring.

lysergic acid /lī súrjik-, li-/ *n* $C_{16}H_{16}N_2O_2$ a crystalline acid, soluble in most organic solvents. Source: ergot fungus. [< LYSO- + ERGOT]

lysergic acid diethylamide *n* full form of **LSD**

lysin /lī́ssin/ *n* an agent, e.g. an enzyme or antibody, that is able to destroy cells by disruption of the bounding membrane (**lysis**) [Early 20C. < LYSIS.]

lysine /lī́ seen/ *n* an essential amino acid [Late 19C. < German *Lysin* < Greek *lusis* 'loosening' (see LYSIS).]

lysis /lī́ssiss/ (*plural* **lyses** /lī́ seez/) *n* **1** the destruction of cells by disruption of the bounding membrane, allowing the cell contents to escape **2** a gradual reduction in severity of a patient's signs and symptoms during the course of a disease [Mid-16C. Via Latin, 'loosening' < Greek *lusis* < *luein* 'to loosen'.]

-lysis *suffix* **1** dissolution, decomposition, disintegration ○ *thermolysis* **2** hydrolysis ○ *proteolysis* [Via Latin < Greek *lusis* (see LYSIS)]

Lysithea /lī síthi ə/ *n* a very small natural satellite of Jupiter, discovered in 1938

lyso- *prefix* lysis ○ *lysosome* [< LYSIS]

lysogen /lī́ssəjən/ *n* **1** a bacterium that is capable of releasing a bacterium-destroying virus (**bacteriophage**) **2** an agent, particularly an antigen, that provokes the production of cell-destroying agents (**lysins**) by cells of the immune system

lysogenic /lī́ssə jénnik/ *adj* describes a bacterium that is capable of producing and releasing a bacterium-destroying virus (**bacteriophage**) in response to certain stimuli

lysogenize /lī sójjə nīz/ (**-nizes, -nizing, -nized**), **lysogenise** (**-nises, -nising, -nised**) *vt* to convert a bacterium to a lysogenic state by infection with a bacterium-destroying virus (**bacteriophage**)

lysogeny /lī sójjəni/ *n* the ability of a bacterial cell to produce and release a bacterium-destroying virus (**bacteriophage**) in response to certain stimuli

lysosome /lī́ssōsōm/ *n* a membrane-bound cavity in living cells that contains enzymes that are responsible for degrading and recycling molecules —**lysosomal** /lī́ssō sṓm'l/ *adj*

lysozyme /lī́ssō zīm/ *n* an enzyme in body secretions that can help destroy bacteria [Early 20C. < LYSO- + ENZYME.]

-lyte *suffix* a substance that can be decomposed by a particular process ○ *electrolyte* [< Greek *lutos* 'soluble' < past participle of *luein* (see LYSIS)] —**lytic** *suffix*

Lytham St Anne's /lítham saynt ánz/ seaside resort in NW England. Population: 40,866 (1991).

lytic /líttik/ *adj* relating to, resulting from, or causing the destruction of cells by disruption of the bounding membrane (**lysis**) [Late 19C. < Greek *lutikos* 'able to loosen' < *luein* (see LYSIS).]

Lyttleton /lítt'ltən/, **Humphrey** (*b.* 1921) British jazz trumpeter, bandleader, broadcaster, and author

-lyze *suffix* to cause or undergo lysis ○ *plasmolyze* [Back-formation < -LYSIS]

Mm

m[1] /em/ (*plural* **m's**), **M** (*plural* **M's** *or* **Ms**) *n* **1** the 13th letter of the English alphabet, representing a consonant sound **2** the Roman numeral for 1,000

m[2] *symbol* **1** em dash **2** magnetic moment **3** mass **4** metre **5** milli- **6** million **7** minute(s) **8** mutual inductance

m[3] *abbr* **1** maiden (over) **2** male **3** married **4** masculine **5** medium **6** mile **7** minute(s) **8** month

M[1] /em/ (*plural* **M's** *or* **Ms**) *n* something shaped like a letter 'M'

M[2] *symbol* em dash

⚡ **M**[3] *abbr* **1** male **2** mass **3** Master (*in degree titles*) **4** medium (*of clothes size*) **5** mega- **6** Member **7** middle term **8** million **9** molar **10** motorway

M. *abbr* **1** *US* Majesty **2** *US* male **3** *US* Manitoba **4** *US* March **5** *US* May **6** *US* medieval **7** *US* middle **8** *US* mill **9** *US* Monday **10** *US* Monsieur **11** *US* mountain

M0 *n* an assessment of the amount of money in public circulation, the money represented by banks' balances, and the money held in banks' tills (**narrow money**)

M1 *n* an assessment of the amount of money in coins, notes, and current and deposit accounts

M-1 rifle *n* a .30 calibre rifle invented by John C. Garand and adopted by the US Army in 1936.

M2 *n* an assessment of the amount of money in coins, currency, current and deposit accounts, savings accounts, and deposits

M3 *n* an assessment of the amount of money in M1, M2, and also large denomination repurchase agreements, institutional money market accounts, and certain Eurodollar time deposits

⚡ **M8** *abbr* mate (*in e-mails*)

ma /maa/ (*plural* **mas**) *n* **1** a word used to refer to a mother or to address your own mother (*informal*) **2** a way of addressing or referring to a woman past middle age (*often considered offensive*) [Early 19C. Shortening of MAMMA.]

mA *symbol* milliampere(s)

MA, M.A. *abbr* **1** Massachusetts **2** Master of Arts **3** mental age **4** Military Academy

ma'am /mam, maam, məm/ *n* **1** used when addressing royal women or other women of high status (*formal*) **2** used when addressing a woman in a polite and respectful way (*dated*) [Mid-17C. Contraction of MADAM.]

ma-and-pa *adj US* = **mom-and-pop**

maar /maar/ (*plural* **maars** *or* **maare** /maàri/) *n* a broad flat volcanic crater formed by a single explosive eruption and often filled with water [Early 19C. Via German dialect, 'crater lake' < Latin *mare* 'sea'.]

Ma'ariv /maàriv/, **Maariv** *n* in Judaism, the evening service of prayer [Late 20C. < Hebrew *ma'ărībh* 'evening prayer'.]

Maasai *n, adj* LANG, PEOPLES = **Masai**

Maastricht /maàstrikht/, **Maestricht** city in SE Netherlands. Population: 122,087 (2000).

Maastricht Treaty /maàstrikht-, -strikht-/ a treaty signed in Maastricht in late 1991 by heads of the 12 member states of the European Community that set out a framework for increased political and economic integration. It was ratified in 1993.

Maat /maat/ *n* in Egyptian mythology, the goddess of the underworld who tests the value of a person's soul after death by weighing the heart on an ostrich feather

maatjes herring *n* ZOOL = matjes herring

Mab /mab/ *n* in Celtic mythology, the god of light, who mediates between humankind and the divine

mabe pearl /máyb-, máybi-/ *n* a cultured pearl with a flat base and a rounded top [< ?]

Mabinogion /mábbi nóggi on/ *n* a collection of ancient Welsh stories of magic and mythology, including stories about King Arthur [< Welsh, plural of *mabinogi* 'youthful career' < *mab* 'youth' < Old Welsh *map* < Celtic, 'son']

Mabo /maàbō/ *n* a 1992 landmark Australian legal case relating to the land rights of Aborigines [Late 20C. After Ernie Koiki MABO.]

Mabo /maàbō/, **Ernie Koiki** (1936–92) Australian land rights campaigner

mac /mak/, **mack** *n* a mackintosh (*informal*) [Early 20C. Shortening.]

Mac /mak/ *n US, Scotland* used as an informal way of addressing a man whose name is not known (*informal*) [Mid-20C. < the Scottish name element *Mac-* or *Mc-*.]

MAC /mak/ *n* a system for transmitting pictures to colour televisions using satellites. Full form **multiplexed analogue component**

macabre /mə kaàbrə, -bə/ *adj* including gruesome and horrific details of death and decay [15C. < French (*danse*) *macabre* 'dance of Death', probably alteration of *danse Macabé* 'dance of the Maccabees'.] —**macabrely** *adv*

macaco /mə kaàkō/ (*plural* **-cos**) *n* a lemur, especially a species of lemur in which the male is black and the female brown [Mid-18C. < French *mococo*.]

macadam /mə káddəm/ *n* a smooth hard road surface made from small pieces of stone, usually mixed with tar or asphalt, in compressed layers [Early 19C. After Scottish civil engineer John Loudon *McAdam*.]

macadamia /máka dáymi ə/ *n* an evergreen tree cultivated for its nuts. Flowers: white, in clusters. Native to: Australia, SE Asia. Genus: *Macadamia*. [Early 20C. < modern Latin, after Scottish-born Australian chemist John *Macadam* (1827–65).]

macadamia nut, macadamia *n* an edible, round, hard-shelled, waxy nut with a mild creamy flavour, produced by the macadamia tree

macadamize /mə káddə mīz/ (**-izes, -izing, -ized**), **macadamise** (**-ises, -ising, -ised**) *vt* to build or surface a road with macadam —**macadamization** /mə káddə mī záysh'n/ *n* —**macadamizer** *n*

Macao /mə ków/ = **Macau**

macaque /mə kaàk, -kák/ (*plural* **-caques** *or* **-caque**) *n* a short-tailed, sturdily built monkey. Native to: Asia, North Africa. Genus: *Macaca*. [Late 17C. Via French < Bantu *makaku* 'some monkeys'.]

macarena /máka ráynə/ *n* a simple solo dance of Spanish origin mainly involving placing the hands on different parts of the body in sequence and swinging the hips [Late 20C. < *Macarena*, song to which it was performed.]

macaroni /máka rốni/ *n* **1** hollow tubular pasta, usually produced in short lengths **2** (*plural* **-nis** *or* **-nies**) an affected, foppish young man of 18th-century Britain who adopted the fashions, manners, and customs of the other countries he had visited [Late 16C. < Italian dialect *maccarone* 'macaroni, dumpling'.]

macaronic /máka rónnik/ *adj* **1** MIXING LANGUAGES IN VERSE describes verse containing words and phrases from everyday language mixed with Latin or other foreign words and phrases, or with vernacular terms with Latinate endings added, usually for comic effect **2** RELATING TO A MIXTURE OF LANGUAGES relating to or involving a combination of two or more languages ■ *n* MACARONIC VERSE a macaronic poem or macaronic poetry in general [Early 17C. Via modern Latin < MACARONI.] —**macaronically** *adv*

macaroni cheese *n* boiled macaroni in a cheese sauce, baked or grilled until golden

macaroon /máka roón/ *n* a biscuit made from sugar and egg whites, with ground almonds or pieces of dried coconut folded in [Late 16C. Via French *macaron* < Italian dialect *maccarone* 'macaroni'.]

Macarthur /mə kaàrthər/, **John** (1767–1834) British-born Australian pioneer and wool merchant

MacArthur /mək aàrthər/, **Douglas, General** (1880–1964) US military commander

Macassar[1] /mə kássər/, **Macassar oil** *n* an oily substance formerly used to make the hair smooth and shiny [Early 19C. After MAKASSAR.]

Macassar[2] /mə kássər/ = **Makassar**

Macau /mə ków/, **Macao** Special Administrative Region in SE China. Population: 497,000 (1996). Area: 23.6 sq. km/9.1 sq. mi.

macaw /mə káw/ (*plural* **-caws** *or* **-caw**) *n* a large parrot with a long tail and brilliant plumage. Native to: Central and South America. Genus: *Anodorhynchus*. [Early 17C. < Portuguese *macao*.]

Macbeth /mək béth/ (c. 1005–57) king of Scotland (1040–57)

Macc. *abbr* Maccabees

Maccabees /máka beez/ *npl* **1** the followers of Judas Maccabeus, who led the revolt of the Jews against Syria in 168 BC **2** four books of Jewish history, the first two of which are included in the Apocrypha [14C. Via Latin *Maccabaeus* < Greek *Makkabaios*, epithet of Judas.] —**Maccabean** /máka beè ən/ *adj*

maccaboy /máka boy/ *n* rose-scented snuff from Martinique

Macclesfield /mák'lz feeld/ town in NW England. Population: 152,604 (1996 estimate).

MacDiarmid /mək dúrmid/, **Hugh** (1892–1978) Scottish poet, editor, and critic. Pseudonym of **Christopher Murray Grieve**

Macdonald /mək dónn'ld/, **Flora** (1722–90) Scottish Jacobite

MacDonald, Ramsay (1866–1937) British statesman and prime minister (1924, 1929–35)

MacDonnell Ranges /mək dónn'l-/ mountain system in the Northern Territory, Australia. Highest peak: Mount Zeil 1,510 m/4,953 ft.

mace[1] /mayss/ *n* **1** CEREMONIAL STAFF OF OFFICE a stick or rod, usually with an ornamental head, carried by certain officials on ceremonial occasions as a symbol of authority **2** SPIKED METAL CLUB a medieval weapon in the form of a heavy club with a round spiked metal head **3** = **macebearer 4** EARLY BILLIARD CUE an early form of the modern billiard cue [13C. Via Old French < Latin *mateola* 'mallet'.]

mace[2] /mayss/ *n* a spice made from the covering of the nutmeg seed, used in the form of dried blades or as a yellow-orange powder [13C. Via Anglo-Norman *macis* < Latin *macir*, an Asian spice.]

macebearer /máyss bairər/ *n* an official who carries a mace on ceremonial occasions

macédoine /mássə dwaán/, **macedoine** *n* **1 MIXED CHOPPED VEGETABLES** a mixture of diced vegetables served hot or cold as a garnish, appetizer, or side dish **2 MIXED CHOPPED FRUITS** a salad of small diced pieces of fruit, often in syrup or jelly **3 MEDLEY** a mixed-up jumble or medley (*literary*) [Early 19C. < French *Macédoine* 'Macedonia'; because ALEXANDER THE GREAT ruled over many different peoples.]

Macedonia /mássə dṓni ə/ **1 Macedonia, Macedon** /mássədən/ ancient kingdom in N Greece, centralized under Philip II, who, with his son, Alexander the Great, created a vast empire in the 4th century BC **2** republic in SE Europe, formerly a constituent republic of Yugoslavia. Capital: Skopje. Population: 1,980,000 (1996). Area: 25,713 sq. km/9,928 sq. mi. Official name **Former Yugoslav Republic of Macedonia 3** mountainous region of NE Greece. Capital: Thessaloniki. Area: 34,177 sq. km/13,200 sq. mi. Population: 2,122,000 (1981). **4** district in SW Bulgaria. Area: 6,465 sq. km/2,496 sq. mi. —**Macedonian** *n, adj*

macerate /mássə rayt/ *vti* (**-ates, -ating, -ated**) **1 SOFTEN BY SOAKING** to soften something by soaking it in liquid or to become soft by soaking in liquid **2 SEPARATE BY SOAKING** to make something break up into pieces or into its various parts by soaking it in liquid, or to break up in this way **3 MAKE SOMETHING THIN OR WASTE AWAY** to make somebody or something thin or lean, or to become thin or lean, especially by starvation or fasting ■ *n* **SOMETHING PRODUCED BY SOAKING** something prepared by soaking in a liquid [Mid-16C. < Latin *macerat-*, past participle of *macere* 'soften'.] —**macerater** *n* —**maceration** /mássə ráysh'n/ *n* —**macerative** /mássərətiv/ *adj*

Macgillicuddy's Reeks /mə gílli kudiz reéks/ mountain range in SW Republic of Ireland. Highest peak: Carrantuohill 1,041 m/3,415 ft.

MacGuffin /mə gúffin/ *n* in a film, play, or book, something that starts or drives the action of the plot but later turns out to be unimportant [Mid-20C. Said to come from a story in which a man pretends to have a macguffin, a Scottish mountain lion, but admits neither exists.]

Mach /maak, mak/ *n* PHYS = **Mach number**

Mach /ma*kh*/, **Ernst** (1838–1916) Austrian physicist and philosopher

mach. *abbr* **1** machine **2** machinery **3** machinist

Machado de Assis /ma sháddoo də a seéss/, **Joachim Maria** (1839–1908) Brazilian novelist, poet, and critic

machair /mákər, má*kh*ər/ *n Scotland* a strip of grassland on a sandy shore, chiefly used for grazing livestock [Late 17C. < Scottish Gaelic.]

machan /mə chaán/ *n* a raised platform, often in a tree, used to watch for tigers and other game in India [Late 19C. < Hindi.]

mache /maash/, **mâche** *n* PLANTS = **lamb's lettuce** [Late 17C. < French.]

Machel /mə shél/, **Samora Moïses** (1933–86) Mozambican statesman

machete /mə shétti, -chétti/ *n* a large heavy broad-bladed knife used as a weapon or as a tool for cutting through vegetation, especially in Central and South America and the Caribbean [Late 16C. < Spanish, 'little sledgehammer' < *macho* 'sledge hammer' < Latin *mateola* 'mallet'.]

Machiavelli /máki ə vélli, má kya-/, **Niccolò** (1469–1527) Italian historian, statesman, and philosopher

Machiavellian /máki ə vélli ən/ *adj* **1** using clever trickery, amoral methods, and expediency to achieve a desired goal, especially in politics **2** relating to or characteristic of the statesman and political philosopher Niccolò Machiavelli —**Machiavellian** *n* —**Machiavellianism** *n* —**Machiavellist** *n, adj*

Machiavellian intelligence *n* in psychology, social intelligence, especially the intelligence that involves deception and the formation of coalitions

machicolate /mə chíkō layt/ (**-lates, -lating, -lated**) *vt* to provide a castle wall with projecting galleries along its top [Late 18C. Via Anglo-Latin < Provençal *machacol* 'neck-crusher'.]

machicolation /mə chíkō láysh'n/ *n* **1 GALLERY ON TOP OF CASTLE WALL** a projecting gallery on top of a castle wall, supported by a row of arches and containing openings through which rocks and boiling oil could be dropped on attackers **2 OPENING IN MACHICOLATION** an opening in the floor of a machicolation **3 ROW OF ARCHES** an ornamental row of supported arches that project from a building

machinate /máki nayt, máshi-/ (**-nates, -nating, -nated**) *vti* to devise secret, cunning, or complicated plans and schemes to achieve a goal or to cause harm to others [Late 16C. < Latin *machinat-*, past participle of *machinari* < *machina* (see MACHINE).] —**machinator** *n*

machination /máki náysh'n, máshi-/ *n* **1** the devising of secret, cunning, or complicated plans and schemes **2** a secret, cunning, or complicated plan or scheme designed to achieve a particular end

machine /mə sheén/ *n* **1 MECHANICAL DEVICE** a device with moving parts, often powered by electricity, used to perform a task, especially one that would otherwise be done by hand ○ *a washing machine* **2 SIMPLE UNPOWERED DEVICE** a simple device used to overcome resistance at one point by applying force at another point, e.g. a lever, pulley, or an inclined plane **3 POWERED FORM OF TRANSPORT** an engine-driven means of transport, e.g. an aircraft, car, or motorcycle **4 GROUP OF PEOPLE IN CONTROL** an organized group of people that controls or directs something, especially a political group ○ *the party machine* **5 COMPLEX SYSTEM** a complex system structured so as to accomplish a specific goal ○ *the war machine* **6 SOMEBODY WHO BEHAVES MECHANICALLY** a person who behaves like a mechanical device, e.g. somebody who is efficient and uncreative ○ *an editing machine* **7 DEVICE TO PRODUCE STAGE EFFECTS** a mechanical device used in the theatre, especially in classical drama, to create special effects such as the entrance of a supernatural being **8 LITERARY DEVICE** a character or factor introduced into a work of literature to produce an effect or to resolve the plot ■ *v* (**-chines, -chining, -chined**) **1** *vti* **WORK WITH POWER-DRIVEN TOOL** to cut, shape, or finish a piece of work using a power-driven tool such as a lathe or drilling device, or to be cut, shaped, or finished in this way **2** *vt* **USE MACHINE ON** to make or do something using a machine [Mid-16C. Via Old French < Latin *machina* 'device' < Greek *mēkhanē* < *mēkhos* 'means'.] —**machinability** /mə sheénə bílləti/ *n* —**machinable** *adj* —**machineless** *adj* —**machine-like** *adj*

machine bolt *n* a bolt with a square or hexagonal head, usually of heavy duty construction for use in aircraft and automobiles

⚡**machine code** *n* COMPUT = **machine language**

machine finish *n* PAPER = **mill finish**

machine gun *n* an automatic weapon that fires rapidly and repeatedly without requiring separate squeezes on the trigger each time

machine-gun *vt* (**-guns, -gunning, -gunned**) **1 SHOOT SOMEBODY WITH MACHINE GUN** to shoot or kill somebody with a machine gun, or to fire a machine gun at somebody or something **2 ADDRESS SOMEBODY RAPIDLY** to speak rapidly to somebody (*informal*) ■ *adj* **STACCATO** rapid, abrupt, and staccato in delivery —**machine-gunner** *n*

⚡**machine language** *n* instructions, usually written in binary code, telling a computer how to process data

machine pistol *n* a light automatic or semiautomatic submachine gun that can be discharged using only one hand

⚡**machine-readable** *adj* in a form that is able to be used directly by a computer

machinery /mə sheénəri/ *n* **1 MECHANICAL PARTS** the aggregate parts that make up a machine or group of machines **2 MACHINES** machines collectively or in general **3 SYSTEM OF MACHINES** a system of machines working together **4 SET OF PROCEDURES** an interconnected series of processes that works like a mechanical system to produce a particular result **5 LITERARY DEVICES** literary devices used for effect, especially in poetry, or to resolve the plot of a play or book

machine screw *n* a slotted or hexagonal-headed screw with a standardized thread used to connect machine parts together

machine shop *n* a workshop where various materials, especially metals, are cut, shaped and worked, often to tight specifications using machine tools

machine tool *n* a machine such as a lathe or grinder, used for shaping and finishing metals and other solid materials —**machine-tooled** *adj*

⚡**machine translation** *n* the translation of text from one language to another by computer

machine-wash *vt* to wash something in a washing machine

machine-washable *adj* able to be washed in a washing machine without being damaged

machinist /mə sheénist/ *n* **1** somebody whose job involves machining something or operating a machine or machine tool, especially in a factory **2** a maker or repairer of machines

machismo /mə chízmō/ *n* an exaggerated sense or display of masculinity, emphasizing characteristics that are conventionally regarded as male, usually physical strength and courage, aggressiveness, and lack of emotional response [Mid-20C. < Mexican Spanish, < *macho* (see MACHO).]

Machmeter /maák meetər, mák-/ *n* an instrument for measuring the Mach number of an aircraft

Mach number *n* the speed of an object relative to the speed of sound [Early 20C. After Ernst MACH.]

macho /máchō/ *adj* having or showing characteristics conventionally regarded as male, especially physical strength and courage, aggressiveness, and lack of emotional response ■ *n* (*plural* **-chos**) a male who displays conventional masculine characteristics [Early 20C. < Mexican Spanish *macho* 'masculine' < Spanish, < Latin *masculus*.] —**machoism** *n*

machree /mə kreé/ *interj Ireland* used as an endearment [Early 19C. < Irish *mo chroidhe* 'of my heart'.]

Machu Picchu /maáchoo peékchoo/ *n* ruined ancient Inca city in the Andes in S Peru

machzor /maak záwr, maa*kh* záwr/ (*plural* **-zorim** /maa*kh* záwrim, maa*kh* zaw reém/), **mahzor** (*plural* **-zorim** *or* **-zors**) *n* a Jewish prayer book that details the rituals prescribed for festivals and holidays [Mid-19C. < Hebrew *mahzōr*.]

Macias Nguema /mə seé əss əng gwáymə/ former name for **Bioko** (1973–79)

macintosh *n* = **mackintosh**

mack *n* = **mac**

Macke /maákə/, **August** (1887–1914) German painter

Mackellar /mə kéllər/, **Dorothea** (1885–1968) Australian poet

Mackenzie /mə kénzi/ river in the Northwest Territories, Canada. Length: 1,800 km/1,120 mi.

Mackenzie, Sir Alexander (1764–1820) Scottish explorer

Mackenzie, Sir Compton (1883–1972) British novelist and playwright

Mackenzie, Sir Thomas (1845–1930) Scottish-born New Zealand statesman

~~mackeral~~ incorrect spelling of **mackerel**

mackerel /mákrəl/ (*plural* **-els** *or* **-el**) *n* **1** a bony oily fish with a greenish-blue body, dark blue bars, and a forked tail, used as a food fish. Native to: North Atlantic coastal waters. *Scomber scombrus*. **2** any fish that is related to the mackerel, e.g. the Spanish mackerel. Family: Scombridae. [13C. < Anglo-Norman.]

mackerel shark *n* a large fierce shark with a pointed snout, related to the great white shark, mako shark, and porbeagle. Family: Lamnidae.

mackerel sky *n* a sky covered with cirrocumulus or altocumulus clouds in a pattern that resembles the markings on a mackerel (*regional*)

Mackerras /mə kérrəss/, **Sir Charles** (*b.* 1925) US-born Australian conductor and musical director

Mackillop /mə kílləp/, **Mary** (1842–1909) Australian nun. Known as **Mother Mary of the Cross**

mackinaw /máki naw/ *n US, Can* **1** a thick heavy woollen cloth, usually with a plaid design **2** a short double-breasted coat made from mackinaw or a similar fabric [Early 19C. After a former trading post in Mackinaw City, Michigan, USA.]

Mackinder /mə kíndər/, **Sir Halford John** (1861–1947) British geographer and politician

Mackinnon /mə kínnən/, **Catherine** (*b.* 1946) US legal scholar

mackintosh /mákin tosh/, **macintosh** *n* **1** a waterproof coat worn for protection against the rain (*dated*) **2** a waterproof fabric, especially rubberized cotton [Mid-

19C. After the Scottish inventor Charles *Macintosh* (1766–1843).]

Charles Rennie Mackintosh

Mackintosh /mákin tosh/, **Charles Rennie** (1868–1928) Scottish architect and interior designer

mackle /mák'l/ *n* a blurred or double impression caused by the movement of paper or type during the printing process ▪ *vti* to cause a printed impression to blur, or to appear blurred [Late 16C. Either directly or via French < Latin *macula* 'spot, stain'.]

Mackmurdo /mac múrdō/, **Arthur Heygate** (1851–1942) British architect and designer

MacLaine /mə kláyn/, **Shirley** (*b.* 1934) US film actor. Born **Shirley MacLean Beaty**

macle /mák'l/ *n* **1** MINERALS = **chiastolite 2** a crystal that is twinned **3** a discoloured spot within a crystal [Early 19C. Via French < Latin *macula* 'spot, mesh'.]

Maclean /mə kláyn/, **Alistair** (1922–87) British novelist

Maclean, Donald (1913–83) British spy for the former U.S.S.R

Macleod /mə klówd/, **John James Rickard** (1876–1935) British physiologist

Macmillan /mək míllən/, **Harold, 1st Earl of Stockton** (1894–1986) British statesman and prime minister (1957–63)

MacMillan /mək míllən/, **Sir Kenneth** (1929–92) British choreographer

MacNeice /mək neéss/, **Louis** (1907–63) British poet and playwright

macon /maà koN, má k-/, **Macon, Mâcon** *n* a red or white wine from the Mâcon area in central France

Macon /máykən/ city in central Georgia. Population: 109,191 (1994).

Mâcon /maa kóN/ city in east-central France. Population: 106,612 (1990).

Macquarie, Lake /mə kwórri/ coastal lake in New South Wales, Australia. Area: 110 sq. km/43 sq. mi.

Macquarie, Lachlan (1762–1824) Australian colonial administrator

Macquarie Harbour harbour in W Tasmania, Australia. Area: 285 sq. km/110 sq. mi.

Macquarie Island uninhabited Australian island in the Southern Ocean, southeast of Tasmania. Area: 123 sq. km/47 sq. mi.

macr- *prefix* = **macro-** (*before vowels*)

macramé /mə kraàmi, -mayl/ *n* pieces of string or cord knotted together to form a coarse ornamental lacy pattern, or something made using this method [Mid-19C. Via Turkish *makrama* 'towel' < Arabic *mikrama* 'bed cover'.]

Macready /mə kreédi/, **William Charles** (1793–1873) British actor

⚡ macro /mákrō/ (*plural* **-ros**) *n* a computer instruction that initiates a series of additional instructions [Mid-20C. < MACRO-.]

macro- *prefix* **1** large, inclusive ○ *macrocyte* ○ *macroclimate* **2** long ○ *macrobiotics* [< Greek *makros* < Indo-European, 'long, thin']

macrobiotics /mákrō bī óttiks/ *n* a vegan diet of seeds, grains, and organically grown fruit and vegetables, said to prolong life and balance the body's systems (+ *singular verb*) [Late 18C. < Greek *makrobiotos* 'long life'.] —**macrobiotic** *adj*

macrocarpa /mákrō kaárpə/ *n* an evergreen tree used as a windbreak. Native to: New Zealand. *Cupressus macrocarpa.* [Early 20C. < modern Latin, < Greek *makros* (see MACRO-) + *karpos* 'fruit'.]

macrocephaly /mákrō séffəli/, **macrocephalia** /mákrō sə fáyli ə/ *n* the condition of having a head that is excessively large —**macrocephalic** /mákrō si fállik/ *adj* —**macrocephalous** *adj*

macroclimate /mákrō klímət/ *n* the general climate of a large region such as a continent —**macroclimatic** /mákrō klī máttik/ *adj* —**macroclimatically** *adv*

macrocosm /mákrō kozəm/ *n* a complex structure such as the world or the universe considered as a single entity that contains numerous similar smaller-scale structures [Early 17C. < medieval Latin *macrocosmus* < Greek *makro-* (see MACRO-) + *kosmos* 'world'.] —**macrocosmic** /mákrō kózmik/ *adj* —**macrocosmically** *adv*

macrocyte /mákrō sīt/ *n* an unusually large red blood cell that commonly occurs in cases of anaemia —**macrocytic** /mákrō síttik/ *adj*

macrocytosis /mákrō sī tōssiss/ *n* the presence of unusually large red cells in the blood —**macrocytotic** /-sī tóttik/ *adj*

macroeconomics /mákrō eekə nómmiks, -ekə-/ *n* a branch of economics that focuses on the general features and processes that make up a national economy and the ways in which different segments of the economy are connected (+ *singular verb*) —**macroeconomic** *adj* —**macroeconomist** /mákrō i kónnəmist/ *n*

macroeconomy /mákrō ikónnəmi/ *n* the economy viewed as a whole and in terms of all those factors that control its overall performance ○ *Employment rates did not respond to the macroeconomy as expected.*

macroevolution /mákrō eévə loòsh'n/ *n* evolution theorized to occur over a long period of time, producing major changes in species and other taxonomic groups —**macroevolutionary** *adj*

macrofossil /mákrō foss'l/ *n* a fossil that is large enough to be observed or examined without the aid of a microscope

macrogamete /mákrō gámmeet/ *n* the larger, usually female, sex cell (**gamete**) in a pair of conjugating cells of a heterogamous species

macroglobulin /mákrō glóbbyŏŏlin/ *n* **1** a soluble protein in the blood with a high molecular weight, typically seen in some diseases **2** a soluble protein in the blood with a normal molecular weight

macroglobulinaemia /mákrō glóbbyŏŏli neèmi ə/ *n* a condition marked by an increase of macroglobulins in the blood

macroglobulinemia *n* US = **macroglobulinaemia**

macrograph /mákrō graaf, -graf/ *n* a drawing, photograph, or other representation in which something appears at its actual size or larger —**macrographic** /mákrō gráffik/ *adj* —**macrography** /mə króggrəfi/ *n*

⚡ macroinstruction /mákrō in strúksh'n/ *n* COMPUT = **macro**

macro lens *n* a lens used for close-up photography that produces a life-size or larger image on film, with a minimum of 1:1 object-to-image ratio

macromere /mákrō meer/ *n* a large yolk-filled cell formed from the unequal splitting of a fertilized egg [Late 19C. < MACRO- + BLASTOMERE.]

macromolecule /mákrō mólli kyool/ *n* a large molecule, e.g. that of a protein or polymer, made up of smaller elements connected to one another —**macromolecular** /mákrō mə lékyóolər/ *adj*

macron /mák ron/ *n* **1** a short horizontal line placed over a vowel sound to indicate that it is long or stressed **2** a stressed syllable in a foot of verse, marked with a macron [Mid-19C. < Greek, 'long thing' < *makros* 'long'.]

macronucleus /mákrō nyóokli əss/ (*plural* **-i** /-kli ī/) *n* the larger of two nuclei in most ciliate protozoans, involved in nonreproductive functions such as feeding and metabolism —**macronuclear** *adj*

macronutrient /mákrō nyoótri ənt/ *n* a chemical element, e.g. nitrogen, carbon, or potassium, needed in large amounts by plants for normal growth and development

macrophage /mákrō fayj/ *n* a large cell that is present in blood, lymph, and connective tissues, removing waste products, harmful micro-organisms, and foreign material from the bloodstream —**macrophagic** /mákrō fájjik/ *adj*

macrophotography /mákrō fə tóggrəfi/ *n* close-up photography that produces images on the film that are life-size or larger than life

macrophysics /mákrō fízziks/ *n* a branch of physics that studies systems and objects large enough to be easily observed (+ *singular verb*)

macrophyte /mákrō fīt/ *n* a plant large enough to be studied and observed using the unaided eye, especially an aquatic plant —**macrophytic** /mákrō fíttik/ *adj*

macropsia /mə krópsi ə/ *n* a condition in which everything perceived by the eye appears to be larger than it really is, often as a result of a retinal disease or a brain disorder [Late 19C. < MACRO- + Greek *opsia* 'seeing'.]

macroscopic /mákrō skóppik/, **macroscopical** /-skóppik'l/ *adj* **1** large enough to be seen and examined without the aid of magnifying equipment **2** relating to or concerned with large units [Late 19C. < MACRO-, after MICROSCOPIC.] —**macroscopically** *adv*

macroscopic anatomy *n* ANAT = **gross anatomy**

macrosociology /mákrō sōssi ólləji/ *n* the branch of sociology concerned with the study and analysis of societies in their entirety —**macrosociological** /-sōssi ə lójjik'l/ *adj*

macrosporangium /mákrōspə ránji əm/ (*plural* **-a** /-ji ə/) *n* BIOL = **megasporangium** [Late 19C. < modern Latin, < MACRO- + Greek *spora* 'spore' + *aggeion* 'vessel'.]

macrospore /mákrō spawr/ *n* BIOL = **megaspore**

macrostructure /mákrō strukchər/ *n* a structure, e.g. that of a metal, large enough to be seen or examined with little or no magnification —**macrostructural** /mákrō strúkchərəl/ *adj*

macula /mákyŏŏlə/ (*plural* **-lae** /-lee/) *n* **1** SMALL SPOT ON SKIN a small pigmented spot on the skin that is neither raised nor depressed **2** YELLOW SPOT NEAR RETINA a small yellowish spot in the middle of the retina that provides the greatest visual acuity and colour perception **3** SUNSPOT a sunspot (*technical*) [14C. < Latin, 'spot, stain'.] —**macular** *adj*

macula lutea /-loòti ə/ (*plural* **maculae luteae** /-ti ee/) *n* ANAT = **macula** **2** [Latin < *luteus* 'yellow']

maculate /mákyŏŏ layt/ *vt* (**-lates, -lating, -lated**) to mark somebody or something with a spot, blotch, or blemish (*literary*) ▪ *adj* **maculate, maculated** marked with spots, blotches, or blemishes (*literary*) [15C. < Latin *maculat-*, past participle of *maculare* < *macula* 'spot'.] —**maculation** /mákyŏŏ láysh'n/ *n*

macule[1] /mákyool/ *n* MED = **macula**. **1** [Mid-19C. Either directly or via French < Latin *macula* 'spot, stain'.]

macule[2] /mákyool/ *n* PRINTING = **mackle** *n*.

Macusi /mə koòssi/, **Macushi** /mə koòshi/ *n* a Cariban language spoken in the border region between Brazil, Guyana, and Venezuela. Native speakers: over 10,000. [Early 20C. < Macusi.] —**Macusi** *adj*

mad /mad/ *adj* (**madder, maddest**) **1** VERY ANGRY affected by great displeasure or anger ○ *She'll go mad when she finds out.* **2** OFFENSIVE TERM an offensive term meaning affected with a psychiatric disorder **3** VERY UNWISE OR RASH lacking common sense and not reasoning logically (*insult; offensive in some contexts*) **4** WILDLY EXCITED completely unrestrained and out of control (*offensive in some contexts*) **5** FRANTIC done with great haste, excitement, or confusion (*offensive in some contexts*) **6** EXCITING very exciting or boisterous (*offensive in some contexts*) **7** SEIZED BY UNCONTROLLABLE EMOTION overcome with a violent emotion (*offensive in some contexts*) **8** PASSIONATE ABOUT very fond of, enthusiastic about, or interested in something, often to the exclusion of everything else (*often in combination, offensive in some contexts*) ○ *I'm not mad about the colour.* ○ *football mad* **9** MARKEDLY AGGRESSIVE unusually aggressive or ferocious (*refers to animals; offensive in some contexts*) **10** RABID having rabies (*refers to animals; offensive in some contexts*) ▪ *adv* UK EXTREMELY used for emphasis (*informal*) ○ *She's not mad keen on the idea.* [Old English *gemǣd* 'deprived of reason' < *gemād* 'irrational' < Indo-European, 'change'] ◇ **like mad** with great speed or energy (*offensive in some contexts*)

MAD /mad/ *abbr* **1** major affective disorder **2** US mutual assured destruction

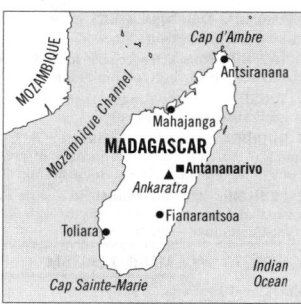

Madagascar

Madagascar /máddə gáskər/ island republic in the Indian Ocean, off the coast of SE Africa. Capital: Antananarivo. Population: 13,671,000 (1996). Area: 587,041 sq. km/226,658 sq. mi. —**Madagascan** adj, n

Madagascar periwinkle n a perennial plant that is poisonous to domestic animals. Flowers: white, pink. Native to: India, Madagascar. Use: production of substances used to treat cancer. Catharanthus roseus.

madam /máddəm/ n 1 (plural **mesdames**) USED TO ADDRESS A WOMAN a polite term of address for a woman, especially a customer in a shop, restaurant, or hotel (formal) 2 WOMAN RUNNING A BROTHEL a woman who manages a brothel 3 PRECOCIOUS GIRL a petulant or self-willed girl who expects everybody to do as she says (informal disapproving) [13C. < Old French ma dame 'my lady' < Latin mea domina.]

Madam /máddəm/ (plural **Mesdames** /máy dam/ or **Madams**) n 1 used at the beginning of a formal letter to a woman, especially one whose name is not known (formal) 2 used before the name of a woman's official position as a term of address ○ Madam President

Madame /máddəm/ (plural **Mesdames** /máy dam/), **madame** (plural **mesdames**) n the title of a Frenchwoman or French-speaking woman, especially if married, used before her name or as a polite term of address

LITERARY LINK *Madame Bovary*, a novel (1857) by French writer Gustave Flaubert. It tells the story of Emma Bovary, a young married woman who seeks refuge from the mundaneness of her provincial life in a series of reckless and ultimately disastrous affairs. The novel's frank depiction of middle-class society and its almost scientific analysis of human behaviour made it a pioneering work of modern realism.

madcap /mád kap/ adj acting or behaving without caring or stopping to think about possible consequences [Late 16C. Cap represents the head.] —**madcap** n

mad cow disease n VET = BSE

madden /mádd'n/ vti 1 to make a person or animal extremely angry, or to become extremely angry (usually passive) 2 to make somebody irrational or furious, or to become irrational or furious

maddening /mádd'ning/ adj 1 causing anger, impatience, or frustration 2 causing intense annoyance and distress —**maddeningly** adv —**maddeningness** n

madder[1] /máddər/ comparative of **mad**

madder[2] /máddər/ n 1 PLANT WITH RED ROOT a perennial plant with a fleshy root. Native to: Europe, Asia. Use: red dye. Rubia tinctorum. 2 RED DYE a red dye formerly obtained from madder roots 3 RED PIGMENT a red pigment obtained from alizarin. Use: dyes, inks, paints. 4 REDDISH-PURPLE a deep reddish-purple colour [Old English mædere < Germanic]

maddest /máddəst/ superlative of **mad**

madding /mádding/ adj acting in a way that suggests or reveals the presence of a psychiatric disorder (literary)

LITERARY LINK *Far from the Madding Crowd*, a novel (1874) by Thomas Hardy. The first of Thomas Hardy's Wessex novels, it is the story of a capricious, forceful young woman, Bathsheba Everdene, and her attempts to improve her social position through marriage.

mad-dog skullcap n a perennial plant. Flowers: two-lipped, blue or white, in clusters. Native to: North America. Use: antispasmodic. Scutellaria lateriflora.

made v 1 past tense of **make** 2 past participle of **make** ■ adj 1 produced by artificial means 2 certain of achieving success

Madeira /mə deérə/ n a sweet or dry wine fortified with brandy, made on the island of Madeira and usually served as a dessert wine or after a meal

Madeira cake n a fine-textured plain cake, similar to a creamed sponge cake, made with fat, butter, and flour and served without filling or icing

Madeira Islands /mə deérə-/ group of islands with many resorts in the E North Atlantic Ocean. Population: 256,000 (1992). Area: 741 sq. km/286 sq. mi.

madeleine /mádd'lin, máddə layn/ n 1 a small light whisked sponge cake baked in an individual shell-shaped tin 2 a sponge cake that is cooked in a small cup-shaped mould, coated in raspberry jam, rolled in desiccated coconut, and topped with a glacé cherry [Mid-19C. Probably after the French pastry cook Madeleine Paulmier.]

mademoiselle /máddəmwə zél/ (plural **mesdemoiselles** /máydə-/ or **mademoiselles**) n 1 a young Frenchwoman or French-speaking woman 2 a woman French teacher or French governess (dated) [15C. < Old French ma demoiselle 'my damsel'.]

Mademoiselle /máddəmwə zél/ n the title of a French woman or French-speaking young or unmarried woman, used before her name or as a polite term of address (sometimes emphatic)

made-to-measure adj made by a tailor to fit a particular person

made-to-order adj 1 US made in accordance with a customer's specifications or requirements 2 perfectly suitable or exactly as required

made-up adj 1 UNTRUE lacking any basis in fact or reality 2 WEARING COSMETICS having applied cosmetics to the face 3 ASSEMBLED completely put together and prepared

madhouse /mád howss/ (plural **-houses** /-howziz/) n 1 an offensive term for a hospital or residential facility for people who have psychiatric disorders 2 a place where there is much noise and activity and little order or control (informal; sometimes offensive)

Madison /máddissən/ 1 capital of Wisconsin, in the south-central part of the state. Population: 209,306 (1998 estimate). 2 town in S Connecticut. Population: 15,485 (1990). 3 city in N New Jersey. Population: 15,828 (1998 estimate).

Madison, James (1751–1836) US statesman and 4th president of the United States (1809–17)

Madison Avenue /máddiss'n-/ n the centre of the US advertising and public-relations industries, or the US advertising industry itself [After the street in New York]

madly /máddli/ adv 1 WILDLY in a wild and uncontrolled way 2 TO NO PURPOSE with great haste or activity but without accomplishing much 3 RASHLY in a rash or thoughtless way 4 WILDLY wildly and with intense emotion 5 OFFENSIVE TERM an offensive term meaning in the manner of somebody who is affected by a psychiatric disorder 6 INTENSELY with an extraordinary degree of intensity or devotion

madman /mádmən/ (plural **-men** /-mən/) n an offensive term for a man with a psychiatric disorder

madness /mádnəss/ n 1 OFFENSIVE TERM an offensive term for a psychiatric disorder 2 RASHNESS rash or thoughtless behaviour 3 ANGER great anger or fury 4 EXCITEMENT great enthusiasm or excitement

Madonna /mə dónnə/ n 1 the Virgin Mary, mother of Jesus Christ 2 **Madonna, madonna** a picture, statue, or other artistic representation of the Virgin Mary [Late 16C. < obsolete Italian ma donna 'my lady' < Latin mea domina.]

Madonna /mə dónnə/ (b. 1959) US pop singer and actor. Born **Madonna Louise Veronica Ciccone**

Madonna lily n a widely cultivated plant. Flowers: white trumpet-shaped. Use: oil used in making perfumes. Native to: E Mediterranean. Lilium candidum. [Traditionally regarded as a symbol of purity, and often included in pictures of the Madonna]

madras /mə draàss, -dráss/ n 1 STRONG FINE CLOTH a strong fine cotton or silk fabric, often with a woven striped or

checked design 2 LIGHT CLOTH a light cotton or rayon fabric. Use: curtains. 3 BRIGHTLY COLOURED SCARF a scarf or handkerchief made from brightly coloured cotton or silk 4 FAIRLY HOT CURRY a fairly hot curried dish made with meat, spices, chillies, and lentils [Early 19C. After MADRAS.]

Madras /mə draàss/ former name for **Chennai**

madrasa /mə draàssə/ n a school for the study of Islamic religion and thought, especially the Koran [Mid-17C. < Arabic, 'place to study'.]

madrepore /máddri pawr/ n a reef-building coral that lives in tropical waters. Genus: Madreporaria. [Mid-18C. Via French or modern Latin < Italian madrepora < madre 'mother' + either poro 'pore' (< late Latin porus) or Latin porus 'calcerous stone' (< Greek poros).] —**madreporal** /máddri páwrəl/ adj —**madreporian** adj —**madreporic** adj —**madreporitic** /-pə ríttik/ adj

madreporite /máddri páw rīt/ n a porous plate in an echinoderm that takes in water to the vascular system [Early 19C. < MADREPORE.]

Madrid /mə dríd/ capital of Spain, in the centre of the country. Population: 3,029,734 (1995).

madrigal /máddrig'l/ n 1 ENGLISH PART SONG a song with parts for several usually unaccompanied voices that was popular in England in the 16th and 17th centuries 2 MEDIEVAL ITALIAN SONG a secular Italian song of the 13th and 14th centuries, written for two or three unaccompanied voices singing in harmony 3 LYRIC POEM a short pastoral or love poem suitable for singing as a madrigal [Late 16C. Via Italian < Latin matricalis 'of the mother' < matrix (see MATRIX).] —**madrigalesque** /máddriga lésk/ adj —**madrigalian** /máddri gálli ən, -gáyli-/ adj —**madrigalist** n

madroña /mə drónya/, **madroño** /-nyō/ (plural **-ños**) n an evergreen tree with smooth crimson peeling bark, glossy leaves, cream flowers, and orange-yellow berries. Native to: North America. Arbutus menziesii. [Mid-19C. < Spanish.]

mad tom n a small common freshwater catfish with poisonous pectoral spines, a long adipose fin, and a rounded dorsal fin. Native to: central United States. Genus: Noturus. [Short for 'mad tom cat', since the fish inflicts nasty wounds with its poisonous spines]

Madura /mə doòrə/ island in SW Indonesia, off the coast of NE Java. Population: 2,832,900 (1989). Area: 5,587 sq. km/2,157 sq. mi.

Madurai /mád yoòrī/ city in S India. Population: 951,696 (1991).

maduro /mə doòrō/ (plural **-ros**) n a dark strong cigar [Late 19C. < Spanish, 'ripe, mature'.]

madwoman /mád woòmən/ (plural **-en** /-wimin/) n an offensive term for a woman with a psychiatric disorder

madwort /mád wurt/ (plural **-worts** or **-wort**) n a low-growing plant of the borage family. Flowers: small, blue. Native to: Europe, Asia. Asperugo procumbens. [Late 16C. Translation of modern Latin alyssum 'removing rabies'; because it was believed to cure the bites of rabid dogs.]

madzoon n = matzoon

Maecenas /mī seé nass/ (plural **-nas**) n a rich patron of the arts (literary)

Maecenas /mī seén ass, mee-/, **Gaius** (74?–8 BC) Roman statesman

maelstrom /máyl strom/ n 1 an exceptionally large or violent whirlpool 2 a situation marked by confusion, turbulence, strong feelings, violence, or destruction [Late 17C. < early modern Dutch, < maalen 'whirl round' + stroom 'stream'.]

Maelstrom /máyl strom/ marine whirlpool in the Lofoten Islands, NW Norway

maenad /meé nad/ n 1 in ancient Greece, a woman who belonged to the cult of Dionysus and took part in orgiastic rites 2 a woman affected by wild, uncontrollable emotion [Late 16C. Via Latin < Greek Mainad-, stem of Mainas < mainesthai 'rave'.] —**maenadic** /mee náddik/ adj —**maenadically** adv —**maenadism** n

maestoso /mī stṑssō/ adv in a dignified or majestic manner (musical direction) ■ n (plural **maestosos**) a section of a piece of music played maestoso [Early 18C. Via Italian, 'majestic' < Latin majestas (see MAJESTY).] —**maestoso** adj

Maestricht = Maastricht

maestro /místrō/ (*plural* **-tros** *or* **-tri** /místri/) *n* an expert in an art or skill, especially an accomplished musician, conductor, or composer [Early 18C. Via Italian, 'master' < Latin *magister*.]

maestro di cappella /-di kə péllə/ (*plural* **maestri di cappella** /místri-/) *n* formerly, especially in 17th-century Italy, the director of a group of musicians, especially a chapel choir or the private orchestra of a royal court or noble household [*Di capella* < Italian, 'of the chapel']

Maeterlinck /máytərlingk/, **Maurice, Comte** (1862–1949) Belgian poet and playwright

Mae West /máy wést/, **mae west** *n* (*informal*) **1** an inflatable life jacket, especially one issued to US pilots during World War II **2** a parachute malfunction in which a suspension line goes over the top of the canopy, creating what appears to be a huge brassiere [Mid-20C. Because the jacket's shape reminded airmen of MAE WEST's large bosom.]

Mafeking former name for **Mafikeng**

MAFF /maf/ *abbr* Ministry of Agriculture, Fisheries, and Food

mafficking /máffiking/ *n* a boisterous and extravagant public celebration (*archaic*) [Early 20C. Based on MAFEKING; from the celebrations after the siege was over in 1900.] —**maffick** *vi* —**mafficker** *n*

mafia /maáfee ə/, **Mafia** *n* a close-knit or influential group of people who work together and protect one another's interests or the interests of a particular person

Mafia /máffi ə/ *n* a secret criminal organization originating in Sicily that spread to mainland Italy and the United States and is involved in international drug-dealing, racketeering, gambling, and prostitution [Mid-19C. < Italian dialect (Sicilian), 'bragging'.]

mafic /máffik/ *adj* relating to dark-coloured minerals or rocks that are high in magnesium and iron [Early 20C. < MAGNESIUM + FERRIC.]

Mafikeng /máffi keng/ town in north-central South Africa, besieged during the Boer War. Population: 6,900 (1994).

Mafioso /máffi óssō, -ózō/ (*plural* **-si** /-ósee, -ee/ *or* **-sos**), **mafioso** *n* a member of the Mafia [Late 19C. < Italian, < *mafia* (see MAFIA).]

mag /mag/ *n* PUBL = **magazine** *n.* 1 (*informal*) [Early 19C. Shortening.]

mag. *abbr* **1** magazine **2** magnesium **3** magnet **4** magnetic **5** magnetism **6** magnitude **7** magnum

magazine /mággə zeén/ *n* **1 PERIODICAL PUBLICATION** a publication issued at regular intervals, usually weekly or monthly, containing articles, stories, photographs, advertisements, and other features, with a page size that is usually smaller than that of a newspaper but larger than that of a book **2 PROGRAMME CONTAINING ASSORTED ITEMS** a television or radio programme made up of an assortment of short factual items, often of interest to a particular group of people **3 BULLET OR CARTRIDGE HOLDER** a detachable container for cartridges or bullets that can be quickly inserted or removed from a gun **4 STOREHOUSE FOR MILITARY SUPPLIES** a structure on land or a part of a ship where weapons, ammunition, explosives, and other military equipment or supplies are stored **5 STOCK OF AMMUNITION** a stock of ammunition or other supplies kept in a storehouse **6 SLIDE HOLDER** a container designed to hold a number of photographic slides and feed them automatically through a projector **7 FILM CONTAINER** a container that is used for loading film into a camera without exposing it to light **8 SUPPLY DEVICE** a device or container attached to a machine that holds or supplies necessary material [Late 16C. Via French *magazin* < Italian *magazzino* < Arabic *makzan* 'storehouse'.]

magdalen /mágdələn/, **magdalene** /mágdə leéni, mágdə leen/ *n* a refuge for reformed prostitutes or an institution where prostitutes are sent to be reformed (*literary*) [14C. < *Mary Magdalen*, reformed sinner, in the Bible.]

Magdalena /mágdə láynə/ river in W Colombia. Length: 1,540 km/957 mi.

Magdalene *n* = **Mary Magdalene**

Magdeburg /mágdə burg/ capital of Saxony-Anhalt State, north-central Germany. Population: 269,500 (1994).

mage /mayj/ *n* a magician or magus (*archaic*) [14C. An anglicization of MAGUS.]

Magellan, Strait of /mə géllən/ channel separating mainland South America and Tierra del Fuego, between the Atlantic and Pacific oceans. Length: 560 km/350 mi.

Magellan, Ferdinand (1480?–1521) Portuguese explorer

Magellanic Cloud /mággi lánnik-, májji-/ *n* either of two small galaxies near the south celestial pole that are irregularly shaped and closest to the Milky Way [Early 17C. After Ferdinand MAGELLAN.]

Magen David /máwgən dáyvid/ *n* JUDAISM = **Star of David** [< Hebrew, 'shield of David']

magenta /mə jéntə/ *n* **1** a brilliant purplish-pink colour that is one of the three subtractive colours **2** CHEM = **fuchsin** ■ *adj* brilliant purplish-pink in colour [Mid-19C. After *Magenta*, N Italy.]

maggid /maágid/ (*plural* **-gidim** /-dim/) *n* a popular teacher travelling among the Ashkenazi Jewish communities of Eastern Europe [Late 19C. < Hebrew *maggīd* 'narrator'.]

maggiore /ma jáw ray/ *n* a section of a fugue or set of variations in the major mode that occurs especially after a section in a minor [Late 19C. < Italian, 'major'.]

Maggiore, Lake /ma jáw ray/ lake on the Italian-Swiss border. Area: 212 sq. km/82 sq. mi.

maggot /mággət/ *n* **1** the worm-shaped larva of various members of the fly family, e.g. the housefly, found in decaying matter and used as bait in fishing **2** a fanciful notion or idea (*archaic*) [14C. < Germanic.]

maggoty /mággəti/ (**-ier, -iest**) *adj* **1** full of or containing maggots **2** extremely intoxicated by alcohol (*slang*)

Magha /múggə/ *n* in the Hindu calendar, the 11th month of the year, made up of 29 or 30 days and occurring around January to February [Late 20C. < Hindi.]

Magherafelt /mákərə félt/ town in NW Northern Ireland. Population: 7,143 (1991).

Maghreb /múgrəb/, **Maghrib** loosely defined region in NW Africa, centred on Algeria, Morocco, and Tunisia

magi plural of **magus**

Magi /máy jī/ *npl* in the Bible, the three wise men, known as Caspar, Melchior, and Balthazar, who came to Bethlehem from the east to celebrate the birth of Jesus Christ. (Matthew 2:1–12). [Plural of MAGUS] —**Magian** /máyji ən/ *adj, n* —**Magianism** *n*

magic /májjik/ *n* **1 SUPPOSED SUPERNATURAL POWER** a supposed supernatural power that makes impossible things happen or that gives somebody control over the forces of nature **2 PRACTICE OF MAGIC** the use of supposed supernatural power to make impossible things happen **3 CONJURING TRICKS** conjuring tricks and illusions that make apparently impossible things seem to happen, usually performed as entertainment **4 INEXPLICABLE THINGS** a special, mysterious, or inexplicable quality, talent, or skill ○ *watched the dancer's feet work their magic* ■ *adj* **1 OF OR FOR MAGIC** relating to magic or used in the working of magic ○ *a magic potion* **2 PARTICULARLY IMPORTANT** particularly important or desirable ○ *reach the magic figure of 100 points* **3 EXCELLENT** very good or enjoyable (*informal*) ○ *a great film and a magic dinner* ■ *vt* (**-ics, -icking, -icked**) **SUBJECT SOMETHING TO MAGIC** to make somebody or something seem to appear, disappear, change, or move by using magic [14C. Via Old French *magique* < Greek *magikē* < *magos* (see MAGUS).] ◇ **like magic 1** rapidly **2** without obstacles or difficulties

LITERARY LINK ***The Magic Mountain***, a novel (1924) by German writer Thomas Mann. It describes young engineer Hans Castorp's lengthy stay in a Swiss TB clinic. The clinic is a microcosm of European society at the time of World War I, with a cosmopolitan group of patients reflecting a range of contemporary political, philosophical, and scientific viewpoints.

magical /májjik'l/ *adj* **1** made or created by or as if by magic **2** so beautiful or pleasing as to seem supernaturally created —**magically** *adv*

magical realism *n* ART = **magic realism**

magic bullet *n* **1** a drug that cures a serious disease with no undesirable side effects on the patient **2** a quick and easy solution for a difficult problem, or a means of accomplishing the impossible

magic carpet *n* in fairy stories, a carpet that flies through the air and is used as a form of transportation

magic eye *n* a tiny cathode-ray tube used in a radio receiver to help tuning

magician /mə jísh'n/ *n* **1 CONJURER OR ILLUSIONIST** an entertainer who performs conjuring tricks and illusions **2 SOMEBODY WHO SUPPOSEDLY PRACTISES SORCERY** a performer of magic who uses supposed supernatural powers **3 SOMEBODY WITH EXCEPTIONAL ABILITY** an extraordinarily skilled or powerful person

Magic Marker *tdmk* a trademark for a highlighting pen that comes in various colours of ink

magic mushroom *n* a fungus that contains a hallucinogenic substance (*informal*)

magic number *n* any of the numbers 2, 8, 20, 28, 50, 82, and 126 that represent the number of protons or neutrons in the nucleus of very stable atomic nuclei

magic realism, **magical realism** *n* a style of art or literature that depicts fantastic or mythological subjects in a realistic manner —**magic realist** *n*

QUICK FACTS ON... **MAGIC REALISM**

Key dates: mid-1950s–late 1980s
Key locations: South and Central America, India, Europe, Australia
Key elements: depiction of supernatural events in realistic, often historical settings; acceptance of implausible occurrences; incorporation of myths, legends, and fables; depiction of influence of public events on private life; surrealism
Key figures: Alejo Carpentier, Gabriel García Márquez, Carlos Fuentes, Isabel Allende, Salman Rushdie, Italo Calvino, Günter Grass, Angela Carter, Peter Carey
Key works: *Our Ancestors* (Calvino) 1960, *One Hundred Years of Solitude* (Márquez) 1967, *Midnight's Children* (Rushdie) 1980, *The House of the Spirits* (Allende) 1982, *Illywhacker* (Carey) 1985
Key developments: postmodernism, historiography as a creative process

magic square *n* a square containing rows and columns of numbers arranged in such a way that each horizontal, vertical, and diagonal line has the same sum

magic wand *n* **1** a small thin stick used by a sorcerer or conjurer to perform magic **2** something fanciful or make-believe that would, if it existed, be able to solve a difficult or impossible problem immediately

magilp *n* ART = **megilp**

Maginot line /mázhi nō-/ *n* **1** a line of fortifications constructed by the French along the border between France and Germany before World War II that failed to stop the German army from invading **2** an ineffective defensive strategy that is relied on with unthinking confidence [Mid-20C. After French war minister André *Maginot* (1877–1932).]

magisterial /májji steéri əl/ *adj* **1 DIGNIFIED** showing great authority and dignity **2 DOMINEERING** behaving in an overbearing or dictatorial way **3 MASTERLY AND AUTHORITATIVE** produced by or characteristic of a teacher, scholar, or expert **4 OF MAGISTRATE** relating to or characteristic of a magistrate —**magisterially** *adv* —**magisterialness** *n*

magisterium /májji steéri əm/ *n* the authority of the church in the Roman Catholic tradition to teach religious doctrine [Late 16C. < Latin, < *magister* 'master'.]

magistracy /májjistrəssi/ (*plural* **-cies**), **magistrature** /-strəchər/ *n* **1 OFFICE OF MAGISTRATE** the position or function of a magistrate **2 MAGISTRATE'S TERM OF OFFICE** the term of office of a magistrate **3 AREA OF MAGISTRATE'S JURISDICTION** the district over which a magistrate has the power and authority to administer justice **4 MAGISTRATES COLLECTIVELY** magistrates considered as a group

magistral /májjistrəl/ *adj* **1 OF MAGISTRATE** relating to or characteristic of a magistrate **2 OF EXPERT** relating to or characteristic of an expert or scholar **3 PRINCIPAL OR DETERMINING** describes a line of fortifications that determines the position of other lines ■ *n* **MAGISTRAL LINE OF FORTIFICATIONS** a line of fortifications that determines the position of other lines —**magistrality** /májji strálləti/ *n* —**magistrally** *adv*

magistrate /májji strayt, -strət/ *n* **1 LOWER COURT JUDGE** a judge in a lower court whose jurisdiction is limited to the trial of misdemeanours and the conduct of preliminary hearings on more serious charges **2 LOCAL LAW OFFICER** a minor law officer or member of a local judiciary with extremely limited powers, e.g. a justice of the peace who deals with moving vehicular violations **3** *Aus* **JUDGE OF AUSTRALIAN LOWER COURT** a judicial officer appointed by the executive government to hear civil and criminal cases in a court of summary jurisdiction [14C. < Latin *magistratus* < *magister* 'master'.] —**magistrateship** *n*

magistrates' court *n* **1** in England, a summary court presided over by a magistrate or two or more justices of the peace who make decisions about minor crimes, some civil actions, and preliminary hearings **2** *Aus* a court of summary jurisdiction in the Australian states of Victoria and Queensland

magistrature *n* LAW = **magistracy**

maglev /mág lev/ *n* an electrically operated high-speed train that glides above a track by means of a magnetic field. ◊ **magnetic levitation** [Late 20C. Blend of MAGNETIC + *levitation*.]

magma /mágmə/ (*plural* **-mas** *or* **-mata** /-mətə/) *n* **1** molten rock deep within the earth from which igneous rock is formed by solidification at or near the earth's surface **2** a soft paste or thick suspension made from fine solid particles mixed with liquid [15C. Via Latin < Greek, < *massein* 'knead'.] —**magmatic** /mag máttik/ *adj*

magma chamber *n* an underground cavity that contains magma, often located below a volcano

Magna Carta /mágnə kaártə/, **Magna Charta** *n* **1** charter establishing the rights of English barons and free citizens, granted by king John at Runnymede in 1215 and regarded as the basis of civil and political liberty in England **2** a document that recognizes or guarantees rights, privileges, or liberties [< Latin, 'great charter']

magna cum laude /mágnə kŏŏm lów day, -di/ *adv, adj* at the second of three levels of commendation for those who achieve excellent grades in coursework, especially graduates of North American universities and colleges that have honours programmes involving theses. ◊ **cum laude, summa cum laude** [< Latin, 'with great praise']

Magna Graecia /mágnə gréessi ə, -gréeshə/ *n* in ancient times, the parts of S Italy and Sicily that contained numerous Greek colonies [< Latin, 'great Greece']

magnanimity /mágnə nímməti/ (*plural* **-ties**) *n* **1** great generosity or noble-spiritedness **2** a generous or noble-spirited act [14C. Via French *magnanimité* < Latin *magnanimitas* < *magnanimus* (see MAGNANIMOUS).]

magnanimous /mag nánniməss/ *adj* very generous, kind, or forgiving [Late 16C. < Latin *magnanimus* < *magnus* 'great' + *animus* 'mind'.] —**magnanimously** *adv* —**magnanimousness** *n*

SYNONYMS See ***generous***.

---

magnate /mág nayt, -nət/ *n* **1** somebody who has a lot of wealth and power, especially somebody in business or industry **2** a high-ranking member of the nobility [15C. < late Latin *magnat-* < Latin *magnus* 'great'.] —**magnateship** *n*

magnesia /mag néeshə, -néezhə/ *n* CHEM = **magnesium oxide** [14C. Via medieval Latin < Greek *magnēsia* 'mineral' < *Magnesia*, Asia Minor.] —**magnesial** *adj* —**magnesian** *adj* —**magnesic** *adj*

magnesite /mágni sīt/ *n* a white or colourless magnesium carbonate mineral. Use: insulation, refractory lining of furnaces refractory, source of magnesium oxide. [Early 19C. < MAGNESIA.]

magnesium /mag néezi əm/ *n* (*symbol* **Mg**) a light silver-white metallic element. Source: magnesite, dolomite, seawater. Use: alloys, metallurgy, photography, fireworks. [Early 19C. < MAGNESIA.]

magnesium carbonate *n* $MgCO_3$ a white crystalline salt. Source: dolomite, magnesite. Use: in antacids, glass, refractories.

magnesium chloride *n* $MgCl_2{\cdot}6H_2O$ a colourless or white crystalline compound. Use: source of magnesium, in fireproofing, paper making, ceramics, fire extinguishers.

magnesium hydroxide *n* $Mg(OH)_2$ a white crystalline powder. Use: antacid, laxative.

magnesium oxide *n* MgO a white powder. Source: periclase. Use: antacid, laxative, refractories, cements, electrical insulation, fertilizers.

magnesium sulphate *n* $MgSO_4$ a colourless crystalline salt. Use: in medicine, fertilizers, manufacturing.

magnet /mágnət/ *n* **1** PIECE OF METAL THAT ATTRACTS METAL a piece of metal, often bar-shaped or U-shaped, that has the power to draw iron or steel objects towards it and to hold or move them **2** ELECTROMAGNET an electromagnet **3** SOURCE OF GREAT ATTRACTION somebody or something that has a great power of attraction over people [15C. Directly or via Old French *magnete* < Latin, < Greek *Magnēs lithos* 'stone from Magnesia', Asia Minor.]

magnetic /mag néttik/ *adj* **1** HAVING POWER OF MAGNET able to attract iron or steel objects **2** ABLE TO BE MAGNETIZED able to be magnetized, or attracted by a magnet **3** RELATING TO MAGNETISM relating to, involving, or produced by magnetism **4** USING MAGNET OR MAGNETISM containing or using a magnet or magnetism **5** OF EARTH'S MAGNETISM relating to the Earth's magnetism **6** POWERFULLY CHARMING having a great power of attraction over people ○ *a magnetic personality* —**magnetically** *adv*

magnetic bottle *n* a strong magnetic field. Use: to confine plasma in nuclear fusion experiments.

⚡**magnetic bubble** *n* a small movable magnetic region in a thin film of magnetic material. Use: to store data in computer memory.

magnetic compass *n* an instrument used to indicate magnetic north and other directions, containing a magnetic needle that swings horizontally around a circle marked in degrees or with the points of the compass

magnetic declination *n* the angle between magnetic north and true north at a particular point on the Earth's surface

⚡**magnetic disk** *n* a computer disk consisting of one or more thin magnetically etched plates

magnetic epoch *n* a long period of geological time between reversals of the Earth's magnetic field

magnetic equator *n* an imaginary line that lies near the geographical equator and passes through all points where a magnetic needle has no dip

magnetic field *n* a region of space surrounding a magnetized body or current-carrying circuit in which the resulting magnetic force can be detected

magnetic flux *n* (*symbol* ϕ) the strength of a magnetic field represented by lines of force

magnetic flux density *n* (*symbol* *B*) the strength of a magnetic field multiplied by the porosity of a medium, measured in teslas or gauss

magnetic head *n* an electromagnetic device to read, write, or erase data on a magnetic medium

magnetic induction *n* PHYS = **magnetic flux density**

magnetic levitation *n* a system of high-speed rail travel using magnetism both to suspend and to propel trains above and along the track. ◊ **maglev**

magnetic meridian *n* an imaginary line around the Earth's surface that passes through both magnetic poles

magnetic mine *n* an underwater mine equipped with magnetic sensors that cause it to detonate when a large metal object, usually a ship, passes into its magnetic field

magnetic mirror *n* PHYS = **magnetic bottle**

magnetic moment *n* (*symbol* *m*) a vector quantity representing the torque experienced by a magnetic system in a magnetic field

magnetic needle *n* thin bar of magnetized metal used in navigational instruments, mounted or suspended so that it swings freely in a horizontal circle and indicates the direction of the Earth's magnetic poles

magnetic north *n* the direction of the north magnetic pole, indicated by the needle of a magnetic compass

magnetic pole *n* **1** either of the two points at the end of a magnet where the magnet's field is most intense **2** either of the two regions on the Earth's surface near the geographic poles where the Earth's magnetic field is most intense

⚡**magnetic recording** *n* **1** the storage of analogue or digital data on a magnetized medium, e.g. audio, video, or computer data on tape, disk, or cards **2** a surface on which information has been magnetically recorded

magnetic resonance imaging *n* an imaging technique that uses electromagnetic radiation to obtain images of the body's soft tissues, e.g. the brain and spinal cord

magnetic reversal *n* the reversal of the Earth's magnetic polarity, which has occurred at irregular intervals averaging approximately one million years

magnetic sense *n* BIOL = **compass sense**

magnetic storm *n* a disturbance in the Earth's magnetic field associated with charged particles from solar flares and sunspot activity

⚡**magnetic stripe, magnetic strip** *n* a strip of magnetic medium on a plastic card such as a credit card, encoded with information

magnetic susceptibility *n* a number that characterizes the magnetization of a substance when it is subjected to a magnetic field

⚡**magnetic tape** *n* a thin ribbon of material, usually plastic, coated with iron oxide and used to record sounds, images, or data

magnetic transition temperature *n* PHYS = **Curie point**

magnetic variation *n* PHYS = **magnetic declination**

magnetise *vti* PHYS = **magnetize**

magnetism /mágnətizəm/ *n* **1** ATTRACTION OF MAGNETS FOR IRON the phenomenon of physical attraction for iron, inherent in magnets or induced by a moving electric charge or current **2** MAGNETIC FIELD FORCE the force exerted by a magnetic field **3** ATTRACTION the strong attractiveness of something, e.g. the power of somebody's personality to influence others ○ *'He was a born boon companion, with a magnetism which drew good humour from all around him'.* (Arthur Conan Doyle, *The Valley of Fear*; 1915)

magnetite /mágnə tīt/ *n* a common black magnetic mineral consisting of iron oxide. Use: source of iron.

magnetize /mágnə tīz/ (**-izes, -izing, -ized**), **magnetise** (**-ises, -ising, -ised**) *v* **1** *vti* to become magnetic, or to make an object or material magnetic **2** *vt* to hold a strong attraction for somebody ○ *prospectors magnetized by the possibility of finding gold in the hills* —**magnetizable** *adj* —**magnetization** /mágnə tī záysh'n/ *n* —**magnetizer** *n*

magneto /mag néetō/ (*plural* **-tos**) *n* a small alternator that uses permanent magnets to generate a spark in an internal-combustion engine, especially in marine and aircraft engines [Late 19C. Shortening of *magneto-electric machine*.]

magneto- *prefix* magnetic field ○ *magnetograph* [< MAGNET]

magnetograph /mag néetō graaf, -graf/ *n* an instrument used to record variations in a magnetic field, usually that of the Earth

magnetohydrodynamics /mag néetō hīdrō dī námmiks/ *n* the study of magnetic and electric fields in relation to the movement of electrically conducting fluids, e.g. plasmas and molten metal (+ *singular verb*) —**magnetohydrodynamic** *adj*

magnetometer /mágnə tómmitər/ *n* a device for measuring the direction and intensity of a magnetic field

magnetomotive /mag néetō mṓtiv/ *adj* relating to or producing a magnetic flux [Late 19C. After ELECTROMOTIVE.]

magnetomotive force /mag néetō mṓtiv-/ *n* (*symbol* $\mathbf{F}_m$) a force that produces magnetic flux

magneton /mágnə ton/ *n* a unit that expresses the combined force and direction of a magnetic field (**magnetic moment**), e.g. the magnetic field of an atom or elementary particle [Early 20C. < MAGNETIC.]

magnetopause /mag néetō pawz/ *n* the region between the magnetosphere and outer space

magnetosphere /mag néetō sfeer/ *n* the region surrounding an astronomical object, e.g. the Earth, in which charged particles are trapped and affected by the object's magnetic field —**magnetospheric** /mag néetō sférrik/ *adj*

magnetotherapy /mag néetō thérrəpi/ *n* the use or wearing of magnets to prevent, alleviate, or remedy medical conditions

magnetron /mágnə tron/ *n* an electronic valve in which the flow of electrons is manipulated by electric and magnetic fields to generate microwaves

magnet school *n US* a state school specializing in particular subjects, e.g. languages or technology, in addition to providing general education, and drawing students from inside and outside the local area

~~**magnificant**~~ incorrect spelling of **magnificent**

Magnificat /mag níffi kat/ *n* **1** the Virgin Mary's hymn of praise to God, taken from and sung or chanted in church **2** any hymn of praise sung or chanted in church [12C. < Latin, '(my soul) magnifies', a form of *magnificare* (see MAGNIFY), from the opening word of the Latin version.]

magnification /mágnifi káysh'n/ *n* **1** INCREASING OF APPARENT SIZE the process of causing an object or image to appear larger than it really is, especially by using a lens or microscope **2** INCREASING OF ACTUAL SIZE the process of increasing the size or magnitude of something **3** GROWTH IN IMPORTANCE the increasing of the importance attributed to somebody or something **4** DEGREE OF ENLARGEMENT the amount by which an image is made bigger **5 ENLARGED COPY** a copy of a map, photograph, or other image that has been made larger than the original **6 RATIO** the size of the image of an object, expressed as a ratio of its actual size

magnificence /mag níffiss'nss/ *n* **1** the impressive beauty or grandeur of somebody or something ○ *the magnificence of the palace and its formal gardens* **2** the great richness and splendour of somebody or something, usually indicating great wealth ○ *the magnificence of a royal wedding* [14C. Directly, or via Old French < Latin *magnificentia* < *magnificent-* (see MAGNIFICENT).]

magnificent /mag níffiss'nt/ *adj* **1 BEAUTIFUL** beautiful, impressive, and splendid in appearance ○ *a magnificent view of Rome from our balcony* **2 EXCEPTIONAL** exceptionally good of its kind ○ *The caterers had laid out a magnificent spread.* **3 VERY GOOD** excellent (*informal*) ○ *The response to the appeal has been magnificent.* [15C. Directly, or via Old French < Latin *magnificent-* 'performing great actions' < *magnus* 'great'.] —**magnificently** *adv*

magnifico /mag níffikō/ (*plural* **-coes**) *n* **1** a rich or powerful person **2** a nobleman of the Venetian Republic [Late 16C. < Italian, 'magnificent'.]

magnify /mágni fī/ (**-fies, -fying, -fied**) *v* **1** *vt* **INCREASE APPARENT SIZE OF** to cause something to appear larger than it is, especially by using a microscope or lens ○ *a virus magnified 50,000 times* **2** *vt* **INCREASE ACTUAL SIZE OF** to increase the size or magnitude of something **3** *vt* **INCREASE IMPORTANCE OF** to increase the importance attributed to somebody or something ○ *The complexities of today's medicine only magnify the need for better hospital management.* **4** *vt* **OVERSTATE IMPORTANCE OF** to cause somebody or something to appear more important than is in fact the case ○ *He tried to magnify his plight by complaining to the media about unfair stories.* **5** *vi* **HAVE ENLARGING ABILITY** to have the ability to increase the size or magnitude of something **6** *vt* **PRAISE GOD** to give praise or thanks to God (*formal*) ○ *'my heart doth magnify his holy name'* (*The Book of Mormon [part 1]*) [14C. Directly, or via Old French *magnifier* < Latin *magnificare* 'make greater' < *magnus* 'great'.] —**magnifiable** *adj* —**magnifier** *n*

magnifying glass *n* a convex lens in a frame with a handle, used to make objects viewed through it appear larger

magniloquent /mag nílləkwənt/ *adj* employing impressive words and an exaggeratedly solemn and dignified style [Mid-17C. < Latin *magniloquus* < *magnus* 'great' + *-loquus* 'speaking'.] —**magniloquence** *n* —**magniloquently** *adv*

Magnitogorsk /mágnitə gáwrsk/ city in SW Siberian Russia. Population: 427,000 (1995).

magnitude /mágni tyood/ *n* **1 GREATNESS OF SIZE** greatness of size, volume, or extent ○ *computing the magnitude of heavenly bodies* **2 IMPORTANCE** the importance or significance of something ○ *the magnitude of the discovery* **3 STATUS** great personal importance or status ○ *a person of her magnitude* **4 MEASURE OF EARTHQUAKE SIZE** a measure of the energy of an earthquake, specified on the Richter scale **5 NUMBER ASSIGNED TO A MATHEMATICAL QUANTITY** a numerical value that describes the amount of something, usually expressed in terms of a multiple of standard units, or the item measured in this way **6 BRIGHTNESS OF AN ASTRONOMICAL OBJECT** a numerical measure of the apparent brightness of an astronomical object, on a scale in which a lower number represents greater brightness [14C. < Latin *magnitudo* < *magnus* 'great'.] —**magnitudinous** /mágni tyóodinəss/ *adj*

magnolia /mag nóli ə/ (*plural* **magnolia** *or* **magnolias**) *n* **1** an evergreen or deciduous tree or bush with typically large simple leaves, widely cultivated as an ornamental. Flowers: yellow, white, pink, green. Native to: North America, Asia. Genus: *Magnolia.* **2** a creamy-white colour [Mid-18C. After Pierre *Magnol* (1638–1715) French botanist.] —**magnolia** *adj*

Magnox /mág noks/ *n* **1** an alloy of magnesium and other metals, especially aluminium, used to make casings for fuel in nuclear reactors **2** an early type of gas-cooled nuclear reactor [Mid-20C. < MAGNESIUM + NO + OXIDATION.]

magnum[1] /mágnəm/ (*plural* **-nums**) *n* **1** a wine bottle that holds approximately 1.5 litres, the equivalent of two normal bottles **2** the volume of liquid contained in a magnum [Late 18C. < Latin, a form of *magnus* 'large'.]

magnum[2] /mágnəm/ *adj* describes firearms cartridges that have a larger charge and casing and are thus more high-powered than other gun cartridges of the same calibre ■ *n* a gun capable of shooting magnum cartridges

magnum opus *n* a great work of art or literature, especially the finest work produced by one individual [< Latin, 'great work']

Magog *n* ♦ **Gog and Magog**

magot /ma gṓ, mággət/ *n* **1** a Barbary ape **2** a crouching, often grotesque figurine in the Japanese or Chinese style [Early 17C. < Old French *magos*, a kind of monkey < *Magog* 'Magog', biblical giant used as an emblem of ugliness in medieval romance.]

magpie /mág pī/ *n* **1 CHATTERING BIRD** a bird of the crow family with black-and-white plumage, a long wedge-shaped tail, and a chattering call. Genus: *Pica.* **2 AUSTRALIAN BIRD** a large black-and-white songbird. Native to: Australia. *Gymnorhina tibicen.* **3 TALKATIVE PERSON** an incurable chatterer (*informal*) **4 AVID COLLECTOR** an enthusiastic or compulsive collector, especially of small objects (*informal*) **5 RING ON A TARGET** the outermost but one ring on a dartboard **6 HIT ON MAGPIE** a hit on the magpie of a target [Late 16C. < *Mag*, shortening of the name *Margaret* + PIE[4].]

Magritte /ma gréet/, **René** (1898–1967) Belgian painter

mag tape *n* magnetic tape (*informal*)

maguey /mə gáy, mág way/ *n* **1** fibre made from the stalk of a tropical plant **2** a tropical plant that yields maguey. Use: pulque alcoholic drink production. Native to: Mexico. Genus: *Agave.* [Mid-16C. Via Spanish < Taino.]

magus /máygəss/ (*plural* **-gi** /máy jī/) *n* **1** a priest in the ancient Persian religion of Zoroastrianism **2** a man with supernatural or magical powers, especially in ancient times [Early 17C. Via Latin < Greek *magos* < Old Persian *maguš.*] —**magian** /máyji ən/ *adj* —**magianism** *n*

LITERARY LINK ***The Magus***, a novel (1966) by John Fowles. The plot concerns a young teacher, Nicholas Urfe, who takes a job on a Greek island and finds himself lured into an elaborate fiction staged by a wealthy resident, Maurice Conchis. Fowles uses this enigmatic story to explore the nature of individual identity and freedom of choice.

Magus (*plural* **-gi** /máy jī/) *n* in the Bible, one of the three wise men who followed a star to Bethlehem to worship the baby Jesus Christ (*literary*)

Magyar /mág yaar/ (*plural* **-yars** *or* **-yar**) *n* **1** a member of the Hungarian people that forms the largest population group of Hungary **2** LANG = **Hungarian** *n.* **2** [Late 18C. < Hungarian.] —**Magyar** *adj*

Mahabharata /mə haa báarətə/ *n* one of India's two great national epic poems, written in Sanskrit from about 300 BC, that tells of the great war in N India between the Pandava and Kaurava families [Late 18C. < Sanskrit, 'the great history of the Bharata dynasty'.]

Mahajanga /máhə zhaángə/ port in NW Madagascar. Population: 100,807 (1993).

maharajah /maáhə raájə/, **maharaja** *n* an Indian prince of a rank above a rajah, especially the ruler of one of the former Native States of India [Late 17C. < Sanskrit, < *mahā* 'great' + *rājān* 'raja'.]

maharani /maáhə raáni/ *n* **1** the wife or widow of a maharajah **2** an Indian princess of a rank above a rani, especially the ruler of one of the former Native States of India [Mid-19C. < Hindi, < Sanskrit *mahā* 'great' + *rājñnī.*]

Maharashtra /maá hə ráshtrə/ state in west-central India. Capital: Mumbai. Population: 85,865,000 (1994). Area: 307,690 sq. km/118,799 sq. mi.

maharishi /maáhə ríshi/ *n* a Hindu religious teacher [Late 18C. < Sanskrit *maharṣi* < *mahā* 'great' + *ṛṣi* 'inspired sage'.]

mahatma /mə haátmə, -hát-/ *n* in India, a title bestowed on somebody who is deeply revered for wisdom and virtue [Late 19C. < Sanskrit *mahātman* < *mahā* 'great' + *ātman* 'soul'.]

Mahavira /maáhə véerə/ (599?–527 BC) Indian founder of Jainism

Mahayana /maáhə yaánə/ *n* the branch of Buddhism that includes Tibetan, Chinese, and Zen Buddhism, developed around AD 1. It stresses compassion for all sentient beings and universal salvation. [Mid-19C. < Sanskrit, < *mahā* 'great' + *yanā* 'vehicle'.]

Mahdi /maádi/ *n* in Islamic belief, a prophet or messiah who is expected to appear in the world sometime before it ends [Early 19C. < Arabic *al-mahdī* 'he who is rightly guided' < *hadā* 'lead in the right way'.] —**Mahdism** *n* —**Mahdist** *n*

Mahdi /maádi/ (1843–85) Sudanese religious leader. Born **Mohammad Ahmad**

Mahé /maa háy/ largest island in the Seychelles, in the W Indian Ocean. Population: 59,500 (1987). Area: 148 sq. km/57 sq. mi.

Mahfouz /maa fóoz/, **Naguib** (*b.* 1911) Egyptian novelist and screenwriter

Mahican /mə héekən/ *n* **1** a member of a Native North American confederacy of peoples who lived in the upper Hudson River Valley of New York State and whose descendants now live in Wisconsin and Oklahoma **2** the Algonquian language of the Mahican people [Early 17C. < Mahican *muhheakunneuw* 'people of the tidal water'.] —**Mahican** *adj*

mahi-mahi /maáhi maáhi/ *n* **1** a tropical sea fish with a bright blue body and long dorsal fin. *Coryphaena hippurus.* **2** the flesh of a mahi-mahi as food [< Hawaiian]

mahjongg /maá jóng/, **mahjong** *n* a game of Chinese origin using 144 small tiles bearing various designs, played by four people around a square table [Early 20C. < Chinese dialect *ma jiang* 'sparrows'.]

Mahler /maálər/, **Gustav** (1860–1911) Czech-born Austrian composer and conductor

Mahmud II /maa móod/ (1785–1839) sultan of the Ottoman Empire (1808–39)

Mahmud of Ghazna /maa móod əv gaáznə/ (971–1030) Afghan sultan

mahogany /mə hóggəni/ (*plural* **-nies**) *n* **1 REDDISH-BROWN HARDWOOD** a hard reddish-brown wood. Use: construction, furniture-making. **2 TROPICAL HARDWOOD TREE** an evergreen hardwood tree cultivated for its timber. Native to: tropical America. Genus: *Swietenia.* **3 REDDISH-BROWN** a dark reddish-brown colour [Mid-17C. < obsolete Spanish *mahogani.*] —**mahogany** *adj*

mahonia /mə hṓni ə/ *n* an evergreen shrub typically with spiny leaflets widely cultivated as an ornamental. Flowers: small, yellow, in clusters. Native to: America, Asia. Genus: *Mahonia.* [Early 19C. After US botanist Bernard *McMahon* (1775–1816).]

mahout /mə hówt/ *n* in South and Southeast Asia, somebody who trains, drives, and looks after elephants [Mid-17C. Via Hindi *mahāut* < Sanskrit *mahāmātra* 'high official' < *mahā* 'great' + *mātra* 'measure'.]

Mahratta *n* PEOPLES = **Maratha**

Mahratti *n* LANG, PEOPLES = **Marathi**

Mahy /máy hi/, **Margaret** (*b.* 1936) New Zealand writer

maid /mayd/ *n* **1 WOMAN SERVANT** a woman servant, e.g. one working in a hotel **2 YOUNG UNMARRIED WOMAN** a young unmarried woman (*archaic or literary; sometimes offensive*) **3 UNMARRIED WOMAN** an unmarried woman past middle age (*often considered offensive*) **4 VIRGIN** a woman who has never had sexual intercourse (*archaic or literary*) [12C. Shortening of MAIDEN.]

maiden /máyd'n/ *n* **1 YOUNG UNMARRIED WOMAN** a young unmarried woman (*sometimes offensive*) **2 VIRGIN** a woman who has never had sexual intercourse (*archaic or literary*) **3 GUILLOTINE** in 16th- and 17th-century Scotland, a guillotine used to execute criminals **4** *N England* **FRAME FOR DRYING CLOTHES** a frame on which wet laundry is hung to dry **5 HORSE YET TO WIN** a horse that has never won a race **6** CRICKET = **maiden over** ■ *adj* **1 FIRST** done for the very first time (*offensive in some contexts*) ○ *a maiden voyage* **2 UNTOUCHED** still in its original, unused, untouched, or unexplored condition (*literary; offensive in some contexts*) **3 FOR HORSES YET TO WIN** for horses that have never won a race [Old English *mægden* < Germanic, 'young woman']

maidenhair fern /máyd'n hair-/ *n* an ornamental fern with slender dark stems and delicate fronds of numerous leaflets. Native to: warm moist regions worldwide. Genus: *Adiantum.*

maidenhair tree *n* TREES = **ginkgo**

maidenhead /máyd'n hed/ *n* (*literary*) **1** the hymen **2** a woman's virginity [13C. < MAIDEN + *-head*, a variant of HOOD[1].]

Maidenhead /máyd'n hed/ town in south-central England. Population: 59,605 (1991).

maidenhood /máyd'n hŏŏd/, **maidhood** /máyd hŏŏd/ *n* the period of a woman's life before marriage or before becoming sexually active (*archaic; sometimes offensive*)

maidenly /máyd'nli/ *adj* of, like, or thought suitable for a maiden —**maidenliness** *n*

maiden name *n* the former surname of a woman who has assumed her husband's surname

maiden over *n* in cricket, an over in which no runs are scored

maidhood *n* = **maidenhood**

maid-in-waiting (*plural* **maids-in-waiting**) *n* a young, usually unmarried lady-in-waiting

Maid Marian /-márri ən/ *n* **1** in English legend, the beautiful young noblewoman loved by Robin Hood **2** a character in morris dancing, played by a man dressed as a woman

maid of all work *n* a maid who does all kinds of domestic work

maid of honour *n* **1 ROYAL ATTENDANT** an unmarried woman of noble birth who attends a queen or princess **2 INDIVIDUAL SPONGE CAKE** a small individual cake with a base of short crust pastry topped with sponge cake and baked until golden **3** *US, Can* **BRIDE'S ATTENDANT** in the United States and Canada, the chief bridesmaid

maidservant /máyd survənt/ *n* a woman servant, especially one working in a large private house (*dated*)

Maidstone /máydstən/ town in SE England. Population: 90,878 (1991).

Maiduguri /máydo góori/ city in NE Nigeria. Population: 312,100 (1995 estimate).

maieutic /may óotik, mī-/, **maieutical** /may óotik'l/ *adj* Socratic (*technical*) [Mid-17C. < Greek *maieutikos* 'acting as midwife' < *maia* 'midwife'.]

maigre /máygər/ *adj* **1** containing no meat and therefore suitable for eating on days when abstinence from meat is prescribed by the Roman Catholic Church **2** describes a day when abstinence from meat is prescribed by the Roman Catholic Church [Late 17C. < French, 'lean'.]

ϟ **mail**[1] /mayl/ *n* **1 ITEMS SENT** the letters, cards, periodicals, and packages that are handled and distributed in a postal system ○ *Is there any mail for me?* **2 POSTAL SYSTEM** the system that handles the collection and delivery of post (*often before nouns*) ○ *send it by mail* **3 SPECIFIC MAIL COLLECTION OR DELIVERY** a particular collection or delivery of letters, cards, periodicals, and packages ○ *It came in yesterday's mail.* **4 VEHICLE DELIVERING MAIL** a car, train, ship, aircraft, or other vehicle used to collect and deliver mail **5 E-MAIL** e-mail (*informal*) ■ *vt US, Can, Aus* **SEND SOMETHING BY MAIL** to send a letter, card, periodical, or package by mail [13C. Via Old French *male* 'bag, trunk' < Germanic, 'bag, wallet'.]

mail[2] /mayl/ *n* **1 ARMOUR** flexible armour made of interlocking metal rings or overlapping plates **2 HARD BODY COVERING** the hard protective body covering of some animals, e.g. turtles and crabs ■ *vt* **COVER WITH MAIL** to cover or protect the body with mail ○ *a mailed torso* [13C. Via French *maille* 'mesh' < Latin *macula* 'spot, holes in a net'.]

mailbag /máyl bag/ *n* **1** a bag used for transporting mail, typically a sack made of coarse material **2** *US* = **postbag** *n.* 1 **3** *US* = **postbag** *n.* 2 [Early 19C. < MAIL[1].]

ϟ **mailbox** /máyl boks/ *n* **1** *US* = **postbox 2** *US, ANZ* a container into which mail is delivered **3** an area of computer memory for messages, especially e-mails ○ *Your online mailbox is empty.* [Early 19C. < MAIL[1].]

mail carrier *n US* a post office employee who delivers post to homes and businesses

maildrop /máyl drop/ *n US* **1** a container into which delivered mail is placed **2** a place where messages or packages can be left for later pick-up by somebody else, often secretly and prearranged

mailed fist *n US* the threat of military force (*literary*) [*Mailed* < MAIL[2]]

mailer /máylər/ *n* **1** a packet or tube for sending objects of a particular kind through the post **2** somebody whose job it is to address, stamp, weigh, and sort items for mailing [Late 19C. < MAIL[1].]

Mailer /máylər/, **Norman** (*b.* 1923) US writer

mailing /máyling/ *adj US* suitable for or associated with mail ○ *a mailing label* ○ *mailing costs* [Late 19C. < MAIL[1].]

mailing list *n* a list, typically computerized, of names and addresses to which advertising material or information can be posted

maillot /mī ṓ/ *n* **1 STRETCHY FABRIC** a soft stretchable jersey fabric **2 LEOTARD OR TIGHTS** a leotard or a pair of tights made of maillot, worn for dancing or gymnastics **3 SWIMSUIT** a woman's one-piece bathing suit made of stretchy fabric, especially one with a high-cut leg **4 CLOSE-FITTING TOP** a tight-fitting knitted top or jersey [Late 19C. < French, < Old French, 'swaddling clothes' < *maille* (see MAIL[2]).]

mailman /máyl man/ (*plural* **-men** /-men, -mən/) *n US* = **postman** [Late 19C. < MAIL[1].]

ϟ **mail merge** *n* the process of creating a series of individual documents on a computer by combining items from a list of names and addresses with a single text

mail order *n* **1** a method of buying and selling goods by post (*hyphenated before nouns*) ○ *a mail-order catalogue* **2** an order for goods to be sent by post

mailroom /máyl room, -rŏŏm/ *n* a room in an organization where mail is sorted, prepared, and distributed [Late 19C. < MAIL[1].]

mailshot /máyl shot/ *n* **1** the sending of unsolicited letters, advertisements, or brochures to a large number of people at one time **2** a letter, advertisement, or brochure sent as part of a mailshot [Mid-20C. < MAIL[1].]

mail slot *n US* = **letterbox** *n.* 1 [Mid-20C. < MAIL[1].]

mailwoman *n US* = **postwoman**

maim /maym/ *vt* to inflict a severe and permanent wound on a person or animal, especially one that renders a limb unable to move ○ *maimed by a land mine* [14C. < Old French *mahaignier.*]

main /mayn/ *adj* **1 PRINCIPAL** greatest in size or importance ○ *the main reason we're here* **2 UTMOST** exerted to the full or the utmost ○ *main force* **3 OF MAINMAST** on or relating to a sailing ship's mainmast ■ *n* **1 LARGE PIPE OR CABLE** a large and important pipe or line for the distribution of water, gas, or electricity ○ *a ruptured water main* **2 SEA** the open sea (*archaic or literary*) [Old English *mægen*, influenced by Old Norse *magn* < Germanic, 'have power'] ◇ **in the main** largely or in general

Main /mīn, mayn/ river in south-central Germany. Length: 523 km/325 mi.

main chance *n* somebody's chief opportunity or best interest ○ *have an eye to the main chance*

main course *n* the most substantial dish eaten at a meal with several courses

main drag *n US* the principal street of a town or city (*informal*)

Maine /mayn/ state in the NE United States. Capital: Augusta. Population: 1,242,051 (1997). Area: 87,389 sq. km/33,741 sq. mi.

Maine coon, Maine coon cat *n* a large, long-haired cat of a breed with a bold striped pattern, usually brown with black stripes. Native to: North America.

ϟ **mainframe** /máyn fraym/ *n* **1** a fast powerful computer with a large storage capacity that can accommodate several users simultaneously **2** a cabinet that houses a mainframe

mainland /máynlənd, -land/ *n* a continent's or country's principal landmass, as distinct from its islands and sometimes excluding peninsulas (*often before nouns*) ○ *a ferry from the mainland* —**mainlander** *n*

Mainland /máynlənd/ **1** largest of the Orkney Islands, NE Scotland. Population: 15,123 (1991). Area: 500 sq. km/195 sq. mi. **2** largest of the Shetland Islands, NE Scotland. Population: 17,562 (1991). Area: 1,053 sq. km/406 sq. mi.

main line *n* **1** a major rail route between two cities, often joined by branch lines along its length **2** a major vein in the arm or leg into which drugs may be injected (*slang*)

mainline /máyn līn/ *vti* (**-lines, -lining, -lined**) (*slang*) **1 TAKE DRUGS INTRAVENOUSLY** to inject an illicit drug, especially heroin or cocaine, intravenously **2** *US* **CONSUME EXCESSIVELY** to consume or be affected by something excessively ■ *adj* **OF A MAIN RAIL LINE** situated on or relating to a main rail line ○ *a mainline station* —**mainliner** *n* —**mainlining** *n*

mainly /máynli/ *adv* to a large extent or in most cases ○ *bacteria that live mainly in the small intestine*

mainmast /máyn maast/ *n* the principal mast on a sailing ship with more than one mast, usually either the foremost mast or the second from the bow

ϟ **main memory** *n* the random access memory of a computer, which executes instructions in real time

mains /maynz/ *npl* the central network of pipes or cables that distribute water, gas, or electricity from a local station to individual buildings in an area (*often used before a noun*) ○ *connected to a mains supply* [Early 17C. Plural of MAIN.]

mainsail /máyn sayl, máynss'l/ *n* the largest and most important sail on a sailing ship

main sequence *n* a grouping of stars that consists of most of the known stars in the universe, represented on a graph of luminosity (**Hertzsprung-Russell diagram**) as a diagonal band

mainspring /máyn spring/ *n* **1** the largest and most important spring in the mechanism of a watch or clock **2** the driving or motive force behind something such as a course of action

main squeeze *n US* somebody's boyfriend or girlfriend (*slang*)

mainstay /máyn stay/ *n* **1** somebody or something that plays the most important role in a particular group, place, or situation ○ *Tourism is the mainstay of the country's economy.* **2** the strong rope that secures the mainmast on a sailing ship

main stem *n* the principal waterway of a river, excluding its tributaries

mainstream /máyn streem/ *n* **MAIN CURRENT OF THOUGHT OR BEHAVIOUR** the ideas, actions, and values that are most widely accepted by a group or society, e.g. in politics, fashion, or music ○ *views well outside those of the mainstream* ■ *adj* **REFLECTING THE NORM** reflecting the most widely accepted views or tastes of a nation or culture and therefore not exceptional, extreme, or avant-garde ○ *The scandal, previously ignored by the mainstream media, is now on the front pages.* ■ *vti* **ENROL SPECIAL STUDENTS IN GENERAL CLASSES** to enrol students with physical disabilities or learning difficulties in general school classes —**mainstreamer** *n*

mainstreaming /máyn streeming/ *n* the practice of educating children with physical or developmental disabilities in regular classes

main street *n* the most important street in a small town

Main Street *n US* people living in small towns, considered as a group and often described as conservative and unsophisticated (*hyphenated when used before a noun*) ○ *Main Street will never accept those fashions.*

maintain /mayn táyn, mən-/ *v* **1** *vt* **MAKE SOMETHING CONTINUE** to make a situation or course of action continue in the same way as before ○ *maintained a semblance of normal procedures even with half the staff out sick* **2** *vt* **KEEP SOMETHING IN WORKING ORDER** to ensure that something continues to work properly by checking it regularly and making repairs and adjustments if required ○ *gives years of service if maintained properly* **3** *vt* **PROVIDE SOMEBODY WITH FINANCIAL SUPPORT** to provide somebody with the money required for a reasonable standard of living ○ *She maintains a big family on a tight budget.* **4** *vt* **KEEP SOMEBODY ALIVE** to keep a person or animal alive by providing food and other basic necessities ○ *maintained the injured animal in a cage over the winter* **5** *vt* **DECLARE SOMETHING TO BE TRUE** to insist on the truth of something in the face of challenge or disbelief ○ *He maintains that she knew all along.* **6** *vt* **SPEAK IN FAVOUR OF** to defend an opinion, idea, or argument against criticism ○ *The governor continues to maintain his position on cleaning up the environment.* **7** *vt* **DEFEND A PLACE** to defend a place against physical attack ○ *The unit maintained its position in spite of heavy enemy shelling.* **8** *vi US* **KEEP GOING** to continue in the present state or situation without losing control (*informal*) ○ *Until the reorganization is complete, we're maintaining, and that's about it.* [13C. < Old French *maintener*, literally 'hold in the hand' < Latin *manus* 'hand'.] —**maintainability** /mayn táynə bíllәti, mən-/ *n* —**maintainable** *adj*

ϟ **maintainer** /mayn táynər/ *n* **1** somebody or something that preserves, upholds, or continues something, e.g. a standard or tradition **2** somebody who is responsible for updating something such as a website or software package

maintenance /máyntənənss/ *n* **1 CONTINUING REPAIR WORK** work that is done regularly to keep a machine, building, or piece of equipment in good condition and working order (*often before nouns*) ○ *We take the car in for maintenance every six months.* **2 CONDITION** working order ○ *a car in a poor state of maintenance* **3 CONTINUATION** the continuation or preservation of something ○ *behaviour that threatens the maintenance of our security* **4 PROVISION OF FINANCIAL SUPPORT** the provision of enough money to enable the things necessary for a decent lifestyle, e.g.

clothes, food, and a place to live ○ *responsible for the maintenance of two retired parents* **5 MEANS OF SUPPORT** the money that somebody has to pay for necessities, e.g. food, clothing, and a place to live ○ *Family maintenance takes a big bite out of our budget.* **6 MONEY PAID TO SUPPORT EX-SPOUSE** a sum of money paid regularly or in a lump sum by a divorced person, usually as part of a divorce settlement, to maintain the normal standard of living of the ex-spouse and any children **7 INTERFERENCE IN LEGAL ACTION** improper or unlawful meddling in a lawsuit by a party typically with no legal standing in the matter

~~**maintenence**~~ incorrect spelling of **maintenance**

Mainz /mīnts/ port in SW Germany. Population: 185,300 (1994).

maiolica *n* CRAFT = **majolica**

maisonette /máyzə nét/, **maisonnette** *n* living accommodation with its own entrance, arranged on two floors of a larger house [Late 18C. < French, 'little house' < *maison* 'house'.]

Maistre /méstrə/, **Roy de** (1894–1968) Australian painter. Full name **Leroy Leveson Laurent de Maistre**

Maitland /máytlənd/ city in E New South Wales, Australia. Population: 45,265 (1991).

maître d' /méttrə dée/ *n* a maître d'hôtel (*informal*)

maître d'hôtel /méttrə dō tél/ (*plural* **maîtres d'hôtel** /méttrə dō-/) *n* **1** a head-waiter in a restaurant or a hotel dining room **2** the senior man servant in a large household, e.g. a royal palace [Mid-16C. < French, 'master of house'.]

maize /mayz/ *n* **1** an annual cereal grass that yields densely packed ears (**cobs**) of yellow grains. Native to: Central and South America. *Zea mays*. US term **corn**[1] *n.* 1 **2** the grain of the maize plant. Use: vegetable, livestock feed, ground for flour, cooking oil. (*often before nouns*) ○ *maize oil.* US term **corn**[1] *n.* 3 [Mid-16C. Directly, or via French *maïs* < Spanish *maíz* < Taino *mahis*.]

Maj. *abbr* Major

majestic /mə jéstik/ *adj* **1** greatly impressive in appearance ○ *a majestic seascape showing the masts of twenty tall ships under full sail* **2** showing great dignity and grandeur ○ *a majestic inclination of the head* —**majestically** *adv*

majesty /májjəsti/ *n* **1 DIGNITY** a deeply impressive dignified quality ○ *a duchess whose majesty was clearly present in her every move* **2 POWER** supreme authority and power ○ *The full majesty of the Crown was brought to bear during the diplomatic mission.* **3 SPLENDOUR** awesomely large size or splendour ○ *the majesty of the Rocky Mountain peaks* [13C. Via Old French *majesté* < Latin *majestas* < the stem of *major* (see MAJOR).]

Majesty (*plural* **-ties**) *n* the title used to address or refer to a king or queen ○ *Her Majesty the Queen*

majlis /májjliss/ *n* an assembly or parliament in various countries in North Africa and the Middle East [Early 19C. < Arabic, 'place of session' < *jalasa* 'be seated'.]

majolica /mə jóllikə, -yólli-/, **maiolica** /mə yóllikə/ *n* Italian earthenware that is coated with a tin oxide glaze and highly decorated [Mid-16C. < Italian, old variant of *Majorca*.]

major /máyjər/ *n* **1 MILITARY RANK** in the US, British, and Canadian armies, the US and Canadian air forces, and the US Marine Corps, an officer of a rank above captain **2 SOMEBODY OF LEGAL AGE** somebody who has reached the age at which a person is deemed fully responsible for his or her actions **3** *US, Can, ANZ* **MAIN SUBJECT** the field of study in which a college or university student chooses to specialize ○ *a major in philosophy* **4** *US, Can, ANZ* **STUDENT IN SPECIALISM** a student studying a particular academic specialism ○ *a math major* **5 MUSICAL KEY** a key or harmony based on a musical scale that has intervals of a semitone between the third and fourth and the seventh and eighth notes (**major scale**) **6 GOAL** in Australian Rules football, a goal ■ *adj* **1 OF HIGH STANDING** greater in importance than most others ○ *a major recording artist* **2 SIGNIFICANT** of considerable degree or significance ○ *major bridge repairs ahead* **3 SERIOUS** of great severity ○ *a major illness* **4 LARGE** great in number or proportion ○ *A major part of the meeting was devoted to agreeing on our report.* **5 OF LEGAL AGE** of the age at which a person is deemed fully responsible for his or her actions **6 OF PRINCIPAL SUBJECT** relating to a subject studied as a specialism **7 DESCRIBES MUSICAL SCALE** describes a musical scale that has intervals of a semitone between the third and fourth and the seventh and eighth notes **8 DESCRIBES MUSICAL INTERVAL** describes the interval between the keynote of a major scale and any other note in it, excluding the perfect intervals ○ *a major sixth* **9 DESCRIBES MUSICAL KEY** describes a key that is based on a major scale ○ *in B major* **10 THE ELDER** in British public schools, used after the surname to refer to the older of two brothers (*dated*) ○ *Hobbs major* ■ *vi US, Can, ANZ* **STUDY AS MAIN SUBJECT** to make a particular subject the main field of study ○ *She majored in economics.* [13C. < Latin, 'greater' < *magnus* 'great'.]

Major /máyjər/, **John** (*b.* 1943) British statesman and prime minister (1990–97)

Major, Dame Malvina (*b.* 1943) New Zealand opera singer

Majorca /mə yáwrkə/, **Mallorca** largest of the Balearic Islands, in the W Mediterranean Sea. Population: 736,885 (1994). Area: 3,624 sq. km/1,399 sq. mi. Spanish **Mallorca** —**Majorcan** *n, adj*

major-domo /-dṓmō/ (*plural* **major-domos**) *n* **1** the chief manservant in a large household, especially a royal or noble household, responsible for managing domestic affairs **2** somebody responsible for managing the affairs of other people, and making arrangements for them (*humorous*) [Late 16C. Via French, Italian, Spanish < medieval Latin *major domus* 'chief of the house' < Latin *magnus* 'great' + *domus* 'house'.]

majorette /máyjə rét/ *n US* a girl or young woman who marches in front of a marching band, twirling a baton

major general *n* in the US, British, and Canadian armies and the US Marine Corps, an officer of a rank above brigadier general

major histocompatibility complex *n* a cluster of genes occurring in humans and other animals that determines the extent to which an individual's immune system will accept or reject tissue from another individual

majoritarian /mə jórri táiri ən/ *adj US* resulting from or based on rule by the majority in any given group ■ *n US* a believer that a group should be ruled in the way chosen by the majority of its members —**majoritarianism** *n*

majority /mə jórrəti/ (*plural* **-ties**) *n* **1 GREATER NUMBER OF PEOPLE OR THINGS** most of the people or things in a large group (+ *singular or plural verb*) ○ *The majority of women now work.* **2 DIFFERENCE IN NUMBER OF VOTES** the number of votes by which the winning party or group beats the opposition ○ *swept to power with an overwhelming majority* **3 GROUP IN POWER** the most powerful party or group voting together in a legislature **4 AGE OF LEGAL RESPONSIBILITY** the age, generally either 18 or 21, at which somebody is legally responsible and can assume civil duties and rights such as serving on a jury or voting **5 RANK OF MAJOR** the military rank of major

LANGUAGE NOTE See ***Collective noun***.

USAGE *majority* as a singular or plural? When you use ***majority*** to refer to a group of people or things as a unit or whole, use a singular verb: *A majority of the House intends to support the motion.* When you use ***majority*** to refer to individuals within the group, use a plural verb: *The majority of our students live on campus, with a minority living in the surrounding neighbourhoods.* In that sentence, each student is under consideration; hence, the plural verb. Ensure that any pronouns referring to ***majority*** are in the same number denoted by ***majority***. Thus, it is incorrect to say *A majority of the House has cast their votes.* Say instead *A majority of the House has cast its vote*, or, if you are speaking of the members of parliament as individuals, say *A majority of the members have cast their votes.*

majority leader *n US* the head of the majority party in a legislature

majority minority *n US* a majority of people in a particular area who belong to a minority group overall ○ *a majority minority district*

majority rule *n* control of an organization or institution according to the wishes or votes of the majority of its members

major league *n* **1 MAIN BASEBALL LEAGUE** either of the two main professional baseball leagues in the United States **2 TOP SPORTS LEAGUE** a top league of professional football, ice hockey, or basketball teams in the United States ■ **major leagues** *npl US* **HIGH PLACES** the highest spheres of influence (*informal*) ○ *a politician operating in the major leagues* —**major-league** *adj* —**major-leaguer** *n*

majorly /máyjərli/ *adv* in a large degree or to a great extent (*informal*) ○ *an account that was majorly overdrawn*

major order *n* in the Roman Catholic Church, one of the higher holy orders of bishop, priest, deacon, or subdeacon

major penalty *n* in sports such as ice hockey and lacrosse, a player's removal from the game for five minutes for a serious violation of the rules

major scale *n* a musical scale with intervals of a semitone between the third and fourth notes and the seventh and eighth notes and whole tones between all other consecutive notes. ◊ **minor scale**

major suit *n* in bridge and some other card games, spades or hearts, owing to their greater scoring potential

Majuba Hill /mə jóobə-/ hill in E South Africa, the site of a battle in 1881 when a Boer force defeated the British

Majuro /mə jóorō/ atoll in central North Pacific Ocean and capital of the Marshall Islands. Population: 19,664 (1988). Area: 10 sq. km/4 sq. mi.

majuscule /májjə skyool/ *n* a large letter used in writing or printing, e.g. a capital letter or any of the large rounded letters (**uncials**) used in ancient manuscripts [Early 18C. Via French < Latin *majuscula (littera)* 'somewhat larger (letters)' < *major* (see MAJOR).] —**majuscular** /mə júskyoolər/ *adj*

Makalu /múkəloo/ mountain in the Himalayas, on the Nepal-China border. Height: 8,481 m/27,824 ft.

makan /má kan/ *n Malaysia, Singapore* food (*informal*) [Early 20C. < Malay.]

Makarios /mə kaári oss/ (1913–77) Cypriot cleric and statesman. Born **Mihail Christodolou Mouskos**

Makarova /mə kaárəvə/, **Natalia** (*b.* 1940) Russian-born US dancer

Makassar /mə kássər/, **Macassar** former name for **Ujung Pandang**

Makassarese /mə kássə réez/ (*plural* **-rese**), **Makasarese** (*plural* **-rese**) *n* **1** a person who was born or brought up in Makassar (now Ujung Pandang) in Sulawesi, Indonesia **2** the Austronesian language of the Makassarese people. Native speakers: 1,600,000. —**Makassarese** *adj*

make /mayk/ *v* (**makes, making, made** /mayd/) **1** *vt* **DO** used with a range of nouns to describe an action, where 'make' is used rather than a more specific verb ○ *She made no effort whatsoever to pass her exams.* **2** *vt* **SAY** to say or deliver a statement or speech ○ *He made an emotional speech about his parents' struggle to get ahead in a new country* **3** *vt* **CONSTRUCT** to assemble something from constituent parts ○ *The exhibit contains items made out of recyclable materials.* **4** *vt* **MANUFACTURE** to manufacture something as a business ○ *The company makes surgical instruments.* **5** *vt* **PRODUCE BY COMBINING INGREDIENTS** to prepare food or drink by mixing and usually cooking a number of ingredients ○ *Let's make soup.* **6** *vt* **FORM WITH MOTION** to form something by performing the movements that it requires ○ *She made the signs for 'I'll see you later'.* ○ *He made a circular motion with his hands.* **7** *vt* **FORMULATE** to form something in the mind ○ *These politicians have made a tacit commitment to try to solve the problem.* **8** *vt* **UNDERSTAND** to comprehend the meaning or truth of something ○ *I couldn't make anything of her last remark.* **9** *vt* **RECKON** to reckon or estimate something ○ *What time do you make it?* **10** *vt* **BRING ABOUT** to cause a condition or situation to arise or exist ○ *The state made it illegal to sell fireworks.* ○ *Some people here have made this a personal issue.* **11** *vt* **CHANGE** to transform somebody or something into something else ○ *They made old clothes into patchwork quilts.* **12** *vt* **APPOINT** to appoint somebody to a particular role or position ○ *She's made me her deputy.* **13** *vt* **PROVIDE** to provide something out of what already exists ○ *Make room for one more.* **14** *vt* **CAUSE SOMEBODY TO ACT** to cause somebody to do something or act in a particular way ○ *I made him realize how wrong he'd been.* ○ *You made me lose my place.* **15** *vt* **FORCE** to force somebody or something to do something or act in a particular way ○ *You can't make me wear that dress.* **16** *vt* **CAUSE TO EXIST FOR REASON** to cause somebody or something to exist for a particular reason (*usually passive*) ○ *She was made to be a star.* **17** *vt* **EARN** to earn or be paid a specified sum of money ○ *He makes fifty thousand a year.* **18** *vt* **CAUSE SOUND TO BE HEARD** to produce or give rise to a sound ○ *She made a choking noise in her throat.* **19** *vt* **ARRANGE FOR USE** to arrange something properly for later use ○ *He made the bed carefully.* **20** *vt* **SCHEDULE MEETING** to fix a meeting or time ○ *Let's make a date for Friday.* **21** *vt* **REPRESENT** to count as one in a series ○ *That makes the third time he's lied to me.* **22** *vt* **AMOUNT TO** to amount to a total ○ *Five and three make eight.* **23** *vt* **HAVE NECESSARY QUALITIES FOR** to have the qualities required to be something ○ *She'll make a very good doctor.* **24** *vt* **DEVELOP RELATIONSHIP** to acquire a friend, enemy, or acquaintance ○ *They made friends straightaway.* **25** *vt* **CAUSE TO SUCCEED** to cause somebody to be successful, or cause something to seem successful ○ *the novel that made her career* **26** *vt* **REACH PLACE** to reach or arrive at a place ○ *I'm not sure we can make the island in this boat.* **27** *vt* **BE IN TIME FOR** to be in time to do something or for something to happen ○ *We can make the 10:05 if we hurry.* **28** *vt* **COVER DISTANCE** to travel a particular distance ○ *They made only five miles a day on the ascent.* **29** *vt* **BE INCLUDED IN** to succeed in being included or mentioned in something ○ *stories that never make the national news* **30** *vi* **SIGNAL INTENTIONS** to act so as to indicate what is coming ○ *They made as if to leave.* **31** *vt* **ACHIEVE SEX WITH** to succeed in having sex with somebody (*dated slang*) **32** *vt* **FULFIL BRIDGE CONTRACT** to fulfil a contract in a game of bridge by winning the required number of tricks **33** *vt* **WIN TRICK IN CARDS** to win a trick in a card game **34** *vt* **CLOSE CIRCUIT** to close an electrical circuit **35** *vi* **MATURE** to dry and mature (*refers to hay*) ■ *n* **1 BRAND** a brand of something, e.g. an appliance, car, or machine ○ *Specify the make and model of the car.* **2 PROCESS AND OUTPUT** the process of making something, or the amount or number made **3 BUILD OR APPEARANCE** the way that something has been made, or the size or shape it naturally has (*literary*) ○ *a woodland cabin of rustic make* **4 IDENTIFICATION** the identification of somebody or something, usually made with the help of police records or information (*slang*) ○ *The police got a make on him from their records.* [Old English *macian* < Indo-European, 'knead-ing'] —**makable** *adj* ◇ **have it made** to be in a position to succeed at something without obstacles or serious problems (*informal*) ◇ **make do (with something)** to use something that is an unsatisfactory substitute or temporary alternative for the real thing ◇ **make it 1** to be successful (*informal*) ○ *You'll never make it as an actor.* **2** to succeed in getting somewhere ○ *We finally made it to the top of the hill.* **3** to be able to attend ○ *I can't make it to the party tonight.* ◇ **make like** to imitate (*informal*) ○ *She made like she was doing the breaststroke.* ◇ **on the make 1** trying hard to gain a profit or advantage, especially using underhand or dishonest means (*informal*) **2** looking for or making efforts to persuade somebody to be a sexual partner (*slang*)

make after *vt* to chase after somebody or something

make away *vi* = **make off**

make away with *vt* **1 STEAL** to steal something and abscond with it ○ *They made away with the week's takings.* **2 ABDUCT** to carry somebody off by force **3 GET RID OF** to destroy or get rid of something incriminating ○ *We think someone's made away with the DNA evidence.* **4 KILL** to kill somebody (*dated*)

make for *vt* **1** to move quickly in the direction of somebody or something ○ *The reporters made for the courtroom.* **2** to result in a particular situation ○ *This plan will make for a successful product launch.*

make off *vi* to leave a place quickly, usually with good reason

make off with *vt* = **make away with**

make out *v* **1** *vt* **SEE OR HEAR INDISTINCTLY** to see or hear somebody or something but not clearly ○ *I could just make out her profile in the darkness.* **2** *vt* **COMPREHEND** to identify or understand something ○ *I can't make out the suspect's motive.* **3** *vt* **COMPLETE IN WRITING** to write necessary information such as the date and the recipient's name on a bill or similar document ○ *The deed is made out in my spouse's name.* **4** *vt* **SUGGEST** to suggest or imply something that may not be true ○ *The kids make him out to be a real tyrant.* **5** *vt* **ARGUE IN SUPPORT OF** to try to prove something is true or valid by giving good reasons ○ *made out a case for keeping the work in-house* **6** *vi* **MANAGE** to perform in a situation (*informal*) ○ *How did you make out on the test?* **7** *vi US* **ENGAGE IN SEXUAL ACTIVITIES WITHOUT INTERCOURSE** to kiss and caress somebody as an expression of sexual desire (*slang*) **8** *vi US* **HAVE SEX** to have sexual intercourse (*slang*)

make over *vt* **1 MAKE SOMEBODY ELSE OWNER OF** to transfer the ownership of money or property to somebody, usually in a legal document ○ *half of her estate was made over to her cousin* **2** *US* **REFASHION GARMENT** to alter or remodel a garment **3 CHANGE APPEARANCE OF** to make major changes to the way somebody or something looks

make up *v* **1** *vt* **MAKE READY** to get something ready, especially by putting a number of items together ○ *I've made up a packed lunch.* **2** *vt* **JOIN TO FORM** to combine with other people or objects to form a whole ○ *a group made up of four men and six women* **3** *vt* **CONSTITUTE** to form part of something ○ *Women make up more than half the country's workforce.* **4** *vt* **INVENT** to invent an excuse, fact, or story ○ *made the whole story up to shock her parents* **5** *vti* **PREPARE FOR PERFORMANCE** to prepare somebody or yourself for an acting performance by applying cosmetics and fitting other accessories, e.g. false hair, necessary for assuming a given role ○ *It takes her two hours to make up for the role.* **6** *vt* **PUT ON FACIAL COSMETICS** to apply cosmetics to your own face or somebody else's face **7** *vt* **COMPLETE** to make a number or amount complete ○ *You three pay £10 each and I'll make up the rest.* **8** *vti* **RESOLVE A QUARREL** to become friends again after a quarrel ○ *Haven't you two made up yet?* **9** *vt* **APPLY SURFACE TO ROAD** to surface a road, e.g. with Tarmac™, concrete, or bitumen **10** *vt* **ARRANGE LAYOUT OF PAGE** to arrange columns of print and illustrations on a page **11** *vi* **COMPENSATE** to compensate for a failing such as a disappointment, deficiency, or shortcoming ○ *I'll buy lunch to make up for being late.*

make up to *vt* **1** to try to gain somebody's favour by behaving in a flattering and attentive way ○ *making up to the general manager's assistant* **2** to flirt with somebody

make with *vt US* to start doing, using, or producing something (*dated slang*) ○ *Hey, let's make with the party, huh?*

Makeba /mə káybə/, **Miriam** (*b.* 1932) South African-born US jazz and folk singer. Born **Sensile Makeba**

make-believe *n* imaginary situations or events that somebody, especially a child playing, pretends are true (*often before nouns*) ○ *watching them in their make-believe world*

make-do *n* (*plural* **make-dos**) *US* a substitute, often an inferior one ■ *adj* temporarily substituting for something else ○ *a make-do dinner service in a furnished flat*

makefast /máyk faast/ *n* a strong ring, post, or buoy to which a boat or ship is moored

make-or-break *adj* likely to result in either complete success or complete failure

makeover /máykōvər/ *n* **1** an alteration of the way somebody looks, usually including changes of hairstyle, make-up, and clothing **2** a remodelling of something that completely changes the way it looks

maker /máykər/ *n* **1 CREATOR OR CAUSE** a creator, source, or cause of something (*often in combination*) ○ *a maker of mischief* **2 PRODUCER OF GOODS** a person or organization that produces goods (*often in combination*) ○ *a maker of mid-priced textiles* **3 SIGNER OF DOCUMENT** somebody who signs a legal document, especially a promissory note

Maker *n* God, regarded as the creator of everything

makeshift /máyk shift/ *adj* providing a temporary and usually inferior substitute ■ *n* a temporary and usually inferior substitute [Mid-16C. < *to make shift* 'try all means'.]

makeup /máyk up/, **make-up** *n* **1 COSMETICS** cosmetic products, especially for the face, e.g. lipstick and mascara (*often before nouns*) **2 THEATRICAL COSMETICS** the cosmetics and other accessories, e.g. false hair, that actors wear to alter their appearance on stage (*often before nouns*) ○ *makeup department* **3 APPLYING ACTORS' COSMETICS** the application of actors' cosmetics and other appearance-altering accessories, e.g. false hair (*often before nouns*) ○ *working in makeup* **4 COMBINATION OF PARTS OR QUALITIES** the way parts or qualities combine or are arranged, especially in somebody's personality ○ *Self-deprecation is an intrinsic part of her makeup.* **5 ARRANGEMENT OF TYPE** the arrangement of typographic elements on a page

makeweight /máyk wayt/ *n* **1** something placed on a scale to bring a weight up to a required level **2** an extra person or object of no intrinsic importance introduced into a situation for the sole purpose of making up the required numbers ○ *invited her cousin along as a makeweight*

make-work *n US* unimportant or needless work assigned merely to keep workers busy

makimono /máki mṓnō/ (*plural* **-nos**) *n* a horizontal Japanese scroll decorated with paintings or calligraphy [Late 19C. < Japanese, 'a scroll', literally 'something rolled up'.]

making /máyking/ *n* **1** the activity of somebody who makes something ○ *during the making of the film* **2** something that causes somebody's success or progress ○ *a book that was the making of her career* ◇ **in the making** in the process of being made, formed, or developed

makings /máykingz/ *npl* **1** the things required to make something, especially a dish of food **2** the qualities required to become a particular thing ○ *has the makings of a good lawyer*

mako shark /maákō-/ *n* a large slender blue-grey shark with a sharp nose and ferocious teeth that is prized as a game fish. Native to: southern oceans. Genus: *Isurus.* [< Maori]

Makurdi /mə kúrdi/ town in east-central Nigeria. Population: 120,110 (1995 estimate).

Mal. *abbr* Malachi

mal- /mə láy/ *prefix* **1** bad, badly ○ *malpractice* **2** abnormal or inadequate ○ *malnutrition* [Via Old French < Latin *malus* 'bad', *male* 'badly']

Malabar Coast /málləbaar-/ coastal region of SW India, extending from Goa southwards, bordering the Arabian Sea

malabsorption /mál əb sáwrpsh'n, -záwrpsh'n/ *n* the inadequate absorption of nutrients from digested food in the alimentary canal, especially by the small intestine in coeliac disease

malac- *prefix* = **malaco-** (*before vowels*)

malacca /mə lákə/, **malacca cane** *n* **1** a walking stick made from the stem of the rattan palm **2** the stem of the rattan palm [Mid-19C. After MALACCA.]

Malacca /mə lákə/ former name for **Melaka**

Malacca, Strait of strait in Southeast Asia between the Malay Peninsula and Sumatra, connecting the Andaman Sea with the South China Sea. Length: 800 km/500 mi.

Malachi /málla kī/ *n* **1** an unidentified Hebrew prophet who wrote in the 5th century BC, usually referred to by this name **2** a book of the Bible containing writings by Malachi

malachite /málla kīt/ *n* a green copper carbonate mineral. Use: decorative stones, source of copper. [14C. Via Old French *melochite* < Greek *molokhitis*, a stone similar in colour to the mallow leaf < *malakhē* 'mallow'.]

malacia /mə láyshi ə/ *n* the abnormal softening of a tissue or organ of the body, e.g. the bones or kidneys, caused by a disease (*often in combination*) [Early 18C. < Greek *malakos* (see MALACO-).]

malaco- *prefix* soft ○ *malacology* [< Greek *malakos* < Indo-European]

malacology /málla kólləji/ *n* the branch of zoology that involves the study of molluscs [Mid-19C. Via French < modern Latin *Malacozoa* 'soft-bodied creatures' < Greek *malakos* (see MALACO-).] —**malacological** /mállәkә lójjik'l/ *adj* —**malacologist** *n*

malacostracan /málla kóstrəkən/ *n* a member of a common group of crustaceans that usually have stalked eyes, a carapace, and a tail fan formed from the rear limbs, e.g. a lobster. Subclass: Malacostraca. [Mid-19C. < modern Latin *Malacostraca* < Greek *malakos* 'soft' + *ostrakon* 'shell'.] —**malacostracan** *adj*

maladapted /málla dáptid/ *adj* unsuitable for or poorly adapted to a particular situation, function, or purpose —**maladaptation** /mál adap táysh'n/ *n*

maladaptive /málla dáptiv/ *adj* **1** unsuitable for or poorly adapted to a particular situation, function, or purpose **2** not facilitating or encouraging adaptation —**maladaptively** *adv*

maladjusted /málla jústid/ *adj* **1** unable to cope with everyday social situations and personal relationships **2** needing to be correctly adjusted —**maladjustment** *n*

maladministration /mállәd minni stráysh'n/ *n* incompetent or dishonest management or administration, especially in public affairs —**maladministrator** /mállәd mínni straytər/ *n* —**maladminister** /-mínnistər/ *vt*

maladroit /málla dróyt/ *adj* clumsy or insensitive in speech or behaviour [Late 17C. < French, 'not adept' < *adroit* (see ADROIT).] —**maladroitly** *adv* —**maladroitness** *n*

malady /mállədi/ (*plural* **-dies**) *n* **1** a physical or psychological disorder or disease (*dated or humorous*) **2** a condition or situation that is problematic and requires a remedy [13C. Via French *maladie* < Latin *male habitus* 'in bad condition'.]

mala fide /málla fīdi/ *adj, adv* done insincerely or dishonestly (*formal*) [Early 17C. < Latin.]

Málaga /máləgə/ port in S Spain, on the Mediterranean Sea. Population: 532,425 (1995).

Malagasy /mállǝ gássi/ (*plural* **-y** or **-ies**) *n* **1** somebody who comes from Madagascar **2** an official language of Madagascar, belonging to the western branch of Austronesian. Native speakers: 12 million. [Mid-19C. Variant of MADAGASCAR.] —**Malagasy** *adj*

Malagasy Republic /mállǝ gássi-/ former name for **Madagascar** (1958–75)

malagueña /mállǝ gáynǝ/ *n* **1** a Spanish dance that is similar to the fandango **2** a Spanish folk melody similar to a fandango [Late 19C. < Spanish, literally 'from Malaga'.]

malaise /ma láyz/ *n* **1** a general feeling of illness or sickness without any specific diagnostic significance **2** a general feeling of worry, discontent, or dissatisfaction, often resulting in lethargy [Mid-18C. < French, 'ill ease' < *aise* (see EASE).]

Malamud /mállǝmood/, **Bernard** (1914–86) US novelist and short-story writer

malamute /mállǝ moot, mállǝ myoot/, **malemute** *n* an Alaskan dog with a thick grey, black, or white coat, used especially for pulling sledges [Late 19C. < Inupiaq *malimiut*, an Alaskan people.]

Malang /mǝ laàng/ city in E Java, Indonesia. Population: 548,193 (1989).

malapert /mállǝ purt/ *adj* impudent or bold in speech or behaviour (*archaic* or *literary*) [15C. < Old French, 'not experienced' < Latin *expertus* (see EXPERT).] —**malapert** *n* —**malapertly** *adv* —**malapertness** *n*

malaprop /mállǝ prop/ *n* LING = **malapropism** *n*. **2**

malapropism /mállǝ propizǝm/ *n* **1** the misuse of a word through confusion with another word that sounds similar, especially when the effect is ridiculous **2** an instance of using malapropism [Early 19C. After Mrs *Malaprop* (< MALAPROPOS), character in Richard Sheridan's play *The Rivals*.] —**malapropist** *n*

malapropos /mál apprǝ pô/ *adj* **OUT OF PLACE** not appropriate to the situation in which something is done or said (*formal*) ■ *adv* **INAPPROPRIATELY OR INOPPORTUNELY** in an inappropriate way or at an inopportune moment (*formal*) ■ *n* **INAPT OR UNTIMELY SPEECH OR ACTION** something that is done or said in an inappropriate way or at an inopportune moment (*formal*) [Mid-17C. < French *mal à propos* 'ill-suited to the purpose'.]

malar /máylǝr/, **malar bone** *adj* relating to the cheek, the cheekbone, or the side of the head ■ *n* the cheekbone [Late 18C. < modern Latin *malaris* < Latin *mala* 'jaw, cheekbone'.]

Mälaren /méllǝren/ lake in SE Sweden. Area: 1,140 sq. km/440 sq. mi.

malaria /mǝ láiri ǝ/ *n* an infectious disease caused by a parasite that is transmitted by the bite of infected mosquitoes [Mid-18C. < Italian *malaria* 'bad air', once thought to be its cause.] —**malarial** *adj* —**malarian** *adj* —**malarious** *adj*

malariology /mǝ láiri ólǝji/ *n* the scientific study of malaria —**malariologist** *n*

malarkey /mǝ laárki/, **malarky** *n* nonsense or rubbish, especially insincere talk (*informal*) [Early 20C. < ?]

malate /mállayt, máy layt/ *n* a chemical compound that is a salt or ester of malic acid

malathion /mállǝ thí on/ *n* $C_{10}H_{19}O_6PS_2$ a colourless solid organophosphorus insecticide [Mid-20C. < MALATE + THIO-.]

Malawi /mǝlaàwi/ republic in SE Africa. Capital: Li-

Malawi

longwe. Population: 9,453,000 (1996). Area: 118,484 sq. km/45,747 sq. mi. —**Malawian** *n, adj*

Malawi, Lake lake in southeast-central Africa, lying between Malawi, Mozambique, and Tanzania. Area: 22,490 sq. km/8,683 sq. mi.

Malay /mǝ láy/ *n* **1** a member of a people that inhabits the Malay Peninsula, Indonesia, and other islands of the Malay Archipelago and the Philippines **2** an Austronesian language spoken in Malaysia, and in parts of Singapore, Borneo, Sumatra, Java, and surrounding areas. Native speakers: 22 million. Other speakers: 100 million. [Late 16C. < Malay *malayu*.] —**Malay** *adj*

Malaya, Federation of /mǝ láy ǝ/ former monarchy in the Malay Peninsula, now part of the Federation of Malaysia —**Malayan** *adj, n*

Malayalam /málli aàlam, mállay-/, **Malayalaam** *n* a Dravidian language that is the official language of the Indian state of Kerala. Native speakers: 30 million. [Early 19C. < Malayalam *Malayālam* 'mountain man'.] —**Malayalam** *adj*

Malay Archipelago largest system of island groups in the world, lying in the South Pacific Ocean between Southeast Asia and Australia, and including Indonesia and the Philippines. Area: 2.8 million sq. km/1.1 million sq. mi.

Malayo-Polynesian /mǝ láyō-/ *n* LANG = **Austronesian** — **Malayo-Polynesian** *adj*

Malay Peninsula peninsula in Southeast Asia between the South China Sea and the Strait of Malacca, including parts of Myanmar, Thailand, and Malaysia. Length: 1,210 km/750 mi.

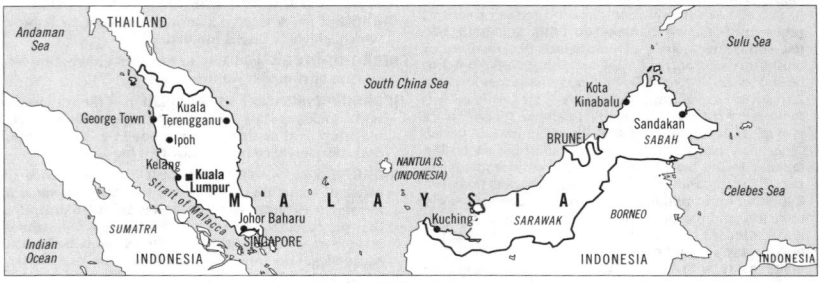

Malaysia

Malaysia /mǝ láyzi ǝ, -zhǝ/ constitutional monarchy in Southeast Asia. Capital: Kuala Lumpur. Population: 17,566,982 (1991). Area: 329,758 sq. km/127,320 sq. mi. —**Malaysian** *n, adj*

Malcolm III /málkǝm/ (c. 1031–93) king of Scotland (1057–93)

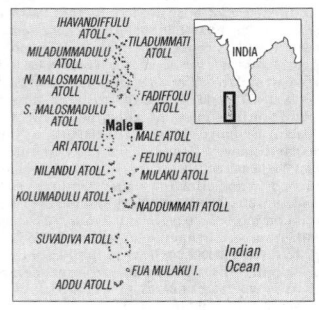

Maldives

Malcolm X (1925–65) US political activist. Born **Malcolm Little**

Popperfoto

Malcolm X

malcontent /mál kǝn tent/ *n* a person who is discontented or dissatisfied with something, e.g. a political system [Late 16C. < French, 'ill contented' < *content* (see CONTENT[2]).] —**malcontent** *adj* —**malcontented** /málkǝn téntid/ *adj* —**malcontentedly** *adv* —**malcontentedness** *n*

mal de mer /mál dǝ máir/ *n* seasickness [Late 18C. < French, 'sea sickness'.]

maldistribution /mál distri byóòsh'n/ *n* unequal and unfair distribution of something, especially resources or wealth

Maldives /máwl divz, mál dívz/ island republic in S Asia, in the N Indian Ocean, SW of Sri Lanka. Capital: Male. Population: 270,758 (1996). Area: 298 sq. km/115 sq. mi. —**Maldivan** *n, adj*

Maldivian /mawl dívvi ǝn, mal-/ *n* **1** a person who was born or brought up in the Maldives off the coast of SW India **2** the Indic language of the Maldives, also spoken in Minicoy Island, India. Native speakers: 200,000. — **Maldivian** *adj*

Maldon /máwldǝn/ town in E England. Population: 15,841 (1991).

male /mayl/ *adj* **1** **PRODUCING SPERM** relating or belonging to the sex that produces sperm to fertilize female eggs **2** **RELATING TO MEN OR BOYS** relating to, involving, or traditionally characteristic of men or boys **3** **FERTILIZING FEMALE SEX CELL** capable of fertilizing a female reproductive cell (**gamete**) during sexual reproduction **4** **BEARING ONLY STAMENS** describes a flower or plant that bears stamens but not pistils and does not produce fruit or seeds **5** **MACHINE PART OR FITTING** describes a projecting part such as a bolt or plug that is designed to fit into a hollow part or socket that is the female counterpart ■ *n* **1** **MALE PERSON OR ANIMAL** a person or animal belonging to the sex that produces sperm **2** **PLANT WITH MALE FLOWERS ONLY** a plant that has only male flowers [14C. Via Old French < Latin *masculus* < *mas* 'male person'.] —**maleness** *n*

Male /maà lay/ **1** atoll in the Maldives in the N Indian Ocean **2** capital of the Maldives, on the Male atoll. Population: 62,973 (1995).

male alto *n* MUSIC = **countertenor**

maleate /málli ayt/ *n* any salt or ester of maleic acid

Malebo Pool /mǝ láybō-/ lake formed by a widening of the River Congo on the border between the Republic of the Congo and the Democratic Republic of Congo. Area: 450 sq. km/174 sq. mi.

male chauvinist *n* a man who believes in the innate superiority of men over women (*disapproving*) —**male chauvinism** *n*

male chauvinist pig *n* an offensive term for a man who believes that men are innately superior to women, especially one who expresses his opinions in an aggressive or offensive way (*dated insult*)

Malecite /málla sīt/ (plural **-cites** or **-cite**), **Maliseet** /-seet/ (plural **-seets** or **-seet**) n the Algonquian language of the Malecite people [Mid-19C. < Mi' kmaq *malisiit* 'somebody who speaks an incomprehensible language'.] —**Malecite** adj

malediction /málli díksh'n/ n (formal) 1 a curse 2 slander or evil talk about somebody [14C. < Latin *malediction*- < *maledicere* 'speak ill of' < *dicere* 'speak'.] —**maledictive** adj

malefactor /málli faktar/ n a wrongdoer, especially a criminal [15C. < Latin, < *male facere* 'do evil'.] —**malefaction** /málli fáksh'n/ n

male fern n a fern whose rhizomes and scaly stalks are used to make a resin that expels tapeworms. *Dryopteris filix-mas.*

malefic /ma léffik/ adj having a harmful or evil effect or influence (literary) [Mid-17C. < Latin *maleficus* 'evil-doing' < *male* 'badly'.]

maleficent /ma léffiss'nt/ adj causing harm or doing evil intentionally, or capable of such acts [Mid-17C. Back-formation from *maleficence* < Latin *maleficentia* 'evil doing' < *male* 'badly'.] —**maleficence** n —**maleficently** adv

maleic acid /ma láyik-/ n $C_4H_4O_4$ a colourless crystalline solid. Use: manufacture of polymers. [< French *maléique*, alteration of *malique* (see MALIC)]

male menopause n a period in middle age when some men experience feelings of insecurity and anxiety about physical decline, sometimes compared to the effects of the menopause in women

malemute n ZOOL = **malamute**

Maler /maàlar/ (plural **-ler** or **-lers**) n 1 a member of a Dravidian people of N India 2 LANG = **Malto** [Early 19C. < Dravidian, 'hill men' < *mala* 'mountain'.] —**Maler** adj

Malevich /mállivich/, **Kasimir** (1878–1935) Russian painter

malevolent /ma lévvalant/ adj 1 having or showing a desire to harm others 2 having a harmful or evil effect or influence [Early 16C. Directly or via Old French < Latin *malevolent*- < *male* 'badly' + *volens*, present participle of *velle* 'wish'.] —**malevolence** n —**malevolently** adv

malfeasance /mal feéz'nss/ n (formal) 1 wrong or illegal conduct, especially in politics or the civil service. ◊ **misfeasance, nonfeasance** 2 an unlawful act, especially one committed by a politician or civil servant [Late 17C. < Anglo-Norman *malfaisance* < Old French *malfaire* 'do ill' < Latin *malefacere*.] —**malfeasant** adj, n

malformation /mál fawr máysh'n/ n abnormality in the shape or structure of something, or an instance of this —**malformed** /mal fáwrmd/ adj

malfunction /mal fúngksh'n/ vi to fail to function in the correct or normal way, or stop working altogether, usually because of a fault or bad design ■ n a breakdown or failure to function in the correct or normal way, usually because of a fault or bad design

Mali

Mali /maàli/ republic in central NW Africa. Capital: Bamako. Population: 9,204,000 (1996). Area: 1,240,192 sq. km/478,841 sq. mi.

malic /mállik, máylik/ adj relating to or derived from malic acid [Late 18C. Directly or via French *malique* < Latin *malum* 'apple'.]

malic acid n $C_4H_6O_5$ a colourless crystalline solid. Source: fruits such as apples.

malice /málliss/ n 1 the desire to cause harm to another or others or to see somebody in pain 2 the intention to commit an unlawful act that will result in harm to others and does not have an excusable cause [Via French < Latin *malitia* < *malus* 'bad'.]

malicious /ma líshass/ adj motivated by or resulting from a desire to cause harm or pain to others —**maliciously** adv —**maliciousness** n

malign /ma lín/ vt to say or write bad or unpleasant things about somebody or something, especially things that are potentially damaging and may not be true ■ adj harmful or evil in nature, effect, or intention [15C. Via French < Latin *malignus* 'of evil kind'.] —**maligner** n —**malignly** adv

SYNONYMS *malign, defame, slander, libel, vilify*

CORE MEANING: to say or write something damaging about somebody

malign to criticize somebody in a spiteful and false or misleading way; **defame** to make an attack on somebody's good name or reputation with a view to damaging or destroying it; **slander** in legal terms, to make spoken false accusations about somebody damaging to the person's reputation; **libel** in legal terms, to make false damaging accusations about somebody in writing, signs, or pictures; **vilify** to make viciously defamatory statements about somebody.

malignancy /ma lígnanssi/ (plural **-cies**) n 1 **malignancy, malignance** the condition or quality of being malignant 2 a tumour that invades surrounding tissue and may spread to distant parts of the body by way of the lymphatic system or the circulation of the blood

malignant /ma lígnant/ adj 1 **WANTING TO DO EVIL** full of hate and showing a desire to harm others 2 **HARMFUL** likely to cause harm 3 **LIKELY TO SPREAD** describes a tumour that invades the tissue around it and may spread to other parts of the body 4 **LIKELY TO CAUSE DEATH** describes a disease or condition that is liable to cause death or serious disablement unless effectively treated [Mid-16C. < late Latin *malignant*- 'plot against' < Latin *malignus* 'of evil kind'.] —**malignantly** adv

malignity /ma lígnati/ (plural **-ties**) n 1 **DESIRE TO DO EVIL** intense hatred and a strong desire to harm others 2 **INTENTIONALLY HARMFUL ACT** an intentionally harmful or evil act 3 **HARMFUL POTENTIAL** potential to cause harm or death

malines /ma leèn/ n thin stiff net with hexagonal holes. Use: dressmaking. [Mid-19C. < French, after *Malines* (Mechlin), Belgium.]

Malines n TEXTILES = **Mechlin**

malinger /ma líng gar/ vi to pretend to be ill, especially in order to avoid work (disapproving) [Late 18C. < French *malingre* 'sickly'.] —**malingerer** n

Malinke /ma língki/ (plural **-ke** or **-kes**) n 1 a member of a people who live in parts of West Africa, especially in the Côte d'Ivoire, Mali, Senegal, and Gambia 2 the Mande language of the Malinke people. Native speakers: 4 million. [Late 19C. < Malinke.] —**Malinke** adj

Malinowski /málli nófski/, **Bronislaw** (1884–1942) Polish-born British social anthropologist

malison /mállliss'n, mállliz'n/ n a curse (archaic) [13C. Via Old French *maleiçon* < Latin *malediction*- (see MALEDICTION).]

mall /mawl, mal/ n 1 **US** = **shopping centre** 2 a sheltered and shady avenue or promenade 3 in former times, an alley used for playing the game of pall-mall [Mid-17C. Shortening of PALL-MALL.]

mallard /máll aard, -ard/ (plural **-lards** or **-lard**) n a wild duck, the male of which has a dark green head with a white ring round the neck. Native to: northern hemisphere. *Anas platyrhynchos.* [14C. < Old French.]

Mallarmé /máll aar may/, **Stéphane** (1842–98) French poet

mall crawl n **US** the act of going to a large number of different shops in a shopping centre (informal)

malleable /málli əb'l/ adj 1 describes a metal or other substance that can be shaped or bent without breaking 2 easily persuaded or influenced by others [14C. < Old French < Latin *malleus* 'hammer'.] —**malleability** /málli ə bílləti/ n —**malleableness** n —**malleably** adv

SYNONYMS See **pliable**.

mallee /málli/ n 1 **SHRUBBY EUCALYPTUS** a low-growing eucalyptus tree. Native to: Australian deserts. Genus: *Eucalyptus.* 2 **THICKET OF MALLEE TREES** a thicket of mallee trees 3 **mallee, Mallee** *Aus* **AREA WITH MANY MALLEE TREES**

land in S Australia where mallee trees are the predominant vegetation [Mid-19C. < Australian Aboriginal.]

Mallee /málli/ region of NW Victoria, Australia. Area: 41,000 sq. km/16,000 sq. mi.

malleolus /ma leè əlass/ (plural **-li** /-lī/) n either of the hammer-shaped bony protuberances at the sides of the ankle joint that project from the lower end of the tibia and fibula [Early 17C. < Latin, 'little hammer' < *malleus* 'hammer'.] —**malleolar** adj

mallet /mállət/ n 1 **TOOL SIMILAR TO HAMMER** a tool with a large usually wooden or metal head that is used for driving another tool such as a chisel or for striking or moulding a material 2 **STICK USED IN CROQUET OR POLO** a long stick with a cylindrical head, used to hit the ball in the games of croquet and polo 3 **HAMMER USED TO PLAY PERCUSSION INSTRUMENT** a small hammer often with a padded head used for playing musical instruments such as the marimba and xylophone [15C. < French *maillet* 'small hammer' < *mail* (see MAUL).]

malleus /málli əss/ (plural **-i** /-ī/) n a hammer-shaped bone, the outermost of three small bones in the middle ear that transmit sound waves from the eardrum to the inner ear. ◊ **incus** n., **stapes** [Mid-17C. < Latin, 'hammer'.]

Mallorca ♦ Majorca

mallow /mállō/ (plural **-lows** or **-low**) n 1 a wild or cultivated plant with fine hairs on its stem and leaves, and disc-shaped fruit. Flowers: pink, purple, white. Genus: *Malva.* 2 a plant resembling or related to the true mallow [Pre-12C. < Latin *malva*.]

malm /maam/ n 1 **TYPE OF LIMESTONE** a limestone that is greyish in colour and crumbles easily 2 **CHALKY SOIL** a chalky soil produced by the crumbling of malm 3 **MIXTURE OF CLAY AND CHALK** a mixture of clay and chalk used to make bricks [Old English *mealm* < Indo-European, 'pound, grind']

Malmesbury /maàmzbari/ town in SW England. Population: 4,439 (1991).

Malmö /málmō/ port in SW Sweden, on the Øresund. Population: 245,699 (1996).

malmsey /maàmzi/ n a dark fortified wine produced in Madeira, the sweetest type of Madeira wine [14C. Via Middle Dutch < medieval Latin *malmasia*, after *Monemvasia*, S Greece.]

malnourished /mal núrrisht/ adj having a diet that leads to physical harm through inadequacy, inappropriateness, or excess —**malnourishment** n

malnutrition /mál nyoo trísh'n/ n a lack of healthy foods in the diet or an excessive intake of unhealthy foods, leading to physical harm

malocclusion /málla klooʒh'n/ n an undesirable relative positioning of the upper and lower teeth when the jaw is closed —**maloccluded** adj

malodorous /mal ódərəss/ adj smelling unpleasant or offensive —**malodorously** adv —**malodorousness** n

malonic acid /ma lónik-, ma lónnik-/ n $C_3H_4O_4$ a colourless crystalline solid. Source: sugar beets. Use: manufacture of pharmaceuticals. [< French *malonique*, alteration of *malique* (see MALIC)]

Malory /mállari/, **Sir Thomas** (d. 1471) English writer and translator

maloti plural of **loti**

Malouf /ma loof/, **David** (b. 1934) Australian writer

Malpighian corpuscle /mal píggi ən-/, **Malpighian body** n a cluster of small blood vessels enclosed in a capsule (**Bowman's capsule**) at the end of each of the tiny urine-secreting tubules (**nephrons**) of the kidney [Mid-19C. After the Italian physician and anatomist Marcello *Malpighi* (1628–94).]

Malpighian layer n the deepest layer of the outermost part of the skin (**epidermis**), now called the basal cell layer [See MALPIGHIAN CORPUSCLE]

Malpighian tubule, Malpighian tube n a narrow tube in the body of an insect that serves as an organ of excretion [See MALPIGHIAN CORPUSCLE]

malposition /mál palpa zísh'n/ n the undesirable position of something, especially a part of the body or a foetus in the womb —**malposed** /mal pózd/ adj

malpractice /mal práktiss/ n 1 **WRONG OR NEGLIGENT CONDUCT OF PROFESSIONAL** illegal, unethical, negligent, or immoral behaviour by somebody in a professional or official position, resulting in a failure to fulfil the duties or responsibilities associated with that position 2 **MEDICAL MISCONDUCT** unethical, illegal, negligent, or immoral behaviour by a physician, resulting in a failure to fulfill the duties and responsibilities required of a physician **3 EXAMPLE OF MALPRACTICE** an act or instance of malpractice —**malpractitioner** /mál prak tísh'nər/ n

Malraux /mal rṓ/, **André** (1901–76) French novelist, art theorist, archaeologist, and public servant

malt /mawlt, molt/ n **1 GRAIN USED TO MAKE ALCOHOLIC DRINKS** grain such as barley that has begun germination by being soaked in water. Use: brewing beer, distilling whisky. **2** BEVERAGES = **malt whisky 3** BEVERAGES = **malt liquor 4** US BEVERAGES = **malted milk** n. **2** ■ adj **CONTAINING MALT** made from or containing malt ■ v **1 CHANGE GRAIN INTO MALT** to make cereal grain into malt by soaking it in water to start germination and then drying it in a kiln, or to undergo this process **2** vt **MAKE OR MIX SOMETHING WITH MALT** to make something with malt, or add malt to something [Old English mealt < Germanic]

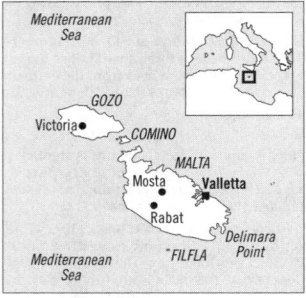

Malta

Malta /máwltə/ island republic in the central Mediterranean Sea. Capital: Valletta. Population: 373,000 (1996). Area: 316 sq. km/122 sq. mi.

Malta fever n MED = **brucellosis**

maltase /máwl tayz, -tayss, mol-, -/ n an enzyme that breaks down maltose into glucose

malted milk, malted n **1** a soluble powder made from dried milk and malted grain **2** a drink made from malted milk, whole milk, ice cream, and flavouring

Maltese /máwl teez, mól-/ (plural **-tese**) n **1** somebody who comes from Malta **2** an official language of Malta, belonging to the Semitic branch of Afro-Asiatic and featuring many words adopted from Italian. Native speakers: 300,000. —**Maltese** adj

Maltese cross n a cross with four arms resembling arrowheads that taper towards the centre

Maltese dog n a small dog of a breed with long white silky hair

malt extract n a sweet sticky substance made from malt. Use: additive in cooking or brewing.

maltha /málthə/ n a black viscous bitumen that is a naturally-occurring mixture of hydrocarbons [Early 17C. Via Latin < Greek, a mixture of pitch and wax.]

Malthus /málthəss/, **Thomas Robert** (1766–1834) British economist —**Malthusian** /mal thyóòzi ən/ adj, n —**Malthusianism** n

malt liquor n an alcoholic drink that is brewed from malt, especially one having a higher alcohol content than most beer or ale

Malto /mál tṓ/ n the Dravidian language of the Maler people. Native speakers: 100,000. [Late 19C. < Malto, 'language of the Maler'.] —**Malto** adj

maltose /máwl tōz, -tōss, mól <tōz/ n a sugar composed of two units of glucose. Source: starch. [Mid-19C. < MALT.]

maltreat /mal treét/ vt to treat somebody or something badly or cruelly, usually through neglect or abuse [Early 18C. < French maltraiter 'treat badly' < traiter (see TREAT).] —**maltreater** n —**maltreatment** n

SYNONYMS See misuse.

maltster /máwltstər, mólt-/ n somebody whose job involves producing or selling malt

malt sugar n BIOCHEM = **maltose**

malt whisky n **1** a whisky distilled from malted barley, often one that is not a blend **2** a drink or measure of malt whisky

malvasia /málvə seé ə/ n the variety of grape that is used to make malmsey wine [Mid-19C. Via Italian < medieval Latin, variant of malmasia (see MALMSEY).] —**malvasian** adj

Malvern Hills /máwlvərn-/ range of hills in west-central England. Highest peak: Worcestershire Beacon 425 m/1,395 ft.

malversation /málvər sáysh'n/ n dishonest or unethical conduct by somebody in a professional position or public office, often involving bribery, extortion, or embezzlement (formal) [Mid-16C. Via French < Latin male versari 'behave badly'.]

mam /mam/ n mother (informal or regional) [Late 16C. Probably < children's first attempts at speech.]

mama /maàmə, mə maà/, **mamma** n **1** mother (dated informal) **2** US a woman, especially somebody's girlfriend or wife (slang; sometimes offensive) [Late 16C. < children's first attempts at speech.]

mama's boy n US = **mummy's boy** (insult)

mamba /mámbə/ n a large venomous snake, especially a green or black snake that lives in trees. Native to: tropical Africa. Genus: Dendroaspis. [Mid-19C. < Zulu imamba.]

mambo /mámbō/ n (plural **-bos**) **1 DANCE RESEMBLING RUMBA** a modern Latin American dance in 4/4 time and originating in Cuba, similar to the rumba **2 MUSIC FOR MAMBO** the music for a mambo ■ vi (**-bos, -boing, -boed**) **DANCE THE MAMBO** to dance the mambo [Mid-20C. < American Spanish.]

Mameluke /mámmi look/ n a member of a former military caste, originally comprising enslaved Turks, that ruled Egypt from the 13th to the 16th centuries, remaining powerful until the early 19th century [Early 16C. Via French < Arabic mamlūk 'enslaved person' < malaka 'possess'.]

Mamet /mámmit/, **David** (b. 1947) US playwright and film director

mamey /ma meé/ (plural **-meys**) n **1** a fruit with red skin, yellow flesh, and poisonous seeds **2** the tree that produces mameys. Native to: Caribbean. Mammea americana. [Late 16C. Via American Spanish mamei < Taino.]

mamilla /ma míllə/ (plural **-lae** /-míllee/) n **1** a nipple or teat **2** a protuberance or organ that resembles a nipple or teat [Late 17C. < Latin, 'little breast' < mamma 'breast'.] —**mamillary** /mámmiləri/ adj —**mamillate** /mámmi layt/ adj —**mamillated** /mámmi laytid/ adj —**mamillation** /mámmi láysh'n/ n

mamm- prefix = **mammo-** (before vowels)

mamma[1] /mámmə/ (plural **-mae** /-mee/) n the milk-secreting organ of female mammals, e.g. a woman's breast or a cow's udder (technical) [Pre-12C. < Latin.] —**mammate** adj —**mammiform** adj

mamma[2] n = **mama**

mammae plural of **mamma**[1]

mammal /mámm'l/ n a class of warm-blooded vertebrate animals that have, in the female, milk-secreting organs for feeding the young [Early 19C. < modern Latin mammalia < Latin mamma 'breast'.] —**mammalian** /mə máyli ən/ adj

mammalogy /ma málləji/ n the branch of zoology that deals with the study of mammals —**mammalogical** /mámmə lójjik'l/ adj —**mammalogist** n

mammaplasty n SURG = **mammoplasty**

mammary /mámməri/ adj relating or belonging to the milk-secreting organ of a female mammal, e.g. the breast or udder [Late 17C. < MAMMA[1].]

mammary gland n a large milk-producing gland in female mammals that consists of a network of ducts and cavities leading to a nipple or teat

mammee /ma meé/ n FOOD, TREES = **mamey** [Variant]

mammee apple n FOOD = **mamey** n. 1

mammie n = **mammy**

mammilla n US = **mamilla**

mammo- prefix breast ○ mammogram [< Latin mamma 'breast']

mammogram /mámmə gram/ n the procedure of taking an X-ray of all or part of the breast [Mid-20C. < Latin mamma 'breast'.]

mammography /ma móggrəfi/ n X-ray examination of the breast, used for the early detection of developing tumours, especially cancerous ones —**mammographic** /mámmə gráffik/ adj

mammon /mámmən/ n wealth and riches considered as an evil and corrupt influence [14C. Via late Latin < Aramaic māmōnā 'riches'.] —**mammonish** adj —**mammonism** n —**mammonist** n

Mammon n the personification of wealth portrayed as a false god in the Bible

mammoplasty /mámmə plasti/ (plural **-ties**), **mammaplasty** (plural **-ties**) n plastic surgery performed on a woman's breast to alter the shape or size, e.g. as reconstruction following a mastectomy or as cosmetic surgery

mammoth /mámməth/ n (plural **-moths** or **-moth**) **1 EXTINCT ELEPHANT** a large extinct elephant that had long curved tusks and was covered with hair. Genus: Mammuthus. **2 SOMETHING ENORMOUS** something that is a particularly large example of its kind ■ adj **VERY LARGE** of very great size or extent [Early 18C. < obsolete Russian mámot.]

mammy /mámmi/ (plural **-mies**), **mammie** n mother (informal; usually by or to children) [Early 16C. Variant of MAMMA[2].]

mammy wagon n in West Africa, a bus with open sides that is used to carry both passengers and goods [< ?]

Mamoré /maa mṓray/ river in N Bolivia, flowing northwards into the River Madeira. Length: 1,900 km/1,200 mi.

Mampruli /-próóli/ n a Niger-Congo language spoken in Ghana and Togo. Native speakers: 200,000. [Mid-20C. < Mampruli.] —**Mampruli** adj

mamzer /mámzər/ (plural **-erim** /-ərim/), **momser** /mómzər/, **momzer** n **1** in Jewish religious law, a child born of an adulterous or incestuous relationship **2** US an offensive term for somebody regarded as untrustworthy or contemptible (slang insult) [Mid-16C. Via late Latin < Hebrew mamzēr.]

man /man/ n (plural **men** /men/) **1 ADULT MALE HUMAN** an adult male human being **2 PERSON** a person, regardless of sex or age (often considered offensive) ○ a six-man crew **3 PARTICULAR TYPE OF MAN** an adult male human being with a particular occupation, responsibility, background, or nationality (usually in combination) ○ the TV repair man ○ I'm not a dogs man. **4 HUMAN RACE** the human race in general (often considered offensive) **5 MODERN OR EARLIER HUMAN BEING** a member of the group that comprises modern humans and their ancestors. Genus: Homo. (sometimes offensive) **6 EMPLOYEE OR WORKER** an employee or worker of either sex (often considered offensive) **7 MALE MEMBER OF ARMED FORCES** a male member of the armed forces, especially one who is not an officer (usually plural) **8 SERVANT** a man who is a servant (dated) **9 VIRILE PERSON** the personification of qualities traditionally associated with the male sex, including courage, strength, and aggression, or somebody with such qualities **10 HUSBAND OR MALE COMPANION** a husband, or a man who is another person's companion or lover (slang) **11 TERM OF ADDRESS** a term of address to a person of either sex (slang; sometimes offensive) ○ Cool it, man! **12 man, Man** US **AUTHORITY FIGURE** somebody in a position of authority, or a group that is seen as having an unfair advantage or undue power over others (slang; sometimes offensive) ○ in trouble with the Man **13 PIECE USED IN BOARD GAMES** a piece used in playing board games such as draughts **14 MEDIEVAL VASSAL** in feudal societies of the early Middle Ages, an adult male human who swore allegiance to a lord in return for help and protection **15 SHIP** a ship, especially one of a particular kind (in combination) ○ man-of-war ■ vt (**mans, manning, manned**) (often considered offensive) **1 SUPPLY WITH WORKERS** to provide something with workers, operators, or military personnel **2 BE READY TO USE** to be ready to operate or defend something ■ interj **USED FOR EMPHASIS** used to add emphasis (slang; sometimes offensive) ○ Man, that was exciting! [Old English man(n) < Indo-European, 'person, man'] —**man-like** adj ◇ **a poor man's...** a cheaper or inferior version of something, especially one that is more widely available than the original ◇ **as a** or **one man** unanimously or without exception (often considered offensive if used of women) ◇ **be your own man** to have the resources or confidence to be responsible for yourself or your actions (often considered offensive if used of women) ◇ **man and boy** throughout somebody's life ○ He's lived in this house for 60 years, man and boy. ◇ **to a man** everyone, without any exceptions (often considered offensive if used of women)

USAGE See person.

Man, Isle of /man/ island in the Irish Sea between England and Northern Ireland, a self-governing Crown dependency of the United Kingdom. Capital: Douglas. Population: 69,788 (1991). Area: 572 sq. km/221 sq. mi.

MAN *abbr* metropolitan area network

Man. *abbr* 1 Manila *or* Manila paper 2 Manitoba

mana /maanə/ *n NZ* a life force associated with ritual power and high social status, especially in Polynesia and Melanesia [Mid-19C. < Maori.]

man about town (*plural* **men about town**) *n* a sophisticated and cultured man who socializes in fashionable circles (*dated*)

manacle /mánnək'l/ *n* either of a pair of metal rings joined by a chain and fastened around the wrists of a prisoner to be restrained (*usually plural*) ■ *vt* (**-cles, -cling, -cled**) to restrain somebody using manacles [14C. Via French *manicle* 'handcuff' < Latin *manicula* < *manus* 'hand'.]

~~managable~~ incorrect spelling of **manageable**

manage /mánnij/ (**-ages, -aging, -aged**) *v* 1 *vti* **ACHIEVE SOMETHING WITH DIFFICULTY** to succeed in doing something, especially something that seems difficult or impossible ○ *I finally managed to open the door.* 2 *vt* **HAVE ENOUGH ROOM FOR** to have enough time or space for something ○ *couldn't manage a whole steak by himself* 3 *vi* **COPE IN DIFFICULT SITUATION** to survive or continue despite difficulties, especially a lack of resources ○ *He manages with very little money.* 4 *vti* **ADMINISTER OR RUN** to be in charge of something such as a shop, department, or project and be responsible for its smooth running and for any personnel employed ○ *manages a department of 25 people* 5 *vt* **HANDLE AND CONTROL** to handle and keep control of something such as a weapon or tool ○ *could manage a computer without difficulty* 6 *vt* **DISCIPLINE OR CONTROL PERSON OR ANIMAL** to keep control of a person or animal, or a number of people or animals, especially when they are wild or unruly 7 *vt* **BE SOMEBODY'S MANAGER** to guide the career and control the business affairs of somebody such as a professional entertainer or athlete [Mid-16C. < Italian *maneggiare* 'train a horse' < Latin *manus* 'hand'.]

manageable /mánnijəb'l/ *adj* able to be handled or controlled without much difficulty —**manageability** /mánnijə bíllәti/ *n* —**manageableness** *n* —**manageably** *adv*

management /mánnijmənt/ *n* 1 **ADMINISTRATION OF BUSINESS** the organizing and controlling of the affairs of a business or a particular sector of a business 2 **MANAGERS AS A GROUP** managers and employers considered collectively, especially the directors and executives of a business or organization 3 **HANDLING OF SOMETHING SUCCESSFULLY** the act of handling or controlling something successfully 4 **SKILL IN HANDLING OR USING** the skilful handling or use of something such as resources —**managemental** /mánnij mént'l/ *adj*

management accounting *n* ACCT = **cost accounting**

⚡**management information system** *n* a system for gathering the financial, production, and other information that managers need to operate a business, especially a system that is computerized

⚡**manager** /mánnijər/ *n* 1 **ORGANIZER OF BUSINESS** a director and controller of the work and staff of a business, or of a department within it 2 **ORGANIZER OF SOMEBODY'S BUSINESS AFFAIRS** an organizer and controller of somebody's business affairs, especially those of a professional entertainer 3 **ORGANIZER OF AFFAIRS OF ATHLETE** an organizer and director of an athlete or of a sports team 4 **COURT APPOINTEE** a person whom a court appoints to manage a business or organization in receivership 5 **ORGANIZER OF PARLIAMENTARY AFFAIRS** in Britain, a member of the House of Commons or the House of Lords appointed to organize matters of concern to both Houses of Parliament 6 **COMPETENT HANDLER** a handler or controller of something, especially somebody who works skillfully 7 **PROGRAM FOR BASIC COMPUTER OPERATIONS** a computer program designed to carry out the basic functions of a computer's operations —**managership** *n*

managerial /mánni jéeri əl/ *adj* involving or characteristic of a manager or management, especially in business —**managerially** *adv*

managerialism /mánni jéeri əlizəm/ *n* the application of the techniques of managing a commercial business to the running of some other organization such as local government or public services —**managerialist** *n*

managing director *n* somebody, usually the head of a board of directors, who has administrative control over a large company or other commercial organization

managing editor *n* an editor of books, newspapers, or other publications who is responsible for the administration of the editorial process

~~managment~~ incorrect spelling of **management**

Managua /mə nágwə/ capital of Nicaragua, in the west of the country. Population: 1,600,600 (1993).

Managua, Lake lake in W Nicaragua. Area: 1,049 sq. km/405 sq. mi.

manakin /mánnəkin/ *n* a small bird with a short bill and bright colourful plumage. Native to: South America. Family: Pipridae. [Early 17C. Variant of MANIKIN.]

Manama /mə naamə/ capital of Bahrain, in the northeastern part of the country. Population: 140,401 (1992 estimate).

mañana /man yaanə/ *adv* 1 on the day following the present day 2 at some unspecified time in the future [Mid-19C. < Spanish, 'morning, tomorrow' < Latin *mane* 'in the morning'.]

Manapouri, Lake /mánnə pòori/ lake in the southwest of the South Island, New Zealand. Area: 142 sq. km/55 sq. mi.

Manassas /mə nássəss/ city in NE Virginia, the site of two Confederate victories at the US Civil War battles of Bull Run in 1861 and 1862. Population: 35,300 (1998).

manat /mánnat/ *n* see table at **currency** [Late 20C. < the Turkic language of Azerbaijan.]

man-at-arms (*plural* **men-at-arms**) *n* a soldier, especially a medieval mounted soldier who was heavily armed

manatee /mánnə tée/ *n* a large plant-eating mammal with front flippers and a broad flattened tail. Native to: warm Atlantic coastal waters. Genus: *Trichechus.* [Mid-16C. Via Spanish *manatí* < Carib *manáti* 'breast'.]

Manaus /mə nówss/ capital of Amazonas State, NW Brazil, on the River Negro. Population: 1,157,357 (1996 estimate).

Manawatu-Wanganui /mánnə waa too wong gə nòoi/ administrative region in the southwest of the North Island, New Zealand. Population: 229,989 (1996). Area: 25,317 sq. km/9,775 sq. mi.

manche /maaNsh/ *n* a sleeve that hangs down (*technical*) [14C. Via French < Latin *manicae* '(long) sleeves' < *manus* 'hand'.]

manchester /mánchistər/ *n ANZ* household linen or cotton goods such as sheets and towels [Mid-16C. After MANCHESTER.]

Manchester /mán chestər/ 1 city in NW England, connected by the Manchester Ship Canal with the Irish Sea. Population: 430,818 (1996 estimate). 2 city in central Connecticut. Population: 51,618 (1990).

Manchester terrier *n* a small terrier with a short-haired coat that is mainly black with tan patches [After MANCHESTER]

manchineel /mánchi néel/ (*plural* **-neels** *or* **-neel**) *n* a tree with poisonous apple-shaped fruit and milky sap that causes blistering. Native to: tropical America. *Hippomane mancinella.* [Mid-17C. Via French *mancenille* < Spanish *manzanilla* 'little apple' < *manzana* 'apple' < Latin *matiana*, a kind of apple, after *Matia*, a Roman gens.]

Manchu /mán chòo/ (*plural* **-chus** *or* **-chu**) *n* 1 a member of a people who invaded China from Manchuria in the 17th century, establishing a dynasty that lasted until the start of the 20th century 2 a Tungusic language spoken in NE People's Republic of China. Native speakers: 20,000. [Late 17C. < Manchu, 'pure'.] —**Manchu** *adj*

Manchuria /man chòori ə/ historical name for a region of NE China comprising Heilongjiang, Jilin, and Liaoning provinces —**Manchurian** *n, adj*

manciple /mánssip'l/ *n* somebody responsible for buying food and other supplies for a college, Inn of Court, or monastery [13C. Via Anglo-Norman < Latin *mancipium* 'purchase, enslaved person'.]

Mancunian /man kyòoni ən/ *n* somebody who comes from Manchester [Early 20C. < Latin *Mancunium* 'Manchester'.] —**Mancunian** *adj*

-mancy *suffix* divination ○ *geomancy* [< Old French *-mancie* < Greek *mantis* (see MANTIC)]

Mandaean /man dée ən/, **Mandean** *n* 1 **ADHERENT OF JOHN THE BAPTIST** a member of a Gnostic religious group who believe themselves to be descendants of John the Baptist 2 **LANGUAGE OF MANDAEANS** a form of Aramaic used in the sacred writings of the Mandaeans ■ *adj* **RELATING TO MANDAEANS** relating to the Mandaeans or their language [Late 18C. < Mandaean *mandaia* 'having knowledge' < *manda* 'knowledge'.] —**Mandaeanism** *n*

mandala /mándələ, man daalə/ *n* 1 a geometric or pictorial design usually enclosed in a circle, representing the entire universe and used in meditation and ritual in Buddhism and Hinduism 2 in Jungian psychology, a symbol representing the self and harmony within the individual [Mid-19C. < Sanskrit *maṇḍalam* 'circle'.] —**mandalic** /man daalik/ *adj*

Mandalay /mándə láy/ city in central Myanmar, on the River Irrawaddy. Population: 532,949 (1983).

mandamus /man dáyməss/ (*plural* **-muses**) *n* an order from a high court to a lower court or to an authority instructing it to perform a specific action or duty. ◊ **certiorari, prohibition** *n.* 3 [Mid-16C. < Latin, 'we command'.]

Mandan /mán dan, mándən/ (*plural* **-dan** *or* **-dans**) *n* 1 a member of a Native American people of North Dakota who lived along the Missouri River and now mainly live near Lake Sakakawea 2 the language of the Mandan people, belonging to the Siouan branch of Hokan-Siouan languages. Native speakers: 1,200. [Late 18C. < North American French *Mandane.*]

mandarin[1] /mándərin/ *n* 1 **FORMER HIGH-RANKING CHINESE OFFICIAL** in the Chinese Empire, a member of any of the nine highest ranks of public officials, attained by examinations 2 **HIGH-RANKING CIVIL SERVANT** a high-ranking civil servant or bureaucrat with wide-ranging powers 3 **INFLUENTIAL MEMBER OF ELITE GROUP** an influential member of an elite group, especially a literary or intellectual group [Late 16C. < Spanish *mandarín*, Portuguese *mandarim* < Sanskrit *mantrin-* 'counsellor' < *mantraḥ* 'counsel'.] —**mandarinate** *n* —**mandarinic** /mándə rínnik/ *adj* —**mandarinism** *n*

mandarin[2] /mándərin/ *n* 1 a small citrus fruit, similar to a tangerine but with easily peelable yellow-orange skin 2 a small citrus tree that bears mandarins. Native to: China. *Citrus reticulata.* [Late 18C. Via French *mandarine* < Spanish *mandarín* (see MANDARIN[1]), so called because of its colour, likened to that of mandarins' yellow robes.]

Mandarin, Mandarin Chinese *n* the official language of the People's Republic of China, belonging to the Chinese branch of Sino-Tibetan languages. Native speakers: 800 million. Other speakers: 100 million. —**Mandarin** *adj*

mandarin collar *n* a narrow collar that stands up from a close-fitting neckline and opens at the front

mandarin duck *n* a duck with a crested head and colourful plumage, the male of which has one enlarged orange feather on each wing for use in displays. Native to: Asia. *Aix galericulata.*

mandarin orange *n* FOOD = **mandarin**[2] *n.* 1

mandatary /mándətəri/ (*plural* **-ies**) *n* a person or state that has been given a mandate

mandate /mán dayt/ *n* 1 **AUTHORITATIVE ORDER** an official command or instruction from an authority 2 **SUPPORT FROM ELECTORATE** the authority bestowed on a government or other organization by an electoral victory, effectively authorizing it to carry out the policies for which it campaigned ○ *The party in power has a clear mandate for reform.* 3 **AGREEMENT FOR FREE SERVICE** a contract by which somebody agrees to perform a service without payment 4 **INSTRUCTION FROM SUPERIOR COURT** an order from a superior court or official to a lower one 5 **INSTRUCTION FOR REGULAR TRANSFER OF FUNDS** an instruction to a bank or building society to arrange for a regular payment such as a salary to be made into a customer's account 6 **REGION RULED BY OUTSIDE POWER** any territory that was placed by the League of Nations under the administration of one of its European member states after World War I 7 **COMMISSION TO ADMINISTER STATE** the power conferred by the League of Nations on a member state to administer a region ■ *vt* (**-dates, -dating, -dated**) 1 **ASSIGN COLONY** to assign a territory or region to a particular nation under a mandate 2 **DELEGATE AUTHORITY** to delegate authority to somebody or require somebody to do something through use of a mandate 3 *US* **MAKE MANDATORY** to require or order something by making it mandatory ○ *The law mandates systematic tracking and reporting of hazardous wastes.* [Early 16C. < Latin *mandatum*

< the past participle of *mandare* 'give into somebody's hand' < Indo-European, 'hand'.] —**mandator** *n*

mandated territory *n* HIST = **mandate** *n*. 6

mandatory /mándətəri/ *adj* **1** COMPULSORY needing to be done, followed, or complied with, usually because of being officially required **2** WITH POWER OF MANDATE resembling or having the power of a mandate **3** AUTHORIZED TO ADMINISTER TERRITORY having a mandate to administer a region or territory ■ *n* POL = **mandatary** —**mandatorily** *adv*

man-day *n* the work done by one person in one day (*offensive in some contexts*)

Mande /maàn day, mán-/ (*plural* **-de** *or* **-des**) *n* **1** a group of around 20 languages spoken in West Africa, especially in Sierra Leone, Mali, Guinea, and the Côte d'Ivoire. It is a branch of the Niger-Congo family of languages. Native speakers: 9 million. **2** a member of a West African group that speaks a Mande language [Late 19C. < Mande, 'little mother'.] —**Mande** *adj*

Mandean *n*, *adj* RELIG, LANG = **Mandaean**

Nelson Mandela

Mandela /man déllə, -dáylə/, **Nelson** (*b*. 1918) South African statesman and president (1994–99)

Mandela, Winnie (*b*. 1934) South African political activist. Born **Nkosikazi Nomzamo Madikizela**

Mandelstam /mánd'l stam/, **Osip Yemilyevich** (1891?–1938?) Russian poet

mandible /mándib'l/ *n* **1** LOWER JAW OF VERTEBRATE the lower jaw of a person or animal, usually containing a single bone (*technical*) **2** BIRD'S BEAK the upper or lower part of a bird's beak **3** INSECT'S MOUTHPART either of a pair of parts in insects and similar animals used for biting and cutting food [Mid-16C. Directly or via Old French < late Latin *mandibula* < Latin *mandere* 'chew'.] —**mandibular** /man díbbyŏŏlər/ *adj* —**mandibulate** /man díbbyŏŏlit, -layt/ *adj*, *n*

Mandingo /man díng gō/ (*plural* **-gos** *or* **-goes** *or* **-go**) *n* **1** a member of any of several peoples who live in parts of West Africa, especially along the Niger River valley **2** a group of Mande languages spoken in parts of West Africa, especially along the Niger River valley. Native speakers: 6 million. [Early 17C. < Mande.] —**Mandingo** *adj*

Mandinka /man díng kə/ (*plural* **-ka** *or* **-kas**) *n* **1** a member of a West African people living in parts of the Gambia, Senegal, and Sierra Leone **2** the Niger-Congo language of the Mandinka people. Native speakers: 700,000. [Mid-20C. < Mande.] —**Mandinka** *adj*

mandir /mún deer/ *n* S *Asia* a Hindu temple [Via Hindi < Sanskrit *mandiram* 'dwelling, mansion']

mandolin /mándə lín/, **mandoline** *n* a stringed instrument of the lute family with a pear-shaped body and four or more pairs of strings, usually played with a plectrum [Early 18C. Via French < Italian *mandolino* 'small lute' < *mandola* 'mandola'.] —**mandolinist** *n*

mandorla /man dáwrlə/ *n* an oval area or panel in painting or sculpture, e.g. the area of light surrounding a representation of Jesus Christ after the resurrection [Late 19C. < Italian, 'almond' < medieval Latin *amandula* (see ALMOND).]

mandragora /man drággərə/ *n* PLANTS = **mandrake** *n*. 1 [Pre-12C. Directly or via French *mandragore* < medieval Latin *mandragora* < Greek *mandragoras*.]

mandrake /mán drayk/ *n* **1** a plant with a forked root resembling a human body that was formerly believed to have magical powers and was made into a drug.

Flowers: yellow, purplish. Native to: Europe, Asia. *Mandragora officinarum*. **2** FOOD = **May apple** *n*. 1 [14C. Alteration of medieval Latin *mandragora*, influenced by MAN, DRAKE 'dragon' (from its emetic and narcotic properties).]

mandrel /mándrəl/, **mandril** *n* **1** TAPERED SHAFT FOR SECURING WORK TO a tapered shaft or arbor to which work is secured during machining or turning, e.g. on a lathe **2** CORE ROD a rod around which materials such as metal or glass are moulded, forged, or shaped **3** SHAFT FOR MOUNTING TOOL a shaft on which a tool such as a dentist's drill or machining tool is mounted **4** PICK a miner's pick [Early 16C. < ?]

mandrill /mándril/ *n* a large baboon with a beard, mane, and crest. The male also has a brilliant ribbed blue, white, and scarlet muzzle. Native to: West Africa. *Mandrillus sphinx*. [Mid-18C. Said to be < MAN + DRILL⁴.]

manducate /mándyŏŏ kayt/ (*-cates, -cating, -cated*) *vt* to chew or eat something (*formal*) [Early 17C. < late Latin *manducare* 'chew'.] —**manducation** /mándyŏŏ káysh'n/ *n* —**manducatory** *adj*

Mandurah /mán dyoorə/ town in SW Western Australia. Population: 35,945 (1996).

mane /mayn/ *n* **1** long hair on the head and neck of an animal such as a lion or horse **2** a large amount of thick long hair on somebody's head (*literary or informal*) [Old English *manu*] —**maned** *adj*

man-eater *n* **1** ANIMAL EATING HUMANS an animal such as a tiger or great white shark that eats or is thought to eat human flesh **2** CANNIBAL an eater of human flesh **3** OFFENSIVE TERM an offensive term for a woman who is thought to pursue men in order to make them her lovers and then discard them —**man-eating** *adj*

maned wolf /maynd-/ *n* a wild South American member of the dog family with long legs, a shaggy yellowish-red coat, and black markings on the neck and legs. *Chrysocyon brachyurus*.

manège /ma náyzh, -nézh/, **manege** *n* **1** ART OF RIDING the art of riding or training horses **2** TRAINED HORSE'S MOVEMENTS the movements that a horse has been trained to make **3** RIDING SCHOOL a school where people are taught to ride and horses trained [Mid-17C. < French, < Italian *maneggio* < *maneggiare* (see MANAGE).]

manes /maà nayz/, **Manes** *n* the revered spirit of a dead person (*literary*; + *singular verb*) ■ *npl* in ancient Roman religious belief, the divine spirits of the dead (+ *plural verb*) [14C. < Latin, 'good ones' < *manus* 'good'.]

Manet /mán ay/, **Édouard** (1832–83) French painter

man Friday (*plural* **man Fridays** *or* **men Friday**) *n* a man acting as an assistant or servant who is loyal and able to do many things [After the servant in *Robinson Crusoe* (1719) by Daniel Defoe]

manful /mánf'l/ *adj* brave, strong, and resolute, as a man is conventionally supposed to be —**manfully** *adv* —**manfulness** *n*

manga /máng gə/ *n* a Japanese style of comic books or animated cartoons, often very violent or erotic

mangabey /máng gə bay/ (*plural* **-beys**) *n* a large agile monkey with a long tail, slender body, and white eyelids. Native to: Africa. Genus: *Cercocebus*. [Late 18C. After the *Mangabey* region in Madagascar.]

Mangalore /máng gə láwr/ port in SW India, on the Arabian Sea. Population: 272,819 (1991).

mangan- *prefix* manganese ○ *manganous* [< MANGANESE]

manganate /máng gə nayt/ *n* any mixed-metal salt containing manganese and oxygen in the form of an anion [Mid-19C. < MANGANESE.]

manganese /máng gə neez/ *n* (*symbol* **Mn**) a brittle greyish-white metallic element. Source: pyrolusite, rhodonite. Use: alloys, strengthening steel. [Late 17C. Via French < Italian, < medieval Latin *magnesia* 'magnesia'.]

manganese nodule *n* a stony nodule rich in manganese, found on the ocean floor

manganese steel *n* steel containing 11 to 14 per cent manganese. Use: manufacture of drills, blades, tools.

manganic /man gánnik/ *adj* containing or derived from manganese, especially with a valency of three or six [Mid-19C. < MANGANESE.]

manganite /máng gə nīt/ *n* a greyish crystalline mineral consisting of manganese hydroxide [Early 19C. < MANGANESE.]

manganous /máng gənəss, man gánnəss/ *adj* containing or derived from manganese, especially with a valency of two

mange /maynj/ *n* an infectious skin disease of animals and sometimes humans that is caused by mites and results in hair loss, scabs, and itching [15C. < French *manjue* 'itch' < Old French *mangier* 'eat' < Latin *manducare* (see MANGER).]

mangel /máng g'l/, **mangel-wurzel** /-wurz'l/, **mangold** /máng gōld/, **mangold-wurzel** *n* a large yellow or reddish variety of beet that is grown as food for livestock [Late 18C. < German *Mangoldwurzel* 'beet root'.]

manger /máynjər/ *n* a trough from which livestock eat [14C. < Old French *mangeoire* < *mangier* 'eat' < Latin *manducare* 'chew' < *mandere*.]

Mangeshkar /man gésh kaar/, **Lata** (*b*. 1929) Indian singer

mangetout /mónj toō, móNzh-/, **mangetout pea** *n* = **snow pea** [Early 19C. < French, 'eat-all'.]

mangey *adj* = **mangy**

mangle¹ /máng g'l/ (*-gles, -gling, -gled*) *vt* **1** to mutilate or disfigure somebody or something by violent tearing, cutting, or crushing **2** to spoil or ruin something through carelessness or ineptitude ○ *a reading that mangled the rhythm of the poem* [14C. < Anglo-Norman *mahangler*.] —**mangler** *n*

mangle² /máng g'l/ *n* a machine for squeezing water out of wet clothes after washing by drawing them between two rotating cylinders. US term **wringer** *n*. [Late 17C. < Dutch *mangelstok* 'mangling roller'.] —**mangle** *vt*

mango /máng gō/ (*plural* **-goes** *or* **-gos**) *n* **1** a red or green fruit with juicy, sweet, orange-yellow pulp and a large stone **2** an evergreen tree that produces mangoes. Native to: tropical Asia. *Mangifera indica*. [Late 16C. Via Portuguese *manga* < Malay *mangga* < Tamil *mānkāy* 'mango-tree fruit'.]

mangold, **mangold-wurzel** *n* AGRIC = **mangel**

mangonel /máng gənəl, máng gə nel/ *n* a medieval military machine used for hurling stones at an enemy [13C. Via Old French *mangonel(le)* < medieval Latin *manganellus* 'little war engine' < Greek *magganon* 'war engine'.]

mangosteen /máng gō steen/ *n* **1** a fruit with a hard reddish-brown rind and sweet juicy pulp **2** an evergreen tree that has leathery leaves and produces mangosteens. Native to: Southeast Asia. *Garcinia mangostana*. [Late 16C. < Malay *manggustan*, alteration of *manggis*.]

Mangrove

mangrove /máng grōv/ *n* an evergreen tree or shrub with straight slender stems and intertwined roots that are exposed at low tide. Native to: tropical coasts. Families: Combretaceae, Verbenaceae, Rhizophoraceae. [Early 17C. Blend of Portuguese *mangue* or Spanish *mangle* (< Taino) + GROVE.]

Mangue /máng gi, máng gwi/ *n* an extinct Native Central American language of Costa Rica, belonging to the Oto-Manguean family of languages [Late 18C. < ?] —**Mangue** *adj*

mangy /máynji/, **mangey** (**-ier, -iest**) *adj* **1** HAVING MANGE affected by or caused by mange **2** SCRUFFY having a dirty or shabby appearance (*informal*) **3** *Ireland* MISERLY reluctant to spend or give money (*informal*) —**mangily** *adv* —**manginess** *n*

manhandle /mán hand'l, man hánd'l/ (**-dles, -dling, -dled**) *vt* **1** to pull or push somebody or something around roughly **2** to move something using human strength alone rather than machinery

Manhattan¹ /man hátt'n/, **manhattan** *n* a cocktail made from vermouth, whisky, and a dash of bitters [Late 19C. After MANHATTAN² 1.]

Manhattan[2] /man hátt'n/ 1 borough of New York City, mainly on Manhattan Island at the northern end of New York Bay. Population: 1,487,536 (1990). Area: 80 sq. km/31 sq. mi. 2 city in NE Kansas. Population: 42,117 (1996).

Manhattan Project *n* the top-secret research and development in several places in the United States that led to the successful construction and detonation of the first atomic bombs [Mid-20C. < *Manhattan District*, the codename it was given.]

manhole /mán hōl/ *n* an opening with a detachable cover that gives access to an enclosed area, especially a sewer, drain, or tank

manhood /mán hòod/ *n* 1 STATE OF BEING A MAN the state of being an adult male human 2 TRADITIONAL MANLINESS the qualities and attributes conventionally thought to be appropriate to a man, especially physical strength, courage, and determination 3 MEN men considered collectively ○ *the nation's manhood* 4 PENIS a man's penis (*literary or humorous*)

manhood suffrage *n* the right to vote given to all adult men

man-hour *n* the amount of work that can be done by one person in one hour, used as a means of assessing requirements, production, and performance (*offensive in some contexts*) ○ *the number of man-hours lost through sickness*

manhunt /mán hunt/ *n* an organized search, especially by the police, for an escaped criminal or other wanted person —**manhunter** *n*

mania /máyni ə/ *n* 1 an excessive and intense interest in or enthusiasm for something 2 psychiatric disorder characterized by excessive physical activity, rapidly changing ideas, and impulsive behaviour [14C. Via late Latin < Greek, 'loss of reason' < *mainesthai* 'to rage'.]

-mania *suffix* excessive enthusiasm for or attachment to ○ *pyromania* [< MANIA]

maniac /máyni ak/ *n* 1 OFFENSIVE TERM an offensive term for somebody who behaves in such an uncontrolled manner as to appear to be affected by mania 2 ENTHUSIAST a person who is obsessively interested in or enthusiastic about something 3 OFFENSIVE TERM an offensive term for somebody affected by mania [Late 16C. Via late Latin *maniacus* < late Greek *maniakos* < *mania* (see MANIA).]

maniacal /mə nī́ ək'l/ *adj* 1 an offensive term meaning so uncontrolled as to appear to be affected by mania 2 an offensive term meaning characteristic of or indicative of mania —**maniacally** *adv*

manic /mánnik/ *adj* 1 RELATING TO MANIA relating to or affected by mania 2 HECTIC extremely or excessively busy (*informal; sometimes offensive*) 3 OVEREXCITED in a state of abnormally high excitement, especially because of tension (*informal*) [Early 20C. < MANIA.] —**manically** *adv*

manic-depressive *n* somebody affected by bipolar disorder ■ *adj* typical of or affected by bipolar disorder

manic-depressive disorder, manic-depressive illness *n* MED = **bipolar disorder**

Manichaeism /mánni kée izəm/, **Manicheism** *n* 1 a religious doctrine based on the separation of matter and spirit and of good and evil that originated in 3rd-century Persia and combined elements of Zoroastrianism, Buddhism, Christianity, and Gnosticism 2 a heretical Christian belief in the separate nature of matter and spirit [Early 17C. < late Latin *Manichaeus* < *Manes*, (216?–276?), its Persian founder.] —**Manichaean** *adj* —**Manichee** /mánni kee/ *n*

manicure /mánni kyoor/ *n* HAND AND NAIL COSMETIC TREATMENT a cosmetic treatment for the hands and nails that usually involves shaping and polishing the fingernails, pushing back the cuticles, and treating rough skin ■ *vt* (**-cures, -curing, -cured**) 1 TREAT HANDS AND NAILS to treat the hands and fingernails by cutting, shaping, and polishing the nails, and softening the hands 2 CUT AND SHAPE SOMETHING CAREFULLY to cut and shape something with great care and precision [Late 19C. Via French < Latin *manus cura* 'hand care'.]

manicurist /mánnikyoorist/ *n* somebody whose job is to give people manicures

manifest /mánni fest/ *adj* OBVIOUS clear to see or understand ■ *v* 1 *vt* SHOW SOMETHING CLEARLY to make something evident by showing or demonstrating it very clearly 2 *vi* APPEAR to appear or be revealed 3 *vt* INCLUDE SOMETHING IN CARGO LIST to include something in a ship's cargo list ■ *n* 1 SHIP'S CARGO LIST a list giving details of a ship's cargo, its destination, and other particulars for customs purposes 2 PLANE OR TRAIN'S CARGO LIST a list of cargo or passengers on a plane or train [14C. Directly or via Old French < Latin *manifestus* 'apprehensible' < *manus* 'hand' + *festus* 'seizable'.] —**manifestable** *adj* —**manifestly** *adv* —**manifestness** *n*

manifestation /mánni fe stáysh'n/ *n* 1 ACT OF SHOWING an act of showing or demonstrating something 2 STATE OF BEING MANIFESTED the condition of being shown or perceptible 3 SIGN an indication that something is present, real, or exists ○ *one of the first manifestations of the disease* 4 PUBLIC DEMONSTRATION a public demonstration, usually over a political issue 5 MATERIALIZATION a supposed appearance in visible form by a spiritual being 6 VISIBLE FORM OF DIVINE BEING a visible form in which a divine being, idea, or person is believed to be revealed or expressed —**manifestational** *adj*

manifest content *n* in dream analysis, the overt meaning of a dream remembered by the dreamer on waking that requires analysis to interpret its latent content or real meaning

Manifest Destiny *n* the 19th-century doctrine according to which the United States was believed to have the God-given right to expand into and possess the whole of the North American continent

manifesto /mánni féstō/ (*plural* **-toes** *or* **-tos**) *n* a public written declaration of principles, policies, and objectives, especially one issued by a political movement or candidate [Mid-17C. < Italian, < *manifestare* 'make evident' < Latin *manifestus* (see MANIFEST).]

manifold /mánni fōld/ *adj* 1 MANY AND VARIOUS of many different kinds ○ *The reasons for the crisis are manifold.* 2 HAVING MANY FORMS having many parts, forms, or applications ○ *a manifold political system* ■ *n* 1 CHAMBER WITH PORTS a chamber or pipe with several openings for receiving or distributing a fluid or gas, such as the intake or exhaust manifolds of an internal-combustion engine 2 TOPOLOGICAL SPACE a topological space or surface satisfying specific conditions ■ *vt* 1 MULTIPLY to multiply something 2 MAKE COPIES OF to make several copies of a book or page [Old English *manigfeald* < earlier forms of MANY + -FOLD] —**manifolder** *n* —**manifoldly** *adv* —**manifoldness** *n*

manikin /mánnikin/, **mannikin** *n* 1 CLOTHING = **mannequin** *n.* 1 2 an anatomical model of the human body, used in teaching art or medicine 3 an offensive term for a very short man [Mid-16C. < Dutch *manneken* 'little man' < *man* 'man'.]

manila /mə níllə/, **Manila** *adj* made of Manila paper ○ *a manila envelope* ■ *n* 1 a cigar made in Manila 2 INDUST = **Manila hemp** 3 PAPER = **Manila paper** [Late 17C. After MANILA.]

Manila /mə níllə/ capital of the Philippines, on the coast of SW Luzon Island. Population: 1,580,924 (1999 estimate).

Manila Bay bay of the South China Sea, on SW Luzon Island in the Philippines. Area: 2,000 sq. km/770 sq. mi.

Manila hemp, Manilla hemp *n* a strong fibre obtained from the Philippine abaca plant. Use: rope, paper. [Mid-19C. After MANILA.]

Manila paper, Manilla paper *n* a strong pale-brown paper with a smooth surface, made from Manila hemp. Use: wrapping, envelopes. [Late 19C. After MANILA.]

manille /mə níl/ *n* the second-best trump in the card games ombre and quadrille [Late 17C. < French, < Spanish *malilla* 'little bad (card)'.]

man in the moon *n* the imaginary being behind the apparent face on the moon when it is full

man in the street *n* the average person, as opposed to an expert, celebrity, or prominent person (*sometimes considered offensive*)

manioc /mánni ok/, **manioca** /mánni ṓkə/ *n* PLANTS, FOOD = **cassava** [Mid-16C. < Tupi *mandioca* (influenced by French *manihot*) < Guarani *mandio*.]

maniple /mánnip'l/ *n* 1 in the ancient Roman army, a subdivision of a legion, containing 60 or 120 men. ◊ **century** *n.* 4 2 a silk band or folded napkin formerly worn on the left arm of somebody administering Communion [Late 16C. < Latin *manipulus* 'handful' < *manus* 'hand'.]

manipular /mə níppyòolər/ *adj* 1 relating to an ancient Roman maniple 2 relating to or constituting manipulation

⚡**manipulate** /mə níppyoo layt/ (**-lates, -lating, -lated**) *vt* 1 OPERATE to operate, use, or handle something ○ *manipulating the crane into position* 2 CONTROL SOMEBODY OR SOMETHING DEVIOUSLY to control or influence somebody or something in a clever or devious way 3 FALSIFY to change or present something in a way that is false but personally advantageous 4 HANDLE NUMBERS to work with data on a computer 5 TREAT BODY PART USING HANDS ONLY to treat a part of the body, or to move a part such as a joint during examination, using the hands only [Early 19C. Back-formation < *manipulation* < French < *manipule* 'handful' < Latin *manipulus* (see MANIPLE).] —**manipulability** /mə níppyòolə bíllәti/ *n* —**manipulable** *adj* —**manipulatable** *adj* —**manipulation** /mə níppyòo láysh'n/ *n* —**manipulator** *n* —**manipulatory** *adj*

manipulative /mə níppyòolətiv/ *adj* 1 using clever, devious ways to control or influence somebody or something ○ *a manipulative personality* 2 relating to or involved in manipulation ○ *a manipulative technique* —**manipulatively** *adv* —**manipulativeness** *n*

manito *n* RELIG = **manitou**

Manitoba /mánni tṓbə/ province in south-central Canada. Capital: Winnipeg. Population: 1,145,200 (1997). Area: 647,797 sq. km/250,116 sq. mi. —**Manitoban** *adj, n*

Manitoba, Lake lake in S Manitoba, Canada. Area: 4,659 sq. km/1,798 sq. mi.

manitou /mánni too/, **manitu, manito** /-tō/ (*plural* **-tos**) *n* a supernatural force or spirit believed by Algonquian peoples to suffuse various living things and inanimate objects [Late 16C. < Narraganset *manittówock*.]

Manitoulin Island /mánni tòolin-/ world's largest freshwater island, in the Manitoulin Islands, Lake Huron, between the United States and Canada. Area: 2,766 sq. km/1,068 sq. mi.

manitu *n* RELIG = **manitou**

Manizales /mánni thàalayss/ city in west-central Colombia. Population: 358,194 (1997 estimate).

mankind /man kī́nd/ *n* 1 human beings considered collectively (*often considered offensive*) 2 men considered collectively, as distinct from women (*dated*)

manky /mángki/ (**-kier, -kiest**) *adj* dirty, greasy, or otherwise unpleasant (*informal*) ○ *that manky old sweater of his* [Mid-20C. < Scots dialect *mank* 'mutilated, defective', via Old French *manc* 'maimed' < Latin *mancus*.]

Manley /mánnli/, **Michael** (1923–97) Jamaican politician and prime minister (1989–92)

manly /mánnli/ (**-lier, -liest**) *adj* 1 having or showing qualities conventionally thought to be characteristic of or appropriate to a man, especially physical strength or courage 2 considered suitable or appropriate for a man —**manliness** *n*

man-made, manmade /mán máyd/ *adj* made by human beings and not occurring naturally (*often considered offensive*)

Mann /man/, **Heinrich** (1871–1950) German writer

Mann, Thomas (1875–1955) German-born US novelist and critic

manna /mánnə/ *n* 1 DIVINELY PROVIDED SUSTENANCE in the Bible, food provided miraculously to feed the Israelites in the wilderness 2 UNEXPECTED BENEFIT something very welcome or of great benefit that comes unexpectedly 3 SWEET SUBSTANCE FROM ASH TREE a pale-yellow sugary gum exuded by the European ash tree. Use: formerly, as a laxative. 4 SWEET SUBSTANCE FROM TAMARISK TREE a sweet substance exuded by a tamarisk tree when its bark is punctured by a scale insect [Pre-12C. Via late Latin < Hebrew *mān*.]

mannan /mán an, mánnən/ *n* a polysaccharide composed of mannose [Late 19C. < MANNOSE.]

Mannar, Gulf of /mə nàar/ inlet of the Indian Ocean between the tip of S India and W Sri Lanka

manned /mand/ *adj* (*often considered offensive*) 1 having a human crew 2 operated or attended by staff

mannequin /mánnikin/ *n* 1 a usually life-size model of the human body used to display or fit clothes 2 a fashion model (*dated*) 3 ARTS = **lay figure** *n.* 1 [Mid-18C. Via French < Dutch *manneken* (see MANIKIN).]

manner /mánnər/ *n* 1 WAY SOMETHING IS DONE the way in which something is done or happens ○ *His manner of doing things is often a little unconventional.* 2 WAY OF BEING the characteristic way in which somebody behaves ○ *had a capricious manner about him* **3 TYPE** a type or kind ○ *What manner of insect makes this hole?* **4 STYLE OF WORK OF ART** the style in which a work of art is executed ○ *painted in the manner of Vermeer* ■ **manners** *npl* **1 SOCIAL BEHAVIOUR** social behaviour, especially in terms of what is considered correct or unacceptable **2 CUSTOMS AND PRACTICES** the customs and practices of a particular society or period in time [12C. < Anglo-Norman *manere* 'way of handling' < Latin *manuarius* 'of the hand' < *manus* 'hand'.] ○ **in a manner of speaking** in some ways, though not exactly or not in all ways ◇ **to the manner born** naturally adapted to something as though accustomed to it from birth

mannered /mánnərd/ *adj* **1** characterized by affected mannerisms ○ *her mannered tones* **2** behaving in a particular way or having manners of a particular kind (*usually in combination*) ○ *an ill-mannered child*

Mannerheim /mánnər hīm/, **Baron Carl Gustaf Emil** (1867–1951) Finnish army officer and statesman

mannerism[1] /mánnərizəm/ *n* **1** a particular gesture, habit, or way of doing something ○ *one of his odd little mannerisms* **2** affected or exaggerated speech, behaviour, or writing —**manneristic** /mánnə rístik/ *adj* —**manneristically** *adv*

mannerism[2], **Mannerism** *n* a style of art and architecture, predominant in Italy in the late 16th century, characterized by stylized and elongated forms and the pursuit of a representation of idealized beauty —**mannerist** *adj*, *n*

QUICK FACTS ON... MANNERISM

Key dates: 1520–1600
Key locations: W Europe, especially Italy
Key elements: rejection of classicism and naturalism; distortion of forms to express grace and beauty; use of complex compositions, dramatic contrasts in scale, and vivid, harsh colours
Key figures: Jacopo da Pontormo, Rosso Fiorentino, Parmigianino, Il Bronzino, El Greco (painting); Benvenuto Cellini (sculpture); Giulio Romano (architecture, painting)
Key works: *Deposition* (Pontormo) 1525, *The Madonna with the Long Neck* (Parmigianino) 1534–40, *The Burial of Count Orgaz* (El Greco) 1586, *Palazzo del Té*, Mantua, (Romano) 1525?–34, *Perseus and Medea* (Cellini) 1545–54
Key developments: baroque and rococo style, expressionism

mannerless /mánnərləss/ *adj* having or showing bad manners —**mannerlessness** *n*

mannerly /mánnərli/ *adj* well-mannered or polite —**mannerliness** *n*

Mannheim /mánn hīm/ city in SW Germany, on the River Rhine. Population: 317,300 (1994).

Mannheim, Karl (1893–1947) Hungarian-born German sociologist

Mannheim school /mánn hīm-/ *n* a style of orchestral and string playing associated with the rise of the Classical period, developed at the court of Mannheim in the 18th century

mannikin *n* = manikin

manning /mánning/ *n* the supplying of people to do jobs (*often considered offensive*)

Manning /mánning/ river in E New South Wales, Australia. Length: 225 km/140 mi.

Manning, Frederic (1892–1935) Australian-born British writer

Manning, Henry, Cardinal (1808–92) British cleric

mannish /mánnish/ *adj* **1** resembling or suitable for a man rather than a woman (*often considered offensive*) **2** considered characteristic of a man —**mannishly** *adv* —**mannishness** *n*

mannitol /mánni tol/, **mannite** /mánnīt/ *n* a sweet white alcohol found in many plants. Source: mannose. Use: sweetener. [Late 19C. < MANNA.] —**mannitic** /mə níttik/ *adj*

Mannix /mánniks/, **Daniel** (1864–1963) Irish-born Australian cleric

mannose /mánnōss, -nōz/ *n* a six-carbon sugar found in many plant cell walls [Late 19C. < mannite.]

manny /mánni/ (*plural* **-nies**) *n* US a young man employed to look after children (*informal*) [Blend of MAN + NANNY]

mano a mano /mánnō ə mánnō/ *n* (*plural* **manos a manos**) US **1 BULLFIGHT IN WHICH MATADORS TAKE TURNS** a bullfight during which two competing matadors take turns fighting several bulls each **2 FACE-TO-FACE CONFRONTATION** a face-to-face confrontation between opposing people or sides ■ *adj, adv* US **COMPETING DIRECTLY** competing directly with somebody or something [Late 20C. < Spanish, 'hand to hand'.]

manoeuvre /mə noŏvər/ *n* **1 SKILLED MOVEMENT** a movement or action that requires skill or dexterity **2 MILITARY MOVEMENT** a planned movement of one or several military or naval units **3 DEVIOUS ACT** an action, especially a devious or deceptive one, done to gain advantage ○ *one of his little manoeuvres to try to stay in total control* **4 CHANGE OF COURSE** a controlled change of course of a vehicle or vessel ■ **manoeuvres** *npl* **MILITARY EXERCISES** large-scale military exercises used for training or practice ■ *v* (**-vres, -vring, -vred**) **1** *vti* **MOVE SKILFULLY** to move or cause something to move skilfully **2** *vti* **DO MILITARY EXERCISES** to perform or cause somebody or something to perform military manoeuvres **3** *vt* **MANIPULATE** to manipulate somebody or something to gain advantage ○ *trying to manoeuvre her into agreeing* **4** *vi* **BEHAVE DEVIOUSLY** to use devious means in order to gain advantage ○ *the various parties manoeuvring for the leadership* [15C. Via French *manoeuvre* 'manipulation' < Old French *maneuvre* 'manual labour' < medieval Latin *manuoperare* 'work with the hands' < Latin *manus* 'hand'.] —**manoeuvrability** /mə noŏvərə bílləti/ *n* —**manoeuvrable** *adj* —**manoeuvrer** /-vərər/ *n*

man of God *n* **1** a man who is a member of the clergy **2** a saint or godly man

man of letters *n* a man who is a writer or scholar (*formal*)

man of straw *n* **1** an issue or person of little importance or relevance, brought up to be shown as an easily defeatable idea or adversary. US term **straw man** *n*. **2 2** somebody who acts as a front for somebody else's questionable or illegal activities. US term **straw man** *n*. **3**

man of the cloth *n* a man who is a member of the clergy

man-of-war /mán əv wáwr/ (*plural* **men-of-war**), **man o'war** /mánnə wáwr/ (*plural* **men o'war** /ménnə-/) *n* **1** a warship **2** MARINE BIOL = **Portuguese man-of-war**

man-of-war bird *n* BIRDS = **frigate bird**

manometer /mə nómmitər/ *n* an instrument used to measure the pressure of a gas [Mid-18C. < Greek *manos* 'thin, rare'.] —**manometric** /mánnə méttrik/ *adj* —**manometrically** *adv* —**manometry** *n*

manor /mánnər/ *n* **1 NOBLE'S HOUSE AND LAND** a house and the land surrounding it, owned by a medieval noble **2 POLICE DISTRICT** the area for which a particular local police station is responsible (*slang*) **3 PERSONAL TERRITORY** somebody's own local area or territory (*slang*) **4 BUILDING** = **manor house** [13C. Via Anglo-Norman *maner* < Old French *maneir* 'dwelling-place' < Latin *manere* 'remain, stay'.] —**manorial** /mə náwri əl/ *adj*

manor house *n* the residence of the lord or lady of a manor

~~manouvre~~ incorrect spelling of **manoeuvre**

man o'war *n* NAVY = **man-of-war**

man-o'-war bird *n* BIRDS = **frigate bird**

manpower /mán powər/ *n* power in terms of the number of people available or needed to do something

manqué /móngk ay, maaN káy/ *adj* having wanted unsuccessfully to be or do something ○ *an artist manqué* [Late 18C. < French, past participle of *manquer* 'fail, lack'.]

mansard /mán saard, -ərd/ *n* the part of a building enclosed by a mansard roof [Mid-18C. < French, after the architect François *Mansard* (1598–1666).] —**mansarded** *adj*

mansard roof *n* a roof that slopes on all four sides, with each side divided into a gentle upper slope and a steeper lower slope

manse /manss/ *n* a house provided for a church minister by some Christian denominations [Late 15C. < medieval Latin *mansus* 'unit of land' < Latin *manere* 'remain'.]

Mansell /mánss'l/, **Nigel** (*b.* 1953) British motor racing driver

manservant /mán survənt/ *n* (*plural* **menservants** /mén survənts/) *n* a man who is a servant, especially somebody's valet

Mansard roof

Mansfield /mánss feeld/ town in central England. Population: 71,858 (1991).

Mansfield, Jayne (1933–67) US film actor. Born **Vera Jayne Palmer**

Mansfield, Katherine (1888–1923) New Zealand-born British writer. Pseudonym of **Katherine Mansfield Beauchamp**

mansion /mánsh'n/ *n* **1 LARGE HOUSE** a large and stately house **2 DIVISION OF ZODIAC** any one of the 28 divisions of the zodiac through which the Moon passes successively each month ■ **mansions** *npl* **LARGE BUILDING DIVIDED INTO FLATS** a large building that is divided up into separate flats (*often in names of buildings*) [14C. < Old French, 'dwelling-place' < Latin *manere* 'remain'.]

mansion house *n* BUILDING = **mansion** *n*. 1

Mansion House *n* the official residence of the Lord Mayor of London

man-sized, man-size *adj* **1** larger than the ordinary size ○ *a man-sized appetite* **2** the same size as or big enough for a man ○ *a man-sized hole in the fence*

manslaughter /mán slawtər/ *n* the unlawful killing of one human being by another without advance planning (**malice aforethought**)

man's man (*plural* **men's men**) *n* a man who prefers the company of other men to that of women (*informal*)

Manson /mánssən/, **Charles** (*b.* 1934) US cult leader and murderer

mansuetude /mánsswi tyood/ *n* a meek or gentle attitude or behaviour (*archaic*) [14C. Via Old French or directly < Latin *mansuetudo* < *mansuetus* 'tame'. < Latin *mansuetudo* < *mansuetus* 'tame', literally 'accustomed to the hand' < *suescere* 'accustom'.]

Mansura /man soŏra/ city in NE Egypt, in the Nile delta. Population: 371,000 (1992).

manta /mántə/ *n* **1** ZOOL = **manta ray 2** Southwest US a square piece of rough cloth. Use: cape, shawl, horse blanket. [Late 17C. < Spanish, 'blanket' (because the ray is traditionally caught in a blanket-like fish-trap).]

manta ray *n* a large warm-water ray with wide pectoral fins, a long tail, and two fins resembling horns that project from the head. Family: Mobulidae. US term **manta** *n*. 1

Mantegna /man ténnyə/, **Andrea** (1431–1506) Italian painter

mantel /mánt'l/, **mantle** *n* an ornamental frame around a fireplace, usually made of stone or wood [15C. < MANTLE.]

mantelpiece /mánt'l peess/, **mantlepiece** *n* the mantel of a fireplace, especially its projecting top

mantelshelf /mánt'l shelf/ (*plural* **-shelves** /-shelvz/), **mantleshelf** (*plural* **-shelves**) *n* the projecting top of the mantel of a fireplace, used as a shelf

manteltree /mánt'l tree/, **mantletree** *n* a stone or beam that acts as a support for the masonry above a fireplace

mantic /mántik/ *adj* relating to or having powers of divination or prophecy [Mid-19C. < Greek *mantikos* < *mantis* 'prophet' < *mainesthai* 'to rage'.] —**mantically** *adv*

mantid *n* INSECTS = **mantis**

mantilla /man tíllə/ *n* **1** a lace scarf that covers the head and shoulders, often worn by women in church, especially in Spain and Latin America **2** a short light cape [Early 18C. < Spanish, 'little mantle'.]

mantis /mántiss/ (*plural* **-tises** *or* **-tes** /-teez/) *n* a large, usually green insect that feeds on other insects and has a long body, large eyes, and strong grasping front legs that it holds up at rest. Family: Mantidae. [Mid-17C. Via modern Latin < Greek, 'prophet' (see MANTIC).]

mantissa /man tíssə/ *n* the fractional part of a logarithm, to the right of the decimal point [Mid-17C. < Latin, 'makeweight'.]

mantis shrimp *n* MARINE BIOL = **squilla**

mantle /mánt'l/ *n* 1 **SLEEVELESS CLOAK** a loose sleeveless cloak 2 **COVERING** something that envelops or covers something else (*literary*) ○ *a mantle of snow* 3 **TRANSFERRED POSITION** a role or position, especially one that can be passed from one person to another (*formal*) ○ *assumed the mantle of the presidency* 4 **WIRE MESH FOR LIGHT** a small circle of wire mesh in a gas or oil lamp that gives out incandescent light when heated by the flame it surrounds 5 **SHELL-PRODUCING GLAND** a layer of epidermis in a mollusc or brachiopod with glands that secrete a shell-producing substance 6 **FEATHERS** the back, inner-wing, and shoulder-area (**scapular**) plumage of a bird 7 **CENTRAL PART OF EARTH** the part of the Earth or another planet that lies between the crust and core 8 ARCHIT = **mantel** ■ *v* (**-tles, -tling, -tled**) 1 *vt* **COVER** to cover something with a mantle or something resembling a mantle ○ *hilltops mantled with snow* 2 *vi* **FLUSH** to become flushed (*refers to the face*) ○ *His puffy face mantled in angry red blotches.* [Pre-12C. Via Old French *mantel* < Latin *mantellum* 'cloak'.]

mantlepiece *n* = **mantelpiece**

mantleshelf *n* = **mantelshelf**

mantletree *n* TREES = **manteltree**

mantling /mántling/ *n* ornamental drapery round a shield on a coat of arms

man-to-man *adj* 1 honest and intimate and treating somebody as an equal ○ *a man-to-man talk* 2 in sports such as soccer, hockey, or basketball, having each defender of one team mark a corresponding attacker of the other team ○ *man-to-man marking* —**man-to-man** *adv*

Mantoux test /mán too-/ *n* a test to determine whether somebody has ever had the tuberculosis infection and so has a measure of immunity to the disease [Mid-20C. After Charles *Mantoux* (1877–1947), French physician.]

mantra /mántrə/ *n* 1 a sacred word, chant, or sound that is repeated during meditation to facilitate spiritual power and transformation of consciousness 2 an expression or idea that is repeated, often without thinking about it, and closely associated with something ○ *the mantra of marketing being 'new, improved'* [Late 18C. < Sanskrit, 'thought' < *man* 'think'.]

mantrap /mán trap/ *n* an illegal trap set to catch poachers or trespassers on private land, usually in the form of a metal device that snaps shut onto somebody's leg

Mantua /mán choo ə/ city in central N Italy. Population: 52,205 (1993).

manual /mánnyoo əl/ *adj* 1 **USING HANDS** relating to, done with, or involving the hands ○ *manual dexterity* 2 **PHYSICAL** involving physical rather than mental exertion ○ *manual tasks* 3 **OPERATED BY PERSON** operated by human effort rather than by a machine, computer, or type of power ○ *switching to manual control* ■ *n* 1 **HANDBOOK** a book that contains information and instructions about the operation of a machine or how to do something 2 **KEYBOARD PLAYED WITH HANDS** an organ or harpsichord keyboard that is played with the hands alone 3 **RIFLE DRILL** a drill or exercise in the use of a hand-held weapon ○ *cadets practising the manual of arms* [15C. Via French *manuel* or directly < Latin *manualis* 'of the hand' < *manus* 'hand'.] —**manually** *adv*

manual alphabet *n* an alphabet in which finger movements and positions stand for letters, used with other hand signs by hearing-impaired people

manual transmission *n* a vehicle transmission that requires the driver to shift gears using a clutch

manubrium /mə nyóobri əm/ (*plural* **-nubria** /-ri ə/ *or* **-nubriums**) *n* a handle-shaped anatomical part, e.g. the upper part of the sternum or part of the inner ear [Mid-17C. < Latin, 'handle' < *manus* 'hand'.] —**manubrial** *adj*

Manuel I Comnenus /man wél kom néenəss/ (1122–80) Byzantine emperor (1143–80)

manuf., **manufac.** *abbr* 1 manufacture 2 manufactured 3 manufacturer

manufactory /mánnyoo fáktəri/ (*plural* **-ries**) *n* a factory (*archaic*) [Early 17C. < MANUFACTURE.]

manufacture /mánnyoo fákchər/ *v* (**-tures, -turing, -tured**) 1 *vti* **PRODUCE SOMETHING INDUSTRIALLY** to make something into a finished product using raw materials, especially on a large industrial scale ○ *built up a business manufacturing lightweight metal goods* 2 *vt* **MAKE BODY CHEMICAL** to produce a substance needed by the body ○ *Bile is manufactured in the liver.* 3 *vt* **PRODUCE MECHANICALLY** to produce something in the manner of a machine, without creativity 4 *vt* **INVENT** to invent or make something up ○ *manufactured an excuse to get out of the meeting* ■ *n* 1 **PRODUCTION OF GOODS** the production of finished goods from raw materials, especially on a large industrial scale ○ *engaged in the manufacture of arms for the military* 2 **PRODUCT** something that has been produced from raw materials, especially on a large industrial scale 3 **MAKING OF BODY CHEMICAL** the production of a substance needed by the body [Mid-16C. Via French < Italian *manifattura* 'something made by hand' < Latin *manu factum* 'made by hand' < *manus* 'hand'.] —**manufacturable** *adj* —**manufactural** *adj*

manufacturer /mánnyoo fákchərər/ *n* a factory, individual, or organization that produces finished goods from raw materials, especially on a large industrial scale

Manukau City /mánnə kow-/ city in the northwest of the North Island, New Zealand. Population: 254,577 (1997).

Manukau Harbour bay in the northwest of the North Island, New Zealand. Area: 350 sq. km/150 sq. mi.

manumit /mánnyoo mít/ (**-mits, -mitting, -mitted**) *vt* to free somebody from slavery (*formal*) [14C. < Latin *manumittere* < *manu emittere* 'send out from your hand'.] —**manumission** /mánnyoo mísh'n/ *n* —**manumitter** *n*

manure /mə nyóor/ *n* 1 **FERTILIZER MADE FROM DUNG** animal excrement, often mixed with straw, used as fertilizer for soil 2 **FERTILIZER** any fertilizer or compost ■ *vt* (**-nures, -nuring, -nured**) **FERTILIZE WITH MANURE** to spread manure on land or soil to fertilize it [14C. Via Anglo-Norman < Old French *manouvrer* 'work with the hands' < medieval Latin *manuoperare* (see MANOEUVRE).] —**manurer** *n*

manus /máynəss/ (*plural* **-nus**) *n* the wrist and hand of humans or the carpus and forefoot of other vertebrates (*technical*) [Early 16C. < Latin, 'hand'.]

manuscript /mánnyooskript/ *n* 1 **HANDWRITTEN BOOK** a book or other text written by hand, especially one written before the invention of printing ○ *rare medieval manuscripts* 2 **AUTHOR'S ORIGINAL TEXT** an author's text for a book, article, or other piece of written work as it is submitted for publication 3 **HANDWRITING** handwriting as opposed to the printed word ○ *a manuscript version of the text* [Late 16C. < medieval Latin *manuscriptus* 'written by hand' < *scribere* 'write'.]

Manx /mangks/ *adj* **OF ISLE OF MAN** relating to the Isle of Man or its people, language, or culture ■ *n* **OLD ISLE OF MAN LANGUAGE** a language formerly spoken on the Isle of Man, belonging to the Goidelic group of Celtic languages ■ *npl* **MANX PEOPLE** the people of the Isle of Man [Early 16C. Alteration of assumed Old Norse *manskr* < Old Irish *Manu* 'Isle of Man'.] —**Manxman** *n* —**Manxwoman** *n*

Manx cat, **manx cat** *n* a short-haired tailless domestic cat [< the origin of the breed in the Isle of Man]

Manx shearwater *n* a seabird with black plumage on its upper parts and white plumage on its underparts that nests in burrows on rocky islands. Native to: Atlantic. *Puffinus puffinus.*

many /ménni/ CORE MEANING: a considerable number of people or things ○ (det) *Many people own their homes.* ○ (det) *Not many people know about this.* ○ (pron) *Many believe that the matter will never come to trial.* ○ (pron) *Many of you may have heard this.* ○ (adj) *He was among the many visitors to this town.*

1 *det, pron* **A CONSIDERABLE NUMBER** a considerable number of people or things ○ (det) *Many children are in the park today.* ○ (pron) *He is a friend to many.* ○ (pron) *Many of us agree with you.* ○ (adj) *Among his many faults is self-importance.* 2 *det, pron* **A LARGE NUMBER** a large number of people or things (*after 'so', 'too', 'not', 'as' or 'that'*) ○ (det) *She has so many clocks, she can't be sure exactly what time it is.* ○ (det) *I've just seen too many government studies that don't move quickly enough.* ○ (det) *There aren't that many people who would agree with you.* ○ (pron) *Help yourself – you can have as many as you like.* 3 *det* **EACH OF A CONSIDERABLE NUMBER** each of a considerable number (*before 'a', 'an' or 'another'*) ○ *The situation has caused them many a sleepless night.* ○ *We did better than many another regiment.* 4 *pron* **THE MAJORITY** the majority of people ○ *All these advantages should be available to the many – not just the few.* [Old English *manig* < Indo-European, 'many, often']

manyfold /ménni fōld/ *adv US* many times over

manyplies /ménni plīz/ (*plural* **-plies**) *n* ZOOL = **omasum** [Late 18C. < MANY + PLY; from its many folds.]

many-sided *adj* having a large number of sides, aspects, or abilities —**many-sidedness** *n*

many-valued logic *n* a system of logic in which propositions may have values in addition to true or false

manzanilla /mánzə níllə/ *n* a pale dry Spanish sherry [Mid-19C. < Spanish, 'camomile', because its smell resembles camomile.]

Manzoni /man zóni, -dzóni/, **Alessandro Francesco Tommaso Antonio** (1785–1873) Italian novelist, poet, and playwright

MAOI *abbr* monoamine oxidase inhibitor

Maoism /mów izəm/ *n* the Marxist-Leninist doctrines, teachings, and policies of the former Chinese Communist leader Mao Zedong —**Maoist** *n, adj*

Mao jacket /mów-/ *n* a plain tunic-style jacket with a stand-up collar worn by Chairman Mao Zedong and the Chinese people under his regime

Maori /mówri/ (*plural* **-ri**) *n* 1 a member of a Polynesian people living in New Zealand and on the Cook Islands 2 the Austronesian language of the Maori people. Native speakers: 300,000. [Mid-19C. < Maori.] —**Maori** *adj*

Maori oven *n NZ* COOK = **hangi** *n.* 1

Mao suit *n* a style of suit consisting of plain loose-fitting trousers and a tunic-style jacket with a stand-up collar worn by Chairman Mao Zedong and the Chinese people under his regime

Mao Zedong /mów tsay tóong/, **Mao Tse-tung** (1893–1976) Chinese statesman. He was chairman of the Chinese Communist Party (1931–76) and president (1949–67). Known as **Chairman Mao**

map /map/ *n* 1 **GEOGRAPHICAL DIAGRAM** a visual representation that shows all or part of the Earth's surface with geographical features, urban areas, roads, and other details 2 **DIAGRAM OF STARS** a representation of the stars or the surface of a planet, usually in the form of a diagrammatic drawing 3 **DRAWING SHOWING ROUTE OR LOCATION** a diagrammatic drawing of something such as a route or area made to show the location of a place or how to get there 4 MATH = **function** *n.* 6 ■ *vt* (**maps, mapping, mapped**) 1 **CREATE MAP OF** to represent a geographical or other defined area on a map ○ *mapping the heavens* 2 **DISCOVER AND SHOW** to discover something and create a visual representation of it 3 **NOTE GENE SEQUENCE** to determine and record the sequence of encoded information on a gene or chromosome 4 **MATCH SET ELEMENTS** to assign an element in one set to an element in another through a mathematical correspondence [Early 16C. < medieval Latin *mappa (mundi)* 'sheet (of the world)' < Latin *mappa* 'towel'.] —**mappable** *adj* —**mapper** *n* ◇ **on the map** so as to be famous or important (*informal*) ◇ **off the map** so as to be no longer famous or important (*informal*)

map out *vt* to construct something such as a plan in detail

Map /map/, **Mapes** /maps, máy peez/, **Walter** (1140?–1210) English cleric and writer

maple /máyp'l/ *n* 1 **DECIDUOUS TREE WITH WINGED SEEDS** a deciduous tree with winged seeds and lobed leaves. Native to: northern temperate regions. Genus: *Acer.* 2 **WOOD OF MAPLE** the hard wood of the maple tree. Use: furniture, flooring. 3 **SUGAR MAPLE FLAVOUR** the flavour of the processed sap of the sugar maple [Old English *mapul-*]

Maple Leaf *n* the Canadian flag, showing a stylized red maple leaf on a white background between vertical red bars

maple sugar *n* a sugar made by boiling down the sap of the sugar maple

maple syrup *n* a sweet syrup made from the sap of the sugar maple, or from various other sugars and artificially flavoured with maple

mapmaker /máp maykər/ *n* a maker of maps —**mapmaking** *n*

mapping /mápping/ *n* 1 the act or process of making maps 2 MATH = **function** *n.* 6

Mapplethorpe /máyp'l thawrp/, **Robert** (1946–89) US photographer

map projection *n* a representation of or way of representing a three-dimensional object on a two-dimensional surface

Mapuche /ma poóchi/ (*plural* **-che** *or* **-ches**) *n* 1 a member of a subgroup of the Araucanian people of central Chile and areas of W Argentina 2 the Araucanian language of the Mapuche people. Native speakers: 400,000. [Early 20C. < Mapuche, 'country people'.] — **Mapuche** *adj*

Maputo /ma poótō/ capital of Mozambique, in the southeast of the country on the Indian Ocean. Population: 1,098,000 (1991 estimate).

maquette /ma két/ *n* a small model of a planned sculpture or architectural work [Early 20C. Via French < Italian *macchietta* 'little spot' < Latin *maculare* 'to spot'.]

maquillage /máki àazh/ *n* make-up, or the art of applying make-up [Late 19C. < French, < *maquiller* 'make up the face' < Old French *masquiller* 'to stain'.]

maquis /ma keé/ (*plural* **-quis**) *n* 1 DENSE COASTAL VEGETATION dense shrubby vegetation of Mediterranean coastal regions 2 **maquis**, **Maquis** FRENCH RESISTANCE the underground French Resistance movement that fought against the German occupying forces during World War II 3 **maquis**, **Maquis** FRENCH RESISTANCE FIGHTER a member of the World War II French Resistance movement [Mid-19C. Via French < Italian *macchia* 'spot' < Latin *macula* (from the vegetation's resemblance to spots).]

Maquisard /máki zaàr, -zaàrd/ *n* HIST = **maquis** *n*. 3 [Mid-20C. < French, < MAQUIS.]

mar /maar/ (**mars, marring, marred**) *vt* to spoil or detract from something [Old English *merran* 'waste, spoil' < Germanic]

mar. *abbr* 1 maritime 2 married

Mar. *abbr* March

mara /ma raà/ *n* a large long-legged member of the cavy family that resembles a hare. Native to: Argentine pampas. *Dolichotis patagonum*. [Mid-19C. < American Spanish *mará*.]

Mara /maàra/ *n* in Buddhism, a force of evil, sometimes conceived of as a being [Late 19C. < Sanskrit *Māra* 'death' < *mr̥*- 'die'.]

marabou /márra boo/, **marabout** *n* 1 LARGE AFRICAN STORK a large carrion stork with dark-grey plumage and a short naked neck with a pink pouch at the front. Native to: Africa. *Leptoptilos crumeniferus*. 2 MARABOU FEATHERS down taken from the tail of the marabou. Use: trimming for clothes. 3 RAW SILK a fine white raw silk [Early 19C. Via French < Arabic *murābit* 'holy man', because the stork was considered holy by Muslims.]

marabout /márra boo/ *n* 1 a Muslim hermit, monk, or holy man, especially in North Africa 2 the tomb or a shrine of a marabout that is often a destination for pilgrims [Early 17C. Via French < Portuguese *marabuto* < Arabic *murābit* < *ribāt* 'frontier post', because hermits would go to such places to gain merit.]

maraca /ma ráka/ *n* a percussion instrument usually shaken in pairs as an accompaniment to Latin American music and consisting of a hollow rattle filled with small pebbles or beans [Early 17C. Via Portuguese *maracá* < Tupi *maráka*.]

Maracaibo, Lake /márra kībō/ largest lake in South America, in NW Venezuela, connected by a channel with the Gulf of Venezuela. Area: 13,300 sq. km/5,140 sq. mi.

Maracay /márra káy/ city in N Venezuela, near Lake Valencia. Population: 354,196 (1990).

Maradona /marra dónna/, **Diego** (*b.* 1960) Argentinian football player

marae /ma rí/ (*plural* **-rae**) *n* NZ a meeting place for Maoris [Late 18C. < Polynesian.]

maraging steel /maà rayjing-/ *n* a strong, low-carbon steel formed by ageing and heating and containing up to 25 per cent nickel with lesser amounts of titanium, aluminium, and niobium [< blend of MARTENSITE + AGE]

Marajó /márra zhō/ island in NE Brazil, in the delta of the River Amazon. Area: 40,100 sq. km/15,500 sq. mi.

Marañón /márra nyōn/ river in N South America, flowing northwards from the Andes into the Amazon River. Length: 1,415 km/879 mi.

maranta /ma ránta/ *n* a tropical plant widely cultivated for its variegated thin leaves. Native to: America. Genus: *Maranta*. [Early 19C. < modern Latin, after Bartolomeo *Maranta*, 16C Italian herbalist.]

marasca /ma ráska/ *n* a cultivated variety of sour cherry tree whose fruit is used to make maraschino. *Prunus cerasus*. [Mid-19C. < Italian, alteration of *amarasca* < *amaro* 'bitter'.]

maraschino /márra skeénō, -sheénō/ (*plural* **-nos**) *n* a sweet liqueur distilled from marasca cherries [Late 18C. < Italian, < *marasca* (see MARASCA).]

maraschino cherry *n* a bright red cherry preserved in a sweet syrup flavoured with maraschino or an imitation of this. Use: in cocktails, cake decoration.

marasmus /ma rázməss/ *n* a gradual wasting away of the body, generally associated with severe malnutrition or inadequate absorption of food and occurring mainly in young children [Mid-17C. < modern Latin < Greek *marasmos* 'decay' < *marainein* 'waste away'.] —**marasmic** *adj*

Marat /má raa/, **Jean-Paul** (1743–93) French journalist and politician

Maratha /ma raàta/, **Maratta, Mahratta** *n* a member of a people living mainly in the Deccan plateau in the Indian state of Maharashtra [Mid-18C. < Marathi *marāthā*, or Hindi *marhattā* < Sanskrit *Mahārāṣṭra* 'great kingdom'.]

Marathi /ma raàti/, **Mahratti** *n* an official language of the Indian state of Maharashtra, belonging to the Indo-Iranian branch of Indo-European. Native speakers: 70 million. ■ *adj* relating to the Indian state of Maharashtra, or its people, language, or culture [Late 17C. < Marathi *marāthī* < Sanskrit *Mahārāṣṭrī* < *Mahārāṣṭra* 'great kingdom'.]

marathon /márrath'n, -thon/ *n* 1 LONG-DISTANCE RACE a long-distance footrace run over a distance of 42.195 km/26 mi. 385 yds 2 LENGTHY AND DIFFICULT TASK a lengthy and difficult task, event, or activity 3 ENDURANCE TEST a test of endurance, especially in a competition ◇ *a dance marathon* [Late 19C. After MARATHON.] —**marathoner** *n*

Marathon /márra thon/ plain in SE Greece that was the site of an important Athenian military victory over the Persians in 490 BC

Maratta *n* PEOPLES = **Maratha**

maraud /ma ráwd/ *vti* to rove around carrying out violent attacks or looking for plunder, or to raid a place in search of plunder [Late 17C. < French *marauder* < *maraud* 'rogue, vagabond'.] —**marauder** *n*

marauding /ma ráwding/ *adj* roving around carrying out violent attacks or looking for plunder ◇ *marauding pirates cruising the high seas*

marble /maàrb'l/ *n* 1 DENSE CRYSTALLIZED ROCK a form of limestone transformed through the heat and pressure of metamorphism into a dense, variously coloured, crystallized rock used in building, sculpture, and monuments 2 MARBLE SCULPTURE a sculpture made from marble ◇ *the Elgin Marbles* 3 SOMETHING RESEMBLING MARBLE something that resembles marble in being cold, hard, smooth, or white (*literary*) 4 SMALL GLASS BALL a small hard ball, usually made of glass, used in the game of marbles ■ **marbles** *npl* 1 GAME WITH GLASS BALLS a game, played mainly by children, in which small hard balls are rolled on the ground with the aim of hitting the opponent's ball (+ *singular verb*) 2 WITS mental abilities or sense of reality (*informal*) ■ *vt* (**-bles, -bling, -bled**) COLOUR SOMETHING WITH MOTTLED STREAKS to colour something, usually paper, with a mottled streaks to give the appearance of marble ◇ *an 18th-century volume with marbled endpapers* [12C. Via Old French *marbre* < Latin *marmor* < Greek *marmaros* 'hard, shiny stone' (influenced by *marmairein* 'shine').] —**marbly** *adv*

Marble Bar town in NW Western Australia. Population: 384 (1991).

marble cake *n* a cake made with two different flavours of sponge, often chocolate and plain, dropped into the same tin and very lightly mixed before baking

Marblehead /maàrb'l hed/ town in NE Massachusetts. Population: 19,971 (1996 estimate).

marblewood /maàrb'l woŏd/ *n* 1 a mottled black-banded wood. Use: cabinet-making. 2 a tree of the ebony family that produces marblewood. Native to: Malaysia. *Diospyros marmorata*.

marbling /maàrbling/ *n* 1 COLOURING LIKE MARBLE colouring or mottling that looks like marble 2 CREATION OF MARBLED EFFECT the process of applying mottled streaks of colour

to paper or other material to create the appearance of marble 3 STREAKS OF FAT IN MEAT streaks of fat in lean meat

Marburg disease /maàr burg-/ *n* a severe viral infection causing high fever, haemorrhaging, rashes, vomiting, and often death [Mid-20C. After *Marburg*, Germany.]

marc /maark/ *n* 1 the skins and pulp remaining after grapes, apples, or other fruit have had their juice pressed out, e.g. for wine-making 2 brandy made from the skins and pulp that remain when grapes and other fruit have had their juice pressed out [Early 17C. < French, < *marcher* 'trample' (see MARCH[1]).]

Marc /maark/, **Franz** (1880–1916) German painter

marcasite /maàrka sīt, -zeét/ *n* 1 a yellowish iron sulphide mineral. Use: jewellery. 2 polished steel or other white metal cut with facets and used in jewellery, or something made from this [15C. Via medieval Latin *marcasita* < Arabic *markaṣīṭa* < Persian or Aramaic.] —**marcasitical** /maàrka síttik'l/ *adj*

marcato /maar kaàtō/ *adv* with a heavy accentuation of individual notes that are often also played in a detached style (*musical direction*) [Mid-19C. < Italian, 'marked, accented'.] —**marcato** *adj*

marc brandy *n* BEVERAGES = **marc** *n.* 2

Marceau /maar sō/, **Marcel** (*b.* 1923) French mime artist

marcel /maar sél/ *n* marcel, marcel wave a women's hairstyle, popular in the 1920s, consisting of regular, deep waves created with curling tongs ■ *vt* (**-cels, -celling, -celled**) to style somebody's hair in a marcel [Late 19C. After the French hairdresser François *Marcel* Grateau (1852–1936).] —**marcelled** *adj* —**marceller** *n*

marcescent /maar séss'nt/ *adj* remaining attached to a plant when withered [Early 18C. < Latin *marcescent-*, present participle of *marcescere* 'begin to wither' < *marcere* 'wither, decay'.]

march[1] /maarch/ *v* 1 *vi* WALK IN MILITARY FASHION to walk with regular formalized movements of the arms and legs at a steady rhythmic pace, often in a military formation 2 *vti* MOVE IN MILITARY-STYLE FORMATION to proceed somewhere, or direct a body of people or troops to proceed somewhere, on foot, in a disciplined military and military-style formation ◇ *marched the troops off to battle* 3 *vi* SET OFF to set off, usually on foot, usually a military campaign or expedition ◇ *Our orders are to march at daybreak.* 4 *vi* WALK WITH DETERMINATION to walk quickly and with an air of determination ◇ *She marched into the shop and demanded to see the manager.* 5 *vt* FORCE SOMEBODY TO GO SOMEWHERE to force somebody to go along with you somewhere, usually by physically taking hold of the person ◇ *She grabbed hold of the boys and marched them into the house.* 6 *vi* WALK TO PROTEST OR PUBLICIZE to take part in a protest march or demonstration ◇ *A huge crowd marched in support of the needy.* 7 *vi* PASS STEADILY to pass steadily or inexorably ◇ *Time marches on.* ■ *n* 1 ACT OR EXTENT OF MARCHING a journey on foot, especially under military discipline or in a military formation ◇ *After a four-hour march, they arrived back at the camp.* 2 MARCHING SPEED a particular speed or style of marching ◇ *The funeral procession advanced at a slow march.* 3 WALK FOR PROTEST OR PUBLICITY a political demonstration or protest, in the form of an organized walk in procession by a group of people to a place in support of a particular cause ◇ *Police estimated that about 20,000 people took part in yesterday's march against world hunger.* 4 MOVEMENT FORWARDS a steady forwards movement or progression ◇ *the march of time* 5 MUSIC IN MARCHING RHYTHM a piece of music especially written or suitable to accompany marching, usually with a regular emphatic beat and in a military style [14C. < Old French *marchier* < Germanic, 'measure off'.] —**marcher** *n* ◇ **on the march** 1 proceeding somewhere on foot, especially purposefully and in a military or military-style formation 2 advancing or making progress ◇ **steal a march on somebody** to do or achieve something before somebody else, thereby gaining an advantage over the person

march[2] /maarch/ *n* 1 BORDER AREA BETWEEN TWO COUNTRIES an area along the border between two countries, especially an outlying area that is subject to territorial disputes and hostile incursions 2 BORDER a border between countries or territories ■ *vi* SHARE BORDER to share a border with a country or territory (*formal*) [13C. < Old French *marche* < Germanic.]

March *n* the third month of the year in the Gregorian calendar, made up of 31 days [< Anglo-Norman, < Latin *Martius (mensis)* '(month) of Mars']

Marches, The /máarchəz/ historical name for the borderlands between England and Scotland, and England and Wales

marchesa /maar káyzə/ (*plural* **-se** /-zay/) *n* an Italian marchioness, holding the title either in her own right or as the wife or widow of a marchese [Late 18C. < Italian, feminine of *marchese* (see MARCHESE).]

marchese /maar káy zay/ (*plural* **marchesi** /-zi/) *n* an Italian marquis, a nobleman of a rank above count [Early 16C. Via Italian < medieval Latin *(comes) marcensis* 'count of the border' < *marca* 'border' < Germanic.]

marching orders *npl* **1** orders to soldiers to set off on a military campaign or expedition **2** a summary dismissal or request to leave (*informal*)

marchioness /máarshə néss, máar shənəss/ *n* in the United Kingdom and Ireland, a noblewoman of a rank above countess, or the wife or widow of a marquess [Late 16C. < medieval Latin *marchionissa* < *marca* 'borderland' < Germanic.]

marchland /máarch land, -lənd/ *n* an area along the border between two countries [Mid-16C. < MARCH[2].]

marchpast /máarch paast/ *n* a formal parade by troops or other people who march in formation past somebody who reviews them from a stand or other vantage point

Marciano /máarssi áanō, -ánnō/, **Rocky** (1923–69) US boxer. Born **Rocco Francis Marchegiano**

Marconi /maar kṓni/, **Guglielmo** (1874–1937) Italian electrical engineer

Marconi rig *n* SAILING = **Bermuda rig** [After Guglielmo MARCONI] —**Marconi-rigged** *adj*

Marcos /máark oss/, **Ferdinand** (1917–89) Philippine national leader and president-dictator of the Philippines (1965–86)

Mardal Waterfall /máardəl-/ waterfall in SW Norway. Height: 517 m/1,696 ft.

Mardi Gras /máardi graá/ (*plural* **Mardis Gras** /máardi graá/) *n* **1** the name given in France and many other countries to Shrove Tuesday, the last day before the beginning of Lent in the Christian calendar **2** in some places, a carnival held or ending on the day before the beginning of Lent in the Christian calendar, often celebrated with costumes, parades, balls, and other festivities [< French, 'fat Tuesday' (the day on which rich foods were used up before Lent)]

Marduk /máardook/ *n* in Babylonian mythology, the god who defeated the great goddess Tiamat and created humankind

mare[1] /mair/ *n* an adult female horse, or adult female of a species closely related to the horse such as the zebra [Old English *mearh* < Indo-European, 'horse']

mare[2] /máa ray/ (*plural* **-ria** /-ri ə/) *n* any large dark plain on the surface of the Moon, or any similar area on Mars [Mid-19C. < Latin, 'sea'.]

mare clausum /máa ray klówssoom/ *n* a sea or other area of water that is under the jurisdiction of one country and closed to all others [< Latin, 'closed sea', title of a work (1635) by John Selden defending the right of a single nation to control parts of the sea]

Mare Crisium /máa ray kríssi əm/ lunar lowland plain visible in the northeast quadrant of the Moon. Area: 170,900 sq. km/66,000 sq. mi.

Mare Fecunditatis /-fe kúndi táatiss/ lunar lowland plain visible in the southeast quadrant of the Moon

Mare Frigoris /-fri gáwriss/ lunar lowland plain visible near the Moon's north pole

Mare Humorum /-hyoo máwrəm/ lunar lowland plain visible in the southwest quadrant of the Moon, approximately 420 km/260 mi. across

Mare Imbrium /-ímbri əm/ lunar lowland plain visible in the northwest quadrant of the Moon, approximately 1,250 km/775 mi. across

mare liberum /máa ray léebəroom/ *n* an area of sea that is open to the ships of all countries [Mid-17C. < Latin, 'free sea', title of a treatise (1609) by Dutch jurist Hugo Grotius, defending free access to the ocean by all nations.]

maremma /mə rémmə/ (*plural* **-me** /-mee/) *n* an area of marshy ground near the sea, especially in Italy [Mid-19C. Via Italian < Latin *maritimus* < *mare* 'sea'.]

Mare Nectaris /-nek táariss/ lunar lowland plain visible in the southeast quadrant of the Moon, approximately 400 km/250 mi. across

mare nostrum /máa ray nóstroom/ *n* an area of sea that is under the jurisdiction of one country or shared by two or more countries [< Latin, 'our sea' (name for the Mediterranean)]

Mare Nubium /-nyóobi əm/ lunar lowland plain visible in the southwest quadrant of the Moon

Mare Orientale /-áwri en táali/ lunar lowland plain on the side of the Moon that is furthest from the Earth

Mare Serenitatis /-sə rénni táatiss/ lunar lowland plain visible in the northeast quadrant of the Moon, approximately 580 by 680 km/360 by 425 mi

mare's nest *n* **1** a discovery at first thought to be important or valuable but subsequently found to be an illusion, a hoax, or valueless **2** a complicated or muddled situation

mare's-tail *n* **1** a long wispy strand of cloud (*usually plural*) **2** a water plant with erect, partially submerged, narrow-leaved stems. *Hippuris vulgaris.*

Mare Tranquillitatis /-trang kwílli táatiss/ lunar lowland plain visible in the northeast quadrant of the Moon, approximately 650 by 900 km/405 by 560 mi. Apollo 11 made the first crewed lunar landing there in 1969.

Mareva injunction /mə ráyvə in j/ *n* an injunction allowing a court to freeze a defendant's assets to prevent them from being transferred abroad [Late 20C. After *Mareva* Compania Naviera SA, first plaintiff to be granted an injunction of this type.]

Marfan syndrome /máar fan-/, **Marfan's syndrome** /máar fans-/ *n* a hereditary disorder that affects the body's connective tissues [Mid-20C. After the French paediatrician A. B. J. *Marfan* (1858–1942).]

marg /maarj/ *n* margarine (*informal*) [Mid-20C. Shortening.]

marg. *abbr* **1** margin **2** marginal

Margaret /máargrət, -ərət/, **St** (1046?–93) queen of Scotland as wife of Malcolm III

Margaret (of Anjou) (1430?–82) queen of England as wife of Henry VI

Margaret, Princess, Countess of Snowdon (*b.* 1930). younger sister of Elizabeth II, queen of the United Kingdom.

margaric /maar gárrik/, **margaritic** /máargə ríttik/ *adj* resembling a pearl or pearls (*formal*) [Early 19C. Via French *margarique* < Greek *margaron* 'pearl'.]

margarine /máarjə réen, máargə-/ *n* a yellow fat that usually consists of a blend of vegetable oils or animal fats mixed with water, flavouring, and other ingredients [Late 19C. < French.]

margarita /máargə réetə/ *n* a cocktail made with tequila, lemon or lime juice, and an orange-flavoured liqueur, typically served in a chilled glass whose rim has been dipped into salt [Early 20C. < Spanish, < the name *Margarita.*]

Margarita /máar gə réetə/ island in N Venezuela, in the Caribbean Sea. Population: 117,700 (1979). Area: 1,072 sq. km/414 sq. mi.

margaritic *adj* = **margaric**

Margasirsa /máargə séersə/ *n* in the Hindu calendar, the ninth month of the year, made up of 29 or 30 days and occurring around November to December

Margate /máar gayt/ town in SE England. Population: 56,734 (1991).

margay /máar gay/ *n* a wild cat slightly larger than a domestic cat with colouring and markings similar to those of a leopard. Native to: rainforests of Central and South America. *Felis wiedi.* [Late 18C. Via French < Portuguese *maracaj'a* < Tupi *marakaya.*]

marge /maarj/ *n* margarine (*informal*) [Early 20C. Shortening.]

margin /máarjin/ *n* **1** BLANK SPACE AT SIDE OF PAGE a blank space on the left or right edge, or the top or bottom, of a written or printed page ○ *comments scribbled in the margin* **2** LINE DOWN SIDE OF PAGE a straight line drawn down the left- or right-hand side of a page to separate a narrow section off from the main part ○ *Draw a margin about one inch from the edge of the paper.* **3** OUTER EDGE the edge of something, especially the outer edge, or the area close to it ○ *dark-green leaves with reddish margins* **4** PART FURTHEST FROM CENTRE that part of anything, e.g. a society or organization, that is least integrated with its centre, least often considered, least typical, or most vulnerable (*often plural*) ○ *people living on the margins of society* **5** LIMIT a boundary indicating the limit beyond which something should not go or below which something should not fall (*often plural*) ○ *beyond the margins of good taste* **6** DIFFERENCE BETWEEN ONE AMOUNT AND ANOTHER the difference between two amounts or scores ○ *She won by a margin of only 270 votes.* **7** ADDITIONAL AMOUNT an amount over and above what is strictly necessary included, e.g. for safety reasons or to allow for mistakes or delays ○ *They left no margin for error.* **8** PROFIT the profit on a transaction, or the amount by which the price of something exceeds its cost ○ *We've cut our margins to the absolute bare minimum.* **9** LOWEST VIABLE PROFIT the minimum profit that a business must make in order to remain viable **10** DIFFERENCE BETWEEN LOAN AND COLLATERAL VALUES the difference between the face value of a loan and the value of the collateral given to secure the loan **11** BROKER'S LOSS COVER the amount deposited with a stockbroker by a client to cover possible losses on transactions made on account **12** *Aus* SUPPLEMENT TO WAGES OR SALARY an additional payment made to a worker in recognition of specific skills or to compensate for extra responsibilities ■ *vt* **1** CREATE MARGIN AROUND to create a margin around something **2** PLACE AS DEPOSIT WITH BROKER to place something such as collateral with a broker as a deposit [14C. < Latin *margin-*.]

marginal /máarjin'l/ *adj* **1** IN A MARGIN written in a margin **2** SMALL IN SCALE very small in scale or importance ○ *You can ignore any marginal discrepancies you find.* **3** IRRELEVANT not of central importance or relevance ○ *In what follows, I have ignored everything that is marginal to my main thesis.* **4** ON THE FRINGE operating or existing on the fringes of a group or movement ○ *a marginal group with no political base* **5** VERY LOW at or close to the lowest acceptable or viable limit ○ *a marginal standard of living* **6** WON BY SMALL MAJORITY won by only a small majority at a previous election and therefore likely to produce a closely fought contest in any subsequent election ○ *a marginal constituency* **7** BARELY COVERING COSTS barely able to cover the costs of production when sold or when producing goods for sale **8** DIFFICULT TO CULTIVATE difficult to cultivate and therefore only brought into use if profits are high enough to make it worth the effort ○ *marginal land* ■ *n* MARGINAL SEAT a marginal political constituency —**marginality** /máarji nálləti/ *n*

marginal cost *n* the additional cost of producing one more item for sale

marginalia /máarji náyli ə/ *npl* notes written in a margin

marginalize /máarjinə līz/ (**-izes, -izing, -ized**), **marginalise** (**-ises, -ising, -ised**) *vt* to take or keep somebody or something away from the centre of attention, influence, or power —**marginalization** /máarjinə lī záysh'n/ *n*

marginally /máarjinəli/ *adv* **1** very slightly **2** only just or barely

marginal utility *n* the increase in utility prompted by one extra unit of a given service or product

marginate /máarji nayt/ *vt* (**-ates, -ating, -ated**) to add a margin to something, or provide something with a margin ■ *adj* **marginate, marginated** with a border or edge of a different colour or pattern ○ *a marginate leaf* —**margination** /máarji náysh'n/ *n*

margin of safety *n* **1** the difference between budgeted output level and the break-even output level **2** the difference, e.g. in terms of time or space, between a dangerous situation and a state of safety ○ *Following another motor vehicle too closely and at high speed diminishes a driver's margin of safety.*

margravate /máargrəvət, -vayt/, **margraviate** /maar gráyvi ət, -ayt/ *n* **1** the territory ruled by a margrave or margravine **2** the rank or position of a margrave or margravine

margrave /máar grayv/ *n* formerly, a German nobleman of a rank equivalent to a British marquess [Mid-16C. < Middle Dutch *markgrave* 'count of the border'.] —**margravial** /maar gráyvi əl/ *adj*

margraviate *n* = **margravate**

margravine /máargrə veen/ *n* formerly, a German noblewoman who was the wife or widow of a margrave or who held the rank in her own right [Late 17C. < Dutch *markgravin*, feminine of *markgraaf* 'margrave'.]

marguerite /máargə réet/ *n* a widely cultivated garden plant with white or pale yellow petals radiating from a yellow centre. Native to: Canary Islands. *Chrysanthemum frutescens.* [Early 17C. < French, < the female name *Marguerite.*]

Mari /máari/ (*plural* **-ri** *or* **-ris**) *n* **1** a member of a people living around western and central stretches of the Volga

River in Russia, and in Kazakhstan **2** the Finno-Ugric language of the Mari people. Native speakers: 700,000. [Early 20C. < Mari.] —**Mari** *adj*

maria plural of **mare**²

mariachi /maári áachi, márri-/ (*plural* **-chis**) *n* **1 MEXICAN STREET BAND** a Mexican street band usually consisting of stringed instruments, especially violins and guitars, but sometimes also including brass instruments and singers **2 MARIACHI BAND MEMBER** a member of a mariachi band **3 MARIACHI MUSIC** traditional Mexican folk music as played by a mariachi band [Mid-20C. < Mexican Spanish.]

~~mariage~~ incorrect spelling of **marriage**

mariage blanc /márri aazh blaaN/ (*plural* **mariages blancs**) *n* a marriage that has not been consummated [< French, 'white marriage']

mariage de convenance /márri aazh də koNvə naaNss/ (*plural* **mariages de convenance**) *n* = **marriage of convenience** [< French, 'marriage for expediency or propriety']

Marian /máiri ən/ *adj* **1 OF VIRGIN MARY** relating to, characteristic of, or devoted to Mary, the mother of Jesus Christ **2 OF MARY** relating to any Mary other than the Virgin Mary, especially Mary Queen of Scots or Queen Mary I of England ■ *n* **DEVOTEE OF VIRGIN MARY** a person who is especially devoted to Mary, the mother of Jesus Christ

Mariana Islands /márri áanə-/ island group in the W North Pacific Ocean, east of the Philippines, comprising Guam and the Commonwealth of the N Mariana Islands. Population: 226,500 (2000). Area: 958 sq. km/370 sq. mi.

Marianao /maárya naá ō/ city in W Cuba. Population: 133,016 (1989).

Mariana Trench /márri áanə-/ deepest ocean trench in the world, in the W Pacific Ocean, east of the Mariana Islands. Depth: 11,000 m/36,200 ft.

Maria Theresa /mə reé ə tə ráyzə/ (1717–80) archduchess of Austria and queen of Hungary and Bohemia (1740–80)

Maria Theresa dollar *n* a silver coin minted in 1780 and used in the Middle East [After MARIA THERESA]

mariculture /márri kulchər/ *n* the cultivation of sea animals and plants in their usual habitats, generally for commercial purposes [Early 20C. < Latin *mari-* (stem of *mare* 'sea') + CULTURE.] —**maricultural** *adj* —**mariculturist** *n*

Marie Antoinette /márri antwə nét/ (1755–93) queen of France as wife of Louis XVI

Marie Byrd Land /maári búrd-/ region of W Antarctica, on the Amundsen Sea, east of the Ross Ice Shelf

Marie de Médicis /mə reé də méddi chee/ (1573–1642) queen and regent of France (1600–17)

Marie Galante /maa reé gaa lóNt/ island in the French West Indies, in the Caribbean Sea, a dependency of Guadeloupe. Population: 3,757 (1982). Area: 158 sq. km/61 sq. mi.

Marie-Louise (of Austria) /mə reé loo eéz-/ (1791–1847) empress of France as wife of Napoleon I

marigold /márri gōld/ *n* a common garden plant with scented stems. Flowers: yellow, orange. Native to: tropical America. Genus: *Tagetes.* [14C. < the name *Mary* (referring to the Virgin Mary) + Old English *golde* 'marigold, corn marigold'.]

marigram /márri gram/ *n* a printed record of tide levels at a particular place [Late 19C. < Latin *mari-*, stem of *mare* 'sea'.]

marigraph /márri graaf, -graf/ *n* an instrument for recording tide levels [Mid-19C. < Latin *mari-*, stem of *mare* 'sea'.]

marijuana /márri waánə, -hwaánə/, **marihuana** *n* **1** the dried flowers and leaves of the Indian hemp plant, smoked or eaten as a drug **2** the Indian hemp plant that is the source of the drugs marijuana and cannabis. *Cannabis sativa.* [Late 19C. < Mexican Spanish *mariguana.*]

marimba /mə rímbə/ *n* a large musical instrument like a xylophone, with resonators made from metal or hollow gourds beneath the bars, used especially in African and Latin American music [Early 18C. < Portuguese, < Bantu.] —**marimbist** *n*

marina /mə reénə/ *n* a harbour specially designed to cater for pleasure boats and their owners [Early 19C. < Italian or Spanish, 'seashore' < Latin *marinus* < *mare* 'sea'.]

marinade /márri náyd, -nayd/ *n* a liquid or paste made with ingredients such as vinegar, wine, oil, spices, and herbs, in which food is soaked or allowed to stand to give extra flavour and tenderness before cooking ■ *vti* COOK = **marinate** [Early 18C. Via French < Italian *marinare* or Spanish *marinar* (see MARINATE).]

marinara /márri naárə/ *adj* **1** made with tomatoes and garlic, often with other ingredients such as onions, parsley, capers, or olives, to serve on pasta or as a pizza topping ○ *marinara sauce* **2** served with marinara sauce ○ *spaghetti marinara* [Mid-20C. < Italian *alla marinara* 'in sailor style' < *marinaro* 'sailor' < *marino* 'marine' < Latin *marinus* < *mare* 'sea'.] —**marinara** *n*

marinate /márri nayt/ (**-nates, -nating, -nated**), **marinade** /-nayd/ (**-nades** *or* **-nading, -naded**) *vti* to soak or stand, or leave food to soak or stand, in a marinade before cooking [Mid-17C. < Italian *marinare* or Spanish *marinar* 'pickle in brine' < Latin *(aqua) marina* 'sea (water)', feminine of *marinus* < *mare* 'sea'.] —**marination** /márri náysh'n/ *n*

Marinduque /márrən dóoki/ island in NW Philippines, south of Luzon and east of Mindoro. Population: 173,715 (1980). Area: 960 sq. km/370 sq. mi.

marine /mə reén/ *adj* **1 OF THE SEA** relating to, found in, or living in the sea **2 NAUTICAL** relating to ships or sailing **3 OF SEAGOING SOLDIERS** relating to soldiers who serve at sea as well as on land ■ *n* **1 marine, Marine SEAGOING SOLDIER** a soldier who serves at sea as well as in the air and on land, e.g. a member of the Royal Marines **2 NATION'S COMMERCIAL FLEET** a fleet of merchant or naval ships and their crews (*formal*) **3 SEA SCENE** a painting or photograph of a seascape, ship, or scene at sea [14C. Via French < Latin *marinus* < *mare* 'sea'.] ◇ **tell that to the marines** used to express disbelief (*slang*)

marine architect *n* somebody specially trained to design ships —**marine architecture** *n*

marine biology *n* the branch of biology that deals with the plants and animals of the oceans —**marine biologist** *n*

Marine Corps *n* a branch of the US armed forces, trained to operate on land, at sea, and in the air, and especially in amphibious assaults

marine engineer *n* a person who attends to the engines and other heavy machinery of a ship or other offshore structure

mariner /márrinər/ *n* a sailor or navigator of vessels at sea [13C. Via Anglo-Norman or French *marinier* < Latin *marinarius* < *marinus* 'marine' < *mare* 'sea'.]

LITERARY LINK ***The Rime of the Ancient Mariner***, a poem (1798) by Samuel Taylor Coleridge. A cautionary tale of sin and redemption, it describes a curse placed on a sailor after he kills an albatross that has led his ship out of danger. The vessel is becalmed and the rest of the crew die of thirst. After his rescue, the sailor is compelled to repeat his story for the remainder of his days.

mariner's compass *n* a navigational ship's compass set within a binnacle, used in manual navigating of a vessel

marine snow *n* small particles of organic and inorganic debris that drift down from the upper layers of the ocean to the bottom

Marinetti /márri nétti/, **Filippo Tommaso** (1876–1944) Italian writer and political activist

marinière /márrini áir/ *adj* cooked with a little wine, herbs, and chopped onion or shallot, in a closed pan, so that the main ingredient, which is usually mussels, is partly poached and partly steamed [< French, 'sailor-style']

Mariolatry /máiri óllətri, márri-/ *n* extreme devotion to Mary, the mother of Jesus Christ [Early 17C. < Latin *Maria* 'Mary'.] —**Mariolater** *n* —**Mariolatrous** *adj*

Mariology /máiri ólləji, márri-/ *n* the study of the doctrines and beliefs concerning Mary, the mother of Jesus Christ [Mid-19C. < Latin *Maria* 'Mary'.] —**Mariological** /máiri ə lójjik'l, márri-/ *adj* —**Mariologist** *n*

marionette /márri ə nét/ *n* a puppet operated by means of strings attached to its hands, legs, head, and body [Early 17C. < French, 'little Mary' < *Marion.*]

mariposa /márri pṓzə, -pṓssə/ *n* a bulbous plant of the lily family. Flowers: brightly coloured, tulip-like. Native to: W North America. Genus: *Calochortus.* [Mid-19C. < Spanish, 'butterfly' (from its brightly coloured flowers).]

Marist /máirist/ *n* **1** a member of either of two Roman Catholic orders, the Society of Mary or Marist Fathers, and the Little Brothers of Mary or Marist Brothers **2** *NZ* a teacher or pupil in a school run by the Marist Brothers [Late 19C. < French *mariste* < *Marie* 'Mary'.] —**Marist** *adj*

Maritain /márri táN, -táyn/, **Jacques** (1882–1973) French philosopher

marital /márrit'l/ *adj* **1** relating to marriage or the marriage of a particular couple **2** relating to a husband or husbands (*formal*) [15C. < Latin *maritalis* < *maritus* 'married'.] —**maritally** *adv*

maritime /márri tīm/ *adj* **1 OF THE SEA** relating to the sea, shipping, sailing in ships, or living and working at sea **2 CLOSE TO SEA** situated or living close to the sea **3 INFLUENCED BY SEA** influenced by the sea, and therefore generally temperate and with relatively small variations in seasonal temperatures [Mid-16C. Directly or via French < Latin *maritimus* < *mare* 'sea'.]

Maritime Provinces /márri tīm-/, **Maritimes** collective name for the E Canadian provinces of New Brunswick, Nova Scotia, and Prince Edward Island —**Maritimer** *n*

Maritsa /mə reétsə/ river in SE Europe, in the Balkan Peninsula. Length: 480 km/300 mi.

Mariupol /məri óopəl/ city in SE Ukraine, on the Sea of Azov. Population: 510,000 (1996).

Marius /márri əss, máiri-/, **Gaius** (157?–86 BC) Roman general and statesman

Marivaux /márri vō/, **Pierre Carlet de Chamblain de** (1688–1763) French playwright and novelist

marjoram /maárjərəm/ *n* a herb with aromatic leaves and small purple or white flowers. Use: seasoning in cookery and salads. Native to: Mediterranean. *Origanum majorana.* [14C. Via Old French *marjorane* < medieval Latin *majorana.*]

mark¹ /maark/ *n* **1 SPOT, SCRATCH, OR DIRT** a coloured, discoloured, or dirty patch, a scratch, dent, or impression, either deliberately or accidentally made, that makes a usually small area of a surface visibly different from the rest ○ *The hot plate left a mark on the table.* **2 SYMBOL** a recognizable sign or symbol used, e.g. to indicate ownership, the quality or origin of goods, or punctuation in a piece of writing (*often in combination*) ○ *a question mark* **3 SUBSTITUTE FOR SIGNATURE** a cross or other symbol used in place of a signature by somebody who cannot write **4 INDICATION OF FEELING** an action, gesture, or other outward sign of somebody's feeling or attitude ○ *a mark of respect* **5 SIGN OF INFLUENCE OR INVOLVEMENT** something that is evidence of somebody's or something's influence on or involvement in something ○ *He left his mark on the firm.* **6 IDENTIFYING FEATURE OR CHARACTERISTIC** a distinctive and identifying feature or characteristic ○ *That perfect finish is the mark of the true professional.* **7 INDICATION OF CORRECTNESS OR QUALITY** a number, letter, or percentage indicating somebody's assessment of something, e.g. the correctness or quality of answers to examination questions or somebody's performance in a gymnastic or ice-skating contest ○ *She always gets top marks in English.* **8 INDICATOR OF POSITION OR EXTENT** any object, sign, or line used to indicate the position, extent, or amount of something ○ *the high-water mark* **9 AMOUNT** the amount, distance, or level reached by something ○ *The temperature is way above the 80 degree mark.* **10 STANDARD** the desired or required standard for something ○ *Your work is simply not up to the mark these days.* **11 TYPE** a model or variety, e.g. of a car, aircraft, or weapon, usually distinguished from earlier or later models by a number **12 TARGET** a target or something that somebody aims at with a weapon ○ *He missed the mark.* **13 GOAL** a goal or standard that somebody wishes to achieve **14 VICTIM OF CRIME** the victim or intended victim of a theft or swindle (*slang*) ○ *a soft mark* **15 GUIDE TO POSITION OR DIRECTION** a conspicuous object or another point of reference that serves as a visual guide to somebody when proceeding in a particular direction or carrying out an action **16 STARTING LINE** the starting line for a race **17 INSTANCE OF PLAYER SHOUTING MARK** in a game of rugby, an instance of a player within his or her 22 m line shouting 'mark' when intercepting the ball from an opponent's kick, entitling him or her to a free kick **18 CATCH OF THE BALL** in Australian Rules football, a catch made after an opponent kicks the ball at least 9 m/10 yds without it touching the ground or another player **19 MIDDLE OF STOMACH** in boxing, the middle of an opponent's stomach **20** SPORTS = **jack**¹ *n.* 5 **21 INDICATOR OF WATER'S DEPTH** a knot or other marker used to indicate intervals of fathoms on a sounding line **22 COMMON**

LAND in medieval Germany and England, land held in common by the members of a community ■ **marks** *npl* RUNNER'S STARTING POSITION a runner's individual starting position for a race ■ *v* 1 *vti* MAKE OR GET SPOTS OR SCRATCHES to make or get a coloured or discoloured patch, dent, scratch, or other mark on something, either accidentally or deliberately ○ *The mugs have marked the table.* 2 *vt* PUT MARK OR SYMBOL ON to put a recognizable sign or symbol or write on something, e.g. to show ownership, to indicate price, or to give a warning or instruction ○ *All items of clothing must be clearly marked with the student's name.* 3 *vt* MAKE CLEARLY IDENTIFIABLE to make something clearly visible, recognizable, or traceable by putting a mark on it ○ *I've marked on the map where our house is.* 4 *vt* INDICATE LOCATION to be an indicator showing where something is situated, how far it extends, or where an event took place ○ *This monument marks their last resting place.* 5 *vt* BE OR INDICATE POINT OF CHANGE to indicate that a significant point in time or in a process has been reached ○ *It marks the end of an era in British theatre.* 6 *vt* GIVE PROMINENCE TO EVENT to do something to celebrate or give prominence to a particular event ○ *a party to mark their 50th anniversary* 7 *vt* SELECT FOR SPECIAL ATTENTION to select or destine somebody or something for particular attention or treatment ○ *He was always marked out for success.* 8 *vt* CHARACTERIZE to characterize, distinguish, or set somebody or something apart in some way ○ *The originality of her approach marks her as a candidate of real distinction.* 9 *vt* ASSESS AND INDICATE QUALITY OR CORRECTNESS to assess the quality or correctness of something and indicate the assessment by means of a mark such as a tick or cross, a letter, number, or percentage ○ *marking exam papers* 10 *vt* ASSESS THE WORK OF to assess the quality or correctness of the work or performance of somebody and indicate the assessment by means of a mark ○ *marked him high on the test* 11 *vt* TAKE NOTICE OF to pay attention to something or somebody (*often a command*) ○ *Mark my words, this'll make them sit up and take notice.* 12 *vt* STAY CLOSE TO PLAYER in games such as football and hockey, to stay close to an attacking player in the opposing team to prevent the player from receiving the ball or scoring 13 *vti* KEEP SCORE to keep a note of the score 14 *vt* MAKE A MARK in Australian Rules football, to catch the ball after it has been kicked at least 9 m/10 yds without having touched the ground or another player ■ *interj* SHOUT FROM RUGBY PLAYER PASSED BALL in a game of rugby, the shout made by a player who catches the ball within his or her own 22 m line in order to gain a free kick [Old English *mearc* 'boundary, marker' < Indo-European, 'boundary'] ◇ **make your mark** to achieve recognition or success, usually in a particular field ◇ **mark you** used to call somebody's attention to a point or remark that you are making ◇ **on your marks** used as a command to runners to take up their starting positions ready for the start of a race ◇ **quick** *or* **slow off the mark** quick *or* slow to begin, react to, or understand something ◇ **up to the mark** of an acceptable standard or quality, or at an acceptable level ◇ **wide of the mark, off the mark** inaccurate or incorrect

SPELLCHECK Do not confuse ***mark*** with ***marque***, which has a similar sound. Beware: your spellchecker will not catch this error.

mark down *vt* 1 MAKE WRITTEN NOTE to make a written note of something somewhere 2 LOWER PRICE to lower the price of something 3 GIVE LOWER MARK to reduce the mark given to something or somebody in a test, examination, or contest ○ *You get marked down for bad spelling.* 4 CHARACTERIZE to form an opinion as to the character or likely behaviour of somebody

mark off *vt* 1 SEPARATE ONE AREA FROM ANOTHER to separate one area from another by means of a boundary line or barrier 2 MAKE DIFFERENT to make somebody or something different from others ○ *Her mathematical ability marks her off from the rest of her class.* 3 PUT A MARK ON to put a mark such as a tick, cross, or line beside, through, or around something, to show that it has been dealt with or to highlight it

mark out *vt* 1 to draw lines or use some other method to indicate the boundaries and divisions of something, especially the playing area for a game or a racecourse 2 to make somebody or something noticeably different from and often superior to others

mark up *vt* 1 INCREASE PRICE to increase the price of something, especially to provide the seller with a profit 2 INCREASE MARKS AWARDED to increase the marks awarded to somebody in a test, examination, or contest 3 MARK CORRECTIONS AND INSTRUCTIONS ON TEXT to prepare a piece of written work for printing or rekeying by making corrections to it or adding instructions to the typesetters or keyboarders

mark[2] /maark/ *n* 1 MONEY = **Deutschmark** 2 a former unit of currency in England and Scotland 3 a former unit of weight for gold and silver [Old English *marc*, a unit of weight < Germanic]

Mark *n* the second of the gospels in the Bible in which the life and teachings of Jesus Christ are described, traditionally attributed to St Mark

Mark /maark/, **St** (*fl.* 1st century) apostle

marka /múrkə/ see table at **currency** [< Serbo-Croatian, < German *Mark* 'mark' (currency)]

Marka /múrkə/ town in SE Somalia, on the Indian Ocean. Population: 70,000 (1985 estimate).

markdown /maárk down/ *n* a reduction in price

marked /maarkt/ *adj* 1 NOTICEABLE very noticeable ○ *a marked contrast* 2 SINGLED OUT singled out for surveillance, suspicion, hostility, or an unpleasant fate ○ *a marked man* 3 WITH MARK ON BACK having a concealed identifying mark that makes it easier to use when cheating in card games or performing conjuring tricks ○ *marked cards* 4 WITH DISTINCTIVE LINGUISTIC FEATURE having an extra or less usual distinctive linguistic feature —**markedness** /maárkidnəss/ *n*

markedly /maárkidli/ *adv* to a significant extent

marker /maárkər/ *n* 1 INDICATOR an object or sign that indicates the position or presence of something or the direction in which somebody is to go 2 SOMETHING THAT MAKES MARKS something used to make marks, especially a felt-tip pen 3 ASSESSOR a person who assesses examination papers or student exercises 4 SCORER a recorder or record of the score in certain games, e.g. snooker and billiards 5 PLAYER MARKING ANOTHER in games such as football and hockey, a player who stays close to an attacking player in the opposing team to prevent the player from receiving the ball or scoring

market /maárkit/ *n* 1 GATHERING FOR BUYING AND SELLING a gathering of people who sell things, especially food or animals, in a place open to the public or other buyers, especially a gathering that is held regularly ○ *a cattle market* 2 MARKET BUILDING OR PLACE a building or open space where a market is regularly held 3 COLLECTION OF SHOPS OR STALLS a number of small shops or stalls, housed in the same building and sometimes all selling the same type of goods, belonging to different, independent traders 4 SHOP a shop, especially one that sells goods or food of a particular type 5 SUPPLY AND DEMAND the whole area of economic activity where buyers are in contact with sellers and in which the laws of supply and demand operate ○ *market forces* 6 BUYING AND SELLING OF PARTICULAR COMMODITY the trade in, or buying and selling of, a particular commodity ○ *the futures market* 7 REGION OR GROUP AS CUSTOMERS a geographical area or a section of the population, considered from the point of view of the amount of goods that can be sold to it ○ *the teenage market* 8 DEMAND the demand for a particular type of goods or service being offered for sale ○ *You've got to go out and create a market if you want to succeed.* 9 TOTAL AMOUNT OF PRODUCT SOLD the total amount of a particular product sold within a particular geographical area or over a particular period of time 10 STOCK MARKET a stock market ○ *Prices rose on the New York and Chicago markets this morning.* 11 TRADING IN STOCKS trading in stocks, shares, and commodities ○ *The market was very slow this morning but picked up later.* 12 PRICES OR EXCHANGE RATES the prices or rates of exchange offered for stocks, shares, or commodities ○ *The market fell this morning but rallied later.* ■ *v* 1 *vt* OFFER FOR SALE to offer something for sale, or sell something, especially by using advertising and other techniques to attract buyers ○ *If this is marketed in the right way, it'll sell very well.* 2 *vi Malaysia, Singapore* SHOP AT A MARKET to go shopping at a market [Pre-12C. Via Old French dialect < Latin *mercatus* < the past participle of *mercari* 'buy' < *merx* 'goods'.] —**marketer** *n* ◇ **come onto the market** to become available for customers to buy ◇ **in the market (for something)** interested in buying or ready to buy something ◇ **on the market** available for customers to buy ◇ **put something on the market** to offer something for sale

marketable /maárkitəb'l/ *adj* 1 SUITABLE FOR SELLING fit to be sold ○ *a highly marketable property* 2 IN DEMAND in demand and therefore relatively easy to sell ○ *skills that are readily marketable* 3 CONVERTIBLE INTO CASH able to be converted into cash quickly, but at a price that is determined by the market in that commodity ○ *marketable value* —**marketability** /maárkitə bílləti/ *n* —**marketableness** *n* —**marketably** *adv*

market basket *n US* 1 a shopping trolley 2 a selection of foods representing the theoretical requirements of a household of 3.2 people or a family of four, the cost of which is a factor in cost-of-living statistics

market economy *n* an economy where prices and wages are determined mainly by the market and the laws of supply and demand, rather than being regulated by a government

marketeer /maárki teér/ *n* 1 a buyer or seller in a market 2 an advocate or supporter of a specific type of market (*usually in combination*) ○ *a free marketeer*

market garden *n* a plot of ground or small farm where fruit, vegetables, and sometimes flowers are grown for sale rather than for the grower's own use —**market gardener** *n* —**market gardening** *n*

marketing /maárkiting/ *n* the business activity of presenting products or services in such a way as to make them desirable

marketing board *n Can, UK* an organization set up by a government to promote and regulate the sale of a particular agricultural product, e.g. grain, dairy products, or poultry

marketing mix *n* the particular mixture of marketing techniques, e.g. pricing, packaging, and advertising, used to promote the sale of a product

market leader *n* a company or brand that has a very large, or the largest, share of the market for a particular product

market maker *n* a dealer who buys and sells securities such as shares

market order *n* an order instructing a broker to buy or sell an asset immediately at the best prevailing price

marketplace /maárkit playss/ *n* 1 OPEN SPACE FOR MARKET an open space where a market is held 2 SPHERE OF TRADING the commercial sphere where buying and selling takes place and the laws of supply and demand operate 3 SET-UP WHERE IDEAS CAN BE DISCUSSED a forum in which ideas are exchanged, discussed, and compete for recognition

market price *n* the price at which something is currently being bought by the majority of customers

market research *n* the gathering and analysis of information about what people want or like or what they actually buy —**market researcher** *n*

market share *n* the proportion of the total sales of a product secured by one particular company or brand

market town *n* a town in which a market is held regularly, usually the chief town of a farming area

market value *n* the amount that a seller could expect to obtain for property or goods sold on the open market

markhor /maár kawr/ (*plural* **-khors** *or* **-khor**) *n* the largest wild goat, which has a reddish-brown coat, spiral horns, and a shaggy beard on the male. Native to: Himalayas. *Capra falconeri.* [Mid-19C. < Persian *mār-kwār* 'serpent-eater'.]

marking /maárking/ *n* 1 MARK OR MARKS a mark or pattern of marks that occurs naturally, e.g. on an animal's coat (*often plural*) 2 AIRCRAFT IDENTIFYING MARK an identifying mark, usually a coloured symbol, on an aircraft (*often plural*) 3 ASSESSMENT AND GRADING OF WRITTEN WORK a teacher's correction and assessment of students' written work 4 WRITTEN WORK TO BE MARKED a quantity of written work that has to be corrected and assessed

marking ink *n* an ink used for writing on such things as clothes and bed linen because it does not wash out

markka /maár kaa, maárkə/ (*plural* **-kaa** /-kaa/) *n* see table at **currency** [Early 20C. Via Finnish < Swedish *marka*.]

Markova /maar kővə/, **Dame Alicia** (*b.* 1910) British ballerina. Born **Lillian Alicia Marks**

Markov chain /maár kof-/ *n* a random process in which events are discrete rather than continuous, and the future development of each event is independent of all historical events, or dependent only on the immediately preceding event [See MARKOV PROCESS]

Markov process /maárkof-/ *n* a continuous random process in which the probability of occurrence of each random event in a series is independent of all historical events, or dependent only on the immediately preceding event [After A. A. *Markov* (1856–1922), Russian mathematician.]

Markownikoff's rule /maar kóvnikofs-/ *n* a rule that describes the order of addition of segments of a halogen acid to an ethylenic compound [After Vladimir Vasilevich *Markownikoff* (1838–1904), Russian chemist]

Marks /maarks/, **Simon, 1st Baron Marks of Broughton** (1888–1964) British retailing magnate

marksman /maárksmən/ (*plural* **-men** /-mən/) *n* **1** an accurate shooter of something, especially a firearm **2** somebody considered from the point of view of his or her ability to shoot accurately —**marksmanship** *n*

markswoman /maárkswoòmən/ (*plural* **-men** /-wimin/) *n* **1** a woman who is able or trained to shoot accurately, especially with a firearm **2** a woman considered from the point of view of her ability to shoot accurately

⚡**mark-up** *n* **1** the difference between the manufacturing cost or wholesale price of an item and its selling price **2** the addition of coding for layout and style to the text in a document

marl[1] /maarl/ *n* a naturally occurring fine crumbly mixture of clay and limestone, often containing shell fragments and sometimes other minerals. Use: fertilizer, water softener. ■ *vt* to add marl to soil as a fertilizer [14C. Via Old French *marle* < medieval Latin *margila* < Latin *marga*, after *argilla* 'white clay'.] —**marlacious** /maar láyshəss/ *adj* —**marly** *adj*

marl[2] /maarl/ *vt* to bind something with a light two-stranded rope [Early 18C. < Dutch *marlen* 'keep binding' < Middle Dutch *marren* 'to bind'.]

Marlborough /maàrlbərə/ **1** town in SW England. Population: 17,771 (1991). **2** administrative region in the NE of the South Island, New Zealand. Population: 40,242 (1996).

Marlborough, John Churchill, 1st Duke of (1650–1722) English general

Marley /maárli/, **Bob** (1945–81) Jamaican musician. Full name **Robert Nesta Marley**

marlin /maárlin/ (*plural* **-lins** *or* **-lin**) *n* **1** a large game fish with a very long thin upper jaw, like a spear. Native to: warm regions of the Atlantic and Pacific oceans. Family: Istiophoridae. **2** the flesh of a marlin as food [Early 20C. Shortening of *marlinspike*; from the shape of its upper jaw.]

marline /maárlin/, **marlin** *n* a light two-stranded rope, used especially for binding around larger ropes to prevent them from fraying [15C. < Dutch *marlijn* 'binding line', *marling* 'binding' < Middle Dutch *marren* 'to bind'.]

marlinespike /maárlin spīk/, **marlinspike** *n* a pointed metal tool used to separate strands of rope that are being spliced [Early 17C. Alteration (influenced by MARLINE) of *marlingspike* < MARL[2] + SPIKE[1].]

marlite /maár līt/ *n* a rock with the same composition as marl but with a harder, more resistant texture [Late 18C. < MARL[1].] —**marlitic** /maar líttik/ *adj*

Marlowe /maárlō/, **Christopher** (1564–93) English playwright

marmalade /maármə layd/ *n* a clear or thick preserve made with citrus fruits, usually containing the shredded rind of the fruit, and traditionally made with bitter Seville oranges ■ *adj* describes cats with orange fur or orange fur streaked with yellow or brown [15C. Via French *marmelade* 'quince jam' < Portuguese *marmelada* < *marmelo* 'quince' < Greek *melimēlon* 'honey-apple', a kind of apple grafted onto the quince.]

marmalade plum *n* FOOD = **sapote** *n.* 2

marmalade tree *n* a tree with brownish edible fruit (**marmalade plums**). Native to: Central America, Mexico, S United States. *Calocarpum sapota.*

Marmara, Sea of /maármərə/, **Marmora, Sea of** inland sea in NW Turkey separating the European and Asian parts of the country, connected with the Black Sea by the Bosporus and with the Aegean Sea by the Dardanelles. Area: 11,350 sq. km/4,382 sq. mi.

marmite /maár mīt/ *n* a deep earthenware or metal cooking pot with a close-fitting lid, used for making soups, stews, or stock [Early 19C. Via French < Old French, 'hypocritical' < *marmouser* 'to murmur' + *mite* 'cat', imitations of sounds.]

Marmora, Sea of = **Marmara, Sea of**

marmoreal /maar máwri əl/ *adj* made of marble, or like marble, especially in being white, cold, or aloof and impressive (*literary*) [Late 18C. < Latin *marmoreus* < *marmor* (see MARBLE).] —**marmoreally** *adv*

marmoset /maármə zét, -zet/ (*plural* **-sets** *or* **-set**) *n* a small monkey that has soft thick fur, tufts of fur around its head and ears, a long tail, and clawed digits. Native to: Central and South America. Family: Callithricidae. [14C. < French *marmouset* 'grotesque figure'.]

marmot /maármət/ (*plural* **-mots** *or* **-mot**) *n* a large brownish stout-bodied rodent of the squirrel family that lives on the ground and in burrows. Native to: North America, Europe, N Asia. Genus: *Marmota.* [Early 17C. < French *marmotte.*]

Marne /maarn/ river in NE France, flowing into the River Seine near Paris. Length: 523 km/325 mi.

marocain /márrə kayn, -káyn/ *n* a ribbed crepe fabric [Early 20C. < French, 'Moroccan'.]

Maronite /márrə nīt/ *adj* belonging or relating to the Christian Uniat Church of the Lebanon, an Eastern Catholic church [Early 16C. < medieval Latin *Maronita*, after the 4C Syrian hermit *Maro.*] —**Maronite** *n*

Maroochydore /maroóchee dawr/ town in SE Queensland, Australia. Population: 36,406 (1996).

maroon[1] /mə roón/ *n* **1** a deep purplish-red colour tinged with brown **2** a small explosive device that makes a loud noise and is used for giving distress or warning signals [Late 18C. Via French *marron* 'large sweet chestnut' < medieval Greek *maraon.*] —**maroon** *adj*

maroon[2] /mə roón/ *vt* **1 LEAVE IN LONELY PLACE** to put somebody ashore on a lonely island or coast and leave the person there with no means of escape **2 LEAVE ISOLATED** to leave somebody somewhere with no means of getting away ■ *n* **1 maroon, Maroon DESCENDANT OF PEOPLE ESCAPED FROM SLAVERY** a descendant of people escaped from slavery in Guyana and the remoter parts of the Caribbean **2 MAROONED PERSON** a person who has been marooned, especially on a desert island [Mid-17C. < French *marron* 'fugitive from slavery', shortening of American Spanish *cimarrón* 'wild, untamed', probably < *cima* 'peak'.]

maroquin /márrə keén, -kin, -kwin/ *n* morocco leather, used especially for bookbindings and shoes [Early 16C. < French, < *Maroc* 'Morocco'.]

Marq. *abbr* **1** Marquess **2** Marquis

marque /maark/ *n* a brand or make of product, especially a make of luxury or high-performance items [Early 20C. < French, < *marquer* 'to mark' < Germanic.]

SPELLCHECK See ***mark***.

marquee /maar keé/ *n* **1 LARGE TENT** a very large tent with straight sides that can be rolled up or removed, used for large gatherings such as parties, meetings, sales, and exhibitions **2** *US, Can* **COVERING LIKE ROOF** a permanent canopy, often of metal and glass, projecting out over the entrance to a large building such as a hotel or theatre ■ *adj US* **HAVING PUBLIC APPEAL** having public appeal or considered in connection with public appeal ○ *a team with no marquee names* ○ *a star with great marquee value* [Late 17C. Alteration of French *marquise* 'canopy over a nobleman's tent' (see MARQUISE).]

Marquesas Islands /maar káyssəss-/ group of volcanic islands in French Polynesia, in the South Pacific Ocean. Population: 7,538 (1988). Area: 1,274 sq. km/492 sq. mi.

marquess /maárkwiss/ *n* in Great Britain and Northern Ireland, a nobleman ranking between a duke and an earl [15C. < Old French *marchis* < *marche* (see MARCH[2]).] —**marquessate** *n*

Marquet /maár kay/, **Albert** (1875–1947) French artist

marquetry /maárkitri/, **marqueterie** *n* **1** designs or pictures made of thin pieces of wood, metal, shell, or other materials, inlaid in a wood veneer and often applied as decoration to pieces of furniture **2** the craft of making marquetry designs or pictures [Mid-16C. < French *marqueterie* < *marqueter* 'variegate' < *marquer* 'to mark'.]

Márquez /maár kez/ ➧ **García Márquez, Gabriel**

marquis /maárkwiss, -keé/ (*plural* **-quises** *or* **-quis** /maar keéz/) *n* **1** in various European countries, a nobleman ranking above a count **2** a marquess [14C. < Old French, alteration of *marchis* (see MARQUESS).] —**marquisate** /maárkwizit, -zayt/ *n*

marquise /maar keéz/ *n* **1 NOBLEWOMAN** in various European countries, a noblewoman ranking above a countess, or the wife or widow of a marquis **2 POINTED OVAL GEM** a gem cut into the shape of a pointed oval and usually faceted **3 RING WITH POINTED OVAL** a ring set with a pointed oval gem or a cluster of stones arranged in a pointed oval shape [Early 17C. < French, feminine of MARQUIS.]

marquisette /maárki zét, maárkwi-/ *n* a fine woven fabric, often cotton or silk. Use: curtains, mosquito nets. [Early 20C. < French, 'little marquise'.]

~~**marrage**~~ incorrect spelling of **marriage**

Marrakesh /márrə késh/, **Marrakech** city in W Morocco. Population: 745,541 (1994).

marram /márrəm/, **marram grass** *n* a variety of grass that grows on sandy shores and is often planted to prevent erosion of sand dunes. Genus: *Ammophila.* [Mid-17C. < Old Norse *marálmr* 'sea haulm'.]

Marrano /mə raánō/ (*plural* **-nos**) *n* in the Middle Ages, a Jew from Spain or Portugal who converted to Christianity under duress and without conviction, and who continued to practise Judaism in secret [Late 16C. < Spanish, 'pig' (from the Jewish prohibition against pork).]

marriage /márrij/ *n* **1 LEGAL RELATIONSHIP BETWEEN SPOUSES** a legally recognized relationship, established by a civil or religious ceremony, between two people who intend to live together as sexual and domestic partners **2 PARTICULAR MARRIAGE RELATIONSHIP** a married relationship between two particular people, or an individual's relationship with their spouse **3 JOINING IN MARRIAGE** the joining together in marriage of two people **4 MARRIAGE CEREMONY** the ceremony in which two people are joined together formally in marriage **5 UNION OF TWO THINGS** a close union, blend, or mixture of two things ○ *Civilization is based on the marriage of tradition and innovation.* **6 KING AND QUEEN OF SAME SUIT** a combination of the king and queen of the same suit, in card games such as pinochle and bezique [13C. < French *mariage* < *marier* (see MARRY).]

marriageable /márrijəb'l/ *adj* suitable or ready for marriage, or old enough to be married —**marriageability** /márrijə bílləti/ *n* —**marriageableness** *n*

marriage bureau *n* an organization that sets up introductions and meetings between single people who are looking for somebody to marry

marriage counselling, marriage guidance *n* advice given by professionals to help married couples who are having difficulties in their relationship

marriage lines *npl* a record of legal marriage, with the names of those marrying, the time and place, and other details (*informal*)

marriage of convenience *n* a marriage between two people that is intended to serve a practical, financial, or political purpose and is not based on their love for each other [Translation of French *mariage de convenance*]

married /márrid/ *adj* **1 HAVING A SPOUSE** having a wife or husband ○ *married people* **2 JOINED IN MARRIAGE** joined together in marriage ○ *get married* **3 RELATING TO MARRIAGE** arising out of or connected with marriage ○ *her married name* **4 COMPLETELY DEDICATED** completely dedicated to something and devoting a lot of time and effort to it ○ *married to her job* ■ **marrieds** *npl* **MARRIED PEOPLE** people who are married ○ *young marrieds*

marron glacé /márron glássay, márroN-/ (*plural* **marrons glacés** /márron glássay, márroN-/) *n* a chestnut cooked and preserved in sugar syrup, drained and then coated with a sugar glaze finish [< French, 'iced chestnut']

marrow /márrō/ *n* **1 LARGE LONG VEGETABLE** a large long cylindrical vegetable with a tough green or green and yellow rind, creamy-white flesh, and a core of seeds that is usually scraped out before it is cooked and eaten. US term **marrow squash** *n.* 1 **2** (*plural* **-rows** *or* **-row**) **MARROW PLANT** a plant in the cucumber family that produces marrows as fruit. *Cucurbita pepo.* US term **marrow squash** *n.* 2 **3 SOFT TISSUE IN BONES** soft red or yellow fatty tissue that fills the central cavities of bones **4 ESSENCE** the essence, core, or key part of something (*literary*) [Old English *mærh* < Indo-European] ◇ **to the marrow (of your bones)** used to emphasize how intensely or deeply somebody is affected by something, especially the cold or an unpleasant experience ○ *I was chilled to the marrow.*

marrowbone /márrō bōn/ *n* a hollow bone that contains edible marrow, traditionally considered to be a culinary delicacy

marrowfat /márrō fat/, **marrowfat pea** *n* a particularly large type of pea, or the pea plant on which it grows [Mid-18C. < MARROW 'substance like tallow, obtained by boiling down marrow', which the pea's texture resembles.]

marrow squash *n US* **1** FOOD = **marrow** *n.* 1 **2** PLANTS = **marrow** *n.* 2

marry /márri/ (**-ries, -rying, -ried**) *v* **1** *vti* **TAKE SOMEBODY IN MARRIAGE** to commit yourself to somebody, or yourselves to each other, formally in marriage **2** vt JOIN IN MARRIAGE to officiate at somebody's marriage ceremony and give legal sanction or a religious blessing to the marriage **3** vt GIVE IN MARRIAGE to give somebody, usually a child or ward, to somebody in marriage, or bring about his or her marriage to somebody **4** vt ACQUIRE BY MARRIAGE to acquire something, especially money, by marrying somebody who has it ○ *wanted to marry wealth and power, and got both* **5** vti COMBINE SUCCESSFULLY to combine successfully, or match things with other things that they combine successfully with ○ *The meat and the spices marry well.* **6** vti = **marry up 7** vt MATCH TWO PIECES OF ROPE TOGETHER to match two pieces of rope together, especially before splicing them together [13C. Via French *marier* < Latin *maritare* < *maritus* 'married person, husband'.] —**marrier** n

marry into vt to become part of something, or gain something, through marriage

marry off vt to find a husband or wife for somebody, especially a child of yours, often to serve your own ends or to free yourself from responsibility for the person

marry up vti to fit and join together, or make two things fit and join together

marrying /márri ing/ adj likely or inclined to get married

Mars /maarz/ n **1** in Roman mythology, the god of war and the father of Romulus, the founder of Rome. Greek equivalent **Ares 2** the third smallest planet in the solar system and the fourth planet from the Sun. See table at **planet**

Marsala /maar saála/ n a sweet or dry dark red fortified wine from Sicily [Early 19C. After the Sicilian port of *Marsala*.]

Marsalis /maar saáliss/, **Wynton** (b. 1961) US musician and bandleader

Marsden /máarzdən/, **Samuel** (1765–1838) British-born Australian cleric and magistrate

Marseillaise /máar say éz, -áyz, máarssə láyz/ n the French national anthem

marseille /maar sáy/, **marseilles** /maar sáy, -sáylz/ n a heavy cotton fabric with a raised pattern. Use: bedspreads. [Mid-18C. After MARSEILLES.]

Marseilles /maar sáy/, **Marseille** port in SE France, on the Gulf of Lions. Population: 1,230,936 (1990).

marsh /maarsh/ n an area of low-lying waterlogged land, often beside water, that is poorly drained and liable to flood, difficult to cross on foot, and unfit for agriculture or building [Old English *merisc* < Germanic] —**marshiness** n —**marshy** adj

Marsh /maarsh/, **Graham** (b. 1944) Australian golfer

Marsh, Dame Ngaio (1899–1982) New Zealand writer and theatre director

Marsh, Rodney (b. 1947) Australian cricketer

marshal /máarsh'l/ n **1** HIGH-RANKING OFFICER the highest-ranking officer in some armed forces **2** SOMEBODY IN CHARGE OF EVENT somebody in charge of or controlling an event or gathering such as a parade, ceremony, race meeting, or sports competition **3** CIRCUIT JUDGE'S ASSISTANT a trained lawyer who assists a judge on circuit **4** HIGH ROYAL COURT OFFICIAL a high official in a royal court, formerly a military adviser and commander for the monarch, but nowadays having a ceremonial role **5** US FEDERAL LAW ENFORCEMENT OFFICER a US federal law enforcement officer who carries out court orders in a federal judicial district **6** CITY LAW OFFICER a municipal law enforcement officer in some US cities **7** SENIOR FIRE OR POLICE OFFICER the head of the fire or police service in some US cities ■ v (**-shals, -shalling, -shalled**) **1** vt ARRANGE to arrange things in an appropriate order so that they can be used effectively ○ *marshal your thoughts* **2** vti GATHER AND ORGANIZE TROOPS to gather troops together and organize them, or gather together and organize, before embarking on a military campaign or expedition **3** vt GATHER TOGETHER to gather people together and organize them into an effective body ○ *marshal your supporters* **4** vt GUIDE OR LEAD to guide or lead somebody carefully or in an officious or ceremonious way **5** vti ACT AS MARSHAL to act as a marshal at something such as a ceremony, parade, or sports event [13C. < Old French *mareschal* 'royal court official' < Germanic, 'groom', literally 'horse-servant'.] —**marshalcy** n —**marshaller** n —**marshalship** n

Marshall /máarsh'l/, **George Catlett** (1880–1959) US military and statesman

Marshall, Sir John Ross (1912–88) New Zealand statesman

marshalling yard n an area occupied by many parallel railway tracks, where railway wagons are made up into trains

Marshall Islands

Marshall Islands island republic in the central N Pacific Ocean, east of the Caroline Islands. Capital: Majuro. Population: 60,652 (1997). Area: 181 sq. km/70 sq. mi.

Marshall Plan /maarsh'l-/ n a programme of loans and other economic assistance provided by the US government between 1947 and 1952 to help W European nations rebuild after World War II [Mid-20C. After George C. MARSHALL.]

Marshal of the Royal Air Force n a Royal Air Force officer of the highest rank

marsh elder n a bush with unisexual flowers and greenish flower heads. Native to: marshes of central and E North America. Genus: *Iva*.

marsh fever n MED = malaria

marsh gas n a mixture of gases, mostly methane, produced by decomposing plant matter in the absence of air

marsh harrier n a long-winged long-tailed hawk, the largest of the harriers, found mainly in marshland and reed-beds. Native to: Europe, Asia. *Circus aeruginosis*.

marsh hen n a wading bird that inhabits marshy areas and belongs to the family of birds that includes the rail, coot, and moorhen. Family: Rallidae.

marshland /máarsh land, -lənd/ n marshy ground, or an area or expanse of it

marsh mallow n a perennial shrubby plant that grows in marshes and has sticky roots that were used in the past to make marshmallow and are still used in some medicines. Flowers: pink. Native to: Europe. *Althaea officinalis*.

marshmallow /maarsh mállō/ n a soft spongy sweet made from sugar syrup, egg whites, flavouring, and other ingredients [Because formerly made from the root of the marsh mallow plant] —**marshmallowy** adj

marsh marigold n a plant of the buttercup family with round or kidney-shaped leaves that grows in swampy areas. Flowers: bright yellow. Native to: Europe, North America. *Caltha palustris*.

Marston /máarstən/, **John** (c. 1575–1634) English playwright and satirist

marsupial /maar syóopi əl, -sóo-/ n a mammal, e.g. a kangaroo, wombat, opossum, or koala, having no placenta and bearing immature young that are developed in a pouch on the mother's abdomen. Order: Marsupialia. [Late 17C. < modern Latin *marsupialis* < *marsupium* (see MARSUPIUM).] —**marsupialian** /maar syóopi áyli ən, -sóo-/ adj —**marsupian** adj

marsupial frog n any one of several species of tree frog in which the female carries the eggs in a pouch on her back

marsupium /maar syóopi əm, -sóopi-/ (plural -**a** /-ə/) n a pouch on the abdomen of most marsupials that encloses the mammary glands and in which the animal's newly born offspring complete their development [Mid-17C. Via Latin *marsupium* < Greek *marsupion* 'pouch', literally 'little purse' < *marsippos* 'purse'.]

mart /maart/ n a market, saleroom, or large shop [15C.

< obsolete Dutch, variant of *markt* < Latin *mercatus* (see MARKET).]

Martaban, Gulf of /máartə baàn-/ inlet of the Andaman Sea in S Myanmar

martagon /máartəgən/, **martagon lily** n an ornamental lily. Flowers: mottled, pinkish-purple, resembling turbans. Native to: Europe, Asia. *Lilium martagon*. [15C. Via French < Turkish *martağān*, a kind of turban, which the flower is thought to resemble.]

martelé /máartə lay/, **martellato** /máartə laàtō/ adv with the strings played in a strongly accented way (*musical direction*) [Late 19C. < French, 'hammered'.]

Martello /maar téllō/ (plural -**los**), **Martello tower** n a fort in the form of a small circular tower, especially one built on the coast for defence against invasion during the Napoleonic Wars [Early 19C. Alteration, influenced by Italian *martello* 'hammer', of Cape *Mortella* in Corsica, where such a tower was captured by the British fleet in 1794.]

marten /máartin/ (plural -**tens** or -**ten**) n a short-legged bushy-tailed mammal with a long slender body that lives in trees. Native to: northern forests. Genus: *Martes*. [13C. Via Middle Dutch *martren* < Old French *martre* < Germanic.]

Martens /máartənz/, **Conrad** (1801–74) British-born Australian painter

martensite /máartin zīt/ n the hard solid solution of iron and carbon used in making hardened steel tools [Late 19C. After the German metallurgist Adolf *Martens* (1850–1914).] —**martensitic** /máart'n zíttik/ adj

Martha /máarthə/ n in the Bible, the sister of Mary and Lazarus, and friend of Jesus Christ (Luke 10: 38–42)

Martha's Vineyard /máarthəz vínnyərd/ island in SE Massachusetts, in the Atlantic Ocean. Population: 8,900 (1990). Area: 280 sq. km/100 sq. mi.

Martí /maartí/, **José Julian** (1853–95) Cuban revolutionary leader and poet

martial /máarsh'l/ adj **1** typical of or suitable for soldiers, the military life, or war **2** warlike and fierce [14C. Directly or via French < Latin *martialis* < *Mars*, the god of war.] —**martialism** n —**martialist** n —**martially** adv —**martialness** n

martial art n a system of combat and self-defence, e.g. judo or karate, developed especially in Japan and Korea and now usually practised as a sport

martial law n the control and policing of a civilian population by military forces and according to military rules, imposed, e.g. in wartime or when the civilian government no longer functions

Martian /máarsh'n/ adj found on, typical of, or originating from the planet Mars ■ n a supposed inhabitant of the planet Mars [14C. Directly or via Old French *martien* < Latin *Martianus* < *Mart-* 'Mars'.]

martin /máartin/ n a bird of the swallow genus with a notched or square tail, e.g. the house martin [15C. < ?]

Martin /máartin/, **St** (316?–397?) Roman monk

Martin V (1368–1431) pope (1417–31)

Martin, Archer (b. 1910) British biochemist

martinet /máarti nét/ n **1** a military officer who demands absolute adherence to military rules and behaviour by subordinates and peers **2** a strict imposer of discipline on others [Late 17C. After Jean *Martinet* (died 1672), who introduced drills into the French army.] —**martinetism** n —**martinettish** adj

martingale /máartin gayl/, **martingal** n **1** PART OF HORSE'S HARNESS a strap of a horse's harness connecting the girth to the reins to keep the horse from throwing its head back **2** martingale, martingale shroud PART OF SHIP'S RIGGING a rope or cable that supports the forward-projecting spar (**bowsprit**) on some sailing ships **3** GAMBLING SYSTEM gambling in which the stakes are doubled after each loss [Late 16C. < French.]

martini /maar teéni/ n a cocktail made of gin or vodka with vermouth [Late 19C. < Italian *Martini*, surname of a winemaker.]

Martini /maar teéni/, **Simone** (1280?–1344?) Italian painter

Martinique /máarti neek/ island department of France in the E Caribbean Sea, one of the Windward Islands. Population: 363,031 (1990). Area: 1,100 sq. km/425 sq. mi.

Martinmas /máartinməss, -mass/ n one of the Scottish

quarter days. Date: 11 November. [13C. < St MARTIN + MASS.]

Martinů /maàrti noo/, **Bohuslav Jan** (1890–1959) Czech composer

martlet /maàrtlət/ n on coats of arms, a footless bird used to represent a fourth son [Early 16C. < French *martelet*, alteration of *martinet*, pet form of the male name *Martin*.]

martyr /maàrtər/ n 1 SOMEBODY PUT TO DEATH a person who chooses to die rather than deny a strongly held belief 2 SOMEBODY WHO MAKES SACRIFICES a person who makes sacrifices or suffers greatly in order to advance a cause or principle 3 SOMEBODY IN PAIN a person who experiences frequent or constant pain from something 4 SOMEBODY SEEKING ATTENTION a frequent complainer who hopes to elicit sympathy from others ■ v 1 vt KILL FOR HOLDING BELIEFS to kill somebody for refusing to deny religious or political beliefs 2 vr MAKE SACRIFICES FOR to make sacrifices or endure hardship for something [Pre-12C. Via ecclesiastical Latin < Greek *martur* 'witness'.] —**martyrdom** n

Maruyama Okyo /márroo yaàma ŏki ŏ/ (1733–95) Japanese artist. Born **Maruyama Mondo**

marvel /maàrv'l/ n 1 WONDERFUL THING something that inspires awe, amazement, or admiration ○ *one of the marvels of the Ancient World* 2 SOMEBODY SKILFUL OR HELPFUL a person skilled in something who often gives much-needed help ■ vi (-vels, -velling, -velled) BE AMAZED to be very impressed, surprised, or bewildered ○ *I could only marvel at her stamina.* [13C. Via French *merveille* < Latin *mirabilis* 'wonderful' < *mirari* (see MIRACLE).]

Marvell /maàrvəl/, **Andrew** (1621–78) English poet and politician

marvellous /maàrvələss/ adj 1 extraordinarily wonderful ○ *a marvellous example of Baroque architecture* 2 very good or pleasing ○ *It was marvellous to see them all again.* —**marvellously** adv —**marvellousness** n

marvelous adj US = marvellous

marvelously adv US = marvellously

Karl Marx

Marx /maarks/, **Karl** (1818–83) German political philosopher —**Marxian** adj

Marx Brothers (fl. early 20th century) US comedians

Marxism /maàrks izəm/ n 1 the political and economic theories of Karl Marx and Friedrich Engels, in which class struggle is a central element in the analysis of social change in Western societies 2 political ideology based on the theories of Karl Marx and Friedrich Engels —**Marxist** n, adj

Marxism-Leninism n Marxism with the inclusion of Lenin's idea that imperialism is the final stage of capitalism, and Lenin's shifting of the focus of class struggle from industrialized to nonindustrialized societies —**Marxist-Leninist** n, adj

Mary /máiri/, **St** mother of Jesus Christ.

Mary (1867–1953) queen of the United Kingdom as wife of George V. Known as **Mary of Teck**

Mary I /máiri/ (1516–58) queen of England and Ireland (1553–58)

Mary II (1662–94) queen of England, Scotland, and Ireland (1689–94)

Mary (Queen of Scots) (1542–87) queen of Scotland (1542–67). Born **Mary Stuart**

Maryborough /máiribərə/ port in SE Queensland, Australia. Population: 21,286 (1996).

Mary Jane /-jáyn/ n US marijuana (*slang*) [Early 20C. < ?]

Maryland /máirilənd/ state in the E United States. Capital: Annapolis. Population: 5,094,289 (1997). Area: 31,849 sq. km/12,297 sq. mi. —**Marylander** n

Mary Magdalene /máiri magdə léni, -mágdələn/ n in the Bible, a follower of Jesus Christ, who cured her of evil spirits (Luke 8:2)

marzipan /maàrzi pan, -pán/ n a sweet paste made of ground almonds and sugar, often with egg whites or yolks, used as a layer in cakes or moulded into ornamental shapes ■ adj relating or belonging to the upper-middle levels of the management hierarchy in an organization, just below the top executives [15C. Via German < Italian *marzapane* 'type of box', originally for sweets or coins.]

Masaccio /mə saàchee ŏ/ (1401?–27) Italian painter. Born **Tommaso Cassai**

Masada /mə saàdə/ ancient ruins of a fortress in SE Israel that was the site of a Roman siege of the Jewish Zealots from 71 to 73 BC

Masai /maà sĩ, maa sĩ́, mássĩ́/ (*plural* -sai or -sais), **Maasai** (*plural* -sai or -sais) n 1 a member of a pastoral people with strong warrior traditions who live in East Africa, mainly in Kenya and Tanzania 2 the Nilotic language of the Masai people. Native speakers: 700,000. [Mid-19C. < Masai.] —**Masai** adj

masala /mə saàla, maa-/ n 1 SPICY PASTE a mixture of spices ground into a paste, used to flavour Indian dishes, or a dish flavoured with such a paste 2 S Asia GOSSIP casual conversation (*informal*) ■ adj S Asia DESCRIBING INDIAN FILMS describes Indian popular films (*informal*) [Late 18C. < Urdu *masālah*.]

Masbate /maas baàti/ island in central Philippines. Population: 599,900 (1990). Area: 4,000 sq. km/1,600 sq. mi.

masc. abbr masculine

Mascagni /mass kánnyi/, **Pietro** (1863–1945) Italian composer

mascara /ma skaàrə, mə-/ n thick coloured paste applied to the eyelashes with a fine brush to darken them and give the appearance of greater length and thickness ■ vt (-as, -aíng, -aed) to apply mascara to eyelashes [Late 19C. Probably < Italian *maschera* 'mask'.]

Mascarene Islands /máskə reèn-/ island group in the Indian Ocean, east of Madagascar, including Réunion, Mauritius, and Rodrigues. Population: 1,798,000 (1996). Area: 4,500 sq. km/1,700 sq. mi.

mascarpone /maàskər pŏni, máskaar-/ n a rich fatty unsalted Italian cream cheese with a spreadable texture [Mid-20C. < Italian, 'rich whey cheese'.]

mascle /másk'l/ n a design on coats of arms in the form of a lozenge with a lozenge-shaped hole in the middle [13C. < Anglo-Norman, < Latin *macula* 'mesh'.]

mascon /máss kon/ n an area of higher-than-normal gravity on the surface of the Moon [Mid-20C. Contraction of *mass concentration*.]

mascot /más kot, máskət/ n a person, animal, or thing that is believed to bring good luck, usually one that becomes the symbol of a particular group, especially a team [Late 19C. Via French *mascotte* < modern Provençal *mascotto* 'little witch'.]

masculine /máskyŏolin/ adj 1 OF MEN AND BOYS relating or belonging to men and boys rather than women and girls 2 OF TRADITIONAL MANLY CHARACTER traditionally associated with men or boys rather than women or girls 3 OF CERTAIN GRAMMATICAL GENDER relating to one of the classes that words and grammatical forms are divided into in some languages 4 CONCLUDING ON AN ACCENTED BEAT ending on a beat that is accented ■ n MASCULINE GENDER the masculine gender, or a word or form in the masculine gender [14C. Via French < Latin *masculinus* < *masculus.*] —**masculinely** adv —**masculineness** n

masculine cadence n a closing section of music (**cadence**) that ends on a strong beat

masculine ending n 1 a stressed syllable that ends a line of poetry 2 an ending that marks a word as belonging to the masculine gender in some languages

masculine rhyme n a rhyme between two monosyllabic words, e.g. 'gab' and 'blab', or between the final stressed syllables of polysyllabic words, e.g. 'connive' and 'survive'

masculinise vt = masculinize

masculinity /máskyŏo línnəti/ n 1 the state of being a man or boy 2 those qualities conventionally supposed to make a man an excellent specimen of manhood, traditionally physical strength and courage

masculinize /máskyŏolin Tz/ (-izes, -izing, -ized), **masculinise** (-ises, -ising, -ised) vt 1 to give something or somebody features conventionally associated with maleness 2 to cause a female animal or a plant to acquire male sexual characteristics, e.g. as a result of administering steroids —**masculinization** /máskyŏolin T záysh'n/ n

Masefield /máyss feeld/, **John** (1878–1967) British poet

maser /máyzər/ n a device used in radar and radio astronomy to boost the strength of microwaves [Mid-20C. Acronym < *Microwave Amplification by Stimulated Emission of Radiation.*]

Maseru /mə sáiroo/ capital of Lesotho, in the west of the country, on the River Mohokare. Population: 130,000 (1992 estimate).

mash /mash/ n 1 GRAIN AND WATER MIX a fermentable mixture of hot water and grain, usually barley or wheat, from which alcohol is brewed or distilled 2 ANIMAL FOOD a mixture of ground feeds for livestock or poultry 3 PULPY MASS the consistency of a soft pulp 4 MASHED POTATOES potatoes that have been reduced to a pulp or puree (*informal*) ■ vt 1 MAKE PULP OF to squash something into a pulpy mass 2 vt SOAK GRAIN to soak grain in hot water to make a mash for brewing or for feeding to animals 3 vt CRUSH to crush or grind something (*informal*) 4 vti BREW TEA to soak tea leaves in hot water until the tea is ready to drink, or infuse in this way (*regional*) [Old English *masc* 'mash for brewing' < Indo-European] —**masher** n

MASH /mash/, **M.A.S.H.** abbr mobile army surgical hospital

mashgiah /mash geè akh/ (*plural* -gihim /-geèkhim/), **mashgiach** (*plural* -gichim) n an Orthodox rabbi, or a man appointed or approved by such a rabbi, who inspects slaughterhouses, meat markets, and restaurants to check that kosher food has been properly prepared and served [Mid-20C. < Hebrew *mašgīaḥ* 'supervisor'.]

mashie /máshi/ n an obsolete golf club similar to the modern five-iron [Late 19C. < ?]

mashie niblick n an obsolete golf club similar to the modern six-iron

masjid n a mosque in an Arab country [Mid-19C. < Arabic, 'place of prostration'.]

mask /maask/ n 1 COVERING FOR FACE a covering for the eyes, mouth, or whole face 2 CONCEALING THING something that conceals or disguises something else, e.g. true motives or feelings 3 ORNAMENT RESEMBLING FACE a representation of a face used as an ornament or decoration 4 ANIMAL'S FACE MARKINGS the face or facial markings of some animals, e.g. foxes and racoons 5 CONCEALMENT FOR TROOPS a natural or artificial feature that hides military troops and installations from an enemy 6 TEMPLATE FOR ELECTRONIC CHIPS a template used to control the pattern of conducting material deposited or etched onto a semiconductor chip 7 BEAUTY TREATMENT a facial preparation used to tighten the skin and remove impurities, applied to the skin as a paste and allowed to dry before being removed 8 PHOTOGRAPHIC GUARD a guard, often a sheet of paper, placed over areas of unexposed photographic film to stop light hitting it ■ vt 1 HIDE to conceal or disguise something, e.g. an unpleasant smell or a true intention 2 SHIELD PART OF to cover part of a surface using masking tape before painting or spraying 3 SHIELD PHOTOGRAPHIC FILM FROM LIGHT to prevent stray or unwanted light from reaching areas of unexposed photographic film, either using hands or a special shield 4 STOP CHEMICAL REACTING to prevent a chemical substance from reacting by the addition of another chemical [Early 16C. Via French *masque* < late Latin *masca* 'ghost, mask'.] —**maskable** adj

masked /maaskt/ adj 1 WEARING A MASK with the face covered in order to prevent recognition 2 NOT DETECTABLE describes diseases and symptoms that are present but not yet perceptible 3 PLANT SCI = **personate**[2] 4 WITH MARKINGS LIKE A MASK with markings on the head or around the eyes that resemble a mask

masked ball n a ball at which people wear masks

masker /maàskər/ n a wearer of a mask at a masked ball

masking /maàsking/ n 1 the hiding or screening of one sensory process, e.g. hearing, by another, e.g. sight

2 scenery that is used to hide a part of the stage from the audience

masking tape *n* easy-to-remove adhesive tape used to cover parts of a surface that are not meant to be painted

masochism /mássəkizəm/ *n* **1 SEXUAL PLEASURE DERIVED FROM HUMILIATION** sexual gratification achieved by humiliation and the acceptance of physical and verbal abuse **2 NEED FOR PAIN** the psychological disorder in which somebody needs to be emotionally or physically abused in order to be sexually satisfied **3 SEARCH FOR ABUSIVE SEXUAL PARTNERS** the active seeking out of sexual partners who will dominate, humiliate, and physically and verbally abuse **4 ENJOYMENT OF HARDSHIP** the tendency to invite and enjoy misery of any kind, especially in order to be pitied by others or perhaps admired for forbearance [Late 19C. After Leopold von Sacher-*Masoch* (1836–95), Austrian novelist.] —**masochist** *n*

masochistic /mássə kístik/ *adj* **1** relating to or experiencing the desire to be humiliated and abused by others in order to feel sexually fulfilled **2** tending to invite and enjoy misery —**masochistically** *adv*

mason /máyss'n/ *n* a maker or dresser of things in stone, e.g. buildings or statues ■ *vt* to build or strengthen something using stone [12C. < Old N French *machun* or Old French *masson*.]

Mason /máyss'n/ *n* FREEMASONRY = **Freemason**

Mason /máyss'n/, **Bruce** (1921–84) New Zealand playwright

mason bee *n* any solitary bee that builds nests of sand or clay held together with saliva

Mason-Dixon Line /máyss'n díks'n-/ *n* the boundary that separates Pennsylvania from Maryland and West Virginia, regarded as the dividing line between free and slave states before the American Civil War [After the 18C surveyors Charles *Mason* and Jeremiah *Dixon*]

masonic /mə sónnik/ *adj* relating to stonemasons or their work —**masonically** *adv*

Masonic /mə sónik/ *adj* relating to Freemasons or Freemasonry

masonry /máyss'nri/ *n* **1** the trade of a mason **2** the stone or brick parts of a building or other structure

Masonry *n* Freemasonry

mason wasp *n* a solitary wasp that builds mud nests or digs out nests in old mortar. Genus: *Odynerus.*

Masorete /mássə reet/, **Masorite** /-rīt/ *n* one of the scholars who produced the traditional text of the Hebrew Bible (**Masoretic text**) [Late 16C. Via French or modern Latin *Massoreta* < a misuse of Hebrew *māsōreṯ*.] —**Masoretic** /mássə réttik/ *adj*

Masoretic text *n* the traditional text of the Hebrew Bible, revised and annotated by Jewish scholars between the 6th and 10th centuries AD

Masqat = **Muscat**

masque /maask/ *n* **1** a dramatic entertainment similar to opera, popular in England in the 16th and 17th centuries, in which masked performers represented mythological or allegorical characters **2** the music and words written for a masque **3** = **masquerade** *n*. 1 [Early 16C. < French (see MASK).]

masquer /maaskər/ *n* = **masker**

masquerade /maàskə ráyd/ *n* **1 PARTY WITH MASKS** a party at which masks and costumes are worn, whether an informal gathering of friends or a formal ball **2 DISGUISING COSTUME** a costume worn to a masquerade **3 DISGUISING PRETENCE** a pretence or disguise ■ *vi* (**-ades, -ading, -aded**) **1 PRETEND** to pretend to be somebody or something else **2 WEAR A COSTUME** to wear a particular costume to a party [Late 16C. Via French *mascarade* < Italian *mascherata* < *maschera* 'mask'.] —**masquerader** *n*

mass /mass/ *n* **1 LUMP** a body of matter that forms a whole but has no definable shape **2 COLLECTION** a collection of many individual parts ○ *The garden is a mass of weeds.* **3 GREAT UNSPECIFIED QUANTITY** a large but unspecified number or quantity ○ *I have masses of work to do.* **4 MAJOR PART** the greater part or majority ○ *The mass of respondents oppose the legislation.* **5 PHYSICAL QUANTITY** (*symbol m*) the property of an object that is a measure of its inertia, the amount of matter it contains, and its influence in a gravitational field **6 AREA OF PAINTING** a large area of a painting where the light, shade, or colour is uniform **7 MIXTURE CONTAINING DRUGS** a thick paste containing drugs that is made into pills **8 DEPOSIT OF ORE** an irregular deposit of ore that does not occur in veins ■ *vti* **COLLECT** to gather or be gathered in a mass ○ *Troops are massing on the border.* ■ *adj* **1 OF LARGE NUMBER** made up of or containing a large number ○ *a mass demonstration* **2 GENERAL** broadly general, in scope or effect ○ *The mass effect is rather disappointing.* [14C. Via French *masse* < Latin *massa* < Greek *maza* 'barley cake'.] ◇ **in the mass** considered as a whole, not as separate entities

mass in *vt* to fill in areas of colour or shade in a drawing or painting

Mass, mass *n* **1** in the Roman Catholic Church and some Protestant churches, the religious ceremony of the Communion **2** a part of the text of a Roman Catholic Mass set to music, to be sung by a choir [Pre-12C. < ecclesiastical Latin *missa* < Latin *mittere* 'send away'.]

Mass. *abbr* Massachusetts

Massachuset /mássə chōōsət/ (*plural* **-set** *or* **-sets**), **Massachusett** (*plural* **-sett** *or* **-setts**) *n* **1** a member of a Native North American people who lived in the Massachusetts Bay area **2** an extinct Algonquian language formerly spoken in E Massachusetts —**Massachuset** *adj*

Massachusetts /mássə chōōssəts/ state in the NE United States. Capital: Boston. Population: 6,117,520 (1997). Area: 23,934 sq. km/9,241 sq. mi.

massacre /mássəkər/ *n* **1 KILLING OF MANY PEOPLE** the vicious killing of large numbers of people or animals **2 BAD DEFEAT** a contest in which one side is badly beaten (*informal*) ■ *vt* (**-cres, -cring, -cred**) **1 KILL IN LARGE NUMBERS** to kill large numbers of people or animals **2 DEFEAT SOMEBODY COMPLETELY** to defeat somebody completely, especially in a sporting contest (*informal*) [Late 16C. < French, 'butchery'.] —**massacrer** *n*

massage /mássaazh, -aaj/ *n* **RUBBING OF BODY** a treatment that involves rubbing or kneading the muscles, either for medical or therapeutic purposes or simply as an aid to relaxation ■ *vt* (**-sages, -saging, -saged**) **1 RUB SOMEBODY'S MUSCLES** to rub or knead somebody's muscles **2 MANIPULATE DECEPTIVELY** to manipulate statistics or other information in order to create a more suitable or falsely impressive result ○ *They massaged the figures.* **3 ENHANCE** to give something a boost with kind or uplifting treatment, especially somebody's ego with flattery [Late 19C. < French, < *masser* 'apply massage to'.] —**massager** *n*

massage parlour *n* **1** a place that provides massages to paying customers **2** a place that offers sex services for money

massasauga /mássə sáwgə/ *n* a small rattlesnake that has variable colouring. Native to: North America. *Sistrurus catenatus.* [Mid-19C. Alteration of *Mississagi*, river in SE Ontario, Canada.]

mass balance *n* a mathematical equation, table, or quantitative chart showing the mass inputs and outputs of a process, plant, or machine, the principle being that what goes in must come out

mass communication, mass communications *n* communication by means of broadcasting and newspapers, that reaches all or most people in society

masscult /máss kult/ *n* culture as it is presented and interpreted by the mass media (*informal*) [Shortening of *mass culture*]

mass defect *n* the difference between the mass of an isotope and the element's mass number

massé /mássi/ *n* a shot in cue games in which the cue is held almost vertically to strike the cue ball off-centre, making it curve round one ball to hit another [Late 19C. < French, < *masse* (see MACE[1]).]

Masséna /ma sáynə/, **André, Prince of Essling and Duke of Rivoli** (1758–1817) French soldier

Massenet /mássə nay/, **Jules Emile Frédéric** (1842–1912) French composer

masses /mássiz, mássəz/ *npl* **1** ordinary people in society, as distinct from political leaders, aristocracy, or educated people **2** large amounts or large numbers (*informal*)

masseter /ma séetər/ *n* a muscle in the cheek that moves the jaws during chewing [Late 16C. < Greek *masētēr* < *masasthai* 'chew'.] —**masseteric** /mássi térrik/ *adj*

masseur /ma súr/ *n* a man who gives massages professionally [Late 19C. < French, < *masser* 'apply massage to'.]

masseuse /ma sőz/ *n* a woman who gives massages professionally [Late 19C. < French, feminine of *masseur* (see MASSEUR).]

mass extinction[1] *n* the destruction of a whole species by force of nature such as climate change, volcanic eruption, or an asteroid collision, thought by many scientists to account for the end of dinosaurs

mass extinction[2] *n* the destruction of a whole species by a force of nature such as climate change, volcanic eruption, or asteroid collision, thought by many scientists to have wiped out the dinosaurs

Massey /mássi/, **William Ferguson** (1856–1925) Irish-born New Zealand statesman

massicot /mássi kot/ *n* a yellow mineral consisting of lead oxide [15C. < French.]

massif /másseef/ *n* **1** a large mountain mass, or a group of connected mountains that form a mountain range **2** a part of the Earth's crust that is surrounded by faults and may be shifted or displaced by tectonic movements [Early 16C. < French (see MASSIVE).]

Massif Central /mássif sen traál/ highland region in south-central France. Area: 93,000 sq. km/36,000 sq. mi.

massive /mássiv/ *adj* **1 BULKY** large, solid, and heavy **2 LARGE-SCALE** extremely large in amount, degree, or scope **3 UNUSUALLY LARGE** large in comparison to what is typical or usual ○ *gained a massive amount of weight* **4 DEVOID OF VISIBLE CRYSTALS** with no visible crystalline structure **5 HOMOGENEOUS** describes rock that is of the same composition throughout, as distinct from being layered [15C. Via French *massif* < Old French *massiz* < Latin *massa* (see MASS).] —**massiveness** *n* —**massively** *adv*

mass leisure *n* the everyday leisure pursuits of the majority of a population, constituting an aspect of popular culture

massless /mássləss/ *adj* with a mass of zero

mass-market *adj* designed for sale to as wide a range of people as possible, rather than to a particular group in society

mass media *n* all of the communications media that reach a large audience, especially television, radio, and newspapers (+ *singular or plural verb*)

mass noun *n* a noun representing something that cannot be counted, e.g. 'water', or something that can only be counted if the meaning is a single type or serving, e.g. 'coffee'. ◊ **noncount noun**

mass number *n* (*symbol A*) the number of protons and neutrons in the nucleus of an atom of a particular substance

mass observation *n* a method of observing how people act in social contexts by collating the subjects' own reports, diaries, and responses to questionnaires

mass-produce *vt* to manufacture a product in very large quantities in factories, especially using mechanization and assembly-line methods —**mass-producer** *n*

mass production *n* the manufacturing of products on a large scale in factories, especially using mechanization and assembly-line methods

mass society *n* a society in which the national or global nature of the influences on life, e.g. mass production and the mass media, has stripped the population of its diversity

mass spectrometer *n* an instrument that separates atoms and molecules according to their mass and that records the resulting mass spectrum

mass spectrum *n* a record of the chemical constituents of a substance separated according to their mass and presented as a spectrum

mass wasting *n* the downward movement of loose rock and soil along a slope

mast[1] /maast/ *n* **1 VERTICAL SUPPORT** a vertical spar that supports sails, rigging, or flags on a ship **2 UPRIGHT POLE** a vertical pole **3 BROADCAST TOWER** a tall broadcasting aerial **4** NAVY = **captain's mast** ■ *vti* **SUBJECT TO CAPTAIN'S MAST** to subject somebody charged with a usually shipboard or on-base crime or infringement to a disciplinary hearing (**captain's mast**), or undergo such a hearing [Old English *mæst* < Indo-European] ◇ **at half mast 1** partway down a flagpole, usually as a sign of respect following a death ○ *flags flying at half mast* **2** partway up or down from the usual position at which something is worn (*informal humorous*) ○ *trousers at half mast* ◇ **before the mast** serving as an ordinary sailor or apprentice seaman

mast[2] /maast/ *n* the nuts of certain trees, such as beech, oak, and chestnut, especially when used as food for pigs [Old English *mæst* 'fodder' < Germanic, 'meat']

mast- *prefix* breast, nipple, mammary gland ○ *mastitis* [< Greek *mastos*]

mastaba /mástəbə/, **mastabah** *n* an ancient Egyptian brick tomb built with a flat base, sloping sides, and a flat roof [Early 17C. < Arabic *maṣṭaba*.]

mastalgia /ma stáljə/ *n* pain in the breast

mast cell *n* a large cell in connective tissue consisting of granules that release histamine and heparin during allergic reactions [< German *Mast* 'fattening, feeding']

mastectomy /ma stéktəmi/ (*plural* **-mies**) *n* the surgical removal of one or both breasts, usually as a treatment for breast cancer [Early 20C. < Greek *mastos* 'breast'.]

ϟ **master** /maástər/ *n* **1 BOSS** especially formerly, a man in a position of authority, e.g. over a business or servants (*sometimes considered offensive*) **2 SOMEBODY IN CONTROL** somebody or something controlling or influencing events or other things (*sometimes offensive*) **3 ABSTRACT CONTROL** an abstract idea or force that is thought of as having control or influence (*sometimes offensive*) **4 OWNER OF ANIMAL** a man who owns or has control of a horse, dog, or other domesticated animal **5 SOMEBODY HIGHLY SKILLED** a person highly skilled at something **6 SKILLED WORKER** somebody who is highly skilled in a trade or craft and is qualified to teach apprentices (*usually in combination*) ○ *master craftsman* **7 PLAYER AT HIGH LEVEL** a player of some games who has reached a high level of achievement, especially in chess or bridge. ◊ **International Master 8 ORIGINAL COPY** an original copy of something such as a recording tape or a stencil, from which other copies can be made **9 MAN TEACHER** a man teacher (*dated*) **10 LEADER** somebody whose philosophy or religious belief has attracted followers (*sometimes offensive*) **11 SHIP'S OFFICER** the captain of a merchant ship **12 LAW COURT OFFICER** a man who serves as officer in the Supreme Court of Judicature, subordinate to a judge **13 VICTOR** a defeater of somebody else (*literary*) **14 CONTROLLING MACHINE** a device or computer that controls the operation of one or more other connected devices or computers (*sometimes offensive*) ■ *adj* (*sometimes offensive*) **1 MAIN** devised to operate on the broadest level ○ *a master plan for flood evacuations* **2 CONTROLLING** controlling the operation of everything or of all others **3 PRINCIPAL** biggest or primary among several ○ *redecorated the master bedroom* ■ *vt* **1 LEARN** to become highly skilled in something or acquire a complete understanding of it **2 CONTROL** to learn to control feelings or behaviour (*sometimes offensive*) **3 MAKE SUBMIT** to break the will of a person or animal (*sometimes offensive*) **4 MAKE MASTER RECORDING** to produce a master recording of something [Pre-12C. < Old English *mægister*, Old French *maistre* < Latin *magister* 'chief' < *magis* 'more'.] —**masterless** *adj*

Master *n* **1 PREFIX TO BOY'S NAME** a title sometimes prefixed to a boy's surname in formal circumstances **2 RELIGIOUS TEACHER** a title used to address a man who is a religious leader or teacher (*sometimes offensive*) **3 SOMEBODY APPOINTED BY ROYALTY** a word that features in the title of various men who perform specific duties as officers in the royal household or who hold senior court positions

master-at-arms (*plural* **masters-at-arms**) *n* a noncommissioned officer aboard a naval vessel who is responsible for maintaining order and enforcing discipline in the ship's company

master builder *n* a self-employed builder who employs others as labour (*sometimes offensive*)

LITERARY LINK ***The Master Builder***, a play (1845) by Norwegian dramatist Henrik Ibsen. It is the story of a successful architect, Halvard Solness, who is disturbed by his continued good fortune. His search for redemption eventually leads to his own death.

master chief petty officer *n US* in the US Navy or Coast Guard, a noncommissioned officer of the highest rank

master class *n* a class given by an acknowledged expert in a particular field (*sometimes offensive*)

master corporal *n* a noncommissioned officer in the Canadian army, senior to a corporal and junior to a sergeant

masterful /maástərf'l/ *adj* **1** demonstrating exceptional skill or ability in a specific area (*sometimes offensive*) **2** showing the ability or tendency to lead others — **masterfully** *adv* —**masterfulness** *n*

master key *n* a key that will open all the locks in a particular set or place

masterly /maástərli/ *adj* demonstrating outstanding skill —**masterliness** *n*

master mariner *n* NAUT = **master** *n.* 10

mastermind /maástər mīnd/ *n* a planner, organizer, and overseer of a complex process

Master of Arts *n* a degree in a nonscience subject, usually awarded after one or two years of postgraduate study, but sometimes awarded as a first degree in place of a bachelor's degree

master of ceremonies *n* a person at a formal event who makes the opening speech and introduces speakers or performers (*sometimes offensive*)

Master of Science *n* a degree in a science subject, usually awarded after one or two years of postgraduate study, but sometimes awarded as a first degree in place of a bachelor's degree

Master of the Rolls *n* the senior judge in England, who sits in the Court of Appeal and also has the official title of Keeper of the Records at the Public Record Office

masterpiece /maástər peess/ *n* **1** an exceptionally good piece of creative work, e.g. a book, film, or performance **2** the best piece of work by a particular artist or craftsperson [Early 17C. After Dutch *meesterstuk* or German *Meisterstück*.]

Master's degree *n* a university degree with the title Master, usually awarded after one or two years of postgraduate study

master sergeant *n US* in the US Army and US Marine Corps, a noncommissioned officer of a rank above sergeant major, and in the US Air Force above technical sergeant

mastersinger /maástər singər/ *n* MUSIC = **Meistersinger** [Early 19C. Anglicization.]

masterstroke /maástər strōk/ *n* a brilliant idea or very clever tactic

Masterton /maástərtən/ town in the south of the North Island, New Zealand. Population: 19,800 (1998 estimate).

masterwork /maástər wurk/ *n* ARTS = **masterpiece** *n.* 1, **masterpiece** *n.* 2

mastery /maástəri/ *n* **1** expert knowledge or outstanding ability **2** total control over somebody or something (*sometimes offensive*)

masthead /maást hed/ *n* **1 MAST'S TOP** the top of a mast **2 NEWSPAPER'S TITLE AS DISPLAYED** the name of a newspaper or magazine as it appears in large letters on the front cover **3 NEWSPAPER INFORMATION** the list that provides information about staff, owners, and circulation in a newspaper or magazine, usually printed on the first page

mastic /mástik/ *n* **1 RESIN** an aromatic resin produced by a Mediterranean tree. Use: manufacture of lacquer, varnish, adhesives, condiments. **2 CEMENT** a flexible cement. Use: filler, adhesive, sealant in woodwork, plaster, brickwork. **3 LIQUOR** a liquor in which mastic gum is used as a flavouring **4** TREES = **mastic tree** *n.* [14C. < French, < Greek *mastikhan* 'grind the teeth'.]

masticate /másti kayt/ (**-cates, -cating, -cated**) *v* **1** *vti* to grind and pulverize food inside the mouth, using the teeth and jaws **2** *vt* to grind or crush something until it turns to pulp [Mid-17C. < the past participle of Latin *masticare* < Greek *mastikhan* 'grind the teeth'.] —**masticable** *adj* —**mastication** /másti káysh'n/ *n* —**masticator** *n*

masticatory /mástikətəri/ *adj* relating to chewing ■ *n* (*plural* **-ries**) a medicine made to be chewed in order to increase the production of saliva

mastic tree *n* a small evergreen bush of the cashew family, grown for its resin. Native to: Mediterranean. *Pistachia lentiscus.*

mastiff /mástif/ *n* a large powerful dog belonging to a breed with smooth-haired often fawn or greyish coats and dark faces [14C. < Old French *mastin* < Latin *mansuetus* 'used to the hand' < *manus* 'hand'.]

mastiff bat *n* a snub-nosed bat. Native to: warm regions. Family: Molossidae.

mastigure /másti gyoor/ *n* a lizard that blocks its burrow with its very spiny tail. Native to: North Africa, Middle East. Genus: *Uromastix.* [Mid-19C. < modern Latin *mastigura* < Greek *mastix* 'whip' + *oura* 'tail'.]

mastitis /ma stítiss/ *n* inflammation of a woman's breast or an animal's udder, usually as a result of bacterial infection [Mid-19C. < Greek *mastos* 'breast'.] —**mastitic** /ma stíttik/ *adj*

mastodon /mástə don, -dən/ *n* a large extinct mammal that resembled an elephant, with shaggy hair and two sets of tusks. Genus: *Mastodon.* [Early 19C. < Greek *mastos* 'breast' + *odōn* 'tooth'.] —**mastodonic** /mástə dónnik/ *adj* —**mastodontic** /-dóntik/ *adj*

mastoid /máss toyd/ *adj* **1** shaped like a nipple or breast **2** relating to the mastoid process ■ *n* ANAT = **mastoid process** [Mid-18C. Via French *mastoïde* or modern Latin *mastoides* < Greek *mastoeidēs* < *mastos* 'breast'.]

mastoid bone *n* ANAT = **mastoid process**

mastoid cell *n* an air-filled space in the mastoid process

mastoidectomy /máss toyd éktəmi/ (*plural* **-mies**) *n* a surgical operation to remove part of an infected mastoid process to allow pus to drain off and prevent infection from spreading to the meninges

mastoiditis /máss toyd ítiss/ *n* inflammation of the mastoid process and mastoid cells

mastoid process *n* a bony protuberance on the skull, found behind the ear in many vertebrates, including humans

Mastroianni /mást roy yánni/, **Marcello** (1924–96) Italian film actor

masturbate /mástər bayt/ (**-bates, -bating, -bated**) *vti* to give oneself or somebody else sexual pleasure by stroking the genitals, usually to orgasm [Mid-19C. < the past participle of Latin *masturbari*.] —**masturbation** /mástər báysh'n/ *n* —**masturbator** *n* —**masturbatory** *adj*

masurium /mə sóori əm/ *n* the metallic element technetium [Early 20C. < German, after *Masuria*, region of NE Poland.]

mat[1] /mat/ *n* **1 PIECE OF CARPET** flat material placed on a floor for decoration or protection or for wiping the feet **2 PIECE OF PADDED MATERIAL** a piece of padded material placed on the floor for use in some sports and activities, e.g. to absorb the impact of falling in judo **3 PROTECTIVE COVER** a piece of fabric or board used to protect surfaces from damage by heat or scratching **4 THICK MASS** any thick or interwoven mass, e.g. a tangle of hair ■ *vti* (**mats, matting, matted**) **FORM TANGLED MASS** to make something into or become a thick tangled mass [Pre-12C. < Latin *matta*.]

mat[2] /mat/ *n* = **matt** *n.* ■ *adj* = **matt** *adj.* [Mid-17th C. < French *mat* 'dull'.]

Matabeleland /máttə beéli land/ region in S Zimbabwe, between the Limpopo and Zambezi rivers. Area: 181,605 sq. km/70,118 sq. mi.

Matadi /mə taádi/ city in the W Democratic Republic of the Congo, on the River Congo. Population: 172,730 (1994).

matador /máttə dawr/ *n* **1 BULLFIGHTER** the main bullfighter, whose job is to kill the bull **2 HIGH CARD** one of the highest playing cards in some games such as skat **3 DOMINO GAME** a variety of the game of dominoes in which the dots on adjacent halves must total seven [Late 17C. < Spanish, < *matar* 'kill'.]

matagouri /máttə goóri/ (*plural* **-ris**) *n* a thorny bush that forms thickets in open areas. Native to: New Zealand. *Discaria toumatou.* [Mid-19C. Alteration of Maori *tumatakuru*.]

Mata Hari /maátə haári/ (1876–1917) Dutch dancer and spy. Born **Margaretha Geertruida Zelle**

matai /maá tī/ (*plural* **-ais**) *n* a coniferous evergreen tree that has bluish bark and yields timber often used for flooring. Native to: New Zealand. *Podocarpus spicatus.* [Mid-19C. < Maori.]

Matamoros /máttə máwrəss/ city in NE Mexico, on the Rio Grande opposite Brownsville, Texas. Population: 266,065 (1990).

Mataura /mə tówrə/ river in S South Island, New Zealand. Length: 240 km/149 mi.

match[1] /mach/ *n* **1 CONTEST** a contest between opponents, especially a sporting contest **2 SOMETHING SIMILAR** a close likeness of somebody or something **3 EQUAL** somebody or something capable of competing equally with another **4 GOOD COMBINER** something that combines well with something else **5 COUNTERPART** a person who or thing that is identical to another or is one half of a pair

6 MARITAL PARTNERSHIP a marriage **7 POTENTIAL PARTNER** an appropriate marriage partner ■ *v* **1** *vt* **BE LIKE** to be similar or identical to somebody or something **2** *vt* **COMPETE EQUALLY** to be as good, or sometimes as bad, as somebody or something else ○ *She knows she can match him for speed any day.* **3** *vti* **COMBINE WELL** to make a suitable or pleasing combination, or put things together to make such a combination **4** *vt* **FIND SOMETHING THAT COMBINES** to find something that makes a suitable accompaniment **5** *vti* **JOIN CLEANLY** to fit or join something smoothly **6** *vt* **PLACE IN OPPOSITION** to provide somebody or something with an opponent **7** *vti* **US TOSS COINS** to toss coins to see which sides land face up to determine a choice or decision [Old English *gemæcca* 'spouse, lover' < Germanic] —**matchability** /mácha bíĺlati/ *n* —**matchable** *adj* —**matcher** *n*

match[2] /mach/ *n* **1** a thin stick of wood whose tip is coated with a combustible material that ignites when scraped against a rough surface, used to light a fire, candle, or gas appliance **2** a slow-burning fuse used in cannons and explosives [14C. Via Old French *meiche* < Greek *muxa* 'lampwick'.]

matchboard /mách bawrd/ *n* a board that has a tongue along one edge and a groove along the other so that it can be fitted together with other boards

matchbook /mách bòok/ *n* a small cardboard folder with safety matches inside and a striking surface usually on the outside

matchbox /mách boks/ *n* a small cardboard box for matches, with a striking surface along one or both sides

matchless /máchlass/ *adj* so outstandingly great as to have no rival —**matchlessly** *adv* —**matchlessness** *n*

matchlock /mách lok/ *n* **1** formerly, a trigger mechanism in guns that ignited the powder with a slow-burning fuse **2** a gun fitted with a matchlock

matchmaker /mách maykar/ *n* an arranger of romantic partnerships or marriages

match play *n* in golf, a method of scoring in which the number of holes won is counted rather than the number of strokes taken —**match player** *n*

match point *n* **1** the final point needed to win a match, especially in tennis and other racket games **2** a unit used for scoring in bridge tournaments

matchstick /mách stik/ *n* **1 STEM OF MATCH** the wooden part of a match ■ *adj* **1 MADE FROM MATCHES** built of matchsticks **2 LIKE STICKS IN THINNESS** in the form of thin strips or simple lines

mate[1] /mayt/ *n* **1 FRIEND** a friend, also used as a friendly, or sometimes hostile, form of address to a man **2 BREEDING PARTNER** each of a pair of animals that breed together **3 PARTNER IN SEX OR WEDLOCK** a sexual or marriage partner (*informal or humorous*) **4 SKILLED WORKER'S HELPER** an assistant to a skilled worker ○ *a plumber's mate* **5 DECK OFFICER** a deck officer of a rank below the master on a merchant ship **6** *US* **PETTY OFFICER** a petty officer in the US Navy who assists a warrant officer **7 SOMETHING THAT MATCHES** each of a pair of things that belong together ■ *v* (**mates, mating, mated**) **1** *vti* **BREED** to come together or be brought together to breed **2** *vi* **HAVE SEX** to engage in sex **3** *vt* **CONNECT TWO OBJECTS** to combine or connect two things **4** *vti* **MARRY** to join or become joined in marriage (*informal or humorous*) [14C. < Middle Low German *gemate*.] —**mateless** *adj*

mate[2] *n*, *vt* (**mates, mating, mated**), *interj* CHESS = **checkmate** *n*. **1**, **checkmate** *v*. **2**, **checkmate** *v*. **1**, **checkmate** *interj*. [14C. See CHECKMATE.]

maté /maa tay, máttay/ *n* **1** a popular South American milky drink that contains caffeine and is made from dried leaves **2** an evergreen tree grown for its leaves, which are used to make maté. Native to: South America. *Ilex paraguariensis.* [Early 18C. Via Spanish < Quechua *mati*.]

mater /máytar/ *n* mother (*dated informal or humorous*) [Late 16C. < Latin, 'mother'.]

materfamilias /máytar fa míĺli ass/ (*plural* **-tresfamilias** /máy trayz-/) *n* a woman described in her role as head of a household or as the mother of her children (*formal*) [Mid-18C. < Latin, 'mother of the family'.]

material /ma teéri al/ *n* **1 SOMETHING USED IN MAKING ITEMS** the substance used to make things **2 INFORMATION** information such as facts, notes, and research, used in the making of a book, film, or other work **3 FABRIC** woven flat cloth or fabric **4 SOMEBODY SUITABLE** somebody regarded in terms of his or her suitability to perform a certain job or do a task ○ *She's certainly executive material.* ■ **materials** *npl* **EQUIPMENT** the tools and other things needed to perform a particular task ■ *adj* **1 PHYSICAL** relating to or consisting of solid physical matter ○ *the material universe* **2 WORLDLY** relating to physical wellbeing rather than emotional or spiritual wellbeing ○ *material comforts* **3 PERTINENT** relevant or important **4 IMPORTANT IN COURT** important to a case that is being tried in court ○ *testimony that is material to the case* **5 OF CONTENT NOT FORM** relating to the substance of reasoning rather than the form it takes [14C. Via French *matériel* < late Latin *materialis* < Latin *materia* (see MATTER).] —**materiality** /ma teéri álláti/ *n* —**materialness** *n*

materialise *vti* = **materialize**

materialism /ma teéri alizam/ *n* **1** the theory that physical matter is the only reality and that psychological states such as emotions, reason, thought, and desire will eventually be explained as physical functions **2** devotion to material wealth and possessions at the expense of spiritual or intellectual values

materialist /ma teéri alist/ *n* **1** a person who values material wealth and possessions rather than spiritual or intellectual things **2** a supporter of the view that physical matter is the only reality and that psychological states can be explained as physical functions ■ *adj* = **materialistic**

materialistic /ma teéri a lístik/ *adj* concerned with material wealth and possessions at the expense of spiritual and intellectual values —**materialistically** *adv*

materialize /ma teéri a líz/ (**-izes, -izing, -ized**), **materialise** (**-alises, -alising, -alised**) *v* **1** *vi* **BECOME REAL** to become real or become fact **2** *vt* **ASSUME PHYSICAL FORM** to assume, or cause a ghost or spirit to assume, a physical form **3** *vi* **APPEAR** to appear suddenly, as if out of nowhere —**materialization** /ma teéri a lí záysh'n/ *n*

materially /ma teéri ali/ *adv* **1** in a real sense or to a significant degree **2** in terms of material wealth and possessions

materials science *n* the study of the features and applications of the different materials used in science and technology such as metals, plastics, and ceramics

matériel /ma teéri él/, **materiel** *n* the supplies, weapons, and equipment associated with a military force [Early 19C. < French (see MATERIAL).]

maternal /ma túrn'l/ *adj* **1 OF OR LIKE MOTHER** belonging or relating to motherhood, a mother, or mothers in general ○ *maternal pride* **2 CARING** kind, caring, and protective in a motherly way ○ *a very maternal person* **3 ON OR FROM** **MOTHER'S SIDE** relating to or inherited from the mother or the mother's side of a family ○ *Her maternal grandfather was Polish.* [15C. < French *maternel* < Latin *maternus* < *mater* 'mother'.] —**maternalism** *n* —**maternalistic** /ma túrna lístik/ *adj* —**maternally** *adv*

maternity /ma túrnati/ *n* **1 MOTHERHOOD** the condition of being a mother (*usually in combination*) ○ *maternity clothes* **2 MOTHERLY CHARACTERISTICS** the characteristics and emotions traditionally associated with being a mother such as loving kindness and protectiveness **3 HOSPITAL SECTION CARING FOR NEWBORNS** a ward, floor, or other section of a hospital where mothers and newborn babies are cared for [Early 17C. < French *maternité* < Latin *maternus* (see MATERNAL).]

maternity benefit, maternity allowance *n* a series of regular payments made by the state to a woman who has a baby, usually covering the 18 weeks around the child's birth

maternity leave *n* paid or unpaid leave from work that a woman is entitled to take before, at, and after the time that she has a child

maternity ward *n* a hospital ward for the care of newly delivered babies and their mothers, often also with beds for pregnant women who need medical attention before having their babies

mateship /máyt ship/ *n* friendship, especially between two men or within a group of men, on terms of equality and mutual support

matey /máyti/, **maty** *adj* (**-ier, -iest**) **FRIENDLY** friendly, especially in a way that is familiar or seems insincere ○ *Those two have been very matey lately.* ■ *n* (*informal*) **1 TERM OF ADDRESS FOR UNKNOWN MAN** used by a man to address another man he does not know and, usually, feels hostile towards **2 FRIEND** a man who is another man's friend and companion —**matily** *adv* —**matiness** *n*

matgrass /mát graass/, **mat grass** *n* a common European grass that grows in dense tufted clumps on peaty moorland. *Nardus stricta.* [Late 18C. < its being likened to thick matting.]

math /math/ *n US* = **maths** (*informal*) [Late 19C. Shortening.]

math. *abbr* **1** mathematical **2** mathematically **3** mathematician **4** mathematics

mathematical /mátha máttik'l/ *adj* **1 OF MATHEMATICS** belonging to, relating to, or used in mathematics **2 ACCURATE** as accurate as if calculated by mathematics ○ *crafted the strategy with mathematical precision* **3 WORKED OUT BY MATHEMATICS** calculated or proved by mathematics ○ *It's a mathematical certainty that two numbers in the set will be the same.* **4 GOOD AT MATHEMATICS** skilled in mathematics ○ *more artistic than mathematical* —**mathematically** *adv*

mathematical expectation *n* STATS = **expected value**

mathematical induction *n* MATH = **induction** *n*. **9**

mathematician /máthama tísh'n/ *n* a student or expert in mathematics, or somebody whose job involves mathematics

mathematics /mátha máttiks/ *n* **1** the study of the relationships among numbers, shapes, and quantities. It uses signs, symbols, and proofs and includes arithmetic, algebra, calculus, geometry, and trigonometry. (+ *singular verb*) **2** the calculations involved in a process, estimate, or plan (+ *plural verb*) ○ *I like the idea, but the mathematics of it are beyond me.*

MATHEMATICAL SYMBOLS

+	plus; positive	#	number	%	per cent	∩	intersection
−	minus; more than	:	is to (used to show ratios)	≠	is not equal to	⊂ ⊆	is a subset of
±	plus or minus; positive or negative; approximate	::	is equal to (used to show equality of ratios)	≡	is identical with	⊃ ⊇	contains as a subset
×	multiplied by	( ), [ ], { }	brackets, square brackets, braces: symbols of grouping or aggregation	≈	is approximately equal to	∈	is a member of
÷	divided by			~	is equivalent to; is similar to	∉	is not a member of
=	equals	/	part of a symbol for a fraction, or used to indicate division	∝	is directly proportional to	∴	therefore
<	is less than			√	square root of	∠	angle
>	is greater than			∞	infinity	≅ ≡	is congruent to
				∪	union	π	pi

mathematize /máthəmə tīz/ (**-tizes, -tizing, -tized**), **mathematise** (**-tises, -tising, -tised**) *vt* to consider something in, or reduce it to, purely mathematical terms —**mathematization** /máthəmə tī záysh'n/ *n*

Mather /máyth̲ər, máth̲-/, **Cotton** (1663–1728) US minister and theologian

~~**mathmatics**~~ incorrect spelling of **mathematics**

maths /maths/ *n* mathematics (*informal*) US term **math** [Early 20C. Contraction.]

Mathura /mu thóorə/ city in north-central India, on the River Yamuna. Population: 226,850 (1991).

Matilda /mə tíldə/ (1102–67) English princess

matin /máttin/, **mattin, matinal** /máttinəl/ *adj* belonging or relating to matins, or taking place during matins [13C. < French *matines* (see MATINS).]

matinée /mátti nay/, **matinee** *n* **1** a performance of a play, concert, or film that is given during the day, especially in the afternoon, often with cheaper seats than the evening performance **2** an event or social occasion taking place at midday or in the afternoon ○ *The Senior Centre holds a matinée dance on the first Saturday of each month.* [Mid-19C. < French, 'morning' < *matin*, singular of *matines* (see MATINS).]

matinée coat, matinée jacket *n* a flared top for a baby. It is usually long-sleeved and knitted and comes down to just on or below the level of the nappy.

matinée idol *n* an actor, especially a good-looking man of the 1930s and 1940s, who was attractive to matinée audiences formed mostly of women (*dated*)

matinée jacket *n* CLOTHING = **matinée coat** (*dated*)

matins /máttinz/, **mattins** *n* **1 MORNING LITURGY** in the Roman Catholic Church, the morning hours of the Divine Office **2 MORNING PRAYER** in the Church of England, the ceremony of morning prayer **3 HOURS BEFORE VIGIL** in some Roman Catholic monastic communities, the hours before a Vigil **4 DAWN CHORUS** a morning song, especially one sung by birds (*literary*) [13C. < French *matines* < Latin *matutinus* 'of the morning' < *Matuta* 'goddess of dawn'.]

Matisse /mə téess/, **Henri** (1869–1954) French artist

matjes herring /máttyəz-/, **maatjes herring** *n* a fillet or fillets of herring, especially of a young herring that has not spawned, that is lightly salted, usually sweetened and flavoured, and eaten raw [Partial translation of Dutch *maatjesharing* 'maiden's herring' < *maatjes* 'maiden's' (from its use for young herring) + *haring* 'herring']

Matlock /mát lok/ town in central England. Population: 14,680 (1991).

Mato Grosso /máttō gróssō/ state in SW Brazil. Capital: Cuiabá. Population: 2,020,581 (1991). Area: 881,000 sq. km/340,000 sq. mi.

matoke /mə tṓki/ *n* banana or plantain flesh boiled and mashed and used in Uganda as a staple food [Mid-20C. < Bantu.]

Matopo Hills /mə tṓpə hilz/ region of SW Zimbabwe. Area: 3,240 sq. km/1,250 sq. mi.

~~**matress**~~ incorrect spelling of **mattress**

matri- *prefix* mother, maternal ○ *matrilineal* ○ *matriarchy* [< Latin *matr-*, stem of *mater* (see MATER)]

matriarch /máytri aark/ *n* **1 WOMAN HEAD OF FAMILY** a woman who is recognized as being the head of a family, community, or people **2 STRONG SENIOR WOMAN** a woman, usually a grandmother, who is highly respected by her family and to whom the family turn for advice and help **3 WOMAN IN POWERFUL POSITION** a woman who holds a position of dominance, authority, or respect [Early 17C. < Latin *matr-* 'mother', after *patriarch*.] —**matriarchal** /máytri áark'l/ *adj* —**matriarchalism** *n* —**matriarchic** *adj*

matriarchate *n* SOC SCI = **matriarchy** *n.* **2**

matriarchy /máytri aarki/ (*plural* **-chies**) *n* **1 SOCIAL ORDER WHERE WOMEN HAVE POWER** a form of social order where women are in charge and are recognized as the heads of families, with power, lineage, and inheritance passing, where possible, from mothers to daughters **2 matriarchy, matriarchate COMMUNITY WHERE WOMEN HAVE POWER** any community, society, or social group that is based on matriarchy **3 ORGANIZATION WHERE WOMEN HAVE POWER** any form of organization or government where women have power [Late 19C. After PATRIARCHY.]

matric /mə trík/ *n* matriculation (*dated informal*) [Late 19C. Shortening.]

matrices plural of **matrix**

matricide /máytri sīd, máttri-/ *n* **1** the act of murdering your own mother **2** a killer of his or her own mother [Late 16C. Directly or via French < Latin *matricidium* < *matr-* 'mother'.] —**matricidal** /máytri sīd'l, máttri-/ *adj*

matriclinous /máttri klīnəss/, **matroclinous** /máttrō-/, **matroclinal** /-klīn'l/ *adj* having obvious characteristics that are inherited predominantly from the woman parent

matriculant /mə tríkyōōlənt/ *n* EDUC = **matriculate** *n.* [Mid-19C. < medieval Latin *matriculant-*, present participle of *matriculare* (see MATRICULATE).]

matriculate /mə tríkyōō layt/ *v* (**-lates, -lating, -lated**) **1** *vt* **ADMIT AS STUDENT** to admit a student to membership of a college or university **2** *vi* **BE ENROLLED AS STUDENT** to be enrolled at a college or university, after meeting the academic standard required to be accepted for a course of further education ■ *n* **SOMEBODY ENROLLED** a person who has matriculated [Late 16C. < medieval Latin *matriculare* < *matricula* 'little list' < *matrix* (see MATRIX).] —**matriculator** *n*

matriculation /mə tríkyōō láysh'n/ *n* **1** the act or process of matriculating at a college or university **2** an examination formerly taken in Britain as a school-leaving qualification ○ *matriculation card*

matrilineal /máttri línni əl/ *adj* **1 FOLLOWING THE FEMALE LINE** describes the line of genealogical relationship or descent that follows the female side of a family **2 RELATED THROUGH MOTHERS** describes a group that is related by descent through mothers **3 COMING THROUGH THE WOMEN'S LINE** inherited or traced through the women's line of descent —**matrilineally** *adv*

matrilocal /máttri lṓk'l/ *adj* **1** describes a form of marriage in which, after the wedding, the bridegroom moves to his new wife's family home **2** describes a culture in which young men live with their brides' families after marriage —**matrilocality** /máttri lō kálləti/ *n* —**matrilocally** *adv*

matrimonial /máttri mṓni əl/ *adj* belonging or relating to marriage or to a particular marriage [15C. Directly or via French < Latin *matrimonialis* < *matrimonium* (see MATRIMONY).] —**matrimonially** *adv*

matrimony /máttriməni/ *n* **1 MARRIED STATE** the state or condition of being married **2 MARRIAGE CEREMONY** the religious ceremony of marriage **3 CARD GAME** a card game in which players try to hold a king and queen [13C. Directly or via Anglo-Norman *matrimonie* < Latin *matrimonium* 'state of motherhood' (because of the association of marriage with parenthood) < *matr-* 'mother'.]

ϟ **matrix** /máytriks/ (*plural* **-trices** /máytri seez/ *or* **-trixes**) *n* **1 CONTAINER SUBSTANCE** a substance in which something is embedded or enclosed **2 SITUATION IN WHICH SOMETHING DEVELOPS** a situation or set of circumstances that allows or encourages the origin, development, or growth of something ○ *The matrix of video and computers is producing new forms of art.* **3 TISSUE-FORMING SUBSTANCE** the substance that exists between cells and from which tissue, e.g. cartilage and bone, develops **4 TISSUE AT BASE OF NAIL** the thickened tissue at the base of a fingernail, toenail, or tooth from which a new nail or tooth grows **5 SOIL OR ROCK CONTAINING** the soil or rock in which something such as a fossil, crystal, or mineral is embedded. ◊ **gangue 6 MAIN PART OF ALLOY** the main metal component in an alloy **7 ARRAY OF MATHEMATICAL ELEMENTS** a rectangular array of mathematical elements, e.g. the coefficients of linear equations, whose rows and columns can be combined with those of other arrays to solve problems **8 NETWORK OF CIRCUIT ELEMENTS** in computing, a network of circuit elements, e.g. transistors and resistors **9 METAL TYPE MOULD** a metal mould from which type is cast in the hot-metal process **10 MOULD MADE FROM RAISED SURFACE** a mould made by taking the impression of a raised surface in a substance such as plastic, used in stereotyping or electrotyping **11 GRAMOPHONE RECORD MOULD** a mould used in the production of gramophone records **12 BED OR SURROUND OF MATERIAL** a bed or surround of material that gives protection or absorbs a force **13 WOMB** the womb (*archaic*) [14C. Directly or via French *matrice* < Latin *matrix* 'womb', later 'list' < *mater* 'mother'.]

matrix sentence *n* the main clause in a complex sentence

matrix trading *n* a bond swap strategy designed to profit from yield curve differentials between bonds of different ratings or classes

matro- *prefix* = **matri-**

matroclinal *adj* GENETICS = **matriclinous**

matroclinous *adj* GENETICS = **matriclinous**

matron /máytrən/ *n* **1 MATURE WOMAN** a woman, especially a married woman of middle age or later, who has had children and is thought of as being mature, sensible, and of good social standing **2 SUPERVISOR** a woman in charge of the medical and housekeeping arrangements in an institution, e.g. a British boarding school **3 HEAD NURSE** a woman who is head of the nursing staff in a hospital, nursing home, or other medical institution, now called the senior nursing officer (*no longer used technically*) **4** *US* **WOMAN WARDEN** a woman who is a warden in a women's correctional institution [14C. Directly or via French *matrone* < Latin *matrona* < *matr-* 'mother'.] —**matronal** *adj* —**matronhood** /máy trən hŏŏd/ *n* —**matronship** *n*

matronly /máytrənli/ *adj* **1 LIKE A MATRON** having qualities associated with a matron, especially dignity and placidity **2 MATURE AND FULL-FIGURED** mature and plump, especially with a large bosom **3 OF A MATRON** relating to or typical of a matron ○ *matronly duties* —**matronliness** *n*

matron of honour *n* a married woman who acts as chief bridesmaid at the wedding of a woman friend or relative

matronymic /máttrə nímmik/, **metronymic** /méttrə-/ *n* a name derived from a mother or a matrilineal ancestor [Late 18C. < Latin *matr-* 'mother'.]

Matsu Islands /mat sóo-/ group of islands in the Taiwan Strait, close to the SE Chinese mainland, administered by Taiwan

matsutake /mátsoo taáki/, **matsutake mushroom** *n* an edible dark brown mushroom with a cinnamon fragrance. Native to: Japan. *Tricholoma matsutake.* [< Japanese, 'pine mushroom']

Matsuyama /mát sōō yaámə/ city on NW Shikoku, Japan. Population: 443,322 (1990).

matt /mat/, **matte, mat** *n* a dull or nonglossy finish, e.g. on paintwork or photographic prints. US term **mat**[2] *n.* ■ *adj* having a matt finish. US term **mat**[2] *adj.* [Mid-17C. < French *mat* 'dull'.]

Matta Echaurren /máttər eCHów ren/, **Roberto** (*b.* 1911) Chilean-born French artist

matte[1] /mat/ *n* **1** a mixture of metal sulphides formed during the smelting of sulphide ores, e.g. ores of copper or nickel **2** a mask used for obscuring part of an image so that another image can be put on top of the original. ◊ **matte shot** [Mid-19C. < French, a form of *mat* 'dull'.]

matte[2] *n, adj* = **matt**

matted /máttid/ *adj* **1** forming a thick tangled mass **2** covered with mats or matting

matter /máttər/ *n* **1 SOMETHING UNDER CONSIDERATION** something that is being considered or needs to be dealt with ○ *This is a matter for serious thought.* **2 SUBSTANCE** a substance or material of a particular kind ○ *reading matter* **3 MATERIAL SUBSTANCE** the material substance of the universe that has mass, occupies space, and is convertible to energy **4 CAUSE OF PROBLEM** the reason why something is wrong or not working properly, or why somebody is annoyed, upset, or not feeling well ○ *What's the matter?* ○ *There's something the matter with the alarm.* **5 PRINTED TEXT** text or other material that is printed ○ *cheaper rates for printed matter* **6 SUBJECT OF SPEECH OR WRITING** the subject that is dealt with in speech or writing, as opposed to its presentation ○ *The subject matter was well presented.* **7 WHAT IS PERCEIVED BY MIND** in Cartesian philosophy, something that is extended in space and persists through time, and is contrasted with mind **8** *US* **SOMETHING TO BE PROVED** a case to be proved or resolved in a court of law ○ *Who is the defendant in this matter?* **9 BODILY DISCHARGE** something such as pus that is discharged from the body ■ **matters** *npl* **CIRCUMSTANCES** the current situation or circumstances ○ *We were both under a lot of stress, which didn't improve matters.* ■ *vi* **1 HAVE IMPORTANCE** to be important ○ *The only thing that matters is for you to get better.* **2 MAKE DIFFERENCE** to make a difference ○ *It doesn't matter how you tell her, just make sure she knows.* **3 PRODUCE PUS** to form or discharge pus [12C. Directly or via Anglo-Norman *mater(i)e*, French *matière* < Latin *materia* 'timber, stuff' < *mater* 'mother'.] ◇ **for that matter** as far as that is concerned ◇ **no matter what** used to express determination ◇ **a matter of opinion** a subject about which there are varying views

SYNONYMS See ***subject***.

Matterhorn

Matterhorn /máttər hawrn/ mountain in the Pennine Alps, on the Italian-Swiss border. Height: 4,478 m/14,692 ft.

matter of fact *n* **1** something that is true and that cannot be denied ○ *Very few people here have jobs – it's a matter of fact.* **2** a question to be decided by a court of law that involves deciding on the truth of a statement ◇ **as a matter of fact 1** used to add a statement that completes what you are saying or emphasizes its truth **2** used to contradict what somebody else has said or to express disagreement

matter-of-fact *adj* **1** straightforward and not fanciful or emotional ○ *I admired her matter-of-fact approach to life.* **2** dealing with facts and not emotions or opinions ○ *The report gave a very matter-of-fact account of the incident.* —**matter-of-factly** *adv* —**matter-of-factness** *n*

matter of law *n* a question to be decided by a court of law that involves the interpretation of a point of law

mattery /máttəri/ *adj* secreting or discharging pus

matte shot *n* in film-making, a visual effect that is achieved by masking out part of an image using a matte and superimposing another image so that it combines with the rest of the original

Matthau /mát ow/, **Walter** (1920–2000) US actor. Born **Walter Matasschanskayasky**

Matthew *n* the first of the gospels of the Bible in which the life and teachings of Jesus Christ are described, traditionally attributed to St Matthew

Matthew /máthyoo/, **St** (*fl.* 1st century) apostle

Matthews /máthyooz/, **Sir Stanley** (1915–2000) British footballer

Matthew Walker /máth yoo wáwkər/ *n* a knot made in the strands at the end of a rope [Mid-19C. Probably after the person who invented or introduced it.]

Matthias /mə thí əss/ *n* in the Bible, the disciple chosen to replace Judas as one of the 12 apostles of Jesus Christ (Acts 1:15–26)

Matthias Corvinus /mə thí əss kawr vínəss/ (1443–90) king of Hungary (1458–90)

mattify /mátti fī/ (**-fies, -fying, -fied**) *vt* to remove or remedy oiliness or shininess of the complexion [< MATT] —**mattifier** *n*

mattin *adj* CHR = **matin**

matting[1] /mátting/ *n* **1 MATERIAL WOVEN FROM NATURAL FIBRES** a coarse material woven from natural fibres. Use: mats, coverings. ○ *coconut matting* **2 MATS** mats, taken collectively ○ *Matting is integral to Japanese interior design.* **3 LAYER OF NATURAL MATERIALS** a bed or layer formed by natural materials, e.g. by fallen leaves in a forest ○ *We walked through the pines on a matting of needles.* **4 MAKING MATS** the process of making a mat or mats

matting[2] /mátting/ *n* **1** a surface that is dull or without sheen **2** the process of giving a surface, especially a metallic one, a dull finish

mattins *n* CHR = **matins**

mattock /máttək/ *n* a tool like a pickaxe with one end of its blade flattened at right angles to its handle and used for loosening soil and cutting through roots [Pre-12C. < ?]

mattress /máttrəss/ *n* **1 PAD FOR SLEEPING ON** a large pad on which to sleep, usually containing springs or a soft springy filling **2 INFLATABLE PAD** a large pad that can be filled with air or water and used as a bed or for floating on, e.g. in a pool **3 FOUNDATION** a slab or platform used as a foundation for a building **4 INTERNAL METAL FRAMEWORK** a metal framework inside reinforced concrete **5** CIV ENG = **blinding** *n.* **6 SHIELD FOR EMBANKMENTS** a closely woven structure made from brushwood and poles and used for protecting dykes, embankments, dams, and other susceptible slopes from erosion [13C. < Old French *materas* < Arabic *al-matrah* 'cushion'; from the practice of sleeping on cushions.]

maturate /máttyŏŏ rayt, máchŏŏ-/ (**-rates, -rating, -rated**) *vti* to mature, ripen, or develop, or develop or ripen something [Mid-16C. Either < Latin *maturare* < *maturus* 'ripe' or a back-formation < MATURATION.] —**maturative** /mə tyŏŏrə tiv/ *adj*

maturation /máttyŏŏ ráysh'n, máchŏŏ-/ *n* **1 PROGRESS TO MATURITY** the process of becoming mature, ripe, or more developed **2 PROCESS OF MAKING SOMETHING MORE MATURE** the process of ripening or developing something or of making it more mature **3 PROCESS OF CELL DEVELOPMENT** the process in which immature cells in the ovary and testes develop into ova and spermatozoa [14C. Directly or via French < medieval Latin *maturation-* < *maturare* < *maturus* 'ripe'.] —**maturational** *adj*

maturation division *n* the process of cell division by which the ova and spermatozoa are developed

mature /mə tyŏŏr, mə chŏŏr/ *adj* **1 ACTING OR SEEMING LIKE ADULT** showing mental, emotional, or physical characteristics that are typical of a fully developed adult person ○ *Philip is only 12 but he's very tall and already quite mature.* **2 EXPERIENCED** showing qualities gained by development and experience ○ *in the author's mature writings* **3 ADULT** adult or fully grown ○ *a mature animal capable of breeding* **4 FULLY DEVELOPED** fully developed to a complete or final stage **5 OLD AND OF GOOD FLAVOUR** old enough to have acquired the maximum flavour ○ *mature Orkney cheddar* **6 IN LATER LIFE** no longer young ○ *the wisdom shown by the mature dramatist* ○ *The role is that of a mature woman with a successful career behind her.* **7 INVOLVING SERIOUS THOUGHT** involving or reached by a period of serious thought ○ *On mature reflection, I feel it would be wiser to sell.* **8 DUE FOR PAYMENT** describes a financial arrangement that has reached a previously set or mutually agreed-on time limit and is therefore due for payment or repayment ○ *mature bonds* **9 NOT SUBJECT TO MAJOR CHANGE** no longer subject to the instability of early development or expansion ○ *Hydroelectric power is a mature industry in the region.* **10 IN MIDDLE OF EROSION CYCLE** describes a natural feature or landform that is in the middle stages of an erosion cycle ■ *v* (**-tures, -turing, -tured**) **1** *vti* **DEVELOP** to go through, or make something or somebody go through, a developmental process ○ *Children begin to mature at different ages.* **2** *vi* **FALL DUE FOR PAYMENT** to reach a previously set or mutually agreed-on time limit and therefore fall due for payment or repayment (*refers to a financial arrangement*) **3** *vti* **DEVELOP INTO SOMETHING FINISHED** to become fully worked out, or work something out fully, especially through long consideration ○ *The plan had matured over the intervening months.* [14C. Directly or via French < Latin *maturus* 'ripe'.] —**maturely** *adv* —**matureness** *n*

mature student *n* a student aged 25 or over who has gone into higher or further education later than is usual, especially after working or raising a family

maturity /mə tyŏŏrəti, mə chŏŏrəti/ *n* **1 FULL GROWTH OR DEVELOPMENT** the state or condition of being fully grown or developed ○ *Girls tend to reach maturity earlier than boys.* **2 TIME FOR REPAYMENT** the time when a financial arrangement falls due for payment or repayment **3 READINESS FOR REPAYMENT** the state of a financial arrangement when it falls due for payment or repayment **4 MATURE STATE** the condition of being ripe, fully aged, or fully grown, especially mentally or emotionally ○ *I'm amazed at the maturity shown by these young people.* **5 MATURE STATE OF LANDFORM** the stage in the development of a landform at which there is maximum relief and drainage is well developed [15C. Directly or via French *maturité* < Latin *maturitas* < *maturus* 'ripe'.]

maturity-onset diabetes *n* MED = **non-insulin-dependent diabetes**

matutinal /máttyŏŏ tín'l/ *adj* relating to or happening in the morning or in the early part of the day (*formal*) [Mid-16C. < late Latin *matutinalis* < *Matuta*, goddess of the dawn.] —**matutinally** *adv*

MATV *abbr* master antenna television

maty *adj, n* = **matey**

matzo /mótsə/, **matzoh** *n* (*plural* **-zos** *or* **-zoth** /mótsōt/; *plural* **-zohs** *or* **-zoth**) unleavened bread traditionally eaten during Passover in commemoration of the unleavened bread eaten by the ancient Hebrews escaping from slavery in Egypt ■ *adj* made from or like matzo, or used to make matzo ○ *matzo meal* ○ *matzo balls* [Mid-19C. Via Yiddish *matse* < Hebrew *maṣṣāh*.]

matzoon /maat sŏŏn/, **madzoon** /maad zŏŏn/ *n* a food similar to yoghurt, made from fermented milk [< Armenian *madzun*]

matzoth plural of **matzo**

mauby /máwbi/ *n Carib* a drink made from the bark of a tree of the buckthorn family [Late 18C. < Carib *mabi* 'sweet potato (drink)'.]

Mauchly /máwkli/, **John W.** (1907–80) US physicist

maudlin /máwdlin/ *adj* tearfully or excessively sentimental, especially because affected by alcohol [Early 16C. Via French *Madeleine* 'Madeleine' < Greek *Mariaē Magdalēnē* 'Mary Magdalene', because she was commonly represented in medieval art weeping in repentance.] —**maudlinism** *n* —**maudlinly** *adv* —**maudlinness** *n*

Mauger /máyjər/, **Ivan Gerald** (*b.* 1939) New Zealand speedway rider

Maui /mówi/ second largest island of Hawaii, between Hawaii and Molokai islands. Population: 100,374 (1990). Area: 1,884 sq. km/727 sq. mi.

maul /mawl/ *vt* **1 ASSAULT** to beat, batter, or tear at a person or animal ○ *He got mauled in the ring by a better boxer.* **2 HANDLE ROUGHLY** to handle somebody or something too roughly or clumsily ○ *Children may need to be taught not to maul their pets.* **3 CRITICIZE FIERCELY** to criticize somebody or something severely or mercilessly ○ *Despite being a box-office success, her new film was mauled by the critics.* ■ *n* **1 IN RUGBY MOVING SCRUM** a loose scrum that members of both teams form around the player holding the ball or trying to run with the ball **2 CROWD** a crowd of people who are pushing, struggling, or fighting ○ *'The maul of medics holding bags and cords around the stretcher'* (Mark Lawson, *Idlewild*; 1995) **3 PILE-DRIVING HAMMER** a large heavy hammer, usually with a wooden head, used for driving in piles, stakes, or wedges **4 LOG-SPLITTING HAMMER** a heavy hammer that has one side of the head shaped like a wedge, making it suitable for splitting logs or wood [13C. Via Old French *mail* 'hammer' < Latin *malleus*.] —**mauler** *n*

Maulana /maw láanə/ *n* a title given to a man who is learned in Persian and Arabic [Mid-19C. < Arabic *mawlānā* 'our master'.]

maulers /máwlərz/ *npl* the hands (*archaic slang*)

Mau Mau /mów mow/ *npl* a secret Kenyan organization set up in 1952 with the aim of forcing European settlers from the land and ending British rule in Kenya [Mid-20C. < Kikuyu.]

mau-mau /mów mow/ (**mau-maus, mau-mauing, mau-maued**) *vt US* to confront somebody, e.g. a public official or bureaucrat, with the intent of gaining concessions, benefits, or advantage through intimidation (*slang*)

maun /maan, mawn/, **man** /mawn, maan/, **mun** /mun/ *v* must (*regional*) ○ *I maun get to the shops afore they shut.* [13C. < Old Norse *man*, a present tense form of *munu* 'intend to'.]

Mauna Kea /máwnə kée ə/ dormant volcano on north-central Hawaii Island, Hawaii, the highest peak in the state 4,205 m/13,796 ft

Mauna Loa /máwnə lṓ ə, mówna-/ active volcano on south-central Hawaii Island, Hawaii. Height: 4,170 m/13,680 ft.

maund /mawnd/ *n* a unit of weight used in South Asia, with a value that varies from place to place but is often equal to 37 kg/82 lbs [Late 16C. < Arabic *mann*.]

maunder /máwndər/ *v* **1** *vti* to talk or say something in a vague, rambling, or incoherent way **2** *vi* to move or act in a vague, aimless, or undirected way [Early 17C. < ?] —**maunderer** *n*

maundy /máwn di/ *n* a ceremony held in some Christian churches on Maundy Thursday that involves an actual or symbolic washing of people's feet in commemoration of Jesus Christ's washing of his disciples' feet (John 13:3–34) [13C. Via Old French *mandé* < Latin *mandatum (novum)* '(new) commandment', first words of an antiphon sung in the ceremony.]

Maundy /máwn di/ *n* the distribution of Maundy money by the British sovereign

Maundy money *n* specially minted silver coins that the British sovereign distributes in a church ceremony on Maundy Thursday

Maundy Thursday *n* a Christian holy day marking the Last Supper. Date: Thursday before Easter Day. ◊ **Holy Thursday**

Maupassant /mó pass oN, mô pass aàN/, **Guy de** (1850–93) French novelist and short-story writer

Mauriac /máw ri ak/, **François** (1885–1970) French poet, novelist, and playwright

Maurist /máwrist/ *n* a member of a group of French Benedictine monks, founded in 1618 and dissolved during the French Revolution, who were renowned for their great scholarship, especially in hagiography [Late 18C. After St *Maur*, 6C disciple of St Benedict.]

Mauritania

Mauritania /mórri táyni ə/ republic in NW Africa, on the Atlantic Ocean. Capital: Nouakchott. Population: 2,333,000 (1996). Area: 1,031,000 sq. km/398,000 sq. mi. —**Mauritanian** *n, adj*

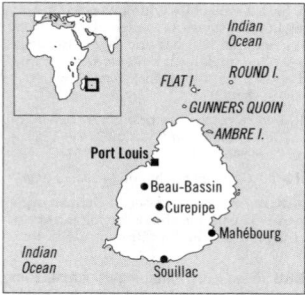

Mauritius

Mauritius /mə ríshəss/ island republic in the SW Indian Ocean, east of Madagascar. Capital: Port Louis. Population: 1,141,000 (1996). Area: 2,040 sq. km/788 sq. mi. —**Mauritian** *n, adj*

Maurya /mówri ə/ *n* an Indian dynasty established in the 4th century BC after invasions by Alexander the Great, members of which included the emperor Ashoka [Late 19C. < Sanskrit, after Candragupta *Maurya*, its founder.]

mausoleum /máwssə leè əm, máwzə-/ (*plural* **-ums** *or* **-a** /-ə/) *n* **1** TOMB a large tomb, especially one that is ornately decorated or made from expensive stone **2** BUILDING CONTAINING TOMBS a building, often a highly decorated or elaborate one, that houses a tomb or several tombs **3** GLOOMY INTERIOR a large gloomy oppressive room or building ○ *I can't study in the library; it's a mausoleum.* [15C. Via Latin < Greek *Mausōleion* 'tomb of Mausolus' (4C BC king of Caria in Asia Minor), built in 353 BC at Halicarnassus (now Bodrum in Turkey).] —**mausolean** *adj*

mauve /mōv/ *n* a pale colour between purple and blue or pink [Mid-19C. Via French < Latin *malva* 'mallow plant'; from the colour of its flowers.] —**mauve** *adj*

maven /máyvən/, **mavin** *n* an expert in about knowledgeable enthusiast of something [Mid-20C. Via Yiddish *meyvn* < Hebrew *mēbīn* 'somebody who understands'.]

maverick /mávvərik/ *n* **1** an independent thinker who refuses to conform to the accepted views on a subject

2 an unbranded animal, especially a calf that has become separated from its mother and herd [Mid-19C. Probably after Samuel Augustus *Maverick* (1803–70), Texas cattle-owner.]

mavin *n* = **maven**

mavis /máyviss/ *n* a song thrush (*literary*) [14C. < French *mauvis*.]

mavourneen /mə voòr neen/, **mavournin** *n Ireland* my darling [Early 19C. < Irish *mo mhuirnín* 'my little love'.]

maw /maw/ *n* **1** ANIMAL'S MOUTH the mouth, jaws, throat, or stomach of an animal, especially a carnivorous animal that devours food greedily **2** GREEDY PERSON'S MOUTH the mouth, throat, or stomach of a greedy person (*informal*) **3** GAPING HOLE anything that seems like a gaping hole that devours things or people ○ *the ravenous maw of readers' expectations* [Old English *maga* 'stomach' < Germanic]

mawkin /máwkin/ *n* **1** a scarecrow (*regional or archaic*) **2** an offensive term that deliberately insults a woman's care for her appearance or her decency of speech and behaviour (*regional insult*) [13C. < the name *Matilda* or *Maud*, literally 'little Matilda'.]

mawkish /máwkish/ *adj* **1** sentimental, especially in a contrived or off-putting way **2** bland or unappetizing in taste or smell [Mid-17C. < *mawk* 'maggot' < Old Norse *maðkr*.] —**mawkishly** *adv* —**mawkishness** *n*

Mawlid al-Nabi /máwlid al naàbi/ *n* in Islam, the celebrations marking the prophet Muhammad's birthday [< Arabic, 'birthday of the prophet']

max /maks/ *n* MAXIMUM the maximum limit or amount of something (*informal*) ○ *I could lend you 50 quid, but that's my max.* ■ *adj* MOST most or highest (*slang*) ○ *Turn up the volume to get the max effect.* ■ *adv* AT THE MOST as a maximum (*slang*) ○ *We were offered £100 max.* [Mid-19C. Shortening of MAXIMUM.]

max out *vti US* to reach a limit in a personal attribute or ability, or reach the limit of a resource (*slang*) ○ *I maxed out my credit card last week.*

max. *abbr* maximum

maxi /máksi/ *n* ANKLE-LENGTH PIECE OF CLOTHING an ankle-length coat, skirt, or dress ■ *adj* **1** ANKLE-LENGTH describes an article of clothing that is ankle-length. ◊ **mini 2** ABNORMALLY LARGE larger than normal ○ *maxi tubs of ice cream* [Mid-20C. < MAXIMUM.]

maxilla /mak sílla/ (*plural* **-lae** /-lee/) *n* **1** either of a pair of bones that are fused at the midline and together form the upper jawbone in vertebrates **2** a mouthpart that is one of one or two pairs behind the mandibles of arthropods [Late 17C. Directly and via Old French *maxille* < Latin *maxilla* 'little jaw' < *mala* 'jaw'.] —**maxillar** *adj* —**maxillary** *adj*

maxillofacial /mak síllō fáysh'l/ *adj* relating to, located in, or affecting the face in the region of the upper jaw [Early 20C. < MAXILLA + FACIAL.]

maxim /máksim/ *n* **1** a succinct or pithy saying that has some proven truth to it **2** a general rule, principle, or truth [15C. Via French < medieval Latin *maxima (propositio)* 'largest (proposition)', a form of *maximus* (see MAXIMUM).]

Maxim *n* ARMS = **Maxim gun**

Maxim /máksim/, **Sir Hiram** (1840–1916) US-born British engineer and inventor

maxima plural of **maximum**

maximal /máksim'l/ *adj* **1** relating to or constituting a maximum **2** the best or greatest possible —**maximally** *adv*

maximalist /máksimalist/ *n* an uncompromising person who is determined to achieve a political aim, directly if necessary [Early 20C. < MAXIMAL after Russian *maksimalist*.] —**maximalist** *adj*

Maximalist *n* a member of a Russian group that, in the early 20th century, advocated terrorist action to get rid of the tsar and the setting up of a temporary proletarian dictatorship

Maxim gun /máksim-/ *n* an early single-barrelled machine gun that was cooled by an outer casing containing water [Late 19C. After Sir Hiram MAXIM.]

Maximilian /máksi mílli ən/ (1832–67) archduke of Austria and emperor of Mexico (1863–67)

Maximilian I (1459–1519) king of Germany (1486–1519) and Holy Roman Emperor (1493–1519)

maximin /máksimin/ *n* **1** the largest of a set of minimum values **2** in game theory, a strategy of attempting to

maximize the smallest possible advantage [Mid-20C. Blend of MAXIMUM + MINIMUM; modelled on MINIMAX.]

⚡**maximize** /máksi mīz/ (**-mizes, -mizing, -mized**), **maximise** (**-mises, -mising, -mised**) *vt* **1** INCREASE SOMETHING TO THE MAXIMUM to make something as great as possible ○ *maximize the chances of success* **2** REGARD SOMETHING AS MOST IMPORTANT to attach the greatest importance to something ○ *Historians maximize the treaty's benefits to trade and tend not to mention its political costs.* **3** FIND A FUNCTION'S LARGEST VALUE to find or work out the largest value of a function **4** MAKE IMAGE LARGER to increase the size of a computer image —**maximization** /máksi mī záysh'n/ *n* —**maximizer** *n*

maximum /máksiməm/ *n* (*plural* **-mums** *or* **-ma** /-mə/) **1** GREATEST POSSIBLE AMOUNT the largest or greatest amount, number, size, or degree possible or allowed ○ *The stadium seats a maximum of 60,000.* **2** HIGHEST AMOUNT OR LEVEL REACHED the largest amount, level, or value that something variable can reach or reaches during a period ○ *Even at its maximum, the noise did not exceed legal levels.* **3** LARGEST NUMBER the largest number in a set **4** FUNCTION'S GREATEST VALUE the greatest value that a continuous function can attain over a specific interval **5** TIME OF STAR'S GREATEST BRIGHTNESS the interval during which a variable star is most luminous **6** VARIABLE STAR'S MAGNITUDE the magnitude of a variable star at its greatest ■ *adj* GREATEST POSSIBLE of the greatest possible or permitted amount or value ○ *visual effects with maximum impact* ○ *Maximum occupancy in this building is 235.* ■ *adv* AT MAXIMUM at the maximum extent ○ *The hall seats 400 maximum.* [Mid-16C. Directly or via French < modern Latin, a form of Latin *maximus* 'greatest' < *magnus* 'great'.]

maximum-minimum thermometer *n* a special type of thermometer that logs the highest and lowest temperatures recorded during the period since it was last set

maximum-security *adj* protected or made secure by the most extensive and elaborate security arrangements that are available or in current use ○ *a maximum-security jail*

maxixe /mə sheèsh, mak seèks/ *n* **1** a Brazilian dance performed in duple time **2** the music for a maxixe [Early 20C. < Brazilian Portuguese.]

maxwell /máks wel/ *n* (*symbol* **Mx**) the centimetre-gram-second unit of magnetic flux, equal to the flux over one square centimetre perpendicular to a magnetic field of one gauss [Late 19C. After James Clerk MAXWELL.]

Maxwell /máks wel, mákswəl/, **James Clerk** (1831–79) Scottish physicist

may[1] /may/ (**may, might** /mīt/) CORE MEANING: a modal verb indicating that something could be true, or could have happened, or will possibly happen in the future ○ *I may not be able to meet you.* ○ *He may have been working too hard.* ○ *A verdict may be announced today.*

v **1** INDICATES POSSIBILITY indicates that something is possibly true ○ *That may be the best way to do it.* **2** INDICATES THAT SOMETHING COULD HAPPEN indicates that something could have happened, or could happen in the future ○ *The crash may well have been caused by faulty brakes.* ○ *The comet may be remembered best for its nonscientific impact.* **3** INDICATES PERMISSION indicates that somebody is asking for permission or giving somebody permission to do something (*formal*) ○ *'May I leave the table'? 'No, you may not'.* **4** INDICATES RIGHT indicates that somebody has a legal or moral right to do something ○ *You may withdraw money from this account at any time.* **5** INDICATES REQUESTS OR SUGGESTIONS indicates polite requests, suggestions, or offers ○ *May I remind you of our earlier agreement?* ○ *May I help you with that bag?* **6** INDICATES WISH indicates that somebody wishes for something very strongly (*formal*) ○ *May God bless us, every one.* [Old English *mæg*, a form of *magan* 'be able' < Indo-European] ◇ **be that as it may** indicates that somebody wants to go on to a new topic after conceding the possible truth of a previous statement ○ *'He doesn't earn much money'. 'Be that as it may, he's been successful in what he set out to do'.*

USAGE may have/might have In Standard English, there is a clear contrast in meaning between *may have* and *might have* when we talk about known and unknown outcomes. When we are uncertain whether something did or did not happen, we generally use *may have*, so *They may have lost the game* means 'Perhaps they did lose the game – we still don't know'. *Might have* can also be used in this way, suggesting perhaps an extra element of uncertainty. But when the possibility no longer exists, and we know what happened, we use *might have*, so *They might have lost the game when* 'There was a possibility that they would lose the game, but they didn't'. In present-day English there is an increasing tendency to use *may have* for known outcomes. This may strike people who are aware of the traditional distinction in usage as deviant, and in extreme cases it can be ambiguous or cause confusion (for example, *The president may have married several times before he met his present wife*), so it is not regarded as Standard English, and is best avoided.

may[2] /may/ *n* PLANT SCI = **hawthorn** [< MAY; from the time it comes into flower]

May *n* the fifth month of the year in the Gregorian calendar, made up of 31 days [12C. Via French *mai* < Latin *Maius*, a form of *Maia* 'Maia' (a fertility goddess).]

May, Cape /may/ cape at the S tip of New Jersey

maya /mí a/ *n* 1 in Hinduism, the material world, considered in reality to be an illusion 2 in Hinduism, the ability to create illusion through supernatural, magical, or sacred power [Late 18C. < Sanskrit *māyā*.] —**mayan** *adj*

Maya[1] /mí a/ (*plural* **-ya** *or* **-yas**) *n* 1 a member of a Native American people of Central America and S Mexico whose classical culture flourished from the 4th to the 8th centuries AD 2 a Mayan language spoken in Mexico, Guatemala, and Belize. Native speakers: 500,000. [Early 19C. Via Spanish < Maya.] —**Maya** *adj*

Maya[2] /mí a/ *n* the mother of the Buddha, by a miraculous virgin birth

Vladimir Mayakovsky

Mayakovsky /mí a kófski/, **Vladimir** (1893–1930) Russian poet and propagandist

Mayan /mí ən/ *n* 1 a member of the Maya people 2 a group of Penutian languages spoken in Mexico, Guatemala, and Belize —**Mayan** *adj*

Mayapán /mí a pán/ ruined ancient Maya city in SE Mexico

May apple *n* 1 an oval yellowish fruit with edible pulp 2 a poisonous plant of the barberry family that produces may apples. Flowers: single, white. Native to: E North America. *Podophyllum peltatum*. [Because the fruit is produced in the month of May]

maybe /máybi, máy bee/ *adv* 1 PERHAPS expresses uncertainty ○ *Maybe I'm being too optimistic, but I really think we can get the best players.* 2 NEITHER YES NOR NO used to give a response that is neither yes nor no ○ *'So do you want to come with us or not'? 'Well, maybe'.* 3 INTRODUCES SUGGESTIONS used to introduce advice or suggestions ○ *Maybe you should ask her what she means before you jump to conclusions.* 4 APPROXIMATELY indicates an approximate estimation, e.g. of frequency or a number ○ *The coastal glacier gives off large icebergs maybe every three or four years.* ○ *The forests in this region are no more than 60, maybe 70, years old.* [14C. < *(it) may be*.]

May beetle *n* 1 = **cockchafer** 2 = **June bug** [Because they appear in late spring]

May bug *n* 1 = **cockchafer** 2 = **June bug** [See MAY BEETLE]

mayday /máy day/ *n* the internationally recognized communications distress call, used especially by ships and aircraft [Early 20C. Representing the pronunciation of French *m'aider* in *venez m'aider* 'come and help me'!]

May Day *n* 1 traditionally, a day for celebrating the coming of spring. Date: 1 May. 2 a national holiday in some countries marking the importance of working people. Date: 1 May.

Mayer /mí ər/, **Sir Robert** (1879–1985) German-born British business executive and philanthropist

mayest *v* = **mayst**

mayflower /máy flowər/ (*plural* **-ers** *or* **-er**) *n* 1 any plant that flowers in May, e.g. the cowslip or marsh marigold 2 the flower of the hawthorn

mayfly /máy flī/ (*plural* **-flies**) *n* 1 an insect that lives as an adult for only a few days, typically having two or four pairs of flimsy wings and two or three long slender tail appendages. Order: Ephemeroptera. 2 a fishing fly that looks like a mayfly [Mid-17C. < mistaken belief that they appear only in May.]

mayhem /máy hem/ *n* 1 absolute chaos or severe disruption (*informal*) ○ *Whenever the teacher left the room, it was mayhem.* 2 under old common law, the disabling or deprivation of a limb or other body part, with the result that the victim is unable to offer any defence or fight his or her adversary (*archaic*) [15C. Via Anglo-Norman *mahem*, Old French *mahaing* 'mutilating injury' < assumed Vulgar Latin *mahagnare* 'injure'.]

Mayhew /máy hyoo/, **Henry** (1812–87) British writer and editor

maying /máying/, **Maying** *n* May Day celebrations, or participation in them

mayn't /maynt, máyənt/ *contr* may not

mayo /máyō/ (*plural* **-os**) *n* mayonnaise (*informal*) [Mid-20C. Shortening.]

Mayo /máyō/ county in NW Republic of Ireland. Area: 5,398 sq. km/2,084 sq. mi.

~~mayonaise~~ incorrect spelling of **mayonnaise**

mayonnaise /máy ə náyz/ *n* a rich creamy sauce or dressing made from egg yolks, vegetable oil, and flavourings [Early 19C. Probably < French.]

Mayon Volcano /ma yón-/ active volcano on SE Luzon, Philippines. Height: 2,421 m/7,943 ft.

mayor /mair/ *n* the person elected to be head of government in a city, town, or borough in many countries including the United States, and in the United Kingdom except for Scotland [13C. Via French *maire* < Latin *major* 'more great' < *magnus* 'great'.] —**mayoral** *adj* —**mayorship** *n*

LITERARY LINK *The Mayor of Casterbridge*, a novel (1886) by Thomas Hardy. It is the tragic story of Michael Henchard, a labourer whose success in business raises him to the position of mayor of his home town, but who then loses his fortune as a result of a petty dispute with his assistant. An instructive character study, it is also a revealing portrait of contemporary rural mores.

---

mayoralty /máirəlti/ (*plural* **-ties**) *n* 1 the official position held by a mayor 2 the length of time that a mayor holds office ○ *a five-year mayoralty*

mayoress /máir ress/ *n* 1 a woman elected to be head of government in a city, town, or borough in many countries including the United States, and in the United Kingdom except for Scotland (*dated*) 2 the wife of a mayor or a woman chosen to assist an unmarried mayor at a social function

Mayotte /ma yáwt/ island in the Comoros Islands, in the W Indian Ocean, an overseas dependency of France. Capital: Mamoudzou. Population: 108,000 (1996). Area: 374 sq. km/144 sq. mi.

maypole /máy pōl/ *n* a tall pole that is traditionally erected for May Day celebrations, usually decorated with flowers and with long coloured ribbons attached at the top

May queen *n* a young woman chosen to reign over a May Day celebration

mayst /mayst/, **mayest** /máyist/ *v* 2nd person present singular of **may**[1] (*archaic*)

may tree *n* TREES = **hawthorn**

mayweed /máy weed/ *n* a straggly weed of the daisy family that has foul-smelling leaves. Flowers: white, daisy-like. *Anthemis cotula*. [Mid-16C. May, alteration of *maythe* 'mayweed, camomile' < Old English *magoþe*.]

mazaltov, mazal tov *interj* JUDAISM = **mazeltov**

Mazarin /mázzərin/, **Jules, Cardinal** (1602–61) Italian-born French clergyman and statesman. Born **Giulio Raimondo Mazzarino**

Mazatlán /máthat lán/ city in central W Mexico, on the Pacific Ocean. Population: 314,345 (1990).

Mazdaism /mázdə izəm/, **Mazdeism** *n* RELIG = **Zoroastrianism** [Late 19C. < Avestan *mazdā* < *Ahura Mazda*, supreme god of ancient Persian religion.]

maze /mayz/ *n* 1 PUZZLE MADE OF CONNECTING PATHS an area of interconnected weaving paths that it is difficult to find a way through, especially one in a garden with hedges between the paths or one designed for laboratory animals 2 ROUTE TRACING PUZZLE a diagrammatic version of a maze, where the object is to arrive at a specific point by tracing a route with a pen or pencil 3 CONFUSING NETWORK OF PATHS a network, especially of paths, streets, or passageways, that a walker or driver might easily become lost in ○ *a maze of narrow cobbled streets* 4 CONFUSING MUDDLE any confusing tangle or muddle, e.g. of regulations or procedures, that is difficult to negotiate ○ *a maze of official rules* [13C. Shortening of AMAZE.]

mazeltov /mázz'l tov/, **mazel tov, mazaltov, mazal tov** *interj* used to express good wishes or congratulations [Mid-19C. < modern Hebrew *mazzāl tōb* 'good star'.]

mazer /máyzər/ *n* a large drinking cup or bowl, usually made from hardwood or metal [13C. Via Old French *masere* 'kind of hardwood, maple' < Germanic.]

mazourka *n* DANCE, MUSIC = **mazurka**

mazuma /ma zoomə/ *n* money, especially cash or loose change (*informal*) [Early 20C. < Yiddish.]

mazurka /ma zúrkə/, **mazourka** *n* 1 a Polish national dance, similar to the polka 2 the music for a mazurka [Early 19C. Probably via Russian < Polish *mazurek* 'dance of an inhabitant of Mazovia (ancient part of Poland)' < *mazur* 'inhabitant of Mazovia'.]

mazy /máyzi/ (**-ier, -iest**) *adj* 1 LIKE A MAZE tangled and interwoven like a maze 2 CONFUSING confusing or complicated 3 GIDDY giddy or confused (*archaic or literary*) —**mazily** *adv* —**maziness** *n*

mazzard /mázzərd/ *n* a wild sweet cherry tree often used as grafting stock for cultivated cherries. *Prunus avium*. [Late 16C. < ?]

Mb *abbr* millibar

⚡**MB** *abbr* 1 Bachelor of Medicine 2 Manitoba 3 Medal of Bravery 4 megabyte 5 message board (*in e-mails*)

MBA *abbr* Master of Business Administration

Mbabane /əmba baáni/ capital of Swaziland, in the west of the country. Population: 46,000 (1990 estimate).

mbaqanga /am baa káng gə/ *n* S Africa a rhythmical form of South African popular music

MBE *abbr* Member of the Order of the British Empire

Mbeki /əm béki/, **Thabo** (*b.* 1942) South African president (1999–). Full name **Thabo Mvuyelwa Mbeki**

mbira /əm béerə/ *n* an African musical instrument with a resonating box, often a hollow gourd, with tuned, attached strips of wood or metal that are plucked [Late 19C. < Shona.]

MBO *abbr* 1 management by objectives 2 management buyout

⚡**Mbps** *abbr* megabytes per second

Mbuji-Mayi /əmbóòja mī ī/ town in south-central Democratic Republic of the Congo. Population: 806,475 (1994).

⚡**Mbyte** /ém bīt/ *abbr* megabyte

MC *abbr* 1 master of ceremonies 2 Medical Corps 3 Midheaven 4 Military Cross

MCA *abbr* merchant certificate authority

McAdam /ma káddəm/, **John Loudon** (1756–1836) British inventor and engineer

McBride /mak brīd/, **Willie John** (*b.* 1940) Irish rugby union player

MCC *abbr* Marylebone Cricket Club

McCahon /ma kaà ən/, **Colin John** (1919–87) New Zealand painter

McCarthy /ma kaárthi/, **Joseph R.** (1908–57) US politician

McCarthy, Mary (1912–89) US writer and critic

McCarthyism /ma kaárthi izəm/ *n* 1 the practice of publicly accusing somebody, especially somebody in government or the media, of subversive or Communist activities or sympathies, especially without real evidence to substantiate this 2 the practice of using unsubstantiated accusations or unfair methods of investigation to discredit people [Mid-20C. After Joseph R. MCCARTHY.] —**McCarthyist** *n, adj* —**McCarthyite** *n, adj*

McCartney /mə kaártni/, **Sir Paul** (b. 1942) British singer and songwriter

McColgan /mə kólgən/, **Liz** (b. 1964) British cross-country and marathon runner. Born **Elizabeth Lynch**

McCormack /mə káwrmək, -ak/, **John** (1884–1945) Irish-born US tenor

McCoy /mə kóy/ (Early 20C. < ?) ◇ **the real McCoy** somebody or something that is genuine (informal)

McCubbin /mə kúbbin/, **Frederick** (1855–1917) Australian painter

McCullers /mə kúllərz/, **Carson** (1917–67) US writer. Born **Lula Carson Smith**

McCulloch /mə kúllok, -okh/, **Warren** (1898–1972) US neurophysiologist

McCullough /mə kúllək, -əkh/, **Colleen Margaretta** (b. 1937) Australian novelist

McEnroe /mákənró/, **John** (b. 1959) US tennis player

McEwen /mə kyoó ən/, **Sir John** (1900–80) Australian statesman

McGrath /mə graáth/, **John** (b. 1935) British playwright

McGraw /mə gráw/, **John Joseph** (1873–1934) US baseball manager. Known as **Little Napoleon**

MCh abbr Master of Surgery [Latin, Magister chirurgiae]

McIndoe /mákindó/, **Sir Archibald Hector** (1900–60) New Zealand plastic surgeon

McKay /mə kí/, **Heather Pamela** (b. 1941) Australian squash player

McKenna /mə kénnə/, **Siobhan** (1923–86) Irish stage and film actor

McKenzie /mə kénzi/, **Sir John** (1838–1901) Scottish-born New Zealand politician

McKinley, Mount /mə kínnli/, **Denali** highest mountain in North America, in the Alaska Range, in south-central Alaska. Height: 6,194 m / 20,320 ft.

McKinley, William (1843–1901) US statesman and 25th president of the United States (1897–1901)

McLaren /mə klárrən/, **Bruce Leslie** (1937–70) New Zealand motor racing driver

McLeish /mə kleésh/, **Henry** (b. 1948) Scottish politician and First Minister of Scotland (2000-)

McLuhan /mə klóoən/, **Marshall** (1911–80) Canadian-born US critic and theorist

McMahon /mak maá ən/, **Sir William** (1908–88) Australian statesman

McMurdo Sound /mak múrdó-/ arm of the Ross Sea in E Antarctica, east of Victoria Land

McNaughten rules /mak náwt'n-/, **McNaghten rules** npl in English law, a legal ruling establishing that a defence of insanity depends on proving that the defendant was unaware or unable to understand that wrong was being done [Mid-19C. After Daniel M'Naghten, acquitted of murder in 1843.]

MCom abbr Master of Commerce

MCP abbr male chauvinist pig (dated informal insult)

McQueen /mə kweén/, **Steve** (1930–80) US actor

⚡ **md** abbr Moldova (in Internet addresses)

Md symbol mendelevium

⚡ **MD** abbr 1 Doctor of Medicine 2 mailed (in e-mails) 3 managing director 4 Maryland 5 memorandum of deposit 6 muscular dystrophy 7 musical director

Md. abbr Maryland

MDF abbr medium density fibreboard

MDMA n the drug Ecstasy. Full form **methylenedioxymethamphetamine**

MDS abbr Master of Dental Surgery

MDT abbr US Mountain Daylight Time

me[1] (stressed) /meé/; (unstressed) /mi/ pron 1 THE SPEAKER OR WRITER used to refer to the speaker or writer ○ asked her to do me a big favour ○ Listen to me! ○ Was it me? 2 PERSONALITY OF THE SPEAKER OR WRITER used to refer to the personality of the speaker or writer, or something that may express it (informal) ○ I don't think I like this hat; it isn't really me. 3 US MYSELF myself (informal) ○ I'll get me a new boyfriend– see if I don't. [Old English mē, me < Indo-European]

USAGE See I[1].

me[2] n MUSIC = **mi**

Me symbol methyl

ME[1] abbr 1 Maine 2 mechanical engineer 3 Methodist Episcopal 4 Middle English 5 mining engineer 6 Most Excellent

ME[2] n chronic fatigue syndrome (informal) Full form **myalgic encephalomyelitis**

Me. abbr Maine

mea culpa /máy ə koôlpə/ interj used to express an admission of your own guilt (formal or humorous) ■ n a formal apology or acknowledgment of responsibility or guilt ○ His grudging mea culpa failed to soothe feelings. [< Latin, '(through) my fault', words in the prayer of confession in the Roman Catholic Church's Latin liturgy]

mead[1] /meed/ n an alcoholic drink made by fermenting honey with water, often with added spices [Old English me(o)du < Indo-European, 'honey, sweet drink']

mead[2] /meed/ n a meadow (archaic or literary) [Old English mæd (see MEADOW)]

Mead /meed/, **Margaret** (1901–78) US anthropologist

Meade /meed/, **George Gordon** (1815–72) US Union general

Meade, James Edward (1907–95) British economist

meadow /méddō/ n 1 a grassy field used for producing hay or for grazing domestic livestock 2 an area of low-lying grassland, especially a marshy one near a river [Old English mædwe, form of mæd < Indo-European, 'cut grass with a scythe'] —**meadowy** adj

meadow brown n a very common brown butterfly that lives in grassy places throughout Europe. The female has an orange tinge to the underside of the wings. Maniola jurtina.

meadow fescue n a perennial grass that has shiny leaves and stem bases that are surrounded by brown sheaths. Native to: Europe, Asia. Festuca pratensis.

meadowland /méddō land/ n a large area of land that is made up of meadows

meadowlark /méddō laark/ (plural **-larks** or **-lark**) n a songbird of the blackbird family with brown speckled feathers, a yellow breast, and a black crescent-shaped mark just under the bill. Native to: North America. Genus: Sturnella.

meadow mouse n a field mouse or vole

meadow mushroom n FUNGI = **field mushroom**

meadow nematode n a parasitic nematode worm that infests and destroys the roots of plants. Genus: Pratylenchus.

meadow rue n a plant related to the buttercup with small yellow flowers. Native to: northern temperate zones. Genus: Thalictrum.

meadow saffron n PLANTS = **colchicum**

meadowsweet /méddō sweet/ (plural **-sweets** or **-sweet**) n 1 a tall perennial plant that grows in damp and marshy places. Flowers: tiny, creamy-white, sweet-smelling, in clusters. Native to: Europe. Filipendula ulmaria. 2 an ornamental shrub. Flowers: small, white, in clusters. Native to: North America. Genus: Spiraea.

Meads /meedz/, **Colin** (b. 1936) New Zealand rugby union player

meager adj US = **meagre**

meagre /meégər/ adj 1 UNSATISFACTORILY SMALL unsatisfactory in quantity, substance, or size ○ a company that is notorious for paying meagre salaries 2 OF BAD QUALITY bad and unsatisfying in quality, strength, or effectiveness ○ The street outside my window furnished meagre entertainment. 3 THIN very thin, especially through malnutrition or illness [14C. Via Anglo-Norman megre, French maigre 'lean, thin' < Latin macr-.] —**meagrely** adv —**meagreness** n

meal[1] /meel/ n 1 a substantial amount of food, often more than one course, that is provided and eaten at one time 2 any occasion, e.g. breakfast or lunch, when a substantial amount of food is provided and eaten [Old English mæl 'measure, mealtime' < Germanic] ◇ **make a meal of something** 1 to put more time or effort into something than is usual or necessary (informal) 2 to exaggerate the importance, intensity, or severity of something (informal)

meal[2] /meel/ n 1 GROUND GRAIN the edible part of a cereal crop that has been ground to a powder 2 GROUND-UP SUBSTANCE any substance ground to a fine or coarse powder ○ fish meal 3 Scotland GROUND OATS ground oats,

especially when used to make porridge [Old English melu < Indo-European, 'crush, grind']

mealie /meéli/ n S Africa an ear of maize. ◇ **mealies** [Early 19C. Via Afrikaans mielie < Latin milium 'millet'.]

mealie pap n S Africa a porridge made from ground maize [Pap < Afrikaans pap 'porridge']

mealie pudding n Scotland FOOD = **white pudding** [Because it is made from oatmeal]

mealies /meéliz/ n S Africa maize (+ singular verb)

meals on wheels n a service, usually provided by a social work department or charity, whereby hot meals are brought to senior citizens, people with disabilities, or housebound people (+ singular verb)

meal ticket n 1 a person who or thing that can be counted on or exploited for money (informal) 2 a voucher that entitles the holder to a meal

mealtime /meél tīm/ n the time when a meal is usually or regularly served

mealworm /meél wurm/ (plural **-worms** or **-worm**) n a larva that feeds on stored grain or flour and can cause severe damage and loss. Genus: Tenebrio.

mealy /meéli/ (**-ier, -iest**) adj 1 LIKE MEAL powdery or granular, like meal or grain ○ mealy potatoes 2 MADE OF MEAL containing, made of, or covered with meal 3 DAPPLED with a spotted or dappled hide or coat 4 PALE exceptionally pale, especially through malnutrition or illness —**mealiness** n

mealy bug n a scale insect that is covered with a white powdery secretion and feeds on plants, often causing significant damage to citrus crops and greenhouse plants. Family: Pseudococcidae.

mealy-mouthed adj wary of speaking plainly or openly, especially of admitting unpleasant truths (disapproving)

mean[1] /meen/ (**means, meaning, meant** /ment/) vt 1 HAVE A PARTICULAR SENSE to indicate or represent a particular sense ○ I don't know what half these words mean. ○ When he raises his hand, it means he's making a bid. 2 INTEND TO EXPRESS to intend or be intended to express a particular idea in speech or writing ○ That's not quite what I meant. ○ Just what's that supposed to mean? 3 INTEND TO DO to have an intention to do something ○ I didn't mean to upset you. ○ I've been meaning to call you for weeks. 4 EXPRESS AN OPINION OR INTENTION to be expressing a definite opinion or intention in what you say ○ She says she's resigning, and I think this time she means it. 5 BE A CAUSE OR SIGN OF to be a cause or indication of something ○ The strike will mean a hard winter for many families. ○ A red sunset means fine weather. 6 GO WITH to accompany or be associated with something ○ For Sam, summer meant golf. [Old English mānan < Indo-European]

mean[2] /meen/ adj 1 UNKIND unkind or malicious ○ You hurt her feelings – that was a mean thing to do. 2 NOT GENEROUS unwilling to spend money on other people ○ the meanest person I know 3 US CRUEL cruel and bad-tempered ○ He can be pretty mean at times. 4 SHABBY shabby and poor-looking ○ streets full of small mean houses 5 US EXCELLENT excellent or skilful (informal) ○ He plays a mean sax. 6 HUMBLE of low social position (archaic) ○ living among the poor and mean 7 UNCOMFORTABLE uncomfortable or disagreeable ○ This is the meanest climate I've ever lived in. [Old English mǣne < gemǣne 'shared by everyone' < Germanic] —**meanly** adv —**meanness** n

mean[3] /meen/ n 1 INTERMEDIATE VALUE a value that is intermediate between other values, e.g. an average or expected value 2 MEDIUM TERM OF A PROPORTION either the second or third term of a proportion 3 MIDDLE WAY a medium or moderate alternative or course of action, in the middle of a range of possibilities ○ We need to find the mean between these extremes. ■ adj 1 MEDIUM medium or intermediate in size, strength, or quality 2 IN AN INTERMEDIATE POSITION occupying an intermediate position in a range ○ Speech was achieved in 74.3% of patients within a mean time interval of 63 days. [14C. Via Old French meien < Latin medianus (see MEDIAN).]

meander /mi ándər/ vi 1 FOLLOW A TWISTING ROUTE to follow an indirect route or course, especially one with a series of twists and turns ○ The river meanders to the sea. 2 WANDER SLOWLY AND AIMLESSLY to move in a leisurely way, especially for pleasure or because of a lack of motivation ○ meandering through the park ■ n 1 RELAXED WALK a slow leisurely walk or journey ○ We went for a meander in the woods. 2 TWIST OR BEND a twist or bend in something, especially a river, path, or street 3 TWISTING ROUTE an indirect course or route, especially one that

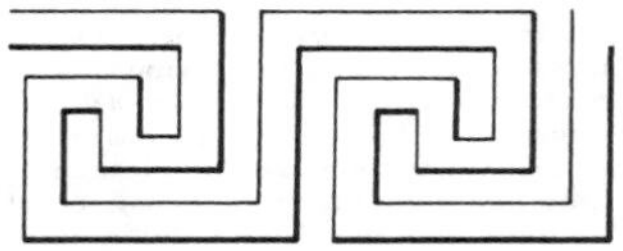

Meander

twists and turns ○ *We followed the meanders of the path.* **4** ORNAMENTAL DESIGN an ornamental design, popular in ancient Greek art and architecture, made by a continuous line that forms square shapes by doubling back on itself [Late 16C. Directly or via French < Latin, 'winding course' < Greek *maiandros*, after a river (now the Büyük Menderes) in Turkey.] —**meanderer** *n* —**meanderingly** *adv* —**meandrous** /mi ándrəss/ *adj*

mean deviation *n* in statistics, the mean of the absolute values of the differences between individual values and the mean or median, used as a measure of dispersion

mean distance *n* the average distance between an orbiting astronomical object and the object it is orbiting

mean free path *n* (*symbol* **λ**) the average distance a gas molecule travels before it collides with another molecule or the containing vessel

meanie /méeni/, **meany** (*plural* **-ies**) *n* an ungenerous or miserly person (*informal*)

meaning /méening/ *n* **1** WHAT SOMETHING MEANS what a word, sign, or symbol means ○ *Do you know the meaning of this word?* **2** WHAT SOMEBODY WANTS TO EXPRESS what somebody intends to express ○ *I want to make my meaning very clear.* **3** WHAT SOMETHING SIGNIFIES what something signifies or indicates ○ *I could not fathom the meaning of their glances.* **4** INNER IMPORTANCE psychological or moral sense, purpose, or significance ○ *an empty life without meaning* ■ *adj* SIGNIFICANT conveying a significance that is not directly expressed ○ *A meaning silence followed these words.* —**meaningly** *adv*

meaningful /méeningf'l/ *adj* **1** WITH MEANING having a discernible meaning ○ *To most, that is not a meaningful expression.* **2** SIGNIFICANT conveying a meaning or significance that is not directly expressed ○ *She gave me a meaningful glance.* **3** ADDING VALUE TO LIFE adding significance, meaning, or purpose to somebody's life ○ *I'm not claiming that we have a deep and meaningful relationship, but we do have fun.* —**meaningfully** *adv* —**meaningfulness** *n*

meaningless /méeningləss/ *adj* **1** having no discernible meaning ○ *a meaningless scrawl* **2** lacking purpose or significance ○ *Offering to help now could be a meaningless gesture* —**meaninglessly** *adv* —**meaninglessness** *n*

mean lethal dose *n* SCI = **median lethal dose**

mean-minded *adj* ungenerous or malicious towards others —**mean-mindedly** *adv* —**mean-mindedness** *n*

means /meenz/ *n* something that is available and makes it possible for somebody to do something (+ *singular or plural verb*) ○ *You can't live out there alone with no means of transport* ■ *npl* the money and other resources that somebody has to live on ○ *It'll be impossible to find a house in this area that's within their means.* [< MEAN³] ◇ **by all means** used as a polite way to give permission ◇ **by no means** used to emphasize a negative ○ *You were by no means the worst player.*

mean sea level *n* the sea level determined and used in mapmaking by the Ordnance Survey

means of production *npl* in Marxism, the raw materials, tools, machinery, and other necessities required in the manufacturing process

mean solar day *n* (*symbol* **d**) the constant interval between two successive transits of the mean sun across the meridian

mean-spirited *adj* malicious or bad-tempered —**mean-spiritedly** *adv* —**mean-spiritedness** *n*

mean square *n* the mean of the squares of a set of values

means test *n* an examination of somebody's income and savings, carried out in order to determine whether the criteria for a benefit or financial aid are met —**means testing** *n*

mean sun *n* in timekeeping, an imaginary sun that moves uniformly in the celestial equator taking the same time to complete a circuit as the real sun takes in the ecliptic

meant past participle, past tense of **mean**¹

mean time *n* time measured with reference to the mean sun crossing a given meridian

meantime /méen tīm/ *n* the intervening period of time between two events, or from now until something else happens ○ *I'll start dinner now and in the meantime you can have an apple.* ○ *I'll come as soon as I can; just wait there for the meantime.* ○ *Repairs will be done tomorrow and meantime please don't use the sink.*

mean value *n* MATH, STATS = **expected value**

meanwhile /méen wīl/ *adv* **1** during the period of time between two events ○ *I'll meet you later; meanwhile I'll leave you to your food.* **2** at the same time as something is happening ○ *I tried to keep everybody calm, meanwhile struggling to open the car door.*

meany *n* = **meanie**

meas. *abbr* **1** measure **2** measurement

measles /méez'lz/ *n* **1** a contagious acute viral disease with symptoms that include a bright red rash of small spots that spread to cover the whole body (+ *singular or plural verb*) **2** the spots that are characteristic of measles [14C. Probably < Middle Low German *masele* or Middle Dutch *masel* 'spot, blemish', and by folk etymology < *mesel* 'leper'.]

measly /méezli/ (**-slier, -sliest**) *adj* **1** ridiculously or disappointingly small or inadequate (*informal*) ○ *He tipped me a measly 5p.* **2** infected with measles

measurable /mézhərəb'l/ *adj* capable of being measured or perceived [13C. Via French *mesurable* < late Latin *mensurabilis* < Latin *mensura* (see MEASURE.] —**measurability** /mézhərə bíllәti/ *n* —**measurableness** *n* —**measurably** *adv*

measure /mézhər/ *n* **1** SIZE the size or extent of something, especially in comparison with a known standard **2** SYSTEM FOR DETERMINING SIZE a particular system used to determine the dimensions, area, volume, or weight of something **3** WAY OF EVALUATING a way of evaluating something, or a standard against which something can be compared **4** ACTION TAKEN an action taken to make something happen or prevent something (*often plural*) ○ *to take precautionary measures* **5** UNIT IN A SYSTEM a unit in a system that is used to determine the dimensions, area, volume, or weight of something (*often used in the plural*) **6** STANDARD AMOUNT OF a standard amount of something, e.g. of a spirit poured into a glass for drinking **7** SOMETHING USED TO DETERMINE QUANTITY something used to determine a quantity, e.g. a ruler, or a spoon or small container that holds a known volume **8** STANDARD USED FOR DETERMINING SIZE a standard used for determining the dimensions, area, volume, or weight of something **9** DEGREE OF an extent or amount that is limited, appropriate, or has its size specified ○ *Their help contributed in no small measure to our success.* **10** LIMITS a limit or limits, especially one that is reasonable or appropriate ○ *His rage had no measure.* **11** LAW a bill to be enacted into law, or a law that has been enacted **12** POETIC METRE the rhythm or metre of a piece of poetry **13** METRICAL FOOT a foot or unit of metre in poetry **14** WIDTH OF TYPE AREA the width of the type area on a page or in a column ○ *In unjustified typesetting, not all lines extend to the full measure.* **15** DANCE a dance (*archaic*) ■ **measures** *npl* ROCK LAYERS strata of rock, especially when they contain a particular material ■ *v* (**-ures, -uring, -ured**) **1** *vt* FIND SIZE, LENGTH, QUANTITY, OR RATE to find out the size, length, quantity, or rate of something using a suitable instrument or device **2** *vt* ASSESS EFFECT OR QUALITY to assess the effect or quality of something, often against a standard ○ *You can't measure a hospital just by its facilities.* **3** *vt* BE A PARTICULAR SIZE, LENGTH, QUANTITY to be a particular size, length, quantity, or rate **4** *vt* DETERMINE SOMEBODY'S SIZE FOR CLOTHES to determine somebody's size in order to make a garment or garments that will fit ○ *She was being measured for her wedding dress.* **5** *vt* COMPARE SIZE OR QUALITY to compare the size, effect, or quality of something with another thing ○ *The champion needs to measure his skill against a worthy challenger.* **6** *vt* ADJUST FOR EFFECT to adjust something so that it is suitable or effective ○ *He measured his punch exactly to catch his opponent on the jaw.* **7** *vi* JOURNEY to travel a particular distance (*archaic*) [12C. Via French *mesure* < Latin *mensura* < *mens-*, past participle of *metiri* 'measure'.] —**measurer** *n* ◇ **beyond measure** very greatly or to an enormous extent ◇ **for good measure** as something extra to the amount required, especially to make sure of something ◇ **get** *or* **have somebody's measure** to arrive at an accurate assessment of somebody's qualities or abilities

LITERARY LINK ***Measure for Measure***, a play (1604) by William Shakespeare. Set in the court of the Duke of Vienna, this tragicomedy tells of a sister's attempts to win clemency for her brother, who has been condemned to death for the relatively minor crime of permissive behaviour. It deals broadly with morality and the nature of justice.

measure off *vt* **1** to determine a particular length of something so that this amount may be cut off **2** to find or mark the limits of an area

measure out *vt* **1** to take a particular amount from a larger amount of something for use **2** to find or mark the limits of an area

measure up *v* **1** *vi* to be good enough to meet a standard ○ *Her new play didn't measure up to expectations.* **2** *vt* to find out the various dimensions of something using a suitable instrument or device

measured /mézhərd/ *adj* **1** UNHURRIED OR REASONABLE slow, deliberate, or carefully considered ○ *spoke in measured tones* **2** ADJUSTED FOR EFFECT adjusted to be suitable or effective ○ *a measured response to the criticism* **3** BY MEASUREMENT determined as a result of measuring ○ *a measured mile* —**measuredly** *adv* —**measuredness** *n*

measureless /mézhərləss/ *adj* too great to be measured (*literary*) ○ *'Through caverns measureless to man'* (Samuel Taylor Coleridge, *Kubla Khan*; 1816) —**measurelessly** *adv* —**measurelessness** *n*

measurement /mézhərmənt/ *n* **1** SIZE OF SOMETHING MEASURED the size, length, quantity, or rate of something that has been measured **2** BODY DIMENSION MEASURED FOR CLOTHING the size of a part of somebody's body, especially used to fit or make clothing (*often plural*) **3** MEASURING an act of measuring something

measuring worm *n* the larva of a geometrid moth that has legs only at each end of its body and moves by bringing its rear forward, forming a loop, then moving its front. US term **inchworm**

meat /meet/ *n* **1** EDIBLE ANIMAL FLESH the flesh of an animal that is considered edible, especially a mammal or bird **2** EDIBLE PART the edible part of anything, e.g. a coconut **3** IMPORTANT PART the essence or important part of something ○ *the meat of the argument* **4** MATERIAL FOR THOUGHT material that is interesting or stimulates thought ○ *There is plenty of meat in the book.* **5** FOOD food or a meal (*archaic or literary*) [Old English *mete* 'food' < Indo-European, 'measure'] —**meatless** *adj* ◇ **meat and drink** something that somebody particularly enjoys

SPELLCHECK Do not confuse ***meat*** with ***meet***, which has a similar sound. Beware: your spellchecker will not catch this error.

meat and potatoes *n US* the most basic or important idea or aspect of something (+ *singular or plural verb*) —**meat-and-potatoes** *adj*

meatball /méet bawl/ *n* **1** minced meat that is shaped into a small round ball, usually with seasonings and a binding ingredient such as breadcrumbs or egg, and then cooked **2** *US, Can* an offensive term that deliberately insults somebody's intelligence or energy (*slang insult*)

ϟ **meatbot** /méet bot/ *n US* a human being (*slang*) [Late 20C. Blend of MEAT + ROBOT.]

Meath /meeth, meeth/ county in E Republic of Ireland. Area: 2,336 sq. km/902 sq. mi.

meathead /méet hed/ *n* an offensive term for somebody who is regarded as unintelligent or imperceptive (*slang insult*)

meat hook *n* a large hook used for hanging carcasses of meat

meat loaf *n* a mixture of minced meat and other ingredients, usually cooked in a loaf tin and served hot or cold

meatus /mi áytəss/ (*plural* **-tuses** *or* **-tus**) *n* a body opening, e.g. the passage in the ear that leads to the

MEASUREMENTS

SI Metric System

The SI (Système Internationale d'Unités) is founded on seven base units that can be multiplied or divided by each other to yield derived units. Values of the base and derived units can be increased or decreased by using SI prefixes indicating decimal multiplication factors. Units and prefixes are assigned internationally accepted symbols.

Base Units

Name	Physical Quantity	Symbol
metre	length	m
kilogram	mass	kg
second	time	s
ampere	electric current	A
kelvin	thermodynamic temperature	K
mole	amount of substance	mol
candela	luminous intensity	cd

Derived Units With Special Names and Symbols

Name	Physical Quantity	Symbol
becquerel	radioactivity	Bq
coulomb	electric charge	C
degree Celsius	temperature	°C
farad	electric capacitance	F
gray	absorbed radiation dose	Gy
henry	inductance	H
hertz	frequency	Hz
joule	energy, work	J
lumen	luminous flux	lm
lux	illumination	lx
newton	force	N
ohm	electric resistance	Ω
pascal	pressure, stress	Pa
radian	plane angle	rad
siemens	electric conductance	S
sievert	radiation dose equivalent	Sv
steradian	solid angle	sr
tesla	magnetic flux density	T
volt	electric potential difference	V
watt	power	W
weber	magnetic flux	Wb

Some Derived Units Without Special Names and Symbols

Name	Physical Quantity	Symbol
ampere per metre	magnetic field strength	A/m
cubic metre	volume	m³
henry per metre	permeability	H/m
joule per kelvin	heat capacity, entropy	J/K
kilogram per cubic metre	mass density	kg/m³
metre per second	linear speed	m/s
metre per second squared	linear acceleration	m/s²
mole per cubic metre	concentration of substance	mol/m³
newton metre	moment of force, torque	N·m
radian per second	angular speed	rad/s
square metre	area	m²
volt per metre	electric field strength	V/m
watt per metre kelvin	thermal conductivity	W/(m·K)
watt per steradian	radiant intensity	W/sr

Prefixes

Multiplication Factor		Name	Symbol
1 000 000 000 000 000 000	or 10^{18}	exa-	E
1 000 000 000 000 000	or 10^{15}	peta-	P
1 000 000 000 000	or 10^{12}	tera-	T
1 000 000 000	or 10^{9}	giga-	G
1 000 000	or 10^{6}	mega-	M
1 000	or 10^{3}	kilo-	k
100	or 10^{2}	hecto-	h
10	or 10^{1}	deca- or deka-	da
0.1	or 10^{-1}	deci-	d
0.01	or 10^{-2}	centi-	c
0.001	or 10^{-3}	milli-	m
0.000 001	or 10^{-6}	micro-	μ
0.000 000 001	or 10^{-9}	nano-	n
0.000 000 000 001	or 10^{-12}	pico-	p
0.000 000 000 000 001	or 10^{-15}	femto-	f
0.000 000 000 000 000 001	or 10^{-18}	atto-	a

Other Units Used With the SI

Some units technically outside of the SI are nevertheless employed with it owing to their practical or special significance or because they are already in wide use. Excepting the electronvolt, litre, tex, and tonne, prefixes are not used with these units. The tonne does not take prefixes indicating a multiplication factor of less than ten.

Name	Symbol	Quantity	SI Equivalent
astronomical unit	–	length	$\approx 1.4960 \times 10^{11}$ m
barn	b	area	$= 10^{-28}$ m²
day, mean solar	d	time	$= 86,400$ s
degree	°	plane angle	$= (\Pi/180)$ rad
electronvolt	eV	energy	$\approx 1.6022 \times 10^{-19}$ J
hectare	ha	area	$= 10,000$ m²
hour, mean solar	h	time	$= 3,600$ s
knot	kn	linear speed	$= 1,852$ m/h
litre	L or l	volume	≈ 1 dm³ or $1,000$ cm³
millibar	mbar	pressure	$= 100$ Pa
minute, mean solar	min	time	$= 60$ s
minute	'	plane angle	$= (\Pi/10,800)$ rad
nautical mile	M	length	$= 1,852$ m
parsec	pc	length	$\approx 3.0857 \times 10^{16}$ m
revolution	r	plane angle	$= 2\Pi$ rad
second	"	plane angle	$= (\Pi/648,000)$ rad
tex	tex	linear density	$= 1$ mg/m
tonne	t	mass	$= 1,000$ kg
unified atomic mass unit	u	mass	$\approx 1.6605 \times 10^{-27}$ kg
year	a	time	$= 3.1536 \times 10^{7}$s (calendar) $= 3.155693 \times 10^{7}$s (solar) $= 3.155815 \times 10^{7}$s (sidereal)

Conversion of Common SI Units

Conversions for some common SI units or those used with the SI to imperial or US customary units are given below.

SI Unit	Conversion
length	
micrometre	$= 0.00003937$ inches
millimetre	$= 0.03937$ inches
centimetre	$= 0.3937$ inches
metre	$= 39.37$ inches or ≈ 1.094 yards
kilometre	≈ 0.621 miles
area	
square millimetre	≈ 0.00155 square inches
square centimetre	≈ 0.155 square inches
square metre	≈ 1.196 square yards or 10.76 square feet
hectare	≈ 2.471 acres
square kilometre	≈ 0.386 square miles
volume or capacity	
cubic millimetre	≈ 0.000061 cubic inches
cubic centimetre or millilitre	≈ 0.0610 cubic inches, 0.0352 Imp. fluid ounces, or 0.0338 US fluid ounces
cubic decimetre or litre	≈ 61.0 cubic inches, 0.880 Imp. quarts, 1.057 US liquid quarts, or 0.908 US dry quarts
cubic metre	≈ 1.308 cubic yards
mass	
gram	≈ 0.0353 oz avoirdupois or 0.0322 oz troy
kilogram	≈ 2.205 pounds avoirdupois
tonne	$\approx 2,205$ pounds avoirdupois
temperature	
degree Celsius	(°C × 1.8) + 32 = degrees Fahrenheit

Foot-Pound-Second and Troy Systems

The imperial and US customary systems are the last foot-pound-second systems still used nationally in everyday trade and commerce, while the troy system of weights continues to find use in the precious metals market, chiefly in North America. All have been supplanted by the SI in scientific and technical work and in nearly all international trade.

Imperial and US Customary System Units

Units of the imperial and US customary systems are equal except for some units of volume and capacity.

Unit	Relation	Conversion
length		
inch	–	$= 25.4$ mm
foot	12 inches	$= 0.3048$ m
yard	3 feet, 36 inches	$= 0.9144$ m
rod	5½ yards, 16½ feet	$= 5.0292$ m
furlong	220 yards, ⅛ mile	≈ 0.201 km
mile (statute)	1,760 yards, 5,280 feet	≈ 1.609 km
area		
square inch	–	$= 645.16$ mm²
square foot	144 sq. inches	$= 929.0304$ cm²
square yard	9 sq. feet	≈ 0.836 m²
acre	4,840 sq. yards	≈ 0.405 ha
volume or capacity		
cubic inch	–	≈ 16.387 cm³
cubic foot	1,728 cubic inches	≈ 28.316 dm³
cubic yard	27 cubic feet	≈ 0.765 m³
(Imperial)		
fluid ounce	–	≈ 28.413 cm³
pint	20 imp fl. oz	≈ 0.568 dm³
quart	2 imp. pints	≈ 1.136 dm³
gallon	4 imp. quarts	≈ 4.546 dm³
peck	8 imp. quarts	≈ 9.092 dm³
bushel	4 imp. pecks	≈ 36.369 dm³
barrel	36 imp. gallons	≈ 163.7 dm³
(US, liquid)		
fluid ounce	–	≈ 29.573 cm³
pint	16 US fl. oz	≈ 0.473 dm³
quart	2 US fl. pints	≈ 0.946 dm³
gallon	4 US fl. quarts	≈ 3.785 dm³
barrel, wine	31½ US gallons	≈ 119.2 dm³
barrel, oil	42 US gallons	≈ 0.159 m³
(US, dry)		
pint	–	≈ 0.551 dm³
quart	2 US dry pints	≈ 1.101 dm³
peck	8 US dry quarts	≈ 8.810 dm³
bushel	4 pecks	≈ 35.239 dm³
weight or mass		
ounce	–	≈ 28.349 g
pound	16 ounces	≈ 0.454 kg
(avoirdupois)		
stone (UK)	14 pounds	≈ 6.350 kg
hundredweight (UK)	112 pounds	≈ 50.80 kg
(long) ton (UK)	2,240 pounds	$\approx 1.016 \times 10^{3}$kg
(short) ton (US)	2,000 pounds	$\approx 0.907 \times 10^{3}$kg
(troy)		
ounce	–	≈ 31.103 g
pound	12 oz troy	≈ 373.242 g
temperature		
degree Fahrenheit	(°F − 32) ÷ 1.8 = degrees Celsius	

Some Volumetric Measurement Comparisons

Imperial Units	In US Units	In SI Units
1 UK fluid ounce	≈ 0.961 US fluid ounce	≈ 28.413 cm³
1 UK pint	≈ 1.201 US liquid pint	≈ 0.568 dm³
1 UK pint	≈ 1.032 US dry pint	≈ 0.568 dm³
1 UK gallon	≈ 1.201 US gallon	≈ 4.546 dm³

US Units	In Imperial Units	In SI Units
1 US fluid ounce	≈ 1.041 UK fluid ounce	≈ 29.573 cm³
1 US liquid pint	≈ 0.833 UK pint	≈ 0.473 dm³
1 US gallon	≈ 0.833 UK gallon	≈ 3.785 dm³
1 US dry pint	≈ 0.969 UK pint	≈ 0.551 dm³

eardrum [15C. < Latin, 'passage', past participle of *meare* 'go, pass'.]

meaty /meéti/ (**-ier, -iest**) *adj* 1 CONTAINING OR TASTING OF MEAT containing a high proportion of meat or tasting strongly of meat 2 INTERESTING AND THOUGHT-PROVOKING full of interesting and thought-provoking material ○ *a meaty role* 3 FLESHY OR MUSCLED big and fleshy or muscular —**meatiness** *n*

mecca /mékə/ *n* a place that is an important centre for a particular activity or that is visited by a great many people

Mecca /mékə/ city in W Saudi Arabia, near the Red Sea. The birthplace of the Prophet Muhammad, it is the holiest city of Islam. Population: 1,500,000 (1994 estimate).

mech. *abbr* 1 mechanical 2 mechanics 3 mechanism

mechan- *prefix* = **mechano-** (*before vowels*)

mechanic /mi kánnik/ *n* 1 a skilled worker who is employed to repair or operate machinery or engines 2 an unskilled worker or labourer (*archaic*) [Mid-16C. Directly or via French *mechanique* < Latin *mechanicus* < Greek *mēkhanē* (see MACHINE).]

mechanical /mi kánni k'l/ *adj* 1 MACHINE-OPERATED operated by or using a machine or mechanism 2 INVOLVING A MACHINE OR ENGINE involving or located in or on a machine or engine ○ *mechanical failure* 3 DONE AS IF BY MACHINE done automatically or as if by a machine instead of a human being ○ *His playing was mechanical.* 4 UNDERSTANDING MACHINES having an aptitude for using or understanding machines ○ *I'm not very mechanical* 5 INVOLVING PHYSICAL FORCES relating to, involving, or done by physical forces ○ *mechanical erosion* 6 OF MECHANICS relating to, involving, or typical of the science of mechanics ○ *mechanical energy* —**mechanically** *adv* —**mechanicalness** *n*

mechanical drawing *n* 1 a drawing done to scale using specialized instruments, e.g. a sketch showing machinery or an architectural plan 2 the process of making mechanical drawings

mechanical engineering *n* the branch of engineering that deals with the design, production, and use of machinery and tools, as well as the generation and transmission of heat and mechanical power —**mechanical engineer** *n*

ϟ **mechanical mouse** *n* a mouse in which the motion of a rotating ball is detected by optical sensors or contact points and translated into cursor movement

mechanical pencil *n* US COMM = **propelling pencil**

mechanical weathering *n* the breakdown of rocks and minerals by physical agents such as frost, wind, and tree roots, with no chemical alteration

mechanician /mékə nísh'n/ *n* a maker of machines or tools

mechanics /mi kánniks/ *n* 1 STUDY OF ENERGY AND FORCES the branch of physics and mathematics that deals with the effect of energy and forces on systems (+ *singular verb*) 2 MAKING AND RUNNING OF MACHINES the application of the science of mechanics to the design, making, and operating of machines (+ *singular or plural verb*) ■ *npl* HOW SOMETHING WORKS OR IS DONE the details of how something works or the way it is done ○ *She's a strategic player who really understands the mechanics of the game.*

mechanise *vt* = **mechanize**

mechanism /mékənizəm/ *n* 1 MACHINE PART a machine or part of a machine that performs a particular task 2 SOMETHING LIKE A MACHINE something that is not a machine but is like one or is studied as if it were one ○ *the fragile mechanism of the planet's ecology* 3 METHOD OR MEANS a method or means of doing something ○ *Interest rates are only one mechanism for controlling inflation.* 4 WAY THAT SOMETHING WORKS the methods, procedures, or processes involved in how something works or is done ○ *the mechanism of international diplomacy* 5 INSTINCTIVE BEHAVIOURAL REACTION a natural unconscious reaction or type of behaviour that comes into action when somebody is faced with a particular situation ○ *defence mechanisms* 6 PHILOSOPHICAL THEORY the philosophical theory that all natural phenomena, including human behaviour, can be explained by physical causes and processes [Mid-17C. < modern Latin *mechanismus* < Greek *mēkhanē* (see MACHINE).]

mechanist /mékənist/ *n* 1 a believer that all natural phenomena, including human behaviour, can be explained by physical causes and processes 2 MECH ENG = **mechanician** [Early 17C. < MECHANIC.]

mechanistic /mékə nístik/ *adj* 1 EXPLAINING BEHAVIOUR MECHANICALLY explaining human behaviour or other natural processes in terms of physical causes and processes 2 LIKE A MACHINE typical of a machine rather than a thinking and feeling human being 3 OF THE SCIENCE OF MECHANICS relating to, involving, or typical of the science of mechanics —**mechanistically** *adv*

mechanize /mékə nīz/ (**-nizes, -nizing, -nized**), **mechanise** (**-nises, -nising, -nised**) *vt* 1 USE MACHINERY TO DO to change a process so that it is performed by machinery rather than human or animal labour 2 EQUIP WITH MACHINERY to equip a place of work or a workforce with machines to do work previously done by human or animal labour 3 EQUIP AN ARMY WITH TRACKED VEHICLES to equip an armed force with tracked armoured vehicles [Late 17C. < MECHANIC.] —**mechanization** /mékə nī záysh'n/ *n* —**mechanized** *adj* —**mechanizer** *n*

mechano- *prefix* 1 mechanical ○ *mechanoreceptor* 2 machinery ○ *mechanize* [< Greek *mēkhanē* (see MACHINE)]

mechanochemistry /mékənō kémmistri/ *n* the branch of chemistry concerned with the conversion of chemical energy into mechanical work —**mechanochemical** *adj*

mechanoreceptor /mékənōri séptər/ *n* a sensory receptor of a nerve that responds to pressure, vibration, or some other mechanical stimulus —**mechanoreception** *n* —**mechanoreceptive** /-séptiv/ *adj*

mechanotherapy /mékənō thérrəpi/ *n* the treatment of injuries through mechanical means such as massage and exercise machines —**mechanotherapist** *n*

Mechlin /méklin/, **Mechlin lace** *n* a type of bobbin lace made at Mechelen, Belgium [15C. After *Mechlin*, former English name for *Mechelen*, Belgium.]

MEcon *abbr* Master of Economics

meconium /mi kṓni əm/ *n* the dark greenish faeces that have collected in the intestines of an unborn baby and are released shortly after birth [Early 17C. Via Latin, 'poppy juice' < Greek *mēkōnion* < *mēkōn* 'poppy'.]

mecopteran /mi kóptərən/ *n* an insect with long legs and wings and a structure resembling a beak at the front of the head, e.g. the scorpion fly. Order: Mecoptera. [< modern Latin *Mecoptera* < Greek *mēkos* 'length' + *ptera* 'wings'] —**mecopterous** *adj*

Med /med/ *n* the Mediterranean Sea (*informal*)

MEd *abbr* Master of Education

med. *abbr* 1 medical 2 medicine 3 medieval 4 medium

médaillon /méddī yóN/ *n* a round thin slice or portion of meat or another food. US term **medallion** *n.* 3 [Early 20C. < French (see MEDALLION).]

medal /médd'l/ *n* 1 PIECE OF METAL GIVEN AS AN AWARD a small flat piece of metal, usually shaped like a coin and stamped with an inscription or design, awarded to somebody for outstanding achievement or bravery or to commemorate something 2 RELIGIOUS IMAGE WORN AS ACCESSORY a cut and shaped piece of metal on which a religious image is often stamped, worn as a brooch or on a chain ■ *vi* (**-als, -alling, -alled**) US WIN A MEDAL to win a medal in a competition ○ *She medalled in the javelin throw.* [Late 16C. Via French < assumed Vulgar Latin *medalia* 'coins worth half the value of a denarius' < late Latin *medialis* 'medial'.] —**medallic** /mi dállik/ *adj*

medalist *n* US = **medallist**

ϟ **medallion** /mə dálli ən/ *n* 1 MEDAL a large medal 2 LARGE DECORATIVE METAL DISC a large decorative metal disc worn on a chain round the neck 3 COOK = **médaillon** 4 ROUND DECORATION a round or oval decoration on something, e.g. a building, vase, or piece of material 5 MICROCHIP INSIDE SMART CARD the microchip inside a smart card [Mid-17C. Via French *médaillon* < Italian *medaglione* 'large medal' < *medaglia* 'medal'.]

medallist /médd'list/ *n* 1 SOMEBODY AWARDED A MEDAL a person who has been awarded a medal, especially in a competition 2 SOMEBODY INVOLVED WITH MEDALS a designer, maker, collector of, or expert on medals 3 WINNER OF A STROKE PLAY TOURNAMENT a golfer who wins a stroke play tournament

Medal of Honor *n* MIL = **Congressional Medal of Honor**

medal play *n* GOLF = **stroke play**

Medan /máy daan/ city on N Sumatra, Indonesia. Population: 1,730,052 (1990).

Medawar /méddəwər/, **Sir Peter** (1915–87) Brazilian-born UK zoologist and immunologist

meddle /médd'l/ (**-dles, -dling, -dled**) *vi* to become involved in somebody else's concerns or with somebody else's property in an intrusive or unwanted way ○ *I don't mean to meddle, only to offer advice.* ○ *Who's been meddling with the settings on my computer?* [13C. < Old French *me(s)dler*, variant of *mesler* < assumed Vulgar Latin *misculare* 'mix thoroughly'.] —**meddler** *n*

meddlesome /médd'lsəm/ *adj* tending to interfere in other people's business —**meddlesomely** *adv* —**meddlesomeness** *n*

Mede /meed/ *n* a member of an Indo-European people who ruled an empire northwest of Persia in ancient times [< Latin *Medi*, plural of *Medus*]

Medea /mə deé ə/ *n* in Greek mythology, a woman with magical powers who was the daughter of the king of Colchis. She helped Jason steal the Golden Fleece and, when he deserted her, killed their children in revenge.

~~**medecine**~~ incorrect spelling of **medicine**

~~**medeival**~~ incorrect spelling of **medieval**

Medellín /méddə yeén/ city in northwest-central Colombia. Population: 1,970,691 (1997 estimate).

medevac /méddi vak/ *n* 1 MEDICAL EVACUATION OF INJURED the removal of injured people, especially military casualties, from the scene of their injury to the nearest hospital or place of treatment 2 US HELICOPTER USED TO EVACUATE INJURED an aircraft, especially a helicopter, used to take injured people, especially military casualties, from the scene of their injury to the nearest hospital or place of treatment ■ *vt* EVACUATE AN INJURED PERSON to evacuate somebody who is injured in order to take them to a hospital or place of treatment [Mid-20C. Blend of MEDICAL + EVACUATION.]

media[1] /meédi ə/ *n* the various means of mass communication thought of as a whole, including television, radio, magazines, and newspapers, together with the people involved in their production (+ *singular or plural verb*) ■ plural of **medium** [Early 20C. Plural of MEDIUM.]

USAGE ***media*** – singular or plural? Even though ***media*** is historically a plural of the Latin word *medium*, in some instances you can safely use ***media*** with a singular verb, depending on what is meant by ***media***. When ***media*** means the broadcast and print press in general, including all its personnel, equipment, and policies, a singular verb is acceptable. The word is also invariably preceded by *the* in such usages: *The media has covered the story ad nauseam.* If the writer's idea is to indicate, using ***media***, various separate journalistic outlets and their activities, a plural verb goes with ***media***: *The media have differed markedly in their approaches to coverage of the scandal.* Avoid using the plural ***media*** to refer to a single system or method of communication; use the singular **medium** instead: *Cable television is a relatively inexpensive advertising medium* [not *media*]. Never use the false plural 'medias' as in 'new medias'. The correct form is ***media***, as in *new media*.

media[2] /meédi ə/ (*plural* **-ae** /-ee/) *n* 1 the middle, muscular layer of the wall of a blood or lymph vessel 2 a primary vein in an insect's wing [Mid-19C. < Latin, 'middle', the feminine of *medius* (see MEDIUM).]

Media /meédi ə/ ancient kingdom in SW Asia, in present-day NW Iran —**Median** *adj, n*

media circus *n* a situation in which members of the media vie with each other in covering an event so that the coverage overwhelms the event and distorts its importance (*informal disapproving*)

mediacy /meédi əssi/ *n* the condition of being intermediate or of having an intermediate effect [Mid-19C. < MEDIATE.]

mediae plural of **media**[2]

mediaeval *adj* = **medieval**

mediaevalism *n* = **medievalism**

mediaevalist *n* = **medievalist**

media event *n* something that attracts great attention from the mass media, often arranged specifically for that purpose

mediagenic /meédi ə jénnik/ *adj* US appealing or attractive when covered by the media and thus highly suitable for media exposure

medial /meédi əl/ *adj* 1 AT THE MIDDLE situated in or towards the middle 2 ORDINARY not extreme or exceptional but average 3 STATS = **median** *adj.* 2 4 NEAR THE MEDIAN PLANE near the median plane of an organism or body part 5 IN THE MIDDLE OF A LANGUAGE UNIT occurring between the first and last positions in a word or linguistic unit (**morpheme**) ■ *n* **SOUND BETWEEN STRONG AND SOFT** a speech sound midway between a strong sound (**fortis**) and a soft sound (**lenis**) [Late 16C. < late Latin *medialis* < Latin *medius* 'middle'.] —**medially** *adv*

median /meédi ən/ *n* **1 MIDDLE POINT** a point, line, part, or plane that is in the middle **2 MIDDLE OF ORDERED VALUES** the middle value in a set of statistical values that are arranged in ascending or descending order **3 MIDPOINT IN A FREQUENCY DISTRIBUTION** the value in a frequency distribution above and below which values with equal total frequencies appear **4 LINE DIVIDING A TRIANGLE** a line connecting a vertex of a triangle and the midpoint of the opposite side **5 LINE DIVIDING A TRAPEZOID** a line connecting the midpoints of the nonparallel sides of a trapezoid ■ *adj* **1 IN, TO, OR THROUGH THE MIDDLE** in, towards, or passing through the middle **2 OF OR AS A STATISTICAL MEDIAN** relating to, involving, or constituting a statistical median **3 IN THE MIDDLE OF A BILATERAL ANIMAL** lying in the plane that divides a bilaterally symmetrical animal into right and left halves [14C. Directly or via French *(veine) médiane* 'median (vein)' < Latin *medianus* 'median' < *medius* 'middle'.] —**medianly** *adv*

median lethal dose *n* the dose of a substance, e.g. a drug or ionizing radiation, that in a specified time period will kill half the experimental animals to whom it is given

median plane *n* a vertical plane that divides a bilaterally symmetrical animal or human body into right and left halves

median strip *n US, Aus* a strip of land down the centre of a road that separates lanes of traffic travelling in opposite directions. ◊ **central reservation**

mediant /meédi ənt/ *n* the third note of a major or minor musical scale, and the harmony built upon this note [Mid-18C. < French *médiante* < late Latin *mediare* 'be in the middle' < Latin *medius* 'middle'.]

mediastinum /meédi ə stīnəm/ (*plural* **-na** /-nə/) *n* in mammals, the region of the chest between the lungs that contains the heart, trachea, and other organs [15C. medieval Latin, form of *mediastinus* 'medial' < Latin, 'common servant' < *medius* 'middle'.] —**mediastinal** *adj*

media studies *n* a field of academic work that examines the role and operation of the mass media (+ *singular or plural verb*)

mediate /meédi ayt/ *v* (**-ates, -ating, -ated**) **1** *vi* **INTERVENE TO RESOLVE CONFLICT** to work with both sides in a dispute in an attempt to help them reach an agreement ○ *mediating between the government and the rebels* **2** *vt* **OVERSEE AGREEMENT** to oversee an attempt to solve a dispute by working with both sides to help them reach an agreement ○ *appointed to mediate the talks* **3** *vt* **ACHIEVE BY AGREEMENT** to achieve a solution, settlement, or agreement by working with both sides in a dispute ○ *Negotiators have mediated a ceasefire.* **4** *vt* **TRANSFER** to act as a medium that transfers something from one place to another **5** *vi* **BE BETWEEN** to be between two stages, ideas, times, or things ■ *adj* **DEPENDING ON INTERMEDIATE ACTION** involving or depending on an intermediary or an intermediate action [15C. < late Latin *mediat-*, past participle of *mediare* 'halve' < Latin *medius* 'middle'.] —**mediately** *adv* —**mediateness** *n* —**mediation** /meédi áysh'n/ *n* —**mediative** /-ətiv/ *adj*

mediatize /meédi ə tīz/ (**-tizes, -tizing, -tized**), **mediatise** (**-atises, -atising, -atised**) *vt* to take control of another country but allow its ruler to retain his or her title and have some role in governing the country [Early 19C. < French *médiatiser* < late Latin *mediare* (see MEDIATE).] —**mediatization** /meédi ə tī záysh'n/ *n*

mediator /meédi aytər/ *n* **1** a person who confers with both sides in a dispute as a way to help them reach an agreement **2** a substance that acts as a medium in transferring something from one place to another in the body [14C. Directly or via French *médiateur* < ecclesiastical Latin *mediator* < late Latin *mediare* (see MEDIATE).] —**mediatorial** /meédi ə táwri əl/ *adj* —**mediatorially** *adv*

medic[1] /méddik/ *n* **1** a doctor or medical student (*informal*) **2** *US* an enlisted or noncommissioned member of a military medical corps [Mid-17C. < Latin *medicus* (see MEDICINE).]

medic[2] *n* PLANTS = **medick**

Medicaid /méddi kayd/ *n* a programme funded by the US and state governments that pays the medical expenses of people who are unable to pay some or all of their own expenses [Mid-20C. Blend of MEDICAL + AID.]

medical /méddik'l/ *adj* relating to, involving, or used in medicine or treatment given by doctors ■ *n* a physical examination by a doctor to check a patient's state of health [Mid-17C. Directly or via French < medieval Latin *medicalis* < Latin *medicus* (see MEDICINE).]

medical certificate *n* a document signed by a doctor giving a judgment on somebody's state of health, especially certifying the person's fitness or unfitness for work

medical food *n* food specially processed or formulated to be given, under medical supervision, to patients who require a special diet

medical jurisprudence *n* MED = **forensic medicine**

⚡**medical telematics** /-téllə máttiks/ *n* the development and use of computer networks for the international exchange and retrieval of medical data (+ *singular verb*)

medicament /mə díkəmənt/ *n* a substance used to treat an illness [15C. Directly or via French < Latin *medicamentum* < *medicari* (see MEDICATE).]

medicare /méddi kair/ *n* in Canada, a government health insurance scheme, which is funded by a tax levy in each province

Medicare /méddi kair/ *n* **1** a health insurance programme in the United States under which medical care and hospital treatment for people over 65 is partially paid by the government **2** in Australia, the national health insurance scheme, which is funded by a tax levy [Mid-20C. Blend of MEDICAL + CARE.]

medicate /méddi kayt/ (**-cates, -cating, -cated**) *vt* **1** to treat a patient with a drug (*often passive*) **2** to add a drug to something, e.g. an antibacterial agent to a soap, or an anaesthetic to a throat lozenge [Early 17C. Either < Latin *medicari* 'heal' < *medicus* (see MEDICINE); or back-formation < MEDICATION.] —**medicated** *adj* —**medicative** /-kətiv/ *adj*

medication /méddi káysh'n/ *n* **1** a drug used to treat an illness **2** treatment of an illness using drugs [15C. Directly or via French < Latin *medicari* (see MEDICATE).]

Medicean /méddi seéən/ *adj* relating to the Medici family and the period of their rule over Florence and Tuscany

Medici /méddichi, mə deéchi/, **Cosimo de'** (1389–1464) Italian banker and statesman. Known as **Cosimo the Elder**

Medici, Cosimo I de' (1519–74) first grand duke of Tuscany

Medici, Lorenzo de' (1449–92) Italian statesman. Known as **Lorenzo the Magnificent**

medicinal /mə díss'nəl/ *adj* **1 CAPABLE OF TREATING ILLNESS** having properties that can be used to treat illness ○ *a medicinal plant* **2 INTENDED TO IMPROVE SOMEBODY'S WELL-BEING** intended to improve somebody's physical or emotional well-being in the way a medicine does ○ *a drink taken for medicinal purposes* **3 LIKE MEDICINE** like medicine, especially in having a bitter taste [14C. Directly or via French < Latin *medicinalis* < *medicina* (see MEDICINE).] —**medicinally** *adv*

medicinal leech *n* a large European freshwater leech that lives on blood, formerly used in bloodletting, and still occasionally used to prevent coagulation. *Hirudo medicinalis.*

medicine /méddss'n, méddiss'n/ *n* **1 DRUG FOR TREATING ILLNESS** a drug or remedy used for treating illness, especially in liquid form ○ *cough medicine* **2 TREATMENT OF ILLNESS** the diagnosis and treatment of illnesses, wounds, and injuries **3 TREATMENT USING DRUGS** the treatment of illness or injury using drugs rather than surgery **4 MEDICAL PROFESSION** the profession of treating illness as a doctor **5 RITUAL PRACTICE OR SACRED OBJECT** a ritual practice or sacred object believed, especially by Native Americans, to control supernatural powers or work as a preventive or remedy of illness [12C. Directly or via Old French < Latin *medicina* 'practice of medicine' < *medicus* 'doctor' < *mederi* 'heal'.] ◇ **a dose** *or* **taste of your own medicine** unpleasant treatment of the same kind that you have given others (*informal*)

medicine ball *n* a large heavy ball that people throw to one another as a strength-building exercise

medicine chest *n* a small cupboard or chest where medicines, bandages, and other things used in treating illness or injury are stored

medicine dance *n* a ceremonial religious dance performed by an aboriginal group or individual to obtain supernatural assistance for something, e.g. to cure illness

medicine lodge *n* a wooden building used by some Native North American peoples for rituals, e.g. ceremonial curing

medicine man *n* a healer believed to make use of supernatural powers, especially among Native North American peoples

medick /méddik/ *n* a plant of the pea family with three-lobed leaves. Use: fodder. Genus: *Medicago.* [14C. Via Latin *medica* < Greek *Mēdikē (poa)* '(poppy) of Media'.]

medico /méddikō/ (*plural* **-cos**) *n* a doctor or medical student (*informal*) [Late 17C. Via Italian < Latin *medicus* (see MEDICINE).]

medieval /méddi eév'l/, **mediaeval** *adj* **1** relating to, involving, belonging to, or typical of the Middle Ages **2** old-fashioned, especially because lacking in modern enlightened attitudes ○ *Some of the working practices in the industry were positively medieval.* [Early 19C. < modern Latin *medium aevum* 'middle age'.] —**medievally** *adv*

medieval Greek *n* the form of Greek used between the 7th and 13th centuries —**medieval Greek** *adj*

medievalism /méddi eév'lizəm/, **mediaevalism** *n* **1 CUSTOMS AND BELIEFS OF THE MIDDLE AGES** the customs, practices, or beliefs of the Middle Ages **2 DEVOTION TO THE MIDDLE AGES** devotion to the spirit or beliefs of the Middle Ages **3 SOMETHING FROM THE MIDDLE AGES** a belief, custom, or style from or like one from the Middle Ages

medievalist /méddi eév'list/, **mediaevalist** *n* a student of or expert in the Middle Ages

medieval Latin *n* the form of Latin used in Europe during the Middle Ages —**medieval Latin** *adj*

medina /me deénə/, **Medina** *n* the oldest part of many North African cities [Early 20C. < Arabic, 'town'.]

Medina /me deénə/ city in west-central Saudi Arabia, site of the Prophet Muhammad's tomb and a holy city of Islam. Population: 500,050 (1990 estimate).

mediocre /meédi ókər/ *adj* adequate but not very good [Late 16C. Directly or via French < Latin *mediocris* 'of middle height' < *ocris* 'rugged mountain'.] —**mediocrely** *adv*

mediocrity /meédi ókrəti/ (*plural* **-ties**) *n* **1** a quality that is acceptable but not very good ○ *His poetry seldom rises above the level of mediocrity.* **2** a person who lacks special skill or flair [15C. Directly or via French *médiocrité* < Latin *mediocritas* < *mediocris* (see MEDIOCRE).]

meditate /méddi tayt/ (**-tates, -tating, -tated**) *v* **1** *vi* **EMPTY OR CONCENTRATE THE MIND** to empty the mind of thoughts, or concentrate the mind on one thing, in order to develop the mind or spirit, aid contemplation, or relax **2** *vi* **THINK CAREFULLY ABOUT** to think about something calmly, seriously, and for some time **3** *vt* **PLAN** to plan or consider doing something [Mid-16C. Either < Latin *meditare* 'keep on measuring', related to *mederi* 'to cure'; or back-formation < MEDITATION.] —**meditator** *n*

meditation /méddi táysh'n/ *n* **1 EMPTYING OR CONCENTRATION OF THE MIND** the emptying of the mind of thoughts, or concentration of the mind on just one thing, in order to aid mental or spiritual development, contemplation, or relaxation **2 PONDERING** the act of thinking about something deeply and carefully, or an instance of such thinking **3 SERIOUS STUDY OF A TOPIC** an extended and serious study of a particular topic [15C. Directly or via French < Latin *meditation-* < *meditari* (see MEDITATE).] —**meditational** *adj* —**meditative** /médditətiv/ *adj* —**meditatively** *adv* —**meditativeness** *n*

Mediterranean /méddi tə ráy ni ən/ *n* **1 MEDITERRANEAN SEA OR SURROUNDING AREA** the Mediterranean Sea or the lands bordering it ○ *holidaying in the Mediterranean* **2 SOMEBODY FROM THE AREA OF THE MEDITERRANEAN SEA** somebody who comes from a region bordering the Mediterranean Sea ■ *adj* **1 IN OR NEAR THE MEDITERRANEAN SEA** in the Mediterranean Sea, or in a region that borders it **2 TYPICAL OF MEDITERRANEANS** typical of the people living in a region that borders the Mediterranean Sea **3 WITH HOT SUMMERS AND WARM WINTERS** having hot summers and warm winters, with most of the rainfall occurring in the winter **4 WITH DARK HAIR AND OLIVE SKIN** resembling people from countries around the Mediterranean Sea, who often have dark hair and olive complexions

Mediterranean fever *n* MED = **brucellosis** [Because it is commonly contracted in that region]

Mediterranean fruit fly *n* a black-and-white two-winged fly that lays its eggs in citrus and other types of fruit, which the maggots then destroy. *Ceratitis capitata.*

Mediterranean Sea inland sea of Europe, Asia, and Africa, linked to the Atlantic Ocean at its western end by the Strait of Gibraltar. Area: 2,510,000 sq. km/969,000 sq. mi.

~~**Mediterranean**~~ incorrect spelling of **Mediterranean**

medium /meédi əm/ *adj* **1 NEITHER LARGE NOR SMALL** of middling size or dimensions, neither large nor small ○ *a man of medium build* **2 NEITHER DARK NOR LIGHT** not particularly dark or particularly light as a shade of a colour **3 BETWEEN RARE AND WELL-DONE** cooked so that the meat is brown on the outside but slightly pink and moist inside ■ *n* (*plural* **-dia** /-di ə/ *or* **-diums**) **1 STATE BETWEEN EXTREMES** an intermediate state or condition halfway between two extremes **2 MEANS OF MASS COMMUNICATION** a means of mass communication such as television, radio, or newspapers **3 VEHICLE FOR IDEAS** a means of conveying ideas or information ○ *French is the medium of instruction in all subjects.* **4 SUBSTANCE CARRIER** a substance through which something is carried or transmitted **5 MEANS TO AN END** the means by which something is carried out or achieved **6 MATERIAL HOLDING DATA** any form of material on which data is stored or printed, e.g. paper, tape, or disk **7 PRESERVING SUBSTANCE** a substance in which specimens of animals and plants are preserved or mounted **8 SUPPOSED RECEIVER OF MESSAGES** a person believed to transmit messages between living people and the spirits of the dead **9 NATURAL ENVIRONMENT** a substance or the environment in which an organism naturally lives or grows **10 TYPE OF ART** a method that an artist uses or a category such as sculpture in which an artist works **11 ARTIST'S MATERIALS** the materials that an artist uses in creating a work **12 SOLVENT** a solvent mixed with a pigment or paint to make it thinner **13 PAPER SIZE** any of several similar sizes of paper, especially 47 cm by 58.5 cm/18.5 in by 23 in ■ **mediums** *npl* **GILT-EDGED SECURITIES** securities that are very safe as an investment [Late 16C. < Latin, the neuter of *medius* 'middle'.]

medium-dated *adj* describes gilt-edged securities redeemable after a period of between 5 and 15 years

medium frequency *n* a radio frequency lying between 300 and 3,000 kilohertz

medium of exchange *n* something commonly recognized in a country or community as a standard of value and used in the same way as money, e.g. gold

medium shot *n* a filmed view, midway between long shot and close-up, that shows a standing person from the waist up or the full body of a sitting person

medium wave *n* a radio wave with a wavelength that lies between 100 and 1,000 metres (*hyphenated before nouns*)

medlar /méddlər/ *n* **1** a small apple-shaped fruit, sometimes eaten raw when overripe. Use: preserves. **2** a small fruit tree that produces medlars. Native to: Europe, Asia. *Mespilus germanica*. [14C. Via Old French *medler* < *medle* 'medlar fruit' (a variant of *mesle*) < Greek *mespilē*.]

medley /méddli/ (*plural* **-leys**) *n* **1 MIXTURE OF THINGS** a mixture or assortment of various things **2 MUSICAL SEQUENCE OF DIFFERENT SONGS** a continuous piece of music consisting of two or more different tunes or songs played one after the other **3 medley, medley relay SWIMMING RACE USING DIFFERENT STROKES** a relay swimming race in which each team member must use a different stroke **4 medley, medley relay RELAY RACE WITH DIFFERENT LENGTHS** a relay race in which each member of a team runs a different length [14C. < Old French *medlee*, variant of *meslee* 'melee' < medieval Latin *misculare* 'mix thoroughly'.]

medulla /mi dúllə/ (*plural* **-lae** /-lee/ *or* **-las**) *n* **1** the innermost area of a part or organ of an animal or plant ○ *the adrenal medulla* **2** ANAT = **medulla oblongata 3** PLANT SCI = **pith** *n.* **2** [14C. < Latin, 'pith'.] —**medullar** *adj*

medulla oblongata /-ób long gaátə/ (*plural* **medullae oblongatae** /mi dúllee ób long gaá tee/ *or* **medulla oblongatas**) *n* the lowermost part of the brain in vertebrates [< Latin, 'prolonged marrow']

medullary sheath *n* ANAT = **myelin sheath**

medullated /médda laytid, mi dúllaytid/ *adj* **1** ANAT = **myelinated 2** having a medulla ○ *medullated fibres*

medulloblastoma /mi dúllō bla stṓmə/ (*plural* **-mas** *or* **-mata** /-mətə/) *n* a rapidly growing malignant tumour of the central nervous system arising in the brain, especially in children [Early 20C. < MEDULLA + BLASTO-.]

medusa /mə dyṓzə/ (*plural* **-as** *or* **-ae** /-zee/) *n* **1** the free-swimming reproductive stage of an animal such as a jellyfish, during which it has a transparent umbrella-shaped body with tentacles **2** ZOOL = **jellyfish** *n.* **1** [Mid-18C. < modern Latin, < Greek *Medousa* 'Medusa'; from the resemblance of the tentacles to the snakes on Medusa's head.] —**medusan** *adj* —**medusoid** *adj, n*

Medusa /mə dyṓzə/ *n* in Greek mythology, a Gorgon who could turn to stone anyone who looked at her —**Medusan** *adj*

Medway /méd way/ river in SE England. Length: 112 km/70 mi.

meek /meek/ *adj* **1** showing mildness or quietness of nature **2** showing submissiveness and lack of initiative or will [12C. < Old Norse *mjúkr* 'soft, pliant'.] —**meekly** *adv* —**meekness** *n*

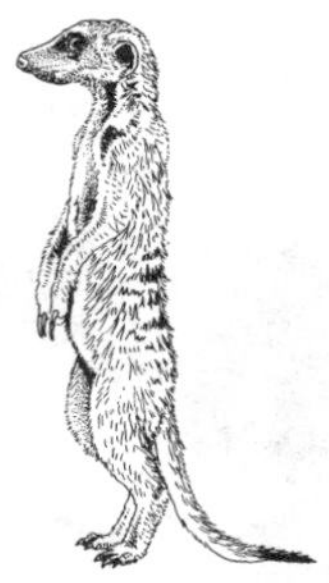

Meerkat

meerkat /meér kat/ *n* a burrowing mongoose with four-toed feet and a greyish coat with faint black markings. Native to: South Africa. *Suricata suricatta*. [Early 19C. Via Afrikaans < Middle Low German *meerkatte* < *meer* 'sea' + *katte* 'cat'.]

meerschaum /meérshəm/ *n* **1** MINERALS = **sepiolite 2 meerschaum, meerschaum pipe** a tobacco pipe with a bowl made of sepiolite [Late 18C. < German, < *Meer* 'sea' + *Schaum* 'foam', translation of Persian *kef-i-daryā*; from its frothy appearance.]

meet[1] /meet/ *v* (**meets, meeting, met** /met/) **1** *vti* **COME ACROSS** to encounter somebody without having arranged to do so beforehand ○ *Guess who I met in the supermarket?* **2** *vti* **GET TOGETHER** to get together with somebody by arrangement ○ *We could meet for lunch tomorrow.* **3** *vti* **ENCOUNTER SOMEBODY FOR FIRST TIME** to encounter somebody or be introduced for the first time ○ *It's exactly a year since they met.* **4** *vt* **GREET** to go somewhere to greet or fetch somebody who is arriving there ○ *I'll come and meet you at the airport.* **5** *vi* **GATHER FOR DISCUSSION** to gather in a place to discuss something ○ *The committee meets monthly.* **6** *vti* **JOIN** to join, cross, or be adjacent to something or each other ○ *where the two roads meet* **7** *vti* **TOUCH** to come into contact with something, or bring two objects into contact ○ *I can't get the two ropes to meet.* **8** *vti* **EXPERIENCE** to experience something, e.g. a difficulty, challenge, or success ○ *All our attempts met with failure.* **9** *vt* **SATISFY** to cope with, satisfy, or fulfil what is required **10** *vt* **AGREE** to come to an agreement on something ○ *I think we can meet you on that price.* **11** *vti* **LOOK AT** to look at or confront something, or look at or confront each other ○ *Their glances met.* **12** *vti* **COMPETE OR FIGHT WITH** to come together to compete or fight with somebody else ○ *The two teams have already met this year.* **13** *vt* **RESPOND IN A PARTICULAR WAY** to respond to a situation with a particular type of behaviour ○ *He met success and failure with equal indifference.* **14** *vi* **OCCUR TOGETHER** to happen or come together in the same place or person ○ *The extremes of creativity and irresponsibility meet in this genius.* ■ *n* **1 SPORTING OCCASION** an occasion at which numbers of competitors and spectators come together **2 GATHERING BEFORE HUNT** the period before a hunt when the riders and hounds gather together [Old English *mētan* 'come upon' < Germanic, 'meeting'] —**meeter** *n*

SPELLCHECK See *meat*.

meet up *vi* to get together with somebody

meet[2] /meet/ *adj* suitable or fitting for a particular situation (*archaic*) [Old English *gemǣte* < Germanic, 'measure'] —**meetly** *adv*

meeting /meéting/ *n* **1 GATHERING OF PEOPLE FOR DISCUSSION** an occasion when people gather together to discuss something **2 GROUP AT A MEETING** the people attending a meeting ○ *The chairman stood up to address the meeting.* **3 OCCASION WHEN SOMEBODY MEETS SOMEBODY ELSE** an occasion when somebody encounters somebody else, either accidentally or by arrangement **4 SPORTING OCCASION** an occasion when people get together for a sporting competition, e.g. a number of horse races **5 OCCASION FOR WORSHIP** a regular occasion when a group of people, especially Quakers, gather for worship

meeting house *n* a room or building where some religious groups, especially Quakers, meet to worship

mefenamic acid /méffə námmik-/ *n* a drug that reduces inflammation. Use: pain relief from rheumatoid arthritis, menstruation. [< METHYL + *-fen-* (alteration and shortening of PHENYL) + *am-* (shortening of *amino-*) + *-ic* (shortening of *benzoic*)]

meg /meg/ *n* a megabyte (*informal*)

meg- *prefix* = **mega-** (*before vowels*)

mega[1] /méggə/ *adj* extremely enjoyable, impressive, excellent, or large (*informal*) [Late 20C. < MEGA-.]

mega[2] /méggə/ *adj* extremely good or successful (*slang*) ○ *This is going to be mega!*

mega- *prefix* **1** (*symbol* **M**) one million (10^6) ○ *megavolt* **2** a binary million (2^{20}) ○ *megabyte* **3** very large ○ *megadose* **4** very great or excellent (*slang*) ○ *megastar* **5** to a great extent (*slang*) ○ *megastar* [< Greek *megas* 'great' < Indo-European, 'large']

megabar /méggə baar/ *n* a unit of pressure equal to one million bars

megabit /méggə bit/ *n* **1** 1,048,576 bits **2** one million bits

megabuck /méggə buk/ *n US, Can* a million dollars (*slang*) ■ **megabucks** *npl US, Can* a large unspecified amount of money (*slang*) ○ *an actor earning megabucks in Hollywood*

megabyte /méggə bīt/ *n* **1** 1,048,576 bytes **2** one million bytes

megacephaly /méggə séffəli/ *n* MED = **macrocephaly** —**megacephalic** /méggəsi fállik/ *adj* —**megacephalous** *adj*

megadeath /méggə deth/ *n* one million deaths, used as a unit for recording deaths in a nuclear war

megadose /méggədōss/ *n* a very large dose of a medical drug or food supplement

Megaera /mə jeérə/ *n* in Greek mythology, one of the Furies. ◊ **Alecto, Tisiphone**

megafauna /méggə fawnə/ *n* all the animals in a certain place that are larger than microscopic size —**megafaunal** *adj*

megaflops /méggə flóps/ *npl* millions of floating-point operations per second (*indicates the speed of a computer*)

megagamete /méggə ga meet/ *n* BIOL = **macrogamete**

megahertz /méggə hurts/ (*plural* **-hertz**) *n* (*symbol* **MHz**) one million hertz

megakaryocyte /méggə kárri ō sīt/ *n* a large cell in bone marrow that fragments to produce blood platelets

megal- *prefix* = **megalo-** (*before vowels*)

megalith /méggə lith/ *n* an enormous stone, usually standing upright or forming part of a prehistoric structure —**megalithic** /méggə líthik/ *adj*

megalo- *prefix* exceptionally large ○ *megalocardia* [< Greek *megal-*, stem of *megas* (see MEGA-)]

megaloblast /méggəlō blast/ *n* an abnormally large red blood cell that has failed to mature properly, found especially in people affected by anaemia

megaloblastic anaemia /méggəlō blástik-/ *n* a form of anaemia in which the red blood cells are abnormally large because they fail to mature properly. It includes the type formerly known as pernicious anaemia. [< MEGALOBLAST]

megalocardia /méggəlō kaárdi ə/ *n* MED = **cardiomegaly**

megalomania /méggəlō máyni ə/ *n* **1** excessive enjoyment of having power over other people and the craving for more of it **2** a psychiatric disorder in which the patient experiences delusions of great power and importance —**megalomaniac** *n, adj* —**megalomaniacal** /méggəlō mə nī́ ək'l/ *adj* —**megalomaniacally** *adv*

megalopolis /méggə lóppə liss/ *n* **1** an area in which there are several large cities whose suburbs meet or nearly meet **2** an extremely large and populous city [Mid-19C. < MEGALO- + Greek *polis* 'city'.] —**megalopolistic** /méggə lóppə lístik/ *adj* —**megalopolitan** /méggə lə póllitən/ *adj*

megalosaur /méggəlō sawr/ *n* a very large carnivorous dinosaur of the Jurassic and early Cretaceous periods. Genus: *Megalosaurus*. [Mid-19C. Anglicization of modern

Latin *megalosaurus* < MEGALO- + Greek *sauros* 'lizard'.] — **megalosaurian** /méggəlō sáwri ən/ *adj*

-megaly *suffix* abnormal enlargement ○ *hepatomegaly* [< modern Latin *-megalia* < Greek *megal-* (see MEGALO-)]

Megan's Law /méggənz-/ *n US* an amendment to the Violent Crime Control and Law Enforcement Act of 1994, requiring community notification when a paroled or released sex offender moves into a locality [Late 20C. After *Megan* Kanka, seven-year-old girl killed by a convicted child molester.]

megaphone /méggə fōn/ *n* a device shaped like a funnel, used to channel the voice in a certain direction and increase its volume —**megaphonic** /méggə fónnik/ *adj* —**megaphonically** *adv*

megaplex /méggə pleks/ *n* **1** a large cinema complex housing at least fifteen screens, often with the same film playing simultaneously in three or four of the theatres **2** a very large complex of buildings

megapode /méggə pōd/ *n* a large ground-dwelling bird that builds a large mound of earth in which to incubate its eggs. Native to: Australasia. Family: Megapodiidae. [Mid-19C. < modern Latin *Megapodius* 'with big feet'.]

Megara /méggərə/ town in east-central Greece. Population: 26,562 (1991).

megaron /méggə ron/ (*plural* **-ra** /-rə/) *n* the largest room in a house built during the Mycenaean period of ancient Greek civilization [Late 19C. < Greek, 'large room'.]

megascopic /méggə skóppik/ *adj* PHYS = **macroscopic** —**megascopically** *adv*

megasporangium /méggə spaw ránji əm/ (*plural* **-a** /-ə/) *n* an organ in seed plants and ferns that produces large spores (**megaspores**) from which female gametophytes develop

megaspore /méggə spawr/ *n* the larger of two kinds of spore produced by seed plants and some ferns that develops into a female gametophyte. ◊ **microspore**

megastar /méggə staar/ *n* an extremely famous person, especially an entertainer

megathere /méggə theer/ *n* a large extinct American ground sloth that lived in the Miocene and Pleistocene epochs. Family: Megatheriidae. [Mid-19C. Anglicization of modern Latin *Megatherium* < Greek *mega-* 'large' + *thērion* 'animal'.] —**megatherian** /méggə theeri ən/ *adj*

megaton /méggə tun/ *n* **1** a unit of explosive power, e.g. in a nuclear weapon, that is equivalent to one million tons of TNT **2** one million tons —**megatonic** /méggə tónnik/ *adj* —**megatonnage** /-ij/ *n*

megavitamin /méggə víttəmin, -vītəmin/ *n* a dose of a vitamin or vitamins that is much higher than the normal dose —**megavitamin** *adj*

megavolt /méggə vōlt/ *n* one million volts

megawatt /méggə wot/ *n* one million watts

Megiddo /mə geédō/ ruined ancient Palestinian city in present-day N Israel, thought to be the site of the biblical battle of Armageddon

megillah /mə gíllə/ (*plural* **-lahs** *or* **-loth** /məgi lót/) *n* **1** a scroll containing part of the Hebrew Bible, especially the scroll containing the Book of Esther **2** an overelaborate and unnecessarily lengthy account of something [Mid-17C. < Hebrew, 'roll, scroll' < *gālal* 'roll'.]

megilp /mə gílp/, **magilp** *n* a mixture of linseed oil and mastic varnish or turpentine. Use: a solvent for oil paints. [Mid-18C. < ?]

megrim[1] /méegrim/ (*plural* **-grims** *or* **-grim**) *n* **1** a marine flatfish related to the turbot. Native to: Europe. *Lepidorhombus whiffiagonis*. **2** the flesh of a megrim used as food [Mid-19C. < ?]

megrim[2] /méegrim/ *n* (*archaic*) **1** MIGRAINE a migraine headache **2** WHIM a sudden change of mind, or something about which somebody is briefly enthusiastic ■ **megrims** *npl* MELANCHOLY a spell of melancholy or low spirits (*archaic*) [15C. Variant of MIGRAINE.]

meibomian cyst /mī bómi ən-/ *n* a painless swelling in the eyelid, somewhat like a pea, caused by blockage of the outlet duct of a meibomian gland and the resulting accumulation of fatty secretion [See MEIBOMIAN GLAND]

meibomian gland /mī bómi ən-/ *n* any sebaceous gland in the eyelid [Early 19C. After Heinrich *Meibom* (1638–1700), German anatomist.]

Meighen /máygən/, **Arthur** (1874–1960) Canadian lawyer, businessman, and statesman

Meiji /máy jee, -jeè/ *n* the reign of the Japanese emperor Meiji Tenno (1867–1912), a period of extensive reform, including the abolition of feudalism [Late 19C. < Japanese, 'enlightened government'.]

Meiji Tenno /máyji ténnō/ (1852–1912) emperor of Japan (1867–1912). Born **Mutsuhito**

meiny /máyni/ (*plural* **meinies**), **meinie** *n* Scotland a crowd of people or a rabble [13C. < Old French *meinée* < Latin *mansion-* (see MANSION).]

meiofauna /mī ō fawnə/ *n* the animal life found on the bed of a river, lake, or sea that is just visible to the naked eye, e.g. tiny mussels and worms [Mid-20C. < Greek *meio-* 'smaller' + FAUNA.]

meiosis /mī ṓsiss/ *n* **1** in organisms that reproduce sexually, a process of cell division during which the nucleus divides into four nuclei, each of which contains half the usual number of chromosomes. ◊ **mitosis 2** LITERAT = **litotes** [Mid-16C. < modern Latin, < Greek *meiōn* 'less'.] —**meiotic** /mī óttik/ *adj*

Golda Meir

Meir /may eèr/, **Golda** (1898–1978) Russian-born Israeli stateswoman

Meissen[1] /míss'n/ *n* CERAMICS = **Dresden china**

Meissen[2] /míssən/ town in east-central Germany, on the River Elbe. Population: 36,800 (1989).

Meissner's corpuscle /mīs nərz-/ *n* ANAT = **tactile corpuscle**

Meistersinger /mísˈtər singər/ (*plural* **-ers** *or* **-er**) *n* a member of a former German guild for poets and musicians in the 14th to 16th centuries [Mid-19C. < German, 'master-singer'.]

Meknés /mek nész/ city in N Morocco. Population: 401,000 (1993).

Mekong /mee kóng/ major river in Southeast Asia, flowing from SE China through the Indochinese peninsula and into the South China Sea in Vietnam. Length: 4,200 km/2,610 mi.

melaena /mə leénə/ *n* a condition characterized by the production of black stools that are caused by bleeding into the bowel and the subsequent chemical changes in the blood effected by the bowel fluids [Early 19C. Via modern Latin < Greek *melaina*, feminine of *melas* 'black'.]

Melaka /mə lákə/ port in W Malaysia, on the SW Malay Peninsula. Population: 295,999 (1991).

melaleuca /méllə lóokə/ *n* a tree or bush of the myrtle family that flourishes in wetlands and has become a pest in certain parts of North America. Native to: Australia. Genus: *Melaleuca*.

melamine /méllə meen/ *n* **1** $C_3H_6N_6$ a white crystalline solid. Use: manufacture of synthetic resins, in leather tanning. **2** a resin made from melamine, or a plastic made from such a resin [Mid-19C. Probably < German *Melamin*, substance obtained from the distillation of ammonium thiocyanate.]

melan- *prefix* = **melano-** (*before vowels*)

melancholia /méllən kṓli ə/ *n* depression as a form of psychiatric disorder (*dated*) [Early 17C. < late Latin (see MELANCHOLY).] —**melancholiac** *n*, *adj*

melancholic /méllən kóllik/ *adj* feeling or tending to feel a thoughtful or gentle sadness (*literary*) [14C. Either < MELANCHOLY, or < French *mélancolique* < Greek *melankholia* (see MELANCHOLY).] —**melancholic** *n* —**melancholically** *adv*

melancholy /méllənkəli/ *adj* feeling or making somebody feel a thoughtful or gentle sadness ■ *n* **1** thoughtful or gentle sadness **2** HIST = **black bile** [14C. Directly or via French *mélancholie* < late Latin *melancholia* < Greek *melankholia* < *melan-* 'black' + *kholē* 'bile'.] —**melancholily** *adv* —**melancholiness** *n*

Melanchthon /mə lángkthən, me lánkh ton/, **Philipp** (1497–1560) German religious reformer. Born **Philipp Schwartzert**

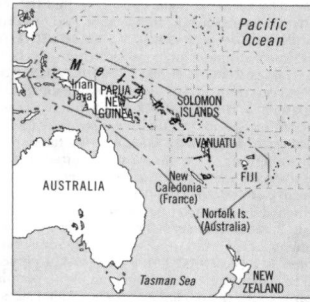

Melanesia

Melanesia /méllə neèzi ə, -neézhə/ ethnographic grouping of Pacific islands, encompassing the islands of the W Pacific Ocean south of the equator, including New Guinea, the Solomon Islands, New Caledonia, Vanuatu, and Fiji

Melanesian /méllə neèzi ən, -neézhən/ *n* **1** a group of Austronesian languages, including Fijian, spoken in Melanesia. Native speakers: 300,000. **2** a member of any people living on the islands of Melanesia —**Melanesian** *adj*

melange /may lṓNzh, -laǎnzh/, **mélange** *n* **1** a collection of things of different kinds (*literary or formal*) **2** a region of rock that consists of a mixture of dissimilar rocky materials [Mid-17C. < French *mélange* < *mêler* 'to mix' < Latin *miscere*.]

melanin /méllənin/ *n* a dark brown or black pigment that is naturally present to varying degrees in the skin, hair, eyes, fur, or feathers of people and animals as well as in plants —**melanoid** *adj*

melanism /méllənizəm/ *n* **1** dark pigmentation of the skin, hair, fur, or feathers in a human being, animal, or plant, resulting from the presence of melanin **2** MED = **melanosis** —**melanic** /mə lánnik/ *adj* —**melanistic** /méllə nístik/ *adj*

melanite /méllə nīt/ *n* a black form of andradite garnet containing titanium —**melanitic** /méllə níttik/ *adj*

melano- *prefix* black, dark ○ *melanocyte* [< Greek *melan-* 'black']

melanoblast /méllənō blast/ *n* a cell that gives rise to either a melanocyte or melanophore, which produces the black or dark brown pigment melanin —**melanoblastic** /méllənō blástik/ *adj*

melanocyte /méllənō sīt/ *n* a cell in the epidermal layer of the skin that produces the black or dark brown pigment melanin

melanocyte-stimulating hormone *n* either of two hormones in vertebrates produced in the pituitary gland that darken the skin by regulating melanin dispersal

melanoma /méllə nṓmə/ (*plural* **-mas** *or* **-mata** /-mətə/) *n* a malignant tumour, most often on the skin, that contains dark pigment and develops from a melanin-producing cell (**melanocyte**)

melanosis /méllə nṓsiss/ *n* an unexpected presence of dark pigmentation in the tissues [Early 19C. < modern Latin, < Greek *melan-* 'black'.] —**melanotic** /méllə nóttik/ *adj*

melanous /méllənəss/ *adj* having a dark complexion and dark hair [Mid-19C. < Greek *melan-* 'black'.] —**melanosity** /méllə nóssəti/ *n*

melatonin /méllə tṓnin/ *n* a hormone derived from serotonin and secreted by the pineal gland that produces changes in the skin colour of vertebrates, reptiles, and amphibians and is important in regulating biorhythms [Mid-20C. Blend of MELANO- + SEROTONIN.]

Melba /mélbə/ ◇ **do a Melba** *ANZ* to announce your retirement from a job or occupation repeatedly without actually leaving

Melba /mélbə/, **Dame Nellie** (1861–1931) Australian opera singer. Born **Helen Porter Mitchell**

Melba toast *n* very thin slices of bread toasted on both sides, sliced horizontally to expose two untoasted sides of bread that are then toasted too, causing the bread to curl [Early 20C. After Nellie MELBA.]

Melbourne /mélbərn/ capital of Victoria, Australia. Population: 2,865,329 (1996).

Melbourne /mél bawrn/, **William Lamb, 2nd Viscount** (1779–1848) British statesman

Melbourne Cup /mélbərn-/ *n* the best-known horse race in Australia, which takes place each year on the first Tuesday in November

Melchite /mél kīt/, **Melkite** *n* a member of any of several Christian churches in the Middle East that use the Greek Orthodox liturgy but acknowledge the authority of the Roman Catholic Pope [Early 17C. Via ecclesiastical Latin < Byzantine Greek *Melkhitai* 'Melkites' < Syriac *malkāyê* 'royalists' < *malkā* 'king'.]

Melchizedek /mel kízzə dek/ *n* in the Bible, a priest and king of Salem who blessed Abraham

meld[1] /meld/ *vti* to cause various things to combine or blend and become one thing or substance, or be combined or blended in this way ■ *n* a combination or blend of various things [Mid-20C. < ?]

meld[2] /meld/ *vti* to show or declare some or all of a hand of cards in order to score points in games such as canasta or pinochle ■ *n* a hand of cards that are shown or declared in order to score points in games such as canasta or pinochle, or an act of showing or declaring these cards [Late 19C. < German *melden* 'announce'.]

Meldrum /méldrəm/, **Max** (1875–1955) British-born Australian painter

melee /méllay/, **mêlée** *n* **1** a noisy confused fight **2** a confused, often noisy mixing of people or things, usually in a public place [Mid-17C. Via French *mêlée* < Old French *meslee*, past participle of *mesler* 'mix' < Latin *miscere*.]

melena *n* US = **melaena**

melic /méllik/ *adj* describes an ancient Greek lyric poem that is meant to be sung rather than recited [Late 17C. Via Latin < Greek *melikos* < *melos* 'song'.]

Méliès /máyl yess/, **Georges** (1861–1938) French film director

Melilla /mə lílla/ Spanish enclave and port in NE Morocco. Population: 64,727 (1995). Area: 14 sq. km/5.5 sq. mi.

melilot /mélli lot/ *n* a plant with compound leaves consisting of three oval leaflets and spikes of small, flared, yellow or white flowers. Genus: *Melilotus*. [14C. Via French < Greek *melilōtos* < *meli* 'honey' + *lōtos* 'lotus, clover'.]

melinite /mélli nīt/ *n* an explosive made from picric acid [Late 19C. < French, < Greek *mēlinos* 'quince-coloured' < *mēlon* 'apple, quince'; from its yellow colour.]

meliorate /meéli ə rayt/ (**-rates, -rating, -rated**) *vti* to become better, or make something better [Mid-16C. < late Latin *meliorare* < Latin *melior* 'better'.] —**meliorable** *adj* —**melioration** /meéli ə ráysh'n/ *n* —**meliorative** *adj* —**meliorator** *n*

meliorism /meéli ərizəm/ *n* the belief that human society has a natural tendency to improve and that people can consciously assist this process [Mid-19C. < Latin *melior* 'better'.] —**meliorist** *n* —**melioristic** /meéli ə rístik/ *adj*

melisma /mə lízmə/ (*plural* **-mata** /-mətə/ *or* **-mas**) *n* **1** a decorative phrase or passage in vocal music, especially one in which one syllable of a plainsong text is sung to a melodic sequence of several notes **2** an embellishment or decoration of a melody **3** MUSIC = **cadenza** [Late 19C. Via modern Latin < Greek, 'tune' < *melizein* 'sing' < *melos* 'song'.] —**melismatic** /mélliz máttik/ *adj*

Melkite *n* = **Melchite**

melli- *prefix* honey ○ *melliphagous* [< Latin *mel* < Indo-European]

melliferous /mə líffərəss/, **mellific** /mə líffik/ *adj* producing or bearing large quantities of honey [Mid-17C. < Latin *mellifer* 'honey-bearing' < *mel* 'honey'.]

mellifluous /mə lífflooəss/, **mellifluent** /mə lífflooənt/ *adj* pleasant and soothing to listen to, and sweet or rich in tone [15C. < late Latin *mellifluus* 'flowing like honey' < Latin *mel* 'honey'.] —**mellifluously** *adv* —**mellifluousness** *n*

mellophone /méllə fōn/ *n* a portable brass musical instrument similar in tone to a French horn, used mainly in brass bands and marching bands [Early 20C. < MELLOW.]

mellow /méllō/ *adj* **1** SOFT IN COLOUR OR TONE comfortingly soft, warm, and rich in colour or tone and lacking any harsh, brash, or jarring quality **2** SMOOTH AND RICH IN TASTE matured to a long-lasting smooth, rich taste **3** FULLY RIPE soft, juicy, fully ripened, and sweet **4** EASY-GOING good-humoured, tolerant, and approachable, especially as a result of long experience or a relaxed atmosphere **5** MILDLY INTOXICATED mildly intoxicated by drink or drugs **6** MOIST AND RICH IN TEXTURE having a moist, rich, loamy texture ■ *vti* **1** BECOME MORE EASY-GOING to become or make somebody more good-humoured, tolerant, and approachable, especially as a result of long experience or a relaxed atmosphere **2** BECOME OR MAKE RICHER IN QUALITY to become or make something richer, smoother, or softer in taste, colour, tone, or atmosphere [15C. < ?] —**mellowly** *adv* —**mellowness** *n*

mellow out *vti US* (*slang*) **1** to become or make somebody more relaxed and friendly **2** to become calm, or make somebody calm

melodeon /mə lṓdi ən/ *n* **1** a small reed organ, similar to a harmonium, that uses suction bellows to draw air through its reeds **2** a small accordion, used especially by German folk musicians [Mid-19C. Probably alteration of *melodium* 'small reed organ' < MELODY after HARMONIUM.]

melodic /mə lóddik/ *adj* **1** consisting of the melody of a piece of music ○ *the melodic line* **2** relating to or characteristic of melody or the composition of melodies **3** = **melodious** —**melodically** *adv*

melodic minor scale *n* a scale with the sixth and seventh notes raised a semitone when played in ascending order but in the natural minor pitch when played in descending order

melodious /mə lṓdi əss/ *adj* **1** tuneful or varied and interesting in tone **2** having the character of a melody —**melodiously** *adv* —**melodiousness** *n*

melodise *vti* = **melodize**

melodist /méllə dist/ *n* **1** a composer of melodies, especially beautiful or memorable melodies for song lyrics **2** somebody who sings sweetly

melodize /méllə dīz/ (**-dizes, -dizing, -dized**), **melodise** (**-dises, -dising, -dised**) *v* **1** *vti* to compose a melody or melodies or compose a melody to which lyrics can be sung **2** *vt* to make something tuneful and pleasing to hear —**melodizer** *n*

melodrama /méllə draamə/ *n* **1** SENSATIONALIZED DRAMATIC OR LITERARY WORK a dramatic or other literary work characterized by the use of stereotyped characters, exaggerated emotions and language, simplistic morality, and conflict **2** DRAMATIC OR LITERARY GENRE melodramas collectively considered as a dramatic or literary genre **3** HISTRIONIC BEHAVIOUR exaggerated behaviour or emotional displays, like those characteristic of a melodrama **4** DRAMA INTERSPERSED WITH MUSIC formerly, a play with a sensational or romantic plot that is interspersed with musical numbers and often has music accompanying the action **5** SPOKEN WORDS WITH MUSICAL ACCOMPANIMENT a piece of poetry or a scene in a dramatic or operatic work in which the text is recited to a musical accompaniment [Early 19C. < French *mélodrame* 'drama with songs' < Greek *melos* 'song'.]

melodramatic /méllədrə máttik/ *adj* **1** behaving, speaking, done, or said in a way that is more dramatic, shocking, or highly emotional than the situation demands **2** relating to or typical of melodrama [Early 19C. < MELODRAMA.] —**melodramatically** *adv*

melodramatics /méllədrə máttiks/ *npl* exaggeratedly theatrical behaviour, speech, or writing

melodramatize /méllə drámmə tīz/ (**-tizes, -tizing, -tized**), **melodramatise** (**-tises, -tising, -tised**) *vti* to treat or react to something in an exaggeratedly theatrical way [Early 19C. < MELODRAMA, after DRAMATIZE.] —**melodramatization** /méllə drámmə tī záysh'n/ *n*

melody /mélladi/ (*plural* **-dies**) *n* **1** TUNE a series of musical notes that form a distinct unit, are recognizable as a phrase, and usually have a distinctive rhythm **2** LINEAR MUSICAL STRUCTURE the linear structure of a piece of music in which single notes follow one another **3** MAIN TUNE the primary and most recognizable part in a harmonic piece of music **4** MUSICALLY EXPRESSIVE QUALITY the musically expressive quality of something, especially poetry **5** MUSICAL LYRIC a poem that lends itself easily to being set to music or sung [12C. Via French *mélodie* < Greek *melōidia* 'choral song' < *melos* 'tune' + *ōidē* 'song'.]

melon /méllən/ *n* **1** ROUND JUICY GOURD FRUIT the round edible fruit of vines belonging to the gourd family, with a tough rind and sweet juicy flesh ranging in colour from pale yellow to deep orange **2** PLANT THAT BEARS MELONS a vine of the gourd family widely grown to yield melons. *Cucumis melo* and *Citrullus lanatus*. **3** SOUND ORGAN a rounded waxy mass found in the head of some dolphins and toothed whales that is thought to play a part in the focusing of sound signals ■ **melons** *npl* OFFENSIVE TERM an offensive term for a woman's breasts, especially when large (*slang*) [14C. Via French < Greek *mēlopepōn*, a kind of gourd < *mēlon* 'apple' + *pepōn* 'gourd'.]

Melos /meé loss/, **Mílos** island in the Cyclades, SE Greece. Population: 4,554 (1981). Area: 158 sq. km/61 sq. mi.

Melpomene /mel pómməni/ *n* in Greek mythology, the muse of tragedy

Melrose /mél rōz/ **1** town in SE Scotland. Population: 2,270 (1991). **2** city in NE Massachusetts. Population: 27,376 (1998 estimate).

melt[1] /melt/ *v* **1** *vti* CHANGE FROM A SOLID TO A LIQUID STATE to change a substance from a solid to a liquid state by heating it, or be changed in this way **2** *vti* DISSOLVE to dissolve something, e.g. sugar, in a liquid or be dissolved in a liquid **3** *vi* DISAPPEAR to disappear gradually and inconspicuously **4** *vi* MERGE INTO to change into, or blend with, something in such a way that the actual point of change or blending is almost imperceptible **5** *vti* BE MOVED EMOTIONALLY to cause somebody to be moved emotionally so as to become gentler and more sympathetic, or be moved in this way **6** *vi* FEEL HOT to feel uncomfortably hot (*informal*) ■ *n* **1** MASS OF MELTED MATERIAL a mass or an amount of melted material, especially metal, produced in a single operation or during a specific period of time **2** MOLTEN MATERIAL a material such as metal or glass in a molten state **3** MELTING the process of melting something **4** LIQUEFACTION the state or condition of being liquefied **5** TOASTED CHEESE-TOPPED OPEN SANDWICH an open toasted sandwich, usually with cheese melted on top —**meltability** *n* —**meltable** *adj* —**melter** *n*

melt down *vti* to liquefy metal or glass by heating in order to reuse it, or to be liquefied in this way

melt[2] /melt/ *n* the spleen of a slaughtered animal, used mainly for animal food (*often plural*) [Late 16C. Variant of MILT.]

meltage /méltij/ *n* **1** the process of melting something **2** a liquefied substance produced by a heating process, or an amount of such a substance

meltdown /mélt down/ *n* **1** MELTING OF NUCLEAR REACTOR FUEL RODS the melting of fuel rods in a nuclear reactor because of overheating that results in the escape of radioactive materials or radiation **2** COMPLETE COLLAPSE OF AN ORGANIZATION a situation of complete collapse of an organization or institution (*informal*) **3** EXTREMELY ANGRY STATE a loss of composure, especially an extremely angry response to something (*informal*) **4** PERSONAL BREAKDOWN a loss of coherence, rationality, or awareness of reality (*informal*)

melting /mélting/ *adj* full of or causing sweet and tender or sentimental emotion —**meltingly** *adv* —**meltingness** *n*

melting point *n* the temperature at which a substance changes from a solid to a liquid form

melting pot *n* **1** CONTAINER FOR MELTING AND MIXING a container in which substances, especially metals, are placed to be liquefied and mixed together **2** SOCIETY COMPOSED OF MANY DIFFERENT CULTURES a place where people of different ethnic groups are brought together and can assimilate, especially a country that takes immigrants from many different ethnic backgrounds **3** PROCESS THAT CREATES SOMETHING NEW a process of mixture and integration of different elements that can produce something new

melton /méltən/ *n* smooth heavy wool cloth. Use: overcoats. [Mid-19C. After MELTON MOWBRAY.]

Melton Mowbray /méltən mṓ bray/ town in central England. Population: 24,348 (1991).

meltwater /mélt wawtər/ *n* water formed by the melting of ice or snow, especially from a glacier

Melville /mélvil/, **Herman** (1818–91) US writer

Melville Island /mélvil-/ island in the Northern Territory, Australia, in the Timor Sea. Population: 2,033 (1996). Area: 5,800 sq. km/2,239 sq. mi.

Melville Peninsula peninsula in central Nunavut, Canada, between the Gulf of Boothia and Foxe Basin. Area: 65,000 sq. km/25,100 sq. mi.

mem /mem/ *n* the 13th letter of the Hebrew alphabet [Early 19C. < Hebrew *mēm* 'water'.]

mem. *abbr* **1** member **2** memoir **3** memorandum **4** memorial

member /mémbər/ *n* **1 ADHERENT OF PARTICULAR GROUP** a belonger to and participant in a specific group by birth or choice **2 member, Member POLITICAL REPRESENTATIVE** somebody elected to a legislative body such as the British Parliament or the US Congress **3 LIMB** a part or organ of a plant or animal body, especially a limb **4 PENIS** a penis (*formal or humorous*) **5 INDIVIDUAL PART** a separate and distinct part of a whole, e.g. an object belonging to a mathematical set, a clause in a sentence, or a proposition in a syllogism **6 STRUCTURAL UNIT IN BUILDING** a beam, wall, or similar structural unit in a building or other construction **7 ELEMENT IN A MATHEMATICAL EQUATION** each of the expressions in a mathematical equation linked by an equals sign [14C. Via French *membre* < Latin *membrum* 'limb, part'.] —**memberless** *adj*

member firm *n* a company trading in securities that belongs to an organized exchange

Member of Congress *n* somebody elected to the US Congress, especially to the House of Representatives

Member of Parliament *n* a person who has been elected to a parliament

membership /mémbərship/ *n* **1** the state or condition of belonging to a particular group, e.g. a species, social class, team, club, or political party **2** the members of a group, e.g. a species, social class, organization, or mathematical set, considered collectively (+ *singular or plural verb*)

membrane /mém brayn/ *n* **1 THIN LAYER OF TISSUE** a thin flexible sheet of tissue connecting, covering, lining, or separating various parts or organs in animal and plant bodies, or forming the external wall of a cell **2 THIN POROUS SHEET** a thin, pliable, and often porous sheet of any natural or artificial material **3 PIECE OF PARCHMENT** a piece of parchment forming part of a roll [15C. Directly or via French < Latin *membrana* 'skin' < *membrum* 'limb, part'.] —**membranaceous** /mémbrə náyshəss/ *adj* —**membranal** /mémbrən'l/ *adj* —**membraned** *adj*

membrane bone *n* a bone that develops directly out of membranous connective tissue rather than from cartilage, e.g. the clavicle and some cranial bones

membrane transport *n* the process by which substances in solution pass through a biological membrane

membranous /mémbrənəss/ *adj* **1** relating to or similar to a membrane, especially in being thin, pliable, and often translucent **2** resulting in the formation of a membrane or of a thin layer similar to a membrane —**membranously** *adv*

membranous labyrinth *n* the structure of fluid-filled sacs in the inner ear that are vital to hearing and balance

memento /mə méntō, mi-/ (*plural* **-tos** *or* **-toes**) *n* an object given or kept as a reminder of or in memory of somebody or something [Mid-18C. < Latin, 'remember!' (originally the first word in prayers for the dead) < *meminisse* 'remember'.]

memento mori /-máw ree/ (*plural* **memento mori**) *n* **1** an object, especially a skull, intended as a reminder of the fact that humans die **2** a reminder of the fact that humans fail and make mistakes (*literary*) [< Latin, 'remember (that you have) to die']

Memling /mémmling/, **Hans** (1435?–94) Flemish painter

Memnon /mém non/ *n* in Greek mythology, the Ethiopian king who fought for the Trojans in the siege of Troy and was killed by Achilles

memo /mémmō/ (*plural* **-os**) *n* **1** a written communication similar to a letter but without the formal address blocks at the beginning, especially one that is circulated to people within an office or organization **2** COMM = **memorandum** *n.* 2 [Early 18C. Shortening of MEMORANDUM.]

memoir /mém waar/ *n* **1 BIOGRAPHY OR HISTORICAL ACCOUNT** a biography or an account of historical events, especially one written from personal knowledge **2 ESSAY ON A SCHOLARLY SUBJECT** a short essay, article, or report on a scholarly subject, usually one in which the writer is a recognized specialist ■ **memoirs** *npl* **1 AUTOBIOGRAPHY** somebody's written account of his or her own life or of events in which he or she took part **2 PROCEEDINGS** the records of the business and discussions of a learned society [Mid-17C. < French *mémoire* 'memory' < Old French *memorie* (see MEMORY).]

memorabilia /mémmərə bílli ə/ *npl* **1** objects associated with a famous person or event, especially considered as collectors' items **2** objects collected as souvenirs of important personal events or experiences [Late 18C. < Latin, 'memorable things' < *memorabilis* (see MEMORABLE).]

memorable /mémmərəb'l/ *adj* **1** sufficiently interesting, exciting, or unusual to be worth remembering or likely to be remembered **2** easy to remember [15C. Via French < Latin *memorabilis* < *memorare* 'bring to mind' < *memor* 'mindful'.] —**memorability** /mémmərə bílləti/ *n* —**memorableness** *n* —**memorably** *adv*

memorandum /mémmə rándəm/ (*plural* **-dums** *or* **-da** /-də/) *n* **1** COMM = **memo** *n.* 1 **2 REMINDER** a note to serve as a reminder of something **3 BRIEF DIPLOMATIC COMMUNICATION** a brief, often unsigned communication circulated among diplomats, especially one that summarizes a country's position on a particular issue **4 SUMMARY OF A LEGAL AGREEMENT** a written statement summarizing the terms of a contract or a similar legal transaction **5 CONSIGNOR'S STATEMENT** a consignor's brief statement about a shipment of returnable goods [15C. < Latin, 'thing to be remembered' < *memorare* 'bring to mind' < *memor* 'mindful'.]

memorial /mə máwri əl/ *n* **1 COMMEMORATIVE OBJECT** something that is intended to remind people of a person who has died or an event in which people died, e.g. a statue, speech, or special ceremony **2 STATEMENT OF FACTS ACCOMPANYING A PETITION** a written statement of facts accompanying a petition presented to somebody in authority ■ *adj* **COMMEMORATIVE** intended as a reminder of a person or event or as a celebration of somebody's life and work [14C. Via French < Latin *memoria* (see MEMORY).] —**memorially** *adv*

Memorial Day *n* in the United States, a public holiday to commemorate soldiers who died in war. Date: last Monday in May, formerly 30 May.

memorialise *vt* = **memorialize**

memorialist /mə máwri əlist/ *n* **1** a writer of memoirs **2** a writer, signer, or presenter of a memorial accompanying a petition

memorialize /mə máwri ə līz/ (**-izes, -izing, -ized**), **memorialise** (**-ises, -ising** *or* **-ised, -ised**) *vt* **1** to serve as a memorial to somebody or something, or provide somebody or something with a memorial **2** to present a written memorial accompanying a petition to somebody or a group in power —**memorialization** /mə máwri ə lī záysh'n/ *n* —**memorializer** *n*

memorize /mémmə rīz/ (**-rizes, -rizing, -rized**), **memorise** (**-rises, -rising, -rised**) *vt* to commit something to memory —**memorizable** *adj* —**memorization** /mémmə rī záysh'n/ *n* —**memorizer** *n*

ϟ**memory** /mémməri/ (*plural* **-ries**) *n* **1 ABILITY TO RETAIN KNOWLEDGE** the ability of the mind or of an individual or organism to retain learned information and knowledge of past events and experiences and to retrieve it **2 SOMEBODY'S STOCK OF RETAINED KNOWLEDGE** an individual's stock of retained knowledge and experience ○ *has a good memory for faces* **3 RETAINED IMPRESSION OF PARTICULAR EVENT** the knowledge or impression that somebody retains of a particular person, event, period, or subject ○ *memories of a happy childhood* **4 RECOLLECTION** the act or a specific instance of remembering **5 PRESERVATION OF KNOWLEDGE** the preservation of knowledge of and, usually, celebration of a deceased person or past event ○ *a poem in memory of her father* **6 POSTHUMOUS IMPRESSION** the knowledge or impression of somebody retained by other people after that person's death **7 TEMPORAL EXTENT OF RECOLLECTION** the period of past time that a person or group is able to remember ○ *within living memory* **8 DATA STORAGE UNIT IN COMPUTER** the part of a computer in which data is stored **9 COMPUTER'S DATA STORAGE CAPACITY** the data storage capacity of a computer **10 ABILITY TO RETURN TO ORIGINAL SHAPE** the ability of some materials, e.g. plastics and metals, to return to their original shape after being subject to deformation [13C. Via Old French *memorie* < Latin *memoria* < *memor* 'mindful'.]

ϟ**memory bank** *n* COMPUT = **memory** *n.* **8**

memory lane *n* the past, especially the past shared and remembered by a group of people, thought of as a path that can be travelled along to visit specific former times

memory span *n* a measure of somebody's memory, often for units of information such as nonsense syllables or sequences of random numbers, over a short period of time

memory trace *n* PSYCHOL = **engram**

Memphis /mém fiss/ **1** ruined city and capital of ancient Egypt, in the Nile delta **2** city in SW Tennessee, on the Mississippi River. Population: 603,507 (1998 estimate). —**Memphian** *n, adj*

Memphremagog, Lake /mémfrə máygog/ lake on the Canada-United States border in S Quebec and N Vermont. Length: 43 km/27 mi.

memsahib /mém saab, mém saab/ *n S Asia* a respectful form of address formerly used by Indians to a European married woman [Mid-19C. < MA'AM + SAHIB.]

men plural of **man**

men- *prefix* = **meno-** (*before vowels*)

menace /ménnəss/ *n* **1 POSSIBLE SOURCE OF DANGER** a possible source of danger or harm **2 NUISANCE** a constant source of trouble and annoyance (*informal*) **3 THREATENING QUALITY** a threatening quality, feeling, or tone **4 THREATENING ACT** a threatening act, gesture, or speech ○ *demanding money with menaces* ■ *v* (**-aces, -acing, -aced**) **1** *vt* **BE DANGEROUS TO** to be a possible or actual source of danger or harm to somebody or something **2** *vti* **MAKE A THREAT AGAINST** to behave towards or speak to somebody in a way that threatens injury or harm (*often passive*) [14C. Via French < Latin *minax* 'threatening' < *minari* 'threaten' < *minae* 'threats', literally 'projecting points'.] —**menacer** *n* —**menacing** *adj* —**menacingly** *adv*

menadione /ménnə dī ōn/ *n* $C_{11}H_8O_2$ a yellow crystalline solid. Use: fungicide, vitamin K supplement in medicines and animal feedstuffs. [Mid-20C. Contraction of METHYL + NAPHTHALENE + DI-[1].]

ménage /máy naazh/ *n* (*formal*) **1** a group of people living together as a household **2** the running of a household [Late 17C. Via French < Latin *manere* 'dwell, stay'.]

ménage à trois /máy naazh aa trwaá/ (*plural* **ménages à trois** /máy naazh-/) *n* a sexual relationship involving three people [< French, 'household for three']

menagerie /mə nájj əri/ *n* **1 WILD ANIMAL EXHIBIT** a collection of wild animals kept in captivity for the curiosity and entertainment of the public, sometimes as part of a travelling show such as a circus **2 WILD ANIMAL ENCLOSURE** an enclosure in which wild animals are kept for public exhibition **3 DIVERSE OR EXOTIC GROUP** a diverse, exotic, or peculiar group of people or things

Menai Strait /ménī stráyt/ narrow channel of the Irish Sea, between NW Wales and Anglesey. Length: 23 km/14 mi.

menarche /me naárki/ *n* the first time that a girl or young woman menstruates [Early 20C. < MENO- + Greek *arkhē* 'beginning'.] —**menarcheal** *adj*

menazon /ménnə zon/ *n* $C_6H_8N_5O_2PS_2$ a colourless crystalline solid. Use: killing aphids. [Mid-20C. Contraction of METHYL + AMINO- + AZO- + *thionate*.]

MENCAP /mén kap/ *abbr* Royal Society for Mentally Handicapped Children and Adults [Contraction of *mental handicap* or *mentally handicapped*]

Mencius /ménshi əss, -shəss/ (371?–289 BC) Chinese philosopher. Born **Meng-tzu**

Mencken /méngkən/, **H. L.** (1880–1956) US journalist and critic. Full name **Henry Louis Mencken**

mend /mend/ *v* **1** *vti* **RESTORE SOMETHING TO SATISFACTORY CONDITION** to work on something that is damaged or defective and return it to its original or a satisfactory condition **2** *vt* **REMOVE A HOLE** to fill, cover, or otherwise remove damage such as a hole or break **3** *vti* **IMPROVE** to improve something or make it more acceptable, or be improved or made more acceptable ○ *You'd better mend your ways.* **4** *vi* **RECOVER OR HEAL** to heal or return to a healthy state after illness or injury ■ *n* **REPAIR** an instance of repair work or a repaired place on a damaged object, especially a darn on a piece of clothing [12C. Partly shortening of AMEND, and partly < Anglo-Norman *mender* (shortening of *amender*; see AMEND).] —**mendable** *adj* —**mender** *n* ◇ **on the mend** recovering or healing after illness or injury

mendacious /men dáyshəss/ *adj* **1** having lied in the past, or prone to lying at any time **2** deliberately untrue [Early 17C. < Latin *mendac-* 'lying'.] —**mendaciously** *adv* —**mendaciousness** *n*

mendacity /men dássəti/ (*plural* **-ties**) *n* **1** deliberate untruthfulness **2** a lie or falsehood [Mid-17C. < French *mendacité* < Latin *mendax* 'lying'.]

Mende /méndi/ (*plural* **-de** *or* **-des**) *n* **1** a member of a people living in Sierra Leone **2** the Niger-Congo language of the Mende people. Native speakers: 1 million. [Mid-18C. < Mende.] —**Mende** *adj*

Mendel /ménd'l/, **Gregor Johann** (1822–84) Austrian monk and scientist —**Mendelian** /men deèli ən/ *adj*

mendelevium /méndə leèvi əm/ *n* (*symbol* **Md**) a synthetic short-lived radioactive element. Source: bombardment of einsteinium atoms with helium particles. [Mid-20C. After Dmitri Ivanovich MENDELEYEV.]

Mendeleyev /méndə láyef/, **Dmitri Ivanovich** (1834–1907) Russian chemist

Mendelism /méndəlizəm/, **Mendelianism** /men deèli ənizəm/ *n* the theory of heredity formulated by Mendel, which explains how certain characteristics are passed on from one generation to the next through genes

Mendel's Laws /ménd'lz-/ *npl* the laws of heredity formulated by Mendel to explain the transmission of characteristics from one generation to the next

Mendelssohn /ménd'lssən/, **Felix** (1809–47) German composer

Menderes /méndə ress/ river in SW Turkey. Length: 584 km/363 mi.

mendicant /méndikənt/ *adj* LIVING ON CHARITY begging for and living on money given by strangers ∎ *n* **1** BEGGAR a beggar, usually in the street (*formal*) **2** FRIAR BEGGING FOR SUPPORT a member of a religious order, e.g. the Franciscans, Dominicans, Carmelites, or Augustinians, that forbids the ownership of property and encourages working or begging for a living [14C. < Latin *mendicare* 'beg' < *mendicus* 'beggar' < *mendum* 'defect'.]

mending /ménding/ *n* articles, especially clothes, to be mended

Mendip Hills /méndip-/ range of hills in SW England. Highest peak: Black Down 326 m/1,068 ft.

Mendoza /men dózə/ city in W Argentina. Population: 1,572,784 (1999 estimate).

Menelaus /ménni láyəss/ *n* in Greek mythology, the king of Sparta and husband of Helen of Troy

Menelik II /ménnəlik/ (1844–1913) emperor of Ethiopia (1889–1909)

Menem /mén em/, **Carlos Saúl** (*b.* 1930) Argentine statesman

menfolk /mén fōk/ *npl* (+ *plural verb*) **1** the men associated with a particular family or group **2** men in general or considered collectively

Mengistu Haile Mariam /meng gístoo híli márri əm/ (*b.* 1937) Ethiopian statesman

menhaden /men háyd'n/ (*plural* **-dens** *or* **-den**) *n* a sea fish of the herring family, used mainly as a source of oil, fertilizer, and bait. Native to: North America. *Brevoortia tyrannus*. [Mid-17C. < ?]

menhir /mén heer/ *n* a large single upright stone, erected by prehistoric people and thought to have been used for astronomical observations, found in the British Isles and N France [Mid-19C. Directly or via French < Breton *maen-hir* < *men* 'stone' + *hir* 'long'.]

Menhir: Le Grand Menhir Dol, Brittany, France

menial /meèni əl/ *adj* **1** UNSKILLED relating to or involving work that requires little skill or training, is not interesting, and confers low social status on the person doing it **2** RELATING TO SERVANTS suitable, typical of, or relating to a servant or servants ∎ *n* **1** DOMESTIC SERVANT a domestic servant, especially one of low status **2** SOMEBODY WHO DOES MENIAL WORK somebody employed to do work that requires no skill or training (*formal*) [14C. < Anglo-Norman, 'of a household' < Latin *mansion-* (see MANSION).] —**menially** *adv*

Ménière's disease /máyn yairz-/, **Ménière's syndrome** *n* a disorder caused by an accumulation of fluid in the labyrinths of the inner ear [Late 19C. After the French physician Prosper Ménière (1799–1862).]

Menindee Lakes /mə níndi-/ group of reservoirs in W New South Wales, Australia, linked with the River Darling

mening- *prefix* = meningo-

meninges /mə nín jeez/ *npl* the three membranes that surround and protect the brain and the spinal cord, called the dura mater, the arachnoid mater, and the pia mater [Early 17C. Via modern Latin < Greek *mēnigg*-'membrane'.] —**meningeal** *adj*

meningi- *prefix* = meningo-

meningioma /mə nínji ōmə/ (*plural* **-mas** *or* **-mata** /-mətə/) *n* a slow-growing benign tumour that affects the meninges of the brain or spinal cord and may cause serious damage by compression [Early 20C. Shortening of *meningothelioma* < MENINGO- + ENDOTHELIOMA.]

meningitis /ménnin jítiss/ *n* a serious, sometimes fatal illness in which a viral or bacterial infection inflames the meninges, causing symptoms such as severe headaches, vomiting, stiff neck, and high fever —**meningitic** /-jíttik/ *adj*

meningo- *prefix* meninges ○ *meningocele* [< Greek *mēnigg*-, stem of *mēnigx* 'membrane']

meningocele /me níng gō seel/ *n* the protrusion of the meninges through a defect in the skull or backbone to form a cyst

meningococcus /mə níng gō kókəss/ (*plural* **-ci** /-sī/) *n* a bacterium that causes cerebrospinal meningitis. *Neisseria meningitidis*. —**meningococcal** *adj* —**meningococcic** /-kóksik/ *adj*

meningoencephalitis /mə níng gō en kéffə lítiss, -séffə-/ *n* an inflammation of the brain and the meninges —**meningoencephalitic** /-líttik/ *adj*

meniscus /mə nískus/ (*plural* **-ci** /-níssī/ *or* **-cuses**) *n* **1** UPPER SURFACE OF LIQUID the curved upper surface of a still liquid in a tube, concave if the liquid wets the walls of the container, convex if it does not, caused by surface tension **2** CARTILAGE DISC a crescent-shaped cartilage disc cushioning the end of a bone where it meets another bone in a joint, especially in the knee **3** CONCAVO-CONVEX LENS a lens that is convex on one side and concave on the other **4** CRESCENT SHAPE a crescent-shaped body or figure [Late 17C. Via modern Latin < Greek *mēniskos* < *mēnē* 'moon'.] —**meniscal** *adj* —**meniscate** *adj* —**meniscoid** *adj* —**meniscoidal** /méniss kóyd'l/ *adj*

Mennonite /ménnə nīt/ *n* a member of a Protestant denomination emphasizing adult baptism and pacifism and rejecting church organization and, in many cases, the holding of public office and the taking of oaths [Mid-16C. < German *Mennonit*, after *Menno* Simons (1496–1561), early Frisian leader of the group.] —**Mennonitism** *n*

meno /ménnō/ *adv* used with a musical direction to mean less quickly or softly [Late 19C. < Italian, 'less'.]

meno- *prefix* menstruation ○ *menopause* [< Greek *mēn(ē)* 'month' < Indo-European]

menology /mi nóllə ji/ (*plural* **-gies**) *n* a church calendar of the months, especially in the Eastern Orthodox Church, that shows saints' days and gives biographies of the saints [Early 17C. Via modern Latin < ecclesiastical Greek *mēnologion* 'month-reckoning' < *mēn* 'month'.]

Menominee /mə nómminee/ (*plural* **-nee** *or* **-nees**), **Menomini** (*plural* **-ni** *or* **-nis**) *n* **1** a member of a Native American people of NE Wisconsin **2** the Algonquian language of the Menominee people [Mid-18C. < Ojibwa *manōminī* 'wild-rice person'.] —**Menominee** *adj*

meno mosso /ménnō móssō/ *adv* at a slower speed (*musical direction*) [< Italian, 'less agitated']

Menon /ménnən/, **V. K. Krishna** (1896–1974) Indian politician

Menorah

menopause /ménnō pawz/ *n* the time in a woman's life when menstruation diminishes and ceases, usually between the ages of 45 and 50 [Late 19C. < MENO- + Greek *pausis* 'pause' < *pausein* 'to stop'.] —**menopausal** /ménnō páwz'l/ *adj* —**menopausic** *adj*

menorah /mə náwrə/ *n* **1** a ceremonial candleholder consisting of a central stem surrounded by six curved branches, used in the Jewish Temple and as an emblem of Judaism and the state of Israel **2** an eight-branched candleholder, lit during the festival of Hanukkah [Late 19C. < Hebrew *mĕnōrāh* 'candlestick'.]

Menorca /mi náwrkə/, **Minorca** island in the Balearic Islands, Spain. Population: 66,900 (1989). Area: 702 sq. km/271 sq. mi. —**Menorcan** *adj*, *n*

menorrhagia /ménnə ráyji ə/ *n* abnormally heavy or prolonged bleeding during menstruation —**menorrhagic** *adj*

menorrhea *n* MED = menorrhoea

menorrhoea /ménnə reè ə/, **menorrhea** *n* normal bleeding during menstruation [Mid-19C. Back-formation < AMENORRHOEA.]

Menotti /mə nótti/, **Gian-Carlo** (*b.* 1911) Italian-born US composer

Mensa /ménssə/ *n* **1** a faint constellation of the southern hemisphere that forms part of the larger Magellanic Cloud **2** an international organization for people with a very high IQ [Mid-20C. < Latin, 'table'.]

mensal[1] /ménss'l/ *adj* occurring monthly [Mid-19C. < Latin *mensis* 'month'.]

mensal[2] /ménss'l/ *adj* used or done at the meal table, or connected with eating meals [15C. < late Latin *mensalis* < Latin *mensa* 'table'.]

mensch /mensh/ (*plural* **menschen** /ménsh'n/ *or* **mensches**), **mensh** (*plural* **menshen** *or* **menshes**) *n* US somebody good, kind, decent, and honourable (*informal*) [Mid-20C. Via Yiddish < Old High German *mennisco* 'manly, human'.]

menses /mén seez/ *n* (*technical*; + *singular or plural verb*) **1** menstruation, or the period of time that it lasts **2** the blood and other matter discharged from the womb during menstruation [Late 16C. < Latin, plural of *mensis* 'month'.]

mensh *n* US = mensch (*informal*)

Menshevik /ménshəvik/ (*plural* **-viks** *or* **-viki** /-víki/) *n* a member of the moderate minority faction of the Marxist Social Democratic Party in prerevolutionary Russia that advocated a gradual approach to social reform, in contrast to the Bolsheviks [Early 20C. < Russian *men'shevik* < *men'she* 'less'; because they favoured less extreme Socialist reform than the Bolsheviks.] —**Menshevism** *n* —**Menshevist** *n*

mens rea /ménz ráyə/ *n* prior intention to commit a criminal act, without necessarily knowing that the act is a crime [< modern Latin, 'guilty mind']

men's room *n* US = gents

mens sana in corpore sano /ménz saànə in káwpəri saànō/ *n* a healthy mind in a healthy body, as an ideal in living [< Latin]

menstrual /mén stroo əl/ *adj* occurring during, or connected with, menstruation

menstrual cycle *n* PHYSIOL = menstruation

menstruate /mén stroo ayt/ (**-ates**, **-ating**, **-ated**) *vi* to discharge blood and other matter from the womb as part of the menstrual cycle [Early 19C. < late Latin *men-*

struare < Latin *menstruus* 'monthly, menstrual' < *mensis* 'month'.]

menstruation /mén stroo áysh'n/ *n* the monthly process of discharging blood and other matter from the womb that occurs between puberty and menopause in women and female primates who are not pregnant

menstruous /mén stroo əss/ *adj* MED = **menstrual**

menstruum /mén stroo əm/ (*plural* **-ums** *or* **-a** /-ə/) *n* a solvent, especially one used to prepare drugs or extract compounds from plant or animal tissue [Early 17C. < medieval Latin, 'menstruation' < Latin *menstruus* (see MENSTRUATE).]

mensurable /ménshərəb'l/ *adj* **1** capable of being measured **2** MUSIC = **mensural** *adj.* **2** [Late 16C. < late Latin *mensurabilis* < Latin *mensura* (see MEASURE).] —**mensurability** /ménshərə bílləti/ *n* —**mensurableness** *n*

mensural /ménshərəl/ *adj* **1** relating to or involving measurement or measurable values **2** describes or relating to notes, particularly in medieval music, that have a fixed length or time value relative to one another [Late 16C. < Latin *mensuralis* < *mensura* (see MEASURE).]

mensuration /ménshə ráysh'n/ *n* **1** the calculation of geometric quantities such as length, area, and volume from dimensions and angles that are already known **2** the act, process, or skill of measuring something (*formal*) [Late 16C. < late Latin *mensuration-* < Latin *mensura* (see MEASURE).] —**mensurational** *adj* —**mensurative** /ménshərətiv/ *adj*

menswear /ménz wair/ *n* **1** clothing designed to be worn by men **2** the department in a shop that sells menswear

-ment *suffix* **1** action, process ○ *arraignment* ○ *betterment* **2** result of an action, or condition resulting from an action ○ *bewilderment* **3** instrument or agent of an action ○ *refreshment* **4** place ○ *emplacement* ○ *escarpment* [Directly and via French < Latin *-mentum*]

mental /mént'l/ *adj* **1** RELATING TO THE MIND relating to, found in, or occurring in the mind ○ *mental stimulation* **2** CARRIED OUT IN THE MIND carried out in the mind without any physical action or the use of any physical aid ○ *mental arithmetic* **3** PRODUCED BY THE MIND produced by the mind and visible only in the mind ○ *mental imagery* **4** OFFENSIVE TERM an offensive term meaning having a psychiatric disorder **5** OFFENSIVE TERM an offensive term meaning extremely unintelligent or silly (*insult*) [15C. Via French < Latin *ment-* 'mind'.] —**mentally** *adv*

mental age *n* a measure of intellectual development developed by the French psychologist Binet, who devised norms against which children could be compared with other children of the same chronological age ○ *a four-year-old with a mental age of seven*

mental block *n* an inability to carry out a mental task such as remembering something, especially when caused by subconscious emotional factors

mental cruelty *n* the infliction of psychological pain on somebody

mental disorder *n* in English law, a psychiatric disorder or impairment of mental faculties

mental handicap *n* an offensive term for an intellectual impairment

mental hospital *n* PSYCHIAT = **psychiatric hospital** (*offensive*)

mental illness *n* any psychiatric disorder of the mind that causes untypical behaviour

mental impairment *n* in English law, a state of mental development that negatively affects somebody's intellectual capacity and ability to function

mentalism /mént'lizəm/ *n* the belief that all objects of knowledge, including the physical universe, ultimately have no existence except as creations of the mind —**mentalist** *n* —**mentalistic** /mént'l ístik/ *adj* —**mentalistically** *adv*

mentality /men tálləti/ (*plural* **-ties**) *n* **1** a habitual way of thinking or interpreting events peculiar to an individual or type of person, especially with reference to the behaviour that it produces **2** somebody's intellectual ability

mentally challenged *adj* affected by a condition that limits the ability to learn and to function independently, as a result of congenital causes, brain injury, or disease

mental reservation *n* a tacit qualification of a statement or oath made when it would be unwise or disadvantageous to express doubt or disagreement openly ○ *agreed to testify without any mental reservation*

mental retardation *n* an offensive term for difficulty in learning or independent functioning (*dated*)

mentation /men táysh'n/ *n* (*formal*) **1** mental activity, especially thinking **2** somebody's state of mind or general attitude [Mid-19C. < Latin *ment-* 'mind'.]

menthol /mén thol/ *n* $CH_3C_6H_9(C_3H_7)OH$ an organic compound having a cool minty taste. Source: peppermint oil. Use: flavourings, perfumes, mild anaesthetic. [Late 19C. < German, 'mint-oil' < Latin *mentha* (see MINT[1]).]

mentholated /ménthə laytid/ *adj* flavoured with or containing menthol

mention /ménsh'n/ *v* **1** *vti* SAY A PARTICULAR WORD OR THING to use a particular word or name when speaking or writing, often in a casual way ○ *I happened to mention your name to her.* **2** *vt* CITE SOMEBODY FOR BRAVERY to refer to somebody by name in an official report as a way of acknowledging exceptional conduct, especially during a military action ■ *n* **1** SPECIFIC REFERENCE the use of a particular word or name, or a reference to a particular person or thing **2** ACKNOWLEDGMENT OF SOMEBODY'S EXCEPTIONAL CONDUCT an acknowledgment, especially in an official report, of somebody's exceptional conduct **3** LINGUISTIC SELF-REFERENCE the use of a word to refer to itself instead of to perform its usual linguistic function [14C. Via French < Latin *mention-* 'calling to mind'.] —**mentionable** *adj* —**mentioner** *n* ◇ **don't mention it** used in reply to an expression of thanks as a polite way of saying that none are necessary ◇ **not to mention** used to emphasize a point by introducing somebody who or something that needs to be taken into consideration and is even more significant than what has been spoken of before

mentor /mén tawr/ *n* **1** EXPERIENCED ADVISER AND SUPPORTER somebody, usually older and more experienced, who provides advice and support to, and watches over and fosters the progress of, a younger, less experienced person **2** TRAINER a senior or experienced person in a company or organization who gives guidance and training to a junior colleague ■ *vt* BE A MENTOR TO to act as a mentor to somebody, especially a junior colleague [Mid-18C. Via French < Greek *Mentōr* 'Mentor'.]

Mentor /mén tawr/ *n* in Homer's *Odyssey*, the friend whom Odysseus left in charge of the household while he was at Troy and who was the teacher and protector of Telemachus, Odysseus' son

mentoring /méntəring/ *n* the task of acting as a mentor to somebody, especially a junior colleague, or the system of appointing mentors

ϟ**menu** /mén yoo/ *n* **1** LIST OF DISHES AVAILABLE a list of the dishes that can be ordered in a restaurant or that are to be served at a formal meal **2** LIST OF PROGRAM OPTIONS a list on a computer screen of the options available to the user **3** LIST OR COLLECTION a list of things available, or a collection of things from which a selection can be made [Mid-19C. < French, 'minute, detailed' < Latin *minutus* (see MINUTE[2]).]

ϟ**menu-driven** *adj* operated by selecting options from menus

Menuhin /ményoo in/, **Yehudi, Baron Menuhin of Stoke d'Abernon** (1916–99) US-born British violinist

Menzies /ménziz/, **Sir Robert** (1894–1978) Australian statesman

meow /mi ów/ *n*, *vi* = **miaow**

MEP *abbr* **1** Member of the European Parliament **2** Master of Engineering Physics

meperidine /mə pérri deen/ *n* PHARM = **pethidine** [Mid-20C. Blend of METHYL + PIPERIDINE.]

Mephistopheles /méffi stóffə leez/, **Mephisto** /mə fístō/ *n* in medieval mythology, a subordinate to the Devil, one of the seven archangels cast out of heaven, to whom Faust sold his soul —**Mephistophelean** /méffistə féeli ən/ *adj*

mephitic /mi fíttik/, **mephitical** /-tik'l/ *adj* relating to or resembling a poisonous or foul smell (*formal*) [Early 17C. < late Latin *mephiticus* 'pestilential' < Latin *mephitis*.] —**mephitically** *adv*

mephitis /mi fítiss/ *n* a foul smell (*literary*) [Early 18C. < Latin.]

meprobamate /mə prṓbə mayt, mépprō bámmayt/ *n* $C_9H_{18}N_2O_4$ a bitter white powder. Use: tranquillizer, muscle relaxant. [Mid-20C. Blend of METHYL + PROPYL + CARBAMATE.]

mer- *prefix* = **mero-**

-mer *suffix* polymer ○ *oligomer* [Back-formation < -MERISM]

Merano /mə raánō/ city in NE Italy. Population: 33,638 (1993).

meranti /mi ránti/ *n* a tree that yields a white, yellow, or red hardwood. Native to: Southeast Asia. Genus: *Shorea*. [Late 18C. < Malay.]

merbromin /mər brṓmin/ *n* $C_{20}H_8Br_2HgNa_2O_6$ a green crystalline solid that forms a red solution when dissolved in water. Use: antiseptic. [Mid-20C. < MERCURIC + BROM-.]

Mercalli scale /mur kálli-/ *n* a scale for measuring the intensity of earthquakes, ranging from 1 to 12, in which 1 denotes a weak earthquake and 12 one that causes complete destruction. ◊ **Richter scale** [Early 20C. After Giuseppe *Mercalli* (1850–1914), Italian geologist.]

mercantile /múrkən tīl/ *adj* **1** used for trade or by merchants, or characteristic of merchants or trading **2** relating to or typical of mercantilism [Mid-17C. < French, < Italian *mercante* 'merchant' < Latin *mercari* (see MERCHANT).]

mercantilism /múrkəntilizəm, múrkən tīlizəm/ *n* **1** an early modern European economic theory and system that actively supported the establishment of colonies that would supply materials and markets and relieve home nations of dependence on other nations **2** the principles and methods of commerce —**mercantilist** *n* —**mercantilistic** /múrkənti lístik, -tī-/ *adj*

mercaptan /mur káp tan/ *n* CHEM = **thiol** [Mid-19C. < modern Latin *(corpus) mercurium captans* '(substance) that seizes mercury'.]

mercaptopurine /mur káptō pyóor een/ *n* $C_5H_4N_4S$ a drug that interferes with the synthesis of purines. Use: treatment of leukaemia, other cancers. [Mid-20C. < MERCAPTAN + PURINE.]

Mercator /mur káytər/, **Gerardus** (1512–94) Flemish geographer, cartographer, and mathematician. Born **Gerhard Kremer**

Mercator Projection *n* a method of making a map of the globe on a flat surface in which the meridians and latitudes are shown as straight lines that cross at right angles [Mid-17C. After Gerardus MERCATOR.]

mercenary /múrss'nəri/ *n* (*plural* **-ies**) **1** PROFESSIONAL SOLDIER a professional soldier paid to fight for an army other than that of his or her country **2** SOMEBODY INTERESTED ONLY IN PROFIT an employee who works only for personal gain ■ *adj* **1** MOTIVATED ONLY BY MONEY motivated solely by a desire for money **2** RELATING TO MERCENARIES paid to serve in a foreign army, or consisting of mercenaries [14C. Directly or via French *mercenaire* < Latin *mercen(n)arius* 'hireling' < *merces* 'wages'.] —**mercenarily** *adv* —**mercenariness** *n*

mercer /múrssər/ *n* a dealer in silks and other fine cloth, especially formerly [13C. < Anglo-Norman, < Latin *merc-* 'merchandise'.]

mercerize /múrssə rīz/ (**-izes, -izing, -ized**), **mercerise** (**-ises, -ising, -ised**) *vt* to treat cotton fabric or thread with an alkali to strengthen it and make it more lustrous and more receptive to dyes [Mid-19C. After John *Mercer* (1791–1866), English calico printer.] —**mercerization** /múrssə rī záysh'n/ *n*

merchandise /múrchən dīz/ *n* GOODS goods bought and sold for profit ■ *v* (**-dises, -dising, -dised**) **1** *vti* TRADE COMMERCIALLY to trade in or buy and sell products for profit **2** *vt* MARKET PRODUCTS to promote a product by developing strategies for packaging, display, and publicity [13C. < French *marchandise* 'goods' < Old French *marchant* (see MERCHANT).] —**merchandisable** *adj* —**merchandiser** *n*

merchandising /múrchən dīzing/ *n* **1** the promotion of a product by developing strategies for packaging, displaying, and publicizing it **2** commercial products that are developed as spin-offs from the success of a film, TV programme, sports team, or event

merchandize /múrchən dīz/ *vti* US COMM = **merchandise** *v.* **1**, **merchandise** *v.* **2**

merchant /múrchənt/ *n* **1** DEALER IN WHOLESALE GOODS a dealer in something, especially as a wholesaler or internationally **2** RETAILER a retail seller of something, especially in a shop or other outlet such as the Internet **3** SOMEBODY NOTED FOR SOME ACTIVITY a person who is noted for an activity or quality (*informal; usually in combination*) ○ *a speed merchant in a souped-up car* ■ *adj* **1** RELATING TO TRADE OR MERCHANTS used for or relating to commerce, wholesalers, or retailers **2 OF A MERCHANT NAVY** relating to, belonging to, or involving a merchant navy ■ *vt* **DEAL IN** to trade or deal in products [12C. < Old French *marchant* < Latin *mercari* 'to trade' < *merc-* 'merchandise'.]

LITERARY LINK *The Merchant of Venice*, a play (1596–97) by William Shakespeare. The story revolves around a loan made by Jewish usurer Shylock to Venetian merchant Antonio, and Shylock's subsequent attempts to claim the pound of flesh he has stipulated as security. Among the more serious issues raised in it are the correct administration of justice and the power conferred by wealth.

Merchant /múrchənt/, **Ismail** (*b.* 1936) Indian film producer and director

merchantable /múrchəntəb'l/ *adj* suitable or of a sufficiently high quality for buying and selling —**merchantability** /múrchəntə bíllәti/ *n*

merchant account *n* a bank account that enables the holder to deposit payments made by credit card, used especially in connection with trading on the Internet

merchant bank *n* a bank that provides financial services mainly for companies and large-scale investors —**merchant banker** *n* —**merchant banking** *n*

merchant certificate authority *n* a certificate authority that provides certificates to merchants

merchantman /múrchəntmən/ (*plural* **-men** /-mən/) *n* SHIPPING = **merchant ship**

merchant marine *n US* = **merchant navy**

merchant navy *n* a country's fleet of merchant ships, or the sailors who serve in them. US term **merchant marine**

merchant prince *n* an extremely wealthy, powerful, and prestigious merchant, especially in Renaissance Italy

merchant ship *n* a seagoing ship designed to carry goods, especially for international trade

Mercia /múrshi ə, múrssi ə/ ancient Anglo-Saxon kingdom of central England —**Mercian** *adj, n*

merciful /múrssif'l/ *adj* **1** showing mercy or compassion to somebody **2** welcome because putting an end to something unpleasant or distressing —**mercifulness** *n*

mercifully /múrssif'li/ *adv* **1** so as to show mercy or compassion **2** fortunately or luckily

merciless /múrssiləss/ *adj* **1 LACKING MERCY** showing no mercy or compassion towards somebody or something **2 STRICT AND INTOLERANT** very strict or harsh in the treatment of other people and extremely intolerant of their weaknesses or mistakes **3 RELENTLESS** continuing at a high level of violence or unpleasantness without pause or relief —**mercilessly** *adv* —**mercilessness** *n*

Merckx /murks/, **Eddy** (*b.* 1945) Belgian bicycle racer

mercur- *prefix* mercury ○ *mercurous* [< MERCURY]

mercurate /múr kyŏŏ rayt/ (**-rates, -rating, -rated**) *vt* to treat or combine something with mercury —**mercuration** /múr kyŏŏ ráysh'n/ *n*

mercurial /mur kyŏŏri əl/ *adj* **1 LIVELY AND UNPREDICTABLE** lively, witty, fast-talking, and likely to do the unexpected **2 CONTAINING MERCURY** containing or caused by mercury ■ *n* **MEDICINE CONTAINING MERCURY** formerly, a drug or chemical preparation containing mercury [14C. Directly and via French *mercuriel* < Latin *mercurialis* < *Mercurius* 'Mercury'.] —**mercuriality** /mur kyŏŏri állәti/ *n* —**mercurially** *adv* —**mercurialness** *n*

Mercurial /mur kyŏŏri əl/ *adj* **1** relating to the Roman god Mercury **2** relating to the planet Mercury

mercurialise *vt* MED = **mercurialize**

mercurialism /mur kyŏŏri əlizəm/ *n* poisoning caused by ingesting mercury

mercurialize /mur kyŏŏri əlīz/ (**-izes, -izing, -ized**), **mercurialise** (**-ises, -ising, -ised**) *vt* to treat somebody or something with mercury or with a compound containing mercury —**mercurialization** /mur kyŏŏri ə lī záysh'n/ *n*

mercuric /mur kyŏŏrik/ *adj* relating to or containing mercury with a valency of 2

mercuric chloride *n* $HgCl_2$ a white crystalline solid that is poisonous and soluble. Use: insecticide, fungicide, wood preservative, in photography.

mercuric oxide *n* HgO a poisonous orange-yellow solid. Use: pigment.

mercuric sulphide *n* HgS a poisonous compound existing as a red or black solid. Use: pigment.

mercurous /múrkyŏŏrəss/ *adj* relating to or containing mercury with a valency of 1

mercurous chloride *n* Hg_2Cl_2 a white poisonous insoluble powder. Use: fungicide, formerly in medicines.

mercury /múrkyŏŏri/ (*plural* **-ries**) *n* **1 LIQUID METALLIC ELEMENT** (*symbol* **Hg**) a poisonous heavy silver-white metallic element that is liquid at room temperature. Source: cinnabar. Use: thermometers, barometers, pharmaceuticals, dental amalgams, lamps. **2 TEMPERATURE OR PRESSURE** the mercury in a weather thermometer or barometer, or the air temperature or pressure it indicates ○ *The mercury rose steadily throughout the early part of the day.* **3 WEEDY PLANT** a weedy plant of the spurge family. Genus: *Mercurialis.* [14C. < Latin *Mercurius* (see MERCURY).]

Mercury /múrkyŏŏri/ *n* **1** the Roman god of commerce and rhetoric, who also acted as a messenger between humans and gods. Greek equivalent **Hermes 2** the smallest planet in the solar system and the one nearest the Sun. See table at **planet** [12C. < Latin *Mercurius* < *merc-* 'merchandise'.]

mercury chloride *n* CHEM = **mercuric chloride**

mercury-vapour lamp *n* an electric lamp whose bluish-green light is generated when electricity is passed through a vapour of low-pressure mercury

mercy /múrssi/ (*plural* **-cies**) *n* **1 COMPASSION** kindness or forgiveness shown to an offender or to somebody a person has power over ○ *The judge showed mercy and imposed the shortest sentence he could.* **2 COMPASSIONATE DISPOSITION** a disposition to be compassionate or forgiving of others ○ *a killer completely without mercy* **3 SOMETHING TO BE THANKFUL FOR** a welcome event or situation that provides relief or prevents something unpleasant from happening ○ *It was a mercy that no one was hurt in the accident.* **4 EASING OF DISTRESS** the easing of distress or pain ○ *The supply convoy was on a mission of mercy.* [12C. Via French *merci* 'thank you' < Latin *merces* 'reward, wages'.] ◇ **at the mercy of somebody** *or* **something** completely unprotected against whatever somebody *or* something does

mercy killing *n* **1** euthanasia regarded as motivated by compassion **2** an act of killing somebody out of compassion, often at that person's request, in order to end his or her pain or distress

mercy seat *n* **1** the gold covering on the Ark of the Covenant, regarded as God's resting place **2** the throne of God in heaven

mere[1] /meer/ (*superlative* **merest**) *adj* **1** just what is specified and nothing more ○ *She was no mere journalist.* **2** by itself and without anything more ○ *The mere mention of his ex-'s name would make him upset.* [14C. Directly or via Anglo-Norman *meer*, Old French *mier* < Latin *merus* 'pure, unmixed'.]

mere[2] /meer/ *n* a body of standing fresh water, especially a lake (*archaic or literary; often in placenames*) [Old English, 'sea' < Indo-European]

mere[3] /mérri/ *n* a short flat curved club used as a weapon by Maoris [Early 19C. < Maori.]

-mere *suffix* part, segment ○ *centromere* [Via French < Greek *meros* 'part']

Meredith /mérrə dith/, **George** (1828–1909) British novelist and poet

merely /méerli/ *adv* only as described and nothing more ○ *merely silly* ○ *merely a temporary setback*

merengue /mə réng gay/ *n* **1** a ballroom dance, originally from Dominica and Haiti, characterized by a shuffling step **2** a piece of music for the merengue [Mid-20C. Via American Spanish < Haitian creole *méringue* 'meringue' < French.]

meretricious /mérrə tríshəss/ *adj* **1 SUPERFICIALLY ATTRACTIVE** attractive in a superficial or vulgar manner but without real value (*formal*) ○ *meretricious extras that don't really add to the car's value* **2 MISLEADINGLY PLAUSIBLE** seemingly plausible or significant, but actually insincere or false ○ *Don't be swayed by this meretricious argument in the project's favour.* **3 OF PROSTITUTES** relating to or like a prostitute (*archaic*) [Early 17C. < Latin *meretricius* < *meretrix* 'prostitute' < *mereri* 'serve for hire'.] —**meretriciously** *adv* —**meretriciousness** *n*

merganser /mur gánssər/ (*plural* **-sers** *or* **-ser**) *n* a fish-eating diving duck with a crested head and a long bill notched like a saw blade. Genus: *Mergus.* [Mid-17C. < modern Latin, < Latin *mergus* 'diver' + *anser* 'goose'.]

merge /murj/ (**merges, merging, merged**) *vti* **1** to combine or unite with something to form a single entity, or make two or more things do this ○ *Two of the country's largest banks have decided to merge.* **2** to blend or make two or more things blend together gradually ○ *The sky and sea seem to merge at the horizon.* [Mid-17C. < Latin *mergere* 'to plunge, dip'.] —**mergence** *n* —**merging** *n*

merger /múrjər/ *n* **1** the joining together of two or more companies or organizations ○ *a merger between two of the country's leading manufacturers* **2** a blending, combining, or joining of something with something else, or the state of being blended, combined, or joined together [Early 18C. < Anglo-Norman, 'incorporate, incorporation' < Latin *mergere* 'to plunge'.]

Mérida /máyri də/ **1** city in W Spain. Population: 52,200 (1987). **2** capital of Yucatán State, SE Mexico. Population: 523,422 (1990).

meridian /mə ríddi ən/ *n* **1 LINE OF LONGITUDE** an imaginary line between the North and South poles that crosses the equator at right angles **2 HALF OF A CIRCLE BETWEEN POLES** either half of the circle of the meridian, from pole to pole **3 CELESTIAL GREAT CIRCLE** a great circle of the celestial sphere that passes through the celestial poles and the zenith of the observer **4 HIGHEST POINT** the peak or a high point, e.g. of development or success (*literary*) ○ *the decade when the empire's power reached its meridian* **5 LINE OF ACUPUNCTURE POINTS** in acupuncture, one of the pathways in the body along which the body's energy is believed to flow and along which acupuncture points are located [14C. Via Old French < Latin *meridianus* < *meridies* 'midday', alteration of *medidies* < *medius* 'middle' + *dies* 'day'.]

meridian circle *n* ASTRON = **transit circle**

meridional /mə ríddi ən'l/ *adj* **1 OF A MERIDIAN** along, belonging to, relating to, or like a meridian **2 OF SOUTHERN REGIONS** typical of or located in the south, especially S Europe **3 OF SOUTHERN PEOPLES** typical of people who live in the south, especially S Europe ■ *n* **SOUTHERN PERSON** somebody who comes from the south, especially S France [14C. Via French < late Latin *meridionalis* < Latin *meridies* (see MERIDIAN).] —**meridionally** *adv*

Mérimée /mérri may/, **Prosper** (1803–70) French writer

meringue /mə ráng/ *n* **1** a mixture of egg whites and sugar beaten until stiff, cooked, and used as a topping for tarts or to make biscuits and shells **2** a cake, biscuit, or shell made of meringue, often with a cream filling [Early 18C. < French.]

merino /mə reénō/ *n* (*plural* **-nos**) **1 merino, merino sheep SHEEP BRED FOR WOOL** a sheep of a breed originally from Spain that is bred for its wool in many parts of the world, especially Australia **2 WOOL** the long fine white wool of the merino sheep **3 YARN OR FABRIC** a fine yarn or fabric made from the wool of the merino sheep, often mixed with cotton ■ *adj* **OF MERINO WOOL** made of merino wool ○ *a merino shawl* [Late 18C. Via Spanish < Arabic (*banū*) *marīn*, a Berber people.]

-merism *suffix* denoting a relationship between chemical constituents ○ *isomerism* [< Greek *meros* 'part']

meristem /mérri stem/ *n* embryonic plant tissue that is actively dividing, such as is found at the tip of stems and roots [Late 19C. < Greek *meristos* 'divided' < *merizein* 'divide' < *meros* 'part'.] —**meristematic** /mérristə máttik/ *adj* —**meristematically** *adv*

meristic /mə rístik/ *adj* **1** divided into or having segments **2** involving a change in the number or arrangement of body parts or segments [Late 19C. < Greek *meris*, *meros* 'part'.] —**meristically** *adv*

merit /mérrit/ *n* **1 VALUE** value that deserves respect and acknowledgment ○ *The film is a work of considerable technical as well as artistic merit.* **2 GOOD QUALITY** a good or praiseworthy characteristic that somebody or something has (*often plural*) **3 ABILITY** proven ability or accomplishment ○ *She got her promotion based on merit.* **4 SPIRITUAL CREDIT** spiritual worthiness achieved by doing good works ■ **merits** *npl* **FACTS OF A CASE** the facts of a matter considered without regard for emotional, procedural, or other issues ○ *to consider a proposal on its merits* ■ *vt* **DESERVE** to be worthy of or earn something ○ *Some people feel the award wasn't merited.* [12C. Via French *mérite* < Latin *meritum* 'price', form of the past participle of *merere* 'earn'.]

meritocracy /mérri tókrəssi/ (*plural* **-cies**) *n* **1 SYSTEM BASED ON ABILITY** a social system that gives opportunities and advantages to people on the basis of their ability rather than, e.g., wealth or seniority **2 ELITE GROUP** an elite group of people who achieved their positions on the basis of ability and accomplishment **3 LEADERSHIP BY ELITE** leadership by an elite group of people who are chosen on the basis of their abilities and accomplishments —**meritocratic** /mérritō kráttik/ *adj*

meritorious /mérri táwri əss/ *adj* deserving honour and recognition ○ *She was awarded a medal for meritorious service.* [15C. < Latin *meritorius* < *merere* 'earn'.] —**meritoriously** *adv* —**meritoriousness** *n*

merle /murl/, **merl** *n* a blackbird (*archaic or literary*) [15C. Via French < Latin *merula*.]

Merleau-Ponty /múrlō pónti/, **Maurice** (1908–61) French philosopher

merlin /múrlin/ *n* a small dark falcon with a broad black band on the end of its tail. Native to: N hemisphere. *Falco columbarius.* [14C. < Anglo-Norman *merilun*, alteration of Old French *esmirillon* 'large merlin' < *esmiril* 'merlin'.]

Merlin *n* a legendary magician and adviser to King Arthur

merlon /múr lon/ *n* a solid part between two openings (**crenels**) in a battlement, e.g. on a castle [Early 18C. Via French < Italian *merlone* 'large battlement' < *merlo* 'battlement'.]

merlot /múrlō/, **Merlot** *n* 1 a red wine made from a variety of black grape **2** a variety of black grape used in winemaking, originally grown in France and now raised in many wine-growing regions worldwide [Early 19C. < French, 'small blackbird' < *merle* 'blackbird', probably from the colour of the grape.]

mermaid /múr mayd/ *n* a mythical sea creature with the head and upper body of a woman and the tail of a fish instead of legs [14C. < MERE[2] + MAID.]

merman /múr man/ *n* (*plural* -**men** /-men/) *n* a mythical sea creature with the head and upper body of a man and the tail of a fish instead of legs [Early 17C. < MERE[2] + MAN.]

mero- *prefix* part, partial ○ *merozoite* ○ *meroplankton* [< Greek *meros* 'part']

merocrine /mérrō krīn/ *adj* relating to or produced by glands that make secretions without cell damage or disintegration [Early 20C. < MERO- + Greek *krinein* 'separate'.]

Meroë /mérrō i/ ruined city in N Sudan, on the River Nile, capital of the ancient kingdom of Cush

meroplankton /mérrō plángktən/ (*plural* -**tons** *or* -**ton**) *n* organisms that are plankton only for part of their life cycle, usually during the larval stage —**meroplanktonic** /mérrō plangk tónnik/ *adj*

-merous *suffix* having a particular number or kind of parts ○ *tetramerous* ○ *heteromerous* [< Greek *meros* 'part']

Merovingian /mérrō vínji ən/ *adj* belonging or relating to a dynasty of Frankish kings that was founded by Clovis I and reigned in Gaul and Germany from about AD 500 to 751 ■ *n* a member of the Merovingian dynasty [Late 17C. < French *mérovingian* < Latin *Meroveus* 'Merowig' (d. 458), grandfather of Clovis.]

merozoite /mérrō zō ĭt/ *n* any protozoan cell produced by the fission of a schizont, e.g. that of the malaria protozoan

Merrick /mérrik/ hill in SW Scotland. Height: 843 m/2,765 ft.

merriment /mérrimənt/ *n* fun and enjoyment marked by noise and laughter

merry /mérri/ (-**rier**, -**riest**) *adj* **1 LIVELY AND CHEERFUL** full of or showing lively cheerfulness or enjoyment ○ *a merry laugh* **2 TIPSY** mildly drunk (*informal*) **3 FUNNY** very funny or amusing (*dated*) ○ *a merry quip* **4 DELIGHTFUL** tending to produce cheerfulness or happiness in people (*archaic*) ○ *the merry month of May* [Old English *myrige* 'pleasant' < Germanic, 'short'] —**merrily** *adv* —**merriness** *n* ○ **make merry** to be amused, or take part in a celebration or festivity

LITERARY LINK *The Merry Wives of Windsor*, a play (1600–01) by William Shakespeare. Written to exploit the popularity of Falstaff, a comic character in *Henry IV*, it tells of Falstaff's attempts to woo two married women in order to gain access to their wealth, the wives' discovery of his plan, and their imaginative revenge.

merry bone *n N England* a bird's wishbone

merry-go-round *n* **1** a fairground or amusement park ride with a rotating circular platform fitted with seats that are usually shaped like animals such as horses and move up and down to music **2** *US* = **roundabout** *n*. **1 3** a busy or continuous cycle of fast-paced activities or events ○ *a merry-go-round of press interviews and promotional events*

merrymaking /mérri mayking/ *n* lively celebration, fun, or enjoyment —**merrymaker** *n*

merry men *npl* somebody's followers (*humorous*)

merse /murss/ *n Scotland* an area of flat, often marshy, alluvial land near a river or estuary [Early 19C. < Old English *mersc*.]

Mersey /múrzi/ river in NW England, flowing into the Irish Sea near Liverpool. Length: 110 km/70 mi.

Mersey beat, **Mersey sound** *n* pop music of the 1960s that originated in the Merseyside area, especially Liverpool, and was performed by groups such as the Beatles

Merseyside /múrzi sīd/ metropolitan county in NW England

Merthyr Tydfil /múrthər tídvil/ town in S Wales. Population: 39,482 (1991).

mes- *prefix* = **meso-** (*before vowels*)

Mesa: Devil's Tower, Wyoming, United States

Library of Congress/Corbis

mesa /máyssə/ *n* a relatively flat elevated area with steep sides that is less extensive than a plateau, found especially in the SW United States. ◊ **butte** [Mid-18C. < Spanish, 'table' < Latin *mensa*.]

mésalliance /me zálli anss/ *n* a marriage with somebody of a lower social position, regarded as a bad match [Late 18C. < French, 'bad alliance' < *alliance* 'alliance' < Old French *aliance*.]

mesarch /méssaark, méz-/ *adj* describes a succession of plant or animal communities (**sere**) that originates in a moist habitat [Late 19C. < MESO- + Greek *arkhē* 'beginning, origin'.]

Mesa Verde National Park /máyssə vúrdi-/ national park in SW Colorado. Area: 211 sq. km/81 sq. mi.

mescal /més kal/ (*plural* -**cals** *or* -**cal**) *n* **1** a colourless Mexican spirit distilled from the fermented sap of some species of agave plant **2** DRUGS, PLANTS = **peyote** [Early 18C. Via Spanish *mezcal* < Nahuatl *mexcalli* 'mescal liquor'.]

Mescalero /méskə láirō/ (*plural* -**ro** *or* -**ros**) *n* a member of a Native North American people who lived in Mexico, New Mexico, and Texas, and now live mainly in S New Mexico [Mid-19C. < Spanish, *mezcal* (see MESCAL).]

mescaline /méskəlin, -leen/, **mescalin** /-lin/ *n* a hallucinogenic drug that is extracted from the button-shaped nodules on the stem of the peyote cactus [Late 19C. < German *Mezcalin* < Spanish *mezcal* (see MESCAL).]

mescla /méskla/ *n* a drug made from the residue of processing cocaine, which is mixed with marijuana and smoked

mesclun /méssklən/ *n* a green salad made from several types of young leaves, typically including rocket, dandelion, radicchio, and endive [< Provençal *mesclar* 'to mix' < Old French *mescler* < Latin *miscere*]

Mesdames /máy dam/ **1** plural of **Madame 2** plural of **Madam 3** plural of **Mrs** [Late 16C. < French, plural of *Madame*.]

mesdemoiselles plural of **mademoiselle**

mesembryanthemum /mi zémbri ánthiməm/ (*plural* -**mums** *or* -**mum**) *n* a succulent plant with thick fleshy leaves, widely grown for its colourful flowers. Native to: southern Africa. Genus: *Mesembryanthemum.* [Late 18C. < modern Latin, < Greek *mesēmbria* 'noon' + *anthemon* 'flower'.]

mesencephalon /méss en séffə lon/ *n* the midbrain (*technical*) —**mesencephalic** /méss enssi fállik/ *adj*

mesenchyme /méss eng kīm/ *n* the cells within the embryo that develop into connective tissue, bone, cartilage, blood, and the lymphatic system [Late 19C. < Greek *mesos* 'middle' + *egkhuma* 'infusion'.] —**mesenchymal** /mi séngkim'l/ *adj* —**mesenchymatous** /méss eng kímmətəss/ *adj*

mesenteritis /me séntə rítiss/ *n* inflammation of the mesentery of the peritoneum

mesenteron /me séntə ron/ (*plural* -**a** /-ə/) *n* the middle section of the embryonic intestine, which develops into the stomach, small intestine, and most of the large intestine —**mesenteronic** /me séntə rónnik/ *adj*

mesentery /méss'ntəri/ (*plural* -**ies**) *n* **1** a membrane that supports an organ or body part, especially the double-layered membrane of the peritoneum attached to the back wall of the abdominal cavity that supports the small intestine **2** a supportive membrane surrounding and giving structure to the inner organs of invertebrates [15C. Via modern Latin *mesenterium* < Greek *mesenterion* 'middle intestine' < *enteron* 'intestine'.] —**mesenteric** /méss'n térrik/ *adj*

mesh /mesh/ *n* **1 MATERIAL LIKE NET** material or a piece of material made of plastic, thread, or wire woven together like a net ○ *wire mesh* **2 OPENING IN A NET** the open space between the threads or wires of a net **3 STRANDS OF NET** the threads or wires that make up a net **4 TRAP** something that holds or entangles like a net or a trap (*often plural*) ○ *caught in the meshes of the criminal underworld* **5 SOMETHING INTERWOVEN** an interwoven or interlinked arrangement or construction ○ *the mesh of the girders against the sky* **6 INTERLOCKING METAL LINKS** a material consisting of interlocking metal links, used in jewellery **7 ENGAGEMENT OF GEARS** engagement of the teeth on gear wheels **8 OPENING IN A SCREEN** a measure of the number of openings in a screen for sorting things into different sizes, usually per inch. A 20-mesh screen has 20 openings per inch. ■ *vti* **1 FIT TOGETHER** to fit or work closely or well together, or make things work closely or well together ○ *Her vision of the company's future meshes perfectly with ours.* **2 CATCH OR ENTANGLE** to catch or entangle somebody or something, or become caught or entangled, in a mesh **3 ENGAGE GEARS** to make gear teeth engage together, or become engaged [14C. Probably < Middle Dutch *maesche* < Indo-European, 'knot'.] —**meshy** *adj*

meshuga /mə shŏŏggə/, **meshugah** *adj* totally unreasonable or thoughtless (*slang insult*) [Late 19C. Via Yiddish *meshuge* < Hebrew *mĕshuggā*.]

meshuggener /mə shŏŏggənər/, **meshugana** *n* somebody considered to be entirely unreasonable or thoughtless (*slang insult*) [Early 20C. Variant of MESHUGA.]

meshwork /mésh wurk/ *n* material consisting of meshes

mesial /méezi al/ *adj* relating to or occurring along the dental arch near the middle of the front of the jaw [Early 19C. < Greek *mesos* 'middle'.] —**mesially** *adv*

mesic[1] /méezik/ *adj* growing in or characterized by moderate moisture [Early 20C. < Greek *mesos* 'middle'.] —**mesically** *adv*

mesic[2] /méezik/ *adj* relating to a meson [Mid-20C. < MESON.]

mesmeric /mez mérrik/ *adj* completely absorbing somebody's attention [Early 19C. < *Mesmer* (see MESMERIZE).] —**mesmerically** *adv*

mesmerise *vt* = **mesmerize**

mesmerism /mézmərizəm/ *n* **1** the power to fascinate somebody in a way that is almost hypnotic **2** hypnotism, formerly believed to involve animal magnetism [Late 18C. < *Mesmer* (see MESMERIZE).] —**mesmerist** *n*

mesmerize /mézmə rīz/ (-**izes**, -**izing**, -**ized**), **mesmerise** (-**ises**, -**ising**, -**ised**) *vt* **1** to fascinate somebody or absorb all of somebody's attention ○ *The speaker mesmerized the audience with his dramatic tale.* **2** to hypnotize somebody, especially formerly in a way believed to involve animal magnetism [Early 19C. After F. A. *Mesmer* (1734–1815),

Austrian physician.] —**mesmerization** /mézmə rī záysh'n/ *n* —**mesmerizer** *n* —**mesmerizingly** *adv*

mesne /meen/ *adj* happening or appearing between two other things, especially assignments of property [Mid-16C. < Legal French, a variant of Anglo-Norman *meen* 'middle'.]

mesne profits *npl* intermediate profits received by a tenant who is in wrongful possession of an estate, which the landlord is entitled to recover

meso- *prefix* middle, intermediate ○ *mesopelagic* [< Greek *mesos*. Ultimately < Indo-European.]

Mesoamerica /méssō ə mérrikə/ *n* a region of Central America and S North America that was occupied by several civilizations, especially the Maya, in pre-Columbian times —**Mesoamerican** *adj, n*

mesoblast /méssō blast/ *n* BIOL = **mesoderm**

mesocarp /méssō kaarp/ *n* the middle layer of a fruit wall (**pericarp**), e.g. the fleshy part of some fruits

mesocratic /méssō kráttik/ *adj* describes igneous rock containing as much as 60 per cent of heavy dark ferromagnesian minerals in its composition

mesoderm /méssō durm/ *n* the middle of the three cell layers in an embryo, from which connective tissue, muscle, blood, dermis, and bone develop —**mesodermal** /méssō dúrm'l/ *adj* —**mesodermic** *adj*

Mesolithic /méssō líthik/, **mesolithic** *n* the middle period of the Stone Age, between the Palaeolithic and Neolithic —**Mesolithic** *adj*

mesomorph /méssō mawrf/ *n* a large muscular body, or somebody who has such a body. ◊ **ectomorph, endomorph** *n.* 1

meson /mée zon/ *n* an elementary particle, e.g. a pion or kaon, that has a rest mass between that of an electron and proton and participates in the strong interaction —**mesonic** /me zónnik/ *adj*

mesopause /méssō pawz/ *n* the upper boundary of the mesosphere, approximately 80 km/50 mi. above the Earth's surface

mesopelagic /méssōpə lájjik/ *adj* found in or relating to the intermediate oceanic depths between approximately 100 and 1,000 m/300 and 3,300 ft

mesophyll /méssōfil/ *n* the soft tissue (**parenchyma**) containing chlorophyll between the epidermal layers of a plant leaf —**mesophyllic** /méssō fíllik/ *adj* —**mesophyllous** /-fílləss/ *adj*

mesophyte /méssō fīt/ *n* a land plant that needs moderate amounts of moisture for growth —**mesophytic** /méssō fíttik/ *adj*

Mesopotamia /méssəpə táymi ə/ ancient region of W Asia, between the rivers Tigris and Euphrates in present-day Iraq. It was the site of several early civilizations, including Babylonia. —**Mesopotamian** *n*

mesosome /méssō sōm/ *n* an indentation in the cell membrane of some bacteria

mesosphere /méssō sfeer/ *n* the layer of the Earth's atmosphere in which temperature decreases rapidly, located between the stratosphere and thermosphere —**mesospheric** /méssō sférrik/ *adj*

mesothelioma /méssō theeli ómə/ (*plural* **-mata** *or* **-mas** /-ómətə/) *n* a benign or malignant tumour of the lining of the lungs, heart, or abdomen, often caused by asbestos exposure

mesothelium /méssō theéli əm/ (*plural* **mesotheliums** *or* **mesothelia** /-ə/) *n* a cell layer derived from mesoderm that lines the body cavity of a vertebrate embryo and develops into epithelia and muscle tissue —**mesothelial** *adj*

Mesozoic /méssō zṓ ik/ *adj* belonging to or dating from an era of geological time 250 to 65 million years ago, between the Permian and Tertiary eras, when dinosaurs, birds, and flowering plants first appeared ■ *n* the Mesozoic era

mesquite /me skeét/ (*plural* **-quite** *or* **-quites**) *n* **1** a hard wood often burned in a barbecue to flavour food **2** a small spiny leguminous tree or shrub with hard wood, the pods of which are sometimes used as fodder. Native to: SW United States, Mexico. Genus: *Prosopis*. [Mid-18C. Via Mexican Spanish *mezquite* < Nahuatl *mizquitl*.]

mess /mess/ *n* **1** UNTIDY CONDITION a dirty or untidy state ○ *The flat was left in a terrible mess after the party.* **2** CHAOTIC STATE a chaotic, confused, or troublesome state or situation ○ *Their business affairs were in a complete mess.* **3** UNTIDY PERSON OR THING somebody or something in a confused, dirty, or untidy state (*informal*) **4** EXCREMENT animal excrement (*informal*) ○ *Someone had tramped dog mess on the front steps.* **5** PLACE FOR COMMUNAL MEALS a place where a group of people, especially members of the armed forces, have meals together **6** PEOPLE WHO EAT TOGETHER a group of people, especially members of the armed forces, who have meals together (*takes a singular or plural verb*) **7** COMMUNAL MEAL a meal eaten together by a group of people, especially members of the armed forces **8** QUANTITY OF FOOD a serving or quantity of food, especially of soft or soggy food ■ *v* **1** *vti* MAKE SOMETHING DIRTY to make something dirty, muddled, or disordered ○ *She messed her jacket while checking the oil.* **2** *vi* MEDDLE to interfere or meddle in something ○ *Don't mess in their business.* **3** *vi* USE SOMETHING CARELESSLY to use something carelessly, causing a problem or damage as a result ○ *Who's been messing with my computer?* **4** *vi* EAT TOGETHER to take meals along with a particular group of people, especially members of the armed forces ○ *I used to mess with the three of them.* [13C. < Old French, 'portion of food' < Latin *mittere* 'send, put'.]

mess around, mess about *v* **1** *vi* WASTE TIME to waste time in an unproductive or aimless manner (*informal*) **2** *vi* RELAX to spend time in a leisurely and pleasant manner (*informal*) **3** *vti* INTERFERE to interfere or meddle in something (*informal*) **4** *vi* ASSOCIATE WITH to associate with somebody, especially somebody who is seen as undesirable (*informal*) ○ *She started messing around with that crowd last summer.* **5** *vi* BEHAVE IN UNSERIOUS WAY to joke or behave playfully (*informal*) ○ *I thought he was just messing around.* **6** *vt* TREAT SOMEBODY BADLY to treat somebody badly or unfairly, e.g. by continual changes of mind or lack of honesty (*informal*) ○ *Neil felt that he was being messed around by his manager.* **7** *vi* BE SEXUALLY UNFAITHFUL to have sexual activity with somebody other than a spouse or regular sexual partner (*slang*)

mess up *v* (*informal*) **1** *vti* RUIN to spoil or bungle something, or make a mistake ○ *The rain messed up our plans to go for a picnic.* **2** *vt* MAKE SOMETHING MESSY to make something dirty or disordered **3** *vt* UPSET to confuse or upset somebody

message /méssij/ *n* **1** COMMUNICATION a communication in speech, writing, or signals **2** MEANING a lesson, moral, or important idea that somebody wants to communicate, e.g. in a work of art **3** ERRAND the mission or errand of a messenger (*dated*) ○ *sent on a message to her grandmother's* **4** *US* ADVERTISEMENT an advertisement, especially one on television, paid for by the sponsors of a programme or event ○ *and now a message from our sponsor* ■ **messages** *npl Scotland* SHOPPING shopping, especially the everyday necessities ○ *I'm away to get the messages.* ■ *vt* (**-sages, -saging, -saged**) **1** COMMUNICATE WITH to send a message to somebody ○ *Can you message me about that?* **2** COMMUNICATE SOMETHING TO to send something as a message ○ *to message the news to your boss* [13C. Via French < Latin *missus*, past participle of *mittere* 'send'.] ◇ **get the message** to take something in and understand it (*informal*)

⚡**message board** *n* ONLINE = **bulletin board** *n.* 2

⚡**message code authentication** *n* the cryptographic verification of the author and integrity of an e-mail message

Messager /méssa zhay/, **André Charles Prosper** (1853–1929) French composer

⚡**messaging** /méssijing/ *n* **1** a system for sending messages to people, e.g. by computer, telephone, or pager **2** the process of sending a message using a messaging system

messaline /méssə leén/ *n* a soft shiny lightweight silk fabric. Use: making dresses. [Early 20C. < French, after Valeria *Messalina*, adulterous wife of the Roman emperor Claudius.]

~~**messanger**~~ incorrect spelling of **messenger**

Messeigneurs plural of **Monseigneur**

messenger /méss'njər/ *n* **1** SOMEBODY CARRYING MESSAGE a carrier of messages between people **2** PAID COURIER an employee who carries and delivers messages, especially a courier **3** SOMEBODY RUNNING ERRAND a person who runs an errand **4 messenger, messenger line** LIGHT ROPE a lightweight rope used to haul a heavier one, e.g. from one ship to another [12C. < French *messager* < *message* (see MESSAGE).]

Messenger /méss'njər/, **Dally** (1883–1959) Australian Rugby League player. Born **Herbert Henry Messenger**

messenger bag *n* a satchel-shaped bag, usually made of synthetic material, used for carrying documents or small items

messenger RNA *n* a form of RNA that is transcribed from a strand of DNA and translated into a protein sequence at a cell ribosome

Messerschmitt /méssər shmit/ *n* a fighter aircraft, especially the Me-109 or the Me-262, used by the German Air Force in World War II

Messerschmitt /méssərshmit/, **Willy** (1898–1978) German aircraft designer. Born **Wilhelm Messerschmitt**

mess hall *n* a building or room where a group of people, especially members of the armed forces, eat their meals together

Messiaen /méssi oN, -ən/, **Olivier** (1908–92) French composer and organist

messiah /mə sī́ ə/ *n* somebody regarded as or claiming to be a saviour or liberator of a country, people, or the world —**messiahship** *n*

Messiah /mə sī́ ə/ *n* **1** in Christianity, Jesus Christ regarded as the Messiah prophesied in the Hebrew Bible **2** in the Hebrew Bible, an anointed king who will lead the Jews back to the land of Israel and establish justice in the world [12C. Via French *Messie* < Greek *Messias* < Aramaic *mĕšīḥā* and Hebrew *māšīăḥ* 'anointed' < *māšhaḥ* 'anoint'.] —**Messiahship** *n*

messianic /méssi ánnik/ *adj* **1 messianic, Messianic** RELATING TO THE MESSIAH belonging or relating to the Messiah **2** OF JUDAIC GOLDEN AGE relating to, belonging to, or constituting a Judaic golden age of peace, truth, and happiness **3** OF A LIBERATOR relating or belonging to an inspirational leader, especially one claiming to be or regarded as a saviour or liberator **4** INVOLVING GREAT ENTHUSIASM done with or showing great enthusiasm or devotion ○ *preaching with messianic fervour* —**messianically** *adv*

messianism /mə sī́ ənizəm/, **Messianism** *n* belief in the coming of the Messiah or a messiah or messianic age

Messieurs plural of **Monsieur**

Messina /me seénə/ city in NE Sicily, Italy, on the Strait of Messina. Population: 234,000 (1994).

Messina, Strait of strait between Sicily and mainland Italy. Length: 32 km/20 mi.

mess jacket *n* a waist-length jacket worn as part of a military uniform, especially on formal occasions

mess kit *n* **1** a compact set of cooking and eating utensils, usually made of metal, used especially by soldiers or campers **2** a dress uniform worn by officers and senior noncommissioned officers at formal dinners

messmate /méss mayt/ *n* somebody with whom somebody regularly eats, especially in a military mess

Messrs plural of **Mr**

messuage /mésswij/ *n* a dwelling with its outbuildings and the surrounding land that is used by the dwelling's occupants [14C. < Anglo-Norman.]

mess-up *n* a complete mistake or totally unsuccessful attempt at something (*informal*)

messy /méssi/ (**-ier, -iest**) *adj* **1** DIRTY OR DISORDERED involving, producing, or marked by dirt or disorder ○ *Repairing a car can be a messy business.* **2** DIFFICULT TO SORT OUT complicated and unpleasant to resolve or deal with **3** CARELESS showing a lack of carefulness or precision ○ *an erroneous conclusion resulting from messy reasoning* —**messily** *adv* —**messiness** *n*

mestiza /mess teézə/ *n* a woman with mixed ancestry, especially a woman in Latin America of both Native American and European ancestry [Late 16C. < Spanish, the feminine of MESTIZO.]

mestizo /mess teézō/ (*plural* **-zos** *or* **-zoes**) *n* a person with mixed ancestry, especially somebody in Latin America of both Native American and European ancestry [Late 16C. Via Spanish < Latin *mixtus*, past participle of *miscere* 'mix'.]

mestranol /méstrə nol/ *n* $C_{21}H_{26}O_2$ a synthetic oestrogen. Use: oral contraceptives. [Mid-20C. < METHYL + OESTRADIOL.]

met past tense, past participle of **meet**[1]

Met /met/ *abbr* **1** Meteorological Office **2** Metropolitan Opera House (in New York) **3** Metropolitan Police

met. *abbr* **1** metallurgy **2** metaphor **3** metaphysics **4** meteorological **5** meteorology **6** metropolitan

met- *prefix* = **meta-** (*before vowels*)

meta- *prefix* **1** later, behind ○ *metaphase* ○ *metathorax* **2** beyond, transcending, encompassing ○ *metagalaxy* ○ *metalanguage* **3** change, transformation ○ *metaplasia* **4** higher, more developed ○ *metaxylem* **5** used in chemical names ○ *metaphosphate* [< Greek *meta* 'beside, after' < Indo-European, 'between']

metabolic /méttə bóllik/ *adj* relating to or typical of metabolism [Mid-19C. < Greek *metabolikos* 'changeable' < *metabolē* (see METABOLISM).] —**metabolically** *adv*

metabolic pathway *n* a sequence of energy-producing biochemical reactions catalysed by enzymes

metabolic rate *n* the speed at which the biochemical reactions of metabolism take place

metabolise *vti* BIOCHEM = **metabolize**

metabolism /mə tábbəlizəm/ *n* **1** the series of processes by which food is converted to the energy and products needed to sustain life **2** the biochemical activity of a particular substance in a living organism [Late 19C. < Greek *metabolē* 'change' < *metaballein* 'throw differently' < *ballein* 'to throw'.]

metabolite /mə tábbə līt/ *n* a by-product of metabolism

metabolize /mə tábbə līz/ (**-lizes, -lizing, -lized**), **metabolise** (**-lises, -lising, -lised**) *vti* to subject something to metabolism [Late 19C. < Greek *metabolē* (see METABOLISM).] —**metabolizable** *adj*

metacarpus /méttə kaárpəss/ (*plural* **-pi** /-pī/) *n* **1** the set of five long bones (**metacarpals**) in the human hand between the wrist and fingers **2** the region between the wrist and digits of the forefoot or hand of a vertebrate animal —**metacarpal** *adj, n* —**metacarpally** *adv*

metacentre /méttə sentər/ *n* the intersection of the vertical line through the centre of buoyancy of an object at equilibrium with the vertical line through the centre of buoyancy when the object is tilted

metacentric /méttə séntrik/ *adj* **1** relating or belonging to a metacentre **2** describes a chromosome whose centromere is located at or near the middle. ◊ **acentric** *adj.* **2**, **acrocentric, telocentric**

metachromatic /méttəkrō máttik/ *adj* **1** taking on a colour atypical of the staining solution **2** able to produce a colour in different shades in tissue or cells [Late 19C. < META- + Greek *khrōmat-* 'colour'.]

metachromatism /méttə krṓmətizəm/ *n* a change in colour caused by a change in physical conditions such as temperature

metacognition /méttə kog nísh'n/ *n* knowledge about your own thoughts and the factors that influence your thinking —**metacognitive** /méttə kógnətiv/ *adj*

meta-ethics /méttə-/ *n* the branch of linguistic philosophy that analyses and seeks to clarify the meaning and use of ethical expressions such as 'good' and 'ought' (+ *singular verb*) —**meta-ethical** *adj*

metafemale /méttə feé mayl/ *n* a female organism with an extra female chromosome

metafiction /méttə fiksh'n/ *n* **1** fiction that emphasizes the nature of fiction, the techniques and conventions used to write it, and the role of the author **2** a work of metafiction —**metafictional** /méttə fíksh'nəl/ *adj* —**metafictionist** /-fíksh'nist/ *n*

metagalaxy /méttə galləksi/ *n* the total of all galaxies making up the universe —**metagalactic** /méttəgə láktik/ *adj*

metage /meétij/ *n* **1** the official measurement of the contents or weight of a load, e.g. of coal or grain **2** a charge for making an official measurement of the contents or weight of a load [Early 16C. < *mete* 'measure'.]

metagenesis /méttə jénnəssiss/ *n* the alternation in the life cycle of an organism between a generation that reproduces sexually and a generation that reproduces vegetatively —**metagenetic** /méttə jə néttik/ *adj* —**metagenetically** *adv* —**metagenic** /méttə jénnik/ *adj*

metagnathous /mə tágnəthəss/ *adj* describes a bird that has the tips of its bill crossed —**metagnathism** *n*

metal /métt'l/ *n* **1** TYPE OF CHEMICAL ELEMENT a chemical element such as copper or iron that is malleable and ductile, usually solid, has a characteristic lustre, and is a good conductor of heat and electricity **2** MIXTURE OF METALS a mixture (**alloy**) of one or more metals **3** HEAVY METAL heavy metal music (*slang*) **4** PRINTING TYPE printer's type made of metal **5** MOLTEN GLASS molten glass for use in glassmaking **6** GOLD OR SILVER gold or silver in heraldry **7** WEIGHT FIRED IN BROADSIDE the collective weight of the projectiles a warship can fire in a broadside **8** TRANSP = **road metal** ■ **metals** *npl* RAILS the rails of a railway track ■ *vt* (**-als, -alling, -alled**) **1** FIT WITH METAL to cover, fit, or provide something with metal **2** MAKE OR MEND ROAD to make or repair a road with broken stones (**road metal**) [13C. Directly or via French < Latin *metallum* 'mine, metal' < Greek *metallon*.]

metal. *abbr* **1** metallurgical **2** metallurgy

metalanguage /méttə lang gwij/ *n* a language or system of symbols used to describe or analyse another language or system of symbols

metal detector *n* **1** DEVICE FOR DETECTING BURIED METAL a portable electronic device with a search head that is swept over the ground and used to detect buried metal objects such as coins **2** DEVICE FOR DETECTING WEAPONS an electronic device that registers the presence of metal, used e.g. to detect metal weapons or to screen passengers at an airport **3** DEVICE FOR DETECTING METAL IN FOOD an electronic device used in the food industry to check for the presence of pieces of metal that might have accidentally got into food during processing

metalinguistic /méttə ling gwístik/ *adj* relating to a metalanguage or to metalinguistics

metalinguistics /méttə ling gwístiks/ *n* (+ *singular verb*) **1** the branch of linguistics that deals with the study of metalanguages **2** the branch of linguistics that deals with the relation between a language and other aspects of a particular culture

metalize *vt* US = **metallize**

metall. *abbr* **1** metallurgical **2** metallurgy

metall- *prefix* = **metallo-** (*before vowels*)

metallic /mə tállik/ *adj* **1** CONTAINING OR BEING METAL made of, containing, or constituting metal or a metal **2** OF METAL typical of a metal **3** SHINY shiny and highly reflective ○ *a sports car with a metallic finish* **4** TASTING OF METAL sharp and bitter to the taste ○ *This water has a slightly metallic taste.* **5** SOUNDING LIKE STRUCK METAL like the sound of two metal objects hitting or knocking against each other **6** HARSH-SOUNDING harsh and unpleasant in tone ○ *speaking with a metallic edge to her voice* —**metallically** *adv*

metallic bond *n* a chemical bond characteristic of metals, in which electrons are shared between atoms and move about in the crystal

metallic lens *n* a device consisting of louvres or slats, used to focus electromagnetic or sound waves

metalliferous /méttə líffərəss/ *adj* containing or yielding metal

metalline /méttə līn/ *adj* **1** resembling a metal **2** containing metal ions

metalling /métt'ling/ *n* **1** TRANSP = **road metal** **2** the process of making or repairing roads with broken stones or other material

metallize /méttə līz/ *vt* to coat or cover something with metal

metallo- *prefix* metal ○ *metallophone* [< Latin *metallum* (see METAL)]

metallography /méttə lóggrəfi/ *n* the study of the composition and microscopic structure of metals —**metallographer** *n* —**metallographic** /mə tállə gráffik/ *adj* —**metallographically** *adv* —**metallographist** /méttə lóggrəfist/ *n*

metalloid /méttə loyd/ *n* NONMETALLIC ELEMENT WITH METAL PROPERTIES a nonmetallic element such as silicon that has properties between those of a metal and nonmetal ■ *adj* **metalloid, metalloidal** **1** OF METALLOID relating to or having the characteristics of a metalloid **2** LIKE METAL resembling a metal

metallophone /me tállə fōn/ *n* a musical instrument resembling a xylophone, with tuned metal bars that are struck with mallets

metallurgy /mə tállurji/ *n* the study of the structure and properties of metals, their extraction from the ground, and the procedures for refining, alloying, and making things from them —**metallurgic** /méttə lúrjik/ *adj* —**metallurgical** *adj* —**metallurgically** *adv* —**metallurgist** /mə tállərjist/ *n*

metalsmith /métt'l smith/ *n* somebody who is skilled at making and repairing metal objects

metalware /métt'l wair/ *n* objects that have been crafted from metal

metalwork /métt'l wurk/ *n* **1** MAKING OF METAL OBJECTS the craft of making objects out of metal **2** METAL THINGS objects made of metal **3** METAL PART OF SOMETHING the metal part of an object —**metalworker** *n* —**metalworking** *n*

metamale /méttə mayl/ *n* a male organism with an extra male chromosome

metamere /méttə meer/ *n* any of the similar segments into which the bodies of animals such as worms or lobsters are divided

metameric /méttə mérrik/ *adj* **1** with a body divided into a series of similar segments (**metameres**) **2** relating to or typical of metamerism —**metamerically** *adv*

metamerism /mə támmərizəm/ *n* the condition of having the body divided into a series of similar segments (**metameres**), or an embryonic stage in which the body is divided in this way

metamorphic /méttə máwrfik/, **metamorphous** /-máwrfəss/ *adj* **1** relating to or having undergone metamorphism **2** relating to or involving a change in physical form, appearance, or character —**metamorphically** *adv*

metamorphism /méttə máwrfizəm/ *n* a change in the physical structure of rock that results from long-term heat and pressure, especially a change that increases the rock's hardness and crystalline structure

metamorphose /méttə máwrfōz/ (**-phoses, -phosing, -phosed**) *v* **1** *vti* CHANGE PHYSICAL FORM to undergo or make somebody or something undergo a complete or marked change of physical form, structure, or substance ○ *The water had metamorphosed into ice.* **2** *vti* CHANGE APPEARANCE OR CHARACTER to undergo or make somebody or something undergo a complete or marked change in appearance, character, or condition **3** *vti* CHANGE SUPPOSEDLY BY MAGIC to undergo or make somebody or something undergo a transformation supposedly by magic **4** *vi* UNDERGO BODILY CHANGES DURING GROWTH to undergo a complete or marked change of bodily form while developing into an adult animal ○ *The tadpole has metamorphosed into a frog.* **5** *vti* CHANGE ROCK STRUCTURE to undergo or make a rock undergo metamorphism [Late 16C. < French *métamorphoser* < *métamorphose* 'metamorphosis' < Latin *metamorphosis* (see METAMORPHOSIS).]

metamorphosis /méttə máwrfəssiss/ (*plural* **-ses** /-seez/) *n* **1** CHANGE OF PHYSICAL FORM a complete or marked change of physical form, structure, or substance ○ *the overnight metamorphosis of the pond water into ice* **2** CHANGE OF APPEARANCE OR CHARACTER a complete or marked change in appearance, character, or condition **3** SUPPOSED SUPERNATURAL TRANSFORMATION a transformation caused by supposed supernatural powers **4** TRANSFORMED PERSON OR THING somebody or something that has gone through a complete or marked change **5** CHANGE IN ANIMAL FORM a complete or marked change in the form of an animal as it develops into an adult, e.g. the change from tadpole to frog or from caterpillar to butterfly [Mid-16C. Via Latin < Greek *metamorphōsis* < *metamorphoun* 'transform' < *morphē* 'form'.]

LITERARY LINK ***The Metamorphosis***, a short novel (1915) by Czech writer Franz Kafka. The protagonist of this bizarre tale, Gregor Samsa, awakens to find himself transformed into an insect, then dies as a result of his family's neglect and his own failure to act. Gregor's metamorphosis can be read as both a portrayal of the author's troubled family life and a metaphor for the artist's power to transform life into art.

LITERARY LINK ***Metamorphoses***, a poem (AD 8) by the Roman poet Ovid. This long narrative work consists of a series of tales in which characters undergo some kind of transformation. The stories were based on Greek myths and legends and are presented in chronological order, but much of their liveliness derives from events, characters, and details invented by the poet.

metamorphous *adj* = **metamorphic**

metanephros /méttə néffross/ (*plural* **-roi** /-néffroy/) *n* an embryonic organ of excretion in reptiles, birds, and mammals that develops into the kidney [Late 19C. < META- + Greek *nephros* 'kidney'.]

metaphase /méttə fayz/ *n* the second stage of cell division, during which chromosomes line up in preparation for separation. ◊ **anaphase, prophase, telophase**

metaphase plate *n* the equatorial plane along which chromosomes line up during the second stage of cell division in preparation for separation

metaphor /méttəfər, -fawr/ *n* 1 IMPLICIT COMPARISON the application of a word or phrase to somebody or something that is not meant literally but to make a comparison, e.g. saying that somebody is a snake 2 FIGURATIVE LANGUAGE all language that involves figures of speech or symbolism and does not literally represent real things 3 SYMBOL one thing used or considered to represent another [15C. < Greek *metaphora* < *metapherein* 'transfer' < *pherein* 'carry'.] —**metaphoric** /méttə fórrik/ *adj* —**metaphorical** *adj* —**metaphorically** *adv*

metaphosphate /méttə fóss fayt/ *n* any salt or ester of metaphosphoric acid

metaphosphoric acid /méttə foss fórrik-/ *n* HPO_3 a glassy solid containing linked phosphate groups. Use: drying agent, in dental cements.

metaphrase /méttə frayz/ *n* LITERAL TRANSLATION a word-for-word translation of something ■ *vt* (**-phrases, -phrasing, -phrased**) 1 TRANSLATE SOMETHING LITERALLY to translate something, especially word for word 2 CHANGE WORDING OF to change the wording of a text [Mid-16C. < Greek *metaphrasis* < *metaphrazein* 'translate', literally 'tell differently' < *phrazein* 'tell'.]

metaphrast /méttə frast/ *n* a changer of the form of a text, e.g. from prose into verse [Early 17C. < Greek *metaphrastēs* < *metaphrazein* (see METAPHRASE).] —**metaphrastic** /méttə fràstik/ *adj* —**metaphrastical** *adj* —**metaphrastically** *adv*

metaphysic *n* PHILOSOPHY = **metaphysics**

metaphysical /méttə fízzik'l/ *adj* 1 RELATING TO METAPHYSICS relating to the philosophical study of the nature of being and beings or a philosophical system resulting from such study 2 SPECULATIVE based on speculative reasoning and unexamined assumptions that have not been logically examined or confirmed by observation ○ *a metaphysical system whose claim to truth is undermined by contradictions* 3 ABSTRACT extremely abstract or theoretical ○ *metaphysical subjects removed from everyday life* 4 INCORPOREAL without material form or substance ○ *the metaphysical realm of pure thought* 5 SUPERNATURAL originating not in the physical world but somewhere outside it ○ *a metaphysical explanation of beauty and goodness* —**metaphysically** *adv*

Metaphysical /méttə fízzik'l/, **metaphysical** *adj* relating to the poetic style of John Donne, George Herbert, and other early 17th-century English poets who used consciously intellectual language and elaborate metaphors that compared dissimilar things ■ *n* a poet of the Metaphysical group

metaphysician /méttə fi zísh'n/ *n* a scholar who specializes in the branch of philosophy concerned with the study of the nature of being, existence, time and space, and causality

metaphysics /méttə fízziks/, **metaphysic** /méttə fízzik/ *n* (+ *singular verb*) 1 PHILOSOPHY OF BEING the branch of philosophy concerned with the study of the nature of being and beings, existence, time and space, and causality 2 UNDERLYING PRINCIPLES the ultimate underlying principles or theories that form the basis of a particular field of knowledge ○ *Symmetry is part of the metaphysics of quantum mechanics.* 3 ABSTRACT THINKING abstract discussion or thinking [Mid-16C. < medieval Latin *metaphysica* (plural) < medieval Greek *(ta) metaphusika* '(the) metaphysics' < *ta meta ta phusika* 'the (works of Aristotle) after the "Physics"'.]

metaplasia /méttə pláyzi ə/ *n* the transformation of one kind of tissue into another undesirable type, as happens in tumour formation [Late 19C. < Greek *metaplassein* 'mould into a new form' < *plassein* 'to mould'.] —**metaplastic** /méttə plástik/ *adj*

metapsychology /méttə sī kólləji/ *n* the philosophical study of those aspects of psychology that cannot be examined experimentally —**metapsychological** /méttə sīkə lójjik'l/ *adj*

metasomatism /méttə sṓmətizəm/, **metasomatosis** /-sṓmə tṓssiss/ *n* the gradual change in rock structure caused by the natural replacement of chemicals through interaction with liquids or gases [Late 19C. < META- + Greek *sōmat-* 'body'.] —**metasomatic** /méttəsō máttik/ *adj* —**metasomatically** *adv*

metastable /méttə stáyb'l/ *adj* 1 in an apparent state of equilibrium, but likely to change to a more truly stable state if conditions change 2 remaining in an excited physical state for a relatively long time —**metastability** /méttəstə bílləti/ *n*

metastasis /me tástəsiss/ (*plural* **-ses** /-seez/) *n* 1 the spread of a cancer from the original tumour to other parts of the body by means of tiny clumps of cells transported by the blood or lymph 2 a malignant tumour that has developed in the body as a result of the spread of cancer cells from the original tumour [Late 16C. < Greek, 'removal, change' < *methistanai* 'remove' < *histanai* 'to place'.] —**metastatic** /méttə státtik/ *adj* —**metastatically** *adv*

metastasize /me tástə sīz/ (**-sizes, -sizing, -sized**), **metastasise** (**-sises, -sising, -sised**) *vi* to spread in the body from the site of the original tumour by means of tiny cells transported by the blood or lymph (*refers to a cancer*)

metatarsus /méttə társsəss/ (*plural* **-si** /-ssī/) *n* 1 the set of five long bones (**metatarsals**) in the human foot between the toes and ankle 2 the region between the ankle and toes of the hind foot in vertebrates —**metatarsal** *adj, n* —**metatarsally** *adv*

metatherian /méttə théeri ən/ *adj* relating or belonging to marsupials ■ *n* a marsupial [Late 19C. < modern Latin *Metatheria* 'wild animals between' < Greek *thēria*, plural of *thērion* 'wild animal'.]

metathesis /me táthəssiss/ (*plural* **-ses** /-seez/) *n* 1 a reversal of the order of two sounds or letters in a word, either as a mispronunciation or as a historical development 2 CHEM = **double decomposition** [Late 16C. < Greek, < *metatithenai* 'transpose' < *tithenai* 'to place'.] —**metathetic** /méttə théttik/ *adj* —**metathetical** *adj* —**metathetically** *adv*

metathesize /me táthə sīz/ (**-sizes, -sizing, -sized**), **metathesise** (**-sises, -sising, -sised**) *vti* to change or make a word change by metathesis

metazoan /méttə zṓ ən/ *n* an animal whose body consists of cells that are separated into different parts such as tissues and organs. Group: *Metazoa*. [Late 19C. < modern Latin *Metazoa* < Greek *meta-* 'beside, after' + *zoion* 'animal'.] —**metazoan** *adj*

mete out *vt* to give out something such as punishment or justice, especially in a way that seems harsh or unfair [*Mete* < Old English *metan* 'measure'. Ultimately < Indo-European.]

metempsychosis /méttem sī kṓssiss/ *n* the passage of somebody's soul after death into the body of another person or an animal [Late 16C. Via late Latin < Greek *metempsukhōsis* < *meta* 'after' + *empsukhos* 'having a soul within'.]

metencephalon /métten séffə lon/ (*plural* **-lons** *or* **-la** /-lə/) *n* the part of an embryo's brain that develops into the cerebellum and the pons —**metencephalic** /métten si fállik/ *adj*

meteor /méeti ə, -awr/ *n* 1 a mass of rock from space that burns up after entering the Earth's atmosphere. ◊ **meteorite** 2 the brief streak of light that a meteor creates, visible in the night sky [Late 16C. Via modern Latin *meteorum* 'atmospheric phenomenon' < Greek *meteōron*, form of *meteōros* 'raised up' < *meta* 'up' + *-aoros* 'lifted'.]

meteoric /méeti órrik/ *adj* 1 relating to or resembling meteors 2 characterized by great speed or brilliance —**meteorically** *adv*

meteoric water *n* water in the ground that has come from the atmosphere as rain or condensation, rather than forming chemically underground

meteorite /méeti ə rīt/ *n* a piece of rock that has reached the Earth from outer space. ◊ **meteor** *n.* 1

meteoritics /méeti ə ríttiks/ *n* the scientific study of meteors and meteorites —**meteoriticist** *n*

meteoroid /méeti ə royd/ *n* a mass of rock in space, often a remnant of a comet, that becomes a meteor when it enters the Earth's atmosphere and a meteorite when it falls to Earth. ◊ **meteor, meteorite** —**meteoroidal** *adj*

meteorology /méeti ə rólləji/ *n* the scientific study of the Earth's atmosphere, especially its patterns of climate and weather [Early 17C. < Greek *meteōrologia* < *meteōron* (see METEOR).] —**meteorological** /-ərə lójjik'l/ *adj* —**meteorologically** /-lójjikli/ *adv* —**meteorologist** *n*

meteor shower *n* a number of meteors seen at regular intervals in a particular area of the sky when a large group of meteors passes through the Earth's atmosphere

meter[1] /méetər/ *n* 1 a device that measures and records the quantity or flow of something such as electricity, gas, water, distance, or time 2 MEASURE = **parking meter** ■ *vt* to measure the amount or flow of something such as electricity or water, using a meter [Early 19C. < ?]

meter[2] *n* US = **metre**

-meter *suffix* measuring device ○ *heliometer* [Via French *-mètre* < Greek *metron* 'measure' (see METRE[2])]

metered mail *n* mail that is franked privately by a machine licensed from the postal service

meter maid *n* a woman employed to report traffic violations (*dated informal*)

meth- *prefix* methyl ○ *methicillin* [Shortening]

methacrylate /meth ákri layt/ *n* an ester derived from methacrylic acid

methacrylic acid /méthə krillik-/ *n* $C_4H_6O_2$ a synthetic, colourless liquid. Use: manufacture of plastic.

methadone /méthə dōn/, **methadon** /-don/ *n* a synthetic narcotic drug similar in its painkilling effect to morphine. Use: substitute for heroin in the treatment of addiction. [Mid-20C. < METH- + AMINO + DI-[1].]

methaemoglobin /met héemə glṓbin, me théemə/ *n* an altered form of haemoglobin that cannot bind oxygen, produced by certain poisons or a genetic disorder

methaemoglobinaemia /met héemə glōbi néemi ə, me théemə-/ *n* the presence in the blood of methaemoglobin

methamphetamine /méth am féttə meen/ *n* $C_{10}H_{15}N$ a form of the stimulant amphetamine

methanal /méthə nal/ *n* CHEM = **formaldehyde** [Late 19C. < METHANE.]

methane /mée thayn/ *n* CH_4 a colourless, odourless, flammable gas that is the main constituent of natural gas. Use: as fuel. [Mid-19C. < METHYL.]

methanoic acid /méthənō ik-/ *n* CHEM = **formic acid** [< METHANE]

methanol /méthə nol/ *n* CH_3OH a colourless, volatile, poisonous, water-soluble liquid. Use: as solvent, fuel, in antifreeze for motor vehicles. [Late 19C. < METHANE.]

methaqualone /méthə kwáylōn/ *n* $C_{16}H_{14}N_2O$ a hypnotic drug that may become habit-forming. Use: treatment of anxiety, sleep disorders. [Mid-20C. < METH- + contraction of *quinazolinon*, a derivative of quinoline.]

methemoglobin *n* US = **methaemoglobin**

methicillin /méthə síllin/ *n* $C_{17}H_{19}N_2NaO_6S$ a synthetic antibiotic. Use: treatment of penicillin-resistant infections. [Mid-20C. < METH- + PENICILLIN.]

methinks /mi thíngks/ (**-thought** /mi tháwt/, **-thought**) *vi* it seems to me (*humorous or archaic*) [Old English *mē þyncþ* 'it seems to me' < *þyncan* 'seem' < Indo-European]

methionine /me thí ə neen, -nīn/ *n* an essential amino acid that contains sulphur [Early 20C. < METH- + THIO-.]

metho /méthō/ (*plural* **-os**) *n Aus* (*informal*) 1 methylated spirits 2 a drinker of methylated spirits

method /méthəd/ *n* 1 WAY OF DOING a way of doing something or carrying something out, especially according to a plan ○ *a successful method of recruitment of new staff* 2 ORDERLINESS orderly thought, action, or technique ○ *There is no method whatsoever in his approach to business.* 3 BODY OF SCIENTIFIC TECHNIQUES the body of systematic techniques used by a particular discipline, especially a scientific one [15C. Via Latin < Greek *methodos* 'pursuit, way' < *meta-* 'after' + *hodos* 'journey'.]

Method *n* a theory and system of acting that involves the actor identifying strongly with the internal motivation of the character being portrayed

methodical /mə thóddik'l/, **methodic** /-dik/ *adj* systematic or painstaking —**methodically** *adv* —**methodicalness** *n*

methodise *vt* = **methodize**

Methodism /méthədizəm/ *n* the doctrines, principles, or organization of the Methodist Church

Methodist /méthədist/ *n* a member of the Methodist Church ■ *adj* relating to Methodism or membership of the Methodist Church. ◊ **Wesleyan** *adj.* [Mid-18C. Originally applied to members of a society founded at Oxford, from the methodical habits of life and worship it promoted.] —**Methodistic** /méthə dístik/ *adj* —**Methodistically** *adv*

Methodist Church *n* a group of Nonconformist Protestant denominations founded in 18th-century England by John Wesley and his followers

methodize /méthə dīz/ (**-izes, -izing, -ized**), **methodise** (**-ises, -ising, -ised**) *vt* to reduce or arrange something according to a method —**methodization** /méthə dī záysh'n/ n —**methodizer** n

methodology /méthə dólləji/ (*plural* -**gies**) n 1 ORGANIZING SYSTEM the methods or organizing principles underlying a particular art, science, or other area of study 2 STUDY OF ORGANIZING PRINCIPLES in philosophy, the study of organizing principles and underlying rules 3 STUDY OF RESEARCH METHODS the study of methods of research — **methodological** /méthədə lójjik'l/ adj —**methodologically** adv —**methodologist** n

methotrexate /méthō trék sayt, meéthō-/ n $C_{20}H_{22}N_8O_5$ a drug that inhibits cellular reproduction. Use: cancer treatment. [Mid-20C. < METH- + -trex- < ?]

methought past participle, past tense of **methinks**

methoxide /mi thók sīd/ n $NaOCH_3$ any chemical derivative of methanol that has some features of a salt, e.g. sodium methoxide [Late 19C. < METH- + OXY-.]

methoxychlor /mi thóksi klawr/ n $C_{16}H_{15}Cl_3O_2$ a white crystalline compound used as an insecticide [Mid-20C. < METH- + OXY- + CHLORINE.]

meths /meths/ n UK methylated spirit (*informal*) [Mid-20C. Contraction.]

Methuselah /mə thyoozələ/ n 1 according to the Bible, a man who was an ancestor of Noah and lived 969 years (Gen 5: 21–27) 2 **Methuselah, methuselah** a wine bottle that holds the equivalent of eight normal bottles, approximately 6 1/208 fl oz

methyl /meé thīl, méth'l/ adj containing the group of atoms CH_3 [Mid-19C. < French méthyle, a back-formation < méthylène (see METHYLENE).] —**methylic** /mə thíllik/ adj

methyl acetate n $C_3H_6O_2$ a fragrant colourless liquid. Use: solvent in paint removers.

methylal /méthi lal/ n $C_3H_8O_2$ a colourless flammable liquid. Use: solvent, manufacture of perfumes and adhesives.

methyl alcohol n CHEM = methanol

methylamine /me thílə meen, mee-/ n CH_5N any of three colourless flammable derivatives of ammonia, especially a gas used in dyes, drugs, and herbicides

methylate /méthi layt/ n = **methoxide** ■ vt (-**ates**, -**ating**, -**ated**) 1 to replace one or more hydrogen atoms in a molecule with the methyl group 2 to mix something with methanol —**methylation** /méthi láysh'n/ n —**methylator** n

methylated spirit, **methylated spirits** n ethanol with methanol added, to make it undrinkable, and coloured with a violet dye. Use: fuel, in solvents.

methylbenzene /meéthīl bén zeen/ n CHEM = **toluene**

methyl bromide n CH_3Br a poisonous colourless gas or liquid. Use: solvent, fumigant, refrigerant.

methylcellulose /meéthīl séllyoō lóss/ n a greyish-white powder derived from cellulose that swells up in water. Use: a food additive, manufacture of paints and cosmetics.

methyl chloride n CH_3Cl a colourless poisonous gas. Use: refrigerant, local anaesthetic.

methyldopa /meé thīl dṓpə/ n $C_{10}H_{13}NO_4$ a white powdered drug. Use: treatment of hypertension.

methylene /méthə leen/ n CH_2 a bivalent group of atoms derived from methane ■ adj CH_2 relating to the group of atoms derived from methane containing one carbon atom and two hydrogen atoms [Mid-19C. < French méthylène < Greek methu 'wine' + hulē 'wood, substance'.]

methylene blue n $C_{16}H_{18}ClN_3S$ a crystalline compound that turns blue when dissolved in water. Use: dye, antiseptic, antidote for cyanide poisoning, stain in laboratories.

methyl isocyanate n CH_3NCO a flammable, colourless, extremely toxic liquid. Use: manufacture of herbicides.

methylmercury /meéthīl múrkyoori/ n an extremely toxic compound, derived from the action of microorganisms on metallic mercury. Use: seed disinfectant.

methyl methacrylate n a colourless flammable liquid that can be converted into clear plastic resins

methylnaphthalene /meéthīl nápthə leen/ n $C_{11}H_{10}$ either of two forms of naphthalene, a liquid used in making diesel fuels or a solid used in making insecticides

methyl orange n an alkaline dye that turns yellow when neutral and pink when acid. Use: chemical indicator.

methylphenidate /meéthīl fénni dayt/ n $C_{14}H_{19}NO_2$ a central nervous system stimulant. Use: treatment of narcolepsy, attention deficit disorder. [Mid-20C. Contraction of METHYL + PHENYL + PIPERIDINE + ACETATE.]

metical /méttik'l/ (*plural* -**cais** /-kísh/ *or* -**cals**) n see table at **currency** [Late 20C. Via Portuguese matical < Arabic miṯḳāl, a unit of weight < ṯakala 'weigh'.]

meticulous /mə tíkyŏŏləss/ adj extremely careful and precise [Late 19C. < Latin meticulosus 'fearful, timid' < metus 'fear'.] —**meticulously** adv —**meticulousness** n

SYNONYMS See *careful*.

métier /métti ay/, **metier** n 1 somebody's occupation or trade 2 an activity that somebody is particularly good at [Late 18C. < French, < Latin ministerium (see MINISTRY).]

Metis /meétiss/ n the innermost known natural satellite of Jupiter, discovered in 1979

metol /meé tol/ n $C_{14}H_{20}N_2O_6S$ a colourless soluble salt. Use: photographic developer. [Late 19C. Arbitrary.]

Metonic cycle /mi tónnik-/ n a cycle of 235 lunar months, after which the phases of the moon occur on the same days of the month as they did at the start of the cycle [Late 17C. After the 5C BC Athenian astronomer Metōn.]

metonym /méttənim/ n a word or phrase used in a figure of speech in which an attribute of something is used to stand for the thing itself, e.g. 'laurels' is used to stand for 'glory' [Late 16C. Back-formation < METONYMY.] —**metonymic** /métta nímmik/ adj —**metonymically** adv

metonymy /me tónnəmi/ n a figure of speech in which an attribute of something is used to stand for the thing itself, e.g. 'laurels' when it stands for 'glory' or 'brass' when it stands for 'military officers' [Mid-16C. Via late Latin < Greek metōnumia 'change of name' < meta- 'beside, different' + onuma 'name'.]

me-too adj (*informal*) 1 using products, methods, or policies copied from somebody else 2 trying to emulate the success of others or to follow a trend —**me-tooer** n —**me-tooism** n

metope /méttōp, méttəpi/ n in a Doric frieze, a square space between two sets of three vertical grooves (**triglyphs**) [Mid-16C. < Greek metopē < meta- 'between' + opē 'hole'.]

metopic /me tóppik/ adj relating to the forehead [Late 19C. < Greek metōpon 'forehead' < meta- 'between' + ōps 'eye'.]

metralgia /mi trálji ə/ n pain in the womb

metre[1] /meétər/ n (*symbol* **m**) the basic SI unit of length, equivalent to approximately 1.094 yd or 39.37 in [Late 18C. Via French < Greek metron (see METRE[2]).]

metre[2] /meétər/ n 1 an arranged pattern of rhythm in a line of verse 2 the pattern of beats that combines to form musical rhythm [Pre-12C. Directly and via French < Latin metrum < Greek metron 'measure'.]

metre-kilogram-second adj using or based on the metre, kilogram, and second as the measuring units of length, mass, and time

metric /méttrik/ adj 1 relating to or using the metric system of measurement 2 LITERAT = **metrical** ■ n a mathematical function defined for a coordinates system that assigns a value to each pair of elements equal to the distance between them, or to a property analogous to distance between points on a line

metrical /méttrik'l/ adj relating to or using poetic metre —**metrically** adv

metricate /méttri kayt/ vt (-**cates**, -**cating**, -**cated**) vt to convert something from nonmetric to metric units of measurement —**metrication** /méttri káysh'n/ n

metric hundredweight n a unit of weight equal to 50 kg

metricize /méttri sīz/ (-**cizes**, -**cizing**, -**cized**), **metricise** (-**cises**, -**cising**, -**cised**) vt to express a measurement in metric units or change it into metric units

metrics /méttriks/ n the art of using metre in poetry (+ singular verb)

metric system n a decimal system of weights and measures based on units such as the kilogram and metre

metric ton n (*symbol* **t**) a unit of weight equal to 1,000 kg

metrify /méttri fī/ (-**fies**, -**fying**, -**fied**) vt to put prose into verse or metre —**metrifier** n

metrist /méttrist/ n a skilled user of poetic metre

metritis /mi trítiss/ n inflammation of the womb

metro /méttrō/ (*plural* -**ros**) n 1 **metro, Metro** SUBWAY an underground railway system in a town or city 2 Can LOCAL GOVERNMENT the metropolitan area or government of a large city 3 METROPOLIS a metropolis (*informal*) [Mid-20C. Shortening of METROPOLITAN.]

metro- prefix womb ○ metrorrhagia [< Greek mētra, related to mētēr 'mother' < Indo-European]

metrology /mi tróllaji/ (*plural* -**gies**) n 1 the scientific study of units of measurement 2 a system of measurement [Early 19C. Via French < Greek metrologie < metron 'measure'.] —**metrologic** /méttra lójjik/ adj —**metrologically** adv —**metrologist** n

metronidazole /méttrō nídazōl/ n $C_6H_9N_3O_3$ a yellow crystalline compound. Use: treatment of vaginal infections. [Mid-20C. Contraction of METHYL + NITRO- + IMIDAZOLE.]

metronome /méttrənōm/ n a device used to indicate a given tempo by means of an aural or visual signal produced electronically or by an adjustable pendulum [Early 19C. < Greek metron 'measure, metre' + nomos 'rule, division'.] —**metronomic** /méttra nómmik/ adj —**metronomically** adv

metronymic n = matronymic

metropolis /mə tróppəliss/ n 1 LARGE CITY a very large city, often the capital or chief urban centre of a country, state, or region 2 CENTRE OF AN ACTIVITY the centre or principal place for a particular activity 3 MAIN DIOCESE in Christianity, the principal diocese or see in an ecclesiastical province [Mid-16C. Via late Latin < Greek mētropolis 'mother city' < mētēr 'mother' + polis 'city'.]

SYNONYMS See *city*.

metropolitan /méttra póllitən/ adj 1 TYPICAL OF A METROPOLIS typical of a metropolis in scale, variety, or sophistication 2 FORMING LARGE CITY constituting a large urban area, usually one that includes a city and its suburbs and outlying areas 3 DOMESTIC AND INTERNAL relating to the home territory of a country rather than its territories elsewhere 4 OF ECCLESIASTICAL METROPOLIS relating to or constituting an ecclesiastical metropolis ■ n 1 METROPOLIS INHABITANT an inhabitant of a metropolis 2 HIGH-RANKING CHURCH OFFICIAL in Christianity, a high-ranking church dignitary such as an archbishop or head of an ecclesiastical province 3 HEAD OF RUSSIAN ORTHODOX CHURCH the head of the Russian Orthodox Church, based in Moscow

metropolitan county n in England, any of the six large urban administrative units in the system of local government between 1974 and 1986

metropolitan district n in England, any of the districts that used to be metropolitan counties. They are the principal units of local government, each with an elected council.

metrorrhagia /meétrō ráyji ə/ n excessive discharge of blood from the womb —**metrorrhagic** adj

-metry suffix measuring ○ cephalometry [< Greek -metria < metron 'measure']

Metternich /métta nikh/, **Klemens Wenzel Nepomuk Lothar von, Prince of Metternich-Winneburg-Beilstein** (1773–1859) German-born Austrian statesman

mettle /métt'l/ n 1 courage, spirit, or strength of character 2 the particular mental and emotional character unique to an individual [Mid-16C. Variant of METAL.] ◇ **on your mettle** ready or determined to do your best

SYNONYMS See *courage*.

mettlesome /métt'lsəm/ adj spirited and courageous

Metz /mets/ city in E France. Population: 123,776 (1999).

Metzinger /métzingər/, **Jean** (1883–1956) French painter

meunière /mōn áir/ adj dredged in flour, fried in butter, and sprinkled with lemon juice and chopped parsley ○ sole meunière [Mid-19C. < French à la meunière 'in the way of a miller's wife'.]

Meursault /múrsō/ n a dry white wine from the Burgundy region of NE France [Mid-19C. < French, a commune in the Côte de Beaune.]

Meuse /möz/ river flowing from NE France through Belgium and the Netherlands into the North Sea. Length: 900 km/560 mi.

MeV, Mev, mev *symbol* million electron volts

mew[1] /myoo/ *n* any common seagull, especially the common gull [Old English *mæw*]

mew[2] /myoo/ *vi* to give out a high-pitched cry (*refers to cats and kittens*) ■ *n* the high-pitched sound a cat or kitten makes [14C. An imitation of the sound.]

mew[3] /myoo/ *n* CAGE FOR HAWKS a cage for keeping hawks in ■ *v* 1 *vt* CONFINE HAWK OR FALCON to confine a hawk or falcon, especially by tying it to a perch 2 *vi* MOULT to shed feathers [14C. < French *mue* < *muer* 'moult' < Latin *mutare* 'to change'.]

mewl /myool/ *vi* to whimper or cry weakly [Early 17C. < ?] —**mewler** *n*

mews /myooz/ *n* a street that originally had stables built on it but is now converted into housing, or the houses themselves (+ *singular or plural verb*) [Early 19C. < MEW[3].]

Mex. *abbr* 1 Mexican 2 Mexico

Mexicali /méksə kaáli/ city in NW Mexico. Population: 601,938 (1990).

Mexican bean *n US* FOOD = **frijol**

Mexican bean beetle *n* a ladybird that feeds on the leaves of bean plants. Native to: North America. *Epilachna varivestis.*

Mexican hairless *n* a tiny, mainly hairless dog, belonging to a breed originating in Mexico

Mexican jumping bean *n* PLANTS = **jumping bean**

Mexican standoff *n* a dispute or argument that cannot be won (*informal*)

Mexican wave *n* the rippling effect produced by rows of spectators at a sporting or musical event standing up, raising their arms, and then sitting down again in sequence. US term **wave**[2] *n*. 11 [Because first used at the World Cup soccer finals in Mexico in 1986]

Mexico

Mexico /méksikō/ federal republic in S North America. Capital: Mexico City. Population: 96,807,451 (1997). Area: 1,964,382 sq. km/758,452 sq. mi. —**Mexican** *adj*, *n*

Mexico, Gulf of arm of the Atlantic Ocean, east of Mexico and south of the United States. Area: 1,812,990 sq. km/700,000 sq. mi.

Mexico City capital of Mexico, in the south-central part of the country. Population: 8,236,960 (1990).

Meyerhof /míy ər hof, -höf/, **Otto Fritz** (1884–1951) German-born US biochemist

Meynell /mə nél/, **Alice** (1847–1922) British poet and literary critic

meze /mézzay/ (*plural* **-zes** *or* **-ze**) *n* an assortment of snacks served with drinks as an appetizer or a light meal in Greece and the Middle East, e.g. stuffed vine leaves, small pastries, or grilled sausages [Early 20C. Via Turkish < Persian *maza* 'taste, relish'.]

mezereon /mə zeeri ən/ *n* a poisonous deciduous bush that flowers before the leaves emerge, and bears crimson berries. Flowers: purple, in clusters. Native to: Europe, Asia. *Daphne mezereum.* [15C. Via medieval Latin < Arabic *māzaryūn.*]

mezuzah /mə zóōzə, -zoó-/ (*plural* **-zahs** *or* **-zoth** /-zōt/) *n* a scroll with biblical passages on one side and a name of God on the other, inserted in a small case attached by religious Jews to doorposts in the home [Mid-17C. < Hebrew *mĕzūzāh* 'doorpost'.]

mezzanine /mézzə neen/ *n* 1 **mezzanine, mezzanine floor** INTERMEDIATE STOREY a low storey, especially one between the ground floor and the first floor in a building 2 *US* THEATRE'S LOWEST BALCONY the lowest balcony in a theatre 3 AREA UNDER STAGE a floor or room beneath the stage in a theatre ■ *adj* WITHIN INTERMEDIATE RANGE OF INVESTMENT describes an intermediate range of funding or investment, such as certain unsecured high-yielding loans [Early 18C. Via French < Italian *mezzanino* 'small one in the middle' < *mezzano* 'middle' < Latin *medianus* (see MEDIAN).]

mezza voce /métsə vôchi, -vô chay/ *adv* with moderate volume from the voice or instrument (*musical direction*) [< Italian, 'half voice'] —**mezza voce** *adj*

mezzo /métsō/ *adv* moderately (*musical direction*) ■ *n* (*plural* **-zos**) MUSIC = **mezzo-soprano** [Mid-18C. Via Italian, 'middle, half' < Latin *medius* (see MEDIUM).]

mezzo forte *adv* moderately loud (*musical direction*) [< Italian] —**mezzo forte** *adj*

mezzo piano *adv* moderately soft (*musical direction*) [< Italian] —**mezzo piano** *adj*

mezzo-relievo /-ri leévō, -ri lyáy/ (*plural* **mezzo-relievos**) *n* SCULPTURE = **half relief** [< Italian, 'half-relief']

mezzo-soprano *n* a woman whose singing voice is between a soprano and a contralto in range [< Italian, 'half soprano']

mezzotint /métsō tint/ *n* 1 ENGRAVING PROCESS an engraving process that involves scraping and burnishing the roughened surface of a copper plate 2 MEZZOTINT PRINT a print produced by the mezzotint process ■ *vt* ENGRAVE PLATE USING MEZZOTINT to engrave a copper plate by using the mezzotint process [Mid-18C. Anglicization of Italian *mezzotinto* 'half-tint'.] —**mezzotinter** *n*

mf *abbr* mezzo forte

mF *abbr* millifarad

MF *abbr* 1 medium frequency 2 Middle French

M/F, m/f *abbr* male or female (*in advertisements*)

MFA *abbr* Master of Fine Arts

mfr *abbr* 1 manufacture 2 manufacturer

mg *symbol* milligram

Mg *symbol* magnesium

MG *abbr* 1 machine gun 2 Major General

MGB *n* the secret police of the former Soviet Union from 1946 to 1954. Full form **Ministerstvo Gosudarstvennoi Bezopasnosti** [Mid-20C. Shortening of Russian, 'Ministry of State Security'.]

mgr *abbr* manager

Mgr *abbr* 1 Monseigneur 2 Monsignor

⚡mh *abbr* Marshall Islands (*in Internet addresses*)

mH *symbol* millihenry

MHA *abbr* Member of the House of Assembly

MHC *n* a group of genes in mammals located next or near to one another that serve to make cells separate and distinguishable from those of other organisms. Full form **major histocompatibility complex**

MHR *abbr* Member of the House of Representatives

MHz *symbol* megahertz

mi /mee/, **me** *n* a syllable that represents the third note in a scale, used for singing solfège [15C. < medieval Latin.]

MI *abbr* 1 Michigan 2 Military Intelligence 3 myocardial infarction

mi. *abbr* mile

MI5 /ém T fív/ *n* a former official and current popular name for Military Intelligence, section five, the British security and counterintelligence service

MI6 /ém T síks/ *n* a former official and current popular name for Military Intelligence, section six, the British secret intelligence and espionage service

MIA *n US* a soldier who is reported missing during a military mission. Full form **missing in action**

Miami /mī ámmi/ city in SE Florida. Population: 368,624 (1998 estimate).

Miami Beach city in SE Florida, on an island opposite Miami. Population: 97,053 (1998 estimate).

Miao /myow/ *n, adj* PEOPLES, LANG = **Hmong** [Early 20C. < Chinese *Miáo* 'people'.]

miaow /mi ów/, **meow** *n* CHARACTERISTIC CRY OF A CAT the characteristic cry made by a domestic cat ■ *vi* UTTER MIAOW to utter a miaow ■ *interj* DESIGNATING A SPITEFUL OR MEAN COMMENT used to indicate that you think somebody's comment is spiteful or malicious (*informal*) [Late 16C. An imitation of the sound.]

miasma /mi ázmə, mī-/ (*plural* **-mata** *or* **-mas** /-mətə/) *n* 1 a harmful or poisonous emanation, especially one caused by burning or decaying organic matter 2 an unwholesome or menacing atmosphere [Mid-17C. Directly or via French *miasme* < Greek *miasma* 'defilement, pollution' < *miainein* 'pollute'.] —**miasmal** *adj* —**miasmatic** /mee əz máttik/ *adj*

Mic. *abbr* Micah

mica /mīkə/ *n* a shiny aluminosilicate mineral belonging to a group having varying compositions. Source: igneous and metamorphic rocks. Use: electrical insulators, heating elements. [Early 18C. < Latin, 'grain, crumb'.]

Micah[1] /mīkə/ *n* in the Bible, a prophet who lived during the 8th century BC

Micah[2] *n* one of the 12 prophetic books of the Bible known as the Minor Prophets, traditionally attributed to the prophet Micah

Micawber /mi káwbər/ *n* a poor and idle person who remains cheerfully optimistic [Mid-19C. After Wilkins *Micawber*, a character in *David Copperfield* (1850) by Charles Dickens.] —**Micawberish** *adj*

mice plural of **mouse**[2]

> **LITERARY LINK** *Of Mice and Men*, a novella (1937) by US author John Steinbeck. With great compassion and realism, Steinbeck recounts the tragic tale of two itinerant labourers, George Milton and Lennie Small. When Lennie, who is mentally ill, accidentally kills a girl, George shoots his friend rather than surrender him to a lynch mob.

micelle /mi sél/ *n* an electrically charged particle formed by an aggregate of ions or molecules in soaps, detergents, and other suspensions [Late 19C. < modern Latin *micella* 'small crumb' < Latin *mica* (see MICA).] —**micellar** *adj*

Mich. *abbr* 1 Michaelmas 2 Michigan

Michael /mík'l/ (*b.* 1921) king of Romania (1927–30, 1940–47)

Michaelmas /mík'lməss/ (*plural* **-mases**) *n* a Christian holy day marking the feast of St Michael the Archangel. Date: 29 September. [Pre-12C. Contraction of *Michael's mass.*]

Michaelmas daisy *n* a common aster that blooms in the autumn. Flowers: purple, pink, or white. Native to: North America.

Michaelmas term *n* the name used for the autumn term at Oxford and Cambridge Universities, the Inns of Court, and some other educational institutions

Michelangelo: Engraving after a 16th-century portrait by Giuliano Bugiardini

Michelangelo /mík'l ánjəlō/ (1475–1564) Italian sculptor, painter, architect, and poet

Michelin /míchəlin, meéshə laN/, **André** (1853–1931) French tyre manufacturer

Michelson /mík'lssən/, **Albert Abraham** (1852–1931) German-born US physicist

Michelson-Morley experiment /mīk'lss'n máwrli-/ *n* an attempt to measure the difference in speed between light beams travelling in different directions by using interference effects [Early 20C. After Albert Abraham MICHELSON and the US physicist Edward *Morley* (1838–1923).]

Michigan[1] /míshigən/ state in the N United States. Capital: Lansing. Population: 9,773,892 (1997). Area: 250,465 sq. km/96,705 sq. mi.

Michigan[2] /míshigən/ *n US* CARDS = **Newmarket**[1] *n.* 1 [Early 20C. After the state of MICHIGAN[1].]

Michigan, Lake lake in the N United States, between Michigan and Wisconsin, one of the Great Lakes. Area: 57,800 sq. km/22,300 sq. mi.

Mick /mik/ *n* highly offensive term that deliberately insults somebody's Irish origin or Roman Catholic faith (*taboo offensive*) [Mid-19C. < *Mick*, nickname for *Michael.*]

mickey /míki/ (*plural* **-eys**) *n* = **Mickey Finn** (*informal*) ◇ **take the mickey** to tease somebody (*informal*)

Mickey Finn /míki fín/ *n* an alcoholic drink to which a strong sedative has been added to make the drinker unconscious (*informal*) [Early 20C. < ?]

Mickiewicz /mits kyáyvich/, **Adam** (1798–1855) Polish poet

mickle /mík'l/ *adj Scotland* abundant or very large ■ *adv Scotland* greatly or much [Old English *micel* < Indo-European]

Micmac *n* PEOPLES, LANG = **Mi'kmaq**

micr- *prefix* = **micro-** (*sometimes used before vowels*)

⚡**micro** /míkrō/ *adj* **SMALL** very small ■ *n* (*plural* **-cros**) (*informal*) **1 MICROPROCESSOR** a microprocessor **2 MICROWAVE OVEN** a microwave oven **3 MICROCOMPUTER** a microcomputer [Mid-19C. < MICRO-.]

micro- *prefix* **1** (*symbol* μ) small, minute ○ *microseism* **2** using a microscope or requiring magnification ○ *microanatomy* **3** (*symbol* μ) one millionth (10^{-6}) ○ *microcurie* **4** of a small area or on a small scale ○ *microhabitat* ○ *microteaching* **5** microfilm, microphotography ○ *microform* [< Greek *mikros* 'small']

microampere /míkrō ám pair/ *n* one millionth part of an ampere

microanalysis /míkrō ə nálləssiss/ (*plural* **-ses**) *n* **1** the chemical analysis of tiny samples of a substance **2** any extremely detailed analysis of something —**microanalyst** /míkrō ánnəlist/ *n* —**microanalytical** /míkrō anə líttik'l/ *adj*

microanatomy /míkrō ə náttəmi/ *n* ANAT = **histology** —**microanatomical** /míkrō anə tómmik'l/ *adj*

microbalance /míkrō balənss/ *n* a balance for precisely weighing extremely small quantities up to 0.1 gm

microbar /míkrō baar/ *n* a unit of pressure equal to one millionth of a bar

microbarograph /míkrō bárrə graaf, -graf/ *n* a barograph that records tiny changes in atmospheric pressure

microbe /míkrōb/ *n* a microscopic organism, especially one that transmits a disease [Late 19C. < French, < Greek *mikros* 'small' + *bios* 'life'.] —**microbial** /mī krṓbi əl/ *adj*

microbiology /míkrō bī ólləji/ *n* the scientific study of microscopic organisms and their effects —**microbiological** /míkrō bī ə lójjik'l/ *adj* —**microbiologically** *adv*

microbrewery /míkrō broo əri/ (*plural* **-ries**) *n* a small, usually independently owned brewery that produces limited quantities of specialized beers, often selling them on the premises —**microbrewer** *n* —**microbrewing** *n*

microburst /míkrō burst/ *n* a strong localized air current that hits the ground and spreads, causing wind to rapidly change direction and speed

microcapsule /míkrō kap syool/ *n* a tiny capsule used to release a drug, flavour, or chemical

microcassette /míkrō kə sét/ *n* a small audiotape cassette designed to fit into a pocket-size tape recorder or dictation machine

microcephaly /míkrō séffəli/ *n* the condition of having a small head or having reduced space for the brain in the skull, often associated with learning difficulties —**microcephalic** /míkrō sə fállik/ *adj*

microchemistry /míkrō kémmistri/ *n* the scientific study of extremely small quantities of substances —**microchemical** *adj* —**microchemist** *n*

⚡**microchip** /míkrō chip/ *n* ELECTRONICS = **chip** *n.* 6

⚡**microcircuit** /míkrō surkit/ *n* ELECTRONICS = **integrated circuit** —**microcircuitry** /míkrō súrkitri/ *n*

microclimate /míkrō klīmət/ *n* the climate of a confined space or small geographical area —**microclimatic** /míkrō klī máttik/ *adj* —**microclimatically** *adv* —**microclimatologic** /míkrō klīmətə lójjik/ *adj* —**microclimatologist** /míkrō klīmə tólləjist/ *n* —**microclimatology** /míkrō klīmə tólləji/ *n*

microcline /míkrō klīn/ *n* a mineral of the feldspar group that contains potassium. Use: making glass, porcelain. [Mid-19C. < German *Mikroklin* < Greek *mikros* 'small' + *klinein* 'lean'; because its angle of cleavage differs only slightly from 90°.]

micrococcus /míkrō kókəss/ (*plural* **-ci** /-róksī/) *n* any mainly harmless spherical bacterium, such as the one that ferments milk. Genus: *Micrococcus.* —**micrococcal** *adj*

⚡**microcomputer** /míkrō kəm pyootər/ *n* a small computer in which the central processing unit is a single silicon chip (**microprocessor**) [Late 20C. After MINICOMPUTER.]

microcontinent /míkrō kontinənt/ *n* a small segment of the Earth's crust with the same overall granitic composition as a continent, but much smaller

microcopy /míkrō kopi/ (*plural* **-ies**) *n* a photographic reproduction of something on microfilm or microfiche

microcosm /míkrō kozəm/ *n* a miniature copy of something, especially when it represents or stands for a larger whole ○ *Our classroom was a microcosm of the university.* [12C. < French *microcosme* < Greek *mikros kosmos* 'little world'.] —**microcosmic** /míkrō kózmik/ *adj* —**microcosmically** *adv*

microcosmic salt *n* a colourless odourless salt obtained from human urine and used to test metallic salts and oxides

microcosmos /míkrō kózmoss/ *n* = **microcosm**

microcrystal /míkrō krist'l/ *n* a crystal that can only be seen under a microscope —**microcrystalline** /míkro krístə līn/ *adj*

microcurie /míkrō kyoori/ *n* a unit of radioactivity equal to a millionth of a curie

microcyte /míkrō sīt/ *n* an unusually small red blood cell —**microcytic** /míkrō síttik/ *adj*

microdissection /míkrō di séksh'n/ *n* dissection carried out using a microscope

microdot /míkrō dot/ *n* **1** a tiny photographic reproduction of something, about the size of a dot or a pinhead **2** a dose of LSD in a tiny tablet (*informal*)

microeconomics /míkrō eekə nómmiks, -ekə-/ *n* the study of specific or localized aspects of an economy (+ *singular verb*) —**microeconomic** *adj*

⚡**microelectronics** /míkrō ilek trónniks, -elek-/ *n* the technology and techniques involved in the design, development, and construction of extremely small electronic circuits, e.g. computers on a single silicon chip (+ *singular verb*) —**microelectronic** *adj* —**microelectronically** *adv*

microelement /míkrō eləmənt/ *n* CHEM = **trace element** *n.* 1

microencapsulate /míkrō in kápsyōō layt/ (**-lates, -lating, -lated**) *vt* to enclose a substance in microcapsules —**microencapsulation** /-in kápsyōō láysh'n/ *n*

microevolution /míkrō eevə lóosh'n, -evə-/ *n* minor change within a species or small group of organisms, usually within a short period of time —**microevolutionary** *adj*

microfarad /míkrō farəd, -rad/ *n* one millionth part of a farad

microfauna /míkrō fawnə/ *npl* animals so small that they can only be seen under a microscope —**microfaunal** *adj*

microfibre /míkrō fībər/ *n* **1** an extremely fine synthetic thread or yarn **2** a wrinkle-resistant, washable, synthetic fabric made of microfibre, used mainly for clothing

microfiche /míkrō feesh/ *n* a sheet of microfilm containing information laid out in a grid pattern [Mid-20C. < French, < Greek *mikros* 'small' + French *fiche* 'slip of paper'.]

microfilament /míkrō fílləmənt/ *n* a thin thread of protein found in muscle and the cytoplasm of all cells —**microfilamentous** /-filə méntəss/ *adj*

microfilaria /míkrō fi láiri ə/ (*plural* **-ae** /-láiri ī/) *n* the early larval stage of a parasitic nematode worm (**filaria**), a cause of heartworm in dogs and elephantiasis in humans —**microfilarial** *adj*

microfilm /míkrō film/ *n* a strip of photographic film on which highly miniaturized reproductions have been recorded ■ *vti* to photograph something on microfilm

microflora /míkrō flawrə/ *npl* plants that can only be seen under a microscope —**microfloral** *adj*

microform /míkrō fawrm/ *n* film or paper that contains miniature reproductions, as microfilm and microfiche do

microfossil /míkrō foss'l/ *n* a fossil that can only be studied with a microscope, e.g. a bacterium fossil

microfungus /míkrō fung gəss/ (*plural* **-gi** /-fung gī/ *or* **-guses**) *n* any fungus that has tiny or unobservable reproductive organs

microgram /míkrō gram/ *n* one millionth part of a gram

micrograph /míkrō graaf, -graf/ *n* **1** a photograph or drawing of something as seen through a microscope **2** a device that can produce engraving or writing using very fine lines —**micrographic** /míkrō gráffik/ *adj* —**micrographically** *adv*

microgravity /míkrō gravəti/ *n* a force of gravity so low that weightlessness occurs, e.g. during space travel

microgroove /míkrō groov/ *n* the narrow spiral groove on a gramophone record

microhabitat /míkrō hábbi tat/ *n* an environment that has a unique set of ecological conditions within a larger habitat and supports distinct flora and fauna

microinch /míkrō inch/ *n* (*symbol* μ**in**) a unit of linear measurement equivalent to one millionth of an inch

microinjection /míkro in jeksh'n/ *n* the injection of a very small amount of liquid into individual cells, using a specialized instrument and a microscope for observation —**microinject** *vti*

⚡**microinstruction** /míkrō in struksh'n/ *n* a single instruction in a low-level computer program

microlepidopteran /míkrō léppi dóptərən/ (*plural* **-a** /-tərə/) *n* a small or medium-sized moth, e.g. a leaf miner, that is of little interest to a collector

microlight /míkrō līt/, **microlight aircraft, microlite, microlite aircraft** *n* a small low-speed lightweight aircraft, often with an open fuselage, that can carry one or two people and is used for flying for pleasure or reconnaissance

microlith /míkrō lith/ *n* a tiny flint tool, usually triangular, found in Mesolithic sites in Europe and dating from 12,000 to 3,000 BC —**microlithic** /míkrō líthik/ *adj*

micromanage /míkrō mannij/ (**-ages, -aging, -aged**) *vt* to manage a business or organization by paying extreme attention to small details —**micromanagement** *n* —**micromanager** *n*

micromanipulator /míkrō mə nípyōō laytər/ *n* a device consisting of geared controls for the manipulation of extremely small dissecting tools or miniature surgical instruments under a microscope —**micromanipulation** /-mə nippyōō láysh'n/ *n* —**micromanipulative** *adj*

micromere /míkrō meer/ *n* either of the small cells (**blastomeres**) formed by the division of a fertilized egg

micrometeorite /míkrō meéti ə rīt/ *n* a particle of cosmic dust that falls to Earth or onto the Moon's surface —**micrometeoritic** /míkrō meéti ə ríttik/ *adj*

micrometeoroid /míkrō meéti ə royd/ *n* an extremely small dust particle found in space that may land on Earth or the Moon as a micrometeorite

micrometeorology /míkrō meéti ə rólləji/ *n* the study of weather conditions in the air immediately above ground level, especially in small areas such as the area around a tree trunk or above a puddle —**micrometeorological** /-meéti ərə lójjik'l/ *adj* —**micrometeorologist** *n*

micrometer[1] /mī krómmitər/ *n* a device for measuring small diameters, thicknesses, distances, or angles to a high degree of accuracy [Late 17C. < French *micromètre.*] —**micrometric** /míkrō méttrik/ *adj* —**micrometrically** *adv* —**micrometry** /mī krómmətri/ *n*

micrometer[2] *n* US = **micrometre**

micrometre /míkrō meetər/ (*plural* **-tres**) *n* (*symbol* μ**m**) a unit of linear measurement equivalent to one millionth of a metre

⚡**microminiaturization** /mīkrō mínnichə rī záysh'n/, **microminiaturisation** *n* the production and use of extremely small electronic components, especially semiconductors —**microminiaturize** /mīkrō mínnichə rīz/ *vt* —**microminiaturized** *adj*

micromole /mīkrō mōl/ *n* (*symbol* μ**mol**) a molecular weight expressed in grams that is equivalent to one millionth of a mole —**micromolar** /mīkrə mólər/ *adj*

micromorphology /mīkrō mawr fóllәji/ *n* the study of the fine detail in the external form and structure of organisms, or of other objects such as metal surfaces —**micromorphological** /mīkrō mawrfə lójjik'l/ *adj*

micron /mī kron/ *n* a unit of linear measurement equivalent to one millionth of a metre [Late 19C. < Greek *mikros* 'small' + -ON[1].]

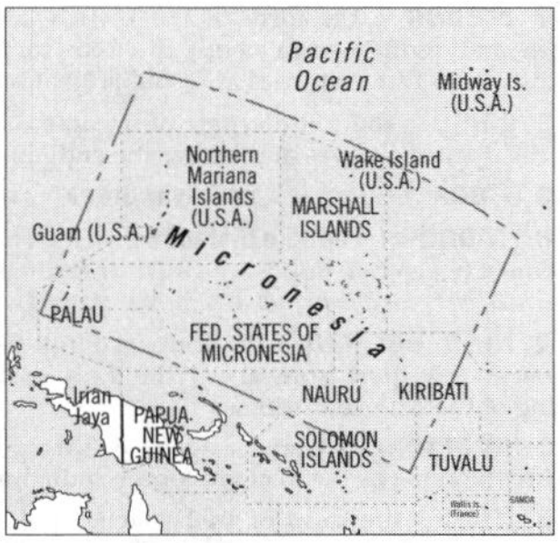

Micronesia

Micronesia[1] /mīkrə néezi ə/ ethnographic grouping of Pacific islands, encompassing the islands of the W Pacific Ocean east of the Philippines and mainly north of the equator —**Micronesian** *adj, n*

Micronesia[2] island nation in the W Pacific Ocean, in the Caroline Islands. Capital: Palikir. Population: 127,616 (1997). Area: 702 sq. km/271 sq. mi.

micronize /mīkrə nīz/ (**-izes, -izing, -ized**), **micronise** (**-ises, -ising, -ised**) *vt* to reduce the particle size of a powder down to a few millionths of a metre [Mid-20C. < ?]

micronucleus /mīkrō nyóokli əss/ (*plural* **-i** /-kli ī/ *or* **-uses**) *n* the smaller of the two nuclei in the cells of ciliate protozoans —**micronuclear** *adj*

micronutrient /mīkrō nyóotri ənt/ *n* a substance such as a vitamin or mineral that an organism requires for normal growth and development but only in very small quantities

microorganism /mīkrō áwrgənizəm/ *n* a tiny organism such as a virus, protozoan, or bacterium that can only be seen under a microscope

micropalaeontology /mīkrō pálli on tólləji/ *n* a branch of palaeontology that studies the microorganisms preserved as fossils in sedimentary rocks —**micropalaeontological** /mīkrō pálli ontə lójjik'l/ *adj* —**micropalaeontologist** /mīkrō pálli on tólləjist/ *n*

micropaleontology *n* US = **micropalaeontology**

microparasite /mīkrō párrə sīt/ *n* a microorganism that lives as a parasite on other organisms —**microparasitic** /-párrə síttik/ *adj*

microphage /mīkrə fayj/ *n* a small white blood cell, part of the immune system, that removes bacteria and other foreign bodies from blood and tissue —**microphagic** /mīkrə fájjik/ *adj*

microphagous /mī króffəgəss/ *adj* feeding on food in the form of microscopic particles, e.g. marine organisms

microphone /mīkrəfōn/ *n* a device that converts sounds to electrical signals by means of a vibrating diaphragm [Late 17C. Originally denoted a device for making faint sounds louder.] —**microphonic** /mīkrə fónnik/ *adj*

microphonics /mīkrə fónniks/ *npl* the sound heard from an electronic device, especially a loudspeaker, caused by the vibration of some mechanical part (+ *plural verb*)

microphotograph /mīkrō fótə graaf, -graf/ *n* **1** a photographic image, e.g. on microfilm, so small that it has to be magnified in order to be viewed **2** a photograph of an object viewed through a microscope —**microphotographer** /mīkrōfə tóggrəfər/ *n* —**microphotographic** /mīkrō fōtə gráffik/ *adj* —**microphotography** /mīkrōfə tóggrəfi/ *n*

microphysics /mīkrō fízziks/ *n* the branch of physics that studies objects and systems such as molecules, atoms, and elementary particles that are observable only microscopically or indirectly (+ *singular verb*) —**microphysical** *adj* —**microphysically** *adv* —**microphysicist** *n*

microphyte /mīkrō fīt/ *n* a plant observable only under a microscope, especially one that is parasitic —**microphytic** /mīkrō fíttik/ *adj*

micropipette /mīkrōpi pet/ *n* a very slender graduated tube that is used to measure, transfer, or remove minute amounts of something

micropower /mīkrō pow ər/ *n* electrical power generated or used in relatively small quantities, usually close to the location where it is needed, avoiding the need for large centralized power stations and distribution networks

microprint /mīkrō print/ *n* printed text, e.g. on microfilm, so small that it has to be magnified in order to be viewed

microprism /mīkrō prizəm/ *n* a small prism that is part of the focusing screen of many single-lens reflex cameras

microprobe /mī krō prōb/ *n* an instrument that focuses a narrow band of radiation on a very small area of a sample in order to excite secondary radiation that yields chemical information for analysis

⚡**microprocessor** /mīkrō prō sessər/ *n* the central processing unit that performs the basic operations in a microcomputer, consisting of an integrated circuit contained on a single chip

QUICK FACTS ON... **MICROPROCESSORS**

Key elements: computing power is a function of the number of transistors, the width of the bus carrying information between devices, and the clock speed of each microprocessor. Moore's law (after a 1965 observation by Gordon Moore, semiconductor pioneer) suggests that the number of transistors per square inch on integrated circuits doubles every 18 months while the price remains the same

Key dates: 1971 first microprocessor, Intel 4004, containing 2,300 transistors and a 4-bit bus, is used in programmable calculators; 1975 Intel 8080 (4,500 transistors, 8-bit bus) becomes the heart of the first personal computer, the Altair 8800; 1977 MOS Technology 6502 (9,000 transistors, 8-bit bus) is featured in the first popular personal computer, the Apple II; 1978 Intel 8088 (29,000 transistors, a 16-bit internal bus, an 8-bit external bus) is incorporated in the IBM PC in 1981, revolutionizing the computer industry; 1984 Motorola 68000 (68,000 transistors, a 32-bit internal bus, 16-bit external bus) is used in Apple's Macintosh personal computer; 1993 Intel Pentium (3.1 million transistors, 32-bit internal bus, 64-bit external bus); 1995 Intel Pentium Pro (5.5 million transistors, a 32-bit internal bus, 64-bit external bus) becomes industry standard; 2000 a 1GHz microprocessor with 22 million transistors on a single chip is produced

Key developments: personal computing, computer games and graphics, portable communications and computer equipment, widespread application of computer control to household appliances

Key publications: *Microprocessor Technology* (J. S. Anderson) 1994, *The Microprocessor: A Biography* (Michael S. Malone) 1995

⚡**microprogram** /mīkrō prō gram/ *n* a built-in program within a microprocessor, consisting of a series of arithmetical and logical steps that enable basic instructions to be carried out

⚡**microprogramming** /mīkrō prō gramming/ *n* a means of programming the central processing unit of a computer by breaking down instructions into a series of small steps

micropropagation /mī krō próppə gáysh'n/ *n* the propagation of plants by cloning a small piece of plant tissue cultured in a growth medium

micropsia /mī krópsi ə/ *n* a vision defect in which the cones of the retina are separated by local swelling, making objects appear smaller than they really are [Mid-19C. < MICRO- + Greek *opsis* 'sight' + -IA.]

micropyle /mīkrō pīl/ *n* **1** a small opening in the covering of the ovule of a plant through which the pollen tube passes prior to fertilization **2** a small pore in the membrane of an insect egg that allows sperm to enter and fertilize the egg [Early 19C. < French, < *micro-* 'micro-' + Greek *pulē* 'gate'.] —**micropylar** /mīkrō pīlər/ *adj*

microradiography /mīkrō ráydi óggrəfi/ *n* a technique that enlarges X-ray radiographs so that fine details can be examined —**microradiograph** /mīkrō ráydi ō graaf, -graf/ *n* —**microradiographic** /mīkrō ráydi ō gráffik/ *adj*

microreader /mīkrō reedər/ *n* a device that projects enlarged images and text from microfilm and microfiche onto a screen for easy reading

microscooter /mīkrō skootər/ *n* a small, often collapsible version of a child's foot scooter, used as a quick way of getting around on the pavements of city streets

microscope /mīkrə skōp/ *n* a device that uses a lens or system of lenses to produce a greatly magnified image of an object

microscopic /mīkrə skóppik/ *adj* **1** VERY SMALL extremely small **2** THOROUGH AND DETAILED very thorough and meticulous **3 microscopic, microscopical** INVISIBLE WITHOUT MICROSCOPE invisible without the use of a microscope **4 microscopic, microscopical** INVOLVING MICROSCOPE using or involving a microscope —**microscopically** *adv*

Microscopium /mīkrō skópi əm/ *n* a small inconspicuous constellation of the southern hemisphere

microscopy /mī króskəpi/ (*plural* **-pies**) *n* **1** the study and design of microscopes **2** an investigation, observation, or experiment that involves the use of a microscope —**microscopist** *n*

microsecond /mīkrō sekənd/ *n* (*symbol* μs) a measurement of time equivalent to one millionth of a second

microseism /mīkrō sīzəm/ *n* a recurrent low-level earth tremor caused by phenomena such as the force of crashing waves rather than by movement of rock masses —**microseismic** /mīkrō sízmik/ *adj* —**microseismicity** /mīkrō sīz míssəti/ *n*

microsmatic /mī kroz máttik/ *adj* having poorly developed olfactory organs [Late 19C. < MICRO- + Greek *osmē* 'smell' + *-atic* (related form of -ATE).]

microsociology /mīkrō sōssi óllәji/ *n* the branch of sociology that studies small groups and units within a larger society

microsome /mīkrōsōm/ *n* a small particle obtained after isolating a cell using centrifugal action, typically consisting of ribosomes associated with fragments of endoplasmic reticulum —**microsomal** /mīkrō sóm'l/ *adj*

microspectrophotometry /mīkrō spéktrō fə tómmətri/ *n* the use of a spectrometer to locate and study biochemical reactions by recording and analysing the colour and energy spectra produced by materials in thin body tissue slices

microsporangium /mīkrō spaw ránji əm/ (*plural* **-a** /-ji ə/) *n* a part of the reproductive structure of certain plants, especially ferns, that produces microspores. ◊ **sporangium** —**microsporangiate** *adj*

microspore /mīkrō spawr/ *n* the smaller of two kinds of spore produced by seed plants and some ferns that develops into a male gametophyte

microstructure /mīkrō strukchər/ *n* the fine structure of a material, usually only visible through a microscope and sometimes after some form of surface preparation, e.g. the etching of metal alloys —**microstructural** /mīkrō strúkchərəl/ *adj*

microsurgery /mīkrō súrjəri/ *n* surgery performed with the aid of miniaturized precision instruments, including scalpels, needles, and a specially designed optical microscope —**microsurgical** *adj*

microswitch /mīkrō swich/ *n* a very small sensitive switch that acts by the movement of a small lever and is used where rapid precise movements are required, especially in keyboards and automatic control devices

microteaching /mīkrō teeching/ *n* a training exercise used in teacher training in which a student or student teacher is video-taped during a class for subsequent analysis and evaluation

microtome /mīkrōtōm/ *n* an instrument that uses a steel blade to cut biological tissues into very thin transparent slices a few millionths of a metre thick for microscopic examination

microtomy /mī króttəmi/ *n* the process of preparing thin slices of biological tissues using a microtome, so that they can be observed under a microscope —**microtomic** /mīkrō tómmik/ *adj* —**microtomist** *n*

microtone /mīkrōtōn/ *n* a musical interval smaller than a semitone, especially a quarter tone —**microtonal** /mīkrō tón'l/ *adj* —**microtonality** /mīkrōtō nálləti/ *n* —**microtonally** *adv*

microtubule /míkrō tyoōb yool/ *n* a hollow tubular structure composed of the protein tubulin that helps to maintain the shape and movement of a living cell and the transport of material within it. ◊ **tubule** —**microtubular** *adj*

microvasculature /míkrō váskyoōləchər/ *n* a part of the circulatory system made up of the smallest vessels such as capillaries, arterioles, and venules —**microvascular** *adj*

microvillus /míkrō vílləss/ (*plural* **-li** /-lī/) *n* a microscopic hair-shaped cell that projects from the surface of the lining of the small intestine, increasing the surface area available for the absorption of nutrients. ◊ **epithelium** —**microvillar** *adj*

microvolt /míkrōvōlt/ *n* (*symbol* **μV**) a unit of electric potential or electromotive force equivalent to one millionth of a volt

microwatt /míkrō wot/ *n* (*symbol* **μW**) a measurement of power equivalent to one millionth of a watt

microwave /míkrə wayv/ *n* **1 HIGH-FREQUENCY ELECTROMAGNETIC WAVE** an electromagnetic wave whose wavelength ranges from 1.0 mm to 30 cm. Use: radar, radio transmissions, cooking or heating devices. **2 OVEN USING ELECTROMAGNETIC RADIATION** an oven that cooks or heats up food or beverages relatively quickly using high-frequency electromagnetic radiation ■ *vt* (**-waves, -waving, -waved**) **HEAT IN A MICROWAVE** to heat or cook food or beverages in a microwave —**microwavable** *adj*

microwave oven *n* HOUSEHOLD = **microwave** *n.* 2

micturate /míktyoō rayt/ (**-rates, -rating, -rated**) *vi* to urinate (*technical*) [Mid-19C. Back-formation < *micturition* 'urination' < Latin *micturire* 'want to urinate' < *mict-*, past participle of *meiere* 'urinate'.] —**micturation** /míktyoō ráysh'n/ *n*

mid /mid/ *adj* **1** being in the centre or halfway through something ○ *cut me off in mid sentence* **2** produced as a vowel with the tongue halfway between the high and low positions, e.g. in the words 'but' or 'bet' [Old English *midd* < Indo-European]

'mid /mid/, **mid** *prep* among a group [15C. Shortening of AMID.]

mid- *prefix* middle ○ *midrange* ○ *midmost* [< MID]

midafternoon /mid àaftər noōn/ *n* the part of the afternoon midway between noon and sunset —**midafternoon** *adj*

midair /mid áir/ *n* a point in the air above the ground or another surface —**midair** *adj*

Midas /mídəss/ *n* in Greek mythology, a Phrygian king who befriended Silenus, a follower of Dionysus, and was rewarded by Dionysus with the gift of making everything he touched turn into gold

Midas touch *n* the ability to make large amounts of money, often with very little apparent effort

mid-Atlantic *adj* influenced by both North America and Britain, especially in behaviour or speech

Mid-Atlantic Ridge submarine mountain range in the Atlantic Ocean, bisecting the ocean from north to south between Iceland and the Antarctic Circle. Its average height is 3,050 m/10,000 ft. Length: 15,000 km/9,300 mi.

Mid-Atlantic States *npl* = **Middle Atlantic States**

midbrain /míd brayn/ *n* the middle part of the three main divisions of either the embryonic or the adult brain in vertebrates. Technical name **mesencephalon**

midcourse /míd káwrss/ *n* the part of a missile's flight between the end of its launch and the beginning of its re-entry ■ *adj* present or occurring partway through a course or course of action

midday /mid dáy/ *n* twelve o'clock noon or the period around the middle of the day

midden /mídd'n/ *n* **1** a pile of dung or refuse **2** ARCHAEOL = **kitchen midden 3** *N England* an earth closet [14C. < N Germanic.]

middle /mídd'l/ *n* **1 MIDWAY PART OR POSITION** the part or position furthest from the sides, edges, or ends of something ○ *the middle finger* **2 PART BETWEEN BEGINNING AND END** the part between or halfway between the beginning and end of a period of time or an event ○ *in the middle of June* ○ *arrived in the middle of a diplomatic crisis* **3 INSIDE PART** the interior or central part of something ○ *in the middle of term* **4 CENTRAL PART OF BODY** the waist, stomach, or central area of the human body (*informal*) **5 VOICE EXPRESSING REFLEXIVE ACTION** the voice of verbs in some languages such as ancient Greek and Sanskrit that expresses the action of a subject on or for itself ■ *adj* **1 CENTRAL AND EQUIDISTANT FROM LIMITS** equidistant from the sides, edges, or ends of something **2 BEING HALFWAY BETWEEN BEGINNING AND END** occurring or located halfway between the start and finish of a period of time, an event, or a series ○ *in the middle years of the 19th century* **3 OCCUPYING INTERMEDIATE POSITION** situated in an intermediate position, e.g. in age or status ○ *below middle height* **4 BEING MIDWAY BETWEEN EXTREMES** lying between two extremes or opposites and, consequently, usually moderate **5 CONCERNING VOICE EXPRESSING REFLEXIVE ACTION** relating to the voice of verbs in some languages such as ancient Greek and Sanskrit that expresses the action of a subject on or for itself ■ *v* (**-dles, -dling, -dled**) **1** *vti* **PUT SOMETHING IN MIDDLE** to place something equidistant from the sides, edges, or ends of something **2** *vti* **FOLD SAIL IN HALF** to fold a sail in half or to be folded in half **3** *vt* **HIT BALL WITH MIDDLE OF BAT** to hit a cricket ball firmly with the middle of the bat [Old English *middel*] ◇ **in the middle of nowhere** in a remote location ◇ **knock somebody into the middle of next week** to hit somebody very hard (*informal*)

Middle *adj* relating to a language or literature between its early and later stages of development

middle age *n* the period in somebody's life when that person is no longer considered young, usually between 40 and 60

middle-aged *adj* **1** no longer considered young, but not yet considered old **2** characterized by the behaviour, attitudes, lifestyle, or interests considered typical of middle age, especially staidness, conventionality, or old-fashionedness

middle-aged spread, middle-age spread *n* the excess fat sometimes accumulated around the waist during middle age (*humorous*)

Middle Ages *n* the period in European history between antiquity and the Italian Renaissance, often considered to be between the end of the Roman Empire in the 5th century and the early 15th century

Middle America *n* **1** a section of the middle class in the United States considered to be politically conservative and to hold traditional social and moral values **2** GEOG = **Midwest 3** *US* the area to the south of the United States and the north of South America that includes Mexico, Central America, and sometimes the Caribbean —**Middle American** *adj, n*

Middle Atlantic States, Mid-Atlantic States *npl US* the states midway along the Atlantic coast of the United States, consisting of New York, New Jersey, and Pennsylvania, and usually Delaware and Maryland

Middleback Ranges /mídd'l bak-/ range of hills in SE South Australia. Highest peak: Mount Middleback450 m/1476 ft.

middlebreaker /mídd'l braykər/ *n* AGRIC = **lister**

middlebrow /mídd'l brow/ *n* a person who has moderate or conventional interests in cultural and intellectual matters (*informal*) [Early 20C. After HIGHBROW and LOWBROW.] —**middlebrow** *adj*

middlebuster /-bustər/ *n* AGRIC = **lister**

middle C *n* a note roughly in the middle of a piano keyboard, written in musical notation on the first ledger line below the treble staff or above the bass staff

middle class *n* the section of society between the poor and the wealthy, including business and professional people and skilled workers —**middle-class** *adj*

middle common room *n* a room in some colleges and universities where postgraduate students can meet and relax

middle distance *n* the portion of space that is farther away from a viewer than the foreground but nearer than the background, especially in a landscape painting or photograph

middle-distance *adj* relating to foot races between 400 m/440 yd and 1,500 m/one mile long

Middle Dutch *n* the form of the Dutch language spoken and written from about the 12th to the beginning of the 16th centuries AD

middle ear *n* the narrow air-filled space between the ear drum and the outer wall of the inner ear containing the three tiny bones that transmit sound vibrations

Middle Earth *n* MYTHOL = **Midgard**

Middle East *n* **1** the region stretching from the E Mediterranean to the western side of the Indian subcontinent, including Egypt, the Arabian Peninsula, Israel, Jordan, Lebanon, Syria, Turkey, Iran, and Iraq **2** formerly, the area extending from Iran to Myanmar, including Afghanistan, India, and Tibet —**Middle Eastern** *adj* —**Middle Easterner** *n*

Middle England *n* a section of the middle class in England considered to be politically conservative and to hold traditional social and moral values

Middle English *n* the form of the English language spoken and written from about the 12th to the beginning of the 16th century AD

middle finger *n* the longest finger of the human hand, next to the index finger

Middle French *n* the form of the French language spoken and written from about the 14th to the beginning of the 17th centuries AD. ◊ **Old French**

middle game *n* the middle part of a game of chess, after the opening moves and before the endgame

Middle Greek *n, adj* LANG = **medieval Greek**

middle ground *n* **1** = **middle distance 2** an intermediate position between two opposing views or factions ○ *The two parties were unable to find any middle ground.*

Middle High German *n* the form of High German spoken and written from about the 12th to the beginning of the 16th centuries AD

middle-income *adj* earning a wage or salary that is roughly the same as the average for a population

Middle Irish *n* the form of Irish Gaelic spoken and written from about the 11th to the beginning of the 15th centuries AD

Middle Kingdom *n* **1 PERIOD OF ANCIENT EGYPTIAN HISTORY** a period of Egyptian history from the late 11th dynasty, approximately 2040 BC, to the 13th dynasty, 1670 BC **2 FORMER CHINESE EMPIRE** the former Chinese Empire, so called because it was supposedly at the centre of the earth **3 CENTRAL TERRITORY OF CHINESE EMPIRE** the central territory held by most Chinese Empires, including the Huang and Yangtze river valleys, and eventually the eighteen inner provinces of China

Middle Low German *n* the form of Low German spoken and written from about the 12th to the beginning of the 16th centuries AD

middleman /mídd'l man/ (*plural* **-men** /-men/) *n* **1** a trader who buys goods from a producer and then sells them to retailers or consumers **2** a negotiator or intermediary

middle management *n* managers who are responsible for relatively small numbers of staff and are involved in the details of running an organization rather than in taking major decisions or setting policy —**middle manager** *n*

middlemost /mídd'l mōst/ *adj* = **midmost**

middle name *n* the name between a first name and a surname ◇ **be somebody's middle name** to possess a great deal of a quality, attribute, or characteristic (*informal*) ○ *Tact's my middle name.*

middle-of-the-road *adj* **1 OCCUPYING INTERMEDIATE POSITION** taking a course of action or adopting a point of view that is midway between two extremes **2 INTENDED TO HAVE BROAD MUSIC APPEAL** intended to be musically appealing to the majority of people and avoiding stylistic extremes, often to the point of blandness ■ *n* **MUSIC AIMING FOR BROAD APPEAL** music intended to appeal to many people and avoiding stylistic extremes —**middle-of-the-roader** *n*

Middle Palaeolithic *n* the period between the Lower and Upper Palaeolithic ages, from about 70,000 to 32,000 years ago

middle passage *n* the journey from W Africa across the Atlantic to the Caribbean or the Americas, undertaken by many slave ships, in former times

Middlesbrough /mídd'lzbərə/ port in NE England. Population: 147,500 (1995).

middle school *n* **1** in Great Britain, a state-run school for children between the ages of about 8 and 13 years **2** in the United States, a school for children between the ages of about 11 and 14 years, depending on the school's location. ◊ **junior high**

Middle Scots *n* the form of the Scots language written and spoken between the late 15th and the early 17th centuries

Middlesex /mídd'l seks/ former county in SE England

middle-sized adj neither very big nor very small

Middle Temple n in England, one of four legal societies of the Inns of Court in London

middle term n a term that appears in both premises of a syllogism but not in the conclusion

⚡ **middleware** /mídd'l wair/ n software that manages the connection between a client and a database

middle watch n the watch from midnight until 4:00 AM aboard a vessel

middleweight /mídd'l wayt/ n 1 PROFESSIONAL BOXER LIGHTER THAN LIGHT HEAVYWEIGHT a professional boxer weighing between 66.5 and 72.5 kg/147 and 160 lb, heavier than a welterweight but lighter than a light heavyweight 2 AMATEUR BOXER LIGHTER THAN LIGHT HEAVYWEIGHT an amateur boxer weighing between 71 and 75 kg/157 and 165 lb 3 WRESTLER OF INTERMEDIATE WEIGHT a contestant in various sports, e.g. wrestling, of approximately the same weight as a middleweight boxer

Middle Welsh n the form of the Welsh language written and spoken from about the 12th to the beginning of the 15th centuries AD

Middle West n US = Midwest —**Middle Western** adj — **Middle Westerner** n

middling /mídd'ling/ adj 1 MEDIUM, MODERATE, OR AVERAGE of average size, quantity, quality, or position 2 ORDINARY AND UNEXCEPTIONAL neither good nor bad, especially in health or mood ■ adv MODERATELY AND UNEXCEPTIONALLY in a moderate and unremarkable way (informal) ■ **middlings** npl 1 THINGS OF AVERAGE QUALITY commodities or resources, such as ore or petrol, that are of average quality, grade, or price 2 POOR-QUALITY FLOUR poor-quality flour made from coarsely ground wheat and bran (+ singular or plural verb) [Late 16C. < MID + -LING².] —**middlingly** adv

Middx abbr Middlesex

middy /mídd/ (plural -dies) n 1 MIDSHIPMAN a midshipman (informal) 2 middy, middy blouse BLOUSE WITH SAILOR COLLAR a loose blouse with a sailor collar worn by women and children 3 Aus HALF A PINT OF BEER a medium-sized beer glass, holding seven to ten ounces

Mideast /míd éest/ n US the Middle East —**Mideastern** adj —**Mideasterner** n

midfield /míd feeld/ n 1 the middle portion of a sports pitch, especially the area midway between the two penalty areas 2 the group of players who contest control of the central area of the pitch between the two penalty areas (+ singular or plural verb)

midfielder /míd feeldər/ n a football player active in the central area of a playing pitch, often both offensively and defensively

Midgard /míd gaard/, **Midgarth** /-gaarth/, **Midgarthr** /-gaarthər/ n in Norse mythology, the home of humankind, midway between Asgard and the underworld, encircled by a huge serpent and formed from the body of the giant Ymir

midge /mij/ n 1 a small slender flying insect that occurs globally, particularly in swarms near bodies of standing water, or a related biting insect that can transmit bloodborne diseases. Family: Chironomidae and Ceratopogonidae. 2 a person or animal of small stature [Old English mycg < Indo-European, probably an imitation of humming]

midget /míjjit/ n 1 OFFENSIVE TERM an offensive term for a very short person whose skeleton and features are of normal proportions 2 VERY SMALL VERSION OF a very small version of something, such as a car or boat ■ adj MINIATURE OR SMALLER THAN USUAL miniaturized or belonging to a class smaller than the ordinary size [Mid-19C. < MIDGE, literally 'little midge'.]

midgut /míd gut/ n 1 PART OF DIGESTIVE TRACT the central section of the digestive tract of a vertebrate, in which the processes of digestion and absorption take place 2 PART OF INVERTEBRATE ALIMENTARY CANAL the middle section of the alimentary canal of an invertebrate 3 PART OF EMBRYO the middle portion of the gut of an embryo that develops into most of the small intestine and part of the large intestine

Midheaven /míd hévv'n/ n the point on the apparent annual path of the Sun in the celestial sphere where the meridian is crossed, or the sign of the zodiac that contains it

midi /míddi/ (plural -is) n a skirt or coat that comes down to just below the knee or halfway down the calf [Mid-

20C. < midi- 'medium-sized', a combining form < MID after MINI- and MAXI-.]

Midi /meédi/ the South of France [French, 'midday']

Midi, Canal du /-kə nál dōō/ canal in S France, linking the Atlantic Ocean and the Mediterranean Sea

⚡ **MIDI** /míddi/ n the interface between an electronic musical instrument and a computer, used in composing and editing music. Abbr of **musical instrument digital interface**

midiron /míd ī ərn/ n in golf, a number 5, 6, 7, or 8 iron, used to give the ball a medium amount of lift

midi system n a compact hi-fi system, usually consisting of a CD-player, tuner, cassette deck, and amplifier, designed as a single unit with separate speakers

midland /mídlənd/ n the middle, inland, or interior part of a country ■ adj relating to or being in the middle or interior of a country

Midland /mídlənd/ n 1 a variety of British English spoken in the Midlands of England 2 US a variety of American English spoken in states south from New Jersey to Georgia, especially in the Appalachian and Piedmont mountains and in the Shenandoah Valley

Midlands /mídləndz/ npl region of central England (+ singular or plural verb) —**Midlander** n

midlife /míd līf/ n = middle age

midlife crisis n feelings of self-doubt and a lack of confidence experienced by some people when they become middle-aged

midline /míd līn/ n a vertical line that divides a bilaterally symmetrical animal or human body into right and left halves

Midlothian /mid lóthi ən/ council area and former county in SE Scotland

midmorning /míd máwrning/ n the middle part of the morning —**midmorning** adj

midmost /mídmōst/ adj situated at or nearest the centre of something ■ adv in the middle or midst of something [Old English midmest]

midnight /míd nīt/ n 1 twelve o'clock at night or the period around the middle of the night 2 a period of intense darkness or gloom (literary) —**midnightly** adj, adv

midnight blue adj of a very dark blue colour —**midnight blue** n

midnight sun n the sun when it is visible from within the Arctic or Antarctic circles at midnight during their respective summer months

mid-ocean ridge n a long underwater mountain range of the Atlantic, Indian, or South Pacific oceans formed from volcanic rock released during the movement of tectonic plates

midpoint /míd poynt/ n 1 the point on a line, journey, or distance that is halfway between the beginning and end 2 the point of time halfway between the beginning and end of an event, course of action, or period of time

midrange /míd raynj/ adj 1 occurring in the middle of a series, array, or range 2 covering a distance midway between a short-range and long-range trajectory

midrash /míd rash/ (plural -rashim) n the technique of interpreting or commenting on the Hebrew Scriptures

Midrash /mídraash/ (plural -rashim) n a body of Rabbinic literature consisting of commentary on and clarification of biblical texts, first compiled before 500 AD [Early 17C. < Hebrew midrāš < dāraš 'expound'.] —**midrashic** /mi dráshik/ adj

midrib /míd rib/ n the thick central vein that runs from the base of a leaf to its apex

midriff /mídrif/ n 1 MIDDLE FRONT AREA OF HUMAN BODY the area of the human body between the chest and the waist 2 DIAPHRAGM the diaphragm (dated) ■ adj 1 NEAR MIDRIFF in the area of the midriff ○ midriff bulge 2 EXPOSING MIDRIFF describes an article of clothing that exposes the midriff ○ a midriff top [Old English midhrif 'diaphragm' < midd (see MID) + hrif 'belly' (< Indo-European, 'body')]

mid-rise adj US relating to or consisting of buildings that are of moderate height, about five to ten storeys ■ n US a building of moderate height, about five to ten storeys

midsagittal /míd sájjit'l/ adj relating to or situated along an imaginary plane that passes through the midline of the body or an organ

midsection /míd seksh'n/ n the middle part of something, especially the area of the human body between the chest and waist

midship /míd ship/ adj relating to or located in the middle section of a ship or vessel ■ n the middle section of a ship or vessel

midshipman /míd shipmən/ (plural -men /-mən/) n 1 an officer in the British or other navies of a rank above naval cadet 2 US a student who is training to be a naval officer, especially at a naval academy [Late 17C. Alteration of midshipman, because originally stationed amidships.]

midships /míd ships/ adv, adj SHIPPING = amidships [Mid-19C. Shortening.]

midsize /míd sīz/, **midsized** /míd sīzd/ adj with a size midway between large and small

midst /midst/ n the middle or central part of something ■ prep amid somebody or something (literary) [15C. Alteration of earlier middes < MID.] ◇ **in the midst of** in the middle of a situation, place, event, or period of time ◇ **in our midst** among us

midstream /míd streem/ n 1 the middle part of a river or stream where the current is often very strong 2 a point after the beginning and before the end of something such as a speech or course of action —**midstream** adv

midsummer /míd súmmər/ n the period of time in the middle of summer

Midsummer Day, Midsummer's Day n the day of the summer solstice in Europe marked by Christians as the feast of St. John the Baptist. It is one of the quarter days in England, Wales, and Ireland. Date: 24 June.

midsummer madness n eccentric, foolish, or frivolous behaviour that is traditionally supposed to occur around the middle of the summer

Midsummer's Day n = Midsummer Day

midterm /míd túrm/ n 1 MIDPOINT OF TERM the middle of an academic term or a term of office 2 PERIOD MIDWAY THROUGH PREGNANCY the period halfway through a pregnancy 3 US, Can EXAM HALFWAY THROUGH ACADEMIC TERM an exam sat halfway through an academic term in North American colleges and universities (often plural) ■ adj IN MIDDLE OF TERM OF OFFICE occurring in the middle of a term of office, especially the term of a president of the United States ○ midterm elections

midtown /míd town/ n US the central area of a city between the uptown and downtown areas, especially in Manhattan

midway /míd wáy/ adv, adj 1 HALF OF THE WAY halfway between two points, parts, or places 2 HALFWAY THROUGH halfway through an event, course of action, or period of time ■ n US, Can AREA OF SIDESHOWS AT FAIR an area in a fair, carnival, or circus for sideshows and other amusements [Old English midweg]

Midway Islands /míd way-/ island group in the NW Hawaiian Islands, administered by the United States. In 1942 it was the site of an important Allied victory in World War II. Area: 5.2 sq. km/2 sq. mi.

midweek /míd week/ n the period of time in the middle of a week ■ adj, adv on a day in the middle of the week —**midweekly** adj, adv

Midweek /míd week/ n the day of Wednesday, so called by members of the Society of Friends

Midwest /míd wést/ n the northern region of the central United States east of the Rocky Mountains, generally including the states of Illinois, Indiana, Iowa, Kansas, Michigan, Minnesota, Missouri, Nebraska, Ohio, and Wisconsin —**Midwestern** adj —**Midwesterner** n

mid-wicket n in cricket, the fielder or fielding position located between square leg and mid-on, usually to the batsman's left

midwife /míd wīf/ n (plural -wives /-wīvz/) 1 SOMEBODY TRAINED TO DELIVER BABIES somebody trained to help deliver babies and offer support and advice to pregnant women 2 CREATOR a creator or producer of something new ■ vt (-wifes, -wifing or -wiving, -wifed or -wived /-wīvd/ US ASSIST IN BIRTH OF to assist in the delivery of a baby [13C. Probably < obsolete mid 'with' + WIFE 'woman'.]

midwifery /míd wiffəri/ n the technique or practice of helping to deliver babies and offering advice and support to pregnant women

midwife toad n a European toad that mates on land. The male carries a band of fertilized eggs wrapped round its back legs until they are ready to hatch. *Alytes obstetricans.*

midwinter /míd wíntər/ *n* the period in the middle of winter

midyear /míd yéer/ *n* the period in the middle of the academic, calendar, or fiscal year

mien /meen/ *n* somebody's appearance, bearing, or posture, especially facial expressions, taken as an indication of mood or character (*formal*) [Early 16C. Probably shortening of obsolete *demeine* 'demeanour' (< Old French, < *demener*; see DEMEAN).]

Mies van der Rohe /méez van dər rṓ ə/, **Ludwig** (1886–1969) German-born US architect and designer

mifepristone /mi féppri stōn/ *n* a drug that blocks the hormone progesterone, which is essential for maintaining pregnancy [Late 20C. Contraction of *aminophenol + propyne + oestradiol.*]

miff /mif/ *vt* to annoy or offend somebody (*informal*) ■ *n* an angry mood or sulk (*informal*) [Early 17C. < ?] —**miffed** *adj*

miffy /míffi/ (**-fier, -fiest**) *adj* **1** easily upset or offended (*informal disapproving*) **2** describes plants that are difficult to propagate because they require very specific environmental conditions —**miffily** *adv* —**miffiness** *n*

MiG /mig/ *n* a high-speed high-altitude fighter aircraft built in Russia [Mid-20C. Acronym < A. I. *Mikoyan* and M. I. *Gurevich*, aircraft designers.]

might[1] /mīt/ CORE MEANING: a modal verb indicating the possibility that something is true or will happen in the future ○ *She said that John might be living abroad now.* ○ *The meeting might be as early as next week.*

vi **1** used as a polite way of making suggestions and giving advice ○ *I thought we might go out tonight.* ○ *You might want to give him a ring first.* **2** used to indicate that somebody ought to do something, often when you are annoyed that the person has not done it ○ *You might at least have told me!* [Old English *mihte, meahte*, the past tense of *magan* (see MAY[1])]

SPELLCHECK Do not confuse ***might*** with ***mite***, which has a similar sound. Beware: your spellchecker will not catch this error.

might[2] /mīt/ *n* **1** great power or influence ○ *up against the might of a huge organization* **2** physical strength and determination ○ *We must push with all our might.* [Old English *miht* < Indo-European, 'to be able']

might-have-been *n* an event or outcome that could have occurred but did not

mightily /mítili/ *adv* **1** to a great extent or degree (*dated*) ○ *mightily relieved* **2** with considerable physical strength and effort

mightn't /mít'nt/ *contr* a spoken form of 'might not'

mighty /míti/ *adj* (**-ier, -iest**) **1 STRONG AND POWERFUL** of great strength and power **2 BIG AND IMPRESSIVE** very impressive in size, scope, or extent ○ *a mighty army* ■ *adv US* **VERY MUCH SO** extremely or to a great degree (*regional*) ○ *mighty fine* [Old English *mihtig* < *miht* (see MIGHT[2])] —**mightiness** *n*

migmatite /mígmə tīt/ (*plural* **-tites** *or* **-tite**) *n* a coarsely crystalline rock composed of a mixture of bands of metamorphic and igneous rocks and found in areas where high-grade metamorphic rocks are partly melted to form igneous rock [Early 20C. < Greek *migmat-*, stem of *migma* 'mixture' + -ITE[1].]

mignon /mín yon/ *adj* very delicate and pretty (*literary*) ■ *n* a small portion of prime beef, especially filet mignon [Mid-16C. < French, alteration of Old French *mignot.*]

mignonette /mínyə nét/ (*plural* **-ettes** *or* **-ette**) *n* a plant with spiky leaves. Flowers: small, fragrant, greenish-white. Native to: the Mediterranean. Genus: *Reseda.* [Early 18C. < French *mignon* 'dainty' (see MIGNON).]

~~**migrain**~~ incorrect spelling of **migraine**

migraine /mée grayn, mí-/ *n* a recurrent, throbbing, very painful headache, often affecting one side of the head and sometimes accompanied by vomiting or by distinct warning signs, including visual disturbances [14C. Via French < Greek *hēmikrania* < *hēmi-* 'half' + *kranion* 'skull'.] —**migrainous** *adj*

migrant /mígrənt/ *n* **1 SOMEBODY MOVING FROM PLACE TO PLACE** a person who moves from one place to another, often for employment or economic improvement **2 MIGRATORY ANIMAL** an animal, especially a bird, that moves from one region to another, often at specific times of the year in order to breed or avoid unsuitable weather conditions **3** *Aus* **RECENT IMMIGRANT** an immigrant, especially one who has entered the country recently [Late 17C. < Latin *migrant-*, present participle of *migrare.*] —**migrant** *adj*

ϟ **migrate** /mī gráyt/ (**-grates, -grating, -grated**) *v* **1** *vi* **MOVE FROM PLACE TO PLACE** to move from one region or country to another, often to seek work or other economic opportunities **2** *vi* **MOVE BETWEEN HABITATS** to move from one habitat or environment to another in response to seasonal changes and variations in food supply **3** *vi* **MOVE POSITION WITHIN ORGANISM** to move within an organism or substance as, e.g., cells do during the growth of an embryo **4** *vt* **MOVE BETWEEN COMPUTER SYSTEMS** to transfer a file from one computer system to another [Early 17C. < Latin *migrat-*, past participle of *migrare.*] —**migrator** *n*

migration /mī gráysh'n/ *n* **1 MOVEMENT FROM ONE PLACE TO ANOTHER** the act or process of moving from one region or country to another **2 PEOPLE OR ANIMALS MIGRATING TOGETHER** a group of people or animals that are moving together from one region or country to another **3 SHIFT OF IONS** the movement of ions under the influence of an electric field **4 MOVEMENT OF ATOMS** the movement of an atom, or a group of atoms or double bonds, from one part of a molecule to another —**migrational** *adj*

migratory /mígrətəri, mī gráytəri/, **migrative** /mígrətiv/ *adj* **1 MOVING TO ANOTHER REGION EVERY YEAR** moving as part of a bird, fish, or other animal population from one region to another every year, usually at specific times in order to breed or avoid unsuitable weather conditions **2 RELATING TO MOVEMENT FROM PLACE TO PLACE** relating to the movement of people or animals from one place to another in order to achieve better living conditions **3 NOT SETTLING DOWN** tending to wander from one region or country to another without settling down in one place for any length of time

mihrab /mée rab, méerəb/ *n* **1** a small niche in a mosque that indicates the direction of Mecca **2** a blank rectangular space in the middle of a prayer rug that faces Mecca during prayer [Early 19C. < Arabic *miḥrāb.*]

mikado /mi kaád ō/ (*plural* **-dos**) *n* formerly, a title of the Japanese emperor [Early 18C. < Japanese, 'honourable gate'.]

Mikasuki /míkə sóoki/ (*plural* **-ki** *or* **-kis**), **Miccosukee** (*plural* **-kee** *or* **-kees**), **Miccosuki** (*plural* **-ki** *or* **-kis**) *n* the Muskogean language of the Mikasuki people [Mid-20C. < the Mikasuki language, after a lake in N Florida where they first settled.] —**Mikasuki** *adj*

mike /mīk/ *n* a microphone (*informal*) ■ *vt* (**mikes, miking, miked**) to supply somebody with or transmit something through a microphone (*informal*) [Early 20C. Shortening.]

Mike /mīk/ *n* a code word used to represent the letter 'm' in international radio communications

Mi'kmaq /mík mak/ (*plural* **-maqs** *or* **-maq**), **Micmac** (*plural* **-macs** *or* **-mac**) *n* **1** a member of a group of Native North American people living in Nova Scotia, New Brunswick, Prince Edward Island, and the Gaspé Peninsula in E Canada **2** an Algonquian language spoken in E Canada. Native speakers: 3,000. [Early 18C. Via French < Mi'kmaq *migmac* 'allies'.] —**Mi'kmaq** *adj*

mikvah /mik vaá, míkvə/, **mikveh, mikve** *n* among Orthodox Jews, a ritual bath for cleansing or purification, especially before the Sabbath or following menstruation, childbirth, or contact with a dead body [Mid-19C. Via Yiddish *mikve* < Hebrew *miqweh* 'mass (of water)'.]

mil[1] /mil/ *n* **1 ONE THOUSANDTH OF INCH** a unit of linear measurement equivalent to 0.0254 mm/one thousandth of an inch, often used in measuring the diameter of wires **2 UNIT OF ANGULAR MEASUREMENT FOR ARTILLERY** a unit of measurement equivalent to the angle subtended by 1/6400th of a circumference, used in aiming artillery **3 ONE MILLILITRE** a unit of volume equivalent to one millilitre or a cubic centimetre [Early 18C. Shortening of Latin *millesimus* 'thousandth' < *mille* 'thousand'.]

ϟ **mil**[2] *abbr* **1** military **2** military organization (*in Internet addresses*) **3** militia

milady /mi láydi/ (*plural* **-dies**), **miladi** (*plural* **-dies**) *n* (*archaic or humorous*) **1** a British gentlewoman or a woman member of the aristocracy **2** a form of address for a gentlewoman or female member of the aristocracy [Late 18C. Via French < English *my lady.*]

milage *n* = **mileage**

Milan /mi lán/ city in N Italy. Population: 1,334,171 (1993). —**Milanese** /míllə néez/ *n, adj*

milch cow /mílch-/ *n* **1** a cow that produces milk (*dated*) US term **milk cow** *n.* 1 **2** a source of easily gained income (*informal*) US term **milk cow** *n.* 2 [*Milch* < Old English *-milce* 'a milking' < Germanic]

mild /mīld/ *adj* **1 NOT HARSH** not severe, or strong ○ *a mild sedative* ○ *mild disagreement* **2 GENTLE AND AMIABLE** gentle, easy-going, and slow to get angry **3 PLEASANT AND TEMPERATE** pleasant and temperate and not excessively hot or cold ○ *one of the mildest winters on record* **4 LIGHTLY FLAVOURED** lightly flavoured and not strong, hot, spicy, or bitter in taste ○ *a mild sauce* **5 NOT DANGEROUS** not serious enough to endanger life ○ *a mild earthquake* ○ *mild to moderate hypertension* **6 NOT CONTAINING HARMFUL CHEMICALS** feeling soft and gentle and not containing any chemicals that might harm the skin or clothes ○ *mild soap* ■ *n* **DRAUGHT BEER** a dark-brown draught beer with a blander taste than bitter [Old English *milde* < Indo-European, 'soft'] —**mildly** *adv* —**mildness** *n*

mildew /mil dyoo/ *n* **1 FUNGAL DISEASE OF PLANTS** a plant disease in which the parasitic fungus is visible as white or grey powdery deposits on the leaves or fruit **2 GREY OR WHITE FUNGUS** a grey or white fungus that grows on walls, paper, leather, and other similar materials in damp conditions ■ *vti* **AFFECT OR BE AFFECTED BY FUNGUS** to become affected or to affect something with a grey or white fungus [Old English *mildēaw* 'honeydew, nectar'. Ultimately < Indo-European 'honey'.] —**mildewed** *adj* —**mildewy** *adj*

mild-mannered *adj* polite and of a gentle disposition

mild steel *n* a strong steel containing a low proportion of carbon [< its being easily worked]

mile /mīl/ *n* **1 UNIT OF DISTANCE** a unit of linear measurement on land, used in English-speaking countries, equivalent to 5,280 ft or 1,760 yd or 1.6 km **2** MEASURE = **nautical mile** *n.* 1 **3 UNIT OF MEASUREMENT COMPARABLE TO MILE** a unit of distance or length used in different historical periods or in non-English-speaking countries, e.g. the Roman mile **4 RACE OVER ONE MILE** a foot race that is a mile long ■ **miles** *npl* **A LONG WAY** a considerable distance (*informal*) ○ *We're miles from anywhere.* ■ *adv* **miles EMPHASIZING DEGREE OR EXTENT OF** emphasizing how much better, longer, farther, or more difficult something is (*informal*) ○ *His car's miles better.* [Old English *mīl* < Latin *milia (passuum)* 'a thousand (paces)' < *mille* 'thousand']

mileage /mílij/, **milage** *n* **1 DISTANCE IN MILES** a distance or length measured in miles **2 NUMBER OF MILES VEHICLE HAS TRAVELLED** the total number of miles a vehicle has travelled **3 MILES VEHICLE TRAVELS ON FUEL** the total number of miles a vehicle can travel on a specified amount of fuel, such as a gallon or a litre **4 TRAVEL ALLOWANCE AT FIXED RATE** a travel allowance, usually set and paid per mile by somebody's employer **5 ADVANTAGE OR USEFULNESS OF** the amount of use, advantage, profit, or service that may be obtained from something (*informal*) ○ *attempts to wring too much emotional mileage out of a melodramatic scene*

~~**milennium**~~ incorrect spelling of **millennium**

mileometer /mī lómmitər/, **milometer** *n* a device built into the dashboard of a vehicle that records distance travelled. US term **odometer**

milepost /míl pōst/ *n* **1** a post on a racecourse one mile from the finishing line **2** *US, Can* a post by the side of a road indicating the number of miles to a certain place, or placed a mile from a similar post

miler /mílər/ *n* an athlete or horse that competes in a one-mile race

Miles /mīlz/, **Bernard, Baron** (1907–91) British stage actor and director

miles gloriosus /mée layz gláwri ṓssəss/ (*plural* **milites gloriosi** /méeli tayz gláwri ṓ sī/) *n* an arrogant, bragging, and often cowardly soldier, especially one who appears as a stock character in comedies (*literary*) [< Latin, 'boastful soldier', the title of a comedy by Plautus]

Milesian /mī léezi ən/ *n* in Irish mythology, a member of a group of people from a royal Spanish family who invaded Ireland about 1300 BC and became the ancestors of the modern Irish [Late 16C. After *Milesius*, the legendary head of the family.]

milestone /míl stōn/ *n* **1** a stone by the side of a road indicating the number of miles to a certain place **2** a significant or important event, e.g. in the history of a country or in somebody's life

Miletus /mə leétəss/ ruined ancient Ionian city in SW Asia Minor, in present-day Turkey

milfoil /míl foyl/ (*plural* **-foils** *or* **-foil**) *n* **1** = **yarrow** **2** = **water milfoil** [13C. Via Old French < Latin *mil(l)efolium* 'thousand-leaf', a translation of Greek *muriophullon*; from the plant's feathery leaves.]

Milford Haven /mílfərd háyv'n/ port in SW Wales. Population: 13,194 (1991).

Milford Sound inlet of the Tasman Sea in SW South Island, New Zealand

Milhaud /meé ō/, **Darius** (1892–1974) French composer and teacher

miliaria /mílli áiri ə/ *n* prickly heat (*technical*) [Early 19C. Via modern Latin < Latin *miliarius* (see MILIARY).] —**miliarial** *adj*

miliary /mílli əri/ *adj* **1** resembling millet seeds **2** consisting of or characterized by small nodules or lesions resembling millet seeds [Late 17C. < Latin *miliarius* < *milium* 'millet'.]

miliary fever *n* a highly infectious illness characterized by a high fever, excessive sweating, and a rash of small fluid-filled spots

miliary tuberculosis *n* an acute form of tuberculosis in which lesions resembling millet seeds occur in the affected organs after bacilli are spread by the blood from one point of infection

milieu /meél yō, meel yǿ/ (*plural* **-lieus** *or* **-lieux**) *n* the particular surroundings or environment that somebody lives in and is influenced by ○ *grew up in an artistic milieu* [Mid-19C. < French, < *mi* 'mid' (< Latin *medius*) + *lieu* 'place'.]

militant /míllitənt/ *adj* **1 AGGRESSIVE** extremely active in the defence or support of a cause, often to the point of extremism **2 INVOLVED IN FIGHTING** engaged in fighting or warfare ■ *n* **SOMEBODY AGGRESSIVE** an aggressive defender or supporter of a cause [15C. Directly or via French < Latin *militant-*, present participle of *militare* 'be a soldier' < *milit-* (see MILITARY).] —**militancy** *n* —**militantly** *adv*

Militant Tendency *n* a former Trotskyite faction of the Labour Party, active in the 1970s and 1980s

militaria /mílli táiri ə/ *n* military objects such as weapons, medals, and uniforms that are collected as a hobby or for historical interest [Mid-20C. < MILITARY.]

militarise *vt* = **militarize**

militarism /míllitərizəm/ *n* **1 PURSUIT OF MILITARY AIMS** the pursuit or celebration of military ideals **2 STRONG INFLUENCE OF MILITARY ON GOVERNMENT** a high level of influence by military personnel and ideals on the government or policies of a country or state **3 GOVERNMENT POLICY OF INVESTING IN MILITARY** a government policy of investing heavily in and strengthening the armed forces

militarist /míllitərist/ *n* **1** a zealous supporter and promoter of military ideals **2** a student of military history and strategy —**militaristic** /míllitə rístik/ *adj* —**militaristically** *adv*

militarize /míllitə rīz/ (**-rizes, -rizing, -rized, -rized**), **militarise** (**-rises, -rising, -rised, -rised**) *vt* **1 EQUIP OR TRAIN FOR WAR** to equip or train a person or group of people for war **2 CONVERT FOR MILITARY USE** to convert something such as a piece of land or a building for military use **3 PERSUADE TO SUPPORT MILITARISM** to persuade somebody to support a policy of aiding and promoting the military —**militarization** /míllitə rī záysh'n/ *n*

military /míllitəri/ *adj* **1 OF WAR OR ARMED FORCES** relating to matters of war or the armed forces **2 OF ARMY** relating to the army, especially as distinguished from the navy or air force **3 TYPICAL OF SOLDIER** characteristic of a soldier or the armed forces ■ *n* **ARMED FORCES OR ITS HIGH-RANKING OFFICERS** the armed forces or high-ranking members of the armed forces [15C. Directly or via French *militaire* < Latin *militaris* < *milit-*, stem of *miles* 'soldier'.] —**militarily** *adv* —**militariness** *n*

military academy *n* a secondary school or college that prepares students to enter the military at officer level, and that typically emphasizes rigorous discipline

military attaché *n* an officer in the armed forces who has been assigned to the official staff of an ambassador in order to gather military intelligence

military honours *npl* ceremonies or ceremonial duties performed by the armed forces on special occasions such as a royal event or a soldier's funeral

military hotel *n S Asia* a restaurant that serves meat, fish, and poultry

military-industrial complex *n US* the military and the defence industries considered as a combined influence on US foreign and economic policy

military intelligence *n* information gathered about another country's military equipment and capabilities by means of observation, exchange of information, surveillance, or spying

military law *n* the legal system, including statutes, regulations, and procedures, that applies to military personnel

military pace *n* the length of a single marching step, taken to be 76 cm/30 in in quick time

military police *n* a police force within the armed forces

military science *n* the academic study of the principles and procedures of warfare

militate /mílli tayt/ (**-tates, -tating, -tated**) *vi* to have an influence, especially a negative one, on something [Late 16C. < Latin *militat-*, past participle of *militare* 'be a soldier, wage war' < *milit-* (see MILITARY).]

USAGE militate or **mitigate**? These two often-confused words have different, mutually exclusive meanings and they function in different ways. ***Mitigate*** needs a noun object and means 'to lessen the impact or degree of seriousness of something undesirable': *A six-month suspended sentence unfairly mitigates the seriousness of the offence. There were mitigating circumstances.* ***Militate*** does not take a noun object, but is followed by a preposition, often *against*, plus a noun. It means 'to have an influence, especially a negative one, on something': *Their unfair accusations militate* [not *mitigate*] *against any conciliatory efforts on our part.*

militia /mə líshə/ *n* **1 SOLDIERS WHO ARE ALSO CIVILIANS** an army of soldiers who are civilians but take military training and can serve full-time during emergencies **2 RESERVE MILITARY FORCE** a reserve army that is not part of the regular armed forces but that can be called up in an emergency **3 UNAUTHORIZED QUASI-MILITARY GROUP** an unauthorized group of people who arm themselves and conduct quasi-military training [Late 16C. < Latin, 'military service, body of soldiers' < *milit-* (see MILITARY).]

militiaman /mə líshəmən/ (*plural* **-men** /-mən/) *n* a man who serves in a militia

militiawoman /mə líshəwŏŏmən/ (*plural* **-en** /-wimmən/) *n* a woman who serves in a militia

milium /mílli əm/ (*plural* **-a** /-li ə/) *n* a whitehead on the skin (*technical*) [Mid-19C. < Latin, 'millet'; so called from the nodule's size and shape.]

milk /milk/ *n* **1 NUTRITIOUS FLUID PRODUCED BY MAMMALS** a nutritious white fluid, rich in protein, fats, lactose, and vitamins, that women and other female mammals produce to feed their young immediately after birth **2 DAIRY PRODUCT** an opaque white fluid produced by cows, sheep, or goats and used by human beings, especially as a food **3 PLANT SAP** a white or off-white liquid from a plant, e.g. the liquid inside a coconut or the sap of certain trees **4 COSMETIC OR PHARMACEUTICAL PRODUCT** a cosmetic or pharmaceutical product that is thick and white ○ *cleansing milk* ■ *v* **1** *vti* **TAKE MILK FROM COW** to draw milk for use as a dairy product from the udder of a cow, goat, or sheep manually or by using a special machine **2** *vi* **PRODUCE MILK** to yield or supply milk (*refers to a dairy animal*) **3** *vt* **REMOVE VENOM OR SAP FROM** to remove the venom from a snake, or drain the sap from a tree **4** *vt* **STEAL IN SLOW STEADY AMOUNTS** to steal money from something such as a fund or an account in small quantities over a period of time (*informal*) **5** *vt* **EXPLOIT** to get as much benefit from something as possible, often in a calculating or unscrupulous way (*informal*) [Old English *milc* < Indo-European, 'to rub, milk']

LITERARY LINK *Under Milk Wood*, a play (1953) by Welsh poet Dylan Thomas. This play for voices, originally written for radio but occasionally presented as a stage play, describes a day in the life of a Welsh fishing village and is noted for its poetic prose, rich humour, and vivid characterization.

Milk /milk/ river in N Montana and S Alberta, Canada. Length: 1,010 km/625 mi.

milk-and-water *adj* weak or bland, especially in expression or sentiment [< the idea of dilution]

milk bar *n* a café or snack bar that specializes in milkshakes and other milk drinks

milk chocolate *n* chocolate that has been made with milk and has a sweet creamy taste

milk cow *n US* **1** AGRIC = **milch cow** *n.* 1 **2** FIN = **milch cow** *n.* 2

milker /mílkər/ *n* **1** an animal that produces milk used for human consumption, especially a cow **2** a milking machine, or somebody who milks animals, especially cows

milk fever *n* **1** mild fever that some new mothers have around the time that they begin to produce breast milk **2** a disease in cows, sheep, and goats that have recently given birth, caused by mineral depletion due to milk production

milkfish /mílk fish/ (*plural* **-fishes** *or* **-fish**) *n* a large toothless silver fish related to herring and salmon. Native to: warm waters of the Pacific and Indian oceans. *Chanos chanos*. [Early 20C. < its colour.]

milk float *n* a small, often electrically powered vehicle used for door-to-door deliveries of milk and other dairy products

milk glass *n* white or translucent whitish glass used in decorative glasswork

milking parlour, milking shed *n* a building with equipment for milking cows, usually part of a farm

milking stool *n* a short simple three-legged stool of a style formerly used when milking cows

milk leg *n* painful leg swelling that some women have following childbirth, caused by inflammation and clotting in the femoral vein

milkmaid /mílk mayd/ *n* a woman or girl who milks cows or does other jobs in a dairy

milkman /mílkmən/ (*plural* **-men** /-mən/) *n* a man who delivers or sells milk door to door

milk pudding *n* a dessert consisting of a sweetened boiled or baked mixture of milk and grain, usually rice, semolina, tapioca, or sago

milk punch *n* a drink consisting of alcoholic spirit, milk, and sometimes sugar or spices

milk round *n* **1** a regular route for door-to-door milk deliveries **2** a regular tour with frequent stops along the way, especially a tour of universities made by companies looking to recruit graduates

milk run *n* a routine trip, especially an airline's regular flight or an uneventful sortie made by a military aircraft (*informal*) [< the routine early-morning trips of milk trains]

milk shake, milkshake /mílk shayk/ *n* a cold drink made by whisking or blending milk and flavouring

milk snake *n* a white or tan nonpoisonous king snake with red, yellow, brown, or black markings. Native to: North America. Genus: *Lampropeltis*. [*Milk* < its colour]

milksop /mílk sop/ *n* a man who is regarded as weak-willed or ineffectual (*dated insult*) [14C. The original meaning was 'bread soaked in milk'.]

milk stout *n* a sweet dark beer that contains lactose and has no bitter aftertaste

milk sugar *n* BIOCHEM = **lactose** *n.* 1

milk thistle *n* **1** PLANTS = **sow thistle** **2** a thistle that has dark-green leaves streaked with white veins. Flowers: purple. Use: in herbal medicine, to treat the liver. *Silybum marianum*. [*Milk* < its milky juice]

milk tooth *n* a tooth in young mammals, including humans, that falls out in early life to be replaced by the adult tooth

milk vetch *n* a plant with seeds in pods that is thought by some to increase milk production in goats. Flowers: yellow, white, or purple. Genus: *Astragalus*.

milkweed /mílk weed/ *n* a flowering plant that secretes a milky latex and has seed pods that burst open to release silky-tufted seeds. Genus: *Asclepias*.

milkweed bug *n* a black crawling insect with red markings that feeds on the juice of the milkweed and is often used in scientific research. *Oncopeltus fasciatus*.

milkwort /mílk wurt/ *n* a plant formerly believed to increase milk production in nursing mothers. Genus: *Polygala*.

milky /mílki/ (**-ier, -iest**) *adj* **1 MILK-COLOURED** like milk in colour or consistency **2 CONTAINING MILK** full of or containing milk **3 OPAQUE** cloudy or translucent, as if milk had been added **4 LACKING COURAGE** lacking courage, strength, or steadfastness (*dated*) —**milkily** *adv* —**milkiness** *n*

Milky Way *n* the spiral galaxy to which the Earth and its solar system belong, appearing as a faint band of light in the night sky [14C. A translation of Latin *via lactea* (compare GALAXY).]

mill[1] /mil/ *n* **1 FLOUR-MAKING FACTORY** a building or group of buildings in which cereal grains are ground to make meal or flour **2 PROCESSING PLANT** a building or group of buildings used for processing raw materials and manufacturing a product such as paper, fabric, or steel **3 ROTARY PROCESSING MACHINE** a machine that processes materials, especially one that grinds, presses, or pulverizes raw materials using a rotary motion **4 SMALL DEVICE FOR GRINDING GRAINS** a small device for grinding something such as coffee, pepper, or salt into granules **5 PROCESSING MACHINE** a machine that repeats a simple manufacturing procedure, e.g. one that stamps or cuts metal **6 METAL ROLLER** a metal roller used for impressing a design on something such as textiles or bank notes **7** INDUST = **milling cutter 8** INDUST = **milling machine 9 SOMETHING WORKING REPETITIVELY OR UNTHINKINGLY** an institution, person, or process that operates in the same automatic, repetitive, or productive manner as a factory ○ *Our family is a regular rumour mill.* **10 TEDIOUS PROCESS** a slow, unpleasant, or tedious process ○ *Getting the book through the editorial mill could take months.* **11 FIGHT** a boxing match or other fist fight (*archaic slang*) ■ *vt* **1 GRIND GRAIN BY MACHINE** to grind grain or seed by machine **2 MANUFACTURE BY MACHINE** to manufacture a product such as paper or fabric from raw materials by machine **3 PROCESS MATERIALS USING ROTARY MACHINERY** to process materials using machinery that grinds, presses, or pulverizes raw materials using a rotary motion **4 SHAPE METAL BY MACHINE** to use a milling cutter or milling machine to cut, shape, or finish metals **5 PUT RIDGES ON COIN EDGE** to cut ridges or grooves into a metal object, especially the edge of a coin **6 MAKE CREAM FROTHY** to whisk or shake something, e.g. cream or chocolate, until it is foamy [Pre-12C. < late Latin *molina* < Latin *molere* 'to grind'.] —**millable** *adj* —**milled** *adj* ◇ **put somebody through the mill** to subject somebody to a difficult or unpleasant ordeal (*informal*)

LITERARY LINK ***The Mill on the Floss***, a novel (1860) by George Eliot. Set in E England in the early 19th century, it describes the intellectual and emotional development of Maggie Tulliver, the daughter of a miller. By contrasting Maggie's independent spirit with the dreary conservatism of most of her family and acquaintances, Eliot highlights the obstacles faced by women in English society at the time.

mill about, mill around *vi* to wander about aimlessly, restlessly, or in confusion

mill[2] /mil/ *n* a million pounds, or some other currency (*informal*) ○ *got over two mill from a bank job in London* [Mid-20C. Shortening of MILLION.]

mill[3] /mil/ *n* a millimetre (*informal*)

mill[4] /mil/ *n* a millilitre (*informal*)

Mill /mil/, **James** (1773–1836) British philosopher and economist

Mill, John Stuart (1806–73) British philosopher and economist

Millais /míl ay, mi láy/, **Sir John Everett** (1829–96) British painter

millboard /míl bawrd/ *n* thick paperboard used in binding books [Early 18C. Alteration of *milled board*.]

milldam /míl dam/ *n* a dam built near a mill in order to raise the water level of a stream so that the flow is strong enough to turn a millwheel

millefeuille /meel fő i, meel fő i/ (*plural* **-feuilles**) *n* a dessert or pastry consisting of several layers of puff pastry with a filling of cream and jam, topped with icing sugar or icing [Late 19C. < French, 'a thousand leaves'.]

millefiori /mílli fi áwri/ *n* decorative glassware made by cutting and arranging cross sections of fused glass rods of varied colour and thickness [Mid-19C. < Italian, 'a thousand flowers'.]

millefleurs /meel flúr/ *adj* covered with a design of small flowers or plants [Early 20C. < French, 'a thousand flowers'.]

millenarian /mílli náiri ən/, **millenary** /mi lénnəri, míllinəri/ *adj* **1 RELATING TO JESUS CHRIST'S SECOND COMING** relating to or believing in doctrines such as Jesus Christ's Second Coming, a final conflict between good and evil, or the end of the world, especially those based on the book of Revelation **2 RELATING TO FUTURE UTOPIA** relating to or expressing belief in the coming of some future utopian age **3 RELATING TO END OF WORLD** relating to or suggesting the end of the world **4 RELATING TO 1,000** relating to units of 1,000, especially 1,000 years [Mid-17C. < Latin *millenarius* < *mille* 'thousand'.] —**millenarian** *n*

millenarianism /mílli náiri ənizəm/ *n* **1 BELIEF IN JESUS CHRIST'S SECOND COMING** belief in doctrines such as Jesus Christ's Second Coming, a final conflict between good and evil, or the end of the world, especially those based on the book of Revelation **2 BELIEF IN COMING UTOPIA** belief in a future utopian age, especially one created through revolution **3 BELIEF IN END OF WORLD** belief that the end of the world is near

millenary /mi lénnəri, míllinəri/ *adj* = **millenarian** ■ *n* (*plural* **-ies**) = **millennium** *n.* 1 [Mid-16C. < Latin *millenarius* (see MILLENARIAN).] —**millenarism** /míllinərizəm/ *n*

mill end *n* either end of a roll of fabric or carpet that is finished rather than cut

~~**millenium**~~ incorrect spelling of **millennium**

millennium /mi lénni əm/ (*plural* **-ums** *or* **-a** /-ə/) *n* **1 1,000 YEARS** a period of 1,000 years, especially a period that begins or ends in a year that is a multiple of 1,000 **2 PROPHESIED RULE BY JESUS CHRIST** the thousand-year period of peace on earth that, according to one interpretation of prophecies in the book of Revelation, will follow the Second Coming of Jesus Christ **3 HOPED-FOR UTOPIAN AGE** an imagined future utopian period of joy, peace, and justice, especially one created through revolution **4 THOUSANDTH ANNIVERSARY** a thousand-year anniversary, especially the one in the year 2000 [Mid-17C. < modern Latin, < Latin *mille* 'thousand' + *annus* 'year' (see ANNUAL).] —**millennial** *adj* —**millennialism** *n* —**millennialist** *n* —**millennially** *adv*

USAGE See ***century***.

ϟ**millennium bug** *n* the problem posed by the year 2000 for computer software coding dates by using only the last two digits of each year (*informal*)

Millennium Dome *n* a large structure by the River Thames in Greenwich, London, built to celebrate the year 2000

millepede *n* INSECTS = **millipede**

millepore /mílli pawr/ *n* a coral that forms white or yellow reefs [Mid-18C. < modern Latin *Millepora* < Latin *mille* 'thousand' + *porus* 'pore' (see PORE[1]).]

miller /míllər/ *n* **1 MILL-OPERATOR** an owner, manager, or operator of a mill **2 MILLING MACHINE** a machine that mills materials **3 MOTH WITH POWDERY WINGS** any moth whose wings have a powdery appearance

Miller /míllər/, **Arthur** (*b.* 1915) US playwright

Miller, George (*b.* 1945) Australian film director

Miller, Glenn (1904–44) US bandleader and composer

Miller, Harry M. (*b.* 1934) New Zealand-born Australian entrepreneur

Miller, Henry (1891–1980) US writer

millerite /míllə rīt/ *n* a nickel sulphide mineral that forms long wiry crystals. Use: source of nickel. [Mid-19C. After W. H. *Miller* (1801–80), British mineralogist.]

miller's thumb *n* a small, flat, spiny freshwater fish. Native to: Europe, North America. Genus: *Cottus*. [< the shape of its body, alluding to the proverbial distrust of millers' methods of measurement]

millesimal /mi léssim'l/ *adj* divided by one thousand or relating to thousandths ■ *n* a thousandth part of something [Early 18C. < Latin *millesimus* 'thousandth' < *mille* 'thousand'.] —**millesimally** *adv*

millet /míllit/ *n* **1 GRAIN** the pale shiny grain of a cereal plant. Use: flour, alcoholic drinks, birdseed, fodder. **2 CEREAL PLANT** a fast-growing cereal plant grown in warm regions for its grain and for fodder. *Panicum miliaceum.* **3 GRASS PLANT** a grass grown for grain that is similar or related to millet, e.g. pearl millet [15C. Via Old French < Latin *milium*.]

Millet /mée ay/, **Jean-François** (1814–75) French painter

mill finish *n* a particularly smooth surface on paper, made by a machine

milli- *prefix* (*symbol* **m**) one thousandth (10^{-3}) ○ *milliroentgen* [< Latin < *mille* 'thousand']

milliampere /mílli ám peer, -ám pair/ *n* a unit of electric current equal to one thousandth of an ampere

milliary /mílli əri/ *adj* indicating or marking a distance of one Roman mile, measured as one thousand paces [Mid-17C. < Latin *milliarius* < *mille* 'thousand' (see MILE).]

millibar /mílli baar/ *n* a unit of atmospheric pressure equal to one thousandth of a bar

millicurie /mílli kyoori/ *n* a unit of radioactivity equal to one thousandth of a curie

millieme /meel yém/ *n* **1** a former minor unit of currency in Egypt and Sudan equal to one thousandth of a pound **2** = **millime** [Early 20C. < French *millième* (see MILLIME).]

millifarad /mílli farəd, -fa rad/ *n* a unit of electrical capacitance equal to one thousandth of a farad

milligram /mílli gram/ *n* a unit of mass and weight equal to one thousandth of a gram

millihenry /mílli henri/ (*plural* **-ries**) *n* a unit of electrical inductance equal to one thousandth of a henry

Millikan /míllikən/, **Robert Andrews** (1868–1953) US physicist

millilambert /mílli lambərt/ *n* a unit of luminance equal to one thousandth of a lambert

milliliter *n* US = **millilitre**

millilitre /mílli leetər/ *n* a unit of volume equal to one thousandth of a litre

millime /mee léem, mílleem/, **millieme** /meel yém/ *n* see table at **currency** [Mid-20C. Via French *millième* 'thousandth' < Latin *millesimus* < *mille* 'thousand'.]

millimeter *n* US = **millimetre**

millimetre /mílli meetər/ *n* a unit of length equal to one thousandth of a metre

millimole /mílli mōl/ *n* a unit used to measure the amount of a chemical substance, equal to one thousandth of a mole —**millimolar** *adj*

milline /míl līn, mil línn/ *n* **1** a unit of advertising copy equal to one column line in agate type in one million copies of a newspaper or magazine **2** COMM = **milline rate** [Late 20C. Blend of MILLION + LINE[1].]

milliner /míllinər/ *n* a designer, maker, or seller of hats for women [Mid-16C. Alteration of earlier *Milaner* 'importer of fancy fabrics and wares from Milan, Italy'.]

milline rate *n* the cost per unit of advertising copy

millinery /míllinəri/ *n* **1** hats and other accessories for women, sold by a milliner **2** the design, manufacture, or sale of women's hats

milling /mílling/ *n* the ridged edge of a coin

milling cutter *n* a rotary tool used for cutting, shaping, and finishing metal objects

milling machine *n* a machine fitted with milling cutters to cut, shape, or finish metal objects

million /míllyən/ *n* **1 THOUSAND THOUSAND** a thousand thousand (10^6). See table at **number 2 LARGE NUMBER** an unspecified very large number (*informal; often plural*) **3 MILLION UNITS OF A CURRENCY** a million units of a currency, especially pounds or dollars **4 SEVENTH DIGIT TO LEFT OF DECIMAL** the seventh digit to the left of the decimal point in the decimal number system ○ *In the number 7654321, the 7 is in the millions place.* ■ **millions** *npl* **MILLION THINGS OR PEOPLE** several million people, things, or currency units ○ *entertainment for the millions* ○ *How did he earn his millions?* [14C. Via French < obsolete Italian *millione* 'great thousand' < Latin *mille* 'thousand'.] —**million** *adj*

millionaire /míllyə náir/ *n* somebody whose net worth or income is more than one million dollars, pounds, or other unit of currency (*often before nouns*) [Early 19C. < French, where it was < *million* (see MILLION).]

millionairess /míllyə náirəss, míllyə náir ess/ *n* a wealthy woman whose net worth or income is more than one million dollars, pounds, or other unit of currency

millionth /míllyənth/ *n* see table at **number** —**millionth** *adj*

millipede /mílli peed/, **millepede** *n* a small plant-eating arthropod with a tubular body made up of segments, most of which have two pairs of legs. Class: Diplopoda. [Early 17C. < Latin *millipeda* 'woodlouse', literally 'with a thousand feet' < *ped-* 'foot' (see PEDAL[1]).]

millisecond /mílli sekənd/ *n* a unit of time equal to one thousandth of a second

millivolt /mílli vōlt/ *n* (*symbol* **mV**) a unit of electrical voltage or potential difference equal to one thousandth of a volt

milliwatt /mílli wot/ *n* (*symbol* **mW**) a unit of electrical power equal to one thousandth of a watt

millpond /míl pond/ *n* a pond created by damming a stream in order to create a flow of water to turn a millwheel

millrace /míll rayss/ n 1 the stream of water that flows through a millwheel, making it turn 2 a channel that directs water to and from a millwheel

millrun /míll run/ n 1 = **millrace** 2 a quantity or quality of mineral yielded by a millrun test 3 a test to determine the quality of a mineral or the mineral content of an ore

Mills /milz/, **Sir John** (b. 1908) British actor

Mills and Boon /mílz ənd boõn/ n tdmk a trademark for popular romantic fiction published by the firm of Mills and Boon

Mills bomb n an oval hand grenade [Early 20C. After the English engineer Sir William Mills (1856–1932).]

millstone /míl stōn/ n 1 either of two large circular stones used to grind grain in a mill 2 a great burden or responsibility

millstream /míl streem/ n 1 a stream from which the water turns a millwheel 2 = **millrace** n. 1

millwheel /míl weel/ n a wheel that powers a mill, typically turned by a flow of water

millwright /míl rīt/ n a designer, builder, or maintainer of mills or mill machinery

Milne /miln/, **A. A.** (1882–1956) British writer. Full name **Alan Alexander Milne**

milo /mílō/ (plural **-los**) n a variety of sorghum grain that resembles millet, known for growing early and resisting drought [Late 19C. < ?]

milometer n = **mileometer**

milord /mi láwrd/ n a form of address for a gentleman or member of the aristocracy [Late 16C. Via French < English my lord.]

Mílos ♦ Melos

Milosevic, Milošević, **Slobodan** (b. 1941) Yugoslavian president of Serbia (1989–97) and the Federal Republic of Yugoslavia (1997–2000)

Miłosz /meé losh, meé wosh/, **Czesław** (b. 1911) Lithuanian-born US writer

Milstein /míl stīn/, **Nathan** (1904–92) Russian-born US violinist

milt /milt/ n 1 the semen and seminal fluid of a fish 2 the testis or sperm duct of a fish [Old English milte 'spleen']

milter /míltər/ n a fertile male fish during the mating season

Milton /míltən/, **John** (1608–74) English poet —**Miltonian** /mil tōni ən/ adj —**Miltonic** /mil tónnik/ adj

Milton Keynes /míltən keénz/ town in S England. Population: 192,900 (1995).

Milwaukee /mil wáwki/ city in SE Wisconsin, on Lake Michigan. Population: 578,364 (1998 estimate). —**Milwaukeean** /-i ən/, n

mim /mim/ adj Scotland excessively or affectedly shy or prim [Late 16C. An imitation of the gesture of pursing the lips.]

Mimas /mí mass, míməss/ n one of the satellites of Saturn, the nearest to the planet

mime /mīm/ n 1 **ACTING USING ONLY GESTURE AND ACTION** a style of performance in which people act out situations or portray characters using only gesture and action (often before nouns) 2 **mime, mime artist PERFORMER WHO USES MIME** a performer who relies on gesture, facial expression, and action rather than using the voice 3 **THEATRICAL PERFORMANCE IN MIME** a theatrical piece performed with gesture, facial expression, and action rather than with words 4 **ANCIENT FARCE** in ancient Greek and Roman theatre, a lewd comedy including dialogue, dance, and gesture ■ vti (**mimes, miming, mimed**) 1 **EXPRESS SOMETHING IN MIME** to express something or act it out using gestures and facial expressions only 2 **MOUTH WORDS** to mouth the words to a song silently [Early 17C. Via Latin mimus < Greek mimos 'imitator, mimic'.] —**mimer** n

mimeograph /mímmi ə graaf, -graf/ n 1 **COPYING MACHINE** a machine that prints copies onto paper from an inked stencil rotated on a cylinder across the pages 2 **MIMEOGRAPHED COPY** a copy made on a mimeograph ■ vt **MAKE COPIES USING MIMEOGRAPH** to make a copy of a document using a mimeograph [Late 19C. Originally a trademark < Greek mimeisthai (see MIMESIS) + -GRAPH.]

mimesis /mi meéssiss, mī-/ n 1 **ART'S IMITATION OF LIFE** the imitation of life or nature in the techniques and subject matter of art and literature 2 BIOL = **mimicry** n. 2 3 **DISEASE SYMPTOMS IN HEALTHY PERSON** the occurrence of a disease's symptoms in somebody who does not have the disease,

often psychosomatically caused 4 **RHETORICAL DEVICE** the rhetorical use of what somebody else might have said [Mid-16C. < Greek mimesis < mimeisthai 'imitate' < mimos 'mime'.]

mimetic /mi méttik, mī-/, **mimetical** /-méttik'l/ adj 1 imitating something, or relating to imitation, e.g. in artistic or literary mimesis 2 relating to mimicry in animals and plants [Mid-17C. < Greek mimētikos < mimēsis (see MIMESIS).] —**mimetically** adv

mimic /mímmik/ vt (**-ics, -icking, -icked**) 1 **MOCK THROUGH IMITATION** to make fun of somebody by imitating him or her in an exaggerated way 2 **IMITATE** to imitate somebody, or copy somebody's voice, gestures, or appearance 3 **COPY** to resemble something in a way that seems like a deliberate copy ○ houses with façades that mimic the Tudor style 4 **RESEMBLE OTHER SPECIES** to take on the appearance of another plant or animal, e.g. to discourage predators ■ n **IMITATOR** somebody who imitates others, especially for comic effect ■ adj 1 **RELATING TO MIMICRY** relating to mime, mimicry, or imitation 2 **SIMULATED** simulated or pretend (literary) 3 **RESEMBLING** imitating or resembling something (literary) [Late 16C. Via Latin mimicus < Greek mimikos < mimos (see MIME).] —**mimicker** n

SYNONYMS See **imitate**.

mimicry /mímmikri/ n 1 **ART OF IMITATION** the imitating of other people's voices, gestures, or appearance, often for comic effect 2 **SIMILARITY OF APPEARANCE IN NATURE** a plant's or animal's resemblance to another species or to a feature of its natural surroundings, evolved as protection from predators 3 **BIRD CALL IMITATION** the ability of some birds to imitate the songs of other species and use them in their own repertoire

miminy-piminy adj = **niminy-piminy** [Early 19C. Alteration of NIMINY-PIMINY.]

Mimir /meé meer/ n in Norse mythology, the god of wisdom, a giant water demon who was said to reside at and drink from the well of wisdom at Yggdrasil

mimosa /mi mṓzə, -mṓssə/ n 1 a tree or bush whose leaves are sensitive to touch. Flowers: white, yellow, or pink, in globular clusters. Native to: warm regions. Genus: Mimosa. 2 TREES = **silk tree** [Mid-18C. < modern Latin < Latin mimus 'imitator' (see MIME), because its leaves seem to flinch when touched, mimicking a recoiling animal.]

mimulus /mímmyoõləss/ n (plural **-lus**) a plant that grows in a number of varieties with yellow or red flowers. Native to: temperate climates. Genus: Mimulus. US term **monkey flower** [Mid-18C. < modern Latin, 'little mime' < Latin mimus (see MIME).]

min /min/ n a minute or a short while (informal) [Late 19C. Shortening of MINUTE.]

min. abbr 1 mineralogical 2 mineralogy 3 minim 4 minimum 5 US minister 6 minor 7 minute[1]

Min. abbr 1 Minister 2 Ministry

Minamata disease /mínnə maátə-/ n a severe degenerative disease of the nervous system caused by mercury contamination, especially from eating mercury-tainted seafood [Mid-20C. After Minamata, a town in Japan.]

Minamoto Yoritomo /mínnəmōtō yórri tṓmō/ (1147–99) Japanese leader

Minaret

minaret /mínnə ret, mínnə rét/ n a tall slender tower attached to a mosque, from which the muezzin calls the

faithful to prayer [Late 17C. Via French and Turkish < Arabic manāra 'lighthouse, minaret'.]

Minas Basin /mínəss-/ tidal inlet on the coast of Nova Scotia, SE Canada. Length: 80 km/50 mi.

Minas Gerais /meénəss zhə ríss/ state in E Brazil. Capital: Belo Horizonte. Population: 15,731,961 (1991). Area: 588,383 sq. km/227,176 sq. mi.

minatory /mínnətəri/, **minatorial** /mínnə táwri əl/ adj menacing or threatening (formal) [Mid-16C. < late Latin minatorius < Latin minari 'threaten' (see MENACE).] —**minatorially** /mínnə táwri əli/ adv —**minatorily** /mínnə táwrəli/ adv

minbar /mín baar/, **mimbar** /mím-/ n a pulpit in a mosque from which the sermon is delivered [Mid-19C. < Arabic, < nabara 'raise'.]

mince /minss/ v (**minces, mincing, minced**) 1 **SHRED FOOD** to chop or grind meat or other food into very small pieces. US term **grind** v. 4 2 vti **WALK DAINTILY** to walk with small light steps in an affectedly dainty way 3 vti **SPEAK DAINTILY** to speak, or say something, in an affectedly dainty way 4 vt **USE TACT** to use words or deal with matters delicately, so as not to offend or upset others (in negatives) ○ She did not mince her words. ■ n **FINELY SHREDDED MEAT** finely shredded or ground meat, especially beef [14C. < Old French mincier < minutus (see MINUTE[1]).] —**mincer** n

mincemeat /mínss meet/ n 1 a mixture of spiced and finely chopped fruits, such as apples and raisins, usually cooked in pies 2 minced meat [Mid-17C. Alteration of minced meat.] ◇ **make mincemeat of somebody** or **something** to defeat somebody or something thoroughly (informal)

mince pie n an individual pie filled with mincemeat and served hot or cold, especially as a Christmas speciality

Minch /minch/, **Minches** /mínchiz/ channel of the Atlantic Ocean separating the Outer Hebrides from NW Scotland. It is divided into North Minch and Little Minch.

Mincha /mínkhə, mín khaa/, **Minchah** n a daily Jewish prayer said in the afternoon [Early 19C. < Hebrew minḥāh 'offering'.]

Minches = **Minch**

Mincho /mín chō, mínchō/ (1352–1431) Japanese artist and Buddhist priest

mincing /mínssing/ adj affectedly dainty or prim —**mincingly** adv

mind /mīnd/ n 1 **SEAT OF THOUGHT AND MEMORY** the centre of consciousness that generates thoughts, feelings, ideas, and perceptions and stores knowledge and memories 2 **THINKING CAPACITY** the capacity to think, understand, and reason ○ has a logical mind 3 **CONCENTRATION** concentration, or the ability to concentrate ○ My mind was wandering. 4 **WAY OF THINKING** an opinion or personal way of thinking about something ○ I've changed my mind about going with you. 5 **STATE OF THOUGHT OR FEELING** the state of thought or feeling that is regarded as normal ○ felt I was going out of my mind 6 **DESIRE** the desire or intention to act or behave in a specified way ○ After such insults, I had a mind to leave right then. 7 **INTELLECTUAL PERSON** somebody considered in terms of his or her intellect or intelligence ○ Einstein was one of the greatest minds of the modern era. 8 **GENERAL TYPE OF PERSON** a pattern of thinking or feeling that is typical of a particular group ○ Who knows what goes through the criminal mind? 9 **NONMATERIAL THINGS** in the philosophy of Descartes, all things that are not matter ■ v 1 vt **PAY ATTENTION TO** to pay attention to something, especially so as to avoid danger or an accident ○ Mind your step! 2 vt **CONTROL** to remain aware of the need to control something 3 vti **OBJECT TO** to object to somebody or something ○ Do you mind if we leave early? 4 vt **TEMPORARILY WATCH OVER** to watch over and look after somebody or something, usually for a short time ○ Will you mind the dog over the weekend? 5 vt **OBEY** to listen to and obey somebody ○ Be sure to mind your father while I'm away. 6 vt **REMEMBER** to remember something ○ Mind what I told you. 7 vt Scotland, US **REMIND** to remind somebody of or about something (regional) 8 vti US **TAKE NOTE OF** to notice or perceive something (regional) ○ Mind the new detour signs or you'll get lost. [Old English gemynd. Ultimately < Indo-European 'to think'.] ◇ **bring something to mind** to remind somebody of something ○ It brings to mind those horse-drawn carts they used to have. ◇ **call something to mind** to remember something ○ I can't quite call to mind the exact date they left. ◇ **do you mind?** used to show that you object to something somebody is doing (informal) ◇ **have it in mind to do something** to intend to do something ◇ **have somebody** *or* **something in mind** to be thinking of somebody or something ◇ **keep something in mind** to remember something because it might be useful later ◇ **mind you** used to qualify something you have just said (*informal*) ◇ **speak your mind** to speak frankly and forthrightly

mind out *vi* to avoid something by keeping watch or being careful

mind-altering *adj* changing perceptions, moods, or thought patterns

Mindanao /mìndə nów/ island in S Philippines. Population: 14,536,000 (1990). Area: 94,630 sq. km/36,540 sq. mi.

mind-bending *adj* **1** mentally overwhelming, e.g. because of great size or complexity (*informal*) **2** changing perceptions, moods, or thought patterns (*dated informal*) —**mind-bender** *n* —**mind-bendingly** *adv*

mind-blowing *adj* (*informal*) **1** extremely exciting, surprising, or shocking **2** changing perceptions, moods, or thought patterns —**mind-blower** *n* —**mind-blowingly** *adv*

mind-body problem *n* the philosophical question of whether the mind is part of the body or separate from it, first formulated as a problem by the French philosopher René Descartes

mind-boggling *adj* mentally overwhelming, e.g. because of great size or complexity (*informal*) —**mind-bogglingly** *adv*

mind candy *n US* something that is entertaining but not intellectually demanding (*slang*) [Late 20C]

minded /mīndid/ *adj* inclined to do a particular thing or act in a particular way

minder /mīndər/ *n* **1 CHILD MINDER** a child minder **2 BODYGUARD** a bodyguard or assistant who accompanies and protects a public figure, celebrity, or criminal (*informal*) **3 ASSISTANT** a public-relations assistant to someone in public life (*informal*)

mind-expanding *adj* **1** changing perceptions, moods, or thought patterns **2** expanding knowledge and awareness

mindful /mīndf'l/ *adj* fully aware of something ○ *was mindful of the difficulties that lay ahead* —**mindfully** *adv* —**mindfulness** *n*

SYNONYMS See ***aware***.

mind game *n* a psychologically manipulative and deceptive practice intended to deceive or confuse somebody (*informal*)

mindless /mīndləss/ *adj* **1 BORING** uninteresting as a result of requiring little mental effort **2 PURPOSELESS** having no apparent purpose or rational cause **3 UNCONCERNED** not careful or concerned —**mindlessly** *adv* —**mindlessness** *n*

mind-numbing *adj* inspiring no interest or thought, especially because of dullness or repetitiveness —**mind-numbingly** *adv*

Mindoro /min dóròʊ/ island in W Philippines. Population: 282,593. Area: 9,738 sq. km/3,760 sq. mi.

mind-reader *n* a person who can sense what others think without being told —**mind-reading** *n*

mindscape /mīnd skayp/ *n* **1** a mental scene constructed from memory or imagination **2** an artistic representation of a mental scene constructed from memory or imagination [< MIND, modelled on LANDSCAPE]

mindset /mīnd set/ *n* a set of beliefs or a way of thinking that determine somebody's behaviour and outlook

mind's eye *n* the mind as a place where visual images are conjured up from memory or imagination ○ *I can see in my mind's eye how the house will look after the renovations.*

mine[1] /mīn/ *n* **1 HOLE IN EARTH FOR EXTRACTING MINERALS** an excavated area from which minerals, often in the form of ore, are extracted **2 MINERAL-EXCAVATING BUSINESS** the industrial and commercial buildings, machinery, and personnel used to work a mine **3 MINERAL DEPOSIT** an area within or on the surface of the earth where there is a deposit of ore, minerals, or precious stones **4 SOURCE** a rich source of something, especially information **5 HIDDEN EXPLOSIVE** an explosive device that is concealed underground or underwater to be detonated by nearby people or vehicles **6 TUNNEL UNDER ENEMY TERRITORY** a tunnel dug under enemy territory in order to gain entry, undermine fortifications, or lay explosives **7 INSECT BURROW** a tunnel made by a burrowing insect or larva, especially in a plant leaf ■ *v* (**mines, mining, mined**) **1** *vti* **REMOVE MINERALS** to extract minerals from the earth **2** *vt* **LAY EXPLOSIVE MINES IN** to place mines throughout an area of ground or water **3** *vt* **DIG TUNNEL BENEATH** to dig a tunnel under the surface of the earth **4** *vt* **MAKE USE OF RESOURCE** to make use of a particular resource ○ *Generations of scholars mined these archives.* [14C. Via Old French < assumed Vulgar Latin *mina*.] —**minable** *adj*

mine[2] /mīn/ *pron* refers to something that belongs or relates to the speaker or writer ○ *He put on his coat, and told me to put mine on too.* ○ *She was a friend of mine.* [Old English *min* < Indo-European, 'me']

mine detector *n* an instrument used for finding explosive mines hidden under the ground or in water

mine dump *n S Africa* a heap of waste material from mines, especially gold mines, that looks like a hill

minefield /mīn feeld/ *n* **1** an area of land or sea in which explosive mines have been placed **2** a situation in which great care is needed to avoid the many hazards that exist

minelayer /mīn layər/ *n* a ship fitted with equipment for laying explosive mines under water

miner /mīnər/ *n* **1 MINEWORKER** a worker in a mine **2 MINERAL-EXTRACTING MACHINE** a machine that extracts minerals, especially coal, from the ground **3** INSECTS = **leaf miner** **4** *Aus* **HONEY-EATER BIRD** a bird of the honey-eater family. Genus: *Manorina*. **5 SOMEBODY LAYING EXPLOSIVE MINES** somebody whose task is to place and set explosive mines

SPELLCHECK Do not confuse ***miner*** with ***minor***, which has a similar sound. Beware: your spellchecker will not catch this error.

mineral /mínnərəl/ *n* **1 INORGANIC SUBSTANCE IN NATURE** a substance that occurs naturally in rocks and in the ground and has its own characteristic appearance and chemical composition **2 MINED SUBSTANCE** any naturally occurring substance that is mined or extracted from the ground **3 INORGANIC NUTRITIVE SUBSTANCE** an inorganic substance that must be ingested by animals or plants in order to remain healthy **4 SOFT DRINK** a soft drink (*dated; usally plural*) [15C. Via medieval Latin *minerale* < Old French *miniere* 'mine' < *mine* (see MINE[1]).] —**mineral** *adj*

mineralize /mínnərə līz/ (**-izes, -izing, -ized**), **mineralise** (**-ises, -ising, -ised**) *v* **1** *vt* to impregnate something, e.g. water or organic matter, with minerals **2** *vti* to transform organic matter into a mineral, as happens in petrification, or to be transformed in this way —**mineralizable** *adj* —**mineralization** /mínnərə lī záysh'n/ *n*

mineralocorticoid /mínnərəlō káwrti koyd/ *n* a hormone (**corticosteroid**), e.g. aldosterone, that controls electrolyte and fluid balance in the body and is secreted by the adrenal cortex [Mid-20C. < MINERAL + CORTICOSTEROID.]

mineralogy /mínnə rálləji/ (*plural* **-gies**) *n* **1** the scientific study of minerals and how to classify, distinguish, and locate them **2** a profile of an area's mineral deposits —**mineralogical** /mínnərə lójjik'l/ *adj* —**mineralogically** *adv* —**mineralogist** *n*

mineral oil *n* **1** *US* = **liquid paraffin** **2** any oil obtained from minerals, especially from petroleum

mineral spring *n* a spring whose water has a high mineral or gas content

mineral tar *n* CHEM = **maltha**

mineral water *n* drinkable water with a high mineral salt or gas content, either obtained from a mineral spring or with minerals added

mineral wax *n* wax made from a mineral, especially a hydrocarbon wax (**ozocerite**) found in veins in sandstone

mineral wool *n* a lightweight fibrous material made from slag or glass. Use: insulation, packing material, filters.

Minerva /mi núrvə/ *n* in Roman mythology, the goddess of wisdom and patron of arts, trade, and the art of war, who was born fully armed from the head of Jupiter

mineshaft /mīn shaaft/ *n* a nearly vertical passageway that provides access or ventilation to an underground mine

minestrone /mínni strṓni/ *n* an Italian vegetable soup [Late 19C. < Italian, < Latin *ministrare* 'serve' < *minister* 'servant' (see MINISTER).]

minesweeper /mīn sweepər/ *n* a ship fitted with equipment for detecting and clearing underwater explosive mines

mineworker /mīn wurkər/ *n* a worker in a mine

Ming /ming/ *n* the Chinese dynasty that ruled from 1364 to 1644, under which arts, trade, and scholarship were greatly developed (*often before nouns*) [Late 18C. < Chinese, 'bright, clear'.]

ϟ **MING** *abbr* mailing (*in e-mails*)

minge /minj/ *n* (*taboo*) **1** a highly offensive term for a woman's genitals **2** a highly offensive term for women collectively [Late 19C. < ?]

minging /mínging/ *adj* unattractive or unpleasant (*slang*) [< ?]

mingle /míng g'l/ (**-gles, -gling, -gled**) *v* **1** *vti* to mix, or mix ingredients, together gently or gradually ○ *Heat gently to allow the flavours to mingle.* **2** *vi* to circulate among a group of people, e.g. guests at a party [15C. Alteration of obsolete *menglen* 'keep mixing' < Old English *mengan* 'to mix'.]

ming tree *n* **1** an evergreen tree used for bonsai, usually in a flat-topped asymmetrical arrangement **2** an artificial bonsai tree [*Ming* < ?]

Mingus /míng gəss/, **Charles** (1922–79) US double bassist and jazz composer

mingy /mínji/ (**-gier, -giest**) *adj* (*informal*) **1** mean or stingy **2** extremely small, ungenerous, or stingy [Early 20C. < ?]

mini /mínni/ *n* something that is small compared to other things of its type, especially a minicomputer or a miniskirt (*informal*) [Mid-20C. < MINI-.]

mini- *prefix* small, short, miniature ○ *ministroke* [Shortening of MINIATURE]

miniature /mínnichər/ *n* **1 SMALLER VERSION** a smaller-than-usual version of something, e.g. a very small model or a smaller version of a particular breed of animal **2 TINY PAINTING** a very small, detailed, and well-finished painting, especially a portrait made to fit inside a locket or other piece of jewellery **3 PAINTING OF MINIATURES** the art of painting miniatures **4 SMALL BOTTLE OF SPIRITS** a small bottle of alcoholic spirits, containing one or two measures only **5 ILLUMINATED MANUSCRIPT ILLUSTRATION** a small picture or decorative initial in an illuminated manuscript ■ *adj* **SMALLER THAN USUAL** smaller in size or scale than others of its type [Late 16C. Via Italian *miniatura* 'illumination' < Latin *minium* 'red lead'.] ◇ **in miniature** on a small scale

miniature golf *n* a novelty version of golf played with a putter on a very small course with obstacles such as tunnels and bridges for the ball to avoid or go through

miniaturist /mínnichərist/ *n* an artist who paints miniatures or small pictures, e.g. in illuminated manuscripts

miniaturize /mínnichə rīz/ (**-izes, -izing, -ized**), **miniaturise** (**-ises, -ising, -ised**) *vt* to make a version of something in a much smaller size or on a greatly reduced scale —**miniaturization** /mínnichə rī záysh'n/ *n*

minibar /mínni baar/ *n* a small refrigerator in a hotel room stocked with alcoholic beverages and often also with soft drinks and snacks

mini-blind *n US* a venetian blind with narrow slits

minibreak /mínni brayk/ *n* a point won against the serve in a tie-break in a tennis match (*informal*)

minibus /mínni buss/ *n* a small bus for carrying around 10 to 15 passengers, usually on short journeys

minicab /mínni kab/ *n* an ordinary car used as a taxi, responding to telephone calls but not generally cruising the streets for business

minicompact /mínni kóm pakt/ *n* a passenger vehicle smaller than a subcompact in size

ϟ **minicomputer** /mínni kəm pyootər/ *n* a computer of a size, speed, and capacity intermediate between a standard personal computer and a mainframe

minidress /mínni dress/ *n* a dress with a hemline above the knee

Minié ball /mínni ay-/ *n* a bullet with a cone-shaped head and a hollow base that expands when fired, used in muzzle-loading rifles of the 19th century [Mid-19C. After Claude-Étienne *Minié* (1804–79), French army officer.]

minify /mínni fī/ (**-fies, -fying, -fied**) *vt* to understate or reduce the size or importance of something [Late 17C. Directly or via medieval Latin < Latin *minimus* 'least' after MAGNIFY.] —**minification** /mínnifi káysh'n/ *n*

minikin /mínnikin/ *adj* small and delicate (*archaic*) [Mid-16C. < Dutch *minneken* 'darling' < *minne* 'love'.]

minim /mínnim/ *n* 1 MUSICAL NOTE a note with the time value of half a semibreve or two crotchets. US term **half note** 2 UNIT OF FLUID MEASURE a unit of fluid measure equal to one sixtieth of a fluid drachm, 0.0616 millilitres or approximately one drop 3 PEN-STROKE a downward vertical stroke of the pen in handwriting [15C. Directly or via medieval Latin *minimus* < Latin 'least'.]

minima plural of **minimum**

minimal /mínnim'l/ *adj* 1 VERY SMALL very small in amount or extent 2 SMALLEST POSSIBLE smallest possible in amount or least possible in extent 3 **minimal, Minimal** RELATING TO MINIMALISM relating to or displaying attributes associated with minimalism [Mid-17C. < Latin *minimus* 'least'.] —**minimality** /minni mállәti/ *n* —**minimally** *adv*

USAGE Strictly speaking, ***minimal*** means 'smallest or least possible', just as *minimize* means 'to reduce something to the lowest possible amount or degree'. Often, however, these words are used more generally: *a minimal amount of noise* may simply be the least amount of noise conveniently possible to make, rather than none at all. If the word is to retain any sense of being a superlative, it should not be used with modifiers such as *rather, somewhat,* and *slightly. Small, limited, reduced,* and *as little as possible* are all suitable alternatives to overextending ***minimal***; and *diminish, lessen,* and *reduce* do the job that *minimize* is sometimes inappropriately asked to do.

minimal art *n* 1 ARTS = **minimalism** *n.* 1 2 minimalist works of art —**minimal artist** *n*

minimalise *vt* = **minimalize**

minimalism /mínnimә lizәm/ *n* 1 simplicity in artwork, design, interior design, or literature, achieved by using a few very simple elements to maximum effect 2 a trend in music towards simplicity of rhythm and tone, including sustained or repeated rhythmic and melodic patterns resulting in a hypnotic effect

minimalist /mínnimәlist/ (*plural* **minimalists** *or* **Minimalists**) *n* 1 **minimalist, Minimalist** somebody whose works of art, literature, or music display the simplicity associated with minimalism 2 an advocate of restricting the power and goals of something, especially somebody who wishes to limit the role of government

Minimalist /mínnәmәlist/, **minimalist** *n* POL = **Menshevik** [Early 20C. Translation of Russian *men'shevik*.]

minimalize /mínnimә līz/, **minimalise** *vt* to reduce something to the minimum —**minimalization** /mínnimә lī záysh'n/ *n*

minimal pair *n* in linguistics, a pair of words or other linguistic expressions that are the same except for one sound, e.g. 'bit' and 'pit'

minimax /mínnimaks/ *n* the lowest of a set of maximum values ■ *adj* describes options or strategies designed to minimize the risk of sustaining maximum loss in any situation that involves conflict or competition [Mid-20C. < MINIMUM + MAXIMUM.]

minimill /mínni mil/ *n US* a small mill, especially a steel mill that processes scrap metal

ϟ **minimize** /mínni mīz/ (**-mizes, -mizing, -mized**), **minimise** (**-mises, -mising, -mised**) *vt* 1 REDUCE SOMETHING TO MINIMUM to reduce something to the lowest possible amount or degree 2 UNDERRATE to play down the extent or seriousness of something 3 MAKE IMAGE SMALLER to reduce the size of a computer image —**minimization** /mínni mī záysh'n/ *n* —**minimizer** *n*

USAGE See ***minimal***.

minimum /mínnimәm/ *n* (*plural* **-mums** *or* **-ma** /-mә/) 1 LOWEST POSSIBLE DEGREE the lowest possible amount or degree of something 2 LOWEST RECORDED DEGREE the lowest recorded amount or degree of something 3 LOWEST PERMISSIBLE DEGREE the lowest amount or degree of something permitted by law, e.g. the lowest speed on a road or the youngest age at which something can be done legally 4 LOWEST NUMBER the lowest number in a finite set 5 FUNCTION'S LOWEST VALUE the smallest value of a continuous function over a particular interval ■ *adj* LOWEST ALLOWED lowest possible, recorded, or allowed [Mid-17C. < Latin, < *minimus* 'least'.]

minimum lending rate *n* the official lowest interest rate at which the Bank of England formerly lent to discount houses, replaced by the base rate in 1981

minimum-security *adj* with security measures appropriate to inmates or patients who are not considered dangerous or who are not likely to try to escape

minimum wage *n* the lowest rate of pay allowed by law or contract, either in general or for a certain type of work

minimus /mínnimәss/ *n* (*plural* **-mi** /-mī/) a very small or insignificant person (*archaic*) ■ *adj* a word sometimes placed after the surname of the youngest of several school pupils with the same surname, especially formerly in public schools (*dated*) [Late 16C. From Latin, 'least'.]

mining /míning/ *n* 1 the process or business of removing minerals from the earth 2 the process of laying explosive mines

minion /mínnyәn/ *n* 1 a servile or slavish follower of somebody generally regarded as important 2 a servant or enslaved person (*archaic or literary*) [Early 16C. < French *mignon* 'darling' (see MIGNON).]

minipill /mínni pil/ *n* an oral contraceptive that contains progesterone but not oestrogen

mini roundabout *n* a small traffic roundabout at junctions of lesser roads, often no more than a white disc painted on the road surface

miniseries /mínni seeriz/ (*plural* **-ries**) *n* a short series of television programmes, often a serialized fictional story, usually broadcast on consecutive nights

miniskirt /mínni skurt/ *n* a skirt with a hemline well above the knee

minister /mínnistәr/ *n* 1 MEMBER OF CLERGY a member of the clergy of a Christian, especially Protestant, church 2 SENIOR POLITICIAN a senior politician who heads a government department, especially in the parliamentary system of government 3 DIPLOMAT RANKED UNDER AMBASSADOR a diplomat representing a country, especially of a rank below ambassador 4 HEAD OF ROMAN CATHOLIC ORDER the superior in some orders in the Roman Catholic Church 5 SPIRITUAL ADVISER a person who sees to the spiritual needs of others 6 BUSINESS REPRESENTATIVE somebody's agent or representative (*formal or literary*) ■ *v* 1 *vi* GIVE HELP to give help to somebody in need (*formal*) 2 *vi* DO RELIGIOUS MINISTER'S WORK to perform the duties of a member of the clergy 3 *vt* GIVE to administer something, e.g. aid, medicine, or a sacrament (*archaic*) [13C. Via Old French < Latin, 'servant'.] —**ministership** *n*

ministerial /mínni stéeri әl/ *adj* 1 RELATING TO CLERGY relating to a religious minister 2 RELATING TO GOVERNMENT MINISTER relating to a government minister or the minister's department 3 REQUIRING FOLLOWING OF INSTRUCTIONS allowing no personal discretion, only the strict following of law 4 INSTRUMENTAL playing an important part in achieving something (*formal*) 5 **ministerial, Ministerial** WITH GOVERNMENT supporting the government rather than the opposition —**ministerially** *adv*

ministerialist /mínni stéeri әlist/, **Ministerialist** *n* a person who sides with the government against the opposition

Minister of State *n* an assistant minister in a government department, who is usually not a member of the Cabinet

Minister of the Crown *n* a senior minister who is head of a government department and a member of the Cabinet

minister without portfolio *n* a senior government minister who is a member of the Cabinet but has no direct responsibility for a government department

ministrant /mínnistrәnt/ *n* somebody who gives aid to others (*literary*) [Mid-16C. < Latin *ministrant-*, present participle of *ministrare* 'serve' < *minister* 'servant' (see MINISTER).]

ministration /mínni stráysh'n/ *n* 1 help, treatment, or service (*formal; often plural*) 2 the service provided by a religious minister [14C. < Latin *ministration-* < *ministrare* (see MINISTRANT).]

ministroke /mínni strōk/ *n* a temporary blockage of blood circulation in some part of the brain, causing short-term stroke symptoms, e.g. dizziness, inability to speak or move, or loss of senses

ministry /mínnistri/ (*plural* **-tries**) *n* 1 **ministry, Ministry** GOVERNMENT DEPARTMENT a government department headed by a minister 2 GOVERNMENT BUILDING the building in which a government department is housed 3 WORK OF RELIGIOUS MINISTER the profession and services of a religious minister 4 PERIOD OF SERVICE a religious minister's career or period of service 5 MINISTERS ministers collectively, especially religious ministers (+ *singular or plural verb*) 6 PRIME MINISTER'S SERVICE the period of government under a prime minister [14C. Via Old French < Latin *ministerium* < *minister* 'servant' (see MINISTER).]

~~**miniture**~~ incorrect spelling of **miniature**

minium /mínni әm/ *n* CHEM = **red lead** [Mid-17C. < Latin.]

minivan /mínni van/ *n* a small van, often with seats that can be removed or rearranged to accommodate cargo

miniver /mínnivәr/ *n* white or light grey fur used as trim on ceremonial costumes [Late 16C. < Old French *menu vair* 'small vair'.]

mink /mingk/ *n* 1 (*plural* **minks** *or* **mink**) WEB-TOED MEMBER OF WEASEL FAMILY a semiaquatic carnivorous member of the weasel family with webbed toes and a bushy tail. Kept for: fur. Native to: North America, Asia, Europe. Genus: *Mustela*. 2 MINK FUR the thick, shiny brown fur of a mink (*often before nouns*) 3 MINK FUR GARMENT a coat, stole, or other garment made of mink fur [15C. < Swedish.]

minke whale /míngkә-, -ki-/ *n* a small grey and white whale with a pointed snout. *Balaenoptera acutorostrata*. [Mid-20C. < Norwegian.]

Minn. *abbr* Minnesota

Minna /mínnә/ capital of Niger State, west-central Nigeria. Population: 133,600 (1995 estimate).

Minneapolis /mínni áppәliss/ city in SE Minnesota, on the Mississippi River, adjacent to St Paul. Population: 351,731 (1998 estimate).

Minnelli /mi nélli/, **Liza** (*b.* 1946) US stage and screen performer

minneola /mínni ṓlә/ *n* an orange-coloured citrus fruit that is a hybrid of a tangerine and a grapefruit [Mid-20C. After the town of *Minneola* in Florida.]

Minnesinger /mínni singәr/, **minnesinger** *n* 1 a German lyric poet and singer of the 12th to 14th centuries 2 a travelling poet-musician in medieval times who wrote and performed songs of courtly love in Germany [Early 19C. Via German < Middle High German, 'love singer'.]

Minnesota /mínnә sṓtә/ 1 state in the north-central United States. Capital: St Paul. Population: 4,685,549 (1997). Area: 225,181 sq. km/86,943 sq. mi. 2 river in S Minnesota. Length: 534 km/332 mi. —**Minnesotan** *adj, n*

Minnesota Multiphasic Personality Inventory *n* a standardized test that uses true-false questions to assess somebody's psychological and social adjustment [After the University of MINNESOTA]

minnow /mínnō/ *n* 1 BAIT FISH any small freshwater fish of the carp family, commonly used as fishing bait. Family: Cyprinidae. 2 SMALL FISH any small silvery freshwater fish 3 INSIGNIFICANT PERSON OR THING a person or organization of relatively low status or little importance [15C. Probably related to Old English *myne* 'minnow'.]

Minoan /mi nṓ әn/ *adj* relating to the Bronze Age civilization on Crete that lasted from around 3000 to 1100 BC ■ *n* somebody who came from the island of Crete during ancient times, especially during the Minoan period [Late 19C. After *Minos*, legendary king of Crete associated with the great palace at Knossos.]

minor /mínәr/ *adj* 1 SMALL relatively small in quantity, size, or degree 2 LOW IN RANK relatively low in rank or importance 3 LOW IN SEVERITY relatively low in severity or danger 4 DESCRIBES MUSICAL SCALE describes a musical scale that has a semitone interval between the second and third, fifth and sixth, and sometimes seventh and eighth notes 5 DESCRIBES MUSICAL INTERVAL describes a musical interval that is a semitone less than a major interval 6 DESCRIBES MUSICAL KEY describes a key that is based on a minor scale ○ *in B minor* 7 NOT LEGALLY ADULT younger than the legal age of adulthood 8 *US* SECONDARY secondary to the major course of study 9 YOUNGER WITH SAME NAME a word sometimes placed after the surname of the younger of two school pupils with the same surname, especially formerly in public schools (*dated*) ■ *n* 1 SOMEBODY NOT LEGALLY ADULT a person who is not yet legally an adult 2 MUSICAL KEY OR HARMONY a key or harmony based on a musical scale whose third and, usually, sixth and seventh notes are lower by a semitone than those in the major scale ■ *vi US* STUDY SECONDARY SUBJECT to have a second specialization in higher education, in addition to a major specialization ○ *She minors in Spanish*. [13C. < Latin, 'lesser'.]

SPELLCHECK See ***miner***.

minor axis *n* the shorter axis of an ellipse

Minorca[1] /mi náwrkə/ *n* a white and black domestic chicken. Native to: Mediterranean. [Mid-19C. After MINORCA.]

Minorca[2] /mi náwrkə/ ♦ **Menorca**

minor element *n* CHEM = **trace element** *n.* 2

minoritarianism /mī nórri tári ənizem/ *n* advocacy or political action on behalf of a minority

Minorite /mínə rīt/ *n* a friar of the Franciscan order [Mid-16C. < *Minor Friars*, translation of medieval Latin *Fratres Minores* 'lesser brethren', because the order stressed the virtue of humility.]

minority /mī nórrəti, mi-/ *n* (*plural* **-ties**) **1** SMALL GROUP a group of people or things that is a small part of a much larger group **2** GROUP WITH INSUFFICIENT VOTES TO WIN a group that has fewer votes in an organization than another group or groups **3** SMALLER SOCIALLY DEFINED GROUP a group of people, within a society, whose members have different ethnic, racial, national, religious, sexual, political, linguistic, or other characteristics from the rest of society **4** NONADULTHOOD the state or period of being younger than the legal age of adulthood ■ *adj* OF A MINORITY relating to or constituting a minority

minor key *n* a key based on a minor scale

minor league *n* in the United States, a league of professional baseball, football, ice hockey, and basketball teams that do not belong to the major leagues

minor-league *adj* **1** relating to or being a team member of a minor sports league in the United States **2** *US* mediocre in quality or position (*informal*)

minor scale *n* a scale whose third and, usually, sixth and seventh notes are lower by a semitone than those in the major scale, giving it a less bright, more emotionally suggestive quality. ◊ **major scale**

minor suit *n* either clubs or diamonds, which in bridge and similar games are ranked below hearts and spades

Minos /mín oss/ *n* in Greek mythology, the king of Crete and the son of Zeus, who kept a monster (**the Minotaur**) in a labyrinth

Minotaur /mínə tawr/ *n* in Greek mythology, a monster with the body of a man and head of a bull that lived in the Cretan labyrinth and was fed human sacrifices until it was killed by Theseus

minoxidil /mi nóksi dil/ *n* an artery-widening drug. Use: treatment of high blood pressure, male-pattern baldness. [Late 20C. < shortening of AMINO- + OXIDE.]

Minsk /minsk/ capital of Belarus, in the north of the country. Population: 1,700,000 (1996).

minster /mínstər/ *n* a large or important cathedral or church, usually one originally connected with a monastery [Old English *mynster* < ecclesiastical Latin *monasterium* (see MONASTERY)]

minstrel /mínstrəl/ *n* **1** a medieval singer, musician, or reciter of poetry who travelled around from place to place giving performances **2** one of a group of entertainers who wore blackface makeup and sang and performed in variety shows (*a form of entertainment now usually considered racist and highly offensive*) [13C. Via Old French *menestral* 'entertainer, handicraftsman' < late Latin *ministerialis* 'official' < *ministerium* (see MINISTRY).]

minstrelsy /mínstrəlssi/ (*plural* **-sies**) *n* **1** MINSTREL'S ART a minstrel's art or performance, or the profession of a minstrel **2** MINSTRELS' POEMS AND SONGS the poems and songs written and performed by minstrels or by a particular minstrel **3** MINSTREL TROUPE a troupe of medieval minstrels [14C. < Old French *menestralsie* < *menestrel* (see MINSTREL).]

mint[1] /mint/ *n* **1** a plant with aromatic leaves. Native to: northern temperate regions. Use: food flavouring. Genus: *Mentha*. **2** a mint-flavoured sweet [Old English *minte*, via Germanic < Latin *mentha* < Greek *minthē*] —**minty** *adj*

mint[2] /mint/ *n* **1** PLACE COINING MONEY a place where the coins used in a currency are manufactured under government control **2** MUCH MONEY a large amount of money (*informal*) ■ *vt* **1** MAKE COINS to make coins by stamping metal **2** INVENT to create or invent something, especially a word or phrase, that is new ■ *adj* IN PERFECT CONDITION in perfect condition as when first made ○ *in mint condition* [Old English *mynet*, via Germanic < Latin *moneta* (see MONEY)] —**minter** *n*

mintage /míntij/ *n* **1** MINTING COINS the minting of coins **2** COINS FROM MINT coins made in a mint, especially a quantity of coins minted at the same time **3** FEE FOR MINTING a fee paid to a mint by a government for minting its coins

mint jelly *n* a jelly made chiefly from mint, green in colour, and served typically as a garnish for roasted lamb

mint julep *n* a drink made by pouring spirits, usually bourbon whiskey, and sugar, over crushed ice and flavouring or garnishing with mint

mintmark /mínt maark/ *n* a letter or symbol stamped on a coin that identifies the mint where it was made

Mintoff /mínt of/, **Dom** (*b.* 1916) Maltese statesman

mint sauce *n* a sauce made from mint, sugar, and vinegar, and traditionally served with roast lamb

minuend /mínnyoo end/ *n* the number from which another number (**subtrahend**) is to be subtracted [Early 18C. < Latin *minuendus* 'be made smaller' < *minuere* 'diminish'.]

minuet /mínnyoo ét/ *n* **1** a slow French court dance of the 17th century, performed in triple time **2** the music for a minuet [Late 17C. < French *menuet* 'small, dainty' < Latin *minutus*; from the steps taken in the dance.]

minus /mínəss/ *prep* **1** LESS reduced by the subtraction of a number ○ *Seven minus four is three.* **2** WITHOUT lacking in or deprived of something ○ *Minus the tools, he cannot do the work required.* ■ *adj* **1** SHOWING SUBTRACTION relating to or showing subtraction ○ *a minus sign* **2** LESS THAN ZERO relating to or showing a value less than zero ○ *Temperatures hovered near minus 20 degrees* ○ *a minus amount* **3** HAVING DETRIMENTAL EFFECT having a negative or detrimental effect ○ *a minus factor in our assessment* **4** SLIGHTLY BELOW STANDARD LEVEL used in marking or assessing something to show that it is slightly below the average standard indicated by a particular symbol ○ *a grade of C minus* ■ *n* **1** MATH = **minus sign** ○ *The minus shows that it's a subtraction* **2** NEGATIVE QUANTITY a quantity below zero ○ *If we take that away we're left with a minus.* **3** DISADVANTAGE something that is detrimental or disadvantageous ○ *The power problem may prove to be a minus.* [15C. < Latin, < *minor* 'less'.]

minuscule /mínnəss kyool/ *adj* **1** EXTREMELY SMALL extremely small or completely insignificant **2** LOWERCASE in lowercase letters ■ *n* **1** SMALL LETTER a lowercase letter **2** MEDIEVAL WRITING STYLE a small cursive style of writing used in medieval manuscripts **3** LETTER WRITTEN IN MINUSCULE a letter of the alphabet written in minuscule style [Early 18C. Via French < Latin *minusculus* 'rather small' < *minus* 'less' (see MINUS).] —**minuscular** /mi núskyŏŏlər/ *adj*

minus sign, minus *n* a symbol, (-), used to indicate subtraction or a negative quantity

minute[1] /mínnit/ *n* **1** 60 SECONDS a period of 60 seconds or a 60th part of an hour **2** VERY SHORT TIME a very short period of time ○ *I'll only be gone a minute.* **3** MOMENT a particular moment ○ *The minute we got there the show began.* **4** SHORT DISTANCE a distance that can be travelled in a minute ○ *The villa is only a couple of minutes from the beach.* **5** UNIT OF ANGULAR MEASURE (*symbol* ′) one 60th of a degree, a unit used in measuring angles **6** BRIEF NOTE a brief note or memorandum ■ **minutes** *npl* RECORD OF A MEETING an official record of what is said or done during a meeting ■ *vt* (**-utes, -uting, -uted**) WRITE DOWN MEETING'S PROCEEDINGS to record or summarize officially what happens during a meeting, or make a note in the minutes of a particular thing that is said or done [14C. Directly or via Old French < Latin *minuta* < *minutus*, past participle of *minuere* 'make small'.] ◇ **up to the minute** aware of, taking account of, or reporting the very latest developments

minute[2] /mī nyŏŏt/ (**-nuter, -nutest**) *adj* **1** VERY SMALL extremely small in size or scope **2** INSIGNIFICANT so very small as not to matter **3** CONCERNED WITH EVERY DETAIL extremely or laboriously thorough and painstaking, and concerned with every detail [Early 17C. < Latin *minutus* (see MINUTE[1]).] —**minuteness** *n*

minute gun /mínnit-/ *n* a gun fired every minute as a distress signal or sign of mourning

minute hand /mínnit-/ *n* the longer pointer on a watch or clock that indicates the minutes

minutely /mī nyŏŏtli/ *adv* **1** IN GREAT DETAIL very thoroughly, carefully, and in great detail **2** TO SMALL EXTENT to a very small extent **3** INTO SOMETHING VERY SMALL into a very small shape or very small pieces

minuteman /mínnit man/ (*plural* **-men** /-men/) *n* an armed fighter in the American War of Independence pledged to be ready to fight for the American cause at a minute's notice

Minuteman (*plural* **-men**), **minuteman** (*plural* **-men**) *n* an intercontinental ballistic missile of the United States armed forces

minute steak /mínnit-/ *n* a piece of frying steak sliced so thinly that it can be cooked very quickly

minutiae /mī nyŏŏshi ee/ *npl* small or trivial details [Mid-18C. < Latin, 'small things' < *minutus* (see MINUTE[1]).]

minx /mingks/ *n* an offensive term that deliberately insults a woman or girl as being impertinent or flirtatious [Mid-16C. < ?] —**minxish** *adj*

Minya, Al- /mínyə-/ city in E Egypt, in the Nile valley. Population: 208,000 (1992).

minyan /mínnyən/ (*plural* **-yanim** /mínnyə ním/ *or* **-yans**) *n* the minimum number, ten, of adult Jewish men required to be present for an orthodox religious service [Mid-18C. < Hebrew, 'count, reckoning'.]

Miocene /mī ə seen/ *n* the epoch of geological time when the great mountain ranges of Europe, Asia, and the Americas were created and the mastodon first appeared, 23.3 to 5.2 million years ago [Mid-19C. < Greek *meiōn* 'less' + *kainos* 'recent' <.] —**Miocene** *adj*

miosis /mī óssiss/ (*plural* **-ses** /-seez/), **myosis** (*plural* **-ses**) *n* a contraction of the pupil of the eye, caused e.g. by a reaction to a drug [Early 19C. < Greek *muein* 'shut the eyes'.] —**miotic, myotic** /mī óttik/ *adj*

MIP *abbr* **1** marine insurance policy **2** monthly investment plan

⚡**MIPS** /mips/, **mips** *abbr* million instructions per second

Miquelon Island ♦ **St-Pierre and Miquelon**

mir /meer/ *n* a peasant commune in tsarist Russia [Late 19C. < Russian.]

Mir *n* a space station launched by the former Soviet Union in 1986, designed to be permanently crewed

mirabile dictu /mi rábbi lay dík too/ *interj* used to introduce the announcement of something the speaker, genuinely or ironically, considers to be amazing [< Latin, 'amazing to relate', literally 'amazing in the saying']

miracidium /mīrə síddi əm/ (*plural* **-a** /-di ə/) *n* the free-swimming first-stage larva of a trematode worm that hatches from an egg and then reproduces asexually [Late 19C. < modern Latin, < Greek *meirakidion* 'little boy'.] —**miracidial** *adj*

miracle /mírrək'l/ *n* **1** ACT OF GOD an event that appears to be contrary to the laws of nature and is regarded as an act of God **2** AMAZING EVENT an event or action that is totally amazing, extraordinary, or unexpected ○ *It'll be a miracle if we get there on time.* **3** MARVELLOUS EXAMPLE OF SKILL something admired as a marvellous creation or example of a particular type of science or skill ○ *a miracle of modern engineering* [12C. Via Old French < Latin *miraculum* 'object of wonder' < *mirari* 'wonder at' < *mirus* 'wonderful'.]

miracle drug *n* a drug, usually a new one, that is extraordinarily effective and seems to represent a breakthrough in the treatment of disease

miracle play *n* a medieval play broadly depicting miracles taken from the life of a saint or a story from the Bible

miraculous /mə rákyŏŏləss/ *adj* **1** REGARDED AS CAUSED BY SUPERNATURAL INTERVENTION apparently contrary to the laws of nature and caused by a supernatural power **2** EXTRAORDINARY totally unexpected, extraordinary, and marvellous **3** ABLE TO PERFORM MIRACLES having the power to perform miracles [15C. Directly or via French *miraculeux* < Latin *miraculum* (see MIRACLE).] —**miraculously** *adv* —**miraculousness** *n*

mirador /mírrə dáwr/ *n* a window, balcony, or turret designed to command a wide view [Late 17C. < Spanish, < *mirar* 'to look' < Latin *mirare* (see MIRAGE).]

Miraflores, Lake /meérə fláwrayz/ lake in central Panama, through which the Panama Canal passes

mirage /mírraazh, mə raázh/ *n* **1** an optical illusion of a sheet of water appearing in the desert or on a hot road, caused by light being distorted by alternate layers of hot and cool air **2** something that is unreal or merely imagined [Early 19C. < French, < *mirer* 'look at' < Latin *mirare* 'wonder at', variant of *mirari* (see MIRACLE).]

Miranda /mi rándə/ *n* one of the satellites of Uranus

Carmen Miranda

Miranda /mi ránda/, **Carmen** (1909–55) Portuguese dancer and singer. Born **Carmo Miranda da Cunha**

MIRAS /míras/ *abbr* mortgage interest relief at source

mire /mīr/ *n* 1 BOG an area of very marshy ground or deep slushy mud 2 THICK MUD thick slimy mud 3 DIFFICULT SITUATION a troublesome or oppressive situation or state that is very difficult to escape from ■ *v* (**mires, miring, mired**) 1 *vti* GET SOMETHING STUCK IN MUD to sink into mud, or make something sink into mud, and become stuck 2 *vt* MAKE MUDDY to make something muddy or dirty 3 *vt* ENTANGLE to involve or entangle somebody or something in difficulties [13C. < Old Norse *myrr* 'bog'.] —**miriness** *n* —**miry** *adj*

mirk *n* = murk

mirky *adj* = murky

Miró /meerō, mee rō/, **Joan** (1893–1983) Spanish painter, sculptor, and printmaker

⚡**mirror** /mírrar/ *n* 1 HIGHLY REFLECTIVE SURFACE a surface such as glass or polished metal that reflects light without diffusing it so that it will give back a clear image of anything placed in front of it 2 GLASS FOR REFLECTING AN IMAGE a piece of reflective material, especially glass coated on one side with metal, mounted in a frame for use, e.g. in the home or a vehicle 3 SOMETHING ACCURATELY REPRODUCING SOMETHING ELSE something that accurately reproduces, describes, or represents something else 4 ONLINE = **mirror site** ■ *vt* 1 REFLECT IN SURFACE to reflect something clearly in a surface (*often passive*) ○ *The mountains were mirrored in the lake.* 2 BE SIMILAR TO to be very similar to or correspond closely with something else, or to reproduce it accurately ○ *These developments are now mirrored on the other side of the world.* 3 to maintain an exact copy of a program, data, or website, usually on another file server [13C. < Old French *mirour* < Latin *mirari* 'wonder at' (see MIRACLE).]

mirror carp *n* a carp with very small scales that give its body a smooth shiny appearance. *Cyprinus carpio.*

mirror image *n* something that, like a reflection in a mirror, is identical to something else but reversed

⚡**mirror site** *n* a copy of a website maintained on a different file server so as to spread the distribution load or to protect data from loss in the event of hardware or software failure

mirth /murth/ *n* happiness or enjoyment, especially accompanied by laughter [Old English *myrgþ* < Germanic, 'pleasant, joyful'] —**mirthful** *adj* —**mirthfully** *adv* —**mirthfulness** *n*

mirthless /múrthlass/ *adj* without, or not expressing, amusement, good humour, or gladness —**mirthlessly** *adv* —**mirthlessness** *n*

MIRV /murv/ *abbr* multiple independently targeted re-entry vehicle

Mirza /múrza/ *n* an Iranian title of respect signifying a learned man or official when placed before a name, or, formerly, a royal prince when placed after a name [Early 17C. < Persian.]

⚡**MIS** *abbr* management information system

mis- *prefix* 1 badly, wrongly ○ *mishandle* 2 bad, wrong ○ *misdeed* 3 opposite, lack, failure ○ *mislike* [Partly Old English, and partly via Old French *mes-* < Germanic, 'wrong']

misaddress /míssa drés/ *vt* to put an incorrect address on an item of mail

misadventure /míssad vénchar/ *n* 1 an unfortunate event, especially something untoward, unlucky, or amusing that happens to somebody 2 an accidental cause of death, not involving a crime or negligence on the part of somebody else [13C. < Old French *mesaventure* < *mesavenir* 'turn out badly' < *avenir* 'happen' < Latin *advenire* 'come to'.]

misalign /míss ə līn/ *vt* to arrange or position something incorrectly in relation to another thing ○ *The caption is misaligned – it should be just under the picture.* —**misalignment** *n*

misalliance /míssa līˈanss/ *n* an unsuitable alliance, especially a marriage between mismatched partners

misallocate /mis álla kayt/ (**-cates, -cating, -cated**) *vt* to allocate something, e.g. money, in a wrong or inappropriate way —**misallocation** /mís alla káysh'n/ *n*

misandry /míss ándri/ *n* hatred of men as a sexually defined group [Early 20C. < Greek *andr-* 'man', after MIS-OGYNY.] —**misandrist** *n* —**misandrous** *adj*

misanthrope /míss'n thrōp/, **misanthropist** /miss ánthrapist/ *n* somebody who hates humanity, or who dislikes and distrusts other people and tends to avoid them [Mid-16C. Via French < Greek *misanthrōpos* < *misein* 'to hate' + *anthrōpos* 'man'.] —**misanthropic** /míss'n thróppik/ *adj* —**misanthropically** *adv* —**misanthropy** /miss ánthrapi/ *n*

misapply /míssa plī/ (**-plies, -plying, -plied**) *vt* to use something badly, incorrectly, or improperly —**misapplication** /miss áppli káysh'n/ *n*

misapprehend /míss apri hénd/ *vt* to fail to understand

misapprehension /míss apri hénsh'n/ *n* a false impression or incorrect understanding, especially of the nature of a situation or somebody's intentions —**misapprehensive** *adj* —**misapprehensively** *adv* —**misapprehensiveness** *n*

misappropriate /míssa própri ayt/ (**-ates, -ating, -ated**) *vt* to take something, especially money, dishonestly, or in order to use it for an improper or illegal purpose —**misappropriation** /míssa própri áysh'n/ *n*

SYNONYMS See *steal.*

misattribute /misa tríbyoot/ (**-utes, -uting, -uted**) *vt* to attribute something to the wrong person or source —**misattribution** /mís attri byoosh'n/ *n*

misbegotten /míssbi gótt'n/ *adj* 1 ILL-CONCEIVED AND GENERALLY BAD from a bad source, badly planned, badly thought out, or generally deplorable from start to finish 2 DISHONESTLY OBTAINED obtained by dishonest means 3 ILLEGITIMATE born to parents who are not married to each other

misbehave /míssbi háyv/ (**-haves, -having, -haved**) *vi* 1 to be naughty and troublesome, or otherwise behave in an unacceptable way 2 to function badly or not at all, or to cause problems (*informal*) —**misbehaved** *adj* —**misbehaver** *n*

misbehavior *n* US = misbehaviour

misbehaviour /míssbi háyvyar/ *n* unacceptable behaviour, especially naughtiness, disobedience, or troublesomeness on the part of somebody

misbelief /míssbi leéf/ *n* a belief that is or is considered to be false or unorthodox

misbelieve /míssbi leév/ (**-lieves, -lieving, -lieved**) *vi* to hold beliefs that are or are considered to be false or unorthodox, especially on religious matters (*disapproving*) —**misbeliever** *n*

misc. *abbr* 1 miscellaneous 2 miscellany

miscalculate /miss kálkyoo layt/ (**-lates, -lating, -lated**) *vti* 1 to calculate something incorrectly 2 to judge or assess something incorrectly, or form false expectations as to the consequences of an action —**miscalculation** /miss kalkyoo láysh'n/ *n* —**miscalculator** *n*

miscall /miss káwl/ *vt* to use the wrong or an inappropriate name for somebody or something —**miscaller** *n*

miscarriage /miss kárrij, míss karij/ *n* 1 an involuntary ending of a pregnancy through the discharge of the foetus from the womb at too early a stage in its development for it to survive. Technical name **abortion** 2 the mishandling or failure of something, such as a plan or project (*formal*)

miscarriage of justice *n* a failure of the legal system to come to a just decision

miscarry /miss kárri/ (**-ries, -rying, -ried**) *vi* 1 HAVE SPONTANEOUS ABORTION to lose a foetus, especially a human foetus, through a miscarriage 2 BE SPONTANEOUSLY ABORTED to be expelled from the womb at too early a stage in development to be able to survive 3 FAIL to result in failure (*formal*) 4 BE LOST IN TRANSIT to be lost or go astray before reaching an intended destination

miscast /míss káast/ (**-casts, -casting, -cast**) *vt* (*often passive*) 1 to choose somebody to play a stage or film part to which he or she is unsuited 2 to give a role in a play or film to an unsuitable actor

miscegenation /míssija náysh'n/ *n* (*offensive when used disapprovingly, as often formerly*) 1 sexual relations between people of different races, especially of different skin colours, leading to the birth of children 2 marriage or cohabitation between people of different races [Mid-19C. < Latin *miscere* 'to mix' + *genus* 'race'.] —**miscegenational** *adj*

~~miscelaneous~~ incorrect spelling of **miscellaneous**

miscellanea /míssa láyni ə/ *npl* miscellaneous things, especially pieces of writing, brought together as a collection [Late 16C. < Latin, < *miscellaneus* (see MISCELLANEOUS).]

miscellaneous /míssa láyni əss/ *adj* 1 made up of many different things or kinds of things that have no necessary connection with each other 2 each being different or having different abilities or qualities from the others ○ *a task force of miscellaneous specialists* [Early 17C. < Latin *miscellaneus* < *miscere* 'to mix'.] —**miscellaneously** *adv* —**miscellaneousness** *n*

miscellanist /mi séllanist/ *n* a compiler or writer of miscellanies

miscellany /mi sélláni/ (*plural* **-nies**) *n* 1 a miscellaneous collection of things 2 a collection of miscellaneous pieces of writing in one volume, often by different authors on various subjects and in different genres [Late 16C. Via French *miscellanées* < Latin *miscellanea* (see MISCELLANEA).]

mischance /miss cha'anss/ *n* 1 the occurrence of unfortunate events by chance 2 something that happens through bad luck [14C. < Old French *mescheance* (see CHANCE).]

~~mischeif~~ incorrect spelling of **mischief**

mischief /mísschif/ *n* 1 NAUGHTY BEHAVIOUR behaviour, especially by children, that is undesirable or troublesome without being wicked 2 TENDENCY TO NAUGHTY BEHAVIOUR a tendency to mildly troublesome or undesirable behaviour such as teasing or practical jokes 3 INJURY OR DAMAGE injury or damage caused by the actions of somebody or something 4 SOURCE OF HARM OR TROUBLE something or somebody that causes serious harm or trouble to others (*dated*) 5 HARMLESS TROUBLEMAKER a causer of harmless trouble (*dated*) [13C. < Old French *meschef* < *meschever* 'meet with misfortune' < *chever* 'come to an end' < *chef* 'head'.]

mischief-maker *n* a troublemaker who sets people against each other, especially by spreading malicious gossip

~~mischievious~~ incorrect spelling of **mischievous**

mischievous /mísschivass/ *adj* 1 PLAYFULLY NAUGHTY OR TROUBLESOME behaving or likely to behave in a naughty or troublesome way, but in fun and not meaning serious harm 2 TROUBLESOME OR IRRITATING intended to tease or cause trouble, though usually in fun or without much malice 3 FULL OF MISCHIEF expressing somebody's intention or inclination to have fun by teasing, playing tricks, or causing trouble 4 DAMAGING causing or meant to cause serious trouble, damage, or hurt (*formal*) —**mischievously** *adv* —**mischievousness** *n*

misch metal /mish-/ *n* an alloy of cerium and rare earth metals used, e.g., in the flints of cigarette lighters [Early 20C. < German *Mischmetall* 'mix-metal'.]

miscible /míssab'l/ *adj* describes two or more liquids that can be mixed together [Late 16C. < medieval Latin *miscibilis* < Latin *miscere* 'to mix'.]

miscommunication /mísska myoóni káysh'n/ *n* 1 failure to communicate something clearly or correctly 2 a communication that is unclear or likely to be misinterpreted

miscomprehend /mís kompri hénd/ *vt* to mistake the meaning or nature of something

misconceive /mísskan seev/ (**-ceives, -ceiving, -ceived**) *vt* to fail to understand something correctly, or to form a false conception of something

misconceived /mísskən séevd/ *adj* resulting from a wrong or faulty understanding or idea of something and consequently doomed to failure

misconception /mísskən sépsh'n/ *n* a mistaken idea or view resulting from a misunderstanding of something

misconduct *n* /miss kóndukt/ **1 IMMORAL, UNETHICAL, OR UNPROFESSIONAL BEHAVIOUR** behaviour that is not in accordance with accepted moral or professional standards **2 INCOMPETENCE** incompetent or dishonest management of something, especially on behalf of others ■ *v* /mísskən dúkt/ **1** *vr* **ACT IMMORALLY** to act in an immoral or improper way **2** *vt* **MANAGE INCOMPETENTLY** to manage something in an incompetent or dishonest way ○ *guilty of misconducting the whole affair*

misconstruction /mísskən strúksh'n/ *n* **1** a faulty understanding or interpretation of something **2** a faulty grammatical construction

misconstrue /mísskən stróo/ (**-strues, -struing, -strued**) *vt* to understand or interpret something incorrectly

miscount *vti* /miss kównt/ to make a mistake when counting something ■ *n* /miss kownt/ an incorrect count or calculation

miscreant /mísskri ənt/ *n* **1** a villain, wrongdoer, or generally wicked and contemptible person (*literary*) **2** an infidel or heretic (*archaic insult*) [13C. < Old French, present participle of *mescroire* 'disbelieve' < Latin *credere* 'believe'.]

miscreate /miskri áyt/ (**-ates, -ating, -ated**) *vt* to make something badly or imperfectly —**miscreation** *n*

miscue /miss kyóo/ *n* **1 FAULTY SHOT IN BILLIARDS** in billiards or snooker, a shot that fails because the cue does not strike the cue ball properly **2 MISTAKE** a mistake, especially one that involves giving somebody the wrong cue to say or begin something or giving a cue at the wrong time (*informal*) ■ *v* (**-cues, -cuing, -cued**) **1** *vti* **MAKE FAULTY SHOT** in billiards or snooker, to fail to strike the cue ball properly, or to play a miscue **2** *vti* **MISS A CUE** to fail to respond to a cue, to give the wrong cue for something, or to give a cue at the wrong time **3** *vi* **ERR** to make a mistake (*informal*)

misdeal /míss deel/ *vti* (**-deals, -dealing, -dealt**) to deal playing cards incorrectly ■ *n* a mistake in the way playing cards are dealt, or an incorrectly dealt hand —**misdealer** *n*

misdeed /miss déed/ *n* a wicked, blameworthy, or unlawful act

misdemeanant /míssdi méenənt/ *n* somebody convicted of a misdemeanour

misdemeanor *n* US = **misdemeanour**

misdemeanour /míssdi méenər/ *n* **1** in the United States and before 1967 in England and Wales, a crime less serious than a felony and resulting in a less severe punishment **2** a relatively minor misdeed

misdial (**-als, -alling, -alled**) *vti* /miss dī́ əl/ to dial a telephone number incorrectly —**misdial** /míss dī əl/ *n*

misdirect /míssdə rékt/ *vt* **1 GIVE WRONG DIRECTIONS** to give somebody wrong directions or instructions **2 WRONGLY ADDRESS MAIL** to put a wrong address on an item of mail **3 AIM INACCURATELY** to aim something, e.g. a punch or bullet, inaccurately, or direct something, e.g. a comment or insult, at the wrong person

mise en scène /meez on sáyn/ (*plural* **mises en scène**) *n* **1** the positioning of actors, scenery, and properties on a stage or film set for a particular scene or particular production **2** the physical environment in which an event takes place [< French, 'putting on stage']

misemploy /misim plóy/ *vt* to employ somebody or use something wrongly or inappropriately —**misemployment** *n*

miser /mī́zər/ *n* **1** somebody who hates spending money and lives as though he or she were poor **2** an ungenerous, greedy, or selfish person [Mid-16C. < Latin, 'unfortunate'.]

miserable /mízzərəb'l/ *adj* **1 VERY UNHAPPY** experiencing a serious lack of contentment or happiness ○ *feeling a bit miserable* **2 VERY UNPLEASANT** causing or accompanied by discomfort, unpleasantness, or unhappiness **3 CONTEMPTIBLE** deserving contempt or condemnation **4 INADEQUATE** inadequate, often insultingly or embarrassingly inadequate, in quantity or quality **5 DIRTY OR SQUALID** dirty, squalid, and lacking any comfort **6** *Scotland, ANZ* **STINGY** mean or stingy [15C. Via Old French < Latin *miserabilis* 'pitiable' < *miser* 'unfortunate'.] —**miserableness** *n* —**miserably** *adv*

LITERARY LINK *Les Misérables*, a novel (1862) by French writer Victor Hugo. Set in mid-19th century France, it tells the story of Jean Valjean, whose attempts to escape his criminal past are dogged by guilt, fate, and persistent police inspector Javert.

---

misère /mi záir/ *n* **1** a call in certain card games, especially solo whist, indicating that a hand is expected to win no tricks **2** a hand that is expected to win no tricks [Early 19C. < French, literally, 'poverty, misery'.]

miserere /mízzə ráiri/ *n* CHR = **misericord** [Late 18C. < Latin, 'have mercy!' < *misereri* 'have mercy' < *miser* 'unfortunate'.]

Miserere /mízzə ráiri/ *n* **1** the 50th or 51st Psalm, depending on the version of the Bible **2** a musical setting of the Miserere [13C. < the first word of the Latin text, beginning *Miserere mei, Deus* 'have mercy on me, O God' (see MISERERE).]

misericord /mi zérri kawrd/ *n* a projecting ledge often with elaborate carving on the underside of a seat in a church stall that, when the seat is turned up, gives a standing person something to rest against [14C. Via Old French < Latin *misericord* 'merciful, compassionate' < *miser* 'unfortunate' + *cor* 'heart'.]

miserly /mī́zərli/ *adj* **1** greedy for money and unwilling to share or to spend it **2** so small as to be insufficient or inadequate —**miserliness** *n*

misery /mízzəri/ (*plural* **-ies**) *n* **1 GREAT UNHAPPINESS** a serious lack of contentment or happiness **2 SOURCE OF GREAT UNHAPPINESS** something that causes great unhappiness **3 POVERTY** a state of extreme poverty and squalor **4 GLOOMY PERSON** a consistently gloomy or brooding person (*informal*) [14C. Directly or via Anglo-Norman *miserie* < Latin *miseria* < Latin *miser* 'unfortunate'.] ◇ **put somebody out of his** *or* **her misery** to put an end to somebody's suspense or anxiety, especially by revealing something that he or she is desperate to know (*humorous*) ◇ **put an animal out of its misery** to kill an animal in order to prevent it suffering further pain

Mises /méessəz/, **Ludwig von** (1881–1973) Austrian-born US economist

⚡**MI-SET** *abbr* merchant initiated SET

misfeasance /missféez'nss/ *n* acting improperly or illegally in performing an action that is in itself lawful. ◊ **malfeasance** *n.* **1, nonfeasance** [Early 17C. < Anglo-Norman *mesfaisance* < *mesfaire* 'misdo' < *mes-* 'wrongly' + *faire* 'to do' < Latin *facere*.] —**misfeasor** *n*

misfire *vi* /miss fī́r/ (**-fires, -firing, -fired**) **1 NOT FIRE PROPERLY** to fail to shoot a bullet or shell when fired **2 FAIL TO OPERATE PROPERLY** to fail to ignite the fuel mixture in the cylinder or to ignite it at the wrong time (*refers to an internal-combustion engine*) **3 GO WRONG** to fail to achieve a planned result ○ *the plot misfired* ■ *n* /míss fīr/ **MALFUNCTION IN FIRING** a failure to fire or function properly

misfit /míss fit/ *n* **1** a person who does not fit comfortably into a situation or environment ○ *a social misfit* **2** something that fits badly

misfortune /miss fáwrchən/ *n* **1** bad luck **2** an undesirable or unhappy event or circumstance

misgive /miss gív/ (**-gives, -giving, -gave** /-gáyv/, **-given** /-gívv'n/) *vt* to feel apprehensive, or to cause a feeling of apprehension or foreboding in somebody (*literary*) [Early 16C. < GIVE in the obsolete sense 'suggest'.]

misgiving /miss gívving/ *n* a feeling of doubt or apprehension, especially about undertaking a course of action (*often plural*) ○ *I had misgivings about the plan from the beginning.*

misgovern /miss gúvvərn/ *vti* to govern somebody or something badly —**misgovernment** *n*

misguide /miss gī́d/ (**-guides, -guiding, -guided**) *vt* to lead somebody in a wrong direction or into making a mistake —**misguidance** *n* —**misguider** *n*

misguided /miss gī́did/ *adj* motivated by or based on ideas that are mistaken, heedless, or inappropriate —**misguidedly** *adv* —**misguidedness** *n*

mishandle /miss hánd'l/ (**-dles, -dling, -dled**) *vt* **1** to deal with something or somebody in an incompetent or ineffective way **2** to treat something or somebody roughly

mishap /míss hap/ *n* **1** an unfortunate accident or piece of bad luck **2** an unfortunate circumstance or set of circumstances (*formal*)

mishear /miss héer/ (**-hears, -hearing, -heard** /-húrd/) *vti* to fail to hear somebody or something correctly

Mishima /míshimə/, **Yukio** (1925–70) Japanese novelist. Pseudonym of **Hiraoka Kimitake**

mishit (**-hits, -hitting, -hit**) *vt* /miss hít/ to hit something badly, e.g. a ball or puck, so that it does not go in the desired direction or has insufficient force behind it —**mishit** /míss hit/ *n*

mishmash /mísh mash/ *n* a disorderly collection or confused mixture of things [15C. < repetition of MASH.]

Mishmi /míshmi/ (*plural* **-mi** *or* **-mis**) *n* **1** a member of a people living in a mountainous region of Assam in NE India **2** the Tibeto-Burman language of the Mishmi people —**Mishmi** *adj*

Mishnah /míshnə/, **Mishna** *n* **1 JEWISH LAW** the primary body of Jewish civil and religious law, forming the first part of the Talmud **2 JEWISH ORAL LAW** Jewish law from the oral tradition, as distinguished from law derived from the scriptures **3 JEWISH LEGAL TEACHING** the teaching of an authority on Jewish law [Early 17C. < Hebrew *mišnāh* 'repetition, teaching'.] —**Mishnaic** /mish náy ik/ *adj*

misidentify /míss ī dénti fī/ (**-fies, -fying, -fied**) *vt* to make a mistake in identifying somebody or something —**misidentification** /míss ī dentifi káysh'n/ *n*

misinform /míssin fáwrm/ *vt* to give incorrect information to somebody —**misinformant** *n* —**misinformation** *n* —**misinformer** *n*

misinterpret /míssin túrprit/ *vt* to understand or explain the meaning of something incorrectly —**misinterpreter** *n*

misinterpretation /míss in túrpri táysh'n/ *n* an incorrect understanding or explanation of the meaning of something

misjoinder /miss jóyndər/ *n* an improper combining of plaintiffs, defendants, or causes of action in a single lawsuit

misjudge /miss júj/ (**-judges, -judging, -judged**) *v* **1** *vti* to make a mistake when judging or assessing something or when attempting to do something that requires accurate judgment **2** *vt* to form an incorrect opinion, especially one that attributes bad qualities to somebody unjustly or mistakenly —**misjudger** *n* —**misjudgment** *n*

miskick /mis kík/ *vti* to fail to kick a ball in the right or intended way

Miskito /mi skéet ō/ (*plural* **-to** *or* **-tos**) *n* **1** a member of a Native Central American people living along the Caribbean coasts of Nicaragua and Honduras **2** the language of the Miskito people [Late 18C. < a Native American language.] —**Miskito** *adj*

Miskolc /méesh kōlts/ city in NE Hungary. Population: 182,000 (1995).

mislay /miss láy/ (**-lays, -laying, -laid** /-láyd/) *vt* to lose something temporarily, especially by forgetting where it was put —**mislayer** *n*

mislead /miss léed/ (**-leads, -leading, -led** /-léd/) *vt* **1 INFORM FALSELY** to cause somebody to make a mistake or form a false opinion or belief, either by employing deliberate deception or by supplying incorrect information ○ *The defendant is trying to mislead the jury.* **2 LEAD INTO BAD ACTIONS** to be responsible for making somebody, especially somebody younger, do wrong or adopt bad habits **3 LEAD IN WRONG DIRECTION** to lead somebody in a wrong direction —**misleader** *n*

misleading /miss léeding/ *adj* likely or deliberately intended to confuse people or give them a false idea of something —**misleadingly** *adv*

misled past participle, past tense of **mislead**

mislike /miss lī́k/ (**-likes, -liking, -liked**) *vt* to dislike somebody or something (*archaic*)

mismanage /miss mánnij/ (**-ages, -aging, -aged**) *vt* to run, organize, or deal with something incompetently —**mismanagement** *n*

mismatch *n* /míss mach/ a pairing or combination of people or things that are incompatible with or apparently ill-suited to each other ■ *vt* /miss mách/ to fail to match or pair suitably (*usually passive*) ○ *They'd been mismatched from the start.*

Misnaged *n* JUDAISM = **Mitnagged**

misnomer /miss nṓmər/ *n* **1** a wrong or unsuitable name or term for something or somebody **2** a use of a wrong or unsuitable name or term to describe something or somebody [15C. < Old French, < *mes-* 'wrongly' + *nommer* 'to name' < Latin *nominare*.]

miso /meéssō/ *n* Japanese fermented soya bean paste used mainly in vegetarian cooking [Early 18C. < Japanese.]

misogamy /mi sóggəmi/ *n* an aversion to marriage and the married state [Mid-17C. < modern Latin *misogamia*, < Greek *misein* 'to hate' + *gamos* 'marriage'.] —**misogamic** /míssə gámmik/ *adj* —**misogamist** *n*

misogyny /mi sójjəni/ *n* the hatred of women, as a sexually defined group [Mid-17C. < Greek *misogunia* < *misein* 'to hate' + *gunē* 'woman'.] —**misogynic** /míssə jínnik/ *adj* —**misogynist** *n* —**misogynistic** /mi sójjə nístik/ *adj* —**misogynistically** *adv*

misology /mi sólləji/ *n* the hatred of reason, logical argument, or enlightenment [Early 19C. < Greek *misologia* < *misein* 'to hate' + *-logia* (see -LOGY).] —**misologist** *n*

misoneism /míssō neé izəm/ *n* the hatred of new things or change [Late 19C. < Italian *misoneismo* < Greek *misein* 'to hate' + *neos* 'new'.] —**misoneist** *n* —**misoneistic** /míssō nee ístik/ *adj*

~~**mispelling**~~ incorrect spelling of **misspelling**

misperceive /míspər seév/ (**-ceives, -ceiving, -ceived**) *vt* to form a mistaken perception of something —**misperception** /-pər sépsh'n/ *n*

mispickel /míss pik'l/ *n* MINERALS = **arsenopyrite** [Late 17C. < German, < ?]

misplace /míss pláyss/ (**-places, -placing, -placed**) *vt* **1 PUT IN WRONG PLACE** to put something in a wrong place or position **2 MISLAY** to lose something, especially temporarily, through forgetting where it was put **3 RELY ON SOMEBODY OR SOMETHING INAPPROPRIATE** to put confidence, faith, or trust in somebody or something unsuitable or unworthy —**misplacement** *n*

misplaced modifier *n* a phrase positioned so that it is unclear what exactly it refers to, e.g. *lying in the gutter* in 'Lying in the gutter, we saw a dead rat'

misplay /míss pláy/ *vt* to play or move something such as a ball or game piece badly or carelessly ■ *n* a bad or unintended play in sport or a game

misplead /míss pleéd/ (**-pleads, -pleading, -pleaded, -plead** *or* **-pled** /-pléd/) *vti* to make or answer an allegation in a lawsuit in a manner not in accordance with procedure or the law

mispleading /míss pleéding/ *n* an error made or contained in the pleading in a lawsuit

misprint *n* /míss print/ an error in the printed copy of a text resulting from a mistake made when the text was being printed ■ *vt* /míss prínt/ to print something wrongly

misprise *vt* = **misprize**

misprision[1] /míss prízh'n/ *n* **1** the failure of somebody who knows of but is not involved in a felony or treason to report it to the authorities **2** *US* neglect or wrong done by a public official in the performance of the duties of his or her office [15C. < Anglo-Norman *mesprisioun* 'error' < Old French *mesprendre* 'make a mistake'.]

misprision[2] /míss prízh'n/ *n* a misunderstanding of something, especially a failure to appreciate the true worth of somebody or something (*archaic*) [Late 16C. < MISPRIZE after MISPRISION[1].]

misprize /míss príz/ (**-prizes, -prizing, -prized**), **misprise** (**-prises, -prising, -prised**) *vt* (*formal*) **1** to fail to appreciate the true worth of something or somebody **2** to consider somebody or something unworthy of respect or admiration [14C. < Old French *mesprisier* 'misestimate value' < *prisier* (see PRIZE[1]).] —**misprizer** *n*

mispronounce /mísspra nówns/ (**-nounces, -nouncing, -nounced**) *vti* to pronounce something incorrectly —**mispronunciation** /mísspra núnssi áysh'n/ *n*

misquote /míss kwṓt/ (**-quotes, -quoting, -quoted**) *vti* to quote somebody or something inaccurately —**misquoter** *n*

misread /míss reéd/ (**-reads, -reading, -read** /-réd/) *vt* **1** to make a mistake in reading something, e.g. reading aloud inaccurately, mistaking one word for another, or misunderstanding the sense of what is written **2** to fail to understand the true meaning or nature of something

misreport /míssri páwrt/ *vt* to report something in an inaccurate or distorted way ■ *n* an inaccurate or distorted report

misrepresent /míss repri zént/ *vt* **1** to give an inaccurate or deliberately false account of the nature of somebody or something **2** not to be truly or typically representative of somebody or something —**misrepresentation** /míss repri zen táysh'n/ *n* —**misrepresentative** *adj* —**misrepresenter** *n*

misrule /míss róol/ *vti* (**-rules, -ruling, -ruled**) **RULE BADLY** to govern a people or place unjustly or inefficiently ■ *n* **1 BAD GOVERNMENT** unjust or inefficient government of a people or place **2 PUBLIC DISORDER** a state of public disorder or anarchy

miss[1] /miss/ *v* **1** *vti* **NOT HIT TARGET** to fail to hit, reach, or make contact with somebody or something that is being aimed at **2** *vt* **NOT ATTEND OR CATCH** to fail to be present or on time for something, or to fail to meet or be on time for somebody **3** *vt* **NOT HEAR, SEE, OR UNDERSTAND** to fail to hear, see, or understand something, e.g. through inattention or being distracted **4** *vt* **NOT TAKE ADVANTAGE OF CHANCE** to fail to take advantage of a chance or opportunity **5** *vti* **FAIL TO ACHIEVE** to fail to achieve a set target or goal **6** *vt* **AVOID** to escape or avoid a potentially harmful, dangerous, or unpleasant situation **7** *vt* **OMIT** to leave something out **8** *vt* **DESIRE SOMEBODY'S PRESENCE** to feel sorry that somebody or something is absent ○ *missed her greatly while she was away* **9** *vt* **DISCOVER ABSENCE OF** to realize that a person or thing is not present at the expected time or in the expected place ○ *He was halfway home before he missed his wallet.* **10** *vi* **MISFIRE** to fail to ignite the fuel mixture in the cylinder (*refers to an internal-combustion engine*) ■ *n* **1 FAILURE TO HIT** a failure to hit, reach, or make contact with somebody or something aimed at **2 A FAILURE** something that does not succeed or fails to impress [Old English *missan* < Germanic, 'go wrong'] —**missable** *adj* ◇ **give something a miss** to choose not to do something or attend something (*informal*)

miss out *v* **1** *vt* to omit or overlook something ○ *You missed out the best bit of the whole story.* **2** *vi* to lose an opportunity of doing something

miss[2] /miss/ *n* **1** a term of address for a girl or young woman, sometimes used in place of her name (*dated*) **2** a girl or young woman [Mid-17C. Shortening of MISTRESS.]

Miss *n* **1 TITLE PRECEDING A NAME** a title placed before the name of a girl or unmarried woman **2 WINNER'S TITLE** used together with a place name or another word in the winner's title awarded in a beauty contest or similar event ○ *Miss Panama* **3 WAY OF ADDRESSING A WOMAN TEACHER** a term of address for or way of referring to a woman teacher

Miss. *abbr* **1** mission **2** missionary **3** Mississippi

missal /míss'l/ *n* a book that contains all the prayers, responses, and hymns used in the Roman Catholic Mass [13C. < medieval Latin *missale* < late Latin *missa* (see MASS).]

missel thrush *n* BIRDS = **mistle thrush**

missense /míss senss/ *n* a genetic mutation in which a genetic coding sequence (**codon**) for one amino acid is changed to one that codes for another

misshapen /míss sháypən/, **misshaped** /-sháypt/ *adj* having an undesirably unusual shape —**misshapenly** *adv* —**misshapenness** *n*

missile /míssīl/ *n* **1** a weapon consisting of a warhead propelled by a rocket **2** any object thrown or launched as a weapon, e.g. a stone or bullet [Early 17C. < Latin *missilis* < *mittere* 'send'.]

missilery /míssīlri/, **missilry** *n* **1** missiles, considered collectively **2** the designing, building, or operating of missiles

missing /míssing/ *adj* **1** not present in an expected place, absent, or lost ○ *There's a page missing from the book.* **2** not yet traced and not known for certain to be alive, but not confirmed as dead ○ *missing persons* ◇ **go missing** to disappear or become lost, untraceable, or unaccounted for ◇ **missing in action** absent after combat and not known to be captured, injured, or dead

missing link *n* **1** an animal theorized or sought as a transitional evolutionary stage between apes and humans **2** something that is absent from a sequence or series and is needed to connect up its various parts and complete it

missiology /míssi ólləji/ *n* the study of Christian missionary work [Mid-20C. < MISSION.]

mission /mísh'n/ *n* **1 ASSIGNED TASK** a particular task given to a person or group to carry out **2 CALLING** an aim or task that somebody believes it is his or her duty to carry out or to which he or she attaches special importance and devotes special care **3 SPACE VEHICLE'S TRIP** a single flight or voyage of a military aircraft or a spacecraft **4 GROUP OF REPRESENTATIVES** a group of people sent to a country to represent their government, a business, or other organization **5** *US* **REPRESENTATION ABROAD** a permanent diplomatic delegation in another country **6 GROUP OF CHURCH WORKERS** a body of people sent by a church to another part of the country or to a foreign country to spread their faith or do medical and social work **7 CHURCH WORK IN THE COMMUNITY** a campaign of religious work, often including community aid at home or abroad, carried out by a church **8 COMMUNICATION OF BELIEFS** the vocation or work of a church or other religious organization or of individuals in communicating their faith in a variety of ways to the wider community **9 HOUSING USED BY MISSIONARIES** a building or group of buildings belonging to a missionary organization **10 MISSIONARY'S TERRITORY** an area assigned to a missionary or missionary group **11 PLACE THAT HELPS THE NEEDY** a centre run by a religious or charitable organization offering food, shelter, aid, and spiritual comfort to needy people **12 MINOR CHURCH** a church that has no permanent clergy and is supported by a larger church ■ *adj* **mission, Mission IN SPANISH MISSION STYLE** relating to or influenced by a style of architecture or heavy dark oak furniture used in early Spanish missions in the SW United States ■ *vt* **1 SEND ON A MISSION** to send somebody on or give somebody a mission **2 OPERATE A MISSION** to establish or conduct a religious mission in a place or among a people [Late 16C. Directly or via French < Latin *mission-* < *mittere* 'send off'.]

missionary /mísh'nəri/ *n* (*plural* **-ies**) **1 SOMEBODY WHO DOES CHURCH WORK ABROAD** somebody sent to another country by a church to spread its faith or to do social and medical work **2 PERSUADER** a person who tries to persuade others to accept or join something ■ *adj* **OF OR LIKE A MISSIONARY** relating to a missionary

missionary position *n* a position for sexual intercourse in which the woman lies on her back and the man lies on top of and facing her [Because missionaries held it to be least reprehensible]

mission creep *n* a tendency of military operations in foreign countries to increase gradually in scope and demand further commitment of personnel and resources as the situation develops

missioner /mísh'nər/ *n* **1** CHR = **missionary** *n*. 1 **2** a person in charge of a mission church in a parish

mission statement *n* a formal document that states the aims of a company or organization

missis /míssiz/, **missus** *n* (*informal*) **1** used as a term of address for a woman, sometimes in place of her name **2** used to refer to a man's wife or woman partner, usually either by the man himself or by another man (*sometimes offensive*) [Late 18C. Alteration of MISTRESS.]

Mississauga /míssi sáwgə/ city in S Ontario, Canada, on Lake Ontario. Population: 544,383 (1996).

Mississippi /míssi síppi/ **1** major river in the United States. It flows southward from N Minnesota to Louisiana, emptying into the Gulf of Mexico. Length: 3,778 km/2,348 mi. **2** state in the SE United States. Capital: Jackson. Population: 2,730,501 (1997). Area: 125,060 sq. km/48,286 sq. mi.

Mississippian /míssi síppi ən/ *n* **1** somebody who comes from the US state of Mississippi **2** the epoch of geological time in North America when large land masses were submerged underwater, 362.5 to 320 million years ago —**Mississippian** *adj*

missive /míssiv/ *n* a letter or written communication [Early 16C. < medieval Latin *missivus* < Latin *mittere* 'send'.]

Missouri /mi zóori/ **1** longest river in the United States. It flows from SW Montana southeastwards to join the Mississippi River in Missouri. Length: 4,128 km/2,565 mi. **2** state in the central United States. Capital: Jefferson City. Population: 5,402,058 (1997). Area: 180,545 sq. km/69,709 sq. mi. —**Missourian** *n, adj*

misspeak /míss speék/ (**-speaks, -speaking, -spoke** /-spṓk/, **-spoken** /-spṓkən/) *v US* **1** *vt* to pronounce something incorrectly **2** *vr* to speak or express yourself in a way that is inappropriate, inaccurate, or unclear ○ *Unfortunately the envoy misspoke himself on that particular issue.*

misspell /míss spél/ (**-spells, -spelling, -spelt** /-spélt/ *or* **-spelled, -spelt** *or* **-spelled**) *vt* to spell a word incorrectly

misspelling /míss spélling/ *n* an incorrect spelling of a word

misspelt past participle, past tense of **misspell**

misspend /miss spénd/ (**-spends, -spending, -spent** /-spént/, **-spent**) *vt* to spend money or time badly or wastefully —**misspender** *n*

misspoke past tense of **misspeak**

misspoken past participle of **misspeak**

misstate /miss stáyt/ (**-states, -stating, -stated**) *vt* to state something incorrectly, e.g. by giving false information or mispronouncing something —**misstatement** *n*

misstep /miss stép/ *n* **1** a bad or awkward step, or a step in a wrong direction **2** an error in judgment or conduct

missus *n* = **missis**

missy /míssi/ (*plural* **-ies**) *n* used as a term of address for a girl or young woman, often expressing affection or reprimand (*informal; sometimes offensive*)

mist /mist/ *n* **1 THIN FOG** a thin grey cloud of water droplets that condenses in the atmosphere just above the ground, limiting the view and making objects appear indistinct **2 CONDENSED WATER VAPOUR** a film of water vapour that has condensed on a surface **3 FINE SPRAY** a fine spray of liquid, e.g. from an atomizer or aerosol **4 LIQUID SUSPENSION IN GAS** a suspension of liquid in a gas **5 OBSCURING THING** something that makes it difficult to see or understand something ■ *v* **1** *vti* **FILM OVER** to cover or obscure something in a mist, or to become covered in or obscured by mist ○ *The windows of the bus had misted over.* **2** *vi* **BECOME BLURRED BY TEARS** to become blurred by tears **3** *vt* **SPRAY** to apply a fine liquid spray to something [Old English. < Indo-European, 'urinate'.]

mistake /mi stáyk/ *n* **1 INCORRECT ACT OR DECISION** an incorrect, unwise, or unfortunate act or decision caused by bad judgment or a lack of information or care ○ *It's an easy mistake to make.* **2 ERROR** something in a piece of work that is incorrect, e.g. a misspelling or a misprint **3 MISUNDERSTANDING** a misunderstanding of something ○ *There must be some mistake, I didn't order this.* ■ *vt* (**-takes, -taking, -took** /-stōōk/, **-taken** /-stáykən/) **1 MISUNDERSTAND** to misunderstand or misinterpret something ○ *I mistook the meaning of the phrase.* **2 IDENTIFY SOMEBODY OR SOMETHING INCORRECTLY** to identify somebody or something incorrectly or fail to recognize somebody or something ○ *We tend to mistake infatuation for real love.* **3 CHOOSE SOMETHING INCORRECTLY** to choose something incorrectly or injudiciously [14C. < Old Norse *mistaka* 'take in error'.] —**mistakable** *adj* —**mistakably** *adv* —**mistaker** *n* ◇ **by mistake** accidentally, without wishing or intending to do something

SYNONYMS ***mistake, error, inaccuracy, slip, blunder, faux pas***

CORE MEANING: something incorrect or improper

mistake an unwise decision or an error resulting from a lack of care; **error** something that unintentionally deviates from a recognized standard or guide; **inaccuracy** something that is incorrect because it has been measured, calculated, copied, or conveyed incorrectly; **slip** a minor mistake or oversight, especially one caused by carelessness; **blunder** a serious or embarrassing mistake, usually the result of carelessness or ignorance; **faux pas** (*literary*) an embarrassing mistake that breaks a social convention.

mistaken /mi stáykən/ *adj* **1** wrong or incorrect in, e.g., an assumption, belief, or your understanding of something ○ *If you think that'll work, then you're sadly mistaken.* **2** based on incorrect information or values ○ *a mistaken sense of loyalty* —**mistakenly** *adv* —**mistakenness** *n*

Mistassini, Lake /místə séeni/ lake in south-central Quebec, Canada. Area: 2,200 sq. km/840 sq. mi.

mister /místər/ *n* **1** used as a term of address for a man, usually in place of his name (*dated*) **2** used to refer to a woman's husband or man partner, either by the woman or by another woman (*informal; sometimes offensive*) [Mid-16C. Alteration of MASTER.]

Mister *n* **1 FORM OF 'MR'** used as the full form of the courtesy title 'Mr' **2 WAY TO ADDRESS JUNIOR OFFICERS** used as the official term of address for men junior officers or warrant officers **3 WAY TO ADDRESS SURGEON** used as the usual title for a surgeon **4 WAY TO ADDRESS MERCHANT NAVY OFFICER** used as the official term of address for any man officer in the merchant navy except the captain of a ship [Mid-18C. < MISTER.]

misterm /miss túrm/ *vt* to call something by a wrong or inappropriate name

misthrow /mis thrṓ/ (**-throws, -throwing, -threw** /-thrōō/, **-thrown** /-thrṓn/) *vti* to throw something, e.g. dice or a ball, in a wrong or invalid way —**misthrow** /mís thrō/ *n*

Misti, Volcán /meésti/ dormant volcano in the Andes, in S Peru. Height: 5,822 m/19,101 ft.

mistime /miss tī́m/ (**-times, -timing, -timed**) *vt* to time something wrongly, usually by missing the precise point of time at which something should be done to be successful

mistle thrush /míss'l-/, **missel thrush** *n* a large thrush with a spotted breast and greyish back that feeds on berries, especially those of mistletoe. Native to: Europe. *Turdus viscivorus.*

mistletoe /míss'ltō/ *n* **1 PARASITIC BUSH** an evergreen bush that grows as a parasite on trees such as apple and oak, has leaves in horseshoe-shaped pairs, and bears white berries in winter. Native to: Europe, Asia. *Viscum album.* **2 PLANT RESEMBLING MISTLETOE** a bush that resembles true mistletoe. Native to: North America. *Phoradendron flavescens.* **3 CHRISTMAS DECORATION** a sprig of mistletoe traditionally used as a decoration and for kissing under at Christmas [Old English *misteltān* < Germanic, 'urine' (because propagated by the droppings of the mistle thrush)]

mistook past tense of **mistake**

mistral /místrəl/ *n* a powerful cold dry northeasterly wind that blows in the south of France [Early 17C. Via French < Latin *magistralis* 'dominant'; from its power.]

mistreat /miss tréet/ *vt* to treat somebody or something badly or roughly

SYNONYMS See ***misuse***.

mistress /místrəss/ *n* **1 EXTRAMARITAL WOMAN LOVER OF MAN** a woman with whom a man has a usually long-term extramarital sexual relationship, often one in which he provides financial support **2 WOMAN OWNER OF A PET** the woman owner of a pet animal **3 ABLE WOMAN** a woman who is highly skilled in a particular activity ○ *a mistress of the art of negotiation* **4 WOMAN TEACHER** a woman teacher **5 PERSONIFICATION AS WOMAN** something that rules or controls, personified as a woman ○ *Venice, once mistress of the seas* **6 WOMAN OWNER OR CONTROLLER** a woman who owns or controls something, e.g. a woman owner of an estate, head of a household, or employer of servants [13C. < Old French *maistresse*, feminine of *maistre* (see MASTER).]

Mistress /místrəss/ *n* used as a courtesy title to address a married woman, usually in front of the surname (*archaic*)

mistress of ceremonies *n* a woman in charge of the proceedings at an event or entertainment

mistrial /miss trī́ əl/ *n* **1** a trial that is invalid because a mistake such as an error in procedure has been made **2** *US* a trial that does not come to a proper conclusion, e.g. because the jury cannot agree on a verdict

mistrust /miss trúst/ *n* suspicion about or lack of confidence in somebody or something ■ *vt* to be suspicious of and unable to trust or rely on somebody or something —**mistruster** *n* —**mistrustful** *adj* —**mistrustfully** *adv* —**mistrustfulness** *n*

misty /místi/ (**-ier, -iest**) *adj* **1 COVERED IN MIST** with a lot of mist in the air or surrounded or covered by mist ○ *a misty mountain* ○ *a misty morning* **2 LIKE MIST** like mist, especially in being in a cloud or spray of fine drops **3 DIM AND INDISTINCT** rather dim and indistinct, as if veiled by mist —**mistily** *adv* —**mistiness** *n*

misty-eyed *adj* **1** with a film of tears in the eyes **2** sentimental or dreamlike

misunderstand /miss undər stánd/ (**-stands, -standing, -stood** /-stōōd/) *vti* to fail to realize the real or intended meaning of something, the true nature of something, or what somebody is really like

misunderstanding /miss undər stánding/ *n* **1** a failure to understand or interpret something correctly **2** a minor disagreement or dispute

misunderstood past participle, past tense of **misunderstand** ■ *adj* not correctly understood, or not properly and sympathetically appreciated ○ *a misunderstood teenager*

misusage /miss yōōssij, miss yōōzij/ *n* **1** a wrong or inappropriate use of language **2** = **misuse** *n.* 1

misuse *n* /miss yōōss/ **1 WRONG USE** the incorrect or improper use of something **2 CRUEL TREATMENT** cruel treatment of a person or animal ■ *vt* /miss yōōz/ (**-uses, -using, -used**) **USE SOMETHING WRONGLY** to use something in an incorrect or improper way or for a dishonest purpose —**misused** *adj*

SYNONYMS ***misuse, abuse, ill-treat, maltreat, mistreat***

CORE MEANING: to treat somebody or something wrongly or badly

misuse to put something to an inappropriate use or purpose, or to treat a person or animal badly or harshly; **abuse** to use in a wrong or inappropriate way something that should be used responsibly, for example a power, privilege, or a substance such as alcohol or a drug. It is also used to refer to cruel or violent treatment of a person or animal, especially on a regular or habitual basis; **ill-treat** or **maltreat** to behave cruelly towards a person or animal, or to treat something roughly and carelessly; **mistreat** to treat a person badly, inconsiderately, or unfairly, not necessarily in a way involving physical cruelty, or to treat something roughly and carelessly.

misuser /miss yōōzər/ *n* an illegal user of a right, privilege, or position of authority

MIT *abbr* Massachusetts Institute of Technology

Mitchell /míchəl/ river in N Queensland, Australia. Length: 560 km/348 mi.

Mitchell, Joni (*b.* 1943) Canadian singer and songwriter. Born **Roberta Joan Anderson**

Mitchell, Margaret (1900–49) US writer

Mitchell, Reginald Joseph (1895–1937) British aircraft designer

Mitchell, Sir Thomas Livingstone (1792–1855) British-born Australian explorer and surveyor

Mitchum /míchəm/, **Robert** (1917–97) US film actor

mite[1] /mīt/ *n* a tiny eight-legged creature related to spiders and ticks. Order: Acarina. [Old English *mīte* < Germanic, 'cut']

SPELLCHECK See ***might***.

mite[2] /mīt/ *n* **1 SMALL CHILD** a small child or animal, especially one that inspires pity (*informal*) **2 SMALL AMOUNT** a small piece or small amount ○ *You could show just a mite of concern.* **3 SMALL COIN** a small coin of little value (*archaic*) [14C. < Middle Low German and Middle Dutch *mīte*, a small Flemish coin, also 'tiny animal'.]

miter *n*, *vt* US = **mitre**

Mitford /mítfərd/, **Jessica** (1917–97) British-born US writer

Mitford, Nancy (1904–73) British writer

Mithraism /mith ray izəm/ *n* a religion originating in Persia and involving worship of the god Mithras —**Mithraic** /mith ráy ik/ *adj* —**Mithraist** *n*

Mithras /mith rass/ *n* the god of light, truth, and goodness in the Zoroastrian tradition and Persian mythology [Mid-16C. Via Latin *Mithras* < Old Persian and Avestan *Mithra*.]

mithridate /mithri dayt/ *n* a substance believed in ancient medicine and folklore to be an antidote to every poison and a cure for every disease [Early 16C. Via medieval Latin *mithridatum* < late Latin *mithridatius* 'relating to Mithridates'.] —**mithridatic** /mithri dáttik/ *adj* —**mithridatism** *n*

miticide /mítti sīd/ *n* a substance that kills mites —**miticidal** /mítti sīd'l/ *adj*

mitigate /mítti gayt/ (**-gates, -gating, -gated**) *vt* **1** to make an offence or crime less serious or more excusable **2** to make something less harsh, severe, or violent [15C. < Latin *mitigat*, past participle of *mitigare* 'make mild' < assumed *mitigus* 'making mild' < *mitis* 'gentle, soft' + *agere* 'make'.] —**mitigable** *adj* —**mitigation** /mítti gáysh'n/ *n*

USAGE See ***militate***.

mitigating /mítti gayting/ *adj* making an offence or a crime seem less serious, or partly excusing it ○ *mitigating circumstances*

mitis /mítiss, méetiss/, **mitis metal** *n* a form of iron made malleable by having a small amount of aluminium added to it [Late 19C. Probably < Latin *mitis* 'mild'.]

Mitnagged /mít naa géd/ (*plural* **-dim** /mít naag dím/), **Mitnaged** (*plural* **-nagdim**), **Misnaged** /míss naa géd/ (*plural* **-dim** /míss naag dím/) *n* in the 18th and 19th centuries, a Jew in central and E Europe who believed in rationalism and opposed Hassidism [Early 20C. < Hebrew *mitnaggēd* 'opponent'.]

mitochondrion /mítō kóndri ən/ (*plural* **-a** /mítō kóndri ə/) *n* a small round or rod-shaped body that is found in the cytoplasm of most cells and produces enzymes for the metabolic conversion of food to energy [Early 20C.

< Greek *mitos* 'thread' + *khondrion* < *khondros* 'granule, lump (of salt)'.] —**mitochondrial** *adj*

mitogen /mítəjən/ *n* a substance or agent that induces mitosis [Mid-20C. < MITOSIS.]

mitomycin /mítō míssin/ *n* an antibiotic produced by a soil bacterium that inhibits DNA synthesis and is used against tumours [Mid-20C. < *mito-* < ?]

mitosis /mī tóssiss/ *n* the process by which a cell divides into two daughter cells, each of which has the same number of chromosomes as the original cell. ◊ **meiosis** *n.* 1 [Late 19C. < Greek *mitos* 'thread'.] —**mitotic** /mī tóttik/

mitrailleuse /míttrī óz/ *n* an early machine gun with 35 barrels that could be fired simultaneously or in sequence, mounted on a carriage drawn by four horses [Late 19C. < French *mitrailler*, < 'fire mitraille' < *mitraille* 'small money, pieces of metal', alteration of Old French *mitaille* < *mite*.]

mitral /mítrəl/ *adj* relating to a bishop's mitre or like it in shape, especially in having separate front and back sections [Early 17C. Via modern Latin *mitralis* < Latin *mitra* (see MITRE).]

mitral stenosis *n* the narrowing of the heart's mitral valve as the result of disease

mitral valve *n* the one-way valve between the upper and lower chambers, or atrium and ventricle, on the left side of the heart [< its shape]

mitre /mítər/ *n* **1 BISHOP'S HAT** the ceremonial headdress of a Christian bishop or abbot, consisting of a tall pointed hat creased across the top, with two ribbons hanging down the back **2** WOODWORK = **mitre joint 3 SURFACES OF A MITRE JOINT** either of the surfaces that are joined together to form a mitre joint **4 DIAGONAL JOIN AT THE CORNER BETWEEN HEMS** in sewing, a diagonal join between the edges of two hems that meet at a corner of a piece of fabric ■ *vt* **1 JOIN PIECES OF WOOD** to join pieces of wood using a mitre joint **2 SHAPE WOOD FOR JOINT** to shape the end of a piece of wood, especially by cutting it off at an angle of 45° when making a corner or mitre joint **3 DIAGONALLY JOIN HEMS AT THE CORNER** in sewing, to make a diagonal join at a corner between two hems **4 GIVE A MITRE TO** to confer a mitre on somebody, indicating promotion to the rank of bishop [14C. Via Old French < Latin *mitra* < Greek, 'belt, turban'.] —**mitrer** *n*

mitre block *n* a block with slots cut in it to guide a handsaw at the appropriate angle when cutting a mitre joint

mitre box *n* a box with open ends that is used to hold wood and guide a handsaw at the appropriate angle when cutting a mitre joint

mitre joint *n* a corner joint in woodwork, usually made by cutting two ends to be joined at 45° angles and gluing or nailing them together into a right angle

mitre square *n* a tool used in cutting wood at an angle that has a bevelled arm either fixed at an angle of 45° or adjustable to any angle

mitrewort /mítər wurt/ (*plural* **mitreworts** *or* **mitrewort**) *n* a plant with seed pods that look a little like a bishop's mitre. Flowers: small, white, in clusters. Native to: Asia, North America. Genus: *Mitella*. [Mid-19C. < the shape of its capsule.]

Mits'twa /mi tséewa/ town and port in N Eritrea. Population: 19,400 (1989).

mitt /mit/ *n* **1 MITTEN** a mitten, especially a child's mitten (*informal*) **2 HAND COVERING** a covering for the hand and fingers, especially one shaped like a mitten ○ *an oven mitt* **3 HAND** a hand, especially when large, clumsy, or dirty (*slang*) **4 BASEBALL PLAYER'S PADDED GLOVE** in baseball, a large fingerless padded glove worn by the catcher or the first baseman **5 GLOVE WITHOUT FINGERS** a woman's glove, popular in the 19th century, that left the fingers uncovered [Mid-18C. Shortening of MITTEN.]

mitten /mítt'n/ *n* a glove with one covering for the thumb and one covering for the four fingers [14C. < French *mitaine*.]

Mitterrand /meétə roN/, **François** (1916–96) French statesman and president (1981–95)

mittimus /míttiməss/ (*plural* **-muses**) *n* an official order to send somebody to prison [15C. < Latin, 'we send', first word of this order in Latin.]

mitzvah /mítsvə/ (*plural* **-vahs** *or* **-voth** /míts vōt/) *n* **1** a Jewish religious duty or obligation, especially one of the commandments of Jewish religious law **2** an act of kindness performed by or to a Jewish person [Mid-17C. < Hebrew *miṣwāh* 'commandment'.]

Miwok /meé wok/ (*plural* **-wok** *or* **-woks**) *n* **1** a member of a Native North American people living in central California from the Sierra Nevada foothills to the San Francisco Bay area **2** the language of the Miwok people, in some classifications belonging to the Penutian family of Native American languages. Miwok is now spoken by very few people. [Late 19C. < Miwok, 'people'.] —**Miwok** *adj*

mix /miks/ *v* **1** *vt* **COMBINE INGREDIENTS** to combine ingredients by putting them together or blending them to make a single new substance ○ *Mix the flour and dried fruit together.* **2** *vi* **BE COMBINED** to become combined, or be capable of becoming combined ○ *Oil and water don't mix.* **3** *vti* **MAKE SOMETHING BY COMBINING** to form or create something by combining separate ingredients ○ *Would you mix me a cocktail?* **4** *vt* **ADD SOMETHING EXTRA** to add something as an extra or later ingredient ○ *Mix the fruit into the batter.* **5** *vt* **COMBINE THINGS** to do something at the same time as something else, or to arrange things next to or alongside each other ○ *mixing browns and golds to create a sense of warmth* **6** *vi* **GO TOGETHER** to go well together ○ *Reds and greens just don't mix.* **7** *vi* **MEET PEOPLE** to meet other people socially, or enjoy being with other people in social situations **8** *vt* **CONSUME THINGS TOGETHER** to consume different drinks or foods on a single occasion **9** *vti* **BLEND MUSICAL SOUNDS** to adjust and blend sounds from prerecorded tracks or live performers to create the desired combination of musical sounds **10** *vt* **CROSSBREED PLANTS OR ANIMALS** to breed one variety of a plant or animal with another in order to create a new variety ■ *n* **1 ACT OF MIXING** an act of mixing something, or an occasion on which it is done ○ *Give all the ingredients a good mix.* **2 COMBINATION** a combination or blend of things ○ *There's an intriguing mix of styles on her latest CD.* **3 SUBSTANCE USED TO PREPARE** a substance, especially a number of dried ingredients in powder form, from which something is prepared ○ *cake mix* **4 MUSICAL BLEND** a balanced blend of live or prerecorded musical sound ○ *He thinks the drums are too low in the mix.* **5 VERSION OF A RECORDING** a version of a musical recording that has been changed in some way to give it a different type of sound ○ *Their last hit has been rereleased in a disco mix.* **6 RATIO OF MORTAR INGREDIENTS** the ratio of sand and cement in mortar, or of sand, cement, and gravel in concrete [15C. < MIXED.] —**mixable** *adj*

mix down *vt* to create a final finished sound recording by blending elements that have been recorded separately

mix up *v* **1** *vt* **MISTAKE THE IDENTITY OF THINGS** to confuse things or people and mistakenly identify one as the other ○ *People always mix her up with her sister.* **2** *vt* **CHANGE THE ORDER OF THINGS** to change the usual or previous order of things, either deliberately or by accident ○ *The pages got mixed up on the way to the printer's.* **3** *vti* **BECOME INVOLVED IN** to involve yourself with a particular group of people or activity, especially something wrong or illegal **4** *vt* **MAKE SOMETHING FROM INGREDIENTS** to prepare or make something by mixing different ingredients **5** *vt* **MAKE SOMEBODY CONFUSED** to make somebody confused and unsure of something ○ *He got mixed up because the street names sounded so similar.*

mixdown /míks down/ *n* **1** the process of converting a multitrack recording, usually a master tape recorded in a studio, into a stereo recording, usually for public release **2** a new recording produced by a mixdown

mixed /mikst/ *adj* **1 WITH DIFFERENT THINGS COMBINED** consisting of different elements or different kinds of things combined **2 INVOLVING BOTH SEXES** intended for, used by, or done by people of both sexes together **3 INVOLVING DIFFERENT RACES** intended for, used by, or done by people of different races together **4 WITH INCONSISTENT ELEMENTS** consisting of inconsistent or conflicting elements ○ *The play has had mixed reviews.* [15C.Via Old French < Latin *mixtus*, past participle of *miscere* 'to mix'.] —**mixedly** /míksidli/ *adv* —**mixedness** *n*

mixed bag *n* a group of people or things of widely differing kinds

mixed blessing *n* something that has both advantages and disadvantages or good points and bad points

mixed doubles *n* a tennis, table tennis, or badminton match played by two pairs, each consisting of a man and a woman (+ *singular verb*)

mixed economy *n* an economy in which some industries and businesses are state-owned and some are privately owned

mixed farming *n* farming that combines growing crops and rearing livestock on the one farm

mixed grill *n* a dish consisting of a grilled meat chop or steak, kidneys, sausage, bacon, mushrooms, and tomatoes

mixed marriage *n* a marriage between people of different racial or religious backgrounds

mixed media *n* **1** the use of different artistic media, e.g. painting combined with photography or collage, in a single composition or work **2** the use of different advertising media together, e.g. billboards, TV, and radio

mixed metaphor *n* a combination of two or more metaphors that together evoke a strange or incongruous image, e.g. 'This thorn in my side has finally bitten the dust'

mixed nerve *n* a nerve that has both motor and sensory fibres, and thus has nerve impulses passing in both directions

mixed number *n* a figure that consists of a whole number and a fraction, such as the figure $2\frac{3}{4}$

mixed-up *adj* (*informal*) **1** in a disorganized state **2** in a state of emotional or psychological confusion

mixed-use *adj US* combining commercial and residential elements in a single property, e.g. a block of flats with offices or shops

mixer /míksər/ *n* **1 MIXING DEVICE** a machine or device for mixing food, cement, or some other substance **2 NONALCOHOLIC DRINK OFTEN MIXED WITH ALCOHOL** a nonalcoholic drink, e.g. fruit juice or soda water, that is often mixed with alcoholic drinks **3 SOCIABLE PERSON** a person considered in terms of his or her ability to socialize ○ *She's a good mixer.* **4 TROUBLEMAKER** a person who constantly causes trouble, especially by gossiping (*informal*) **5 ELECTRONIC DEVICE FOR MIXING SOUNDS** an electronic device used to adjust and combine various inputs, e.g. performed or broadcast sounds, to create a single output **6 SOMEBODY CREATING SOUND FOR FILM** somebody who combines various sound recordings to create the final soundtrack of a film

mixer tap *n* a tap with separate controls for hot and cold water and a single outlet that combines both flows

mixte /míksti/, **mixte frame** *adj* describes a frame for bicycles designed for women, consisting of two horizontal tubes connecting to the back axle without a crossbar [Late 20C. < French, 'mixed'.]

Mixtec /meéss tek/ (*plural* **-tecs** *or* **-tec**), **Mixtecan** /meess téc ən/ (*plural* **-ans** *or* **-an**) *n* **1** a member of a Native American people who originally lived in S Mexico and are now spread throughout Mexico **2** an Oto-Manguean language spoken in Mexico. Native speakers: 400,000. [Late 18C. Via Spanish < Nahuatl *mixtecah* 'person from a cloudy place'.] —**Mixtec** *adj*

mixte frame *adj* CYCLING = **mixte**

mixter-maxter /míkstər mákstər/ *adj Scotland* in a disorganized or confused state (*informal*) ■ *n Scotland* a confused or disorganized collection of things (*informal*) [Late 18C. < reduplication of *mixt*, variant of MIXED.]

mixture /míkschər/ *n* **1 BLEND OF INGREDIENTS** a substance containing several ingredients combined or blended together ○ *cough mixture* **2 DIFFERENT THINGS COMBINED** a number of different elements brought or existing together ○ *an interesting mixture of people* ○ *a mixture of old and new styles* **3 LIQUID MEDICINE** a medicinal preparation consisting of an insoluble solid suspended in a liquid, often with added flavouring and colouring **4 SUBSTANCE FORMED WITHOUT CHEMICAL REACTION** a substance consisting of two or more substances that have been combined without chemical bonding taking place **5 FUEL AND AIR MIX** the combination of petrol vapour and air in an internal-combustion engine **6 ACT OF MIXING** the combining or mixing of different ingredients or elements (*formal*) [15C. Directly or via French < Latin *mixtura* < *mixt-*, past participle of *miscere*.]

SYNONYMS ***mixture, blend, combination, compound, alloy, amalgam***

CORE MEANING: something formed by mixing materials

mixture a number of elements or ingredients brought together; **blend** something formed by putting together two or more different kinds of things, especially in a skilled way, to form a new whole in which the original elements lose their distinctness; **combination** something formed by the association of two or more things that retain their distinctness; **compound** a technical word for a chemical formed from two or more elements, also used generally to describe anything composed of two or more separate parts; **alloy** a technical word for a metal such as steel that is formed by combining two or more different metallic elements; **amalgam** a technical word for an alloy formed by combining mercury with another metal, also used generally to describe something that is a mixture of two or more elements or characteristics.

---

mix-up *n* a state of confusion, or an error resulting from confusion ○ *an administrative mix-up*

Mizar /mī́ zaar/ *n* a multiple star in the constellation Ursa Major [< Arabic *Mi'zar* 'cloak, veil']

mizuna /mi zóonə/, **mizuma** /-mə/ *n* a mildly flavoured Japanese salad vegetable with a delicate texture [Late 20C. < Japanese.]

mizzen /mízz'n/ *n* **1** a sail on a mizzenmast **2** SAILING = **mizzenmast** ■ *adj* relating to or used on a mizzenmast or its sail [15C. < French *misaine* 'foresail, foremast' < Latin *medianus* 'of the middle, median'.]

mizzenmast /mízz'n maast/ *n* **1** on a ship with three or more masts, the third mast from the front **2** on a boat such as a ketch or yawl, the mast nearest the back

mizzle /mízz'l/ *n* very fine rain (*regional*) ■ *vi* (**-zles, -zling, -zled**) to rain lightly in fine drops (*regional*) [15C. < ?] —**mizzling** *adj* —**mizzly** *adj*

⚡**mk**[1] *abbr* Macedonia (*in Internet addresses*)

mk[2] *abbr* **1** mark **2** markka

Mk *abbr* **1** Mark **2** mark

mks, MKS *abbr* metre-kilogram-second

mks units *npl* the metric system of measurement, which has the metre, the kilogram, and the second as its basic units of length, mass, and time

ml[1] *symbol* mile

ml[2] *abbr* millilitre

mL *abbr* **1** millilambert **2** millilitre

⚡**ML** *abbr* more later (*in e-mails*)

MLA *abbr* **1** Master of Landscape Architecture **2** Member of the Legislative Assembly **3** Modern Language Association

MLD *abbr* minimum lethal dose

MLF *abbr* multilateral (nuclear) force

MLitt /ém lít/ *abbr* Master of Letters [Latin *Magister Litterarum*]

Mlle *abbr* Mademoiselle

MLR *abbr* minimum lending rate

mm *abbr* millimetre

MM *abbr* **1** Messieurs **2** Military Medal

Mme *abbr* Madame

mmf *abbr* magnetomotive force

mmHg *n* a unit for measuring atmospheric pressure. Full form **millimetre of mercury**

MMR vaccine *n* a vaccine that is routinely given to small children to protect them against measles, mumps, and rubella

MMus *abbr* Master of Music

⚡**mn** *abbr* Mongolia (*in Internet addresses*)

Mn *symbol* manganese

MN *abbr* **1** magnetic north **2** Merchant Navy **3** Minnesota

MNA *abbr* Member of the National Assembly (of Quebec)

mnemonic /ni mónnik/ *n* MEMORY AID a short rhyme, phrase, or other mental technique for making information easier to memorize ■ *adj* **1** ACTING AS MNEMONIC acting as a memory aid **2** RELATING TO MNEMONICS relating to the practice of improving the memory, or to systems designed to improve the memory [Mid-18C. < MNEMONICS, or < Greek *mnēmonikos* 'relating to memory' < *mnēmon-* 'mindful'.]

mnemonics /ni mónniks/ *n* the practice of improving or helping the memory, or the systems used to achieve this (*+ singular verb*) [Early 18C. < Greek *mnēmonika*, neuter plural of *mnēmonikos* (see MNEMONIC).]

Mnemosyne /nee mózzini, -mόssini/ *n* in Greek mythology, the goddess of memory and mother of the Muses [Via Latin < Greek *Mnēmosunē*]

mo /mō/ (*plural* **mos**) *n* a moment or short while (*informal*) ○ *I'll be there in half a mo.* [Late 19C. Shortening.]

Mo *symbol* molybdenum

MO *abbr* **1 m.o.** mail order **2** Medical Officer **3** Missouri **4 MO, m.o.** money order

mo. *abbr* month

Mo. *abbr* Missouri

m.o. = **MO**

M.O., m.o. *abbr* modus operandi

-mo *suffix* used after numerals to indicate the number of pages made by folding a sheet of paper ○ *16mo* [< *12mo*, abbreviation of Latin *(in) duodecimo* '(in) a twelfth'; < *duodecimus* 'twelfth']

moa /mṓ ə/ *n* a large flightless bird similar to the ostrich that became extinct at the end of the 18th century. Native to: New Zealand. Family: Dinornithidae. [Mid-19C. < Maori.]

Moab[1] /mṓ ab/ *n* the son of Lot and his eldest daughter, whose descendants were the enemies of Israel

Moab[2] /mṓ ab/ ancient kingdom situated to the east of the Dead Sea, in modern-day Jordan —**Moabite** /mṓ ə bīt/ *n, adj*

moan /mōn/ *v* **1** *vi* MAKE LOW SOUND EXPRESSING PAIN to make a long low sound that expresses pain or misery **2** *vti* COMPLAIN to complain about something, especially unreasonably or needlessly (*informal*) ○ *What's he moaning on about?* **3** *vt* SPEAK IN PAINED VOICE to say something in a voice that expresses pain or misery ○ *'Oh no!', she moaned* **4** *vi* MAKE NOISE LIKE SOMEBODY IN PAIN to make a long low noise that sounds like somebody expressing pain ○ *the wind moaning in the trees* ■ *n* **1** SOUND OF PAIN a long low sound made by somebody expressing pain or misery **2** SOUND LIKE MOAN a long, low sound that resembles an expression of pain or misery, made by something such as the wind **3** COMPLAINING SESSION a period of time during which somebody has an opportunity to complain about a particular thing or about things in general (*informal*) ○ *had a good moan* **4** COMPLAINT a complaint, especially one that is unreasonable or trivial (*informal*) [12C. Via assumed Old English *mān* 'complaint' < Germanic.] —**moaner** *n* —**moanful** *adj*

moat /mōt/ *n* **1** DITCH AROUND A CASTLE a wide water-filled ditch around a castle or fort, dug to give protection from invaders **2** DITCH ACTING AS A BARRIER a water-filled ditch dug to prevent access or escape, e.g. to confine animals in a zoo **3** *Ireland* = **motte** ■ *vt* PUT A MOAT AROUND A CASTLE to surround a castle or other fortified place with a moat [14C. < Old French *mote* 'mound' or medieval Latin *mota*.]

mob /mob/ *n* **1** NOISY CROWD a large and unruly crowd of people **2** GROUP OF PEOPLE a particular group of people (*informal*) **3** ORDINARY PEOPLE ordinary people, especially when thought of collectively as unintelligent or irrational (*informal*) ■ *vt* (**mobs, mobbing, mobbed**) **1** CROWD ROUND to crowd round somebody or something noisily and excitedly **2** CROWD INTO PLACE to crowd into and fill a place **3** ATTACK to attack somebody in a large group **4** ATTACK PREDATOR among animals that are preyed upon, to surround and harass a potential predator [Late 17C. Shortening of archaic *mobile* < Latin *mobile (vulgus)* 'excitable (crowd)'.] —**mobbed** *adj* —**mobber** *n* —**mobbish** *adj*

Mob *n* a group of people who are involved in organized crime, or the world of organized crime (*informal*)

mobcap /mób kap/ *n* **1** a loose-fitting frilly cap women often wore indoors in the 18th and early 19th centuries **2** a soft hat that is shaped like a mobcap and worn especially by small children and babies [Mid-18C. < obsolete *mob* 'prostitute, negligé', variant of *mab* 'promiscuous woman' < ?]

mob-handed *adj* in a large, often threatening, group of people (*informal*)

mobile /mṓ bīl/ *adj* **1** EASY TO MOVE able to move freely or easily ○ *She's mobile again after her skiing accident.* **2** OPERATING FROM VEHICLE operating from or set up in a vehicle that travels from place to place **3** CHANGING EXPRESSION changing expressions quickly and easily ○ *a mobile face* **4** PREPARED FOR CHANGE able or willing to change job, move home, or alter other arrangements at short notice if necessary **5** CHANGING SOCIALLY moving or able to move from one social or professional class or group to another, e.g. by changing jobs or moving to a new neighbourhood **6** WITH OWN TRANSPORT able to go somewhere because you have transport available (*informal*) ○ *He's got his wife's car for the evening, so we're mobile.* ■ *n* **1** HANGING DECORATION a hanging sculpture or decoration whose parts are balanced to move in response to air currents **2** MOBILE TELEPHONE a mobile phone (*informal*) [15C. Via French < Latin *mobilis* 'movable' < *movere* 'to move'.]

Mobile /mō béel/ city in SW Alabama. Population: 202,181 (1998 estimate).

-mobile *suffix* automobile, vehicle ○ *bloodmobile* ○ *snowmobile* [< AUTOMOBILE]

mobile home *n* a large caravan that can be transported on the back of a lorry but is usually connected to utilities and left on a single site

mobile library *n* a library operating from a bus or van and travelling from place to place, e.g. in rural areas

mobile phone *n* a portable telephone that works using a series of locally based cellular radio networks

Mobilian /mō bílli ən/ *n* a pidgin trading language containing elements of Choctaw that was used before the 20th century as a lingua franca in the Mississippi Valley and Gulf Coast [Mid-19C. < *Mobile*, town in Alabama.] —**Mobilian** *adj*

mobilise *vti* = **mobilize**

mobility /mō bíllәti/ *n* **1** ABILITY TO MOVE the ability to physically move about, especially to do work or take exercise **2** MOVEMENT TO ANOTHER SOCIAL GROUP the ability of people to move from one social group or class to another **3** BEING MOBILE the quality of being mobile

mobility housing *n* housing built or adapted for people who use wheelchairs for whom walking requires effort

mobilize /mṓbə līz/ (**-lizes, -lizing, -lized**), **mobilise** (**-lises, -lising, -lised**) *vti* to organize people or resources to be ready for action, or to take action, especially in a military or civil emergency [Mid-19C. < French *mobiliser* < *mobile* 'movable' (see MOBILE).] —**mobilizable** *adj* —**mobilization** /mṓbə lī záysh'n/ *n*

Möbius strip /mṓbi əss-/ *n* a continuous single-sided surface formed by rotating one end of a strip through 180° and joining it to the other end [Early 20C. After August Ferdinand *Möbius* (1790–1868), German mathematician.]

mobocracy /mo bókrəssi/ (*plural* **-cies**) *n* **1** CONTROL BY A MOB political control exercised by a mob (*disapproving*) **2** PLACE RUN BY A MOB a place where a mob has political control **3** MOB THAT RULES a mob that rules in a mobocracy —**mobocrat** /móbbə krat/ *n* —**mobocratic** /-kráttik/ *adj* —**mobocratical** *adj*

mobster /móbstər/ *n US* a participant in organized crime (*informal*)

Mobutu Sese Seko /mə bóotoo séss e sékō/ (1930–97) Congolese soldier and president of Zaïre (Democratic Republic of the Congo) (1965–97). Born **Joseph Désiré Mobutu**

Moçâmedes /mə saámədish/ former name for **Namibe**

~~**mocassin**~~ incorrect spelling of **moccasin**

moccasin /mókəssin/ *n* **1** a Native North American heelless shoe made of deerskin or other soft leather wrapped around over the foot and stitched on top **2** a low-heeled leather shoe whose side panels are joined to the upper panel using prominent stitching to form a raised puckered seam **3** ZOOL = **water moccasin** *n.* 1 [Early 17C. < Virginia Algonquian *mockasin*.]

moccasin telegraph *n Can* the exchange of news or information through social networks, especially by casual conversation (*informal; sometimes offensive*) [Because such information was originally transmitted by a Native North American runner]

mocha /mókə/ *n* **1** STRONG ARABIAN COFFEE a dark-brown strong-tasting coffee from Yemen and some other countries on the Arabian peninsula **2** FLAVOURING a flavouring made by mixing coffee and cocoa, used in baking **3** LEATHER soft suede leather made from sheepskin or goatskin, originally from Africa ■ *adj* DARK BROWN of a dark brown colour, like mocha coffee [Late 18C. After MOCHA.]

Mocha /mṓkə, mókə/ port in SW Yemen. Population: 1,163 (1977 estimate).

mochaccino /mṓkə chéen ō/ *n* a cappuccino made from a mixture of coffee and chocolate

mock /mok/ *v* **1** *vti* TREAT SOMETHING WITH SCORN to treat somebody or something with scorn or contempt **2** *vt* MIMIC to imitate people in a way that is intended to make them appear silly or ridiculous **3** *vt* PREVENT to prevent something from succeeding in a way that causes frustration or humiliation ○ *the wind mocking his efforts to light a fire* ■ *adj* **1** IMITATION made to appear like something else, usually something older or more expensive ○ *mock leather* **2** PRETEND done as an act, especially in order to amuse people ○ *frowned in mock disapproval* 3 PRACTICE done as practice for the real thing ○ *mock exams* ■ *n* 1 AN IMITATION something made as an imitation 2 OBJECT OF SCORN something or somebody ridiculed by others (*dated*) ■ **mocks** *npl* PRACTICE EXAMINATIONS the practice examinations given to school pupils in England and Wales to prepare them for examinations such as GCSEs and A-Levels [15C. < Old French *mocquer*.] —**mockable** *adj* —**mocker** *n* —**mocking** *adj* —**mockingly** *adv*

mock up *vt* to make a full-scale model of something, e.g. a working model of a machine to undergo testing

mockernut /mókər nut/ *n* 1 a large sweet hard-shelled nut, commonly gathered in the wild 2 a hickory tree that produces mockernuts. Native to: North America. *Carya tomentosa*.

mockery /mókəri/ (*plural* **-ies**) *n* 1 SCORN words or behaviour intended to make something or somebody look silly or ridiculous 2 SOMETHING INADEQUATE something that is ridiculously inadequate or wholly unsuccessful ○ *the survey was a mockery from start to finish* 3 OBJECT OF SCORN somebody or something that is treated with scorn or contempt and made to look silly or ridiculous

mock-heroic *adj* describes poetry that satirizes the heroic style by using it to describe something trivial ■ *n* verse written in the mock-heroic style

mockingbird /móking burd/ *n* a long-tailed greyish bird that incorporates the songs and calls of other birds into its own song. Native to: North America. *Mimus polyglottus*.

LITERARY LINK ***To Kill a Mockingbird***, a novel (1960) by US writer Harper Lee. Set in the southern United States, it tells the story of a white lawyer who agrees to defend an African American man wrongly accused of the rape of a white girl. The events are narrated from the point of view of the lawyer's six-year-old daughter, Scout.

mock moon *n* ASTRON = **paraselene**

mock orange /mok/ *n* 1 an ornamental shrub or tree. Flowers: fragrant, white, resembling those of an orange tree. Genus: *Philadelphus*. 2 any shrub or tree that resembles an orange tree

mock sun *n* ASTRON = **parhelion**

mock turtle *n US* 1 = **turtleneck** *n*. 3 2 = **turtleneck** *n*. 4

mock turtle soup *n* an old-fashioned soup made in imitation of turtle soup, using meat from a calf's head to replace the flesh of the green turtle

mock-up *n* 1 a full-sized model of something, built to scale and with working parts, used especially for testing or research 2 a preliminary layout of a newspaper, magazine, or other publication, showing the size and arrangement of material to be included

mod[1] /mod/, **Mod** *n* a member of a youth group in 1960s Britain remembered especially for their fashionable dress, motor scooters, and fights with motorcycle gangs (**rockers**) [Mid-20C. Shortening of MODERN or MODERNISM.]

mod[2] /mod/, **Mod** *n* a festival of Gaelic music and poetry held annually in Scotland, usually in the Highlands [Late 19C. Via Gaelic *mòd* 'assembly, court' < Old Norse *mót*.]

MoD *abbr* Ministry of Defence

mod. *abbr* 1 moderate 2 moderato 3 modern

modal /mṓd'l/ *adj* 1 EXPRESSING GRAMMATICAL MOOD describes verbs and auxiliary verbs expressing a grammatical mood, e.g. possibility or necessity. ◊ **modal auxiliary** 2 RELATING TO MUSICAL MODES relating to or using a mode, especially instead of a major or minor scale 3 DESCRIBING LOGICAL MODALITIES describes propositions involving necessity or probability, and those relating to knowledge, belief, and obligation [Mid-16C. Directly or via French < medieval Latin *modalis* < Latin *modus* 'measure'.] —**modally** *adv*

modal auxiliary *n* a verb used with other verbs to express such ideas as permission, possibility, and necessity. The modal auxiliaries in English grammar are 'can', 'could', 'may', 'might', 'must', 'ought to', 'shall', 'should', 'will', and 'would'. Some classifications also include 'dare', 'need', and 'used'.

modality /mō dálləti/ (*plural* **-ties**) *n* 1 WHAT MODAL VERB EXPRESSES the idea or concept that a modal auxiliary verb expresses 2 PROPOSITIONS OF NECESSITY OR POSSIBILITY the purely logical classification of propositions that relate to necessity or possibility 3 TREATMENT something used in the treatment of a disorder, e.g. surgery or chemotherapy [Early 17C. Directly or via French *modalité* < medieval Latin *modalitas* < *modalis* < Latin *modus* 'measure'.]

modal logic *n* the branch of logic that studies the relations between modal propositions

mod cons /mód kónz/ *npl* the facilities that make modern life easier and more comfortable such as central heating, hot water, telecommunications, and household appliances (*informal*) [Mid-20C. Shortening of *modern conveniences*.]

mode /mōd/ *n* 1 MANNER OR FORM a way, manner, or form, e.g. a way of doing something, or the form in which something exists 2 STYLE OR FASHION a style or fashion, e.g. in art or in dress 3 MACHINE SETTING a setting or function on a machine such as a computer 4 TYPE OF AUTOMATIC BEHAVIOUR a way of behaving, especially one that is instinctive, familiar, or habitual (*informal humorous*) 5 MUSICAL SCALE a musical scale that is one of the seven patterns of notes that can be played over an octave using only the white notes of the piano keyboard 6 MOST FREQUENT VALUE the value that has the highest frequency within a statistical range 7 MODAL STATUS OF PROPOSITION the modal status of a proposition, e.g. its being necessary or merely possible 8 RADIO FREQUENCY one of the radio frequencies characteristic of a given resonator or oscillator 9 COMBINATION OF IDEAS a combination of ideas that cannot be worked out merely by analysis of its components [14C. < Latin *modus* 'measure'.]

model /módd'l/ *n* 1 COPY OF OBJECT a copy of an object, especially one made on a smaller scale than the original (*often before nouns*) 2 PARTICULAR VERSION OF MANUFACTURED ARTICLE a particular version of a manufactured article ○ *had traded in her car for the latest model* 3 SOMETHING COPIED something that is copied or used as the basis for a related idea, process, or system 4 SOMEBODY PAID TO WEAR CLOTHES a person who is paid to wear clothes or demonstrate merchandise, e.g. in fashion shows or in photographs 5 SIMPLIFIED VERSION a simplified version of something complex used, e.g., to analyse and solve problems or make predictions ○ *a financial model* 6 PERFECT EXAMPLE an excellent example that deserves to be imitated 7 ARTIST'S SUBJECT a poser for a painter, sculptor, photographer, or other artist 8 SMALL VERSION OF SCULPTURE a small version of a sculpture, from which a finished work is copied 9 ANIMAL COPIED BY ANOTHER ANIMAL an animal species repellent to predators that another animal mimics for protection 10 INTERPRETATION an interpretation of a theory arrived at by assigning referents in such a way as to make the theory true 11 EXCLUSIVE GARMENT the first sewn example of a couturier's or clothing manufacturer's design, from which a new line of garments is produced ■ *v* (**-els, -elling, -elled**) 1 *vti* WORK AS FASHION MODEL to work as a fashion model, wearing clothes, make-up, and other items in order to display them to others 2 *vi* BE ARTIST'S MODEL to sit as a model for somebody such as a painter or photographer 3 *vt* BASE ONE THING ON SOMETHING ELSE to base something, especially somebody's appearance or behaviour, on that of another person ○ *She modelled herself on her older sister.* 4 *vt* SHAPE to make something by shaping a substance or material, e.g. clay or wood 5 *vti* MAKE SIMPLIFIED VERSION OF PROCESS to make a model of a process or system as a way of analysing and solving problems or making predictions [Late 16C. Via French *modèle* < Italian *modello* 'model' < Latin *modulus* 'measure' < *modus*.] —**modeller** *n*

model home *n US* = **show house**

modeling *n* US = **modelling**

modelling /móddling/ *n* 1 FASHION MODEL'S WORK the work of a fashion model 2 MAKING MODELS the activity or hobby of making models 3 DEMONSTRATION OF BEHAVIOUR the demonstration of a way of behaving to somebody, especially a child, in order for that behaviour to be imitated

model theory *n* the branch of logic that deals with providing models for theories —**model-theoretic** *adj*

ϟ **modem** /mṓ dem/ *n* an electronic device that connects computers via a telephone line [Mid-20C. Blend of MODULATE + DEMODULATE.]

Modena /mo déenə/ city in north-central Italy. Population: 176,972 (1992).

moderate *adj* /móddərət/ 1 SMALL OR SLIGHT not large, great, or severe ○ *a moderate portion* 2 REASONABLE not excessive or unreasonable ○ *a moderate eater* 3 MIDDLE-OF-THE-ROAD not extreme or radical ○ *moderate views* 4 AVERAGE neither particularly good nor particularly bad ○ *moderate results* ■ *n* SOMEBODY WITH MODERATE VIEWS a person who holds views, especially political views, that are not extreme ■ *vti* /móddə rayt/ (**-ates, -ating, -ated**) 1 MAKE OR BECOME LESS EXTREME to become, or make something become, less great, extreme, violent, or severe 2 PRESIDE OVER to chair or preside over something such as a meeting or discussion 3 ACT AS EXAM MODERATOR to act as a moderator in school examinations 4 *Scotland* PRESIDE OVER CHURCH ASSEMBLY in the Presbyterian denominations of the Christian church, to preside over a formal meeting or assembly [14C. < Latin *moderat-*, past participle of *moderari* 'regulate'.] —**moderately** *adv* —**moderateness** *n*

moderate breeze *n* a wind that measures force four on the Beaufort scale, with a speed of between 13 and 18 mph or 20.9 and 29 kph

moderate gale *n* a wind that measures force seven on the Beaufort scale, with a speed of between 32 and 38 mph or 51.5 and 61.2 kph

moderation /móddə ráysh'n/ *n* 1 BEING MODERATE the state in which something remains moderate rather than becoming extreme or excessive ○ *moderation in all things* 2 MAKING SOMETHING MODERATE the limiting, controlling, or restricting of something so that it becomes or remains moderate 3 ACTING AS MODERATOR the position or function of moderating something ◇ **in moderation** within reasonable limits, and never to excess

Moderations /móddə ráysh'nz/ *npl* EDUC = **Honour Moderations**

moderato /móddə raàtō/ *adv* at a moderate tempo (*musical direction*) [Early 18C. < Italian, < Latin *moderat-* (see MODERATE).]

ϟ **moderator** /móddə raytər/ *n* 1 SOMEBODY IN CHARGE OF DISCUSSIONS a presider over an assembly, especially a legislative assembly, or a mediator in discussions or negotiations 2 PRESIDING MINISTER in the Presbyterian denominations of the Christian church, a minister presiding over a church court or other assembly 3 *Scotland* PRESIDING MINISTER IN CHURCH OF SCOTLAND in the Church of Scotland, the minister chosen to preside for one year over the General Assembly of the Church of Scotland and perform ceremonial duties 4 NEUTRON ABSORBER a substance, e.g. graphite or beryllium, that slows neutrons in a nuclear reactor so that they can bring about the fission of uranium 5 EXTERNAL EXAMINER an official responsible for making sure that standards of marking in public examinations are consistent from region to region 6 MAILING LIST MANAGER a manager of a moderated mailing list or Usenet newsgroup —**moderatorship** *n*

modern /módd'n/ *adj* 1 BELONGING TO PRESENT DAY relating or belonging to the present period in history 2 OF LATEST KIND of the latest, most advanced kind, or using the most advanced equipment and techniques available ○ *modern medicine* 3 USING LATEST STYLES relating to or using ideas and techniques that have only recently been developed or are still considered experimental 4 OF LANGUAGE'S LATEST STAGE relating or belonging to the most recent stage in the development of a language ■ *n* 1 MODERN PERSON somebody living in the present period, especially somebody whose tastes and attitudes are regarded as nontraditional or strikingly new 2 TYPEFACE a typeface with heavy vertical strokes and straight serifs [Early 16C. Directly or via French *moderne* < Latin *modernus* < *modo* 'just now, in a (certain) manner' < *modus* 'measure'.] —**modernly** *adv* —**modernness** *n*

SYNONYMS See ***new***.

Modern Apprenticeship *n* work-based training for 16-to-17-year-olds, intended to include the achieving of an NVQ (National Vocational Qualification) at level 3 within three years

modern dance *n* a free style of theatrical dancing that developed in the early 20th century

modern-day *adj* 1 resembling a particular person or thing from the past 2 relating to, belonging to, or existing in the present time

moderne /mə dáirn/ *adj* describes a style of architecture and design popular in the 1920s and 1930s and characterized by streamlined and curved forms [Mid-20C. < French *moderne* (see MODERN).]

Modern English *n* the English language from about 1500, when it began to develop a more standardized form compared with the dialects of Middle English. ◊ **Old English, Middle English** —**Modern English** *adj*

modern Greek *n* the form of Greek spoken since around

1453, the year of the fall of Byzantium —**modern Greek** *adj*

Modern Hebrew *n* the form of the Hebrew language, a revival of the ancient form, that is the official language of the state of Israel —**Modern Hebrew** *adj*

modern history *n* the study of the period of history that extends from the end of the Middle Ages in Europe, around the middle of the 15th century, to the present day

modernise *vti* = **modernize**

modernism /módd'nizəm/ *n* **1 LATEST THINGS** the latest styles, tastes, attitudes, or practices **2 MODERN STYLES IN ART** the revolutionary ideas and styles in art, architecture, and literature that developed in the early 20th century as a reaction to traditional forms **3 MOVEMENT WITHIN ROMAN CATHOLICISM** a movement in European Roman Catholicism in which scholars and theologians attempt to accommodate the contemporary world view within Roman Catholic theology and doctrine —**modernist** *n, adj* —**modernistic** /-ístik/ *adj* —**modernistically** *adv*

QUICK FACTS ON... **MODERNISM**

Key dates: 1870s–1960s
Key locations: W Europe, especially Paris and Germany; United States, especially New York
Key elements: abandonment of conventional techniques and forms of representation; autonomy of artwork; formalism; experimentation; originality; fascination with technology; influence of non-European cultures
Key figures: Claude Monet, Pablo Picasso, Piet Mondrian, Marcel Duchamp, Jackson Pollock (painting and sculpture); T.S. Eliot, James Joyce, Virginia Woolf, Samuel Beckett (literature); Walter Gropius, Le Corbusier, Ludwig Mies van der Rohe (architecture); Arnold Schoenberg, Igor Stravinsky (music)
Key works: *Impression, Sunrise* (Monet) 1874, *Les Demoiselles d'Avignon* (Picasso) 1907, *The Waste Land* (Eliot) 1922, *Ulysses* (Joyce) 1922, Bauhaus Building, Dessau (Gropius) 1926, *The Rite of Spring* (Stravinsky) 1913
Key developments: avant-gardism, abstraction, Art Deco, moderne design, cubism, Dada, surrealism, 12-tone music and serialism, abstract expressionism, International Style, brutalism, postmodernism, conceptual art, performance art

modernity /mo dúrnəti/ (*plural* **-nities**) *n* **1 QUALITY OF BEING MODERN** the quality of being modern or up-to-date **2 SOMETHING MODERN** a modern thing **3 PERIOD SINCE ENLIGHTENMENT** the historical period from the Enlightenment to the present day, associated with the search for rational explanation of the universe and all things in it

modernize /módd'n īz/ (**-izes, -izing, -ized**), **modernise** (**-ises, -ising, -ised**) *vti* to change something in order to make it conform to modern tastes, attitudes, or standards —**modernization** /módd'n ī záysh'n/ *n* —**modernizer** *n*

modern jazz *n* a style of jazz that developed in the early 1940s, with rhythms and harmonies much more complex than those of traditional jazz

modern pentathlon *n* an athletics competition consisting of the five events of swimming, horse riding and jumping, cross-country running, fencing, and pistol shooting

modest /móddist/ *adj* **1 HUMBLE** not having or expressing a high opinion of your own achievements or abilities **2 SHY** not confident or assertive, and tending to be easily embarrassed in company **3 REASONABLE** not large, extreme, or excessive ○ *a modest income* **4 SIMPLE** not showy, elaborate, or pretentious ○ *a modest dwelling* **5 NOT OVERTLY SEXUAL** not drawing attention to or discussing sexuality, and so unlikely to offend or arouse others [Mid-16C. Partly a back-formation < MODESTY, partly via French *modeste* < Latin *modestus* 'kept within due measure'.] —**modestly** *adv*

modesty /móddisti/ *n* **1 HUMILITY** unwillingness to draw attention to your own achievements or abilities **2 SEXUAL RESERVE** reserve about nudity or sexual matters, especially a preference for clothes that keep much of the body covered **3 SHYNESS** lack of confidence when speaking to others or stating opinions, and the tendency to be uneasy or embarrassed in company **4 SIMPLICITY** lack of grandeur or ostentation **5 MODERATION** moderation in size, scale, or extent

modicum /móddikəm/ *n* a small amount, especially of something abstract, such as a particular quality ○ *It only requires a modicum of common sense.* [Late 15C. < Latin, 'little way, short time', a form of *modicus* 'moderate' < *modus* 'measure'.]

modif. *abbr* **1** modification **2** modifier

modification /móddifi káysh'n/ *n* **1 CHANGE** a slight change or alteration made to improve something or make it more suitable ○ *made a few modifications to the original design* **2 ACT OF MODIFYING** the act or process of modifying something, or the condition of having been modified ○ *in need of modification* **3 SOMETHING MODIFIED** something that has been modified ○ *The new version is a modification and is based on existing software.* **4 GRAMMATICAL RELATIONSHIP WITH A MODIFIER** in grammar, the relationship between a modifier and what it modifies [15C. Directly or via French < Latin *modificatio(n)-*, past participle of *modificare* (see MODIFY).] —**modificative** /móddifi kaytiv/ *adj* —**modificator** *n* —**modificatory** *adj*

modifier /móddi fī ər/ *n* **1** somebody or something that makes slight changes to something, especially to improve it **2** a word or phrase that affects the meaning of another, usually describing it or restricting its meaning. 'Pink' in the phrase 'the pink ribbon', 'fire' in the compound 'fire alarm', and 'in the morning' in the sentence 'She always goes jogging in the morning' are modifiers.

modify /móddi fī/ (**-fies, -fying, -fied**) *v* **1** *vti* **MAKE CHANGES TO** to make a slight change or alteration to something, or to change slightly **2** *vt* **LESSEN** to make something less extensive, severe, or extreme **3** *vt* **AFFECT WORD'S MEANING** to affect the meaning of a word, usually by describing or limiting it, by adding an adjective, noun, or phrase **4** *vt* **CHANGE VOWEL SOUND** to change the sound of a vowel by adding an umlaut [14C. Via French *modifier* < Latin *modificare* 'limit' < *modus* 'measure' + form of *facere* 'make'.] —**modifiability** /móddi fī ə bílləti/ *n* —**modifiable** *adj* —**modifiableness** *n*

SYNONYMS See *change*.

Modigliani /móddil yaáni/, **Amedeo** (1884–1920) Italian painter and sculptor

modillion /mə díllyən/ *n* a small curved ornamental bracket under the corona of a Corinthian or Composite column [Mid-16C. Via French < Italian *modiglione* < Latin *mutulus* 'mutule'.]

modiolus /mō dī ələss/ (*plural* **-li** /-ə lī/) *n* the bony central pillar of the cochlea in the inner ear [Late 17C. < Latin, 'nave of a wheel', < *modius* 'measure'.]

modish /mṓdish/ *adj* in or conforming to the very latest fashions or styles, especially those considered extreme or outrageous —**modishly** *adv* —**modishness** *n*

modiste /mō deést/ *n* a designer, maker, or seller of fashionable women's clothes (*dated*) [Mid-19C. < French, < *mode* 'fashion'.]

Modred /mṓdrid/, **Mordred** /máwdrid/ *n* in Arthurian legend, a knight of the Round Table who killed his uncle, King Arthur

Mods /modz/ *npl* Honour Moderations (*informal*) [Mid-19C. Shortening of MODERATIONS.]

modular /móddyòolər/ *adj* **1** made up of separate modules that can be rearranged, replaced, or interchanged easily ○ *modular construction techniques* **2** relating to or resembling a modulus, or made up of moduli ○ *a modular course structure* [Late 18C. < modern Latin *modularis* < Latin *modulus* (see MODULUS).] —**modularity** /móddyòo lárrəti/ *n* —**modularly** *adv*

modular arithmetic *n* a branch of arithmetic that deals with the remainders of whole numbers after the numbers have been divided by a modulus

modularized /móddyòolə rīzd/, **modularised** *adj* made up of separate parts or modules that can be rearranged, replaced, or interchanged easily

modulate /móddyòo layt/ (**-lates, -lating, -lated**) *v* **1** *vt* **CHANGE SOUND** to change the tone, pitch, or volume of sound, e.g. of a musical instrument or the human voice **2** *vt* **ALTER** to make alterations in something to make it less strong, forceful, or severe **3** *vti* **CHANGE KEY** in tonal music, to change from one key to another through a harmonic progression **4** *vt* **VARY WAVE CHARACTERISTICS** to vary the frequency, amplitude, or other characteristics of a radio wave or another carrier wave in order to transmit information [Mid-16C. < Latin *modulat-*, past participle of *modulari* 'measure, adjust to rhythm' < *modulus* (see MODULUS).] —**modulability** /móddyòolə bílləti/ *n* — **modulable** *adj* —**modulation** /móddyòo láysh'n/ *n* —**modulative** *adj* —**modulator** *n* —**modulatory** *adj*

module /móddyool/ *n* **1 INDEPENDENT INTERCHANGEABLE UNIT** a unit that is combined with others to form a larger structure or system and is self-contained enough to be easily rearranged, replaced, or interchanged to form different structures or systems **2 SHORT COURSE OF STUDY** a short course of study that forms part of a larger academic course or training programme, e.g. any of the elements that form part of a degree course **3 PART OF A SPACE VEHICLE** one of the self-contained units or craft that make up a space vehicle **4 UNIT OF MEASUREMENT** a unit of measurement or a standard, used especially in measuring architectural elements [Late 16C. Directly or via French < Latin *modulus* (see MODULUS).]

modulo /móddyòolō/ *prep* with respect to a particular modulus ○ *9 and 30 are congruent modulo 7 because both leave the same remainder if they are divided by 7.* [Late 19C. < Latin, form of *modulus* (see MODULUS).]

modulus /móddyòoləss/ (*plural* **-li** /-lī/) *n* **1 COEFFICIENT** a coefficient expressing the degree to which a substance exhibits a particular property **2 LOGARITHM FACTOR** the factor by which a logarithm of one base must be multiplied to become the logarithm of another base **3 ABSOLUTE VALUE** the absolute value of a complex number **4 DIVISION NUMBER** a number by which two other numbers can be divided so that both give the same remainder [Mid-16C. < Latin, 'small measure' < *modus* 'measure'.]

modus operandi /mṓdəss óppə rán dee, -dī/ (*plural* **modi operandi** /mṓ dee óppə rán dee, mṓ dī óppə rán dī/) *n* a particular way of doing things [< Latin, 'mode of operating']

modus vivendi /mṓdəss vi vén dee, -dī/ (*plural* **modi vivendi** /mṓ dee vi vén dee, mṓ dī vi vén dī/) *n* **1** a practical arrangement that allows conflicting people, groups, or ideas to coexist **2** the way that a particular person or group of people lives [< Latin, 'mode of living']

ϟ **MOF, MorF** *abbr* male or female (*in e-mails*)

mog /mog/ *n* a cat (*informal*) [Early 20C. Shortening of MOGGY.]

Mogadishu /mogə dísho͞o/ capital of Somalia, in the southeast of the country. Population: 982,000 (1995 estimate).

Mogen David /mṓgən-/ *n* JUDAISM = **Star of David**

moggy /móggi/ (*plural* **-gies**), **moggie** (*plural* **-gies**) *n* a cat (*slang*) [Late 17C. Variant of *Maggie* < *Mag*, shortening of *Margaret*.]

Moghul *n* HIST = **Mughal**

Mogollon /mṓgə yṓn/ (*plural* **-lons** *or* **-lon**) *n* a member of a Native North American people whose civilization in Arizona and New Mexico lasted from around the 2nd century BC to the 13th century AD [After places in Arizona and New Mexico, after Juan Ignacio Flores *Mogollon*, governor of New Mexico (1712–15)]

mogul[1] /mṓg'l/ *n* an important or powerful person, especially somebody working in the media [Late 17C. < MOGUL.]

mogul[2] /mṓg'l/ *n* a mound of hard compacted snow formed as an obstacle on a ski slope [Mid-20C. < ?]

Mogul *n* HIST = **Mughal**

mohair /mṓ hair/ *n* **1** the soft silky wool of the Angora goat **2** the silky yarn made from mohair [Late 16C. Alteration of *mocayre* < Arabic *mukayyar* 'cloth of goat's hair' < past participle of *kayyara* 'prefer'.]

Mohammed ISLAM = **Muhammad**

Moharram *n* ISLAM = **Muharram**

Mohave /mō haávi/ (*plural* **-ves** *or* **-ve**), **Mojave** (*plural* **-ves** *or* **-ve**) *n* the Yuman language of the Mohave people [Mid-19C. < Mohave *hàmakhá:v.*] —**Mohave** *adj*

mohawk /mṓ hawk/ *n US* = **mohican** [Late 19C. < MOHAWK.]

Mohawk /mṓ hawk/ (*plural* **-hawks** *or* **-hawk**) *n* **1** a member of an Iroquois people who lived along the Mohawk and Hudson rivers, and who now live mainly in Ontario and New York State **2** an Iroquoian language spoken in Quebec, Ontario, and N New York. Native speakers: 3,000. [Mid-17C. < Narragansett *mohowawog* 'man-eaters'.]

Mohegan /mō heégən/ (*plural* **-gans** *or* **-gan**) *n* **1** a member of a Native North American people who lived in E Connecticut, and who now live mainly in SE Connecticut and Wisconsin **2** an Algonquian language spoken in Connecticut and Wisconsin. Native speakers: 1,000. [Variant of MOHICAN] —**Mohegan** *adj*

mohel /mó hel, -el/ (plural **-helim** /-he leem/) n a person who is qualified under Jewish religious law to carry out circumcisions [Mid-17C. < Hebrew môhēl.]

Mohenjo-daro /mahen jō daărō/ ruined ancient city of the Indus Valley civilization, in modern-day S Pakistan

mohican /mō heĕkan, mō ikan/ n a hairstyle in which the sides of the head are shaved and the remaining hair is worn sticking up. US term **mohawk** n. [Mid-20C. < the topknots worn in Last of the Mohicans (1826), a novel by James Fenimore COOPER.]

Mohican (plural **-cans** or **-can**) n a Mahican, or the Mahican language (dated) —**Mohican** adj

Moho /mŏhō/ n GEOG = **Mohorovicic discontinuity** [Mid-20C. Shortening.]

Moholy-Nagy /mō hōli nój/, László (1895–1946) Hungarian-born US artist

Mohorovicic discontinuity /mōĥa rŏvichich-/ n the boundary between the Earth's crust and the mantle, occurring on average at 8 km/5 mi. under the oceans to 35 km/22 mi. under the continents [Mid-20C. After A. Mohorovičić (1857–1936), Yugoslav seismologist.]

Mohs scale /mōz-/ n a scale used to measure the hardness of minerals, with talc at zero and diamond at 10 [Late 19C. After Friedrich Mohs (1773–1839), German mineralogist.]

mohur /mŏhər/ n a gold coin worth 15 rupees used in British India in the 19th and early 20th centuries [Late 17C. < Persian and Urdu muhr 'seal'.]

moidore /mŏy dáwr/ n an obsolete Portuguese or Brazilian gold coin [Early 18C. < Portuguese moeda d'ouro 'coin of gold'.]

moiety /mŏy əti/ (plural **-ties**) n 1 either of the two parts, not necessarily equal, into which something is divided (formal) 2 among Native South Americans and Aboriginal Australians, one of two halves into which society is divided for ritual and marriage purposes [15C. Via French moitié 'half' < late Latin medietas < Latin medius 'middle'.]

moil /moyl/ n (archaic) 1 TURMOIL a state of agitation or confusion 2 DRUDGERY hard work ■ vi WORK HARD to work very hard ○ toiling and moiling [14C. Via Old French moillier 'moisten, paddle in mud' < Latin mollire 'soften' < mollis 'soft'.] —**moiler** n

Moirai /mŏy ree/ npl in Greek mythology, the Fates. Roman equivalent **Parcae** [< Greek]

moire /mwaar/, **moiré** /mwaà ray/ n a moiré fabric, especially silk but also, formerly, mohair [Mid-17C. < French, later form of mouaire 'mohair'.]

moiré /mwaà ray/ adj WITH A WAVY PATTERN describes fabric with a shiny or wavy pattern on the surface ■ n 1 WAVY PATTERN ON FABRIC a shiny finish and wavy pattern on fabric, especially silk, created by using engraved rollers 2 WAVY PATTERN the wavy or blurred effect created by superimposing one geometric pattern on a similar or identical pattern that is slightly out of alignment with the first [Early 19C. < French moiré, past participle of moirer 'to water' < moire 'moiré fabric', probably alteration of MOHAIR.]

moiré effect n TEXTILES = **moiré** n. 2

moiré pattern n TEXTILES = **moiré** n. 2

moist /moyst/ adj 1 DAMP slightly wet or damp 2 FRESH pleasantly fresh, rather than dry or stale ○ a rich, moist fruitcake 3 TEARFUL full of tears ○ moist eyes 4 RAINY humid or rainy, especially with light rain or drizzle [14C. Via Old French moiste < Latin mucidus 'mouldy' < mucus 'slime', probably influenced by musteus 'new'.] —**moistly** adv —**moistness** n

SYNONYMS See **wet.**

moisten /mŏyss'n/ vti to make something moist or to become moist ○ Moisten the mixture with a little beaten egg. —**moistener** n

moisture /mŏyss chər/ n wetness, especially droplets of condensed or absorbed liquid, or in a vapour [14C. < Old French moistour < moiste (see MOIST).]

moisturize /mŏyss chə rīz/ (**-izes, -izing, -ized**), **moisturise** (**-ises, -ising, -ised**) v 1 vti to apply a cosmetic cream or lotion to the skin, especially on the face, to help prevent the skin drying out 2 vt to make something moist or more moist

moisturizer /mŏyss chər īzər/ n a cosmetic cream or lotion used to make the skin, especially on the face, feel less dry

Mojave Desert /mō haǎvi-/ dry region in S California. Area: 39,000 sq. km/15,000 sq. mi.

mojo /mŏjō/ (plural **-joes** or **-jos**) n US (slang) 1 witchcraft or magic, or some powerful influence 2 an object believed to have magical powers, especially the power to keep away evil spirits [Early 20C. Probably of African origin.]

moke /mōk/ n a donkey (slang) [Mid-19C. Probably from a personal name.]

moko /mŏkō/ (plural **-kos**) n NZ 1 tattooing practised by Maoris, especially on the face 2 a pattern of tattoos used by the Maori [Mid-19C. < Maori.]

moksha /mŏksha/ n in Hinduism, the spiritual goal of release from reincarnation [Late 18C. < Sanskrit mokṣa < muc 'set free, release'.]

mol symbol mole

mol. abbr 1 molecular 2 molecule

mola /mŏla/ (plural **-las** or **-la**) n ZOOL = **sunfish** n. 1 [Late 17C. < French mole.]

molal /mŏlal/ adj describes a solution consisting of one mole of dissolved substance (**solute**) per 1,000 grams of solution

molality /mo lálləti/ (plural **-ties**) n the concentration of a solution, expressed as the number of moles of a dissolved substance (**solute**) that can be found in 1,000 grams of solvent

molar[1] /mŏlər/ n a large back tooth in humans and other mammals, used for chewing and grinding [14C. < Latin molaris 'of a mill; grindstone, molar tooth' < mola 'mill'.]

molar[2] /mŏlər/ adj 1 RELATING TO A MOLE describes something that relates to or is a mole of a substance ○ the molar volume of hydrogen 2 CONTAINING ONE MOLE PER LITRE containing one mole of substance per litre of solution 3 RELATING TO A WHOLE RATHER THAN PARTS relating to a body of matter rather than the properties of its molecules or atoms [Mid-19C. < MOLE[4] (chemical senses); partly < Latin moles 'mass'.] —**molarity** /mə lárrəti/ n

molar mass n the weight of one mole of any chemical substance

molasses /mō lássiz/ n 1 the thick dark bitter residue produced at the end of the sugar refining process 2 US FOOD = **treacle** n. 1 [Late 16C. Via Portuguese melaço < late Latin mellaceum 'new wine, must' < Latin mel 'honey'.]

mold n, vt US = **mould**

Mold /mōld/ town and administrative centre of Flintshire, Wales. Population: 9,168 (1991).

Moldavia /mol dáyvi ə/ region and former principality of E Europe, in modern-day Romania and Moldova — **Moldavian** n, adj

moldboard n US = **mouldboard**

molder vi US = **moulder**

molding n US = **moulding**

Moldova

Moldova /mol dŏvə/ republic in SE Europe. Capital: Chisinau. Population: 4,372,000 (1996). Area: 33,700 sq. km/13,000 sq. mi. —**Moldovan** n, adj

moldy adj US = **mouldy**

mole[1] /mōl/ n 1 BURROWING MAMMAL a small mammal that usually lives underground and has large forelimbs for digging, no external ears, minute eyes, and dense velvety fur. Family: Talpidae. 2 SPY somebody employed by a group or organization such as a government ministry who discloses sensitive information while keeping his or her own identity secret 3 TUNNELLING

MACHINE a machine designed for boring through hard materials such as rock [14C. Probably < Middle Dutch mol.]

mole[2] /mōl/ n a small dark, sometimes raised, growth on the human skin, sometimes with a hair or hairs growing from it [Old English māl 'discoloured mark' < Germanic, 'spot, mark']

mole[3] /mōl/ n 1 a massive wall, usually made of stone, that extends into the sea and encloses or protects a harbour 2 a harbour enclosed or protected by a mole [Mid-16C. Via French môle and medieval Greek molos < Latin moles 'mass, massive structure'.]

mole[4] /mōl/ n (symbol **mol**) the basic SI unit of amount of substance equal to the amount containing the same number of elementary units as the number of atoms in 12 grams of carbon-12 [Early 20C. < German Mol, shortening of Molekul 'molecule'.]

mole[5] /mŏli/ n a spicy Mexican sauce made with unsweetened chocolate and a variety of chillies and spices, used especially for cooking poultry [Mid-20C. Via Mexican Spanish < Nahuatl molli 'sauce, stew'.]

Molech n BIBLE = **Moloch**

mole cricket n a cricket with a heavy body and short wings that burrows in the ground using front legs that are adapted for digging. Family: Gryllotalpidae.

molecular /mə lékyŏolar/ adj 1 relating to or made up of molecules 2 relating to or organized from simpler parts —**molecularity** /mə lekyŏo lárrəti/ n —**molecularly** adv

molecular biology n the branch of biology concerned with the nature and function, at the molecular level, of biological phenomena, such as RNA and DNA, proteins, and other macromolecules

molecular distillation n a technique of vacuum distillation in which the molecules of the distilled substance reach the condenser before colliding with each other

molecular film n SCI = **monolayer** n. 1

molecular formula n a chemical formula that specifies which atoms and how many of each atom there are in a molecule of a compound

molecular genetics n the branch of genetics that studies genes, chromosomes, and the transmission of hereditary characteristics at the molecular level (+ singular verb)

molecular sieve n a crystalline compound with molecule-sized pores that can be used in separating larger molecules from smaller ones

molecular volume n the volume occupied by one mole of a substance when in the form of a gas

molecule /mólli kyool/ n 1 the smallest physical unit of a substance that can exist independently, consisting of one or more atoms held together by chemical forces 2 a very small amount of something [Late 18C. Via French molécule < modern Latin molecula 'small mass' < Latin moles 'mass'.]

mole fraction n the ratio of the number of moles of one substance present in a mixture or solution to the total number of moles of all constituents [< MOLE[4]]

molehill /mŏl hil/ n a small mound of earth on the surface of the ground dug up by a burrowing mole

mole rat n 1 a tailless rodent that digs burrows with its enlarged incisors and powerful head. Native to: E Europe, Middle East. Genus: Spalax. 2 a rodent that has large protruding incisors for digging burrows. Native to: sub-Saharan Africa. Family: Bathyergidae.

mole run n a part of a network of tunnels and underground rooms built to provide shelter during a nuclear war (informal)

moleskin /mŏl skin/ n 1 FUR OF MOLE the short dense soft fur of a mole 2 CLOTHING FABRIC a strong heavy cotton fabric with a brushed surface. Use: clothing. ■ n **moleskins** npl MOLESKIN CLOTHING clothing, especially trousers, made of moleskin fabric

molest /mō lést/ vt 1 to force unwanted sexual attentions on somebody, especially a child or physically weaker adult (disapproving) 2 to pester, bother, or disturb a person or animal [14C. Directly or via Old French molester < Latin molestare < molestus 'troublesome'.] —**molestation** /mŏ le stáysh'n/ n —**molester** n

Molière /mólli air/ (1622–73) French dramatist. Pseudonym of **Jean-Baptiste Poquelin**

moline /mō lēen/ adj describes a heraldic cross that has arms of equal length that broaden at the ends by forking and curving backwards [Mid-16C. Probably via Anglo-Norman < *molin* 'mill' < late Latin *molinum*.]

Molinism /mólənizəm/ n the doctrine in Christianity formulated by Luis Molina, that a person has a choice in accepting divine grace [Mid-17C. After Luis *Molina* (1535–1600), Spanish Jesuit.] —**Molinist** n

Molinos /mō lēen oss/, **Miguel de** (1628–96) Spanish cleric and mystic

moll /mol/ n (slang) 1 the woman companion of a gangster 2 a woman prostitute [Early 17C. Shortening of *Molly*, a pet form of *Mary*.]

mollie n ZOOL = **molly**

mollify /mólli fī/ (-fies, -fying, -fied) vt 1 PACIFY to calm or soothe somebody who is angry or upset 2 TEMPER to make something less intense or severe 3 SOFTEN to make something less hard, rigid, or stiff [15C. Directly or via French *mollifier* < Latin *mollificare* < *mollis* 'soft'.] —**mollifiable** adj —**mollification** /mólli káysh'n/ n —**mollifier** n —**mollifyingly** adv

mollusc /mólləsk/ n an invertebrate with a soft unsegmented body, usually protected by a shell in one, two, or three pieces, e.g. snails and octopuses. Phylum: Mollusca. [Late 18C. Via French *mollusque* < Latin *molluscus* 'thin-shelled nut' < *mollis* 'soft'.] —**molluscan** adj, n

molluscicide /mə lúski sīd/ n a chemical that kills molluscs —**molluscicidal** /mə lúski sīd'l/ adj

molluscum contagiosum /mə lúskəm kən táyji óssəm/ n a benign viral skin infection characterized by numerous small round dimpled pearly-white nodules [Early 19C. < modern Latin, 'contagious fungus'.]

mollusk n US = **mollusc**

Mollweide projection /mól vīdə-/ n a projection of a map of the world showing lines of latitude as straight lines and lines of longitude as elliptical lines, used to show the distribution of land masses and oceans [Early 20C. After the German mathematician Karl B. *Mollweide* (1774–1825).]

molly /mólli/ (plural -lies), **mollie** n a fish that bears live young and is often kept in aquariums. Native to: Central and South America. Genera: *Poecilia* and *Mollienesia*. [Mid-20C. Shortening of modern Latin *Mollienisia*, after Count F. N. *Mollien* (1758–1850), French statesman.]

mollycoddle /mólli kod'l/ vt (-dles, -dling, -dled) to treat somebody in an overprotective and overindulgent way ■ n a child, especially a boy, who is spoilt and overprotected [Mid-19C. < the name *Molly* (used for an effeminate boy or man) + CODDLE.] —**mollycoddler** n

Molnár /mól naar, mōl-/, **Ferenc** (1878–1952) Hungarian playwright and novelist

Moloch

moloch /mō lok/ (plural -lochs) n a lizard with large spiny scales covering its head and back. Native to: plains and deserts of central and southern Australia. *Moloch horridus*. [Mid-19C. Via late Latin < Greek *Molokh* < Hebrew *Mōlek*, a Canaanite idol.]

Moloch /mō lok/, **Molech** /mō lek/ n 1 in the Bible, a Semitic deity to whom children were sacrificed 2 somebody or something that requires a costly and painful sacrifice [Early 17C. Via late Latin < Greek *Molokh* < Hebrew *mōlek*.]

Molotov /mólla táwf/, **Vyacheslav Mikhailovich** (1890–

1986) Soviet statesman. Born **Vyacheslav Mikhailovich Scriabin**

Molotov cocktail /mólla tof-/ n a crude bomb, usually made of a bottle filled with a flammable liquid such as petrol and a wick that is set alight just before it is thrown [Mid-20C. After V. M. *Molotov*.]

molt vi, n US = **moult**

molten /mōltən/ adj 1 MELTED changed into liquid form by heat 2 MOULDED produced by melting a material and then shaping it in a mould 3 GLOWING glowing with great heat [13C. Originally past participle of MELT[1].]

Moltke /móltkə/, **Helmuth Johannes Ludwig, Count** (1848–1916) German military commander

molto /móltō/ adv used for emphasis before or after a musical direction derived from Italian [Early 19C. Via Italian < Latin *multus* 'much'.]

Moluccas /mə lúkəz/ group of islands in E Indonesia, between Sulawesi and New Guinea. Population: 1,741,800 (1998). Area: 74,500 sq. km/28,800 sq. mi. —**Moluccan** n, adj

moly /mōli/ (plural -lies) n 1 in Homer's *Odyssey*, a magic herb with milky-white flowers and black roots that Hermes gave to Odysseus to protect him from Circe's spells 2 a plant of the garlic family. Flowers: yellow. Native to: S Europe. *Allium moly*. [Mid-16C. Via Latin < Greek *mōlu*.]

molybdate /mə lib dayt/ n any salt of molybdenum [Late 18C. < MOLYBDIC.]

molybdenite /mə lībdə nīt/ n a greyish mineral consisting of molybdenum sulphide. Use: source of molybdenum. [Late 18C. < modern Latin *molybdenum* (see MOLYBDENUM).]

molybdenous /mə lībdənəss/ adj relating to or containing molybdenum, especially with a valency of 2 [Late 18C. < modern Latin *molybdenum* (see MOLYBDENUM).]

molybdenum /mə lībdənəm/ n (symbol Mo) a very hard silvery metallic element. Use: strengthening steel alloys. [Early 19C. Via modern Latin < Greek *molubdaina* 'piece of lead' < *molubdos* 'lead'.]

molybdenum sulphide, molybdenum disulphide n MoS[2] a black crystalline powder that is insoluble in water and is used as a lubricant

molybdic /mə lībdik/ adj relating to or containing molybdenum, especially with a valency of 6 [Late 18C. < modern Latin *molybdenum* (see MOLYBDENUM).]

molybdous /mə lībdəss/ adj relating to or containing molybdenum, especially with a valency lower than 6 [Late 18C. < modern Latin *molybdenum* (see MOLYBDENUM).]

mom /mom/ n US = **mum**[1] n. (informal) [Late 19C. Shortening of MOMMA.]

mom-and-pop, ma-and-pa adj US describes a business that is owned and operated by a family, especially by a husband and wife ○ *a mom-and-pop store*

Mombasa /mom bássə/ port in SE Kenya, on the Indian Ocean. Population: 465,000 (1989).

moment /mōmənt/ n 1 UNSPECIFIED SHORT TIME a very short period of time ○ *Wait a moment.* 2 SPECIFIC INSTANT a specific instant in time ○ *At that moment she walked in the door.* 3 PRESENT the present time ○ *busy at the moment* ○ *There are no vacancies at this moment in time.* 4 SIGNIFICANT PERIOD an important or significant time or occasion ○ *great moments in world history* 5 SHORT PERIOD OF EXCELLENCE a brief period of excellence or interest (often plural) ○ *It's not a great opera, but it has its moments.* 6 IMPORTANCE special importance or significance (formal) ○ *a decision of great moment* 7 SPECIFIC STAGE a specific stage or aspect of something 8 MOMENTUM a momentum (dated) 9 TENDENCY TO PRODUCE ROTATION a tendency to cause motion, especially rotation 10 PRODUCT OF FORCE TIMES DISTANCE the product of a quantity, e.g. force, multiplied by its perpendicular distance from a given point 11 MEAN IN FREQUENCY DISTRIBUTION the expected value of the deviations of a variable, compared to a fixed value, raised to a given power [14C. Via French < Latin *momentum* 'movement' < *movere* 'to move'.]

momentarily /mōməntərəli/ adv 1 BRIEFLY for a brief period of time 2 US, Can VERY SOON within a very short period of time ○ *He'll be here momentarily.* 3 PROGRESSIVELY with every passing moment

momentary /mōməntəri/ adj 1 VERY BRIEF lasting for a very short time 2 CONSTANT present or happening at every moment 3 WITH SHORT LIFE living or continuing for only a relatively short time —**momentariness** n

momently /mōməntli/ adv US 1 PROGRESSIVELY with every passing moment ○ *to grow momently more uneasy* 2 VERY SOON within a very short period of time 3 FOR AN INSTANT for a very short period of time

moment of inertia n (symbol I) a measure of resistance to changes in angular speed, calculated as the sum of the products of the component masses of an object multiplied by the square of their distance from the axis

moment of truth n 1 a point in time when a crucial decision has to be taken or when somebody or something is put to an important test 2 in a bullfight, the point at which the bull is about to be killed with the final blow

momentous /mō méntəss/ adj extremely important or crucial, especially in its effect on the future course of events —**momentously** adv —**momentousness** n

momentum /mō méntəm/ (plural -ta /-tə/ or -tums) n 1 CAPACITY FOR PROGRESSIVE DEVELOPMENT the power to increase or develop at an ever-growing pace ○ *The project was in danger of losing momentum.* 2 FORWARD MOVEMENT the speed or force of forward movement of an object ○ *the momentum gained on the downhill stretches of the course* 3 MEASURE OF MOVEMENT (symbol p) a quantity that expresses the motion of a body and its resistance to slowing down. It is equal to the product of the body's mass and velocity. 4 BASIC ELEMENT an essential part of a whole [Early 17C. < Latin *momentum* (see MOMENT).]

MOMI /mómi/ abbr Museum of the Moving Image (London)

momma /mómmə/ n US, Can somebody's mother (informal) [Early 19C. Alteration of MAMA.]

Mommsen /mómz'n/, **Theodor** (1817–1903) German historian

mommy /mómmi/ (plural -mies) n US = **mummy**[2] (informal) [Early 20C. Alteration of MAMMY.]

mommy track n US a career route taken by a woman whereby she risks reducing her chances of career advancement by working flexitime or fewer hours in order to look after a child or children (informal)

momser n = **mamzer**

Momus /mōməss/ n the god of fault-finding and mockery in Greek mythology [Late 16C. Via Latin < Greek *Mōmos*.]

momzer n = **mamzer**

Mon /món/ (plural Mon or Mons) n 1 a member of a people that lives in adjacent parts of Thailand and Myanmar 2 a Mon-Khmer language that is spoken in adjacent parts of Thailand and Myanmar. Native speakers: 700,000. [Late 18C. < Mon.] —**Mon** adj

mon. abbr 1 monastery 2 monetary

Mon. abbr 1 Monday 2 Monsignor

mon- prefix = **mono-** (before vowels)

mona /mōnə/ n a West African monkey that has a dark back and white or yellow front and is capable of moving at speed through the trees. *Cercopithecus mona*. [Late 18C. Via Spanish < Portuguese < Italian *monna* 'monkey'.]

monachal /mónnək'l/ adj relating to a monastery or monks, or resembling monastic life [Late 16C. Directly or via French *monacal* < ecclesiastical Latin *monachalis* < late Latin *monachus* (see MONK).] —**monachism** n —**monachist** adj, n

monacid n CHEM = **monoacid** ■ adj CHEM = **monoacidic**

monacidic adj CHEM = **monoacidic**

Monaco /mónnəkō, mə naákō/ independent principality

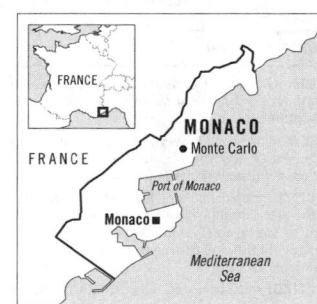
Monaco

in S Europe on the Mediterranean Sea, forming a coastal enclave in SE France. Capital: Monaco. Population: 31,719 (1996). Area: 2 sq. km/0.75 sq. mi. —**Monacan** *n, adj*

monad /mónnad/ *n* **1 BASIC ENTITY IN METAPHYSICS OF LEIBNITZ** in the metaphysics of Leibnitz, an indivisible indestructible unit that is the basic element of reality and a microcosm of it **2 SINGLE-CELLED MICROORGANISM** a microorganism consisting of just one cell, especially a flagellate protozoan. Genus: *Monas.* **3 ATOM WITH VALENCY OF ONE** an atom or chemical group that has a valency of one [Mid-16C. Directly or via French *monade* < late Latin *monad-* < Greek *monos* 'single'.] —**monadic** /mo náddik/ *adj* —**monadical** *adj* —**monadically** *adv* —**monadism** /mónnadizəm/ *n*

monadelphous /mónnə délfəss/ *adj* **1** describes stamens that have all the filaments united to form a single bundle in the shape of a tube **2** describes a flower that has monadelphous stamens [Early 19C. < MONO- + Greek *adelphos* 'brother'.]

monadnock /mə nád nok/ *n* an isolated mountain or rock that has resisted the process of erosion and stands alone in an otherwise flat area [Late 19C. After such a peak in New Hampshire, US.]

Monaghan /mónnəhən/ county in NE Republic of Ireland. Area: 1,291 sq. km/498 sq. mi.

monandrous /mo nándrəss/ *adj* **1 WITH ONE MALE LOVER** having a sexual relationship with only one man during a period of time **2 WITH ONE STAMEN** describes a flower that has a single stamen **3 WITH MONANDROUS FLOWERS** describes a plant that has monandrous flowers

monandry /mo nándri/ *n* **1** the practice of having only one husband at a time **2** the practice of having a sexual relationship with only one man during a period of time

Mona Passage /mṓnə-/ area of sea separating the islands of Hispaniola and Puerto Rico, linking the Atlantic Ocean to the Caribbean Sea

monarch /mónnərk/ *n* **1 SUPREME RULER** somebody, especially a king or queen, who rules a state or territory, usually for life and by hereditary right **2 EXCEPTIONALLY POWERFUL PERSON** a possessor of exceptional power or influence in an area of activity (*literary*) **3 SOMETHING OUTSTANDING OR PREDOMINANT** something that occupies a pre-eminent or predominant position (*literary*) **4** INSECTS = **monarch butterfly** [15C. Directly or via French *monarque* < late Latin *monarcha* < Greek *monarkhos* 'rule alone' < MONO- 'alone' + *arkhein* 'to rule'.] —**monarchal** /mə naárk'l/ *adj* —**monarchally** *adv*

monarch butterfly *n* a large migrating orange and black butterfly whose caterpillars feed on milkweed plants. Native to: North America. *Danaus plexippus.*

monarchic /mə naárkik/, **monarchical** /mə naárkik'l/ *adj* relating to a monarch or monarchy —**monarchically** *adv*

monarchism /mónnərkizəm/ *n* **1** belief in or support for monarchy as a system of government **2** the system of government in which a monarch rules

monarchist /mónnərkist/ *n* an advocate or supporter of a system of monarchy ■ *adj* favouring or supporting a system of monarchy

monarchy /mónnərki/ (*plural* **-chies**) *n* **1 SYSTEM OF RULE BY MONARCHS** a political system in which a state is ruled by a monarch **2 ROYAL FAMILY** a monarch and his or her family **3 STATE RULED BY A MONARCH** a country ruled by a monarch

monarda /mə naárdə/ *n* an aromatic plant of the mint family. Native to: North America. Genus: *Monarda.* [Late 18C. < modern Latin.]

Monash /mó nash/, **Sir John** (1865–1931) Australian military commander, engineer, and administrator

monastery /mónnəstəri/ (*plural* **-ies**) *n* **1** a building or buildings with grounds in which a group of people observing religious vows, especially monks, live together **2** a group of people, especially monks, living together and observing religious vows [14C. Via ecclesiastical Latin *monasterium* < Greek *monazein* 'live alone' < *monos* 'alone'.] —**monasterial** /mónnə steéri əl/ *adj*

monastic /mə nástik/ *adj* **monastic, monastical 1 OF MONKS, NUNS, OR MONASTERIES** relating to monks, nuns, or their way of life or the buildings in which they live ○ *monastic rule* **2 RECLUSIVE OR AUSTERE** characteristic of the life of a monk, especially in being reclusive, self-denying, or austere ■ *n* **MONK** somebody, especially a monk, who lives with others in a monastery and observes religious vows [15C. Directly or via French *monastique* < late Latin *monasticus* < Greek *monazein* (see MONASTERY).] —**monastically** *adv*

monasticism /mə nástissizəm/ *n* the way of life typical of monks or nuns, in which they withdraw entirely or in part from society to devote themselves to prayer, solitude, and contemplation

~~**monastry**~~ incorrect spelling of **monastery**

monatomic /mónnə tómmik/, **monoatomic** /mónnō ə tómmik/ *adj* **1** having only one atom in the molecule **2** with one atom or chemical group that can be replaced during a chemical reaction **3** CHEM = **monovalent** *adj.* 1 —**monatomically** *adv*

monaural /mo náwrəl/ *adj* **1** relating to or involving the hearing of sound by one ear **2** ELECTRONICS = **monophonic** —**monaurally** *adv*

monazite /mónnə zīt/ *n* a reddish-brown phosphate mineral that contains cerium, lanthanum, and some thorium [Mid-19C. < Greek *monazein* 'be alone' < *monos* (see MONO-), because of its rare occurrence.]

Monck /mungk/, **George, 1st Duke of Albemarle** (1609–70) English soldier

Moncton /múngktən/ city in SE New Brunswick, Canada. Population: 59,313 (1996).

mondain /mon dáyn, moN dáN/ *n* a man who belongs to fashionable society ■ *adj* = **mondaine** [Late 19C. < French (see MUNDANE).]

mondaine /mon dáyn, moN dén/ *n* a woman who belongs to fashionable society ■ *adj* **mondaine, mondain** relating to fashionable society, especially in being worldly or sophisticated [Late 19C. < French, feminine of *mondain* (see MUNDANE).]

Monday /mún day, -di/ *n* the first day of the traditional working week, coming after Sunday and before Tuesday [Old English *mōnandæg* < Germanic, translation of Latin *lunae dies* 'day of the moon']

Monday Club *n* a club for right-wing Conservatives, founded in 1961

Mondays /mún dayz, -diz/ *adv* every Monday

mondial /móndi əl/ *adj* relating to or involving the entire world [Early 20C. Via French < *monde* 'world' < Latin *mundus.*]

Mondrian /móndri aan, móndri aan/, **Piet** (1872–1944) Dutch painter. Born **Pieter Cornelis Mondriaan**

monecious *adj* PLANT SCI = **monoecious**

Monégasque /mónnə gásk/ *n* somebody who comes from Monaco ■ *adj* relating to Monaco, or its people or culture [Late 19C. Via French < *Mounegue* 'Monaco'.]

Monet /món ay/, **Claude** (1840–1926) French painter

monetarism /múnnitərizəm/ *n* **1** the theory that inflation and other economic variations are caused by changes in the money supply **2** the policy of controlling an economic system by increasing or decreasing the money supply, especially in a gradual manner —**monetarist** *n, adj*

QUICK FACTS ON... **MONETARISM**

Key dates: late 20th century
Key locations: Austria, United Kingdom, United States
Key elements: regulation of money supply by gradually raising or lowering interest rates to prevent recession or inflation; increased money supply regarded as leading to inflation, not improved output; private enterprise and business spending, not government intervention and public spending, regarded as the basis of balanced economic growth
Key figures: Ludwig von Mises, Friedrich von Hayek, Milton Friedman
Key works: *The Road to Serfdom* (Hayek) 1944, *A Monetary History of the United States, 1867–1960* (Friedman) 1963
Key developments: privatization of formerly nationalized industries, deregulation of industries formerly controlled by government, emergence of 'new' parties of the left in UK and USA

monetary /múnnitəri/ *adj* **1** relating to or involving money **2** relating to a national currency ○ *The monetary unit of the US is the dollar.* [Early 19C. Directly or via French *monétaire* < late Latin *monetarius* < Latin *moneta* (see MONEY).] —**monetarily** *adv*

monetary unit *n* the standard unit in a nation's currency system, e.g. the pound in the United Kingdom or the dollar in the United States

monetize /múnni tīz/ (**-tizes, -tizing, -tized**), **monetise** (**-tises, -tising, -tised**) *vt* **1 MAKE SOMETHING LEGAL TENDER** to make something the legal tender of a country **2 COIN METAL** to convert a metal into coins **3 CONVERT DEBT INTO AVAILABLE MONEY** to convert a government debt into available currency, especially by issuing securities [Late 19C. < Latin *moneta* (see MONEY).] —**monetization** /múnni tī záysh'n/ *n*

money /múnni/ *n* **1 SOMEBODY'S COINS AND BANKNOTES** the amount of coins and banknotes in somebody's possession at any one time **2 SAVINGS OR CREDIT** the amount of money held in a bank account or available on credit to somebody **3 WAGES OR SALARY** the amount somebody is paid for working **4 CONVERTIBLE ASSETS** assets or property that can be converted into cash **5 NATIONAL CURRENCY** the official currency of a country **6 OFFICIAL MEDIUM OF EXCHANGE** a commodity, usually gold, that is an official medium of exchange and a measure of value **7 UNOFFICIAL MEDIUM OF EXCHANGE** a medium of exchange that can be used to purchase goods and services **8 RICH PEOPLE** a rich individual, family, or class ○ *She married money.* ■ **monies** *npl* **SUMS OF MONEY** specific individual sums of money (*formal*) ○ *all monies payable* [13C. Via Old French *monie* < Latin *moneta* 'mint, money' < *Moneta* (epithet of the goddess Juno, in whose temple coins were minted).] ◇ **for somebody's money** in somebody's opinion ◇ **in the money** having a lot of money ◇ **on the money** *US* correct or accurate ◇ **put your money where your mouth is** to take action to show that you truly mean what you have said (*informal*) ◇ **throw good money after bad** to put more money, better used elsewhere, into a bad investment ○ *If you have the car repaired again, you'll just throw good money after bad.*

money-back *adj* refunding money paid for something if the product or service is unsatisfactory ○ *It comes with a money-back guarantee.*

moneybags /múnni bagz/ (*plural* **-bags**) *n* a conspicuously rich person (*informal; + singular verb*)

moneychanger /múnni chaynjər/ *n* an exchanger of currencies, usually for a commission

moneyed /múnnid/, **monied** *adj* **1** possessing a great deal of money **2** consisting of or resulting from money

moneygrubber /múnni grubbər/ *n* somebody bent on making money from every possible opportunity (*disapproving*) —**moneygrubbing** *adj, n*

moneylender /múnni lendər/ *n* a lender of money in exchange for interest on the amount borrowed —**moneylending** *n*

moneymaker /múnni maykər/ *n* **1** a person who is skilled at making money **2** a business, product, or project that makes a lot of money —**moneymaking** *n, adj*

moneyman /múnni man/ (*plural* **-men**) *n* *US* an expert on finance and economics (*informal*)

money market *n* the trade in low-risk securities that have a life of one year or less

money of account *n* a monetary unit that is used to keep accounts

money order *n* an order for a specific sum of money, usually purchased with cash at a bank or post office, that can be used to make payments.

money shell *n* the shell of the butter clam, formerly used as money by Native Americans on the western coast of North America

money spider *n* a tiny brownish spider. Family: Linyphiidae. [< the folk belief that money will come to those on whom the spider crawls]

money-spinner *n* = **moneymaker** *n.* 2 (*informal*)

money supply *n* the total amount of money available in a given economy

money wages *npl* wages considered only in terms of how much money is paid and not in terms of what that money can buy. US term **nominal wages**

moneywort /múnni wurt/ *n* PLANTS = **creeping Jennie**

mong /mung/ *n* *Aus* **1** a dog, especially a mongrel (*informal*) **2** an offensive term for somebody regarded as unintelligent (*slang*) [Mid-20C. Shortening.]

-monger *suffix* seller, dealer, promoter ○ *fashionmonger* [Old English *mangere*, via Germanic < Latin *mango* 'peddler, swindler']

mongo[1] /móng gō/ (*plural* **-go** *or* **-gos**) *n* see table at **currency** [Mid-20C. < Mongolian *möngö* 'silver'.]

mongo[2], **mongoe** *n* = **mungo**

mongol /móng g'l/ *n* a former term for somebody affected by Down's syndrome, now considered highly offensive (*dated offensive*)

Mongol /móng g'l, -gol/ *adj* **1** OF MONGOLIA relating to Mongolia, its people, or its culture **2** RELATING TO MONGOLIAN LANGUAGE relating to the Mongolian language ■ *n* SOMEBODY FROM MONGOLIA a member of the originally nomadic peoples who inhabit Mongolia and established the Mongol Empire in the 13th century [Late 17C. < Mongolian.]

Mongolia

Mongolia /mong góli ə/ republic in Central Asia. Capital: Ulaanbaatar. Population: 2,538,211 (1997). Area: 1,566,500 sq. km/604,830 sq. mi.

Mongolian /mon góli ən/ *n* **1** PEOPLES = **Mongol** *n*. **2** a group of languages or dialects of the Altaic family spoken in Mongolia and in the Chinese region of Inner Mongolia —**Mongolian** *adj*

Mongolic /mon góllik/ *n* GROUP OF ALTAIC LANGUAGES an Altaic group of languages that includes Mongolian, Buryat, and Santa ■ *adj* **1** RELATING TO MONGOLOID RACIAL GROUP belonging or relating to Mongoloid racial group (*dated*) **2** RELATING TO MONGOLIC LANGUAGE relating to the Mongolic languages

mongolism /móng gəlizəm/ *n* a former term for Down's syndrome, now considered highly offensive (*dated offensive*)

mongoloid /móng gə loyd/ *adj* a former term meaning affected by Down's syndrome, now considered highly offensive (*dated offensive*)

Mongoloid /móng gə loyd/ *adj* relating to or belonging to the racial group that includes the peoples of E Asia, the Inuit, and the Native Americans (*no longer used technically*) —**Mongoloid** *n*

mongoose /móng gooss/ (*plural* -**gooses**) *n* a small short-legged carnivorous mammal that resembles a ferret and is noted for its ability to kill poisonous snakes. Native to: S Asia. Genus: *Herpestes*. [Late 17C. < Marathi *maṅgūs*.]

mongrel /múng grəl/ *n* **1** DOG THAT IS a dog that is a mixture of different breeds **2** ANIMAL OR PLANT OF MIXED BREED an animal or plant that is a mixture of different breeds or strains **3** OFFENSIVE TERM an offensive term for somebody who is of mixed racial ancestry **4** STRANGE MIXTURE a combination or mixture of different people or things, especially one that seems particularly strange ■ *adj* MIXED IN ORIGIN OR CHARACTER of mixed breed, descent, type, or character (*offensive in some contexts*) [15C. Probably < Germanic, 'to mix'.] —**mongrelism** *n* —**mongrelly** *adj*

mongrelize /múng grə līz/ (-**izes**, -**izing**, -**ized**), **mongrelise** (-**ises**, -**ising**, -**ised**) *vt* to make something or somebody become mongrel or mixed in character, type, or race (*offensive when used of a person*) —**mongrelization** *n*

'mongst /mungst/ *prep* amongst (*literary*) [Late 16C. Variant of *amongst*, a variant of AMONG.]

Monicagate /mónikə gáyt/ *n* US the 1998–99 sex scandal involving US President William Jefferson Clinton and a former White House intern, culminating in his impeachment and subsequent acquittal (*slang*) [< Monica S. Lewinsky, the intern.]

monicker *n* = **moniker** (*slang*)

monied *adj* = **moneyed**

monies plural of **money**

moniker /mónnikər/, **monicker** *n* somebody's name or nickname (*slang*) [Mid-19C. < ?]

moniliform /mə nílli fawrm/ *adj* describes a plant root or insect antenna that resembles a string of beads [Early 19C. Directly or via French *moniliforme* < modern Latin *moniliformis* < Latin *monile* 'necklace'.] —**moniliformly** *adv*

monism /mónnizəm/ *n* **1** the theory that reality is a unified whole and is grounded in a single basic substance or principle **2** a theory or point of view that attempts to explain everything in terms of a single principle —**monist** *n*, *adj* —**monistic** /mo nístik/ *adj* —**monistically** *adv*

monition /mə nísh'n/ *n* **1** WARNING OF DANGER a warning, especially a warning of danger **2** EXHORTATION TO CAUTION a piece of advice counselling caution **3** SUMMONS an order to appear in court **4** WARNING FROM A BISHOP an official warning from a bishop to refrain from doing something [14C. < French, < Latin *monit-*, past participle of *monere* 'warn'.]

⚡ **monitor** /mónnitər/ *n* **1** CLOSED-CIRCUIT TELEVISION SET a receiving device used in a closed-circuit television or video system **2** VDU a video device that displays data or images generated by a computer or terminal **3** STAGE LOUDSPEAKER a loudspeaker on a stage during a concert used to let performers hear what they are playing ○ *playing a guitar solo with one foot up on the monitor* **4** SOMEBODY WHO CHECKS FOREIGN BROADCASTS a person who listens to and checks broadcasts for a client or employer **5** SOMEBODY ENSURING PROPER CONDUCT a person who checks for incorrect or unfair conduct **6** PUPIL GIVEN SPECIAL DUTY a pupil who helps a teacher by being given a particular responsibility or special duty (*dated*) **7** VIEWING DEVICE IN STUDIO a receiver in a studio that enables the audience to watch the recorded portions of a show or performers to view parts of a programme **8** LARGE LIZARD a large tropical carnivorous lizard, found in Asia, Africa, and Australia. Family: Varanidae. US term **monitor lizard 9** COMPUTER PROGRAM a computer program that observes and controls other programs in a system **10** NOZZLE a jointed device with a rotating nozzle that controls and aims a jet of water **11** 19C WARSHIP a heavily armoured warship with gun turrets used in the 19th century in coastal manoeuvres ■ *vt* **1** CHECK REGULARLY FOR DEVELOPMENTS to check something at regular intervals in order to find out how it is progressing or developing **2** LISTEN TO BROADCASTS OR TELEPHONE CONVERSATIONS to use an electronic receiver to listen in on broadcasts or telephone conversations, especially in order to discover secret or illegal plans and activities **3** CHECK QUALITY OF TRANSMITTED SIGNALS to use an electronic receiver to check the quality of transmitted audio or visual signals **4** WATCH OVER TO CHECK CONDUCT to watch over somebody or something, especially in order to ensure that good order or proper conduct is maintained [Early 16C. < Latin, < *monit-* (see MONITION).] —**monitorial** /mónni táwri əl/ *adj* —**monitorially** *adv* —**monitorship** *n*

monitor lizard *n* ZOOL = **monitor** *n*. 8 [< the belief that they warn of the proximity of crocodiles]

monitory /mónnitəri/ *adj* communicating a warning ■ *n* (*plural* -**ries**) a letter, usually from a bishop, that warns somebody to refrain from doing something

monk /mungk/ *n* a man who withdraws entirely or in part from society and goes to live in a religious community to devote himself to prayer, solitude, and contemplation [Old English *munuc*, via Germanic < late Latin *monachus* < Greek *monos* 'alone']

Monk /mungk/, **Meredith** (*b.* 1942) US performer, choreographer, dancer, and musician

Monk, Thelonious (1917–82) US jazz pianist and composer

monkery /múngkəri/ (*plural* -**ies**) *n* (*disapproving*) **1** the way of life led by monks in a monastery **2** monks as a group

monkey /múngki/ *n* (*plural* -**keys**) **1** NONHUMAN PRIMATE a medium-sized primate found mostly in tropical areas, belonging to a group including baboons, marmosets, capuchins, macaques, guenons, and tamarins, but excluding apes, lemurs, and tarsiers **2** MISCHIEVOUS CHILD somebody, usually a child, who behaves badly, annoyingly, or high-spiritedly (*informal*) ○ *Did you hear what that cheeky monkey said?* **3** PILE-DRIVER RAM the ram of a pile-driver **4** DUPE a person who has been made to look foolish (*informal*) ○ *Nobody makes a monkey out of me.* **5** £500 the sum of £500, especially in betting (*slang*)

■ *vt* (-**keys**, -**keying**, -**keyed**) MIMIC to copy or imitate somebody or something (*archaic*) [Mid-16C. < ?] ◇ **have a monkey on your back** US to have an addiction to drugs (*slang*) ◇ **I'll be a monkey's uncle** used to express surprise (*dated informal*) ◇ **not give a monkey's (about somebody** *or* **something)** not to care at all about somebody or something (*informal*)

monkey around, **monkey about** *vi* to behave in a silly, casual, or careless way

monkey with *vt* to touch or move something casually or carelessly

monkey bars *npl* US a structure, usually freestanding, consisting of metal or wooden poles and bars that children can climb on to play

monkey bread *n* **1** the gourd-shaped fruit of the baobab tree, whose pulp is eaten by monkeys **2** **monkey bread**, **monkey bread tree** TREES = **baobab**

monkey business *n* (*informal*) **1** silly or mischievous behaviour **2** illegal, dishonest, or dubious activity

monkey flower *n* PLANTS = **mimulus** [Because spots on the flowers form a pattern reminiscent of a monkey's face]

monkey in the middle *n* US = **piggy in the middle** *n*. 1

monkey jacket *n* a tight-fitting waist-length jacket, especially one worn by a sailor or as part of a military dress uniform [Because like the kind worn by an organ grinder's monkey]

monkey nut *n* a peanut while still in its shell (*informal*)

monkey orchid *n* a European orchid. Flowers: white and pink. *Orchis simia*. [Because the shape of the lip of the flower is reminiscent of a monkey]

monkeypot /múngki pot/ *n* **1** SEED POD a large bulbous woody seed pod of a tropical tree **2** TROPICAL AMERICAN TREE WITH LARGE PODS a tree that bears monkey pots. Native to: tropical America. Genus: *Lecythis*. **3** GLASSMAKING POT a melting pot used in the manufacture of flint glass

monkey puzzle, **monkey puzzle tree** *n* a coniferous evergreen tree with spreading branches, sharp stiff leaves, and edible seeds. Native to: Chile. *Araucaria araucana*. [Probably because of its long intertwining limbs and leaves]

monkeyshines /múnki shīnz/ *npl* US = **monkey tricks** (*informal*)

monkey suit *n* (*dated slang*) **1** a suit worn by a man as part of formal evening wear **2** a uniform, especially a military one

monkey's wedding *n* S Africa a simultaneous occurrence of sunshine and a light shower (*informal*) [< *The monkey and the moon are getting married*, suggesting the union of two very different things]

monkey tricks *npl* silly or mischievous behaviour (*informal*) US term **monkeyshines**

monkey wrench *n* a spanner with a jaw that can be adjusted so that it can be used to turn nuts of different sizes

monkfish /múnk fish/ (*plural* -**fish** *or* -**fishes**) *n* **1** a large bottom-dwelling anglerfish. Native to: Atlantic waters of Europe and Africa. *Lophius piscatorius*. **2** ZOOL = **angel shark 3** the flesh of a monkfish as food [Early 17C. < ?]

Mon-Khmer *n* an Austro-Asiatic group of languages that includes Mon and Khmer, spoken in Southeast Asia —**Mon-Khmer** *adj*

Thelonious Monk

monkish /múngkish/ *adj* 1 relating to monks or their way of life 2 characteristic of the life of a monk, especially in being reclusive, self-denying, or austere —**monkishly** *adv* —**monkishness** *n*

monk's cloth *n* a heavy cotton fabric with a basket weave. Use: curtains, bedcovers.

monk seal *n* a small dark brown subtropical seal that is now endangered. Native to: the waters of the Hawaiian Islands and the Mediterranean. Genus: *Monachus.*

monkshood /múngks hood/ (*plural* **-hood** *or* **-hoods**) *n* 1 a poisonous perennial plant. Flowers: purplish. Native to: N Europe. *Aconitum napellus.* 2 PHARM = **aconite** *n.* 3 [Late 16C. < the shape of its flowers.]

Monmouth /mónməth/ town in SE Wales. Population: 7,246 (1991).

Monmouthshire /mónməthshər/ county in SE Wales. Area: 1,375 sq. km/530 sq. mi.

Monnet /món ay/, **Jean** (1888–1979) French diplomat and financier

mono /mónnō/ *n* monophonic sound reproduction [Mid-20C. Shortening.]

mono- *prefix* 1 one, single, alone ○ *monoculture* 2 containing a single atom, radical, or group ○ *monoxide* 3 monomolecular ○ *monolayer* [Via Old French and Latin < Greek *monos*]

monoacid /mónnō-/, **monacid** /mon-/ *n* an acid that has only one replaceable hydrogen atom

monoacidic /mónnō ə síddik/, **monacidic** /mónnə síddik/, **monacid** /mon ássid/ *adj* describes a chemical base or alcohol that has only one hydroxyl group that can react with an acid

monoamine /mónnō áy meen/ *n* an amine compound that contains one amino group, especially the neurotransmitters adrenaline and serotonin

monoamine oxidase *n* an enzyme that breaks down monoamine neurotransmitters

monoamine oxidase inhibitor *n* a drug that blocks the breakdown of monoamines by monoamine oxidase in the brain. Use: antidepressant.

monoatomic *adj* CHEM = **monatomic**

monobasic /mónnō báyssik/ *adj* describes an acid that has only one replaceable hydrogen atom in each molecule

monocarboxylic /mónnō kaar bok síllik/ *adj* COOH describes an acid that has only one group

monocarpellary /mónnō kaarpələri/ *adj* 1 describes a flower that has only one carpel 2 describes a plant gynoecium that consists of only one carpel

monocarpic /mónnō kaarpik/ *adj* describes a plant that flowers and bears fruit only once before dying

monocarpous /mónnō kaarpəss/ *adj* 1 = **monocarpic** 2 = **monocarpellary**

Monoceros /mə nóssərəss/ *n* a constellation near the celestial equator. See illustration at **constellation** [Late 18C. Via French < Greek *monokerōs* 'having one horn'.]

monochasium /mónnō káyziə m/ (*plural* **-a** /-ə/) *n* a flower cluster in which each branch bears one other branch and ends in a single flower [Late 19C. < MONO- + Greek *khasis* 'separation'.] —**monochasial** *adj*

monochord /mónnə kawrd/ *n* an ancient acoustical device consisting of a single string stretched over an oblong sounding box, used to determine mathematical intervals between musical tones

monochromat /mónnō krō mat/, **monochromate** /-krō mayt/ *n* a person who cannot perceive colours and sees only shades of grey [Early 20C. Back-formation < MONOCHROMATIC.]

monochromatic /mónnōkrō máttik/ *adj* 1 WITH ONLY ONE COLOUR having only one colour 2 WITH ONLY ONE WAVELENGTH consisting of radiation that has only one wavelength, like the light of a laser 3 IN ONE COLOUR painted or printed in a single colour 4 RELATING TO TOTAL COLOUR BLINDNESS relating to or having total colour blindness (**monochromatism**) —**monochromatically** *adv* —**monochromaticity** /mónnōkrōmə tíssəti/ *n*

monochromatism /mónnō krómətizəm/ *n* a defect of vision in which the retina cannot distinguish any colours and a person sees only shades of grey

monochrome /mónnə krōm/ *adj* 1 IN SHADES OF ONE COLOUR using or displaying only shades of one colour or black and white 2 CONSISTING OF ONE COLOUR painted or drawn in shades of a single colour 3 DULL dull, insipid, and lacking interest or distinctiveness ■ *n* 1 BLACK-AND-WHITE IMAGE a black-and-white photograph or transparency 2 BLACK-AND-WHITE COLORATION the condition of being only in black and white 3 ARTWORK IN ONE COLOUR a painting, drawing, or print in shades of a single colour 4 ART TECHNIQUE USING ONE COLOUR the art of painting or drawing in shades of a single colour 5 CONDITION OF HAVING ONE COLOUR the condition of being painted, drawn, or printed in shades of a single colour [Mid-17C. < medieval Latin *monochroma* < Greek *monokhrōmatos* 'of one colour' < *khrōma* 'colour'.] —**monochromic** /mónnə krómik/ *adj* —**monochromist** *n*

monocle /mónnək'l/ *n* a lens for correcting the vision of one eye, held in position by the muscles around the eye socket [Mid-19C. Via French < late Latin *monoculus* 'single-eyed' < Greek *mono-* 'single' + Latin *oculus* 'eye'.]

monocline /mónnō klīn/ *n* a rock structure in which all the strata slope in one direction [Late 19C. < MONO- + Greek *klinein* 'to lean'.] —**monoclinal** /mónnō klīn'l/ *adj* —**monoclinally** *adv*

monoclinic /mónnō klínnik/ *adj* describes a type of crystal that has three unequal axes, with one pair not at right angles [Mid-19C. < MONO- + Greek *klinein* 'to lean'.]

monoclinous /mónnō klīnəss/ *adj* describes a flower that has both pistils and stamens [Early 19C. < French *monocline* or modern Latin *monoclinus* 'in a single bed' < Greek *klinē* 'bed'.]

monoclonal /mónnō klōn'l/ *adj* describes cells or products of cells that are formed or derived from a single clone

monoclonal antibody *n* an antibody with unique amino acid sequences derived from a single cell clone or cell line

monocoque /mónnō kok/ *n* 1 the metal outer shell of an aircraft, boat, or rocket that absorbs most of the stresses to which the craft is subjected 2 a design of motor vehicle in which the body and frame are integrated [Early 20C. < French, 'having a single shell' < *coque* 'shell'.]

monocot /mónnō kot/ *n* a monocotyledon (*informal*)

monocotyledon /mónnō kotə leéd'n/ *n* a flowering plant that has a single leaf in the seed and floral parts in multiples of three. Class: Monocotyledones. —**monocotyledonous** *adj*

monocracy /mo nókrəssi/ (*plural* **-cies**) *n* a form of government in which one person alone rules —**monocrat** /mónnə krat/ *n* —**monocratic** *adj*

monocular /mo nókyoolər/ *adj* relating to, affecting, or having only one eye ■ *n* an optical device such as a field glass or a microscope designed for use with one eye only [Mid-17C. < late Latin *monoculus* (see MONOCLE).] —**monocularly** *adv*

monoculture /mónnō kulchər/ *n* the practice of growing a single crop plant in a field or a larger area, e.g. a cereal crop such as wheat —**monocultural** /mónnō kúlchərəl/ *adj*

monocycle /mónnə sīk'l/ *n* TRANSP = **unicycle**

monocyclic /mónnō síklik/ *adj* 1 WITH A SINGLE-RING MOLECULAR STRUCTURE describes a chemical compound that has a molecular structure in which there is only one ring 2 FORMING ONE WHORL forming a single whorl as, e.g., the petals of a flower do 3 LIVING DURING ONE YEAR describes a plant that completes its life cycle within a single year

monocyte /mónnō sīt/ *n* a large circulating white blood cell, formed in the bone marrow and in the spleen, that has a single well-defined nucleus and consumes large foreign particles and cell debris —**monocytic** /mónnō síttik/ *adj* —**monocytoid** /mónnō sī toyd/ *adj*

monocytosis /mónnō sī tōssiss/ *n* an abnormal increase in the numbers of a type of white blood cell (**monocyte**)

monodisperse /mónnō di spúrss/ *adj* describes a colloid that contains particles that are all of a uniform size

monodrama /mónnō draamə/ *n* a dramatic piece written for one actor —**monodramatic** /mónnōdrə máttik/ *adj*

monody /mónnədi/ (*plural* **-dies**) *n* 1 ODE SUNG BY ONE ACTOR in Greek tragedy, an ode for one actor to sing alone 2 ELEGY a poem that mourns somebody's death 3 17C ITALIAN VOCAL MUSIC Italian vocal music of the 17th century for solo voice with instrumental accompaniment 4 MUSIC WITH SINGLE MELODIC LINE a piece of music that has a single melodic line [Early 17C. < late Latin *monodia* < Greek *monōdos* 'singing alone' < *ōidē* 'song'.] —**monodic** /mə nóddik/ *adj* —**monodically** *adv* —**monodist** *n*

monoecious /mo neéshəss/, **monecious, monoicous** /mo nóykəss/ *adj* describes a plant that has separate male and female flowers on the same plant [Mid-18C. < modern Latin *Monoecia*.] —**monoeciously** *adv*

monoethnic /mónnō éthnik/ *adj* belonging or relating to the same ethnic group

monofilament /mónnə fílləmənt/ *n* an untwisted continuous single strand of natural or artificial fibre. Use: fishing lines.

monogamy /mə nóggəmi/ *n* 1 PRACTICE OF HAVING ONE SEXUAL PARTNER the practice of having a sexual relationship with only one partner during a period of time 2 MARRIAGE TO ONE PERSON the practice of being married to only one person at a time 3 PRACTICE OF HAVING ONE MATE the practice of having only one mate at a time or during a lifetime [Early 17C. < French *monogamie* < Greek *monogamos* 'monogamous' < *gamos* 'marriage'.] —**monogamist** *n* —**monogamous** *adj* —**monogamously** *adv*

monogenean /mónnə jeéni ən/ *n* a parasitic flatworm that spends its entire life cycle on the outside of the same fish. Order: Monogenea. [Mid-20C. < modern Latin *Monogenea* 'single generation' < Greek *genea* 'generation'.]

monogenesis /mónnō jénnəssiss/ *n* 1 the theory that all living organisms are ultimately descended from a single cell 2 reproduction that does not involve the fusion of male and female gametes —**monogenous** /mə nójjənəss/ *adj*

monogenetic /mónnōjə néttik/ *adj* 1 relating to or involving monogenesis 2 describes a nematode that spends its entire life cycle as a parasite on the outside of the same fish

monogenic /mónnə jénnik/ *adj* 1 describes a characteristic that is controlled by one gene or one pair of genes 2 producing offspring that are all of the same sex —**monogenically** *adv*

monoglot /mónnō glot/ *n* a speaker of only one language [Mid-19C. < Greek *monoglōttos* 'one tongue' < *glōtta* 'tongue'.] —**monoglot** *adj*

monoglyceride /mónnō glíssə rīd/ *n* a compound derived from glycerol in which one hydroxyl group has been esterified

monogram /mónnə gram/ *n* a design of one or more letters, usually the initials of a name, used to decorate or identify an object —**monogram** *vt* —**monogrammatic** /mónnəgrə máttik/ *adj* —**monogrammed** *adj*

monograph /mónnə graaf, -graf/ *n* a scholarly article, paper, or book on a single topic —**monographer** /mə nóggrəfər/ *n* —**monographic** /mónnə gráffik/ *adj* —**monographically** *adv*

monogyny /mə nójjəni/ *n* 1 the practice of having only one wife at a time 2 the practice of having a sexual relationship with only one woman during a period of time —**monogynist** *n* —**monogynous** *adj*

monohull /mónnō hul/ *n* a boat that has a single hull

monohybrid /mónnō hībrid/ *n* a hybrid from parents that are different only with respect to a single gene pair

monohydrate /mónnō hī drayt/ *n* a salt that is combined with one molecule of water

monohydric /mónnə hīdrik/ *adj* describes an alcohol that contains one replaceable atom of hydrogen

monohydroxy /mónnō hī dróksi/ *adj* describes a compound that contains one hydroxyl group

monolatry /mə nóllətri/ *n* the practice of worshipping only one god without, however, denying the existence of other gods —**monolater** *n* —**monolatrous** *adj*

monolayer /mónnō layər/ *n* 1 a film or other coating of a compound that is one molecule thick 2 a cultured layer of cells that is one cell thick

monolingual /mónnō língwəl/ *adj* 1 able to speak only one language 2 written, spoken, or produced in only one language —**monolingualism** *n*

monolith /mónnə lith/ *n* 1 PILLAR OF ROCK a tall block of solid stone standing by itself, whether a natural rock feature or a stone column shaped and erected by people, e.g. as a monument 2 LARGE BLOCK OF BUILDING MATERIAL a large uniform block of a single building material such as concrete pieced together with others to form a building or other structure 3 SOMETHING LARGE AND IMMOVABLE something massive and unchanging, especially a large and long-established organization that is slow to change, uniform in character, and difficult to deal with on a human level

monolithic /mónnə líthik/ *adj* 1 **IN THE FORM OF A LARGE STONE BLOCK** consisting of or formed into a tall column of solid stone 2 **BUILT USING LARGE BLOCKS** constructed using massive stones or solid blocks of material 3 **LARGE AND UNCHANGING** massive, uniform in character, and slow to change —**monolithically** *adv*

monolithic technology *n* a technology in electronic manufacturing in which all circuit components, e.g. resistors, capacitors, and diodes, are mounted on a single uniform piece of material

monologue /mónnə log/ *n* 1 **ACTOR'S LONG SPEECH** a long passage in a play or film spoken by one actor, or an entire play for one actor only 2 **SOMEBODY'S LONG UNINTERRUPTED SPEECH** a long tedious uninterrupted speech during a conversation 3 **PERFORMANCE BY COMEDIAN** a set of jokes or humorous stories following one another without a break, told by a solo entertainer —**monologic** /mónnə lójjik/ *adj* —**monologist** /mónnə logist, mə nólləjist/ *n* —**monologize** /mə nóllə jīz/ *vti*

monomania /mónnō máyni ə/ *n* an obsessive interest in a single thing, or a preoccupation with a single idea or thought —**monomaniac** *n* —**monomaniacally** /mónnō mə nī əkli/ *adv*

monomark /mónnə maark/ *n* an identifying set of numbers or letters marked on an individual item, especially by a retailer ■ *vt* to put a monomark on something

monomer /mónnəmər/ *n* a relatively light, simple organic molecule that can join in long chains with other molecules to form a more complex molecule or polymer —**monomeric** /mónnə mérrik/ *adj*

monometallic /mónnō mə tállik/ *adj* 1 describes a currency or monetary system that uses one type of metal, especially gold or silver, as a monetary standard 2 made of one type of metal only

monometallism /mónnō mètt'lizəm/ *n* the use of just one metal, especially gold or silver, as a basic monetary standard

monomial /mo nṓmi əl/ *n* 1 an expression in algebra consisting of a single term, e.g. 3y, as distinct from one that contains two or more terms, e.g. 3x + 5y 2 a scientific name that consists of one element only, as do the names of most families of plants and animals [Early 18C. < MONO- after *binomial*.] —**monomial** *adj*

monomolecular /mónnō mə lékyōōlər/ *adj* 1 relating to or involving single molecules 2 describes a surface film that has a thickness of only one molecule —**monomolecularly** *adv*

monomorphic /mónnō máwrfik/, **monomorphous** /-máwrfəss/ *adj* 1 describes an organism or species that exists in a single discrete form, as distinct from one that changes form, as a caterpillar does when it becomes a butterfly 2 exhibiting only a single crystalline form —**monomorphism** *n*

Monongahela /mə nóng gə heélə/ river in West Virginia and Pennsylvania. Length: 206 km/128 mi.

mononuclear /mónnō nyóokli ər/ *adj* 1 describes a cell that has a single nucleus 2 describes an organic compound with a molecular structure containing only one ring of atoms

mononucleosis /mónnō nyóokli ṓssiss/ *n* 1 a significant rise in the number of atypical lymphocytes in the blood 2 MED = **infectious mononucleosis**

mononucleotide /mónnō nyóokli ə tīd/ *n* a nucleotide that contains a phosphate group, a sugar, and a nitrogenous base

monophagous /mo nóffəgəss/ *adj* feeding on a single type of plant or animal —**monophagy** /mo nóffəji, mə-/ *n*

monophonic /mónnō fónnik/ *adj* using only one channel to carry sound from the source to the loudspeaker, as distinct from, e.g., stereophonic sound that transmits across multiple channels to give some auditory perspective —**monophonically** *adv*

monophthong /mónnəf thong, mónnəp-/ *n* a vowel sound that keeps the same quality for the whole syllable [Early 17C. < Greek *monophthoggos* < *phthoggos* 'sound'.] —**monophthongal** /mónnəf thóng g'l, mónnəp-/ *adj*

monophyletic /mónnō fī léttik/ *adj* describes a group of plants or animals that are descended from a single stock or ancestral form —**monophyletically** *adv* —**monophyletism** /mónnō fílətizəm/ *n*

Monophysite /mo nóffi sīt/ *n* a believer that Jesus Christ has a single inseparable nature that is both human and divine [Late 17C. Via ecclesiastical Latin *Monophysita* < ecclesiastical Greek *monophusitēs* < *phusis* 'nature' (see PHYSICS).] —**Monophysitic** /mónnō fi síttik, mə nóffə síttik/ *adj* —**Monophysitism** *n*

monoplane /mónnō playn/ *n* an aeroplane that has just one pair of wings

monoplegia /mónnō pleéji ə/ *n* inability to move a single limb or a single group of muscles —**monoplegic** *adj*

monopod /mónnə pod/ *adj* describes a structure whose only support is one central pillar ■ *n* a single-legged adjustable support used to steady a camera

monopode /mónnə pōd/ *n* 1 PLANT SCI = **monopodium** 2 a person or animal with a single foot, especially a member of a mythical African race of one-legged people [Early 19C. Via Latin *monopodius* < Greek *monopodios* < *pod-* 'foot'.] —**monopodially** /mónnə pṓdi əli/ *adv*

monopodium /mónnə pṓdi əm/ (*plural* **-a** /-di ə/) *n* the main axis of some plants such as the pine tree that extends to the tip of the plant and produces lateral branches

monopole /mónnə pōl/ *n* 1 **SINGULAR MAGNETIC POLE OR ELECTRIC CHARGE** an electric charge or hypothetical magnetic pole isolated from its opposite charge or pole 2 **HYPOTHETICAL MAGNETICALLY CHARGED ELEMENTARY PARTICLE** a theoretical elementary particle that has only one magnetic pole, instead of the two present in ordinary magnetic bodies 3 **RADIO ANTENNA** a radio antenna made of an electrically charged conducting rod with an electrical connection at one end

monopolise *vt* = **monopolize**

monopolist /mə nóppə list/ *n* 1 a controller of a monopoly 2 a supporter of policies that favour monopolies —**monopolistic** /mə nóppə lístik/ *adj* —**monopolistically** *adv*

monopolize /mə nóppə līz/ (**-lizes, -lizing, -lized**), **monopolise** (**-lises, -lising, -lised**) *vt* 1 to have complete control of an industry or service and prevent other companies or people from participating or competing in it 2 to demand or take all of something such as somebody's time, attention, or affections, in a selfish way —**monopolization** /mə nóppə lī záysh'n/ *n* —**monopolizer** *n*

monopoly /mə nóppəli/ (*plural* **-lies**) *n* 1 **CONTROL OF MARKET SUPPLY** a situation in which one company controls an industry or is the only provider of a product or service 2 **BUSINESS CORPORATION WITH EXCLUSIVE CONTROL** a company with a commercial monopoly 3 **EXCLUSIVE COMMODITY OR AREA OF CONTROL** a product or service whose supply is controlled by only one company 4 **EXCLUSIVE LEGAL RIGHT** a legal right to the exclusive control of an industry or service, as granted by a government 5 **PERSONAL AND EXCLUSIVE POSSESSION** an exclusive right to have or do something ○ *He seems to think he has a monopoly on common sense.* [Mid-16C. Via Latin < Greek *monopōlion* < *pōlein* 'sell'.] —**monopolism** *n*

Monopoly *tdmk* a trademark for a property trading board game

monopsony /mə nópsəni/ (*plural* **-nies**) *n* a situation in which a particular type of product or service is only being bought or used by one customer [Mid-20C. < MONO + Greek *opsōnein* 'purchase provisions'.] —**monopsonist** *n* —**monopsonistic** *adj*

monopteros /mo nóptə ross/ (*plural* **-oi** /-roy/), **monopteron** /mo nóptə ron/ (*plural* **-a** /-rə/) *n* a circular classical temple surrounded by a single ring of columns [Late 17C. Via Latin < Greek, 'having one wing' < *pteron* 'wing'.] —**monopteral** *adj*

monorail /mónnə rayl/ *n* a passenger transport system in which the carriages straddle or are suspended from a single beam

monosaccharide /mónnō sákə rīd, -rid/ *n* a simple sugar such as glucose or fructose that cannot be broken down into simpler sugars

monosemy /mo nóssəmi, mónnō seemi/ *n* the linguistic feature or fact of having only one meaning [Mid-20C. < MONO-, after POLYSEMY.]

monoski /mónnō skee/ *n* a broad single ski on which a skier stands with both feet —**monoskier** *n* —**monoskiing** *n*

monosodium glutamate /mónnə sṓdi əm glóotə mayt/ *n* a sodium salt of glutamic acid. Use: flavour enhancer.

monosome /mónnə sōm/ *n* 1 an abnormal isolated chromosome, especially an unpaired X-chromosome 2 a single protein-manufacturing particle (**ribosome**) combined with messenger RNA —**monosomic** /mónnə sṓmik/ *adj* —**monosomy** /-sōmi/ *n*

monosyllabic /mónnō si lábbik/ *adj* 1 saying very little, often in a way that gives an impression of unfriendliness or lack of intelligence 2 consisting of one syllable only —**monosyllabically** *adv* —**monosyllabicity** /mónnō silə bíssəti/ *n*

monosyllable /mónnō silləb'l/ *n* a word or sentence consisting of only one syllable, e.g. 'Yes' or 'me'

monotheism /mónnə thee izəm/ *n* the belief that there is only one God, found, e.g., in Judaism, Christianity, and Islam —**monotheist** *n, adj* —**monotheistic** /mónnə thi ístik/ *adj* —**monotheistically** *adv*

monotint /mónnə tint/ *n* ART = **monochrome** *n.* 3

monotone /mónnə tōn/ *n* 1 **ONE UNCHANGING SOUND TONE** a sound, especially a speech sound, that does not rise and fall in pitch, but stays on the same tone 2 **SERIES OF IDENTICAL SOUNDS** a sequence of sounds, such as a piece of speech, singing, or music, that stays at exactly the same pitch throughout 3 **UNVARYING QUALITY** complete lack of variety in colour, expression, or style 4 **SINGER WITH NO SENSE OF PITCH** a person who cannot produce, or distinguish between, sounds of varying pitches when singing ■ *adj* 1 **WITH UNVARYING QUALITY** lacking variety in pitch, colour, or another quality 2 **monotone, monotonic ASCENDING OR DESCENDING IN SEQUENCE** describes a function or a sequence of real numbers that steadily increases or decreases —**monotonicity** /mónnə to níssəti/ *n*

monotonous /mə nóttənəss/ *adj* 1 uninteresting or boring as a result of being repetitive and unvaried 2 uttered or performed in one unvaried tone —**monotonously** *adv* —**monotonousness** *n*

monotony /mə nóttəni/ *n* 1 boredom or dullness arising from the fact that nothing different ever happens 2 repetitiousness or lack of variation in pitch or tone, especially in relation to music or speech

monotreme /mónnō treem/ *n* a mammal such as the duck-billed platypus or echidna that lays eggs and has a single opening for the discharge of faeces and urine. Order: Monotremata. [Mid-19C. < MONO- + Greek *trēma* 'hole'.]

monotropy /mónnə trōpi/ *n* a form of allotropy in which one form of an element is stable at all temperatures and pressures

monotype /mónnə tīp/ *n* 1 a plant or animal that is the only member of the taxonomic category to which it belongs 2 an artwork created by pressing on paper laid on an inked metal plate or sheet of glass —**monotypic** /mónnə típpik/ *adj*

Monotype *tdmk* a trademark for a typesetting machine that is run from a keyboard activating a unit that sets type by individual characters

monounsaturated /mónnō un sáchə raytid/ *adj* describes a fatty acid with only one carbon double bond

monovalent /mónnō váylənt/ *adj* 1 describes a chemical element or isotope that has a valency of one 2 containing only one type of antibody —**monovalence** *n* —**monovalency** /-váylənsee/ *n*

monoxide /mo nók sīd/ *n* a chemical compound with molecules that consist of one atom of oxygen and one or more atoms of another element

monozygotic /mónnō zī góttik/ *adj* describes twins derived from a single fertilized egg (**zygote**), e.g. human identical twins

Monroe /mən rṓ/, **James** (1758–1831) US statesman and 5th president of the United States (1817–25)

Monroe, Marilyn (1926–62) US actor. Born **Norma Jean Mortenson**

Monroe doctrine *n* the political principle, as stated by President James Monroe in 1823, that Europe should no longer involve itself in the American continent by exerting influence [Mid-19C. After James MONROE.]

Monrovia /mon rṓvi ə/ capital of Liberia, in the northwest of the country on the Atlantic Ocean. Population: 421,058 (1984).

mons /monz/ (*plural* **montes** /món teez/) *n* a fleshy body part that sticks out, especially the one formed by a pad of flesh at the juncture of the pubic bones. ◊ **mons pubis** [Mid-20C. Shortening of MONS PUBIS.]

Marilyn Monroe

Mons /moNs/ city in SW Belgium. Population: 92,260 (1996).

Monseigneur /móN see nyúr, -say-/ (plural **Messeigneurs** /máy see-, -say-/) n a title given to some dignitaries, especially bishops and princes, in France and French-speaking countries [Early 17C. < French, < mon 'my' + seigneur 'lord' < Latin senior 'older'.]

Monsieur /mə syúr/ (plural **Messieurs** /may syúr/), **monsieur** (plural **messieurs**) n 1 a title for a man in France or a French-speaking country, if he has no other special title 2 a form of address used when speaking or referring to a French or French-speaking man whose name is not known [Early 16C. < French, < mon 'my' + sieur 'lord' < Latin senior 'older'.]

Monsignor /mon seényər, -nyawr/ (plural **-gnors** or **-gnori** /món see nyáwri/) n a title used when speaking or referring to certain clerics of the Roman Catholic Church, especially bishops and officials of the papal court [Late 16C. Via Italian < French monseigneur (see MONSEIGNEUR).] —**Monsignorial** /món see nyáwri əl/ adj

monsoon /mon soón/ n 1 WINDS THAT REVERSE DIRECTION SEASONALLY a large-scale wind system that seasonally blows in opposite directions and determines the climate of large regions 2 RAINY SEASON, ESPECIALLY IN S ASIA any period of heavy rainfall, especially during the summer over South and Southeast Asia 3 HEAVY RAINFALL a very heavy fall of rain (informal) [Late 16C. Via obsolete Dutch monssoen < Portuguese monção < Arabic mawsim 'season'.] —**monsoonal** adj

mons pubis /-pyóobiss/ (plural **montes pubis** /món teez-/) n a prominence caused by the pad of fat that overlies the junction of the pubic bones in women and girls [Late 19C. < Latin, 'mount of the pubes'.]

monster /mónstər/ n 1 UGLY TERRIFYING CREATURE any large, ugly, terrifying animal or person found in mythology or created by the imagination, especially something fierce that kills people 2 EVIL PERSON somebody whose perceived inhumanity or vicious behaviour terrifies and disgusts people 3 HUGE THING something extraordinarily or unusually large (informal; often before nouns) 4 IMPROPERLY FORMED FOETUS a foetus that is markedly improperly formed, especially one that cannot live outside the uterus (offensive in some contexts) 5 OFFENSIVE TERM an offensive term for a person, animal, or plant that is undesirably formed (archaic) [13C. Via French monstre < Latin monstrum 'monster, divine omen' < monere 'warn, remind'.]

monstrance /mónstranss/ n a large gold or silver container in which the Host is placed and then shown to the congregation for adoration in a Roman Catholic Mass [13C. < medieval Latin monstrantia < Latin monstrare 'to show' < monstrum (see MONSTER).]

monstrosity /mon stróssət/ (plural **-ties**) n 1 an object, animal, or person that is very unpleasant or frightening to look at, often because it is large and strangely shaped 2 frightening size, shape, and ugliness ○ a figure of overwhelming monstrosity [Mid-16C. < late Latin monstrositas < monstruosus (see MONSTROUS).]

monstrous /mónstrəss/ adj 1 SHOCKING AND MORALLY UNACCEPTABLE wicked, cruel, or unpleasant to an extent that is morally unacceptable, often in a way that seems ugly and frightening 2 EXTREMELY LARGE extremely large, often in a way that seems ugly and frightening 3 LIKE A MONSTER resembling a monster of the type found in folklore and fairy tales [14C. Via Old French < Latin monstruosus < monstrum (see MONSTER).] —**monstrousness** n

monstrously /mónstrəssli/ adv in a way or to an extent that shocks or offends other people

mons veneris /-vénnəriss/ (plural **montes veneris** /món teez-/) n ANAT = **mons pubis** [Early 17C. < Latin, 'the mount of Venus'.]

Mont. abbr Montana

montage /mon taázh/ n 1 ARTWORK CREATED FROM MANY SMALL PIECES a picture or other work of art composed by assembling, overlaying, and overlapping many different materials or pieces collected from different sources, e.g. photographs, magazines, and other pictures 2 CREATION OF IMAGE FROM COLLECTED BITS the technique of creating a montage 3 SEQUENCE OF OVERLAPPING FILM CLIPS a film sequence consisting of a series of dissolves, superimpositions, or cuts used to condense time or to suggest memories or hallucinations 4 FILM-MAKING STYLE a style of film-making that makes extensive use of cuts, camera movements, and changes of camera position, particularly to set up new meanings not conveyed by the filmed action itself [Early 20C. < French, < monter 'to mount' (see MOUNT[1]).]

Montagnais /mónta nyáy/ (plural **-gnais**) n the Algonquian language of the Montagnais. Native speakers: 4,000. [Early 18C. < French, < montagne 'mountain'.] —**Montagnais** adj

Montagnard /mónta nyaárd, -nyaár/ (plural **-gnard** or **-gnards**) n a member of a people who live in the border region between Vietnam, Laos, and Cambodia [Mid-19C. < French, 'mountaineer' < montagne 'mountain'.]

Montaigne /mon táyn, mon tényə/, **Michel de Eyquem** (1533–92) French essayist

Montana /mon taána/ state in the NW United States. Capital: Helena. Population: 878,810 (1997). Area: 380,847 sq. km/147,046 sq. mi. —**Montanan** n, adj

montane /món tayn/ adj growing or living in mountainous regions [Mid-19C. < Latin montanus < mont- 'mountain'.]

montan wax /món tan-/ n a brittle, white to dark brown wax extracted from lignite and substituted in polishes and candles for carnauba and beeswax [Early 20C. < Latin montanus (see MONTANE), because extracted from lignite, a mountain rock.]

Mont Blanc /móN blaáN/ highest mountain in the Alps and W Europe, in E France, on the Italian border. Height: 4,807 m/15,771 ft.

Montcalm /mont kaám, moN kálm/, **Louis-Joseph de, Marquis de Montcalm** (1712–59) French soldier

monte /móntí/ n a game in which a player chooses between two cards and bets on being dealt a card of that same suit before being dealt a card of the other suit [Early 19C. Via Spanish < Latin mont- 'mountain'; from the heap of cards on the table.]

Monte Carlo /móntí kaárlō/ city in Monaco. Population: 13,154 (1982).

Montego Bay /mon teegō-/ 1 inlet of the Caribbean Sea in NW Jamaica 2 city in NW Jamaica. Population: 83,446 (1991).

monteith /mon teéth/ n a silver or pewter basin with notches around the edge, made to hold punch, or to cool punch glasses by resting their bases over the scalloped edge [Late 17C. Probably after a Scotsman Monteith, known for his capes with scalloped hems.]

Montélimar /món tay li maár/ town in central France. Population: 31,386 (1990).

Montenegro /mónta neégrō/ constituent republic of the Federal Republic of Yugoslavia, in the southwest of the country. Capital: Podgorica. Population: 635,442 (1996). Area: 13,812 sq. km/5,333 sq. mi. —**Montenegrin** n, adj

Monterey /mónta ráy/ city in W California. Population: 31,106 (1998 estimate).

Monterey Jack n a semihard cheese that is mild when young and becomes stronger and drier as it ages [Mid-20C. After Monterey County, California.]

Monterey pine n a widely planted pine tree. Native to: Monterey Peninsula of California. Use: timber. Pinus radiata.

Monte Rosa /móntí rōzə/ massif in the Pennine Alps, on the Swiss-Italian border. Highest peak: Dufourspitze 4,633 m/15,200 ft.

Monterrey /mónta ráy/ capital of Nuevo Leon State, NE Mexico. Population: 1,064,197 (1990).

Montes Alpes /món tayz ál páyz/ lunar mountain range visible in the northeastern quadrant of the Moon

Montes Apenninus /-áppa nínəss/ lunar mountain range visible in the northeastern quadrant of the Moon

Montes Jura /-jóora/ lunar mountain range visible in the northwestern quadrant of the Moon. Height: 4,500 m/15,000 ft.

Montesquieu /món təskyə, -təskyoo/, **Charles Louis de Secondat, Baron de la Brède et de** (1689–1755) French jurist and writer

Montessori /mónta sáwri/, **Maria** (1870–1952) Italian physician and educationalist

Montessori method /mónta sáwri-/ n a system of educating young children that was initiated by Maria Montessori in 1952 and aims to develop the child's natural interests and activities rather than use formal teaching methods

Monteverdi /mónti váirdi/, **Claudio** (1567–1643) Italian composer

Montevideo /móntivi dáyō/ capital of Uruguay, in the south of the country. Population: 1,251,647 (1985).

Montez /mon téz/, **Lola, Baroness Rosenthal and Countess of Lansfeld** (1818–61) Irish dancer. Pseudonym of Marie Dolores Eliza Rosanna Gilbert

Montezuma II /móntí zóoma/ (1466–1520) Aztec emperor

Montezuma's revenge n an offensive term for diarrhoea and sickness experienced when visiting another country, originally Mexico, and eating unfamiliar food (informal) [Mid-20C. After MONTEZUMA II.]

Montfort /móntfart/, **Simon de, Earl of Leicester** (1200?–65) English aristocrat and soldier

Montgolfier /mont gólfi ər, moN gólfyay/, **Jacques Etienne** (1745–99) French industrialist and inventor

Montgomery /mənt gómməri/ 1 town in E Wales. Population: 1,035 (1981). 2 capital of Alabama, in the centre of the state. Population: 196,363 (1996).

Montgomery, Bernard Law, 1st Viscount Montgomery of Alamein (1887–1976) British military commander

Montgomeryshire /mənt gómmərishər/ former county in central Wales

month /munth/ n 1 MAJOR DIVISION OF YEAR any major named division of the year in various calendar systems, e.g. in the Gregorian calendar there are 12 months, varying in length from 28 to 31 days 2 FOUR WEEKS OR 30 DAYS a period of time equivalent to about four weeks or 30 days 3 INTERVAL BETWEEN DATES IN CONSECUTIVE MONTHS a time lasting from a specified date in one calendar month until the same date in the next calendar month 4 ASTRON = **solar month** 5 ASTRON = **lunar month** 6 ASTRON = **sidereal month** ■ **months** npl LONG PERIOD OF TIME a long time, often an excessively or unacceptably long time [Old English mōnap < Indo-European, 'to measure'.] ◇ **not** or **never in a month of Sundays** used to emphasize that you think that something will never happen (informal)

monthly /múnthli/ adj 1 HAPPENING EACH MONTH done, held, or arranged once every month ○ a monthly meeting 2 PRODUCED EVERY MONTH published or issued once a month ○ a monthly periodical 3 LASTING A MONTH valid for one month ○ a monthly pass ■ adv ONCE A MONTH at intervals of one month ■ n (plural **-lies**) 1 MAGAZINE ISSUED EVERY MONTH a publication or periodical that is produced once a month 2 WOMAN'S MENSTRUAL PERIOD a woman's monthly menstruation (informal; usually plural)

monticule /mónti kyool/ n mound or small hill [Late 18C. Via French < late Latin monticulus < Latin mont- 'mountain'.]

Montmorency /móntmə rénssi/ river in S Quebec, Canada. Length: 97 km/60 mi.

Montmorency Falls highest waterfall in Quebec, Canada, near the mouth of the Montmorency River. Height: 84 m/275 ft.

montmorillonite /móntmə rílla nīt, -reè ə nīt/ n a soft clay mineral. Source: bentonite clays. [Mid-19C. After Montmorillon, France.] —**montmorillonitic** /móntmə rílla níttik, -reè ə-/ adj

Montpelier /mont peélyər/ capital of Vermont, in the north-central part of the state. Population: 7,734 (1998 estimate).

Montpellier /moN pə lyáy/ city in S France. Population: 225,392 (1999).

Montreal /móntri áwl/ city in S Quebec, Canada. Population: 1,016,376 (1996).

Montreux /mon trō/ area in W Switzerland, on Lake Geneva

Mont-Saint-Michel /móN saN mi shél/ granite islet off the coast of NW France, known for its Benedictine abbey

Montserrat /móntsə rát/ island in the Leeward Islands, in the E Caribbean Sea, a dependency of the United Kingdom. Population: 12,771 (1996). Area: 102 sq. mi./39 sq. mi.

monument /mónnyōōmənt/ *n* **1 LARGE STONE STATUE OR CARVING** something designed and built as a lasting public tribute to a person, a group of people, or an event **2 FAMOUS PLACE OR BUILDING** a site or structure that is preserved because of its historical, cultural, or aesthetic importance **3 CARVED HEADSTONE** a tombstone, plaque, or ornamental stone structure placed on somebody's grave **4 WORTHY REMINDER** something that remains as a reminder of something, especially something fine or distinguished **5 MEMORIAL TRIBUTE** a memorial to somebody in the form of a written or spoken tribute **6 BOUNDARY MARKER** an object such as a stone that marks a boundary [13C. Via French < Latin *monumentum* < *monere* 'remind'.]

monumental /mónnyōō mént'l/ *adj* **1 LARGE** huge in size, importance, or intensity **2 DESERVING SPECIAL ADMIRATION** so important or enduring that people cannot fail to notice or be impressed **3 MAKING CARVED HEADSTONES** related to or involved in the making of tombstones and memorial items to go in cemeteries and churches **4 OF MONUMENTS** relating to monuments or taking the form of a monument —**monumentality** /mónnyōō men tálləti/ *n* —**monumentally** *adv*

Monument Valley /mónnyōōmənt -/ region of NE Arizona and SE Utah, notable for its scenic rock formations

monuron /mónnyōō ron/ *n* a white crystalline odourless solid. Use: herbicide. [Mid-20C. Blend of MONO- + UREA.]

Monza /móntsa, mónzə/ city in N Italy. Population: 120,054 (1992).

monzonite /mónzə nīt/ *n* a visibly crystalline, granular igneous rock composed chiefly of equal amounts of two feldspar minerals, plagioclase and orthoclase, and small amounts of a variety of coloured minerals [Late 19C. After Mount *Monzoni* in the Tyrol.] —**monzonitic** /mónzə níttik/ *adj*

moo /moo/ *vi* (**moos, mooing, mooed**) **MAKE NOISE LIKE COW** to produce the deep drawn-out sound that a cow makes ■ *n* (*plural* **moos**) **1 NOISE THAT COW MAKES** a deep drawn-out sound made by a cow, or by somebody imitating this sound **2 OFFENSIVE TERM** an offensive term that deliberately insults a woman's intelligence and usefulness [Mid-16C. An imitation of the sound.]

⚡**MOO** *n* a virtual space in which several participants can meet online at a given time to discuss a given topic. Full form **multi-user domain, object-oriented**

mooch /mooch/ *v* **1** *vti* **GET THINGS FOR NOTHING FROM OTHERS** to get something for nothing from somebody by asking directly for it, without making any personal effort for it (*informal*) ○ *He's always mooching off friends.* **2** *vi* **WANDER AIMLESSLY** to wander or linger in an aimless way (*slang*) ○ *just mooching about* **3** *vi US* **SNEAK AROUND SUSPICIOUSLY** to move around or wait somewhere quietly and secretly, trying not to be noticed (*slang*) [15C. < Old French *muchier* 'to hide'.] —**moocher** *n*

mood[1] /mood/ *n* **1 STATE OF MIND** a state of mind that somebody experiences at a particular time ○ *a good mood* **2 GENERAL FEELING OF GROUP** the way a group of people think and feel about something at a particular time ○ *The mood of the country after the war was generally optimistic.* **3 BAD TEMPER** a feeling or display of sullen anger or irritability, especially one that begins suddenly or lasts a relatively short time ○ *He's in a mood.* [Old English *mōd* 'mind, courage' < Germanic] ◇ **in the mood** in the right or best state of mind for a particular activity or experience

mood[2] /mood/ *n* **1** a group of verb forms expressing a particular attitude. English has the indicative mood, expressing factual statements, the imperative mood, expressing commands, and the subjunctive mood, expressing possibilities and wishes. **2** LOGIC = **mode** *n.* **7** [Mid-16C. Alteration of MODE.]

mood swing *n* a sudden and extreme change in a person's mood

moody /mōōdi/ (**-ier, -iest**) *adj* **1 UNPREDICTABLY GRUMPY OR GLOOMY** tending to change mood unpredictably from cheerful to bad-tempered **2 CHANGEABLE** unusually changeable or difficult to predict **3 DISPLAYING PARTICULAR MOOD** displaying particular emotions, especially unhappiness or anger, clearly and intensely —**moodily** *adv* —**moodiness** *n*

Moody /mōōdi/, **Dwight Lyman** (1837–99) US evangelist

moola /mōōlə, mōō laa/, **moolah** *n US* money (*slang dated*) [Mid-20C. < ?]

mooli /mōōli/ (*plural* **-lis** *or* **-li**) *n* a large long white radish that can be eaten raw, cooked, or pickled and is typically used in Japanese, Chinese, and other Asian cuisines. US term **daikon** [Mid-20C. < Hindi *mūlī*.]

moon /moon/ *n* **1** ASTRON = **Moon 2 PLANET'S NATURAL SATELLITE** any natural satellite revolving around a planet **3 MOON'S SHAPE AS SEEN FROM EARTH** a form or view of the Moon, called its phase, at a specific point in the lunar cycle **4 SYMBOLIC REPRESENTATION OF MOON** a simple or stylized representation of the Moon, usually in the form of a circle or crescent **5 PERIOD OF TIME** a month, either as a rough estimate of time or as the time it takes for the Moon to complete its cycle of the Earth (*archaic or literary*) **6 MOONLIGHT** light given out by the Moon ■ *v* **1** *vi* **WANDER AIMLESSLY** to wander around in a dreamy or listless state, unable to concentrate on anything **2** *vi* **YEARN FOR LOVED ONE** to be stricken with longing for an absent loved one, and rendered listless and dreamy as a result (*literary or humorous*) **3** *vti* **BARE BUTTOCKS** to bend over and deliberately expose the bare buttocks to somebody, either as a rude joke or as an act of defiance and disrespect (*informal*) [Old English *mōna* < Germanic]

Moon *n* the Earth's only natural satellite

Moon /moon/, **William** (1818–94) British inventor

moonbeam /mōōn beem/ *n* a pale, milky, or iridescent beam of light reflected to the Earth by the Moon at night

moon blindness *n* periodic episodes of impaired vision in horses that often lead to permanent loss of sight

mooncalf /mōōn kaaf/ (*plural* **-calves** /-kaavz/) *n* somebody regarded as unintelligent or thoughtless (*archaic insult*) [Mid-16C. Originally 'shapeless fleshy mass in the womb', thought to be caused by the influence of the moon.]

moon daisy *n* PLANTS = **daisy** *n.* **2**

moon dog *n* ASTRON = **paraselene**

moon-faced *adj* with a large round face

moonfish /mōōn fish/ (*plural* **-fish** *or* **-fishes**) *n* **1** a slender deep-bodied silvery or golden fish, sometimes caught for food. Native to: W Atlantic or Pacific oceans. Genus: *Selene.* **2** a slender deep-bodied fish with large dorsal and anal fins. Native to: coastal and estuarine waters of Africa, Indian Ocean, adjacent parts of Pacific. Family: Monodactylidae.

moonflower /mōōn flowər/ *n* a name given to various plants whose flowers open at night, especially climbing plants related to the morning glories

Moonie /mōōni/ *n* a member of the Unification Church (*informal; often considered offensive*) [Late 20C. After Sun Myung *Moon*, the church's founder.]

moonlight /mōōn līt/ *n* the pale cool light that shines from the Moon on a clear night, often considered eerie or romantic. Moonlight is light from the Sun reflected from the Moon's surface. ■ *vi* to have a second job in addition to a main job, often one done at night and kept secret for purposes of tax evasion (*informal*) —**moonlighting** *n*

moonlight flit *n* an act of secretly abandoning a rented house during the night, in order to avoid paying rent that is owed (*informal*)

moonlit /mōōn lit/ *adj* brightened or illuminated by light from the Moon

Moonlite /mōōn līt/, **Captain** (1842–80) Irish-born Australian bushranger. Born **Andrew George Scott**

moon pool *n* an open shaft in a deep-sea drilling vessel, usually located in the centre of the hull, through which the drilling takes place

moonraker /mōōn raykər/ *n* a small sail sometimes set above the skysail on a square-rigged ship [Early 19C. Probably < its great height.]

moonrise /mōōn rīz/ *n* **1** the time of day when the Moon rises over the horizon **2** the Moon's rising in the sky over the horizon

moonscape /mōōn skayp/ *n* **1** the general appearance of the surface of the Moon as seen or portrayed **2** a view or place that looks as rough, grey, and bleak as the surface of the Moon

moonset /mōōn set/ *n* **1** the time of day when the Moon disappears below the horizon **2** the disappearance of the Moon below the horizon [Mid-19C. < MOON after *sunset*.]

moon shell *n* a carnivorous marine mollusc with a smooth rounded shell. Family: Naticidae.

moonshine /mōōn shīn/ *n* **1 ILLEGALLY MADE ALCOHOL** whisky or other strong spirits produced and sold illegally (*informal dated or humorous*) **2 NONSENSE** talk, opinions, or ideas dismissed as senseless (*informal*) **3 MOONLIGHT** moonlight. US term **moonlight** —**moonshiner** *n*

moonshot /mōōn shot/ *n* the launch of a crewed or uncrewed spacecraft to orbit or land on the Moon

moonstone /mōōn stōn/ *n* a semiprecious lustrous bluish-white stone that is a translucent variety of feldspar. Use: gems.

LITERARY LINK ***The Moonstone***, a novel (1868) by Wilkie Collins. The first British detective novel, it involves the disappearance of a priceless Indian diamond and a subsequent puzzling murder. All the classic elements of the genre are present, including red herrings, alibis, and sufficient clues for the reader to solve the crime ahead of its hero, Sergeant Cuff of Scotland Yard.

moonstruck /mōōn struk/ *adj* **1** acting in a rather irrational, dreamy, confused way, often out of love (*informal humorous*) **2** behaving in a wild or confused way (*dated literary*)

moonwalk /mōōn wawk/ *n* **INSTANCE OF WALKING ON MOON** an exploratory walk or expedition across part of the Moon's surface, carried out by an astronaut ■ *vi* **1 GO ON FOOT ACROSS MOON'S SURFACE** to walk away from a spacecraft for some distance across the surface of the Moon **2 PERFORM GLIDING DISCO DANCE** to perform a disco dance with gliding movements of the feet and legs —**moonwalker** *n*

moony /mōōni/ (**-ier, -iest**) *adj* **1** in a distracted or dreamy state, with little energy or concentration (*informal*) **2** relating to or resembling the Moon —**moonily** *adv* —**mooniness** *n*

moor[1] /moor, mawr/ *n* a large uncultivated treeless stretch of land covered with bracken, heather, coarse grasses, or moss (*often plural*) [Old English *mōr* < Germanic]

moor[2] /moor, mawr/ *vti* to fix a boat, ship, or aircraft to one place with cables, chains, or an anchor, or be secured in this way [15C. Probably < Middle Low German *mōren*.]

Moor /moor, mawr/ *n* a member of a nomadic people of Arab and Berber descent whose civilization flourished in North Africa from the 8th to the 15th centuries [14C. Via Old French *More* < Latin *Maurus* < Greek *Mauros*.]

moorage /mōōrij, máwrij/ *n* **1** NAUT, AIR = **mooring** *n.* **1 2** the fee charged for mooring somewhere

Moore /moor, mawr/, **Bobby** (1941–93) British footballer. Full name **Robert Frederick Moore**

Moore, Dudley (*b.* 1935) British actor, comedian, and pianist

Moore, G.E. (1873–1958) British philosopher. Full name **George Edward Moore**

Moore, Gerald (1899–1987) British pianist

Moore, Henry (1898–1986) British sculptor and print-maker

Moore, Michael Kenneth (*b.* 1949) New Zealand states-man

Moore, Patrick (*b.* 1923) British astronomer

moorhen /mōōr hen, máwr-/ *n* a medium-sized water bird with black plumage and a red bill found in marshy areas. *Gallinula chloropus.*

Moorhouse /mōōr howss, máwr-/, **Frank Thomas** (*b.* 1938) Australian writer

mooring /mōōring, máwr-/ *n* **1 PLACE FOR SECURING WATERCRAFT OR AIRCRAFT** a place where a boat, ship, or aircraft can be moored **2 CABLE SECURING WATERCRAFT OR AIRCRAFT** a rope, cable, or chain used to stop a watercraft or aircraft from drifting away **3 PHYSICAL OR EMOTIONAL TIE** something such as a family bond that gives a feeling of emotional or physical security (*usually plural*)

mooring tower *n* a permanent structure built as a place to moor airships

Moorish /mo͝orish, máwr-/ *adj* **1** relating to the Moors or their culture **2** built or designed in an architectural style popular in Spain between the 8th and the 16th centuries, noted for its use of ornate curving decoration

Moorish idol *n* a tropical marine fish that lives near Indo-Pacific reefs and has broad black and yellow stripes on its sides. *Zanclus canescens.* [Because its markings resemble those found in Moorish art]

moorland /mo͝orlənd, máwr-/ *n* countryside, or a piece of countryside, consisting of a moor

moose /mooss/ (*plural* **moose**) *n US* ZOOL = **elk** *n.* 1 [Early 17C. < Abenaki *mos.*]

moot /moot/ *adj* **1 ARGUABLE** open to argument or dispute ○ *Whether natural therapies actually aid recovery in such cases is a moot point.* **2 NOT RELEVANT** irrelevant or unimportant ○ *Her resignation was a moot issue, since she was going to have to leave her employment in any case.* **3 NOT LEGALLY RELEVANT** legally insignificant because of having already been decided or settled ○ *Whether he was entitled to do business under that name or not was moot, because his company had in fact ceased trading.* ■ *v* **1** *vt* **SUGGEST FORMALLY** to offer an idea for consideration or a topic for discussion (*usually passive*) **2** *vi* **HAVE FORMAL ARGUMENT** to take part in a debate, especially one organized as an academic exercise, e.g. a hypothetical case argued among law students ■ *n* **1 DEBATE ON HYPOTHETICAL ISSUE** an academic discussion in which people such as law students argue hypothetically or plead a hypothetical legal case **2 ANGLO-SAXON LOCAL COURT** in Anglo-Saxon England, a formal gathering for settling legal and administrative matters [Old English *mōt* 'assembly' < Germanic, 'meeting'] —**mootness** *n*

moot court *n* a court in which imaginary legal cases are conducted and tried by law students as part of their training

mop /mop/ *n* **1 TOOL FOR WASHING FLOORS** a long-handled tool for washing floors, with a washing head consisting of a large sponge or a thick mass of absorbent threads or fabric strips **2 TOOL FOR WASHING DISHES** a short-handled tool for washing dishes with a head consisting of a mass of twisted cotton threads **3 UNTIDY MASS** a thick or scruffy-looking tangle of hair ■ *vt* (**mops, mopping, mopped**) **1 WASH WITH MOP** to use a mop to wipe a floor surface clean **2 WIPE PERSPIRATION** to wipe perspiration from a part of the body [15C. < ?]

mop up *v* **1** *vti* **GET RID OF LIQUID WITH CLOTH** to wipe or rub a piece of material over a liquid to soak it up **2** *vt* **DEAL WITH REMAINING ENEMY FORCES** to capture or kill remaining enemy troops in order to secure an area after a decisive victory **3** *vt* **FINISH OFF** to complete or carry out the final details of a task (*informal*)

MOP *n* somebody who has assets, such as shares, that are nominally worth a million but that may never be realizable in cash. Full form **millionaire on paper**

mopboard /móp bawrd/ *n US* CONSTR = **skirting board**

mope /mōp/ *vi* (**mopes, moping, moped**) **1 BE MISERABLE** to be full of self-pity or sulky unhappiness and lose interest in everything else **2 WANDER ABOUT SADLY** to show self-pity and sulky unhappiness, especially by listless or aimless lingering or with a self-consciously slumping gait ■ *n* **MISERABLE PERSON** a person who tends to mope and who depresses others (*informal*) ■ **mopes** *npl* **GLOOMY MOOD** a bout of melancholy or sulkiness (*informal*) [Mid-16C. Probably < N Germanic.] —**moper** *n* —**mopy** *adj*

moped /mō ped/ *n* a lightweight pedalled motorcycle with an engine of less than 50cc [Mid-20C. Blend of MOTOR + PEDAL[1].]

moppet /móppit/ *n* a small child, or a term of endearment for a child (*informal*) [Early 17C. < obsolete *mop* 'baby, doll' < ?]

moquette /mo két, mō két/ *n* thick velvety fabric. Use: carpeting, upholstery. [Mid-19C. < French.]

MOR *abbr* middle-of-the-road (*in radio programming*)

Mor. *abbr* **1** Moroccan **2** Morocco

moraine /mə ráyn/ *n* a mass of earth and rock debris carried by an advancing glacier and left at its front and side edges as it retreats [Late 18C. Via French < French dialect *morena* 'mound'.] —**morainal** *adj* —**morainic** *adj*

moral /mórrəl/ *adj* **1 INVOLVING RIGHT AND WRONG** relating to issues of right and wrong and to how individuals should behave **2 DERIVED FROM PERSONAL CONSCIENCE** based on what somebody's conscience suggests is right or wrong, rather than on what the law says should be done **3 IN TERMS OF NATURAL JUSTICE** regarded in terms of what is known to be right or just, as opposed to what is officially or outwardly declared to be right or just ○ *a moral victory.* **4 ENCOURAGING GOODNESS AND RESPECTABILITY** giving guidance on how to behave decently and honourably **5 GOOD BY ACCEPTED STANDARDS** good or right, when judged by the standards of the average person or society at large **6 TELLING RIGHT FROM WRONG** able to distinguish right from wrong and to make decisions based on that knowledge **7 BASED ON CONVICTION** based on an inner conviction, in the absence of physical proof ■ *n* **1 VALUABLE LESSON IN BEHAVIOUR** a conclusion about how to behave or proceed drawn from a story or event **2 FINAL SENTENCE OF STORY GIVING ADVICE** a short, precise rule, usually written in a rather literary style as the conclusion to a story, used to help people remember the best or most sensible way to behave ■ **morals** *npl* **STANDARDS OF BEHAVIOUR** principles of right and wrong as they govern standards of general or sexual behaviour [14C. < Latin *moralis* < *mor-*, stem of *mos* 'custom', in plural 'morals'.] —**morally** *adv*

morale /mə ráal/ *n* the general level of confidence or optimism felt by a person or group of people, especially as it affects discipline and willingness [Mid-18C. Via French *moral* < Latin *moralis* (see MORAL).]

moralise *vti* = **moralize**

moralising *n* = **moralizing**

moralism /mórrəlìzəm/ *n* **1 PIECE OF MORAL ADVICE** a conventional moral maxim or saying **2 MORAL BEHAVIOUR** behaviour conforming to a system of moral standards that do not depend on religion **3 MORALIZING** criticism of other people's moral standards (*formal or dated*)

moralist /mórrəlist/ *n* **1 SOMEBODY GIVING ADVICE ON MORAL STANDARDS** a critic or teacher of moral standards **2 SOMEBODY WITH HIGH MORAL STANDARDS** a follower of a strict moral code **3 SPECIALIST WHO STUDIES MORALITY** a student or teacher of morals as an academic discipline —**moralistic** /mórrə lístik/ *adj* —**moralistically** *adv*

morality /mə rálləti/ (*plural* **-ties**) *n* **1 ACCEPTED MORAL STANDARDS** standards of conduct that are accepted as right or proper **2 HOW RIGHT OR WRONG SOMETHING IS** the rightness or wrongness of something as judged by accepted moral standards **3 MORAL LESSON** a lesson in moral behaviour

morality play *n* a play intended to teach a moral lesson, in which the characters embody human virtues and vices, e.g. Mercy and Lust, especially a medieval play written in verse

moralize /mórrə līz/ (**-izes, -izing, -ized**), **moralise** (**-ises, -ising, -ised**) *v* **1** *vi* **CRITICIZE MORALS OF OTHERS** to criticize other people's conduct or standards of behaviour, or give advice on how general moral standards should be improved **2** *vt* **ANALYSE IN TERMS OF MORALITY** to consider and explain something in terms of its moral significance **3** *vt* **MAKE MORE MORAL** to change something to make it conform, or conform better, with society's ideas of what is good, right, or decent —**moralization** /mórrə lī záysh'n/ *n* —**moralizer** *n* —**moralizing** *n* —**moralizingly** *adv*

moral philosophy *n* PHILOSOPHY = **ethics** *n.* 1

moral theology *n* the academic study of moral and ethical questions from a Christian viewpoint

Morant /mə ránt/, **Breaker** (1864?–1902) British-born Australian soldier and poet. Born **Edwin Henry Murrant**

morass /mə ráss/ *n* **1** an area of low-lying ground that is soft and wet to a great depth and therefore difficult to walk on **2** a frustrating, confusing, or unmanageable situation that makes any kind of progress extremely slow [Mid-17C. Via Dutch *moeras* < French *marais.*]

moratorium /mórrə táwri əm/ (*plural* **-ums** *or* **-a** /-ri ə/) *n* **1** a formally agreed period during which a specific activity is halted or a planned activity is postponed **2** a period during which a person, usually a debtor, has the right to postpone meeting an obligation [Late 19C. < modern Latin, < late Latin *moratorius* 'delaying' (see MORATORY).]

moratory /mórrətəri/ *adj* giving somebody the right to delay making payments on a debt [Late 19C. < late Latin *moratorius* 'delaying' < Latin *morat-*, past participle of *morari* 'to delay' < *mora* 'delay'.]

Morava /mə ráavə/ river in the east-central Federal Republic of Yugoslavia. Length: 160 km/100 mi.

Moravia /mə ráyvi ə/ historic region of E Czech Republic

Moravian /mə ráyvi ən/ *n* **1 SOMEBODY FROM MORAVIA** somebody who comes from Moravia **2 MORAVIAN CHURCH MEMBER** a member of the Moravian Church **3 DIALECT OF CZECH** the dialect of the Czech language spoken in Moravia —**Moravian** *adj*

Moravian Church *n* a Protestant church founded in Moravia in 1722 whose members place a strong emphasis on evangelism, ecumenism, and the authority of the Bible

moray /mórr ay, mo ráy/, **moray eel** *n* a brightly coloured sharp-toothed voracious eel that has no pectoral fins. Native to: rocky crevices or reefs of tropical coastal waters. Family: Muraenidae. [Early 17C. Via Portuguese *moréia* < Latin *murena* < Greek *muros* 'sea eel'.]

Moray /múrri/ council area in NE Scotland

Moray Firth arm of the North Sea, on the NE coast of Scotland

morbid /máwrbid/ *adj* **1 INTERESTED IN GRUESOME SUBJECTS** showing a strong interest in unpleasant or gloomy subjects such as death, murder, or accidents **2 GRISLY** inspiring disgust or horror **3 RELATING TO DISEASE** relating to or resulting in illness [Early 17C. < Latin *morbidus* 'diseased' < *morbus* 'sickness'.] —**morbidly** *adv* —**morbidness** *n*

morbidity /mawr bíddəti/ *n* **1** the presence of illness or disease **2** the relative frequency of occurrence of a particular disease in a particular area (*often before nouns*)

morceau /máwr sō, mawr sṓ/ (*plural* **-ceaux** /máwr sō, mawr sṓ/) *n* **1** a short musical or literary composition **2** a tiny piece, e.g. a small mouthful of food [Mid-18C. Via French < Old French *morsel* (see MORSEL).]

mordacious /mawr dáyshəss/ *adj* **1** deliberately bitter or critical, and intended to hurt somebody's feelings (*formal or literary*) **2** capable of biting, or tending to bite (*archaic or literary*) [Mid-17C. < Latin *mordac-* 'biting' < *mordere* 'to bite'.] —**mordaciously** *adv* —**mordaciousness** *n* —**mordacity** /-dássəti/ *n*

mordant /máwrd'nt/ *adj* **1 SARCASTIC** sharply sarcastic or bitingly critical **2 CORROSIVE** having a corrosive effect ■ *n* **1 SUBSTANCE THAT FIXES DYES** a substance that fixes a dye in and on textiles and leather by combining with the dye to form a stable insoluble compound (**lake**) **2 ACID USED IN ETCHING** a corrosive substance used to etch treated areas on a metal plate ■ *vt* **APPLY MORDANT TO** to apply a mordant to fabric in order to fix a dye [15C. Via French < Vulgar Latin variant of Latin *mordere* 'to bite'.] —**mordancy** *n* —**mordantly** *adv*

mordent /máwrd'nt/ *n* a musical embellishment, similar to a short trill, in which either the note above or the note below the written note is played as well as the principal note [Early 19C. Via German < Italian *mordente* < *mordere* 'to bite' < Latin.]

Mordred *n* MYTHOL = **Modred**

Mordvin /máwrdvin/ (*plural* **-vin** *or* **-vins**) *n* **1** a member of a Finnish people who live mainly in the middle of the Volga region of W Russia **2** the Finno-Ugric language of the Mordvin. Native speakers: 1 million. [Mid-18C. < Russian.] —**Mordvin** *adj*

more /mawr/ CORE MEANING: a grammatical word, the comparative of 'much' and 'many', used to indicate a greater number of something, either a greater number than before, than average, or than something else ○ (det) *a need for more adult education programs* ○ (pron) *As benefits go, this job offers me more.*

1 *adv* **TO GREATER EXTENT** having a larger amount or a greater extent of a particular quality (*forming the comparative of some adjectives and adverbs*) ○ (adv-attrib) *This problem is more complex than the other one.* **2** *adv* **FOR LONGER TIME** doing something or happening for a longer time ○ *We chatted a bit more.* **3** *adv, pron* **WITH GREATER FREQUENCY OR INTENSITY** used as the comparative of 'much' to mean 'with greater frequency or intensity' ○ (adv-degree) *We go out more than we used to.* ○ (adv-degree) *It inspires me more now than ever.* ○ (pron) *The more you listen, the more you hear.* **4** *det, pron* **ADDITIONAL** additional or further (*pronoun + singular or plural verb*) ○ (det) *I need more light.* ○ (pron) *There aren't any more of these.* ○ (pron) *No more is expected.* [Old English *māra* < Germanic] ◇ **(all the) more so** to an even greater extent or degree ◇ **more or less 1** approximately **2** essentially or basically ◇ **no** *or* **neither more nor less (than)** simply, or exactly ◇ **the more** *Ireland* although (*nonstandard*) ◇ **what is more** used to introduce an additional or reinforcing point

More /máwri/, **Moore** /mo͝o əri/ *n* LANG = **Mossi** *n.* **2** [< Mossi] —**More** *adj*

More /mawr/, **Sir Thomas, St** (1478–1535) English statesman and scholar

Moreau /mo rṓ/, **Gustave** (1826–98) French painter

Morecambe /máwrkəm/ town in NW England. Population: 46,657 (1991).

Moree /maw reé/ town in N New South Wales, Australia. Population: 9,270 (1996).

moreen /mo reén/ n a thick ribbed curtain material made of wool, cotton, or a mixture of both [Mid-17C. < ?]

moreish /máwrish/, **morish** adj so good to eat or drink that you keep wanting more of it (informal)

morel /mo rél/ n an edible mushroom with a brown pitted spongy cap. Genus: Morchella. [Late 17C. < French morille.]

morello /mə réllō/ (plural **-los**) n a small sour cultivated cherry with dark red skin [Mid-17C. < ?]

morendo /mə réndō/ adv growing continuously softer and sometimes slower (musical direction) [Early 19C. < Italian, 'dying', form of morire 'die'.] —**morendo** adj

moreover /mawr ṓvər/ adv used to add a further piece of information that supports a previous statement

morepork /máwr pawrk/ a small owl native to New Zealand. Ninox novaeseelandiae. [An imitation of its call]

mores /máwr ayz, máwr eez/ npl the customs and habitual practices, especially as they reflect moral standards, that a particular group of people accept and follow [Late 19C. < Latin, plural of mos 'manner, custom'.]

Moresque /maw résk/ adj ARCHIT = **Moorish** adj. 2 [Early 17C. Via French < Italian moresco < Moro 'Moor' < Latin Maurus (see MOOR).]

Moreton Bay /máwrt'n báy/ bay in E Australia. Area: 800 sq. km/309 sq. mi.

Moreton Bay fig n a large fig tree that has massive buttresses at the foot of its trunk and huge spreading roots. Native to: E Australia. Ficus macrophylla.

Moreton Island island off the coast of E Queensland, Australia. Population: 455 (1996). Area: 170 sq. km/66 sq. mi.

~~morgage~~ incorrect spelling of **mortgage**

morgan /máwrgən/ n unit of chromosome length [Early 20C. After Thomas Hunt Morgan (1866–1945), US geneticist and zoologist.]

Morgan /máwrgən/ n a black, bay, brown, or chestnut horse with a full mane and tail, short deep body, and slender legs, belonging to a US breed popular for hunting, jumping, and recreation [Mid-19C. After Justin Morgan.]

Morgan, Sir Henry /máwrgən/ (1635?–88) Welsh buccaneer

Morgan, John Pierpont (1837–1913) US financier

Morgan, Thomas Hunt (1866–1945) US geneticist and biologist

morganatic /máwrgə náttik/ adj describes a marriage in which neither the spouse of lower social rank nor any children of the marriage may inherit the title or possessions of the higher-ranking spouse [Mid-19C. Directly or via French or German < medieval Latin (matrimonium ad) morganaticam '(marriage for the) morning-gift' (the bridegroom's gift to the bride, which relieved him of further responsibility).] —**morganatically** adv

morganite /máwrgə nīt/ n a pink gemstone that is a variety of beryl [Early 20C. After J. P. MORGAN.]

Morgan le Fay /máwrgən lə fáy/ n in Arthurian legend, an evil sorceress who was the half-sister and enemy of King Arthur

morgen /máwrgən/ n a unit of measurement for land area formerly used in various parts of the world and still in use in South Africa [Early 17C. < Dutch and German, 'area of land that can be ploughed in a morning'.]

morgue /mawrg/ n 1 PLACE FOR DEAD BODIES a room or building in which dead bodies are kept until a post mortem has been carried out or until they are buried or cremated 2 COLLECTION OF INFORMATION a room or file in a newspaper office containing miscellaneous pieces of information kept for future reference, e.g. for writing obituaries 3 DISMAL PLACE a gloomy place that lacks warmth or cheer (informal) [Mid-19C. < French Morgue, building in Paris.]

LITERARY LINK The Murders in the Rue Morgue, a novel (1841) by US writer Edgar Allan Poe. Regarded as the world's first detective story, it begins with the brutal murder of an old woman and her daughter. Amateur sleuth C. Auguste Dupin comes to their aid, providing an explanation based on a brilliant analysis of scattered clues.

MORI /máwri, mórri/, **Mori** abbr Market and Opinion Research Institute

moribund /mórri bund/ adj 1 DYING nearly dead 2 STAGNANT having lost all sense of purpose or vitality 3 OBSOLESCENT becoming obsolete [Early 18C. < Latin moribundus < mori 'die'.] —**moribundity** /mórri búndati/ n —**moribundly** adv

Moriori /mórri áwri/ (plural **-i** or **-is**) n the extinct Austronesian language of the Moriori [Mid-19C. < Polynesian.] —**Moriori** adj

Morisco /mə rískō/ (plural **-cos** or **-coes**), **Moresco** /mə réskō/ (plural **-cos** or **-coes**) n 1 a Muslim of medieval Spain who was forcibly converted to Christianity and often continued the surreptitious practice of Islam, or a descendant of such a person 2 a morris dance or morris dancer [Mid-16C. < Spanish, < Moro 'Moor'.] —**Morisco** adj

morish adj = **moreish**

Morisot /mórri sṓ/, **Berthe** (1841–95) French painter

Morley /máwrli/, **Thomas** (1557–1603) English composer

Mormon /máwrmən/ adj relating to the Church of Jesus Christ of Latter-Day Saints, its members, or its doctrines and beliefs [Mid-19C. After the prophet said to be the author of the Book of Mormon, a sacred history of the Americas.] —**Mormonism** n

morn /mawrn/ n 1 a morning (literary) 2 Scotland tomorrow [Old English morgen < Germanic]

mornay /máwr nay/ adj served in a white sauce containing grated cheese ◇ cod mornay [Early 20C. Probably after Philip de Mornay (d. 1623), a French writer.]

morning /máwrning/ n 1 EARLY PART OF DAY the early part of the day, from dawn until noon or lunchtime 2 MIDNIGHT TO MIDDAY the part of the day between midnight and midday 3 DAWN dawn or daybreak 4 EARLY PART the beginning of something ■ interj GOOD MORNING good morning (informal) [13C. < MORN + -ing, after EVENING.]

morning-after pill n an emergency contraceptive pill designed to be taken after sexual intercourse

morning coat n a man's jacket, usually black, cut away at the front below the waist and with a long divided tail, worn on formal occasions as part of morning dress

morning dress n a man's suit worn to formal daytime events such as weddings, consisting of a black morning coat, striped black trousers, usually a waistcoat, and sometimes a top hat

morning glory n a climbing plant of the bindweed family. Flowers: trumpet-shaped, blue, purple, pink, or white, closing in the evening. Genus: Ipomoea.

morning line n a list of entrants and their odds for a race, estimated by a bookmaker and posted before betting begins, usually on the morning of the race

Morning Prayer n the morning service of worship in the Anglican Church

morning roll n Scotland a plain bread roll made from white flour

mornings /máwrningz/ adv during the morning, or every morning (informal)

morning sickness n nausea and vomiting experienced by many pregnant women, usually in the morning and during the early months of pregnancy

Morningside /máwrning sīd/ n Scotland an anglicized accent of Scottish English, often considered affected. ◊ **Kelvinside** [Late 19C. After a district of Edinburgh.]

morning star n a planet, especially Venus, seen in the eastern sky around dawn

Mornington Island /máwrningtən-/ island in the Wellesley Islands, N Australia. Population: 1,114 (1996). Area: 1,002 sq. km/387 sq. mi.

Mornington Peninsula peninsula in S Victoria, Australia

morning watch n the period of watch between four o'clock and eight o'clock in the morning

Moro /máwrō/, **Aldo** (1916–78) Italian statesman

morocco /mə ró kō/, **morocco leather** n a soft leather made from goatskin, used especially for covering books and for shoes, or any similar leather made in imitation of it from sheepskin or calfskin [Mid-17C. After MOROCCO.]

Morocco

Morocco /mə rókō/ kingdom in NW Africa. Capital: Rabat. Population: 27,020,000 (1996). Area: 453,730 sq. km/175,186 sq. mi. —**Moroccan** n, adj

morocco leather n INDUST = **morocco**

moron /máwr on/ n 1 an offensive term that deliberately insults somebody's intelligence (insult) 2 an offensive term for somebody with significant learning difficulties and difficulty in carrying out usual social functions [Early 20C. < Greek mōron 'unintelligent, thoughtless'.] —**moronic** /mə rónnik/ adj —**moronically** adv —**moronism** n —**moronity** /mə rónnati/ n

Moroni /mə rṓni/ capital of Comoros. Population: 23,432 (1990 estimate).

morose /mə rṓss/ adj having a withdrawn gloomy personality [Mid-16C. < Latin morosus 'peevish' < mos 'manner, disposition'.] —**morosely** adv —**moroseness** n —**morosity** /mə róssati/ n

Morpeth /máwrpəth/ town in NE England. Population: 14,500 (1992).

morph¹ /mawrf/ n an element of speech or writing that represents and expresses one or more morphemes [Mid-20C. Shortening of MORPHEME.]

morph² /mawrf/ n one of two or more variant forms of an animal or plant [Mid-20C. < Greek morphē 'form'.]

⚡ **morph³** /mawrf/ vti 1 to transform one graphic image on screen into another or others, through the use of sophisticated computer software, or be transformed in this way 2 to cause something to change its outward appearance completely and instantaneously, or undergo this process [Late 20C. < METAMORPHOSIS.]

morph. abbr 1 morphological 2 morphology

-morph suffix something that has a particular form, shape, or structure ◇ mesomorph [< Greek morphē 'form'] —**-morphic** suffix —**-morphism** suffix —**-morphous** suffix —**-morphy** suffix

morphactin /mawrf áktin/ n a substance affecting plant growth and development [Mid-20C. Probably < morph- + ACTIVE.]

morpheme /mawr feem/ n the smallest meaningful element of speech or writing [Late 19C. < French, < Greek morphē 'form', after English phoneme.] —**morphemic** /mawr feémik/ adj —**morphemically** adv

morphemics /mawr feémiks/ n (+ singular verb) 1 the way in which morphemes combine to form words in a language 2 the study and description of the ways in which morphemes combine in languages

Morpheus /máwr fi ass, -fyooss/ n in Greek mythology, the god of dreams and sleep, and son of Hypnos [14C. < Latin.] —**Morphean** adj

morphia /máwrfi ə/ n morphine (dated) [Early 19C. < MORPHEUS.]

morphine /máwr feen/ n an alkaloid drug that may become addictive with prolonged use. Source: opium. Use: relief of severe pain. [Early 19C. < French, < Morphée < Latin Morpheus 'Morpheus'.]

morphinism /máwrfinizəm/ n addiction to morphine and the related health problems of such addiction (dated) —**morphinist** n

morpho /máwrfō/ (plural **-phos**) n a large butterfly with iridescent blue wings. Native to: tropical America. Genus: Morpho. [Mid-19C. Via modern Latin < Greek Morphō, epithet of APHRODITE.]

morpho- *prefix* form, shape, structure ○ *morphogenesis* [< Greek *morphē*]

morphogen /máwrfəjən, máwrfə jen/ *n* a substance that influences the differentiation and growth of embryonic cells

morphogenesis /máwrfō jénnəssiss/ *n* **1** the origin and development of an organism or of some part of one, as it grows from embryo to adult **2** the development of an organism or of some part of one, as it changes as a species —**morphogenetic** /máwrfōjə néttik/ *adj* —**morphogenetically** *adv* —**morphogenic** *adj*

morphol. *abbr* **1** morphological **2** morphology

morpholine /máwrfə leen/ *n* C_4H_9NO a colourless liquid with a smell resembling ammonia. Use: solvent, manufacture of emulsifying agents, prevention of corrosion. [Late 19C. < MORPHINE + -OL[1].]

morphology /mawr fólləji/ (*plural* **-gies**) *n* **1 STRUCTURE OF ORGANISM** the form and structure of an organism or of any part of an organism **2 STUDY OF STRUCTURE OF ORGANISMS** the study of the form and structure of organisms **3 STRUCTURE OF WORDS** the structure of words in a language, including patterns of inflections and derivation **4 STUDY OF WORD FORMATION** the study of the structure of words in a language **5 STRUCTURE OTHER THINGS** the structure of something, or the study of the structure of something —**morphologic** /máwrfə lójjik/ *adj* —**morphological** *adj* —**morphologically** *adv* —**morphologist** *n*

morphometry /mawr fómmətri/ *n* the measurement of the outside of something —**morphometric** /máwrfə méttrik/ *adj* —**morphometrically** *adv*

morphosis /mawr fóssiss/ (*plural* **-ses** /-seez/) *n* a variation in the pattern of development (**morphogenesis**) of an organism as a result of changes in the external environment [Late 17C. < Greek *morphōsis* 'a shaping' < *morphē* 'form'.] —**morphotic** /mawr fóttik/ *adj*

morris /mórriss/ *n* DANCE = **morris dance** [15C. < Old French *morois* 'Moorish' < *More* 'Moor', because perhaps of Moorish origin.]

Morris /mórriss/, **William** (1834–96) British artist, poet, and social activist

Morris chair *n* a light carved wooden armchair with removable cushions and a reclining back that can be set at varying angles [After William MORRIS]

morris dance *n* an English folk dance, traditionally performed by men who wear white costumes and use small bells, sticks, and handkerchiefs. US term **morris** —**morris dancer** *n* —**morris dancing** *n*

Morrison /mórriss'n/, **Herbert Stanley, Baron Morrison of Lambeth** (1888–1965) British politician

Morrison, James (*b.* 1962) Australian jazz musician

Morrison, Jim (1943–71) US rock singer and songwriter. Full name **James Douglas Morrison**

Toni Morrison

Morrison, Toni (*b.* 1931) US writer. Born **Chloe Anthony Wofford**

Morrison, Van (*b.* 1945) British singer and songwriter. Born **George Ivan Morrison**

morro /mórrō/ (*plural* **-ros**) *n* a hill or headland with a rounded outline [< Spanish]

morrow /mórrō/ *n* **1** the day after today or after a particular day (*archaic or literary*) **2** the period of time following an event or occurrence (*literary*) [13C. < earlier form of MORN.]

Mors /mawrz/ *n* in Roman mythology, the god of death. Greek equivalent **Thanatos** [< Latin, 'death']

Morse /mawrss/, **Morse code** *n* a system for representing letters and numbers by signs consisting of one or more short or long signals of sound or light that are printed out as dots and dashes [Mid-19C. After Samuel F. B. MORSE.]

Morse /mawrss/, **Helen** (*b.* 1946) British-born Australian actor

Morse, Samuel F. B. (1791–1872) US inventor and artist. Full name **Samuel Finley Breese Morse**

Morse code *n* COMMUNICATIONS = **Morse**

morsel /máwrss'l/ *n* **1** a small piece of something, especially of food **2** a small amount of something [13C. < Old French, 'little bite' < *mors* 'bite' < past participle of Latin *mordere* 'to bite'.]

Mort /mawrt/, **Thomas Sutcliffe** (1816–78) British-born Australian merchant and shipbuilder

mortadella /máwrtə déllə/ *n* a smoked, fried, or steamed Italian sausage consisting of pork and beef flavoured with wine, garlic, and pepper [Early 17C. < Italian, < Latin *murtatum* '(sausage) seasoned with myrtle berries'.]

~~**mortagage**~~ incorrect spelling of **mortgage**

mortal /máwrt'l/ *adj* **1 EVENTUALLY DYING** certain to die eventually **2 HUMAN** relating to human beings **3 FATAL** causing death ○ *a mortal blow* **4 CONTINUING UNTIL SOMEBODY DIES** continuing, or intended to continue, until somebody dies ○ *mortal combat* **5 OF DEATH** relating to or accompanying death ○ *in mortal agony* **6 EXTREMELY HATED** being the object of somebody's unrelenting hatred ○ *his mortal enemy* **7 INTENSE** intensely felt ○ *mortal fear* **8 CONCEIVABLE** being within the bounds of what is imaginable or possible ○ *What mortal reason could there be for him to leave like that?* **9 BORING** tedious and dull (*slang*) ■ *adj, adv* **USED FOR EMPHASIS** used for emphasis, and sometimes indicating that the speaker is frustrated or annoyed (*dated*) ■ *n* **1 HUMAN BEING** a human being, who will eventually die **2 PERSON** a person (*informal*) [14C. Directly or via Old French < Latin *mortalis* < *mors* 'death'.]

SYNONYMS See ***deadly***.

mortality /mawr tálləti/ *n* **1 CERTAINTY TO DIE** the condition of being certain to die eventually **2 NUMBER OF DEATHS** the number of deaths that occur at a given time, in a given group, or from a given cause **3 MANY DEATHS** great loss of life **4 RATE OF FAILURE** the rate of failure of something, e.g. businesses or farms **5 HUMAN BEINGS** the human race

mortality rate *n* the number of deaths in a particular place or group compared with the total number of residents in that place or members of that group

mortality table *n* a table listing the life expectancy and death rate for various ages or occupations and based on mortality statistics over the course of a number of years

mortally /máwrt'li/ *adv* **1** so badly that death follows **2** in an extreme or intense way

mortal sin *n* in the Roman Catholic Church, a sin considered to be so wicked that it causes a complete loss of grace and leads to damnation unless it is absolved. ◊ **venial sin**

mortar /máwrtər/ *n* **1 CEMENT, SAND, AND WATER** a mixture of sand, water, and cement or lime that becomes hard like stone. Use: in building to hold bricks and stones together. **2 CANNON** a cannon with a relatively short and wide barrel, used for firing shells at a high angle over a short distance **3 GUN FIRING LIFELINE** a gun for firing something other than a bullet, e.g. a rope to somebody in need of rescue **4 BOWL USED FOR GRINDING** a hard heavy bowl designed to hold substances to be ground into small pieces or powder by means of a club-shaped tool (**pestle**) **5 BOWL FOR CRUSHING ORE** a cast-iron bowl in which ore is crushed ■ *vt* **1 FIRE AT** to fire at somebody or something with a mortar **2 FIX WITH MORTAR** to hold stones and bricks together with mortar [Pre-12C. Via French *mortier* 'bowl for mixing' < Latin *mortarium* 'bowl, substance prepared in it'.]

mortarboard /máwrtər bawrd/ *n* **1** a hat often worn on formal academic occasions, consisting of a round cap with a hard square flat top and usually a tassel **2** a square board with a handle in the centre of the underside, used by bricklayers for carrying mortar

mortgage /máwrgij/ *n* **1 LOAN AGREEMENT FOR PROPERTY** an agreement by which somebody borrows money from an organization and gives that organization the right to take possession of property given as security if the loan is not repaid **2 CONTRACT BETWEEN BORROWER AND LENDER** a written contract describing the agreement between a borrower and a lender by which a loan is given against security **3 TOTAL MONEY BORROWED** the total amount of money lent to a borrower by a money-lending organization, with some of the borrower's property being given as security **4 LOAN INSTALMENT TO BE REPAID** the money paid by a borrower, usually monthly, to a bank or building society until the entire sum borrowed by a mortgage agreement has been repaid ■ *vt* (**-gages, -gaging, -gaged**) **1 GRANT CLAIM TO OWNERSHIP OF PROPERTY** to give a claim to legal possession of property to a money-lending organization such as a bank or building society as security for a loan **2 PLEDGE RISKILY** to pledge something when risk is involved (*informal*) [14C. < Old French, < *mort* 'dead' + *gage* 'pledge', because property pledged as security may be lost.] —**mortgageable** *adj*

mortgagee /máwrgi jée/ *n* an organization such as a bank or building society that lends money to a borrower by a mortgage agreement

mortgager *n* FIN = **mortgagor**

mortgage rate *n* the interest rate charged by organizations such as banks and building societies on mortgage loans

mortgagor /máwrgi jáwr, -jər/, **mortgager** /máwrgijər/ *n* a borrower of money under a mortgage agreement

mortice *n* CONSTR, PRINTING = **mortise**

mortician /mawr tísh'n/ *n* US = **undertaker** *n*. 1 [Late 19C. < Latin *mort-* 'death'.]

mortification /máwrtifi káysh'n/ *n* **1 SHAME** deep shame and humiliation **2 SOMETHING CAUSING MORTIFICATION** something that causes a feeling of shame and humiliation **3 SELF-IMPOSED HARDSHIP** the use of self-imposed discipline, hardship, abstinence from pleasure, and especially self-inflicted pain in an attempt to control or put an end to desires and passions, especially for religious purposes **4 DEATH AND DECAY OF LIVING TISSUE** the death and decaying of a part of a living body, e.g. because the blood supply to it has been cut off [14C. Directly and via Old French < late Latin *mortificatio(n-)* 'destruction' < Latin *mortificat-* past participle of *mortificare* (see MORTIFY).]

mortify /máwrti fī/ (**-fies, -fying, -fied**) *v* **1** *vt* **SHAME** to make somebody feel ashamed and humiliated **2** *vt* **IMPOSE HARDSHIP ON** to use self-imposed discipline, hardship, abstinence from pleasure, and especially self-inflicted pain in an attempt to control or put an end to desires and passions, especially for religious purposes **3** *vi* **DECAY** to decay and die (*refers to living tissue*) [14C. Via Old French *mortifier* < Latin *mortificare* 'kill' < *mort-* 'death'.] —**mortifier** *n* —**mortifying** *adj* —**mortifyingly** *adv*

Mortimer /máwrtimər/, **Roger de, 8th Baron of Wigmore, 1st Earl of March** (1287?–1330) English courtier

mortise /máwrtiss/, **mortice** *n* **1 HOLE CUT TO HOLD OTHER PART** a hole or slot cut into a piece of wood, stone, or other material, for a projecting part (**tenon**) to be inserted into it, in order to form a tight joint **2 HOLE IN PRINTING PLATE** a hole cut in a printing plate to receive type or another plate ■ *vt* (**-tises, -tising, -tised; -tices, -ticing, -ticed**) **1 CUT MORTISE IN** to cut a mortise in something **2 JOIN BY MORTISE AND TENON** to join two things or parts by means of a mortise and tenon **3 CUT HOLE IN PRINTING PLATE** to cut a hole in a printing plate [14C. < Old French, probably < Arabic *murtaj* 'locked'.] —**mortiser** *n*

mortise lock *n* a lock inserted into a hole (**mortise**) cut into the side edge of a door so that when the door is closed the lock cannot be seen or removed

mortmain /máwrt mayn/ *n* the perpetual, nontransferable, and nonsaleable ownership of property by organizations such as churches [13C. Via Anglo-Norman, Old French < medieval Latin *mortua manus* 'dead hand'.]

Morton /máwrt'n/, **Jelly Roll** (1885–1941) US pianist and composer. Born **Ferdinand Joseph La Menthe**

mortuary /máwrchoo əri/ *n* (*plural* **-ies**) a room or building in which dead bodies are kept until a post mortem has been carried out or until they are buried or cremated ■ *adj* relating to death or funerals [14C. Directly or via Anglo-Norman *mortuarie* < Latin *mortuarius* < *mortuus* 'dead', past participle of *mori* 'die'.]

morula /máwryoolə/ (*plural* **-las** *or* **-lae** /-lee/) *n* an early stage in the development of an animal embryo, consisting of a solid ball of cells derived by cleavage of the fertilized egg (**zygote**) [Mid-19C. < modern Latin, 'little mulberry' < *morum* 'mulberry'.] —**morular** *adj* —**morulation** /máwryŏŏ láysh'n/ *n*

Morwell /máwrwəl/ town in SE Victoria, Australia. Population: 15,423 (1991).

morwong /máwr wong/ (*plural* **-wongs** *or* **-wong**) *n* **1** a large marine fish with a thick-lipped head, sharply tapering body, and extended dorsal fin. Native to: Australia, Asia. Family: Cheilodactylidae. **2** the flesh of a morwong used as a food [Late 19C. Probably < Aboriginal.]

mosaic /mŏ záy ik/ *n* **1** PICTURE MADE WITH SMALL COLOURED PIECES a picture or design made with small pieces of coloured material such as glass or tile stuck onto a surface **2** MAKING OF MOSAICS the art of making mosaics **3** SOMETHING CONSISTING OF VARIETY OF ELEMENTS something consisting of a number of things of different types, forms, or colours **4** LIGHT-SENSITIVE SURFACE IN TV CAMERA a light-sensitive surface on a television camera tube, consisting of a thin sheet covered by particles that convert incoming light into an electric charge for scanning by an electron beam **5** VIRAL PLANT DISEASE a plant disease, often caused by a virus, in which the foliage develops irregular patches of discoloration **6** PLANT DISCOLORATION a pattern of light-green or yellowish mottling on the foliage of a plant, usually caused by a viral infection **7** GENETICS = **chimera** *n.* 2 ◾ *vt* (**-ics, -icking, -icked**) DECORATE WITH MOSAIC to make something into, or decorate something with, a mosaic [14C. < Old French, < Latin *Musa* 'Muse'; from the decorations of medieval shrines dedicated to the Muses.]

Mosaic /mŏ záy ik/, **Mosaical** /-ik'l/ *adj* relating to the biblical figure Moses [Mid-17C. Directly or via French < Latin *Mosaicus* < *Moses* 'Moses' < Hebrew *Mŏsheh*.]

mosaic disease *n* PLANT SCI = **mosaic** *n.* 5

mosaic gold *n* **1** tin disulphide used in gilding **2** an alloy of copper and either zinc or tin that looks like gold. Use: to decorate such things as furniture and jewellery.

mosaicism /mŏ záy issizəm/ *n* the occurrence of genetically distinct cells within tissue or an individual organism

Mosaic Law *n* the ancient code of law of the Hebrews, beginning with the Ten Commandments, believed to have been set down by Moses and contained in the Pentateuch

mosasaur /mŏssə sawr/, **mosasaurus** /-sáwrəss/ (*plural* **-sauri** /-sáw rī/) *n* an extinct marine lizard that had a long slender body with limbs resembling paddles for steering, and a long flexible tail for propulsion. Family: Mosasauridae. [Mid-19C. < modern Latin *Mosaurus* < Latin *Mosa*, the River Meuse.]

moschatel /móska tél/ (*plural* **-tels** *or* **-tel**) *n* a low-growing plant found in moist places. Flowers: small, yellowish-green, in cube-shaped clusters. Native to: northern temperate regions. *Adoxa moschatellina*. [Mid-18C. Via French < Italian *Moscatella* < *moscato* 'musk', from the scent of the flowers.]

Moscow /móss kŏ/ **1** capital of Russia, located in the west-central European part of the country. Population: 10,666,935 (1995). **2** city in NW Idaho. Population: 19,312 (1998 estimate).

Moseley /mŏzli/, **Henry Gwyn-Jeffreys** (1887–1915) British physicist

Moselle[1] /mŏ zél/ *n* a light dry to sweet white wine from the Moselle valley in Germany

Moselle[2] /mŏ zél/ river in NE France and NW Germany. Length: 515 km/320 mi.

Moses /mŏziz/ *n* in the Bible, a Hebrew prophet and the brother of Aaron who led the Israelites from slavery in Egypt to the Promised Land and is believed to have written down the Ten Commandments (Exodus 20)

Moses, Grandma (1860–1961) US artist. Born **Anna Mary Robertson Moses**

Moses basket *n* a portable wicker or straw cot for a baby [Because Moses was placed in such a basket (Exodus 2)]

mosey /mŏzi/ (**-seys, -seying, -seyed**) *vi* to walk somewhere at a leisurely unhurried pace (*informal*) [Early 19C. < ?]

mosh /mosh/ (**moshes, moshing, moshed**) *vt* to dance to rock music in a frenzied way (*informal*) [Late 20C. Probably alteration of MASH.]

Grandma Moses

moshav /mŏ sháav/ (*plural* **-shavim** /-shaa vém/) *n* in Israel, a cooperative settlement consisting of independent small farms, or land farmed by the whole community with each family having its own house and garden [Mid-20C. < modern Hebrew *mŏšāḇ* 'dwelling, colony'.]

mosh pit *n* an area in front of the stage at a rock concert where people dance in a frenzy (*informal*)

Moslem /mózləm, mŏozləm/ *n* (*plural* **-lems** *or* **-lem**), *adj* an offensive term for a Muslim (*dated*) [Variant] — **Moslemic** /moz lémmik, mŏoz-/ *adj* —**Moslemism** *n*

Mosley /mŏzli/, **Sir Oswald Ernald** (1896–1980) British politician

mosque /mosk/ *n* a building in which Muslims worship [15C. Via French < Arabic *masjid* 'place of worship' < *sajada* 'bow down'.]

mosquito /mə skeēt ŏ, mo-/ (*plural* **-toes** *or* **-tos**) *n* a small slender fly that feeds on the blood of mammals, including humans, and transmits diseases such as malaria, yellow fever, and dengue. Native to: tropics. Family: Culicidae. [Late 16C. Via Spanish, 'little fly' < *mosca* 'fly' < Latin *musca*.]

mosquito boat *n* NAVY = **motor torpedo boat**

mosquito coil *n* incense in the form of a coil that is lit at night to repel mosquitoes

mosquito fern *n* a small fern that has branched stems with small leaves resembling scales that floats on fresh-water ponds and lakes. Genus: *Azolla*.

mosquito net *n* a curtain of fine netting hung over a bed or across a window as a protection against mosquitoes

moss /moss/ *n* **1** SIMPLE NONFLOWERING PLANT a simple nonflowering plant (**bryophyte**) that has short stems bearing small leaves arranged in a spiral and resembling scales, and inhabits moist shady sites. Class: Musci. **2** PLANT RESEMBLING MOSS a plant that in some way resembles a true moss, e.g. a variety of seaweed known as Irish moss **3** MARSHY AREA in Scotland and Northern England, an area of marshy ground or moorland, especially a peat bog (*often in placenames*) [Old English *mos* 'swamp' < Germanic]

Moss /moss/, **Stirling** (b. 1929) British racing driver

Mossad /móssad/ *n* the intelligence service of Israel, established in 1951 (*takes a singular or plural verb*) [Mid-20C. < Hebrew *mosad* 'institution'.]

moss agate *n* a whitish agate containing dark-green patterns resembling moss

moss animal *n* MARINE BIOL = **bryozoan**

mossback /móss bak/ (*plural* **-backs** *or* **-back**) *n* **1** US, Can an old turtle, shellfish, or fish with algae growing on its back **2** US an offensive term for a person regarded as old-fashioned or conservative (*insult*)

Mössbauer effect /móss bowər-/ *n* the emission or absorption of a gamma ray by a nucleus within a crystal in which the recoil is shared between atoms in the crystal [Mid-20C. After Rudolf *Mössbauer* (b. 1929), German physicist.]

moss campion *n* a plant of the pink family that forms tufts of leaves resembling moss. Flowers: solitary, pink. Native to: cool alpine regions. *Silene acaulis*.

moss green *adj* of a dull yellowish-green colour — **moss green** *n*

mossgrown /móss grōn/ *adj* **1** covered with moss **2** old-fashioned or out-of-date

---

Mossi /móssi/ (*plural* **-si** *or* **-sis**) *n* **1** a member of a people living in West Africa, especially in Burkina Faso **2** the Gur language of the Mossi. Native speakers: 6 million. [Mid-19C. African name.] —**Mossi** *adj*

mossie *n* INSECTS = **mozzie**

mosso /móssŏ/ *adv* in a quick and lively way (*musical direction*) ◊ **meno mosso** [Late 19C. < Italian, past participle of *muovere* 'to move'.]

moss pink, moss phlox *n* a garden plant of the pink family with spreading mats of tiny leaves. Flowers: lavender, pink, or white. Native to: E North America. *Phlox subulata*.

moss rose *n* a rose with a mossy calyx and flower stalk. Flowers: fragrant, pink. *Rosa centifolia* var. *muscosa*.

moss stitch *n* a basic knitting stitch consisting of alternating knit and purl stitches in one row, then alternating purl and knit stitches in the next row, producing a regular raised design

moss-trooper *n* in the 17th century, somebody involved in raiding, especially cattle-raiding, in the area around the Scottish-English border [< MOSS 'marshy area']

mossy /móssi/ (**-ier, -iest**) *adj* **1** COVERED WITH MOSS covered or overgrown with moss **2** RESEMBLING MOSS similar to moss, e.g. in texture or colour **3** OLD-FASHIONED old-fashioned or out-of-date (*informal*) —**mossiness** *n*

mossy zinc *n* a form of zinc with a grainy texture. Source: pouring melted zinc into water.

most /mŏst/ CORE MEANING: a grammatical word indicating nearly all or the majority of the people or things mentioned ◊ *Most people enjoy watching a good film.* ◊ *We'd finished off most of the work by lunchtime.*

1 *det, pron* GREATEST greatest in number, amount, extent, or degree ◊ (*det*) *He won the most seats in the election.* ◊ (*pron*) *The most I can lend you is 50 pounds.* **2** *adv* TO THE GREATEST EXTENT in or to the greatest extent (*forming the superlative of some adjectives and adverbs*) ◊ *the most expensive suit I'd ever bought* ◊ *It works most effectively if you heat it gently first.* **3** *adv* SUPERLATIVE OF 'MUCH' the superlative of 'much' ◊ *What I like most about him is his easygoing attitude.* **4** *adv* VERY in a high degree ◊ *a most enjoyable day* **5** *adv* US, Can ALMOST nearly but not entirely ◊ *Most everyone was invited.* [Old English *mæst* < Indo-European, 'big'] ◇ **at (the) most** at the maximum ◊ *It'll take you two hours at the most.* ◇ **make the most of something** to take full advantage of something ◇ **the most** the best of all (*dated slang*) ◊ *That song is the most!*

-most *suffix* **1** nearest to or toward ◊ *endmost* **2** most ◊ *nethermost* [Old English *-mest* < Germanic, taken as < MOST]

Mostaganem /mə stággə ném/ city in NW Algeria. Population: 114,037 (1987).

Mostar /móss taar/ city in S Bosnia-Herzegovina. Population: 126,000 (1991).

most favoured nation *n* a nation accorded the most favourable trading terms by another nation —**most-favoured-nation** *adj*

Most Honourable *adj* in the United Kingdom, a title given to marquesses and marchionesses, and to members of the Order of the Bath

mostly /mŏstli/ *adv* **1** almost entirely ◊ *The audience was mostly made up of younger fans.* **2** on most occasions ◊ *I swim mostly at weekends.*

Most Reverend *adj* a title given to Anglican and Roman Catholic archbishops, to Irish Roman Catholic bishops, to the Anglican Bishop of Meath, and to the Primus of the Episcopal Church in Scotland

mot /mot/ *n* Ireland a girl or young woman, especially a regular woman companion (*slang*) [Mid-16C. < ?]

MOT *n* **1** ROADWORTHINESS TEST an inspection of a vehicle to test its roadworthiness **2** MOT, MOT certificate ROADWORTHINESS CERTIFICATE a certificate of roadworthiness awarded to a vehicle that has passed its MOT test. Full form **Ministry of Transport** ◾ *vt* CARRY OUT MOT ON A VEHICLE to carry out an MOT test on a vehicle [Late 20C. Abbreviation of *Ministry of Transport*, which administers the test.]

MOTD *abbr* message of the day (*in e-mails*)

mote /mŏt/ *n* a tiny speck or particle [Old English *mot* < ?]

motel /mŏ tél/ *n* a hotel intended to provide short-term accommodation for travelling motorists, usually situated close to a main road and having rooms accessible from the parking area [Early 20C. Blend of MOTOR + HOTEL.]

~~**moter**~~ incorrect spelling of **motor**

motet /mō tét/ *n* a vocal composition with parts for different voices, usually based on a sacred text [14C. < Old French, 'little word' < Latin *muttire* 'to murmur'.]

moth /moth/ *n* an insect resembling a butterfly, typically with a duller colour and differently shaped antennae, active at night. Order: Lepidoptera. [Old English *moþþe* < ?]

mothball /móth bawl/ *n* **MOTH-REPELLENT CHEMICAL BALL** a small ball of a strong-smelling chemical such as camphor or naphthalene, used for keeping clothes moths away from clothing and other materials ■ *vt* **1 PUT SOMETHING OFF INDEFINITELY** to postpone work or discussion on something for an indefinite time ○ *We'll mothball the expansion plans until we have the financing.* **2 TAKE A FACTORY OUT OF OPERATION** to take a factory out of operation but protect the equipment in it so that it can be used again at some time in the future **3 SEAL A CRAFT UP FOR STORAGE** to seal all the openings in a ship or aircraft in order to protect it from corrosion while it is not in use ◇ **in mothballs** put aside or stored and not in use

moth bean *n* **1** a yellowish-brown edible bean seed **2** a plant of the pea family. Flowers: small, yellow. Use: forage, fertilizer, food. Native to: tropical regions, especially South Asia. *Phaseolus aconitifolius.*

moth-eaten *adj* **1 EATEN BY MOTH LARVAE** damaged by clothes moth caterpillars **2 WORN-OUT** old and worn-out from use **3 OUTDATED** no longer usable or appropriate (*informal*)

mother[1] /mú̲thər/ *n* **1 FEMALE PARENT** a woman who has a child, or a female animal that has produced young **2 WOMAN ACTING AS PARENT** a woman who acts as the parent of a child to whom she has not given birth **3 CHARACTERISTICS OF A MOTHER** the qualities or feelings that are traditionally associated with being a mother ○ *brought out the mother in her* **4 ORIGINATOR** a woman regarded as the creator, instigator, or founder of something **5 ORIGIN OF** the cause, source, or origin of something ○ *Necessity is the mother of invention* **6 PROTECTOR** something that protects and nourishes like a mother **7 GOOD OR BAD EXAMPLE** something very big, good, bad, or extreme, or particularly noteworthy in some other way (*slang; sometimes offensive*) ○ *a real mother of a headache* **8 US TABOO TERM** a highly offensive term for somebody regarded as objectionable or contemptible (*taboo*) ■ *vt* **1 LOOK AFTER SOMEBODY WITH CARE** to look after somebody with great care and affection, sometimes to an excessive degree **2 GIVE BIRTH TO BABY** to give birth to and bring up a baby **3 BRING SOMETHING ABOUT** to give rise to something [Old English *modor* < Indo-European] —**motherhood** *n* ◇ **at your mother's knee** in early childhood ◇ **be mother** to pour out tea from a teapot for those present (*humorous*) ◇ **every mother's son** every man or boy (*dated*)

mother[2] /mú̲thər/ *n* a slimy mass of bacteria and yeast cells that forms on the surface of alcohol being converted into acetic acid [Mid-16C. Probably < obsolete Dutch *moeder* < Middle Dutch *moeder* 'female parent'; from its part in the production of vinegar.]

Mother *n* **1** used as a title or form of address for a senior nun in a religious community **2 Mother, mother** used as a title of respect for a woman past middle age (*archaic; sometimes offensive*)

ϟ **motherboard** /mú̲thər bawrd/ *n* a circuit board in a minicomputer or microcomputer through which all signals are directed

Mother Carey's chicken /-káiriz-/ *n* a storm petrel (*dated*) [Probably < alteration of medieval Latin *mater cara* 'Virgin Mary']

mother cell *n* a cell that gives rise to other cells by cell division

mother church *n* a church from which other churches derive their authority

mother country *n* **1** the country of origin of people who have left to found a colony or colonies elsewhere **2** the country that somebody was born and grew up in

mother figure *n* a woman who embodies the qualities traditionally associated with a mother, especially support, advice, and affection

motherfucker /mú̲thər fukər/ *n* US a highly offensive term of abuse for somebody regarded as objectionable or contemptible (*taboo*) —**motherfucking** *adj*

Mother Goose *n* the supposed author of a collection of nursery rhymes first published in the 18th century

mother hen *n* an overprotective person who fusses over others

motherhouse /mú̲thər howss/ *n* a monastery or convent from which monks or nuns have gone out to found new monasteries and convents

Mothering Sunday *n* Mother's Day

mother-in-law (*plural* **mothers-in-law**) *n* the mother of your spouse

mother-in-law apartment *n* US = **granny flat**

mother-in-law's tongue *n* PLANTS = **sansevieria** [< its long pointed leaves]

motherland /mú̲thər land/ *n* the country that somebody was born and grew up in

motherless /mú̲thərləss/ *adj* without a mother, or having lost a mother through bereavement ■ *adv Australian* completely or thoroughly ○ *motherless broke*

mother lode *n* **1** the main vein of ore in a mine **2** a plentiful supply of something

motherly /mú̲thərli/ *adj* having or showing qualities traditionally considered to be typical of a mother, especially kindness and protectiveness —**motherliness** *n*

mother-naked *adj* US completely nude

Mother Nature *n* the forces of nature conceived of as a wilful being

Mother of God *n* a title given to Mary, the mother of Jesus Christ, especially by Catholics

Mother of Parliaments *n* the British parliament, thought of as the model for the parliaments of many other countries

mother-of-pearl *n* the hard pearly internal layer of the shells of some molluscs. Use: decorative inlays. [Early 16C. Translation of obsolete French *mère perle*.]

mother of the chapel *n* in trade unions in the printing and publishing industries, the woman head of a workplace section (**chapel**) of a union

mother-of-thousands (*plural* **mothers-of-thousands** *or* **mother-of-thousands**) *n* a creeping or trailing plant that produces masses of small flowers, especially the ivy-leaved toadflax or the strawberry geranium

mother of vinegar *n* BIOL = **mother**[2]

Mother's Day *n* the fourth Sunday in Lent, when people traditionally give cards and presents to their mothers

mother ship *n* **1 SHIP SERVICING SMALLER SHIPS** a ship or spaceship that provides services and supplies for a number of other, usually smaller ships **2** an organization that oversees, or a place that acts as a base for, other activities (*informal*) **3** a person's mother (*slang*)

mother superior (*plural* **mother superiors** *or* **mothers superior**) *n* the head of a convent or community of Christian nuns

mother-to-be (*plural* **mothers-to-be**) *n* a woman who is expecting a baby

mother tongue *n* **1** the first language somebody learns as a child at home **2** a language from which other languages have developed

Motherwell /mú̲thərwel/ town in central Scotland. Population: 30,717 (1991).

Motherwell /mú̲thərwəl, -wel/, **Robert** (1915–91) US artist

mother wit *n* natural intelligence or good sense

motherwort /mú̲thər wurt/ (*plural* **-worts** *or* **-wort**) *n* a plant with deeply lobed leaves. Flowers: white or pink, purple-spotted. Use: formerly, as a medicinal herb during childbirth. Native to: Europe, Asia. *Leonurus cardiaca.* [14C. < obsolete sense of MOTHER, 'womb'.]

moth fly *n* a tiny insect with wings covered with hairs that resembles an extremely small moth. Family: Psychodidae.

mothproof /móth proof/ *adj* treated with a substance designed to prevent damage by clothes moths —**mothproof** *vt* —**mothproofer** *n*

mothy /móthi/ (**-ier, -iest**) *adj* **1** damaged by the action of clothes moths **2** full of or infested by moths

motif /mō téef/ *n* **1 REPEATED DESIGN** a repeated design, shape, or pattern **2 SEWN OR PRINTED DECORATION** a repetitive decorative design sewn into or printed on something such as a piece of clothing, or a single example of the pattern **3 THEME IN LITERATURE** an important and sometimes recurring theme or idea in a work of literature **4 PROMINENT SEQUENCE OF NOTES** a short prominent sequence of notes forming the basis for development in a piece of music **5 CAR DECORATION** a decoration on a car that serves to identify the manufacturer [Mid-19C. < French (see MOTIVE).]

motile /mó tīl/ *adj* capable of or demonstrating movement by independent means [Mid-19C. < Latin *motus* 'motion' < past participle of *movere* 'to move'.] —**motility** /mō tílləti/ *n*

motion /mósh'n/ *n* **1 ACT OF MOVING** the act or process of moving, or the way in which somebody or something moves ○ *walked with a swaying motion* **2 A MOVEMENT** a movement, action, or gesture ○ *made a quick motion of the wrist* **3 POWER OF MOVEMENT** the power or ability to move something **4 PROPOSAL** a proposal put forward for discussion at a meeting **5 APPLICATION TO A JUDGE OR COURT** an application made to a court or judge for an order or ruling in a legal proceeding **6 PASSING OF SOLID WASTE FROM THE BODY** the passing of solid waste matter out of the body through the anus **7 ACT OF EMPTYING BOWELS** a single act of emptying of the bowels, or the matter emptied (*dated; often plural*) **8 MOVEMENT FROM ONE NOTE TO ANOTHER** the movement from one note to the next by a voice or instrument ■ *vti* **SIGNAL TO** to gesture or signal something such as a request or intention to somebody ○ *motioned me over and told me to sit down* [14C. Via Old French < Latin *motion-* < past participle of *movere* 'to move'.] ◇ **go through the motions** to do something in a perfunctory or mechanical way, without enthusiasm or commitment ◇ **put** *or* **set something in motion** to cause something to start moving, functioning, or happening

motionless /mósh'nləss/ *adj* not moving —**motionlessly** *adv* —**motionlessness** *n*

motion picture *n* US, Can a film (*technical*)

motion sickness *n* = **travel sickness**

motion study *n* INDUST = **time and motion study**

motivate /mṓti vayt/ (**-vates, -vating, -vated**) *v* **1** *vt* **GIVE SOMEBODY AN INCENTIVE** to give somebody a reason or incentive to do something **2 MAKE SOMEBODY WILLING** to make somebody feel enthusiastic, interested, and committed to something **3** *vt* **CAUSE SOMEBODY'S BEHAVIOUR** to be the cause or driving force behind something that somebody does ○ *motivated purely by greed* [Mid-19C. < MOTIVE, after French *motiver* 'motivate'.] —**motivated** *adj* —**motivator** *n*

motivation /mṓti váysh'n/ *n* **1 GIVING OF A REASON TO ACT** the act of giving somebody a reason or incentive to do something **2 ENTHUSIASM** a feeling of interest or enthusiasm that makes somebody want to do something, or something that causes such a feeling **3 REASON** a reason for doing something or behaving in some way **4 FORCES DETERMINING BEHAVIOUR** the biological, emotional, cognitive, or social forces that activate and direct behaviour —**motivational** *adj* —**motivationally** *adv* —**motivative** /mṓti vaytiv/ *adj*

motivational research, motivation research *n* the study of the motivation of consumers in their buying practices, used to plan marketing and sales

motive /mṓtiv/ *n* **1 REASON** the reason for doing something or behaving in a particular way **2** LITERAT, ARTS = **motif** *n.* **1, motif** *n.* **3** ■ *adj* **1 CAUSING MOTION** capable of causing or producing motion **2 DRIVING SOMEBODY** tending to make somebody want or be willing to do something ■ *vt* (**-tives, -tiving, -tived**) **MOTIVATE** to make somebody want or be willing to do something [14C. Via Old French *motif* < late Latin *motivus* < past participle of Latin *movere* 'to move'.]

SYNONYMS ***motive, incentive, inducement, spur, goad***

CORE MEANING: something that prompts action

motive the reason for doing something or behaving in a particular way; **incentive** something external, often some kind of reward, that inspires extra enthusiasm or effort; **inducement** something external that persuades or attracts somebody to a particular course of action, especially something that is offered as a reward; **spur** something such as the hope of a reward or the fear of punishment that encourages action or effort or energy; **goad** a stimulus that motivates somebody or stirs somebody into action, often against his or her will.

motiveless /mṓtivləss/ *adj* having no reason for doing something or behaving in a particular way ○ *a motiveless crime*

motive power *n* **1** the power or energy that drives a piece of machinery, or the source of that power or energy **2** the driving force behind an action or activity

motivic /mō tívvik/ *adj* relating to a musical motif or motifs

motivity /mō tívvəti/ *n* the power to move or to make something move

mot juste /mṓ zhóost/ (*plural* **mots justes** /mṓ zhóost/) *n* exactly the right word or words to express something [< French]

motley /mótli/ *adj* (**-lier, -liest**) **1 MADE UP OF DIFFERENT TYPES** consisting of people or things that are very different from one another and do not seem to belong together **2 OF VARIED COLOURS** made up of different colours ■ *n* (*plural* **-lies**) **1 JESTER'S COSTUME** the multicoloured clothing worn by medieval jesters **2 VARIED GROUP** a group of people or things that are very different from one another and do not seem to belong together [14C. < ?]

motmot /mót mot/ *n* a bird with a broad downward-curved bill, long tail, and usually greenish plumage with a black patch on the chest. Native to: Central and South America. Family: Momotidae. [Mid-19C. < American Spanish, an imitation of its call.]

motocross /mṓtō kross/ *n* a motorcycle race, or the sport of racing motorcycles, over a rough course with steep hills, wet or muddy areas, and turns of varying difficulty. ◊ **autocross** [Mid-20C. < French, < *moto* 'motorcycle' + English CROSS-COUNTRY.]

motoneuron /mṓtō nyóor on/ *n* ANAT = **motor neuron** [Early 20C. < MOTOR.] —**motoneuronal** *adj*

motor /mṓtər/ *n* **1 MACHINE THAT CREATES MOTION** a machine that converts energy into motion and can be used as a power source, e.g. to drive another machine or to move some form of transport **2 CAR** a vehicle, especially a car, powered by a motor (*slang*) ■ *adj* **1 OF VEHICLES** relating to vehicles, especially cars, powered by a motor **2 MOTOR-DRIVEN** powered by a motor **3 CAUSING MOTION** causing or producing motion **4 OF MUSCLE ACTIVITY** relating to muscle activity, especially voluntary muscle activity, and the consequent body movements ■ *vi* **1 DRIVE IN CAR** to travel by car or some other form of private vehicle, especially for pleasure (*formal*) **2 MOVE FAST** to move or progress at a fast pace (*informal*) **3 PROCEED SMOOTHLY** to be moving towards an objective, e.g. in work, with the desired degree of speed and momentum (*slang*) ○ *Now we're really motoring!* [15C. < Latin, 'mover' < *movere* 'to move'.]

motorable /mṓtərəb'l/ *adj* being a suitable surface on which to drive motor vehicles

motorbicycle /mṓtər bīssik'l/ *n* a motorcycle or moped

motorbike /mṓtər bīk/ *n* = **motorcycle**

motorboat /mṓtər bōt/ *n* a small boat powered by an engine —**motorboater** *n* —**motorboating** *n*

motorbus /mṓtər buss/ *n* a passenger bus (*dated*)

motorcade /mṓtər kayd/ *n* a procession of cars or other vehicles, especially one forming an escort for somebody important [Early 20C. < MOTOR + CAVALCADE.]

motor camp *n NZ* a drive-in campsite for motorists with tents or caravans

motor car *n* a car (*dated or formal*)

motor caravan *n* a vehicle with cooking, living, and sleeping facilities like those of a caravan. US term **motor home**

motor cortex *n* the region of the outer surface of the brain (**cortex**) where nervous impulses controlling voluntary muscle activity are initiated

motorcycle /mṓtər sīk'l/ *n* a two-wheeled road vehicle powered by an engine ■ *vi* (**-cles, -cling, -cled**) to ride or travel on a motorcycle —**motorcyclist** *n*

motor drive *n* a motorized mechanism to advance film in a camera

motor home *n US* = **motor caravan**

motoric /mō tórrik/ *adj* relating to voluntary muscle movement —**motorically** *adv*

motorise *vt* = **motorize**

motorist /mṓtərist/ *n* a driver of a motor vehicle

motorize /mṓtə rīz/ (**-izes, -izing, -ized**), **motorise** (**-ises, -ising, -ised**) *vt* **1** to fit something with a motor **2** to provide troops with motor vehicles —**motorization** /mṓtə rī záysh'n/ *n*

motorman /mṓtərmən/ (*plural* **-men** /-mən/) *n* the driver of a tramcar or electric train

motormouth /mṓtər mowth/ (*plural* **-mouths** /-mowthz/) *n* an unduly talkative or rapid speaker (*informal insult*)

motor neuron, motor neurone *n* a nerve cell (**neuron**) that conveys nerve impulses from the spinal cord or brainstem away from the central nervous system towards a muscle or gland

motor neuron disease *n* a progressive degenerative disease involving the motor neurons and causing weakness and wasting of the muscles

motor neurone *n* = **motor neuron**

motor park *n W Africa* a car park

motor pool *n US* BUSINESS, TRANSP = **car pool** *n.* 2

motor racing *n* racing in motor vehicles, especially in cars that are specially designed to travel at high speeds. US term **auto racing**

motor rhythm *n* a rhythmic motif in a piece of music maintaining a constant pulse, usually at a fast tempo, for an extended period

motorsailer /mṓtər saylər/ *n* a sailing boat equipped with a motor

motor scooter *n* a light motorcycle with small wheels, an enclosed engine, and a framework that includes a protective front plate and support for the rider's feet

motor ship *n* a ship powered by an engine

motorsport /mṓtər spawrt/ *n* a sport in which participants race motor vehicles, usually around a track

motor torpedo boat *n* a highly manoeuvrable vessel, 18 to 30 m/60 to 100 ft in length, carrying light armament and used to torpedo enemy shipping. US term **PT boat**

motor unit *n* a motor neuron and the muscle fibres it acts on

motor vehicle *n* a car, lorry, or other road vehicle powered by an engine

motor vessel *n* a ship powered by an engine

motorway /mṓtər way/ *n UK* a limited-access road usually consisting of three lanes for vehicles moving in both directions, intended for travelling relatively fast over long distances

Motown /mṓ town/ *tdmk* a trademark for a music company based in Detroit whose music, consisting of elements of pop, soul, and gospel, was especially popular during the 1960s and 1970s

motser /mótsər/, **motza** /mótsə/ *n Aus* a large sum of money, especially a gambling win (*informal*) [20C. < ?]

motte /mot/ *n* a mound on which a castle was built [Late 19C. < French.]

motte and bailey (*plural* **mottes and baileys**) *n* a fortification consisting of a fortified courtyard (**bailey**) overlooked by a wooden castle built on a mound of earth (**motte**)

MOT test *n* CARS = **MOT** *n.* 1

mottle /mótt'l/ *vt* (**-tles, -tling, -tled**) **MARK SOMETHING WITH DIFFERENT COLOURS** to mark something with an irregular pattern of patches or spots of different colours ■ *n* **1 IRREGULAR PATTERN OF COLOURS** an irregular pattern of patches or spots of different colours **2 PATCH OF COLOUR** a patch or spot of colour that forms part of an irregular pattern [Late 17C. Probably back-formation < MOTLEY.]

mottled enamel *n* tooth enamel that is mottled as a result of swallowing excessive amounts of fluoride at the age when teeth harden

motto /móttō/ (*plural* **-toes** *or* **-tos**) *n* **1 RULE TO LIVE BY** a short saying that expresses a rule to live by ○ *'I heartily accept the motto, "That government is best which governs least"; and I should like to see it acted up to more rapidly and systematically'.* (Henry David Thoreau, *Civil Disobedience*; 1849) **2 SAYING ON COAT OF ARMS** a short saying that forms part of a coat of arms and expresses something about the family or place whose coat of arms it is **3 SAYING OR QUOTATION** a saying or quotation printed on a small piece of paper, generally one of the contents of a cracker **4 QUOTATION AT BEGINNING OF WRITING** a short quotation at the beginning of a piece of writing, e.g. a book, a chapter of a book, or a poem, related in some way to its contents **5** MUSIC = **motif** *n.* 4 [Late 16C. < Italian, probably < assumed Vulgar Latin, 'word'.]

Motu /mṓ too/ (*plural* **-tu** *or* **-tus**) *n* **1** a member of a Melanesian people of Papua New Guinea who live in the central province in and around Port Moresby **2** the Austronesian language of the Motu. Native speakers: 14,000. [Late 19C. < Melanesian.] —**Motu** *adj*

motu proprio /mṓ too prōpri ō/ (*plural* **motu proprios**) *n* a decree issued by a pope acting independently and on his own initiative [< Latin, 'on your own initiative']

motza *n Aus* = **motser** (*informal*)

moue /moo/ *n* a look of discontent with the lips pressed together and forward [Mid-19C. < French.]

mouflon /moo flon/ *n* a reddish-brown wild sheep with prominent curved horns. Native to: Sardinian, Corsica. *Ovis musimon.* [Late 18C. Via French < Italian *muflone.*]

mouillé /mwee ay/ *adj* describes a consonant pronounced with the tongue touching the palate [Mid-19C. < French, past participle of *mouiller* 'wet, moisten'.]

moulage /moo laázh/ *n* **1** the process of making a mould or cast of something, e.g. a footprint, in the course of a criminal investigation **2** a mould or cast made in the course of a criminal investigation [Early 20C. < French, 'moulding, moulded copy' < Old French *mouler* 'to mould'.]

mould[1] /mōld/ *n* **1 CONTAINER FOR MAKING A SHAPE** a container that gives a shape to a molten or liquid substance poured into it to harden **2 FRAME** a frame on which something is formed or built **3 OBJECT MADE IN A MOULD** an object that was formed using a mould **4 DISTINCTIVE TYPE** a particular type that has a distinctive character or nature ○ *a leader in the heroic mould* **5 SET OF ASSUMPTIONS** a fixed pattern or framework of assumptions, especially when regarded as restricting ○ *negotiators who break out of the traditional diplomatic mould* **6** ARCHIT = **moulding** *n.* 1 ■ *v* **1** *vt* **MAKE SOMETHING IN MOULD** to shape or form something in a mould **2** *vt* **GIVE SOMETHING SHAPE** to shape or give form to something **3** *vt* **INFLUENCE SOMEBODY'S CHARACTER** to guide or influence the growth or development of somebody or something ○ *the childhood experience that helped mould her personality* **4** *vti* **FIT THE CONTOURS OF** to fit closely by following the contours or acquiring the shape of something **5** *vt* **MAKE A MOULD FROM** to make a material into a mould to be used in casting metal **6** *vt* **PUT MOULDING ON** to decorate something with a moulding [12C. Via Old French *modle* < Latin *modulus* 'little measure' < *modus* 'measure'.] —**mouldable** *adj*

mould[2] /mōld/ *n* **1 FUNGUS** a fungus that causes organic matter to decay **2 GROWTH OF MOULD** a growth of mould on the surface of something, or the discoloration caused by the growth of mould ■ *vi* **BECOME COVERED WITH MOULD** to become covered with or affected by mould [15C. < obsolete *moul* 'go mouldy' < assumed Old Norse *mugla.*]

mould[3] /mōld/ *n* **1 SOIL RICH IN HUMUS** soil that is rich in humus and easily worked or crumbled **2 EARTH** the earth or ground (*literary*) **3 THE GROUND** the ground, especially the earth of the grave (*literary*) [Old English < Indo-European 'to grind']

mouldboard /mṓld bawrd/ *n* **1 BLADE OF A PLOUGH** the curved metal blade of a plough that turns over the soil **2 BLADE OF A BULLDOZER OR SNOWPLOUGH** the large curved blade on the front of a bulldozer or snowplough that pushes the soil or snow **3 SIDE OF A CONCRETE MOULD** a board that forms one side or one surface of a concrete mould

moulder[1] /mṓldər/ *vti* to crumble or decay because of natural processes, or to make something crumble or decay [Mid-16C. < *mold* 'loose soil' < Germanic, 'grind'.]

moulder[2] /mṓldər/ *n* a person who moulds things or makes moulds

moulding *n* **1** a strip of wood or some other material that is used to decorate or finish a surface of a wall or a piece of furniture **2** something that is produced using a mould

mouldy /mṓldi/ (**-ier, -iest**) *adj* **1 WITH MOULD** with mould growing on or inside it **2 STALE FROM AGE OR ROT** stale and unpleasant from old age, neglect, or fungal growth **3 OLD** old-fashioned or out-of-date (*informal*) **4 BORING** dull, boring, or contemptible (*informal*) —**mouldiness** *n*

moules marinières /mool mari nyér/ *npl* a dish of mussels cooked and served in their shells with a wine sauce [< French]

moulin /moolin/ *n* an almost vertical shaft in a glacier, created by meltwater and debris boring into a crack in the surface of the ice [Mid-19C. Via French, 'mill' < late Latin *molinum.*]

moult /mōlt/ *vti* **LOSE FEATHERS, FUR, OR SKIN** to shed feathers, hair, or skin periodically, especially seasonally, to allow replacement of what is lost with new growth ■ *n* **1 LOSS OF FEATHERS, FUR, OR SKIN** the process or time during which a bird or animal casts off all or part of its feathers, fur, or skin **2 SHED FEATHERS, FUR, HAIR, OR SKIN** the material shed during moulting [Pre-12C. < Latin *mutare* 'to change'.] —**moulter** *n*

mound /mownd/ *n* **1 SMALL HILL** a small hill **2 CONSTRUCTED PILE** a pile of earth, stones, or other material built up for some purpose, e.g. to provide shelter, defence, or concealment **3 PILE OF OBJECTS** an untidy heap or pile of objects ○ *a mound of dirty laundry on the floor* **4 LARGE AMOUNT** a large amount of something ○ *a mound of mashed potatoes* ■ *vt* **MAKE INTO A MOUND** to form something into a mound [Early 16C. < ?]

moundbird /mównd burd/ *n* BIRDS = **megapode** [Mid-19C. < its custom of depositing its eggs in a mound.]

mound-builder *n* BIRDS = **megapode** [See MOUNDBIRD]

mount¹ /mownt/ *v* **1** *vt* **BEGIN COURSE OF ACTION** to put into operation a course of action such as a campaign, rescue, or attack **2** *vt* **ORGANIZE ARTS PRODUCTION** to organize something such as an exhibition or production of a play **3** *vi* **INCREASE** to become greater, stronger, or more intense ○ *tension was mounting* **4** *vti* **GET ONTO TO RIDE** to get onto an animal or a form of transport such as a bicycle **5** *vt* **PUT SOMEBODY ON FORM OF TRANSPORT** to put somebody onto an animal or a form of transport such as a bicycle **6** *vt* **GET ONTO SOMETHING HIGHER** to get up onto a platform or other raised position **7** *vti* **CLIMB** to climb up something such as stairs or a hill **8** *vi* **GO UP INTO THE AIR** to move upwards into the air **9** *vt* **SECURE TO SOMETHING ELSE** to fix something securely to something, e.g. a picture into a frame, a specimen onto a slide, a stamp into an album, or an exhibit onto a stand or support **10** *vt* **PUT SOMETHING FOR USE** to put something onto a support or into a particular position so that it is ready for use ○ *mount a camera* **11** *vt* **CLIMB ONTO ANIMAL IN ORDER TO COPULATE** to climb onto a female animal or bird in order to copulate (*technical; refers to male animals or birds*) ■ *n* **1** **SOMETHING FOR FIXING SOMETHING IN PLACE** something such as a stand, support, frame, or backing on which or with which something can be mounted **2** **ANIMAL FOR RIDING** an animal, e.g. a horse, used for riding **3** **SOMETHING FOR MOUNTING STAMP** an envelope or card on which to mount a stamp [13C. < Old French *monter* 'go up' < Latin *mont-* 'mountain'.] —**mountable** *adj* —**mounter** *n*

mount² /mownt/ *n* a mountain (*archaic or literary; often in placenames*) [Pre-12C. Via Old French *mont* < Latin *mont-* 'mountain'.]

mountain /mówntin/ *n* **1** **HIGH POINT OF LAND** a high and often rocky area of a land mass with steep or sloping sides ○ *a plateau surrounded by mountains* **2** **LARGE PILE** a large pile or heap of something ○ *a mountain of books* **3** **mountain, mountains** LARGE AMOUNT a large amount of something (*informal*) ○ *a mountain of work* **4** **SURPLUS** a large surplus of a particular commodity (*informal; usually in combination*) ○ *a butter mountain*. ◊ **lake**¹ *n*. **2** [13C. Via Old French *montaigne* < Latin *mont-, mons*.] ◊ **make a mountain out of a molehill** to treat something that is not important as if it were

mountain ash *n* TREES = **rowan** *n*. 1

mountain avens *n* a small trailing plant of the rose family. Flowers: white. Native to: temperate mountainous and arctic areas. *Dryas octopetala*.

mountain beaver *n* a large thick-set rodent that lives in colonies made up of extensive burrows in NW North America. *Aplodontia rufa*.

mountain bike *n* a bicycle built for rough terrain with wide thick tyres, straight handlebars, a strong frame, and more gears than a standard bicycle

mountain cat *n* any feline animal that lives in mountainous areas, e.g. the lynx or puma

mountain chain *n* a range of mountains or a string of adjacent mountain peaks

mountain devil *n* Aus ZOOL = **moloch**

mountaineer /mównti neèr/ *n* **1** **MOUNTAIN CLIMBER** a climber of mountains for sport **2** **MOUNTAIN INHABITANT** an inhabitant of a mountainous area (*archaic*) ■ *vi* **CLIMB MOUNTAINS** to climb mountains for sport

mountaineering /mównti neèring/ *n* the sport or pastime of climbing mountains

mountain goat *n* a large white wild goat with a woolly coat. Native to: North American, above the timberline in mountains from Alaska to Colorado. *Oreamnus americanus*.

mountain laurel *n* an evergreen shrub with shiny poisonous leaves. Flowers: pink or white, darker stamens. Native to: E North America. *Kalmia latifolia*.

mountain lion *n* ZOOL = **puma**

mountainous /mówntinəss/ *adj* **1** characterized by many mountains **2** very large in height, shape, or size ○ *The ship was battered by mountainous waves.* —**mountainousness** *n*

WORLD'S HIGHEST MOUNTAINS

World order

1	Everest	*Himalayas*
Height	[29,028 ft / 8,848 m]	
2	K2	
	Himalayas	
Height	[28,251 ft / 8,611 m]	
3	Kanchenjunga	*Himalayas*
Height	[28,209 ft / 8,598 m]	
4	Lhotse	*Himalayas*
Height	[27,940 ft / 8,516 m]	
5	Makalu	*Himalayas*
Height	[27,824 ft / 8,481 m]	
6	Cho Oyu	*Himalayas*
Height	[26,906 ft / 8,201 m]	
7	Dhaulagiri	*Himalayas*
Height	[26,811 ft / 8,172 m]	
8	Manaslu	*Himalayas*
Height	[26,781 ft / 8,163 m]	
9	Nanga Parbat	*Himalayas*
Height	[26,657 ft / 8,125 m]	
10	Annapurna	*Himalayas*
Height	[26,545 ft / 8,091 m]	

Highest by continent

Europe

1	Mont Blanc
Location	*Alps, France-Italy*
Height	[15,771 ft / 4,807 m]

Africa

1	Kilimanjaro
Location	*Kibo Peak, Tanzania*
Height	[19,340 ft / 5,895 m]

North America

1	McKinley
Location	*Alaska Range, United States*
Height	[20,320 ft / 6,194 m]

South America

1	Aconcagua
Location	*Andes, Argentina-Chile*
Height	[22,834 ft / 6,960 m]

Oceania/Australasia

1	Puncak Jaya
Location	*Sudirman Range, Indonesia*
Height	[16,502 ft / 5,030 m]

---

mountain range *n* a series of adjacent or interconnected mountains forming a distinct group and usually dating from the same geological period

mountain rescue *n* an organization of experienced climbers who go to the aid of people who get into difficulties in a mountainous place

mountain sheep *n* any wild sheep that lives in mountainous areas, e.g. the bighorn

---

mountain sickness *n* MED = **altitude sickness**

mountainside /mówntən sīd/ *n* the sloping side of a mountain

Mountain Standard Time, **Mountain Time** *n* the standard time in the time zone centred on longitude 105° W, which includes the Rocky Mountain region of North America

mountaintop /mówntən top/ *n* the summit of a mountain

mountainy /mówntini/ *adj* having many mountains, or forming part of a mountainous area

Mount Aspiring National Park national park in the SW of the South Island, New Zealand. Area: 2,873 sq. km / 1,109 sq. mi.

Mountbatten /mownt bátt'n/, **Louis, 1st Earl Mountbatten of Burma** (1900–79) British naval commander and diplomat

mountebank /mównti bangk/ *n* (*literary*) **1** somebody who deceives other people **2** formerly, somebody who sold ineffective medicines in public places [Late 16C. < Italian *montambanco* < *monta in banco* (command) 'get up onto the bench'; from the quacks' practice of hocking goods from a platform.] —**mountebankery** *n*

mounted /mówntid/ *adj* **1** riding on a horse ○ *mounted police* **2** fixed onto something for use or display

Mount Gambier /-gámbi ər/ town in SE South Australia. Population: 22,037 (1996).

Mountie /mównti/, **Mounty** (*plural* **-ies**) *n* a member of the Royal Canadian Mounted Police (*informal*) [Early 20C. < MOUNTED.]

mounting /mównting/ *n* a support onto which another thing is fixed ■ *adj* becoming greater in size, number, or intensity ○ *We listened to the news with mounting alarm.*

mounting block, **mounting-block** *n* a block of stone on which somebody stands to get onto a horse

Mount Isa /-ízə/ city in W Queensland, Australia. Population: 21,751 (1996).

Mount Lofty Ranges /-lófti/ range of hills in SE South Australia. Highest peak: Mount Bryan 932 m / 3,058 ft.

Mount Rainier National Park /-ráyni ər/ national park in W Washington State. Area: 953 sq. km / 368 sq. mi.

Mount Vernon /-vúrnən/ city in SE New York State. Population: 67,112 (1996).

Mounty *n* CRIME = **Mountie**

mourn /mawrn/ *v* **1** *vti* **EXPRESS SADNESS AT SOMEBODY'S DEATH** to feel and show sadness because somebody has died ○ *mourning the loss of his father* **2** *vti* **WEAR MOURNING CLOTHES** to wear mourning clothes or other things that indicate grief over a death **3** *vi* **EXPRESS SADNESS AT SOMETHING LOST** to feel and show sadness because something has been lost or no longer exists ○ *She mourned the loss of her independence.* [Old English *murnan* < Indo-European, 'remember'] —**mourner** *n*

Mourne Mountains /máwrn-/ mountain range in SE Northern Ireland. Highest peak: Slieve Donard 852 m / 2,796 ft.

mournful /máwrnf'l/ *adj* **1** expressing or feeling deep sadness ○ *a youth with a mournful face* **2** causing or suggesting deep sadness ○ *a mournful anniversary* — **mournfully** *adv* —**mournfulness** *n*

mourning /máwrning/ *n* **1** **SHOW OF SADNESS** the feeling or showing of deep sadness following somebody's death ○ *was still in mourning over the death of her mother* **2** **CLOTHING FOR SOMEBODY WHO IS MOURNING** clothing of a particular style, fabric, or colour, e.g. black in Christian cultures, worn as a sign of sorrow following somebody's death ○ *wore mourning for a year* **3** **PERIOD OF SADNESS** the period during which somebody's death is mourned ○ *The family observed a period of 40 days' mourning.* —**mourningly** *adv*

LITERARY LINK *Mourning Becomes Electra*, a play (1931) by US dramatist Eugene O'Neill. This 13-act drama, lasting six hours, is a somewhat Freudian reworking of the *Oresteia* trilogy by Greek author Aeschylus. Set in New England during the American Civil War, it portrays Lavinia Brant's attempts to avenge her mother's infidelity by turning the rest of the family against her.

mourning band *n* a band of black cloth worn on the arm as a sign of mourning

mourning cloak *n* US INSECTS = **Camberwell beauty**

mourning dove *n* a common dove with greyish-brown feathers, a long pointed tail, and a mournful call. Native to: North America. *Zenaida macroura.*

mouse[1] /mowss/ *abbr* minimum orbital unmanned satellite of the earth

ϟ **mouse**[2] /mowss/ *n* (*plural* **mice** /mīss/) **1 SMALL RODENT** a small rodent that has a brown or greyish-brown coat and a long mostly hairless tail. Family: Muridae and Cricetidae. **2** (*plural* **mouses** *or* **mice**) **COMPUTER CONTROLLING DEVICE** a hand-held input device with control buttons that is moved across a mat to control the movement of a cursor on a computer screen or is clicked to transmit instructions **3 COWARD** a timid or cowardly person (*insult*) **4 BLACK EYE** a dark swelling under the eye that is caused by a blow (*dated slang*) ■ *vi* (**mouses, mousing, moused**) **HUNT MICE** to hunt for and kill mice, as cats do [Old English *mūs* < Indo-European]

mousebird /mówss burd/ *n* BIRDS = **coly** [Early 19C. < its soft hairlike plumage.]

ϟ **mouse button** *n* a push button, typically one of two or three, on a computer mouse that transmits instructions to the computer

mouse-coloured *adj* of a dull nondescript brown or grey colour

mouse deer *n* ZOOL = **chevrotain** [< the animal's small size and its similarity to a deer]

mouse-ear, mouse-ear chickweed *n* a variety of chickweed or hawkweed with short hairy leaves resembling mouse ears. Genus: *Cerastium.*

ϟ **mouse mat** *n* a small thin piece of material that provides a surface for a computer mouse to be moved on. US term **mouse pad**

ϟ **mouse potato** *n* a person who spends much time sitting at a computer (*slang*) [Late 20C. After COUCH POTATO.]

mouser /mówssər/ *n* a domestic animal such as a dog or cat that catches mice

mousetrap /mówss trap/ *n* a trap for catching and often killing mice

mousey *adj* = **mousy**

mousing /mówssing/ *n* a cord or bar across the opening of a hook to prevent its load from slipping

moussaka /moo saákə/ *n* a Greek baked dish with alternating layers of aubergine and minced meat in a tomato sauce, topped with a savoury white sauce [Mid-20C. Via Turkish *musakka* < Arabic *musakkā*.]

mousse /mooss/ *n* (*plural* **mousses**) **1 LIGHT FOOD** a light rich dish consisting mostly of whipped cream, eggs, or gelatine that is sweetened to serve as a dessert, or flavoured with vegetables, meat, or fish **2 FOAMY HAIR PRODUCT** a foamy substance used to set or style hair ■ *vt* (**mousses, moussing, moussed**) **STYLE HAIR** to apply mousse to hair in order to style it [Mid-19C. < French, 'moss, foam' < Germanic.]

mousseline /mooss léen/ *n* **1** a loosely woven fine fabric of natural or synthetic fibres, resembling muslin **2** delicate blown glass **3** COOK = **mousseline sauce** [Late 17C. Via French < Italian *mussolina*, after *Mosul*, Iraq.]

mousseline de laine /-də lén/ *n* a thin lightweight woollen fabric, often with a printed pattern [< French, literally 'muslin of wool']

mousseline de soie /-də swaá/ *n* a thin plain-woven rayon or silk fabric [< French, literally 'muslin of silk']

mousseline sauce *n* hollandaise sauce to which whisked egg white or whipped cream has been added

moustache /mə staásh/ *n* **1** facial hair allowed to grow on somebody's upper lip and often down the sides of the mouth or onto the cheeks **2** hair, bristles, or feathers around the mouth or beak of an animal [Late 16C. Via French < Italian *mostaccio* < Greek *mustak-* 'upper lip, moustache'.] —**moustached** *adj*

moustache cup *n* an old-fashioned cup with a partial cover to prevent the contents from getting onto a drinker's moustache

Mousterian /moo stéeri ən/ *n* a prehistoric culture of the Palaeolithic period in Europe, North Africa, and the Middle East associated with the Neandertals and marked by the use of flint tools [Late 19C. < French *moustérien*, after *Le Moustier*, cave in SW France.]

mousy /mówssi/ (**-ier, -iest**), **mousey** (**-ier, -iest**) *adj* **1 DULL BROWN** dull brown in colour **2 TIMID** shy or uncommunicative, especially boringly or irritatingly so **3 FULL OF MICE** overrun with mice **4 RESEMBLING MOUSE** having features that resemble a mouse, e.g. big front teeth or a pointed nose —**mousily** *adv* —**mousiness** *n*

mouth *n* /mowth/ (*plural* **mouths** /mowt͟hz/) **1 FOOD AND VOICE ORGAN** in people and animals, the opening in the head and its surrounding lips, gums, tongue, and teeth, through which food is taken in and through which sounds come out **2 FACE FEATURE** the part of the mouth visible to others, including the lips and the opening between them ○ *She kissed him on the mouth.* **3 SPEECH ORGAN** the mouth regarded as the organ of speech ○ *You wouldn't believe some of the things that came out of his mouth.* **4 WAY OF SPEAKING** a particular way of using language that other people think is inappropriate or offensive (*disapproving*) ○ *a foul mouth* **5 BACK TALK** impudent challenging speech in response to a question or order (*informal*) ○ *All I got from them was a lot of mouth.* **6 WATER JUNCTION** the place where a stream or river enters a sea or lake **7 OPENING IN GROUND** an opening to a cave, tunnel, mineshaft, or volcano **8 CONTAINER OPENING** the opening of a container such as a jar, tube, or bottle **9 OPENING BETWEEN PARTS OF TOOL** the opening between the two sides of a device that can be closed to hold something, e.g. in a vice or clamp **10 GRIMACE** a facial expression that shows displeasure, distaste, or sulkiness ○ *She made a mouth at him and quickly turned away.* **11 PIPE OPENING** the slit in the pipe of a pipe organ **12** *vti* **FLUTE OPENING** the hole in a flute that the player blows into ■ *vt* /mowt͟h/ (**mouths, mouthing, mouthed**) **1 SAY INSINCERELY** to speak or say something in a loud, affected, or insincere way ○ *How can you get up there and mouth such clichés?* **2 FORM WORDS** to form words with the tongue and lips without making a sound, usually in order to avoid being heard or to pretend to speak or sing something ○ *She mouthed a warning to the girl opposite as the teacher entered the room.* **3 PUT IN MOUTH** to put and hold something in the mouth as babies and young animals do **4 CARESS WITH MOUTH** to touch or caress something with the mouth **5 TRAIN A HORSE** to train a horse to get used to a bit and bridle [Old English *mūþ* < Indo-European, 'to project'] ◇ **a mouth to feed** a person who must be provided for, especially fed ◇ **be all mouth** to boast about doing something but never actually do it (*informal*) ◇ **down in the mouth** looking sad or gloomy (*informal*) ◇ **foam at the mouth** to produce foam from the mouth as a result of exertion, illness, or anger ◇ **give mouth to something** to express something in speech or writing (*formal*)

mouthbreeder /mówth breedər/, **mouthbrooder** /-broodər/ *n* a freshwater fish that carries its eggs and young in its mouth. Genus: *Haplochromis* and *Tilapia.*

-mouthed *suffix* **1** with a particular kind of mouth ○ *wide-mouthed* **2** speaking in a particular way ○ *foul-mouthed*

mouthful /mówthfòol/ (*plural* **-fuls**) *n* **1 QUANTITY OF FOOD OR DRINK** the amount of food or drink that can comfortably be held in the mouth at one time **2 SMALL AMOUNT OF FOOD** only a very little amount to eat ○ *You can't go all day on a mouthful of food like that.* **3 HARD-TO-PRONOUNCE WORD OR PHRASE** a word or phrase that is hard to pronounce because of its unfamiliar sound combinations ○ *Her last name's a mouthful!* **4 OFFENSIVE SPEECH** something said that is offensive or cheeky ○ *If you complain about the noise you only get a mouthful from them.*

mouth guard *n* US SPORTS = **gumshield**

mouth organ *n* MUSIC = **harmonica**

mouthpart /mówth paart/ *n* a body part near the mouth of an insect or other arthropod that it uses to gather or chew food

mouthpiece /mówth peess/ *n* **1** a part of a musical instrument, telephone, or other device that is held to or in the mouth **2** a person or publication that expresses the views of an organization (*sometimes offensive*) ○ *He is the mouthpiece for big business in this city.*

mouth-to-mouth, mouth-to-mouth resuscitation *n* a method of reviving somebody who is not breathing in which the rescuer places his or her mouth over the mouth of the person not breathing and inflates the lungs with air

mouth ulcer *n* a small white ulcer that appears in groups in the mouth and on the tongue as a result of the fungal condition thrush (*usually plural*) Technical name **aphtha**

mouthwash /mówth wosh/ *n* a medicated liquid that is gargled and swilled around the mouth to cleanse it and to freshen the breath

mouthwatering /mówth wawtəring/ *adj* stimulating the appetite by having a delicious smell or appearance —**mouthwateringly** *adv*

mouthy /mówt͟hi, mówthi/ (**-ier, -iest**) *adj* tending to talk rudely, loudly, or too much (*informal*) —**mouthiness** *n*

mouton /móo ton/ *n* sheepskin processed to resemble a fur such as seal or beaver [Mid-20C. < French.]

movable /móovəb'l/, **moveable** *adj* **1 EASILY MOVED** able to move or be moved easily **2 CHANGING DATE FROM YEAR TO YEAR** falling on a different date from year to year ■ *n* **PROPERTY** something that can be easily moved from one place to another, especially personal property such as an item of furniture (*often plural*) —**movability** /móovə bílləti/ *n* —**movableness** *n* —**movably** *adv*

movable feast *n* a religious festival that is not fixed but falls on a different day from year to year, as does Easter in the Christian calendar

move /moov/ *v* (**moves, moving, moved**) **1** *vti* **CHANGE POSITION** to change position or location, or change the position or location of something ○ *Something moved behind that tree.* **2** *vti* **CHANGE YOUR RESIDENCE, JOB, OR SCHOOL** to change your place of residence, work, or study, or make somebody change one of these ○ *move to the other side of town* **3** *vti* **TAKE ACTION** to take action, or make somebody act ○ *It's due next week so we need to move quickly.* **4** *vti* **CHANGE YOUR VIEW** to change a view or opinion, or cause somebody to do so ○ *She has moved to a more moderate position.* **5** *vti* **IMPROVE OR PROGRESS** to make progress, or start to go in the desired direction ○ *Finally things have started moving.* **6** *vi* **ASSOCIATE WITH A GROUP** to associate with a particular group ○ *She moves among the yachting set.* **7** *vi* **PROPOSE ACTION** to propose formally that something should happen or be done ○ *I move that the meeting be adjourned.* **8** *vt* **STIR SOMEBODY'S EMOTIONS** to make somebody feel something, especially tender feelings ○ *Her performance moved all of us.* **9** *vti* **TAKE A TURN IN A GAME** to take a turn in a board game ○ *Have you moved yet?* **10** *vti* **SELL** to sell well or effectively, or sell something well or effectively ○ *The souvenir mugs aren't really moving.* **11** *vti* **EMPTY THE BOWELS** to empty the bowels ■ *n* **1 ACT OF MOVING** an act or instance of moving ○ *One false move and we're done for.* **2 STEP IN SERIES** an action considered as one of a series ○ *Keep your rivals guessing what your next move will be.* **3 SOMEBODY'S TURN TO PLAY** somebody's turn in a board game ○ *It's your move.* **4 CHANGE OF LOCATION** a change of residence or location ○ *I'm considering a move across town.* **5 MANOEUVRE** a manoeuvre or particular way of doing something ○ *If you're interested in martial arts, I could show you a few moves.* [13C. Via Anglo-Norman *mover* < Latin *movere*.] ◇ **get a move on** start doing something right away, or do something faster (*informal*) ◇ **make a move on somebody** to proposition somebody sexually (*slang*) ◇ **on the move 1** going from one place to another **2** busy doing one thing after another **3** going forward, or making progress

move in *v* **1** *vti* to begin living or doing business in a place **2** *vi* to approach closer to somebody or something, especially to make an attack ○ *move in for the kill*

move in on *vt* **1** US **INTRUDE ON** to intrude on somebody **2 ATTEMPT TO TAKE CONTROL** to attempt to take control of somebody or something, or take over from somebody ○ *He's trying to move in on our department* **3 APPROACH TO ATTACK** to approach closer to somebody or something, especially to make an attack ○ *The guards are moving in on the intruders.*

move into *vt* **1** to begin living in a particular place ○ *move into a new flat* **2** to begin dealing with something or doing business in a particular field ○ *The company is set to move into home banking.*

move on *vi* **1** to leave a place and go somewhere else ○ *I think I'll be moving on.* **2** to stop doing or dealing with something and start doing something else ○ *Let's move on to the next item on the agenda.*

move out *vi* to leave a place of residence or business, or help somebody do this

move over *vti* to move to one side in order to make room, or help or make somebody do this ○ *If you move over I'll be able to sit down.*

moveable *adj*, *n* = **movable**

movement /móovmənt/ *n* **1 ACT OF MOVING** an act of changing location or position ○ *an instrument to detect subtle movements* **2 WAY OF MOVING** the way in which somebody or something moves ○ *the awkward movement of an injured arm* **3 EFFORT BY MANY TO ACHIEVE** a collective effort by a large number of people to try to achieve something, especially a political or social reform ○ *the civil rights movement* **4 PEOPLE ORGANIZED TO EFFECT CHANGE** the people who organize themselves in order to achieve some political or social reform **5 MOVING PARTS** the parts of a clock or watch mechanism that drive and regulate it **6 CHANGE IN PRICE** a change in the prices of traded securities

○ *upward movement before the close of trading* **7 PLOT EVENTS** developments in the plot of a literary work ○ *no movement in the plot for three chapters* **8 SUGGESTED MOTION** the illusion or suggestion of motion in a work of art, e.g. a sculpture or painting **9 SECTION OF MUSICAL WORK** one of several self-contained sections that make up a large-scale musical work, often differentiated from one another by different tempos and characters ○ *the concerto's third movement* **10 TACTICAL CHANGE OF POSITION** a tactical change in the position or location of a military unit **11 RHYTHM** the cadence or rhythm of a piece of poetry **12 ACT OF EMPTYING BOWELS** an act of emptying of the bowels, or the matter emptied ■ **movements** *npl* **ACTIVITIES AND LOCATION** what somebody does and where he or she goes, noted over a period of time ○ *The accused was asked to describe his movements on the day in question.*

mover /moóvər/ *n* **1 SOMEBODY OR SOMETHING THAT CAUSES MOTION** somebody or something that causes movement or accomplishes something ○ *She's the mover behind the project.* **2** *US* **MOVING COMPANY** a company or individual whose work is to transport the personal property of households or businesses from one location to another **3 INTRODUCER OF MOTION** a proposer of a motion during a meeting ○ *Does the mover of the motion consent to the amendment?*

movers and shakers *npl* people in society who are powerful or influential ○ *one of the industry's movers and shakers*

movie /moóvi/ *n US* **CINEMA** = **film** *n.* 1 ■ **movies** *npl US* **1** the film industry, treated as a whole **2** the showing of a film in a cinema [Early 20C. Shortening of *moving picture*.]

movie camera *n US* = **cine camera**

movie film *n US* = **cine film**

moviegoer /moóvi gò ər/ *n US* **CINEMA** = **filmgoer**

movie house *n US* a cinema

moviemaker /moóvi maykər/ *n US* **CINEMA** = **filmmaker** — **moviemaking** *n*

movie star *n* **CINEMA** = **film star**

moving /moóving/ *adj* **1 MAKING PEOPLE FEEL EMOTION** making people feel deep emotions, especially sadness or compassion ○ *After such a moving speech we were all in tears.* **2 MOVABLE** able to move ○ *moving parts* **3 IN MOTION** in a state of movement (*usually in combination*) ○ *slow-moving* **4 CAUSED BY CHANGING PLACES** involved in or caused by a change of residence or business location

---

SYNONYMS *moving, pathetic, pitiful, poignant, touching, heartwarming, heartrending*

CORE MEANING: arousing emotion

moving causing deep feelings, especially of sadness or compassion; **pathetic** arousing feelings of compassion and pity, often centred on somebody who is vulnerable, helpless, or unfortunate; **pitiful** arousing compassion and pity, or arousing contempt or derision; **poignant** causing strong, often bittersweet feelings of sadness, pity, or regret; **touching** causing feelings of warmth, sympathy, and tenderness; **heartwarming** inspiring warm or kindly feelings, usually by showing life and human nature in a positive and reassuring light; **heartrending** causing intense sadness or distress, especially in sympathy with somebody else's unhappiness or hardship because it involves tragic or tragic events.

---

moving-coil *adj* describes an electromechanical device or instrument having a conducting coil freely suspended in a magnetic field

movingly /moóvingli/ *adv* in a way that makes people feel deep emotions, especially tender ones ○ *She spoke movingly about their plight.*

moving pavement *n* an endlessly circulating motor-driven belt that conveys people over a flat expanse of ground, e.g. in an airport. US term **moving sidewalk**

moving picture *n* a cinematographic film (*dated*)

moving sidewalk *n US* = **moving pavement**

moving spirit *n* an energetic person who inspires others about or to do something ○ *She was one of the moving spirits behind the campaign.*

moving staircase *n* = **escalator** *n.* 1

moving van *n US* = **removal van**

mow[1] /mō/ (**mows, mowing, mowed, mown** /mōn/ *or* **mowed**) *v* **1** *vti* to cut tall grass, hay, or grain with a scythe or machine **2** *vt* to cut the grass, hay, or grain growing in a particular place ○ *Mow the front lawn today, please.* [Old English *māwan* < Germanic]

mow down *vt* **1** to kill people quickly and in large numbers **2** to knock somebody or something down by force

mow[2] /mō/ *n* **1** the part of a barn where hay or grain is stored when it has been harvested **2** a pile of hay or grain, especially in a barn [Old English *mūga* < ?]

mower /mó ər/ *n* a lawn mower

mown past participle of **mow**[1]

MOX /moks/ *n* reactor fuel made from plutonium that has been separated from spent nuclear fuel by chemical reprocessing and mixed with natural or depleted uranium [Blend of MIXED + OXIDE]

moxie /móksi/ *n US* courage combined with inventiveness (*slang*) [Mid-20C. After a brand of soft drink originally marketed as a 'nerve tonic'.]

Moynihan /móynihan/, **Daniel Patrick** (*b.* 1927) US academic and politician

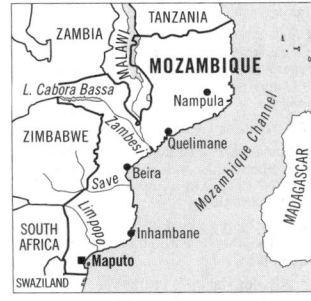

Mozambique

Mozambique /mó zam beék/ republic in SE Africa. Capital: Maputo. Population: 18,028,000 (1996). Area: 799,380 sq. km/308,642 sq. mi. —**Mozambican** *n, adj*

Mozarab /mō zárrab/ *n* a Christian living in Moorish Spain who adopted some Arab customs without converting to Islam [Early 17C. Via Spanish *mozárabe* < Arabic *musta'rib* 'becoming an Arab'.] —**Mozarabic** *adj*

Mozart /móts aart/, **Wolfgang Amadeus** (1756–91) Austrian composer

mozetta *n CHR* = **mozzetta**

mozzarella /mótsə réllə/ *n* a rubbery white unsalted Italian cheese used in salads, cooking, and especially on pizza [Early 20C. < Italian, < *mozza*, type of cheese < *mozzare* 'cut off'.]

mozzetta /mō zéttə/, **mozetta** *n* a short hooded cape worn by the pope and other senior Roman Catholic clergymen [Late 18C. Via Italian < medieval Latin *almutia*.]

mozzie /mózzi/, **mossie** *n* a mosquito (*informal*) [Mid-20C. Shortening and alteration.]

mp[1] *abbr* **1** melting point **2** mezzo piano

mp[2] *abbr* Northern Mariana Islands (*in Internet addresses*)

MP *abbr* **1** Member of Parliament **2** Metropolitan Police **3** military police **4** mounted police

MP3 *n* a computer file standard facilitating the download of compressed music from the Internet, playable on a multimedia system with appropriate software. Full form **Motion Picture Experts Group, Audio Layer 3**

M.P.A. *abbr US* **1** Master of Professional Accounting **2** Master of Public Administration **3** Master of Public Accounting

MPD *abbr* multiple personality disorder

MPEG /ém peg/ *n* a computer file standard for compressing, storing, and transmitting digital video and audio. Full form **Moving Pictures Experts Group**

mpg *abbr* miles per gallon

mph *abbr* miles per hour

MPhil /ém fil/ *abbr* Master of Philosophy

Mpumalanga /am poomə láng gə/ province in NE South Africa. Capital: Nelspruit. Population: 3,007,100 (1995). Area: 78,370 sq. km/30,259 sq. mi.

mq *abbr* Martinique (*in Internet addresses*)

mr *abbr* Mauritania (*in Internet addresses*)

Mr /místər/ *n* **1 MAN'S TITLE** the customary title of courtesy used before the name or names of a man ○ *Mr Smith*

2 JOB OR FUNCTION TITLE a courtesy title used for a man before the name of his position or function ○ *Mr President* **3 DESCRIPTIVE TITLE** a humorous title used for a man before a place, thing, or description that he is supposed to typify or represent ○ *He's not exactly Mr Personality, is he?* **4 SURGEON'S TITLE** a title used before a surgeon's surname, rather than 'Dr' **5 JUNIOR OFFICER'S TITLE** a title used to address a junior naval officer, a warrant officer, or a cadet in a service academy [15C. Contraction of *maister*, form of MASTER.]

MR *abbr* Master of the Rolls

Mr Big *n US* a powerful or important man, e.g. the chief of a criminal organization (*slang*)

MRBM *abbr* medium-range ballistic missile

MRC *abbr* Medical Research Council

Mr Clean *n US* somebody, especially a public figure, who is seen as being admirably upright, honest, and moral (*informal*) [Mid-20C. After a cleaning solution trademark.]

MRCS *abbr* Member of the Royal College of Surgeons

MRCVS *abbr* Member of the Royal College of Veterinary Surgeons

MRE *abbr* meal, ready to eat

MRI *abbr* magnetic resonance imaging

mridanga /mri dúng gə/, **mridang** /mri dúng/, **mridangam** /-gəm/ *n* an Indian drum that is shaped like a barrel and is made in various sizes [Late 19C. < Tamil.]

mRNA *abbr* messenger RNA

MRP *abbr* manufacturer's recommended price

Mr Right *n* somebody seen as being a perfect romantic or marriage partner for somebody else (*informal*) ○ *One day Mr Right will come along.*

Mrs /míssiz/ *n* **1** a customary title of courtesy for a married or widowed woman, used before her name or names ○ *Mrs Wright* **2** a title used for a woman before a place name, thing, or description that she is supposed to typify or represent ○ *Mrs Cheerful* [Early 17C. Contraction of MISTRESS.]

MRSA *n* a strain of bacteria that has become resistant to antibiotic drugs and is therefore a hazard in places such as hospitals. Full form **multiply resistant Staphylococcus aureus**

Mrs Grundy /-gründi/ *n* a very narrow-minded and prudish person (*informal*) [Late 18C. After a character in the play *Speed the Plough*, by Thomas Morton (1764–1838).]

Mrs Mop /-móp/, **Mrs Mopp** *n* a woman employed to do domestic cleaning (*dated informal*)

ms *abbr* **1** millisecond **2** Montserrat (*in Internet addresses*)

Ms /məz, miz/ *n* a customary title of courtesy used before the name or names of a woman without making a distinction between married and unmarried status ○ *Ms Bennett* **2** a title used for a woman before a place, name, thing, or description that she is supposed to typify or represent ○ *Ms Efficiency* [Mid-20C. Blend of MISS + MRS.]

MS *abbr* **1** Master of Surgery **2** Mississippi **3** more (of the) same (*in e-mails*) **4** motor ship **5** multiple sclerosis **6** sacred to the memory of (*on gravestones*)

ms. *abbr* ms., MS. manuscript

MSB *abbr* most significant bit

MSc *abbr* Master of Science [< Latin *Magister Scientiae*]

MS-DOS /ém ess dóss/ *tdmk* a trademark for a widely used computer operating system

msec *abbr* millisecond

Mses plural of **Ms**

MSF *abbr* Manufacturing, Science, and Finance (Union)

MSG *abbr* monosodium glutamate

Msgr *abbr* **1** Monseigneur **2** Monsignor

MSGT *abbr US* Master Sergeant

M.Sgt. *abbr US* Master Sergeant

MSP *abbr* Member of the Scottish Parliament

Ms Right *n* somebody seen as being the perfect romantic or marriage partner for somebody else ○ *tired of waiting for Ms Right to come along*

mss., MSS *abbr* manuscripts

MST *abbr* Mountain Standard Time

mt *abbr* **1** Malta (*in Internet addresses*) **2** mount **3** mountain

Mt *abbr* 1 Matthew 2 Mount 3 Mountain

MT *abbr* 1 megaton 2 metric ton 3 Montana 4 Mountain Time

mt. *abbr* 1 megaton 2 mount 3 mountain

Mtarazi Falls /əm tə ra̋atsi-/ waterfall in east-central Zimbabwe. Height: 762 m/2,500 ft.

MTB *abbr* motor torpedo boat

MTBE *n* a lead-free antiknock petrol additive. Full form **methyl tertiary-butyl ethyl**

⚡ **MTBF** *abbr* mean time between failures

mtDNA *abbr* mitochondrial DNA

MTech /ém ték/ *abbr* Master of Technology

M-theory *n* a theory describing the forces and matter that make up the universe that incorporates existing string theories and suggests the existence of 11 dimensions

mts., Mts. *abbr US* 1 mountains 2 mounts

⚡ **MTTR** *abbr US* mean time to repair

mu[1] /myoo/ *n* the 12th letter of the Greek alphabet [Late 19C. < Greek.]

⚡ **mu**[2] *abbr* Mauritius (*in Internet addresses*)

MU *abbr* 1 Mothers' Union 2 Musicians' Union

muah muah *n* = **mwah mwah**

Mubarak /mō͝o ba̋arək, moo ba̋arək/, **Hosni** (*b.* 1928) Egyptian statesman

muc- *prefix* = **muco-**

much /much/ *adv* 1 LARGELY used to indicate that something exists or is true to a great extent, intensity, or degree (*often in combination*) ○ *She hasn't changed much over the years.* ○ *It's a much more difficult game than the other.* ○ *a much-loved figure in British political life* 2 OFTEN happening often or frequently ○ *I don't get out much these days.* ○ *Do you see your children much over the holidays?* 3 NEARLY nearly or practically ○ *One day is much like the next when you're ill.* ○ *It's much the same problem all over again.* ■ *pron, det* LARGE AMOUNT a large amount or degree ○ (det) *He doesn't have much free time due to the demands of work.* ○ (pron) *Much remains to be done.* ○ (pron) *She does much of her writing at home.* ■ *pron* IMPRESSIVE something impressive, important, or unusual ○ *The house isn't much to look at, but it's very comfortable.* [13C. Shortening of Old English *mycel* < Germanic.] ◇ **as much** precisely that ○ *I wasn't surprised when she said she'd taken the money, as I'd suspected as much from the start.* ◇ **(as) much as** although, or even though ○ *As much as I'd like to join you, I'm afraid I can't.* ◇ **much as** to almost the same degree, or in a similar manner ○ *You cook it much as you would a potato.* ◇ **not much of a** not particularly good at something or not a very good example of something ○ *It's not been much of a celebration, has it?* ◇ **not up to much** 1 of a low standard (*informal*) 2 *US* not very active (*informal*)

muchness /múchnəss/ *n* greatness in quantity, extent, or degree (*archaic*) ◇ **much of a muchness** amounting to or being practically the same (*informal*)

muci- *prefix* = **muco-**

mucic acid /myoóssik-/ *n* $C_4H_4(OH)_4(COOH)_2$ a colourless crystalline solid. Source: lactose. Use: manufacture of chemicals.

muciferous /myoo síffərəss/ *adj* producing or containing a lot of mucus

mucigen /myoóssijən/ *n* a substance in mucous cells that is converted into mucin

mucilage /myoóssilij/ *n* 1 a thick water-based solution used as an adhesive 2 a gummy substance secreted by some plants such as seaweed that contains protein and carbohydrates [14C. Via French < late Latin *mucillago* 'mouldy juice' < Latin *mucus*.]

mucilaginous /myoóssi lájjinəss/ *adj* 1 relating to or producing mucilage 2 moist and sticky like glue —**mucilaginously** *adv* —**mucilaginousness** *n*

mucin /myoóssin/ *n* a complex protein present in mucus —**mucinous** *adj*

muck /muk/ *n* 1 STICKY DIRT soft moist dirt or filth (*informal*) 2 MANURE moist manure or compost, especially when used to fertilize land 3 RUBBISH something that is distasteful, disgusting, or of very poor quality (*informal*) ○ *don't know how they can publish such muck* 4 MINE WASTE waste material from mining, e.g. earth or rubble ■ *vt* 1 FERTILIZE LAND to fertilize land with manure or compost (*informal*) 2 CLEAN OUT A PLACE to clean the muck out of a place such as a stable or barn 3 MAKE SOMETHING DIRTY to pollute something or make something dirty (*informal*) [13C. < N Germanic < Germanic, 'soft'.]

muck about *v* 1 *vi* to waste time instead of doing something useful or important (*informal*) ○ *We'd get this job finished sooner if you two stopped mucking about.* 2 *vt* to waste somebody's time or fail to deal with somebody in a serious way ○ *The car people keep mucking me about.*

muck in *vi* to share something, especially work or accommodation, with other people (*informal*) ○ *It won't take long if everyone mucks in.* ○ *The house is a little overcrowded but we all just muck in together.*

muck up *vt* (*informal*) 1 to ruin or make a mess of something ○ *She's really mucked up her chances now.* 2 to soil or stain something ○ *He fell in the mud and mucked up his trousers.*

muckamuck *n US* = **high-muck-a-muck** (*informal*)

mucker /múkər/ *n* 1 a friend (*dated slang*) ○ *This is my old mucker Charlie.* 2 somebody whose job is to remove rocky mine waste

muckle /múk'l/ *adj Scotland* LARGE very big or great ○ *a muckle stone* ■ *adv Scotland* MUCH much or greatly ○ *not muckle clever* ■ *n Scotland* A LOT a large amount of something ○ *Many a mickle makes a muckle.* [Old English *mycel* (see MUCH)]

muckluck *n* CLOTHING = **mukluk**

muckrake /múk rayk/ *vi* (**-rakes, -raking, -raked**) to seek out and publicize misconduct by prominent people ■ *n* a rake used to spread manure or compost —**muckraker** *n* —**muckraking** *n*

muck sweat *n* heavy sweating, or a condition in which somebody does this (*informal*) ○ *I've been in a muck sweat over that lost file.*

mucky /múki/ (**-ier, -iest**) *adj* 1 FILTHY very dirty or covered with muck (*informal*) 2 RUDE rude or obscene 3 RAINY rainy or stormy —**muckily** *adv* —**muckiness** *n*

muco-, muc-, muci- *prefix* mucus, mucous membrane ○ *mucocutaneous* [< Latin *mucus*]

mucocutaneous /myoókō kyoo táyni əss/ *adj* involving both skin and mucous membrane

mucolytic /myoókō líttik/ *adj* able to break down mucus

mucopeptide /myoókō pép tīd/ *n* BIOCHEM = **peptidoglycan**

mucopolysaccharide /myoókō pólli sákə rīd/ *n* a complex polysaccharide containing amino groups, found in connective tissues

mucoprotein /myoókō prō teen/ *n* a complex protein found in mucous secretions

mucopurulent /myoókō pyoórələnt/ *adj* containing both mucus and pus

mucosa /myoo kóssə/ (*plural* **-sae** /-see/) *n* ANAT = **mucous membrane** [Late 19C. < modern Latin *(membrana) mucosa* 'mucous membrane'.]

mucous /myoókəss/ *adj* containing, secreting, resembling, or covered with mucus [Mid-17C. < Latin *mucosus* < *mucus*.]

mucous membrane *n* a moist lining in the body passages of all mammals that contains mucus-secreting cells and is open directly or indirectly to the external environment

mucro /myoókrō/ (*plural* **-cros**) *n* a sharp point projecting from an organ or plant part [Mid-17C. < Latin, 'sharp point, sword'.]

mucronate /myoókrə nayt/, **mucronated** /myoókrə naytid/ *adj* ending in a sharp point —**mucronation** /myoókrə náysh'n/ *n*

mucus /myoókəss/ *n* the clear slimy lubricating substance consisting mostly of mucins and water that coats and protects mucous membranes [Mid-17C. < Latin.] —**mucoid** /myoó koyd/ *adj*

mud /mud/ *n* 1 earth that is very wet, soft, and gummy 2 defamatory things said or written about somebody [14C. Probably < Middle Low German *mudde*.] ◇ **(as) clear as mud** not clear or understandable at all (*informal*) ◇ **here's mud in your eye!** used as a drinking toast (*informal*) ◇ **sling** *or* **throw mud at somebody** *or* **something** to make defamatory statements about somebody or something (*informal*)

⚡ **MUD** /mud/ *n* a virtual online space in which several participants can contribute to a communal project, e.g. a collaboratively written story or a game for several players. Full form **multiuser domain**

mudbath /múd baath/ (*plural* **-baths** /-baat͟hz/) *n* 1 a bath in heated mud, thought to tone the skin and organs 2 something such as a football game that takes place outdoors in very muddy conditions (*informal*)

mud dauber *n* a wasp that builds multicellular nests with mud. Family: Sphecidae. US term **mud wasp**

muddle /múdd'l/ *v* (**-dles, -dling, -dled**) 1 *vt* MIX THINGS TOGETHER IN DISORDER to mix things together in a confused or disordered way ○ *The disks have been carefully filed, so don't muddle them.* 2 *vt* CONFUSE THINGS to confuse things in the mind (*often passive*) ○ *They look so alike that it's easy to muddle them up.* 3 *vti* CONFUSE OR BE CONFUSED to be confused or bemused or to cause somebody to be so ○ *Tell me again slowly – you're muddling me.* ■ *n* 1 CONFUSED STATE something that is in such a confused condition that it is hard to organize or understand ○ *How did our records get into such a muddle?* 2 MIX-UP a misunderstanding arising from or causing a confused situation or state ○ *There's been a muddle over the bookings.* [Mid-16C] —**muddled** *adj* —**muddler** *n* —**muddly** *adj*

muddle through *vi* to succeed or manage to keep going despite being disorganized ○ *I expect we'll muddle through somehow.*

muddleheaded /múdd'l héddid/ *adj* 1 unable to think clearly 2 not clearly thought out —**muddleheadedly** *adv* —**muddleheadedness** *n*

muddy /múddi/ *adj* (**-dier, -diest**) 1 MARKED WITH MUD full of, covered in, or dirtied with mud 2 RESEMBLING MUD like mud in being cloudy or thick 3 LACKING CLARITY lacking clarity, brightness, or transparency ○ *a muddy colour* 4 CONFUSED hard to understand or lacking in logical reasoning ■ *vt* (**-dies, -dying, -died**) 1 MAKE SOMETHING MUDDY to make something muddy 2 MAKE SOMETHING UNCLEAR to make something confused and unclear —**muddily** *adv* —**muddiness** *n*

Mudéjar /moo dáy haar/ *n* (*plural* **-jares** /-haa ress/) a Moor who was allowed to stay in a part of Spain after it had been recaptured by the Christians ■ *adj* relating to the Mudéjares, especially their style of architecture [Mid-19C. < Spanish, < Arabic *mudajjan*, past participle of *dajjana* 'permit to stay'.]

mudfish /múd fish/ (*plural* **-fish** *or* **-fishes**) *n US* a fish that lives in muddy waters, especially the bowfin

mud flap *n* a flap attached behind the wheel of a vehicle to prevent mud and water from splashing up onto the vehicle, or on to the vehicles following. US term **splashguard**

mudflat /múd flat/, **mud flat** *n* an area of low muddy land that is underwater only at high tide, especially one near an estuary

mudflow /múd flō/ *n* a fast-moving downhill flow of mud and soil loosened by rainfall or melting snow

mudguard /múd gaard/ *n* a curved rigid arch above the wheel of a bicycle or motorcycle designed to cut down the amount of water or mud thrown up by the wheel. US term **fender** *n.* 5

mudlark /múd laark/ *n* a child who lives on the streets and makes money by selling objects found in tidal mud (*archaic*) [Late 18C. < MUD + LARK[1].]

mudpack /múd pak/ *n* a beauty treatment for the face made of fuller's earth and additives that is allowed to dry before being removed

mud pie *n* a mass of mud shaped by children as a game

mud puppy, mudpuppy /múd puppi/ (*plural* **-pies**) *n* a salamander that lives on muddy banks and has dark red external gills. Native to: E North American. Genus: *Necturus*.

mudra /mə dra̋a/ (*plural* **-dras**) *n* any of the symbolic positions in which the hands are held in Indian dancing and ritual [Early 19C. < Sanskrit *mudrā* 'seal, sign'.]

mudskipper /múd skipər/ *n* a tropical fish of the goby family that uses its pectoral fins to leave the water to feed. Native to: Asia, Africa. Genus: *periophthalmadon*.

mudslide /múd slīd/ *n* a slow-moving and often destructive mass of mud flowing down a slope

mudslinging /múd slinging/ *n* the making of defamatory remarks about somebody, especially a political opponent or other competitor ○ *The level of debate in this election has seldom risen above petty mudslinging.* —**mudslinger** *n*

mudstone /múd stōn/ *n* a grey sedimentary rock formed from mud, similar to shale but with less developed lamination

mud turtle *n* a small freshwater turtle that lives at the bottom of muddy ponds and streams. Native to: North and Central America. Genus: *Kinosternon*.

⚡MUD virtual *n* a virtual space in which several participants can contribute to a communal project, e.g. a collaboratively written story or a game for several players

mud volcano *n* a conical mound of mud that forms around a hot spring or geyser

mud wasp *n US* INSECTS = **mud dauber**

Mueller /múllər, mŭllər/, **Sir Ferdinand Jakob Heinrich von, Baron** (1825–96) German-born Australian botanist and explorer

Muenster /múnstər, mŏŏnstər/, **muenster, Munster, munster** *n* a white to yellow semisoft mildly flavoured cheese that typically has an orange edible rind [Early 20C. After *Munster*, town in NE France.]

muesli /myŏŏzli/ *n* a mixture of cereal flakes and rolled oats with dried fruit and nuts, eaten with milk for breakfast [Mid-20C. < Swiss German, 'little purée' < German *Mus* 'purée'.]

muezzin /moo ézzin, myoo-/ *n* a mosque official who calls Muslims to prayer from a minaret five times a day [Late 16C. < dialect variant of Arabic *mu'aḏḏin*, form of *'aḏḏana'* 'call to prayer' < *'uḏn'* 'ear'.]

muff[1] /muf/ *n* **1** an open-ended cylinder of fur or cloth used for keeping hands warm, one hand going in at each end **2** either of the tufts of feathers on each side of the face of some fowl [Late 16C. < Dutch *mof*, shortening of Middle Dutch *moffel* < medieval Latin *muffula* 'glove'.]

muff[2] /muf/ *vt* **1 FAIL TO CATCH** to fail to catch a ball or make a shot ○ *He got right under the ball and still muffed it.* **2 DO SOMETHING BADLY** to do something badly or awkwardly ○ *The play got off to a bad start when the actors muffed the opening lines.* ■ *n* **1 FAILED ACTION** a badly performed catch, shot, or action **2 BUNGLER** a clumsy or bungling person [Mid-19C. < ?]

muffin /múffin/ *n* **1** a small round thick savoury cake (**griddlecake**) made from yeasted batter and usually served split, toasted, and buttered **2** a small round cake for one person made from a thick batter and often containing fruit or nuts [Early 18C. < ?]

muffle[1] /múff'l/ *vt* (**-fles, -fling, -fled**) **1 WRAP SOMETHING TO STIFLE SOUND** to wrap or pad something with material in order to deaden the sound it makes **2 MAKE SOMETHING LESS LOUD** to make a sound less loud ○ *He put his hands over his ears to muffle the noise of the sirens.* **3 PREVENT SOMETHING BEING EXPRESSED** to prevent something from being said or written ○ *a government that sought to muffle all opposition* **4 KEEP SOMEBODY WARM** to wrap somebody or a part of somebody's body in a garment or cloth for warmth ○ *She muffled herself up in a thick shawl.* ■ *n* **1 SOMETHING MUFFLING SOUND** something used to muffle a sound **2 TYPE OF KILN** a kiln in which objects being fired are protected from direct contact with the flames [15C] —**muffled** *adj*

muffle[2] /múff'l/ *n* the moist fleshy hairless upper lip of some rodents and ruminants [Early 17C. < French *mufle*.]

muffler /múfflər/ *n* **1** a scarf worn around the neck for warmth **2** *US, ANZ* a device attached to a car's exhaust pipe to reduce the amount of noise made by the engine **3** ACOUSTICS = **muffle[1]** *n.* 1

mufti /múfti, mŏŏfti/ *n* ordinary clothes when worn by somebody who is normally in uniform [Early 19C. < ?]

Mufti /múfti, mŏŏfti/ *n* an expert on Islamic religious law [Late 16C. < Arabic *muftī*, past participle of *aftā* 'decide a legal point'.]

mufti day *n* a day on which school students are permitted to wear casual clothes rather than uniform, as a fundraising exercise

mug[1] /mug/ *n* **1** a large round straight-sided cup typically made of earthenware and having a handle **2** what a mug has in it, or the amount of liquid it can hold ○ *a mug of hot soup* [Early 16C. < ?] —**mugful** /múgfŏŏl/ *n*

mug[2] /mug/ *n* (*slang*) **1 SOMEBODY'S FACE** somebody's face or mouth **2 UNINTELLIGENT PERSON** an unintelligent or easily deceived person ■ *v* (**mug, mugging, mugged**) **1** *vt* **ROB** to attack and rob somebody, especially a pedestrian in a public place **2** *vi* **MAKE FACES** to make exaggerated facial expressions when performing or posing for a camera ○ *The actors were playing it for laughs, mugging in every scene.* ◇ **a mug's game** something only gullible people would take part in (*informal*)

Mugabe /mŏŏ gaábi/, **Robert** (*b.* 1924) Zimbabwean national leader and president (1987–) of Zimbabwe

muggar *n* ZOOL = **mugger[2]**

mugger[1] /múggər/ *n* a public attacker and robber

mugger[2] /múggər/, **muggar, muggur** *n* a freshwater crocodile. Native to: India and Sri Lanka. *Crocodylus palustris*. [Mid-19C. < Hindi *magar*.]

mugging /múgging/ *n* the crime of attacking and robbing somebody

muggins /mugginz/ *n* **1** somebody regarded as gullible (*humorous insult*) **2** a name people use to refer to themselves when they believe they are acting gullibly (*informal humorous*) ○ *I suppose muggins will have to come and pick you up?* [Mid-19C. < ?]

muggur *n* ZOOL = **mugger[2]**

muggy /múggi/ (**-gier, -giest**) *adj* unpleasantly hot and humid [Mid-18C. < obsolete *mug* 'rain lightly' < N Germanic.] —**muggily** *adv* —**mugginess** *n*

Mughal /mŏŏg'l/, **Mogul** /mṓg'l/, **Moghul** /mŏŏg'l/ *n* **1** a member of the Muslim dynasty of Mongol origin that ruled large parts of India from 1526 to 1857 **2** the Mughal emperor of Delhi [Late 16C. Via Urdu *muġal* < Persian *muġul* 'Mongol'.]

mug shot, mugshot /múg shot/ *n* a photograph of somebody's face, especially one of a suspected criminal's face or profile taken by police

mug up *vti* to study hard at a particular subject, especially in preparation for an exam (*informal*)

mugwort /múg wurt/ *n* a herbaceous perennial wormwood with aromatic leaves. Flowers: small, pale green. Native to: temperate regions of N hemisphere. *Artemisia vulgaris*. [Old English *mucgwyrt* < earlier forms of MIDGE + WORT[1]]

mugwump /múg wump/ *n US* a person who takes an independent or neutral position, especially in politics [Mid-19C. < Massachuset *mugquomp* 'war leader'.] —**mugwumpery** *n* —**mugwumpish** *adj* —**mugwumpism** *n*

Muhammad /mə hámmid/, **Mohammed** (570?–632) Arabian founder of Islam

Muhammad Ali /mə hámmid aáli/ (1769–1849) Albanian-born viceroy of Egypt (1805–49)

Muharram /moo hárrəm/, **Moharram** /mō-/ *n* the first month of the Islamic calendar, made up of 30 days [Early 19C. < Arabic *muḥarram* 'inviolable', past participle of *ḥarrama* 'forbid'.]

Muir /myoor/, **Edwin** (1887–1959) British poet, translator, and critic

Muir, Jean Elizabeth (1933–96) British fashion designer

Muir Glacier /myoor-/ glacier in SE Alaska, flowing down Mount Fairweather and into Glacier Bay. It is nearly 3 km/2 mi. long and 40 to 65 m/135 to 210 ft high.

mujaheddin /mŏŏjəhə deén/, **mujahedeen, mujahideen, mujahidin** *npl* Islamic guerrillas based in Iran and Pakistan who fought a holy war (**jihad**) against the Soviet forces occupying Afghanistan in the late 1970s and the 1980s [Mid-20C. < Persian or Arabic *mujāhidīn*, plural of *mujāhid* 'somebody who fights a jihad'.]

mukluk /múk luk/, **muckluck** *n* **1** *US* a waterproof boot made of animal skin or canvas that is large enough to be worn over shoes or several pairs of socks **2** a sealskin boot originally worn by the Inuit [Mid-19C. < Yupik *maklak* 'bearded seal', misunderstood as 'sealskin'.]

mulatto /myŏŏ láttō, mŏŏ-/ (*plural* **-tos** *or* **-toes**) *n* (*dated*) **1** an offensive term for somebody who has one Black and one white parent **2** an offensive term for somebody who has both Black and white ancestors [Late 16C. < Spanish *mulato* 'young mule' < *mulo* 'mule' < Latin *mulus*.]

mulberry /múlbəri/ *n* (*plural* **-ries**) **1 PURPLE FRUIT** a small sweet fruit resembling a berry **2 TREE WITH EDIBLE FRUIT** a small deciduous tree, one species of which bears edible fruit and another species leaves that are fed to silkworms. Genus: *Morus*. **3 PURPLE COLOUR** a dark purple colour tinged with red or grey ■ *adj* **OF DARK PURPLE** of a dark purple colour tinged with red or grey [Old English *mōrberie* < *mōr-* < Latin *morum* 'mulberry']

mulch /mulch/ *n* a protective covering of organic material laid over the soil around plants to prevent erosion, retain moisture, and sometimes enrich the soil ■ *vti* to cover soil with mulch ○ *mulch with newspaper* [Mid-17C. < ?]

mulct /mulkt/ *vt* **1 FINE** to fine somebody as a penalty **2 CHEAT** to cheat somebody out of something (*archaic*) ■ *n* **PENALTY** a fine or penalty [15C. < Latin *mulctare* < *mulcta* 'fine'.]

Muldoon /mul dŏŏn/, **Sir Robert David** (*b.* 1921) New Zealand statesman

mule[1] /myool/ *n* **1 CROSS BETWEEN HORSE AND DONKEY** the offspring of a female horse and a male donkey **2 HYBRID PLANT OR ANIMAL** the sterile offspring of two closely related species of animal or plant **3 STUBBORN PERSON** a stubborn or intractable person (*informal*) **4 DRUG COURIER** a transporter of illegal drugs for a dealer (*slang*) **5 SPINNING MACHINE** a machine that draws and spins cotton fibres into yarn and winds it onto spindles [Old English *mūl*, probably via Germanic < Latin *mulus*]

mule[2] /myool/ *n* a backless slipper or shoe [Mid-16C. Via French < Latin *mulleus (calceus)* 'reddish-purple (shoe)'.]

mule deer *n* a large deer that has a greyish-brown coat, some white underparts, a black tail, and long ears. Native to: of W North America. *Odocoileus hemionus*.

muleta /myoo léttə/ (*plural* **-tas**) *n* a short red cape attached to a stick that a matador uses instead of the full cape in the final stages of a bullfight [Mid-19C. < Spanish, diminutive of *mula* 'female mule' < Latin *mulus* 'mule'.]

muleteer /myŏŏlə teér/ *n* somebody whose occupation is driving mules [Mid-16C. < French *muletier* < *mulet*, diminutive of Old French *mul* 'mule' < Latin *mulus*.]

muley /myŏŏli/ *adj* having no horns ■ *n* (*plural* **-leys**) an animal that does not have horns [Late 16C. Probably < Irish *maol* or Welsh *moel* 'bald' < Indo-European, 'to cut'.]

mulga /múlgə/ *n* **1** an acacia bush or small tree that forms dense thickets. Native to: arid regions of Australia. Genus: *Acacia*. **2** *Aus* an arid part of Australia where mulgas are the dominant vegetation ○ *His car broke down out in the mulga.* [Mid-19C. < Aboriginal.]

mulga snake *n* a large aggressive brown or tan snake. Native to: Australian interior. *Pseudechis australis*.

Mulhacén /mŏŏla tháyn/ mountain in S Spain. Height: 3,478 m/11,411 ft.

Mulhouse /mü lŏŏz/ city in NE France. Population: 110,359 (1999).

muliebrity /myŏŏli ébbriti/ *n* (*literary*) **1** the condition of being a woman **2** the qualities conventionally associated with women [Late 16C. < Latin *muliebritas* < *mulier* 'woman'.]

mulish /myŏŏlish/ *adj* obstinate and unwilling to cooperate or listen to suggestions —**mulishly** *adv* —**mulishness** *n*

mull[1] /mul/ *n* a period of deep thought [Mid-19C. < ?]
mull over *vti* to consider something thoroughly

mull[2] /mul/ *vt* to heat, sweeten, and flavour wine, beer, or cider [Early 17C. < ?]

mull[3] /mul/ *n* soft cotton muslin used in dresses [Late 17C. Shortening of Hindi *malmal*.]

mull[4] /mul/ *n* nonacidic humus on a forest floor that eventually integrates into the soil beneath it [Early 20C. < Danish *muld* 'mould'.]

mull[5] /mul/ *n Scotland* a promontory (*often in placenames*) [14C < Celtic or Old Norse]

Mull /mul/ island in the Inner Hebrides, W Scotland. Population: 2,078 (1991). Area: 925 sq. km/353 sq. mi.

mullah /múllə, mŏŏlə/ *n* **1** in Iran and Central Asia, a Muslim cleric who specializes in the interpretation of Islamic religious law **2** used in Iran and Central Asia as a term of respect for a Muslim man who is thought to be very wise [Early 17C. Via Persian or Urdu *mullā* < Arabic *mawlā*.]

mullein /múllin/ *n* a tall plant with hairy leaves. Flowers: yellow, lavender, or white, in spikes. Native to: Europe, Asia, naturalized in the United States. Genus: *Verbascum*. [15C. < Old French *moleine*.]

muller /múllər/ *n* a heavy smooth object made of stone, metal, wood, or glass, used for grinding paints or drugs on a flat surface [14C. < ?]

Müller /múllər, myŏŏlər/, **Paul Hermann** (1899–1965) Swiss chemist

Müllerian mimicry /moo leéri ən-/ *n* mimicry in which two or more animals that are inedible or harmful assume one another's appearance so that predators will leave them alone [Late 19C. After J. F. T. *Müller* (1821–97), German-born Brazilian zoologist.]

Müller-Lyer illusion /mo͝olər lĭ́ ər-/ *n* an optical illusion in which a line with inward-pointing arrows is seen as longer than one of equal length with outward-pointing arrows [Late 19C. After Franz Carl *Müller-Lyer* (1857–1916), German sociologist and philosopher.]

mullet /múllit/ *n* **1** (*plural* **-lets** *or* **-let**) SPINY FISH a common spiny small-mouthed fish that lives in fresh or salt water. Family: Mugilidae and Mullidae. **2** (*plural* **-lets** *or* **-let**) *US* = **grey mullet 3** MULLET AS FOOD the flesh of a mullet used as food **4** LONG HAIRSTYLE a hairstyle that is long at the back and short at the front and sides [15C. < Old French *mulet* < *mul* < Latin *mullus* 'red mullet' < Greek *mullos*, a sea fish.]

mulligan /mŭlligən/ *n US* a shot that, against the rules, a golfer allows an opponent to take again [Mid-20C. Probably < the name *Mulligan*.]

mulligan ballot *n US* a second ballot paper used if a voter records his or her vote wrongly at the first attempt (*informal*)

mulligatawny /mŭlligə táwni/ (*plural* **-nies**) *n* a spicy meat and vegetable soup originally from E India [Late 18C. < Tamil *milaku-tanni* 'pepper-water'.]

Mulliken /mŭllikən/, **Robert Sanderson** (1896–1986) US chemist

Mullingar /mŭlling gáar/ town in the central Republic of Ireland. Population: 8,003 (1991).

mullion /mŭllyən/ *n* a vertical piece of stone, metal, or wood that divides the panes of a window or the panels of a screen [Mid-16C. Alteration of obsolete *monial* 'mullion' < Anglo-Norman *moinel* 'middle (part)' < *moien* 'in the middle, median'.] —**mullioned** *adj*

mullite /mŭllīt/ *n* a colourless mineral consisting of crystalline aluminium silicate [Early 20C. < MULL.]

Mulroney /mul rṓni/, **Brian** (*b.* 1939) Canadian statesman and prime minister (1984–93) of Canada

mult- *prefix* = **multi-**

Multan /mo͝ol taán/, **Multān** city in E Pakistan. Population: 1,257,000 (1995).

multi- *prefix* many, multiple, more than one or two ○ *multilevel* ○ *multiparous* [Via Old French < Latin *multus* 'much, many']

ϟ **multiaccess** /múlti áksess/ *adj* relating to a computer system that allows several users to access it at the same time

multibillion /múlti bíllyən/ *adj* involving or costing many billions of dollars, pounds, or other currency unit

ϟ **multicasting** /múlti kaasting/ *n* the process of sending data across a network to several recipients simultaneously —**multicast** *vt*

multicellular /múlti séllyo͝olər/, **multicelled** /-séld/ *adj* consisting of many cells —**multicellularity** /múlti séllyo͝o lárrəti/ *n*

multicentre bond *n* a chemical bond that consists of three or more atoms instead of the usual two, e.g. as found in boranes

multichannel communication /múlti chánn'l-/ *n* the existence or use of two or more communication channels over the same path, e.g. in radio transmission or within a communication cable

multicolour /múlti kulər/, **multicoloured** /-kulərd/ *adj* of many different colours

multicultural /múlti kúlchərəl/ *adj* **1** relating to, consisting of, or participating in the cultures of different countries, ethnic groups, or religions **2** advocating or encouraging the integration of people of different countries, ethnic groups, and religions into all areas of society —**multiculturalism** *n* —**multiculturalist** *n*

multidimensional /múlti di ménsh'nəl, -dī-/ *adj* **1** relating to or having more than three dimensions **2** having several different aims, qualities, or aspects —**multidimensionality** /múlti di ménshə nálləti, -dī-/ *n*

multidirectional /múltidi réksh'nəl, -dī-/ *adj* **1** having several aims or covering several aspects of a situation **2** going, operating, or pointing in several different directions

multidisciplinary /múlti díssə plinəri/, **multidiscipline** /-plin/ *adj* studying or using several specialized subjects or skills

multiethnic /múlti éthnik/ *adj* relating to or including several different ethnic groups

multifaceted /múlti fássitid/ *adj* **1** with many different talents, qualities, or features **2** having many facets or cut surfaces

multifactorial /múlti fak táwri əl/, **multifactor** /múlti fáktər/ *adj* **1** involving several different factors or elements **2** relating to inheritance depending on more than one gene —**multifactorially** *adv*

multifarious /múlti fáiri əss/ *adj* including parts, things, or people of many different kinds [Late 16C. < Latin *multifarius* 'varied, diverse' < *multi-* 'many' + *-farius* 'doing'.] —**multifariously** *adv* —**multifariousness** *n*

multifid /múltifid/, **multifidous** /mul tíffidəss/ *adj* having many lobe-shaped segments

multiflora rose /múlti fláwrə-/ *n* a wild climbing rose that is the origin of many cultivated roses. Flowers: small, fragrant. Native to: Asia. *Rosa multiflora.*

multiflorous /múlti fláwrəss/ *adj US* having many flowers [Mid-18C. < late Latin *multiflorus* < Latin *multi-* 'many' + *flor-* 'flower'.]

multifoil /múlti foyl/ *n* in architecture, a flat shape, opening, or decorative design with many lobes or scallops at its edges

multiform /múlti fawrm/ *adj* including or existing in many different shapes or kinds [Early 17C. < French *multiforme* or Latin *multiformis.*] —**multiformity** /múlti fáwrməti/ *n*

multifunctional /múlti fúngksh'nəl/, **multifunction** /múlti fúngksh'n/ *adj* having various different purposes or uses

multigenerational /múlti jénnə ráysh'nəl/ *adj US* including or affecting several generations

multigrade oil /múlti grayd-/, **multigrade** *n* engine oil that has a range of viscosities and is therefore effective over a range of temperatures

multigrain /múlti grayn/ *adj* describes bread that is made from several different types of grain

multigravida /múlti grávvidə/ *n* a pregnant woman who has had at least one previous pregnancy. ◊ **primigravida**

multigym /múlti jim/ *n* an exercise apparatus with a range of weights, used for muscle toning

multihued /múlti hyo͞od/ *adj* = **multicolour**

multihull /múlti hul/ *n* a sailing vessel with two or more hulls

multilateral /múlti láttərəl/ *adj* **1** involving more than two parties or countries **2** having many sides [Late 17C. < medieval Latin *multilateralis* < Latin *multi-* 'many' + *lateralis* (see LATERAL).] —**multilaterally** *adv*

multilateralism /múlti láttərə lizəm/ *n* the principle or belief that several nations should be cooperatively involved in the process of achieving a goal, especially nuclear disarmament —**multilateralist** *n, adj*

multilevel /múlti levv'l/ *adj* **multilevel, multilevelled** having or operating on several or many different levels ■ *n* a building or structure with several or many levels

multilevelled *adj* = **multilevel**

multilingual /múlti líng gwəl/ *adj* **1** able to speak more than two languages fluently **2** relating to the use of more than two languages —**multilingualism** *n* —**multilingually** *adv*

multilocular /múlti lókyo͝olər/ *adj* consisting of or having several different chambers or cavities

ϟ **multimedia** /múlti me͞edi ə/ *n* **1** SOUND AND VIDEO ON COMPUTERS programs, software, and hardware capable of using a wide variety of media such as film, video, and music as well as text and numbers **2** USE OF VARIOUS MATERIALS AND MEDIA the use in art, especially the plastic arts, of different kinds of materials and media such as television, sound, and text (*often before nouns*) **3** USE OF ALL COMMUNICATIONS MEDIA the use in advertising of a combination of media such as television, radio, and the press (*often before nouns*) **4** USE OF MEDIA IN TEACHING the use of film, video, and music in addition to more traditional teaching materials and methods (*often before nouns*)

multimeter /múlti meetər/ *n* an instrument that reads and measures the values of several different electrical parameters such as current, voltage, and resistance

multimillion /múlti míllyən/ *adj* costing or involving many millions of pounds, dollars, or other units of currency

multimillionaire /múlti míllyə náir/ *n* somebody with money or assets worth several million pounds, dollars, or other units of currency

multinational /múlti násh'nəl/ *adj* **1** OPERATING IN SEVERAL COUNTRIES operating or having investments in several countries **2** INVOLVING PEOPLE FROM SEVERAL COUNTRIES relating to or including people from more than two countries ■ *n* LARGE COMPANY OPERATING IN SEVERAL COUNTRIES a large company that operates or has investments in several different countries —**multinationalism** *n*

multinomial /múlti nṓmi əl/ *n, adj* MATH = **polynomial**

multinuclear /múlti nyo͞okli ər/, **multinucleate** /-ət/ *adj* having more than two nuclei

multipack /múlti pak/ *n* a packet that contains more than two of a particular item of consumer goods, e.g. batteries, and is sold at a reduced price

multipara /mul típpərə/ (*plural* **-rae** /-ree/) *n* a woman who has borne a live child from each of two or more pregnancies [Mid-19C. < form of modern Latin *multiparus* (see MULTIPAROUS).]

multiparous /mul típpərəss/ *adj* **1** describes an animal, especially a mammal, that normally gives birth to two or more offspring at one time **2** describes a woman who has borne a child from each of two or more pregnancies, each pregnancy lasting for at least 20 weeks [Mid-17C. < modern Latin *multiparus* < Latin *multi-* 'many' + *-parus* '-bearing' (see -PAROUS).] —**multiparity** /múlti párrəti/ *n*

multipartite /múlti paar tīt/ *adj* **1** divided into many sections **2** involving more than two parties or countries

multipath /múlti paath/ *adj* relating to television or radio signals that use more than one route from the transmitter to the receiver, causing picture or sound distortion

multiphase /múlti fayz/ *adj* ELEC ENG = **polyphase** —**multiphasic** /múlti fáyzik/ *adj*

multiplane /múlti playn/ *n* an aircraft with more than one pair of wings

multiple /múltip'l/ *adj* INVOLVING SEVERAL THINGS involving or including several things, people, or parts ■ *n* **1** NUMBER DIVISIBLE BY ANOTHER a number that can be divided exactly by a particular smaller number **2** SYSTEM WITH MANY POSSIBLE ACCESS POINTS a system of wiring so arranged that a group of communication lines are accessible at a number of points **3** COMM = **chain store** [Mid-17C. Via French < late Latin *multiplus*, alteration of Latin *multiplex* (see MULTIPLEX).]

multiple alleles *npl* three or more different forms of a gene

multiple-choice *adj* requiring the choice of the correct answer or answers out of several possible suggested answers ○ *a multiple-choice question*

multiple factor *n* a polygene

multiple fission *n* a form of asexual reproduction occurring in some single-celled organisms such as malaria parasites in which a single parent cell breaks up to yield numerous daughter cells

multiple fruit *n* a fruit such as a pineapple or fig that is produced from the ovaries of several flowers that merge to form a single structure

multiple myeloma, multiple myelomatosis *n* a form of cancer of the bone marrow characterized by swellings, deformities, and fractures of various bones and accompanied by pain, anaemia, and weight loss

multiple personality *n* a psychological disorder, typically associated with childhood trauma, in which somebody appears to have two or more distinct personalities that are present at different times and dominate behaviour. Now called **dissociative disorder**

multiple sclerosis *n* a serious progressive disease of the central nervous system, occurring mainly in young adults and thought to be caused by a malfunction of the immune system

multiple shop *n* COMM = **multiple store**

multiple star *n* a group of three or more stars, usually with the same gravitational centre, that appears as one star to the naked eye

multiple store, multiple shop, multiple *n* COMM = **chain store**

multiplet /múlti plet/ *n* **1** a line in a spectrum made up of two or more component lines, caused by slight variations in atomic or molecular energy levels **2** a group of elementary particles that have a different electric charge but have otherwise similar properties [Early 20C. < MULTIPLE, after DOUBLET, TRIPLET.]

multiple unit *n* a passenger train with engines or motors in or beneath the coaches that require no separate locomotive

multiple voting *n* the fraudulent practice of voting in more than one constituency in an election

ϟ **multiplex** /múlti pleks/ *n* **1** CINEMA COMPLEX a large cinema complex that has several separate units with screens as well as other facilities such as a restaurant or bar **2** MULTIPLE TRANSMISSION the simultaneous transmission of two or more signals along one communications channel **3** SYSTEM FOR SIMULTANEOUS TRANSMISSION a transmission system that carries two or more individual channels over a single communication path ■ *adj* COMPLEX involving or including several different things, parts, or factors ■ *vti* SEND BY MULTIPLEX to send two or more messages or signals along one communications channel at the same time [Mid-16C. < Latin, < *multi-* 'many' + *-plex* '-fold'.]

ϟ **multiplexer** /múlti pleksər/, **multiplexor** *n* **1** a device for sending several data streams down a communications line and for splitting a received multiple stream into components **2** a device for transferring projected film to video

multiplicand /múltipli kánd/ *n* a number that is multiplied by another number (**multiplier**). The number 2 is the multiplicand in the statement 2 × 4 = 8. [Late 16C. < medieval Latin *multiplicandus*, form of Latin *multiplicare* (see MULTIPLY[1]).]

multiplicate /múltipli kayt/ *adj* containing many elements or parts [15C. < Latin *multiplicat-*, past participle of *multiplicare* (see MULTIPLY[1]).]

multiplication /múltipli káysh'n/ *n* **1** ARITHMETIC OPERATION a mathematical operation, symbolized by ×, that for integers is equivalent to adding a number to itself a particular number of times **2** MATHEMATICAL OPERATION a mathematical operation equivalent to multiplication extended to expressions that are not numbers, e.g. functions or matrices **3** INCREASE a marked increase in number or amount ○ *a multiplication of claims* **4** REPRODUCTION the act or process of reproduction in animals, plants, or people —**multiplicational** *adj* —**multiplicative** /múlti plíkətiv/ *adj* —**multiplicatively** *adv*

multiplication sign *n* the symbol × or ·, used to indicate that one number is to be multiplied by another

multiplication table *n* a table giving a number from 1 to 10 or 12 multiplied by all the numbers from 1 to 10 or 12 in turn

multiplicity /múlti plíssəti/ (*plural* **-ties**) *n* **1** GREAT VARIETY a considerable number or variety ○ *Her style was shaped by a multiplicity of influences.* **2** COMPLEXITY the state of being multiple or varied **3** NUMBER OF MOLECULAR ENERGY LEVELS the number of energy levels of a molecule, atom, or nucleus that result from interactions between angular momenta **4** PARTICLES IN A MULTIPLET the number of elementary particles that form a multiplet [15C. < late Latin *multiplicatus* < Latin *multiplic-*, stem of *multiplex* (see MULTIPLEX).]

multiplier /múlti plī ər/ *n* **1** a person who or thing that multiplies or increases **2** the number by which another number (**multiplicand**) is multiplied, e.g. the number 4 is the multiplier in the statement 2 × 4 = 8 **3** PHYS = **photomultiplier**

multiply[1] /múlti plī/ (**-plies, -plying, -plied**) *v* **1** *vti* PERFORM MULTIPLICATION to perform the mathematical operation of multiplication **2** *vti* INCREASE IN AMOUNT to increase or make something increase by a considerable number, amount, or degree **3** *vi* BREED to increase in number by breeding [12C. Via French *multiplier* < Latin *multiplicare* < *multiplic-* (see MULTIPLICITY).] —**multipliable** *adj* —**multiplicable** /múlti plikəb'l/ *adj*

multiply[2] /múltipli/ *adv* many times or in many different ways

multipoint /múlti póynt/ *n US* TELECOM = **multiple** *n.* 2

multipolar /múlti pólər/ *adj* **1** describes a nerve cell with more than two connecting fibres that carry impulses into the cell body **2** having several poles —**multipolarity** /-pō lárrəti/ *n*

ϟ **multiport** /múlti pawrt/ *adj* describes a computer network with more than one point of access or connection

multipotent /mul típpətənt/, **multipotential** /múltipə ténsh'l/ *adj* capable of developing into various types of cell, depending on the surrounding conditions

ϟ **multiprocessing** /múlti prō sessing/ *n* the operation of a computer in which two or more processing units work on separate parts of the same program or set of instructions to reduce processing time

ϟ **multiprocessor** /múlti prō sessər/ *n* a system of linked central processing units on which two or more programs can be run simultaneously by parallel processing

multipronged /múlti próngd/ *adj* **1** involving several different approaches or elements **2** having several prongs

multipurpose /múlti púrpəss/ *adj* designed or able to be used for several different purposes

multiracial /múlti ráysh'l/ *adj* relating to, made up of, or involving people from several races ○ *a multiracial society* —**multiracially** *adv*

multiracialism /múlti ráysh'l izəm/ *n* the principle or practice of ensuring that people of various races are fully integrated into a society —**multiracialist** *adj*

multirole /múlti rōl/ *adj* having several roles or functions

multiscreen /múlti skreen/ *adj* with several screens for showing films, videos, or slides

multisense /múlti senss/ *adj* having many different meanings

multisensory /múlti sénssəri/ *adj* relating to or involving two or more of the senses

multistage /múlti stayj/ *adj* **1** divided into or taking place in several separate stages **2** having several propulsion units, each of which operates sequentially ○ *a multistage rocket*

multistage rocket *n* a rocket with two or more propulsion units that are used and discarded in succession

multistorey /múlti stáwri/ *adj* having several storeys ■ *n* (*plural* **-storeys**) a car park constructed on several levels (*informal*)

multitasking /múlti taasking/ *n* the simultaneous management of two or more tasks by a computer or a person

multitiered /múlti teérd/ having many layers or levels placed one above the other

multiton /múlti tun/ *adj US* weighing or capable of carrying several tons

multitrack /múlti trak/ *adj* using, capable of, or produced by the separate recording of several different tracks

multitude /múlti tyood/ *n* **1** CROWD a large crowd of people **2** LARGE NUMBER a very large number of things or people (*often plural*) **3** MAJORITY the majority of ordinary people [14C. Via French < Latin *multitudo* < *multus* 'much, many'.]

multitudinous /múlti tyoódinəss/ *adj* **1** VERY NUMEROUS very great in number **2** FULL OF VARIETY with many parts, great in number, or existing in many varieties **3** CROWDED crowded with people (*archaic*) [Early 17C. < Latin *multitudin-*, stem of *multitudo* (see MULTITUDE).] —**multitudinously** *adv* —**multitudinousness** *n*

multiuse /múlti yooss/ *adj* having a variety of uses

ϟ **multiuser** /múlti yoózər/ *adj* capable of being used by several people at the same time

ϟ **multiuser domain, object-oriented** ONLINE = **MOO**

multivalent /múlti váylənt/ *adj* **1** = **polyvalent** *adj.* 1 **2** with several meanings or values —**multivalence** *n*

multivariate /múlti váiri ət/, **multivariable** /-váiri əb'l/ *adj* describes or relating to a statistical distribution that involves a number of random but often related variables

multiversity /múlti vúrssəti/ (*plural* **-ties**) *n* a university that has many affiliated or associated institutions such as research centres and colleges [Mid-20C. < MULTI- + UNIVERSITY.]

multivibrator /múlti vī bráytər/ *n* an oscillating electronic circuit consisting of pairs of tubes, transistors, or other components, whose oscillation is sustained by coupling the output of one to the input of the other

multivitamin /múlti vittəmin/ *n* a tablet or capsule containing several vitamins and sometimes minerals —**multivitamin** *adj*

multivocal /múlti vők'l/ *adj* with many different and valid meanings or interpretations

multivolume /múlti vóllyoom/ *adj* published in several volumes

multiyear /múlti yeer/ *adj US* existing, valid, or taking place over several years ○ *a multiyear agreement*

multum in parvo /mőoltōom in paárvō/ *n* the quality or fact of containing, implying, or expressing much in a little space or time [< Latin, 'much in little']

mum[1] /mum/ *n* mother (*informal*) US term **mom** [Mid-17C. Partly (especially in early use) a variant of MAM and partly shortening of MUMMY[2].]

mum[2] /mum/ *adj* saying nothing, especially about a sensitive piece of information (*informal*) [15C. An imitation of the sound made when the lips are closed.]

mum[3] /mum/ (**mums, mumming, mummed**), **mumm** *vi* **1** to act in a masked folk play or mime **2** to participate in festivities wearing a mask or disguise [Mid-16C. < French *momer* 'act in a mime'.]

mum[4] /mum/ *n* a chrysanthemum (*informal*) [Late 19C. Shortening.]

Mumbai /mōōm bī/ port and capital of Maharashtra, west-central India. Population: 9,925,891 (1991).

mumble /múmb'l/ *vti* (**-bles, -bling, -bled**) **1** MUTTER to speak or utter something quietly and unclearly without opening the mouth very much **2** CHEW WITH DIFFICULTY to chew food with difficulty ■ *n* INDISTINCT SPEECH an indistinct and quiet utterance [14C. < obsolete *mum* 'make an indistinct sound with closed lips'.] —**mumbler** *n* —**mumbling** *adj* —**mumblingly** *adv*

mumbo jumbo /múmbō júmbō/ *n* **1** CONFUSING LANGUAGE complicated and confusing language, especially technical jargon, that is difficult to understand (*informal*) **2** WORTHLESS RELIGIOUS BELIEF OR RITUAL religious beliefs, language, or rituals that appear pointless or meaningless to the speaker (*offensive in some contexts*) **3** OBJECT BELIEVED SUPERNATURAL an object or effigy that is believed to hold supernatural powers [Mid-18C. < ?]

mu meson *n* PHYS = **muon**

mumm *vt* = **mum**[3]

mummer /múmmər/ *n* **1** ACTOR one of a group of actors in a pantomime, folk play, or mime show **2** SOMEBODY WHO CELEBRATES IN DISGUISE a participant in festivities who wears a mask or disguise **3** MIME ARTIST an artist who performs in mimes **4** ACTOR an actor (*humorous*) [15C. < Old French *momeur* < *momer* 'act in a mime'.]

Mummerset /múmmər set/ *n* a stereotypical West Country accent used in drama [Mid-20C. Probably blend of MUMMER + *Somerset*, county in the west of England.]

mummery /múmməri/ (*plural* **-ies**) *n* **1** a performance by a group of mummers **2** a showy or hypocritical ceremony (*disapproving*)

mummify /múmmi fī/ (**-fies, -fying, -fied**) *v* **1** *vt* PRESERVE CORPSE FOR BURIAL to preserve the corpse of a person or animal for burial by embalming it and wrapping it in cloth **2** *vti* SHRIVEL to dry out and shrivel, or cause something to dry out and shrivel **3** *vt* PRESERVE AGAINST NATURAL TENDENCY to preserve something such as an old custom or an institution just for the sake of it and without making any effort to keep it alive [Early 17C. < MUMMY[1] after French *momifier.*] —**mummification** /múmmifi káysh'n/ *n*

mummy[1] /múmmi/ (*plural* **-mies**) *n* **1** the body of a person or animal that has been embalmed and wrapped in cloth, especially as was the custom in ancient Egypt **2** the body of an organism preserved by natural processes, e.g. by burial in peat or ice [Early 17C. Via Old French *momie* < Arabic *mūmiyā* 'embalmed body'.]

mummy[2] /múmmi/ (*plural* **-mies**) *n* mother (*usually used by or to children*) US term **mommy** [Late 18C. Dialectal variant of MAMMY.]

mummy's boy *n* an offensive term that deliberately insults a man's strength of character, courage, or independence (*insult*) US term **mama's boy**

mumps /mumps/ *n* an acute contagious disease, usually affecting children, that causes a fever with swelling of the salivary glands (+ *singular or plural verb*) [Late 16C. Plural of obsolete *mump* 'grimace', an imitation of the sounds made with a closed mouth.]

mumsy /múmzi/ (**-sier, -siest**) *adj* **1** unfashionable and dowdy (*informal*) **2** kind and motherly in a gentle sweet-natured way [Late 19C. < MUM[1].]

mun *v* = **maun** (*regional*)

munch /munch/ *vti* to chew food purposefully, usually with visible movements of the jaw and sometimes with a crunching sound [14C. < ?] —**muncher** *n*

Munch /mōongk/, **Edvard** (1863–1944) Norwegian painter

Münchausen /múnch owz'n/ *n* **1** a fantastic story full of exaggeration, told to impress people **2** an inventor or teller of fantastic stories [Mid-19C. After the eponymous hero, Baron *Münchausen*, of a book of impossible adventures (1785) written in English by the German author Rudolf Eric Raspe.]

Münchausen syndrome /mún chowz'n-/ *n* a psychological disorder in which somebody pretends to have a serious illness in order to undergo testing or treatment or to be admitted to hospital

munchies /múnchiz/ *npl* a craving for snack food (*informal*)

munchkin /múnchkin/ *n* US (*informal*) **1** a small child **2** an insignificant person who keeps busy with trivial matters [Late 20C. < creatures invented by L. Frank Baum in *The Wizard of Oz* (1900).]

Muncie /múnssi/ city in E Indiana. Population: 67,476 (1998 estimate).

Munda /móondə/ *n* **1** one of the four major Indian language groups spoken throughout India. Native speakers: 5 million. **2** somebody who speaks Munda as a native language [Mid-19C. < Munda *Muṇḍā*.] —**Munda** *adj*

mundane /mun dáyn/ *adj* **1** commonplace, not unusual, and often boring **2** relating to matters of this world [15C. Via French < late Latin *mundanus* < Latin *mundus* 'world'.] —**mundanely** *adv* —**mundaneness** *n*

mung bean /múng-/ *n* **1** a small green or yellow bean that is dried and sometimes split **2** a plant that produces mung beans. Native to: E Asia. *Vigna radiata*. [< Hindi *mūng*]

mungo /múng gō/ (*plural* **-gos** *or* **-goes**), **mongo** (*plural* **-gos** *or* **-goes**), **mongoe** *n* a cheap fabric made from waste wool and rags [Mid-19C. < ?]

Mungo, Lake /múng gō/ dry lake in W New South Wales, Australia

Munich /myóonikh/ capital of Bavaria, SE Germany. Population: 1,251,100 (1994).

municipal /myoo níssip'l/ *adj* relating to a town, city, or region that has its own local government [Mid-16C. Directly or via French < Latin *municipalis* < *municip-* 'holder of a civic office' < *munus* 'gift, service, duty' + *capere* 'take'.] —**municipalism** *n* —**municipalist** *n* —**municipally** *adv*

municipal bond *n* US a bond or security issued by a city or other local government, usually to pay for public improvements

municipalise *vt* = municipalize

municipality /myoo níssi pállət/ (*plural* **-ties**) *n* **1** a city, town, or other region that has its own local government **2** the appointed or elected members of a local government

SYNONYMS See *city*.

municipalize /myoo níssipə līz/ (**-izes**, **-izing**, **-ized**), **municipalise** (**-ises**, **-ising**, **-ised**) *vt* **1** to bring something such as a public service or area of land under the ownership or control of a city, town, or region with its own local government **2** to grant a city, town, or region powers of government on local matters —**municipalization** /myoo níssipə lī záysh'n/ *n*

munificent /myoo níffiss'nt/ *adj* **1** very generous in giving **2** characterized by generosity ○ *a munificent award* [Late 16C. < Latin *munificent-* < *munificus* 'generous' < *munus* 'gift, service, duty'.] —**munificence** *n* —**munificently** *adv*

SYNONYMS See *generous*.

muniments /myóonimənts/ *npl* documents by which a claim to property or rights is supported, e.g. the title deeds to land [15C. < Latin *munimentum* 'fortification' < *munire* (see MUNITION).]

munition /myoo nísh'n/ *vt* to supply somebody or a group with arms and ammunition ■ **munitions** *npl* military supplies such as weapons and ammunition [Early 16C. Via French < Latin *munition-* < *munire* 'fortify' < *moenia* 'defensive walls'.] —**munitioner** *n*

Munnings /múnningz/, **Sir Alfred James** (1878–1959) British painter

Munro /mən rṓ/ (*plural* **-ros**) *n* a mountain peak over 3,000 ft high, either in Scotland only or in any part of the British Isles [Early 20C. After Sir H. *Munro*, compiler of a list of mountains.]

Munro /mən rṓ/, **Alice** (b. 1931) Canadian writer. Pseudonym of **Alice Anne Laidlaw**

Munsee /múnsee/ (*plural* **-see** *or* **-sees**), **Munsi** (*plural* **-si** *or* **-sis**) *n* the Algonquian language of the Delaware people —**Munsee** *adj*

Munster[1] *n* FOOD = Muenster

Munster[2] /múnstər/ historic province in SW Republic of Ireland

Münster /múnstər/ inland port in NW Germany. Population: 265,500 (1994).

munt /móont/ *n* S Africa an offensive term for a black African person (*dated slang insult*) ■ *vi* to drink alcohol or take drugs for pleasure (*slang*) [Mid-20C. < Bantu *umuntu* 'person', singular of *abantu*.]

munter /múntər/ *n* a person considered unattractive (*slang insult*) [< ?]

muntin /múntin/ *n* a strip of wood or metal that separates and holds in place the panes of a window [Early 17C. Old French *montant* 'upright' < present participle of *monter* (see MOUNT[1]).]

muntjac /múnt jak/ (*plural* **-jacs** *or* **-jac**), **muntjak** (*plural* **-jaks** *or* **-jak**) *n* a small deer with a reddish-brown coat, a cry like a dog's bark, and small antlers. Native to: Southeast Asia. Genus: *Muntiacus*. [Late 18C. < Sundanese *minchek*, Malay *menjangan* 'deer'.]

Muntz metal /múnts-/ *n* brass containing two parts of zinc to three parts of copper. Use: casting, extrusion. [Mid-19C. After the English metallurgist George Frederick *Muntz* (1794–1857).]

muon /myóo on/ *n* an elementary particle with a mass about 200 times that of an electron [Mid-20C. Contraction of MU MESON.] —**muonic** /myoo ónnik/ *adj*

muon neutrino *n* a lepton that exists in association with a muon

muppet /múppit/ *n* a person considered silly or stupid (*slang insult*) [After the puppets in *The Muppet Show*]

Murad IV /myoor ad/ (1609–40) sultan of the Ottoman Empire (1623–40)

mural /myóorəl/ *n* a usually large picture painted directly onto an interior or exterior wall ■ *adj* applied to or relating to a wall [Mid-16C. Via French < Latin *muralis* < *murus* 'wall'.] —**muralist** *n*

muramic acid /myoo rámmik-/ *n* an amino sugar found in the cell walls of blue-green algae [< Latin *murus* 'wall' + AMINE]

Murasaki /moor aa saáki/, **Shikibu** (978?–1031?) Japanese court lady and writer

Murat /myoor a, mü rá/, **Joachim** (1767–1815) French military commander and king of Naples (1808–15)

Murchison /múrchiss'n/ river in W Western Australia. Length: 800 km/500 mi.

Murchison /múrchiss'n/, **Sir Roderick Impey** (1792–1871) British geologist

Murcia /múr shə, múrssi ə/ capital of Murcia Province, SE Spain. Population: 344,904 (1995).

murder /múrdər/ *n* CRIME OF KILLING the crime of killing another person deliberately and not in self-defence or with any other extenuating circumstance recognized by law ■ *v* **1** *vti* KILL SOMEBODY ILLEGALLY to kill another person deliberately and not in self-defence or with any other extenuating circumstance recognized by law **2** *vt* DESTROY to put an end to or destroy something (*informal*) ○ *The fire murdered their chances of selling the house.* **3** *vt* SPOIL to spoil something such as a song or a piece of writing by performing it badly or changing it (*informal*) **4** *vt* DEFEAT COMPLETELY to defeat a person or team completely, especially in a sporting contest (*informal*) **5** *vt* PUNISH to punish or be very angry with somebody (*informal*) ○ *My mother will murder me if I'm not on time.* [Old English *morþor*. < Indo-European.] ◇ **be murder** to be very difficult or unpleasant and involve great effort or hardship (*informal*) ○ *Driving in this morning was murder.* ◇ **get away with murder** to escape punishment for or detection of wrongdoing —**murderee** /múrdə rée/ *n* —**murderer** *n* —**murderess** *n*

murderous /múrdərəss/ *adj* **1** LIKELY TO MURDER capable of, guilty of, or likely to commit murder **2** LIKELY TO CAUSE DEATH violent and likely to result in bloodshed or murder **3** DIFFICULT very difficult, unpleasant, or dangerous (*informal*) —**murderously** *adv* —**murderousness** *n*

Murdoch /múr dok/, **Dame Iris** (1919–99) Irish-born British novelist and philosopher

Murdoch, **Sir Keith Arthur** (1885–1952) Australian journalist and newspaper proprietor

Murdoch, **Rupert** (b. 1931) Australian-born US media proprietor

murein /myóor een/ *n* BIOCHEM = peptidoglycan [Mid-20C. < Latin *murus* 'wall' after PROTEIN; from its forming the walls of cells.]

murex /myóor eks/ (*plural* **-rices** /-ri seez/) *n* a marine invertebrate animal that typically has a spiny shell. Native to: tropical waters. Genus: *Murex*. [Late 16C. < Latin.]

muriatic acid /myóori áttik-/ *n* CHEM = hydrochloric acid [< Latin *muriaticus* 'pickled in brine' < *muria* 'brine']

muricate /myóorikət/, **muricated** /-kaytid/ *adj* covered in short spines or points [Mid-17C. < Latin *muricatus* 'shaped like a murex' < *murex*.]

Murillo /myoo rílló/, **Bartolomé Esteban** (1617–82) Spanish painter

murine /myóor īn/ *adj* **1** OF MOUSE AND RAT FAMILY relating to or belonging to the family of long-tailed rodents that includes rats and mice. Family: Muridae. **2** LIKE A RODENT like a mouse or a rat **3** SPREAD BY RODENTS caused or transmitted by mice or rats [Early 17C. < Latin *murinus* < *mur-* 'mouse'.]

murine typhus *n* a relatively mild form of typhus that is transmitted from rats to humans by fleas or lice

murk /murk/, **mirk** *n* **1** GLOOMY DARKNESS gloomy darkness caused by mist, smoke, or cloud **2** N England MIST a mist or thin fog (*informal*) ■ *adj* MURKY murky (*archaic or literary*) [Old English *mirce, myrce* < N Germanic]

murky /múrki/ (**-ier, -iest**), **mirky** (**-ier, -iest**) *adj* **1** GLOOMY dark and gloomy **2** HARD TO SEE THROUGH thick with fog, cloud, smoke, or dirt, and difficult to see through **3** OBSCURE unclear and difficult to understand ○ *offered several murky excuses* **4** DISHONEST involving dishonesty or illegal activities —**murkily** *adv* —**murkiness** *n*

Murmansk /mur mánsk/ port in NW Russia. Population: 472,000 (1990).

~~murmer~~ incorrect spelling of murmur

murmur /múrmər/ *n* **1** CONTINUOUS HUM a continuous low sound that often seems to be coming from some distance away **2** SOMETHING SAID QUIETLY something said that is either very quiet or sounds indistinct **3** COMPLAINT a complaint, especially one that is not made openly **4** SYMPTOMATIC SOUND IN CHEST a soft blowing or fluttering sound, usually heard via a stethoscope, that originates from the heart, lungs, or arteries and may indicate disease or structural concerns ■ *v* **1** *vti* SAY SOMETHING SOFTLY to say something very softly so that it can hardly be heard **2** *vi* COMPLAIN DISCREETLY to complain in a discreet or secretive way **3** *vi* MAKE CONTINUOUS LOW SOUND to make a continuous low sound, as if from a distance [14C. Via French *murmurer* < Latin *murmurare*.] —**murmurer** *n* —**murmuringly** *adv* —**murmurous** *adj* —**murmurously** *adv*

murmuration /múrma ráysh'n/ *n* **1** an act or sound of murmuring **2** a flock of starlings

murmurings /múrməringz/ *npl* quiet and subdued expressions of discontent

murphy /múrfi/ (*plural* **-phies**) *n* a potato (*dated informal*) [Early 19C. < the Irish surname *Murphy*; from the stereotypical prominence of the potato in the Irish diet.]

Murphy /múrfi/, **Graeme** (b. 1950) Australian dancer and choreographer

Murphy bed *n* US a bed that can be folded or swung into a cupboard or wall recess when not in use [Early 20C. After William *Murphy* (1876–1959), American inventor.]

Murphy's Law /múrfiz-/ *n* = Sod's Law (*informal*) [Mid-20C. After Edward *Murphy* (b. 1917), American engineer.]

murragh /múrrə/ (*plural* **-raghs** *or* **-ragh**) *n* a caddis fly to which trout are particularly attracted. *Phryganea grandis*. [< ?]

murrain /múrrin/ *n* **1** an infectious disease such as anthrax that affects cattle **2** an infectious and fast-spreading disease (*archaic or humorous*) [14C. < Anglo-Norman *moryn*, Old French *morine* < *mourir* 'die' < Latin *mori*.]

Murray /múrri/ river in SE Australia. Length: 2,520 km/1,566 mi.

Murray, Gilbert (1866–1957) British scholar

Murray, Sir James Augustus Henry (1837–1915) British philologist and lexicographer

Murray, Les (b. 1938) Australian poet and critic

Murray Bridge town in SE South Australia. Population: 12,740 (1991).

Murray cod *n* a large freshwater fish. Native to: Australian inland waterways. *Maccullochella peeli.*

murre /mur/ *n US, Can* an auk with black plumage and white markings. Genus: *Uria*. [Late 16C. < ?]

murrelet /múrlit/ (*plural* **-lets** *or* **-let**) *n* a small diving bird related to the auk. Genera: *Brachyramphus* and *Synthliboramphus*.

murrhine glass /múrrīn-/ *n* glassware made from fluorspar and decorated with flecks of metal

Murrumbidgee /múrrəm bíji/ river in New South Wales, Australia. Length: 1,600 km/980 mi.

Murry /múrri/, **John Middleton** (1889–1957) British writer and literary critic

murther /múrthər/ *n* murder, or a murder (*archaic*) [14C. Variant.]

mus. *abbr* **1** museum **2** music **3** musical **4** musician

Musaf /mōō sáf/ *n* in Judaism, a group of additional prayers that is included in morning services on Sabbaths, festivals, and Rosh Chodesh [< Hebrew, 'addition']

MusB, MusBac *abbr* Bachelor of Music [Latin *Musicae Baccalaureus*]

Musca /múskə/ *n* a small constellation of the southern hemisphere. See illustration at **constellation**

muscadel, muscadelle *n* WINE = **muscatel**

Muscadet /múskə day/ *n* a dry white wine from the Loire Valley in France [Early 20C. < French, < *muscade* 'nutmeg' < *musc* 'musk' (see MUSK).]

muscadine /múskə dīn/ *n* **1** a grapevine that is the ancestor of cultivated varieties used for wine making. Native to: SE United States. *Vitis rotundifolia*. **2** a purple grape from the muscadine vine with a thick skin and musky smell. Use: wine making. [Mid-16C. Probably variant of MUSCATEL.]

muscae volitantes /múski vólli tán teez/ *npl* specks that appear to float before the eyes (*technical*) [Mid-18C. < Latin, 'flies flying about'.]

muscarine /múskərin/ *n* a toxic substance, found in fly agaric and certain other fungi, that affects the nervous system when ingested [Late 19C. < modern Latin *Muscaria*, species the fly agaric < Latin *musca* 'fly'.] —**muscarinic** /múskə rínnik/ *adj*

muscat /múskət/ *n* **1** a grapevine producing sweet white grapes **2** WINE = **muscatel** *n*. [Mid-16C. Via French < Provençal, < *musc* < Latin *muscus* (see MUSK).]

Muscat /mús kat/, **Masqat** /máss gat/ capital of Oman, on the northeastern coast of the country. Population: 622,506 (1993).

muscatel /múskə tél/, **muscadel** /-dél/, **muscadelle, muscat** *n* a sweet white wine made from muscat grapes [Mid-16C. Via Old French < Provençal, 'little muscat' < *muscat* (see MUSCAT).]

muscavado *n* FOOD = **muscovado**

muscid /mússid/ *n* any fly of the family that includes the housefly and the stable fly. Family: Muscidae. [Late 19C. Back-formation < modern Latin *Muscidae* < Latin *musca* 'fly'.] —**muscid** *adj*

muscle /múss'l/ *n* **1 BODY TISSUE PRODUCING MOVEMENT** a tissue that is specialized to undergo repeated contraction and relaxation, thereby producing movement of body parts, maintaining tension, or pumping fluids within the body **2 ORGAN COMPOSED OF MUSCLE TISSUE** an organ composed of bundles or sheets of muscle tissue, bound together with connective tissue and with tendons by which the contracting part is attached to the bones that it moves **3 INFLUENCE** power and influence, especially in the realm of politics, finance, or the military **4 STRENGTH** physical strength (*informal*) ○ *put some muscle into it* ■ *vti* (**-cles, -cling, -cled**) **MOVE BY USING STRENGTH** to move, or make somebody or something move, using strength and force or effort (*informal*) [14C. Via French < Latin *musculus* literally 'small mouse' < *mus* 'mouse'; from the resemblance of certain muscles to mice moving under the skin.] —**muscly** *adj*

SPELLCHECK Do not confuse ***muscle*** with ***mussel***, which has a similar sound. Beware: your spellchecker will not catch this error.

muscle in *vi* to become involved in or interfere in something by disregarding other people's wishes or by using strength, power, or influence (*informal*)

muscle-bound *adj* **1** with muscles so bulky that they restrict movement **2** too large, powerful, or overdeveloped to be capable of flexibility or a swift response

muscle candy *n US* a dietary supplement used by athletes to enhance bursts of high performance (*slang*)

muscle fibre *n* a basic contracting unit of striated muscle, e.g., in arm and leg muscles. Each is a microscopic thread-like structure, formed from several fused cells.

muscleman /múss'l man/ (*plural* **-men** /-men/) *n* **1** a man with highly developed muscles who is very strong **2** a strong man hired by a criminal or gangster for protection and to intimidate enemies

muscle mary *n* an offensive term for a homosexual man with a very muscular physique (*slang*)

muscle sense *n* = **kinaesthesia**

muscovado /múskə vaádō/, **muscavado** *n* a raw or unrefined sugar made by evaporating the molasses from sugar-cane juice [Early 17C. < Portuguese *mascabado* 'made badly'.]

muscovite /múskə vīt/ *n* a common mica mineral, consisting of potassium aluminium silicate. Source: igneous and sedimentary rocks. [Mid-19C. < *Muscovy glass* 'mica' (from its being obtained from Russia).]

Muscovite /múskə vīt/ *n* somebody who comes from Moscow, Russia ■ *adj* Russian (*archaic*) [Mid-16C. < modern Latin *Muscovia* < Russian *Moskva* 'Moscow'.]

Muscovy /múskəvi/ former principality of Moscow, W Russia

Muscovy duck /múskəvi-/ *n* a large duck with greenish-black plumage, white markings, and heavy red wattles. Kept for: food. Native to: Central America. *Cairina moschata*. [Alteration (by association with archaic *Muscovy* 'of Moscow') of MUSK DUCK]

muscular /múskyōōlər/ *adj* **1 OF THE MUSCLES** consisting of, relating to, or affecting muscles **2 STRONG** physically strong and with well-developed muscles **3 VIGOROUS** having considerable power or strength but sometimes lacking subtlety [Late 17C. < obsolete *musculous*, directly or via French < Latin *musculosus* < *musculus* (see MUSCLE).] —**muscularity** /múskyōō lárrəti/ *n* —**muscularly** *adv*

muscular dystrophy *n* a medical condition in which there is gradual wasting and weakening of skeletal muscles

musculature /múskōōləchər/ *n* **1** the way a person's or animal's muscles are arranged in a limb or organ **2** an organism's entire muscular system [Late 19C. < French, < Latin *musculus* (see MUSCLE).]

musculo- *prefix* muscle, muscular ○ *musculocutaneous* [< Latin *musculus* (see MUSCLE)]

musculocutaneous /múskyōōlō kyōō táyni əss/ *adj* relating to or supplying the muscles and skin

musculoskeletal /múskyōōlō skéllit'l/ *adj* relating to or involving the muscles and the skeleton

MusD, MusDoc *abbr* Doctor of Music [Latin *Musicae Doctor*]

muse¹ /myooz/ *v* **1** *vti* **THINK ABOUT** to think about something in a deep and serious or dreamy and abstracted way **2** *vti* **SAY SOMETHING THOUGHTFULLY** to say something in a thoughtful or questioning way **3** *vi* **GAZE THOUGHTFULLY** to gaze at somebody or something thoughtfully or abstractedly ■ *n* **THOUGHTFUL STATE** a state of deep thought (*literary*) [14C. < Old French *muser* 'meditate'.] —**museful** *adj* —**musefully** *adv* —**muser** *n* —**musingly** *adv*

muse² /myooz/ *n* **1 SOMEBODY WHO INSPIRES ARTIST** a source of inspiration for an artist, especially a poet **2 ARTIST'S INSPIRATION** the source of inspiration that stimulates an artist, especially a poet **3 ARTIST'S PARTICULAR TALENT** the particular gift or talent of an artist, especially a poet ○ *'With Donne, whose muse on dromedary trots/ Wreathe iron pokers into true-love knots'* (Samuel Taylor Coleridge, *On Donne's Poetry*; 1818) [14C. Directly or via French < Latin *musa* < Greek *mousa*.]

Muse *n* in Greek mythology, one of the nine daughters of Zeus and Mnemosyne, goddess of memory. The Muses inspired and presided over the creative arts.

museology /myoōzi óllәji/ *n* the study of how museums are designed, organized, and managed —**museological** /myoōzi ə lójjik'l/ *adj* —**museologically** *adv* —**museologist** *n*

musette /myoo zét/ *n* **1** French bagpipes that make a relatively soft sound **2** a piece of pastoral dance music that imitates the sound of bagpipes or has bagpipes playing the bass line [14C. < French, 'little bagpipes' < *muse* 'bagpipes'.]

museum¹ /myoo zée əm/ *n* a building or institution where objects of artistic, historical, or scientific importance and value are kept, studied, and put on display [Early 17C. Via Latin, 'library, academy' < Greek *mouseion* 'place of the Muses' < *mousa* 'muse'.]

ϟ **museum**² *abbr* museum (*in Internet addresses*)

museum piece *n* **1** an object that is so valuable, interesting, or old that it could be in a museum **2** somebody or something considered very old-fashioned (*informal*)

Musgrave Ranges /múss grayv-/ mountain range in central Australia. Highest peak: Mount Woodroffe 1,435 m/4,708 ft.

mush¹ /mush/ *n* **1 PULP** a soft pulpy mass **2 SENTIMENTAL STUFF** overly romantic and sentimental words or ideas, e.g. in a book or film **3 INTERFERENCE** radio interference, especially a hissing noise **4** *US* **PORRIDGE** a thick mixture made from cornmeal and milk or water ■ *vt US* **MASH** to mash something into a soft pulpy mass [Late 17C. Probably variant of MASH.] —**mushily** *adv* —**mushiness** *n* —**mushy** *adj*

mush² /mush/ *interj US, Can* **COMMAND TO SLED DOGS** used to make sled dogs start pulling or moving faster ■ *n US, Can* **DOGSLED JOURNEY** a journey on a dogsled ■ *vti US, Can* **TRAVEL BY DOGSLED** to travel on a dogsled, or drive a dogsled or team of dogs [Mid-19C. < *Mush on!*, probably < French *marchons* 'let us march' < *marcher* 'to march'.] —**musher** *n*

mush³ /mōōsh/ *n* somebody's face or mouth (*dated slang*) [Mid-20C. < ?]

mush⁴ /mōōsh/ *n* a familiar or disrespectful way of addressing somebody, usually a man (*slang*) [Mid-20C. < ?]

mush area *n* a region where two or more radio signals overlap, causing interference

mushroom /músh room, -rōōm/ *n* **1 UMBRELLA-SHAPED FUNGUS** the typically umbrella-shaped spore-producing body of a fungus that consists of a usually fleshy cap on a stalk. Class: Basidiomycetes. **2 EDIBLE FUNGUS** an edible mushroom, especially the field mushroom **3 FAST-GROWING THING** something that grows very fast ■ *vi* **1 GROW QUICKLY** to grow or develop very rapidly **2 BECOME MUSHROOM-SHAPED** to swell into a shape like a mushroom **3 PICK MUSHROOMS** to go mushroom picking [15C. Via French *mousseron* < late Latin *mussirion-* a type of mushroom.] —**mushroomy** *adj*

mushroom cloud *n* the large mushroom-shaped cloud of dust and debris caused by an explosion, especially a nuclear explosion

music /myoōzik/ *n* **1 SOUNDS THAT PRODUCE EFFECT** sounds, usually produced by instruments or voices, that are arranged or played in order to create a particular effect **2 ART OF ARRANGING SOUNDS** the art of arranging or making sounds, usually those of musical instruments or voices, so as to create a particular effect **3 TYPE OF MUSIC** music of a particular type, place, time, instrument, or style ○ *rock-and-roll music* **4 WRITTEN MUSIC** written notation indicating the pitch, duration, rhythm, and tone of notes to be played **5 PLEASING SOUND** a sound or group of sounds that creates a desired effect ○ *the music of the wind in the trees* [13C. Via French *musique* < Greek *mousikē* 'art of the Muse, music' < *mousikos* 'of a Muse' < *mousa* 'muse'.] ◇ **face the music** to deal with a pressing, difficult, or unpleasant situation arising from something you have done previously

musical /myoōzik'l/ *adj* **1 OF OR FOR MUSIC** relating to or producing music **2 PLEASANT-SOUNDING** sounding pleasant and melodious **3 GOOD AT MUSIC** having a talent for or a keen interest in music **4 WITH MUSIC** set to, consisting of, or involving music ■ *n* **FILM OR PLAY WITH SONGS** a lighthearted film or play that has singing, music, and often dancing in it as important elements in developing the story and portraying the emotions of the characters —**musically** *adv* —**musicalness** *n*

musical box *n* a box that contains a mechanical device that plays music. US term **music box**

musicale /myoōzi kaál/ *n US* a social occasion in which music is the featured entertainment

musicality /myoōzi kálləti/ *n* musical ability, especially a particular knowledge of or sensitivity to music

music box *n US* = **musical box**

music centre *n* a one-piece hi-fi unit that has a turntable, amplifier, cassette deck, radio, and speakers (*dated*)

KEY DATES IN WESTERN CLASSICAL MUSIC

Western music is one of several separate, highly developed musical cultures, each of which has its own specific theoretical base that encompasses, among other things, its own system of tunings and scales, its preferred timbres (tone colours), its particular approach to musical form, and its characteristic musical textures. This table is concerned with 'art' or 'classical' music, composed and performed by trained professionals originally under the patronage of courts and religious establishments. This is one of several established genres of Western music, standing alongside other major forms such as folk, jazz, and pop music.

Century	Movement	Development	Principal composers
6th–13th	Early medieval	earliest use of polyphony	anonymous plainsong Gregorian chants, troubadours' songs
14th	Late medieval	birth of madrigal	anonymous ars nova, chansons, madrigals, masses
15th–16th	Renaissance	first printed music	Dunstable, Josquin Desprez, Palestrina, Byrd
16th–18th	Baroque	birth of opera; age of complex counterpoint	Monteverdi, Purcell, Scarlatti, Vivaldi, Bach, Handel
18th	Classical	rise of sonata, symphony, solo concerto	Haydn, Mozart, Beethoven
19th	Romantic	greater use of programmatic music	Schubert, Berlioz, Schumann, Chopin, Liszt, Verdi, Wagner, Brahms, Tchaikovsky, Mahler
20th	Neoclassical	return to clarity and structure of form	Stravinsky, Prokofiev, Shostakovich, Copland, Carter
20th	Serialist	birth of electronic and recorded music	Schoenberg, Berg, Webern, Messiaen, Boulez, Stockhausen, Babbitt, Berio
20th	Indeterminate	non-traditional notation; improvisation	Anderson, Ives, Xenakis
late 20th	Minimalist	extensive repeated patterns with minimal variations	Cage, Glass, Reich, Adams

music drama *n* a type of opera, first composed by Richard Wagner in the late 19th century, in which the dramatic and musical content are intended to be of equal importance

music hall *n* 1 a type of entertainment, popular in the late 19th and early 20th centuries, that consisted of a variety of singing, dancing, and comic acts. US term **vaudeville** *n*. 1 2 a theatre in which music hall shows were staged

musician /myoo zísh'n/ *n* a player, performer, conductor, or composer of music —**musicianly** *adj* —**musicianship** *n*

music of the spheres *n* the perfect but inaudible music that Pythagoras and other later philosophers believed was created by the movement of the celestial bodies

musicology /myoōzí kóllǝji/ *n* the academic study of music and its history —**musicological** /myoōzikǝ lójjik'l/ *adj* —**musicologically** *adv* —**musicologist** *n*

music paper *n* paper with staves printed on it that is used for writing down music

music roll *n* a roll of paper with carefully positioned holes in it, used for controlling a mechanical instrument such as a player piano

music stand *n* a height-adjustable frame for holding printed music that is being performed

music video *n* a short video or film made to accompany a song or piece of popular music, often as a cinematic or dramatic interpretation of it

Musil /moōss'l/, **Robert** (1880–1942) Austrian novelist

musings /myoōzingz/ *npl* thoughts, especially when aimless and unsystematic o *philosophical musings*

musique concrète /myoo zeék kong krét/ *n* recorded music composed by electronically combining and enhancing natural and musical sounds [Mid-20C. < French, 'concrete music'.]

musk /musk/ *n* 1 GLANDULAR SECRETION OF DEER a pungent and greasy secretion from a gland in the male musk deer. Use: perfume manufacture. 2 SUBSTANCE LIKE MUSK a secretion similar to musk from other animals such as the civet or otter, or a synthetic substance with similar properties 3 PLANT WITH MUSKY SCENT a plant that has a musky scent 4 SMELL OF MUSK the smell of musk, or a similar smell [14C. Via Latin *muscus* < Persian *mušk*.]

musk deer *n* a small mountain-dwelling deer, the male of which lacks antlers and possesses long canine teeth. Native to: central and NE Asia. *Moschus moschiferus.*

musk duck *n* BIRDS = Muscovy duck [< its smell]

muskeg /músk eg/ *n* 1 US, Can an area of swamp or boggy land covered in sphagnum moss, leaves, and a mass of dead plant matter resembling peat 2 the dead plant matter resembling peat that covers areas of muskeg [Early 19C. < Cree *maske:k.*]

muskellunge /múska lunj/ (*plural* -**lunges** or -**lunge**), **muskelunge** (*plural* -**lunges** or -**lunge**) *n* 1 US, Can a large predatory freshwater fish of the pike family, caught when young for game. Native to: Great Lakes region of North America. *Esox masquinongy.* 2 the flesh of a muskellunge used as food [Late 18C. < Ojibwa *maskinonje* 'big fish'.]

musket /múskit/ *n* a shoulder gun of the 16th to 18th centuries, with a long barrel and a smooth bore [Late 16C. Via French *mousquet* < Italian *moschetto* 'crossbow bolt' < *mosca* 'fly' < Latin *musca.*]

musketeer /múska teer/ *n* 1 an infantryman armed with a musket 2 a member of a company of musketeers in the French royal household's personal troops in the 17th and 18th centuries

LITERARY LINK *The Three Musketeers*, a novel (1844) by French writer Alexandre Dumas. Set in France during the reign of Louis XIII, this historical romance tells the story of a young adventurer, D'Artagnan, who is taken under the wing of three musketeers, Athos, Porthos, and Aramis. The four become embroiled in a series of adventures involving love, politics, swordsmanship, and the machinations of the evil Cardinal Richelieu.

musketry /múskitri/ *n* 1 a group of muskets or musketeers 2 the technique or practice of using small arms

Muskhogean *n, adj* LANG = Muskogean

musk mallow *n* a plant of the mallow family with a hairy and often purple-spotted stem and a slight musky scent. Flowers: pink. Native to: Europe, North Africa. *Malva moschata.*

muskmelon /músk mellǝn/ *n* 1 a fruit with a ribbed or rough rind and white, yellow, or green flesh with a sweet full flavour and a pleasant, slightly musky, smell 2 a trailing vine that bears muskmelon. *Cucumis melo.*

Muskogean /mus kógi ǝn/, **Muskhogean** *n* a Hokan-Siouan branch of languages, including Chickasaw, Choctaw, and Creek —**Muskogean** *adj*

Muskogee /mus kógi/ (*plural* -**gee** or -**gees**) *n* a member of a Native North American people who lived in SE North America [Late 18C. < Creek *ma:skó:ki.*]

musk orchid *n* a small orchid. Flowers: musk-scented, greenish-yellow, in dense spikes. Native to: Europe, Asia. *Herminium monorchis.*

musk ox *n* a large wild ox with a black or brown shaggy coat and flat downward-curving horns. Native to: N Canada, Greenland. *Ovibos moschatus.*

muskrat /músk rat/ (*plural* -**rats** or -**rat**) *n* 1 a large amphibious rodent, closely related to the vole and the lemming, with a thick brown coat and musk glands. Native to: North America, Europe. *Ondatra zibethica.* 2 the fur of the muskrat [Early 17C. < Algonquian *muscasus* 'it is red' (from the animal's colour), by association with MUSK and RAT.]

musk rose *n* a rose that is widely cultivated for its musk-scented flowers. Native to: the Mediterranean. *Rosa moschata.*

musk thistle *n* a thistle with leaves divided into narrow spine-tipped lobes. Flowers: single, drooping, reddish-purple. Native to: temperate regions of Europe and Asia. *Carduus nutans.*

musk turtle *n* a small freshwater turtle that gives off a pungent smell. Native to: E United States, Canada. Genus: *Sternotherus.*

musky /múski/ (-**ier**, -**iest**) *adj* with a sweet pungent smell similar to that of musk —**muskily** *adv* —**muskiness** *n*

~~musle~~ incorrect spelling of **muscle**

Muslim /moōzlǝm/ *n* a person whose religion is Islam ■ *adj* relating to the followers of Islam or to areas, cultures, or activities in which followers of Islam are especially numerous [Early 17C. < Arabic 'somebody who surrenders (to God)', (see MOUSSELINE) of '*aslama* (see ISLAM).] —**Muslimism** *n*

Muslim Brotherhood *n* an Egyptian nationalist movement founded by Hasan al-Bannah in 1928 that is committed to the Islamic fundamentalist cause and opposes Western influence

Muslim League *n* a Muslim political organization founded in India in 1906 that was instrumental in achieving the creation of Pakistan in 1947

muslin /múzlin/ *n* a thin plain-weave cotton cloth. Use: curtains, sheets, dresses. [Early 17C. Via French *mousseline* < Italian *mussolina*, < Arabic *mawsiliy* 'of Mosul', Iraqi city.]

MusM *abbr* Master of Music [Latin *Musicae Magister*]

muso /myoōzō/ (*plural* -**sos**) *n* (*informal*) 1 a musician, especially in a pop group, who pays too much attention to technique 2 Aus somebody who plays a musical instrument [Mid-20C. Shortening of MUSICIAN.]

musquash /múss kwosh/ *n* ZOOL = muskrat [Early 17C. < W Abenaki *mòskwas.*]

muss /muss/ *vt* US to make something, especially somebody's hair or clothes, untidy or ruffled (*informal*) ■ *n* US a state of untidiness or disorder (*informal*) [Mid-19C. Probably variant of MESS.]

mussel /múss'l/ *n* 1 an edible marine bivalve mollusc with a blue-black shell that lives attached to objects in the sea. *Mytilus edulis.* 2 a freshwater bivalve mollusc whose shell is a source of mother of pearl. Family: Unionidae. [Pre-12C. < assumed Vulgar Latin *muscula*, alteration of Latin *musculus* 'small mouse' (see MUSCLE); from the mussel's supposed resemblance in shape and colour to a mouse.]

SPELLCHECK See ***muscle.***

Mussolini /mŏŏssə leéni/, **Benito** (1883–1945) Italian fascist leader. Known as **Il Duce**

Mussulman /múss'lmən/ (*plural* **-men** /-mən/ or **-mans**) *n* a Muslim (*archaic literary*) [Late 16C. < Persian *musulmān* 'Muslim' (adjective) < Arabic *muslim* (see MUSLIM).]

mussy /mússi/ (**mussier, mussiest**) *adj US* not tidy or in an orderly state (*informal*) —**mussily** *adv* —**mussiness** *n*

must[1] (*stressed*) /must/; (*unstressed*) /məst, məss/ (**must,** *plural* **musts**) CORE MEANING: a modal verb indicating that somebody is compelled to do something because of a rule or law, or that it is necessary or advisable to do something ○ *Accidents causing injury must be reported immediately.* ○ *Employment decisions must be based on ability.* ○ *We must improve our schools.* ○ *You must give him a chance to state his case.*

1 *v* **BE COMPELLED** to be compelled to do something because of a rule or law ○ *You must stop when the light is red.* ○ *All guests must vacate their rooms by 12 noon.* **2** *v* **BE NECESSARY** to be important or necessary to do something ○ *Henceforth, he said, the central organizing principle of all governments must be the environment.* ○ *Health care insurance must be affordable.* **3** *v* **BE CERTAIN** indicates that somebody is sure that something is the case ○ *This must seem strange to you.* ○ *Those must be your footprints in the garden.* **4** *v* **INDICATES BELIEF** indicates that somebody concludes that something is the case, based on the available evidence ○ *Palaeontologists know that primates must have immigrated to South America sometime before 28 million years ago.* **5** *v* **INTEND** to intend or be determined to do something ○ *I must be going.* ○ *I must telephone my brother.* **6** *v* **USED TO MAKE SUGGESTIONS** used to make suggestions or invitations or to give advice ○ *You must see a doctor.* ○ *You must come round for dinner one evening.* **7** *n* **SOMETHING ESSENTIAL** something that is essential or obligatory ○ *Formal attire is a must at a state dinner.* [Old English *mōste*, past tense of assumed *mōtan* 'have to, be able to' < Germanic]

must[2] /must/ *n* the juice from grapes or other fruit that is to be fermented into wine [Pre-12C. < Latin *mustum*, form of *mustus* 'new, fresh'.]

must[3] /must/ *n* the condition of being musty or mouldy [Early 17C. Back-formation < MUSTY.]

must[4] *n* = **musth**

mustache *n* US = **moustache**

mustachio /mə staáshi ō/ (*plural* **-chios**) *n* a moustache that is thick or trimmed into a fancy shape (*archaic or humorous; often plural*) [Mid-16C. Blend of Spanish *mostacho* + Italian *mostaccio* (see MOUSTACHE).] —**mustachioed** *adj*

mustang /mús tang/ *n* a small hardy wild horse living on the plains of North America, descended from Arab horses brought to the continent by Spanish soldiers [Early 19C. Via Mexican Spanish *mestengo* < Spanish, 'ownerless' < *mesta* 'ranchers who appropriated wild cattle' < Latin *mixta* 'mixed'.]

mustard /mústərd/ *n* **1 SPICY CONDIMENT** powdered seeds of a brassica plant, or a hot spicy paste made from these, or sometimes whole seeds, water, and other ingredients, eaten in small quantities as a condiment **2 PLANT WITH PUNGENT SEEDS** a plant with long thin seed pods containing mustard seeds. Flowers: small, yellow. Genus: *Brassica.* **3** *US* **ENTHUSIASM** enthusiasm or zest (*informal*) **4 DARK YELLOW COLOUR** a dark brownish-yellow colour, like that of mustard [12C. < Old French *mo(u)starde* < Latin *mustum* 'must, new wine' (originally mixed with the crushed seeds).] —**mustard** *adj* —**mustardy** *adj* ◇ **cut the mustard** to be up to the desired standard of performance, ability, or quality (*informal*)

mustard and cress *n* a salad of seedlings of white mustard and garden cress, cultivated indoors in small containers

mustard gas *n* $(CH_2CLCH_2)_2S$ an oily liquid that evaporates to a poison gas [Because its smell resembles mustard]

mustard oil *n* an oil obtained from mustard seeds that is used in making soap

mustard plaster *n* a paste made from black mustard seeds and applied to the skin. Use: formerly, to stimulate blood flow and counter inflammation.

musteline /músti līn, -lin/ *adj* belonging to, relating to, or typical of the group of mammals that includes weasels, otters, badgers, and skunks. Family: Mustelidae. [Mid-17C. < Latin *mustelinus* < *mustel* 'weasel'.]

muster /mústər/ *v* **1** *vti* **ASSEMBLE PEOPLE** to bring together a group of soldiers or the members of a crew for a particular reason, e.g. inspection, or assemble in this way **2** *vt* **GATHER PEOPLE OR THINGS** to gather people or things together for a particular reason **3** *vt* **CALL UP** to summon up something such as strength or courage that will help in doing something **4** *vt ANZ* **ROUND UP LIVESTOCK** to round up animals, especially cattle or sheep ■ *n* **1 MILITARY ASSEMBLY** a gathering of soldiers or a crew for a particular reason, e.g. inspection **2** MIL = **muster roll** **3** *ANZ* **ROUNDUP OF ANIMALS** a roundup of animals, especially cattle or sheep **4 GATHERING OR COLLECTION** any gathering of people or collection of things [14C. Via Old French *mo(u)strer* 'to show', *moustre* 'showing' < Latin *monstrare* < *monstrum* '(evil) omen, sign'.] ◇ **pass muster** to measure up to set standards or to expectations

muster in *vti US* to enrol somebody or be enrolled for military service

muster out *vti US* to discharge somebody, or be discharged, from military service

muster roll *n* a list of the members of a military or naval unit

musth /must/, **must** *n* a state of increased sexual activity, accompanied by aggression, in large male land mammals, especially male elephants, lasting 2 to 3 months [Late 19C. Via Urdu *mast* < Persian, 'drunk, intoxicated'.]

must-have *n* something that is considered to be essential (*often before nouns*) ○ *a list of this year's must-have accessories*

Mustique /mu steék, mŏŏ-/ island in St Vincent and the Grenadines, in the E Caribbean Sea, one of the Windward Islands

mustn't /múss'nt/ *contr* must not ○ *You mustn't worry.*

must-see *n* something such as a place, film, or work of art that is considered so important, beautiful, or excellent that everyone should see it (*often before nouns*)

musty /músti/ (**-ier, -iest**) *adj* **1 WITH OLD DAMP SMELL** smelling old, damp, and stale because of not having been used or exposed to fresh air for a long time **2 STALE** tasting old, stale, and mouldy **3 OUTDATED AND UNINTERESTING** no longer relevant or interesting because of being old-fashioned [Early 16C. < ?] —**mustily** *adv* —**mustiness** *n*

Muswellbrook /mússəl brŏŏk/ town in E New South Wales, Australia. Population: 10,156 (1991).

mutable /myŏŏtəb'l/ *adj* **1 CHANGEABLE** tending or likely to change **2 CAPABLE OF CHANGE** capable of changing, or subject to change **3 TENDING TO UNDERGO MUTATION** describes a gene or organism that has a tendency to undergo mutation **4 OF GEMINI, VIRGO, SAGITTARIUS, AND PISCES** describes the signs of the zodiac Gemini, Virgo, Sagittarius, and Pisces, thought to be characterized by adaptability. ◊ **cardinal, fixed** [14C. < Latin *mutabilis* < *mutare* 'to change'.] —**mutability** /myŏŏtə bíllәti/ *n* —**mutableness** *n* —**mutably** *adv*

mutagen /myŏŏtəjən/ *n* an external agent, e.g. radiation or some chemicals or viruses, that increases the rate of mutation of cells or organisms [Mid-20C. < MUTATION + -GEN.] —**mutagenic** /myŏŏtə jénnik/ *adj* —**mutagenically** *adv* —**mutagenicity** /myŏŏtəjə níssəti/ *n* —**mutagenesis** /myŏŏtə jénnəssiss/ *n*

mutant /myŏŏt'nt/ *n* **1 SOMETHING THAT HAS MUTATED** an animal, organism, cell, or gene that has mutated **2 ODD-LOOKING PERSON** an offensive term for a person who looks or appears strange (*slang insult*) **3 ODD THING** a strange-looking thing or animal ■ *adj* **1 RESULTING FROM MUTATION** undergoing or resulting from genetic mutation **2 APPEARING STRANGE** with an odd appearance or other qualities regarded as strange (*slang*) [Early 20C. < Latin *mutant-*, present participle of *mutare* 'to change'.]

Mutare /moo taári/ capital of Manicaland Province, east-central Zimbabwe. Population: 131,367 (1992).

mutase /myŏŏ tayz/ *n* an enzyme that promotes a change in the shape of a molecule [Early 20C. < Latin *mutare* 'to change'.]

mutate /myoo táyt/ (**-tates, -tating, -tated**) *vti* to undergo or make something undergo mutation [Mid-18C. Partly back-formation < MUTATION; partly < Latin *mutat-*, past participle of *mutare* 'to change'.] —**mutative** /myŏŏtətiv, myoo táytiv/ *adj*

mutation /myoo táysh'n/ *n* **1 CHANGE IN GENETIC MATERIAL** a random change in a gene or chromosome resulting in a new trait or characteristic that can be inherited **2** BIOL = **mutant** *n.* **1** **3 ALTERATION** the action or process of changing something or of being changed **4** LING = **umlaut** *n.* **1** **5 PHONETIC CHANGE** a phonetic change found in Celtic languages in which the initial consonant of a word changes according to the preceding word —**mutational** *adj* —**mutationally** *adv*

mutation stop *n* a stop that controls a set of organ pipes that do not play the tones of the written notes but usually a fifth or third above them

mutatis mutandis /moo taátiss moo tandiss/ *adv* with the necessary changes having been made [< Latin]

Mutazilite /moo taázi līt/ *n* a member of an ancient Muslim religious group who subsequently became part of the Shia group [Early 18C. < Arabic, 'those who keep to themselves'.]

mute /myoot/ *adj* **1 UNABLE TO SPEAK** unwilling or unable to speak **2 MAKING NO SOUND** saying nothing, or making no sound **3 NOT EXPRESSED IN WORDS** felt or expressed without speech **4 REFUSING TO ANSWER CHARGE** refusing to answer a charge brought in a court of law **5** PHON = **plosive** *adj.* **6 NOT PRONOUNCED** not pronounced, like the final 'e' in 'cheese' ■ *n* **1 OFFENSIVE TERM** an offensive term for somebody who is unable or unwilling to speak (*dated*) **2 SOMEBODY REFUSING TO ANSWER CHARGE** a person who refuses to answer a charge in a court of law **3** PHON = **plosive** *n.* **4 SILENT LETTER** a letter that is not pronounced **5 DEVICE TO ALTER INSTRUMENT'S TONE** a pad, clip, or other device used to reduce or alter in some way the tone of a brass or stringed instrument **6 HIRED MOURNER** a person who was formerly paid to act as a mourner at a funeral ■ *vt* (**mutes, muting, muted**) **1 TURN DOWN SOUND** to moderate the volume of a sound **2 MAKE SOMETHING LESS BRIGHT** to make a colour or light less bright or harsh **3 ALTER INSTRUMENT'S TONE** to reduce or alter in some way the tone of a brass or stringed instrument using a pad, clip, or other device [14C. < French *muet* 'slightly mute' < Old French *mu* < Latin *mutus.*] —**mutely** *adv* —**muteness** *n*

muted /myŏŏtid/ *adj* **1 NOT BRIGHT OR INTENSE** not bright, intense, or harsh in colour or tone **2 NOT LOUD** not loud or distinct enough to be heard clearly **3 UNDERSTATED** subdued and understated rather than forceful or enthusiastic **4 MADE BY INSTRUMENT FITTED WITH MUTE** fitted with a mute, or produced by an instrument fitted with a mute —**mutedly** *adv*

mute swan *n* a large white swan with an orange bill. Native to: Europe, Asia. *Cygnus olor.*

muti /mŏŏti/ *n S Africa* medicine, in particular herbal medicine [Late 19C. < Zulu *umuthi* 'tree, plant'.]

mutilate /myŏŏti layt/ (**-lates, -lating, -lated**) *vt* **1 REMOVE OR DESTROY BODY PART** to inflict serious injury on a person or animal or part of somebody or something's body by removing or destroying parts of it **2 RUIN BY REMOVING PARTS** to damage or spoil something such as a piece of writing or a film by removing important parts of it **3 DAMAGE SERIOUSLY** to inflict serious damage on something [Mid-16C. Partly < Latin *mutilat-*, past participle of *mutilare* 'cut or lop off' < *mutilus* 'maimed'; partly < obsolete *mutilate* 'mutilated'.] —**mutilation** /myŏŏti láysh'n/ *n* —**mutilative** *adj* —**mutilator** *n*

mutineer /myŏŏti neér/ *n* somebody who rebels against the legal authority of others, especially a soldier or sailor [Early 17C. < French *mutinier* < Old French *mutin* 'rebellious' (see MUTINY).]

mutinous /myŏŏtinəss/ *adj* **1** plotting, participating in, or typical of a mutiny **2** refusing to obey or submit to control, especially military control [Late 16C. < Old French *mutineus* < *mutin* 'rebellious' (see MUTINY), or < English *mutine.*] —**mutinously** *adv* —**mutinousness** *n*

mutiny /myŏŏtəni/ *n* (*plural* **-nies**) a rebellion against legal authority, especially by soldiers or sailors refusing to obey orders and, often, attacking their officers ■ *vi* (**-nies, -nying, -nied**) to take part in a rebellion against legal authority [Mid-16C. Via obsolete *mutine* 'rebellion' < French *mutiner* < Old French *mutin* 'rebellious' < *muete* 'revolt', via assumed Vulgar Latin *movitus* < Latin *motus* 'moved'.]

mutism /myŏŏtizəm/ *n* **1** an offensive term for the inability to speak (*dated*) **2** a refusal to speak either at all times or at some, which may indicate trauma or stress

muton /myŏŏt on/ *n* the smallest known unit of DNA in which mutation can take place, either spontaneously or caused by an external agent [Mid-20C. < MUTATION.]

mutt /mut/ *n* **1** a dog that is of mixed or unknown breed (*slang*) **2** an offensive term that deliberately insults somebody's intelligence or knowledge (*slang insult*) [Late 19C. Shortening of MUTTONHEAD.]

mutter /múttər/ v 1 *vti* SAY SOMETHING QUIETLY to speak or say something quietly and indistinctly 2 *vi* GRUMBLE to say something in a quiet voice, especially as a complaint or in annoyance ■ *n* SOMETHING SAID QUIETLY an act of saying something quietly and indistinctly, or something said in this way [14C. < ?]

mutton /múttʼn/ *n* the flesh of a fully grown sheep, eaten as food [13C. Directly or via Old French *molton* 'ram, wether, sheep' < medieval Latin *multon-*.] —**mutton dressed as lamb** an offensive term for a woman who dresses or behaves in a way considered to be more suitable for a younger one

mutton bird *n* a seabird of the shearwater family, traditionally hunted by the Maori for food. Native to: Australasia. family: procellaridae. [Because its cooked flesh is said to resemble mutton]

muttonchops /múttʼn chops/ *npl* facial hair trimmed into a narrow strip beside each ear, broadening out along the lower cheek and stopping at the side of the chin, which is kept bare [< the shape]

muttonhead /múttʼn hed/ *n* an offensive term that deliberately insults somebody's intelligence or knowledge (*dated insult*) —**muttonheaded** *adj*

mutual /myoōchoo əl/ *adj* 1 FELT AND EXPRESSED BY EACH done, felt, or expressed by each towards or with regard to the other 2 WITH SAME FEELINGS OR RELATIONSHIP with the same feelings, or in the same relationship to each other 3 SHARED BY TWO PEOPLE OR GROUPS shared by or common to two or more people or groups 4 OF MUTUAL INSURANCE relating to mutual insurance [15C. < French *mutuel* < Latin *mutuus* 'borrowed, reciprocal, done in exchange'.] —**mutuality** /myoōchoo álləti/ *n* —**mutually** *adv* —**mutualness** *n*

mutual assured destruction *n* the enormous reciprocal damage that the superpowers and their allies would inflict on each other in the event of a nuclear war

mutual fund *n US* FIN = unit trust

mutual inductance *n* (*symbol* **M**) a measure of the change in the electromotive force of a circuit caused by a change in the current flowing through an associated circuit

mutual induction *n* the production of an electromotive force in a circuit resulting from a change in the current flowing through another circuit to which it is magnetically linked

mutual insurance *n* a method of insurance in which the customers buying policies own the company, pay premiums into a common fund to cover claims, and share in the profits

mutualise *vti* = mutualize

mutualism /myoōchoo əlizəm/ *n* a relationship between two organisms of different species that benefits both and harms neither —**mutualist** *n* —**mutualistic** /myoōchoo ə lístik/ *adj*

mutualize /myoōchoo ə līz/ (**-izes, -izing, -ized**), **mutualise** (**-ises, -ising, -ised**) *vti* to become mutual, or make something mutual —**mutualization** /myoōchoo ə lī záyshʼn/ *n*

mutual savings bank *n* a bank without shareholders in which the depositors are technically the owners

mutuel /myoōtyoo əl/ *n US* GAMBLING = pari-mutuel [Early 20C. Shortening.]

mutule /myoō tyool/ *n* a projecting block that holds a conical ornament (**gutta**) under a Doric cornice [Mid-17C. Via French < Latin *mutulus*.]

muumuu /moō moo/ (*plural* **-muus**), **mumu** (*plural* **-mus**) *n* a loose shapeless Hawaiian dress made of brightly coloured fabric [Early 20C. < Hawaiian *mu'u mu'u* 'cut off' (because there was originally no yoke).]

⚡**mux** /muks/ *n* a multiplexer (*informal*) [Late 20C. Contraction.]

Muzak /myoō zak/ *tdmk* a trademark for recorded background music played in shops, restaurants, lifts, and other public places

muzhik /moo zhík/ *n* a Russian peasant, especially during the tsarist era [Mid-16C. < Russian, 'small man' < *muzh* 'man, husband'.]

Muzorewa /moōzzə ráywə/, **Abel Tendekayi** (*b.* 1925) Zimbabwean cleric and statesman

muzzle /múzzʼl/ *n* 1 ANIMAL'S NOSE AND JAWS the projecting part of an animal's face, made up of its nose and jaws 2 RESTRAINING DEVICE FOR ANIMAL a device that is strapped over the nose and jaws of an animal to prevent it from opening its mouth, e.g. to bite, bark, or eat 3 END OF GUN BARREL the front open end of the barrel of a firearm 4 SOMETHING THAT PREVENTS FREE EXPRESSION something that is meant to prevent free expression ■ *vt* (**-zles, -zling, -zled**) 1 PUT MUZZLE ON ANIMAL to put a muzzle over the nose and jaws of an animal 2 PREVENT SOMEBODY'S FREE EXPRESSION to prevent a person or group from publicly expressing particular views or opinions 3 TAKE IN SAIL to roll up and secure a sail [14C. < Old French *musel* 'small muzzle' < *muse* 'muzzle'.] —**muzzler** *n*

muzzleloader /múzzʼl lōdər/ *n* a firearm that is loaded through its muzzle

muzzle velocity *n* the speed of a bullet or other projectile as it leaves the muzzle of a firearm

muzzy /múzzi/ (**-zier, -ziest**) *adj* 1 thinking in a confused way, especially as a result of illness or drinking alcohol 2 vague and confused [Early 18C. < ?] —**muzzily** *adv* —**muzziness** *n*

⚡**MV** *abbr* 1 Maldives (*in Internet addresses*) 2 mezza voce

mV *abbr* millivolt

MV *abbr* 1 megavolt 2 merchant vessel 3 motor vessel 4 muzzle velocity

m.v. *abbr* 1 market value 2 mean variation

MVD *n* the Ministry for Internal Affairs in the former Soviet Union from 1946 to 1960, acting as secret police. Full form **Ministerstvo vnutrennikh dyel**

MVO *abbr* Member of the Royal Victorian Order

⚡**mw** *abbr* Malawi (*in Internet addresses*)

mW *abbr* milliwatt

MW *abbr* 1 medium wave 2 megawatt 3 molecular weight

mwah mwah /mwaà mwaà/, **muah muah** *n* used as a humorous representation of the sound of ritual social kissing, which does not involve physical contact

⚡**mx** *abbr* Mexico (*in Internet addresses*)

Mx *abbr* maxwell

my[1] /mī/ *det* belonging or relating to the speaker (*first person possessive determiner*) ○ *You can borrow my car.* ○ *I always keep my promises.* ■ *interj* used to express sudden emotion such as surprise, fright, concern, or pleasure ○ *My! What a mess!* [12C. Shortening of MINE[2], originally only before consonants other than 'h'.]

⚡**my**[2] *abbr* 1 Malaysia (*in Internet addresses*) 2 million years

MY *abbr* motor yacht

my- *prefix* = myo- (*before vowels*)

myalgia /mī álji ə/ *n* pain or tenderness in a muscle or group of muscles —**myalgic** *adj*

myalgic encephalomyelitis /mī áljik-/ *n* full form of ME[1]

myalism /mī əlizəm/ *n* witchcraft practised in the Caribbean [Mid-19C. < *myal* 'myalism' < ?] —**myalist** *n*

Myall Lake /mī əl-/ coastal lake in E New South Wales, Australia. Area: 310 sq. km/120 sq. mi.

Myanmar

Myanmar /mee ən maar/ republic in Southeast Asia, formerly Burma. Capital: Yangon. Population: 45,570,000 (1996). Area: 676,552 sq. km/261,218 sq. mi.

myasthenia /mī əss theeni ə/, **myasthenia gravis** /-graàviss/ *n* an autoimmune disease characterized by chronic muscle weakness —**myasthenic** /-thénnik/ *adj*

my bad *interj US* used to apologize for a mistake (*slang*) ○ *Whoops, my bad! You were right after all.*

mycelium /mī seeli əm/ (*plural* **-a** /-li ə/) *n* a loose network of the delicate filaments (**hyphae**) that form the body of a fungus, consisting of the feeding and reproducing hyphae [Mid-19C. < modern Latin, < Greek *mukēs* 'fungus' after *epithelium* (see EPITHELIUM).] —**mycelial** *adj* —**myceloid** /mīssə loyd/ *adj*

Mycenae /mī see nee/ ancient Greek city in the Peloponnese that was a centre of Bronze Age culture until its destruction around 1100 BC —**Mycenaean** *n, adj*

mycet- *prefix* = myceto- (*before vowels*)

-mycete *suffix* a fungus [Via modern Latin *-mycetes* < Greek *mukētes*, plural of *mukēs* 'fungus']

myceto- *prefix* fungus, fungi ○ *mycetophagous* [Via modern Latin < Greek *mukēt-*, stem of *mukēs*]

mycetoma /mīssi tōmə/ (*plural* **-mas** *or* **-mata** /-mətə/) *n* an inflammation of tissues caused by a fungal or bacterial infection, usually of the feet or legs, which swell and develop pus-discharging nodules [Late 19C. < modern Latin, < Greek *mukēt-*, stem of *mukēs* 'fungus'.] —**mycetomatous** /-tómmətəss/ *adj*

-mycin *suffix* a substance derived from a bacterium ○ *streptomycin* [< MYCO- + -IN; because the bacteria were originally thought to be fungi]

myco- *prefix* fungus, fungi ○ *mycotoxin* [< Greek *mukēs* < Indo-European, 'slimy']

mycobacterium /mīkō bak teeri əm/ (*plural* **-a** /-ri ə/) *n* a rodlike Gram-positive aerobic bacterium that can form branching structures resembling filaments. Genus: *Mycobacterium*. —**mycobacterial** *adj*

mycology /mī kólləji/ *n* 1 STUDY OF FUNGI a branch of botany that specializes in the scientific study of fungi 2 FUNGI OF PARTICULAR AREA the fungi that live in a particular area 3 CHARACTERISTICS OF INDIVIDUAL FUNGUS the characteristics of a particular fungus —**mycologic** /mīkə lójjik/ *adj* —**mycological** *adj* —**mycologically** *adv* —**mycologist** *n*

mycophagist /mī kóffəjist/ *n* an animal that eats fungi [Mid-19C. < *mycophagy*.]

mycophagous /mī kóffəgəss/ *adj* feeding on fungi —**mycophagy** /-kóffəji/ *n*

mycoplasma /mīkō plázmə/ *n* a microorganism of a genus considered to be the smallest known living cells. Genus: *Mycoplasma*. —**mycoplasmal** *adj*

mycoprotein /mīkō prō teen/ *n* a food made from the heated, drained, and textured fermentation product of the fungus *Fusaria graminearum*, used as a meat substitute

mycorrhiza /mīkō rízə/ (*plural* **-zas** *or* **-zae** /-rí zee/), **mycorhiza** (*plural* **-zas** *or* **-zae**) *n* a mutually beneficial association of a fungus and the roots of a plant such as a conifer or an orchid, in which the plant's mineral absorption is enhanced and the fungus obtains nutrients [Late 19C. < modern Latin < *myco-* (see MYCO-) + Greek *rhiza* 'root'.] —**mycorrhizal** *adj*

mycosis /mī kóssiss/ (*plural* **-ses** /-seez/) *n* any disease or infection of human beings or animals caused by a fungus

mycotoxin /mīkō tóksin/ *n* a poisonous substance produced by a fungus. Mycotoxins may affect foods such as peanuts.

mycotrophic /mīkō tróffik, -tróffik/ *adj* describes a plant that lives in association with a fungus, as do various orchids in which the fungus lives on the roots

mydriasis /mī drí əssiss, mi-/ *n* excessive dilation of the pupils of the eye, usually caused by prolonged drug therapy, coma, or injury to the eye [Early 19C. Via Latin < Greek *mudriasis*.]

myel- *prefix* = myelo- (*before vowels*)

myelencephalon /mī ə len séffə lon/ *n* a part of the embryonic hindbrain formed by an extension of the spinal cord into the skull —**myelencephalic** /-mī ə len sə fállik/ *adj*

myelin /mī əlin/ *n* a whitish material made up of protein and fats that surrounds some nerve cells in concentric sheaths, insulating adjacent nerve fibres and enabling transmission of nerve impulses

myelinated /mī əli naytid/ *adj* describes nerve fibres that are surrounded by a sheath of myelin

myelin sheath *n* a layer of myelin that insulates some nerve cells. In multiple sclerosis, the myelin sheath is damaged and the nerve impulse is impaired.

myelitis /mī ə lītiss/ *n* inflammation of the spinal cord or bone marrow

myelo- *prefix* **1** bone marrow ○ *myelofibrosis* **2** spinal cord, spinal column ○ *myelencephalon* [Via modern Latin < Greek *muelos* 'marrow']

myeloblast /mī əlō blast/ *n* a cell that develops into a type of white blood cell (**granulocyte**) and that is normally seen only in the bone marrow where blood is formed —**myeloblastic** /mī əlō blástik/ *adj*

myelocyte /mī əlō sīt/ *n* an immature form of a type of white blood cell (**granulocyte**), normally found in the blood-forming tissue of the bone marrow —**myelocytic** /mī əlō síttik/ *adj*

myelofibrosis /mī əlō fī brṓssiss/ *n* a progressive disease in which the cells of the bone marrow that produce fibre rather than blood cells proliferate, leading to anaemia and enlargement of the spleen and liver —**myelofibrotic** /-fī bróttik/ *adj*

myelogenous /mī ə lójjənəss/, **myelogenic** /mī əlō jénnik/ *adj* originating in or produced by the bone marrow

myelogenous leukaemia *n* MED = **myeloid leukaemia**

myelogram /mī əlō gram, mī éllō-/ *n* a radiographic image created by injecting an X-ray-opaque liquid into the spinal cord, to diagnose disorders of the spine including slipped discs or tumours —**myelography** /mī ə lóggrəfi/ *n*

myeloid /mī ə loyd/ *adj* relating to, involving, or derived from bone marrow or the spinal cord

myeloid leukaemia *n* a variety of leukaemia in which some types of white blood cells, originating in the myeloid tissue of the bone marrow, proliferate and suppress healthy red and white blood cells

myeloma /mī ə lṓmə/ (*plural* **-mas** *or* **-mata** /-mətə/) *n* a malignant tumour that develops in the cells of the bone marrow that produce blood cells —**myelomatoid** *adj*

Myer /mī ər/, **Sidney Baevski** (1878–1934) Russian-born Australian retailer. Born **Simcha Baevski Myer**

myiasis /mī əssiss/ (*plural* **-ses** /-seez/) *n* an infestation of living tissue or an organism by maggots such as fly larvae [Mid-19C. < modern Latin, < Greek *muia* 'fly'.]

My Lai /mī lī, mee-/ village in Vietnam that was the site of a massacre of civilians by US troops in 1968 during the Vietnam War

mylonite /mílə nīt, míllə-/ *n* a fine-grained layered metamorphic rock, formed where the movement of rocks against each other causes crushing and grinding [Late 19C. < Greek *mulōn* 'mill'.]

mynah /mínə/, **mynah bird, myna** *n* a medium-sized bird of the starling family, some varieties of which are known for their ability to mimic human speech. Native to: Southeast Asia, Australia. Genera: *Acridotheres* and *Gracula*. [Mid-18C. < Hindi *mainā*.]

Mynheer /mə neer/ *n* **1** a title used to address a Dutch man, equivalent to 'Mr' when used before a surname and to 'sir' when used alone **2 Mynheer, mynheer** a Dutchman (*informal*) [Mid-17C. < Dutch *mijnheer* 'my lord' < *heer* 'lord, master'.]

myo- *prefix* muscle ○ *myofibril* [Via modern Latin < Greek *mus* < Indo-European, 'mouse']

myocardial /mī ō kaárdi əl/ *adj* relating to or affecting the thick muscular wall of the heart [Late 19C. < MYOCARDIUM.]

myocardial infarction *n* the death of a segment of heart muscle, caused by a blood clot in the coronary artery interrupting blood supply

myocarditis /mī ō kaar dítiss/ *n* acute or chronic inflammation of the heart muscle

myocardium /mī ō kaárdi əm/ (*plural* **-a** /-di ə/) *n* the thick muscular wall of the heart [Late 19C. < MYO- after PERICARDIUM.]

myoclonus /mī óklənəss/ *n* a sudden muscular contraction, or a series of these, that usually indicates a disorder of the nervous system if experienced persistently —**myoclonic** /mī ō klónnik/ *adj*

myoelectric /mī ō i léktrik/, **myoelectrical** /-trik'l/ *adj* **1** relating to or involving the electrical properties of muscle **2** using the detection of electrical impulses in muscle to activate a bionic part such as an artificial limb

myofascial release /mīō fáysh'l-/ *n* a form of gentle massage involving the stretching and manipulation of the tough connective tissue (**fascia**) that surrounds the body

myofibril /mī ō fíbril/ *n* a structure resembling a thread running through a muscle cell that enables the muscle to contract

myofilament /mī ō fílləmənt/ *n* any one of the filaments that make up a myofibril, either the thicker filaments composed of the protein myosin or the thinner filaments composed of the proteins actin or troponin

myogenic /mī ō jénnik/ *adj* originating in or able to form in muscle cells, as are the contractions of heart muscle fibres that are spontaneous and do not depend on nerve stimulation

myoglobin /mī ō glṓbin/ *n* an iron-containing protein resembling haemoglobin, found in muscle cells, that takes oxygen from the blood, releasing it to the muscles during strenuous exercise

myograph /mī ə graaf, -graf/ *n* an instrument that produces a tracing corresponding to muscle contractions —**myographic** /mī ə gráffik/ *adj* —**myographically** *adv*

myology /mī ólləji/ *n* the study of the structure, function, and diseases of muscle [Mid-17C. Directly or via French *myologie* < modern Latin *myologia* < *myo-* (see MYO-) + *-logia* (see -LOGY).] —**myologic** /mī ə lójjik/ *adj* —**myologist** *n*

myoma /mī ṓmə/ (*plural* **-mas** *or* **-mata** /-mətə/) *n* a benign tumour of the muscle tissue —**myomatous** *adj*

myometrium /mī ō meétri əm/ *n* the muscle wall of the womb [Early 20C. < MYO- + Greek *mētra* 'womb'.]

myoneural /mī ō nyóorəl/ *adj* relating to or involving both muscles and nerves

myopathy /mī óppəthi/ (*plural* **-thies**) *n* any disease of the muscles or muscle tissues, either inherited like muscular dystrophy or acquired like polio —**myopathic** /mī ə páthik/ *adj*

myope /mī ōp/ *n* somebody affected by myopia [Early 18C. Via French < Latin *myop-*, stem of *myops* 'short-sighted' < Greek *muōps* (see MYOPIA).]

myopia /mī ṓpi ə/ *n* **1** a common condition in which light entering the eye is focused in front of the retina and distant objects cannot be seen sharply **2** lack of foresight or long-term planning [Early 18C. Via modern Latin < late Greek *muōpia* < Greek *muōps* 'short-sighted' < *muein* 'blink'.]

myopic /mī óppik/ *adj* **1** affected by myopia **2** showing a lack of foresight or long-term planning —**myopically** *adv*

myosin /mī əssin/ *n* a protein in muscles that helps them contract [Mid-19C. < MYO- + -OSE[2].]

myosis *n* MED = **miosis**

myositis /mī ə sítiss/ *n* muscle inflammation and soreness [Early 19C. < modern Latin, < Greek *muos*, form of *mus* 'mouse, muscle'.]

myosotis /mī ə sṓtiss/ (*plural* **-tes**), **myosote** /mī ə sōt/ *n* a plant of the borage family with hairy leaves and stems, e.g. the forget-me-not. Flowers: small, pink at first and then blue. Genus: *Myosotis*. [Early 17C. Via modern Latin < Latin, 'mouse-ear (a plant)' < Greek *muōsotis* < *mus* 'mouse, muscle' + *ous* 'ear'.]

myotome /mī ə tōm/ *n* **1** any cell in early embryos that gives rise to muscle in the body **2** a muscle that is supplied by a nerve of the spine

myotonia /mī ə tṓni ə/ *n* a muscle condition that results in the muscles maintaining contractions for much longer than normal and having difficulty in relaxing [Late 19C. < modern Latin, < *myo-* (see MYO-) + Greek *tonos* 'tone'.] —**myotonic** /-tónnik/ *adj*

myriad /mírri əd/ *adj* **1 TOO NUMEROUS TO COUNT** so many that they cannot be counted **2 OF MANY DIFFERENT ELEMENTS** made up of many different elements ■ *n* **1 LARGE NUMBER** a huge number **2 TEN THOUSAND** ten thousand (*archaic*) [Mid-16C. Directly or via Old French < late Latin *myriad-* < Greek *muriad-* < *murios* 'countless'.]

myriapod /mírri ə pod/ *n* an arthropod such as a centipede or millipede with a head, a long segmented body, and at least nine pairs of legs. Class: Myriapoda. [Early 19C. < modern Latin *Myriapoda* 'with a myriad of feet' < Greek *murias* 'myriad'.]

myrica /mi ríkə/ *n* a tonic made from the root bark of the bayberry tree. Use: treatment of diarrhoea. [Early 18C. Via Latin, 'tamarisk' < Greek *murikē*.]

myristic acid /mi rístik-/ *n* a fatty acid found in plants and animals. Use: soap manufacture, flavourings, cosmetics, perfumes. [< modern Latin *Myristica* (genus name of trees) < medieval Latin *(nux) myristica* 'nutmeg' < Greek *murizein* 'anoint']

myrmecology /múrmi kólləji/ *n* the scientific study of ants [Late 19C. < Greek *murmēk-* 'ant'.] —**myrmecologic** /múrmikə lójjik/ *adj* —**myrmecologist** *n*

myrmidon /múrmidən, -don/ *n* a faithful follower who obeys orders unquestioningly [Mid-17C. < MYRMIDON.]

Myrmidon *n* in Greek mythology, a member of a legendary people who lived in Thessaly and were led by Achilles in the Trojan War [15C. Via Latin *Myrmidones* (plural) < Greek *Murmidones* < *murmēkes* 'ants', (from which they were created, according to legend).]

myrobalan /mī róbbələn, mi-/ *n* **1** the dried fruit of a tropical bush that resembles a plum. Use: dyeing, making ink. **2** = **cherry plum** [Mid-16C. Directly or via French < Latin *myrobalanum* < Greek *murobalanon* < *muron* 'balsam, ointment' + *balanos* 'acorn'.]

myrrh /mur/ *n* **1** an aromatic resinous gum obtained from various trees and shrubs that are native to Africa and S Asia. Use: in perfume, incense, and medicinal preparations. **2** PLANT SCI = **sweet cicely** *n*. **2** [Pre-12C. Via Latin *myrrha* < Greek *murra* < Semitic.]

myrtle /múrt'l/ *n* a commonly cultivated evergreen shrub with blue-black fruit. Flowers: fragrant, white or pink. Native to: Mediterranean region, W Asia. *Myrtus communis*. [14C. Directly or via Old French < medieval Latin *myrtilla* 'small myrtle tree' < Latin *myrtus* 'myrtle tree' < Greek *murtos* < Semitic.]

Myrtle Beach /múrt'l-/ city in E South Carolina. Population: 25,456 (1996).

myself /mī sélf/ *pron* **1 REFERS BACK TO SPEAKER** refers to the speaker or writer (*first person reflexive pronoun, used when the object of a verb or preposition refers to the same person as the subject of the verb*) ○ *I didn't enjoy myself very much.* ○ *Of all the people I am hard on, I am hardest on myself.* **2 REFERS EMPHATICALLY TO SPEAKER** refers emphatically to the speaker or writer ○ *I'm curious about that myself.* ○ *I can't expect you to be able to read my writing; I myself can't read it.* **3 MY NORMAL SELF** my normal or usual self ○ *I haven't been myself since the accident.* [Old English *mēseolf* 'me self' (*self* in the obsolete sense of 'same')]

USAGE The use of ***myself*** and other *-self* pronouns (reflexive pronouns) when they do not refer to the subjects of sentences is not appropriate in formal contexts. Write: *The team coach chose Sarah and me* [not *myself*]. Yet another problem is the use of ***myself*** in sentences like these: *On behalf of my wife and myself, I want to thank you for your support. My wife and myself are pleased to have served you* instead of *My wife and I want to thank you for your support.* In the second sentence ***myself***, in the objective, or object, case, cannot form part of a compound subject. The writer should have used *My wife and I are pleased to have served you.*

Mysore /mī sáwr/ city on the western coast of S India. Population: 480,006 (1991).

mystagogue /místə gog/ *n* **1** somebody who instructs candidates for initiation into sacred mysteries **2** a believer in and disseminator of mystical doctrines [Mid-16C. Directly or via French < Latin *mystagogus* < Greek *mustagōgos* 'leader of candidates for initiation' < *mustēs* 'initiated person' (see MYSTERY[1]).] —**mystagogic** /místə gójjik/ *adj* —**mystagogically** *adv* —**mystagogy** *n*

mysterious /mi steéri əss/ *adj* **1 ABOUT WHICH LITTLE IS KNOWN** about whom or which little is known or explained **2 DIFFICULT TO UNDERSTAND** difficult to understand or explain **3 FULL OF MYSTERY** full of or suggesting mystery [Late 16C. < French *mystérieux* < *mystère* 'mystery' < Latin *mysterium* (see MYSTERY[1]).] —**mysteriously** *adv* —**mysteriousness** *n*

mystery[1] /místəri/ *n* (*plural* **-ies**) **1 PUZZLING EVENT OR SITUATION** an event or situation that is difficult to understand or explain **2 SOMEBODY UNKNOWN** an unknown, secret, or hidden person or thing **3 STRANGENESS** the quality of being strange, secret, or puzzling **4 STORY ABOUT PUZZLING EVENT** a book, play, or film about a puzzling event, especially an unsolved crime, that makes great use of suspense **5 SOMETHING KNOWN BY DIVINE REVELATION** a Christian belief or truth that is considered to be beyond human understanding and can be made known only by divine revelation **6 INCIDENT FROM LIFE OF JESUS CHRIST** an incident in the life of Jesus Christ that Christians believe to have particular spiritual significance, especially, in Roman Catholicism, one of 15 events including the Annunciation and the Crucifixion **7 CHRISTIAN SACRAMENT** one of the Christian sacraments, especially Communion **8 RELIGIOUS GROUP** a religious group having secret rites, especially one of the ancient Mediterranean religions, e.g. of the Romans **9 RELIGIOUS RITE** a secret rite or ceremony performed by a religious group, especially belonging to one of the ancient Mediterranean religions (*often plural*) **10** ARTS = **mystery play** ■ **mysteries** *npl* **1 SECRET KNOWLEDGE** special knowledge known only to people skilled or involved in a particular activity, group, or subject **2 CONSECRATED BREAD AND WINE** in Christianity, the consecrated bread and wine used in the sacrament of Communion [14C. Directly or via Anglo-Norman < Latin *mysterium* < Greek *mustērion* 'secret rite' < *mustēs* 'initiated person' < *muein* 'close the eyes or lips, initiate'.]

mystery² /místəri/ (*plural* **-ies**) *n* a handicraft or trade (*archaic*) [13C. < medieval Latin *misterium* 'service, office', contraction (influenced by Latin *mysterium* 'mystery') of Latin *ministerium* < *minister* 'servant'.]

mystery play *n* a medieval drama staged by a craft guild and often based on stories from the Bible such as the Flood or incidents from the life of Jesus Christ

mystery tour *n* a pleasure trip, especially by bus, to a destination that is not made known to the passengers beforehand

mystic /místik/ *n* a person who practises or believes in mysticism ■ *adj* = **mystical** [14C. Directly or via French *mystique* (adjective) < Latin *mysticus* < Greek *mustikos* < *mustēs* 'initiated person' (see MYSTERY¹).]

mystical /místik'l/ *adj* **1 WITH DIVINE MEANING** with a divine meaning beyond human understanding **2 OF MYSTICISM** relating to, involving, or typical of mysticism or mystics **3 WITH SUPERNATURAL SIGNIFICANCE** with supernatural or spiritual significance or power **4 MYSTERIOUS** mysterious or difficult to understand —**mystically** *adv* —**mysticalness** *n*

mysticism /místisizəm/ *n* **1 BELIEF IN INTUITIVE SPIRITUAL REVELATION** the belief that personal communication or union with the divine is achieved through intuition, faith, ecstasy, or sudden insight rather than through rational thought **2 SPIRITUAL SYSTEM** a system of religious belief or practice that people follow to achieve personal communication or union with the divine **3 CONFUSED AND VAGUE IDEAS** vague or unsubstantiated thought or speculation about something

mystify /místi fī/ (**-fies, -fying, -fied**) *vt* **1** to put somebody in a position of being unable to understand or explain something **2** to make something mysterious or unclear [Early 19C. < French *mystifier* < *mystère* 'mystery' (< Latin *mysterium*; see MYSTERY¹) or *mystique* 'mystic' (see MYSTIC).] —**mystification** /místifi káysh'n/ *n* —**mystifier** *n* —**mystifying** *adj* —**mystifyingly** *adv*

mystique /mi steék/ *n* a special quality or air that makes

somebody or something appear mysterious, powerful, or desirable [Late 19C. Via French < Greek *mustikos* < *mustēs* 'initiated person' (see MYSTERY¹).]

myth /mith/ *n* **1 ANCIENT STORY** a traditional story about heroes or supernatural beings, often explaining the origins of natural phenomena or aspects of human behaviour **2 MYTHS COLLECTIVELY** myths considered as a group or a type of story **3 SYMBOLIC CHARACTER OR STORY** a character, story, theme, or object that embodies a particular idea or aspect of a culture **4 SOMEBODY OR SOMETHING FICTITIOUS** somebody or something whose existence is or was widely believed in, but who is fictitious **5 ALLEGORY OR PARABLE** a story that has a hidden meaning, especially one that is meant to teach a lesson [Mid-19C. Directly or via French *mythe* < modern Latin *mythus* < Greek *muthos* 'speech, myth'.]

myth. *abbr* **1** mythological **2** mythology

mythical /míthik'l/, **mythic** /míthik/ *adj* **1 TYPICAL OF MYTH** relating to, appearing in, based on, or typical of myth **2 IMAGINARY** not true or real, but existing only in somebody's imagination **3 LIKE MYTH** like a myth, especially in being widely known or considered wonderful — **mythically** *adv*

mythicize /míthi sīz/ (**-cizes, -cizing, -cized**), **mythicise** (**-cises, -cising, -cised**) *vt* **1** to make somebody or something into a myth **2** to see or explain an event or person as a myth —**mythicization** /míthi sī záysh'n/ *n* —**mythicizer** *n*

mythmaker /míth maykər/ *n* a creator of myths —**mythmaking** *n*

mythography /mi thóggrəfi/ (*plural* **-phies**) *n* **1** a collection of myths **2** the representation of a mythical subject in a work of art

mythoi plural of **mythos**

mythol. *abbr* **1** mythological **2** mythology

mythological /míthə lójjik'l/, **mythologic** /-ik/ *adj* **1** relating to, typical of, or appearing in myth **2** not real, but existing only in the imagination —**mythologically** *adv*

mythologise *vti* = **mythologize**

mythologize /mi thóllə jīz/ (**-gizes, -gizing, -gized**), **mythologise** (**-gises, -gising, -gised**) *v* **1** *vt* **MAKE INTO MYTH** to make somebody or something into a myth **2** *vti* **EXPLAIN MYTHS** to explain or relate myths **3** *vi* **CREATE MYTHS** to create or make up myths —**mythologization** /mi thóllə jī záysh'n/ *n* —**mythologizer** *n*

mythology /mi thóllə ji/ (*plural* **-gies**) *n* **1 BODY OF MYTHS** a group of myths that belong to a particular people or culture and tell about their ancestors, heroes, gods and other supernatural beings, and history **2 BODY OF STORIES** a body of stories, ideas, or beliefs that are not necessarily true about a particular place or individual

3 MYTHS COLLECTIVELY myths considered as a group **4 STUDY OF MYTHS** the study of myths, or the branch of knowledge that deals with myths [15C. Directly or via French < late Latin *mythologia* < Greek *muthologia* 'science of myths' < *muthos* ('speech, myth').] —**mythologer** *n* —**mythologist** *n*

mythomania /míthō máyni ə/ *n* a very strong tendency to tell lies or exaggerate, which may be symptom of a disorder —**mythomaniac** *n*

mythopoeia /míthō peé ə/, **mythopoesis** /-pō eéssis/ *n* the creating of myths [Mid-19C. Directly or via late Latin < Greek *muthopoiia* < *muthos* ('speech, myth') + *poiein* 'make'.] —**mythopoeist** *n*

mythopoeic /míthō peé ik/ *adj* relating to, involving, or engaged in the production of myths [Mid-19C. < Greek *muthopoios* < *muthos* ('speech, myth') + *poiein* 'make'.]

mythos /mí thoss, mí-/ (*plural* **-thoi**) *n* **1** the interrelated set of beliefs, attitudes, and values held by a society or cultural group **2** a myth or mythology [Mid-18C. < Greek *muthos* 'speech, myth'.]

myx- *prefix* = **myxo-** (*before vowels*)

myxo- *prefix* mucus ○ *myxomycete* [Via modern Latin < Greek *muxa* 'slime, mucus']

myxoedema /míksə deèma/ *n* **1** a disease caused by an underactive or atrophied thyroid gland, characterized by sluggishness and weight gain **2** dry swelling of the skin and subcutaneous tissues, associated with an underactive thyroid gland —**myxoedematous** /-démmətəss, -deè-/ *adj* —**myxoedemic** /-démmik/ *adj*

myxoma /mik sṓma/ (*plural* **-mas** *or* **-mata** /-mətə/) *n* a benign tumour composed of mucus and gelatinous material embedded in connective tissue, typically in the heart where it can obstruct blood flow and lead to sudden unconsciousness —**myxomatous** /-sómmətəss/ *adj*

myxomatosis /míksəmə tṓssiss/ *n* a highly infectious disease of rabbits caused by a virus, leading to swelling of the mucous membranes and the formation of tumours similar to myxomas [early 20C. < modern Latin, < *myxomat-*, stem of *myxoma* < *myxo-* (see MYXO-).]

myxomycete /míksō mī seét/ *n* MICROBIOL = **slime mould** [Late 19C. < modern Latin *Myxomycetes* < *myxo-* (see MYXO-) + Greek *mukētes*, plural of *mukēs* 'fungus'.]

myxovirus /míksō vírəss/ *n* a group of RNA-containing viruses including those that cause diseases of the respiratory tract such as influenza, and those that cause measles and mumps (**paramyxoviruses**)

⚡ mz *abbr* Mozambique (*in Internet addresses*)

mzungu /mə zoóng goo/ (*plural* **-us**) *n E Africa* a white person [< Kiswahili]

n[1] /en/ (*plural* **n's**), **N** (*plural* **N's** *or* **Ns**) *n* the 14th letter of the English alphabet, representing a consonant sound

n[2] /en/ *n* an indefinite whole number

n[3] *symbol* **1** amount of substance **2** en dash **3** nano- **4** neutron **5** refractive index

n[4] *abbr* **1** net **2** neuter **3** nominative **4** noon **5** north **6** northern **7** note **8** noun **9** number

n' /ən/, **'n'** *conj* and (*informal*)

N[1] *symbol* **1** Avogadro's number **2** en dash **3** newton **4** nitrogen

N[2] /en/ (*plural* **N's** *or* **Ns**) *n* something shaped like a letter 'N'

N[3] *abbr* **1** knight **2** neutral (*on gear sticks*) **3** New (*in place names*) **4** Norse **5** November

n- *prefix* normal

⚡na *abbr* Namibia (*in Internet addresses*)

Na *symbol* sodium [Shortening of modern Latin *natrium* < Greek *nitron* 'nitre']

n/a *abbr* **1** not applicable **2** not available

NAACP *abbr* National Association for the Advancement of Colored People

NAAFI /náffi/, **Naafi** *n* **1** an organization that provides canteens and shops for people who work in the armed forces. Full form **Navy, Army, and Air Force Institutes 2** (*plural* **NAAFIs** *or* **Naafis**) a canteen or shop provided by the NAAFI

naan /naan/, **naan bread** *n* FOOD = **nan**[1]

naartje /naárchi/ *n* S Africa FOOD = **nartjie**

Naas /nayss/ town in E Republic of Ireland. Population: 11,141 (1991).

nab /nab/ (**nabs, nabbing, nabbed**) *vt* **1** to seize, snatch, or take something suddenly **2** to catch and arrest a criminal or fugitive (*informal*) [Late 17C. Probably variant of *nap* < N Germanic.]

Nabataean /nábbə teé ən/, **Nabatean** *n* the extinct language of the Nabataeans, a dialect of Aramaic [Early 17C. < Latin *Nabat(h)aeus*.] —**Nabataean** *adj*

Nabis /naábi/ *npl* a group of 19th-century French artists, including Bonnard, who embraced symbolism rather than the naturalism of the impressionist painters [Mid-20C. Plural of *nabi* 'member of the Nabis' < Hebrew *nābī* 'prophet'.]

Nablus /naáblɒss/ = **Nabulus**

nabob /náy bob/ *n* **1** a rich or powerful person (*informal*) **2** formerly, a person from Europe who had made a fortune in the East, especially in India **3** HIST = **nawab** *n*. **1** [Early 17C. Via Portuguese *nababo* or Spanish *nabab* < Urdu *nawwāb* 'deputy governor'.]

Nabokov /nə bók of, -bók-, nábbə kof/, **Vladimir** (1899–1977) Russian-born US writer

Nabulus /nábbəlōoss/, **Nablus, Nābulus** city in the West Bank territory. Population: 106,944 (1987).

nacelle /nə sél/ *n* a separate streamlined enclosure on an aircraft for crew, cargo, or engines [Early 20C. Via French, 'dinghy, gondola' < late Latin *navicella* 'boat' < Latin *navis* 'ship'.]

nachos /náchōz/ *npl* a hot snack of tortilla chips covered with melted cheese, chili sauce, or another savoury topping [Mid-20C. < ?]

NACODS /náy kodz/ *abbr* National Association of Colliery Overmen, Deputies, and Shotfirers

nacre /náykər/ *n* CRAFT = **mother-of-pearl** [Late 16C. Via French < Italian *naccaro* < Arabic *nāqūr* 'hunting horn'.]

nacreous /náykri əss/ *adj* **1** relating to, typical of, or made of mother-of-pearl **2** with the iridescent quality of mother-of-pearl

nacreous cloud *n* an iridescent cloud that looks like a cirrus and appears especially in the winter at high latitudes

NACRO /nákrō/, **Nacro** *abbr* National Association for the Care and Resettlement of Offenders

NAD *n* a coenzyme that plays a role in the electron transport chain, where it is vital in the production of energy. Full form **nicotinamide adenine dinucleotide**

Na-Dene /naá dáyni, nə deèn/, **Na-Déné** *n* a group of Native North American languages spoken in parts of Alaska, Canada, and the SW United States. Native speakers: 200,000. [Early 20C < Athabaskan *na* + *dene* 'people'] —**Na-Dene** *adj*

Nader /náydər/, **Ralph** (*b.* 1934) US attorney and consumer-protection advocate

NADH *n* the reduced form of NAD that reverts to NAD during the generation of cellular energy [Mid-20C. < NAD + *H* 'hydrogen'.]

nadir /náy deer, nád-/ *n* **1** the lowest possible point ○ *the nadir of despair* **2** the point on the celestial sphere directly below the observer and opposite the zenith [14C. Via French and medieval Latin < Arabic *nazīr (as-samt)* 'opposite (the zenith)'.]

NADP *n* a coenzyme involved in anabolism, consisting of NAD with an extra phosphate group. Full form **nicotinamide adenine dinucleotide phosphate**

nae /nay/ *adv* Scotland **1** no **2** not

naevi *plural of* **naevus**

naevus /neévəss/ (*plural* **-i** /-ī, -eé/) *n* a birthmark, mole, or any other kind of growth or mark on the skin that a person is born with [Mid-19C. < Latin *naevus*.]

naff /naf/ *adj* lacking real or fashionable stylishness and appearing boring, tasteless, or unattractive (*informal*)

naff off *vi* used as a rude way of telling somebody to go away (*informal*)

NAFTA /náftə/ *n* a free trade agreement signed between the United States and Canada in 1989, and extended to include Mexico in 1994. Full form **North American Free Trade Agreement**

nag[1] /nag/ *v* (**nags, nagging, nagged**) **1** *vti* ASK REPEATEDLY to ask or urge somebody persistently and annoyingly to do something ○ *He keeps nagging me to go and see the doctor.* **2** *vti* KEEP CRITICIZING to complain repeatedly to somebody in an irritating way, e.g. about some aspect of their behaviour or appearance **3** *vi* BE PERSISTENTLY PAINFUL OR BOTHERSOME to be a persistent cause of discomfort, anxiety, or unease ○ *My conscience had been nagging me all week.* ○ *a nagging pain* ■ *n* SOMEBODY WHO NAGS somebody, especially a woman, who is regarded as having a tendency to nag (*insult*) [Early 19C. < ?] —**nagger** *n* —**nagging** *n* —**naggingly** *adv*

SYNONYMS See *complain*.

nag[2] /nag/ *n* **1** OLD HORSE an old horse, especially one that is worn out **2** RACEHORSE a horse, especially a racehorse

(*slang*) **3** SMALL HORSE a small horse for riding (*archaic*) [15C. < ?]

Naga /naágə/ (*plural* **-ga** *or* **-gas**) *n* the Tibeto-Burman language of the Naga people. Native speakers: 120,000. [Mid-19C. < ?] —**Naga** *adj*

Nagaland /naágə land/ state in NE India. Capital: Kohima. Area: 16,579 sq. km/6,400 sq. mi. Population: 1,410,000 (1994).

nagana /nə gaánə/, **n'gana** /əng gaánə/ *n* an often fatal disease caused by trypanosome protozoan parasites that affects hoofed animals such as cattle, horses, and goats in tropical Africa and is transmitted by the tsetse fly [Late 19C. < Zulu *nakane*.]

Nagano /nə gaánō/ port on central Honshu, Japan. Population: 347,036 (1990).

Nagari /naágəri/ *n* **1** a set of alphabets used in languages of the Indian subcontinent, including Sanskrit and Hindi **2** LING = **Devanagari** [Late 18C. < Sanskrit *nagari* 'script of the city'.]

Nagarjuna /nág aar jōonə/ (*fl.* AD mid-2nd or 3rd century) Indian philosopher

Nagasaki /nággə saáki/ city on W Kyushu, Japan. Population: 445,000 (1990).

Nagoya /na góy yə/ city on S Honshu, Japan. Population: 2,091,000 (1990).

Nagpur /nag poòr/ city in central India, on the Deccan Plateau. Population: 1,622,225 (1991).

Nagy /nóddjə/, **Imre** (1896–1958) Hungarian statesman and prime minister (1953–55 and 1956)

nah /na, naa/ *interj* no (*nonstandard*) [Early 20C. Alteration of NO[1].]

Nah. *abbr* Nahum

Nahanni National Park /nə haáni-/ national park and preserve in SW Northern Territories, Canada. Area: 4,766 sq. km/1,840 sq. mi.

Nahuatl /naá waat'l, naa waát'l/ (*plural* **-tl** *or* **-tls**), **Nahua** /naá waa, naa waá/ (*plural* **-hua** *or* **-huas**) *n* **1** a member of a Native Central American people who live in S Mexico and Central America **2 Nahuatl, Nahua, Nahuatlan** the Uto-Aztecan language of the Nahuatl people. Native speakers: 1 million. [Early 19C. Via Spanish < Nahuatl, singular of *Nahua* 'the Nahuatl people'.] —**Nahuatl** *adj*

Nahum /náyhəm/ *n* **1** a Hebrew prophet who lived in the 7th century BC **2** a book of the Bible that records the prophecies of Nahum, including the prophecy foretelling the siege and sack of the Assyrian capital of Nineveh in 612 BC

naiad /ní ad/ (*plural* **-ads** *or* **-ades** /ní ədeez/) *n* **1** GREEK WATER NYMPH in Greek mythology, a nymph of lakes, rivers, springs, and fountains **2** AQUATIC LARVA the immature water-dwelling form (**larva**) of a dragonfly, damselfly, mayfly, or stonefly **3** AQUATIC PLANT an underwater plant with narrow leaves. Flowers: small, white. Genus: *Najas*. [14C. Via Latin *naiad-* < Greek, 'water nymph' < *naein* 'to flow'.]

Naiad /ní ad/ *n* the innermost known natural satellite of Neptune, discovered in 1989 by Voyager 2

naïf *adj* naive [Late 16C. < French *naïf* (see NAIVE).]

nail /nayl/ *n* **1** SHORT POINTED METAL ROD a strong metal pin with a flat round head and a pointed end that is hammered into wood or masonry and used to fasten objects together or hang something on **2** SOMETHING LIKE

NAIL something that is like a nail in its shape, in being sharp, or in the way it is used **3 HARD AREA ON FINGER OR TOE** in humans and other primates, the thin horny covering that grows on the upper surface of the end of each finger and toe **4 CLAW** the claw of a bird, mammal, or reptile **5 UNIT OF MEASURE** an old unit of measure for cloth that was equal to 5.7 cm/2.25 in ■ *vt* **1 ATTACH WITH NAILS** to fasten, attach, or secure something using nails **2 FIX STEADILY** to keep something fixed or focussed on something ○ *His gaze was nailed to the astonishing scene.* **3 CATCH OR CONVICT GUILTY PERSON** to catch somebody who is guilty of an offence, prove the person's guilt, or have the person convicted (*informal*) ○ *It took them five years to nail him for insider trading.* **4 EXPOSE UNTRUTH** to prove that something is not true or valid and so stop others from believing it (*informal*) **5 HIT WITH BULLET OR PROJECTILE** to hit or bring down somebody or something with a bullet or a projectile **6 STOP** to stop somebody and speak to him or her (*informal*) ○ *nailed me in the corridor and demanded an explanation* **7** *US* **DO PRECISELY OR WELL** to catch, hit, seize, or execute something adroitly or precisely (*informal*) **8** *US* **IDENTIFY** to identify somebody or establish something precisely (*informal*) ○ *I nailed him as a fraud as soon as he started talking about his wealthy background.* [Old English *nægl* < Indo-European, 'fingernail, toenail'] —**nailable** *adj* —**nailer** *n* ◇ **a nail in somebody's coffin** an event or action that further weakens the position of somebody or something already in decline ◇ **hit the nail on the head** to be absolutely correct or accurate ◇ **on the nail** immediately, or paid immediately

nail down *v* **1** *vt* to make somebody be definite about something **2** to establish something clearly and conclusively ○ *an investigation that will attempt to nail down what really happened here*

nail bed *n* the layer of tissue at the base of a fingernail or toenail from which new nail material develops

nail-biter *n* **1** a situation or contest that is extremely tense and exciting because its outcome remains uncertain until the end (*informal*) **2** a habitual biter of the ends of his or her fingernails [< the stereotype of nail-biting as a sign of anxiety]

nail-biting *n* the habit of biting off the ends of the fingernails, especially out of anxiety, tension, or boredom ■ *adj* extremely tense and exciting because the outcome is uncertain [See NAIL-BITER]

nail bomb *n* a bomb packed with nails to cause widespread injuries among people who are near it when it goes off

nailbrush /náyl brush/ *n* a small brush used for cleaning the fingernails, with short stiff bristles on one or both sides

nail clippers *npl* a small pair of clippers used for trimming fingernails and toenails

nail enamel *n* = **nail polish**

nail file *n* a small file used for smoothing and shaping the ends of the fingernails

nailhead /náyl hed/ *n* a decorative design that resembles the round head of a nail, used on furniture and leather

nail polish *n* a fast-drying coloured or transparent varnish used to decorate fingernails or toenails

nail punch, nail set *n* a tool that pushes a nail level with or lower than the surrounding surface

nail scissors *npl* small scissors, sometimes with curved blades, used for trimming fingernails or toenails

nail set *n* CONSTR = **nail punch**

nail varnish *n* = **nail polish**

nainsook /náynssòok, nán-/ *n* a lightweight cotton fabric. Use: babywear, lingerie. [Late 18C. < Hindi *nainsukh* 'pleasure to the eye'.]

Naipaul /nī pawl/, **V. S.** (*b.* 1932) Trinidadian-born British novelist. Full name **Sir Vidiadhar Surajprasad Naipaul**

naira /nīrə/ *n* see table at **currency** [Late 20C. < Nigerian English, alteration of NIGERIA.]

Nairnshire /náirnshər/ former county in N Scotland

Nairobi /nī rṓbi/ capital of Kenya, in the south-central part of the country. Population: 1,346,000 (1989).

Nairobi National Park national park in south-central Kenya. Area: 115 sq. km/44 sq. mi.

NAIRU /náy roo/ *abbr* nonaccelerating inflation rate of unemployment

naissance /náyss'nss/ *n* the birth or origination of something or somebody (*formal*) [15C. < French, < *naissant* (see NAISSANT).]

naissant /náyss'nt/ *adj* in heraldry, describes a beast figure shown in the top half of a shield with only the upper part of its body visible [Late 16C. < French, present participle of *naître* 'be born'.]

naive /nī éev/, **naïve** *adj* **1 EXTREMELY SIMPLE AND TRUSTING** having or showing an excessively simple and trusting view of the world and human nature, often as a result of youth and inexperience **2 NOT SHREWD OR SOPHISTICATED** showing a lack of sophistication and subtlety or of critical judgment and analysis ○ *a politically naive statement* **3 ARTLESS** admirably straightforward and uncomplicated or refreshingly innocent and unaffected **4 REJECTING SOPHISTICATED TECHNIQUES IN ART** not using the conventional styles and techniques of trained artists, e.g. in the treatment of perspective or light and shade **5 NOT PREVIOUSLY EXPERIMENTED ON** not previously used in any scientific tests or experiments or not having previously used a particular drug ○ *naive laboratory mice* [Mid-17C. < French *naïve*, feminine of *naïf* < Latin *nativus* 'born'.] —**naively** *adv* —**naiveness** *n*

naive realism *n* the theory of perception that holds that when we look at an object what we see is the actual object, not a mental representation of it

naivety /nī éevə tay/ (*plural* **-ties**), **naivety** /nī éevəti/ *n* **1** a naive quality or naive behaviour **2** a naive action or remark [Late 17C. < French.]

Najd /najd, nejd/ plateau region in central Saudi Arabia. Area: 1,158,000 sq. km/447,100 sq. mi. Population: 1,200,000.

⚡**NAK** /nak/, **nak** *n* an ASCII control code used to indicate to the sender that a transmitted message has not been properly received. Full form **negative acknowledgment**

Nakasone Yasuhiro /nákə sṓni yássoo héerō/ (*b.* 1918) Japanese statesman and prime minister (1982–87)

naked /náykid/ *adj* **1 WITH NO CLOTHES ON** not covered by clothing, especially having no clothing on any part of the body **2 LACKING COVERING** without the usual covering or protection ○ *a naked flame* ○ *a naked light bulb* **3 NOT CONCEALED** openly displayed or expressed and often threatening or disturbing ○ *naked aggression* **4 UNADORNED** plain and lacking any decoration or embellishment ○ *the naked truth* **5 UNARMED** unarmed and defenceless ○ *'If you carry this resolution you will send Britain's Foreign Secretary naked into the conference chamber'.* (Aneurin Bevan, 1957) **6 DEVOID** without or unaccompanied by a particular quality or thing ○ *naked of all pretensions to grandeur* **7 WITHOUT NATURAL COVERING** without any natural covering in the form of earth, vegetation, or foliage **8 WITHOUT HAIR, FUR, OR FEATHERS** without hair, fur, scales, shell, or feathers **9 WITH NO GROWTH** without a covering of leaves or hairs ○ *naked stems* **10 NOT ENCLOSED IN OVARY** describes conifer seeds that are not enclosed in an ovary **11 WITHOUT SEPALS OR PETALS** describes flowers that have no sepals or petals [Old English *nacod* < Indo-European] —**nakedness** *n*

LITERARY LINK ***The Naked and the Dead***, a novel (1948) by US writer Norman Mailer. Set on a Pacific island during World War II, it is both a powerful account of the experience of war and, through its presentation of the principal characters, a portrayal of some of the tensions in contemporary US society.

naked eye *n* human sight without the aid of a microscope, telescope, or other optical instrument

naked ladies (*plural* **naked ladies**) *n* = **autumn crocus** (+ *singular verb*) [< its leafless flower stems]

nakedly /náykidli/ *adv* without any attempt at disguise or concealment ○ *a description of the state as a nakedly repressive machine*

naked option *n* a stock or commodity option sold by somebody who does not own the underlying asset, and who is exposed to considerable risk if the price of the underlying asset changes adversely

nakfa /nák fə/ *n* see table at **currency** [After *Nakfa*, town in N Eritrea]

Nakh /naak/ *n* a language family of the North Caucasian group of Caucasian languages, including Chechen and Ingush [Mid-20C. < ?] —**Nakh** *adj*

Nakuru /nə kòo roo/ capital of Rift Valley Province, west-central Kenya. Population: 124,200 (1994).

Nakuru, Lake lake in west-central Kenya. Area: 62 sq. km/24 sq. mi.

nalbuphine /nal béw feen/ *n* $C_{21}H_{27}NO_4$ a drug resembling morphine. Use: relief of moderate to severe pain. [Mid-20C. Blend of NALORPHINE + BUTYL.]

nalidixic acid /náyli díkssik-/ *n* $C_{12}H_{12}N_2O_3$ an antibacterial drug. Use: treatment of urinary infections. [< NAPHTHALENE + DI- + *carboxylic*]

nalorphine /na láwrfeen/ *n* $C_{19}H_{21}NO_3$ a white crystalline drug. Source: morphine. Use: diagnosis of narcotics addiction, reversal of effects of narcotics poisoning. [Mid-20C. Contraction of *N-allylnormorphine*.]

naloxone /nə lókssōn/ *n* $C_{19}H_{21}NO_4$ a drug resembling morphine. Use: diagnosis of narcotics addiction, reversal of effects of narcotics poisoning. [Mid-20C. Contraction of *N-allylnoroxymorphone*.]

Nam /nam, naam/ *n* *US* a name for Vietnam, used particularly by veterans of the war there during the 1960s and 1970s (*informal*) [Mid-20C. Shortening.]

N. Am. *abbr* **1** North America **2** North American

Nama /naámə/ (*plural* **-ma** *or* **-mas**), **Namaqua** /nə maákwə/ (*plural* **-qua** *or* **-quas**) *n* **1** a member of a Khoikhoi people who live in SW Africa **2** the San language of the Nama people. Native speakers: 25,000. [Mid-19C. < Nama.] —**Nama** *adj*

namable *adj* = **nameable**

Namaqualand /nə maákwə land/ coastal region of SW Africa, divided between S Namibia and South Africa. Area: 47,962 sq. km/18,518 sq. mi.

namaste /númmə stay/, **namaskar** /nummə skaár/ *n* a polite bow of greeting or farewell used by Hindus, made with the hands held at chest height and both palms pressed together [Mid-20C. < Hindi, 'bowing to you'.]

Namatjira /námmət jéerə/, **Albert** (1902–59) Australian Aboriginal painter

Nambour /nám bòor/ town in SE Queensland, Australia. Population: 12,205 (1996).

Nambu /námboo/, **Yoishiro** (*b.* 1921) Japanese physicist

namby-pamby /námbi pámbi/ *adj* (*informal*) **1 WEAK** feeble, childish, and weak **2 SILLY** silly, sentimental, or overly sensitive ■ *n* (*plural* **namby-pambies**) **NAMBY-PAMBY PERSON** a weak or silly person (*informal insult*) [Mid-16C. < nickname for the English poet *Amb(rose)* Philips (1674–1749).]

name /naym/ *n* **1 WHAT SOMEBODY OR SOMETHING IS CALLED** a word, term, or phrase by which somebody or something is known and distinguished from other people or things **2 UNCOMPLIMENTARY DESCRIPTION** a usually uncomplimentary or abusive word or phrase used to describe somebody's character ○ *called him names behind his back* **3 REPUTATION** the reputation or standing of somebody or something ○ *She's made quite a name for herself in the music world.* **4 FAMOUS PERSON** a famous person ○ *All the big Hollywood names were there.* **5 MEMBER OF LLOYD'S** a member of Lloyd's, the London insurance house, who provides capital for a syndicate but is not involved in how it is run ■ *adj* **RESPECTED** having an established and good reputation ○ *name brands at discount prices* ■ *vt* (**names, naming, named**) **1 GIVE A NAME TO** to give somebody or something a name ○ *They named the dog Sport.* **2 IDENTIFY BY NAME** to identify somebody or something by giving his, her, or its name ○ *He says he can name all 50 state capitals.* **3 DECIDE ON** to decide upon or specify something, such as a date, time, or price ○ *would not name a figure* **4 APPOINT TO OFFICE** to choose somebody for a particular office or honour ○ *They haven't yet named her successor.* **5 BAN MP FROM COMMONS** to refer formally by name to a Member of Parliament who has behaved in an unparliamentary manner, thereby temporarily banishing that MP from the House of Commons [Old English *nama* < Indo-European] —**namable** *adj* —**namer** *n* ◇ **a name to conjure with** a person or organization considered to be influential, powerful, or extremely famous ◇ **in name only** supposedly or officially, but not in any real sense ◇ **in the name of 1** by the authority of **2** for the sake of something ◇ **name names** to mention the names of specific people in order to blame or accuse them of an error or of wrongdoing ◇ **somebody's name is mud** somebody is in trouble or the object of another's or others' disapproval ◇ **name and shame** to reveal the name of a person or organization that has been unsatisfactory or done something illegal or immoral in order to cause embarrassment and so provoke an improvement in performance or behaviour ◇ **the name of the game** what something is all about, its most important element or the kind of thing that most commonly happens in it (*informal*) ◇ **to some-**

body's name credited or belonging to somebody ○ *hasn't got a penny to his name* ◇ **you name it** used to suggest that an enormous number of options are involved or an enormous number of options are possible (*informal*) ○ *They experienced cold, chills, and frostbite–you name it!*

nameable /náymə'l/, **namable** *adj* able to be identified by name

name-calling *n* verbal abuse, especially as a substitute for reasoned argument in a dispute

name day *n* in the Roman Catholic and Eastern Orthodox Churches, the feast day of the saint that somebody is named after

name-dropping *n* the practice of frequently mentioning the names of famous or influential people as friends or acquaintances in order to impress people — **name-drop** *vi* —**name-dropper** *n*

nameless /náymləss/ *adj* **1 LACKING A NAME** not having a name **2 ANONYMOUS** having a name that is unknown or not revealed **3 INDESCRIBABLE** defying accurate description ○ *a nameless fear* **4 DISTRESSING BEYOND WORDS** too unpleasant or disgusting to be described or mentioned **5 ILLEGITIMATE** illegitimate or not legally entitled to a name —**namelessly** *adv* —**namelessness** *n*

namely /náymli/ *adv* used to introduce a specific description or explanation of something just referred to in a more general way ○ *She was given a new post, namely that of head of department.*

nameplate /náym playt/ *n* a plate or plaque, e.g. on a door, bearing a name and associating the named person with the place or thing that the plate is attached to

namesake /náym sayk/ *n* somebody or something with the same name as somebody or something else [Mid-17C. Probably < *for your name's sake*.]

name tag *n* a small piece of metal or plastic with somebody's name on, attached to his or her clothing for purposes of identification at work or social functions

name tape *n* a small strip of cloth with somebody's name on, sewn onto the inside of his or her clothing as proof of ownership

Namib Desert /nə míb-/ desert in SW Africa, stretching along the Atlantic coast from Angola to South Africa. Length: 1,500 km/930 mi.

Namibe /nə meéb/ port and capital of Namibe Province, SW Angola. Population: 100,000 (1981 estimate).

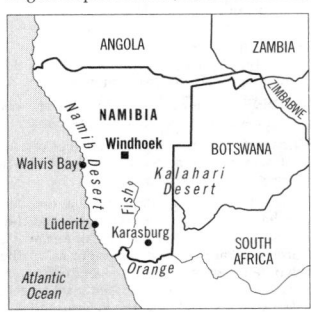

Namibia

Namibia /nə míbbi ə/ republic in SW Africa, on the Atlantic coast. Capital: Windhoek. Population: 1,709,000 (1996). Area: 824,269 sq. km/318,252 sq. mi. —**Namibian** *n, adj*

Namoi /nám oy/ river in NE New South Wales, Australia. Length: 845 km/525 mi.

Nampa /námpə/ city in SW Idaho. Population: 37,558 (1996).

nam pla /nám plàa/ *n* a thin sauce of fermented fish with a strong flavour and smell and a salty taste, widely used in Southeast Asian cookery [< Thai]

Namur /nə moòr-/ capital of Namur Province, SE Belgium. Population: 104,986 (1998 estimate).

nan[1] /naan, nan/, **naan** *n* a flat round or oval bread served with Indian food [Early 20C. < Persian, Urdu *nān*.]

nan[2] *n* = **nana** (*informal*)

nana /nánnə/, **nanna**, **nan** /nan/ *n* somebody's grandmother (*informal*)

Nanaimo /nə nímõ/ city in British Columbia, Canada, on SE Vancouver Island. Population: 85,585 (1996).

Nanak /naának/ (1469–1539) Indian religious leader. Known as **Guru Nanak**

nance *n* = **nancy**

Nanchang /nan chúng/ capital of Jiangxi Province, SE China. Population: 1,350,000 (1991).

nancy /nánssi/ (*plural* **nancies**), **nancy boy**, **nance** /nanss/ (*plural* **nances**) *n* an offensive term for an effeminate man or a homosexual man (*slang*)

Nancy /noN seé/ city in NE France. Population: 102,410 (1990).

✦ **NAND** /nand/ (*plural* **NANDs**), **NAND gate** *n* a logic operator used in computing that produces an output signal only if at least one of its inputs has no signal, thus being the inverse of an AND operator [Mid-20C. Blend of NOT + AND.]

Nanda Devi /núndə deèvi/ mountain in the W Himalayas, in N India. Height: 7,817 m/25,646 ft.

nandrolone /nándrə lōn/ *n* a muscle-building anabolic steroid that athletes are banned from using by the rules of the International Amateur Athletics Federation [Late 20C. Contraction < NOR- + ANDRO- + -l- + -ONE.]

Nanga Parbat /núng gə pàar baat/ mountain in the W Himalayas, in NW Kashmir. Height: 8,125 m/26,657 ft.

Nanjing /nan jíng/ capital of Jiangsu Province, E China, on the River Yangtze. Population: 2,090,204 (1990).

nankeen /nan keén/ *n* a durable yellowish-brown cotton fabric [Mid-18C. After *Nanking* (NANJING).]

nankeen kestrel *n* a small falcon with reddish-brown upper parts and cream-coloured underparts. Native to: Australia, New Guinea. *Falco cenchroides.* [Because the colour of nankeen cloth]

Nanking /nan kíng/ = **Nanjing**

nanna *n* = **nana**

nannie *n* = **nanny**

Nanning /nan níng/ capital of Guangxi Zhuangzu Autonomous Region, SE China. Population: 788,393 (1991).

nannofossil *n* PALAEONT = **nanofossil**

nanny /nánni/, **nannie** *n* (*plural* **-nies**) **1 SOMEBODY EMPLOYED TO WATCH A FAMILY'S CHILDREN** a person who is paid to take care of one or more children in a family home, often living there **2 GRANDMOTHER** somebody's grandmother (*informal*) ■ *vt* (**-nies, -nying, -nied**) **BE FUSSY AND OVERPROTECTIVE** to behave in an overprotective and patronizing way towards others, not allowing them to make their own decisions (*disapproving*) [Early 18C. Pet-form of *Ann(e)*.]

nanny goat *n* a female domestic goat

nanny state *n* a government that brings in legislation that it considers is in the people's best interests but that is regarded by some as interfering and patronizing

nano- *prefix* **1** (*symbol* **n**) extremely small ○ *nanofossil* ○ *nanotechnology* **2** (*symbol* **n**) one thousand millionth (10⁻⁹) ○ *nanosecond* [< Greek *nan(n)os* 'dwarf, little old man']

nanobacteria /nánnō bak teeri ə/ *npl* microorganisms much smaller in diameter than usual bacteria and coated with a mineralized shell

nanobot /nánnō bot/ *n* US a robot of microscopic proportions built using nanotechnology (*informal*) [Blend of NANO- + ROBOT]

nanofossil /nánnō foss'l/, **nannofossil** *n* a very small fossil, especially of nanoplankton

nanogram /nánnō gram/ *n* one billionth (one thousand-millionth) of a gram

nanometre /nánnō meetər/ *n* one billionth (one thousand-millionth) of a metre

nanoplankton /nánnō plangktən/, **nannoplankton** *n* very small plankton including bacteria, algae, and protozoa

nanosecond /nánnō sekənd/ *n* one billionth (one thousand-millionth) of a second

nanotechnology /nánnō tek nólləji/ (*plural* **-gies**) *n* the art of manipulating materials on a very small scale in order to build microscopic machinery

Nansen /nánss'n/, **Fridtjof** (1861–1930) Norwegian explorer and statesman

Nantes /noNt/ city in W France, on the Loire. Population: 243,247 (1994).

Nantong /nan toòng/ city in SE Jiangsu Province, E China. Population: 343,341 (1990).

Nantucket /nan túkət/ island in SE Massachusetts, on Nantucket Sound. Population: 6,012 (1990). Area: 148 sq. km/57 sq. mi.

Nantwich /nántwich/ town in NW England. Population: 11,695 (1991).

Nanuet /nánnyoŏ ət/ city in SE New York State. Population: 14,065 (1996 estimate).

Naomi /náyəmi/ *n* in the Bible, the mother-in-law of Ruth (Ruth 1:2)

naos /náyoss/ (*plural* **-oi** /-oy/) *n* ARCHIT = **cella** [Late 18C. < Greek, 'temple'.]

nap[1] /nap/ *n* **1 SHORT SLEEP** a period of short light sleep, especially during the day ■ *vi* (**naps, napping, napped**) **1 SLEEP LIGHTLY** to have a short period of light sleep **2 BE OFF GUARD** to be inattentive or off guard ○ *caught napping* [Old English *hnappian* < ?]

nap[2] /nap/ *n* the small soft fibres that stick up slightly from the surface of a fabric such as velvet and that usually all lie in one direction ■ *vt* (**naps, napping, napped**) to raise the nap of a fabric by brushing it [15C. < Middle Low German, Middle Dutch *noppe* < Germanic.]

nap[3] /nap/ *n* **1 CARD GAME** a card game similar to whist, played with hands of five cards, in which players bid for the number of tricks they will take. **2 BID IN NAP** a bid to win all five tricks in the game of nap. **3 A GOOD TIP IN RACING** in horse racing, a tip for a horse that is likely to win ■ *vt* (**naps, napping, napped**) **NAME LIKELY WINNER** to name a horse as a likely winner of a race [Early 19C. Shortening of NAPOLEON.]

napa = **nappa**

Napa /náppə/ city in west-central Florida. Population: 66,548 (1998 estimate).

napalm /náy paam, náp-/ *n* **1 JELLY USED FOR FIRE BOMBS** a highly flammable jelly produced by mixing a thickening agent with petrol. Use: in flamethrowers and fire bombs. **2 THICKENING AGENT FOR JELLIED PETROL** a thickening agent, consisting of aluminium soap. Use: manufacture of jellied petrol. ■ *vt* **ATTACK WITH NAPALM** to attack or destroy something with napalm [Mid-20C. Blend of NAPHTHENE + PALMITATE.]

Napa Valley region of west-central California, northeast of San Francisco, famous for its vineyards

nape /nayp/ *n* the back part of the neck [13C. < ?]

Naperville /náypərvil/ city in NE Illinois. Population: 117,091 (1998 estimate).

napery /náypəri/ *n* tablecloths and napkins, collectively (*archaic*) [14C. < Old French *naperie* < *nappe* (see NAPKIN).]

nap hand *n* a situation that appears to be favourable for taking risks

Naphtali /náftə lī/ *n* in the Bible, the son of Jacob and Rachel's handmaid, Bilhah (Genesis 30: 7–8)

naphtha /náfthə, nápthə/ *n* a clear colourless flammable mixture of light hydrocarbons. Source: petroleum. Use: raw material for many petrochemicals and plastics. [Late 16C. Via Latin < Greek.]

naphthalene /náfthə leen, nápth-/ *n* $C_{10}H_8$ a white crystalline hydrocarbon. Source: coal tar. Use: moth repellent, in solvents, in the manufacture of dyes, resins, plasticizers, polyesters, and explosives. [Early 19C. < NAPHTHA + -AL³.] —**napthalenic** /náfthə lénnik, nápthə-/ *adj*

naphthene /náf theen, náp-/ *n* a cycloalkane obtained from petroleum [Late 19C. < NAPHTHA.] —**naphthenic** *adj*

naphthol /náfthol, nápth-/ *n* $C_{10}H_7OH$ either of two derivatives of naphthalene that are isomers. Use: antiseptics, manufacturing. [Mid-19C. < NAPHTHA.]

Napier /náypi ər/ city in the eastern part of the North Island, New Zealand. Population: 55,044 (1996).

Napier, John (1550–1617) Scottish mathematician

Napier, Robert Cornelis, 1st Baron Napier of Magdala (1810–90) British field marshal

Napierian logarithm /nə peéri ən-/ *n* MATH = **natural logarithm** [Early 19C. After John NAPIER.]

Napier's bones /náypi ərz-/ *npl* a set of graduated rods based upon the principles of logarithms, formerly used to perform multiplication and division but now used primarily for educational purposes [Mid-17C. After John NAPIER.]

napiform /náypi fawrm/ *adj* shaped like a turnip in being conical at one end and spherical at the other [Mid-19C. < Latin *napus* 'turnip'.]

napkin /nápkin/ *n* **1** a usually square piece of cloth or tissue paper used at mealtimes to protect clothes and wipe the mouth **2** full form of **nappy** (*formal*) [14C. < French *nap(p)e* 'tablecloth' < Latin *mappa* 'napkin, cloth'.]

Naples /náyp'lz/ **1** capital of Campania Region, S Italy, on the Bay of Naples. Population: 1,061,583 (1993). **2** city in SW Florida. Population: 19,505 (1990).

napoleon /nə pṓli ən/ *n* **1** a gold coin formerly used in France, equivalent to 20 francs **2** CARDS = **nap**³ [Early 19C. After NAPOLEON I.]

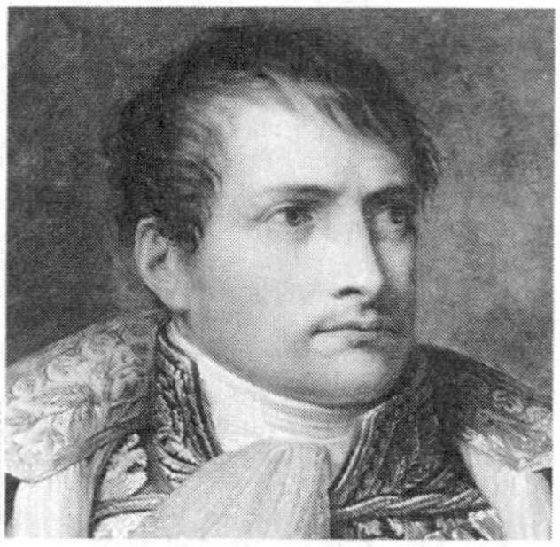

AKG London

Napoleon I, Emperor of the French: Portrait (1807) by Andrea Appiani

Napoleon I /nə pṓli ən/ (1769–1821) emperor of the French (1804–14, 1815). Born **Napoleon Bonaparte** —**Napoleonic** /nə pṓli ónnik/ *adj*

nappa /náppə/, **napa** *n* a soft leather made from sheep or kid's skin [Late 19C. After *Napa*, county, town, and valley in California, USA.]

nappe /nap/ *n* **1 SHEET OF WATER** a sheet of water flowing over a dam or a weir **2 SHEET OF ROCK** a large arch-shaped sheet of rock that has been forced over underlying rocks by internal stresses **3 PART OF CONE** either of the two parts, or sheets, of a conical or pyramidal surface that are separated by a line through the vertex [Late 19C. < French (see NAPKIN).]

napper /náppər/ *n* a person's head (*dated informal*) [Late 18C. < ?]

nappy /náppi/ (*plural* **-pies**) *n* a piece of soft absorbent material, usually made of paper or cloth, that is wrapped around a baby's bottom and between its legs to absorb urine and excrement. US term **diaper** *n.* **1** [Early 20C. Shortening and alteration of NAPKIN.]

nappy rash *n* a sensitive red area on a baby's skin around the genitals and buttocks caused by irritation from urine or faeces

naproxen /nə próks'n/ *n* a drug that reduces inflammation and pain. Use: treatment of arthritis. [Late 20C. < *methoxynaphthylpropionic (acid).*]

Nara /naárə/ city on S Honshu, Japan. Population: 349,349 (1990).

Naracoorte /nárrə kawrt/ town in South Australia. Population: 4,718 (1991).

Narayan /nə rī́yən/, **Jayaprakash** (1902–79) Indian politician

Narayan, R. K. (*b.* 1906) Indian writer. Full name **Rasipuram Krishnaswamy Narayan**

narc /naark/ *vi US* = **nark** *v.* **3** (*slang*) [Mid-19C. < Romany *nāk* 'nose'.]

narcissism /naárssissizəm/ *n* **1** excessive self-admiration and self-centredness **2** in psychiatry, a personality disorder characterized by the patient's overestimation of his or her own appearance and abilities and an excessive need for admiration [Early 19C. After NARCISSUS.] —**narcissist** *n* —**narcissistic** /nárssi sístik/ *adj* —**narcissistically** *adv*

narcissus /naar síssəss/ (*plural* **-suses** *or* **-si** /-síssī/) *n* a spring-blooming plant with narrow leaves that grows from a bulb. Flowers: yellow or white, with a cup-shaped centre. Genus: *Narcissus*. [Mid-16C. Via Latin < Greek *narkissos* < *narkē* 'numbness'; from its narcotic properties.]

Narcissus *n* in Greek mythology, a youth who was punished for repulsing Echo's love by being made to fall in love with his own reflection in a pool

narco-¹ *prefix* sleep, stupor ○ *narcolepsy* [< Greek *narkoun* 'make numb' < *narkē* 'numbness']

narco-² *prefix* relating to illicit narcotics and the narcotics trade (*informal*)

narcoanalysis /naárkō ə nálləssiss/ *n* psychoanalysis using drugs to induce a state akin to sleep

narcolepsy /naárkō lepsi/ *n* a condition characterized by frequent, brief, and uncontrollable bouts of deep sleep, sometimes accompanied by hallucinations and inability to move —**narcoleptic** /naárkō léptik/ *adj, n*

narcosis /naar kṓssiss/ *n* a state of unconsciousness or stupor caused by a narcotic or other drug [Late 17C. < Greek *narkōsis* < *narkoun* (see NARCOTIC).]

narcotic /naar kóttik/ *n* **1 DRUG** a typically addictive drug, especially one derived from opium, that may produce effects ranging from pain relief and sleep to stupor, coma, and convulsions **2** *US* **ILLEGAL DRUG** a drug whose use is illegal, whether it is addictive or not **3 SOOTHING THING** something that soothes, induces sleep, relieves pain or stress, or causes a sensation of mental numbness ■ *adj* **1 CAUSING SLEEP** able to induce drowsiness, sleep, or stupor, or alter mental states through its chemical properties **2 SOOTHING** having a generally soothing, numbing, or soporific effect **3 OF NARCOTICS** relating to narcotic drugs and their use **4 OF ADDICTS** relating to people addicted to narcotics [14C. Via French and medieval Latin < Greek *narkōtikos* 'numbing' < *narkoun* 'make numb' < *narkē* 'numbness'.] —**narcotically** *adv*

narcotise *vt* = **narcotize**

narcotization /naárkə tī záysh'n/ *n US* the process by which a society falls under the control of drugs, drug traffickers, and the illegal drug business (*informal*)

narcotize /naárkə tīz/ (**-tizes, -tizing, -tized**), **narcotise** (**-tises, -tising, -tised**) *vt* **1** to treat somebody with a narcotic **2** to induce stupor in somebody, especially by administering a narcotic drug

nard /naard/ *n* = **spikenard** *n.* **1**, **spikenard** *n.* **2** [14C. Via Latin *nardus* < Greek *nardos*, probably < Sanskrit *naladam* 'Indian spikenard'.]

nares /náir eez/ *npl* openings or passages leading out of the nose or naval cavity [Late 17C. < Latin, plural of *naris* 'nostril'.]

narghile /naárgə lay/, **nargileh** *n* DRUGS = **hookah** [Mid-18C. Directly and via French and Turkish < Persian *nārgīl* 'coconut, hookah' < Sanskrit *nārikela* 'coconut'.]

Narita /nə reétə/ city on SE Honshu, Japan. Population: 86,708 (1990).

nark /naark/ *v* **1** *vt* **ANNOY** to irritate, offend, or annoy somebody (*informal*) **2** *vi* **COMPLAIN** to complain in an irritating way (*informal*) **3** *vi* **ACT AS INFORMER** to act as an informer, especially for the police (*slang*) US term **narc** *v.* ■ *n* **POLICE INFORMER** a person who acts as a decoy or informer, especially an ex-criminal who is working for the police (*slang*) [Mid-19C. < Romany *nāk* 'nose'.]

Narrabri /nárrə brī/ town in NE New South Wales, Australia. Population: 7,075 (1991).

Narraganset /nárrə gánssət/ (*plural* **-sets** *or* **-set**), **Narragansett** (*plural* **-setts** *or* **-sett**) *n* **1** a member of a Native North American people who lived in W Rhode Island **2** the extinct Iroquoian language of the Narraganset people [Early 17C. < Narraganset.] —**Narraganset** *adj*

Narragansett /nárrə gánssət/ town in SE Rhode Island. Population: 3,658 (1996 estimate).

Narragansett Bay inlet of the Atlantic Ocean in SE Rhode Island. Length: 42 km/26 mi.

narrate /nə ráyt/ (**-rates, -rating, -rated**) *vt* **1** to be the teller of a story, or to give an account of something in detail **2** to provide the narration for a film or television programme [Mid-17C. < Latin *narrat-*, past participle of *narrare* < *gnarus* 'knowing'.] —**narratable** *adj*

narration /nə ráysh'n/ *n* **1 ACT OF NARRATING** the act of telling a story or giving an account of something **2 SOMETHING NARRATED** a narrative or story **3 SOUNDTRACK VOICED BY ACTOR** the voiced soundtrack of a broadcast or film when given by an actor or commentator who does not appear —**narrational** *adj*

narrative /nárrətiv/ *n* **1 STORY** a story or an account of a sequence of events in the order in which they happened **2 PROCESS OF NARRATING** the art or process of telling a story or giving an account of something **3 STORY IN LITERARY WORK** the part of a literary work that is concerned with telling the story ■ *adj* **1 TELLING A STORY** having the aim or purpose of telling a story ○ *narrative poetry* **2 RELATING TO NARRATION** relating to or involving the art of storytelling —**narratively** *adv*

narrator /nə ráytər/ *n* **1 STORYTELLER** a teller of a story or account **2 TALKING CHARACTER** a character in a work of fiction who is presented as telling the story and who refers to himself or herself as 'I' **3 COMMENTATOR** a person who provides a narration, e.g. for a television programme

narrow /nárrō/ *adj* **1 SMALL IN WIDTH** having a small width, especially in comparison to height or length ○ *a narrow gap* **2 LIMITED IN SIZE** limited or restricted in size or scope ○ *a narrow range of options* **3 NARROW-MINDED** limited and usually inflexible in outlook ○ *a narrow view of events* **4 JUST ENOUGH FOR SUCCESS** only just sufficient for success ○ *a narrow victory* ○ *a narrow escape* **5** *US* **NOT GENEROUS** mean and stingy **6 THOROUGH** close and thorough, leaving nothing uninvestigated **7 MEAGRE** small or limited in quantity ○ *a narrow provision* **8** PHON = **tense**¹ *adj.* **4** **9 HIGH IN PROTEIN** describes animal feed that is very rich in protein ■ *n* **NARROW PASSAGE** a narrow place or passage. ◊ **narrows** ■ *vti* **1 MAKE OR BECOME NARROW** to make something, or to become, narrow or narrower **2 CONTRACT OR BE CONTRACTED** to restrict or limit the scope or extent of something, or to become restricted or limited in scope or extent ○ *narrowed the focus of their investigation to two individuals* [Old English *nearu* < Germanic] —**narrowness** *n*

narrow down *vt* = **narrow** *v.* **2**

narrowband /nárrō band/ *adj* functioning within a narrow band of broadcasting frequencies

narrowboat *n* a long canal barge with a width not exceeding 2.1 m/7 ft

narrowcast /nárrō kaast/ (**-casts, -casting, -cast** *or* **-casted**) *vt* to aim a radio or television transmission at a limited group of people such as cable subscribers or a particular target audience

narrow gauge *n* **1** a distance between the two rails of a railway track that is less than the 143.5 cm/4 ft 8.5 in distance of the standard gauge railways **2** a railway line with track of a narrow gauge, or a carriage or locomotive designed to run on one —**narrow-gauge** *adj*

narrowly /nárrōli/ *adv* **1 BY SMALL MARGIN** by a very small margin or distance ○ *narrowly avoided capture* **2 INTENTLY** in a very concentrated, searching, or detailed way ○ *eyed him narrowly* **3 WITHIN NARROW LIMITS** in a way that allows little freedom or scope ○ *narrowly circumscribed*

narrow-minded /-mī́ndid/ *adj* having or showing a limited and often prejudiced or intolerant outlook —**narrow-mindedly** *adv* —**narrow-mindedness** *n*

narrow money *n* money usable as a means of exchange, especially notes and coins, but also some bank balances

narrows /nárrōz/ *n* a narrow section of a river, or a narrow stretch of sea usually between two larger bodies of water (+ *singular or plural verb*) ◊ **narrow**

narthex /naár theks/ *n* **1** an entrance hall at the west end of a Christian church between the porch and the nave **2** an area at the west end of the nave of an early Christian church separated off by a screen or railing behind which women, catechumens, or penitents were admitted [Late 17C. < late Greek *narthēx* 'giant fennel', later 'casket' (because the plant was used to make boxes).]

nartjie /naárchi/, **naartje** *n S Africa* a small sweet tangerine [Late 18C. Via Afrikaans < Tamil *nārattai* 'citrus'.]

narwhal /naár wayl/ (*plural* **-whal** *or* **-whals**), **narwal** (*plural* **-wal** *or* **-wals**), **narwhale** (*plural* **-whale** *or* **-whales**) *n* a small arctic whale, about 6m/20 ft long, with a spotted body, short flippers, and, in the male, a long twisted ivory tusk, formerly hunted for oil and ivory. *Monodon monoceros*. [Mid-17C. < Danish or Norwegian *narhval*.]

nary /náiri/ *adj* not a single (*archaic or regional*) ○ *Nary a word was said.* [Mid-18C. Contraction of *ne'er a* 'never a'.]

NASA /nássə/ *n* the US government agency responsible for nonmilitary programmes in the exploration and scientific study of space. Full form **National Aeronautics and Space Administration**

nasal /náyz'l/ *adj* **1 OF THE NOSE** forming part of or relating to the nose **2 PRONOUNCED THROUGH NOSE** pronounced with breath escaping mainly through the nose rather than the mouth. ◊ **oral** *adj.* **5** **3 WITH NASAL SOUNDS** characterized by nasal sounds ○ *a nasal accent* ■ *n* **1 NASAL SOUND** a nasal sound or a letter that represents it **2 HELMET**

PART the nosepiece of a helmet [Mid-17C. Directly or via French < medieval Latin *nasalis* < Latin *nasus* 'nose'.] —**nasality** /nay zálləti/ *n* —**nasally** *adv*

nasal concha *n* ANAT = **turbinate** *n*. 1

nasalize /náyzə līz/ (**-izes, -izing, -ized**), **nasalise** (**-ises, -ising, -ised**) *vti* to make a sound nasal by lowering the soft palate so that air flows through the nose — **nasalization** *n*

nascent /náss'nt, náyss-/ *adj* **1** in the process of emerging, being born, or starting to develop **2** in the process of being created in a reaction medium, often in a highly active form [Early 17C. < Latin *nascent-*, present participle of *nasci* 'be born'.] —**nascence** *n* —**nascency** *n*

NASDAQ /náz dak/ *n* in the United States, an electronic communications system that links all over-the-counter securities dealers to form a single market. Full form **National Association of Securities Dealers Automated Quotation System**

naseberry /náyz berri/ (*plural* **-ries**) *n* TREES = **sapodilla** *n*. 2 [Late 17C. < Spanish *nispero* or Portuguese *nespera* < Latin *mespilus* 'medlar', by association with BERRY.]

~~**nash**~~ incorrect spelling of **gnash**

Nash /nash/, **John** (1752–1835) British architect

Nash, **Ogden** (1902–71) US writer and lyricist

Nash, **Paul** (1889–1946) British painter

Nash, **Sir Walter** (1882–1968) British-born New Zealand statesman

Nashua /náshōŏ ə/ city in S New Hampshire. Population: 79,662 (1990).

Nashville /násh vil/ capital of Tennessee, in the north-central part of the state. Population: 510,274 (1998 estimate).

nasi goreng /naássi gə réng/ *n* a Malaysian dish of fried rice with other ingredients, usually including meat or fish [< Malay, 'fried rice']

nasion /náyzi ən/ *n* the point where the bridge of the nose meets the forehead [Late 19C. < French, < *nasal* 'nasal', after INION.] —**nasial** *adj*

naso- *prefix* nose, nasal ○ *nasogastric* [< Latin *nasus* < Indo-European, 'nose']

nasofrontal /náyzō frúnt'l/ *adj* relating to the nasal and the frontal bones jointly

nasogastric /náyzō gástrik/ *adj* passing through the nose to the stomach

nasolacrimal /náyzō lákrim'l/, **nasolachrymal** *adj* relating to or connecting the nose and the tear-producing sacs

nasopharyngeal /náyzō fə rínji əl/ *adj* relating to the nose and pharynx or to the nasopharynx

nasopharynx /náyzō fárringks/ (*plural* **-pharynges** /-fə rínjeez/ *or* **-pharynxes**) *n* the upper part of the pharynx, behind and above the soft palate, continuous with the nasal passages

Nasruddin /názrōŏ deen/ *n* a trickster who appears in Islamic folklore [Mid-20C. < Turkish.]

Nassau /nássaw/ capital of the Bahamas, on NE New Providence Island. Population: 171,542 (1990).

AKG London
Gamal Abdel Nasser

Nasser /nássər/, **Gamal Abdel** (1918–70) Egyptian statesman and president of Egypt (1956–70)

Nastase /nə stássi/, **Ilie** (*b.* 1946) Romanian tennis player

nastic /nástik/ *adj* relating to the movement of the parts of a plant in response to external stimuli such as the opening of a crocus flower in response to temperature [Early 20C. < Greek *nastos* 'pressed together' < *nassein* 'to press'.]

nasturtium /nə stúrshəm/ *n* a plant with shield-shaped pungent edible leaves. Flowers: yellow, orange, red. Genus: *Tropaeolum*. [12C. < Latin.]

nasty /naásti/ *adj* (**-tier, -tiest**) **1** SPITEFUL showing spitefulness, malice, or ill-nature ○ *a nasty trick to play on someone* **2** REPUGNANT TO SENSES repugnant or disgusting to the senses ○ *a nasty smell* **3** UNPLEASANT generally disagreeable, unpleasant, or causing discomfort ○ *The weather turned nasty.* **4** SERIOUS likely to cause harm or to be painful ○ *a nasty accident* ○ *a nasty bump on the head* **5** MORALLY OFFENSIVE morally offensive or obscene (*informal*) **6** DIFFICULT difficult to solve or deal with (*informal*) ■ *n* (*plural* **-ties**) UNPLEASANT PERSON OR THING somebody or something that is very disagreeable, harmful, or offensive (*informal*) [14C. < ?] —**nastily** *adv* —**nastiness** *n*

-nasty *suffix* nastic response ○ *thermonasty* [< Greek *nastos* (see NASTIC)]

NAS/UWT *abbr* National Association of Schoolmasters/Union of Women Teachers

Nat /nat/ *n* ANZ, S Africa a member of the National Party in Australia, New Zealand, or South Africa, or a member of parliament belonging to the National Party (*informal*) [Mid-20C. Shortening of *Nationalist*.]

nat. *abbr* **1** national **2** native **3** natural

natal[1] /náyt'l/ *adj* **1** relating to birth or to the time and place of birth **2** native (*literary*) [14C. < Latin *natalis* < *nasci* 'be born'.]

natal[2] /náyt'l/ *adj* relating to the buttocks [Late 19C. < Latin *natis* 'buttock'.]

Natal /nə taál/ **1** capital of Rio Grande do Norte State, NE Brazil. Population: 606,541 (1991). **2** former province of E South Africa

natality /nay tálləti, nə-/ *n* = **birthrate**

natant /náyt'nt/ *adj* floating or swimming in water (*technical*) [15C. < Latin *natant-*, present participle of *natare* (see NATATORY).]

Nataraja /naátə raája/ *n* the Hindu god Shiva when represented as a dancing figure with several arms and legs [Early 20C. < Hindi, 'prince of dancers'.]

natation /nə táysh'n/ *n* the action or skill of swimming (*formal*) [Mid-16C. < Latin *natation-* < *natare* (see NATATORY).] —**natational** *adj*

natatory /nə táytəri/, **natatorial** /náttə táwri əl/ *adj* relating to or adapted for swimming (*formal*) [Late 18C. < late Latin *natatorius* < Latin *natator* 'swimmer' < *natare* 'keep on swimming' < *nare* 'to swim'.]

natch /nach/ *adv* naturally or of course (*informal*) [Mid-20C. Shortening.]

Natchitoches /nákə tosh/ city in W Louisiana. Population: 17,267 (1996).

nates /náy teez/ *npl* the buttocks [Late 17C. < Latin, plural of *natis* 'buttock, rump'.]

NATFHE /nát fee/ *abbr* National Association of Teachers in Further and Higher Education

Nathan /náyth'n/ *n* in the Bible, a prophet at David's court (2 Samuel 7:1–17, 12:1–15)

Natick /náttik/ town in E Massachusetts. Population: 31,310 (1996).

nation /náysh'n/ *n* **1** PEOPLE IN LAND UNDER SINGLE GOVERNMENT a community of people or peoples living in a defined territory and organized under a single government **2** PEOPLE OF SAME ETHNICITY a community of people who share a common ethnic origin, culture, historical tradition, and, frequently, language, whether or not they live together in one territory or have their own government **3** NATIVE AMERICAN PEOPLE OR FEDERATION a Native American people or a federation of peoples ○ *the Apache nation* **4** LAND OF NATIVE AMERICAN NATION a territory occupied by a Native American people or federation **5** GROUP WITH COMMON INTEREST a group of people united by a common interest ○ *the hip-hop nation* [13C. Via French < Latin *nation-* 'birth, race' < *nat-*, past participle of *nasci* 'be born'.] —**nationhood** *n* —**nationless** *adj*

Nation /náysh'n/, **Carry** (1846–1911) US temperance leader

national /násh'nəl/ *adj* **1** OF A NATION relating or belonging to, or representing a nation, especially a nation as a whole rather than any particular part of it or section of its territory ○ *the national team* **2** FOR WHOLE NATION relating or applicable to or representing a whole nation ○ *the chairman of a national search committee* **3** CHARACTERISTIC OF PEOPLE OF PARTICULAR NATION relating to or characteristic of the people of a particular nation ○ *the British national character* **4** OWNED OR CONTROLLED BY CENTRAL GOVERNMENT owned, maintained, or controlled by the central government of a nation ○ *a national film museum* **5** REFERRING TO COALITION GOVERNMENT describes a coalition government consisting of members of all the major political parties ■ *n* **1** CITIZEN OF PARTICULAR NATION a citizen of a particular nation, especially when living in another country **2** MEDIA = **national newspaper** **3** COMPETITION INVOLVING CONTESTANTS FROM WHOLE COUNTRY a sports contest involving participants from every part of a country (*often plural*)

National *n* the Grand National (*informal*)

national anthem *n* a nation's official hymn or song, expressing patriotic sentiments and played or sung on public occasions

national assembly *n* a legislative body consisting of the elected representatives of a particular nation or country

National Assembly *n* the first legislative assembly set up during the French Revolution and ruling from 1789 to 1791

national bank *n* **1** a bank that acts as banker to a government and performs duties relating to national finances, especially the country's fiscal and monetary policy **2** US a bank in a system of privately owned commercial banks in the United States, operating under federal charter and legally required to be a member of the Federal Reserve System

National City city in SW California. Population: 54,249 (1990).

national colours *npl* the colours of a country's flag

national consciousness *n* the ideas, beliefs, and attitudes regarded as characteristic of a nation

national costume *n* CLOTHING = **national dress**

National Curriculum *n* the curriculum for pupils aged 5 to 16 taught in state schools in England and Wales following the Education Reform Act of 1988

national debt *n* the total amount of money owed by a nation's central government as a result of borrowing

national dress *n* clothes of a distinctive design that are, or were, typical of the people of a particular country

national emblem *n* an object that a country has adopted as its symbol, e.g. Canada's maple leaf or Scotland's thistle

National Gallery *n* a museum in Trafalgar Square, London, that contains more than 2,000 paintings from the national collection

National Gallery of Art *n* a museum in Washington, D.C. that contains the national collection of paintings, prints, drawings, sculptures, photographs, and other works of art

National Gallery of Australia *n* a museum in Canberra that contains the national collection of Aboriginal, modern Australian, and world art. Formerly called **Australian National Gallery**

National Gallery of Canada *n* a museum in Ottawa that contains the national collection of Canadian and European art

national grid *n* **1** a network of high-voltage electric power lines linking major power stations throughout the United Kingdom **2** a system of metric coordinates, shown as vertical and horizontal lines on maps, used for map reference purposes by the Ordnance Survey and other map-producing organizations

national guard *n* a military organization that operates as a national defence or police force

National Guard *n* in the United States, the military reserve units controlled by individual states and equipped by the federal government that can be called into service by either federal or state governments

National Health Service *n* in the United Kingdom, the state system for providing free or subsidized medical care, established in 1948 and financed mainly by taxation and national insurance

National Hunt racing, national hunt racing *n* horse-racing over distances up to 6.5 km/4½ mi. in which horses jump over movable hurdles or fixed fences, as opposed to flat racing

national income *n* the total money earned or gained by all residents of a country over a particular period of time, including income from rent, profits, interest, government benefits, salaries, and wages

National Insurance *n* in the United Kingdom, a state system based on compulsory contributions from employees and employers that provides medical and financial assistance, including pensions, to people who are ill, retired, or unemployed

National Insurance number *n* in the United Kingdom, a unique reference number assigned to each person within the state insurance system

national interest *n* whatever will benefit a nation, or a nation's concern for its own survival and prosperity

nationalise *vt* = **nationalize**

nationalism /násh'nəlizəm/ *n* **1** DESIRE FOR POLITICAL INDEPENDENCE the desire to achieve political independence, especially by a country under foreign control or by a people with a separate identity and culture but no state of their own **2** PATRIOTISM proud loyalty and devotion to a nation **3** EXCESSIVE DEVOTION TO NATION excessive or fanatical devotion to a nation and its interests, often associated with a belief that one country is superior to all others —**nationalist** *n, adj*

nationalistic /násh'nə lístik/ *adj* relating to or supporting nationalism, especially the kind that emphasizes fervent devotion to one nation and its interests above all others —**nationalistically** *adv*

nationality /náshə nálləti/ (*plural* **-ties**) *n* **1** CITIZENSHIP OF PARTICULAR NATION the status of belonging to a specific nation by origin, birth, or naturalization **2** PEOPLE FORMING NATION-STATE a people with a common origin, tradition, and often language, who form or are capable of forming a nation-state **3** ETHNIC GROUP WITHIN A LARGER ENTITY an ethnic group that is part of a larger entity such as a state **4** NATIONHOOD political independence as a separate nation **5** NATIONAL CHARACTER the character of a nation of people

nationalize /násh'nə līz/ (**-izes, -izing, -ized**), **nationalise** (**-ises, -ising, -ised**) *vt* **1** to transfer a business, property, or industry from private to governmental control or ownership **2** to make something national or to give a national character to something **3** = **naturalize** *v.* 1 —**nationalization** *n* —**nationalized** *adj* —**nationalizer** *n*

National Liberation Front *n* a radical nationalist movement in Algeria that launched a guerrilla war against France in the 1950s, leading to Algeria's independence in 1958

National Library of Australia *n* the national library of Australia, in Canberra, established as an independent institution by an Act of Parliament in 1960

National Library of Canada *n* the national library of Canada, founded in Ottawa in 1953

National Library of New Zealand *n* the national library of New Zealand, in Wellington, created in 1966 by combining the collections of the General Assembly Library, the Alexander Turnbull Library, and the National Library Service

nationally /násh'nəli/ *adv* in, to, or throughout an entire nation

national media *n* the nationally distributed or marketed broadcast and print products of a country such as major newspapers and television programming

national newspaper *n* a newspaper that is distributed to and sold in all parts of a country

national park *n* a large area of public land chosen by a government for its scenic, recreational, scientific, or historical importance and usually given special protection

National Party *n* **1** *Aus* AUSTRALIAN POLITICAL PARTY in Australia, a conservative political party that has strong support in rural areas and has usually formed a coalition with the Liberal Party of Australia **2** *NZ* NEW ZEALAND POLITICAL PARTY in New Zealand, a conservative political party **3** SOUTH AFRICAN POLITICAL PARTY in South Africa, a conservative political party that developed from the Afrikaner nationalist movement, came to power in 1948, was largely responsible for instituting apartheid, and relinquished power in 1994

national product *n* the total value of all goods and services produced by a nation during a specified, usually annual, period

National Record of Achievement *n* a record of a young person's achievements that, together with portfolios of evidence, will help in making a decision about the young person's future education, training, or employment

National Savings *n* in the United Kingdom, a savings bank that operates through local post offices and offers a variety of government-backed savings and investment schemes (+ *singular verb*)

national security *n* the protection of a nation from attack or other danger by maintaining adequate armed forces and guarding state secrets

National Security Council *n* in the United States, a council consisting of the President, the Secretary of State, and top military and intelligence officers that decides on policies and measures to maintain national security

national service *n* compulsory service in the armed forces or in a civilian role, as prescribed in some countries

national socialism, National Socialism *n* the ideology and practices of the Nazi Party, in Germany's Third Reich, which included national expansion, state control of the economy, the totalitarian principle of government, and anti-Semitism —**national socialist** *n, adj*

National Trust *n* **1** a charitable organization in England, Wales, and Northern Ireland, concerned with the preservation of areas of great natural beauty and historic buildings and monuments for the benefit of the public **2** an organization in Australia concerned with the preservation of areas of natural beauty and historic monuments

National Trust for Scotland *n* a Scottish charitable organization, established in 1931, concerned with the preservation of areas of natural beauty and historic buildings and monuments for the benefit of the public

National Vocational Qualification *n* full form of **NVQ**

Nation of Islam *n* a movement of African Americans founded in 1930 whose members follow Islamic religious practice, because of a belief that Black Americans have Islamic origins

nation-state *n* an independent state recognized by and able to interact with other states, especially one composed of people who are of one, as opposed to several, nationalities

nationwide /náysh'n wíd/ *adj* applying to, happening in, or found in all parts of a nation ○ *a nationwide advertising campaign* ■ *adv* covering the whole nation or throughout the nation

ϟ **native** /náytiv/ *adj* **1** INBORN existing in or belonging to someone by nature ○ *her native intelligence* **2** BORN OR ORIGINATING SOMEWHERE born or originating in a particular place **3** RELATING TO SOMEBODY BECAUSE OF BIRTH relating or belonging to somebody or something because of the place or circumstances of birth **4** INDIGENOUS originating, produced, growing, or living naturally in a place **5** LOCAL, ESPECIALLY ABORIGINAL, INHABITANTS characteristic of, belonging to, or relating to the indigenous inhabitants of a particular place, particularly those with a traditional culture **6** NOT EXTERNALLY AFFECTED unaffected by artificial or outside influences **7** OCCURRING NATURALLY found in nature, especially in a pure or unadulterated form ○ *native copper* **8** RAISED IN BRITISH WATERS describes oysters raised in British waters, especially in artificial beds **9** FOR A PARTICULAR COMPUTER SYSTEM designed exclusively for a particular computer operating system ■ *n* **1** SOMEONE BORN IN PARTICULAR PLACE someone born or brought up in a particular place ○ *a native of Birmingham* **2** INDIGENOUS INHABITANT an original indigenous inhabitant of a place **3** OFFENSIVE TERM an offensive term for an original inhabitant of a place belonging to an indigenous non-white people with a traditional culture, as distinct from a colonial settler and immigrant (*dated*) **4** LONG-TERM LOCAL RESIDENT an established permanent local resident as opposed to a visitor, temporary resident, or newcomer (*humorous*) **5** INDIGENOUS PLANT OR ANIMAL SPECIES a plant or animal species that originates from a particular area **6** OYSTER RAISED IN BRITISH WATERS an oyster raised in British waters, especially in an artificial bed [14C. Directly or via French *natif* < Latin *nativus* 'born' < *nasci* 'be born'.] —**natively** *adv* —**nativeness** *n* ◇ **go native** to take up the customs and culture of the foreign place where you have settled (*humorous*)

SYNONYMS ***native, aboriginal, indigenous, autochthonous***

CORE MEANING: originating in a particular place

native born or originating in a particular place; **aboriginal** existing in a region from the earliest known times; **indigenous** originating in and typical of a region or country; **autochthonous** originating where currently found, especially used of rocks and minerals that were formed in their present position, or flora, fauna, or inhabitants descended from those present in a region from earliest times.

Native American *n* a member of any of the indigenous peoples of North, South, or Central America, belonging to the Mongoloid group of peoples ■ *adj* relating to any of the indigenous American peoples, their languages, or their cultures

USAGE See ***Indian***.

native-born *adj* belonging to a place by birth

native land *n* the land to which somebody belongs by birth

native speaker *n* a speaker of a language learned in infancy

native tongue *n* the first language that somebody learns to speak

nativism /náytivizəm/ *n* **1** POLICY OF FAVOURING NATIVE INHABITANTS a policy, especially in the United States, of favouring the interests of the native inhabitants of a country over those of immigrants **2** POLICY OF REAFFIRMING INDIGENOUS CULTURE a policy of protecting and celebrating traditional cultures **3** DOCTRINE OF INNATE IDEAS the belief that the mind possesses some ideas that are inborn and not derived from external sources **4** THEORY CLAIMING PERSONALITY IS INNATELY DETERMINED a theory claiming that personality and behaviour are determined from within, not externally —**nativist** *n, adj* —**nativistic** /náyti vístik/ *adj*

nativity /nə tívvəti/ (*plural* **-ties**) *n* **1** birth or origin, especially the place, process, or circumstances of being born **2** a horoscope based on the time of somebody's birth [14C. Via Old French < Latin *nativitas* < *nativus* (see NATIVE).]

Nativity (*plural* **-ties**) *n* **1** BIRTH OF JESUS CHRIST the birth of Jesus Christ, which is celebrated by Christians at Christmas **2** REPRESENTATION OF JESUS CHRIST'S BIRTH an artistic representation, especially a painting, of the events surrounding the birth of Jesus Christ **3** CHRISTMAS the festival of Christmas

nativity play *n* a play, usually performed by children at Christmastime, that tells the story of the birth of Jesus Christ

NATO /náytō/, **Nato** *n* an international organization established in 1949 to promote mutual defence and collective security that was the primary Western alliance during the Cold War. Full form **North Atlantic Treaty Organization**

natrium /náytri əm/ *n* a name for sodium, which gave it its chemical symbol of Na [Mid-19C. < NATRON.]

natriuresis /náytriyōō réessiss/ *n* the excretion of sodium in urine, especially in excessive amounts [Mid-20C. < NATRIUM + Greek *ourēsis* 'urination'.] —**natriuretic** /-réttik/ *adj*

natrolite /náttrə līt/ *n* a white sodium aluminosilicate mineral of the zeolite group [Early 19C. < NATRON.]

natron /náytrən, -tron/ *n* a white, yellow, or grey hydrous sodium carbonate mineral. Source: salt deposits. Use: formerly, embalming. [Late 17C. Via French, Spanish, and Arabic < Greek *nitron* 'potassium or sodium nitrate'.]

natter /náttər/ *vi* to talk about not very serious matters, often rapidly and at length and sometimes in an irritating way (*informal*) ■ *n* a trivial or gossipy conversation (*informal*) [Early 19C. < ?]

natterjack /náttər jak/ *n* a rare West European toad that inhabits sandy areas and has short hind legs and a skin colour ranging from yellow-green to olive-grey. *Bufo calamita.* [Mid-18C. < ?]

natty /nátti/ (**-tier, -tiest**) *adj* neat and smart in appearance or dress [Late 18C. < ?] —**nattily** *adv* —**nattiness** *n*

natural /náchərəl/ *adj* **1** OF NATURE relating to nature **2** CONFORMING WITH NATURE in accordance with the usual course of nature ○ *natural symptoms of aging* **3** PRODUCED BY NATURE present in or produced by nature, rather than being artificial or created by people ○ *a natural sapphire* **4 OF PHYSICAL WORLD** relating to the physical rather than the spiritual world **5 LIKE HUMAN NATURE** in accordance with human nature ○ *It's only natural that they should want to be independent.* **6 INNATE** inborn, rather than acquired ○ *lots of natural charm* **7 BEING SOMETHING BY NATURE** having a particular character by nature ○ *a natural leader* **8 NOT AFFECTED** behaving in a sincere and unaffected way and not affected or adopted for a particular purpose **9 NOT ARTIFICIAL** not artificially coloured or treated **10 LIKE REAL LIFE** representing something in a way that seems true to life **11 ILLEGITIMATE** born of unmarried parents (*archaic*) ○ *a natural child* **12 BIOLOGICAL** related by blood, rather than adoption ○ *her natural mother* **13 NOT SHARP OR FLAT** describes a note in music that is neither sharp nor flat **14 WITHOUT SHARPS OR FLATS** describes a musical key or scale containing no sharps or flats **15 WITHOUT JOKER OR WILD CARD** not made using a joker or a wild card ○ *a natural flush* ■ *n* **1 SOMEBODY WITH INNATE SKILLS OR ABILITIES** a person who has seemingly innate skills or abilities ○ *a natural at bowling* **2 MUSICAL SIGN CANCELLING SHARP OR FLAT** a sign placed before a musical note in order to cancel a previous sharp or flat **3 NOTE AFFECTED BY NATURAL SIGN** a musical note affected by a natural sign **4 STAKE-WINNING RESULT OR COMBINATION** a result or combination in certain card and dice games such as craps and pontoon, that immediately wins the stake **5 LIGHT COLOUR** a nearly white colour with tints of grey, yellow, or brown, like that of undyed fibres [13C. Via French < Latin *naturalis* < *natura* (see NATURE).] —**naturalness** *n*

natural childbirth *n* childbirth with little or no medication or medical intervention, in which the mother uses special techniques and exercises in order to minimize pain and assist in the delivery

natural death *n* death caused by disease or old age rather than by an act of violence or an accident

natural disaster *n* a disaster such as an earthquake caused by natural forces rather than by human action

natural fibre *n* a fibre such as cotton, wool, or silk that forms naturally

natural gas *n* a mixture of combustible hydrocarbon gases, mostly methane and ethane, found trapped in the pore spaces of certain sedimentary rocks, often along with petroleum deposits

natural history *n* **1 STUDY AND DESCRIPTION OF NATURE** the study and description of living things, especially their behaviour and how they relate to one another **2 NATURAL PHENOMENA OF TIME OR PLACE** the natural phenomena, especially plants and animals, of a particular time or place **3 NATURAL DEVELOPMENT** the natural development of something such as an organism or a disease over a period of time ○ *the natural history of the leech* **4 WRITTEN ACCOUNT OF ASPECT OF NATURE** a written account of a particular aspect of the natural world

naturalise *vti* = **naturalise**

naturalism /náchərəlizəm/ *n* **1 MOVEMENT OR SCHOOL ADVOCATING REALISTIC DESCRIPTION** in art or literature, a movement or school advocating factual or realistic description of life including its less pleasant aspects **2 BELIEF IN RELIGIOUS TRUTH FROM NATURE** a belief that all religious truth is derived from nature and natural causes, and not from revelation **3 DOCTRINE REJECTING SPIRITUAL EXPLANATIONS OF WORLD** a system of thought that rejects all spiritual and supernatural explanations of the world and holds that science is the sole basis of what can be known

naturalist /náchərəlist/ *n* **1 SOMEBODY STUDYING NATURAL HISTORY** a student of or expert in natural history, especially botany or zoology **2 ADVOCATE OF NATURALISM** a believer in or adherent of naturalism, especially in the arts ■ *adj* **RELATING TO BELIEFS OF NATURALISM** relating to or in accordance with the beliefs of naturalism

naturalistic /náchərə lístik/ *adj* **1 REPRODUCING EFFECTS OF NATURE** imitating or reproducing nature or perceived reality in a very exact and faithful way **2 RELATING TO BELIEFS OF NATURALISM** relating to, characteristic of, or in accordance with the tenets of naturalism, especially in art or literature **3 OF NATURALISTS** relating to naturalists or natural history —**naturalistically** *adv*

naturalize /náchərə līz/ (**-izes, -izing, -ized**), **naturalise** (**-ises, -ising, -ised**) *v* **1** *vti* **GRANT CITIZENSHIP TO** to grant citizenship to somebody of foreign birth, or to acquire citizenship in an adopted country **2** *vt* **INTRODUCE SOMETHING FOREIGN INTO GENERAL USE** to introduce something foreign such as a word or custom into general use or into the language of a community **3** *vti* **ACCLIMATIZE PLANT OR ANIMAL** to cause a plant or animal from another region to become established in a new environment or to adapt successfully to new environmental conditions **4** *vt* **EXPLAIN IN NATURAL TERMS** to explain a phenomenon in terms of natural as opposed to supernatural causes **5** *vt* **MAKE NATURAL** to make something natural or lifelike —**naturalization** *n* —**naturalized** *adj* —**naturalizer** *n*

natural killer cell *n* a white blood cell (**lymphocyte**) that can recognize microbes and tumour cells as 'foreign', without requiring prior exposure to them, and destroy them

natural language *n* **1** a naturally evolved human language as opposed to a created language such as a computer language **2** naturally evolved human languages considered collectively

⚡**natural language processing** *n* the branch of computational linguistics concerned with the use of artificial intelligence to process natural languages, as in machine translation

natural law *n* **1 LAW OF MORALITY** a law of morality believed to be derived from human beings' inherent sense of right and wrong, rather than from revelation or the legislation produced by society **2 LAW OF NATURE** a law that governs the behaviour of natural phenomena **3 BELIEF IN UNIVERSAL JUSTICE SYSTEM** the belief that general laws of nature can be applied as a system of justice for all societies, regardless of their individual culture or customs

natural light *n* light from a natural source, usually the sun, as opposed to artificial light

natural logarithm *n* a logarithm with the irrational number *e* as a base

naturally /náchərəli/ *adv* **1 AS EXPECTED** as might be expected ○ *They naturally objected to being treated in this way.* **2 OF COURSE** without any question or doubt ○ *'You'll go then?' 'Naturally'.* **3 BY NATURE** as a result of a natural feature, talent, or quality that somebody possesses ○ *a naturally gifted player* ○ *Writing seems to come naturally to her.* **4 IN NORMAL WAY** in a normal and unaffected manner ○ *People seldom act naturally when being filmed.* **5 WITHOUT ARTIFICIAL AID OR TREATMENT** occurring as a natural feature or quality without artificial aid **6 REALISTICALLY** in a manner that faithfully represents nature

natural medicine *n* MED = **naturopathy**

natural number *n* any whole number greater than zero

natural philosophy *n* the study of nature and natural phenomena (*archaic*)

natural resource *n* a naturally occurring material such as coal or wood that can be exploited by people

natural scale *n* a musical scale that has no sharps or flats

natural science *n* any science such as biology, chemistry, and physics that deals with phenomena observable in nature —**natural scientist** *n*

natural selection *n* the process, according to Darwin, by which organisms best suited to survival in a particular environment achieve greater reproductive success, thereby passing advantageous genetic characteristics on to future generations. ◊ **artificial selection**

natural theology *n* a theology that holds that knowledge of God can be derived by human reason alone, not requiring divine revelation

natural virtue *n* in theology, one of the four virtues of which people are capable without direct assistance from God, specifically fortitude, justice, prudence, and temperance

natural wastage *n* a gradual reduction in the workforce of an organization achieved by not replacing staff who leave through retirement or resignation

natural world *n* natural phenomena collectively, as opposed to supernatural or paranormal phenomena or those created by human activity

nature /náychər/ *n* **1 PHYSICAL WORLD** the physical world including all natural phenomena and living things **2 nature, Nature FORCES CONTROLLING PHYSICAL WORLD** the forces and processes collectively that control the phenomena of the physical world independently of human volition or intervention. ◊ **Mother Nature 3 COUNTRYSIDE** the countryside or the environment in a condition relatively unaffected by human activity or as the home of living creatures other than human beings **4 TYPE** a type or sort of thing ○ *a detective novel or something of that nature* **5 INTRINSIC CHARACTER OF PERSON OR THING** the intrinsic or essential character of somebody or something ○ *It's not in her nature to be spiteful.* **6 TEMPERAMENT** disposition or temperament in a person ○ *It's just not part of his nature to act unkindly.* **7 REAL APPEARANCE OR ASPECT** the appearance or aspect of a person, place, or thing that is considered to reflect reality ○ *The portrait was remarkably true to nature.* **8 PRIMITIVE EXISTENCE** a basic state of existence, untouched and uninfluenced by civilization **9 NATURAL STATE OF HUMANKIND** the natural and original condition of humankind, as distinguished from a state of grace **10 UNIVERSAL HUMAN BEHAVIOUR** the patterns of behaviour or the moral standards that are considered to be universally found and recognized among human beings **11 INHERITED CHARACTERISTICS** the inherited characteristics of an organism, as opposed to what is learnt from experience or the environment ○ *nature versus nurture* [13C. Via Old French < Latin *natura* 'birth, nature' < *nasci* 'be born'.] ◇ **by nature** as a part of somebody's or something's essential character ○ *optimistic by nature* ◇ **in the nature of something** in the category of something ○ *Have you got anything in the nature of a computer table?*

-natured *suffix* having or showing a particular nature or disposition ○ *good-natured* —**-naturedly** *adv*

nature reserve, nature preserve *n* a managed and protected area of land usually containing rare or endangered plants or animals

nature strip *n Aus* a strip of vegetation, such as trees, grass, or other plants, along the edge of a pavement or between the lanes of a main road or highway

nature trail *n* a route through a natural area that is specially designed to draw attention to interesting natural features

naturism /náychərizəm/ *n* **1** the practice of going without clothes, usually in a communal setting or in designated areas, in the belief that nudity is a healthy natural state **2** worship of nature in general, or of objects of nature such as trees and mountains —**naturist** *n* —**naturistic** /naychə rístik/ *adj* —**naturistically** *adv*

naturopathy /náychə róppəthi/ *n* a system of medicine founded on the belief that diet, mental state, exercise, breathing, and other natural factors are central to the origin and treatment of disease —**naturopath** /náychərō path/ *n* —**naturopathic** /náychərō páthik/ *adj* —**naturopathically** *adv*

Naugatuck /náwgə tuk/ **1** river in SW Connecticut. Length: 105 km/65 mi. **2** town in SW Connecticut. Population: 30,625 (1990).

naught /nawt/ *n* **1** *US* = **nought** *n*. 1 **2** nothing at all (*archaic or literary*) ○ *Their efforts were all for naught.* [Old English *nāwiht* < *nā* NO[1] + *wiht* 'thing, being' (see WIGHT)]

naughty /náwti/ (**-tier, -tiest**) *adj* **1 BADLY BEHAVED** badly behaved, especially by being mischievous or disobedient **2 MILDLY INDECENT** mildly indecent or improper (*humorous*) ○ *standing with his hands over his naughty parts* ○ *a naughty smile* **3 SINFUL** mildly sinful (*humorous*) ○ *Would it be naughty of me to have another chocolate?* [14C. Literally 'having naught, poor'.] —**naughtily** *adv* —**naughtiness** *n*

Nauman /nówmən/, **Bruce** (*b.* 1941) US sculptor

nauplius /náwpli əss/ (*plural* **-i** /-pli ī/) *n* a free-swimming larva that is produced by many different crustaceans, with an unsegmented body, three pairs of limbs, and a single eye [Mid-19C. Via Latin, kind of shellfish < Greek *nauplios*.]

Nauru /nə rōō/ island republic in the central Pacific Ocean, just south of the Equator. Capital: Yaren. Population: 10,273 (1996). Area: 21 sq. km/8.2 sq. mi. —**Nauruan** *n*, *adj*

nausea /náwzi ə, -si ə/ *n* **1** the unsettling feeling in the stomach that accompanies the urge to vomit **2** deep disgust (*literary*) [15C. Via Latin < Greek *nausia* < *naus* 'ship'.]

nauseate /náwzi ayt, -si ayt/ (**-ates, -ating, -ated**) *vti* **1** to have, or make somebody have, the unsettling feeling in the stomach that accompanies the urge to vomit **2** to feel, or make somebody feel, deep disgust

USAGE ***Nauseous, nauseating,*** or ***nauseated***? If you feel sick, you are ***nauseated***, though some people do use ***nauseous*** in this sense. If you experience something sickening, that thing is ***nauseous*** or ***nauseating***, as in *a nauseous/nauseating odour in the barn.*

nauseating /náwzi ayting, -si ayting/ *adj* **1** producing the unsettling feeling in the stomach that accompanies the urge to vomit **2** deeply disgusting —**nauseatingly** *adv*

nauseous /náwzi əss, -si əss/ *adj* **1** producing the unsettling feeling in the stomach that accompanies the urge to vomit **2** ⚠ suffering from the unsettling feeling in the stomach that accompanies the urge to vomit — **nauseously** *adv* —**nauseousness** *n*

USAGE See ***nauseate***.

naut. *abbr* nautical

nautch /nawch/ *n* a professional performance of traditional Indian dancing [Early 19C. Via Hindi *nāc* < Sanskrit *nṛt* 'dance'.]

nautical /náwtik'l/ *adj* relating to sailors, ships, or seafaring [Mid-16C. Via Latin < Greek *nautikos* < *nautēs* 'sailor' < *naus* 'ship'.] —**nautically** *adv*

nautical mile *n* **1** (*symbol* **M**) an international unit of measurement of distance at sea equal to 1.852 km **2** a measurement of distance at sea used in the UK and taken to be equal to 1.8532 km or about 6,076 ft

nautiloid /náwti loyd/ *n* a mollusc that belongs to the group that includes the nautiluses and many fossil species. Subclass: Nautiloidea. [Mid-19C. < NAUTILUS.]

nautilus /náwtiləss/ (*plural* **-luses** *or* **-li** /-ti lī/) *n* **1** a mollusc with numerous tentacles, a horny beak, and a spiral shell with gas-filled chambers for buoyancy. Native to: South Pacific and Indian Oceans. Genus: *Nautilus*. **2** MARINE BIOL = **paper nautilus** [Early 17C. Via Latin < Greek *nautilos* 'sailor, nautilus' < *nautēs* (see NAUTICAL).]

NAV *abbr* net asset value

nav. *abbr* **1** naval **2** navigable **3** navigation

Navajo /návvəhō/ (*plural* **-jo** *or* **-jos** *or* **-joes**), **Navaho** (*plural* **-ho** *or* **-hos** *or* **-hoes**) *n* **1** a member of a Native North American people living mainly in N New Mexico and Arizona **2** the Athabaskan language of the Navajo people. Native speakers: 225,000. [Late 18C. Via Spanish *(Apaches de) Navajó* '(Apaches of) Navajó' < Tewa *navahū* 'fields adjoining a ravine'.] —**Navajo** *adj*

naval /náyv'l/ *adj* relating or belonging to a navy or to warships —**navally** *adv*

SPELLCHECK Do not confuse ***naval*** with ***navel***, which has a similar sound. Beware: your spellchecker will not catch this error.

naval architect *n* a designer of ships —**naval architecture** *n*

naval dockyard *n* a navy-owned shipyard where warships are built and repaired. US term **navy yard**

naval stores *npl* products used in shipbuilding, especially, formerly, turpentine and pitch

Navarre /nə vaár/ autonomous region in NE Spain. Capital: Pamplona. Population: 519,227 (1991). Area: 10,421 sq. km/4,024 sq. mi.

nave[1] /nayv/ *n* the long central hall of a cross-shaped church, often with pillars on each side, where the congregation sits [Late 17C. Via medieval Latin < Latin *navis* 'ship'.]

nave[2] /nayv/ *n* the hub of a wheel [Old English *nafu* < Germanic]

navel /náyv'l/ *n* a small rounded hollow on the surface of the human stomach, where the end of the umbilical cord was tied after being cut. Technical name **umbilicus** [Old English *nafela* < Indo-European] ◇ **examine** *or* **contemplate your navel** to spend too much time in pointless self-analysis (*informal humorous*)

SPELLCHECK See ***naval***.

navel-gazing *n* pointless self-analysis as opposed to considering broader issues or making a decision

navel orange *n* a sweet seedless orange with a small navel-shaped depression or bump at its blossom end enclosing a smaller secondary fruit. *Citrus sinensis*.

navelwort /náyv'l wurt/ *n* PLANTS = **pennywort** *n*. 1 [15C. < the navel-shaped indentation on its leaves.]

navicular /nə víkyŏŏlər/ *n* ANAT = **navicular bone** *n*. 1 ■ *adj* **1** shaped like a boat (*formal*) **2** relating to a navicular bone [15C. < late Latin *navicularis* < Latin *navicula* 'small ship' < *navis* 'ship'.]

navicular bone *n* **1** a small boat-shaped bone in the human wrist or ankle **2** a small bone in a horse's hoof. It is prone to disease (**navicular disease**), causing lameness.

⚡**navigable** /návvigəb'l/ *adj* **1** PASSABLE BY SHIP passable by ship or boat, especially deep enough and wide enough to allow ships or boats to sail through **2** STEERABLE able to be steered or otherwise controlled **3** FOLLOWABLE THROUGH LINKS designed in such a way that the user can move between or through sections by clicking on usually highlighted computer links ○ *This website is navigable in English and Spanish.* —**navigability** /návvigə bílləti/ *n* — **navigably** *adv*

⚡**navigate** /návvi gayt/ (**-gates, -gating, -gated**) *v* **1** *vti* FIND A ROUTE to find a way through a place, or direct the course of something, especially a ship or aircraft, using a route-finding system ○ *navigating by the stars* **2** *vt* PASS THROUGH A PLACE to follow a correct or satisfactory course along a route ○ *Even a champion paddler would have difficulty navigating those rapids.* **3** *vi* KEEP A CAR ON THE RIGHT ROUTE to have responsibility for keeping a car on the right route, e.g. by following a map and giving the driver instructions **4** *vt* FIND YOUR WAY to find a way to a place, usually with difficulty (*informal*) ○ *managed to navigate his way through the fog* **5** *vti* FOLLOW THROUGH LINKS to move between the different areas of a website by using the links provided in it [Late 16C. < Latin *navigat-*, past principle of *navigare* 'to sail' < *navis* 'ship' + *agere* 'drive'.]

navigation /návvi gáysh'n/ *n* **1** SCIENCE OF NAVIGATING the science of plotting and following a course from one place to another and of determining the position of a moving ship, aircraft, or other vehicle **2** DIRECTING OF A VEHICLE'S COURSE the plotting and directing of the course of a ship, aircraft, or other vehicle **3** MOVEMENT THROUGH A PLACE the act or task of moving through a place or along a route, e.g. along a river or through a range of mountains —**navigational** *adj* —**navigationally** *adv*

navigation light *n* any one of a number of lights on the outside of a ship or aircraft that alerts others to its position and direction

navigation satellite *n* an artificial satellite, used as an aid to navigation, that follows a fixed orbit made known to navigators on ships and aircraft

navigator /návvi gaytər/ *n* **1** a person who navigates something, especially a ship or aircraft **2** a passenger of a motor vehicle who gives a driver information about a route

Navratilova /na vrátti lṓvə/, **Martina** (*b.* 1956) Czech-born US tennis player

navvy /návvi/ *n* (*plural* **-vies**) an unskilled labourer, especially somebody who does the heavy digging work involved in the building of roads, railways, and canals (*dated*) ■ *vi* (**-vies, -vying, -vied**) to work as a navvy [Early 19C. Shortening of NAVIGATOR ('canal labourer').]

navy /náyvi/ *n* (*plural* **-vies**) **1** the branch of a country's armed forces that crews, maintains, and fights on warships **2** a fleet of ships, especially one belonging to a country **3** COLOURS = **navy blue** ■ *adj* COLOURS = **navy blue** [14C. < Old French *navie* 'fleet' < Latin *navis* 'ship'.]

navy bean *n* a small white variety of kidney bean [< its former use as a food staple in the US Navy]

navy blue *n* a dark blue colour ■ *adj* of a dark blue colour (*hyphenated before nouns*) ○ *a navy-blue dress* [< the colour of the British naval uniform]

navy cut *n* tobacco that has been cut into fine slices from a large block

navy yard *n US* = **naval dockyard**

nawab /nə waáb/ *n* **1** a title used for a local nobleman in India during the Mughal empire **2** a distinguished Muslim man in Pakistan [Mid-18C. Via Urdu *nawāb* < Arabic *nā'ib* 'deputy'.]

nay /nay/ *n* NO VOTE a vote of no or somebody who votes no ■ *adv* INTRODUCING CORRECTION used to introduce a phrase that corrects something just said, often a phrase that states the truth in stronger terms (*archaic or literary*) ○ *It was a disappointing, nay, humiliating, outcome.* ■ *interj* NO no (*archaic*) [12C. < Old Norse *nei* < *ne* 'not' + *ei* 'ever'.]

naysay /náy say/ (**-says, -saying, -said**) *vt US* to refuse, oppose, or criticize a proposal (*literary*)

naysayer /náy sayər/ *n US* a voter or speaker against something (*literary*)

Nazarene /názzə reén/ *n* **1** SOMEBODY FROM NAZARETH somebody who comes from Nazareth **2** MEMBER OF PROTESTANT CHURCH a member of the Church of the Nazarene, a modern Protestant denomination **3** JESUS CHRIST Jesus Christ, as connected with Nazareth (*literary*) [13C. Via late Latin < Greek *Nazarēnos* < *Nazaret* 'Nazareth'.]

Nazareth /názzərəth/ town in N Israel. Population: 49,800 (1992).

Nazarite /názzə rīt/, **Nazirite** *n* a member of a Jewish religious group in biblical times whose members made various vows of abstinence, including a vow not to drink wine or cut their hair [Mid-16C. < late Latin *Nazaraeus* < Greek *Nazōraios* < *Nazaret* 'Nazareth'.]

Nazca Lines *n* a group of long straight lines representing birds, fish, animals, or geometrical figures carved into the desert near Nazca, S Peru, in pre-Inca times and only visible from the air

Nazi /naátsi/ *n* **1** FOLLOWER OF HITLER a member of the German National Socialist Party that came to power under the leadership of Adolf Hitler in 1933 (*often before nouns*) **2** RACIST somebody regarded as having right-wing political views, especially on race and immigration (*insult*) **3** **Nazi, nazi** BOSSY PERSON an authoritarian or dictatorial person (*insult; offensive in some contexts*) [Mid-20C. < German, shortening of *Nationalsozialist* 'national socialist' or *Nationalsozialismus* 'national socialism'.] —**Nazification** /naàtsifi káysh'n/ *n* — **Nazify** /naátsi fī/ *vt*

Nazirite *n* RELIG = **Nazarite**

Nazism /naátsizəm/ *n* the philosophy of the German National Socialist Party under the leadership of Adolf Hitler

nb *abbr* no ball

Nb *symbol* niobium

NB, N.B. *abbr* New Brunswick

N.B., NB, n.b., nb *interj* used to draw somebody's attention to something particularly important, usually an addition to or qualification of a previous statement. Full form **nota bene**

NBA *abbr* **1** National Basketball Association **2** National Boxing Association **3** Net Book Agreement

NBC *abbr* **1** National Broadcasting Company **2** nuclear, biological, and chemical (*refers to weapons or warfare*)

⚡**NBD** *abbr* no big deal (*in e-mails*)

NBG, nbg *abbr* no bloody good (*informal*)

⚡**NBTD** *abbr* nothing better to do (*in e-mails*)

⚡**nc** *abbr* New Caledonia (*in Internet addresses*)

NC[1] *n* a UK qualification in a vocational subject that is roughly equivalent to a GCSE. Full form **National Certificate**

NC[2] *abbr* **1** no charge **2** **NC, N.C.** North Carolina **3** **NC, N.C.** National Curriculum

NCC *abbr* **1** National Consumer Council **2** National Curriculum Council **3** Nature Conservancy Council

NCO *abbr* noncommissioned officer

NCT *abbr* National Childbirth Trust

Nd *symbol* neodymium

ND[1] *n* a UK vocational qualification that is roughly equivalent to two A levels. Full form **National Diploma**

ND[2], **N.D.** *abbr* North Dakota

n.d., ND *abbr* no date

N. Dak. *abbr* North Dakota

Ndebele /əndə beéli, -báyli/ (*plural* **-le** *or* **-les**) *n* **1** a member of a South African people who originated in NE South Africa, but now live mainly in S Zimbabwe **2** the Bantu language of the Ndebele people, which has distinct forms in Zimbabwe and South Africa. Native speakers: over 1 million. [Late 19C. < Nguni.] —**Ndebele** *adj*

NDP *abbr* net domestic product

NDT *abbr* Newfoundland Daylight Time

⚡**ne** *abbr* Niger (*in Internet addresses*)

né /nay/ *adj* **1** used to introduce a man's former or original name, e.g. the name of a newly titled peer ○ *Lord Healey, né Denis Healey* **2** *US* used to introduce the name that something was formerly known under ○ *Zimbabwe, né Rhodesia* [Mid-20C. < French.]

Ne *symbol* neon

NE *abbr* **1** Nebraska **2** **NE, N.E.** New England **3** northeast **4** northeastern

Neagh, Lough /nay/ lake in central Northern Ireland, the largest lake in the British Isles. Area: 396 sq. km/153 sq. mi.

Neandertal /ni ándər taal/, **Neanderthal** /ni ándər thaal/ *adj* **1** RELATING TO NEANDERTAL MAN relating to Neandertal man **2 Neandertal, neandertal** OFFENSIVE TERM an offensive term used to describe somebody perceived as displaying the lack of intellect, lack of sensitivity, and boorishness traditionally associated with cave dwellers (*insult*) **3 Neandertal, neandertal** OFFENSIVE TERM an offensive term meaning very old-fashioned or conservative (*insult*) ■ *n* **Neandertal, neandertal** OFFENSIVE TERM an offensive term for somebody who is regarded as crude, primitive, or excessively old-fashioned (*insult*) [Mid-19C. After a valley in W Germany.]

Neandertal man *n* an extinct subspecies of human beings that populated Europe, North Africa, and W Asia in the early Stone Age

Neanderthal *adj*, *n* = **Neandertal**

neap /neep/ *n* GEOG = **neap tide** ■ *adj* relating to or associated with a neap tide [15C. < Old English nēp-.]

Neapolitan /neè əpóllitən/ *adj* relating to the Italian city of Naples, or its people or culture ■ *n* somebody who comes from Naples [15C. < Latin *Neapolitanus* < Greek *Neapolis*, literally 'new town'.]

Neapolitan ice cream *n* ice cream made in differently coloured and flavoured layers, usually served in a slice

neap tide *n* a tide that shows the least range between high and low and occurs twice a month between the first and third quarters of the moon

near /neer/ CORE MEANING: at or to a point that is not far away in distance ○ (*prep*) *The art exhibition is near here.* ○ (*adv*) *He took a step nearer to the water.* ○ (*adv*) *as the car drew nearer* ○ (*adj*) *There must be a restaurant nearer than that.* ○ (*adj*) *Can you tell me where the nearest telephone is?* **1** *adv*, *prep*, *adj* SHORT TIME AWAY at or to a time not far away ○ (*adv*) *as the time for her to leave drew near* ○ (*prep*) *He should arrive near the end of the week.* ○ (*adj*) *We shall be moving in the very near future.* **2** *adv*, *adj* CLOSE at a point that is not far away in state, resemblance, or number ○ (*adv*) *It was nearer two hours before he got through customs.* ○ (*adv*) *He felt a sensation that was near to fear.* ○ (*adj*) *the nearest thing to a champion this country has ever had* **3** *adv*, *adj* ALMOST almost the state or situation mentioned ○ (*adv*) *I damn near fainted.* ○ (*adv*) *near total failure* ○ (*adj*) *living in near poverty* **4** *adj*, *n* ON THE LEFT on the left side, especially of an animal or a horse-drawn vehicle ○ *the near foreleg* **5** *adj* CLOSELY RELATED closely related to somebody (*archaic*) **6** *adj* MISERLY reluctant to give or spend money (*archaic*) **7** *vti* APPROACH to approach, or approach a particular place, time, or state ○ *The project is nearing completion.* ○ *With the big event nearing, everyone was working hard.* [12C. < Old Norse *nær* 'nearer' < *nā* 'near'.] —**nearness** *n* ◇ **near the bone** *or* **knuckle** rather vulgar or indecent (*informal*)

⚡**NEAR** *n* a binary operator used in text searches that returns true if its operands (usually two words) occur within a specified proximity to each other, and false otherwise

nearby /neèr bí/ *adj*, *adv* in, at, or to a place a short distance away ○ *a nearby grocer* ○ *His mother was waiting nearby.*

Nearctic /ni áarktik/ *adj* relating to or located in the region of plant and animal life in the Arctic and temperate areas of Greenland and North America [Mid-19C. < NEO-.]

near-death experience *n* a sensation that people on the brink of death have described as leaving their own bodies and observing them as though they were bystanders

near-earth object *n* an asteroid or comet that can approach, or is on course to approach, within 28 million miles of the Earth's orbit

Near East *n* **1** = **Middle East** *n*. **1 2** the countries on the Balkan peninsula, comprising Greece, Albania, Romania, Bulgaria, the states of the former Yugoslavia, and the European part of Turkey (*dated*)

near gale *n* METEOROL = **moderate gale**

⚡**near letter quality** *adj* describes the printing quality of a computer printer that produces printed characters as clear as a typewriter's

nearly /neèrli/ *adv* **1** almost but not quite the case ○ *We waited for nearly an hour.* **2** closely, in time, proximity, or relationship ○ *Brennan described to the police the man he*

saw in the window and then identified Oswald as the person who most nearly resembled the man he saw'. (Earl Warren et al, *The Report of the Warren Commission*; 1964) ◇ **not nearly** used to emphasize that something stated, implied, or assumed is very far from being the case ○ *not nearly enough time to answer all the questions*

near miss *n* **1** SHOT NEAR TARGET a shot or strike that comes very close to a target but does not quite hit it **2** NEAR COLLISION a situation in which two vehicles only narrowly avoid colliding with each other **3** BARELY AVERTED DISASTER something, especially something undesirable, that is only narrowly avoided or averted (*informal*)

near point *n* the point nearest the eye at which an object remains in focus

nearside /neèr síd/ *n* **1** the side of a vehicle that is opposite the driver's side and close to the kerb **2** the left side of an animal's body (*often before nouns*) ○ *the nearside foreleg*

nearsighted /neèr sítid/ *adj* US OPHTHALMOL = **short-sighted** —**nearsightedly** *adv* —**nearsightedness** *n*

near thing *n* something only just avoided or only just achieved (*informal*)

neat[1] /neet/ *adj* **1** ORDERLY IN APPEARANCE orderly and in a clean condition **2** ORDERLY BY NATURE tending to keep things in an orderly and clean condition ○ *My husband's very neat in the kitchen.* **3** UNDILUTED not diluted with water, ice cubes, or a mixer **4** ELEGANT simple, effective, and elegant ○ *a neat solution to a complex problem* **5** SKILFULLY PERFORMED performed with skill, ingenuity, and apparent ease ○ *a neat pirouette* **6** COMPACT appealingly regular or compact ○ *She stood admiring her own neat little figure in the mirror.* **7** US EXCELLENT used as a general term of approval ○ *Her parents are really neat.* [Mid-16C. Via French *net* < Latin *nitidus* 'shiny' < *nitere* 'to shine'.] —**neatness** *n*

neat[2] /neet/ *n* (*plural* **neats** *or* **neat**) *n* an animal in the cattle family, e.g. a cow or ox (*archaic*) [Old English *nēat* < Germanic, 'to use']

neaten /neét'n/ *vt* to make something neat or orderly

neath /neeth/, **'neath** *prep* beneath (*literary*) [Late 18C. Shortening.]

Neath /neeth/ town in S Wales. Population: 45,965 (1991).

neatly /neétli/ *adv* **1** CAREFULLY with care, order, and some precision ○ *a pile of clothes neatly folded* **2** ELEGANTLY simply, effectively, and elegantly **3** SKILFULLY with skill, ingenuity, and apparent ease

neat's-foot oil *n* a pale yellow oil. Source: feet and shinbones of cattle. Use: treatment of leather. [< NEAT[2]]

neb /neb/ *n* **1** Scotland or N England SOMEBODY'S NOSE somebody's nose (*informal or humorous*) ○ *told him to keep his neb out of my business* **2** N England ANIMAL'S NOSE an animal's bill, beak, nose, or snout (*informal*) **3** POINT OR PROJECTION something that sticks out, e.g. an overhanging rock or peak (*archaic*) [Old English *nebb* < Germanic]

NEB *abbr* **1** National Enterprise Board **2** New English Bible

Neb. *abbr* US Nebraska

nebbish /nébbish/ *n* an offensive term that deliberately insults somebody's courage, personality, and initiative (*insult*) [Late 19C. < Yiddish *nebekh* 'poor thing' < assumed Slavic *ne-bogŭ* 'poor'.]

Nebr. *abbr* US Nebraska

Nebraska /nə bráskə/ state in the central United States. Capital: Lincoln. Population: 1,656,870 (1997). Area: 200,356 sq. km/77,358 sq. mi. —**Nebraskan** *n*, *adj*

Nebuchadnezzar II /nébbyoŏkəd nézzər/ (*fl.* 6th century BC) Babylonian king (605–562 BC)

nebula /nébbyoŏlə/ (*plural* **-lae** /-lee/ *or* **-las**) *n* **1** SPACE DUST a region or cloud of interstellar dust and gas appearing variously as a hazy bright or dark patch **2** FLAW ON EYEBALL a faint cloudy area or scar on the cornea **3** CLOUDY URINE cloudiness in the urine **4** LIQUID FOR SPRAYING liquid prepared for use in any kind of atomizing sprayer, especially a nebulizer [Mid-17C. < Latin, 'mist, vapour'.] —**nebular** *adj*

nebular hypothesis *n* a formerly held theory that the solar system evolved as a hot rotating flattened gaseous nebula

nebulise *vti* = **nebulize**

nebuliser *n* = **nebulizer**

nebulize /nébbyoŏ līz/ (**-lizes, -lizing, -lized**), **nebulise** (**-lises, -lising, -lised**) *vt* to reduce a liquid to a fine spray for medical use —**nebulization** /nébbyoŏ līzáysh'n/ *n*

nebulizer /nébbyoŏ līzər/, **nebuliser** *n* a device, with a face mask attached, for administering a medicinal liquid in the form of a fine spray that is breathed in through the mouth or nose

nebulosity /nébbyoŏ lóssəti/ (*plural* **-ties**) *n* ASTRON = **nebula** *n*.1

nebulous /nébbyoŏləss/ *adj* **1** not clear, distinct, or definite **2** relating to or resembling a nebula —**nebulously** *adv* —**nebulousness** *n*

NEC *abbr* **1** National Exhibition Centre (Birmingham) **2** National Executive Committee

~~neccesary~~ incorrect spelling of **necessary**

~~neccessary~~ incorrect spelling of **necessary**

necessarily /néssəsərəli, néssə sérrəli/ *adv* **1** inevitably, or in every case ○ *This route isn't necessarily the best one.* **2** following as an unavoidable result or consequence ○ *Voting was a necessarily slow and complex process.*

necessary /néssəsəri/ *adj* **1** REQUIRED needed, essential, or required by authority or convention ○ *Is it really necessary to contact the police?* **2** FOLLOWING INEVITABLY inevitable given what has happened previously ○ *No doubt they will draw the necessary conclusion.* **3** LOGICALLY TRUE logically true because of being impossible to be false ■ *n* (*informal*) **1** (*plural* **-ies**) SOMETHING ESSENTIAL an essential item ○ *I've packed the necessaries.* **2** SOMETHING NEEDED the thing that is needed, especially a sum of money or a particular action ○ *Tell him to do the necessary.* [14C. Via Anglo-Norman < Latin *necessarius* < *necesse* 'unyielding' < *cess-* (see CESSION).]

SYNONYMS *necessary, essential, vital, indispensable, requisite, needed*

CORE MEANING: *describes something that is required*

necessary important in order to achieve a desired result, or required by authority or convention; **essential** of the highest importance for achieving something; **vital** extremely important for the survival or continuing effectiveness of something; **indispensable** absolutely essential, or extremely desirable or useful; **requisite** (*formal*) necessary for a particular purpose; **needed** required or desired.

necessary condition *n* something that must happen or exist in order for something else to happen or exist

necessary evil *n* something that is unpleasant or undesirable but is needed to achieve a desired result

necessitarian /ni séssi táiri ən/ *n* a believer that all events are determined by previous causes —**necessitarianism** *n*

necessitate /nə séssi tayt/ (**-tates, -tating, -tated**) *v* **1** *vti* to make something necessary or inescapable ○ *a dry climate that necessitates water conservation* **2** *vt* to force or oblige somebody to do something (*formal*) —**necessitation** /nə séssi táysh'n/ *n* —**necessitative** *adj*

necessitous /nə séssitəss/ *adj* **1** in a state of poverty (*literary*) ○ *'grew necessitous, pawn'd his cloaths, and wanted bread'* (Benjamin Franklin, *The Autobiography of Benjamin Franklin*; 1788) **2** pressingly necessary (*archaic*) —**necessitously** *adv* —**necessitousness** *n*

necessity /nə séssəti/ (*plural* **-ties**) *n* **1** SOMETHING ESSENTIAL something that is essential, especially a basic requirement ○ *food, shelter, and the other necessities of life* **2** COMPELLING CIRCUMSTANCES circumstances that create a need or an obligation ○ *The decision was taken out of necessity.* **3** NEED the condition of being needed or required ○ *We'll hire new staff when the necessity arises.* **4** NECESSARY QUALITY the quality of being necessary or of not being able to be otherwise [14C. Via French *nécessité* < Latin *necessitas* < *necesse* (see NECESSARY).]

neck /nek/ *n* **1** PART BETWEEN HEAD AND BODY the part of the body that joins the head to the rest of the body **2** GARMENT PART ROUND NECK the part of a garment that goes round or lies below the wearer's neck **3** CUT OF MEAT a cut of meat from the neck of an animal, especially a sheep **4** LONG OPENING a long narrow opening ○ *a bottle with a long neck* **5** STRIP OF LAND OR WATER a long narrow strip of land or stretch of water **6** LONG NARROW FINGERBOARD the long narrow fingerboard that projects out of the body or sound box of a hand-held string instrument such as a guitar or violin **7** WINNING MARGIN in horseracing, a narrow winning margin equal to the distance between a horse's nose and its shoulder **8** SOMETHING IMPORTANT RISKED OR SAVED somebody's life, job, reputation, or other important asset that has been placed at risk or saved from danger (*informal*) ○ *I'm not going to lie to save your neck again.* **9 CHEEK** impudence or cheek (*informal*) ○ *had the neck to ask another favour* **10 SOLIDIFIED LAVA** a plug of solidified lava or igneous rock filling the vent of an extinct or dormant volcano **11** MARINE BIOL = **siphon** *n.* 3 **12 BAND AROUND PILLAR** a narrow band around the top of a pillar ■ *v* **1** *vi* **KISS AND CUDDLE** to kiss and embrace sexually, usually sitting or lying with clothes on (*dated informal*) ○ *teenagers necking in the car* **2** *vt* **KILL POULTRY** to kill a bird to be cooked by breaking its neck or chopping its head off (*informal*) [Old English *hnecca* 'nape' < Indo-European, 'high point, ridge'] —**necked** *adj* ◇ **be breathing down somebody's neck 1** to be close behind somebody **2** to be putting pressure on somebody to do something more quickly ◇ **be in something up to your neck** to be very much involved in something, often something dishonest or illegal ◇ **break your neck** to try very hard to achieve something (*informal*) ◇ **get it in the neck** to be punished or scolded severely (*informal*) ◇ **neck and neck** level in a competition and with an equal chance of winning (*informal*) ◇ **neck of the woods** a particular area or part of the country (*informal*) ◇ **neck or nothing** risking everything, or prepared to risk everything (*informal*) ◇ **stick your neck out** to take a risk by saying or doing something that could bring blame or censure (*informal*)

neckband /nék band/ *n* the part of a garment that fits or wraps round the neck

neckcloth /nék kloth/, **neck-cloth** *n* a cravat or scarf worn round the neck rather than round the collar by men between the 17th and mid-19th centuries

neckerchief /nékər chif, -cheef/ (*plural* **-chiefs** *or* **-chieves** /nékər cheevz/) *n* a square of cloth worn tied round the neck as a scarf [14C. < NECK + KERCHIEF.]

necking /néking/ *n* **1** kissing and embracing sexually while sitting or lying with clothes on (*dated informal*) **2** a moulding at the top of a pillar, below the capital

necklace /nékləss/ *n* a decorative chain or string of jewels worn around the neck

necklet /néklət/ *n* a small plain necklace

neckline /nék līn/ *n* the line formed by the edge of a garment at or under the neck, especially at the front

neckpiece /nék peess/ *n* a garment like a scarf, especially one made of fur

neck ring *n* a rigid necklace or ornamental band that fits snugly round the neck

necktie /nék tī/ *n US* a shaped strip of cloth tied around the collar of a man's shirt, with the ends hanging down the front

neckwear /nék wair/ *n* garments or fashion accessories worn round the neck, e.g. ties, cravats, and scarves

necr- *prefix* = **necro-** (*before vowels*)

necro- *prefix* death, the dead, dead body ○ *necrophobia* [< Greek *nekros* 'corpse' < Indo-European]

necrobiosis /nékrō bī óssiss/ *n* the degeneration and death of the body's cells from natural processes. ◊ **necrosis** —**necrobiotic** /-bī óttik/ *adj*

necrolatry /ne króllətri/ *n* the worshipping of the dead —**necrolatrous** *adj*

necrology /ne króllәji/ (*plural* **-gies**) *n* (*formal*) **1** a list of people who have died recently or during a particular period **2** a notice of somebody's death —**necrological** /nékrə lójjik'l/ *adj* —**necrologist** *n*

necromancy /nékrō manssi/ *n* **1** the practice of attempting to communicate with the spirits of the dead in order to predict or influence the future **2** witchcraft or sorcery in general (*literary*) [13C. Alteration of *nigromancie*, via Old French < medieval Latin *nigromantia* < late Latin *necromantia* (influenced by Latin *niger* 'black') < Greek *nekromanteia* < *nekros* 'corpse' + *manteia* 'divination'.] —**necromancer** *n* —**necromantic** /nékrō mántik/ *adj* —**necromantically** *adv*

necrophilia /nékrō fílli ə/ *n* sexual feelings for or sexual acts with dead bodies —**necrophiliac** *n* —**necrophilic** *adj*

necrophobia /nékrō fṓbi ə/ *n* an irrational fear of death or of dead bodies —**necrophobe** /nékrō fōb/ *n* —**necrophobic** *adj*

necropolis /nə króppəliss/ (*plural* **-lises** *or* **-leis** /nə króppə layss/) *n* a cemetery, especially a large, elaborate, or ancient one [Early 19C. < Greek, < *nekros* 'corpse' + *polis* 'city'.]

necropsy /nékropsi/ (*plural* **-sies**) *n* MED = **autopsy** *n.* 1 [Mid-19C. < NECRO- + AUTOPSY.]

necrosis /ne krṓssiss/ (*plural* **-ses** /ne krṓ seez/) *n* the death of cells in a tissue or organ caused by disease or injury. ◊ **necrobiosis** [Mid-17C. < modern Latin, < Greek *nekrōsis* 'deadness' < *nekros* 'corpse'.] —**necrotic** *adj*

necrotising *adj* = **necrotizing**

necrotising fasciitis *n* = **necrotizing fasciitis**

necrotizing /nékrō tīzing/, **necrotising** *adj* causing or undergoing the death of cells (**necrosis**) ○ *necrotizing bacteria* [Late 19C. < *necrotize* 'become affected with necrosis' < *necrotic* 'of necrosis' < Greek *nekroun* 'to kill'.]

necrotizing fasciitis /nékrō tīzing fáshi ītiss/, **necrotising fasciitis** *n* a severe bacterial infection that causes cell tissue to decay rapidly

nectar /néktər/ *n* **1 PLANT LIQUID** the sweet liquid that flowering plants produce as a way of attracting the insects and small birds that assist in pollination **2 DRINK OF THE GODS** in Greek and Roman mythology, the drink of the gods that sustained their beauty and immortality **3 ENJOYABLE DRINK** an enjoyable or much appreciated drink (*informal*) **4** *US* **PULPY JUICE** a thick drink made from pureed fruit ○ *mango nectar* [Mid-16C. Via Latin < Greek *nektar* 'drink of the gods'.] —**nectarous** *adj*

nectarine /néktə reen/ *n* **1** a variety of peach with a smooth skin **2** a tree that produces nectarines. *Prunus persica.*

nectary /néktəri/ (*plural* **-ries**) *n* the nectar-producing organ of a flowering plant —**nectarial** /nek táiri əl/ *adj* —**nectaried** *adj*

neddy /néddi/ (*plural* **-dies**) *n* **1** a child's name for a donkey (*babytalk*) **2** *Aus* a horse, particularly a racehorse (*informal*) [Mid-16C. < *Ned*, nickname for the name *Edward*.]

née /nay/, **nee** *adj* used to introduce a married woman's maiden name ○ *Jane Smith née Jones* [Mid-18C. < French form of *né*, past participle of *naître* 'be born' < Latin *nasci*.]

need /need/ *v* **1** *vti* **REQUIRE** used to indicate that something is required in order to have success or achieve something ○ *Do you need any money?* ○ *He told me that I didn't need to know.* **2** *vi* **BE UNNECESSARY** used to indicate that a course of action is not desirable or not necessary (*in negatives*) ○ *You don't need to thank me; I'm happy to help whenever I can.* ○ *Studying medicine need not mean you can't study architecture later.* **3** *vti* **DESERVE** to deserve a particular, usually punishing treatment (*informal*) ○ *That little boy needs to be given a good talking to.* ○ *Those troops need to be shown who's boss.* **4** *vi* **BE ESSENTIAL** to be essential or necessary to something (*archaic*) ○ *'I think that we are all agreed in this matter, and therefore there needs no more words about it'.* (John Bunyan, *Pilgrim's Progress*; 1678) ■ *n* **REQUIREMENT** something that is a requirement or is wanted ○ *an economic system that recognizes the need for financial security* ○ *His needs are small.* [Old English *nē(o)d* < Indo-European] ◇ **in need 1** not having enough of things essential for an adequate standard of living ○ *children in need* **2** needing something ◇ **no need to** *or* **for something** no reason or justification for something

SPELLCHECK Do not confuse ***need*** with ***knead***, which has a similar sound. Beware: your spellchecker will not catch this error.

SYNONYMS See ***necessary.***

needful /neédf'l/ *adj* **1 REQUIRING** lacking or requiring (*formal*) ○ *a situation needful of common sense* **2 REQUIRED** necessary or required (*formal or archaic*) ■ *n* **SOMETHING NEEDED** something that is needed, especially the sum of money required or the action that needs to be taken (*informal*) ○ *Make sure you bring the needful.* —**needfully** *adv* —**needfulness** *n*

needle /neéd'l/ *n* **1 SEWING TOOL** a small sharp metal pin used for sewing, with a hole at the blunt end for holding thread **2 KNITTING TOOL** a pointed rod used in knitting **3 STYLUS** the stylus on a record player **4 POINTER** a pointed indicator on a dial, scale, or scientific instrument such as a compass or a car's speedometer **5 SYRINGE** a hypodermic syringe, or its hollow pointed end **6 ACUPUNCTURE TOOL** a small sharp metal pin used in acupuncture to stimulate points on the body **7 CONIFER LEAF** a small pointed leaf of a conifer tree ○ *pine needles* **8 POINTED PART** a long thin pointed part of an animal's body, e.g. a porcupine quill or a sea urchin spine **9 POINTED CRYSTAL** a long thin pointed crystal **10 OBELISK** a tall stone pillar **11 ENGRAVING TOOL** a sharp tool used in engraving **12 SUPPORTING BEAM** a beam that passes through a wall as a temporary support **13 ENMITY** a feeling of antagonism or hostility (*informal*) ■ *vt* (**-dles, -dling, -dled**) **1 PROVOKE** to tease or provoke somebody, especially repeatedly in an indirect way (*informal*) **2 USE A NEEDLE ON** to sew, prick, or pierce something with a needle [Old English *nǣdl* < Indo-European, 'sew'] —**needler** *n*

needlecord /neéd'l kawrd/ *n* corduroy fabric with very fine ribs

needlecraft /neéd'l kraaft/ *n* sewing as a skill or craft

needle exchange *n* a public health programme that allows drug addicts to exchange used hypodermic needles for new ones in an effort to stop the spread of disease and infection

needlefish /neéd'l fish/ *n* a carnivorous marine fish with a very long slender body and long jaws with sharp teeth. Native to: tropical and subtropical waters. Family: Belonidae.

needle grass *n* PLANTS = **feather grass**

needle match *n* a bitterly fought contest between two competitors or teams who bear each other a grudge (*informal*)

needlepoint /neéd'l poynt/ *n* **1** embroidery done with thick coloured threads on canvas or plain cloth, usually in uniform diagonal stitches (*often used before a noun*) US term **tapestry** *n.* 2 **2** lace made with a needle and a paper pattern (*often before nouns*)

Needles, The /neéd'lz/ group of three chalk rocks in SW England, in the English Channel off the W Isle of Wight. Height: 30 m/100 ft.

needless /neédləss/ *adj* without reason or justification —**needlessly** *adv* —**needlessness** *n*

needle time *n* the amount of time that a radio station spends playing music [< the use of a record player]

needle valve *n* a valve in which the flow of a fluid or gas is precisely controlled by a needle-shaped insert in a conical seat

needlewoman /neéd'l wŏŏmən/ (*plural* **-en** /-wimin/) *n* = **seamstress**

needlework /neéd'l wurk/ *n* **1** a craft such as sewing, needlepoint, embroidery, quilting, crochet, or knitting, that involves the use of a needle **2** an example or piece of work done with a needle in a craft such as sewing, needlepoint, embroidery, quilting, crochet, or knitting —**needleworker** *n*

needn't /neéd'nt/ *contr* need not

needs /needz/ *adv* used before or after 'must' to reinforce necessity, urgency, or inevitability (*archaic*) ○ *'any abstract ideas that are once true must needs be eternal'* (John Locke, *An Essay Concerning Human Understanding*; 1690)

needy /neédi/ (**-ier, -iest**) *adj* **1** living in poverty (*dated*) ○ *gifts for needy children* **2** feeling or showing a strong need for affection, love, or other emotional support —**needily** *adv* —**neediness** *n*

neem /neem/ *n* a tall evergreen tree grown for its bark, resin, and seed oil. Native to: South Asia. *Azadirachta indica.* [Early 19C. Via Hindi *nīm* < Sanskrit *nimba*.]

neep /neep/ *n Scotland, N England* a turnip [Pre-12C. < Latin *napus*.]

ne'er /nair/ *adv* never (*archaic or literary*) [13C. Contraction.]

Ne'erday /náir day/ *n Scotland* New Year's Day [Mid-19C. Contraction.]

ne'er-do-well *n* a lazy and irresponsible person (*dated*) ■ *adj* lazy and irresponsible (*dated*)

nefarious /ni fáiri əss/ *adj* utterly immoral or wicked [Early 17C. < Latin *nefarius* < *nefas* 'sin' < *ne* 'not' + *fas* 'divine law'.] —**nefariously** *adv* —**nefariousness** *n*

Nefertiti /néffər teétitae/ ancient Egyptian queen

neg. *abbr* negative

negate /ni gáyt/ *vt* (*formal*) **1** to deny the truth of something, or prove something to be false ○ *a theory that negates all previous research* **2** to declare officially that something is invalid or render it invalid ○ *Failure to disclose such a change of circumstances would automatically negate the policy.* [Early 17C. < Latin *negat-*, past participle of *negare* 'deny'.] —**negator** *n*

SYNONYMS See ***nullify.***

negation /ni gáysh'n/ *n* **1 DENIAL OR ANNULMENT** the denying, disproving, or nullifying of something **2 LOGICAL DENIAL** a statement of denial or contradiction, especially an assertion that a particular proposition is false **3 NEGATIVE**

the opposite of something regarded as positive, or the absence of such a thing ○ *The existence of happiness implies its negation.*

negative /néggətiv/ *adj* **1 INDICATIVE OF 'NO'** indicating 'no', or refusing or denying something ○ *a negative response* **2 BAD** unhappy, discouraging, angry, or otherwise detracting from a happy situation ○ *You seem to have very negative feelings towards him.* **3 PESSIMISTIC** pessimistic, or tending to have a pessimistic outlook ○ *Don't be so negative; cheer up!* **4 SHOWING THAT SOMETHING IS NOT PRESENT** showing the absence of a particular disease or condition that is being tested for ○ *The test for cancer is negative.* **5** MED = **Rh negative 6 LESS THAN ZERO** indicating a quantity that is less than zero ○ *a negative number* **7 OPPOSITE TO POSITIVE** describes something, e.g. a quantity or angle, of the same magnitude as, but opposite to, something considered positive **8 HAVING SAME CHARGE AS ELECTRON** with the same electric charge as that of an electron, shown by the symbol – **9 SHOWING DIRECTION OF CURRENT** indicating the direction toward which current flows in an external circuit **10 WITH TONES AND COLOURS REVERSED** describes photographic film that has been exposed to light, used as a basis for preparing final prints **11 OPPOSING** denying or contradicting a statement, proof, or argument **12 MOVING AWAY** moving or growing away from a source of stimulation, e.g. heat or light ○ *negative tropism* ■ *n* **1 PHOTOGRAPHIC IMAGE** a photographic image, or the film containing it, that shows black and white tones reversed and colours as complementary **2 ANSWER OF 'NO'** an answer meaning 'no' ○ *The general answered in the negative.* **3 WORD IMPLYING 'NO'** any word that expresses the idea 'no', e.g. the words 'not', 'nothing', and 'never' **4 NEGATING PROPOSITION** a statement that contradicts, denies, or disproves something **5 DESTINATION OF ELECTRONS** the part of an electric circuit to which the electrons flow, e.g. a terminal or the cathode where negative ions are formed in electrolytic applications **6 SOMETHING OR SOMEBODY UNDESIRABLE** a person, thing, or situation, that is bad, undesirable, discouraging, or otherwise detracts from satisfaction (*informal*) ○ *The area's harsh winters will be a negative for anyone who doesn't like snow.* **7 QUANTITY OPPOSITE TO POSITIVE** a number or quantity, e.g. speed, angle, or direction, that is less than zero or considered to be the opposite of positive ■ *interj* **NO** used to say 'no' to something or somebody (*formal*) ■ *vt* (**-tives, -tiving, -tived**) **1 SAY 'NO'** to refuse, reject, deny, cancel, or forbid something (*formal*) ○ *'a polite request that Elizabeth would lead the way, which the other politely and more earnestly negatived'* (Jane Austen, *Pride And Prejudice*; 1813) **2 DISPROVE PROPOSITION** to contradict or invalidate a proposition (*informal*) —**negativeness** *n* —**negativity** /néggə tívvəti/ *n*

negative equity *n* a situation in which, as a result of falling prices, a piece of property is worth less than the amount of money that was borrowed to buy it

negative feedback *n* in an electronic or mechanical system, the redirecting of part of the output back to the input as a way of improving the quality of the output

negatively /néggətivli/ *adv* **1 SAYING 'NO'** in a way that means 'no' **2 ADVERSELY** in an adverse way ○ *patients reacting negatively to the medication* **3 PESSIMISTICALLY** in a pessimistic or defeatist way **4 WITH NEGATIVE ELECTRICAL CHARGE** with the same electric charge as that of one or more electrons, shown by the symbol –

negative reinforcement *n* encouragement of a desired response by giving an unpleasant stimulus when the response is absent, or discouragement of an undesired response by an unpleasant stimulus when the response is present

negative staining *n* staining of an area around a biological subject, rather than the subject itself, so that the subject can be clearly seen against it

negativism /néggətivizəm/ *n* **1** a strong tendency to be pessimistic, to assess situations in the worst light, or to be unreasonably sceptical about generally accepted beliefs **2** persistent defiance of authority and refusal to obey instructions —**negativist** *n* —**negativistic** /néggəti vístik/ *adj* —**negativistically** *adv*

Negeri Sembilan /néggri sem béelən/ state in SW Malaysia. Capital: Seremban. Population: 691,150 (1991). Area: 6,500 sq. km/2,510 sq. mi.

Negev /néggev/, **Negeb** /néggeb/ desert region in Israel, comprising the southern half of the country. Area: 12,800 sq. km/4,940 sq. mi.

neglect /ni glékt/ *vt* **1 NOT CARE FOR SOMETHING PROPERLY** to fail to give the proper or required care and attention to somebody or something **2 FAIL TO DO** to fail to do something, especially because of carelessness or forgetfulness ○ *I neglected to tell you that I won't be here next week.* ■ *n* **1 WITHHOLDING OF PROPER CARE** the failure to give proper care or attention to somebody or something ○ *parents charged with criminal neglect* **2 LACK OF CARE** lack of proper care or attention ○ *Soon the business began to suffer from neglect.* [Early 16C. < Latin *neglect-*, past participle of *neglegere* < *legere* 'choose'.] —**neglecter** *n* —**neglectful** *adj* —**neglectfully** *adv* —**neglectfulness** *n*

SYNONYMS ***neglect, forget, omit, overlook***

CORE MEANING: to fail to do something

neglect to fail to give the the proper or required care and attention to somebody or something, or to fail to do something, especially because of carelessness, forgetfulness, or indifference; **forget** to fail, or fail to remember, to give due attention to somebody or something; **omit** to fail to do something, either deliberately or accidentally; **overlook** to fail to notice or check something as a result of inattention, preoccupation, or haste.

negligée /néggli zhay/, **negligé** /négli zhay/ *n* **1** a woman's nightdress made of thin silky often see-through fabric **2** informal dress (*dated formal*) [Mid-18C. < French *négligé*, past participle of *négliger* (see NEGLIGIBLE).]

negligence /négglijənss/ *n* **1 CONDITION OF BEING NEGLIGENT** the condition or quality of being negligent **2 CIVIL WRONG CAUSING INJURY OR HARM** a civil wrong (**tort**) causing injury or harm to another person or to property as the result of doing something or failing to provide a proper or reasonable level of care. ◊ **contributory negligence 3 CASUALNESS** casualness in matters of dress or general appearance, whether regarded as stylish or slovenly (*dated formal*) ○ *'clad in an artist's velvet, but with none of an artist's negligence'* (G. K. Chesterton, *The Wisdom of Father Brown*; 1914)

negligent /négglijənt/ *adj* **1 HABITUALLY CARELESS** habitually careless or irresponsible **2 GUILTY OF NEGLIGENCE** guilty of failing to provide a proper or reasonable level of care **3 CASUAL IN APPEARANCE** casual in matters of dress or general appearance, whether considered stylish or slovenly (*literary*) [14C. Via French < Latin *negligent-*, present participle of *negligere*, variant of *neglegere* (see NEGLECT).] —**negligently** *adv*

negligible /négglijəb'l/ *adj* too small or unimportant to be worth considering [Early 19C. < obsolete French *négligible* < *négliger* 'to neglect' < Latin *neglegere* (see NEGLECT).] —**negligibility** /négglijə bílləti/ *n* —**negligibleness** *n* —**negligibly** *adv*

negotiable /ni góshəb'l, -góshi əb'l/ *adj* **1 OPEN TO DISCUSSION** not fixed but able to be established or changed through discussion and compromise ○ *Salary is negotiable, according to age and experience.* **2 EXCHANGEABLE FOR MONEY** describes financial instruments, e.g. cheques and securities, that can be transferred to another person in exchange for money **3 NAVIGABLE** able to be crossed, passed, or successfully dealt with ■ *n* **SOMETHING EXCHANGEABLE FOR MONEY** a negotiable financial instrument (*usually plural*) —**negotiability** /ni góshə bílləti, -góshi ə-/ *n* —**negotiably** *adv*

negotiate /ni góshi ayt/ (**-ates, -ating, -ated**) *v* **1** *vti* **DISCUSS TERMS OF AGREEMENT** to attempt to come to an agreement on something through discussion and compromise **2** *vt* **SELL** to transfer ownership of a financial instrument, e.g. a cheque or security, to somebody else in exchange for money **3** *vt* **NAVIGATE SUCCESSFULLY** to manage to get past or deal with something that constitutes a hazard or obstacle ○ *A canoe can negotiate these waters when the wind is calm.* [Late 16C. < Latin *negotiat-*, past participle of *negotiari* 'do business' < *negotium* 'business' < *neg-* 'not' + *otium* 'leisure'.] —**negotiator** *n*

negotiation /ni góshi áysh'n/ *n* **1 RESOLVING OF DISAGREEMENTS** the reaching of agreement through discussion and compromise ○ *matters still under negotiation* **2 NAVIGATION** the tackling of a hazard or problem (*formal*) ■ **negotiations** *npl* **DISCUSSION SESSIONS** one or more meetings at which attempts are made to reach agreement through discussion and compromise ○ *Negotiations are already under way between the opposing factions.*

Negress /néegress, -grəss/ *n* an offensive term for a Black woman [Late 18C. < French *négress* < *négre* < Latin *nigr-* 'black'.]

Negrillo /ni gríllō/ (*plural* **-los** *or* **-loes**) *n* a member of a people of central and southern Africa [Mid-19C. < Spanish, 'small Black person' < *negro* (see NEGRO).]

Negrito /ni gréetō/ (*plural* **-tos** *or* **-toes**) *n* a member of some of the peoples of Austronesia [Early 19C. < Spanish, 'small Black person' < *negro* (see NEGRO).]

negritude /néggri tyood/ *n* identity as a Black person, especially awareness of a distinct Black history and culture as something to be proud of [Mid-20C. Via French *négritude* < Latin *nigritudo* < *nigr-* 'black'.]

Negro /née grō/ (*plural* **-groes**) *n* a now usually offensive term for a Black person [Mid-16C. < Spanish and Portuguese, < Latin *nigr-* 'black'.]

Negro, Río /néggrō/ **1** river in NW South America that rises in E Colombia and flows southeastwards to empty into the Amazon in N Brazil. Length: 2,253 km/1,400 mi. **2** river in central Argentina flowing eastwards into the Atlantic Ocean. Length: 644 km/400 mi.

Negroid /née groyd/ *adj* an offensive term meaning belonging or relating to a group, in a former classification of humankind, that originated in Africa (*dated*)

negrophile /néegrō fīl/ *n* an offensive term for a person who favours the interests of Black people —**negrophilia** /néegrō fílli ə/ *n* —**negrophilism** /ni gróffilizəm/ *n*

Negro spiritual *n* = **spiritual** *n.* 1

negus /néegəss/ *n* a hot drink made of port or sherry with water, sugar, lemon juice, and spices [Mid-18C. After Francis *Negus* (died 1732), English colonel.]

Negus /née gəss/ *n* a title formerly used for the king or emperor of Ethiopia [Late 16C. < Amharic *n'gus* 'kinged, king'.]

Neh. *abbr* Nehemiah

Nehemiah[1] /née i mī ə/ *n* in the Bible, a Jewish leader and governor of Judea

Nehemiah[2] *n* a book of the Bible, recounting the rebuilding of Jerusalem in the 5th century BC and the reforms undertaken after its completion, traditionally attributed to Nehemiah

Nehru /náir oo/, **Jawaharlal** (1889–1964) Indian statesman and first prime minister of independent India (1947–64)

Nehru jacket *n* a long narrow jacket with a high stand-up collar [Mid-20C. After Jawaharlal NEHRU.]

~~**neice**~~ incorrect spelling of **niece**

neigh /nay/ *n* the long high-pitched sound that a horse makes ■ *vi* to make the high-pitched sound characteristic of a horse [Old English *hnǣgan* < ?]

neighbor *n*, *vt* US = **neighbour**

neighborhood *n* US = **neighbourhood**

neighboring *adj* US = **neighbouring**

neighborly *adj* US = **neighbourly**

neighbour /náybər/ *n* **1 SOMEBODY LIVING NEARBY** a person who or thing that lives or exists nearby **2 SOMETHING OR SOMEBODY NEARBY** a person, place, or thing located next to another or very nearby ○ *the Spanish and their Portuguese neighbours* **3 FELLOW HUMAN** a fellow human being (*archaic or literary*) ■ *vti* **BE CLOSE TO** to be very close to something or somebody [Old English *nēahgebūr* < *nēah* 'near' + *gebūr* 'dweller']

neighbourhood /náybər hŏŏd/ *n* **1 COMMUNITY** a local community with characteristics that distinguish it from the areas around it **2 APPROXIMATION OF AMOUNT** an approximate amount, size, or range (*informal*) ○ *expenses in the neighbourhood of £175,000* **3 SURROUNDING POINTS** the set of all points within a given distance from a specified point

neighbourhood watch *n* a nationwide scheme to raise awareness of crime and crime prevention within local communities, with members taking part in various initiatives, including keeping watch on one another's homes

neighbouring /náybəring/ *adj* situated or located nearby

neighbourly /náybərli/ *adj* friendly, helpful, and kind, especially to a neighbour —**neighbourliness** *n*

Neill /neel/, **Sam** (*b.* 1948) New Zealand actor. Born **Nigel Neill**

neither /nī̄thər, née-/ CORE MEANING: a grammatical word used to indicate that each of two things or people is included when making a negative statement ○ (det) *Neither shirt looks good on you.* ○ (pron) *Neither of the boys wants to go.* ○ (pron) *'Would you like pork or fish'? 'Neither, thank you'.*

1 *conj* used preceding two alternatives joined by 'nor' to indicate that both did not happen or are not true ○ *Neither my boss nor his wife can cook.* **2** *adv* used to indicate people or things that can also be included in a statement just made (*in response to no, not, or another negative*) ○ '*We've never been to Paris*'. '*Neither have I.*' ○ *She doesn't want to go? Me neither!* ○ *She can't play today, and neither can her brother.* [12C. Alteration (influenced by EITHER) of Old English *nawþer*, contraction of *nāhwæþer < nā* 'not' + *hwæþer* 'which of two'.]

USAGE Neither meaning **none** Do not substitute **neither** for the pronoun **none** in the sense 'not one of several', as in *Neither of these (four) options has any appeal*. Say instead: *None* [or *Not one*] *of these (four) options has any appeal*. When you use **neither** as a conjunction, follow it with **nor**, not *or*, and make the verb agree with the nearest noun: *Neither rain nor snow* [not *or snow*] *is* [not *are*] *going to stop mail delivery*.

nekton /nék ton/ *n* an organism, e.g. a fish, that lives in water and can actively swim against currents, as opposed to microorganisms that are simply carried along [Late 19C. < Greek *nēkton*, form of *nēktos* 'swimming' < *nēkhein* 'to swim'.] —**nektonic** /nek tónnik/ *adj*

nelly /nélli/ (*plural* **-lies**), **nellie** *n* **1** a man or boy who is regarded as weak or cowardly (*dated informal insult*) **2** an offensive term for an effeminate or homosexual man [Mid-20C. < pet form of the name *Helen* or *Eleanor*.] ◇ **not on your nelly** absolutely not (*dated informal*)

nelson /nélss'n/ *n* a wrestling hold in which one arm (**half nelson**) or both arms (**full nelson**) are passed through the opponent's arms from behind and pulled back, levering against the opponent's back [Late 19C. < ?]

Nelson /nélss'n/ **1** town in NW England. Population: 29,120 (1991). **2** city and port on N South Island, New Zealand. Population: 52,100 (1998 estimate). **3** region of N South Island, New Zealand. Population: 42,073 (1996). Area: 1,114 sq. km/430 sq. mi.

Nelson, Horatio, Viscount (1758–1805) British admiral

nemat- *prefix* = **nemato-** (*before vowels*)

nematic /ni máttik/ *adj* describes a phase of liquid crystals in which the axes of the molecules become parallel in response to a magnetic field [Early 20C. < Greek *nēmat-* 'thread'.]

nematicide *n* BIOCHEM = **nematocide**

nemato- *prefix* **1** thread, threadlike ○ *nematocyst* **2** nematode ○ *nematocide* [< Greek *nēmat-* 'thread' < Indo-European, 'spin']

nematocide /ne máttō sīd/, **nematicide** *n* a substance that destroys nematodes —**nematocidal** /ne máttō sīd'l/ *adj*

nematocyst /némmə tō sist/ *n* a sting found in animals of the jellyfish family

nematode /némmə tōd/ *n* a worm, often microscopic, with a cylindrical unsegmented body protected by a tough outer skin (**cuticle**). Phylum: Nematoda. [Mid-19C. < modern Latin *Nematoda* < Greek *nēmat-* (see NEMATO-).]

nematology /némmə tóllaji/ *n* the branch of zoology that is concerned with the study of nematodes —**nematological** /némmətə lójjik'l/ *adj* —**nematologically** *adv* —**nematologist** *n*

nem. con. /ném kón/ *adv* without opposition ○ *The motion was carried nem. con.* [< Shortening of Latin *nemine contradicente* 'with no one contradicting']

Nemean lion /ni mée ən-/ *n* in Greek mythology, the huge lion that Heracles killed as the first of his twelve labours [Late 16C. After *Nemea*, district in ancient Greece.]

nemertean /ni múrti ən/ *n* a burrowing marine worm with a long flat unsegmented body. Phylum: Nemertia. [Mid-19C. < modern Latin *Nemertes* < Greek *Nemertēs* 'Nereid'.]

nemesis /némməssiss/ (*plural* **nemeses** /-seez/) *n* (*literary*) **1** a person or force that inflicts punishment or revenge **2** punishment that is deserved, especially when it results in somebody's downfall [Late 16C. < Greek, 'Nemesis, righteous indignation' < *nemein* 'distribute what is due'.]

Nemesis /némməssiss/ *n* the ancient Greek goddess of just punishment or vengeance

nene /náy nay/ *n* a rare wild goose with a greyish-brown body and a black face. Native to: Hawaiian Islands. *Branta sandvicensis*. [Early 20C. < Hawaiian.]

NEO *abbr* near-earth object

neo- *prefix* new, recent ○ *neotype* ○ *neo-Darwinism* [< Greek *neos* < Indo-European]

Neoclassical: Front porch of Monticello, Charlottesville, Virginia (begun 1770)

CORBIS/G. E. Kidder Smith

neoclassical /née ō klássik'l/, **neoclassic** /-klássik/ *adj* **1** OF NEOCLASSICISM relating to neoclassicism or created in the style of neoclassicism (*literary*) **2** OF CLASSICAL REVIVAL relating to or typical of the European revival of Greek and Roman literary form **3** OF FORMAL MUSICAL STYLE relating to a movement in the late 19th and early 20th centuries that favoured the more formal style of composers before the Romantic movement **4** OF MACRO-ECONOMIC MONETARIST THEORY relating to macroeconomic monetarist theories that emphasize the need for the free operation of market forces

neoclassicism /née ō klássisizəm/ *n* a style of art and architecture prevalent in the late 18th and early 19th centuries, characterized by the simple, symmetrical forms of ancient Greek and Roman art —**neoclassicist** *n*

QUICK FACTS ON... **NEOCLASSICISM**

Key dates: 1750–1830
Key locations: W Europe, especially Rome
Key elements: austerity, order, clarity; abandonment of illusionism; classical subjects, static poses
Key figures: Johann Winckelmann (theory); Robert Adam, Charles Percier and Léonard Fontaine, Thomas Jefferson (architecture); Anton Raphael Mengs, Jacques-Louis David, John Flaxman (graphic arts); Antonio Canova, Bertel Thorvaldsen (sculpture)
Key events: excavation of Herculaneum 1738, excavation of Pompeii 1748, arrival of Elgin Marbles in London 1806
Key works: Panthéon, Paris (Soufflot) 1757–90, Arc de Triomphe, Paris (Chalgrin) 1806, *Parnassus* (Mengs) 1761, *Oath of the Horatii* (David) 1784–88, *Theseus and the Dead Minotaur* (Canova) 1781–82
Key developments: Empire style, Regency style, Federal style, Greek revival style (architecture and furniture); Greek-vase style painting; Etruscan style, Louis XVI style (decorative arts)

neocolonial /née ō kə lṓni əl/ *adj* **1** relating to the domination of an economically weaker nation by another wealthier and politically more powerful nation **2** being or suggesting domination by another, more powerful, nation

neocolonialism /née ō kə lṓni əlizəm/ *n* the domination by a powerful, usually Western nation of another nation that is politically independent but has a weak economy greatly dependent on trade with the powerful nation —**neocolonialist** *n*

neoconservative /née ō kən súrvətiv/ *n* somebody who, during the mid-1980s, began to support conservatism in society, and in politics in particular, as a reaction to the social freedoms sought throughout the 1960s and early 1970s —**neoconservatism** *n* —**neoconservative** *adj*

neocortex /née ō káwr teks/ (*plural* **-tices** /-káwrt seez/ *or* **-texes**) *n* the roof of the cerebral cortex that forms the part of the mammalian brain that has evolved most recently and makes possible higher brain functions such as learning —**neocortical** /-káwrtik'l/ *adj*

neo-Darwinism *n* a theory of evolution that combines Darwin's theory and modern genetics, especially with regard to variations in populations as a result of genetic mutations —**neo-Darwinian** *adj* —**neo-Darwinist** *n, adj*

neodymium /née ō dímmi əm/ *n* (*symbol* **Nd**) a silvery-white or yellowish metallic element that is one of the lanthanide series of rare-earth elements. Source: monazite, bastnaesite. Use: lasers, glass manufacture. [Late 19C. < NEO- + DIDYMIUM.]

neo-expressionism *n* a 20th-century art movement, begun in Germany, Italy, and the United States, and based on expressionism, that focuses on the artist's inner experiences and often produces violent or erotic paintings —**neo-expressionism** *n, adj*

neofascism /née ō fáshizəm/ *n* **1** the modern-day revival of Fascist beliefs of the 1930s and 1940s, which assume that a supposed Aryan race is superior to all others and attempt to justify genocide **2** the views or actions of any modern-day white group or movement that holds racist views, especially anyone involved in the violent intimidation of non-white people —**neofascist** *adj, n*

neo-Freudianism *n* a theory of psychoanalysis that modifies Freudian theory by emphasizing social and cultural influences on personality development —**neo-Freudian** *adj, n*

Neogene /née ō ə jeen/ *n* an interval of geological time that includes both the Miocene and Pliocene epochs [Late 19thC. < NEO- + Greek *-genēs* 'born'.]

neogenesis /née ō jénnassiss/ *n* the regrowth of living tissue —**neogenetic** /-jə néttik/ *adj* —**neogenetically** *adv*

neo-Gothic *adj* based on the Gothic Revival in architecture —**neo-Gothic architecture** *n*

neoimpressionism /née ō im présh'nizəm/ *n* the 19th-century movement in painting, led by the pointillist Georges Seurat, that favoured stricter and more formal techniques of composition —**neoimpressionist** *adj, n*

QUICK FACTS ON... **NEOIMPRESSIONISM**

Key dates: 1884–1900
Key locations: France
Key elements: plein-air painting; precision; formal composition; pointillism (divisionism); positivism
Key figures: Georges Seurat, Paul Signac, Camille Pissarro, Maximilien Luce
Key works: *Bathers at Asnières* (Seurat) 1884, *A Sunday Afternoon on the Island of La Grande Jatte* (Seurat) 1884–86
Key developments: fauvism, futurism, op art

Neo-Latin *n, adj* LANG = **New Latin** ■ *adj* relating to a language that has developed from Latin

neoliberalism /née ō líbbərəlizəm/ *n* the political view, arising in the 1960s, that emphasizes the importance of economic growth and asserts that social justice is best maintained by minimal government interference and free market forces —**neoliberal** *adj, n*

neolith /née ō lith/ *n* a stone tool from the Neolithic period

Neolithic /née ō líthik/ *n* the latest period of the Stone Age, between about 8000 BC and 5000 BC, characterized by the development of settled agriculture and the use of polished stone tools and weapons —**Neolithic** *adj*

neologise *vi* = **neologize**

neologism /ni óllajizəm/, **neology** /ni óllaji/ (*plural* **-gies**) *n* **1** a recently coined word or phrase, or a recently extended meaning of an existing word or phrase **2** the practice of coining new words or phrases, or of extending the meaning of existing words or phrases [Early 19C. < French *néologisme* < *néo-* 'new' + Greek *logos* 'word'.] —**neologist** *n* —**neologistic** /ni óllə jístik/ *adj* —**neologistically** *adv* —**neologize** *vi*

neology *n* = **neologism**

neo-Melanesian *n* a creole language based on English with borrowings from other languages that is used in island groups of the SW Pacific —**neo-Melanesian** *adj*

neomycin /née ō míssin/ *n* a broad-spectrum antibiotic. Source: the bacterium *Streptomyces fradiae*. Use: treatment of skin, eye, and intestinal infections.

neon /née on, -ən/ (*plural* **-ons** *or* **-on**) *n* **1** (*symbol* **Ne**) a colourless odourless gaseous element that occurs in very small quantities in the air and glows orange when electricity is passed through it **2** lighting produced by neon lights or by lamps containing similar gases such as argon or krypton **3** ZOOL = **neon tetra** [Late 19C. < Greek, form of *neos* 'new'.]

neonate /née ō nayt/ *n* a newborn child, especially one less than one month old [Early 20C. < NEO- + Latin *natus*, past participle of *nasci* 'be born'.] —**neonatal** /née ō nayt'l/ *adj*

neonatology /née ō nay tólləji/ *n* the branch of medicine that deals with the care and development of newborn babies and the treatment of their diseases —**neonatological** /née ō náyta lójjik'l/ *adj* —**neonatologist** *n*

neo-Nazi /née/ *n* **1** a member of a modern-day movement that promotes the idea that a supposed race of Aryans is superior to all others, and that genocide is justifiable **2** a member of any modern-day group or movement of white people who hold racist views, especially those involved in violent attacks on non-white people —**neo-Nazism** *n*

neon light, neon lamp *n* a light with a bulb, usually tube-shaped, containing neon gas, which glows red when a high-voltage electric current is passed through it

neon tetra *n* a small iridescent blue and red fish, often kept in aquariums. Native to: River Amazon. *Hyphessobrycon innesi*. [< its bright colours like neon glowing]

neoorthodoxy /née ō áwrthə doksi/ *n* an early 20th-century Protestant movement connected with the theology of Karl Barth that emphasizes ethics and the teachings of the Bible —**neoorthodox** *adj*

neophilia /née ō fílli ə/ *n* a liking for new things, change for the sake of change, or novelty —**neophile** /née ō fíl/ *n* —**neophiliac** *n, adj*

neophyte /née ō fít/ *n* **1** BEGINNER a beginner or novice at some task, work, or endeavour **2** RECENT CONVERT a recent convert to a religion **3** RELIGIOUS NOVICE a new resident of a religious community who has not yet taken vows [14C. Via late Latin *neophytus* < Greek *neophutos* 'newly planted' < *phuein* 'plant, cause to grow'.] —**neophytic** /née ō fíttik/ *adj*

neoplasia /née ō pláyzi ə/ *n* the formation or existence of tumours

neoplasm /née ō plazəm/ *n* a tumour or tissue containing an abnormal growth [Late 19C. < NEO- + Greek *plasma* 'formation' < *plassein* 'to form'.]

neoplasticism /née ō plástissizəm/ *n* a style of abstract painting, as found in the work of Mondrian, using black, grey, white, and the primary colours and horizontal and vertical lines and planes —**neoplastic** *adj*

neoplasty /née ō plasti/ *n* the surgical construction of new tissue, or the repair of damaged tissue —**neoplastic** /née ō plástik/ *adj*

neo-Platonism /née ō pláytənizəm/, **Neoplatonism** *n* a philosophical system combining Platonism with mysticism and Judaic and Christian ideas and positing one source for all existence, developed by Plotinus and his followers in the 3rd century AD —**neo-Platonic** *adj* —**neo-Platonist** /née ō pláytənist/ *n*

neoprene /née ō preen/ *n* a synthetic material resembling rubber but slower to perish and more resistant to oil. Use: in the manufacture of equipment for which waterproofing is important. [Mid-20C. < NEO- + CHLOROPRENE.]

neorealism /née ō reé alizəm/ *n* a style of cinema developed in Italy in the 1940s by directors such as Rossellini and De Sica, dealing typically with the problems of ordinary working-class life —**neorealist** *n, adj* —**neorealistic** /née ō reé ə lístik/ *adj*

neo-Scholasticism *n* a late 19th-century Roman Catholic movement that used the writings of the early scholastic theologians such as Anselm as the basis for its teachings —**neo-Scholastic** *adj*

neostigmine /née ō stíg meen/ *n* a white crystalline compound. Use: treatment of myasthenia. [Mid-20C. < NEO- + PHYSOSTIGMINE.]

neoteny /ni óttəni/ *n* the existence of juvenile features in an adult animal, e.g. the retention of gills in certain salamanders [Late 19C. < NEO- + Greek *teinein* 'stretch, extend'.]

neoteric /née ō térrik/ *adj* having a contemporary origin [Late 16C. Via Latin < Greek *neōterikos* 'youthful'.]

Neotropical /née ō tróppik'l/, **Neotropic** /-tróppik/ *adj* relating to a geographic area of plant and animal distribution east, south, and west of Mexico's central plateau that includes Central and South America and the West Indies

neotype /née ō tīp/ *n* a specimen of a plant or animal selected to replace an original representative example used in classification (**holotype**) that has been lost or destroyed —**neotypical** /née ō típpik'l/ *adj*

Nepal

Nepal /nə páwl/ kingdom in South Asia, on the NE border of India, in the Himalayas. Capital: Katmandu. Population: 22,090,000 (1996). Area: 147,181 sq. km/56,827 sq. mi. —**Nepalese** *n, adj*

Nepali /ni páwli/ (*plural* -**i** *or* -**is**) *n* **1** the Indic official language of Nepal, also spoken in Bhutan and NE India **2** somebody who comes from Nepal —**Nepali** *adj*

nepenthe /ni pénthi/ *n* **1** a supposed substance that people took in ancient times to forget their sadness or troubles, or the plant that produced the substance **2** something that eases pain or makes people forget their troubles (*literary*) ○ *'respite and nepenthe from thy memories of Lenore'* (Edgar Allan Poe, *The Raven*; 1845) [Late 16C. < Greek *nēpenthēs* 'banishing pain' < *nē* 'not' + *penthos* 'grief'.] —**nepenthean** *adj*

neper *n* (*symbol* Np) a unit for comparing two currents, voltages, or related quantities, equal to the natural logarithm of the ratio of the quantities

nepheline /néffəlin, -leen/, **nephelite** /-līt/ *n* a white aluminosilicate of potassium and sodium. Source: igneous rocks. Use: manufacture of glass and ceramics. [Early 19C. < French, < Greek *nephelē* 'cloud'.]

nephelinite /néffali nīt/ *n* a fine-grained igneous rock that has nepheline and pyroxene as its main mineral ingredients

nephelite *n* MINERALS = **nepheline**

nephelometer /néffə lómmitər/ *n* **1** an instrument that uses reflected light to measure the size or density of solid particles present in a liquid **2** an instrument used to measure the degree of cloudiness in the sky [Late 19C. < Greek *nephelē* 'cloud'.] —**nephelometric** /néffəlō méttrik/ *adj* —**nephelometry** *n*

nephew /néffyoo, névvyoo/ *n* the son of somebody's brother, sister, brother-in-law, or sister-in-law [13C. Via French *neveu* < Latin *nepot-* 'sister's son, grandson'.]

nephogram /néffō gram/ *n* a photograph of a cloud

nephograph /néffō graf, -graf/ *n* a device for taking photographs of clouds

nephology /ne fóllaji/ *n* the branch of meteorology concerned with the study of clouds —**nephological** /néffə lójjik'l/ *adj* —**nephologist** *n*

nephoscope /néffə skōp/ *n* an instrument for measuring the altitude, speed, and direction of movement of clouds

nephr- *prefix* = **nephro-** (*before vowels*)

nephralgia /ni frálja/ *n* pain in the kidneys

nephrectomy /ni fréktəmi/ *n* (*plural* -**mies**) the surgical removal of a kidney

nephric /néffrik/ *adj* relating to or affecting the kidneys

nephridiopore /ni fríddi ō pawr/ *n* the external opening of an excretory organ (**nephridium**), found in worms, snails, and various other invertebrate animals, through which bodily wastes are discharged [Late 19C. < Greek *nephrion* 'little kidney' (< *nephros* 'kidney') + PORE[1].]

nephridium /ni fríddi əm/ *n* (*plural* -**a** /-di ə/) *n* **1** a simple tube-shaped organ in earthworms and many other invertebrate organisms for releasing waste matter into the gut or out of the body **2** the organ that develops into the kidney in a vertebrate animal's embryo [Late 19C. < NEPHRO- + modern Latin *-idium* 'small one' (< Greek *-idion*).] —**nephridial** *adj*

nephrite /néf rīt/ *n* a variety of jade that ranges in colour from white to dark green, containing calcium, magnesium, and iron

nephritic /ni fríttik/ *adj* **1** relating to or affected by nephritis **2** relating to or affecting the kidneys

nephritis /ni fríttiss/ *n* severe inflammation of the kidney, caused by infection, degenerative disease, or disease of the blood vessels

nephro- *prefix* kidney ○ *nephrogenous* [< Greek *nephros*]

nephrogenous /ni frójjənəss/, **nephrogenic** /néffrō jénnik/ *adj* **1** located in or moving into a kidney **2** capable of developing into kidney tissue

nephrology /ni fróllaji/ *n* the branch of medicine concerned with the study and diseases of the kidneys —**nephrological** /néffrō lójjik'l/ *adj* —**nephrologist** *n*

nephron /néf ron/ *n* a fine tubule in the kidneys of vertebrates that filters and excretes waste materials from the blood and produces urine

nephropathy /ni fróppathi/ *n* (*plural* -**thies**) *n* a disease or medical disorder of the kidney —**nephropathic** /néffrō páthik/ *adj*

nephroscope /néffrō skōp/ *n* a tube-shaped instrument inserted into an incision in the body wall in order to examine a patient's kidneys

nephrosis /ni frōssiss/ *n* a disease that causes the kidneys to degenerate without inflaming them, especially one that affects the nephrons —**nephrotic** /ni fróttik/ *adj*

nephrotomy /ni fróttəmi/ *n* (*plural* -**mies**) *n* a surgical incision into a kidney

ne plus ultra /náy plóōss ōōl traa, née pluss úl tra/ *n* the highest level of excellence, or something that reaches it [Late 17C. < Latin, 'not farther beyond', supposed to have been inscribed on the Pillars of Hercules.]

nepotism /néppətizəm/ *n* favouritism shown by somebody in power to relatives and friends, especially in appointing them to good positions [Mid-17C. < French *népotisme* < Latin *nepot-* 'grandson, sister's son'.] —**nepotist** *n* —**nepotistic** /néppə tístik/ *adj* —**nepotistically** *adv*

Neptune /néptyoon/ *n* **1** the eighth planet from the Sun in our solar system. See table at **planet 2** in Roman mythology, the god of the sea, son of Saturn, brother of Jupiter and Pluto. Greek equivalent **Poseidon** [15C. Directly or via French < Latin *Neptunus*.]

neptunium /nep tyóoni əm/ *n* (*symbol* Np) a silvery radioactive metallic element. Source: uranium ores, a by-product of plutonium production in nuclear reactors. Use: neutron detection. [Late 19C. After the planet NEPTUNE, discovered after uranium (named after Uranus).]

NERC /nurk/ *abbr* Natural Environment Research Council

nerd /nurd/ *n* **1** an offensive term deliberately insulting somebody's physical appearance or social skills (*slang insult*) **2** an enthusiast whose interest is regarded as too technical or scientific and who seems obsessively wrapped up in it (*often in combination; offensive in some contexts*) [Mid-20C. < ?] —**nerdish** *adj* —**nerdy** *adj*

Nereid[1] /néeri id/ (*plural* -**ides** /nə reé ə deez/) *n* in Greek mythology, a sea nymph, one of the 50 daughters of the sea god Nereus [Late 17C. Via Latin < Greek *Nērēid-* < *Nēreus*, a Greek sea god.]

Nereid[2] /néeri id/ *n* the outermost known natural satellite of Neptune, discovered in 1949

Nereides *plural* of **Nereid**[1]

nereis /néeri iss/ (*plural* -**ides** /nə reé ə deez/ *or* -**ises**) *n* a large segmented worm usually found living in saltwater, e.g. the ragworm. Genus: *Nereis*. [Mid-18C. Via modern Latin < Latin, < Greek *Nēreus*, a Greek sea god.]

neritic /nə ríttik/ *adj* relating to or found in shallow coastal waters [Late 19C. < Latin *nerita*, type of shellfish of shallow seas < Greek *Nēreus*, a Greek sea god.]

Nernst /nairnst/, **Walther Hermann** (1864–1941) German physical chemist

Nernst equation /núrnst-/ *n* an equation that shows the dependence of the electromotive force in a dry cell on the activities of the reacting chemicals and the temperature [After Walther Hermann NERNST]

Nero /néerō/ (AD 37–68) Roman emperor. Born **Lucius Domitius Ahenobarbus**

nerol /néer ol, nérr-/ *n* a colourless alcohol. Source: neroli and other essential oils. Use: perfumes. [Early 20C. < NEROLI.]

neroli /néerəli/, **neroli oil** *n* an oil distilled from the flowers of orange trees, especially the Seville orange. Use: aromatherapy, perfumes, food flavouring. [Late 17C. Via French < Italian, after an Italian princess who supposedly discovered the oil.]

Neruda /ne róodə, -róothə/, **Pablo** (1904–73) Chilean poet and diplomat. Pseudonym of **Neftalí Ricardo Reyes y Basoalto**

Nerva /núrvə/, **Marcus Cocceius** (AD 35?–98) Roman emperor

nerve /nurv/ *n* 1 **FIBRE BUNDLE TRANSMITTING IMPULSES** a bundle of fibres forming a network that transmits messages, in the form of impulses, between the brain or spinal cord and the body's organs 2 **SENSITIVE PULP IN TOOTH** the sensitive tissue inside the roots of a tooth 3 **COURAGE** courage or self-assurance ○ *lost his nerve* 4 **BOLDNESS** boldness or impudence ○ *You've got a nerve!* 5 **LEAF VEIN** a vein in a leaf 6 **VEIN IN INSECT'S WING** a thin rib visible inside an insect's wing ■ **nerves** *npl* 1 **STRESS THRESHOLD** somebody's ability to tolerate emotional stress or excitement ○ *My nerves are shattered.* 2 **NERVOUSNESS** a state of emotional agitation (*informal*) ○ *He had a bad case of nerves before every performance.* ■ *vt* **STEEL YOURSELF** to gather all your courage or self-control in preparation for dealing with something difficult, stressful, or frightening [14C. Directly or via Old French *nerf* 'sinew' < Latin *nervus* 'nerve, sinew, tendon'.]

SYNONYMS See ***courage***.

nerve block *n* use of a local anaesthetic to numb a part of the body, thereby preventing the transmission of pain messages to the brain

nerve cell *n* ANAT = **neuron**

nerve centre *n* 1 a place from which a large organization, system, or network is controlled 2 a cluster of interconnected nerve cells that performs a specific function in the body

nerve cord *n* a strand of nerve tissue, e.g. the spinal cord, that runs the length of the body and forms a principal part of an animal's nervous system

nerve fibre *n* one of the long thin extensions of a neuron such as an axon or dendrite

nerve gas *n* a poisonous gas used as a weapon of war that attacks the central nervous system and stops people breathing

nerve impulse *n* a rapid and momentary change in electrical activity that passes along a nerve fibre to other neurons, muscles, or other body organs and signals instructions or information

nerveless /núrvləss/ *adj* 1 **NUMB** having no sensation or strength 2 **FEARLESS** showing calmness, courage, or confidence, especially in a dangerous situation 3 **COWARDLY** lacking courage or determination —**nervelessly** *adv* —**nervelessness** *n*

nerve net *n* a simple nervous system, found in some invertebrates such as jellyfish, consisting of interconnecting nerve cells but lacking a control centre such as a brain

nerve-racking, nerve-wracking *adj* causing great anxiety or distress

nerve trunk *n* a bundle of nerve fibres surrounded by a sheath of connective tissue that forms the main stem of a nerve

nerve-wracking *adj* = **nerve-racking**

Nervi /náirvi/, **Pier Luigi** (1891–1979) Italian architect and engineer

nervous /núrvəss/ *adj* 1 **UNEASY** having a feeling of dread or apprehension ○ *feeling nervous about meeting his parents* 2 **TIMID** easily worried or frightened ○ *people of a nervous disposition* 3 **AFFECTING THE NERVES** relating to somebody's ability to tolerate anxiety and stress ○ *a nervous illness* 4 **OF NERVES** relating to or located in nerves or the nervous system ○ *nervous tissue* [14C. Originally 'sinewy'.] —**nervosity** /nur vóssəti/ *n* —**nervously** *adv* —**nervousness** *n*

nervous breakdown *n* a psychiatric disorder, usually caused by intense stress or anxiety, in which somebody becomes incapable of coping with daily life and exhibits low self-esteem or depression

nervous system *n* the network of nerve cells and nerve fibres in most animals that conveys sensations to the brain and motor impulses to organs and muscles

nervous tic *n* an involuntary twitch of a muscle, especially of the face, that is sometimes a symptom of nervousness or a nervous disease

nervure /núr vyoor/ *n* 1 a supporting structure resembling a rod that is visible inside an insect's wing 2 PLANT SCI = **vein** *n.* 3 [Early 19C. < French, 'strap' < Latin *nervus* 'nerve'.]

nervy /núrvi/ (**-ier, -iest**) *adj* 1 feeling, or easily becoming, worried, upset, or frightened (*informal*) 2 extremely strong (*archaic*) —**nervily** *adv* —**nerviness** *n*

Nesbit /nézbit/, **E.** (1858–1924) British novelist and poet

nesh /nesh/ *adj* (*regional*) 1 very sensitive to cold temperatures 2 lacking courage or self-confidence [Old English *hnesce*]

ness /ness/ *n* a section of coastline that projects into the sea (*often in placenames*) [Old English *næs(s)* < Indo-European]

Ness, Loch /ness/ lake in N Scotland, forming part of the Caledonian Canal. Length: 39 km/24 mi.

-ness *suffix* state, condition, quality ○ *callousness* [Old English *-nes* < Germanic]

nesselrode /néss'l rōd/, **Nesselrode** *n* a creamy frozen dessert containing puréed chestnuts, candied fruit, and usually a sweet wine or liqueur [Mid-19C. After Karl-Robert *Nesselrode* (1780–1862), Russian statesman, whose chef invented it.]

nest /nest/ *n* 1 **BIRD OR ANIMAL'S DWELLING** a structure that birds and other animals such as mice build to shelter themselves and their young, using available natural materials such as grass, twigs, and mud 2 **COMMUNITY OF ANIMALS** the community of animals living in a nest 3 **SOMETHING SHAPED LIKE BIRD'S NEST** something shaped more or less like a bird's nest, especially something that encloses or contains things ○ *a meringue nest* 4 **COSY PLACE** a cosy, protected, or secluded place 5 **BAD PLACE** a place where something bad, such as crime or treason, flourishes ○ *a nest of vice* 6 **CRIMINALS' SECRET PLACE** a hideaway for criminals, or a group of criminals hiding away there ○ *a nest of thieves* 7 **SET OF THINGS** a set of things such as tables or wooden eggs that fit one inside the other 8 **GUN EMPLACEMENT** a protected or camouflaged place from which a gun or other weapon is fired ■ *v* 1 *vi* **BUILD NEST** to make or live in a nest, especially in preparation for giving birth to young 2 *vi* **MAKE PLACE MORE HOME-LIKE** to make a place more comfortable and home-like (*informal*) 3 *vt* **PUT THINGS TOGETHER** to put one thing inside another, or group things together into a single unit, e.g. items in a reference book into a single entry or under a main heading 4 *vi* **LOOK FOR BIRDS' NESTS** to go looking for birds' nests in order to take the eggs [Old English < Indo-European 'place where a bird sits down']

nest box, nesting box *n* a box of the appropriate size, depending on the species, placed in a park, forest, or other place for wild birds to use for breeding

nest-building *n* 1 a bird's construction of a nest in preparation for having young 2 the process of making a place more comfortable and home-like, often for an expected baby (*informal*)

nest egg *n* 1 a sum of money put aside for future expenses or emergencies 2 a real or artificial egg that is put in a hen's nest to encourage it to continue laying after the other eggs have been removed

nesting box *n* = **nest box**

nestle /néss'l/ *v* 1 *vti* **SETTLE INTO COMFORTABLE POSITION** to settle into a position that feels comfortable, warm, and safe, or lay a part of the body in such a position 2 *vt* **CUSHION SOMETHING WITH SOFT MATERIAL** to put something such as delicate china or glassware in a protected cushion of soft material 3 *vi* **BE SECLUDED** to be in a sheltered or secluded place [Old English *nestlian* < Germanic] —**nestler** *n*

nestling /néstling/ *n* a young bird that does not yet have its flight feathers, and is therefore not yet able to leave the nest [Late 14C. < NEST or NESTLE.]

Nestorian /ne stáwri ən/ *adj* relating to an Asian Christian denomination that believes that two distinct persons, one divine and the other human, existed in Jesus Christ [15C. < late Latin *Nestorianus*, after *Nestorius* (AD 428–31), patriarch of Constantinople.]

⚡**net**[1] /net/ *n* 1 **MESH** material made from threads or wires knotted, twisted, or woven to form a regular pattern with spaces between the threads 2 **MESHWORK BAG** a piece of meshwork fabric in a shape resembling a bag that is used for holding, carrying, trapping, or confining something ○ *a fishing net* 3 **LIGHT MESHWORK FABRIC** a fine light cotton or synthetic fabric with an open weave ○ *net curtains* 4 **SELECTING OR RESTRICTING SYSTEM** a plan or system designed to select or restrict somebody or something ○ *those who slip through the net* 5 **STRIP OF MATERIAL ACROSS PLAYING AREA** a strip of meshwork material that divides a court into halves in some sports, e.g. tennis and volleyball, and over which the players must hit a ball or shuttlecock 6 **GOAL IN SOME SPORTS** a goal in some sports, e.g. soccer and water polo, with a backing made of meshwork material 7 **PART OF BASKETBALL NET** an open-bottomed piece of meshwork material attached to the hoop of the basket in basketball 8 **PRACTICE CRICKET PITCH** in cricket, an indoor or outdoor practice pitch surrounded on three sides by nets that contain the ball after it has been hit (*often plural*) 9 **CRICKET PRACTICE SESSION** in cricket, a session on a practice pitch (*often plural*) 10 **TELEVISION NETWORK** a television or radio network 11 **TELEPHONE OR COMPUTER NETWORK** a telecommunications or computer network ■ *v* (**nets, netting, netted**) 1 *vt* **TRAP IN NET** to catch or snare something in a net 2 *vt* **GET** to manage to obtain or achieve something (*informal*) ○ *We may net ourselves several new clients this way.* 3 *vt* **PROTECT WITH NET** to cover something with a net in order to keep something out or away ○ *Net the cherry trees to keep birds out.* 4 *vi* **MAKE NET** to make a net by knotting, twisting, or weaving threads or wires together 5 *vt* **HIT BALL INTO NET TO SCORE** to score by hitting the ball into the net in games such as soccer and hockey 6 *vt* **SERVE BALL INTO NET** to lose a serve, and sometimes a point, by hitting the ball into the net in games such as tennis and volleyball [Old English < Indo-European, 'to bind, tie'] —**netless** *adj* —**netlessly** *adv*

net[2] /net/, **nett** *adj* 1 **LEFT AFTER DEDUCTIONS** remaining from an amount, especially of money, after all necessary deductions have been made 2 **RELATING TO CONTENTS** relating to contents only, excluding the container or the packaging 3 **HAVING ALL THINGS CONSIDERED** general or overall when positive and negative features have been weighed against each other ■ *vt* (**nets, netting, netted**) **EARN PROFIT** to earn or provide a sum of money as pure profit after all necessary deductions have been made ■ *n* 1 **NET AMOUNT** a net profit or weight 2 **GOLFER'S SCORE** a golfer's final score after his or her handicap has been deducted [15C. Via Italian *netto* < Latin *nitidus* (see NEAT[1]).]

⚡**net**[3] *abbr* network organization (*in Internet addresses*)

⚡**Net** /net/, **net** *n* the Internet (*informal*) [Late 20C. Shortening.]

Netanyahu /nétt'n yaáhoo/, **Binyamin** (*b.* 1949) Israeli politician

net asset value *n* the value of the securities owned by a mutual fund, calculated as the total value of assets minus the total amount of liabilities divided by the number of shares issued

netball /nét bawl/ *n* an indoor or outdoor game usually played by girls or women, who can hand or throw the ball to each other but not run with it

Net Book Agreement *n* an agreement in the British book trade, ended in 1995, that prevented booksellers from selling books at prices lower than those fixed by the publishers

net cord *n* 1 a tennis shot, especially a serve, that touches the net before landing on the opponent's side 2 the wire that holds up the net on a tennis court

net domestic product *n* the gross sum of domestic production minus the cost of depreciation of capital goods

nether /néthər/ *adj* located in a low or lower position or under something [Old English *neoþera* < Indo-European, 'down']

Netherlands /néthər ləndz/ constitutional monarchy in NW Europe, on the North Sea. Capital: Amsterdam. Population: 15,451,000 (1995). Area: 41,526 sq. km/16,033 sq. mi. —**Netherlander** *n* —**Netherlandish** *adj*

Netherlands Antilles two island groups in the West Indies, in the Caribbean Sea, an overseas territory of the Netherlands. Capital: Willemstad. Population: 202,244 (1994). Area: 800 sq. km/309 sq. mi.

nethermost /néthərmōst/ *adj* lowest or farthest down

nether world *n* 1 **HELL** hell or the place where evil spirits live in the belief system of some cultures (*formal*) 2 **ABODE OF DEAD SOULS** in Greek and Roman mythology, the place below the earth's surface where the souls of the dead live 3 **CRIMINAL UNDERWORLD** the world of organized crime, or the people involved in it (*literary*)

Netherlands

⚡ netiquette /nétti ket, -kət/ *n* a set of empirically derived rules for getting along harmoniously in the electronic communication environment (*informal*) [Late 20C. Blend of NET + ETIQUETTE.]

⚡ Netizen /néttizən/ *n* a frequent user of the Internet (*informal*) [Late 20C. Blend of NET + CITIZEN.]

net national product *n* the amount left after subtracting a depreciation allowance for capital goods from the gross national product

⚡ netphone /nétfōn/ *n* a phone that uses the Internet to make connections and carry voice messages

net present value *n* the value of an investment project found by adding the present value of expected future cash flows and the cost of the initial investment

net profit *n* gross profit minus all the costs incurred by a business

net realizable value, net realisable value *n* the value an asset would have if sold, allowing for the costs of bringing it to a condition for sale and making the sale

netsuke /nétski, -kay, nétsōóki, -kay/ *n* a carved wooden or ivory ornamental toggle worn at the end of a cord that holds a kimono closed, originally used to fasten a purse or pouch [Late 19C. < Japanese.]

⚡ Net surfing *n* browsing through the information and sites available on the Internet, especially casually

nett /net/ *adj* 1 = net[2] 2 *Malaysia, Singapore* describes a price that cannot be changed by bartering

⚡ netter /néttər/ *n* somebody with an Internet address (*slang*)

netting /nétting/ *n* fabric made from threads or wires knotted, twisted, or woven to form a regular pattern with spaces between the threads

nettle /nétt'l/ *n* 1 PLANT WITH STINGING LEAVES a wild plant with serrated-edged leaves covered with fine hairs or spines that sting when touched. Genus: *Urtica*. 2 NON-STINGING PLANT RESEMBLING NETTLE a wild plant with serrated leaves like a stinging nettle, but without the stinging hairs, especially a dead nettle. Genus: *Lamium*. ■ *vt* (-tles, -tling, -tled) 1 IRRITATE to irritate or annoy somebody (*informal*) 2 STING to sting somebody [Old English *netele* < Indo-European, 'to tie']

nettle rash *n* MED = urticaria

net ton *n* MEASURE = ton[1] *n*. 1 [< NET[2]]

net weight *n* the weight of the contents only, excluding the weight of the container or packaging [< NET[2]]

net-winged *adj* describes the wings of beetles and midges that have a network of veins

⚡ network /nét wurk/ *n* 1 SYSTEM OF INTERCONNECTED LINES a pattern or system that looks like a series of branching or interconnecting lines 2 COORDINATED SYSTEM OF PEOPLE OR THINGS a large and widely distributed group of people or things such as shops, colleges, or churches, that communicate with one another and work together as a unit or system 3 GROUP OF BROADCASTING CHANNELS a group of radio or television channels with a core of programmes that they all broadcast at the same time, with local or regional variations at other times 4 SYSTEM OF ELECTRICAL CIRCUITS a system of interconnected electrical circuits or components 5 SYSTEM OF LINKED COMPUTERS a system of two or more computers, terminals, and communications devices linked by wires, cables, or a telecommunications system, in order to exchange data 6 NETTING net or netting ■ *v* 1 *vi* MAINTAIN RELATIONSHIPS WITH PEOPLE to build up or maintain informal relationships,

especially with people whose friendship could bring advantages such as job or business opportunities 2 *vt* LINK COMPUTERS to link a group of computers or their users so that information can be mutually accessed or exchanged 3 *vt* BROADCAST SOMETHING SIMULTANEOUSLY to broadcast a programme simultaneously on all the channels that form a network

⚡ networking /nét wurking/ *n* 1 the linking of computers so that users can exchange information or share access to a central store of information 2 the building up or maintaining of informal relationships, especially with people whose friendship could bring advantages such as job or business opportunities —**networker** *n*

Neumann /nyoómən/, **Balthasar** (1687–1753) German architect

Neumann, John von (1903–57) Hungarian-born US mathematician

neume /nyoom/, **neum** *n* during the Middle Ages in Europe, an early kind of musical notation that sometimes indicated only the approximate shape of a melody [15C. Via French < Greek *pneuma* 'breath'.] —**neumatic** /nyoo máttik/ *adj*

neur- prefix = **neuro-** (before vowels)

neural /nyoórəl/ *adj* relating to or located in a nerve or the nervous system —**neurally** *adv*

neural arch *n* a bony or cartilaginous arch enclosing the spinal cord on the outward-facing side of a vertebra

⚡ neural computer *n* COMPUT = neurocomputer

neural crest *n* a ridge of cells in the ectoderm of the vertebrate embryo that develops into cranial, spinal, and autonomic ganglia

neuralgia /nyoo rálja/ *n* intermittent and often severe pain in a part of the body that a particular nerve runs through, especially when there is no physical change in the nerve itself —**neuralgic** *adj*

⚡ neural net *n* a system of electrical circuits designed to perform like the human nervous system, especially a computer system mimicking the human brain

⚡ neural network *n* 1 an interconnecting system of nerve cells such as the system that makes the brain function 2 COMPUT = neural net

neural spine *n* a projection that points backwards from the neural arch of a vertebra

neural tube *n* the hollow tube of tissue in the embryo of humans and other vertebrates that develops into the spinal cord and brain

neural tube defect *n* a disorder such as spina bifida that is present at birth and is caused by failure of the neural tube to close completely, resulting in loss of muscle function and various medical disorders

neurasthenia /nyoorass theéni ə/ *n* a condition marked by chronic mental and physical fatigue and depression (*dated*) —**neurasthenic** /-thénnik/ *adj* —**neurasthenically** *adv*

neurectomy /nyoo réktəmi/ (*plural* -mies) *n* the removal of part of a nerve using surgery, e.g. as a treatment for neuralgia

neurilemma /nyoóri lémmə/, **neurolemma** /nyoórō-/ *n* the outermost layer of the myelin sheath that surrounds the axon of a myelinated nerve cell [Early 19C. < NEUR- + Greek *eilēma* 'covering'.] —**neurilemmal** *adj* —**neurilemmally** *adv*

neurilemmoma /nyoóri le mōmə/ (*plural* -mas *or* -mata /-mətə/) *n* MED = neurofibroma

neurinoma /nyoóri nōmə/ (*plural* -mas *or* -mata /-mətə/) *n* MED = neurofibroma [Early 20C]

neuritis /nyoo rítiss/ *n* inflammation of a nerve, accompanied by pain, loss of reflexes, and muscle shrinkage —**neuritic** /-rittik/ *adj*

neuro- prefix nerve, neural ○ *neurosurgery* [< Greek *neuron* 'nerve']

neuroactive /nyoórō áktiv/ *adj* having an effect on neural tissue or the nervous system

neuroanatomy /nyoórō ə náttəmi/ *n* 1 the structure of the nervous system 2 the branch of anatomy that studies the structure of the nervous system —**neuroanatomical** /-ánnə tómmik'l/ *adj* —**neuroanatomically** *adv* —**neuroanatomist** /-ə náttəmist/ *n*

neurobiology /nyoórō bī ólləji/ *n* BIOL = **neuroscience** *n*. 2 —**neurobiological** /-bī ə lójjik'l/ *adj* —**neurobiologically** *adv* —**neurobiologist** /-bī ólləjist/ *n*

neuroblast /nyoórō blast/ *n* an embryonic cell that develops into a nerve cell

neuroblastoma /nyoórō bla stōmə/ (*plural* -mas *or* -mata /-mətə/) *n* a malignant tumour of embryonic nerve cells (**neuroblasts**)

neurochemistry /nyoórō kémmistri/ *n* the study of the chemical composition and reactions within the nervous system —**neurochemical** *adj* —**neurochemically** *adv* —**neurochemist** *n*

⚡ neurocomputer /nyoórō kəm pyootər/ *n* a computer designed to imitate the human brain's ability to identify patterns, learn by trial and error, and find relationships in information —**neurocomputational** /nyoórō kómpyoó táysh'nal/ *adj* —**neurocomputing** *n*

neurodegenerative /nyoórō di jénnərativ/ *adj* causing a loss of structure or function in nerve cells, their connections, or supportive tissue

neuroendocrine /nyoórō éndō krīn, -krin/ *adj* relating to or involving a nerve cell that releases a chemical messenger, especially a neurohormone, directly into the bloodstream

neuroendocrinology /nyoórō éndōkri nóllaji/ *n* the study of the interrelationships between the nervous system, the endocrine system, and hormones —**neuroendocrinological** /-krínnə lójjik'l/ *adj* —**neuroendocrinologically** *adv* —**neuroendocrinologist** /-éndōkri nóllajist/ *n*

neurofibril /nyoórō fíbril/ *n* a microscopic thin strand that occurs inside the cell body, axon, and dendrites of a nerve cell —**neurofibrillary** /nyoórō bríllari/ *adj*

neurofibroma /nyoórō fī brōmə/ (*plural* -mas *or* -mata /-mətə/) *n* a usually benign tumour arising from the sheath of a nerve

neurofibromatosis /nyoórō fī brōmə tóssiss/ *n* an inherited disorder marked by coffee-coloured patches on the skin and neurofibromas formed along nerves, causing visual and hearing defects, other nervous disorders, and sometimes major deformities

neurogenesis /nyoórō jénnəsiss/ *n* the formation and development of nerve cells —**neurogenetic** /-jə néttik/ *adj* —**neurogenetically** *adv*

neurogenetics /nyoórō jə néttiks/ *n* the branch of medicine that studies the genetic influences involved in neurological disorders (+ *singular verb*) —**neurogeneticist** *n*

neurogenic /nyoórō jénnik/ *adj* 1 causing or relating to the growth of nerve tissue 2 arising in or stimulated by nerve tissue or the nervous system —**neurogenically** *adv*

neuroglia /nyoo róggli ə/ *n* ANAT = **glia** [Mid-19C. < NEURO- + Greek *glia* 'glue'.] —**neuroglial** *adj*

neurohormone /nyoórō háwrmōn/ *n* any hormone secreted by specialized nerve cells —**neurohormonal** /-hawr mōn'l/ *adj* —**neurohormonally** *adv*

neurohumour /nyoórō hyoómər/ *n* BIOL = **neurotransmitter** —**neurohumoral** /nyoórō hyoómərəl/ *adj*

neurohypophysis /nyoórō hī póffississ/ (*plural* -ses /-seez/) *n* the posterior lobe of the pituitary gland that secretes hormones such as vasopressin —**neurohypophyseal** /nyoórō hīpō fízzi əl, -hī póffi seé əl/ *adj*

neurol. *abbr* 1 neurological 2 neurology

neurolemma *n* MED = neurilemma

neuroleptic /nyoórō léptik/ *adj* reducing nerve activity and producing a tranquillizing effect ■ *n* a tranquillizing drug that works by reducing nerve activity. Use: treatment of delirium, behavioural disturbances. [Mid-20C. < NEURO- + Greek *lēptikos* 'seizing' < *lambanein* 'seize, take'.] —**neuroleptically** *adv*

neurolinguistic programming /nyoórō ling gwístik-/ *n* 1 a theory and model of human behaviour and communication based on linguistic insights into how people avoid change and how to assist them in changing 2 a system of therapy in which the brain is viewed as a computer that can be reprogrammed to think and feel in a way that helps achieve specific goals

neurolinguistics /nyoórō ling gwístiks/ *n* the branch of linguistics that explores how the brain encodes language (+ *singular verb*) —**neurolinguist** /nyoórō ling gwist/ *n* —**neurolinguistic** *adj* —**neurolinguistically** *adv*

neurology /nyoo róllaji/ *n* the branch of medicine that deals with the structure and function of the nervous system and the treatment of the diseases and disorders that affect it —**neurologic** /nyoórō lójjik/ *adj* —**neuro-**

logical *adj* —**neurologically** *adv* —**neurologist** /nyoo róllәjist/ *n*

neuroma /nyoo rómә/ (*plural* **-mata** /-mәtә/ *or* **-mas**) *n* MED = **neurofibroma**

neuromuscular /nyóorō múskyoolәr/ *adj* **1** relating to or affecting both nerve and muscle tissue **2** having features common to both nerve and muscle tissue —**neuromuscularly** *adv*

neuromuscular junction *n* the connection between a nerve cell and a muscle, where nerve impulses are transmitted to initiate contraction of the muscle

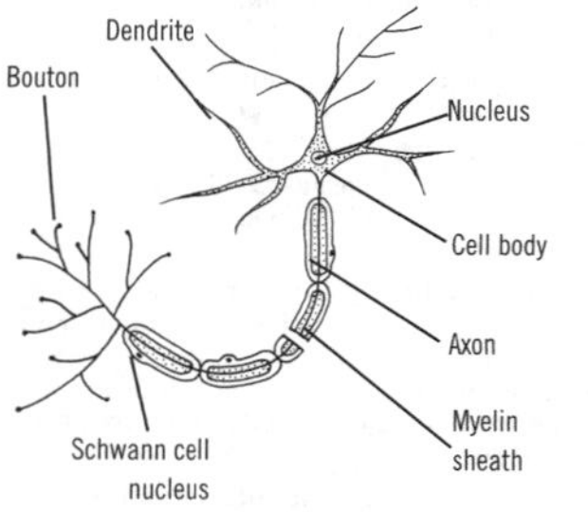

Neuron

neuron /nyóor on/, **neurone** /nyóor ōn/ *n* a cell, typically consisting of a cell body, axon, and dendrites, that transmits nerve impulses and is the basic functional unit of the nervous system [Late 19C. Via German < Greek *neuron* 'sinew, cord, nerve'.] —**neuronal** /nyoo rṓn'l/ *adj* —**neuronally** /-rṓn'li/ *adv*

neuropath /nyóorō path/ *n* somebody affected by a disorder of the nervous system

neuropathology /nyóorō pә thóllәji/ *n* the branch of medicine that studies diseases and disorders of the nervous system —**neuropathological** /nyóorō páthә lójjik'l/ *adj* —**neuropathologically** *adv* —**neuropathologist** *n*

neuropathy /nyoo róppәthi/ (*plural* **-thies**) *n* a disease or disorder, especially a degenerative one, that affects the nervous system —**neuropathic** /nyóorō páthik/ *adj* —**neuropathically** *adv*

neuropeptide /nyóorō pép tīd/ *n* any peptide released by the nervous system and acting as a neurotransmitter

neuropharmacology /nyóorō faarmә kóllәji/ *n* the branch of medicine that studies the effects of drugs on the nervous system —**neuropharmacological** /nyóorō faarmәkә lójjik'l/ *adj* —**neuropharmacologically** *adv* —**neuropharmacologist** *n*

neurophysiology /nyóorō fízzi óllәji/ *n* the branch of physiology that studies how the nervous system functions —**neurophysiological** /-fízzi ә lójjik'l/ *adj* —**neurophysiologically** *adv* —**neurophysiologist** *n*

neuropsychiatry /nyóorō sī kī́ ətri/ *n* the study of the neurological aspects of psychiatric disorders —**neuropsychiatric** /nyóorō sīki áttrik/ *adj* —**neuropsychiatrically** *adv* —**neuropsychiatrist** /-sī kī́ ətrist/ *n*

neuropsychology /nyóorō sī kóllәji/ *n* the branch of neurology that studies behaviour, especially in disorders such as epilepsy, memory loss, or speech impairment —**neuropsychological** /nyóorō sīkә lójjik'l/ *adj* —**neuropsychologically** *adv* —**neuropsychologist** *n*

neuropteran /nyoo róptәrәn/, **neuropteron** (*plural* **-tera** /-tәrә/) *n* an insect such as the ant lion or lacewing that has two large pairs of veined wings and mouthparts adapted for chewing. Order: Neuroptera. —**neuropterous** *adj*

neuroradiology /nyóorō ráydi óllәji/ *n* the use of X-rays to diagnose and treat physiological disorders and diseases of the nervous system, or the branch of medicine that deals with their use —**neuroradiological** /nyóorō ráydi ә lójjik'l/ *adj* —**neuroradiologically** *adv* —**neuroradiologist** *n*

neuroscience /nyóorō sī әnss/ *n* **1** a scientific discipline such as neuroanatomy or neurophysiology that studies nerve cells or the nervous system, or all such disciplines collectively **2** the scientific study of the molecular and cellular levels of the nervous system, of systems within the brain such as vision and hearing, and behaviour produced by the brain —**neuroscientific** /nyóorō sī әn tíffik/ *adj* —**neuroscientifically** *adv* —**neuroscientist** /nyóorō sī әntist/ *n*

neurosensory /nyóorō sénssәri/ *adj* relating to the sensory activity of nerve cells or the nervous system —**neurosensorily** *adv*

neurosis /nyoo róssiss/ (*plural* **-ses** /nyoo ró seez/) *n* a mild psychiatric disorder characterized by anxiety, depression, and hypochondria

neurosurgery /nyóorō súrjәri/ *n* surgery on any part of the nervous system, including the brain —**neurosurgeon** *n* —**neurosurgical** *adj* —**neurosurgically** *adv*

neurotic /nyoo róttik/ *adj* **1 AFFECTED BY NEUROSIS** relating to, involving, affected by, or typical of a mild mental disorder characterized by depression, anxiety, and hypochondria **2 OVERANXIOUS OR OBSESSIVE** overanxious, oversensitive, or obsessive about everyday things (*often considered offensive*) ■ *n* **1 SOMEBODY AFFECTED BY NEUROSIS** somebody diagnosed as affected by neurosis **2 SOMEBODY WHO IS EXTREMELY SENSITIVE** an overanxious, oversensitive, or obsessive person (*often considered offensive*) [Mid-17C. < Greek *neuron* 'nerve'.] —**neurotically** *adv* —**neuroticism** *n*

neurotomy /nyoo róttәmi/ (*plural* **-mies**) *n* a surgical operation to cut a nerve, especially in order to relieve pain

neurotoxin /nyóorō tóksin/ *n* a substance that damages, destroys, or impairs the functioning of nerve tissue —**neurotoxic** *adj* —**neurotoxically** *adv* —**neurotoxicity** /nyóorō tok síssәti/ *n*

neurotransmitter /nyóor ō tranz míttәr/ *n* a chemical that carries messages between different nerve cells or between nerve cells and muscles, e.g. to trigger or prevent an impulse in the receiving cell

neurotropic /nyóorō tróppik/ *adj* affecting or having an affinity with nerve tissue —**neurotropically** *adv* —**neurotropism** /nyoo róttrәpizәm, nyoorә trṓpizәm/ *n*

neurula /nyóoryoolә/ (*plural* **-rulae** /-lee/ *or* **-ralas**) *n* a vertebrate embryo in an early stage during which the nervous system begins to develop [Late 19C. < NEURO- + Latin *-ula* 'small' after BLASTULA, SCROFULA.] —**neurulation** /nyóoryoo láysh'n/ *n*

neuston /nyóost'n/ *n* minute organisms that float or swim on the surface of water [Early 20C. < German, < a form of Greek *neustos* 'swimming' < *nein* 'to swim'.]

neuter /nyóotәr/ *vt* **REMOVE TESTICLES OR OVARIES** to remove the testicles or ovaries of an animal ■ *adj* **1 WITHOUT SEX ORGANS** with undeveloped, nonfunctioning, or no sexual organs **2 NOT INDICATING SEX OR OTHER CHARACTERISTICS** not indicating the sex of a person, the qualities of a thing, or an attitude towards somebody or something **3 GRAMMATICALLY NEITHER MASCULINE NOR FEMININE** describes nouns and adjectives in languages such as Latin or German belonging to a separate gender that is neither masculine nor feminine **4 INTRANSITIVE** describes a verb that is neither active nor passive ■ *n* **1 CASTRATED OR SPAYED ANIMAL** an animal that has been castrated or spayed **2 GRAMMATICALLY NEUTER WORD** a grammatically neuter noun, adjective, or verb **3 INSECT WITH UNDEVELOPED SEXUAL ORGANS** an insect with undeveloped sexual organs, e.g., a worker bee **4 FLOWER WITHOUT STAMEN OR PISTIL** an asexual flower without a stamen or pistil [14C. < Latin, < *ne* 'not' + *uter* 'which of two'.]

neutral /nyóotrәl/ *adj* **1 TAKING NO SIDES** belonging to, favouring, or assisting no side in a war, dispute, contest, or controversy **2 WITHOUT DISTINCTIVE QUALITIES** possessing no particular quality or revealing no particular attitude or feeling ○ *She was careful to explain the problem in neutral terms.* **3 WITHOUT HUE** describes a colour such as white, black, or grey that is not in the spectrum **4 NOT STRONGLY COLOURED** not strongly or strikingly coloured and thus relatively inconspicuous **5** PHYSIOL = **neuter** *adj.* **1 6 NOT ACID NOT ALKALINE** neither acidic nor alkaline **7 WITH ZERO ELECTRIC CHARGE** with zero electric charge or potential **8 WITH NO MOTION TRANSMITTED** in which no motion is transmitted **9 PRONOUNCED WITH TONGUE MIDWAY** describes a vowel articulated with the tongue relaxed and in the mid-central position, as, e.g., in the first syllable of 'away' ■ *n* **1 NONALIGNED PERSON OR THING** a person who or a country that remains neutral in a war or dispute **2 GEAR WITH NO MOTION TRANSMITTED** a gear in which no power is transmitted from the engine to the moving parts [15C. < Latin *neutralis* 'of neuter gender' < *neuter* (see NEUTER).] —**neutrally** *adv*

neutral corner *n* either of the two corners of a boxing ring that are not used by boxers between rounds

neutralise *vt* = **neutralize**

neutralism /nyóotrәlizәm/ *n* the policy of remaining neutral in wars and other disputes, or support for this policy —**neutralist** *n, adj* —**neutralistic** /nyóotrә lístik/ *adj* —**neutralistically** *adv*

neutrality /nyoo trállәti/ *n* the state of being neutral, especially as regards noninvolvement in wars and disputes, not taking sides, and not joining alliances

neutralize /nyóotrә līz/ (**-izes, -izing, -ized**), **neutralise** (**-ises, -ising, -ised**) *vt* **1 RENDER INEFFECTIVE** to make something ineffective, especially by removing its ability to act as a threat or obstacle **2 MAKE NONALIGNED** to make or declare a country unaligned in an international dispute or war **3 MAKE NEITHER ACID NOR ALKALINE** to render a substance neither acid nor alkaline **4 GIVE ZERO CHARGE TO** to make the electric charge or potential of something zero —**neutralization** /nyóotrә lī záysh'n/ *n* —**neutralizer** *n*

neutral spirits *n* US alcohol distilled at or above 190 proof. Use: in blending alcoholic drinks. (+ *singular or plural verb*)

neutral zone *n* in sport, the space between the areas of two competing teams, especially the area between the linemen of American football teams or the middle area of an ice hockey rink between the two blue lines

neutrino /nyoo treén ō/ (*plural* **-nos**) *n* any of three stable neutral elementary particles of the lepton family with a zero rest mass and no charge [Mid-20C. < NEUTRAL + Italian *-ino* 'small'.]

neutron /nyóo tron/ *n* a neutral elementary particle of the baryon family with a zero electrical charge and a mass approximately equal to that of a proton [Early 20C. < NEUTRAL.] —**neutronic** /nyoo trónnik/ *adj*

neutron bomb *n* a nuclear bomb designed to kill all life by a heavy bombardment with neutrons but to cause little blast damage and leave relatively low radioactive contamination

neutron star *n* an astronomical object consisting entirely of a very dense compact mass of neutrons, the remnant of a star that has collapsed under its own gravity

neutrophil /nyóotrә fil/ *adj* describes cells or tissues, e.g. white blood cells, that are readily stainable only with chemically neutral dyes ■ *n* **neutrophil, neutrophile** the most common type of white blood cell in vertebrates, responsible for protecting the body against infection and stainable with neutral dyes [Late 19C. < Latin *neutr-*, stem of *neuter* (see NEUTER).] —**neutrophilic** /nyóotrә fíllik/ *adj*

Nev. *abbr* Nevada

Nevada /nә vaádә/ state in the W United States. Capital: Carson City. Population: 1,676,809 (1997). Area: 286,367 sq. km/110,567 sq. mi. —**Nevadan** *n, adj*

névé /névvay/ (*plural* **-vés**) *n* **1** compact granular snow, found at the top of a glacier, that has not yet become ice **2** a field of compacted granular snow at the top of a glacier [Mid-19C. < Swiss French, < Latin *nivatus* 'snow-cooled' < *niv-* 'snow'.]

never /névvәr/ CORE MEANING: an adverb indicating that something will not happen at any time, or that somebody will definitely not do something ○ *The details will never be known.* ○ *I would never do anything to harm or hurt her.*

1 *adv* **AT NO TIME** at no time in the past or the future ○ *The bird has never been seen in Iceland before. It may never appear there again.* **2** *adv* **CERTAINLY NOT** not in any circumstances at all ○ *I would never turn my back on them.* **3** *interj* **EXCLAMATION OF SURPRISE** an exclamation indicating surprise or shock ○ *'She's come top again'.'Never!'* [Old English, < *ne* 'not' + EVER] ◇ **never ever** used as an emphatic expression for 'never' (*informal*) ◇ **something will** *or* **would never do** indicates that something is not appropriate or suitable in the circumstances ◇ **well I never** used to express surprise or shock ○ *Well I never! You've done it again!*

never-ending *adj* continuing on and on and seeming unlikely ever to stop —**never-endingly** *adv*

nevermore /névvәr máwr/ *adv* never again (*literary*)

never-never *n* **1** hire purchase (*dated informal*) ○ *They bought a three-piece suite on the never-never.* **2** *Aus* the remote arid parts of central Australia

never-never land *n* an unreal or imaginary place, especially one where wonderful things happen ○ *The Opposition's budget policy springs from the same never-*

never land as their employment policy. [< Never Never Land in J. M. Barrie's *Peter Pan* (1904).]

nevertheless /névvərthə léss/ *adv* despite a situation or comment

Nevin /névvin/, **Robyn Anne** (*b*. 1942) Australian actor

Nevis /néeviss/ island in St Kitts and Nevis, in the Caribbean Sea, one of the Leeward Islands. Population: 8,794 (1991). Area: 93 sq. km/36 sq. mi.

Nevis, Ben ♦ Ben Nevis

nevus (*plural* -**i**) *n* US = **naevus**

new /nyoo/ *adj* **1 RECENTLY MADE** recently made, created, or invented ○ *a new drug* **2 FIRST-HAND** not yet used by anyone else ○ *And motorists will continue paying higher registration fees for new cars.* **3 AS REPLACEMENT** a recent or innovative replacement for something ○ *new rules to enhance security* **4 RECENTLY DISCOVERED** recently discovered or noticed ○ *The new comet will be visible at the beginning of July this year.* **5 AT START OF PERIOD** at the beginning of another day, month, or year ○ *I will come to visit you in the new year.* **6 WITH RECENTLY ACQUIRED STATUS** having recently acquired a particular status or position ○ *a new mother* ○ *the new medical school graduates* **7 RECENTLY INTRODUCED** recently introduced and previously unfamiliar ○ *The city was completely new to me.* **8 UNACQUAINTED** recently introduced to a place or situation ○ *He's not new to this city.* **9 CHANGED** changed, especially for the better ○ *I felt as if I had slept, and had now just awakened – a new woman, with a new mind.* **10 EARLY** appearing early in the season ○ *new potatoes* [Old English *nēowe* < Indo-European]

SYNONYMS new, fresh, modern, newfangled, novel, original
CORE MEANING: never experienced before or having recently come into being
new recently invented, discovered, made, bought, experienced, or not previously known or encountered; **fresh** excitingly or refreshingly different from what has been done or experienced previously; **modern** of the latest kind, or characterized by up-to-date ideas, techniques, design, or equipment; **newfangled** puzzlingly or worryingly new or different, especially because it seems gimmicky or over-complicated; **novel** new and different, often in an interesting, unusual, or inventive way; **original** unique and not copied or derived from anything else.

NEW *abbr* nonexplosive warfare

New Age *adj* relating to a cultural movement dating from the 1980s that emphasizes spiritual consciousness, and often involves belief in reincarnation and astrology and the practice of meditation, vegetarianism, and holistic medicine ■ *n* **New Age, New Age music** a style of instrumental music with simple repetitive melodies, often synthesized or reproducing natural sounds, that is intended to promote mental tranquillity —**New Ager** *n*

New Age traveller *n* a member of a New Age cultural movement who travels, often in a group, to gather in spiritually significant places

Newark /nyoo árk/ **1** city in NE New Jersey. Population: 267,823 (1998 estimate). **2** city in W California. Population: 43,134 (1998 estimate). **3** city in N Delaware. Population: 28,000 (1998 estimate).

Newark-on-Trent town in central England. Population: 35,129 (1991).

new arrival *n* **1** a person who or thing that is the latest to arrive ○ *She's a new arrival at the firm.* **2** a recently born baby (*informal*) ○ *I hear there's been a new arrival in the family.*

New Bedford /nyoo-/ port in SE Massachusetts. Population: 96,903 (1996).

⚡**newbie** /nyoobi/, **Newbie** *n* a new user of online computer services, especially the Internet ○ *most users welcome newbies*

new blood *n* a person or group bringing fresh ideas and enthusiasm to a place, situation, or organization

newborn /nyoo bawrn/ *adj* **1 BORN RECENTLY** born very recently **2 NEWLY DISCOVERED OR RECOVERED** recently discovered, or recovered afresh ○ *newborn faith* ■ *n* **NEW BABY** a newborn child

New Britain 1 largest island in Papua New Guinea, in the W Pacific Ocean. Population: 311,955 (1990). Area: 36,520 sq. km/14,100 sq. mi. **2** city in central Connecticut. Population: 75,491 (1990).

new broom *n* a newly arrived person in a place or organization who is keen to make changes and improvements [< the saying *new brooms sweep clean*]

New Brunswick province in SE Canada, bordering the Gulf of St Lawrence and the Bay of Fundy. Capital: Fredericton. Population: 738,133 (1996). Area: 72,908 sq. km/28,150 sq. mi.

Newbury /nyoobəri/ town in S England. Population: 33,273 (1991).

New Caledonia island in the SW Pacific Ocean, east of Australia, with nearby islands an overseas territory of France. Capital: Nouméa. Population: 183,200 (1994). Area: 19,103 sq. km/7,376 sq. mi.

Newcastle /nyoo kaass'l/ city in E New South Wales, Australia. Population: 270,324 (1996).

Newcastle, Thomas Pelham-Holles, 1st Duke of (1693–1768) British statesman. Born **Thomas Pelham**

Newcastle disease *n* a highly infectious viral disease that affects poultry and other birds, attacking the lungs and nervous system [Early 20C. After NEWCASTLE UPON TYNE.]

Newcastle upon Tyne /nyoo kaassəl ə pon tín/ port in NE England. Population: 283,600 (1994).

Newcombe /nyoo kəm/, **John** (*b*. 1944) Australian tennis player

Newcomen /nyoo kumən/, **Thomas** (1663–1729) English inventor

newcomer /nyoo kummər/ *n* a person who or thing that has recently arrived, appeared, or been introduced

New Country *n* a form of country-and-western music, originating in the 1980s, that typically features bland lyrics and smooth arrangements and is designed to appeal to an urban audience

New Deal *n* **1** the policies of social and economic reform introduced in the United States in the 1930s under the presidency of Franklin D. Roosevelt. **2** the period during which Franklin D. Roosevelt's policies of social and economic reform were implemented. —**New Dealer** *n*

New Delhi capital of India, in the north-central part of the country. Population: 301,000 (1991).

New Economic Policy *n* a programme implemented in the Soviet Union between 1921 and 1928 that permitted some private enterprise although the state retained overall economic control

new economy *n* the post-industrial economy considered by some to have emerged in the late 20th century, characterized by global competition, the exploitation of information technology, and the valuing of intangible assets such as ideas and knowledge

newel /nyoo al/ *n* **1** a vertical pillar to which the steps of a spiral staircase are attached **2 newel, newel post** a post supporting the handrail of a staircase at the top or bottom or on a landing [14C. Via French *novel* 'knob' < assumed Vulgar Latin *nodellus* 'little knot'.]

New England region of the NE United States, comprising the states of Maine, New Hampshire, Vermont, Massachusetts, Rhode Island, and Connecticut —**New Englander** *n*

New England Range mountain range in NE New South Wales, Australia. Highest peak: Ben Lomond 1,550 m/5,100 ft.

New English Bible *n* a version of the Bible in modern English translated by British scholars from various denominations and published in 1970

Newf. *abbr* Newfoundland

newfangled /nyoo fáng g'ld/ *adj* puzzlingly or suspiciously new or novel [15C. < past participle of Old English *fōn* 'capture'.] —**new-fangledness** *n*

SYNONYMS See new.

new-fashioned *adj* up to date or modern (*informal*) [After OLD-FASHIONED]

New Forest area of heathland and forest in England. Area: 340 sq. km/130 sq. mi.

New Forest pony *n* a hardy pony with a short neck and sturdy body belonging to a breed originating from the New Forest region of England

newfound /nyoo fownd/ *adj* recently discovered or met

Newfoundland /nyoofəndlənd/ *n* a large sturdy dog with a long straight back and a dense, usually black, coat, belonging to a breed formerly used in water rescues

Newfoundland, Island of /nyoofəndlənd/ island in the Atlantic Ocean, east of the Gulf of St Lawrence, part of the Canadian province of Newfoundland and Labrador. Population: 538,099 (1991). Area: 108,860 sq. km/42,031 sq. mi. —**Newfoundlander** *n*

Newfoundland and Labrador easternmost province in Canada, comprising the island of Newfoundland and part of Labrador. Capital: St John's. Population: 551,792 (1996). Area: 405,720 sq. km/156,649 sq. mi.

New Georgia island group in the SW Pacific Ocean, in the central Solomon Islands. Area: 1,300 sq. km/500 sq. mi.

New Granada former Spanish colony in NW South America, in present-day Colombia, Ecuador, Venezuela, and Panama

New Guinea island in the W Pacific Ocean, north of Australia, divided between Irian Jaya in the west and Papua New Guinea in the east. Population: about 5,300,000 (1995). Area: 808,510 sq. km/312,170 sq. mi. —**New Guinean** *n, adj*

New Hampshire state in the NE United States. Capital: Concord. Population: 1,172,709 (1997). Area: 24,043 sq. km/9,283 sq. mi.

New Harmony /-haˈarməni/ town in SW Indiana, site of two utopian communities in the 19th century. Population: 846 (1990).

Newhaven /nyoo hayv'n/ town and port in SE England. Population: 11,208 (1991).

New Haven city in S Connecticut. Population: 123,189 (1998 estimate).

New Hebrides former name for **Vanuatu**

Ne Win /náy wín/ (*b*. 1911) Burmese national leader. Born **Maung Shu Maung**

New Ireland island in NE Papua New Guinea, in the SW Pacific Ocean. Population: 87,194 (1990). Area: 8,650 sq. km/3,340 sq. mi.

New Jersey state on the eastern coast of the United States. Capital: Trenton. Population: 8,052,849 (1997). Area: 21,277 sq. km/8,215 sq. mi. —**New Jerseyan** *n, adj* —**New Jerseyite** *n*

New Kingdom *n* a period in the history of ancient Egypt, from the 18th to the 20th dynasty (approximately 1580 to 1090 BC)

New Labour *n* the Labour Party as it evolved in the late 20th century, characterized by abandonment of the principle of state ownership and greater acceptance of the free-market economy. ◊ **Old Labour**

Newlands /nyoolandz/, **John** (1837–98) British chemist

New Latin *n* the form of the Latin language used since about the beginning of the 16th century AD especially for scientific and taxonomic classification —**New Latin** *adj*

New Left *n* a political movement, chiefly among students and intellectuals in the United States and Europe during the 1960s and 1970s, that sought radical social and economic change —**New Leftist** *n*

new look *n* a radical change in appearance, design, or style —**new-look** *adj*

New Look *n* a style in women's clothes introduced in 1947 by the designer Christian Dior that featured broad shoulders, narrow waists, and long full skirts

newly /nyooli/ *adv* **1 LATELY** recently or lately **2 AGAIN** again or once more **3 DIFFERENTLY** in a different or new way

newlywed /nyooli wed/ *n* a person who has recently been married —**newlywed** *adj*

Newman /nyoomən/, **Barnett** (1905–70) US painter

Newman, John Henry, Cardinal (1801–90) British theologian

Newman, Paul (*b*. 1925) US stage and film actor

New Man *n* modern man characterized by emotional sensitivity, recognition of women as equals, and a desire to share in domestic chores and the work associated with child rearing

Newmarket[1] /nyoo maarkit/ *n* **1** a card game in which players win by playing cards that match those already on the table. US term **Michigan**[2] **2** a long double-breasted close-fitting jacket with a full skirt worn in the 19th century as a riding coat or overcoat [Late 17C. After NEWMARKET[2].]

Newmarket[2] /nyoò maarkət/ town in E England. Population: 16,498 (1991).

new maths n a method of teaching mathematics, devised in the 1960s, in which children are introduced to elementary set theory at an early stage

New Mexico state in the SW United States. Capital: Santa Fe. Population: 1,729,751 (1997). Area: 314,937 sq. km/121,598 sq. mi. **—New Mexican** n, adj

new money n recently acquired wealth, or people who have it ○ It's largely new money that's buying this kind of property these days.

new moon n **1 MOON AS NARROW CRESCENT** the Moon at the beginning of its cycle, when it is invisible from Earth or when only a narrow crescent on the right-hand side of its surface as seen from Earth is visible **2 PERIOD OF NEW MOON** the period during which there is a new moon **3 PHASE OF MOON** one of the four phases of the Moon, during which it is directly between Earth and the Sun and invisible or seen only as a narrow crescent

New Netherland /-néthər land/ former Dutch colony in E North America, in present-day New York and New Jersey

New Orleans /-áwrleenz, -áwrlinz/ port in SE Louisiana, between Lake Pontchartrain and the Mississippi River. Population: 465,538 (1998 estimate).

New Plymouth city in SW North Island, New Zealand. Population: 48,871 (1996).

Newport /nyoò pawrt/ **1** town in SE Wales. Population: 137,200 (1996). **2** town in S England, on the Isle of Wight. Population: 25,033 (1991). **3** city in SE Rhode Island. Population: 24,279 (1998 estimate).

Newport News /-nyoòz/ city in SE Virginia. Population: 178,615 (1998 estimate).

Newquay /nyoò kee/ town in SW England. Population: 17,390 (1991).

New Quebec region in N Quebec, Canada, between Hudson Bay and Labrador. Area: 777,000 sq. km/300,000 sq. mi.

New Right n a conservative political movement that arose in the United States during the late 1960s and affirmed a commitment to established religion, patriotism, and smaller, less interventionist government

Newry /nyoòri/ port in S Northern Ireland. Population: 22,975 (1991).

Newry and Mourne local government district in S Northern Ireland. Area: 894 sq. km/345 sq. mi.

news /nyooz/ n **1 RECENT INFORMATION** information about recent events or developments ○ I phoned the hospital, and the news is good. **2 CURRENT EVENTS** information about current events printed in newspapers or broadcast by the media ○ She has been in the news a lot lately. **3 PROGRAMME** a radio or television broadcast presenting the important events or developments that have taken place on a particular day ○ I heard about it on the radio news. **4 SOMEBODY OR SOMETHING INTERESTING** somebody or something considered as being of interest to people in general ○ The reporters considered that the Royal Family were always news. **5 SOMETHING PREVIOUSLY UNKNOWN** something previously unknown to somebody that he or she is surprised to hear about [15C. Plural of NEW.]

news agency n an organization that gathers information about current events and supplies it to the media

newsagent /nyoòz ayjənt/ n somebody who keeps a shop or stall selling newspapers and magazines, often together with confectionery, tobacco, and other items. US term **newsdealer**

newsboy /nyoòz boy/ n a boy who sells newspapers in the street or delivers them to houses

newsbreak /nyoòz brayk/ n US, Can **1** a short pause in a radio or television programme during which two or three news items are broadcast **2** something that is newsworthy

newscast /nyoòz kaast/ n a television or radio broadcast consisting of news

newscaster /nyoòz kaastər/ n = **newsreader**

news conference n MEDIA = **press conference**

newsdealer /nyoòz deelər/ n US = **newsagent**

news desk n an area of a newspaper office or a radio or television studio where news is prepared for publication or broadcasting

news flash n a brief item of urgent news, often broadcast at short notice interrupting a scheduled programme

newsgirl /nyoòz gurl/ n a girl who sells newspapers in the street or delivers them to houses

⚡newsgroup /nyooz groop/ n a discussion group maintained on a computer network such as the Internet in which people leave messages on topics of mutual interest

New Siberian Islands uninhabited island group in NE Russia, in the Arctic Ocean. Area: 38,000 sq. km/14,700 sq. mi.

newsletter /nyooz letər/ n a printed report or letter containing news of interest to a particular group, e.g. the members of a society or employees of an organization, and circulated to them periodically

news magazine n US **1** a magazine, usually published weekly, containing news and news analysis from the preceding week **2** a weekly radio or television programme of interviews, investigative reportage, features, and commentary on the news

newsman /nyoòz man, -man/ (plural -**men** /-mən, -men/) n a man journalist or broadcaster who reports news

newsmonger /nyooz mung gər/ n a gatherer and spreader of gossip **—newsmongering** n

New South Wales state in SE Australia, bordering on the Pacific Ocean. Capital: Sydney. Population: 6,204,000 (1996). Area: 801,600 sq. km/309,500 sq. mi.

newspaper /nyoòss paypər, nyoòz-/ n **1 PRINTED ACCOUNT OF NEWS** a publication, usually appearing daily or weekly, containing news and comment on current events, together with features and advertisements, and printed on large sheets of paper that are folded together **2 ORGANIZATION** an organization that produces a newspaper **3 PAPER FROM A NEWSPAPER** a sheet or sheets of the printed paper from a newspaper when used for a purpose other than reading

newspaperman /nyoòss paypər man, nyoòz-/ (plural -**men** /-men, -/) n **1** a man who writes or edits for a newspaper ○ Although he eventually built up a global media empire he remained a newspaperman at heart. **2** a man who owns or publishes a newspaper

newspaperwoman /nyoòss paypər woomən, nyoòz-/ (plural -**en** /-wimin, -/) n **1** a woman who writes or edits for a newspaper **2** a woman who owns or publishes a newspaper

newspeak /nyoò speek/ n language that is ambiguous and designed to conceal the truth, especially that sometimes used by bureaucrats and propagandists ○ She said that to call sacking workers 'rationalization' was typical of modern newspeak. [After the language of propaganda in Nineteen Eighty-Four, by George ORWELL, 1949]

newsperson /nyoòz purss'n/ (plural -**persons** or -**people** /-peep'l/) n US a journalist or broadcaster who reports news

newsprint /nyoòz print/ n a relatively cheap and low-quality paper made from recycled materials or wood pulp and used for printing newspapers

newsreader /nyoòz reedər/ n somebody who reads the news on a television or radio broadcast. US term **newscaster**

newsreel /nyoòz reel/ n a short cinema film about recent news events, formerly often shown before a feature film

news release n MEDIA = **press release**

newsroom /nyoòz room, -roòm/ n a room in a radio or television studio or newspaper office where news is prepared for publication or broadcasting

news service n MEDIA = **news agency**

newssheet /nyoòz sheet/ n = **newsletter**

newsstand /nyoòz stand/ n a stall or booth where newspapers and magazines are sold

New Style n the reckoning of dates by the Gregorian calendar

newsvendor /nyoòz vendər/ n UK, Can a seller of newspapers

⚡newswire /nyoòz wīr/ n an Internet service providing the latest information on current events

newswoman /nyoòz woomən/ (plural -**en** /-wimin/) n a woman journalist or broadcaster who reports news

newsworthy /nyoòz wurthí/ (-**thier**, -**thiest**) adj interesting or important enough to be reported in the media **— newsworthily** adv **—newsworthiness** n

newswriting /nyoòz rīting/ n the craft of writing news stories **—newswriter** n

newsy /nyoòzi/ (-**ier**, -**iest**) adj filled with news and gossip **—newsily** adv **—newsiness** n

newt /nyoot/ n a small amphibian of the salamander family with short legs and a well-developed tail. Family: Salamandridae. [15C. < mistaken division of an ewte, ewte being a form of EFT.]

New Territories /-térrətəriz/ area of Hong Kong situated mostly on the Chinese mainland north of Kowloon. Area: 950 sq. km/365 sq. mi.

New Testament n the second section of the Christian Bible dealing with the life and teachings of Jesus Christ, containing the Gospels, the Acts of the Apostles, the Epistles, and the Book of Revelations

newton /nyoòt'n/ n (symbol **N**) an SI unit of force equivalent to the force that produces an acceleration of one metre per second on a mass of one kilogram [Early 20C. After Sir Isaac NEWTON.]

Newton /nyoòt'n/, **Sir Isaac** (1642–1727) English scientist **—Newtonian** /nyoo tóni ən/ adj

Newtonian telescope n a reflecting telescope in which mirrors transfer an image to an eyepiece in the side of the telescope's body

Newton-John /nyoòt'n jón/, **Olivia** (b. 1948) Australian singer and actor

Newton's cradle /nyoòt'nz-/ n a toy consisting of five metal balls hanging side by side in a frame, in which swinging the ball at one end transmits force along the line so the other end ball swings away [After Sir Isaac NEWTON]

Newton's law of gravitation n the principle that any two particles attract each other with a force that is proportional to the product of their masses and inversely proportional to the square of their separation [After Sir Isaac NEWTON]

Newton's laws of motion npl three fundamental principles describing the motion of objects moving at speeds that are not comparable with the speed of light [After Sir Isaac NEWTON]

Newton's rings n a pattern of light interference created by the contact of a convex lens with a glass plate, appearing as a series of alternating bright and dark rings [After Sir Isaac NEWTON]

new town n a complete self-contained town with all the usual facilities, created with government funding on an open site, usually to accommodate excess population from existing urban areas

Newtown /nyoò town/ new town in central Wales. Population: 10,548 (1991).

Newtownabbey /nyoòt'n ábbi/ town in NE Northern Ireland. Population: 57,103 (1991).

Newtownards /nyoòtənərdz/ industrial town in E Northern Ireland. Population: 24,301 (1991).

Newtown St Boswells /-sənt bózwəlz/ town in S Scotland. Population: 1,102 (1991).

new university n one of the former UK polytechnics or colleges of higher education designated as a university in the 1990s

new variant CJD n a form of Creutzfeldt-Jakob disease that has a much shorter incubation period than previously recognized types but is clinically identical ◊ **Creutzfeldt-Jakob disease**

new wave n **1 INNOVATIVE ARTS MOVEMENT** any new and innovative movement in the arts **2 POST-PUNK ROCK MUSIC** rock music made in the late 1970s after the punk rock era **3 FORM OF FRENCH CINEMA** a form of film-making originating in France during the 1950s that emphasized spontaneity, unconventionality, and the individual styles of directors

---

QUICK FACTS ON... NEW WAVE

Key dates: late 1950s–mid-1960s
Key locations: France
Key elements: rejection of filmmaking conventions; freshness; emphasis on role of director; use of quasi-documentary style, real locations, and innovative techniques such as jump-cuts
Key figures: Claude Chabrol, François Truffaut, Jean-Luc Godard, Jacques Rivette (directors); Jeanne Moreau, Jean-Paul Belmondo (actors)
Key works: Le Beau Serge (Bitter Reunion) (Chabrol) 1958,

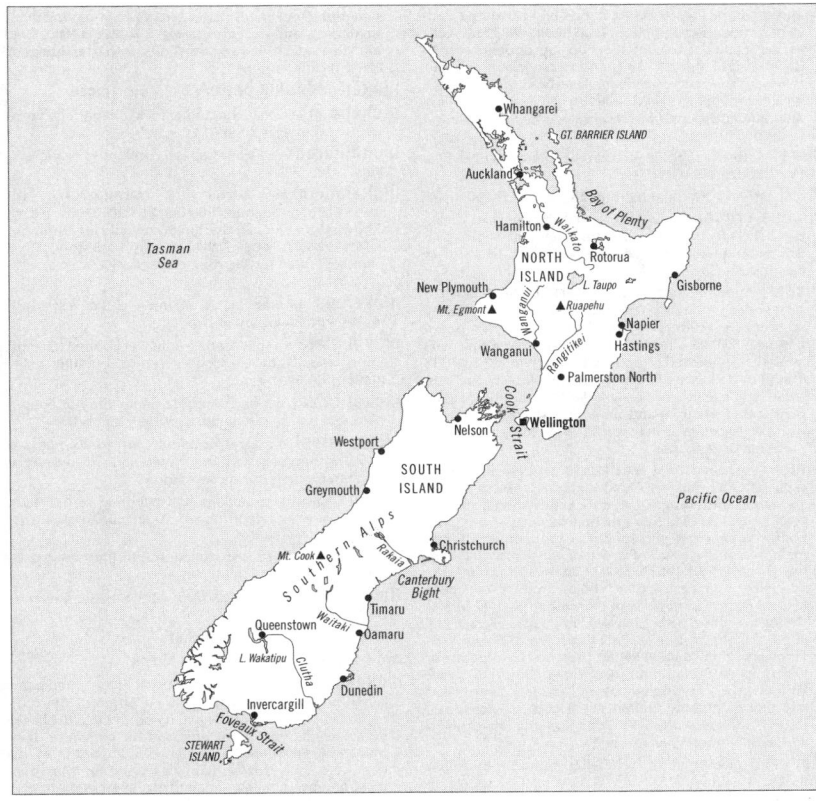

New Zealand

Les Quatre Cents Coups (The 400 Blows) (Truffaut) 1959, A Bout de Souffle (Breathless) (Godard) 1960
Key developments: auteur theory, Czech new wave

New World *n* North and South America as considered by Europeans following Columbus's discovery of the Americas (*dated*) ◇ **Old World**

new year *n* the year following the current year, especially the early part of it ○ *We hoped that things would be better in the new year.*

New Year *n* the first day or first few days of a calendar year

New Year's Day *n* the first day of the year in the Gregorian calendar, widely celebrated as a public holiday. Date: 1 January.

New Year's Eve *n* the last day of the year in the Gregorian calendar, or the evening of that day. Date: 31 December.

New Year's resolution *n* a decision to do or stop doing something, made or announced at the New Year, which is traditionally considered a time for a fresh start

New York 1 **New York, New York City** city in SE New York State, at the mouth of the Hudson River. It comprises the boroughs of Manhattan, Queens, Brooklyn, the Bronx, and Staten Island. Population: 7,420,166 (1998 estimate). **2** state in the NE United States. Capital: Albany. Population: 18,137,226 (1997). Area: 139,831 sq. km/53,989 sq. mi. —**New Yorker** *n*

New York Bay inlet of the Atlantic Ocean in SE New York State and NE New Jersey, lying at the mouth of the Hudson River and forming the harbour of New York City

New York English *n* a variety of English spoken in New York

new zaïre *n* MONEY = **zaïre**

New Zealand /-zeeland/ country in the SW Pacific Ocean, southeast of Australia, comprising mainly the North Island and the South Island. Capital: Wellington. Population: 3,681,546 (1996). Area: 270,534 sq. km/104,454 sq. mi. —**New Zealander** *n*

New Zealand English *n* a variety of English spoken in New Zealand

New Zealand Time *n* the standard time in the time zone with an eastern border of 180° longitude that includes New Zealand

next /nekst/ CORE MEANING: a grammatical word indicating that something is close to something else, e.g. in space or time ○ (adj) *He lives next door to me.* ○ (adj) *When I returned, my next patient was waiting.* ○ (adv) *Which patient do you want to see next?*
1 *adj, adv* IMMEDIATELY FOLLOWING following immediately after the present or previous one ○ (adj) *Our next meeting is on April 2nd.* ○ (adv) *Are you wondering what to do next?* **2** *det* FOLLOWING THIS ONE describes the day, month, or year following this one ○ *The case is scheduled for trial next month.* ○ *There is no way of predicting whether this might happen next year or in 300 years.* **3** *adj* ADJOINING the one that is nearest ○ *My colleague in the next office called.* **4** *adj* CLOSEST closest to in degree ○ *It's 40 times heavier than the next heaviest quark.* **5** *adj* Malaysia, Singapore SECOND describes somebody or something that follows the next one ○ *Take the next left turn, not the first.* [Old English *nēhsta* 'most near' < Germanic, 'near'] ◇ **next to** 1 adjacent to or beside something or somebody ○ *Come and sit next to me.* **2** closest to, in comparison with something else ○ *Cleanliness, he said, was next to godliness.* **3** almost, but not completely (*in negatives*) ○ *I have spent many days trying to figure out a good alternative, and it's next to impossible.* ◇ **the next best thing** the option to be preferred if a first choice is not available ○ *For healthier eating the next best thing to chocolate is carob.*

next door *adv* 1 IN NEXT HOUSE OR ROOM in or into the house or room next to the one somebody is in ○ *Go next door and see if their phone's working.* **2** VERY CLOSE a very short

distance away ■ *adj* IMMEDIATELY ADJACENT situated immediately beside or very close to the one somebody is in or at, or living in the adjoining house or flat (*hyphenated before nouns*) ◇ **next door to** almost, or virtually the same thing as

next friend *n* a person who acts for somebody who is not legally allowed to act independently, e.g. a child

next of kin *n* somebody's nearest relative or relatives (*takes a singular or plural verb*)

nexus /néksəss/ (*plural* **-us** *or* **-uses**) *n* 1 CONNECTION a connection or link associating two or more people or things **2** CONNECTED GROUP a group or series of connected individuals or things **3** CENTRE the centre or focus of something **4** SPECIALIZED PART OF CELL MEMBRANE a specialized area of the cellular membrane that helps cells to communicate or adhere [Mid-17C. < Latin *nex-*, past participle of *nectere* 'bind'.]

Nez Percé /nez púrss, -páir say/ (*plural* **Nez Percés** *or* **Nez Percé**) *n* 1 a member of a Native North American people who lived along the Snake River, and who now live mainly in W Idaho and NE Washington state **2** the Sahaptin-Chinook language of the Nez Percé. Native speakers: 5,000. [< French, 'pierced nose'] —**Nez Percé** *adj*

⚡ **nf** *abbr* Norfolk Island (*in Internet addresses*)

NF *abbr* 1 National Front **2** Newfoundland **3** NF, N/F no funds **4** Norman French

Nfd. *abbr* Newfoundland

NFL *abbr US* National Football League

Nfld *abbr* Newfoundland

⚡ **NFS** *abbr* 1 National Fire Service **2** network file service **3** network file system **4** not for sale

NFT *abbr* 1 National Film Theatre **2** Newfoundland Standard Time

NFU *abbr* National Farmers' Union

⚡ **ng** *abbr* Nigeria (*in Internet addresses*)

ngaio /ní ó/ (*plural* **-os**) *n* an evergreen tree that has white wood and leaves dotted with oil glands. Native to: New Zealand. *Myoporum laetum*. [Mid-19C. < Maori.]

n'gana *n* VET = **nagana**

Ngata /naátə, əng gaátə/, **Sir Apirana Turupa** (1874–1950) New Zealand Maori leader and politician

NGO *abbr* nongovernmental organization

Ngo Dinh Diem /n'g gŏ din deèm/ (1901–63) South Vietnamese statesman

ngoma /əng gŏmə/ *n* E Africa 1 a traditional African drum **2** a social gathering for dancing [Early 20C. < Kiswahili, 'dance, music'.]

Ngoni /əng góni/ (*plural* **-ni** *or* **-nis**) *n* 1 a member of a people of E Africa, now mostly living in Malawi **2** the language of the Ngoni, a dialect of Zulu or Swazi **3** PEOPLES, LANG = **Nguni** [Late 19C. < Bantu.] —**Ngoni** *adj*

ngultrum /əng goòltrəm/ *n* see table at **currency** [Late 20C. < Tibetan.]

Nguni /əng goòni/ (*plural* **-ni** *or* **-nis**) *n* 1 a member of a group of Bantu-speaking peoples living in S Africa that includes the Zulu, Swazi, Xhosa, and Ndebele **2** a group of closely related Bantu languages spoken by the Nguni peoples and including Zulu, Swazi, and Xhosa [Early 20C. < Zulu.] —**Nguni** *adj*

ngwee /əng gwáy/ (*plural* **ngwee**) *n* see table at **currency** [Mid-20C. < Bantu.]

NH, N.H. *abbr* New Hampshire

NHS *abbr* National Health Service

⚡ **ni** *abbr* Nicaragua (*in Internet addresses*)

Ni *symbol* nickel

NI *abbr* 1 National Insurance **2** Northern Ireland **3** NZ North Island

niacin /ní əssin/ *n* a B complex vitamin found in meat and dairy products. Use: prevention and treatment of pellagra. [Mid-20C. < NICOTINE + ACID.]

niacinamide /ní ə sínnə mīd/ *n* a B complex vitamin that is an amide of niacin

Niagara /ní ágrə, ní ággərə/ river in NE North America, flowing from Lake Erie into Lake Ontario and forming part of the US-Canadian border. Length: 56 km/35 mi.

Niagara Falls waterfall in the Niagara River, divided by Goat Island into American Falls and Horseshoe, or Canadian Falls. Height: 55–57 m/182–187 ft.

Niamey /nyaa máy/ capital of Niger, in the southwest of the country. Population: 398,265 (1988).

Niarchos /ni aárk oss/, **Stavros Spyros** (1909–96) Greek shipowner

~~niave~~ incorrect spelling of **naive**

nib /nib/ n 1 METAL WRITING TIP OF PEN a shaped detachable metal tip on the end of a pen such as a fountain pen, by means of which the ink is transferred to the paper 2 SHARP POINT a sharp point or tip, especially the sharpened end of a quill pen 3 BEAK a bird's beak [Late 16C. Variant of NEB.]

nibble /níbb'l/ v (-bles, -bling, -bled) 1 vti TAKE SMALL QUICK BITES to take a series of small quick bites at something, or eat something in a series of small quick bites ○ She nibbled an apple while she read. 2 vti EAT SOMETHING DAINTILY OR CAUTIOUSLY to take dainty, cautious, or reluctant little bites of something, or eat something in this way taking a very small amount at a time ○ The mouse had nibbled the cheese. 3 vti BITE PLAYFULLY AND CARESSINGLY to take gentle playful little bites at part of somebody's body as a form of caress ○ The lion cubs nibbled at each other playfully. 4 vi REDUCE GRADUALLY to reduce or wear away something gradually by taking a small amount at a time ○ These day-to-day expenses nibble away at our funds. 5 vi SHOW MILD INTEREST to show a tentative interest in something ○ Lower the price a little and the buyers will start to nibble. ■ n 1 ACT OF NIBBLING a series of small quick or gentle bites at something 2 TINY AMOUNT OF FOOD a tiny amount of some type of food (informal) 3 EXPRESSION OF MILD INTEREST an expression of tentative interest ○ I've been trying to make a sale all day but not a nibble so far. ■ nibbles npl SMALL THINGS TO EAT small pieces of food intended as appetizers, snacks, or party food, e.g. nuts or canapés ○ Help yourself to some nibbles while I put away your coat. [Early 16C. < ?] —**nibbler** n

Nibelung /néebəloong/ n in German mythology, a member of a race of dwarfs who owned a hoard of treasure that was captured by the heroic prince Siegfried [Mid-19C. < German.]

niblick /níbblik/ n a golf club that has a short iron head with a steeply sloping face, used to give extra lift, e.g. when playing out of a bunker (dated) [Mid-19C. < ?]

nibs /nibz/ n used as a kind of mock title when referring to an important or self-important person (informal) ○ His nibs will doubtless be expecting the red carpet treatment. [Early 19C. < ?]

nicad /ní kad/, **nicad battery** n a dry cell battery with electrodes of nickel and cadmium in an alkaline electrolyte [Mid-20C. < NICKEL + CADMIUM.]

Nicaea /nī seè ə/ ancient Byzantine city of Asia Minor, on the site of present-day İznik, NW Turkey

Nicaragua

Nicaragua /ní kə rággyoô ə/ republic and largest nation in Central America, situated between the North Pacific Ocean and the Caribbean Sea. Capital: Managua. Population: 4,272,000 (1996). Area: 129,494 sq. km/49,998 sq. mi. —**Nicaraguan** n, adj

niccolite /níka lît/ n a nickel arsenide mineral. Use: source of nickel. [Mid-19C. < modern Latin niccolum 'nickel'.]

nice /nīss/ (**nicer, nicest**) adj 1 PLEASANT pleasant or enjoyable 2 KIND kind, or showing courtesy, friendliness, or consideration ○ It was a nice gesture to return the money. 3 RESPECTABLE respectable, or of an acceptable social or moral standard ○ She's made some nice friends at work. 4 GOOD-LOOKING good-looking, or pleasing to look at ○ What a nice hat you're wearing! 5 ACCOMPLISHED skilful

and accomplished 6 SUBTLE subtle and involving delicacy or fine discrimination 7 FASTIDIOUS AND FUSSY very concerned and careful about choosing, or being seen to do, the right thing ○ You can't be too nice about your methods if you want to get the job done. [13C. Via Old French < Latin nescius 'ignorant'.] —**nicely** adv —**niceness** n ◇ **nice and** sufficiently or pleasingly ○ It's nice and warm by the fire.

Nice /neess/ city in SE France, on the Mediterranean Sea. Population: 338,166 (1994).

NICE /nīs/ abbr National Institute of Clinical Excellence

Nicene creed /nī seen-/ n a formal statement of Christian beliefs formulated at a council held in Nicaea in AD 325, subsequently altered and expanded, and still in use in most Christian churches

nicety /níssəti/ (plural **-ties**) n 1 REFINEMENT OR DETAIL a subtle distinction or point, or a small detail, especially of proper procedure or social etiquette (often plural) 2 REFINED FEATURE a feature that makes something particularly refined and pleasurable (often plural) 3 SUBTLETY a subtle, delicate, or fastidious quality, especially in somebody's feelings or taste 4 PRECISION the ability to be precise and accurate and make fine distinctions ○ the nicety of his powers of judgment ◇ **to a nicety** with great precision or exactness

niche /neesh, nich/ n 1 WALL RECESS a recess in a wall, especially one made to hold a statue 2 RECESS IN ROCK any recess or hollow, e.g. in a rock formation 3 SUITABLE PLACE a position or activity that particularly suits somebody's talents and personality or that somebody can make his or her own ○ She carved out her own niche in the industry. 4 SPECIALIZED MARKET an area of the market specializing in a particular type of product ○ designed to undercut the competition in the same niche 'Thanks to the Internet, small niche companies can reach mass markets in a heartbeat'. (Forbes Global Business and Finance; November 1998) 5 PLACE IN NATURE the role of an organism within its natural environment that determines its relations with other organisms and ensures its survival ■ vt (**niches, niching, niched**) PUT IN NICHE to place something in a niche [Early 17C. < Old French nichier 'build a nest, nestle' < Latin nidus 'nest'.]

Nichiren /neéch ee ren/ (1222–82) Japanese Buddhist monk

Nicholas /níkələss/, **St** (fl. 4th century) prelate and saint from Asia Minor

Nicholas I (1796–1855) tsar of Russia (1825–55)

Nicholas II (1868–1918) tsar of Russia (1894–1917)

Nicholas of Cusa /ník'ləss əv kyooza/ (1401–64) German cardinal and scholar

Nicholson /ník'lss'n/, **Ben** (1894–1982) British painter and sculptor

Nicholson, Jack (b. 1937) US film actor

nick /nik/ n 1 NOTCH a small V-shaped cut or indentation in an edge or surface 2 SMALL CUT a small cut on the skin 3 GROOVE ON TYPE a groove on the side of a piece of metal printing type, used to identify and orient it 4 POLICE STATION a police station (slang) 5 PRISON prison (slang) ○ He spent ten years in the nick. 6 CONDITION the particular condition of something or somebody (slang) ○ What kind of nick is your motor in? ■ vt 1 NOTCH OR CUT SLIGHTLY to make a notch, indentation, or small cut in something ○ The scythe blade had been nicked by a stone. 2 STEAL to steal something (slang) ○ Somebody's nicked my bike. 3 ARREST to place somebody under arrest (slang) ○ A copper's job is to nick villains. 4 US CHEAT to cheat or defraud somebody (slang) 5 INCISE HORSE'S TAIL to make a cut in the tendons at the root of a horse's tail to make the tail stick up [15C. < ?] ◇ **in the nick of time** at the critical or last possible moment

SYNONYMS See **steal**.

nickel /ník'l/ n 1 SILVERY WHITE METALLIC ELEMENT (symbol Ni) a hard, corrosion-resistant, silvery-white metallic element. Source: sulphide and oxide ores. Use: in alloys, batteries, electroplating, catalyst. 2 US, Can FIVE-CENT COIN a coin worth five cents ■ vt (**-els, -elling, -elled**) COAT WITH NICKEL to plate something with nickel [Mid-18C. Shortening of German Kupfernickel 'copper nickel' < nickel 'mischievous demon', because the ore yielded no copper.]

nickel-and-dime adj US 1 LOW-PAID paying or involving only a small amount of money (slang) 2 MINOR small-scale, or of little importance (informal) ■ vt (**nickel-and-dimes, nickel-and-diming, nickel-and-dimed**) US 1 IMPOVERISH THROUGH SMALL EXPENSES to get somebody or

something into financial trouble by accumulating many small costs and expenses (slang) 2 BOTHER IN MANY SMALL WAYS to hinder or harass somebody with trivialities and insignificant matters

nickel-cadmium battery n ELEC ENG = **nicad**

nickelic /ni kéllik/ adj containing nickel, especially nickel with a valency of three

nickeliferous /níkə líffərəss/ adj containing or yielding nickel

nickelodeon /níkə lôdi ən/ n US 1 EARLY JUKEBOX an early variety of coin-operated jukebox 2 5-CENT CINEMA an early 20th-century cinema, charging five cents for admission 3 COIN-OPERATED PLAYER PIANO an early variety of player piano operated by inserting coins [Early 20C. < NICKEL + MELODEON.]

nickelous /níkələss/ adj containing nickel, especially nickel with a valency of two

nickel plate n a thin coating of nickel applied to something, usually by electrolysis —**nickel-plated** adj —**nickel-plating** n

nickel silver n a hard durable white alloy of copper, zinc, and nickel. Use: making cutlery and wire.

nickel steel n a steel containing up to six per cent nickel, sometimes with other metal added, usually to assist hardening during formation

nicker[1] /níkər/ vi to make a soft neighing sound ○ The pony nickered and shook its head. [Late 16C. An imitation of the sound.] —**nicker** n

nicker[2] /níkər/ (plural **-er**) n a pound sterling (slang) [Early 20C. < ?]

Nicklaus /ník lowss/, **Jack** (b. 1940) US golfer. Known as **Golden Bear**

~~nickle~~ incorrect spelling of **nickel**

nick-nack n HOUSEHOLD = **knick-knack**

nickname /ník naym/ n 1 INVENTED NAME an invented name for somebody or something, used humorously or affectionately instead of the real name and usually based on a conspicuous characteristic of the person or thing involved 2 SHORT NAME a shortened or altered form of a name, e.g. 'Billy' for 'William' or 'Peggy' for 'Margaret' ■ vt (**-names, -naming, -named**) CALL BY NICKNAME to give a nickname to somebody or something ○ They nicknamed him 'Spuds' because of his fondness for potatoes. [15C. < mistaken division of an eke name 'an additional name'.] —**nicknamer** n

Nicobarese /níkəbə reéz/ (plural **-ese**) n 1 a person who comes from the Nicobar Islands 2 a group of Austro-Asiatic languages spoken in the Nicobar Islands. Native speakers: fewer than 20,000. —**Nicobarese** adj

Nicobar Islands /níkə baar-/ island group in the Indian Ocean, east of Sri Lanka, part of the Indian union territory of the Andaman and Nicobar Islands. Population: 39,022 (1991). Area: 1,841 sq. km/711 sq. mi.

Nicol prism /ník'l-/ n a device for producing light polarized in a plane, consisting of two specially shaped calcite prisms cemented together with Canada balsam [Mid-19C. After William Nicol (1768–1851), Scottish physicist and geologist.]

Nicosia /níkə seè ə/ capital of Cyprus, in the north-central part of the island. Population: 194,000 (1997 estimate).

nicotiana /ni kôshi áana, níkəti áana/ (plural **-as** or **-a**) n a perennial or annual flowering plant of a genus that includes the tobacco plant. Flowers: fragrant, white, yellow, or purple. Genus: Nicotiana. [Early 17C. After Jacques Nicot (1530–1604), French ambassador to Lisbon, who introduced tobacco to France.]

nicotinamide /níkə tínnə mīd/ n BIOCHEM = **niacinamide**

nicotinamide adenine dinucleotide n full form of **NAD**

nicotinamide adenine dinucleotide phosphate n full form of **NADP**

nicotine /níkə teen/ n 1 $C_{10}H_{14}N_2$ a toxic alkaloid. Source: tobacco. Use: insecticide. 2 tobacco products, or the smoking of them (informal) [Early 19C. Shortening of NICOTIANA.] —**nicotinic** /níkə tínnik/ adj

nicotine gum n chewing gum containing nicotine, used as a substitute for tobacco by people who are trying to give up smoking

nicotine patch n a small patch that when placed on the skin releases nicotine directly into the bloodstream, used by people who are trying to give up smoking

nicotinic acid /nikə tínnik-/ n BIOCHEM = **niacin**

nicotinism /níkə tee nizəm/ n poisoning caused by an excessive intake of nicotine through smoking

nictitate /níkti tayt/ (-**tates**, -**tating**, -**tated**), **nictate** /nik táyt, níkt ayt/ (-**tates**, -**tating**, -**tated**) vti to blink or wink (technical) [Early 19C. < medieval Latin nictitat-, past participle of nictitare 'wink repeatedly' < Latin nictare 'to wink'.] —**nictation** /nik táysh'n/ n —**nictitation** /níkti táysh'n/ n

nictitating membrane /níkti tayting-/ n a thin transparent layer of skin underneath the eyelid that can cover the eye surface of birds, reptiles, and some mammals to moisten and protect it

Nidderdale /níddər dayl/ Area of Outstanding Natural Beauty in N England. Area: 603 sq. km/233 sq. mi.

nidi plural of **nidus**

nidicolous /ni díkələss/ adj describes young birds that remain in the nest for some time after hatching [Early 20C. < Latin nidus 'nest'.]

nidificate vi BIOL = **nidify** [Early 19C. < Latin nidificat-, past participle of nidificare (see NIDIFY).]

nidifugous /ni díffyoogəss/ adj describes young birds that leave the nest a short time after hatching [Early 20C. < Latin nidus 'nest' + fugere 'flee'.]

nidify /níddi fī/ (-**fies**, -**fying**, -**fied**) vi to build a nest [Mid-17C. < Latin nidificare 'build a nest' < nidus 'nest'.] —**nidification** /níddifi káysh'n/ n

nidus /nídəss/ (plural -**duses** or -**di** /-dī/) n 1 SPIDER OR INSECT NEST a nest in which spiders or insects deposit eggs 2 FOCUS OF INFECTION a site in the body at which an infection develops 3 SPORE-DEVELOPING PLANT PART a place in a plant where its spores develop [Early 18C. < Latin, 'nest'.]

niece /neess/ n a daughter of somebody's brother, brother-in-law, sister, or sister-in-law [13C. Via Old French < Latin neptis 'granddaughter, niece'.]

~~nieghbour~~ incorrect spelling of **neighbour**

niello /ni éllō/ n (plural -**li** /-élli/ or -**los**) 1 BLACK ALLOY USED AS INLAY a deep black alloy of sulphur and silver, lead, or copper, used to fill lines inlaid as decoration on a metal surface 2 USE OF NIELLO the process of using niello to decorate a metal surface 3 SOMETHING DECORATED WITH NIELLO something decorated with niello as an inlay ■ vt (-**los**, -**loing**, -**loed**) DECORATE WITH NIELLO to decorate something using niello as an inlay [Early 19C. Via Italian < Latin nigellus 'blackish', diminutive of niger 'black'.] —**niellist** n

nielsbohrium /neelz báwri əm/ n an artificially produced radioactive element with the atomic number 105 [Late 20C. After Niels BOHR.]

Nielsen /neéls'n/, **Holger Bech** Danish theoretical physicist

Niemeyer /neé mī ər/, **Oscar** (b. 1907) Brazilian architect

~~niether~~ incorrect spelling of **neither**

Nietzsche /neétshə/, **Friedrich Wilhelm** (1844–1900) German philosopher —**Nietzschean** n, adj —**Nietzscheanism** n

nieve /neev/ n Scotland a fist [13C. < Old Norse hnefi.]

nifedipine /nī féddi peen/ n $C_{17}H_{18}N_2O_6$ a drug that stops the heart muscles from taking up calcium. Use: treatment of high blood pressure, angina pectoris. [Late 20C. < NITRO- + fe (shortening and alteration of PHENYL) + DI-1 prefix. 1 + pine (contraction of PYRIDINE).]

niff /nif/ n an unpleasant smell or odour (slang) ■ vi to have an unpleasant or strong smell (slang) [Early 20C. < ?] —**niffiness** n —**niffy** adj

nifty /nífti/ (-**tier**, -**tiest**) adj (informal) 1 AGILE good, quick, and clever at doing something or using something 2 STYLISH AND GOOD-LOOKING fashionable and good-looking 3 VERY GOOD very good or effective [Mid-19C. < ?] —**niftily** adv —**niftiness** n

Nig. abbr 1 Nigeria 2 Nigerian

nigella /nī jéllə/ n a flowering plant of the buttercup family, such as love-in-a-mist. Flowers: white, blue, or yellow. Native to: the Mediterranean, W Asia. Genus: Nigella. [14C. < modern Latin, feminine of nigellus (see NIELLO).]

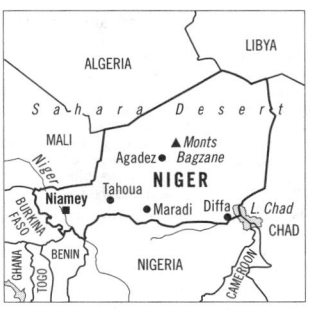

Niger

Niger[1] /nījər/ republic in NW Africa, north of Nigeria and south of Libya. Capital: Niamey. Population: 9,465,000 (1996). Area: 1,267,000 sq. km/489,191 sq. mi.

Niger[2] river in W Africa, rising in S Guinea and flowing through Mali, Niger, and Nigeria into the Gulf of Guinea. Length: 4,180 km/2,600 mi.

Niger-Congo n a large family of languages spoken in central and southern parts of Africa. Native speakers: 200 million. —**Niger-Congo** adj

Nigeria /nī jeéri ə/ republic in West Africa. Capital: Abuja. Population: 103,912,000 (1996). Area: 923,768 sq. km/356,669 sq. mi. —**Nigerian** n, adj

Nigerian English n a variety of English spoken in Nigeria

niggard /níggərd/ n a stingy or miserly person [14C. Alteration of nigon, perhaps < nig 'stingy' < N Germanic.]

niggardly /níggərdli/ adj (-**lier**, -**liest**) 1 NOT GENEROUS very reluctant to give or spend anything 2 SMALL OR INADEQUATE very small or inadequate in quantity ■ adv IN A STINGY WAY in a miserly or stingy way —**niggardliness** n

nigger /níggər/ n (taboo) 1 a highly offensive term for a Black person 2 a highly offensive term for a dark-skinned person [Late 17C. Alteration of NEGRO.]

USAGE This term is arguably the single most racially offensive term in the English language. The fact that Black people sometimes use this word in reference to themselves (sometimes as nigga) does not excuse its present-day use by members of other ethnic groups. White students may be accustomed to hearing it in its pop culture context. They should avoid using it, even in fictional dialogue. The term of choice is Black person. See also **insult**.

niggle /nígg'l/ v (-**gles**, -**gling**, -**gled**) 1 vi CRITICIZE IN PETTY WAY to criticize or find fault continually, especially about small matters 2 vi BE PREOCCUPIED WITH DETAILS to be preoccupied with petty details 3 vt WORRY to be a source of worry and irritation to somebody, especially in a small way over a long period of time ■ n UK, Can 1 PETTY CRITICISM a petty or carping criticism ○ Once we have a broad agreement, we can sort out these niggles. 2 NAGGING WORRY a small but continuing source of annoyance or worry [Early 17C. < ?] —**niggler** n

niggling /níggling/ adj 1 petty or too preoccupied with details 2 irritating, painful, or worrying, especially in a small but persistent way —**nigglingly** adv

nigh /nī/ adv, adj near in place or time (literary) ○ (adv) Daybreak drew nigh. ○ (adj) Morning was nigh. ■ adv nearly ○ We talked for nigh on two hours. [Old English nēah < Germanic]

night /nīt/ n 1 DAILY PERIOD OF DARKNESS the period of darkness occurring each day in most parts of the world, or the entire period between sunset and sunrise 2 TIME BETWEEN BEDTIME AND WAKING the time between somebody's going to sleep in the evening and waking the next morning 3 PERIOD OF EVENING ACTIVITIES the period between sunset and bedtime, especially when spent in entertainment or some other activity ○ We had a great night at her birthday party. 4 night, Night EVENING DEVOTED TO SPECIAL ACTIVITY any period after sunset devoted to a special activity, function, or observance ○ Tomorrow night is Burns Night. 5 NIGHTFALL the period of time just after the sun goes down, when it gets dark 6 DARK OR DARKENED STATE a dark or darkened state, or an absence of light, consciousness, or enlightenment (literary) 7 SAD OR BAD PERIOD a period marked by grief, gloom, ig-norance, or obscurity ○ Europe slipped into the long night of the Dark Ages. ○ adj 1 OCCURRING AT NIGHT occurring, appearing, or visible at night ○ night terrors 2 USED AT NIGHT used chiefly at night ○ Use the night entrance. 3 WORKING AT NIGHT working at night in a job also done during the day ○ the night porter 4 ACTIVE AT NIGHT awake or active at night ○ night feeders ■ interj GOODNIGHT goodnight (informal) [Old English niht < Indo-European]

SPELLCHECK See **knight**.

night blindness n an inability to see clearly in dim light while having normal vision in clear light. Technical name **nyctalopia** —**night-blind** adj

nightcap /nīt kap/ n 1 DRINK BEFORE SLEEP a drink, often alcoholic, taken before going to bed 2 CAP USED AS NIGHTWEAR a soft cap worn in bed to keep the head warm, in use mainly until the late 19th century 3 US LAST EVENT the last event of a day of sports, especially the second game of a baseball double-header

nightclothes /nīt klōthz/ npl any clothes designed to be worn in bed

nightclub /nīt klub/ n a place of entertainment open late at night, offering music, dancing, and drinks, and sometimes serving food and providing a floor show

nightclubbing /nīt klubing/ n LEISURE = **clubbing** n. 1

night depository n US BANKING = **night safe**

nightdress /nīt dress/ n a loose dress of light material worn in bed by women and girls. US name **nightgown**

nightfall /nīt fawl/ n the time of evening at which it becomes dark and night begins ○ Be home by nightfall.

night fighter n a fighter aircraft designed to fly at night

nightglow /nīt glō/ n a dim light from the upper atmosphere seen at night

nightgown /nīt gown/ n 1 = **nightdress** 2 = **nightshirt**

nighthawk /nīt hawk/ n 1 a nightjar that has long pointed wings and black, white, and buff plumage. Native to: North America. Genus: Chordeiles. 2 = **night owl** (informal)

night heron n a stocky heron with short legs and a thick bill that is active at night or twilight. Genus: Nycticorax.

nightie /níti/, **nighty** (plural -**ies**) n a nightdress (informal) [Late 19C. Shortening and alteration.]

nightingale /nīting gayl/ n a migratory songbird of the thrush family with brownish plumage, the male of which is particularly known for its song. Luscinia megarhynchos. [13C. Alteration of Old English nihtegala < Germanic, 'night-singer']

LITERARY LINK Ode to a Nightingale, a poem (1819) by John Keats. The poet recounts how on hearing the joyful song of the nightingale he is filled with an intense joy that provides an escape from his woes. But, as he considers the fact that the bird's song has been an inspiration throughout history, the sound fades and he is suddenly returned to reality.

Florence Nightingale

Nightingale /níting gayl/, **Florence** (1820–1910) British nursing pioneer

nightjar /nīt jaar/ n a bird with a short bill, large gaping mouth, and dark plumage that is active at night and twilight and feeds on insects caught in flight. Family: Caprimulgidae. [< JAR2 'quivering sound']

night latch n a door lock operated from inside by a knob and from outside by a key

nightlife /nít līf/ *n* the entertainment or social life that goes on in a place in the evenings ○ *Let's go out and check out the local nightlife.*

nightlight /nít līt/ *n* a small lamp or candle lit to give a dim light during the night, especially in a child's bedroom

nightlong /nít lóng/ *adj* lasting or occurring throughout the entire night —**nightlong** *adv*

nightly /nítli/ *adj* **1 OCCURRING AT NIGHT** typically occurring at night **2 HAPPENING EVERY NIGHT** taking place every night ■ *adv* **EVERY NIGHT** on or during each and every night ○ *The band is playing nightly this week.*

nightmare /nít mair/ *n* **1 BAD DREAM** a frightening or upsetting dream **2 TRAUMATIC EXPERIENCE** a traumatic, very upsetting, or extremely difficult and troublesome experience or situation **3 DREADED EVENT** a situation or event that somebody particularly fears **4 EVIL SPIRIT** a malign spirit formerly believed to suffocate or haunt people during sleep ■ *adj* **EXTREMELY FRIGHTENING OR DIFFICULT** extremely frightening, upsetting, or difficult to deal with [13C. Literally 'night goblin'; *mare* < Old English, < Germanic.] —**nightmarish** *adj* —**nightmarishly** *adv*

night owl *n* a person who stays up late at night, especially to work or socialize (*informal*)

nights /nīts/ *adv* during the night, or every night ○ *They work nights.*

night safe *n* a safe in the wall of a bank that can be opened from outside to allow people to deposit money at times that the bank is closed. US term **night depository**

night school *n* a school or college that holds classes in the evening, especially for people who are at work during the day

nightscope /nít skōp/ *n* an optical device, e.g. using infrared radiation, that gives better vision in the dark ○ *The police surveillance team used a nightscope after dark.*

nightshade /nít shayd/ *n* a wild plant, related to potatoes, tomatoes, and aubergines, with flowers that have five petals, and small berries. Family: Solanaceae.

night shift *n* **1** a set period of work during the night ○ *The manager asked if anyone wanted to work a night shift.* **2** a group of people who work during a set period at night (*+ a singular or plural verb*) ○ *The night shift finish at seven in the morning.*

nightshirt /nít shurt/ *n* a long loose garment resembling a shirt, worn in bed by men

nightside /nít sīd/ *n* the side of a planet or moon that is not lit by the Sun

night sight *n* an infrared sight on a rifle used for taking aim in darkness

night soil *n* human excrement collected at night from toilets or cesspools, especially for use as fertilizer

nightspot /nít spot/ *n* LEISURE = **nightclub**

nightstand /nít stand/ *n* US FURNITURE = **night table**

nightstick /nít stik/ *n* US a club carried by a police officer [Because traditionally carried especially at night]

night table *n* US, *Can* a bedside table or stand

night terror *n* a sudden awakening from sleep in a condition of extreme fear that is not associated with a dream or nightmare

nighttime /nít tīm/ *n* the period of each day when it is dark, or the time between sunset and sunrise

night vision *n* somebody's ability to see in the dark ○ *They say eating carrots improves your night vision.*

night watch *n* **1** a guard or watch kept during the night ○ *I'm on night watch this week.* **2** = **night watchman** *n.* 1

night watchman *n* **1** a person who guards or watches over something at night, especially at a building site or factory **2** in cricket, a lower-order batsman who is sent in out of order if a wicket falls near the end of a day's play, to play defensively and prevent the loss of another more important wicket

nightwear /nít wair/ *n* clothes for people to wear while sleeping. US term **sleepwear**

nighty *n* CLOTHING = **nightie**

nigrescence /nī gréss'nss/ *n* the process of becoming black or dark [Mid-19C. < Latin *nigrescent-*, present participle of *nigrescere* 'grow black' < *niger* 'black'.] —**nigrescent** *adj* —**nigrescently** *adv*

nigrosine /nígrə seen, -sin/, **nigrosin** /-sin/ *n* a black aniline pigment or dye. Use: ink, polish, textile dye. [Late 19C. < Latin *niger* 'black'.]

nihilism /nī i lizəm, nīhi-/ *n* **1 TOTAL REJECTION OF SOCIAL MORES** the general rejection of established social conventions and beliefs, especially of morality and religion **2 BELIEF THAT NOTHING IS WORTHWHILE** a belief that life is pointless and human values are worthless **3 DISBELIEF IN OBJECTIVE TRUTH** the belief that there is no objective basis for truth **4 BELIEF IN DESTRUCTION OF AUTHORITY** the belief that all established authority is corrupt and must be destroyed in order to rebuild a just society [Early 19C. < German *Nihilismus* < Latin *nihil* 'nothing'.] —**nihilist** *n* —**nihilistic** /nī i lístik, nīhi-/ *adj* —**nihilistically** *adv*

Nihilism *n* a political movement in late 19th-century Russia that sought to bring about a just new society by destroying the existing one through acts of terrorism and assassination

nihility /nī híllәti, nee-/ *n* the condition of being nothing [Late 17C. < medieval Latin *nihilitas* < Latin *nihil* 'nothing'.]

nihil obstat /nīhil ób stat, níhil-/ *n* **1** a statement by a Roman Catholic Church official that a publication is not offensive to religion or morals **2** any official statement of nonopposition [Mid-20C. < Latin, 'nothing hinders'.]

Niigata /nyi ə gaátə/ port on N Honshu, Japan. Population: 486,097 (1990).

Nijinsky /ni jínski/, **Vaslav** (1890–1950) Russian ballet dancer

-nik *suffix* somebody associated with or characterized by ○ *refusenik* [Directly and via Yiddish < Russian]

Nikkei Index /ní kay-/ *n* an index of 225 leading shares traded on the Tokyo Stock Exchange [Late 20C. Abbreviation of Japanese *Nihon Keizai Shimbun* 'Japanese Economic Journal'.]

Nikko /neékō/ city on central Honshu, Japan. Population: 20,128 (1990).

nil /nil/ *n* nothing or zero , often used in the scores of games or to indicate that something is nonexistent or at the lowest possible level ○ *Our team won two-nil.* [Early 19C. Contraction of Latin *nihil* 'nothing'.]

Nile

Nile /nīl/ river in NE Africa, rising in Lake Victoria, Uganda, and flowing northwards to empty into the Mediterranean Sea in Egypt. Length: 6,695 km/4,160 mi.

Nile blue *adj* of a pale greenish-blue colour —**Nile blue** *n*

Nile crocodile *n* a crocodile that was once found along the entire length of the Nile but is now confined to the upper Nile. Native to: Africa, Madagascar. *Crocodylus niloticus.*

Nile green *adj* of a yellowish-green colour —**Nile green** *n*

Nile perch *n* a large predatory fish. Native to: lakes and rivers of Central and North Africa. *Lates niloticus.*

nilgai /níl gī/ (*plural* **-gai** *or* **-gais**), **nilgau** /-gaw/ (*plural* **-gau** *or* **-gaus**), **nilghau** (*plural* **-ghau** *or* **-ghaus**) *n* a large antelope of India, the male of which is bluish-grey and horned, the female brownish and hornless. *Boselaphus tragocamelus.* [Late 18C. < Hindi *nīlgāe* < Sanskrit *nīla* 'blue' + *-gāvī* 'cow'.]

Nilo-Saharan /nīlō-/ *n* a large family of languages spoken in central Africa. Native speakers: 15 million. —**Nilo-Saharan** *adj*

Nilotic /nī lóttik/ *adj* **1 RELATING TO THE NILE** relating to, involving, or living beside the River Nile **2 OF NILOTIC PEOPLE OR LANGUAGE** relating to a Nilotic people or language ■ *n* **NILE VALLEY LANGUAGE GROUP** a Nilo-Saharan group of languages spoken in parts of the Nile valley, mainly in Uganda and Sudan. Native speakers: 3 million. [Mid-17C. < Greek *Neilos* 'Nile'.]

nim /nim/ *n* a game in which players remove small, differently arranged items from piles, the winner being the player who takes, or sometimes does not take, the final item [Early 20C. < ?]

nimble /nímb'l/ (**-bler, -blest**) *adj* **1** agile, fast, and light in movement **2** able to think quickly and cleverly [Old English *nǣmel*, *numol* 'quick at grasping' < *niman* 'to take'] —**nimbleness** *n* —**nimbly** *adv*

nimbostratus /nímbō stráytəss, -straátəss/ (*plural* **-ti** /-tī/) *n* a low dark layer of rain-bearing cloud covering all of the sky. ◊ **stratus** [Late 19C. < NIMBUS.]

nimbus /nímbəss/ (*plural* **-buses** *or* **-bi** /-bī/) *n* **1 DARK RAIN-BEARING CLOUD** a dense, dark rain-bearing cloud **2 CLOUD OF LIGHT AROUND DEITY** a cloud of light believed to surround a god or goddess while on earth or a saint or holy person **3 IMAGE OF HALO** a bright halo or disc around the head of a deity, saint, or sovereign in a painting, icon, or medal **4 AURA OF SPLENDOUR** an aura or atmosphere of splendour surrounding somebody or something [Early 17C. < Latin, 'cloud, rain'.] —**nimbused** *adj*

NIMBY[1] /nímbi/ (*plural* **-BYs**), **Nimby** (*plural* **-bys**) *n* **1** an objector to something unattractive or potentially dangerous being located near his or her home (*informal*) **2** the attitude of a NIMBY [Late 20C. Acronym < *not in my backyard.*] —**Nimbyism** *n*

ϟ **NIMBY**[2] *abbr* not in my backyard (*in e-mails*)

niminy-piminy /nímmәni pímmәni/, **miminy-piminy** /mímmәni-/ *adj* affected and mincing [Late 18C. Based on NAMBY-PAMBY.]

nimrod /ním rod/ *n* any skilful or enthusiastic hunter (*literary*) [Mid-16C. < *Nimrod* as a 'mighty hunter' (Genesis 10:9).]

Nin /nin/, **Anaïs** (1903–77) French writer

nincompoop /níngkəm poop/ *n* an offensive term that deliberately insults somebody's intelligence or competence (*insult*) [Late 17C. Alteration of *nicompoop* < ?] —**nincompoopery** *n* —**nincompoopish** *adj*

nine /nīn/ *n* **1** see table at **number 2** a team of nine baseball players **3** half of the total number of holes on a golf course, usually specified as the front nine or the back nine [Old English *nigon* < Indo-European] —**nine** *adj, pron* ◇ **dressed (up) to the nines** very elaborately or formally dressed

ninebark /nín baark/ *n* a shrub with bark that separates into many layers. Native to: E North America. Genus: *Physocarpus.*

nine days' wonder, nine day wonder *n* something that, or somebody who, briefly arouses great interest or excitement but is soon forgotten again [Refers to Lady Jane Grey (1537–54), who was proclaimed Queen of England in 1553 but was deposed after nine days and subsequently beheaded]

ninefold /nín fōld/ *adj* **1 BY NINE TIMES** of nine times the original figure ○ *a ninefold rise* **2 WITH NINE PARTS** made up of nine parts ○ *The problem is ninefold.* ■ *adv* **BY NINE TIMES AS MUCH** by nine times as much or as many ○ *The numbers increased ninefold.*

ninepin /nín pin/ *n* = **skittle**

nineteen /nín teén/ *n* see table at **number** [Old English *nigontȳne* < Germanic, 'nine-ten'] —**nineteen** *adj, pron*

nineteenth /nín teénth/ *n* see table at **number** —**nineteenth** *adj, pron*

nineteenth hole *n* a place, especially the bar of a clubhouse, where players can drink and socialize after a round of golf (*slang*) [As after the conventional 18 holes]

nineteenth man *n* in an Australian Rules football team, the first of two substitutes that can be used during a regular match

~~**nineth**~~ incorrect spelling of **ninth**

ninetieth /nínti əth/ *n* see table at **number** —**ninetieth** *adj, pron*

nine-to-five *adj* requiring regular attendance, e.g. at an office job, especially between 9 a.m. and 5 p.m. (*informal*) ○ *without the self-discipline to hold down a nine-to-five job*

nine-to-fiver *n* US a worker at regular hours, especially from 9 a.m. to 5 p.m. (*informal*) ○ *She took the morning train with the rest of the nine-to-fivers.*

ninety /nínti/ *n* (*plural* **-ties**) see table at **number** ■ **nineties** *npl* **1** the numbers between 90 and 99, particularly as a range of Fahrenheit temperatures **2** the years from 90 to 99 in a century or somebody's life —**ninety** *adj*

Nineveh /nínnəvə/ ancient capital of the Assyrian Empire, on the River Tigris opposite present-day Mosul, N Iraq

Ningbo /ning bṓ/ city in NE Zhejiang Province, China. Population: 1,145,219 (1991).

Ninian /nínni ən/, **St** (360?–432?) Scottish bishop and missionary

ninja /nínjə/ (*plural* **-jas** *or* **-ja**) *n* a member of a group of mercenaries in feudal Japan who were trained in stealth and the martial arts and employed as spies, saboteurs, or assassins [Mid-20C. < Japanese, 'spy'.]

ninjitsu /nin jít soo/ *n* a Japanese martial art that emphasizes stealth in movement and camouflage [Mid-20C. < Japanese, 'stealth art'.]

ninny /nínni/ (*plural* **-nies**) *n* an offensive term that deliberately insults somebody's intelligence, common sense, or effectiveness (*insult*) [Late 16C. < ?] —**ninnyish** *adj*

ninon /neé non, nī́-/ *n* a sturdy sheer silk or synthetic fabric [Early 20C. < French.]

ninth /nīnth/ *n* **1** see table at **number** **2** a musical tone separated from another by an interval of an octave and a second, or the interval of this tone —**ninth** *adj*, *pron*

ninth chord *n* a musical chord containing four thirds, including the ninth, added above the root

~~**ninty**~~ incorrect spelling of **ninety**

niobic /nī ṓbik/ *adj* concerning or containing niobium with a valency of five

niobite /nī́ ə bīt/ *n* MINERALS = **columbite**

niobium /nī ṓbi əm/ *n* (*symbol* **Nb**) a lustrous light grey ductile metallic element that is a superconductor chemically resembling tantalum. Source: columbite. Use: steel alloys. [Mid-19C. < its association with tantalum, *Tantalus* being the father of *Niobe*.]

niobous /nī ṓbəss/ *adj* concerning or containing niobium with a valency less than five

nip[1] /nip/ *v* (**nips, nipping, nipped**) **1** *vt* **PINCH** to take hold of something and squeeze or compress it, often painfully, between two surfaces, e.g. to pinch skin between a forefinger and thumb **2** *vti* **TAKE BRIEF BITE AT** to bite something briefly, often painfully, but without doing much damage **3** *vt* **SEVER** to remove something by pinching, biting, or clipping ○ *She nipped off the growing point of the plant to encourage bushiness.* **4** *vt* **AFFECT SOMEBODY WITH COLD** to sting or chill a person or part of the body painfully with cold ○ *As she struggled with the car door the frost began to nip her fingers.* **5** *vt* **INJURE GROWTH OF** to halt or destroy the growth of something **6** *vt* **MAKE SOMETHING NARROWER** to make something narrower or tighter ○ *The dress is nipped in at the waist.* **7** *vt US* **STEAL** to steal or snatch something (*informal*) **8** *vi* **GO QUICKLY** to go somewhere quickly or briefly (*informal*) ○ *She nipped down to the shop for bread.* ■ *n* **1 SHARP SQUEEZE** a sharp or painful squeeze with the fingers or between two surfaces **2 SMALL BRIEF BITE** a small bite with the teeth that may be painful but does not do much damage ○ *The dog tried to give my ankle a nip as I passed.* **3 SMALL CUT-OUT PIECE** a small piece cut from something **4 CHILL** a chilly feeling caused by a marked drop in temperature ○ *There's a nip in the air tonight.* **5 SHARP FLAVOUR** a sharp or pungent flavour [14C. < Middle Low German *nipen*.] ◇ **nip and tuck** *US* very closely and evenly contested so that the outcome remains in doubt (*informal*)

nip[2] /nip/ *n* a small portion or drink of something alcoholic ■ *vti* (**nips, nipping, nipped**) to drink an alcoholic beverage in small sips [Late 18C. < ?]

nipa /neépə, nī́pə/ *n* **1** (*plural* **-pas** *or* **-pa**) **ASIAN PALM TREE** a palm tree with long feathery leaves and edible fruit. Native to: South Asia. *Nipa fruticans.* **2 LEAVES OF PALM TREE** the long feathery leaves of the nipa palm. Use: thatching, basketry. **3 DRINK FROM PALM SAP** an alcoholic drink made from the sap of the nipa palm [Late 16C. < Malay *nipah*.]

Nipigon, Lake /níppi gon/ lake in west-central Ontario, Canada. Area: 4,848 sq. km/1,872 sq. mi. Depth: 165 m/540 ft.

Nipissing, Lake /níppi sing/ lake in SE Ontario, Canada. Area: 832 sq. km/321 sq. mi.

nipper /níppər/ *n* **1 PINCER** a large claw of a crustacean, especially a lobster or crab **2 CHILD** a small child (*informal*) ■ **nippers** *npl* **PLIERS** a tool, such as pliers, used to squeeze or clip something

nipping /nípping/ *adj* **1** very cold and biting **2** bitingly sarcastic —**nippingly** *adv*

nipple /nípp'l/ *n* **1** a small knob in the centre of the breast that in females is the outlet for the ducts that provide young mammals with milk **2** *US* BABYWARE = **teat** *n.* **2** **3** a small knob on a device that is the outlet for fluid such as oil or grease [Mid-16C. < ?]

nipplewort /nípp'l wurt/ (*plural* **-worts** *or* **-wort**) *n* an annual plant with milky juice. Flowers: small, yellow. Native to: Europe, naturalized in E North America. Use: formerly, herbal remedy for breast tumours. *Lapsana communis.*

Nippon /níppon/ Japanese name for Japan —**Nipponese** /níppə neéz/ *adj*

nippy /níppi/ (**-pier, -piest**) *adj* **1 CHILLY** rather chilly **2 SMALL AND FAST** small, quick, and easy to manoeuvre **3 TENDING TO BITE** inclined to attempt to bite people or animals —**nippily** *adv* —**nippiness** *n*

N. Ire. *abbr* Northern Ireland

NIREX /nī́ reks/ *abbr* Nuclear Industry Radioactive Waste Executive

nirvana /neer vaánə, nur-/ *n* **1** **nirvana, Nirvana** in Hinduism, Buddhism, and Jainism, the attainment of enlightenment and freeing of the spiritual self from attachment to worldly things, ending the cycle of birth and rebirth **2** an ultimate experience of some pleasurable emotion such as harmony or joy [Mid-19C. < Sanskrit, < *nirvā-* 'be extinguished' < *nis-* 'out' + *vā-* 'to blow'.]

Nisan /neé saan/ *n* in the Jewish calendar, the seventh month of the civil year and first of the religious year

Nisga'a /níss gaa/ (*plural* **-ga'a** *or* **-ga'as**), **Nishga** /nísh-/ (*plural* **-ga** *or* **-gas**) *n* **1** a member of an Aboriginal people whose traditional territory is in the Nass River Valley in NW British Columbia **2** the Tsimshian language of the Nisga'a people [Late 19C. < Tsimshian.] —**Nisga'a** *adj*

nisi /nī́ sī, neéssi/ *adj* scheduled to take effect on a specified date unless some cause can be shown for cancelling or changing the date [Mid-19C. < Latin, 'unless'.]

Nissen hut /níss'n-/ *n* a temporary shelter made of corrugated steel in the shape of a half cylinder that was first used by the British during World War I [Early 20C. After Lt-Col. Peter Norman *Nissen* (1871–1930).]

nit /nit/ *n* **1** the egg or larva of a parasitic insect, especially a louse **2** an offensive term that deliberately insults somebody's common sense or intelligence (*insult*) [Old English *hnitu* < Indo-European.] —**nitty** *adj*

SPELLCHECK See ***knit***.

nite /nīt/ *n* a spelling of the word 'night', not appropriate for use in formal writing (*informal*)

Niten /neét en, nee tén/ (1584–1645) Japanese artist and soldier. Born **Miyamoto Musashi**

niter *n* US = **nitre**

Niterói /neetə róy/ city in SE Brazil. Population: 416,123 (1991).

nitpick /nít pik/ *vti* to find fault, often unjustifiably, with insignificant details of something —**nitpicker** *n* —**nitpicky** *adj*

SYNONYMS See ***criticize***.

nitpicking /nít piking/ *n* trivial, unnecessary, detailed, and often unjustified faultfinding

nitr- *prefix* = **nitro-** (*before vowels*)

nitrate /nī́ trayt/ *n* **1 CHEMICAL GROUP** a salt or an ester of nitric acid **2 FERTILIZER** a fertilizer that consists of sodium nitrate, potassium nitrate, or ammonium nitrate ■ *vt* (**-trates, -trating, -trated**) **USE NITRATE ON** to treat something with a nitrate or nitric acid, usually in order to change an organic compound into a nitrate [Late 18C. < French, < *nitre* 'nitre'.] —**nitration** /nī tráysh'n/ *n*

nitrazepam /nī trázzi pam/ *n* $C_{15}H_{11}N_3O_{35}$ a tranquillizer used in some sleeping pills [Mid-20C. < NITRO + AZO- + *-epine* + AMIDE.]

nitre /nī́tər/ *n* **1** = **potassium nitrate** **2** = **sodium nitrate** [14C. Via Old French < Latin *nitrum* < Greek *nitron*.]

nitric /nī́ trik/ *adj* made from or containing nitrogen, especially in a high valency state

nitric acid *n* HNO_3 a corrosive colourless or yellowish liquid that is a highly reactive oxidizing agent. Use: manufacture of explosives, fertilizers, and rocket fuels.

nitric oxide *n* NO a colourless poisonous gas. Source: ammonia, atmospheric nitrogen.

nitride /nī́ trīd/ *n* a compound made up of nitrogen and another more electropositive element such as phosphorus or a metal [Mid-19C. < NITROGEN.]

nitrify /nī́tri fī/ (**-fies, -fying, -fied**) *vt* **1 TREAT WITH NITROGEN** to treat or combine something with nitrogen or nitrogen compounds **2 FERTILIZE SOIL** to introduce nitrogen or nitrogen compounds into the soil in order to increase fertility **3 OXIDIZE AMMONIA IONS** to oxidize ammonia ions into nitrite or nitrate ions [Early 19C. < French *nitrifier* < *nitre* (see NITRE).] —**nitrification** /nītrifi káysh'n/ *n* —**nitrifier** *n*

nitrifying bacterium *n* a soil bacterium that converts ammonia to nitrites and nitrates, making nitrogen available to plants

nitrile /nī́trəl, -trīl/ *n* an organic cyanide

nitrite /nī́ trīt/ *n* a salt or ester of nitrous acid

nitrite bacterium *n* a nitrobacterium that converts ammonia to nitrites by oxidation

nitro /nī́ trō/ *n* nitroglycerine (*informal*) [Early 20C. Shortening.]

nitro- *prefix* **1** nitrogen ○ *nitrify* **2** nitre, nitrate ○ *nitrogen* **3** containing a univalent NO_2 group ○ *nitroparaffin* [< Latin *nitrum* (see NITRE)]

nitrobacterium /nī́trō bak teéri əm/ (*plural* **-a** /-ə/) *n* MICROBIOL = **nitrifying bacterium**

nitrobenzene /nī́trō bén zeen/ *n* $C_6H_5NO_2$ a poisonous organic compound that occurs either as bright yellow crystals or an oily liquid that smells like almonds. Use: manufacture of polishes and insulating compounds.

nitrocellulose /nī́trō séllyōō lōss, -lōz/ *n* a chemical compound produced by the reaction of nitric and sulphuric acids on cellulose. Use: manufacture of plastics, explosives, and lacquers.

nitrochloroform /nī́trō klórrə fawrm/ *n* CHEM = **chloropicrin**

nitrogen /nī́trəjən/ *n* (*symbol* **N**) a nonmetallic element that occurs as a colourless odourless almost inert gas and makes up four-fifths of the Earth's atmosphere by volume. Use: manufacture of ammonia, explosives, fertilizers. [Late 18C. < French *nitrogène* < *nitre* (see NITRE) + *-gène* (see -GEN).] —**nitrogenous** /nī trójjənəss/ *adj*

nitrogenase /nī trójjə nayz, -nayss/ *n* an enzyme found in nitrogen-fixing bacteria that catalyses the conversion of nitrogen to ammonia

nitrogen balance *n* **1** the difference between the amount of nitrogen taken into the body and the amount excreted **2** the difference between the amount of nitrogen absorbed by the soil and the amount lost

nitrogen cycle *n* the series of processes by which nitrogen is converted from a gas in the atmosphere to nitrogen-containing substances in soil and living organisms, then reconverted to a gas

nitrogen dioxide *n* NO_2 a highly poisonous brown gas often present in smog and exhaust from vehicles. Use: manufacture of nitric and sulphuric acids.

nitrogen fixation *n* **1** the natural conversion of atmospheric nitrogen by certain bacteria found in the nodules of legumes into compounds in the soil that plants and other organisms can use **2** an industrial process in which nitrogen from the atmosphere is changed into compounds such as ammonia by chemical agents. Use: manufacture of fertilizers. —**nitrogen-fixer** *n* —**nitrogen-fixing** *adj*

nitrogenize /nī trójjə nīz/ (**-izes, -izing, -ized**), **nitrogenise** (**-ises, -ising, -ised**) *vt* to combine or treat something with nitrogen or one of its compounds —**nitrogenization** /nī trójjə nī záysh'n/ *n*

nitrogen mustard *n* a compound similar to mustard gas in which the sulphur is replaced by amino nitrogen. Use: treatment of some cancers.

nitrogen narcosis *n* light-headedness, confusion, or exhilaration caused by increased nitrogen in the blood

nitroglycerine /nī́trō glíssərin, -reen/, **nitroglycerin** /-rin/ *n* $C_3H_5N_3O_9$ a colourless thick oily flammable and explosive liquid. Use: manufacture of explosives, treatment of angina pectoris

nitrohydrochloric acid /nítrō hídrō klórrik-/ *n* CHEM = **aqua regia**

nitromethane /nítrō mee-/ *n* CH_3NO_2 a poisonous colourless oily slightly water-soluble liquid. Use: manufacture of dyes, resins, and rocket fuels, as a solvent and petrol additive.

nitroparaffin /nítrō párrəfin/ *n* a colourless simple hydrocarbon containing the chemical group NO_2

nitrosamine /nī trṓzə meen/ *n* R_2NNO an organic carcinogenic compound found in various foods [Late 19C. < Latin *nitrosus* 'nitrous'.]

nitrous /nítrəss/ *adj* made from or containing nitrogen, especially in a low valency state

nitrous acid *n* HNO_2 a weak inorganic acid found only in solution or in the form of its salts

nitrous oxide *n* N_2O a colourless nonflammable sweet-smelling, sweet-tasting gas. Use: anaesthetic.

nitty-gritty /nítti grítti/ *n* BASICS the basic and most important details of something (*informal*) ■ *adj* (*informal*) **1** BASIC AND IMPORTANT concerning or involving the most important aspects of a subject **2** PRACTICAL useful and direct in a practical down-to-earth way ○ *a nitty-gritty approach to teaching* [Mid-20C. < ?]

nitwit /nít wit/ *n* somebody thought to be silly or unintelligent (*insult*) [Early 20C. < ?]

Niue /nee óo ay/ island in the central South Pacific Ocean, east of Tonga, a self-governing territory of New Zealand. Population: 2,244 (1991). Area: 263 sq. km / 101 sq. mi.

Niuean /nee óo ay ən/ *n* **1** a member of a Polynesian people who inhabit the Pacific island of Niue **2** the Polynesian language of Niue —**Niuean** *adj*

nival /nív'l/ *adj* growing in or under the snow [Mid-17C. < Latin *nivalis* < *niv-* 'snow'.]

niveous /nívvi əss/ *adj* resembling snow in colour [Early 17C. < Latin *niveus* < *niv-* 'snow'.]

nix[1] /niks/ *n* US nothing (*dated slang*) ■ *vt* US to refuse, forbid, or veto something (*slang*) [Late 18C. < German, variant of *nichts* 'nothing'.]

nix[2] /niks/ *n* MYTHOL = **nixie** [Mid-19C. < German.]

nixie /níksi/ *n* in German mythology, a female water spirit that can appear in human form or as half-human, half-fish [Early 19C. < German *Nixe*, feminine of *Nix*.]

Nixon /níks'n/, **Richard Milhous** (1913–94) 37th president of the United States (1969–74)

Nizhniy Novgorod /nízhniy nóvgərət/ port in W Russia. Population: 1,440,600 (1992).

Nizhny Tagil /nízhni taa gíl/ city in W Siberian Russia. Population: 437,000 (1992).

NJ, **N.J.** *abbr* New Jersey

Nkomo /əng kṓmō/, **Joshua** (1917–99) Zimbabwean nationalist leader and statesman

Nkrumah /'n kroómə, 'ng kroómə/, **Kwame** (1909–72) Ghanaian statesman and first prime minister (1957–60) and president (1960–66) of Ghana

NKVD *n* the Soviet secret police from 1934 to 1946. Full form **Narodny Kommissariat Vnutrennikh Del** [Russian, 'People's Commissariat of Internal Affairs']

⚡ **nl** *abbr* Netherlands (*in Internet addresses*)

NL, **N.L.** *abbr* **1** Netherlands (*international vehicle registration*) **2** New Latin

⚡ **NLB** *abbr* nonlinear behaviour (*in e-mails*)

⚡ **NLP** *abbr* **1** neurolinguistic programming **2** natural language processing

nm *abbr* **1** nanometre **2** nautical mile **3** nuclear magneton

NM *abbr* **1** NM, N.M. New Mexico **2** nautical mile

N. Mex. *abbr* New Mexico

NMR *abbr* nuclear magnetic resonance

NNE *abbr* north-northeast

NNP *abbr* net national product

NNW *abbr* north-northwest

no[1] /nō/ *interj* **1** indicates a negative response, used to refuse, deny, or disagree with something ○ *'Will you be taking the car?' – 'No, not today'.* ○ *'Would you like a coffee?' – 'No, I'm fine, thanks'.* **2** ACKNOWLEDGING A NEGATIVE STATEMENT used to express acceptance or understanding of a negative statement made by somebody else ○ *'Nobody seems to have the time to really listen these days'. – 'No, they don't'.* **3** INDICATING DISBELIEF used to indicate shock, disbelief, or disappointment at something somebody has said ○ *'The car's going to be in the garage for another week'. – 'Oh no!'* ■ *n* **1** (*plural* **noes** *or* **nos**) ANSWER OR VOTE an answer or vote of 'no' ○ *They all gave resounding noes to the proposition.* **2** SOMEBODY VOTING 'NO' a person who answers 'no' to a question or votes against something [Old English *nā* < *ne* 'not' + *ā* 'ever'] ◇ **say no** to express disagreement or refusal ◇ **the noes have it** used to indicate that the majority have voted against something

---

SPELLCHECK See ***know***.

---

no[2] /nō/ CORE MEANING: a determiner used to indicate that there is not any or not one person or thing ○ *There is nothing within walking distance: no post office, no bank.* ○ *I had no choice in the matter.* ○ *They pay no attention to me.*
det **1** used to indicate that somebody or something does not have any of the characteristic or identity mentioned ○ *She's no fool.* **2** not exceeding a particular amount or quality (*with comparative adjectives and adverbs*) ○ *The issue was no less important to us than you.* [12C. Shortening of NONE.]

⚡ **no**[3] *abbr* Norway (*in Internet addresses*)

No[1] /nō/, **Noh** *n* a form of Japanese drama that presents a story in a highly stylized fashion, using music, dance, and elaborate costumes [Late 19C. < Japanese *nō* 'talent, ability'.]

No[2] *symbol* nobelium

no., No. *abbr* **1** north **2** northern **3** number

n.o. *abbr* not out

no-account, **no-'count** *adj* US without any redeeming or useful qualities (*informal*)

Noachian /nō áyki ən/, **Noachic** /-áykik/, **Noachical** /-áykik'l/ *adj* **1** typical of or relating to Noah or his time **2** long out-of-date [Late 19C. < *Noach*, form of *Noah*.]

Noah /nṓ ə/ *n* in the Bible, a Hebrew patriarch who, at God's command, built an ark and saved himself, his family, and a pair of every kind of animal from the Flood (Genesis 6–9)

Noah's ark *n* BIBLE = **ark** *n.* **1**

nob[1] /nob/ *n* a rich or socially powerful person (*informal*) [Late 17C. < ?]

nob[2] /nob/ *n* **1** the human head (*slang*) **2** in cribbage, the jack of the suit that the dealer turns up, which scores one point for the player who holds it [Late 17C. < ?]

no ball *n* in cricket, a ball that has been bowled in a way not permitted by the rules of the game

nobble /nóbb'l/ (**-bles, -bling, -bled**) *vt* (*informal*) **1** FIND AND PERSUADE to make contact with somebody else, especially in order to persuade that person to do something **2** WIN SOMEBODY OVER to get somebody to do something using lies, threats, or bribes **3** DISABLE A RACEHORSE to prevent a racehorse from winning a race by drugging or disabling it **4** CHEAT to swindle or defraud somebody **5** STEAL to steal something **6** SEIZE to seize hold of somebody **7** KIDNAP to kidnap somebody [Mid-19C. < ?] —**nobbler** *n*

nobbut /nóbbət/ *adv* N England just or only [14C. < NO[1] + BUT[1].]

nobby /nóbbi/ *adj* fashionable or elegant (*informal*) [Late 18C. < NOB[1].]

Nobel /nō bél/, **Alfred** (1833–96) Swedish chemist and inventor of dynamite, who established the original Nobel Prizes

Nobelist /nō béllist/ *n* a winner of a Nobel Prize

nobelium /nō béeli əm/ *n* (*symbol* **No**) a radioactive element. Source: produced artificially from curium. [Mid-20C. After Alfred NOBEL.]

Nobel Prize /nṓ bel-/ *n* any of six international awards made annually for outstanding achievement in the fields of chemistry, literature, physics, physiology or medicine, economics, and for promoting world peace [Early 20C. After Alfred NOBEL.] —**Nobel prizewinner** *n* —**Nobel-prizewinning** *adj*

nobiliary /nō bílli əri/ *adj* relating to the nobility

nobiliary particle *n* a preposition, such as 'de' in French or 'von' in German, used before a title or surname as a mark of rank

nobility /nō bíllәti/ (*plural* **-ties**) *n* **1** ARISTOCRATS a noble class or people of noble rank in a country **2** NOBLE RANK aristocratic social position or rank **3** NOBLE CHARACTER high ideals or excellent moral character **4** MAGNIFICENCE impressiveness or magnificence [14C. Directly or via French < Latin *nobilitas* < *nobilis* 'noble'.]

noble /nṓb'l/ *adj* (**-bler, -blest**) **1** HAVING EXCELLENT MORAL CHARACTER possessing high ideals or excellent moral character **2** RELATING TO HIGH MORAL PRINCIPLES based on high ideals or revealing excellent moral character **3** MAGNIFICENT impressive in quality or appearance **4** ARISTOCRATIC belonging or relating to an aristocratic social or political class **5** NONREACTIVE chemically inactive or inert ■ *n* **1** ARISTOCRAT a titled aristocrat **2** FORMER ENGLISH COIN a gold coin worth half a mark, formerly used in England [13C. Via French < Latin *(g)nobilis*.] —**nobleness** *n* —**nobly** *adv*

noble gas *n* a chemically inert rare gas belonging to group 18 of the periodic table, including helium, neon, argon, krypton, xenon, and radon

nobleman /nṓb'lmən/ (*plural* **-men** /-mən/) *n* a man who belongs to a titled aristocracy

noble metal *n* a metal, such as gold, silver, or platinum that is resistant to oxidation

noble rot *n* a parasitic fungus that shrivels ripe grapes, increasing the proportion of sugar to liquid in them. *Botrytis cinerea.*

noble savage *n* somebody belonging to a nontechnological culture whose life is, according to an idea popularized by Rousseau, purer because it is closer to nature (*offensive in some contexts*)

noblesse /nō bléss/ *n* **1** aristocratic social position or rank **2** the members of an aristocracy, especially the French aristocracy [13C. < French, 'nobility' < *noble* (see NOBLE).]

noblesse oblige /-ōbleézh/ *n* the idea that people born into the nobility or upper social classes must behave in an honourable generous way towards those less privileged [< French, 'nobility obliges']

noblewoman /nṓb'l wòomən/ (*plural* **-en** /-wimin/) *n* a woman who belongs to a titled aristocracy

nobody /nṓbədi, -bodi/ *pron* not one single person ○ *Nobody can order the attack except the general.* ■ *n* (*plural* **-ies**) an unimportant or insignificant person ○ *I felt like a nobody among so many important scientists.*

LITERARY LINK ***The Diary of a Nobody***, a fictional journal (1892) by George and Weedon Grossmith. Originally published in serial form in 'Punch', it is the diary of Charles Pooter, an anxious and hypersensitive middle-aged man who lives in the suburbs and works in the city of London. The text provides an amusing insight into the everyday life of the lower middle classes in late 19th-century London.

---

no-brainer *n* US something such as an idea or question that is so easily understood or done that it requires little or no thought (*slang*)

nocent /nṓss'nt/ *adj* causing harm, injury, or damage [15C. < Latin *nocent-*, present participle of *nocere* 'to hurt'.] —**nocently** *adv*

nociceptive /nóssi séptiv/ *adj* **1** describes a stimulus that causes pain **2** caused by or reacting to pain [Early 20C. < Latin *nocere* 'to hurt'.] —**nociceptively** *adv*

nociceptor /nóssi septər/ *n* a nerve ending that responds selectively to painful stimuli, causing the sensation of pain [Early 20C. < Latin *nocere* 'to hurt'.]

nock /nok/ *n* **1** GROOVE ON BOW one of the grooves at either end of a bow that holds the bowstring **2** NOTCH ON ARROW the notch at the end of an arrow that holds it on the bowstring ■ *vt* **1** PREPARE TO FIRE ARROW to place an arrow on a bowstring **2** CUT NOTCH IN BOW OR ARROW to put a notch in a bow or an arrow [14C. Probably < Middle Dutch *nocke* 'projection, tip'.]

no claims bonus, **no claim bonus, no claims discount** *n* a discount or reduction on an insurance premium, especially for a car, applied when the insured has not made a claim on the insurance during a specified period of time

noct- *prefix* = **nocti-** (*before vowels*)

nocti- *prefix* night, at night ○ *noctilucent* [< Latin *noct-* 'night' < Indo-European]

noctiluca /nókti loókə/ (*plural* **-cae** /-kī/) *n* a plankton that produces light. Genus: *Noctiluca*. [Mid-19C. < Latin, 'moon, lantern'.]

noctilucent /nókti loóss'nt/ *adj* describes high clouds that are visible at night [Late 19C. < NOCTI- + Latin *lucere* 'to shine'.]

noctuid /nóktyoo id/ *n* a dull-coloured moth whose larvae, called army worms and cutworms, are destructive to young plants. Family: Noctuidae. [Late 19C. < Latin *noctua* 'night-owl'.] —**noctuid** *adj*

noctule /nók tyool/ *n* a large reddish-brown bat, common in Europe and Asia, that eats insects. *Nyctalus noctula*. [Late 18C. Via French < Italian *nottola* 'bat'.]

nocturn /nók turn/ *n* one of the three divisions of the Roman Catholic service of matins, the first service of the day, previously held at midnight but now usually at daybreak [14C. Directly or via French *nocturne* < ecclesiastical Latin *nocturnus* < Latin, 'of the night' < *noct-* 'night'.]

nocturnal /nok túrn'l/ *adj* **1 AT NIGHT** occurring at night, as opposed to during the day **2 ACTIVE AT NIGHT** describes animals that are active at night rather than during the day **3 FLOWERING AT NIGHT** describes flowers that open at night and close during the day —**nocturnally** *adv*

nocturne /nók turn/ *n* **1** a musical composition, especially for the piano, that suggests a tranquil, dreamy mood **2** a painting of a night scene [Mid-19C. < French (see NOCTURN).]

nocuous /nókyoo əss/ *adj* likely to cause injury or damage [Mid-17C. < Latin *nocuus* < *nocere* 'to hurt'.] —**nocuously** *adv* —**nocuousness** *n*

nod /nod/ *v* (**nods, nodding, nodded**) **1** *vti* **MOVE HEAD IN AGREEMENT** to lower and then raise the head quickly in order to show agreement or recognition or to give a signal ○ *He nodded discreetly to a man who was standing by the door.* **2** *vi* **DOZE** to let the head fall forward because of sleepiness **3** *vi* **LOSE CONCENTRATION** to be momentarily careless or negligent **4** *vi* **MOVE IN WIND** to droop, bend, or sway in a breeze ■ *n* **1 MOVEMENT OF HEAD TO SHOW AGREEMENT** a quick lowering and raising of the head in order to show agreement or recognition **2 ACKNOWLEDGMENT** a gesture, especially a token one, in recognition of something such as a convention or requirement ○ *an upbeat slogan that was a nod to the vogue for mission statements* [14C. < ?] —**nodder** *n* ◇ **a nod's as good as a wink (to a blind horse)** used to indicate that something expressed indirectly has been understood and that no further explanation is required ◇ **give somebody** *or* **something the nod** to select or approve somebody or something ◇ **be on nodding terms (with somebody)** to know somebody slightly ◇ **on the nod** agreed without formal discussion or procedures (*informal*)

nod off *vi* to fall asleep unintentionally or go into a drug-induced state of semiconsciousness

nod through *vt* **1** to approve something without discussing it and voting on it **2** to consider an MP as having voted in the House of Commons when he or she is unable to do so

nodding acquaintance *n* a slight familiarity with or knowledge of somebody or something

nodding donkey *n* a pump for extracting oil

noddle /nódd'l/ *n* the human head or brain (*dated informal*) [15C. < ?]

noddy /nóddi/ (*plural* **-dies**) *n* **1 TROPICAL SEABIRD** a dark-coloured tern. Native to: tropical coastal waters in N and S hemispheres. Genera: *Anous* and *Micranous*. **2 OFFENSIVE TERM** an offensive term that deliberately insults somebody's intelligence or common sense (*dated insult*) **3 FOOTAGE OF INTERVIEWER NODDING** a short piece of film of a television interviewer nodding as if listening to the person interviewed that is spliced in with the main film of the person interviewed (*informal*) [Early 16C. < ?]

noddy suit *n* a protective suit worn by military personnel likely to be exposed to nuclear, biological, or chemical weapons (*slang*)

ϟ**node** /nōd/ *n* **1 LUMP, BULGE OR SWELLING** a lump, knob, knot, or other kind of swelling that sticks out **2 POINT ON PLANT STEM** the place on a plant stem where a leaf is attached or has been attached **3 POINT ON WAVE** in physics, a place in a standing wave that has little or no amplitude **4 POINT OF INTERSECTION** a point where lines meet or intersect in a diagram or graph **5 POINT WHERE PARTS OF CURVE INTERSECT** in geometry, a place on a curve where it crosses itself **6 POINT WHERE ORBIT INTERSECTS ECLIPTIC** either of the two points where an orbit, e.g. that of a planet, crosses the ecliptic plane **7 TERMINAL OR POINT IN NETWORK** a terminal or other point in a computer network where a message can be created, received, or repeated **8 POINT IN SENTENCE STRUCTURE** in transformational grammars, a point in a sentence diagram where a category label, indicating the part of speech, appears and from which further branches may lead off [14C. < Latin *nodus* 'knot'.] —**nodal** *adj* —**nodally** *adv*

node of Ranvier /-raánvi ay/ *n* a short gap in the myelin sheath that occurs at intervals along the length of a nerve fibre [After Louis Antoine *Ranvier* (1835–1922), French histologist]

nodose /nṓd ōss, nō dṓss/ *adj* having many points at which leaves join the stem —**nodosity** /nō dóssəti/ *n*

nodule /nóddyool/ *n* **1 SMALL LUMP** a small protruding knob, lump, or swelling on something **2 ROOT PROTUBERANCE** a swelling or knob on the roots of legumes that contains bacteria **3 CELL OR TISSUE MASS** a small mass of cells or tissue, which may be a normal part of the body or a growth such as a tumour **4 LARGE ROUNDED MINERAL FORM** a form of a mineral that is massive with a rounded outer surface [15C. < Latin *nodulus* 'small knot' < *nodus* 'knot'.] —**nodular** *adj* —**nodulose** *adj*

Noel /nō éll/, **Noël** *n* Christmas, especially in carols or greetings

noetic /nō éttik/ *adj* typical of, coming from, or understood by the human mind [Mid-17C. < Greek *noētikos* < *noein* 'think' < *nous* 'mind'.] —**noetically** *adv*

no-fault *adj* **1** relating to a system of motor vehicle insurance in which insurance companies compensate accident victims without determining who is responsible for the accident **2** relating to a form of divorce in which no blame is placed on either party for the breakdown of the marriage

no-fly-zone *n* **1** an area over which aircraft, especially those of another country, are forbidden to fly, and in which they will be attacked if they enter it **2** *US* a topic of questioning or conversation that is off-limits (*slang*) ○ *The press secretary declared that issue to be a no-fly-zone for reporters.*

no-frills *adj* relating to a kind of service or establishment that does not offer extra or special treatment (*informal*)

no-fuss *adj* involving little bother or few difficulties for the user

nog[1] /nog/ *n* **1** a block of wood inserted into masonry or brickwork so that something can be nailed to it **2** a wooden peg or pin [Early 17C. < ?]

nog[2] /nog/ *n* **1** BEVERAGES = **eggnog** **2** a strong ale once brewed in Norfolk [Early 17C. < ?]

noggin /nóggin/ *n* **1 ONE-FOURTH OF PINT** a measure of spirits equivalent to 0.148 litres/$\frac{1}{4}$ of a pint (*dated*) **2 CUP** a small cup or mug (*dated*) **3 HEAD** the human head (*dated informal*) [Mid-17C. < ?]

nogging /nógging/ *n* **1** small stones, bricks, or bits of masonry used to fill the spaces between studs in a wall or partition **2** one of the pieces of wood that are inserted between the main timbers of a half-timbered wall

no-go *n* an event or situation that is not going to occur because of adverse conditions (*informal*) ■ *adj* no longer going to happen or scheduled to occur

no-go area *n* **1** a district where people are frightened or unable to go because of the violence and crime there **2** an area that unauthorized people are forbidden to enter

no-good *adj* considered as lacking merit, virtue, worth, or morals (*insult*) ■ *n* somebody or something considered to lack merit, virtue, worth, or morals (*insult*)

Noguchi /naw go͝ochi/, **Hideyo** (1876–1928) Japanese bacteriologist

Noguchi, Isamu (1904–88) US sculptor

Noh *n* THEATRE = **No**[1]

no-hit *adj* relating to a baseball or softball game in which the opponents do not get a hit

no-hitter *n* a baseball or softball game in which the pitcher does not allow opponents a hit

no-holds-barred *adj* happening, or engaged in something, without restraint or control (*informal*) [< a wrestling match in which any hold is permitted]

no-hoper *n* an offensive term that deliberately insults somebody's achievements and likelihood of future success

nohow /nṓ how/ *adv* not in any way (*nonstandard*)

noil /noyl/ *n* short fibres separated during combing from the long fibres of cotton, wool, or another material [Early 17C. Probably < Old French *noel* < medieval Latin *nodellus* 'small knot' < Latin *nodus* 'knot'.]

ϟ**noise** /noyz/ *n* **1 UNPLEASANT SOUND** a loud, surprising, irritating, or unwanted sound **2 ANY SOUND** any sound or combination of sounds **3 OUTCRY** a loud clamour or commotion concerning something **4 COMPLAINT** a complaint or protest about something (*informal*) **5 RUMOUR** idle talk, rumour, or gossip (*informal*) **6 ELECTRIC DISTURBANCE** a random disturbance in an electric circuit that makes clear reception of a signal difficult **7 MEANINGLESS DATA** unwanted or meaningless data intermixed with the relevant information in the output from a computer ■ *vt* (**noises, noising, noised**) **SPREAD GOSSIP** to spread a rumour or gossip ○ *an ugly story that was being noised about in newsrooms* [13C. Via French, 'uproar, brawl' < Latin *nausea* 'seasickness' < Greek *naus* 'ship'.] ◇ **make noises** to do or say something intended to attract attention or indicate an intention ○ *He's making noises about a career change.*

noise abatement *n* the reduction of noise pollution —**noise-abating** *adj*

noiseless /nóyzləss/ *adj* not making any noise —**noiselessly** *adv* —**noiselessness** *n*

noisemaker /nóyz maykər/ *n* *US* a device such as a rattle or horn used to make noise at a party or a celebration

noise pollution *n* irritating, distracting, or physically dangerous noise to which people are exposed in their environment and over which they usually have no control

noisette /nwaa zét/ *n* a piece of boned and rolled meat, especially the neck or loin of lamb [Late 19C. < French, 'little nut'; from its shape.]

noisome /nóyssəm/ *adj* **1** so offensive, especially to the senses, as to arouse feelings of disgust or repulsion **2** extremely harmful [14C. < obsolete *noy*, shortening of ANNOY.] —**noisomely** *adv* —**noisomeness** *n*

noisy /nóyzi/ (**-ier, -iest**) *adj* **1** making a loud and annoying racket **2** full of or characterized by loud sounds —**noisily** *adv* —**noisiness** *n*

Nok /nok/ *n* a civilization located in the forests of central Nigeria that flourished between 500 BC and AD 300. It is known for its highly developed art style.

Sir Sidney Nolan

Nolan /nṓlən/, **Sir Sidney Robert** (1917–92) Australian painter

Nolde /nóldə/, **Emil** (1867–1956) German artist

nolens volens /nṓ lenz vṓ lenz/ *adv* whether willing or not willing [< Latin, 'unwilling willing']

noli-me-tangere /nṓli may táng gəri, -tánjəri/ *n* **1 PROHIBITION AGAINST TOUCHING** a warning not to touch or interfere with somebody or something **2 SOMEBODY OR SOMETHING NOT FOR TOUCHING** a person who or thing that must not be touched or interfered with **3 PAINTING OF JESUS CHRIST AND MARY MAGDALENE** a depiction in art of Jesus Christ appearing to Mary Magdalene after his resurrection [< Latin, 'do not touch me'; from Jesus Christ's words to Mary Magdalene (John 20:17)]

nolle prosequi /nólli próssi kwī/ *n* an entry made in a court record when a plaintiff or a prosecutor decides not to proceed further with a case or action [< Latin, 'be unwilling to pursue']

nolo /nṓlō/ (*plural* **-los**) *n* *US* a nolo contendere (*informal*) [Shortening]

nolo contendere /nṓlō kon téndəri/ *n* *US* in law, a plea entered by a defendant that does not explicitly admit guilt, but subjects the defendant to punishment, while allowing denial of the alleged facts in other proceedings [< Latin, 'I do not wish to contend']

no-lose *adj* certain to result in success or be beneficial, regardless of the outcome ○ *a no-lose proposition*

nol. pros. /nól próss/ *abbr* nolle prosequi

nom. *abbr* nominative

noma /nṓmə/ *n* a severe gangrenous inflammation of the mouth or genitals, usually occurring in children who are malnourished or otherwise debilitated [Mid-19C. < modern Latin alteration of Latin *nome* < Greek *nom-*, stem of *nemein* 'to feed'.]

nomad /nṓ mad/ *n* **1** a member of a people who move seasonally from place to place to search for food and water or pasture for their livestock **2** a person who wanders from place to place [Late 16C. < French *nomade* < Greek *nomas* 'wandering about to find pasture' < *nemein* 'to pasture'.] —**nomadic** /nō máddik/ *adj* —**nomadically** *adv* —**nomadism** *n*

no-man's-land *n* **1** TERRITORY BETWEEN OPPOSING FORCES the area of land that lies between two opposing armies and is held by neither side **2** UNCLAIMED TERRITORY any area of land that no one has established a claim to **3** BAD POSITION ON TENNIS COURT in tennis and other court games, an area on a court in which a player is tactically at a disadvantage **4** AMBIGUOUS AREA any indefinite or ambiguous situation in which boundaries, rules, or authority are unclear or unfamiliar

nomarchy /nóm aarki/ (*plural* **-chies**) *n* any of the administrative provinces into which modern Greece is divided [Mid-17C. < Greek *nomarkhia* < *nomos* (see NOME) + *-arkhia* 'government'.]

nombril /nómbril/, **nombril point** *n* in heraldry, the midpoint of the lower half of an escutcheon, halfway between the fess point and the base point [Mid-16C. < French, 'navel'.]

nom de guerre /nóm də gáir/ (*plural* **noms de guerre** /nóm-/) *n* an assumed name that somebody uses in certain situations, e.g. when fighting [< French, 'name of war']

nom de plume /nóm də plóom/ (*plural* **noms de plume** /nóm-/) *n* LITERAT = **pen name** [< French, 'name of pen']

nome /nōm/ *n* **1** a province of ancient Egypt **2** POL = **nomarchy** [Early 18C. < Greek *nomos* < *nemein* 'divide'.]

nomen /nṓ men/ (*plural* **nomina** /nó minə/) *n* in ancient Rome, a citizen's second name, which indicated the clan to which he or she belonged [Early 18C. < Latin, 'name'.]

nomenclator /nṓ men klaytər/ *n* an assigner of names in a scientific classification system (**taxonomy**) [Mid-16C. < Latin, < *nomen* 'name' + *calare* 'to call'.]

nomenclature /nō méngklәchәr, nṓmәn klaychәr, -kláychәr/ *n* **1** the assigning of names to organisms in a scientific classification system (**taxonomy**) **2** a system of names assigned to objects or items in a particular science or art [Early 17C. Via French < Latin *nomenclatura* < *nomen* 'name' + *calare* 'to call'.] —**nomenclatural** /nṓmən kláychərəl/ *adj*

nomenklatura /nṓ men kla tóorə/ *n* **1** in Communist governments, the elite, privileged class consisting of the people holding positions of authority in the bureaucracy (+ *plural verb*) **2** the system in the former Soviet Union and other Communist countries, controlled by committees in the Communist Party, for assigning senior positions in the bureaucracy (+ *singular verb*) [Mid-20C. Via Russian < Latin *nomenclatura* (see NOMENCLATURE).]

nomina plural of **nomen**

nominal /nómmin'l/ *adj* **1** SO-CALLED acting or being something in name only, but not in reality **2** VERY LOW IN COST representing very little cost when compared with the actual value received **3** RELATING TO CURRENT PRICES considered in terms of the stated or original value only, and ignoring changes due to inflation and other factors **4** OF NOUN relating to a noun or a group of words that functions as a noun **5** BEARING SOMEBODY'S NAME assigned to a named person, and bearing that person's name **6** OF NAMES relating to or consisting of a name or names ■ *n* NOUN OR NOUN GROUP a word or group of words that functions as a noun [15C. Directly or via French < Latin *nominalis* < *nomen* 'name'.] —**nominally** *adv*

nominalise *vt* = **nominalize**

nominalism /nómminəlizəm/ *n* the philosophical doctrine that there are no realities other than concrete individual objects —**nominalist** *n, adj* —**nominalistic** *adj* —**nominalistically** *adv*

nominalize /nómminə līz/ (**-izes, -izing, -ized**), **nominalise** (**-ises, -ising, -ised**) *vt* **1** to change a part of speech into a noun by the addition of a suffix **2** to change an underlying clause by a syntactic process or series of rules so that it functions like a noun —**nominalization** /nómminə lī záysh'n/ *n*

nominal quote *n* an approximate price given for a security when there is no firm bid or asking price

nominal value *n* FIN = **par value**

nominal wages *npl* = **money wages**

nominate /nómmi nayt/ (**-nates, -nating, -nated**) *vt* **1** PROPOSE to suggest somebody for appointment or election to a position or for an honour or award **2** APPOINT to appoint somebody to a position, or make somebody responsible for a duty **3** ENTER HORSE FOR RACE to enter a horse in a race [Mid-16C. < Latin *nominat-*, past participle of *nominare* 'to name' < *nomin-* 'name'.] —**nominator** *n*

nomination /nómmi náysh'n/ *n* **1** PROPOSAL a suggestion of somebody for appointment or election to a position or for receiving an honour or award **2** SOMEBODY OR SOMETHING PROPOSED somebody or something suggested for appointment or election to a position or for receiving an honour or award **3** APPOINTMENT the appointment of somebody to a position, or assignment of somebody to a duty

nominative /nómminətiv/ *n* **1** GRAMMATICAL FORM the grammatical case in some languages of a noun functioning as a subject of a sentence or clause, and of some other words agreeing with the noun **2** INSTANCE OF NOMINATIVE a word or phrase in the nominative ■ *adj* **1** OF NOMINATIVE relating to the nominative **2** APPOINTED TO OR PROPOSED FOR OFFICE appointed or suggested for election to an office or position **3** WITH OWNER'S NAME having the name of the owner specified on it [14C. Directly or via French *nominatif* < Latin *nominativus (casus)* 'nominative (case)' < *nominat-* (see NOMINATE).]

nominee /nómmi née/ *n* **1** a person who has been proposed for a position, honour, or office **2** a person or group that holds title to a security or property but is not actually the holder or owner [Mid-17C. < NOMINATE.]

nomograph /nómmə graaf, nṓmə-, -graf/, **nomogram** /-gram/ *n* **1** a graph with three lines graduated so a straight line intersecting any two of the lines at their known values intersects the third at the value of the related variable **2** any graph that represents numerical relationships [Mid-18C. < Greek *nomos* 'law, custom'.] —**nomographic** /nómmə gráffik, nṓmə-/ *adj* —**nomography** /no móggrəfi, nō-/ *n*

nomothetic /nómmə théttik, nṓmə-/, **nomothetical** /-théttik'l/ *adj* **1** relating to the enactment of laws **2** relating to the discovery of universal laws, e.g. those principles that explain how some aspects of personality affect behaviour. ◊ **idiographic** [Early 17C. < Greek *nomothetikos* < *nomothetēs* 'lawgiver' < *nomos* 'law'.] —**nomothetically** *adv*

-nomy *suffix* system of rules, laws, or knowledge about a particular field ○ *gastronomy* [< Greek *-nomia* < *nomos* 'law, custom'] —**-nomic** *suffix* —**-nomical** *suffix* —**-nomically** *suffix*

non-[1] *prefix* not, without, the opposite of ○ *nonconducting* ○ *nondiscrimination* [Via Old French < Latin *non* < Indo-European]

non-[2] *prefix* = **nona-** (*before vowels*)

non-A, non-B hepatitis *n* an acute chronic viral disease of the liver, similar to hepatitis B but caused by neither the hepatitis A nor the hepatitis B virus

nona- *prefix* nine ○ *nonagon* [< Latin *nonus* 'ninth' < Indo-European, 'nine']

nonacademic /nón ákə démmik/ *adj* **1** NOT TEACHING working at a university or college but not involved in teaching or research **2** NOT STUDIOUS lacking an aptitude for studying **3** VOCATIONAL practical or vocational in content

nonaccelerating /nón ək séllə rayting/ *adj* having the property of remaining at rest unless acted on by a directional force

nonacceptance /nónnək séptənss/ *n* the act of refusing or rejecting something such as the terms of a contract

nonaccidental /nón aksi dént'l/ *adj* not occurring accidentally ○ *nonaccidental injuries*

nonacid /non ássid/ *adj* not containing or having the properties of an acid

nonacidic /nón ə síddik/ *adj* not forming an acid in water

nonaddictive /nón ə díktiv/ *adj* not causing addiction in the user

nonadjacent /nón ə jáyss'nt/ *adj* **1** not adjoining or next to one another ○ *nonadjacent houses* **2** not having common edges or a common vertex ○ *nonadjacent vertices*

nonaerial /non áiri əl/ *adj* not relating to, consisting of, living in, or moving through the air

nonaerobic /nón air rṓbik/ *adj* not increasing respiration and heart rates or otherwise relating to aerobics

nonage /nṓnij, nón-/ *n* **1** the status of being under the requisite age for some legal entitlement (*formal*) **2** any time of immaturity [14C. < Anglo-Norman *nounage*, variant of Old French *nonage* 'not (the full) age' < *age* (see AGE).]

nonagenarian /nṓnəjə náiri ən, nón-/ *n* somebody 90 years of age or between 90 and 100 years old ■ *adj* 90 years of age or between 90 and 100 years old [Early 19C. < Latin *nonagenarius* 'consisting of ninety' < *nonaginta* 'ninety' < *nonus* 'ninth'.]

nonaggression /nónnə grésh'n/ *n* a policy of not attacking other countries ○ *The two countries have signed a nonaggression pact.*

nonaggressive /nón ə gréssiv/ *adj* showing or feeling no aggression or aggressiveness

nonagon /nónnə gon, nṓn-/ *n* a plane geometric figure with nine angles and sides —**nonagonal** /no nággən'l, nō-/ *adj*

nonalcoholic /nón álkə hóllik/ *adj* containing no alcohol, or an extremely low amount of alcohol

nonaligned /nónnə línd/ *adj* not allied with any major world power —**nonalignment** *n*

nonalphabetical /nón alfə béttik'l/ *adj* **1** not arranged in the customary order of the letters of the alphabet ○ *a nonalphabetical list* **2** not based on or using an alphabet ○ *The password must contain at least one nonalphabetical character.*

nonanalytic /nón annə líttik/, **nonanalytical** /-líttik'l/ *adj* **1** NOT ANALYTIC not relating to, involving, or using analysis **2** NOT TRUE BY MEANING ALONE not true by definition or by virtue of the meaning of the words used ○ *a nonanalytic statement* **3** NOT DIFFERENTIABLE AT ALL POINTS describes a function of a complex variable that is not differentiable at all points in its domain

nonanoic acid /nónnə nṓ ik-/ *n* $CH_3(CH_2)_7COOH$ a colourless to yellow oil. Source: beets, potatoes. Use: in plastics, pharmaceuticals, synthetic flavours, additive in petrol. US term **pelargonic acid** [< *nonane* 'straight chain hydrocarbon containing nine carbon atoms',]

nonappearance /nónnə péeranss/ *n* failure to appear or attend, especially the failure of an accused person or witness to turn up for a court appearance

nonaquatic /nónnə kwáttik/ *adj* **1** not living or growing in water **2** NOT RELATING TO WATER not relating to, consisting of, or dependent upon water **3** NOT LIVING IN WATER not living or growing in water ○ *nonaquatic species* **4** NOT DONE IN WATER not played or performed in or on water ○ *nonaquatic games*

nonarable /non árrəb'l/ *adj* not suitable for or used in the cultivation of crops ○ *nonarable land*

nonaromatic /nón arrə máttik/ *adj* not relating to or belonging to the class of organic chemical compounds that contain one or more rings of carbon atoms and undergo chemical reactions that are characteristic of benzene

nonarrival /nón ə rív'l/ *n* a failure to arrive or be delivered —**nonarriver** *n*

nonassessable /nónnə séssəb'l/ *adj* impossible to estimate or determine ○ *nonassessable losses*

nonastronaut /non ástrə nawt/ *n* a person such as a scientist who is a passenger on a spacecraft rather than a member of the flight crew

nonattendance /nón ə téndənss/ *n* failure to go to or be present at a place or event ○ *Although they say the meeting is voluntary, nonattendance will certainly be counted against you.* —**nonattender** /nón ə téndər/ *n*

nonattributable /nón ə tríbbyootəb'l/ *adj* being such that a cause, source, or explanation cannot be assigned to it —**nonattributably** *adv*

nonbank /nón bángk/ *n* a financial enterprise that is not a bank but performs a number of the functions of a bank —**nonbanking** *adj*

nonbaryonic /nón bari ónnik/ *adj* not relating to or belonging to the group of subatomic particles that have a mass greater than or equal to that of a proton

nonbeing /non bée ing/ *n* the state of not existing or not being alive

nonbelief /nón bi léef/ *n* an absence of belief in something, especially a religion

nonbeliever /nónbi léevər/ *n* a person who has no religious beliefs —**nonbelieving** *adj*

nonbelligerent /nón bə líjjərənt/ *adj* **1 NOT HOSTILE OR AGGRESSIVE** not hostile, ready to start a fight, or ready to go to war **2 NOT ENGAGED IN WARFARE** not taking part in warfare, especially in a war recognized by the law of nations ■ *n* **NONBELLIGERENT PERSON OR NATION** a person or country that is not a participant in a war or fight, especially a war recognized by the law of nations —**nonbelligerency** /nónbə líjjərənssi/ *n* —**nonbelligerent** *n* —**nonbelligerently** *adv*

nonbiting /non bíting/ *adj* describes an insect that does not have the habit of biting or sucking the blood of other organisms ○ *nonbiting gnats*

non-black, non-Black *adj* relating to a person or to people with light skin tones, ultimately of European ancestry ■ *n* a light-skinned person whose ancestry can be traced ultimately to Europe

nonbook /nón bòok/ *adj* kept in a permanent form other than as books, e.g. as video tapes ○ *the library's nonbook holdings*

nonbreaking /nón bráyking/ *adj* designed so as not to break ○ *a nonbreaking windscreen*

nonbreeding /nón bréeding/ *adj* not kept for breeding purposes

nonbroadcast /non bráwd kaast/, **nonbroadcasting** /-kaasting/ *adj* not relating to, suitable for, or transmitted by radio or television ○ *nonbroadcast media*

nonbusiness /nón bíznəss/ *adj* personal and not relating to business ○ *details of nonbusiness expenditure*

noncancerous /non kánssərəss/ *adj* not affected or caused by cancer or a malignant tumour

noncanonical /nón kə nónnik'l/ *adj* **1 NOT INCLUDED IN A CANON** not included in the biblical canon or that of other religions, or a canon of artistic works accepted as genuine and complete **2 NOT CONFORMING TO CANON LAW** not authorized by or conforming to canon law **3 NOT CONFORMING TO GENERAL PRINCIPLES** not conforming to accepted principles or standard practice

noncarbon /non kaárbən/ *adj* not containing or relating to the chemical element carbon ○ *noncarbon atoms*

noncarbonate /non kaárbə nayt, -nət/ *n* a sedimentary rock of a relatively rare type that does not contain carbonate minerals

nonce[1] /nonss/ *n* the present time (*archaic*) [12C. < misdivision of *for then anes* 'for the one (occasion)'.] ◇ **for the nonce 1** for the present occasion **2** for the time being

nonce[2] /nonss/ *n* a committer of a sexual offence against a child (*slang insult*) [Late 20C. < ?]

noncellular /non séllyoolər/ *adj* not consisting of, involving, or organized into cells

nonce word *n* a word that is coined for a single occasion

nonchalant /nónshələnt/ *adj* calm and unconcerned about things [Mid-18C. < French, 'not being concerned' < *chalant*, present participle of *chaloir* 'be concerned' < Latin *calere* 'be hot or roused'.] —**nonchalance** *n* —**nonchalantly** *adv*

nonchemical /non kémmik'l/ *adj* not composed of or involving chemicals

noncitizen /non síttiz'n/ *n* a person who does not have the rights and responsibilities of citizenship of a particular country although he or she may be permitted to live there

noncitrus /non síttrəss/ *adj* belonging to or produced by trees or fruit other than those classified as citrus

nonclassical /non klássik'l/ *adj* not classical in form, content, or function ○ *nonclassical civilizations* ○ *nonclassical music*

nonclimbing /non klíming/ *adj* describes plants that form bushes or grow along the ground

noncling /nón klíng/ *adj* made of a material that prevents the garment clinging to the wearer's body

nonclinical /nón klínnik'l/ *adj* not relating to or involved in the medical care of patients

noncoding /non kóding/ *adj* describes a segment of DNA that does not transcribe genetic information to messenger RNA

noncollegiate /nónkə léeji ət/ *adj* **1** describes a university that does not consist of colleges **2** not associated with or belonging to a particular college within a university

noncom /nón kom/ *n* a noncommissioned officer (*informal*) [Late 19C. Shortening.]

noncombat /non kóm bat/ *adj* not actively involved in the fighting during a war ○ *noncombat personnel such as army chaplains and medical staff*

noncombatant /non kómbətənt/ *n* **1** person who is not in the armed forces during a war **2** a chaplain, medical officer, or other member of the armed forces who does not take part in battle

noncombustible /nón kəm bústəb'l/ *adj* not able or likely to catch fire ■ *n* a substance or material that is not likely to catch fire or burn

noncommercial /nón kə múrsh'l/ *adj* not run or produced with the intention of making a profit

noncommissioned officer /nónkə mísh'nd-/ *n* a subordinate officer in any of the armed forces, e.g. a sergeant or corporal, who, instead of being given a commission, has been appointed from the lower ranks

noncommittal /nónkə mítt'l/ *adj* not making clear any personal opinions or feelings about something —**noncommittally** *adv*

non-Communist /non kómmyoonist/ *adj* not having the beliefs or characteristics associated with Communism ○ *non-Communist countries* ■ *n* somebody who does not have Communist beliefs or membership of a Communist political party

noncompetitive /nónkəm péttətiv/ *adj* **1 WITHOUT BUSINESS RIVALRY** not characterized by competition between rival businesses or organizations **2 UNABLE TO COMPETE COMMERCIALLY** unable to compete commercially against rival businesses or organizations **3 NEITHER CHEAP NOR GOOD ENOUGH** neither low enough in price nor high enough in quality to compete in the marketplace **4 UNAMBITIOUS** not having the type of personality that makes somebody want to compete against and beat other people **5 NOT INVOLVING COMPETING SPORTSPEOPLE** not involving competition between athletes, players, or teams

noncompliance /nónkəm plí ənss/ *n* a refusal or failure to obey a law, rule, contractual agreement, or a doctor's order for medicine-taking —**noncompliant** *adj*

noncomplying /nón kəm plí ing/ *adj* not conforming to or obeying a rule, law, wish, request, prescription, or regulation

non compos mentis /nón kómpəss méntiss/ *adj* in law, not mentally competent to understand what is happening and to make important decisions [< Latin, 'not having control of (your) mind']

noncompulsory /nónkəm púlssəri/ *adj* not required by law or an authority

nonconcentric /nón kən séntrik/ *adj* describes circles and spheres of different sizes that do not have the same middle point

noncondensing /nón kən dénssing/ *adj* **1** not changing from a vapour into a liquid, or not employing such a change ○ *a noncondensing engine* **2** not bonding together to form a larger denser molecule

nonconductive /nón kən dúktiv/ *adj* **1** not able to transmit energy, especially heat or electricity ○ *nonconductive surfaces* **2** not belonging to the class of cells that allow nerve impulses to pass through them

nonconductor /nónkən dúktər/ *n* a substance that does not conduct heat, electricity, or sound —**nonconducting** *adj*

nonconforming /nón kən fáwrming/ *adj* failing or refusing to conform to an accepted set of rules or behavioural patterns, or to an established religion or ideology

nonconformist /nónkən fáwrmist/ *adj* **UNCONVENTIONAL** not conforming to an established pattern of behaviour ■ *n* **1 UNCONVENTIONAL PERSON** a person who does not conform to an accepted pattern of behaviour **2 nonconformist, Nonconformist MEMBER OF DISSENTING PROTESTANT CHURCH** a member of a Protestant church not adhering to the doctrines or usage of a national or established church —**nonconformism** *n*

nonconformity /nónkən fáwrməti/ *n* **1** the practice of not conforming to an established pattern of behaviour **2** the state of being in disagreement with something

nonconsecutive /nón kən sékyootiv/ *adj* **1** not following one another without interruption or break ○ *You are allowed three nonconsecutive weeks off.* **2** not following a logical or chronological sequence

noncontagious /nón kən táyjəss/ *adj* not capable of being transmitted by direct or indirect contact from one person to another or from one member of a species to another member of the same species

noncontiguous /nón kən tíggyoo əss/ *adj* **1** not next to one another or something else or not sharing a common boundary **2** not forming an unbroken sequence or an uninterrupted expanse

noncontributory /nónkən tríbbyootəri/ *adj* **1** describes a health insurance or pension scheme that does not require contributions from an employee or member **2** not contributing to a health insurance or pension scheme

nonconventional /nón kən vénsh'nəl/ *adj* not conforming to established customs or using well-established methods

nonconvertible /nón, kən vúrtəb'l/ incapable of being changed from one form, function, or use to another

noncooperation /nónkō óppə ráysh'n/ *n* **1** refusal or failure to cooperate **2** the practice of refusing to pay taxes or otherwise obey government decrees, as a means of protest —**noncooperative** /nónkō óppərətiv/ *adj*

noncorporate /non káwrpərət/ *adj* **1** not relating to, belonging to, or typical of a corporation **2** not relating to or involving a group as a whole (*formal*)

noncount noun /nón kownt-/ *n* a noun that refers to a mass of something or a quality rather than one thing and that cannot usually be used with 'a' or 'an', with a number, or in the plural. Examples of English noncount nouns are 'milk', 'freight', and 'unhappiness'. ◊ **mass noun**

noncriminal /non krímmin'l/ *adj* **1** not specified or punishable as a crime under the law ○ *noncriminal offences* **2** not relating to crime or criminals ○ *noncriminal law*

noncrystalline /non krístə l-n/ *adj* having a homogeneous structure that is not made up of crystals

noncumulative /non kyoomyoolətiv/ *adj* not cumulative in form, content, or function

noncustodial /nón ku stódi əl/ *adj* not involving imprisonment or detention in custody

nondairy /nón dáiri/ *adj* describes ingredients or foods that contain no dairy products and can be substituted for them, e.g. some kinds of margarine

nondeductible /nóndi dúktəb'l/ *adj* not allowed to be deducted, especially as an allowance against income taxes

nondegradable /nóndi gráydəb'l/ *adj* not subject to decomposition by biological or chemical means

nondegree /nón di grée/ *adj* not relating to or leading to a higher education qualification classed as a degree ○ *nondegree courses*

nondelivery /nón di lívvəri/ *n* a failure to deliver something

nondemocratic /nón demə kráttik/ *adj* not following a democratic system of government or a democratic procedure for making decisions —**nondemocratically** *adv*

nondenominational /nóndi nómmi náysh'nəl/ *adj* not associated with or restricted to a particular religious denomination

nondescript /nóndiskript/ *adj* with no interesting or remarkable characteristics ■ *n* somebody with no interesting or remarkable characteristics [Late 17C. < NON- + Latin *descriptus*, past participle of *describere* (see DESCRIBE).]

nondestructive /nón di strúktiv/ *adj* not causing or capable of causing destruction

nondestructive testing /nóndi strúktiv-/ *n* any technique used to test for flaws in materials, components, and joints without causing damage or destruction

⚡**nondigital** /non díjjit'l/ *adj* **1 NOT INVOLVING COMPUTERS OR INTERNET** not relating to or using the Internet, computers, or other digital technology ○ *advertising in the nondigital world* **2 NOT REPRESENTING DATA BY NUMBERS** not processing, operating on, storing, transmitting, representing, or displaying data in the form of numerical digits **3 NOT REPRESENTING SOUND WAVES AS NUMBERS** not representing a varying physical quantity, such as sound or light waves, by means of discrete signals interpreted as numbers

nondirective /nóndə réktiv, -dt́-/ adj describes a form of psychotherapy or counselling in which the patient is encouraged to speak freely with minimal input from the therapist

nondisclosure agreement /nón diss kló̄zhər-/ n 1 an agreement, often required of new or departing employees, not to disclose any confidential or secret information relating to their new or previous employer 2 a contract that prohibits the signor from sharing information about a specified project or other matter except under specified terms

nondiscretionary /nóndi skrésh'nəri/ adj subject to specific rules and not giving the freedom to make a decision according to individual circumstances

nondiscrimination /nóndi skrímmi náysh'n/ n 1 the practice of treating different people or groups fairly, equally, and without prejudice 2 the absence of discrimination —**nondiscriminatory** /nóndi skrímminətəri/ adj

nondisjunction /nóndiss júngksh'n/ n a failure of paired chromosomes or sister chromatids to separate during cell division —**nondisjunctional** adj —**nondisjunctionally** adv

nondisposable /nón di spó̄zəb'l/ adj 1 not designed to be thrown away after use 2 not available to be used as money or an asset

nondistinctive /nóndi stíngktiv/ adj describes features of speech sounds that do not distinguish meanings

non dit /nón deè/ n US a taboo subject or fact that remains unspoken or is not discussed ○ *His absence was a non dit.* [Late 20C. < French le non-dit 'what is left unsaid'.]

nondomestic /nón də méstik/ adj 1 not relating to the home, the family, or a country or its internal affairs ○ *nondomestic politics* 2 not kept as a farm animal or a pet ○ *nondomestic animals*

nondramatic /nón drə máttik/ adj not written or suitable for performance in the theatre

nondrinker /nón dríngkər/ n a person who does not drink alcoholic beverages —**nondrinking** adj

nondrip /nón dríp/ adj not likely to drip while being applied

nondual /non dyoò əl/ adj not having two different parts, functions, elements, or aspects

nondualism /non dyoò əlizəm/ adj a Vedantic doctrine that denies that the relationship between the individual self and ultimate reality is dualistic

nonduality /nón dyoo álləti/ n the state or quality of not consisting of two opposed or complementary parts

none /nun/ pron 1 not one person ○ *Wealth that is free for all is valued by none.* ○ *None of us wanted the situation to continue.* 2 not any of something, or any part of something ○ *None of it seemed to matter any more.* ○ *We wrote last week demanding some answers, but so far have received none.* [Old English nān 'not one' < ne 'not' + ān, form of ONE] ◇ **have none of something** to refuse to tolerate something (informal) ○ *We asked him to explain himself, but he would have none of it.* ◇ **none the** in no degree (in front of comparative adjectives) ○ *I'm still none the wiser.* ◇ **none too** not very

---

USAGE none Does the pronoun have a singular or plural verb? When ***none*** refers to a singular uncountable noun, a singular verb is the only choice: *We were desperate for information, but none was available.* When ***none*** refers, as it often does, to a plural noun (none of the buses, none of my friends) or to a singular countable noun, it can take either a singular or a plural verb, depending on what exactly is meant. The traditional view is that since ***none*** means 'not one', and one takes a singular verb, none should take a singular verb. If you write *None of my friends was able to come* or *I'd have liked a sandwich, but none was left*, you mean 'Not one of my friends was able to come; I'd have liked a sandwich, but not a single one was left'. But none can also mean 'not any', indicating a countable number of persons, animals, or things, and thus requiring a plural verb. In contexts like these, use of the plural also allows the writer to avoid gender tagging, that is, use of his or her in sentences such as this one: *None of the class have handed their work in yet.*

USAGE See ***neither***. See ***one***.

noneconomic /nón ekə nómmik, -eekə-/ adj 1 not relating to economics or the economy 2 not making or capable of making a profit

nonedible /non éddib'l/ adj not able to be eaten by human beings, or unfit or unsuitable for eating

noneffective adj 1 having, exhibiting, or promising no effectiveness or usefulness 2 unfit or unsuitable for military service —**noneffectiveness** n

nonelect /nón i lékt/ adj not chosen or favoured by God, especially not chosen for salvation ■ npl those not chosen or favoured by God, especially those not chosen for salvation

nonelected /nón i léktid/ adj holding a position or office without having been elected to it

nonelective /nón i léktiv/ adj 1 NOT RELATING TO VOTING not involving or concerned with voting 2 NOT REQUIRING ELECTION not chosen by a vote, or whose holder is not chosen by a vote ○ *a nonelective assembly* ○ *held a nonelective office* 3 COMPULSORY essential or compulsory ○ *a nonelective Caesarean Section* ■ n COMPULSORY COURSE a required academic course ○ *nonelectives such as history and maths*

nonelectric /nón i léktrik/ adj 1 not powered by electricity 2 unable to sustain an electric field

nonelectrolyte /nón i léktrə līt/ n a substance that does not ionize readily in solution or in the molten state and is therefore a bad conductor of electricity

nonentity /no néntəti/ n (plural -ties) 1 INSIGNIFICANT PERSON an unimportant, powerless, or insignificant person 2 SOMETHING NONEXISTENT something that does not exist in reality 3 NOT EXISTING the condition of being nonexistent

nonenzyme /non énzīm/ n a substance that is not an enzyme or does not contain an enzyme

nonequilibrium /nón eekwi líbbri əm, -ekwi-/ n the state or condition of imbalance between different forces or processes

nonequivalence /nón i kwívvələnss/ n 1 the state of not being equal or equivalent 2 a situation in which two propositions can have different truth values —**nonequivalent** adj

nones /nōnz/ n (+ singular or plural verb) 1 the ninth day before the ides of each month in the ancient Roman calendar 2 the fifth canonical hour of prayer, originally held at the ninth hour after sunrise [15C. '9th day' via French < Latin nonas, plural of nonus 'ninth'. 'Prayer hour' plural of none < Latin nona, feminine of nonus.]

nonessential /nón i sénsh'l/ adj 1 not absolutely necessary 2 manufactured by the body and therefore not essential in the diet —**nonessential** n —**nonessentially** adv

nonestablished /nón i stáblisht/ adj not granted legal recognition or financial support as an official national institution ○ *the nonestablished churches*

nonet /no nét/ n 1 a piece of music composed for nine voices or instruments 2 a group of nine singers or instrumentalists [Mid-19C. < Italian nonetto 'small ninth' < nono 'ninth' < Latin nonus.]

nonetheless /núnthə léss/ adv = nevertheless

non-Euclidean adj describes or relating to any branch of geometry not based on the postulates of Euclid

non-European n a person who is not of European descent ■ not being of European descent or not originally from Europe

nonevent /nón i vént/ n an occasion that is disappointingly unexciting

nonexchangeable /nón iks cháynjəb'l/ adj not able to be exchanged for another or something else

nonexclusive /nónnik skloössiv/ adj not exclusive, limited, or restricted

nonexecutive director /nón ig zékyoötiv-/ n a director of a business organization who is not a full member of staff but whose duty is to advise the other directors

nonexempt /nón ig zémpt/ adj subject to something such as a duty, tax, or military service that others do not have to do or pay

nonexistent /nón ig zístənt/ adj not in existence —**nonexistence** n

nonexpansion /nón ik spánsh'n/ n the state or condition of not expanding or increasing in size, volume, extent, or scope

nonexperimental /nón ik spérri mént'l/ adj 1 relating to or employing only old or tried methods, materials, or ideas ○ *nonexperimental drama* 2 not relating to, involved

in, or based on scientific experiment ○ *nonexperimental psychology*

nonexpert /non éks purt/ n somebody who has no specialist skill, knowledge, or training in a particular field or activity —**nonexpert** adj

nonexplosive /nón ik splóssiv/ adj incapable of exploding, or unlikely to explode

nonexposure /non ik spó̄zhər/ n the condition or fact of not being exposed to or by somebody or something

nonfading /non fáyding/ adj not likely to lose brightness or colour

nonfat /nón fát/ adj without fat solids, or with the fat content removed

nonfatal /non fáyt'l/ adj not causing or leading to death ○ *nonfatal injuries* —**nonfatally** adv

nonfeasance /nón feè'nss/ n failure to do something that is legally obligatory. ◊ **malfeasance** n. 1, **misfeasance** [Early 17C. < obsolete feasance 'doing' < Anglo-Norman fesa(u)nce, French faisance < fais-, present stem of faire 'to do' < Latin facere.]

nonfederal /non féddərəl/ adj not relating to or having a federal form of government

nonferrous /nón férrəss/ adj 1 not composed of or containing iron 2 being a metal other than iron

nonfiction /non fíksh'n/ n prose literature that consists of factual information rather than works of the imagination ○ *her first nonfiction work* —**nonfictional** adj

nonfighting /non fíting/ adj not actively engaged in combat

nonfigurative /nón fíggərətiv/ adj 1 LITERAT = literal adj. 2 ARTS = nonrepresentational

nonflammable /nón flámmab'l/ adj difficult to burn or ignite

nonflowering /non flówəring/ adj describes plants such as mosses, liverworts, ferns, and conifers that never produce flowers

nonfood /non foòd/ adj describes something that is sold in a supermarket that is not for eating or drinking

nonformal /non fáwrm'l/ adj not formal in nature or character —**nonformally** adv

nonfraying /non fráying/ adj not likely to wear away through friction and in threads

nonfreehold /non freè hōld/ adj not having the legal status of freehold property

nonfuel /non fyoò əl/ n a naturally occurring mineral, such as gypsum or potash, that is not a fuel but usually has economic importance

nonfulfilment /nón foòl fílmənt/ n failure to carry out a duty or obligation

nonfunctional /non fúngksh'nəl/ adj 1 not having any specific purpose ○ *The knob at the top is nonfunctional but it looks nice.* 2 not currently in working order ○ *Half the checkouts are nonfunctional this afternoon.*

nonfunctioning /non fúngksh'ning/ adj not operating or in good working order

nongloss /non glóss/ adj having or providing a matt appearance, surface, or texture

nonglossy /non glóssi/ adj not having a shiny and smooth surface or texture

nongonococcal urethritis /nón gonō kók'l-/ n US MED = nonspecific urethritis

nongovernmental /nón gúvv'rn mént'l/ adj not run by or associated with a government ○ *nongovernmental organizations*

nongraded /nón gráydid/ adj not sorted into different sizes ○ *nongraded rocks*

nongranular /non gránnyoòlər/ adj not consisting of or having the texture of small grains or particles

nongraphic /non gráffik/ adj not relating to or consisting of writing, pictures, graphs, graphics, or the graphic arts

nongrasping /non gráasping/ adj not able or not designed to grip something

non grata /nón graàtə/ adj not welcome [< PERSONA NON GRATA]

nongreen /non greèn/ adj describes a plant, alga, or other organism that does not have green photosynthetic pigment

nonhazardous /non házzərdəss/ adj not potentially dangerous to human beings or the environment

nonhereditary /nón hə rédditəri/ adj 1 not passed down or capable of being passed down genetically from one generation to the next ○ *nonhereditary diseases* 2 not handed or handing down, or not legally capable of handing or being handed down through generations by inheritance ○ *nonhereditary peerages*

non-Hodgkin's lymphoma n a cancer of the lymph nodes that is distinguished from Hodgkin's disease by the absence of a particular type of cell with double nuclei

nonhomogeneous /nón hōmə jeéni əss, -homə-/, **nonhomogenous** /nón hə mójjənəss/ adj 1 not having the same kind of constituent elements, or being dissimilar in nature 2 having a composition or structure that is not uniform

nonhuman /non hyóomən/ adj relating to a thing or being that does not belong to the human race

nonhydrogen /non hídrəjən/ adj not containing the chemical element hydrogen

nonidentical /nón ī déntik'l/ adj 1 not the same 2 BIOL = fraternal adj. 4

nonideologue /non ídi ə log/ n somebody who is not intellectually dogmatic or polemical or not a particularly zealous or doctrinaire supporter of an ideology

nonillion /nō níllyən/ n the number equal to 10⁵⁴, written as 1 followed by 54 zeros [Late 17C. < French, < Latin *nonus* 'ninth' + *-illion* as in MILLION.] —**nonillionth** adj, n

nonimage /non ímmij/ adj blank and outside the area containing an image that is to be printed ○ *the nonimage area of the printing surface*

nonimitative /non ímmitətiv/ adj not involving or practising imitation ○ *nonimitative behaviours*

nonimmigrant /non ímmigrənt/ n 1 a person who enters a country for a temporary stay 2 a person who returns to his or her own country after some time spent in another country

nonimpact /non ímpakt/ adj 1 not having been caused or created by the force of collision ○ *nonimpact rocks* 2 using a printing method that does not press the ink onto the paper but uses the technology of laser or ink-jet printers ○ *a nonimpact printer*

nonimportation /nón im pawr táysh'n/ n the condition or fact of not importing goods or services from another country, or of not being imported ○ *nonimportation laws*

noninclusion /nón in klōózh'n/ n failure to include somebody or something, or to be included

nonindependent /nón indi péndənt/ adj not having independence

nonindigenous /nón in díjinəss/ adj not originating in or typical of a region or country ○ *Nonindigenous species have been successfully introduced.*

nonindustrial /nón in dústri əl/ adj 1 not having a large number of highly developed industries ○ *nonindustrial nations* 2 not relating to, used by, or created by industry ○ *nonindustrial injuries*

nonindustrialized /nón in dústri ə līzd/, **nonindustrialised** adj 1 not having developed or not dominated by large-scale industry 2 not using or having been adapted to industrial methods of production and manufacturing

⚡**noninfected** /nón in féktid/ adj 1 not infected with a disease ○ *noninfected crops* 2 not infected with a computer virus

noninfectious /nón in fékshəss/ adj not capable either of communicating or being used to communicate illness to another person or part of the body

noninflammable /nónin flámməb'l/ adj CHEM = **nonflammable**

noninflammatory /nón in flámmətəri/ adj not caused or characterized by inflammation

noninheritable /nón in hérritəb'l/ adj 1 not able to be passed down genetically from parent to offspring ○ *noninheritable qualities* 2 not able to be passed on to an heir by the laws of inheritance

noninjury /nón ínjəri/ n RELIG = **ahimsa**

non-insulin-dependent diabetes n a type of diabetes mellitus that does not require insulin for its treatment

noninterference /nón intər feérənss/ n the practice or policy of not interfering or intervening in political or other matters —**noninterfering** adj

nonintervention /nón intər vénsh'n/ n the policy and practice of a nation's abstaining from involvement in the affairs of another state or population group —**noninterventionism** n —**noninterventionist** n, adj

noninvasive /nón in váyssiv/ adj 1 not involving cutting into the body or entry into a body cavity, e.g. the colon or stomach 2 not spreading or likely to spread to other parts of the body

noninvolvement /nón in vólvmənt/ n the practice of not participating in something or not being associated with something

nonionizing /non í ə nīzing/ adj not undergoing or causing something to undergo ionization

noniron /non í ərn/ adj not needing to be ironed

nonirrigated /non írri gaytid/ adj not provided with a supply of water to compensate for natural dryness, especially in cultivating crops

nonirritant /non írritənt/ adj not causing irritation

nonissue /non íssyoo, -íshyoo/ n something that is so unimportant that it is not worth considering or discussing

nonjoinder /non jóyndər/ n failure to include a party in a lawsuit who should have been included

nonjudgmental /nón juj mént'l/, **nonjudgemental** adj not making or involving moral judgments —**nonjudgmentally** adv

nonjuror /non jóorər/ n somebody who refuses to take an oath, especially a member of the Church of England clergy who refused to take an oath of allegiance to William and Mary in 1689 —**nonjuring** adj

nonjury /nón jóori/ adj describes a trial where the verdict is not the responsibility of a jury but of a judge

nonlegal /non leég'l/ adj 1 not relating to the law, courts of law, or lawyers 2 not established under the law, or by common law or legislation —**nonlegally** adv

SYNONYMS See *unlawful.*

nonlethal /non leéth'l/ adj not causing or able to cause death ○ *nonlethal weapons*

nonlife /non líf/ n the world of nonliving things, composed of inorganic matter and dead organisms

nonlinear /non línni ər/ adj 1 NOT IN A LINE not lying on the same straight line 2 NOT PREDICTABLE FROM PAST varying markedly as a result of individual factors or circumstances and so difficult to anticipate or likely to depart from previous patterns 3 NOT IN DIRECT PROPORTION describes a relationship or function that is not strictly proportional

nonlinguistic /nón ling gwístik/ adj not relating to language or linguistics ○ *nonlinguistic communication*

nonliteral /non líttərəl/ adj not adhering strictly to the meaning or form of an original word or text, but subjecting it to interpretation, alteration, or elaboration —**nonliterally** adv

nonliterate /non líttərət/ adj 1 not having the ability to read and write 2 not having a written language

nonliturgical /nón li túrjik'l/ adj not forming part of a liturgy or relating to formal religious worship ○ *nonliturgical prayers*

nonliving /non lívving/ adj dead, inanimate, or no longer used or existing

non-loadbearing /non lōd bairing/ adj not supporting the gravitational force exerted on a structure or part of one ○ *a non-loadbearing wall*

nonlocal /non lōk'l/ adj relating to or typical of a widespread or general area as opposed to a specific one —**nonlocally** adv

nonluminous /nón lōóminəss/ adj emitting or reflecting no light

nonmagnetic /nón mag néttik/ adj not able to attract iron or steel objects or be attracted by a magnet

nonmainstream /non máyn streem/ adj not reflecting the most widely accepted views or tastes of a culture or society ○ *nonmainstream broadcasting*

nonmalignant /nón mə lígnənt/ adj describes a tumour that does not invade surrounding tissue and spread to other parts of the body

nonmammalian /nón mə máyli ən/ adj not belonging to the class of warm-blooded vertebrates in which the female has milk-secreting organs for feeding the young

nonmanagement /non mánnijmənt/ n the employees or sections of an organization or business who are not involved in its management —**nonmanagement** adj

nonmanipulative /non mə níppyōōlətiv/ adj not relating to or involved in manipulation

nonmanual /non mánnyoo əl/ adj not involving physical effort, or not doing work that requires physical effort

nonmanufacturing /nón manyōō fákchəring/ adj not relating to or involved in the large-scale industrial manufacture of finished goods from raw materials ○ *nonmanufacturing industries*

nonmarketable /non maárkitəb'l/ adj 1 NOT ABLE TO BE MARKETED not suitable for sale or easy to sell ○ *nonmarketable goods* 2 NOT CONVERTIBLE INTO CASH not able to be quickly converted into cash ○ *nonmarketable securities* 3 NOT CAPABLE OF ACCEPTANCE incapable of winning wide acceptance ○ *a nonmarketable tax*

nonmatching /non máching/ adj not similar or identical to something else, or not belonging to a set of matching things

nonmaterial /nón mə teéri əl/ adj not relating to physical matter or to material comforts

nonmathematical /nón mathə máttik'l/ adj 1 not relating to mathematics 2 not skilled at mathematics

nonmedia /non meédi ə/ adj not relating to or forming part of the electronic or print media or other means of mass communication ○ *nonmedia sources*

nonmedical /non méddik'l/ adj not involving or used in medicine or medical treatment

nonmedicinal /nón mə díss'nəl/ adj not used to treat illnesses, or not having properties capable of treating illness

nonmember /non mémbər/ n a person, group, or nation that does not belong to a particular organization

nonmetal /nón méttl'/ n a chemical element that does not have the chemical and physical properties of a metal, e.g. carbon or oxygen

nonmetallic /nón mə tállik/ adj not made of, containing, or constituting metal or a metal

nonmetalliferous /nón metə lífferəss/ adj not containing or yielding metal

nonmetric /non méttrik/ adj not relating to or using the metric system of measurement

nonmetropolitan /nón mettrə póllitən/ adj not relating to, constituting, or typical of a large urban area

nonmigratory /non mígrətəri, nón mī gráytəri/, **nonmigrating** /non mī gráyting/ adj not moving from one habitat to another in order to breed or in response to seasonal changes and variations in food supply

nonmilitary /non míllitəri/ adj not concerned with, involving, intended for, or being a member of the armed forces

nonmonastic /nón mə nástik/ adj unrelated to monks and nuns, their way of life, or the buildings in which they live ○ *nonmonastic priests*

nonmoral /non mórrəl/ adj 1 neither immoral nor moral, but unrelated to moral or ethical considerations 2 not having or showing moral principles

nonmotile /non mō tīl/ adj describes a cell or organism that does not have the ability to move independently

nonmotorized /non mōtə rīzd/ adj 1 not fitted with a motor 2 not owning or not having been supplied with a motor vehicle or vehicles

nonmusical /non myoözik'l/ adj 1 not relating to, producing, or containing music 2 not having a talent for or particular appreciation of music

non-narcotic /non naar kóttik/ adj describes a drug that does not induce sleep, drowsiness, or dullness of the senses

non-national /non násh'nəl/ adj not relating or belonging to a nation ■ n somebody who is not a citizen of a particular country

non-native /non náytiv/ adj 1 not born in, originating in, or growing naturally in a particular place ○ *These orchids are a non-native species introduced 10 years ago.* 2 not learnt as a first language, or not learning a particular language first ○ *You'd never think she was a non-native speaker.*

non-naturalistic /nón nacharə lístik/ *adj* **1 NOT REPRODUCING EFFECTS OF NATURE** not imitating or reproducing nature or perceived reality in a very exact and faithful way **2 NOT RELATING TO NATURALISM** not relating to, characteristic of, or in accordance with the beliefs of the naturalism movement in the arts and literature **3 BELIEVING IN INDEPENDENCE OF MORAL QUALITIES** relating to the theory of ethics that claims that moral properties such as goodness exist independently of natural, supernatural, or metaphysical properties

non-naval /non náyv'l/ *adj* not relating or belonging to a navy or the ships in it

nonnegative /nón néggətiv/ *adj* in mathematics, relating to or being a real quantity that is positive or zero

non-negotiable /nón ni gṓshəb'l, -shi əb'l/ *adj* **1** not open to negotiation or arbitration **2** not legally transferable from one owner to another

nonnuclear /nón nyoókli ər/ *adj* not using nuclear power or weapons

non-numerical /nón nyoo mérrik'l/, **non-numeric** /-mérrik/ *adj* not relating to, using, or consisting of numbers

non-nutrient /non nyoótri ənt/ *n* something that does not provide nourishment as food —**nonnutrient** *adj*

no-no /nṓnō/ (*plural* **no-nos**) *n* something that is not allowed or is disapproved of (*informal*)

nonobjective /nónnəb jéktiv/ *adj* **1** based on somebody's opinions or feelings, rather than on facts or evidence **2** ARTS = **nonrepresentational** —**nonobjectivity** /nón ob jek tívvəti/ *n*

nonobservance /nónnəb zúrv'nss/ *n* a failure to comply with something such as a law or practice, especially a religious practice —**nonobservant** *adj*

no-nonsense *adj* **1** direct and practical in dealing with things or people **2** basic and offering no extras, frills, or luxuries

nonoperatic /nón opə ráttik/ *adj* not relating to or characteristic of opera ○ *nonoperatic arias*

nonoperational /nón opə ráysh'nəl/ *adj* **1** not functioning or not being in effect **2** not involved in combat or active duties

nonordained /nón awr dáynd/ *adj* **1** not having been officially appointed as a priest, rabbi, or minister of religion **2** not established formally by law or other authority

nonorganic /nón awr gánnik/ *adj* **1 UNRELATED TO LIVING THINGS** not relating to, derived from, or characteristic of living things **2 NOT ORGANICALLY GROWN** relating to or employing agriculture practices that use synthetic chemicals, pesticides, and other growing aids

nonorthodox /non áwrthə doks/ *adj* not following the established rules or practices of a society, religion, or profession

nonoxynol-9 /non óksi nol nī́n/ *n* a spermicide particularly used with barrier contraceptives such as diaphragms to improve their efficiency [< NONA- (in *nonyl*) + OXY- + PHENOL + 9 (because the compounds contained have an average of nine ethylene oxide groups per molecule)]

nonparallel /non párrə lel/ *adj* not parallel with one another

nonparametric /nón parrə méttrik/ *adj* relating to statistical methods that do not require assumptions about the form of the underlying distribution

nonparasitic /nón parrə síttik/ *adj* not living in or on another organism

nonpareil /nónpə ráy'l/ *n* **1 SOMEBODY OR SOMETHING UNPARALLELED** a person or thing without an equal **2 SIX-POINT TYPE** a size of printers' type equivalent to six point (*dated*) ■ *adj* **PEERLESS** having no equal [15C. < French, 'not (having) equal' < *pareil* 'equal' < popular Latin *pariculus*, diminutive of Latin *par* 'equal'.]

nonparticipant /nón paar tíssipənt/ *n* somebody who is not a participant in an event or activity —**nonparticipant** *adj*

nonparticipating /nón paar tíssi payting/ *adj* **1** not involved in or taking part in an event or activity **2** not having the right to receive a dividend from an insurance company or a share in the distribution of the company's surplus ○ *a nonparticipating insurance policy*

nonparticipation /nón paartissi páysh'n/ *n* the condition or fact of taking no part in an activity ○ *a policy of nonparticipation in the political process*

nonpartisan /nón paárti zán/, **nonpartizan** *adj* not belonging to, supporting, or biased in favour of any political party —**nonpartisan** *n*

nonparty /non paárti/ *adj* not belonging to or having any allegiance to a particular political party

nonpayer /non páy ər/ *n* somebody who does not pay for something or is not eligible for or responsible for payment —**nonpaying** *adj*

nonpayment /non páymənt/ *n* a refusal or failure to pay money owed

nonpenetrative /nón pénnitrətiv/ *adj* not involving penetration of the vagina or anus by the penis

nonperishable /nón pérrishəb'l/ *adj* describes food products that remain edible, without spoiling, for long periods without special storage, e.g. in a refrigerator —**nonperishable** *n*

nonpermanent /non púrmənənt/ *adj* not lasting forever or for a very long time

nonpersistent /nón pər sístənt/ *adj* describes pesticides and other chemicals that decompose within a short time, thus limiting environmental damage

nonperson /nón púrss'n/ *n* **1** a person who is ignored or not mentioned, usually because his or her views are disapproved of **2** somebody of no importance or significance

nonpetroleum /nón pə trṓli əm/ *adj* not relating to, derived from, or containing petroleum ○ *Bahrain's nonpetroleum industries*

nonphysical /non fízzik'l/ *adj* not involving tangible objects or the body —**nonphysically** *adv*

non placet /nón pláyssət, nṓn-/ *n* a negative vote in an ecclesiastical or academic assembly [< Latin, 'it does not please']

nonplant /non plaánt/ *adj* not included in the plant kingdom

nonplaying /nón pláy ing/ *adj* not playing in a game or competition, but usually having a coaching or advisory role

nonplus /non plúss/ *vt* (**-plusses, -plussing, -plussed**) to make somebody feel confused and unable to decide what to do ■ *n* a state of confusion and nervousness (*dated*) [Late 16C. < Latin *non plus* 'no more'.] —**nonplussed** *adj*

nonpoint source /non póynt-/ *n* a source of radiation or pollution that is diffuse rather than highly localized

nonpoisonous /non póyz'nəss/ *adj* not containing or producing poison, or not acting as a poison

nonpolar /non pṓlər/ *adj* describes a molecule in which an electrical charge is spherically symmetrical so that there are no opposed poles, e.g. in methane

nonporous /non páwrəss/ *adj* **1** not having a surface that contains pores or a body that contains cavities **2** not permitting the movement of fluids or gases through pores or other passages

nonprecious /non préshəss/ *adj* not having great worth or financial value

nonpredatory /non préddətəri/ *adj* **1** not hunting, killing, and eating other animals in order to survive **2** not greedily eager to steal from or destroy others for gain

nonpregnant /non prégnənt/ *adj* not carrying unborn offspring inside the body

nonprescription /nónpri skrípsh'n/ *adj* PHARM = **over-the-counter** *adj.* 1

nonprint /non prínt/ *adj* relating to or produced by media other than those that publish in print ○ *nonprint media*

nonprinting /nón prínting/ *adj* relating to characters used in word-processing programs to format the text on screen or on the printed page that are usually invisible on the computer screen and do not themselves print out

nonproductive /nón prə dúktiv/ *adj* **1 NOT PRODUCING GOOD RESULTS** not producing adequate or satisfactory results **2 NOT INVOLVED IN PRODUCING GOODS** not directly involved in producing goods **3 NOT YIELDING** not producing crops or a natural resource **4 NOT PRODUCTIVE OF PHLEGM** describes a cough that does not produce phlegm —**nonproductively** *adv* —**nonproductiveness** *n*

nonprofessional /nón prə fésh'nəl/ *n* a person without professional status ■ *adj* not having professional status —**nonprofessional** *adj* —**nonprofessionally** *adv*

nonprofit /nón próffit/ *adj* US = **nonprofitmaking**

nonprofitmaking /nón próffit mayking/ *adj* not operated with the primary aim of making a profit. US term **nonprofit** *adj.*

nonprogrammer /non prṓ gramər/ *n* somebody working with computers who does not write computer programs

nonproliferation /nón prə líffə ráysh'n/ *n* the practice of limiting the production or spread of something, especially nuclear weapons (*often before nouns*) ○ *nonproliferation agreements*

nonpros /nón prṓs/ *n* (*plural* **-prosses**) LAW = **non prosequitur** (*informal*) ■ *vt* (**-prosses, -prossing, -prossed**) to enter a judgment against a plaintiff who fails to appear in court (*informal*) [Late 17C. < shortening of NON PROSEQUITUR.]

non prosequitur /nónprō sékwitər/ *n* a judgment in the defendant's favour when the plaintiff fails to appear in court [< Latin, 'he or she does not prosecute']

nonprotein /non prṓ teen/ *adj* not relating to, consisting of, or containing protein ■ *n* a substance that is not a protein or that does not contain protein

nonpsychotic /nón sī kóttik/ *adj* relating to psychiatric conditions in which a person has full insight into his or her own mental state and an awareness of reality, together with fairly severe psychological or behavioural problems

nonpublic /non púbblik/ *adj* **1** not relating to, concerning, or open to all members of a community **2** relating to or involving private companies or industry rather than government and governmental agencies

nonracial /non ráysh'l/ *adj* not relating to race, or not taking people's racial origins into account in any way

nonradioactive /nón raydi ō áktiv/ *adj* not producing or using radiation

nonrational /non rásh'nəl/ *adj* **1** not governed by or in accordance with reason **2** lacking the ability to think rationally

nonreactive /nón ri áktiv/ *adj* **1** not reacting to events, situations, or stimuli **2** not taking part in a chemical reaction

nonreader /non reédər/ *n* a person who does not or cannot read, especially a child who has difficulty in learning to read

nonrealistic /nón ree ə lístik/ *adj* not representing or simulating what is considered to be real life

nonrecombinant /nón ri kómbinənt/ *adj* not produced by artificially manipulating genetic material

nonreflection /nón ri fléksh'n/ *n* the quality or fact of being unable to reflect light, sound, or other forms of energy

nonreflective /nón ri fléktiv/ *adj* unable to reflect light, heat, or other forms of energy

nonrefundable /nón ri fúndəb'l/ *adj* **1** for which payment cannot be claimed back ○ *a nonrefundable air ticket* **2** describes a debt, usually in the form of a bond, that is not subject to refunding by the lender, to take advantage of lower prevailing interest rates

nonrelative /non réllətiv/ *adj* not considered, measured, valued, or established in relation to something else ■ *n* somebody who is not a member of the same family through birth, adoption, or marriage

nonrelativistic /nón rélləti vístik/ *adj* not affected by the effects of relativity —**nonrelativistically** *adv*

nonreligious /nón ri líjjəss/ *adj* not relating to, believing in, or having the characteristics of a religion

nonrenewable /nón ri nyoó əb'l/ *adj* **1** not able to be sustained or renewed indefinitely, because supply is limited or regrowth impossible ○ *Trees are a nonrenewable resource.* **2** not able to be renewed for a longer period once the agreed term has expired ○ *The lease was nonrenewable, and we had to find a new home.*

nonrepeating /nón ri peéting/ *adj* **1 OCCURRING ONLY ONCE** not happening or being said or performed more than once **2 NOT RECURRING INDEFINITELY** describes a decimal number that is not a repeating decimal but has a definite and limited number of digits after the decimal point **3 FIRING ONE SHOT AT A TIME** describes a firearm that is not a repeater but has to be reloaded after every shot

nonrepresentational /nón réppri zen táysh'nəl/ *adj* in art, not aiming to depict an object but focusing on internal structure and form —**nonrepresentationalism** n —**nonrepresentationally** adv

nonreproductive /nón reeprə dúktiv/ adj not relating to, taking part in, or enabling the production of new offspring or individuals

nonresident /nón rézzidənt/ adj 1 not living or staying in a particular place 2 not involving living at the place of work —**nonresidence** n —**nonresidency** n —**nonresident** n —**nonresidential** /nón rezi dénsh'l/ adj

nonresistant /nón ri zístənt/ adj 1 unable to withstand something, especially a disease 2 exhibiting passive obedience to people in authority —**nonresistance** n

nonresonant /non rézzənənt/ adj not producing or increasing the amplification of sound or echoes

nonrestrictive /non ri stríktiv/ adj with few or no restrictions

nonrestrictive clause n a relative clause that gives additional information about a noun or pronoun in the main clause but that is not essential to the understanding of the main clause. A nonrestrictive clause is usually separated from the rest of the sentence by commas, e.g. 'My partner, who is an artist, comes from Edinburgh'.

nonreturn /nón ri túrn/ adj permitting a flow of air or liquid through a pipe or similar conduit in one direction only

nonreturnable /nón ri túrnəb'l/ adj not able to be returned to the place of purchase for refund of a deposit

nonreturn valve /nón ri túrn-/ n TECH = **check valve**

nonrigid /nón ríjjid/ adj 1 not stiff 2 describes airships such as balloons or dirigibles that have a flexible gas container held in shape by the internal gas pressure

nonrotating /nón rō táyting/ adj 1 not turning on an axis or around a fixed point ○ a nonrotating planet 2 not replacing one person or thing with another, or being replaced, in rotation

nonrun /nón rún/ adj designed not to ladder easily ○ nonrun tights

nonrunner /non rúnnər/ n a nonstarter in a race

nonsaleable /non sáyləb'l/, **nonsalable** adj not suitable for selling or capable of being sold

nonscheduled /nón shéddyoold/ adj 1 not planned to happen as part of a schedule 2 operating according to demand, rather than on a published schedule

nonschool /non skóol/ adj not relating or belonging to a school or schools

nonscience /non sī ənss/ n a discipline or area of study that is not regarded as a science

nonscientific /nón sī ən tíffik/ adj not relating to, employing the techniques of, or skilled in science

nonscientist /non sī əntist/ n somebody who is not a scientist, does not have scientific qualifications, or does not use recognized scientific methods

nonscriptural /non skrípchərəl/ adj not relating to, contained in, or according to sacred writings, especially the biblical scriptures

nonsectarian /nón sek táiri ən/ adj 1 not relating to a group or denomination within a wider religion or disputes between such groups 2 not restricted to members of one religious denomination, but open to all

nonsense /nónssənss/ n 1 MEANINGLESS LANGUAGE OR BEHAVIOUR pointless or meaningless language or behaviour 2 POINTLESS ACT OR UTTERANCE an instance of pointless or meaningless language or behaviour ○ To pay more than the price would be a nonsense. 3 IRRITATING BEHAVIOUR disrespectful, obnoxious, or irritating behaviour ○ the kind of judge who won't stand for any nonsense from barristers 4 LITERAT = **nonsense verse** 5 nonsense, nonsense codon DNA SECTION PRODUCING NO AMINO ACID a triplet of nucleotides, or codon, in a DNA molecule that does not code for any amino acid but is thought to signal the beginning and end of the synthesis of particular protein molecules ■ interj EXPRESSION OF CONTRADICTION used to contradict what somebody has said or written ◇ **make (a) nonsense of something** to make something seem pointless or absurd

nonsense verse n poetry that is written in deliberately absurd language for humorous effect, mainly for children

nonsense word n a word with no meaning, usually created for humorous effect

nonsensical /non sénssik'l/ adj 1 having no sense or meaning 2 deserving ridicule —**nonsensicality** /non sénssi kálləti/ n —**nonsensically** adv —**nonsensicalness** n

nonseptate /non sép tayt/ adj describes filaments (hyphae) in fungi that are not divided by thin partitions (septa)

non sequitur /nón sékwitər/ n 1 a statement that appears unrelated to a statement that it follows 2 a conclusion that does not follow from its premises [< Latin, 'it does not follow']

nonsexist /nón séksist/ adj avoiding or not involving discrimination, limitation, or stereotypes based on gender

nonsexual /non sékshoo əl/ adj not involving sex, sexual reproduction, or sexual relations —**nonsexually** adv

nonshrink /nón shríngk/ adj resistant to shrinking when washed

nonskid /nón skíd/ adj designed to prevent or lessen skidding

nonslave /non sláyv/ n somebody who is free and not an enslaved person ■ adj not relating to or using enslaved people or the system based on enslaved labour ○ nonslave states ○ nonslave labour

nonslip /non slíp/ adj designed to prevent people from slipping

nonsmoker /non smókər/ n 1 a person who does not smoke tobacco products 2 a carriage or compartment in a train in which smoking is not allowed

nonsmoking /nón smóking/ adj 1 RESTRICTED TO NONSMOKERS reserved for people who do not want to smoke cigarettes, cigars, or pipes 2 NOT SMOKING not smoking cigarettes, cigars, or a pipe ■ n AREA WHERE SMOKING IS FORBIDDEN an area of, e.g. a restaurant or an aircraft, where smoking is not permitted ○ Do you want smoking or nonsmoking?

non-Socialist n somebody who is not a Socialist or is opposed to Socialism ■ adj not relating to, based on, or supporting Socialism

nonsoldier /non sóljər/ n somebody who is not a soldier in an army —**nonsoldier** adj

nonsoluble /no sóllyŏob'l/ adj incapable of being dissolved in a liquid

nonspeaking /non speeking/ adj 1 not having the ability to speak 2 not involving speech or speaking ○ a nonspeaking part in a play

nonspecialist /non spéshəlist/ n a person who is not qualified or expert in a specific occupation or field of study, though perhaps having a wide range of knowledge —**nonspecialist** adj

nonspecific /nón spə siffik/ adj 1 not particular or detailed 2 not attributable to a specific medical cause or condition

nonspecific urethritis n inflammation of the urethra not caused by any identified infection. US term **nongonococcal urethritis**

nonspiritual /non spírrityoo əl/ adj not relating to the soul or spirit or to religious or sacred matters

nonsporting /non spáwrting/ adj 1 NOT SUITABLE FOR HUNTING not having suitable characteristics for use as a hunting dog ○ nonsporting breeds 2 NOT INVOLVED IN SPORT not relating to, used in, or participating in sports activities 3 UNSPORTING behaving in a manner unbecoming to a sportsperson or athlete

nonstandard /non stándərd/ adj 1 not conforming to an accepted standard 2 not conforming to a standard accepted as grammatically correct by educated native speakers

nonstanzaic /non stan záy ik/ adj not written in groups of lines that form separate units within a poem

nonstarter /nón staártər/ n 1 SOMETHING OR SOMEBODY UNLIKELY TO SUCCEED something that or somebody who is obviously going to be unsuccessful right from the beginning (informal) 2 HORSE THAT DOES NOT COMPETE a horse that does not run in a race in which it has been entered 3 COMPETITOR WHO WITHDRAWS BEFORE START a competitor who does not start a race, event, or competition in which he or she has been entered

nonstatutory /non státtyŏotəri/ adj not relating to, controlled by, or covered by a statute or statutes

nonsteroid /nón steér oyd, -stér-/ n a drug that does not

contain steroids —**nonsteroid** adj —**nonsteroidal** /-ste róyd'l/ adj

nonstick /nón stík/ adj with a coating or surface that prevents food sticking during cooking

nonstinging /non stínging/ adj not having the ability to sting ○ nonstinging insects

nonstoichiometric /nón stóyki ə méttrik/ adj describes a solid chemical compound in which the numbers of component atoms are not in a simple numerical ratio

nonstop /nón stóp/ adj, adv 1 continuing without a stop ○ a nonstop flight 2 continuing without interruption or rest ○ a weekend of nonstop partying

nonstriker /non stríkər/ n 1 a worker or employee who does not take part in a strike 2 in cricket, a person who is batting but not being bowled at

nonstructural /non strúkchərəl/ adj not constituting an important or essential part of a structure ○ nonstructural columns

nonsugar /non shŏoggər/ n a substance that is not a sugar

nonsuit /nón sŏot, -syŏot/ n the dismissal of a suit by a judge when the plaintiff fails to make out a legal case or to produce adequate evidence

nonsupport /nón sə páwrt/ n failure or refusal to supply legally required financial support, usually for a child or ex-spouse

nonsurgical /non súrjik'l/ adj not relating to, involving, or accomplished by surgery ○ nonsurgical therapies

nonsynchronous /non síngkrənəss/ adj 1 not happening at the same time or moving at the same rate 2 not having the same period and phase of oscillation or cyclical movement

nonsystematic /nón sistə máttik/ adj not constituting or based on a system

nontangible /non tánjəb'l/ adj 1 UNABLE TO BE TOUCHED not capable of being perceived through the sense of touch 2 NOT REAL OR REALIZABLE not able to be regarded as real, actual, or realizable ■ n SOMETHING WITHOUT A PHYSICAL FORM something that does not have a physical form

nontarget /nón taárgit/ adj describes cells, tissues, or organisms that are not intended for treatment, e.g. by drugs or radiation, but may be affected by such treatment aimed elsewhere

nontaxable /nón táksəb'l/ adj not subject to taxation

nontechnical /non téknik'l/ adj 1 not expressed in or using specialist language 2 not relating to, having, or employing technical skills —**nontechnically** adv

nontechnological /nón teknə lójjik'l/ adj not relating to or using technology ○ nontechnological societies

nontectonic /nón tek tónnik/ adj not produced by or not involving structural change caused by movement and deformation of the Earth's crust

nonterminal /non túrminəl/ adj describes a medical condition that does not lead to the death of the person affected by it

nonterminating /non túrmi nayting/ adj 1 having an infinite number of digits after the decimal point in a decimal fraction 2 not having or coming to an end (formal)

nontext /non tékst/ adj not relating to, or designed for use with, words in written or printed form

nontextile /nón ték stíl/ adj not relating to or made from cloth that is woven, knitted, or otherwise manufactured

nontheatrical /nón thi áttrik'l/ adj not relating to or having the characteristics of the theatre or dramatic performance ○ documentaries and other nontheatrical films

nontheistic /nón thee ístik/ adj not believing or relating to belief in the existence of God or of deities

nonthematic /nón thi máttik/ adj not relating to, constituting, or having a theme

nontherapeutic /nón therrə pyóotik/ adj not used in the treatment of diseases or disorders or for maintaining health

nonthermal /non thúrm'l/ adj not involving or caused by heat or changes of temperature

nonthreatening /non thrétt'ning/ adj not being or seeming to be a threat —**nonthreateningly** adv

nontitle /nón tít'l/ adj not competed in to win a sports title or championship ○ a nontitle fight

nontoxic /nón tóksik/ adj not containing a poison or toxin, especially when this is contrary to appearance or belief —**nontoxicity** /nón tok síssəti/ n

nontraditional /nón trə dísh'nəl/ *adj* not relating to or based on tradition

nontransferable /nón transs fúr əb'l/, **nontransferrable** *adj* relating to a ticket, licence or voucher that cannot be transferred to or used by anyone other than the person to whom it is sold or assigned

nontransparent /nón transs párrənt/ *adj* not allowing light to pass through so that objects on the other side can be easily seen

non troppo /non tróppō/ *adv, adj* not too much (*musical direction*) [< Italian]

non-U /nón yóo/ *adj* not belonging to or characteristic of the upper classes (*dated informal*) ○ *a non-U word for 'napkin'* [*U* abbreviation of *upper (class)*]

nonuniform /non yóoni fawrm/ *adj* not all the same, regular, or constant

nonunion /nón yóonyən/ *adj* **1 NOT IN UNION** not belonging to a trade union **2 NOT USING UNION MEMBERS** not employing trade-union members **3 NOT MADE BY UNION MEMBERS** not produced by trade-union members —**nonunionized** *adj*

nonuser /non yóozər/ *n* somebody who does not use something, especially somebody who does not take addictive drugs

nonvascular /non váskyoolər/ *adj* **1** describes body tissue that contains no arteries, veins, or capillaries **2** describes body tissue that has suffered loss of blood vessels as a result of disease

nonvegetable /non véjjətəb'l/ *adj* not consisting of, made from, or using vegetables or plants in general

nonvenomous /non vénnəməss/ *adj* having or producing no venom

nonverbal /nón vúrb'l/ *adj* not using or involving words —**nonverbally** *adv*

nonverbal communication *n* methods of communicating other than by using words, e.g. facial expressions, hand gestures, and tone of voice

nonviable /nón vī́ əb'l/ *adj* **1** incapable of growing and developing independently **2** not capable of succeeding

nonvintage /nón víntij/ *adj* not belonging to an especially good year for a wine and not identified by year

nonviolence /nón vī́ ələnss/ *n* **1** the principle of refraining from using violence, especially as a means of protest **2** the absence of or freedom from violence —**nonviolent** *adj* —**nonviolently** *adv*

nonvisible /non vízzəb'l/ *adj* not visible to the aided or unaided eye

nonvital /non vī́t'l/ *adj* not indispensable to survival or effectiveness, or not required for the continuation of life

⚡**nonvolatile** /non vóllə tīl/ *adj* **1** not prone to evaporation at normal temperatures **2** able to store data when the power is off, e.g. in read-only memory

nonvoter /non vṓtər/ *n* a person who does not or is not entitled to vote

nonvoting /nón vṓting/ *adj* describes a share that does not give the holder the right to vote at company meetings

non-white, **non-White** *n* a person whose ancestry cannot be traced ultimately to Europe (*sometimes offensive*) —**non-white** *adj*

nonwoody /non wóoddi/ *adj* **1** not made of or containing wood or a material resembling wood **2** describes a plant that does not form a woody stem

nonwork /non wúrk/ *adj* not relating to the world of paid employment ○ *He's quite different in a nonwork situation.*

nonworker /non wúrkər/ *n* a person who does not work, or an animal that is not put to work

nonwoven /nón wṓv'n/ *adj* describes a material that is made of fibres that have been bonded or interlocked by mechanical, chemical, thermal, or solvent methods

nonwritten /non rítt'n/ *adj* not having been written down ○ *nonwritten laws*

nonzero /nón zéerō/ *adj* greater or less than zero in value or quantity

noodle[1] /nóod'l/ *n* a long thin strip of pasta (*often plural*) [Late 18C. < German *Nudel*.]

noodle[2] /nóod'l/ *n* **1** *US* the head or mind (*slang*) **2** a term that deliberately, though perhaps affectionately, insults somebody's intelligence or common sense (*dated informal*) [Mid-18C. < ?]

noodle[3] /nóod'l/ (**-dles, -dling, -dled**) *vti* to improvise on a musical instrument in a random, meandering fashion, often in order to warm up (*slang*) [Mid-19C. Probably from likening such playing to the disorganized appearance of a dish of noodles.]

nook /nòok/ *n* **1** a quiet private place **2** a corner or small recess in a room [13C. Probably < Old Norse.] ◇ **every nook and cranny** every tiny part of a place

nookie /nóoki/, **nooky** *n* sexual intercourse (*slang; sometimes offensive*) [Early 20C. < ?]

noon /noon/ *n* **1** 12 o'clock in the middle of the day **2** the most important period of something (*literary*) [Pre-12C. < Latin *nona (hora)* 'ninth (hour) (of the Roman day, counted from sunrise)', feminine of *nonus*.]

noonday /nóon day/ *adj* relating to or happening at midday (*literary*) —**noonday** *n*

no one *pron* no person at all

noontide /nóon tīd/ *n* noontime (*literary*)

noontime /nóon tīm/ *n* the middle of the day, around 12 o'clock

Noonuccal /noo núk'l/, **Oodgeroo** (1920–93) Australian poet. Born **Kath Walker**

noose /nooss/ *n* **1 LOOP IN ROPE** a loop, tied with a knot, at the end of a rope that permits tightening and slackening, and is used for trapping animals or hanging people **2 SOMETHING THAT TRAPS** something that traps somebody in an unpleasant or unwanted situation ■ *vt* (**nooses, noosing, noosed**) **1 CATCH WITH A NOOSE** to catch somebody or something with a noose **2 TIE IN A NOOSE** to tie a rope or cord in a noose [15C. Probably via Old French *nos* (singular), *nous* (plural) < Latin *nodus* 'knot'.]

noosphere /nṓ ə sfeer/ *n* the totality of information and human knowledge that is collectively available to people [Mid-20C. < French *noösphere* < Greek *noos* 'mind'.]

Nootka /nóotkə, nóot-/ (*plural* **-kas** *or* **-ka**) *n* **1** a member of a Native North American people of the coast of W Vancouver Island, British Columbia, and Cape Flattery, on the Olympic Peninsula in Washington State **2** the Wakashan language of the Nootka people [Early 19C. After *Nootka* Sound, an inlet on the coast of Vancouver Island, British Columbia, Canada.] —**Nootka** *adj*

nopal /nṓp'l/ (*plural* **-pals** *or* **-pal**) *n* **1** a cactus that is a host plant to the cochineal insect. Flowers: red, with long stamens. *Nopalea cochinellifera*. **2** the edible fruit of a nopal cactus. Use: Mexican cookery. [Mid-18C. Via French < Nahuatl *nopalli* 'cactus'.]

no-par, **no-par-value** *adj* describes a security without a par or face value

nope /nōp/ *interj* indicates a negative response refusing, denying, or disagreeing with something (*slang*) [Late 19C. Alteration of NO[1] (probably imitating the lips' emphatic closure).]

no-questions-asked *adj* given or granted unconditionally, whatever the reason or circumstances ○ *a no-questions-asked refund*

nor /nawr/ *conj* **1 AND NOT** used to introduce an alternative, after a first alternative that is preceded by 'neither' (*in negatives*) ○ *Neither he nor his wife had profited in any way from the crime.* **2 AND NOT EITHER** used to indicate that what has just been said also applies to somebody or something else, or to add extra information to what has just been said (*after negative statements and followed by 'have', 'do', or 'be'*) ○ *He doesn't want to move to another town, and nor do I.* ○ *No surrounding tissue was damaged, nor did the infection spread.* ■ *prep* **THAN** than (*nonstandard*) ■ *conj* **NEITHER** neither (*literary*) [13C. Contraction of obsolete *nouther* 'neither, nor'.]

⚡**NOR** /nawr/ *n* a logical operator with two arguments that returns true if, and only if, both arguments are false [Mid-20C. Blend of NOT + OR[1].]

Nor. *abbr* **1** North **2** Norway

nor- *prefix* an unaltered parent compound ○ *nornicotine* [Shortening of NORMAL]

noradrenaline /náwrə drénnəlin/, **noradrenalin** *n* a hormone, secreted by the adrenal gland and similar to adrenaline, that is also the principal neurotransmitter of sympathetic nerve endings supplying the major organs and skin. US term **norepinephrine**

noradrenergic /náwr adrə núrjik/ *adj* releasing or involving noradrenaline in the transmission of nerve impulses

⚡**NOR circuit** *n* a computer circuit with two inputs and one output where the output is on only when both inputs are off

Nordic /náwrdik/ *adj* **1 SCANDINAVIAN** relating to the countries of NW Europe, especially the Scandinavian countries and Iceland **2 TALL, FAIR, AND BLUE-EYED** tall, blonde, fair-skinned and blue-eyed, in a way that is considered to be typical of people from Scandinavian countries **3 Nordic, nordic INVOLVING CROSS-COUNTRY SKIING OR JUMPING** describes or relating to ski events involving either cross-country racing or ski jumping or both ■ *n* **SOMEBODY FROM SCANDINAVIA** somebody from a Nordic country or of Nordic appearance [Late 19C. < French *nordique* < *nord* 'north' < Germanic.]

Nord-Ostsee Kanal /náwrt óst zay kə nál/ = **Kiel Canal**

nor'easter /náwr éestər/ *n* METEOROL = **northeaster** [Mid-19C. Alteration.]

norepinephrine /náwr eppi néffrin/ *n US* MED = **noradrenaline**

norethisterone /náwr e thístərōn/ *n* a progestogen drug. Use: oral contraceptives, hormone replacement therapy, treatment of premenstrual syndrome, menstrual disorders, endometriosis, and cancer.

Norfolk /náwrfək/ county in E England, bordering on the North Sea. Area: 5,360 sq. km/2,069 sq. mi.

Norfolk Island island in the SW Pacific Ocean northeast of Sydney, a dependency of Australia. Population: 2,756 (1995). Area: 35 sq. km/13 sq. mi.

Norfolk Island pine *n* a tall symmetrical pine tree. Native to: Norfolk Island, off E Australia, but now found on the mainland. *Araucaria heterophylla*.

Norfolk jacket *n* a loose jacket with a belt and box pleats, first worn by men and later adapted to women's fashions [After NORFOLK]

⚡**NOR gate** *n* = **NOR circuit**

nori /náwri/ *n* an edible preparation of dried pressed seaweed, often used to wrap sushi [Late 19C. < Japanese.]

noria /náwri ə/ *n* a series of buckets on a water wheel, used for raising water from a stream [Late 18C. Via Spanish < Arabic *nāʻūra*.]

Noriega /nórri áygə/, **Manuel** (*b.* 1934) Panamanian general and head of state (1983–89)

nork /nawrk/ *n Aus* an offensive term for a woman's breast (*slang*) [Mid-20C. < ?]

norm /nawrm/ *n* **1 STANDARD PATTERN OF BEHAVIOUR** a standard pattern of behaviour that is considered normal in a particular society **2 USUAL SITUATION** the usual situation or circumstances **3 REQUIRED ACHIEVEMENT LEVEL** a required level of achievement **4 EXPECTED RANGE OF FUNCTIONING** the range of functioning that can be expected of members of a particular population, e.g. babies of nine months or ten-year-old children **5 REAL-VALUED FUNCTION** the magnitude of a vector expressed as the square root of the sum of the squares of the absolute values of the components of the vector **6** MATH = **mode** *n.* 6 [Early 19C. Latin *norma* 'carpenter's square, rule'.]

Norm *n Aus* an Australian man who enjoys watching sports on television while consuming large quantities of beer (*slang*) ○ *It's Grand Final week, so your average Norm will be glued to the box.* [< the forename *Norm*, short for *Norman*, influenced by NORM, NORMAL]

norm. *abbr* normal

Norma /náwrmə/ *n* a small faint constellation of the southern hemisphere

normal /náwrm'l/ *adj* **1 USUAL** conforming to the usual standard, type, or custom **2 HEALTHY** physically, mentally, and emotionally healthy **3 OCCURRING NATURALLY** maintained or occurring in a natural state **4 CONTAINING ONE GRAM PER LITRE** describes a chemical solution containing an equivalent weight of solute in grams per litre of solution (*dated*) **5 UNBRANCHED** describes aliphatic hydrocarbons with unbranched chains of carbon atoms **6** MATH = **perpendicular** *adj.* 3 ■ *n* **1 USUAL STANDARD** the usual standard, type, or custom **2 PERPENDICULAR LINE OR PLANE** a line or plane that is perpendicular to another line or plane [15C. Directly or via French < Latin *normalis* 'made according to the square' < *norma* 'carpenter's square'.] —**normalness** *n*

normal curve *n* the symmetrical bell-shaped curve of a normal distribution

normalcy /náwrm'lssi/ *n US* = **normality**

normal distribution *n* a probability frequency distribution for a random variable that theoretically takes on a bell shape symmetrical about the mean

normal fault *n* a geological fault in which the upper side of the inclined plane appears to have slipped downwards relative to the lower

normalise *vti* = **normalize**

normality /nawr mállәti/ *n* the way things are under normal circumstances

normalize /náwrmә līz/ (**-izes, -izing, -ized**), **normalise** (**-ises, -ising, -ised**) *v* **1** *vti* **MAKE OR BECOME NORMAL** to make something normal or return something to normal, or become or return to normal **2** *vt* **MAKE CONFORM** to make something or somebody conform to a standard **3** *vt* **HEAT STEEL** to heat steel above a particular temperature and then cool it in order to reduce internal stress —**normalization** /náwrmә lī záysh'n/ *n*

normally /náwrm'li/ *adv* **1** as a custom or habit ○ *Normally, we go swimming on Sundays.* **2** in the usual or standard way ○ *The trains are running normally again.*

normal school *n* a school or college for training teachers, especially in France and, formerly, in England, the United States, and Canada [Mid-19C. After French *école normale*; from the first French school so named being considered a model for others.]

Norman /náwrmәn/ *n* **1 MEDIEVAL INHABITANT OF NORMANDY OR ENGLAND** a member of a Viking people who raided and then settled in the French province later known as Normandy and who invaded England in 1066 **2 SOMEBODY FROM NORMANDY** a person who comes from the French region of Normandy **3** LANG = **Norman French** *n.* 1 **4 STYLE OF MEDIEVAL ARCHITECTURE** a style of Romanesque architecture developed by the Normans in the Middle Ages, characterized by vaults separated by groins, heavy walls, and deeply recessed portals [13C. < Old French *Normans*, plural of *Normant* < Old Norse *Norðmaðr* (plural *Norðmenn*), < *norð* 'north'.] —**Norman** *adj*

Norman /náwrmәn/, **Greg** (*b.* 1955) Australian golfer. Full name **Gregory John Norman**. Known as **Great White Shark**

Norman, Jessye (*b.* 1945) US soprano

Norman Conquest *n* the invasion and conquest of England by the Normans, led by William the Conqueror, in 1066

Normandy /náwrmәndi/ region of NW France, bordering on the English Channel. Capital: Rouen.

Norman French *n* **1** a variety of French spoken by the Normans in the Middle Ages **2** the French dialect spoken in modern Normandy —**Norman French** *adj*

normative /náwrmәtiv/ *adj* (*formal*) **1** relating to standards **2** tending to create or prescribe standards [Late 19C. < French, < Latin *norma* 'carpenter's square'.] —**normatively** *adv* —**normativeness** *n*

norming /náwrming/ *n* US the practice of adjusting the scores on standardized tests in order to compensate for the possible effects that ethnic and cultural differences may have on the test results

normotensive /náwrmō ténssiv/ *adj* having or indicating normal blood pressure ■ *n* a person with normal blood pressure [Mid-20C. < NORM or NORMAL.]

normothermia /náwrmō thúrmi ә/ *n* the state of having a normal body temperature —**normothermic** *adj*

norm-referenced *adj* using a comparison of a pupil's performance in a test with the performance of other children in the same test

norm-referencing *n* the comparing of a pupil's performance in a test with the performance of other children in the same test

Norse /nawrss/ *adj* **1 OF OLD SCANDINAVIA** relating to ancient or medieval Scandinavia, or its people or culture **2 OF N GERMANIC LANGUAGES** relating to the North Germanic languages ■ *npl* **1 VIKINGS** the Viking people of medieval Scandinavia **2 SCANDINAVIANS** the people of Scandinavia **3 N GERMANIC NATIVE SPEAKERS** the people who speak one of the North Germanic languages as their native language ■ *n* **N GERMANIC LANGUAGE** a North Germanic language, especially Danish, Icelandic, or Norwegian in their earlier forms [Late 16C. Via Dutch *Noorsch* < *noordsch* 'northern'.]

Norseman /náwrssmәn/ (*plural* **-men** /-mәn/) *n* a member of a medieval Scandinavian group, especially a Viking

north /nawrth/ *n* **1 DIRECTION** the direction that lies directly to the left of somebody facing the rising sun or that is located towards the top of a conventional map of the world **2 COMPASS POINT** one of the cardinal points on a compass. North is 90 degrees anticlockwise from east. **3 north, North AREA IN THE NORTH** the part of an area, region, or country that is situated in or towards the north **4 LEFT-HAND SIDE OF CHURCH** the left-hand side of a church as you face the altar from the central section of the building **5 north, North POSITION EQUIVALENT TO NORTH** the position equivalent to north in any diagram consisting of four points at 90-degree intervals ■ *adj* **1 IN THE NORTH** situated in, facing, or coming from the north of a place, region, or country **2 FROM THE NORTH** blowing from the north ○ *a north wind* ■ *adv* **TOWARDS THE NORTH** in or towards the north [Old English *norþ* < Germanic]

North /nawrth/, **Frederick, 8th Baron North** (1732–92) British statesman. Known as **Lord North**

North Africa northern part of the African continent, comprising Morocco, Mauritania, Algeria, Tunisia, Libya, and Egypt —**North African** *adj, n*

Northallerton /náwrth állәrt'n/ town in N England. Population: 13,774 (1991).

Northam /náwrthәm/ town in SW England. Population: 8,715 (1981).

North America continent in the western hemisphere, extending northwards from NW South America to the Arctic Ocean. It comprises Central America, Mexico, the United States, Canada, and Greenland. Population: 405,000,000 (2000). Area: 23,700,000 sq. km/9,200,000 sq. mi. —**North American** *adj, n*

Northampton /náwr thámptәn/ city in central England. Population: 189,700 (1995).

Northamptonshire /nawr thámptәnshәr/ county in central England. Area: 2,370 sq. km/915 sq. mi.

Northants /náwrth ants/ *abbr* Northamptonshire

North Atlantic drift *n* the relatively warm current, originating in the Gulf of Mexico, that flows across the surface of the North Atlantic Ocean from Newfoundland to NW Europe, influencing the latter's climate

North Atlantic Treaty Organization *n* full form of **NATO**

North Ayrshire council area in west-central Scotland. Area: 884 sq. km/341 sq. mi.

North Borneo former name for **Sabah**

northbound /náwrth bownd/ *adj* leading, going, or travelling towards the north

north by east *n* the direction or compass point midway between north and north-northeast —**north by east** *adj, adv*

north by west *n* the direction or compass point midway between north and north-northwest —**north by west** *adj, adv*

North Cape promontory on Magerøya Island, N Norway, on the Barents Sea

North Carolina state on the coast of the E United States. Capital: Raleigh. Population: 7,425,183 (1997). Area: 136,420 sq. km/52,672 sq. mi. —**North Carolinian** *adj, n*

North Channel strait between the Atlantic Ocean and the Irish Sea, separating Northern Ireland and Scotland. Width: 37 km/23 mi.

northcountryman /náwrth kúntrimәn/ (*plural* **-men** /-mәn/) *n* a man who was born or brought up in the north of England

North Dakota state in the W north-central United States. Capital: Bismarck. Population: 640,883 (1997). Area: 183,123 sq. km/70,704 sq. mi. —**North Dakotan** *adj, n*

North Downs range of chalk hills in S England

northeast /náwrth éest/; *nautical usage* /náwr éest/ *n* **1 COMPASS POINT BETWEEN N AND E** the direction or compass point midway between north and east **2 northeast, Northeast AREA IN THE NORTHEAST** the part of an area, region, or country that is situated in or towards the northeast ■ *adj* **1 northeast, Northeast IN THE NORTHEAST** situated in, facing, or lying towards the northeast of a region, place, or country **2 FROM NORTHEAST** blowing from the northeast ○ *a northeast wind* ■ *adv* **TOWARDS THE NORTHEAST** in or towards the northeast

Northeast *n* **1** NE England, especially the area from the River Tees northwards including Tyneside, Northumberland, and Durham **2** *US* a region of the NE United States, usually thought of as consisting of the New England states, sometimes together with E New York, Pennsylvania, and New Jersey

northeast by east *n* the direction or compass point midway between northeast and east-northeast —**northeast by east** *adj, adv*

northeast by north *n* the direction or compass point midway between northeast and north-northeast —**northeast by north** *adj, adv*

northeaster /náwrth éestәr/; *nautical usage* /náwr éestәr/ *n* a storm or wind that blows from the northeast

northeasterly /náwrth éestәrli/; *nautical usage* /náwr éestәrli/ *adj* **1** situated in or towards the northeast **2** blowing from the northeast ○ *a northeasterly wind* ■ *n* (*plural* **-lies**) METEOROL = **northeaster** —**northeasterly** *adv*

northeastern /náwrth éestәrn/; *nautical usage* /náwr éestәrn/ *adj* **1 IN THE NORTHEAST** situated in the northeast of a region or country **2 COMING FROM OR FACING NORTHEAST** coming or blowing from, or facing towards the northeast **3 northeastern, Northeastern OF THE NORTHEAST** relating or native to the northeast of a region or country —**northeasterner** *n* —**northeasternmost** *adj*

Northeast Passage sea passage extending along the coast of N Europe and Asia, connecting the Atlantic and Pacific oceans

northeastward /náwrth éestwәrd/; *nautical usage* /náwr éestwәrd/ *adj* **IN THE NORTHEAST** towards or in the northeast ■ *n* **POINT IN THE NORTHEAST** a direction towards or a point in the northeast ■ *adv* **EAST OF NORTH** towards or from east of due north —**northeastwardly** *adj, adv* —**northeastwards** *adv*

northerly /náwrthәrli/ *adj* **1 IN THE NORTH** situated in or towards the north **2 FROM THE NORTH** blowing from the north ○ *a northerly wind* ■ *n* (*plural* **-lies**) **WIND FROM THE NORTH** a wind blowing from the north —**northerly** *adv*

northern /náwrthәrn/ *adj* **1 IN THE NORTH** situated in the north of a region or country **2 NORTH OF EQUATOR** lying north of the equator or north of the celestial equator **3 FACING NORTH** situated on the north side of something or facing north **4 northern, Northern OF THE NORTH** relating or native to the north of a region or country **5 FROM THE NORTH** blowing from the north ○ *a northern wind*

Northern Cross *n* a cross formed by six stars in the constellation Cygnus

Northern Crown *n* ASTRON = **Corona Borealis**

northerner /náwrthәrnәr/, **Northerner** *n* a person who comes from the northern part of a country or region

northern harrier *n US* BIRDS = **hen harrier**

northern hemisphere *n* **1** the half of the Earth that lies to the north of the equator **2** the half of the celestial sphere north of the celestial equator

Northern Ireland province of the United Kingdom, in NE Ireland. Capital: Belfast. Population: 1,641,700 (1994). Area: 13,483 sq. km/5,206 sq. mi.

Northern Isles *npl* the Orkney and Shetland islands

Northernism /náwrthәrnizәm/ *n* a pronunciation, word, or other linguistic construction typical of the northern region of a country

northern lights *npl* ASTRON = **aurora borealis**

Northern Mariana Islands /-marri ánnә-/ island group in the Mariana Islands, in the W Pacific Ocean, a self-governing commonwealth of the United States. Population: 71,912 (2000). Area: 457 sq. km/176 sq. mi.

northernmost /náwrthәrn mōst/ *adj* situated farthest north

northern oriole *n* an oriole with two subspecies, the Baltimore oriole and Bullock's oriole, the males of each having black and orange plumage. Native to: North America. *Icterus galbula*.

Northern Paiute, Northern Piute *n* **1** a member of a Native North American people of Oregon, Nevada, and NE California ◊ **Southern Paiute 2** a Uto-Aztecan language spoken in Oregon, Nevada, and NE California. Native speakers: 6,000. ◊ **Southern Paiute** —**Northern Paiute** *adj*

northern pike *n* ZOOL = **pike**[1] *n.* 1

Northern Territory territory of north-central Australia. Capital: Darwin. Population: 182,000 (1996). Area: 1,346,200 sq. km/519,770 sq. mi.

North Germanic *n* a group of Germanic languages that includes Danish, Faroese, Icelandic, Norwegian, and Swedish. Native speakers: 20 million. —**North Germanic** *adj*

northing /náwrthing, -thing/ *n* **1** MOVEMENT NORTH distance covered or movement made in a northerly direction, especially as measured by the difference in latitude between two points **2** PROGRESS NORTH progress made in a northern direction **3** LATITUDINAL GRID LINE ON MAP a grid line on a map that runs from east to west. ◊ **easting** **4** DISTANCE NORTHWARDS the distance northwards from a particular east-west grid line shown in the second half of a map reference

North Island northernmost principal island in New Zealand. Population: 2,749,980 (1996). Area: 115,777 sq. km/44,689 sq. mi.

North Korea /-kə rèë ə/ country in NE Asia, in the north of the Korean Peninsula. Capital: Pyongyang. Population: 23,904,124 (1996). Area: 120,538 sq. km/46,540 sq. mi. —**North Korean** *n, adj*

North Lanarkshire council area in S Scotland. Area: 474 sq. km/183 sq. mi.

northland /náwrth land/ *n* the northern part of a country

Northland[1] /náwrth land/ Scandinavian peninsula comprising Norway and Sweden

Northland[2] administrative region of N New Zealand. Area: 30,105 sq. km/11,624 sq. mi.

north magnetic pole *n* the point on the Earth's surface to which the north-seeking pole of a compass needle is attracted

Northman /náwrthmən/ (*plural* **-men** /-mən/) *n* = **Norseman**

north-northeast *n* the direction or compass point midway between north and northeast ■ *adj, adv* in, from, facing, or towards the north-northeast —**north-northeasterly** *adj, adv*

north-northwest *n* the direction or compass point midway between north and northwest ■ *adj, adv* in, from, facing, or towards the north-northwest —**north-northwesterly** *adj, adv*

North Pennines /-pénnīnz/ Area of Outstanding Natural Beauty in N England. Area: 1,983 sq. km/773 sq. mi.

north pole *n* **1** north pole, North Pole NORTHERN END OF EARTH'S AXIS the northern end of the Earth's axis at a latitude of 90° N **2** NORTH END OF AXIS OF ROTATION the north end of the axis of rotation of a planet or other celestial body **3** = **north magnetic pole 4** POINT AT NORTHERN EXTENSION OF EARTH'S AXIS the point at infinity along the northern extension of one end of the Earth's axis of rotation

North Riding /-rīding/ division of the former county of Yorkshire, N England

North Saskatchewan river in Alberta and Saskatchewan, Canada. Length: 1,200 km/760 mi.

North Sea arm of the Atlantic Ocean lying between the NE United Kingdom and continental Europe. Area: 575,000 sq. km/222,000 sq. mi.

North-South Divide *n* a term used to describe the political and economic differences between the northern and the southern regions of England

North Star *n* ASTRON = **Polaris** *n.* **1**

North Stradbroke Island /-strád brook-/ island in Moreton Bay, SE Queensland, Australia. Population: 2,290 (1994). Area: 319 sq. km/123 sq. mi.

North Uist /-yoó ist/ island in the Outer Hebrides, NW Scotland. Population: 1,404 (1991).

Northumberland /nawr thúmbərland/ northernmost county of England. Area: 5,033 sq. km/1,944 sq. mi.

Northumberland National Park national park in NE England. Area: 1,030 sq. km/398 sq. mi.

Northumbria /nawr thúmbri ə/ ancient Anglo-Saxon kingdom in N Great Britain —**Northumbrian** *adj, n*

northward /náwrthwərd/ *adj* towards or in the north ■ *n* a direction towards or a point in the north ■ *adv* = **northwards** —**northwardly** *adj, adv*

northwards /náwrthwərdz/, **northward** /náwrthwərd/ *adv* in a northerly direction

North Wessex Downs Area of Outstanding Natural Beauty in S England. Area: 1,730 sq. km/675 sq. mi.

northwest /náwrth wést/; *nautical usage* /náwr wést/ *n* **1** COMPASS POINT BETWEEN N AND W the direction or compass point midway between north and west **2** northwest, Northwest AREA IN THE NORTHWEST the part of an area, region, or country that is situated in or towards the northwest ■ *adj* **1** northwest, Northwest IN THE NORTHWEST

situated in, facing, or lying towards the northwest of a region, place, or country **2** FROM NORTHWEST blowing from the northwest ○ *a northwest wind* ■ *adv* TOWARDS THE NORTHWEST in or towards the northwest

Northwest /náwrth wést/ *n* **1** AREA OF ENGLAND the northwestern region of England, especially Cumbria and Lancashire and including the Lake District **2** US NW UNITED STATES the northwestern area of the United States, including the states of Washington, Oregon, and Idaho **3** US FORMER AREA OF THE UNITED STATES formerly, a region of the United States west of the Mississippi River and north of the Missouri River **4** Can CANADIAN REGION the area of Canada north and west of the Great Lakes

northwest by north *n* the direction or compass point midway between northwest and north-northwest —**northwest by north** *adj, adv*

northwest by west *n* the direction or compass point midway between northwest and west-northwest —**northwest by west** *adj, adv*

northwester /náwrth wéstər/; *nautical usage* /náwr wéstər/ *n* a wind blowing from the northwest

northwesterly /náwrth wéstərli/; *nautical usage* /náwr wéstərli/ *adj* **1** situated in or towards the northwest **2** blowing from the northwest ○ *a northwesterly wind* —**northwesterly** *n*

northwestern /náwrth wéstərn/; *nautical usage* /náwr wéstərn/ *adj* **1** IN THE NORTHWEST situated in the northwest of a region or country **2** FACING NORTHWEST coming or blowing from, or facing towards the northwest **3** OF THE NORTHWEST relating to or native to the northwest of a region or country —**northwesterner** *n* —**northwesternmost** *adj*

Northwest Passage sea passage along the coast of N North America, connecting the Atlantic and Pacific oceans

Northwest Territories territory of NW Canada, extending north of the provinces between Yukon Territory and Hudson Bay. Capital: Yellowknife. Population: 64,402 (1996). Area: 1,346,106 sq. km/519,734 sq. mi.

Northwest Territory historic territory of the north-central United States, extending from the Ohio and Mississippi rivers northwards to the Great Lakes, comprising present-day Ohio, Indiana, Illinois, Michigan, Wisconsin, and E Minnesota

northwestward /náwrth wéstwərd/; *nautical usage* /náwr wéstwərd/ *adj* towards or in the northwest ■ *n* a direction towards or a point in the northwest —**northwestwardly** *adj, adv* —**northwestwards** *adv*

Northwich /náwrth wich/ town in NW England. Population: 34,520 (1991).

North York Moors National Park national park in N England. Area: 1,432 sq. km/533 sq. mi.

North Yorkshire county in N England. Area: 8,321 sq. km/3,213 sq. mi.

nortriptyline /nawr trípti leen/ *n* $C_{19}H_{21}N$ a tricyclic drug. Use: antidepressant, tranquillizer, pain reliever. [Mid-20C. < NOR- + TRI- + *ptyl* (shortening of *heptyl*).]

Norw. *abbr* **1** Norway **2** Norwegian

Norway

Norway /náwr way/ monarchy in N Europe, in W Scandinavia. Capital: Oslo. Population: 4,369,957 (1996). Area: 385,639 sq. km/148,896 sq. mi.

Norway maple *n* a maple with broad five-lobed green or reddish leaves, widely grown as a shade tree. Native to: central and N Europe. *Acer platanoides.*

Norway rat *n* ZOOL = **brown rat**

Norway spruce *n* a spruce tree with drooping branches and long cones, widely grown for its timber and as an ornamental. Native to: central and N Europe. *Picea abies.*

Norwegian /nawr wéëj'n/ *n* **1** somebody who comes from Norway **2** the North Germanic language that is the official language of Norway. Native speakers: 5 million. [Early 17C. < medieval Latin *Norvegia* 'Norway' < Old Norse *Norvegr*.]

nor'wester /náwr wéstər/ *n* **1** METEOROL = **northwester 2** a strong alcoholic drink (*slang*)

Norwich /nórrich/ city in E England. Population: 120,895 (1991).

Norwich terrier *n* a small short-legged dog with wiry fur and erect ears, belonging to a breed that originated in East Anglia

nos., Nos. *abbr* numbers

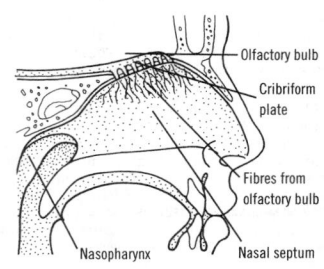

Nose: Cross-section of the human nose

Olfactory bulb
Cribriform plate
Fibres from olfactory bulb
Nasopharynx
Nasal septum

nose /nōz/ *n* **1** ORGAN OF SMELL the part of the face or head through which a person or animal breathes and smells **2** SENSE OF SMELL the sense of smell, especially the ability to recognize things by smell or to follow a scent **3** TALENT FOR DISCOVERY an intuitive ability to discover, detect, or recognize something **4** PART RESEMBLING NOSE a part that resembles the nose of a person or animal in appearance or function **5** PROJECTING FRONT PART OF VEHICLE the pointed or rounded front end of an aircraft, spacecraft, boat, car, or other vehicle **6** DISTINCTIVE SMELL the characteristic aroma of something, e.g. wine or tobacco ■ *v* (**noses, nosing, nosed**) **1** *vi* PRY OR SNOOP to try to make discoveries by searching or asking questions in an inquisitive, impertinent, or intrusive manner (*informal*) **2** *vi* SEARCH FOR BY SCENT to try to find something by smelling or sniffing **3** *vti* ADVANCE WITH CAUTION to move forward slowly, carefully, or cautiously, or make something move in this way **4** *vt* TOUCH SOMETHING WITH NOSE to touch, rub, or push somebody or something with the nose (*refers to animals*) **5** *vt* SMELL to smell or sniff something [Old English *nosu* < Indo-European] —**noseless** *adj* ◊ **follow your nose 1** to go or continue straight ahead in the direction you are facing **2** to act in accordance with your instincts or intuition ◊ **keep your nose clean** to avoid getting into trouble (*informal*) ◊ **keep** *or* **have your nose to the grindstone** to keep working hard without taking a break ◊ **look down your nose at somebody** *or* **something** to regard somebody or something arrogantly or disdainfully as inferior or not worth your attention ◊ **nose to tail** so close together that the front of one vehicle almost touches the rear end of another ◊ **on the nose 1** US absolutely on target, with total accuracy, or completely correctly (*informal*) ○ *at 10 o'clock on the nose* **2** in betting on horse racing, for a horse to win only, not to be placed second or third (*slang*) **3** Aus foul-smelling (*informal*) ◊ **put somebody's nose out of joint** to make somebody feel thwarted or offended ◊ **thumb your nose at somebody** *or* **something** to express defiance or contempt, especially by putting the thumb to the nose and extending the fingers ◊ **turn up your nose at something** to refuse to accept something because you feel it is inferior or unworthy of you (*informal*) ◊ **under somebody's nose** in full view of or very close to somebody

nose around, nose about *vti* to look or search through a place in an inquisitive and often intrusive way (*informal*) **nose out** *v* **1** *vt* FIND SOMETHING OUT BY PRYING to discover something by thorough and often cunning or intrusive searching or questioning **2** *vt* NARROWLY DEFEAT OPPONENT to defeat an opponent by a very narrow margin **3** *vi* **DRIVE CAUTIOUSLY FORWARDS** to move a vehicle very slowly and cautiously forwards out of a place **4** *vt* **FIND SOMETHING BY SCENT** to discover something by smelling or sniffing, or as if by following a scent

nosebag /nṓz bag/ *n* a cylindrical or bucket-shaped bag containing a horse's food that can be hung around its head, over its nose. US term **feedbag** *n.* 2

noseband /nṓz band/ *n* the part of a horse's bridle that goes over its nose

nosebleed /nṓz bleed/ *n* a flow of blood from the nose. Technical name **epistaxis** ■ *adj US* extremely high or excessive, e.g. in price or profit level (*informal*)

nose candy *n US* cocaine (*slang*)

nose cone *n* the pointed front section of a missile, rocket, spacecraft, aircraft, or racing car, designed for aerodynamic efficiency

nose dive *n* **1** an extremely steep sudden plunge by an aircraft towards the earth **2** a sudden very significant fall or decline in price, value, amount, or quality

nose-dive *vi* **1** to fall vertically or almost vertically with the front end pointing downward (*refers to aircraft*) **2** to experience a sudden very significant fall or decline in price, value, amount, or quality —**nose-diver** *n*

nose drops *npl* medicated liquid applied by a dropper into the nostrils

nose flute *n* a wind instrument of the South Pacific Islands, usually played by being breathed into through one nostril while the other one is plugged

nosegay /nṓz gay/ *n* a small bouquet of flowers [< GAY 'ornament']

noseguard /nṓz gaard/ *n US* in American football, a defensive lineman who plays opposite the centre in the offensive line

nose job *n* a surgical operation to improve the shape or size of the nose (*informal*)

nose ornament *n* a decorative ring or stud worn through the nostril or septum

nosepiece /nṓz peess/ *n* **1** **PART OF SPECTACLES** the part of a pair of spectacles that fits over the nose and connects the lenses **2** **PART OF MICROSCOPE** the end piece of a microscope to which one or more objective lenses are attached **3** **PROTECTION FOR NOSE** the part of a helmet or piece of armour that protects the nose **4** RIDING = **noseband**

nose rag *n* a handkerchief (*slang*)

nose ring *n* **1** a ring put through an animal's nose to lead or control it **2** a ring worn for adornment through a hole pierced in the nostril or septum

nose stud *n* a small stud worn for adornment in a hole pierced in the nostril or septum

nose tackle *n US* FOOTBALL = **noseguard**

nose wheel *n* a landing-gear wheel at the front end of an aircraft

nosey *adj* = **nosy**

nosh /nosh/ *n* (*informal*) **1** **MEAL** a meal **2** **FOOD** prepared food ■ *vt* **EAT** to eat something (*informal*) [Early 20C. < Yiddish *nashen* 'to nibble' < Middle High German *naschen*.] —**nosher** *n*

no-show *n* a person who fails to appear or arrive when expected, without giving notice

nosh-up *n* a large, satisfying, and enjoyable meal (*informal*)

no-side *n* the end of a rugby match, as signalled by the referee's whistle

nosing /nṓzing/ *n* **1** **PROJECTING EDGE OF STAIR TREAD** the rounded edge of a stair tread that projects horizontally **2** **PROTECTION FOR NOSING** a shield that protects a nosing on a staircase **3** **PROJECTING EDGE OF MOULDING** the rounded projecting edge of a moulding

no-smoking *adj* where smoking is not allowed, or that prohibits smoking

noso- *prefix* disease ○ *nosophobia* [< Greek *nosos*]

nosocomial /nóssō kṓmi əl/ *adj* describes a disease or infection that originates or occurs in a hospital [Mid-19C. < Greek *nosokomos* 'somebody who tends the sick' < *nosos* 'sickness'.]

nosography /no sóggrəfi/ (*plural* **-phies**) *n* a detailed classification and description of known diseases —**nosographer** *n* —**nosographic** /nóssə gráffik/ *adj* —**nosographically** *adv*

nosology /no sólləji/ (*plural* **-gies**) *n* **1** the branch of medicine concerned with the classification and description of known diseases **2** a completed classification of known diseases —**nosological** /nóssə lójjik'l/ *adj* —**nosologically** *adv* —**nosologist** *n*

nosophobia /nóssō fṓbi ə/ *n* an irrational fear of catching diseases

nostalgia /no stáljə, -ji ə/ *n* **1** **SENTIMENTAL RECOLLECTION** a mixed feeling of happiness, sadness, and longing when recalling a person, place, or event from the past, or the past in general **2** **THINGS THAT AROUSE NOSTALGIA** something, or things, intended to arouse a feeling of nostalgia or to evoke the past nostalgically **3** **HOMESICKNESS** a longing for home or family when away from either (*dated*) [Late 18C. < modern Latin, 'homesickness' < Greek *nostos* 'homecoming' + *algos* 'pain'.] —**nostalgic** *adj* —**nostalgically** /no stáljikli/ *adv*

nostoc /nóss tok/ *n* a freshwater microorganism that lives in spherical colonies as coiled filaments and fixes atmospheric nitrogen. Genus: *Nostoc.* [Mid-17C. < modern Latin, invented.]

nostology /no stólləji/ *n* MED = **gerontology** [Mid-20C. < Greek *nostos* 'return home' (from the former idea that later life is like a return to early years).] —**nostologic** /nóstə lójjik/ *adj* —**nostologically** *adv* —**nostologist** /no stólləjist/ *n*

Nostradamus /nóstrə daámass, -dáymass/ (1503–66) French astrologer and physician. Born **Michel de Notredame**

nostril /nóstrəl/ *n* either of the two openings at the end of the nose of a person or animal [Old English *nosþyrl* < *nosu*, form of NOSE + *þyrl* 'hole' < *þurh*, form of THROUGH]

nostrum /nóstrəm/ *n* **1** a remedy for a social, political, or economic problem, especially an idea or scheme that is often suggested but never proved to be successful **2** a medicine prepared or prescribed by an unqualified person whose claims for its effectiveness have no scientific basis [Early 17C. < Latin *nostrum (remedium)* 'our (remedy)'.]

nosy /nṓzi/ (**-ier, -iest**), **nosey** (**-ier, -iest**) *adj* too curious about other people's affairs (*informal*) —**nosily** *adv* —**nosiness** *n*

nosy parker /-paárkər/ *n* somebody who pries into other people's affairs, especially an impertinent or intrusive questioner (*informal*) [Said to refer to Elizabeth I's Archbishop of Canterbury, Matthew *Parker*, who was noted for detailed inquiries concerning ecclesiastical affairs]

not /not/ *adv* **1** **FORMING NEGATIVES** a negative adverb used to form structures indicating that something is to no degree or in no way the case or conveying the general notion 'no' (*often contracted in spoken and informal written English to 'n't'*) ○ *Don't you think you've done enough?* ○ *Not every household has a dishwasher.* ○ *There's nothing in my account; not one penny.* ○ *Not only was the meal expensive, the service was bad too.* **2** **SENTENCE SUBSTITUTE** used as a sentence substitute when indicating denial, refusal, or negation, in order to avoid repetition ○ *'Won't you come with us?' 'Certainly not'.* ○ *I don't think I'll be late, at least I hope not.* **3** **INDICATING OPPOSITE** tagged onto the end of a statement to indicate that the truth is the opposite of what has been stated (*humorous*) ○ *You're really going to enjoy this – not!* [14C. Contraction of NOUGHT.] ◇ **not at all** used as a polite way of acknowledging somebody's thanks ◇ **not that** used to introduce a clause that explicitly denies something that the listener might infer from a previous or subsequent statement ○ *I'm actually seeing her tonight. Not that it's any of your business!*

SPELLCHECK See ***knot***.

⚡**NOT** /not/ *n* a NOT circuit

nota bene /nṓtə bénni, -nay/ *interj* used to draw somebody's attention to something particularly important, usually an addition to or qualification of a previous statement (*formal*) [< Latin, < *nota*, imperative form of *notare* 'mark' + *bene* 'well']

notability /nṓtə bílləti/ (*plural* **-ties**) *n* **1** a particularly important or distinguished person **2** the importance of somebody or something, or the quality that makes somebody or something worth paying attention to

notable /nṓtəb'l/ *adj* **1** **WORTHY OF NOTE** significant or great enough to deserve attention or to be recorded ○ *a notable contribution to our understanding of this complex phenomenon* **2** **INTERESTING** interesting, significant, and worth calling attention to ○ *more notable for what it leaves out than for what it includes* **3** **DISTINGUISHED** particularly important, distinguished, or famous ■ *n* **SOMEBODY IMPORTANT** a particularly important or distinguished person [14C. < Old French, < Latin *notare* 'to note'.] —**notableness** *n*

notably /nṓtəbli/ *adv* **1** especially or in the most significant case ○ *There has been much opposition, notably from the farming community.* **2** extremely or remarkably ○ *She seems notably unimpressed by all their arguments.*

notarial /nō táiri əl/ *adj* relating to or done by a notary public —**notarially** *adv*

notarize /nṓtə rīz/ (**-rizes, -rizing, -rized**), **notarise** (**-rises, -rising, -rised**) *vt* to certify something, e.g. a signature on a legal document, as authentic or legitimate by affixing a notary's stamp and signature —**notarization** /nṓtə rī záysh'n/ *n*

notary /nṓtəri/ (*plural* **-ries**) *n* LAW = **notary public** [14C. Via Old French *notarie* < Latin *notarius* 'shorthand writer, clerk'.]

notary public (*plural* **notaries public**) *n* a person who is legally authorized to certify the authenticity of signatures and documents

notate /nō táyt/ (**-tates, -tating, -tated**) *vt* to write something down using notation, especially musical notation [Early 20C. Back-formation < NOTATION.]

notation /nō táysh'n/ *n* **1** **SYMBOLIC REPRESENTATION** a set of written symbols used to represent something, e.g. the length and pitch of musical notes **2** **USE OF NOTATION** the process of using a system of notation **3** **NOTING** the act of making a note or writing something down **4** **NOTE** a note or annotation [Late16C. Directly or via Old French < Latin *notation-* < *notat-*, past participle of *notare* 'to note'.]

notch /noch/ *n* **1** **NICK OR INDENTATION** a small V-shaped cut in the edge or on the surface of something **2** **NICK USED AS TALLY** cut made to record a score, a debt, or the number of times something has been done **3** **DEGREE ON SCALE** a level or step on a scale, especially one measuring quality or achievement ○ *raise the tension on the wire another notch* ■ *vt* **1** **MAKE V-SHAPED CUT IN** to make a notch in or on something **2** **RECORD WITH NOTCHES** to record a score or debt by making a series of cuts in a surface **3** **ACHIEVE OR SCORE** to achieve a victory or success, or score a point or goal (*informal*) ○ *notched up one more win* [Mid-16C. < ?] —**notchy** *adj*

⚡**NOT circuit** *n* a logic circuit, used especially in computers, that produces a high-voltage output signal if the input signal is low or a low-voltage output signal if the input signal is high

note /nōt/ *n* **1** **JOTTED RECORD OR SUMMARY** something written down, often in abbreviated form, as a record or reminder ○ *Fortunately, I'd made a note of her phone number.* **2** **INFORMAL LETTER** a short written message or informal letter **3** **OFFICIAL LETTER** a formal communication in writing, especially between governments **4** **DOCUMENT** a short official document **5** **ITEM OF SUPPLEMENTARY INFORMATION** a piece of additional information about something in a printed text, usually given at the bottom of the page or at the end **6** **WRITTEN COMMENT** a short written comment or item of information, e.g. written in the margin of a book or piece of work **7** **BANKNOTE** a banknote. US term **bill**[1] *n.* 7 **8** FIN = **promissory note** **9** **MUSICAL OR VOCAL SOUND** a sound of a distinct pitch, quality, or duration produced by a musical instrument or by the voice **10** **SYMBOL IN MUSIC** in written or printed music, a symbol representing a particular sound **11** **KEY ON KEYBOARD** a black or white key of a piano or other keyboard instrument **12** **INDICATION OF MOOD** a tone in the voice or in writing, or an attitude or atmosphere, that indicates feelings or mood ○ *a note of urgency* ○ *The meeting closed on an optimistic note.* **13** **DISTINCTION** distinction or excellence ○ *a writer of note* ■ **notes** *npl* **SUMMARY FOR FUTURE REFERENCE** a summary of important facts or points written down by a listener, e.g. by a student during a lesson ■ *vt* (**notes, noting, noted**) **1** **OBSERVE** to notice or remember something by paying particular attention to it **2** **PERCEIVE** to notice or become aware of something **3** **MENTION** to mention something important **4** **WRITE SOMETHING DOWN** to write down something important as a record or reminder [13C. Via Old French *note* 'sign' < Latin *nota* 'sign, mark'.] —**noteless** *adj* —**noter** *n*

~~**noteable**~~ incorrect spelling of **notable**

⚡**notebook** /nṓt bòòk/ *n* **1** a small book in which to write, containing blank or lined pages **2** a small thin portable personal computer

note card *n US* = **notelet**

notecase /nṓt kayss/ *n* a wallet (*dated*)

noted /nṓtid/ *adj* **1** well-known and especially distinguished by or admired for a particular thing or quality ○ *He is not noted for his generosity.* **2** significant or distinctive enough to be noticeable —**notedly** *adv* —**notedness** *n*

notelet /nṓtlət/ *n* a folded sheet of paper or thin card with a picture on the front, used for writing short informal letters. US term **note card**

note of hand *n* FIN = **promissory note**

notepad /nṓt pad/ *n* a number of small sheets of blank or lined paper on which to write, fastened together in a way that makes it easy to detach a single page

notepaper /nṓt paypər/ *n* paper for writing letters or making notes on

note row *n* MUSIC = **tone row**

noteworthy /nṓt wurthi/ (**-thier, -thiest**) *adj* deserving notice or attention, usually because of particular significance, excellence, uniqueness, or interest —**noteworthily** *adv* —**noteworthiness** *n*

ϟ **NOT gate** *n* COMPUT = **NOT circuit**

nothing /núthing/ *pron* **1** NOT ANYTHING an indefinite pronoun indicating that there is not anything, not a single thing, or not a single part of a thing ○ *There is nothing more annoying than people who can't keep their personal lives private.* **2** SOMETHING OF NO IMPORTANCE a thing or matter of no importance or significance ○ *It's nothing to me whether they win or lose.* **3** NOT HAVING A QUALITY used to indicate the complete lack of the quality mentioned in somebody or something ○ *He wore an ordinary dark-blue jacket, with nothing special about it.* ○ *Nothing of any consequence was said.* **4** ZERO AMOUNT a zero quantity or zero ○ *We won, three–nothing.* **5** STATE OF NONEXISTENCE a condition of nonexistence, or the absence of any perceptible qualities ○ *vanished into nothing* ■ *n* SOMEBODY OR SOMETHING COMPLETELY UNIMPORTANT a totally unimportant person or thing ■ *adj* COMPLETELY UNDISTINGUISHED completely lacking in distinguishing qualities, interest, or significance (*informal*) ○ *a nothing product, despite all the hype* [Old English *nāðinc* < earlier forms of NO[1] + THING] ◇ **not for nothing** for a very good reason ◇ **nothing but** only ◇ **nothing doing** used to indicate a complete refusal to do something or to cooperate (*informal*) ◇ **nothing for it** used to indicate that there is no other course of action open to somebody ○ *There was nothing for it but for us to admit our error.* ◇ **nothing if not** definitely, undoubtedly, or at the very least ○ *He's nothing if not fair.* ◇ **nothing less than, nothing short of** used to emphasize forcefully that something truly, definitely, or amazingly is as described ◇ **nothing like** having no resemblance to somebody or something else ◇ **there's nothing to it** used to indicate that something is very easy

USAGE ***Nothing*** – a singular or a plural? ***Nothing*** is a singular indefinite pronoun, and so should be treated as a singular even if followed by a phrase introduced by words like *but* and *except for* and a plural noun: *Nothing but truthful answers is* [not *are*] *acceptable on this questionnaire. Nothing except for your boxes and bags has* [not *have*] *been removed from the apartment.* Moving the subject closer to its verb, however, reduces the chance of grammatical error and more closely follows the natural flow of speech: *Except for your boxes and bags, nothing has been removed from the apartment.*

nothingness /núthingnəss/ *n* **1** ABSENCE OF EVERYTHING the absence of life, existence, and all discernible qualities **2** EMPTY SPACE space with nothing in it **3** COMPLETE WORTHLESSNESS complete worthlessness or insignificance **4** SOMEBODY OR SOMETHING COMPLETELY WORTHLESS somebody or something without any worth or significance **5** LACK OF APPARENT MEANING the condition of lacking any apparent meaning

~~**noticable**~~ incorrect spelling of **noticeable**

notice /nṓtiss/ *n* **1** PUBLIC SIGN a sign in a public place giving information, instructions, or a warning **2** WRITTEN ANNOUNCEMENT a written or printed announcement or statement of information, often displayed on a board or wall or published in a newspaper or magazine **3** WARNING advance warning or notification of something ○ *gave us notice that the system would be changed* **4** PERIOD OF WARNING the period of time between the giving of a warning or notification and its taking effect ○ *a day's notice of repairs to the water mains* **5** WARNING OF END OF EMPLOYMENT official notification of the exercise of a right, especially the right to terminate employment, or the amount of time in advance that such notification is given **6** ATTENTION somebody's attention, observation, or consideration ○ *How can such a glaring error possibly have escaped your notice?* **7** CRITICAL REVIEW a written or published review of a book, play, or film ■ *v* (**-tices, -ticing, -ticed**) **1** *vti* OBSERVE to see or catch sight of somebody or something and register the fact in the mind ○ *Did you notice what he had in his hand?* **2** *vti* PERCEIVE to become aware of something or somebody and register the fact in the mind ○ *I noticed that he avoided mentioning her name.* **3** *vt* MENTION to mention or remark on something **4** *vt* RECOGNIZE to recognize somebody, or indicate that you recognize somebody **5** *vt* TREAT POLITELY to treat somebody with polite attention **6** *vt* WRITE ARTS REVIEW to write or publish a review of a book, play, or film **7** *vt* GIVE OFFICIAL NOTICE TO to give official notice to somebody (*formal*) [15C. Via Old French < Latin *notitia* 'fame, knowledge' < *notus* 'known'.]

noticeable /nṓtissəb'l/ *adj* **1** easy to see, hear, feel, or detect **2** important, distinctive, or worthy of comment —**noticeability** /nṓtissə bílləti/ *n* —**noticeableness** *n* —**noticeably** *adv*

noticeboard /nṓtiss bawrd/ *n* a board fixed to a wall on which notices, announcements, or advertisements can be fastened for temporary display. US term **bulletin board** *n.* 1

notifiable /nṓti fī əb'l/ *adj* describes an infectious disease of people or animals that must be reported to the appropriate authority when it occurs so that control or preventive measures can be taken

notify /nṓti fī/ (**-fies, -fying, -fied**) *vt* **1** to inform or warn somebody officially about somebody or something **2** to announce or report something officially, or make something officially known [14C. Via Old French *notifier* < Latin *notificare* 'make known' < *notus* 'known'.] —**notification** /nṓtifi káysh'n/ *n* —**notifier** *n*

no-tillage *n* a method of farming in which crops are planted in narrow slit trenches, without any ploughing, and weeds are controlled with chemical weedkillers

notion /nṓsh'n/ *n* **1** IDEA an idea, opinion, or concept **2** IMPRESSION a vague understanding or impression **3** DESIRE a sudden desire or whim ■ **notions** *npl US* ITEMS FOR NEEDLEWORK small items used in sewing, e.g. needles, pins, thread, and buttons [14C. < Latin *notion-* 'concept' < *not-*, past participle of *noscere* 'know'.]

notional /nṓsh'nəl/ *adj* **1** IMAGINARY OR HYPOTHETICAL existing only as an idea or in theory, not in reality **2** ABSTRACT OR SPECULATIVE relating to or characteristic of ideas or concepts **3** USED WITH DEFINITE MEANING used in a particular, concrete sense, like, e.g., 'did' in 'We did (= carried out) the work', as opposed to expressing a grammatical relationship, like 'did' in 'Why didn't she come?' ◊ **relational** —**notionally** *adv*

notochord /nṓtə kawrd/ *n* a long flexible rod of cells that supports the body of chordates and vertebrate embryos and is in effect a primitive backbone [Mid-19C. < Greek *nōton* 'back' + CHORD[2] 'line'.] —**notochordal** /nṓtə káwrd'l/ *adj*

notoriety /nṓtə rī əti/ *n* the condition of being well-known for some unsavoury or undesirable reason [Mid-16C. Directly or via French < medieval Latin *notorietas* < *notorius* (see NOTORIOUS).]

USAGE See ***fame***.

notorious /nō táwri əss/ *adj* well-known for some undesirable feature, quality, or act [Mid-16C. < medieval Latin *notorius* < Latin *notus*, past participle of *noscere* 'know'.] —**notoriously** *adv* —**notoriousness** *n*

notornis /nō táwrniss/ (*plural* **-nes** /-neez/) *n* a rare flightless bird, especially a takahe. Native to: New Zealand. Genus: *Notornis*. [Mid-19C. < modern Latin, < Greek *notos* 'south' + *ornis* 'bird'.]

not proven *adj Scotland* used as a verdict in Scottish courts as an alternative to guilty or not guilty, when there is a strong suspicion of guilt but not enough evidence to prove it

no trump, no trumps *n* a bid or contract to play a hand of cards without a trump suit, especially in bridge —**no-trump** *adj*

Nottingham /nóttingəm/ city in central England. Population: 284,000 (1996).

Nottinghamshire /nóttingəmshər/ county in central England. Area: 2,165 sq. km/835 sq. mi.

Notts /nots/ *abbr* Nottinghamshire

notwithstanding /nót with stánding/ *prep* DESPITE in spite of (*formal; often after nouns*) ○ *Its democratic structures, notwithstanding inevitable flaws, are among the most solid on the continent.* ○ *The lack of a decent catalogue notwithstanding, the exhibition contains much to marvel at.* ■ *adv* NEVERTHELESS nevertheless or in spite of this (*formal*) ○ *They, notwithstanding, persisted in their inquiries.* ■ *conj* ALTHOUGH in spite of the fact that (*formal*) ○ *Notwithstanding they were provoked, they ought not to have reacted so violently.* [14C. After Old French *non obstante* 'being of no hindrance'.]

ϟ **notwork** /nótwurk/ *n* a computer network that is non-functional (*slang humorous*) [Late 20C. Blend of NOT + NETWORK.]

nougat /nóo gaa/ *n* a chewy sweet made with egg whites, honey, and usually chopped nuts or dried fruit [Early 19C. < Provençal *nogat* < *noga* 'nut' < Latin *nux*.]

nought /nawt/ *n* **1** the number zero. US term **naught** *n.* 1 **2** = **naught** *n.* 2 (*archaic*) ■ *adv* = **naught** *adv.* (*archaic*) ■ *adj* = **naught** *adj.* (*archaic*) [Old English *nōwiht* < *ne* 'not' + *ōwiht* 'anything', form of AUGHT]

Noughties /náwtiz/ *npl* the years from 2000 to 2009 (*humorous*) [< NOUGHT, 'zero']

noughts and crosses *n* a game in which two players alternately write '0' or 'X' on a grid of nine squares, until one player gets three of the same symbols in a line (*takes a singular verb*) US term **tick-tack-toe**

Nouméa /noo máyə/ capital of New Caledonia, on SW New Caledonia Island, in the SW Pacific Ocean. Population: 65,110 (1989).

noumenon /nóomənən, -non, nów-/ (*plural* **-na** /-nə/) *n* **1** something beyond the tangible world that can only be known or identified by the intellect, not by the senses **2** in Kantian philosophy, something that exists independently of intellectual or sensory perception of it, e.g. the soul in some beliefs [Late 18C. Via German < Greek, < the present participle of *noien* 'apprehend, conceive'.] —**noumenal** *adj* —**noumenally** *adv*

noun /nown/ *n* a word or group of words used as the name of a class of people, places, or things, or of a particular person, place, or thing [14C. Via Anglo Norman, 'name, noun' < Old French *nom* < Latin *nomen* 'name'.]

LANGUAGE NOTE Singular English ***nouns*** can be classified into two types: those which can have a plural and those which cannot. Nouns which can be pluralized are called *countable nouns*: *one shirt, two shirts*; *one mouse, two mice*; *one alumnus, two alumni*. Words like singular *sheep*, which have no separate form for the plural (the plural is also *sheep*), are also considered as *countable nouns*: *one sheep in the north pasture; a hundred sheep in the south pasture.* Nouns which cannot be pluralized are known as *uncountable nouns*: *music*; *happiness*; *fuss*. An *uncountable noun* denoting something unquantifiable is called a *mass noun*: *envy*; *trouble*. One feature of *mass nouns* is that they can be preceded by words such as *some*, *any*, and *no*. Many *mass nouns* are capable of being used as *countable nouns* when they refer to a particular *type* or *quantity* of what they denote: *French cheeses*; *Two coffees and five teas, please.* See Correct Usage note at ***Collective noun***.

noun phrase *n* a word or group of words that functions syntactically as a noun, e.g. as the subject, object, or topic, in a clause or sentence

nourish /núrrish/ *vt* **1** GIVE FOOD TO to give people, animals, or plants the substances they require to live, grow, or remain fit and healthy **2** SUPPORT OR FOSTER to encourage or strengthen a feeling or idea **3** HELP TO DEVELOP to help something to grow or develop [13C. < Old French *norriss-*, a stem of *norir* < Latin *nutrire* 'suckle'.] —**nourisher** *n*

nourishing /núrrishing/ *adj* providing people, animals, or plants with a substantial quantity of the substances they require to live, grow, or remain fit and healthy —**nourishingly** *adv*

nourishment /núrrishmənt/ *n* **1** food, or the valuable substances in food that a person, animal, or plant requires to live, grow, or remain fit and healthy **2** something that provides a stimulating and healthy emotional or intellectual environment for people or animals

nous /nowss/ *n* **1** COMMON SENSE good sense or intelligence (*informal*) **2** INTELLECTUAL ABILITY in ancient Greek philosophy, the capacity to reason and acquire knowledge, as distinguished from sensation **3** INTELLECT the part of the human spirit that is capable of rational thought [Late 17C. < Greek, 'intelligence'.]

nouveau /noóvō/ *adj* having recently appeared or become fashionable (*humorous*) [Early 20C. < French.]

nouveau riche /noóvō reésh/ (*plural* **nouveaux riches** /noóvō reésh/) *n* a person with recently acquired wealth who likes to display it. ◊ **arriviste** [Early 19C. < French, 'new rich'.] —**nouveau riche** *adj*

nouveau roman /noó vō rō maaN/ (*plural* **nouveaux romans** /noóvō rō maaN/) *n* LITERAT = **antinovel** [Mid-20C. < French, 'new novel'.]

nouvelle cuisine /noó vel kwi zeén/ *n* a style of French cooking consisting of beautifully presented dishes made from fresh lightly cooked ingredients in less rich sauces than in traditional French cookery [Late 20C. < French, 'new cooking'.]

Nouvelle Vague /noó vel vaág/ *n* CINEMA = **new wave** *n.* 3 [Mid-20C. < French, 'new wave'.]

Nov., Nov *abbr* November

nova /nṓvə/ (*plural* **-vas** *or* **-vae** /-vī/) *n* a star that suddenly increases dramatically in brightness and then fades to its original luminosity over a short period of months or years [Late 19C. < Latin, form of *novus* 'new'.]

Nova Scotia /nṓvə skṓshə/ province in E Canada, bordering the Atlantic Ocean and comprising a mainland peninsula and Cape Breton Island. Capital: Halifax. Population: 909,282 (1996). Area: 55,284 sq. km/21,345 sq. mi. —**Nova Scotian** *adj*

novation /nō váysh'n/ *n* the replacement of an old contract or obligation with a new one [Early 16C. < late Latin *novation-* < Latin *novare* 'make new' < *novus* 'new'.]

novel1 /nóvv'l/ *n* **1** a fictional prose work with a relatively long and often complex plot, usually divided into chapters, in which the story traditionally develops through the thoughts and actions of its characters **2** novels considered collectively as a literary genre [15C. Via Old French < Latin *novellus* < *novus* 'new'.]

novel2 /nóvv'l/ *adj* new, original, and different, and often particularly interesting or unusual as well [15C. Via Old French < Latin *novellus* 'slightly new' < *novus* 'new'.]

SYNONYMS See ***new***.

novel3 /nóvv'l/ *n* in Roman law, a new decree or something that changes an existing statute [Early 17C. < late Latin *novella (constitutio)* 'new (constitution)', < a form of Latin *novellus* (see NOVEL2).]

novelese /nóvvə leéz/ *n* a style of writing or language that is typical of inferior novels (*disapproving*)

novelette /nóvvə lét/ *n* **1 SENTIMENTAL NOVEL** a light romantic novel, especially one that is considered trite or sentimental **2 SHORT NOVEL** a long story or short novel **3 SHORT LYRICAL MUSICAL COMPOSITION** a short piece of music written in a free lyrical style, usually for the piano —**novelettist** *n*

novelettish /nóvvə léttish/ *adj* having the qualities of an inferior piece of writing, especially triteness or sentimentality

novelise *vt* = **novelize**

novelist /nóvvə list/ *n* a writer of novels

novelistic /nóvvə lístik/ *adj* characteristic of a novel, especially in the treatment of real people or historical events —**novelistically** *adv*

novelize /nóvvə līz/ (**-izes, -izing, -ized**), **novelise** (**-ises, -ising, -ised**) *vt* **1** to write the story of a film, play, or television series in the form of a novel **2** to retell a true story in the form of a novel, sometimes adding fictional details —**novelization** /nóvvə lī záysh'n/ *n*

novella /nō véllə/ *n* a fictional prose work that is longer than a short story but shorter than a novel [Early 20C. < Italian *(storia) novella* 'new (story)' < Latin *novellus* (see NOVEL2).]

novelty /nóvvəlti/ (*plural* **-ties**) *n* **1 NEW THING OR EXPERIENCE** something new, original, and different that is interesting or exciting, though often for only a short time **2 NEWNESS AND ORIGINALITY** the quality of being new, original, and different **3 SMALL TOY OR TRINKET** a small inexpensive toy, ornament, piece of jewellery, or trinket

November /nō vémbər/ *n* **1** the 11th month of the year in the Gregorian calendar, made up of 30 days **2** a code word for the letter 'N', used in international radio communications [13C. Via Old French < Latin *November*, ninth month of the Roman calendar < *novem* 'nine'.]

novena /nō veénə/ (*plural* **-nas** *or* **-nae** /-nee/) *n* in the Roman Catholic Church, the recitation of prayers for nine consecutive days to achieve a particular purpose [Mid-19C. < medieval Latin, form of *novenus* 'ninefold' < *novem* 'nine'.]

novercal /nō vúrk'l/ *adj* relating to or said to be typical of a stepmother (*formal*) [Early 17C. < Latin *novercalis* < *noverca* 'stepmother'.]

Novgorod /nóvgə rod/ city in NW Russia. Population: 288,910 (1995).

novice /nóvviss/ *n* **1** a person who is beginning or learning an activity and has acquired little skill in it **2** a person who has joined a religious order but has not yet taken final vows [14C. Via Old French < late Latin *novicius* < Latin *novus* 'new'.]

SYNONYMS See ***beginner***.

novitiate /nō víshi ət/, **noviciate** *n* **1** the period of time during which somebody is a novice, especially in a religious order **2** the part of a monastery or convent where novices live **3** RELIG = **novice** *n.* 2 [Early 17C. < French *noviciat*, or medieval Latin *noviciatus* < late Latin *novicius* (see NOVICE).]

novocaine /nṓvō kayn/ *n* = **procaine** [Early 20C. < Latin *novus* 'new' + *-caine* as in COCAINE.]

Novosibirsk /nóvvəssə beérsk/ city in south-central Russia. Population: 1,428,141 (1995).

Novyy Margelan /nóvvi maar jéllən/ former name for **Fergana**

now /now/ *adv* **1 AT PRESENT TIME** at the present time, often as opposed to in the past or in the future ○ *I've never done this before, and I'm not starting now.* **2 IMMEDIATELY** at once or at this exact time ○ *We'll miss our train if we don't go now.* **3 GIVEN THE CURRENT SITUATION** under the present circumstances ○ *She asked me not to tell anyone, but now I don't suppose she'll mind.* **4 UP TO THE PRESENT TIME** used with statements of time to indicate that something has been happening for a particular length of time up to the present ○ *For six months now, I've been telling you to clean this room.* **5 USED TO PREFACE OR CLARIFY REMARK** used to preface a remark, to clarify a statement, to get somebody's attention, or for emphasis ○ *Now, what would you like to drink?* **6 USED IN HESITATION** used in speech when hesitating and thinking of what to say next (*informal*) ○ *Now, where was I?* ■ *conj* **SINCE** since or in view of the fact that this is the present situation ○ *She can afford a decent car now that she's working.* ■ *n* **PRESENT TIME** the present time or moment ○ *Now would be a good time to tell her.* ■ *adj* **FASHIONABLE** in the latest fashion (*informal*) ○ *the now look in menswear* [Old English *nu* < Indo-European] ◇ **(every) now and then, (every) now and again** occasionally ◇ **for now** for the time being, as a temporary measure ◇ **just** *or* **right now 1** a short time ago ○ *I was talking to her just now.* **2** at the present moment ○ *Go away, I'm busy right now.* ◇ **now now 1** used as a friendly way of trying to comfort somebody **2** used to warn or reprimand somebody gently ◇ **now then 1** used to warn or reprimand somebody gently **2** = **now** *adv.* **5**, **now** *adv.* **6** ◇ **up to** *or* **up till** *or* **until now** up to the present time

NOW /now/ *abbr* National Organization for Women

nowadays /nów ə dayz/ *adv* in the present, or in the times in which we are now living, usually in contrast to the past [14C. < NOW + *adayes* 'during the day' < DAY.]

noway /nṓ way/ *interj* **noway, no way** used to express emphatic refusal or denial (*informal*) ■ *adv* in no way or not at all

nowhere /nṓ wair/; *occasional unstressed form* /nṓ wər/ *adv* not in or to any place ○ *Nowhere does it mention any side-effects.* ■ *n* a remote or insignificant place ◇ **get** *or* **go nowhere** to fail to make any progress with something you are trying to do ◇ **nowhere near** not at all, or a long way from being as specified (*informal*)

no-win *adj* in which there is no chance of a successful outcome for a participant (*informal*)

nowise /nṓ wīz/ *adv* in no manner or by no means at all

nowt /nowt, nōt/ *pron N England* nothing [Variant of NOUGHT]

noxious /nókshəss/ *adj* **1 PHYSICALLY HARMFUL** harmful to life or health, especially by being poisonous **2 MORALLY HARMFUL** likely to cause moral, spiritual, or social harm or corruption **3 DISGUSTING** very unpleasant ○ *a noxious smell* [15C. < Latin *noxius* 'hurtful, damaging'.] —**noxiously** *adv* —**noxiousness** *n*

ϟ **NOYB** *abbr* none of your business (*in e-mails*)

Noyce /noyss/, **Phillip Roger** (*b.* 1950) Australian film director

nozzle /nózz'l/ *n* **1** a narrow or tapering part at the end of a tube or pipe, used to direct or control the flow of a liquid or gas **2** a short tapered tube that directs or accelerates the flow of a fluid, e.g. in a jet engine [Early 17C. Literally 'noselike appliance' < NOSE + *-le*.]

ϟ **np** *abbr* Nepal (*in Internet addresses*)

Np *symbol* **1** neper **2** neptunium

NP *abbr* **1** *ANZ, S Africa* National Party **2** neuropsychiatry **3** new paragraph **4** notary public **5** noun phrase

NPA *abbr* Newspaper Publishers' Association

NPL *abbr* National Physical Laboratory

NPN *abbr* nonprotein nitrogen

NPV *abbr* **1** net present value **2** no par value

ϟ **NQA** *abbr* no questions asked (*in e-mails*)

ϟ **nr** *abbr* **1** Nauru (*in Internet addresses*) **2** near

NRA *abbr* **1** National Rivers Authority **2** *US* National Rifle Association

NRDS *abbr* neonatal respiratory distress syndrome

NRMA *n* the largest motoring organization in Australia, providing roadside assistance, travel information, and other motor-related services to its members, as well as insurance and travel services to the general public. Full form **National Roads and Motorists Association**

ϟ **NRN** *abbr* no reply necessary (*in e-mails*)

ns *abbr* nanosecond

NS, N.S. *abbr* **1** New Style **2** not sufficient (*funds*) **3** *US* Nova Scotia **4** nuclear ship

n.s. *abbr* **1** nearside **2** new series **3** not specified

n/s *abbr* **1** nonsmoker **2** nonsmoking **3** not sufficient (funds)

N/S *abbr* nonsmoker

NSA *abbr US* National Security Agency

NSAID *n* a nonsteroid, anti-inflammatory drug taken orally or applied externally. Use: relief of headaches, muscular and joint pain and inflammation. Full form **nonsteroid anti-inflammatory drug**

NSB *abbr* National Savings Bank

NSC *abbr* **1** National Safety Council **2** *US* National Security Council

nsec *abbr* nanosecond

NSPCC *abbr* National Society for the Prevention of Cruelty to Children

NST *abbr Can* Newfoundland Standard Time

NSU *abbr* nonspecific urethritis

NSW *abbr Aus* New South Wales

NT *abbr* **1** National Trust **2** New Testament **3** Nome Time **4** *Aus* Northern Territory **5 NT, N.T.** *Can* Northwest Territories **6** no trump **7** Nunavut

nth /enth/ *adj* **1** describes a very large, but unspecified, ordinal number, usually one that is the largest in a series of values **2** last or latest in a long and often tedious series of similar occurrences (*informal*) [Mid-19C. < N2 'indefinitely large or small amount'.]

ϟ **NTIM** *abbr* not that it matters (*in e-mails*)

ϟ **NTL** *abbr* (*in e-mails*) **1** nevertheless **2** nonetheless

NTP *abbr* normal temperature and pressure

NTSC *abbr* National Television Systems Committee

ϟ **NTW** *abbr* not to worry (*in e-mails*)

nt wt, nt. wt. *abbr* net weight

n-type *adj* **1** describes conductivity in a semiconductor due mainly to the movement of electrons **2** describes a semiconductor in which there are more electrons free to transport charge than mobile lattice holes [Mid-20C. *N* abbreviation of NEGATIVE.]

nu1 /nyoo/ (*plural* **nus**) *n* the 13th letter of the Greek alphabet [Via Greek < Semitic]

ϟ **nu**2 *abbr* Niue (*in Internet addresses*)

Nu /nyoo/, **U** (1907–95) Burmese politician

nuance /nyoó aanss, noó oNss/ *n* **1** a very slight difference in meaning, feeling, tone, or colour **2** the use or awareness of subtle shades of meaning or feeling, especially in artistic expression or performance [Late 18C. < French, 'slight difference of tone' < *nuer* 'shade' < Latin *nubes* 'cloud'.] —**nuanced** *adj*

nub /nub/ n **1** CENTRAL ISSUE the main point or most important part of a problem or argument **2** SMALL LUMP a small lump or chunk **3** SMALL PROJECTION a small protuberance **4** FIBRE KNOT a knot of fibres in yarn [Late 16C. < Middle Low German *knubbe*, variant of *knobbe* 'knob'.] —**nubbiness** n —**nubby** adj

Nuba /nyōōba/ (*plural* **-ba** *or* **-bas**) n a member of a people inhabiting the mountains of central Sudan

nubbin /núbbin/ n US a small undeveloped part of a fruit or vegetable, e.g. an ear of corn [Late 17C. Literally 'small nub' < NUB.]

nubble /núbb'l/ n a small lump or knob —**nubbliness** n —**nubbly** adj

nubecula /nyoo békyōōla/ (*plural* **-lae** /-lī/) n a Magellanic Cloud (*technical*) [Late 17C. < Latin, 'small cloud' < *nubes* 'cloud'.]

Nubia /nyōōbi ə/ region of NE Africa, in S Egypt and N Sudan, in the River Nile valley —**Nubian** n, adj

nubile /nyōō bīl/ adj **1** describes a young woman who is physically mature enough to have sexual intercourse and therefore suitable for marriage (*dated*) **2** young and sexually desirable (*informal*) [Mid-17C. < Latin *nubilis* < *nubere* 'take a husband'.] —**nubility** /nyoo billəti/ n

nucellus /nyoo séllass/ (*plural* **-li** /-lī/) n the central part of a plant ovule in which the embryo develops [Late 19C. < modern Latin, probably alteration of Latin *nucleus* (see NUCLEUS).]

nucha /nyōōka/ (*plural* **-chae** /nyōōkī/) n the nape of the neck (*technical*) [14C. < Arabic *nukā* 'spinal marrow'.] —**nuchal** /nyōōk'l/ adj

nucl- *prefix* = **nucleo-** (before vowels)

nuclear /nyōōkli ər/ adj **1** OF AN ATOM NUCLEUS relating to the nucleus of an atom **2** OF NUCLEAR WEAPONS relating to or using weapons that produce a nuclear explosion **3** OF NUCLEAR ENERGY relating to, using, or producing nuclear energy through fission or fusion **4** OF A CELL NUCLEUS relating to, involving, or contained in the nucleus of a cell **5** FORMING A NUCLEUS forming or resembling a nucleus [Mid-19C. < NUCLEUS.]

nuclear bomb n a bomb in which the explosive potential is controlled by nuclear fission or fusion. ◊ **atom bomb, hydrogen bomb**

nuclear chemistry n the branch of chemistry in which nuclear reactions are studied

nuclear deterrent n the nuclear weapons possessed by a country or an alliance thought of as a means of discouraging enemy attack

nuclear disarmament n the reduction or elimination of a nation's nuclear weapons or its capacity to manufacture them

nuclear emulsion n a photographic emulsion used to identify and show the paths of subatomic particles after development

nuclear energy n the energy released by nuclear fission or fusion

nuclear envelope n PLANT SCI = **nuclear membrane**

nuclear family n a social unit that consists of a mother, a father, and their children. ◊ **extended family**

nuclear fission n PHYS = **fission** n. 2

nuclear force n PHYS = **strong interaction**

nuclear-free zone n an area, usually within a country, where all activities involving nuclear weapons or nuclear power are officially banned

nuclear fuel n a substance such as an isotope of uranium that undergoes fission in a nuclear reactor and is used to provide power for electricity and submarines

nuclear fusion n the process in which light atoms such as those of hydrogen and deuterium combine and form heavier atoms, releasing a great amount of energy, that primarily manifests itself in the form of heat

nuclearize /nyōōkli ə rīz/ (**-izes, -izing, -ized**), **nuclearise** (**-ises, -ising, -ised**) vt to provide or equip a military force with nuclear weapons —**nuclearization** /nyōōkli ə rī záysh'n/ n

nuclear magnetic resonance n the energy pulse released by an atomic nucleus exposed to high-frequency radiation in a magnetic field, which is used to provide data about the atom that can be transformed into an image by computer techniques

nuclear medicine n the branch of medicine in which radioactive materials are used to diagnose and treat diseases

nuclear membrane n a two-layered membrane surrounding the nucleus of a cell

nuclear physics n the branch of physics in which the structure, forces, and behaviour of the atomic nucleus are studied —**nuclear physicist** n

nuclear pore n any of thousands of complex openings in a nuclear membrane

nuclear power n the power, usually electrical or motive power, produced by nuclear fission or fusion —**nuclear-powered** adj

nuclear power station, **nuclear power plant** n a power station in which the heat for producing steam to drive electric turbogenerators is derived from a nuclear reactor

nuclear reaction n a process in which energy is produced by either the splitting of heavy atoms (**nuclear fission**) or the combining of light atoms (**nuclear fusion**)

nuclear reactor n a device in which controlled nuclear fission takes place to produce heat energy

nuclear reprocessing plant n a facility in which various useful isotopes are removed from used rods of nuclear reactors

nuclear sap n the colourless liquid in the nucleus of a cell

nuclear submarine n **1** a submarine in which a nuclear reactor produces steam to drive turbines for propulsion **2** a submarine that carries nuclear weapons

nuclear threshold n the point in a war being fought with conventional weapons when one of the opposing forces decides to use nuclear weapons

nuclear warhead n the forward part of a missile or other projectile whose explosive device derives its power from nuclear fission or fusion

nuclear waste n unwanted, often radioactive, material that is produced by nuclear reactors and reprocessing plants

nuclear weapon n a military weapon that derives its explosive power from nuclear fission or fusion

nuclear winter n a period of continual cold and darkness believed to follow a nuclear war, caused by the blocking of the Sun's rays by high-altitude dust clouds, with disastrous environmental consequences

nuclease /nyōōkli ayz/ n an enzyme that breaks down nucleic acids [Early 20C. < shortening of *nucleic*.]

nucleate adj /nyōōkli ət, -ayt/, **nucleated** /nyōōkli aytid/ having a nucleus or nuclei ■ vti /nyōōkli ayt/ (**-ates, -ating, -ated**) to come together as a nucleus, or to bring things together to form a nucleus [Mid-19C. < shortening of NUCLEAR.] —**nucleator** n

nucleation /nyōōkli áysh'n/ n **1** the process by which ice crystals and rain drops form in clouds round a solid core **2** the formation of crystals from a melt, often round a core of solid material

nuclei plural of **nucleus**

nucleic acid /nyōō klée ik-, -kláy-/ n an acid of high molecular weight, e.g. DNA or RNA, consisting of nucleotide chains that convey genetic information and are found in all living cells

nuclein /nyōōkli in/ n BIOCHEM = **nucleoprotein**

nucleo- *prefix* **1** nucleus, nuclear ○ *nucleoplasm* **2** nucleic acid ○ *nucleocapsid* [< NUCLEUS]

nucleocapsid /nyōōkli ō kápsid/ n the basic viral structure consisting of a core of nucleic acid surrounded by a protein coat

nucleoid /nyōōkli oyd/ n the aggregated DNA of a bacterium, seen as a distinct region inside the cell ■ adj resembling a nucleus

nucleolar organizer n a segment of a chromosome at which a nucleolus forms

nucleolus /nyōōkli ōlass/ (*plural* **-li** /-lī/) n a small round body inside a cell nucleus, composed of protein and RNA and associated with the formation of ribosomes and ribosomal RNA [Mid-19C. < late Latin, 'little nucleus' < Latin *nucleus* (see NUCLEUS).] —**nucleolar** adj —**nucleolate** /nyōōkli ō layt/ adj

nucleon /nyōōkli on/ n a proton or neutron, especially when part of an atomic nucleus

nucleonics /nyōōkli ónniks/ n the branch of physics dealing with the properties of nucleons and the atomic nucleus (+ *singular verb*)

nucleon number n PHYS = **mass number**

nucleophile /nyōōkli ō fīl/ n a substance that becomes an electron donor in bonding during a chemical reaction —**nucleophilic** /nyōōkli ō fillik/ adj

nucleoplasm /nyōōkli ō plazəm/ n the matter (**protoplasm**) contained in a cell nucleus

nucleoprotein /nyōōkli ō prō teen/ n a nucleic acid combined with a protein, as in a chromosome

nucleoside /nyōōkli ə sīd/ n a compound consisting of a purine or pyrimidine base linked to a sugar, especially ribose or deoxyribose [Early 20C. < NUCLEO- + GLYCOSIDE.]

nucleosome /nyōōkli ə sōm/ n a structural unit of chromosomes, containing DNA

nucleosynthesis /nyōōkli ō sínthəssiss/ n the synthesis of heavier elements from lighter elements by fusion reactions within stars

nucleotide /nyōōkli ə tīd/ n a component of RNA and DNA, consisting of a nucleoside linked to a phosphate group [Early 20C. Alteration of NUCLEOSIDE.]

nucleus /nyōōkli əss/ (*plural* **-i** /-li ī/ *or* **-uses**) n **1** IMPORTANT ELEMENT a central or most important item or part that has others grouped or built around it **2** CENTRAL REGION OF AN ATOM the positively charged central region of an atom, consisting of protons and neutrons and containing most of the mass **3** STABLE ATOMS IN A MOLECULE a stable group of atoms in a molecule, e.g. a benzene ring, that forms the base structure of many compounds and remains unchanged in chemical reactions **4** CENTRAL PART OF A LIVING CELL the central body, usually spherical, within a eukaryotic cell, which is a membrane-encased mass of protoplasm containing the chromosomes and other genetic information necessary to control cell growth and reproduction **5** STARCH GRANULE'S CENTRE the central part of a starch granule **6** INNER KERNEL OF A NUT the central kernel of a nut seed **7** GROUP OF NERVE CELLS a group of nerve cells in the central nervous system or a small mass of grey matter in the brain that has a specialized function **8** CORE OF A COMET'S HEAD the central core in the head of a comet, consisting of ice, frozen gases, and dust **9** CENTRAL PORTION OF A NEBULA OR GALAXY the central brighter portion of a nebula or galaxy **10** MOST RESONANT PART OF A SYLLABLE the most resonant part of a syllable, usually the vowel [Early 18C. < Latin, 'kernel' < *nuc-'nut'*.]

nuclide /nyōō klīd/ n one or more atomic nuclei identifiable as being of the same element by having the same number of protons and neutrons and the same energy content [Mid-20C. < NUCLEUS.]

nucular incorrect spelling of **nuclear**

nuddy /núddi/ n nude (*informal*) [Mid-20C. Alteration of NUDE.]

nude /nyood/ adj (**nuder, nudest**) **1** UNCLOTHED wearing no clothes ○ *the nude figure of a man* **2** FOR UNCLOTHED PEOPLE intended for, or done by, people wearing no clothes **3** PLAIN bare or plain, with no covering or decoration **4** LACKING A LEGAL REQUISITE lacking a legal requisite such as supporting evidence or a contract ■ n UNCLOTHED FIGURE an unclothed person, especially an unclothed figure in a painting or other artistic work [Mid-16C. < Latin *nudus*.] —**nudely** adv —**nudeness** n ◊ **in the nude** without clothes

nudge /nuj/ v (**nudges, nudging, nudged**) **1** vt PUSH SOMEBODY OR SOMETHING GENTLY to push or poke somebody gently, usually with a motion of the elbow **2** vt MOVE SOMETHING GENTLY to move something gently, especially by pushing it slowly and carefully **3** vt APPROACH A LEVEL to have very nearly reached a particular level or standard ○ *Their profits are nudging the 100 million mark.* **4** vt GENTLY PERSUADE to persuade somebody into an action, gently and delicately **5** vi MOVE SLOWLY to move slowly or little by little ■ n **1** GENTLE PUSH a gentle push to get somebody's attention **2** PERSUASIVE ACT a gentle act of persuasion [Late 17C. < ?] ◊ **nudge nudge (wink wink)** used to hint or suggest that something is slightly lewd or sexually improper

nudism /nyōōdizəm/ n LEISURE = **naturism** n. 1

nudist /nyōōdist/ n a person who prefers not to wear clothes, especially somebody who does so in designated areas or communities —**nudist** adj

nudist colony n a place, especially a holiday camp, where the wearing of clothes is not allowed, intended for people who believe nudity is a healthy natural state

nudity /nyōōdəti/ n **1** the state of having no clothes on **2** bareness or plainness, with no covering or decoration

nuée ardente /noò ay aar daànt/ *n* a thick, rapidly moving, deadly gaseous cloud produced by a volcano and consisting of steam, ash, and rock segments [< French, 'burning cloud']

Nuevo Laredo /nwáyvō lə ráydō/ city in NE Mexico, opposite Laredo, Texas. Population: 217,912 (1990).

nuevo sol /nwáyvō sol/ (*plural* **nuevos soles** /nwáyvōs sólays/) *n* MONEY = **sol**[4]

Nuffield /núf eeld/, **William Richard Morris, 1st Viscount** (1877–1963) British automobile manufacturer and philanthropist

nugatory /nyoógətəri/ *adj* **1** of no importance whatsoever **2** with no legal force [Early 17C. < Latin *nugatorius* < *nugae* 'trifling matters'.] —**nugatorily** *adv*

nugget /núggit/ *n* **1 LUMP OF PRECIOUS METAL** a lump of gold or other precious metal in its natural state, dug up out of the ground **2 SMALL PRECIOUS THING** any small item or piece, especially of something abstract such as knowledge or information, regarded as very precious **3 SMALL ROUND PIECE OF FOOD** a small piece of food, usually coated with breadcrumbs and fried or baked in an oven [Mid-19C. Probably < an English dialect word, 'lump'.]

nuggety /núggiti/ *adj* **1** occurring as nuggets **2** ANZ having a broad and strong-looking physique, and usually short in stature (*informal*)

nuisance /nyoóss'nss/ *n* **1** an annoying or irritating person or thing **2** something not allowed by law because it causes harm or offence, either to people in general (**public nuisance**) or to a private individual [15C. < Old French, < Latin *nocere* 'injure'.]

SYNONYMS *nullify*, *abrogate*, *annul*, *repeal*, *invalidate*, *negate*

CORE MEANING: to put an end to the effective existence of something

nullify to make something legally invalid or ineffective, or to cancel something out; **abrogate** (*formal*) to end an agreement or contract formally and publicly; **annul** to declare something officially or legally invalid or ineffective; **repeal** to end a law officially; **invalidate** to deprive something of its legal force or value, e.g., by failing to comply with certain terms and conditions; **negate** (*formal*) to render something ineffective, e.g., by doing something that counterbalances its force or effectiveness.

nullipara /nu líppərə/ (*plural* **-ras** *or* **-rae** /-ree/) *n* a woman who has never given birth to a child [Late 19C. < Latin *nullus* 'none' + English *-para* 'woman who has given birth' < Latin *parere* 'give birth'.]

nullity /núllati/ *n* **1** the state of being legally invalid **2** lack of effectiveness or usefulness

NUM *abbr* National Union of Mineworkers

num. *abbr* **1** number **2** numeral

Num. *abbr* Numbers

numb /num/ *adj* **1 WITH NO FEELING** unable to feel or have sensations, e.g. as a result of extreme cold or the application of a local anaesthetic **2 EMOTIONLESS** unable to feel emotions ▪ *vt* **1 TAKE SENSATION AWAY FROM** to take away from a part of the body the power to feel or have sensations, or to take away the sensations themselves **2 TAKE AWAY SOMEBODY'S FEELINGS** to make somebody incapable of feeling emotion, or deaden somebody's emotions or feelings [15C. Past participle of Old English *niman* 'take'.] —**numbly** *adv* —**numbness** *n*

number /númbər/ *n* **1 COUNTING, OR FIGURES USED TO COUNT** the concept of calculating quantities of individual things, or any of the words, figures, or symbols used in doing this **2 IDENTIFYING FIGURE** any figure or group of figures identifying somebody or something, e.g. a set of figures identifying somebody as a telephone subscriber, or a figure identifying a sports player or competitor ○ *What's your fax number?* **3 TOTAL** a total or estimated total of countable individuals or things ○ *The number of people treated has risen to over 3 million.* **4 QUANTITY** an unspecified quantity, often a large one ○ *We have received a number of complaints.* **5 SINGLE THING IN A SERIES** a single one of a series of things produced in sequence, especially a single issue of a magazine **6 PIECE OF MUSIC** a self-contained piece of popular music, especially one of several that feature in a performance **7 GARMENT** an item of clothing, especially women's clothing (*informal*) ○ *a little silk number* **8 THING** a thing of any kind, especially something that gives pleasure or impresses (*informal*) **9 PERSON** somebody regarded in sexual terms (*informal*; *sometimes offensive*) **10 CANNABIS CIGARETTE** a cannabis cigarette (*slang*) **11 GRAMMATICAL QUANTITY** quantity expressed, in some languages, by the form of a word ○ *The qualifying adjective agrees with the noun in gender and number.* ▪ *v* **1** *vt* **IDENTIFY BY A NUMBER** to give something or somebody an identifying number ○ *Don't forget to number the pages.* **2** *vt* **INCLUDE** to include somebody or something as one of a group ○ *It is numbered among the world's most prestigious hotels.* **3** *vti* **ACHIEVE A TOTAL** to reach a particular total amount ○ *Supporters numbered over 300, while there were only 15 dissenters.* [13C. < Anglo-Norman *numbre* < Latin *numerus*.] —**numberer** *n* ◇

somebody's days are numbered somebody's life or career is about to come to an end ◇ **do a number on somebody** US to treat somebody unfairly or harshly, e.g. by deliberate and systematic criticism or ridicule (*slang*) ◇ **have (got) somebody's number** to understand somebody's true motives or character and so be well placed to deal with him or her

USAGE **number** or **quantity**? Careful writers distinguish between **quantity** ('an amount of something') and **number** ('a total or estimated total of persons or things that can be individually counted'), as in *A large number* [better than *quantity*] *of people had gathered in the square.* **Quantity** is best reserved for references to inanimate objects or inanimate noncount nouns, as in *a huge quantity of rotten wheat; a large quantity of fuel oil.*

USAGE See *amount*.

USAGE **number** – singular or plural? **Number** is a collective noun that can take a singular or plural verb depending on how you use it. If you put the definite article *the* in front of **number**, you are stipulating one particular number, even if *of* and *a* series of things comes next. Therefore, you must use a singular verb with **number** preceded by 'the': *The number of lab coats available is limited.* On the other hand, if you put the indefinite article *a* before **number**, you must use a plural verb: *A number of lab coats are available.*

⚡number-cruncher *n* (*slang*) **1** a computer designed to perform large quantities of complex numerical calculations **2** somebody whose job consists of performing large quantities of arithmetical calculations —**number-crunching** *n*

NUMBERS

Words for numbers have the following basic numerical meanings (sample shown below for *five* and *fifth*). Other special meanings are covered at the individual entries.

Cardinal numbers (used as nouns, pronouns, and adjectives)			
five	the number 5	a group of five objects or people: *a table set for five*	number five in a series: *the five of hearts*

Ordinal numbers (used as nouns, adjectives, and adverbs)			
fifth	the ordinal number assigned to item number 5 in a series: *the fifth of March; in fifth place; came fifth in the race*		one of five equal parts of something: *a fifth of the population*

nuisance call *n* a usually anonymous telephone call made to annoy, harass, upset, or scare somebody

nuisance value *n* the relative usefulness of something based on its potential to cause problems or difficulties for somebody

NUJ *abbr* National Union of Journalists

nuke /nyook/ *vt* (**nukes**, **nuking**, **nuked**) **1 ATTACK PEOPLE** to attack people or places with nuclear weapons (*slang*) **2 MICROWAVE** to cook something in a microwave oven (*informal*) ▪ *n* **NUCLEAR WEAPON** a nuclear weapon (*slang*) [Mid-20C. Shortening of NUCLEAR.]

Nukualofa /nookoo ə lófə/ capital of Tonga on Tongatapu Island in the S Pacific Ocean. Population: 34,000 (1990).

~~nukular~~ incorrect spelling of **nuclear**

null /nul/ *adj* **1 INVALID** having no legal validity **2 VALUELESS** having no value or importance **3 AMOUNTING TO NOTHING** amounting to nothing in terms of context or character **4 AT ZERO LEVEL** at the level of zero or nothing **5 RELATING TO ZERO** equal to or relating to zero **6 EMPTY** describes a mathematical set containing no elements ○ *the null set* **7 ENDING IN ZERO** converging to zero ○ *a null sequence* **8 INDICATING A READING OF ZERO** indicating a reading of zero when a measured quantity is undetectable or equal to zero in a comparison ▪ *n* **ZERO** a zero (*literary*) [Mid-16C. Via Old French *nul* < Latin *nullus* 'not any'.] ◇ **null and void** not legally valid

nullah /núlla/ *n* S Asia a ditch or ravine [Late 18C. < Hindi *nālā*.]

Nullarbor Plain /núllər bawr-/ dry plateau in S South Australia. Area: 300,000 sq. km/116,000 sq. mi.

nullify /núlli fī/ (**-fies**, **-fying**, **-fied**) *vt* **1** to make something legally invalid or ineffective **2** to have the effect of cancelling something out —**nullifier** *n*

numbered account *n* a bank account identified by a number only, allowing the account holder to keep his or her identity secret

numberless /númbərləss/ *adj* **1** too numerous to be counted **2** not given a number or marked with a number

number one *n* **1 FIRST THING** the first one in a series of things or people ○ *She's number one among the top candidates.* **2 BESTSELLING RECORD** a recording in a particular category that has sold the most copies in a given week **3 SELF** yourself and your own interests (*informal*) **4 IMPORTANT PERSON** the leader or the most important person in a group or organization (*informal*) **5 URINATION** the act or an instance of urinating, or urine (*babytalk*) ◊ **number two** *n.* **2** ▪ *adj* **1 MOST IMPORTANT** first, best, or most important **2 EXCELLENT** of a very high standard or quality (*informal*)

Number One *n* the first officer or first mate on a ship (*informal*)

number plate *n* a metal or plastic plate on the front and back of a motor vehicle, carrying the vehicle's registration number. US term **license plate**

numbers /númbərz/ *n* US an illegal form of gambling in which people bet on an unpredictable number to be drawn or determined later (+ *singular or plural verb*)

Numbers *n* the fourth book of the Bible

numbers game *n* GAMBLING = **numbers** *n*.

Number Ten *n* 10 Downing Street, the official London home of the prime minister

number theory *n* the branch of mathematics that deals with the properties of integers and relationships between integers

number two *n* **1** somebody's deputy or second-in-command (*informal*) **2** the act or an instance of defecating, or faeces (*babytalk*) ◊ **number one** *n.* **5**

numbing /númming/ *adj* **1** causing numbness in part of the body **2** temporarily taking away somebody's ability to feel or think, e.g. as a result of shock

numbles /númb'lz/ *npl* the edible inside organs of an animal, especially a deer, including the heart, liver, and lungs (*archaic*) [14C. < Old French, < Latin *lumbulus* 'small loin' < *lumbus* 'loin'.]

numbskull /núm skul/, **numskull** *n* an offensive term that deliberately insults somebody's intelligence (*insult*) [Early 18C. < NUMB.]

numdah /núm daa/ *n* an embroidered rug made from felt, in a style from South Asia and the Middle East [Early 19C. Via Urdu *namdā* < Persian *namad* 'felt, carpet'.]

numen /nyoó men/ (*plural* **-mina** /-minə/) *n* **1** a god or spirit believed to inhabit a place or living object such as a tree **2** any guiding force or influence [Early 17C. < Latin, 'nod, command, divine power'.]

numerable /nyoómərəb'l/ *adj* able to be counted

numeracy /nyoómərəssi/ *n* competence in the mathematical skills needed to cope with everyday life and the understanding of information presented in mathematical terms like graphs, charts, or tables [Mid-20C. < NUMERATE.]

numeral /nyoómərəl/ *n* a symbol or set of symbols used to represent a number, e.g. the Arabic numeral 5, the equivalent Roman numeral V, and the equivalent binary numeral 101 ■ *adj* relating to numbers or representing a number or numbers [14C. < late Latin *numeralis* < Latin *numerus* 'number'.] —**numerally** *adv*

numerary /nyoómərəri/ *adj* relating to numbers [Early 18C. Via medieval Latin *numerarius* < Latin *numerus* 'number'.]

numerate *adj* /nyoómərət/ **1** able to do arithmetical calculations **2** having a basic understanding of mathematics [Early 18C. < Latin *numeratus*, past participle of *numerare* 'count' < *numerus* 'number'.]

numeration /nyoómə ráysh'n/ *n* **1** the naming of numbers, e.g. by schoolchildren, or the giving of numbers to items in a set or group **2** a system of symbols used for counting or numbering things

numerator /nyoómə raytər/ *n* the part of a common fraction appearing above the line, representing the number of parts of the whole that are being considered

numerical /nyoo mérrik'l/, **numeric** *adj* **1** using numbers or consisting of numbers **2** in terms of the number of people or things [Early 17C. < Latin *numerus* 'number'.]

numerical analysis *n* a branch of mathematics dealing with the use of repeatedly used quantitative approximations to solve problems, and the measurement of the errors involved —**numerical analyst** *n*

numerical control *n* an often computerized technique for controlling machine tools where the position or action of a tool, e.g. the depth of a drill, is determined by a numerical value

numerically /nyoo mérrikli/ *adv* in terms of the numbers of people or things involved ◊ *His forces were numerically superior to those of the enemy.*

numerical order *n* an ordering of people or things identified by number from the lowest to the highest

numerical taxonomy *n* a procedure that involves comparing a large number of characteristics of one organism with the same characteristics of another

numeric control *n* ENG = **numerical control**

⚡**numeric keypad** *n* a section of a computer keyboard, usually to the right of the main keypad, containing numbered keys in the same layout as the numbers on a calculator

numerology /nyoómə rólləji/ *n* the study of the occult use and supposed influence of numbers —**numerological** /nyoómərə lójjik'l/ *adj* —**numerologically** *adv* —**numerologist** *n*

numero uno /noómərō oónō/ *n* (*informal humorous*) **1** = **number one** *n*. **3 2** the leader or most important person in a group or organization [Late 20C. < Spanish or Italian, 'number one'.]

numerous /nyoómərəss/ *adj* many in number [15C. < Latin *numerosus* < *numerus* 'number'.] —**numerously** *adv* —**numerousness** *n*

Numidia /nyoo míddiə/ ancient kingdom in NW Africa, roughly corresponding to present-day Algeria —**Numidian** *adj, n*

Numidian crane *n* BIRDS = **demoiselle** *n*. 1

numina *plural of* **numen**

numinous /nyoóminəss/ *adj* **1** MYSTERIOUSLY ASSOCIATED WITH A DEITY having a mysterious power that suggests the presence of a spirit or god (*formal*) **2** HOLY filled with inextricable associations with God (*formal*) **3** OF NUMINA relating to numina, the spirits or gods believed in some cultures to inhabit places or things [Mid-17C. < Latin *numin-* 'deity'.] —**numinously** *adv* —**numinousness** *n*

numismatic /nyoómiz máttik/ *adj* relating to the study or collecting of coins and medals [Late 18C. < French *numismatique* < Greek *nomisma* 'coin, currency' < *nomizein* 'have in use' < *nomos* 'custom'.] —**numismatically** *adv*

numismatics /nyoómiz máttiks/ *n* the study and collecting of coins and medals (+ *singular verb*) —**numismatist** /nyoo mízmatist/ *n*

nummary /númməri/ *adj* relating to coins, or to coins and banknotes [Early 17C. < Latin *nummarius* < *nummus* 'coin'.]

nummular /númmyóoíər/ *adj* shaped like a coin or disc (*formal*) [Mid-18C. < Latin *nummulus* 'small coin' < *nummus* 'coin'.]

nummulite /númmyoo līt/ *n* a fossil shaped like a flat disc that is commonly found in limestone in the Mediterranean and dates from between 56.5 million and 5.2 million years ago [Early 19C. < modern Latin *Nummulites* < Latin *nummulus* (see NUMMULAR); from its shape.] —**nummulitic** /númmyoo líttik/ *adj*

numnah /núm naa/ *n* a pad placed under a saddle [Mid-19C. Variant of NUMDAH.]

nun[1] /nun/ *n* **1** a member of a religious community of women who dedicate their lives to religious devotion and undertake not to marry **2** a variety of domestic pigeon with black-and-white feathers all over and a ring of white feathers round its neck and head resembling a nun's headdress [Pre-12C. Via Old French *nonne* < ecclesiastical Latin *nonna* < *nonnus* 'old man, monk'.]

nun[2] /noòn/ *n* the 14th letter of the Hebrew alphabet [Early 19C. < Hebrew *nûn*.]

nunatak /núnnə tak/ *n* a mountain peak surrounded by glacial ice, originally in Norway and Greenland [Late 19C. < Inuit *nunataq*.]

Nunavut /noónnə voòt/ territory of N Canada, situated east of Northwest Territories and extending northwards to comprise most of Arctic Canada. Capital: Iqaluit. Population: 22,000 (1997). Area: 2,000,000 sq. km/770,000 sq. mi.

nun buoy *n* a buoy with a rounded middle and tapering ends, used to mark the right-hand side of a harbour channel [Early 18C. < *nun* 'child's top' < ?]

Nunc Dimittis /núngk di míttiss, noóngk-/ *n* a hymn or canticle with a text from Luke 2:29–32, starting in Latin with 'Nunc dimittis servum tuum', in English meaning 'Lord, now you are dismissing your servant in peace'

nunchaku /nun chaà koo/ *n* a martial arts weapon consisting of two thick sticks joined at their ends by an untanned leather strip, a rope, or a chain [Late 20C. < Japanese dialect.]

nunciature /núnssi əchər/ *n* the rank or position of a nuncio, or the period of time somebody spends as a nuncio [Early 17C. < Italian *nunciatura* < *nuncio* (see NUNCIO).]

nuncio /núnssi ō, noòn-, -shi ō/ (*plural* **-os**) *n* **1** somebody appointed by the pope to represent him in a country, with the diplomatic status of an ambassador **2** somebody sent by a person to act on his or her behalf, especially a person regarded as self-important or authoritarian (*formal humorous*) [Early 16C. Via Italian < Latin *nuntius* 'messenger'.]

nuncle /núngk'l/ *n* an uncle (*archaic*) [Late 16C. < *mine uncle* or *an uncle*.]

nuncupative /núngkyoo paytiv, -pətiv/ *adj* given or declared orally by somebody making a will, and written down later by somebody else [Mid-16C. < late Latin *nuncupativus* < Latin *nuncupare* 'name, declare' < *nomen* 'name' + *capere* 'to take'.]

Nuneaton /nun eét'n/ town in central England. Population: 66,715 (1991).

nunnery /núnnəri/ (*plural* **-ies**) *n* a convent

Nupe /noó pay/ (*plural* **-pe** *or* **-pes**) *n* **1** a member of a Nigerian people who live between the rivers Benue and Niger **2** the Benue-Congo language of the Nupe people. Native speakers: 1 million. [Early 19C. After a former kingdom at the junction of the Niger and Benue.]

nuptial /núpsh'l, -chəl/ *adj* **1** relating to marriage or weddings. ◊ **nuptials 2** relating to mating or breeding in animals [15C. < Old French, < Latin *nuptiae* 'wedding' < *nubere* 'take a husband'.] —**nuptially** *adv*

nuptial plumage *n* the distinctive feathers that some birds grow during their mating season

nuptials /núpsh'lz, -chəlz/ *npl* a wedding ceremony (*formal*)

Nuremberg /nyoórəm búrg/ city in SE Germany. Population: 497,496 (1992).

CORBIS/Bettmann

Rudolf Nureyev

Nureyev /nyoóri ef, nyoo ráy-/, **Rudolf** (1938–93) Russian-born ballet dancer and choreographer

Nuristan /noòri staàn/ administrative province of E Afghanistan. Area: 13,000 sq. km/5,000 sq. mi.

Nurmi /núrmi/, **Paavo** (1897–1973) Finnish athlete. Known as **the Flying Finn**

nurse /nurss/ *n* **1** SOMEBODY CARING FOR PATIENTS somebody trained to look after ill and injured people, especially somebody who works in a hospital or clinic, administering the care and treatment that a doctor prescribes **2** NANNY a nanny (*dated*) **3** = **wet nurse 4** NURSERY NURSE somebody professionally qualified to look after young children in a nursery, nursery school, or crèche **5** INSECT LOOKING AFTER YOUNG an insect that looks after the young or the larvae in a colony of social insects such as ants or bees ■ *v* (**nurses, nursing, nursed**) **1** *vt* CARE FOR A SICK PERSON to take care of somebody who is ill or injured **2** *vi* WORK AS A NURSE to do the work of a nurse, especially professionally in a hospital **3** *vt* TREAT A HEALTH PROBLEM to take care of yourself while ill or injured ◊ *nursing a broken leg* **4** *vt* KEEP A FEELING to keep a feeling in the mind for a long time and perhaps indulge in it, allowing it to grow or deepen ◊ *nursing his resentment* **5** *vt* HOLD to hold something precious with love or care **6** *vt* MANAGE SOMEBODY OR SOMETHING CAREFULLY to manage, guide, or supervise somebody or something with care and devotion **7** *vt* CONSUME SOMETHING SLOWLY to consume something, especially a drink, very slowly in order to make it last **8** *vt* HOLD SOMEBODY IN YOUR ARMS to hold somebody, especially a child, affectionately or protectively in your arms, or hold a part of somebody's body in this way **9** *vti* BREAST-FEED to breast-feed a baby, or suckle at a mother's breast [13C. Via Old French *norrice* < Latin *nutricia* 'wet nurse' < *nutrix*.] —**nurser** *n*

nursemaid /núrss mayd/ *n* a woman employed to look after somebody's children when they are young (*dated*)

nurse practitioner *n* a registered nurse trained in primary health care to assume certain responsibilities once assumed only by a doctor, e.g. the diagnosis and treatment of minor illnesses

nursery /núrssəri/ (*plural* **-ies**) *n* **1** EDUC = **nursery school 2** CHILD'S ROOM a child's bedroom or playroom in a house **3** PLACE GROWING PLANTS COMMERCIALLY a place where plants are grown commercially, either for sale direct to the public or to other retailers **4** FOSTERING PLACE a place where talents or abilities are allowed or encouraged to develop and flourish (*literary*) [14C. < Old French *norricerie* < *norrice* (see NURSE).]

nursery class *n* a school class for children under five years of age, especially one in a school where the majority of children are older

nurserymaid /núrssəri mayd/ *n* a woman employed to look after somebody's children when they are young (*dated*)

nurseryman /núrssərimən/ (*plural* **-men** /-mən/) *n* a man who works in or owns a nursery where plants are grown commercially

nursery rhyme *n* a short song or poem for young children, especially one that has become traditional

nursery school, nursery *n* a school for children between the ages of three and five, staffed wholly or partly by qualified teachers who encourage and supervise educational play rather than simply providing childcare

nursery slopes *npl* the gentlest slopes in a ski resort or complex, designed for beginners to use. US term **bunny slopes**

nurse's aide *n US* MED = **healthcare assistant**

nurse shark *n* a warm-water shark that has a bristle (**barbel**) hanging from its jaw and a deep groove on either side of its mouth. Family: Orectolobidae. [Because it tends its eggs until they hatch]

nursing /núrssing/ *n* **1** the profession or task of looking after people who are ill or injured **2** breast-feeding, or the period of time that a mother spends breast-feeding her baby

nursing assistant *n* MED = **healthcare assistant**

nursing auxiliary *n* a healthcare assistant

nursing bra *n* a bra with cups that can be removed or opened, worn by breast-feeding mothers

nursing home *n* a long-term hospital or home that provides full-time care and medical treatment for people who are unable to take care of themselves

nursling /núrssling/ *n* (*literary*) **1 BREAST-FED INFANT** a baby that is being breast-fed **2 CHILD BEING CARED FOR** a baby or child that somebody is looking after or bringing up, especially somebody else's child **3 SOMETHING FOSTERED** something fostered or developed by a person, a place, or a set of circumstances

nurture /núrchər/ *vt* (**-tures, -turing, -tured**) **1 CARE FOR A YOUNG THING** to give tender care and protection to a child, a young animal, or a plant, helping it to grow and develop **2 ENCOURAGE TO FLOURISH** to encourage somebody or something to grow, develop, thrive, and be successful ○ *an agent who nurtured several budding young playwrights* **3 KEEP A FEELING** to keep a feeling in the mind for a long time, allowing it to grow or deepen ■ *n* **1 CARE OR ENCOURAGEMENT** care and protection given to a young child, animal, or plant, or support and encouragement given to something to help it develop **2 ENVIRONMENTAL INFLUENCE** environmental influence on an organism, especially when contrasted with what is determined genetically [14C. Via Old French < late Latin *nutritura* < Latin *nutrire* 'suckle'.] —**nurturer** *n*

NUS *abbr* **1** National Union of Seamen **2** National Union of Students

Nusa Tenggara /nóossə teng gaárə/ island group in S Indonesia, in the Indian Ocean, east of Java. Population: 7,237,600 (1995). Area: 73,144 sq. km/28,241 sq. mi.

nut /nut/ *n* **1 HARD FRUIT** the fruit of a plant, especially a tree, with a hard outer shell containing the seed **2 EDIBLE KERNEL** the hard seed of a nut, especially when it is edible **3 PEANUT** a roasted peanut **4 HARD FRUIT OF SOME PLANTS** the hard dry one-seeded fruit of various plants, which does not split open to scatter its seed when it is mature **5 FASTENING SCREWED ONTO A BOLT** a piece of metal, usually square or hexagonal, with a hole in the middle, screwed on the end of a bolt as a fastening for it **6 PART OF A STRINGED INSTRUMENT** a ridge at the top end of the fingerboard of a stringed instrument that the strings pass over before reaching the tuning pegs **7 PART OF AN INSTRUMENT'S BOW** a device like a screw at one end of a bow for a musical instrument that is turned to tighten the hairs of the bow **8 SMALL PIECE** a small piece of something hard or solid ○ *a nut of coal* **9 HUMAN HEAD** a person's head (*informal*) **10 OFFENSIVE TERM** an offensive term for somebody with a psychiatric disorder **11 ENTHUSIAST** somebody with a deep interest in something (*informal*) ○ *a film nut* **12** PRINTING = **en** ■ *v* (**nuts, nutting, nutted**) **1** *vi* **GATHER NUTS** to gather edible nuts from trees **2** *vt* **HIT SOMEBODY WITH HEAD** to use the head to hit somebody, usually in the face (*informal*) [Old English *hnutu* < Indo-European]

NUT *abbr* National Union of Teachers

nutation /nyoo táysh'n/ *n* **1 WOBBLY ROTATION** the wobbly rotation of a spinning object, especially a planet, caused by a temporary shift in the position of its axis **2 PLANT'S IRREGULAR GROWTH** a spiral movement of a plant part caused by varying growth rates on each side **3 NODDING** the nodding of somebody's head (*formal*) [Early 17C. < Latin *nutation-* < the past participle of *nutare* 'nod'.] —**nutational** *adj*

nut-brown *adj* dark brown or reddish-brown in colour

nut butter *n* nuts ground to a fine paste or spread, usually with oil and seasonings added and sometimes sugar

nutcase /nút kayss/ *n* an offensive term for somebody with a psychiatric disorder (*informal*)

nutcracker /nút krakər/ *n* **1** a tool for cracking hard nutshells, usually consisting of two hinged metal arms between which the nut is squeezed **2** a bird of the crow family that feeds mainly on nuts and the seeds of pines. Native to: Europe, Asia, W North America. Genus: *Nucifraga*.

nut cutlet *n* a vegetarian cake, patty, or burger made from chopped nuts and other vegetable ingredients mixed together and sometimes shaped into a meat chop or cutlet form

nutgall /nút gawl/ *n* a hollow nut-shaped growth on the trunks of oak and other trees caused by the gall wasp, which uses the growth as a shelter for its larvae

nuthatch /nút hach/ *n* a small bird with a blue-grey back that usually hangs upside down on a tree trunk and works its way down, eating insects, seeds, and nuts. Family: Sittidae. [14C. < NUT + *hache* 'hatchet, axe' < Old French (see HATCHET), from its habit of hacking at nuts with its beak.]

nuthouse /nút howss/ *n* (*slang*) **1** an offensive term for psychiatric hospital **2** a place full of noisy, boisterous, chaotic activity

nutlet /nútlət/ *n* **1** a small nut, especially a small hard dry one-seeded fruit of various plants **2** the stone of fruits such as cherry and plum

nutmeg /nút meg/ *n* **1 SPICE** an aromatic spice made by grinding or grating the large hard seed of a nutmeg tree **2 TROPICAL EVERGREEN TREE** an evergreen tree widely grown in tropical regions for its seeds, which yield nutmeg and mace. Native to: E India. *Myristica fragrans.* **3 KICK OF BALL THROUGH OPPONENT'S LEGS** in soccer, a move in which the ball is kicked between an opponent's legs and often regained behind him or her (*informal*) ■ *adj* **LIGHT BROWN** of a light greyish-brown colour ■ *vt* (**-megs, -megging, -megged**) **KICK BALL THROUGH OPPONENT'S LEGS** to kick the ball through the open legs of an opponent (*informal*) [13C. Probably < medieval Latin *nux muscata* 'nut smelling like musk' < *nux* 'nut' + late Latin *muscus* (see MUSK).]

nutraceutical /nóotrə sóotik'l/, **nutriceutical, neutraceutical** *n* PHARM = **functional food** [Late 20C. < Latin *nutrire* 'to nourish' + PHARMACEUTICAL.]

nutria /nyóotri ə/ *n* **1** ZOOL = **coypu 2** the light brown fur of the coypu [Early 19C. Via Spanish < Latin *lutra* 'otter'.]

nutrient /nyóotri ənt/ *n* any substance that provides nourishment, e.g. the minerals that a plant takes from the soil or the constituents in food that keep a human body healthy and help it grow ■ *adj* providing nourishment [Mid-17C. < Latin *nutrient-*, present participle of *nutrire* 'nourish'.]

nutriment /nyóotrimənt/ *n* nourishment or nourishing substances [Mid-16C. < Latin *nutrimentum* < *nutrire* 'nourish'.]

nutrition /nyoo trísh'n/ *n* **1 PROCESSING OF FOOD** the process of absorbing nutrients from food and processing them in the body in order to keep healthy or to grow **2 SCIENCE OF FOOD** the science that deals with foods and their effects on health **3 FOODS** foods, or the minerals, vitamins, and other nourishing substances that they contain [Mid-16C. Via Old French < Latin *nutrition-* < *nutrire* 'nourish'.] —**nutritional** *adj* —**nutritionally** *adv*

nutritional therapy *n* the alleviation of symptoms by dietary changes, sometimes using vitamin and mineral pills

nutritionist /nyoo trísh'nist/ *n* a student of or expert in nutrition

nutritious /nyoo tríshəss/ *adj* containing minerals, vitamins, and other substances that promote health —**nutritiously** *adv* —**nutritiousness** *n*

nutritive /nyóotrətiv/ *adj* **1** providing nutrients **2** relating to nutrition [15C. Via Old French < medieval Latin *nutritivus* < the past participle of *nutrire* 'nourish'.] —**nutritively** *adv*

nut roast *n* a savoury vegetarian loaf made from chopped or ground-up nuts with onions, herbs, and seasonings, bound with breadcrumbs and baked

nuts /nuts/ *adj* (*slang*) **1 OFFENSIVE TERM** an offensive term meaning having a psychiatric disorder **2 ENTHUSIASTIC** wildly enthusiastic about something, or extremely fond of somebody (*offensive in some contexts*) ■ *npl* **OFFENSIVE TERM** an offensive term for testicles (*slang*) ■ *interj* **EXPRESSION OF ANNOYANCE** used to express annoyance, disbelief, or contempt (*slang; offensive in some contexts*)

nuts and bolts *npl* the most basic components, elements, or constituents of something (*informal*)

nutshell /nút shel/ *n* the hard outer shell of a nut that surrounds the edible inner seed ◇ **in a nutshell** in very few words, getting right to the main point

nutter /núttər/ *n* an offensive term that deliberately insults somebody's mental condition or way of behaving (*informal*)

nutty /nútti/ (**-tier, -tiest**) *adj* **1 WITH NUTS** containing a large amount of nuts **2 LIKE NUTS** like nuts in taste, appearance, texture, or smell **3 nutty, nutsy OFFENSIVE TERM** an offensive term meaning having a psychiatric disorder (*informal*) —**nuttily** *adv* —**nuttiness** *n*

Nuuk /nook/ capital of Greenland, on the SW coast of the island. Population: 12,483 (1994).

nux vomica /núks vómmikə/ (*plural* **nux vomica**) *n* **1 MEDICINE** a medicine or homeopathic remedy made from the poisonous seeds of a South Asian tree **2 POISONOUS SEEDS** the seeds of a South Asian tree, which contain strychnine and other poisonous substances **3 ASIAN TREE** a tree with orange-red berries and poisonous seeds. Native to: South Asia. *Strychnos nux-vomica.* [< medieval Latin, 'emetic nut']

nuzzle /núzz'l/ *v* (**-zles, -zling, -zled**) **1** *vti* **RUB SOMETHING WITH THE NOSE** to rub or push something gently with the nose, especially as a way of showing affection **2** *vi* **RUB SOMETHING WITH THE FACE** to make affectionate rubbing or stroking movements with the face ■ *n* **RUBBING MOVEMENT** a rubbing or stroking movement with the nose or face [15C. < ?] —**nuzzler** *n*

NV *abbr* **1** Nevada **2** non-voting

nvCJD *abbr* new variant CJD

NVQ *n* a UK qualification in a technical or vocational subject certifying the holder's proficiency in a range of work-related activities, awarded at a variety of levels. Full form **National Vocational Qualification**

NW *abbr* **1** northwest **2** northwestern

Nwfld *abbr* Newfoundland

n.wt. *abbr* net weight

N.W.T. *abbr Can* Northwest Territories

NY, N.Y. *abbr* New York

nyala /nyaálə/ (*plural* **-la** *or* **-las**) *n* **1** an antelope with vertical white stripes on its sides and, on the male, spiral horns. Native to: central Africa. *Tragelaphus angasi.* **2** an antelope with spiral horns on the male. Native to: mountainous regions in NE Africa. *Tragelaphus buxtoni.* [Late 19C. < Zulu *i-nyala*.]

Nyasaland /ni ássə land, nī-/ former name for **Malawi**

⚡**nybble** /níbb'l/ *n* half of one byte or four bits in size [Humorous play on the idea of a small bite]

NYC *abbr* New York City

nyctalopia /níktə lṓpi ə/ *n* the state of being unable to see well at night (*technical*) [Late 17C. < late Latin, < Greek *nuktalōps* 'sightless at night' < *nukt-* 'night' + *alaos* 'sightless' + *ōps* 'eye'.] —**nyctalopic** /-lóppik/ *adj*

nyctinasty /níkti nasti/ (*plural* **-ties**) *n* a movement of a plant or plant part in response to the onset of darkness, e.g. the shutting of the petals of a flower at night [Mid-20C. < Greek *nukt-* 'night'.]

nyctitropism /nik títtrəpizəm/ *n* the movement of parts of a plant in response to light and temperature differences between night and day, such as the opening and closing of flowers and the folding together of leaves at night [Late 19C. < Greek *nukt-* 'night'.] —**nyctitropic** /níktə trṓpik, -tróppik/ *adj*

nyctophobia /níktə fṓbi ə/ *n* an irrational fear of the night or of darkness in general [Early 20C. < Greek *nukt-* 'night'.] —**nyctophobic** *adj* —**nyctophobically** *adv*

⚡ **nyetwork** *n* = **notwork** (*slang humorous*) [Late 20C. Blend of Russian *nyet* 'no' + NETWORK.]

nylon /nī lon/ *n* a tough synthetic material. Use: food containers, brush bristles, clothing. ■ **nylons** *npl* stockings made of a synthetic fibre such as nylon [Mid-20C. < ?]

NY-LON *adj* relating to a transatlantic lifestyle divided between New York and London, as lived by successful business executives [< the abbreviations for NEW YORK and LONDON]

NYMEX /nī meks/ *abbr* New York Mercantile Exchange

nymph /nimf/ *n* **1 SPIRIT OF NATURE** a minor goddess or spirit of nature in mythology, inhabiting areas of natural beauty such as woods, mountains, and rivers and traditionally regarded as a beautiful young woman **2 WOMAN** a beautiful young woman (*literary*) **3 INSECT LARVA** the larva of some insects, e.g. mayflies, dragonflies, and grasshoppers, that resembles the adult and develops into the adult insect directly, without passing through the intermediate pupa stage [14C. Via Old French < Greek *nymphē* 'bride, nymph'.]

nympha /nímfə/ (*plural* **-phae** /-fee/) *n* either of the small inner folds of skin (**labia minora**) that form the opening to the vagina [Late 17C. Via Latin < Greek *nymphē* 'nymph'.]

nymphalid /nímfəlid/ *adj* belonging to a family of butterflies that has brightly coloured wings and includes the tortoiseshell butterfly and the red admiral. Family: Nymphalidae. [Late 19C. Via modern Latin *Nymphalidae* < Latin *nympha* (see NYMPHA).]

nymphet /nímfit, nim fét/, **nymphette** /nim fét/ *n* a sexually aware and sexually desirable young woman, especially a woman in her early teens

nympho /ním fō/ (*plural* **-phos**) *n* an offensive term for a woman who is very active sexually, especially when she is regarded with distaste (*slang*) [Mid-20C. Shortening of NYMPHOMANIAC.]

nymphomania /nímfə máyni ə/ *n* a woman's compulsive desire to have sex with many different men, theorized to occur in some women (*often considered offensive*)

nymphomaniac /nímfə máyni ak/ *n* **1** a woman supposed to have a compulsive desire to have sex with many different men **2** an offensive term for a woman who is very active sexually, especially when she is regarded with distaste (*informal*) —**nymphomaniacal** /nímfōmə ní ək'l/ *adj*

NYSE *abbr* New York Stock Exchange

nystagmus /ni stágməss/ *n* an involuntary rhythmic movement of somebody's eyes, usually from side to side, caused by some illnesses that affect the nerves and muscle behind the eyeball [Early 19C. Via modern Latin < Greek *nustagmos* 'drowsiness' < *nustazein* 'nod, be sleepy'.]

nystatin /nístətin/ *n* an antibiotic drug. Use: treatment of fungal infections, especially thrush. [Mid-20C. < *N(ew) Y(ork) Stat(e)*.]

Nyungar /nyoŏngər/, **Nyunga** *n* an Aboriginal language of SW Australia, now extinct [Mid-19C. < Nyungar *nungar* 'a man'.] —**Nyungar** *adj*

⚡ **nz** *abbr* New Zealand (*in Internet addresses*)

Oo

o¹ /ō/ (*plural* **o's**), **O** (*plural* **O's** *or* **Os**) *n* the 15th letter of the English alphabet, representing a vowel sound

o² *abbr* **1** ocean **2** octavo **3** old **4** order **5** out **6** over(s) **7** pint [Shortening of modern Latin *octarius*]

o' (*stressed*) /ō/; (*unstressed*) /ə/ *contr* of

⚡**O¹** *abbr* over (completion of communication) (*in e-mails*)

O² (*plural* **O's** *or* **Os**) *n* **1** something shaped like a letter 'O' **2** a human blood type of the ABO system containing the O antigen

O³ /ō/ *interj* **1** used to address a person or topic or at the start of a plea or wish **2** used to express surprise or great wonderment (*literary*) [12C. Natural exclamation.]

O⁴ *symbol* oxygen

O⁵ *abbr* **1** ocean **2** octavo **3** old **4** order **5** out **6** over(s)

-o *suffix* **1** used to form abbreviated words ○ *aggro* ○ *demo* ○ *hypo* **2** somebody or something associated with or having the characteristics of something ○ *dumbo* [< ?]

oaf /ōf/ *n* somebody regarded as unintelligent, clumsy, or uncultured (*insult*) [Early 17C. < Old Norse *álfr* 'elf'.]

oafish /ōfish/ *adj* resembling an oaf, e.g. in clumsiness, or lack of intelligence or refinement (*insult*) —**oafishly** *adv* —**oafishness** *n*

Oahu /ō áà hoo/ island in central Hawaii, between Kauai and Molokai islands. Population: 870,761 (1995). Area: 1,546 sq. km/597 sq. mi.

oak /ōk/ *n* **1 TREE BEARING ACORNS** a deciduous or evergreen tree with acorns as fruit and leaves with several rounded or pointed lobes. Genus: *Quercus*. **2 BUSH WITH LOBED LEAVES** a bush with lobed leaves like those of the oak tree, e.g. a Jerusalem oak or poison oak **3 HARD WOOD OF OAK TREE** the hard wood of the oak tree. Use: furniture-making, flooring. **4 OAK WREATH OR GARLAND** a decoration made from the leaves of an oak tree, especially a wreath or garland ■ *adj* **OF RICH BROWN COLOUR** of a rich brown colour, similar to the colour of oak wood [Old English *āc*]

oak apple *n* a rounded hollow growth on the trunk of an oak tree caused by infestation with gall wasps, which use the growths as shelters for their larvae

oaken /ōkən/ *adj* made of oak wood (*literary*)

oak fern *n* a light green woodland fern found in northern climates. *Thelypteris dryopteris*.

Oakham /ōkəm/ town in central England. Population: 8,691 (1991).

Oakland /ōklənd/ city in W California. Population: 372,242 (1990).

oak leaf cluster *n* a small decoration shaped like a bunch of oak leaves and acorns, added to another military decoration to show that it has been awarded to the wearer more than once

Oakley /ōkli/, **Annie** (1860–1926) US sharpshooter. Full name **Phoebe Anne Oakley Moses**

oakmoss /ōk moss/ *n* any lichen that grows on oak trees and produces a resin used in the making of some perfumes. *Evernia prunastri*.

oakum /ōkəm/ *n* hemp or jute fibres, especially from old ropes unravelled and soaked in tar. Use: formerly, sealant for gaps between the planks in a wooden boat's hull. [Old English *ācumba* 'broken fibers', literally 'off-combing' < Indo-European, 'tooth']

Oakville /ōkvil/ town in SE Ontario, Canada. Population: 114,670 (1991).

oak wilt *n* a disease of oak trees caused by a fungus that kills their leaves

Oamaru /ómmə roo/ port on E South Island, New Zealand. Population: 13,695 (1996).

O & M *abbr* organization and method

OAP *n* a person who draws a pension from a government on reaching a specified age

oar /awr/ *n* **1 POLE USED TO PROPEL BOAT** a wooden pole with one broad flat end, used either singly or in pairs to propel a boat by dipping the broad end in the water **2 SOMEBODY ROWING** a rower of a boat, especially in a team of rowers ■ *vti* **TO ROW** to row a boat [Old English *ār*]

SPELLCHECK Do not confuse *oar* with *or* or *ore*, which have similar sounds. Beware: your spellchecker will not catch this error.

---

oarfish /áwr fish/ (*plural* **-fish** *or* **-fishes**) *n* a long, eel-shaped fish that grows up to 7 m/23 ft, with a dazzling red head fin and dorsal fin. Native to: tropical Atlantic waters. *Regalecus glesne*. [Mid-19C. < the shape of its body.]

oarlock /áwr lok/ *n US* ROWING = **rowlock** [Old English *ārloc* < *ār* 'oar' + *loc* 'lock']

oarsman /áwrzmən/ (*plural* **-men** /-mən/) *n* a man who rows a boat, especially as part of a team of rowers —**oarsmanship** *n*

oarswoman /áwrz wŏŏmən/ (*plural* **-en** /-wimmən/) *n* a woman who rows a boat, especially as part of a team of rowers

oarweed /áwr weed/ *n* FUNGI = **tangle²** *n*.

OAS *abbr US* Organization of American States

oasis /ō áyssiss/ (*plural* **-ses** /-seez/) *n* **1** fertile ground in a desert where the level of underground water rises to or near ground level, where plants grow and travellers can replenish water supplies **2** a place or period that gives relief from a troubling or chaotic situation [Early 17C. Via late Latin < Greek.]

oast /ōst/ *n* a kiln used for drying hops, especially hops used to flavour beer **2** = **oasthouse** [Old English *āst* 'kiln' < Indo-European, 'be hot, burn']

oasthouse /ōst howss/ (*plural* **-houses** /ōst howziz/) *n* a building that was built to contain hop-drying kilns and typically has conical or pyramid-shaped towers

oat /ōt/ *n* a grass that has edible seeds and is grown in numerous northern countries as a cereal crop. *Avena sativa*. ■ **oats** *npl* the seeds of the oat grown as a cereal crop and used to make foods such as porridge and as a livestock feed [Old English *āte*]

oatcake /ōt kayk/ *n* a hard unsweetened biscuit made from oatmeal, eaten with cheese and other savoury foods

oat-cell *adj* relating to a highly malignant form of lung cancer (**oat-cell carcinoma**) characterized by the rapid growth of undifferentiated small round cells [Because the cells look like grains of oats]

oaten /ōt'n/ *adj* made from oats, oatmeal, or oat straw

oater /ōtər/ *n* a film about cowboys, Native North Americans, and settlers in the American West (*humorous slang*) [Mid-20C. < the staple food of the horses featured.]

Oates /ōts/, **Joyce Carol** (*b*. 1938) US writer

Oates, Titus (1649–1705) English conspirator

oat grass *n* a wild grass that looks like the cultivated oat. Genera: *Arrhenatherum* and *Danthonia*.

oath /ōth/ (*plural* **oaths** /ōthz/) *n* **1 SOLEMN PROMISE** a formal or legally binding pledge to do something such as tell the truth in a court of law, made formally and often naming God or a loved one as a witness ○ *took a solemn oath of loyalty* **2 WORDS OF PROMISE** the words said when making a formal pledge, especially when reciting a conventional formula such as that used in a court of law **3 SWEARWORD** a swearword, especially one that uses the name of God or another sacred name in a disrespectful way [Old English *āþ*] ◇ **my oath** *ANZ* used to express strong confirmation or agreement (*slang*)

oatmeal /ōt meel/ *n* **1** oat grains ground or crushed into flakes or powder, used to make various foods such as porridge, flapjacks, and oatcakes ○ *oatmeal biscuits* **2** *US FOOD* = **porridge** *n*. **1** ■ *adj* of a light greyish-brown colour

OAU *abbr* Organization of African Unity

⚡**OAUS** *abbr* on an unrelated subject (*in e-mails*)

Oaxaca /wə haáka/ capital of Oaxaca State, S Mexico. Population: 212,818 (1990).

Ob' /ob/ river in W Siberian Russia that flows northwards into the Gulf of Ob'. Length: 3,680 km/2,290 mi.

OB *abbr* **1 OB, ob.** obstetric **2 OB, ob.** obstetrician **3 OB, ob.** obstetrics **4** outside broadcast

ob. *abbr* **1** obstetric **2** obstetrics **3** obstetrician **4** oboe **5** he or she died ['He or she died', shortening of Latin *obiit*]

ob- *prefix* inverse, inversely ○ *obvolute* [< Latin *ob* 'in the way, against, towards']

oba /ōbə/ *n* a ruler among the Yoruba people of West Africa [Early 20C. < Yoruba.]

Obad. *abbr* Obadiah

Obadiah /ōbə dí ə/ *n* **1** in the Bible, a minor Hebrew prophet of the 6th century BC **2** a book of the Bible containing the prophecies of Obadiah

Oban /ōbən/ town and port in W Scotland. Population: 8,134 (1981).

obb. *abbr* obbligato

obbligato /óbbli gaà tō/, **obligato** *adj* not to be omitted from a musical piece, either as an instrumental part in the piece or as an instrumental accompaniment to a singer (*musical direction*) ■ *n* (*plural* **-tos** *or* **-ti** /-tee/) a musical part or accompaniment that is not to be left out [Early 18C. Via Italian, 'obliged' < Latin *obligare* < OBLIGATE.]

obconic /ob kónnik/, **obconical** /ob kónnik'l/ *adj* cone-shaped and attached to a plant by the pointed end ○ *an obconic fruit*

obcordate /ob káwr dayt/ *adj* heart-shaped and attached to a plant by the pointed end

obdurate /óbdyŏŏrət/ *adj* **1** not easily persuaded or influenced **2** not influenced by emotions, especially not inclined to feel sympathy or pity [15C. < late Latin *obduratus*, past participle of *obdurare* 'be hard' < *durus* 'hard'.] —**obduracy** *n* —**obdurately** *adv* —**obdurateness** *n*

OBE *abbr* Officer of the (Order of the) British Empire

obeah /ṓbi ə/, **obi** /ṓbi/ *n* **1** a religion that involves witchcraft, originally practised in Africa and surviving now in parts of the Caribbean **2** an object believed to have magical powers, used in practising obeah [Mid-18C. < Twi *ōbayifo*.]

obedience /ə beédi'nss/ *n* **1** the action or condition of obeying authority **2** the religious authority of a church or of a priest or other member of the clergy, or the people who are under this authority

obedient /ə beédi'nt/ *adj* carrying out or willing to carry out what is demanded or ordered, particularly by somebody in authority [13C. < Old French < Latin *oboediens*, present participle of *oboedire* (see OBEY).]

obeisance /ō báyss'nss, ō beéss'nss/ *n* **1** a gesture of respect or deference, e.g. a bow of the head (*formal*) **2** the attitude or behaviour of somebody who pays respect or homage to somebody or something [14C. < Old French, < *obeir* (see OBEY).]

obeli plural of **obelus**

obelia /ō beéli ə/ (*plural* **-lias**) *n* an ocean hydrozoan polyp that forms colonies that resemble moss on rocks, ships' hulls, and pilings. Genus: *Obelia*. [Late 19C. < modern Latin, < Greek *obelias* 'leaf baked on a spit' < *obelos* 'spit'.]

obelise *vt* = **obelize**

obelisk /óbbə lisk/ *n* **1** a pillar of stone, especially one built as a monument, that has a square base and sides that taper like a pyramid towards a pointed top **2** PRINTING = **dagger** *n.* **3** [Mid-16C. Via Latin *obeliscus* < Greek *obeliskos* < *obelos* (see OBELUS).] —**obeliskoid** /óbbə lísk oyd/ *adj*

obelize /óbbə līz/ (**-lizes, -lizing, -lized**), **obelise** (**-lises, -lising, -lised**) *vt* to mark a written or printed word or passage with a dagger or obelus [Mid-17C. < Greek *obelizein* < *obelos* 'spit'.]

obelus /óbbələss/ (*plural* **-li** /-lī/) *n* **1** PRINTING = **dagger** *n.* **3** **2** a printed mark (†) used in modern editions of ancient manuscripts to indicate that the passage marked is thought not to be genuine [14C. Via late Latin < Greek *obelos* 'spit, obelisk'.]

obento /ō béntō/ (*plural* **-tos**), **bento** (*plural* **-tos**) *n* a Japanese meal that is packaged in a partitioned lacquer box [Late 20C. < Japanese.]

Oberammergau /ṓbər ámmər gow/ town in SE Germany, famous for producing a Passion Play every ten years. Population: 5,425 (1991).

Oberon /ṓbə ron/ *n* second-largest natural satellite of Uranus, 1,522 km in diameter

obese /ō beéss/ *adj* so overweight as to be at risk from several serious illnesses, including diabetes and heart disease, if action is not taken to control the weight [Mid-17C. < Latin *obesus*, past participle of assumed *obedere* 'eat until overweight' < *edere* 'eat'.] —**obesely** *adv* —**obeseness** *n*

obesity /ō beéssəti/ *n* a condition in which somebody's weight is more than 20% higher than is recommended for that person's height

obey /ə báy/ (**obeys, obeying, obeyed**) *vti* **1** to follow instructions or behave in accordance with a law, rule, or order **2** to be controlled by somebody or something [13C. Via Old French *obeir* < Latin *oboedire* 'listen to' < *audire* 'hear'.] —**obeyer** *n*

obfuscate /ób fuss kayt, óbfəss-/ (**-cates, -cating, -cated**) *v* **1** *vti* to make something obscure or unclear, especially by making it unnecessarily complicated **2** *vt* to make somebody confused [Mid-16C. < late Latin *obfuscat-*, past participle of *obfuscare* 'darken' < *fuscus* 'dark'.] —**obfuscation** /ób fu skáysh'n, óbfə-/ *n* —**obfuscator** *n* —**obfuscatory** /óbfəs káytəri/ *adj*

ob-gyn /ṓ bee jeé wī én/, **Ob-Gyn** *n US* (*informal*) **1** the branch of medicine that deals with obstetrics and gynaecology **2** a specialist in obstetrics and gynaecology

obi[1] /ṓbi/ (*plural* **obis** *or* **obi**) *n* a silk sash worn by a Japanese person in traditional dress to fasten the kimono [Late 19C. < Japanese, 'belt, band, girdle'.]

obi[2] /ṓbi/ *n* RELIG = **obeah**

Ob'-Irtysh /ób eer tísh/ river system in W Siberian Russia, incorporating the rivers Irtysh and Ob'. Length: 5,410 km/3,362 mi.

obit /ṓbit, ō bít/ *n* an obituary (*informal*) [14C. Via French < Latin *obitus* 'death' < (*mortem*) *obire* 'die', literally 'meet (death)' < *ire* 'go'.]

obiter dictum /óbbitər díktəm, ṓbitər-/ (*plural* **obiter dicta** /-díktə/) *n* **1** an observation made by a judge that is incidental to the case being tried and, while being authoritative, is not binding on future courts under the doctrine of precedent **2** a comment made in passing [Early 19C. < Latin, 'said by the way, said in passing'.]

obituary /ə bíchoo əri/ *n* (*plural* **-ies**) an announcement, especially in a newspaper, of somebody's death, often with a short biography ■ *adj* relating to or recording a death [Early 18C. < medieval Latin *obituarius* < Latin *obitus* (see OBIT).]

obj. *abbr* **1** object **2** objection **3** objective

⚡**object** *n* /óbb jikt/ **1** SOMETHING VISIBLE OR TANGIBLE something that can be seen or touched **2** FOCUS a focus of somebody's attention or emotion **3** AIM an aim or purpose **4** SOMEBODY OR SOMETHING RIDICULOUS somebody or something ridiculous or pitiable (*informal*) **5** NOUN AFFECTED BY VERB a noun, pronoun, or noun phrase denoting somebody or something that is acted on by a verb or affected by the action of a verb **6** NOUN GOVERNED BY PREPOSITION a noun, pronoun, or noun phrase that is governed by a preposition **7** SOMETHING PERCEIVED AND NAMED AS SEPARATE something that is perceived as an entity and referred to by a name ○ *mental objects* **8** SOURCE OF LIGHT RAYS the point or series of points that appear to be the source of light rays in an optical system **9** UNIT OF INFORMATION a block of information such as a text or graphics document or a part of a document that can be linked to and embedded in other documents **10** UNIT OF COMPUTER PROGRAMMING a collection of variables, data structures, and procedures stored as an entity and forming a basic building block of object-oriented programming ■ *v* /əb jékt/ **1** *vi* BE OPPOSED to be opposed to something, or express opposition to it ○ *I object to being treated like a lackey.* **2** *vt* STATE AS OBJECTION to state something as a reason for being opposed to something [14C. < medieval Latin *objectum* 'thing presented (to the sight)' < Latin *obicere* 'present, throw against' < *jacere* 'to throw'.] —**objector** *n* ◇ **something is no object** used in order to say that something is not a concern or difficulty ○ *I want the best room you have – money's no object.*

SYNONYMS ***object, protest, demur, remonstrate, expostulate***

CORE MEANING: to indicate opposition to something

object to be opposed or averse to something, or express opposition to it; **protest** to express strong disapproval of or disagreement with something, or to refuse to obey or accept something, often by making a formal statement or taking action in public; **demur** to raise objections in a hesitant or tentative way; **remonstrate** to reason or argue forcefully with somebody about something; **expostulate** to express disagreement or disapproval vehemently, or to attempt to dissuade somebody from doing something.

object ball *n* in billiards, pool, or snooker, the ball that a player intends to hit with the cue ball in a particular shot

⚡**object code** *n* the binary version of a computer program that is used by the computer to run the program. ◊ **source code**

object complement *n* a noun, pronoun, or adjective that is a complement of a verb and qualifies its direct object, e.g. *angry* in 'He makes me angry'. US term **objective complement**

object glass *n* OPTICS = **objective** *n.* **5**

objectify /əb jékti fī/ (**-fies, -fying, -fied**) *vt* **1** to think of or represent an idea or emotion as if it were something that actually exists **2** to reduce somebody, or something that is complex and multifaceted, to the status of a simple object

objection /əb jéksh'n/ *n* **1** a feeling or expression of opposition ○ *Several people raised very pertinent objections to the plan.* **2** a reason for a feeling or expression of opposition

objectionable /əb jéksh'nəb'l/ *adj* causing disapproval, offence, or opposition ○ *an objectionable habit* —**objectionability** /əb jéksh'nə bílləti/ *n* —**objectionableness** *n* —**objectionably** *adv*

objective /əb jéktiv/ *adj* **1** FREE OF BIAS free of any bias or prejudice caused by personal feelings **2** BASED ON FACTS based on facts rather than thoughts or opinions **3** OBSERVABLE describes disease symptoms that can be observed by somebody other than the person who is ill **4** EXISTING INDEPENDENTLY OF MIND existing independently of the individual mind or perception **5** BEING OBJECT OF VERB in or constituting the grammatical case of a noun or pronoun that is the object of a verb ■ *n* **1** AIM an aim or goal **2** MILITARY TARGET the target or goal of a military operation **3** OBJECTIVE CASE the objective grammatical case **4** NOUN IN OBJECTIVE CASE a noun or pronoun in the objective case **5** LENS NEAREST OBJECT the lens or combination of lenses in an optical instrument nearest to and facing the object being viewed —**objectiveness** *n*

objective complement *n* GRAM = **object complement**

objective correlative *n* something in a written or performed work that is associated with a particular emotion and used to evoke it in the reader or audience

objective lens *n* OPTICS = **objective** *n.* **5**

objectively /əb jéktivli/ *adv* **1** without being influenced by personal feelings **2** on the basis of fact, experience, or some measurable quality ○ *objectively derived measures such as test scores*

objectivise *vt* = **objectivize**

objectivism /əb jéktivizəm/ *n* **1** the emphasizing of external realities rather than beliefs or feelings in literature or art **2** a philosophical belief that moral truths or external objects exist independently of the individual mind or perception —**objectivist** *n, adj*

objectivity /ób jek tívvəti/ *n* **1** ABILITY TO VIEW THINGS OBJECTIVELY the ability to perceive or describe something without being influenced by personal emotions or prejudices **2** ACTUAL EXISTENCE the actual existence of something, without reference to people's impressions or ideas **3** ACCURACY the quality of being accurate and independent of individual perceptions

objectivize /əb jékti vīz/ (**-vizes, -vizing, -vized**), **objectivise** (**-vises, -vising, -vised**) *vt* = **objectify** *v.* **1**

⚡**object language** *n* **1** the language that a computer interprets in running programs **2** = **target language** *n.* **3**

object lens *n* OPTICS = **objective** *n.* **5**

object lesson *n* an incident that provides an opportunity for learning something, especially the best way to do something ○ *an object lesson in tact*

⚡**object-oriented graphics** *npl* graphics images present in a computer as actual instructions to draw objects and not as bit maps

⚡**object-oriented programming** *n* a form of computer programming based on objects arranged in a branching hierarchy

object permanence *n* the knowledge that objects have an existence in time and space, independent of whether or not they can be seen or touched

object relations *npl* a psychoanalytic theory that sees an individual as motivated by a desire to form bonds with appropriate objects or people, rather than merely satisfying impulses in order to discharge tension

objet d'art /ób zhay daár/ (*plural* **objets d'art** /ób zhay daár/) *n* an object that has artistic value, especially a small piece [Mid-19C. < French, 'object of art'.]

objet trouvé /ób zhay troó vay/ (*plural* **objets trouvés** /ób zhay troó vay/) *n* a natural or everyday object such as a pebble from a beach, treated as something of artistic value or incorporated into a work of art [Mid-20C. < French, 'found object'.]

objurgate /ób jur gayt/ (**-gates, -gating, -gated**) *vt* to scold somebody angrily (*literary*) [Early 17C. < Latin *objurgat-*, past participle of *objurgare* 'quarrel against' < *jurgium* 'quarrel'.] —**objurgation** /ób jur gáysh'n/ *n* —**objurgator** *n* —**objurgatorily** *adv* —**objurgatory** /ob júrgətəri/ *adj*

oblast /ób laast, óbbləst/ *n* a subdivision of a republic of the former Soviet Union [Late 19C. < Russian *óblast* 'authority on' < *vlast* 'authority, power'.]

oblate[1] /ób layt, o bláyt/ *adj* shaped like a sphere but with the length of the diameter at the equator greater than the length from pole to pole [Early 18C. < modern Latin *oblatus* 'brought against' < Latin *latus*, past participle of *ferre* 'bring'.] —**oblately** *adv* —**oblateness** *n*

oblate[2] /ób layt/ *n* in the Roman Catholic Church, a lay person who is part of a religious community [Late 17C. Via French < medieval Latin *oblatus* 'brought to' < the past participle of Latin *offerre* (see OFFER).]

oblation /o bláysh'n/ *n* **1** OFFERING OF GIFT TO DEITY the offering of a gift or sacrifice to a deity **2** COMMUNION OFFERING the offering of bread and wine to God during the Christian service of Communion **3** RELIGIOUS OR CHARITABLE GIFT something offered in a religious rite or as a charitable gift [15C. Directly or via Old French < late Latin *oblation-* < Latin *offerre* (see OFFER).] —**oblational** *adj*

obligate /óbbli gayt/ *vt* (**-gates, -gating, -gated**) to compel somebody to do something as a legal or moral duty ■ *adj* describes an organism that can exist only in a particular role or under particular environmental conditions. ◊ **facultative** *adj.* 3 [15C. < Latin *obligatus*, past participle of *obligare* (see OBLIGE).] —**obligable** /óbbligəb'l/ *adj* —**obligately** /-gaytli/ *adv* —**obligator** /-gaytər/ *n*

obligation /óbbli gáysh'n/ *n* **1 STATE OF OWING** the state or condition of being obligated **2 DUTY** something that must be done because of legal or moral duty **3 SOMETHING OWED** something such as assistance or a debt that somebody owes in return for something given **4 BINDING LEGAL AGREEMENT** a legal agreement by which somebody is bound to do something, especially pay money, or to refrain from doing something **5 LEGAL CONTRACT** a legal contract that contains a penalty for nonfulfilment —**obligational** *adj*

obligato *adj, n* MUSIC = **obbligato**

obligatory /ə blíggətəri/ *adj* **1** required by law or by a moral or religious rule **2** compulsory rather than optional —**obligatorily** *adv*

oblige /ə blíj/ (**obliges, obliging, obliged**) *v* **1** *vt* **REQUIRE SOMEBODY TO DO** to bind somebody morally or legally to do something **2** *vt* **FORCE SOMEBODY TO DO** to make it necessary for somebody to do something **3** *vt* **CAUSE SOMEBODY TO FEEL INDEBTED** to cause somebody to feel indebted by doing something for that person **4** *vt* **DO FAVOUR FOR** to do a favour or service for somebody ○ *Would you oblige me by closing the door?* **5** *vi* **BE HELPFUL** to do something necessary or helpful ○ *was only too happy to oblige* [13C. Via Old French *oblig(i)er* < Latin *obligare* 'tie to' < *ligare* 'to tie'.] —**obliger** *n*

obligee /óbbli jeé/ *n* somebody to whom another person is legally or morally bound, e.g. by a financial debt or obligation to do something

obligement /ə blíjmənt/ *n* *Scotland* a favour done for or owed to somebody else

obliging /ə blíjing/ *adj* willing to be helpful or do favours —**obligingly** *adv* —**obligingness** *n*

obligor /óbbli gáwr/ *n* a person who legally agrees to do or pay something

oblique /ə bleék/ *adj* **1 SLOPING** sloping or joining something at an angle that is not a right angle **2 INDIRECT** not straightforward or direct ○ *an oblique reference to the lateness of the hour* **3 NOT PARALLEL OR PERPENDICULAR** neither perpendicular nor parallel to another line or plane **4 NOT RIGHT-ANGLED** not being or containing a right angle or a multiple of a right angle **5 NOT BEING SUBJECT** being a grammatical case other than the nominative or vocative **6 WITH SIDES OF DIFFERENT LENGTH** describes leaves that have sides of different length **7 NOT BEING ON ANATOMICAL PLANE** slanting away from any of the anatomical planes of the body, e.g. the horizontal or perpendicular plane **8 BEING AT TANGENT TO EARTH'S SURFACE** describes a map projection based on a plane of projection that is at a tangent to the Earth's surface at a point between the poles and the equator ■ *adv* **CHANGING DIRECTION AT 45°** changing direction to or at an angle of 45° ■ *n* **1 SOMETHING SLANTING** something that is oblique, e.g. a slanting line **2** PRINTING = **slash** *n.* 6 **3 COURSE CHANGE OF LESS THAN 90°** a change of course of less than 90° ■ *vi* (**obliques, obliquing, obliqued**) **1 TAKE OBLIQUE DIRECTION** to move or slant in an oblique direction **2 ADVANCE IN OBLIQUE DIRECTION** to move forward at an angle in a military formation [15C. < Latin *obliquus* 'slanting, sidelong'.] —**obliqueness** *n*

obliquely /ə bleékli/ *adv* **1** in a way that is not direct or straightforward **2** at an angle that is not a right angle

oblique projection *n* a map projection based on a plane of projection that is at a tangent to the Earth's surface at a point between the poles and the equator

obliquity /ə blíkwəti/ (*plural* **-ties**) *n* **1 STATE OF BEING OBLIQUE** the condition of being oblique **2 DEVIATION FROM PLANE** a deviation from the horizontal or perpendicular **3 CHARACTER FLOW** a departure from morality or reason **4 LACK OF DIRECTNESS** a lack of directness or straightforwardness in speech or conduct **5 obliquity, obliquity of the ecliptic ANGLE BETWEEN EARTH'S ORBIT AND EQUATOR** the angle between the plane of the Earth's equator and the plane of the Earth's orbit around the sun, approximately 23.5°

obliquity of the ecliptic *n* ASTRON = **obliquity** *n.* 5

obliterate /ə blíttə rayt/ (**-ates, -ating, -ated**) *vt* **1** to destroy something so utterly that nothing is left **2** to erase or obscure something completely, leaving no trace [Late 16C. < Latin *oblitterat-*, past participle of *oblitterare* 'remove letters' < *littera* 'letter'.] —**obliteration** /ə blíttə ráysh'n/ *n* —**obliterative** /ə blíttərətiv/ *adj* —**obliterator** /-raytər/ *n*

oblivion /ə blívvi ən/ *n* **1 STATE OF BEING FORGOTTEN** a state of being utterly forgotten **2 STATE OF FORGETTING** a state of forgetting everything or of being unaware of surroundings **3 OVERLOOKING OF PAST OFFENCES** the deliberate overlooking of past offences [14C. Via Old French < Latin *oblivion-* < *oblivisci* 'forget'.]

oblivious /ə blívvi əss/ *adj* **1** unaware of or paying no attention to somebody or something **2** forgetting about somebody or something —**obliviously** *adv* —**obliviousness** *n*

oblong /óbb long/ *adj* having a shape that is considerably longer than it is wide, especially a rectangular or roughly elliptical shape ■ *n* something with a length greater than its width, especially a rectangle or distorted circle [15C. < Latin *oblongus* 'rather long' < *longus* 'long'.]

obloquy /óbbləkwi/ *n* (*formal or literary*) **1** statements that severely criticize or defame somebody **2** a state of disgrace brought about by being defamed [15C. < late Latin *obloquium* 'talking against' < *loqui* 'to talk'.]

obnoxious /əb nókshəss/ *adj* very offensive and unpleasant ○ *obnoxious stench* [Late 16C. < Latin *obnoxius* 'vulnerable to harm' < *noxa* 'harm'.] —**obnoxiously** *adv* —**obnoxiousness** *n*

o.b.o. *abbr* or best offer (*in advertisements*)

oboe /óbō/ *n* a woodwind instrument that produces a penetrating high sound and consists of a slim tube of conical bore with a double reed and keys operated by the fingers [Late 17C. Via Italian < French *hautbois* (see HAUTBOY).] —**oboist** *n*

oboe da caccia /óbō də kácha/ *n* an early form of oboe from which the cor anglais was developed [Late 19C. < Italian, 'hunting oboe'.]

oboe d'amore /-da máwray/ *n* an oboe used mainly in baroque music that has a lower pitch than the standard instrument [Late 19C. < Italian, 'oboe of love'.]

Obon /ō bón/ *n* in Japan, a Buddhist festival celebrating All Souls. Date: 13 to 31 July.

Obote /o bṓt ay, o bṓti/, **Milton** (*b.* 1925) Ugandan statesman

obovate /ob ṓ vayt/ *adj* describes leaves that are oval with the narrow end at the base

obs. *abbr* **1** obscure **2** observation **3 obs., Obs.** observatory **4** obsolete **5** obstetrics

obscene /əb seén/ *adj* **1 INDECENT** offensive to conventional standards of decency, especially by being sexually explicit **2 LIKELY TO DEPRAVE AND CORRUPT** describes publications that are considered likely to deprave and corrupt people **3 DISGUSTING** disgusting and morally offensive, especially because of showing total disregard for other people [Late 16C. Via Old French < Latin *obscenus* 'ill-omened'.] —**obscenely** *adv*

obscenity /əb sénnəti/ (*plural* **-ties**) *n* **1 INDECENCY** offensiveness to conventional standards of decency, especially as a result of sexual explicitness **2 OBSCENE EXPRESSION** a word, phrase, or statement that is offensive, especially because of being sexually explicit **3 SOMETHING OBSCENE** something that is disgusting and morally offensive

obscurantist /ób skyoŏ rántist/, **obscurant** /əb skyoŏrənt/ *adj* opposing or hindering the spread of new ideas and new social or political developments —**obscurant** /əb skyoŏrənt/ *adj, n* —**obscurantism** *n* —**obscurantist** *n*

obscure /əb skyoŏr/ *adj* **1 HARD TO UNDERSTAND** difficult to understand because of not being fully or clearly expressed ○ *an obscure passage in the manuscript* **2 INDISTINCT** not able to be seen or heard distinctly **3 UNIMPORTANT OR UNKNOWN** not important or well-known ○ *an obscure portrait painter* **4 KNOWN TO FEW PEOPLE** unknown to most people, e.g. because of being hidden or remote **5 DARK** dark, shadowy, or clouded ○ *an obscure corner of the hall* **6 UNSTRESSED** describes a vowel that has a neutral, unstressed pronunciation (*technical*) ■ *vt* (**-scures, -scuring, -scured**) **1 MAKE UNCLEAR** to make something unclear, indistinct, or hidden **2 DARKEN** to make something dark or cover something with cloud [14C. Via Old French < Latin *obscurus* 'covered over' < *-scurus* 'covered'.] —**obscuration** /ób skyoŏ ráysh'n/ *n* —**obscureness** *n*

SYNONYMS ***obscure, abstruse, recondite, arcane, cryptic, enigmatic***

CORE MEANING: difficult to understand

obscure difficult to understand because it is expressed in a complicated way or because it involves areas of knowledge or study that are not known to most people; **abstruse** not easy to understand, often because it involves specialist knowledge or is expressed in specialist language; **recondite** requiring a high degree of scholarship or specialist knowledge to be understood; **arcane** requiring information that is secret or known only to a few people in order to be understood; **cryptic** deliberately mysterious or ambiguous and seeming to have a hidden meaning; **enigmatic** having a quality of mystery and ambiguity that makes it difficult to understand or interpret.

obscurely /əb skyoŏrli/ *adv* **1 UNCLEARLY** in a way that is not clear, definite, or easy to understand **2 DIMLY** dimly or indistinctly **3 AWAY FROM PEOPLE'S ATTENTION** in a place or position that is remote, secluded, or not prominent or well-known

obscurity /əb skyoŏrəti/ (*plural* **-ties**) *n* **1 STATE OF BEING UNKNOWN** a state of being unknown or inconspicuous ○ *plucked from obscurity to star in a Broadway musical* **2 UNCLEARNESS** difficulty in being understood or unclearness of meaning **3 SOMEBODY OR SOMETHING OBSCURE** an obscure person or thing

~~**obsene**~~ incorrect spelling of **obscene**

obsequies /óbssi kwiz/ *npl* rites or ceremonies carried out at a funeral [14C. Via Anglo-Norman < late Latin *obsequiae*, alteration (influenced by *obsequium* 'compliance') of *exequiae* 'those following out (to the grave)' < *exsequi* (see EXECUTE).]

obsequious /əb seékwi əss/ *adj* excessively eager to please or to obey all instructions [15C. < Latin *obsequiosus* < *obsequium* 'compliance'.] —**obsequiously** *adv* —**obsequiousness** *n*

observable /əb zúrvəb'l/ *adj* able to be seen or detected ■ *n* something such as temperature that can be measured or observed directly —**observability** /əb zúrvə bílləti/ *n*

observably /əb zúrvəbli/ *adv* in a way or to an extent that can be seen or detected

observance /əb zúrvənss/ *n* **1 COMPLIANCE** the execution of or compliance with laws, instructions, or customs **2 RITUAL** a custom, ritual, or ceremony, especially a religious one **3 PERFORMANCE OF RELIGIOUS CEREMONIES** the celebration of a religious occasion, or the practice of a religious rite, ceremony, or action **4 RELIGIOUS RULE** a rule of a religious order **5 OBSERVATION** careful watching or close attention

USAGE observance or **observation**? These two words share the meaning 'close attention', though ***observation*** is much more common: *our observation of the habits of the condor; the child's observance of the waving flags.* If you refer to 'compliance', 'ritual', 'celebration of religious rites', or 'a rule of a religious order', the only word to use is ***observance***, as in *observance* [not *observation*] *of the law; church observances* [not *observations*] *such as baptism and Communion; followed the observances* [not *observations*] *of the Jesuit order.* If you refer to 'a remark or comment' or 'a record of something seen or studied', ***observation*** is the correct choice: *made a few casual observations* [not *observances*] *about the foul weather; astronomical observations* [not *observances*] *in one volume.*

observant /əb zúrvənt/ *adj* **1** paying such careful attention that little or nothing is unnoticed **2** carrying out rituals or obeying laws, especially religious ones —**observantly** *adv*

observation /óbzər váysh'n/ *n* **1 PAYING ATTENTION** the attentive watching of somebody or something **2 OBSERVING OF DEVELOPMENTS IN** the careful observing and recording of something that is happening, e.g. a natural phenomenon **3 REMARK OR COMMENT** a remark or comment on something that has been noticed **4 RECORD OF SOMETHING SEEN OR NOTED** the result or record of observing something such as a natural phenomenon and noting developments **5 ACT OF OBSERVING OR OBEYING** the act of observing a religious occasion or ritual or of obeying a law or rule **6 SIGHTING WITH NAVIGATIONAL INSTRUMENT** a sighting with a navigational instrument to establish the observer's position in relation to an astronomical object such as the Sun **7 NAVIGATIONAL INSTRUMENT READING** the reading taken from a navigational instrument that has been used to find the observer's position in relation to an astronomical object —**observational** *adj* —**observationally** *adv*

USAGE See ***observance***.

observation car *n* a railway carriage fitted with extra or larger windows and often a partly transparent roof to allow passengers a better view of passing scenery

observation post *n* a position from which soldiers can watch enemy movements and direct artillery fire

observatory /əb zúrvətəri/ (*plural* **-ries**) *n* **1** a building, station, or artificial satellite used for scientific observation of natural phenomena such as astronomical objects, the weather, or earthquakes **2** a place or building that commands an expansive view

observe /əb zúrv/ (**-serves, -serving, -served**) *v* **1** *vt* **NOTICE** to see or notice something, especially while watching carefully **2** *vti* **WATCH ATTENTIVELY** to watch somebody or something attentively, especially for scientific purposes **3** *vti* **BE FORMAL WITNESS** to be a formal witness to something **4** *vi* **BE SPECTATOR** to watch something without taking part **5** *vt* **COMMENT** to make a comment or remark on something seen or noticed **6** *vt* **COMPLY WITH** to carry out or comply with something such as a law or custom **7** *vt* **CELEBRATE FESTIVAL** to celebrate or keep a religious or traditional festival [14C. Via Old French *observer* < Latin *observare* 'watch towards' < *servare* 'to watch'.]

observer /əb zúrvər/ *n* **1 SOMEBODY WHO SEES OR WATCHES** a person who observes something that is happening **2 NONPARTICIPATING WITNESS** a person who acts as a witness, often by arrangement **3 SOMEBODY OBSERVING CEREMONY OR OBEYING LAW** a person who duly celebrates a religious ceremony or ritual, or complies with a rule or law **4 AIRCRAFT IDENTIFIER** somebody trained in identifying aircraft **5 WATCHER OF ENEMY MOVEMENTS** a soldier who watches enemy movements or directs artillery fire

observingly /əb zúrvingli/ *adv* in an attentive or considering manner

obsess /əb séss/ *v* **1** *vt* to occupy somebody's thoughts constantly and exclusively ○ *The desire for vengeance obsesses him.* **2** *vi* *US* to think or worry about something constantly and compulsively [Early 16C. < Latin *obsess-*, past participle of *obsidere* 'besiege', literally 'sit opposite to' < *sedere* 'sit'.]

obsession /əb sésh'n/ *n* **1 PREOCCUPATION** an idea or feeling that completely occupies the mind **2 STATE OF BEING OBSESSED** the state of being obsessed by somebody or something ○ *Their devotion to each other borders on obsession.* **3 UNCONTROLLABLE PERSISTENCE OF IDEA** the uncontrollable persistence of an idea or emotion in the mind, sometimes associated with psychiatric disorder —**obsessional** *adj* —**obsessionally** *adv*

obsessive /əb séssiv/ *adj* **1** amounting to an obsession or as strong as an obsession **2** worrying compulsively about a particular thing or things generally —**obsessive** *n* —**obsessively** *adv* —**obsessiveness** *n*

obsessive-compulsive *adj* with or characteristic of obsessive-compulsive disorder such as hand-washing ■ *n* somebody with obsessive-compulsive disorder

obsessive-compulsive disorder *n* a psychiatric disorder characterized by obsessive thoughts and compulsive behaviour, e.g. continual washing of the hands prompted by a feeling of uncleanliness

obsidian /ob síddi ən/ *n* a jet-black volcanic glass, chemically similar to granite and formed by the rapid cooling of molten lava, that was used by early civilizations for manufacturing tools and ceremonial objects [14C. < Latin *(lapis) Obsidianus*, copyist's error for *Obsianus* '(stone) of Obsius', a Roman who discovered this or a similar stone.]

obsolesce /óbssə léss/ (**-lesces, -lescing, -lesced**) *vi* to become obsolete by being replaced by something new [Late 19C. < Latin *obsolescere* (see OBSOLESCENT).]

obsolescent /óbssə léss'nt/ *adj* becoming obsolete or disappearing from use or existence by being replaced by something new [Mid-18C. < Latin *obsolescent-*, present participle of *obsolescere* 'wear out' < *solere* 'be accustomed'.] —**obsolescence** *n* —**obsolescently** *adv*

obsolete /óbssə leet, óbssə léet/ *adj* **1 NOT USED ANY MORE** no longer in use because replaced by something new **2 OUT-OF-DATE** superseded by something newer, though possibly still in use **3 UNDEVELOPED** describes a part or organ of an animal or plant that is undeveloped or no longer functional [Late 16C. < Latin *obsoletus*, past participle of *obsolescere* (see OBSOLESCENT).] —**obsolete** *vt* *US* —**obsoletely** *adv*

obstacle /óbstək'l/ *n* **1 HINDRANCE** somebody or something that hinders or prevents progress **2 SOMETHING IN WAY** something that blocks or impedes a road, passage, or somebody's way **3 HURDLE** a fence or hedge set up for horses to jump over in showjumping [14C. Via Old French < Latin *obstaculum* < *obstare* 'stand in the way' < *stare* 'to stand'.]

obstacle course *n* **1** *US* MIL = **assault course** **2** an area similar to a military assault course, used by competitors in an obstacle race

obstacle race *n* a race in which competitors have to get past a range of obstacles

obstet. *abbr* **1** obstetric **2** obstetrics

obstetric /ob stéttrik/ *adj* relating to childbirth or obstetrics [Mid-18C. < Latin *obstetricius* 'of a midwife' < *obstetric-* 'midwife', literally 'woman who is present, stands before' < *stare* 'stand'.]

obstetrician /óbstə trísh'n/ *n* a doctor who specializes in pregnancy, delivering babies, and the care of women after childbirth

obstetrics /ob stéttriks/ *n* the branch of medicine that deals with the care of women during pregnancy and childbirth, and for some six weeks following delivery (+ *singular verb*)

obstinate /óbstinət/ *adj* **1 STUBBORN** determined not to agree to other people's wishes or accept their suggestions **2 REFUSING TO CHANGE** unwilling to change or give up something such as an idea or attitude **3 DIFFICULT TO CONTROL** difficult to control, get rid of, solve, or cure ○ *an obstinate blockage in the pipe* [14C. < Latin *obstinatus*, past participle of *obstinare* 'be resolved', literally 'stand by' < *stare* 'to stand'.] —**obstinacy** *n* —**obstinately** *adv* —**obstinateness** *n*

obstipation /óbsti páysh'n/ *n* severe constipation, often caused by a blockage in the intestines [Late 16C. < late Latin *obstipation-* 'pressing in the way of' < *stipare* 'to press'.]

obstreperous /əb stréppərəss/ *adj* **1** noisily and aggressively boisterous **2** strongly objecting to something or noisily refusing to be controlled [Late 16C. < Latin *obstreperus* 'clamorous', literally 'rattling against' < *strepere* 'to rattle'.] —**obstreperously** *adv* —**obstreperousness** *n*

SYNONYMS See ***unruly***.

obstruct /əb strúkt/ *vt* **1 BLOCK** to block a road, course, or passage **2 HINDER** to hinder or impede somebody or something **3 IMPEDE VIEW** to be in the way and prevent a clear view [Early 17C. < Latin *obstructus*, past participle of *obstruere* 'build up against' < *struere* 'heap up, pile'.] —**obstructor** *n*

SYNONYMS See ***hinder***.

obstruction /əb strúksh'n/ *n* **1 BLOCK OR HINDRANCE** somebody or something that causes or forms a blockage or hindrance **2 ACT OF BLOCKING** an act of blocking or hindering of somebody or something **3 STATE OF BEING BLOCKED** the state of being obstructed **4 DELAYING OF** the deliberate delaying of the business of something such as a legislative body **5 UNFAIR IMPEDING OF OPPONENT** in football and other sports, the unfair impeding of an opposing player

obstructionist /əb strúksh'nist/ *adj* deliberately causing delay or impeding progress —**obstructionism** *n* —**obstructionist** *n* —**obstructionistic** /əb strúksh'n ístik/ *adj*

obstruction of justice *n* *US* the criminal offence of obstructing the administration and process of the law

obstructive /əb strúktiv/ *adj* **1** hindering or preventing the progress of something **2** relating to or caused by the obstruction of a passage in the body —**obstructively** *adv* —**obstructiveness** *n*

obstructive sleep apnoea *n* cessation or restriction of breathing during sleep that results in loud snoring

obstruent /óbb stroo ənt/ *adj* **1 OBSTRUCTING PASSAGE IN BODY** obstructing or closing a passage in the body, e.g. the intestinal tract **2 PRODUCED BY CUTOFF OF AIR** describes a speech sound produced by a stoppage of air from the lungs ■ *n* **1 OBSTRUCTION** something that obstructs or closes a passage in the body **2 SOUND PRODUCED BY CUTOFF OF AIR** a speech sound produced by a stoppage of air from the lungs [Mid-17C. < Latin *obstruent-*, present participle of *obstruere* (see OBSTRUCT).]

obtain /əb táyn/ *v* **1** *vt* **GET** to get possession of something, especially by making an effort or having the necessary qualifications **2** *vi* **BE ESTABLISHED** to be established, valid, or current ○ *under the regulations that obtained at the time* **3** *vi* **RESULT** to follow as a result (*formal*) ○ *the unfortunate situation that obtains when such diverse elements are forced together* [15C. Via Old French *obtenir* < Latin *obtinere* 'hold to' < *tenere* 'to hold'.] —**obtainer** *n* —**obtainment** *n*

SYNONYMS See ***get***.

obtainable /əb táynəb'l/ *adj* able to be obtained or reached —**obtainability** /əb táynə bílləti/ *n*

obtrude /əb tróod, ob tróod/ (**-trudes, -truding, -truded**) *v* **1** *vti* **IMPOSE** to impose something such as opinions or yourself on other people **2** *vt* **PUSH OUT** to push something out or forwards **3** *vi* **APPEAR UNWELCOME** to appear or be present in a way that is unwelcome but cannot be ignored ○ *'Not a leaf stirred; not a sound obtruded upon great Nature's meditation'.* (Mark Twain, *The Adventures of Tom Sawyer*; 1875) [Mid-16C. < Latin *obtrudere* 'thrust against' < *trudere* 'to thrust'.] —**obtruder** *n* —**obtrusion** /əb tróozh'n/ *n*

obtrusive /əb tróossiv/ *adj* **1 ANNOYING** tending to force your presence or opinions on other people ○ *plagued by an obtrusive photographer* **2 HIGHLY NOTICEABLE** highly noticeable, often with a bad or unwelcome effect **3 STICKING OUT** projecting or sticking out [Mid-17C. < Latin *obtrusus*, past participle of *obtrudere* (see OBTRUDE).] —**obtrusively** *adv* —**obtrusiveness** *n*

obtund /ob túnd/ *vt* to blunt, dull, or deaden something (*dated*) [14C. < Latin *obtundere* 'strike against' < *tundere* 'to strike'.] —**obtundent** *adj*

obturator /óbtyoo raytər/ *n* **1 obturator, obturator muscle** one of a pair of muscles at the front of the human body, on either side of the pelvis, used to move the hip and thigh **2** an object, device, or body part that closes or obstructs an opening or access to a cavity [Early 18C. < medieval Latin, < Latin *obturat-*, past participle of *obturare* < *ob-* (see OB-) + *turare* 'close up'.]

obtuse /əb tyóoss/ *adj* **1 SLOW TO UNDERSTAND** slow to understand or perceive something **2 BETWEEN 90° AND 180°** describes an angle greater than 90° and less than 180° **3 WITH INTERNAL ANGLE GREATER THAN 90°** describes a triangle with one internal angle greater than 90° **4 BLUNT** not sharp or pointed **5 WITH ROUNDED OR BLUNT TIP** describes a leaf that has a rounded or blunt tip [Early 16C. < Latin *obtusus* 'blunted', past participle of *obtundere* (see OBTUND).] —**obtusely** *adv* —**obtuseness** *n*

ϟ **OBTW** *abbr* oh, by the way (*in e-mails*)

obverse /óbvurss/ *n* **1 MAIN SIDE OF COIN OR MEDAL** the side of a coin or medal that has the more important design on it, especially a head. ◊ **reverse** *n.* 3 **2 COUNTERPART** a counterpart, complement, or opposite **3 EQUIVALENT CATEGORICAL PROPOSITION** a proposition derived from another proposition by denying it and then negating the predicate, e.g. 'Everything is possible' becomes 'Nothing is impossible' ■ *adj* **1 VISIBLE** facing an observer **2 BEING A COUNTERPART** forming a counterpart to something else **3 NARROWER AT BASE** describes a leaf that is narrower at the base than the tip [Mid-17C. < Latin *obversus*, past participle of *obvertere* (see OBVERT).]

obversion /ob vúrsh'n/ *n* **1** the process of turning something so that the other side is seen **2** the process of forming the obverse of a proposition

obvert /ob vúrt/ *vt* **1** to turn something such as a coin or medal so that the other side is seen **2** to convert a proposition to its obverse [Early 17C. < Latin *obvertere* 'turn toward' < *vertere* 'to turn'.]

obviate /óbvi ayt/ (**-ates, -ating, -ated**) *vt* **1** to render something unnecessary (*formal*) **2** to avoid an anticipated difficulty by doing something to prevent its arising [Late 16C. < Latin *obviat-*, past participle of *obviare* 'withstand', literally 'stand in the way of' < *via* 'way'.] —**obviation** /óbvi áysh'n/ *n*

USAGE obviate the need for: Because one of the meanings of ***obviate*** is 'to make unnecessary', it is sometimes argued that *obviate the need* (or *necessity*) *for* is redundant. An older but still current meaning, however, is 'to avoid an anticipated difficulty'. In a sentence like *Addressing these issues early can obviate any need for a joint resolution*, the need can be perceived as a difficulty — or early consideration can make the resolution unnecessary, in which case *any need for* is indeed redundant. There is little reason to prefer either interpretation to the other, except that the meaning 'to make unnecessary' allows much the same thought to be expressed with fewer words.

obvious /óbvi əss/ *adj* **1** easy to see or understand because not concealed, or ambiguous **2** lacking subtlety or any attempt at concealment [Late 16C. < Latin *obvius* 'in the way' < *via* 'way'.] —**obviousness** *n*

obviously /óbvi əssli/ *adv* **1** in a way or to an extent that is obvious **2** used to suggest that there can be no doubt or uncertainty about something ○ *They want you to do it, obviously.*

obvolute /óbvə loot/ *adj* describes leaves or petals that are folded so as to overlap each other [Mid-18C. < Latin *obvolutus*, past participle of *obvolvere* 'wrap round' < *volvere* 'to roll'.] —**obvolution** /óbvə loósh'n/ *n* —**obvolutive** /óbvə lootiv/ *adj*

OC *abbr* **1** Officer Commanding **2** original cover

oca /ókə/ *n* a plant grown for its edible tubers. Native to: South America. Genus: *Oxalis*. [Early 17C. Via Spanish < Quechua *ócca*.]

O Canada *n* the title of the national anthem of Canada

ocarina /ókə reénə/ *n* a simple wind instrument related to the flute that has an oval body, finger holes, and a protruding mouthpiece [Late 19C. < Italian, 'little goose' (< its shape) < *oca* 'goose' < Latin *avis* 'bird'.]

ocasionally incorrect spelling of **occasionally**

occ. *abbr* **1** occident **2** occupation

Occam's razor /óckəmz-/ *n* PHILOS, SCI = **Ockham's razor**

occas. *abbr* **1** occasional **2** occasionally

occasion /ə káyzh'n/ *n* **1** PARTICULAR TIME a particular time, especially a time when something happens **2** CAUSE OR REASON a cause of or reason for something ○ *He has no occasion to criticize me.* **3** CHANCE OR OPPORTUNITY a chance or opportunity to do something ○ *You might never have another occasion to do it.* **4** NEED the need for something or to do something ○ *has never had occasion to use it* **5** IMPORTANT EVENT an important or special event ■ *vt* CAUSE to cause or lead to something [14C. Via Old French < Latin *occasion-* 'falling down, happening' < *cadere* 'to fall'.] ◇ **on occasion** from time to time

occasional /ə káyzh'nəl/ *adj* **1** INFREQUENT happening, seen, used, or doing something from time to time but not regularly or frequently **2** RELATING TO SPECIAL EVENT done for or connected with a special event ○ *occasional verse* **3** DESIGNED FOR USE FROM TIME TO TIME intended for use as needed, but not essential or in constant use ○ *an occasional table* **4** CAUSING serving as the cause of something (*formal*)

SYNONYMS See *periodic*.

occasionally /ə káyzh'nəli/ *adv* from time to time, but not regularly or frequently

occident /óksidənt/ *n* the west (*formal*) [14C. Via Old French < Latin *occident-*, present participle of *occidere* 'fall down, set (of the sun)' < *cadere* 'to fall'.]

Occident the western hemisphere, especially the countries of Europe and America (*dated*) ◇ **Orient**

occidental /óksi dént'l/ *adj* western (*formal*)

Occidental *adj* relating to a country of the Occident, or its people or culture ■ *n* somebody who comes from the West

occidentalize /óksi déntə līz/ (**-izes**, **-izing**, **-ized**), **Occidentalize**, **occidentalise** *vt* to make somebody or something conform to the culture of the West

occipita plural of **occiput**

occipital /ok síppit'l/ *adj* relating to or located at the back of the head or skull ■ *n* ANAT = **occipital bone** [Mid-16C. < medieval Latin *occipitalis* < Latin *occiput* (see OCCIPUT).]

occipital bone *n* the saucer-shaped bone at the rear of the skull that connects with the spinal column and has an opening at its base through which the spinal cord passes

occipital lobe *n* the pyramid-shaped area at the back of each hemisphere of the brain that deals with the interpretation of vision

occiput /óksi put, óksipət/ (*plural* **-ciputs** *or* **-cipita** /-síppitə/) *n* the back part of the head or skull [14C. < Latin, 'back of the head' < *caput* 'head'.]

occlude /ə kloōd/ (**-cludes**, **-cluding**, **-cluded**) *v* **1** *vt* STOP UP to block or stop up something such as a passage **2** *vt* CUT OFF FLOW OF to cut off or prevent the flow or passage of something such as light or liquid **3** *vti* ALIGN TEETH PROPERLY to align the upper and lower teeth in the proper position for chewing or for being in normal contact when the mouth is closed **4** *vt* ABSORB OR ADSORB to absorb

or adsorb a liquid or gas on the surface of or within a solid **5** *vti* FORM OCCLUDED FRONT to form an occluded front or to undercut a mass of warm air so that it is no longer in contact with the Earth's surface [Late 19C. < Latin *occludere* 'close up' < *claudere* 'to close'.]

occluded front *n* a composite front formed when a cold air mass meets and undercuts a warm air mass, and forces the warm air upwards and away from contact with the Earth's surface

occlusal /ə klooz'l/ *adj* relating to the biting surface of a molar or premolar tooth

occlusion /ə kloōzh'n/ *n* **1** ACT OF OCCLUDING an act of occluding or the condition of being occluded **2** OBSTRUCTION something that obstructs or occludes **3** METEOROL = **occluded front 4** MEETING OF UPPER AND LOWER TEETH the relation between the upper and lower teeth when the jaw is closed and their surfaces come in contact **5** CLOSURE OF HOLLOW ORGAN the closure of a hollow organ such as the vocal tract in articulating a speech sound **6** ABSORPTION OR ADSORPTION OF LIQUID the absorption or adsorption of a liquid or gas on or in a solid [Mid-17C. < Latin *occlus-*, past participle of *occludere* (see OCCLUDE).]

occlusive /ə kloōssiv/ *adj* relating to, involving, or producing an occlusion ■ *n* a speech sound that involves a closure of the vocal tract

occult *adj* /ókult, o kúlt/ **1** SUPPOSEDLY SUPERNATURAL OR MAGIC relating to, involving, or typical of the supposed supernatural, magic, or witchcraft **2** NOT UNDERSTANDABLE not capable of being understood by ordinary human beings **3** SECRET secret or known only to the initiated **4** HIDDEN describes a diseased condition that is hidden or difficult to detect **5** DIFFICULT TO SEE not visible to the naked eye, and only detectable by microscope or chemical testing ■ *n* /ókult, o kúlt/ THE SUPPOSED SUPERNATURAL the realm of the supposed supernatural, magic, or witchcraft ■ *vti* /o kúlt/ **1** TEMPORARILY HIDE ASTRONOMICAL OBJECT to hide an astronomical object temporarily by moving between it and an observer, or to be hidden in this way **2** HIDE OR BE HIDDEN to hide something from view or be hidden from view [Early 16C. < Latin *occultus*, past participle of *occulere* 'conceal'.] —**occultation** /ókul táysh'n, ó kul-/ *n* —**occultly** /ó kultli, o kúltli/ *adv* —**occultness** /ó kultnəss, ó kúltnəss/ *n*

occultism /ókultizəm, ók'ltizəm, o kúltizəm/ *n* the belief in and study of the supposed supernatural, magic, or witchcraft —**occultist** *n*

occupancy /ókyoōpənssi/ (*plural* **-cies**) *n* **1** ACT OF OCCUPYING the act or state of occupying something such as a building or an official position **2** LEVEL OF OCCUPATION the level of occupation of a place ○ *a block of flats with high occupancy* **3** TIME OF OCCUPYING the period of time during which somebody occupies something such as a building or an official position **4** USE WITHOUT OWNERSHIP the use and possession of property without claiming ownership of it **5** POSSESSION OF UNOWNED PROPERTY the act of taking possession of property, especially land, that has no owner, with the intention of becoming its owner

occupant /ókyoōpənt/ *n* **1** a resident of a place or holder of a position **2** a person who takes possession of unclaimed property, especially land, with the intention of becoming its owner

occupation /ókyoō páysh'n/ *n* **1** JOB the job by which somebody earns a living **2** ACTIVITY an activity on which time is spent **3** ACT OF OCCUPYING an act of occupying or the state of being occupied **4** INVASION the invasion and control of a country or area by enemy forces **5** TIME OF OCCUPYING the period of time during which something is occupied

occupational /ókyoō pásh'nəl/ *adj* relating to or caused by somebody's job —**occupationally** *adv*

occupational disease *n* a disease that is directly caused by the conditions of somebody's work

occupational hazard *n* a risk associated with a particular type of work

occupational medicine *n* the branch of medicine that deals with work-related diseases and injuries incurred at work

occupational pension *n* a pension paid to an employee or former employee from a scheme set up by an employer, not the state

occupational therapy *n* the use of regular periods of suitable productive activity as part of the treatment of illness or medical condition —**occupational therapist** *n*

occupation groupings *npl* the categories, e.g. C1 or C2, that people can be put into according to their occupation, formerly used in the advertising industry to define target markets

occupy /ókyoō pī/ (**-pies**, **-pying**, **-pied**) *vt* **1** LIVE IN PLACE to live in or be the established user of a place such as a home or office **2** ENGAGE SOMEBODY'S ATTENTION to take up somebody's time or attention (*often passive*) **3** FILL SPACE OR TIME to take up a space or an amount of time (*often passive*) **4** TAKE OVER PLACE to invade and take control of a country, area, or building **5** HOLD POSITION to hold a post or rank [14C. Via Old French *occuper* < Latin *occupare* 'take over' < *capere* 'to take'.] —**occupier** *n*

occur /ə kúr/ (**-curs**, **-curring**, **-curred**) *vi* **1** HAPPEN to happen or come about **2** EXIST to exist or be present **3** ENTER MIND to come into somebody's mind ○ *It didn't occur to him to lock the door.* [Early 16C. < Latin *occurrere* 'run against' < *currere* 'to run'.]

occurance incorrect spelling of **occurrence**

occured incorrect spelling of **occurred**

occurence incorrect spelling of **occurrence**

occurrence /ə kúrrənss/ *n* **1** something that happens **2** the fact or act of something happening —**occurrent** *adj*

OCD *abbr* obsessive-compulsive disorder

WORLD'S LARGEST OCEANS AND SEAS

1	Pacific Ocean	
Area	[64 million sq. mi. / 165 million sq. km]	
2	Atlantic Ocean	
Area	[31.7 million sq. mi. / 82 million sq. km]	
3	Indian Ocean	
Area	[28.3 million sq. mi. / 73.4 million sq. km]	
4	Arctic Ocean	
Area	[5.4 million sq. mi. / 14 million sq. km]	
5	Mediterranean Sea	
Area	[0.97 million sq. mi. / 2.5 million sq. km]	
6	Bering Sea	
Area	[0.87 million sq. mi. / 2.26 million sq. km]	
7	Caribbean Sea	
Area	[0.75 million sq. mi. / 1.94 million sq. km]	
8	Sea of Okhotsk	
Area	[0.59 million sq. mi. / 1.53 million sq. km]	
9	Sea of Japan	
Area	[0.39 million sq. mi. / 1 million sq. km]	
10	Hudson Bay	
Area	[0.28 million sq. mi. / 0.73 million sq. km]	

ocean /ósh'n/ *n* **1** LARGE SEA a large expanse of salt water, especially any of the Earth's five main seas, the Atlantic, Pacific, Indian, Arctic, and Antarctic oceans **2** EARTH'S SEAS TOGETHER the whole body of salt water on the Earth **3** SEA the sea (*literary*) **4** LARGE AMOUNT a vast amount or expanse of something [13C. Via Old French < Latin *oceanus* < Greek *ōkeanos*, the river surrounding the disc of the Earth.]

oceanarium /óshə náiri əm/ (*plural* **-ums** *or* **-a** /-ə/) *n* a large saltwater aquarium for observing and exhibiting marine animals and plants [Mid-20C. Blend of OCEAN + AQUARIUM.]

oceanaut /ṓshə nawt/ *n* an underwater swimmer in an ocean who uses an aqualung [Mid-20C. Blend of OCEAN + AQUANAUT.]

oceanfront /ṓsh'n frunt/ *n* **1** land along the seashore (*often before nouns*) ○ *oceanfront property* **2** the point at which two oceanic water masses of different thermal characteristics meet

oceangoing /ṓsh'n gō ing/ *adj* built, equipped, or used for travel on the ocean

ocean greyhound *n* a fast ocean liner

Oceania /ṓssi áania, ṓshi-/ the smaller islands of the central and S Pacific Ocean, including Micronesia, Melanesia, and Polynesia, and sometimes Australasia —**Oceanian** *n, adj*

oceanic /ṓshi ánnik, ṓssi-/ *adj* **1 IN OR FROM OCEAN** living, situated in, produced by, or taking place in an ocean, especially the depths of the open sea **2 VOLCANIC** resulting from volcanic activity in the ocean ○ *oceanic island* **3 IMMENSE** immense, vast, or overwhelming

Oceanic /ṓshi ánnik, ṓssi-/ *n* an Austronesian group of languages spoken mainly on the Pacific islands lying to the north and east of Australia. Native speakers: 2 million.

oceanic ridge *n* any section of a range of underwater mountains, found in all major oceans

oceanic trench *n* a long narrow deep furrow in the earth's crust at the bottom of an ocean

Ocean Island former name for **Banaba**

oceanography /ṓshə nóggrəfi, ṓshi ə-/ *n* the scientific study of oceans, including their chemistry, biology, and geology —**oceanographer** *n* —**oceanographic** /ṓsh'nə gráffik, ṓshi ənə-/ *adj* —**oceanographically** *adv*

oceanology /ṓshə nólləji, ṓshi ə-/ *n* the branch of oceanography that studies how oceans may be used for economic or technological purposes —**oceanological** /ṓsh'nə lójjik'l, ṓ shi ənə-/ *adj* —**oceanologically** *adv*

ocean tramp *n* NAUT = **tramp steamer**

Oceanus Procellarum /ṓssi áanəss próssə láarəm/ lunar lowland plain visible in the northwest quadrant of the Moon. Area: over 2,000,000 sq. km/775,000 sq. mi.

ocellus /ō sélləss/ (*plural* **-li** /-lī/) *n* **1 SIMPLE EYE IN INVERTEBRATES** a simple eye in some insects and other invertebrates that is sensitive to light but unable to focus clearly **2 EYE-SHAPED SPOT ON FEATHERS** an eye-shaped spot on the feathers of some birds such as the peacock **3 EYE-SHAPED SPOT ON LEAF** an enlarged discoloured eye-shaped spot on a leaf **4 EYE-SHAPED SPOT ON FISH** an eye-shaped spot on a fish, usually dark-ringed with a lighter colour inside, believed to deceive predators [Early 19C. < Latin, 'small eye' < *oculus* 'eye'.]

ocelot /óssə lot, -lot/ (*plural* **-lots** *or* **-lot**) *n* a small wildcat with dark spots on a light brownish coat. Native to: S United States, Central and South America. *Felis pardalis.* [Late 18C. Via French < Nahuatl *tlatlocelotl* 'field jaguar'.]

och /okh/ *interj Scotland, Ireland* an exclamation used to express disgust, disapproval, regret, weariness, or exasperation (*informal*) ○ *Och, it's too late now.* [Early 16C. Natural exclamation.]

oche /óki/ *n* the line behind which a darts player must stand when throwing [Mid-20C. < ?]

ocher *n, adj* US = **ochre**

ochlocracy /ok lókrəssi/ (*plural* **-cies**) *n* POL = **mobocracy** *n.* 1 [Late 16C. Via French *ochlocratie* < Greek *okhlokratia* < *okhlos* 'mob'.] —**ochlocrat** /óklə krat/ *n* —**ochlocratic** /óklə kráttik/ *adj* —**ochlocratically** /-kráttikli/ *adv*

ochre /ṓkər/ *n* a brownish-yellow colour [14C. Via French *ocre* < Latin *ochra* < Greek *ōkhros* 'pale, yellow'.] —**ochre** *adj* —**ochreous** *adj* —**ochry** /ṓkəri/ *adj*

ochrea *n* PLANT SCI = **ocrea**

-ock *suffix* something small or worthless ○ *hillock* [Old English *-oc, -uc*]

ocker /ókər/ *n Aus* an Australian regarded as boorish, uncultivated, and chauvinistic, especially a man with traditional views (*slang insult*) ■ *adj ANZ* displaying the boorish, uncultivated, or chauvinistic attitudes sometimes thought to be characteristic of some Australian men (*slang insult*) [Late 20C. Alteration of the forename *Oscar*, a character in an Australian television series.]

Ockham /ókəm/, **William of** (1285?–1349) English philosopher

Ockham's razor /ókəmz ráyzər/, **Occam's razor** *n* the philosophical and scientific rule that simple explanations should be preferred to more complicated ones, and that the explanation of a new phenomenon should be based on what is already known [Mid-19C. After William of OCKHAM.]

o'clock /ə klók/ *adv* **1** in telling the time, used to indicate an exact hour of the day or night, rather than some minutes past or before the hour ○ *woke up at six o'clock in the morning* **2** describes a position or direction of something by comparing it to the positions of numbers on a clock face, with the observer at the centre of the clock ○ *Look at the man sitting to your right, at three o'clock.* [15C. Contraction of *of the clock*.]

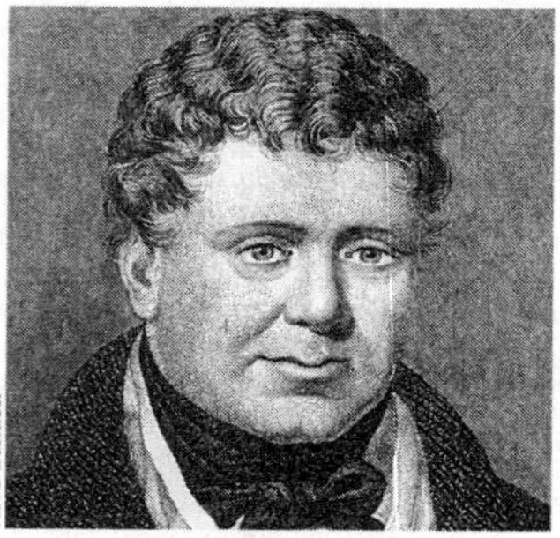

AKG London

Daniel O'Connell

O'Connell /ō kónn'l/, **Daniel** (1775–1847) Irish politician, supporter of Irish independence

ocotillo /ókə teélyō, ókə teé ō/ (*plural* **-los** *or* **-lo**) *n* a spiny bush with red flowers at the tip of each branch. Native to: dry parts of SW United States, Mexico. *Fouquieria splendens.* [Mid-19C. < American Spanish, 'small ocote' < *ocote* 'Mexican pine tree' < Nahuatl *ocotl* 'torch'.]

⚡**OCR** *abbr* **1** optical character reader **2** optical character recognition

ocrea /ókri ə/ (*plural* **-ae** /-ri ee/), **ochrea** (*plural* **-ae**) *n* a cup-shaped sheath formed by appendages at the base of a leaf, as in rhubarb [Mid-19C. < Latin, 'soldier's leg-armour'.]

oct. *abbr* octavo

Oct. *abbr* October

oct- *prefix* = **octo-** (*before vowels*)

octa- *prefix* = **octo-**

octad /ók tad/ *n* a group or series of eight [Mid-19C. < Greek *oktad-* < *oktō* (see OCTO-).] —**octadic** /ok táddik/ *adj*

octagon /óktəgən/ *n* a closed plane figure that has eight sides and eight angles —**octagonal** /ok tággən'l/ *adj*

octahedron /óktə heédrən/ (*plural* **-drons** *or* **-dra** /-drə/) *n* a three-dimensional figure that has eight faces —**octahedral** *adj* —**octahedrally** *adv*

⚡**octal** /óktəl/ *adj* using or having a number system based on eight instead of ten ■ *n* **1** = **octal notation** **2** a number with eight as its base

⚡**octal notation** *n* a number system used in writing computer programs that is based on eight and uses numerals 0 to 7, one octal unit equalling three bits

octameter /ok támmitər/ *n* a line of verse with eight metrical units or feet

octane /ók tayn/ *n* **1** C_8H_{18} a liquid hydrocarbon found in petroleum that exists in 18 structurally different forms **2** CARS = **octane number** [Late 19C. < OCTO-; from the number of carbon atoms in the hydrocarbon.]

octane number, octane rating *n* a number that measures the ability of a liquid motor fuel such as petrol to prevent preignition or knocking

Octans /ók tanz/ *n* a faint constellation of the southern hemisphere incorporating the south celestial pole. See illustration at **constellation**

octant /óktənt/ *n* **1 EIGHTH OF AN ASTRONOMICAL CIRCLE** the position of one body in the sky one-eighth of a circle (45°) from another **2 EIGHTH OF A CIRCLE** one-eighth of a circle, with or without the enclosed area **3 REGION OF SPACE IN CARTESIAN SYSTEM** any one of the eight regions into which space is divided by the three planes of the Cartesian coordinate system [Late 17C. < Latin *octant-* 'half-quadrant' < *octo* (see OCTO-).] —**octantal** /ok tánt'l/ *adj*

octapeptide /óktə pép tīd/ *n* a peptide consisting of eight amino acids

octavalent /óktə váylənt/ *adj* describes an element, atom, or group that has a valency of eight

octave /óktiv/ *n* **1 INTERVAL ON MUSICAL SCALE** an interval between two notes consisting of eight notes inclusive or seven steps on the diatonic scale **2 NOTE AT EACH END OF OCTAVE** the note at each end of an octave, especially the higher one, considered in relation to the note at the other end **3 NOTES AT END OF OCTAVE TOGETHER** the two notes at each end of an octave played together **4 ALL NOTES INCLUDED WITHIN OCTAVE** the series of notes that fall within an octave, including the octave on each end, or the strings, keys, or other musical devices that produce these notes **5 ORGAN STOP FOR PRODUCING HIGHER NOTES** an organ stop that causes tones to be produced an octave higher than the keys played alone **6 EIGHT LINES OF POETRY** a group of eight lines of verse, especially the first eight lines of a sonnet, or a poem that consists of eight lines **7 CHRISTIAN FEAST DAY AND FOLLOWING WEEK** in Christianity, a feast day and the week following it **8 EIGHTH DAY AFTER FEAST DAY** the eighth day after an octave feast day when the feast day is counted as one **9 EIGHTH DEFENSIVE POSITION IN FENCING** the eighth of eight basic defensive positions in fencing, known as a rotating perry **10 EIGHTH ITEM** the eighth in a series **11 SET OF EIGHT** a set or series of eight [14C. Via French < Latin *octava*, the feminine of *octavus* 'eighth' < *octo* 'eight'.]

octave coupler *n* a mechanism on an organ or harpsichord that allows somebody simultaneously to play one note and another one an octave higher or lower

Octavia /ok táyvi ə/ (69?–11 BC) Roman aristocrat

octavo /ok táyvō, -taávō/ (*plural* **-vos**) *n* a book size of about 16 by 23 cm/6 by 9 in, or a book of this size [Late 16C. < Latin, 'in an eighth (of a sheet)' < *octavus* (see OCTAVE) from the folding of a sheet eight times.]

octennial /ok ténni əl/ *adj* **1** occurring at intervals of eight years **2** lasting for a period of eight years [Mid-17C. < late Latin *octennium* 'period of eight years' < Latin *octo* 'eight'.] —**octennially** *adv*

octet /ok tét/ *n* **1** a group of eight, especially eight singers or instrumentalists **2** a musical composition for a group of eight voices or instruments **3** LITERAT = **octave** *n.* 6 [Mid-19C. Alteration of Italian *otteto* (< Latin *octo* 'eight').]

octet rule *n* CHEM = **Lewis rule of eight**

octo- *prefix* eight ○ *octosyllable* [< Latin *octo* and Greek *oktō*. Ultimately from the Indo-European word for 'eight' that is also the ancestor of English *eight*.]

October /ok tṓbər/ *n* the tenth month of the year in the Gregorian calendar, made up of 31 days [Pre-12C. < Latin, 'eighth month' < *octo* 'eight'.]

octocentenary /óktō sen teénəri/ (*plural* **-naries**) *n* an 800th anniversary

octodecimo /óktō déssimō/ (*plural* **-mos**) *n* a book size of about 10 by 16 cm/4 by 4 $\frac{1}{4}$ in, or a book of this size [Mid-19C. < Latin, 'in an eighteenth (of a sheet)' < *octodecim* 'eight and ten'; from the folding of a sheet 18 times.]

octogenarian /óktō jə náiri ən/ *n* a person between 80 and 89 years of age [Early 19C. < Latin *octogenarius* < *octoginta* 'eighty', literally 'eight times ten'.]

⚡**octonary** /óktənəri/ *adj* **1 BASED ON EIGHT** based on the number eight **2 CONSISTING OF EIGHT** consisting of eight things ■ *n* (*plural* **-ies**) **1 GROUP OF EIGHT** a group or set of eight things **2** COMPUT = **octal** *n.* 2 [Mid-16C. < Latin *octonarius* 'containing eight' < *octo* (see OCTO-).]

octoploid /óktə ployd/ *n* a cell nucleus or an organism, especially a plant, containing eight haploid sets of chromosomes

octopod /óktə pod/ *n* a shell-less mollusc such as the octopus with a large head and eyes and eight tentacles. Order: Octopoda. [Early 20C. < modern Latin *Octopoda* < Greek *oktōpod-*, stem of *oktōpous* (see OCTOPUS).] —**octopodous** /októ pōdəss/ *adj*

octopus /óktəpəss/ (*plural* **-puses** *or* **-pi** /-pī/ *or* **-pus**) *n* **1** a sea animal with a big head, a soft oval body, well-developed eyes, and eight arms containing rows of suckers. Genus: *Octopus.* **2** something, especially an organization, that has many branches and forms of influence or control **3** = **spider** *n.* 3 [Mid-18C. < modern Latin, < Greek *oktōpous* 'eight feet' < *oktō* 'eight'.]

octoroon /óktə roón/ *n* an offensive term for somebody who has one Black great-grandparent and no other

Black ancestors (*archaic*) [Mid-19C. < OCTO- after QUADROON.]

octosyllable /óktə siləb'l/ *n* a language unit of eight syllables, usually a complete line of verse but occasionally just a word —**octosyllabic** /óktə si lábbik/ *adj*

octroi /ók trwaa/ *n* formerly, especially in France and Italy, a local tax levied on goods entering a town or city [Late 16C. Via French < medieval Latin *auctorizare* (see AUTHORIZE).]

octuple /óktyoop'l, ok tyóop'l/ *adj* **1 EIGHT TIMES AS LARGE** eight times as large or effective **2 WITH EIGHT PARTS** consisting of eight parts ■ *vti* **MULTIPLY BY EIGHT** to multiply something by eight or to be multiplied by eight ■ *n* **QUANTITY EIGHT TIMES GREATER** an amount that is eight times more than another amount

ocul- *prefix* = **oculo-** (*before vowels*)

ocular /ókyoolər/ *adj* relating to, perceived by, or performed by the eye ■ *n* an eyepiece in an optical instrument [Late 16C. Via French *oculaire* < late Latin *ocularis* < Latin *oculus* 'eye'.]

oculist /ókyoolist/ *n* an optometrist or ophthalmologist (*dated*)

oculo- *prefix* eye ○ *oculomotor* [< Latin *oculus*]

oculogyric /ókyoolō jírrik/ *adj* relating to the movement of an eyeball in its socket

oculomotor /ókyoolō mṓtər/ *adj* relating to or causing movement of the eyeball

oculomotor nerve *n* either of the third pair of cranial nerves that carry nerve fibres from the brain to the eye muscles and eyelids

~~ocupation~~ incorrect spelling of **occupation**

~~ocurred~~ incorrect spelling of **occurred**

~~ocurrence~~ incorrect spelling of **occurrence**

Od /od/ *interj* used euphemistically as an oath to mean 'God' (*archaic*) [Late 16C. Alteration of GOD.]

OD[1] *abbr* **1** overdraft **2** overdrawn **3** Officer of the Day **4** Doctor of Optometry **5** Old Dutch **6** olive drab **7** ordnance datum

OD[2] /ō deé/ *vi* to take a dangerous amount of a drug, often causing hospitalization or death (*informal*) ■ *n* an overdose (*informal*) [Mid-20C. Shortening of OVERDOSE.]

o.d. *abbr* **1** outside diameter **2** on demand **3** olive drab **4** right eye [Shortening of Latin *oculus dexter*]

O/D, o/d *abbr* **1** overdraft **2** overdrawn

odalisque /ódə lisk, ódda-/, **odalisk** *n* **1** an enslaved woman or concubine, especially, formerly, in a Turkish harem **2** a representation of an odalisque in art [Late 17C. Via French < Turkish *ōdalik* 'somebody who works in a chamber' < *ōda* 'chamber'.]

Oda Nobunaga /ṓdə nóbbyoo naágə/ (1534–82) Japanese feudal lord

odd /od/ *adj* **1 UNUSUAL** peculiar, unusual, or out of the ordinary ○ *There's something very odd about the letter.* **2 NOT DIVISIBLE EXACTLY BY 2** being a number such as 1, 3, 5, 7, 9, or 11 that, when divided by 2, leaves a remainder of 1. ◊ **even**[1] *adj.* 9 **3 LEFTOVER** leftover, and usually few in number ○ *a few odd coins* **4 SEPARATED FROM PAIR OR SET** left on its own without the other member or members of its pair, set, or series ○ *a number of odd socks in the drawer* **5 IRREGULAR** irregular or occasional ○ *We get the odd day off here and there.* **6 SLIGHTLY GREATER THAN STATED NUMBER** used after a number to mean a little more than the number stated ○ *I figured on paying 50-odd pounds for it.* **7 REMOTE** not usually visited or reached by many people ○ *We found the papers lying about in odd corners of the house.* **8 HAVING CHANGING MATHEMATICAL SIGNS** used to refer to a function that changes sign but not value when the sign of each independent variable is changed at the same time ■ *n* **SOMETHING ODD IN NUMBER** something that is odd in number or numerical order [14C. < Old Norse *oddi* 'third or odd number'.] —**oddish** *adj* —**oddly** *adv* —**oddness** *n*

oddball /ód bawl/ *n* a person who is thought to be unusual or unconventional, but usually in a harmless way (*informal insult*)

odd bod *n* = **oddball** (*informal*)

Odd Fellow *n* a member of the Independent Order of Odd Fellows, a secret international social and charitable fraternity founded in England in the 18th century [< ODD 'remote, out-of-the-way'; from the Order's mystic practices]

oddity /óddəti/ (*plural* **-ties**) *n* somebody or something unique, unusual, or unconventional

odd job *n* any unspecialized job such as household repairs, usually done casually and for low pay (*often plural*) ○ *does odd jobs for a living*

odd-job (**odd-jobs, odd-jobbing, odd-jobbed**) *vi* to work at one or more odd jobs ○ *odd-jobbed around town* —**odd-jobber** *n*

odd lot *n* a quantity or number of shares that is smaller than the usual trading unit, e.g. fewer than 100 shares when traded on a stock exchange, or less than one whole share when liquidated

odd man out *n* = **odd one out**

oddment /ódmənt/ *n* something left over when most of something has been used or disposed of (*usually plural*) ○ *By the time she arrived there were only oddments left in the sale.* [Late 18C. < ODD after FRAGMENT.]

odd one out (*plural* **odd ones out**), **odd man out** (*plural* **odd men out**) *n* somebody in a group who differs from the rest of the group in some way, or who is not treated as part of the group

odds /odz/ *npl* **1 CHANCES OF SOMETHING HAPPENING** the likelihood or probability that something will occur, sometimes expressed as a ratio such as 10 to 1 ○ *The odds are that you'll never make it.* **2 PREDICTED CHANCES IN BETTING** a ratio of probability given to people placing a bet, usually the likelihood of a specific event happening, or of a competitor, team, or animal winning ○ *The horse was given odds of four to one.* **3 HANDICAP OR ADVANTAGE USED IN COMPETITION** an advantage or handicap given to a person, animal, or team in a sporting contest, to equalize the chances of winning **4 PERCEIVED ADVANTAGE OR DISADVANTAGE** a perceived advantage or disadvantage, especially one that one person is believed to have over another in a competition [Early 16C. Plural of ODD.] ◇ **at odds (with somebody)** in disagreement with somebody ◇ **at odds (with something)** in conflict with something ◇ **over the odds** more than is usual or necessary ◇ **what's the odds?** used to indicate that something is of no importance

odds and ends *npl* a group of miscellaneous items ○ *The top drawer is where I keep my odds and ends.*

odds and sods *npl* miscellaneous people or items (*informal*)

oddsmaker /ódz maykər/ *n* an official calculator of betting odds

odds-on *adj* likeliest to win, succeed, or happen (*informal*) ○ *It was odds-on that he would succeed his father.*

ode /ōd/ *n* **1** a lyric poem, usually expressing exalted emotion in a complex scheme of rhyme and metre **2** an ancient Greek song written either for a chorus or for a solo singer [Late 16C. Via French < Greek *ōidē* 'song'.]

-ode *suffix* **1** electrically conducting element ○ *electrode* **2** electrode ○ *tetrode* [< Greek *hodos* 'way']

Odense /ṓth'nssə/ port in south-central Denmark. Population: 182,617 (1995).

odeon *n* ARCHIT = **odeum**

Oder /ṓdər/ river in north-central Europe, flowing northwards from the Czech Republic into the Baltic Sea. Length: 906 km/563 mi.

Odessa /ō déssə/, **Odesa** city and port in south-central Ukraine, on the Black Sea. Population: 1,060,000 (1995).

odeum /ṓdi-/ (*plural* **-a** /-ə/), **odeon** /ṓdi ən/ (*plural* **-a**) *n* an ancient Greek or Roman building in which musical performances were held [Early 17C. Directly or via French < Latin *odeum* < Greek *ōideion* < *ōidē* (see ODE).]

odious /ṓdi əss/ *adj* inspiring hatred, contempt, or disgust [14C. Via Old French < Latin *odiosus* < *odium* (see ODIUM).] —**odiously** *adv* —**odiousness** *n*

~~odissey~~ incorrect spelling of **odyssey**

odium /ṓdi əm/ *n* **1** intense dislike, repugnance, or contempt for somebody or something ○ *incurred scorn and odium for his actions* **2** the state of being hateful, contemptuous, or disgusting [Early 17C. < Latin.]

odometer /ō dómmitər, o-/ *n* US TRANSP = **mileometer** [Late 18C. Via French *odomètre* or directly < Greek *hodos* 'way'.]

odonate /ṓdə nayt/ *n* an insect belonging to the order of insects that includes the dragonfly and damselfly. Order: Odonata. [Early 20C. < modern Latin *Odonata* < Greek *odōn*, a variant of *odous* 'tooth'.]

odont- *prefix* = **odonto-** (*before vowels*)

-odont *suffix* having a particular kind of teeth ○ *acrodont* [< Greek *odont-*, stem of *odous* (see ODONTO-)]

odontalgia /óddon tálji ə/ *n* toothache (*technical*)

-odontia *suffix* condition or treatment of teeth ○ *anodontia* [< Greek *odont-*, stem of *odous* (see ODONTO-)]

odonto- *prefix* tooth, teeth ○ *odontology* [< Greek *odont-* 'tooth' < Indo-European, 'tooth']

odontoblast /o dóntə blast/ *n* one of a layer of cells lining the pulp cavity of a tooth and taking part in the formation of dentine —**odontoblastic** /o dóntə blástik/ *adj*

odontoglossum /o dóntə glóssəm/ *n* a variety of orchid that grows on other plants and is widely cultivated for its clusters of brightly coloured flowers. Native to: mountainous areas from Bolivia to Mexico. Genus: *Odontoglossum*. [Late 19C. < modern Latin, 'tooth tongue' < Greek *odont-* 'tooth' + *glōssa* 'tongue'; from the toothlike projection on the end of the flower.]

odontoid /o dónt oyd/ *adj* resembling a tooth, especially in shape

odontoid process *n* a tooth-shaped peg that projects upwards from the second neck vertebra to engage with the first, acting as a pivot for side-to-side movements of the head

odontology /óddon tólləji/ *n* the branch of science that studies the teeth and their anatomy, development, and diseases —**odontological** /o dóntə lójjik'l/ *adj* —**odontologically** *adv* —**odontologist** /óddon tólləjist/ *n*

odor *n* US = **odour**

odorant /ṓdərənt/ *n* something that gives a characteristic smell to a product

odoriferous /ṓdə ríffərəss/ *adj* having or diffusing a strong odour (*technical*) —**odoriferously** *adv* —**odoriferousness** *n*

odorous *adj* = **odoriferous** (*literary*) —**odorously** *adv* —**odorousness** *n*

odour /ṓdər/ *n* **1** smell or scent, whether pleasant or unpleasant ○ *the delicious odour of baking bread* **2** a quality or attitude that suggests or resembles a particular thing ○ *They had an odour of propriety.* ○ *odour of sanctity* [13C. Via Anglo-Norman and Old French *odor, odur* < Latin *odor* 'smell'.] ◇ **be in bad** *or* **good odour (with somebody)** to be out of *or* in favour with somebody

SYNONYMS See ***smell***.

odourless /ṓdərləss/ *adj* having no smell that is strong enough to be detected by the human nose —**odourlessness** *n*

Odysseus /ō díssee əss/ *n* in Greek mythology, the king of Ithaca who is the main character in Homer's epic poem the *Odyssey*. ◊ **Ulysses**

odyssey /óddissi/ (*plural* **-seys**) *n* a long series of travels and adventures [Late 19C. < the *Odyssey*, < Greek *Odusseia*, < ODYSSEUS.]

LITERARY LINK ***The Odyssey***, an epic poem (?8th century BC) by the Greek writer Homer. The oldest surviving source of Greek mythology along with the *Iliad*, it describes Odysseus's ten-year journey home to Ithaca after the Trojan War. It provides both an insight into a long-lost civilization and a gripping narrative rich in evocative details, complex characters, and universal themes.

Oe *symbol* oersted

OE *abbr* Old English

OECD *abbr* Organization for Economic Cooperation and Development

oedema /i deémə/ (*plural* **-mas** *or* **-mata** /-mətə/) *n* **1** an abnormal buildup of serous fluid between tissue cells **2** an abnormal swelling in a plant, chiefly caused by a buildup of excess water [15C. < Greek *oidēma* 'swelling tumour' < *oidein* 'swell'.] —**oedematous** /i démmətəss, i deémətəss/ *adj*

Oedipus /eédipəss/ *n* in Greek mythology, a son of Jocasta and Laius, king of Thebes, who unwittingly killed his father and married his mother —**Oedipal** *adj*

Oedipus complex /eédipəss-/ *n* according to the psychoanalytic theory of Sigmund Freud, feelings or desires originating when a child, especially a son, unconsciously seeks sexual fulfilment with the parent of the opposite sex. ◊ **Electra complex** [Early 20th C. After OEDIPUS.]

OEIC /oyk/ *abbr* open-ended investment company

Ōe Kenzaburō /ṓ ay kénzə bóorō/ (*b.* 1935) Japanese writer

OEM *abbr* original equipment manufacturer

oenomel /éenə mel/ *n* (*literary*) **1** a drink of wine and honey made in ancient Greece **2** words or ideas that combine strength and sweetness [Late 16C. Via late Latin *oenomeli* < Greek *oinomeli* 'honey wine' < *oinos* 'wine' + *meli* 'honey'.]

oenophile /éenə fīl/ *n* a lover of or expert on wine [Mid-20C. < French < *oeno-* < Greek *oinos* 'wine'.]

o'er /ṓ ər, awr/ *prep, adv* over (*literary*) ○ *The sun rose o'er the mountain.* [14C. Contraction.]

oersted /-sted/ *n* (*symbol* **Oe**) the unit measure of magnetic field strength in the centimetre-gram-second system [Late19C. After H.C. Hans Christian OERSTED.]

Oersted /úrstid, őrstid/, **Hans Christian** (1777–1851) Danish physicist and chemist

oesophagus (*plural* **-gi** /-gī/) *n* the passage down which food moves between the throat and the stomach [14C. Via medieval Latin *isophagus* < Greek *oisophagos*.] —**oesophageal** /isóffə jée əl/ *adj*

oestradiol /éestrə dī ol, éstrə-/ *n* $C_{18}H_{24}O_2$ an oestrogenic hormone produced in the ovaries and synthesized for use in treating oestrogen deficiency and breast cancer [Mid-20C. < OESTRUS + DI-[1] + -OL.]

oestriol /éestri ol, és-/ *n* an oestrogen hormone produced in the ovaries and secreted in the urine during pregnancy [Early 20C. < OESTRUS + TRI- + -OL.]

oestrogen /éestrəjən, éstrəjən/ *n* any steroid hormone produced mainly in the ovaries that stimulates oestrus and the development of female secondary sexual characteristics [Early 20C. < OESTRUS + -O- + -GEN.] —**oestrogenic** /éestrə jénnik, éstrə-/ *adj*

oestrone /éestrōn, és-/ *n* $C_{18}H_{22}O_2$ an oestrogenic hormone produced in the ovaries and synthesized for use in treating oestrogen deficiency and breast cancer [Early 20C. < OESTRUS + -ONE.]

oestrous cycle *n* a hormonally controlled reproductive cycle occurring in most female mammals, marked by a period of heat followed by ovulation and changes in the womb lining

oestrus /éestrəss, és-/ *n* a regular period of sexual excitement in many female mammals during which the animal is receptive to mating [Late 19C. Via Latin *oestrus* 'frenzy' < Greek *oistros* 'gad-fly'.] —**oestrous** *adj* —**oestral** *adj*

oeuvre /úrvrə, urvr/ *n* a work of art or literature, or such works considered as a unit, especially the complete work of a single artist [Late 19C. Via French < Latin *opera*, the plural of *opus* 'work'.]

of (*stressed*) /ov/; (*unstressed*) /əv, ə/ CORE MEANING: used between two nouns, the second providing more information about the first ○ *Most software has complex sets of commands and options.* ○ *She let out a little squeal of delight.*

prep **1 AFFECTED BY ACTION** used to indicate the person or thing affected by or performing an action ○ *the promotion of junior staff* ○ *the death of her father* **2 USED IN MEASURING QUANTITIES** used after words or phrases expressing quantities to indicate the substance or thing being measured ○ *millions of dollars* ○ *a herd of cows* ○ *10 gallons of oil* **3 CONNECTED WITH** used to indicate the place that somebody or something belongs to or is connected with ○ *the president of France* **4 CONTAINING** containing the substance mentioned ○ *a mug of coffee* ○ *a busload of schoolchildren* **5 PART OF** used to indicate a part of something that is normally considered as a whole ○ *a slice of cake* ○ *a square of fabric* **6 MADE FROM** made from or used as a material to form something ○ *ruled with a rod of iron* ○ *a paste of flour and water* **7 INDICATING RELATIONSHIP OR ASSOCIATION** used to indicate a relationship, association, or cause ○ *I'll be thinking of you.* ○ *accused of negligence* **8 RELATING TO** used after words describing feelings and qualities to indicate the person or thing they relate to ○ *He's very sure of himself.* ○ *It's very kind of you to come.* **9 INDICATING A PARTICULAR TYPE** describes somebody or something in terms of a particular type or kind ○ *one heck of a gymnast* **10 HAVING A PARTICULAR QUALITY** used to indicate a quality that somebody or something has, or the person or thing having a particular quality ○ *announcements of a general nature* ○ *a musician of great talent* ○ *the gentleness of his manner* **11 INDICATING AMOUNT** used to indicate an amount, age, or value ○ *There is a limit of eight characters in a computer user name.* ○ *a young boy of 12* **12 EVERY** used to indicate a day or other period of time when an activity regularly occurs (*informal*) ○ *We usually go out for a meal of a Friday.* **13** US **BEFORE** before the hour of ○ *It was a quarter of ten before she returned.* [Old English < Germanic]

off /of/ CORE MEANING: a grammatical word used to indicate separation or distance between two points, especially movement away from the speaker ○ (adv) *He ran off before I could stop him.* ○ (prep) *The bottle rolled off the ledge and fell to the floor.*

1 *prep, adv* **SO AS TO LEAVE** so as to come out of or leave a bus, train, or plane ○ *Check you have all your belongings before getting off the bus.* ○ *He got off at the next stop.* **2** *prep, adv* **SO AS TO KEEP AWAY FROM** so as to keep away from, avoid stepping on, or be at a distance from or to the side of ○ *The sign said 'Please keep off the grass'.* ○ *I stepped off the kerb.* **3** *prep, adv* **AWAY FROM WORK** away from work or usual duties owing to illness, holidays, or normal nonwork time ○ *trying to get time off work to visit her in hospital* ○ *I didn't see Jane – it must be her night off.* **4** *prep, adv* **REDUCED BY** so as to be reduced by the amount indicated ○ *10 per cent off all swimwear this week* ○ *She knocked £10 off for the slight stain on the sleeve.* **5** *prep, adv* **IN THE FUTURE** a particular distance away in the future ○ *My fortieth birthday is only two years off!* **6** *prep, adv* **SO AS TO REMOVE** so as to eliminate or remove something from view ○ *The dirt should wash off easily.* ○ *He was rubbing something off the board when I came in.* **7** *adv* **TO A DISTANT PLACE** so as to be away from the present location ○ *He hopped in the car, started it up, and took off.* **8** *adv* **AWAY** at a particular physical distance away ○ *The nearest stop's about two miles off.* **9** *adv* **MEASURED** so as to be divided or measured ○ *Measure the gap, mark it off with a pencil, and cut the wood to size.* **10** *adv* **TO COMPLETION** to the point of completion ○ *We're trying to get our bills paid off.* **11** *adv* **INTO A PARTICULAR STATE** into a particular state, especially an unconscious state ○ *The baby dozed off on the way over here.* **12** *adv* **REQUIRED NUMBER** indicating the number of items required or produced (*preceded by a number*) **13** *prep* **ABSTAINING FROM** no longer participating in or using ○ *stay off caffeine for a week* **14** *prep* **NOT LIKING** no longer inclined towards ○ *I'm really off horror movies at the moment.* **15** *prep* **ON A DIET OF** using as a means of subsistence ○ *living off vegetables from our garden* **16** *prep* **LEADING AWAY FROM** near or next to, and leading or branching away from ○ *He lives in an apartment block just off the high street.* **17** *prep* **FROM** used to show the object of an action (*nonstandard*) ○ *I got these sunglasses off my sister for my birthday.* **18** *adv, adj* **NOT IN OPERATION** not functioning or in use ○ *Shall I switch the engine off?* ○ *He was always constantly checking to make sure the lights were off.* **19** *adv, adj* **CANCELLED** so as to be no longer taking place ○ *The deal's off.* **20** *adj* **NO LONGER FRESH** smelling and tasting bad because of being no longer fresh ○ *We had to throw the fish away – it was going off.* **21** *adj* **NOT ON THE MENU** no longer on the menu in a restaurant, not being served at the moment ○ *I'm sorry sir, the steak is off.* **22** *adj* **IN PARTICULAR CONDITION** in a particular condition with regard to something ○ *How are you off for cash?* **23** *adj* **NOT CORRECT** in error or out of alignment **24** *adj* **ON RIGHT OF** situated on the right side of a vehicle, farthest away from the kerb **25** *adj* **UNACCEPTABLE** unacceptable or disappointing, not up to normal standards (informal) ○ *'She turned up two hours late'.'Well I think that's a bit off'.* **26** *n* **PART OF CRICKET FIELD** the side of the cricket field facing the batsman taking strike [Old English. Originally an emphatic variant of OF.] ◇ **off and on** occasionally

USAGE There are two usages of ***off*** that should be avoided in formal writing. The first involves ***off*** plus *of*: *The actors stepped off* [not *off of*] *the stage.* The second problem involves the use of ***off*** after certain verbs like *buy* or *borrow*, which mean 'to obtain something from a source': *I bought the computer from* [not *off*] *my flatmate.*

off. *abbr* **1** office **2** officer **3** official

Offa /óffə/ (730?–796) Anglo-Saxon king of Mercia (757–96)

off-air *adj* spoken or occurring in broadcasting studios but not used during a broadcast —**off air** *adv*

offal /óff'l/ *n* **1** the edible, mainly internal organs of an animal, e.g. the heart, liver, brains, and tongue, sometimes regarded as unpalatable or even inedible **2** something discarded as refuse [14C. < OFF + FALL.]

Offaly /óffəli/ county in the central Republic of Ireland. Area: 1,998 sq. km/771 sq. mi.

Offa's Dyke /óffəz-/ ancient earthwork along the England-Wales border, constructed in the 8th century. Length: 240 km/150 mi.

offbeat /óf beet/ *adj* not conforming to convention or to expectations

off beat *n* any unaccented beat in a bar of music

off-Broadway *n* in New York City, professional theatre productions, sometimes experimental or innovative in nature, that are staged outside the principal theatre district of Broadway. ◊ **off-off-Broadway**

off-camera *adj* out of sight of the camera —**off camera** *adv*

off-campus *adj* done, taking place, or existing outside the area of a university, college, or other campus —**off campus** *adv*

off-centre *adj* **1** not at the centre and therefore sometimes causing a lack of symmetry, balance, or evenness of movement **2** slightly unconventional or eccentric —**off centre** *adv*

off chance, off-chance *n* a slight or remote possibility ◇ **on the off chance** just in case something happens

off-colour *adj* **1 ILL** ill or not very well ○ *I'm feeling a bit off-colour today.* **2 SLIGHTLY SMUTTY** mildly sexually indecent or suggestive (*informal*) **3 NOT COLOURED NORMALLY** not having the usual or desired colour

off-course *adj* occurring somewhere other than a racecourse. US term **off-track**

offcut /óf kut/ *n* a remnant left after the main pieces of something such as fabric or paper have been cut

off day *n* Malaysia a day on which somebody does not have to work

Offenbach /óff'n baak/ city in west-central Germany. Population: 116,700 (1994).

Offenbach, Jacques (1819–80) German-born French composer. Born **Jacob Eberst**

offence /ə fénss/ *n* **1 LEGAL OR MORAL CRIME** an official crime, or a crime against moral, social, or other accepted standards ○ *He was convicted of a motoring offence* **2 ATTACK** an attack or assault, usually in the military or in sports ○ *The army launched its great offence that spring.* **3 ATTACKING PLAYERS ON A TEAM** the players making up the part of a team that attempts to score in a game, as distinct from the defence that tries to stop the other team from scoring ○ *We lacked a good offence last spring.* **4 ANGER OR RESENTMENT** anger, resentment, hurt, or displeasure ○ *'Please don't take offence'.* ○ *His remarks caused great offence.* **5 CAUSE OF DISPLEASURE OR ANGER** something that causes displeasure, humiliation, anger, resentment, or hurt ○ *The request was an offence to their dignity.* [14C. Via French < Latin *offens-*, past participle of *offendere* (see OFFEND).]

offend /ə fénd/ *v* **1** *vti* to hurt somebody's feelings, or cause resentment, irritation, anger, or displeasure ○ *The book offended too many people.* **2** *vi* to violate a law or code of conduct ○ *he offended against the club's rules of proper dress* [14C. Directly or via Old French *offendre* < Latin *offendere* 'to strike'.] —**offender** *n* —**offending** *adj*

offense *n* US = **offence**

offensive /ə fénssiv/ *adj* **1 UPSETTING, INSULTING, OR IRRITATING** causing anger, resentment, or moral outrage ○ *removed the offensive material from the play* **2 UNPLEASANT TO THE SENSES** causing physical repugnance ○ *an offensive smell* **3 AGGRESSIVE** demonstrating aggression ○ *warned that this would be seen as an offensive action* **4 USED WHEN ATTACKING** used, or designed to be used, when attacking ○ *an offensive weapon* ■ *n* **ATTACK OR ASSAULT** an attack, assault, or siege ○ *The platoon braced itself for the dawn offensive.*

offer /óffər/ *vt* **1 PRESENT SOMETHING FOR ACCEPTANCE OR REJECTION** to attempt to give somebody something that may be taken or refused, usually something desirable ○ *They offered me the job.* **2 HAVE SOMETHING FOR THE USE OF OTHERS** to provide something, or make something available for those who want it ○ *The town offered many amenities.* **3 VOLUNTEER TO DO** to suggest doing something yourself as a favour for somebody else ○ *I offered to bring the salad.* **4 HAVE SOMETHING FOR SALE OR HIRE** to present or have something for sale or hire ○ *the first gym to offer professional trainers at a low cost* **5 GIVE AS WORSHIP** to present something to God, often as part of worship ○ *We offer hymns of praise to God.* **6 EXHIBIT A QUALITY** to exhibit or demonstrate a particular quality ○ *The city offered little resistance against the army.* ○ *a plan that offers hope to millions* **7 MAKE A BID** to make a bid or financial proposal for something ○ *They offered 40 pence a share.* **8 PRESENT PERFORMANCE** to present an exhibition or performance ○ *They offered two films each night.* ■ *n* **1 PROPOSAL OF A SUGGESTED GIFT OR ACTION** a suggestion from somebody to give something or do something for somebody else ○ *A home-cooked meal and a place to stay: that's the best offer I've had all day!* **2 FINANCIAL PROPOSAL OR BID** a sum of money suggested as payment for something such as a house ○ *They made an offer for the house but we refused it.* **3 REDUCED PRICE** a reduced price for something ○ *this week's special offer* **4 PROPOSAL LEADING TO A BINDING CONTRACT** a proposal that, if accepted, creates a binding contract [Old English *offrian*. Via Germanic < Latin *offerre* 'bring to' < *ferre* 'bring'.] —**offerer** *n*

offer up *vt* RELIG = **offer** *v.* 5

offering /óffəring/ *n* **1 CONTRIBUTION** something that is offered, or the act of offering ○ *The restaurant had some pretty awful offerings.* **2 GIFT FOR GOD** something offered as a sacrifice to a deity **3 MONEY GIVEN DURING A CHURCH SERVICE** a financial contribution to a church, often made during a church service [Old English *offrung*]

offer price *n* the price at which something, especially a share of a stock or mutual fund, is offered for sale

~~**offerred**~~ incorrect spelling of **offered**

offertory /óffərtəri/ (*plural* **-ries**) *n* **1 OFFERING OF COMMUNION BREAD AND WINE** the offering of the bread and wine during the Christian service of Holy Communion **2 CHURCH COLLECTION** the offering of money or gifts made by a church congregation **3 PART OF A CHRISTIAN SERVICE** a part of a church service during which prayers are said or sung while offerings are received [14C. Via ecclesiastical Latin *offertorium* 'offering place' < Latin *offerre* (see OFFER).]

off-glide *n* a sound produced by the vocal organs prior to their making another sound or assuming a neutral position

off-guard *adj* not paying attention or being prepared for possible attack (*not hyphenated after verbs*) ○ *caught the enemy offguard*

offhand /of hánd/ *adv* **1 CASUALLY** casually, thoughtlessly, or spontaneously **2 WITHOUT PREPARATION** without preparation or research ○ *Offhand, I'd say there must be 50 people in there.* ■ *adj* **offhand, offhanded 1 UNCONCERNED AND UNCARING** so casual, uninterested, or blunt as to appear impolite or uncaring ○ *She was pretty offhand about the whole affair.* **2 CASUALLY DONE** taken or made casually or without planning, usually on the spur of the moment ○ *Only through her offhand comment did I realize who she was.* —**offhandedly** *adv* —**offhandedness** *n*

off-hour *n* **1** US **TIME OUTSIDE THE RUSH HOUR** a period of time that is not crowded with cars or people (*informal; often before nouns*) ○ *We try to visit the zoo during off-hours.* **2** US **TIME OUTSIDE WORKING HOURS** a period of time outside normal business hours (*informal*) **3** US **GOVERNMENT AGENCY OR SUBDIVISION** a US government agency or subdivision, especially of the Federal Government

office /óffiss/ *n* **1 ROOM USED FOR BUSINESS ACTIVITY** a room in which business or professional activities take place, often occupied by a single person or a single section of the business **2 PLACE OF BUSINESS** the quarters in which a commercial, professional, or government organization carries out its activities **3 OFFICIAL ORGANIZATION** a commercial or professional organization **4 STAFF IN OFFICE** the people who work in an office ○ *get-well cards from the office* **5 BRITISH GOVERNMENT DEPARTMENT** a department in the British Government ○ *He works for the Home Office.* **6 US GOVERNMENT AGENCY OR DEPARTMENT** a US government agency or subdivision, especially of the federal government **7 POSITION OF RESPONSIBILITY** an official post or position of duty, trust, or responsibility ○ *The mayor has been in office four years now.* **8 PLACE FOR TICKETS OR INFORMATION** a booth or other place where tickets or information may be obtained **9 SET FORM OF CHRISTIAN SERVICE** the prescribed order or form of a Christian church service, or of daily prayers **10 TASK OR ASSIGNMENT** a task, assignment, or chore (*formal; usually plural*) ■ **offices** *npl* **1 SOMETHING DONE ON BEHALF OF ANOTHER** something said or done by somebody to or for another person (*formal*) ○ *I got the job through her kind offices.* **2 AREAS OR BUILDINGS WHERE SERVANTS WORK** the outbuildings or parts of a house in which the servants work (*dated*) [13C. Via French < Latin *officium* 'doing work' < *opus* 'work' + *facere* 'do'.]

office-bearer *n* somebody who holds office in a society, club, or voluntary organization, e.g. the President or Treasurer. US = **office holder**

office block *n* a large building holding offices

office boy *n* a boy or man who does errands around an office (*dated*)

office building *n* US = **office block**

office-free *adj* US relating to or involving a workforce that is not required to work from or at an office

office holder *n* **1** an official in a government position **2** = **office-bearer**

office hours *npl* the regular times during which a business or profession, or business as a whole, is conducted

office junior *n* a young office-worker entrusted only with minor clerical tasks

officer /óffissər/ *n* **1 SOMEBODY OF RANK IN ARMED FORCES** somebody in a military force authorized to command others **2** = **police officer 3 SOMEBODY IN AUTHORITY ON SHIP** somebody with a position of authority on a civilian ship **4 ELECTED OR APPOINTED OFFICIAL** an official who holds an administrative position ■ *vt* **SUPPLY SOMETHING WITH OFFICERS** to provide something such as a military unit or a ship with officers

officer of arms *n* a herald, especially one who devises, grants, or confirms coats of arms

official /ə físh'l/ *n* **SOMEBODY HOLDING OFFICE** a holder of office in an organization, corporation, or government department ■ *adj* **1 OF GOVERNMENTAL OR ORGANIZATIONAL OFFICE** relating to or concerned with a governmental or organizational office ○ *official rules and regulations* **2 AUTHORIZED BY SOME AUTHORITY** approved, recognized, or issued by some authority ○ *No official statement has been issued.* **3 FORMAL** formal or ceremonial ○ *invited to attend the official opening* —**officially** *adv*

official birthday *n* in the United Kingdom, a date in June chosen as the occasion on which to celebrate the sovereign's birthday, with formal ceremonies taking place in London

officialdom /ə físh'ldəm/ *n* bureaucracy and those who work within it, especially when viewed as inefficient or pompous (*informal*) ○ *caught up in the red tape of officialdom*

officialese /ə físhə léez/ *n* unclear, pedantic, and verbose language considered characteristic of official documents

officialism /ə físh'lizəm/ *n* excessive respect or adherence to official routines and regulations, considered to be characteristic of officials (*informal*)

Official Receiver *n* an official appointed to manage a bankrupt's property prior to the appointment of a trustee

Official Referee *n* in England and Wales, a circuit judge with authority from the High Court to try cases involving examination of accounts or other documents

Official Solicitor *n* in England and Wales, an officer of the Supreme Court of Judicature with special responsibilities for protecting the interests of people with disabilities

officiary /ə físhi əri/ *adj* derived from the holding of an office, or having a title that is derived from an office held ○ *an officiary title* ■ *n* (*plural* **-ies**) an official or an organized group of officials [Early 17C. Via medieval Latin *officiarius* < Latin *officium* (see OFFICE).]

officiate /ə físhi ayt/ *vi* to preside in an official capacity, especially at a religious ceremony [Mid-17C. Via medieval Latin *officiat-*, past participle of *officiare* 'conduct sacred service' < Latin *officium* (see OFFICE).] —**officiant** *n*

officinal /o físsinəl, óffi sínəl/ *adj* having medicinal properties, especially those recognized by a pharmacopoeia (*archaic*) [Late 17C. Via medieval Latin *officinalis* < *officina* 'workshop' (later 'storeroom for medicines') < Latin *officium* (see OFFICE).] —**officinally** *adv*

officious /ə físhəss/ *adj* **1** characteristic of somebody who is eager to give unwanted help or advice ○ *whisked away our unfinished meal in an officious manner* **2** unofficial or informal, especially in political or diplomatic dealings [Late 15C. < Latin *officiosus* < *officium* (see OFFICE).] —**officiously** *adv* —**officiousness** *n*

offing /óffing/ *n* the more distant part of the sea seen from the shore [Early 17C. Probably < OFF.] ◇ **in the offing** expected or likely in the future

offish /óffish/ *adj* standoffish (*informal*)

off-key *adj* (*not hyphenated after verbs*) **1 OUT OF TUNE** not having the correct pitch **2 INAPPROPRIATE** not usual, conventional, or appropriate ■ *adv* **OUT OF TUNE** above or below the correct pitch

off-label *adj* US using or involving the use of a prescription drug to treat a condition for which the drug has not been approved by the US Food and Drug Administration

off-licence *n* UK a shop or a pub where bottles or cans of alcoholic beverages may be bought for consumption elsewhere

off-limits *adj* to which entry is forbidden or barred ○ *That part of town was off-limits to us.*

⚡ **off-line** *adj* **1** describes a computer terminal or peripheral device that is disconnected or is functioning separately from an associated computer or computer network ○ *The printer was taken off-line for repairs.* ◊ **online 2** involved in preparing but not transmitting material for broadcasting ○ *off-line editing* —**off line** *adv*

⚡ **off-line newsreader** *n* software that allows a user to read newsgroup articles when the computer is not connected to the Internet

⚡ **offload** /of lód, óf lōd/ *v* **1** *vti* **UNLOAD GOODS** to unload goods or a cargo from a vehicle or container ○ *ships waiting to offload* **2** *vt* **GET RID OF** to get rid of something unwanted by passing it on to somebody else ○ *managed to offload some of the work onto colleagues* **3** *vti* **UNBURDEN YOURSELF** to relieve yourself of a stressful emotion such as anxiety or frustration by talking to someone (*informal*) **4** *vti* **TRANSFER DATA** to transfer data from one computer to another to create spare capacity

off-message *adj* not following the official policy of a political party or other organization ○ *off-message MPs*

off-off-Broadway *n* in New York City, theatre productions that are considered to be fringe, experimental, or avant-garde. ◊ **off-Broadway**

off-peak *adj* relating to the periods outside that of maximum use, frequency, or demand —**off peak** *adv*

off-piste *adj* relating to or taking place on fresh trackless snow that is away from the regular skiing runs —**off piste** *adv*

off-plan *adj* based only on the plans of a building that has not yet been built —**off plan** *adv*

off-price *adj* **1** US **CUT-PRICE** offering goods at low prices, or being sold at a discount (*informal*) **2 OF BRAND NAMES SOLD CHEAP** relating to brand name merchandise that is sold by retail establishments at below normal prices **3** US **SOLD CHEAPLY** sold by retailers at below normal prices

offprint /óf print/ *n* a separate printing of a single article from a periodical, often given in small quantities to each individual contributor

off-putting *adj* arousing irritation, repugnance, or mild unease —**offputtingly** *adv*

off-ramp *n* US a one-way road serving as an exit from a main highway

off-rhyme *n* a partial or near rhyme

off-road *adj* designed, manufactured, or used for travel off public roads, especially over rough terrain

off-road vehicle *n* a motorized vehicle designed or used for travel away from public roads or on rough terrain

off-sales *npl* the sales within a pub of alcoholic beverages for consumption elsewhere ○ *Off-sales amounted to about 10% of gross takings.*

offscourings /óf skowringz/ *npl* the leftover or discarded parts of something

off-screen *adj* **1 NOT VISIBLE ON A SCREEN** not visible on a television or cinema screen ○ *an off-screen commentator* **2 OCCURRING IN ORDINARY LIFE** occurring in ordinary life, not as fiction on television or in a film ○ *Her off-screen life was just as exciting.* ■ *adv* **IN ORDINARY LIFE** aside from television or film performances ○ *Off-screen, he mostly played golf.*

off-season *n* a time of year when activity or business is at a low level (*often before nouns*) ○ *Hotel rooms were cheaper in the off-season.* ■ *adv* during the off-season ○ *He liked to travel off-season.*

offset *n* /óf set/ **1 SOMETHING COUNTERBALANCING SOMETHING ELSE** something that counterbalances or compensates, or an allowance made in order to counterbalance something (*often before nouns*) **2 BEGINNING** the beginning of something (*dated*) **3 SOMETHING SET APART** anything set apart from something else (*often before nouns*) **4 OFFSHOOT CAPABLE OF PROPAGATION** an offshoot or runner from the base of a plant that can propagate the plant **5 PRINTING PROCESS USING INK TRANSFER** a method of printing in which inked impressions are transferred onto paper from another surface (*often before nouns*) **6 UNINTENTIONAL MARKING FROM WET INK** an accidental transfer of ink, usually from one piece of paper to another (*often before* nouns) **7 SPUR IN A MOUNTAIN RANGE** a projecting spur or ridge in a mountain range (*often before nouns*) **8 HORIZONTAL DISPLACEMENT OF ROCK** the horizontal displacement that occurs as a result of the movement of a rock mass along a fault **9** ARCHIT = **setback** *n.* **2 10 SURVEYING LINE** a short distance measured at right angles from a main survey line, used in finding the area of a piece of land **11 ABRUPT BEND IN A STRAIGHT LINE** an abrupt bend put into an otherwise straight bar or pipe in order to avoid an obstruction **12 OFFSHOOT OR DESCENDANT** something that has developed from something else, e.g. a collateral descendant or group of descendants of a family ■ *v* /of sét, óf sét/ (**-sets, -setting, -set**) **1** *vt* COUNTERACT to balance or make up for something (*often passive*) ○ *These improved sales were offset by last month's losses.* **2** *vti* PRINT SOMETHING BY TRANSFER to print something by offset printing, or to accidentally transfer ink by an offset **3** *vti* FORM OR BE AN OFFSET IN to make an offset in something such as a wall or pipe, or to be formed into an offset —**offset** /of sét/ *adv*

offshoot /óf shoot/ *n* **1** a branch or shoot growing from the main stem of a plant **2** something that springs or spreads from or that is a subsidiary of a main source or origin ○ *The company was an offshoot of their leisure empire.*

offshore *adv* /of sháwr/ **1 FROM WATER TO LAND** on or over land that is near water, especially from a body of water ○ *An icy wind blew offshore.* **2 IN WATER SOME WAY FROM SHORE** in a body of water at some distance from the shore ○ *anchored offshore* ■ *adj when attributive* /óf shawr/ **1 BLOWING FROM WATER TO LAND** blowing or moving from water to land ○ *offshore breezes* **2 AT SEA SOME WAY FROM SHORE** located at sea a considerable distance from shore **3 IN FOREIGN COUNTRY** based in a foreign country, usually in order to avoid taxes

offside *adj when attributive* /óf sīd/ illegally beyond or in advance of a ball or puck during play ■ *n* /óf sīd/ the side of a motor vehicle away from the edge of the road, which when driving on the left of the road, as in the United Kingdom, is the right side of the vehicle ○ *The offside wing mirror had been knocked off.* —**offside** /óf sīd/ *adv*

offsider /of sīder/ *n* Aus an assistant ○ *Tony, my offsider, will meet you at the airport.*

offsite /óff sīt/ *adj* not based or occurring in an organization's principal place of activity

offspring /óf spring/ (*plural* **-spring** *or* **-springs**) *n* **1** the descendants of people, animals, or sometimes plants **2** the product, consequence, or effect of something

offstage /óf stáyj/ *adv* **1 OUTSIDE ACTING AREA** away from the area of the stage used for a performance, usually out of the view of the audience **2 IN PRIVATE LIFE** in private life, especially as opposed to the character an actor plays or the personality a performer projects **3 OUT OF PUBLIC VIEW** unseen by the public and media ■ *adj* **1 HAPPENING OFFSTAGE** happening or situated outside the area of the stage visible to the audience **2 PRIVATE** occurring in or characteristic of somebody's private life **3 HAPPENING UNSEEN** occurring out of the gaze of the public and the media

off-street *adj* not in a street but in a car park, driveway, or another place

off-the-books *adj* US **1** not recorded in the accounts of a company **2** not registered for the purposes of paying income tax

off-the-cuff *adj* delivered spontaneously or without preparation or notice [< the custom of scribbling extempore remarks on a starched shirt cuff] —**off the cuff** *adv*

off-the-peg *adj* ready-made and sold in standard sizes, not tailored for the individual customer —**off the peg** *adv*

off-the-record *adj* not intended for publication or to be attributed by name to the person who said it —**off the record** *adv*

off-the-shelf *adj* **1** readily obtainable or taken from an existing stock of merchandise or supplies ○ *a mix of components that were both cheap and off the shelf* **2** officially registered with the Registrar of Companies solely in order to be sold (*not hyphenated after verbs*) —**off the shelf** *adv*

off-the-wall *adj* unusual or unconventional in a way that is particularly bizarre (*informal*) [< ?] —**off the wall** *adv*

off-track *adj* US HORSERACING = **off-course**

off-white *adj* of a very pale colour that is a shade or two away from white —**off-white** *n*

OFGAS /óff gass/, **Ofgas** *n* a regulatory body set up to supervise the gas industry in the United Kingdom after privatization and deregulation. Full form **Office of Gas Supply**

O'Flaherty /ō fláhəti, ō flaà-/, **Liam** (1896–1984) Irish novelist

OFSTED /óff sted/, **Ofsted** *n* the government department that monitors educational quality in schools and colleges in England and Wales. Full form **Office for Standards in Education**

oft /oft/ *adv* often (*archaic or literary; often used in combination*) [Old English]

OFT *abbr* Office of Fair Trading

OFTEL /óf tel/, **Oftel** *n* a regulatory body set up to supervise the telecommunications industry in the United Kingdom after privatization and deregulation. Full form **Office of Telecommunications**

often /óff'n, óftən/ *adv* at short intervals or repeatedly [13C. Alteration of OFT.] ◊ **every so often** regularly but with fairly long intervals between each occurrence ◊ **more often than not, as often as not** fairly frequently, or in a majority of instances

oftentimes /óff'n tīmz, óftən-/, **ofttimes** /óft tīmz/ *adv* frequently (*archaic or literary*)

OFWAT /óff wot/, **Ofwat** *n* a regulatory body set up to supervise water services in the United Kingdom after privatization and deregulation. Full form **Office of Water Services**

OG *abbr* **1** Officer of the Guard **2** original gum

o.g. *abbr* own goal

ogam *n* LING = **ogham**

Ogbomosho /ógbə mōsh ō/ city in SW Nigeria. Population: 711,900 (1995 estimate).

Ogdon /ógdən/, **John** (1937–89) British pianist and composer

ogee /ō jee/ *n* **1** a decorative double curve like an elongated and flattened S **2** a decorative moulding with an ogee-shaped profile **3** ARCHIT = **ogee arch** [Late 17C. Alteration of OGIVE.]

Ogee arch

ogee arch *n* an arch whose sides curve gently inwards near the top and then curve upwards steeply to meet in a point

Ogen melon /ógen-/ *n* a small variety of melon with a green skin and sweet pale green flesh [After *Ogen*, a kibbutz in Israel]

ogham /óggəm/, **ogam** *n* **1 ANCIENT CELTIC WRITING SYSTEM** an ancient British and Irish Celtic alphabet consisting of twenty characters **2 CELTIC LETTER** any character used in the ogham alphabet **3 CELTIC INSCRIPTION** an inscription written in ogham, or something bearing such an inscription [Early 18C. Via modern Irish < Old Irish *ogam*, after *Ogma*, the Celtic god who supposedly invented it.]

ogive /ō jīv/ *n* **1 RIB IN GOTHIC VAULT** a diagonal rib in a Gothic vault **2 POINTED ARCH** an arch that rises to a sharp point **3 CUMULATIVE FREQUENCY GRAPH** a graph or curve that represents the cumulative frequencies of a set of values [< ?]

Oglala /og laálə/ (*plural* **-la** *or* **-las**) *n* a member of a Native North American people, a branch of the Teton, who live mainly in South Dakota [Mid-19C. < Dakota.]

ogle /óg'l/ *vti* (**ogles, ogling, ogled**) to look at somebody for sexual enjoyment or as a way of showing sexual interest ■ *n* a prolonged flirtatious or lustful look at somebody [Late 17C. < ?] —**ogler** *n*

SYNONYMS See *gaze*.

Ogooué /o gṓ way/ river in west-central Africa. Length: 970 km/603 mi.

O grade *n* the lower-level examination for the Scottish Certificate of Education, now replaced by Standard grade. Full form **Ordinary grade**

ogre /ṓgər/ *n* **1** a wicked giant or monster in fairy tales, especially one who eats people **2** a person who is particularly unpleasant and frightening —**ogreish** *adj*

ogress /ṓgriss/ *n* **1** a wicked female giant or monster in fairy tales, especially one who eats people **2** an offensive term that deliberately insults a woman's appearance and temperament

Ogun /ṓ gōōn/ state in SW Nigeria. Capital: Abeokuta. Population: 2,338,570 (1991). Area: 16,762 sq. km/6,472 sq. mi.

oh /ō/ *interj* **1 USED TO EXPRESS STRONG EMOTION** used to express a strong emotional reaction to something, e.g. surprise, shock, pain, or extreme pleasure ○ *Oh! That's wonderful news!* **2 USED TO INTRODUCE STRONG REACTION** used to introduce short phrases that express a strong emotion, e.g. anger, shock, delight, or triumph ○ *Oh what a fool I've been* **3 USED TO INTRODUCE RESPONSE** used to introduce a response to what somebody has just said or asked ○ *Oh, I'm fine. How are you?* **4 USED TO SHOW THOUGHT** used to indicate thought or hesitation concerning what will be said next ○ *We've got, oh, fifteen minutes before the bus is due.* **5 USED TO ATTRACT ATTENTION** used to attract somebody's attention or call attention to something ○ *Oh, John, can you come over here a minute?* [Mid-16C. Alteration of O³.]

OH *abbr* Ohio

O'Higgins /ō hígginz/, **Bernardo** (1778–1842) Chilean leader. Known as **the Liberator of Chile**

Ohio[1] /ō hí ō/ state in the north-central United States. Capital: Columbus. Population: 11,186,331 (1997). Area: 116,104 sq. km/44,828 sq. mi. —**Ohioan** *adj*

Ohio[2] river in the E United States, flowing southwestwards from Pittsburgh into the Mississippi River. Length: 1,580 km/981 mi.

ohm /ōm/ *n* (*symbol* Ω) the SI unit of electrical resistance, equal to the resistance between two points on a conductor when a potential difference of 1 volt produces a current of 1 ampere [Mid-19C. After Georg Simon OHM.]

Ohm /ōm/, **Georg Simon** (1787–1854) German physicist

ohmage /ṓ mij/ *n* electrical resistance measured in ohms

ohmmeter /ṓm meetər/ *n* an instrument that measures electrical resistance in ohms

OHMS *abbr* On Her (or His) Majesty's Service

Ohm's law *n* the law of physics that states that electric current is directly proportional to the voltage applied to a conductor and inversely proportional to that conductor's resistance [After Georg Simon OHM]

oho /ō hṓ/ *interj* used to express surprise or exultation, e.g. at making a discovery [14C. < O³ + HO².]

OHP *abbr* overhead projector

OHV *abbr* **1** off-highway vehicle **2** OHV, o.h.v. overhead valve

OIC *abbr* oh, I see (*in e-mails*)

-oid *suffix* like, resembling, related to ○ *toxoid* ○ *cylindroid* [< Greek *-oeidēs* < *eidos* 'form, shape' (see IDOL)]

oidium /ō íddi əm/ (*plural* **-a** /ō íddi ə/) *n* a thin-walled eggshaped fungal spore produced by the fragmentation of a hypha [Mid-19C. Via modern Latin < Greek *ōion* 'egg' (see OO-).]

oik /oyk/ *n* somebody, usually a man, who is considered to be ill-mannered, ignorant, and socially inferior (*informal insult*) [< ?]

oil /oyl/ *n* **1 THICK GREASY LIQUID** a liquid fat obtained from plant seeds, animal fats, mineral deposits, and other sources that does not dissolve in water and will burn **2 PETROLEUM** petroleum, the crude product that is distilled and refined to produce industrial oils and oil-based products (*often before nouns*) ○ *oil prices* **3 PETROLEUM DERIVATIVE** any liquid extracted from petroleum, e.g. paraffin and motor oil, that is used as a domestic fuel or as a machinery and engine lubricant (*often before nouns*) **4 PETROLEUM INDUSTRY** the worldwide industry that is based on petroleum extraction and refining (*often before nouns*) ○ *oil companies* **5 THICK LIQUID CONTAINING OIL** a thick liquid containing oil or with the consistency of oil, especially a cosmetic **6** ART = **oil paint** (*usually plural*) **7 OIL PAINTING** a painting done in oil paints ■ v **1** vt **APPLY OIL TO** to put oil into or onto something in order to lubricate, polish, preserve, or soften it ○ *oiling the rusty gears* **2** vti **FUEL** to take on oil as a fuel, or supply a ship with oil **3** vti **TURN INTO OIL** to become an oily liquid, or turn a solid fat, e.g. butter or lard, into an oily liquid [12C. < Old French, via Latin *oleum* 'olive oil' < Greek *elaion* < *elaia* 'olive'.] —**oiled** *adj* ◇ **burn the midnight oil** to work or study until very late at night

oil beetle *n* a beetle that emits a foul-smelling oily substance from the joints of its legs to deter predators. Family: Meloidae.

oilbird /ˈoyl burd/ *n* a bird whose young have fatty flesh formerly used as a source of oil for cooking and lighting. Native to: Central and South America. *Steatornis caripensis.*

oil cake *n* the solid residue remaining after extraction of the oil from some seeds, e.g. cottonseed and linseed. Use: livestock feed.

oilcan /ˈoyl kan/ *n* a metal container with a long thin spout, used to squirt lubricating oil into machinery

oilcloth /ˈoyl kloth/ *n* cloth that has been treated with oil or a synthetic resin to make it waterproof. Use: table coverings.

oil-cooled *adj* with a cooling system that uses oil

oil drum *n* a large metal cylinder designed for transporting and storing oil

oiler /ˈoylər/ *n* **1 REFUELLING TANKER** an oil tanker, especially one that refuels ships at sea **2 OIL-FUELLED SHIP** a ship that uses oil as fuel **3 OIL WELL** an oil well (*informal*)

oil field /ˈoyl feeld/, **oilfield** *n* an area of land or sea under which there are substantial reserves of petroleum, especially one that is being exploited

oil-fired *adj* burning oil as a fuel

oil gland *n* a gland at the base of a bird's tail that secretes an oily substance that the bird uses to preen and waterproof its feathers

oilman /ˈoyl man, ˈoylmən/ (*plural* -**men** /-men, -mən/) *n* **1** an executive in the petroleum industry **2** a worker in an oil field

oil of cloves *n* an essential oil extracted from clove flowers. Use: relief of dental pain, component of temporary fillings.

oil of wintergreen *n* an aromatic oil extracted from a North American evergreen shrub. Use: in liniments, as flavouring.

oil paint *n* a paint that consists of pigment mixed with a drying oil

oil painting *n* **1** a picture painted with oil paints **2** the art of painting with oil paints ◇ **be no oil painting** an offensive term meaning to lack appealing physical features, especially facial ones

oil palm *n* a palm tree widely cultivated for its fruit and seeds, which yield palm oil. Native to: West Africa. *Elaeis guineensis.*

oil pan *n* US AUTOMOT = **sump** *n.* 2

oil rig *n* the equipment used for drilling for oil, including the platform that supports the drilling equipment

oilseed /ˈoyl seed/ *n* a seed that is rich in oil, especially one grown as a crop for oil extraction, e.g. linseed, groundnut, or cottonseed ○ *fields of oilseed rape*

oil shale *n* a black or dark brown type of shale from which petroleum can be extracted by distillation

oilskin /ˈoyl skin/ *n* **1 WATERPROOF FABRIC** cotton fabric that has been treated with oil to make it waterproof **2 WATERPROOF GARMENT** a garment, especially a coat, made of oilskin ■ **oilskins** *npl* **WATERPROOF CLOTHING** waterproof overgarments consisting of a coat and trousers made of oilskin

oil slick *n* a film of oil covering part of the surface of something, especially a large expanse of oil floating on the sea following a spillage of oil from an oil tanker

oilstone /ˈoyl stōn/ *n* a fine-grained stone that is lubricated with oil and used to sharpen cutting tools

oil trap *n* a set of conditions within rock strata that

blocks the upward movement of oil or gas, causing it to accumulate

oil well *n* a shaft drilled into the earth or the bottom of the sea, through which petroleum is extracted

oily /ˈoyli/ (-**ier**, -**iest**) *adj* **1 DIRTY WITH OIL** covered, smeared, or dirtied with oil ○ *don't want to get my hands oily* **2 CONTAINING OIL** containing or producing a lot of oil **3 LIKE OIL** reminiscent of oil in texture, smell, or taste **4 INGRATIATING** unpleasantly eager to please or charm, or distressingly expert at doing this (*disapproving*) — **oiliness** *n*

oink /oyngk/ *interj, n* a word used for the nasal grunting sound made by a pig ■ *vi* to make the nasal grunting sound of a pig [Mid-20C. An imitation of the sound.]

ointment /ˈoyntmənt/ *n* a smooth greasy substance used on the skin to soothe soreness or itchiness, help wounds heal, or make the skin softer [13C. Via Old French *oignement* < Latin *unguentum*.]

OIRO *abbr* offers in the region of

Oise /waz/ river in S Belgium and N France. Length: 299 km/186 mi.

Oita /ˈoytə/ city on NE Kyushu, Japan. Population: 417,051 (1992).

OJ, oj *abbr* orange juice

Ojibwa /ō jíbbwə/ (*plural* -**was** *or* -**wa**), **Ojibway** /ō jíb way/ (*plural* -**ways** *or* -**way**) *n* **1** a Native North American people who originally lived north of Lake Huron and who later moved into territories ranging from Saskatchewan across to Michigan **2** the Algonquian language of the Ojibwa people [Early 18C. < Ojibwa *ojibwe.*] —**Ojibwa** *adj*

OK¹ /ō káy/, **okay** *interj* (*informal*) **1 INDICATING AGREEMENT** used to indicate agreement to or approval of what somebody said or did ○ *'Can you help?' 'OK. What do you want me to do?'* **2 USED TO CHECK FOR APPROVAL** used at the end of a statement to inquire whether somebody understood and agrees with or approves of what was said ○ *It's your job to make the arrangements, OK?* **3 USED TO INDICATE FINISHING** used to indicate that something is finished and that something else will now be done or discussed ○ *OK, let's move to the next item on the agenda.* ■ *adj* (*informal*) **1 PASSABLE** acceptable or tolerable but not exceptional ○ *OK for a first effort.* **2 RATHER GOOD OR PLEASANT** better than just satisfactory or acceptable ○ *Her parents are OK; we get on quite well.* **3 PHYSICALLY WELL** in good health or condition ○ *I'll be OK if I can just sit down for a minute.* **4 ALLOWABLE** acceptable to somebody or permissible ○ *Is it OK for me to call home on the office phone?* ■ *adv* **FAIRLY WELL** in an acceptable, tolerable, or satisfactory manner (*informal*) ○ *Everything's going OK, except that we're a little bit behind schedule.* ■ *vt* (**OK's, OK'ing, OK'ed**) (*informal*) **1 GIVE APPROVAL FOR** to approve of or consent to something ○ *I just need you to OK the agenda.* **2 OBTAIN SOMEBODY'S CONSENT** to obtain somebody's approval of or consent to something ○ *I'll need to OK that with my boss.* ■ *n* (*plural* **OK's**) **APPROVAL** approval to do something or consent to something (*informal*) ○ *As soon as she gives the OK, we'll start work.* [Mid-19C.]

OK² *abbr* Oklahoma

Okanagan, Lake /ˈōkə naˈagən/ lake in S British Columbia, Canada. Area: 352 sq. km/136 sq. mi.

okapi /ō kaˈapi/ (*plural* -**pis** *or* -**pi**) *n* a plant-eating mammal of central Africa that resembles a small giraffe without a long neck. *Okapia johnstoni.* [Early 20C. < an African language.]

Okavango /ōkə váng gō/ river in south-central Africa, flowing from central Angola to N Botswana. Length: 1,800 km/1,120 mi.

Okavango Swamp inland delta in NW Botswana. Area: 16,800 sq. km/6,500 sq. mi.

okay *interj, adj, adv, vt, n* = **OK¹**

Okayama /ōkə yaˈamə/ city on W Honshu, Japan. Population: 593,730 (1990).

Okeechobee, Lake /ōki chóbi/ lake in S Florida, in the N Everglades. Area: 1,717 sq. km/663 sq. mi.

O'Keefe /ō keˈef/, **Johnny** (1935–78) Australian singer. Full name **John Michael O'Keefe**

Georgia O'Keeffe

O'Keeffe /ō keˈef/, **Georgia** (1887–1986) US artist

Okefenokee Swamp /ōkifi nóki-/ swamp in SE Georgia and NE Florida. Area: 1,710 sq. km/660 sq. mi.

okeydokey /ˈōki dóki/, **okeydoke** /ˈōki dók/ *interj* OK (*informal humorous*) [Mid-20C. Alteration of OK¹.]

Okhotsk, Sea of /ō kótsk, ō khótsk/ arm of the NW Pacific Ocean, lying off the coast of E Siberia. Area: 1,530,000 sq. km/590,000 sq. mi.

Okie /ˈōki/ *n* US **1** an offensive term for a migrant farm labourer in the United States, especially one from Oklahoma or neighbouring Dust Bowl states during the 1930s (*slang insult*) **2** somebody who comes from Oklahoma (*slang*)

Okinawa /ˈōki naˈawə/ **1** city on south-central Okinawa Island, Japan. Population: 105,845 (1990). **2** largest of the Ryukyu Islands, SW Japan. Population: 1,229,000 (1991). Area: 1,176 sq. km/454 sq. mi.

Okla. *abbr* Oklahoma

Oklahoma /ˈōklə hómə/ state in the south-central United States. Capital: Oklahoma City. Population: 3,317,091 (1997). Area: 181,048 sq. km/69,903 sq. mi. —**Oklahoman** /ˈōklə hómən/ *adj, n*

Oklahoma City capital of Oklahoma, in the central part of the state. Population: 472,221 (1998 estimate).

okra /ˈōkrə, ókrə/ (*plural* **okra** *or* **okras**) *n* **1** a green fingerlength seed pod, cooked and eaten as a vegetable or used to thicken soups and stews **2** a tall tropical plant that produces okra pods. Native to: Asia. *Abelmoschus esculentus.* [Early 18C. Of West African origin, related to Igbo *okuro.*]

okta /ˈōktə/ *n* a unit of measure used to specify the amount of cloud cover, especially over an airfield, equivalent to enough cloud to cover one eighth of the sky [Mid-20C. Alteration of OCTO-.]

-ol¹ *suffix* compound containing hydroxyl, especially an alcohol or phenol ○ *glycerol* [< ALCOHOL]

-ol² *suffix* = **-ole**

Olaf II /ō laf/, **Olav II** (995–1030) king of Norway (1015–1028)

Öland /ˈö land/ island in SE Sweden, in the Baltic Sea. Population: 25,781 (1994). Area: 1,342 sq. km/518 sq. mi.

Olav II = **Olaf II**

old /ōld/ *adj* (**older, oldest**) **1 HAVING LIVED LONG** having lived for many years compared to others **2 ORIGINATING YEARS AGO** made, produced, or originating many years ago and still in existence **3 ELDERLY** showing physical or mental characteristics sometimes associated with long life **4 WISE** showing the understanding, wisdom, or behaviour that results from long experience of life ○ *She acts much older than she is.* **5 EXISTING FOR SPECIFIED TIME** having lived or existed for a particular amount of time (*usually in combination*) ○ *The day was only a few hours old.* **6 ANCIENT** from the remote past ○ *the remains of an old civilization* **7 FORMER** from an earlier period of something such as somebody's life ○ *We drove past my old school.* **8 FAMILIAR** familiar from past experience ○ *She always makes the same old excuses.* **9 EXISTING OR USED OVER TIME** having existed or been used for a long time, especially if showing wear or age ○ *Change into old clothes before gardening.* **10 Old, Old EARLIER** existing before one or all of the other stages, forms, or instances of something ○ *Old English words* **11 USED FOR EMPHASIS** used as an intensifier (*informal*) ○ *any old reason* **12 EXPRESSING**

FAMILIARITY used to express affection or familiarity (*informal*) ○ *Good old Charlie!* **13** *US* **ANNOYINGLY FAMILIAR** annoyingly familiar, especially as a result of repetition (*informal*) ○ *the kind of routine that gets old fast* **14 ERODED** reduced through erosion and weathering **15 SLOWER-MOVING** characterized by slower moving water and broad, flat floodplains ■ *n* **1 PERSON OF PARTICULAR AGE** somebody of a particular age (*in combination*) ○ *childcare for three- and four-year-olds* **2 OLD THINGS** things or customs that are old ○ *to balance the old with the new* ■ *npl* **OFFENSIVE TERM** an offensive term for people who have lived a long time [Old English *eald*] —**oldness** *n*

USAGE See *age*.

USAGE See *elder*.

old age *n* the latter years of somebody's life lived out to its full term. ◊ **middle age**

Old Bill *n* the police, or an individual police officer or a group of police (*slang*) ○ *Better watch it, lads, here come the Old Bill.* [Probably from a cartoon character created by Captain Bruce Bairnsfather (1887–1959), who was used in a recruitment campaign for London's Metropolitan Police]

old boy *n* **1 FORMER STUDENT** a former student at a boys' or men's school, especially a British public school or college **2 OFFENSIVE TERM** an offensive term for a man who has reached an advanced age **3 FAMILIAR ADDRESS TO MAN** used as a familiar way of addressing a man or boy (*dated informal*) ○ *See here, old boy, you can't enter this club uninvited.*

old-boy network *n* a system of informal contacts between men who belong to a particular group, especially former members of a school or university, and use their influence to help one another

Old Church Slavonic *n* the earliest written Slavonic language, used in religious services in some Eastern Orthodox Churches

old country *n* an immigrant's country of origin

Old Dart *n Aus* Britain, especially England (*informal humorous*) [*Dart* from a dialect pronunciation of DIRT]

old dear *n* an offensive term that patronizes a woman of advanced age

olden /óldən/ *adj* in or from the distant past (*archaic or literary*) [14C. < OLD + -EN.]

Oldenburg /óldən burg/, **Claes** (*b.* 1929) Swedish-born US sculptor

Old English *n* **1** the earliest form of the English language, used up to about AD 1150. ◊ **Middle English, Modern English 2** a form of black-letter typeface used by English printers up to the 18th century —**Old English** *adj*

Old English sheepdog *n* a large dog with a long shaggy coat and dark grey and white markings [Because they were originally bred in England]

olde-worlde /óldi wúrldi/ *adj* quaintly historical in a way that may or may not be genuine [An alteration to resemble early English spellings]

old face *n* a typeface that shows little difference between light and heavy strokes and has slanting serifs. It originated in the 18th century. US term **old style**

oldfangled /óld fáng g'ld/ *adj* antiquated or out of date [Mid-19C. After NEWFANGLED.]

old fart *n* an offensive term for somebody, usually a person in authority, who is regarded as being set in his or her ways and lacking a sense of humour or fun (*slang insult*)

old-fashioned *adj* **1 OUT OF DATE** typical of or belonging to a time in the past and no longer considered fashionable or suitable for the present ○ *an old-fashioned car with a running board* **2 MAINTAINING OLD-STYLE WAYS** favouring or deliberately maintaining ideas, behaviour, or ways of doing things from an earlier time ■ *n* **WHISKY COCKTAIL** a cocktail made with whisky, bitters, sugar, and lemon peel and garnished with fruit

old-fashioned look *n* a quizzical or reproving look directed at somebody who has done or said something amiss

Old French *n* the earliest form of the French language, used until about AD 1400 or, in some analyses, AD 1600. ◊ **Middle French** —**Old French** *adj*

old girl *n* **1 FORMER STUDENT** a former student at a girls' or women's school, especially a British public school or college **2 OFFENSIVE TERM** an offensive term for a woman who has reached an advanced age **3 FAMILIAR ADDRESS TO WOMAN** used as a familiar way of addressing a woman or girl (*dated informal*) ○ *Sorry, old girl, didn't mean to lose my temper like that.*

old-girl network *n* a system of informal contacts between women who belong to a particular group, especially former members of a school or university, and use their influence to help one another

Old Glory *n* a nickname for the flag of the United States

old gold *adj* of a dark dull yellow colour —**old gold** *n*

old growth *n* a long-established forest or woodland that contains some large old trees and has a relatively stable and diverse community of plants and animals (*hyphenated before nouns*)

old guard, Old Guard *n* the members of a group or organization who have been in it longest, are the staunchest defenders of its traditions, and are the least amenable to change (+ *singular or plural verb*)

Oldham /óldəm/ town in NW England. Population: 103,931 (1991).

old hand *n* a person who is throughly experienced in a field of activity

old hat *adj* boringly familiar or old-fashioned (*informal*)

Old High German *n* the form of German used in written documents up to about AD 1200 —**Old High German** *adj*

oldie /óldi/ *n* something old, especially an old popular song (*informal*)

Old Kingdom *n* the period of ancient Egyptian history that comprises the third to sixth dynasties, from around 2700 to 2150 BC, when the capital was at Memphis and the great pyramids were built

Old Labour *n* the British Labour Party as it evolved during the greater part of the 20th century, characterized by adherence to traditional socialist principles such as state ownership and opposition to the free market economy. ◊ **New Labour**

old lady *n* (*slang*) **1** an offensive term for somebody's mother **2** an offensive term for a man's wife or woman partner

old-line *adj* in existence for a long time and having a high social status or good reputation that has endured

old maid *n* **1 OFFENSIVE TERM** an offensive term for a woman in or past middle age who has never been married and seems unlikely ever to marry **2 OFFENSIVE TERM** an offensive term for a man or woman insulted as being excessively prim and fussy **3 CARD GAME** a card game played with a pack from which one card has been removed **4 LOSER IN OLD MAID** the losing player in a game of old maid —**old-maidish** *adj*

old man *n* **1 OFFENSIVE TERM** an offensive term for somebody's father (*slang*) **2 OFFENSIVE TERM** an offensive term for a woman's husband, or the man whom she lives with (*slang*) **3 COMMANDING OFFICER** a man in a position of authority, especially a commanding officer (*slang*) ○ *The old man is on the bridge, mad as can be.* **4 FAMILIAR ADDRESS TO MAN** used a familiar way of addressing another man (*dated informal*) ○ *Look here, old man, I'm in a spot of bother and wonder if you could help me out.*

old man's beard *n* a plant that has trailing or hanging whitish growths, e.g. traveller's joy, Spanish moss, or the fringe tree

old master *n* **1** any great European painter of the period dating roughly from the late Middle Ages to the 18th century **2** a picture painted by an old master

Old Nick *n* a nickname for the Devil (*dated slang*)

Old Norse *n* the Germanic language from which the modern Scandinavian languages are derived, in use in Scandinavia from about AD 700 to 1350 —**Old Norse** *adj*

Old Red Sandstone *n* a sedimentary rock, usually red in colour, formed during the Devonian period and found in Britain and NW Europe

old rose *adj* of a deep greyish-pink colour —**old rose** *n*

old salt *n* a sailor who has years of experience at sea

Old Saxon *n* LANG = **Saxon** *n.* **2**

old school *n* a group of people who adhere to traditional or old-fashioned values and practices ○ *As a disciplinarian of the old school, he was horrified at the laxity of the new regime.* —**old-school** *adj*

old school tie *n* **1** a tie whose colours indicate which school, especially which British public school, the wearer attended **2** the shared attitudes, traditions, and loyalties attributed to people who attended the same school, especially the same public school

old soldier *n* **1** an experienced and long-serving soldier, or a former soldier **2** somebody with a great deal of experience

oldsquaw /óld skwáw/, **old-squaw, old squaw** *n* BIRDS = **long-tailed duck** [Mid-19C. Probably from its gabbling voice.]

old stager /-stáyjər/ *n* somebody with long experience in a particular activity

oldster /óldstər/ *n* an offensive term for somebody who has reached an advanced age [Early 19C. After YOUNGSTER.]

old style *n* **1** *US* PRINTING = **old face 2** a modern typeface that imitates the characteristics of old face

Old Style *adj* used to indicate a date recorded according to the Julian calendar

old-style *adj* typical of the past but now superseded by something else

old sweat *n* a veteran soldier (*informal*)

Old Testament *n* the first part of the Christian Bible, corresponding to the Hebrew Bible, that recounts the creation of the world and the history of ancient Israel and contains the Psalms and the prophetic books

old-time *adj* **1** typical of or dating from a time in the past ○ *the old-time music hall* **2** in existence for a long time ○ *the old-time families of the town*

old-timer *n* **1** *US* a senior citizen, especially a man (*sometimes offensive*) **2** a resident or worker who has been at a particular place for a long time

Olduvai Gorge /óldə vī-/ ravine in N Tanzania, where fossil remains of early humans and hominids have been found. Length: 50 km/30 mi. Depth: 91 m/300 ft.

old wives' tale *n* a traditional belief or story, passed down by word of mouth, that is now considered untrue or superstitious ○ *Do what your doctor tells you and don't listen to old wives' tales.* [< *old wife*, an old woman]

old woman *n* (*slang*) **1** an offensive term for somebody's mother **2** an offensive term for a man's wife or woman partner **3** an offensive term for a man that deliberately insults his courage and decisiveness —**old-womanish** *adj*

Old World *n* the part of the world that was known to Europeans before Columbus's first voyage to the Americas, comprising Europe, Asia, and Africa. ◊ **New World**

old-world *adj* considered to be typical of a former and more gracious age

Old World monkey *n* any monkey closely related to the great apes, with close-set nostrils and nongrasping tails, such as the baboon or mandrill. Family: Cercopithecidae.

olé /ō láy/ *interj* used to express triumph, excited approval, or encouragement in Spanish ■ *n* a cry or shout of olé [Early 20C. < Spanish.]

⚡**OLE** *abbr* object linking and embedding

ole- *prefix* = **oleo-** (*before vowels*)

-ole *suffix* **1** a chemical compound containing a five-membered, usually heterocyclic ring ○ *carbazole* **2** a chemical compound, usually an ether, that does not contain hydroxyl ○ *anisole* [Via French < Latin *oleum* (see OIL)]

olea plural of **oleum**

oleaginous /óli ájjənəss/ *adj* **1 CONTAINING OIL** containing or producing oil **2 LIKE OIL** similar to oil in nature or consistency **3 INGRATIATING** unpleasantly eager to please, charm, or be of service to people ○ *the oleaginous concierge* [Mid-17C. Directly and via Old French *oleagineux* < Latin *oleaginus* 'of an olive tree, oily' < *olea* 'olive tree', alteration of *oliva* (see OLIVE).] —**oleaginously** *adv* —**oleaginousness** *n*

oleander /óli ándər/ (*plural* **-ders** *or* **-der**) *n* a poisonous evergreen bush with leathery lance-shaped leaves and long seed pods. Flowers: sweet-smelling white, pink, or purple. Native to: Mediterranean region. *Nerium oleander.* [Mid-16C. < medieval Latin.]

oleaster /óli ástər/ (*plural* **-ters** *or* **-ter**) *n* **1** an evergreen or deciduous bush with glossy leaves, silvery underneath. Flowers: small, white, greenish yellow. Genus: *Elaeagnus.* **2** the fruit of an oleaster, which resembles an olive [14C. Via Latin < *olea* 'olive tree', alteration of *oliva* (see OLIVE).]

oleate /ṓli ayt/ *n* a salt or ester of oleic acid

olecranon /ō lékrə non/ *n* the upper end of the ulna bone that extends beyond the joint of the elbow to form the elbow's hard projecting point [Early 18C. < Greek *ōlekranon* < *ōlenē* 'elbow' + *kranion* 'head'.]

olefin /ṓlə fin/, **olefine** *n* **1 olefin, olefin fibre** any synthetic fibre that is a long chain of polymers **2** CHEM = **alkene** [Mid-19C. < French *(gaz) oléfiant* 'oil-forming (gas)' < Latin *oleum* 'oil' (see OIL).]

oleic /ō lée ik/ *adj* **1** derived from or relating to oil **2** derived from or relating to oleic acid

oleic acid *n* $C_{18}H_{34}O_2$ a colourless oily liquid. Source: animal and vegetable fats. Use: manufacture of soap, ointments, cosmetics, and lubricating oils.

olein /ṓli in/, **oleine** *n* a yellow oily liquid that occurs naturally in most fats. Use: textile lubricant.

oleo /ṓli ō/ (*plural* **-os**) *n* an oleograph (*informal*)

oleo- *prefix* **1** oil, oily ○ *oleograph* **2** oleic acid ○ *oleate* [Via French *oléo-* < Latin *oleum* (see OIL)]

oleograph /ṓli ə graaf, -graf/ *n* a coloured lithographic print made on canvas with oil colours in order to imitate an oil painting —**oleographic** /ṓli ə gráffik/ *adj*

oleo oil *n* a yellow fatty substance extracted from beef fat. Use: manufacture of margarine, soap.

oleoresin /ṓli ō rézzin/ *n* a mixture of a resin and an essential oil, either obtained naturally from plants or produced synthetically

oleum /ṓli əm/ (*plural* **-a** /ṓli ə/ *or* **-ums**) *n* a solution of sulphur trioxide in sulphuric acid [Early 20C. < Latin, 'oil' (see OIL).]

O level *n* a subject studied, an examination taken, or a pass obtained at O level [Shortening of ORDINARY]

olfaction /ol fáksh'n/ *n* **1** the sense of smell **2** the smelling of something [Mid-19C. < Latin *olfacere* 'to smell'.]

olfactometer /ól fak tómmitər/ *n* an instrument for measuring the keenness of somebody's sense of smell [Late 19C. < OLFACTION + -METER.]

olfactory /ol fáktəri/ *adj* used in smelling or relating to the sense of smell [Mid-17C. Via assumed Latin *olfactorius* 'used for smelling' < *olfacere* 'to smell' < *olere* + *facere* 'do'.]

Olgas /ólgəz/ group of monolithic rocks in SW Northern Territory, Australia. Highest peak: Mount Olga 3,516 ft/1,072 m.

olibanum /o líbbənəm/ *n* CHEM = **frankincense** [14C. Via medieval Latin *olibanum* and Greek *libanos* < Arabic *al-lubān* 'storax'.]

oligarch /ólli gaark/ *n* a ruler or leader in an oligarchy [Early 17C. < Greek *oligarkhēs* < *oligos* 'few' + -ARCH.]

oligarchy /ólli gaarki/ (*plural* **-chies**) *n* **1** SMALL GOVERNING GROUP a small group of people who together govern a nation or control an organization, often for their own purposes **2** ENTITY RULED BY OLIGARCHY a nation governed or an organization controlled by an oligarchy **3** GOVERNMENT BY SMALL GROUP government or control by a small group of people [Late 15C. < Greek *oligarkhia* < *oligos* 'few' + *-arkhia* '-archy' (see -ARCH).] —**oligarchic** /ólli gáarkik/ *adj*

oligo- *prefix* few ○ *oligophagous* [< Greek *oligos* 'small, little, few']

Oligocene /ólligō seen/ *n* the third geological period of the Tertiary Era, from 40 to 25 million years ago, when primates first appeared —**Oligocene** *adj*

oligochaete /ólli gō keet/ *n* a freshwater or terrestrial worm such as an earthworm that has a body consisting of numerous similar segments with projections resembling bristles. Class: Oligochaeta. [Late 19C. < modern Latin *Oligochaeta* 'small or few bristles'.]

oligoclase /ólligō klayss/ *n* a white, bluish, or reddish-yellow feldspar mineral of the plagioclase series. Source: igneous and metamorphic rocks. [Mid-19C. < OLIGO- + Greek *klasis* 'breaking' < *klan* 'break' (see CLASTIC), from its imperfect cleavage.]

oligomer /ólli gōmər/ *n* a polymer consisting of less than five monomer units —**oligomeric** /ólligə mérrik/ *adj* —**oligomerization** /ólli gōmə rī záysh'n/ *n*

oligonucleotide /ólligō nyóokli ə tīd/ *n* a polymeric chain containing ten nucleotides or fewer

oligopeptide *n* a peptide consisting of fewer than ten amino acids

oligophagous /ólli góffəgəss/ *adj* feeding on a restricted range of foodstuffs, usually a small number of different plants

oligopoly /ólli góppəli/ (*plural* **-lies**) *n* an economic condition in which there are so few suppliers of a particular product that one supplier's actions can have a significant impact on prices and on its competitors [Late 19C. < OLIGO- + MONOPOLY.] —**oligopolistic** /ólli góppə lístik/ *adj*

oligopsony /ólli gópsəni/ (*plural* **-nies**) *n* an economic condition in which there are so few buyers for a particular product that one buyer's actions can have a significant impact on prices and the market in general [Mid-20C. < OLIGO- + MONOPSONY.] —**oligopsonistic** /ólli gopsə nístik/ *adj*

oligosaccharide /ólligō sákə rīd/ *n* a carbohydrate made up of a relatively small number of linked monosaccharides. ◊ **polysaccharide**

oligotrophic /ólligō trṓfik, -tróffik/ *adj* containing relatively little plant life and nutrients in its waters but rich in dissolved oxygen

olingo /o líng gō/ (*plural* **-gos**) *n* a small tree-dwelling nocturnal mammal similar in appearance to a slim sleek raccoon. Native to: tropical South and Central America. *Bassaricyon gabbii*. [Early 20C. < American Spanish.]

olio /ṓli ō/ (*plural* **-os**) *n* **1** SPICED STEW a highly spiced stew made from a variety of meats and vegetables **2** ASSORTMENT a miscellaneous collection of things **3** MISCELLANY OR MEDLEY something made up of works of various kinds or works by different people, e.g. a literary miscellany or a musical medley [Mid-17C. Alteration of Spanish *olla* 'pot, stew', (see OLLA).]

Oliphant /óllifənt/, **Sir Mark** (*b.* 1901) Australian physicist

olive /ólliv/ *n* **1** GREEN OR BLACK FRUIT a small oval bitter fruit with a stone, green when unripe and black when ripe, that yields olive oil **2** OLIVE TREE a widely cultivated evergreen tree that produces olives. Native to: Mediterranean region. *Olea europaea*. (*often before nouns*) **3** OLIVE WOOD the wood of the olive tree. Use: decorative work. **4** TREE RESEMBLING OLIVE a tree or bush that resembles the olive tree **5** COLOURS = **olive green** [12C. Via Latin *oliva* < Greek *elaiwa*, a variant of *elaia* 'olive, olive oil'.] —**olive** *adj*

olive branch *n* **1** a gesture or offer intended to bring about a reconciliation **2** a branch of an olive tree used as a symbol of peace [< Genesis 8:11]

olive drab *n* **1** GREYISH GREEN a greyish-green colour **2** *US* GREEN CLOTH cloth dyed in an olive drab colour. Use: military uniforms. **3** GREEN MILITARY UNIFORM a military uniform made of olive drab cloth —**olive drab** *adj*

olive green *n* a deep yellowish-green colour —**olive-green** *adj*

olivenite /o lívvi nīt/ *n* a rare, olive-green, hydrated copper arsenate mineral [Early 19C. < German *Olivenit* < *Olive* 'olive'; from its colour.]

olive oil *n* monounsaturated oil with a distinctive flavour extracted from olives. Use: salad dressings, cooking, manufacture of soap and cosmetics.

Oliver /ólliver/, **Isaac** (1560?–1617?) English painter of miniatures

Olives, Mount of /óllivz/ ridge of hills in the West Bank Territory, east of Jerusalem, the site of many events in Christian history. Height: 834 m/2,737 ft.

Olivier /ə lívvi ay/, **Laurence, 1st Baron Olivier of Brighton** (1907–89) British actor and director

olivine /ólli veen/ *n* an olive-green magnesium-iron silicate mineral. Source: igneous rocks. Use: refractories, gems. —**olivinic** /ólli vínnik/ *adj* —**olivinitic** /óllivə níttik/ *adj*

olla /óllə/ *n* **1** a large, usually unglazed pot with a spherical body and a wide mouth, used in Latin America and the SW United States for storing water and for cooking **2** FOOD = **olla podrida** *n.* 1 [Early 17C. Via Spanish < Latin *aulla* 'pot'.]

olla podrida /-po dréedə/ (*plural* **olla podridas** *or* **ollas podridas**) *n* **1** a traditional Spanish and Latin American stew of meat and vegetables, usually containing sausage and chickpeas, and highly seasoned **2** a miscellaneous mixture or assortment of things [< Spanish, 'rotten pot']

Olley /ólli/, **Margaret Hannah** (*b.* 1923) Australian painter

Olmec /ól mek/ (*plural* **-mecs** *or* **-mec**) *n* **1** a Central American civilization that arose around AD 1200, before the Maya civilization (*often before nouns*) **2** a member of a people in the Olmec civilization [Late 18C. < Nahuatl *olmecatl* 'somebody who lives in the rubber country'.]

ology /óllə ji/ (*plural* **-gies**) *n* any science or academic field, especially one whose name ends in '-ology' (*informal*) ○ *people studying ologies you've never heard of* [Early 19C. < -LOGY.]

oloroso /óllə rṓssō/ (*plural* **-sos**) *n* a golden-coloured full-bodied sherry, typically medium-sweet [Late 19C. Via Spanish, 'fragrant' < Latin *olere* 'to smell'.]

Olsen /ólss'n/, **John Henry** (*b.* 1928) Australian painter

Olympia /ə límpi ə/ plain in SW Greece, the site of the ancient Olympic Games

Olympiad /ə límpi ad/ *n* **1** a holding of the modern Olympic Games **2** a four-year interval between one holding of the Olympic Games and the next, used by the ancient Greeks as a way of calculating dates [14C. Via Latin < Greek *Olumpia*, where the games were held.]

Olympian /ə límpi ən/ *adj* **1** RELATING TO MOUNT OLYMPUS relating to Mount Olympus, the home of the gods in Greek mythology **2** ALOOF OR SUPERIOR so superior or grand as to be above everyday events and concerns ○ *his Olympian indifference to petty squabbles* **3** ENORMOUS extraordinarily great or demanding **4** OF OLYMPIA relating to ancient Olympia **5** LIKE GREEK DEITY characteristic of a Greek god or goddess, or resembling one in power, majesty, or beauty (*literary*) ■ *n* **1** GREEK DEITY any one of the twelve major Greek gods or goddesses who had their home on Mount Olympus **2** OLYMPIC ATHLETE a competitor in the Olympic Games **3** SUPERIOR PERSON a person whose status is superior to everyday events and concerns **4** SOMEBODY FROM OLYMPIA somebody who lived in ancient Olympia [15C. < Greek *olumpios*.]

Olympic /ə límpik/ *adj* relating to the Olympic Games

Olympic Games, Olympic games *npl* **1** a large-scale international sports contest intended to promote international goodwill **2** an ancient Greek religious festival held every four years at Olympia in honour of Zeus, with athletic, literary, and musical contests involving participants from throughout Greece

Olympics /ə límpiks/ *npl* the modern Olympic Games

Olympus, Mount /ə límpəss/ highest mountain in Greece, in the north of the country, the mythological home of the Greek gods. Height: 2,917 m/9,570 ft.

Olympus Mons /ə límpəss mónz/ volcano near the equator of Mars, the highest volcano in the solar system. Height: 26 km/16 mi.

ϟ **om** *abbr* Oman (*in Internet addresses*)

Om /ōm/, **Aum** *n* a sacred syllable that is chanted in Hindu and Buddhist prayers and mantras

OM *abbr* Order of Merit

-oma *suffix* tumour ○ *encephaloma* [Directly and via modern Latin < Greek *-ōma*]

Omagh /ṓmə, ōm aa/ town in central Northern Ireland. Population: 17,280 (1991).

Omaha[1] /ṓmə haa/ (*plural* **-has** *or* **-ha**) *n* **1** a member of a Native North American people who live in NE Nebraska **2** the Siouan language of the Omaha people [Early 19C. < Omaha *umonhon* 'upstream people'.] —**Omaha** *adj*

Omaha[2] /ṓmə haa/ city in E Nebraska, on the Missouri River. Population: 371,291 (1998 estimate).

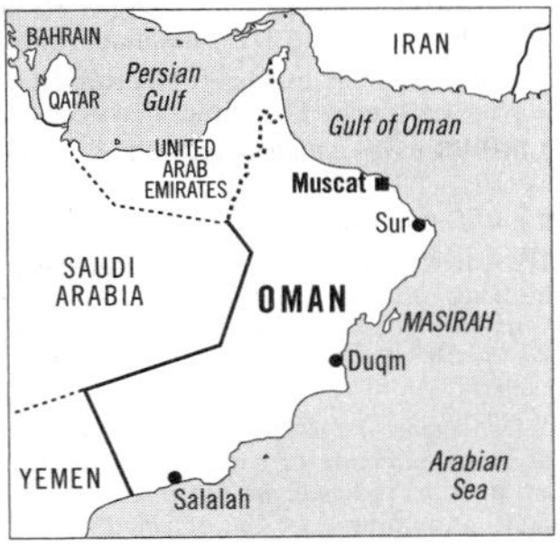

Oman

Oman /ō máan/ sultanate on the SE Arabian Peninsula, on the Gulf of Oman. Capital: Muscat. Population:

2,251,000 (1996). Area: 309,500 sq. km/119,500 sq. mi. —**Omani** /ō maáni/ *adj, n*

Oman, Gulf of /ō maán/ arm of the Arabian Sea, situated between Oman and SE Iran

Omar Khayyam /ō maar kī aám, -ám/ (1050?–1122) Persian poet, mathematician, and astronomer

omasum /ō máyssəm/ (*plural* **-sa** /-sə/) *n* the third compartment of the stomach of a cow or other ruminant, situated between the abomasum and the reticulum [Early 18C. < Latin, 'bullock's tripe'.]

Omayyad *n* HIST, ISLAM = **Umayyad**

ombre /ómbər/ *n* a card game, popular in the 18th century, for three players using forty cards, with one player competing against the other two [Mid-17C. < Spanish *hombre* 'man, ombre' < Latin *homo* 'man'.]

ombro- *prefix* rainfall, precipitation ○ *ombrogenous* [< Greek *ombros*]

ombrogenous /om brójjinəss/ *adj* describes a peat-forming plant community that derives all its water, and hence dissolved nutrients, from rainfall and other precipitation as opposed to watercourses or below-ground drainage

ombudsman /ómbōōdzmən/ (*plural* **-men** /-mən/) *n* **1** somebody responsible for investigating and resolving complaints from consumers or other members of the public against a company, institution, or other organization **2** a government official responsible for impartially investigating citizens' complaints against a public authority or institution and trying to bring about a fair settlement [Mid-20C. Via Swedish < Old Norse *umboðsmaðr* 'manager, deputy' < *umboð* 'commission' + *maðr* 'man'.] —**ombudsmanship** *n*

ombudsperson /ómbōōdz purs'n/ *n* somebody responsible for investigating or resolving complaints from consumers or other members of the public against a company, institution, or other organization [After OMBUDSMAN] —**ombudspersonship** /ómbōōdz purs'n ship/ *n*

ombudswoman /ómbōōdz wōōmən/ (*plural* **-en** /-wimmin/) *n* **1** a woman responsible for investigating and resolving complaints from consumers or other members of the public against a company, institution, or other organization **2** a woman government official responsible for impartially investigating citizens' complaints against a public authority or institution and trying to bring about a fair settlement [Mid-20C. After OMBUDSMAN.] —**ombudswomanship** /ómbōōdz wōōmən ship/ *n*

Omdurman /óm dur maán/ city in east-central Sudan. Population: 1,267,077 (1993).

-ome *suffix* mass ○ *trichome* [Via modern Latin < Greek *-ōma*]

omega /ṓmigə/ *n* **1** the 24th and final letter of the Greek alphabet **2** the end, or the last thing in a series (*literary*) [Early 16C. < Greek *ō mega* 'great (long) o', as opposed to 'small (short) o', 'o mikron'.]

omega-3 oil *n* a long-chain polyunsaturated oil with a double bond at the third carbon, obtained mainly from fish and believed to have health benefits for conditions such as high cholesterol, heart disease, and arthritis

omega-6 oil *n* a long-chain polyunsaturated oil with a double bond at the sixth carbon, obtained mainly from certain plants and seeds, deficiency of which can cause skin problems and hormonal imbalances

omega hyperon *n* a negatively charged elementary particle with a rest mass 3,272 times that of an electron

omega meson *n* an extremely short-lived neutral meson with a rest mass 1,532 times that of an electron

omega minus *n* PHYS = **omega hyperon** [< the symbol for the particle]

omelet *n* US = **omelette**

omelette /ómlət/ *n* a dish consisting of beaten eggs fried over high heat until set, often served folded in half over a savoury filling such as cheese or mushrooms [Early 17C. Via French < Latin *lamella* 'small thin plate' < *lamina* 'thin plate'.]

omen /ṓ men, ṓmən/ *n* a happening that is regarded as a sign of how somebody or something will fare in the future ■ *vti* to indicate the future course of events relating to something [Late 16C. < Latin.]

omentum /ō méntəm/ (*plural* **-ta** /-tə/) *n* any fold of the peritoneum, especially the fold that covers the intestines (**greater omentum**) or the fold that connects to the liver (**lesser omentum**) [Mid-16C. < Latin.]

Omer /ṓmər/ *n* in Judaism, a seven-week period between the second day of Passover and the first day of Shavuoth, observed as a period of mourning, except on one day

omerta /ō mair taá/, **omertà** *n* the code requirement alleged to apply to members of the Mafia, requiring that they remain silent about any crimes of which they have knowledge [Late 19C. < Italian dialect < Latin *humilitas* 'humility' < *humilis* 'humble'.]

omicron /ō mī kron/ *n* the 15th letter of the Greek alphabet [Mid-17C. < Greek *o mikron* 'small (i.e. short) o', as opposed to 'great (long) o', 'ō mega'.]

ominous /ómminəss/ *adj* suggesting or indicating that something bad is going to happen or be revealed ○ *I think it's rather ominous that they haven't replied to your letter.* [Late 16C. < Latin *ominosus* 'of an omen' < *omen* 'omen'.] —**ominously** *adv* —**ominousness** *n*

omission /ō mísh'n/ *n* **1** something that has been deliberately or accidentally left out or not done ○ *errors and omissions excepted* **2** the omitting of something or the state of being omitted ○ *The omission of those three words changed the sense of the whole paragraph.* [14C. Via Old French < late Latin *omission-* < *omittere* 'OMIT'.]

omit /ō mít/ (**omits, omitting, omitted**) *vt* **1** to fail to include or mention somebody or something, either deliberately or accidentally **2** to fail or forget to do something, either deliberately or accidentally [15C. < Latin *omittere* < *ob-* 'away' + *mittere* 'send'.] —**omissible** /ō míssəb'l/ *adj*

SYNONYMS See ***neglect***.

~~**ommission**~~ incorrect spelling of **omission**

~~**ommited**~~ incorrect spelling of **omitted**

~~**ommitted**~~ incorrect spelling of **omitted**

omni- *prefix* all ○ *omnicompetent* [< Latin *omnis*. Ultimately < Indo-European 'abundance, to produce' that is also the ancestor of English *opulent, copy, optimum*, and *operate*.]

omnibus /ómnibəss/ *n* **1** BOOK COLLECTING SEPARATE WORKS a single book containing several works, usually by the same author, involving the same main character, or on the same subject, previously published separately **2** **omnibus, omnibus edition** SINGLE BROADCAST OF PROGRAMMES a single continuous broadcast consisting of several radio or television programmes previously broadcast separately, e.g. instalments of a serial or soap opera **3** BUS a bus (*archaic or formal*) ■ *adj* WITH MANY DIFFERENT THINGS bringing many different things together as a single unit ○ *an omnibus education bill* [Early 19C. Via French and directly < Latin, 'for all' < *omnis* 'all' (see OMNI-).]

omnibus survey *n* a survey in which data on a wide variety of subjects is collected during the same interview

omnicompetent /ómni kómpitənt/ *adj* **1** able to deal successfully with any task or situation **2** competent to judge or try any kind of case

omnidirectional /ómnidi réksh'nəl, -dī-/ *adj* able to transmit or receive radio or sound waves in or from any direction

omnidirectional radio range *n* MEDIA = **omnirange**

omnipotent /om níppətənt/ *adj* possessing complete, unlimited, or universal power and authority [13C. Via Old French < Latin *omnipotent-* < *omnis* 'all' + *potens*, present participle of *posse* 'be able'.] —**omnipotence** *n* —**omnipotently** *adv*

Omnipotent *n* a word sometimes used to refer to God

omnipresent /ómni prézz'nt/ *adj* **1** continuously and simultaneously present throughout the whole of creation **2** present or seemingly present all the time or everywhere [Early 17C. < medieval Latin *omnipraesent-* < *omni-* 'omni-' + *praesens* 'present'.] —**omnipresence** *n*

omnirange /ómni raynj/ *n* a very-high-frequency radio navigation network that enables aircraft pilots to choose and fly any bearing relative to a transmitter on the ground

omniscient /om níssi ənt/ *adj* knowing or seeming to know everything [Early 17C. < medieval Latin *omniscient-* < Latin *omni-* 'omni-' + *scire* 'know' (see SCIENCE).] —**omniscience** *n* —**omnisciently** *adv*

omnium-gatherum /ómni əm gáthə rəm/ (*plural* **omnium-gatherums**) *n* a collection of many different, often unsorted ideas or items (*humorous*) [< Latin *omnium* 'of all' + pseudo-Latin *gatherum*, alteration of 'gathering']

omnivore /ómni vawr/ *n* **1** an animal that will feed on any kind or many different kinds of food, including both plants and animals. ◊ **carnivore** *n*. 1, **herbivore 2** a person who has wide interests and will read or study many things [Late 19C. Via modern Latin *Omnivora* 'omnivores' < Latin *omnivorus* (see OMNIVOROUS).]

omnivorous /om nívvərəss/ *adj* **1** eating any kind or many different kinds of food, including both plants and animals **2** wide-ranging and often undiscriminating in interests and tastes [Mid-17C. < Latin *omnivorus* < *omni-* (see OMNI-) + *-vorus* 'devouring'.] —**omnivorously** *adv*

OMOV /ṓmov/, **Omov** *abbr* one member one vote

omphalos /ómfə loss/ *n* **1** a conical stone with sacred significance in ancient Greek religion, especially the one at Delphi that was believed to mark the centre of the world **2** the central or focal point, around which everything else revolves (*literary*) [Mid-19C. < Greek, 'navel'.]

Omsk /omsk/ city in SW Russia. Population: 1,437,781 (1995).

on /on/ *prep* **1** INDICATES POSITION describes something in a position above and in contact with the surface of something else ○ *sitting on the bed* **2** ATTACHED TO used to indicate attachment to or suspension from a surface or object ○ *a wooden wheel mounted on the wall* **3** SUPPORTING WEIGHT used to indicate what part of the body is supporting somebody's weight ○ *They sat there leaning on their elbows.* **4** CARRYING carrying something that is therefore readily accessible ○ *I didn't have any cash on me at the time.* **5** IN THE VICINITY OF located in a place or situated close to or alongside a place ○ *a town on the coast of Trinidad* **6** AT A TIME used to indicate when something happens ○ *just before noon on Tuesday* **7** RELATING TO concerned with or relating to a particular subject, thing, or activity **8** WHERE SOMETHING IS AVAILABLE used to indicate that specific information is currently available from a machine or instrument ○ *a comedy show on the radio* **9** AS MEANS OF FUNCTIONING used to indicate the means by which somebody or something subsists or functions ○ *animals that feed on the leaves of the trees* **10** BY MEANS OF using something as a means of transport ○ *They arrived on horseback.* **11** DURING engaged in an activity ○ *My assistant is away on a course.* **12** ACCORDING TO used to indicate that something is grounds for a statement, way of thinking, or action ○ *allowing them to compete on an equal basis* **13** IN CURRENT RANK OR POSITION used to indicate somebody's current status or position in an organization or institution ○ *My sister is on the committee.* **14** DIRECTED TOWARDS used to indicate that something is directed towards somebody or something ○ *I shone my torch on the inscription.* **15** CHARGED TO used to indicate that the cost of drinks or a meal is charged to a particular person ○ *The drinks are on me.* ■ *adv* **1** IN CONTACT WITH in contact with, attached to, or supported by something ○ *an envelope with a stamp on* **2** INTO CONDITION OF ATTACHMENT OR SUSPENSION into a condition of being attached to or suspended from something ○ *sewing a button on* **3** INTO OPERATION into the condition of operating or functioning ○ *turned the television on* **4** WITH CLOTHING wearing clothes or placing clothing over a part of the body ○ *I pulled my tee-shirt on.* **5** PERSISTENTLY in a continuous or persistent way ○ *decided to stay on in Cambridge* **6** IN PROGRESS in activity or performance at the present time or at some implied time ○ *putting a play on* **7** INDICATING RUNNER'S POSITION in baseball, used to indicate whether an offensive player is on the bases ○ *left three runners on* **8** WAGERED wagered as a bet ○ *put a bet on* ■ *adj* **1** TAKING PLACE happening or being performed at the present time ○ *There's nothing good on tonight.* ○ *I've got a lot on at the moment.* **2** ARRANGED OR PLANNED indicating that an activity is arranged and will happen ○ *Are we still on for tomorrow?* **3** FUNCTIONING indicating that a machine or device is functioning or in use ○ *Is the oven on?* **4** BOWLING indicating that a particular bowler is bowling **5** OF LEG SIDE indicating or relating to the leg side of a cricket pitch **6** IN CRICKET FIELDING POSITION indicating certain fielding positions on the leg side [Old English, < Indo-European] ◇ **be on about** used to indicate what somebody is talking about or what he or she means (*informal*) ◇ **be on to somebody** *or* **something** to have information on or be aware of the real nature of somebody or something (*informal*) ◇ **it's not on** used to indicate that something is unacceptable ◇ **on and off** occasionally ◇ **on and on** in a continuous, persistent way ◇ **you're on** used to indicate that somebody is agreeing to do something proposed by somebody else (*informal*)

ON *abbr* Ontario

-on[1] *suffix* **1** subatomic particle ○ *fermion* **2** chemical substance ○ *fenuron* **3** fundamental hereditary unit ○ *muton* **4** unit, quantum ○ *chronon* **5** inert gas ○ *radon* [< ION, influenced by the Greek neuter present participle *on* 'being' or neuter noun ending *-on*]

-on[2] *suffix* = **-one** [Alteration of -ONE]

on-again, off-again *adj US* happening or continuing intermittently, and thus difficult to predict (*informal*)

onager /ónnəjər/ (*plural* **-gers** *or* **-gri** /ónnə grī/) *n* **1** a wild ass that is dark yellow with a stripe along its back. Native to: N Iran and bordering areas. Genus: *Equus hemionus.* **2** in former times, a war machine used to throw stones [14C. Via Latin < Greek *onagros* < *onos* 'ass' + *agrios* 'wild'.]

onanism /ṓnənizəm/ *n* (*literary*) **1** masturbation **2** coitus interruptus [Early 18C. After *Onan*, a character in the Bible (Genesis 38:9), who spilled his semen onto the ground rather than impregnate his deceased brother's wife.] —**onanist** *n* —**onanistic** /ṓnə nístik/ *adj*

onboard /ón báwrd/ *adj* carried or available on an aircraft, ship, or other vehicle or vessel [Mid-20C. *Board* < BOARD 'side of a ship'.]

once /wunss/ *adv* **1** AT A TIME IN THE PAST used to indicate that something happened or was the case at some time in the past ○ *The place must have been nice once.* ○ *a once comfortable lifestyle* **2** MULTIPLIED BY ONE indicating that a number is multiplied by one ○ *once three is three* **3** BY ONE STEP distant by one place or degree ○ *a cousin once removed* ■ *conj* AS SOON AS happening when or whenever something else has happened ○ *Once he got started, it was clear we were dealing with an expert.* ◇ **all at once** **1** happening suddenly, often unexpectedly ○ *I felt really sick all at once.* **2** happening all at the same time ○ *She could not read the books all at once.* ◇ **at once** **1** immediately ○ *Tell him at once.* **2** happening all at the same time ○ *It's a lot to take in at once.* ◇ **for once** happening on this particular occasion, if or but at no other time ○ *For once my strategy worked.* ◇ **once and away** **1** conclusively **2** occasionally ◇ **once and for all** completely or finally ◇ **once or twice** *or* **once and again** a few times, but not often ○ *pausing once and again to listen*

once-over *n* a rapid inspection or examination of somebody or something (*informal*) ○ *I'll give the car a quick once-over.*

onchocerciasis /óngkōsur kī́ əssiss/ *n* a disease caused by infestation with worms, especially a tropical disease of humans caused by a parasitic worm and transmitted by blackflies, causing skin nodules, lesions, and blindness [Early 20C. < modern Latin *Onchocerca* < Greek *ogkos* 'barb' + *kerkos* 'tail' < their shape.]

onco- *prefix* tumour ○ *oncolysis* [< Greek *onkos* 'mass']

oncogene /óngkō jeen/ *n* a gene that can cause a cell to become malignant

oncogenesis /óngkō jénnəssiss/ *n* the development of a tumour or tumours

oncogenic /óngkō jénnik/, **oncogenous** /ong kójjənəss/ *adj* relating to or causing the formation and growth of tumours —**oncogenicity** /óngkōjə níssəti/ *n*

oncology /ong kólləji/ *n* the branch of medicine that deals with the study and treatment of malignant tumours —**oncological** /óngkə lójjik'l/ *adj* —**oncologist** *n*

oncolysis /ong kólləssiss/ *n* the destruction of tumour cells, either spontaneously or, more usually, in response to drug or radiographic treatment

oncoming /ón kuming/ *adj* heading directly towards somebody or something ■ *n* the approach of something that is soon to occur

oncornavirus /ong káwrnə vī́rəss/ *n* a virus containing single-stranded RNA and capable of causing cancer [Late 20C. < ONCO- + RNA + VIRUS.]

oncost /ón kost/ *n* the general recurring expense of running a business, e.g. rent, maintenance, and utilities

Ondaatje /on dáatyə/, **Michael** (*b.* 1943) Sri Lankan-born Canadian writer

Ondes Martenot /óNd maártənō/ *n* an electronic musical instrument that can be played on a keyboard or with a finger slider, producing a sliding sound [< French *Ondes (musicales)* '(musical) waves', its original name + *(Maurice) Martenot*, 1898–1980, French inventor]

on dit /oN dée/ (*plural* **on dits** /oN dée/) *n* a piece of gossip [< French, 'they say']

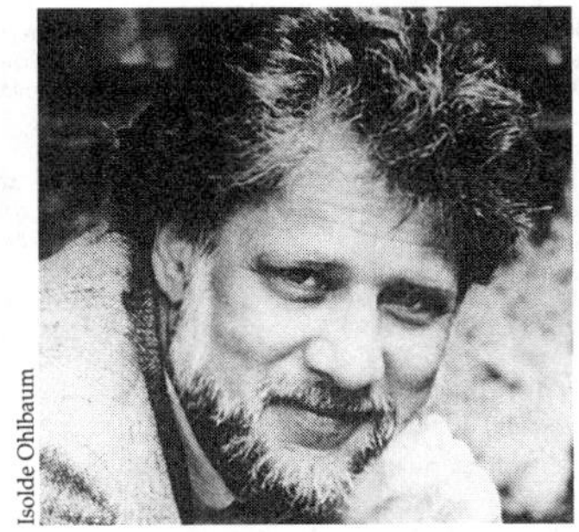

Isolde Ohlbaum

Michael Ondaatje

one /wun/ CORE MEANING: a grammatical word indicating a single thing or unit, and not two or more ○ (det) *just one accident out of thousands* ○ (det) *a one-legged man* ○ (pron) *Central Newark, once home to several bank branches, now has one.* ○ (pron) *Bill got one of his boxing gloves off.*

1 *det, pron* UNIQUE distinct from all others ○ *the one exception to this* **2** *det, pron* USED TO DISTINGUISH distinct from all others of its kind in a comparison ○ *from one thought to the next* **3** *det* A NONSPECIFIC TIME relating to an unspecified time in the past or future ○ *one August afternoon* **4** *det* USED FOR EMPHASIS used instead of 'a' and 'an' to emphasize a following adjective or expression (*informal*) ○ *She's written one great novel!* **5** *det* PARTICULAR introducing the name of somebody who is not known to the speaker ○ *a letter from one Thomas Atherton of Southport* **6** *pron* TYPICAL INDIVIDUAL used to refer to people in general (*formal*) ○ *One can eat well here.* **7** *pron* SOMEBODY OR SOMETHING UNSPECIFIED used to indicate somebody or something not specifically identified (*dated*) ○ *the voice of one crying in the wilderness* **8** *pron* PREVIOUSLY MENTIONED used instead of a preceding noun to indicate somebody or something already mentioned ○ *nothing but an old vase, and a cracked one at that* **9** *pron* JOKE OR STORY used to refer to a question, joke, or remark ○ *That's a good one!* **10** *n* see table at **number** **11** *n US* DOLLAR BILL a one-dollar bill (*informal*) **12** *n* TIME MEASURE used to indicate the time as one hour after twelve midday or midnight ○ *We'll stop for lunch at one.* **13** *n* MUSICAL NOTATION the numeral 1 used as the bottom figure in a time signature to indicate that the beat is measured in semibreves [Old English *ān* < Indo-European] ◇ **as one** doing something at the same time or in the same way ◇ **all one** not important enough to be of any consequence to somebody ○ *It's all one to me.* ◇ **at one** in harmony with somebody or something ◇ **one and all** everyone in a group ◇ **one and only** **1** unique and without comparison (*often used to introduce a performer on a show*) **2** the person that somebody loves ◇ **one by one** happening individually in sequence ◇ **one or two** a few people or things

USAGE one of those people who is or **one of those people who are**? Sense determines whether the verb in a construction of this type should be singular or plural, and in any given case one choice is right and the other wrong. To decide which verb form to choose, start with the *of.* For example, *He is one of those people who is/are always trying to impress* is not equivalent in meaning to *Of those people, he is one who is always trying to impress.* Rather, the idea is *Of those people who are always trying to impress, he is one.* Here the form of the verb *to be* is not governed by *one* but by *people*, and therefore *one of those people who are* is right. In the following example the choice of the form of 'to be' is governed by 'only': *He is the only one of those people who is worth talking to.* Here the idea is *Of those people, he is the only one who is worth talking to*, so in this case *one of those people who is* is right.

-one *suffix* ketone or related compound ○ *quinone* [< ?]

one-acter *n* a play that consists of only one act

one another *pron* each of several members of a group to the others ○ *neighbours helping one another*

one-armed bandit *n* a gambling machine that is operated by inserting a coin or token in a slot and pulling down a lever on one side (*informal*)

one-dimensional *adj* **1** existing in or possessing only one dimension **2** presenting or perceiving only the most superficial aspects of something

Onega, Lake /o náygə/ lake in NW Russia, the second-largest lake in Europe. Area: 9,700 sq. km/3,745 sq. mi.

one-horse *adj* **1** VERY SMALL AND BORING small, dull, and insignificant ○ *a one-horse town* **2** HAVING ONE LIKELY WINNER fielding only one candidate or competitor who is likely to win ○ *a one-horse race* **3** DRAWN BY SINGLE HORSE drawn by only one horse

Oneida[1] /ō nī́də/ (*plural* **-das** *or* **-da**) *n* **1** a member of a Native North American people who originally occupied lands in New York State and whose members now live mainly in Ontario, New York State, and Wisconsin **2** the Iroquoian language of the Oneida people [Mid-17C. < Oneida *onē̃yote*, the main Oneida settlement.] —**Oneida** *adj*

Oneida[2] /ō nī́də/ city in central New York State. Population: 10,850 (1990).

O'Neill /ō neél/, **Eugene** (1888–1953) US playwright

oneiric /ō nī́ ərik/ *adj* relating to, experienced in, or similar to a dream or dreams [Mid-19C. < Greek *oneiros* 'dream'.]

oneiromancy /ō nī́ ərō manssi/ *n* the practice of divining the future through the interpretation of dreams [Mid-17C. < Greek *oneiros* 'dream' + -MANCY.] —**oneiromancer** *n*

one kind *adj Malaysia, Singapore* different from others in a way that makes somebody or something worthy of note

one-liner *n* a short joke or funny remark in one sentence

one-man *adj* consisting of, designed for, featuring, or performed by only one person ○ *a one-man tent*

one-man band *n* **1** a street performer who carries and plays several musical instruments at once **2** a business or organization in which one person does all or most of the work

oneness /wúnn nəss/ *n* **1** SINGLENESS the quality of being one as opposed to many **2** UNIQUENESS the quality of being unique **3** AGREEMENT the condition of being united or agreed **4** SAMENESS the quality of being the same or monotonous

one-night stand *n* **1** a sexual encounter that lasts for only one night (*informal*) **2** a single performance given at any one place for one night only

one-note *adj US* limited in ability, scope, or range (*informal*) ○ *a one-note writer*

one-off *adj* happening only once, not as part of a series ■ *n* a unique and unrepeatable or unrepeated thing or event

one-on-one *adj US* = **one-to-one** *adj.* **1** —**one-on-one** *adv*

one-person *adj* consisting of, designed for, featuring, or performed by only one person

one-piece *adj* consisting of a single, not two or more, components ■ *n* a bathing suit consisting of a single piece

oner /wúnnər/ *n* a unique or extraordinary person or thing (*informal*)

onerous /ṓnərəss, ónnərəss/ *adj* **1** representing a great burden or much trouble **2** involving obligations that are more disadvantageous than advantageous [14C. Via Old French *onéreux* < Latin *onerosus* < *oner-*, stem of *onus* 'burden'.] —**onerously** *adv* —**onerousness** *n*

oneself /wun sélf/ *pron* (*formal*) **1** REFERRING TO THE SUBJECT used as a pronoun, the reflexive form of 'one', meaning a person's own self ○ *The aim is to improve oneself and one's ability.* **2** WITHOUT HELP FROM OTHERS used to indicate that something is done without help or interference from others ○ *One should always try and manage things oneself.* **3** NORMAL SELF your usual or normal self ○ *In such situations one never feels oneself.* [Mid-16C. < *one's self.*]

one-shot *adj* (*informal*) **1** taking effect after only one application or attempt ○ *a one-shot solution to financial problems* **2** *US* happening or doing something only once

one-sided *adj* **1** UNFAIRLY WEIGHTED dominated by or favouring one side more than the other in a competition **2** BIASED presenting or considering one side of a matter whilst ignoring other aspects of it **3** BIGGER ON ONE SIDE larger, more prominent, or more developed on one side than the other **4** BEING ON ONE SIDE having or occurring on only one side —**one-sidedly** *adv* —**one-sidedness** *n*

one-step *n* **1** BALLROOM DANCE a ballroom dance similar to the foxtrot, in 2/4 time **2** DANCE MUSIC the music for a one-step ■ *vi* DANCE ONE-STEP to perform the one-step

one-stop *adj* offering a wide variety of services or goods in one location so that a customer has to go to only one place ○ *a one-stop home design centre*

one-tailed *adj* describes a statistical test in which all values of the critical region either fall below or exceed a given value, but not both

onetime *adj* **1** having been something or played a particular role at a previous time ○ *the one-time world champion* **2** **one-time** done or occurring only once and unlikely to happen again

one-to-one *adj* **1** INDIVIDUAL involving contact or communication between only two people ○ *I find it much easier to teach one-to-one.* US term **one-on-one** *adj.* **2** MATCHING with one part that corresponds to or matches another **3** WITH PAIRINGS THAT LEAVE NO REMAINDER describes a mathematical set with members such that each member can be paired with one of another set leaving no remainder —**one-to-one** *adv*

one-track *adj* focused on, obsessed with, or restricted to only one issue or subject ○ *a one-track mind*

one-two *n* **1** TWO SUCCESSIVE PUNCHES a punch with one hand followed by a punch from the side (**cross**) with the other hand ○ *I gave him the one-two.* US term **one-two punch** *n.* 1 **2** QUICK SEQUENTIAL ACTIONS OR EVENTS two actions or events producing an effect because delivered or happening quickly and in sequence ○ *The incumbent could not survive the one-two of a sex scandal and defections by supporters.* US term **one-two punch** *n.* 2 **3** PASS TO ANOTHER PLAYER THEN BACK a pass made to another player on the same team who then immediately passes to a new position taken up by the original passer

one-two punch *n US* **1** BOXING = **one-two** *n.* 1 **2** = **one-two** *n.* 2

one-up (**one-ups, one-upping, one-upped**) *vt US* to gain an advantage over an opponent (*informal*) ○ *Looks like I've been one-upped again.*

one-upmanship /-úpmənship/ *n* the practice of attempting to outdo or show yourself to be superior to a rival or opponent

one-way *adj* **1** GOING IN ONE DIRECTION moving or allowing movement in one direction only ○ *a one-way street* **2** NOT ALLOWING A RETURN allowing somebody to travel to a destination but not to return ○ *a one-way ticket* **3** INVOLVING ONLY ONE OF TWO PEOPLE agreed on, felt, or involving a contribution from one person or party only ○ *a one-way agreement* **4** ALLOWING VIEWING FROM ONE SIDE made in such a way that it can be looked through from one side but not from the other ○ *one-way glass* ■ *n* ONE-WAY ROAD SYSTEM a one-way road system (*informal*)

one-way mirror *n US* = **two-way mirror**

one-woman *adj* consisting of, designed for, featuring, or performed by one woman ○ *a one-woman show*

ongoing /ónn gō ing, -gṓ-/ *adj* having existed or been in progress for some time and continuing to do so

onion /únnyən/ *n* **1** EDIBLE BULB a rounded edible bulb with hard pungent flesh in concentric layers beneath a flaky brown skin eaten raw or cooked as a vegetable **2** PLANT WITH PUNGENT BULBS plant of the lily family that produces onions. Flowers: greenish-white. Native to: Asia. *Allium cepa.* **3** PLANT RELATED TO ONION any plant related to the onion, e.g. the Welsh onion [12C. < Latin *unio* 'onion' < ?] —**oniony** *adj*

onion dome *n* a rounded dome resembling an onion in shape, typical of Russian and Byzantine church architecture

onionskin /únnyən skin/ *n* smooth thin translucent paper. Use: formerly, carbon copies.

Onitsha /ō níchə/ city in SE Nigeria. Population: 336,600 (1992).

-onium *suffix* a complex cation ○ *diazonium* [< AMMONIUM]

onium ion /ṓni əm-/ *n* NH_4^+ a positively charged ion (**cation**) that is analogous to the ammonium ion

on-label *adj US* using or involving the use of a prescription drug to treat a condition for which the drug is approved by the US Food and Drug Administration

onlay *vt* /on láy/ (**-lays, -laying, -laid**) LAY SOMETHING ON A SURFACE to lay something on a surface, especially for decorative reasons, so that it stands in relief ■ *n* /ónlay/ **1** SKIN GRAFT a skin graft surgically transferred to the surface of an organ or other part of the body **2** INLAY IN A TOOTH an inlay fixed to the biting surface of a tooth [15C. < ON + LAY[1] (verb).]

ϟ **online** /ón lín/ *adj* **1** CONNECTED VIA COMPUTER attached to or available through a central computer or computer network. ◊ **off-line** **2** DIRECTLY CONNECTED TO MEASURABLE PROCESS describes an instrument or sensor that is connected directly to a process being measured, thus obviating the need to take samples for analysis in a laboratory or elsewhere **3** *US* ONGOING currently going on or being done ■ *adv* WHILE CONNECTED TO COMPUTER while under the control of a computer or connected to a computer network ■ *adj* CONNECTED TO COMPUTER NETWORK attached to or available through a central computer or computer network

ϟ **online banking** *n* a banking service accessed from a commercial online network

ϟ **onliner** /ón līnər/ *n* a user or a supplier of online computer services

onload /on lṓd/ *vti* to load freight onto a vehicle

onlooker /ón lòòkər/ *n* a watcher of an event who does not take part in it —**onlooking** *adj*

only /ónli/ CORE MEANING: an adverb used to indicate the one thing or person that solely or exclusively happens or is involved in a situation ○ *facilities for club members only* ○ *I will act only in the best interests of our country.* ○ *The regulations apply only to new firms.*

1 *adv* INDICATING CONDITION used to indicate the condition that exists for something to happen or be true ○ *I'll go to the party, but only if you come with me.* **2** *adv* MERELY merely the situation, level, or amount stated ○ *I could only stand and look.* ○ *That's only part of the picture.* **3** *adv* NO MORE AND NO LESS just the particular amount specified ○ *There are only 3.3 people at work for every person retired.* **4** *adv* AS RECENTLY AS considered as happening very recently ○ *only last March* **5** *adv* INDICATING EVENT HAPPENING IMMEDIATELY AFTER used to introduce a surprising or unpleasant event that happens immediately after the one mentioned ○ *We rushed the cat to the vet, only to find there was nothing wrong with it.* **6** *adv Ireland* EMPHASIZING used to emphasize a statement ○ *It was only terrible.* **7** *adj* THE SINGLE PERSON OR THING used to indicate the single person or thing involved in a situation ○ *the only Democratic candidate* ○ *the only barrier between himself and the job* **8** *adj* WITH NO SIBLINGS with no brothers or sisters ○ *an only child* **9** *conj* BUT but or except ○ *It's the same product, only better.* [Old English *ānlic* < *ān* 'one' (see ONE)] ◇ **only too** used to emphasize the extent to which something is true ○ *Scenes like this are getting only too familiar.*

USAGE Avoid ambiguity in the placement of the limiting adverb ***only***. The position of ***only*** within a sentence can determine the meaning of the entire sentence. As a general rule, put it next to the word you want it to modify: *She had only a pound. Only she had a pound. She only had a pound.* Avoid putting ***only*** between a subject and a verb and between an auxiliary verb and a main verb: *He only does these things to get attention* where *He does these things only to get attention* is better. Similarly, *I will only stop the car once on the way there* is less desirable than *I will stop the car only once on the way there.*

on-message *adj* following the official policy of a political party or other organization ○ *The views expressed were most definitely not on-message.*

Ono /ṓnō/, **Yoko** (*b.* 1933) Japanese-born US artist

o.n.o. *abbr* or nearest offer (*in advertisements*)

onomasiology /ónnō máyssi óllәji/ *n* **1** the branch of linguistics that studies how meaning is expressed **2** LING = **onomastics** *n.* 1 [Early 20C. < Greek *onomasia* 'name' + -LOGY.]

onomastic /ónnə mástik/ *adj* relating to, connected with, or explaining names [Late 16C. Via French < Greek *onomastikos* < *onoma* 'name'.]

onomastics /ónnə mástiks/ *n* (+ *singular verb*) **1** the study of proper names, their origins, and their formation **2** the system underlying the creation and use of proper names in a specialized field

onomatopoeia /ónnō matə pée ə/ *n* the formation or use of words that imitate the sound associated with something, e.g. 'hiss' and 'buzz' [Late 16C. Via late Latin < Greek *onomatopoiia* 'making of words' < *onoma* 'name' + *poiein* 'make' (see POEM).]

onomatopoeic /ónnə matə pée ik/ *adj* imitative of the sound associated with the thing or action denoted by a particular word —**onomatopoeically** *adv*

Onondaga /ónnən dáagə/ (*plural* **-gas** *or* **-ga**) *n* **1** a member of a Native North American people that originally occupied lands in central New York State and whose members mainly continue to live there as well as in Ontario **2** the Iroquoian language of the Onondaga people [Late 17C. < Onondaga *onõtà'ke*, the main Onondaga settlement.] —**Onondaga** *adj*

Onondaga, Lake /ónnən dáagə/ lake in central New York State. Area: 13 sq. km/5 sq. mi.

onrush /ón rush/ *n* a forward rush or push ○ *the onrush of enemy soldiers* ○ *the onrush of events* —**onrushing** *adj*

on-screen *adj, adv* appearing on the screen in a television programme or film and therefore visible to the audience ○ *Their private life was very different from their on-screen relationship.*

onset /ón set/ *n* **1** the beginning of something, especially of something difficult or unpleasant ○ *the onset of winter* **2** an initial attack or assault in battle [Early 16C. < SET[1] (noun).]

onshore /ón sháwr/ *adj* **1** on land as opposed to at sea ○ *onshore drilling* **2** towards land from the sea ○ *onshore breeze* —**onshore** *adv*

onside /ón síd/ *adj, adv* in a position that is allowed within the rules of the game, e.g. in soccer or hockey

on-site *adj, adv* taking place or provided at the location where work or some other activity is being carried out

onslaught /ón slawt/ *n* **1** a powerful attack or force that overwhelms somebody or something **2** a very large quantity of people or things that is difficult to deal with or process ○ *faced with an onslaught of junk mail* [Early 17C. Via Dutch *aanslag* < Middle Dutch *aenslach* 'blow on' < *slach* 'blow'.]

onstage /ón stáyj/ *adj, adv* performing, happening, or existing on the stage as opposed to in the wings, backstage, or somewhere not visible to the audience

on-stream *adj, adv* in or into production or operation ○ *when the new system comes on-stream*

Ont. *abbr* Ontario

ont- *prefix* = **onto-** (*before vowels*)

-ont *suffix* cell, organism ○ *schizont* [< Greek *ont-* 'being' (see ONTO-)]

Ontario /on táiri ō/ province of east-central Canada. Capital: Toronto. Population: 10,753,573 (1996). Area: 1,076,395 sq. km/415,598 sq. mi. —**Ontarian** *n, adj*

Ontario, Lake smallest of the Great Lakes, on the border between NW New York State and SE Ontario, Canada. Area: 19,011 sq. km/7,340 sq. mi.

on-the-job *adj* provided or obtained while working at a job ○ *on-the-job training*

ontic /óntik/ *adj* relating to real existence [Mid-20C. < the Greek stem *ont-* 'being' (see ONTO-).]

onto (*stressed*) /ón too/; (*unstressed*) /óntə, óntòò/ CORE MEANING: a preposition indicating that somebody or something is located on something, or moves towards it so as to be on it ○ *I splashed water onto my face.* ○ *hop onto a bus* ○ *shine a flashlight onto the wall* ○ *loading the data onto a disk* ○ *come onto the market*

prep **1** making or about to make a discovery, often about something secret or illegal ○ *I'm really onto something big here.* ○ *The police were onto them.* **2** in contact with a person or organization ○ *Get onto the suppliers.* [Early 18C. < ON + TO.]

onto- *prefix* **1** being, existence ○ *ontology* **2** organism ○ *ontogeny* [< Greek *ont-*, present participle of *einai* 'be' < Indo-European]

ontogeny /on tójjəni/, **ontogenesis** /óntə jénnəssiss/ *n* the development of an individual from a fertilized ovum to maturity, as contrasted with the development of a group or species (**phylogeny**) —**ontogenic** /óntə jénnik/ *adj* —**ontogenically** *adv*

ontological argument /óntə lójjik'l-/ *n* an argument made by St Anselm and others to prove the existence of God by pointing to God's essence as a perfect, necessary being

ontology /on tólləji/ (*plural* **-gies**) *n* **1** the most general branch of metaphysics, concerned with the nature of being **2** a particular theory of being [Early 18C. < modern Latin, 'study of being' < the Greek stem *ont-* 'being' (see ONT-).] —**ontological** /óntə lójjik'l/ *adj* —**ontologically** *adv* —**ontologist** *n*

onus /ṓnəss/ *n* **1** BURDEN a duty or responsibility ○ *The onus is on her to make the first move.* **2** BLAME the blame for something ○ *He'll always bear the onus of having caused the accident.* **3** BURDEN OF PROOF OR PROCEEDING the burden of proof or responsibility for acting in a legal proceeding [Mid-17C. < Latin, 'burden, load'.]

onward /ónwərd/ *adj* directed or moving forward in space, time, or development ○ *the great onward march of organization and life* ■ *adv* **onward, onwards** moving towards a point or position ahead in space, time, or development

onycholysis /ónni kólləssiss/ *n* the separation of all or part of a fingernail or thumbnail from its bed, associated with psoriasis or a fungal skin condition [< modern Latin < Greek *onukh-*, stem of *onux* 'nail, claw']

onychophoran /ónni kóffərən/ *n* a small land invertebrate that has many pairs of unjointed legs and captures insects and similar prey by spraying them with adhesive mucus. Phylum: Onychophora. [Late 19C. < modern Latin *Onychophora* < Greek *onukh-* 'claw' + *-phoros* 'bearing'; from the curved claws.]

-onym *suffix* name, word ○ *pseudonym* [< Greek *onuma* (see ONOMASTIC)]

onymous /ónniməss/ *adj* having a name rather than being anonymous [Late 18C. < ANONYMOUS.]

onyx /ónniks/ *n* a semiprecious stone that is a fine-grained variety of chalcedony with bands of different colours. Use: gems, cameo work. [13C. Directly and via Old French and Latin < Greek *onux* 'fingernail, claw'.]

oo- *prefix* ovum, egg ○ *oospore* [< Greek *ōion* < Indo-European, 'egg']

oocyte /ṓ ə sīt/ *n* a cell that develops into a female reproductive cell **(ovum)**

oodles /óod'lz/ *npl* a large amount or number of something (*informal*) ○ *She has oodles of friends.* [Mid-19C. < ?]

⚡**OOG** *abbr* object-oriented graphics

oogamete /ō óggə meet/ *n* a female reproductive cell **(ovum)**

oogamy /ō óggəmi/ *n* reproduction in which a small motile male sex cell fuses with a large immobile female sex cell, as happens, e.g., when a sperm fuses with an egg —**oogamous** *adj*

oogenesis /ṓ ə jénnəssiss/ *n* the formation and development of an ovum —**oogenetic** /ṓ əjə néttik/ *adj*

oogonium /ṓ ə gṓni əm/ (*plural* **-a** /-i ə/ *or* **-ums**) *n* **1** a cell in the ovary that develops into an oocyte **2** the female sex organ of some algae and fungi that contains oospheres [Mid-19C. < OO- + Greek *gonos* 'generation, seed'.] —**oogonial** *adj*

ooh /oo/ *interj* USED TO EXPRESS SURPRISE used as an exclamation of surprise, excitement, pleasure, or pain (*informal*) ■ *vi* EXPRESS SURPRISE OR AWE to exclaim in surprise, excitement, pleasure, or pain, especially on first encountering something ○ *When they went into the royal chambers, you could hear them oohing and aahing.* ■ *n* EXCLAMATION OF SURPRISE an exclamation of surprise, excitement, pleasure, or pain [Early 20C. Natural exclamation.] ◇ **ooh la la** used to show pleasant surprise or approval, or, humorously, to suggest that something is scandalous

oolite /ṓ ə līt/ *n* **1** a sedimentary rock, often shale, clay, or sandstone, that is made up of small spherical grains consisting of concentric layers **2** any small spherical grain in oolite [Early 19C. Via French *oölithe* < modern Latin *oolites* < Greek *ōion* 'egg' + *lithos* 'stone'.] —**oolitic** /ṓ ə líttik/ *adj*

oolith /ṓ ə lith/ *n* GEOL = **oolite** *n.* 2

oolong /óo long/ *n* a dark Chinese tea that is partly fermented before being dried [Mid-19C. < Chinese (Mandarin) *wulong* < *wu* 'black' + *long* 'dragon'.]

oompah /óo mpaa/, **oompah-pah** /óom paa paa/ *n* a representation of the sound made by a bass brass instrument, considered typical of some kinds of band music (*often before nouns*) ○ *an oompah band* [Late 19C. An imitation of the sound.]

oomph /óomf/ *n* **1** energy or enthusiasm ○ *Put some oomph into it!* **2** *US* strong or obvious sexual attractiveness (*slang*) [Mid-20C. < ?]

oophorectomy /ṓ əfə réktəmi/ (*plural* **-mies**) *n* SURG = **ovariectomy** [Late 19C. < modern Latin *oophoron* 'ovary', literally 'egg-bearer' < Greek *ōion* 'egg'.]

oophoritis /ṓ əfə rítiss/ *n* ovary inflammation [Late 19C. < modern Latin *oophoron* 'ovary' (see OOPHORECTOMY).]

oops /óops, oops/ *interj* used as an exclamation when you drop something, bump into somebody, or do something in a clumsy or awkward manner (*informal*) ○ *She dropped the entire tray? Oops!* [Mid-20C. Natural exclamation.]

Oort cloud /áwrt-, óort-/ *n* a huge, roughly spherical, orbiting collection of comets thought to exist at the edge of the solar system [Late 20C. After Jan Hendrix *Oort* (1900–92), Dutch astronomer.]

oose /ooss/ *n* Scotland fluff from textiles (*informal*)

oosphere /ṓ ə sfeer/ *n* an unfertilized female reproductive cell in algae and fungi [Late 19C. < OO- + SPHERE.]

oospore /ṓ ə spawr/ *n* a fertilized female reproductive cell in algae and fungi [Mid-19C. < OO- + SPORE.] —**oosporic** /ṓ ə spórrik/ *adj* —**oosporous** /ō óspərəss/ *adj*

⚡**OOTB** *abbr* (*in e-mails*) **1** out of the blue **2** out of the box

ooze[1] /ooz/ *v* (**oozes, oozing, oozed**) **1** *vti* FLOW OR LEAK SLOWLY to exude a liquid substance slowly and in small quantities, or to flow in this way ○ *Resin oozed from the trunk.* **2** *vti* OVERFLOW WITH SOME QUALITY OR EMOTION to possess a quality in abundance or express an emotion intensely, or to be expressed in an intense or overpowering way ○ *oozing charm and self-confidence* **3** *vi* MOVE SLOWLY BUT STEADILY to move slowly but steadily forward or outward ○ *The huge crowd oozed through the streets.* **4** *vi* EBB to disappear or decline slowly and gradually ■ *n* **1** VERY SLOW FLOW a slow and gradual leakage or flow **2** TANNING SOLUTION an infusion used in tanning, made from oak bark and other plant materials [Old English *wōs* 'juice, sap']

ooze[2] /ooz/ *n* **1** SLUDGE thick mud or slime that is found at the bottom of a river or lake **2** BOG OR MARSH a soft or muddy area such as a bog or marsh **3** SEDIMENT ON THE OCEAN FLOOR a layer of muddy sediment on the seafloor consisting mainly of the remains of microscopic organisms such as plankton [Old English *wāse*]

ooze leather *n* a soft leather with a velvety finish [*Ooze* < OOZE[1] 'tanning solution']

oozy[1] /óozi/ (**-ier, -iest**) *adj* leaking moisture [Old English; < OOZE[1]]

oozy[2] /óozi/ (**-ier, -iest**) *adj* wet and muddy [Old English; < OOZE[2]]

op /op/ *n* a surgical operation (*informal*)

OP *abbr* **1** organophosphate **2** order of preachers (*a title used by the Dominican order of friars*) **3** observation post **4** out of print

op. *abbr* **1** **op., Op.** opus **2** operation **3** opposite **4** optical **5** opera

opacify /ō pássi fī/ (**-fies, -fying, -fied**) *vti* to become opaque or turn or make something opaque [Early 20C. < OPACITY.] —**opacifier** *n*

opacity /ō pássəti/ (*plural* **-ties**) *n* **1** BEING OPAQUE the quality, condition, or degree of being opaque **2** OBSCURITY the quality of being obscure in meaning **3** ABILITY OF MATERIAL TO STOP LIGHT the capacity of a material such as photographic film to stop light, expressed as a comparison between light striking the material and light transmitted **4** PROPOSITIONS NOT ADHERING TO LEIBNIZ'S LAW propositions containing modal notions such as necessity or belief in which principles of logic such as Leibniz's law do not obtain [Mid-16C. Via French < Latin *opacus* 'shaded, dark'.]

opah /ṓpə/ *n* a brightly coloured sea fish that can be up to 1.8 m/6 ft long. *Lampris regius.* [Mid-18C. < a West African language.]

opal /ṓp'l/ *n* a semiprecious stone that is a variously coloured noncrystalline variety of silica. Use: gems. [Late 16C. < French *opale* or Latin *opalus* < ?]

opalesce /ṓpə léss/ (**-esces, -escing, -esced**) *vi* to display shimmering milky colours (*refers to opals*) [Early 19C. < OPAL + Latin *-esce* 'assuming a certain state'.]

opalescent /ṓpə léss'nt/ *adj* showing or possessing shimmering milky colours —**opalescence** *n*

opaleye /ṓp'l ī/ (*plural* **-eyes** *or* **-eye**) *n* a common greenish omnivorous sea fish with two white spots on its back. Native to: coast of California and Mexico. *Girella nigricans.* [< the opalescent appearence of its eyes]

opaline /ṓpə līn, -leen/ *adj* = **opalescent** ■ *n* a semi-translucent glass made by adding fluorides

opaque /ō páyk/ *adj* **1** NOT TRANSPARENT OR TRANSLUCENT impervious to light, so that images cannot be seen through it **2** NOT SHINY dull and without lustre **3** HARD TO UNDERSTAND obscure and unintelligible in meaning **4** IMPENETRABLE BY RADIATION impenetrable by a specified form of radiation ■ *n* MATERIAL THROUGH WHICH LIGHT CANNOT PASS something opaque, especially a photographic pigment [15C. Directly or via French < Latin *opacus* 'shaded, dark'.] —**opaquely** *adv* —**opaqueness** *n*

op art *n* a 20th-century school of abstract art that uses geometric patterns and colour to create the illusion of movement (*often before nouns*) ○ *op art designs* [Shortening of OPTICAL ART, modelled on POP ART] —**op artist** *n*

QUICK FACTS ON... **OP ART**

Key dates: 1960s
Key locations: France, United Kingdom, United States
Key elements: geometric patterns, strong colour contrasts; grand scale; goal of provoking visual disturbance and impression of movement
Key figures: Victor Vasarély, Josef Albers, Bridget Riley, Richard Anuszkiewicz, Larry Poons
Key works: *On Late Sky* (Albers) 1962, *Fall* (Riley) 1963, *VEGA PER* (Vasarély) 1969
Key developments: minimalism, kinetic art

op. cit. *abbr* in the text or texts quoted (*in footnotes to refer to a source just mentioned*) [Shortening of Latin *opus citatum* or *opere citato*]

ope /ōp/ *adj* open (*archaic or literary*) ■ *vti* (**opes, oping, oped**) to open, or open something (*archaic or literary*) [< OPEN]

OPEC /ṓ pek/ *n* an organization of oil-producing countries that share the same policies regarding the sale of petroleum. Full form **Organization of Petroleum Exporting Countries**

op-ed /óp éd/ *n* **1** a newspaper page, usually opposite the editorial page, that features signed articles expressing personal opinions (*often before nouns*) **2** an article expressing a personal viewpoint written for the op-ed section of a newspaper [Shortening of *opposite editorial (page)*]

open /ṓpən/ *adj* **1** NOT CLOSED OR LOCKED allowing people or things to pass through freely ○ *an open window* **2** ALLOWING ACCESS TO THE INSIDE with the lid, cork, or other device removed or in a position that allows access to the inside ○ *an open box* **3** NOT SEALED not sealed, fastened, or wrapped ○ *an open envelope* **4** APART OR WIDE with a part of the body widened or apart ○ *The kitten's eyes were open.* **5** UNFOLDED OR APART having been unfolded, extended, or left apart ○ *A newspaper lay open on the table.* **6** FRANK AND HONEST not trying to hide anything or deceive anyone ○ *open hostility* **7** PUBLIC conducted in a public manner ○ *open hearings* **8** RECEPTIVE ready and willing to accept or listen to something, e.g. new ideas or suggestions ○ *I'm always open to suggestions.* **9** VULNERABLE in a position where blame, criticism, or attack are likely ○ *That remark left him open to criticism.* **10** NOT ENCLOSED having no boundaries or enclosures ○ *open countryside* **11** NOT COVERED having no cover or roof ○ *an open fire* **12** AVAILABLE TO DO BUSINESS ready for business and available for use by customers or clients ○ *The garage is still open.* **13** FREELY ACCESSIBLE accessible to all, with no restrictions on entry, membership, or acceptance ○ *an open meeting* **14** ACCESSIBLE TO PARTICULAR GROUP accessible to a particular group of interested people ○ *This competition is open to all students under the age of 18.* **15** VACANT ready for or available to applicants ○ *The vacancy is no longer open.* **16** *US* TURNED ON switched on and ready to use ○ *an open microphone* **17** NOT PREDETERMINED OR DECIDED remaining undecided or unresolved ○ *I'm trying to keep my options open.* **18** ALERT in a state of focused attention and alertness ○ *Keep your eyes and ears open.* **19** WITH NO TIME RESTRICTION with no restrictions on the period of use ○ *an open ticket* **20** *US* GENEROUS very free or generous, especially with money ○ *She gave to charity with an open hand.* **21** *US* NOT HAVING LEGAL RESTRICTIONS not having restrictions that limit activities such as gambling or drinking ○ *an open town* **22** UNGUARDED unprotected by the assigned player ○ *He left the goal wide open.* **23** UNPROTECTED BY SKIN unprotected and exposed, with the skin cut, torn, or missing ○ *an open wound* **24** NOT BLOCKED free from blockage and therefore allowing unobstructed passage **25** HAVING GAPS with small gaps or intervals between the stitches or threads ○ *an open weave* **26** FREE FROM ICE OR OTHER HAZARDS not covered by ice or containing objects dangerous to shipping ○ *open water* **27** NOT CLOSED OR MUTED not closed off at the end, stopped by a finger, or covered with a mute ○ *an open organ pipe* **28** FROSTLESS mild and free of frost **29** KNOWN TO BE UNDEFENDED publicly declared not to be garrisoned or defended in wartime ○ *an open city* **30** AVAILABLE WITHOUT LIMITATIONS freely available without restrictions ○ *open credit* **31** CURRENTLY ACTIVE active and with transactions being made ○ *an open bank account* **32** HAVING UNUSUALLY

WIDE SPACES with wide spacing between printed lines **33 ENDING IN A VOWEL** describes a syllable that ends in a vowel **34 HAVING SEPARATE ELEMENTS** describes a compound word formed by two or more words that are spelled separately and without hyphenation **35 WITHOUT PAWNS** not having pawns as part of a file **36 HAVING THE FRONT FOOT BACK** in sports, having the front foot farther from the line along which the ball is to be hit than the back foot ○ *Adopting an open stance, he began hitting the ball to the opposite field.* **37 CONTAINING NO ENDPOINTS** describes a mathematical interval that contains neither of a set's endpoints **38 REFERRING TO SET QUALITY** describes a mathematical set that has at least one neighbourhood of every point within the set **39 SERVING AS A COMPLEMENT TO A CLOSED SET** describes a mathematical set that is in a complementary relation to a closed set ■ *v* **1** *vti* **UNFASTEN FROM LOCKED OR CLOSED POSITION** to change position or move so as to allow access, or change the position of or move something such as a door or window in order to allow access **2** *vt* **UNSEAL OR UNFASTEN** to remove or unseal the lid, cork, or other device that keeps something such as a container closed **3** *vt* **UNWRAP** to reveal the contents of something, e.g. by removing its wrapping ○ *I opened the parcel.* **4** *vti* **UNFOLD TO SHOW INSIDE** to unfold something or spread it apart so that the inner part is revealed ○ *Open your books at page 75.* **5** *vti* **PART THE LIPS OR EYELIDS** to move apart, or move the lips or eyelids apart **6** *vti* **START TRADING** to start selling, trading, or doing business, or allow clients or customers access in order to buy, trade, or do business **7** *vti* **GET UNDER WAY** to start something formally ○ *She opened the meeting with a speech about the environment.* **8** *vt* **START AN ACCOUNT** to start an active banking or investment account **9** *vt* **DECLARE TO BE IN OPERATION OR SESSION** to make an official and usually public declaration that something is now ready for use or in session ○ *The sports centre was officially opened by the mayor.* **10** *vi* **BEGIN SHOWING TO THE PUBLIC** to start being shown to or performed for the general public for the first time ○ *The show opens on Friday.* **11** *vt* **BECOME ACCESSIBLE TO THE PUBLIC** to be visited by the public, or become accessible to the public ○ *The house opens to the public in August.* **12** *vt* **REMOVE OBSTRUCTIONS** to allow people free access when formerly this was denied or obstructed ○ *The country had finally opened its borders to the West.* **13** *vi* **GIVE ACCESS TO A PLACE** to provide access directly to another place (*refers to part of a building*) ○ *The bedroom opened onto a large living room.* **14** *vti* **BE READY FOR NEW IDEAS** to become or make somebody ready to accept new ideas ○ *Try opening your mind a bit.* **15** *vi* **BEGIN TO RAIN** to produce a downpour ○ *The heavens opened.* **16** *vi* **UNFOLD** to open out fully (*refers to flowers or leaves*) ○ *The daffodils will open soon.* **17** *vt* **EMPTY BOWELS** to cause the bowels to evacuate **18** *vi* **START TRADING AT A PARTICULAR VALUE** to have a particular value at the start of a day's trading on a stock exchange **19** *vt Malaysia, Singapore, Philippines* **SWITCH SOMETHING ON** to switch on something such as a light or an electrical appliance ■ *n* **1 COMPETITION ANYONE CAN ENTER** a competition or championship in which anybody, amateur or professional, can compete **2 OUTSIDE** a large and unobstructed outdoor space ○ *in the open* **3 UNCONCEALED STATE** the state of being no longer hidden or held back ○ *It's good to get all the facts out in the open.* [Old English, < Indo-European, 'up from under, over'] —**openness** *n*

open out *v* **1** *vi* **WIDEN** to become wider ○ *The track opened out into a clearing.* **2** *vti* **UNFOLD** to unfold or spread out something, or be unfolded or spread out **3** *vi* **DEVELOP FROM BUD TO FLOWER** to uncurl from a bud into a fully open flower or leaf, or cause a bud to do this **4** *vi* **BECOME LESS INTROVERTED** to become more sociable, outgoing, and communicative

open up *v* **1** *vi* **UNFOLD** to expand or unfold, e.g. before a viewer **2** *vti* **MAKE SOMETHING ACCESSIBLE** to make something more accessible or available to a wider range of people **3** *vt* **MAKE AN OPENING IN** to make an opening in something, especially in order to get access **4** *vt* **REMOVE A COVER OR OBSTRUCTION FROM** to remove the wrapping, restrictions, obstructions, or covering from something **5** *vti* = **open** *v.* 6 ○ *A new video store is opening up next week* **6** *vi* **SPEAK FREELY** to speak honestly, especially about personal feelings or experiences ○ *She opens up when she gets to know you.* **7** *vi* **TELL WHAT YOU KNOW** to confess to a crime or give information about a crime under coercion (*informal*) **8** *vi* **START SHOOTING A WEAPON** to start firing or cause a gun or other weapon to start firing **9** *vti* **OPEN BUSINESS FOR THE TRADING** to unlock something, especially a shop or business premises, so that trading can begin **10** *vi* **MAKE A VEHICLE GO FASTER** to cause a motor vehicle to accelerate, or travel at an accelerated speed (*informal*) **11** *vti* **BECOME OR MAKE SOMETHING MORE EXCITING** to become, or cause something to become, more interesting or exciting ○ *After the first goal the match opened up.*

open adoption *n* an arrangement when a child has been adopted by which contact between the child's adoptive and biological parents is maintained

open-air *adj* situated or happening outside a building

open-and-shut *adj* simple and easily resolved ○ *an open-and-shut case*

open bar *n US* a bar at a party, wedding, or other social function where the drinks are served free of charge

open book *n* somebody or something that is very easy to understand or about which everything is known

open-cast *adj* describes a method of mining in which minerals or other materials are excavated from the surface rather than deep underground ○ *open-cast mining*

open chain *adj* an arrangement of atoms in a molecule in which the atoms are not joined at the ends to form a ring

open cluster *n* a loosely scattered group of related and typically relatively young stars, e.g. the Pleiades

open court *n* a trial or court that is open to members of the public, and whose proceedings are recorded

open day *n* a day on which an institution such as a school or university is open to the public for visitors to view aspects of its work and activities. US term **open house** *n.* 2

open door *n* (*hyphenated before nouns*) **1** a policy whereby a nation allows free and unrestricted trade with all other nations **2** free and unrestricted access at all times ○ *open-door management*

open-end *adj US* LAW = **open-ended** *adj.* 4

open-ended *adj* **1 WITH NO PREARRANGED END** with no planned or defined end **2 EASILY MODIFIED** not definite and easily changed ○ *We'd left everything pretty open-ended about the holidays.* **3 NEEDING MORE THAN ONE WORD ANSWER** requiring or allowing an answer that is fuller than a simple yes or no ○ *an open-ended question* **4 HAVING NO LIMITS** not having a fixed limit in either time or amount ○ *an open-ended contract.* US term **open-end** *adj.* —**open-endedly** *adv* —**open-endedness** *n*

opener /ṓpənər/ *n* **1 OPENING DEVICE** a device for opening containers such as tins, cans, or bottles **2 INITIAL EVENT** somebody or something that begins a discussion or event (*informal*) **3 OPENING PLAYER** an opener of the bidding, betting, or play in a card game **4 FIRST GAME** the first game in a series or season ■ **openers** *npl* **STARTING POINT** a starting position or point, e.g. cards that allow somebody to begin the betting in some card games ◇ **for openers** used to open a statement or discussion (*informal*)

open-eyed *adj* **1 WATCHFUL** alert to all that is happening **2 WITH EYES WIDE IN WONDER** with the eyes wide open in wonder or surprise **3 ASSESSING REALISTICALLY** realistic in knowing and accepting all aspects of a situation

open-faced *adj* with a face that suggests an honest, straightforward, and sincere character

open-faced sandwich *n US* FOOD = **open sandwich**

openhanded /ṓpən hándid/ *adj* generous with money or other material things —**openhandedly** *adv* —**openhandedness** *n*

openhearted /ṓpən haártid/ *adj* sincere and generous in spirit towards other people —**openheartedly** *adv* —**openheartedness** *n*

open-hearth *adj* describes a steel-making process that uses a furnace with a shallow hearth and a low roof (**reverberatory furnace**) to produce high-quality steel

open-heart surgery *n* heart surgery during which the heart is exposed and blood is circulated outside the body by mechanical means

open house *n* **1** a situation or occasion when visitors are welcome at any time ○ *It's open house here – come over whenever you like!* **2** *US* EDUC = **open day**

opening /ṓpəning/ *n* **1 GAP** a gap or hole in something, especially one through which you can see or through which people or animals can pass ○ *We found an opening in the fence.* **2 FIRST PART** the first part of something ○ *The movie has a wonderful opening.* **3 FIRST TIME OF USE** the often formal occasion when something new such as a building or road is used for the first time, or when something starts again after stopping for some time (*often before nouns*) ○ *the opening ceremony* **4 FIRST PERFORMANCE FOR THE GENERAL PUBLIC** the first public performance or showing of a play, exhibition, or other production (*often before nouns*) **5 OPPORTUNITY** an opportunity to do something ○ *It gave her an opening to say how delighted she was.* **6 VACANCY** a job that is available ○ *We have an opening for a young person with drive and enthusiasm.* **7 ACT OF OPENING** the act of opening something **8** *US* **CLEARING IN WOODS** an area in a wood or forest in which trees do not grow **9 BEGINNING OF A GAME** the first moves of a game, especially in chess and draughts **10 FIRST STATEMENT BY COUNSEL IN TRIAL** the initial statement made by the prosecuting and defending barristers in a trial, before witnesses are called to give evidence

opening night *n* ARTS = **first night**

opening time *n* the time at which pubs in the United Kingdom are legally allowed to start serving alcohol

open interval *n* in mathematics, a set of real numbers consisting of all numbers between but excluding its endpoints, usually written (a,b) or]a,b[

open-jaw *adj* describes a flight or flight booking that goes to one destination and returns from another and is booked as a round-trip ticket

open learning *n* a system of further education that allows people to learn on a flexible part-time basis (*often before nouns*) ○ *open learning courses*

open letter *n* a letter that is addressed to an individual or organization but is intended for everybody to read and is published in a newspaper or magazine

openly /ṓpənli/ *adv* without making any attempt at concealment ○ *Many members were openly hostile to the proposed plan.*

open market *n* a market with no commercial restrictions that allows free competition between buyers and sellers

open marriage *n* a marriage in which each partner agrees to allow the other to engage in sexual relationships with other people

open-minded *adj* free from prejudice and receptive to new ideas —**open-mindedly** *adv* —**open-mindedness** *n*

open-mouthed *adj* **1** with the mouth wide open in surprise or wonder **2** loudly and persistently demanding or complaining —**open-mouthedly** *adv* —**open-mouthedness** *n*

open-necked *adj* with the top button unfastened ○ *an open-necked shirt*

open-plan *adj* having a large space left open rather than divided up into smaller units, especially in a workplace

open prison *n* a prison with security measures that are appropriate to inmates who are not dangerous and are unlikely to try to escape

open punctuation *n* minimal punctuation, especially minimal use of commas

open sandwich *n* a sandwich consisting of a single slice of bread with filling on it but no second piece of bread on top, sometimes eaten with a knife and fork. US term **open-faced sandwich**

open season *n* **1** a period during the year when certain restrictions concerning the hunting and killing of game or the catching of fish are lifted **2** a period of unrestrained attack or criticism (*informal*) ○ *It seems to be open season on lawyers at the moment.*

open secret *n* something that is supposed to be secret but in actual fact is widely known

open sentence *n* a formula containing a free variable, e.g. 'X is human', that cannot be said to be true or false because the referent of the variable is not determined

open sesame /-séssəmi/ *n* a sure means of gaining access to or obtaining something [< the magical words used by Ali Baba, a character in the *Arabian Nights*, to open the door of the robbers' cave]

open set *n* a mathematical set that is included within a particular topology

open shop *n* a workplace where being a member of a union, or of a specified union, is not a condition of being employed. ◊ **closed shop, union shop**

open side *n* in rugby, the side of the field that lies between a scrum and the farther touchline. ◊ **blind side** *n.* 2 —**open-side** *adj*

open-skies, open-sky *adj* allowing aircraft belonging to any nation the freedom to fly over an area, and therefore placing no restrictions on aerial surveillance of military installations

open slather *n ANZ* a situation in which there are no limits or constraints on behaviour (*informal*)

open society *n* a society in which there is freedom of thought, ideas, speech, and communication

⚡**open system** *n* a computer design system with uniform industry standards, compatible with any similar type of system or part

open-toe, open-toed *adj* describes a shoe, especially a sandal, that is not closed at the front, allowing the toes to be seen

open-top, open-topped *adj* describes cars and buses that have no roof or that have the roof removed

⚡**open trading protocol** *n* a standardized computer protocol for payment-related transactions such as purchase agreements, receipts, and payment methods (*in e-commerce*)

Open University *n* a university, founded in 1969, offering degree courses primarily by correspondence to mature students studying part-time and having many classes that are broadcast on TV and radio (*often before nouns*) ◊ **distance learning**

open verdict *n* in a coroner's court, the verdict given when the cause of death is not clear and no charge of murder or manslaughter can therefore be brought

open water *n* **1** an expanse of water that is not enclosed or obstructed **2** *Can* the springtime melting of ice on rivers and lakes, or the time when this happens

openwork /ṓpən wurk/ *n* **1** decorative items that make use of patterns of holes, e.g. wrought-iron work, fretwork, or lace **2** an embroidery technique in which holes are formed in a fabric by cutting or pulling threads and embellishing with various stitches, or embroidery made in this way

opera[1] /óppərə/ *n* **1 MUSICAL DRAMA** a dramatic work where music is a dominant part of the performance **2 OPERAS IN GENERAL** operas thought of collectively or as an art form **3 OPERATIC SCORE** the musical score or libretto of an operatic work **4** MUSIC = **opera house** [Mid-17C. Via Italian < Latin, 'works' < *opus* (see OPUS).]

opera[2] plural of **opus**

operable /óppərəb'l/ *adj* **1** capable of being treated by surgery **2** capable of being done or put into practice —**operability** /óppərə bílləti/ *n* —**operably** /óppərəbli/ *adv*

opéra bouffe /óppərə bóof/ (*plural* **opéras bouffes** /óppərə bóof/) *n* **1** an opera with a comic or farcical theme **2** opéra bouffes thought of collectively or as an art form [< French, 'comic opera'; translation of Italian *opera buffa*]

opera buffa /óppərə bóofə/ (*plural* **opera buffas** *or* **opere buffe** /óppə ray bóo fay/) *n* a comic opera of the kind that originated in Italy in the 18th century, using themes or characters from everyday life and usually having a happy ending [< Italian, 'comic opera']

opéra comique /óppərə ko méek/ (*plural* **opéras comiques**) *n* an opera on a light-hearted theme with spoken dialogue, especially popular in 19th-century France [< French, 'comic opera']

opera glasses *npl* small decorative low-powered binoculars for use by people in the audience at theatrical, operatic, or ballet performances

operagoer /óppərə gō ər/ *n* a regular attender at opera performances

opera hat *n* a man's collapsible top hat that is spring-operated

opera house *n* a theatre that is designed for putting on operas, often grander in style than an ordinary theatre

⚡**operand** /óppə rand/ *n* **1** a quantity, function, or other entity that is to have a mathematical operation performed on it **2** the portion of a computer instruction that specifies the location in memory of the data to be manipulated [Late 19C. < Latin *operandum* 'thing to be worked on' < *operari* (see OPERATE).]

operant /óppərənt/ *n* **1 PERFORMER OF AN OPERATION** somebody or something that operates or that carries out some kind of operation **2 VOLUNTARY ACTION** in learning theory, an action or other unit of behaviour that does not appear to have a stimulus ■ *adj* **HAVING EFFECT** producing a specified effect [Early 17C. < Latin *operant-*, present participle of *operari* (see OPERATE).] —**operantly** *adv*

operant conditioning *n* a form of learning that takes place when an instance of spontaneous behaviour is either reinforced by a reward or discouraged by punishment

opera seria /óppərə séeri ə/ (*plural* **opere serie** /óppəray séeri ay/) *n* **1** an opera that has a serious theme, often one taken from classical mythology, and usually a tragic ending **2** opere serie thought of collectively or as an art form [< Italian, 'serious opera']

operate /óppə rayt/ (**-ates, -ating, -ated**) *v* **1** *vti* **DO OR FUNCTION** to function or work, or make something function or work **2** *vti* **MANAGE OR BE MANAGED** to exist as a working business or organization, or oversee the running of a working business or organization **3** *vi* **PERFORM SURGERY** to perform surgery on a person or animal **4** *vi* **EXERT AN EFFECT** to have an effect or influence on somebody or something **5** *vi* **PERFORM MILITARY MANOEUVRES** to carry out military manoeuvres **6** *vi* **TRADE IN THE FINANCIAL MARKET** to trade or deal in securities or commodities on the stock exchange **7** *vi* **ENGAGE IN ILLEGAL ACTIVITIES** to be active in some illegal or underhand business [Early 17C. < Latin *operat-*, past participle of *operari* 'work' < *oper-*, stem of *opus* 'work'.]

~~**operater**~~ incorrect spelling of **operator**

operatic /óppə ráttik/ *adj* **1** belonging or relating to opera **2** overly or flamboyantly extravagant, especially in behaviour [Mid-18C. < OPERA[1], after DRAMATIC.] —**operatically** *adv*

operatics /óppə ráttiks/ *n* flamboyantly exaggerated or extravagant behaviour (+ *singular or plural verb*)

operating cycle *n* the period of time from when somebody purchases a product to when proceeds from its sale are received

operating room, operating suite *n US* MED = **operating theatre**

⚡**operating system** *n* the essential program in a computer that maintains disk files, runs applications, and handles devices such as the mouse and printer

operating table *n* a table on which somebody undergoing a surgical operation lies

operating theatre *n* a room in a hospital where surgical operations are performed. US term **operating room**

⚡**operation** /óppə ráysh'n/ *n* **1 CONTROL** the controlling of something, or the managing of the way it works **2 FUNCTIONING STATE** the state of functioning or of being in effect ○ *The ban is to be put into operation from next week.* **3 SOMETHING DONE** something that is carried out, especially something difficult or complex ○ *the tricky operation of removing the sting* **4 SURGICAL INTERVENTION** any surgical procedure, e.g. one carried out to repair damage to a body part **5 ORGANIZED ACTION** an organized campaign, manoeuvre, or other form of action, especially one carried out by a rescue team **6 operation, Operation MILITARY ACTION** an action conducted by military forces that can range in scope from a reconnaissance mission to an entire campaign (*often before nouns*) ○ *Operation Desert Storm* **7 MATHEMATICAL PROCESS** a mathematical process such as subtraction, multiplication, or differentiation in which certain entities are derived from others through the application of rules **8 SINGLE PART OF COMPUTER PROGRAM** a series of actions performed by a computer, defined by an instruction and forming part of a computer program **9 BUSINESS DEAL** a business deal or financial transaction **10 ILLEGAL BUSINESS** an illegal, dishonest, or underhand business ■ **operations** *npl* **CONTROLLING OF ORGANIZED ACTIVITIES** the supervising, monitoring, and coordinating of the activities of a military or civilian organization (*often before nouns*)

operational /óppə ráysh'nəl/ *adj* **1 ABLE TO BE USED** in proper working order and able to be used ○ *The new transport link will be fully operational next month.* **2 OF OPERATING** relating to the operating of something or to the way it operates **3 COMBAT-READY** ready for combat or manoeuvres —**operationally** *adv*

operational amplifier *n* an amplifier with high gain and high stability that is controlled by way of externally connected negative-feedback circuits

operationalism /óppə ráysh'nəlizəm/, **operationism** /-sh'nizəm/ *n* the view that terms for scientific concepts should be defined in terms of the scientific operations, e.g. measuring or observing, performed to establish or disprove them —**operationalist** *n, adj* —**operationalistic** /óppə ráysh'nə lístik/ *adj*

operational research *n* MANAGEMT = **operations research**

operationism *n* PHILOS = **operationalism**

operations research *n* analysis of the problems that exist in complex systems such as those used to run a business or a military campaign, designed to give a scientific basis for decision-making

operatise *vt* = **operatize**

operative /óppərətiv/ *adj* **1 IN EFFECT** in place and having an effect, especially the right or desired effect **2 SIGNIFICANT** carrying a special meaning or significance **3 OF SURGERY** relating to or resulting from a surgical procedure ■ *n* **1 SKILLED WORKER** a skilled worker, especially in a manufacturing industry **2 WORKER** somebody who performs a particular task or who works in a particular field (*formal or humorous*) ○ *a rodent operative* **3 POLITICAL WORKER** an employee of a political party who works in any behind-the-scenes capacity, e.g. political troubleshooting or manipulation of media stories **4** *US* **DETECTIVE** a private detective **5** *US* **SPY** a spy or secret agent —**operatively** *adv* —**operativeness** *n* —**operativity** /óppərə tívvəti/ *n*

operatize /óppərə tīz/ (**-tizes, -tizing, -tized**), **operatise** (**-tises, -tising, -tised**) *vt* to make an opera out of an existing novel, play, or other text [Mid-19C. < OPERA[1], after DRAMATIZE.]

operator /óppə raytər/ *n* **1 SOMEBODY OPERATING** a person who operates machinery, an instrument, or other equipment **2 BUSINESS OWNER OR MANAGER** an owner or manager of a business or other commercial enterprise **3 STOCK-EXCHANGE DEALER** a dealer on the stock exchange or in a money market, especially somebody who is aggressive or speculative **4 MANIPULATIVE PERSON** a person who behaves in a devious or manipulative way, especially in order to gain something (*informal*) ○ *a smooth operator* **5 SOMETHING EFFECTING MATHEMATICAL OPERATION** a mathematical symbol, term, or other entity that performs or describes an operation, e.g. a multiplication or subtraction sign

operculum /ō púrkyŏoləm/ (*plural* **-la** /-lə/ *or* **-lums**) *n* **1 MUCUS PLUG IN CERVIX** the plug of mucus that fills the opening of a woman's cervix while she is pregnant **2 GILL-COVERING FLAP** the flexible bony flap covering the gills of bony fishes **3 FLAP IN MOSSES AND FUNGI** a flap covering an aperture in the spore capsules of mosses and some fungi **4 SEAL ON MOLLUSC'S SHELL** a rounded plate that seals the mouth of the shell of some gastropod molluscs when the animal's body is inside [Early 18C. < Latin, 'lid' < *operire* 'to cover'.] —**opercular** *adj* —**operculary** *adv* —**operculate** /-lət/ *adj* —**operculated** /-laytid/ *adj*

opere buffe plural of **opera buffa**

opere serie plural of **opera seria**

operetta /óppə réttə/ *n* a theatrical production, usually with a comic theme, similar to opera but with much spoken dialogue and usually some dancing [Late 18C. < Italian, 'small opera' < *opera* (see OPERA[1]).] —**operettist** *n*

operon /óppə ron/ *n* in bacteria, a segment of a chromosome containing the genes that specify the structure of a given protein, alongside the genes that regulate its manufacture [Mid-20C. < French *opéron* < *opérer* 'to work' < Latin *operari* (see OPERATE).]

operose /óppə rōss/ *adj* (*formal*) **1** requiring a lot of effort **2** busy, active, or hard working [Late 17C. < Latin *operosus* < *oper-*, stem of *opus* (see OPUS).] —**operosely** *adv* —**operoseness** *n*

Ophelia /ə féeli ə/ *n* a very small inner natural satellite of Uranus

ophicleide /óffi klīd/ *n* a musical instrument resembling and superseded by the bass tuba [Mid-19C. < French *ophicléide* < Greek *ophis* 'snake' + *kleid-* 'key'; from its resemblance to an earlier instrument called a 'serpent'.]

ophidian /ō fíddi ən/ *adj* **1** belonging or relating to snakes **2** resembling a snake in appearance, habits, or movement [Early 19C. < modern Latin *Ophidia* < Greek *ophid-* 'snake'.] —**ophidian** *n*

ophiolite /óffi ə līt/ *n* any igneous and metamorphic rock that was formed from deep-sea sediment [Mid-19C. < Greek *ophis* 'snake' + -LITE; from its snaky texture.]

Ophiuchus /o fyóokəss/ *n* a large constellation near the celestial equator. See illustration at **constellation**

ophthal. *abbr* **1** ophthalmologist **2** ophthalmology

ophthalm- *prefix* = **ophthalmo-** (*before vowels*)

ophthalmia /of thálmi ə/ *n* inflammation of the eye, especially of the conjunctiva and surrounding area [14C. < late Latin, < Greek, from *ophthalmos* 'eye' (see OPHTHALMO-).]

ophthalmic /of thálmik/ *adj* relating to the eyes, or located in the region of the eye

ophthalmic optician *n* = **optician** *n.* 1

ophthalmitis /óf thal mítiss/ *n* inflammation of the eye

ophthalmo- *prefix* eye, eyeball ○ *ophthalmoscope* [< Greek *ophthalmos* < Indo-European, 'see']

ophthalmol. *abbr* 1 ophthalmologist 2 ophthalmology

ophthalmology /óf thal mólləji/ *n* the branch of medicine that is concerned with the diagnosis and treatment of eye diseases and conditions —**ophthalmological** /of thálmə lójjik'l/ *adj* —**ophthalmologically** *adv* —**ophthalmologist** *n*

ophthalmoscope /of thálmə skōp/ *n* a medical instrument used for examining the inside of the eye to detect changes to the retina, e.g. those associated with diabetes and hypertension —**ophthalmoscopy** /óf thal móskəpi/ *n* —**ophthalmoscopic** /of thálmə skóppik/ *adj* —**ophthalmoscopically** *adv*

Ophuls /óff'lz/, **Opüls, Max** (1902–57) German-born French film director. Born **Maximilian Oppenheimer**

-opia *suffix* condition or defect of vision ○ *hyperopia* ○ *protanopia* [< Greek, < *ops* 'eye, face' < Indo-European, 'see']

opiate /ópi ət/ *n* 1 **OPIUM-CONTAINING DRUG** a drug such as morphine or heroin that contains opium or an opium derivative 2 **SLEEP-INDUCING SUBSTANCE** a drug, hormone, or other substance capable of inducing sleep-like effects similar to those of opium or its derivatives 3 **SOMETHING WITH DULLING EFFECT** something that has a relaxing, pacifying, or dulling effect ■ *adj* 1 **CONTAINING OPIUM** containing opium or an opium derivative 2 **BORING** mind-numbingly unexciting, especially because of being simplistic, cliché-ridden, or formulaic ■ *vt* (**-ates, -ating, -ated**) 1 **TREAT WITH OPIATE** to treat somebody, or somebody's symptoms, with an opiate 2 **DEADEN OR DULL** to dull or deaden pain, anguish, or some other unwanted condition [15C. < medieval Latin *opiatus* < Latin *opium* (see OPIUM).]

opine /ō pín/ (**opines, opining, opined**) *vti* to express an opinion (*formal*) [15C. < Latin *opinari* 'suppose, believe'.]

opinion /ə pínnyən/ *n* 1 **PERSONAL VIEW** the view somebody takes about a certain issue, especially when it is based solely on personal judgement ○ *In my opinion it's all a waste of time.* 2 **ESTIMATION** a view regarding the worth of somebody or something ○ *They had a pretty low opinion of me.* 3 **EXPERT VIEW** an expert assessment of something ○ *I told the doctor I wanted a second opinion.* 4 **BODY OF GENERALLY HELD VIEWS** general assessment, judgement, or evaluation ○ *pundits and other opinion formers* 5 **CONCLUSION OF FACT** a conclusion drawn from observation of the facts [14C. Via French < Latin *opinion-* < *opinari* 'suppose'.] ◇ **be a matter of opinion** to be open to dispute or debate ◇ **be of the opinion that** to think that something is the case

opinionated /ə pínnyə naytid/ *adj* always ready to express opinions and tending to hold to them stubbornly, unreasonably dismissing other people's views —**opinionatedly** *adv* —**opinionatedness** *n*

opinionative /ə pínnyənətiv/ *adj* (*formal*) 1 relating to opinions or to the stating of them 2 = **opinionated** —**opinionatively** *adv* —**opinionativeness** *n*

opinion poll *n* a survey carried out to discover what the general public think about something

opioid /ópi oyd/ *n* any opium-containing substance that is produced naturally in the brain ■ *adj* similar in effect or properties to opium but not derived from opium [Mid-20C. < OPIUM.]

opioid peptide *n* a naturally occurring peptide that has pain-relieving and sedative effects

opisthobranch /ə pís thə brangk/ *n* any marine gastropod mollusc that has gills, a small or nonexistent shell, and tentacles [Mid-19C. < modern Latin *Opisthobranchiata* < Greek *opisthen* 'behind' + *bragkhia* 'gills', because the gills are behind the heart.]

opisthognathous /óppiss thógnəthəss/ *adj* having jaws that slope backwards or mouthparts that face backwards [Mid-19C. < Greek *opisthen* 'behind'.] —**opisthognathism** *n*

opisthosoma /o píss thə sṓmə/ *n* the rear section of the body of a spider or other arachnid [< Greek *opisthen* 'behind' + *sōma* 'body']

opium /ṓpi əm/ *n* 1 a brownish gummy extract from the unripe seed pods of the opium poppy that contains several highly addictive narcotic alkaloid substances, e.g. morphine and codeine 2 something that has a stupefying, numbing, or sleep-inducing effect ○ *soap operas dismissed as the opium of a bored populace* [14C. Via Latin < Greek *opion* 'poppy juice' < *opos* 'vegetable juice'.]

opium den *n* a place where opium is sold and smoked, especially one that has facilities where people using the drug can stay while under its influence

opium poppy *n* a poppy with greyish-green leaves, grown as a source of opium. Flowers: pink, red, or white. Native to: Europe, Asia. *Papaver somniferum.*

~~**oponent**~~ incorrect spelling of **opponent**

Oporto = **Porto**

~~**oportunity**~~ incorrect spelling of **opportunity**

~~**oposite**~~ incorrect spelling of **opposite**

opossum /ə póssəm/ (*plural* **-sums** *or* **-sum**) *n* 1 a small nocturnal tree-dwelling marsupial with dense fur, a long snout, and a hairless prehensile tail. Native to: United States, Central and South America. *Didelphis marsupialis.* 2 any one of several similar marsupials that are mostly nocturnal plant-eating tree-dwellers. Native to: Australia, New Zealand. Family: Phalangeridae. [Early 17C. < Virginia Algonquian *opassom* < *op* 'white' + *assom* 'dog, doglike creature'.]

opossum shrimp *n* a crustacean that resembles a shrimp, the female of which carries the eggs and newly-hatched young in a brood pouch just below the thorax. Order: Mysidacae.

opp. *abbr* opposite

Oppenheimer /óppən hīmər/, **J. Robert** (1904–67) US nuclear physicist, leader of the team that developed the atomic bomb. Full name **Julius Robert Oppenheimer**

~~**opperation**~~ incorrect spelling of **operation**

Opperman /óppərmən/, **Sir Hubert Ferdinand** (1904–96) Australian cyclist

OPP film *n* plastic film used for packaging. Abbr of **oriented polypropylene**

oppidan /óppidən/ *adj* belonging to, relating to, or found in a town, often the town in which a university is sited as distinct from the university itself (*formal*) ■ *n* a resident of a town (*formal*) [Mid-16C. < Latin *oppidanus* < *oppidum* 'fort, town'.]

oppilate /óppi layt/ (**-lates, -lating, -lated**) *vt* to block up a body passage such as a duct or a body opening such as a pore [15C. < Latin *oppilat-*, past participle of *oppilare* 'stop up' < *pilare* 'heap up' < *pila* 'heap of stones'.] —**oppilation** /óppi láysh'n/ *n*

~~**oppinion**~~ incorrect spelling of **opinion**

opponent /ə pṓnənt/ *n* 1 **RIVAL IN CONTEST** a person or team faced in a competition, debate, battle, or other contest 2 **SOMEBODY OPPOSING** a person who opposes a course of action, or a cause or belief ○ *a fierce opponent of reform of the voting system* 3 **OPPOSING MUSCLE** any muscle that counteracts the motion of another ■ *adj* 1 **CONTRARY** working or arguing against something 2 **CONTRADICTORY** serving to contradict something [Late 16C. < Latin *opponent-*, present participle of *opponere* 'set against' < *ponere* 'to place'.] —**opponency** *n*

opportune /óppər tyoon/ *adj* suitable for a purpose, or occurring at just the right time [15C. Via French < Latin *opportunus* 'favourable' (used of the wind) < *ob portum veniens* 'coming towards port'.] —**opportunely** *adv* —**opportuneness** *n*

opportunist /óppər tyóonist/ *n* a person who takes advantage of something, especially somebody who does so in a devious, unscrupulous, or unprincipled way ■ *adj* = **opportunistic** —**opportunism** *n*

opportunistic /óppərtyoo nístik/, **opportunist** /óppər tyóonist/ *adj* 1 resourcefully taking advantage of all opportunities or situations, especially in a devious, unscrupulous, or unprincipled way 2 describes a microorganism or relatively minor disease that is not normally serious but that can become pathogenic or life-threatening when the host has a low level of immunity ○ *opportunistic infections* —**opportunistically** *adv*

opportunity /óppər tyóonəti/ (*plural* **-ties**) *n* 1 a chance, especially one that offers some kind of advantage 2 a combination of favourable circumstances or situations

opportunity cost *n* the cost of a commercial decision regarded as the value of the alternative that is forgone

opportunity shop *n ANZ* full form of **op shop**

opposable /ə pṓzəb'l/ *adj* 1 **RESISTIBLE** capable of being opposed or resisted 2 **ABLE TO BE PLACED OPPOSITE** capable of being put in a position that is opposite something else 3 **TOUCHING THE END OF ANOTHER DIGIT** describes a thumb or big toe that can face and touch the end of one or more of the other digits of the same hand or foot —**opposability** /ə pṓzə bílləti/ *n* —**opposably** *adv*

oppose /ə pṓz/ (**-poses, -posing, -posed**) *v* 1 *vti* **STAND IN OPPOSITION** to be against something or to take an active stance against something ○ *would not state openly that they oppose violence* 2 *vt* **SET IN CONTRAST TO** to set something up as a contrast to something else 3 *vt* **PUT OPPOSITE TO** to put one thing in a position directly facing another 4 *vt* **COMPETE WITH AS OPPONENTS** to be in competition, conflict, or battle with another person, team, or fighting force [14C. < French *opposer*, an alteration (influenced by *poser* 'place') of Latin *opponere* (see OPPONENT).] —**opposer** *n* —**opposing** *adj*

opposed /ə pṓzd/ *adj* disagreeing with or taking an active stance against somebody or something ○ *a government opposed to change of any sort* ◇ **as opposed to** used to introduce something that is in contrast or is distinct

opposed-cylinder engine *n* an engine in which cylinders or banks of cylinders are mounted on opposite sides of the crankcase in the same plane, with their connecting rods mounted on a common crankshaft

opposite /óppəzit/ *adj* 1 **ON THE FACING SIDE** on the side that faces something, or at the farthest distance possible from something 2 **FACING AWAY** pointing, facing, or moving away from each other 3 **TOTALLY DIFFERENT** of the same general class yet completely different 4 **LEVEL WITH ON THE OTHER SIDE** describes plant parts, especially pairs of leaves or flowers, that grow at the same level on a stem but on either side of it 5 **FACING AN ANGLE** describes the side of a triangle facing a specified angle 6 **FACING EACH OTHER GEOMETRICALLY** describes sides or angles in an even-sided polygon that face each other ■ *n* 1 **SOMEBODY OR SOMETHING DIFFERENT FROM ANOTHER** somebody or something that is completely different from another or from what is expected 2 **ANTONYM** a word that has an opposite meaning ■ *adv* **IN THE OPPOSITE POSITION** in or into a position that is opposite ○ *They live directly opposite.* ■ *prep* 1 **ACROSS FROM** facing or across from something or somebody ○ *They moved to a house opposite the museum.* 2 **IN A COMPLEMENTING ACTING ROLE TO** in an acting role that corresponds to or complements another, especially when the two roles are played by people of different genders ○ *excited to be playing opposite the great star* [14C. Via French < Latin *oppositus*, past participle of *opponere* (see OPPONENT).] —**oppositely** *adv* —**oppositeness** *n*

opposite number *n* a person with a similar job or post as somebody else, especially in another department or organization

opposite prompt *n* in a theatre, the side of a stage that is to the actors' right when they face the audience. ◊ **stage right**

opposite sex *n* women when thought of collectively as opposed to men, or men when thought of collectively as opposed to women

opposition /óppə zísh'n/ *n* 1 **ACTIVELY HOSTILE ATTITUDE** an actively hostile attitude towards something, or a resistant stance against something ○ *Public opposition to the plan was growing.* 2 **SPORTS OPPONENT** a person or team that plays against another (*takes a singular or plural verb*) 3 **opposition, Opposition OUT-OF-POWER POLITICAL PARTY** a political party that is not in power (*often before nouns; takes a singular or plural verb*) 4 **LINGUISTIC CONTRAST** in linguistics, the contrast between two or more similar elements in a language 5 **PHONETIC CONTRAST BETWEEN SOUNDS** in phonetics, the contrast between two sounds that are articulated in a similar place in the mouth, e.g. between the voiced consonant /v/ and the voiceless consonant /f/ 6 **CHESS ADVANTAGE** a situation towards the end of a game of chess in which the two kings are in such a position that the opponent must make a king move and is therefore at a disadvantage 7 **RELATIONS BETWEEN LOGICAL PROPOSITIONS** the way in which logical propositions relate to each other 8 **MOON OR PLANET POSITION** the position of the Moon or one of the outer planets when it is on the opposite side of the Earth as seen from the Sun 9 **ASTRONOMICAL OBJECT ALIGNMENT** the position of two astronomical objects when they are diametrically opposite on the celestial sphere 10 **ASTROLOGICALLY OPPOSING PLANETARY POSITION** in astrology, a situation when two planets are 180° from each other, believed to cause friction or symbolize confrontation —**oppositional** *adj*

opposition research *n US* research done in order to discover damaging or detrimental information about somebody

oppress /ə préss/ *vt* **1** to subject a person or a people to a harsh or cruel form of domination **2** to be a source of worry, stress, or trouble to somebody [14C. < French *oppresser* < Latin *oppress-*, past participle of *opprimere* 'press against' < *premere* 'to press'.] —**oppression** *n* —**oppressor** *n*

oppressive /ə préssiv/ *adj* **1 DOMINATING HARSHLY** imposing a harsh or cruel form of domination ○ *an oppressive regime* **2 HIGHLY STRESSFUL** exerting a worrying, troubling, or burdensome pressure on somebody **3 STIFLING** so hot and humid as to make people feel tired, irritable, or sluggish —**oppressively** *adv* —**oppressiveness** *n*

opprobrium /ə próbri əm/ (*plural* **-a**) *n* **1 SCORN** scorn, contempt, or severe criticism **2 DISGRACE** shame or disgrace that stems from disreputable behaviour **3 SOURCE OF SHAME** something or somebody that brings shame or disgrace (*archaic*) ○ *'would render him an object of scorn and an opprobrium of the religion with which he had diligently associated himself'* (George Eliot, *Middlemarch*; 1872) [Mid-17C. < Latin, 'infamy, reproach' < *opprobare* 'to reproach' < *probrum* 'disgrace'.] —**opprobrious** *adj* —**opprobriously** *adv* —**opprobriousness** *n*

oppugn /ə pyóon/ *vt* to question the validity or truthfulness of something (*formal*) [15C. < Latin *oppugnare* 'fight against' < *pugnare* 'to fight'.] —**oppugner** *n*

~~**opression**~~ incorrect spelling of **oppression**

ops /ops/ *npl* the controlling of organized military or civilian activities (*informal; often before nouns*) ○ *Who's in the ops room tonight?* [Early 20C. Shortening of *operations*.]

op shop *n ANZ* a charity shop selling second-hand goods donated by members of the public (*informal*) [Shortening of opportunity shop]

opsin /ópsin/ *n* a light-sensitive pigment found in the rod cells of the eye [Mid-20C. Back-formation < RHODOPSIN.]

opsonic /op sónnik/ *adj* relating to or involving opsonins

opsonic index *n* a measure of the number of bacteria destroyed by certain blood cells, expressed as the ratio of opsonin in the infected patient's blood to the amount found in a healthy person's blood

opsonify *vt* BIOL = **opsonize**

opsonin /ópsənin/ *n* a protein fragment in blood that binds to the surface of an invading antibody and promotes its destruction by white blood cells [Early 20C. < Latin *opsonare* 'cater, buy provisions' < Greek *opsōnein* 'condiment'.]

opsonize /ópsə nīz/ (**-nizes, -nizing, -nized**), **opsonise** (**-nises, -nising, -nised**), **opsonify** /op sónni fī/ (**-fies, -fying, -fied**) *vt* to make foreign bodies such as bacteria susceptible to destruction by certain blood cells by coating them with opsonin —**opsonization** /ópsə nī záysh'n/ *n*

-opsy *suffix* examination ○ *biopsy* [< Greek *-opsia* 'sight' < *opsis* < Indo-European, 'see']

opt /opt/ *vi* to choose something or choose to do something, usually in preference to other available alternatives [Late 19C. Via French *opter* < Latin *optare* 'choose, desire'.]

opt out *vi* **1** to decide not to join in something or not to go along with something (*informal*) **2** to choose to manage financial and administrative affairs without any input or control from the relevant local authority (*refers to schools and hospitals*)

opt. *abbr* **1** optative **2** optical **3** optician **4** optics **5** optimum **6** optional

optative /óptətiv/ *adj* **1 OF CHOICE-MAKING** relating to the making of choices (*formal*) **2 OF GRAMMATICAL MOOD** describes a grammatical mood in Greek and some other languages that expresses wishes or desires, or a verb in this mood **3 CONTAINING A VERB EXPRESSING A WISH** describes a clause or sentence containing a verb expressing a wish or desire and in the subjunctive or optative mood ■ *n* **1 OPTATIVE MOOD** the optative mood of a verb **2 VERB IN THE OPTATIVE MOOD** a verb in the optative mood [Mid-16C. Via French < Latin *optativus* < *optare* 'choose, desire'.] —**optatively** *adv*

~~**opthalmology**~~ incorrect spelling of **ophthalmology**

optic /óptik/ *adj* **OF EYES** belonging or relating to the eyes, or situated in or near the eye ■ *n* **1 INSTRUMENT'S LENS** any lens or reflecting part in an optical instrument **2 EYE** an eye (*archaic*) [14C. Via French or medieval Latin < Greek *optikos* < *optos* 'seen, visible'.]

optical /óptik'l/ *adj* **1 OF VISIBLE LIGHT** relating to or producing light that can be seen **2 OF VISION** belonging or relating to the sense of sight **3 OF CORRECTIVE LENSES** describes a lens designed to correct or enhance faulty vision **4 LIGHT-SENSITIVE** describes an instrument or device that is sensitive to light **5 OF OPTICS** belonging or relating to the science of optics —**optically** *adv*

optical activity *n* the property of a crystal or a chemical solution of rotating the plane of polarized light that passes through it

optical art *n* full form of **op art**

optical brightener *n* a chemical substance used to make the whiteness or colour of fabrics brighter, e.g. in washing powders and liquids

ϟ **optical character reader** *n* a device for inputting material into a computer by digitizing the image of a printed page, identifying the characters, and storing them as machine code for further processing

ϟ **optical character recognition** *n* the use of light-sensing methods to identify printed and handwritten material and encode it in machine-readable form for inputting into a computer

ϟ **optical computer** *n* a proposed computer that uses optical switches, fibres, and laser light instead of wires, transistors, and printed circuits to achieve processing speeds far higher than those of conventional computers

ϟ **optical disk, optical disc** *n* a rigid computer storage disk with data stored as tiny pits in the plastic coating, readable by laser beam

optical double star *n* a pair of stars that appear to lie close together as viewed from the Earth

optical fibre *n* a fibre made of very pure glass or plastic that is used in modern communications systems to transmit information in the form of pulses of laser light. ◊ **fibre optics**

optical glass *n* any high-quality glass used in lenses for its superior refractive quality

optical illusion *n* **1** a visual experience in which there is some kind of false perception of what is actually there **2** something that causes an optical illusion, especially something drawn or designed deliberately to fool the eye

optical isomerism *n* the property exhibited by a pair of molecules that differ only in being mirror images of each other and rotate plane-polarized light in opposite directions when in solution —**optical isomer** *n*

ϟ **optical mouse** *n* a computer mouse that registers a change in position by detecting reflected light from a pair of light-emitting diodes and translating it into cursor movement

optical rotation *n* the rotation of plane-polarized light as it passes through an optically active medium

ϟ **optical scanner** *n* COMPUT = **scanner** *n.* **3**

optical sound *n* a form of sound reproduction in films that employs a photographed pattern of light on the film that is read by a lamp in the projector

optic axis *n* a line passing through a lens, a curved mirror, or a crystal along which light can travel without undergoing double refraction

optic chiasma *n* the X-shaped nerve tract beneath the brain where the optic nerves from each eye meet and that enables certain of their constituent nerve fibres to cross sides

optic cup *n* a two-walled depression in a human embryo that develops into the retina

optic disc *n* a small light-sensitive area of the retina marking the point where nerve fibres from the retinal cells converge to form the optic nerve

optician /op tísh'n/ *n* **1 QUALIFIED EYE EXAMINER** somebody who is qualified to examine eyes and prescribe corrective lenses. US term **optometrist 2 SHOP SELLING SPECTACLES** a shop where eye examinations are carried out, corrective lenses are prescribed, and spectacles and contact lenses are supplied and fitted **3** *US* **MAKER AND SELLER OF LENSES** a fitter and supplier of spectacles and contact lenses who does not examine eyes or prescribe corrective lenses

optic nerve *n* either of the paired second cranial nerves whose nerve fibres transmit visual light signals from the eye to the brain

optics /óptiks/ *n* the study of light or electromagnetic radiation in the visible, infrared, and ultraviolet regions (+ *singular verb*) ■ *npl* instruments used for detecting electromagnetic radiation and for attaining highly accurate long-range vision (+ *plural verb*)

optic vesicle *n* a fold of the embryonic forebrain that develops into the retina and optic nerve

optima plural of **optimum**

optimal /óptim'l/ *adj* most desirable or favourable ○ *waited for optimal weather conditions* [Late 19C. < Latin *optimus* 'best'.] —**optimality** /ópti mállәti/ *n* —**optimally** /óptim'li/ *adv*

optimise *vt* = **optimize**

optimism /óptimizəm/ *n* **1 TENDENCY TO EXPECT THE BEST** the tendency to believe, expect, or hope that things will turn out well **2 CONFIDENCE** the attitude of somebody who feels positive or confident **3 DOCTRINE THAT OUR WORLD IS BEST** a philosophical doctrine, first proposed by Leibnitz, that ours is the best of all possible worlds **4 BELIEF IN THE POWER OF GOOD** the belief that things are continually getting better and that good will ultimately triumph over evil [Mid-18C. < French *optimisme* < Latin *optimum* (see OPTIMUM).]

optimist /óptimist/ *n* **1** a person who tends to feel hopeful and positive about future outcomes **2** a follower of a philosophical doctrine of optimism

optimistic /ópti místik/ *adj* tending to take a hopeful and positive view of future outcomes —**optimistically** *adv*

ϟ **optimize** /ópti mīz/ (**-mizes, -mizing, -mized**), **optimise** (**-mises, -mising, -mised**) *vt* **1 ENHANCE EFFECTIVENESS OF** to make something function at its best or most effective, or use something to its best advantage **2 SOLVE IN BEST WAY POSSIBLE** to find the best possible solution to a technical problem in which there are a number of competing or conflicting considerations **3 WRITE PROGRAM CONCISELY** to write computer programming instructions for a task in as few lines as possible to maximize the speed and efficiency of program execution [Early 19C. < Latin *optimus* 'best'.] —**optimization** /ópti mī záysh'n/ *n*

optimum /óptiməm/ *n* (*plural* **-ma** /-mə/ *or* **-mums**) the best out of a number of possible options or outcomes ■ *adj* most desirable or favourable ○ *optimum trading conditions* [Late 19C. < Latin, 'best thing' < *optimus* 'best'.]

option /ópsh'n/ *n* **1 CHOICE** a choice that is or can be taken ○ *Several options were ruled out right away.* **2 FREEDOM OF CHOICE** the right, power, or freedom to make a choice ○ *I'd no option but to refuse.* **3 OPPORTUNITY AVAILABLE FOR A LIMITED TIME** an opportunity, usually a commercial opportunity, that has been made available for a limited period only **4 RIGHT TO BUY OR SELL** the right to buy or sell something, especially a stock-market commodity, at a specified price during a specified time period **5** POL = **local option 6 PIECE OF NONSTANDARD EQUIPMENT** an item of nonstandard equipment that can be purchased separately, e.g. on a car ■ *vt* **HAVE OR GIVE A RIGHT TO** to give or acquire an exclusive right to something [Mid-16C. Via French < Latin *option-* < *optare* 'choose, desire'.] ◇ **keep** *or* **leave your options open** to put off making a decision or selection until a later time

optional /ópsh'nəl/ *adj* left to individual choice ○ *It comes with optional air conditioning.* —**optionally** *adv*

opto- *prefix* **1** eye, vision ○ *optometry* **2** optical ○ *optoelectronics* [< Greek *optos* 'seen, visible']

optoelectronics /óptō i lek trónniks, -ellek-/ *n* the branch of electronics dealing with devices that generate, modulate, transmit, and sense electromagnetic radiation in the visible-light, infrared, and ultraviolet ranges (+ *singular verb*) [Mid-20C. < Greek *optos* 'seen, visible'.] —**optoelectronic** *adj*

optometrist /op tómmətrist/ *n* OPHTHALMOL = **optician** *n.* **1**

optometry /op tómmətri/ *n* the practice of examining eyes in order to determine levels of vision and then prescribing and supplying any necessary corrective lenses [Late 19C. < Greek *optos* 'seen, visible' (see OPTIC) + -METRY.] —**optometer** *n* —**optometric** /óptə méttrik/ *adj*

~~**optomist**~~ incorrect spelling of **optimist**

~~**optomistic**~~ incorrect spelling of **optimistic**

optophone /óptə fōn/ *n* a device used especially by blind or visually impaired people that can convert written text into sounds [Early 20C. < Greek *optos* 'seen, visible'.]

opt-out *n* a decision taken by the administration of a hospital or school to remove itself from local authority control and administer its own affairs (*often before nouns*)

opulent /óppyōōlənt/ *adj* **1** characterized by an obvious or lavish display of wealth or affluence **2** in richly abundant supply [Mid-16C. < Latin *opulentus* 'producing much'.] —**opulence** *n* —**opulency** *n* —**opulently** *adv*

Opüls ◊ **Max Ophuls**

opuntia /ō púnshi ə/ *n* a cactus, e.g. the prickly pear or cholla, with orange, orange-red, or yellow flowers and oval fruits. Native to: North and South America. Genus: *Opuntia.* [Early 17C. < modern Latin, < *Opunt-*, stem of *Opus*, city in Greece.]

opus /ṓpəss/ (*plural* **opuses** *or* **opera** /óppərə/) *n* **1** a musical work, especially one of a numbered series by the same composer arranged to show the order in which they were written or catalogued **2** a creative piece of work in any field of the arts. ◊ **magnum opus** [Early 18C. < Latin, 'work'.]

opus anglicanum /-ang gli kaánəm/ *n* a form of English embroidery that was popular in the Middle Ages, usually seen on ecclesiastical robes [Mid-19C. < medieval Latin, 'English work'.]

opuscule /ō pús kyool/, **opusculum** /əpsskyóoləm/ (*plural* **-la** /-lə/) *n* a minor or insignificant creative work, especially a musical or literary work [Mid-17C. Via French < Latin *opusculum* 'little work' < *opus* 'work'.]

or[1] (*stressed*) /awr/; (*unstressed*) /ər/ CORE MEANING: a conjunction used to link two or more alternatives. In a series of alternatives, it is usually used only before the last alternative. ○ *Which do you prefer, butter or low fat spread?* ○ *factors that may trigger or exacerbate the illness*
conj **1 FOLLOWING 'EITHER' OR 'WHETHER'** used to join two alternatives when the first is introduced by 'either' or 'whether' ○ *Either you typed the wrong name, or something is wrong with the equipment.* **2 INDICATING APPROXIMATION** used between two numbers to indicate an approximate quantity or to imply a few of something ○ *Hit the return key every three or four seconds until you get a greeting message.* **3 REPHRASING STATEMENT** used to introduce a rephrasing synonym or correction of a statement just made ○ *foetal oxygen deprivation, or hypoxia* **4 OTHERWISE** used to give an explanation of a statement just made ○ *You'd better leave or you'll be late.* **5 WHETHER OR EITHER** a poetic word for 'either' or 'whether', preceding the first of two alternatives, with 'or' also preceding the second alternative (*archaic or literary*) ◇ **or other** used to show that the preceding words you use are not exact or definite ○ *For some reason or other, the house was crowded that night.* ◇ **or so** approximately ○ *I haven't seen her for a year or so*

SPELLCHECK See ***oar***

or[2] /awr/ *adj* describes an element of a coat of arms or other heraldic insignia that is coloured gold [15C. Via French < Latin *aurum* 'gold'.]

⚡**OR**[1] /awr/ *n* a binary operator in Boolean algebra whose result is true if one or both of its operands are true and false otherwise. ◊ **AND, NOT**

OR[2] *abbr* **1** operations research **2** Oregon **3** other ranks **4** owner's risk

-or[1] *suffix* somebody or something that does or performs ○ *conductor* [Via Old French *-eor*, *-eur* and Anglo-Norman *-(o)ur* < Latin *-or* and *-ator*]

-or[2] *suffix* condition, state, activity ○ *horror* [Via Old French *-eur* < Latin *-or*]

ora plural of **os**[1]

orache /órrəch/, **orach** *n* a wild plant with greyish-green edible leaves resembling spinach leaves. Flowers: tiny, green, in spikes. Native to: Europe. Genus: *Atriplex.* [13C. Via Anglo-Norman *arasche* < Greek *atraphaxus* < ?]

oracle /órrək'l/ *n* **1 SOURCE OF WISDOM** somebody or something considered to be a source of knowledge, wisdom, or prophecy **2 WISE SAYING** a wise or prophetic statement **3 SHRINE OF ANCIENT GOD** in ancient Greece and Rome, a shrine dedicated to a particular god where people went to consult a priest or priestess in times of trouble or uncertainty **4 GREEK OR ROMAN DEITY** an ancient Greek or Roman deity that a priest or priestess would consult for advice on behalf of troubled or uncertain people **5 ADVICE FROM GREEK OR ROMAN DEITY** a piece of advice, often in the form of a puzzle or an enigmatic statement, handed down by a Greek or Roman deity **6 GOD-GIVEN MESSAGE** a message believed to come from God in response to a request, plea, or petition **7 AREA OF BIBLICAL TEMPLE** the most sacred area in either of the biblical Temples, often referred to as the Holy of Holies ■ **oracles** *npl* **SCRIPTURE** the books of the Bible [14C. Via French < Latin *oraculum* < *orare* 'speak' (see ORATE).]

oracular /o rákyóolər/ *adj* **1 OF OR AS AN ORACLE** relating to oracles, or in the form of an oracle **2 WISE** knowing, wise, or prophetic **3 MYSTERIOUS** puzzling, ambiguous, or enigmatic [Mid-17C. < Latin *oraculum* (see ORACLE).] —**oracularity** /o rákyoo lárrəti/ *n* —**oracularly** *adv*

oracy /áwrəssi/ *n* the ability to speak fluently and articulately and to understand and respond to what other people say [Mid-20C. < ORAL, after LITERACY.]

ora et labora /áwrə et lə báwrə/ a Latin phrase meaning 'pray and work'

oral /áwrəl/ *adj* **1 OF MOUTH** relating to or belonging to the mouth ○ *oral hygiene* **2 FOR MOUTH** designed for use in the mouth **3 SPOKEN** existing in spoken form as distinct from written form **4 ADMINISTERED BY MOUTH** describes medicines that are taken by mouth **5 WITH RELEASE OF AIR THROUGH MOUTH** describes a speech sound that is produced by means of an airstream that escapes through the mouth only, with the nasal cavity sealed off by the velum. ◊ **nasal** *adj.* 2 **6 DERIVING PLEASURE VIA MOUTH** in Freudian analysis, describes a stage in child development when erotic pleasure is derived from mouth-associated sensations, especially through feeding, thumb-sucking, and putting objects into the mouth **7 DEPENDENT AND AGGRESSIVE** in Freudian analysis, describes a dependent, selfish and aggressive personality type with a tendency to derive pleasure from mouth-related activities such as eating, drinking, or smoking **8 WHERE MOUTH IS SITED** describes the surface of the body of an animal such as the underside of a starfish, on which the mouth is situated ■ *n* **TEST REQUIRING SPOKEN ANSWERS** an examination or test that involves candidates giving spoken answers to spoken questions, as distinct from one where the questions and answers are in written form [Early 17C. < late Latin *oralis* < Latin *or-*, stem of *os* 'mouth'.] —**orally** *adv*

SYNONYMS See ***verbal.***

USAGE See ***aural.***

oral contraceptive *n* a pill that is taken daily to prevent conception, especially one that combines an oestrogen and a progestogen

oral history *n* **1** the personal recollections of people who participated in historical events, recorded on audio or video tape or told to a younger generation **2** the branch of history that deals with personal accounts of historical events or periods —**oral historian** *n*

oral hygiene *n* DENT = **dental hygiene** —**oral hygienist** *n*

Oral Law, Oral Torah *n* Jewish religious law that developed out of interpretations of the Torah and was originally passed on orally by rabbis and sages before being recorded in writing, principally in the Mishnah and Talmud

oral sex *n* sexual activity that involves using the mouth and tongue to stimulate a partner's genitals

oral society *n* a community in which people do not read or write

Oral Torah *n* JUDAISM = **Oral Law**

oral tradition *n* a community's cultural and historical background preserved and passed on from one generation to the next in spoken stories and song, as distinct from being written down

Oran /ə rán/ port in NW Algeria. Population: 590,000 (1987).

orange /órrinj/ *n* **1 CITRUS FRUIT** a round or oval citrus fruit with thick orange skin and juicy segmented flesh (*often before nouns*) **2 TREE YIELDING JUICY FRUIT** an evergreen tree with glossy leaves that bears oranges. Flowers: white, fragrant. Native to: Southeast Asia. Genus: *Citrus.* **3 COLOUR** the bright colour of the skin of an orange, a mixture of red and yellow **4** INDUST = **orangewood 5 TREE WITH FRUITS SIMILAR TO ORANGE** a tree or bush that produces flowers or fruits similar to a true orange tree, e.g. mock orange or Osage orange **6 ORANGE-COLOURED BUTTERFLY** a butterfly with predominantly orange coloration, e.g. the sulphur butterfly. Family: Pieridae. **7 ORANGE-COLOURED OBJECT** something that is coloured orange [13C. < Old French *pomme d'orenge* < Italian *melarancia* 'orange fruit', via Arabic *nāranj* and Persian *nārang* < Sanskrit *nāraṅgaḥ.*] —**orange** *adj* —**orangey** *adj*

Orange /órrinj/ *n* **DUTCH ROYAL HOUSE** the princely family that became the royal house of the Netherlands in 1815. William of Orange became King William III of Great Britain and Ireland in 1689. ■ *adj* **1 OF HOUSE OF ORANGE** relating to or belonging to the house of Orange **2 OF ORANGE ORDER** relating to or belonging to the Orange Order [Mid-17thC. After ORANGE in SE France.]

Orange 1 river in South Africa, flowing westwards from Lesotho into the Atlantic Ocean. Length: 2,090 km/1,300 mi. **2** town in SE France. Population: 26,964 (1996). **3** town in central New South Wales, Australia. Population: 29,647 (1991).

orangeade /órrinj áyd/ *n* a still or fizzy nonalcoholic drink flavoured with orange or tasting like oranges [Early 18C. < ORANGE, after LEMONADE.]

orange badge *n* an official sign displayed on vehicles of drivers with disabilities, entitling them to use reserved parking places

Orange lodge *n* a local branch of the Orange Order, or the building in which the branch has its headquarters

Orangeman /órrinjmən/ (*plural* **-men** /-mən/) *n* **1** a member of the Orange Order **2** an Irishman of the Protestant faith [Late 18C. After the ORANGE ORDER.]

Orange Order *n* a Protestant organization formed in 1795 with the aim of celebrating and defending Protestantism in Northern Ireland [Because it was formed out of loyalty to William of *Orange* (WILLIAM III)]

orange peel *n* the thick dimpled skin of an orange

orange-peel *adj* having a dimpled surface caused, e.g. by open pores or cellulite ○ *orange-peel skin*

orange-peel fungus *n* a widespread fungus that has an orange cup with a rough white underside resembling dry, curled-up orange peel. *Aleuria aurantia.*

orange pekoe *n* a high-quality black tea grown in South Asia and made using only the small, young, tender leaves growing at the tips of the stems

orangery /órrinjəri/ (*plural* **-ries**) *n* a building where orange trees are grown, especially a large greenhouse for use in cooler climates

orange squash *n* a sweet nonalcoholic drink made from oranges or tasting of oranges

orange stick *n* a small stick used for manicuring the fingernails and cuticles that is usually wooden or plastic, with one pointed end and one rounded end [Because it is usually made from ORANGEWOOD]

orange-tip *n* a common European butterfly with predominantly white wings, mottled underneath, and the outer part of the forewing tipped with orange in the males. *Anthocaris cardamines.*

orangewood /órrinj wòod/ *n* the yellowish hard fine-grained wood of the orange tree. Use: furniture, carved objects.

orang-utan /aw rángə táng, -tán, ə rángə-/, **orang-utang** *n* a large tailless ape with reddish-brown coarse shaggy hair and long powerful arms. Native to: forests of Borneo and Sumatra. *Pongo pygmaeus.* [Late 17C. < Malay *orang hutan* 'forest person'.]

orate /aw ráyt/ (**orates, orating, orated**) *vi* **1** to make a speech, especially a public, formal, or ceremonial speech (*formal*) **2** to speak in a pompous or boring way or for an inappropriately long time [Early 17C. < Latin *orat-* (see ORATOR).]

oration /aw ráysh'n/ *n* **1 FORMAL PUBLIC SPEECH** a speech, lecture, or other instance of formal or ceremonial public speaking **2 POMPOUS SPEECH** a speech that is considered pompous, boring, or inappropriately long **3 PUBLIC SPEECH SHOWING RHETORICAL SKILLS** an academic speech that is designed to show the speaker's rhetorical skills, especially a speech given as an exercise in public speaking, often in a public speaking contest **4 STYLE OF SPEECH DELIVERY** the way in which a speech is delivered, or a way of speaking [14C. < Latin *oration-* < *orat-* (see ORATOR).]

orator /órrətər/ *n* **1** a giver of speeches, especially somebody skilled in giving formal, ceremonial, or persuasive public addresses **2** a pompous, boring, or overlong speaker [14C. Via Anglo-Norman < Latin 'speaker, pleader' < *orat-*, past participle of *orare* 'speak, pray'.]

oratorio /órrə táwri ō/ (*plural* **-os**) *n* **1** a musical composition for voices and instruments that has a religious theme, often telling a sacred story but not using costumes, scenery, or dramatic staging **2** oratorios as a musical genre [Mid-17C. < Italian, after the *Oratory* of St Philip Neri in Rome.]

oratory[1] /órrətəri/ *n* **1 ART OF PUBLIC SPEAKING** the art of speaking in public with style, cogency, and grace **2 RHETORICAL SKILL AND ELOQUENCE** eloquence in public speaking, especially of the kind that shows the speaker's rhetorical skills **3 POMPOSITY IN SPEECH** pompous, boring, or inappropriately long speech [Early 16C. < Latin *(ars) oratoria* '(art) of speaking' < *orator* (see ORATOR).] —**oratorical** /órrə tórrik'l/ *adj* —**oratorically** /-tórrikli/ *adv*

oratory[2] /órrətəri/ (*plural* **-ries**) *n* a place for private prayer or worship such as a small secluded chapel, usually set aside in a church [14C. Via Anglo-Norman *oratorie* < Latin *orare* 'speak, pray'.]

Oratory *n* a religious society that has secular priests and is a branch of the Roman Catholic Church [Mid-17C. < ORATORY[2].]

orb /awrb/ *n* **1 KING'S OR QUEEN'S JEWELLED SPHERE** a small sphere usually made from a precious metal set with jewels and with a cross fixed to the top of it that forms part of a sovereign's ceremonial regalia. ◊ **sceptre** *n*. 1 **2 SPHERE** a sphere or spherical object **3 EYE** an eye (*literary*) **4 AREA OF INTEREST** a sphere of interest, influence, or activity (*literary*) **5 CONCENTRIC PLANET-HOLDING SPHERE** any of the concentric spheres that were formerly believed by astronomers to hold the planets in their orbital paths ■ *v* **1** *vt* **ENCIRCLE** to encircle something (*literary*) **2** *vti* **MAKE OR BECOME CIRCULAR** to become circular, or make something circular (*archaic*) [14C. < Latin *orbis* 'wheel, circle'.]

orbicular /awr bíkyŏŏlər/, **orbiculate** /-lət/ *adj* **1** in the form of a circle or sphere (*formal*) **2** describes plant parts, especially leaves, that are flat and round or roundish [14C. < late Latin *orbicularis* < Latin *orbiculus* 'small globe' < *orbis* 'globe'.] —**orbicularity** /awr bíkyŏŏ lárrəti/ *n* —**orbicularly** /awr bíkyŏŏlərli/ *adv* —**orbiculately** /-lətli/ *adv*

orbit /áwrbit/ *n* **1 PATH OF A PLANET, SATELLITE, OR MOON** the path that an astronomical object such as a planet, moon, or satellite follows around a larger astronomical object such as the Sun **2 ASTRONOMICAL OBJECT'S REVOLUTION** a single revolution of an astronomical object around a larger body **3 AREA OF INTEREST** a sphere of interest, influence, or activity **4 EYE SOCKET** a round cavity in which an eye is located in the skull of a vertebrate **5 ELECTRON'S PATH AROUND AN ATOM'S NUCLEUS** the path that an electron takes as it moves around the nucleus of an atom ■ *v* **1** *vti* **MOVE AROUND AN ASTRONOMICAL OBJECT** to move around an astronomical object in a path dictated by the force of gravity exerted by that body **2** *vt* **PUT INTO ASTRONOMICAL ORBIT** to send something, especially a spacecraft or an artificial satellite, into orbit **3** *vi* **FOLLOW A REGULAR PATH** to move regularly or repeatedly along the same path, especially a circular path [Mid-16C. < Latin *orbita* 'wheel-track'.]

orbital /áwrbit'l/ *adj* belonging to or relating to an orbit ■ *n* **1** a subdivision of the available space within an atom for an electron to orbit the nucleus **2** TRANSP = **ring road** —**orbitally** *adv*

orbital space station *n* a spacecraft orbiting the Earth, designed to be occupied by a crew for extended periods and used as a base for the exploration, observation, and research of space

orbital space vehicle *n US* a vehicle that transports payloads to and from points in space having different orbits such as a space station, a satellite, and the Moon

orbiter /áwrbitər/ *n* a spacecraft or satellite designed to orbit an astronomical object but not to land on it

orb weaver *n* a spider that weaves a broad intricate web of silk to entrap its prey

orca /áwrkə/ *n* ZOOL = **killer whale** [Mid-19C. Via modern Latin < Latin *orca* 'large sea creature'.]

Orcadian /awr káydi ən/ *n* somebody who lives on or was born or brought up on Orkney, a group of islands lying to the north of Scotland [Mid-17C. < Latin *Orcades* 'Orkney Islands'.] —**Orcadian** *adj*

orcein /áwrsi in/ *n* a brown dye. Source: orcinol. Use: as a biological stain. [Mid-19C. < *orcin* 'orcinol' < modern Latin *orcina* 'orchil'.]

orch. *abbr* **1** orchestra **2** orchestrated by

orchard /áwrchərd/ *n* **1** an area of land on which fruit or nut trees are grown, especially commercially **2** all the fruit or nut trees growing in a particular area, planted for commercial reasons [Old English *ortgeard* < *ort* < ? + YARD[2]]

LITERARY LINK ***The Cherry Orchard***, a play (1903–04) by the Russian dramatist Anton Chekhov. It depicts the decline of the Ranyevskayas, a family of upper-class landowners, who despite being faced with bankruptcy refuse to contemplate merchant Lopakhin's suggestion that they sell their beloved cherry orchard.

orchardist /áwrchərdist/ *n* an owner or manager of an orchard

orchestra /áwrkistrə/ *n* **1 LARGE GROUP OF CLASSICAL MUSICIANS** a large group of musicians playing classical music, consisting of sections of string, woodwind, brass, and percussion players, and directed by a conductor **2 GROUP OF MUSICIANS** a group of musicians, especially a fairly large group usually but not always playing classical music **3** *US* THEATRE = **orchestra pit 4 PLACE FOR THE CHORUS** the semicircular area in front of the stage in ancient Greek theatres, reserved for the chorus [Early 17C. Via Latin, 'space in front of the stage where the chorus danced' < Greek *orkhēstra* < *orkheisthai* 'to dance'.]

orchestral /awr késtrəl/ *adj* relating to orchestras, or intended for an orchestra, especially a symphony orchestra —**orchestrally** *adv*

orchestra pit *n* the part of a theatre where the musicians sit, immediately in front of the stage or under the front part of the stage. US term **orchestra** *n*. 3

orchestra stalls *npl* the front seats on the lower floor of a theatre, situated just in front of the orchestra

orchestrate /áwrki strayt/ (**-trates, -trating, -trated**) *vt* **1** to arrange or compose music to be played by an orchestra **2** to organize a situation or event unobtrusively so that a desired effect or outcome is achieved ○ *The press conference had clearly been carefully orchestrated.* —**orchestration** /áwrki stráysh'n/ *n* —**orchestrator** *n*

orchestrion /awr késtri ən/, **orchestrina** /áwrki streénə/ *n* a mechanical musical instrument resembling a barrel organ, imitating the sounds of an orchestra [Mid-19C. < ORCHESTRA after *accordion*.]

orchid /áwrkid/ *n* any of a large and varied family of perennial plants, many of which grow on other plants and have striking flowers. Native to: tropical climates. Family: Orchidaceae. [Mid-19C. < Latin *orchid-*, mistakenly < *orchis* (see ORCHIS).] —**orchidaceous** /áwrki dáyshəss/ *adj*

orchiectomy /áwrki éktəmi/ (*plural* **-mies**), **orchidectomy** /áwrki déktəmi/ (*plural* **-mies**) *n* surgical removal of one or both testicles [Late 19C. < Greek *orkhis* 'testicle'.]

orchil /áwrkil, -chil/ *n* **1** a reddish dye derived from a lichen, obtained by treating the lichen with aqueous ammonia **2** a lichen that yields orchid. Genera: *Roccella* and *Lecanora*. [15C. Via Spanish *orchilla* < Catalan *orxella* < Arabic.]

orchis /áwrkiss/ *n* an orchid with a fleshy tuber and spikes of small flowers with spurred lips. Genus: *Orchis*. [Mid-16C. Via Latin < Greek *orkhis* 'testicle' (from the tuber's shape).]

orchitis /awr kítiss/ *n* inflammation of one or both testicles, usually caused by infection [Late 18C. < modern Latin, < Greek *orkhis* 'testicle'.] —**orchitic** /awr kíttik/ *adj*

orcinol /órsinawl/ *n* $CH_3C_6H_3(OH)_2$ a colourless substance found in many lichens. Use: litmus dyes. [Late 19C. < modern Latin *orcina* 'orchil'.]

⚡**OR circuit** /áwr-/ *n* a logic circuit, used especially in computers, that gives a high-voltage output if all or one of its inputs carries a high voltage and a low-voltage output otherwise

Ord /awrd/ river in N Western Australia. Length: 320km/200 mi.

ord. *abbr* **1** order **2** ordinal **3** ordinance **4** ordinary **5** ordnance

ordain /awr dáyn/ *vt* **1** to order or establish something formally, especially by law or by another authority ○ *laws of commercial transactions that had long been ordained by the government* **2** to appoint somebody officially as a priest, minister, or rabbi [13C. Via Old French *ordener* < Latin *ordinare* 'set in order' < *ordo* 'order'.] —**ordainer** *n*

ordeal /awr deél, áwr deel/ *n* **1** a very difficult or harrowing experience, especially one lasting a long time **2** formerly, a trial that involved subjecting a defendant to life-threatening danger, e.g. from fire or water, with the outcome regarded as reflecting divine judgment [Old English *ordāl* 'trial, judgment' < Germanic, 'share out']

order /áwrdər/ *n* **1 INSTRUCTION** an instruction to do something **2 ARRANGEMENT OF ITEMS** the way in which several items are arranged, as an indication of their relative importance or size or when each will be dealt with ○ *I will announce the winners in reverse order.* **3 NEATNESS** an organized condition, with elements arranged properly, neatly, or harmoniously ○ *We all need a little order in our lives.* **4 ABSENCE OF CRIME** a peaceful condition in which laws are obeyed and misbehaviour or crime is not present or is prevented ○ *the establishment of law and order* **5 FUNCTIONING CONDITION** the condition something is in when it is functioning properly **6 INSTRUCTION TO PROVIDE SOMETHING** an instruction to bring or supply something, e.g. a spoken instruction to a waiter or waitress, or a written instruction to a manufacturer or supplier of goods ○ *Can I take your order now?* **7 SOMETHING PROVIDED** something provided in response to an instruction ○ *If you are not completely satisfied, you may return your order.* **8 SOCIAL GROUPING** the arrangement of society into groups or classes and the relationships between them ○ *a new world order* **9 SOCIAL GROUP** any one of the groups or classes into which a society is divided (*often plural*) **10 SET OF RELATED FAMILIES** a taxonomic classification made up of related families of organisms ○ *the cat family, in the order Carnivora* **11 TYPE** a kind or type of something, often one judged on importance or worth ○ *Exactly what order of stupidity are we dealing with?* **12 COURT'S INSTRUCTION** an instruction issued by a judge or a court of law **13 FINANCIAL INSTRUCTION** a written instruction to pay money **14 order, Order RELIGIOUS COMMUNITY** a religious community in which members live according to principles that are often based on the writings of a particular saint ○ *the Order of Saint Francis* **15 RELIGIOUS RANK** any one of the grades into which the ministry is divided in some Christian denominations, including deacons, priests, bishops, and archbishops **16 RELIGIOUS SERVICE** a form of Christian religious service used on specific occasions **17 order, Order GROUP OF HONOURED PEOPLE** a prestigious group consisting of people who have been awarded an honour for services to their country, or the decoration indicating such an honour ○ *the Order of the Garter* **18 ARCHITECTURAL STYLE** any one of the five major styles of classical architecture, the Doric, Ionic, Corinthian, Tuscan, and Composite **19 NUMBER OF ROWS AND COLUMNS** the number of rows and columns in a matrix **20 GROUP MEMBERS** the number of elements in a finite group **21** SCI = **order of magnitude 22 NUMBER OF TIMES VARIABLE IS DIFFERENTIATED** the number of times differentiation must be applied to a mathematical expression to obtain a specified derivative **23 NUMBER OF DIFFERENTIATIONS NEEDED IN EQUATION** in a differential equation, the number of successive differentiations required to reach the highest-order derivative **24 CLASSIFICATION OF CHEMICAL REACTIONS** a classification of chemical reactions based on the mathematical relationship between the rate of a given chemical reaction and the concentration of the reacting chemical compounds ■ **orders** *npl* RELIG = **holy orders** ■ *v* **1** *vt* **GIVE SOMEBODY INSTRUCTIONS** to command somebody to do something ○ *The colonel ordered the troops to move out.* **2** *vt* **PRESCRIBE** to give an instruction for something to be done **3** *vti* **REQUEST** to give an instruction for something to be provided, e.g. food in a restaurant or goods from a manufacturer or supplier **4** *vt* **ARRANGE ITEMS** to arrange items in a particular way, especially in the sequence in which they are to be dealt with ○ *addresses ordered by postcode* **5** *vt* **ARRANGE THINGS NEATLY** to put things into a neat, well organized state or into the required state ○ *ordered her business affairs prior to leaving for the summer* ■ *interj* **CALL FOR CALM** used to request calm or observance of correct procedure, e.g. by a person chairing a debate [13C. Via French *ordre* < Latin *ordin-*, stem of *ordo*.] —**orderer** *n* ◇ **a tall order** a request that is very difficult to fulfil (*informal*) ◇ **in order 1** in a correct sequence or arrangement ○ *Put them in order alphabetically.* **2** in a condition of being correct or appropriate ○ *The customs official was checking that the paperwork was in order.* ◇ **in order to** *or* **that** with the object or purpose of ◇ **on order** requested but not yet supplied or delivered ◇ **out of order 1** not working properly or at all **2** not in the correct sequence or place within a sequence **3** not done or behaving in a fair, appropriate, or tolerable way (*informal*)

order about, order around *vt* to subject somebody to domineering or bullying treatment ○ *Don't think you can order me about.*

order arms *n* an act of bringing a weapon, usually a rifle, from the shoulder to a resting position on the ground alongside the right leg, performed as part of a military drill ■ *interj* used as a command in a military drill to assume the order arms position

orderly /áwrdərli/ *adj* **1** WELL-BEHAVED well-behaved or peaceful ○ *The meeting passed off in an orderly fashion.* **2** NEATLY ARRANGED arranged or organized in a neat, sensible, or proper way ○ *orderly bookshelves* ■ *n* (*plural* **-lies**) **1** ASSISTANT WORKING IN HOSPITAL a hospital worker with no medical training who is employed to do various ancillary jobs such as transporting patients **2** SOLDIER WITH MINOR DUTIES a soldier acting as a senior officer's personal assistant who carries out a variety of minor duties such as carrying messages —**orderliness** *n*

Order of Australia *n* an order awarded in Australia to individuals who are seen to have made an outstanding contribution to society

order of battle *n* the way that military forces are organized in preparation for a battle

order of business *n* the order in which a number of items are to be discussed or dealt with, e.g. at a meeting

order of magnitude *n* the difference in size, usually expressed in powers of 10, between two quantities ○ *The mass of the Earth is an order of magnitude greater than that of Mars.*

Order of Merit *n* a British honour awarded for eminence in any field

order of the day *n* **1** a programme of items to be discussed or dealt with on a particular day, e.g. by a legislative assembly **2** something that is regularly done, offered, chosen, or experienced during a particular period ○ *Heroism was the order of the day during the last big battle of the war.*

Order of the Garter *n* the highest British order of knighthood

order paper *n* a printed list given out daily to British MPs showing the order and nature of business to be dealt with in Parliament

ordinal /áwrdin'l/ *adj* **1** SHOWING POSITION showing the relative position in a sequence of numbers **2** RELATING TO BIOLOGICAL ORDERS relating to a biological order in the classification of plants and animals ■ *n* **1** MATH = **ordinal number** *n.* 1 **2** CATHOLIC BOOKLET in the Roman Catholic Church, an instruction booklet that lists the order of services in church worship **3** CHRISTIAN BOOKLET an instruction booklet that outlines rules and ceremony for the ordination of Christian ministers [Late 16C. < late Latin *ordinalis* 'ordered' < Latin *ordin-* (see ORDER).]

ordinal number *n* **1** a number used to show the relative position of something or somebody in a sequence **2** a measure of the size of an ordered set in addition to the order of its elements

ordinal scale *n* a list that shows only the relative positions of items on a scale, giving no measure of the difference between them

ordinance /áwrdinənss/ *n* **1** a law or rule made by an authority, e.g. a local council **2** something regularly done because it is formally prescribed, especially a religious ceremony such as Communion (*formal*) [14C. Via Old French < Latin *ordinare* (see ORDAIN).]

> **SPELLCHECK** Do not confuse ***ordinance*** with ***ordnance***, which has a similar sound. Beware: your spellchecker will not catch this error.

ordinand /áwrdi nand/ *n* a candidate for ordination as a Christian minister [Mid-19C. < Latin *ordinandus* < *ordinare* (see ORDAIN).]

ordinarily /áwrd'nərəli/ *adv* usually or normally

ordinary /áwrd'nəri/ *adj* **1** COMMON of a common everyday kind **2** UNREMARKABLE not remarkable or special in any way, and therefore uninteresting and unimpressive ○ *He's just a pretty ordinary kind of guy.* **3** USUAL usual or customary **4** WITH IMMEDIATE JURISDICTION with immediate jurisdiction, as opposed to jurisdiction by delegation or deputation **5** WITH TWO VARIABLES relating to a differential equation that has only two variables ■ *n* (*plural* **-ies**) **1** JUDGE a judge who acts in his or her own right **2 ordinary, Ordinary** CLERIC WITH JUDGE'S POWERS a member of the clergy, especially a bishop, whose position brings with it the power to act as a judge in some ecclesiastical matters **3 ordinary, Ordinary** UNCHANGING PARTS OF THE RELIGIOUS MASS in the Roman Catholic Church, the parts of the daily Mass that do not change from day to day **4 ordinary, Ordinary** FORM FOR A RELIGIOUS SERVICE in the Roman Catholic Church, the correct form that a religious service, especially Mass, should take, or a book that sets out the correct form **5** SIMPLE DESIGN any one of the simpler shapes or designs used on coats of arms **6** EATING HOUSE an eating establishment or a dining room in a tavern (*archaic*) [14C. Via Old French < medieval Latin *ordinarius* 'following the usual course' < Latin *ordin-* (see ORDER).] —**ordinariness** *n* ◇ **out of the ordinary** unusual or extraordinary

Ordinary grade *n Scotland* full form of **O grade**

Ordinary level *n* full form of **O level**

ordinary seaman *n* a Royal Navy sailor of the lowest rank

ordinary shares *npl* shares that entitle the holder to a dividend in line with the company's profits, as distinct from preference shares that give the holder priority when dividends are paid. US term **common stock**

ordinate /áwrd'nət/ *n* the vertical or y-coordinate of a point on a two-dimensional graph or diagram in which pairs of numbers denote distances along fixed horizontal and vertical axes. ◊ **abscissa** [Late 17C. < Latin *ordinare* (see ORDAIN).]

ordination /áwrdi náysh'n/ *n* an official investiture as a Christian priest or minister, or as a rabbi, or a ceremony during which somebody is consecrated as a priest, minister, or rabbi [15C. Directly or via French < Latin *ordination-* < *ordinare* (see ORDAIN).]

ordnance /áwrdnənss/ *n* **1** military weapons systems, including supplies for their use and equipment for their maintenance **2** the army or government department that has responsibility for military weapons and supplies [14C. Variant of ORDINANCE.]

> **SPELLCHECK** See ***ordinance***.

ordnance datum *n* the sea-level standard adopted by the Ordnance Survey for mapmaking purposes. It is established as the sea level at Newlyn, in Cornwall.

Ordnance Survey *n* the government body responsible for mapmaking in the United Kingdom

ordo /áwrdō/ (*plural* **-dos** *or* **-dines** /-di neez/) *n* in the Roman Catholic Church, a calendar detailing the forms of Mass and other services to be followed for each day in the year [Mid-19C. < Latin, 'order'.]

ordonnance /áwrdənənss/ *n* the general arrangement of elements in architecture and in works of art and literature (*formal*) [Mid-17C. < French, alteration of Old French *ordenance* 'ordinance'.]

Ordovician /áwrdō víshi ən/ *adj* belonging to or dating from the second oldest period of the Palaeozoic era, approximately 500 to 440 million years ago [Late 19C. < Latin *Ordovices*, ancient Celtic people of N Wales.]

ordure /áwr dyoor/ *n* **1** excrement or dung (*formal*) **2** obscene or otherwise morally corrupting material or behaviour, or an example of it (*literary*) [14C. Via Old French < Latin *horridus* 'frightful' < *horrere* (see HORROR).]

ore /awr/ *n* a naturally occurring mineral from which particular constituents, especially metals, can be profitably extracted [Old English *ōra*, *ār* 'brass, bronze']

> **SPELLCHECK** See ***oar***

öre /úrrə/ (*plural* **öre**) *n* see table at **currency** [Early 18C. Via Swedish < Old Norse *aurar*.]

øre /úrrə/ *n* see table at **currency** [Early 18C. Via Danish or Norwegian < Old Norse *aurar*.]

Ore. *abbr* Oregon

oread /áwri ad/ *n* in Greek mythology, a mountain nymph [14C. Via Latin *Oread-* < Greek *Oreias* < *oros* 'mountain'.]

Örebro /úrrə broō/ city in central Sweden. Population: 119,635 (1995).

ore dressing *n* the separation of the mineral content of an ore from the unwanted rock or earth

Oreg. *abbr* Oregon

oregano /órri gaánō/ *n* **1** the fresh or dried leaves of an aromatic herb, used as a flavouring **2** a variety of wild marjoram that produces oregano. Native to: Mediterranean. *Origanum vulgare.* [Late 18C. Via Spanish < Greek *origanon* 'wild marjoram'.]

Oregon /órrigən/ state in the NW United States. Capital: Salem. Population: 3,243,487 (1997). Area: 251,571 sq. km/97,132 sq. mi. —**Oregonian** /órri gṓni ən/ *n, adj*

Oregon Trail *n* a 19th-century route to the W United States extending from W Missouri to N Oregon that was used by pioneers and settlers

Ore Mountains /áwr-/ mountain range along the Czech-German border. Highest peak: Klinovec 1,244 m/4,080 ft.

Orenburg /órrən burg/ city in SW Siberian Russia. Population: 686,289 (1995).

Orense /aw rénss e/ capital of Orense Province, NW Spain. Population: 110,796 (1995).

Öresund /úrrə sún, -soŏnd/, **Øresend** strait between SW Sweden and E Denmark. Length: about 105 km/65 mi.

Oreti /ō ráyti/ river in the south of the South Island, New Zealand. Length: 203 km/126 mi.

orf /awrf/ *n* a pox caused by a virus, affecting sheep and goats, and also transmittable to humans, in which pus-filled blisters form on the animals' lips [Mid-19C. Probably < Old Norse *hrufa*.]

Orff /awrf/, **Carl** (1895–1982) German composer

orfray *n* HANDICRAFT = **orphrey**

ϟ **org** *abbr* private organization (*in Internet addresses*)

org. *abbr* **1** organic **2** organization **3** organized

organ /áwrgən/ *n* **1** MUSICAL KEYBOARD INSTRUMENT a large musical keyboard instrument producing sounds at different volumes using compressed air passed through pipes **2** INSTRUMENT SIMILAR TO ORGAN a musical instrument that make sounds resembling the organ without using pipes, e.g. electronically or with reeds **3** BODY PART a complete and independent part of a plant or animal that has a specific function ○ *the organs of the digestive system* **4** MEANS OF COMMUNICATION a newspaper or magazine regarded as a means of communication, especially one communicating the views of a particular group such as a political party (*formal*) ○ *the daily organ of left-of-centre politics* **5** AGENCY an organization or body acting on behalf of a larger institution, especially a government (*formal*) ○ *There were no secrets about the institute's role as an organ of the business community.* **6** PENIS a penis (*euphemistic*) [13C. Via Old French *organe* and Latin *organum* < Greek *organon* 'tool, instrument'.]

organa plural of **organum**

organdie /áwrgəndi, awr gándi/ (*plural* **-dies**) *n* a lightweight transparent cotton fabric, often stiffened. Use: dressmaking. [Early 19C. < French *organdi*.]

organelle /áwrgə nél/ *n* a specialized part of a cell, e.g. the nucleus or the mitochondrion, that has its own particular function [Early 20C. < modern Latin *organella* 'small organ' < Latin *organum* (see ORGAN).]

organ grinder *n* a street musician who plays a barrel organ, traditionally accompanied by a small monkey who circulates to collect money from bystanders [< the hand-cranked barrel organ]

organic /awr gánnik/ *adj* **1** OF LIVING THINGS relating to, derived from, or characteristic of living things **2** DEVELOPING NATURALLY occurring or developing gradually and naturally, without being forced or contrived **3** INTRINSIC forming a basic and inherent part of something and largely responsible for its identity or makeup **4** WITH ELEMENTS EFFICIENTLY COMBINED consisting of elements that exist together in a seemingly natural relationship that makes for organized efficiency ○ *need to integrate the various functions of the department into an organic whole* **5** AVOIDING SYNTHETIC CHEMICALS relating to or employing agricultural practices that avoid the use of synthetic chemicals in favour of naturally occurring pesticides, fertilizers, and other growing aids **6** PRODUCED WITHOUT SYNTHETIC CHEMICALS grown or reared without the use of synthetic chemicals ○ *a wide range of organic produce* **7** OF BODY'S ORGANS relating to the organs of the body, specifically to basic changes in them brought about by physical disorders **8** BASED ON CARBON belonging to a family of compounds having chains or rings of carbon atoms that are linked to atoms of hydrogen and sometimes oxygen, nitrogen, and other elements ■ *n* ORGANIC SUBSTANCE an organic substance, especially a fertilizer or pesticide —**organicity** /áwrgə níssəti/ *n*

organically /awr gánnikli/ *adv* **1** in a natural or seemingly natural way ○ *paintings with elements organically arranged* **2** without the use of synthetic chemicals, especially fertilizers and pesticides ○ *organically raised chickens*

organic brain syndrome *n* a psychiatric disorder caused by a permanent or temporary physical change in the brain

organic chemistry *n* the scientific study of carbon-based compounds, originally limited to compounds that are the natural products of living things, now including the study of synthetic carbon compounds such as plastics. ◊ **inorganic chemistry**

organic disease *n* a disorder associated with physical changes in one or more organs of the body

organicism /awr gánnissizəm/ *n* **1** the theory that all diseases are due to structural changes in the body's organs **2** the theory that society is analogous to, or shares characteristics with, living organisms —**organicist** *n* —**organicistic** /awr gánni sístik/ *adj*

organisation *n* = **organization**

organise *vti* = **organize**

organised *adj* = **organized**

organiser *n* = **organizer**

organism /áwrgənizəm/ *n* **1** a living thing such as a plant, animal, virus, or bacterium **2** a functioning system of interdependent parts that resembles a living creature ○ *'Like any organism, public libraries and the people who run them must adapt and respond to change'* (Laurence Arnold, *Pulse of the People*; 1997) —**organismal** /áwrgə nízm'l/ *adj* —**organismic** /-nízmik/ *adj* —**organismically** *adv*

organist /áwrgənist/ *n* a musician who plays the organ

organization /áwrgə nī záysh'n/, **organisation** *n* **1 GROUP** a group of people identified by shared interests or purpose, e.g. a business ○ *Each news organization sent its own photographer.* **2 COORDINATION OF ELEMENTS** the coordinating of separate elements into a unit or structure ○ *in charge of the organization of international conferences* **3 RELATIONSHIP OF ELEMENTS** the relationships that exist between separate elements arranged into a coherent whole ○ *changes to the organization of the party* **4 EFFICIENCY IN ARRANGEMENT** efficiency in the way separate elements are arranged into a coherent whole ○ *Your working method lacks organization.* —**organizational** *adj* —**organizationally** *adv*

organizational psychology *n* PSYCHOL, INDUST = **industrial psychology**

organization theory *n* the branch of sociology that deals with the structure of organizations and the systems and processes that operate within them

organize /áwrgə nīz/ (**-izes, -izing, -ized**), **organise** (**-ises, -ising, -ised**) *v* **1** *vti* **FORM** to form or establish something such as a club, by coming together or bringing people together into a structured group (*often passive*) **2** *vt* **COORDINATE** to oversee the coordination of the various elements of something **3** *vt* **ARRANGE ELEMENTS** to arrange the elements of something in a way that creates a particular structure ○ *a society organized along democratic lines* ○ *candidates organized into groups of three* **4** *vt* **MAKE MORE EFFECTIVE** to apply or impose efficient working methods in order to work effectively or make somebody else work effectively ○ *Mature students are not necessarily better at organizing themselves.* **5** *vti* **FORM TRADE UNION** to recruit the workers in a place or industry into a trade union, or come together to form a trade union [15C. Via French < medieval Latin *organizare* 'provide with bodily organs' < Latin *organum* (see ORGAN).]

organized /áwrgə nīzd/, **organised** *adj* **1** existing on a large scale and involving the systematic coordination of many different elements ○ *organized religion* **2** working in a systematic and efficient way ○ *a motivated and organized self-starter*

organized crime *n* a powerful ruthless large-scale network of professional criminals, or such networks in general

⚡**organizer** /áwrgə nīzər/, **organiser** *n* **1 SOMEBODY WHO ORGANIZES** a person who sets up or organizes projects and motivates others to take part **2 DIARY** a small portable calendar and diary used for planning, or a hand-held computerized device with a simple database for managing appointments and other information **3 CONTAINER WITH COMPARTMENTS** a container with compartments for storing items in neat groups, e.g. a desktop container with compartments for pens, pencils, and other items of stationery **4 EMBRYO PART** a part of an embryo that controls the differentiation of cells, eventually leading to the formation of organs and all the other specialized parts that make up an individual organism

organo- *prefix* **1** organ ○ *organography* **2** organic ○ *organophosphate* [< Greek *organon* 'tool, instrument']

organ of Corti /-káwrti/ *n* a part of the cochlea of the inner ear that transforms sound energy into nerve impulses and sends those impulses to the brain [Late 19C. After Alfonso *Corti* (1822–88), Italian anatomist.]

organogenesis /awr gánnō jénnəssiss, áwgənō-/ *n* the formation and development of animal or plant organs that takes place during the development of an embryo —**organogenetic** /awr gánnō jə néttik, áwrgənō-/ *adj* —**organogenetically** *adv*

organography /áwrgə nóggrəfi/ *n* the scientific description of the organs and other main structures of plants and animals —**organographic** /áwrgənō gráffik/ *adj* —**organographical** /-gráffik'l/ *adj* —**organographically** /-gráffikli/ *adv* —**organographist** /áwrgə nóggrəfist/ *n*

organoleptic /awr gánnō léptik, áwrgənō-/ *adj* affecting an organ, especially a sense organ [Mid-19C. < French *organoleptique* < Greek *organon* 'instrument' + *lēptikos* 'receptive'.] —**organoleptically** *adv*

organology /áwrgə nóllə ji/ *n* the study of plant and animal organs —**organological** /áwrgənō lójjik'l/ *adj* —**organologist** /áwgə nólləjist/ *n*

organometallic /awr gánnō me tállik, áwrgənō-/ *adj* relating to an organic compound containing one or more metal atoms, e.g. the petrol additive tetraethyl lead

organophosphate /awr gánnō fóss fayt/ *n* an organic compound containing phosphate groups, which may be toxic. Use: pesticides, fertilizers.

organophosphorous compound /órganō fóssfərəss-/ *n* an organic compound containing phosphorus

organotherapy /awr gánnō thérrəpi/ (*plural* **-pies**) *n* treatment of diseases by administering substances derived from animal organs, e.g. bovine insulin, which is used to treat diabetes in humans —**organotherapeutic** /awr gánnō thérrə pyóotik/ *adj*

organ-pipe cactus *n* a tall branched cactus. Native to: SW United States, N Mexico. *Lemaireocereus marginatus.* [< its tall pipe-shaped stems]

organ screen *n* an ornamental wooden or stone partition that separates the nave from the choir in a church or cathedral

organ stop *n* **1** a set of pipes on a musical organ, used to vary the tone and sometimes to imitate the sounds of other instruments **2** a knob or handle that controls the flow of air to an organ stop

organum /áwrgənəm/ (*plural* **-na** /-nə/ *or* **-nums**) *n* **1** a style of composition in western music of the late medieval period that combines plainsong melody with other melodies **2** a piece of music in the organum style [Early 17C. < Latin (see ORGAN).]

organza /awr gánzə/ *n* a stiff transparent fabric, usually silk, rayon, or nylon. Use: dressmaking. [Early 19C. < ?]

organzine /áwrgən zeen, awrgán zeen/ *n* yarn made from strands of silk twisted together, or fabric made from the yarn [Late 17C. Via French *organsin* < Italian *organzino*.]

orgasm /áwr gazəm/ *n* the climax of sexual excitement, consisting of intense muscle tightening around the genital area experienced as a pleasurable wave of tingling sensations through parts of the body ■ *vi* to experience sexual orgasm [Late 17C. Via French or modern Latin < Greek *orgasmos* < *organ* 'swell, be excited'.] —**orgasmic** /awr gázmik/ *adj* —**orgasmically** *adv* —**orgastic** /-gástik/ *adj* —**orgastically** *adv*

⚡**OR gate** *n* COMPUT = **OR circuit**

orgeat /áwrji ət/ *n* a cooling drink made from almonds and orange-flower water [15C. < French < Latin *hordeum* 'barley'.]

orgiastic /áwrji ástik/ *adj* **1** full of a spirit of wild revelry ○ *orgiastic gatherings* **2** showing extravagance or lack of restraint ○ *orgiastic shopping sprees* [Late 17C. < Greek *orgiastikos* < *orgiazein* 'celebrate secret rites' < *orgia* 'secret Dionysian rites'.] —**orgiastically** *adv*

orgone /áwrgōn/ *n* a life force that is purported to exist in all living things [Mid-20C. Probably < ORGANISM or ORGASM after HORMONE.]

orgy /áwrji/ *n* **1 GROUP SEX PARTY** a gathering at which a group of people indulge in promiscuous sexual activity **2 DEBAUCHED PARTY** a wild party or celebration characterized by excessive drinking and eating, with or without sexual promiscuity **3 PERIOD OF INDULGENCE** a period of indulgence in a particular activity or emotion, especially something that is disapproved of ○ *an orgy of self-pity* **4 WORSHIP OF ANCIENT GODS** in ancient Greece and Rome, a secret worshipping of the gods of pleasure, especially Bacchus or Dionysus, that involved much dancing, drinking, and singing (*often plural*) [Mid-16C. Via French < Greek *orgia* 'secret Dionysian rites'.]

oribi /órribi/ (*plural* **-bis** *or* **-bi**) *n* a small fawn-coloured antelope with long legs and, in the male, short horns. Native to: plains of S and E Africa. *Ourebia ourebi.* [Late 18C. Via Afrikaans < Khoikhoi.]

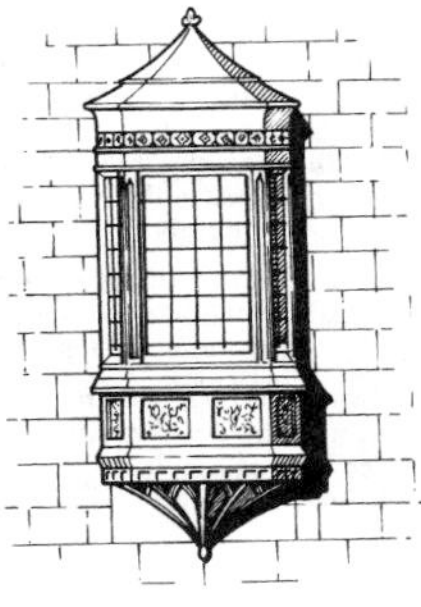

Oriel

oriel /áwri əl/ *n* **1 oriel, oriel window** a bay window projecting from an outside wall and supported from beneath by a bracket **2** a recess or small room formed by an oriel [15C. Via Old French *oriol* 'porch' < medieval Latin *oriolum* 'upper chamber'.]

orient /áwri ənt, órri-/ *v* **1** *vt* **PUT IN POSITION** to position somebody or something so that the person or thing faces in a particular direction ○ *old stone buildings oriented north-south* **2** *vr* **FIND YOUR POSITION** to work out where you are and in which direction you need to travel ○ *the seaman's skill of orienting himself by the stars* **3** *vt* **DIRECT** to direct something in a particular way, e.g. towards a particular objective or audience ○ *advertising oriented towards teenage girls* **4** *vt* **MAKE FAMILIAR** to accustom somebody or yourself to a new situation or set of surroundings ○ *It might take you a few weeks to orient yourself.* **5** *vt* **POSITION TOWARDS EAST** to position something so that it faces east, especially to build a church so that its length lies east to west, with the main altar at the eastern end ■ *n* (*archaic*) **1 PEARL'S LUSTRE** the lustre of a pearl, especially a pearl of high quality **2 PEARL** a pearl, especially one of high quality ■ *adj* **1 EASTERN** eastern (*archaic*) **2 RISING** rising in the sky (*archaic or literary*) **3 WITH GOOD LUSTRE** describes pearls having an exceptionally rich lustre (*archaic*) ○ *'These pearls are orient, but they yield in whiteness to your teeth'.* (Walter Scott, *Ivanhoe*; 1819) [14C. Via Old French < Latin *orient-*, present participle of *oriri* 'rise'; because the sun rises in the east.]

Orient /áwri ənt, órri ənt/, **orient** the countries of E Asia, especially China, Japan, and their neighbours (*dated*) ◊ **Occident**

Oriental /áwri ént'l, órri-/, **oriental** *adj* **1 RELATING TO E ASIA** relating to the countries and peoples of E Asia, especially to China, Japan, and their neighbouring countries (*dated*) **2 HIGH IN QUALITY** describes high quality, valuable pearls and gems ○ *an oriental ruby* ■ *n* **TABOO TERM** a highly offensive term for somebody from E Asia (*dated*)

Orientalia /áwri en táyli ə, órri-/, **orientalia** *n* artefacts from countries in E Asia [Early 20C. < Latin, 'things from the Orient'.]

orientalism /áwri ént'lizəm, órri-/, **Orientalism** *n* **1** a cultural feature associated with the countries, peoples, or cultures of E Asia **2** the study of the civilizations of E Asia —**orientalist** *n* —**orientalistic** /áwri entə lístik, órri-/ *adj*

Oriental poppy *n* a perennial poppy, widely cultivated as a garden plant. Flowers: large, deep red. Native to: SW Asia. *Papaver orientale.*

Oriental rug *n* a brightly coloured and patterned carpet traditionally made by hand from high-quality wool in the Middle East and East Asia, and now often factory-made from a variety of materials

orientate /áwri ən tayt/ (**-tates, -tating, -tated**) *vt* to orient somebody or something or be oriented. [Mid-19C. Back-formation < ORIENTATION.]

orientation /áwri ən táysh'n, órri-/ *n* **1 POSITIONING** the positioning of something, or the position or direction in which something lies ○ *slopes with a southerly orientation* **2 DIRECTION OF DEVELOPMENT** the direction in which something, e.g. a scheme, is developed or focused ○ *the programme's clear orientation towards the white middle class*

3 LEANING the direction in which somebody's thoughts, interests, or tendencies lie ○ *irrespective of sexual orientation* **4 BECOMING ACCUSTOMED** the process of becoming accustomed to a new situation or set of surroundings **5 BRIEFING MEETING** a meeting at which introductory information or training is provided to people embarking on something new, e.g. a course of study **6 MOLECULE ARRANGEMENT** the arrangement of atoms, ions, radicals, or groups relative to each other in crystals or molecules **7 REACTION TO STIMULUS** movement or direction of growth in response to a stimulus, e.g. the way a plant grows in response to light —**orientational** *adj*

oriented /áwri entid, órri-/ *adj* openly supporting or favouring a particular point of view or set of beliefs (*often in combination*) ○ *a Marxist-oriented approach to economics*

orienteering /áwri ən téering, órri-/ *n* a sport that combines map-reading and cross-country running [Mid-20C. Anglicization of Swedish *orientering* < *orientera* 'to orient' < French *orienter* < Latin *orient* (see ORIENT).] —**orienteer** *n, vi*

orifice /órrə fiss/ *n* an opening, especially the mouth, anus, vagina, or other opening into a cavity or passage in the body [Mid-16C. Via Old French < Latin *orificium* 'making a mouth' < *or-* 'mouth' + *-fic-*, stem of *facere* 'make'.]

oriflamme /órri flam/ *n* a red banner or flag that was adopted as the national flag of France in the Middle Ages [15C. < French *oriflambe* < ?]

orig. *abbr* **1** origin **2** original **3** originally

origami /órri gaámi/ *n* the Japanese art of paper folding [Mid-20C. < Japanese, 'fold paper'.]

origin /órri jin/ *n* **1 STARTING POINT** a starting point or first cause (*often plural*) ○ *the origins of the universe* **2 SOURCE** the thing from which something develops, or the place where it comes from (*often plural*) ○ *the uncertain origin of the expression* **3 ANCESTRY** the ethnic group, social class, or country that somebody belongs to or that somebody's family comes from (*often plural*) ○ *a great family whose origins stretch back to the Middle Ages* **4 MUSCLE ATTACHMENT** the place where a muscle is attached **5 ANATOMICAL ROOT** the root of a nerve or blood vessel **6 INTERSECTION OF AXES** the point of intersection of all axes in a coordinate system [Mid-16C. Directly or via French < Latin *origin-* < *oriri* 'arise'.]

LITERARY LINK ***On the Origin of Species by Means of Natural Selection***, a treatise (1859) by Charles Darwin. A highly controversial work, it challenged the established belief in the divine creation of life on earth. Darwin put forward the theory that species evolved slowly in the struggle for existence: those best adapted to life in a particular environment would survive and reproduce by natural selection.

SYNONYMS ***origin, source, derivation, provenance, root***

CORE MEANING: the beginning of something

origin the beginning of something in terms of the time, place, situation, or idea from which it arose, or somebody's ancestry, social background, or country; **source** the place, person, or thing through which something has come into being or from which it has been obtained; **derivation** the origin or source of something, especially a word, phrase, or name; **provenance** the place of origin of something, or the source and ownership history of a work of art or archaeological artefact; **root** the fundamental cause, basis, or origin of something, especially a feeling or a problem.

original /ə ríjj'nəl/ *adj* **1 FIRST** existing first, from the beginning, or before other people or things ○ *The original plan was to turn the site into a shopping centre.* **2 NEW** completely new, and so not copied or derived from something else ○ *She doesn't have a single original idea in her head.* **3 CREATIVE** possessing or demonstrating the ability to think creatively ○ *blessed with an original mind* **4 NOT TRADITIONAL** representing a departure from traditional or previous practice ○ *a refreshingly original interpretation of the classics* **5 SOURCE FOR COPIES** relating to or being something from which a copy or alternative version has been made ○ *the original document* ■ *n* **1 FIRST VERSION** the first or unique item from which copies or alternative versions are made ○ *The meaning of the original has been lost in translation.* **2 AUTHENTIC PIECE OF ART** a genuine work of art, and so not a copy or forgery ○ *verified as an original* **3 ECCENTRIC PERSON** an unusual or eccentric person **4 CREATIVE PERSON** a person of outstanding creativity or revolutionary thinking [14C. Directly or via Old French < Latin *originalis* < *origin-* (see ORIGIN).]

SYNONYMS See ***new***.

originality /ə ríjjə nálləti/ *n* **1 NEWNESS** the quality of newness that exists in something not done before or not derived from anything else ○ *Improvised music lives on the tension between tradition and originality.* **2 CREATIVITY** the ability to think creatively and depart from traditional or previous forms **3** (*plural* **-ties**) **ORIGINAL THING** something original, e.g. a new idea or approach ○ *'That's always the case with my originalities – they are original to nobody but myself'.* (Thomas Hardy, *A Pair of Blue Eyes*; 1889)

originally /ə ríjj'nəli/ *adv* **1** at first or from the beginning ○ *Originally a ballet dancer, she trained to become a circus acrobat.* **2** in a creative or innovative way ○ *thoughtfully assembled and originally presented*

original sin *n* the sinful state, deriving from the disobedience of Adam and Eve, that Christians believe all people are born into

originate /ə ríjjə nayt/ (**-nates, -nating, -nated**) *v* **1** *vi* **HAVE ORIGIN** to begin or develop somewhere or from something ○ *a custom that originated in the 19th century* **2** *vt* **INVENT** to invent something, or bring something into being ○ *Einstein originated the theory of relativity.* **3** *vt* **CREATE FILM OF SOMETHING FOR REPRODUCTION** to reproduce an image on film from which printing plates will be made ○ *Colour plates originated by Smith and Jones, plc.* [Mid-17C. < medieval Latin *originat-*, past participle of *originare* < Latin *origin-* (see ORIGIN).] —**origination** /ə ríjjə náysh'n/ *n* —**originator** /ə ríjjə naytər/ *n*

originative /ə ríjjənətiv/ *adj* with the ability to think of new ways of doing things —**originatively** *adv*

orinasal /áwri náyz'l/ *adj* describes a speech sound pronounced with both oral and nasal passages open, as the nasal vowels in French are [Mid-19C. < Latin *ori-* < *or-* 'mouth' + NASAL.] —**orinasal** *n* —**orinasally** *adv*

O-ring /ṓ ring/ *n* a plastic or rubber ring used in machinery as a seal against air, oil, or high pressure [Mid-20C. < its shape.]

Orinoco /óri nṓkō/ river in Venezuela, flowing northwards into the Atlantic Ocean. Length: 2,560 km/1,590 mi.

oriole /áwri ōl/ *n* **1** a songbird with bold black and yellow markings. Native to: forests of Europe, Asia, Africa. Family: Oriolidae. **2** a brightly coloured songbird, especially the Baltimore oriole. Native to: North America. Family: Icteridae. [Late 18C. Via medieval Latin *oriolus* < Latin *aureolus* < *aurum* 'gold'.]

Orion /ə rī́ ən/ *n* **1** in Greek mythology, a giant and hunter, the son of the sea god Poseidon, who was killed by the goddess Artemis and transformed into a constellation **2** a constellation near the celestial equator containing the Great Nebula and more than 200 stars visible to the naked eye. See illustration at **constellation**

Orissa /o ríssə/ state in NE peninsular India. Capital: Bhubaneswar. Population: 33,795,000 (1994). Area: 155,782 sq. km/60,148 sq. mi.

Oriya /o reé ə/ (*plural* **-ya**) *n* **1** a member of a people who live mainly in Orissa and neighbouring Indian states **2** an Indo-Iranian language spoken in E India, especially in Orissa and neighbouring states on the Bay of Bengal. Native speakers: 36 million. [Early 19C. Via *Oriya* < Sanskrit *Oḍra* 'Orissa'.] —**Oriya** *adj*

Orkney Islands /áwrkni-/ island group and council area in NE Scotland. Population: 19,612 (1991). Area: 905 sq. km/349 sq. mi.

Orlando /awr lánd ō/ city in N Florida. Population: 164,693 (1990).

orle /awrl/ *n* a border that runs inside and parallel to the edge of the shield of a coat-of-arms [Late 16C. < French, < Latin *ora* 'border, edge'.]

Orleanist /awr leé ənist/ *n* a supporter of the family of the duke of Orléans and of their claim to the French throne, especially a supporter of King Louis-Philippe, who reigned 1830 to 1848 [Mid-19C. < French *Orléaniste* < *Orléans*, 'Orléans'.]

Orléans /awr leé ənz/ capital of Loire Department, north-central France. Population: 107,965 (1990).

Orléans /awr leé ənz, awr lay aáN/, **Louis Philippe Joseph, Duc d'** (1747–93) French nobleman. Known as **Philippe Égalité**

Orly /áwrli/ city in north-central France, the location of an international airport. Population: 21,824 (1990).

Ormandy /áwrməndi/, **Eugene** (1899–1985) Hungarian-born US conductor. Born **Eugene Blau**

Ormazd /áwrməzd/ *n* RELIG = **Ahura Mazda**

ormer /áwrmər/ *n* an edible marine mollusc (**gastropod**) that has a large ear-shaped shell. *Haliotis tuberculata.* [Mid-17C. Via Channel Islands French < Latin *auris maris* 'sea ear'; from its shape.]

ormolu /áwrmə loo/ *n* a gold-coloured alloy of copper, zinc, and sometimes tin. Use: decorating furniture, jewellery, mouldings. [Mid-18C. < French *or moulu* 'ground gold'.]

ornament *n* /áwrnəmənt/ **1 DECORATIVE OBJECT** a small decorative object displayed for its beauty **2 DECORATION** decoration or decorative quality ○ *manuscript pages entirely without ornament* **3 SOMETHING THAT DECORATES** a thing that decorates or adds beauty to something else **4 EMBELLISHING NOTE** a note or set of notes added to embellish a melody or harmony **5 VALUED PERSON** somebody whose presence is a source of pride or honour (*archaic or literary*) ■ *vt* /áwrnəment/ **DECORATE** to make something richer by adding decorative elements or items to it ○ *a stone facade ornamented with gargoyles* [14C. Via Old French < Latin *ornamentum* < *ornare* 'equip'.] —**ornamented** /-mentid/ *adj*

ornamental /áwrnə mént'l/ *adj* **1 DECORATIVE** serving as a decoration, as opposed to having any practical use ○ *The hitching post in the front yard was strictly ornamental.* **2 GROWN FOR SHOW** describes plants grown for beauty as distinct from food ○ *an ornamental border* ■ *n* **ORNAMENTAL PLANT** a plant that is grown for its beauty —**ornamentally** *adv*

ornamentation /áwrnə men táysh'n/ *n* **1 ADDITION OF DECORATIVE ELEMENTS** the addition of elements that enhance beauty or visual appeal, especially in the arts **2 DECORATIVE ELEMENT ADDED** one or more elements added to enhance beauty or visual appeal, especially in the arts **3 ADDITION OF EMBELLISHING NOTES** the addition of a note or set of notes that embellishes a melody or harmony

ornate /awr náyt/ *adj* **1** with elaborate or excessive decoration **2** using or consisting of elaborate language, especially language that is designed to impress with its flair or literary quality ○ *expressions that are far too ornate for a TV soap opera* [Early 16C. < Latin *ornatus*, past participle of *ornare* 'equip'.] —**ornately** *adv* —**ornateness** *n*

ornery /áwrnəri/ *adj US* (*informal*) **1** uncooperative and irritable **2** meagre, whether out of poverty or lack of generosity [Early 19C. Dialectal variant of ORDINARY.] —**orneriness** *n*

ornith. *abbr* **1** ornithological **2** ornithology

ornith- *prefix* = **ornitho-** (*before vowels*)

ornithine /áwrni theen/ *n* an amino acid formed in the liver as an intermediate in the manufacture of urea [Late 19C. < its presence in birds' urine.]

ornithischian /áwrni thíski ən/ *adj* belonging or relating to an order of dinosaurs that had a backward-rotating pelvis similar to that of birds. Order: Ornithischia. ■ *n* an ornithischian dinosaur, e.g. an ankylosaur [Early 20C. < modern Latin *Ornithischia* < Greek *ornith-* 'bird' + *iskhion* 'hip joint'.]

ornitho- *prefix* bird ○ *ornithology* [< Greek *ornith-*, stem of *ornis* 'bird']

ornithology /áwrni thólləji/ *n* the branch of zoology that deals with the scientific study of birds —**ornithological** /áwrnithə lójjik'l/ *adj* —**ornithologically** *adv* —**ornithologist** *n*

ornithopod /awr níthə pod/ *n* a plant-eating dinosaur, e.g. the hadrosaur and the iguanadon, that had hind feet similar to those of birds. Suborder: Ornithopoda. [Late 19C. < modern Latin *ornithopoda* < Greek *ornith-* 'bird' + *pod-* 'foot'.]

ornithopter /áwrni thoptər/ *n* an early flying machine that operated using flapping wings [Early 20C. < French *ornithoptère* < Greek *ornith-* 'bird' + *pteron* 'wing'.]

ornithosis /áwrni thṓssiss/ *n* the bacterial disease psittacosis, especially when contracted by humans from birds

oro- *prefix* mountain ○ *orography* [< Greek *oros*]

orogenesis /órrō jénnəssiss/ *n* GEOL = **orogeny** —**orogenetic** /órrō jə néttik/ *adj* —**orogenetically** /-néttikli/ *adv*

orogenic belt /órrō jénnik-/ *n* a large linear feature on the Earth's surface that has undergone tectonic compression and uplift to form mountain ranges such as the Andes and the Alps

orogeny /o rójjəni/ *n* the folding, faulting, and uplift of the Earth's crust to form mountain ranges, often accompanied by volcanic and seismic activity —**orogenic** /órrə jénnik/ *adj* —**orogenically** *adv*

orography /o róggrəfi/ *n* the branch of physical geography involved with the study and mapping of variations in the Earth's surface, including mountains and mountain ranges

oroide /áwrō īd/ *n* an alloy of copper, zinc, tin, and iron that has a lustre similar to gold. Use: manufacture of inexpensive jewellery. [Late 19C. < French, 'goldlike' < *or* 'gold' (see OR[2]).]

orology /o róllәji/ *n* GEOG = **orography** —**orological** /órrə lójjik'l/ *adj* —**orologically** /-lójjikli/ *adv* —**orologist** *n*

⚡**OROM** /ō rom/ *abbr* optical read-only memory

Oromo /o rṓmō/ (*plural* **-mos** *or* **-mo**) *n* **1** a member of a people who originally occupied lands in Somalia, and whose members now live in parts of E Africa, especially in Ethiopia and Kenya **2** the Cushitic language of the Oromo people. Native speakers: 7 million. [Late 19C. < Oromo.] —**Oromo** *adj*

Orontes /ə rónt eez/ **1** mountain in W Iran. Height: 3,548 m/11,640 ft. **2** river in SW Asia, flowing from Lebanon through Syria and Turkey into the Mediterranean Sea. Length: 571 km/355 mi.

oropharynx /órrō fárringks/ (*plural* **-pharynxes** *or* **-pharynges** /-fə rín jeez/) *n* the part of the throat that is located below the soft palate and above the larynx [Late 19C. < Latin *or-* 'mouth' (see ORAL) + PHARYNX.] —**oropharyngeal** /órrō fə rínji əl/ *adj*

orotund /órrō tund/ *adj* (*formal*) **1** loud, clear, and strong, as in tone or voice timbre **2** pompous or bombastic in speech or prose [Late 18C. < Latin *ore rotundo* 'with a round mouth'.] —**orotundity** /órrō túndəti/ *n*

orphan /áwrf'n/ *n* **1** CHILD WITHOUT PARENTS a child whose parents are both dead or who has been abandoned by his or her parents, especially a child not adopted by another family **2** ANIMAL WITHOUT MOTHER a young animal whose mother is dead or has abandoned it **3** STRANDED FIRST LINE an opening line of a paragraph that is also the last line on a page, cut off from the rest of the paragraph by the page break. ◊ **widow** *n.* 3 ■ *vt* DEPRIVE OF PARENTS to make somebody an orphan ○ *a young boy orphaned by the war* ■ *adj US* **1** DESCRIBES MEDICAL CONDITION describes rare medical conditions that affect only a small number of people and for which it is not commercially viable to develop drugs or therapies **2** DESCRIBES PRODUCT describes products that are not developed or marketed, often because of their perceived limited commercial potential ○ *orphan technologies* [14C. Via late Latin < Greek *orphanos* 'orphaned'.] —**orphanhood** *n*

orphanage /áwrfənij/ *n* a home or other institutional setting for orphans, often operated by a local government or charitable organization

orphan assets *npl* assets held by life assurance and pension companies that are surplus to amounts needed to cover current or future payouts [Because deriving from policyholders who have died without making a claim, or a full claim]

orphan drug *n US* a US category for a medication used to treat rare conditions or diseases that affect only a small number of people [< the idea that the drug is of little economic interest to a manufacturer]

orphan site *n* an area of contaminated land for which neither polluter nor owner will take responsibility

orpharion /awr fárri ən/ *n* a large lute, popular during the Renaissance, played by plucking or strumming the strings [Late 16C. After ORPHEUS and *Arion*, musician in Greek mythology.]

Orpheus /áwrfyooss, áwrfi əss/ *n* in Greek mythology, a poet and musician, who descended to the underworld to seek his wife, Eurydice, after her death but failed to bring her back —**Orphean** *adj*

Orphic /áwrfik/ *adj* **1** relating to the poems and mystical writings associated with Orpheus **2** mystical or magical (*literary*)

Orphism /áwrfizəm/ *n* an artistic movement within Cubism that flourished briefly at the beginning of the 20th century, concentrating on achievement of harmony of colour [Late 19C. < ORPHEUS.] —**Orphist** *n* —**Orphistic** /awr fístik/ *adj*

orphrey /áwrfri/ (*plural* **-phreys**), **orfray** (*plural* **-frays**) *n* elaborate embroidery, often done in gold [13C. Via Old French *orfreis* < medieval Latin *aurifrigium* 'Phrygian gold'.]

orpiment /áwrpi mənt/ *n* a bright yellow arsenic sulphide mineral. Use: dyeing, tanning. [14C. Via French < Latin *auripigmentum* 'gold pigment'.]

orpine /áwr pīn/, **orpin** /-pin/ *n* a low-growing succulent plant. Flowers: pink or purple. *Sedum telephium.* [14C. < French *orpin* < *orpiment* (see ORPIMENT).]

Orpington /áwrpingtən/ *n* a heavy deep-chested domestic fowl with a single comb. Native to: England. [Late 19C. After the town of *Orpington* in Kent, England.]

orrery /órrəri/ (*plural* **-ries**) *n* a mechanical model of the solar system that shows the orbits of the planets around the sun at the correct relative velocities [Early 18C. After Charles Boyle, fourth Earl of *Orrery* (1676–1731), who had one made for him.]

orris /órriss/ (*plural* **-ris** *or* **-rises**) *n* **1** an iris with a fragrant root. *Iris germanica.* **2** PLANT SCI = **orrisroot** [Mid-16C. Probably alteration of IRIS.]

orrisroot /órriss root/ (*plural* **-roots** *or* **-root**), **orris root** *n* the fragrant rootstock of the orris. Use: perfumes, cosmetics.

ortanique /áwrtə neék/ *n* a hybrid fruit produced by crossing an orange with a tangerine [Mid-20C. Contraction < ORANGE + TANGERINE + UNIQUE.]

orth. *abbr* **1** orthopaedic **2** orthopaedics

orthicon /áwrthi kon/ *n* a television camera tube in which the image is projected onto a transparent plate that is scanned from behind by an electron beam to produce the output signal [Mid-20C. < ORTHO- + shortening of ICONOSCOPE.]

ortho- *prefix* **1** correct; correction, straightening ○ *orthography* ○ *orthodontics* **2** straight, upright, vertical ○ *orthotropous* **3** perpendicular ○ *orthorhombic* **4** fully hydrated or hydroxylated ○ *orthophosphate* [Via Old French and Latin < Greek *orthos* 'straight, right']

orthocentre /áwrthō sentər/ *n* the point at which the three altitudes of a triangle intersect

orthochromatic /áwrthō krə máttik/ *adj* describes film that is sensitive to all the visible colours except red

orthoclase /áwrthō klayz, áwrthō klayss/ *n* a variously coloured type of feldspar. Source: igneous rock.

orthodontics /áwrthō dóntiks/, **orthodontia** /-dónti ə/ *n* the area of dentistry concerned with the prevention and correction of irregularities of the teeth —**orthodontic** *adj* —**orthodontist** *n*

orthodox /áwrthə doks/ *adj* following the established or traditional rules of a political or religious belief, a philosophy, or a way of life [Late 16C. Via French *orthodoxe* and late Latin < Greek *orthodoxos* 'having the correct opinion' < *doxa* 'opinion'.] —**orthodoxly** *adv*

Orthodox /áwrthə doks/ *adj* **1** relating to the Eastern Orthodox Church **2** relating to Orthodox Judaism

Orthodox Church *n* a Christian church that originated in the Byzantine Empire and recognizes the Patriarch of Constantinople as primate rather than the Pope

Orthodox Judaism *n* the branch of Judaism that accepts without reservation that the Torah was directly handed down from God to Moses

orthodoxy /áwrthə doksi/ *n* the practice of observing established social customs and definitions of appropriateness

Orthodoxy /áwrthə doksi/ *n* **1** the beliefs and practices of the Eastern Orthodox Church **2** the beliefs and practices of Orthodox Judaism

orthoepy /áwrthō epi/ *n* **1** the study of the ways that words are pronounced **2** the usual pronunciation of words [Mid-17C. < ORTHO- + Greek *epe-* 'word, tale'.] —**orthoepic** /áwrthō éppik/ *adj* —**orthoepically** *adv* —**orthoepist** /áwthō epist/ *n*

orthogenesis /áwrthō jénnəsiss/ (*plural* **-ses** /-seez/) *n* an obsolete theory that evolution can proceed in a specific direction determined by internal genetic factors rather than the external forces of natural selection —**orthogenetic** /áwrthō jə néttik/ *adj* —**orthogenetically** *adv*

orthogonal /awr thóggən'l/ *adj* **1** relating to or composed of right angles **2** describes a set of axes all at right angles to each other in a crystal structure —**orthogonality** /awr thóggə nálləti/ *n* —**orthogonally** /awr thóggən'li/ *adv*

orthogonal matrix *n* a matrix in which two rows or two columns are vectors whose scalar product is zero

orthogonal projection *n* a way of providing a two-dimensional graphic view of an object in which the projecting lines are drawn at right angles to the plane of projection

orthograde /áwrthō grayd/ *adj* describes primates that carry the body upright (*refers to primates*) [Early 20C. < ORTHO- + Latin *gradus* 'walking'.]

orthographic /áwrthə gráffik/, **orthographical** /-gráffik'l/ *adj* **1** RELATING TO SPELLING relating to the study of spelling **2** SPELT CORRECTLY correctly spelt **3** MADE UP OF VERTICAL LINES composed of vertical lines —**orthographically** *adv*

orthographic projection *n* ENG = **orthogonal projection**

orthography /awr thóggrəfi/ (*plural* **-phies**) *n* **1** STUDY OF CORRECT SPELLING the study of established correct spelling **2** STUDY OF HOW LETTERS ARE ARRANGED the language study concerned with the letters of an alphabet and how they occur sequentially in words **3** RELATIONSHIP BETWEEN SOUNDS AND LETTERS the way letters and diacritic symbols represent the sounds of a language in spelling

orthomorphic /áwrthō máwrfik/ *adj* GEOG = **conformal** *adj.* 2

orthopaedic /áwrthə peédik/, **orthopedic** *adj* **1** relating to or used in orthopaedics **2** relating to or marked by disorders of the bones, joints, ligaments, or muscles [Mid-19C. < French *orthopédique* 'of correct child-rearing' < Greek *paideia* 'child-rearing' < *paid-* 'child'.] —**orthopaedically** *adv* —**orthopaedist** *n*

orthopaedics /áwrthə peédiks/, **orthopedics** *n* the branch of medicine concerned with the nature and correction of disorders of the bones, joints, ligaments, or muscles (+ *singular verb*)

orthopedic *adj* MED = **orthopaedic**

orthopedics *n* MED = **orthopaedics**

orthophosphate /áwrthō fóss fayt/ *n* any salt or ester of phosphoric acid

orthophosphoric acid /áwrthō foss fórrik-/ *n* CHEM = **phosphoric acid** *n.* 1

orthopsychiatry /áwrthō sī kī́ atri/ *n* a cross-disciplinary method of diagnosing, preventing, and treating childhood psychological problems that involves psychiatrists, child psychologists, paediatricians, and social workers —**orthopsychiatric** /áwrthō sīki áttrik/ *adj* —**orthopsychiatrist** *n*

orthopteran /awr thóptərən/, **orthopteron** *n* any member of the order Orthoptera of primitive winged insects, including cockroaches, mantises, locusts, and crickets ■ *adj* INSECTS = **orthopterous** [Late 19C. < modern Latin *Orthoptera* (plural) 'those with straight wings' < Greek *pteron* 'wing'.]

orthopterous /awr thóptərəss/ *adj* relating to the order Orthoptera of primitive winged insects, including cockroaches, mantises, locusts, and crickets

orthoptics /awr thóptiks/ *n* the study of eye disorders and their detection and correction, especially using nonsurgical treatments, e.g. eye exercises (+ *singular verb*) —**orthoptic** *adj* —**orthoptist** *n*

orthopyroxene /áwrthō pī rók seen/ *n* a member of a subgroup of the pyroxene silicate minerals

orthorhombic /áwrthō rómbik/ *adj* relating to a crystal system with three axes of different lengths that cross at right angles

orthoscopic /áwrthō skóppik/ *adj* **1** able to see normally, without any visual distortion of images **2** describes an optical instrument that gives normal vision

orthostatic /áwrthə státtik/ *adj* associated with or caused by standing in an upright position ○ *orthostatic hypotension* ○ *orthostatic intolerance*

orthotics /awr thóttiks/ *n* the branch of medical engineering concerned with the design and fitting of devices, e.g. braces, in the treatment of orthopaedic disorders (+ *singular verb*) [Mid-20C. < *orthosis* 'artificial external device' < Greek *orthōsis* 'making straight' < *orthos* 'straight'.] —**orthotic** *adj* —**orthotist** *n*

ortolan /áwrtələn/ (*plural* **-lan** *or* **-lans**) *n* a small brownish bunting with a yellow throat, known for its territorial display flight. Native to: Europe, Asia, Africa. Latin name: *Emberiza hortulana.* [Early 16C. Via French < Provençal, 'gardener' < Latin *hortulanus* < *hortus* 'garden'.]

Orvieto /áwrvi áytō/ (*plural* **-tos**) *n* a light white wine produced in the region of Orvieto, Italy

Orwell /áwr wel/, **George** (1903–50) British writer. Born **Eric Arthur Blair** —**Orwellian** /awr wélli ən/ *adj*

-ory *suffix* **1** of or relating to ○ *conclusory* **2** place or thing connected with or used for ○ *crematory* [Via Anglo-Norman and Old French dialect *-orie* < Latin *-orius* and *-orium*]

oryx /órriks/ (*plural* **oryx** *or* **oryxes**) *n* an antelope that has long horns, bold black and white markings on the face, and a hump above the shoulders. Native to: Africa, Arabia. Genus: *Oryx*. [14C. Via Latin < Greek *orux* 'spike, pickaxe, oryx'.]

orzo /áwrzō/ (*plural* **-zos**) *n* pasta that is the size and shape of rice grains, often served with lamb in Greek cooking [Early 20C. Via Italian, 'barley' < Latin *hordeum*.]

os[1] /oss/ (*plural* **ora**) *n* a mouth or similar opening in an organism [Mid-18C. < Latin, 'mouth, face, head' (stem *or-*).]

os[2] /oss/ (*plural* **ossa**) *n* a bone (*technical*) [Mid-16C. < Latin, 'bone' (stem *oss-*).]

Os *symbol* osmium

ϟ **OS** *abbr* **1** Old Saxon **2** old series **3** Old Style **4** operating system **5** ordinary seaman **6** Ordnance Survey **7** out of stock **8** outsize **9** outstanding

o.s. *abbr* **1** left eye **2** old series **3** out of stock **4** outstanding

O/s *abbr* **1** out of stock **2** outstanding

Osage /ō sáyj, ō sayj/ (*plural* **Osage** *or* **Osages**) *n* **1** a member of a Native North American people who originally lived in Ohio, Missouri, and Kansas, and who now live mainly in Oklahoma **2** the Siouan language of the Osage people. Native speakers: 1,000. [Late 17C. Alteration of Osage *Wazhazhe*, one of the three Osage bands.] —**Osage** *adj*

Osage orange *n* **1** a pulpy inedible fruit of a spiny tree **2** a spiny tree that bears Osage oranges. Native to: south-central United States. *Maclura pomifera*.

Osaka /ō saáka/ port on SE Honshu, Japan. Population: 2,481,000 (1994).

Osborne /ózbən, óz bawrn/, **John** (1929–94) British playwright and screenwriter

Oscan /óskən/ *n* an extinct Italic language formerly spoken in S Italy [Late 16C. < Latin *Oscus* 'Oscan'.] — **Oscan** *adj*

Oscar /óskər/ *n* a code word for the letter 'O', used in international radio communications

Oscar II /óskər/ (1829–1907) king of Sweden (1872–1907) and Norway (1872–1905)

OSCE *abbr* Organization for Security and Cooperation in Europe

oscillate /óssi layt/ (**-lates, -lating, -lated**) *v* **1** *vi* **MOVE BACKWARDS AND FORWARDS** to swing between two points with a rhythmic motion **2** *vi* **BE INDECISIVE** to be unable to decide which is the better of two positions, points of view, or courses of action **3** *vti* **CAUSE TO CHANGE PREDICTABLY** to cause or produce rhythmic, predictable variations between two extremes, usually within a set period of time [Early 18C. < Latin *oscillat-*, past participle of *oscillare* 'to swing' < *oscillum* 'swing, mask' (of Bacchus hung as a charm on a tree to swing) < *os* 'mouth, face, head'.] — **oscillation** /óssi láysh'n/ *n* —**oscillational** *adj* —**oscillator** *n* —**oscillatory** *adj*

oscillogram /o síllə gram/ *n* the record produced by an oscillograph or oscilloscope [Early 20C. < shortening of OSCILLOGRAPH.]

oscillograph /o síllə graaf, -graf/ *n* a device that produces a visual record of variations between two points or states, e.g. of electric current [Late 19C. < French *oscillographe* 'that which swings while writing' < Latin *oscillare* 'swing' (see OSCILLATE).] —**oscillographic** /o síllə gráffik/ *adj* —**oscillographically** *adv* —**oscillography** /óssi lóggrəfi/ *n*

oscilloscope /o síllə skōp/ *n* a device that uses a cathode ray tube to produce a visual record of an electrical current on a fluorescent screen [Early 20C. < shortening of *oscillation*.] —**oscilloscopic** /o síllə skóppik/ *adj*

oscine /óss īn, óssin/ *adj* relating to, typical of, or belonging to the large suborder of passerine birds that includes most songbirds [Late 19C. < modern Latin *Oscines* < Latin *oscen* 'songbird' < *canere* 'sing'.]

oscitancy /óssitənssi/ (*plural* **-cies**), **oscitance** /-tənss/ *n* (*technical*) **1** the act of yawning **2** a state of drowsiness or dullness [Early 17C. < Latin *oscitant-*, present participle of *oscitare* 'yawn' < *os* 'mouth, face, head' + *citare* 'put in motion'.] —**oscitant** *adj*

Osco-Umbrian /óskō-/ *n* a group of extinct Italic languages, including Oscan, Umbrian, and Faliscan, spoken in Italy during ancient times —**Osco-Umbrian** *adj*

oscular /óskyōōlər/ *adj* **1** relating to or characteristic of an osculum **2** relating to the mouth or activities of the mouth, e.g. kissing (*technical*) [Early 19C. < Latin *osculum* (see OSCULUM).]

osculate /óskyōō layt/ (**-lates, -lating, -lated**) *v* **1** *vt* **KISS** to kiss (*formal or humorous*) **2** *vi* **TOUCH AT TANGENCY POINT** to touch at a point of common tangency to a line passing between two branches of a curve, each branch continuing in both directions of the line (*refers to arcs*) **3** *vi* **MAKE CONTACT** to make contact or come together (*technical*) [Mid-17C. < Latin *osculatus*, past participle of *osculari* 'kiss' < *osculum* (see OSCULUM).] —**osculant** *adj* — **osculation** /óskyōō láysh'n/ *n* —**osculatory** *adj*

osculum /óskyōōləm/ (*plural* **-la** /-lə/) *n* an opening like a mouth, through which a sponge expels water [Early 17C. Via modern Latin < Latin, 'little mouth, kiss' < *os* 'mouth'.]

-ose[1] *suffix* full of, having the qualities of, resembling ○ *frondose* [< Latin *-osus*]

-ose[2] *suffix* **1** carbohydrate, sugar ○ *maltose* **2** product of primary hydrolysis ○ *proteose* [< GLUCOSE]

ϟ **OSF** *abbr* **1** Order of Saint Francis **2** Open Software Foundation

O'Shane /ō sháyn/, **Pat** (*b.* 1941) Australian lawyer. Full name **Patricia June O'Shane**

Oshawa /óshəwə/ city in SE Ontario, Canada. Population: 268,773 (1996).

Oshkosh /ósh kosh/ city in E Wisconsin. Population: 55,006 (1990).

Oshogbo /ə shóg bō/ capital of Osun State, SW Nigeria. Population: 465,000 (1995 estimate).

ϟ **OSI** *abbr* open systems interconnection

osier /ōzi ər/ *n* **1** a willow tree with long flexible stems used in making baskets and furniture. *Salix viminilis* and *Salix purpurea*. **2** a branch or twig from a willow tree [14C. Via French < medieval Latin *auseria*.]

Osiris /ō sīriss/ *n* in Egyptian mythology, the god of the underworld and the dead, husband of Isis and father of Horus

-osis *suffix* **1** abnormal or diseased condition ○ *chlorosis* **2** condition, action, or process ○ *osmosis* **3** formation of or increase in ○ *thrombosis* [Via Latin < Greek]

Oslo /óz lō/ capital of Norway, in the southeast of the country. Population: 499,693 (1998).

Osman I /oz maán, ózmən/, **Othman** /óthmən, oth maán/ (1258–1324) Turkish warrior

Osmanli /oz mánli/ *n* (*plural* **-lis** *or* **-li**) **1 SUBJECT OF OTTOMAN EMPIRE** a subject of the Ottoman Empire **2 TURKISH LANGUAGE OF OTTOMAN EMPIRE** the Turkish language spoken in the Ottoman Empire, especially when written in Arabic script ■ *adj* **RELATING TO OTTOMAN EMPIRE** relating to the Ottoman Empire [Late 18C. < Turkish *Osmānli* < *Osman* 'Osman'.]

osmatic /oz máttik/ *adj* having or characterized by a sensitive sense of smell [Late 19C. < French *osmatique* < Greek *osmē* 'smell, odour'.]

osmic /ózmik/ *adj* **1** connected with or containing the element osmium, especially in a high valence state **2** relating to odours or the sense of smell (*technical*)

osmic acid *n* CHEM = **osmium tetroxide**

osmiridium /ózmi ríddi əm/ *n* a very hard white or grey naturally occurring alloy of osmium and iridium, often with platinum and other metals. Use: pen nibs. [Late 19C. < German, blend of OSMIUM + IRIDIUM.]

osmium /ózmi əm/ *n* (*symbol* **Os**) a hard white crystalline metallic element, the densest known. Source: osmiridium. Use: catalyst, alloyed with iridium for pen nibs. [Early 19C. < modern Latin, < Greek *osmē* 'smell' (from the pungent smell of osmium oxides).]

osmium tetroxide *n* OsO_4 a colourless or yellow crystalline solid with an unpleasant smelling, poisonous vapour. Use: biological stain.

osmoconformer /ózmō kən fáwrmər/ *n* an ocean organism that varies the concentration of dissolved substances inside its body in accordance with that of the surrounding seawater [Mid-20C. < OSMOSIS.]

osmometer /oz mómmitər/ *n* an instrument that measures osmotic pressure [Mid-19C. < OSMOSIS.] —**osmometric** /ózmə méttrik/ *adj* —**osmometry** /oz mómmətri/ *n*

osmoregulation /ózmō réggyōō láysh'n/ *n* the control of the concentration of dissolved substances in the cells and body fluids of an animal [Mid-20C. < OSMOSIS.] — **osmoregulatory** /-réggyōōlətəri/ *adj*

osmoregulator /ózmō réggyoo laytər/ *n* an organism that can maintain a concentration of dissolved substances inside its body that is different from that of its surroundings [Mid-20C. < OSMOSIS.]

osmose /oz mōz/ (**-moses, -mosing, -mosed**) *vti* to cause or undergo osmosis [Mid-19C. shortening of obsolete *endosmose*, *exosmose*, both < French, < Greek *ōsmos* 'pushing'.]

osmosis /oz mṓssiss/ *n* **1** the diffusion of solvent through a semipermeable membrane from a dilute to a more concentrated solution **2** the gradual, often unconscious, absorption of knowledge or ideas through continual exposure rather than deliberate learning ○ *She seemed to have picked up a working knowledge of Greek by osmosis.* [Mid-19C. Latinization of OSMOSE.] —**osmotic** /oz móttik/ *adj*

osmotic pressure *n* the pressure that must be applied to a solution to stop osmosis

osmunda /oz múndə/ (*plural* **-das** *or* **-da**) *n* a fern with large spreading fronds, e.g. the royal and cinnamon ferns. Genus: *Osmunda*. [13C. < modern Latin *Osmunda* < Old French *osmunde*.]

osnaburg /óznə burg/ *n* a heavy coarse cotton cloth. Use: grain sacks, upholstery, draperies. [Mid-16C. After *Osnaburg*, *Osnabrück*, NW Germany.]

osprey /óss pray, óspri/ (*plural* **-preys** *or* **-prey**) *n* a fish-eating hawk that has long wings and a white head with a dark strip around the eyes. *Pandion haliaetus*. [15C. Probably via assumed Old French *ospreit* < Latin *avis predae* 'bird of prey'.]

Ossa, Mount /óssə/ mountain in N Tasmania, Australia. Height: 1,617 m/5,305 ft.

ossature /óssə tyoor, -chər/ *n* the underlying structure or framework that supports a building or sculpture [Late 19C. < French, < *os* 'bone', after MUSCULATURE.]

ossein /óssi in/ *n* the protein component of bone [Mid-19C. < OSSEOUS.]

osseous /óssi əss/ *adj* made of or resembling bone [Late 17C. < Latin *osseus* 'bony' < *os* 'bone'.]

Osset /óssit/, **Ossete** /ósseet/ *n* a member of a people who live in parts of S European Russia and Georgia, especially Ossetia [Early 19C. < Russian *osetin* < Georgian *osetci* 'Ossetia'.]

Ossetia /o seéshə/ region in central Caucasia, now divided between Russia and Georgia

Ossetic /o séttik/, **Ossetian** /o seésh'n/ *n* the Iranian language of the Ossets. Native speakers: 300,000. ■ *adj* relating to the Ossets, their language, or culture

ossia /o seé ə, óssi ə/ *conj* used to introduce an alternative version given by a composer of a piece of music, often in order to solve technical difficulties in the original version [Late 19C. < Italian *o sia* 'or let it be'.]

Ossian /óssi ən/ *n* a legendary Gaelic hero and poet supposed to have lived in the 3rd century AD —**Ossianic** /óssi ánnik/ *adj*

ossicle /óssik'l/ *n* a small bone, especially one of three bones of the middle ear in humans [Late 16C. < Latin *ossiculum* 'little bone, ossicle' < *os* 'bone'.] —**ossicular** /o síkyōōlər/ *adj* —**ossiculate** /-lət, -layt/ *adj*

ossification /óssifi káysh'n/ *n* **1 PROCESS OF BONE FORMATION** the natural process of forming bone **2 HARDENING OF SOFT TISSUE** the hardening of soft tissue as a result of impregnation with calcium salts **3 BONY MASS** a mass or deposit of bony material in the human body **4 PROCESS OF BECOMING INFLEXIBLE** the process of becoming set and inflexible in behaviour, attitudes, and actions **5 INFLEXIBLE CONFORMITY** rigid, unthinking acceptance of social conventions

ossify /óssi fī/ (**-fies, -fying, -fied**) *vti* **1** to change or be changed from soft tissue, e.g. cartilage, into bone as a result of impregnation with calcium salts **2** to become or make somebody become rigidly set in a conventional pattern of behaviour, beliefs, and attitudes [Early 18C. < French *ossifier* 'turn into bone' < Latin *os* 'bone'.]

Ossining /óss'ning/ town in SE New York State. Population: 23,010 (1998 estimate).

osso buco /óssō bṓōkō/ (*plural* **osso bucos** *or* **osso buchi** /óssō bóokee/) *n* an Italian veal casserole, traditionally served with risotto [< Italian, 'bone marrow']

ossuary /óssyoo əri/ (*plural* **-ies**) *n* an urn or a vault used to hold the bones of the dead (*formal*) [Mid-17C. < late Latin *ossuarium* < Latin *os* 'bone'.]

ost- *prefix* = **osteo-**

osteal /ósti əl/ *adj* **1** made of, containing, or resembling bone **2** relating to bones or the skeletons of mammals [Late 19C. < Greek *osteon* 'bone'.]

osteitis /ósti ítiss/ *n* inflammation of a bone or bony tissue, caused by infection or injury

Ostend /o sténd/ port in W Belgium. Population: 68,635 (1996). Flemish **Oostende**

ostensible /o sténssəb'l/ *adj* presented as being true, or appearing to be true, but usually hiding a different motive or meaning [Mid-18C. Via French < medieval Latin *ostensibilis* < Latin *ostensus*, past participle of *ostendere* 'show' < *tendere* 'stretch, spread'.]

ostensibly /o sténssəbli/ *adv* apparently for a particular reason, but not really for that reason ○ *He left the room, ostensibly to go and use the phone.*

ostensive /o sténssiv/ *adj* = **ostensible** [Early 17C. < late Latin *ostensivus* < Latin *ostensus* (see OSTENSIBLE).] —**ostensively** *adv*

ostensorium /óss ten sáwri əm/ (*plural* **-a** /-ə/), **ostensory** /o sténssəri/ (*plural* **-ries**) *n* CHR = **monstrance** [Late 18C. < medieval Latin, < past participle of Latin *ostendere* (see OSTENSIBLE).]

ostentation /óss ten táysh'n/ *n* conspicuous or vulgar display of wealth and success, especially designed to impress people [15C. Via Old French < Latin *ostentation-* < *ostentare* 'display, exhibit' < *ostendere* (see OSTENSIBLE).] —**ostentatious** /óstən táysh əss/ *adj* —**ostentatiously** *adv* —**ostentatiousness** *n*

osteo- *prefix* bone ○ *osteotomy* [< Greek *osteon* < Indo-European]

osteoarthritis /ósti ō aar thrítiss/ *n* a form of arthritis characterized by gradual loss of cartilage of the joints, usually affecting people after middle age

osteoblast /ósti ō blast/ *n* a cell from which bone develops —**osteoblastic** /ósti ō blástik/ *adj*

osteoclasis /ósti ókləssiss/ (*plural* **-ses** /-seez/) *n* **1** **osteoclasis, osteoclasia** the process of disintegration and assimilation of bony tissue that occurs during normal growth of bone or as part of healing at a fracture site **2** a surgical procedure in which a bone is broken in order to correct a natural deformity or a badly healed fracture [Early 20C. < OSTEO- + Greek *klasis* 'breaking' < *klan* 'to break'.]

osteoclast /ósti ō klast/ *n* **1** a large cell with many nuclei, found in growing bone **2** an instrument used to break bones during surgery to correct a deformity [Late 19C. < OSTEO- + Greek *klastas* 'broken' < *klan* 'to break'.] —**osteoclastic** /ósti ō klástik/ *adj*

osteogenesis /ósti ō jénnəsiss/ *n* the formation of bone in the body

osteogenesis imperfecta /-ímpər féktə/ *n* a rare hereditary disease in which abnormal connective tissue development causes fragile, brittle bones

osteogenic sarcoma *n* MED = **osteosarcoma**

osteoid /ósti oyd/ *adj* resembling or having the characteristics of bone ■ *n* the tissue from which bone develops, especially before it has hardened

osteology /ósti óllәji/ (*plural* **-gies**) *n* **1** the branch of anatomy concerned with the study of the structure and functions of bones **2** the bone structure or skeleton of an animal —**osteological** /ósti ə lójjik'l/ *adj* —**osteologically** /-lójjikli/ *adv* —**osteologist** /ósti óllәjist/ *n*

osteolysis /ósti óllәssiss/ *n* the gradual disintegration of bone caused by disease

osteoma /ósti ṓmə/ (*plural* **-mata** /-mətə/ *or* **-mas**) *n* a benign tumour made of bone, usually on the skull

osteomalacia /ósti ō mə láyshi ə/ *n* a disease occurring mainly in women that results from a lack of vitamin D or calcium, causing softening of the bones and resulting pain and weakness

osteomyelitis /ósti ō mī ə lítiss/ *n* inflammation of bone and bone marrow, caused by infection

osteopathy /ósti óppəthi/ *n* a system of medicine based on the theory that many diseases are caused by incorrect alignments of bones, ligaments, and muscles, and that correcting these through manipulation can cure the problems —**osteopath** *n* —**osteopathic** /ósti ə páthik/ *adj* —**osteopathically** *adv*

osteophyte /ósti ə fīt/ *n* a small abnormal outgrowth of bone that occurs within joints or at other sites where there is degeneration of cartilage, e.g. due to osteoarthritis —**osteophytic** /ósti ə fíttik/ *adj*

osteoplastic /ósti ə plástik/ *adj* **1** relating to or typical of bone surgery **2** relating to or important in the process of bone development

osteoplasty /ósti ə plásti/ *n* the surgical repair or correction of distortions of bones

osteoporosis /ósti ō pə rṓssiss/ (*plural* **-ses**) *n* a disease occurring among women after the menopause in which the bones become very porous, break easily, and heal slowly [Mid-19C. < OSTEO- + Greek *poros* 'passage'.]

osteosarcoma /ósti ō saar kṓmə/ (*plural* **-mata** *or* **-mas**) *n* a malignant bone tumour

osteosis /ósti ṓssiss/ *n* the presence of bone-making nodules in the skin

osteotome /ósti ə tōm/ *n* a surgical instrument used to cut or divide bone

osteotomy /ósti óttəmi/ (*plural* **-mies**) *n* a surgical procedure in which bone is divided or sectioned —**osteotomist** *n*

Ostia /ósti ə/ ancient Roman port in west-central Italy, at the mouth of the River Tiber

ostiary /ósti əri/ (*plural* **-ies**) *n* a doorkeeper in a Roman Catholic church [15C. < Latin *ostiarius* 'doorkeeper' < *ostium* 'opening'.]

ostinato /ósti naátō/ (*plural* **-tos**) *n* a short musical phrase or melody that is repeated over and over, usually at the same pitch [Late 19C. < Italian, 'stubborn, obstinate'.]

ostiole /ósti ōl/ *n* a small pore or opening in some algae or fungi, through which reproductive spores pass [Mid-19C. < Latin *ostiolum* 'little door' < *ostium* 'opening'.]

ostium /ósti əm/ (*plural* **-a** /ósti ə/) *n* **1** a small pore or opening in a passage or organ of the body **2** a pore or small opening in a sponge through which water passes [Mid-17C. < Latin, 'mouth of a river, opening'.]

ostler /ósslər/, **hostler** /hósslər/ *n* formerly, a person employed to look after horses at an inn [14C. Variant of HOSTELLER.]

ostomate /óstə mayt/ *n* a person who has had a stoma created, allowing the intestine to open at the body surface [Mid-20C. < OSTOMY.]

ostomy /óstəmi/ (*plural* **-mies**) *n* a surgical procedure such as a colostomy or ileostomy, in which an artificial opening for excreting waste matter is created [Mid-20C. < terms like COLOSTOMY, ILEOSTOMY.]

-ostosis *suffix* formation of bone ○ *hyperostosis* [< Greek *osteon* 'bone']

ostracize /óstrə sīz/ (**-cizes, -cizing, -cized**), **ostracise** (**-cises, -cising, -cised**) *vt* **1** to banish or exclude somebody from society or from a particular group, either formally or informally ○ *She was ostracized by all her former friends.* **2** to banish somebody by a popular vote because that person is regarded as dangerous to society, as was the practice in ancient Greece [Mid-19C. < Greek *ostrakizein* < *ostrakon* 'pottery fragment'.] —**ostracism** *n*

ostracod /óstrə kod/ (*plural* **-cod** *or* **-cods**) *n* a tiny crustacean that lives inside a hard outer shell made of two hinged halves. Subclass: Ostracoda. [Mid-19C. < modern Latin *Ostracoda* < Greek *ostrakōdēs* 'like a pottery fragment' < *ostrakon* 'shell'.]

ostracoderm /o strákə durm/ *n* an extinct, jawless, mainly freshwater fish, dating from the Silurian and Devonian periods, that had a flat body encased in a layer of protective bony plates and scales [Late 19C. < Greek *ostrakon* 'hard shell'.]

Ostrava /óstrava/ city in NE Czech Republic. Population: 325,827 (1994).

ostrich /óstrich/ (*plural* **-triches** *or* **-trich**) *n* **1** a two-toed fast-running bird with a long bare neck, small head, and fluffy drooping feathers. It cannot fly, and is the largest living bird. Native to: Africa. *Struthio camelus.* **2** a person who tries to avoid unpleasant situations by refusing to acknowledge that they exist (*informal*) [13C. < Old French *ostrusce* < Latin *avis* 'bird' + Greek *strouthiōn-* < *strouthos* 'sparrow'.]

Ostrogoth /óstrə goth/ *n* a member of the eastern branch of Gothic peoples who invaded Italy, where they ruled from the end of the 5th to the middle of the 6th centuries. ◊ **Visigoth** [14C. < late Latin *Ostrogothi* (plural) 'Ostrogoths' < Germanic.] —**Ostrogothic** /óstrə góthik/ *adj*

Ostyak /ósti ak/ (*plural* **-aks** *or* **-ak**), **Ostiak** (*plural* **-aks** *or* **-ak**) *n* the Finno-Ugric language of the Ostyak people. Native speakers: 15,000. [Early 18C. Via Russian < Tartar *ustyak* 'one of another tribe'.] —**Ostyak** *adj*

Oswald /ózzwəld/, **St** (605?–642) Anglo-Saxon king of Northumbria (634–41)

Oswald, Lee Harvey (1939–63) US alleged assassin of President John F. Kennedy.

Oswestry /ózwəstri/ town in west-central England. Population: 15,612 (1991).

OT *abbr* **1** occupational therapy **2** Old Testament **3** overtime

ot- *prefix* = **oto-** (*before vowels*)

Otago /ō taágō/ administrative region in the southeastern part of the South Island, New Zealand. Population: 193,132 (1996). Area: 38,638 sq. km/14,918 sq. mi.

Otago Peninsula peninsula in the southeastern part of the South Island, New Zealand. Length: 25 km/16 mi.

otalgia /ō tálji ə, -jə/ *n* pain in the ear (*technical*) [Mid-17C. < Greek *ōtalgia* < *ōt-*, stem of *ous* 'ear'.]

OTC *abbr* **1** Officers' Training Corps **2** over-the-counter

OTE *abbr* on-target earnings (*in advertisements for jobs that pay commission*)

other /úthər/ CORE MEANING: a grammatical word used to show that a thing, person, or situation is additional or different ○ (adj) *He does much to help the homeless and other people in need.* ○ (adj) *They met plenty of other children there.* ○ (adj) *I went on ahead, and the other climbers struggled on behind.* ○ (pron) *This is one problem, but there are many others.* ○ (pron) *As much as I demand of others, I am much more demanding of myself.*

1 *adj, pron* **FURTHER** refers to an additional or further person or thing of the type already mentioned ○ (adj) *Let me make one other suggestion.* ○ (pron) *A couple of students failed the exam, but many others passed.* **2** *adj, pron* **DIFFERENT** refers to a different thing or things from that or those already specified ○ (adj) *Banks are unlike any other business.* ○ (adj) *Are there any other items you'd like to take home?* ○ (pron) *This problem, more than any other, has divided the critics.* **3** *adj, pron* **THE REMAINING** refers to the remaining people or things in a group, apart from the one specified ○ (adj) *She left earlier, with the other kids.* **4** *adj, pron* **SECOND OF TWO THINGS** refers to the second of two things when the first is known or understood ○ (adj) *He threw his other glove out of the window.* ○ (pron) ○ *She had a cup in one hand and a glass in the other.* ○ (pron) *It goes in one ear and out the other.* **5** *pron* **others OTHER PEOPLE OR THINGS** other people or things ○ *Others may think differently* ○ *Put the others in the drawer* [Old English *ōðer* < Indo-European] ◇ **other than** indicates an exception to a statement ○ *Was anyone there other than the two of you?* ◇ **the other day** *or* **night** a few days or nights ago ○ *A funny thing happened the other day.*

other-directed *adj* more concerned with what other people think than with your own values and standards —**other-directedness** *n*

otherness /úthərnəss/ *n* the condition of being perceived as strange or different

otherwise /úthər wīz/ *adv* **1 OR ELSE** if things had been different ○ *'I overslept', said Joe, 'otherwise you would have heard from me earlier'.* **2 DIFFERENTLY** different from or opposite to something stated ○ *You may take your hand luggage with you unless otherwise requested.* **3 IN OTHER WAYS** in any other ways ○ *An otherwise dull day was enlivened by her arrival.* [Old English *(on) ōðre wīsan* '(in) (an)other wise or manner']

otherworld /úthər wurld/ *n* a world or life that is beyond the conventional perception of reality —**otherworldliness** /úthər wúrldlinəss/ *n* —**otherworldly** /úthər wúrldli/ *adj*

Othman = **Osman I**

otic /ṓtik, óttik/ *adj* relating to or located near the ear [Mid-17C. < Greek *ōtikos* < *ōt-*, stem of *ous* 'ear'.]

-otic *suffix* **1** relating to a particular condition, action, or process ○ *hypnotic* **2** having a particular abnormal or diseased condition ○ *psychotic* [Via French and Latin < Greek *-ōtikos*]

otiose /ṓti ōss, -ōz/ *adj* **1 NOT EFFECTIVE** with no useful result or practical purpose **2 WORTHLESS** with little or no value **3 LAZY** unwilling or uninterested in working or being active (*archaic*) [Late 18C. < Latin *otiosus* 'at leisure, idle' < *otium* 'leisure'.] —**otiosely** *adv* —**otiosity** /ōti óssəti/ *n*

otitis /ō títiss/ *n* inflammation of the ear, caused by infection

otitis media /-méedi ə/ *n* a painful inflammation of the middle ear that can cause dizziness and temporary hearing loss

⚡**OTL** *abbr* out to lunch (*in e-mails*)

oto- *prefix* ear ○ *otolith* [Via modern Latin < Greek *ōt-*, stem of *ous*]

otocyst /ótō sist/ *n* **1** the structure from which the adult inner ear develops **2** ZOOL = **statocyst**

otolaryngology /ótō lárring góllәji/ *n* a branch of medicine concerned with the treatment and diagnosis of diseases of the ear, nose, and throat —**otolaryngological** /ótō lә ríng gә lójjik'l/ *adj* —**otolaryngologist** *n*

otolith /ótō lith/ *n* **1** a particle of calcium carbonate found in the inner ear of vertebrates and involved in sensory perception **2** ZOOL = **statolith** *n.* 1

otology /ō tóllәji/ *n* the branch of medicine concerned with the structure and function of the ear, its diseases, and their treatment —**otological** /ótә lójjik'l/ *adj* —**otologist** *n*

Oto-Manguean /ótō máng gee әn, -gwee әn/, **Otomanguean** *n* a family of about 30 Native Central American languages spoken in a region extending from N Mexico to Nicaragua [< OTOMI + MANGUE] —**Oto-Manguean** *adj*

Otomi /ótә méé/ (*plural* **-mi** *or* **-mis**) *n* **1** a member of a Native Central American people of central Mexico **2** the Oto-Manguean language of the Otomi people. Native speakers: 200,000. [Late 18C. Via American Spanish < Nahuatl *otomih* 'unknown'.] —**Otomi** *adj*

O'Toole /ō tóol/, **Peter** (*b.* 1932) Irish-born British actor

otorhinolaryngology /ótō rínō lárring góllәji/ *n* MED = **otolaryngology** —**otorhinolaryngological** /ótō rínō lә ríng gә lójjik'l/ *adj* —**otorhinolaryngologist** /ótō rínō lárring góllәjist/ *n*

otosclerosis /ótō sklә róssiss/ *n* a hereditary disease of the inner ear in which spongy bone growth leads to progressive hearing impairment

otoscope /ótō skōp/ *n* an instrument incorporating a light and a magnifying lens, used to examine the external canal of the ear and the eardrum —**otoscopic** /ótō skóppik/ *adj*

ototoxic /- tóksik/ *adj* toxic to the ear and hence impairing hearing or balance —**ototoxicity** /- tok síssәti/ *n*

⚡**OTP** *abbr* open trading protocol (*in e-commerce*)

Otranto, Strait of /o tránt ō/ sea passage between the Adriatic and Ionian seas, separating SE Italy from W Albania. Length: 69 km/43 mi.

OTT *abbr* over the top (*informal*)

ottava /ō taávә/ *adj* sung or played at an octave higher or lower than the notes written on the staff, indicated by a sign placed above or below the staff [Early 19C. < Italian, 'octave, eighth' < *otto* 'eight' < Latin *octo.*]

ottava rima /-réemә/ *n* a verse form made up of eight lines in iambic pentameter with the rhyme scheme abababcc [Early 19C. < Italian, 'eighth rhyme'.]

Ottawa /óttәwә/ **1** river in Ontario and Quebec, Canada, flowing into the St Lawrence River. Length: 1,270 km/790 mi. **2** capital of Canada, in SE Ontario. Population: 323,340 (1996).

otter /óttәr/ (*plural* **-ter** *or* **-ters**) *n* **1** an aquatic fish-eating mammal with smooth dark brown fur and webbed feet. Family: Mustelidae. **2** the fur of the otter [Old English *ot(t)or* < Indo-European, 'water']

Otterburn /óttәr burn/ village in NE England, where the Scots defeated the English in the Battle of Otterburn in 1388

otter hound *n* a large dog of an English breed used in otter hunting

otto /óttәō/ *n* PHARM, INDUST = **attar** [Variant]

Otto cycle /óttō-/ *n* a thermodynamic process for the conversion of heat into work, e.g. the sequential suction, compression, ignition, and expulsion in a four-stroke engine [Late 19C. After Nikolaus August *Otto* (1832–91), German engineer and inventor.]

ottoman /óttәmәn/ *n* **1** LONG SEAT an upholstered sofa that has no arms and is usually backless **2** STOOL FOR FEET a low upholstered stool used for resting the feet or as a seat **3** HEAVY FABRIC a heavy corded silk or rayon fabric. Use: coats, trimmings. [Late 16C. Via French or Italian < medieval Latin *ottomanus* < Arabic *'Uṯmān* 'Osman'.]

Ottoman /óttәmәn/ *n* a member of a Turkish people who conquered Asia Minor in the 13th century —**Ottoman** *adj*

Ottoman Empire *n* a Turkish empire established in the late 13th century in Asia Minor, eventually extending throughout the Middle East and ending in 1922

Otway Ranges /ót way ráynjiz/ range of hills in S Victoria, Australia. Highest peak: Mount Cowley 686 m/2,251 ft.

ou /ō/ *n S Africa* a man (*slang*) [Mid-20C. < Afrikaans < ?]

OU *abbr* Open University

ouabain /waá bay in, -bayn/ *n* a poisonous crystalline compound. Source: seeds of certain trees. Use: medicinally as a heart stimulant. *Strophanthus gratus.* [Late 19C. Via French *ouabaïo* < Somali *wabayo* 'arrow poison'.]

Ouagadougou /waágә dóog oo/ capital of Burkina Faso, in the centre of the country. Population: 634,479 (1991 estimate).

oubaas /ō baass/ *n S Africa* a person who is above somebody else in age or rank [Mid-19C. < Afrikaans, 'old boss' < ?]

oubliette /óobli ét/ *n* a dungeon made so that the only way in or out is through a trap door at the top [Early 19C. < French, < *oublier* 'forget' < Latin *oblitus*, past participle of *oblivisci.*]

ouch /owch/ *interj* an exclamation used to express sudden pain [Mid-19C. < ?]

oud /ood/ *n* a stringed instrument of SW Asia and North Africa that resembles a lute or a mandolin [Mid-18C. < Arabic *al-'ūd* 'the wood'.]

ought[1] /awt/ CORE MEANING: a modal verb indicating what somebody should do ○ *It seems to me that we ought to support their initiative.* ○ *You ought to tell her how you feel.*
v **1** BE MORALLY RIGHT indicates that somebody has a duty or obligation to do something or that it is morally right to do something ○ *You ought to be ashamed of what you have done.* **2** BE IMPORTANT indicates that something is important or a good idea ○ *You ought to see a doctor as soon as possible.* **3** BE PROBABLE indicates probability or expectation ○ *We ought to be there by now.* **4** BE WISHED FOR indicates a desire or wish ○ *You ought to come to dinner sometime.* **5** BE THE CASE indicates that something should be the case but may not be ○ *That ought to be easy.* [Old English *āhte*, past tense of OWE]

USAGE Avoid in formal writing the regional constructions (called *double modal auxiliaries*) ***hadn't ought*** or ***shouldn't ought***, as in *They hadn't ought to have done that.* Use instead: *They ought not to have done that.* The same holds with the regional *might could*, as in *We might could get there by three if we hurry*, which is also inappropriate in standard English.

ought[2] *n* zero [Mid-18C. < erroneous division of *a nought.*]

ouguiya /oo géé yә/ *n* see table at **currency** [Late 20C. Via French < Mauritanian Arabic *ūgiyya* < Greek *ougkia* < Latin *uncia* (see OUNCE[1]).]

Ouija /wéejә/, **Ouija board** *tdmk* a trademark for a board with letters and a pointer or planchette by which answers to questions are spelt out, supposedly by spiritual forces

ould /owld/ *adj Ireland* used to represent the Irish pronunciation of 'old', especially its use as an intensifier

Oulu /ó ōol ōō/ port in west-central Finland, on the Gulf of Bothnia. Population: 109,094 (1995).

ouma /ó maa/ *n S Africa* **1** a grandmother **2** an elderly woman [Early 20C. < Afrikaans, 'grandmother' < *ou* 'old' + *ma* 'mother'.]

ounce[1] /ownss/ *n* **1** UNIT OF WEIGHT a unit of weight equal to one-sixteenth of a pound in the avoirdupois system **2** FLUID OUNCE a unit for measuring liquid, equal to 0.0284 of a litre **3** SMALL AMOUNT a small amount of something ○ *Anyone with an ounce of common sense would take an umbrella on a day like this.* [14C. Via Old French *unce* < Latin *uncia* 'twelfth part, inch, ounce' < *unus* 'one'.]

ounce[2] /ownss/ (*plural* **ounce** *or* **ounces**) *n* ZOOL = **snow leopard** [14C. < Old French *once*, variant of *lonce* (the *l* being mistaken for the definite article) < Latin *lync-* 'lynx'.]

oupa /ó paa/ *n S Africa* **1** a grandfather **2** an elderly man [Early 20C. < Afrikaans, 'grandfather' < *ou* 'old' + *pa* 'father'.]

our /owr/ *det* **1** BELONGING TO US indicates that something belongs to or is associated with the speaker or writer and at least one other person (*first person plural possessive determiner*) ○ *Where are all our bags?* ○ *Our house is just a few hundred yards from yours.* **2** BELONGING TO EVERYONE indicates that something belongs to or is associated with people in general ○ *the dreams that inspire us to do our best* **3** REFERS TO MEMBER OF FAMILY refers to a member of the speaker's family (*informal*) ○ *Our John is an electrician now.* [Old English *ūre* 'of us', genitive plural of WE]

SPELLCHECK See ***hour.***

Our Father *n* CHR = **Lord's Prayer**

Our Lady *n* a title for the Virgin Mary

ours /owrz/ *pron* refers to something or somebody that belonging to or associated with the speaker and at least one other person (*first person plural possessive pronoun*) ○ *It's no surprise that their team is ahead of ours.* [13C. < OUR + -'s 'belonging to'.]

ourselves /owr sélvz, aar sélvz/ *pron* **1** BELONGING TO US refers to the speaker or writer and at least one other person, sometimes emphatically (*used as the object of a verb or preposition when the subject refers to the same people*) ○ *We ourselves can't work it out, so we don't expect others to be able to.* **2** REFERS TO PEOPLE IN GENERAL refers to people in general ○ *Many of us have secrets that we find difficult to admit even to ourselves.* **3** REFERS EMPHATICALLY TO US refers emphatically to the speaker or writer and at least one other person ○ *These papers are of no interest to anyone but ourselves.* **4** OUR USUAL SELVES our usual selves ○ *At home with the family, we can really be ourselves.*

-ous *suffix* **1** full of, having the qualities of ○ *virtuous* ○ *traitorous* **2** having a lower valence than a corresponding compound or ion the name of which ends in *-ic* ○ *chromous* [Via Old French < Latin *-osus* and *-us*]

Ouse /ooz/ **1** river in E England, emptying into the Wash. Length: 257 km/160 mi. **2** river in NE England, emptying into the Humber estuary. Length: 92 km/57 mi. **3** river in SE England, emptying into the English Channel. Length: 48 km/30 mi.

oust /owst/ *vt* **1** to use force to remove somebody from a place **2** to remove or force somebody from an office or position [15C. Via Old French *oster* < Latin *obstare* 'stand in the way' < *stare* 'to stand'.]

ouster /ówstәr/ *n* **1** the act of removing or forcing somebody out of a place or position **2** the illegal removal or forceful dispossession of somebody's property

out /owt/ CORE MEANING: a grammatical word indicating that somebody or something is away from a place or removed from somewhere ○ (adv) *The child ran out and got back onto the bike.* ○ (adv) *She took out her laptop.* ○ (adj) *She's been out late every night.*
1 *adv* OUTSIDE outside a place rather than inside ○ *It's cold out.* **2** *adv* IN ANOTHER PLACE in another place, usually far away ○ *She's out in Australia, I think.* **3** *adv* INDICATES END POINT indicates a goal or objective achieved in the action specified by the verb ○ *Stick it out – never give up.* **4** *adv* IN EXISTENCE that there is in existence ○ *It's one of the best albums out.* **5** *adj, adv* AWAY FROM HOME away from home or your place of work ○ (adj) *He's not answering the doorbell – he must be out.* ○ (adv) *She's not answering the phone – she must have gone out.* **6** *adj, adv* FARTHER AWAY refers to the tide when the sea moves away from the shore ○ (adj) *We can cross to the island when the tide is out.* ○ (adv) *The tide goes out at around five o'clock.* **7** *adj, adv* NO LONGER BURNING of a light or a fire, no longer alight or no longer burning ○ (adj) *The fire is out.* ○ (adv) *The fire has gone out.* **8** *adj, adv* IN FLOWER in flower ○ (adj) *The daffodils are out at last.* ○ (adv) *All the wild flowers are coming out.* **9** *adj, adv* AVAILABLE of a book, CD, or similar publication or release, available for people to buy ○ (adj) *Her new book is out in paperback at last.* ○ (adv) *Their new album came out last week.* **10** *adj, adv* ON STRIKE on strike ○ (adj) *The miners have been out for a month now.* ○ (adv) *500 workers came out in protest over the benefit cuts.* **11** *adj* NO LONGER IN A GAME unable to take part any longer in a game or sport **12** *adj* CONSIDERING A VERDICT of a jury, considering its verdict **13** *adj* INCORRECT inaccurate or incorrect ○ *Look – the figures are way out.* **14** *adj* UNACCEPTABLE unacceptable, or not worth considering ○ *That possibility is out, I'm afraid.* **15** *adj* UNFASHIONABLE no longer in fashion **16** *adj* INTENT determined or intent on ○ *He's just out for what he can get.* **17** *adj* UNCONSCIOUS unconscious ○ *She was out cold.* **18** *adj* USED UP used up or exhausted ○ *All our rations are out.* **19** *adj* NOT IN GOVERNMENT not in power or office **20** *adj* FINISHED completed or concluded ○ *before the year is out* **21** *adj* NOT WORKING not working ○ *All the phones are out.* **22** *adj* OPENLY HOMOSEXUAL open about being homosexual ○ *He isn't out*

to his parents. **23** *interj* **AWAY FROM HERE!** a command for somebody to leave a place ○ *Out!* **24** *vt* **EXPOSE SOMEBODY AS HOMOSEXUAL** to expose somebody, especially a public figure or famous person, as a homosexual ○ *The action group has outed many prominent celebrities.* **25** *n US* **WAY OF AVOIDING BAD CONSEQUENCE** a way of escaping from a predicament or avoiding the undesirable consequences of something (*informal*) ○ *What's my out if things go wrong?* [Old English *ūt* < Germanic] ◇ **out of 1** indicates that somebody leaves a place ○ *Three men came out of the store.* **2** indicates that somebody removes something from a place ○ *In her enthusiasm, she pulled the drawer right out of the desk.* **3** towards the outside ○ *She looked longingly out of the window.* **4** no longer available or in somebody's possession ○ *We're out of butter.* **5** using as a source or material ○ *Plastic products are made out of petroleum.* **6** indicates proportion that something is true of ○ *This applies to one out of five adults.* **7** indicates that somebody gains an advantage from something ○ *I think I got a lot out of the course.* **8** indicates that somebody is sheltered from the weather ○ *Remember to keep out of the sun, or at least use sunblock.* **9** beyond the range of a sound ○ *I called her, but she was out of earshot.* **10** indicates the motivation behind an action ○ *He only did it out of spite.* **11** indicates that somebody is not or is no longer in a situation ○ *A police officer warned them to stay out of trouble.* ◇ **out of it** very drunk, or under the influence of drugs (*informal*) ○ *You were totally out of it last night!* ◇ **out with it** a command to somebody to let something be known immediately ○ *Come on, what's going on? Out with it!*

outa *prep* = **outta**

outage /ówtij/ *n* **1** an amount of something that is missing after delivery or storage **2** a temporary loss of function or interruption of a power source, especially a loss of electric power

out-and-out *adj* being a thorough, uncompromising, or unapologetic example of something

out-and-outer *n* a person who goes to extremes in some activity or endeavour

outback *n* /ówt bak/ a sparsely inhabited or wilderness region of a country, especially of Australia —**outback** *adj*

outbalance /owt bállənss/ (**-ances, -ancing, -anced**) *vt* to go beyond something in effect, influence, or importance

outbid /owt bíd/ (**-bids, -bidding, -bidded**) *vt* to offer to pay more money for something than somebody else

outboard /ówt bawrd/ *adj* **1 ON THE OUTSIDE OF A BOAT** located on the outside of the hull of a ship or boat **2 LOCATED TOWARDS BOAT'S HULL** positioned away from the centre of a ship or boat **3 AWAY FROM THE FUSELAGE** away from the main body of an aircraft and towards the wing tips ■ *adv* **TOWARDS OUTSIDE OF SHIP** in a direction away from the centre of a ship or aircraft ■ *n* **1 BOAT WITH OUTBOARD MOTOR** a boat with an engine mounted outside the stern **2** NAUT = **outboard motor**

outboard motor *n* a small or medium-sized engine with a propeller that can be mounted outside the stern of a boat

outbound /ówt bownd/ *adj* travelling away from rather than towards a particular place ○ *an outbound journey*

out-box *n US* COMM = **out-tray**

outbrave /owt bráyv/ *vt* (*archaic*) **1** to face a threat with defiance **2** to be braver than somebody else

outbreak /ówt brayk/ *n* a sudden occurrence, usually of something unpleasant or dangerous such as illness or fighting ○ *the outbreak of war*

outbreed /owt bréed/ (**-breeds, -breeding, -bred** /-bréd/, **-bred**) *vti* to bring together distantly related members of a species in order to breed genetically varied offspring, or reproduce in this way [Early 20C. After INBREED.]

outbuilding /ówt bilding/ *n* a barn, shed, or other structure that is situated away from the main building on a property

outburst /ówt burst/ *n* **1** a sudden display of strong emotion ○ *an outburst of grief* **2** a sudden burst of energy or growth

outcall /ówt kawl/ *n* a visit made by a doctor or other professional to the home of a client or patient

outcast /ówt kaast/ *n* a person who has been rejected by a group or by society ○ *a social outcast* —**outcast** *adj*

outcaste /ówt kaast/ *n* **1** in South Asia, somebody who has been expelled from a Hindu caste for violating its rules or customs **2** somebody in South Asia who does not belong to a caste

outclass /owt klaáss/ *vt* to be so much better than others as to seem to be in a separate class altogether

outcome /ówt kum/ *n* the way that something turns out in the end

outcrop /ówt krop/ *n* the part of a rock formation that is exposed on the surface of the ground ■ *vi* (**-crops, -cropping, -cropped**) to stick out of the ground as an outcrop [Mid-18C. < *crop out*.]

outcross *vt* /owt kross/ to mate two plants or animals not closely related but usually of the same breed in order to produce offspring ■ *n* the process of outcrossing plants or animals, or the progeny produced as a result

outcry /ówt krī/ (*plural* **-cries**) *n* **1** a strong and widespread public reaction against something **2** a loud cry from a crowd of people

outdated /owt dáytid/ *adj* old-fashioned or out-of-date ○ *outdated notions about how to raise children*

outdistance /owt dístənss/ (**-tances, -tancing, -tanced**) *vt* **1** to be faster than others in a race and leave other competitors behind **2** to be considerably more successful than others

outdo /owt dóo/ (**-does, -doing, -did** /-díd/, **-done** /-dún/) *vt* to do more or better than other people, or better than previously

outdoor /ówt dáwr/ *adj* **1** located in, belonging in, or suited to the open air ○ *outdoor activities* **2** enjoying activities that take place in the open air

outdoor relief *n* HIST = **out relief**

outdoors /owt dáwrz/ *adv* outside, or in the open air ■ *n* the open air, especially when away from populated areas [Early 19C. < *out of doors*.]

outdoorsman /owt dáwrzmən/ (*plural* **-men** /-mən/) *n* a man who spends much time doing outdoor activities such as camping, hunting, and fishing

outdoorsperson /owt dáwrz purss'n/ (*plural* **-people** /-peep'l/) *n* a person who spends much time doing outdoor activities such as camping, hunting, and fishing

outdoorswoman /owt dáwrz wŏŏmmən/ (*plural* **-en** /-wimmin/) *n* a woman who spends much time doing outdoor activities such as camping, hunting, and fishing

outdoorsy /owt dáwrzi/ *adj* suited to or fond of the open air (*informal*)

outdraw /owt dráw/ (**-draws, -drawing, -drew** /-dróo/, **-drawn** /-dráwn/) *vt* **1** to draw a handgun faster than another person **2** to attract a larger audience than another performer or performance

outer /ówtər/ *adj* **1 ON THE OUTSIDE** on or around the outside of something ○ *the outer surface of the spacecraft* **2 AWAY FROM THE CENTRE** on the edge or away from the centre of something ○ *the outer islands* **3 ABOUT BODY RATHER THAN SPIRIT** concerning or belonging to external or worldly things rather than the life of the mind or spirit

outer bar *n* in England and Wales, all the junior barristers practising at the bar. ◊ **inner bar**

Outer Hebrides island group in NW Scotland, comprising the westernmost islands of the Hebrides

outermost /ówtər mōst/ *adj* farthest away from the centre [14C. < OUTER, after INNERMOST.]

outer planet *n* any of the five planets, Jupiter, Saturn, Uranus, Neptune, and Pluto, that have orbits lying beyond the asteroid belt

outer space *n* all space in the universe beyond the Earth and its atmosphere, especially interplanetary and interstellar space, but including the region where astronauts walk and satellites orbit the earth

outerwear /ówtər wair/ *n* clothing that is designed to be worn outdoors over other clothing

outface /owt fáyss/ (**-faces, -facing, -faced**) *vt* **1** to win a confrontation with somebody, especially by staring or not looking away **2** to confront somebody boldly or confidently

outfall /ówt fawl/ *n* the outlet of a sewer, drain, or stream, especially where it empties into a larger body of water

outfield /ówt feeld/ *n* **1 OUTER PART OF CRICKET PITCH** the part of a cricket pitch farthest from the bowler and the player who is batting **2 AREA BEYOND THE INFIELD** the part of a baseball or softball field beyond the diamond marked by the bases **3 PLAYERS IN OUTFIELD** the players in baseball or softball whose positions are in the outfield —**outfielder** *n*

outfit /ówt fit/ *n* **1 SET OF CLOTHES** a set of clothes worn together **2 EQUIPMENT** a set of tools or equipment for a particular task or occupation ○ *a diving outfit* **3 SMALL ORGANIZATION** a team or group of people who work closely together, e.g. a military unit (*informal*) ■ *vt* (**-fits, -fitting, -fitted**) **1 EQUIP** to provide somebody with all the equipment that is needed to do a particular job **2 DRESS** to provide somebody with a set of clothes

outfitter /ówt fittər/ *n* a shop that sells men's clothes

outflank /owt flángk/ *vt* **1** to go around the main body of an enemy force and attack it from the side or from behind **2** to outwit or bypass an opponent or competitor

outflow /ówtflō/ *n* the flow, movement, or transfer of something such as gas, water, or money away from a place

outfox /owt fóks/ *vt* to defeat somebody by being more cunning

outgas /owt gáss/ (**-gases, -gassing, -gassed**) *vti* to remove or release trapped or absorbed gas, or be released as gas

outgeneral /owt jénnərəl/ (**-als, -alling, -alled**) *vt* to defeat somebody in battle through better leadership

outgo /owt gṓ/ *vt* (**-goes, -going, -went** /-wént/, **-gone** /-gón/) **OUTDO** to go beyond or surpass somebody or something ■ *n* **1 EXPENDITURE** something that goes out, especially money that is paid out **2 SOMETHING THAT FLOWS OUT** something that is flowing out

outgoing /owt gō ing/ *adj* **1 LEAVING OR GOING OUT** in the process of departing or going out of a building or place ○ *outgoing flights* **2 LEAVING A JOB** in the process of departing or being sent away after a period of office ○ *a dinner for the outgoing president* **3 SOCIABLE** confident and friendly in social situations ○ *a cheerful, outgoing child* —**outgoingness** *n*

outgoings /owt gō ingz/ *npl* money paid out, especially on a regular basis

outgrew past tense of **outgrow**

out-group *n* a group of people excluded from another group with higher status

outgrow /owt grṓ/ (**-grows, -growing, -grew** /-gróo/, **-grown** /-grṓn/) *vt* **1 GET TOO LARGE** to grow too large for something **2 MOVE BEYOND PREVIOUS INTERESTS** to change so that old ideas, interests, or ways of behaving are lost in favour of new ones **3 OUTSTRIP** to grow larger or faster than other things or people

outgrowth /ówt grōth/ *n* **1** a natural development or result of something else **2** something that is growing out from the main part

outguess /owt géss/ *vt* to get an advantage over somebody by anticipating what that person is thinking or planning to do

outgun /owt gún/ (**-guns, -gunning, -gunned**) *vt* **1** to have more guns or firepower than somebody else **2** to defeat a rival or competitor by being stronger or having better resources (*informal*)

outhaul /ówt hawl/ *n* a rope used to pull a sail taut along a spar or boom

out-Herod (**out-Herods, out-Herodding, out-Herodded**) *vt* to behave more excessively than somebody else ○ *out-Herod Herod* [After HEROD (THE GREAT), presented in medieval mystery plays as an overdramatic character]

outhouse /ówt howss/ (*plural* **-houses** /-howziz/) *n* **1** a small building situated near the main building on a property **2** *US* an outdoor toilet consisting of a small building that encloses a seat with a hole in it built over a pit

outing /ówting/ *n* **1 EXCURSION** a short pleasure trip usually lasting no more than a day **2 TAKING PART IN EVENT** an appearance at or participation in a public event, especially an athletic competition **3 DECLARING SOMEBODY TO BE HOMOSEXUAL** the practice of making public the fact that somebody is homosexual when that person wants the information kept private

outjockey /owt jóki/ (**-eys, -eying, -eyed**) *vt* to get an advantage over somebody by cleverness or trickery

outlander /ówt landər/ *n* somebody from another country or from a different region, and thus a stranger [Late 16C. After Dutch *uitlander*, German *Ausländer*.]

outlandish /owt lándish/ *adj* 1 extremely unusual or bizarre 2 alien or foreign (*archaic*) —**outlandishly** *adv* —**outlandishness** *n*

outlast /owt laáast/ *vt* to last or exist longer than somebody or something else

outlaw /ówt law/ *n* 1 **FUGITIVE** a notorious criminal, especially one on the run 2 **SOMEBODY WITHOUT LEGAL RIGHTS** somebody, often a criminal, who has been officially deprived of legal rights and so is not protected by the law 3 **REBEL** somebody who is rebellious or flouts the law 4 **VICIOUS ANIMAL** a savage or uncontrollable animal ■ *vt* 1 **BAN** to make something illegal 2 **TAKE AWAY SOMEBODY'S LEGAL RIGHTS** to deprive somebody officially of all their legal rights [12C. < Old Norse *útlagi* 'person outside the law' < *útlagr* 'outlawed, banished'.]

outlawry /ówt lawri/ *n* 1 refusal to obey the law 2 a state in which somebody has been deprived of his or her legal rights and is no longer protected by the law, or the legal process by which this happens

outlay *n* /ówt lay/ 1 **SPENDING** the expending of resources or spending of money 2 **MONEY SPENT** an amount of money spent ■ *vt* /owt láy/ (**-lays, -laying, -laid** /-láyd/) **SPEND MONEY** to spend money on something

outlet /ówt let, -lət/ *n* 1 **VENT** a passage or opening for letting something out, e.g. water or steam 2 **RELEASE FOR EMOTIONS** a way of releasing emotions or impulses 3 **STORE** a place where something is sold, often a shop that sells the products of a particular manufacturer 4 **MARKET FOR GOODS** a market providing goods or services for purchasers 5 *US* ELEC = **socket** *n*. 2 6 **HOLE ON ELECTRICAL DEVICE FOR PLUG** a hole on a piece of electrical equipment into which a plug fits 7 **MOUTH OF RIVER** the lower end of a river where it flows into a lake or the sea 8 **STREAM DRAINING LAKE** a stream or channel flowing from a larger body of water

outlier /ówt lī ər/ *n* 1 **ROCK FORMATION** an outcrop of rock that is separated from a main formation 2 **OUTLYING PART** a separate part of a system, organization, or body that is at some distance from the main part 3 **SOMEBODY LIVING AT DISTANCE FROM WORK** a person who lives far from his or her workplace

outline /ówt līn/ *n* 1 **LINE THAT SHOWS SHAPE** the edge or outer shape of something 2 **LINE DRAWN ROUND** a line drawn around the outside edge of something 3 **DRAWING WITHOUT SHADING** a style or example of drawing in which an object or figure is represented only by an outline 4 **ROUGH PLAN** a list of the main points of a subject to be written about, or a rough idea of a proposed plan ■ *vt* (**-lines, -lining, -lined**) 1 **DRAW MAIN FEATURES** to draw a line showing or emphasizing the shape of something 2 **GIVE ESSENTIAL ELEMENTS** to give the main points of an argument or plan

outlive /owt lív/ (**-lives, -living, -lived**) *vt* 1 to live longer than somebody else 2 to continue to exist beyond or last through something ○ *The policy has outlived its usefulness.*

outlook /ówt löök/ *n* 1 **ATTITUDE** an attitude or point of view 2 **LIKELY FUTURE** expectations for the future, especially for the way a particular situation will develop 3 **VIEW** a view seen from a particular place

out loud *adv* aloud, rather than silently in somebody's head

outlying /ówt lī ing/ *adj* far from the central part of a particular place or region

outman /owt mán/ (**-mans, -manning, -manned**) *vt* to have a larger force of people than an opponent has

outmanoeuvre /owt mə nóovər/ (**-vres, -vring, -vred**) *vt* to get the better of somebody by using skill or cunning

outmatch /owt mách/ *vt* to prove stronger or better than somebody else

outmoded /ówt mṓdid/ *adj* 1 no longer fashionable or widely used 2 having been superseded by something newer or more efficient [Early 20C. Translation of French *démodé*.] —**outmodedness** *n*

outmost /ówt mōst/ *adj* farthest away from the centre or main area [14C. Alteration of UTMOST.]

outnumber /owt númbər/ *vt* to be more numerous than another group or set of things

out-of-body *adj* describes an experience in which a person's consciousness appears to have an existence separate from the body, enabling the subject to see his or her own body from the outside

out of bounds *adj, adv* in or indicating a place that is beyond the established or official boundaries

out-of-court *adj* arranged without going to court or without completing a court case, usually in an effort to avoid a long court case or to minimize costs

out-of-date *adj* old-fashioned or no longer current

out-of-doors *adv* = **outdoors** *adv.*

out of order *adj* 1 **NOT FUNCTIONING** describes a machine that is not working properly 2 **NOT OBEYING RULES OF SPEAKING** describes somebody who is not following the official procedures of a court or parliament, e.g. by speaking when told not to 3 **BEHAVING BADLY** not acceptable, or behaving in an unacceptable way (*informal*) ○ *What he said was well out of order.*

out-of-pocket *adj* 1 **HAVING LOST MONEY** with less money than before, after spending some on something that did not produce good results ○ *I was seriously out-of-pocket.* 2 **REQUIRING SOMEBODY TO SPEND CASH** describes expenses paid for with cash 3 **WITH NO MONEY** with no money to spend

out-of-the-way *adj* 1 far from a populated area or difficult to get to 2 uncommon or unconventional

out-of-town *adj* coming from or happening in another town or city

outpace /owt páyss/ (**-paces, -pacing, -paced**) *vt* to do better or go faster than something or somebody else

outpatient /ówt paysh'nt/ *n* a patient who receives treatment at a hospital without staying overnight

outperform /ówt pər fáwrm/ *vt* to perform better than somebody or something else

outplacement /ówt playssmənt/ *n* a service offered by a company to help employees who are being dismissed find new jobs

outplay /owt pláy/ *vt* to play better than an opponent

outpoint /owt póynt/ *vt* 1 to sail closer to the wind than another ship 2 to score more points than somebody else

outport /ówt pawrt/ *n* a secondary port near another port but in deeper water, used for larger vessels

outpost /ówt pōst/ *n* 1 **TROOPS APART FROM MAIN FORCE** a small group of troops stationed at a distance from the main body of an army and assigned to guard a particular place or area 2 **MILITARY BASE** a small military base in a remote area or different country 3 **BASE** a settlement in unfamiliar territory or on a frontier

outpour *vti* /owt páwr/ to flow out quickly or make something flow out quickly ■ *n* /ówt pawr/ something that flows out freely, or the act of flowing out

outpouring /ówt pawring/ *n* something that pours or floods out, e.g. lava or a strong emotion

⚡**output** /ówt pŏŏt/ *n* 1 **PRODUCTION** the act of producing 2 **YIELD** an amount of something produced or manufactured, especially during a fixed period of time 3 **CREATIVE OR ARTISTIC PRODUCTION** creative or intellectual work produced by somebody ○ *her literary output* 4 **ENERGY PRODUCED** energy or power produced by a system 5 **ELECTRICAL POWER** the electrical energy, measured in watts, delivered by a generator or consumed by an electronic circuit 6 **INFORMATION FROM COMPUTER** information produced by a computer ■ *vt* (**-puts, -putting, -put** *or* **-putted**) **PRODUCE COMPUTER INFORMATION** to display information from a computer on a monitor, or direct it to a printer or other device

outrace /owt ráyss/ (**-races, -racing, -raced**) *vt* to do something better or faster than others

outrage /ówt rayj/ *n* 1 **VIOLENT ACT** an extremely violent or cruel act 2 **OFFENSIVE ACT** a very offensive or insulting act 3 **FURY** intense anger and indignation aroused by a violent or offensive act ■ *vt* (**-rages, -raging, -raged**) 1 **ATTACK OR VIOLATE** to commit a vicious crime against somebody 2 **AROUSE ANGER IN** to make somebody feel intense anger or indignation 3 **RAPE** to rape somebody (*literary*) [13C. Via French, 'excess, atrocity' < Old French *outrer* 'exceed' < Latin *ultra* 'beyond'.]

outrageous /owt ráyjəss/ *adj* 1 **EXTRAORDINARY AND UNCONVENTIONAL** extravagant or unconventional, and likely to shock people 2 **MORALLY SHOCKING** violating accepted standards of decency or morality 3 **EXCESSIVE** exceeding the bounds of what is reasonable or expected ○ *outrageous prices* 4 **VIOLENT OR CRUEL** violent or unrestrained in mood or action —**outrageously** *adv* —**outrageousness** *n*

~~**outragious**~~ incorrect spelling of **outrageous**

~~**outragous**~~ incorrect spelling of **outrageous**

outrange /owt ráynj/ (**-ranges, -ranging, -ranged**) *vt* to have a greater range than something else of the same class, e.g. a firearm or missile

outrank /owt rángk/ *vt* to have a higher rank or status than somebody else

outré /óo tray/ *adj* passing well beyond what is usual, normal, or generally acceptable [Early 18C. Via French < Old French, past participle of *outrer* (see OUTRAGE).]

outreach *vt* /owt réech/ 1 **REACH FARTHER** to reach or extend farther than somebody or something else 2 **EXCEED** to exceed or go beyond a limit ■ *n* /ówt reech/ 1 **PROVISION OF COMMUNITY SERVICES** the provision of information or services to groups in society who might otherwise be neglected ○ *an outreach programme for people who cannot read* 2 **EXTENT OF REACH** the length or extent of the reach of somebody or something ○ *the outreach of a communications network*

out relief *n* formerly, money given by the state to people who needed financial support but were not living in a workhouse

outride /owt ríd/ (**-rides, -riding, -rode** /-rṓd/, **-ridden** /-rídd'n/) *vt* 1 to ride better, farther, or faster than somebody else 2 to survive the violence of the wind and waves during a storm

outrider /ówt rīdər/ *n* 1 a rider in front of or at the side of a carriage, motor vehicle, or race horse, who acts as an escort 2 a person who precedes a group and acts as a scout

outrigger /ówt riggər/ *n* 1 **PART OF A BOAT** a beam or framework sticking out from the side of a boat, used to extend a rope or sail or as a brace for an oarlock 2 **FRAMEWORK ON CANOE** a long float attached to a framework that projects from the side of a seagoing canoe to prevent it from capsizing 3 **KIND OF BOAT OR CANOE** a boat or canoe fitted with an outrigger 4 **STRUCTURE ON AIRCRAFT** a projection attached to an aircraft or other vehicle or machine to stabilize it or to support something [Mid-18C. < ?]

outright *adv* /ówt rít/ 1 **WHOLLY** wholly and completely ○ *He now owns the business outright.* 2 **INSTANTLY** immediately or instantly ○ *They refused our offer outright.* 3 **CANDIDLY** openly and without reservation ○ *I told him outright that he was making a big mistake.* ■ *adj* /ówt rīt/ 1 **ABSOLUTE** complete or total ○ *an outright lie* 2 **WITHOUT QUALIFICATIONS** without restrictions or limitations ○ *The car was an outright gift from the corporation.*

outrival /owt rív'l/ (**-vals, -valling, -valled**) *vt* to surpass somebody or something in a particular respect

outrun /owt rún/ (**-runs, -running, -ran** /-rán/, **-run**) *vt* 1 **RUN FASTER** to run faster or farther than somebody else 2 **RUN AWAY** to escape by or as if by running faster than a pursuer ○ *outrun the bill collectors* ○ *The hare outran the wolf.* 3 **EXCEED** to develop faster than or exceed something ○ *Demand for petrol began to outrun supply.*

outsell /owt sél/ (**-sells, -selling, -sold** /-sṓld/, **-sold**) *vt* 1 to be sold faster or in greater quantities than something else 2 to sell more than another salesperson

outset /ówt set/ *n* the beginning or initial stage of an activity

outshine /owt shín/ (**-shines, -shining, -shone** /-shón/, **-shone**) *vt* 1 to shine brighter than something else 2 to surpass somebody or something else, especially in terms of excellence or quality

outshoot *vt* /owt shóot/ (**-shoots, -shooting, -shot** /-shót/) to shoot a weapon better than somebody else ■ *n* /ówt shoot/ something that projects or shoots out

outside /ówt síd/ CORE MEANING: a grammatical word indicating the outer surface or appearance of something ○ (noun) *Grill the chicken wings until the outsides are crisp.* ○ (adv) *The house still needs to be painted outside.*

1 *adv, prep, adj* **OUT OF DOORS** in the open air rather than inside a building ○ (adv) *We should head outside soon if we're going to start the barbecue.* ○ (prep) *I'll meet you outside the post office.* ○ (adj) *an outside toilet* 2 *adj, adv, prep* **BEYOND IMMEDIATE ENVIRONMENT** happening, existing, or originating in places, people, or groups other than your own or what you are used to ○ (adj) *It was claimed that most of the substandard work had been done by outside contractors.* ○ (adv) *in the world outside* ○ (prep) *married outside her religion* 3 *adj* **SLIGHT** slight or remote ○ *There's an outside chance we may still be able to get tickets.* 4 *adj* **MAXIMUM** the most extreme possible or probable ○ *an outside estimate of three months to complete the job* 5 *adj* **FARTHEST FROM SIDE OF ROAD** farthest from the side of a road or centre of a race track ○ *coming up fast in the outside lane* 6 *prep* **BEYOND THE SCOPE OF** not included in the range or scope of something ○ *Such behaviour is completely outside my comprehension.* 7 *n* **EXISTENCE NOT IN AN INSTITUTION** existence in the community and not in an

institution such as prison or a psychiatric hospital ○ *We wondered what life was like on the outside.* **8** *n* **AREA FARTHEST FROM SIDE OF ROAD** the part farthest from the side of a road or centre of a race track ○ *Large crowds of shoppers forced her to walk on the outside of the pavement.* **9** *n* **HEAVILY POPULATED AREA OF CANADA** the most populous areas of Canada along the coasts ◇ **at the outside** at the maximum amount or time that can be expected ◇ **outside of** other than the person or thing mentioned

outside broadcast *n* a radio or television programme not recorded or filmed in a studio. US term **remote** *n.* 3

outsider /owt sídər/ *n* **1** a person who is not part of a group or organization **2** a competitor or candidate who is considered unlikely to win

LITERARY LINK ***The Outsider***, a novel (1942) by French writer Albert Camus. This classic existentialist work, also known as *The Stranger*, is set in Algiers and recounts how a young man's extreme sense of alienation leads him to commit murder. During his trial, however, the absurdities of the judicial process compel him to acknowledge the value of human life.

outsight /owt sīt/ *n* the ability to take note of or judge external things [Early 17C. After INSIGHT.]

outsize /ówt sīz, ówt sīz/ *n* a size that is larger than usual ■ *adj* **outsize, outsized** much larger, heavier, or more extensive than is usual or expected ○ *an outsize ego*

outskirts /ówt skurts/ *npl* the areas at the edge of a town or city, farthest from the centre

outsmart /owt smaárt/ *vt* to use cunning or cleverness to get an advantage over somebody

outsold past participle, past tense of **outsell**

outsource /ówt sawrss/ (**-sources, -sourcing, -sourced**) *vt* to buy labour or parts from a source outside a company or business, usually as a means of cutting costs or to employ expertise not available within the company

outspan *n* /ówt span/ *S Africa* a place kept available on a farm for people travelling to stop to rest their animals ■ *vti* /owt spán/ (**-spans, -spanning, -spanned**) *S Africa* to remove a yoke or harness from an animal [Early 19C. Via Afrikaans *uitspan* 'unyoke, unharness' < Middle Dutch *uitspannen*.]

outspend /owt spénd/ (**-spends, -spending, -spent** /-spént/, **-spent**) *vt* **1** to spend more than somebody else **2** to exceed fixed limits for something in spending ○ *outspent our budget*

outspoken /owt spṓkən/ *adj* expressing opinions directly, frankly, and fearlessly —**outspokenly** *adv* —**outspokenness** *n*

outspread *adj* /ówt spred/ **STRETCHED OUT** extended or spread out flat ■ *vt* /owt spréd/ (**-spreads, -spreading, -spread**) **EXTEND** to stretch out or extend something ■ *n* **ACT OF SPREADING OUT** the act or an example of extending outwards

outstand /owt stánd/ (**-stands, -standing, -stood** /-stŏŏd/, **-stood**) *vi* to stand out or be prominent

outstanding /owt stánding/ *adj* **1** **UNUSUALLY EXCELLENT** excellent, and superior to others in the same group or category ○ *outstanding work* **2** **NOT YET RESOLVED** not yet paid, resolved, or dealt with ○ *outstanding debts* **3** **JUTTING OUT** jutting outwards or upwards **4** **PUBLICLY SOLD** publicly issued and sold as securities —**outstandingly** *adv*

outstare /owt stáir/ (**-stares, -staring, -stared**) *vt* to make somebody look away or submit by staring hard

outstation /ówt stayshʼn/ *n* a post or station in a remote unsettled spot ■ *adv Malaysia* in, at, or to a place that is not where you normally live or work, often one that is in a more rural area

outstay /owt stáy/ *vt* **1** to stay longer than other people, or beyond the limit of something ○ *outstayed their welcome* **2** to show greater endurance than somebody ○ *outstayed their rivals*

outstep /owt stép/ (**-steps, -stepping, -stepped**) *vt* **1** to go beyond a limit or boundary ○ *a remark that overstepped the bounds of free speech* **2** to achieve more than somebody, or be better than something ○ *felt outstepped by his predecessor*

outstood past participle, past tense of **outstand**

outstretch /owt stréch/ *vt* to hold out or extend something

outstrip /owt stríp/ (**-strips, -stripping, -stripped**) *vt* **1** to achieve more or go faster than somebody, especially a competitor **2** to be greater than something ○ *Demand for their products has already outstripped supply.*

outswing /ówt swing/ *n* the movement of a bowled cricket ball from the leg side to the off side

outta /ówttə/, **outa** *prep* out of (*informal*) ○ *I'm outta here.* [Mid-20C. Representing a pronunciation.]

outtake /ówt tayk/ *n* **1** a recorded scene or sequence that is not included in the final version of a film or television programme, usually because it contains mistakes ○ *The outtakes were funnier than the movie itself.* **2** a recording not used in the final version of an album

out-there *adj US* outgoing and positively involved with life and the world (*slang*)

outthink /owt thíngk/ (**-thinks, -thinking, -thought** /-tháwt/, **-thought**) *vt* to think better, faster, or more intelligently than another person

outthrust /ówt thrúst/ *adj* extending out beyond something ○ *the dog's outthrust paw*

out-tray *n* a tray or container in an office for mail ready to be sent and completed items ready to be filed

outturn /ówt turn/ *n* the amount produced during a specific period [Late 18C. < *turn out.*]

outvote /owt vṓt/ (**-votes, -voting, -voted**) *vt* to defeat other candidates or a proposal by a majority of votes

outward /ówtwərd/ CORE MEANING: a grammatical word indicating that something is outside or on or towards the exterior of something, or relates to the exterior of something ○ *the rustic balustrading that bounded the arbour on the outward side*

1 *adj* **VISIBLE** clearly observable ○ *She gave no outward indication that she was upset.* **2** *adj* **RELATING TO THE PHYSICAL BODY** relating to the physical body rather than the mind or spirit ○ *his outward appearance reflected his inner turmoil* **3** *adj* **APPARENT** apparent or superficial ○ *can't judge by outward appearances* **4** *adj* **OUTBOUND** heading away from a place **5** *adv* = **outwards** **6** *n* **MATERIAL WORLD** the reality of the external world (*literary*) —**outwardness** *n*

outward-bound *adj* making an outgoing journey or passage

outwardly /ówtwərdli/ *adv* in appearance rather than in reality

outwards /ówtwərdz/, **outward** *adv* towards the outside and away from the inside or middle

outwash /ówt wosh/ *n* sand and gravel deposited by streams that are flowing away from a glacier

outwear /owt wáir/ (**-wears, -wearing, -wore** /-wáwr/, **-worn** /-wáwrn/) *vt* to last longer or wear better than something else

outweigh /owt wáy/ *vt* **1** to be more important or valuable than something else **2** to weigh more than somebody or something else

outwit /owt wít/ (**-wits, -witting, -witted**) *vt* to use cunning or trickery to get an advantage over somebody

outwith /ówt wíth/ *prep Scotland* outside or beyond ○ *working outwith normal hours*

outwore past tense of **outwear**

outwork *vt* /owt wúrk/ **WORK HARDER THAN** to work harder or faster than somebody ■ *n* /ówt wurk/ **1** **MILITARY OUTPOST** a trench or fortification built beyond the main line of defence **2** **WORK DONE AT HOME** work done for a company outside the company's premises

outworker /ówt wurkər/ *n* a company employee who works from home rather than on the company's premises

outworn /ówt wáwrn/ *adj* outdated or no longer useful ■ past participle of **outwear**

ouzel /óozʼl/ *n* a small bird of the thrush family with dark plumage and a white band across its throat. Native to: Europe. *Turdus torquatus.* [Old English *ōsle* 'blackbird' < Indo-European]

ouzo /óozō/ (*plural* **-zos**) *n* a colourless Greek alcoholic spirit flavoured with aniseed [Late 19C. < modern Greek.]

ova plural of **ovum**

oval /ṓvʼl/ *adj* shaped like an egg ■ *n* something shaped like an egg [Late 16C. < medieval Latin *ovalis* < Latin *ovum* 'egg'.] —**ovally** *adv* —**ovalness** *n*

ovalbumin /ōv álbyŏŏmin, ṓv al byŏŏmin/ *n* the main crystalline protein or albumin found in egg whites [Mid-19C. < Latin *ovi albumen* 'white of egg' < *ovum* 'egg' + *albumen* (see ALBUMEN).]

Oval Office *n* **1** an oval-shaped room in the White House that is the private office used by the president of the United States **2** the power and authority of the president of the United States

oval window *n* a membranous opening between the middle ear and the inner ear that transmits sound vibrations

Ovambo /ō vámbō/ (*plural* **-bo** *or* **-bos**) *n* **1** a member of a people who live in parts of southern Africa, especially in Angola and Namibia **2** the Bantu language of the Ovambo people. Native speakers: 700,000. [Mid-19C. < Bantu, 'people of leisure'.] —**Ovambo** *adj*

ovariectomy /ō váiri éktəmi/ (*plural* **-mies**) *n* the surgical removal of one or both ovaries

ovariotomy /ō váiri óttəmi/ (*plural* **-mies**) *n* **1** a surgical incision into an ovary **2** SURG = **ovariectomy**

ovaritis /ṓvə rítiss/ *n* MED = **oophoritis**

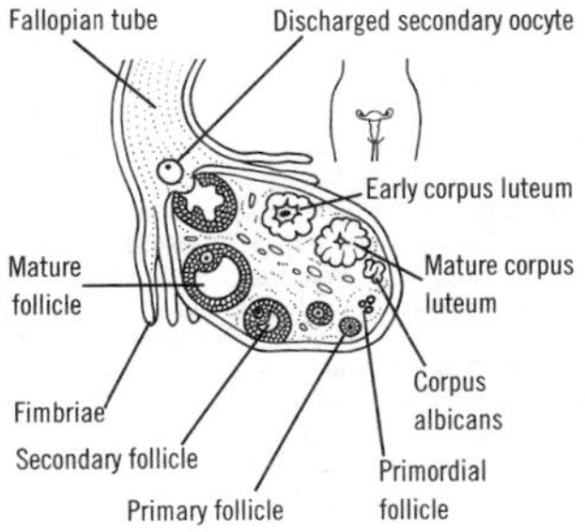

Ovary

ovary /ṓvəri/ (*plural* **-ries**) *n* **1** either of the two female reproductive organs that produce eggs and, in vertebrates, also produce the sex hormones oestrogen and progesterone **2** the lower part of a pistil that bears ovules and ripens into a fruit [Mid-17C. < modern Latin *ovarium* < Latin *ovum* 'egg'.] —**ovarian** /ō váiri ən/ *adj*

ovate /ṓ vayt/ *adj* **1** shaped like an egg **2** describes a leaf or petal that is broad and rounded at the base and tapers towards the tip [Mid-18C. < Latin *ovatus* 'egg-shaped' < *ovum* 'egg'.] —**ovately** *adv*

ovation /ō váyshʼn/ *n* **1** enthusiastic applause or cheering, especially from a crowd or large group of people **2** an ancient Roman victory ceremony for a returning military hero [Mid-16C. Via Latin *ovation-* < *ovare* 'rejoice'; from an imitation of the sound of exulting.] —**ovational** *adj*

oven /úvvʼn/ *n* a compartment warmed by a heat source and used for baking, roasting, or drying [Old English *ofen* < Indo-European, 'cooker']

ovenable /úvvʼnəbʼl/ *adj* heat-resistant, or in heat-resistant packaging and ready to be cooked without further preparation ○ *ovenable food packaging*

ovenbird /úvvʼn burd/ *n* **1** a warbler with a shrill call that builds a dome-shaped nest on the ground. Native to: North America. *Seiurus aurocapillus.* **2** a small brown bird that builds a dome-shaped nest from clay and dried leaves. Native to: South America. Genus: *Furnarius.* [Early 19C. < the shape of the birds' nests.]

oven glove *n* a padded hand covering used as protection when putting hot dishes into, and taking them out of, an oven

ovenproof /úvvʼn proof/ *adj* capable of being used in an oven without being damaged by the heat

oven-ready *adj* already prepared and ready to be cooked or heated before eating

ovenware /úvvʼn wair/ *n* heat-resistant dishes that can be used for baking or roasting as well as for serving

over /ṓvər/ CORE MEANING: a grammatical word used to indicate a position directly above something, either resting on the top of something, or above the upper surface of something with a space in between ○ (prep) *a framed portrait over the fireplace* ○ (prep) *He wore a red flannel shirt over a T-shirt.* ○ (prep) *Julia was bent over the sink washing glasses.* ○ (adv) *flocks of geese flying over* ○ (adv) *Heat the milk and pour it over.*

1 *prep, adv* **ON OR TO OTHER SIDE OF** positioned on or moving to the other side of something such as a barrier, obstacle, or area of land ○ (prep) *To see the cathedral you need to cross over the river.* ○ (adv) *He climbed over into the next* *field.* **2** *prep, adv* **THROUGHOUT** throughout the whole extent of ○ (prep) *travelling over Europe* ○ (prep) *In the past few years, fifties diners have sprung up all over town.* ○ (adv) *People are the same the world over.* **3** *prep, adv* **MORE THAN** more than a particular amount, measurement, or age ○ (prep) *go over your quota* ○ (adv) *people 30 and over* **4** *adv* **ACROSS INTERVENING SPACE** positioned in or moving to a point across intervening space ○ *She reached over and turned off the TV.* ○ *Jim sent a couple of guys over to help out.* **5** *adv* **SO AS TO FALL** so as to change position, especially from being upright ○ *knocked over a pile of books* ○ *He rolled over and turned out the light.* **6** *adv* **REMAINING** remaining or surplus after what was needed has been used ○ *There was plenty of food left over from the party.* **7** *adv US* **AGAIN** doing something again, or again from the beginning ○ *If you make a mistake you'll just have to start over.* **8** *prep* **BY MEANS OF** by means of a device for communication such as a radio or telephone ○ *talk over the phone* **9** *prep* **ABOUT** on the subject of or related to ○ *grieving over the loss of her husband* **10** *prep* **AFFECTING** as an effect or influence upon somebody or something ○ *exercise more control over file access.* **11** *prep* **DURING** happening during or throughout a period of time or an occasion ○ *We can discuss this over lunch.* **12** *prep* **RECOVERED FROM** having recovered from the bad effects of something such as an illness ○ *get over a virus* **13** *prep* **IN PREFERENCE TO** in preference to something else ○ *I'd choose steak over fish every time.* **14** *adj* **FINISHED** finished, or no longer in progress ○ *When all this is over I'm going on holiday.* **15** *adv* **VERY** to a great extent or degree ○ *He's not over happy at the moment* **16** *interj* **INDICATING SOMEBODY'S TURN TO SPEAK** used when communicating via radio to indicate that somebody has finished talking and it is the other person's turn to speak **17** *n US* **SCORE ABOVE PARTICULAR NUMBER IN WAGER** in a wager, the score above a particular number of points, or an amount above a particular total ○ *bet the over in the play-off* **18** *n* **BOWLING OF SIX BALLS** a series of six correctly bowled balls in cricket, or the play during this **19** *vt* **CARRY AGENDA ITEM FORWARD** to postpone dealing with an item on an agenda until a later meeting [Old English *ofer* < Indo-European] ◇ **over again** once more ◇ **over against** **1** opposite to **2** in contrast with, or in opposition to ◇ **over and above** in addition to or in excess of something ○ *benefits over and above the basic salary* ◇ **over and done with** completely finished or at an end ◇ **over and over** repeatedly, or a great deal

overabundance /ṓvər ə búndənss/ *n* an amount greater than what is needed or appropriate —**overabundant** *adj*

overachieve /ṓvər ə chéev/ (**-chieves, -chieving, -chieved**) *vi* to perform better or be more successful than expected —**overachievement** *n* —**overachiever** *n*

overacid /ṓvər assid/ *n* in in-line skating, a trick by which the skater grinds with the trailing foot on a ledge, with the front foot pointing in the opposite direction

overact /ṓvər ákt/ *vti* to exaggerate movements or emotions, especially when acting in a performance

overactive /ṓvər áktiv/ *adj* excessively or abnormally active —**overactivity** /ṓvər ak tívvəti/ *n*

overage[1] *adj* /ṓvər áyj/ **1** older than the age fixed as a standard or considered appropriate for a particular activity **2** of too great an age to be useful (*offensive if used of people*)

overage[2] /ṓvərij/ *n* money, goods, or something else in excess of what is proper or shown in the records

overall *adj* /ṓvər awl/, *adv* /ṓverawl/ **1** **END TO END** from one extremity to the other **2** **TOTAL** including everything ■ *adj* /ṓvər awl/ **GENERAL** considered as a whole ○ *an overall impression* ■ *adv* /ṓveráwl/ **ON THE WHOLE** in general, or as a whole ○ *Overall, we were disappointed with the results.* ■ *n* /ṓvər awl/ **PROTECTIVE GARMENT** a loose-fitting lightweight piece of clothing like a coat, worn over ordinary clothes to protect them ■ **overalls** *npl* **1** **ONE-PIECE PROTECTIVE GARMENT** a one-piece garment with long sleeves and trousers worn to protect a worker's clothes from dirt or wear **2** **WORK TROUSERS WITH BIB** loose-fitting trousers that have a bib and shoulder straps, originally worn over ordinary clothing as a protection from dirt and wear

overall majority *n* a majority of votes in an election when measured against the total combined votes of all other competing political parties

overambitious /ṓvər am bíshəss/ *adj* excessively, inappropriately, or unrealistically ambitious —**overambitiously** *adv* —**overambitiousness** *n*

overanxious /ṓvər ángkshəss/ *adj* more anxious than is usual or appropriate —**overanxiously** *adv*

overarch /ṓvər aarch/ *vt* to form an arch over something or somewhere

overarching /ṓvər aarching/ *adj* embracing or overshadowing everything

overarm /ṓvər aarm/ *adj* **1** **WITH ARM ABOVE SHOULDER** thrown or done with the arm raised above the shoulder and rotating forward **2** **WITH ARM RAISED** beginning a stroke in swimming with the arm raised above the shoulder and rotating forward ■ *adv* **WITH HAND ABOVE SHOULDER** with the hand coming forward in a semicircular motion from behind and above the shoulder. US term **overhand** *adv*

overate past tense of **overeat**

overawe /ṓvər áw/ (**-awes, -awing, -awed**) *vt* to make somebody feel subdued or inhibited by inspiring respect and some fear

overbalance /ṓvər bállənss/ *v* (**-ances, -ancing, -anced**) **1** *vti* **LOSE BALANCE** to lose balance, or make somebody or something lose balance **2** *vt* **BE MORE IMPORTANT THAN** to have greater weight or importance than something else ■ *n* **PREPONDERANCE** an excess of an amount, quantity, or weight

overbear /ṓvər báir/ (**-bears, -bearing, -bore** /-báwr/, **-borne** /-báwrn/) *v* **1** *vt* **OVERPOWER** to defeat somebody by having superior weight or strength **2** *vt* **OUTWEIGH** to be more important than other considerations **3** *vi* **PRODUCE TOO MUCH** to produce too much fruit or too many offspring

overbearing /ṓvər báiring/ *adj* arrogant and tending to order people around —**overbearingly** *adv* —**overbearingness** *n*

overbid *v* /ṓvər bíd/ (**-bids, -bidding, -bid, -bidden** *or* **-bid**) **1** *vti* **BID MORE THAN WORTH OF** to bid more than something is worth **2** *vi* **BID FOR TOO MANY TRICKS** in bridge, to bid for more tricks than can be won ■ *n* /ṓvərbid/ **HIGHER BID** a bid that is higher than somebody else's bid —**overbidder** /ṓvər bíddər/ *n*

overbite /ṓvər bīt/ *n* a faulty alignment of the teeth in which the upper front teeth project too far over the lower teeth when the mouth is closed

overblanket /ṓvər blangkit/ *n* an electric blanket designed to be placed over somebody in bed rather than on the mattress

overblouse /ṓvər blowz/ *n* a blouse designed to be worn outside the waistband of a skirt or trousers

overblow /ṓvər blṓ/ (**-blows, -blowing, -blew** /-blóo/, **-blown** /-blṓn/) *vti* to blow a wind instrument with extra force so as to produce an overtone

overblown /ṓvər blṓn/ *adj* **1** **EXAGGERATED** done to excess and seeming exaggerated ○ *overblown stories that are barely credible* **2** **PRETENTIOUS** showing pomposity or pretentiousness ○ *His style of writing is overblown and excessively wordy.* **3** **PAST BEST** past full bloom and beginning to die ○ *an overblown rose*

overboard /ṓvər bawrd, ṓvər báwrd/ *adv* over the side of a ship and into the water [Old English *ofer bord* 'over the side']

overbook /ṓvər bóok/ *vti* to take more reservations than there are seats or places available in a place

overbore past tense of **overbear**

overborne, overborn past participle of **overbear**

overbought /ṓvər báwt/ *adj* characterized by high prices on the stock exchange as the result of recent heavy trading, and so not likely to rise further in the near future. ◊ **oversold** *adj.*

overbridge /ṓvər brij/ *n* a bridge built to carry people or vehicles over a road, railway line, or canal. ◊ **overpass**

overbuild /ṓvər bíld/ (**-builds, -building, -built** /-bílt/) *v* **1** *vti* **BUILD TOO MUCH** to construct more buildings than are necessary or desirable in an area **2** *vti* **BUILD OVERAMBITIOUSLY** to construct something that is too large or elaborate **3** *vt* **BUILD ON SOMETHING ELSE** to build something on top of a particular place or thing

overburden *vt* /ṓvər búrd'n/ **OVERLOAD** to place too much weight or worry on somebody or something ○ *overburdened with debt* ■ *n* /ṓvər burd'n/ **1** **EXCESSIVE BURDEN** an excessive or onerous burden **2** **SOIL LAYERED OVER ROCK** soil or other material layered over bedrock or over a geological deposit

overcall *vti* /ṓvər káwl/ in bridge, to bid higher than an opponent before a partner has made a positive bid —**overcall** *n*

overcame past tense of **overcome**

overcapacity /ṓvər kə pássəti/ *n* an ability to produce goods or provide services that exceeds demand

overcapitalize /ṓvər káppit'l īz/ (**-izes, -izing, -ized**), **overcapitalise** (**-ises, -ising, -ised**) *vt* **1** to provide a business with more capital than is justified by its condition or its ability to make profits **2** to give a corporation a nominal value that is higher than its fair market value

overcast *adj* /ṓvər kaast/ **1** **CLOUDY** very cloudy, with no sun showing **2** **SEWN WITH LONG STITCHES** sewn along the edge with long loose stitches that prevent a piece of fabric from unravelling ■ *n* /ṓvər kaast/ **1** **HEAVY CLOUD COVER** a heavy covering of clouds in the sky **2** **MINE ARCH** an arch in a mine supporting a passage above it ■ *v* /ṓvər káast/ **1** *vi* **BECOME CLOUDY** to become cloudy or dull **2** *vt* **SECURE WITH LOOSE STITCHES** to sew the edge of a piece of fabric with an overcast stitch

overcasting /ṓvər kaasting/ *n* long slanting stitches sewn loosely across the edge of a piece of fabric to prevent it from unravelling

overcautious /ṓvər káwshəss/ *adj* more cautious than is appropriate or necessary —**overcaution** *n* —**overcautiously** *adv*

overcharge *v* /ṓvər cháarj/ **1** *vti* **CHARGE TOO MUCH** to charge somebody too much money for something **2** *vt* **PUT EXCESSIVE POWER INTO** to charge a battery or circuit with more electricity than it can safely hold **3** *vt* **OVERFILL OR OVERLOAD** to fill or load something with more than it can hold or bear **4** *vt* **EXAGGERATE** to make something seem greater or more important than it actually is (*literary*) ■ *n* /ṓvər chaarj/ **1** **EXCESSIVE CHARGE** an excessively high charge for something **2** **ACT OF CHARGING TOO MUCH** an act of charging too much for something

overcloud /ṓvər klówd/ *vti* **1** to cover something, or become covered, with clouds **2** to become, or to make something become, dim and gloomy (*formal*)

overcoat /ṓvər kōt/ *n* **1** a heavy coat worn over other outer clothes **2** **overcoat, overcoating** an additional protective layer of something such as paint or varnish on top of a treated surface

overcome /ṓvər kúm/ (**-comes, -coming, -came** /ṓvər káym/, **-come**) *v* **1** *vt* **MAKE SOMEBODY HELPLESS** to make somebody incapacitated or helpless, or break down somebody's normal self-control (*usually passive*) ○ *completely overcome with emotion* **2** *vt* **SURMOUNT DIFFICULTY** to struggle successfully against a difficulty or disadvantage **3** *vti* **DEFEAT** to defeat somebody or something, especially in a conflict or competition (*formal*) **4** *vi* **WIN DESPITE OBSTACLES** to win or be successful, especially in spite of obstacles

overcommit /ṓvər kə mít/ (**-mits, -mitting, -mitted**) *vti* to undertake, or make somebody or yourself undertake, more than can be accomplished (*often passive*)

overcompensate /ṓvər kómpən sayt/ (**-sates, -sating, -sated**) *vti* **1** to try too hard to make up for a disadvantage or shortcoming and fall into a fault of another kind **2** to pay somebody too much in recompense or compensation for something done —**overcompensation** /-kómpən sáysh'n/ *n* —**overcompensatory** *adj*

overconfident /ṓvər kónfidənt/ *adj* excessively confident or self-assured —**overconfidence** *n* —**overconfidently** *adv*

overconsumption /ṓvər kən súmpsh'n/ *n* the using, eating, or drinking of too much of something, especially the use of an excessive amount of a valuable resource

overcook /ṓvər kóok/ *vt* to cook something so long that it loses its flavour and texture

overcorrect /ṓvər kə rékt/ *vti* to do too much when trying to correct a mistake or fault, usually so that a further mistake is made ■ *adj* excessively exact or proper

overcorrection /ṓvər kə réksh'n/ *n* **1** LING = **hypercorrection** **2** the fact of overcorrecting a mistake or fault

overcritical /ṓvər kríttik'l/ *adj* judging or criticizing somebody or something too harshly or too fastidiously —**overcriticalness** *n*

overcrop /ṓvər króp/ (**-crops, -cropping, -cropped**) *vt* to make soil infertile by removing its nutrients through continuous cultivation

overcrowd /ṓvər krówd/ *vt* to put more people or things into an area than it is comfortably able to hold —**overcrowded** *adj* —**overcrowding** *n*

overcut /ṓvər kút/ (**-cuts, -cutting, -cut**) *vti* to cut timber in amounts that are in excess of annual growth or of a prescribed quota

overdevelop /ṓvər di vélləp/ *vt* **1** to develop something to excess **2** to exceed the amount of time, temperature, or strength of solution required to develop a photographic film, thereby producing too much contrast —**overdevelopment** *n*

overdo /ṓvər dóo/ (**-does** /-dúz/, **-doing, -did** /-díd/, **-done** /-dún/) *vt* **1** OVERCOOK to cook food for too long **2** SPOIL EFFECT BY EXAGGERATION to spoil the effect of something by exaggerating it ○ *You rather overdid the sympathetic friend act on that occasion.* **3** DO SOMETHING TO EXCESS to do something too much, often with a harmful effect —**overdoer** *n* ◇ **overdo it** *or* **things 1** to work too hard and tire yourself **2** to do something to excess

overdone past participle of **overdo**

overdosage /ṓvər dṓssij/ *n* **1** a drug quantity substantially in excess of the standard amount for a person's weight and age **2** the prescribing, administering, or ingesting of an overdosage

overdose *n* /ṓvər dōss/ a dangerously large dose of a drug, especially a narcotic, causing hospitalization or death ■ *vti* /ṓvər dṓss/ (**-doses, -dosing, -dosed**) to take or give somebody an overdose

overdraft /ṓvər draaft/ *n* **1** the amount that an account holder owes a bank because the balance in the account does not cover the amount that he or she has withdrawn from or debited to it **2** a limit up to which an account holder may borrow from a bank when there are no funds in his or her current account **3** *US* = **overdraught**

overdramatic /ṓvər drə máttik/ *adj* excessively dramatic in manner or style —**overdramatically** *adv*

overdramatize /ṓvər drámmə tīz/ (**-tizes, -tizing, -tized**), **overdramatise** (**-tises, -tising, -tised**) *vti* to behave, or treat something, in an excessively dramatic way, e.g. by exaggerating the strength of your feelings or the gravity of a situation

overdraught /ṓvər draaft/ *n* a current of air passed over a fire, e.g. in a furnace or kiln. US term **overdraft** *n.* 3

overdraw /ṓvər dráw/ (**-draws, -drawing, -drew** /-dróo/, **-drawn** /-dráwn/) *v* **1** *vti* LACK ENOUGH FUNDS IN BANK ACCOUNT to withdraw or have debited more money from a bank account than it has credited to it, so that money is owed to the bank **2** *vt* EXAGGERATE to exaggerate in describing or telling about something **3** *vti* PULL BOW TOO TIGHT in archery, to pull a bow too tight

overdrawn /ṓvər dráwn/ *adj* owing money to a bank because an account has had more money withdrawn or debited from it than credited to it

overdress *vti* /ṓvər dréss/ to dress, or dress somebody, more formally or elaborately or in more clothes than the situation requires ■ *n* /ṓvər dress/ a dress that is intended to be worn over other outer clothing —**overdressed** *adj*

overdrew *v* past tense of **overdraw**

overdrive *n* /ṓvər drīv/ **1** HIGHEST ENGINE GEAR the highest gear in the engine of a motor vehicle that is used at high speeds for fuel economy and to save engine wear **2** EXTRA HARD LEVEL OF ACTIVITY a particularly intense and productive mode of activity, usually possible only for short periods (*informal*) ○ *Production has gone into overdrive.* ■ *vt* /ṓvər drīv/ DRIVE TOO HARD to drive somebody, something, or yourself too hard

overdub /ṓvər dub/ *vti* (**-dubs, -dubbing, -dubbed**) to add supplementary sound or music to a recording ■ *n* a supplementary layer of sound or music added onto a recording

overdue /ṓvər dyóo/ *adj* late or after the scheduled time, especially in arriving, occurring, or being paid ○ *The library said the books were overdue.*

overdye /ṓvər dī/ (**-dyes, -dying, -dyed**) *vt* **1** to use too much dye on something **2** to dye a fabric with another colour over the original one

overeager /ṓvər éegər/ *adj* more eager than is usual or appropriate —**overeagerly** *adv* —**overeagerness** *n*

overeat /ṓvər éet/ (**-eats, -eating, -ate** /-áyt, -ét/, **-eaten** /-éet'n/) *vi* to eat too much food, especially habitually —**overeater** *n* —**overeating** *n*

overelaborate *adj* /ṓvər i lábbərət/ excessively elaborate, fussy, or detailed ■ *vti* /ṓvər i lábbə rayt/ (**-rates, -rating, -rated**) to add or give too much elaboration or detail to something —**overelaborately** /-rətli/ *adv* —**overelaborateness** *n* —**overelaboration** /-ráysh'n/ *n*

overemotional /ṓvər i mṓsh'nəl/ *adj* affected by or expressing feelings more openly than is thought usual or appropriate —**overemotionally** *adv*

overemphasis /ṓvər émfəssiss/ *n* an emphasis that is stronger than is thought usual or appropriate —**overemphatic** /ṓvər im fáttik/ *adj*

overemphasize /ṓvər émfə sīz/ (**-sizes, -sizing, -sized**), **overemphasise** (**-sises, -sising, -sised**) *vt* to give something too much importance, attention, or force

overenthusiasm /ṓvər in thyóozi azəm/ *n* more enthusiasm than is thought usual or appropriate

overenthusiastic /ṓvər in thyoozi ástik/ *adj* more enthusiastic than is thought usual or appropriate —**overenthusiastically** *adv*

overestimate *vt* /ṓvər ésti mayt/ (**-mates, -mating, -mated**) **1** CALCULATE SOMETHING TOO HIGHLY to calculate the amount, value, or quantity of something at too high a level **2** GIVE EXCESSIVE MERIT OR IMPORTANCE TO to judge somebody or something to be better, greater, or more important than he, she, or it actually is ■ *n* /ṓvər éstimət, -ésti mayt/ EXCESSIVELY HIGH ESTIMATE an estimate that is too high —**overestimation** /-ésti máysh'n/ *n*

overexaggerate /ṓvər ig zájjə rayt/ (**-ates, -ating, -ated**) *vti* to overstate something, especially to a considerable degree (*informal*)

overexcite /ṓvər ik sī́t/ (**-cites, -citing, -cited**) *vt* to excite or stimulate a person or animal too much —**overexcitement** *n*

overexert /ṓvər ig zúrt/ *vr* to make a greater physical or mental effort than is necessary or desirable ○ *Don't overexert yourself in the garden during the heat of the day.* —**overexertion** /ṓvər ig zúrsh'n/ *n*

overexpansion /ṓvər ik spánsh'n/ *n* the process of increasing excessively, or increasing something excessively, in size, extent, scope, or number

overexpose /ṓvər ik spṓz/ (**-poses, -posing, -posed**) *vt* **1** to expose a photographic medium such as film to too much light or for too long a time, so that the colours or tones in the resulting photograph are too light **2** to allow somebody, or expose somebody to, too much of something, especially to allow somebody to appear in public or in the media too often —**overexposure** /-ik spṓzhər/ *n*

overextend /ṓvər ik sténd/ *v* **1** *vt* STRETCH LIMITS OF RESOURCES to force somebody, something, or yourself beyond a safe or reasonable limit **2** *vt* PROLONG SOMETHING BEYOND EXPECTED DURATION to prolong something beyond its normal or expected duration **3** *vr* RISK FINANCIAL RUIN to risk financial ruin by borrowing excessively, spending too much, or overcommitting resources

overfamiliar /ṓvər fə mílli ər/ *adj* **1** more friendly, informal, or intimate than is appropriate **2** used so much or so well known as to be boring or ineffective —**overfamiliarity** /-fə mílli árrəti/ *n*

overfeed /ṓvər féed/ (**-feeds, -feeding, -fed** /-féd/) *vt* to give a person, animal, or plant an excessive amount of food

overfill /ṓvər fíl/ *vti* to become, or make somebody or something become, too full

overfish /ṓvər físh/ *vti* to take too many fish from a body of water and so deplete its population

overflew past tense of **overfly**

overflight /ṓvər flīt/ *n* the flight of an aircraft over an area

ϟ **overflow** *v* /ṓvər flṓ/ **1** *vti* FLOW OR POUR OVER to pour out over the limits or edge of a container because the container is too full of liquid **2** *vt* FLOOD to flood, cover, or flow over the surface of something **3** *vt* SPREAD BEYOND LIMITS OF to spread beyond the area intended to contain it ○ *The crowd overflowed the hall into the street outside.* **4** *vi* BE OVERWHELMED BY EMOTION to be so full of an emotion as to feel the need to express it ○ *overflowing with happiness* ■ *n* /ṓvər flō/ **1** EXCESS LIQUID CONTENTS excess liquid that flows or pours over the edge of something **2** EXCESS PEOPLE OR THINGS people or things that cannot be contained in the space originally set aside for them **3** OUTLET THAT PREVENTS FLOODING an outlet that allows something, usually a liquid, to escape before it runs over the top of its container, e.g. water in a cistern **4** AMOUNT IN EXCESS OF LIMIT the amount by which a limit is exceeded **5** COMPUTER'S INABILITY TO HANDLE LARGE DATA the inability of a location in computer memory to handle data of an excessively large magnitude, or an instance of this ○ *an overflow error.* ◊ **underflow**

overfly /ṓvər flī́/ (**-flies, -flying, -flew** /-flóo/, **-flown** /-flṓn/) *vti* **1** to fly over an area **2** to fly past a specific point ○ *The plane has overflown the runway.*

overfold /ṓvər fōld/ *n* a geological fold that has turned over on itself so that both sides dip in the same direction, causing the middle strata to be upside down

overfull /ṓvər fóol/ *adj* full beyond the normal or practical capacity ○ *an overfull suitcase impossible to close*

overfunding /ṓvər fúnding/ *n* the policy of selling more securities than are needed to finance government spending

overgarment /ṓvər gaarmənt/ *n* an article of clothing such as an outer garment or protective wear worn on top of other clothes

overgeneralize /ṓvər jénnərə līz/ (**-izes, -izing, -ized**), **overgeneralise** (**-ises, -ising, -ised**) *vti* to draw too general a conclusion about something on the basis of limited or incomplete evidence —**overgeneralization** /-jennərə lī záysh'n/ *n*

overgenerous /ṓvər jénnərəss/ *adj* more generous than is thought appropriate or desirable

overglaze *n* /ṓvər glayz/ **1** EXTRA GLAZE ON POTTERY an additional coat of glaze applied to pottery or porcelain **2** TOP LAYER OF DECORATION ON POTTERY a decoration applied to pottery or porcelain on top of the glaze ■ *vt* /ṓvər gláyz/ (**-glazes, -glazing, -glazed**) APPLY GLAZE OR OVERGLAZE TO POTTERY to apply a glaze or overglaze to pottery or porcelain ■ *adj* /ṓvər glayz/ APPLIED ON TOP OF GLAZE applied on top of a ceramic glaze ○ *overglaze colours*

overgraze /ṓvər gráyz/ (**-grazes, -grazing, -grazed**) *vt* to graze land to the point that vegetation is harmed and as a consequence can no longer support stock (*often passive*)

overground /ṓvər grównd/ *adj, adv* on or above ground level

overgrow /ṓvər grṓ/ (**-grows, -growing, -grew** /-gróo/, **-grown** /-grṓn/) *vti* to grow so large, dense, or extensive as to cover the area of ground or container it is planted in and hinder the growth of other plants —**overgrowth** /ṓvər grōth/ *n*

overgrown /ṓvər grṓn/ *adj* **1** COVERED WITH VEGETATION GROWING WITHOUT CHECK covered with plants or weeds that have been allowed to grow without check **2** GROWN TOO MUCH FOR ALLOTTED SPACE grown too dense, large, or extensive for the area of ground or container in which it is planted **3** IMMATURE grown to a large or adult size, but remaining immature ○ *behaving like an overgrown schoolboy*

overhand /ṓvər hand/ *adj* **1** made with the hand coming forward in a semicircular motion from behind and above the shoulder **2** sewn with small vertical stitches passing over the two edges that are being joined together to make a seam ■ *adv US* SPORTS = **overarm** *adv.*

overhand knot *n* a knot formed by passing one end of a cord or rope through a loop formed on another part of it, often used to prevent an end from fraying

overhang *v* /ṓvər háng/ (**-hangs, -hanging, -hung** /-húng/) **1** *vti* PROJECT OVER to project or extend over something leaving a sheltered space beneath **2** *vt* LOOM OVER to threaten or loom over somebody or something ■ *n* /ṓvər hang/ **1** PROJECTION something, e.g. part of a rock face or the edge of a roof, that projects out over the space beneath **2** EXTENT OF PROJECTION the degree or amount by which something projects or extends over something **3** HALF DIFFERENCE IN WINGSPAN half the difference in the span of the two wings of a biplane **4** DISTANCE TO WING END ON MONOPLANE the distance from the last outer strut to the end of a monoplane's wing

overharvest /ṓvər haárvist/ *vt* to harvest a crop or a population of organisms to such an extent that their numbers are depleted ○ *laws prohibiting trawlers from overharvesting shrimp in the bay*

overhaul *vt* /ṓvər háwl/ **1** LOOK FOR MECHANICAL DEFECTS to examine a piece of machinery thoroughly to identify defects **2** REPAIR MACHINE EXTENSIVELY to carry out comprehensive repairs and adjustments to a piece of machinery **3** REVISE SOMETHING THOROUGHLY to examine and revise something thoroughly **4** GRADUALLY OVERTAKE to catch up with and overtake somebody or something **5** SLACKEN OR RELEASE to slacken or release something such as a rope or the blocks of a tackle ■ *n* /ṓvər hawl/ COMPREHENSIVE REPAIR a comprehensive examination and repair of something —**overhauler** /ṓvər hawlər, -háwlər/ *n*

overhead *adv* /ṓvər hed/ DIRECTLY ABOVE directly above somebody or something, especially up in the air ■ *adj* /ṓvər hed/ **1** POSITIONED DIRECTLY ABOVE positioned directly above somebody or something **2** HIT WITH RACQUET ABOVE HEAD describes a stroke in racquet games played hard and downwards, with the racquet held high above the head **3** RELATING TO ONGOING COSTS relating to the general recurring costs of running a business, e.g. rent, maintenance, and utilities ■ *n* /ṓvər hed/ **1** SHOT IN RACQUET GAMES a shot in racquet games played hard and downwards, with the racquet held above head height **2** SOMETHING LOCATED ABOVE something such as a light that is mounted or located in an overhead position ■ *n* /ṓvər hed/ **1** = **overhead projection** *n.* 1 **2** EXTRA SPACE IN COMPUTER extra capacity for support, checking, or memory to run programs in a computer operating system ■ **overheads** *npl* ONGOING BUSINESS COSTS the general recurring costs of running a business, excluding the costs of labour and materials, e.g. rent, maintenance, and utilities

overhead camshaft, overhead cam *n* a camshaft in an internal-combustion engine that is mounted above the cylinder heads and controls the operation, opening, and closing of the cylinder's valves

overhead compartment *n* a luggage compartment above the passenger seats for holding luggage in an aeroplane

overhead projection *n* **1** a transparent sheet placed on an overhead projector so that its enlarged image can be projected on a screen or other surface **2** the use or the image produced by the use of an overhead projector

overhead projector *n* a projector with a flat transparent top on which a transparent sheet carrying an image is placed for projection onto a screen or other surface

overhead-valve engine *n* an internal-combustion engine with the inlet and exhaust valves located in the cylinder head above the pistons. US term **valve-in-head engine**

overhear /ṓvər hēer/ (**-hears, -hearing, -heard** /ṓvər húrd/, **-heard**) *vti* to hear what somebody is saying, either deliberately or accidentally, without the speaker's knowledge

overheat /ṓvər hēet/ *vti* **1** BECOME OR MAKE TOO HOT to become, or make somebody or something become, too hot **2** GROW TOO QUICKLY to experience too rapid growth in demand with a resultant increase in inflation, or cause too rapid growth in an economy **3** MAKE OR BECOME TOO EXCITED to become, or make somebody become, too excited, agitated, or angry —**overheated** *adj*

overhit /ṓvər hít/ (**-hits, -hitting, -hit**) *vti* to hit a ball too hard, or put too much force into a stroke

overhung past tense, past participle of **overhang**

overhunt /ṓvər húnt/ *vti* to hunt an animal species to such an extent that the stock of the species is depleted

overhype /ṓvər hīp/ (**-hypes, -hyping, -hyped**) *vt* to praise and publicize somebody or something excessively or misleadingly (*informal*)

~~**overide**~~ incorrect spelling of **override**

overimprovement /ṓvər im prōōvmənt/ *n* improvement in the performance of a business or asset that exceeds what is expected or needed

overindulge /ṓvər in dúlj/ (**-dulges, -dulging, -dulged**) *v* **1** *vti* to give in to a desire for something too lavishly or too often, especially to eat or drink too much **2** *vt* to allow somebody to do or have what he or she wants too much —**overindulgence** *n* —**overindulgent** *adj* —**overindulgently** /ṓvər in dúljəntli/ *adv*

overinvestment /ṓvər in véstmənt/ *n* the act or process of investing an excessive amount of something, especially money, in a venture, project, or company

overjoyed /ṓvər jóyd/ *adj* extremely delighted

overkill /ṓvər kil/ *n* **1** EXCESS action that far exceeds what is needed in order to achieve a result **2** GREATER DESTRUCTIVE CAPACITY THAN NEEDED the capacity of weaponry, especially nuclear weapons, to cause greater damage or destruction than is necessary to accomplish a mission ■ *vti* DESTROY WITH EXCESS OF WEAPONS to use excessive force, especially far more nuclear weapons than necessary, to destroy an enemy or place

overladen /ṓvər láyd'n/ *adj* carrying too heavy a physical or emotional load

overland /ṓvər land/ *adv* BY LAND by or across land ■ *adj* ACROSS LAND travelling across land ○ *take the overland route* ■ *vti Aus* DRIVE LIVESTOCK to drive cattle or sheep long distances across land —**overlander** *n*

overlap *v* /ṓvər láp/ (**-laps, -lapping, -lapped**) **1** *vti* PLACE OR BE OVER to position things in such a way that the edge of one thing is on top of and extending past the edge of another, or be positioned in this way ○ *The roofers overlapped the slates.* **2** *vt* EXTEND BEYOND to cover something such as a boundary or edge, and extend beyond it ○ *The tablecloth overlapped the table by several inches.* **3** *vti* COINCIDE to coincide or correspond in part with something in time, function, or purpose, or make something coincide or correspond with something else ○ *Her area of responsibility to some extent overlaps mine.* ■ *n* /ṓvər lap/ **1** PARTIAL OVERLAY an edge that partly covers or is covered by something else **2** EXTENT OF OVERLAP the amount by which something overlaps something else ○ *It needs an overlap of six centimetres.* **3** PARTIAL COINCIDENCE OR CORRESPONDENCE a partial coincidence or correspondence of two things in time, function, or purpose [Early 18C. < LAP².]

overlay[1] *vt* /ṓvər láy/ (**-lays, -laying, -laid** /-láyd/) **1** PLACE SOMETHING AS COVERING to place a covering or covering layer of something on top of something else **2** COVER to cover the surface of something with something else **3** APPLY DECORATION TO SURFACE to apply a decorative material to a surface (*often passive*) **4** EQUALIZE PRESSURE OVER to affix a piece of paper to the surface of a press to help make a uniform impression on a forme or plate ■ *n* /ṓvər lay/ **1** COVERING a covering or covering layer laid on top of something else **2** EXTRA DECORATIVE LAYER an layer of decorative material applied to a surface **3** ADDITIONAL TRANSPARENCY LAID ON TOP a transparent sheet containing additional details, e.g. a chart or map, that is placed on top of another transparency in an overhead projector during a presentation or lecture **4** PAPER TO EQUALIZE PRINTING PRESSURE in traditional methods of printing, a piece of paper used to equalize the pressure on a forme or printing plate before printing

overlay[2] past tense of **overlie**

overleaf /ṓvər lēef/ *adv* on the other side of the page

overlie /ṓvər lī/ (**-lies, -lying, -lay** /-láy/, **-lain** /-láyn/) *vt* **1** to lie on top of somebody or something **2** to kill a newborn baby or animal by accidentally lying on and smothering it

overload *vt* /ṓvər lṓd/ **1** PUT EXCESSIVE LOAD ON to put too large or heavy a load on somebody or something or in something **2** FUSE ELECTRICAL SYSTEM to use more current than an electrical system can handle, e.g. by using too many electrical appliances simultaneously **3** OVERBURDEN to give somebody too much work, stress, or other difficulty ■ *n* /ṓvər lōd/ **1** EXCESSIVE ELECTRICAL LOAD a greater amount of electrical current than an electrical system can handle **2** EXCESSIVE PHYSICAL WEIGHT something that is physically too heavy or too much to carry **3** EXCESSIVE MENTAL OR EMOTIONAL BURDEN something that is mentally or emotionally too difficult to cope with **4** US MENTAL OR EMOTIONAL EXHAUSTION the condition of having an excessive mental or emotional burden (*informal*) ○ *I'm in overload right now.*

overlock /ṓvər lok/ *n* a sewing technique using an invisible hem stitch made by a sewing machine or a special device

overlong /ṓvər lóng/ *adj* too long in extent or duration ■ *adv* for too long a time

overlook /ṓvər lŏŏk/ *vt* **1** MISS to miss or fail to notice something **2** IGNORE to choose to disregard or ignore a shortcoming or fault **3** LOOK DOWN AT to look at something from above **4** PROVIDE VIEW OF to provide a view of something, especially from above **5** BE ABOVE to be located high above something **6** EXAMINE to look at something with care

SYNONYMS See ***neglect***.

overlord /ṓvər lawrd/ *n* **1** a ruler with overall power, usually over several subservient rulers, and especially somebody who ruled over other lords in a feudal system **2** somebody of great power or influence —**overlordship** *n*

overloud /ṓvər lówd/ *adj* unpleasantly or inappropriately loud in tone, volume, or hue

overly /ṓvərli/ *adv* to an extreme or excessive degree

overman *vt* /ṓvər mán/ (**-mans, -manning, -manned**) HR = **overstaff** ■ *n* /ṓvər man/ (*plural* **-men** /-men/) in the thought of Friedrich Nietzsche, a man whose superior powers of creativity and insight enable him to live beyond standards of good and evil —**overmanning** *n*

overmantel /ṓvər mant'l/ *n* an ornamental shelf above a mantelpiece

overmaster /ṓvər maástər/ *vt* to conquer somebody's resistance or break down somebody's self-control and take control of him or her (*formal*) ○ *an overmastering urge to tell her precisely what I thought of her*

overmatch *vt* /ṓvər mách/ *US* **1** DEFEAT to be superior enough to defeat or surpass somebody or something **2** PROVIDE WITH SUPERIOR OPPONENT to provide somebody with an opponent who is likely to defeat him or her easily ■ *n* /ṓvər mach/ *US* UNEQUAL CONTEST a contest in which one competitor is far superior to another

overmatter /ṓvər matər/ *n* copy typeset in excess of the space available for it

overmedicate /ṓvər méddi kayt/ (**-cates, -cating, -cated**) *vt* to give somebody or yourself too much medication —**overmedication** /-méddi káysh'n/ *n*

overmiked /ṓvər mīkt/ *adj* sounding too loud or artificial because of an imperfectly positioned or adjusted microphone

overmuch /ṓvər múch/ *adv* EXCESSIVELY to an excessive degree ■ *adj* EXCESSIVE too much ■ *n* EXCESSIVE QUANTITY an excessive quantity or amount

overnight /ṓvər nīt/ *adv* **1** THROUGHOUT THE NIGHT for the duration of the entire night **2** DURING NIGHT at some point in the course of the night **3** VERY QUICKLY within a very short time ○ *It became a bestseller overnight.* ■ *adj* **1** LASTING ONE NIGHT lasting throughout a night **2** SPENDING NIGHT resident for the night **3** OCCURRING AT NIGHT taking place during the night **4** USED WHEN SPENDING A NIGHT used when staying overnight somewhere **5** EXTREMELY SUDDEN happening in a very short time ○ *an overnight success* **6** *US* INTENDED FOR NEXT-DAY DELIVERY guaranteed to get to the intended destination by the next day ■ *vi* SPEND NIGHT to stay somewhere for the night

overnight bag, overnight case *n* a small piece of luggage used to carry necessities for a stay lasting one night

overnighter /ṓvər nītər/ *n* **1** a stay lasting one night (*informal*) **2** a person who takes an overnight trip or stays somewhere overnight

overoptimistic /ṓvər opti místik/ *adj* unrealistically hopeful about the future —**overoptimism** /ṓvər óptimizəm/ *n* —**overoptimistically** *adv*

overpass *n* /ṓvər paass/ *US, Can, ANZ* a road, bridge, or passage that crosses over another route. ◊ **overbridge**

overpay /ṓvər páy/ (**-pays, -paying, -paid** /-páyd/, **-paid**) *vti* **1** to pay somebody at a rate that is too high for the job **2** to pay somebody too much for something as a result of an error

overperform /ṓvər pər fáwrm/ *vi* to produce a result that is better than expected

overpersuade /ṓvər pər swáyd/ (**-suades, -suading, -suaded**) *vt* to persuade somebody to act contrary to his or her inclination or judgment

overpitch /ṓvər pích/ *vti* to bowl a ball in cricket so that it lands too close to the batsman

overplay /ṓvər pláy/ *v* **1** *vti* OVERDO to play a part or role in an exaggeratedly dramatic or theatrical way **2** *vt* OVERSTATE to exaggerate the importance or strength of something **3** *vt* HIT TOO HARD OR FAR to hit or kick a ball too hard or too far

overplus /ṓvər pluss/ *n* a larger amount than is needed or appropriate [14C. Translation of French *surplus*.]

overpopulate /ṓvər póppyōō layt/ (**-lates, -lating, -lated**) *v* **1** *vt* to increase the population of a place so much that the amount of space, food, water, or other resources available to support it is insufficient **2** *vi* to increase to unsustainable or undesirable numbers by excessive reproduction —**overpopulated** *adj* —**overpopulation** /-póppyōō láysh'n/ *n*

overpotted /ṓvər póttid/ *adj* growing in a pot too large for healthy development

overpower /ṓvər pów ər/ *vt* **1** SUBDUE PHYSICALLY to use superior strength or force to defeat somebody, especially to make somebody physically helpless and unable to fight **2** OVERWHELM MENTALLY to have so strong an effect on somebody that he or she is unable to resist or control it **3** GIVE EXCESSIVE POWER to supply something, especially a car, with more power than necessary, especially mechanical or electrical power

overpowering /ṓvər pów əring/ *adj* **1** impossible to resist or control ○ *an overpowering urge to laugh* **2** with overwhelmingly superior physical strength —**overpoweringly** *adv*

overpraise /ṓvər práyz/ (**-praises, -praising, -praised**) *vt* to praise somebody or something more than is deserved or reasonable

overprescribe /ṓvər pri skríb/ (**-scribes, -scribing, -scribed**) *vti* to prescribe too much medication for somebody ○ *The doctor was prone to overprescribe for his patients.* —**overprescription** /-pri skrípsh'n/ *n*

overpressure /ṓvər preshər/ *n* the amount by which atmospheric pressure exceeds normal levels, e.g. in a shock wave from an explosion or an accelerating aircraft

overprice /ṓvər príss/ (**-prices, -pricing, -priced**) *vt* to charge too high a price for something (*often passive*)

overprint *vti* /ṓvər prínt/ **ADD PRINTING TO** to print something additional on an already printed surface, especially in order to add text, numbers, or another colour ■ *n* /ṓvər print/ **1 ADDITIONAL PRINTING** an additional printing on a surface, especially text, numbers, or another colour **2 OVERPRINTED POSTAGE STAMP** a postage stamp with additional information printed on its surface

overprivileged /ṓvər prívvilijd/ *adj* having too many advantages in life

overprize /ṓvər príz/ (**-prizes, -prizing, -prized**) *vt* to regard something as more valuable and important than it really is

overproduce /ṓvər prə dyóoss/ (**-duces, -ducing, -duced**) *vti* to produce more of something, e.g. a product or crop, than is wanted or needed —**overproducer** *n* —**overproduction** /-prə dúksh'n/ *n*

overproof /ṓvər próof/ *adj* higher in alcohol content than proof spirit is

overproportion /ṓvər prə páwrsh'n/ *vt* to make something larger than is usual or needed and out of proportion to other things —**overproportionately** *adv*

overprotect /ṓvər prə tékt/ *vt* to protect somebody or something more than is necessary or wise, especially to shield a child too much from the realities of life —**overprotection** *n* —**overprotective** *adj* —**overprotectively** *adv* —**overprotectiveness** *n*

overpublicize /ṓvər púbbli sīz/ (**-cizes, -cizing, -cized**), **overpublicise** (**-cises, -cising, -cised**) *vt* to publicize somebody or something so widely that the effect is counterproductive

overqualified /ṓvər kwólli fīd/ *adj* with more academic or vocational qualifications or experience than is necessary or desirable for a job

overrate /ṓvər ráyt/ (**-rates, -rating, -rated**) *vt* to regard somebody as better or more capable, or something as greater, than is in fact the case —**overrated** *adj*

overreach /ṓvər réech/ *v* **1** *vr* **FAIL THROUGH OVERAMBITION** to fail through trying to do things that are beyond your abilities **2** *vti* **EXTEND TOO FAR OR BEYOND** to reach or extend too far or beyond something **3** *vti* **DEFEAT BY TRICKERY** to get the better of somebody by trickery or deception **4** *vt* **OVERTAKE** to catch up with and pass somebody or something **5** *vi* **HURT ONE FOOT WITH ANOTHER** to strike and injure the forefoot with the hind foot while walking or running (*refers to a horse*) **6** *vi* **SAIL ON TACK LONGER THAN NECESSARY** to sail on a tack longer than is wanted or needed

overreact /ṓvər ri ákt/ *vi* to react to something with disproportionate action or excessive emotion —**overreaction** *n* —**overreactive** *adj*

overrefine /ṓvər ri fín/ *vti* to make something more refined, subtle, or fastidious than is desirable or appropriate, especially to make too many subtle points or distinctions in presenting an argument —**overrefinement** *n*

overregulate /ṓvər réggyoo layt/ (**-lates, -lating, -lated**) *vt* to impose too many regulations on somebody or something, especially an industry

overrepresented /ṓvər réppri zéntid/ *adj* having too many representatives, or represented by too many examples in proportion to the total ○ *His earlier work is rather overrepresented in this collection.* —**overrepresentation** /ṓvər réppri zen táysh'n/ *n*

override *vt* /ṓvər ríd/ (**-rides, -riding, -rode** /-rṓd/, **-ridden** /-rídd'n/) **1 CANCEL** to cancel or change an action or decision taken by somebody else **2 OUTWEIGH** to be more important than and take priority over something else **3 TAKE MANUAL CONTROL OF** to take manual control of an automatic control system **4 RIDE HORSE OVER** to ride a horse over or across an area **5 RIDE HORSE TOO HARD** to tire a horse by riding it too hard **6 OVERLAP** to extend over something, especially by overlapping it ■ *n* /ṓvər ríd/ **1 ASSUMPTION OF MANUAL CONTROL** the condition, process, or action of temporarily taking manual control of an automatic system **2 SWITCH FOR MANUAL CONTROL** a switch or some other manual control that temporarily cancels or reverses the effect of an automatic system

overrider /ṓvər rīdər/ *n* either of a pair of projections on the bumper of a motor vehicle, designed to prevent damage in a collision with the bumper of another vehicle

overriding /ṓvər ríding/ *adj* highest in priority —**overridingly** *adv*

overripe /ṓvər ríp/ *adj* too ripe, and past its best flavour and texture —**overripeness** *n*

overrode past tense of **override**

overruff /ṓvər rúf/ *vti* CARDS = **overtrump**

overrule /ṓvər róol/ (**-rules, -ruling, -ruled**) *vt* **1 RULE AGAINST SOMEBODY'S ARGUMENT** to rule authoritatively that somebody's argument is unsound, especially in the case of a judge disallowing a barrister's arguments ○ *Objection overruled!* **2 DECIDE AGAINST** to decide against somebody, or overturn a decision taken by somebody with lesser authority **3 EXERCISE CONTROL OVER** to exercise dominion or control over somebody or something (*literary*)

overrun *v* /ṓvər rún/ (**-runs, -running, -ran** /-rán/, **-run**) **1** *vt* **SPREAD RAPIDLY AND INFEST** to arrive in such large numbers or spread so rapidly in a place that it becomes infested or overcrowded (*often passive*) ○ *The cathedral square was overrun with tourists.* **2** *vt* **CONQUER ENEMY AND TERRITORY** to attack an enemy force, defeat it conclusively, and take over the territory occupied by it ○ *The rebels overran the government forces.* **3** *vti* **EXCEED LIMIT** to continue beyond a predetermined limit, especially a time limit or fixed budget **4** *vt* **OVERSHOOT** to go on beyond an intended stopping point such as a boundary line or the end of an airport runway **5** *vti* **OVERFLOW** to overflow or spill over something **6** *vt* **PRINT MORE THAN PLANNED** to print extra copies of a publication **7** *vt* **MOVE TYPESET MATERIAL** to transfer set type or illustrated material from one column, page, or line to another **8** *vi* **RUN WITH THROTTLE CLOSED** to run at higher revolutions than the throttle setting dictates ■ *n* /ṓvər run/ **1 ACT OF OVERRUNNING** an instance of somebody or something overrunning, especially of going on beyond the intended stopping point **2 AMOUNT EXCEEDING ESTIMATE** the amount by which something exceeds a preset limit, an estimated cost, or a budget **3 EXTRA QUANTITY PRODUCED** an extra quantity of something produced, e.g. manufactured items or copies of printed matter **4 EXTRA AREA AT END OF RUNWAY** a cleared level area at the end of a runway, available in case a plane overshoots

overrun brake *n* a brake on a vehicle being towed, to prevent it from running into the back of the vehicle towing it

oversaw past tense of **oversee**

⚡**overscan** *adj* describes an image that extends beyond the viewing boundary of a computer screen

overscore /ṓvər skáwr/ (**-scores, -scoring, -scored**) *vt* to draw a line over or through written text, usually so as to cancel or revise it

oversea /ṓvər sée/ *adj* = **overseas** *adj.* 1, **overseas** *adj.* 2 —**oversea** *adv*

overseas /ṓvər séez/ *adv* **ACROSS THE SEA** across or beyond a sea, especially in another country ○ *They live overseas.* ■ *adj* **overseas, oversea 1 RELATING TO PLACE ACROSS SEA** relating to, located in, or coming from, a foreign country or place beyond a sea ○ *overseas visitors* **2 TRAVELLING ACROSS SEA** involving travel across a sea ○ *an overseas assignment* ■ *n* **SOMEWHERE BEYOND SEA** a foreign country, or foreign countries and places beyond the sea collectively (+ *singular verb*) ○ *come from overseas*

oversecretion /ṓvər si kréesh'n/ *n* the secretion of too much of a substance, especially of an excessive amount of a hormone by a gland

oversee /ṓvər sée/ (**-sees, -seeing, -saw** /-sáw/, **-seen** /-séen/) *vt* **1** to watch over, manage, and direct somebody or a task done by somebody **2** to observe something covertly or secretly while it is happening

overseer /ṓvər seer/ *n* a supervisor of work

oversell /ṓvər sél/ (**-sells, -selling, -sold** /-sṓld/, **-sold**) *v* **1** *vt* **PRAISE TOO HIGHLY** to exaggerate the value or worth of somebody, something, or yourself to an implausible extent **2** *vti* **SELL TOO AGGRESSIVELY** to use excessively aggressive sales techniques when selling a product **3** *vti* **SELL TOO MUCH OF** to sell too much of a product, especially more than can be produced or supplied

oversensitive /ṓvər sénssətiv/ *adj* more sensitive than is thought appropriate or desirable —**oversensitiveness** *n* —**oversensitivity** /-senssə tívvəti/ *n*

overset /ṓvər sét/ (**-sets, -setting, -set**) *v* **1** *vti* **TYPESET TOO MUCH COPY** to set too much type or copy for the available space **2** *vt* **TIP OVER** to tip or turn something over (*archaic*) **3** *vt* **DISTURB** to disturb or upset somebody (*archaic*)

oversew /ṓvər sṓ/ (**-sews, -sewing, -sewed, -sewn** /-sṓn/) *vt* to sew two edges together, with small stitches overlapping both edges

oversexed /ṓvər sékst/ *adj* having an excessive preoccupation with or need for sex

overshadow /ṓvər sháddō/ *vt* **1** to take attention away from somebody or something by appearing more important or interesting **2** to cast a physical shadow over something, or make something become gloomy

overshoe /ṓvər shoo/ *n* a shoe, usually made of rubber or plastic, that is worn over an ordinary shoe to protect it from dampness or dirt

overshoot *v* /ṓvər shóot/ (**-shoots, -shooting, -shot** /-shót/) **1** *vti* **SEND OR GO FARTHER THAN INTENDED** to shoot a projectile beyond the target that was being aimed at, or be shot in this way **2** *vti* **MISS TARGET** to miss a target by missing or being shot too far **3** *vti* **RUN OFF END OF RUNWAY** to fail to complete a takeoff or landing before reaching the end of the runway and run off the end of it **4** *vti* **EXCEED LIMIT** to exceed a fixed or prearranged limit **5** *vt* **MOVE QUICKLY OVER** to move at a high speed over something ■ *n* /ṓvər shoot/ **1 ACT OF OVERSHOOTING** an instance of somebody or something overshooting an intended stopping point, especially the end of an airport runway **2 AMOUNT OF EXCESS** an instance of something exceeding a prearranged limit, or the amount or extent by which it exceeds it

overshot /ṓvər shot/ *adj* **1** describes a jaw with an upper part that is longer than and sticks out over the lower part **2** describes a water wheel driven by water flowing onto it from above

oversight /ṓvər sīt/ *n* **1** a mistake, especially as a result of a failure to do or notice something **2** the responsibility of supervising something (*formal*)

oversimplify /ṓvər símpli fī/ (**-fies, -fying, -fied**) *vt* to reduce something to such a level of simplicity that it becomes distorted or falsified —**oversimplification** /-sim plif i káy shən/ *n*

oversize *adj* /ṓvər síz/ **oversize, oversized UNUSUALLY LARGE** larger than is usual or necessary ■ *n* /ṓvər sīz/ **1 UNUSUALLY LARGE SIZE** a size that is larger than usual **2 EXTRA-LARGE ARTICLE** an article that comes in a larger size than usual

overskirt /ṓvər skurt/ *n* a skirt that is worn on top of another garment, often revealing part of the lower one

oversleep /ṓvər sléep/ (**-sleeps, -sleeping, -slept** /-slépt/, **-slept**) *vi* to continue sleeping for longer than desired or intended

oversold /ṓvər sṓld/ past participle, past tense of **oversell** ■ *adj* available at or characterized by prices that are excessively low as a result of previous heavy selling on the stock market. ◊ **overbought**

overspecialized /ṓvər spéshə līzd/, **overspecialised** *adj* concentrating too much on a specific area of interest or field of study or on too few such areas —**overspecialization** /-spéshə lī záysh'n/ *n*

overspend *v* /ṓvər spénd/ (**-spends, -spending, -spent** /-spént/) **1** *vti* **SPEND TOO MUCH** to spend more money than can be afforded **2** *vt* **EXHAUST** to tire somebody or something out completely ■ *n* /ṓvər spend/ **1 EXTRAVAGANCE** an act or instance of spending more money than can be afforded **2 AMOUNT OVERSPENT** an amount by which somebody overspends

overspill *n* /ṓvər spil/ **1 SOMETHING SPILLED** something that spills or has spilled over from something **2 PEOPLE MOVING FROM CITY TO OUTSKIRTS** the part of a crowded city's population that leave to live in new housing areas outside it ■ *vti* /ṓvər spíl/ (**-spills, -spilling, -spilled** *or* **-spilt** /-spílt/) **SPILL OVER** to spill over, or make something spill over

overspread /ṓvər spréd/ (**-spreads, -spreading, -spread**) *vt* to spread widely over or cover the surface of something

overspun /ṓvər spun/ *adj* describes a string of a musical instrument that has a thin coil of metal wire, usually copper, wound around it

overstaff /ṓvər staáf/ *vt* to supply a workplace with too large a staff (*usually passive*)

overstate /ṓvər stáyt/ (**-states, -stating, -stated**) *vt* to exaggerate something in talking or writing about it —**overstatement** *n*

overstay /ṓvər stáy/ *vti* to remain beyond the expected, planned, or desired time

oversteer *vi* /ṓvər steér/ to turn more sharply than expected, especially in a motor vehicle ○ *We oversteered and landed in a ditch.* ■ *n* /ṓvər steer/ the tendency of a motor vehicle to turn more sharply than expected

overstep /ṓvər stép/ (**-steps, -stepping, -stepped**) *vt* to go beyond the limit of something

overstimulate /ṓvər stímmyoo̅ layt/ (**-lates, -lating, -lated**) *vt* to stimulate a person or animal to an extent that is thought inappropriate or undesirable —**overstimulation** /-stimmyoo̅ láysh'n/ *n*

overstock *v* /ṓvər stók/ **1** *vti* **STOCK IN EXCESS** to stock more of something than is necessary or desirable **2** *vt* **KEEP TOO MANY ANIMALS ON** to graze an area with more livestock than it can support ■ *n* /ṓvər stok/ *US* **EXCESS** an excessively large supply of something

overstored /ṓvər stáwrd/ *adj US* having more retail outlets than are required to meet consumer demand

overstrain /ṓvər stráyn/ *vti* to try to force somebody, something, or yourself to perform beyond capacity, especially so that damage, injury, or breakdown results

overstress *vt* /ṓvər stréss/ **1 PUT EXCESSIVE EMPHASIS ON** to put too much emphasis on something **2 PUT UNDER TOO MUCH STRESS** to subject somebody to too much mental or emotional pressure **3 DEFORM AS RESULT OF EXCESSIVE FORCE** to deform material permanently by exerting too much force on it ■ *n* /ṓvər stress/ **EXCESSIVE EMPHASIZING** the putting of too much emphasis on something

overstretch /ṓvər stréch/ *v* **1** *vti* **STRETCH SOMETHING TOO FAR** to stretch something such as a muscle too much, so as to cause injury or damage **2** *vt* **STRETCH RESOURCES TOO FAR** to try to do too much with the resources available, with consequent strain on those resources and, usually, poor performance (*often passive*) ○ *Absenteeism is often a sign that employees are overstretched.* **3** *vt* **STRETCH OVER** to extend or stretch over something

overstrung /ṓvər strúng/ *adj* **1 TOO NERVOUS** excessively nervous and tense **2 WITH DOUBLE SET OF STRINGS** describes a piano fitted with two sets of strings, one crossing the other at an angle **3 STRUNG TOO TIGHTLY** in archery, describes a bow with the bowstring fixed too tightly

overstuff /ṓvər stúf/ *vt* **1** to stuff a cavity or object with too much material **2** to upholster a piece of furniture using a large amount of padding to make it soft, deep, and comfortable

oversubscribe /ṓvər səb skrī́b/ (**-scribes, -scribing, -scribed**) *vt* to apply to participate in something in numbers in excess of the available number of places (*usually passive*) ○ *The course on modern poetry was heavily oversubscribed.* —**oversubscription** /-səb skrípsh'n/ *n*

oversupply *n* /ṓvər sə plī́/ (*plural* **-plies**) an excessive supply of something ■ *vti* /ṓvər sə plī́/ (**-plies, -plying, -plied**) to provide somebody or something with an excessive supply of something

overt /ō vúrt/ *adj* **1** done openly and without any attempt at concealment **2** done openly and intentionally, and therefore able to be taken as a sign of criminal intent [14C. < Old French, past participle of *ovrir* 'open' < Latin *aperire* (see APERTURE).] —**overtly** *adv* —**overtness** *n*

overtake /ṓvər táyk/ (**-takes, -taking, -took** /-tóok/, **-taken** /-táyk'n/) *v* **1** *vti* **GO PAST** to draw level with and pass a person or vehicle travelling in the same direction **2** *vt* **DO BETTER THAN** to reach and then surpass a level achieved by somebody or something **3** *vt* **COME OVER SOMEBODY SUDDENLY** to come over somebody suddenly, or catch somebody by surprise ○ *Sleep overtook them.* **4** *vt* **CATCH UP WITH** to go after and catch up with somebody

overtax /ṓvər táks/ *vt* **1** to impose too great a strain on somebody, something, or yourself **2** to levy more tax on somebody or something than is justified or considered fair

over-the-air *adj* transmitted by radio or television —**over the air** *adv*

over the counter *adv* directly to a customer, without requiring a doctor's prescription

over-the-counter *adj* **1 BUYABLE WITHOUT PRESCRIPTION** sold directly to the public without a doctor's prescription **2 BOUGHT AND SOLD ELECTRONICALLY** not quoted as a security on an exchange, but bought and sold electronically **3 DEALING IN OVER-THE-COUNTER SECURITIES** relating to or dealing in over-the-counter securities

over-the-hill *adj* **1** past the point at which talent, energy, or physical performance is at its peak **2** an offensive term for no longer young [< the idea of being past your peak]

over-the-shoulder shot *n* a cinematographic shot taken from over the shoulder of a character whose back can be seen at the side of the frame

over-the-top *adj* so exaggerated as to appear ridiculous or outrageous (*informal*)

overthrow *vt* /ṓvər thrṓ/ (**-throws, -throwing, -threw** /-thróo/, **-thrown** /-thrṓn/) **1 REMOVE FROM POWER BY FORCE** to remove a person or group of people from a position of power by force **2 THROW BALL TOO FAR OR HARD** to throw a ball too far so that it goes beyond the player or target it was intended to reach ■ *n* /ṓvər thrō/ **1 REMOVAL FROM POWER BY FORCE** the removal of a person or group of people from a position of power by force **2 THROW THAT GOES TOO FAR** a throw of a ball that goes beyond the player or target, e.g. the stumps in cricket, it was intended to reach **3 ADDITIONAL RUN FROM OVERTHROW** an additional run scored as a result of an overthrow by a fielder

overtime /ṓvər tīm/ *n* **1 ADDITIONAL TIME WORKED** extra time worked beyond the normal hours of employment **2 PAY FOR ADDITIONAL TIME WORKED** payment, usually at a higher rate, for time worked beyond the normal hours of employment **3** *US, Can* SPORTS = **extra time** ■ *adv* **1 BEYOND NORMAL LENGTH OF TIME** beyond the normal or contracted length of time **2 VERY HARD** using a great deal of energy and effort (*informal*) ○ *been working overtime to try and make them see sense*

overtire /ṓvər tī́r/ (**-tires, -tiring, -tired**) *vt* to make somebody more tired than is advisable or desirable —**overtired** *adj* —**overtiredness** *n*

overtone /ṓvər tōn/ *n* **1** a subtle additional meaning, nuance, or quality **2** a higher tone produced at the same time as the lowest tone that helps to determine the overall quality of the sound

overtook past tense of **overtake**

overtop /ṓvər tóp/ (**-tops, -topping, -topped**) *vt* **1 RISE ABOVE** to rise above somebody or something **2 SURPASS** to surpass somebody or something **3 OVERRIDE** to be more important than somebody or something

overtrade /ṓvər tráyd/ (**-trades, -trading, -traded**) *vi* to trade beyond the level that can be supported by the trader's financial means or the market involved

overtrading /ṓvər tráyding/ *n* expansion of a business to a point where it cannot finance itself through its available cash resources

overtrain /ṓvər tráyn/ *vti* to train or exercise, or make somebody train or exercise, excessively, especially before a competition, with a resulting decrease in effectiveness —**overtraining** *n*

overtrick /ṓvər trik/ *n* a trick taken in bridge in addition to the number needed to make a contract

overtrump /ṓvər trúmp/ *vti* to play a higher trump card than one already played by another player in a trick

overtunic /ṓvər tyoonik/ *n* a tunic that is worn on top of other clothes

overture /ṓvər tyoor, -chər/ *n* **1 MUSICAL INTRODUCTION** a single orchestral movement that introduces an opera, play, ballet, or longer musical work, often including the work's themes **2** MUSIC = **concert overture** **3 INTRODUCTORY PROPOSAL OR INITIATIVE** an introductory proposal or initiative made to mark the beginning of a discussion, agreement, or relationship ○ *make overtures to someone* **4 INTRODUCTION TO A POEM** an introduction to a written work such as a poem or play [15C. Via Old French, 'opening' < Latin *apertura* (see APERTURE).]

overturn *v* /ṓvər túrn/ **1** *vti* **TIP OVER** to turn somebody or something upside down **2** *vt* **OVERTHROW** to remove a person or a group of people from a position of power **3** *vt* **REVERSE PREVIOUS DECISION** to reverse a previous decision, ruling, or law by using legal or legislative procedures —**overturn** /ṓvər turn/ *n*

over-under *n US* a wager that the final score in a game will be above or below a particular number of points

overuse *n* /ṓvər yóoss/ the excessive use of something ■ *vt* /ṓvər yóoz/ (**-uses, -using, -used**) to use something excessively, often wearing it out or making it ineffective

overvalue /ṓvər vállyoo/ (**-ues, -uing, -ued**) *vt* to set too high a value or price on something —**overvaluation** /-vállyoo áysh'n/ *n*

overview /ṓvər vyoo/ *n* **1** a general or comprehensive outline of something **2** a brief summary of something

overvoltage /ṓvər vōltij/ *n* a voltage that is in excess of the normal voltage for which an electrical circuit or system was designed and may sometimes cause damage to components

overwater /ṓvər wáwtər/ *vt* to water something such as a plant or area of grass to an extent that damages growth

overweening /ṓvər weéning/ *adj* **1** intolerably arrogant or conceited **2** excessive, especially in an arrogant and conceited way [14C. < *ween* 'think, believe'.] —**overweeningly** *adv*

overweigh /ṓvər wáy/ *vt* **1** = **outweigh** *v.* 2 **2** to oppress or burden somebody heavily

overweight *adj* /ṓvər wáyt/ **1 TOO HEAVY FOR GOOD HEALTH** with more weight than is considered healthy for somebody of a specific height, build, or age **2 ABOVE WEIGHT LIMIT** heavier than the allowed weight limit ○ *an overweight letter* ■ *vt* /ṓvər wáyt/ **1 OVEREMPHASIZE** to give too much emphasis or consideration to something **2 OVERLOAD** to weigh something down with an excessive load ■ *npl* **OVERWEIGHT PEOPLE** people who weigh too much for their height, build, or age (*sometimes offensive*)

overwhelm /ṓvər wélm/ *vt* (*often passive*) **1 OVERPOWER EMOTIONALLY** to affect somebody's emotions in a complete or irresistible way **2 OVERCOME PHYSICALLY** to use superior strength, force, or numbers to defeat somebody, especially an enemy, completely **3 SURGE OVER AND COVER** to flow over the top of and submerge or cover somebody or something **4 PROVIDE WITH HUGE AMOUNT OF** to supply somebody with a very large or excessive amount of something

overwhelming /ṓvər wélming/ *adj* **1 EMOTIONALLY OVERPOWERING** having such a great effect as to be emotionally overpowering **2 PHYSICALLY OVERPOWERING** overpowering in strength, force, or numbers **3 EXTREMELY LARGE** extremely large in amount or proportion —**overwhelmingly** *adv*

overwind /ṓvər wī́nd/ (**-winds, -winding, -wound** /-wównd/, **-wound**) *vt* to wind up the spring of a clockwork device, especially a watch or clock, too tightly, so that it will not operate or the spring breaks

overwinter /ṓvər wíntər/ *v* **1** *vti* to keep livestock or plants alive through the winter by sheltering them, or be kept alive in this way **2** *vi* to spend the winter by taking up residence in a particular place

overwork *v* /ṓvər wúrk/ **1** *vti* **DO TOO MUCH WORK** to work, or make somebody, yourself, or an animal work, excessively **2** *vt* **OVERUSE** to use something too often, especially a word or expression **3** *vt* **DECORATE SURFACE OF** to apply decoration to the surface of something **4** *vt* **WORK TOO MUCH ON** to expend too much effort on something, especially so as to reduce its quality or effectiveness ■ *n* /ṓvər wurk/ **EXCESSIVE WORK** too much work

overwound past participle, past tense of **overwind**

⚡ **overwrite** /ṓvər rī́t/ (**-writes, -writing, -wrote** /-rṓt/, **-written** /-rítt'n/) *v* **1** *vti* **REPLACE COMPUTER FILE** to replace data or a program in memory or on a disk with a new file of the same name **2** *vti* **WRITE TOO ELABORATELY** to make a piece of writing too elaborate, polished, or decorative **3** *vt* **COVER WRITING WITH MORE WRITING** to cover a piece of writing by writing on top of it

overwrought /ṓvər ráwt/ *adj* **1 VERY UPSET** extremely upset, emotional, or agitated **2 TOO ELABORATE** fashioned or decorated too elaborately **3 ORNAMENTED ON SURFACE** ornamented on the surface with something

overzealous /ṓvər zélləss/ *adj* too enthusiastic or eager, especially in carrying out a duty, and usually causing trouble or annoyance as a result —**overzealously** *adv*

ovi- *prefix* egg, ovum ○ *oviform* [< Latin *ovum* 'egg']

Ovid /óvvid/ (43 BC–AD 17) Roman poet —**Ovidian** /o víddi ən/ *adj*

oviduct /óvi dukt/ *n* either of a pair of tubes in the body that transport eggs from the ovary to the uterus

Oviedo /óvi áyd ō/ capital of Oviedo Province, NW Spain. Population: 202,421 (1995).

oviform /óvi fawrm/ *adj* shaped like an egg

ovine /ō vīn/ *adj* relating to or like a sheep [Early 19C. < late Latin *ovinus* < Latin *ovis* 'sheep'.]

oviparous /ō vípparəss/ *adj* **1** describes birds, fish, reptiles, and insects that reproduce by means of eggs that develop and hatch outside the mother's body. ◊ **viviparous** *adj*. ↑ **2** relating to the production of eggs that develop and hatch outside the mother's body — **oviparously** *adv*

oviposit /óvi pózzit/ *vi* to lay eggs (*refers usually to insects*) [Early 19C. < OVI- + Latin *posit-*, past participle of *ponere* 'to place'.]

ovipositor /óvi pózzitər/ *n* a tubular organ at the end of the abdomen of some female fish or animals, especially insects, that is used to deposit eggs

ovo- *prefix* = ovi-

ovoid /ō voyd/ *adj* **1** WITH FORM OF EGG with the solid form of an egg **2** SHAPED LIKE AN EGG describes a fruit or similar plant part that is shaped like an egg ■ *n* SOMETHING EGG-SHAPED something with the shape or form of an egg [Early 19C. < French *ovoïde* < Latin *ovum* 'egg'.]

ovolactovegetarian /óvō láktō vejjə táiri ən/ *n* a vegetarian who eats eggs and dairy products, but no products that involve the killing of animals

ovolo /óvvəlō/ (*plural* -**li** /-lī/) *n* a convex moulding that resembles a quarter-circle or ellipse when viewed in cross section [Mid-17C. < Italian, 'little egg' < Latin *ovum* 'egg'.]

ovonic /ō vónnik/ *adj* relating to, consisting of, or using glassy materials that can rapidly and reversibly become electrical conductors after a minimum voltage is applied [Mid-20C. < OVSHINSKY EFFECT + ELECTRONIC.]

ovonics /ō vónniks/, **Ovonics** *n* the study or use of glassy materials that can rapidly and reversibly become electrical conductors after a minimum voltage is applied (+ *singular verb*)

ovoviviparous /óvō vī víppərəss/ *adj* describes insects, fish, and reptiles that reproduce by means of eggs that develop within the female, deriving some nutrition from her but remaining encased within an egg membrane —**ovoviviparously** *adv*

Ovshinsky effect /ov shínski-/ *n* an effect that occurs in thin films of glass containing selenium and tellurium in which the resistance of the material drops rapidly when a particular voltage is applied across it [Mid-20C. After Stanford R. *Ovshinsky* (b. 1922), US physicist.]

ovulate /óvvyō layt/ (-**lates**, -**lating**, -**lated**) *vi* to ripen and release an egg or eggs from the ovary for possible fertilization [Late 19C. < OVULE.] —**ovulation** /óvvyōō láysh'n/ *n* —**ovulatory** *adj*

ovule /óvvyool/ *n* **1** a small structure in a seed plant that contains the embryo sac and develops into a seed after fertilization **2** a small or immature egg [Early 19C. Via French < modern Latin *ovulum* 'little egg' < Latin *ovum* 'egg'.] —**ovular** *adj*

ovum /óvəm/ (*plural* **ova** /óvə/) *n* a female reproductive cell [Early 18C. < Latin, 'egg'.]

ow /ow/ *interj* used to represent an involuntary expression of pain [Early 20C. Natural exclamation.]

owe /ō/ (**owes**, **owing**, **owed**) *v* **1** *vt* BE OBLIGATED TO PAY SOMEBODY MONEY to be under an obligation to pay or repay somebody an amount of money ○ *She owed the bank a lot of money.* **2** *vti* BE FINANCIALLY IN DEBT to be financially in debt to somebody or for something ○ *She claims she doesn't owe anyone.* **3** *vt* BE INDEBTED FOR to have something, usually some desirable thing, only because of something or somebody else ○ *I owe my success to my father.* **4** *vt* FEEL THAT RESPONSE IS DESERVED to feel that something should be given to or done for somebody in recompense for something ○ *She owes you an explanation.* ○ *I owe myself a night out.* **5** *vt* BEAR GRUDGE TOWARDS to feel a particular emotion, especially a grudge, towards somebody ○ *owed me a grudge* [Old English *āgan* < Indo-European, 'to own']

Owen /ō in/, **Robert** (1771–1858) British social reformer

Owen, Wilfred (1893–1918) British poet

Jesse Owens: Photographed in the long jump competition at the Berlin Olympics (1936)

Barnaby's

Owens /ō inz/, **Jesse** (1913–80) US athlete. Born **James Cleveland Owens**

Owerri /ə wérri/ capital of Imo State, S Nigeria. Population: 35,010 (1983).

owing /ō ing/ *adj* due to be given, especially in payment or repayment of a debt ○ *amounts still owing* ◊ **owing to** as a result or consequence of something

owl /owl/ *n* **1** HOOTING BIRD OF PREY a predatory, usually nocturnal bird with a large head, large front-facing eyes, hooked and feathered talons, a small curved beak and a distinctive hooting call. Order: Strigiformes. **2** FANCY PIGEON a domestic pigeon belonging to a breed resembling an owl **3** SOMEBODY RESEMBLING OWL a person whose habits or qualities resemble those attributed to owls, e.g. wisdom, solemnity, or staying up late [Old English *ūle* < Germanic]

owl butterfly *n* a South American butterfly that has a spot like an owl's eye on the underside of each hind wing. Genus: *Caligo*.

owlet /ówl ət/ *n* a young or baby owl

owlet moth *n* INSECTS = noctuid ['Owlet' < the fact that its eyes shine in the dark when light strikes them]

owlet nightjar *n* a bird related to the nightjar but resembling a small owl, that swoops down on insects from a perch. Native to: Australia, Papua New Guinea. Family: Aegothelidae.

owlish /ówlish/ *adj* physically resembling an owl, or displaying a characteristic attributed to owls, e.g. wisdom, contemplativeness, solemnity, or staying up all night — **owlishly** *adv* —**owlishness** *n*

owl parrot *n* BIRDS = kakapo

own /ōn/ *adj, pron* **1** EMPHASIZES POSSESSIVE a grammatical word emphasizing that somebody or something belongs to a particular person or thing and not to somebody or something else ○ (*adj*) *I always wanted to have my own business.* ○ *Her own mother wouldn't have recognized her.* ○ (*pron*) *That's my paintbrush – get your own.* ○ *At last he had a house of his own.* **2** INDICATES THAT SOMEBODY DOES SOMETHING UNAIDED with something without help or interference ○ (*adj*) *She made her own dress.* ○ *I can make my own decisions.* ○ (*pron*) *I'd rather make my own than buy them ready-made.* ■ *v* **1** *vt* HAVE AS PROPERTY to have something as your property ○ *He owns a chain of hotels.* **2** *vti* ACKNOWLEDGE to acknowledge or admit something (*formal*) ○ *He owned that the struggle had been hard.* **3** *vt* TAKE RESPONSIBILITY FOR to acknowledge full personal responsibility for something ○ *encourage team members to own the project* [Old English *āgnian* < *āgen* 'one's own', past participle of *āgan* (see OWE)] ◊ **come into your own** to start to be really effective, useful, or successful ◊ **hold your own 1** put up effective resistance in an argument or contest **2** remain in a stable condition after an illness or injury, often when it might not be expected ◊ **on your own 1** alone **2** without help or interference

own up *vi* to admit to having done something

own brand *n* an item for sale that has the trademark or label of the retailer, usually a large supermarket chain, instead of that of the manufacturer (*hyphenated when used before a noun*)

owner /ónər/ *n* a person who owns something

owner-occupied *adj* used as a residence by the person who owns it

owner-occupier *n* a person who owns or is buying the residence he or she is living in

ownership /ónər ship/ *n* **1** the legal right of possessing something **2** the fact or condition of being an owner of something

own goal *n* **1** a goal scored by mistake for the opposing team, usually by being miskicked or mishit by, or deflected off, a defender **2** an action, especially one intended to damage somebody, that ends up harming its initiator (*informal*)

own label *n* COMM = own brand (*hyphenated when used before a noun*)

⚡**OWTTE** *abbr* or words to that effect (*in e-mails*)

ox /oks/ (*plural* **oxen** /óks'n/) *n* **1** BOVINE DRAUGHT ANIMAL an adult castrated bull, sometimes used for pulling heavy loads and ploughs. Genus: *Bos*. **2** COW OR BULL a male or female bovine mammal, especially one belonging to a domestic breed **3** SOMEBODY UNINTELLIGENT AND CLUMSY somebody who is regarded as unintelligent and clumsy, especially somebody with a large build (*insult*) [Old English *oxa* < Germanic]

ox- *prefix* oxygen ○ *oxime* [< OXYGEN]

oxacillin /óksə síllin/ *n* an antibiotic used to treat bacterial infections that are resistant to penicillin [Mid-20C. < *isoxazole* + PENICILLIN.]

oxalate /óksə layt/ *n* a salt or ester of oxalic acid

oxalic acid /ok sállik-/ *n* $H_2C_2O_4$ a colourless poisonous acid. Source: plants, also made synthetically. Use: bleaching, dyeing, cleaning. [< Latin *oxalis* 'wood sorrel' (see OXALIS), because it occurs mainly in the plant's leaves]

oxalis /ok sálliss, óksaliss/ *n* a plant such as wood sorrel with leaves similar to those of clover. Genus: *Oxalis*. [Early 17C. Via Latin < Greek, 'wood sorrel' < *oxus* 'sour', because of the taste of its leaves.]

oxaloacetate /óksilō ássə tayt/ *n* a negatively charged ion (**anion**) of oxaloacetic acid that plays an important role in the Krebs cycle [< OXALIC ACID.]

oxaloacetic acid /óksalō ə settik-/ *n* $C_4H_4O_5$ a crystalline organic acid important in metabolism [Mid-20C. < OXALIC ACID.]

oxazepam /ok sázzə pam/ *n* $C_{15}H_{11}ClN_2O_2$ a tranquillizer used to manage anxiety, insomnia, and alcohol withdrawal [Mid-20C. < HYDROXY + BENZODIAZEPINE + AMINE.]

oxblood /óks blud/, **oxblood red** *adj* of a dark brownish-red colour —**oxblood** *n*

oxbow /óks bō/ *n* **1** a collar for an ox used as a draught animal, consisting of a U-shaped piece of wood attached to a yoke **2** a bend in a river shaped like an oxbow, or the land found in the bend of a river **3** GEOG = oxbow lake

oxbow lake *n* a small curved lake developed on a river floodplain by a river abandoning its original meandering course and cutting a new channel

Oxbridge /óksbrij/ *n* the universities of Oxford and Cambridge, seen as forming an institution distinct from all the other more recently established universities in England [Mid-19C. Blend of OXFORD + CAMBRIDGE.]

oxcart /óks kaart/ *n* a cart drawn by oxen, for transporting heavy goods

oxen *plural of* ox

oxeye /óks ī/ *n* **1** a plant of the daisy family. Flowers: yellow. Native to: Europe, Asia, North America. Genera: *Buphthalum* and *Heliopsis*. **2** PLANTS = daisy *n.* 2

ox-eyed *adj* with big round eyes like those of an ox

oxeye daisy *n* PLANTS = daisy *n.* 2

Oxfam /óks fam/ *n* an international charity dedicated to providing poverty and disaster relief

oxford /óksfərd/, **Oxford** *n* a sturdy leather shoe that laces over the instep [Late 19C. After OXFORD.]

Oxford /óksfərd/ city in south-central England. Population: 137,343 (1996 estimate).

Oxford accent *n* a way of speaking using the pronunciation associated with Oxford English

Oxford bags *npl* trousers with extremely loose baggy legs, popular during the 1920s [After *Oxford* University]

Oxford blue *adj* ◊ **Cambridge blue** DARK BLUE a dark blue colour. ■ *n* **1** DARK BLUE COLOUR a dark blue colour **2** OXFORD UNIVERSITY SPORTSPERSON a student who has represented Oxford University in a sporting competition

Oxford English *n* a variety of English, associated with Oxford University, that uses a form of Received Pronunciation, the standard educated speech of S England

Oxford Movement *n* a movement in the Church of England that began in Oxford in the 1830s and advocated a renewal of Roman Catholic doctrine and practices

Oxfordshire /óksfərdshər/ county in south-central England. Area: 2,610 sq. km/1,010 sq. mi.

oxidant /óksidənt/ *n* **1** a substance that oxidizes other substances **2** a substance in a bipropellant rocket fuel that contains oxygen to support the combustion of another substance, usually liquid oxygen, hydrogen peroxide, or nitric acid [Late 19C. < French, < *oxide* (see OXIDE).]

oxidase /óksi dayz, -dayss/ *n* an enzyme that catalyses oxidation [Late 19C. < OXIDATION.]

oxidation /óksi dáysh'n/ *n* **1** a chemical reaction in which oxygen is added to an element or compound **2** the process of losing electrons from a chemical element or compound [Late 18C. < French, < *oxide* (see OXIDE).] —**oxidative** /óksi daytiv, óksidátiv/ *adj*

oxidation number *n* CHEM = **oxidation state**

oxidation-reduction *n* a chemical reaction in which one component loses electrons or is oxidized and another gains electrons or is reduced

oxidation state *n* the positive or negative difference between the number of electrons associated with an atom in a chemical compound and the same atom in an element

oxidative phosphorylation *n* the production of ATP from ADP and phosphate in the final stages of aerobic respiration

oxidative stress *n* the impaired performance of cells, caused by the presence of too many oxygen molecules in them

oxide /óks īd/ *n* any compound containing oxygen, especially in combination with a metal [Late 18C. < French, < *oxygène* 'oxygen', after *acide* 'acid'.]

oxidise *vt* CHEM = **oxidize**

oxidiser *n* CHEM = **oxidant**

oxidize /óksi dīz/ (**-dizes, -dizing, -dized**), **oxidise** (**-dises, -dising, -dised**) *vti* **1** REACT OR MAKE REACT WITH OXYGEN to react or cause a chemical to react with oxygen, e.g. in forming an oxide **2** LOSE OR MAKE LOSE ELECTRONS to lose electrons, or cause a chemical element or compound to lose electrons **3** COVER WITH OXIDE COATING to form an oxide coating, or cover something with an oxide coating —**oxidizable** /óksi dīzəb'l/ *adj* —**oxidization** /óksi dī záysh'n/ *n*

oxidizer /óksi dīzər/, **oxidiser** *n* CHEM = **oxidant**

oxidizing agent *n* a substance that oxidizes other substances and undergoes reduction in the process

oxidoreductase /óksidō ri dúk tayss, -tayz/ *n* an enzyme that catalyses the oxidation of one compound and reduction of another

oxime /óks eem, -īm/ *n* an organic compound containing a hydroxyl group bonded to a nitrogen atom [Late 19C. < OXY- + IMIDE.]

oximeter /ok símmitər/ *n* an instrument that measures the amount of oxygen in something, especially in blood [Mid-19C. < OXY-.] —**oximetric** /óksi méttrik/ *adj* —**oximetrically** *adv* —**oximetry** *n*

oxlip /ókslip/ *n* a woodland plant. Flowers: small, yellow, in clusters. Native to: Europe, Asia. *Primula elatior*. [Old English *oxanslyppe* 'ox dung' < *oxa* 'ox' + *slyppe* 'slime' (see SLIP³)]

Oxon. *abbr* Oxfordshire ◼ *adj* of the University of Oxford (*after titles of academic awards*) ◊ **Cantab.** [Shortening of Latin *Oxoniensis*]

Oxonian /ok sṓni ən/ *adj* **1** relating to or typical of Oxford University, or its students and staff **2** relating to the city of Oxford or its inhabitants [Mid-16C. < *Oxonia*, Latinized form of Old English *Oxe(n)aford* 'Oxford'.] —**Oxonian** *n*

oxonium ion /ok sṓni əm-/ *n* a cation consisting of an oxygen atom covalently bound to three other atoms or groups of atoms [< OXY- after AMMONIUM]

oxpecker /óks pekər/ *n* a starling that climbs on the back of wild and domestic mammals and eats parasites from their skin. Native to: Africa. Genus: *Buphagus*.

oxtail /óks tayl/ *n* the tail of a beef animal, skinned and chopped into short lengths and simmered for a long time to make rich soups or stews

oxter /ókstər/ *n* a person's armpit (*regional*) [Old English *ōxta* < Indo-European, 'axis']

oxtongue /óks tung/ *n* a plant with bristly leaves. Flowers: yellow like those of a dandelion. Native to: Europe, Asia. Genus: *Picris*. [14C. < the shape of its leaves.]

oxy- *prefix* oxygen ○ *oxyacid* [Shortening]

oxyacetylene /óksi ə séttə leen, -lin/ *n* a mixture of oxygen and acetylene. Use: cutting and welding metal.

oxyacid /óksi assid/ *n* an acid that contains oxygen

oxycephaly /óksi séffəli/ *n* a condition in which the skull becomes slightly pointed as a result of the premature closure of some connective bones (**sutures**) [Late 19C. < Greek *oxukephalos* < *oxus* 'sharp' + *kephalē* 'head'.]

oxygen /óksijən/ *n* (*symbol* **O**) a colourless odourless gas that is the most abundant element, forms compounds with most others, and is essential for plant and animal respiration [Late 18C. < French, 'acid-former' (because it was thought to be a basic component of acids) < Greek *oxus* 'sharp, sour'.] —**oxygenic** /óksi jénnik/ *adj*

oxygenase /óksijə nayz, -nayss/ *n* an enzyme that promotes the addition of oxygen to a compound

oxygenate /óksijə nayt, ok síjjə nayt/ *vti* (**-ates, -ating, -ated**) to combine something, or be combined, with oxygen ◼ *n* a substance added to fuels, especially petrol, to make them burn more efficiently

oxygen bar *n* a place similar to a café where customers can pay to breathe in oxygen through a face mask for its reviving effects

oxygen debt *n* the amount of oxygen needed to replenish the stores the body uses for its normal physiological processes after these have been depleted during strenuous physical exercise

oxygen demand *n* BIOCHEM = **biochemical oxygen demand**

oxygen mask *n* a device fitting closely over the nose and mouth through which oxygen is supplied to assist breathing, e.g. at high altitudes

oxygen tent *n* a structure enclosing a patient in bed and resembling a transparent plastic tent, into which oxygen can be pumped to assist breathing

oxygen therapy *n* the inhaling of oxygen under pressure, often inside a pressurized chamber, as a treatment for respiratory conditions

oxyhaemoglobin /óksi heèmə glṓbin/ *n* the bright red form of haemoglobin containing bound oxygen molecules

oxyhydrogen /óksi hī drə gən/ *adj* using a mixture of oxygen and hydrogen gases, thus allowing hydrogen to burn in an oxygen atmosphere and giving a flame temperature of 2,400°C ○ *oxyhydrogen welding*

oxymetazoline /óksi méttə zṓlīn/ *n* a nasal decongestant, usually administered as a spray

oxymoron /óksi máwron, óksi máwrən/ *n* (*plural* **-ra**) a phrase in which two words of contradictory meaning are used together for special effect, e.g. 'wise fool' or 'legal murder' [Mid-17C. < Greek *oxumōron*, form of *oxumōros* < *oxus* 'sharp' + *mōros* 'foolish'.]

oxyntic /ok síntik/ *adj* producing or secreting acid ○ *oxyntic cells* [Late 19C. < Greek *oxunteos* < *oxunein* 'sharpen, make acidic' < *oxus* 'sour'.]

oxysulphide *n* any compound in which a chemical element is combined with sulphur and oxygen

oxytetracycline /óksi téttrə sī kleen/ *n* a yellow crystalline compound. Source: the soil bacterium *Streptomyces rimosus*. Use: broad-spectrum antibiotic.

oxytocic /óksi tṓssik/ *adj* inducing or speeding up childbirth by causing contractions in the muscles of the womb ◼ *n* a drug that induces or speeds up childbirth [Mid-19C. < Greek *oxutokia* 'sharp birth' < *tokos* 'birth'.]

oxytocin /óksi tṓssin/ *n* a pituitary hormone that stimulates uterine contractions during childbirth and triggers lactation

oxytone /óksi tōn/ *adj* **1** WITH ACUTE ACCENT ON LAST SYLLABLE describes a classical Greek word with an acute accent on the final syllable **2** WITH STRESS ON FINAL SYLLABLE describes a word with the stress on the final syllable ◼ *n* WORD STRESSED ON FINAL SYLLABLE an oxytone word or

syllable [Mid-18C. < Greek *oxutonos* 'sharp pitch' < *tonos* 'pitch, force'.]

oyer and terminer /óyər ənd túrminə/ *n* **1** a commission from the British Crown empowering a judge to try cases in English courts of assize, abolished along with the assize system in 1972 **2** a high court with general criminal jurisdiction in some states of the United States [Partial translation of Anglo-Norman *oyer et terminer* 'hear and determine']

oyez /ṓ yéz, -yéss, -yáy/, **oyes** *interj* used, usually three times in succession, to call for silence and indicate that an official announcement is about to be made, e.g. in court or by a town crier ◼ *n* a cry of 'oyez' [< Anglo-Norman, imperative plural ('hear ye!') of *oyer* 'hear' < Latin *audire*]

oyster /óystər/ *n* **1** SHELLFISH a shellfish with a rough irregularly shaped shell in two parts. Native to: sea bed of coastal waters. Genera: *Ostrea* and *Crassostrea*. **2** SHELLFISH SIMILAR TO OYSTER any shellfish similar to an edible oyster, e.g. a pearl oyster **3** OYSTER AS FOOD the flesh of an oyster as food **4** SLIGHTLY GREYISH OFF-WHITE a pale greyish beige or pink colour **5** PIECE OF DARK MEAT IN FOWL a small piece of dark meat found in a hollow on either side of the pelvic bone of a fowl such as a chicken or turkey ◼ *vi* GATHER OYSTERS to grow or gather oysters [Via Old French *oistre* < Latin *ostrea, ostreum* < Greek *ostreon*, related to *ostrakon* 'shell']

oyster bed *n* an area of seabed where oysters grow or are grown

oystercatcher /óystər katshər/ *n* a common large shore bird, found worldwide, with a long flat almost chisel-shaped red bill and black or black-and-white plumage, living on shellfish and worms. Genus: *Haematopus*.

oyster crab *n* a small soft-bodied crab that lives harmlessly inside the shell of a live oyster or other mollusc. *Pinnotheres ostreum*.

oysterman /óystər mən/ (*plural* **-men** /-mən/) *n* **1** a grower, harvester, or seller of oysters **2** a boat used in gathering oysters

oyster mushroom *n* an edible mushroom that grows on dead wood and has a soft flavourful grey cap. *Pleurotus ostreatus*.

oyster plant *n* **1** FOOD = **salsify** *n*. **1 2** PLANTS = **salsify** *n*. **2 3** PLANTS = **lungwort** *n*. **2**

oyster sauce *n* a salty bottled sauce flavoured with oysters, used in Chinese cooking

oyster shell scale *n* an insect pest of shade trees and shrubs that in its wingless and eyeless adult form lives under an impenetrable white shell and sucks the sap of its host. *Lepidosaphes ulmi*.

oz[1] *abbr* ounce [< Italian *ōz*, abbreviation of *onza* 'ounce' < Latin *uncia* 'twelfth part' (see OUNCE¹)]

⚡oz[2] *abbr* Australia (*in Internet addresses*)

Oz /oz/ *n* Australia (*informal*)

Özal /ṓ zaàl/, **Turgut** (1927–93) Turkish statesman

Ozark Plateau /ṓ zaark-/, **Ozarks** /ṓ zaarks/, **Ozark Mountains** mountainous region of the south-central United States, extending from SW Missouri across NW Arkansas and E Oklahoma. Area: 130,000 sq. km/50,000 sq. mi.

AKG London

Seiji Ozawa

Ozawa /ṓ zaàwə/, **Seiji** (*b.* 1935) Japanese conductor

ozocerite /ṓzō sírrit/, **ozokerite** /-kírrit/ *n* a waxy hydrocarbon substance occurring naturally in irregular veins in sandstone rock, ranging in colour from brown to jet black. Use: making candles, wax paper, polishes. [Mid-19C. < German *Ozokerit* < Greek *ozein* 'to smell' + *kēros* 'beeswax'.]

ozone /ố zōn, ố zŏn/ *n* 1 O$_3$ a gaseous form of oxygen with three oxygen atoms per molecule, formed by electrical discharge in oxygen. Use: water purification. 2 fresh pure air, especially sea air (*informal*) [Mid-19C. Via German *Ozon* < Greek *ozon*, neuter present participle of *ozein* 'smell'; from its pungent smell.]

ozone-friendly *adj* causing no harm to the ozone layer

ozone hole *n* an area of the upper atmosphere where the ozone layer is absent or has become unusually thin

ozone layer *n* the layer of the upper atmosphere, from 15 to 50 km/10 to 30 miles above the Earth's surface, where most atmospheric ozone collects, absorbing harmful ultraviolet radiation from the Sun

ozonide /ố zōnīd/ *n* an explosive organic compound formed by the addition of ozone to any organic compound with a double or triple carbon bond

ozonize /ố zōnīz/ (**-nizes, -nizing, -nized**),   **ozonise** (**-nises, -nising, -nised**) *vt* 1 to convert oxygen into ozone 2 to treat something with ozone, or add ozone to an organic compound with a double or triple carbon bond —**ozonization** /ốzō nī záysh'n/ *n*

ozonizer /ốzən īzzər/ *n* a device that produces ozone from oxygen gas

ozonolysis /ốzō nóllassis/ *n* the technique of using ozone to oxidize an organic material in the process of identifying double bonds or synthesizing chemicals

ozonosphere /ō zŏnə sfeer, ō zónnə-/ *n* METEOROL = **ozone layer**

Pp

p[1] /pee/ (*plural* **p's**), **P** (*plural* **P's** *or* **Ps**) *n* the 16th letter of the English alphabet, representing a consonant ◇ **mind your p's and q's** to be careful to be polite, tactful, and well-behaved

p[2] *symbol* 1 pence 2 penny 3 piano (*musical direction*)

p[3] *abbr* 1 page 2 part 3 participle 4 past 5 per 6 pint 7 pipe 8 population 9 purl

P[1] /pee/ (*plural* **P's** *or* **Ps**) *n* something shaped like a letter 'P'

P[2] *symbol* 1 peseta 2 pataca 3 peso 4 phosphorus 5 pula

P[3] *abbr* 1 parity 2 park (*on gear sticks*) 3 Pastor 4 pawn 5 played (*in sports tables*) 6 power 7 President 8 pressure 9 Priest 10 Prince

⚡**P2P** *adj* 1 describes payments or linkups made between two individuals via the Internet. Full form **person-to-person** 2 describes software enabling commercial or private users of the Internet communicate or share resources without the use of intermediaries such as servers. Full form **peer-to-peer**

pa[1] /paa/ (*plural* **pa's** *or* **pas**) *n* father (*informal*) [Early 19C. Shortening of PAPA.]

⚡**pa**[2] *abbr* Panama (*in Internet addresses*)

pa[3] /paa/ (*plural* **pa**), **pah** (*plural* **pah**) *n* a fortified Maori settlement on a hilltop [Mid-18C. < Maori *pà* < *pā* 'block up'.]

Pa *symbol* 1 pascal 2 protactinium

PA[1] *abbr* 1 particular average 2 Pennsylvania 3 personal account 4 personal appearance 5 personal assistant 6 *US* physician's assistant 7 Post Adjutant 8 power of attorney 9 press agent 10 Press Association 11 *US* prosecuting attorney

PA[2] *n* an electronic amplification system used to increase the sound level of speech or music in a large or open space such as a stadium or auditorium. Full form **public-address system**

Pa. *abbr* Pennsylvania

p.a. *abbr* yearly

P/A *abbr* power of attorney

pa'anga /paàng gə, paa aàng-/ *n* see table at **currency** [Mid-20C. < Polynesian.]

PABA /pábbə, paàbə/ *n* a form of aminobenzoic acid that is part of the B vitamin complex. Use: sunscreen. Full form **para-aminobenzoic acid**

pablum /pábbləm/ *n* LITERAT = **pabulum** *n*. 2

Pabst /paapst/, **G. W.** (1885–1967) Austrian film director

pabulum /pábbyŏoləm/ *n* 1 a source of nourishment in an easily absorbable liquid, especially the nutrient intake of plants and lower animals 2 material whose intellectual content is thin, trite, bland, or generally unsatisfying (*literary*) [Mid-17C. < Latin < stem of *pascere* 'feed'.]

PABX *abbr* private automatic branch exchange

paca /paàkə, páka/ *n* a large burrowing plant-eating rodent with a large head and brown fur with white spots. Native to: rainforests of South and Central America. Genus: *Cuniculus*. [Mid-17C. Via Spanish and Portuguese < Tupi.]

pace[1] /payss/ *n* 1 SPEED OF MOVEMENT the particular speed at which somebody or something moves, especially when walking or running ○ *She quickened her pace.* 2 SPEED OF EVENTS the rate or speed at which things happen or develop ○ *the pace of modern life* 3 SPEED IN PERFORMANCE the degree of urgency, sharpness, or speed in the writing, composition, or performance of a dramatic or musical work 4 STEP a step taken when walking or running 5 DISTANCE COVERED IN A STEP the distance covered in a single step or stride 6 UNIT OF LENGTH any unit of distance, ranging from .76 to 1.52 m/30 to 60 in, based on the length of one or two human strides 7 WAY OF WALKING a particular manner or style of walking 8 GAIT OF HORSE a distinctive way in which a four-legged animal walks or runs at different speeds, e.g. a walk, trot, or canter, especially as executed by a trained horse 9 2-BEAT GAIT a two-beat gait of a four-legged animal where both legs on one side of the body move and are put down together ■ *v* (**paces, pacing, paced**) 1 *vti* WALK TO AND FRO to walk to and fro within a restricted area, especially in a state of nervous anxiety or deep thought ○ *paced up and down all night worrying* 2 *vti* WALK ALONG to walk along or through something with regular strides 3 *vti* MEASURE BY COUNTING STEPS to measure a distance by counting the paces taken to cover it ○ *I paced out the width of the room.* 4 *vt* SET THE SPEED OF to set the speed at which somebody runs, moves, or does something ○ *I helped her train for the marathon by pacing her on a bicycle.* 5 *vr* DO SOMETHING AT CONTROLLED RATE to run or work at an even controlled speed so as not to waste energy ○ *Learn to pace yourself.* 6 *vi* MOVE AT A PACE to move at a pace (*refers to horses*) [13C. Directly or via French *pas* 'step' < Latin *passus* 'stretch (of the leg)' < *pandere* 'stretch, extend'.] ◇ **at somebody's own pace** at the rate that is natural or comfortable for somebody ◇ **force the pace** to do something to force somebody to go faster or to make something happen more quickly ◇ **off the pace** behind the leader or the score of the leading competitor ◇ **put something through its paces** to make something demonstrate its capabilities, as a test or in order to impress other people ◇ **set the pace** to go at a speed or establish a standard that others have to keep up with ◇ **stand** *or* **stay the pace** to be able to keep up with other people, especially when the pace is fast, the standard high, or the competition fierce

pace[2] /páyssi, paà chay/ *prep* used in front of a name or title as a gesture of real or ironic respect to somebody who is mistaken and about to be corrected ○ *Pace the critic of this newspaper, the character's name is Prospero, not Prosperus.* [Late 18C. < Latin, 'with peace, with permission', form of *pax* 'peace'.]

PACE *abbr* Police and Criminal Evidence Act

pace bowler *n* a fast bowler in cricket

pace car *n* a car that leads the competitors in a motor race through a pace lap before the start of a race but does not participate in the race itself

pace lap *n* a lap of the course driven by all the competitors in a motor race before the race begins, to warm up the engines

pacemaker /páyss maykər/ *n* 1 COMPETITOR WHO SETS THE PACE a competitor in a race who sets the speed at which the whole or part of the race is run 2 = **pacesetter** *n*. 1 3 DEVICE THAT REGULATES THE HEARTBEAT a battery-operated electrical device inserted into the body to deliver small regular shocks that stimulate the heart to beat in a normal rhythm 4 NATURAL HEARTBEAT REGULATOR a small area of specialized heart-muscle tissue in the wall of the upper right chamber of the heart that sends out rhythmic electrical impulses to regulate the heartbeat

pacer /páyssər/ *n* 1 SPORTS = **pacemaker** *n*. 1 2 a horse trained to move at a pace in races

pacesetter /páyss setər/ *n* 1 a person or group regarded as being a leader in any field and one whom others may emulate 2 SPORTS = **pacemaker** *n*. 1

pacey /páyssi/ (**pacier, paciest**), **pacy** (**-ier, -iest**) *adj* with fast-moving action or a fast-moving, exciting plot ○ *a pacey story*

pacha *n* HIST = **pasha**

pachisi /pə cheèzi, paa-/ *n* an ancient Indian four-handed game similar to backgammon, played on a cross-shaped board with six cowrie shells used as dice [Early 19C. < Hindi *pac(c)īsī* '(throw of) 25' (the highest in the game).]

pachycephalosaur /páki séffələ sawr/, **pachycephalosaurus** /páki seffələ sáwrəss/ *n* a plant-eating dinosaur of the late Cretaceous and Jurassic periods that walked on its hind legs and had a very thick skull covered with knobs or spikes. Suborder: Pachycephalosauria. [Mid-20C. < modern Latin *Pachycephalosauria* < Greek *pakhus* 'thick' + *kephalē* 'head, skull' + *sauros* 'lizard'.]

pachyderm /páki durm/ *n* a large mammal with a thick skin, especially the elephant, rhinoceros, or hippopotamus [Mid-19C. < French *pachyderme* < Greek *pachydermos* 'thick-skinned' < *pachys* 'thick' + *derma* 'skin'.] — **pachydermal** /páki dúrm'l/ *adj*

pachydermatous /páki dúrmətəss/ *adj* 1 having the thick skin or some other physical characteristic typical of a pachyderm 2 insensitive to other people and unworried by criticism or attack (*literary or humorous*) [Early 19C. < Greek *pakhus* 'thick' + *dermat-* 'skin'.]

pachysandra /páki sándrə/ (*plural* **-dras** *or* **-dra**) *n* a low-growing evergreen bush with toothed leaves and tiny white flowers, often used as ground cover. Genus: *Pachysandra*. [Early 19C. < modern Latin, < Greek *pakhus* 'thick' + *andr-* 'man, male'; from the thick stamens.]

pachytene /páki teen/ *n* the third stage of cell division, during which the paired chromosomes become shorter and thicker and divide into four chromatids [Early 20C. < French *pachytène* < Greek *pakhus* 'thick' + French *-tène* 'ribbon' (< Greek *tainia*).]

pacific /pə síffik/ *adj* 1 BRINGING PEACE leading to or promoting peace and an end to conflict 2 HAVING A PEACEFUL TEMPERAMENT calm and peaceful by nature 3 UNAGGRESSIVE avoiding the use of force [Mid-16C. Directly or via French *pacifique* < Latin *pacificus* < *pac-*, stem of *pax* 'peace'.]

Pacific /pə síffik/ *n* the Pacific Ocean ■ *adj* relating to the Pacific Ocean, or to the territories that surround it or are surrounded by it

Pacific Islands Melanesia, Micronesia, and Polynesia —**Pacific Islander** *n*

Pacific Islands, Trust Territory of the former UN trust territory in the W Pacific Ocean administered by the United States, comprising 2,000 islands including the Caroline, Marshall, and Mariana islands

Pacific Northwest *n* a region of the NW United States on the Pacific coast that includes the states of Washington and Oregon and sometimes SW British Columbia, in Canada

Pacific Ocean largest ocean in the world, stretching from the Arctic Ocean in the north to Antarctica in the south, and from North and South America in the east to East Asia, the Malay Archipelago, and Australia in the west. Area: 165,000,000 sq. km/64,000,000 sq. mi.

Pacific Rim *n* the countries that border the Pacific, especially the countries of East Asia, considered as a political or economic unit

Pacific Standard Time, Pacific Time *n* the standard time for the coastal regions of W North America, one hour behind Mountain Time and eight hours behind Greenwich Mean Time

pacifier /pássi fī ər/ *n* **1** somebody or something that calms a person or situation **2** *US* BABYWARE = **dummy** *n.* 4

pacifism /pássi fizəm/ *n* **1 BELIEF IN THE PEACEFUL RESOLUTION OF CONFLICTS** a belief that violence, war, and the taking of lives are unacceptable ways of resolving disputes **2 REFUSAL TO PARTICIPATE IN WAR** the refusal to take up arms or participate in war because of moral or religious beliefs **3 BELIEF IN DIPLOMACY OVER WAR** a belief that international conflicts should be settled by negotiation rather than war

pacifist /pássi fist/ *n* **1** a believer in or advocate or practitioner of pacifism **2** a person who refuses to perform military service or take part in a war —**pacifist** *adj* —**pacifistic** /pássi fístik/ *adj* —**pacifistically** /-fístikli/ *adv*

pacify /pássi fī/ (**-fies, -fying, -fied**) *vt* **1** to calm somebody who is angry or agitated, or soothe violent or angry feelings **2** to bring peace to an area, people, or situation, often by using military force to end conflict or unrest [15C. Directly or via French *pacifier* < Latin *pacificare* 'make peace' < *pac-*, stem of *pax* 'peace'.] —**pacifiable** *adj* —**pacification** /pássifi káysh'n/ *n*

Pacinian corpuscle /pə sínni ən-/ *n* a pressure-sensitive nerve ending resembling a tiny white onion that is connected to the end of nerve fibres in the skin, especially of the hands and feet, and in connective tissue [Mid-19C. After Filippo *Pacini* (1812–83), Italian anatomist.]

Pacino /pə cheénō/, **Al** (*b.* 1940) US actor. Full name **Alfredo Pacino**

⚡**pack**[1] /pak/ *v* **1** *vti* **PUT BELONGINGS INTO A CONTAINER** to put personal belongings into a bag or other container for transporting **2** *vti* **PUT PRODUCTS IN CONTAINERS** to put something into a container or fill a container with something for sale, transport, or storage **3** *vt* **MAKE SOMETHING INTO A PARCEL OR BUNDLE** to make up a parcel or bundle, or to wrap or roll something up in one **4** *vt* **FILL SOMETHING WITH A LARGE QUANTITY** to fill something, especially a limited space, tightly (*often passive*) ○ *a book packed with useful information* **5** *vti* **CROWD INTO OR FILL A PLACE** to crowd into a place so that it is full or overfull, or to fill a place with people **6** *vt* **FIT SOMETHING INTO A LIMITED TIME** to fit many different activities or events into a limited period of time ○ *packed a lot of sightseeing into one weekend* **7** *vt* COMPUT = **compress** *v.* 3 **8** *vti* **COMPACT SOMETHING OR BECOME COMPACTED** to compact a substance such as snow or soil into a dense mass, or to become densely compacted **9** *vt* **PRESS SOMETHING ROUND AN OBJECT** to wrap or press something in around an object to hold it firmly or protect it **10** *vt* **USE A PACK ON A WOUND** to apply a medical pack to a wound or insert one into a body cavity **11** *vt* **APPLY A COMPRESS TO A BODY PART** to apply cold compresses to part of a patient's body in order to control body temperature **12** *vt* **SEAL SOMETHING TO PREVENT LEAKAGE** to seal a mechanical joint by inserting a layer of compressible material between the moving parts to prevent leakage of fluid **13** *vt* **FILL A CAVITY WITH GREASE** to fill a cavity containing bearings with grease **14** *vti US* **CARRY A GUN** to carry a weapon, especially a gun (*informal*) **15** *vt* **POSSESS SOMETHING AS A FORCEFUL CAPABILITY** to be capable of delivering something that has a powerful or devastating effect (*informal*) **16** *vt* **LOAD BAGGAGE ONTO AN ANIMAL** to put goods or belongings onto a horse, donkey, or other animal in order to transport them **17** *vti* **CARRY A LOAD** to carry a load **18** *vi* **FORM SCRUM OR MAUL** to get into a compact group for a scrum or maul ■ *n* **1 COMMERCIAL CONTAINER** a container or piece of packaging holding several products or items of the same kind, or such a container and its contents **2 COLLECTION OF THINGS IN A PACKAGE** a set of documents or other materials relating to a subject that are packaged together ○ *a free information pack* **3 AMOUNT CONTAINED IN A PACK** the contents of a pack, or the amount of something that can be contained in a pack **4 LARGE AMOUNT** a large amount of something ○ *a pack of lies* **5 BAG CARRIED ON THE BACK** a bag or bundle, especially one designed to be carried on a person's or animal's back **6 SOLDIER'S BAG FOR EQUIPMENT** a soldier's canvas or nylon bag with shoulder straps used to carry personal clothing and equipment in the field **7 PARACHUTE IN A CONTAINER** a parachute, rigged, folded, and in its container ready for use **8 SET OF CARDS** a set of 52 playing cards, including the four suits plus jokers ○ *a pack of cards* **9 GROUP OF ANIMALS** a group of animals that live and hunt together, especially wolves or dogs ○ *a pack of wolves* **10 LARGE GROUP OF PEOPLE ACTING TOGETHER** a group of people who behave in the same way, especially a group whose behaviour appears to be threatening, predatory, or criminal ○ *always followed by a pack of photographers* **11 GROUP OF BROWNIES OR CUBS** a local organized unit of Brownie Guides or Cub Scouts **12 RUGBY TEAM'S FORWARDS** the forwards playing for a particular rugby team, or the forwards from both sides during a match, especially when involved in a scrum or maul **13 MAIN BODY OF COMPETITORS** the main body of competitors in a race or competition **14 GROUP OF SUBMARINES OR AIRCRAFT** a number of submarines, aircraft, or other military units who hunt and fight the enemy as a group **15 COMPRESS USED IN SURGERY** a wad of soft absorbent material applied to a wound or temporarily inserted into a body cavity to control bleeding or keep tissues dry during surgery **16 MEDICINAL COMPRESS** a compress placed on the body for medicinal purposes **17 COSMETIC PASTE** a quantity of moist material applied to part of the body, especially the face, for cosmetic purposes ○ *a mud pack* **18** GEOG = **pack ice** **19 AMOUNT OF FOOD PRESERVED** an amount of food canned or preserved in a particular year or season [12C. < Dutch or Low German *pakken*.] —**packable** *adj*

pack in *v* **1** *vt* **ATTRACT IN LARGE NUMBERS** to attract very large audiences ○ *The show has been running three years and is still packing them in night after night.* **2** *vti* **STOP DOING** to stop or give up doing something (*informal*) ○ *She's packed in her job.* **3** *vt* **END RELATIONSHIP WITH** to end a sexual or romantic relationship with somebody (*informal*) ◇ **pack it in** to stop doing something (*informal; often used as a command*)

pack off *v* **1** *vt* to send somebody away unceremoniously to another place (*informal*) ○ *They were packed off to boarding school at the age of seven.* **2** *vi* to leave or to go somewhere hastily or unceremoniously ○ *They packed off home as soon as the work was done.*

pack up *v* **1** *vti* **STOP DOING** to stop doing something **2** *vi* **STOP WORKING** to stop working properly (*informal*) ○ *The washing machine has packed up.* **3** *vi* **FINISH WORK** to finish work for the day (*informal*) ○ *I'm packing up and going home.*

pack[2] /pak/ *vt* to ensure that a group such as a jury or committee is made up wholly or mainly of supporters of a particular side [Early 16C. Probably alteration of PACT.]

⚡**package** /pákij/ *n* **1 PARCEL** an object or set of objects, wrapped, boxed, or tied in a bundle for transportation or mailing **2 DIFFERENT THINGS CONSTITUTING A SINGLE ITEM** a number of different components intended to constitute a single item **3 PIECE OF GENERAL ADAPTABLE COMPUTER SOFTWARE** a piece of computer software that can be used for a range of related purposes, such as word processing or financial analysis **4** LEISURE = **package holiday** ■ *vt* (**-ages, -aging, -aged**) **1 PUT SOMETHING INTO PACKAGE** to put things into or wrap them up as a package **2 PRODUCE ATTRACTIVE PACKAGING FOR** to create suitable or attractive packaging in which a product is to be sold **3 PROMOTE OR PRESENT** to present somebody or something to others in a way intended to ensure appeal and acceptance ○ *It wasn't so much the policy that was wrong as the way it was packaged.* **4 GROUP SOMETHING AS A PACKAGE** to group or offer several different items together in a package **5 PRODUCE SOMETHING FOR OTHERS TO MARKET** to produce a book or television programme or series in finished form ready to be published or broadcast by another company —**packager** *n*

package deal *n* a proposal or agreement comprising a number of different items that must all be accepted together

package holiday *n* a holiday or tour organized in advance by a travel company to whom the holidaymaker pays a single fee covering transport, accommodation, board, and often entertainment. US term **package tour**

package tour *n US* LEISURE = **package holiday**

packaging /pákijing/ *n* **1 WRAPPING OR CONTAINER** the wrapping or container in which an item is presented for sale, or the materials used to make it **2 DESIGN OR STYLE OF WRAPPING** the design or style of the wrapping or container in which something is offered for sale, especially from the point of view of its appeal to buyers **3 PRESENTATION** the manner in which something or somebody is presented to the public in order to create a favourable image or impression **4 WORK OF PACKAGER** the work done by a packager

pack animal *n* **1** an animal that is used to carry goods or equipment, e.g. a horse, donkey, or mule **2** an animal that lives in a pack

pack drill *n* a military punishment in which the offender has to march carrying a full load of equipment

packed /pakt/ *adj* **1 FULL OF PEOPLE** full of people and extremely crowded ○ *played to a packed house every night* **2 CONTAINING A LOT OF** containing or offering something in excitingly large quantities (*often in combination*) ○ *a fun-packed adventure* **3 COMPRESSED** pressed together to form a compact mass ○ *packed snow*

packed lunch *n* a lunch that has been prepared and put into a container to be eaten later, usually on a picnic or excursion. US term **box lunch** *n.*

packed out *adj* crowded with or completely full of people (*informal*)

packer /pákər/ *n* **1** a person or machine that packs goods in containers or in packaging **2** a person or company involved in the processing and packing of goods, especially meat or fresh produce, for the wholesale market

Packer /pákər/, **Sir Frank** (1906–74) Australian journalist and newspaper proprietor

Packer, Kerry (*b.* 1937) Australian media proprietor

⚡**packet** /pákit/ *n* **1 SMALL CONTAINER FOR GOODS** a small box, envelope, or bag in which goods are sold or stored **2 CONTENTS OR QUANTITY IN PACKET** the contents of a packet, or the quantity of goods contained in a packet ○ *still have half a packet of crisps* **3 SMALL PARCEL** a small parcel or package **4 DATA UNIT IN A COMPUTER NETWORK** a message or part of a message packaged as a fixed-size unit of data for transmission through a computer network **5 packet, packet boat BOAT ON A REGULAR SHORT RUN** a small ship that provides a regular service carrying passengers, freight, and mail over a fixed short route ■ *vt* **PUT SOMETHING IN A PACKET** to put something into a packet or wrap it up as a parcel [15C. Probably 'small pack' < PACK[1].] ◇ **catch** *or* **cop** *or* **get a packet** to be seriously injured (*slang*) ◇ **cost a packet** to cost a great deal of money (*informal*)

⚡**packet switching** *n* the transmitting and routing of data as packet segments sent rapidly and sequentially over a channel that is occupied only during the actual transmission

packframe /pák fraym/ *n* a lightweight frame with shoulder straps to which equipment or unwieldy loads can be strapped to be carried on a person's back

packhorse /pák hawrss/ *n* a horse used for carrying goods or equipment

pack ice *n* floating ice, especially in polar regions, that has formed itself into a solid mass covering a wide area

packing /páking/ *n* **1 ACT OF PUTTING THINGS INTO CONTAINERS** the task of putting things into containers, usually for storage or transport **2 MATERIAL FOR PROTECTING A PACKED OBJECT** material used to surround and protect something packed inside a container **3 WATERTIGHT OR AIRTIGHT MATERIAL** material used to fill or surround something such as a joint in a pipe in order to make it watertight or airtight **4 PROCESSING AND PACKAGING OF FOOD** the processing and packaging of food such as meat or produce for sale **5 ABSORBENT MATERIAL FOR MEDICAL PACKS** absorbent material such as gauze for insertion in body cavities or wounds **6 SPACERS BETWEEN CLAMPED SURFACES** shims, washers, or other pieces of metal used to adjust the distance between component surfaces before they are secured

packing case *n* a large wooden box or crate in which objects are packed for transportation or storage

pack rat *n* a rat that lives in woodlands and collects and carries away objects to its nest, the best-known species of which has a long bushy tail and cheek pouches. Native to: North America. *Neotoma cinerea.*

packsack /pák sak/ *n US* a bag with shoulder straps that can be carried on the back

packsaddle /pák sad'l/ *n* a saddle for carrying loads on a pack animal

packthread /pák thred/ *n* strong twine used for sewing up packages wrapped in sacking

pact /pakt/ *n* an agreement made between two or more groups or individuals, either formally or informally, to do something together or for each other [15C. Via French *pacte* < Latin *pactum*, form of *pactus*, past participle of *pacisci* 'agree'.]

pacy *adj* = **pacey**

pad[1] /pad/ *n* 1 **PIECE OF SOFT MATERIAL** a piece of soft material used to protect something or give it shape, to clean or polish articles, or to absorb moisture 2 **PROTECTIVE MATERIAL WORN BY SPORTS PLAYERS** a specially shaped covering of impact-absorbing material used to protect part of the body, especially when playing a sport 3 **BLOCK OF PAPER SHEETS** a number of sheets of paper of the same size fastened together along one edge 4 **INK-FILLED MATERIAL** a thick firm piece of material saturated with ink onto which a rubber stamp is pressed so that ink is transferred onto it 5 **AREA FOR TAKING OFF AND LANDING** a place where a helicopter can land and take off or from which a rocket is launched 6 **SANITARY TOWEL** a strip of absorbent material used externally during menstruation 7 **BACKING MATERIAL** a firm backing or support for something that is laid on a surface 8 **FLESHY CUSHION OF AN ANIMAL'S PAW** a small rounded fleshy cushion on the underside of an animal's paw 9 **FLESHY TIP OF A FINGER OR TOE** the rounded fleshy part at the end of a human finger or toe 10 **LIVING QUARTERS** somebody's flat or house (*slang dated*) 11 **WATER LILY LEAF** the broad leaf of an aquatic plant such as a water lily that floats on the surface of the water 12 **SET OF RESISTORS** a fixed configuration of resistors designed to reduce the strength of an electrical signal without distorting the signal itself ■ *vt* (**pads, padding, padded**) 1 **LINE OR COVER SOMETHING WITH SOFT MATERIAL** to use soft material to give something shape, to make it more comfortable, or to protect it 2 **ADD UNNECESSARY MATERIAL TO** to add unnecessary material to something, especially a piece of writing or a speech, in order to lengthen it ○ *padded out the speech with anecdotes* 3 **INFLATE SOMETHING BY ADDING BOGUS EXPENSES** to add extra charges to a bill or expense account to make it higher than it should be [Mid-16C. < ?]

pad[2] /pad/ *vti* (**pads, padding, padded**) 1 **WALK QUIETLY** to walk, or to walk along or through somewhere, with soft or silent steps ○ *She padded along in her slippers.* 2 **WALK SLOWLY** to walk along a route very slowly ■ *n* **SOUND OF FOOTSTEPS** the sound of soft steady footsteps [Mid-16C. < ?]

padded cell *n* formerly, a room in a psychiatric hospital with its walls and floor covered with padding to prevent a patient from doing himself or herself physical harm

padding /pádding/ *n* 1 **THICK SOFT MATERIAL** thick soft material used as a protective lining or covering or to fill and give shape to things 2 **UNNECESSARY ADDITIONS TO SPEECH OR WRITING** unnecessary or irrelevant material added to a piece of writing or speech to make it longer 3 **BOGUS ADDITIONS TO BILL** extra charges added to a bill or expense account to make it higher than it should be

paddle[1] /pádd'l/ *n* 1 **SHORT FLAT-BLADED OAR** a short oar with a flat blade at one or both ends used to propel a canoe or small boat 2 **BLADE OF A PADDLE WHEEL** a blade of a paddle wheel 3 *US* **TABLE TENNIS BAT** a round wooden bat with a short handle used in table tennis 4 *US* **PIECE OF WOOD FOR SPANKING** a usually short piece of wood with a flattened end used for physical punishment 5 ZOOL = **flipper** *n.* 1 6 **FLAT-BLADED STIRRING TOOL** a tool with a flat blade used for shaping, stirring, or beating 7 **EARLY INPUT DEVICE FOR VIDEO GAMES** an input device for early video games with a dial that allowed the user to move an on-screen object either up and down or from side to side ■ *v* (**-dles, -dling, -dled**) 1 *vti* **PROPEL A CANOE WITH A PADDLE** to propel a canoe or small boat through water using a paddle 2 *vt* **CARRY IN A CANOE** to carry somebody or something somewhere in a canoe or paddleboat 3 *vt US* **SPANK** to spank somebody with a paddle or with the hand 4 *vt* **STIR WITH PADDLE** to stir, beat, or shape something using a paddle 5 *vti* **ROW AT AN EASY PACE** to row a boat at an easy pace [15C. < ?] —**paddler** *n*

paddle[2] /pádd'l/ *v* (**-dles, -dling, -dled**) 1 *vi* **WALK ABOUT IN SHALLOW WATER** to walk or play, usually with bare feet, in shallow water 2 *vti* **DABBLE IN WATER** to move the hands or feet about gently in shallow water 3 *vi* **WADDLE** to walk along unsteadily like a very small child ■ *n* **ACT OF PLAYING IN WATER** an act or period of walking or playing in shallow water ○ *go for a paddle* [Mid-16C. < ?] —**paddler** *n*

paddleball /pádd'l bawl/ *n* a game for two to four players played by hitting a ball against a wall with small paddles, or the ball used in this game

paddleboard /pádd'l bawrd/ *n* a long narrow surfboard used especially in rescuing swimmers

paddleboat /pádd'l bōt/ *n* a boat propelled by one or more paddle wheels

paddlefish /pádd'l fish/ (*plural* **-fishes** *or* **-fish**) *n* a large freshwater fish with a long flat snout and a cartilaginous skeleton. Native to: Mississippi River valley, Yangtze River. Family: Polyodontidae.

paddle steamer *n* a steamship propelled by paddle wheels on each side of the hull or by a single paddle wheel at the stern. US term **paddle wheeler**

paddle wheel *n* a wheel with flat blades fixed all round its edge, attached to the hull of a ship and usually turned by an engine to propel the ship through water

paddle wheeler *n US* SHIPPING = **paddle steamer**

paddock[1] /páddək/ *n* 1 **ENCLOSED FIELD FOR HORSES** a small field near a house or stable with grazing for horses 2 **AREA FOR MOUNTING RACEHORSES** an area on a racecourse where the racehorses are paraded before a race and the jockeys mount 3 **AREA FOR CARS BEFORE A RACE** an area near the pits on a motor-racing track where cars are worked on before a race 4 *ANZ* **FENCED AREA OF LAND** a field or other fenced-off area of land 5 *ANZ* **PLAYING AREA** the playing area for a sport, e.g. a football pitch ■ *vt* **KEEP HORSES IN PADDOCK** to keep animals, especially horses, in a paddock [Early 17C. Alteration of *parro(c)k* < Old English *pearroc* 'fence, enclosed land' < Germanic.]

paddock[2] /páddək/, **puddock** /púddək/ *n* a frog or toad (*regional*) [14C. < Old Norse *padda* 'toad'.]

paddy[1] /páddi/ (*plural* **-dies**) *n* 1 **paddy, paddy field** a field, usually kept covered with shallow water, in which rice is grown 2 rice as a crop in the field or when harvested but not yet processed [Early 17C. < Malay *padi.*]

paddy[2] /páddi/ (*plural* **-dies**) *n* a fit of rage or bad temper (*informal*) [Late 19C. < PADDY.]

Paddy /páddi/ (*plural* **-dies**) *n* an offensive term for an Irish person (*slang*) [Late 18C. < the pet form of Irish *Pádraig* 'Patrick'.]

paddy field *n* AGRIC = **paddy**[1] *n.* 1

paddymelon *n* ZOOL = **pademelon**

paddy wagon *n US, ANZ* a patrol wagon (*informal*) [Late 19C. *Paddy* probably referred to Irish policemen in New York and New England.]

pademelon /páddi melən/ (*plural* **-ons** *or* **-on**), **paddymelon** (*plural* **-ons** *or* **-on**) *n* a small wallaby that lives at the edges of forests in Australia. Genus: *Thylogale.* [Early 19C. Alteration of an Aboriginal name.]

padlock /pád lok/ *n* a detachable lock with a movable semicircular bar at the top, the free end of which is usually passed through a hasp and then locked shut ■ *vt* to secure something using a padlock [15C. < ?]

padre /paádri, -dray/ *n* 1 a Christian clergyman who ministers to the armed forces 2 used to address or refer to a Roman Catholic priest in a country where Spanish, Italian, or Portuguese is spoken [Late 16C. Via Italian, Spanish, or Portuguese < Latin *pater* 'father'.]

padrone /pə drṓni/ (*plural* **-nes** *or* **-ni** /-nee/) *n* the owner or manager of an Italian business, especially a restaurant or café [Late 17C. Via Italian < Latin *patronus* 'protector, patron' < *pater* 'father'.] —**padronism** *n*

padsaw /pádd saw/ *n* a small narrow saw with a handle at one end only, used for cutting curves. US term **keyhole saw** [Late 19C. < PAD[1] 'handle into which different tools can be fitted'.]

Padua /páddyoō ə/ capital of Padua Province, NE Italy. Population: 213,656 (1992). Italian name **Padova**

paduasoy /páddyoo ə soy/ *n* a rich heavy silk fabric [Late 16C. Alteration (influenced by *Padua*) of French *pou-de-soie.*]

paean /peé ən/ *n* a written, spoken, or musical expression of enthusiastic praise or rapturous joy [Late 16C. Via Latin, 'religious hymn (originally in honour of Apollo)' < Greek *paian* < *Paian*, name for Apollo.]

paed- *prefix* = **paedo-** (*before vowels*)

paederast *n* = **pederast**

paederasty *n* = **pederasty**

paediatrics /peédi áttriks/, **pediatrics** *n* the branch of medicine concerned with the care and development of children and with the prevention and treatment of children's diseases (+ *singular verb*) US term **pediatrics** —**paediatric** *adj* —**paediatrician** /peédi ə trísh'n/ *n*

paedo- *prefix* child, children ○ *paedophile.* US term **pedo-**[2] [< Greek *paid-*, stem of *pais* 'child, boy'. Ultimately < Indo-European 'little', which is also the ancestor of English *poor.*]

paedodontics /peédə dóntiks/, **pedodontics** *n* the branch of dentistry concerned with dental care and treatment for children (+ *singular verb*)

paedology /pi dólləji/ (*plural* **pedology**) *n* the scientific study of the physical and mental development of children —**paedologic** /peédə lójjik/ *adj* —**paedological** /-lójjik'l/ *adj*—**paedologically** /-lójjikli/ *adv*—**paedologist** /pi dólləjist/ *n*

paedomorphosis /peédə máwrfəsiss, péddə máwrfəsiss/ *n* ZOOL = **neoteny**

paedophile /peédə fīl/, **pedophile** *n* an adult who has sexual desire for children or who has committed the crime of sex with a child —**paedophilic** /peédə fíllik/ *adj*

paedophilia /peédə fílli ə/, **pedophilia** *n* sexual desire felt by an adult for children, or the crime of sex with a child —**paedophiliac** /-fílli ak/ *n, adj*

paella /pī éllə/ *n* 1 a Spanish dish made of saffron-flavoured rice with chicken, shellfish, and other ingredients that vary from region to region 2 a large shallow frying pan, with a handle on each side, that allows rice to cook in a shallow depth of liquid that evaporates quickly and evenly [Late 19C. Via Catalan < Latin *patella* 'small dish' < *patina* 'shallow dish'.]

paeon /peé ən/ *n* a metrical foot consisting of one long and three short syllables arranged in any order [Early 17C. Via Latin < Greek *paiōn*, variant of *paian* (see PAEAN).]

paeony *n* PLANTS = **peony**

Paestum /péstəm/ ancient Greek and Roman city in S Italy, on the Gulf of Salerno

pagan /páygən/ *n* 1 **FOLLOWER OF A LESS POPULAR RELIGION** a religious adherent who does not follow one of the world's main religions, especially somebody who is not a Christian, Muslim, or Jew (*sometimes offensive*) 2 **POLYTHEIST OR PANTHEIST** a follower of an ancient polytheistic or pantheistic religion 3 **HEATHEN** a person without a religion (*disapproving*) ■ *adj* 1 **OF A LESS POPULAR RELIGION** believing in or relating to a religion that is not one of the world's main religions 2 **FOLLOWING POLYTHEISTIC OR PANTHEISTIC RELIGION** believing in or relating to an ancient polytheistic or pantheistic religion 3 **NONRELIGIOUS** having no religion (*sometimes offensive*) [14C. Via late Latin *paganus* < Latin, 'villager, civilian' < *pagus* 'rural district'.] —**paganism** *n* —**paganistic** /páygə nístik/ *adj*

Paganini /pággə neéni/, **Niccolò** (1782–1840) Italian composer and violinist

ϟ**page**[1] /payj/ *n* 1 **ONE SIDE OF SHEET OF PAPER** one side of a single sheet of paper, especially one bound into a book, newspaper, or magazine, or forming part of a piece of written work 2 **SINGLE SHEET IN A BOOK** a single sheet of paper, especially one bound into a book, newspaper, or magazine ○ *a book with some pages missing* 3 **AMOUNT OF WRITING ON A PAGE** the amount of writing or printed matter that can be contained on a page 4 **COMPUTER DATA PRINTING OUT AS A PAGE** the amount of text or graphics in a computer document that will print out as a single page 5 **SCREENFUL OF COMPUTER DISPLAY** the portion of text or graphics that can be seen on a computer screen at one time 6 **NOTEWORTHY PERIOD OR EVENT** a period or event, especially a noteworthy one, in the history of something or somebody's life ○ *Antibiotics wrote an important page in the history of medical research.* ■ *v* (**pages, paging, paged**) 1 *vi* **LOOK THROUGH PAGES** to turn and look over the pages of something 2 *vt* LITERAT = **paginate** [Late 16C. < French, shortening of *pagene* < Latin *pagina* '(strips of papyrus) fastened together'.]

page[2] /payj/ *n* 1 **BOY ATTENDANT** a youth acting as an attendant to somebody on a ceremonial occasion, e.g. to a bride at her wedding 2 **BOY WHO RUNS ERRANDS** a youth employed to run errands or carry messages for guests in a hotel or club 3 **BOY SERVANT IN MEDIEVAL TIMES** a youth who acted as a personal or household servant to somebody, especially a royal or noble person, in medieval times 4 **BOY APPRENTICED TO KNIGHT** a youth who acted as the personal servant to a knight in medieval times as the first stage of his training to become a knight 5 **ERRAND RUNNER IN US CONGRESS** a person employed as a messenger, guide, and assistant in the US Congress ■ *vt* (**pages, paging, paged**) 1 **SUMMON BY NAME** to summon somebody by calling out his or her name, e.g. over a loudspeaker system 2 **CONTACT ON A PAGER** to try to contact somebody on his or her pager 3 **ACT AS PAGE TO** to serve somebody in the capacity of page [13C. < French.]

Page /payj/, **Sir Earle** (1880–1961) Australian statesman

pageant /pájjənt/ *n* **1** a large-scale stage production representing historical or legendary events, especially local ones, in scenes or tableaux in which dramatic interest is less important than spectacle **2** an elaborate and colourful procession, display, or ceremonial occasion [14C. Alteration of earlier *pagyn* 'scene, stage' < Anglo-Latin *pagina*.]

pageantry /pájjəntri/ *n* highly colourful, splendid, and stately display or ceremonies, usually with a historical or traditional flavour

pageboy /páyj boy/ *n* **1** = **page**[2] *n.* 1 **2** a hairstyle in which the hair is cut to one length, usually jaw-length, and curls under slightly at the ends, with a fringe at the front

⚡**page break** *n* a code or symbol on a computer screen that shows where a printer will start a new page, e.g. in a word processing document

~~**pagent**~~ incorrect spelling of **pageant**

pager /páyjər/ *n* a small electronic message-receiving device, often with a small screen, that beeps, flashes, or vibrates to let the user know that somebody is trying to contact him or her

Page Three *tdmk* a trademark for the page on which the *Sun* newspaper prints a large photograph of a bare-breasted woman

Paget's disease /pájjəts-/ *n* **1** a disease in which the bones become enlarged and weakened and subject to fracture **2 Paget's disease, Paget's cancer** a cancerous inflammatory condition of the nipple and areola, associated with breast cancer [Late 19C. After Sir James *Paget* (1814–99), English surgeon.]

page-turner *n* a book with a very gripping plot

paginal /pájjin'l/ *adj* **1** exactly duplicating a previous edition or version, so that the same text appears on the same page in both **2** consisting of, relating to, or like a page or pages [Mid-17C. < late Latin *paginalis* < Latin *pagina* (see PAGE[1]).]

paginate /pájji nayt/ (**-nates, -nating, -nated**) *vt* to number the pages of a book or document [Late 19C. Probably back-formation < PAGINATION.]

pagination /pájji náysh'n/ *n* **1** the sequential numbers given to pages in a book or document **2** the process or work of numbering pages [Mid-19C. < French < Latin *pagina* (see PAGE[1]).]

⚡**paging**[1] /páyjing/ *n* the movement of a fixed-size block of data between faster main and slower auxiliary memories to optimize performance without the user being aware that the transfer has taken place

paging[2] /páyjing/ *n* a facility that enables somebody to be contacted via a pager (*often before nouns*) ○ *a paging service*

Paglia /páyli ə/, **Camille** (*b.* 1947) US writer

Pagnol /pán yol/, **Marcel** (1895–1974) French playwright and film director

pagoda /pə gṓdə/ *n* **1** a Buddhist temple building, especially one in the form of a tower with several storeys, each with an upward curving roof that tapers slightly towards the top **2** a building that is shaped like a Buddhist pagoda but has a decorative rather than a religious purpose [Late 16C. < Portuguese *pagode*.]

pagoda tree *n* a tree whose contorted branches can form a shape resembling a pagoda. Flowers: creamy-white, in clusters. Native to: China. *Sophora japonica*.

pah /paa/ *interj* used to show disgust, contempt, or annoyance [Late 16C. Natural exclamation.]

Pahlavi /páyləvi/, **Pehlevi** *n* a literary form of classical Persian used especially in Zoroastrian and Manichaean texts [Late 18C. < Persian *pahlawī* < *pahlav* < *parthava* 'Parthia (country of ancient Asia)'.] —**Pahlavi** *adj*

Pahlavi /pa̋aləvi/, **Muhammad Reza Shah** (1919–80) shah of Iran (1941–79)

Pahlavi, Reza Shah (1877–1944) shah of Iran (1925–41)

pahoehoe /pə hṓ i hō i/ *n* a smooth dark-coloured glassy basaltic rock formed from lava flow [Mid-19C. < Hawaiian.]

paid /payd/ past participle, past tense of **pay**[1] ■ *adj* given money in return for work, or done for the purpose of earning money

paid-up *adj* (*not hyphenated after verbs*) **1 NOT OWING ANYTHING** having paid all the money owed to an organization or individual **2 COMMITTED** enthusiastic and committed **3 FULLY PAID FOR** for which the full price or all instalments have been paid ○ *paid-up shares* **4 RECEIVED FROM SHAREHOLDERS** constituting the amount of a company's capital that has actually been received from its shareholders ○ *paid-up capital*

Paik /peek/, **Nam June** (*b.* 1932) Korean-born US artist

pail /payl/ *n* a bucket [14C. < Old French *paielle* 'warming pan, liquid measure'.]

paillasse /pal yáss/ *n* FURNITURE = **palliasse**

paillette /pal yét, pálli ét/ *n* a sequin or spangle sewn onto a piece of clothing [Mid-19C. < French, 'small straw' < *paille* 'straw, chaff' < Latin *palea*.]

pain /payn/ *n* **1 UNPLEASANT PHYSICAL SENSATION** the acutely unpleasant physical discomfort experienced by somebody who is violently struck, injured, or ill in certain ways ○ *cried out in pain* **2 FEELING OF DISCOMFORT** a sensation of pain in a particular part of the body (*often plural*) ○ *was complaining of pains in the lower abdomen* ○ *back pain* **3 EMOTIONAL DISTRESS** severe emotional or mental distress ○ *the pain of rejection* **4 SOMEBODY OR SOMETHING TROUBLESOME** somebody or something that is extremely annoying or causes many problems (*informal*) ■ **pains** *npl* **1 TROUBLE TAKEN TO DO** conscientious effort or trouble taken, usually in tackling a piece of work **2 LABOUR PAINS** the painful spasms experienced by a woman during childbirth, caused by the contraction of the womb ■ *v* **1** *vt* **SADDEN** to make somebody feel saddened or distressed ○ *It pains me to hear you speak like that.* **2** *vti* **CAUSE OR FEEL PAIN** to cause physical pain to somebody, or experience pain [13C. Via French *peine* < Latin *poena* 'penalty, punishment' < Greek *poinē* 'penalty'.] ◇ **a pain in the arse** *or* **backside** an offensive term for somebody or something that is considered to be extremely annoying or troublesome (*slang*) ◇ **a pain in the neck** somebody or something that is considered extremely annoying or troublesome (*informal*) ◇ **on** *or* **under pain of something** risking or threatened with something, e.g. death or instant dismissal, as punishment

SPELLCHECK Do not confuse ***pain*** with ***pane***, which has a similar sound. Beware: your spellchecker will not catch this error.

pain barrier *n* the point at which pain reaches its peak and begins to diminish, especially as experienced by an athlete

Paine /payn/, **Thomas** (1737–1809) British-born American writer, political philosopher, and revolutionary

pained /paynd/ *adj* expressing wounded feelings or a sense of being disappointed or offended by something that somebody has done ○ *a pained expression*

painful /páynf'l/ *adj* **1 CAUSING PAIN** causing acute physical discomfort ○ *a painful cut* **2 HURTING** hurting as a result of an injury or disease ○ *My arm's still quite painful.* **3 CAUSING DISTRESS** causing emotional or mental distress ○ *painful memories* **4 DIFFICULT** accomplished with laborious effort ○ *making painful progress with the work* **5 VERY BAD** embarrassingly bad ○ *Her performance was painful to watch.* —**painfully** *adv* —**painfulness** *n*

painkiller /páyn kilər/ *n* something, especially a drug, that reduces pain —**painkilling** *adj*

painless /páynləss/ *adj* **1** not causing any pain **2** involving little or no difficulty or effort ○ *a painless solution to our problem* —**painlessly** *adv* —**painlessness** *n*

painstaking /páynz tayking/ *adj* involving or showing great care and attention to detail —**painstakingly** *adv*

SYNONYMS See ***careful***.

paint /paynt/ *n* **1 COLOURED LIQUID APPLIED TO A SURFACE** a coloured liquid applied to a surface in order to decorate or protect it, or in order to create a painting **2 DRIED PAINT ON A SURFACE** a film of dried paint on a surface (*often before nouns*) ○ *paint remover* **3 SOLID PIGMENT** a solid block of pigment that forms liquid paint when moistened or dissolved **4 FACIAL MAKEUP** makeup for the face (*informal*) **5** THEATRE = **greasepaint** ■ *v* **1** *vti* **COVER SOMETHING WITH PAINT** to cover the surface of something with paint in order to decorate or protect it **2** *vti* **CREATE A PICTURE USING PAINT** to create a picture, or create a picture of something, by applying paint in different colours to paper, canvas, or some other surface **3** *vt* **ADD SOMETHING TO A SURFACE USING PAINT** to mark designs or words on a surface using paint ○ *The words 'No Parking' were painted on the wall.* **4** *vt* **APPLY LIQUID WITH A BRUSH** to apply a liquid to a surface using a brush, e.g. to brush a medicated liquid onto the skin ○ *My father used to paint iodine onto our grazed knees.* **5** *vt* **APPLY COSMETICS TO THE FACE OR NAILS** to apply makeup to the face or lips, or varnish to the nails **6** *vt* **DESCRIBE IN WORDS** to describe something in words, especially to give a vivid description of something ○ *In his autobiography, he paints his uncle's home as a palace.* [12C. < French *peint*, past participle of *peindre* < Latin *pingere* 'to paint'.]

paintball /páynt bawl/ *n* a team game in which each player has a gun that fires gelatin capsules filled with water-soluble marking dye, the object being to shoot members of the opposing team —**paintballer** *n* —**paintballing** *n*

paintbrush /páynt brush/ *n* a brush for putting paint onto surfaces or painting pictures

Painted Desert plateau region of north-central Arizona, noted for its vividly coloured rocks. Area: 19,000 sq. km/7,500 sq. mi.

painted lady *n* a widely distributed migratory butterfly with reddish-brown, black, and orange wings. *Vanessa cardui*.

painted turtle *n* a turtle found near slow-moving water that has red or yellow stripes on its legs, head, and tail and red markings on the margins of its shell. Native to: North America. *Chrysemys picta*.

painter[1] /páyntər/ *n* **1** an artist who paints pictures ○ *a portrait painter* **2** somebody whose job is to cover surfaces with paint, especially to paint and decorate the interiors of buildings

painter[2] /páyntər/ *n* a rope attached to the front of a boat that is used to tie it to something such as a mooring [14C. Probably < Old French *penteur* 'rope running from masthead' < *pendre* 'hang' < Latin *pendere*.]

painterly /páyntərli/ *adj* **1** characterized by the use of colour rather than line to represent shapes or to structure a composition **2** typical of a good painter and his or her work

painting /páynting/ *n* **1** a picture made using paint **2** the art or work of applying paint to surfaces

paintwork /páynt wurk/ *n* the painted surfaces of something, e.g. a vehicle's bodywork or the interior of a building

pair /pair/ *n* **1 2 SIMILAR THINGS USED TOGETHER** two matching objects that are designed to be used together ○ *a pair of socks* **2 THING WITH TWO JOINED PARTS** a garment or article consisting of two matching or identical parts joined together ○ *a pair of binoculars* **3 2 PEOPLE TOGETHER** two people who are doing something together, or who are considered together because there is some connection between them **4 COUPLE** two people in a relationship such as a marriage **5 2 MATING ANIMALS** a male and female animal of the same species who are together for mating **6 ONE OF TWO MATCHED ARTICLES** one of two matched articles such as shoes or gloves ○ *lost the pair to his cuff link* **7 2 HORSES HARNESSED TOGETHER** two horses harnessed together to pull a carriage ○ *a coach and pair* **8 2 PLAYING CARDS** two playing cards that have the same value ○ *a pair of aces* **9 2 OPPOSING MEMBERS MAKING A VOTING AGREEMENT** two members from opposing sides in a legislative body who each agree not to vote on issues if the other is not present and able to vote **10 AGREEMENT TO FORM A PAIR** an arrangement between two members on opposing sides in a legislative body to form a pair **11** ROWING = **pair-oar** **12 SET OF 2 ELEMENTS IN ORDER** a set consisting of two elements in order **13 ELECTRON BOND** two electrons forming a bond between atoms **14 ZERO IN BOTH INNINGS** a score of zero in both innings of a match ■ **pairs** *npl* HOBBIES = **pelmanism** ■ *v* **1** *vti* **PUT INTO GROUP OF 2** to form a pair with somebody, or to partner somebody with somebody else, for some shared activity or for romance or friendship **2** *vt* **MATCH 2 THINGS TOGETHER** to put two matching articles together **3** *vt* **FORM A LEGISLATIVE PAIR** to arrange a pair between two members of a voting assembly or to form a pair with another member **4** *vi* **FORM A MATING PAIR** to form a mating pair [13C. Directly or via French *paire* < Latin *paria* 'equals', a plural of *par* 'equal, a pair'.]

SPELLCHECK Do not confuse ***pair*** with ***pare*** or ***pear***, which sound similar. Beware: your spellchecker will not catch this error.

USAGE Pair as a singular or a plural: If ***pair*** means a unit, set, or whole, it takes a singular verb: *A pair of new leather riding boots is expensive.* If the people or things constituting the ***pair*** are regarded individually and not as a set, a plural verb is used: *A pair of volunteers are walking up and down various streets and alleys, picking up rubbish.* Here, the two people are thought of as working not only together on one

KEY MOVEMENTS IN WESTERN PAINTING

Century	Movement	Principal artists
4th–15th	Byzantine	anonymous icons and illuminated manuscripts
12th–15th	Gothic	Limbourg brothers, Giotto, van Eyck
15th–16th	Renaissance	Masaccio, Piero della Francesca, Botticelli, Leonardo da Vinci, Michelangelo, Raphael, Titian, Bosch, Bruegel, Dürer
16th–17th	Mannerist	Giulio Romano, Il Bronzino, Artemisia Gentileschi, Tintoretto, El Greco
16th–18th	Baroque	Caravaggio, Rubens, Velázquez, Rembrandt
18th	Rococo	Wattteau, Boucher, Fragonard, Chardin, Hogarth, Gainsborough
late 18th	Neoclassical	David, West, Ingres, Angelica Kauffman
18th–19th	Romantic	Blake, Turner, Constable, Allston, Géricault, Delacroix, Cole
19th	Realist	Daumier, Millet, Courbet, Eakins
19th	Pre-Raphaelite	Rossetti, Millais, Holman Hunt, Burne-Jones, Morris
19th–20th	Art nouveau	Klimt, Toulouse-Lautrec, Beardsley
19th–20th	Impressionist	Pissarro, Manet, Degas, Monet, Renoir, Cassatt, Berthe Morisot
19th–20th	Expressionist	Schiele, Kokoschka, Kirchner, Kandinsky, Klee, Munch
early 20th	Postimpressionist	Matisse, Gauguin, Cézanne, van Gogh, Seurat
early 20th	Cubist	Picasso, Braque, Gris, Léger
early 20th	Surrealist	de Chirico, Man Ray, Ernst, Miró, Magritte, Dali
mid-20th	Abstract expressionist	Rothko, de Kooning, Kline, Pollock, Newman
mid-late 20th	Pop art	Lichtenstein, Oldenburg, Warhol, Johns, Rauschenberg, Hockney
late 20th	Neoexpressionist	Baselitz, Chia, Clemente, Schnabel

street but separately on any of various other streets and alleys. If **pair** comes after a number over *one* (as in *16 pairs of boots*), *16 pairs*, not *16 pair*, is correct.

pair-oar *n* a racing shell in which two rowers with one oar each sit one behind the other

pair production *n* the creation of a negative particle (**electron**) and a positive particle (**positron**) when a fast particle (**photon**) passes through a strong electric field such as that surrounding an atomic nucleus

paisa /pī saa/ (*plural* **-se** *or* **-sa**) *n* see table at **currency** [Late 19C. < Hindi *paisā*.]

paisley /páyzli/ (*plural* **-leys**) *n* 1 a distinctive bold design consisting of multicoloured curving shapes, stylized cones, and feathers 2 a fabric with a paisley design, especially a type of woollen shawl popular in the 19th century [Early 19C. After PAISLEY.] —**paisley** *adj*

Paisley /páyzli/ town in central Scotland. Population: 75,526 (1991).

País Vasco /pa eèss váskõ/ ♦ **Basque Country**

Paiute /pī oot/ (*plural* **-utes** *or* **-ute**), **Piute** /pī oot, pī yoòt, pī oot/ (*plural* **-utes** *or* **-ute**) *n* 1 a member of either of two Native North American peoples, the Northern Paiutes and the Southern Paiutes 2 the Uto-Aztecan language of the Paiute people. Native speakers: 12,000. [Early 19C. < Spanish *payuchi* < ?] —**Paiute** *adj*

pajamas *npl* US = **pyjamas**

pak choi /pák chóy/ *n* a type of Chinese vegetable with tender wide white stems and bright green leaves, similar to Swiss chard in appearance. US term **bok choy** [< Chinese (Cantonese) *paàk ts'oi* 'white vegetable']

pakeha /paà ki haa/ (*plural* **-ha** *or* **-has**) *n* NZ 1 a white New Zealander 2 a person who is not Maori, especially a white person [Early 19C. < Maori.]

Paki /páki/ (*plural* **-is**) *n* (*taboo*) 1 a highly offensive term for somebody from Pakistan or with ancestors from Pakistan 2 a highly offensive term for any person from the Indian subcontinent [Mid-20C. Shortening.]

Pakistan

Pakistan /paàki staàn/ republic in S Asia, bordering the Arabian Sea. Capital: Islamabad. Population: 132,185,388 (1997). Area: 796,095 sq. km / 307,374 sq. mi. —**Pakistani** *n*, *adj*

pakora /pə káwrə/ *n* a deep-fried Indian fritter made by dipping pieces of vegetable, meat, or shellfish in a chickpea-flour batter and generally eaten as a snack [Mid-20C. < Hindi *pakoṛā*.]

pal /pal/ *n* (*informal*) 1 FRIEND a friend 2 AGGRESSIVE FORM OF ADDRESS used to address somebody, often in an unfriendly or aggressive way ○ *Listen, pal, you'd better watch out!* ■ *vi* (**pals, palling, palled**) BECOME FRIENDS WITH to become friends with and spend time with somebody [Late 17C. Via English Romany, 'pal, brother' < Sanskrit *bhrātṛ* 'brother'.]

pal around *vi* to become friends with and spend time with somebody (*informal*)

pal up *vi* to form a friendship or friendly partnership (*informal*)

PAL *n* the system used for broadcasting television programmes in the United Kingdom and many other European countries. Full form **phase alternation line**

palace /pálləss/ *n* 1 a grand and imposing building that is the official residence of a king or queen, a head of state such as a president, or a high-ranking aristocrat or church dignitary 2 a large public or private building with an imposing ornate style, used for entertainment or exhibitions ○ *an old movie palace fallen into disrepair* [13C. Via Old French *palais*, after *Palatium* 'Palatine Hill', where the emperor Augustus built a house.]

palace revolution *n* the overthrow of a ruler by those who are already in the ruling group, often carried out with little violence

paladin /pálladin/ *n* 1 MEDIEVAL CHAMPION a champion or hero, especially in medieval legend or history 2 CHAMPION OF A CAUSE somebody known for championing a cause 3 ONE OF CHARLEMAGNE'S COMPANIONS any one of the 12 legendary companions of Charlemagne [Late 16C. Via French < Latin *palatinus* (see PALATINE[1]).]

Palaearctic /páyli aàrktik, -aàrtik, pálli-/, **Palearctic** *adj* relating to the biogeographic region of the Arctic and immediately adjacent temperate regions of Europe, Asia, and Africa, or to a species within that range such as the Eurasian sparrowhawk.

palaeo- *prefix* 1 ancient, prehistoric ○ *palaeozoology* 2 primitive, early ○ *paleoethnology* [< Greek *palaios* < *palai* 'long ago']

palaeoanthropology /páyli ō ánthrə pólləji, pálli-/, **paleoanthropology** *n* the study of early human beings and related species through fossil evidence. —**palaeoanthropological** /páyli ō ánthrəpə lójjik'l, pálli-/ *adj* —**palaeoanthropologist** *n*

Palaeo-Asiatic *adj* LANG = **Palaeo-Siberian**

palaeobiochemistry /páyli ō bío kémmistri, pálli-/, **paleobiochemistry** *n* 1 the study of the evolution of biochemical processes from evidence in fossils 2 the biological chemicals found in fossils of ancient organisms

palaeobotany /páyli ō bóttəni, pálli-/, **paleobotany** *n* the study of prehistoric plants on the basis of fossil evidence. —**palaeobotanical** /páyli ō bə tánnik'l, pálli-/ *adj* —**palaeobotanist** *n*

Palaeocene /páyli ō seen, pálli-/, **Paleocene** *n* the epoch of geological time when placental mammals first appeared, 65 to 55 million years ago. [Late 19C. < PALAEO- + Greek *kainos* 'new'.] —**Palaeocene** /páyli ō seen, pálli-/ *adj*

palaeoclimatology /páyli ō klímə tólləji, pálli-/, **paleoclimatology** *n* the study of prehistoric climates on a global or regional scale from evidence preserved in glacial deposits, sedimentary structures, and fossils. —**palaeoclimatologist** *n*

palaeoecology /páyli ō i kólləji, pálli-/, **paleoecology** *n* the study of the interaction of prehistoric life forms and their environments —**palaeoecological** /páyli ō eèkə lójjik'l, pálli-, -ékə-/ *adj* —**palaeoecologist** *n*

palaeoethnobotany /páyli ō éthnō bóttəni, pálli-/, **paleoethnobotany** *n* the study of fossilized seeds and grain in order to gain information about prehistoric patterns of cereal growth.

Palaeogene /páyli ə jeen, pálli-/, **Paleogene** *n* the early part of the Tertiary period of geological time, comprising the Palaeocene, Eocene, and Oligocene epochs. —**Palaeogene** *adj*

palaeogeography /páyli ō ji óggrəfi, pálli-/, **paleogeography** *n* the study of the geographical features of past epochs. —**palaeogeographer** *n* —**palaeogeographic** /páyli ō jeè ə gráffik, pálli-/ *adj* —**palaeogeographical** *adj* —**palaeogeographically** *adv*

palaeography /páyli óggrəfi, pálli-/, **paleography** *n* 1 the study of ancient handwriting and manuscripts 2 an ancient manuscript or piece of handwriting —**palaeographic** /páyli ə gráffik, pálli-/ *adj* —**palaeographical** *adj* —**palaeographer** /páyli óggrəfər/ *n*

Palaeo-Indian, **Paleo-Indian** *adj* relating to the earliest inhabitants of the Americas, who arrived from Asia by the Bering land bridge that connected Alaska and Siberia. —**Palaeo-Indian** *n*

palaeolith /páyli ə lith, pálli-/, **paleolith** *n* a stone tool from the Palaeolithic age.

Palaeolithic /páyli ə líthik, pálli-/, **Paleolithic** *n* the early part of the Stone Age, when early human beings made chipped-stone tools, from 750,000 to 15,000 years ago — **Palaeolithic** *adj*

Palaeolithic man *n* a member of any of the various peoples who lived in the Palaeolithic period, such as Neanderthal, Cro-Magnon, or Java man.

palaeomagnetism /páyli ō mágnitizəm, pálli-/, **paleomagnetism** *n* **1** the polarity and intensity of residual magnetism in ancient rock. **2** the study of changes in the intensity and direction of the Earth's magnetic field throughout geological time —**palaeomagnetic** /páyli ō mag néttik, pálli-/ *adj*

palaeontography /páyli on tóggrəfi, pálli-/, **paleontography** *n* the branch of palaeontology concerned with describing fossils. —**palaeontographic** /páyli óntə gráffik, pálli-/ *adj* —**palaeontographical** *adj*

palaeontology /páyli on tólləji, pálli-/, **paleontology** *n* the study of life in prehistoric times by using fossil evidence. —**palaeontological** /páyli óntə lójjik'l, pálli-/ *adj* —**palaeontologically** *adv* —**palaeontologist** *n*

Palaeo-Siberian *adj* relating to a small group of languages spoken in E Siberia, including Chukchi, that do not belong to any of the major language families

Palaeozoic /páyli ə zō ik, pálli-/, **Paleozoic** *n* the era of geological time when fish, insects, amphibians, reptiles, and land plants first appeared, about 600 million to 230 million years ago. —**Palaeozoic** *adj*

palaestra (*plural* **-tras** *or* **-trae** /-tree/), **palestra** *n* a public sports ground or gymnasium in ancient Greece. [14C. Via Latin < Greek *palaistra* < *palaiein* 'wrestle'.]

palanquin /pállən keén/ *n* a covered seat carried on poles held parallel to the ground on the shoulders of two or four people, formerly used to transport an important person, especially in E Asia [Late 16C. Via Portuguese *palanquim* < Sanskrit *palyaṅka* 'bed, litter'.]

palatable /pállətəb'l/ *adj* **1** having a good enough taste to be eaten or drunk **2** acceptable to somebody's sensibilities —**palatability** /pállətə bílləti/ *n*

palatal /pállət'l/ *adj* **1 FACING OR RELATING TO THE PALATE** occurring at, facing, or relating to the palate **2 PRONOUNCED WITH THE TONGUE AT THE PALATE** describes a consonant sound that is produced by raising the tongue to or near the hard palate ○ *The 'sh' sound is a palatal fricative.* **3 PRONOUNCED WITH THE TONGUE FORWARD** describes a vowel sound that is produced with the tongue moved forward in the mouth ○ *The vowel in 'meet' is palatal.* ■ *n* **PALATAL SPEECH SOUND** a speech sound pronounced with the tongue at or near the hard palate or with the tongue pushed forward, especially a palatal consonant —**palatally** *adv*

palatalise *vt* LING = **palatalize**

palatalize /pállətə līz/ (**-izes, -izing, -ized**), **palatalise** (**-ises, -ising, -ised**) *vt* **1** to make a speech sound by raising the tongue to or towards the hard palate **2** to alter a speech sound in pronunciation by placing the tongue closer to the hard palate, rather than to the teeth, alveolar ridge, or velum —**palatalization** /pállətə lī záysh'n/ *n*

palate /pállət/ *n* **1 ROOF OF THE MOUTH** the roof of the mouth that separates it from the nasal cavity **2 SENSE OF TASTE** a personal sense of taste and flavour **3 AESTHETIC TASTE** intellectual or aesthetic tastes or sensibilities [14C. < Latin *palatum*.]

SPELLCHECK Do not confuse ***palate*** with ***palette*** or ***pallet***, which sound similar. Beware: your spellchecker will not catch this error.

palatial /pə láysh'l/ *adj* **1** grand or luxurious ○ *palatial mansions* **2** appropriate for a palace [Mid-18C. < Latin *palatium* (see PALACE).] —**palatialness** *n*

palatinate /pə látti nayt, -nət/ *n* the territory, office, or responsibilities of a feudal palatine

palatine[1] /pállə tīn/ *n* **1 POWERFUL FEUDAL LORD** a feudal lord in central Europe with sovereign powers within his territory **2 IMPERIAL COURT OFFICIAL** a court official in the late Roman and Byzantine empires ■ *adj* **1 SUITABLE FOR A PALACE** relating to or suitable for a palace **2 HAVING POWER OVER TERRITORY** describes an official or feudal lord who had sovereign power over a territory **3 RULED BY LORD** describes a territory that is ruled by a sovereign feudal lord [15C. Via French *palatine* < Latin *palatinus* 'of the palace, palace official' < *palatium* (see PALACE).]

palatine[2] /pállə tīn/ *adj* relating to the palate ■ *n* either of the two bones that form the hard palate

Palatine /pállə tīn/ *n* the central hill of the seven on which Rome was built, considered the oldest and the site of many of the imperial palaces

Palau /pə lów/ republic in the W Pacific Ocean comprising a group of islands that are part of the Caroline Islands. Capital: Koror. Population: 17,000 (1996). Area: 488 sq. km/188 sq. mi.

palaver /pə laávər/ *n* **1 INCONVENIENT BOTHER** irritating and time-consuming activity and bother **2 EMPTY TALK** idle, flattering, or time-wasting talk **3 CONFERENCE BETWEEN DIFFERENT PARTIES** a conference or meeting between different parties (*humorous*) ■ *vi* **1 TALK IDLY** to talk idly, emptily, or with the intention of flattering (*archaic*) **2 CONFER** to confer or hold a conference (*humorous*) [Mid-18C. Via Portuguese *palavra* 'speech' < Latin *parabola* (see PARABLE).]

palazzo /pə látsō/ (*plural* **-zos** *or* **-zi** /-tsee/) *n* a large ornate building such as a museum or official residence, especially in Italy [Mid-17C. Via Italian < Latin *palatium* (see PALACE).]

palazzo pants *npl* women's loose-fitting lightweight trousers with flared legs

pale[1] /payl/ *adj* (**paler, palest**) **1 LACKING COLOUR** lacking in colour or intensity ○ *pale blue* **2 PALLID FROM ILLNESS** unusually light in skin complexion because of illness, shock, or worry **3 PRODUCING LITTLE LIGHT** producing or reflecting little light **4 INADEQUATE** inadequate or faint ○ *a pale version of his former flamboyant self* ■ *v* (**pales, paling, paled**) **1** *vi* **BECOME WHITER** to become whiter or lose brilliance **2** *vi* **BECOME LESS IMPORTANT** to be or become less important, remarkable, or intense, especially in comparison to something more important or serious **3** *vt* **CAUSE TO LOSE COLOUR** to cause somebody or something to lose colour or brilliance [14C. Via Old French < Latin *pallidus* (see PALLID).] —**palely** *adv* —**paleness** *n*

pale[2] /payl/ *n* **1 FENCE STAKE** a pointed slat of wood for a fence **2 FENCE** a fence marking a boundary **3 FENCED-IN AREA** an area fenced in or its boundary **4 VERTICAL STRIPE ON A SHIELD** a wide vertical band down the centre of a shield ■ *vt* (**pales, paling, paled**) **FENCE IN** to fence in an area [12C. Via French *pal* < Latin *palus* 'stake'.] ◇ **beyond the pale** outside the limits of what is considered to be acceptable

Pale *n* **1** formerly, a restricted area in Imperial Russia where Jews were allowed to settle **2** the area of Ireland, based around Dublin, that was controlled by England from the 12th century until the final conquest of the entire country in the 16th century

palea /páyli ə/ (*plural* **-ae** /-li ee/) *n* **1** a dry membranous leaf with a single flower (**bract**) on a flowering grass **2** a dry membranous scale on the head of a composite flower such as a sunflower [Mid-18C. < Latin, 'chaff'.]

Palearctic /páyli aárktik, pálli-/ *adj* GEOG = **Palaearctic**

paleethnology *n* US = **palaeethnology**

paleface /páyl fayss/ *n* an offensive term for a white person

paleo- US = **palaeo-** [< Greek *palaios*]

paleoanthropology *n* US = **palaeoanthropology**

paleobiochemistry *n* US = **palaeobiochemistry**

paleobiogeography *n* US = **palaeobiogeography**

paleobotany *n* US = **palaeobotany**

Paleocene *adj, n* US = **Palaeocene**

paleoclimatology *n* US = **palaeoclimatology**

paleocurrent *n* US = **palaeocurrent**

paleoecology *n* US = **palaeoecology**

paleoethnobotany *n* US = **palaeoethnobotany**

Paleogene *adj, n* US = **Palaeogene**

paleogeography *n* US = **palaeogeography**

paleography *n* US = **palaeography**

Paleo-Indian *n, adj* US = **Palaeo-Indian**

paleolith *n* US = **palaeolith**

Paleolithic *adj, n* US = **Palaeolithic**

paleomagnetism *n* US = **palaeomagnetism**

paleontography *n* US = **palaeontography**

paleontology *n* US = **palaeontology**

paleopathology *n* US = **palaeopathology**

Paleozoic *adj, n* US = **Palaeozoic**

paleozoology *n* US = **palaeozoology**

Palermo /pə láirm ō/ port on NW Sicily, Italy. Population: 694,749 (1993).

Palestine /pállə stīn/ **1** historical region in SW Asia on the coast of the E Mediterranean Sea, the biblical land of Canaan **2** former country in SW Asia, between the Dead Sea and the Mediterranean Sea, divided in 1947 between Israel and Jordan. In 1993 Palestinians gained limited self-rule in Israeli-held territories in the Gaza Strip and on the West Bank of the River Jordan. —**Palestinian** /pallə stíni ən/ *n, adj*

palestra *n* US = **palaestra**

Palestrina /pális treénə/, **Giovanni Pierluigi da** (1525–94) Italian composer

palette /pállət/ *n* **1 BOARD FOR ARTIST'S PAINTS** a board or tray on which an artist arranges and mixes paints **2 RANGE OF COLOURS USED BY AN ARTIST** the assortment of colours on a palette, in a painting, or typical of an artist's work **3 COLOUR RANGE OF A COMPUTER DISPLAY** the range of colours that can be reproduced on a computer display **4 QUALITIES IN NONGRAPHIC ART** a range of qualities or elements in a nongraphic art such as music or literature [Late 18C. Via French (see PALLET[1]).]

SPELLCHECK See ***palate***.

palette knife *n* **1** a kitchen implement with a long flexible blunt-edged blade for lifting and turning food or for spreading, particularly when filling or icing cakes **2** a spatula-shaped implement with a slender flexible metal blade and a handle, used by an artist to mix and apply thick paints

palfrey /páwlfri, pól-/ (*plural* **-freys**) *n* a horse for everyday riding, especially one for a woman to ride (*archaic*) [12C. Via Old French *palefrei* < late Latin *paraveredus* 'extra horse' < Latin *veredus* 'light horse used by couriers' < Gaulish.]

Pali /paáli/ *n* an ancient Indo-European language derived from Sanskrit and formerly spoken in India, surviving in Hinayana Buddhist scriptures [Late 18C. < Pali *pāli* 'canonical text' (as opposed to the commentary), shortening of Sanskrit *pāli-bhāsā* 'language of the line'.] —**Pali** *adj*

palimony /pállimәni/ (*plural* **-nies**) *n* *US* a maintenance allowance for an ex-lover or member of an unmarried couple, when required by a court of law [Late 20C. Blend of PAL + ALIMONY.]

palimpsest /pállimp sest/ *n* a manuscript written over a partly erased older manuscript in such a way that the old words can be read beneath the new ■ *adj* describes a document that has been overwritten [Mid-17C. Via Latin *palimpsestus* < Greek *palimpsestos* 'something rubbed smooth again'.]

palindrome /pállin drōm/ *n* **1** a word, phrase, passage, or number that reads the same forwards and backwards, e.g. 'Anna', 'Draw, o coward', or '23832' **2** a segment of DNA in which the nucleotide sequence in one strand read from one end is the same as the sequence in the complementary strand read from the opposite end [Early 17C. < Greek *palindromos* 'running back again'.] —**palindromic** /pállin drómmik/ *adj*

paling /páyling/ *n* **1** a fence formed by a line of pointed stakes planted in the ground **2** CONSTR = **pale**[2] *n*. 1

palingenesis /pállin jénnəssiss/ *n* **1** BIOL = **recapitulation** *n*. 2 **2** spiritual rebirth by means of baptism **3** the supposed transmigration of the soul of somebody who has died into the body of another person or animal [Early 19C. < Greek *palin* 'again' + *genesis* 'birth'.] —**palingenetic** /pállin jə néttik/ *adj* —**palingenetically** *adv*

palinode /pálli nōd/ *n* **1** a poem in which a poet retracts something written in a previous poem **2** a formal retraction of a statement [Late 16C. Directly or via French < Latin *palinodia* < Greek *palinōdia* < *palin* 'again, back' + *ōidē* song.]

palisade /pálli sayd/ *n* **1 FENCE** a fence made of pales driven into the ground **2 FENCE PALE** a pale in a fence ■ *vt* (**-sades, -sading, -saded**) **FENCE IN** to provide a place with a fence of pales as a means of defence [Early 17C. < French *palissade* < Latin *palus* 'stake'.]

palisade layer, **palisade mesophyll, palisade parenchyma** *n* a layer of long cells under the upper epidermis of a leaf that are full of specialized chlorophyll-containing cell parts (**chloroplasts**)

Palk Strait /páwk-, páwlk-/ inlet of the Bay of Bengal, separating SE India from NW Sri Lanka. Length: 137 km/85 mi.

pall[1] /pawl/ *n* **1 DARK COVERING** a covering that makes a place dark and gloomy ○ *a pall of thick black smoke* **2 GLOOMY ATMOSPHERE** a prevailing gloomy mood or oppressive atmosphere ○ *Her departure cast a pall over the weekend.* **3 COFFIN COVERING** a cloth covering for a coffin, bier, hearse, or tomb **4 COFFIN** a coffin, especially when being carried in a funeral **5 CHALICE COVER** a square cover for a communion chalice, especially a linen-covered board **6 PALLIUM** a pallium (*archaic*) **7 HERALDIC BEARING** a heraldic bearing representing an archbishop's pallium in the form of three bands in a Y-shape, charged with crosses ■ *vt* **COVER WITH A PALL** to cover somebody or something with a pall or with something that resembles a pall [Pre-12C. < Latin *pallium* 'covering'.]

pall[2] /pawl/ *vi* to be or become uninteresting, unsatisfying, or insipid ○ *The music soon began to pall on us.* [14C. Alteration of APPAL.]

palladia plural of **palladium**[2]

Palladian[1] /pə láydi ən/ *adj* typical of or similar to the classical architectural style developed by Andrea Palladio in the 16th century

Palladian[2] /pə láydi ən/ *adj* **1** relating to the goddess Pallas Athena **2** relating to wisdom or knowledge [Mid-16C. < Latin *palladium* (see PALLADIUM[2]).]

Palladio /pə laádi ō, -laádee-/, **Andrea** (1508–80) Italian architect. Born **Andrea di Pietro della Gondola**

palladium[1] /pə láydi əm/ *n* (*symbol* **Pd**) a malleable silvery-white metallic element resembling platinum. Source: ores of copper, gold, platinum. Use: catalyst, in electrical contacts, jewellery, dental alloys, medical instruments. [Early 19C. < *Pallas* (see PALLADIUM[2]), asteroid discovered before the metal.] —**palladic** /pə láddik, -láy-/ *adj* —**palladous** /pə láydəss, pálləddəss/ *adj*

palladium[2] /pə láydi əm/ (*plural* **-ums** *or* **-a** /pə láydi ə/) *n* **1** a protection or safeguard, especially one protecting social and civic institutions **2 palladium, Palladium** an object believed to have the power to protect a city or nation, especially the statue of Pallas Athena that was believed to protect Troy [14C. Via Latin < Greek *palladion* < *Pallas*, epithet of Athena.]

Pallas /pálləss/ *n* **1** the second largest asteroid, discovered in 1802. It has an average diameter of approximately 530 km/330 mi. **2 Pallas, Pallas Athena** MYTHOL = **Athena**

Pallas's cat *n* a small wild cat of mountainous Tibet and Siberia, with small ears and luxurious grey fur with dark stripes. *Felis manul*. [After the German naturalist Peter *Pallas* (1741–1811)]

pallbearer /páwl bairər/ *n* a bearer or escort of a coffin at a funeral or burial

pallet[1] /pállət/ *n* **1 PLATFORM FOR LOADS** a standardized platform or open-ended box, usually made of wood, that allows mechanical handling of bulk goods during transport and storage **2 CLAY-WORKING TOOL** a wooden tool similar to a knife, used to mix and shape ceramic clay **3 BOARD FOR DRYING CERAMICS** a board on which ceramic pieces are dried **4 REGULATING LEVER IN A TIMEPIECE** a lever that regulates a ratchet wheel, especially one that regulates the movement of the balance wheel or pendulum in a timepiece by transmitting movements from the escape wheel **5 GILDING TOOL** a tool for manipulating gold leaf in gilding **6 VALVE ON ORGAN** a valve on an organ that opens in order to let air into a pipe **7** ART = **palette** *n.* 1 [15C. Via French *palette* 'small blade or spade' < Latin *pala* 'spade, shovel'.]

SPELLCHECK See *palate*.

---

pallet[2] /pállət/ *n* **1** a straw-filled mattress **2** a temporary and usually uncomfortable bed, made from materials at hand [14C. < Anglo-Norman *paillete* < *paille* 'straw' < Latin *palea*.]

palletize /pállə tīz/ (**-tizes, -tizing, -tized**), **palletise** (**-tises, -tising, -tised**) *vt* to put, transport, or store a load of something on a standardized platform

pallia plural of **pallium**

palliasse /pálli ass, -áss/ *n* a straw-filled mattress. US term **paillasse**

palliate /pálli ayt/ (**-ates, -ating, -ated**) *vt* **1 ALLEVIATE** to alleviate a symptom without curing the underlying medical condition **2 MITIGATE** to reduce the intensity or severity of something **3 PARTIALLY EXCUSE** to make an offence seem less serious by providing excuses or mitigating evidence [15C. < Latin *palliat-* past participle of *palliare* 'cover or hide' < *pallium* 'covering'.] —**palliation** /pálli áysh'n/ *n* —**palliator** /pálli aytər/ *n*

palliative /pálli ətiv/ *adj* **1 TREATING SYMPTOMS ONLY** alleviating pain and symptoms without eliminating the cause **2 SOOTHING** soothing anxieties or other intense emotions ■ *n* **SYMPTOM-TREATING MEDICINE** something that palliates, especially a medicine that treats symptoms only —**palliatively** *adv*

palliative care *n* the treatment and relief of mental and physical pain without curing the causes, especially in patients suffering from a terminal illness

pallid /pállid/ *adj* **1** having an unhealthily pale complexion **2** lacking colour, spirit, or intensity [Late 16C. < Latin *pallidus* < *pallere* 'be pale'.] —**pallidity** /pə líddəti/ *n* —**pallidly** /pállidli/ *adv*

Palliser, Cape /pállissər/ southernmost point of the North Island, New Zealand

pallium /pálli əm/ (*plural* **-a** /-ə/ *or* **-ums**) *n* **1 VESTMENT WORN BY A POPE OR ARCHBISHOP** a white vestment that rests on the shoulders with pendants hanging at its front and back, worn by a pope, all Roman Catholic archbishops, and some bishops **2** MARINE BIOL = **mantle** *n.* 5 **3** BIRDS = **mantle** *n.* 6 **4 CEREBRAL CORTEX** the cerebral cortex (*technical*) **5 PART OF THE BRAIN** the layer of grey matter forming the surface of the cerebral cortex **6 ANCIENT CLOAK** a man's rectangular cloak worn in ancient Rome [Late 16C. < Latin, 'covering'.] —**pallial** *adj*

pall-mall /páll máll/ *n* **1** a 17th-century game in which players used a mallet to hit a wooden ball through an iron hoop suspended at the end of a long alley **2** an alley in which pall-mall is played [Mid-16C. Via obsolete French *palle maille* < Italian *pallamaglio* < *balla* 'ball' + *maglio* 'mallet'.]

pallor /pállər/ *n* an unhealthy-looking paleness of complexion [14C. < Latin, < *pallere* 'be pale'.]

pally /pálli/ (**-lier, -liest**) *adj* having a friendly relationship (*informal*)

palm[1] /paam/ *n* **1 INNER SURFACE OF THE HAND** the inner surface of the hand, extending from the base of the fingers to the wrist **2 UNDERSIDE OF A MAMMAL'S FOREFOOT** the part of a mammal's forefoot that is most often in contact with the ground **3 HAND-SIZED MEASURE** a unit of length, based on the length or width of a hand **4 COVERING FOR THE PALM OF THE HAND** something that covers the palm of the hand, e.g. the inner hand surface of a glove **5 FLAT PART OF A BRANCHED STRUCTURE** the broad flat lobe of a branched structure such as the antler of a moose or deer or a cactus stalk **6 OAR BLADE** the blade of an oar **7 INNER FACE OF AN ANCHOR POINT** the inner face of an anchor's point ■ *vt* **1 HIDE IN THE HAND** to hide something in the hand, especially as part of a trick **2 TAKE STEALTHILY** to take something secretly by hiding it in the hand **3 TOUCH WITH THE PALM** to touch something with the palm **4 HOLD INSTEAD OF DRIBBLING** to let a basketball come to rest in the hands during a dribble, thereby committing a foul [Old English, via Germanic < Latin *palma* 'palm of the hand'] ◇ **have somebody** *or* **something in the palm of your hand** to have complete power or influence over somebody or something

palm off *vt* **1** to shift something into another's possession in a deceitful way ○ *The crooks needed a way to palm off the stolen CDs on unsuspecting buyers.* **2** to give or pass on something unwanted to somebody else ○ *Don't try to palm off that old armchair on me!*

palm[2] /paam/ *n* **1** PLANT SCI = **palm tree** **2** a leaf from a palm tree, used as a symbol of victory or success **3** a small decoration shaped like a palm leaf that is added to a military decoration to show that it has been awarded to the wearer more than once [12C. Via French *paume* < Latin *palma* 'palm of the hand, palm tree'.]

Palma /pálmə/ port on SW Majorca, Spain, on the Bay of Palma. Population: 323,138 (1995). Full name **Palma de Mallorca**

palmar /pálmər/ *adj* relating to the palm of the hand or to the underside of an animal's forefoot

palmate /pál mayt, -mət/ *adj* **1 palmate, palmated** /pál maytəd/ forming a branching pattern that spreads like fingers from a hand **2** having three toes that are connected by webbing [Mid-18C. < Latin *palmatus* < *palma* (see PALM[1]).] —**palmately** *adv*

Palm Beach /paam beéch/ town in SE Florida. Population: 9,814 (1990).

palm civet *n* a tree-dwelling mammal of Africa and Asia, with short legs and sharp claws. Family: Viverridae.

palmcorder /paám kawrdər/ *n* a small portable video camera and recorder that fits in the palm of the hand [Late 20C. Blend of PALM[1] + RECORDER.]

Palme /pálmə/, **Olof** (1927–86) Swedish statesman

palmer /paámər/ *n* a pilgrim, especially a medieval Christian pilgrim who carried or wore palm leaves as proof of a visit to the Holy Land [14C. Via Anglo-Norman < medieval Latin *palmarius* < *palma*.]

Palmer /paámər/, **Arnold** (*b.* 1929) US golfer

Palmer, Sir Geoffrey (*b.* 1942) New Zealand statesman

Palmerston /paámərstən/, **Henry John Temple, 3rd Viscount** (1784–1865) British statesman

Palmerston North /paámərstən-/ city in the south of the North Island, New Zealand. Population: 75,700 (1998 estimate).

palmette /pal mét/ *n* a stylized palm leaf used as an ornament or in a decoration [Mid-19C. < French, 'small palm' < Latin *palma*.]

palmetto /pal méttō/ (*plural* **-tos** *or* **-toes**) *n* **1** a low-growing palm plant with fan-shaped leaves, especially the cabbage palmetto **2** the blade of a palmetto leaf. Use: weaving. [Mid-16C. < Spanish *palmito* 'small palm' < Latin *palma*.]

palmist /paámist/ *n* a person who practises palmistry

palmistry /paámistri/ *n* the practice of examining the features of somebody's palms in order to predict that person's destiny

palmitate /pálmi tayt/ *n* a salt or ester of palmitic acid

palmitic acid /pal míttik-/ *n* $C_{15}H_{31}COOH$ a waxy acid. Source: plant and animal fats and oils. Use: manufacture of soap, candles, food additives. [< French *palmitique* < *palme* (see PALMITIN)]

palmitin /pálmitin/ *n* an ester of palmitic acid and glycerol. Source: animal fats, palm oil. Use: soap-making. [Mid-19C. < French *palmitine* < *palme* 'palm tree' < Old French *paume* (see PALM[2]).]

palm oil *n* a yellowish oil extracted from the fruit of oil palms. Use: lubricants, soap, cosmetics, foods.

Palm Springs city in S California. Population: 40,181 (1990).

palm sugar *n* sugar made from palm tree sap

Palm Sunday *n* a Christian religious day marking Jesus Christ's triumphal entry into Jerusalem through a crowd waving palm branches. Date: Sunday before Easter.

ϟ **palmtop** /paám top/ *n* a computer with a miniature keyboard and screen that fits into the palm of the hand

palm tree *n* a tree, bush, or plant typically with a trunk without branches and a crown of pinnate or palmate leaves on top. Native to: tropics, subtropics. Family: Palmae.

palm wine *n* an alcoholic drink made from fermented palm sap, common in parts of Africa

palmy /paámi/ (**-ier, -iest**) *adj* **1** relating to, consisting of, or abundant in palm trees **2** prosperous or flourishing (*literary*) ○ *in her palmy days*

palmyra /pal mīrə/ (*plural* **-ras** *or* **-ra**) *n* a tall fan-leafed palm tree whose fronds, wood, and sap are harvested for various uses. Native to: Asia. *Borassus flabellifer*. [Late 17C. Alteration (influenced by *Palmyra*, ancient city in Syria) of Portuguese *palmeira* 'palm tree' < Latin *palma* (see PALM[2]).]

Palo Alto /pállō áltō/ city in W California. Population: 59,098 (1998 estimate).

Palomar, Mount /pállə maar/ mountain in S California, site of an astronomical observatory. Height: 1,871 m/6,138 ft.

palomino /pállə meénō/ (*plural* **-nos**) *n* a golden-coloured horse with a pale mane and tail, originally bred in the SW United States [Early 20C. Via American Spanish < Latin *palumbinus* 'like a dove'.]

palooka /pə loókə/ *n US* **1** somebody considered to be very clumsy and unintelligent (*slang insult*) **2** an easily beaten athlete, especially a boxer (*slang*) [Early 20C. < ?]

paloverde /pállō vúrdi/ (*plural* **-des** *or* **-de**) *n* TREES = **Jerusalem thorn** [Early 19C. < American Spanish, 'green tree'.]

palp /palp/ *n* a sensory appendage situated near the mouth of many invertebrate animals, used to assess or manipulate food before it is eaten [Mid-19C. Via French *palpe* < Latin *palpus* < *palpare* 'touch gently, palpate'.]

palpable /pálpəb'l/ *adj* **1 INTENSE** so intense as to be almost able to be felt physically ○ *the palpable tension in the room* **2 OBVIOUS** obvious or easily observed ○ *a palpable need for change* **3 ABLE TO BE FELT** able to be felt by the hands, especially in a medical examination ○ *a palpable lump in the abdomen* [14C. < late Latin *palpabilis* < Latin *palpare* 'touch gently, palpate'.] —**palpability** /pálpə bílləti/ *n* —**palpableness** /pálpəb'lnəss/ *n* —**palpably** *adv*

palpate /pal páyt/ (**-pates, -pating, -pated**) *vt* to examine a part of the body [15C. < Latin *palpatus* < *palpare* 'touch gently'.]

palpation /pal páysh'n/ *n* a method of clinical examination using gentle pressure of the fingers to detect growths, changes in the size of underlying organs, and unusual tissue reactions to pressure [Late 15C. < Latin *palpation-* 'flattery, stroking' < *palpare* 'touch gently palpate'.]

palpebral /pálpəbrəl/ *adj* relating to the eyelids [Mid-19C. < Latin *palpebra* 'eyelid'.]

palpi plural of **palpus**

palpigrade /pálpi grayd/ *n* a tropical arachnid with a long structure resembling a whip at the tip of the abdomen. Order: Palpigradi. [< PALPUS + Latin *-gradus* < *gradi* 'walk']

palpitate /pálpi tayt/ (**-tates, -tating, -tated**) *vi* to beat in an irregular or unusually rapid way, either because of a medical condition or because of exertion, fear, or anxiety (*refers to the heart*) [15C. < Latin *palpitatus*, past participle of *palpitare* < *palpare* 'touch gently, palpate'.] —**palpitant** *adj*

palpitation /pálpi táysh'n/ *n* an irregular or unusually rapid beating of the heart, either because of a medical condition or because of exertion, fear, or anxiety (*usually plural*)

palpus /pálpəss/ (*plural* **-pi** /-pee/) *n* ANAT = **palp** [Early 19C. < Latin (see PALP).]

palsgrave /páwlz grayv/ *n* a count palatine, especially in Germany [Mid-16C. < Early Dutch *paltsgrave* < *palts* 'palatinate' + *grave* 'count'.]

palstave /páwl stayv/ *n* a metal axe that fits into a split handle, especially one of a distinctive bronze type found in ancient Europe [Mid-19C. < Danish *paalstav*.]

palsy /páwlzi/ *n* muscular inability to move part or all of the body (*archaic*) [13C. Via Old French *paralisie* < Latin *paralysis* (see PARALYSIS).]

palsy-walsy /pálzi wálzi/, **palsy** *adj* very friendly, often in an insincere or unpleasant way (*slang*) [Based on PAL]

palter /páwltər/ *vi* to act or talk insincerely or deceitfully (*archaic*) [Mid-16C. < ?] —**palterer** *n*

paltry /páwltri, pól-/ (**-trier, -triest**) *adj* **1** insignificant or unimportant ○ *a paltry sum of money* **2** low and contemptible [Mid-16C. Probably < Scots, N English dialect *pelt* 'coarse cloth, rubbish'.] —**paltrily** *adv* —**paltriness** *n*

paludal /pə lyóod'l, pállyòod'l/ *adj* relating to or living in swamps or marshes [Early 19C. < Latin *palud-*, stem of *palus* 'marsh'.]

paludism /pállyòodizəm/ *n* malaria (*not in technical use*) [Late 19C. < Latin *palud-* (see PALUDAL).]

paly /páyli/ *adj* describes a heraldic shield that is divided into equal-sized sections by vertical lines [< French *palé* < *pal* (see PALE[2])]

palynology /pálli nólləji/ *n* the study of spores and pollen, including the study of fossilized spores and pollen [Mid-20C. < Greek *palunein* 'sprinkle'.] —**palynological** /pállinə lójjik'l/ *adj* —**palynologist** /pálli nólləjist/ *n*

Pama-Nyungan /paámə nyóongən/ *n* a large family of Aboriginal languages spoken in Australia. Native speakers: 100,000. —**Pama-Nyungan** *adj*

~~**pamflet**~~ incorrect spelling of **pamphlet**

Pamirs /pə méerz/ mountainous region of central Asia, located mainly in Tajikistan and extending to NE Afghanistan and NW China. Highest peak: Ismail Samani Peak, 7,495 m/24,590 ft.

pampas /pámpəss, -pəz/ *n* treeless grassy plains in temperate South America, especially Argentina (+ *singular or plural verb*) [Early 18C. Via Spanish *pampa* < Quechua, 'plain'.] —**pampean** /pámpi ən, pam pée ən/ *adj*

pampas grass *n* a tall grass with silky white flower plumes, often grown in parks and gardens. Native to: South America, naturalized in S United States. *Cortaderia selloana*.

pamper /pámpər/ *vt* **1** to lavish attention on somebody, indulging his or her taste for luxury **2** to indulge or gratify a desire or need [14C. Probably < Low German or Dutch.] —**pamperer** *n*

pampero /pam páirō/ (*plural* **-ros**) *n* a strong, cold, dry wind that blows southwest from the Andes to the Atlantic, across the South American pampas [Late 18C. < Spanish < *pampa* 'plain'.]

pamphlet /pámflət/ *n* a small leaflet or paper booklet, usually unbound and coverless, that gives information or supports a position [14C. < *Pamphilet* or *Pamflet*, variants of *Pamphilus, seu de Amore* 'Pamphilus, or about Love', 12C Latin love poem.]

pamphleteer /pámflə téer/ *n* a writer of opinionated pamphlets ■ *vi* to write material for pamphlets, especially political ones

pamphrey /pámfri/ (*plural* **-phreys**) *n Ireland* a cabbage, especially a variety of dark-green, open-leaved spring cabbage [< ?]

Pamplona /pam plṓnə/ city in NE Spain. Population: 181,776 (1995).

pan[1] /pan/ *n* **1 COOKING POT** a cooking pot, usually metal and with a handle, for use on the hob of a cooker **2 CONTAINER FOR WASTE** a shallow container that household waste is put into for easy disposal **3 SHALLOW, OPEN CONTAINER** any shallow open container used to store, catch, or heat liquids or other substances **4 DISH FOR SORTING MINERALS** a flat metal dish, shaped like a pie plate, used to separate precious minerals, especially gold, from loose soil, gravel, or sediment **5 SCALE DISH** either of the dishes suspended in a balance scale **6 CONCAVITY IN EARTH** a natural shallow sink or basin in the ground, usually filled with rainwater or mud **7 SHALLOW AREA FOR EVAPORATING BRINE** a natural or artificial concavity in the earth, in which brine is evaporated, leaving behind salt **8** TRANSP = **hardpan 9 THIN ICE FLOE** a small, flat, thin ice floe of the type that forms near a shore or in a bay **10 PRIMING CONTAINER IN GUN** the hollow part of a flintlock gun, into which the gunpowder is loaded **11 STEEL DRUM** a metal drum played in steel bands ■ *v* (**pans, panning, panned**) **1** *vt* **CRITICIZE SEVERELY** to criticize somebody or something severely, especially in a review (*informal*) **2** *vi* **SORT THROUGH DIRT FOR MINERALS** to use a shallow dish to separate valuable minerals from loose soil, gravel, or sediment by washing or shaking **3** *vi* **YIELD PRECIOUS METALS** to yield valuable metals when separating minerals and leavings by means of washing or shaking using a shallow dish [Old English *panne* < Germanic]

pan out *vi* (*informal*) **1** to turn out or result ○ *After all our careful planning, it's a shame that things didn't pan out as we had hoped.* **2** to turn out well or successfully ○ *Her new career never panned out.* [< the practice of panning for gold]

pan[2] /pan/ *vti* (**pans, panning, panned**) to move a camera horizontally from a stationary point in order to capture a broad view of a scene or to film or photograph a moving object ■ *n* a horizontal movement of a camera from a fixed point, or the resulting filmed shot [Early 20C. Shortening of PANORAMA.]

pan[3] /paan/ *n* **1** a leaf of the betel plant **2** a leaf of the betel plant rolled and filled with spices and lime, chewed for its flavour and as a stimulant in SW Asia [Early 17C. < Hindi *pān*.]

Pan[1] /pan/ *n* in Greek mythology, the god of nature, pastures, flocks, and forests, believed to have a human torso and head, and the hind legs, ears, and horns of a goat. Roman equivalent **Faunus**

Pan[2] /pan/ *n* the innermost known natural satellite of Saturn, discovered in 1990. It is approximately 20 km/12 mi. in diameter.

pan- *prefix* all, any, everyone ○ *panchromatic* ○ *Pan-Slavism* [< Greek, a form of *pas* 'all']

panacea /pánnə sée ə/ *n* a supposed cure for all diseases or problems [Mid-16C. Via Latin < Greek *panakeia* < *panakēs* 'all-healing' < *akos* 'remedy'.] —**panacean** *adj*

panache /pə násh/ *n* **1** a sense or display of spirited style and self-confidence **2** a plume or tuft of feathers, especially on a hat or helmet [Mid-16C. Via French < Italian *pennacchio* 'plume of feathers' < Latin *pinna* 'feather'.]

panada /pə naádə/ *n* a very thick paste of flour or some other starchy ingredient and a liquid such as milk or stock. Use: base for sauces, binding for stuffing. [Late 16C. Via Spanish or Portuguese < Latin *panis* 'bread'.]

Pan-African *adj* relating to the nations of Africa, collectively or in cooperation with one another, or advocating freedom and independence for African people —**Pan-Africanism** *n*

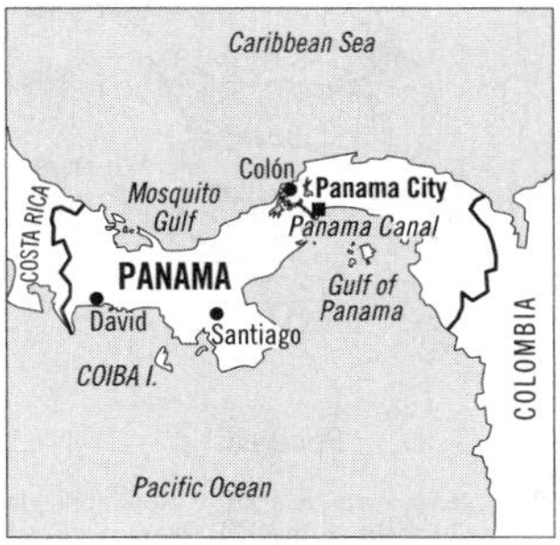

Panama

Panama /pánnə maa, -maá/ republic in Central America. It has the Caribbean Sea to its north and the Pacific Ocean to its south, connected by the Panama Canal, and is situated between Costa Rica and Colombia. Capital: Panama City. Population: 2,674,490 (1996). Area: 75,517 sq. km/29,157 sq. mi. —**Panamanian** /pánnə máyni ən/ *n, adj*

Panama, Isthmus of /pánnə maa, -maá/ isthmus connecting North and South America, and separating the Pacific Ocean and the Caribbean Sea

Panama Canal canal across the Isthmus of Panama, connecting the Pacific Ocean and the Caribbean Sea. Length: 64 km/40 mi.

Panama City capital of Panama, on the southern coast of the country. Population: 668,927 (1996 estimate).

Pan-American *adj* relating to the nations of North, South, and Central America, collectively or in cooperation with one another —**Pan-Americanism** *n*

Pan-Arabism *n* a movement for greater cooperation among and self-reliance within Arab or Islamic nations —**Pan-Arab** *n, adj* —**Pan-Arabic** *adj* —**Pan-Arabist** *n, adj*

panatella /pánnə téllə/, **panatela** *n* a long thin cigar that does not bulge in the middle [Mid-19C. Via American Spanish, 'long thin biscuit' < Italian *panatello* 'small loaf' < Latin *panis* 'bread'.]

pancake /pán kayk/ *n* **1 THIN FRIED CAKE** a thin flat cake made by pouring batter onto a hot greased flat pan, and cooking it on both sides **2** *Scotland* **DROP SCONE** a drop scone **3** AIR = **pancake landing** ■ *v* (**-cakes, -caking, -caked**) **1** *vti* **MAKE PANCAKE LANDING** to make a pancake landing or cause an aircraft to make such a landing **2** *vt US* **FLATTEN** to turn something parallel to the ground, especially a tennis racquet in the course of a stroke

Pancake Day *n* CHR = **Shrove Tuesday** [< the practice of making pancakes to use up eggs and fat before Lent]

pancake ice *n* a small flat thin piece of sea ice that drifts out into deeper water from near the shore or the bay in which it was formed

pancake landing *n* an aeroplane landing in which the aircraft drops abruptly straight to the ground from a low altitude, usually due to engine failure

pancake tortoise *n* a Tanzanian turtle with a flattened flexible shell. It can slip between rocks and narrow crevices and then slightly inflate to resist being pulled out. *Malachersus tornieri*.

Pancake Tuesday *n* CHR = **Shrove Tuesday**

pancetta /pan chéttə/ *n* a salt-cured and spiced form of unsmoked belly of pork, used in Italian dishes [Mid-20C. < Italian, 'little belly' < Latin *pantix* 'bowel, intestine'.]

panchayat /pun chī ət/ *n S Asia* a village council in India [Early 19C. Via Hindi *pañcāyat* < Sanskrit *pañcāyatta* 'depending on five' (the original number of members).]

Panchen Lama /púnchən-/ *n* in Tibetan Buddhism, a lama of the second highest rank [< Tibetan, contraction of *pandi-tachen-po* 'great learned one']

panchromatic /pán krō máttik/ *adj* describes photographic film that is sensitive to all visible colours and some ultraviolet light

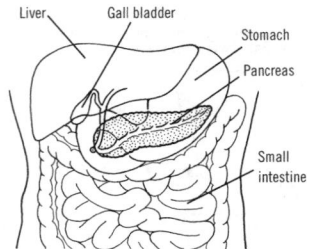

Pancreas

pancreas /pángkri əss/ n a large elongated glandular organ lying near the stomach. It secretes juices into the small intestine and the hormones insulin, glucagon, and somatostatin into the bloodstream. [Late 16C. Via modern Latin < Greek *pagkreas* < *kreas* 'flesh'.] —**pancreatic** /pángkri áttik/ adj

pancreat- prefix pancreas ○ pancreatitis [< Greek *pankreat*-, stem of *pankreas* (see PANCREAS)]

pancreatectomy /pángkri ə téktəmi/ (plural **-mies**) n whole or partial removal of the pancreas by surgery

pancreatic duct n a duct that carries pancreatic juice and, in human beings, runs from the pancreas to join the common bile duct, which empties into the small intestine

pancreatic juice, pancreatic fluid n a watery alkaline fluid secreted by the pancreas

pancreatin /pángkri ətin, pan krée ətin/ n 1 a digestive aid made from a mixture of pancreatic enzymes extracted from domestic animals 2 the mixture of digestive enzymes produced by the pancreas, including amylase, lipase, and trypsin

pancreatitis /pángkri ə títiss/ n inflammation of the pancreas

pancreozymin /pángkri ŏ zímin/ n BIOCHEM = **cholecystokinin** [Mid-20C. < PANCREAS + *zymin*.]

pancytopenia n MED = **aplastic anaemia**

panda /pándə/ n 1 a large bamboo-eating mammal with bold black-and-white markings, including black patches over the eyes. Native to: central China. *Ailuropodia melanoleuca*. 2 ZOOL = **red panda** [Mid-19C. Via French < the Nepalese name for the red panda.]

panda car n a police patrol car (informal) [< the resemblance of its colour scheme to the giant panda's markings]

pandanus /pan dáynəss/ (plural **-nuses** or **-nus**) n a tropical plant resembling a palm, with prop roots and a crown of narrow leaves often used to make mats. Genus: *Pandanus*. [Mid-19C. Via modern Latin < Malay *pandan*.]

Pandean /pan deé ən/ adj relating to the mythological Greek god Pan

pandect /pán dekt/ n 1 a set of documents containing all the laws of a country or society 2 a comprehensive treatise on a subject [Mid-16C. Directly or via French < Latin *pandecta* < Greek *pandektēs* 'all-receiving' < *dekhesthai* 'receive'.]

pandemic /pan démmik/ adj existing in the form of a widespread epidemic that affects people in many different countries ■ n a disease or condition that is found in a large part of a population [Mid-17C. < Greek *pandēmos* 'of all the people' < *dēmos* 'people'.]

pandemonium /pándə mŏni əm/ n 1 wild uproar and chaos 2 a place or situation that is noisy and chaotic [Mid-17C. < modern Latin *Pandaemonium* < Greek *daimōn* (see DEMON).] —**pandemoniac** adj —**pandemonic** /-mónnik/ adj

pander /pándər/ vi 1 INDULGE WEAKNESSES to indulge somebody's weaknesses or questionable wishes and tastes ○ *tired of pandering to their children's demands* 2 PROCURE SEXUAL FAVOURS to procure sexual favours for somebody (disapproving) ■ n 1 **pander, panderer** SOMEBODY WHO INDULGES ANOTHER'S WEAKNESSES an indulger of somebody else's weaknesses or questionable wishes and tastes (disapproving) 2 **pander, panderer** ROMANTIC GO-BETWEEN a go-between in an illicit or secret romantic or sexual relationship (disapproving) 3 **PIMP** a pimp (archaic) [14C. < *Pandare*, character in Chaucer's *Troilus & Criseyde* who procures Criseyde for Troilus.]

P and H, p. and h., p&h abbr US postage and handling

pandit /pándit/ n a wise or learned man in India, especially a Brahman who is an expert in Hindu culture, law, and philosophy

P & L abbr profit and loss

Pandora[1] /pan dáwrə/ n in Greek mythology, the first woman, who was sent by the gods with a jar full of evils in order to avenge Prometheus's theft of fire

Pandora[2] /pan dáwrə/ n a small inner natural satellite of Saturn, discovered in 1980 by Voyager 2. It is irregular in shape with a maximum dimension of 110 km/68 mi.

Pandora's box n 1 in Greek mythology, the jar, later referred to as a box, from which Pandora allowed all the world's evils to escape 2 the source of a great collection of ills that need not be faced unless an unwise action is taken ○ *If you criticize her work, you'll be opening a real Pandora's box.*

pandowdy /pan dówdi/ (plural **-dies**) n US a dish made of sliced apples and spices covered with a biscuit crust and baked in a deep pan [Mid-19C. Probably < PAN[1] + a variant of DOUGH.]

p & p abbr postage and packing

pane /payn/ n 1 GLAZED SECTION OF A WINDOW a glazed section of a window or door 2 PIECE OF GLASS IN A WINDOW a piece of plate glass in a window or door 3 SECTION OF SURFACE a distinct section of a surface such as a door or wall 4 SURFACE OF A FACETED OBJECT a surface on a faceted object, e.g. a metal nut or cut jewel 5 SECTION OF A SHEET OF STAMPS rectangular section into which a sheet of postage stamps is divided before being sold [13C. Via French *pan* < Latin *pannus* 'piece of cloth'.]

SPELLCHECK See *pain*.

panegyric /pánnə jírrik/ n extravagant praise delivered in formal speech or writing [Early 17C. Via French *panegyrique* < Latin *panegyricus* 'public eulogy' < Greek *panēguris* 'public assembly' < *aguris* 'assembly, marketplace'.] —**panegyrical** adj —**panegyrically** adv —**panegyrist** n

⚡**panel** /pánn'l/ n 1 FLAT RECTANGULAR PART a flat rectangular piece of hard material that serves as a part of something such as a door or wall, often raised above or sunk in the surface 2 FENCE SECTION a section between two posts in a fence or gate 3 STRIP OF FABRIC IN GARMENT a vertical section of fabric sewn onto other such sections in a flowing garment or drapery 4 WOODEN SURFACE FOR PAINTING a thin piece of wood used as a surface for oil painting, or the painting on it 5 COMIC STRIP FRAME a section depicting a single scene in a comic strip 6 PART OF AN AIRCRAFT WING a section or surface of an aeroplane wing 7 CLUSTER OF PERFORMANCE-MEASURING INSTRUMENTS a surface on which performance-measuring instruments such as gauges, dials, lights, and digital displays are clustered 8 CONTROL AREA OF A COMPUTER the collection of lights, digital displays, and switches used to monitor and control the operation of a computer 9 DISPLAY ON A COMPUTER SCREEN a display of related information on a computer screen, often a list of options 10 GROUP OF JUDGES OR SPEAKERS a group of people who publicly discuss or judge something, usually in a situation where they sit in a row to face an audience or a competition arena 11 LIST OF PEOPLE FOR JURY DUTY a list of people summoned as potential jurors, or the people themselves 12 JURY a jury in a court proceeding 13 *Scotland* ACCUSED PERSON an accused person or group of accused people brought into court to face charges ■ vt (**-els, -elling, -elled**) 1 SUPPLY WITH PANELS to furnish, cover, or decorate something with panels, especially wooden panelling for walls 2 EMPANEL to make a list of potential jurors or select a jury from such a list 3 *Scotland* INDICT to indict somebody for a crime [14C. Via Old French < *pan* 'piece of cloth'.]

panel beater n a person or business that repairs car bodies, especially by beating out dents

panel heating n a domestic heating system in which heating elements are housed in panels attached to walls or floors

paneling n US = **panelling**

panelist n US = **panellist**

panelling /pánn'ling/ n 1 thin boards or sheets of wood for covering walls, especially as decoration 2 a panel-covered wall or other surface

panellist /pánn'list/ n a member of a panel

panel truck n US a small delivery van that is entirely enclosed, with access to the storage area from the driver's seat

panel van n ANZ a small van with rear doors, used for carrying goods and tools

panettone /pánnə tŏni/ (plural **-ettones** or **-nettoni**) n a tall Italian yeast cake flavoured with vanilla and dried and candied fruits, traditionally eaten at Christmas [Early 20C. < Italian, < *pane* 'bread' < Latin *panis*.]

Pan-European adj relating to all the nations of Europe, collectively or in cooperation with one another

pan fish n US any small freshwater food fish, considered too small to be classed as a game fish, that is the right size to fry whole in a frying pan

pan-fry (**pan-fries, pan-frying, pan-fried**) vt to fry food, usually fish or meat, in a frying pan with a little fat

pang /pang/ n 1 a short sharp pain 2 a sudden, intense, and usually distressing feeling [15C. < ?]

panga /páng gə/ n an African knife with a long, broad, and heavy blade, often used for cutting down sugar cane [Mid-20C. < Kiswahili.]

Pangaea /pan jeě ə/ n hypothetical ancient supercontinent thought to have incorporated all the Earth's major landmasses before the beginning of continental drift

Pangasinan /pán gassi naán/ (plural **-nan** or **-nans**) n 1 a member of a people who live in the province of Pangasinan in central Luzon in the Philippines 2 the Austronesian language spoken by Pangasinan people [Mid-19C. < Pangasinan, 'region of salty ponds'.] —**Pangasinan** adj

Panglossian /pan glóssi ən/ adj excessively and inappropriately optimistic (literary) [Mid-19C. After Dr *Pangloss*, a philosopher in Voltaire's *Candide* (1759).]

Pangolin

pangolin /páng gəlin, pang gŏlin/ n an African and Asian mammal with horny scales, a long tapering snout and tail, and a long sticky tongue for catching ants and termites. Order: Pholidota. [Late 18C. < Malay *pengguling* 'roller', because it rolls itself up when frightened.]

panhandle[1] /pán hand'l/ n 1 the handle of a cooking pan 2 **panhandle, Panhandle** US a narrow section of land shaped like the handle of a cooking pan that extends away from the body of the US state or territory it belongs to ○ *the Texas Panhandle*

panhandle[2] /pán hand'l/ (**-dles, -dling, -dled**) v US 1 BEG MONEY FROM STRANGERS to beg for money on the street by approaching and talking to passers-by 2 vt GET BY BEGGING to get money from a stranger by approaching him or her in the street and begging 3 vt BEG MONEY FROM to approach and beg for money from somebody [Late 19C. Probably so called from the beggar's outstretched arm, thought to resemble the handle of a pan.] —**panhandler** n

Panhellenic /pán he lénnik/ adj relating to all Greek peoples or all of Greece

Panhellenism /pan héllənizəm/ n a philosophy or movement advocating a single political system for all Greek people

panic[1] /pánnik/ n OVERPOWERING FEAR OR ANXIETY a sudden feeling of fear or anxiety, especially among many people, that comes on suddenly, is overwhelming, appears to be uncontrollable, and may seem to be unfounded ■ *adj* **INVOLVING OR RESULTING FROM PANIC** relating to, responding to, or resulting from panic or possible panic ○ *panic selling on the stock market* ■ *vti* (**-ics, -icking, -icked**) **BE OR MAKE SOMEBODY EXTREMELY AFRAID** to feel panic, or make a person or animal feel panic [Early 17C. Via French *panique* and modern Latin *panicus* 'terrified' < Greek *Pan*, Greek god of nature, thought to inspire fear.] —**panicky** /pánniki/ *adj*

panic[2] *n* PLANTS = **panic grass**

Panic *adj* relating to Pan, a god in Greek mythology

panic attack *n* a sudden overpowering feeling of fear or anxiety that prevents somebody from functioning, often triggered by a past or present source of anxiety

panic bolt *n* a bolt released by a waist-high bar that is fitted on emergency exit doors in buildings used by large numbers of people

panic button *n* an alarm to call security staff or summon help in an emergency ◇ **hit** *or* **press** *or* **push the panic button** to react to a perceived emergency or crisis by panicking and responding too hastily (*informal*)

panic buying *n* the buying of a particular product or products in quantity by a large number of people who fear a possible shortage

panic disorder *n* a condition in which somebody has recurrent panic attacks

panic grass, panic, pannick *n* a grass, e.g. millet, used for grain fodder and as a cereal. Genus: *Panicum*. [*Panic* < Latin *panicum* 'foxtail millet']

panicle /pánnik'l/ *n* **1** a cluster of flowers on a plant consisting of a number of individual stalks (**racemes**) each of which has a series of single flowers along its length **2** a loose branching pyramid-shaped cluster of flowers [Late 16C. < Latin *panicula* 'little ear of millet' < *panus* 'swelling, ear of millet'.] —**paniculate** /pə níkyŏŏlət/ *adj*

panicmonger /pánnik mung gər/ *n* a creator of panic in others

panic stations *n* a state of panic, confusion, and commotion immediately following an unexpected event that requires immediate action (*informal; + singular verb*)

panic-stricken, panic-struck *adj* suddenly affected by or characterized by panic

Panislamism /pán iz laámizəm, pan ízləmizəm/ *n* a movement that aims to unify Islamic countries and spread the Islamic religion —**Panislamic** /pániz lámmik/ *adj* —**Panislamist** /pán iz laámist, pan ízləmist/ *n, adj*

Panjabi *n, adj* LANGUAGE, PEOPLES = **Punjabi**

panjandrum /pan jándrəm/ (*plural* **-drums** *or* **panjandra** /-drə/) *n* somebody, especially an official, who is pompous or pretentious [Mid-18C. Nonsense word.]

AKG London

Emmeline Pankhurst

Pankhurst /pángk hurst/, **Emmeline** (1858–1928) British suffragette

panleucopenia /pán lookō peéni ə/, **panleukopenia** *n* feline distemper (*technical*)

pan loaf *n* a baker's loaf of white bread with a thin soft crust all the way round it that is baked individually in a tin (*regional*) ■ *adj, adv Scotland* with an affected way of speaking (*informal humorous*) [*Pan* because it is baked in a pan]

panmixia /pan míksi ə/, **panmixis** /-míksiss/ *n* random breeding and free interchange of genes within a population [Late 19C. Via modern Latin < German *Panmixie* 'all mixing' < Greek *mixis* 'mixing, mingling'.] —**panmictic** *adj*

panne /pan/ *n* a lightweight silk or rayon fabric resembling velvet [Late 18C. < French.]

pannick *n* PLANT SCI = **panic grass**

pannier /pánni ər/ *n* **1 BASKET ON BACK OF ANIMAL** a large basket, often one of a pair, that is placed on the back of a horse, donkey, or other pack animal **2 BAG ON BACK OF BICYCLE** one of a pair of bags carried on either side of the back or front wheel of a bicycle or motorcycle **3 FRAMEWORK TO WIDEN SKIRT** a framework of cane worn by women in the 18th century at each side of the hips to widen a skirt **4 OVERSKIRT LOOPED UP AT HIPS** an overskirt looped up at the hips to show the underskirt and give the impression of fullness, worn in the second half of the 19th century [13C. Via Old French *pannier* < Latin *panarium* 'breadbasket' < *panis* 'bread'.]

pannikin /pánnikin/ *n* a small metal drinking cup [Early 19C. < PAN[1], after CANNIKIN 'cup'.]

Panoan /pan ő ən/ *n* a group of languages spoken in Peru and W Brazil [Early 20C. < American Spanish *Pano*, a people of the upper Amazon basin.] —**Panoan** *adj*

panoply /pánnəpli/ (*plural* **-plies**) *n* **1 FULL ARRAY** an impressive and magnificent display or array of something **2 FULL CEREMONIAL DRESS** ceremonial dress with all the necessary accessories **3 FULL ARMOUR** a full suit of armour and equipment for a warrior **4 PROTECTIVE COVERING** a covering that protects something [Late 16C. Via French < Greek *panoplia* 'all weapons' < *hopla* 'weapons'.] —**panoplied** *adj*

panoptic /pan óptik/, **panoptical** /-óptik'l/ *adj* taking in or showing everything in a single view [Early 19C. < Greek *panoptos* 'seen by all', and *panoptēs* 'all-seeing', both < *optos* 'visible'.] —**panoptically** *adv*

panorama /pánnə raámə/ *n* **1 ALL-ROUND VIEW** an unobstructed view extending in all directions, especially of a landscape **2 COMPREHENSIVE SURVEY** an all-encompassing survey of a particular topic or issue **3 PICTURE WITH A WIDE VIEW** a picture or photograph that has a wide view, especially one that is unrolled gradually in front of the spectator **4** ARTS = **cyclorama** *n.* 1 [Late 18C. < PAN- + Greek *horama* 'view' < *horan* 'see'.] —**panoramic** /-rámmik/ *adj* —**panoramically** *adv*

panoramic sight *n* a sight on a military weapon that gives the user a wide-angled view of the target area

panpipes /pán pīps/ *npl* a set of reeds of different lengths that are bound together in a row and played by blowing across the top of each pipe [Early 19C. After the Greek god *Pan*.]

pansexual /pán sékshoo əl/ *adj* relating to a sexuality that expresses itself in many different forms —**pansexuality** /pán sekshoo állati/ *n*

Pan-Slavism *n* a 19th-century political and cultural movement advocating the union of all Slav people —**Pan-Slavic** *adj* —**Pan-Slavist** *n, adj*

panspermia /pan spúrmi ə/ *n* a theory of biogenetics that states that the universe is full of spores that germinate when they find a favourable environment [Mid-19C. < Greek, 'doctrine that the elements are made of all the seeds of things' < *sperma* 'seed'.]

pansy /pánzi/ (*plural* **-sies**) *n* **1 FLOWER WITH BRIGHT VELVETY PETALS** a plant with brightly coloured velvety flowers that usually have black or dark centres. Native to: Europe. Genus: *Viola* and *Achimenes*. **2 OFFENSIVE TERM** an offensive term for a homosexual or effeminate man or boy (*dated*) **3 DEEP VIOLET** a deep violet colour [15C. < French *pensée* 'thought' (from its lowered head), feminine past participle of *penser* 'think'.] —**pansy** *adj*

pant[1] /pant/ *v* **1** *vi* **TAKE SHORT FAST SHALLOW BREATHS** to take short fast shallow breaths, especially when excited, hot, or after physical exertion **2** *vt* **SAY SOMETHING BREATHLESSLY** to say something while trying to catch your breath **3** *vi* **YEARN** to have a strong desire and yearning for somebody or something **4** *vi* **PULSATE QUICKLY** to throb at a fast rhythm ■ *n* **SHALLOW BREATH** a short fast shallow breath [15C. < assumed Anglo-Norman, 'gasp' < Vulgar Latin *phantasiare* 'gasp in horror' < Latin *phantasia* 'apparition'.]

pant[2] /pant/ *n US* a pair of trousers [Late 19C. Back-formation < PANTS.]

pant- *prefix* = **panto-** (*before vowels*)

pantalets /pántə léts/, **pantalettes** *npl* **1** long underpants extending below the skirt, usually with a frill round the bottom of each leg, worn by women in the first half of the 19th century **2** a pair of frills, one at the bottom of each leg, on a pair of pantalets [Mid-19C. < PANTALOON.]

pantaloon /pántə lóon/ *n* a character in pantomime who is the victim of the clown's jokes and tricks [Late 16C. Via French *pantalon* < Italian *Pantalone* (see PANTALOON).]

Pantaloon /pántə lóon/ *n* a character in Italian commedia dell'arte, a very thin man of advanced years who is easily tricked and who wears pantaloons and slippers [Late 16C. Probably after *San Pantaleone* 'Saint Pantaleon', patron saint of Venice.]

pantaloons /pántə lóonz/ *npl* **1 WIDE TROUSERS GATHERED AT ANKLE** loose-fitting trousers that are gathered at the ankle **2 BAGGY TROUSERS** trousers that fit very loosely (*informal humorous*) **3 TIGHT-FITTING MEN'S TROUSERS** tight-fitting men's trousers fastened with buttons or ribbons at the ankle and sometimes held with a strap under the instep, worn in the early 19th century **4 17C ENGLISH TROUSERS** men's wide ankle-length breeches, worn especially in England during the reign of Charles II [Mid-17C. Plural of PANTALOON.]

pantechnicon /pan téknikən/ *n* a large furniture-removal van [Mid-19C. After a building in London used as a bazaar < PAN- + Greek *tekhnikos* 'artistic'.]

pantheism /pánthi izəm/ *n* **1** the belief that God and the material world are one and the same thing and that God is present in everything **2** the belief in and worship of all or many deities [Mid-18C. < PAN- + Greek *theos* 'god' + -ISM.] —**pantheist** *n* —**pantheistic** /pánthi ístik/ *adj* —**pantheistically** /-ístikli/ *adv*

pantheon /pánthi ən, pan theé-/ *n* **1 TEMPLE** a temple dedicated to all deities **2 ALL DEITIES OF SPECIFIC RELIGION** all the deities of a particular religion considered collectively **3 MEMORIAL TO DEAD HEROES** a monument or public building commemorating the dead heroes of a nation **4 GROUP OF IMPORTANT PEOPLE** a group of people who are the most famous or respected in a particular field [15C. Via Latin < Greek *pantheion* 'of all the gods' < *theos* 'god'.]

Pantheon /pánthi ən, pan theé ən/ *n* a circular temple in Rome that was completed in 27 BC and dedicated to all the deities but which has been used as a Christian church since AD 609

panther /pánthər/ (*plural* **-thers** *or* **panther**) *n* **1** a leopard, especially in its black unspotted phase **2** *US* ZOOL = **puma** [13C. Via Old French *pantere* < Greek *panthēr*.]

pantie girdle /pánti-/, **panty girdle** *n* a woman's undergarment with a sewn-in crotch like underpants, but made of elasticated material in order to give the abdomen a flatter appearance

panties /pántiz/ *npl* short light fitted underpants for women or girls (*informal*) [Mid-19C. < PANTS.]

pantihose *npl* CLOTHING = **pantyhose**

pantile /pán tīl/ *n* a roof tile made in an S shape so that the downcurving tail of the S overlaps the upcurving head of the S of the tile next to it [Mid-17C. < PAN[1] + TILE.]

pantisocracy /pánti sókrəssi/ (*plural* **-cies**) *n* a planned Utopian community in which everyone shares power and is equal [Late 18C. < PANTO- + Greek *isokratia* 'equality of power'.]

panto /pántō/ (*plural* **-tos**) *n* pantomime (*informal*) [Mid-19C. Shortening.]

panto- *prefix* all ○ *pantograph* [< Greek *pant-*, stem of *pas*]

pantograph /pántə graaf, -graf/ *n* **1 COPYING INSTRUMENT** an instrument that consists of a set of adjustable interconnected bars forming a parallelogram and is used to copy line drawings or maps to any scale **2 FRAME OR BRACKET** a device shaped like a pantograph and used as a frame or bracket **3 CURRENT-SUPPLY DEVICE FOR ELECTRIC TRAIN** a device on the roof of electric trains and locomotives for picking up electric current from overhead wires —**pantographer** /pan tóggrəfər/ *n* —**pantographic** /pántə gráffik/ *adj* —**pantographically** /-gráffikli/ *adv*

pantomime /pántə mīm/ *n* **1 HUMOROUS THEATRICAL ENTERTAINMENT** a style of theatre, or a play in this style, traditionally performed at Christmas, in which a folktale or children's story is told with jokes, songs, and dancing **2 LUDICROUS SITUATION** a ridiculous and farcical situation that results from confusion and misunderstanding (*informal*) **3 MIME ARTIST** a person who acts without speaking, using gesture and expression **4 ROMAN THEATRICAL PERFORMANCE** a theatrical performance in ancient Rome by one masked actor who played all the characters, using only dance, gesture, and expression, and no words, while a chorus narrated the story **5 ROMAN ACTOR** an actor in a Roman pantomime [Late 16C. Via Latin *pantomimus* 'mime artist' < Greek *pantomōmos* 'complete imitator' < *mōmos* 'imitator'.] —

pantomimic /pántə mímmik/ *adj* —**pantomimist** /-mīmist/ *n*

pantomime dame *n* the role in a pantomime of an ill-tempered comic woman of advanced years, traditionally played by a man

pantomime horse *n* a comic character in a pantomime played by two actors in a horse costume, with one occupying the front half of the horse and the other the back half

pantothenate /pántə thénnayt, pan tóthə nayt/ *n* an ester of pantothenic acid [Mid-20C. < PANTOTHENIC ACID.]

pantothenic acid /pántə thénnik-/ *n* a B complex vitamin that is present in many foods and is essential for growth [< Greek *pantothen* 'from every side', because it is widely found]

pantoum /pan tóom/ *n* a form of verse in which the second and fourth lines of each four-line verse are repeated as the first and third lines of the following verse [Late 18C. Via French < Malay *pantun*.]

pantropic /pan trṓpik, -tróppik/, **pantropical** /-trṓpik'l, -tróppik'l/ *adj* found throughout the tropics

pantry /pántri/ (*plural* **pantries**) *n* **1** a small closed space connected to a kitchen, often with a door, in which food and utensils for food preparation can be stored **2** a highly ventilated cold small room or walk-in cupboard with shelves and a marble surface used for storing food [13C. < Old French *paneterie* 'cupboard for bread' < late Latin *panarius* 'breadseller' < Latin *panis* 'bread'.]

pants /pants/ *npl* **1** an item of clothing worn next to the skin that covers the buttocks and genital area **2** *US, Can, Aus* an item of clothing that covers the part of the body from the waist to the ankles or, sometimes, the knees, each leg having a separate tubular piece [Mid-19C. Shortening of PANTALOONS.] ◇ **beat the pants off somebody** to defeat somebody decisively (*informal*) ◇ **bore** *or* **scare** *or* **charm the pants off somebody** to bore, scare, or charm somebody very much (*informal*) ◇ **caught with your pants down** caught in an unprepared or embarrassing position ◇ **wear the pants** *US, Can, ANZ* to be the boss

panty girdle *n* CLOTHING = **pantie girdle**

pantyhose /pánti hōz/, **pantihose** *npl US* CLOTHING = **tights** *npl.* 1

pantyliner /pánti līnər/ *n* a light, thin sanitary towel

pantywaist /pánti wayst/ *n US* **1** an offensive term for a man that deliberately insults his courage and masculinity (*slang*) **2** a piece of clothing for children, consisting of a shirt and trousers that are buttoned together at the waist (*dated*)

panzer /pánzər/ *n* an armoured vehicle such as a tank, especially a German armoured vehicle used in World War II [Mid-20C. Shortening of German *Panzerdivision* 'armoured unit' < Old French *pancier* 'armour for the belly' < *pance* 'belly' (see PAUNCH).]

Paolozzi /pow lótsi/, **Sir Eduardo** (*b.* 1924) Scottish sculptor

pap[1] /pap/ *n* **1** soft semiliquid food, usually mashed or pulped, especially for babies or sick people **2** something, especially a book, film, television programme, or idea, that is so lacking in depth and substance that it is considered worthless [14C. Via Old French *papa* < Latin *pappa*, a children's word, 'food'.] —**pappy** /páppi/ *adj*

pap[2] /pap/ *n* **1** a nipple or teat (*archaic*) **2 pap, Pap** a round, conical hill (*often in placenames*) [12C. < ?]

papa /pə paá/ *n* **1** a father (*dated*) **2** a code word for the letter 'P', used in international radio communications [Late 17C. Via French < Latin < Greek *pappas* 'father'.]

papacy /páypəssi/ (*plural* **-cies**) *n* **1 PAPAL POWER OR STATUS** the power or position of the pope **2 POPE'S PERIOD IN POWER** the period of office of a pope **3 PAPAL GOVERNMENT** the system of government in the Roman Catholic Church with the pope as the head [14C. < medieval Latin *papatia* < late Latin *papa* 'pope'.]

Papa Doc /páppə dók/ ♦ **François Duvalier**

Papago /páppə gō/ (*plural* **-go** *or* **Papagos**) *n* **1** a member of a Native North American people who lived in central Arizona, and now live mainly in N Mexico and S Arizona **2** the Uto-Aztecan language of the Papago people, closely related to Pima. Native speakers: 9,000. [Mid-19C. Via Spanish *pápago* < a Pima-Papago word.] —**Papago** *adj*

papain /pə páy in, -pī́-/ *n* an enzyme found in the juice of papaya and used as a meat tenderizer and in medicine to promote digestion and healing of wounds [Late 19C. < PAPAYA.]

papal /páyp'l/ *adj* relating to the pope or the papacy [14C. Via Old French < medieval Latin *papalis* < late Latin *papa* 'pope' (see POPE).] —**papally** *adv*

papal cross *n* a cross consisting of a long upright and three crossbars of successively decreasing length, with the shortest at the top

Papal States former territory in central Italy that was under the direct rule of the pope between AD 754 and 1870

Papandreou /páppən dráy oo/, **Andreas** (1919–96) Greek statesman

Papanicolaou test /páppə níkə loo-/, **Papanicolaou smear** *n US* a smear test [Mid-20C. After G. N. *Papanicolaou* (1883–1962), Greek-born US anatomist.]

paparazzo /páppə ráts ō/ (*plural* **-zi** /páppə rátsi/) *n* a freelance photographer who follows famous people hoping to catch a newsworthy story, especially something shocking or scandalous (*often plural*) [Mid-20C. < Italian, surname of a photographer in the film *La Dolce Vita*, 1959, by Federico Fellini.]

papaverine /pə pávvə reen, -páyvə-/ *n* $C_{20}H_{21}O_4N$ a toxic white crystalline nonaddictive alkaloid. Source: opium, derived synthetically. Use: antispasmodic to treat asthma and colic. [Mid-19C. < Latin *papaver* 'poppy'.]

papaya /pə pī́ ə/ *n* **1** a large spherical or elongated fruit with yellow pulp and numerous seeds, eaten fresh or in salads and desserts **2** a tropical evergreen tree with a crown of broad leaves, widely cultivated to produce papayas. *Carica papaya.* [Late 16C. < Spanish *papaya* < Carib or Arawak.]

paper /páypər/ *n* **1 THIN FLAT MATERIAL FROM WOOD PULP** a thin material consisting of flat sheets made from pulped wood, cloth, or fibre. Use: for writing and printing on, for wrapping things in, for covering walls. **2 SHEET OR SHEETS OF PAPER** one or more pieces or sheets of paper, for writing or drawing on **3** MEDIA = **newspaper** *n.* 1 **4 EXAMINATION** a set of examination questions prepared on paper **5 SET OF EXAM ANSWERS** a written set of answers by a student to a set of examination questions **6 ACADEMIC ARTICLE OR TALK** an essay or article, particularly an academic one, read at a conference or to a society, or submitted for publication **7 STUDENT'S ESSAY** an essay written by a student for a class **8 WALLPAPER** wallpaper (*informal*) **9 WRAPPER** a piece of paper, especially one used to wrap a sweet or a cigarette (*often plural*) **10 GOVERNMENT DOCUMENT** a white paper, green paper, or command paper **11 COMMERCIAL NEGOTIABLE DOCUMENT** a negotiable document, e.g. a bill of exchange or promissory note **12 FREE THEATRE TICKET** a free ticket that is given out in order to fill up a theatre (*slang*) **13 THEATREGOERS WITH FREE TICKETS** members of the audience who have been given free tickets in order to fill up a theatre (*slang*) ■ **papers** *npl* **1 PERSONAL IDENTITY DOCUMENTS** a document or documents, such as a passport, showing somebody's identity or status **2 ASSORTMENT OF DOCUMENTS** a collection of documents relating to a particular issue or subject ○ *official papers in the archives* **3 SOMEBODY'S PERSONAL WRITINGS** somebody's diaries, letters, and other personal writings **4 SHIP'S PAPERS** ship's papers ■ *adj* **1 MADE OF PAPER** consisting of or made of paper **2 RESEMBLING PAPER** similar to paper, e.g. in flimsiness **3 EXISTING IN DOCUMENTARY FORM** written in a document but not necessarily effective or useful in reality **4 IN WRITING** conducted in writing ■ *vt* **1 COVER WITH WALLPAPER** to cover a wall or room with wallpaper **2 COVER WITH PAPER** to cover something with paper **3 FILL UP THEATRE** to fill up a theatre by giving out free tickets (*slang*) [14C. Via Old French *papier* and Anglo-Norman *papir* < Latin *papyrus* (see PAPYRUS).] —**paperer** *n* ◇ **on paper 1** in theory, but not in fact **2** in writing

paper over *vt* **1** to cover something up with paper, especially to cover a wall's imperfections or old paint with wallpaper **2** to conceal something without resolving it, especially mistakes, disagreements, or faults

paperback /páypər bak/ *n* **SOFTCOVER BOOK** a book that has a thin flexible cover instead of a hard cover ■ *adj* **WITH FLEXIBLE COVER** with a thin flexible cover, instead of a hard cover ■ *vt* **PUBLISH AS PAPERBACK** to publish a book in paperback form —**paperbacker** *n*

paperbark /páypər baark/ *n* a tree with pale thin papery bark that peels off in large sheets. Native to: Australia. Genus: *Melaleuca.* [< the colour and texture of the bark]

paper birch *n* a birch tree with white peeling bark that was formerly used to cover canoes. Native to: North America. *Betula papyrifera.* [< the white colour of the bark]

paperboard /páypər bawrd/ *n* thick cardboard

paperboy /páypər boy/ *n* a boy who delivers newspapers to people's homes, or who sells newspapers

paper chase *n* **1** an intense searching and collation of files, books, or documents **2** a cross-country race in which runners follow a trail of shredded paper that has been left by an earlier runner or runners

paperclip /páypər klip/ *n* a clip designed to be slipped over two or more sheets of paper to hold them together, especially a piece of wire that is bent into a long flat oval spiral

paper-cutter *n* **1** a machine or device for cutting paper, especially a flat platform with a long arm containing a blade that can be raised and lowered in order to cut straight edges **2** *US* HOUSEHOLD = **paperknife**

papergirl /páypər gurl/ *n* a girl who delivers newspapers to people's homes, or who sells newspapers

paperhanger /páypər hangər/ *n* **1** a hanger of wallpaper, especially as a professional **2** *US* somebody who regularly passes bad cheques (*slang*) —**paperhanging** *n*

paper jam *n* a situation in which paper becomes jammed in a printer or photocopier, causing it to stop working

paperknife /páypər nīf/ (*plural* **paperknives** /páypər nīvz/) *n* a blunt knife for slitting open envelopes, or for slitting folded paper, especially leaves of books

paperless /páypərləss/ *adj* using records or means of communication that are electronic rather than on paper ○ *the age of the paperless office*

paper money *n* currency in the form of banknotes, as opposed to coins

paper mulberry *n* a common shade tree whose inner bark was once used for making paper. Native to: Asia. *Broussonetia papyrifera.*

paper nautilus *n* a cephalopod mollusc, the female of which has a thin delicate shell. Genus: *Argonauta.* ◊ **pearly nautilus** [< the delicacy and whiteness of its shell]

paper profit *n* a profit that is not generated from the normal trading of a business and may or may not be realized (*often plural*)

paper-pusher *n* somebody with a routine clerical job involving much paperwork (*informal*)

paper round *n* **1** the job of delivering newspapers to people's homes. US term **paper route** *n.* 1 **2** the course followed from house to house by somebody delivering newspapers. US term **paper route** *n.* 2

paper route *n US* **1** = **paper round** *n.* 1 **2** = **paper round** *n.* 2

paper-thin *adj* extremely thin, like paper ■ *adv* extremely thinly

paper tiger *n* a person or thing, especially an organization or a nation, that appears to be very strong and powerful but is in fact weak and ineffectual

paper trail *n* a sequence of documents that reflects the stages in the actions of a person or organization, especially as the object of an investigation (*informal*)

paper wasp *n* a large slender wasp known for its elaborate nest that is made up of individual cells built of papery material. Genus: *Polistes.*

paperweight /páypər wayt/ *n* a small heavy, usually ornamental, object that is used to hold down papers and keep them in place

paperwork /páypər wurk/ *n* routine work that involves tasks such as filling in forms, keeping files up to date, or writing reports and letters

papery /páypəri/ *adj* similar to paper in texture or thickness —**paperiness** *n*

Paphian /páyfi ən/ *adj* **1 RELATING TO PAPHOS** relating to the village of Paphos **2 RELATING TO APHRODITE** relating to the deity Aphrodite, who, in Greek mythology, rose fully formed from the sea at Paphos **3 CONCERNING SEXUAL ACTIVITY** relating to sexual love (*literary*) ■ *n* **Paphian, paphian PROSTITUTE** a prostitute (*literary*)

Paphos[1] /pá foss/ town in SW Cyprus, on the site of an ancient city. Population: 38,000 (1997).

Paphos[2] /páy foss/, **Paphus** /páyfəss/ *n* in Greek mythology, a king of Cyprus who was the son of Pygmalion and Galatea

Papiamento /páppi ə méntō/ n a Spanish-based creole of the Netherlands Antilles, derived from a Portuguese pidgin and including many Dutch words. Native speakers: 200,000. [Mid-20C. < Spanish < Papiamento *papya* 'talk' + *-mentu* '-ment'.] —**Papiamento** adj

papier collé /páppi ay kóllay/ n scraps of paper and other objects that are glued onto a sheet as an abstract artistic composition [< French, 'glued paper']

papier-mâché /páppi ay máshay, páypər-/ n sheets of paper pulp and glue stuck together in layers, usually onto a frame or mould, used to make various objects such as boxes, bowls, and masks [< French, 'mashed paper'] —**papier-mâché** adj

papilla /pə píllə/ (plural **papillae** /-lee/) n 1 NIPPLE a nipple or teat (technical) 2 SMALL LUMP OF TISSUE a small nipple-shaped protuberance, e.g. on the tongue enclosing the taste buds, or at the root of a hair or feather 3 SMALL PROJECTION ON PETAL OR LEAF a small elevated pad on the surface of a stigma, petal, or leaf 4 SMALL PROJECTION RESEMBLING NIPPLE a very small projection like a nipple on the surface of something [Late 17C. < Latin, 'little swelling' < papula 'swelling'.] —**papillary** adj —**papillate** adj —**papilliferous** /páppi lífferəss/ adj —**papilliform** /pə pílli fawrm/ adj

papilloma /páppi lṓmə/ (plural **-mata** or **-mas** /-mətə/) n a benign tumour of the skin or mucous membrane projecting from a surface, e.g. a wart —**papillomatous** adj

papillon /páppi lon/ n a small spaniel with a silky coat and heavily fringed tail and ears [Early 20C. < French, 'butterfly', because its pointed ears resemble the shape of a butterfly's wings.]

papist /páypist/ n an offensive term for a member of the Roman Catholic Church [Mid-16C. Directly or via French < modern Latin papista < ecclesiastical Latin papa 'pope'.] —**papism** n —**papistic** /pə pístik/ adj —**papistry** /páypistri/ n

papoose /pə pooss/, **pappoose** n 1 an offensive term for a Native North American baby or young child 2 a bag that fits over the shoulders, used for carrying a baby, especially in front of the body [Mid-17C. < Algonquian, 'very young'.]

papovavirus /pə pṓvə vīrəss/ n a DNA-containing virus, of a group that can cause cancers in animals, including those responsible for warts [Mid-20C. < PAPILLOMA + POLYOMA + VACUOLATION + VIRUS.]

pappardelle /páppər délli/ npl pasta in the shape of broad flat ribbons [< Italian, < pappare 'eat ravenously']

pappus /páppəss/ (plural **-pi** /-pī/) n a covering of scales, bristles, and feathery hairs that surrounds the fruit of plants such as dandelions and thistles and helps to disperse the fruits [Early 18C. Via Latin < Greek pappos 'grandfather'.] —**pappose** /páppŏss/ adj

pappy /páppi/ (plural **-pies**) n US a father (dated regional) [Mid-18C. < PAPA.]

paprika /pápprikə, pə preékə/ n 1 MILD RED SPICE FROM SWEET PEPPER a mild red spice made from various sweet red peppers and used especially in Hungarian cooking 2 SWEET RED PEPPER a sweet red pepper 3 PEPPER PLANT a plant on which sweet red peppers grow. Genus: Capsicum. 4 REDDISH-ORANGE COLOUR a bright reddish-orange colour [Late 19C. Via Hungarian < Serbian pàpar 'pepper' < Latin piper 'pepper'.] —**paprika** adj

Pap smear /páp-/, **Pap test** n US MED = **cervical smear** [Pap shortening of Papanicolaou (see PAPANICOLAOU TEST)]

Papuan /páppōō ən/ n 1 somebody who comes from Papua New Guinea 2 a group of languages spoken in Papua New Guinea and nearby islands, unrelated to the Austronesian languages. Native speakers: 2 million. —**Papuan** adj

Papua New Guinea /páppōō ə nyōō gínni/ nation in the SW Pacific Ocean, comprising E New Guinea and several hundred smaller islands. Capital: Port Moresby. Population: 4,394,537 (1996). Area: 462,840 sq. km/178,704 sq. mi. —**Papua New Guinean** n, adj

papule /páppyool/ n a small hard round protuberance on the skin [Early 18C. < Latin papula.] —**papular** /páppyŏolər/ adj —**papuliferous** /páppyŏo lífferəss/ adj

papyrology /páppə róllǝji/ n the study of ancient papyrus manuscripts —**papyrological** /páppərə lójjik'l/ adj —**papyrologist** /páppə róllǝjist/ n

papyrus /pə pírəss/ (plural **-ri** /-rī/ or **papyruses**) n 1 MATERIAL RESEMBLING PAPER writing material made from the pith of the stem of an aquatic plant that was used by the ancient Egyptians, Greeks, and Romans 2 PAPYRUS DOCUMENT an ancient manuscript written on papyrus 3 TALL MARSH PLANT a tall aquatic plant. Flowers: small, like umbrellas. Use: writing material. Native to: S Europe, Nile valley. Cyperus papyrus. [14C. Via Latin < Greek papuros 'papyrus plant'.]

par /paar/ n 1 AVERAGE LEVEL a level or standard considered to be average or normal 2 ACCEPTED VALUE OF CURRENCY the accepted value of one country's currency in terms of the currency of another country that uses the same metal standard 3 COMM = **par value** 4 ALLOCATED STANDARD SCORE the standard score assigned to each hole on a golf course, or to the sum total of these holes ■ adj AVERAGE average or normal ■ vt (**pars, parring, parred**) SCORE PAR ON to score the equivalent of the par on a hole or course [Late 16C. < Latin, 'equal'.] ◇ **be feeling below par** to feel slightly unwell or out of sorts (informal) ◇ **be on (a) par (with somebody or something)** to be on the same level as somebody or something, or generally have the same status or value ◇ **be par for the course** to be usual or to be expected under the circumstances (informal)

par. abbr 1 paragraph 2 parallel 3 parenthesis 4 parish

par- prefix = **para-**[1]

para[1] /párrə/ n a paratrooper (informal; usually plural) [Mid-20C. Shortening.]

para[2] /paərə/ (plural **-ras** or **-ra**) n see table at **currency** [Late 17C. Via Turkish < Persian pāra 'piece, para'.]

para-[1] prefix 1 beside, near, along with ◇ parataxis 2 beyond ◇ paranormal 3 isomeric or related compound ◇ paraldehyde 4 resembling ◇ paramyxovirus 5 faulty, undesirable ◇ paraphasia 6 assistant, auxiliary ◇ paralegal 7 occupying the para position in the benzene ring ◇ para-radichlorobenzene [< Greek para 'beside' < Indo-European, 'next to, in front of']

para-[2] prefix parachute ◇ paraskiing [< PARACHUTE]

-para suffix a woman who has given birth to a particular number of children ◇ nullipara [< Latin < parere 'give birth']

para-aminobenzoic acid /párrə ə mī̆nō ben zṓik-/ n full form of PABA

para-aminosalicylic acid /párrə ə mee̅ nō sállisilik-, -mī̆-/ n a drug similar to aspirin. Use: treatment of tuberculosis.

parabasis /pə rábbəsiss/ (plural **parabases** /-seez/) n in classical Greek comedy, a speech to the audience that is made by the chorus [Early 19C. < Greek, < parabainein 'go aside' < bainein 'to step'.]

parabiosis /párrə bī ṓssiss/ (plural **-ses** /-seez/) n 1 the state in which two individuals are joined together and share the same circulation of blood 2 the temporary suppression of nerve conduction [Early 20C. < PARA-[1] + Greek biōsis 'way of life' < bios 'life'.] —**parabiotic** /-bī óttik/ adj

parablast /párrə blast/ n the yolk of a fertilized egg [Mid-19C. < PARA-[1] + Greek blastos 'a bud, shoot'.] —**parablastic** /párrə blástik/ adj

parable /párrəb'l/ n 1 a short simple story intended to illustrate a moral or religious lesson 2 a parable that appears in the Bible, as told by Jesus Christ [14C. Via Old French parabole and Latin parabola < Greek paraballein 'put beside' (< ballein 'throw').]

Papua New Guinea

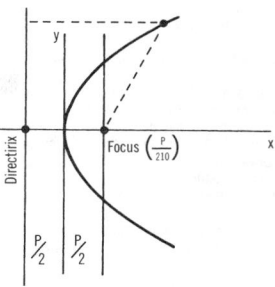

Parabola

parabola /pə rábbələ/ n a curve formed by the intersection of a cone with a plane parallel to its side [Late 16C. Via modern Latin < Greek parabolē 'application, comparison'; from the relationship between the section of a cone that forms the parabola and part of the cone's surface.]

parabolic[1] /párrə bóllik/ adj 1 relating to, resembling, or having the form of a parabola 2 with the form of a paraboloid

parabolic[2] /párrə bóllik/, **parabolical** /párrə bóllik'l/ adj relating to or resembling a parable [15C. Via late Latin parabolicus < late Greek parabolikos 'figurative' < parabolē (see PARABLE).] —**parabolically** adv

parabolic aerial n COMMUNICATION = **dish aerial**

parabolize /pə rábbə līz/ (**-lizes, -lizing, -lized**), **parabolise** (**-lises, -lising, -lised**) vt to explain something or tell a story by means of a parable [Early 17C. < medieval Latin parabolizare 'speak in parables' < Latin parabola (see PARABLE).]

paraboloid /pə rábbə loyd/ n a mathematical surface in which intersections with planes produce parabolas, ellipses, or hyperbolas —**paraboloidal** /pə rábbə lóyd'l/ adj

para boots npl high-lacing boots worn by paratroopers that are popular in various street fashions

parabuntal /párrə búnt'l/ n fine straw made from the leaves of a palm tree. Use: hatmaking.

Paracelsus /párrə sélssəss/, **Philippus Aureolus** (1493?–1541) German physician and alchemist. Pseudonym of **Theophrastus Bombastus von Hohenheim**

paracentesis /párrə sen teéssiss/ (plural **-ses**) n MED = **thoracentesis** [Late 16C. Via Latin, 'the removing of a cataract' < Greek parakentein 'pierce at the side' < kentein 'prick, stab'.]

paracetamol /párrə seètə mol, -séttə-/ (plural **-mol** or **-mols**) n 1 a drug sold in tablet form. Use: relief of pain, fever. US term **acetaminophen** n. 1 2 a tablet or capsule containing paracetamol. US term **acetaminophen** n. 2 [Mid-20C. < par(a-)acet(yl)am(inophen)ol.]

parachronism /pə rákrənizəm/ n an error in assigning a date to something, especially when the date given is later than it should be [Mid-17C. < PARA-[1] + Greek khronos 'time', or alteration of ANACHRONISM.]

parachute /párrə shoot/ n 1 a device consisting of a canopy fitted to a harness that is used to slow the speed at which a person or object drops from an aircraft 2 ZOOL = **patagium** n. 1 ■ vti (**-chutes, -chuting, -chuted**) to drop, or allow somebody or something to drop, from an aircraft by parachute [Late 18C. < French, 'protection against a fall' < chute 'a fall'.] —**parachutist** n

parachute spinnaker n a very large light triangular sail used on a racing yacht

Paraclete /párrə kleet/ n in Christianity, the Holy Spirit [13C. Via French paraclet 'somebody called to assist' < Greek parakalein 'call to your side' < kalein 'to call'.]

parade /pə ráyd/ n 1 CELEBRATORY PROCESSION an organized procession of people celebrating a special occasion and often including decorated vehicles or floats, a marching band, people twirling batons, and people on horseback 2 DISPLAY a long moving line of people or things intended to be publicly displayed 3 SUCCESSION a large number of people or things in succession ◇ a parade of visitors to the palace 4 PROCESSION OF TROOPS a march by troops along the streets or in a large area such as a square, usually as a celebration of an important event 5 GATHERING OF TROOPS IN FORMATION a formal gathering of a troop of soldiers in a regimented formation for a ceremonial march, inspection, or training **6 PARADE GROUND** a parade ground **7 PEOPLE IN PARADE** people marching in a parade **8 FLAMBOYANT OR FLAUNTING EXHIBITION** a showy or ostentatious exhibition or display of something **9 parade, Parade STREET** a street with a row of shops (often in placenames) **10 PARRY** a parry in fencing ■ v **1** vti **GO ON FESTIVE PROCESSION** to march in a festive public parade **2** vti **USE IN FESTIVE PARADE** to use something or be used in a festive public parade **3** vti **ASSEMBLE FOR MILITARY PARADE** to gather for and march in a military parade **4** vt **SHOW SOMEBODY OR SOMETHING OFF** to display or show somebody or something, especially proudly and ostentatiously **5** vi **WALK ABOUT TO BE SEEN** to walk or stroll about in public, especially in order to be seen or admired **6** vti **CLAIM TO BE SOMETHING ELSE** to claim to be other than you really are, or claim that one person or thing is another person or thing ◇ *parading old ideas as new reforms* [Mid-17C. Via French < Spanish *parada* 'stopping (a horse)' < Latin *parare* 'prepare'.] ◇ **rain on somebody's parade** US to spoil things for somebody (*informal*)

parade ground *n* a place where troops regularly gather in formation for inspection or training

~~paradice~~ incorrect spelling of **paradise**

paradichlorobenzene /párrə dī kláw rō bén zeen/ *n* $C_6H_4Cl_2$ a white crystalline compound. Use: moth repellent.

paradiddle /párrə did'l/ *n* a drum roll in which left and right drumsticks alternate [Early 20C. An imitation of the sound.]

paradigm /párrə dīm/ *n* **1 TYPICAL EXAMPLE** a typical example of something **2 MODEL THAT FORMS BASIS** an example that serves as a pattern or model for something, especially one that forms the basis of a methodology or theory **3 SET OF ALL FORMS OF WORD** a set of word forms giving all of the possible inflections of a word **4 RELATIONSHIP OF IDEAS TO ONE ANOTHER** in the philosophy of science, a generally accepted model of how ideas relate to one another, forming a conceptual framework within which scientific research is carried out [15C. Via late Latin < Greek *paradeigma* 'example' < *paradeiknunai* 'show beside' < *deiknunai* 'to show'.] —**paradigmatic** /párrədig máttik/ *adj* —**paradigmatically** *adv*

paradigm shift *n* a radical change in somebody's basic assumptions or approach to something

paradise /párrə dīss/ *n* **1 PLACE OR STATE OF PERFECT HAPPINESS** a place, situation, or condition in which somebody finds perfect happiness **2 PLACE IDEALLY SUITED** a place where there is everything that a particular person needs for his or her interest (*informal*) ◇ *a surfer's paradise* **3 paradise, Paradise HEAVEN** in religions such as Christianity, Islam, and Judaism, the place where good people are believed to go or the state they are believed to attain after death **4 paradise, Paradise GARDEN OF EDEN** according to the Bible, the perfect garden where Adam and Eve were placed at the Creation [12C. Via Old French and late Latin *paradisus* < Greek *paradeisos* 'enclosed place, park' < Avestan *pairidaeza* 'to form around' < *diz* 'to form'.] —**paradisaical** *adj* —**paradisaically** *adv* —**paradisal** /párrə dīss'l/, -díz'l/ *adj* —**paradisiacal** *adj* —**paradisiacally** *adv*

LITERARY LINK *Paradise Lost*, an epic poem (1667) by John Milton. This monumental work describes Satan's rebellion against God, his corruption of Adam and Eve, and their subsequent expulsion from the Garden of Eden. The sustained brilliance of its language, structure, characterization, and imagery makes it arguably the greatest epic poem in English literature. A sequel, *Paradise Regained*, was published in 1671.

paradise duck *n* a large duck, the male of which is dark-coloured with a black head, while the female is chestnut-coloured with a white head and wing patches. Native to: New Zealand. *Tadorna variegata*. [< its bright colours]

paradise flycatcher *n* a brightly coloured flycatcher, the male of which has a very long slender forked tail. Native to: Asia. Genus: *Terpsiphone*.

parador /párrə dawr/ *n* **1** a tourist hotel in Spain, operated by the national government and usually located in a castle, monastery, convent, or other historic site **2** a privately owned and operated hotel or resort in Latin America [Mid-19C. < Spanish, < *parar* 'stop, stay' < Latin *parare* 'prepare'.]

parados /párrə doss/ *n* a bank built up behind a trench or other fortification that gives protection from attack from the rear [Mid-19C. < French, 'defend the back' < *dos* 'back'.]

paradox /párrə doks/ *n* **1 SOMETHING ABSURD OR CONTRADICTORY** a statement, proposition, or situation that seems to be absurd or contradictory, but in fact is or may be true **2 SELF-CONTRADICTORY STATEMENT** a statement or proposition that contradicts itself **3 PERSON OF OPPOSITES** a person with seemingly self-contradictory qualities [Mid-16C. Via Latin *paradoxum* < Greek *paradoxos* 'contrary to opinion' < *doxa* 'opinion' < *dokein* 'think'.] —**paradoxical** /párrə dóksik'l/ *adj* —**paradoxically** /-dóksikli/ *adv* —**paradoxicalness** *n*

paradoxical frog *n* a frog of the Amazon forest and the island of Trinidad. The adult frog is less than a third the size of the tadpole. *Pseudis paradoxa*.

paradoxical sleep *n* MED = **REM sleep** [Because its electrical brain patterns resemble those of the waking state]

paradrop /párrə drop/ *n* the delivery of personnel, materials, provisions, or other supplies to a place by attaching them to a parachute and dropping them from an aircraft ■ vt to deliver somebody or something to a place by paradrop

paraesthesia /párress theezi ə/ *n* an abnormal or unexplained tingling, pricking, or burning sensation on the skin [Late 19C. < PARA-1 + Greek *aesthēsis* 'feeling'.]

paraffin /párrəfin/ *n* **1** a mixture of liquid hydrocarbons obtained from petroleum and used as a domestic heating fuel and as fuel for aircraft. ◊ **kerosene 2** CHEM = **alkane 3** INDUST = **paraffin wax 4** vt to treat something by saturating, impregnating, or coating it with paraffin or paraffin wax [Mid-19C. < Latin *parum* 'little' + *affinis* 'related', because it is not closely related to any other substance.] —**paraffinic** /párrə fínnik/ *adj*

paraffin oil *n* INDUST = **paraffin** *n*. 1

paraffin wax *n* a white waxy solid mixture of hydrocarbons. Source: petroleum. Use: in making candles, pharmaceuticals, and cosmetics, as a sealing agent.

~~parafin~~ incorrect spelling of **paraffin**

paraformaldehyde /párrə fawr máldi hīd/, **paraform** /párrə fawrm/ *n* a white combustible polymer of formaldehyde. Use: disinfectant, fungicide, in contraceptive creams.

paragliding /párrə glīding/ *n* a sport in which a person jumps from an aircraft or an elevation wearing a rectangular parachute that allows control of direction in the descent to the ground [< PARA2] —**paraglider** *n*

paragoge /párrə gog/, **paragogue** *n* the addition of a letter, sound, or syllable at the end of a word as a word develops, e.g. the 's' in 'towards' [Mid-16C. Via late Latin < Greek *paragōgē* 'carrying beyond' < *agōgē* 'carrying'.] —**paragogic** /párrə gójjik/ *adj* —**paragogically** /-gójjikli/ *adv*

paragon /párrəgon/ *n* **1** somebody or something that is the very best example of something **2** a perfect diamond that weighs at least 100 carats [Mid-16C. Via archaic French < Italian *paragone*, originally 'touchstone to test gold' < medieval Greek *parakonan* 'sharpen against'.]

paragraph /párrə graaf, -graf/ *n* **1 SECTION OF WRITING** a piece of writing that consists of one or more sentences, begins on a new and often indented line, and contains a distinct idea or the words of one speaker **2 SHORT NEWS STORY** a short item of news or editorial comment in a newspaper ■ vt **1 SET OUT IN PARAGRAPHS** to arrange something in a series of paragraphs **2 WRITE NEWS IN A PARAGRAPH** to report news or a story in a short paragraph [15C. Via Old French < Greek *paragraphos* 'stroke marking a line in which there is a break in sense', literally 'writing beside' < *graphein* 'write'.] —**paragrapher** *n*

paragraphia /párrə gráffi ə, -graafi-/ *n* the writing of words or letters different from the ones intended, as a result of a stroke or disease [Late 19C. < PARA-1 + Greek *-graphia* 'writing'.]

Paraguay[1] /párrə gwī/ republic in south-central South America. Capital: Asunción. Population: 5,504,146 (1996). Area: 406,752 sq. km/157,048 sq. mi. —**Paraguayan** *n*, *adj*

Paraguay[2] river in SW Brazil and Paraguay. Length: 2,550 km/1,580 mi.

Parahyba /párrə eébə/ former name for **João Pessoa**

parahydrogen /párrə hídrəjən/ *n* a form of molecular hydrogen in which the two atomic nuclei spin in opposite directions

Paraguay

para-influenza virus *n* any of four viruses, similar to the influenza virus, that cause respiratory illnesses, especially in children, with symptoms of severe sore throat, croup, and pneumonia

parakeet /párrə keet/ *n* a small tropical parrot that has a long tail and is usually very brightly coloured [Mid-16C. Anglicization of Old French *paraquet*.]

paralanguage /párrə lang gwij/ *n* nonverbal vocal elements in communication that may add a nuance of meaning to language as it is used in context, e.g. tone of voice or whispering

paraldehyde /pə ráldi hīd/ *n* $C_6H_{12}O_3$ a colourless liquid polymer of acetaldehyde. Use: sedative, solvent.

paralegal /párrə leèg'l/ *n* somebody with specialist legal training who assists a fully qualified lawyer ■ *adj* relating to a paralegal or the work of a paralegal

~~paralel~~ incorrect spelling of **parallel**

paralinguistics /párrə ling gwístiks/ *n* the study of paralanguage (+ *singular verb*) —**paralinguistic** *adj*

paralipomena /párrə lī pómmənə/ *npl* material added to a literary work as a supplement [Late 17C. Via late Latin (plural) < Greek *paralipomena* '(things) left out' < *leipein* 'leave'.]

Paralipomena /párrə lī pómmənə/ *npl* the title used for the Book of Chronicles in the Vulgate (*sometimes singular*) [14C. Via ecclesiastical Latin < Greek *paraleipein* 'leave to one side' (because it contains material omitted from the Books of Kings).]

Paralipomenon singular of **Paralipomena**

paralipsis /párrə lípsiss/ (*plural* **paralipses** /-seez/), **paraleipsis** /-lípsiss/ (*plural* **paraleipses** /-seez/) *n* a rhetorical technique of emphasizing a topic by saying in some way that you will not talk about it, e.g. by using the phrase 'not to mention' [Mid-16C. Via late Latin < Greek *paraleipsis* 'omission' < *paraleipein* 'leave on one side' < *leipein* 'leave'.]

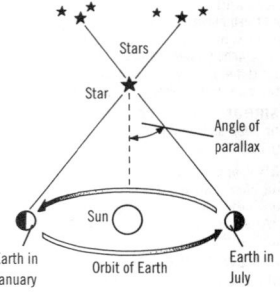
Parallax

parallax /párrə laks/ *n* **1** an apparent change in the position of an object when the person looking at the object changes position **2** the angle between two imaginary lines from two different observation points meeting at a star or astronomical object, that is used to measure its distance from the Earth [Late 16C. Via French < Greek *parallaxis* 'alternation, angle between two lines' < *parallassein* 'alter' < *allos* 'other'.] —**parallactic** /párrə láktik/ *adj* —**parallactically** /-láktikli/ *adv*

parallel /párrə lel/ *adj* **1 ALWAYS SAME DISTANCE APART** relating to or being lines, planes, or curved surfaces that are always the same distance apart and therefore never meet **2 RESEMBLING EACH OTHER** relating to two things that are comparable because they are similar and share many characteristics **3 OF IDENTICAL SYNTACTIC CONSTRUCTIONS** describes two or more phrases or clauses in a single sentence that have identical syntactic constructions **4 USING SEVERAL ITEMS OF INFORMATION SIMULTANEOUSLY** relating to a computer that processes several items of information at the same time. ◊ **serial** *adj.* 3 **5 KEEPING SAME MUSICAL INTERVAL THROUGHOUT** describes the movement of two voices or melodies that match each other exactly in pitch, while preserving the same interval between them ■ *n* **1 PARALLEL LINE OR PLANE** any of a set of parallel geometric forms, especially lines or planes **2 SOMEBODY OR SOMETHING EQUIVALENT** somebody or something that is very similar to another, sharing many characteristics **3 COMPARISON** a comparison between two things that reveals their similarity ○ *It's easy to draw a parallel between their two careers* **4 LINE PARALLEL TO THE EQUATOR** an imaginary line round the Earth that lies parallel to the equator and represents a particular degree of latitude from the equator **5 LINE ON MAP** a line on a map representing a parallel of latitude **6 CONFIGURATION OF ELECTRICAL COMPONENTS** the way in which electrical components or circuits are connected so that the same voltage is applied across each component or circuit ○ *connected in parallel* ■ *vt* **1 BE PARALLEL** to be or run parallel to something **2 MAKE SOMETHING PARALLEL TO** to make something be or run parallel to something else **3 CORRESPOND TO** to be similar to something else, especially in following a similar course of events **4 COMPARE SOMETHING TO SOMETHING ELSE** to compare something with, or show something to be similar to, something else **5 MATCH** to be equal to or as good as somebody or something else ■ *adv* **ALONGSIDE** in a parallel manner so as to keep the same distance away from something and never meet it [Mid-16C. Via French and Latin < Greek *parallēlos* 'beside each other' < *allēlōn* 'each other' < *allos* 'other'.] ◇ **in parallel (with somebody *or* something)** in conjunction with and at the same time as somebody or something else

parallel bars *npl* a piece of gymnastic equipment consisting of two horizontal bars parallel to each other and supported on vertical posts ■ *n* an event in a gymnastics competition that uses the parallel bars (*+ singular verb*)

parallel broadcast *n* a broadcast that is transmitted simultaneously by radio or television and over the Internet

parallel cousin *n* a cousin who is the child of your mother's sister or your father's brother. ◊ **cross cousin**

parallelepiped /párrə lellə pí ped, -le léppi-/ *n* a polyhedron consisting of six faces that are parallelograms [Late 16C. < Greek *parallēlepipedon* 'parallel surface' < *epipedon* 'surface' < *pedon* 'ground'.]

paralleling /párrə leling/ *n* the exploitation of differences in commercial markets by buying an expensive product in a place where prices are relatively low and selling it on in a place where prices are higher

parallelism /párrə lelizəm/ *n* **1 PARALLEL STATE** the condition of being parallel **2 REPETITION FOR EFFECT** in writing, the deliberate repetition of particular words or sentence structures for effect **3 THEORY OF MIND-BODY RELATIONSHIP** the philosophical theory that mind and body do not interact but follow separate parallel tracks, without any relationship of cause and effect existing between the two —**parallelist** *n*

parallel of latitude *n* GEOG = **parallel** *n.* 4

parallelogram /párrə lélla gram/ *n* a four-sided plane figure in which both pairs of opposite sides are parallel and of equal length, and the opposite angles are equal [Late 16C. Via late Latin < Greek *parallēlogrammon* < *parallēlos* 'parallel'.]

parallel play *n* play in which two or more children who are in close proximity and possibly involved in similar activities do not interact with each other socially

parallel port *n* a connection point through which a computer sends and receives data simultaneously by means of a number of separate wires, commonly used for connecting a printer or external storage device [Because it transfers data over more than one channel at the same time]

parallel processing *n* the use of two or more processors to run different parts of the same computer program concurrently and merge the results, with significantly faster program execution [Because instructions are sent to multiple processors at the same time]

parallel ruler *n* a ruler designed for drawing parallel lines, constructed with two linked straight edges that remain parallel although the distance between them may be varied

parallel turn *n* a skiing turn executed by shifting the body weight and keeping the skis parallel, rather than by adjusting the line of the skis

paralogism /pə rállәjizəm/ *n* in logic, an invalid argument that is unintentional or that has gone unnoticed [Mid-16C. Via late Latin *paralogismus* < Greek *paralogos* 'contrary to reason' < *logos* 'reason'.] —**paralogist** *n* —**paralogistic** /pə rállə jístik/ *adj*

Paralympic Games /párrə límpik-/, **Paralympics** /párrə límpiks/ *npl* an international sports competition for disabled athletes —**Paralympian** *n*

paralyse /párrə līz/ (**-lyses, -lysing, -lysed**) *vt* **1 DEPRIVE OF VOLUNTARY MOVEMENT** to cause somebody to lose the ability to move a part of the body, either by damaging nerve or muscle function, or through the use of a drug **2 MAKE TEMPORARILY UNABLE TO MOVE** to make somebody temporarily unable to move, e.g. with fear **3 BRING SYSTEM TO STANDSTILL** to bring a system or network to a stop or prevent it from functioning effectively [Late 18C. Via French *paralyser* < Latin *paralysis* (see PARALYSIS).]

paralysis /pə rálləssiss/ *n* **1** loss of voluntary movement as a result of damage to nerve or muscle function **2** failure to take action or make progress [Pre-12C. Via Latin < Greek *paralusis* < *paraluesthai* 'be disabled' < *para-* 'on one side' + *luein* 'release'.]

paralysis agitans /-ájji tanz/ *n* MED = **Parkinson's disease** [*Agitans* < Latin, present participle of *agitare* 'shake']

paralytic /párrə líttik/ *adj* **1 DRUNK** extremely drunk (*informal*) **2 OF PARALYSIS** relating to loss of voluntary movement ■ *n* **OFFENSIVE TERM** an offensive term for somebody affected by loss of voluntary movement [14C. Via Old French and Latin < Greek *paralutikos* < *paralusis* (see PARALYSIS).] —**paralytically** *adv*

paralyze *vt* US = **paralyse**

paramagnetic /párrə mag néttik/ *adj* describes a substance that is weakly magnetized so that it will lie parallel to a magnetic field. ◊ **ferromagnetic** —**paramagnetism** /párrə mágnətizəm/ *n*

Paramaribo /párrə márribō/ capital of Suriname, in the north of the country. Population: 180,000 (1994).

paramatta /párrə máttə/, **parramatta** *n* a lightweight fabric made from wool blended with silk or cotton [Early 19C. After the settlement of *Parramatta* in New South Wales, Australia.]

paramecium /párrə meéssi əm/ (*plural* **paramecia** /-si ə/ *or* **-ums**) *n* a single-celled microscopic aquatic organism (**protozoan**) with fine appendages (**cilia**) around its body that it uses to move around and to capture bacteria. Genus: *Paramecium.* [Mid-18C. < modern Latin < Greek *paramēkēs* 'oval'; from its shape.]

paramedic /párrə méddik/ *n* **1** somebody trained to perform emergency medical procedures in the absence of a doctor, especially a member of an ambulance crew **2** somebody whose work supports that of doctors and nurses, e.g. a radiologist or a laboratory technician —**paramedical** *adj*

parameter /pə rámmitər/ *n* **1 LIMITING FACTOR** a fact or circumstance that restricts how something is done or what can be done ○ *working within the parameters of cost and manpower* **2 VARIABLE QUANTITY DETERMINING OUTCOME** a measurable quantity, e.g. temperature, that determines the result of a scientific experiment and can be altered to vary the result **3** ⚠ **NOTABLE CHARACTERISTIC** a distinguishing feature or notable characteristic. **4 VARIABLE MATHEMATICAL VALUE** in a mathematical expression, a variable value that, when it changes, gives another different but related mathematical expression from a limited series of such expressions **5 OVERALL QUANTITY** a general quantity that relates to an entire population, as distinct from an individual statistic that relates to a sample [Mid-17C. < modern Latin *parametrum* < PARA-[1] + Greek *metron* 'measure'.] —**parametric** /párrə méttrik/ *adj*

USAGE ***Parameter***, which has special meanings in science, mathematics, and statistics, has taken on a general sense 'a limiting factor', as in *had to adhere to all the parameters of tax law with regard to the establishment of family trusts and foundations.* This meaning, along with the others, is acceptable. Some people, however, object to yet another general meaning of the word, 'a distinguishing feature or notable characteristic', as in *An important parameter in their culture is vegetarianism*, where *characteristic* or *feature* would be more precise and less pompous. Avoid confusing ***parameter*** with *perimeter* ('boundary'): *Guards patrolled the perimeter* [not *parameter*] *of the military installation.*

parametric equalizer *n* a device used with audio equipment to cut or boost selected frequencies of an output signal by continuously widening or narrowing the filtered frequencies of the signal. ◊ **graphic equalizer**

parametric equations *npl* a set of mathematical equations in which coordinates of points are explicitly expressed in terms of independent parameters

paramilitary /párrə míllitəri/ *adj* **1 USING MILITARY TECHNIQUES** using military weapons and tactics to fight within a country against the official ruling power **2 MILITARY IN STYLE** similar to or modelled on the military but not belonging to it **3 ASSISTING OFFICIAL MILITARY FORCES** organized and staffed by civilians to provide support for the regular military services ○ *a paramilitary unit* ■ *n* (*plural* **-ies**) **UNOFFICIAL SOLDIER** a member of a paramilitary organization, especially one fighting against the official ruling power

paramnesia /párram neézi ə/ *n* **1** false memories of events that did not really take place **2** an inability to recall the meanings of common words

paramorph /párrə mawrf/ *n* a mineral formed by the conversion of one crystalline form (**polymorph**) into another —**paramorphism** /párrə máwrfizəm/ *n*

paramount /párrə mownt/ *adj* greatest in importance or significance [Mid-16C. < Anglo-Norman *paramont* < *par* 'by' + *amont* 'above'.] —**paramountcy** *n* —**paramountly** *adv*

paramour /párrə moor/ *n* a lover, especially one in a relationship with a married person (*literary*) ○ *'found thee out even in the arms of thy paramour'* (Sir Walter Scott, *Ivanhoe*; 1819) [14C. < *par amur* 'passionately' < Anglo-Norman *par amour* 'by way of love'.]

paramyxovirus /párrə míksō vīrəss/ *n* a virus belonging to the group that includes the mumps and measles viruses and the parainfluenza virus

Paraná /párrə naá/ **1** river flowing southwards from SW Brazil through east-central South America into the Río de la Plata in Argentina. Length: 2,800 km/1,740 mi. **2** city in NE Argentina. Population: 206,848 (1991).

parang /paá rang/ *n* a large knife with a short straight-edged blade, used in Malaysia and Indonesia as a weapon and as a tool [Mid-19C. < Malay.]

paranoia /párrə nóy ə/ *n* **1** extreme and unreasonable suspicion of other people and their motives **2** a psychiatric disorder involving systematized delusion, usually of persecution [Early 19C. < Greek, 'out of one's mind' < *nous* 'mind'.]

paranoiac /párrə nóy ak/ *adj* characteristic of or resembling paranoia ■ *n* a person affected by paranoia

paranoid /párrə noyd/ *adj* **1 DISTRUSTFUL** obsessively anxious about something, or unreasonably suspicious of other people and their thoughts or motives **2 SHOWING CHARACTERISTICS OF PARANOIA** relating to or showing the characteristics of paranoia ■ *n* **PARANOID PERSON** a person who is paranoid (*dated*)

paranormal /párrə náwrm'l/ *adj* unable to be explained or understood in terms of scientific knowledge ■ *n* paranormal events or phenomena —**paranormally** *adv*

paraparesis /párrəpə reéssiss/ *n* a medical condition in which both legs, and often the bladder, have little voluntary control —**paraparetic** /párrəpə réttik/ *adj*

parapet /párrəpət, -pet/ *n* **1** a low protective wall built where there is a sudden dangerous drop, e.g. along the edge of a balcony, roof, or bridge **2** a bank of earth, rubble, or sandbags piled up along the edge of a military trench for protection from enemy fire [Late 16C. Via French < Italian *parapetto* < *parare* 'protect' + *petto* 'chest' < Latin *pectus*.]

paraph /párrəf, pə ráff/ *n* a decorative flourish written under a signature to finish it off or, formerly, to protect against forgery [Late 16C. Via French < medieval Latin *paragraphus* 'paragraph'.]

~~**paraphanalia**~~ incorrect spelling of **paraphernalia**

paraphasia /párrə fáyzi ə/ *n* a speech defect of neurological origin in which the speaker's words are jumbled unintelligibly. ◊ **aphasia**

paraphernalia /párrəfər náyli ə/ *n* **1** assorted objects or items of equipment, often things that seem amusing, strange, or irritating **2** formerly, items of property given to a wife on her wedding day by her new husband and regarded by law as belonging to her [Mid-17C. Via medieval Latin < Greek *parapherne* 'beside the dowry' < *pherne* 'dowry'.]

paraphilia /párrə filli ə/ *n* the need for an extreme or dangerous stimulus, e.g. a sadistic or masochistic practice, in order to achieve sexual arousal or orgasm — **paraphiliac** *n*

paraphrase /párrə frayz/ *vt* (**-phrases, -phrasing, -phrased**) to restate something using other words, especially in order to make it simpler or shorter ■ *n* written or spoken material that is rephrased and simplified through being made shorter [Mid-16C. Via French < Greek *paraphrazein* 'explain alongside' < *phrazein* 'explain'.] —**paraphraser** *n* —**paraphrastic** /párrə frástik/ *adj*

paraplegia /párrə pleéjə/ *n* total inability to move both legs and usually the lower part of the trunk, often as a result of disease or injury of the spine. ◊ **hemiplegia, quadriplegia** [Mid-17C. Via modern Latin < Greek *paraplēgiē* 'stroke on one side' < *paraplēssein* 'strike on one side' < *plessein* 'to strike'.] —**paraplegic** *adj, n*

paraprofessional /párrəprə fésh'nəl/ *n US* a trained assistant to a professional person

parapsychology /párrə sī kólləji/ *n* the study of supposed mental phenomena that cannot be explained by known psychological or scientific principles, e.g. extrasensory perception and telepathy —**parapsychological** /párrə sīkə lójjik'l/ *adj* —**parapsychologist** /</ *n*

paraquat /párrə kwot/ *n* a widely used, fast-acting weedkiller that destroys green plant tissue on contact

parasailing /párrə sayling/ *n* a sport in which a waterskier wearing a parachute or holding onto a type of hang-glider is towed along behind a motorboat and rises up into the air [Mid-20C. < PARA-² + SAIL.]

parascending /párrə sending/ *n* a sport in which somebody wearing an open parachute is towed along by a speedboat or land vehicle, rises into the air, and descends independently using the parachute [Late 20C. < PARA-² + ASCEND.]

parascience /párrə sī ənss/ *n* the study of phenomena that cannot be explained or tested by conventional scientific methods

paraselene /párrəsi leéni/ (*plural* **-nae** /-nee/) *n* an image of the Moon seen within a lunar halo [Mid-17C. < PARA-¹ + Greek *selēnē* 'moon'.] —**paraselenic** /párrəsi lénnik/ *adj*

parasexual /párrə sékshoo əl/ *adj* describes a type of reproduction, seen in certain fungi, in which the recombination of parental chromosomes takes place without the usual formation of sex cells by cell division (**meiosis**) —**parasexuality** /párrə sekshoo álləti/ *n*

Parashah /párrə shaa/ (*plural* **Parashoth** /-shōt/) *n* in Judaism, a passage from the Torah read during traditional weekly worship at the synagogue [Early 17C. < Hebrew *pārāšāh* 'division'.]

parasite /párrə sīt/ *n* **1** a plant or animal that lives on or in another, usually larger, host organism in a way that harms or is of no advantage to the host **2** a person who exploits others without doing anything in return [Mid-16C. Via Latin < Greek *parasitos* 'one who eats from another's table' < *sitos* 'grain, food'.]

parasitic /párrə síttik/, **parasitical** /párrə síttik'l/ *adj* **1** living in or on another host organism, usually causing it harm **2** living off the generosity of others without offering anything in return —**parasitically** *adv*

parasiticide /párrə sítti sīd/ *adj* used or designed to destroy parasites ■ *n* a substance used to destroy parasites —**parasiticidal** /párrə sítti sīd'l/ *adj*

parasitise *vt* = **parasitize**

parasitism /párrə sītizəm/ *n* **1** symbiosis in which one organism lives as a parasite in or on another organism **2** VET = **parasitosis**

parasitize /párrəssi tīz, -sī tīz/ (**-izes, -izing, -ized**), **parasitise** (**-ises, -ising, -ised**) *vt* to infest an animal or plant as a parasite, or to live on it as a parasite

parasitoid /párrəssi toyd, -sī toyd/ *adj* describes an insect that lays its eggs inside the living body of another animal or insect. The hatched newborns feed off the body, eventually killing the host. ■ *n* an insect that lays its eggs within a host, eventually causing the death of the host

parasitology /párrə sī tólləji/ *n* the scientific study of plants and animals that live as parasites —**parasitological** /párrə sītə lójjik'l/ *adj*

parasitosis /párrə sī tōsiss/ (*plural* **-ses** /-seez/) *n* a disease that develops as a result of infestation by parasites

paraskiing /párrə skee ing/ *n* the sport of skiing off high mountains and descending through the air using a light steerable parachute made of inflatable tubes of fabric [Mid-20C. < PARA² + SKI.]

parasol /párrə sol/ *n* an umbrella made to provide shade from the sun [Early 17C. Via French < Italian *parasole* < *parare* 'protect' + *sole* 'sun'.]

parastatal /párrə stáyt'l/ *adj* performing a function usually associated with a government and under its indirect control ■ *n* a parastatal organization, business, or industry

parasuicide /párrə soó i sīd/ *n* **1** a suicide attempt or act of self-injury that is motivated by a desire to draw attention to other personal problems rather than by a genuine wish to die **2** a person who carries out a parasuicide

parasympathetic /párrə simpə théttik/ *adj* relating or belonging to the parasympathetic nervous system

parasympathetic nervous system *n* one of the two divisions in the part of the nervous system that controls involuntary and unconscious bodily functions (**autonomic nervous system**). ◊ **sympathetic nervous system**

parasynthesis /párrə sínthississ/ (*plural* **-ses** /-seez/) *n* the formation of words by a combination of smaller words and additional elements —**parasynthetic** /párrəsin théttik/ *adj*

parasyntheton /párrə sínthi ton/ (*plural* **-ta** /-tə/) *n* a word formed by the combination of smaller words and additional elements

parataxis /párrə táksiss/ *n* the combination of clauses or phrases without the use of conjunctions such as 'and' or 'so', e.g. in 'He saved my life – he deserves a medal'. ◊ **asyndeton** [Mid-19C. < Greek < *paratassein* 'place side by side' < *tassein* 'arrange'.] —**paratactic** /párrə táktik/ *adj* —**paratactically** *adv*

paratha /pə raátə/ *n* a flat unleavened bread of Indian origin, made from flour, water, and clarified butter [Mid-20C. < Hindi *parāṭhā*.]

parathion /párrə thī on/ *n* $C_{10}H_{14}NO_5PS$ a colourless highly toxic oil. Use: insecticide. [Mid-20C. < PARA-¹ + *thiophosphate* + -ON¹.]

parathormone /párrə tháwr mōn/ *n* PHYSIOL = **parathyroid hormone** [Early 20C. Contraction.]

parathyroid /párrə thī royd/ *adj* **1** relating to or produced by the parathyroid glands **2** in the area around the thyroid gland ■ *n* PHYSIOL = **parathyroid gland**

parathyroid gland *n* any of four small glands that lie in or near the walls of the thyroid gland and secrete a hormone that controls the depositing of calcium and phosphorus in bones

parathyroid hormone *n* a hormone secreted by the parathyroid glands that controls calcium and phosphorus balance in the body

paratrooper /párrə troopər/ *n* a soldier trained to go into battle by parachute, especially one who is also a member of an airborne unit —**paratroop** *adj* —**paratroops** *npl*

paratyphoid fever /párrə tī foyd-/ *n* an infectious bacterial disease similar to typhoid but with much less severe symptoms, usually limited to a pink rash, diarrhoea, and some abdominal pain

paravane /párrə vayn/ *n* a torpedo-shaped device with sharp fins at the front, towed by a ship to cut the moorings of submerged mines [Early 20C. < *para-* 'protector' (after PARASOL) + VANE.]

par avion /-ávvi on/ *adv* by air mail [< French, 'by aeroplane']

paraxial /pə ráksi əl/ *adj* describes rays of light that are close to the axis of an optical system [Mid-19C. < PARA-¹ + AXIS¹, after AXIAL.]

parazoan /párrə zō ən/ (*plural* **-a** /-ə/) *n* a member of the subkingdom of invertebrate animals that includes sponges. Subkingdom: *Parazoa*. [Early 20C. < modern Latin, < PARA-¹ after PROTOZOAN, METAZOAN.]

parboil /paár boyl/ *vt* to boil something, especially a vegetable, until it is partly cooked, usually before frying or roasting it [15C. Via Old French *parboillir* 'boil thoroughly' < Latin *bullire* 'boil'.]

parbuckle /paár buk'l/ *n* a rope sling for lifting or lowering barrels, logs, or similar objects [Early 17C. < ?]

Parcae /paár see/ *npl* in Roman mythology, the Fates. Greek equivalent **Moirai** [Late 16C. < Latin.]

parcel /paárss'l/ *n* **1** SOMETHING WRAPPED UP one or more things wrapped up together in paper or other packaging **2** PORTION any of the portions into which something is divided, especially a piece of land that was originally part of a larger area **3** BATCH OF COMMERCIAL GOODS a specific quantity of wholesale merchandise, or a sales transaction involving such a batch ■ *vt* (**-cels, -celling, -celled**) **1** MAKE PARCEL OF to wrap something or a group of things into a parcel **2** PROTECT ROPE to bind canvas tightly round rope or cable to protect it [14C. Via Old French < Latin *particula* 'small part'.]

parcel out *vt* to divide and distribute something between a number of people

parcel-gilt *adj* partly gilded, often on the inside but not on the outside

parcel post *n* a postal service that collects, processes, and delivers parcels

parch /paarch/ *vt* to make somebody or something extremely dry through water deprivation or exposure to heat [14C. < ?]

parched /paarcht/ *adj* **1** very thirsty (*informal*) **2** completely lacking in moisture because of hot conditions or lack of rainfall

SYNONYMS See ***dry***.

parchment /paárchmənt/ *n* **1** FORMER WRITING MATERIAL a creamy or yellowish material made from dried and treated sheepskin, goatskin, or other animal hide, used in former times for books and documents **2** DOCUMENT a manuscript or other work written, drawn, or painted on a sheet of parchment **3** HIGH-QUALITY PAPER strong, smooth or textured, usually off-white paper used for special documents, letters, or artwork [13C. < Old French *parchemin*, via Latin *pergamena* < Greek *Pergamon*, the city of Pergamum in Asia Minor.]

parclose /paár klōz/ *n* a screen or railing that separates or encloses a side chapel, private tomb, or other special area within a large church [15C. < Old French, past participle of *parclore* 'close off' < Latin *claudere* 'to close'.]

parcourse /paár kawrss/ *n US* a training circuit in a park or other open space, where people can walk or run between stations carrying equipment and instructions for specific fitness exercises [Partial translation of French *parcours* 'course', loan translation of medieval Latin *percursus* 'running through' < *percurrere* 'run through']

pard¹ /paard/ *n* a large cat, especially a leopard or a panther (*archaic*) [13C. Via Old French < Greek *pardos*, < Iranian.]

pard² /paard/ *n US* = **pardner** (*slang*) [Mid-19C. Shortening.]

pardner /paárdnər/ *n US* used to address a friend, in imitation of the cowboy's supposed pronunciation of the word 'partner' (*slang*)

pardon /paárd'n/ *vt* **1** FORGIVE SOMEBODY FOR WRONGDOING to pronounce the official release from punishment of somebody who has committed a crime or other wrongdoing, or the official forgiving of a crime or wrongdoing **2** EXCUSE SOMEBODY FOR SOMETHING IMPOLITE to excuse somebody for doing something impolite, or to excuse something impolite, such as interrupting or contradicting somebody ■ *n* **1** RELEASE FROM PUNISHMENT the act of officially releasing somebody guilty of a crime or wrongdoing from facing punishment **2** PAPER AUTHORIZING FREEDOM FROM PUNISHMENT an official document stating that somebody may be released without receiving any, or any further, punishment **3** ACT OF EXCUSING the excusing of an impolite act or the forgiving of the person committing it **4** INDULGENCE an indulgence (*dated informal*) ■ *interj* **1** WHAT DID YOU SAY? used as a request to somebody to repeat something that has just been said **2** EXPRESS APOLOGY used as an apology for doing something impolite or wrong [13C. Via Old French *pardun* (noun) and *pardoner* (verb) 'grant thoroughly' < Latin *donare* 'give, grant'.] —**pardonable** *adj* —**pardonably** *adv* ◇ **pardon me 1** used as an apology for doing something impolite or wrong **2** *US* used as a request to somebody to repeat something that has just been said

pardoner /paárd'nər/ *n* **1** a granter of a pardon **2** somebody who, in medieval times, made a living by selling papal indulgences that were believed to free people from their sins

pare /pair/ (**pares, paring, pared**) *vt* **1** to trim something such as fingernails or toenails **2** to remove the skin or outer layer of something such as a vegetable or fruit thinly and neatly [13C. Via Old French *parer* 'prepare, trim' < Latin *parare*.]

SPELLCHECK See *pair*.

pare down *vt* to reduce a total amount or number, usually an amount of money or a number of workers, slowly and steadily

paregoric /párrə górrik/ *n* a camphorated tincture of opium, once a major source of opium addiction. Use: formerly, a nonprescription painkiller. ■ *adj* soothing or painkilling [Late 17C. Via late Latin < Greek *parēgorikos* 'soothing' < *para* 'beside' + *agoreuein* 'speak'.]

parenchyma /pə réngkimə/ *n* **1** PLANT TISSUE soft plant tissue made up of thin-walled cells that forms the greater part of leaves, stem pith, roots, and fruit pulp **2** SPECIALIZED ORGAN TISSUE the tissue that makes up the specialized parts of particular organs, rather than the blood vessels and connective or supporting tissue **3** WORM TISSUE the loose meshwork of cells that surrounds internal organs and fills spaces inside the body of animals such as flatworms [Mid-17C. Via modern Latin < Greek *paregkhuma* 'soft tissue' < *paregkhein* 'pour in beside' < *khein* 'pour'.] —**parenchymatous** /párren kímmətəss/ *adj*

parent /páirənt/ *n* **1** MOTHER OR FATHER somebody's mother, father, or legal guardian **2** ORIGIN OF SOMETHING ELSE something from which one or more similar and separate things have developed, or to which they are attached (*often before nouns*) ○ *money transferred from the parent fund* **3** EARLIER ATOMIC FORM an atom, molecule, or ion that undergoes change to become a new product. The starting components in a chemical reaction are the parent molecules. (*often before nouns*) **4** PARTICLE'S EARLIER FORM a radioactive particle that disintegrates to give a new particle (**nuclide**) as a subsequent member of a radioactive decay series (*often before nouns*) ■ *vt* ACT AS PARENT TO to be or act as a parent to somebody or something [15C. Via Old French < Latin *parent-*, present participle of *parere* 'give birth'.] —**parenthood** *n*

parentage /páirəntij/ *n* **1** the parents or ancestors of a particular person, especially when regarded in terms of social characteristics ○ *tends to determine his parentage* ○ *of Irish parentage* **2** the particular origins or sources that something has developed from

parental /pə rént'l/ *adj* **1** relating to, belonging to, or provided by parents **2** describes the original generation of individuals from which all subsequent generations have been bred —**parentally** *adv*

parental leave *n* time off from work, granted to a parent to care for a newborn or newly adopted child

parenteral /pa réntərəl/ *adj* **1** describes drug administration other than by the mouth or the rectum, e.g. by injection, infusion, or implantation **2** describes drugs that are administered by injection, infusion, or implantation [Early 20C. < PARA-[1] + Greek *enteron* 'intestine'.] —**parenterally** *adv*

parenthesis /pə rénthississ/ (*plural* **-ses** /-seez/) *n* **1** PRINTING = **bracket** *n.* **1 2** BRACKETED MATTER a word or phrase that comments on or qualifies part of the sentence in which it is found and is isolated from it by brackets or dashes **3** DEPARTURE FROM TOPIC a piece of speech or writing that wanders off from the main topic **4** INTERVAL something that acts as a pause or break in something (*formal*) [Mid-16C. Via late Latin < Greek, < *parentithenai* 'insert' < *tithenai* 'to place'.] ◇ **in parenthesis** as an additional qualifying, explanatory, or otherwise separate comment

parenthesize /pə rénthə sīz/ (**-sizes, -sizing, -sized**), **parenthesise** (**-sises, -sising, -sised**) *v* **1** *vt* PUT SOMETHING IN BRACKETS to enclose part of a written or printed passage in brackets **2** *vt* ADD SOMETHING AS EXTRA COMMENT to add a word, phrase, or opinion as an extra comment that is not wholly related to what is being said **3** *vti* INSERT EXTRA COMMENTS to break up speech or writing with extra comments added throughout

parenthetical /párrən théttik'l/, **parenthetic** /párrən théttik/ *adj* **1** added as an extra comment or parenthesis **2** describes writing that uses or contains additional comments or notes added as parentheses —**parenthetically** *adv*

parenting /páirənting/ *n* the experiences, skills, qualities, and responsibilities involved in being a parent and in teaching and caring for a child (*often before nouns*) ○ *parenting skills*

parent metal *n* in welding, the metal of any of the components that are to be welded together

parents' evening *n* an evening meeting at which teachers make themselves available in school for parents to discuss their children's progress

Parent-Teacher Association *n* a school body run by teachers and parents to organize fundraising and social events and encourage cooperation and understanding

Parer /párrər/, **Damien Peter** (1912–44) Australian photographer and film director

parergon /pə rúr gon/ (*plural* **-ga** /-gə/) *n* one thing that exists as an addition or as an additional detail to something else, especially an employment or activity that is subsidiary to a person's main occupation (*archaic or literary*) [Early 17C. < Greek, < *para* 'beside' + *ergon* 'work'.]

paresis /pə réessiss, párrississ/ *n* muscular weakness or partial inability to move caused by disease of the nervous system [Late 17C. < Greek, 'letting go' < *para* 'aside' + *hienai* 'to throw'.]

paresthesia *n* US = **paraesthesia**

pareu /paa ráy oo/ *n* a length of fabric worn wrapped round the hips by both men and women in Polynesian countries [Mid-19C. < Tahitian.]

pareve /paárəvə/, **parveh** /paárvə/, **parve** *adj* describes a food that, under Jewish law, is neither a dairy nor a meat product and can therefore be eaten with either as part of the same meal. ◊ **fleishig** [Mid-20C. < Yiddish.]

par excellence /paar éksə laaNss, -éksə laáNss, -éksələnss/ *adj* of the very best kind or highest quality [< French, 'by virtue of preeminence']

parfait /paar fáy/ (*plural* **-faits** *or* **-fait**) *n* a rich dessert consisting of frozen whipped cream or rich ice cream flavoured with fruit [Late 19C. Via French, 'perfect' < Latin *perfectus*.]

parfleche /paár flesh/ *n US, Can* **1** the hide of an animal, soaked and scraped to remove the hair, then stretched and dried, but not tanned **2** a shield, bag, or other item made of parfleche [Early 19C. < Canadian French, < French *parer* 'defend' + *flèche* 'arrow'.]

parget /paárjit/ *n* **1** PLASTER FOR WALLS OR CHIMNEYS plaster, whitewash, roughcast, or any similar material used to coat walls or line chimneys **2** PLASTERWORK ornamental plasterwork on a wall ■ *vt* COAT SOMETHING WITH PARGET to cover walls, line chimneys, or decorate a surface with parget [14C. Alteration (influenced by Old French *parjeter* 'throw about') of Old French *porgeter* 'plaster a wall' < *jeter* 'to throw'.] —**pargeting** *n*

parhelia plural of **parhelion**

parhelic circle /paar héelik-, -héllik-/ *n* a luminous horizontal band in the sky that passes through the Sun and is caused by the Sun's rays reflecting off ice crystals in the atmosphere

parhelion /paar héeli ən/ (*plural* **-a** /-li ə/) *n* a bright coloured spot on a parhelic circle, often seen in pairs and caused by ice crystals in the atmosphere diffracting light [Mid-17C. Via Latin < Greek *parēlion* < *para* 'beside' + *hēlios* 'sun'.] —**parheliacal** /paárhə lī́ ək'l/ *adj* —**parhelic** /paar héelik, -héllik/ *adj*

pari- *prefix* equal ○ *parisyllabic* [< Latin < *par* 'equal']

pariah /pə rī́ ə/ *n* **1** a despised and avoided person **2** in India and Myanmar, a member of a caste that is lower than the four main Hindu castes, usually doing domestic or agricultural work [Early 17C. < Tamil *paraiyan* 'drummer' < *parai* 'festival drum', because hereditary drummers belonged to this caste.]

pariah dog *n* = **pye-dog** [Because it is seen as belonging to the fringes of society]

Parian /páiri ən/ *adj* **1** OF MARBLE FROM PAROS describes a fine white marble that was mined on the Greek island of Paros in ancient times **2** OF PORCELAIN FROM PAROS describes a variety of fine porcelain used mainly to make figures and originally from the Greek island of Paros **3** OF PAROS relating to the Greek island of Paros ■ *n* SOMEBODY FROM PAROS somebody who comes from the Greek island of Paros [Mid-16C. < Latin *Parius*.]

parietal /pə rī́ ət'l/ *adj* **1** OF WALLS OF HOLLOW PART relating to the walls of any hollow part of a plant or animal such as a plant's ovary or an animal's skull **2** *US* OF IN-COLLEGE RESIDENCE relating to residence within a college ■ *n* PARIETAL PART a parietal part of a plant or animal [Early 16C. Directly or via French < late Latin *parietalis* < *paries* 'wall'.]

parietal bone *n* either of two bones, one on each side of the skull, that form a part of the sides and roof of the skull

parietal cell *n* any of the cells that make up the peptic glands of the stomach and secrete hydrochloric acid

parietal lobe *n* the middle region of each of the two hemispheres of the brain, lying beneath the crown of the skull

pari-mutuel /párri myóotyoo əl/ (*plural* **pari-mutuels** *or* **paris-mutuels**) *n US* a system of betting on horse races using an electronic machine that totals all bets, deducts management charges and taxes, and determines the final odds and payouts. ◊ **tote**[2] [< French, 'mutual wager']

paring /páiring/ *n* something such as a thin slice of fruit or vegetable peel that has been pared or cut off something larger

paring knife *n* a short tapered knife with a sharp blade designed for removing the outer skin of vegetables or fruit

pari passu /párri pássoo, paári-/ *adv* **1** at an equal rate or in an otherwise fair way, with no one person or group taking precedence over another **2** together, step for step (*literary*) [< Latin, 'with equal step']

Paris[1] /párriss/ *n* in Greek mythology, a Trojan prince whose abduction of Helen, the wife of Menelaus, started the Trojan War [Via Latin < Greek]

Paris[2] /párriss/; *French* /pa rée/ capital of France, in the north-central part of the country. Population: 2,125,246 (1999). —**Parisian** /pə rízzi ən/ *adj, n*

Paris Commune *n* the Commune of 1871, established in Paris in opposition to the national government and to what it regarded as the humiliating peace terms it negotiated to end the Franco-Prussian War

Paris green *n* $(CuO)_3As_2O_3.Cu(Cu_2H_3O_2)_2$ a bright blue-green toxic powder. Use: pigment in paints, insecticide, wood preserver. [Mid-19C. After PARIS[2].]

parish /párrish/ *n* **1** DISTRICT WITH OWN CHURCH in the Anglican, Roman Catholic, and some other churches, a division of a diocese that has its own church and clergy member (*often before nouns*) ○ *the parish priest* **2** PEOPLE OF PARISH the people who live in a particular parish **3** SMALL LOCAL GOVERNMENT UNIT the smallest defined area of local government in rural areas of England, containing a village with its own elected council [13C. Via Old French *parroche* and ecclesiastical Latin *parochia* < Greek *paroikos* 'neighbour', literally 'dwelling nearby' < *oikos* 'dwelling'.]

parish council *n* in England, a local government body that meets regularly to make decisions concerning a civil parish

parishioner /pə rísh'nər/ *n* a resident of a religious or civil parish [15C. < *parishon* < Old French *parochien* < *parroche* (see PARISH).]

parish pump *adj* of interest only to a small group in a particular area [*Parish* because use of the pump is limited to members of the local parish]

parish register *n* a book in which the births, baptisms, marriages, and burials in a parish are recorded

ϟ **parity**[1] /párriti/ *n* **1** EQUALITY equality of status or position, especially in terms of pay or rank **2** SIMILARITY BETWEEN THINGS the quality of being similar or identical **3** RELATIONSHIP BETWEEN NUMBERS a relationship of oddness or evenness between two numbers (**integers**). If two numbers are both odd or both even, they are said to have the same parity. **4** EQUALITY OF EXCHANGE RATE equivalence in the rate of exchange between several currencies **5** INTEGRITY OF TRANSMITTED DATA equivalence between computer data transmitted, e.g. by fax or e-mail, and the data received [Late 16C. Directly or via Old French *parite* < late Latin *paritas* < *par* 'equal' (see PAR).]

parity[2] /párriti/ *n* **1** the condition or fact of having given birth **2** the number of children that a particular woman has given birth to [Late 19C. < PAROUS + *-ity*.]

park /paark/ *n* **1** AREA FOR PUBLIC RECREATION a publicly owned area of land, usually with grass, trees, paths, sports fields, playgrounds, picnic areas, and other features for recreation and relaxation **2** PROTECTED AREA OF COUNTRYSIDE an area of land reserved and managed so that it remains unspoilt, undeveloped, and as natural as possible **3 PRIVATE AREA OF LAND** a large area of land attached to a country louse that forms a private estate **4 PRIVATELY OWNED RECREATION FACILITY** an area of privately owned land, developed to offer recreation or amusements to paying customers **5 BUSINESS SITE** an area of land developed for a group of related commercial enterprises ○ *a science park* **6** *US, Can* **STADIUM OR SPORTS FIELD** a sports stadium or sports field ○ *a ball park* **7 ROAD OR DISTRICT** a street or district, especially in a suburban area (*often in placenames*) **8 FOOTBALL PITCH** a football pitch (*informal*) **9 POSITION ON AUTOMATIC GEARBOX** a position on the gear selector of an automatic gearbox that acts as a brake when parking a motor vehicle **10 AREA HOUSING MILITARY VEHICLES** a designated area where military vehicles are kept, within a military base ■ *v* **1** *vti* **STOP AND LEAVE VEHICLE** to stop a motor vehicle beside or off the road and leave it there for some time **2** *vti* **MANOEUVRE MOTOR VEHICLE INTO SPACE** to manoeuvre a motor vehicle into a space in order to park it **3** *vt* **SETTLE SOMEWHERE** to sit down somewhere, usually with the intention of staying there for some time (*informal*) ○ *Just park yourself over there.* **4** *vt* **LEAVE SOMETHING SOMEWHERE** to place or leave something somewhere temporarily, especially something heavy, bulky, or unwanted (*informal*) **5** *vi US* **KISS IN PARKED CAR** to kiss and cuddle in a parked car in a quiet and secluded location (*slang*) **6** *vt* **PLACE SPACECRAFT IN ORBIT** to place a spacecraft or satellite in orbit, usually temporarily **7** *vt* **PUT ON HOLD** to stop pursuing or dealing with something temporarily ○ *I suggest we park that proposal and move on.* [13C. Via Old French *parc* < medieval Latin *parricus* < Germanic, 'enclosure'.]

LITERARY LINK ***Mansfield Park***, a novel (1814) by Jane Austen. It tells the story of young Fanny Price, who is sent to live with her wealthy relatives, the Bertrams. Fanny's warmth and moral strength, which are contrasted with her uncle's stern traditionalism and the irresponsible flirtations of her neighbours Mary and Henry Crawford, eventually win her the respect of the family and the hand of her cousin Edmund.

Park /paark/, **Sir Keith** (1892–1975) New Zealand air marshal

Park, Mungo (1771–1806) Scottish explorer

Park, Ruth (*b.* 1923) New Zealand-born Australian novelist

parka /pa̋arkə/ *n* **1** a warm, knee- or thigh-length jacket with a hood that is often lined with fur or imitation fur **2** a thick, fur-lined, hooded outer garment for Arctic conditions, pulled on over the head. Traditionally, parkas are made of animal hide and worn by the Inuit and Aleut people. [Late 18C. < Russian, 'pelt, skin jacket', < Nenets.]

park-and-ride *n* a transport scheme, designed to reduce car use in city centres, in which motorists drive to out-of-town car parks from which buses or trains run regularly into the city

park day *n US* a day on which a group of people, usually parents and children, meet for communal activities in a public park

Parker /pa̋arkər/, **Charlie** (1920–55) US jazz musician and composer. Known as **Yardbird, Bird**

Parker, Dorothy (1893–1967) US writer, critic and humorist

Parker, Theodore (1810–60) US clergyman and reformer

Parkes /paarks/ town in central New South Wales, Australia. Population: 10,094 (1996).

Parkes, Sir Henry (1815–96) Australian statesman

parkie /pa̋arki/ *n* a park keeper (*informal*)

parkin /pa̋arkin/ (*plural* **-kins** *or* **-kin**) *n N England, Scotland, NZ* a heavy moist dark ginger cake made with oatmeal and treacle [Early 19C. < ?]

parking /pa̋arking/ *n* **1 SPACE TO LEAVE VEHICLES** spaces in which vehicles may be parked **2 STOPPING AND LEAVING VEHICLE** the action of driving a road vehicle into a position beside or off the road and leaving it there **3** *US* **KISSING IN PARKED CAR** kissing and cuddling in a parked car in a quiet and secluded location (*slang*)

parking light *n* either of the two small lights on a motor vehicle used in conditions where light is poor, but not poor enough to warrant the use of headlights

parking lot *n US, Can* an open area of ground in which people can park their cars

parking meter *n* a coin-operated roadside meter that displays the length of time for which a vehicle may remain legally parked in a parking space

parking orbit *n* a temporary orbit of a spacecraft during which preparations are made for the next step in its programme

Parkinsonism /pa̋arkins'nizəm/ *n* a nervous disorder, e.g. Parkinson's disease, marked by symptoms of trembling limbs and muscular rigidity

Parkinson's disease /pa̋arkins'nz-/ *n* a progressive nervous disorder marked by symptoms of trembling hands, lifeless face, monotone voice, and a slow, shuffling walk [Late 19C. After James *Parkinson* (1755–1824), British physician.]

Parkinson's law *n* the observation that work always expands to fill the time set aside for it [Mid-20C. After the C. Northcote *Parkinson* (1909–93), British historian.]

park keeper *n* a public official who patrols, supervises, and maintains a public park

parkland /pa̋ark land/ *n* the land contained within a park, especially when the grassland contains shrubs and trees

Popperfoto

Rosa Parks

Parks /paarks/, **Rosa** (*b.* 1913) US civil rights leader

parkway /pa̋ark way/ *n US, Aus* a wide stretch of public highway with grassy areas on both sides, often divided by a grassy central reservation

parky /pa̋arki/ (**-ier, -iest**) *adj* cold or chilly (*informal*) ○ *It does get a bit parky at night.* [Late 19C. < ?]

Parl. *abbr* **1** Parliament **2 Parl., parl.** parliamentary

~~**parlament**~~ incorrect spelling of **parliament**

parlance /pa̋arlənss/ *n* **1** the style of speech or writing used by people in a particular context or profession **2** speech, especially in a conversation [Late 16C. < Old French, < *parler* 'speak'.]

parlando /paar lándō/ *adv* in a style of singing that suggests speech, usually without pitch or with less clear pitch (*musical direction*) [Late 19C. < Italian, 'speaking'.] — **parlando** *adj*

parlay /pa̋arli, -lay/ *vt* (**-lays, -laying, -layed**) *US, Can* **1 BET WINNINGS ON** to stake an original bet and its winnings on a subsequent bet **2 USE ADVANTAGE** to make good use of an asset or advantage to obtain success ■ *n US, Can* **INSTANCE OF BETTING WINNINGS** a bet in which winnings from a previous bet are gambled [Late 19C. Alteration of obsolete *paroli*, via French and Italian < Italian *parare* 'place a bet' < Latin, 'prepare'.]

parley /pa̋arli/ *vi* (**-leys, -leying, -leyed**) to talk or negotiate, especially with an enemy ■ *n* (*plural* **-leys**) a round of talks or negotiations, especially between opposing military forces [Late 16C. < Old French *parlee* < *parler* 'speak' < late Latin *parabolare* < *parabola* 'talk'.]

parliament /pa̋arləmənt/ *n* **1 LEGISLATIVE BODY** a nation's legislative body, made up of elected and sometimes non-elected representatives **2 ASSEMBLY OR CONFERENCE** an assembly or conference held to make laws or discuss something **3 ASSEMBLY OF PARLIAMENT** an assembly of a parliament, created following a general election and dissolved before the next general election [13C. < Old French *parlement* < *parler* 'speak'.]

Parliament *n* the supreme legislative body in various countries. In the United Kingdom, Parliament consists of the House of Commons and the House of Lords.

parliamentarian /pa̋arlə men táiri ən/ *n* **1** a member of a parliament **2** an expert in parliamentary procedures and parliamentary history

Parliamentarian *n* during the English Civil War, a supporter or member of Oliver Cromwell's parliamentary army against King Charles I

parliamentarianism /pa̋arlə men táiri ənizəm/ *n* government of a country by a parliament, or support for this kind of government

parliamentary /pa̋arlə méntəri/ *adj* **1** relating to parliaments, or in the form of a parliament ○ *parliamentary government* **2** describes language and behaviour considered to conform to the standards that apply to a parliament

Parliamentary Commissioner, Parliamentary Commissioner for Administration *n* POL = **ombudsman** *n.* **2**

parliamentary private secretary *n* in the United Kingdom, a member of parliament who acts as an assistant to a government minister in parliamentary dealings, especially dealings with other members of parliament

parliamentary secretary *n* in the United Kingdom, a Member of the British parliament, especially one appointed as a junior minister, who assists a Minister of the Crown in the running of a government department

~~**parliment**~~ incorrect spelling of **parliament**

parlor *n* US = **parlour**

parlour /pa̋arlər/ *n* **1 WORK PREMISES** a room or set of rooms equipped and used to provide particular goods or services (*often in combination*) ○ *a beauty parlour* **2 LIVING ROOM FOR ENTERTAINING GUESTS** a living room that is set aside for entertaining guests **3 SMALL QUIET ROOM** a room in a hotel or pub that offers more privacy and comfort than the main or public bar areas (*dated*) [13C. < Old French, < *parler* 'to talk'.]

parlour car *n* in the United States and Canada, a railway carriage containing individual reserved seats

parlour game *n* a game that can be played indoors (*dated or formal*)

parlous /pa̋arləss/ *adj* very unsafe, uncertain, or difficult (*archaic or humorous*) ■ *adv* used to emphasize the extreme or excessive nature of something (*archaic*) [14C. Shortening and alteration of *perilous*.] —**parlously** *adv* —**parlousness** *n*

Parma /pa̋armə/ city in north-central Italy. Population: 167,487 (1997 estimate).

Parmenides /paar ménni deez/ (*fl.* 500 BC) Greek philosopher

Parmesan /pa̋armi zan, -zən, -zán/ (*plural* **-sans** *or* **-san**) *n* a pale-yellow hard Italian cheese, often served grated as a garnish on pasta dishes [Mid-16C. Via French < Italian *parmigiano* 'from the city of Parma'.]

parmigiana /pa̋armi jáanə/ *adj* describes a dish that has been prepared using Parmesan cheese ○ *veal parmigiana* [Late 19C. < Italian, feminine of *parmigiano* (see PARMESAN).]

Parmigianino /pa̋armi ja néenō/, **Parmigiano** /pa̋armi jáanō/ (1503–40) Italian painter

Parnassian[1] /par nássi ən/ *adj* found in poetry or associated with poetic works (*literary*) [Mid-17C. < Latin *Parnassius* < Greek *Parnasos* 'Parnassus'.]

Parnassian[2] *n* a poet of a late 19th-century French school that advocated emotional detachment and purity of metrical form [< *Le Parnasse contemporain* (1866), a poetry anthology]

Parnassus /paar nássəss/ mountain in central Greece, north of the Gulf of Corinth. Height: 2,457 m/8,061 ft.

Parnell /paar nél/, **Charles Stewart** (1846–91) Irish politician

parochial /pə rṓki əl/ *adj* **1** concerned only with narrow local concerns without any regard for more general or wider issues **2** relating to or belonging to a parish, or to parishes [14C. Via Old French < ecclesiastical Latin *parochia* 'parish'.] —**parochialism** *n* —**parochialist** *n* —**parochially** *adv*

parochial school *n US* a private school affiliated with a church that provides children with religious instruction as well as a general education

parody /párrədi/ *n* (*plural* **-dies**) **1 AMUSING IMITATION** a piece of writing or music that deliberately copies another work in a comic or satirical way **2 PARODIES IN GENERAL** parodies as a literary or musical style or genre **3 POOR IMITATION** an attempt or imitation that is so poor that it seems ridiculous ■ *vt* (**-dies, -dying, -died**) **IMITATE COMICALLY** to write or perform a parody of somebody or something [Late 16C. Via late Latin < Greek *parōidia* < *para* 'secondary, indirect' + *ōidē* 'song'.] —**parodic** /pə róddik/ *adj* —**parodical** *adj* —**parodist** *n*

parol /pə rōl, párrəl/ *adj* describes a legal contract that is made by word of mouth only, rather than in writing ■ *n* a legal contract that is made orally only [15C. Via Anglo-Norman < Latin *parabola* 'speech, talk' (see PARABLE).]

parole /pə rōl/ *n* **1 CONDITIONAL RELEASE OF PRISONER** the early release of a prisoner, with conditions such as good behaviour and regular reporting to the authorities applying for a stated period of time ○ *He's out on parole.* **2 PRISONER'S PROMISE** the promise to fulfil set conditions, given by a prisoner released on parole **3 CONDITIONAL PERIOD** the period after a prisoner's release on parole during which the conditions of release continue to apply **4** *US* **PRISONER OF WAR'S PROMISE** a promise, given by a prisoner of war as a condition of release, either not to escape or not to take up arms again **5 REAL-WORLD LANGUAGE** language considered as the utterances of real people, as distinct from the system of language (**langue**) that governs how those utterances are constructed. ◊ **competence** *n.* **4**, **performance** *n.* **8** ■ *vt* (**-roles, -roling, -roled**) **GIVE PRISONER PAROLE** to release a prisoner on parole [15C. Via French < Latin *parabola* 'speech, talk' (see PARABLE).] —**parolable** *adj*

paronomasia /párrənō máyzi ə/ *n* a play on words, especially a pun [Late 16C. < Latin, < Greek *paronomazein* 'name differently' < *onomazein* 'to name'.] —**paronomastic** /párrənō mástik/ *adj* —**paronomastically** *adv*

paronym /párrənim/ *n* a word derived from the same root as another word, e.g. 'folly' is a paronym of 'fool' [Mid-19C. < Greek *parōnumon* < *para-* 'beside' + *onuma* 'name'.] —**paronymic** /párrə nímmik/ *adj* —**paronymous** /pə rónniməss/ *adj* —**paronomously** *adv*

parotic /pə róttik/ *adj* situated close to or beside the ear [Mid-19C. < Greek *ōt-* 'ear'.]

parotid /pə róttid/ *adj* **1** situated close to or beside the ear **2** relating to the parotid gland ■ *n* ANAT = **parotid gland** [Late 17C. Via French < Greek *parōtid-* 'beside the ear' < *ōt-* 'ear'.]

parotid gland *n* a salivary gland located below the ear in humans

parotitis /párrə tītiss/, **parotiditis** /pə rótti dítiss/ *n* inflammation of a parotid gland or the parotid glands —**parotitic** /párrə títtik/ *adj*

parous /párrəss/ *adj* having given birth on at least one occasion [Late 19C. < -PAROUS.]

-parous *suffix* giving birth to, producing ○ *uniparous* [< Latin *-parus* < *parere* 'give birth']

Parousia /pə róossi ə/ *n* RELIG = **Second Coming** [Late 19C. < Greek, 'presence' < the present participle of *pareinai* < *einai* 'be'.]

paroxysm /párrək sizəm/ *n* **1** a sudden and uncontrollable expression of emotion ○ *paroxysms of grief* **2** a sudden onset or intensification of a pathological symptom or symptoms, especially when recurrent [Late 16C. < medieval Latin < Greek *paroxunein* 'irritate', literally 'sharpen beyond' < *oxus* 'sharp'.] —**paroxysmal** /párrək sízm'l/ *adj* —**paroxysmally** *adv* —**paroxysmic** *adj*

paroxytone /pə róksi tōn/ *n* **1 WORD WITH PENULTIMATE STRESS** a word in which the main stress is on the second-last syllable **2 GREEK WORD CATEGORY** in ancient Greek, a word with an acute accent on the second-last syllable ■ *adj* **WITH STRESSED PENULTIMATE SYLLABLE** with the main stress on the second-last syllable [Mid-18C. < Greek *paroxutonos* < *para-* 'beside' + *oxutonos* 'oxytone'.] —**paroxytonic** /pə róksi tónnik/ *adj*

parp /paarp/ *n* a honking noise emitted by the horn of a vehicle [Mid-20C. An imitation of the sound.] —**parp** *vti*

parpen /paárpən/, **parpend** /paár pənd/ *n* a stone or brick built into a wall to go from one side of the wall to the other and act as a binder. US term **perpend** [15C. Via Old French < medieval Latin *parpannus*.]

parquet /paár kay, paárki/ *n* flooring consisting of blocks of wood laid in a decorative pattern ■ *vt* to cover a floor in parquet [Early 19C. < French, 'small enclosed space' < *parc* 'enclosure' (see PARK).]

parquetry /paárkitri/ *n* flooring or a decorative inlay for furniture made with blocks of wood

parr /paar/ (*plural* **parrs** *or* **parr**) *n* **1** a young salmon up to two years old that has dark transverse bands (**parr marks**) and lives in fresh water **2** the young of some fishes other than the salmon, e.g. the trout [Early 18C. < ?]

Parr /paar/, **Catherine** (1512–48) sixth wife of Henry VIII of England (1543–47)

~~**parrallel**~~ incorrect spelling of **parallel**

parramatta *n* TEXTILES = **paramatta**

Parramatta /párrə máttə/ city in E New South Wales, Australia. Population: 142,993 (1996).

parrel /párrəl/, **parral** *n* a ring, loop, or band that secures a boom to a mast while allowing it to move up and down [15C. Shortening and alteration of APPAREL 'rigging'.]

parricide /párri sīd/ *n* **1** the murder of a parent or close relative **2** somebody who murders his or her parent or close relative [Mid-16C. < Latin *parricidium* 'kin-slaying', *parricida* 'kin-slayer' < assumed *parri-* 'relative'.] —**parricidal** /párri sīd'l/ *adj* —**parricidally** *adv*

Parrish /párrish/, **Maxfield** (1870–1966) US artist

parrot /párrət/ *n* **1 BRIGHTLY COLOURED TROPICAL BIRD** a bird with a stout hooked bill and variously coloured, often brilliant plumage, some species of which can mimic speech. Native to: tropics, subtropics. Order: Psittaciformes. **2 SOMEBODY WHO COPIES OTHERS** a repeater of something that somebody else has said, without thought or understanding ■ *vt* **COPY OTHER PEOPLE** to repeat what somebody else says or writes without having thought about it or understood it [Early 16C. Probably < French dialect *Perrot* 'little Pierre'.] —**parroter** *n*

parrot-fashion *adv* mechanically and with no apparent understanding (*informal*) US term **parrotlike**

parrot fever *n* MED = **psittacosis** [Because humans can contract it from pet birds such as parrots]

parrotfish /párrət fish/ (*plural* **-fish** *or* **-fishes**) *n* a brightly coloured marine fish with jaws shaped like a parrot's beak that it uses for scraping coral. Native to: tropics. Family: Scaridae.

parrotlike *adv US* = **parrot-fashion**

parry /párri/ *v* (**-ries, -rying, -ried**) **1** *vti* **TURN BLOW ASIDE** to block or deflect the damaging effect of a blow or weapon **2** *vt* **AVOID ANSWERING** to evade a question by cleverly saying something that does not answer it ■ *n* (*plural* **-ries**) **ACT OF EVADING** an act of evading a blow, criticism, or question [Late 17C. Probably via French *parez* 'defend (yourself)'! < Latin *parare* 'prepare' (see PARE).]

Parry, Cape /párri/ promontory in the NW Northwest Territories, Canada, between Franklin and Darnley bays

Parry, Sir William Edward (1790–1855) British explorer

⚡**parse** /paarz/ (**parses, parsing, parsed**) *v* **1** *vti* **DESCRIBE GRAMMATICAL ROLE OF WORD** to describe the grammatical role of a word in a sentence, or to undergo this process **2** *vti* **ANALYSE GRAMMATICAL STRUCTURE OF SENTENCE** to analyse and describe the grammatical structure of a sentence, or to undergo this process **3** *vt* to analyze computer input in a specified language against the formal grammar of that language, both to validate the input and to create an internal representation of it for use in subsequent processing [Mid-16C. Probably < *pars* 'part of speech' < Latin, 'part'.] —**parsable** *adj*

parsec /paár sek/ *n* (*symbol* **pc**) an astronomical unit of distance equal to 3.262 light years [Early 20C. < PARALLAX + SECOND[2].]

Parsee /paár see, paar seé/, **Parsi** *n* a member of a Zoroastrian group living mainly in W India, descended from Persian refugees of the 7th and 8th centuries [Early 17C. < Persian *Pārsī* < *Pārs* 'Persia'.] —**Parsee** *adj* —**Parseeism** *n*

⚡**parser** /paárzər/ *n* **1** a program that parses computer input **2** somebody or something that analyses something into its component parts

Parsi *n, adj* RELIG = **Parsee**

parsimonious /paárssi mṓni əss/ *adj* very frugal or ungenerous —**parsimoniously** *adv* —**parsimoniousness** *n*

parsimony /paárssiməni/ *n* **1** great frugality or unwillingness to spend money **2** economy in the use of means to achieve something, especially the principle of endorsing the simplest explanation that covers a case [15C. < Latin *parsimonia* < *pars-*, past participle of *parcere* 'spare'.]

parsley /paárssli/ *n* a widely cultivated plant of the carrot family with small compound leaves. Use: in cooking, as a garnish. *Petroselinum crispum.* [Pre-12C. < late Latin *petrosilium* < Greek *petroselinon* < *petra* 'rock' + *selinon* 'parsley'.]

parsley fern *n* a bright green fern with leaves that look like parsley leaves. Native to: Europe. *Cryptogramma crispa.*

parsley piert /-peert/ *n* a small plant of the rose family with three-lobed leaves. Flowers: green, tiny. *Aphanes arvensis.* [Late 16C. Alteration of French *perce-pierre* 'stone-piercer'.]

parsnip /paárssnip/ *n* **1** a long tapering cream-coloured root eaten cooked as a vegetable **2** a plant of the carrot family that produces parsnips. *Pastinaca sativa.* [14C. Alteration (influenced by *neep* 'turnip') of Old French *pasnaie* < Latin *pastinaca* < *pastinum* 'gardening fork', probably from its shape.]

parson /paárs'n/ *n* **1** an Anglican parish priest **2** a member of the clergy, especially of the Protestant Church [13C. < Old French *persone* 'person' (see PERSON).] —**parsonic** /paar sónnik/ *adj* —**parsonical** *adj*

parsonage /paárss'nij/ *n* the house, usually provided by the parish, where a parson lives

Parsons /paárss'nz/, **Sir Charles Algernon** (1854–1931) British engineer

Parsons, Geoffrey Penwill (*b.* 1930) Australian pianist

parson's nose *n* the fatty piece of flesh at the rear end of a cooked chicken, turkey, or other bird, to which the tail feathers were attached. US term **pope's nose**

part /paart/ *n* **1 PORTION OR DIVISION** a portion or section of something ○ *the early part of the century* **2 EQUAL PORTION** any of several equal portions that make up something such as a mixture ○ *pastry that is one part fat to three parts flour* **3 COMPONENT** a separable piece or component of something such as a machine, system, or device ○ *a motor with only three moving parts* **4 IMPORTANT ELEMENT** an integral and essential feature or component of something ○ *She wants to be part of the community.* **5 ACTOR'S ROLE** a role in a dramatic performance ○ *played the part of Hamlet in the school play* **6 INVOLVEMENT IN AN EVENT** somebody's participation in or influence on something ○ *What part did he have to play in all this?* **7 SIDE** somebody's side or viewpoint ○ *You're always taking her part.* **8 ORGANIC CONSTITUENT** an organ, system, or other discrete element of an organism ○ *the part of the plant that carries out photosynthesis* **9 SEPARATE MUSICAL ROLE** the score for a single voice or instrument in a symphonic, orchestral, or choral work **10 LOGICAL DIVISION** a logical division of something such as a report, book, or presentation ○ *Part three of the paper deals with environmental issues.* **11** *US* HAIR = **parting** *n.* **3** ■ **parts** *npl* **1 AREA** a region or area (*informal*) ○ *That's unheard of in these parts.* **2 ABILITIES** intellectual abilities or talents (*literary*) ○ *a man of parts* ■ *v* **1** *vti* **SEPARATE** to move apart, or to move two things or people in different directions so that there is a space between them ○ *They had to part the children to keep them from fighting.* ○ *The curtains parted.* **2** *vti* **DIVIDE INTO PARTS** to divide something into parts, or to undergo division into parts **3** *vti* **DIVIDE HAIR** to make a line in the hair by combing in opposite directions from it, or to separate naturally in this way **4** *vi* **END RELATIONSHIP** to finish a relationship with somebody ○ *We parted on bad terms.* **5** *vi* **GO AWAY** to go away from somebody ○ *They parted at the corner of the street.* ■ *adj* **PARTIAL** partial or less than the whole ○ *part owner of a beach house* ■ *adv* **PARTIALLY** to some extent but not completely ○ *She's part Irish, part French.* [13C. Noun < Old French, verb via French *partir* < Latin *partire* < *part-*.] ◇ **for the most part** in general, or mostly ○ *She does OK at school, for the most part.* ◇ **in good part** without taking offence or becoming angry ◇ **in part** to an extent but not completely ◇ **on the part of** as far as somebody is concerned, or with regard to somebody ◇ **part and parcel** an essential, indivisible element of something ◇ **part company** to go away in separate directions (*refers to two or more people*) ○ *They chatted for a while before parting company.* ◇ **take part (in something)** to be actively involved in something, usually as a member of a group

USAGE The idiom ***part and parcel***, meaning 'an essential component of something else', is correctly worded as shown here, e.g. *Walking is part and parcel of a postman's occupation. 'Part and partial'* is incorrect.

part with *vt* to give something up or to give something away, especially unwillingly

partake /paar táyk/ (**-takes, -taking, -took** /-tóok/, **-taken** /-táykən/) *vi* **1 EAT OR DRINK** to have something to eat or drink (*formal*) **2 HAVE OR SEEM TO HAVE** to have or appear to have a certain amount of some quality or characteristic (*formal*) **3 PARTICIPATE** to share in or take part in something

○ *How many students partake in sports activities?* [Mid-16C. Back-formation < *partaker* < *part-taker*, translation of Latin *particeps* (see PARTICIPATE).] —**partaker** *n*

partan /paárt'n/ *n Scotland* an edible crab [15C. Probably < Scottish Gaelic *partan* 'red'.]

parted /paártid/ *adj* **1 IN PARTS** divided into parts **2 SEPARATED** separated or kept separate ○ *with parted lips* **3 DIVIDED BY A PARTING** having a parting ○ *a hairstyle parted on the left* **4 DIVIDED TO BASE** describes a leaf or plant part that is separated or cleft nearly to the base

parterre /paar táir/ *n* an ornamental garden laid out in a formal pattern that is usually marked out with low evergreen hedges and filled in with annual bedding plants [Early 17C. < French, 'ornamental garden' < *par terre* 'on the ground'.]

part exchange *n* a payment method by which a buyer gives an article he or she owns to a seller as part payment for a more expensive article

part-exchange *vt* to accept or give goods as part payment for something being bought

parthenogenesis /paàthənō jénnəssiss/ *n* a form of reproduction, especially in plants, insects, and arthropods, in which a female gamete develops into a new individual without fertilization by a male gamete [Mid-19C. < Greek *parthenos* 'virgin'.] —**parthenogenetic** /paàrthinō jə néttik/ *adj* —**parthenogenetically** *adv*

AKG London

Parthenon, Athens, Greece

Parthenon *n* a large fifth-century temple to the goddess Athena on the Acropolis in Athens

Parthian /paárthi ən/ *n* somebody who came from Parthia, an ancient country in Asia that ruled an empire until the 3rd century —**Parthian** *adj*

Parthian shot *n* a final hostile remark or gesture made while leaving [< the Parthians' legendary tactic of firing arrows over their shoulders while retreating]

partial /paársh'l/ *adj* **1 INCOMPLETE** not complete or total ○ *only a partial success* **2 AFFECTING PARTS** affecting a part or parts but not the whole ○ *a partial restoration of the building* **3 FOND OF** having a particular liking for something ○ *very partial to chocolate cake* **4 BIASED** showing an unfair preference for one person or thing over another ■ *n* **1** MATH = **partial derivative 2** MUSIC = **overtone** *n.* 2 [15C. Via Old French *parcial* < late Latin *partialis* < *part-* 'part'.] —**partialness** *n*

partial derivative *n* the derivative of a function of two or more mathematical variables calculated with respect to one of the variables and on the assumption that the others are fixed

partial differential equation *n* a differential equation that involves partial derivatives of more than one variable

partial eclipse *n* an eclipse in which only part of something such as the Sun or Moon is covered or darkened

partial fraction *n* any of a set of simpler fractions, the sum of which comprises a more complex fraction

partiality /paàrshi állәti/ (*plural* **-ties**) *n* **1** a liking for something **2** an unfair preference for one person or thing over another

partially /paársh'li/ *adv* **1** to a degree but not completely **2** in a way that shows an unfair preference for one person or thing over another

partially sighted *adj* having a visual impairment that cannot be completely corrected by the use of glasses or contact lenses

partial pressure *n* the pressure that one gas in a mixture of gases would exert if it were the only gas present

partial product *n* the result when a mathematical quantity is multiplied by one digit of a number with two or more digits

partible /paártəb'l/ *adj* able to be divided ○ *a partible inheritance* [Mid-16C. Via late Latin *partibilis* < Latin *partire* 'part' (see PART).]

participant /paar tíssipənt/ *n* a person who takes part in something ■ *adj* taking part in something [Mid-16C. < French, present participle of *participier* < Latin *participare* (see PARTICIPATE).]

participate /paar tíssi payt/ (**-pates, -pating, -pated**) *v* **1** *vi* to take part in an event or activity **2** to have a particular quality (*archaic*) [15C. < Latin *participare* < *particeps* 'taking part' < *part-* 'part'.] —**participation** /paar tíssi páysh'n/ *n* —**participative** *adj* —**participator** *n* —**participatory** *adj*

participating insurance *n* insurance in which the policyholders are entitled to a dividend from the insurance company's profits

participial /paàrti síppi əl/ *adj* having the form or function of a verb that can be used as both adjective and verb [Late 16C. < Latin *participialis* < *participium* (see PARTICIPLE).] —**participially** *adv*

participle /paárti sip'l, paar tíssip'l/ *n* a form of a verb that is used to form complex tenses, as in 'was loving' and 'has loved' in English, and may also be used as an adjective [14C. Via Old French < Latin *participium* < *particeps* 'sharing' (see PARTICIPATE), because it shares qualities of both adjectives and verbs.]

USAGE English verbs have two participles: a ***present participle*** and a ***past participle***. The present participle ends in *-ing*: *rush, rushing* (the present participle of *rush*). The past participle of most verbs ends in *-ed*: *rushed*. But there are some irregular verbs that have a special form for the past participle: *sing* becomes *sung*; *go* becomes *gone*. The present participle is used in forming progressives: *You're lying!* The present participle of many verbs can also be used as an adjective: *a working model*; *a growing economy*. The past participle is used with the auxiliary verb *have* to form the perfect of verbs: *You have never played so well*; *I hadn't heard the news*. The past participle of many verbs can also be used as an adjective: *a diverted stream*; *a broken arm*.

~~particlar~~ incorrect spelling of **particular**

particle /paártik'l/ *n* **1 TINY PIECE** a very small piece of something ○ *airborne particles* **2 TINY AMOUNT** a very small amount of something ○ *There wasn't a particle of truth in anything he said.* **3 BODY WITH FINITE MASS** a minute body that is considered to have finite mass but negligible size **4 BASIC UNIT OF MATTER** any of the basic units of matter, e.g. a molecule, atom, or electron **5 SUBATOMIC UNIT** a unit of matter smaller than the atom or its main components **6 PART OF MULTIWORD VERB** an adverb or preposition that occurs as part of a multiword verb, such as 'up' in 'blow up' **7 PIECE OF CONSECRATED BREAD OR WAFER** in the Roman Catholic Mass, a small piece of consecrated bread or wafer [14C. < Latin *particula* 'small part' < *part-* 'part'.]

particle accelerator *n* PHYS = **accelerator** *n.* 2

particle beam *n* a very narrow concentrated stream of charged particles such as electrons or protons, produced by a particle accelerator or a particle-beam weapon

particleboard /paártik'l bawrd/ *n US, NZ* a wood board made from sawdust or wood particles bonded with a resin binder

particle bombardment *n* a technique for inserting DNA from one organism into another by bombarding embryogenic cell cultures with DNA-coated metal particles

particle physics *n* the branch of physics that deals with the study of subatomic particles, particularly the many unstable particles produced in particle accelerators and high-energy collisions (+ *singular verb*)

parti-coloured /paárti-/ *adj* having different parts in different colours [< PARTY 'multi-coloured']

particular /pər tíkyŏŏlər/ *adj* **1 ONE OUT OF SEVERAL** relating to one person or thing out of several ○ *Which particular dress do you prefer?* **2 PERSONAL** belonging to one person and different from other people's **3 EXCEPTIONAL** great or more than usual ○ *took particular care over it* **4 SPECIAL** special and worth mentioning ○ *had no particular objection to the plan* **5 FUSSY** having or demanding high standards ○ *She's very particular about standards of hygiene.* **6 CHOOSY** taking great care when making a choice **7 DETAILED** going into great detail about something (*formal*) **8 NOT DEALING WITH ALL** describes a proposition in logic that deals with some but not all members of a class ■ *n* **1 ITEM** an individual fact, item, or detail (*often plural*) ○ *noted down his particulars* **2 SINGLE INSTANCE** an individual case or instance, as opposed to a more general theory **3 REAL THING** an entity with definite spatial and temporal properties [14C. Via Old French < Latin *particularis* 'concerned with small parts or details' < *particula* 'small part'.] ◇ **in particular** specifically or especially

particularise *vti* = **particularize**

particularism /pər tíkyŏŏlərizəm/ *n* **1 COMMITMENT TO ONE GROUP** exclusive commitment to one particular group, especially when detrimental to the interests or well-being of a larger group **2 SELF-RULE PRINCIPLE** a policy of allowing political divisions within a state or federation to be self-governing, without regard to what effect this may have on the larger body **3 BELIEF THAT GOD BESTOWS GRACE INDIVIDUALLY** the belief that God chooses to bestow grace and salvation on particular individuals —**particularist** *n* —**particularistic** /pər tíkyŏŏlə rístik/ *adj*

particularity /pər tíkyŏŏ lárrəti/ (*plural* **-ties**) *n* (*formal*) **1 EXACTITUDE** attention to detail and concern for accuracy **2 FASTIDIOUSNESS** the practice of taking great care when making a choice **3 USE OF DETAIL** the use of great detail in describing something **4** = **particular** *n.* 1 **5 SOMETHING CHARACTERISTIC** a peculiarity or characteristic **6 INDIVIDUALITY** the condition of being peculiar to an individual rather than a group

particularize /pər tíkyŏŏlə rīz/ (**-izes, -izing, -ized**), **particularise** (**-ises, -ising, -ised**) *v* **1** *vt* **FOCUS ON INDIVIDUAL** to make something become particular, e.g. by focusing on a particular person or thing **2** *vt* **PROVIDE WITH SPECIFIC EXAMPLES** to provide something with specific examples **3** *vti* **GO INTO DETAIL** to go into detail about something —**particularization** /pər tíkyŏŏlə rī záysh'n/ *n* —**particularizer** *n*

particularly /pər tíkyŏŏlərli/ *adv* **1 VERY MUCH** to a great degree **2 MORE THAN USUALLY** more than usually or more than in other cases **3 SPECIFICALLY** as a specific example **4 IN DETAIL** with great attention to detail

particulate /paar tíkyŏŏlət, -layt/ *adj* relating to or consisting of separate particles ■ *n* a substance that consists of separate particles, especially airborne pollution [Late 19C. < Latin *particula* 'small part'.]

parting /paárting/ *n* **1 LEAVING** the act of leaving somebody or something, especially if the separation is sad or upsetting **2 SEPARATION** the process or action of separating or dividing **3 DIVIDING LINE IN HAIR** the line in a hairstyle from which the hair is combed or brushed in different directions. US term **part** *n.* 11 **4 BREAKING OF CRYSTAL ALONG PLANE** the tendency of some crystals to break along a plane of weakness ■ *adj* **1 DONE WHILE LEAVING** done, made, or given when leaving ○ *a parting remark* **2 DEPARTING** leaving or coming to an end (*literary*) ○ *'The curfew tolls the knell of parting day...'* (Thomas Gray, *Elegy Written in a Country Churchyard*; 1751) **3 DIVIDING** used to divide or separate something

parting shot *n* a final, often hostile, remark or gesture made by somebody who is leaving

parti pris /paárti preé/ (*plural* **partis pris** /paárti preé/) *n* a preconceived opinion or bias [< French, 'side taken']

partisan[1] /paárti zán/, **partizan** *n* **1 BIASED SUPPORTER** a strong supporter of a person, group, or cause, especially one who does not listen to other people's opinions **2 RESISTANCE FIGHTER** a member of a group that has taken up armed resistance against occupying enemy forces ■ *adj* **SHOWING UNREASONING SUPPORT** showing strong and usually biased support for a cause, especially a political one [Mid-16C. Via French and Italian dialect *partisano* < Italian *parte* 'part, side' < Latin *part-*.] —**partisanship** *n*

partisan[2] /paárti zán/, **partizan** *n* a weapon with a long shaft and a blade, used in the 16th and 17th centuries [Mid-16C. Via obsolete French < obsolete Italian *partesana*, variant of *partigiana (arma)* 'partisan (weapon)', feminine of *partigiano* < *parte* (see PARTISAN[1]).]

partita /paar teétə/ (*plural* **-te** /-teé tay/ *or* **-tas**) *n* a suite or set of musical variations, especially in baroque music [Late 19C. Via Italian, 'composition divided into parts' < Latin *partire* 'divide'.]

partite /paár tīt/ *adj* **1** describes a plant part such as a leaf that is split almost to its base **2** divided into or consisting of two or more parts (*usually in combination*)

○ *tripartite negotiations* [Late 16C. < Latin *partitus*, past participle of *partire* 'divide'.]

partition /paar tísh'n/ *n* **1 SOMETHING THAT DIVIDES SPACE** a structure that divides a space, e.g. a wall built to make two rooms out of one **2 DIVISION OF COUNTRY** the division of a country into two or more separate states or countries ○ *the partition of India* **3 DIVIDING UP** the division of something into parts, or the state of being divided into parts (*formal*) ■ *v* **1** *vt* **DIVIDE WITH A PARTITION** to divide or separate an area such as a room by means of a partition **2** *vti* **SPLIT A COUNTRY** to divide a country into two or more separate states **3** *vt* **DIVIDE** to divide something into separate parts [15C. Via Old French < Latin *partire* 'divide'.] —**partitioner** *n* —**partitionist** *n* —**partitionment** *n*

partitive /paártətiv/ *adj* **1 SEPARATING** separating or dividing something (*formal*) **2 EXPRESSING PART** describes a grammatical construction expressing a part of something, such as 'of' in 'a lump of coal' or the possessive form in 'the dog's tail' ■ *n* **PARTITIVE CONSTRUCTION** a partitive construction [14C. Via Old French < Latin *partit-*, past participle of *partire* 'divide' (see PART).] —**partitively** *adv*

partizan *n, adj* MIL = **partisan**[1] ■ *n* ARMS = **partisan**[2]

partly /paártli/ *adv* to some extent, but not completely ○ *The road was partly blocked by a heavy snowfall.*

partner /paártnər/ *n* **1 SOMEBODY WHO SHARES ACTIVITY** a sharer of an activity or undertaking ○ *his partner in crime* **2 MEMBER OF RELATIONSHIP** either member of an established couple in a relationship **3 FELLOW PARTICIPANT IN SEXUAL ACTIVITY** either of two people who have or have had sex together **4 ASSOCIATE IN DANCE OR GAME** a person who dances with somebody else, or plays with somebody else on the same side in a game **5 BUSINESS ASSOCIATE** an owner of part of a company, usually a company he or she works in, who shares both the financial risks and the profits of the business **6 SOMETHING RELATED** something that is related in some way to something else **7 SUPPORTING TIMBER ON SHIP** one of the timbers on a ship underneath the deck that is used to support the mast (*often plural*) ■ *vt* **BE SOMEBODY'S PARTNER** to be somebody's partner, e.g. in a game or dance [14C. Alteration (influenced by PART) of *parcener*, via Anglo-Norman 'sharer' < Latin *partition-* 'sharing' < *partire* 'divide'.]

partnership /paártnər ship/ *n* **1 RELATIONSHIP BETWEEN PARTNERS** the relationship between two or more people or organizations that are involved in or share the same activity **2 COOPERATION** cooperation between people or groups working together ○ *scientists working in close partnership with colleagues overseas* **3 GROUP OF PEOPLE WORKING TOGETHER** an organization formed by two or more people or groups to work together for some purpose **4 COMPANY OWNED BY PARTNERS** a company set up by two or more people who put money into the business and share the financial risks and profits **5 PARTNERS IN BUSINESS** the people who make up a partnership, collectively

part of speech *n* a grammatical category or word group in a language to which words may be assigned on the basis of how they are used in sentences [Translation of Latin *pars orationis*]

parton /paár ton/ *n* a postulated elementary particle, proposed as a constituent of neutrons and protons [Mid-20C. < PARTICLE.]

Parton /paárt'n/, **Dolly** (*b.* 1946) US singer, songwriter, and actor

partook past tense of **partake**

partridge /paártrij/ *n* **1** a medium-sized, ground-nesting bird with variegated plumage, related to pheasants and grouse. Native to: Europe, Asia. Genera: *Alectoris* and *Perdix*. **2** the flesh of the partridge as food [13C. Via Old French *perdriz* < Greek *perdix*.]

partridgeberry /paártrij beri/ (*plural* **-ries**) *n* a trailing evergreen plant with rounded leaves, that bears scarlet berries. Flowers: small, white, fragrant. Native to: E North America. *Mitchella repens*. [Early 18C. Because partridges eat the berries.]

part song, part-song *n* a vocal musical composition with parts for different voices, usually performed without accompaniment

part-time *adj, adv* for less than the usual amount of time associated with a particular activity ○ *a part-time job* —**part-timer** *n*

parturient /paar työóri ənt/ *adj* **1 GIVING BIRTH** about to give birth (*technical*) **2 RELATING TO CHILDBIRTH** relating to the process or time of childbirth **3 ABOUT TO PRODUCE** on the verge of producing something or coming forth (*literary*) [Late 16C. < Latin *parturient-*, present participle of *parturire* (see PARTURITION).] —**parturiency** *n*

parturifacient /paar työóri fáysh'nt/ *n* a drug that induces birth or makes it easier to give birth [Mid-19C. < Latin *parturire* 'be in labour' (see PARTURITION) + -FACIENT.] —**parturifacient** *adj*

parturition /paártyoo rísh'n/ *n* the act of giving birth to offspring (*formal*) [Mid-17C. Via late Latin *parturition-* < Latin *parturire* 'be in labour' < *parere* 'give birth'.]

partway /paárt way/, **part way** *adv* some but not all of the way

partwork /paárt wurk/, **part work** *n* a series of magazines on a particular topic or area of interest, published in weekly, fortnightly, or monthly instalments and intended to be collected to form a complete volume

party /paárti/ *n* (*plural* **-ties**) **1 SOCIAL GATHERING FOR FUN** a social gathering to which people are invited in order to enjoy themselves and often celebrate something ○ *Are you coming to my birthday party?* **2 GROUP ACTING TOGETHER** a group of people who are doing something together ○ *a search party* **3 POLITICAL ORGANIZATION** a nationally based organization of people who share the same broad political views and goals, usually one attempting to have members elected to government **4 GROUP OF SOLDIERS** a detachment of soldiers given a particular task **5 ONE SIDE IN AGREEMENT OR DISPUTE** a person or a group of people acting together and forming one side in an agreement, contract, dispute, or lawsuit **6 PERSON** an individual (*formal*) ■ *vi* (**-ties, -tying, -tied**) **BE AT PARTY** to socialize and have fun at a party or similar occasion (*informal*) ■ *adj* **OF TWO COLOURS** divided into parts of two different colours [13C. Via French *partie* 'part, side', and Old French *parti* 'political faction' < Latin *partitus*, past participle of *partire* 'divide'.] —**partyer** *n* ◇ **be (a) party to something** to participate or be involved in a particular activity

party animal *n* a regular and enthusiastic participant in informal social events, especially parties (*informal*)

partygoer /paárti gō ər/ *n* an attender of a party or parties

party line *n* **1** the official policy of a political party or other organization ○ *always toed the party line* **2** a telephone line shared by more than one subscriber

party man *n* a man who is a loyal member or supporter of a political party

party piece *n* the usual song or turn that a person performs when called on to entertain people

party political broadcast *n* a short television or radio programme in which a political party is allowed to comment on political issues or to campaign, especially during an election

party politics *n* political activity as carried on by political parties, especially when devoted to furthering their own interests rather than the public's (+ *singular or plural verb*) —**party-political** *adj*

party pooper /-poopər/ *n* a spoiler of other people's fun, or an unenthusiastic person (*informal*)

party wall *n* a wall separating adjoining homes, buildings, or pieces of land

parulis /pə róoliss/ (*plural* **-lides** /-deez/) *n* a gumboil (*technical*) [< modern Latin, 'beside the gums' < Greek *oulon* 'gums']

parure /pə róor/ *n* a matching set of jewellery that includes earrings, a brooch, ring, necklace, and bracelet, and sometimes other items such as buckles [Early 19C. < French, < *parer* 'adorn' (see PARE).]

par value *n* the value printed on a security such as a share certificate or bond at the time of issue. ◊ **market value**

Parvati /paárvəti/ *n* a Hindu mother and fertility goddess, the wife of Shiva

parve, parveh *adj* JUDAISM = **pareve**

parvenu /paárvə nyoo/ (*plural* **-nus**) *n* a person who has recently gained wealth or social status but who is still considered as inferior [Early 19C. Via French, 'somebody who has arrived' < Latin *pervenire* 'arrive' < *venire* 'come'.]

parvis /paárviss/, **parvise** *n* an enclosed area or portico at the front of a building, especially a church [14C. Via Old French < late Latin *paradisus* 'garden' (see PARADISE).]

parvovirus /paárvō vīrəss/ *n* **1** any of a group of viruses that have a single strand of DNA, especially those causing disease in mammals **2** a contagious disease of dogs caused by a parvovirus and marked by fever, loss of appetite, and diarrhoea [Mid-20C. < Latin *parvus* 'small'.]

pas /paa/ (*plural* **pas** /paa/) *n* a step in dancing, especially in ballet [Early 18C. Via French < Latin *passus* 'step' (see PACE[1]).]

Pasadena /pássə deénə/ **1** city in SW California. Population: 134,587 (1998 estimate) **2** city in SE Texas. Population: 133,964 (1998 estimate).

pascal /pásk'l, pa skál/ *n* (*symbol* **Pa**) a unit of pressure or stress equal to one newton per square metre [Mid-20C. After Blaise PASCAL.]

ϟ **Pascal** /pa skál, pásk'l/ *n* a high-level general-purpose computer language designed to encourage structured programming [Mid-20C. Acronym for *programme appliqué à la sélection et la compilation automatique de la littérature*; also after Blaise PASCAL.]

Pascal /pa skaál/, **Blaise** (1623–62) French philosopher and mathematician

Pascal's triangle *n* a triangular arrangement of numbers with a 1 at the top and at the beginning and end of each row, with each of the other numbers being the sum of the two numbers above it [After Blaise PASCAL]

paschal /pásk'l/ *adj* **1** relating to Easter **2** relating to Passover (*archaic*) [15C. Via Old French *pascal* < ecclesiastical Latin *pascha* < Greek *paskha*, via Aramaic < Hebrew *pesaḥ*.]

pas de deux /paa də dố/ (*plural* **pas de deux** /paa də dố/) *n* a dance or dance sequence for two dancers [< French, 'step for two']

paseo /paa sáy ō/ (*plural* **-os**) *n* the procession of matadors and other bullfighters into an arena before a bullfight begins [Mid-19C. Via Spanish < Latin *passus* 'step'.]

pasha /paáshə, páshə/, **pacha** *n* formerly, in Turkey and other Middle Eastern countries, an official of high rank [Mid-17C. < Turkish *paşa*.]

pashm /páshəm/ *n* the fine soft wool of some goats, especially the Kashmir goat. Use: cashmere shawls, other garments. [Late 19C. < Persian *pašm* 'wool'.]

pashmina /pash meénə/ (*plural* **-nas**) *n* **1** a fine woollen fabric made from the hair of goats raised in N South Asia **2** a shawl made from pashmina [Late 19C. < Persian *pašm* 'wool'.]

Pashto /púsh tō/ (*plural* **-to** *or* **-tos**), **Pushto** /púsh too/ (*plural* **-to** *or* **-tos**), **Pushtu** (*plural* **-tu** *or* **-tus**) *n* **1** an official language of Afghanistan, also spoken in NW Pakistan, belonging to the Indo-Iranian branch of Indo-European. Native speakers: 21 million. **2** somebody who speaks Pashto as a native language [Late 18C. < Pashto *paṣ̌tō*.] —**Pashto** *adj*

Pasiphaë /pə síffi ee/ *n* **1** in Greek mythology, the wife of Minos, King of Crete, who fell in love with a bull and gave birth to the Minotaur **2** the eighth moon of Jupiter [Via Latin < Greek, 'all-shining']

paso doble /pássō dố blay/ (*plural* **paso dobles** /pássō dốblayz/) *n* **1** a quick ballroom dance using Latin American marching movements **2** the music for a paso doble [Early 20C. < Spanish, 'double step'.]

Pasolini /pássō leéni/, **Pier Paolo** (1922–75) Italian film director

pas op /páss op/ *interj S Africa* used to warn another person to look out (*informal*) [Mid-19C. < Cape Dutch, < Dutch *oppassen* 'be on guard'.]

pasqueflower /pásk flowər, paásk-/ *n* a small spring-flowering perennial plant with hairy leaves. Flowers: blue, purple, white. Genus: *Anemone*. [Late 16C. Anglicization and alteration (influenced by French *pasque* 'Easter', because it blooms in the spring) of French *passefleur*.]

pasquinade /pásskwi náyd/ *n* an often anonymous lampoon or satire that was traditionally displayed in a public place (*archaic*) [Late 16C. Via French < Italian *pasquinata* < *Pasquino*, statue in Rome where lampoons were posted.] —**pasquinader** *n*

pass /paass/ *v* **1** *vti* **MOVE PAST** to move past or through a place or past a person ○ *We passed several groups of refugees on our way.* ○ *dark clouds passing overhead* **2** *vti* **OVERTAKE** to overtake and leave behind somebody or something **3** *vti* **THROW OR KICK BALL TO PLAYER** to throw, kick, or hit a ball or other object to another player during a game **4** *vt* **HAND OVER** to hand something to somebody ○ *Could you pass me the salt, please?* **5** *vti*

TRANSFER to transfer something such as property, authority, or responsibility to somebody, or to be transferred in this way ○ *The house will pass to his daughter when he dies.* **6** *vti* **MOVE INTO DIFFERENT PLACE OR CONDITION** to move somebody or something move, or move from one place or condition to another **7** *vti* **MOVE IN A PARTICULAR WAY** to move, or move something in a particular way in relation to something else ○ *He passed his hand along the banister.* **8** *vt* **GUIDE** to guide something into a particular position ○ *Pass the wire over that hook.* **9** *vi* **EXTEND PAST** to extend through, in front of, or along something such as a road or area ○ *The road passes by the cemetery.* **10** *vi* **CHANGE** to go from one condition, stage, or state to another ○ *It sheds its skin before it passes to the pupal stage.* **11** *vt* **SPEND TIME** to use up time doing something ○ *We passed the time playing cards.* **12** *vi* **ELAPSE** to elapse or go by ○ *Time passes quickly.* **13** *vi* **END** to come to an end ○ *The storm finally passed.* **14** *vti* **BE SUCCESSFUL IN AN EXAM** to be successful in a test or examination, or officially decide that somebody has been successful in a test or examination **15** *vti* **SUCCEED IN SUBJECT** to meet the requirements of a course of study **16** *vi* **BE ACCEPTABLE** to be of an acceptable standard ○ *It's not the best but it will pass.* **17** *vti* **APPROVE MEASURE OR BE APPROVED** to approve something such as a law, measure, or proposal, or to get official approval **18** *vi* **DIE** to stop living (*formal*) ○ *She passed from this life in 1967.* **19** *vi* **HAPPEN BETWEEN PEOPLE OR THINGS** to happen or be exchanged between two or more people or things ○ *A look passed between them.* **20** *vi* **NOT DO** to decide not to do something that is suggested or accept something that is offered **21** *vi* **NOT RAISE BID** to stop raising a bid in a card game **22** *vt* **EXCRETE** to process and excrete something from the body ○ *had been passing blood* **23** *vt* **GIVE JUDGMENT** to give a judgment or opinion ○ *pass judgment* **24** *vt* **STATE** to say something or give an opinion ○ *She didn't pass any comment at all.* **25** *vt* **CIRCULATE FAKE MONEY** to use fake money to pay for something ○ *passing counterfeit bills* ■ *n* **1 DOCUMENT GIVING PRIVILEGES** a document that entitles the holder to do something such as enter a place ○ *a press pass* **2 ACT OF THROWING TO PLAYER** an act of throwing, kicking, or hitting a ball or other object to another player in a sport **3 SUCCESSFUL GRADE** a successful outcome in a test, examination, or course of study **4 WAY THROUGH MOUNTAINS** a way through or over mountains (*often in placenames*) **5 ATTEMPT TO KISS OR TOUCH** an uninvited attempt to kiss or touch somebody in a sexual way ○ *made a pass at her* **6 ACT OF GOING BY** an instance of something going past, through, over, or round a place **7 MOVEMENT** a particular movement of something such as the hand **8 OPERATION** a single cycle or complete operation of something such as machinery **9 DOCUMENT EXCUSING SOMEBODY** a document that excuses the holder from normal activities **10 FAILURE TO BID** an instance of not bidding or raising the bid in a card game **11 STATE OF AFFAIRS** a particular and usually undesirable state of affairs ○ *How did we let things get to such a pass?* **12 SWORD THRUST** a thrust with a sword ■ *interj* **I DON'T KNOW** used to indicate that you do not know the answer to a question or do not want to give an answer (*informal*) ○ *'Guess who I've just seen'. – 'Pass!'* ○ *'How would you rate him as a manager?' – 'Pass!'* [13C. < Old French *passer* < Latin *passus* 'step'.] —**passer** *n* ◇ **let something pass** to make no comment or intervention ○ *It was a deliberate lie, but I let it pass.*

pass as *vt* = **pass for**

pass away *vi* **1** to stop living (*often used as a euphemism for 'die'*) **2** to come to an end or no longer exist

pass by *vt* to leave somebody or something unaffected or uninvolved ○ *The usual troubles of adolescence seemed to pass her by.*

pass for, pass as *vt* to be so like somebody or something as to be easily mistaken for the real person or thing

pass off *v* **1** *vt* **MAKE ACCEPTED UNDER FALSE IDENTITY** to cause somebody or something to be accepted under a different, false identity **2** *vi* **HAPPEN** to have a particular outcome (*refers to a planned event*) ○ *The ceremony passed off uneventfully.* **3** *vi* **DIMINISH** to end or disappear gradually

pass on *v* **1** *vi* to stop living (*often used as a euphemism for 'die'*) **2** *vt* to convey or transmit something that has been received to somebody else

pass out *v* **1** *vi* **FAINT** to lose consciousness **2** *vt* **DISTRIBUTE** to distribute things among a number of people **3** *vi* **COMPLETE TRAINING** to complete a course of training, especially as a military officer

pass over *vt* **1 IGNORE** to ignore somebody's right to be considered for something, especially a job or a promotion **2 DISREGARD** to fail to consider or include somebody or something **3 DIE** to stop living (*dated*)

pass up *vt* to decide not to take advantage of an opportunity

passable /pa̋assəb'l/ *adj* **1** adequate or good enough **2** capable of being crossed or travelled on —**passably** *adv*

passacaglia /pássə ka̋alyə/ *n* a baroque musical composition in slow triple time over a repeated bass line [Mid-17C. Via Italian < Spanish *pasacalle* < *pasar* 'to pass' + *calle* 'street', because it was often played in the streets.]

passade /pə sáyd/ *n* a movement in dressage in which a horse is made to move forwards and back again on the same spot [Mid-17C. Via French < Italian *passata* < Latin *passus* 'step'.]

passado /pə sa̋adō/ (*plural* **-dos** *or* **-does**) *n* in fencing, a thrust made while stepping forwards [Late 16C. Alteration of Spanish *pasada* or French *passade* < Latin *passus* 'step'.]

passage[1] /pássij/ *n* **1 CORRIDOR OR PATHWAY** a corridor in an enclosed area or a path enclosed on both sides ○ *an underground passage* **2 WAY THROUGH** a path made for somebody through an obstruction such as a crowd of people **3 PIECE OF WRITING OR MUSIC** a section of a piece of writing, speech, or music **4 CHANGE OF PLACE OR CONDITION** the act of going from one place to another or changing from one condition to another (*formal*) ○ *the team responsible for easing the passage of the new President-elect into power* **5 PROCESS OF TIME PASSING** the process of time going by ○ *the passage of time* **6 JOURNEY** a journey, especially one made by sea or air **7 RIGHT TO TRAVEL** the right to come and go, travel, or pass through somewhere ○ *The guides ensured our safe passage.* **8 APPROVAL OF NEW LAW** official approval of a new law or other proposal **9 TUBE IN THE BODY** a tube or channel in the body **10 SEA CHANNEL** a sea channel or strait (*often in placenames*) **11 BOWEL MOVEMENT** the act or process of expelling something from the body, e.g. emptying the bowels or the bladder **12 INTERCHANGE** an exchange of words, blows, or information between people or parties (*formal*) **13 BIOLOGICAL TECHNIQUE** the technique of introducing a microorganism or cell into a host organism or culture medium as part of the process of maintaining or modifying it ■ *vt* (**-sages, -saging, -saged**) **TRANSFER BIOLOGICAL MATERIAL** to use the biological technique of passage [13C. < Old French, < Latin *passus* 'step'.]

LITERARY LINK ***A Passage to India***, a novel (1924) by E. M. Forster. In Forster's last novel, an Englishwoman travelling in colonial India accuses a local doctor of assaulting her during a visit to the mysterious Marabar Caves. The conflicting responses of English expatriates and local Indians to the subsequent trial highlight the limitations of their belief systems and the problems of human understanding.

---

passage[2] /pássij, pə sa̋a<u>zh</u>/ *n* either of two movements in dressage, one being a sideways walk and the other a slow deliberate trot ■ *vti* (**-sages, -saging, -saged**) to perform a passage or make a horse do this [Late 18C. Via French *passager* < Latin *passus* 'step' (see PACE).]

passage hawk, passager hawk /pássijər-/ *n* a hawk or falcon captured while in its first plumage

passageway /pássij way/ *n* = **passage**[1] *n.* 1

passagework /pássij wurk/ *n* **1** parts of a musical work that are thematically unrelated to the whole but enable a performer to display virtuosity **2** the performance or execution of passagework

passant /páss'nt/ *adj* in heraldry, describes an animal shown walking to the left or right [15C. < French, present participle of *passer* (see PASS).]

passback /pa̋ass bak/ *n* the act of passing the ball or puck to another player who is closer to the home goal

pass band *n* the range of frequencies that an electronic filter will allow to pass without attenuation

passbook /pa̋ass bŏŏk/ *n* **1 RECORD OF BANK TRANSACTIONS** a book in which a record is kept of the money put into and taken out of a bank account or a building society account **2 BOOK RECORDING CREDIT PURCHASES** a book in which a trader records the items a customer has bought on credit **3 IDENTITY DOCUMENT** a mandatory identification document issued to Black people in South Africa during apartheid that gave details of their ancestry and spelt out restrictions on their movement [Early 19C. *Pass* < ?]

Passchendaele /pásh'n dayl/, **Passendale** /páss'n dayl/ village in W Belgium that was the scene of heavy fighting during World War I in October and November 1917

passé /pássay, pa̋a-/ *adj* **1** out-of-date or no longer fashionable **2** no longer in prime condition [Late 18C. < French, past participle of *passer* 'pass' (see PASS).]

passed past participle of **pass**

USAGE passed or **past**? Do not confuse these two words. Consider these examples: *He passed me at 80 mph; She is the past president of our student union.* In the first example, the past tense of the verb *pass*, which is ***passed***, is required: *He passed me. . . .* In the second sentence the adjective ***past*** ('one-time, former') is required: *She is the past president. . . .*

---

passed pawn *n* in chess, a pawn with no opposing pawn in front of it on its own or on either adjacent file that could become a queen

passementerie /pass méntri/ *n* **1** a decorative trimming for clothing made, e.g. of beads, braid, or lace **2** the craft of making fringes, tassels, and cords to embellish soft furnishings and upholstery [Early 17C. < French < *passement* 'decorative lace or braid', literally 'passing (over one another)' < *passer* (see PASS).]

Passendale ♦ **Passchendaele**

passenger /pássinjər/ *n* **1** a traveller in a motor vehicle, aircraft, train, or ship who is not a driver or crew member **2** somebody in a team who does not do his or her fair share of the work [14C. Alteration of Old French *passageor* 'one who makes a passage' < *passage* (see PASSAGE[1]).]

passenger pigeon *n* a migratory pigeon that was abundant until it was hunted to extinction in the 19th century. Native to: North America. *Ectopistes migratorius.* [*Passenger* 'migrating bird', because of its long migrations in huge flocks]

passenger seat *n* the seat in the front of a vehicle next to the driver's seat

passe-partout /páss paar tōō/ (*plural* **passe-partouts** /-tōō/) *n* **1 MASTER KEY** something such as a master key that gives unrestricted access to a building or area **2 PICTURE FRAME** a decorated mat round a framed picture **3 ADHESIVE TAPE OR GUMMED PAPER** adhesive tape or gummed paper used to fix pictures to mats before framing [< French, 'pass everywhere']

passer-by /pássər-/ (*plural* **passers-by**) *n* a person who happens to be going past a place, especially on foot

passerine /pássə rīn, -reen/ *adj* relating or belonging to an order of mainly perching songbirds, the largest order of birds comprising more than half of all species. Order: Passeriformes. [Late 18C. < late Latin *passerinus* 'of sparrows' < *passer* 'sparrow'.] —**passerine** *n*

pas seul /pa̋a sől/ (*plural* **pas seuls** /pa̋a sől/) *n* a dance or passage performed by a single dancer [< French, 'solo step']

pass-fail *adj US* relating to a system of marking in which a student simply passes or fails, without a grade such as A, B, or C being awarded

passible /pássəb'l/ *adj* sensitive to feeling emotions, especially when this causes pain (*formal*) [14C. Via Old French < Latin *passibilis* < *pass-*, past participle of *pati* 'feel, suffer' (see PATIENT).] —**passibility** /pássə bíllәti/ *n* — **passibly** *adv*

passim /pássim/ *adv* used especially in footnotes to indicate that what is being referred to occurs in various places in a book or other text [Early 19C. < Latin, 'scatteredly' < *passus*, past participle of *pandere* 'spread out'.]

passing /pa̋assing/ *adj* **1 GOING PAST** moving past ○ *a passing car* **2 TRANSITORY** lasting only a short time **3 BRIEF AND WITHOUT MUCH ATTENTION** done briefly and without much attention being paid ○ *a passing interest* ■ *n* **1 CEASING TO EXIST** the fact or process of something becoming obsolete or ceasing to exist **2 PLACE WHERE IT IS POSSIBLE TO PASS** a place where it is possible to pass or cross something **3 PROCESS OF TIME GOING BY** the elapsing of time **4 DEATH** death (*used euphemistically*)

passing bell *n* a bell rung to mark a death or a funeral

passing lane *n* a lane designated for passing slower traffic

passing note *n* a note played between two chords or pitches to provide a melodic transition from one to the other

passing out *n* the successful completion of a course of training, especially as a military officer (*hyphenated before nouns*)

passing shot *n* in racket games such as tennis, a winning shot that passes beyond the reach of an opponent at the net

passion /pásh'n/ *n* **1 INTENSE EMOTION** intense or overpowering emotion such as love, joy, hatred, or anger ○ *Try and play it with a little more passion.* **2 STRONG SEXUAL DESIRE** strong sexual desire and excitement **3 OUTBURST OF EMOTION** a sudden outburst of an emotion such as rage, hatred, or jealousy ○ *He flew into a passion.* **4 INTENSE ENTHUSIASM** a keen interest in a particular subject or activity ○ *a passion for music* **5 OBJECT OF ENTHUSIASM** the object of somebody's intense interest or enthusiasm ○ *Orchids are my passion.* ■ **passions** *npl* **EMOTIONS** strong emotions, especially as distinct from reason or intellect ○ *a meeting at which passions were running high* [12C. Via French < the ecclesiastical Latin stem *passion-* 'suffering, affection' < *pati* 'suffer'.]

SYNONYMS See ***love***.

Passion *n* **1 SUFFERING OF JESUS CHRIST** the sufferings of Jesus Christ from the Last Supper until his crucifixion **2 STORY OF JESUS CHRIST'S SUFFERING** an account of the Passion in the Gospels **3 MUSICAL SETTING OF GOSPEL STORY** a musical work based on one of the Gospel accounts of the Passion

passional /pásh'nəl/ *adj* relating to passion or arising from passion (*literary*) ■ *n* a book that tells of the sufferings of Christian saints and martyrs [15C. < Latin *passionalis* < *passion-* (see PASSION).]

passionate /pásh'nət/ *adj* **1 SHOWING SEXUAL DESIRE** expressing or showing strong sexual desire ○ *a passionate kiss* **2 SHOWING INTENSE EMOTION** expressing intense feeling ○ *a passionate speech on human rights* **3 ENTHUSIASTIC** having a keen enthusiasm or intense desire for something ○ *a passionate golfer* **4 HAVING STRONG EMOTIONS** tending to have strong feelings, especially of love, desire, or enthusiasm ○ *a fiery, passionate personality* **5 QUICK-TEMPERED** easily made angry —**passionately** *adv*

passionflower /pásh'n flow ər/ *n* a climbing vine with large flowers and edible fruit. Native to: Central, South America. Genus: *Passiflora*. [Mid-17C. Because parts of the flower are taken as symbols of Jesus Christ's Passion.]

passion fruit *n* the edible fruit of a passionflower, especially a granadilla

passionless /pásh'nləss/ *adj* **1** empty of romantic or sexual love ○ *a passionless film* **2** feeling or expressing no emotion —**passionlessness** *n*

Passion play *n* a play that tells the story of the sufferings and crucifixion of Jesus Christ

Passion Sunday *n* **1** the fifth Sunday in Lent, or the second Sunday before Easter, when Passiontide begins **2** = **Palm Sunday**

Passiontide /pásh'n tīd/ *n* the last two weeks of Lent, from Passion Sunday to Easter

Passion Week *n* **1** the second week before Easter, from Passion Sunday to the Sunday before Easter **2** Holy Week (*archaic*)

passivate /pássi vayt/ (**-vates, -vating, -vated**) *vt* to coat the surface of a metal with a substance that protects it against corrosion

passive /pássiv/ *adj* **1 NOT ACTIVELY TAKING PART** tending not to participate actively, and usually letting others make decisions **2 OBEYING READILY** tending to submit or obey without arguing or resisting **3 NOT OPERATIONAL** not working or operating **4 INFLUENCED BY SOMETHING EXTERNAL** influenced, affected, or produced by something external ○ *passive solar heat gain* **5 EXPRESSING ACTION DONE TO THE SUBJECT** indicating that the apparent subject of a verb is the person or thing undergoing, not performing, the action of the verb, as in 'We were given work to do'. ◊ **active** *adj.* 7 **6 UNREACTIVE** chemically inactive or resistant to corrosion **7 LACKING A POWER SOURCE** describes an electronic circuit or device that does not contain a source of energy **8 NOT PRODUCING INTEREST** describes a form of investment that does not produce interest ■ *n* **PASSIVE VOICE** the passive voice, or a verb in the passive voice [14C. Directly or via French < Latin *passivus* < *pati* (see PASSION).] —**passively** *adv* —**passiveness** *n* —**passivism** *n* —**passivist** *n*

LANGUAGE NOTE In the active voice, the subject of the verb is the one who does the action described by the verb, and the object is the one acted upon: *The waiters will collect the plates.*

In the passive voice, this situation is reversed: the subject of the verb is the one acted upon by the verb, and the one who does the action – if mentioned at all – is relegated to a separate phrase, typically beginning with by: *The plates will be collected by the waiters.*

The passive can be used for a variety of purposes; for example, if the identity of the doer of the action is unknown, if the writer desires to conceal the identity of the doer of the action, as in *The vase was broken*, or if the writer wants to put special emphasis on what is affected by the action rather than on the doer of the action, as in *The bomb was defused by experts.*

Formal writing uses the passive more frequently than informal writing, and the passive is normal style in some scientific and technical writing. However, in many contexts too much use of the passive can seem wordy or pompous and the active is more direct and preferable. Compare: *Electrical goods may be found on the fourth floor* with *You can find electrical goods on the fourth floor*, or *Electrical goods are on the fourth floor.*

Avoid mixing passive and active voices in sentences like this: *Our commuter railway needs more money for major improvements and it will probably be raised by fare increases.* Say instead: *Our commuter railway needs more money for major improvements and will probably raise it by fare increases.*

A less commonly encountered but awkward construction is called the *double passive*. The writer has inserted two passive constructions close together in the same sentence: *No legal remedy was sought to be obtained by the victim.* Avoid such constructions and say instead *The victim did not seek to obtain any legal remedy*, or even *The victim did not seek any legal remedy.*

passive-aggressive *adj* describes a personality type or way of behaving that seeks to manipulate others indirectly and resist their demands rather than confronting or opposing directly —**passive-aggression** *n*

passive immunity *n* immunity from disease acquired by the transfer of antibodies from one person to another, e.g. through injections or between a mother and a fetus through the placenta

passive resistance *n* resistance to authority using only nonviolent methods such as peaceful demonstration or noncooperation —**passive resister** *n*

passive smoking *n* the involuntary breathing in of other people's tobacco smoke

passivity /pa sívvəti/ *n* the quality of being passive, or passive behaviour

passkey /paass kee/ (*plural* **-keys**) *n* **1** a key that gives the holder access via a restricted entrance **2** = **skeleton key**

pass law *n* a law operating in South Africa before the abolition of apartheid restricting the movement of Black people within the country

Passmore /paass mawr/, **John** (1904–84) Australian painter

Passmore, John Arthur (*b.* 1914) Australian philosopher and historian

Passover /paass ōvər/ *n* a Jewish festival marking the exodus of the Hebrews from captivity in Egypt. Date: seven or eight days from 14th day of Nisan. [Mid-16C. Translation of Hebrew *pesaḥ* 'pass without affecting'; because God passed over the Israelites' firstborn (Exodus 12:11–27).]

passport /paass pawrt/ *n* **1 OFFICIAL IDENTIFICATION DOCUMENT** an official document issued by the government of a country to a citizen that identifies the bearer and gives permission to travel to and from that country **2 ANY AUTHORIZATION TO TRAVEL** any authorization or official permission to travel in or through a country **3 MEANS OF ACCESS** something that grants somebody access to something ○ *Education can be the passport to a more fulfilling life.* [15C. < French *passeport* 'pass the seaport'.]

pass-through *n US* = **serving hatch**

~~**passtime**~~ incorrect spelling of **pastime**

⚡**password** /paass wurd/ *n* **1** a secret word or phrase that must be used by somebody who wants to be allowed in somewhere **2** a sequence of characters that must be keyed in to gain access to all or part of a computer system or program ○ *Don't let anyone know your password.*

past[1] /paast/ CORE MEANING: a grammatical word describing movement that involves passing or going beyond somebody or something ○ (prep) *Walk past the library and you'll arrive at the park.* ○ (adv) *She walked right past without saying a word to us.*

1 *prep, adv* **LATER** later than a particular time ○ *It's twenty past seven.* ○ *It's past your bedtime.* ○ *It's half past.* **2** *prep* **ON THE FARTHER SIDE OF** on the farther side of or beyond something ○ *We prefer the bakery that's just past the school.* **3** *prep* **BEYOND A NUMBER, AMOUNT, OR POINT** beyond a particular number, amount, or point, especially a point at which something can be done ○ *Do what you like; I'm past caring.* **4** *adv Scotland* **AWAY** away, for the sake of tidiness or for future use (*informal*) ○ *Be a good wee soul and put your toys past.* [13C. Originally past participle of PASS.] ◇ **not put it past somebody** to believe that somebody is quite capable of doing something, usually something disreputable or outrageous (*informal*) ◇ **past it** an offensive term meaning not as effective or capable of doing something as in former times (*informal*)

USAGE See ***passed***.

past[2] /paast/ *adj* **1 ELAPSED** gone by ○ *the past few days* **2 RELATING TO AN EARLIER TIME** having existed or occurred in a previous time ○ *in a past job* **3 ONE-TIME** having formerly occupied a particular position ○ *a gathering of past presidents* ○ *a past love of his* **4 EXPRESSING ACTION THAT TOOK PLACE PREVIOUSLY** describes the verb tense used for an action that took place previously ■ *n* **1 TIME BEFORE THE PRESENT** the time before the present and the events that happened then **2 PAST TENSE** the past tense of a language, or a verb form in the past tense **3 SOMEBODY'S PREVIOUS HISTORY** everything that has happened previously to somebody or something ○ *She has a mysterious past.* **4 SHAMEFUL HISTORY** a shameful or scandalous earlier period in somebody's life [13C. Originally past participle of PASS.] —**pastness** *n*

pasta /pástə/ *n* **1** a fresh or dried food that is usually made from a dough of flour, eggs, and water formed into a variety of shapes, e.g. macaroni or spaghetti **2** a dish made with cooked pasta [Late 19C. Via Italian < late Latin (see PASTE[1]).]

⚡**paste**[1] /payst/ *n* **1 ADHESIVE MIXTURE** a soft mixture of flour and water or starch and water used as an adhesive, especially for sticking paper to something **2 SEMISOLID MIXTURE** a soft mass or mixture with a consistency between a liquid and a solid **3 PASTRY DOUGH** pastry dough usually made with shortening and used especially to make pie crusts **4 FOOD SPREAD** a soft food product that can be spread on something such as bread ○ *anchovy paste* **5 GLASS FOR IMITATION GEMS** a hard, brilliant glass used to make imitation jewels **6 PORCELAIN CLAY** the clay mixture used to make porcelain ■ *vt* (**pastes, pasting, pasted**) **1 GLUE SOMETHING TO SOMETHING ELSE** to stick things together using paste **2 COVER A SURFACE WITH PASTE** to cover a surface by sticking things to it with paste **3 PLACE TEXT IN DOCUMENT ELECTRONICALLY** to place text, data, or an image into a document electronically as an addition or alteration from another location [13C. Via Old French < late Latin *pasta* < Greek *passein* 'to sprinkle'.] —**paster** *n*

paste up *vt* to take printed pages or proofs and stick them onto separate sheets of paper so that they can be read and amended

paste[2] /payst/ (**pastes, pasting, pasted**) *vt* to give somebody a severe beating or defeat somebody heavily (*informal*)

pasteboard /páyst bawrd/ *n* a stiff board made either of sheets of paper pasted together or of layers of paper pulp pressed together ■ *adj* not of good quality, or not very substantial ○ *pasteboard houses*

pastel /pást'l, pa stél/ *adj* **PALE IN COLOUR** having a pale soft colour ■ *n* **1 PALE COLOUR** a pale soft colour **2 PASTE USED FOR MAKING CRAYONS** a paste of powdered pigment and gum, used for making crayons **3 CRAYON** a crayon for doing pastel drawings **4 DRAWING** something drawn using pastel crayons **5 ART USING PASTELS** the technique or process of drawing with pastels [Late 16C. Directly or via French < Italian *pastello* 'small amount of paste' < *pasta* 'paste' < late Latin (see PASTE[1]).] —**pastellist** *n*

pastern /pástərn/ *n* **1** the part of a horse's foot between the fetlock and the top of the hoof **2** either of two bones in a horse's foot that connect the hoof with the fetlock [13C. Via Old French *pasturon* < *pasture* 'hobble for pastured animal' < Latin *pascere* 'to feed'.]

paste-up *n* **1 SHEETS WITH PAGES FOR CHECKING** a number of sheets of paper onto which printed pages or proofs have been pasted for checking **2 PREPARATION FOR PRINTING PLATES** cards on which pieces of typesetting or artwork have been pasted to be photographed for making printing plates **3 TECHNIQUE OF MAKING PASTE-UPS** the technique or process of making paste-ups (*often before nouns*) ○ *a paste-up artist*

Pasteur /pa stúr/, **Louis** (1822–95) French scientist

pasteurisation *n* = **pasteurization**

pasteurise *vt* = **pasteurize**

pasteurize /pa̋aschə rīz, páschə-/ (**-izes, -izing, -ized**), **pasteurise** (**-ises, -ising, -ised**) *vt* to treat a liquid such as milk by heating it in order to destroy harmful bacteria [Late 19C. After Louis PASTEUR.] —**pasteurization** /pa̋aschə rī záysh'n, páschə-/ *n* —**pasteurizer** *n*

pasticcio /pa stíchō/ (*plural* **-ci** /-chi/ *or* **pasticcios**) *n* a pastiche [Mid-18C. Via Italian, 'pie, pasty' < late Latin *pasta* (see PASTE[1]).]

pastiche /pa stéesh/ *n* 1 IMITATIVE WORK a piece of creative work, e.g. in literature, drama, or art, that imitates and often satirizes another work or style 2 MIXTURE a piece of creative work, e.g. in literature, drama, or art, that is a mixture of things borrowed from other works 3 USE OF PASTICHE the creation or use of a pastiche [Late 19C. Via French < Italian *pasticcio* (see PASTICCIO).]

pastille /pást'l/ *n* 1 a small flavoured or medicated sweet 2 a substance, usually in tablet or paste form, that is burnt to scent or fumigate a room [Mid-17C. Via French < Latin *pastillus* 'little loaf' (from the shape) < *panis* 'loaf'.]

pastime /pa̋ass tīm/ *n* an interest or activity that somebody pursues in his or her spare time [15C. < PASS + TIME.]

pasting /páysting/ *n* a severe beating or a complete defeat (*informal*)

pastis /pa stéess/ *n* a yellowish French liqueur flavoured with aniseed, often drunk as an aperitif [Early 20C. Via French, 'muddle, mixture' < late Latin *pasta* (see PASTE[1]).]

past master *n* 1 a person with great experience and skill in doing something 2 a former holder of the position of master, e.g. in the Freemasons

pastor /pa̋astər/ *n* 1 MINISTER a Christian minister or priest in charge of a congregation 2 SPIRITUAL ADVISER somebody who is not a minister or priest but who gives spiritual advice to a group of people 3 ASIAN STARLING a starling with a black head and wings and a pink body that often feeds on the parasites that live on sheep. Native to: Asia. *Sturnus roseus*. [14C. Via Old French *pastre* < Latin *pastor* 'herdsman, shepherd' < *past-*, past participle of *pascere* 'feed or graze'.] —**pastorship** *n*

pastoral /pa̋astərəl/ *adj* 1 RURAL relating to the countryside or to rural life ○ *pastoral living* 2 IDEALIZING RURAL LIFE presenting an idealized image of rural life and nature ○ *pastoral poetry* 3 OF CLERGY relating to ministers of religion or priests or their duties 4 USED FOR PASTURE describes land that is used as pasture 5 GIVING ADVICE TO STUDENTS relating to the duties of a teacher who gives personal advice and support to students rather than just teaching them 6 OF SHEEP OR CATTLE relating to or keeping sheep or cattle ■ *n* 1 DESCRIPTION OF RURAL LIFE a literary work or painting that portrays rural life in an idealized way 2 MUSIC = **pastorale** 3 LETTER FROM A MINISTER a letter written by a minister of religion to his or her congregation 4 BISHOP'S STAFF a staff carried by a bishop as a symbol of office [15C. < Latin *pastoralis* < *pastor* (see PASTOR).] —**pastorally** *adv*

pastorale /pástə ra̋al, pástə ra̋ali/ (*plural* **-rales** *or* **-rali** /-ra̋ali/) *n* 1 an opera with a rural story and setting, popular in the 16th and 17th centuries 2 a piece of music with a pastoral theme [Early 18C. Via Italian, 'pastoral' < Latin *pastor* (see PASTOR).]

Pastoral Epistles *n* in the Bible, the three epistles, two to Timothy and one to Titus, traditionally attributed to St Paul

pastoralism /pa̋astrəlizəm/ *n* 1 LIVESTOCK RAISING the raising of livestock, especially by traditional methods, as the main economic activity of a society 2 WAY OF LIFE DEPENDENT ON LIVESTOCK a way of life that depends on raising livestock and living on its milk and meat 3 ARTISTIC TREATMENT OF RURAL LIFE a style in literary work or painting that portrays rural life, especially that of shepherds, in an idealized way

pastoralist /pa̋astrəlist/ *n* 1 somebody who has a pastoral way of life 2 *Aus* a cattle or sheep farmer, especially the owner of a large area of land in the Australian outback

pastorate /pa̋astərət/ *n* 1 the office, term of office, or jurisdiction of a pastor 2 pastors considered as a group

past participle *n* a participle that expresses past time or a completed action

past perfect *n* a verb tense formed with 'had' that expresses an action completed at a specified or implied time in the past ■ *adj* being in or relating to the past perfect tense

pastrami /pə stra̋ami/ *n* smoked and strongly seasoned beef, usually prepared from a shoulder cut, that is served cold in thin slices [Mid-20C. Via Yiddish < Romanian *pastramă*.]

pastry /páystri/ (*plural* **-tries**) *n* 1 DOUGH FOR PIES a dough made with flour, water, and shortening, used to make a base or covering for pies 2 FOODS MADE FROM PASTRY sweet baked food made from pastry 3 SOMETHING MADE WITH PASTRY a pie or small cake made with pastry [15C. < PASTE[1].]

pastry fork *n* a small delicate fork for eating pastries and cakes

past tense *n* a verb tense expressing something that happened or was done in the past. In the sentence 'I felt very proud of them', the verb 'felt' is in the past tense.

pasturage /pa̋aschərij/ *n* 1 AGRIC = **pasture** *n.* 1 2 the grazing of livestock, or the right to graze livestock on a particular area of land

pasture /pa̋aschər/ *n* 1 LAND FOR GRAZING grass-covered land used for grazing livestock 2 PLANTS FOR GRAZING grass and other growing plants that are suitable food for livestock ■ *vti* (**-tures, -turing, -tured**) GRAZE to graze, or to put livestock somewhere to graze [13C. Via Old French < late Latin *pastura* < *past-*, past participle of Latin *pascere* 'feed'.] ◇ **pastures new** somewhere different to work or live (*informal*) ◇ **put somebody out to pasture** to impose early retirement on somebody (*informal*)

pastureland /pa̋aschər land/ *n* an area of land that is used for grazing livestock

~~**pasturized**~~ incorrect spelling of **pasteurized**

pasty[1] /pásti/ (*plural* **-ties**) *n* a pie made from a folded-over round of pastry with a savoury or sweet filling in the middle [Via Old French *pasté(e)* < late Latin *pasta* (see PASTE[1])]

pasty[2] /páysti/ *adj* (**-ier, -iest**) 1 UNHEALTHILY PALE having a pale unhealthy appearance 2 RESEMBLING PASTE resembling paste in consistency, colour, or texture ■ *n* (*plural* **-ies**) NIPPLE COVERING either of a pair of small adhesive coverings for a woman's nipples, worn usually by erotic dancers [Early 17C. < PASTE[1].] —**pastily** *adv* —**pastiness** *n*

pat[1] /pat/ *vt* (**pats, patting, patted**) 1 STRIKE LIGHTLY to strike something lightly with the palm of the hand or something flat 2 LAY THE HAND ON SOMETHING REPEATEDLY to touch somebody or something repeatedly with the palm of your hand, e.g. to show affection or to congratulate somebody ○ *I patted the child's curly head.* 3 SHAPE SOMETHING WITH THE HANDS to shape or smooth something with the hands or with a flat object ○ *patted the dough into shape* ■ *n* 1 LIGHT BLOW a light blow with the palm of the hand or with a flat object 2 LIGHT TOUCH a light, usually repeated, touch with the hand to show affection or to congratulate somebody 3 SOFT SOUND the sound made by a light blow with the hand or with a flat object, or by a light footstep 4 SMALL PIECE a small piece of a soft substance, especially butter [14C. Imitative of the sound of patting.] ◇ **a pat on the back** an expression of praise or congratulation (*informal*) ○ *You deserve a pat on the back for getting the work done so quickly.* ◇ **pat somebody on the back** to praise or congratulate somebody (*informal*)

pat[2] /pat/ *adv* 1 EXACTLY in an exact, accurate, or fluent way ○ *He has his lines off pat.* 2 OPPORTUNELY at the most appropriate time or place ■ *adj* 1 GLIB so easily and readily produced as to suggest lack of proper thought ○ *pat answers* 2 NOT TO BE IMPROVED describes a poker hand that is not likely to be improved by drawing additional cards [Late 16C. Probably 'hitting the mark' < PAT[1].]

Pat *n* an offensive term for an Irishman [Early 19C. Shortening of the name *Patrick*, common in Ireland.]

pat. *abbr* 1 patent 2 patented

pataca /pə ta̋akə/ *n* see table at **currency** [Mid-19C. Via Portuguese < Arabic *abū ṭāqah*, a kind of coin.]

patagium /pə táyji əm/ (*plural* **-a** /-ə/) *n* 1 a loose fold of skin between the fore and hind limbs in some mammals, e.g. bats and flying lemurs, used as an aid to flying or gliding 2 a thin fold of skin between a bird's wing and its shoulder [Early 19C. < Latin, 'gold edging on a tunic'.]

Patagonia /páttə gṓni ə/ region of S Argentina, between the Andes Mountains and the South Atlantic Ocean. Area: 670,000 sq. km/260,000 sq. mi. —**Patagonian** *n, adj*

ϟ **patch** /pach/ *n* 1 SOMETHING THAT COVERS OR MENDS a piece of material used to cover, strengthen, or mend a hole in something ○ *an elbow patch* 2 SMALL AREA a small area of something within a larger one ○ *a patch of ice* 3 SMALL GROWING AREA a small area of land used for growing a particular crop ○ *a cabbage patch* 4 PERIOD a period of time in which a particular situation exists ○ *a relationship going through a rough patch* 5 AREA OF CONTROL an area under somebody's control or jurisdiction ○ *They warned him to stay off their patch.* 6 EYE SHIELD a pad worn over an injured or missing eye ○ *an eye patch* 7 COVER FOR WOUND a piece of material used to cover a wound 8 SEWN-ON BADGE a cloth badge sewn onto clothing as identification, a sign of rank, or to commemorate something 9 SOFTWARE BUG CORRECTOR OR UPDATE a fragment of program code made available to fix a bug in a software application or to add a new feature before an updated version of the application is released ○ *a patch available on the Internet* 10 DRUG-IMPREGNATED MATERIAL a drug-impregnated adhesive pad worn on the skin to allow gradual absorption of the drug ○ *a nicotine patch* 11 ARTIFICIAL BEAUTY SPOT a small piece of black silk or velvet worn on the face by men and women as an adornment in the 17th and 18th centuries ■ *vt* 1 REPAIR WITH MATERIAL to cover or mend a hole in something or to strengthen a weak place using cloth or some other material 2 MAKE FROM CLOTH PIECES to make something by sewing together pieces of fabric 3 AMEND A PROGRAM USING A PATCH to fix or update software using a patch 4 CONNECT A CALL to connect one telephone or radio caller with another or transfer a call to somewhere else ○ *Patch me through to headquarters.* [14C. < ?] —**patcher** *n* ◇ **hit** *or* **strike a bad patch** go through a period of misfortune or difficulty ◇ **not a patch on somebody** *or* **something** not nearly as good as somebody or something (*informal*)

patch up *vt* 1 MEND SOMETHING HURRIEDLY to mend or assemble something hurriedly or as a temporary measure 2 BECOME FRIENDS AGAIN to become friends with somebody again after an argument 3 GIVE TREATMENT TO to give somebody medical treatment for an injury (*informal*)

patch board, patch panel *n* an electrical panel with numerous sockets into which electrical cords (**patch cords**) can be plugged to form temporary circuits

patchouli /páchŏŏli, pə chŏŏli/ *n* 1 an aromatic oil obtained from a tropical mint. Use: perfumes, aromatherapy. 2 a bush of the mint family whose leaves produce patchouli. Native to: tropical Asia. *Pogostemon cablin.* [Mid-19C. < Tamil *paccuḷi*.]

patch panel *n* TELECOM = **patch board**

patch pocket *n* a pocket made by sewing a patch of fabric onto the outside of a garment

patch test *n* a test for allergies in which small pads impregnated with allergens are applied to somebody's skin to check whether there is any negative reaction

patchwork /pách wurk/ *n* 1 needlework in which pieces of fabric are sewn together to make a decorative cover ○ *a patchwork quilt* 2 something made up of many different elements ○ *a patchwork of fields*

patchy /páchi/ (**-ier, -iest**) *adj* 1 occurring only in patches rather than throughout an area, or consisting only of patches rather than a large expanse ○ *patchy fog* 2 good only at times or in places —**patchily** *adv* —**patchiness** *n*

patd *abbr* patented

pate /payt/ *n* the head, especially the top of the head (*archaic or humorous*) [14C. < ?]

pâté /páttay, pátti/ *n* a paste made from meat, fish, or vegetables, often served as an appetizer [Mid-19C. Via French < Old French *paste* (see PASTE[1]).]

pâté de foie gras /páttay də fwa̋a gra̋a, pátti-/ (*plural* **pâtés de foie gras** /páttay də fwa̋a gra̋a, pátti-/) *n* a rich pâté made from the livers of geese that are fattened specifically for this purpose [< French, 'pâté of fatty liver']

patella /pə téllə/ (*plural* **-lae** /-lee/ *or* **-las**) *n* a kneecap (*technical*) [15C. < Latin, 'small shallow dish' (from the shape) < *patina* (see PATEN).] —**patellar** *adj* —**patellate** *adj*

paten /pátt'n/ *n* a shallow metal plate, often made of gold or silver, used to carry the bread at the celebration of the Christian ceremony of Communion [13C. Directly or via French *patène* < Latin *patina* 'shallow dish' < Greek *patanē* 'plate'.]

patency /páyt'nssi/ *n* **1** the obvious nature of something **2** the naturally open and unblocked state of an artery, duct, or other tube in the body

patent /páyt'nt, pátt'nt/ *n* **1 EXCLUSIVE RIGHT TO MARKET AN INVENTION** an exclusive right officially granted by a government to an inventor to make or sell an invention **2 DOCUMENT GRANTING A PATENT** an official document setting out the terms of a patent **3 INVENTION PROTECTED BY PATENT** an invention for which a patent has been granted **4 DOCUMENT GRANTING A RIGHT** any official document that grants a right to somebody ■ *adj* **1 CLEAR OR OBVIOUS** very obvious and not being open to doubt ○ *his patent discomfiture* **2 OPEN FOR INSPECTION** describes a legal document that is accessible to anyone for inspection **3 OF PATENTS** relating to or dealing in patents ○ *a patent lawyer* **4 PROTECTED BY PATENT** protected by a patent from being copied or sold by somebody else **5 UNBLOCKED** describes an artery, duct, or other tube in the body that is naturally open and unblocked **6 SPREADING** describes plant parts that spread out widely from a centre ■ *vt* **PROTECT RIGHTS TO SOMETHING BY PATENT** to obtain a patent on or for something, especially an invention [14C. Directly or via French < Latin *patent-*, present participle of *patere* 'lie open'.]

patentee /páyt'n teé, pátt'n-/ *n* a person or group to whom a patent has been granted

patent leather *n* leather that has been treated with lacquer to give it a hard, glossy surface [< the idea of protection]

patent log *n* an instrument that measures a ship's speed or the distance it has travelled by means of fins that rotate as the instrument is dragged through the water behind the vessel [Because it was patented]

patently /páyt'ntli, pátt-/ *adv* in a way that can easily be seen or understood ○ *She was patently ill at ease.*

patent medicine *n* a medicine protected by a patent or trademark that can be bought without a prescription

Patent Office *n* a government office that evaluates patent claims and grants patents

patentor /páyt'n táwr, pátt'n-/ *n* a person or office that grants a patent

patent right *n* the exclusive right to make or sell something that is granted to somebody by a patent

Patent Rolls *npl* the register of patents granted in the United Kingdom

patent still *n* an alcohol still using steam heat and running continuously that produces very pure spirit [Because it was patented by Geneas Coffey (1830)]

pater /páytər/ *n* somebody's father (*dated slang or humorous*) [14C. < Latin, 'father'.]

Pater /páytər/, **Walter** (1839–94) British essayist and philosopher

paterfamilias /páytərfə mílli ass, páttər-/ (*plural* **patresfamilias** /paá trayz-/) *n* a man in the role of father and head of a household [15C. < Latin, 'father of a family'.]

paternal /pə túrn'l/ *adj* **1 OF FATHERS OR FATHERHOOD** relating to fathers or typical of a father **2 RELATED THROUGH A FATHER** being on a father's side of a family ○ *her paternal grandfather* **3 INHERITED FROM A FATHER** inherited or deriving from a father [15C. Via late Latin *paternalis* < Latin *pater* 'father'.] —**paternally** *adv*

paternalism /pə túrn'lizəm/ *n* a style of government or management, or an approach to personal relationships, in which the desire to help, advise, and protect may neglect individual choice and personal responsibility —**paternalist** *n* —**paternalistic** /pə túrnə lístik/ *adj* —**paternalistically** *adv*

paternity /pə túrnəti/ *n* **1 FATHERHOOD** a man's role or status as a father **2 ANCESTRY** descent from a father **3 ORIGIN** the origin or authorship of something (*literary*) [15C. Directly or via French *paternité* < late Latin *paternitas* < Latin *pater* 'father'.]

paternity leave *n* time off work that an employer grants to a man whose partner has just had, or is about to have, a baby

paternity suit *n* a lawsuit brought by a woman against a man whom she claims is the father of her child and therefore liable for contributing to the child's financial support

paternity test *n* a medical test using DNA fingerprinting or other genetic information to determine whether or not a man is the father of a particular child

paternoster /páttər nóstər, -nostər/ *n* **1 paternoster, Paternoster LORD'S PRAYER** in Roman Catholicism, the Lord's Prayer, or a recitation of it **2 LARGE BEAD IN A ROSARY** in Roman Catholicism, a large bead in a rosary, used to indicate when the Lord's Prayer is to be recited **3 WORDS IN PRAYER OR ATTEMPTED MAGIC** a set form of words used in prayer or in attempting magic **4 NONSTOP LIFT** a doorless lift in which compartments move continuously and people step on and off as they wish [Pre-12C. < Latin *pater noster* 'our father', the first two words of the Lord's Prayer.]

Paterson /páttərss'n/, **Banjo** (1864–1941) Australian poet. Born **Andrew Barton Paterson**

ϟ **path** /paath/ *n* **1 TRODDEN TRACK** a track that has been worn by the continual passage of feet **2 SURFACED TRACK** a surfaced track made for walking or cycling **3 COURSE** a route along which something moves ○ *the path of the Earth's orbit round the Sun* **4 COURSE OF ACTION** a course of action or a way of living ○ *her path to freedom and independence* **5 ROUTE TO A COMPUTER FILE** the route that a computer operating system follows through the directories on a disk to locate a file, or the sequence of keyed characters that identifies this route [Old English *pæþ* < Indo-European, 'to tread'] ◇ **lead somebody up the garden path** to deceive or mislead somebody, often over a period of time (*informal*)

-path *suffix* **1** somebody with a particular disorder ○ *neuropath* **2** somebody who practices a particular type of remedial treatment ○ *osteopath* **3** somebody who possesses a particular ability ○ *telepath* [Back-formation < -PATHY]

Pathan /pə taán/ (*plural* **-than** *or* **-thans**) *n* a member of a people who live in Afghanistan, where Pathans are the largest ethnic group, and in parts of Pakistan [Mid-17C. < Hindi *Paṭhān*.]

pathetic /pə théttik/ *adj* **1** provoking or expressing feelings of pity **2** so inadequate as to be laughable or contemptible (*informal*) [Late 16C. Via French *pathétique* < Greek *pathētikos* 'sensitive' < *pathos* 'feeling'.] —**pathetically** *adv*

SYNONYMS See ***moving***.

---

pathetic fallacy *n* the attribution of human characteristics to nature or to inanimate objects, as in the phrase 'the angry waves'

pathfinder /paáth fìndər/ *n* a discoverer of a route, especially through unmapped territories or uncharted areas of knowledge —**pathfinding** *n*

patho- *prefix* disease ○ *pathogen* [< Greek *pathos* (see PATHOS)]

pathogen /páthəjən, -jen/ *n* something that can cause disease, such as a bacterium or a virus

pathogenesis /páthə jénnəssiss/ *n* the cause, development, and effects of a disease —**pathogenetic** /páthəjə néttik/ *adj*

pathogenic /páthə jénnik/ *adj* **1** causing disease, or able to cause disease **2** relating to the causes and development of diseases

pathognomonic /páthəgnə mónnik/ *adj* describes a symptom or sign that indicates almost beyond doubt the correct diagnosis of a disease [Early 17C. < Greek *pathognōmonikos* < *pathos* 'disease' + *gnōmōn* 'judge'.]

pathological /páthə lójjik'l/ *adj* **1 OF PATHOLOGY** relating to pathology or used in pathology **2 DISEASE** relating to disease or arising from disease **3 EXTREME** uncontrolled or unreasonable ○ *a pathological fear of heights* [Late 17C. < Greek *pathologikos* < *pathos* 'disease'.] —**pathologically** *adv*

pathology /pə thólləji/ (*plural* **-gies**) *n* **1 STUDY OF DISEASE** the scientific study of the nature, origin, progress, and cause of disease ○ *plant pathology* **2 PROCESSES OF A PARTICULAR DISEASE** the processes of a particular disease, observable either with the naked eye or by microscopy, or, at a molecular level, as inferred from biochemical tests ○ *the pathology of cholera* **3 DISEASE** a diseased condition ○ *a scan showing the area of suspected pathology* ○ *evidence of intestinal pathology* **4 CONDITION THAT IS NOT NORMAL** any condition that is a deviation from the normal [Late 16C. Directly or via French *pathologie* < medieval Latin *pathologia* < Greek *pathos* 'disease'.] —**pathologist** *n*

pathophysiology /páthō fízzi ólləji/ *n* the disturbance of function that a disease causes in an organ, as distinct from any changes in structure that might be caused

pathos /páy thoss/ *n* **1** the quality in something that makes people feel pity or sadness **2** feelings of pity, especially when they are expressed in some way [Late 16C. < Greek, 'feeling, disease'.]

pathway /paáth way/ *n* **1** a path or route **2** a sequence of biochemical reactions involved in a metabolic process

-pathy *suffix* **1** disorder, disease ○ *retinopathy* **2** remedial treatment ○ *hydropathy* **3** feeling, perception ○ *telepathy* [< Greek *-patheia* < *pathos* (see PATHOS)] —**-pathic** *suffix*

patience /páysh'nss/ *n* **1** the ability to endure waiting, delay, or provocation without becoming annoyed or upset, or to persevere calmly when faced with difficulties ○ *I was beginning to run out of patience.* **2** a card game for one player. US term **solitaire** *n.* **2** [12C. Via French < Latin *patientia* < *patient-* (see PATIENT).]

patient /páysh'nt/ *adj* able to endure waiting, delay, or provocation without becoming annoyed or upset or to persevere calmly when faced with difficulties ■ *n* a person who receives medical treatment [14C. Via French < Latin *patient-*, present participle of *pati* 'suffer'.] —**patiently** *adv*

patina /páttinə/ *n* **1 THIN GREEN LAYER ON COPPER** a thin layer formed by corrosion on the surface of some metals and minerals, especially the green layer that covers copper and bronze and is valued for its colour **2 SURFACE SHEEN** a pleasing surface sheen that develops on an object with age or frequent handling **3 SUPERFICIAL LAYER** any thin or superficial layer on something [Mid-18C. Via Italian < Latin (see PATEN).] —**patinated** /pátti naytid/ *adj*

patio /pátti ō/ (*plural* **-os**) *n* **1** a paved area adjoining a house, used for outdoor dining and recreation **2** a roofless inner courtyard typical of a Spanish-style house [Early 19C. < Spanish, 'courtyard of a house'.]

patio doors *npl* a pair of glazed doors in an outside wall of a house that open onto a patio

patisserie /pə teéssəri, -tíssəri/ *n* **1** a bakery that specializes in pastries and cakes **2** sweet pastries or cakes collectively [Late 16C. < French *pâtisserie* < *patissier* 'pastry chef' < late Latin *pasta* (see PASTE[1]).]

Pátmos /pát moss/ Greek island in the SE Aegean Sea, one of the Dodecanese group. Population: 2,650 (1995). Area: 34 sq. km/13 sq. mi.

Patna /pátnə/ capital of Bihar State, NE India. Population: 916,980 (1991).

Patna rice /pátnə-/ *n* a variety of long-grained rice, used in savoury dishes [Mid-19C. After PATNA.]

Pat. Off. *abbr* Patent Office

patois /pát waa/ (*plural* **patois** /pát waaz/) *n* **1** a regional form of a language, used informally and usually containing nonstandard elements **2** the jargon used by a particular group [Mid-17C. < French, 'native speech'.]

Patois /pát waa/ *n* LANG = **Creole** *n.* **3**

pat. pend. *abbr* patent pending

patr- *prefix* = **patri-** (*before vowels*)

Patras /pə tráss, pátrəss/ port in S Greece, on the NW Peloponnese. Population: 152,570 (1991).

patresfamilias plural of **paterfamilias**

patri- *prefix* father, paternal ○ *patrilineal* [< Latin and Greek *patr-* 'father']

patriachal incorrect spelling of **patriarchal**

patrial /páytri əl, páttri əl/ *n* formerly, a person entitled to enter and stay in the United Kingdom without being regarded as an immigrant, e.g. somebody from a Commonwealth country [Early 17C. < French or medieval Latin *patrialis* 'of your country' < Latin *pater* 'father'.]

patriarch /páytri aark, páttri-/ (*plural* **-archs**) *n* **1 HEAD OF A FAMILY** a man who is the head of a family or group **2 RESPECTED ELDERLY MAN** a respected and experienced elderly man within a group or family **3 BIBLICAL ANCESTOR** in the Bible, a figure mentioned as the ancestor of the whole human race, e.g. Adam or Noah **4 HEBREW LEADER** in the Hebrew Scriptures, especially the book of Genesis, any ancestor or religious leader of the Hebrew people, e.g. Abraham, Isaac, or Jacob **5 OLDEST MEMBER** the oldest male member of something such as a community of people or a herd of livestock **6 FOUNDER** a man who is a founder of something **7 EASTERN ORTHODOX BISHOP** in the Eastern Orthodox Church, a bishop of the sees of Constantinople, Alexandria, Antioch, or Jerusalem, and also of Russia, Romania, or Serbia **8 SENIOR ROMAN CATHOLIC BISHOP** in the Roman Catholic Church, a leading bishop in a Uniat church **9 DIGNITARY OF THE LATTER-DAY**

SAINTS a high dignitary of the Church of Latter-Day Saints with the power to invoke blessings [12C. Directly and via French < ecclesiastical Latin < Greek *patriarkhēs* 'head of a family' < *patria* 'family'.]

patriarchal /páytri aárk'l, pátri-/ *adj* 1 **RELATING TO A PATRIARCH** relating to or held to be characteristic of a patriarch 2 **CHARACTERISTIC OF A CULTURE RULED BY MEN** relating to or characteristic of a culture in which men are the most powerful members 3 **RULED BY A BISHOP** in Roman Catholicism, governed by a bishop —**patriarchally** *adv*

patriarchal cross *n* a Christian cross with a second and shorter horizontal bar above the main bar

patriarchalism /páytri aárkəlizəm, páttri-/ *n* institutionalized domination by men, with women being regarded as socially or constitutionally inferior

patriarchate /páytri aarkət, páttri-/ *n* 1 the office, term of office, area of jurisdiction, or residence of a patriarch of a Christian church 2 SOC SCI = **patriarchy** [Early 17C. Via medieval Latin *patriarchatus* < ecclesiastical Latin *patriarcha* (see PATRIARCH).]

patriarchy /páytri aarki, páttri-/ (*plural* **-chies**) *n* 1 a social system in which men are regarded as the authority within the family and society, and in which power and possessions are passed on from father to son 2 a society based on a system of patriarchy [Mid-16C. Via medieval Latin *patriarchia* < Greek *patriarkhēs* (see PATRIARCH).]

patrician /pə trísh'n/ *n* 1 **ARISTOCRATIC ROMAN** a member of an aristocratic family of ancient Rome whose privileges included the exclusive right to hold certain offices 2 **NONHEREDITARY BYZANTINE TITLE** a nonhereditary honorary title bestowed by Byzantine emperors on people who had been of great service to the empire 3 **ARISTOCRAT** a member of an aristocracy 4 **SOMEBODY WITH UPPER-CLASS CHARACTERISTICS** a person with the qualities and manners traditionally associated with the upper class ■ *adj* 1 **OF PATRICIANS** relating to patricians, or belonging to a class of patricians 2 **ARISTOCRATIC** characteristic of aristocrats or the upper class 3 **OPPOSED TO DEMOCRACY** opposed to the idea that people in all social classes should have voting rights [15C. Via French *patricien* < Latin *patricius* 'of a noble father' < *pater* 'father'.]

patriciate /pə tríshi ət/ *n* 1 the position or rank of a patrician 2 the social class to which patricians belong [Mid-17C. < Latin *patriciatus* < *patricius* (see PATRICIAN).]

patricide /páttri sīd, páytri-/ *n* 1 the murder of a father by his child or children 2 somebody who murders his or her own father [Late 16C. < late Latin *patricidium* < Latin *pater* 'father'.] —**patricidal** /páttri sīd'l, páytri-/ *adj*

Patrick /páttrik/, **St** (389?–461?) British-born Irish churchman. Known as **the Apostle of Ireland**

patriclinous /pə tríklinəss/, **patroclinous** *adj* descended or inherited from the male line [Early 20C. < PATRI- + Greek *klinein* 'lean'.]

patrilineal /páttrə línni əl/, **patrilinear** /-ər/ *adj* describes family relationships traced through the male line, or societies in which only such relationships are recognized —**patrilineally** *adv*

patrilocal /páttri lṓk'l/ *adj* describes a custom in which a wife goes to live with her husband's family or people after marriage, or a society in which this custom prevails —**patrilocally** *adv*

patrimony /páttriməni/ (*plural* **-nies**) *n* 1 **INHERITANCE FROM A FATHER** an inheritance from a father or male ancestor 2 **HERITAGE** the objects, traditions, or values that one generation has inherited from its ancestors 3 **ESTATE BELONGING TO A CHURCH** an estate or endowment that belongs to a church [14C. Via French < Latin *patrimonium* < *pater* 'father'.] —**patrimonial** /páttri mṓni əl/ *adj* —**patrimonially** *adv*

patriot /páttri ət, páy-/ *n* a proud supporter or defender of his or her country and its way of life [Late 16C. Via French < late Latin *patriota* 'fellow countryman' < Greek *patris* 'fatherland'.] —**patriotic** /páttri óttik, páytri-/ *adj* —**patriotically** *adv* —**patriotism** *n*

patristic /pə trístik/, **patristical** /pə trístik'l/ *adj* relating to the early Christian writers such as St Augustine or St Ambrose whose works have helped to shape the Christian Church [Mid-19C. < German *Patristik* < Latin *pater* 'father'.] —**patristically** *adv*

patristics /pə trístiks/ *n* the study of the writings and lives of the early Christian theologians (+ *singular verb*) [Mid-19C. Via German *Patristik* < Latin *pater*.]

patro- *prefix* = **patri-**

Patroclus /pə trókləss/ *n* in Greek mythology, a friend of Achilles and a warrior in the Trojan War

patrol /pə trṓl/ *n* 1 **REGULAR TOUR MADE BY A GUARD** a regular tour made of a place in order to guard it or to maintain order 2 **SOMEBODY CARRYING OUT A PATROL** a person or group that carries out a patrol 3 **MILITARY UNIT ON A MISSION** a military unit sent on a particular mission, e.g. to carry out an attack or reconnaissance 4 **SUBDIVISION OF A SCOUT TROOP** a subdivision of a troop of Scouts or Guides ■ *vti* (**-trols, -trolling, -trolled**) **GO ON PATROL** to guard or protect a place ○ *troops patrolling the border* [Mid-17C. Directly or via German *Patrolle* < French *patrouillier*, originally 'walk through mud in a military camp' < Old French *patte* 'paw'.]

patrol car *n* = **squad car**

patrolman /pə trṓlmən/ (*plural* **patrolmen** /-mən/) *n* 1 an employee of a motoring organization who patrols an area and responds to calls from members 2 *US* a police officer who patrols a beat

patrology /pə trólləji/ *n* the study of the writings of the Fathers of the Christian Church [Early 17C. < Greek *patēr* 'father'.] —**patrological** /páttrə lójjik'l/ *adj* —**patrologist** *n*

patrol wagon *n US, ANZ* an enclosed police vehicle for transporting prisoners

patrolwoman /pə trṓl wòomən/ (*plural* **patrolwomen** /-wimmən/) *n US* a policewoman who patrols a beat

patron /páytrən/ *n* 1 **SPONSOR** a giver of money or other support to somebody or something, especially in the arts 2 **REGULAR CUSTOMER** a customer, especially a regular one, of a shop or business 3 RELIG = **patron saint** 4 **ROMAN SLAVE MASTER** a slave master in ancient Rome who had freed a slave but retained some rights over him or her 5 **SOMEBODY ABLE TO MAKE CHURCH APPOINTMENTS** a holder of the right to appoint a member of the clergy to an ecclesiastical benefice in the Church of England [14C. Via French < Latin *patronus* 'one who protects' < *pater* 'father'.] —**patronal** /pə trṓn'l/ *adj* —**patronly** /páytrənli/ *adj*

SYNONYMS See ***backer***.

patronage /páttrənij/ *n* 1 **SUPPORT OF A PATRON** the encouragement, financial support, or influence of a patron 2 *US* = **custom** *n.* 3 3 **BUSINESS PROVIDED BY CUSTOMER** the trade that a regular customer brings to a shop or business (*formal*) 4 **CONDESCENDING KINDNESS** support or kindness offered in a condescending way 5 **POWER TO MAKE APPOINTMENTS** the political power to grant privileges or appoint people to positions 6 **APPOINTMENTS ASSIGNED BY A POLITICIAN** the appointments or privileges that a politician can give to loyal supporters 7 **RIGHT OF ECCLESIASTICAL APPOINTMENT** the right to appoint a member of the clergy to an ecclesiastical benefice in the Church of England [14C. < French < *patron* (see PATRON).]

patronise *vti* = **patronize**

patronising *adj* = **patronizing**

patronize /páttrə nīz/ (**-izes, -izing, -ized**), **patronise** (**-ises, -ising, -ised**) *v* 1 *vti* **BE CONDESCENDING TO** to treat somebody as if he or she were less intelligent or knowledgeable than yourself 2 *vt* **BE A REGULAR CUSTOMER OF** to be a regular customer of a particular shop or business (*formal*) 3 *vt* **SUPPORT** to give money or other material support to somebody or something, especially in the arts —**patronizer** *n*

patronizing /páttrə nīzing/, **patronising** *adj* treating somebody as if he or she is less intelligent or knowledgeable than yourself —**patronizingly** *adv*

patron saint *n* a saint who is believed to be a special guardian, especially of a country, trade, or group of people

patronymic /páttrə nímmik/ *adj* describes a name derived from a male ancestor's name, especially one that adds a prefix, e.g. 'Mac-', or a suffix, e.g. '-son', to the earlier name ■ *n* a patronymic name [Early 17C. Via late Latin *patronymicus* < Greek *patrōnumikos* < *patrōnumos* 'father's name'.]

patsy /pátsi/ (*plural* **-sies**) *n* an easily victimized, cheated, or manipulated person (*informal insult*) [Late 19C. < ?]

pattée /páttay, pátti/ *adj* describes a cross with triangular arms that widen towards the ends [15C. < French < *patte* 'paw'.]

patter[1] /páttər/ *vi* 1 **MAKE A QUICK TAPPING SOUND** to make a quick light tapping sound on something ○ *The rain pattered against the window.* 2 **STEP LIGHTLY** to move or run with short quick light steps ○ *She pattered across the floor in her pyjamas.* ■ *n* **TAPPING NOISE** a quick light tapping sound [Early 17C. < PAT[1].]

patter[2] /páttər/ *n* 1 **GLIB AND RAPID TALK** the fast well-prepared talk of someone such as a comedian or salesperson 2 **JARGON** the language of a specific group or class of people 3 **SMALL TALK** meaningless empty chatter ■ *v* 1 *vi* **TALK QUICKLY** to speak rapidly and glibly 2 *vt* **REPEAT SOMETHING RAPIDLY** to repeat something quickly in a mechanical way [14C. Shortening of PATERNOSTER.]

pattern /páttərn/ *n* 1 **DESIGN** a repeated decorative design, e.g. on fabric ○ *a zigzag pattern* 2 **REGULAR FORM** a regular or repetitive form, order, or arrangement ○ *a predictable pattern of behaviour* ○ *local variations in voting patterns* 3 **PROTOTYPE** an original design or model from which exact copies can be made 4 **PLAN OR MODEL** a plan or model used as a guide for making something ○ *a knitting pattern* 5 **GOOD EXAMPLE** a model that is considered to be worthy of imitation 6 **REGULAR MANNER OF PERFORMANCE** a regular or standard way of moving or behaving ○ *the flight patterns of birds* 7 **SAMPLE** a specimen of a piece of fabric, wallpaper, or other material 8 **MODEL USED FOR MAKING A MOULD** a wood, plaster, or metal shape used to make a mould for casting in a foundry 9 **GUNSHOTS ON TARGET** marks made by shots from a gun on a target 10 **SPREAD OF SPENT PROJECTILES** the dispersal of projectiles such as artillery shells and shrapnel on the ground around a target ■ *vt* 1 **MIMIC** to imitate the design of something 2 **PUT A PATTERN ON** to make something into, or decorate something with, a repeated decorative design [14C. Via Old French *patron* 'pattern, patron' < Latin *patronus* 'patron'.]

patter song *n* a comic song, especially in the works of Gilbert and Sullivan, that consists of words sung together in rapid succession

USMA Archives, West Point

George S. Patton

Patton /pátt'n/, **George S.** (1885–1945) US general. Full name **George Smith Patton, Jr**

patty /pátti/ (*plural* **-ties**) *n* 1 a small flat individual cake made from minced meat, vegetables, or other food 2 a small pie or pasty [Mid-17C. Anglicization of French *pâté*, influenced by PASTY[1].]

pattypan squash *n* a variety of wheel-shaped summer squash with a ribbed edge. *Cucurbita pepo.* [< PATTY + PAN[1]]

patulous /páttyòoləss/ *adj* describes branches that spread or expand from a central point [Early 17C. < Latin *patulus* 'standing open' < *patere* 'be open'.] —**patulously** *adv* —**patulousness** *n*

Patwa /pát waa/ *n* LANG = **Creole** *n.* 3

patzer /pátsər, paátsər/ *n US* an inept player of chess (*informal insult*) [Mid-20C. < ?]

Pau /pō/ city in SW France. Population: 83,928 (1990).

PAU *abbr* Pan American Union

paua /pów ə/ (*plural* **-as** *or* **-a**) *n ANZ* an edible abalone with an iridescent shell. Use: ornaments, jewellery. Native to: New Zealand. *Haliotis iris.* [Mid-19C. < Maori.]

paucity /páwssəti/ *n* 1 an inadequacy or lack of something 2 a small number of something [14C. Via Old French *paucité* < Latin *paucitas* < *paucus* 'few, little'.]

Paul /pawl/, **St** (AD 3?–62?) early Christian missionary. Known as **Saul of Tarsus** —**Pauline** /páwl īn/ *adj*

pauldron /páwldrən/ *n* a piece of armour consisting of a metal plate worn on the shoulder [Late 16C. < Old French *espauleron* < *espoule* 'shoulder' < late Latin *spatula* 'shoulder blade'.]

Paul VI (1897–1978) pope (1963–78). Born **Giovanni Batista Montini**

Pauli exclusion principle /pówli-/ *n* a law of quantum physics stating that no two identical particles of a particular type (**fermions**) may occupy the same quantum state at the same time [Early 20C. After Wolfgang *Pauli* (1900–58), Austrian-born US physicist.]

Pauling /páwling/, **Linus** (1901–94) US chemist and peace activist

Paul Jones (*plural* **Paul Joneses**) *n* a dance in which partners are exchanged in a prearranged pattern [Early 20C. After John *Paul Jones* (1742–92), a Scottish naval officer.]

paulownia /paw lṓni ə/ (*plural* **-as** *or* **-a**) *n* a deciduous tree with large heart-shaped leaves. Flowers: purple, white, bell-shaped, in clusters. Native to: China. *Paulownia tomentosa.* [Mid-19C. < modern Latin, after Anna *Paulowna* (1795–1865), wife of William II of the Netherlands and daughter of Tsar Paul I of Russia.]

paunch /pawnch/ *n* **1** a large round protruding stomach **2** ZOOL = **rumen 3** a thick rope mat that protects against chafing [14C. Via Old French *pance, panche* < Latin *panticem* 'belly, bowels'.] —**paunchiness** *n* —**paunchy** *adj*

pauper /páwpər/ *n* **1** an impoverished person **2** formerly, an impoverished person who was eligible to receive aid from public funds (*archaic*) [15C. < Latin, 'getting little' < *paucus* 'little' + *parare* 'get'.] —**pauperism** *n*

pauperize /páwpə rīz/ (**-izes, -izing, -ized**), **pauperise** (**pauperises, pauperising, pauperised**) *vt* to make somebody become impoverished

pauropod /páwrə pod/ *n* a small eyeless invertebrate with eleven segments and nine pairs of legs. Class: Pauropoda. [Late 19C. < modern Latin *pauropoda* 'small-footed' < Greek *pauros* 'small'; from its tiny feet.]

pause /pawz/ *v* (**pauses, pausing, paused**) **1** *vi* **STOP BRIEFLY** to stop doing something before carrying on ○ *He paused for a moment and then continued eating.* **2** *vi* **STAY BRIEFLY** to stop somewhere for a short time ○ *I paused to glance into a shop window.* **3** *vi* **HESITATE** to hesitate before doing or saying something **4** *vt* **CAUSE SOMETHING TO PAUSE** to cause something such as a machine to stop temporarily, e.g. by pressing a pause button ○ *Can you pause the video for a moment?* ■ *n* **1 BRIEF STOP** a temporary break in an activity **2 SHORT SILENCE** a brief moment of silence between words, sounds, or musical notes **3 HESITATION** a brief moment of hesitation or uncertainty before something happens or is done **4 MUSICAL SYMBOL FOR TIME EXTENSION** a musical symbol indicating that a note, chord, or pause is to be held longer than the indicated time value. It is represented by a full stop with an upside-down 'u' above it. **5** LITERAT = **caesura** *n.* 1 **6 pause, pause button** a control on an electronic or mechanical device such as a video recorder that brings it temporarily to a halt [15C. Via Middle French, and Latin *pausa* 'stopping, cessation' < Greek *pauein* 'stop, cease'.] —**pausal** *adj* —**pauser** *n* ◇ **give somebody pause** to make somebody hesitate or reconsider

SYNONYMS See *hesitate*.

pavane /pə ván, -vaán/ *n* **1** a slow court dance of the 16th and 17th centuries **2** the music for a pavane [Mid-16C. Via French < Italian *pavana* 'Paduan' < *Pavo*, a dialect name for the city of Padua.]

Pavarotti /pávvə rótti/, **Luciano** (*b.* 1935) Italian tenor

pave /payv/ (**paves, paving, paved**) *vt* **1** to cover a surface with stone, brick, concrete, or other hard materials in order to make it suitable for walking or travelling on **2** to cover a surface with a flat, uniform material, e.g. leaves or flowers [14C. Via Old French *paver* < Latin *pavire* 'beat, tread down'.] ◇ **pave the way (for something)** to prepare for and facilitate the progress of something

pavé /pávvay/ *n* a jewel setting in which small stones are set very close together so as to cover the surface of the piece and obscure the metal base [Late 19C. < French, 'paved'.]

pavement /páyvmənt/ *n* **1 PATH FOR PEDESTRIANS** a paved path for pedestrians alongside a street. US term **sidewalk 2** *US* **ASPHALT SURFACE** an asphalt surface, especially of a road **3 LEVEL AREA OF ROCK** a level area of bare rock that resembles a pavement **4 MATERIAL FOR PAVEMENTS** material such as concrete or stone that is used to make a pavement **5 LAYERED SURFACE OF A PATH** the layered structure that forms the surface of a path, road, carriageway, or aircraft runway [13C. Via Old French < Latin *pavimentum* 'beaten floor' < *pavire* 'beat, tread down'.]

paver /páyvər/ *n* a stone or slab used to pave an area such as a patio

pavilion /pə vílli ən/ *n* **1 OUTDOOR STRUCTURE** a summer house or other ornamental building in a garden, **2 SPORTS CLUBHOUSE** a building at a cricket or other sports ground where players can change and where refreshments are served **3 EXHIBITION TENT** a large tent or other temporary structure used for displaying or exhibiting things **4 BIG TENT** a large and often extremely ornate tent **5 ANNEX** a detached building that forms part of a complex for a hospital or other large public building **6 FACET OF A GEM** a facet of a brilliant-cut gem that comes below the girdle ■ *vt* **1 SET IN A PAVILION** to enclose or house something inside a pavilion **2 ENCLOSE** to enclose or completely surround something (*literary*) ○ *'Pavilioned in splendour, And girded with praise'* (Sir Robert Grant, *O Worship the King*; 1833) **3 CONSTRUCT A PAVILION FOR** to construct a pavilion for something [Pre-12C. < Old French *pavilloun* < Latin *papilio* 'butterfly, tent', because a tent was thought to resemble a butterfly's wings.]

~~**pavillion**~~ incorrect spelling of **pavilion**

paving /páyving/ *n* **1 SURFACE FOR PATH, ROAD, ETC.** a surface of paved stone, brick, concrete, or other material **2 MATERIAL FOR MAKING A HARD SURFACE** material such as concrete or stones used for making a firm surface, e.g. for a path or road **3 CONSTRUCTION OF PAVED SURFACE** the act of making a paved surface

paving stone *n* a large flat rectangular slab, usually made from concrete or stone, used in making a paved surface

paviour /páyvyər/, **pavior** *n* **1** somebody whose occupation is laying external paving **2** a stone, slab, or block used to pave an outdoor area such as a patio

Pavlov /páv lof/, **Ivan Petrovich** (1849–1936) Russian physiologist

pavlova /pav lṓvə/ *n* a dessert consisting of a large meringue shell filled with cream and fruit [Early 20C. After Anna PAVLOVA, in whose honour the dish was created.]

Pavlova /pav lṓvə, pávləvə/, **Anna** (1882–1931) Russian ballet dancer

Pavlovian /pav lṓvi ən/ *adj* **1** produced involuntarily in response to a stimulus **2** relating to Ivan Pavlov and his work [Mid-20C. After Ivan Petrovich PAVLOV.]

Pavlovian conditioning *n* PSYCHOL = **classical conditioning**

Pavo /paávō/ *n* a constellation of the southern hemisphere containing the bright star Peacock. See illustration at **constellation**

pavonine /pávvə nīn/ *adj* resembling a peacock, especially the colours and design of its tail (*literary*) [Mid-17C. < Latin *pavoninus* 'peacock'.]

paw /paw/ *n* **1 ANIMAL'S FOOT** the foot of a four-legged mammal, usually having claws or nails **2 HUMAN HAND** a human hand, especially one that is large or clumsy (*informal*) ■ *vti* **1 STRIKE REPEATEDLY WITH THE HOOF** to scrape or strike something repeatedly with a paw or hoof **2 TOUCH CLUMSILY** to touch or caress somebody roughly or rudely with the hands [13C. Via Old French *powe* < Germanic.]

pawky /páwki/ (**-ier, -iest**) *adj* witty or shrewd in a dry or sly manner (*regional*) [Mid-17C. < *pawk* 'trick'.] —**pawkily** *adv* —**pawkiness** *n*

pawl /pawl/ *n* a hinged or pivoted catch, often spring-controlled, designed to engage with the teeth of a ratchet wheel to prevent reverse motion [Early 17C. < ?]

pawn[1] /pawn/ *n* **1** a chess piece of the lowest value that can move one square forward at a time, with an optional first move of two squares **2** somebody or something that is being used for the advantage of another person or thing [14C. Via Anglo-Norman *poun*, Old French *peon* < medieval Latin *pedon-* 'footsoldier' < Latin *ped-* 'foot'.]

pawn[2] /pawn/ *vt* **1 DEPOSIT WITH A PAWNBROKER** to leave something with a pawnbroker as security against money borrowed **2 TO STAKE** to stake or pledge your honour, life, or word on something ■ *n* **1 OBJECT DEPOSITED AS SECURITY** an object that is left as security with a pawnbroker in exchange for a loan of money **2 HOSTAGE** a person who is held as security, usually as a hostage **3 ACT OF PAWNING** the act of pawning something [15C. Via Old French *pan(d)* 'pledge' < Germanic.] —**pawnage** *n* —**pawner** *n* ◇ **in pawn** left or held as security with a pawnbroker in exchange for a loan of money

pawnbroker /páwn brōkər/ *n* somebody who lends money at a fixed rate of interest in exchange for articles of personal property that are left as security

Pawnee /paw neé/ (*plural* **-nee** *or* **-nees**) *n* **1** a member of a confederation of Native North American peoples who lived in Nebraska and Kansas and who are now mainly dispersed **2** the Caddoan language of the Pawnee people. Native speakers: 3,000. [Late 18C. Via Canadian French *Pani* < a Native North American language.] —**Pawnee** *adj*

pawnshop /páwn shop/ *n* a shop where articles or personal property may be left as security in exchange for a loan of money

pawn ticket *n* a ticket that serves as a receipt for something that has been pawned

pawpaw /páw paw/, **papaw** /páw paw, pə páw/ *n* **1** a yellow medium-sized oval fruit with sweet flesh and black seeds **2** a deciduous tree with purple flowers that bears pawpaws. Native to: North America. *Asimina triloba.* **3** TREES, FOOD = **papaya** *n.* 2 [Early 17C. Alteration of PAPAYA.]

pax /paks/ *interj* **SCHOOLCHILDREN'S TRUCE** a call for a truce or a break in a game used by children and usually signalled by holding up crossed fingers (*informal*) ■ *n* **1 KISS OF PEACE IN CHURCH** a kiss or other greeting given as a sign of peace during the Christian ceremony of Communion, especially in the Roman Catholic Mass **2 TABLET KISSED AT CHRISTIAN COMMUNION** a tablet bearing a representation of the Crucifixion that is kissed by participants in the Christian ceremony of Communion, especially during the Roman Catholic Mass [Pre-12C. < Latin, 'peace'.]

PAX *abbr* private automatic exchange

Pax Romana /-rō maánə/ *n* the long period of peace and stability that existed under the Roman Empire, especially in the 2nd century AD [< Latin, 'peace of the Romans']

pax vobiscum /-vō bískoōm/ *interj* peace be with you [< Latin]

pay[1] /pay/ *v* (**pays, paying, paid** /payd/, **paid**) **1** *vti* **GIVE MONEY FOR** to give somebody a particular amount of money for work done or for goods or services provided ○ *They were paid a small fortune for it.* ○ *a well-paid job* **2** *vti* **SETTLE A DEBT** to settle a debt or other obligation **3** *vti* **BRING IN MONEY** to bring in a certain amount of money ○ *How much will the job pay?* **4** *vti* **BE PUNISHED** to be punished or suffer the bad consequences of something you have done ○ *He's paid dearly for what he did.* **5** *vt* **YIELD INTEREST** to yield a particular amount as a return on a sum of money invested ○ *The account pays 12% interest.* **6** *vi* **GIVE A POSITIVE RESULT** to be profitable or beneficial ○ *Crime doesn't pay.* **7** *vt* **BESTOW** to give something, e.g. attention or a compliment, to somebody or something ○ *pay a compliment* **8** *vt* **VISIT** to make a visit or call to see somebody **9** *vt* = **pay out** *v.* 2 **10** *vt* **LET GO LEEWARD** to allow a vessel to make leeway ■ *n* **1 MONEY GIVEN IN RETURN FOR WORK** money that is given in return for work or services provided, especially in the form of a salary or wages **2 REWARD** reward, recompense, or recognition granted to somebody **3** MIN EXTRACT = **pay dirt** *n.* 2 ■ *adj* **1 NEEDING THE INSERTION OF A COIN TO FUNCTION** requiring the insertion of coins or a card in order to function ○ *pay TV* **2 RICH IN METALS** yielding metal or minerals valuable enough to make mining them profitable [12C. Via Old French *payer* 'pacify' < Latin *pacare* < *pax* 'peace'.] ◇ **in the pay of somebody** employed by somebody, especially for a dishonest or criminal purpose ◇ **pay your way** to pay your share of expenses ◇ **put paid to** to put an end to or ruin something (*informal*)

SYNONYMS See *wage*.

pay back *vt* **1** to repay money that has been lent ○ *I'll pay you back on Friday.* **2** to revenge yourself on somebody

pay down *vt US* to reduce the amount of a debt by repaying some of the money that has been borrowed ○ *'...should have paid down its debt or invested in microchip technology...'* (*Newsweek*; November 1998)

pay for *vt* to undergo the bad consequences of something you have done

pay in *vt* to deposit money in a bank or other account

pay off *v* **1** *vt* **REPAY IN FULL** to repay the full amount of a bill, debt, or other financial obligation, especially one that has been paid in instalments **2** *vt* **BRIBE** to give somebody money as a bribe, usually to prevent that person from causing trouble (*informal*) **3** *vt* **PAY AND LAY OFF WORKERS** to give employees or workers the money owing to them for work performed before dismissing them **4** *vi* **BE SUCCESSFUL** to be successful or profitable ○ *All that preparation paid off in the end.* **5** *vt* **TAKE REVENGE ON** to take revenge on somebody for something he or she has done to you **6** *vi* **MAKE LEEWAY** to make leeway **pay out** *v* **1** *vti* **PAY MONEY** to spend or pay money **2** *vt* **UNWIND** to release a rope or cable gradually by hand **3** *vt* **TAKE REVENGE** to take revenge on somebody **pay over** *vt* to transfer money to somebody officially **pay up** *vi* to pay money that is due

pay² /pay/ *vt* to make a ship's hull waterproof with pitch or tar [Early 17C. Via Old French *peier* < Latin *picare* < *pix* 'pitch'.]

payable /páy əb'l/ *adj* **1** due or needing to be paid **2** requesting payment to be made to a particular person ○ *Shall I make the cheque payable to you or to Jean?*

pay and display *n* a parking system in which motorists buy tickets from a machine to cover the amount of time they intend to leave their vehicles in a car park

pay-as-you-earn *n* full form of **PAYE**

pay-as-you-go *n* the practice or system of paying debts or costs as they are incurred

payback /páy bak/ *n* **1** **RETURN ON INVESTMENT** a financial return on an investment equalling the initial capital invested **2** **TIME REQUIRED TO RECOVER OUTLAY** the period of time required to recover the return on an initial investment **3** **REVENGE** revenge or retaliation (*informal*)

pay cheque *n* **1** a cheque issued to an employee as payment for salary or wages **2** wages or salary

payday /páy day/ *n* the day on which employees are paid their wages or salary

pay dirt *n* **1** *US* a discovery or idea that is likely to be useful or profitable **2** gravel, sand, earth, or ore that is worth mining

paydown /páy down/ *n* *US* the reduction of a debt by paying back some of the money borrowed

PAYE *n* a system in which income tax is deducted as wages are earned. Full form **pay-as-you-earn**

~~payed~~ incorrect spelling of **paid**

payee /pay eé/ *n* a person to whom money is being paid or is due, especially in a transaction such as the payment of a cheque or money order

pay envelope *n* = **pay packet** *n*. **1**, **pay packet** *n*. **2**

payer /páyər/ *n* **1** a person who pays somebody or something **2** the person named as responsible for the payment of a cheque, money order, or other financial paper when it is redeemed

paying guest *n* a person who pays to stay in another person's home for a temporary period, e.g. during a holiday

payload /páy lōd/ *n* **1** **QUANTITY OF CARGO** the quantity of cargo or load that a plane, train, or other vehicle can carry, often expressed as weight or volume **2** **PLANE PASSENGERS AND EQUIPMENT** the passengers and instruments carried by an aircraft or spacecraft **3** **EXPLOSIVE CHARGE** the explosive charge of a rocket or missile or the total explosive charge of the bomb load carried by an aircraft

paymaster /páy maastər/ *n* the person who is responsible for paying wages or salaries in a business or government organization

Paymaster-General (*plural* **Paymasters-General**) *n* the government minister who heads the office that acts as paying agent for government departments

payment /páymənt/ *n* **1** **MONEY PAID** an amount of money that is paid or is due to be paid **2** **REWARD** a reward or punishment given in return for something **3** **ACT OF PAYING** the act of paying money, or fact of being paid ○ *Payment will be made at the end of the month.* [14C. < Old French *paiement* < *payer* (see PAY¹).]

payment by results *n* a system of payment in which the salary paid depends on how well an employee does a job

⚡ **payment gateway** *n* a server or organization acting as an interface between the payment systems of retail seller, acquirer, and issuer with regard to Internet payments (*in e-commerce*)

⚡ **payment gateway certificate authority** *n* a body issuing, renewing, or revoking certificates identifying an Internet payment gateway (*in e-commerce*)

paynim /páynim/ *n* (*archaic*) **1** a pagan **2** a person who is not a Christian, especially a Muslim [13C. Via Old French

pai(e)nime < ecclesiastical Latin *paganismus* 'paganism' < *paganus* 'pagan'.]

payoff /páy of/ *n* **1** **FULL PAYMENT** full payment of a salary, wages, or a debt **2** **TIME FOR FULL PAYMENT** the time when full and final payment of a debt, salary, or wage is due **3** **SETTLEMENT** a final settlement, reward, or reckoning **4** **CLIMAX OF NARRATIVE** the final climax of a narrative or sequence of events **5** **REVENGE** final retribution or revenge **6** **BRIBE** a payment made to someone as a bribe (*informal*) **7** **HIDDEN BENEFIT OF NEGATIVE BEHAVIOUR** an often unconscious or hidden benefit of a negative thought pattern or action

payola /pay ólə/ (*plural* **-las** *informal*) *n* *US* a payment given in exchange for promoting a commercial product, or the system of making such payments, especially to disc jockeys [Mid-20C. < PAY¹.]

payout /páy owt/ *n* the act of paying out money or the sum of money paid

pay packet *n* **1** an envelope containing an employee's wages. US term **pay envelope** *n*. **1 2** wages received for a job or service. US term **pay envelope** *n*. **2**

pay-per-view *n* a cable or satellite television system in which individual programmes can be watched for a fee

payphone /páy fōn/ *n* a public telephone that operates only when coins or a card are used to pay for calls

payroll /páy rōl/ *n* **1** a list of employees and their salaries or wages **2** the total sum of money to be paid to employees at a given time

payslip /páy slip/ *n* a printed statement of the amount an employee is paid, showing deductions for tax, pensions, and National Insurance. US term **paystub**

paystub /páy stub/ *n* *US* = **payslip**

pay television *n* a system in which television programmes are transmitted in a scrambled form that can be decoded by viewers who have paid for the appropriate equipment

paytrain /páy trayn/ *n* a train on which passengers pay fares to the guard because there are no ticket offices open on the stations

pay TV *n* = **pay television**

⚡ **payware** /páy wair/ *n* commercial software as opposed to freeware or shareware

Octavio Paz

Paz /pass, paz/, **Octavio** (1914–98) Mexican writer

Pb *symbol* lead

PB *abbr* **1** personal best **2** Pharmacopoeia Britannica **3** power brakes **4** prayer book

PBB *abbr* polybrominated biphenyl

PBX *abbr* private branch exchange

pc¹ *abbr* **1** per cent **2** postcard

pc² *abbr* after meals (*in prescriptions*) [< Latin *post cibum* 'after food']

PC¹ *abbr* **1** Parish Council **2** Parish Councillor **3** Past Commander **4** Police Constable **5** politically correct **6** Post Commander **7** Prince Consort **8** printed circuit **9** Privy Council **10** Privy Councillor

⚡ **PC²** *n* **1** COMPUT = **personal computer 2** a computer compatible with IBM PCs and DOS [Abbreviation of PERSONAL COMPUTER]

p.c., p/c *abbr* **1** petty cash **2** price current

PCB *n* a compound derived from biphenyl and containing chlorine that is a hazardous pollutant. Use: in

electrical insulators, flame retardants, plasticizers. Full form **polychlorinated biphenyl**

⚡ **PCI** *n* a specification for extending the internal circuitry (**bus**) that transmits data from one part of a computer to another by inserting circuit boards. Full form **peripheral component interconnect**

pcm *abbr* **1** per calendar month **2** pulse code modulation

⚡ **PCMCIA** *n* **1** a specification for extending the internal circuitry (**bus**) that transmits data from one part of a computer to another, adding memory. Full form **personal computer memory card interface adapter 2** an international organization that has developed a standard for adding memory to personal computers and credit-card size devices. Full form **Personal Computer Memory Card International Association**

PCP *abbr* **1** phencyclidine **2** pneumocystis carinii pneumonia

PCR *abbr* polymerase chain reaction

PCV *abbr* passenger carrying vehicle

pd *abbr* paid

Pd *symbol* palladium

PD *abbr* **1** police department **2** postal district

p.d., P.D. *abbr* **1** per diem **2** potential difference

⚡ **PDA** *abbr* personal digital assistant

⚡ **pdf** *n* a format for a computer document file that enables a document to be processed and printed on any computer using any printer or word-processing program. Full form **portable document format**

⚡ **PDN** *abbr* public data network (*in e-mails*)

⚡ **pdq** *adv* at once or immediately (*informal*) Full form **pretty damn quick**

PDR *abbr* price-dividend ratio

P-D ratio *abbr* price-dividend ratio

PDSA *abbr* People's Dispensary for Sick Animals

PDT *abbr* Pacific Daylight Time

pe¹ /pay/ *n* the 17th letter of the Hebrew alphabet [Early 19C. < Hebrew *pē*.]

⚡ **pe²** *abbr* **1** Peru (*in Internet addresses*) **2** printer's error

PE¹ *abbr* **1** Peru (*international vehicle registration*) **2** physical education **3** potential energy **4** Present Era **5** probable error **6** Protestant Episcopal

PE² *abbr* Prince Edward Island

p.e. *abbr* printer's error

pea /pee/ *n* **1** **SEED AS A VEGETABLE** a round green seed that grows in a pod, eaten as a vegetable **2** **LEGUMINOUS PLANT WITH EDIBLE SEEDS** an annual vine of the legume family with compound leaves that is widely grown for its peas. Flowers: small, white. Native to: Europe, Asia. *Pisum sativum.* **3** **PLANT RELATED TO THE PEA** a plant related to or similar to the pea, e.g. the chickpea, sweet pea, or cowpea **4** **SOMETHING RESEMBLING A PEA** something resembling a pea in form or size [Mid-17C. Back-formation < *pease* (singular but thought to be plural) < Latin *pisa*.]

Peabody /peé bodi/, **George** (1795–1869) US businessman and philanthropist

~~peacable~~ incorrect spelling of **peaceable**

peace /peess/ *n* **1** **FREEDOM FROM WAR** freedom from war, or the time when a war or conflict ends ○ *the signing of the peace agreement* **2** **MENTAL CALM** a state of mental calm and serenity, with no anxiety **3** **PEACE TREATY** a treaty agreeing to an end of hostilities between two warring parties **4** **LAW AND ORDER** the absence of violence or other disturbances within a state ○ *Peace reigned throughout the land.* **5** **STATE OF HARMONY** freedom from conflict or disagreement among people or groups of people ■ *interj* **BE CALM OR SILENT** used to tell somebody to be calm or silent or as a greeting or farewell [12C. Via Anglo-Norman *pes* < Latin *pax* 'peace'.] ◇ **at peace 1** in a state of friendship and freedom from conflict **2** dead (*used euphemistically*) **3** in a state of calm and serenity ◇ **hold your peace** to refrain from speaking (*dated*) ◇ **keep the peace** to refrain from or prevent conflict or violence ◇ **make peace** to bring a disagreement or war to an end ◇ **make your peace with somebody** to become friends with somebody again after an argument

SPELLCHECK Do not confuse **peace** with **piece**, which has a similar sound. Beware: your spellchecker will not catch this error.

peaceable /peessəb'l/ adj 1 inclined towards peace and avoiding contentious situations 2 tranquil and free from strife and disorder —**peaceableness** n —**peaceably** adv

peace camp n a camp set up by antiwar demonstrators, usually in the vicinity of a military establishment

Peace Corps n a US government organization that trains volunteers to work in developing countries on educational and agricultural projects. ◊ **VSO**

peaceful /peessf'l/ adj 1 QUIET AND CALM quiet, calm, and tranquil ○ a peaceful atmosphere 2 MENTALLY CALM serene and untroubled in the mind 3 APPROPRIATE FOR PEACETIME appropriate for a time of peace rather than war —**peacefully** adv —**peacefulness** n

SYNONYMS See **calm**.

peacekeeping /peess keeping/ n the preservation of peace, especially as a military mission in which troops attempt to keep formerly warring armed forces from starting to fight again —**peacekeeper** n

peacemaker /peess maykər/ n a person who brings peace and reconciliation to others —**peacemaking** n

peace offering n something done for or given to an enemy or somebody you have quarrelled with in the hope of bringing about a reconciliation

peace officer n US somebody such as a justice of the peace, police officer, or sheriff whose main duty is to preserve public order

peace pipe n a long-stemmed ceremonial pipe used by some Native North American peoples

peace sign n a sign used to indicate peaceful intentions, made by holding the palm upright and outwards and forming a V with the middle and index fingers

peacetime /peess tīm/ n a time when there is no war

peach[1] /peech/ n 1 LARGE FRUIT WITH STONE a sweet round juicy fruit with yellow flesh, a single stone, and a soft downy orange-yellow skin 2 TREE WITH EDIBLE FRUIT a tree that bears peaches, widely grown in temperate regions. Flowers: pink. Native to: China. Prunus persica. 3 SOMEBODY OR SOMETHING EXCELLENT somebody or something that is particularly good or pleasing (informal) ○ That was a peach of a throw! 4 CREAMY ORANGE-YELLOW COLOUR a creamy yellowish-orange colour [13C. Via Old French < medieval Latin persica, alteration of earlier persicum < mālum Persicum 'Persian apple'.] —**peach** adj

peach[2] /peech/ vi to inform against somebody, especially an accomplice (dated informal) [15C. Shortening of appeach, via Anglo-Norman < late Latin impedicare (see IMPEACH).] —**peacher** n

peach melba n a dessert made with fresh or canned peaches, vanilla ice cream, and a raspberry sauce

peach palm n a dense spiny palm with an edible heart. Native to: Amazon basin. Bactris gasipaes.

peachy /peechi/ (-ier, -iest) adj 1 resembling a peach in colour, taste, or texture 2 excellent or wonderful (informal) [Late 16C. < PEACH[1].] —**peachily** adv —**peachiness** n

peacock /pee kok/ n 1 MALE PEAFOWL a male peafowl with a crested head and a large fan-shaped tail with brilliantly coloured blue and green spots 2 PEAFOWL a peafowl, either male or female 3 VAIN PERSON a conspicuously vain person, especially as shown by behaviour and dress [14C. Pea < an Old English word, 'peacock' < Latin pavo.] —**peacockish** adj

peacock blue adj of a brilliant greenish-blue colour, like a peacock's plumage —**peacock blue** n

peacock butterfly n a European butterfly with bold iridescent colours and eyespots on its wings. Nymphalis io.

peacock ore n a copper ore such as bornite that becomes iridescent as it tarnishes

peafowl /pee fowl/ (plural -fowls or -fowl) n a large pheasant, the male of which holds up its brilliant iridescent tail like a fan in courtship displays. Native to: India, Southeast Asia. Pavo cristatus and Pavo muticus. [Early 19C. < pea (see PEACOCK).]

pea green adj of a medium yellowish-green colour —**pea green** n

peahen /pee hen/ n a female peafowl, with much plainer plumage than the peacock [14C. < pea (see PEACOCK).]

pea jacket n a heavy double-breasted jacket or short coat, made of mohair or thick wool and originally worn by sailors [By folk etymology < Dutch pijjakker, pijjekker 'coarse cloth jacket' < pij 'coarse cloth' (by association with PEA) + jekker 'jacket']

peak /peek/ n 1 MOUNTAIN TOP the pointed summit of a mountain 2 MOUNTAIN a mountain with a pointed summit 3 POINTED PART a sharp projecting pointed part of something, e.g. the brim of a cap 4 HIGHEST POINT the point of greatest success, development, or strength of a process or activity ○ She's at the peak of her career. 5 TOP OF CURVE the highest point in a curve, especially the curve of a wave 6 HAIR = widow's peak 7 MAXIMUM VALUE OF QUANTITY a point at which a variable physical quantity such as temperature or voltage changes from rapidly increasing to rapidly decreasing, or the value of the quantity at such a point 8 EXTREME END OF HULL narrow part at the front or back end of a boat's hull 9 CORNER OF FORE-AND-AFT SAIL the top rear corner of a fore-and-aft sail 10 GAFF END the outermost end of a gaff sail ■ v 1 vi REACH HIGHEST POINT to reach the point of greatest success, development, intensity, or strength ○ Sales peaked in July. 2 vi FORM PEAK to form a peak or peaks ○ The waves peaked as the storm grew. 3 vt CAUSE PEAK IN to cause something to come to a high point or peak ■ adj 1 HIGHEST being at a maximum or highest point ○ peak efficiency 2 OF GREATEST USE relating to the maximum use of something or the maximum demand on something ○ peak viewing time [Mid-16C. Back-formation < PEAKED[1], a variant of PICKED 'pointed'.]

SPELLCHECK Do not confuse **peak** with **peek** or **pique**, which sound similar. Beware: your spellchecker will not catch this error.

peak out vi to reach a peak or its highest level, often before beginning to decline

Peak District /peek distrikt/ region in central England forming the southern part of the Pennine Hills

Peak District National Park national park in N England. Area: 1,404 sq. km/542 sq. mi.

peaked[1] /peekt/ adj having a peak or point —**peakedness** n

peaked[2] /peekt/ adj US = peaky

peak hour n ANZ the rush hour, when the greatest number of people are travelling to or from work

peak load n the maximum instantaneous rate of power consumption in a load circuit

peak season n LEISURE = high season

peaky /peeki/ (-ier, -iest) adj thin, pale, and sickly in appearance. US term **peaked**[2] adj. [Early 19C. < peak 'be sickly' <?]

peal /peel/ n 1 RINGING OF BELLS a ringing of bells, especially a change or series of changes rung on bells 2 GROUP OF BELLS a set of tuned bells 3 NOISY OUTBURST a loud repetitive sound, e.g. of thunder or laughter ■ v 1 vti RING to ring a bell loudly and sonorously, or to be rung in this way 2 vt SAY LOUDLY to say something loudly and sonorously [14C. Variant of APPEAL 'call, request'.]

SPELLCHECK Do not confuse **peal** with **peel**, which has a similar sound. Beware: your spellchecker will not catch this error.

pean /peen/ n sable fur spotted with a gold or yellow colour [Mid-16C. <?]

peanut /pee nut/ n 1 OILY EDIBLE SEED an oily edible seed with a thin shell that grows underground and is a source of vegetable oil 2 PLANT PRODUCING PEANUTS a low-growing annual plant of the legume family whose seeds are peanuts. Arachis hypogaea. ■ **peanuts** npl SMALL AMOUNT OF MONEY a very small amount of money, especially when smaller than would be expected (informal) ○ They're paid peanuts! [Early 19C. < PEA (from the similarity of peanuts to peas, because peanuts also grow in a pod) + NUT.]

peanut brittle n a hard sweet made of toffee and peanuts

peanut butter n an oily paste made from ground roasted peanuts and usually spread on bread or used in cooking

peanut oil n a combustible yellow oil extracted from peanuts. Use: cooking, medicine, soaps.

pear /pair/ n 1 a sweet juicy fruit with a usually green skin, firm white flesh, and roughly teardrop shape, eaten fresh or canned 2 a tree with fine-toothed glossy leaves, widely grown to produce pears. Native to: Europe. Pyrus communis. [Pre-12C. Via assumed Vulgar Latin pira < Latin pirum.]

SPELLCHECK See **pair**.

pearl[1] /purl/ n 1 GEM FORMED IN MOLLUSC a small lustrous sphere of calcium carbonate that forms round a grain of sand in a mollusc such as an oyster, and is valued as a gem 2 CRAFT = mother-of-pearl 3 SOMEBODY OR SOMETHING MUCH VALUED somebody or something highly esteemed or valued 4 PALE GREYISH-WHITE COLOUR a pale greyish-white colour tinged with blue ■ v 1 vi HARVEST PEARLS to fish or dive for pearls 2 vi MAKE BEADS to form a pearl or pearl-shaped drops 3 vt DECORATE WITH PEARLS to decorate something with pearls or with things that resemble pearls [14C. < Old French perle 'little mollusc whose feet resemble hams in shape' < Latin perna 'ham'.] —**pearl** adj

pearl[2] /purl/ n HANDICRAFT = purl[1] n. 2, purl[1] n. 3

pearl ash n the commercial form of potassium carbonate

pearl barley n grains of barley that have been polished and are used in soups and stews

pearler /purlər/ n 1 a diver for or dealer in natural pearls 2 a boat used for pearl-diving or for trading pearls

pearlescent /pur léss'nt/ adj with a lustrous surface like a pearl [Mid-20C. < PEARL and -ESCENT]

pearl grey n of a pale blue-grey colour —**pearl grey** adj

Pearl Harbor /purl-/ inlet of the Pacific Ocean on S Oahu, Hawaii. Japanese planes attacked the US naval base there on 7 December, 1941, prompting the United States' entry into World War II.

pearlised adj = pearlized

pearlite /purl īt/ n a microstructure of steel or cast iron made up of bands (lamellae) of pure iron (ferrite) and iron carbide (cementite) [Late 19C. < PEARL[1] + -ITE[1].] —**pearlitic** /pur líttik/ adj

pearlized /purl īzd/, **pearlised** adj having a pearly iridescent lustre

pearl millet n a tall cereal grass widely grown for its whitish seeds. Pennisetum americanum.

pearl onion n a very small white onion that is often pickled

pearl oyster n a tropical marine mollusc that is a source of pearls. Genus: Pinctada.

pearly /purli/ adj (-ier, -iest) 1 RESEMBLING PEARL resembling pearls or mother-of-pearl, particularly in having an iridescent lustre 2 DECORATED WITH PEARLS adorned or decorated with pearls or mother-of-pearl 3 PALE GREYISH-WHITE of a pale greyish-white colour tinged with blue ■ n (plural -ies) COCKNEY WEARING PEARL-DECORATED COSTUME a member of a Cockney family who, on ceremonial occasions, traditionally wears a special costume covered with pearl buttons arranged in ornamental patterns. ◊ pearly king, pearly queen —**pearliness** n

pearly everlasting n a North American plant with woolly leaves and white flower heads. Anaphalis margaritacea.

Pearly Gates npl in Christianity, the gates of heaven (informal)

pearly king n a man from one of the Cockney families traditionally entitled to wear a pearl-covered costume, who is chosen as the one with the finest costume

pearly nautilus n a mollusc that has a spiral pearl-coloured multi-chambered shell. Genus: Nautilus. ◊ paper nautilus [< the colour of its shell]

pearly queen n a woman from one of the Cockney families traditionally entitled to wear a pearl-covered costume, who is chosen as the one with the finest costume

pearmain /páir mayn/ (plural -mains or -main) n a variety of red-skinned apple [13C. Via Old French parmaine < Latin Parmensis 'from Parma' (in Italy).]

Pears /peerz/, **Sir Peter** (1910–86) British tenor

Pearse /peerss/, **Patrick Henry** (1879–1916) Irish nationalist leader

Pearse, Richard William (1877–1953) New Zealand inventor

pear-shaped adj having a shape similar to that of a pear with a rounded bottom part and narrower top part ◊ **go pear-shaped** to get out of control or go wrong (informal)

Pearson /peérss'n/, **Lester** (1897–1972) Canadian statesman

peart /peert/ *adj* lively and brisk [15C. Variant of PERT.]

Peary /peéri/, **Robert** (1856–1920) US explorer

peasant /pézz'nt/ *n* **1 AGRICULTURAL LABOURER OR SMALL FARMER** a member of a class of people living in rural areas who are engaged in agricultural labouring or are small farmers **2 RURAL PERSON** a country-dweller or rustic **3 OFFENSIVE TERM** an offensive term for somebody considered to be ill-mannered or uneducated [15C. Via Anglo-Norman *paisant*, Old French *païsant* < Latin *pagus* 'rural district'.]

peasantry /pézz'ntri/ *n* **1** peasants as a class in society **2** the status or characteristic behaviour of a peasant

pease-brose /peéz brōz/ *n Scotland* a thick porridge made from dried peas [< *pease*, an earlier form of PEA, + *brose*, originally a Scottish dialect word]

pease pudding /peéz-/ *n* a thick puree made from dried peas and served usually with ham, pork, or bacon [*Pease* an earlier form of PEA]

peashooter /peé shootər/ *n* a toy in the form of a pipe through which dried peas or similar small pellets can be blown

pea soup *n* **1** soup made with fresh or dried peas **2** *US* = **peasouper** *n.* 1 (*informal*)

peasouper /pee soópər/ *n* **1** an extremely thick fog (*informal*) US term **pea soup** *n.* 2 **2** *Can* an offensive term for a French Canadian (*slang*)

peat /peet/ *n* **1** a compacted deposit of partially decomposed organic debris, usually saturated with water **2** a cut and dried piece of peat used as fuel [14C. Via Anglo-Latin < a Celtic word, 'bit'.] —**peaty** *adj*

peat bog *n* an area of land composed primarily of peat

peat moss *n* a moss that grows in wet places, and whose partially decomposed remains form peat. Genus: *Sphagnum.*

peau de soie /pṓ də swaá/ *n* a silk or artificial fabric with a smooth texture and a fine grainy or ribbed surface [< French, 'silk skin']

peavey /peévi/ (*plural* **-veys**), **peavy** (*plural* **-vies**) *n* a pointed lever with a hinged hook, used for handling logs [Late 19C. After Joseph *Peavey*, US inventor.]

pebble /pébb'l/ *n* **1 SMALL ROUND STONE** a small rounded stone that has been worn smooth by erosion **2 ROCK FRAGMENT** a rock fragment with a diameter between 4 mm/0.16 in and 64 mm/2.51 in **3 QUARTZ USED FOR LENSES** a colourless form of quartz (**rock crystal**) used for making lenses **4 CRYSTAL LENS** a lens made from colourless rock crystal **5 IRREGULAR SURFACE** a rough grainy surface, especially of leather ■ *adj* **THICK AND DISTORTING** being or containing lenses that make the eyes of the wearer seem very large and distorted (*informal*) ○ *wearing thick pebble glasses* ■ *vt* (**-bles, -bling, -bled**) **1 COVER WITH PEBBLES** to cover or pave something with pebbles **2 GIVE IRREGULAR SURFACE TO** to give a rough grainy surface to something [Old English *papolstān*] —**pebbly** *adj*

pebbledash /pébb'l dash/ *n* a finish for exterior walls, consisting of small stones set in plaster

pec /pek/ *n* a pectoral muscle (*informal; often plural*) ○ *exercises to strengthen the pecs* [Mid-20C. Shortening.]

pecan /peékən, pi kán/ *n* **1** an edible nut resembling a long walnut with a thin dark red shell **2** a large hickory tree that has deeply furrowed bark and produces pecans. Native to: S United States, Mexico. *Carya illinoensis.* [Late 18C. Via French *pacane* < Algonquian *pakani*.]

peccadillo /pékə díllō/ (*plural* **-loes** *or* **-los**) *n* a petty or unimportant offence or fault [Late 16C. Via Spanish, 'little fault' < *peccado* 'sin' < Latin *peccare* 'to sin'.]

peccant /pékənt/ *adj* (*formal*) **1** guilty of a sin **2** violating a rule or practice [Late 16C. < Latin *peccant-*, present participle of *peccare* 'to sin'.] —**peccancy** *n* —**peccantly** *adv*

peccary /pékəri/ (*plural* **-ries**) *n* a wild pig with a rudimentary tail and small tusks on the upper jaw that grow downwards. Native to: Mexico, South America. Genus: *Tayassu.* [Early 17C. < Carib *pakira*.]

peccavi /pe kaá vee/ (*plural* **-vis**) *n* an admission of sin or guilt (*literary*) [Early 16C. < Latin, 'I have sinned'.]

pech /pekh/ *n Scotland* a short, fast, and forceful breath ■ *vi Scotland* to pant or struggle for breath from exertion [15C. An imitation of the sound of breathing heavily.]

Pechora /pi cháwrə/ river in NW Russia, flowing northwards into the Barents Sea. Length: 1,809 km/1,124 mi.

peck[1] /pek/ *v* **1** *vt* **PICK UP WITH BEAK** to take small bits of food using a beak **2** *vti* **STRIKE WITH BEAK** to strike somebody or something with a beak **3** *vt* **MAKE HOLE IN** to make a hole in something by repeatedly striking it with a beak **4** *vi* **NIBBLE** to eat small quantities of food with little interest ○ *She just pecked at her food.* **5** *vt* **KISS LIGHTLY** to kiss somebody lightly and briefly ■ *n* **1 SWIFT BITE WITH BEAK** a quick light stroke, blow, or bite with a beak **2 HOLE MADE BY BEAK** a mark or hole made by a beak or pointed object **3 LIGHT KISS** a quick light kiss (*informal*) [14C. Probably variant of PICK[1].]

peck[2] /pek/ *n* **1 UNIT OF DRY MEASURE** a unit of dry measure equal to 9.09 litres/8 quarts **2 CONTAINER FOR PECK** a container that holds a peck of material **3 LARGE QUANTITY** a large amount or number of something (*informal*) [13C. < ?]

pecker /pékər/ *n* **1** something that pecks, especially a woodpecker **2** *US* a penis (*slang; sometimes offensive*) ◇ **keep your pecker up** used to tell somebody to keep his or her spirits up (*informal*)

pecking order *n* **1** a social hierarchy in which some members of a group are established as superior to others **2** a social hierarchy among domestic fowl in which each member maintains its place by dominance over the lower members ['Pecking' < PECK[1] 'strike with beak']

peckish /pékish/ *adj* slightly hungry (*informal*)

Pecksniffian /pek snífi ən/ *adj* hypocritical and making a show of having high moral principles [Mid-19C. After *Pecksniff*, character in *Martin Chuzzlewit* (1844) by Charles Dickens.]

pecorino /pékə reénō/ (*plural* **-nos**) *n* a hard pungent Italian cheese made from ewe's milk [Mid-20C. < Italian *pecora* 'sheep'.]

Pécs /paych/ city in SW Hungary. Population: 172,177 (1994).

pectate /pék tayt/ *n* a salt or ester of pectic acid [Mid-19C. < PECTIC ACID.]

pectic acid /péktik-/ *n* an insoluble component of pectin [*Pectic* < Greek *pēktikos* < *pēktos* 'curdled' < *pēgnunai* 'make solid']

pectin /péktin/ *n* a mixture of polysaccharides found in plant cell walls. Use: gelling agent. [Mid-19C. Via French < Greek *pektos* (see PECTIC ACID).] —**pectic** *adj* —**pectinaceous** /-náyshəss/ *adj* —**pectinous** *adj*

pectinesterase /pékti néstə rayz, -rayss/ *n* an enzyme that catalyses the breakdown of pectin [Mid-20C. < PECTIN + ESTERASE.]

pectize /pék tīz/ (**-tizes, -tizing, -tized**), **pectise** (**-tises, -tising, -tised**) *vt* to change something into a gel —**pectizable** *adj* —**pectization** /pék tī záysh'n/ *n*

pectoral /péktərəl/ *adj* **1 OF THE CHEST** relating to or located in or on the chest **2 WORN ON CHEST** worn on the chest ○ *a pectoral medal* ■ *n* **1 CHEST MUSCLE** a chest muscle or organ ○ *an exercise for the pectorals* **2** ZOOL = **pectoral fin** **3 BREASTPLATE** something that is worn on the chest as a decoration or ornament **4 CHEST MEDICINE** a medicine for chest or respiratory disorders (*dated*) [15C. Via French *pectorale* 'something worn on the chest' < Latin *pectorale* 'breastplate' and *pectoralis* 'of the chest' < *pectus* 'chest'.] —**pectorally** *adv*

pectoral fin *n* either of a pair of fins of a fish located either directly behind the gill openings or below them

pectoral girdle *n* the part of the skeleton of a vertebrate animal that consists of bone or cartilage and provides attachment and support for the forelimbs

pectoral muscle *n* any of four flat muscles, two on each side of the front of the chest, that help to move the upper arm and shoulder

peculate /pékyoo layt/ (**-lates, -lating, -lated**) *vt* to appropriate money or property by embezzlement or theft (*formal*) [Mid-18C. < Latin *peculari* < *peculium* (see PECULIAR).] —**peculator** *n* —**peculation** /pékyoo láysh'n/ *n*

peculiar /pi kyoóli ər/ *adj* **1 UNUSUAL** unusual, strange, or unconventional ○ *The situation was very peculiar.* **2 UNIQUE** belonging exclusively to or identified distinctly with somebody or something ■ *n* **CHURCH EXEMPT FROM DIOCESAN JURISDICTION** a church or parish that is exempt from the jurisdiction of the diocese in which it is situated [15C. < Latin *peculiaris* 'of private property' < *peculium* 'private property' < *pecus* 'cattle'.] —**peculiarly** *adv*

peculiarity /pi kyoóli árrəti/ (*plural* **-ties**) *n* **1** a characteristic or trait that belongs distinctively to a particular person, place, or thing **2** the quality or state of being unusual or strange

~~**peculier**~~ incorrect spelling of **peculiar**

pecuniary /pi kyoóni əri/ *adj* **1** relating to or involving money **2** involving a financial penalty such as a fine ○ *a pecuniary offence* [Early 16C. < Latin *pecuniarius* < *pecunia* 'money, wealth in cattle' < *pecus* 'cattle'.] —**pecuniarily** *adv*

pecuniary advantage *n* in law, a financial benefit gained by fraud or deception

ped- *prefix US* = **pedo-** (*before vowels*)

-ped *suffix* foot ○ *biped* [< Latin *ped-*, *pes* 'foot']

pedagogue /péddə gog/ *n* **1** an educator or schoolteacher **2** a teacher who teaches in a particularly pedantic or dogmatic manner [14C. Via Latin *paedagogus* < Greek *paidagōgos* 'slave who leads a child to school' < *pais* 'child'.]

pedagogy /péddə goji/ *n* the science or profession of teaching [Mid-16C. Via French *pédagogie* < Greek *paidagōgia* 'duties of a pedagogue'.] —**pedagogic** *adj* —**pedagogical** *adj* —**pedagogically** *adv*

pedal[1] /pédd'l/ *n* **1 FOOT-OPERATED LEVER FOR MACHINE** a lever operated by the foot that powers a mechanism such as a bicycle, sewing machine, or the foot controls of a car **2 FOOT-OPERATED LEVER FOR MUSICAL INSTRUMENT** a foot-operated lever used in playing the piano, organ, and other musical instruments **3** MUSIC = **pedal point** ■ *vti* (**-als, -alling, -alled**) **1 MAKE BICYCLE MOVE** to use the pedals to make a bicycle or other vehicle move forward **2 OPERATE OR PLAY INSTRUMENT USING FOOT MECHANISM** to operate the pedals of something such as a piano, organ, or machine in order to make it work [Early 17C. Via French < Latin *pedalis* 'of the foot' < *ped-*, *pes* 'foot'.] —**pedaller** *n*

SPELLCHECK Do not confuse ***pedal*** with ***peddle***, which has a similar sound. Beware: your spellchecker will not catch this error.

pedal[2] /peéd'l, pédd'l/ *adj* relating to the foot or feet [Early 17C. < Latin *pedalis* 'of the foot'.]

pedalfer /pi dálfər/ *n* soil without a layer of accumulated calcium carbonate, but in which iron and aluminium have tended to accumulate [Early 20C. Blend of PEDO- + ALUMINIUM, and Latin *ferrum* 'iron'.]

pedalo /péddəlō/ (*plural* **-los** *or* **-loes**) *n* a small pleasure boat that is powered by paddles and operated by pedals [Mid-20C. < PEDAL[1].]

pedal point *n* a note, usually in the bass, that is sustained while other musical parts and harmonies continue

pedal pushers *npl* calf-length trousers for women, originally designed for cycling

pedal steel, pedal steel guitar *n* an electrically amplified floor-mounted guitar that is fretted with a steel bar and usually has ten strings, whose pitch can be varied by the use of pedals

pedant /pédd'nt/ *n* **1** a person who unduly emphasizes unimportant details and rules **2** an ostentatious displayer of learning [Late 16C. Via French *pédant* < Italian *pedante* < ?]

pedantic /pi dántik/ *adj* too concerned with what are thought to be correct rules and details, e.g. in language —**pedantically** *adv*

pedantry /pédd'ntri/ (*plural* **-ries**) *n* a pedantic attitude or an example of pedantic behaviour

~~**pedastal**~~ incorrect spelling of **pedestal**

~~**pedastool**~~ incorrect spelling of **pedestal**

peddle /pédd'l/ (**-dles, -dling, -dled**) *v* **1** *vti* **SELL GOODS** to sell goods, especially while travelling from place to place **2** *vt* **SELL DRUGS** to sell something illegal, especially drugs (*dated*) **3** *vt* **PROMOTE IDEA** to promote an idea or belief insistently [Mid-16C. Back-formation < PEDDLER.]

SPELLCHECK See ***pedal***.

peddler /péddlər/ *n* **1** a dealer in something, especially illegal drugs **2** *US* = **pedlar** [14C. Alteration of *pedder*.]

pederast /péddə rast/, **paederast** *n* a man who has sex with a boy (*formal*) [Mid-17C. < Greek *paiderastēs* 'lover of boys'.]

pederasty /péddə rasti/, **paederasty** n sexual relations between a man and a boy (formal) —**pederastic** /péddə rástik/ adj

pedestal /péddist'l/ n 1 BASE OF COLUMN a base or support for a column or statue 2 SUPPORTING BASE the column-shaped base of a piece of furniture such as a table or washbasin 3 POSITION OF BEING EXALTED OR ADMIRED a position in which somebody admires another person so much that he or she thinks that person is perfect ○ I don't want to be put on a pedestal – I just want to be treated as a normal person! ■ vt (-tals, -talling, -talled) PUT SOMETHING ON PEDESTAL to provide somebody or something with a pedestal [Mid-16C. Via French piédestal < Italian piedestallo 'foot of a stall'.]

pedestrian /pə déstri ən/ n a traveller on foot, especially in an area also used by cars ■ adj ordinary, unimaginative, or uninspired [Early 18C. Directly or via French pédestre < Latin pedester 'going on foot' < pes 'foot'.] —**pedestrianism** n —**pedestrianly** adv

pedestrian crossing n a place marked on a road as a place for people to cross. US term **crosswalk**

pedestrianize /pə déstri ə nīz/ (-izes, -izing, -ized), **pedestrianise** (-ises, -ising, -ised) vt to change a street into an area for pedestrians only by banning motor vehicles —**pedestrianization** /pə déstri ə nī záysh'n/ n

Pedi /péddi/ (plural -dis or -di) n 1 a member of a people who live in South Africa, mainly in Transvaal 2 the Bantu language of the Pedi people. Native speakers: 3 million. —**Pedi** adj

pedi- prefix foot, feet ○ pedipalp [< Latin ped-, stem of pes (see PEDAL¹)]

pediatrics n MED = paediatrics

pedicab /péddi kab/ n a pedal-operated tricycle with a seat in front for the driver and a passenger seat behind covered by a hood, available for hire in some Southeast Asian countries

pedicel /péddi sel, -s'l/, **pedicle** /péddik'l/ n 1 STALK OF INDIVIDUAL FLOWER a stalk bearing a single flower or spore-producing body within a cluster 2 STALK-SHAPED BODY PART an anatomical part that resembles a stem or stalk 3 NARROW SEGMENT a narrow anatomical part such as the waist between the thorax and abdomen of wasps and related insects [Late 17C. < modern Latin pedicellus < Latin pediculus 'footstalk' < pes 'foot'.] —**pedicellar** /péddi séllar/ adj —**pedicellate** /-séllit, -layt/ adj

pediculicide /péddi kyóoli sīd/ n a chemical substance that kills lice, used to treat infestations of humans and animals [Early 20C. < Latin pediculus 'louse' + -CIDE.]

pediculosis /pi díkyōō lṓssiss/ n infestation with lice, specifically the head and body louse Pediculus humanus [Early 19C. < Latin pediculus 'louse'.] —**pediculous** /pi díkyōōlass/ adj

pedicure /péddi kyoor/ n 1 MEDICAL CARE OF FEET medical treatment of the feet, e.g. the removal of corns 2 COSMETIC TREATMENT OF FEET cosmetic treatment of the feet, e.g. the application of nail varnish 3 SESSION OF TREATMENT FOR FEET a session of cosmetic or medical treatment of the feet ■ vt (-cures, -curing, -cured) TREAT FEET OF to give a pedicure to somebody [Mid-19C. < French pédicure < Latin ped- 'foot' + cura 'care'.] —**pedicurist** n

pedigree /péddi gree/ n 1 LINE OF ANCESTORS the line of ancestors of an individual animal or person, especially a pure-bred animal 2 LIST OF ANIMAL'S ANCESTORS a document recording the line of ancestors of an animal, especially a pure-bred animal 3 FAMILY TREE a table showing the line of ancestors of a person, especially an aristocratic or upper class person 4 BACKGROUND the background, history, or origin of something, especially a group ■ adj PURE-BRED descended from a line of animals whose purity of breed has been recorded over several generations [15C. < Anglo-Norman pe de gru 'crane's foot'.] —**pedigreed** adj

pediment /péddimənt/ n 1 a broad triangular or segmental gable surmounting a colonnade as the major part of a facade 2 a broad flat rock surface of low relief adjacent to a steeper slope in a dry region, e.g. that of a mountain range, often covered with rock debris [Late 16C. < ?] —**pedimental** /péddi mént'l/ adj

pedipalp /péddi palp/ n either of a pair of appendages that are part of the mouths of spiders and other arachnids, used for various functions including manipulating food [Early 19C. < modern Latin pedipalpi < Latin pes 'foot' and palpus 'palp'.]

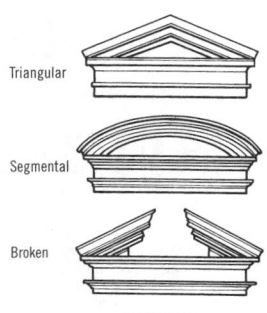

Triangular

Segmental

Broken

Pediment

pedlar /péddlər/ n somebody who travels from place to place or from door to door selling goods. US term **peddler** n. 2 [14C. Alteration of pedder < ?]

SPELLCHECK Do not confuse **pedlar** with **peddler**, which has a similar sound. Beware: your spellchecker will not catch this error.

pedo-¹ prefix soil ○ pedology [< Greek pedon 'ground']

pedo-² prefix US = **paedo-** [< Greek paid-, stem of pais 'child, boy'. Ultimately < Indo-European 'little', which is also the ancestor of English poor.]

pedodontics n US = paedodontics

pedogenesis /péedə jénnississ/ n the natural process of soil formation, including erosion and leaching —**pedogenetic** /péedǝjə néttik/ adj —**pedogenic** /-jénnik/ adj

pedology¹ n US = paedology

pedology² /pi dóllaji/ n the scientific study of soil properties and the classification of soil types —**pedologic** /péedə lójjik/ adj —**pedological** /-lójik'l/ adj —**pedologically** /-lójjikli/ adv —**pedologist** /pi dóllajist/ n

pedometer /pi dómmitar/ n an instrument that measures the distance covered by a walker by recording the number of steps taken [Early 18C. < French pédomètre < Latin ped- 'foot' + French pédomètre '-meter'.]

pedophile n US = paedophile

pedophilia n US = paedophilia

Pedro I /péddrō/ (1798–1834) emperor of Brazil (1822–31)

Pedro II (1825–91) emperor of Brazil (1831–89)

peduncle /pi dúngk'l/ n 1 the stalk of a plant 2 a part resembling a stalk in shape or function, e.g. the base of a fish's tail or a structure attaching an invertebrate animal to the place where it lives [Mid-18C. < modern Latin pedunculus 'a small foot' < Latin pes 'foot'.] —**peduncled** adj —**peduncular** /pi dúngkyōōlar/ adj —**pedunculate** /pi dúngkyōōlət/ adj

pee /pee/ vi (pees, peeing, peed) URINATE to pass urine (informal; often considered offensive) ■ n (informal; often considered offensive) 1 URINE urine 2 URINATION an act of urinating [Late 18C. < the first letter of PISS.]

Peebles /peeb'lz/ town in S Scotland. Population: 7,065 (1991).

peek /peek/ vi to take a quick look at something, especially in a secretive way or at something you should not be looking at ○ I peeked at the name at the foot of the letter. ■ n a quick or secret look at something [14C. < ?]

SPELLCHECK See **peak**

peekaboo /péekə bṓo, péekə boo/ n CHILDREN'S GAME a game played to amuse small children, in which the face is hidden in the hands and then suddenly uncovered as 'peekaboo!' is shouted ■ interj WORD SAID IN GAME OF PEEKABOO the word used when playing a game of peekaboo ■ adj HAVING HOLES having holes or gaps intended to reveal parts of the body [Late 16C. < PEEK + BOO.]

Peekskill /péek skil/ city in SE New York State. Population: 21,111 (1998 estimate).

peel¹ /peel/ v 1 vt REMOVE OUTER LAYER OF to cut away or pull off the skin or outer layer of something, especially a fruit or vegetable 2 vi HAVE REMOVABLE SKIN to have a skin that can be removed 3 vt PULL SOMETHING OFF to pull or strip off something, especially something that is stuck to a surface 4 vi LOSE OUTER LAYER to lose or shed an outer layer or covering, e.g. of paint or sunburnt skin ○ The skin on her nose was peeling. 5 vi COME OFF IN THIN PIECES to come off in flakes, small pieces, or thin strips 6 vt PUT BALL THROUGH CROQUET HOOP to make another player's ball go through a hoop in croquet ■ n FRUIT OR VEGETABLE SKIN the rind or skin of a fruit or vegetable ○ apple peel [13C. < Latin pilare 'deprive of hair' < pilus 'hair'.] —**peelable** adj

SPELLCHECK See **peal**.

peel² /peel/ n a shovel with a long handle, used by bakers to move bread in and out of an oven [14C. Via Old French pele < Latin pala 'spade'.]

peel³ /peel/ n a fortified tower of the type built in the border counties of Scotland and England in the 16th century to withstand raids [13C. Via Anglo-Norman pel < Latin palus 'stake'.]

Peel /peel/, **Sir Robert** (1788–1850) British statesman

peeler /péelar/ n 1 a device for removing the skin from fruit or vegetables, usually a hand-held utensil with a blade 2 US a striptease dancer (slang)

peelie-wallie adj Scotland = peely-wally (informal)

peeling /péeling/ n a piece of something, especially fruit or vegetable skin, that has been peeled off (often plural) ○ potato peelings

peely-wally /péeli wólli/, **peelie-wallie** adj Scotland pale, sickly, or feeling ill (informal) [Mid-19C. < ?]

peen /peen/ n the end of a hammer head opposite the flat face, often rounded or wedge-shaped, and used for bending and shaping ■ vt to bend or shape something by striking it with the peen of a hammer [Late 17C. < ?]

peep¹ /peep/ v 1 vi LOOK QUICKLY OR SECRETLY to look quickly or secretly, e.g. through a small opening or from a hiding place 2 vti EMERGE OR MAKE SOMETHING EMERGE to become or make something become partly visible or visible only for a short time ■ n 1 QUICK LOOK a quick or secret look at something 2 THE FIRST SIGHT OF the first appearance or sight of something [15C. < ?]

peep² /peep/ vi 1 MAKE A SHORT, HIGH-PITCHED NOISE to make a high-pitched little noise like a baby bird or a mouse 2 SPEAK IN HIGH OR QUIET VOICE to speak in a quiet, weak, or high-pitched voice 3 MAKE QUIET NOISE to make the quietest possible noise or remark ■ n 1 SHORT HIGH-PITCHED SOUND a high-pitched sound like that of a baby bird or a mouse 2 SMALLEST SOUND a very quiet utterance ○ I don't want to hear another peep out of any of you! [15C. An imitation of the sound.]

peeper¹ /péepar/ n 1 a person who looks secretly at somebody or something 2 somebody's eye (dated slang; often plural)

peeper² /péepar/ n AMPHIB = spring peeper

peephole /péep hṓl/ n 1 a small crack or hole that somebody can look through 2 a small hole or opening in a door that allows somebody to see people on the other side without being observed

Peeping Tom, **peeping Tom** n a man who gets sexual pleasure from secretly watching somebody undressing or sexual activity between other people [Early 19C. After a tailor in English legend who was the only person to look at Lady Godiva riding naked.]

peepshow /péep shṓ/, **peep show** n 1 an erotic or pornographic film or show viewed from individual booths 2 a sequence of pictures viewed through a hole or lens in a box, regarded as a form of entertainment in former times

peep sight n a metal tab at the rear of a rifle barrel, containing a small circular opening through which the user looks to align the front sight with the target

peepul n TREES = pipal

peer¹ /peer/ vi 1 to look very carefully or hard, especially at somebody or something that is difficult to see, often with narrowed eyes 2 to be partially visible or appear briefly [Late 16C. < ?]

SPELLCHECK Do not confuse **peer** with **pier**, which has a similar sound. Beware: your spellchecker will not catch this error.

peer² /peer/ n 1 a person who is the equal of somebody else, e.g. in age or social class 2 a member of the nobility in Great Britain and Northern Ireland [13C. Via Old French < Latin par 'equal'.]

peerage /péerij/ n 1 NOBLES AS A GROUP peers considered as a class or group 2 NOBLE RANK the rank, status, or title of a peer 3 LIST OF NOBLES a book listing the members of the nobility and giving information about their families

peeress /peer éss/ n 1 a woman who is a peer 2 the wife or widow of a peer

peer group n a social group consisting of people who are equal in such respects as age, education, or social class ○ *Teenagers usually prefer to spend time with their own peer group.*

peerie /peeri/ adj Scotland small [Early 19C. < ?]

peerless /peerlass/ adj incomparable, matchless, or without equal —**peerlessly** adv —**peerlessness** n

peer of the realm n in Great Britain and Northern Ireland, a member of the nobility who has the right to sit in the House of Lords

peer pressure n social pressure on somebody to adopt a particular type of behaviour, dress, or attitude in order to be accepted as part of a group

peer review n an assessment of an article, piece of work, or research by people who are experts on the subject

peer-review vt to assess an article, piece of work, or research as an expert on the subject —**peer-reviewed** adj

⚡ **peer-to-peer** adj full form of **P2P**

peeve /peev/ vt (**peeves, peeving, peeved**) ANNOY to make somebody feel annoyed, irritated, or resentful (*informal*) ■ n (*informal*) 1 SOMETHING THAT ANNOYS something that annoys or irritates somebody 2 BAD MOOD an irritated or resentful mood [Early 20C. Back-formation < PEEVISH.]

peevish /peevish/ adj bad-tempered, irritable, or tending to complain [14C. < ?] —**peevishly** adv —**peevishness** n

peewee[1] /pee wee/ n somebody or something that is extremely or exceptionally small, especially a small child ■ adj very small [Late 19C. Reduplication of WEE[1].]

peewee[2] /pee wee/ n BIRDS = **pewee** [Late 19C. Imitation of its cry.]

peewit /pee wit/ n BIRDS = **lapwing** [Early 16C. Imitation of its cry.]

~~perform~~ incorrect spelling of **perform**

peg /peg/ n 1 PIN FOR FASTENING OR MARKING a small piece of metal, plastic, or wood used to secure or mark something or to join two parts together 2 HOOK FOR HANGING THINGS a hook or projecting piece of wood or metal that is attached to a surface such as a door or wall and used to hang things on, especially clothes 3 FASTENER FOR CLOTHES ON WASHING LINE a hinged piece of wood or plastic used to fasten washing to a clothes line 4 PART FOR TUNING STRING a screw or pin around which a string is wound in the head (**pegbox**) of a stringed instrument 5 REASON FOR DOING an excuse or reason for doing something, or a support for an argument 6 DEGREE OR STEP a degree, notch, or step, especially in somebody's opinion of a person or thing 7 SMALL DRINK OF SPIRITS a small drink of spirits such as brandy or whisky (*dated informal*) 8 FAST THROW in baseball, a fast low throw of the ball that puts a base runner out 9 CROQUET PIN in croquet, a post that must be hit with a ball in order for a player to win the game ■ vt (**pegs, pegging, pegged**) 1 SECURE WITH PEGS to fasten something with one or more pegs 2 PUT A PEG IN to insert a peg into something 3 MARK WITH PEG to mark something, such as the score in a game, with a peg or pegs 4 FIX AT CERTAIN LEVEL to fix the cost or value of something at a certain level 5 US CATEGORIZE to classify somebody or something, especially as having a particular character 6 THROW A BASEBALL to throw something, especially a low and fast baseball (*informal*) [15C. Probably < obsolete Dutch *pegge*.] ◊ **a square peg in a round hole** a person who is unsuited to the situation he or she is in ◊ **bring** or **take somebody down a peg (or two)** to make somebody more humble ◊ **off the peg** ready to wear, not tailor-made

peg away vi to persist or continue working at something

peg down vt to fasten something down with pegs, e.g. a tent

peg out v 1 vi COLLAPSE FROM EXHAUSTION to collapse from exhaustion or to be too exhausted to continue (*informal*) 2 vt FASTEN CLOTHES TO WASHING LINE to attach wet clothes to a washing line with pegs 3 vt SECURE SOMETHING WITH PEGS to fasten something, such as a tent, with pegs 4 vi DIE to die (*informal*) 5 vt MARK OUT LAND WITH PEGS to mark out a piece of land with pegs 6 vi WIN CROQUET GAME in croquet, to hit the peg, thereby winning the game 7 vt EXCLUDE OPPONENT'S BALL IN CROQUET to make an opponent's croquet ball hit the peg, thereby causing it to be out of the game 8 vi SCORE WINNING POINT IN CRIBBAGE to score the winning point in cribbage

Pegasus /péggəssəss/ n 1 in Greek mythology, a horse with wings, born of the shed blood of Medusa 2 a large constellation of the northern hemisphere. See illustration at **constellation**

Pegasus Bay /péggəssəss-/ bay on the east of the South Island, New Zealand

pegboard /peg bawrd/ n 1 a board with a pattern of holes into which pegs are placed in games such as solitaire 2 a board with a pattern of holes into which pegs are placed to keep the score in some games, especially card games such as cribbage

pegbox /peg boks/ n the portion of a stringed instrument that holds the tuning pegs

peg leg n 1 a prosthetic leg, especially a simple wooden one fitted at the knee (*offensive*) 2 an offensive term for somebody who has a prosthetic leg

pegmatite /pégmə tīt/ n a coarse-grained igneous rock, usually granite, that is characterized by large well-formed crystals and often contains rare elements [Mid-19C. < the Greek stem *pegmat-* 'something joined together'.] —**pegmatitic** /-títtik/ adj

peg top n a spinning top that is thrown from the hand and is caused to spin as a string quickly unwinds from around a central metal peg ■ **peg tops** npl trousers that are full and gathered at the hips and narrow at the ankle (*dated*)

peg-top adj describes a garment, especially a skirt or pair of trousers, that is wide at the hips and narrow at the hem (*dated*)

Pegu /pe goo/ city in S Myanmar. Population: 150,447 (1983).

Pehlevi n, adj LANG = **Pahlavi**

Popperfoto

I. M. Pei

Pei /pay/, **I. M.** (b. 1917) Chinese-born US architect. Full name **Ieoh Ming Pei**

PEI abbr Prince Edward Island

~~peice~~ incorrect spelling of **piece**

peignoir /páyn waar/ n a woman's loose-fitting dressing gown, bathrobe, or negligée [Mid-19C. < French < *peigner* 'comb' < Latin *pecten* 'to comb'.]

~~peir~~ incorrect spelling of **pier**

Peirce /peerss/, **Charles Sanders** (1839–1914) US philosopher and physicist

pejoration /peejə ráysh'n/ n 1 a worsening, deterioration, or decline in quality, status, or value (*formal*) 2 a change over time in the meaning of a word so that it becomes less favourable or more negative [Mid-17C. < medieval Latin *peioration-* < late Latin *peiorare* 'worsen' < Latin *peior* 'worse'.]

pejorative /pi jórrətiv/ adj expressing criticism or disapproval (*formal*) ■ n a word, expression, or affix that expresses criticism or disapproval [Late 19C. Via French *péjoratif* < late Latin *peiorare* (see PEJORATION).] —**pejoratively** adv

peke /peek/, **Peke** n a Pekingese dog (*informal*) [Early 20C. Shortening.]

Pekinese n, adj DOGS, LANG = **Pekingese**

Peking /pee king/ former name for **Beijing**

Peking duck n 1 a Chinese dish in which small portions of duck meat, strips of crisp duck skin, cucumber, and spring onions are rolled in thin pancakes 2 *Hong Kong* a student who is expected to deal with a large amount of school work and learn by rote

Pekingese /peeki neez/, **Pekinese** n (*plural* **-ese**) 1 SMALL CHINESE DOG a small pet dog of a Chinese breed with a short flat nose, a long straight silky coat, and a tail that curls over its back 2 MANDARIN CHINESE Mandarin Chinese (*dated*) 3 SOMEBODY FROM BEIJING somebody who comes from Beijing ■ adj OF BEIJING relating to Beijing, or its people or culture

Peking man n the fossilized remains of an extinct human species that lived 400,000 to 500,000 years ago, originally classified as Pithecanthropus and now regarded as a subspecies of Homo erectus [Early 20C. After PEKING because its remains were discovered in China.]

pekoe /peekō/ n a high-quality black tea [Early 18C. < Chinese *pekho* 'white down'.]

pelage /péllij/ n a mammal's coat of fur, hair, or wool (*technical*) [Early 19C. Via French < Latin *pilus* 'hair'.]

Pelagianism /pi láyji ənizəm/ n the belief of the heretical Christian Pelagius that people can earn salvation through their own efforts, without relying on the grace of God, and the rejection of the concept of original sin [Late 16C. After PELAGIUS.]

pelagic /pə lájjik/ adj 1 FOUND IN OPEN SEA living, occurring, or deposited in the deep waters of the ocean or the open sea as opposed to near the shore 2 FOUND IN SURFACE WATERS living, occurring, or found in the surface waters of the ocean or the open sea 3 DEPOSITED ON OCEAN BED describes sediments deposited beneath deep ocean waters that are rich in the remains of microscopic organisms [Mid-17C. Via Latin < Greek *pelagikos* < *pelagos* 'sea'.]

Pelagius /pi láyji əss/ (360?–420?) Romano-British monk —**Pelagian** adj, n

pelargonic acid /pélaar gonnik-/ n CHEM = **nonanoic acid**

pelargonium /péllə gōni əm/ (*plural* **-ums** or **-um**) n a flowering plant with rounded or lobed leaves. Flowers: red, pink, white, in clusters. Native to: southern Africa. Genus: *Pelargonium*. [Early 19C. < modern Latin < Greek *pelargos* 'stork'.]

Pelasgian /pi lázji ən, -lázgi-/ n a member of an ancient people who lived in Greece and the Aegean Islands before the arrival of the Bronze Age Hellenic peoples ■ adj **Pelasgian, Pelasgic** relating to the Pelasgian peoples or their cultures [15C. < Latin *Pelasgus* < Greek *Pelasgos*, the Pelasgians' mythical founder.]

Express Newspapers

Pelé

Pelé /pél ay/ (b. 1940) Brazilian football player. Born **Edson Arantes do Nascimento**

pelecypod /pi léssipod/ n MARINE BIOL = **bivalve** [Late 19C. < modern Latin *Pelecypoda* < Greek *pelekus* 'axe' + *-podos* 'footed'.]

Pele's hair /péllayz-/ n fine threads of volcanic glass formed by the action of the wind on jets of lava erupting into the air [Mid-19C. Translation of Hawaiian *lauoho o Pele*.]

Peleus /peeli əss, peel yooss/ n in Greek mythology, the king of the Myrmidons in Thessaly

pelf /pelf/ n money, wealth, or riches, especially if obtained dishonestly (*archaic*) [14C. Via Anglo-Norman < Old French *pelfre* 'booty' < ?]

pelham /péllam/ n a bit for a horse's bridle that is midway between the simple snaffle bit and the harsher curb bit [Mid-19C. < the surname *Pelham*.]

pelican /péllikan/ n a large water bird that has webbed feet and a large flat bill with a hanging pouch that can be expanded to catch and store fish. Native to: warm-water coasts. Family: Pelecanidae. [Pre-12C. Via late Latin *pelicanus* < Greek *pelekan* < ?]

pelican crossing *n* a pedestrian crossing where people wishing to cross the road can stop the traffic by pressing a button that controls traffic lights at the side of the road [Acronym < *pedestrian light controlled*]

pelisse /pə léess/ *n* **1** a cloak, coat, or jacket lined or trimmed with fur, often worn as part of a military uniform, e.g. by members of the Hussar regiments **2** a woman's long fitted coat or dress that opens at the front and is often trimmed with fur [Early 18C. Via French and late Latin *pellicia* < Latin *pellis* 'skin'.]

pelite /pée līt/, **pelyte** *n* aluminium-rich metamorphic rock formed by the action of temperature and pressure on clay-rich sedimentary rocks [Late 19C. < Greek *pēlos* 'clay'.] —**pelitic** /pi líttik/ *adj*

pellagra /pə lággrə, pə láygrə/ *n* a disease caused by a dietary deficiency of niacin and marked by dermatitis, diarrhoea, and disorder of the central nervous system [Early 19C. < Italian < *pelle* 'skin' + *agra* 'rough' or *-agra* 'seizure'.] —**pellagrous** *adj*

pellet /péllət/ *n* **1 SMALL BALL OF COMPRESSED MATERIAL** a small ball or a piece of material that has been pressed tightly together, e.g. for animal feed or a medicine **2 SMALL BULLET** a small bullet or ball of metal fired from a gun **3 IMITATION BULLET** an imitation bullet for use in a toy gun **4 STONE MISSILE FOR CANNON OR CATAPULT** a ball, usually made of stone, formerly used as a cannonball or as a missile fired from a catapult **5 UNDIGESTED MATTER REGURGITATED BY PREDATORY BIRDS** an undigested mass of food, mostly bone and hair, that is regurgitated by owls and other birds of prey **6 ANIMAL FAECES** a small round piece of the faeces of some animals such as sheep or rabbits ■ *vt* **1 STRIKE WITH PELLETS** to bombard or hit somebody or something with pellets **2 MAKE PELLETS OF** to make or form something into pellets [14C. < French *pelote* 'small ball' < Latin *pila* 'ball'.] —**pelletization** /péllə tī záysh'n/ *n* —**pelletize** /péllə tīz/ *vt* —**pelletizer** *n*

pellicle /péllik'l/ *n* **1** a thin film, membrane, or skin **2** a multilayered flexible sheath that lies immediately beneath the cell membrane of many protozoans [Mid-16C. Via French *pellicule* < Latin *pellicula* 'a small skin' < *pellis* 'skin'.] —**pellicular** /pə líkyŏŏlər/ *adj*

pellitory /péllitəri/ (*plural* **-ries**) *n* a Mediterranean plant whose oil was formerly used for the relief of toothache. *Anacyclus pyrethrum*. [Mid-16C. Via Old French *peletre* < Latin *pyrethrum* (see PYRETHRUM).]

pell-mell /pél mél/ *adv* **1 IN A DISORDERLY RUSH** in a disorderly frantic rush **2 UNTIDILY** in a confused, jumbled, or untidy manner ■ *adj* **DISORDERLY** confused, frantic, or disorderly ■ *n* **CONFUSION OR DISORDER** a confused or disorderly condition or situation [Late 16C. Via French *pêle-mêle* < Old French *pesle mesle* < *mesler* 'to mix'.]

pellucid /pə lŏŏssid/ *adj* **1** allowing all or most light to pass through (*literary*) **2** easy to understand or clear in meaning (*formal*) [Early 17C. < Latin *pellucidus* < *pellucere* 'shine through' < *lucere* 'to shine'.] —**pellucidity** /péllyoo síddəti/ *n* —**pellucidly** /pə lŏŏssidli/ *adv* —**pellucidness** /-sidnəss/ *n*

Pelly /pélli/ river in W Yukon Territory, Canada. Length: 530 km/329 mi.

pelmanism /pélmənizəm/, **Pelmanism** *n* a game in which a pack of cards is laid face down on a table and players try to select matching pairs by remembering their positions from previous attempts [Early 20C. After Christopher Louis *Pelman*, English psychologist.]

pelmet /pélmət/ *n* a narrow piece of fabric or board fitted above a window for decoration and to hide the curtain rail [Early 20C. Probably alteration of French *palmette* 'small palm'.]

pelobatid /péllō báttid, péelō-/ *n* a frog with the backbone development of more primitive frogs and the leg-muscle structure of more advanced ones. The European spadefoot toad is a pelobatid. Family: Pelobatidae. [Mid-20C. < Greek *pelos* 'mud' + *bates* 'walker' + -ID.]

Peloponnese /péllәpә neess/ peninsula forming the southern part of mainland Greece. Area: 21,439 sq. km/8,278 sq. mi. —**Peloponnesian** /péllәpә néezh'n, -néesh'n/ *n, adj*

Pelops /pée lops/ *n* in Greek mythology, the son of Tantalus, killed by his father and served up as a meal to the gods

pelorus /pi láwrəss/ *n* a device used to measure bearings relative to the direction in which a boat is travelling [Mid-19C. < ?]

pelota /pə lóttə, -lṓtə/ *n* **1** a fast court game of Basque origin, in which two players use long wickerwork baskets strapped to their wrists to hurl a ball against a marked wall and catch it. ◊ **jai alai 2** the ball used in pelota [Early 19C. Via Spanish, 'ball' < Latin *pila* (see PELLET).]

pelt[1] /pelt/ *n* **1 ANIMAL SKIN WITH FUR** the skin of an animal with the fur, hair, or wool still attached **2 ANIMAL SKIN READY FOR TANNING** the skin of an animal with the fur, hair, or wool removed so that it is ready for tanning into leather ■ *vt* **REMOVE ANIMAL'S SKIN** to remove the skin of an animal [15C. < ?]

pelt[2] /pelt/ *v* **1** *vt* **THROW THINGS AT** to bombard somebody or something with many blows or missiles **2** *vt* **BEAT AGAINST** to beat against something continuously **3** *vi* **RAIN HEAVILY** to fall fast and hard as hail or rain **4** *vi* **MOVE QUICKLY** to hurry or move quickly ■ *n* **A BLOW** a strong blow [15C. < ?] —**pelter** *n* ◇ **at full pelt** extremely fast

peltate /pél tayt/ *adj* describes a leaf that has its stalk attached to the lower surface in the centre rather than at the edge [Mid-18C. Via Latin, 'armed with a light shield' < Greek *peltē* 'a small light shield'.] —**peltately** *adv* —**peltation** /pel táysh'n/ *n*

Peltier effect /pélti ay-/ *n* the production or absorption of heat at the junction of two metals when an electric current is passed from one metal to another [Mid-19C. After J. C. A. *Peltier* (1785–1845), French scientist.]

Pelton wheel /pélt'n-/ *n* an impulse turbine in which cup-shaped buckets on the edge of a rotor are hit with a high-pressure jet of water, causing the rotor to turn [Late 19C. After L. A. *Pelton* (1829–1908), US engineer.]

peltry /péltri/ *n* the skins of animals collectively, especially when the fur is still attached [15C. Via Anglo-Norman *pelterie* < Old French *pel* (see PELT[1]).]

pelves *n* plural of **pelvis**

pelvic /pélvik/ *adj* relating to, involving, or located in or near the pelvis

pelvic fin *n* either of a pair of fins on the lower surface of a fish that have skeletal support and are analogous to the hind limbs of land animals

pelvic inflammatory disease *n* an inflammation of a woman's reproductive organs in the pelvic area, which can cause infertility

pelvimetry /pel vímmətri/ *n* measurement of the inlet and outlet diameters of the pelvis, usually to assess whether there will be any difficulty during childbirth

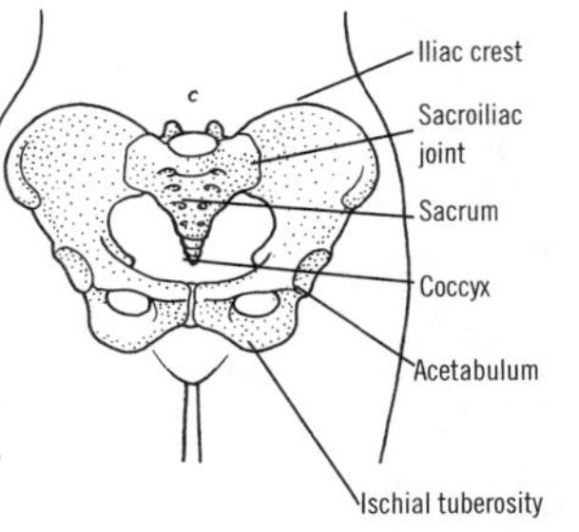
Iliac crest
Sacroiliac joint
Sacrum
Coccyx
Acetabulum
Ischial tuberosity

Pelvis

pelvis /pélviss/ (*plural* **-vises** *or* **-ves** /-veez/) *n* **1** the strong basin-shaped ring of bone near the bottom of the spine formed by the hip bones on the front and sides, and the triangular sacrum on the back **2** any basin- or cup-shaped anatomical cavity such as the region of the kidney into which urine is discharged before its passage into the ureter [Early 17C. < Latin, 'basin'.]

pelycosaur /péllikə sawr/ *n* a large extinct reptile that was common in Europe and North America during the Permian period, 245 to 290 million years ago. Order: Pelycosauria. [Mid-20C. < the Greek stem *peluk-* 'bowl' + *-saur*.]

pelyte *n* GEOL = **pelite**

Pemba /pémbə/ island in NE Tanzania, in the Indian Ocean. Population: 265,039 (1988). Area: 984 sq. km/380 sq. mi.

Pembroke /pém brŏŏk, pémbrək/ town in SW Wales. Population: 15,820 (1991).

Pembrokeshire /pém brŏŏkshər/ county in SW Wales. Area: 1,591 sq. km/614 sq. mi.

Pembroke table, pembroke table *n* a small four-legged table with a top that folds down on two sides and one or two drawers [Late 18C. < ?]

pemmican /pémmikən/, **pemican** *n* **1** a traditional Native North American food made with strips of lean dried meat pounded into paste, mixed with melted fat and dried berries or fruits, and pressed into small cakes **2** a nutritious food adapted from traditional Native North American pemmican and used as emergency rations, e.g. by explorers [Late 18C. < Cree *pimihkan* < *pimiy* 'fat'.]

pemoline /pémmə leen/ *n* $C_9H_8N_2O_2$ a synthetic stimulant of the central nervous system. Use: treatment of depression, attention deficit disorder in children. [Mid-20C. < parts of *phenyliminooxooxazolidine*.]

pemphigus /pémfigəss/ *n* a disease characterized by large blisters on the skin and mucous membranes, often accompanied by itching or burning sensations [Late 18C. Via modern Latin < the Greek stem *pemphig-* 'pustule'.]

pen[1] /pen/ *n* **1 INSTRUMENT FOR WRITING IN INK** a long thin instrument used for writing or drawing with ink **2 WRITING** the written word considered as a means of expression ○ *They say the pen is mightier than the sword.* **3 STYLE OF WRITING** a particular style of writing **4 SOMETHING WRITTEN BY** something written by a particular person **5 SQUID'S INTERNAL SHELL** the internal feather-shaped horny shell of a squid ■ *vt* (**pens, penning, penned**) **WRITE** to write something (*formal*) [13C. Via French *penne* < Latin *penna* 'feather'.] —**penner** *n*

pen[2] /pen/ *n* **1 SMALL ENCLOSURE FOR ANIMALS** a small fenced area of land, or an enclosure within a building, used to keep farm animals in **2 ANIMALS KEPT IN PEN** the farm animals kept in a pen **3 AREA THAT CONFINES** an enclosed area where somebody or something is confined or controlled **4 FORTIFIED DOCK FOR REPAIRING SUBMARINES** a heavily fortified dock for repairing or servicing submarines ■ *vt* (**pens, penning, penned** *or* **pent** *archaic*) **CONFINE** to keep or shut somebody or something in a pen or other enclosed area ○ *animals kept penned up in a tiny space* [Old English *penn*]

pen[3] /pen/ *n* a female swan [Mid-16C. < ?]

pen[4] /pen/ *n US, Can* a state, provincial, or federal prison (*slang*) [Late 19C. Shortening of PENITENTIARY.]

PEN /pen/ *abbr* International Association of Poets, Playwrights, Editors, Essayists, and Novelists

Pen. *abbr* Peninsula (*in placenames*)

penal /péen'l/ *adj* **1 OF PUNISHMENT** relating to, forming, or prescribing punishment, especially by law ○ *the penal system* **2 PUNISHABLE BY LAW** subject to punishment under the law **3 USED AS PLACE OF PUNISHMENT** used as a place of imprisonment and punishment ○ *a penal institution* **4 PAYABLE AS PENALTY** required to be paid as a penalty [15C. Via French *pénal* < Latin *poenalis* < *poena* 'penalty'.]

penal code *n* a body or system of laws concerned with the punishment of crime

penal colony *n* a place of imprisonment and punishment at a remote location

penalize /péenə līz/ (**-izes, -izing, -ized**), **penalise** (**-ises, -ising, -ised**) *vt* **1 SUBJECT SOMEBODY OR SOMETHING TO PENALTY** to impose a penalty on somebody or something for breaking a law or rule **2 PUT SOMEBODY OR SOMETHING AT DISADVANTAGE** to put somebody or something at a disadvantage or treat him or her unfairly **3 PUNISH PLAYER FOR BREAKING RULE** to punish a team or player for breaking a rule by giving an advantage to the opposing team or player **4 MAKE ACT PUNISHABLE** to make something punishable by a law or rule —**penalization** /péenə lī záysh'n/ *n*

penal servitude *n* confinement in a penal colony as a result of conviction of a crime

penalty /pénn'lti/ (*plural* **-ties**) *n* **1 LEGAL PUNISHMENT FOR COMMITTING CRIME** a legal or official punishment such as a fine or imprisonment for committing a crime or other offence **2 LEGAL PUNISHMENT FOR BREAKING CONTRACT** a punishment such as a fine for failing to fulfil the terms of a legal agreement **3 UNPLEASANT CONSEQUENCE** something unpleasant suffered as the result of an unwise action **4 DISADVANTAGE FOR BREAKING RULE** a disadvantage imposed on a player or team for breaking a rule in a sport or game, e.g. a free shot at the goal awarded to the opposing side **5** SOCCER = **penalty kick** *n.* 1 **6 GOAL FROM PENALTY** a goal scored from a penalty in football

penalty area *n* a rectangular area in front of a football goal within which the goalkeeper is allowed to handle the ball

penalty box *n* **1** SOCCER = **penalty area 2** an area with a bench beside an ice-hockey rink where penalized players must stay during the period they have to serve as a time penalty

penalty kick *n* **1** in football, a free kick from the penalty spot at the opposing team's goal, which is defended only by its goalkeeper **2** in rugby, a kick worth three points that can be aimed at the goal after a serious foul by a member of the opposing side

penalty rates *npl ANZ* rates of pay that are higher than normal rates and that are paid for work performed outside normal working hours

penalty shoot-out *n* SOCCER = **shoot-out** *n.* **2**

penalty shot *n* SPORTS = **penalty** *n.* **4**

penalty spot *n* **1** a designated spot on a football field, 11 m/12 yd from the goal line, from which penalty kicks are taken **2** in hockey, a designated spot 7 m/23 ft from the goal line from which the shot is taken

penance /pénnənss/ *n* **1 SELF-PUNISHMENT FOR COMMITTING SIN** self-punishment or an act of religious devotion performed to show sorrow for having committed a sin **2 CHRISTIAN SACRAMENT OF RECONCILIATION** a sacrament in some Christian churches in which a person confesses sins to a priest and is forgiven after performing a religious devotion or duty such as praying or fasting **3 DUTY IMPOSED BY PRIEST** a duty or religious devotion imposed by a priest during the sacrament of confession in some Christian churches ■ *vt* (**-ances, -ancing, -anced**) **IMPOSE PENANCE ON** to make somebody do penance for a sin [13C. Via Old French < Latin *paenitentia* 'regret' < *paenitere* 'to regret'.]

Penang /pə náng/, **Pinang** state in NW Malaysia. Capital: George Town. Population: 1,065,075 (1990). Area: 1,031 sq. km/398 sq. mi.

penannular /pen ánnyŏŏlər/ *adj* in the shape of an almost complete circle [Mid-19C. < *pene-* < Latin *paene* 'almost' + ANNULAR.]

penates /pə naá teez, -náy-/, **Penates** *npl* in ancient Roman religious belief, the gods of a household or state [Early 16C. < Latin < *penus* 'provisions'.]

pence plural of **penny**

pencel /péns'l/, **pensil** *n* a small narrow flag (**pennon**) or streamer, especially one carried at the end of a lance [13C. Via Anglo-Norman < Old French *penoncel* 'a small pennon'.]

penchant /póN shoN/ *n* a strong liking, taste, or tendency for something [Late 17C. < French, present participle of *pencher* 'incline' < Latin *pendere* (see PENDANT).]

pencil /péns'l/ *n* **1 INSTRUMENT FOR DRAWING AND WRITING** a thin cylindrical instrument used for drawing or writing. It consists of a rod of graphite or some other erasable marking material inside a wooden or metal shaft. **2 SOMETHING RESEMBLING PENCIL** something that has a similar shape, structure, or function to a pencil, e.g. a stick for applying cosmetics ○ *an eyebrow pencil* **3 NARROW CYLINDER OF LIGHT** a long narrow cylinder or cone of light with a small angle of convergence **4 SET OF LINES THROUGH A POINT** the set of all lines passing through a fixed point or of all lines parallel to a given line **5 ARTIST'S INDIVIDUAL STYLE** the individual drawing style or technique of an artist ■ *vt* (**-cils, -cilling, -cilled**) **DRAW OR WRITE SOMETHING WITH PENCIL** to draw, mark, write, or colour something with a pencil [14C. Via Old French *pincel* < Latin *peniculus* 'brush', literally 'a small tail' < *penis* 'tail'.]

pencil in *vt* to note or enter something provisionally, e.g. the time of a proposed engagement in an appointments book or on a calendar

pencil case *n* a small container for somebody's pens, pencils, and rubbers, used especially by school, college, and university students

pencil moustache *n* a very thin moustache

pencil pusher *n US* = **penpusher** (*informal*)

⚡**pen computer** *n* a computer using pattern-recognition circuitry or software to enable it to accept handwriting as data input

pend[1] /pend/ *vi* **1** to remain unsettled or wait to be judged **2** to hang [15C. Probably < French *pendre* (see PENDANT).]

pend[2] /pend/ *n Scotland* a vaulted or arched passageway, especially from the street to the back of a group of houses [15C. Directly or via French *pendre* < Latin *pendere* (see PENDANT).]

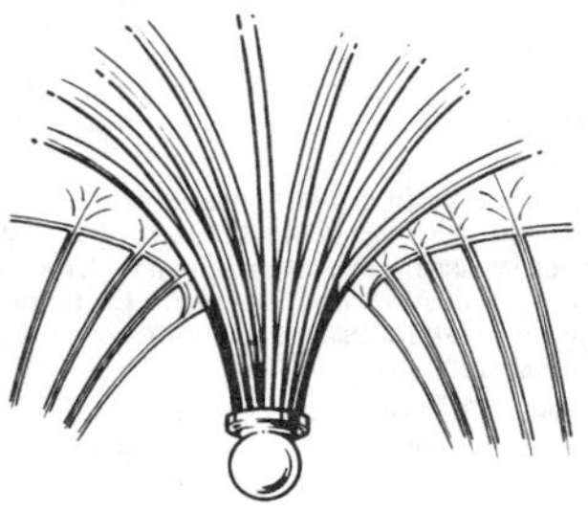

Pendant

pendant /péndənt/ *n* **1 HANGING ORNAMENT OR JEWELLERY** an ornament or a piece of jewellery that hangs from a necklace, bracelet, or earring **2 NECKLACE WITH HANGING ORNAMENT** a necklace with a hanging ornament attached to it **3 HANGING LIGHT** a lamp, chandelier, or other lighting fixture that hangs from the ceiling **4 ORNAMENT HANGING FROM CEILING** an architectural ornament hanging from a vaulted ceiling or roof **5 ONE OF MATCHING PAIR** a piece of art that matches or goes with another piece **6 LENGTH OF WIRE OR ROPE** a length of wire or rope attached at the upper end to a spar or similar part and at the lower end to a block and tackle ■ *adj* = **pendent** [14C. < French, present participle of *pendre* 'hang' < Latin *pendere*.]

pendent /péndənt/ *adj* **pendent, pendant 1 HANGING OR SUSPENDED** dangling, hanging, or suspended (*formal or literary*) **2 OVERHANGING** jutting, overhanging, or sticking out (*formal or literary*) **3 GRAMMATICALLY INCOMPLETE** describes an incomplete grammatical structure **4 PENDING** not yet dealt with, decided, or settled (*formal or literary*) ■ *n* = **pendant** [13C. Variant of PENDANT.] —**pendency** *n* —**pendently** *adv*

pendentive /pen déntiv/ *n* a sloping triangular piece of vaulting between the arches that support a dome and its rim [Early 18C. Via French *pendentif* < Latin *pendere* 'hang'.]

Penderecki /péndə rétski/, **Krzysztof** (*b.* 1933) Polish composer

pending /pénding/ *adj* **1 NOT YET TAKEN CARE OF** not yet dealt with, decided, or settled **2 ABOUT TO HAPPEN** about to happen or come into effect ■ *prep* **1 UNTIL** until or while waiting for ○ *pending further enquiries* **2 DURING** during something [Mid-17C. Anglicization of French *pendant* (see PENDANT).]

pendragon /pen drággən/, **Pendragon** *n* a supreme leader of the ancient Britons [15C. < Welsh < *pen* 'head' + *dragon* 'military standard' (< Latin *draco*).] —**pendragonship** *n*

pendular /péndyŏŏlər/ *adj* swinging to and fro with the motion of a pendulum

pendulous /péndyŏŏləss/ *adj* **1** hanging loosely or swinging freely **2** undecided or wavering in making a decision [Early 17C. < Latin *pendulus* (see PENDULUM).] —**pendulously** *adv* —**pendulousness** *n*

pendulum /péndyŏŏləm/ *n* **1 WEIGHT SWINGING FREELY FROM A FIXED POINT** a weight hung from a fixed point so that it can swing freely to and fro under the influence of gravity **2 SWINGING ROD CONTROLLING A CLOCK MECHANISM** a rod with a weight at its base that swings from side to side and controls the mechanism of a clock **3 SOMETHING THAT CHANGES REGULARLY** something that changes its direction or position regularly, often alternating between two extremes ○ *The pendulum has swung back to more traditional teaching methods.* [Mid-17C. Via modern Latin < Latin *pendulus* 'hanging' < *pendere* (see PENDANT).]

Penelope /pə néllәpi/ *n* in Greek mythology, the wife of Odysseus, who waited for his return from the Trojan War and was the mother of his son, Telemachus

peneplain /peéni playn/, **peneplane** *n* an area of nearly flat featureless land that is the result of a prolonged period of erosion —**peneplanation** /peénipla náysh'n/ *n*

penes plural of **penis**

penetralia /pénni tráyli ə/ *npl* the innermost parts of a place, especially a sanctuary within a temple (*formal*) [Mid-17C. < Latin < *penetralis* 'innermost' < *penetrare* (see PENETRATE).] —**penetralian** *adj*

penetrance /pénnitrənss/ *n* the frequency with which a particular hereditary characteristic, e.g. a genetic disease, occurs among individuals carrying the gene or genes for that characteristic [Mid-20C. < German *Penetranz*.]

penetrant /pénnitrənt/ *n* **1** a substance that encourages a liquid to penetrate a porous material by lowering the surface tension of the liquid **2** somebody or something that penetrates

penetrate /pénni trayt/ (**-trates, -trating, -trated**) *v* **1** *vti* **ENTER OR PASS THROUGH** to enter or pass through something, such as by piercing it or forcing a way in ○ *The aim of the mission was to penetrate deep into enemy territory.* **2** *vt* **SPREAD THROUGH** to enter and spread through something ○ *The fumes had penetrated the entire building.* **3** *vt* **GET A SHARE OF A MARKET** to succeed in getting a share of a particular market **4** *vt* **INFILTRATE A GROUP** to enter something such as an organization or country, usually secretly, in order to influence or gather information from within **5** *vt* **SEE INTO** to see into or through something that is dark or obscuring **6** *vt* **DECIPHER A MEANING** to understand or discover the meaning of something ○ *an enigma few were able to penetrate* **7** *vi* **BE UNDERSTOOD** to be understood or taken in by the mind ○ *It took a few seconds for the news to penetrate.* **8** *vt* **INSERT THE PENIS INTO** to insert the penis into a vagina or anus [Mid-16C. < Latin *penetrat-*, past participle of *penetrare* 'penetrate' < *penitus* 'inner, innermost'.] —**penetrability** /pénnitrə bílləti/ *n* —**penetrable** *adj* —**penetrably** *adv* —**penetrator** *n*

penetrating /pénni trayting/ *adj* **1 ABLE OR TENDING TO PENETRATE** strong enough to enter or spread through something ○ *a penetrating odour* **2 PIERCING OR PROBING** apparently able to see or understand things that are hidden ○ *a penetrating glance* **3 LOUD AND PIERCING** loud, piercing, shrill, or unpleasant to the ears **4 SHARP OR PERCEPTIVE** able to understand or accurately identify something ○ *a penetrating observation*

penetration /pénni tráysh'n/ *n* **1 ENTERING OR PASSING THROUGH** the action of penetrating, entering, or passing through something ○ *Penetration of the foundations by torrential rain resulted in structural damage.* **2 ABILITY TO PENETRATE** the ability or power to penetrate, enter, or pass through something **3 UNDERSTANDING** the ability to understand or perceive something **4 ATTACK THAT ENTERS ENEMY TERRITORY** an attack that succeeds in penetrating an enemy's territory or defences **5 DEPTH PROJECTILE GOES INTO A TARGET** a measure of the depth a projectile reaches beneath the surface of its target **6 DEGREE OF SUCCESS IN A MARKET** the extent to which a commercial product or service is recognized or bought in a particular market ○ *The launch of the new product should improve the company's market penetration.* **7 INSERTION OF PENIS** the insertion of the penis into a vagina or anus

penetrative /pénnitrətiv, -traytiv/ *adj* **1 PENETRATING** piercing something or able to get through something **2 KEEN** mentally perceptive or insightful **3 INVOLVING INSERTION OF PENIS** describes sexual activity that involves putting the penis into a vagina or anus

penetrometer /pénni trómmitər/ *n* **1** an instrument for measuring the penetrating power of forms of electromagnetic radiation such as X-rays by comparing the transmission through standard absorbers **2** an instrument for measuring the penetrability of a solid material by measuring the depth to which it may be pierced with a standard needle [Early 20C. < PENETRATION + -METER.]

pen friend *n* a person, especially one living in another country, with whom you establish a friendship through an exchange of letters and who you may never meet in person. US term **pen pal**

penguin /péng gwin/ *n* an upright web-footed seabird with contrasting black-and-white plumage that cannot fly but uses its flipper-shaped wings for swimming. Native to: cold regions of the S hemisphere. Family: Spheniscidae. [Late 16C. < ?]

penholder /pén hōldər/ *n* **1** a handle for a pen point or nib, consisting of a metal, plastic, or wooden rod **2** a holder for a pen or pens in the form of, e.g. a beaker, rack, or stand

-penia *suffix* deficiency ○ *thrombocytopenia* [Via modern Latin < Greek *penia* 'poverty, want']

penicillamine /pénni síllə meen/ *n* a chelating agent. Source: penicillin. Use: removal of toxic metals from the body. [Mid-20C. Blend of PENICILLIN + AMINE.]

penicillate /pénni síllət/ *adj* having or resembling a tuft of hair [Early 19C. < Latin *penicillus* (see PENICILLIUM).] —**penicillately** *adv* —**penicillation** /pénnissi láysh'n/ *n*

penicillin /pénni síllin/ *n* an antibiotic belonging to a group originally derived from mould of the genus *Penicillium* but now produced synthetically [Early 20C. < PENICILLIUM.]

penicillinase /pénni sílli nayz, -nayss/ *n* an enzyme produced by some bacteria that inactivates penicillin. Use: treatment of adverse penicillin reactions.

penicillium /pénni sílli əm/ *n* a bluish-green fungus that grows on stale or ripening food. Use: in cheese-making, as a source of penicillin. Genus: *Penicillium*. [Mid-19C. < modern Latin < Latin *penicillus* 'paintbrush' < *peniculus* (see PENCIL).]

penile /peé nīl/ *adj* relating to, affecting, or resembling the penis

penillion /pe nílli ən/ *npl* Welsh songs, often improvised, sung to a set harp accompaniment [Late 18C. < Welsh, 'verses' < *pen* 'head'.]

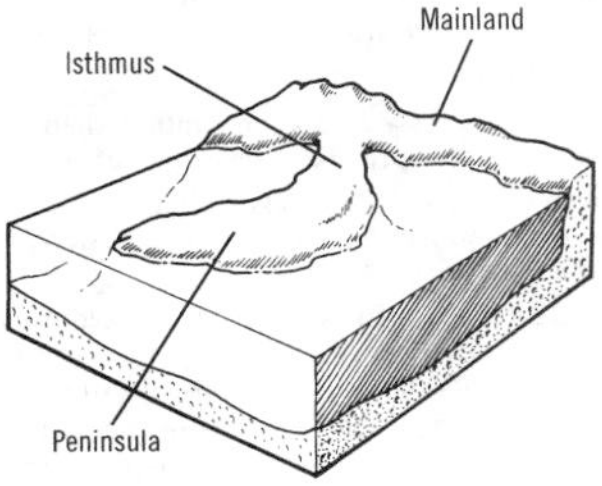

Peninsula

peninsula /pə nínsyŏŏlə/ *n* a narrow piece of land that juts out from the mainland into a sea or lake [Mid-16C. < Latin *paeninsula* < *paene* 'almost' + *insula* 'island'.] —**peninsular** *adj*

penis /peéniss/ (*plural* **-nises** *or* **-nes** /-neez/) *n* the external male organ of copulation, used to transfer semen to the female. In most mammals, it is also used to expel urine from the body. [Late 17C. < Latin, 'tail, penis'.]

penis envy *n* in Freudian psychoanalysis, the theory that some girls' and women's psychological problems stem from a sense of deprivation about not having a penis

penitent /pénnitənt/ *adj* **FEELING REGRET FOR SINS** expressing or feeling regret or sorrow for having committed sins or misdeeds ■ *n* **1 SOMEBODY REGRETTING HIS OR HER SINS** a sinner or wrongdoer who feels regret or sorrow for misdeeds **2 SOMEBODY DOING PENANCE AFTER CONFESSION** a person who does a penance as directed by a priest or minister after confessing his or her sins [14C. Via French *pénitent* < Latin *paenitere* (see PENANCE).] —**penitence** *n* —**penitently** *adv*

penitential /pénni ténsh'l/ *adj* constituting or expressing penance or penitence —**penitentially** *adv*

penitentiary /pénni ténshəri/ *n* (*plural* **-ries**) **1** *US, Can* **PRISON** a prison, especially for people who have been convicted of serious crimes **2 ROMAN CATHOLIC OFFICIAL GRANTING ABSOLUTION** a high official in the Roman Catholic Church who can grant absolution in extraordinary cases **3 ROMAN CATHOLIC TRIBUNAL** a tribunal of the Roman Catholic Church dealing with penance ■ *adj* **1 OF PENANCE** relating to penance **2 CONCERNING PUNISHMENT OR REFORM OF OFFENDERS** involving or used for the punishment or reform of offenders **3** *US* **PUNISHABLE BY IMPRISONMENT IN A PENITENTIARY** punishable by a term of imprisonment in a penitentiary [15C. Via medieval Latin *paenitentiaria* < Latin *paenitentia* (see PENANCE).]

penknife /pén nīf/ (*plural* **-knives** /-nīvz/) *n* a small knife with one or more blades that can be folded back into the handle. US term **pocketknife** [15C. < its original use for making quill pens.]

penlight /pén līt/ *n* a small electric torch that is similar in size and shape to a fountain pen

penman /pénmən/ (*plural* **-men** /-mən/) *n* **1 SOMEBODY SKILLED AT WRITING** a person who is skilled, or has reached a specific level of skill, at handwriting, especially with a pen **2 AUTHOR** an author or writer **3 SCRIBE** a writer or copier of documents as a profession

penmanship /pénmən ship/ *n* **1** the art, skill, or technique of writing by hand **2** the manner, quality, or style of somebody's handwriting

Penn /penn/, **William** (1644–1718) English-born American Quaker reformer and colonialist

Penn. *abbr* Pennsylvania

penna /pénnə/ (*plural* **-nae** /-nee/) *n* a feather that helps to form the outer contour of a bird's plumage, as opposed to a down feather [< Latin, 'feather'] —**pennaceous** /pe náyshəss/ *adj*

pennae plural of **penna**

pen name *n* a name used by a writer instead of his or her real name

pennant /pénnənt/ *n* **1 TRIANGULAR FLAG DISPLAYED ON A SHIP** a small narrow triangular flag displayed on boats and ships for identification and signalling **2 FLAG RESEMBLING A SHIP'S PENNANT** a flag that has a shape similar to a ship's pennant **3** NAUT = **pendant** *n.* **6 4** *US, Can, Aus* **FLAG SYMBOLIZING A SPORTS CHAMPIONSHIP** a flag that symbolizes a championship in some sports, especially baseball **5** *US, Can, Aus* **CHAMPIONSHIP SYMBOLIZED BY A PENNANT** a championship that is symbolized by a pennant [Early 17C. Blend of PENNON + PENDANT.]

pennate /pénnayt/, **pennated** /pénnaytid/ *adj* **1** having feathers or wings **2** describes diatoms in the class Pennales, which are bilaterally symmetrical **3** PLANT SCI = **pinnate**

penne /pénnay/ *n* short tube-shaped pasta cut diagonally at the ends [Late 20C. < Italian, the plural of *penna* 'feather, quill pen'.]

Penney /pénni/, **William George, Baron** (1909–91) British physicist

penni /pénni/ (*plural* **-nia** /pénni ə/ *or* **-nis**) *n* see table at **currency** [Late 19C. < Finnish.]

penniless /pénniləss/ *adj* very poor or without any money —**pennilessly** *adv* —**pennilessness** *n*

Pennine Hills /pén īn-/ range of hills in N England, forming the 'spine' of England. Highest peak: Cross Fell 893 m/2,930 ft.

penninite /pénni nīt/, **pennine** /pénīn/ *n* a green-blue mineral of the chlorite group, containing magnesium and iron. Source: metamorphic rocks. [Mid-19C. After the *Pennine* Alps, on the Swiss-Italian border.]

pennon /pénnən/ *n* **1** a long narrow flag, usually triangular, tapering, or divided at the end, originally carried on a lance by a medieval knight **2** NAUT = **pennant** *n.* **1 3** a bird's wing or the pinion of a wing (*literary*) [14C. Via French *penon* 'a large feather' < Latin *penna* 'feather'.]

Pennsylvania /pénss'l váyni ə/ state in the NE United States. Capital: Harrisburg. Population: 12,019,661 (1997). Area: 119,290 sq. km/46,058 sq. mi.

Pennsylvania Dutch *npl* **GERMAN AND SWISS IMMIGRANTS IN PENNSYLVANIA** a group of people who emigrated from Germany and Switzerland to E Pennsylvania in the 17th and 18th centuries, or their descendants ■ *n* **1 Pennsylvania Dutch, Pennsylvania German GERMAN DIALECT SPOKEN IN PENNSYLVANIA** a dialect of German mixed with some English that is spoken in E Pennsylvania by the Pennsylvania Dutch. Native speakers: 70,000. **2 FOLK ART THAT USES STYLIZED FIGURES** folk art developed by the Pennsylvania Dutch that uses stylized figures of people, plants, and animals, primarily in the decoration of household objects and in needlework [Mid-18C. Alteration of German *Deutsch* 'German'.] —**Pennsylvania Dutch** *adj*

Pennsylvanian /pénss'l váyni ən/ *n* **1** somebody who was born in or lives in Pennsylvania **2** the period of geological time in North America when the climate was relatively warm and damp and the major coal beds were formed, 290 to 320 million years ago —**Pennsylvanian** *adj*

penny /pénni/ (*plural* **pennies** *or* **pence** /penss/) *n* **1 SMALL BRITISH COIN** (*symbol* **p**) a subunit of currency in the United Kingdom and the Republic of Ireland. See table at **currency 2 COIN IN UNITED STATES AND CANADA** a US and Canadian coin worth one cent **3 COIN WITH LOW VALUE** a coin or monetary unit with a low value in some countries **4 VERY SMALL AMOUNT OF MONEY** a very small amount of money ○ *It won't cost you a penny.* [Old English *penig* < Germanic] ◇ **a penny for your thoughts** used to ask somebody what he or she is thinking about ◇ **cost a pretty penny** to cost a great deal of money ◇ **in for a penny, in for a pound** if you decide to do something, you should do it wholeheartedly and boldly, and accept any resulting problems or difficulties ◇ **penny wise and pound foolish** economical with regard to small items of expenditure but extravagant with regard to large items ◇ **spend a penny** to urinate (*informal; euphemistic*) ◇ **the penny dropped** used to say that you suddenly understood or realized something ◇ **turn up like a bad penny** to keep making unwelcome appearances ◇ **two** *or* **ten a penny** very numerous or common, and therefore of little value

penny ante *n* **1 TYPE OF POKER** a game of poker in which the bets are limited to small sums of money **2** *US* **BUSINESS TRANSACTION INVOLVING VERY LITTLE MONEY** any business arrangement that involves very little money or is inconsequential (*informal*) ○ *We're talking penny ante here.* ■ *adj* **penny-ante** *US* **INVOLVING VERY LITTLE MONEY** involving a very small amount of money (*informal*) —**penny-ante** *adj*

penny arcade *n US* LEISURE = **amusement arcade**

penny black, Penny Black *n* the first adhesive postage stamp, issued by Britain in 1840, printed in black with a portrait of Queen Victoria and a cost of one penny

pennycress /pénnee kress/ *n* a plant with round flat seed pods, naturalized throughout the United States. Native to: Europe, Asia. Genus: *Thlaspi*.

penny dreadful *n* a cheap book or comic containing lurid stories of adventure, crime, or passion

penny-farthing *n* an early type of bicycle with a very large front wheel carrying the pedals and a small rear wheel, used in Britain in the 19th century

penny pincher *n* a person who is mean or unduly careful with his or her money (*informal*)

pennyroyal /pénnee róyəl/ *n* **1** a plant of the mint family. Flowers: small, purple, in clusters. Use: medicines, insect repellent. Native to: Europe, Asia. *Mentha pulegium*. **2** an aromatic plant of the mint family, especially a variety with bluish flowers. Native to: E North America. *Hedeoma pulegioides*. [Mid-16C. Alteration of Anglo-Norman *puliol real* 'royal thyme'.]

penny shares *npl* securities that sell on a stock exchange at less than 20p a share

pennyweight /pénnee wayt/ *n* a unit of weight in the troy system, equal to 1.555 g/1/20 oz [Old English *penega gewiht*]

penny whistle *n* a small high-pitched flute with six finger holes, similar to a recorder but made of metal and very inexpensive to buy

penny-wise *adj* extremely careful about spending even small amounts of money

pennywort /pénnee wurt/ *n* **1 ROCK PLANT** a rock plant with rounded leaves. Flowers: whitish-green, tubular. Native to: Europe, Asia. *Umbilicus rupestris*. **2 MARSH PLANT** a plant with rounded leaves that grows in marshy areas. Flowers: greenish-pink. Native to: Europe, North America. *Hydrocotyle vulgaris*. **3 PLANT WITH ROUNDED LEAVES** a plant of the gentian family with rounded leaves. Flowers: small, white, purplish. Native to: North America. *Obolaria virginica*.

pennyworth /pénnee wurth, pénnərth/ *n* **1** (*plural* **-worths** *or* **-worth**) **AMOUNT COSTING A PENNY** the amount of something that can be bought for a penny (*dated*) **2 SMALL AMOUNT** a small amount or the slightest amount (*dated*) **3 COMMENT OR OPINION** somebody's comment or opinion, especially an unwelcome one (*informal*)

penology /pee nólləji/, **poenology** *n* the theory, scientific study of, and practice of how crime is punished, how prisons are managed, and how rehabilitation is handled [Mid-19C. < Latin *poena* (see PENAL).] —**penological** /peénə lójjik'l/ *adj* —**penologically** *adv* —**penologist** /-nólləjist/ *n*

pen pal *n US* = **pen friend**

penpusher /pén pooshər/ *n* somebody who has a boring administrative job (*informal*) US term **pencil pusher** —**penpushing** *adj, n*

Penrith /pén rith, pen ríth/ town in NW England. Population: 12,049 (1991).

Penrose /pénnrōz/, **Sir Roger** (*b.* 1931) British mathematician

pensil *n* HIST = **pencel**

pensile /pén sīl/ *adj* **1** hanging or suspended ○ *a pensile nest* **2** describes a bird such as the Baltimore Oriole that builds a hanging nest [Early 17C. Via Latin *pensilis* <

pens-, past participle of *pendere* (see PENDANT).] —**pensileness** *n* —**pensility** /pen sílləti/ *n*

pension[1] /pénsh'n/ *n* **1 RETIREMENT PAY** a fixed amount of money paid regularly to somebody during retirement by the government, a former employer, or an insurance company **2 REGULAR SUM PAID** a sum of money paid regularly as compensation, e.g. for an injury sustained on a job, or as a reward for service, e.g. to an ex-soldier ■ *vt* **PAY A PENSION** to pay a pension to somebody [14C. Via French < Latin *pension-* 'payment' < *pens-*, past participle of *pendere* (see PENDANT).] —**pensionary** *adj*

pension off *vt* **1** to force somebody into retirement with a pension, e.g. as a cost-cutting measure or because of age **2** to get rid of something because it is useless or no longer needed (*informal*)

pension[2] /paànsyáwn/ *n* **1** a boarding house or small inexpensive hotel in continental Europe, especially in France **2** = **full board**

pensionable /pénsh'nəb'l/ *adj* entitled to or relating to entitlement to receive a pension —**pensionability** /pénsh'nə bílləti/ *n*

pensioner /pénsh'nər/ *n* **1** a recipient of a pension, especially somebody who has retired from work on the grounds of age **2** a student at Cambridge University who does not have a scholarship

pensive /pénssiv/ *adj* thinking deeply about something, especially in a sad or serious manner [14C. Via French < *penser* 'think' < Latin *pensare* 'keep on weighing' < *pendere* 'weigh'.] —**pensively** *adv* —**pensiveness** *n*

penstemon /pénstimən, pen stéemən/, **pentstemon** *n* a plant belonging to the figwort family. Flowers: large, brightly coloured, with five stamens, one of which is sterile. Native to: North America. Genus: *Pentstemon* and *Penstemon*. [Mid-18C. < modern Latin, 'five stamens' < Greek *penta-* 'five'.]

penstock /pén stòk/ *n* a sluice, channel, or pipe used to control water flow or supply water to something such as a hydroelectric plant [Early 17C. < PEN[2] 'enclosure'.]

pent- *prefix* = **penta-** (*before vowels*)

penta- *prefix* five ○ *pentagon* [< Greek *pente* 'five' < Indo-European]

pentachlorophenol /péntə klawrə fée nol/ *n* C_6Cl_5OH a white chemical compound. Use: in fungicides, disinfectants, wood preservatives.

pentacle /péntək'l/ *n* MATH = **pentagram** [Late 16C. < medieval Latin *pentaculum* 'little five' < Greek *penta-* (see PENTA-).]

pentad /pén tad/ *n* **1 GROUP OF FIVE** any group or series of five **2 ATOM WITH VALENCY OF FIVE** an atom or chemical group with a valency of five **3 5 DAYS** a period of five days [Mid-17C. < Greek < *pente* (see PENTA-).]

pentadactyl /péntə dákt'l/ *adj* having five fingers on each hand or five toes on each foot —**pentadactylism** *n*

pentagon /péntəgən/ *n* a geometrical figure that has five sides and five angles [Late 16C. Via late Latin *pentagonum* < Greek *pentagōnos* 'five-angled' < *penta-* (see PENTA-).] —**pentagonal** /pen tággən'l/ *adj* —**pentagonally** *adv*

Pentagon /péntəgən/ *n* the US Department of Defense, or the five-sided main building that houses it

pentagram /péntə gram/ *n* a star-shaped geometrical figure with five points, especially one used as a magical or occult symbol [Mid-19C. < Greek *pentagrammon*, a form of *pentagrammos* 'of five lines'.]

pentahedron /péntə héedrən/ (*plural* **-drons** *or* **-dra** /-héedrə/) *n* a solid geometrical figure that has five faces —**pentahedral** *adj*

pentamerous /pen támmərəss/ *adj* **1** divided into or having five similar parts **2** describes flowers that have petals or other parts such as sepals or stamens arranged in groups of five —**pentamerism** *n*

pentameter /pen támmitər/ *n* a line of poetry that is made up of five units of rhythm, e.g. five pairs of stressed and unstressed syllables [Early 16C. Via Latin < Greek *pentametros* 'having five measures' < *penta-* (see PENTA-) + *metron* (see METRE[2]).]

pentamidine /pen támmi deen, -din/ *n* $C_{19}H_{24}N_4O_2$ a drug effective against protozoal infections. Use: treatment of African sleeping sickness, pneumonia in Aids patients. [Mid-20C. < PENTANE + *amidine*.]

pentane /pén tàyn/ *n* C_5H_{12} an organic chemical belonging to the group containing only hydrogen and carbon (**hydrocarbons**). Use: solvent. [Late 19C. < PENTA-.]

pentangle /pént ang g'l/ *n* MATH = **pentagram**

pentanoic acid /péntə nō ik-/ *n* CHEM = **valeric acid**

pentapeptide /péntə pép tīd/ *n* a peptide with five amino acids in its molecules

pentaploid /péntə ployd/ *adj* having five times the basic number of each chromosome ■ *n* a cell, nucleus, or organism that has five times the basic number of each chromosome

pentaprism /péntəprizəm/ *n* a prism with five faces that deviates light at a 90-degree angle, making it useful in correctly presenting an image in the viewfinder of a single-lens reflex camera

pentaquine /péntə kween, -kwin/, **pentaquin** /-kwin/ *n* $C_{18}H_{27}N_3O$ a synthetic drug. Use: with quinine in the treatment and prevention of malaria. [< PENTA- + QUINOLINE]

pentastich /péntəstik/ *n* a poem or section of a poem consisting of five lines [Mid-17C. Via modern Latin < Greek *pentastikhos* 'having five rows' < *penta-* (see PENTA-).]

Pentateuch /péntə tyook/ *n* the first five books of the Bible, traditionally regarded as having been written by Moses. ◊ **Heptateuch, Hexateuch** [15C. Via ecclesiastical Latin < Greek *pentateukhos* 'having five books' < *penta-* (see PENTA-).] —**Pentateuchal** *adj*

pentathlete /pen táthleet/ *n* an athlete who takes part in a pentathlon

pentathlon /pen táthlən/ *n* **1** SPORTS = **modern pentathlon** **2** the Olympic competition consisting of five track and field events, usually sprinting, hurdling, long jumping, and discus and javelin throwing. ◊ **triathlon, heptathlon, decathlon** [Early 17C. < Greek, 'contest of five' < *penta-* (see PENTA-).]

pentatomic /péntə tómmik/ *adj* having five atoms in a molecule

pentatonic scale /péntə tonnik-/ *n* any musical scale that has five notes to an octave, especially a major scale in which the fourth and seventh tones are omitted [*Pentatonic* < PENTA- + TONIC]

pentavalent /péntə váylənt/ *adj* describes chemical elements that have a valency of five

pentazocine /pen tázzō seen/ *n* $C_{19}H_{27}NO$ a synthetic narcotic drug. Use: painkiller. [Mid-20C. < PENTA- + AZO- + OCTA- + -INE.]

Pentecost /pénti kost/ *n* **1** a Christian festival that commemorates the descent of the Holy Spirit upon the apostles, or the day on which it is celebrated. Date: 7th Sunday after Easter. **2** JUDAISM = **Shavuoth** [Pre-12C. Via late Latin < Greek *pentēkonta* 'fifty' (because it falls fifty days after the second day of the Passover) < *pentē* 'five'.]

Pentecostal /pénti kóst'l/ *adj* **1 EMPHASIZING THE HOLY SPIRIT** belonging or relating to any Christian denomination that emphasizes the workings of the Holy Spirit, interprets the Bible literally, and adopts an informal demonstrative approach to religious worship **2 OF PENTECOST** relating to the Christian festival of Pentecost ■ *n* **MEMBER OF A PENTECOSTAL DENOMINATION** a member of a Pentecostal denomination —**Pentecostalism** *n* —**Pentecostalist** *n, adj*

pentene /pén teen/ *n* C_5H_{10} a colourless flammable liquid with several isomers. Use: manufacture of organic compounds.

penthouse /pént howss/ (*plural* **-houses** /-howziz/) *n* **1 ROOFTOP DWELLING** an expensive and comfortable flat on the top floor of a building or built on the roof (*often before nouns*) ○ *a penthouse apartment* **2 HOUSING FOR SERVICE EQUIPMENT** a structure on the roof of a building to house lift machinery, a water tank, or other service equipment **3 ADJOINING ROOF OR SHED** a sloping roof, or a shed with a sloping roof, built against the outer wall of a building **4 ROOFED CORRIDOR** in real tennis, a roofed corridor that runs along three sides of a court [14C. Alteration (influenced by HOUSE) of Anglo-Norman *pentiz* 'lean-to', via Old French *apentis* < Latin *appendere* 'hang onto' < *pendere* 'hang'.]

pentimento /pént méntō/ (*plural* **-ti** /-ti/) *n* **1** the technique of removing a top layer of paint to reveal a painting or part of a painting that has been painted over **2** a painting or part of a painting that is revealed by pentimento [Early 20C. Via Italian, 'correction', literally 'repentance' < Latin *paenitere* 'repent'.]

Pentland Firth /péntlənd-/ sea passage in NE Scotland, separating the Orkney Islands from the mainland, and linking the North Sea to the Atlantic Ocean. Length: 32 km/20 mi.

pentlandite /péntlən dīt/ *n* a brownish-yellow sulphide mineral containing iron and nickel. Use: source of nickel. [Mid-19C. After Joseph B. *Pentland* (1797–1873), Irish scientist.]

pentobarbital sodium /péntō baárbit'l-/ *n* US PHARM = **pentobarbitone sodium**

pentobarbitone sodium /péntō baárbitōn-/ *n* $C_{11}H_{17}N_2O_3Na$ a barbiturate drug. Use: hypnotic, sedative. US term **pentobarbital sodium**

pentode /pén tōd/ *n* an electronic valve that has five electrodes. They are a cathode, an anode, and three grids. ■ *adj* describes a transistor that has three electrodes at the base or gate [Early 20C. < PENTA-.]

pentosan /péntə san/ *n* a plant polysaccharide composed of linked pentose units

pentose /péntōss, -tōz/ *n* a five-carbon sugar such as ribose

pentose phosphate pathway *n* a series of biochemical reactions in which glucose is converted into other molecules such as those needed to synthesize nucleic acids

pentoxide /pen tók sīd/ *n* a chemical element whose oxides contain five atoms of oxygen in each molecule

pentstemon *n* PLANTS = **penstemon**

pent-up *adj* repressed or stifled rather than being released or freely expressed ○ *pent-up emotions*

pentyl /pén tīl, péntil/ *adj* C_5H_{11} relating to a chemical group containing carbon and hydrogen, deriving from pentane [Late 19C. < PENTA-.]

pentyl acetate *n* $CH_3COOC_5H_{11}$ a colourless combustible liquid. Use: solvent for paints, in extracting penicillin, in photographic film, flavouring.

pentylenetetrazol /péntə leen téttrə zol/ *n* $C_6H_{10}N_4$ a white crystalline powder. Use: stimulant for the central nervous system. [Mid-20C. < PENTA- + METHYLENE + *tetrazole*.]

penuchle, penuckle *n* CARDS = **pinochle**

penult /pe núlt, pénnult/ *n* the second to last item in a series of things, especially the second to last syllable of a word [15C. Shortening of Latin *penultima*, the feminine of *paenultimus* (see PENULTIMATE).]

penultimate /pe núltimət/ *adj* **1** second to last in a series or sequence ○ *the penultimate chapter* **2** relating to a penult [Late 17C. < Latin *paenultimus* < *paene* 'almost' + *ultimus* 'last' (see ULTIMATE).] —**penultimately** *adv*

penumbra /pə númbrə/ (*plural* **-brae** /-bree/ *or* **-bras**) *n* **1 PARTIAL SHADOW** a partial outer shadow that is lighter than the darker inner shadow (**umbra**), e.g. the area between complete darkness and complete light in an eclipse **2 EDGE OF A SUNSPOT** a greyish area surrounding the dark centre of a sunspot **3 INDETERMINATE AREA** an indistinct area, especially a state in which something is unclear or uncertain [Mid-17C. < modern Latin, < Latin *paene* 'almost' + *umbra* 'shadow'.] —**penumbral** *adj* —**penumbrous** *adj*

penurious /pə nyóori əss/ *adj* (*literary*) **1 POOR** having very little money **2 NOT GENEROUS** not generous with money **3 BARREN** barren or yielding little —**penuriously** *adv* —**penuriousness** *n*

penury /pényoori/ *n* extreme poverty [15C. < Latin *penuria* < ?]

Penutian /pi nyóoti ən, -nyóosh'n/ *n* in some language classifications, a grouping (**phylum**) of Native American languages of California, sometimes also including some Central and South American languages, and sometimes Sahaptin-Chinook as a separate branch [Early 20C. < Yokuts *pen* 'two' + Miwok *uti* 'two'.] —**Penutian** *adj*

Penzance /pen zánss/ port in SW England. Population: 17,500 (1994 estimate).

Penzias /péntsi əss/, **Arno** (*b.* 1933) German-born US astrophysicist

peon /pée ən/ *n* **1 LABOURER** in Latin America and the S United States, a farm labourer, especially formerly, who was forced to work for a creditor until a debt was paid off **2 LOW-PAID WORKER** formerly, in India and Sri Lanka, a low-paid office worker, soldier, or public servant **3 DRUDGE** a worker at boring menial tasks [Early 17C. Via Spanish *peón* and Portuguese *peão* 'foot soldier' < medieval Latin *pedon-* < Latin *pes* 'foot'.]

peonage /pée ənij/ *n* **1** a former system used in Latin America and the S United States under which a debtor was forced to work for a creditor until a debt was paid **2** the status or condition of being a peon

peony /peé əni/ (*plural* **-nies**), **paeony** (*plural* **-nies**) *n* a large ornamental shrubby plant. Flowers: large, globe-shaped, red, white, pink. Native to: Europe, Asia, North America. Genus: *Paeonia*. [Old English *peonie*. Via medieval Latin < Greek *paiōnia* < *Paiōn* 'Paian', the physician of the deities.]

people /peép'l/ *n* (*plural* **-ples**) **NATION** a nation, community, ethnic group, or nationality ○ *a proud people* ■ *npl* **1 HUMAN BEINGS COLLECTIVELY** human beings considered collectively or in general ○ *People tend not to mind if you ask them for help.* **2 SUBORDINATES** persons such as employees, subjects, or followers who are under the authority or leadership of somebody or something ○ *I'll get one of my people to phone them.* **3 FAMILY MEMBERS** the members of somebody's family, especially somebody's close family (*informal*) ○ *My people were farmers.* **4 ORDINARY MEN AND WOMEN** the general population, as distinct from the government or higher social classes ○ *the will of the people* **5 POLITICAL UNIT** a group of persons comprising a political unit, electorate, or group ■ *vt* (**-ples, -pling, -pled**) **POPULATE AREA** to populate an area (*usually passive*) ○ *mountain regions that are sparsely peopled* [13C. Via Anglo-Norman < Latin *populus*, of Etruscan origin.]

USAGE In most cases, ***people*** behaves like a plural, as in *People are funny; you never know what they will do.* However, when ***people*** means 'a group of human beings sharing one specific nationality, culture, or language', it is regarded as a singular and when used in the plural, takes an *s* plural ending: *a Native American people of the Southwest, one of several such peoples noted for their peaceableness.* The possessive of ***people*** is formed by adding an apostrophe + *s* if one people is stipulated: *the people's choice of a new Prime Minister.* If many peoples are stipulated, the possessive is formed by adding an apostrophe after the *s*: *various Caribbean peoples' representatives at the conference.* ***People*** is the preferred form in designating human beings in the plural generally: *Thousands of people* [not *persons*] *jammed the stadium. What on earth will people* [not *persons*] *think if you do that?* Use ***persons*** only in certain narrow, typically legalistic or otherwise official, contexts: *the Bureau of Missing Persons; the arrest of three suspicious persons loitering outside the gates of Downing Street.*

people carrier *n* a versatile passenger vehicle for large families, resembling a van in shape and with three rows of seats

peoplehood /peép'l hŏŏd/ *n* identity as a member of a particular people, especially a nation or ethnic group

people mover *n* any automated means of transporting large numbers of people over short distances

people person *n* a sociable and communicative person

people's republic *n* a Socialist or Communist republic

Peoria /pi áwri·ə/ city in S Arizona. Population: 87,048 (1998 estimate).

pep /pep/ *n* liveliness or vigour (*informal*) [Early 20C. Shortening of PEPPER.] —**peppily** *adv* —**peppiness** *n* —**peppy** *adj*

pep up *vt* to make somebody or something more lively, energetic, or interesting (*informal*)

PEP /pep/ *n* a tax-free investment plan that allows small investors to own shares in UK companies. Full form **Personal Equity Plan**

peperomia /péppə rṓmi ə/ *n* a tropical or subtropical plant often cultivated as a house plant for its heavily veined foliage. Genus: *Peperomia*. [Late 19C. < modern Latin *Peperomia* < Greek *peperi* < Sanskrit *pippalī* 'peppercorn'.]

pepino /pə peénō/ (*plural* **-nos**) *n* **1 OVAL FRUIT** an aubergine-shaped purple-streaked fruit that has a flavour like that of a melon **2 SPINY PLANT** a plant with spiny foliage, that bears pepinos. Flowers: bright blue. Native to: Peru. *Solanum muricatum*. **3 CONE-SHAPED HILL** a steep conical hill, especially in Puerto Rico [Mid-19C. Via American Spanish < Latin *pepo* (see PUMPKIN).]

pepla plural of **peplum**

peplos /pépplәss/ (*plural* **peploses**) *n* a loose-fitting garment worn by women in ancient Greece, draped in folds around the shoulders and reaching the waist [Late 18C. < Greek.]

peplum /pépplәm/ (*plural* **-lums** *or* **-la** /-plә/) *n* a short flared ruffle attached to the waist of a jacket or blouse [Late 17C. < Latin < Greek *peplos* (see PEPLOS).]

pepo /peé pō/ (*plural* **-pos**) *n* a fruit of the gourd family such as a melon, squash, pumpkin, or cucumber that typically has a firm or hard rind, a large number of flat seeds, and soft watery flesh [Mid-19C. < Latin (see PUMPKIN).]

pepper /péppər/ *n* **1 SEASONING** a hot condiment or seasoning made from the ground dried berries of a tropical climbing plant **2 PLANT WITH BERRIES** a tropical climbing plant such as betel, cubeb, or kava whose berries are dried for use as pepper. Genus: *Piper*. **3 HOLLOW VEGETABLE** a green, red, or yellow fruit that is hollow with firm walls containing seeds and has mild or pungent flesh that can be eaten either raw or cooked as a vegetable **4 PLANT WITH EDIBLE PODS** a tropical plant of the nightshade family that produces mild or pungent peppers. Genus: *Capsicum*. **5 PUNGENT CONDIMENTS** condiments such as chilli sauce or cayenne pepper made from the more strongly pungent peppers ■ *v* **1** *vt* **SPRINKLE WITH PEPPER** to add or sprinkle pepper as a seasoning onto something **2** *vt* **ASSAIL** to bombard somebody or something with something **3 SPRINKLE AROUND** to scatter things liberally onto or among something (*often passive*) ○ *manuscripts peppered with typing errors* **4** *vt* **MAKE LIVELY** to liven up something such as a speech with wit [Old English *piper*, via W Germanic < Latin *piper* < Sanskrit *pippalī* 'berry, peppercorn']

pepper-and-salt *adj* flecked with dark and light colours ○ *pepper-and-salt hair*

pepperbox /péppər boks/ *n* **1** a cylindrical turret or cupola **2** a small 18th-century pistol with several short revolving barrels

peppercorn /péppər kawrn/ *n* a small dried tropical berry that is ground to make pepper [Old English *piporcorn*]

peppered moth *n* a moth that is grey and speckled when found in rural areas and black in smoke-darkened industrial regions. *Biston betularia*.

pepper mill *n* a kitchen utensil for storing and grinding peppercorns

peppermint /péppər mint/ *n* **1 FLAVOURING** a flavouring prepared from the aromatic oil of a mint plant. Use: food industry, pharmaceuticals. (*often before nouns*) **2 PEPPERMINT SWEET** a sweet flavoured with peppermint **3 PUNGENT HERB** a plant of the mint family whose dark-green downy leaves yield peppermint. *Mentha piperita*.

pepperoni /péppə rṓni/ *n* a hard dry Italian sausage spiced with pepper, or a slice of this, often used on pizzas [Mid-20C. Via Italian *peperone* 'red pepper' < Latin *piper* (see PEPPER).]

pepper pot *n* **1** a small cylindrical container for ready-ground pepper with a perforated top for sprinkling. US term **peppershaker 2** a Guyanese or Caribbean stew made with meat, rice, and vegetables and seasoned with cassava syrup

peppershaker /péppər shaykər/ *n* US HOUSEHOLD = **pepper pot** *n.* 1

pepper steak *n* a steak coated with crushed peppercorns before being fried or grilled

pepper tree *n* a tree of the cashew family that is cultivated for its bright red fruits. Native to: subtropical South America. Genus: *Schinus*.

pepperwort /péppər wurt/ *n* **1** a freshwater fern with floating leaves and slender tangled stems that grows in marshes and ponds. Genus: *Marsilea*. **2** a plant of the mustard family whose pungent lower leaves are used in salads and to season dishes. Genus: *Lepidium*.

peppery /péppəri/ *adj* **1 CONTAINING PEPPER** strongly flavoured with pepper, or tasting of pepper **2 ANGRY** angry and critical **3 EASILY ANNOYED** easily annoyed —**pepperiness** *n*

pep pill *n* any pill that contains a stimulant drug, especially an amphetamine (*dated informal*)

pepsin /pépsin/ *n* an enzyme produced in the stomach that breaks down proteins into simpler compounds [Mid-19C. < Greek *pepsis* 'digestion' < *peptein* (see PEPTIC).]

pepsinogen /pep sínnəjən/ *n* a substance produced by stomach glands that is converted into pepsin after contact with hydrochloric acid during digestion

pep talk *n* a short speech designed to give advice and generate enthusiasm, e.g. in a sports team or among a company's employees (*informal*)

peptic /péptik/ *adj* **1 HELPING DIGESTION** relating to or helping digestion **2 INVOLVING PEPSIN** relating to, caused by, or producing pepsin **3 OF THE STOMACH** relating to or involving the stomach, especially any digestive actions or their results [Mid-17C. Via Latin < Greek *peptikos* 'capable of digesting' < *peptein* 'to digest'.]

peptic ulcer *n* erosion of the mucous membrane that lines the upper digestive tract, caused by excess secretion of acid in the stomach

peptidase /pépti dayz, -dayss/ *n* an enzyme that splits amino acids from peptides

peptide /pép tīd/ *n* a linear molecule made up of two or more linked amino acids [Early 20C. < German *Peptid*, a back-formation < *Polypeptid* (see POLYPEPTIDE).] —**peptidic** /pep tíddik/ *adj*

peptide bond *n* a linkage formed between the amino group of one amino acid and the carboxylic acid group of another

peptidoglycan /pep tídə glī kan/ *n* a large structural molecule found in the cell walls of bacteria

peptize /pép tīz/ (**-tizes, -tizing, -tized**), **peptise** (**-tises, -tising, -tised**) *vt* to disperse fine particles of one substance evenly throughout another substance to create a state intermediate between a suspension and a solution (**colloid**) [Mid-19C. < PEPTONE.] —**peptizable** *adj* —**peptization** /pép tī záysh'n/ *n* —**peptizer** /pép tīzər/ *n*

peptone /péptōn/ *n* a fragment of protein formed by enzyme action in the first stages of digestion [Mid-19C. Via German < Greek *peptos* 'digested' < *peptein* (see PEPTIC).]

peptonize /péptə nīz/ (**-nizes, -nizing, -nized**), **peptonise** (**-tonises, -tonising, -tonised**) *vt* to digest protein using an enzyme —**peptonization** /péptə nī záysh'n/ *n* —**peptonizer** *n*

Pepys /peeps/, **Samuel** (1633–1703) English diarist

Pequot /peé kwot/ (*plural* **-quot** *or* **-quots**) *n* **1** a member of a Native North American people of E Connecticut **2** the Algonquian language of the Pequot people. Native speakers: 7,000. [Mid-17C. < Narragansett *Pequtôog* 'Pequot people'.] —**Pequot** *adj*

per /pər/ *prep* **1** for each or for every thing mentioned ○ *50 miles per hour* **2** by, through, or according to something ○ *per instructions* [14C. < Latin.]

per- *prefix* **1** through ○ *peroral* **2** containing a large proportion of an element ○ *peroxide* **3** containing an element in its highest oxidation state ○ *perchlorate* **4** containing a peroxide group ○ *peracid* [< Latin *per* (see PER)]

peracid /pər ássid/ *n* an acid such as perchloric acid or permanganic acid in which one element is in its highest possible state of oxidation —**peracidity** /pérrə síddəti/ *n*

peradventure /púrəd vénchər/ *adv* possibly or perhaps (*archaic*) ■ *n* chance, doubt, or uncertainty (*literary*) [13C. < Old French *per aventure* 'by chance'.]

perambulate /pə rámbyŏŏ layt/ (**-lates, -lating, -lated**) *vti* to walk about a place (*formal*) [Mid-16C. < Latin *perambulare* < *ambulare* 'to walk'.] —**perambulation** /pə rámbyŏŏ láysh'n/ *n* —**perambulatory** *adj*

perambulator /pə rámbyŏŏ laytər/ *n* **1** a baby's pram (*formal*) **2** a device consisting of a wheel on a long handle, used to measure distance while walking [Early 17C. Originally 'somebody who walks'.]

per annum /pər ánnəm/ *adv* in or for every year, or by the year [< modern Latin, 'by the year']

per ardua ad astra /pər aárdyoo ə ad ástrə/ by endeavour to the stars [< Latin]

p/e ratio *abbr* price-earnings ratio

perborate /pər báw rayt/ *n* a salt compound of borate. Use: bleaching agent in washing powder.

percale /pər káyl/ *n* a smooth-textured closely woven cotton or polyester fabric. Use: sheets, clothing. [Early 17C. < French < ?]

per capita *adv, adj* by or for each person ○ *earnings per capita* [< modern Latin, 'per head']

perceive /pər seév/ (**-ceives, -ceiving, -ceived**) *vt* **1** to notice something, especially something that escapes the notice of others **2** to understand something in a particular way [13C. Via Anglo-Norman and Old French variants of *perçoivre* < Latin *percipere* 'seize completely' < *capere* 'seize'.] —**perceivable** *adj* —**perceivably** *adv* —**perceiver** *n*

per cent, percent /pər sént/ *adv* **AS EXPRESSED IN HUNDREDTHS** used to express a proportion of an amount in hundredths, sometimes represented by the symbol % ■ *n* (*plural* **per cent**; *plural* **-cent**) **1 ONE HUNDREDTH** one hundredth part of something **2 PERCENTAGE** a part or percentage [< Latin *per centum* 'by a hundred']

USAGE ***per cent*** – singular or plural? If ***per cent*** stands alone without a subsequent prepositional phrase, you can use a singular or a plural verb with it: *Sixty per cent is accounted for; Sixty per cent are accounted for.* If a prepositional phrase following ***per cent*** contains a noun or pronoun object regarded as a unit or a whole, use a singular verb: *Sixty per cent of the electorate is accounted for.* If the object of the preposition in such a phrase is regarded as a number of people or things, use a plural verb: *Sixty per cent of the votes are accounted for.*

percentage /pər séntij/ *n* **1 PROPORTION IN ONE-HUNDREDTHS** a proportion stated in terms of one-hundredths that is achieved by multiplying an amount by a per cent **2 PROPORTION** a proportion of a larger group or set ○ *A larger percentage of pupils are choosing to go on to college.* **3 COMMISSION OR CUT** an amount charged that is based on the total amount involved, e.g. a commission charged on a sale, especially the commission that an agent charges a client (*informal*) **4 ADVANTAGE** advantage or benefit (*informal*) ○ *There's no percentage in accepting the proposal.*

USAGE ***Percentage*** – singular or plural? If you put the definite article *the* before ***percentage***, you are stipulating just one percentage and thus you must use a singular verb: *The percentage of errors in this term paper is large.* If you put the indefinite article *a* before ***percentage***, use a plural verb when the noun or pronoun in any subsequent prepositional phrase is regarded as a countable plural, not a unit or a whole: *A large percentage of the errors are found in this text.* If the noun or pronoun object in such a phrase is singular or is regarded as a unit or a whole, use a singular verb: *A large percentage of the electorate remains undecided.*

percentile /pər sén tīl/ *n* a value on a scale of one hundred that indicates whether a distribution is above or below it

percept /púr sept/ *n* something that is perceived by the senses [Mid-19C. < Latin *perceptum* 'something perceived', past participle of *percipere* (see PERCEIVE).]

perceptible /pər séptəb'l/ *adj* large enough, great enough, or distinct enough to be noticed ○ *a perceptible difference* —**perceptibility** /pər séptə bílləti/ *n* —**perceptibly** *adv*

perception /pər sépsh'n/ *n* **1 PERCEIVING** the process of using the senses to acquire information about the surrounding environment or situation ○ *the range of human perception* **2 RESULT OF PERCEIVING** the observation or result of the process of perception ○ *After watching the experiment closely, he noted his perceptions in his lab notebook.* **3 IMPRESSION** an attitude or understanding based on what is observed or thought ○ *a news report that altered the public's perception of the issue* **4 POWERS OF OBSERVATION** the ability to notice or discern things that escape the notice of most people **5 NEUROLOGICAL PROCESS OF OBSERVATION AND INTERPRETATION** any neurological process of acquiring and mentally interpreting information from the senses [14C. Via Old French < Latin *perception-* < *percipere* (see PERCEIVE).] —**perceptional** *adj*

perceptive /pər séptiv/ *adj* **1** quick to understand or discern things or showing understanding of a person or situation **2** relating to perception or capable of perceiving —**perceptively** *adv* —**perceptiveness** *n* —**perceptivity** /púr sep tívvəti/ *n*

perceptual /pər sépchoo əl/ *adj* relating to perception with the senses —**perceptually** *adv*

Perceval /púrssiv'l/, **John de Burgh** (*b.* 1923) Australian painter and ceramicist

Perceval, Spencer (1762–1812) British statesman

perch[1] /purch/ *n* **1 PLACE FOR BIRD TO SIT** a place for a bird to land or rest on such as a branch or a pole in a cage **2 RESTING PLACE** any temporary resting place for a person or thing **3 SOLID MEASURE FOR STONE** a unit of measure for the volume of stone, equal to about 0.7 cu m/24 cu ft **4 UNIT OF LENGTH** a unit of length equal to 5.03 m/$5\frac{1}{2}$ yd **5 UNIT OF AREA** a unit of area equal to 25.3 m^2/$30\frac{1}{4}$ sq. yd **6 INSPECTION FRAME** a frame that woven fabric is laid on to be inspected after weaving ■ *v* **1** *vt* **SIT PRECARIOUSLY** to sit or stand somewhere awkwardly and precariously ○ *He was perched on a high stool.* **2** *vt* **PUT IN A HIGH PLACE** to situate something in a place high up ○ *the ruins of a castle perched on the cliffs* **3** *vi* **BE ON A PERCH** to land or rest on a perch ○ *A pair of doves perched on the apple tree.* [13C. Via Old French < Latin *pertica* 'pole, stick'.] —**percher** *n* ◇ **fall off your perch** to die (*informal*) ◇ **knock somebody off his** *or* **her perch** to make somebody feel less proud or superior

perch[2] /purch/ (*plural* **perches** *or* **perch**) *n* **1** a bony freshwater fish with rough scales and two dorsal fins, one spiny and one soft. Native to: North America, Europe. Genus: *Perca.* **2** the flesh of a perch used as food [14C. Via Old French < Greek *perkē*.]

perchance /pər cháanss/ *adv* (*archaic or literary*) **1** possibly or perhaps **2** by chance [14C. < Anglo-Norman *par chance* 'by chance'.]

Percheron /púrshə ron/ *n* a large black or grey draught horse of a breed that originated in France [Late 19C. < French, 'of the Percheron breed', after *le Perche*, a region of France.]

perchlorate /pər kláw rayt/ *n* a salt or ester of perchloric acid

perchloric acid /pər kláwrik-/ *n* $HClO_4$ a colourless acid of chlorine that is explosive under some conditions. Use: oxidizing agent in laboratory work.

perchloride /pər kláw rīd/ *n* a chloride of an element that contains more chlorine than all other chlorides of the same element

perchloroethylene /pər kláwrō éthə leen/ *n* C_2Cl_4 a colourless toxic organic solvent. Use: in dry-cleaning fluid.

perciatelli /púrchə télli/ *n* pasta in the form of long thin tubes, thicker than spaghetti [< Italian dialect, 'little pierced thing' < *perciato*, past participle of *perciare* 'pierce' < Old French *percer* (see PIERCE)]

Percier /pursi áy/, **Charles** (1764–1838) French architect

~~**percieve**~~ incorrect spelling of **perceive**

percipient /pər síppi ənt/ *adj* perceptive, observant, or discerning ■ *n* somebody or something capable of perceiving [Mid-17C. < Latin *percipere* (see PERCEIVE).] —**percipiently** *adv*

percoid /púr koyd/ *adj* belonging or relating to a large suborder of bony spiny-finned fishes that includes the perch, sea bass, sunfishes, and red mullet. Suborder: Percoidea. [Mid-19C. < modern Latin *Percoidea* < Latin *perca*.] —**percoid** *n*

percolate /púrkə layt/ (**-lates, -lating, -lated**) *v* **1** *vti* **PASS THROUGH A FILTER** to make a liquid or gas pass through a filter or porous substance, or filter through in this way **2** *vi* **PASS THROUGH SLOWLY** to pass slowly through something or spread throughout a place ○ *I let the idea percolate through my mind.* **3** *vti* **MAKE COFFEE** to prepare coffee in a percolator, or undergo preparation in a percolator [Early 17C. < Latin *percolare* 'sieve through' < *colare* 'to sieve' < *colum* 'sieve'.] —**percolable** /púrkələb'l/ *adj* —**percolation** /púrkə láysh'n/ *n* —**percolative** /púrkələtiv/ *adj*

percolator /púrkə laytər/ *n* a coffeepot in which boiling water rises repeatedly through a narrow stem, spills over into a sieve-like basket containing coffee grounds, mixes with them, and returns to the water below

per contra /pər kóntrə/ *adv* on the other hand or by way of contrast [< Italian, 'by the opposite side']

per curiam /pər kyóori am/ *adj* relating to a unanimous decision or opinion by a court of law [< Latin *per curiam* 'by the court']

percuss /pər kúss/ *vt* to gently tap a part of a patient's body in order to diagnose an illness or condition [Mid-16C. < Latin *percuss-*, past participle of *percutere* 'strike hard' < *quatere* 'to strike'.] —**percussor** *n*

percussion /pər kúsh'n/ *n* **1 INSTRUMENTS THAT ARE HIT** the group of instruments that produce sound by being struck, including drums and cymbals, or the section of the orchestra playing such instruments **2 TAPPING OF THE BODY** examination of part of a patient's body by tapping with the fingers to assess the presence of fluid, the enlargement of organs, or the solidification of normally hollow parts **3 IMPACT** the impact of one object striking another, or the noise or shock created when two objects hit each other (*formal*) **4 ACT OF DETONATING A PERCUSSION CAP** the striking or detonating of a percussion cap in a firearm [Mid-16C. < Latin *percussion-* < *percussus*, past participle of *percutere* (see PERCUSS).]

percussion cap *n* a detonator consisting of a thin metal cap or strip of paper containing explosive powder, formerly used to fire some pistols

percussion instrument *n* a musical instrument such as a drum, cymbal, or triangle that is hit to produce sound

percussionist /pər kúsh'nist/ *n* a musician who plays a percussion instrument

percussion lock *n* a mechanism on a gun that fires by striking a percussion cap

percussion tool *n* any power tool that delivers repeated heavy blows, e.g. a pneumatic drill

percussive /pər kússiv/ *adj* having the effect of an impact or a blow —**percussively** *adv* —**percussiveness** *n*

percutaneous /púrkyoo táyni əss/ *adj* administered or absorbed through the skin as an injection or, e.g. ointment —**percutaneously** *adv*

Percy /púrssi/, **Sir Henry** (1366–1403) English military leader. Known as **Harry Hotspur**

per diem /pər dée em, -dī em/ *adv, adj* by the day or every day ■ *n* a daily payment or allowance [< Latin, 'by the day']

perdition /pər dísh'n/ *n* **1** in some religions, the state of everlasting punishment in Hell that sinners endure after death **2** Hell itself as a location [14C. Via Old French < Latin *perdere* 'put to destruction' < *dare* 'put'.]

père /pair/ *n* **1** the title given to Roman Catholic priests in France and French-speaking countries **2** in France and French-speaking countries, used after a man's surname to distinguish him from his son ○ *M. Doucet père.* ◊ **fils**[2] [Early 17C. Via French < Latin *pater* (see PATERNAL).]

Père David's deer *n* a large reddish-grey deer that survives in captivity only. Native to: China. *Elaphurus davidianus.* [Late 19C. After *Père* Armand *David* (1826–1900), French missionary and naturalist.]

peregrinate /pérrəgri nayt/ (**-nates, -nating, -nated**) *vti* to travel around a place or from place to place (*literary*) [Late 16C. < Latin *peregrinari* < *peregrinus* (see PEREGRINE).] —**peregrinator** *n*

peregrination /pérrəgri náysh'n/ *n* a journey or voyage (*literary*) [15C. Directly or via French < Latin < *peregrinari* 'to travel' < *peregrinus* (see PEREGRINE).]

peregrine /pérrəgrin/ *n* BIRDS = **peregrine falcon** ■ *adj* coming from another region or country (*archaic*) [14C. Via French < Latin *peregrinus* 'travelling' < *pereger* 'through fields' < *ager* 'field'.]

peregrine falcon *n* a large falcon with a blue-grey back and whitish underparts that hunts other birds on the wing. Family: Falconidae. [Because they were captured full-grown while migrating, rather than taken from their nests while young]

peremptory /pə rémptəri/ *adj* **1 DICTATORIAL** expecting to be obeyed and unwilling to tolerate disobedience **2 CLOSED TO FURTHER CONSIDERATION OR ACTION** ending, or not open to, discussion, debate, or further action **3 EXPRESSING URGENCY** communicating urgency, command, or instruction [13C. Via Anglo-Norman < Latin *perimere* 'take away completely' < *emere* 'to buy'.] —**peremptorily** *adv* —**peremptoriness** *n*

Perendale /pérrən dayl/ *n* a sheep of a New Zealand breed that is a cross between a Romney Marsh and a Cheviot

~~**perenial**~~ incorrect spelling of **perennial**

perennate /pérrə nayt, pə rénnayt/ (**-nates, -nating, -nated**) *vi* to survive from one growing season to the next with reduced or arrested growth between seasons [Early 17C. < Latin *perennare* 'last for years' < *perennis* (see PERENNIAL).] —**perennation** /pérrə náysh'n/ *n*

perennial /pə rénni əl/ *adj* **1 LASTING OVER 2 YEARS** describes a plant that lasts for more than two growing seasons, either dying back after each season, as some herbaceous plants do, or growing continuously, as some bushes do **2 RECURRING OR ENDURING** constantly recurring, or lasting for an indefinite time ○ *the perennial problem of litter* ■ *n* **PERENNIAL PLANT** a plant that lasts for more than two growing seasons [Mid-17C. < Latin *perennis* 'through the year' < *annus* 'year'.] —**perennially** *adv*

perentie /pə rénti/, **perenty** (*plural* **-ties**) *n* a large burrowing lizard that has brown skin with yellow patches and can reach 2.5 m/8 ft in length. Native to: semidry and desert regions of central and N Australia. *Varanus giganteus.* [Early 20C. Of Aboriginal origin, probably < Diyari *pirindi*.]

perestroika /pérrə stróykə/ *n* the political and economic restructuring in the former Soviet Union initiated by Mikhail Gorbachev from about 1986. The stated aims included decentralized control of industry and agriculture and some private ownership. ◊ **glasnost** [Late 20C. < Russian, 'rebuilding, reconstruction'.]

Pérez de Cuéllar /pé ress də kwáy yaar/, **Javier** (*b.* 1920) Peruvian diplomat

perf. *abbr* 1 perfect 2 perforated 3 performance

perfect *adj* /púrfikt/ 1 **WITHOUT FAULTS** without errors, flaws, or faults ○ *in perfect condition* 2 **COMPLETE AND WHOLE** complete and lacking nothing essential ○ *We had a perfect day together.* 3 **EXCELLENT OR IDEAL** excellent or ideal in every way ○ *That's the perfect word to describe him.* 4 **ESPECIALLY SUITABLE** having all the necessary or typical characteristics required for a given situation ○ *the perfect candidate for the job* 5 **UTTER OR ABSOLUTE** used to emphasize the extent or degree of something ○ *a perfect nuisance* 6 **EXACT AS A REPRODUCTION** exactly reproducing an original ○ *a perfect likeness* 7 **WITH STAMENS AND PISTILS TOGETHER** describes a flower that has functional stamens and pistils in the same flower 8 **EXACTLY DIVISIBLE** exactly divisible into equal roots 9 **WITH THE VERB ACTION FINISHED** describes a verb or verb aspect for an action that is brought to a close 10 **OF MUSICAL INTERVALS** describes the differences in pitch between the fourth, the fifth, and the octave, common to both major and minor scales 11 **WITH SEXUAL AND ASEXUAL REPRODUCTION** describes a fungus that reproduces both sexually and asexually during its life cycle 12 **SEXUALLY MATURE** describes an insect that is sexually mature and completely differentiated ■ *vt* /pər fékt/ 1 **BRING TO COMPLETION** to make something as good as possible, or bring something to completion ○ *They perfected the process last year.* 2 **PRINT THE REVERSE SIDE OF** to complete a printed page by printing its reverse side ■ *n* /púrfikt/ 1 **PERFECT ASPECT OF VERB** the perfect aspect of a verb 2 **VERB IN THE PERFECT ASPECT** a verb that is in the perfect aspect [13C. Directly and via Old French *parfit* < Latin *perfecere* 'make completely, finish' < *facere* 'to make'.] —**perfecter** *n* —**perfectibility** /pər féktə bílləti/ *n* —**perfectible** /pər féktəb'l/ *adj* —**perfectness** *n*

perfecta /pər féktə/ *n* a type of bet, especially on dogs or horses, that pays if the two entries chosen come in first and second in the order predicted. US term **exacta** [Late 20C. < American Spanish *quiniela perfecta* 'perfect quinella'.]

perfect binding *n* a method of bookbinding in which a book's pages are cut and then bound to the spine with glue, as opposed to being stitched uncut —**perfect bound** *adj*

perfect competition *n* a market condition in which a product is traded freely by buyers and sellers in large numbers without any individual transaction affecting the price

perfect game *n* a game of bowling in which 12 consecutive strikes occur

perfect gas *n* PHYS, CHEM = **ideal gas**

perfection /pər féksh'n/ *n* 1 **PERFECT NATURE** the quality of something that is as good or suitable as it can possibly be ○ *to strive for perfection as a goal* 2 **PROCESS OF PERFECTING** the process of becoming or making something perfect ○ *The perfection of the technique will require another two years' research.* 3 **EXAMPLE OR INSTANCE OF BEING PERFECT** somebody or something that reaches the highest attainable standard, or an instance of this ○ *His cooking that evening was sheer perfection* ◇ **to perfection** perfectly ○ *The piece showed off her talent as a pianist to perfection.*

perfectionism /pər féksh'nizəm/ *n* 1 the doctrine that perfection is possible in human beings 2 rigorous rejection of anything less than perfect

perfectionist /pər féksh'nist/ *n* 1 a demander of nothing less than perfection 2 a believer in the philosophical doctrine of perfectionism

perfective /pə féktiv/ *adj* 1 **TOWARDS PERFECTION** tending towards perfection 2 **DESCRIBES COMPLETED ACTION** describes a verb that reports a completed action as opposed to an incomplete or continuing one ■ *n* **PERFECTIVE VERB OR ASPECT** a verb in the perfective aspect, or the aspect itself —**perfectively** *adv* —**perfectiveness** *n* —**perfectivity** /púr fek tívvəti/ *n*

perfectly /púrfiktli/ *adv* 1 in exactly the way desired or required ○ *That will suit her perfectly.* 2 used to emphasize the degree or extent of something ○ *They're perfectly capable of managing on their own.*

perfect number *n* a positive whole number that is equal to the sum of the numbers that can be multiplied to give it as a result, excluding itself

perfecto /pər féktō/ (*plural* **-tos**) *n* a medium-sized cigar with tapered ends and a thick centre [Late 19C. < Spanish, 'perfect'.]

perfect participle *n* GRAM = **past participle**

perfect pitch *n* MUSIC = **absolute pitch** *n.* 1

perfect rhyme *n* 1 a rhyme of two words that are pronounced the same but spelt differently and have different meanings, e.g. 'flew' and 'flue' 2 a rhyme in which the stressed vowel and consonants following it are the same, e.g. 'alive' and 'contrive'

perfect square *n* a rational number equal to the square of another rational number

perfervid /pur fúrvid/ *adj* extremely passionate or enthusiastic (*literary*) [Mid-19C. < modern Latin *perfervidus* 'extremely vehement' < Latin *fervidus* (see FERVID).] —**perfervidly** *adv* —**perfervidness** *n*

perfidy /púrfidi/ *n* treachery or deceit (*formal*) [Late 16C. < Latin *perfidia* < *perfidus* 'through faith' (< *per fidem decipere* 'deceive through trustingness') < *fides* 'faith'.] —**perfidious** /pər fíddi əss/ *adj* —**perfidiously** *adv* —**perfidiousness** *n*

perfin /púrfin/ *n* a postage stamp with initials perforated in it by a business or other organization to prevent misuse [Mid-20C. Blend of PERFORATED + INITIAL.]

perfoliate /pər fóli ət/ *adj* describes a leaf that encloses a stem so that the stem seems to pass through it [Late 17C. < modern Latin *perfoliatus* 'through a leaf' < Latin *folium* 'leaf'.] —**perfoliation** /pər fóli áysh'n/ *n*

perforate *v* /púrfə rayt/ (**-rates, -rating, -rated**) 1 *vt* **PUNCTURE** to make a hole or holes in something 2 *vt* **MAKE HOLES FOR TEARING** to make a line of small holes in paper to make tearing it easier 3 *vi* **PENETRATE** to penetrate or pass through something ■ *adj* /púrfərət/ 1 **WITH SMALL HOLES** dotted with small holes 2 **WITH TRANSPARENT SPOTS** dotted with transparent spots 3 STAMPS = **perforated** *adj.* 1 [Mid-16C. < Latin *perforare* 'bore through' < *forare* 'to bore'.] —**perforable** /púrfərəb'l/ *adj* —**perforative** /-rətiv/ *adj* —**perforator** /-raytər/ *n* —**perforatory** /-rətəri/ *adj*

perforated /púrfə raytid/ *adj* 1 **perforated, perforate** pierced with a hole or holes, especially with a line of small holes designed to make tearing easy 2 in which a hole has developed ○ *a perforated eardrum*

perforation /púrfə ráysh'n/ *n* 1 **HOLE** a hole made in something 2 **MAKING HOLES OR HAVING THEM** the act of making a hole or holes in something or the state of being perforated 3 **HOLES FOR TEARING** a small hole or series of holes punched into a piece of paper to make tearing easy 4 **FORMATION OF A HOLE** the formation of a hole in an organ, tissue, or tube, usually as a consequence of disease

perforce /pər fáwrss/ *adv* unavoidably or as forced by circumstances (*archaic or literary*) [14C. < Old French *par force* 'by force'.]

perforin /púrfərin/ *n* a substance produced by cytotoxic T-cells and natural killer cells that attacks and kills foreign cells by forming pores in their membranes [Late 20C. < PERFORATE + -IN.]

perform /pər fáwrm/ *v* 1 *vt* **ACCOMPLISH** to carry out an action or accomplish a task ○ *the surgeon who performed the operation* 2 *vt* **FULFIL** to do what is stated or required 3 *vti* **PRESENT AN ARTISTIC WORK** to present or enact an artistic work such as a piece of music or a play to an audience 4 *vi* **FUNCTION OR BEHAVE** to function, operate, or behave in a particular way or to a particular standard ○ *athletes who perform best under pressure* [14C. < Anglo-Norman *parformer*, alteration of Old French *parfornir* 'accomplish completely' < *fournir* 'accomplish'.] —**performable** *adj* —**performer** *n*

performance /pər fáwrmənss/ *n* 1 **ARTISTIC PRESENTATION** a presentation of an artistic work to an audience, e.g. a play or piece of music 2 **MANNER OF FUNCTIONING** the manner in which something or somebody functions, operates, or behaves 3 **WORKING EFFECTIVENESS** the effectiveness of the way somebody does his or her job (*often before nouns*) 4 **DISPLAY OF BEHAVIOUR** a public display of behaviour that others find distasteful, e.g. an angry outburst that causes embarrassment (*informal*) 5 **IRRITATING PROCEDURE** an irritating or troublesome procedure (*informal*) 6 **THING ACCOMPLISHED** something that is carried out or accomplished 7 **ACCOMPLISHMENT OF** the act of carrying out or accomplishing something such as a task or action 8 **LANGUAGE PRODUCED** the language that a speaker or writer actually produces, as distinct from his or her understanding of the language. ◊ **competence** *n.* 4, **parole** *n.* 5

performance art *n* art that combines two or more artistic media, a traditionally static medium, e.g. sculpture or photography, and a dramatic medium, e.g. recitation or improvisation —**performance artist** *n*

QUICK FACTS ON... **PERFORMANCE ART**

Key dates: late 1950s–mid-1970s
Key locations: United States, W Europe
Key elements: mixed media; live performance, spontaneity, improvisation, audience participation; uncertainty; unusual settings; blurring of art and life
Key figures: Allan Kaprow, Vito Acconci, Joseph Beuys, Nam June Paik, Gilbert and George, Yoko Ono, Meredith Monk, Pina Bausch, Laurie Anderson
Key works: *18 Happenings in 6 Parts* (Kaprow) 1959, *How to Explain Pictures to a Dead Hare* (Beuys) 1965, *TV Bra for Living Sculpture* (Paik) 1969, *Underneath the Arches* (Gilbert and George) 1969, *Juice* (Monk) 1969
Key developments: happenings; body art, video art, action art; mixed-means theatre

performance enhancer *n* any one of various dietary supplements used by athletes to enhance bursts of high performance

performative /pər fáwrmətiv/ *adj* describes speech that constitutes an act of some kind, e.g. the phrase 'I promise I'll do my best', that constitutes a promise in itself ■ *n* a performative utterance [Mid-20C. < PERFORM.] —**performatively** *adv*

performing arts /pər fáwrming-/ *npl* the forms of art that involve theatrical performance, especially drama, dance, and music

perfume /púr fyoom/ *n* 1 **FRAGRANT LIQUID** a fragrant liquid that is sprayed or rubbed on the skin or clothes to give a pleasant smell 2 **PLEASANT SCENT** a pleasant smell ■ *vt* (**-fumes, -fuming, -fumed**) **GIVE SOMETHING PLEASANT SCENT** to give something a pleasant smell [Mid-16C. Via French *parfum* < obsolete Italian *parfumare* 'smoke through' < *fumare* 'to smoke'.] —**perfumed** /púr fyoomd, pər fyóomd/ *adj* —**perfumey** /púrf yoomi/ *adj*

SYNONYMS See ***smell***.

perfumer /pər fyóomər/ *n* a manufacturer or seller of perfumes

perfumery /pər fyóoməri/ (*plural* **-ies**) *n* 1 **PERFUMES IN GENERAL** perfumes generally 2 **PLACE MAKING OR SELLING PERFUMES** a place of business where perfumes are manufactured or sold 3 **MAKING OF PERFUMES** the manufacture of perfumes, or the art of making perfumes

perfunctory /pər fúngktəri/ *adj* 1 done as a matter of duty or custom, without thought, attention, or genuine feeling ○ *a perfunctory kiss* 2 done hastily or superficially ○ *a perfunctory search* [Late 16C. Via late Latin *perfunctorius* < *perfungi* 'work through' < *fungi*.] —**perfunctorily** *adv* —**perfunctoriness** *n*

perfuse /pər fyóoz/ (**-fuses, -fusing, -fused**) *vt* 1 to spread throughout something, or spread a substance or quality, e.g. liquid, light, or colour, throughout something 2 to introduce a liquid into tissue or an organ by circulating it through blood vessels or other channels within the body [Early 16C. < Latin *perfus-*, past participle of *perfundere* 'pour over' < *fundere* 'pour'.] —**perfused** *adj* —**perfusion** *n* —**perfusive** /pər fyóoziv/ *adj*

Pergamum /púrgəməm/ ancient Greek and Roman city in NW Asia Minor, in present-day W Turkey

pergola /púrgələ/ *n* a frame structure consisting of colonnades or posts with a latticework roof, designed to support climbing plants [Late 17C. Via Italian < Latin *pergula*.]

perhaps /pər háps/; *informal* /praps/ CORE MEANING: an adverb expressing uncertainty, or indicating that something is possibly true or may possibly happen, often used to make remarks appear less definite ○ *Perhaps it will be warmer later.* ○ *He wondered if perhaps he had been mistaken.* ○ *Perhaps his best-known ceramic work is his public mural 'Voyage'.*
adv 1 used to show approximation ○ *The house is perhaps five miles from here.* 2 used in requests and suggestions in order to sound more polite ○ *Perhaps we should help Dad in the kitchen.* [15C. < PER 'by' + an earlier form of *hap* 'chance'.]

peri /péeri/ *n* 1 in Persian mythology, a beautiful supernatural being descended from the fallen angels 2 a graceful and beautiful girl or woman (*literary*) [Late 18C. < Persian *perī*.]

peri- *prefix* 1 around, surrounding ○ *pericarp* 2 near ○ *perilune* ○ *perinatal* [< Greek *peri* 'around, about' < Indo-European]

perianth /pérri anth/ *n* the outer structure of a flower, made up of the corolla, the calyx, or both [Early 19C. Via French < modern Latin *perianthium* 'around a flower' < Greek *peri* 'around' + *anthos* 'flower'.]

periapsis /pérri ápsiss/ (*plural* **-sides** /-ápsi deez/) *n* the point in an orbit that is nearest to the centre of gravitational attraction

periapt /pérri apt/ *n* a charm worn to protect the wearer from harm [Late 16C. Via French < Greek *periapton* 'something fastened around' < *peri* 'around' + *haptein* 'fasten'.]

periastron /pérri ás tron/ *n* the points in space and time in the orbits of two stars in a binary system at which they are closest together [Mid-19C. < PERI- + Greek *astron* 'star', after *perihelion*.]

pericarditis /pérri kaar dítiss/ *n* inflammation of the pericardium —**pericarditic** /-díttik/ *adj*

pericardium /pérri kaárdi əm/ (*plural* **-a** /-di ə/) *n* a fibrous membrane that forms a sac surrounding the heart and attached portions of the main blood vessels [Late 16C. Via medieval Latin < Greek *perikardion* 'around the heart' < *peri* 'around' + *kardia* 'heart'.] —**pericardiac** *adj* —**pericardial** *adj*

pericarp /pérri kaarp/ *n* the part of a fruit that surrounds the seed or seeds, including the skin, flesh, and, e.g. in apples, the core —**pericarpial** /pérri kaárpi əl/ *adj* —**pericarpic** /-kaárpik/ *adj*

perichondrium /pérri kóndri əm/ (*plural* **-a** /-dri ə/) *n* the fibrous membrane that covers the surface of cartilage except at joints [Mid-18C. Via modern Latin, 'around the cartilage' < Greek *peri* 'around' + *khondros* 'cartilage'.] —**perichondrial** *adj*

periclase /pérri klayss/ *n* a colourless, grey, green, or yellow magnesium oxide mineral. Source: limestones. [Mid-19C. Directly or via German *Periklas* < modern Latin *periclasia* < Greek *peri* 'around' + *klasis* 'breaking'; from its perfect cleavage.] —**periclastic** /pérri klástik/ *adj*

Pericles /pérri kleez/ (495?–429? BC) Athenian statesman —**Periclean** /pérri kleé ən/ *adj*

periclinal /pérri klín'l/ *adj* **1** describes a fold in sedimentary rocks that appears as a regular dome on the surface of the earth **2** describes cell walls that are parallel to the outer surface of a plant part [Late 19C. < Greek *periklinēs* 'sloping all around' < *peri* 'all around' + *klinein* 'slope'.]

pericline /pérri klīn/ *n* **1** a dome-shaped fold in sedimentary rock **2** a variety of the mineral albite that forms long white crystals [Mid-19C. < Greek *periklinēs*.]

pericope /pə ríkəpi/ *n* an extract from a book, especially a passage from the Bible selected for reading during a Roman Catholic Mass [Mid-17C. Via late Latin < Greek *perikopē* 'cutting around' < *peri* 'around' + *koptein* 'to cut'.] —**pericopic** /pérri kóppik/ *adj*

pericranium /pérri kráyni əm/ (*plural* **-a** /-ni ə/) *n* the membrane of connective tissue that surrounds the skull [Early 16C. Via modern Latin < Greek *perikranion* 'round the skull' < *peri* 'round' + *kranion* 'skull'.] —**pericranial** *adj*

pericycle /pérri sīk'l/ *n* the outer layer of plant tissue surrounding the inner tissues in the roots and stems of plants (**stele**) that conducts moisture and nutrients around the plant [Late 19C. Via French < Greek *perikuklos* 'circling around' < *peri* 'around' + *kuklos* 'circle'.] —**pericyclic** /pérri síklik/ *adj*

periderm /pérri durm/ *n* the outer layer of plant tissue in woody roots and stems —**peridermal** /pérri dúrm'l/ *adj* —**peridermic** /-dúrmik/ *adj*

peridium /pə ríddi əm/ (*plural* **-a** /-di ə/) *n* the covering of the spore-bearing organ in many kinds of fungi [Early 19C. Via modern Latin < Greek *pēridion* 'small leather wallet' < *pēra* 'wallet'.]

peridot /pérri dot/ *n* a semiprecious stone that is a pale green or yellowish-green transparent form of olivine. Use: gems. [Early 18C. < French.]

peridotite /pérri dō tīt/ *n* a coarse-grained igneous rock rich in iron and magnesium —**peridotitic** /-dō títtik/ *adj*

perigee /pérri jee/ *n* the point in the orbit of a satellite, moon, or planet at which it comes nearest to the object it is orbiting [Late 16C. Via French < late Greek *perigeios* 'close round the earth' < *peri* 'close round' + *gaia* 'earth'.] —**perigeal** /pérri jeé əl/ *adj* —**perigean** /-jeé ən/ *adj*

periglacial /pérri gláysh'l/ *adj* relating to or found in a region that borders on a glacier

Périgueux /pérri gö/ town in SW France. Population: 32,848 (1990).

perigynous /pə ríjjinəss/ *adj* describes a flower that has petals, stamens, and sepals arranged around a cup-shaped receptacle that contains the ovary, e.g. the flowers of cherries and roses —**perigyny** *n*

perihelion /pérri heéli ən/ (*plural* **-a** /-li ə/) *n* the point in the orbit of a planet or other astronomical body at which it comes closest to the Sun [Mid-17C. Via modern Latin *perihelium* 'close round the sun' < Greek *peri* 'close round' + *hēlios* 'sun', after PERIGEE.] —**perihelial** *adj*

perikaryon /pérri kárri ən/ (*plural* **-a** /-ə/) *n* the part of a nerve cell that contains cytoplasm —**perikaryal** *adj*

peril /pérrəl/ *n* **1 EXPOSURE TO RISK** exposure to risk of harm **2 DANGER** a source of possible harm ■ *vt* (**-ils, -illing, -illed**) **IMPERIL** to expose somebody or something to the risk of harm (*archaic*) [13C. Via French < Latin *periculum* 'experiment, risk'.] —**perilous** *adj* —**perilously** *adv* —**perilousness** *n*

perilune /pérri loon/ *n* the point at which a planet or other body orbiting the Moon comes closest to the Moon's surface [Mid-20C. < PERI- + Latin *luna* 'moon', after APOLUNE.]

perilymph /pérri limf/ *n* the fluid that fills the space between the membranous labyrinth and the bony labyrinth in the inner ear [Mid-19C. < PERI- + LYMPH.]

perimeter /pə rímmitər/ *n* **1 BOUNDARY ENCLOSING AN AREA** a boundary that encloses an area **2 CURVE ENCLOSING AREA** a curve enclosing an area on a plane, or the length of such a curve **3 OUTER EDGE OF TERRITORY** the outer edge of an area of defended territory [Late 16C. Via Latin < Greek *perimetros* 'measuring around' < *peri* 'around' + *metron* 'measure'.] —**perimetric** /pérri méttrik/ *adj* —**perimetrical** /-méttrik'l/ *adj* —**perimetrically** /-méttrikli/ *adv*

perimysium /pérri mízzi əm/ (*plural* **-a** /-zi ə/) *n* the sheath of connective tissue that surrounds bundles of muscle fibres [Mid-19C. < PERI- + Greek *mus* 'muscle'.]

perinatal /pérri náyt'l/ *adj* relating to or occurring during the period around childbirth, specifically from around week 28 of pregnancy to around one month after the birth —**perinatally** *adv*

perinatology /pérri nay tólləji/ *n* a medical speciality concerned with the care and treatment of mother and infant immediately prior to, during, and following childbirth —**perinatologist** *n*

perinephrium /pérri néffri əm/ (*plural* **-a** /-fri ə/) *n* the fatty tissue that surrounds the kidney [Late 19C. < PERI- + Greek *nephros* 'kidney'.] —**perinephric** *adj*

perineum /pérri neé əm/ (*plural* **-a** /-neé ə/) *n* the region of the abdomen surrounding the urogenital and anal openings [Mid-17C. Via late Latin < Greek *perinaion* 'near to where excretion takes place' < *peri* 'near to' + *inan* 'excrete'.] —**perineal** *adj*

perineurium /pérri nyoóri əm/ (*plural* **-a** /-ri ə/) *n* the sheath of connective tissue that surrounds a bundle of nerve fibres [Mid-19C. < PERI- + NEURO-.] —**perineurial** *adj*

period /peéri əd/ *n* **1 INTERVAL OF TIME** an interval of time **2 IDENTIFIABLE TIME** an interval of time that is identified by what happens or exists during it **3 TIMETABLE SECTION** a division of a schedule or timetable, e.g. a portion of the school day **4 MENSTRUATION TIME** an occurrence of menstruation (*often before nouns*) **5 UNIT OF GEOLOGICAL TIME** a division of geological time shorter than an era and longer than an epoch **6** *US* GRAM = **full stop** *n.* 1 **7 DIVISION OF GAME** a division of playing time in some sports **8 TIME FOR SINGLE CYCLE** (*symbol T*) the time required for one complete cycle of a repetitive system, e.g. the rotation of a star or the movement of an electromagnetic wave **9 INTERVAL BETWEEN EQUAL VALUES** the interval between the points at which the values of a periodic function are equal **10 ROW IN PERIODIC TABLE** any of the horizontal rows of elements in the periodic table **11 UNIT OF POETIC RHYTHM** one of the longer units in the classical system of analyzing the rhythms of poetry **12 MUSICAL PASSAGE** a long passage of music consisting of two or more contrasting musical phrases ■ *interj* **SHOWING FINALITY** a word added to the end of a statement to emphasize that the speaker will not discuss it further (*informal*) ■ *adj* **RELATING TO PARTICULAR HISTORICAL TIME** belonging to or intended to suggest a particular historical time ○ *actors in period costume* [14C. Via French < Greek *periodos* 'way around' < *hodos* 'way'.]

periodic /peéri óddik/ *adj* **1 OCCASIONAL** recurring or reappearing from time to time **2 REGULAR** occurring or appearing at regular intervals or in regular cycles **3 INVOLVING PERIODS** associated with or occurring in periods [Mid-17C. Via French and Latin < Greek *periodikos* < *periodos* (see PERIOD).] —**periodically** *adv*

SYNONYMS ***periodic, intermittent, occasional, sporadic***

CORE MEANING: recurring over a period of time

periodic recurring or reappearing from time to time with a degree of regularity; **intermittent** occurring at irregular intervals; **occasional** occurring infrequently at irregular intervals; **sporadic** occurring irregularly and unpredictably.

periodic acid *n* any strongly oxidizing acid of iodine [< PER- + IODIC]

periodical /peéri óddik'l/ *n* **MAGAZINE** a magazine or journal published at regular intervals such as weekly, monthly, or quarterly ■ *adj* **1 PUBLISHED REGULARLY** published at regular intervals **2 OCCASIONAL** recurring or reappearing from time to time

periodic function *n* a mathematical function whose value is the same at regular intervals

periodicity /peéri ə díssəti/ *n* **1** recurrence at regular intervals **2** similarity between the properties of chemical elements that are close to each other in the periodic table

periodic law *n* the law stating that chemical elements fall into groups sharing similar properties when they are arranged according to atomic number

periodic sentence *n* in rhetoric, a complex sentence in which the main clause is left unfinished until the end in order to create the effect of anticipation or suspense

periodic system *n* the system of arranging chemical elements in a table according to the periodic law

periodic table *n* a table of the chemical elements arranged according to their atomic numbers

periodization /peéri ə dī záysh'n/, **periodisation** *n* the dividing of history into distinct and identifiable periods

periodontal /pérri ō dónt'l/ *adj* relating to or affecting the tissues that surround the neck and root of a tooth [Mid-19C. < PERI- + Greek *odont-* 'tooth'.] —**periodontally** *adv*

periodontics /pérri ō dóntiks/, **periodontology** /pérri ō don tólləji/ *n* the branch of dentistry concerned with the treatment of diseases of the gums and other periodontal tissues —**periodontic** *adj* —**periodontical** *adj* —**periodontically** *adv* —**periodontist** *n*

period piece *n* something, especially a curio or a work of art, that dates from or evokes a particular historical period, often something with no other value

perionychium /pérri ō níki əm/ (*plural* **-a** /-ki ə/) *n* the areas of skin that surround a fingernail or toenail [Early 20C. < modern Latin, 'round the nail' < Greek *onux* 'nail'.]

periosteum /pérri ósti əm/ (*plural* **-a** /-ti ə/) *n* the sheath of connective tissue that surrounds all bones except those at joints [Late 16C. Via modern Latin < Greek *periosteon* 'around the bone' < *osteon* 'bone'.] —**periosteal** *adj*

periostitis /pérri o stítiss/ *n* inflammation of the periosteum —**periostitic** /-stíttik/ *adj*

periostracum /pérri óstrəkəm/ (*plural* **-ca** /-kə/) *n* the hard outer layer of the shell of some molluscs, especially freshwater molluscs [Mid-19C. < modern Latin, 'shell around' < Greek *ostrakon* 'shell'.]

periotic /pérri ṓtik/ *adj* involving the area around the ear, especially the bones around the inner ear

peripatetic /pérripə téttik/ *adj* travelling from place to place, especially working in several establishments and travelling between them ■ *n* a peripatetic worker, especially a teacher who travels between schools [Early 17C. Via French or Latin < Greek *peripatētikos* < *peripatein* 'walk around' < *patein* 'to walk'.] —**peripatetically** *adv*

Peripatetic /pérripə téttik/ *adj* belonging or relating to the school of philosophy founded by Aristotle, who gave lectures while walking about the Lyceum in Athens ■ *n* a member of the Aristotelian school of philosophy

peripatus /pə ríppətəss/ *n* ZOOL = **onychophoran** [Mid-19C. Via modern Latin < Greek *peripatos* 'way around' < *peripatos* 'way'.]

ϟ **peripheral** /pə ríffərəl/ *adj* **1 AT THE EDGE** at or relating to the edge of something, as opposed to its centre **2 NOT**

PERIODIC TABLE

Chemical elements are indicated by their symbols. The numbers above the elements are the atomic numbers, and those below are the atomic weights (those in parentheses are for the longest-lived isotopes, while those for Np, Pa, and Tc are for the most technologically important isotopes). The lanthanides and actinides do not fit easily into any group and are thus shown separate from the main table.

Group → Period ↓	1	2	3	4	5	6	7	8	9	10	11	12	13	14	15	16	17	18
1	1 H 1.01																	2 He 4.00
2	3 Li 6.94	4 Be 9.01											5 B 10.81	6 C 12.01	7 N 14.01	8 O 16.00	9 F 19.00	10 Ne 20.18
3	11 Na 22.99	12 Mg 24.31											13 Al 26.98	14 Si 28.09	15 P 30.97	16 S 32.06	17 Cl 35.45	18 Ar 39.95
4	19 K 39.10	20 Ca 40.08	21 Sc 44.96	22 Ti 47.90	23 V 50.94	24 Cr 52.00	25 Mn 54.94	26 Fe 55.85	27 Co 58.93	28 Ni 58.71	29 Cu 63.55	30 Zn 65.38	31 Ga 69.72	32 Ge 72.59	33 As 74.92	34 Se 78.96	35 Br 79.90	36 Kr 83.80
5	37 Rb 85.47	38 Sr 87.62	39 Y 88.91	40 Zr 91.22	41 Nb 92.91	42 Mo 95.94	43 Tc 98.91	44 Ru 101.07	45 Rh 102.91	46 Pd 106.40	47 Ag 107.87	48 Cd 112.40	49 In 114.82	50 Sn 118.69	51 Sb 121.75	52 Te 127.60	53 I 126.90	54 Xe 131.30
6	55 Cs 132.91	56 Ba 137.34	57 * La 138.91	72 Hf 178.49	73 Ta 180.95	74 W 183.85	75 Re 186.2	76 Os 190.2	77 Ir 192.22	78 Pt 195.09	79 Au 196.97	80 Hg 200.59	81 Tl 204.37	82 Pb 207.20	83 Bi 208.98	84 Po 209	85 At (210)	86 Rn (222)
7	87 Fr (223)	88 Ra (226)	89 ** Ac (226)	104 Rf (261)	105 Db (262)	106 Sg (266)	107 Bh (264)	108 Hs (269)	109 Mt (268)	110 Uun (269)	111 Uuu (272)	112 Uub (277)	113 Uut	114 Uuq	115 Uup	116 Uuh	117 Uus	118 Uuo

Lanthanides *	57 La 138.91	58 Ce 140.12	59 Pr 140.91	60 Nd 144.24	61 Pm (145)	62 Sm 150.40	63 Eu 151.96	64 Gd 157.25	65 Tb 158.93	66 Dy 162.50	67 Ho 164.93	68 Er 167.26	69 Tm 168.93	70 Yb 173.04	71 Lu 174.97
Actinides **	89 Ac (226)	90 Th 232.04	91 Pa 231.04	92 U 283.04	93 Np 237.05	94 Pu (244)	95 Am (243)	96 Cm (247)	97 Bk (247)	98 Cf (251)	99 Es (254)	100 Fm (257)	101 Md (258)	102 No (255)	103 Lr (256)

SIGNIFICANT minor or incidental in importance or relevance **3 NEAR THE SURFACE** near the surface of an organ or the body ■ *n* **PERIPHERAL PIECE OF HARDWARE** a piece of computer hardware such as a printer or a disk drive that is external to but controlled by a computer's central processing unit —**peripherally** *adv*

peripheral nervous system *n* the part of the nervous system that lies outside the brain and spinal cord

periphery /pə riffəri/ (*plural* **-ies**) *n* **1 BOUNDARY** the area around the edge of a place **2 SURFACE** the surface of an object **3 POSITION OF LITTLE INVOLVEMENT** the position or state of having only a minor involvement in something [Late 16C. Via late Latin < Greek *peripherēs* 'carrying around' < *pherein* 'carry'.]

periphrasis /pə riffrassiss/ (*plural* **-ses** /-seez/) *n* **1** the use of excessively long or indirect speech in order to

say something **2** an expression that states something indirectly [Mid-16C. Via Latin < Greek *periphrazein* 'explain around' < *phrazein* 'explain'.]

periphrastic /pérri frástik/ *adj* **1** concerning or using periphrasis **2** formed using two or more words rather than an inflected form, especially used to describe a verb tense formed using an auxiliary verb rather than by inflecting the main verb [Early 19C. < Greek *periphrastikos* < *periphrazein* (see PERIPHRASIS).] —**periphrastically** *adv*

periphyton /pə riffi ton/ *n* aquatic plants and animals that live attached to rocks and other submerged objects [Mid-20C. Probably < PERI- + Greek *phuton* 'plant', after *plankton*.]

periplasm /pérri plazəm/ *n* the area of a cell that lies immediately inside the cell wall but outside the plasma membrane

periplast /pérri plast/ *n* a cell wall or cell membrane

periproct /pérri prokt/ *n* the area surrounding the anus of some invertebrate animals such as sea urchins [Late 19C. < PERI- + Greek *prōktos* 'anus'.]

peripteral /pə ríptərəl/ *adj* describes a classical building that has a single row of columns on all sides [Early 19C. < Greek *peripteros* 'with a wing around' < *pteron* 'wing'.]

perique /pə reek/ *n* a strongly-flavoured tobacco grown in Louisiana [Late 19C. < Louisiana French.]

periscope /pérri skōp/ *n* a long tubular optical instrument, e.g. on a submarine, that uses lenses, prisms, and mirrors to allow a viewer to see objects not in a direct line of sight

periscopic /pérri skóppik/ *adj* **1** describes a lens that has a wide field of view **2** relating to or using a periscope —**periscopically** *adv*

perish /pérrish/ *v* **1** *vi* **DIE** to die, e.g. because of harsh conditions or accident (*literary*) **2** *vi* **DISAPPEAR** to come to an end or cease to exist (*formal*) **3** *vti* **DECAY** to deteriorate or decay, or to make a material, e.g. rubber, deteriorate or decay [13C. Via French *périss-*, stem of *périr* < Latin *perire* 'go completely' < *ire* 'to go'.]

perishable /pérrishəb'l/ *adj* liable to decay, rot, or spoil ■ *n* something that is perishable, especially an item of food —**perishability** /pérrishə bíllәti/ *n* —**perishableness** *n* —**perishably** /pérrishəbli/ *adv*

perished /pérrisht/ *adj* feeling extremely cold (*informal*)

perisher /pérrishər/ *n* an annoying person, especially a naughty child (*dated informal*)

perishing /pérrishing/ *adj* **1** extremely cold **2** used to emphasize how annoying something or somebody is (*dated informal*) ○ *a perishing nuisance* —**perishingly** *adv*

perisperm /pérri spurm/ *n* nutritive tissue from a plant nucleus that surrounds the seed embryo —**perispermal** /pérri spúrm'l/ *adj*

perissodactyl /pə rissō dáktil/ *n* a large mammal that belongs to the order of mammals with hooves and an odd number of toes, which includes horses, rhinoceroses, and tapirs. Order: Perissodactyla. [Mid-19C. < modern Latin *Perissodactyla* 'uneven finger or toe' < Greek *perissos* 'uneven' + *daktulos* 'finger, toe'.] —**perissodactyl** *adj* —**perissodactylous** *adj*

peristalsis /pérri stálssiss/ (*plural* **-ses** /-seez/) *n* the waves of involuntary muscle contractions that transport food, waste matter, or other contents through a tube-shaped organ such as the intestine [Mid-19C. Via modern Latin < Greek *peristaltikos* 'clasping, compressing' < *peristellein* 'place around' < *stellein* 'to place'.] —**peristaltic** *adj* —**peristaltically** *adv*

peristome /pérri stōm/ *n* the mouthparts of an invertebrate such as an earthworm or echinoderm —**peristomal** /pérri stṓm'l/ *adj* —**peristomial** /-stṓmi əl/ *adj*

peristyle /pérri stīl/ *n* **1** a line of columns (**colonnade**) that encircles a building or a courtyard **2** a building or courtyard that has a peristyle [Early 17C. Via French < Greek *peristulos* 'having columns around' < *stulos* 'column'.] —**peristylar** /pérri stī́lər/ *adj*

peritoneum /pérritō nee əm/ (*plural* **-a** /-nee ə/ *or* **-ums**) *n* a smooth transparent membrane that lines the abdomen and doubles back over the surfaces of the internal organs to form a continuous sac [Mid-16C. Via late Latin < Greek *peritonos* 'stretched around' < *teinein* 'to stretch'.] —**peritoneal** *adj* —**peritoneally** *adv*

peritonitis /pérritō nī́tiss/ *n* inflammation of the membrane that lines the abdomen (**peritoneum**) —**peritonitic** /-níttik/ *adj*

peritrack /pérri trak/ *n* AIR = **taxiway** [Late 20C. < PERIMETER + TRACK.]

peritrich /pérri trik/ (*plural* **-tricha** /pə ríttrikə/) *n* a simple microscopic invertebrate (**protozoan**) covered in tiny filaments (**cilia**) that it uses to move around [Early 20C. Shortening of modern Latin *peritricha* 'hair around' < Greek *peri* 'around' + *trikh-*, stem of *thrix* 'hair'.] —**peritrichous** /pə ríttrikəss/ *adj*

periwig /pérri wig/ *n* a wig, especially of the kind that men wore in the 17th and 18th centuries [Early 16C. Alteration of an earlier form of PERUKE.]

periwinkle[1] /pérri wingk'l/ *n* MARINE BIOL = **winkle** [Mid-16C. < ?]

periwinkle[2] /pérri wingk'l/ *n* a trailing evergreen plant with dark-green glossy leaves. Flowers: blue, white. Native to: Europe, Asia. Genus: *Vinca*. ■ *adj* of a pale bluish-purple colour [Pre-12C. < late Latin *pervinca* < Latin *vincapervinca*.]

perjink /pər jíngk/ *adj* *Scotland* caring too much about neatness or unimportant details (*humorous*) [Early 19C. < ?]

~~**perjorative**~~ incorrect spelling of **pejorative**

perjure /púrjər/ (**-jures, -juring, -jured**) *vr* to tell a lie in a court of law and therefore be guilty of perjury [15C. Via French < Latin *perjurare* 'swear falsely' < *jurare* (see JURY).] —**perjurer** *n*

perjured /púrjərd/ *adj* **1** guilty of telling a lie in a court of law and therefore of committing perjury **2** containing lies and therefore breaking an oath to tell the truth in a court of law

perjury /púrjəri/ (*plural* **-ries**) *n* **1** the telling of a lie after having taken an oath to tell the truth, usually in a court of law **2** a lie told in a court of law by somebody who has taken an oath to tell the truth [14C. Via Anglo-Norman < Latin *perjurium* < *perjurare* (see PERJURE).] —**perjurious** /pər jóori əss/ *adj* —**perjuriously** /-əssli/ *adv* —**perjuriousness** /-əssnəss/ *n*

perk[1] /purk/ *n* **1** a benefit given to an employee in addition to a salary, e.g. the use of a car or membership of a club **2** anything that somebody gains incidentally or as a consequence of something else ○ *Taking time off whenever you want is one of the perks of being self-employed.* [Early 19C. Shortening of PERQUISITE.]

perk[2] /purk/ *vti* to percolate, or to percolate coffee (*informal*) [Mid-20C. Shortening.]

Perkins /púrkinz/, **Charles Nelson** (*b.* 1936) Australian Aboriginal activist

perk up /purk-/ *vti* **1** to become or make somebody more cheerful, positive, or active **2** to stick up or make something stick up, especially quickly ○ *saw the dog's ears perk up* [Mid-20C. Probably < *perk* 'perch' (now dialectal) < Old French *perche* (see PERCH[1]).]

perky /púrki/ (**-ier, -iest**) *adj* **1** lively, cheerful, and energetic **2** irritatingly self-confident —**perkily** *adv* —**perkiness** *n*

perlite /púr līt/ *n* a greyish volcanic glass in the form of grains that resemble pearls —**perlitic** /pur líttik/ *adj*

Perlman /púrlmən/, **Itzhak** (*b.* 1945) Israeli-born US violinist

perlocution /púr lō kyoósh'n/ *n* the effect that a speaker's words have on somebody [Mid-20C. < PER + LOCUTION.] —**perlocutionary** *adj*

perm[1] /purm/ *n* a hair treatment that uses chemicals to give hair long-lasting curliness or waviness ■ *vt* to treat hair chemically to give it long-lasting curliness or waviness [Early 20C. Shortening of PERMANENT.]

perm[2] /purm/ *n* the selection of possible winners made by somebody making a bet, especially, in football pools, a selection of matches that are thought likely to end in a score draw (*informal*) ■ *vt* to select a number of possible winners to bet on from a larger field, especially, in football pools, a number of matches thought likely to end in a score draw (*informal*) [Mid-20C. Shortening of PERMUTATION.]

Perm /purm/, **Perm'** city in E European Russia. Population: 1,098,600 (1992).

permaculture /púrmə kulchər/ (*plural* **-tures** *or* **-ture**) *n* a system of agriculture that uses a mix of trees, shrubs, other perennial plants, and livestock to create a self-sustaining ecosystem that yields crops and other products [Late 20C. Blend of PERMANENT + AGRICULTURE.]

permafrost /púrmə frost/ *n* underlying soil or rock that remains permanently frozen, found mainly in the polar regions [Mid-20C. < PERMANENT + FROST.]

permalloy /pur málloy/ *n* a nickel-iron alloy belonging to a group of alloys that are highly valued in the electronics industry because they allow magnetic fields to pass through them [Early 20C. < PERMEABLE + ALLOY.]

~~**permanant**~~ incorrect spelling of **permanent**

permanence /púrmənənss/, **permanency** /púrmənənssi/ *n* existence in the same form for ever or for a very long time [15C. Directly or via French or medieval Latin *permanentia* < Latin *permanent-* (see PERMANENT).]

permanent /púrmənənt/ *adj* **1 EVERLASTING** lasting for ever or for a very long time, especially without undergoing significant change **2 UNCHANGING** never changing or not expected to change ■ *n* *US* **PERM** a perm (*formal*) [15C. Directly or via French < Latin *permanere* 'remain through' < *manere* 'remain'.] —**permanently** *adv* —**permanentness** *n*

permanent health insurance *n* health insurance that provides a regular income in cases of absence from work owing to long-term illness

permanent magnet *n* a magnet that retains its properties after the magnetizing force has been removed from it —**permanent magnetism** *n*

permanent press *n* a chemical process used to give fabric shape and make it resistant to wrinkling (*hyphenated before nouns*)

permanent tooth *n* any of the second and final set of teeth, 32 in human adults, that grow to replace the milk teeth

permanent wave *n* a perm

permanent way *n* a railway track intended for long-term public use, laid with sleepers on a prepared bed of ground and supported by stones, as opposed to a lightweight or temporary track

permanganate /pər máng gə nayt/ *n* a chemical compound that is a salt of permanganic acid [Mid-19C. < MANGANESE.]

permanganic acid /púr man gánnik-/ *n* $HMnO_4$ an unstable acid that exists only in dilute solution [*Permanganic* < PERMANGANATE]

permeability /púrmi ə bíllәti/ (*plural* **-ties**) *n* **1 PERMEABLE NATURE** the property of being permeable **2 RATE SUBSTANCE PASSES THROUGH POROUS MEDIUM** the rate at which something such as a liquid or a magnetic field passes through a membrane or other medium **3 MAGNETIC PROPERTY** (*symbol* μ) the property of a material to alter a magnetic field in which it is placed, or a measure of this property

permeable /púrmi əb'l/ *adj* allowing liquids, gases, or magnetic fields to pass through —**permeably** *adv*

permeance /púrmi ənss/ *n* **1** the act of passing through a porous substance or membrane **2** the ability of a magnetic component or assembly to be magnetized, measured in henries and calculated by dividing the magnetic flux by the magnetomotive force —**permeant** *adj, n*

permease /púrmi ayz, -ayss/ *n* a protein in bacterial cell membranes that allows a solute to enter the cell [Mid-20C. < PERMEATE.]

permeate /púrmi ayt/ (**-ates, -ating, -ated**) *vti* **1** to enter something and spread throughout it, so that every part or aspect of it is affected **2** to pass through the minute openings in a porous substance or membrane, or make something such as a liquid pass through [Mid-17C. < Latin *permeare* 'pass through' < *meare* 'to pass'.] —**permeation** /púrmi áysh'n/ *n* —**permeative** /púrmi ətiv/ *adj*

~~**permenent**~~ incorrect spelling of **permanent**

Permian /púrmi ən/ *n* the period of geological time when reptiles flourished, 290 million to 245 million years ago [Late 16C. After the province of *Perm* in E Russia.] —**Permian** *adj*

per mille /pər mílay/, **per mil** *adv* in every thousand or by the thousand [*Mill* < Latin *mille* 'thousand']

~~**permissable**~~ incorrect spelling of **permissible**

permissible /pər míssəb'l/ *adj* allowable or permitted [15C. < French, < Latin *permiss-* (see PERMISSION).] —**permissibility** /pər míssə bíllәti/ *n* —**permissibly** /pər míssəbli/ *adv*

permission /pər mísh'n/ *n* agreement to allow something to happen or be done ■ *vt* to give explicit permission for something, e.g. for marketing information to be sent automatically [15C. < French, < Latin *permiss-*, past participle of *permittere* (see PERMIT).]

permissive /pər míssiv/ *adj* **1 ALLOWING FREEDOM OF BEHAVIOUR** allowing or enjoying the freedom to behave in ways others might consider unacceptable, particularly in sexual matters **2 GIVING PERMISSION** granting permission **3 OPTIONAL** not required (*archaic*) [15C. < French, < Latin *permiss* (see PERMISSION).] —**permissively** *adv* —**permissiveness** *n*

permit *v* /pər mít/ (**-mits, -mitting, -mitted**) **1** *vti* **ALLOW** to allow something or give permission for it **2** *vti* **MAKE SOMETHING POSSIBLE** to allow somebody the possibility of doing something **3** *vr* **ALLOW YOURSELF** to allow yourself to have or do something, especially as a luxury or for a special occasion ■ *n* /púrmit/ **1 DOCUMENT GIVING PERMISSION** an official document or certificate giving permission for something **2 PERMISSION** permission granted, especially in written form (*formal*) [15C. < Latin *permittere* 'let go through' < *mittere* 'let go'.] —**permittee** /púrmi tée/ *n* —**permitter** /pər míttər/ *n*

permittivity /púrmi tívvəti/ (*plural* **-ties**) *n* (*symbol* υ) the measure of the ability of a nonconducting material to retain electric energy when placed in an electric field [Late 19C. < PERMIT, after *conductivity*.]

permutate /púrmyoŏ tayt/ (**-tates, -tating, -tated**) *vt* to change the order of items in a group, especially to rearrange them in every possible way [Late 16C. < Latin *permutare* (see PERMUTE).]

permutation /púrmyoŏ táysh'n/ *n* **1 ARRANGEMENT** an arrangement of items created by moving or reordering them **2 REARRANGING** the reordering or rearranging of items in a group **3 TRANSFORMATION** a change or transformation **4 ORDER OF MATHEMATICAL ELEMENTS** an ordered arrangement of elements from a set **5 PERM** a perm (*formal*) —**permutational** *adj*

permute /pər myoōt/ (**-mutes, -muting, -muted**) *vt* **1** to change the order of items in a group, especially to rearrange them in every possible way **2** to reorder the elements in a mathematical set [Late 19C. < Latin *permutare* 'change completely' < *mutare* 'to change'.] —**permutability** /pər myoōtə bílləti/ *n* —**permutable** /pər myoōtəb'l/ *adj* —**permutably** /-əbli/ *adv*

pernicious /pər níshəss/ *adj* **1** wicked or meaning to cause harm **2** causing great harm, destruction, or death [Early 16C. Via Old French < Latin *pernicies* 'complete destruction' < *nec-*, stem of *nex* 'destruction'.] —**perniciously** *adv* —**perniciousness** *n*

pernicious anaemia *n* a severe form of anaemia, found mostly in older adults, that results from the body's inability to absorb vitamin B_{12}

pernickety /pər níkəti/ *adj* (*informal*) **1** excessively concerned about unimportant details. US term **persnickety** *adj.* **1 2** requiring precise attention to detail. US term **persnickety** [Early 19C. < ?: perhaps thought to suggest small pieces.] —**pernicketiness** *n*

~~**perogative**~~ incorrect spelling of **prerogative**

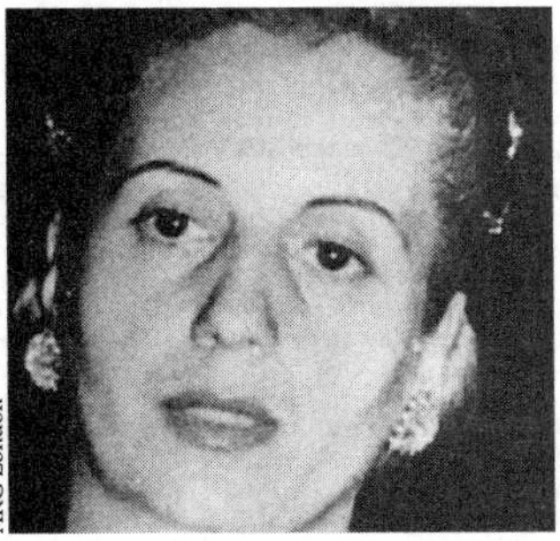

AKG London

Eva de Perón

Perón /pə rón/, **Eva de** (1919–52) Argentinian political figure. Born **María Eva Duarte**. Known as **Evita**

Perón, Isabel de (*b.* 1931) Argentinian politician. Born **María Estela Martínez Cartas**

Perón, Juan (1895–1974) Argentinian statesman — **Peronist** /pə rónnist/ *n, adj*

peroneal /pérrə neé əl/ *adj* relating to the narrower of the two bones in the lower leg (**fibula**) [Mid-19C. < Greek *peronē* 'pin of a brooch, fibula'.]

perorate /pérrə rayt/ (**-rates, -rating, -rated**) *vi* (*formal*) **1** to finish a speech by summarizing its main points **2** to speak at length, especially in a formal or pompous way [Early 17C. < Latin *perorare* 'speak all the way through' < *orare* 'speak'.]

peroration /pérrə ráysh'n/ *n* **1** a conclusion to a speech in which the main points of the speech are summarized (*formal*) **2** a long speech making much use of rhetorical devices —**perorational** *adj*

perovskite /pe róv skīt/ *n* a black, yellow, or brown calcium titanate mineral. Use: superconductive materials. [Mid-19C. After L. A. *Perovski* (1792–1856), Russian mineralogist.]

peroxidase /pə róksi dayz, -dayss/ *n* an enzyme in animals and plants that helps neutralize harmful peroxides

peroxide /pə rók sīd/ *n* **1 CHEMICAL COMPOUND** a chemical compound such as hydrogen peroxide that contains oxygen atoms in the group $-O_2-$ **2 HAIR COLOURING SUBSTANCE** a solution of hydrogen peroxide used as a hair lightener (*often before nouns*) ○ *a peroxide blonde* ■ *vt* (**-ides, -iding, -ided**) **1 BLEACH HAIR WITH PEROXIDE** to bleach hair using peroxide **2 TREAT SOMETHING WITH PEROXIDE** to treat something with peroxide or hydrogen peroxide

peroxisome /pə róksi sōm/ *n* a tiny part within a cell containing enzymes that oxidize toxic substances such as alcohol and prevent them from doing any harm [Mid-20C. < PEROXIDE + -SOME.]

perp /purp/ *n US* somebody responsible for a crime (*slang*) [Late 20C. Shortening of *perpetrator*.]

perpend /púr pend/ *n* BUILDING = **parpen** [15C. Variant of PARPEN.]

perpendicular /púrpən díkyoōlər/ *adj* **1 VERTICAL** perfectly vertical **2 STEEP** very steep **3 AT RIGHT ANGLES** at right angles to a line or plane **4 perpendicular, Perpendicular IN LATE GOTHIC STYLE** relating to or typical of a style of Gothic architecture whose characteristic elements are tall narrow facades, windows, and doors, and vaulted ceilings ■ *n* **1 PERPENDICULAR LINE** a perpendicular line or plane **2 DEVICE FINDING THE VERTICAL** any device used to establish a vertical line such as a spirit level or a plumb line **3 perpendicular, Perpendicular ARCHITECTURAL STYLE** the perpendicular style of architecture **4 SHEER ROCK** a sheer rock face [14C. Via Old French < Latin *perpendiculum* 'plumb line', literally 'something weighed thoroughly' < *perpendere* 'weigh thoroughly' < *pendere* 'weigh'.] —**perpendicularity** /-díkyoō lárrəti/ *n* —**perpendicularly** /-díkyoōlərli/ *adv*

perpetrate /púrpi trayt/ (**-trates, -trating, -trated**) *vt* to commit or be responsible for something, usually something criminal or morally wrong [Mid-16C. < Latin *perpetrare* 'completely bring about' < *patrare* 'bring about' < *pater* 'father'.] —**perpetration** /púrpi tráysh'n/ *n* —**perpetrator** /púrpi traytər/ *n*

perpetual /pər péchoo əl/ *adj* **1 LASTING FOR EVER** lasting for all time **2 LASTING INDEFINITELY** lasting for an indefinitely long time **3 OCCURRING REPEATEDLY** occurring over and over **4 BLOOMING THROUGHOUT SEASON** describes flowers or flowering plants that bloom throughout the season [14C. Via French < Latin *perpes* 'going towards throughout' < *petere* 'go towards'.]

perpetual calendar *n* a calendar set out in such a way that it can be used for several years or for any year

perpetual check *n* a situation in chess in which one player's king is placed in check with every move the other player makes, resulting in a draw

perpetually /pər péchoo əli/ *adv* **1** for ever or for a very long time **2** repeatedly at very short intervals, and so appearing to be continuous

perpetual motion *n* **1** the hypothetical continuous operation of a mechanism without the introduction of energy from an external source, known as perpetual motion of the first kind **2** the hypothetical operation of a mechanism that would convert heat directly into work, known as perpetual motion of the second kind

perpetuate /pər péchoo ayt/ (**-ates, -ating, -ated**) *vt* **1** to make something continue, usually for a very long time **2** to make something or somebody be remembered [Early 16C. < Latin *perpetuare* < *perpetuus* (see PERPETUAL).] —**perpetuation** /-péchoo áysh'n/ *n* —**perpetuator** /pər péchoo aytər/ *n*

perpetuity /púrpi tyoō əti/ (*plural* **-ties**) *n* **1 PERPETUAL CONDITION** the state of continuing for a long time or indefinitely **2 ETERNITY** eternity or the rest of time ○ *a sacrifice honoured in perpetuity* **3 TRANSFER OF PROPERTY FOR EVER** the transfer of property for an unlimited period of time, restricted in law by the rule against perpetuity **4 INVESTMENT** an investment designed to pay an annual return indefinitely, having no maturity date [15C. Via French < Latin *perpetuus* (see PERPETUAL).]

perphenazine /pər fénnə zeen, -zin/ *n* $C_{21}H_{26}ClN_3OS$ a crystalline drug. Use: treatment of anxiety, tension, nausea. [Mid-20C. < PIPERIDINE + PHENYL + AZINE.]

Perpignan /púrp een yaaN/ city in S France. Population: 108,049 (1990).

perplex /pər pléks/ *vt* **1** to puzzle or confuse somebody, especially causing doubt **2** to make something excessively complicated or intricate [15C. Earliest as *perplexed*, via French < Latin *perplexus* 'completely woven together' < *plexus*, past participle of *plectere* 'weave together'.] —**perplexed** *adj* —**perplexedly** /-sidli/ *adv*

perplexing /pər pléksing/ *adj* disconcertingly difficult to understand or come to terms with —**perplexingly** *adv*

perplexity /pər pléksəti/ (*plural* **-ties**) *n* **1 BEING PERPLEXED** the state of being perplexed **2 PERPLEXING THING** something that is difficult to understand, especially because it is complex or part of a complicated whole (*often plural*) **3 COMPLEX NATURE** the nature of something that is disconcertingly complex

per pro /pər prṓ/ *prep* a fuller form of the abbreviation 'pp' that is written in formal correspondence by somebody who is signing on behalf of another person [Shortening of Latin *per procurationem* 'by proxy']

perquisite /púrkwizit/ *n* **1 PERK** a perk (*formal*) **2 CUSTOMARY TIP** a tip that is customary on some occasions **3 A RIGHT** something considered to be an exclusive right [Early 18C. < medieval Latin *perquisitum* 'something searched for' < *perquirere* 'seek for' < *quaerere* 'seek'.]

Perrault /pérrō/, **Charles** (1628–1703) French writer and collector of fairy stories

~~**perrenial**~~ incorrect spelling of **perennial**

perron /pérrən/ *n* **1** a raised platform at an entrance that is not at ground level **2** an external stairway leading up to a perron [14C. < French, 'large stone' < Latin *petra* 'stone'.]

perry /pérri/ (*plural* **-ries**) *n* a drink made from fermented pear juice, similar to cider or wine [14C. Via Old French *pere* < Latin *pirum* (see PEAR).]

Perry /pérri/, **Fred** (1909–95) British tennis player

perse /purss/ *adj* of a dark bluish-grey or purplish-black colour [14C. Via French < medieval Latin *persus*.] —**perse** *n*

per se /pər sáy/ *adv* in itself, by itself, or intrinsically [< Latin, 'by itself']

Perse /purss/, **Saint-John** (1887–1975) French poet and diplomat. Pseudonym of **Alexis Saint-Léger Léger**

persecute /púrssi kyoot/ (**-cutes, -cuting, -cuted**) *vt* **1** to systematically subject a race or group of people to cruel or unfair treatment, e.g. because of their ethnic origin or religious beliefs **2** to make somebody the victim of continual pestering or harassment [15C. Via French < Latin *persecut-*, past participle of *persequi* 'keep following' < *sequi* 'follow'.] —**persecutee** /púrssi kyoo teé/ *n* —**persecutive** /púrssi kyootiv/ *adj* —**persecutor** /-kyootər/ *n* —**persecutory** /-kyootəri/ *adj*

persecution /púrssi kyoōsh'n/ *n* **1** the subjecting of a group of people to cruel or unfair treatment, e.g. because of their ethnic origin or religious beliefs **2** the suffering felt by persecuted people

Perseid /púrsi id/ *n* a meteor in a meteor shower that appears around 12 August and seems to originate from near the constellation Perseus

Persephone /pər séffəni/ *n* in Greek mythology, the daughter of Demeter and Zeus who was abducted by Hades, king of the underworld. Roman equivalent **Proserpina**

Persepolis /pər séppəliss/ ruined ancient Persian city in present-day SW Iran

Perseus[1] /púrssi əss, púr syooss/ *n* a constellation of the northern hemisphere. See illustration at **constellation**

Perseus[2] /púrs yooss, púrsi əss/ *n* in Greek mythology, the son of Zeus and Danae

perseverance /púrssi veérənss/ *n* **1 DETERMINED CONTINUATION** steady and continued action or belief, usually over a long period and especially despite difficulties or setbacks **2 CALVINIST CONCEPT OF DIVINE GRACE** in Calvinism, the belief that God's grace brings selected people, the elect, to salvation **3 ROMAN CATHOLIC BELIEF IN GOD'S GRACE** in the Roman Catholic Church, the belief that God's grace lasts to the end of somebody's life if that person has maintained his or her good works and faith —**perseverant** *adj*

perseveration /pə sévvə ráysh'n/ *n* a tendency to repeat the response to an experience in later situations where it is not appropriate [Early 20C. < Latin *perseverare* (see PERSEVERE).]

persevere /púrssi veér/ (**-veres, -vering, -vered**) *vi* to persist steadily in an action or belief, usually over a long period and especially despite problems or difficulties [14C. Via French *persévérer* < Latin *perseverare* 'follow strictly' < *perseverus* 'very strict' < *severus* (see SEVERE).] —**persevering** *adj* —**perseveringly** *adv*

~~**perseverence**~~ incorrect spelling of **perseverance**

Pershing /púrshing/ *n* a two-stage US Army ballistic missile capable of delivering a nuclear warhead [Mid-20C. After J. J. PERSHING.]

Pershing /púrshing/, **John J.** (1860–1948) US general. Full name **John Joseph Pershing**

Persia /púrshə, púrzhə/ **1** former name for **Iran 2** ancient empire in SW Asia that stretched eastwards from the E Mediterranean Sea to the River Indus in present-day Pakistan

Persian /púrsh'n, púrzhn/ *n* **1 RESIDENT OR NATIVE OF IRAN** somebody who comes from Iran **2** LANG = **Farsi 3 PEOPLE OF ANCIENT PERSIA** a member of a people who lived in ancient Persia and who founded an empire around 500 BC **4 LANGUAGE OF ANCIENT PERSIANS** the language spoken by the ancient Persians —**Persian** *adj*

Persian carpet, Persian rug *n* a carpet consisting of a woven backing to which wool or silk threads have been hand-knotted, made in the Middle East and typically having rich colours and strong designs

Persian cat *n* a domestic cat with long silky hair belonging to a breed originally from the Middle East

Persian Gulf /púrsh'n-/ arm of the Arabian Sea, between the NE Arabian Peninsula and SW Iran. Area: 233,000 sq. km/90,000 sq. mi.

Persian lamb *n* **1** the soft curled usually black fur from the karakul lamb **2** a lamb of the karakul sheep

Persian rug *n* TEXTILES = **Persian carpet**

Persian wool *n* a loosely twisted three-strand wool yarn used in needlepoint, each strand being two-ply

persiflage /púrssi flaa<u>zh</u>/ *n* **1** light or teasing good-natured talk **2** light-heartedness or frivolity in the treatment of something [Mid-18C. < French, < *persifler* 'to banter' < *siffler* 'to whistle', via Old French < Latin *sibilare* (see SIBILANT).]

persimmon /pər símmən/ *n* **1** a juicy smooth-skinned orange-red fruit that is sweet only when fully ripe **2** a tree that has hard wood and bears persimmons. Native to: Asia, Europe, E North America. Genus: *Diospyros*. [Early 17C. Alteration of Virginia Algonquian *pessemmins*.]

persist /pər síst/ *vi* **1 KEEP CARRYING ON** to continue steadily or obstinately despite problems, difficulties, or obstacles **2 CONTINUE TO BE BELIEVED WRONGLY** to continue being widely believed or accepted despite evidence or proof to the contrary ○ *a view that persists to this day* **3 CONTINUE** to continue happening [Mid-16C. < Latin *persistere* 'stand through' < *sistere* 'make stand' < *stare* (see STATION).] —**persister** *n*

~~**persistant**~~ incorrect spelling of **persistent**

persistence /pər sístənss/, **persistency** /-tənssi/ *n* **1 QUALITY OF PERSISTING** the quality of continuing steadily despite problems or obstacles **2 ACT OF PERSISTING** the action of somebody who persists with something **3 LONG CONTINUANCE** continuance of an effect after its cause has ceased or been removed **4 RESILIENCE OF ORGANISM** the ability of a living organism to resist being disturbed or altered

persistent /pər sístənt/ *adj* **1 CONTINUING DESPITE PROBLEMS** tenaciously or obstinately continuing despite problems or difficulties **2 INCESSANT OR UNRELENTING** existing or continuing for a long time **3 PERSISTING BEYOND MATURATION** describes a plant part such as a scale on a pine cone that lasts beyond maturity without falling off **4 SUSTAINING CONTINUAL GROWTH** describes a body part such as a tooth that grows throughout life **5 ABLE TO REMAIN IN THE ENVIRONMENT** describes a chemical or a living organism that remains in the environment for months or years, usually because of resistance to attack by oxygen, light, and micro-organisms —**persistently** *adv*

persistent vegetative state *n* a medical condition in which a patient has severe brain damage and as a result is unable to stay alive without the aid of a life-support system, showing no response to stimuli

persnickety /pər saníkəti/ *adj US* = **pernickety** [Early 20C. Alteration of PERNICKETY.] —**persnicketiness** *n*

person /púrss'n/ (*plural* **people** /peép'l/ *or* **persons** *formal*) *n* **1 HUMAN BEING** an individual human being **2 HUMAN'S BODY** a human being's body, often including the clothing ○ *objects found on her person* **3 HUMAN'S APPEARANCE** an individual human being's general appearance (*formal*) **4 FORM OF VERB AND PRONOUN** any one of three forms of verbs and pronouns used to denote the speaker, the person addressed, or somebody else being referred to **5 OBJECT WITH SPECIAL MORAL VALUE** an object with special moral value because of some spiritual status, autonomous nature, or importance for other people **6 INDIVIDUAL OR BODY OF INDIVIDUALS** a living human being or a group, either or both having legal rights and responsibilities [12C. Via Old French < Latin *persona* 'mask worn by an actor, character'.] —**person** *suffix* —**personhood** *n* ◇ **in person** personally, rather than being represented by somebody or something else

USAGE Terms that are not gender-specific have increasingly grown in prominence, and ones incorporating the suffix ***-person*** are now common (*chairperson, spokesperson*). The terms that have taken hold most strongly tend to be those that do not simply replace *-man* (or *-woman*) with ***-person*** but are more subtly neutral with respect to sex: *chair* rather than *chairperson*, *customer adviser* rather than *salesperson*. Despite the powerful trend towards inclusive terms, however, it remains true that when the members of the group at issue are predominantly male, the traditional term incorporating *-man* tends to be used more frequently (*chairman, fisherman*). Forms with *-woman* are also seen, though in most cases these are now less common than the form incorporating ***-person***. Choose gender-neutral words when they are available.

USAGE See ***individual*** and ***people***.

Person /púrss'n/ *n* in Christianity, the Father, the Son, or the Holy Spirit, together being the Trinity

persona /pər sṓnə/ (*plural* **-nae** /-nee/ *or* **-nas**) *n* **1 CHARACTER IN LITERATURE** a character in a literary work, especially a play (*often plural*) **2 ASSUMED IDENTITY OR ROLE** an identity or role that somebody assumes **3 PERSONAL FAÇADE** the image of character and personality that somebody wants to show the outside world [Early 20C. < Latin (see PERSON).]

personable /púrss'nəb'l/ *adj* having a pleasant personality and appearance —**personableness** *n* —**personably** *adv*

personage /púrss'nij/ (*plural* **-ages**) *n* (*formal*) **1** a distinguished, important, or famous person **2** a historical figure, or a character in a work of literature [15C. < Old French < *persone* (see PERSON).]

persona grata /pər sṓnə graátə/ (*plural* **personae gratae** /-nee graá tee/) *n* a person who is acceptable to others, especially as a diplomat. ◊ **persona non grata** [< late Latin, 'acceptable person'] —**persona grata** *adj*

personal /púrss'nəl/ *adj* **1 RELATING TO SOMEBODY'S PRIVATE LIFE** relating to the parts of somebody's life that are private **2 RELATING TO ONE PERSON** relating to a particular person **3 BELIEVED BY INDIVIDUAL PERSON** believed by or originating from an individual person ○ *personal opinion* **4 DONE BY ONE PERSON ONLY** done by a particular person rather than by that person's delegate ○ *that personal touch* **5 INTENDED FOR PARTICULAR PERSON** intended for or owned by a particular person rather than anyone else **6 REFERRING OFFENSIVELY TO PARTICULAR PERSON** referring, especially in an offensive way, to somebody's beliefs, actions, or physical characteristics ○ *That personal remark was definitely uncalled for.* **7 UNFAIRLY REMARKING OR QUESTIONING ABOUT OTHERS** making unacceptable remarks or being too probing about other people ○ *There's no need to get personal.* **8 OF THE BODY** relating to somebody's body **9 CONSCIOUS AND INDIVIDUAL** having the character or nature of a conscious and individual entity **10 OF MOVABLE PROPERTY** relating to or constituting an person's movable property ■ *n US* MEDIA = **personal ad** (*often plural*)

personal ad *n* a usually classified newspaper or magazine advertisement in which somebody expresses interest in meeting others or sends a message of a personal nature to somebody else. US term **personal**

personal allowance *n* an amount of money a person is entitled to earn before paying tax

personal appearance *n* **1** the visual aspect of somebody, especially with regard to personal cleanliness and tidiness of clothing **2** the participation in, or performance at, a public event of an important or famous person

personal assistant *n* somebody employed to perform secretarial and administrative tasks for somebody such as an executive who has many responsibilities

personal column *n* a section of a newspaper or magazine in which personal ads are printed

⚡**personal computer** *n* a computer with its own operating system and a wide selection of software, intended to be used by one person

QUICK FACTS ON... **PERSONAL COMPUTERS**

Key elements: increasing speed, memory, storage capability, and ease of use; decreasing size and weight with the goal of creating a mobile computing environment

Key dates: 1975 Altair, first personal computer marketed, aimed primarily at hobbyists; 1977 Apple II, first commercially successful assembled personal computer; 1981 IBM PC launched, creating a market for its clones, using Microsoft operating system; 1984 Macintosh introduced, with a pioneering graphical user interface; 1985 the first successful laptop computer; 1993 the first personal digital assistant (PDA)

Key publications: *Fire in the Valley: The Making of the Personal Computer* (Paul Feinberg and Michael Swain, 2nd ed.) 1999, *Remembering the Future: Interviews from Personal Computer World* (Wendy M. Grossman) 1997

⚡**personal digital assistant** *n* a small hand-held computer with a built-in notebook, diary, and fax capability, usually operated using a stylus rather than a keyboard

personal effects *npl* possessions that somebody carries or wears either regularly or at a particular time

Personal Equity Plan *n* full form of **PEP**

personal foul *n* a foul, especially one committed in football or basketball, involving illegal physical contact with an opponent during a game and also sometimes involving unnecessary roughness

⚡**personal identification device** *n* a device, such as a magnetic card, containing machine-readable information that allows access to a computer system

⚡**personal identification number** full form of **PIN**

⚡**personal information manager** *n* a piece of software that organizes random notes, contacts, and appointments for fast access

personal injury *n US* an actionable injury to an individual person, whether involving physical contact or not and whether fatal or not, but causing pain, discomfort, or injury

personalise *vt* = **personalize**

personalism /púrss'nəlizəm/ *n* a quirky or highly individualistic mode of expression or behaviour —**personalist** *n, adj* —**personalistic** /púrss'nə lístik/ *adj*

personality /púrssə nálləti/ (*plural* **-ties**) *n* **1 SOMEBODY'S SET OF CHARACTERISTICS** the totality of somebody's attitudes, interests, behavioural patterns, emotional responses, social roles, and other individual traits that endure over long periods of time **2 CHARACTERISTICS MAKING SOMEBODY APPEALING** the distinctive or very noticeable characteristics that make somebody socially appealing ○ *a partner with real personality* **3 SOMEBODY REGARDED AS EPITOMIZING TRAITS** an individual regarded as epitomizing particular character traits **4 FAMOUS PERSON** a famous person, especially an entertainer or athlete **5 UNUSUAL PERSON** a distinctive and unusual person **6 QUALITY OF BEING A PERSON** the quality of existing as a person ○ *Do you think that computers will ever achieve personality?* **7 DISTINGUISHING CHARACTERISTICS** the distinguishing characteristics of a place or situation

personality disorder *n* a psychiatric disorder in attitude or behaviour that makes it difficult for somebody to get along with other people or to succeed at work or in social situations but that does not involve loss of touch with reality

personality test *n* a standardized psychological test in which the subject is given questions about various aspects of personality, the answers supplying a character-trait profile unique to that individual

personality type *n* a set of categories based on attitudes or behavioural tendencies into which people are grouped, e.g. introvert and extrovert

personalize /púrss'nə līz/ (**-izes, -izing, -ized**), **personalise** (**-ises, -ising, -ised**) *vt* **1 PUT INITIALS OR NAME ON** to mark something such as a wallet, pen, or item of clothing with somebody's initials or name **2 CHANGE SOMETHING TO REFLECT OWNER'S PERSONALITY** to change or modify something showing that it obviously originated from or belonged to a particular person **3 TAKE REMARK PERSONALLY** to take a remark in a personal way **4** = **personify** *v.* 3 —**personalization** /púrss'nə lī záysh'n/ *n*

personally /púrss'nəli/ *adv* **1 AS OWN OPINION** in one's own experience or showing one's own opinion ○ *Personally, I would have given it back.* **2 AS AN INDIVIDUAL** as a particular individual **3 WITHOUT OTHERS** without intervention or assistance from others ○ *I'll handle it personally.* **4 AS PERSON IN SOCIAL CONTEXT** as a person, considered in a social context ○ *personally likable but professionally inept* **5 AS SOMEBODY ONE HAS MET** by personal contact rather than by reputation ○ *I never knew your brother personally.*

⚡**personal organizer** *n* **1** a diary that also contains personal information and has replaceable pages so that it can be kept up to date **2** a hand-held computer with a small keyboard and display that can function as a diary, an address book, a scheduler, and a calculator

personal pronoun *n* a pronoun such as 'I', 'you', or 'she' that refers to a speaker, somebody being addressed, or another person

personal property *n* in law, the tangible movable property of an individual, exclusive of land and including items such as automotive vehicles, boats, and money

personal stereo *n* a small audio cassette or CD player used with earphones, designed to be carried in a pocket or worn attached to a belt

personalty /púrss'nəlti/ (*plural* **-ties**) *n* LAW = **personal property** [Mid-16C. Via Anglo-Norman < late Latin *personalitas* (see PERSONALITY).]

personal unconscious *n* in Jungian and related forms of psychotherapy, a section of an individual's unconscious mind that contains impulses, fears, and memories that have been repressed

ϟ**personal video recorder** *n* a video recorder with a digital hard drive that can record TV programmes independently and offers facilities such as instant replay during live programmes

personal watercraft *n US* a jet-propelled vehicle for one or two people, used for travelling on water

persona non grata /pər sṓnə non graátə/ (*plural* **personae non gratae** /-nee non graá tee/) *n* **1** an unwelcome or unacceptable person. ◊ **persona grata 2** a diplomat who is unacceptable to the country to which he or she is sent [< late Latin, 'unacceptable person'] —**persona non grata** *adj*

personate[1] /púrssə nayt/ (**-ates, -ating, -ated**) *vt* **1** to play a dramatic role, especially in a play **2** to impersonate somebody in order to deceive or defraud [Late 16C. < late Latin *personare* < Latin *persona* (see PERSON).] —**personation** /púrssə náysh'n/ *n* —**personative** /púrss'nətiv/ *adj* —**personator** /púrssə naytər/ *n*

personate[2] /púrssə nayt/ *adj* describes a flower such as a snapdragon that has two lips, with one lip curling over the other to close the opening between them [Late 16C. < Latin *personatus* 'masked' < *persona* (see PERSON).]

~~**personel**~~ incorrect spelling of **personnel**

~~**personell**~~ incorrect spelling of **personnel**

person-hour *n* a unit that measures the amount of work that can be done by one person in one hour and the cost of that hour's work

personification /pər sónnifi káysh'n/ *n* **1 SOMEBODY WHO EMBODIES SOMETHING** an embodiment or perfect example of something **2 REPRESENTATION IN HUMAN FORM** a representation of an abstract quality or notion as a human being, especially in art or literature **3 ATTRIBUTION OF HUMAN QUALITIES TO ABSTRACTS** the attribution of human qualities to objects or abstract notions

personify /pər sónni fī/ (**-fies, -fying, -fied**) *vt* **1 BE PERFECT EXAMPLE OF** to be an embodiment or perfect example of something **2 REPRESENT SOMETHING ABSTRACT AS HUMAN** to represent an abstract quality as a human being, especially in art or literature **3 ASCRIBE HUMAN QUALITIES TO NONHUMAN** to ascribe human qualities to an object or abstract notion —**personifiable** *adj* —**personifier** *n*

personnel /púrssə nél/ *n* the department of an organization or business that deals with employing staff and staffing issues generally ■ *npl* the people employed in an organization, business, or armed force [Early 19C. < French, < *personne* 'person'.]

person-to-person *adj* **1** *US* describes a telephone call chargeable only when a particular person is reached **2** ONLINE, COMPUT full form of **P2P**

perspective /pər spéktiv/ *n* **1 PARTICULAR EVALUATION OF** a particular evaluation of a situation or facts, especially from one person's point of view **2 MEASURED ASSESSMENT OF SITUATION** a measured or objective assessment of a situation, giving all elements their comparative importance ○ *He's having trouble keeping things in perspective right now.* **3 APPEARANCE OF DISTANT OBJECTS TO OBSERVER** the appearance of objects to an observer allowing for the effect of their distance from the observer **4 ALLOWANCE FOR ARTISTIC PERSPECTIVE WHEN DRAWING** the theory or practice of allowing for artistic perspective when drawing or painting **5 VISTA** a vista or view [14C. Via Old French < late Latin *perspectivus* 'optical' < Latin *perspicere* 'look closely' < *specere* (see SPECTACLE).] —**perspectively** *adv*

Perspex /púr speks/ *tdmk* a trademark for a tough transparent acrylic plastic that can be used in place of glass

perspicacious /púrspi káyshəss/ *adj* penetratingly discerning, perceptive, or astute [Early 17C. < Latin *perspicac-*, stem of *perspicax* < *perspicere* (see PERSPECTIVE).] —**perspicaciously** *adv* —**perspicaciousness** *n*

perspicacity /púrspi kássəti/ *n* acuteness of discernment or perception

perspicuity /púrspi kyoó əti/ *n* **1** = **perspicacity 2** the quality of being perspicuous

perspicuous /pər spíkyoo əss/ *adj* clearly expressed and therefore easily understood [Late 16C. < Latin *perspicuus* < *perspicere* (see PERSPECTIVE).] —**perspicuously** *adv* —**perspicuousness** *n*

perspiration /púrspə ráysh'n/ *n* **1** fluid lost from the body both in the form of sweat secreted by the sweat glands and as water that diffuses through the skin **2** the process or act of excreting sweat secreted by the sweat glands or fluid that diffuses through the skin —**perspiratory** /pər spīrətəri/ *adj*

perspire /pər spīr/ (**-spires, -spiring, -spired**) *vti* to secrete fluid from the sweat glands through the pores of the skin [Mid-17C. Via obsolete French *perspirer* < Latin *perspirare* 'breathe through' < *spirare* 'breathe' (see SPIRIT).] —**perspiringly** *adv*

persuade /pə swáyd/ (**-suades, -suading, -suaded**) *vt* **1** to successfully urge somebody to perform a particular action, especially by reasoning, pleading, or coaxing **2** to make somebody believe something, especially by giving good reasons for doing so [Early 16C. < Latin *persuadere* 'urge strongly' < *suadere* 'to urge'.] —**persuadability** /pər swáydə bílləti/ *n* —**persuadable** *adj* —**persuader** /pər swáydər/ *n*

USAGE See ***convince***.

persuasion /pər swáyzh'n/ *n* **1 ACT OF PERSUADING** the act of persuading somebody to do something **2 ABILITY TO PERSUADE** the ability to persuade somebody **3 SET OF BELIEFS** a set of beliefs, e.g. a set of religious or political beliefs **4 GROUP WITH PARTICULAR BELIEFS** a group whose members share a particular set of beliefs or views or a particular lifestyle [14C. Via Old French < Latin *persuas-*, past participle of *persuadere* (see PERSUADE).]

USAGE See ***conviction***.

persuasive /pər swáyssiv/ *adj* having the ability to persuade people or the effect of persuading them [Late 16C. Via French or medieval Latin < Latin *persuas-*, past participle of *persuadere* (see PERSUADE).] —**persuasively** *adv* —**persuasiveness** *n*

~~**persue**~~ incorrect spelling of **pursue**

~~**persuit**~~ incorrect spelling of **pursuit**

pert /purt/ *adj* **1 AMUSINGLY CHEEKY** cheeky and lively in a pleasant or amusing way **2 JAUNTY** jaunty and stylish in design ○ *a pert hat* **3 SMALL AND WELL-SHAPED** small, well-shaped, and pretty ○ *a pert nose* [13C. Via Old French *apert* 'open, frank' < Latin *apertus* 'open' (see APERTURE).] —**pertly** *adv* —**pertness** *n*

PERT /purt/ *n* a method of charting and scheduling a complex set of interrelated activities that identifies the most time-critical events in the process. Full form **programme evaluation and review technique**

pertain /pər táyn/ *vi* **1 RELATE OR HAVE RELEVANCE** to relate to something or have relevance, reference, or a connection to it **2 BE APPROPRIATE** to be appropriate, fitting, or suitable **3 BE PART OR BELONG** to be part of something or belong to something, especially as an attribute or accessory [14C. Via Old French *partenir* < Latin *pertinere* 'hold to' < *tenere* (see TENANT).]

Perth /purth/ **1** city in central Scotland. Population: 41,453 (1991). **2** capital of Western Australia, on the southwestern coast of the state. Population: 1,096,829 (1996).

Perth and Kinross council area in north-central Scotland. Area: 5,321 sq. km/2,019 sq. mi.

pertinacious /púrti náyshəss/ *adj* **1** determinedly resolute in purpose, belief, or action **2** highly persistent [Early 17C. < Latin *pertinac-*, stem of *pertinax* 'very tenacious' < *tenax* (see TENACIOUS).] —**pertinaciously** *adv* —**pertinaciousness** *n* —**pertinacity** /-nássəti/ *n*

pertinent /púrtinənt/ *adj* relevant to the matter being considered [14C. Via Old French < Latin *pertinere* (see PERTAIN).] —**pertinence** *n* —**pertinently** *adv*

perturb /pər túrb/ *vt* **1** to disturb and trouble or worry somebody **2** to cause a small deviation in the behaviour of a physical system, e.g. in the orbit of an electron or a planet [14C. Via Old French < Latin *perturbare* 'disturb thoroughly' < *turbare* 'disturb' < *turba* 'turmoil' (see TURBID).] —**perturbable** *adj* —**perturbably** *adv* —**perturbing** *adj* —**perturbingly** *adv*

perturbation /púrtə báysh'n/ *n* **1 BEING PERTURBED** the act of being disturbed and troubled, or a disturbed and troubled state **2 CAUSE OF TROUBLE** something causing disruption, trouble, or disorder **3 SECONDARY INFLUENCE ON A SYSTEM** a slight disturbance of a system by a secondary influence within it **4 DEVIATION IN ORBIT CAUSED BY GRAVITY** a deviation in an astronomical object's orbit or path caused by the gravitational attraction of another astronomical object —**perturbational** *adj*

pertussis /pər tússiss/ *n* whooping cough (*technical*) [Late 18C. < modern Latin < *per-* 'extreme' + *tussis* 'cough' (see TUSSIS).] —**pertussal** *adj*

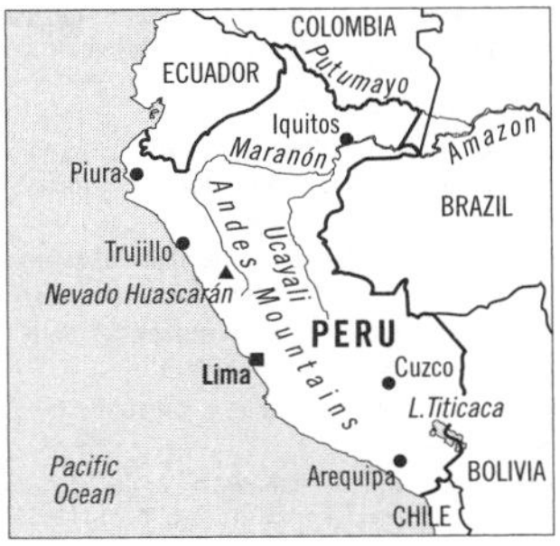

Peru

Peru /pə roó/ republic in W South America. Capital: Lima. Population: 24,523,408 (1996). Area: 1,285,216 sq. km/496,225 sq. mi. —**Peruvian** /pə roóvi ən/ *adj, n*

Perugia /pə roójə/ capital of Umbria Region, central Italy. Population: 146,160 (1992).

peruke /pə roók/ *n* a periwig (*archaic*) [Mid-16C. Via French *perruque* < Italian *perrucca* 'head of hair'.]

peruse /pə roóz/ (**-ruses, -rusing, -rused**) *vt* to read or examine something in a leisurely or careful way [Mid-16C. Originally 'use thoroughly' < USE[1].] —**perusable** *adj* —**perusal** *n* —**peruser** *n*

Perutz /pə roóts/, **Max Ferdinand** (*b.* 1914) Austrian-born British biochemist

Peruvian balsam *n* PHARM = **balsam of Peru**

Peruvian bark *n* the bark of a cinchona tree. Use: formerly, to make quinine. [Because the trees grew in Peru]

perv /purv/, **perve** *n* **1 PERVERT** a pervert (*slang insult*) **2** *ANZ* **LUSTFUL LOOK** a voyeuristic glance or look (*slang*) ■ *vi* (**pervs, perving, perved; perves, perving, perved**) *ANZ* **LEER** to give somebody a lustful look (*slang*) [Mid-20C. Shortening of PERVERT.] —**pervy** *adj*

pervade /pər váyd/ (**-vades, -vading, -vaded**) *vt* to spread through or be present throughout something [Mid-17C. < Latin *pervadere* 'go throughout' < *vadere* 'to go'.] —**pervader** *n* —**pervasion** /-váyzh'n/ *n*

pervasive /pə váyssiv/ *adj* spreading widely [Mid-18C. < Latin *pervas-*, past participle of *pervadere* (see PERVADE).] —**pervasively** *adv* —**pervasiveness** *n*

perve *n, vi ANZ* = **perv** (*informal*)

perverse /pər vúrss/ *adj* **1 PURPOSELY BEING UNREASONABLE** purposely deviating from what is accepted as good, proper, or reasonable **2 UNREASONABLY STUBBORN** unreasonably stubborn, contrary, or awkward **3 WILFULLY DOING WRONG** wilfully persisting in what is wrong **4 PERVERTED** perverted (*archaic*) [14C. Via Old French < Latin *perversus*, past participle of *pervertere* (see PERVERT).] —**perversely** *adv* —**perverseness** *n*

perversion /pər vúrsh'n/ *n* **1** a sexual practice regarded as abnormal **2** the changing of something good, true, or correct into something bad or wrong, or a situation in which the change has occurred (*disapproving*) ○ *perversion of justice*

perversity /pər vúrssəti/ (*plural* **-ties**) *n* **1** being unreasonable or wilfully persisting in doing wrong **2** something such as an action or activity that is perverse

pervert *vt* /pər vúrt/ **1 LEAD AWAY FROM GOOD** to lead somebody or something away from what is considered good, normal, moral, or proper **2 MISINTERPRET OR DISTORT** to misinterpret or distort something such as a piece of text **3 USE IMPROPERLY** to use something incorrectly or improperly **4 DEBASE** to bring something into a state regarded as morally inferior or reprehensible ■ *n* /púr vurt/ **OFFENSIVE TERM** an offensive term for somebody whose sexual behaviour is considered unusual (*insult*) [14C. Via Old French *pervertir* < Latin *pervertere* 'turn wrong' < *vertere* (see VERSE).] —**perverter** /pər vúrtə/ *n* —**pervertible** *adj*

perverted /pər vúrtid/ *adj* **1 DEVIATING FROM WHAT IS PROPER** deviating greatly from what is accepted as right, normal, or proper **2 RELATING TO UNUSUAL SEXUAL ACTIVITIES** relating to or practising sexual activities considered abnormal (*disapproving*) **3 DISTORTED** misinterpreted or distorted —**pervertedly** *adv* —**pervertedness** *n*

pervious /púrvi əss/ *adj* **1** able to be penetrated or permeated **2** open to ideas, suggestions, and change [Early 17C. < Latin *pervius* < *per-* 'through' + *via* 'way'.] —**perviously** *adv* —**perviousness** *n*

pes /pays, peez/ (*plural* **pedes** /peé deez/) *n* **1** the foot or a part resembling a foot **2** a hind foot of a four-footed vertebrate [Mid-19C. < Latin, 'foot'.]

Pesach /páy saakh/ *n* the Passover festival [Early 17C. < Hebrew *pesaḥ* < *pāsaḥ* 'pass over'.]

peseta /pə sáytə/ *n* see table at **currency** [Early 19C. < Spanish, 'small peso' < *peso* (see PESO).]

pesewa /pay sáy waa/ *n* see table at **currency** [Mid-20C. < Fanti and Twi, 'penny'.]

Peshawar /pə shaáwər/, **Peshāwar** city in N Pakistan, near the Khyber Pass. Population: 1,676,000 (1995).

Peshitta /pə sheétə/, **Peshitto** /pə sheétō/ *n* the Syriac version of the Bible, written around the 4th century [Late 18C. < Syriac *pšīṭtā* 'the simple one'.]

pesky /péski/ (**-kier, -kiest**) *adj US, Can* troublesome or irritating (*informal*) [Late 18C. Probably < alteration of PEST.] —**peskily** *adv* —**peskiness** *n*

peso /páyssō/ (*plural* **-sos**) *n* see table at **currency** [Mid-16C. Via Spanish < Latin *pensum* 'weight' < past participle of *pendere* 'weigh' (see PENSIVE).]

pessary /péssəri/ (*plural* **-ries**) *n* **1** a plastic device such as a ring placed in the vagina to keep the womb in position following a prolapse due to weakened ligaments **2** a suppository containing medication for insertion into the vagina [14C. Via late Latin *pessarium* < Greek *pessos*, originally an oval stone used in board games.]

pessimism /péssəmizəm/ *n* **1** a tendency to see only the negative or worst aspects of all things and to expect only bad or unpleasant things to happen **2** a doctrine that all things become evil or that evil outweighs good in life [Late 18C. < French *pessimisme* < Latin *pessimus* 'worst'.]

pessimist /péssə mist/ *n* a person who always expects the worst to happen —**pessimistic** /pessə místik/ *adj* —**pessimistically** /-místikli/ *adv*

pest /pest/ *n* **1** an organism that is damaging to livestock, crops, humans, or land fertility **2** somebody or something that is a nuisance (*informal*) [Mid-16C. Via French, 'pestilence' < Latin *pestis*.]

Pestalozzi /péstə lótsi/, **Johann Heinrich** (1746–1827) Swiss educator

pester /péstər/ *vt* to be a constant source of annoyance to somebody, e.g. by harassing him or her with demands [Mid-16C. < French *empestrer* 'embarrass' (influenced by PEST).] —**pesterer** *n* —**pesteringly** *adv*

pesthouse /pést howss/ (*plural* **-houses** /-howziz/) *n* a hospital where patients suffering from infectious disease were once treated [Early 17C. < PEST 'contagious disease'.]

pesticide /pésti sīd/ *n* a chemical substance used to kill pests, especially insects [Mid-20C. < PEST + -CIDE.] —**pesticidal** /pésti sīd'l/ *adj*

pestiferous /pə stíffərəss/ *adj* **1 ANNOYING** troublesome or annoying **2 CAUSING INFECTIOUS DISEASE** breeding or spreading a virulently infectious disease **3 CORRUPTING** wicked and corrupting (*formal*) [15C. < Latin *pestifer* 'plague-carrying' < *pestis* 'plague'.] —**pestiferously** *adv* —**pestiferousness** *n*

pestilence /péstilənss/ *n* an epidemic of a highly contagious or infectious disease such as bubonic plague (*archaic*)

pestilent /péstilənt/ *adj* **1 DEADLY** causing or tending to cause death **2 DAMAGING** very harmful morally or socially (*archaic*) **3 ANNOYING** annoying or infuriating (*literary or humorous*) [14C. Via Old French < Latin *pestilent-* < *pestis* 'plague'.] —**pestilential** /pésti lénsh'l/ *adj* —**pestilentially** *adv* —**pestilently** *adv*

pestle /péss'l/ *n* a rod-shaped object made from hard material with a rounded end that is used for crushing or grinding substances in a mortar ■ *vti* (**-tles, -tling, -tled**) to crush, grind, or pound a substance or object using a pestle [14C. Via Old French < Latin *pistillum*.]

pesto /péstō/ *n* **1** a sauce or paste made by crushing together basil leaves, pine nuts, oil, Parmesan cheese, and garlic **2** a pureed or finely minced paste of herbs and vegetables, tomatoes, or olives [Mid-20C. < Italian < the past participle of *pestare* 'pound, crush', via late Latin *pistare* < Latin *pinsere* 'to beat'.]

pet[1] /pet/ *n* **1 ANIMAL KEPT AT HOME** an animal kept for companionship, interest, or amusement **2 FAVOURITE PERSON** an indulged or pampered person **3 LOVED PERSON** a person whom others find lovable, often used as a term of endearment in direct address ■ *adj* **1 KEPT AS PET** kept as a pet **2 SPECIAL OR FAVOURITE** cherished by, special, or favourite to somebody ○ *a pet topic* ■ *v* (**pets, petting, petted**) **1** *vt* **STROKE ANIMAL** to pat or stroke an animal, or touch a child similarly **2** *vt* **TREAT INDULGENTLY** to treat a person or animal indulgently **3** *vi* **TOUCH FOR SEXUAL PLEASURE** to touch each other in a way that causes sexual pleasure [Early 16C. < ?] —**petter** *n*

pet[2] /pet/ *n* a fit of sulkiness or peevishness ■ *vi* (**pets, petting, petted**) to be peevish or sulky [Mid-16C. < ?]

PET /pet/ *abbr* **1** polyethylene terephthalate **2** positron emission tomography

Pet. *abbr* Peter

peta- *prefix* (*symbol* **P**) one thousand million million (10^{15}) [< PENTA-, after 'tera-' (as if < 'tetra-'); so called because it represents 1,000 to the fifth power]

ϟ **petabyte** /péttə bīt/ *n* one thousand million million bytes

petal /pétt'l/ *n* one of the showy coloured parts that form the outer part of a flower, that together are the corolla [Early 18C. Via modern Latin *petalum* < Greek *petalon* 'leaf'.] —**petaline** /péttə līn/ *adj* —**petalled** /pétt'ld/ *adj* —**petaloid** *adj*

-petal *suffix* moving toward ○ *centripetal* [< modern Latin *-petus* < Latin *petere* 'seek' (see PETITION)]

pétanque /pay tóngk/ *n* GAMES = **boules** [Mid-20C. < French.]

petard /pe taárd/ *n* **1** a small explosive charge or grenade used to blow a hole in a door, wall, or fortification **2** a powerful firecracker [Mid-16C. Via French < Latin *pedere* 'break wind'.] ◇ **be hoist with your own petard** to be the victim of your own attempt to harm somebody else

Petavius /pə táyvi əss/ lunar crater visible in the SE quadrant of the Moon, 177 km/110 mi. in diameter

petcock /pét kok/ *n* a small manually operated valve or tap used to drain off waste material or excess fluid from the cylinder of an internal combustion engine [Mid-19C. < *pet* < ? + COCK 'spout'.]

petechia /pi teéki ə/ (*plural* **-ae** /-teéki ee/) *n* a tiny purplish-red spot on the skin caused by the release into the skin of a very small quantity of blood from a capillary [Late 18C. Via modern Latin < Italian *petecchie* 'spots on the skin' < Latin *impetigo* (see IMPETIGO).] —**petechial** *adj*

peter[1] /peétər/ *vi* to become less [Early 19C. < ?] **peter out** *vi* to dwindle and finally stop or disappear

peter[2] /peétər/ *n* (*slang*) **1 CASH BOX** a safe or cash box **2 WITNESS BOX IN COURT** the witness box in a court **3** *US* **PENIS** a penis (*considered offensive by some people*)

peter[3] /peétər/ *vi* in bridge and whist, to play a high card first, followed by a low card [Late 19C. Shortening of an obsolete sense of BLUE PETER, a higher card than necessary, played as a signal to one's partner.]

Peter /peétər/ *n* two books in the Bible, in the form of epistles traditionally attributed to St Peter

Peter /peétər/, **St** (*d.* AD 64?). one of the 12 disciples of Jesus Christ. Born **Simon**

Peter (the Great) (1672–1725) tsar of Russia (1682–1725)

Peterborough /peétərbərə/ **1** city in east-central England. Population: 160,000 (1996). **2** city in SE Ontario, Canada. Population: 69,535 (1996).

Peterhead /peétər héd/ port in east-central Scotland. Population: 18,674 (1991).

Peterlee /peétər leé/ town in NE England. Population: 31,139 (1991).

peterman /peétərmən/ (*plural* **-men** /-mən/) *n* a burglar who specializes in breaking safes (*slang*) [Early 19C. < PETER[1].]

Peter Pan *n* a man who looks very young or behaves in a boyish way (*informal*) [Early 20C. After the hero of J. M. Barrie's play *Peter Pan, or The Boy Who Wouldn't Grow Up* (1904).]

Peter Pan collar *n* a flat collar attached to a round neck with rounded ends visible at the front

Peter Principle *n* the theory that all members of an organization will eventually be promoted to a level at which they are no longer competent to do their job [Mid-20C. After Laurence Johnston *Peter* 1919–90, US author.]

Peters /peétərz/, **Winston Raymond** (*b.* 1945) New Zealand politician

petersham /peétərshəm/ *n* a strong ribbed ribbon used to reinforce parts of garments such as waistbands [Early 19C. After Viscount *Petersham* (1790–1851), British army officer.]

Peterson /peétərss'n/, **Oscar** (*b.* 1925) Canadian jazz pianist

Peter's pence *n* **1** a voluntary financial contribution made by some Roman Catholic dioceses to the Papal See **2** a tax of one penny per household paid to the Papal See in medieval times until it was abolished by Henry VIII [< the tradition that the papacy was founded by Saint PETER]

Peters' projection *n* a form of map projection that represents the relative size of land masses more accurately than Mercator's projection [Late 20C. After Arno *Peters* (1916–), German historian.]

pethidine /péthi deen/ *n* $C_{15}H_{21}NO_2$ a white crystalline compound. Use: painkiller, sedative. US term **meperidine** [Mid-20C. Blend of P(IPER)IDINE + ETH(YL).]

pétillant /pétti oN, péttilənt/ *adj* describes wine that is slightly sparkling [Late 19C. < French, 'effervescent', literally 'passing gas'.]

petiolar /pétti ōlər/ *adj* relating to the growth of petioles

petiole /pétti ōl/ *n* a leafstalk (*technical*) [Mid-18C. < modern Latin *petiolus*, a variant of Latin *peciolus* 'little foot' (see PEDICEL).] —**petiolate** /pétti ə layt/ *adj*

petit bourgeois /pétti boórzhwaa/ (*plural* **petits bourgeois** /pétti boórzhwaa/) *n* a member of the lower middle class [< French, 'little citizen']

petite /pə teét/ *adj* **1** having a small and delicate build ○ *a petite woman* **2** designed to fit smaller women or girls [Mid-16C. < French, feminine of *petit* 'little'.]

petite bourgeoisie /pə teét boor zhwaa zeé/ (*plural* **petites bourgeoisies**) *n* people in the lower middle class, a group traditionally including small business operators and tradespeople

petit four /pétti fáwr/ (*plural* **petits fours** /pétti fáwr, -fáwrz/) *n* any one of a mixture of bite-size sweet biscuits or cakes served at the end of a meal with coffee [< French, 'little oven']

petition /pə tísh'n/ *n* **1 DEMAND FOR ACTION WITH SIGNATURES** a written request signed by many people demanding a particular action from an authority or government **2 APPEAL OR REQUEST TO HIGHER AUTHORITY** an appeal or request to a higher authority or being **3 SOMETHING REQUESTED** something requested or appealed for **4 ACT OF PETITIONING** the act of making a petition **5 DOCUMENT INITIATING LEGAL ACTION** a written application for a legal action to be taken, particularly at the start of divorce proceedings ■ *v* **1** *vti* **GIVE PETITION TO** to give or address a petition to somebody, especially somebody in authority or a representative of an organization **2** *vi* **MAKE DEMAND USING PETITION** to urge for or against a course of action by presenting a petition **3** *vi* **MAKE FORMAL REQUEST** to request formally, using a petition [14C. Via Old French < Latin *petere* 'seek, go toward'.] —**petitionary** *adj* —**petitioner** *n*

petitio principii /pə tíshi ō prin kíppi ī, -síppi ī/ *n* logically fallacious reasoning in which what has to be proved is already assumed [< Latin, 'assuming the first thing']

petit larceny /pétti-/, **petty larceny** *n* the theft of something whose value lies below a particular standard in a particular jurisdiction

petit mal /pétti mál/ *n* a form of epilepsy marked by episodes of brief loss of consciousness without convulsions or falling. ◊ **grand mal** [< French, 'small illness']

petit point /pétti póynt/ (*plural* **petits points**) *n* **1** a small stitch used in needlepoint when creating details **2** work embroidered using small stitches [< French, 'small stitch']

petits pois /pétti pwaá/ *npl* small sweet green peas [< French, 'small peas']

pet name *n* a name showing endearment used for a family member or special friend

petnapping /pét naping/ *n* the stealing or kidnapping of a pet animal [Late 20C. After 'kidnapping'.] —**petnapper** *n*

Petra /péttrə/ ancient ruined city of Edom in present-day SW Jordan

Petrarch /pét raark/ (1304–74) Italian poet and scholar. Born **Francesco Petrarca** —**Petrarchan** *adj*

Petrarchan sonnet /pə traákən-/ *n* a form of poetry that has an eight line stanza with the rhyme scheme abbaabba followed by six lines with various rhyme schemes, usually cdcdcd or cdecde [Early 19C. After Francesco PETRARCH.]

petrel /péttrəl/ *n* a seabird such as the storm petrel, the diving petrel, or the fulmar. Families: Hydrobatidae and Pelecanoididae and Procellariidae. [Early 17C. < ?]

petri- *prefix* = **petro-**

Petri dish /péttri-, peétri-/ *n* a shallow flat-bottomed dish with a loose cover, used especially to grow bacterial cultures in the laboratory [After Julius *Petri* (1852–92), German bacteriologist]

Petrie /peétri/, **Sir Flinders** (1853–1942) British archaeologist

petrifaction /péttri fáksh'n/, **petrification** /péttrifi káysh'n/ *n* **1** the process in which the porous structure of organic material such as bones, shell, and wood is infiltrated by salt-bearing ground water, which preserves the structure when it solidifies **2** the condition of being turned into stone

Petrified Forest National Park national park in E Arizona. Area: 379 sq. km/146 sq. mi.

petrify /péttri fī/ (**-fies, -fying, -fied**) *v* **1** *vt* **IMMOBILIZE SOMEBODY WITH FEAR** to cause a person or animal to become immobile with terror **2** *vti* **CAUSE PETRIFICATION** to cause or bring about the process by which something organic is turned into stone **3** *vti* **MAKE OR BECOME DEADENED OR STIFF** to become or cause something to become dull, stiff, or deadened [15C. < French *pétrifier* or medieval Latin *petrificare*, both < Latin *petra* 'stone' < Greek *petra* (see PETRO-).] —**petrifier** *n*

Petrine /peé trīn/ *adj* **1** relating to or associated with St. Peter, the Apostle. **2** in the Roman Catholic Church, describes a dissolved marriage between somebody who has been baptized and somebody who has not [Mid-19C. < ecclesiastical Latin *Petrus* 'Peter'.]

petro- *prefix* **1** rock, stone ○ *petrography* **2** petroleum ○ *petrodollar* [< Greek *petros* 'a stone' and *petra* 'a rock']

petrochemical /péttrō kémmik'l/ *n* a substance derived from petroleum or natural gas, such as petrol or paraffin wax ■ *adj* relating to or derived from petrochemicals —**petrochemically** *adv*

petrochemistry /péttrō kémmistri/ *n* **1** the branch of chemistry that is concerned with petroleum and derivatives of petroleum **2** the chemistry of rocks, especially with reference to their composition

petrodollar /péttrō dolər/ *n* a unit of foreign currency earned by an oil-exporting country

petrogenesis /péttrō jénnəssiss/ *n* the origin, formation, and history of rocks

petroglyph /péttrōglif/ *n* a prehistoric drawing done on rock [Late 19C. < French < Greek *petros* 'stone' + *glyphē* 'carving'.]

Petrograd /péttrə grád/ former name for **St Petersburg**

petrography /pə tróggrəfi/ *n* the systematic description of the texture of rocks and the minerals they contain, often using microscopy of thin slices of the rock to determine the mineral content —**petrographer** *n* —**petrographic** /péttrə gráffik/ *adj* —**petrographically** /-gráffikli/ *adv*

petrol /pétrəl/ *n* a volatile flammable liquid made from petroleum, used as fuel in internal-combustion engines. US term **gasoline** [Mid-16C. Via French *pétrole* < medieval Latin *petroleum* (see PETROLEUM).]

petrol blue *adj* of a greyish-blue colour tinged with green —**petrol blue** *n*

petrol bomb *n* a crude bomb usually made of a bottle filled with a flammable liquid such as petrol with a rag for a wick that is lighted just before it is thrown ■ *vt* to use a petrol bomb on a target —**petrol bomber** *n*

petrol cap *n* a sealing device for the pipe that leads to the petrol tank of a motor vehicle

petroleum /pə trṓli əm/ *n* crude oil that occurs naturally in sedimentary rocks and consists mainly of hydrocarbons. A wide variety of commercially important petrochemicals, such as petrol and paraffin, are derived from it. [Early 16C. < medieval Latin < Latin *petra* 'rock' + *oleum* (see OIL).]

petroleum jelly *n* a greasy gelatinous substance. Source: petroleum. Use: ointment base, lubricant, protective covering.

petrology /pə tróllәji/ *n* the study of sedimentary, igneous, and metamorphic rocks with respect to their occurrence, structure, origin, history, and mineral content —**petrological** /péttrə lójjik'l/ *adj* —**petrologically** /-lójjikli/ *adv* —**petrologist** /pe tróllәjist/ *n*

petrol pump *n* a device usually located at a petrol station for delivering fuel to a vehicle

petrol station *n* a place at which drivers can buy fuel, oil, and other motoring supplies. US term **gas station**

petronel /pétrə nel/ *n* a short firearm with a curved butt whose length was between that of a long pistol and a short carbine, used mostly by cavalry in the 16th and 17th centuries [Late 16C. Via French *petrinal* < Latin *pectus* 'chest'; because the butt-end rested against the chest when the gun was fired.]

petrosal /pə trṓss'l/ *adj* affecting or belonging to the hard (**petrous**) portion of the temporal bone surrounding the inner ear [Mid-18C. < Latin *petrosus* (see PETROUS).]

petrous /péttrəss/ *adj* **1** relating to or resembling rock or stone **2** describes the hard portion of the temporal bone surrounding the inner ear [Mid-16C. < Latin *petrosus* 'rocky' < *petra* 'rock' (see PETRIFY).]

PET scan /pét-/ *n* an image of a bodily cross-section, usually of the brain, that reveals metabolic processes and that is obtained by means of positron emission tomography —**PET scanner** *n* —**PET scanning** *n*

petticoat /pétti kōt/ *n* **1 WOMAN'S UNDERGARMENT** a woman's undergarment that is sometimes decorated and consists of an underskirt with or without a bodice **2 SKIRT UNDER SARI** a long skirt worn under a sari **3 OFFENSIVE TERM** an offensive term for a woman or girl, or women in general (*dated*) [15C. < PETTY 'small' + COAT.]

pettifogger /pétti fogər/ *n* a person who argues or fusses about petty details [Mid-16C. Probably < PETTY + *fogger* < ?] —**pettifog** *vi* —**pettifoggery** *n*

pettifogging /pétti foging/ *adj* **1** petty or trivial ○ *pettifogging details* **2** quibbling or fussing over trivial matters (*insult*)

petting /pétting/ *n* touching between people that causes sexual pleasure but does not include sexual intercourse (*dated informal*)

pettish /péttish/ *adj* peevish, irritable, or sulky [Late 16C. < PET².] —**pettishly** *adv* —**pettishness** *n*

petty /pétti/ (**-tier, -tiest**) *adj* **1 INSIGNIFICANT** of little importance **2 NARROW-MINDED** narrow-minded in nature **3 MEAN** spiteful in character **4 OF LITTLE IMPORTANCE** subordinate in rank or importance [14C. < Old French *peti*, a variant of *petit* 'small' < ?] —**pettily** *adv* —**pettiness** *n*

Petty /pétti/, **Bruce Leslie** (*b.* 1929) Australian cartoonist and filmmaker

petty cash *n* a small amount of money kept, e.g. in an office, and used to cover minor everyday expenses

petty larceny *n* CRIME = **petit larceny**

petty officer *n* a naval officer of a rank in the US Navy or Coast Guard above seaman, in the British Navy above leading seaman, and in the Canadian Navy above master seaman

petty sessions *n* a court of summary jurisdiction in the United Kingdom, no longer used formally

petulant /péttyŏŏlənt/ *adj* ill-tempered or sulky in a peevish manner [Late 16C. Via French < Latin *petulans* 'insolent' < *petere* 'seek, assail' (see PETITION).] —**petulance** *n* —**petulantly** *adv*

petunia /pə tyóoni ə/ *n* a flowering plant with sticky stems. Flowers: brightly coloured, funnel-shaped. Native to: tropical America. Genus: *Petunia*. ■ *adj* of a dark purple or violet colour [Early 19C. Via modern Latin < Portuguese *petum* 'tobacco' < Tupi or Guarani; because it is related to tobacco.]

petuntse /pi túntsi, -tóontsi/, **petunze** *n* a variety of feldspar that can be melted. Use: Chinese porcelain. [Early 18C. < Chinese (Mandarin) *báidūnzi* 'white stone block'.]

Pevsner /pévsnər/, **Antoine** (1886–1962) Russian-born French sculptor

pew /pyoo/ *n* **1** a usually wooden bench with a straight back and often a kneeling bench attached to the one in front of it, used by worshippers in a church or synagogue **2** a seat (*informal humorous*) ○ *take a pew* [14C. Via Old French *puie* 'balcony' < Latin *podium* (see PODIUM).]

pewee /peé wee/, **peewee** *n* a drab medium-sized flycatcher with a plaintive song. Genus: *Contopus*. [Late 18C. An imitation of its call.]

pewit /peé wit/ *n* BIRDS = **lapwing** [Early 16C. An imitation of its call.]

pewter /pyóotər/ *n* **1 TIN AND LEAD ALLOY** a silver-grey alloy of tin and lead sometimes containing antimony and copper **2 PEWTER OBJECTS COLLECTIVELY** articles made from pewter **3 DARK GREYISH COLOUR** a dark dull grey colour tinged with blue or purple [14C. Via Old French *peutre* < assumed Vulgar Latin *peltrum*.] —**pewter** *adj* —**pewterer** *n*

peyote /pay ṓti/ *n* **1** a spineless globe-shaped cactus that has small rounded nodules containing mescaline. Native to: Mexico, SW United States. *Lophophora williamsii*. **2 peyote, peyote button** any one of the button-shaped nodules on the stem of the peyote cactus that contain mescaline [Mid-19C. Via American Spanish < Nahuatl *peyotl*.]

⚡**pf** *abbr* French Polynesia (*in Internet addresses*)

pF *symbol* picofarad

pf. *abbr* **1** perfect **2** pfennig

PFD *abbr* **1** personal flotation device **2** preferred (*of shares*)

pfennig /fénnig/ (*plural* **-nigs** *or* **pfennige**) *n* see table at **currency** [Mid-16C. < German.]

⚡**pg** *abbr* Papua New Guinea (*in Internet addresses*)

PG¹ *adj* describes a film that would be inappropriate for children, unless accompanied by a parent. Full form **parental guidance**

PG² *abbr* postgraduate

P.G. *abbr* paying guest

PGA *abbr* Professional Golfers' Association

⚡**PGCA** *abbr* payment gateway certificate authority (*in e-commerce*)

PGCE *n* in the United Kingdom, a teaching qualification taken by somebody who has already graduated from a university or college with a first degree. Full form **Postgraduate Certificate of Education**

⚡**PGP** *n* a program to encrypt data for security purposes when transmitting over public networks like the Internet (*in e-commerce*) Full form **Pretty Good Privacy**

PGR *adj ANZ* describes a film that would be inappropriate for children, unless accompanied by a parent. Full form **parental guidance recommended**

⚡**ph** *abbr* Philippines (*in Internet addresses*)

pH *n* a measure of acidity or alkalinity in which the pH of pure water is 7 with lower numbers indicating acidity and higher numbers indicating alkalinity. Full form **potential of hydrogen**

Ph *symbol* phenyl group

phacoemulsification /fákō i múlssifi káysh'n/ *n* an ultrasonic technique using microsurgical instruments that allows a cataract-affected lens to be liquefied and removed by suction using a very small incision near the edge of the cornea [Late 20C. < Greek *phakos* 'lentil' (because of the shape of the lens) + *emulsification*.]

phaeton /fáytən/ *n* a small light four-wheeled carriage, usually with two seats and usually drawn by two horses [Late 16C. Via French < Greek *Phaethōn*, the son of Helios, who was killed by Zeus while trying to drive his father's chariot across the sky.]

phage /fayj/ (*plural* **phages**) *n* MICROBIOL = **bacteriophage** [Early 20C. Shortening.]

-phage *suffix* something that eats ○ *xylophage* [< Greek *-phagos* < *phagein* 'eat']

phagedaena /fájjə deénə/, **phagedena** *n* an ulcer that spreads rapidly [Late 16C. Via Latin < Greek *phagedaina*.]

-phagia *suffix* eating ○ *aerophagia* ○ *hyperphagia* [< Greek < *phagein* 'eat' (see PHAGO-)]

phago- *prefix* eating, consuming ○ *phagocyte* [< Greek *phagein* 'eat' < Indo-European, 'share out']

phagocyte /fággə sīt/ *n* a cell in the body's bloodstream and tissues such as a white blood cell that engulfs and ingests foreign particles, cell waste material, and bacteria —**phagocytic** /fággə síttik/ *adj*

phagocytosis /fággə sī tṓsiss/ *n* the engulfing and ingesting of foreign particles or waste matter by phagocytes —**phagocytotic** /-sī tóttik/ *adj*

phagosome /fággə sōm/ *n* a membranous sac formed within some types of cells that contains the microorganisms or other small particles that the cell has engulfed in order to destroy them —**phagosomal** /fággə sṓm'l/ *adj*

-phagous *suffix* eating ○ *polyphagous* [< Latin *-phagus*, via Greek *-phagos* < *phagein* 'eat' (see PHAGO-)]

-phagy *suffix* = **-phagia**

Phalange /fə lánj/ *n* a Lebanese Christian paramilitary group [Mid-20C. Variant of *Falange* < Spanish, 'phalanx'.] —**Phalangist** *n, adj*

phalanger /fə lánjər/ *n* a small tree-dwelling marsupial with dense woolly fur and a long tail. Native to: Australia and nearby islands. Family: Phalangeridae. [Late 18C. Via modern Latin < the Greek stem *phalagg-* 'toe bone', because of the webbed or fused toes on its hind feet.]

phalanx /fállanks/ (*plural* **-lanxes** *or* **-langes** /fə lán jeez/) *n* **1 TIGHT GROUP** a group of people, animals, or objects that are moving or standing closely together **2 BODY OF TROOPS** especially in ancient Greece, a group of soldiers that attacks in close formation, protected by their overlapping shields and projecting spears **3** (*plural* **-langes**) **FINGER AND TOE BONE** a finger or toe bone of a human being or vertebrate animal [Mid-16C. Via Latin (stem *phalang-*) < Greek *phalagx* 'line of battle, finger, or toe bone'.] —**phalangeal** /fe lánji əl/ *adj*

phalarope /fállə rōp/ *n* a small wading bird that is related to the sandpiper but has lobed toes adapted for swimming. Genus: *Phalaropus.* [Late 18C. Via French < modern Latin *Phalaropus* < Greek *phalaris* 'coot' + *pous* 'foot'.]

Phalguna /fúl goonə/ *n* in the Hindu calendar, the 12th month of the year, made up of 29 or 30 days and occurring about the same time as February or March

phalli plural of **phallus**

phallic /fállik/ *adj* **1 OF A PHALLUS** relating to or resembling a phallus **2 RELATING TO THEORETICAL STAGE OF DEVELOPMENT** in psychoanalytic theory, relating to a stage of psychosexual development during which a young child's sexual feelings are concentrated on the genitals **3 OF PHALLICISM** relating to phallicism [Late 18C. < Greek *phallikos* < *phallos* (see PHALLUS).]

phallicism /fállisizəm/ *n* the worshipping of the reproductive forces of life as symbolized by the penis —**phallicist** *n*

phallocentric /fállō séntrik/ *adj* centred on men or showing a preference for traditionally masculine qualities rather than traditionally feminine ones [Early 20C. < PHALLUS + -CENTRIC.]

phallus /fálləss/ (*plural* **-luses** *or* **-li** /-lī/) *n* **1** a picture, sculpture, or other representation of a penis, especially one regarded as a symbol of the reproductive force of life **2** the human penis, especially when erect [Early 17C. Via late Latin < Greek *phallos.*]

-phan *suffix* = **-phane**

-phane *suffix* a substance having the appearance or qualities of ○ *cymophane* [< Greek *-phanēs* < *phainesthai* 'appear' < *phainein* 'bring to light']

Phanerozoic /fánnərə zṓ ik/ *adj* relating to or belonging to the aeon of geological time that consists of the Palaeozoic, Mesozoic, and Cenozoic eras ■ *n* the Phanerozoic aeon of geological time [Late 19C. < Greek *phaneros* 'visible' + *zōē* 'life'.]

phantasm /fán tazəm/ *n* **1** a supposed being such as a ghost or a disembodied spirit that can be seen but does not have physical substance **2** an understanding or perception that is not based on reality [13C. Via Old French *fantasme* < Greek *phantasma* < *phantazesthai* 'appear' (see FANTASTIC).] —**phantasmal** /fan tázm'l/ *adj* —**phantasmally** /-m'li/ *adv* —**phantasmic** /-tázmik/ *adj* —**phantasmically** /-tázmikli/ *adv*

phantasmagoria /fán tazmə gáwri ə/, **phantasmagory** /fan tázmə gawri/ (*plural* **-ries**) *n* **1** a series or group of strange or bizarre images seen as if in a dream **2** a scene or view that encompasses many things and changes constantly [Early 19C. < French *fantasmagorie* 'art of making optical illusions' < *fantasme* (see PHANTASM).] —**phantasmagoric** /-górrik/ *adj* —**phantasmagorical** /-górrik'l/ *adj* —**phantasmagorically** /-górrikli/ *adv*

phantasy /fántəssi/ (*plural* **-sies**) *n* fantasy (*archaic*)

phantom /fántəm/ *n* **1 UNREAL BEING OR SENSATION** something that can be seen or heard or whose presence can be felt, but that is not physically present **2 ILLUSION** somebody or something that does not exist, or whose existence is difficult to prove **3 APPARENT POWER** somebody or something that appears to have power over somebody but has no reality ○ *The phantom of disaster seemed to threaten their success.* ■ *adj* **NOT REAL** appearing to be real but not actually existing ○ *The local branch of the organization turned out to have a lot of phantom members.* [13C. Via Old French *fantosme* < Greek *phantasma* (see PHANTASM).]

phantom limb *n* the powerful sensation that an amputated limb remains attached

phantom limb pain *n* pain that appears to come from an amputated limb

phantom pregnancy *n* a condition in which a woman has the delusional belief that she is pregnant and suffers symptoms and displays signs of pregnancy. US term **false pregnancy**. Technical name **pseudocyesis**

-phany *suffix* a manifestation of something ○ *epiphany* [< Greek *phan-*, stem of *phainesthai* 'appear' < *phainein* 'bring to light']

Pharaoh /fáirō/, **pharaoh** *n* **1** the ancient Egyptian title for a ruler of Egypt **2** somebody in a position of authority, especially somebody who is harsh, gives unreasonable orders, and expects unquestioning obedience [Pre-12C. Via ecclesiastical Latin and Greek *Pharaō* and Hebrew *par'ōh* < Egyptian *pr-'o* 'great house'.] —**Pharaonic** /fair rónnik/ *adj*

Pharaoh ant, **Pharaoh's ant** *n* a small yellowish-red ant that is a household pest in many tropical countries. *Monomorium pharaonis.* [*Pharaoh* because it is common in warm parts of the world such as Egypt]

Pharisaic /fárri sáy ik/, **Pharisaical** /fárri sáy ik'l/ *adj* **1** relating to or characteristic of the Pharisees **2 Pharisaic, pharisaic, Pharisaical, pharisaical** acting with hypocrisy, self-righteousness, or obsessiveness with regard to the strict adherence to rules and formalities (*disapproving*) [Early 17C. Via ecclesiastical Latin *pharisaïcus* < Greek *pharisaios* (see PHARISEE).] —**Pharisaically** *adv* —**Pharisaicalness** *n*

Pharisaism /fárri say izəm/ *n* **1** the beliefs and practices of the Pharisees, especially the great attention they paid to the detailed rules of everyday life **2 Pharisaism, Phariseeism, pharisaism, phariseeism** hypocritical, self-righteous, or obsessive behaviour or attitudes towards the observing of rules and formalities (*disapproving*) [Late 16C. Via French < Greek *pharisaios* (see PHARISEE).]

Pharisee /fárri see/ *n* **1** a member of an ancient Jewish religious group who followed the Oral Law in addition to the Torah and attempted to live in a constant state of purity **2 Pharisee, pharisee** a self-righteous, hypocritical, or sanctimonious person (*disapproving*) [Pre-12C. Via ecclesiastical Latin < Greek *pharisaios* < Aramaic *prīšayyā* 'those who are separate'.] —**Phariseeism** *n*

pharm /faarm/ *vt* to produce human proteins of value in medicine in the milk of genetically modified cows and sheep

Pharm., **pharm.** *abbr* **1** pharmacist **2** pharmacopoeia **3** pharmaceutical **4** pharmacy

pharmac- *prefix* = **pharmaco-** (*before vowels*)

pharmaceutical /faarmə syóotik'l/ *adj* involved in or related to the manufacture, preparation, dispensing, or sale of drugs used in medicine ■ *n* a drug used in medicine (*usually plural*) [Mid-17C. < late Latin *pharmaceuticus* < Greek *pharmakeutēs* 'one who prepares drugs' < *pharmakon* 'drug'.] —**pharmaceutically** *adv*

pharmaceutics /faarmə syóotiks/ *n* the science of the preparation and dispensing of prescribed drugs (+ *singular verb*) ■ *npl* drugs prescribed as medicines

pharmacist /faarməsist/ *n* somebody trained and licensed to dispense medicinal drugs and to advise on their use [Mid-19C. < PHARMACY.]

pharmaco- *prefix* drugs, medicine ○ *pharmacodynamics* [< Greek *pharmakon* 'drug, poison']

pharmacodynamics /faarməkō dī námmiks/ *n* the study of the effects of drugs on living organisms (+ *singular verb*) —**pharmacodynamic** *adj*

pharmacogenomics /faarməkō ji nṓmiks/ *n* the study of the relationship between an individual's genetic makeup and response to drug treatments

pharmacognosy /faarmə kógnəssi/ *n* the branch of pharmacology that deals with active substances found in plants [Mid-19C. < PHARMACO- + Greek *gnōsis* 'knowledge' (see GNOSIS).] —**pharmacognosist** *n* —**pharmacognostic** /faarmə kog nóstik/ *adj*

pharmacokinetics /faarməkō ki néttiks, -kī-/ *npl* the body's reaction to drugs, including their absorption, metabolism, and elimination (+ *plural verb*) ■ *n* the study of the body's reaction to drugs (+ *singular verb*)

pharmacology /faarmə kólləji/ (*plural* **-gies**) *n* **1** the science or study of drugs, including their sources, chemistry, production, use in treating diseases, and side effects **2** the effects that a drug has when taken by somebody, especially as a medical treatment —**pharmacological** /faarməkə lójjik'l/ *adj* —**pharmacologically** /-lójjikli/ *adv* —**pharmacologist** /faarmə kólləjist/ *n*

pharmacopoeia /faarməkə pée ə/, **pharmacopeia** *n* **1** a book or database listing medicinal drugs and their composition, preparation, use, dosages, effects, and side effects, especially one published as an official guide **2** a stock or collection of drugs [Early 17C. Via modern Latin < Greek *pharmakopoiia* 'preparing of drugs' < *pharmakon* 'drug'.] —**pharmacopoeial** *adj* —**pharmacopoeic** *adj* —**pharmacopoeist** *n*

pharmacotherapy /faarməkō thérrəpi/ (*plural* **-pies**) *n* the use of drugs to treat conditions, especially psychiatric disorders

~~**pharmacuetical**~~ incorrect spelling of **pharmaceutical**

pharmacy /faarməssi/ (*plural* **-cies**) *n* **1** the science or profession of dispensing medicinal drugs **2** a place where medicinal drugs are dispensed or sold [14C. Via Old French *farmacie* < Greek *pharmakeia* 'use of drugs' < *pharmakon* 'drug'.]

pharynges plural of **pharynx**

pharyngeal /fə rínji əl, fárrin jée əl/ *adj* found in, affecting, or relating to the throat [Early 19C. < modern Latin *pharyngeus* < *pharyng-* (see PHARYNX).]

pharyngitis /fárrin jítiss/ *n* inflammation of the pharynx, commonly known as a sore throat

pharyngo- *prefix* pharynx ○ *pharyngoscope* [Via modern Latin < Greek, stem of *pharugx* 'throat' (see PHARYNX)]

pharyngology /fárring gólləji/ *n* the branch of medicine concerned with the throat, its diseases, and their treatment —**pharyngological** /fárring gə lójjik'l/ *adj* —**pharyngologist** /-gólləjist/ *n*

pharyngoscope /fə ríng gə skōp/ *n* a medical instrument for examining the throat —**pharyngoscopic** /fə ríng gə skóppik/ *adj* —**pharyngoscopy** /fárring góskəpi/ *n*

pharynx /fárringks/ (*plural* **pharynges** /fə rín jeez/ *or* **pharynxes**) *n* **1** the throat, the region of the alimentary canal in humans and in vertebrate animals that lies between the mouth and oesophagus **2** a region between the mouth and the digestive system in sea anemones, worms, insects, and other invertebrate animals [Late 17C. Via modern Latin (stem *pharyng-*) < Greek *pharugx* 'throat'.]

phase /fayz/ *n* **1 STAGE OF DEVELOPMENT** a clearly distinguishable period or stage in a process, in the development of something, or in a sequence of events **2 PATTERN OF BEHAVIOUR** a period of time when a situation or particular pattern of behaviour persists and is often annoying or worrying **3 PART OR ASPECT** one of the many parts or aspects of something ○ *We needed to restructure all phases of our business.* **4 RECURRING SHAPE OF MOON** a recurring form of the Moon or a planet seen in the sky **5 PART OF REPEATING CYCLE** a part of a repeated uniform pattern of occurrence of a phenomenon or process, relative to a fixed starting point or time **6 STATE OF MATTER** a state in which matter can exist, depending on temperature and pressure, e.g. the solid, liquid, gaseous, and plasmatic state **7 VARIATION IN ANIMAL FORM** an alternative stage, appearance, or colouring that distinguishes a group of animals from most of their kind, or that a particular animal adopts under specific conditions **8 STAGE IN ORGANISM'S LIFE CYCLE** a stage in the life cycle of an organism ■ *vt* (**phases, phasing, phased**) **1 DO IN STAGES** to plan or arrange something so that it is carried out in stages (*often passive*) ○ *a takeover that is being phased to minimize disruption* **2 SYNCHRONIZE** to cause two or more things to happen or operate simultaneously or in a coordinated way ○ *to phase the departure of one train with the arrival of another* [Early 19C.

Partly via French, partly a back-formation < modern Latin *phases* 'moon phases' < Greek *phasis* 'appearance' < *phainein* 'to show'.] —**phaseal** /fáyzi əl/ *adj* —**phasic** *adj* ◇ **in phase** in the same phase at the same time, or operating in a synchronized or coordinated way ◇ **out of phase** not in the same phase, or not synchronized or coordinated with each other

SPELLCHECK See ***faze***.

phase in *vt* to introduce something in stages over a period of time
phase out *vt* to bring something to an end or remove it in stages over a period of time

phase alternation line *n* full form of **PAL**

phase angle *n* the difference in angle between two sinusoidally varying quantities that have the same frequency

phase diagram *n* a graph on which parameters of a property, such as temperature or pressure, are plotted on perpendicular axes in such a way that a curve corresponds to a transition between physical states

phase modulation *n* a method of transmitting a voice or other signal in which the phase of a radio carrier wave is varied in accordance with the signal

phase music *n* a musical composition, associated with minimalism, in which the different parts use the same material at the same time but only sometimes in phase with each other

-phasia *suffix* speech disorder ○ *aphasia* [< Greek *phasis* 'utterance' < *phanai* 'to say' < Indo-European, 'speak']

phasmid /fázmid/ *n* a tropical plant-eating insect that has a body that looks like a twig with long legs and antennae. Stick insects and leaf insects are phasmids. Family: Phasmidae. ■ *adj* belonging or relating to the phasmids [Late 19C. Via modern Latin *Phasmida* < Greek *phasma* 'apparition' < *phainein* 'to show'.]

phasor /fáyzər/ *n* a rotating vector that can be used to represent a sinusoidally varying quantity, especially an alternating current or voltage [Mid-20C. < PHASE + -OR[1].]

phat /fat/ *adj* of a very high quality or standard (*slang*) ○ *'music... set to the phat beats of hip-hop'* (*The New York Times*; November 1998) [Late 20C. < ?]

phatic /fáttik/ *adj* spoken in order to share feelings, create goodwill, or set a pleasant social mood, rather than to convey information [Early 20C. < Greek *phatos* 'spoken' < *phanai* 'to say' (see -PHASIA).]

PhB *abbr* Bachelor of Philosophy [Latin, *Philosophiae Baccalaureus*]

PhD *abbr* Doctor of Philosophy [Latin, *Philosophiae Doctor*]

pheasant /fézz'nt/ (*plural* **-ants** *or* **-ant**) *n* **1** a large bird, the male of which has a long curved tail and is often brightly coloured. Native to: Asia, Europe, North America. Family: Phasianidae. **2** the meat obtained from a pheasant [13C. Via Old French *fesan* < Greek *phasianos (ornis)* '(bird) from the river Phasis' in W Georgia, its supposed place of origin.]

pheasant's eye (*plural* **pheasant's eyes** *or* **pheasant's eye**) *n* **1** a plant of the buttercup family with very narrow twiggy leaves. Flowers: deep red with a dark centre or yellow and cup-shaped. Genus: *Adonis*. **2** a variety of narcissus with white petals surrounding a red-rimmed cup. *Narcissus poeticus*.

phen- *prefix* CHEM = **pheno-**

phenacaine /fénnə kayn/ *n* $C_{18}H_{22}N_2O_2$ a white crystalline compound used as a local anaesthetic in ophthalmology [Early 20C. < *phen-*, variant of PHENO- + -CAINE.]

phenacetin /fə nássətin/ (*plural* **-tin** *or* **-tins**) *n* **1** $C_{10}H_{13}NO_2$ a white crystalline analgesic having toxic side effects. Use: formerly, pain reliever. **2** a tablet containing phenacetin [Late 19C. Alteration of *acetophenetidin*.]

phenacite /fénnə kīt, fénnə sīt/, **phenakite** /fénnə kīt/ *n* a colourless glassy mineral consisting of beryllium silicate. Use: gems. [Mid-19C. < Greek *phenak-*, stem of *phenax* 'impostor', because it was mistaken for quartz.]

phenanthrene /fə nánth reen/ *n* $C_{14}H_{10}$ a colourless crystalline aromatic hydrocarbon. Use: manufacture of dyes, drugs, and explosives. [Late 19C. Contraction of PHENO- + ANTHRACENE.]

phencyclidine /fen síkli deen, -síkli-/ *n* $C_{17}H_{25}N$ a drug used as an anaesthetic in veterinary medicine and illegally as a hallucinogen [Mid-20C. < *phen-* (variant of PHENO-) + CYCLO- + PIPERIDINE.]

phenetics /fi néttiks/ *n* a system of biological classification based on overall similarities between organisms rather than on their genetic or developmental relationships (+ *singular verb*) [Mid-20C. < Greek *phainesthai* (see -PHANE).] —**phenetic** /fi néttik/ *adj* —**phenetically** *adv* —**pheneticist** *n*

pheno- *prefix* **1** containing phenyl ○ *phenobarbitone* **2** related to or derived from benzene ○ *phenol* **3** appearing ○ *phenocryst* [< Greek *phainein* 'to show']

phenobarbital /feénō baárbit'l/ *n* US MED = **phenobarbitone**

phenobarbitone /feénō baárbitōn/ *n* $C_{12}H_{12}N_2O_3$ a crystalline barbiturate used as a sedative, hypnotic, and anticonvulsant. US term **phenobarbital**

phenocopy /feénō koppi/ (*plural* **-ies**) *n* a noninheritable change in an organism induced by its response to its environment but resembling a genetic mutation [Mid-20C. Blend of PHENOTYPE + COPY.]

phenocryst /feénə krist, fénnə-/ *n* a large embedded crystal in a porphyritic rock [Late 19C. < French *phénocryste* < *phéno-* 'pheno-' (see PHENO-) + Greek *krustallos* 'crystal' (see CRYSTAL).] —**phenocrystic** /feénə krístik, fénnə-/ *adj*

phenol /feénol/ *n* **1** C_6H_5OH a poisonous caustic crystalline compound. Source: coal, wood tar, benzene. Use: manufacture of resins, dyes, and pharmaceuticals, antiseptic, disinfectant. **2** a chemical compound that has one or more hydroxyl groups attached to a benzene ring [Mid-19C. < *phen-*, variant of PHENO-, + -OL[1].]

phenolic /fi nóllik/ *n* **phenolic, phenolic resin** a resin that has high temperature stability. Use: in plastics, paints, adhesives. ■ *adj* derived from or containing phenol

phenology /fi nólləji/ (*plural* **-gies**) *n* **1** the study of regularly recurring biological phenomena such as animal migrations or plant budding, especially as influenced by climatic conditions **2** the relationship between a regularly recurring biological phenomenon and climatic or environmental factors that may influence it [Late 19C. < PHENOMENON + -LOGY.] —**phenological** /feénə lójjik'l/ *adj* —**phenologist** /fi nólləjist/ *n*

phenolphthalein /feé nol thálleen, -tháy-/ *n* $C_{20}H_{14}O_4$ a colourless or yellowish compound. Use: chemical indicator, laxative.

phenol red *n* a red dye. Use: acid-base indicator, testing kidney function.

phenom /fə nóm/ *n* an outstanding or unusual person or thing (*slang*) [Late 19C. Shortening of PHENOMENON.]

phenomena plural of **phenomenon**

phenomenal /fə nómminəl/ *adj* **1 REMARKABLE** remarkable, especially if remarkably and impressively good or great ○ *a phenomenal talent* **2 GREAT** very great in extent or degree (*informal*) ○ *a phenomenal success* **3 PERCEIVED BY SENSES** perceived by or perceptible to the senses, rather than the mind, and thus having at least an apparent external existence **4 OF A PHENOMENON** constituting or relating to a phenomenon —**phenomenally** *adv*

phenomenalism /fə nómminəlizəm/ *n* a philosophical theory stating that knowledge of the external world is limited to appearances so that we know what our senses tell us about things (**sense-data**), not what they are in themselves —**phenomenalist** *n, adj* —**phenomenalistically** /fə nómminə lístikli/ *adv*

phenomenology /fə nómmi nólləji/ *n* **1** in philosophy, the science or study of phenomena, things as they are perceived, as opposed to the study of being, the nature of things as they are **2** the philosophical investigation and description of conscious experience in all its varieties without reference to the question of whether what is experienced is objectively real —**phenomenological** /fə nómminə lójjik'l/ *adj* —**phenomenologically** /-lójjikli/ *adv* —**phenomenologist** /-ólləjist/ *n*

phenomenon /fə nómminən/ (*plural* **-na** /-nə/ *or* **-nons**) *n* **1 SOMETHING EXPERIENCED** a fact or occurrence that can be observed **2 SOMETHING NOTABLE** something that is out of the ordinary and excites people's interest and curiosity ○ *a strange phenomenon* **3 EXTRAORDINARY PERSON OR THING** somebody or something that is, or that is considered to be, truly extraordinary and marvellous **4 OBJECT OF PERCEPTION** something perceived or experienced, especially an object as it is apprehended by the human senses as opposed to an object as it intrinsically is in itself [Late 16C. Via late Latin < Greek *phainomenon* 'that which appears' < the past participle of *phainein* 'bring to light'.]

USAGE Usage varies for the plural ending of nouns derived from Latin and Greek. For ***phenomenon*** never use the false singular *phenomena* as in *This phenomena occurs only in the southern hemisphere*; say instead *This phenomenon occurs...* Similarly, never attach an *-s* plural to the already-plural ***phenomena***, as in *These physiological phenomenas are fascinating*. Say instead *These physiological phenomena are...* The variant plural *phenomenons* is appropriate only outside scientific and philosophical contexts with the meaning 'extraordinary people, events, or things', as in *The dot.coms are one of the most interesting 21st-century phenomenons*. Do not overuse ***phenomenon*** in nonscientific, nonphilosophical contexts. Restrict it to people, events, and things that are extraordinary, not merely interesting or vaguely out of the ordinary.

phenothiazine /feénō thí ə zeen, fénnō-/ *n* **1** $C_{12}H_9NS$ a yellowish crystalline compound used in veterinary medicine to destroy intestinal worms and as an insecticide **2** a derivative of phenothiazine used as a tranquillizer and in the treatment of schizophrenia

phenotype /feénō tīp/ *n* the visible characteristics of an organism resulting from the interaction between its genetic makeup and the environment [Early 20C. < German *Phänotypus* 'type that shows' < Greek *phainein* (see PHENOMENON).] —**phenotypic** /feénō típpik/ *adj* —**phenotypical** /-típpik'l/ *adj* —**phenotypically** /-típpikli/ *adv*

phenoxide /fi nók sīd/ *n* a chemical compound that is a salt of phenol

phenyl /feé nīl, fénn'l/ *n* C_6H_5 a chemical group derived from benzene by removing a hydrogen atom, thus having a valency of one [Mid-19C. < French *phényle* < Greek *phainein* 'to show'; because it was used to name compounds formed from lighting gas.]

phenylalanine /feé nīl állə neen, fénn'l-/ *n* an essential amino acid found in many proteins

phenylbutazone /feé nīl byóotəzōn, fénn'l-/ *n* $C_{19}H_{20}N_2O_2$ an anti-inflammatory drug. Use: to treat arthritis, bursitis, and gout

phenylenediamine /feé nīl énnə dí ə meen/ *n* $C_6H_8N_2$ a white or dark-yellow crystalline solid. Use: manufacture of photographic developers and dyestuffs

phenylketonuria /feé nīl keétə nyóori ə, fénn'l-/ *n* a condition, resulting from a genetic mutation, in which the body lacks the enzyme to metabolize phenylalanine which, if untreated, results in developmental deficiency, seizures, and tumours

phenylpropanolamine /feé nīl prōpə nóllə meen, fénn'l-/ *n* $C_9H_{13}NO$ a drug that constricts blood vessels. Use: as a nasal and bronchial decongestant, appetite suppressant

phenylthiocarbamide /feé nīl thí ō kaárbə mīd, fénn'l-/, **phenylthiourea** /feé nīl thí ō yoóri ə, fénn'l-/ *n* a crystalline compound that tastes extremely bitter to people who possess a particular dominant gene. Use: testing for that gene.

phenytoin /fénni tō in/ *n* $C_{15}H_{12}N_2O_2$ an anticonvulsant drug. Use: to treat epilepsy

pheromone /férrəmōn/ *n* a chemical compound, produced and secreted by an animal, that influences the behaviour and development of other members of the same species [Mid-20C. < Greek *pherein* 'carry' (see -PHORE) + HORMONE.] —**pheromonal** /férrə mōn'l/ *adj*

phew /fyoo/ *interj* used to express tiredness, relief, surprise, or disgust [Early 17C. An imitation of blowing through partly closed lips.]

phi /fī/ (*plural* **phis**) *n* the 21st letter of the Greek alphabet [Mid-20C. Via late Greek < Greek *phei*.]

phial /fí əl/ *n* = **vial** [14C. Via Old French *fiole* < Greek *phialē* 'broad flat vessel'.]

Phi Beta Kappa *n* **1** an honorary society of American college and university students showing high academic achievement **2** a member of Phi Beta Kappa

ϟ **PHIGS** /figz/ *abbr* programmers' hierarchical interactive graphics standard

phil. /fil/ *abbr* **1** philological **2** philology **3** philosopher **4** philosophical **5** philosophy

Phil. *abbr* **1** Philharmonic **2** Philippians **3** Philippines

phil- *prefix* = **philo-** (*before vowels or h*)

-phil *suffix* = **-phile**

Philadelphia /fíllə délfi ə/ port in SE Pennsylvania. Population: 1,436,287 (1998 estimate).

philadelphus /fíllə délfəss/ *n* TREES = **mock orange** *n.* 1 [Late 18C. Via modern Latin < Greek *philadelphos* 'loving one's brother' < *philos* 'loving' + *adelphos* 'brother'.]

Philae /fí ee/ submerged island in the River Nile, SE Egypt, the former site of ancient temples that were moved when the island was covered by Lake Nasser after dam construction

philander /fi lándər/ *vi* to flirt with and have casual sexual affairs with women, especially when married to another woman (*disapproving*) [Late 17C. < Greek *philandros* 'loving men' < *andr-* 'man'.] —**philanderer** *n*

philanthropic /fillən thróppik/, **philanthropical** /-pik'l/ *adj* **1** showing kindness, charitable concern, and generosity towards other people **2** devoted to helping other people, especially through giving charitable aid —**philanthropically** *adv*

philanthropy /fi lánthrəpi/ *n* **1** a desire to improve the material, social, and spiritual welfare of humanity, especially through charitable activities **2** general love for, or benevolence towards, the whole of humankind (*formal*) [Early 17C. Via late Latin < Greek *philanthrōpos* 'humane' < *philos* 'loving' + *anthrōpos* 'human being'.] —**philanthropist** *n*

philately /fi láttəli/ *n* the collection and study of postage stamps and related items [Mid-19C. < French *philatélie* < Greek *philos* 'loving' + *ateleia* 'exemption from tax' < *telos* 'tax'; from the freedom from charges that a stamped letter provides.] —**philatelic** /fíllə téllik/ *adj* —**philatelically** /-téllikli/ *adv* —**philatelist** /fi láttəlist/ *n*

Philby /fílbi/, **Kim** (1912–88) British intelligence agent and Soviet spy. Born **Harold Adrian Russell Philby**

-phile *suffix* **1** one that loves or has an affinity for ○ *nucleophile* ○ *Europhile* **2** loving or having an affinity for ○ *homophile* [Via Latin *-philus* < Greek *philos* 'loving'] —**-philic** *suffix* —**-philous** *suffix* —**-phily** *suffix*

Philemon /fi lée mən/ *n* a book in the Bible, written by St Paul, appealing to Philemon to take pity on his slave who had escaped and converted to Christianity

philharmonic /fíl haar mónnik, fíllər-/, **Philharmonic** *adj* describes an orchestra or choir that performs music or a society that promotes the study, performance, and appreciation of music ■ *n* a symphony orchestra, choir, or musical society that has the word 'philharmonic' in its title [Mid-18C. Via French *philharmonique* < Greek *philos* 'loving' + *harmonia* 'harmony' (see HARMONY).]

philhellene /fíl he leen, fil hélleen/, **philhellenist** /fil héllənist/ *n* an admirer of Greece, Greek history and culture, or the Greeks [Early 19C. < Greek *philellēn* < *philos* 'loving' + *Hellēn* 'a Greek'.] —**philhellenic** /fíl he léenik, -lénnik/ *adj* —**philhellenism** /fil héllənizəm/ *n* —**philhellenistic** /fil héllə nístik/ *adj*

-philia *suffix* **1** intense or abnormal attraction to ○ *neophilia* ○ *zoophilia* **2** tendency toward ○ *basophilia* [Via modern Latin < Greek *philia* 'fondness' < *philos* 'loving'] —**-philiac** *suffix*

philibeg *n* = **filibeg**

Philip /fíllip/, **St** (*fl.* AD 1st century) one of the disciples of Jesus Christ

Philip I (1478–1506) duke of Burgundy and king of Castile (1504–06). Known as **Philip the Handsome**

Philip II (382–336 BC) king of Macedonia (359-336 BC)

Philip IV (1268–1314) king of France (1285–1314). Known as **Philip the Fair**

Philip V (1683–1746) king of Spain (1700–46)

Philip, Prince, Duke of Edinburgh (*b.* 1921) husband of Queen Elizabeth II

~~**Philipines**~~ incorrect spelling of **Philippines**

Philippi /fi líp ī, fílli pī/ ancient town of Macedonia, in present-day NE Greece, the site of a battle in 42 BC in which forces led by Antony and Augustus defeated Brutus and Cassius

Philippians /fi líppi ənz/ *n* a book of the Bible consisting of a letter (**Epistle**) from St Paul to the Christian church at Philippi (*+ singular verb*)

philippic /fi líppik/ *n* a verbal attack on somebody or something delivered in the most savage, bitter, and insulting terms, usually as a speech [Late 16C. Via Latin *philippicus* < Greek *philippikos*, the speech of the fourth-century BC Greek orator Demosthenes urging the citizens of Athens to rise up against Philip of Macedon (see PHILIP II).]

Philippine /fíllәpeen/ *adj* **1** relating to the Philippines or its people or culture **2** PEOPLES = **Filipino** *adj.*

Philippine English *n* a variety of English spoken in the Philippines

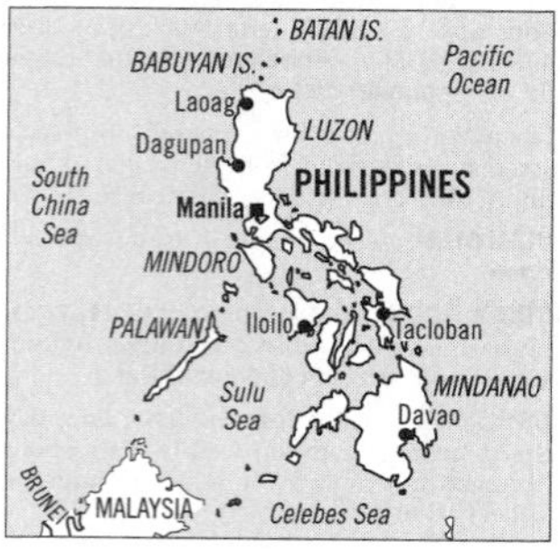

Philippines

Philippines /fílləpeenz/ republic in E Asia, comprising over 7,000 islands in the W Pacific Ocean. Capital: Manila. Population: 68,614,612 (1995). Area: 300,000 sq. km/115,831 sq. mi.

Philippine Sea /fílləpeen-/ section of the W Pacific Ocean, between S Japan and NE Philippines. Area: 5,000,000 sq. km/2,000,000 sq. mi.

Philistine /fíllistīn/ *n* **1** SOMEBODY FROM ANCIENT PHILISTIA a member of a people who settled in ancient Philistia in S Palestine around the 12th century BC **2 philistine, Philistine** SOMEBODY WHO DOES NOT APPRECIATE ART a materialistic person who is indifferent to artistic and intellectual achievements and values (*disapproving*) ■ *adj* **1** RELATING TO PHILISTINES relating to the ancient Philistines or their culture **2 philistine, Philistine** UNCULTURED ignorant, uncultured, and indifferent or hostile to artistic and intellectual achievement [14C. Via late Latin and Greek < Hebrew *Pĕlištī* 'people of Philistia' in Palestine.] —**philistinism** /fíllistinizəm/ *n*

Phillip /fíllip/, **Arthur** (1738–1814) British naval officer

~~**Phillipines**~~ incorrect spelling of **Philippines**

~~**Phillippines**~~ incorrect spelling of **Philippines**

Phillips screw /fíllips-/ *tdmk* a trademark for a screw with a cross-shaped slot on its head

Phillips screwdriver *tdmk* a trademark for a screwdriver that has a cross-shaped tip so that it can be used to turn a Phillips screw

phillumenist /fi lyóomənist/ *n* a collector of matchboxes and matchbooks as a hobby [Mid-20C. < PHILO- + Latin *lumen* 'light' (see LUMEN).] —**phillumeny** *n*

philo- *prefix* loving, having an attraction to or affinity for ○ *philoprogenitive* [< Greek *philos* 'loving']

Philoctetes /fíllək tée teez, fi lók ti teez/ *n* in Greek mythology, a friend of Achilles and the slayer of the Trojan prince Paris

philodendron /fíllə déndrən/ (*plural* **-drons** *or* **-dra** /-drə/) *n* a climbing plant of the arum family, grown as a house plant for its evergreen leaves. Native to: tropical America. Genus: *Philodendron.* [Late 19C. Via modern Latin < Greek *philodendros* 'loving trees' (because it climbs trees in its native habitat) < *dendron* 'tree' (see DENDRON).]

philogyny /fi lójjəni/ *n* a positive and admiring attitude towards women in general (*archaic*) —**philogynist** *n* —**philogynous** *adj*

philology /fi lólləji/ *n* **1** the scientific study of the relationship of languages to one another, and their history, especially based on the analysis of texts **2** the study and analysis of ancient texts, especially as an approach to the cultural history of a period or people [14C. Via Latin *philologia* < Greek *philologos* 'fond of words' < *philos* 'loving' + *logos* 'word'.] —**philological** /fíllə lójjik'l/ *adj* —**philologically** /-lójjikli/ *adv* —**philologist** /fi lólləjist/ *n*

philoprogenitive /fíllō prō jénnitiv/ *adj* **1** producing a large number of offspring (*formal*) **2** loving children, especially your own offspring (*literary*)

philosopher /fi lóssəfər/ *n* **1** STUDENT OF LIFE AND REALITY a person who seeks to understand and explain the principles of existence and reality **2** THINKING PERSON a thinker who deeply and seriously considers human affairs and life in general **3** CALM AND RATIONAL PERSON a person who calmly and rationally reacts to events, especially adversity [14C. < Old French *philosophe* via Latin < Greek *philosophos* 'lover of knowledge' < *sophia* 'learning, wisdom'.]

philosopher's stone, philosophers' stone *n* a substance that medieval alchemists believed could be used to convert other metals into gold

philosophical /fíllə sóffik'l, -zóffik'l/, **philosophic** /-sóffik, -zóffik/ *adj* **1** RELATING TO STUDYING NATURE OF REALITY concerned with the study of the nature of life and reality, or of related areas such as ethics, logic, or metaphysics **2** CONCERNED WITH DEEP QUESTIONS OF LIFE concerned with or given to thinking about the larger issues and deeper meanings in life and events **3** SHOWING CALMNESS AND RESIGNATION showing calmness, restraint, or resignation, especially reacting to adversity in a restrained or resigned way —**philosophically** *adv*

philosophize /fi lóssə fīz/ (**-phizes, -phizing, -phized**), **philosophise** (**-phises, -phising, -phised**) *v* **1** *vi* DISCUSS NATURE OF REALITY to comment on or attempt to explain the nature of life and reality, or some part of it such as logic, ethics, knowledge, or existence **2** *vi* EXPLAIN OR MORALIZE IN SUPERFICIAL WAY to express opinions of a supposedly philosophical nature in a superficial, tedious, or moralistic way **3** *vt* DEAL WITH SOMETHING FROM PHILOSOPHICAL STANDPOINT to consider, explain, or deal with something from a philosophical standpoint —**philosophization** /fi lóssə fī záysh'n/ *n* —**philosophizer** /fi lóssə fīzər/ *n*

philosophy /fi lóssəfi/ (*plural* **-phies**) *n* **1** EXAMINATION OF BASIC CONCEPTS the branch of knowledge or academic study devoted to the systematic examination of basic concepts such as truth, existence, reality, causality, and freedom **2** SYSTEM OF THOUGHT a particular system of thought or doctrine **3** GUIDING OR UNDERLYING PRINCIPLES a set of basic principles or concepts underlying a particular sphere of knowledge **4** SET OF BELIEFS OR AIMS a precept, or set of precepts, beliefs, principles, or aims, underlying somebody's practice or conduct **5** CALM RESIGNATION restraint, resignation, or calmness and rationality in a person's behaviour or response to events [14C. Via Old French *filosofie* < Greek *philosophia* < *philosophos* 'philosopher' (see PHILOSOPHER).]

philter *n* US = **philtre**

philtre *n* a magical potion or charm, especially one that causes somebody to fall in love (*literary*) [Late 16C. Via French < Greek *philtron* < *philein* 'to love' < *philos* 'loving'.]

phimosis /fī mósiss/ *n* an abnormal narrowing of the opening in the foreskin to the extent that it cannot be drawn back over the penis [Late 17C. Via modern Latin < Greek *phimōsis* 'muzzling'.]

phi phenomenon *n* an optical illusion in which the rapid appearance and disappearance of two stationary objects, e.g. flashing lights, is perceived as the movement back and forth of a single object

~~**phisical**~~ incorrect spelling of **physical**

phiz /fiz/, **phizog** /fízzog, fi zóg/ *n* a person's face (*slang*) [Late 17C. Shortening of PHYSIOGNOMY.]

phleb- *prefix* = **phlebo-** (*before vowels*)

phlebitis /fli bítiss/ *n* inflammation of the wall of a vein

phlebo- *prefix* vein ○ *phlebotomy* [< Greek *phleb-*, stem of *phleps* 'blood vessel']

phlebography /fli bóggrəfi/ *n* MED = **venography**

phlebotomize /fli bóttə mīz/ (**-mizes, -mizing, -mized**), **phlebotomise** (**-mises, -mising, -mised**) *vt* to make an incision into somebody's vein, formerly done to release blood from a vein as a therapeutic treatment

phlebotomy /fli bóttəmi/ (*plural* **-mies**) *n* a surgical incision made in a vein, or a puncture made by a needle to draw blood for testing. ◊ **bloodletting** —**phlebotomist** *n*

phlegm /flem/ *n* **1** THICK MUCUS the thick mucus secreted by the walls of the respiratory passages, especially during a cold **2** UNFLAPPABILITY calmness or composure that is not easily disturbed **3** BODILY FLUID DETERMINING HEALTH AND EMOTIONS in medieval medicine, one of the four basic bodily fluids (**humours**). Phlegm was believed to be cold and moist in nature and to cause sluggishness and apathy. [14C. Via Old French *fleume* < Greek *phlegma* 'heat' < *phlegein* 'to burn'.] —**phlegmy** *adj*

phlegmatic /fleg máttik/, **phlegmatical** /-máttik'l/ *adj* characterized by a lack of emotion or emotional display, and not easily worried, excited, or annoyed [14C. Via Old French *fleumatique* and Latin *phlegmaticus* < Greek

KEY MOVEMENTS IN MODERN WESTERN PHILOSOPHY

Period	School of thought	Principal ideas	Principal philosophers
16–17th centuries	Materialism	belief that material substance is the fundamental reality	Bacon, Hobbes
early 17th century	Rationalism	belief that genuine knowledge comes only through reason	Descartes
17–18th centuries	Empiricism	belief that all knowledge comes from experience	Hume, Locke
17–18th centuries	Idealism	to exist means to be perceived; to exist when one is not observing them, things must continue to be perceived by God	Leibniz, Berkeley
18th century	Critical idealism	combines rationalism and empiricism with idea that metaphysical beliefs are matters of faith, not philosophy	Kant
18th–19th centuries	Utilitarianism	idea of good equated with 'the greatest happiness of the greatest number'	Bentham, Mill
18th–19th centuries	Romanticism	emphasis on the individual; divinity of nature	Schelling, Rousseau
19th century	Absolute idealism	belief that source of all reality is absolute spirit	Hegel, Bradley
19th century	Nietzscheanism	belief that human behaviour is motivated by will to power; rejection of religion	Nietzsche
19th–20th centuries	Pragmatism	defined truth as the capacity of a belief to guide one to successful action	Peirce, James
19th–20th centuries	Logical positivism	rejects metaphysics as a meaningless game of words, insists on the definition of all concepts in terms of observable facts	Russell, Moore, Wittgenstein
19th–20th centuries	Existentialism	humans project themselves out of nothingness by asserting their own values and thus assume moral responsibility for their acts	Kierkegaard, Heidegger, Sartre
20th–21st centuries	Poststructuralism	basic human ideas are historically relative, and ideologies and social structures are fluid	Foucault, Derrida

phlegmatikos < *phlegma* (see PHLEGM).] —**phlegmatically** *adv*

SYNONYMS See *impassive*.

phloem /flố em/ *n* one of the two main types of tissue in the more highly developed plants, that conducts synthesized foodstuffs to all parts of the plant [Late 19C. < German, < Greek *phloos* 'bark'.]

phlogiston /flə jístən, -gístən/ *n* a hypothetical element that some early scientists, before the discovery of oxygen, believed to be present in all combustible substances to make them burn [Mid-18C. < Greek, 'inflammable thing' < *phlogizein* 'set on fire' < *phlox* 'flame' (see PHLOX).] —**phlogistic** /flə jístik, -gístik/ *adj*

phlogopite /flốggə pīt/ *n* a yellowish-brown or reddish-brown mineral form of mica. Source: marble, dolomite. [Mid-19C. < Greek *phlogōpos* 'fiery-faced' < *phlox* 'flame'; from its highly reflective flat crystals.]

phlox /floks/ (*plural* **phlox** *or* **phloxes**) *n* a common garden plant that has slim stems with oval narrow leaves. Flowers: scented, white, red, purple, in clusters. Native to: North America. Genus: *Phlox*. [Early 18C. Via modern Latin < Greek, 'flame'; from its brightly coloured flowers.]

Phnom Penh /nóm pén/ capital of Cambodia, in the south of the country. Population: 369,000 (1990 estimate).

-phobe *suffix* fearing or disliking something or somebody ○ *computerphobe* [Via French < Greek *phobos* 'fear']

phobia /fốbi ə/ *n* an irrational or very powerful fear and dislike of something, e.g. spiders or confined spaces [Late 18C. < -PHOBIA.]

-phobia *suffix* an exaggerated or irrational fear ○ *claustrophobia* [Via Latin < Greek *phobos* 'fear']

phobic /fốbik/ *adj* 1 having or showing an intense fear and dislike of something 2 affected with or arising out of a phobia —**phobic** *n*

-phobic *suffix* with a strong or irrational fear or dislike of somebody or something ○ *claustrophobic*

Phobos /fố boss/ *n* the innermost of the two natural satellites of Mars, both of which are small

phocine /fố sīn/ *adj* relating to or resembling seals [Mid-19C. < modern Latin *Phocinae* < Greek *phōkē* 'seal'.]

phocomelia /fốkō méeli ə/ *n* a condition, present at birth, characterized by an absent or underdeveloped upper section of a limb, with a normal-sized hand or foot attached to the trunk by a short, broad, flat limb [Late 19C. < Greek *phōkē* 'seal' + *melos* 'limb'; from the short limbs of seals.]

phoebe /féebi/ *n* a bird of the flycatcher family that has greyish-brown plumage, a yellowish-white breast, and is noted for the flicking of its tail. Native to: E North America. Genus: *Sayornis*. [Early 18C. An imitation of its song (influenced by the name PHOEBE).]

Phoebe /féebi/ *n* 1 in Greek mythology, a Titan goddess who later became identified with the goddess of the moon, Artemis 2 a personification of the moon (*literary*) [14C. Via Latin < Greek *Phoibē*, feminine of *phoibos* 'bright, shining'.]

Phoebe /féebi/ *n* the outermost known natural satellite of Saturn, discovered in 1898. It is irregular in shape and has a maximum dimension of approximately 230 km.

Phoebus /féebass/ *n* 1 **Phoebus Apollo** in Greek mythology, the god Apollo when identified with the sun 2 a personification of the sun (*literary*) [14C. Via Latin < Greek *phoibos* 'bright, shining'.]

Phoenician /fə nísh'n, fə néesh'n/ *n* 1 a member of an ancient people who occupied Phoenicia, coastal lands in present-day Syria, where they established trading ports 2 an extinct Semitic language spoken in ancient Phoenicia —**Phoenician** *adj*

phoenix /féeniks/ *n* 1 in ancient mythology, a bird resembling an eagle that lived for 500 years and then burned itself to death on a pyre from whose ashes another phoenix arose 2 a supremely beautiful, rare, or unique person or thing (*literary*) ○ *a phoenix of princes* [Pre-12C. Via Old French < Greek *phoinix*.]

Phoenix /féeniks/ *n* a constellation of the southern hemisphere. See illustration at **constellation**

Phoenix /féeniks/ capital of Arizona, in the south of the state. Population: 1,198,064 (1998 estimate).

phon /fon/ *n* a unit of subjective measure of loudness level. The level in phons is equal in number to the sound intensity of a 1,000-hertz reference sound, measured in decibels, judged to be the same loudness as the measured sound.

phon- *prefix* = **phono-** (*before vowels*)

phonate /fố nayt, fō náyt/ (**-nates, -nating, -nated**) *v* 1 *vti* to make a voiced sound or make a sound voiced by vibrating the vocal cords 2 *vi* to produce sounds, especially speech sounds, with the voice —**phonation** /fố náysh'n/ *n* —**phonatory** /-náytəri/ *adj*

phone /fōn/ *n* TELEPHONE a telephone ■ **phones** *npl* EARPHONES a set of earphones (*informal*) ■ *v* (**phones, phoning, phoned**) 1 *vti* CALL SOMEBODY BY TELEPHONE to call somebody on the telephone 2 *vt* REPORT SOMETHING BY TELEPHONE to report or communicate something using a telephone [Late 19C. Shortening.]

phone /fōn/ *n* a single basic speech sound [Mid-19C. See -PHONE.]

-phone *suffix* 1 a device that emits or receives sounds, e.g. a musical instrument ○ *diaphone* ○ *hydrophone* ○ *sousaphone* 2 a telephone ○ *speakerphone* 3 a speech sound ○ *isophone* 4 a speaker of a particular language ○ *Francophone* [< Greek *phōnē* (see PHONO-)] —**phonic** *suffix* —**-phony** *suffix*

phone book *n* a telephone directory

phone booth *n US* TELECOM = **phone box**

phone box *n* a telephone box. US term **phone booth**

phonecard /fốn kaard/ *n* a rectangular plastic card that can be used instead of money when making calls from some public telephones

phone-in *n* a radio or television programme in which audience members call in to discuss topics with the host and guest. US term **call-in** *n*

phoneme /fố neem/ *n* a speech sound that distinguishes one word from another, e.g. the sounds 'd' and 't' in the words 'bid' and 'bit'. A phoneme is the smallest phonetic unit. [Late 19C. Via French < Greek *phōnēma* 'sound produced' < *phōnein* 'produce a sound' < *phōnē* 'sound, voice'.]

phonemic /fə néemik, fō-/ *adj* 1 OF PHONEMES relating to a phoneme 2 OF DIFFERENT PHONEMES relating to speech sounds that belong to different phonemes rather than being different ways of pronouncing the same phoneme 3 OF PHONEMICS relating to the branch of linguistics that studies phonemes —**phonemically** *adv*

phonemics /fə néemiks, fō-/ *n* the branch of linguistics involved in the classification and analysis of the phonemes of a language (+ *singular verb*) —**phonemicist** /fə néemissist, fō-/ *n*

⚡ **phone phreak** /fốn freek/ *n* an intruder into telephone systems, often in order to make free long-distance telephone calls (*slang*)

phoner /fốnər/ *n* 1 an interview conducted by telephone, especially on a radio or TV programme (*informal*) 2 somebody who makes a telephone call

phone sex *n* the act of talking in an erotic and explicit way to another person on the telephone for mutual or individual sexual pleasure

phonetic /fə néttik, fō-/ *adj* 1 OF SPEECH SOUNDS belonging to or associated with the sounds of human speech 2 SHOWING PRONUNCIATION representing the sounds of human speech in writing, often with special symbols or unconventional spelling 3 OF PHONETICS relating to the science of phonetics [Early 19C. Via modern Latin < Greek *phōnētikos* 'spoken' < *phōnein* (see PHONEME).] —**phonetically** *adv*

phonetic alphabet *n* 1 a set of letters and symbols used to represent the sounds of human speech in writing 2 a set of words representing alphabetical letters, e.g. 'Delta' for D and 'Tango' for T, used in radio or telephone communications

phonetics /fə néttiks, fō-/ *n* (+ *singular verb*) 1 the scientific study of speech sounds and how they are produced 2 the system or pattern of speech sounds used in a particular language —**phonetician** /fōnə tísh'n, fónnə-/ *n*

phoney /fṓni/, **phony** *adj* (-nier, -niest) 1 NOT GENUINE not genuine and used to deceive 2 GIVING A FALSE IMPRESSION putting on a false show of something such as sincerity or expertise ■ *n* (*plural* -neys *or* -nies) SOMEBODY OR SOMETHING PHONEY a phoney person or thing [Late 19C. < ?] —**phonily** *adv* —**phoniness** *n*

phoney war *n* a period when enemies are officially at war but not actively engaged in armed conflict, e.g. the period of relative calm at the beginning of World War II

phonic /fónnik/ *adj* 1 USING PHONICS using or involving phonics as a method of teaching people to read 2 OF SOUND associated with sound or the scientific study of sound 3 OF SPEECH SOUNDS relating to the sounds used in speech [Early 19C. < Greek *phōnē* 'sound, voice'.] —**phonically** *adv*

phonics /fónniks/ *n* a method of teaching reading in which people learn to associate letters with the speech sounds they represent, rather than learning to recognize the whole word as a unit (+ *singular verb*) [Late 17C. < Greek *phōnē* 'sound, voice'.]

phono- *prefix* 1 sound, speech, voice ○ *phonogram* 2 telephone ○ *phonecard* [< Greek *phōnē* 'sound' < Indo-European, 'speak']

phonocardiogram /fṓnō kaárdi ə gram/ *n* a visual record of heart sounds and murmurs made by a phonocardiograph

phonocardiograph /fṓnō kaárdi ə graaf, -graf/ *n* an instrument that amplifies heart sounds and converts them into a visual display —**phonocardiographic** /-kaárdi ə gráffik/ *adj* —**phonocardiography** /-kaárdi óggrəfi/ *n*

phonochemistry /fṓnō kémmistri/ *n* a branch of science and technology dealing with the effect of sound and ultrasonic waves on chemical reactions

phonogram /fṓnə gram/ *n* 1 a symbol that represents a word, part of a word, or an individual speech sound 2 a sequence of letters that have the same pronunciation in several different words, e.g. 'ear' in 'earth', 'heard', and 'learn' —**phonogramic** /fṓnə grámmik/ *adj* —**phonogramically** /-grámmikli/ *adv*

phonograph /fṓnə graaf, fṓnə graf/ *n US* a record player

phonography /fə nóggrəfi/ *n* 1 the use of symbols to represent speech sounds in writing 2 a method of writing in shorthand that uses symbols to represent speech sounds —**phonographer** *n* —**phonographic** /fṓnə gráffik/ *adj* —**phonographically** /-gráffikli/ *adv* —**phonographist** /fə nóggrəfist/ *n*

phonolite /fṓnə līt/ *n* a fine-grained light-coloured volcanic rock characterized by the presence of alkali feldspar and nepheline [Early 19C. < PHONO- + -LITE; from the resonance of the rock when hit with a hammer.] —**phonolitic** /fṓnə líttik/ *adj*

phonology /fə nólləji, fō-/ (*plural* -gies) *n* 1 the scientific study of the system or pattern of speech sounds used in a particular language or in language in general 2 the system or pattern of speech sounds used in a particular language —**phonological** /fṓnə lójjik'l, fónnə-/ *adj* —**phonologically** /fṓnə lójjikli, fónnə lójjikli/ *adv* —**phonologist** /fə nólləjist, fō-/ *n*

phonon /fṓ non/ *n* a quantum of vibrational or acoustic energy in a crystal lattice

phonoscope /fṓnə skōp/ *n* a device that visually represents the vibrations of sound waves, used especially with musical instruments

phonotactics /fṓnō táktiks, fṓnə-/ *n* the study of the sounds it is possible to put together to form words and parts of words in a language (+ *singular verb*)

phony *adj, n* = **phoney**

phooey /fóo i/ *interj* used to express contempt, disbelief, disgust, or disappointment (*informal*) [Early 20C. Natural exclamation.]

phorate /fáwr ayt/ *n* $C_7H_{17}O_2PS_3$ an organophosphorous compound used as an insecticide to control crop pests [Mid-20C. Shortening of *phosphorodithioate* < PHOSPHORUS + DI- + THIO- + -ATE.]

-phore *suffix* something that carries ○ *sporophore* [< Greek *-phoros* 'bearing' < *pherein* 'carry'. Ultimately < Indo-European.] —**-phorous** *suffix*

-phoresis *suffix* transmission ○ *diaphoresis* [< Greek *phorēsis* < *phorein* 'keep carrying' < *pherein* (see -PHORE)]

phoresy /fórrəssi/ *n* a method of dispersal used by some animals in which they cling to the surface of another animal to be carried to a new site, e.g. in search of food [Early 20C. Via French *phorésie* < Greek *phorēsis* 'being carried'.]

phoronid /fórrənid/ *n* a marine tube worm with a mouth surrounded by an array of tentacles that it extends to capture plankton and detritus. Native to: coastal regions. Phylum: Phoronida. [< modern Latin *Phoronida*, ultimately probably < Greek *Phorōneus*, the son of Inachus, mythological king of Argos]

phosgene /fóss jeen, fóz-/ *n* $COCl_2$ a highly toxic colourless gas. Use: chemical weapons in World War I, manufacture of pesticides, plastics, and dyes.

phosgenite /fóssji nīt, fózji-/ *n* a rare greyish fluorescent crystalline mineral consisting of a carbonate and chloride of lead [Mid-19C. < PHOSGENE, because the minerals are formed from the same substances as phosgene gas.]

phosph- *prefix* = **phospho-** (*before vowels*)

phosphatase /fóssfə tayz, -tayss/ *n* an enzyme that catalyses the hydrolysis of phosphate esters and the transfer of phosphate groups [Early 20C. < PHOSPHATE + -ASE.]

phosphate /fóss fayt/ *n* a salt or ester formed by the reaction of a metal, alcohol, or other radical with phosphoric acid [Late 18C. < French *phosphate* < *phosphore* 'phosphorus'.] —**phosphatic** /foss fáttik/ *adj*

phosphate rock *n* a sedimentary rock with a naturally high phosphate concentration. Use: fertilizer, manufacture of phosphorus compounds.

phosphatide /fóssfə tīd/ *n* BIOCHEM = **phospholipid** —**phosphatidic** /fóssfə tíddik/ *adj*

phosphatidylcholine /fóssfəti dīl kṓ leen/ *n* BIOCHEM = **lecithin** [Mid-20C. < PHOSPHATIDE + -YL + CHOLINE.]

phosphatidylethanolamine /fóssfəti dīl éthə nóllə meen/ *n* BIOCHEM = **cephalin** [Mid-20C. < PHOSPHATIDE + -YL + ETHANOLAMINE.]

phosphatize /fóssfə tīz/ (-tizes, -tizing, -tized), **phosphatise** (-tises, -tising, -tised) *v* 1 *vt* to treat something with phosphoric acid or with a phosphate, typically to protect ferrous metal against corrosion 2 *vti* to convert something or be converted into a phosphate or phosphates —**phosphatization** /fóssfə tī záysh'n/ *n*

phosphene /fóss feen/ *n* a sensation of seeing light caused by pressure or electrical stimulation of the eye [Late 19C. < modern French *phosphène* < Greek *phōs* 'light' + *phainein* 'to show'.]

phosphide /fóss fīd/ *n* a compound of phosphorus with a more electropositive element, e.g. a metal

phosphine /fóss feen/ *n* PH_3 a colourless inflammable gas with a fishy smell. Use: pesticide.

phosphite /fóss fīt/ *n* any salt or ester of phosphorous acid

phospho- *prefix* 1 phosphorus ○ *phosphate* 2 phosphate ○ *phosphocreatine* [< PHOSPHORUS]

phosphocreatine /fóssfō kree ə teen/, **phosphocreatin** /-tin/ *n* a phosphate of creatine found in muscles, providing energy for muscle contraction

phosphofructokinase /fóssfō frúktō kī nayz, -kī nayz, -kee nayss/ *n* an enzyme that catalyses the transfer of phosphate to a fructose compound during the metabolism of glucose

phosphoglucomutase /fóssfō glóokō myoo tayz, -tayss/ *n* an enzyme that catalyses both the breakdown and synthesis of glycogen, providing energy that can be used or stored

phospholipase /fóssfō lī payz, fóssfō lī payss/ *n* an enzyme that catalyses the hydrolysis of phospholipids in cell membranes

phospholipid /fóssfō líppid/ *n* a phosphorus-containing lipid found in double-layered cell membranes

phosphonic acid /foss fónnik-/ *n* CHEM = **phosphorous acid** *n.* 1

phosphonium /foss fṓni əm/ *n* PH_4 a univalent radical derived from phosphene [Late 19C. < PHOSPHO- + ending of AMMONIUM.]

phosphor /fóssfər/ *n* a substance that can emit light when irradiated with particles of electromagnetic radiation [Early 17C. < Latin *phosphorus* (see PHOSPHORUS).]

phosphorate /fóssfə rayt/ (-ates, -ating, -ated) *vt* to treat, combine, or impregnate something with phosphorus

phosphor bronze *n* any one of several alloys containing copper, tin, and phosphorus that are resistant to wear and corrosion and are used in bearings, gears, and components exposed to sea water

phosphoresce /fóssfə réss/ (-resces, -rescing, -resced) *vi* to continue to emit light without accompanying heat after exposure to and removal of a source of stimulating radiation

phosphorescence /fóssfə réss'nss/ *n* the continued emission of light without heat after exposure to and removal of a source of electromagnetic radiation —**phosphorescent** *adj* —**phosphorescently** *adv*

phosphoric /foss fórrik/ *adj* containing phosphorus with a valency state higher than that of the phosphorus ion or radical in an analogous phosphorous compound

phosphoric acid *n* 1 H_3PO_4 a water-soluble transparent solid acid. Use: fertilizer, rust-proofing, in soft drinks, pharmaceuticals, and animal feeds. 2 any of the acids formed by the combination of phosphorus pentoxide with water, each having one more oxygen atom than the corresponding phosphorous acid

phosphorite /fóssfə rīt/ *n* 1 a mineral deposit consisting of apatite and other phosphates 2 GEOL = **phosphate rock** —**phosphoritic** /fóssfə ríttik/ *adj*

phosphorolysis /fóssfə róllississ/ *n* a process in which a phosphate group is added to a molecule, which then splits into two simpler fragments [Mid-20C. Blend of PHOSPHORUS or *phosphorylation* + HYDROLYSIS.]

phosphorous /fóssfərəss/ *adj* relating to phosphorus with a valency state lower than that of the phosphorus ion or radical in an analogous phosphoric compound [Late 18C. < PHOSPHORUS + -OUS.]

phosphorous acid *n* 1 H_3PO_3 a white or yellowish crystalline solid that absorbs water from the atmosphere. Use: reducing agent, production of phosphite salts. 2 any of the acids formed by the combination of phosphorus pentoxide with water, each having one less oxygen atom than the corresponding phosphoric acid

phosphorus /fóssfərəss/ *n* a phosphorescent substance or object [Early 17C. Via modern Latin < Greek *phōsphoros* 'morning star', literally 'light-bringing' < *phōs* 'light'.]

phosphorus pentoxide, **phosphorus oxide** *n* P_2O_5 a flammable hygroscopic white solid. Source: burning phosphorus in air. Use: manufacture of phosphoric acid.

phosphoryl /fóssfəril/ *n* a chemical group, usually with a valence of three, consisting of one phosphorus atom and one oxygen atom

phosphorylase /foss fórri layz, -layss/ *n* an enzyme that catalyses the phosphorolysis of a molecule

phosphorylate /foss fórri layt/ (-ates, -ating, -ated) *vt* to add a phosphate group to an organic molecule —**phosphorylation** /fóss forri láysh'n/ *n* —**phosphorylative** /foss fórrilətiv/ *adj*

phot /fōt, fot/ *n* a unit of illumination in the centimetre-gram-second system equal to one lumen per square centimetre [Late 19C. Via French < Greek *phōt-*, stem of *phōs* 'light'.]

phot- *prefix* = **photo-** (*before vowels*)

photic /fṓtik/ *adj* 1 relating to light, especially when produced by living organisms 2 describes the area of the ocean where light penetrates and photosynthesis occurs [Mid-19C. < PHOT.]

Photius /fṓti əss/ (820?–891?) Byzantine churchman and scholar

photo /fṓtō/ *n* (*plural* **-tos**) PHOTOGRAPHY = **photograph** *n.* ■ *vt* (**-tos, -toing, -toed**) to take a photograph or photographs of somebody or something [Mid-19C. Shortening.]

photo- *prefix* **1** light, radiant energy ○ *photochemistry* **2** photographic ○ *photomontage* **3** photoelectric ○ *photocurrent* [< Greek *phōt-* 'light' < Indo-European, 'to shine']

photoactinic /fṓtō ak tínnik/ *adj* emitting radiation similar to visible and ultraviolet light in its chemical effects on such substances as photographic emulsions

photoactive /fṓtō áktiv/ *adj* exhibiting a reaction to electromagnetic radiation, especially visible light, either by chemical reaction or photoelectrically

photoautotroph /fṓtō áwtō trof/ *n* an organism that derives its energy exclusively from light and uses it to synthesize food —**photoautotrophic** /fṓtō áwtō tróffik/ *adj* —**photoautotrophically** /-tróffikli/ *adv*

photobiology /fṓtō bī óllәji/ *n* a branch of biology concerned with the interaction of living organisms with light —**photobiological** /fṓtō bī ə lójjik'l/ *adj* —**photobiologist** /fṓtō bī óllәjist/ *n*

photobiotic /fṓtō bī óttik/ *adj* describes organisms that need light in order to live and grow

photocall /fṓtō kawl/ *n* **1** an occasion when celebrities pose for the press and other photographers, usually for publicity purposes **2** PHOTOGRAPHY = **photo opportunity**

photocatalysis /fṓtō kə tállississ/ *n* the acceleration or deceleration of the speed at which a chemical reaction occurs, caused by electromagnetic radiation and especially visible light

photocathode /fṓtō káthōd/ *n* an electrode that emits electrons when exposed to electromagnetic radiation such as light

ϟ**photo CD** *n* a compact disc that stores images from photographs that can be displayed on a computer or television screen

photocell /fṓtō sel/ *n* TECH = **photoelectric cell**

photochemical smog /fṓtō kémmik'l-/ *n* air pollution caused by the effect of strong sunlight on nitrogen dioxide and hydrocarbons emitted by motor vehicles, creating a harmful haze of minute droplets in the air

photochemistry /fṓtō kémmistri/ *n* a branch of chemistry that studies the effect of radiation, especially of visible and ultraviolet light, on chemical reactions and of the emission of radiation by chemical reactions —**photochemical** *adj* —**photochemically** *adv* —**photochemist** *n*

photochromic /fṓtō krṓmik/ *adj* changing colour or becoming darker or lighter in colour as light increases or decreases in intensity

photocoagulation /fṓtō kō ággyoō láysh'n/ *n* the use of a high-energy light source such as a laser to harden tissue for surgical repair, especially in eye injuries

photocomposition /fṓtō kómpə zísh'n/ *n* PRINTING = **filmsetting** —**photocompose** /fṓtō kəm pṓz/ *vt* —**photocomposer** /-pṓzər/ *n*

photoconduction /fṓtō kən dúksh'n/ *n* the conduction of electricity resulting from the absorption of electromagnetic radiation, especially visible light

photoconductivity /fṓtō kón duk tívvəti/ *n* an increase in the electrical conductivity of a substance on exposure to electromagnetic radiation, especially visible light —**photoconductive** /fṓtō kən dúktiv/ *adj* —**photoconductor** /-dúktər/ *n*

photocopier /fṓtə kopi ər/ *n* a machine that uses a photographic process to produce an almost instant copy of something printed, written, or drawn

photocopy /fṓtə kopi/ *n* (*plural* **-ies**) a copy of something printed, written, or drawn that is produced almost instantly by a photographic process in a machine designed for this purpose ■ *vti* (**-ies, -ying, -ied**) to make a photocopy of something, or be photocopied

photocurrent /fṓtō kurrənt/ *n* an electric current that is produced by and varies with the intensity of illumination

photodecomposition /fṓtō dee kómpə zísh'n/ *n* the breakdown of a chemical compound into simpler substances by means of incident electromagnetic energy, especially visible light

photodegradable /fṓtō di gráydəb'l/ *adj* able to be decomposed into simpler substances through prolonged exposure to incident electromagnetic energy, especially ultraviolet light

photodiode /fṓtō dī ōd/ *n* a semiconductor device in which the flow of current is controlled by the intensity of light and which can therefore be used to detect light

photodisintegration /fṓtō diss ínti gráysh'n/ *n* the ejection of a proton, neutron, or other elementary particle from an atomic nucleus as a result of its absorption of a photon, usually in the form of gamma radiation —**photodisintegrate** /-diss ínti grayt/ *vti*

photodynamic /fṓtō dī námmik/ *adj* **1** OF PHOTODYNAMICS relating to photodynamics or to the energy of light **2** INVOLVING AN ADVERSE REACTION TO LIGHT bringing about or enhancing the toxic effects of some wavelengths of light, especially ultraviolet, on living tissue **3** OF A LASER CANCER TREATMENT relating to or used to describe a cancer treatment in which the drug used is activated by a laser beam —**photodynamically** *adv*

photodynamics /fṓtō dī námmiks/ *n* a branch of biology dealing with the effects of light on living organisms (+ *singular verb*)

photoelectric /fṓtō i léktrik/, **photoelectrical** /-trik'l/ *adj* relating to any electrical effects that are due to the action of electromagnetic radiation, especially visible light —**photoelectrically** *adv* —**photoelectricity** /fṓtō ilek tríssəti, -éllek-/ *n*

photoelectric cell *n* a solid-state device sensitive to varying levels of light that is used to generate or control an electric current, e.g. in burglar alarms, smoke detectors, and exposure meters

photoelectron /fṓtō i lék tron/ *n* an electron released from the surface of a substance that has been struck by a photon of electromagnetic radiation

photoemission /fṓtō i mísh'n/ *n* the release of electrons from a substance by incident electromagnetic radiation —**photoemissive** /fṓtō i míssiv/ *adj*

photoengraving /fṓtō ingráyving/ *n* **1** PROCESS OF ETCHING A PRINTING PLATE the process of making a printing plate by photographing an image onto a metal plate and then etching the image **2** PRINTING PLATE MADE BY PHOTOENGRAVING a printing plate made by photographing an image onto a metal plate **3** PRINT MADE BY PHOTOENGRAVING a print made using a photoengraved printing plate

~~**photoes**~~ incorrect spelling of **photos**

photo finish *n* **1** the end of a race in which two or more contestants are so close that the result must be determined from a photograph taken as they cross the finish line **2** a race or competition won by a very small margin

photofission /fṓtō físh'n/ *n* fission of an atomic nucleus induced by collision with a high-energy photon, e.g. a gamma ray

Photofit /fṓtō fit/ *tdmk* a trademark for a way of constructing a photograph of somebody using photographs of individual facial features arranged to fit a description closely

photoflood /fṓtō flud/ *n* a very bright incandescent lamp used in photography and filming

photofluorogram /fṓtō flóorə gram/ *n* a photograph of an image produced using X-rays

photofluorography /fṓtō floor róggrəfi/ *n* a technique that photographs an X-ray image onto a fluorescent screen for diagnostic purposes —**photofluorographic** *adj*

photog /fə tóg/ *n* a photographer (*informal*)

photogenic /fṓtə jénnik/ *adj* **1** LOOKING ATTRACTIVE IN PHOTOGRAPHS tending to look good in photographs **2** PRODUCING LIGHT describes an organism that produces its own light, especially by phosphorescence **3** CAUSED BY LIGHT caused or aggravated by light, as, e.g., an epileptic episode may be brought about by blinking lights [Mid-19C. < PHOTO- + *-genic*.] —**photogenically** *adv*

photogeology /fṓtō ji óllәji/ *n* the study and identification of landforms and other geological features by means of aerial and satellite photographs —**photogeologic** /fṓtō jee ə lójjik/ *adj* —**photogeological** *adj* —**photogeologist** /fṓtōji óllәjist/ *n*

photogram /fṓtə gram/ *n* **1** a photographic image produced without a camera, usually by placing an object on or near a piece of film or light-sensitive paper and exposing it to light **2** a photograph, especially an artistic one (*archaic*)

photogrammetry /fṓtō grámmətri/ *n* the making of measurements or scale drawings from photographs, especially using aerial photography in the construction of maps —**photogrammetric** /fṓtōgrə méttrik/ *adj* —**photogrammetrist** /fṓtō grámmətrist/ *n*

photograph /fṓtə graaf, -graf/ *n* PICTURE PRODUCED WITH A CAMERA an image produced on light-sensitive film or array inside a camera, especially a print or slide made from the developed film or from a digitized array image, or a reproduction in a newspaper, magazine, or book ■ *v* **1** *vti* TAKE A PHOTOGRAPH OF to produce an image of something by pointing a camera at it and allowing light briefly to fall on the film inside **2** *vi* BE PHOTOGRAPHED WITH A PARTICULAR RESULT to be able to be photographed, or to have a particular quality or appearance in a photograph ○ *Scenes like this photograph best in bright sunlight.* —**photographer** /fə tóggrəfər/ *n*

photographic /fṓtə gráffik/ *adj* **1** relating to, used in, or produced by photography **2** as accurate and detailed as a photograph —**photographically** *adv*

photographic magnitude *n* the magnitude of a star determined by measuring its size on a photographic plate

photographic memory *n* the ability to recall information, especially visual images, with great accuracy and clarity

photography /fə tóggrəfi/ *n* **1** the art, hobby, or profession of taking photographs, and developing and printing the film or processing the digitized array image **2** the process of recording images by exposing light-sensitive film or array to light or other forms of radiation

photogravure /fṓtō grə vyóor/ *n* the process of using photography to make a printing plate with an image engraved into it [Late 19C. < French < *photo* + *gravure* 'engraving' < *graver* 'engrave'.]

photoinduced /fṓtō in dyóost/ *adj* initiated through exposure to light —**photoinduction** /fṓtō in dúksh'n/ *n* —**photoinductive** /-dúktiv/ *adj*

photoionization /fṓtō í ə nī záysh'n/ *n* the removal of one or more electrons from an atom or molecule by absorption of a photon of electromagnetic radiation, especially visible or ultraviolet light —**photoionize** /-í ə nīz/ *vti*

photojournalism /fṓtō júrnəlizəm/ *n* a form of journalism in which photographs play a more important role than the accompanying text —**photojournalist** *n* —**photojournalistic** /-júrnə lístik/ *adj*

photokinesis /fṓtō ki néessiss, -kī-/ *n* the movement of an organism when stimulated by light —**photokinetic** /-ki néttik, -kī-/ *adj* —**photokinetically** /-néttikli/ *adv*

photolithography /fṓtō li thóggrəfi/ *n* **1** the process of creating lithographs using photographic methods **2** a process of producing integrated circuits and printed circuit boards by photographing the circuit pattern on a photosensitive substrate and then chemically etching away the background —**photolithograph** /fṓtō líthə graaf, -graf/ *n* —**photolithographer** *n* —**photolithographic** /fṓtō líthə gráffik/ *adj* —**photolithographically** /-gráffikli/ *adv*

photoluminescence /fṓtō lóomi néss'nss/ *n* the emission of light from a substance as a result of the absorption of electromagnetic radiation —**photoluminescent** /fṓtō lóomi néss'nt/ *adj*

photolysis /fō tóllәssiss/ *n* the irreversible decomposition of a chemical compound as a result of the absorption of electromagnetic radiation, especially visible light —**photolytic** /fṓtō líttik/ *adj* —**photolytically** /-líttikli/ *adv*

photomap /fṓtō map/ *n* a map produced by marking placenames, grid lines, and other information on an aerial photograph ■ *vti* (**-maps, -mapping, -mapped**) to make a photomap of an area

photomask /fṓtō maask/ *n* ELECTRONICS = **mask** *n.* 6

photomechanical /fṓtō mi kánnik'l/ *adj* describes a method of producing printed text or images that uses photographic methods —**photomechanically** *adv*

photometry /fō tómmətri/ *n* **1** the measurement of the luminous intensities of visible light sources **2** the branch of physics concerned with the measurement of the intensity of light —**photometer** *n* —**photometric** /fṓtə méttrik/ *adj* —**photometrically** /-méttrikli/ *adv* —**photometrist** /fō tómmətrist/ *n*

photomicrograph /fṓtō míkrə graaf, -graf/ *n* a photograph made of something seen through a microscope —

photomicrographic /fōtō mīkrə gráffik/ *adj* —**photomicrography** /fōtō mī krógrəfi/ *n*

photomontage /fōtō mon táazh/ *n* **1** the technique of combining a number of photographs or parts of photographs to form a composite picture, used especially in art and advertising **2** a composite picture made up of many photographs or parts of photographs, used especially in art and advertising

photomosaic /fōtō mō záy ik/ *n* a large picture made up of many photographs, e.g. one combining aerial photographs to produce a detailed picture of an area

photomultiplier /fōtō múlti plīʹ ər/, **photomultiplier tube** *n* an evacuated electronic device used to convert low-intensity electromagnetic radiation, especially visible light, into an electrical current, and to amplify this current significantly

photon /fō ton/ *n* a quantum of visible light or other form of electromagnetic radiation demonstrating both particle and wave properties —**photonic** /fō tónnik/ *adj*

photonegative /fōtō néggətiv/ *adj* **1** describes a conductive material whose electrical conductivity decreases in response to increasing illumination **2** describes organisms that move away from a source of light

photonics /fō tónniks/ *n* the study or use of light as a means of information transmission (+ *singular verb*)

photonuclear /fōtō nyóokli ər/ *adj* relating to a nuclear reaction caused by the absorption of a photon, usually in the form of gamma radiation, by an atomic nucleus

photo-offset *n* a method of offset printing in which plates are created using photographic methods

photo opportunity, photo op *n* an opportunity for the media to photograph a politician or other public figure doing something newsworthy, especially when this is deliberately staged to produce favourable publicity

photoperiod /fōtō peʹeri əd/ *n* the daily cycle of light and darkness that affects the behaviour and physiological functions of organisms —**photoperiodic** /fōtō peʹeri óddik/ *adj* —**photoperiodically** /-óddikli/ *adv*

photoperiodism /fōtō peʹeri ədizəm/ *n* the influence of the daily cycle of light and darkness on the physiology and behaviour of an organism

photophobia /fōtō fóbi ə/ *n* **1** very low tolerance of the eye for light, sometimes a symptom of disease or migraine **2** an irrational fear and avoidance of light or lighted spaces

photophobic /fōtō fóbik/ *adj* **1** AFFECTED BY PHOTOPHOBIA relating to or having a condition in which the eye has very low tolerance to light **2** HAVING A FEAR OF LIGHT being abnormally afraid of light **3** GROWING WELL IN REDUCED LIGHT describes an organism such as a plant that grows well in reduced light

photophore /fōtə fawr/ *n* a luminous light organ on many deep-sea and some nocturnal fish, squids, and shrimps

photophosphorylation /fōtō fóss fórri láysh'n/ *n* the process in photosynthesis that converts light energy to stored energy

photopia /fō tōpi ə/ *n* normal vision during daylight, when the activity of the cones in the retina enables the eye to perceive colour —**photopic** /fō tóppik, fō tōpik/ *adj*

photopolymer /fōtō póllimər/ *n* a light-sensitive plastic whose physical properties change on exposure to visible or ultraviolet light

photopositive /fōtō pózzətiv/ *adj* **1** describes a conductive material whose electrical conductivity increases in response to increasing illumination **2** describes organisms that move towards a light source

photorealism /fōtō reeʹ əlizəm/ *n* an artistic style, e.g. in painting or sculpture, that produces an accurate and detailed representation of the subject without attempting to conceal any unattractive aspects —**photorealist** *adj*, *n* —**photorealistic** /-reeʹ ə lístik/ *adj*

photoreception /fōtō ri sépsh'n/ *n* the perception, absorption, and use of light, e.g. for vision in animals or photosynthesis in plants —**photoreceptive** *adj*

photoreceptor /fōtō rə séptər/ *n* a cell or organ that responds to light

photoreconnaissance /fōtō ri kónniss'nss/ *n* reconnaissance undertaken using cameras, usually from an aircraft or drone

photoresist /fōtō ri zist, -zíst/ *n* a photosensitive material that is applied to a surface, exposed to visible or ultra-

violet light, and developed prior to chemical etching during the photolithographic process

photorespiration /fōtō respi ráysh'n/ *n* a pathway in photosynthesis in some plants in which oxygen is absorbed and carbon dioxide released

photosensitise *vt* = **photosensitize**

photosensitive /fōtō sénssətiv/ *adj* reacting to incident electromagnetic radiation, especially visible, infrared, and ultraviolet light —**photosensitivity** /fōtō sénssə tívvəti/ *n*

photosensitize /fōtō sénssə tīz/ (**-tizes, -tizing, -tized**), **photosensitise** (**-tises, -tising, -tised**) *vt* to increase the sensitivity of an organism or substance to electromagnetic radiation, especially visible light —**photosensitization** /fōtō sénssə tī záysh'n/ *n* —**photosensitizer** /fōtō sénssə tīzər/ *n*

photosphere /fōtə sfeer/ *n* the intensely bright gaseous outer layer of a star, especially the Sun —**photospheric** /fōtə sférrik/ *adj*

Photostat /fōtō stat/ *tdmk* a trademark for a kind of photocopier

photo story *n* a collection of photographs in a magazine or book, often accompanied by a short commentary, that tells a story

photosynthesis /fōtō sínthəssiss/ *n* a process by which green plants and other organisms turn carbon dioxide and water into carbohydrates and oxygen, using light energy trapped by chlorophyll —**photosynthetic** /fōtō sin théttik/ *adj* —**photosynthetically** /-théttikli/ *adv*

photosynthesize /fōtō sínthə sīz/ (**-sizes, -sizing, -sized**), **photosynthesise** (**-sises, -sising, -sised**) *vti* to produce carbohydrates and oxygen by photosynthesis [Early 20C. < PHOTOSYNTHESIS.]

photosystem /fōtō sistəm/ *n* either of two reactions in the light phase of photosynthesis involving chlorophyll molecules that trap light, the first (**photosystem I**) proceeding best with longer wavelengths of light, the second (**photosystem II**) with shorter

phototaxis /fōtō táksiss/, **phototaxy** /fōtō táksi/ *n* movement of an organism either towards or away from a source of light —**phototactic** /-táktik/ *adj* —**phototactically** /-táktikli/ *adv*

phototherapy /fōtō thérrəpi/, **phototherapeutics** /fōtō thérrə pyóotiks/ *n* the use of light of particular wavelengths, especially ultraviolet light, in the treatment of disease —**phototherapeutic** /fōtō thérrə pyóotik/ *adj*

phototoxic /fōtō tóksik/ *adj* making the skin unusually sensitive to and subject to damage by light, e.g. by sunburn —**phototoxicity** /fōtō tok síssəti/ *n*

phototransistor /fōtō tran zístər/ *n* a light-sensitive junction transistor that amplifies the base current as the illumination increases

phototrophic /fōtō trófik, -tróffik/ *adj* describes organisms that can utilize light as a source of energy —**phototroph** /fōtō trof/ *n*

phototropism /fōtō trópizəm/ *n* the tendency of an organism to grow towards or away from a source of light [Late 19C. < Greek *tropikos* 'relating to turning' < *tropē* 'to turn'.]

phototropy /fōtō trópi/ *n* a property of some solids whereby they change colour in relation to the wavelength of the incident electromagnetic radiation, especially visible light

phototube /fōtō tyoob/ *n* an electron tube that uses a cathode to convert visible light into electrical current at a rate proportional to the intensity of the illumination

phototypesetting /fōtō tīp seting/ *n* PRINTING = **filmsetting** —**phototypesetter** *n*

photovoltaic /fōtō vol táy ik/ *adj* able to generate a current or voltage when exposed to visible light or other electromagnetic radiation

photovoltaic cell *n* a photoelectric cell that detects and measures light intensity using the potential difference that arises between dissimilar materials when they are exposed to electromagnetic radiation

photovoltaic effect *n* the production of a potential difference across the junction of dissimilar materials or in a nonhomogeneous semiconductor material by the absorption of visible light or other electromagnetic radiation

phrasal verb *n* a verb followed by an adverb, a preposition, or both, used with an idiomatic meaning that

is often quite different from the literal meaning of the individual words

phrase /frayz/ *n* **1** GRAMMATICAL UNIT a string of words that form a grammatical unit, usually within a clause or sentence **2** FIXED EXPRESSION a string of words that are used together and have an idiomatic meaning **3** SHORT UTTERANCE a short expression **4** WORDS SPOKEN AS GROUP a group of words that form a unit of meaning or rhythm in prose or poetry, often separated by punctuation in writing and by pauses in speech **5** MELODIC DIVISION a sequence of notes that form a unit of melody within a piece of music **6** PART OF A CHOREOGRAPHIC PATTERN a short sequence of dance movements ■ *v* (**phrases, phrasing, phrased**) **1** *vt* EXPRESS IN PARTICULAR WAY to express something with a particular pattern of words **2** *vt* SEPARATE TEXT INTO PHRASES to show clearly in speech which groups of words belong together, usually by pausing in appropriate places or by stress and intonation **3** *vt* SEPARATE MUSIC INTO PHRASES to show clearly which sequences of notes belong together in a piece of music, especially when performing it [Mid-16C. Via Latin < Greek *phrasis* 'speech, way of speaking' < *phrazein* 'show, explain'.] —**phrasal** *adj* —**phrasally** *adv*

phrase book *n* a book of useful words and phrases in a foreign language with translations for visitors to a country or region where that language is spoken

phrasemaker /fráyz maykər/ *n* a maker of impressive phrases in speech or writing —**phrasemaking** *n*

phrase marker *n* a representation of the structure of a sentence, usually in the form of a tree diagram

phraseogram /fráyzi ə gram/ *n* a symbol used to represent a particular phrase in shorthand

phraseograph /fráyzi ə graaf, -graf/ *n* a phrase that is or can be represented by a symbol, usually in shorthand

phraseology /fráyzi óllaji/ *n* **1** the phrases used in a particular sphere of activity **2** the way words and phrases are chosen or used [Mid-17C. < modern Latin *phraseologia* < Greek *phrasis* 'speech' (see PHRASE).] —**phraseological** /fráyzi ə lójjik'l/ *adj* —**phraseologist** /fráyzi óllajist/ *n*

phrase-structure grammar *n* a grammar that describes the structure and linear sequence of a sentence in terms of the phrases of which it is made up

phrasing /fráyzing/ *n* **1** the way words are chosen and put together for a particular purpose, or the words themselves **2** the way sequences of notes are grouped together to form units of melody in a piece of music, especially when it is played or sung

phratry /fráytri/ (*plural* **-tries**) *n* **1** a group of clans claiming descent from a common ancestor **2** a kinship group in ancient Greece [Mid-19C. < Greek *phratria* < *phratēr* 'clansman, brother'.] —**phratric** *adj*

⚡**phreak** /freek/ *vi* to use computer and telecommunications skills illegally to break into a telephone system to make free long-distance calls (*slang*) [Late 20C. Alteration of FREAK[1] after PHONE[1].] —**phreaking** *n*

phreatic /fri áttik/ *adj* **1** relating to or used to describe the soil or rock below the water level, where all the pores and intergranular spaces are full of water **2** relating to an explosion caused by ground water coming into contact with ascending magma, e.g. in a volcano [Late 19C. < Greek *phreat-*, stem of *phrear* 'well, cistern'.]

phrenic /frénnik/ *adj* **1** belonging to or supplying the diaphragm **2** belonging to or associated with the mind [Early 18C. < French *phrénique* < Greek *phrēn* 'mind, heart, diaphragm'.]

phrenology /frə nólləji/ *n* the study of the bumps on the outside of the skull, based on the now discredited theory that these bumps reflect somebody's character —**phrenological** /frénnə lójjik'l/ *adj* —**phrenologist** /frə nólləjist/ *n*

Phrygia /fríjji ə/ ancient country in Asia Minor, in present-day west-central Turkey

Phrygian /fríjji ən/ *n* **1** somebody who came from ancient Phrygia **2** an extinct Anatolian language spoken in ancient Phrygia —**Phrygian** *adj*

PHS *abbr* Public Health Service

phthalein /tháy leen, tháy li in, thálleen, thálli in/ *n* an organic dye obtained by reacting phthalic anhydride with a phenol [Late 19C. < PHTHALIC ACID.]

phthalic acid /thállik-/ *n* $C_6H_4(CO_2H)_2$ one of three isomers obtained by the oxidation of benzene derivatives. Use: dyes, perfumes, pharmaceuticals, synthetic fibres. [*Phthalic* < shortening of NAPHTHALENE]

phthalic anhydride *n* $C_6H_4(CO)_2O$ a white crystalline organic compound. Source: naphthalene. Use: manufacture of dyes, insecticides, and plastics.

phthalocyanine /thállō sí ə neen, thály lō-/ *n* **1** $(C_6H_4C_2N_4)_4N_4H_2$ a bright greenish-blue crystalline compound. Source: phthalic anhydride. Use: pigment, coating for CD-ROMs, anticancer agent. **2** a blue or green pigment developed as a metal-substituted form of phthalocyanine. Use: in enamels, plastics, printing inks, wallpaper, linoleum.

phthiriasis /thi rí əssiss/ *n* an infestation of the pubic hair of human beings with lice whose bite can irritate the skin [Late 16C. Via Latin < Greek *phtheiriasis* < *phtheirian* 'be infested with lice' < *phtheir* 'louse'.]

phthisic /thí sik, tí sik/ *n* MED = **phthisis** n. **1** ■ *adj* **phthisic, phthisical** relating to or having phthisis [14C. Via Old French *tisike*, later *ptisique* < Greek *phthisikos* 'consumptive' < *phthisis* (see PHTHISIS).]

phthisis /thíssiss, tíssiss/ *n* **1** a disease or condition marked by wasting of the body **2** a disease of the respiratory system, especially asthma or tuberculosis (*archaic*) [Mid-16C. Via Latin < Greek *phthisis* 'consumption' < *phthinein* 'waste away'.]

phut /fut/ *n* a sound like a small explosion or a sudden expulsion of air (*informal*) [Late 19C. < ?] ◇ **go phut 1** to stop working suddenly or break down completely (*informal*) **2** to collapse or come to nothing (*informal*)

phyco- *prefix* relating to seaweed or algae [< Greek *phukos* 'seaweed']

phycobilin /fíkō bílin/ *n* the blue pigment that occurs naturally in cyanobacteria and gives these organisms their characteristic colour [Mid-20C. < PHYCO- + BILE + -IN.]

phycocyanin /fíkō sí ənin/ *n* a protein pigment in cyanobacteria

phycoerythrin /fíkō érrithrin/ *n* a red protein pigment in red algae

phycology /fī kólləji/ *n* PLANT SCI = **algology** —**phycological** /fíkə lójjik'l/ *adj* —**phycologist** /fī kólləjist/ *n*

phycomycete /fíkō mí seet, fíkō mī seèt/ *n* a mould resembling algae. Class: Phycomycetes. [Mid-20C. < Greek *phukos* 'seaweed' + *mukētes*, plural of *mukēs* 'fungus'.] —**phycomycetous** /-mī seètass/ *adj*

phyl- *prefix* = **phylo-** (*before vowels*)

phyla plural of **phylum**

phylactery /fi láktəri/ (*plural* **-ies**) *n* **1** either of two small leather boxes containing slips of paper with scriptures written on them, traditionally worn by Jewish men during morning weekday prayers as reminders of their religious duties (*often plural*) ◇ **tefillin 2** a reminder of something important [14C. Via Latin *phylacterium* < Greek *phulaktērion* 'amulet' < *phulaktēr* 'guard' < *phulassein* 'to guard'.]

phyletic /fī léttik/ *adj* relating to the hereditary descent of a species or its evolutionary development [Late 19C. < Greek *phuletikos* < *phulē* 'tribe'.] —**phyletically** *adv*

phyll- *prefix* = **phyllo-** (*before vowels*)

-phyll *suffix* leaf ○ *chlorophyll* [< Greek *phyllon* (see PHYLLO-)] —**phyllous** *suffix*

phyllite /fíllīt/ *n* a fine-grained metamorphic rock with a distinctive shiny surface, containing large quantities of mica and resembling slate or schist [Early 19C. < Greek *phullon* 'leaf' (see PHYLLO-) + -ITE¹.] —**phyllitic** /fi líttik/ *adj*

phyllo /féelō/, **phyllo pastry** *n* US COOK = **filo** [Mid-20C. Via modern Greek, 'leaf, sheet' < Greek *phullon* 'leaf' (see PHYLLO-).]

phyllo- *prefix* leaf ○ *phyllotaxis* [< Greek *phullon*. Ultimately < Indo-European.]

phyllode /fíllōd/, **phyllodium** /filṓdi əm/ (*plural* **-a** /-ə/) *n* a flat leaf stalk that functions as a leaf in certain plants, such as the acacia [Mid-19C. < modern Latin *phyllodium* < Greek *phullōdēs* 'leaflike' < *phullon* (see PHYLLO-).] —**phyllodial** *adj*

phylloquinone /fíllō kwi nṓn/ *n* BIOCHEM = **vitamin K**$_1$ [Mid-20C. < PHYLLO- + QUINONE.]

phyllotaxis /fíllō táksis/ (*plural* **-es**), **phyllotaxy** /-táksi/ (*plural* **-ies**) *n* **1** the way the leaves on a particular plant are arranged in relation to one another **2** the study of the factors that determine the growth patterns and arrangement of plant leaves —**phyllotactic** /fíllō táktik/ *adj*

phylloxera /fi lóksərə/ (*plural* **-ra** *or* **-ras** *or* **-rae** /-rī/) *n* an aphid that is a major pest in wine-producing areas. *Viteus vitifolii.* [Mid-19C. < modern Latin < PHYLLO- + Greek *xeros* 'dry'; from the insect's effect on leaves.]

phylo- *prefix* race, kind, tribe, phylum ○ *phylogeny* [< Greek *phulon* (see PHYLUM)]

phylogenetics /fílō jə néttiks/ *n* a system of classification of organisms based on their developmental relationships rather than their overall similarity of form (+ *singular verb*) —**phylogenetic** *adj* —**phylogenetically** *adv* —**phylogeneticist** *n*

phylogeny /fī lójjəni/ (*plural* **-nies**), **phylogenesis** /fílō jénnəsiss/ (*plural* **-ses** /-seez/) *n* the evolutionary history of a species, genus, or group, as contrasted with the development of an individual (ontogeny) —**phylogenetic** /fílō jé néttik/ *adj* —**phylogenetically** /fílō jə néttikli/ *adv* —**phylogenetics** /-jə néttiks/ *n* —**phylogenic** /fílō jénnik/ *adj* —**phylogenically** *adv*

phylum /fíləm/ (*plural* **-la** /-llə/) *n* **1** a major taxonomic group into which animals are divided, made up of several classes **2** a large group of languages or language stocks thought to be historically related, e.g. Afro-Asiatic or Indo-European [Late 19C. Via modern Latin < Greek *phulon* 'race'.]

physalis /fī sáyliss/ (*plural* **-ises** *or* **-es** /-leez/) *n* a tropical plant of the nightshade family that bears edible yellow berries. Native to: the Americas. *Physalis peruviana.* US term **Cape gooseberry** [Early 19C. Via modern Latin < Greek *phusallis* 'bladder'.]

physi- *prefix* = **physio-** (*before vowels*)

physiatrics /fízzi áttriks/ *n* US MED = **physical medicine** (+ *singular verb*) [Mid-19C. < Greek *phusis* 'nature' (see PHYSICS) + *iatrikos* 'medical'.]

physic /fízzik/ *n* (*archaic*) **1** PROFESSION OF MEDICINE medicine or healing as an art or profession **2** A MEDICINE a medicine, especially a purgative ■ *vt* (**-ics, -icking, -icked**) TREAT to treat somebody or something with a medicine or

AKG London

Phylactery

cure (*archaic*) [13C. Directly or via Old French *fisique* < Latin *physica* (see PHYSICS).]

physical /fízzik'l/ *adj* **1** OF THE BODY relating to the body, rather than to the mind, the soul, or the feelings **2** REAL AND TOUCHABLE existing in the real material world, rather than as an idea or notion, and able to be touched and seen **3** NEEDING BODILY STRENGTH involving or needing a lot of bodily strength or energy **4** WITH BODILY CONTACT involving a lot of bodily contact or aggression ○ *Some of the players were a little too physical.* **5** INVOLVING TOUCHING tending to touch people or involving touching, especially in an affectionate or sexual way (*informal*) **6** NOT SOCIAL OR BIOLOGICAL describes sciences such as physics and chemistry that deal with nonliving things such as energy and matter ○ *the physical sciences* ■ *n* PHYSICAL EXAMINATION a physical examination (*informal*) ■ **physicals** *npl* TANGIBLE GOODS items of trade or commerce that can be bought and used, as distinct from items bought and sold in a futures market —**physicality** /fízzi kálləti/ *n* —**physicalness** /fízzik'lnəss/ *n*

physical anthropology *n* the branch of anthropology that studies the evolutionary development of human physical characteristics and the differences in appearance among the peoples of the world, as distinct from cultural differences

physical challenge *n* **1** an inability to perform some or all of the tasks of daily life **2** a medically diagnosed condition that makes it difficult to engage in the activities of daily life

physical chemistry *n* the branch of chemistry that studies the physical and thermodynamic properties of substances in relation to their structures and chemical reactions

physical education *n* gymnastics, athletics, team sports, and other forms of physical exercise taught to children at school

physical examination *n* a doctor's general examination to determine somebody's state of physical health and fitness, sometimes as a requirement for a specific job or activity

physical geography *n* the branch of geography that studies the natural features of the Earth's surface as well as their formation

physicalism /fízzik'lizəm/ *n* in philosophy, a form of materialism that explains the phenomena of reality, including perceptual and intellectual processes, in terms of the physical —**physicalist** *n*, *adj* —**physicalistic** /fízzikə lístik/ *adj*

physicalize /fízzikə līz/ (**-izes, -izing, -ized**), **physicalise** (**-ises, -ising, -ised**) *vt* **1** to express or exhibit something such as emotion with the body **2** to represent something abstract in the form of a physical or concrete thing

physical jerks *npl* physical exercises of the kind done regularly to keep fit, such as press-ups (*dated informal*) [*Jerks* is the plural of JERK¹.]

physically /fízzikli/ *adv* **1** in terms of what is real or what exists in the material world, as opposed to what is theoretical or exists only in the mind ○ *physically impossible* **2** relating to somebody's body or appearance ○ *physically unattractive*

physically challenged *adj* describes somebody with a condition that makes it difficult to perform some or all of the basic tasks of daily life

physical medicine *n* the branch of medicine concerned with the diagnosis and treatment of injuries or physical disabilities and their treatment by external means, including heat, massage, or exercise, rather than by medication or surgery

physical science *n* a science such as physics and chemistry that studies nonliving things. See chart overleaf.

physical therapy *n* US MED = **physiotherapy** —**physical therapist** *n*

physician /fi zísh'n/ *n* a doctor who diagnoses and treats diseases and injuries using methods other than surgery [13C. < Old French *fisicien* < *fisique* (see PHYSIC).]

physician-assisted suicide *n* MED = **doctor-assisted suicide**

physicist /fízzissist/ *n* a student of physics or a scientist who specializes in physics [Mid-19C. < PHYSICS + -IST.]

KEY DATES IN THE PHYSICAL SCIENCES

See also table at *astronomy*

3rd century BC	Greek mathematician Archimedes discovers principle of buoyancy and principle of lever
1010–30	Arabian physicist Alhazen accounts for action of lenses
1604	Italian scientist Galileo Galilei discovers that a falling body increases its distance as a square of time
1637	French philosopher and mathematician René Descartes' *Discourse on Method* includes law of refraction and cause of rainbows
1640	Italian scientist Evangelista Torricelli applies laws of motion to liquids
1662	English scientist Robert Boyle formulates law on relationship of pressure and volume of gas
1687	English scientist Isaac Newton publishes three laws of motion
1714	German physicist Gabriel Fahrenheit develops mercury thermometer and temperature scale
1738	Dutch-born Swiss scientist Daniel Bernoulli proposes principle of velocity of flow of liquids and gases
1752	American statesman and scientist Benjamin Franklin demonstrates that lightning is electricity
1772–74	British chemist Joseph Priestley and French chemist Antoine Lavoisier discover and name oxygen
1779–1848	Swedish chemist Jöns Jakob Berzelius introduces modern chemical symbols, classifies organic and inorganic chemicals
1785	French physicist Charles Coulomb describes attraction and repulsion of positive and negative electrical charges
1800	Italian scientist Alessandro Volta invents first battery
1802	French scientist Joseph Gay-Lussac formulates law on relation of temperature and pressure of gas
1807	British chemist Humphry Davy uses electrolysis to identify sodium and potassium
1808–10	Davy publishes atomic theory of matter
1811	Italian scientist Amedeo Avogadro proposes law of constant number of molecules in equal volumes of gas
1821	British scientist Michael Faraday demonstrates electromagnetic field of force – basic principle of electric motor
1826	German physicist Georg Simon Ohm proposes law for measuring electric current
1833	British scientist Michael Faraday formulates law of electrolysis
1842	Austrian physicist Christian Doppler describes Doppler effect
1850	French physicist Jean Foucault establishes speed of light
1869	Russian chemist Dmitry Mendeleyev publishes first periodic table
1887	Swedish chemist Svante Arrhenius introduces theory of ions carrying electric charges
1895	German physicist Wilhelm Roentgen discovers X-rays
1896	French scientist Henri Becquerel discovers radioactivity
1898	French chemists Marie and Pierre Curie discover radium and polonium
1900	German physicist Max Planck formulates quantum theory
1905	German-born US physicist Albert Einstein proposes special theory of relativity
1909	Belgian-US chemist Leo Hendrik Baekeland invents Bakelite, first synthetic plastic
1916	Theory of shared electrons developed
1932	British scientists split atom
1938	Nylon and Teflon first manufactured by US scientists
1985	US chemists Robert Curl and Richard Smalley and British chemist Harold Kroto discover fullerenes
1986	Quantum jumps shown in single atom

physicochemical /fízzikō kémmik'l/ *adj* **1** relating to both physical and chemical characteristics **2** relating to physical chemistry [Mid-17C. < Greek *physikos* (see PHYSICS) + CHEMICAL.] —**physicochemically** *adv*

physics /fízziks/ *n* the scientific study of matter, energy, force, and motion, and the way they relate to each other (+ *singular verb*) ■ *npl* the physical processes, interactions, qualities, properties or behaviour of something [15C. < PHYSIC; translation of Latin *physica* (plural) < Greek *phusika*, plural of *phusikos* 'of nature' < *phusis* 'nature' < *phuein* 'make grow'.]

physio /fízzi ō/ (*plural* **-os**) *n* (*informal*) **1** a physiotherapist **2** MED = **physiotherapy** [Mid-20C. Shortening of PHYSIO-THERAPY.]

physio- *prefix* physical ○ *physiotherapy* [< Greek *phusis* 'nature']

physiochemical /fízzi ō kémmik'l/ *adj* relating to the underlying molecular organization of life that is manifested as chemical and energy transformations

physiognomy /fízzi ónnəmi/ (*plural* **-mies**) *n* **1** FACIAL FEATURES the features of somebody's face, especially when they are used as indicators of that person's character or temperament **2** JUDGMENT OF CHARACTER FROM FACIAL FEATURES the use of facial features to judge somebody's character or temperament **3** CHARACTER OR APPEARANCE the character or outward appearance of something, e.g. the physical features of a landscape [13C. Via Old French < Greek *phusiognōmonia* < *phusis* 'nature' (see PHYSICS) + *gnomon* 'judge' (see GNOMON).] —**physiognomic** /fízzi ə nómmik/ *adj* —**physiognomically** *adv* —**physiognomist** /fízzi ónnəmist/ *n*

physiography /fízzi óggrəfi/ *n* physical geography (*dated*) —**physiographer** *n* —**physiographic** /fízzi ə gráffik/ *adj* —**physiographically** /fízzi ə gráffikli/ *adv*

physiological /fízzi ə lójik'l/, **physiologic** /fízzi ə lójjik/ *adj* **1** relating to the way that living things function, rather than to their shape or structure **2** relating to physiology —**physiologically** *adv*

physiological saline *n* an aqueous salt solution used to keep cells alive and to administer medication intravenously

physiology /fízzi ólləji/ *n* **1** the branch of biology that deals with the internal workings of living things, including such functions as metabolism, respiration, and reproduction, rather than with their shape or structure **2** the way a particular body or organism works [Mid-16C. Via French *physiologie* or Latin *physiologia* < *phusiologia* < *phusis* 'nature' (see PHYSICS) + *-logia* see -LOGY).] —**physiologist** *n*

physiotherapy /fízzi ō thérrəpi/, **physical therapy** *n* the treatment of injuries and physical disabilities by a trained person under the supervision of a specialist in physical medicine. US term **physical therapy** —**physiotherapeutic** /fízzi ō therə pyóotik/ *adj* —**physiotherapeutically** *adv* —**physiotherapist** /-thérrəpist/ *n*

physique /fi zéek/ *n* the shape and size of somebody's body [Early 19C. < French < *physique* 'physical' < Greek *phusikos* (see PHYSICS).]

physostigmine /físsō stíg meen/, **physostigmin** /-min/ *n* $C_{15}H_{12}N_3O_2$ a crystalline alkaloid. Source: dried leaves of the vine that produces Calabar beans. Use: treatment of glaucoma, to counteract adverse effects of anticholinergic drugs on the central nervous system. [Mid-19C. < modern Latin *Physostigma* < Greek *phusa* 'bladder' + *stigma* (see STIGMA).]

phyt- *prefix* = **phyto-** (*before vowels*)

-phyte *suffix* **1** plant ○ *saprophyte* **2** pathological growth ○ *osteophyte* [< Greek *phuton* (see PHYTO-)]

phyto- *prefix* plant ○ *phytohormone* [Via modern Latin < Greek *phuton* < *phuein* 'make grow' < Indo-European, 'to be']

phytoalexin /fítō ə léksin/ *n* a chemical produced by a plant to protect it from infection by a pathogen or exposure to some agents of stress

phytochemistry /fítō kémmistri/ *n* the chemistry of plants —**phytochemical** *adj* —**phytochemically** *adv* —**phytochemist** *n*

phytochrome /fítōkrōm/ *n* a light-sensitive pigment in plants that controls flowering and germination of seeds [Late 19C. < PHYTO- + Greek *khrōma* 'colour'.]

phytogenic /fítō jénnik/, **phytogenous** /fítójənəss/ *adj* describes substances, such as coal, that are formed from plants

phytogeography /fítōji óggrəfi/ *n* the study of the geographical distribution of plants —**phytogeographer** *n* —**phytogeographic** /-jee ə gráffik/ *adj* —**phytogeographically** /-gráffik'li/ *adv*

phytohormone /fítō háwrmōn/ *n* PLANT SCI = **plant hormone**

phytol /fí tol/ *n* an alcohol derived from chlorophyll from which plants synthesize vitamins E and K

phytology /fí tólləji/ *n* botany (*archaic*)

phyton /fí ton/ *n* the smallest part of a plant, usually a leaf and its stem, that can grow when it has been cut from the parent plant [Mid-19C. < French < Greek *phuton* (see -PHYTE).]

phytopathology /fítō pə thólləji/ *n* the branch of botany that studies plant diseases —**phytopathological** /fítō pathə lójjik'l/ *adj* —**phytopathologically** /-lójjikli/ *adv* —**phytopathologist** /fítō pə thólləjist/ *n*

phytophagous /fī tóffəgəss/ *adj* describes animals, especially insects, that feed on plants —**phytophagy** /fī tóffəji/ *n*

phytoplankton /fítō plángktən/ *n* very small free-floating aquatic plants such as one-celled algae, found in plankton. ◊ **zooplankton** —**phytoplanktonic** /-plangk tónnik/ *adj*

phytoremediation /fítō ri meédi áysh'n/ *n* the process of decontaminating soil by using plants to absorb heavy metals or other pollutants

phytotoxic /fítō tóksik/ *adj* poisonous to plants —**phytotoxicity** /fítō tok síssəti/ *n*

phytotoxin /fítō tóksin/ *n* **1** a poisonous substance obtained from plants such as the drug digitalis **2** something that is poisonous to plants

pi[1] /pī/ *n* **1** the 16th letter of the Greek alphabet **2** a number approximately equal to 3.14159 that is the ratio of the circumference of a circle to its diameter and is represented by the symbol π [Early 19C. < Greek.]

pi[2] /pī/, **pie** *n* **1 JUMBLE OF PRINTER'S TYPE** a pile of printer's type that has been mixed up together **2 DISORDERED MIXTURE** a disorganized combination of things ■ *v* (**pies, piing, pied; pies, pieing, pied**) **1** *vt* **JUMBLE TYPE** to mix printer's type up together **2** *vti* **MAKE OR BECOME JUMBLED** to mix things up in a confusing way or to become mixed up or confused [Mid-17C. < ?]

pi[3] /pī/ *adj* pretending to be very religious or virtuous (*archaic informal*) [Mid-19C. Shortening of PIOUS.]

PI *abbr* **1** Philippines (*international vehicle registration*) **2** *US* private investigator

pia *n* ANAT = **pia mater** —**pial** *adj*

PIA *abbr* peripheral interface adaptor

Piacenza /pya chéntsa/ city in N Italy. Population: 102,161 (1992).

piacular /pī ákyŏŏlər/ *adj* **1** done or offered in order to make up for a sin or sacrilegious action **2** wicked or sinful and requiring the offender or sinner to atone [Early 17C. < Latin *piacularis* < *piaculum* 'atonement' < *piare* 'appease'.]

Piaf /peé af/, **Édith** (1915–63) French singer. Born **Édith Giovanna Gassion**

piaffe /pi áf/ *n* **piaffe, piaffer** a dressage movement performed by a horse in which it trots in one place and raises its legs very high ■ *vi* (**piaffes, piaffing, piaffed**) to perform a dressage movement that involves trotting on the spot with the legs raised high [Mid-18C. < French, < *piaffer* 'to strut'.]

Piaget /pi ázh ay/, **Jean** (1896–1980) Swiss psychologist

pia mater /pía máytər/ *n* the innermost and most delicate of the three membranes (**meninges**) that surround the brain and the spinal cord [14C. < Latin, 'tender mother', translated < Arabic *al-'umm ar-rakika*.]

pianism /peé ənizəm/ *n* piano-playing skill or technique —**pianistic** /peé ə nístik/ *adj*

pianissimo /peé ə níssimō/ *adv* very softly and quietly (*musical direction*) ■ *n* (*plural* **-mos** *or* **-mi** /-mee/) a part of a musical composition that is played very softly [Early 18C. < Italian, 'very quiet' < *piano* (see PIANO[2]).] —**pianissimo** *adj*

pianist /peé ənist/ *n* a player of the piano

piano[1] /pi ánnō/ *n* (*plural* **-os**) **MUSICAL INSTRUMENT WITH KEYBOARD** a large musical instrument with a wooden case and interior containing stretched wires that are played by pressing keys, each attached to a small hammer that strikes the strings. ◊ **grand piano, upright piano** ■ *adj* **1 OF OR FOR PIANO** relating to or played on a piano ○ *a piano sonata* **2 OF OR FOR ENSEMBLE CONTAINING PIANIST** relating to a small musical ensemble that contains a pianist, and usually a violinist and cellist ○ *a piano trio* [Early 19C. < Italian, shortening of PIANOFORTE.]

piano[2] /pyaánō/ *adv* softly and quietly (*musical direction*) ■ *n* (*plural* **-nos** *or* **-ni** /-nee/) a part of a musical composition that is played softly [Late 17C. Via Italian < Latin *planus* 'soft, flat'.] —**piano** *adj*

piano accordion *n* an accordion with a keyboard on one side to play the notes of the melody on —**piano accordionist** *n*

pianoforte /pi ánnō fáwrti/ (*plural* **-tes**) *n* a piano [Mid-18C. < Italian, < *gravecembalo col piano e forte* 'harpsichord with soft and loud'.]

piano hinge *n* a long narrow hinge that has a pin running the length of its joint

piano nobile /pyaánō nóbili/ *n* the first floor of a large residence or public building [< Italian, 'noble floor', because it is high above the ground]

piano quartet *n* an ensemble consisting of a piano and three other instruments, usually a violin, viola, and cello, or a piece of music written for this combination

piano roll *n* a roll of paper with patterns of perforations whose positions determine the sequence of notes played on a player piano

piano stool *n* an adjustable stool for a pianist to sit on and often having a hollow compartment under the seat for storing sheet music

piassava /peé ə saávə/, **piassaba** /-saábə/ *n* **1** a coarse fibre obtained from a Brazilian tree. Use: rope, brooms, brushes. **2** a palm tree that produces piassava. Native to: Brazil. *Attalea funifera* and *Leopoldinia piassaba*. [Mid-19C. Via Portuguese < Tupi *piaçába*.]

piastre /pi ástə/ *n* see table at **currency** [Late 16C. Via French < Italian *piastra (d'argento)* '(silver) plate' < Latin *emplastrum* (see PLASTER).]

Piave /pyaáv e/ river in NE Italy. Length: 220 km/137 mi.

piazza /pi átsə/ (*plural* **-zas**) *n* **1** (*plural* **-ze**) **ITALIAN PUBLIC SQUARE** a large open square, especially one in an Italian town **2 OPEN-SIDED PASSAGEWAY** a covered passageway that has arches on one or both sides and is usually attached to a building, e.g. along the inner walls of a courtyard or quadrangle **3** *US* **PORCH** a veranda or porch, especially one attached to a house (*dated regional*) [Late 16C. Via Italian < Latin *platea* 'open space' (see PLACE).]

pi bond *n* a covalent bond between two atoms and a pair of electrons having orbitals whose greatest overlap is along a plane perpendicular to a line connecting the nuclei of the atoms —**pi-bonding** *adj*

pibroch /peéb rokh/ *n* a piece of music written for the Scottish Highland bagpipes, consisting of a theme and variations, often with a mournful tone [Early 18C. < Gaelic *piobaireachd* 'the art of piping' < English *pipe*.]

pic /pik/ (*plural* **pics** *or* **pix** /piks/), **pick** *n* a picture, especially a photograph, illustration, or cinema film (*informal*) [Late 19C. Shortening of PICTURE.]

pica[1] /píkə/ *n* **1** a unit of measurement for printing type, equal to 12 points or 0.422 cm/0.166 in **2** a linear measure used in typography, equal to about 0.422 cm/0.166 in [15C. < Anglo-Latin, 'church almanac'.]

pica[2] /píkə/ *n* indiscriminate craving for and eating of substances such as paint chips, clay, plaster, or dirt [Mid-16C. < Latin, 'magpie', translation of Greek *kissa*.]

Picabia /pi cábbi ə/, **Francis** (1879–1953) French painter

picador /píkə dawr/ *n* a bullfighter on horseback, who attacks the bull with a spear early in the fight, making it easier for the main bullfighter (**matador**) to kill with his sword [Late 18C. < Spanish < *picar* 'prick, pierce'.]

pica em *n* PRINTING = **pica**[1] *n.* 1

picante /pi kán tay/ *adj* spicy, especially in being served with a sauce that contains tomatoes, onions, peppers, vinegar, and spices [< Italian *piccante* < present participle of *piccare* 'to sting']

Picard /píkaard/ *n* **1** a person who was born or brought up in Picardy in N France **2** the dialect of French spoken in Picardy [14C. < French.] —**Picard** *adj*

picaresque /píkə résk/ *adj* **1 TYPICAL OF ROGUES** relating to or typical of rogues or scoundrels **2 HAVING ROGUE AS HERO** belonging to or characteristic of a type of prose fiction that features the adventures of a roguish hero and usually has a simple plot divided into separate episodes ■ *n* **PICARESQUE FICTION** prose fiction featuring the adventures of a roguish hero [Early 19C. Via French < Spanish *picaresco* < *picaro* 'rogue' < assumed Vulgar Latin *piccare* 'to prick'.]

picaroon /píkə róon/, **pickaroon** *n* a rogue (*archaic literary*) ■ *vi* to live the adventurous life of a pirate, thief, swindler, or scoundrel (*archaic literary*) [Early 17C. < Spanish *picaron* 'great rogue' < *picaro* (see PICARESQUE).]

Picasso /pikássō/, **Pablo** (1881–1973) Spanish painter and sculptor

picayune /píkə yóon/ *adj US, Can* (*informal*) **1 TRIFLING** of very little importance **2 SMALL-MINDED** tending to fuss about unimportant things and to be childishly spiteful ■ *n* **1** *US, Can* **TRIFLING THING** something unimportant or of little value (*informal*) **2** *US* **SMALL COIN** a low-value coin, especially a five-cent piece (*archaic informal*) [Early 19C. Via French *picaillon*, a Piedmontese coin < Provençal *picaioun*.]

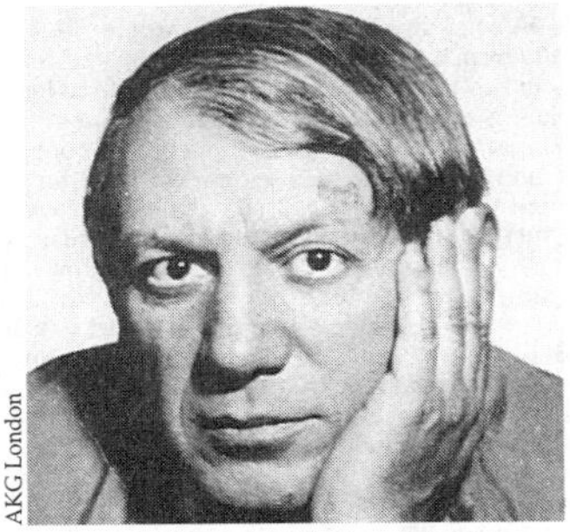

Pablo Picasso: Photographed in 1933 by Man Ray

piccalilli /píkə lílli/ *n* pickle consisting of mixed vegetables, especially cauliflower, small whole onions, and cucumber, in a sauce containing mustard and vinegar [Mid-18C. Probably < PICKLE + CHILLI.]

piccaninny /píkə nínni/ (*plural* **-nies**) *n* (*taboo*) **1** a highly offensive term for a small Black child **2** *Aus* a highly offensive term for an Aboriginal child [Mid-17C. < Caribbean creole, probably < Portuguese *pequenino* 'very small' < *pequeno* 'small'.]

Piccard /pík aar/, **Auguste** (1884–1962) Swiss physicist

piccata /pi kaátə/ *adj* describes meats sautéed in slices and served in a spicy lemon and butter sauce ○ *veal piccata* [Via Italian < French *piqué*, past participle of *piquer* 'attach ingredients, to lard', literally 'to prick']

piccolo /píkəlō/ (*plural* **-los**) *n* a musical instrument, the smallest member of the flute family, with a range one octave higher than the standard flute [Mid-19C. < Italian, 'small'.]

pichiciego /píchissi áygō/ (*plural* **-go** *or* **-gos**), **pichiciago** (*plural* **-go** *or* **-gos**) *n* **1** a very small silky-haired armadillo with pink armour. Native to: Argentina. *Chlamyphorus truncatus*. **2** a large armadillo with yellowish-brown armour and coarse whitish hair. Native to: South America. *Burmeisteria retusa*. [Early 19C. < Spanish *pichiego*, probably < Guarani *pichey*, a type of armadillo, literally 'small' + Spanish *ciego* 'sightless' < Latin *caecus*.]

pick[1] /pik/ *v* **1** *vt* **REMOVE SOMETHING FROM PLANT** to remove something, especially in quantity and by hand, from a plant on which it has grown ○ *picking strawberries* **2** *vt* **STRIP SOMETHING OF FRUIT OR FLOWERS** to strip a plant or all the plants in a particular place of fruit or flowers ○ *The bushes nearest the path had already been picked.* **3** *vt* **CHOOSE** to take or decide to take one or more things or people from a larger number ○ *Pick three people for your team.* **4** *vt* **REMOVE SOMETHING IN SMALL PIECES** to remove something bit by bit from the surface or middle of something using a sharp or pointed object such as a fingernail or a beak **5** *vt* **SCRAPE BODY PART WITH FINGERNAIL** to use a fingernail to loosen and remove something, or to loosen and remove something attached to the surface of a part of the body ○ *pick a scab* **6** *vt* **OPEN SOMETHING WITHOUT PROPER KEY** to use a special device or pointed instrument to open a lock, usually illegally ○ *pick a lock* **7** *vt* **UNDO** to loosen, unfasten, or separate something into disconnected parts, especially something that was sewn together ○ *pick a seam apart* **8** *vi* **FIND FAULT** to be petty or fault-finding **9** *vt* **START FIGHT OR QUARREL** to begin a fight or quarrel with somebody, usually deliberately **10** *vt* **PLUCK OR PLAY BY PLUCKING** to pluck the strings of a stringed instrument or to play a tune on such an instrument in this way ■ *n* **1 CHOICE** the act or right of choosing somebody or something ○ *I was first so I got to take my pick.* **2 BEST** the very best of a wide selection of people or things ○ *the pick of the bunch* **3 CROP PORTION** the amount of a crop gathered by hand at one time [13C. Probably < assumed Old English *pīcian* 'to prick', Old Icelandic *pikka*.] —**pickable** *adj* —**picker** *n* ◇ **pick and choose** to select, or be in a position to select, the best of several choices ◇ **pick your way** to step very carefully through a dirty, untidy, or dangerous area of ground

pick at *vt* **1 EAT LITTLE FOOD** to eat very little of a meal ○ *He only picked at his breakfast.* **2 SCRAPE SOMETHING WITH FINGERNAILS** to scrape away surface pieces of something with the fingernails **3 NAG** to nag or criticize somebody in a petty way (*informal*)

pick off *vt* to shoot a number of targets one by one, usually from a distance
pick on *vt* **1** to blame, criticize, or bully somebody repeatedly in a way that is considered unfair or unkind **2** to choose somebody or something from among others
pick out *vt* **1 CHOOSE** to choose or select something from among others ○ *She picked out her favourite chocolate.* **2 IDENTIFY FROM CROWD OR BACKGROUND** to recognize or distinguish somebody or something from among others or against a background that makes this difficult ○ *I couldn't pick him out in the crowd.* **3 MAKE STAND OUT** to make something stand out against its background, especially by giving it a strikingly different colour (*often passive*) ○ *The design was picked out in green.* **4 PLAY NOTE BY NOTE** to play a tune slowly, note by note
pick over *vt* to go through something, selecting the best items or discarding unwanted items
pick up *v* **1** *vt* **LIFT** to take hold of and raise or remove something or somebody **2** *vti* **GATHER DROPPED THINGS** to collect things that have been dropped or have fallen to the ground **3** *vr* **REGAIN UPRIGHT OR STRONGER POSITION** to stand up after falling down, or recover strength, courage, or sense of purpose after a setback **4** *vti* **TAKE ON PASSENGERS** to stop a vehicle and let a passenger or passengers in ○ *picked up a hitchhiker* **5** *vt* **CLAIM** to collect something such as items left for repair or goods ordered from a shop ○ *pick up a library book* **6** *vt* **PAY FOR** to take on the responsibility for providing payment for something such as a bill **7** *vt* **BUY SOMETHING ON IMPULSE** to buy something in a casual or unplanned way **8** *vt* **ACQUIRE SOMETHING CHEAPLY OR EASILY** to get or buy something easily or cheaply **9** *vt* **ACQUIRE SOMETHING CASUALLY** to acquire something casually, without meaning to and without knowing it ○ *has picked up some bad habits* **10** *vt* **CATCH A DISEASE** to become infected with a disease **11** *vt* **NOTICE** to notice something or become aware of it **12** *vt* **FIND** to find and follow something, such as a scent or trail ○ *pick up the scent* **13** *vt* **UNDERSTAND** to understand something that is communicated indirectly **14** *vt* **LEARN** to learn something in a casual or unsystematic way, e.g. by frequently hearing it, seeing it done, or trying to do it **15** *vi* **BECOME BETTER** to improve after being ill, injured, bad, or unsuccessful (*informal*) ○ *He picked up quickly* **16** *vti* **ACCELERATE** to increase in strength, speed, or intensity, or to cause something to increase ○ *Her speed picked up.* **17** *vti* **RETURN TO SOMETHING AGAIN** to continue something at a later time, usually after an interruption or break, or to be continued in this way ○ *She wanted to pick up her career.* **18** *vt* **FIND SEXUAL PARTNER** to make the acquaintance of a stranger, often in a public place, usually for sexual purposes (*informal*) ○ *picked him up in a pub* **19** *vt* **ARREST** to arrest somebody (*informal*) ○ *He was picked up on a burglary charge.* **20** *vt* **RECEIVE SIGNAL** to receive something such as a radio or television signal or a radar image on a piece of equipment
pick up on *vt* (*informal*) **1** to notice something, and perhaps mention or question it **2** to criticize somebody for an action or behaviour, often in a condescending way

pick² /pik/ *n* **1 TOOL FOR BREAKING UP HARD SURFACES** a tool used for breaking up hard surfaces, consisting of a long handle and a curved metal head that is pointed at one or both ends **2 SMALL TOOL FOR BREAKING INTO PIECES** a small tool used to break up something into smaller pieces (*often in combination*) **3 SHARP TOOL FOR PICKING** a sharp tool for cleaning something such as the teeth or for getting into small places, as in a lock (*often in combination*) **4** MUSIC = **plectrum** ■ *vi* **WORK WITH PICK** to use a pick or do labouring work with a pick [14C. Variant of PIKE².]

pick³ /pik/ *n* = **pic** (*informal*)

pickaback /píkə bak/ *n, adj, adv* a piggyback (*dated*)

pickaninny *n* US = **piccaninny** (*taboo offensive*)

pickaxe /pík aks/ *n* a tool consisting of a long handle and a metal head that usually has one pointed end and one flattened end, used for breaking up something hard or cutting something [13C. Middle English *pikois* < Old French *picois* (ultimately < Latin *picus* 'woodpecker'), altered in the 15C by association with AXE.]

pickerel /píkərəl/ (*plural* **-el** *or* **-els**) *n* **1** a predatory fish of the pike family, popular as a game fish. Native to: North America. *Esox niger.* **2** a young pike [14C. Literally 'small pike'; partly after Anglo-Latin *picerellus*.]

picket /píkit/ *n* **1 POINTED POST STUCK IN THE GROUND** a post or plank with a pointed end that is hammered into the ground, e.g. as a marker, as a support for a fence, or to tether an animal **2 picket, picquet, piquet SOLDIER OR SOLDIERS ON GUARD** a soldier or small body of troops used to occupy ground of tactical importance **3 PROTESTER OR PROTESTERS OUTSIDE BUILDING** a person or group of people demonstrating or protesting outside a building, e.g. a striking worker who tries to persuade other people not to enter during a strike ■ *v* **1** *vt* **ENCLOSE OR MARK SOMETHING WITH STAKES** to enclose or mark something with wooden stakes driven into the ground, or enclose it with a picket fence **2** *vt* **POST GUARDS** to post troops as guards **3** *vt* **GUARD** to patrol or guard a place, especially a military site or position **4** *vti* **HOLD PROTEST OUTSIDE PLACE** to hold a demonstration or protest outside a place, e.g. as part of a strike, in order to persuade others not to enter a place of business **5** *vt* **TETHER ANIMAL** to tether a horse or other animal [Late 17C. < French *piquet* 'pointed stake' < *piquer* 'prick, pierce' (see PICK¹).] —**picketer** *n*

picket fence *n* a fence made of pointed stakes or posts driven into the ground and connected by one or more horizontal bars

picket line *n* a line of people who are protesting outside a building, e.g. striking workers outside their workplace, who attempt to persuade other people not to enter

Pickford /píkfərd/, **Mary** (1893–1979) Canadian-born US actor and producer. Born **Gladys Marie Smith**. Known as **America's Sweetheart**

pickings /píkingz/ *npl* things available to be earned or taken in a particular place ○ *easy pickings*

pickle /pík'l/ *n* **1 SAVOURY PRESERVE** a lumpy mixture of chopped vegetables, typically cauliflower, onions, cucumbers, and gherkins, preserved in vinegar or brine to give it a sharp or spicy flavour and eaten with other foods **2 VEGETABLE PRESERVED IN VINEGAR** a small vegetable, such as an onion or gherkin, that has acquired a sharp taste by being preserved in vinegar or brine, usually with added spices (*usually plural*) **3 LIQUID FOR PRESERVING FOOD** liquid, usually brine or a vinegar solution, used to preserve cold foods such as vegetables or fish **4 CLEANING OR PROCESSING SOLUTION** an industrial or commercial solution used to clean or process something **5 AWKWARD SITUATION** a difficult or problematic situation (*informal*) **6 TROUBLESOME PERSON** a mildly troublesome person, especially a naughty child (*informal*) **7 pickle, puckle** *Scotland* **SMALL AMOUNT** a small amount (*informal*) ■ *vt* (**-les, -ling, -led**) **1 PRESERVE FOOD** to preserve food, especially vegetables or fish, in vinegar, brine, or another solution **2 DIP OR SOAK SOMETHING IN LIQUID** to clean or process something by dipping or soaking it in a liquid [14C. < Middle Low German *pekel* < ?] —**pickler** *n*

pickled /pík'ld/ *adj* **1** preserved in vinegar, brine, or another liquid **2** inebriated (*informal*)

picklock /pík lok/ *n* **1** a tool used to open locks without using the key **2** an opener of locks without using a key, especially a burglar

pick-me-up *n* something that lifts the spirits and energizes somebody, especially a stimulating drink (*informal*)

pick 'n' mix /píkən míks/ *n* a wide range of items, especially sweets, cheeses, or salads, from which you choose whatever combination you want (*hyphenated before nouns*)

pickoff /pík of/ *n* an electronic device that senses movement used, e.g. in the guidance system of an aircraft or as part of a surveillance system

pickpocket /pík pokit/ *n* a thief who steals from people's pockets and bags in public places, usually unnoticed —**pickpocketing** *n*

pick-up *n* **1 LIFTING OR COLLECTING** the raising, gathering, collection, or removal of something to be taken somewhere else **2 SOMEBODY OR SOMETHING TAKEN SOMEWHERE** somebody or something that is moved from one place to another **3 HITCHHIKER** a hitchhiker (*informal*) **4** AUTOMOT = **pick-up truck** **5 IMPROVEMENT OR INCREASE** an improvement or increase (*informal*) **6** BEVERAGES = **pick-me-up** **7 PROSPECTIVE SEXUAL PARTNER** somebody met casually with the aim of developing a sexual relationship (*informal*) **8 ARREST** the taking of somebody into custody by a police officer (*informal*) **9** *US* **POWER TO ACCELERATE** the ability of a vehicle to accelerate quickly (*informal*) **10 TONE ARM** the tone arm of a record player **11 pick-up, pick-up arm PART OF TONE ARM** a device inside the tone arm of a record player that converts the stylus's vibrations into electrical signals that are converted into sound **12 CONVERTER OF VIBRATIONS ON MUSICAL INSTRUMENT** an electromagnetic device that converts the vibrations from the strings of an electric guitar or other amplified instrument into electrical signals that are amplified into sound **13 RECEIVING OF LIGHT OR SOUND WAVES** the receiving and gathering of light or sound waves that are to be converted into electrical impulses **14 RECEIVER FOR LIGHT OR SOUND WAVES** a device used to receive light or sound waves ■ *adj US* **INFORMAL AND IMPROMPTU** informally organized on the spot and made up of or involving people available at the time

pick-up truck, pick-up *n* a light truck with a low-sided open back and a tailgate that drops down for easy loading and unloading

Pickwickian /pik wíki ən/ *adj* **1** generous, naive, or benevolent **2** not literal or typical in usage or meaning [Mid-19C. < the character of Mr Pickwick in Charles Dickens' novel *The Pickwick Papers* (1837).]

picky /píki/ (**-ier, -iest**) *adj* having specific and inflexible likes and dislikes and, therefore, hard to please or satisfy [Mid-19C. < PICK¹.] —**pickily** *adv* —**pickiness** *n*

pick-your-own *adj* describes crops that can be picked directly by customers, or such a service offered to customers

picloram /píklə ram/ *n* $C_6H_3Cl_3N_2O_2$ a herbicide permitted for use on plants other than crops, such as the grass of playing fields [Mid-20C. < PICOLINE + CHLOR- + AMINE.]

picnic /píknik/ *n* **1 MEAL TAKEN AND EATEN OUTDOORS** an informal meal prepared for eating in the open air or the food that makes up such a meal **2 EASY OR PLEASANT THING** something easy to do or pleasant to experience (*informal*) ○ *Moving house was no picnic.* ■ *vi* (**-nics, -nicking, -nicked**) **HAVE A PICNIC** to eat an informal meal outdoors [Mid-18C. < French *pique-nique*.] —**picnicker** *n*

~~**picnicing**~~ incorrect spelling of **picnicking**

picnic races *npl Aus* horseraces for amateur riders, usually local farmers or farmhands, that are major social events in rural areas of Australia

pico- *prefix* **1** (*symbol* **p**) one million millionth (10^{-12}) ○ *picofarad* **2** very small ○ *picornavirus* [Via Spanish *pico* 'beak, small amount' < Latin *beccus*; ultimately of Celtic origin]

Pico della Mirandola /peékō déllə mi rándōlə/, **Giovanni, Count** (1463–94) Italian humanist philosopher

picofarad /peékō farəd, -farad/ *n* (*symbol* **pF**) one million millionth of a farad

picogram /peékō gram/ *n* one million millionth of a gram

picoline /píkə leen/ *n* C_6H_7N a colourless liquid. Source: coal tar, bone oil. Use: solvent, in organic synthesis. [Mid-19C. < Latin *pic-* 'pitch' + *oleum* 'oil' + -INE.] —**picolinic** /píkə línnik/ *adj*

picomole /peékōmōl/ *n* one million millionth of a mole

picornavirus /pi káwrnə vīrəss/ *n* a small infectious virus, such as the virus that causes polio or the common cold. Family: Picornaviridae. [Mid-20C. < PICO- + RNA + VIRUS.]

picosecond /peékō sekənd/ *n* a million millionth of a second

picot /peékō/ *n* a loop that forms a pattern with others, e.g. in lace ■ *vt* to embroider small loops on fabric [Early 17C. < French, 'small point' < *pic* 'peak, point' < *piquer* 'to prick' (see PICK¹).]

picotee /píkə teé/ *n* a flower, especially a carnation or tulip, that has petals edged with a different, usually darker colour [Early 18C. < French *picotée*, feminine past participle of *picoter* 'to prick' < *picot* (see PICOT).]

picowave /peékō wayv/ (**-waves, -waving, -waved**) *vt* to expose food to radiation in order to kill insects, worms, or bacteria

picquet *n* **1** MIL = **picket** *n.* **2** **2** CARDS = **piquet**

picr- *prefix* = **picro-** (*before vowels*)

picrate /pík rayt/ *n* a salt or ester of picric acid [Mid-19C. < Greek *pikros* 'bitter' + -ATE.]

picric acid /píkrik-/ *n* $C_6H_3N_3O_7$ a strong toxic yellow crystalline acid. Use: dyes, antiseptics, high explosives. [< Greek *pikros* 'bitter' + -IC]

picrite /pík rīt/ *n* a dark-coloured igneous rock made up primarily of coarse grains of olivine and other ferromagnesian minerals [Early 19C. < Greek *pikros* 'bitter' + -ITE¹.]

picro- *prefix* **1** bitter ○ *picrotoxin* **2** picric acid ○ *picrate* [< Greek *pikros* 'sharp' < Indo-European, 'to cut']

picrotoxin /píkrə tóksin/ *n* $C_{30}H_{34}O_{13}$ a bitter crystalline compound. Source: seeds of an Indian vine. Use: antidote to barbiturate poisoning.

Pict /pikt/ *n* a member of an ancient people who occupied lands north of the Forth and Clyde Rivers in Scotland from the 1st to the 4th centuries [Pre-12C. < late Latin *Picti* (plural) < ?]

Pictish /píktish/ *adj* relating to the Picts, their culture, or their language ■ *n* an extinct language spoken in Scotland [Late 16C]

pictograph /píktō graaf, -graf/, **pictogram** /-gram/ *n* **1** a graphic symbol or picture representing a word or idea in some writing systems **2** a chart or diagram that uses symbols or pictures to represent values [Mid-19C. < Latin *pictus* (see PICTURE) + -GRAPH.] —**pictographer** /pik tóggrəfər/ *n* —**pictographic** /píktə gráffik/ *adj* —**pictographically** /-gráffikli/ *adv* —**pictography** /pik tóggrəfi/ *n*

Picton /píktən/ town in the NE of the South Island, New Zealand. Population: 3,061 (1996).

Pictor /píktər/ *n* an inconspicuous constellation of the southern hemisphere. See illustration at **constellation**

pictorial /pik táwri əl/ *adj* **1 OF PICTURES** relating to, composed of, or shown by pictures **2 ILLUSTRATED** containing illustrations or photographs, as opposed to writing or text **3 DESCRIPTIVE** describes language that conjures up vivid images ■ *n* **HIGHLY ILLUSTRATED PERIODICAL** a newspaper or magazine that has many pictures in it, especially one with far more pictures than text [Mid-17C. < late Latin *pictorius* < Latin *pictor* 'painter' < *pictus* (see PICTURE).] —**pictoriality** /pik táwri állati/ *n* —**pictorially** /pik táwri əli/ *adv* —**pictorialness** *n*

picture /píkchər/ *n* **1 SOMETHING DRAWN OR PAINTED** a shape or set of shapes and lines drawn, painted, or printed on paper, canvas, or some other flat surface, especially shapes that represent a recognizable form or object **2 PHOTO** a photograph **3 TV IMAGE** the image on a television screen **4 FILM** a cinema film or motion picture **5 MENTAL IMAGE** a vivid image or impression in the mind of how somebody or something looks **6 ARTISTIC DESCRIPTION OR REPRESENTATION** a description or representation of something in writing, in a film, in music, or some other art form **7 OBSERVED SITUATION** a situation in its context ○ *get the picture* **8 EMBODIMENT OR EPITOME** a typical or perfect example of the way something looks, or somebody or something that embodies a quality or state perfectly ○ *They're the picture of the happily married couple.* **9 SOMEBODY WHO CLOSELY RESEMBLES ANOTHER** a person who closely resembles somebody else ○ *The daughter was the absolute picture of the grandmother.* **10 BEAUTIFUL THING** something that is beautiful to look at ■ **pictures** *npl* **CINEMA** the cinema as entertainment, rather than an industry (*informal dated*) ■ *vt* (**-tures, -turing, -tured**) **1 IMAGINE** to imagine or have an image of somebody or something in mind **2 DESCRIBE** to describe somebody or something in a particular way **3 FEATURE PICTURE OF** to feature a picture, especially a photograph, of somebody or something in a newspaper, magazine, or book (*often passive*) [15C. < Latin *pictura* < *pictus*, past participle of *pingere* 'to paint'.]

LITERARY LINK ***The Picture of Dorian Gray***, a novel (1890) by Oscar Wilde. In Wilde's update of the Faust legend, the decadent young gentleman Dorian Gray trades his soul for eternal youth and beauty, but is subsequently tormented by a portrait of himself that constantly changes to reflect the ravages of time and of his debauched lifestyle.

picture book *n* a highly illustrated book, especially one for children, written in a simple style

picture card *n* CARDS = **court card**

picture hanger *n* HOUSEHOLD = **picture hook**

picture hat *n* a woman's elaborately decorated hat with a very broad brim, of the kind often featured in informal portraits of women painted in the 18th century

picture hook *n* a hook that is nailed to a wall or suspended from a rail fixed to the wall and used to hang a picture

picture house *n* a cinema (*dated*)

picture library *n* a place where photographs and other images are stored, from which they may be borrowed for use in books, magazines, and newspapers

picture moulding *n* carved or moulded wood used to make picture frames

picture palace *n* a cinema (*dated*)

picture postcard *n* a postcard with a picture, often a photograph of a landmark or landscape, on one side (*dated*)

picture-postcard *adj* very attractive, like the scenes typically photographed for picture postcards

picture rail *n* a strip of wood or plaster, usually a cornice-like moulding, fixed high up around the walls of a room, from which you can hang pictures

picture researcher *n* somebody whose job is finding the photographs, drawings, and other illustrative material for a book or magazine, using picture libraries and other sources

picturesque /píkchə résk/ *adj* **1 VERY ATTRACTIVE** visually pleasing enough to be the subject of a painting or photograph **2 VIVID** so accurate or detailed as to evoke a clear mental image of what has been described **3 OBSCENE** containing a lot of swearwords (*used euphemistically*) **4 DISTINCTIVE** having a pleasingly distinctive or unusual atmosphere ○ *We ate lunch in a picturesque fishing village.* ■ *n* **PLEASING OR DISTINCTIVE THINGS** things that are unusually pleasing or distinctive, spoken of collectively [Early 18C. Anglicization (after PICTURE) of French *pittoresque* < Italian *pittoresco* < *pittore* 'painter' < Latin *pictor* (see PICTORIAL).] —**picturesquely** *adv* —**picturesqueness** *n*

picture tube *n* MEDIA = **tube** *n.* 7

picture window *n* a large window, usually with a single pane of glass, especially one that has a pleasant view

picture writing *n* **1** a writing system such as that of Chinese that uses symbols or pictures to represent whole words or ideas rather than individual sounds **2** the reporting of an event or telling of a story using pictures instead of words, e.g. in ancient cave paintings

picul /pík'l/ *n* a unit of weight used in Southeast Asia, especially a Chinese unit equal to 60 kg/133 lb [Late 16C. < Malay and Javanese *pikul* 'load'.]

piculet /píkyoolət/ (*plural* **-let** *or* **-lets**) *n* a very small tropical woodpecker. Genus: *Picumnus*. [Mid-19C. Literally 'small small woodpecker' < Latin *picus* 'woodpecker'.]

ϟ**PID** *abbr* **1** pelvic inflammatory disease **2** personal identification device

piddle /pídd'l/ *v* (**-dles, -dling, -dled**) **1** *vi* **URINATE** to urinate (*informal; usually by or to children*) **2** *vti* **DO THINGS HAPHAZARDLY** to do something in a casual, unhurried, or disorganized way, often spending time on unimportant things ■ *n* (*plural* **-dles**) **URINATION** an act of urinating (*informal; usually by or to children*) [Late 18C. < ?] —**piddler** *n*

piddling /pídd'ling/ *adj* very small, insignificant, or trivial (*informal*) [Mid-16C. < PIDDLE.] —**piddlingly** *adv*

piddock /píddək/ *n* a saltwater mollusc that has a hinged shell, like the mussel or clam, but with serrated edges that it uses to bore into rock and wood. Family: Pholadidae. [Mid-19C. < ?]

pidgin /píjjin/ *n* a simplified language made up of elements of two or more languages, used as a communication tool between speakers whose native languages are different [Early 19C. < Chinese, alteration of BUSINESS.] —**pidginization** /píjji nī záysh'n/ *n* —**pidginize** /píjji nīz/ *vt*

pidgin English *n* a pidgin containing elements of English, especially one formerly used between Chinese people and Europeans, or one currently spoken in West Africa and some Pacific islands

pi-dog *n* ZOOL = **pye-dog**

PIDS *abbr* primary immune deficiency syndrome

pie¹ /pī/ *n* **1** a baked dish consisting of a filling such as chopped meat or fruit enclosed in or covered with pastry and usually cooked in a container **2** something regarded as a resource to be shared or divided up ○ *Our competitors are always looking for a larger piece of the overseas pie.* [14C. < ?] ◇ **pie in the sky** something described very attractively that is not likely to happen or materialize

pie² /pī/ *n* PRINTING = **pi**²

pie³ /pī/ (*plural* **pie** *or* **pies**) *n* a magpie (*archaic*) [14C. Via French < Latin *pica* 'magpie'.]

piebald /pī bawld/ *adj* used to describe a horse whose coat has patches of two or more contrasting colours, especially black and white. US term **pinto** *adj.* ■ *n* (*plural* **-bald** *or* **-balds**) a piebald horse. US term **pinto** *n.* [Late 16C. < PIE³ (from the resemblance to a magpie's plumage) + BALD.]

piece /peess/ *n* **1 PART DETACHED FROM LARGER WHOLE** a part that has been broken, torn, or cut from a larger whole **2 PORTION OR SERVING** a portion or serving from a larger block or whole **3 INDIVIDUAL ITEM OR ARTICLE** an item or article of a particular kind or class ○ *an expensive piece of equipment* **4 INTERCONNECTING PART** any of a set of parts that fit together to form a whole or unit ○ *a 500-piece jigsaw* ○ *took the radio to pieces* **5 EXAMPLE** an instance or example of something, often something abstract such as luck **6 DECLARATION OF OPINION** a statement of opinion on a particular subject, event, or situation ○ *At least I said my piece.* **7 ARTISTIC WORK** a single artistic work, e.g. a musical composition, play, or painting ○ *a piano piece* ○ *a piece of music* **8 PUBLISHED ARTICLE** an article in a newspaper or magazine ○ *a piece of writing* **9 COIN** a coin of a specified value ○ *a fifty-pence piece* **10 OBJECT MOVED IN BOARD GAME** an object that a player of board games moves on the board **11 FIREARM** a gun, especially a handgun (*slang*) **12 OFFENSIVE TERM** an offensive term for a woman (*slang*) **13** *US* **OFFENSIVE TERM** an offensive term for sexual intercourse (*slang*) **14** *US, Can* **ESTIMATE OF DISTANCE** an unspecified distance (*informal*) ○ *You go down the road a piece and then you come to the bridge.* **15 SLICE OF BREAD OR SNACK** a slice of bread, a sandwich, or a snack taken to be eaten somewhere, especially school or work (*regional*) **16** *ANZ* **FLEECE** a fragment of fleece (*often plural*) ■ *vt* (**pieces, piecing, pieced**) **1 WORK OUT** to put something together gradually, bit by bit ○ *We finally managed to piece together the events of that night.* **2 MEND** to mend something by patching it [12C. < Old French *piece*, probably of Gaulish origin.] ◇ **fall** *or* **go to pieces 1** to become broken into small bits **2** to become unable to cope ◇ **pull somebody** *or* **something to pieces** to criticize somebody or something severely

SPELLCHECK See ***peace***.

piece out *vt* to share or dispense something, such as food, in a makeshift, piecemeal way

pièce de résistance /pi éss de re zís toNss/ (*plural* **pièces de résistance** /pi éss de re zís toNss/) *n* **1** the most impressive thing or something that brings the greatest pride or satisfaction **2** the most important dish served at a meal (*formal*) [Late 18C. < French, 'piece of resistance', originally applied to the most substantial dish in a meal.]

piece-dyed *adj* dyed after being woven

piece goods *npl* fabrics made and sold in standard lengths

piecemeal /peéss meel/ *adv* **1 GRADUALLY** little by little **2 IN PARTS** in separate parts or fragments ■ *adj* **DONE BIT BY BIT** done in a disorganized or fragmentary way ○ *His novel is a ragtag, piecemeal work.* [13C. < PIECE + obsolete *-meal* 'measure' < Old English *mǣl* 'measure, meal' (see MEAL¹).]

piece of cake *n* something that is very easy to do (*informal*) [< the easiness of eating cake, a soft food]

piece of eight *n* an old Spanish gold coin worth eight reals

piece of piss *n* an offensive term for something that is very easy to do (*slang*)

piece of work *n* somebody or something remarkable or outstanding

piecework /peéss wurk/ *n* work that is paid by the amount rather than by the time spent doing it

piechart /pī chaart/ *n* a diagrammatic representation of a group shown as a circle divided into sections by straight lines from its centre with areas proportional to the relative size of the quantity represented

pied-à-terre /pi áyd aa taír, peé edaa táir/ (*plural* **pieds-à-terre**) *n* a small flat or house used as a second home for holidays or business purposes [< French, 'foot to earth']

piedmont /peéd mont/ *n* a region at the base of a mountain range ■ *adj* lying or formed at the base of a mountain range [Mid-19C. < *Piedmont*, hilly region of the eastern US, after *Piemonte*, region of NW Italy.]

Piedmont Plateau /peéd mont-/ upland region of the E United States, extending from New York State to Alabama between the Appalachian Mountains and the Atlantic Coastal Plain

Pied Piper /pīd pīpər/ *n* **1** a visiting piper in German folklore whose entrancing music rid the town of Hamelin of its rats **2 Pied Piper, pied piper** somebody who attracts supporters and followers, especially by making unrealistic promises

LITERARY LINK ***The Pied Piper of Hamelin***, a poem (1842) by Robert Browning. Based on a medieval legend, it tells the story of a piper who successfully rids a town of rats by luring the animals into a river with his music. When the citizens refuse to pay him for his services, he uses the same technique to abduct their children. The term *pied piper*, a charismatic leader who makes attractive but false promises, is taken from the title and main character of this poem.

pied wagtail *n* 1 a small bird with black-and-white plumage and a long black tail. Native to: Europe. *Motacilla alba yarrellii.* 2 a long-tailed black-and-white bird. Native to: Africa. *Motacilla aguimp.*

pie-eyed *adj* very drunk (*informal*)

pier /peer/ *n* 1 **SEASIDE STRUCTURE** a platform built on stilts jutting out into a body of water, used as a boat jetty, a place from which to fish, or as an entertainment centre 2 **VERTICAL STRUCTURAL SUPPORT** a pillar, especially a rectangular one supporting the end of an arch, lintel, or vault 3 **BRIDGE SUPPORT** a vertical structural support between two spans of a bridge 4 **WALL BETWEEN ADJACENT DOORS** an area of wall between two adjacent doors, windows, or other openings 5 **COLUMN PROJECTING FROM WALL** a column of masonry projecting from a wall 6 **WALL REINFORCEMENT** a vertical structure, usually of masonry, built against a wall to support it 7 **BREAKWATER** a barrier built out to sea to protect a harbour from heavy waves [12C. < Anglo-Latin *pera*.]

SPELLCHECK See *peer*.

pierce /peerss/ (**pierces, piercing, pierced**) *v* 1 *vti* **BORE INTO** to penetrate through or into something with a sharp pointed object 2 *vt* **PUT HOLE IN** to make a hole through something ○ *She had her ears pierced.* 3 *vti* **PENETRATE A BARRIER** to break through a barrier of some kind, e.g. a defensive line or security system 4 *vti* **GAIN SIGHT OR KNOWLEDGE** to perceive something with the eyes or the mind 5 *vti* **PENETRATE SOMETHING WITH SOUND OR LIGHT** to sound or shine suddenly and sharply through something, such as silence or darkness ○ *A dreadful scream pierced the silence.* 6 *vt* **AFFECT DEEPLY** to have a sudden intense, often painful effect on somebody ○ *A stab of fear pierced his heart.* [13C. Via French *percer* < Latin *pertundere* 'bore through' < *tundere* 'to bore'.] —**piercer** *n*

Pierce /peerss/, **Franklin** (1804–69) US statesman

piercing /peérssing/ *adj* 1 **PENETRATING** with an unpleasantly intense quality ○ *a piercing cry* 2 **PERCEPTIVE** capable of perceiving acutely ○ *her piercing gaze* 3 **INTENSELY COLD** with a sharp deeply chilling cold ○ *a piercing wind* ■ *n* 1 **MAKING HOLES FOR RINGS IN BODY** the practice of piercing holes in parts of the body so that rings or studs can be inserted ○ *body piercing* 2 **HOLE FOR RING IN BODY** a hole pierced in a part of the body to take a ring or stud ○ *She had piercings on her eyebrow and nose.* —**piercingly** *adv*

Pierian Spring /pī eéri ən-/ *n* in Greek mythology, the spring at Pieria in ancient Macedonia that was sacred to the Muses, who lived there, and gave poetic inspiration to anyone who drank from it

Piero della Francesca /pyáirō déllə fran chéskə/ (1420?–92) Italian painter

Pierre /peer/ capital of South Dakota, in the central part of the state. Population: 13,267 (1998 estimate).

Pierrot /peérō/ *n* 1 a character in traditional French pantomime. He is a white-faced clown with a white costume and pointed hat, and is often represented as sad or crying. 2 **pierrot, Pierrot** any clown with a white face and a baggy white costume [Mid-18C. < French, 'little Peter' < *Pierre* 'Peter'.]

Pietà /peé e taá/, **pietà** *n* a painting or sculpture of the Virgin Mary mourning over Jesus Christ's dead body [Mid-17C. Via Italian < Latin *pietas* (see PIETY).]

Pietermaritzburg /peétər márrits burg/ capital of Kwazulu-Natal Province, South Africa. Population: 156,473 (1991).

pietism /pī ətizəm/ *n* 1 devotion to a deity or deities and observance of religious principles in everyday life 2 excessive or insincere religious devotion [Early 19C. < PIETISM.] —**pietist** /pī ətist/ *n* —**pietistic** /pī ə tístik/ *adj* —**pietistically** /-tístikli/ *adv*

Pietism *n* a German Protestant movement in the 17th and 18th centuries that changed the focus of Lutheranism from ritual and church government to personal piety [Late 17C. Via German *Pietismus* < Latin *pietas* (see PIETY).]

Pietro da Cortona /pi éttrō də kawr tṓnə/ (1596–1669) Italian architect and painter

piety /pī ə ti/ (*plural* **-ties**) *n* 1 **RELIGIOUS DEVOTION** strong respectful belief in a deity or deities and strict observance of religious principles in everyday life 2 **DEVOUT ACT** an action inspired by devout religious principles 3 **INSINCERE ATTITUDE** a conventional or hypocritical statement or observance of a belief [14C. Via Old French *piete* < Latin *pietas* < *pius* 'devout'.]

piezo- *prefix* pressure ○ *piezoelectric crystal* [< Greek *piezein* 'to press' < Indo-European, 'sit']

piezoelectricity /peézō i lék tríssəti, -éllek-/ *n* the electric current produced by some crystals and ceramic materials when they are subjected to mechanical pressure —**piezoelectric** /peézō i léktrik/ *adj*

piezometer /pee zómmitər/ *n* an instrument for measuring the compressibility of a material or fluid under pressure —**piezometric** /peézō méttrik/ *adj* —**piezometrically** /-méttrikli/ *adv*

piffle /píff'l/ *n* silly talk or ideas (*informal*) ○ *Don't talk piffle!* ■ *vi* (**-fles, -fling, -fled**) to behave in a silly or ineffective way (*dated informal*) [Mid-19C. < ?]

piffling /píff'ling/ *adj* of little use, value, or importance (*informal*)

pig /pig/ *n* 1 **FARM ANIMAL WITH BROAD SNOUT** a sturdy short-legged mammal with a broad snout, especially a domesticated pig, commonly kept as a farm animal and traditionally represented as fat and pink with a curly tail. *Sus scrofa.* 2 **PORK** the meat of a pig 3 **GREEDY PERSON** somebody who is regarded as slovenly, greedy, or gluttonous (*informal insult*) 4 **COARSE PERSON** somebody who is thought to behave in a coarse, discourteous, or brutal manner (*informal insult*) 5 **SOMETHING UNPLEASANT** a thing or situation that is difficult or unpleasant (*informal*) ○ *a pig of a job* 6 **BLOCK OF METAL** a casting of metal in a basic shape suitable for storage or transportation 7 **METAL MOULD** a basic mould for casting metal, especially iron 8 **OFFENSIVE TERM** an offensive term for a member of the police force (*slang*) ■ *v* (**pigs, pigging, pigged**) 1 *vi* **GIVE BIRTH TO PIGS** to give birth to a litter of pigs 2 *vt* **EAT GREEDILY** to eat gluttonously or excessively (*informal*) ○ *Who's pigged all the chocolate biscuits?* [Assumed Old English *picga*. Originally in the sense 'young pig'.] ◇ **a pig in a poke** something that is bought or obtained without being inspected to see if it is worth having ◇ **make a pig's ear of something** to do something very badly (*informal*)

pig out *vi* to eat greedily or gluttonously (*informal*)

pigeon[1] /píjjən/ *n* 1 a medium-sized bird with a stocky body and short legs, especially a domesticated variety of the rock dove, commonly seen in cities and throughout most of the world, or trained for racing and carrying messages. *Columba livia.* 2 somebody who is easily swindled or deceived (*informal*) [14C. Via Old French *pijon* 'young bird' < a Vulgar Latin alteration of late Latin *pipio* < an imitation of cheeping.]

pigeon[2] /píjjən/ *n* a matter of concern or responsibility to somebody in particular ○ *Matters of this kind are not my pigeon.* [Early 19C. Alteration of PIDGIN, in allusion to pigeon-fancying.]

pigeon breast, pigeon chest *n* a condition in which the sides of the chest are flattened and the centre protrudes like the keel of a boat —**pigeon-breasted** *adj*

pigeonhole /píjjən hōl/ *n* 1 **PLACE TO PUT MESSAGES** any of a series of small compartments in a desk or wall unit into which papers or messages can be sorted or placed 2 **BROAD CATEGORY** a category or label assigned to somebody or something without a great deal of thought ○ *the tendency to put writers into pigeonholes* 3 **PIGEON'S NESTING COMPARTMENT** a small nesting hole in a shelter for domestic pigeons ■ *vt* 1 **PUT IN BROAD CATEGORY** to categorize somebody or something without a great deal of thought 2 **POSTPONE** to put something off for a while

pigeonite /píjjə nīt/ *n* a yellow-green aluminosilicate mineral of the pyroxene group, containing iron, magnesium and calcium. Source: basic igneous rocks. [Early 20C. After *Pigeon* Point, Minnesota, where the mineral occurs in significant quantities.]

pigeon pea *n* 1 a small nutritious seed that is popular in Caribbean cookery 2 a woody plant of the pea family with three-lobed leaves, cultivated in tropical regions to produce pigeon peas. Flowers: yellow, orange. Native to: Africa. *Cajanus cajan.* [< the use of its seeds as pigeon-feed]

pigeon-toed *adj* tending to walk or stand with the toes turned inwards

piggery /píggəri/ (*plural* **-ies**) *n* 1 a farm or a building on a farm where pigs are bred and raised 2 coarse, greedy, or otherwise distasteful behaviour

piggish /píggish/, **piggy** /píggi/ *adj* 1 eating too much too fast 2 behaving in a stubborn, uncooperative, or obstructive way —**piggishly** *adv* —**piggishness** *n*

piggy /píggi/ *n* (*plural* **-gies**) (*informal babytalk*) 1 a pig or piglet 2 a toe, especially a small child's toe ■ *adj* (**-gier, -giest**) = **piggish**

piggyback /píggi bak/ *n* 1 **RIDE ON SOMEBODY'S BACK** a ride on somebody's back or shoulders 2 **HAULING OF ONE VEHICLE BY ANOTHER** the transporting of one vehicle by another, e.g. cars by lorry or lorry trailers by railway wagon ■ *adj, adv* 1 **ON SOMEBODY'S BACK** carried on the back or shoulders of another person 2 **ON OTHER VEHICLE** transported on another vehicle 3 **AS AN ADDITION** linked with or added onto something larger or more important ■ *v* 1 *vt* **CARRY ON BACK** to carry somebody on the back or shoulders 2 *vt* **TRANSPORT** to transport one vehicle on another 3 *vti* **ATTACH ONE THING TO ANOTHER** to link or add something to a larger or more important item, or to become linked or added to something else [Mid-16C. < ?]

piggy bank *n* a child's money box, especially but not necessarily one in the shape of a pig

piggy in the middle *n* 1 a game played by children, in which two people throw a ball to each other and a third person stands in the middle and tries to intercept it. US term **monkey in the middle** 2 somebody who is uncomfortably caught up in a disagreement between two people or groups

pigheaded /píg héddid/ *adj* stubbornly adhering to a belief, decision, or course of action —**pigheadedly** *adv* —**pigheadedness** *n*

pig iron *n* a crude form of iron made in a blast furnace and shaped into rough blocks for storage or transportation [< PIG]

pig Latin *n* any joke dialect coined and used by children, especially one in which first consonants are moved to the end of the words and extra syllables added

piglet /píglət/ *n* a newborn or immature pig

pigment *n* /pígmənt/ 1 **COLOURING SUBSTANCE** a substance that is added to give something, such as paint or ink, its colour 2 **NATURAL PLANT COLOURING** a natural substance in plant or animal tissue that gives it its colour ■ *vt* /pig mént/ **GIVE COLOUR TO** to impart colour to something [Pre-12C. < Latin *pigmentum* < *pingere* 'to paint'.] —**pigmentary** /pígməntəri/ *adj*

pigmentation /pígmen táysh'n/ *n* 1 the natural colour of plants and animals 2 abnormal colouring in plant or animal tissue that occurs as a result of disease

Pigmy /pígmi/ *n* ANTHROP = **Pygmy**

pignut /píg nut/ *n* 1 the roundish edible tuber of a woodland plant 2 a plant found in woods and the shaded sides of fields whose underground tubers are pignuts. *Conopodium majus.*

pigpen /píg pen/ *n* 1 *US* AGRIC = **pigsty** *n.* 1 2 an indoor enclosure in which pigs are kept on a modern pig farm, as distinct from the traditional outdoor pigsty 3 *US* = **pigsty** *n.* 2

Pigs, Bay of /pigz/ ➧ **Bay of Pigs**

pigskin /píg skin/ *n* the skin of a pig, especially when made into leather ■ *adj* made of leather prepared from the skin of a pig

pigsty /píg stī/ (*plural* **-sties**) *n* 1 a building or enclosure where pigs are kept, especially a traditional outdoor enclosure. US term **pigpen** *n.* 1 2 a dirty or disorderly place. US term **pigpen** *n.* 3

pigswill /píg swil/ *n* waste food and kitchen scraps that are fed to pigs

pigtail /píg tayl/ *n* 1 **PLAIT** a plait or bunch, often in pairs, into which the hair is either plaited or gathered 2 HAIR = **queue** *n.* 4 3 **TOBACCO STRAND** a thin twisted piece of tobacco 4 **BRAIDED WIRE** a short length of flexible electrical cable or wire, usually braided, connecting two terminals —**pigtailed** *adj*

pigweed /píg weed/ *n* 1 a hairy-leaved weed of the amaranth family. Flowers: green, in spikes. Native to: North America. *Amaranthus retroflexus.* 2 *US* PLANTS = **fat hen**

pika /pīkə/ (*plural* **-kas** *or* **-ka**) *n* a small short-eared burrowing mammal that is related to the rabbit and lives in rocky mountainous regions of W North

America and Asia. Family: Ochotonidae. [Early 19C. < Tungus *piika*.]

pike[1] /pīk/ (*plural* **pikes** *or* **pike**) *n* **1** a large predatory freshwater fish with a long body, long broad snout, and sharp teeth, popular as a game fish. Native to: northern waters. *Esox lucius.* **2** a fish that resembles the pike or belongs to the same family, especially the muskellunge and the pickerel [14C. < PIKE[3]; from its long pointed jaws.]

pike[2] /pīk/ *n* a weapon, formerly used by foot soldiers, consisting of a long pole with a pointed metal head ■ *vt* (**pikes, piking, piked**) to stab or kill somebody with a pike [Early 16C. < French *pique* < *piquer* (see PIQUE[1]).] —**pikeman** *n*

pike[3] /pīk/ *n* a sharp pointed object of any kind [Old English *pic*]

pike[4] /pīk/ *n N England* a pointed rugged summit of a steep hill or mountain [13C. Either < PIKE[3] , or < N Germanic.]

pike[5] /pīk/ *n* TRANSP = **turnpike** *n.* 1 [Early 19C. Shortening of TURNPIKE.]

pike[6] /pīk/ *n* a diving or gymnastic position in which the body is bent at the hips with the head tucked under and the hands touching the toes or behind the knees [Early 20C. < ?] —**piked** *adj*

pike[7] /pīk/ (**pikes, piking, piked**) *vi Aus* to let somebody down by breaking an arrangement or commitment (*slang*) ○ *We're playing this evening, but no doubt John will pike on us.* [Late 19C. < *pike* 'leave quickly'.]

pikelet /pīklət/ *n* **1** a soft flat yeast cake, traditionally made in N England, and usually eaten buttered **2** *ANZ* a small thick pancake made of batter [Late 18C. < Welsh *pyglyd* 'pitchy', in the phrase *bara pyglyd* 'pitchy bread'.]

pikeperch /pīk purch/ (*plural* **-perches** *or* **-perch**) *n* ZOOL = **walleye** *n.* 4

piker /pīkər/ *n* **1** *US* **CAUTIOUS GAMBLER** somebody who gambles cautiously with little money (*informal*) **2** *US* **STINGY PERSON** somebody who is stingy with money (*informal*) **3** *US* **PETTY PERSON** somebody who does things in a small-minded or petty way (*informal*) **4** *Aus* **UNRELIABLE PERSON** a person who is undependable by not honouring agreements or commitments (*slang*)

pikestaff /pīk staaf/ *n* **1** the wooden shaft of a pike, which forms the handle **2** a walking stick with a pointed metal end

pilaf *n* FOOD = **pilau**

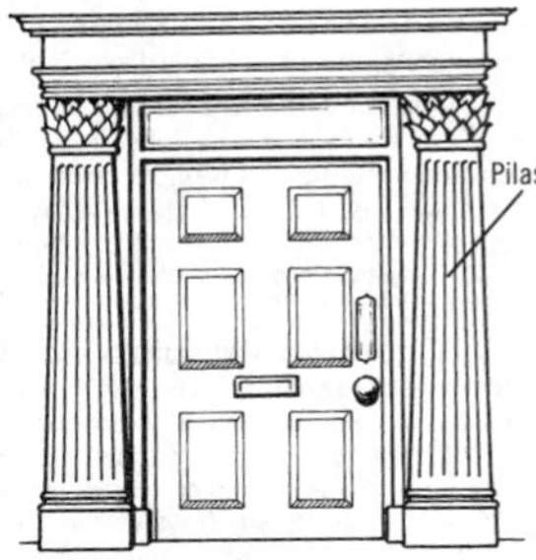

Pilaster

pilaster /pi lástər/ *n* a vertical structural part of a building that projects partway from a wall and is made to resemble an ornamental column by adding a base and capital [Late 16C. Via French *pilastre* < Italian *pilastro* or medieval Latin *pilastrum* < Latin *pila* 'pillar'.] —**pilastered** *adj*

Pilate /pīlət/, **Pontius** (*fl.* 1st century) Roman administrator

Pilates /pi laátayz/ *n* a holistic form of exercise and postural therapy that emphasizes the development of the deep abdominal muscles to control body movement and protect the back [Mid-20C. After Joseph H. *Pilates* (1880–1967), German fitness trainer.]

pilau /pee low/, **pilaf** /pee laf/ *n* a dish of spiced rice, often with chopped vegetables, fish, or meat added [Early 17C. < Turkish *pilâv* 'cooked rice'.]

Pilbara /pílbrə/ region of W Western Australia. Area: 440,000 sq. km/170,000 sq. mi.

pilchard /pílchərd/ (*plural* **-chards** *or* **-chard**) *n* **1** a small marine fish of the herring family with a rounded body and large scales. Native to: Europe. *Sardinia pilchardus.* **2** the flesh of a pilchard used as food [Mid-16C. < ?]

pile[1] /pīl/ *n* **1** **MOUND OF THINGS** a number of things heaped or stacked one on top of another **2** **LARGE QUANTITY** a very large amount of something (*informal; often plural*) ○ *I've got piles of work to do.* **3** **FORTUNE** a very large amount of money, especially one large enough to retire on (*informal*) ○ *He'd already made his pile by the age of 30.* **4** **BUILDING** a large impressive building **5** **PYRE** a funeral pyre (*archaic*) **6** ELEC = **voltaic pile** **7** **NUCLEAR REACTOR** a nuclear reactor (*dated*) ■ *v* (**piles, piling, piled**) **1** *vt* **MAKE INTO A MOUND** to heap or stack things one on top of another **2** *vt* **PLACE LARGE AMOUNTS ON** to heap a large amount of something somewhere ○ *plates piled high with mussels* **3** *vi* **GO AS A CROWD** to move hurriedly in a large disorganized group ○ *We all piled into the car and headed for the seaside.* [15C. Via French < Latin *pila* 'pillar'.]

pile on *vt* to add more and more of something on a continual basis ○ *Our team piled on the pressure in the second half.* ◇ **pile it on (thick)** to exaggerate something, especially its intensity or severity (*informal*)

pile up *vti* **1** to accumulate, or accumulate something, rapidly, forming a large amount **2** to crash a vehicle, or to collide with other vehicles, starting a chain of collisions

pile[2] /pīl/ *n* **1** **SUNKEN SUPPORT FOR BUILDING** a vertical wood, metal, or concrete support for a building or other structure that is driven into the ground **2** **HERALDIC SYMBOL** a heraldic figure in the shape of an arrowhead, usually displayed with the point downwards **3** **ARROWHEAD** the pointed head of an arrow (*technical*) **4** **ANCIENT ROMAN JAVELIN** a javelin used by foot soldiers in ancient Rome ■ *vt* (**piles, piling, piled**) **SUPPORT A STRUCTURE WITH PILES** to use piles as a support for a building or other structure [Pre-12C. < Latin *pilum* 'javelin'.]

pile[3] /pīl/ *n* **1** the surface of a carpet or of a fabric such as velvet that is formed of short, sometimes cut, loops of fibre **2** the fine soft fur or hair of an animal [Mid-16C. Probably via Anglo-Norman *peile* < Latin *pilus* 'hair'.]

pilea plural of **pileum**

pileated woodpecker /pílli aytid-/ *n* a large black-and-white woodpecker with a tall red crest. Native to: North America. *Dryocopus pileatus.*

pile-driver *n* **1** a large mechanical hammering device that uses steam, compressed air, or gravity to drive construction piles into the ground **2** a very strong blow or kick (*informal*)

pilei plural of **pileus**

piles /pīlz/ *npl* haemorrhoids (*informal*) [15C. Probably < Latin *pila* 'ball'; from their shape.]

pileum /píli əm/ (*plural* **-a** /píli ə/) *n* the top of a bird's head from the base of the bill to the nape of the neck [Late 19C. Via modern Latin < Latin *pileus* 'felt cap'.]

pile-up *n* **1** a collision involving several vehicles (*informal*) **2** an accumulated number or amount of things such as tasks

pileus /píli əss/ (*plural* **-i** /píli ī/) *n* **1** **CAP OF MUSHROOM** the top cap-shaped part of a mushroom or other fungus **2** **JELLYFISH'S BODY** the part of the body of a jellyfish that resembles an opened umbrella **3** **ROMAN SKULLCAP** a close-fitting brimless cap worn by ancient Romans [Mid-18C. < Latin *pileus* 'felt cap'.]

pilewort /pīl wurt/ (*plural* **-worts** *or* **-wort**) *n* a flowering plant of the buttercup family such as the lesser celandine. Use: remedy for haemorrhoids. [15C. *Pile* the singular of PILES.]

pilfer /pílfər/ *vti* to steal small items of little value, especially habitually [14C. < Anglo-Norman *pelfrer* 'rob' < ?] —**pilferage** *n* —**pilferer** *n* —**pilfering** *n*

SYNONYMS See ***steal***.

pilgrim /pílgrim/ *n* **1** a traveller who journeys to a holy place for religious reasons **2** a person who makes a special journey (*literary*) [12C. Via Provençal *pelegrin* < Latin *peregrinus* (see PEREGRINE).]

LITERARY LINK ***The Pilgrim's Progress***, a story (1678, 1684) by John Bunyan. An allegorical account of religious conversion, it describes the journey of a man called Christian from the City of Destruction (the contemporary, corrupt world) to the Celestial City (a state of religious grace). Much of its lasting popularity can be attributed to the author's skill in rendering complex abstract issues immediate, entertaining, and accessible.

Pilgrim /píll grim/ *n* one of the English Puritans who founded Plymouth Colony in Massachusetts in 1620

pilgrimage /pílgrimij/ *n* **1** a journey to a holy place, undertaken for religious reasons **2** a journey to a place with special significance ○ *Thousands of fans make the pilgrimage to Elvis's birthplace every year.* [13C. < Provençal *pelegrinatge* < Latin *peregrinus* (see PEREGRINE).]

Pilgrims' Way prehistoric track in S England, between Winchester and Canterbury. Length: 195 km/120 mi.

pili plural of **pilus**

Pilipino /pílli peénō/ *n, adj* LANG = **Filipino**

pill /pil/ *n* **1** **ROUND TABLET OF MEDICINE** a round solid tablet of medicine to be taken orally **2** **pill, Pill** **ORAL CONTRACEPTIVE** a contraceptive taken orally **3** **SOMETHING ROUND** something round such as a ball, bullet, or bomb (*informal*) **4** **TIRESOME PERSON** an unpleasant or boring person (*dated slang*) ■ **pills** *npl* **TESTICLES** a man's testicles (*slang*) ■ *v* **1** *vi* **FORM LITTLE BALLS WHEN RUBBED** to become covered in small balls of matted fibre because of rubbing (*refers to fabrics*) **2** *vt* **EXCLUDE** to reject somebody either by vote or consensus (*dated slang*) [15C. < Middle Low German or Middle Dutch *pille* < ?] ◇ **a bitter pill (to swallow)** something that is difficult or painful to accept ◇ **sugar** *or* **sweeten the pill** to make something unpalatable easier to accept or deal with

pillage /píllij/ *vti* (**-lages, -laging, -laged**) **1** **PLUNDER A PLACE** to rob a place using force, especially during a war **2** **STEAL PEOPLE'S POSSESSIONS** to steal goods using force, especially during a war ■ *n* **1** **STEALING OF SOMEBODY'S POSSESSIONS** theft of goods from a place using force, especially during a war **2** **STOLEN POSSESSIONS** goods that are stolen using force, especially during war [14C. < French < *piller* 'to plunder'.] —**pillager** *n*

pillar /píllər/ *n* **1** **COLUMN USED FOR SUPPORT OR DECORATION** a vertical column that is part of a building or other structure and can be either a support or decoration **2** **SOMETHING TALL AND NARROW** something that is tall and slender like a pillar **3** **CENTRAL FIGURE** a mainstay of an organization or society ○ *She was a pillar of the community.* ■ *vt* **SUPPORT WITH PILLARS** to support or strengthen something with pillars [13C. Via Anglo-Norman *piler* < Latin *pila* 'pillar'.] ◇ **from pillar to post** from one place to another

pillar box *n* a tall round red postbox where letters can be posted for collection

pillar-box red *adj* of a bright red colour, like a British letter box —**pillar-box red** *n*

Pillars of Hercules ancient name of two promontories at the E end of the Strait of Gibraltar, the Rock of Gibraltar, in Europe, and Jebel Musa, in Africa

Pillars of Islam, Five Pillars of Islam *npl* the basic tenets of Islam, which are a belief in Allah and in Muhammad as his prophet, in prayer, in charity, in fasting, and in making a pilgrimage to Mecca

pillbox /píl bokss/ *n* **1** **PILL-CONTAINER** a small container for pills **2** **pillbox, pillbox hat** **WOMAN'S BRIMLESS HAT** a woman's shallow brimless hat with a flat top **3** **GUN SHELTER** a small fortified shelter with a flat roof

pill bug *n* INSECTS = **woodlouse** [Because it is able to roll itself into a ball]

pilled-up /píld úp/ *adj* affected by or high on drugs, especially drugs taken in tablet form (*slang*)

pillion /pílli ən/ *n* a seat for a passenger behind the driver of a motorbike or the rider of a horse ■ *adv* seated behind the driver of a motorbike or the rider of a horse [15C. < Gaelic *pillean* and Irish *pillin* 'little couch' < *pell* 'couch' < Latin *pellis* 'skin'.]

pilliwinks /pílli wingks/ *n* an instrument of torture used on the fingers and thumbs in medieval times (+ *singular or plural verb*) [15C. < ?]

pillock /píllək/ *n* an offensive term for a person who is regarded as behaving in a thoughtless or unintelligent way (*slang insult*) [Mid-16C. Contraction of earlier *pillicock* 'penis' + COCK.]

pillory /píllәri/ *n* (*plural* **-ries**) **OLD PUNISHMENT DEVICE** a device formerly used as a means of public punishment, in the form of a wooden frame with holes into which somebody's head and hands could be locked ■ *vt* (**-ries, -rying, -ried**) **1** **RIDICULE** to scorn or ridicule somebody or something openly, or expose somebody or something to scorn or ridicule **2** **PUNISH IN PILLORY** to put somebody into a pillory as a public punishment [13C. Via Anglo-Latin *pillorium* < Old French *pillorie* < ?]

pillow /píllō/ *n* **1** CUSHION FOR HEAD a sealed fabric bag stuffed with feathers or a synthetic filling used as a soft support for the head in bed **2** CRAFT, HANDICRAFT = **cushion** *n.* 7 **3** SOMETHING LIKE A PILLOW something that is similar to a pillow in appearance or use ■ *vt* **1** CUSHION THE HEAD to rest the head on a pillow or something else that is soft and comfortable **2** ACT AS PILLOW FOR to provide a soft comfortable surface on which to rest something [Pre-12C. Via W Germanic < Latin *pulvinus*.]

pillowcase /píllō kayss/ *n* a fabric cover for a pillow

pillow lace *n* lace made using bobbins and a firm pad or pillow as a base, as distinct from lace made with a needle and a paper pattern

pillow lava *n* lava that has solidified into pillow-shaped masses, formed from underwater lava flows or from lava flowing into water from land

pillow sham *n US* a decorative covering for a pillow on a bed

pillowslip /píllō slip/ *n* HOUSEHOLD = **pillowcase**

pillow talk *n* the discussion of intimate or private matters in bed with a sexual partner

pilm /pilm/ *n Wales* dust

pilocarpine /pīlō kaar pīn, -pin/ *n* a poisonous alkaloid. Source: leaves of jaborandi trees. Use: formerly, to induce sweating, treat glaucoma. [Late 19C. < modern Latin *Pilocarpus*.]

piloerection /pīlō i réksh'n/ *n* the raising of the hairs on the surface of the skin, e.g. to conserve heat [Mid-20C. < Latin *pilus* 'hair'.]

pilose /pīlōss/, **pilous** /pīləss/ *adj* describes plant parts that are covered with soft hair [Late 18C. < Latin *pilosus* 'hairy' < *pilus* 'hair'.] —**pilosity** /pī lóssəti/ *n*

pilot /pīlət/ *n* **1** SOMEBODY WHO FLIES PLANE a person who pilots an aircraft or spacecraft **2** SOMEBODY STEERING SHIPS THROUGH DIFFICULT AREA somebody with local knowledge whose job is to navigate ships in and out of a harbour or through a particular stretch of water **3** STEERER OF SHIP a steerer of a ship or boat **4** LEADER a leader or guide **5** TELEVISION PROGRAMME a television or radio programme made as a prototype for a projected series **6** TRIAL RUN a test of something, e.g. a proposed manufacturing process, to discover and solve problems before full implementation **7** TECH = **pilot light** *n.* 1 **8** MACHINE GUIDE a guiding part of a tool or machine ■ *vt* **1** FLY AN AIRCRAFT to fly an aircraft or spacecraft **2** NAVIGATE to navigate a ship **3** BE IN CHARGE OF to direct the course of something, e.g. a project or a programme of research **4** RUN A TRIAL to test something, e.g. a proposed manufacturing process, to discover and solve problems before full implementation [Early 16C. Via French *pilote* < medieval Latin *pilotus*, alteration of *pedota* < Greek *pēdon* 'oar'.]

pilotage /pīlətij/ *n* **1** PILOTING OF CRAFT the controlling of a ship, aircraft, or spacecraft **2** HARBOUR OR RIVER PILOT'S FEE the fee paid to a harbour or river pilot for steering a ship along a short difficult stretch **3** MANUAL NAVIGATION the navigation of an aircraft using landmarks and maps, rather than an aircraft's own navigation systems

pilot balloon *n* a small balloon launched to study the speed and direction of winds at high altitudes

pilot fish *n* a small striped marine fish, often found swimming with sharks, mantas, and other large fishes, where it finds stray scraps of food. *Naucrates ductor.*

pilot house *n* an enclosed control room on or near the bridge of a ship, containing the steering wheel and navigational and communication equipment

pilot lamp *n* a small light in an electric circuit to show if the power is on or if an electrical device is operating

pilot light *n* **1** **pilot light, pilot** a small gas flame that remains lit in order to ignite a burner when it is turned on **2** ELEC = **pilot lamp**

pilot officer *n* a commissioned officer in the Royal Air Force of the lowest rank

pilot whale *n* a large black toothed whale with a bulbous head, found in warm seas. Genus: *Globicephala.*

pilous *adj* BIOL = **pilose**

Pils /pilz/ (*plural* **Pils**) *n* any kind of lager beer similar to Pilsner [Mid-20C. Shortening of PILSNER.]

Pilsener *n* BEVERAGES = **Pilsner**

Pilsner /pílznər/, **Pilsener** *n* lager beer with a strong hops flavour, originally and especially made in Pilsen in the Czech Republic [Late 19C. < German, 'of Pilsen' < *Pilsen* (Czech *Plzeň*), province in the Czech Republic.]

Piłsudski /pil sóōtski/, **Józef Klemens** (1867–1935) Polish statesman

Piltdown man /pilt down-/ *n* a supposed primitive form of human being represented by remains of bones found in Sussex in 1912, shown in 1953 to be a hoax [Early 20C. After the village in Sussex.]

pilus /pīləss/ (*plural* **-li** /pī lī/) *n* any part of a plant or animal organism that looks like a hair [Mid-20C. < Latin, 'hair'.]

ϟ**PIM** /pim/ *abbr* **personal information manager**

Pima /péemə/ *n* **1** a member of a Native North American people who lived in southern and central Arizona, and who now live mainly in central Arizona **2** the Uto-Aztecan language of the Pima people. Native speakers: 15,000. [Early 19C. < Spanish, shortening of *Pimahito* < Pima *pimahaitu* 'nothing'.] —**Pima** *adj*

Pima-Papago /péemə páppə gō/ *n* the Pima and Papago languages regarded together. They are closely-related members of the Uto-Aztecan family of Native North and Central American languages. —**Pima-Papago** *adj*

pimento /pi méntō/ *n* **1** FOOD = **pimiento** **2** TREES, COOK = **allspice** [Late 17C. Via Spanish *pimiento* < Latin *pigmentum* (see PIGMENT).]

pi meson /pī meezon/ *n* = **pion**

pimiento /pim yén tō, pi méntō/ (*plural* **-tos**) *n* **1** a large sweet red pepper. Use: paprika, olive stuffing, garnish. **2** a European plant that produces pimientos. *Capsicum annuum.* [Mid-17C. < Spanish (see PIMENTO).]

pimp /pimp/ *n* a man who finds customers for a prostitute in return for a portion of the prostitute's earnings [Late 16C. < ?]

pimpernel /pímpər nel/ (*plural* **-nels** *or* **-nel**) *n* a small plant with long trailing stems. Flowers: small, red, white, purple. Genus: *Anagallis.* [15C. Via Old French *pimpernelle* 'burnet' (the plant) < *piprenelle* < Latin *piper* 'pepper', because its fruit resembles peppercorns.]

pimple /pímp'l/ *n* a small inflamed or pus-filled spot on the skin [14C. Related to Old English *piplian* 'break out in spots'.] —**pimpled** *adj* —**pimply** *adj*

pimpmobile /pímp mō beel/ *n US* a very showy large car, typical of one that might be used by a pimp (*informal*)

ϟ**pin** /pin/ *n* **1** THIN POINTED METAL STICK a small thin metal stick with a sharp point and a rounded head used for holding pieces of fabric together **2** POINTED METAL FASTENER any fastener that has a sharp metal point designed to pierce the things it is fastening **3** = **safety pin** *n.* 1, **safety pin** *n.* 2 **4** SOMETHING DECORATIVE ATTACHED TO CLOTHING a badge, piece of jewellery, or other decorative item that attaches to clothing by means of a sharp metal point or a clasp **5** HAIR = **hairpin** *n.* 1 **6** MECH ENG = **cotter pin** **7** PART OF ELECTRICAL CONNECTOR a thin metal terminal extending from an electrical or electronic device such as a plug or a valve, used to connect the device by socket to other circuitry ○ *a three-pin plug* **8** ROD TO JOIN BROKEN BONE a thin metal rod used to hold the ends of a fractured bone together **9** PEG USED IN DENTISTRY a peg used to attach a crown to the root of a tooth **10** KEY PART ENTERING LOCK the part of a key that inserts into a lock **11** PEG HOLDING INSTRUMENT STRING a peg on a stringed instrument such as a piano that holds the strings and can be turned to tighten or loosen them to tune the instrument **12** SAFETY CLIP ON GRENADE the safety clip on a hand grenade that must be removed before the grenade can be detonated **13** SKITTLE a club-shaped target used in various games of bowling **14** HOLE MARKER IN GOLF a pole with a flag on it, used to mark each hole on a golf course **15** WRESTLING FALL a fall in wrestling in which an opponent's shoulders are made to touch the mat **16** BEER CASK a small beer barrel holding 4.5 gallons **17** GUIDE ON COMPUTER PRINTER any of the pegs that guide the paper through a computer printer **18** PART OF PRINTHEAD THAT FORMS LETTERS any of the tiny wires on the printhead of a dot matrix printer that form one dot of a letter or symbol ■ **pins** *npl* LEGS somebody's legs (*informal*) ○ *He's a bit unsteady on his pins.* ■ *vt* (**pins, pinning, pinned**) **1** FASTEN WITH PINS to fasten, attach, or secure something with a pin **2** KEEP FROM MOVING to hold somebody or something immobile, e.g. on the ground ○ *The beam fell across his back, pinning him to the ground.* **3** RESTRICT OPPONENT'S CHESS PIECE to make it impossible for a chess opponent to move a piece without exposing the king to check or a valuable piece to capture **4** HOLD WRESTLING OPPONENT DOWN to hold a wrestling opponent's shoulders to the mat [12C. < Latin *pinna* 'feather, pointed peak'.] —**pinner** *n*

pin down *vt* **1** IDENTIFY PRECISELY to determine something with certainty ○ *Can you pin down the time of death?* **2** FORCE TO DECIDE to force somebody to keep a commitment or come to a decision ○ *I haven't managed to pin him down to a date for our meeting yet.* **3** PREVENT SOMEBODY FROM MOVING to prevent somebody from going anywhere ○ *The platoon was pinned down by enemy fire.*

ϟ**PIN** /pin/ (*plural* **PINs**), **PIN number** *n* a multidigit number unique to an individual that is used to gain access to an account at a cashpoint machine, a computer, or a telephone system. Abbr of **personal identification number**

~~**pinacle**~~ incorrect spelling of **pinnacle**

piña colada /péenə kō laadə, péenyə-/ *n* a cocktail made from pineapple juice, rum, and coconut [< Spanish, 'strained pineapple']

pinafore /pínnə fawr/ *n* **1** DRESS WORN OVER SOMETHING ELSE a sleeveless dress, usually worn over a blouse or sweater. US term **jumper**[2] *n.* 2 **2** APRON an apron, usually one with a bib (*dated*) **3** GIRL'S OVERGARMENT a sleeveless collarless garment formerly worn by girls over a dress and fastened at the top of the back [Late 18C. < PIN + AFORE, because it was originally used for a garment pinned to the front of a dress.]

pinafore dress *n* CLOTHING = **pinafore** *n.* 1

Pinang /pə náng/ = **Penang**

pinaster /pī nástər/ *n* a pine tree with long paired needles and clusters of long cones. Native to: Mediterranean. *Pinus pinaster.* [Mid-16C. < Latin < *pinus* (see PINE[1]).]

piñata /peen yaa tə/ *n US* a decorated container of sweets or small gifts that is hung from the ceiling and is hit and broken by blindfolded people with sticks, traditionally during Latin American festivals [Late 19C. < Spanish, 'jug'.]

Pinatubo, Mount /pinnə tóōbō/ active volcano on central Luzon, Philippines. Height: 1,780 m/5,840 ft.

pinball /pínn bawl/ *n* a game played on an electronic table fitted with obstacles, targets, and pivoted flippers. The player controls the flippers to keep a ball in play, hitting targets to score points. (*often before nouns*)

pince-nez /pánss náy/ (*plural* **pince-nez** /pánss náyz/) *n* a pair of spectacles without side arms, held in place by a clip that fits over the nose [< French, 'pinch the nose']

pincer movement /pínssər-/ *n* a military manoeuvre that attempts to surround an enemy by simultaneous attack from the front and two side columns that curve around the enemy and back towards each other

pincers /pínssərz/ *npl* **1** the front claws of some crustaceans and arachnids, e.g. the lobster and scorpion, used for grasping things **2** a tool, resembling a pair of pliers or scissors, with curved pivoted jaws that are used to grip something, e.g. a nail, when they are closed [14C. < Anglo-Norman, a variation of Old French *pincier* (see PINCH).]

pinch /pinch/ *v* **1** *vti* GRIP SOMETHING BETWEEN FINGER AND THUMB to grip or squeeze something tightly between finger and thumb or between two hard objects or edges **2** *vti* BE TOO TIGHT AND PAINFUL to painfully constrict or squeeze a part of the body ○ *These shoes are pinching my feet.* **3** *vt* REMOVE SHOOTS TO ENCOURAGE BUSHY GROWTH to remove new shoots and buds from a plant to make it become more bushy **4** *vt* WITHER to make somebody or something become shrunken or withered, especially through harsh conditions like cold or hunger ○ *a face pinched with grief and pain* **5** *vti* STEAL to steal something or take something without permission (*informal*) ○ *Who's pinched my pen?* **6** *vt* ARREST to arrest somebody (*informal*) **7** *vt* IMPOSE HARDSHIP ON to put somebody in financial difficulty ○ *Unexpected expenses have really pinched me this month.* **8** *vt* SAIL A VESSEL INTO THE WIND to sail a sailing vessel too close to the wind, so that it loses wind from its sails **9** *vi* NARROW AND DISAPPEAR to become gradually narrower, eventually disappearing entirely (*refers to a vein of ore*) ■ *n* **1** PAINFUL SQUEEZE a painful squeeze or nip, especially with the thumb and finger ○ *a pinch on the arm* **2** VERY LITTLE a very small amount of a substance, especially the amount held between the thumb and first finger ○ *add a pinch of salt* **3** ROBBERY a robbery (*informal*) **4** AN ARREST an arrest made by the police (*informal*) **5** CRITICAL TIME an emergency or critical situation ○ *If it comes to the pinch, we'll have to sell the house.* [13C. Via assumed Anglo-Norman *pincher*, a variant of Old French *pincier* < assumed Vulgar Latin *pinctiare* 'to prick'.] ◇ **at a**

pinch if absolutely necessary, although preferably not ◇ **feel the pinch** to have financial problems

SYNONYMS See ***steal***.

pinch bar *n* a crowbar with a pointed end and a projection that provides a fulcrum, used as a lever, often having a notch, or claw, at the other end

pinchbeck /pínch bek/ *n* **1 GOLD-COLOURED METAL ALLOY** an alloy of copper and zinc used as imitation gold in inexpensive jewellery **2 CHEAP COPY** an inferior imitation ■ *adj* **1 MADE OF PINCHBECK** made from pinchbeck alloy **2 IMITATION** made in imitation of something and usually of inferior quality [Mid-18C. After Christopher *Pinchbeck*, (*d.* 1732), English watchmaker.]

pinch effect *n* the narrowing of a beam of charged particles caused by the interaction of each particle with the magnetic field generated by the movement of the beam

pinch hit *n* in baseball, a hit made by a substitute batter

pinch-hit (**pinch-hits, pinch-hitting, pinch-hit**) *vi* **1** to replace the scheduled batter at bat in baseball, especially when a hit is needed **2** *US* to take somebody else's place at something —**pinch hitter** *n*

pinchpenny /pínch peni/ *adj* unwilling to spend or give money ■ *n* (*plural* **-nies**) a miser

pinchpoint /pínch poynt/ *n* **1** a narrow area between two surfaces that is likely to trap or catch objects and so is a potential safety hazard **2** a point in a system or process that is likely to experience or cause delays

pinch runner *n* in baseball, a runner who replaces a batter who has successfully reached base, usually because the batter is slow or injured

pin curl *n* a flat curl in hair, made by winding strands of hair into a circle and securing it with a clip or hairpin

pincushion /pín kòosh'n/ *n* a small stuffed pad used for sticking dressmaking pins into when they are not being used

Pindar /píndər/ (*fl.* 522? BC–443 BC) Greek poet —**Pindaric** /pin dárrik/ *adj*

Pindaric ode *n* a form of ode with three-stanza sections, the first and second stanzas having one metrical form and the third having a different form

pine[1] /pīn/ *n* **1 WOOD FROM PINE** the wood from an evergreen tree, varying from soft to hard. Use: furniture-making, construction, finishing material. **2 EVERGREEN TREE** an evergreen coniferous tree with needle-shaped leaves and woody cones, often grown for its wood or resin, or for ornament. Genus: *Pinus*. (*often before nouns*) **3 TREE RESEMBLING THE PINE** a coniferous tree or shrub that resembles a true pine, e.g. the Norfolk Island pine [Pre-12C. < Latin *pinus* < ?] —**piney** *adj*

pine[2] /pīn/ (**pines, pining, pined**) *vi* **1** to long for somebody or something, especially somebody or something unattainable **2** to become weak and lose vitality as a result of grief or longing [Pre-12C. Probably < Latin *poena* 'penalty' < Greek *poinē*.]

pineal /pínni əl, pī neé əl/ *adj* **1** relating to or secreted by the pineal gland **2** shaped like a pine cone [Late 17C. Via French *pinéal* < Latin *pinea* 'pine cone' (from its pine-cone-like shape) < *pinus* (see PINE[1]).]

pineal gland, pineal body *n* a small cone-shaped organ of the brain that secretes the hormone melatonin into the bloodstream

pineapple /pī nap'l/ *n* **1 JUICY YELLOW FRUIT** a large fruit with juicy yellow flesh, a thick lumpy yellowish-brown skin, and a tuft of tough pointed leaves at the top **2** (*plural* **-ples** *or* **-ple**) **PLANT ON WHICH PINEAPPLES GROW** a plant that produces pineapples. Native to: tropical America. *Ananas comosus*. **3 GRENADE WITH PATTERNED SURFACE** a hand grenade with a surface of raised geometric shapes (*slang*) [14C. Originally 'pine cone'.]

pineapple weed *n* a plant with greenish-yellow flower heads that smell like pineapple when crushed. Native to: Asia. *Matricaria matri.*

pine cone *n* a pine tree's seed case, usually woody, oval, and scaly

pine kernel *n* FOOD = **pine nut**

pine leaf scale *n* an insect with a tough outer covering that attaches itself to pine needles and seriously inhibits their growth. *Chionaspis pinifoliae.*

pine marten *n* a woodland animal similar in appearance to a weasel, with a dark-brown coat and yellow throat. It is native to Asia, N Europe, and N North America. Genus: *Martes.*

pinene /pī́n een/ *n* $C_{10}H_{16}$ each of two colourless liquid compounds. Source: turpentine, eucalyptus. Use: manufacture of plastics, solvent. [Late 19C. < Latin *pinus* 'pine' + -ENE.]

pine needle *n* the needle-shaped leaf of a pine tree

pine nut *n* a small sweet seed of some pine trees, especially a piñon

pinery /pī́nəri/ (*plural* **-ies**) *n* **1** a plantation or heated glasshouse where pineapples are grown commercially **2** a pine forest, especially one planted for timber production

pinesap /pī́n sap/ (*plural* **-saps** *or* **-sap**) *n* a fleshy red or yellowish plant that resembles the Indian pipe and grows as a parasite on tree roots. Native to: North America. *Montropa hypopithys.*

pine snake *n* a large bull snake with black-and-white markings. Native to: pine forests in the E United States. *Pituophis melanoleucus.*

pine tar *n* a thick sticky brown to black substance obtained by the destructive distillation of pine wood and used in making roofing materials, paints, medicines, and shampoos

pinewood /pī́n wòod/ *n* **1** the wood of a pine tree (*often before nouns*) **2** a small forest of pine trees (*often plural*)

pinfeather /pínn fethər/ *n* a feather only recently emerged from a bird's skin and still surrounded by a horny sheath

pinfish /pínn fish/ (*plural* **-fishes** *or* **-fish**) *n* a small marine fish of the porgy family with a thin dark-green body and sharp dorsal spines. Native to: S Atlantic coast of the United States. *Lagodon rhomboides.*

pinfold /pínn fōld/ *n* **1** an enclosure for stray animals, especially farm animals **2** any place or situation that confines [Pre-12C. < Alteration of earlier *pund-* 'enclosure' + FOLD[2].]

ping /ping/ *n* **1 SOUND** a single short ringing sound **2** *US* AUTOMOT = **knock** *n.* **3 3 SONAR PULSE** a brief sonic or ultrasonic pulse emitted by a sonar, the reflection or echo of which is used in detecting submarines or shoals of fish ■ *v* **1** *vti* **RING** to make a single short ringing sound, or to make something such as a bell produce a ringing sound **2** *vi* **DETECT UNDERWATER OBJECTS** to detect submarines or shoals of fish by emitting and receiving the echo of a brief sonic or ultrasonic pulse [Mid-18C. An imitation of the sound.]

pinger /píngər/ *n* (*informal*) **1** a device that produces pinging noises, especially one used as part of underwater detection equipment **2** a timer that makes pinging noises as an alarm after a set amount of time

pingo /píng gō/ (*plural* **-gos**) *n* a large mound of soil-covered ice forced up by the pressure of water in permafrost [Mid-20C. < Inuit (Eskimo) *pinguq*.]

Ping-Pong /píng pong/ *tdmk* a trademark for table tennis

pinguid /píng gwid/ *adj* containing a lot of fat, oil, or grease [Mid-17C. < Latin *pinguis* 'fat'.] —**pinguidity** /ping gwíddəti/ *n*

pinhead /pín hed/ *n* **1 BLUNT END OF PIN** the rounded head of a pin **2 SMALL THING** something that is very small or trivial **3 OFFENSIVE TERM** an offensive term that deliberately insults somebody's intelligence (*informal insult*) —**pinheaded** *adj*

pinhole /pín hōl/ *n* a tiny hole or puncture of the size made by a pin

pinhole camera *n* a basic form of camera with a tiny hole for the aperture, and no lens

pinion[1] /pínnyən/ *n* **BIRD'S WING** a bird's wing, especially the tip of the wing where the stiff flight feathers are found, containing the carpus, metacarpus, and phalanx bones ■ *vt* **1 RESTRAIN** to restrain or immobilize somebody, especially by tying his or her arms **2 KEEP FROM FLYING** to prevent a bird from flying by removing or binding its wing feathers [15C. Via French *pignon* < Latin *pinna* (see PIN).]

pinion[2] /pínnyən/ *n* a small gear wheel that engages with a larger gear or with a rack, e.g. in a vehicle steering system [Mid-17C. Via French *pignon*, alteration of earlier *pignol* < Latin *pinea* 'pine cone' < *pinus* (see PINE [1]).]

pinite /pínnīt, pī nīt/ *n* a grey-green mixture of the minerals mica and chlorite. Source: alteration of cordierite. [Early 19C. < German *Pinit*, after *Pini*, a mine in Saxony.]

pink[1] /pingk/ *n* **1 PALE REDDISH COLOUR** a pale reddish colour that, as a pigment, is formed by mixing red and white **2 PLANT WITH FRAGRANT FLOWERS** a plant with narrow greyish-green leaves. Flowers: fragrant, especially pink, white, or red. Genus: *Dianthus*. **3 PLANT SIMILAR TO TRUE PINK** a plant that is similar but not related to the pink, e.g. the wild pink or moss pink **4 HIGHEST FORM** the highest degree or perfect example of something ○ *the pink of perfection* **5 RED HUNTING JACKET** the scarlet riding coat traditionally worn by fox hunters **6** POL = **pinko** ■ *adj* **1 COLOURED PINK** of the colour pink **2 SLIGHTLY LEFT-WING** relating to or holding political views that tend towards the left (*informal disapproving*) **3 RELATING TO HOMOSEXUALS** relating to homosexuals (*informal; sometimes offensive*) [Late 16C. Probably < Dutch *pinck* 'small' < *pinck oogen* 'small eyes'.] —**pinkish** *adj* —**pinkness** *n* ◇ **in the pink** in excellent physical health (*dated*)

pink[2] /pingk/ *vt* **1 CUT WITH PINKING SHEARS** to cut fabric with pinking shears to make a zigzag edge that will not easily fray **2 STAB** to prick somebody's skin with a sword or other pointed weapon **3 DECORATE WITH LITTLE HOLES** to make a pattern on leather or other material by punching little holes in the surface [14C. < ?]

pink[3] /pingk/ *n* a sailing ship with a narrow overhanging stern [Late 15C. < Middle Dutch *pincke*.]

pink[4] /pingk/ *vi* AUTOMOT = **knock** *v.* **8** [Early 20C. Imitation of the sound.]

pink-collar *adj* *US* relating to jobs, especially clerical jobs, traditionally associated with women. ◊ **blue-collar, white-collar**

pink dollar *n* *US* COMM = **pink pound**

pink elephants *npl* hallucinations in any form that are sometimes experienced by somebody who has over-indulged in alcohol or drugs (*informal humorous*)

pinkeye /píngk ī/ *n* **1** a contagious form of acute conjunctivitis in human beings and some domestic animals marked by inflammation of the eyelid and eyeball **2** an eye infection of cattle, caused by any of several different viruses or bacteria

pink gin *n* gin that has Angostura™ bitters added to it, giving it a pale pinkish colour and an aromatic spicy flavour

pinkie /píngki/, **pinky** (*plural* **-ies**) *n* *US, Can, Scotland* the little finger (*informal*) [Late 16C. Probably < Dutch *pinkje* < *pink* 'little finger'.]

pinking shears, pinking scissors *npl* scissors for cutting cloth that have one blade or both blades serrated, so that whatever they cut has a zigzag edge, either for decoration or to prevent fraying [< PINK[2]]

pink lady *n* a cocktail that is made by mixing gin, brandy, lemon or lime juice, egg white, and grenadine

pink money *n* money belonging to or provided by the gay and lesbian community (*informal; sometimes offensive*)

pinko /píngkō/ (*plural* **-os** *or* **-oes**) *n* a person who favours the political left (*slang disapproving*) [Early 20C. < PINK, alluding to RED in the sense 'communist'.]

pink pound *n* the collective spending power of homosexual men and lesbians, especially when targeted as consumers (*informal; sometimes offensive*) US term **pink dollar**

pink salmon *n* **1** a small salmon, the male of which has a pinkish body and a distinctive hump on the back at breeding times. Native to: N Pacific waters. *Oncorhynchus gorbuscha*. **2** the pink flesh of the pink salmon used as food, often tinned

pink slip *n* *US* a termination of employment notice that an employer gives to an employee in the United States (*informal*) [< the traditional colour of such notices]

pinky *n* ANAT = **pinkie**

pin money *n* **1 MONEY FOR BUYING PERSONAL THINGS** money that is earned, put aside, or used for buying personal, often nonessential, things **2 NOT MUCH MONEY** a small amount of money **3 MONEY THAT MAN GIVES TO WIFE** money that a man gives to his wife, woman partner, or daughter for personal use (*dated*)

pinna /pínnə/ (*plural* **-nae** /-nee/ *or* **-nas**) *n* **1** a feather, wing, fin, or other similarly shaped body part or appendage **2** any one of the several leaflets that make up a pinnate compound leaf **3** ANAT = **auricle** *n.* 1 [Late 18C. < Latin *penna* 'feather'.] —**pinnal** *adj*

pinnace /pínnəss/ *n* a small boat such as a sailing boat carried by a larger vessel and used as a gig or a tender [Mid-16C. Via French < Latin *pinus* 'pine' (see PINE[1]).]

pinnacle /pínnək'l/ *n* **1 HIGHEST POINT** the highest or topmost point or level of something ○ *at the pinnacle of a career* **2 MOUNTAIN PEAK** a natural peak, especially a distinctively pointed one on a mountain or in a mountain range **3 POINTED ORNAMENT** a pointed ornament on top of a buttress or parapet ■ *vt* (**-cles, -cling, -cled**) **1 ADD PINNACLE TO** to provide something with a pinnacle **2 PUT SOMETHING ON PINNACLE** to put or set something on a pinnacle or on something resembling a top or peak [13C. Via Old French < late Latin *pinnaculum* 'little feather' < Latin *pinna* 'feather' (see PINNA).]

pinnae plural of **pinna**

pinnate /pínnayt/, **pinnated** /pínnaytid/, **pennate** /pénnayt/, **pennated** /-naytid/ *adj* resembling a feather in appearance or structure, especially in having a central axis or stem with parts branching off it [Early 18C. < Latin *pinnatus* < *pinna* (see PINNA).] —**pinnately** *adv* —**pinnation** /pi náysh'n/ *n*

pinnati- *prefix* like a feather ○ *pinnatifid* [< Latin *pinnatus* (see PINNATE)]

pinnatifid /pi náttifid/ *adj* describes leaves that have a central axis with parts branching off it [Mid-18C. < PINNATI- + -FID.] —**pinnatifidly** *adv*

pinniped /pínni ped/, **pinnipedian** /pínni péedi ən/ *n* any sea-dwelling mammal such as a walrus, sea lion, or seal that has a streamlined body and four flippers and eats fish and other meat. Suborder: Pinnipedia. [Mid-19C. < modern Latin *Pinnipedia* < Latin *pinna* 'wing, fin' + *pes* 'foot'.] —**pinniped** *adj*

pinnule /pín yool/, **pinnula** /pínnyoolə/ (*plural* **-lae** /pínnyoolee/) *n* **1** a small fin or fin-shaped part of an organ or organism **2** a small division or lobe of a leaf that has a central axis with parts branching off it [Late 16C. < Latin *pinnula* 'little feather' < PINNA.] —**pinnular** *adj*

ϟPIN number *n* TECH = **PIN**

pinny /pínni/ (*plural* **-nies**) *n* an apron (*informal*) [Mid-19C. Shortening of PINAFORE.]

Pinochet /péenō shay/, **Augusto** (*b.* 1915) Chilean general and national leader (1973–90)

pinochle /pée nuk'l/, **pinocle, penuchle, penuckle** *n* **1** a card game for two or four players using two packs of cards that do not include two to eight. Certain combinations of cards score points, as do tricks taken. **2** a combination of the queen of spades and the jack of diamonds in the game of pinochle [Mid-19C. < ?]

pinocytosis /péenō sī tóssiss/ *n* the ingestion of fluid into a cell by turning a portion of the cell membrane inwards to form a sheath that is then pinched off to form an internal vesicle [Late 19C. < Greek *pinein* 'to drink'.] —**pinocytotic** /-tóttik/ *adj* —**pinocytotically** /-tóttikli/ *adv*

pinole /pi nóli/ *n US* a flour that is made by mixing lightly roasted cornflour with ground mesquite beans and sometimes other ingredients [Mid-19C. Via American Spanish < Aztec *pinolli*.]

piñon /pi nyón, pínnyən/ (*plural* **-ñons** *or* **-ñones** /pi nyó neez/), **pinyon** *n* **1 piñon, piñon nut** a small sweet nut produced by a pine tree **2** a low-growing pine that bears piñons. Native to: SW United States. *Pinus edulis* and *Pinus monophylla*. [Mid-19C. Via Spanish *piñón* < Latin *pineus* 'of pines' < *pinus* (see PINE[1]).]

Pinot Grigio /péenō gríjjō/ (*plural* **Pinot Grigios**) *n* **1** a white grape grown in Italy, used for making wine **2** a crisp dry white wine made from the Pinot Grigio grape [< Italian, 'grey Pinot', a grape variety (from French; see PINOT NOIR)]

Pinot Noir /péenō nwáar/ *n* **1** a black grape grown in the Burgundy area of France and also in Australia, the United States, and elsewhere, used for making wine **2** red wine made from the Pinot Noir grape [< French, 'black Pinot' (a grape variety) < *pin* 'pine cone']

pinpoint /pín poynt/ *vt* **IDENTIFY SOMETHING CORRECTLY** to identify or locate something accurately ■ *n* **1 SOMETHING SMALL OR TRIVIAL** something small or trivial and with no value or consequence **2 PIN'S POINT** the sharp end of a pin or something that resembles it ■ *adj* **PRECISELY EXACT** reflecting exact meticulous precision

pinprick /pín prik/ *n* **1 SMALL HOLE MADE BY PIN** a small puncture, especially to the skin, made by a pin or something with a similarly sharp end **2 SLIGHT WOUND** a very minor wound **3 MINOR IRRITANT** a minor annoyance, nuisance, or distraction **4 SMALL MARK** a very small dot or mark of something ■ *vt* **PUNCTURE SOMETHING WITH PIN** to puncture something, especially the skin, with a pin or something with a similarly sharp end

pins and needles *n* a tingling sensation, especially in the feet or hands, sometimes experienced when a temporarily restricted blood flow to the affected body parts returns to normal (*+ singular or plural verb*)

Pinsk /pinsk/ city in SW Belarus. Population: 107,729 (1996 estimate).

pinstripe /pín strīp/ *n* **1 NARROW LINE IN FABRIC** any one of many very narrow lines, especially in a fabric **2 MATERIAL WITH VERY NARROW LINES** material that has very narrow lines in it. Use: business suits. (*often before nouns*) **3 PINSTRIPE SUIT** a suit made of pinstripe fabric (*often plural*) —**pinstriped** *adj*

pint /pīnt/ *n* **1 UNIT OF LIQUID MEASURE** a unit of liquid measure equal to one eighth of a gallon, which is equal to 0.568 litre in the United Kingdom and 0.473 litre in the United States **2 UNIT OF DRY MEASURE** a unit of dry measure equal to one eighth of a gallon, which is equal to 0.568 litre in the United Kingdom and 0.551 litre in the United States **3 CONTAINER** a container or measure that has the capacity of a pint **4 PINT OF LIQUID** a pint of a liquid, especially of beer or milk (*informal*) **5** *UK* **DRINK SERVED IN PUB** a drink of beer or some similar alcoholic drink in a pub or bar perhaps, but not necessarily, a single or exact pint (*informal*) [14C. < French *pinte* < ?]

pinta /píntə/ *n* an infectious bacterial skin disease of tropical America that is marked by the formation and eruption of papules, loss of pigmentation, and thickening of the skin [Early 19C. Via Spanish, 'painted spot' < assumed Vulgar Latin *pincta*.]

pintado petrel /pin taadō-/, **pintado** (*plural* **-dos** *or* **-does**) *n* BIRDS = **Cape pigeon** [Via Portuguese *pintado* 'guinea fowl', literally 'painted' (from its black-and-white colouring) < Latin *pingere* (see PAINT)]

pintail /pín tayl/ (*plural* **-tails** *or* **-tail**) *n* a slender duck that has a long pointed tail and brown and white plumage. Native to: N hemisphere. *Anas acuta*. [< the pointed tip of the male bird's tail]

Pinter /píntər/, **Harold** (*b.* 1930) British playwright and director —**Pinteresque** /píntə résk/ *adj*

pintle /pínt'l/ *n* a pin or bolt, especially one used as a vertical pivot or hinge, e.g. on a rudder [Old English *pintle* 'peg, penis' < Germanic]

pinto /píntō/ *adj US, Can* ZOOL = **piebald** *adj.* ■ *n* (*plural* **-tos**) *US, Can* ZOOL = **piebald** *n.* [Mid-19C. Via Spanish, 'painted' < Latin *pingere* 'to paint'.]

pinto bean *n* **1** a mottled brown and pink kidney-shaped bean, cooked and eaten as a vegetable or used as fodder **2** a variety of kidney bean that produces pinto beans [*Pinto* < Spanish, 'painted, mottled']

pint-size, pint-sized *adj* very small, especially smaller than usual or than expected (*informal*)

pin tuck *n* a narrow vertical fold stitched in place and used for decoration, especially on the front of clothes —**pin-tucked** *adj*

pin-up *n* **1** a photograph or poster of a sexually attractive person, especially one in which the person is posing in a seductive way and scantily clothed or naked **2** somebody considered attractive enough to appear in a pin-up picture

pinwheel /pín weel/ *n US, Can* **1** = **windmill** *n.* 4 **2** = **Catherine wheel** *n.* 1

pinwork /pín wurk/ *n* the delicate stitches that are raised above the main design in the embroidery of needlepoint lace

pinworm /pín wurm/ *n* **1** a thread-shaped nematode worm that occurs as a parasite in the intestines of vertebrate animals, including human beings. Family: Oxyuridae. **2** an infestation of pinworms

Pinyin /pín yín/ *n* a system for transliterating written Chinese characters into the Roman alphabet, introduced in 1959 and adopted by the People's Republic of China in 1979 [Mid-20C. < Mandarin Chinese *pīnyīn* 'spell sound'.]

pinyon *n* TREES = **piñon**

piolet /pée ə lay/ *n* a double-headed ice axe used by mountaineers [Mid-19C. < French dialect < *piola* 'small axe'; ultimately < Germanic.]

pion /pī on/ *n* any of the group of three mesons that have either single positive, negative, or zero charge, a mass approximately 270 times that of the electron, and spin zero [Mid-20C. < *pi meson*.]

pioneer /pī ə néer/ *n* **1 INVENTOR OR INNOVATOR** a person or group that is the first to do something or that leads in developing something new **2 FIRST PERSON TO EXPLORE TERRITORY** an explorer or settler of a territory previously unclaimed by his or her country of origin **3 SOLDIER WHO BUILDS THINGS** a foot soldier whose duties include going ahead of the main company to construct things to pave the way for them **4 FIRST SPECIES TO GROW SOMEWHERE** the first species of plant or animal life to begin living in a previously unoccupied site, e.g. a moss beginning to grow on otherwise bare rock ■ *v* **1** *vt* **INVENT NEW THING** to experiment with or develop something new **2** *vt* **GO INTO UNEXPLORED TERRITORY** to go into previously uncharted or unclaimed territory with the aim of exploring it and possibly settling there **3** *vi* **ACT AS PIONEER** to act as a pioneer in a specified field [Early 16C. Via French *pionnier* < medieval Latin *pedon-* 'foot soldier' < Latin *ped-*, stem of *pes* 'foot'.]

pious /pī əss/ *adj* **1 RELIGIOUS** devoutly religious **2 RELIGIOUSLY REVERENT** characterized by religious reverence **3 ACTING IN FALSELY MORALIZING WAY** talking or acting in a falsely, hypocritically, or affectedly moralizing way **4 HOLY OR SACRED** holy or sacred, especially as distinct from worldly **5 PRAISEWORTHY** deserving to be praised **6 SHOWING DUE RESPECT** showing appropriate respect, especially towards parents (*archaic*) [15C. < Latin *pius* 'dutiful'.] —**piously** *adv* —**piousness** *n*

pip[1] /pip/ *n* **1 SEED OF FRUIT** a small hard seed of an edible fruit such as an apple, pear, or orange **2 SECTION OF PINEAPPLE SKIN** any one of the many irregular diamond-shaped sections on the outer skin of a pineapple **3 ROOTSTOCK OR FLOWER** a rootstock or flower of certain plants, especially the lily of the valley [Late 18C. Shortening of PIPPIN.]

pip[2] /pip/ *n* **1 SPOT ON DIE OR DOMINO** a single spot on a die or domino **2 MARK ON PLAYING CARD** a single symbol of a club, diamond, heart, or spade on a playing card **3 SHORT HIGH-PITCHED SOUND** a short, usually high-pitched sound, especially of the kind used in broadcasting as a time signal **4 SOMETHING INDICATING RANK** something such as a diamond-shaped insignia on the shoulder of a British Army officer's uniform that indicates rank (*informal*) **5 SPECK** a very small mark or piece of something ■ *v* (**pips, pipping, pipped**) **1** *vi* **CHEEP** to make a cheeping sound, especially when newly hatched (*refers to birds*) **2** *vti* **USE BEAK TO BREAK SHELL** to use the beak to break through the shell during hatching (*refers to birds*) **3** *vi* **MAKE SHRILL NOISE** to make or emit a short shrill noise [Late 16C. < ?]

pip[3] /pip/ *n* **1 CONTAGIOUS POULTRY DISEASE** a contagious disease of birds, especially domestic ones, characterized by the presence of a thick crust in the mouth and throat, caused by an abnormal secretion of mucus **2 MINOR AILMENT** a slight ailment in humans (*informal dated*) ■ *vt* (**pips, pipping, pipped**) **IRRITATE** to make somebody annoyed or upset (*informal dated*) [14C. Via Middle Dutch *pippe* < Latin *pituita* 'phlegm'.] ◇ **give somebody the pip** to annoy or irritate somebody (*dated informal*)

pip[4] /pip/ (**pips, pipping, pipped**) *vt* (*informal*) **1** to beat somebody in competition, especially when it looked as though the other person was going to stay ahead **2** to wound or kill a person or animal with a bullet from a gun [Late 19C. < ?]

pipa[1] /péepə/ *n* a completely aquatic American toad that has a flattened body, large webbed feet, and no eyelids or tongue. Genus: *Pipa*. [Early 18C. Probably < Galibi.]

pipa[2] /pée paa/ *n* a plucked four-stringed Chinese instrument with a fretted fingerboard like a guitar's [Mid-19C. < Chinese *píba* 'loquat'; from its shape.]

pipal /péep'l/, **peepul** *n* TREES = **bo tree** [Late 18C. < Hindi *pīpal*.]

pipe[1] /pīp/ *n* **1 TUBE FOR TRANSPORTING LIQUID OR GAS** a long cylindrical tube that water, oil, gas, or other such material passes through **2 TUBE OF ANY KIND** an object in tubular form **3 DEVICE FOR SMOKING TOBACCO** a small bowl with a hollow stem coming from it, used for smoking tobacco or other substances **4 AMOUNT IN SMOKER'S PIPE** the amount of tobacco or other substance that the bowl of a smoker's pipe holds **5 HOLLOW BODY PART** a tubular part or organ in a plant or animal, especially one in an animal's respiratory system **6 TUBULAR MUSICAL INSTRUMENT** a tubular musical instrument that is played by blowing air into it **7 TUBULAR PART OF MUSICAL ORGAN** an upright tubular part of a musical organ that produces sound when air is blown into it **8 WIND INSTRUMENT OF MIDDLE AGES** a three-holed wind instrument of the Middle Ages, played with one hand while the other hand beats on a small drum **9 SAILOR'S WHISTLE** a small whistle used for signalling orders to a crew, usually by a boatswain **10 CYLINDER-SHAPED GEOLOGICAL FORMATION** a vertical cylinder-shaped geological formation such as a vein of ore **11 PASSAGE THROUGH WHICH LAVA FLOWS** a vertical passage through which molten lava flows **12 HOLE IN CAST METAL** a conical cavity in the middle of a piece of metal, produced by gas escaping as the metal cools **13 HIGH-PITCHED NOISE** a high-pitched or shrill noise such as a birdcall ■ **pipes** *npl* **1 BAGPIPES** the bagpipes **2 HUMAN RESPIRATORY SYSTEM** the human respiratory system or vocal cords (*slang*) ■ *v* (**pipes, piping, piped**) **1** *vt* **CARRY BY PIPE** to carry something, especially water, gas, or a semisolid, by means of a pipe, pipeline, or system of pipes ○ *The company pipes crude oil to the refinery.* **2** *vti* **INSTALL AND CONNECT PIPES** to equip something with pipes, or install pipes and their connections in something **3** *vt* **PLAY TUNE ON PIPE** to play a tune on a musical pipe **4** *vt* **SEND PIPED MUSIC THROUGH PLACE** to play prerecorded music in a public place or workplace to create a soothing atmosphere **5** *vt* **SIGNAL SOMETHING USING PIPE** to signal the arrival or departure of somebody or something using a pipe **6** *vt* **ORDER CREW USING BOATSWAIN'S PIPE** to give orders to a crew using a boatswain's pipe **7** *vt* **DECORATE GARMENT WITH PIPING** to add decorative piping to a garment or to soft furnishing **8** *vt* **DECORATE FOOD WITH PIPING** to add decorative piping to food, especially by forcing it out of a bag that has a nozzle designed to create the various decorative forms **9** *vti* **MAKE HIGH-PITCHED NOISE** to make a high-pitched or shrill noise, or speak in a squeaky voice [Old English *pīpe*, via Vulgar Latin *pipa* < Latin *pipare* 'to peep, cheep', ultimately an imitation of the sound] —**pipeful** *n*

pipe down *vi* to stop talking or become less noisy or boisterous (*informal*)

pipe up *vi* **1** to say something, often as an interruption or a clarification **2** to begin to sing or play a musical instrument

pipe[2] /pīp/ *n* **1 LARGE CONTAINER FOR LIQUID** a large container for wine, oil, or some other liquid **2 UNIT OF LIQUID CAPACITY** a unit of liquid measure for wine, equal to four barrels, two hogsheads, or 105 gallons **3 CASK** a cask that has the capacity of four barrels, two hogsheads, or 105 gallons [14C. Via Anglo-Norman < Vulgar Latin *pipa* (see PIPE[1]).]

pipe band *n* a marching or military band with bagpipes, drums, and often a drum major, typically playing traditional Scottish music

pipe bomb *n* a bomb made of a length of pipe that is filled with explosives and is capped at its ends

pipeclay /pīp klay/ *n* a very fine white pure clay used in the manufacture of pottery and smokers' pipes, and for whitening leather and other materials ■ *vt* to use pipeclay for whitening leather or some other, usually natural, material

pipe cleaner *n* a flexible wire covered with fluffy material that is used for cleaning the stems of smokers' pipes and other things that are difficult to access

piped music *n* prerecorded, usually easy-listening music played through speakers in public places and some workplaces to create a soothing atmosphere

pipe dream *n* an aim, hope, idea, or plan so fanciful that it is very unlikely to be realized [< the dreams caused by smoking opium]

pipefish /pīp fish/ (*plural* **-fish** *or* **-fishes**) *n* a mainly marine fish with a long slender body protected by bony rings, a long tubular snout, and a small mouth. Native to: warm and temperate regions. Family: Syngnathidae.

pipefitting /pīp fiting/ *n* **1 BRANCH OF PLUMBING INVOLVING PIPES** the branch of plumbing that involves measuring, cutting, bending, and joining lengths of pipe, either in installation or repairs **2 ACT OR PROCESS OF PIPE INSTALLATION** an act or process of installing or connecting pipes **3 SOMETHING USED IN CONNECTING PIPES** something that is used in the connection or joining of pipes —**pipefitter** *n*

pipeline /pīp līn/ *n* **1 LONG PIPE SYSTEM FOR TRANSPORTING** a pipe or system of pipes designed to carry something such as oil, natural gas, or other petroleum-based products over long distances, often underground **2 CHANNEL OF COMMUNICATIONS** a channel of communications, especially a private one among several people within a single organization **3 SYSTEM FOR SUPPLYING** a system for the supply or transfer of something, especially goods or information ■ *vt* (**-lines, -lining, -lined**) **1 SEND SOMETHING BY PIPE SYSTEM** to send, connect, or carry something by way of a long system of pipes **2 FIT SOMETHING WITH LONG PIPE SYSTEM** to fit or supply something with a long system of pipes ◇ **in the pipeline** in preparation but not yet ready

pipe major *n* a noncommissioned officer in charge of a regiment's pipe band

pip-emma /píp émmə/ *adv* in the afternoon (*dated informal*) [Early 20C. < the former code names for the letters 'p' and 'm'.]

pipe of peace *n* = **peace pipe**

pipe organ *n* a musical organ that uses pipes to produce the sound, as opposed to a reed organ or an electric organ. Most church organs are pipe organs.

piper /pīpər/ *n* **1** a player of the bagpipes **2** a player of a pipe ◇ **he who pays the piper calls the tune** used to say that the person who is paying for something will control what happens

piperazine /pi pérrə zeen/ *n* $C_4H_{10}N_2$ a colourless crystalline compound. Use: parasiticide, insecticide. [Late 19C. Blend of PIPERIDINE + AZINE.]

piperidine /pi pérri deen/ *n* $C_5H_{11}N$ a colourless liquid compound that has a peppery odour resembling ammonia. Use: manufacture of rubber and epoxy resins. [Mid-19C. < PIPERINE + -IDINE.]

piperine /píppə reen/ *n* $C_{17}H_{19}NO_3$ a white crystalline alkaloid compound that is the chief active component of pepper [Early 19C. < Latin *piper* (see PEPPER).]

piperonal /píppərō nal/ *n* $C_{19}H_{63}$ a white crystalline compound that has an odour resembling heliotrope. Use: in perfumes and flavourings. [Mid-19C. < German < *Piperin* 'piperine'.]

pipe snake *n* a tropical snake with a fused inflexible skull, vestiges of hind limbs, and two unequally-sized lungs. Family: Anillidae.

pipes of Pan *npl* MUSIC = **panpipes**

pipestem /pīp stem/ *n* the long, slender stem of a pipe for smoking tobacco ■ *adj* US long, narrow, and very skinny ○ *his pipestem legs*

pipestone /pīp stōn/ *n* a reddish or pinkish stone resembling clay in consistency that some Native North Americans harden and use for decorative objects and long, often ornate pipes

pipette /pi pét/ *n* a small glass tube that liquid is drawn into so that it can be measured, often before delivering it to another container, e.g. in experiments or in medication doses ■ *vt* (**-pettes, -petting, -petted**) to measure or deliver an accurate amount of liquid using a pipette [Mid-19C. < French, 'little pipe' < *pipe* 'pipe' < Vulgar Latin *pipa* (see PIPE[1]).]

pipi /píppee/ (*plural* **-pi** *or* **-pis**) *n* ANZ an edible shellfish [Mid-19C. < Maori.]

piping /pīping/ *n* **1 PIPES COLLECTIVELY** pipes thought of collectively, especially when they form a connected plumbing system in a house or other building **2 DECORATIVE TWISTED CORD** a twisted cord covered with fabric inserted into a seam as a decoration. Use: clothes, soft furnishings. **3 DECORATIVE EFFECT ON FOOD** a decorative effect used on food, especially strands or swirls of icing in a contrasting colour **4 SKILL OF PLAYING MUSICAL PIPE** the art, technique, or skill of playing the bagpipes or another kind of musical pipe **5 SOUND OF MUSICAL PIPE** the sound of bagpipes or some other musical pipe **6 SHRILL NOISE** a shrill, high-pitched, or whistling noise ■ *adj* **SHRILLY PITCHED** shrill and very high in pitch, as some voices are

pipistrelle /píppi strél/, **pipistrel** *n* a small brown insect-eating bat found throughout the world. Genus: *Pipistrellus*. [Late 18C. Via French and Italian < Latin *vespertilio* 'bat' < *vesper* 'evening'.]

pipit /píppit/ *n* a small songbird in the wagtail family with brown speckled plumage and a long tail. Family: Motacillidae. [Mid-18C. An imitation of the bird's call.]

pipkin /pípkin/ *n* a small cooking pot, usually made of metal or earthenware and with a handle going across the top [Mid-16C. < ?]

pippin /píppin/ *n* **1 VARIETY OF APPLE** a variety of cultivated eating or cooking apples **2 PIP OR SEED** a pip or seed, especially an apple pip **3 DESIRABLE OR ADMIRABLE PERSON OR THING** somebody or something that is particularly desirable or admirable (*dated informal*) [14C. < French *pepin*.]

pipsissewa /pip síssəwə/ (*plural* **-was** *or* **-wa**) *n* an evergreen plant with jagged astringent leaves that are used medicinally as a diuretic. Flowers: white or pinkish. Genus: *Chimaphila*. [Late 18C. < Abenaki *kpi-pskwàhsawe* 'flower of the woods'.]

pipsqueak /píp skweek/ *n* somebody or something that is small or insignificant, but nevertheless often annoying or troublesome (*informal*) [Early 20C. Thought to suggest smallness and insignificance.]

piquant /peékənt, -kaant/ *adj* **1 SPICY OR SAVOURY** having a flavour, taste, or smell that is spicy or savoury, often with a slightly tart or bitter edge to it **2 SHARPLY STIMULATING OR PROVOCATIVE** refreshingly interesting, stimulating, or provocative **3 SHARPLY CRITICAL AND BITING** excessively severe or hurtful, e.g. in tone or content [Early 16C. < French, present participle of *piquer* 'to prick, sting' (see PIQUE[1]).] —**piquancy** *n* —**piquantly** *adv* —**piquantness** *n*

pique[1] /peek/ *n* **BAD MOOD** a bad mood or feeling of resentment, especially when brought on by an insult, hurt pride, or loss of face ■ *v* (**piques, piquing, piqued**) **1** *vt* **PUT SOMEBODY IN BAD MOOD** to cause somebody to be in a bad mood or to feel resentful **2** *vt* **AROUSE SOMEBODY'S INTEREST** to cause a feeling of interest, curiosity, or excitement in somebody **3** *vr* **TAKE PRIDE IN** to take pride in something, especially a personal attribute or ability [Mid-16C. Via French *piquer* 'prick, irritate' < assumed Vulgar Latin *piccare*.]

SPELLCHECK See ***peak***

pique[2] /peek/ *n* in the game of piquet, a score of 30 points to an opponent's 0 from the hand as dealt ■ *vti* (**piques, piquing, piqued**) in the game of piquet, to score a pique against an opponent [Mid-17C. < French *pic* < ?]

piqué /peé kay/ *n* a closely woven ribbed fabric produced from natural fibres. Use: clothes. [Mid-19C. < French, past participle of *piquer* 'to prick, stitch' (see PIQUE[1]).]

piquet /pi két, -káy/, **picquet** *n* a card game for two players using a deck that does not include two to six [Mid-17C. < French < ?]

piracy /pīrəssi/ *n* **1 ROBBERY ON HIGH SEAS** robbery on the high seas, especially the stealing of a ship's cargo **2 ROBBERY ON ANY FORM OF TRANSPORT** robbery committed on board any form of transport, especially an aircraft **3 HIJACKING** the hijacking of an aircraft or another form of transport **4 USE OF COPYRIGHT MATERIAL WITHOUT PERMISSION** the taking and using of copyright or patented material without authorization or without the legal right to do so **5 ILLEGAL BROADCASTING** the unauthorized or illegal broadcasting of TV or radio programmes [Mid-16C. < medieval Latin *piratia* < Latin *pirata* (see PIRATE).]

Piraeus /pī reé əss/ city in east-central Greece, the port of Athens. Population: 182,671 (1991).

piragua /pi raágwə, pi rággwə/ *n* = **pirogue** [Early 17C. Via American Spanish < Carib, 'dugout'.]

piraña *n* ZOOL = **piranha**

Pirandello /pírrən déllō/, **Luigi** (1867–1936) Italian playwright

Piranesi /pírrə náyzi/, **Giovanni Battista** (1720–78) Italian artist

piranha /pi raánə/ (*plural* **-nhas** *or* **-nha**), **piraña** (*plural* **-ñas** *or* **-ña**) *n* a small freshwater fish that has sharp teeth, strong jaws, and is a dangerous predator when attacking in large numbers. Native to: South America. Genus: *Serrasalmo*. [Mid-18C. Via Portuguese < Tupi *piráya*.]

pirate /pīrət/ *n* **1 ROBBER AT SEA** a robber who operates on an ocean or seas **2 SHIP USED BY SEA ROBBERS** a ship used by people who rob or otherwise attack shipping on the high seas **3 SOMEBODY USING COPYRIGHT MATERIAL WITHOUT PERMISSION** an unauthorized or illegal duplicator or user of copyright or patented material **4 SOMEBODY INVOLVED IN ILLEGAL BROADCASTING** somebody who takes part in or manages the unauthorized or illegal broadcasting of TV or radio programmes ■ *v* (**-rates, -rating, -rated**) **1** *vti* **ROB SOMETHING ON HIGH SEAS** to rob a vessel or commit robbery on the high seas **2** *vt* **USE COPYRIGHT MATERIAL WITHOUT PERMISSION** to duplicate or use copyright or patented material without authorization or without the legal right to do so [13C. Via Latin *pirata* < Greek *peiratēs* < *peiran* 'to attack'.] —**piratic** /pī ráttik/ *adj* —**piratically** /-ráttikli/ *adv*

pirog /pi rṓg/ (*plural* **-rogi** /-rṓgi/ *or* **-roghi**) *n* a large rectangular pie that has a pastry crust top and bottom, filled with chopped meat or cabbage, onions, and hard-boiled eggs [Mid-19C. < Russian.]

pirogue /pi rṓg/ *n* a canoe made from a hollowed-out tree trunk [Early 17C. Via French < Carib *piragua* 'dugout'.]

piroshki *n* FOOD = **pirozhki**

pirouette /pírroo ét/ *n* a spin of the body, especially one performed in ballet on tiptoe or on the ball of one foot [Mid-17C. Via French < Old French, 'spinning top' < ?]

pirozhki /pi róshki/, **piroshki** *npl* very small fried or baked pastries, usually filled with finely chopped meat or cabbage and onions (+ *singular or plural verb*) [Early 20C. < Russian, 'little pirog' < PIROG.]

Pisa /peéza/ city in west-central Italy. Population: 97,872 (1993). ◊ **Leaning Tower of Pisa**

pis aller /peéz állay/ (*plural* **pis allers** /peéz állay/) *n* something that is done as a last resort or when no other option is available [< French < *pis* 'worse' + *aller* 'to go']

Pisano /pi zaánō/, **Giovanni** (1250?–1314?) Italian sculptor

Pisano, Nicola (1220?–84?) Italian sculptor

piscary /pískəri/ (*plural* **-ries**) *n* **1** a place where people fish or are allowed to fish **2** the legal right to fish in a particular place even if it belongs to another person [15C. Via medieval Latin *piscaria* < Latin *piscis* 'fish' (see PISCI-).]

piscatorial /pískə táwri əl/, **piscatory** /pískətəri/ *adj* relating to fish, fishing, or people who fish (*formal*) [Early 19C. Via Latin *piscatorius* < *piscis* 'fish' (see PISCI-).] —**piscatorially** *adv*

Pisces /pí seez/ (*plural* **-sces**) *n* **1 12TH SIGN OF ZODIAC** the 12th sign of the zodiac, represented by two fishes and lasting from approximately 19 February to 20 March **2 SOMEBODY BORN UNDER PISCES** somebody whose birthday falls between 19 February and 20 March **3 ZODIACAL CONSTELLATION BETWEEN AQUARIUS AND PISCES** a large faint zodiacal constellation of the northern hemisphere. See illustration at **constellation** [Pre-12C. < Latin, plural of *piscis* 'fish'.] —**Pisces** *adj* —**Piscean** /píssi ən/ *n*

pisci- *prefix* fish ○ *housekeeping* *pisciform* [< Latin *piscis* < Indo-European]

pisciculture /píssi kulchər/ *n* the controlled breeding, hatching, and rearing of fish, especially for scientific or commercial purposes [Mid-19C. < Latin *piscis* 'fish' (see PISCI-).] —**piscicultural** /píssi kúlchərəl/ *adj* —**pisciculturally** /-kúlchərəli/ *adv* —**pisciculturist** /-kúlchərist/ *n*

piscina /pi seénə/ (*plural* **-nas** *or* **-nae** /-nee/) *n* **1** in some Christian churches, a sacred container or basin that holds holy water, used to carry it away after ablutions have been completed **2** the place where a priest can wash his hands and the sacred containers used in Mass, located in the sacristy, especially in a Roman Catholic church [Late 16C. Via medieval Latin, 'fish pond' < *piscis* 'fish' (see PISCI-).] —**piscinal** /píssin'l/ *adj*

piscine /píssīn/ *adj* relating to, characteristic of, or resembling fish (*formal*) [Late 18C. Via medieval Latin *piscinus* < Latin *piscis* 'fish' (see PISCI-).]

Piscis Austrinus /píssiss o strínəss, píssiss-/ *n* a small constellation of the southern hemisphere. See illustration at **constellation**

piscivorous /pi sívvərəss/ *adj* feeding habitually or mainly on fish

pisé /peé zay/, **pisé de terre** /-də táir/ *n* compressed earth or clay used for making floors or walls [Late 18C. < French *pisé de terre* 'beaten earth'.]

pish /pish/ *interj* used to express contempt, annoyance, or impatience (*dated*) [Late 16C. Natural exclamation.]

pishogue /pi shṓg/, **pishoge** *n Ireland* **1** superstition or old-fashioned nonsense **2** a superstitious belief or practice [Early 19C. < Irish *piseog*.]

pisiform /píssi fawrm/ *adj* resembling a pea in shape or size ■ *n* ANAT = **pisiform bone** [Mid-18C. < Latin *pisum* 'pea'.]

pisiform bone *n* the small knobbly bone at the place where the inner bone of the forearm (**ulna**) joins the wrist (**carpus**)

pismire /píss mīr/ *n* an ant (*archaic or informal*) [14C. < PISS (from the smell of formic acid) + obsolete *mire* 'ant'.]

pisolite /píssō līt/ *n* an inorganic limestone consisting of individual spherical concretions (**pisoliths**) [Early 18C. < Greek *pisos* 'pea' + -LITE.] —**pisolitic** /píssō líttik/ *adj*

pisolith /píssəlith/ *n* a spherical concretion with concentric laminations that with others makes up an inorganic limestone. Pisoliths can be up to 10 cm/4 in in diameter. [Late 18C. < Greek *pisos* 'pea' + -LITH.]

piss /piss/ *v* (*slang*) **1** *vi* an offensive term meaning to urinate **2** *vt* an offensive term meaning to discharge a substance, e.g. blood, when urinating **3** *vt* an offensive term meaning to urinate on or into something ■ *n* (*slang*) **1** an offensive term for urine **2** an offensive term for an act or instance of urinating [13C. Via French *pisser* < assumed Vulgar Latin *pissiare*, ultimately an imitation of the sound.] ◇ **on the piss** an offensive phrase meaning taking part in a heavy alcohol-drinking session (*slang*) ◇ **piss and vinegar** *US* an offensive phrase for feisty strength of character and physical vigour (*slang*) ◇ **piss yourself (laughing)** an offensive phrase meaning to laugh uncontrollably (*slang*) ◇ **take the piss** an offensive phrase meaning to ridicule or mock somebody or something (*slang*)

piss about, piss around *v* (*slang*) **1** *vt* an offensive term meaning to annoy somebody or waste somebody's time, especially deliberately **2** *vi* an offensive term meaning to behave in a silly or childish way, especially by wasting time

piss away *vt* an offensive term meaning to waste or squander something, e.g. money or time (*slang*)

piss down *vi* an offensive term meaning to rain heavily (*slang*)

piss off *v* (*slang*) **1** *vt* an offensive term meaning to annoy, irritate, or upset somebody **2** *vi* an offensive term often used as a command to tell somebody to go away and stop being annoying

pissant /píss ant/, **piss ant** *n US* **1** an offensive term for somebody who pays too much attention to small details **2** an offensive term for somebody regarded as being of no importance, significance, or consequence ■ *adj US* **1** an offensive term meaning paying too much attention to small details **2** an offensive term meaning regarded as being of no importance, significance, or consequence [Mid-17C. < PISS + ANT.]

Pissarro /pi saárō/, **Camille** (1830–1903) French painter

piss artist *n* (*slang*) **1** an offensive term for somebody who regularly drinks a lot of alcohol or who regularly gets drunk **2** an offensive term for somebody who is regarded as completely incompetent or who is thought to exaggerate his or her competence

pissed /pist/ *adj* **1** an offensive term meaning extremely drunk (*slang*) **2** *US* = **pissed off** (*slang offensive*)

pissed off *adj* an offensive term meaning very annoyed or angry (*slang*) US term **pissed** *adj.* 2

pisser /píssər/ *n* an offensive term for a situation that is extremely annoying or disappointing (*slang*)

pisshead /píss hed/ *n* an offensive term for somebody who frequently or habitually gets very drunk (*slang*)

pissoir /píss waar/ *n* a public urinal, especially one on the streets of some European cities, with a circular screen round it [Early 20C. < French < *pisser* (see PISS).]

pisspot /píss pot/ *n US* an offensive term for somebody regarded as ill-tempered and generally mean (*slang*) [Originally 'chamber pot']

piss-take *n* an offensive term for a parody, especially one that involves mockery or ridicule (*slang*) —**piss-taker** *n* —**piss-taking** *n*

piss-up *n* (*slang*) **1** an offensive term for a heavy alcohol-drinking session **2** an offensive term for a deplorable mess or mix-up

pistachio /pi staáshi ō, pi stásh-/ *n* **1 pistachio** (*plural* **-os**), **pistachio nut** a nut with a small green kernel that is eaten fresh and also yields an edible oil **2** (*plural* **-os** *or* **-o**) a tree of the cashew family that produces pistachios. Native to: W Asia. *Pistachia vera*. [15C. Via Old French *pistace* and Italian *pistacchio* < Greek *pistakion* < *pistakē* 'pistachio tree'.]

pistachio green *adj* of a pale whitish-green colour, like a pistachio kernel —**pistachio green** *n*

pistachio nut *n* FOOD = **pistachio** *n.* 1

piste /peest/ *n* **1** a downhill track or area of densely packed snow that provides good skiing conditions **2** a rectangular area, sometimes cordoned off, where a contest, especially a fencing bout, takes place [Early 18C. Via French, 'track' < Latin *pinsere* 'to beat'.]

pistil /pístil/ *n* a carpel or group of fused carpels forming the female reproductive part of a flower and including the ovary, style, and stigma [Early 18C. Directly or via French *pistile* < Latin *pistillum* 'pestle', because of its shape.]

pistillate /písti layt/ *adj* having one or more pistils but usually without stamens

pistol /píst'l/ *n* a small short-barrelled gun designed to be held in one hand ■ *vt* (**-tols, -tolling, -tolled**) to shoot somebody or something using a pistol [Mid-16C. Via French *pistole* < Czech *pišt'ala* 'pipe' < *pištěti* 'whistle', ultimately an imitation of the sound.]

pistole /pis tṓl/ *n* a gold coin used in some European countries during the 17th and 18th centuries [Late 16C. < French, shortening of *pistolet* < ?]

pistoleer /pístə leér/ *n* somebody, especially a soldier, who carries or uses a pistol (*archaic*)

pistol grip *n* a handle that resembles the butt of a pistol, especially in being shaped to fit the hand

pistol-whip *vt* to hit or beat somebody or something with the butt or barrel of a pistol

piston /píst'n/ *n* **1** a metal cylinder that slides up and down inside a tubular housing, receiving pressure from or exerting pressure on a fluid, e.g. in an internal-combustion engine **2** the valve mechanism in a brass musical instrument that is used to alter its pitch [Early 18C. Via French < Italian *pestone* 'large pestle' < *pestare* 'to crush'.]

piston ring *n* a metal ring or series of rings fitted round a piston to ensure a tight seal with the cylinder wall and prevent gaseous leakage

piston rod *n* a rod connected to a piston that transmits the motion of the piston to a pump or an engine

pistou /peé too/ *n* a sauce from Provence made of basil, garlic, and olive oil, similar to Italian pesto [Mid-20C. Via French < Provençal, past participle of *pestar* 'to crush' < late Latin *pistare* (see PESTO).]

pit[1] /pit/ *n* **1 BIG HOLE IN GROUND** a large hole in the ground **2 HOLE IN GROUND FOR MINING** a deep hole in the ground that gives access to a mining resource, especially coal **3 MINESHAFT** a shaft that gives access to a mine **4 SMALL INDENTATION LEFT BY ILLNESS** a small indentation in the skin, usually permanent, left by a disease such as chickenpox or by a skin disorder such as acne **5 SERVICING AREA FOR RACING CARS** an area, or section of an area, off the side of a motor-racing track where vehicles can get fuel, fresh tyres, and repairs (*often plural*) **6 SUNKEN AREA FOR EXAMINING CARS** a sunken area, especially in a garage, where the undersides of cars and other motor vehicles can be inspected and repaired **7 SANDY AREA WHERE JUMPERS LAND** a soft sandy area where a long-jumper, triple-jumper, or pole-vaulter can land safely **8 UNTIDY PLACE** an extremely untidy or dirty place (*informal*) **9 NATURAL HOLLOW** a natural hollow, especially on the surface of a body part **10 CONCAVE SPOT ON PLANT WALL** a tiny concavity or thin-walled area in the wall of a plant serving to help transport water and nutrients **11 LOWEST PART** the very bottom of something **12 AREA CONTAINING PARTICULAR SUBSTANCE** an area filled with a particular material or substance ○ *a tar pit* **13** THEATRE = **orchestra pit 14** = **pitfall** *n.* 2 **15 AREA IN CASINO** the area in a casino where the gambling takes place **16** *US* **AREA ON FLOOR OF EXCHANGE** the area of the floor of an exchange where commodities trading takes place **17 ARENA FOR FIGHTING** an arena that is cordoned off for bouts of fighting, especially illegal fighting between cocks or dogs **18 BED** a bed (*slang*) ■ **pits** *npl* **WORST POSSIBLE THING, PERSON, OR PLACE** the worst or most unpleasant thing, person, or place it is possible to find (*informal*) ■ *vt* (**pits, pitting, pitted**) **1 SET UP IN OPPOSITION** to set somebody or something up in opposition to somebody or something else **2 MARK SURFACE WITH SMALL HOLES** to cause small holes or indentations to form in a surface **3 PUT SOMEBODY OR SOMETHING INTO DEEP HOLE** to put or bury somebody or something in a deep hole [Old English *pytt* < Germanic < Latin *puteus* 'pit, well']

pit[2] /pit/ *n US* the kernel or stone of a fruit ■ *vt* (**pits, pitting, pitted**) *US* to remove the kernel or stone from a fruit [Mid-19C. Probably < Dutch < Germanic.]

pita[1] /píttə, peétə/ *n* a plant such as the agave that yields a strong fibre. Use: paper, cordage. [Late 17C. Via American Spanish < Taino.]

pita[2], **pita bread** *n* FOOD = **pitta**

pitapat /píttə pát/ *adv* **WITH TAPPING SOUND** with quick light tapping noises ■ *n* **SERIES OF TAPPING NOISES** a series of quick light tapping noises, especially those made by light, running feet ■ *vi* (**-pats, -patting, -patted**) **MAKE SERIES OF TAPPING NOISES** to make a series of quick light tapping noises [Early 16C. An imitation of the sound.]

pit bull terrier, pit bull *n* a large bull terrier similar to the Staffordshire bull terrier but more muscular and powerful

Pitcairn Island /pít kairn-/ island in the central South Pacific Ocean, the main island of a group forming a dependency of the United Kingdom. Population: 61 (1991). Area: 36 sq. km/14 sq. mi.

pitch[1] /pich/ *v* **1** *vti* **THROW** to throw or hurl something **2** *vt* **SET UP TEMPORARY STRUCTURE** to set up a camp, tent, marquee, or other temporary structure **3** *vt* **SECURE IN GROUND** to secure, embed, or implant something in the ground **4** *vti* **FALL OR MAKE FALL DOWN** to fall or stumble, or cause somebody or something to fall or stumble, especially headfirst **5** *vi* **SLANT IN PARTICULAR WAY** to slant or slope in a particular way or to a particular level **6** *vi* **WOBBLE UP AND DOWN** to move with the front and rear being alternately uppermost, e.g. in rough water or turbulent air currents (*refers especially to ships and aircraft*) **7** *vt* **SET AT PARTICULAR INTELLECTUAL LEVEL** to put, set, or have something at a particular intellectual level **8** *vt* **BOWL BALL TO BATSMAN** to bowl a ball so that it hits the ground at a particular spot or distance from the batsman **9** *vti* **THROW BALL TO BATTER** to throw a baseball from the mound to the batter **10** *vti* **HIT GOLF BALL HIGH** to hit a high ball, usually onto the green and often with some backspin so that it does not roll too much on landing **11** *vt* **TRY TO SELL OR PROMOTE** to try to sell or promote something such as a product, personal viewpoint, or potential business venture, often in an aggressive way **12** *vt* **SET INSTRUMENT TO PARTICULAR KEY** to set a musical instrument to a particular key **13** *vt* **LEAD CARD TO ESTABLISH TRUMPS** to lead a card of a particular suit in order to establish that suit as trumps for the trick **14** *vi US, Can* **GIVE ENTHUSIASTIC SUPPORT** to provide enthusiastic support for somebody or something ■ *n* **1 PARTICULAR DEGREE** a particular degree or level of something ○ *What drove him to such a pitch of anxiety?* **2 DEGREE OF SLOPE** the degree, angle, or extent of the slope of something, especially a hill, road, or other feature **3 FIELD FOR GAME** a playing area for a team ball game **4 AREA BETWEEN CRICKET STUMPS** the area between the two sets of stumps **5 PLACE WHERE BALL BOUNCES** the point a cricket ball lands on when it is bowled **6 THROW OF BALL** in baseball, the act or an instance of pitching the ball in baseball **7 WAY OF THROWING** a particular way or manner of throwing something, especially a ball **8 HIGHEST OR LOWEST POINT ON FEATURE** the highest or lowest point on a feature such as an arch **9 DEGREE OF ELEVATION OF ROOF** the degree of elevation of a roof, usually expressed in terms of the ratio between its height and its span **10 DISTANCE BETWEEN SIMILAR FORMS** the spacing between adjacent forms on an object that has repeated elements, e.g. the distance between threads on a screw thread **11 PARTICULAR FREQUENCY OF SINGLE NOTE** the level of a sound in a scale, according to its frequency **12 ANGLE OF PROPELLER** the angle formed between the plane of a propeller blade and the plane of rotation of the propeller **13 TOSSING MOTION** an act or instance of pitching up and down, e.g. in rough water or air turbulence **14 PLACE WHERE STALL IS ERECTED** a place where a stall is erected, especially in a street market **15 AGGRESSIVE SPEECH AIMING TO PERSUADE** an aggressive speech given, often more than once, in order to try to persuade somebody to accept or buy something (*informal*) **16 TILT OF GEOLOGICAL FORMATION** the inclination from the horizontal of a geological formation or structure, e.g. a vein or stratum **17 DISTANCE SEPARATING CLIMBERS** the distance between climbers making an ascent or descent using the same ropes, equal to one rope length or less **18 HIGH GOLF SHOT** a golf shot, especially one from fairway to green, in which the ball lofts high in the air, often with some backspin, so that it does not roll too far on landing [12C. < ?] ◇ **queer somebody's pitch** to spoil somebody's plans or prevent somebody from doing something (*informal*)

pitch in *vi* **1** to help or cooperate, especially in a very willing way **2** to begin to do or participate in something, especially with great enthusiasm

pitch into *vt* to begin to attack somebody, either verbally or physically (*informal*)

pitch up *vi* to arrive at a place (*informal*)

pitch[2] /pich/ *n* **1 SUBSTANCE OBTAINED FROM TAR** a dark sticky substance obtained from tar and used in the building trade, especially for waterproofing roofs **2 NATURAL TARRY SUBSTANCE** a sticky dark substance such as asphalt, found naturally **3 RESIN** resin that is obtained from the sap of certain pine trees ■ *vt* **SPREAD PITCH ON SURFACE** to coat a surface with pitch [Partly Old English *pic*, and partly < Anglo-Norman *piche*, both ultimately < Latin *pix*]

pitch-and-putt *n* **1** a game similar to regulation golf, but played on a much shorter course, in which players use only two clubs, an iron and a putter **2** a course for pitch-and-putt, with holes shorter than those for regulation golf

pitch-and-toss *n* a game of skill and luck that involves each player throwing a coin towards a designated spot

pitchbend /pích bend/ *n* an instrumental and vocal technique by which the pitch of a note is modified by raising or lowering it slightly

pitch-black *adj* extremely dark, especially when dark enough to make seeing difficult or impossible

pitchblende /pích blend/ *n* a dark-coloured form of the mineral uraninite. Use: source of uranium and radium. [Late 18C. < German *Pechblende* < *Pech* 'pitch' + *Blende* (see BLENDE).]

pitch-dark *adj* = **pitch-black**

pitched battle *n* **1** a fierce battle, usually involving a large number of people and fought between two sides who take up prearranged positions in close proximity to each other **2** a large-scale, usually bitter conflict or confrontation, often including people who have no direct involvement with the matter

pitcher[1] /píchər/ *n* **1** a large single-handled water jug, usually wide around the middle, gradually narrowing towards the neck, and flaring out at the lip or spout **2** a modified urn-shaped leaf of the pitcher plant [13C. Via Old French *pichier* < medieval Latin *bicarium* < an assumed Vulgar Latin word.]

pitcher[2] /píchər/ *n* **1** in baseball, the player on the fielding side who stands on the mound and throws the ball in the direction of the batter, attempting to cause the batter to make an out **2** a paving stone, especially one made of granite [Early 18C. < PITCH[1].]

pitcher plant *n* a plant with leaves that are pitcher-shaped to attract, trap, and digest insects. Family: Sarraceniaceae.

pitchfork /pích fawrk/ *n* **PRONGED FARMING TOOL** a farming implement, usually with a long handle and two or three widely spaced, slightly curved prongs, that is used for stacking, turning, and moving hay ■ *vt* **1 USE PITCHFORK TO MOVE HAY** to use a pitchfork to lift, turn, or move hay **2 THRUST SOMEBODY INTO DIFFICULT SITUATION** to cause somebody to become involved in a situation that is extremely difficult and unwanted [13C. Alteration of *pickfork* (influenced by PITCH[1]) < PITCH[1].]

pitch pine *n* a pine tree that yields pitch or turpentine. Native to: E North America. *Pinus rigida.*

pitchy /píchi/ (**-ier, -iest**) *adj* **1** covered with or full of pitch **2** resembling pitch, especially in colour, smell, or consistency —**pitchiness** *n*

piteous /pítti əss/ *adj* deserving pity or bringing out feelings of pity [13C. Via Old French *piteus* 'full of pity' < Latin *pietas* 'compassion'.] —**piteously** *adv* —**piteousness** *n*

pitfall /pít fawl/ *n* **1** a potential disaster or difficulty, often one that is unexpected or cannot be anticipated **2** a deep hole in the ground disguised in some way, often with a canopy of foliage covering its top opening and sides so steep that escape is impossible

pith /pith/ *n* **1 TISSUE UNDER RIND OF CITRUS FRUITS** the soft whitish fibrous tissue that lies under the outer rind of citrus fruits **2 TISSUE INSIDE STEM OF PLANT** the central spongy tissue of the stem of a vascular plant **3 CENTRAL PART OF** the central or most important or significant part of something such as an argument or discussion **4 SPONGY INTERIOR OF BODY PART** the soft spongy inner material of a part of the body such as a hair shaft or bone **5 VIGOUR** vigour, stamina, weight, or substance ■ *vt* **1 CUT LABORATORY ANIMAL'S SPINAL CORD** to cut or destroy the spinal cord of a vertebrate as part of a laboratory experiment **2 KILL ANIMALS BY CUTTING SPINAL CORD** to kill animals, especially cattle, by cutting through the spinal cord **3 REMOVE PITH FROM PLANT STEM** to remove the pith from the centre of a plant stem [Old English *piþa* < Germanic]

pithead /pít hed/ *n* the top part of a mineshaft, including the machinery, equipment, and buildings

Pithecanthropus /píthi kánthrəpəss/ (*plural* **-pi** /-pī/) *n* the original genus name of Java Man, now classified as Homo erectus [Late 19C. < modern Latin, < Greek *pithēkos* 'ape' + *anthrōpos* 'human being'.] —**pithecanthropic** /píthi kan thróppik/ *adj* —**pithecanthropine** /píthi kánthrə pīn/ *adj* —**pithecanthropoid** /-kánthrə poyd/ *adj*

pith helmet *n* a lightweight hat made from dried pith or some other material, worn in hot climates to protect the head, face, and the back of the neck from strong sunlight

pithos /píth oss, pī́-/ (*plural* **-oi** /-thoy/) *n* a large jar, usually made of pottery, used in ancient Greece for storing oil or grain [Late 19C. < Greek.]

pithy /píthi/ (**-ier, -iest**) *adj* **1** brief yet forceful and to the point, often with an element of wit **2** relating to, full of, or resembling pith —**pithily** *adv* —**pithiness** *n*

pitiable /pítti əb'l/ *adj* **1** arousing or deserving pity or compassion **2** arousing or deserving contempt or derision —**pitiableness** *n* —**pitiably** *adv*

pitiful /píttif'l/ *adj* **1** arousing or deserving pity or compassion **2** arousing or deserving contempt or derision —**pitifully** *adv* —**pitifulness** *n*

pitiless /píttiləss/ *adj* **1** lacking in pity, mercy, or sympathy **2** severe to the highest degree possible ○ *the blazing, pitiless sun* —**pitilessly** *adv* —**pitilessness** *n*

Pitjantjatjara /píchənchə chárrə/ (*plural* **-ra** *or* **-ras**), **Pitjantjara** /píchən járrə/ (*plural* **-ra** *or* **-ras**) *n* **1** a member of an Australian Aboriginal people who live in the desert regions in the south of the continent **2** the Pama-Nyungan language of the Pitjantjatjara people. Native speakers: 2,000. [< Pitjantjatjara]

pitlane /pít layn/ *n* a part of a motor racing circuit's track that leads into the pits or from the pits back to the main track

Pitlochry /pit lókhri, pit lókri/ town in central Scotland. Population: 2,541 (1991).

pitman /pítmən/ (*plural* **-men** /-mən/) *n* a worker in a mine, especially somebody who works at a coalface

piton /peé ton/ *n* a metal spike for driving into ice or a rock crevice, with an eye at the other end so that a rope can be passed through it and then secured [Late 19C. < French, 'eye-bolt'.]

Pitot-static tube /peétō staáttik-/ *n* a device consisting of a Pitot tube and a static tube, used to measure fluid velocity and especially as an air speed indicator in aircraft [Early 20C. See PITOT TUBE.]

Pitot tube /peétō-/ *n* **1** an instrument placed in a moving fluid and used along with a manometer to measure fluid velocity **2** = **Pitot-static tube** [Late 19C. After Henri *Pitot* (1695–1771), French physicist.]

pit stop *n* **1 REFUELLING STOP FOR CAR DURING RACE** a stop in the pits to allow a racing car to be refuelled and serviced during a race **2 BRIEF STOP DURING ROAD JOURNEY** a brief stop during a journey by road to rest, refuel, use a toilet, or buy refreshments (*informal*) **3 PLACE TO MAKE PIT STOP** a place to make a pit stop during a road journey (*informal*)

Pitt /pít/, **William, 1st Earl of Chatham** (1708–78) British statesman and prime minister (1766–68). Known as **Pitt the Elder**

Pitt, William (1759–1806) British statesman and prime minister (1783–1801 and 1804–06). Known as **Pitt the Younger**

pitta /píttə, peétə/, **pita, pitta bread, pita bread** *n* a flat round Middle Eastern unleavened bread that can be opened to insert a filling [Mid-20C. < modern Greek *pētta, pit(t)a* 'bread, pie'.]

pittance /pítt'nss/ *n* a very small amount of something, especially a very small sum of money, wage, or allowance [13C. Via Old French *pietance* < medieval Latin *pietantia* 'pious or charitable gift' < Latin *pietas* 'piety'.]

pitter-patter /píttər patər/ *n* **LIGHT CONTINUOUS TAPPING SOUND** a light, rapid, and continuous tapping sound, similar to the sound of raindrops falling on something ■ *vi* **MAKE LIGHT CONTINUOUS TAPPING SOUND** to make or move with a light, rapid, and continuous tapping sound ■ *adv* **WITH LIGHT CONTINUOUS TAPPING SOUND** with a light, rapid, and continuous tapping sound [15C. An imitation of the sound.]

pittosporum /pi tóspərəm, píttə spawrəm/ *n* an evergreen shrub with leathery leaves, often planted for hedges in warm regions. Flowers: white, purple, or greenish-yellow. Native to: Australasia, Southeast Asia, southern Africa. Genus: *Pittosporum.* [Late 18C. < modern Latin < Greek *pitta* 'pitch' + *sporos* 'seed'; from the resinous pulp around the seeds.]

Pitts /pits/, **Walter** (1923–69) US mathematician

Pittsburgh /píts burg/ city in SW Pennsylvania. Population: 340,520 (1998 estimate).

pituitary /pi tyóo itəri/ *n* (*plural* **-ies**) **1** PHYSIOL = **pituitary gland** **2** PHARM = **pituitary extract** ■ *adj* relating to or produced by the pituitary gland [Early 17C. < Latin *pituitarius* 'of slime or mucus' < *pituita* 'slime'.]

pituitary extract *n* a pharmaceutical preparation made from substances obtained from the pituitary gland that is rich in beneficial hormones

pituitary gland, pituitary body (*plural* **pituitary bodies**), **pituitary** (*plural* **-ies**) *n* a small oval gland at the base of the brain in vertebrates, producing hormones that control other glands and influence growth of the bone structure, sexual maturing, and general metabolism

pit viper *n* a venomous American snake that has heat-sensitive pits below its eyes used to detect prey. Rattlesnakes and copperheads are pit vipers. Family: Crotalidae.

pity /pítti/ *n* **1 FEELING OF SYMPATHY** a feeling of sadness because somebody else is in trouble or pain, or the capacity to feel this **2 REGRETTABLE THING** a sad or regrettable thing ○ *It's a pity you couldn't make it.* **3 MERCY** a willingness to help or to forgive somebody who is in pain or who has done wrong ■ *vt* (**-ies, -ying, -ied**) **FEEL PITY FOR** to feel pity for somebody or for somebody's pain or trouble ■ *interj* **EXPRESSION OF SYMPATHY OR REGRET** used to express sympathy or regret about something (*informal*) [13C. Via Old French *pité* < Latin *pietas* 'piety, dutifulness, compassion' (see PIETY).] —**pitying** *adj* —**pityingly** *adv* ◇ **have** *or* **take pity on somebody** to feel pity for somebody or for somebody's pain or trouble, or show mercy to somebody ◇ **(the) more's the pity** used to express regret, disappointment, or annoyance that something is the case (*informal*)

pityriasis /pítti rí əssiss/ *n* a skin disease affecting humans and animals in which the skin comes off in dry flakes [Late 17C. Via modern Latin < Greek *pituriasis* < *pituron* 'corn husks'.]

più /pyoo/ *adv* more or increasingly (*musical direction*) [Early 18C. Via Italian < Latin *plus* (see PLUS).]

piupiu /peé oo pee oo/ *n* a skirt worn by Maori men and women for traditional ceremonies and dances, made from the leaves of the New Zealand flax [Late 19C. < Maori.]

Pius IX /pí əss/ (1792–1878) pope (1846–78). Born **Giovanni Maria Mastai-Ferretti**

Pius XI (1857–1939) pope (1922–39). Born **Ambrogio Damiano Achille Ratti**

Pius XII (1876–1958) pope (1939–58). Born **Eugenio Pacelli**

Pius X, St (1835–1914) pope (1903–14). Born **Giuseppe Melchiorre Sarto**

pivot /pívvət/ *n* **1 OBJECT ON WHICH LARGER OBJECT TURNS** a small object such as a bar or pin that supports a larger object and lets it turn or swing **2 CRUCIAL PERSON OR THING** the one person or thing that is essential to the success or effectiveness of something **3 TURNING MOVEMENT** a turning movement carried out by pivoting on something **4 CENTRE POINT OF WHEELING MOVEMENT** a person, a group of people, or point that acts as the centre around which a military formation carries out a wheeling movement **5 BASKETBALL POSITION OR PLAYER** an offensive position in basketball in which a player faces away from the opposing basket, relays passes, and screens other members of the team, or a player in this position ■ *v* **1** *vi* **TURN ON PIVOT** to turn or swing supported by a pivot **2** *vi* **DEPEND ON** to depend on somebody or something, usually a single person, thing, or factor **3** *vt* **PROVIDE WITH PIVOT** to provide something with a pivot on which it can turn or swing [< French < ?]

pivotal /pívvət'l/ *adj* **1** vitally important, especially in determining the outcome, progress, or success of something **2** relating to or functioning as a pivot

pivotman /pívvət man/ *n* **1** a person who acts as a pivot in an organization or formation **2** BASKETBALL = **pivot** *n.* **5**

pix[1] /piks/ plural of **pic**

pix[2] /piks/ *n* CHR = **pyx**

⚡**pixel** /píks'l/ *n* an individual tiny dot of light that is the basic unit from which images on computer or television screens are made [Mid-20C. < PIX[1] + ELEMENT.]

pixie /píksi/, **pixy** (*plural* **-ies**) *n* a fairy or elf often depicted as having pointed ears, wearing a long pointed hat, and being cheerful and rather mischievous [Mid-17C. < ?]

pixilated[1] /píksi laytid/, **pixillated** *adj* **1** feeling bewildered because unable to understand what is happening **2** drunk (*slang*) [Mid-19C. Coined humorously < PIXIE + *-lated* (as in English words such as 'elated' and 'titillated').] —**pixilation** /píksi láysh'n/ *n*

⚡**pixilated**[2] /píksi laytid/, **pixillated** *adj* describes an image on a computer or television screen that is made up of pixels, especially one that is unclear or distorted [Mid-20C. < PIXEL + *-ated*.]

pixy *n* MYTHOL = **pixie**

Pizarro /pi zaárō/, **Francisco** (1476?–1541) Spanish conquistador

pizazz *n* = **pizzazz**

pizza /peétsə/ *n* a flat round piece of bread dough baked with a variety of toppings, often including tomato sauce and cheese [Late 19C. < Italian, 'pie' < ?]

pizzazz /pə záz/, **pizazz, pizzaz, pzazz** *n* an attractive and exciting vitality, especially when combined with style and glamour (*informal*) [Mid-20C. < ?]

pizzeria /peétsə reé ə/ (*plural* **-as**) *n* a restaurant that specializes in making and serving pizzas [Mid-20C. < Italian *pizzeria* < PIZZA.]

pizzicato /pítsi kaátō/ *adv* by using the fingers to pluck the strings of an instrument that is normally played with a bow, especially a violin (*musical direction*) ■ *n* (*plural* **-tos** *or* **-ti** /-ti/) a piece of music, or a section of a piece, played pizzicato [Mid-19C. < Italian < *pizzicare* 'pluck' < *pizzare* 'to prick, sting' < *pizza* 'point'.] —**pizzicato** *adj*

pizzle /pízz'l/ *n* the penis of an animal, especially a bull (*archaic; sometimes offensive*) [Late 15C. < Low German *pēsel* 'little penis' < Middle Low German *pēse* 'penis'.]

pk[1] *abbr* **1** pack **2** park **3** peak **4** peck

⚡**pk**[2] *abbr* Pakistan (*in Internet addresses*)

PK *abbr* psychokinesis

⚡**PKI** *abbr* public key infrastructure (*in e-commerce*)

PKU *abbr* phenylketonuria

Pky, pky, Pkwy *abbr* parkway

pl[1] *abbr* plural

⚡**pl**[2] *abbr* Poland (*in Internet addresses*)

PL *abbr* **1 PL, pl** plural **2** public law

Pl. *abbr* Place (*in addresses*)

⚡**PL/1** *abbr* high level computer programming language specially designed for both business and scientific applications. Full form **programming language 1**

PLA *abbr* Port of London Authority

placard /plákaard/ *n* **1 NOTICE DISPLAYED IN PUBLIC** a large piece of card or board with something written or printed on it, displayed to be read by the public or carried by somebody such as a demonstrator **2 SMALL CARD OR METAL PLAQUE** a small card or metal plaque such as a doorplate, with a name or some other piece of writing on it ■ *vt* **1 PUT PLACARDS ON** to put up placards on or in something **2 ADVERTISE OR ANNOUNCE WITH PLACARDS** to display something on or advertise something with placards, or in a very conspicuous way [Late 15C. < French < Old French *plaquier* 'flatten, plaster' < Middle Dutch *placken* 'flatten, patch'.]

placate /plə káyt/ (**-cates, -cating, -cated**) *vt* to make somebody less angry, upset, or hostile, usually by doing or saying things to please him or her [Late 17C. < Latin *placat-*, past participle of *placare* 'to calm'.] —**placation** *n* —**placatory** *adj*

place /playss/ *n* **1 AREA OR PORTION OF SPACE** an area, position, or portion of space that somebody or something can be in ○ *This is a good place to plant the sapling.* **2 LOCALITY** a particular geographical locality such as a town, country, or region ○ *People come here to work from lots of different places.* **3 AREA IN TOWN** a relatively open area in a town, e.g. a public square or a short street **4 DWELLING** the house or other type of accommodation where somebody lives ○ *a place of our own* **5 AREA WHERE SOMETHING HAPPENS** a building or area where something in particular happens or is located ○ *the firm's place of business* ○ *their regular place of worship* **6 PARTICULAR POINT IN** a particular point in something, e.g. a book, film, or story ○ *I lost my place when you interrupted me.* **7 PROPER POSITION** the position or location where somebody or something belongs ○ *A place for everything, and everything in its place.* **8 OPPORTUNITY TO STUDY** an opportunity to study at school or university ○ *hoping for a place at Oxford.* **9 STATUS** somebody's social position or rank in an organization ○ *know your place* **10 RESPONSIBILITY** somebody's responsibility or right, especially one arising from who the person is or the status he or she has ○ *It's not your place to tell me what to do.* **11 JOB** a job or position ○ *offered a place on the board* **12 SOMEWHERE TO SIT** somewhere for somebody to sit, e.g. at a table during a meal or in the audience of a theatre ○ *I'll keep a place for you next to me.* **13 POSITION IN RANK** the position of somebody or something in a rank, sequence, or series ○ *She finished in second place.* **14 WINNING, SECOND, OR THIRD POSITION** the winning, second, or third position in a race, especially a horse race **15** *US* **SECOND POSITION** second position in a race, especially a horse race **16 POSITION OF DIGIT IN NUMBER** the relative position of a particular digit in a number ■ *vt* (**places, placing, placed**) **1 PUT SOMEWHERE** to put something or somebody in a particular location or position ○ *placed the box on the table* **2 PUT IN PARTICULAR STATE** to cause somebody or something to be in a particular state or condition ○ *Your actions placed all of us in danger.* **3 SEE SOMEBODY IN PARTICULAR WAY** to see or treat somebody or something as having a particular value or character ○ *He placed his family above everything else in his life.* **4 REMEMBER** to be able to recognize or remember somebody or something ○ *I know the face but I can't place the name.* **5 ASSIGN** to assign somebody to a job, position, home, or the care of somebody else ○ *I'll see if I can place you with the sales team.* **6 AIM SOMETHING CAREFULLY** to aim or calculate something carefully so that it lands in a particular spot or has a desired effect ○ *The champion's experience showed in the way he placed his punches.* **7 HAVE SOMETHING ACCEPTED** to have something accepted and dealt with by somebody else ○ *placed an order for a new car* **8 WIN OR BE SECOND OR THIRD** to finish or cause to finish in the winning, second, or third position in a contest, especially a horse race (*usually passive*) ○ *This horse has been placed in its last three outings.* [Pre-12C. Via French < Latin *platea* 'broad way' < the Greek phrase *plateia hodos*.] ◇ **all over the place 1** everywhere (*informal*) **2** in a state of disorder or confusion (*informal*) ◇ **a place in the sun** a position of success, happiness, or prosperity ◇ **give place (to)** to make room for somebody or something or allow somebody or something to take precedence ◇ **go places** to be successful (*informal*) ◇ **in place 1** where somebody or something belongs or ought to be **2** in position or ready for use ◇ **in place of** instead of or as a replacement for somebody or something ◇ **out of place 1** not where something or somebody should be **2** inappropriate or incongruous ◇ **put somebody in his** *or* **her place** to humble somebody who is behaving in an arrogant, presumptuous, or insolent way (*informal*) ◇ **take place** to happen ◇ **take the place of** to be a substitute for or replace something or somebody

SPELLCHECK Do not confuse ***place*** with ***plaice***, which has a similar sound. Beware: your spellchecker will not catch this error.

placebo /plə seébō/ (*plural* **-bos** *or* **-boes**) *n* **1 PRESCRIPTION WITHOUT PHYSICAL EFFECT** something prescribed for a patient that produces a psychological improvement rather than having a physical effect **2 INACTIVE SUBSTANCE** a preparation containing no active ingredients given to a patient participating in a clinical trial in order to assess the performance of a new drug **3 SOMETHING DONE TO PLACATE** something done or said simply to placate or reassure somebody that has no actual effect on whatever is causing his or her problems or anxiety **4 VESPERS OF OFFICE FOR DEAD** in the Roman Catholic Church, the vespers of the office for the dead [13C. < Latin, 'I shall please' (first word in the Vulgate text of Psalm 114:9, used in the Roman Catholic service for the dead) < *placere* 'please' (see PLEASE).]

placebo effect *n* a sense of benefit felt by a patient that arises solely from the knowledge that treatment has been given

place card *n* a small card with somebody's name on it, put on a table to show where that person is to sit, especially for a formal meal

placeholder /pláyss hōldər/ *n* a symbol in a mathematical or logical expression used to show a pattern, e.g. by representing a term in an equation or a statement in an argument

place kick *n* a kick to resume play after a stoppage, especially in American football or rugby, for which the ball is propped or held up on the ground

place-kick *vt* to kick the ball or to score a goal or points by kicking the ball while it is propped up on the ground —**place-kicker** *n*

placeman /pláyssmən/ (*plural* **-men** /-mən/) *n* somebody appointed to public office as a reward for services to a political party or who uses public office to satisfy personal greed or ambition

place mat *n* a protective mat set out for the plate of someone eating at a table

placement /pláyssmənt/ *n* **1 PLACING OR BEING PLACED** the act of placing or arranging something in a particular place or position, or the fact of being placed or arranged in this way **2 MATCHING SOMEBODY TO PARTICULAR SITUATION** the task of finding something such as jobs or accommodation for people, or of assigning people to particular jobs, classes, or accommodation, or an instance of doing so **3 WORK EXPERIENCE AS PART OF STUDY** a period of work for practical experience as part of an academic course. US term **practicum** **4 SKILFUL PLAYING OF BALL** a player's skill in accurately playing the ball in a sport such as tennis or rugby **5** *US* **PLACE FROM WHICH BALL IS KICKED** a place kick for a field goal or point after touchdown in American football or the positioning of the ball for such a kick

placename /pláyss naym/ *n* the name of a geographical area or feature such as a town, settlement, hill, or body of water

placenta /plə séntə/ (*plural* **-tas** *or* **-tae** /-tee/) *n* **1 ORGAN IN UTERUS OF PREGNANT MAMMAL** a vascular organ that develops inside the uterus of most pregnant mammals to supply food and oxygen to the foetus through the umbilical cord **2 PART OF OVARY OF PLANT** the part of the ovary in a flowering plant that bears ovules **3 SPORE-BEARING MASS OF TISSUE** the tissue in a nonflowering plant where the sporangia or spores develop [Late 17C. Via Latin, 'cake' < Greek *plakous* 'flat cake' < *plak-* 'flat surface'.] —**placental** *adj, n* —**placentary** *adj*

placentation /plássen táysh'n/ *n* **1 FORMATION OR ATTACHMENT OF PLACENTA** the process of forming a placenta during pregnancy, or the way in which the placenta is attached to the wall of the uterus **2 WAY OVULES ARE ATTACHED** the way in which ovules are attached to the ovary of a plant **3 PLACENTA TYPE** the form, structure, or type of a placenta

place of safety order *n* a court order in the United Kingdom enabling somebody to remove a child or young person temporarily to a place of safety from actual or likely abuse or neglect

placer /pláyssər/ *n* a deposit of river sand or gravel containing particles of gold or some other valuable mineral [Early 19C. < American Spanish, 'shoal'.]

place setting *n* the set of items such as cutlery, plates, and glasses arranged on a table to be used by one person at a meal, or the cutlery or plates alone

place value *n* the value of the place that a digit occupies in a numeral

placid /plássid/ *adj* calm and tending not to become excited, upset, or disturbed, or appearing so [Early 17C. Directly or via French *placide* < Latin *placidus* 'gentle' < *placere* 'to please' (see PLEASE).] —**placidity** /plə síddəti/ *n* —**placidly** /plássidli/ *adv*

SYNONYMS See ***calm***.

placing /pláyssing/ *n* the issuing of securities to the public through a stockbroker or another intermediary

placket /plákit/ *n* **1** an opening in a woman's garment such as a skirt or blouse, either where it fastens or at a pocket **2** a piece of cloth sewn in behind an opening in a woman's garment [Early 17C. Alteration of PLACARD.]

placoderm /plákə durm/ *n* an extinct creature resembling a fish that was covered with bony plates and lived in the Palaeozoic era. Class: Placodermi. [Mid-19C. < the Greek stem *plak-* 'flat stone' (see PLACENTA) + -DERM.]

placoid /plák oyd/ *adj* describes fish scales that have a flat base and a sharp projecting spine tipped with enamel. The subclass of fish that includes sharks, rays, and skates have placoid scales. [Mid-19C. < the Greek stem *plak-* 'flat stone' (see PLACENTA) + -OID.]

plafond /plə fón, pla fóN/ *n* a ceiling, especially one that is highly ornamented [Mid-17C. < French, 'flat bottom'.]

plagal /pláyg'l/ *adj* **1** describes a musical cadence or harmonic progression in which the subdominant chord is immediately followed by the tonic chord **2** relating to or being a musical mode beginning on the note a fourth below the keynote of its equivalent authentic mode but ending on the same final note [Late 16C. < medieval Latin *plagalis* < medieval Greek *plagios hēkhos* 'plagal mode'.]

plage /plaazh/ *n* a mark on the Sun's surface often associated with sunspots [Via Old French, 'region' < Greek *plagos* 'side' (see PLAGAL)]

plagiarise *vti* = **plagiarize**

plagiarism /pláyjərizəm/ *n* **1** copying what somebody else has written or taking somebody's else's idea and trying to pass it off as original **2** something copied from somebody else's work, or somebody else's idea that somebody presents as his or her own —**plagiarist** *n* —**plagiaristic** /pláyjə rístik/ *adj*

plagiarize /pláyjə rīz/ (**-rizes, -rizing, -rized**), **plagiarise** (**-rises, -rising, -rised**) *vti* to take something that somebody else has written or thought and try to pass it off as original —**plagiarizer** *n*

plagio- *prefix* **1** oblique, offset ○ *plagiotropism* **2** disturbance ○ *plagioclimax* [< Greek *plagios* 'sideways' < *plagos* 'side' < Indo-European, 'to be flat']

plagioclase /pláyji ə klayz/ *n* a feldspar consisting of sodium calcium aluminosilicate [Mid-19C. < PLAGIO- + Greek *klasis* 'breaking'.] —**plagioclastic** /pláyji ə klástik/ *adj*

plague /playg/ *n* **1 EPIDEMIC DISEASE** a disease that spreads very rapidly, infecting very large numbers of people and killing a great many of them, or an outbreak of such a disease **2 BUBONIC PLAGUE** the bubonic plague **3 APPEARANCE OF SOMETHING IN LARGE NUMBERS** the appearance of something harmful or annoying such as vermin in abnormally large numbers or with abnormal frequency **4 SOMEBODY OR SOMETHING TROUBLESOME** an affliction or extremely troublesome or annoying person or thing ■ *vt* (**plagues, plaguing, plagued**) **1 AFFLICT** to occur or recur frequently, causing a great deal of trouble, difficulty, or pain to somebody or something (*often passive*) **2 ANNOY SOMEBODY CONSTANTLY** to harass or annoy somebody constantly, usually by asking questions or making requests or demands [14C. Via Latin *plaga* 'blow, stroke, wound'.]

plaguy /pláygi/, **plaguey** (**-guier, -guiest**) *adj* causing trouble or irritation (*archaic informal*) —**plaguily** *adv*

plaice /playss/ (*plural* **plaice**) *n* **1 LARGE FLAT SEA FISH** a large flat-bodied sea fish with brown skin and red or orange spots. Native to: European waters. *Pleuronectes platessa*. **2 FLATFISH OF N AMERICAN ATLANTIC** a fish similar and related to the European plaice. Native to: North American Atlantic. *Hippoglossoides platessoides*. **3 PLAICE AS FOOD** the flesh of a plaice as food [13C. Via Old French *plaïs* < late Latin *platessa* 'flatfish' < Greek *platus* 'broad'.]

SPELLCHECK See ***place***.

plaid /plad/ *n* **1 TARTAN CLOTH WORN OVER SHOULDER** a long rectangular piece of tartan material worn draped over the shoulder as part of traditional Scottish Highland dress **2 TARTAN FABRIC** a woollen fabric woven in a tartan or chequered pattern **3 TARTAN PATTERN** a tartan or checked pattern [Early 16C. Via Gaelic < Middle Irish < ?]

Plaid Cymru /plīd kúmri/ *n* the Welsh Nationalist Party [Mid-20C. < Welsh, 'party of Wales'.]

plain /playn/ *adj* **1 SIMPLE AND ORDINARY** simple and ordinary in nature or appearance and without additions or decorations ○ *plain homely food* ○ *a plain brown envelope* **2 CLEARLY VISIBLE** not blocked or obscured by anything, so as to be clearly visible ○ *in plain view* **3 CLEAR IN MEANING** quite clear in meaning and easy to recognize or understand ○ *The plain fact is that they lied to us.* **4 FRANK** stating the truth clearly without concealing anything or sparing somebody's feelings ○ *The time has come for plain speaking.* **5 PURE** not combined with any other substances ○ *plain water* **6 LACKING PATTERN OR COLORATION** uncoloured or unpatterned ○ *plain fabric* **7 NOT PRETTY** not pretty or striking in looks ○ *plain looks* **8 IN SIMPLEST KNITTING STYLE OR STITCH** done in the simplest knitting style or stitch ■ *adv* **1 ABSOLUTELY** used to emphasize an adjective or adverb ○ *just plain wrong* **2 CLEARLY** in a clear or distinct way ○ *I'll tell you plain, I've had enough of this.* ■ *n* **1 FLAT EXPANSE OF LAND** a large expanse of fairly flat dry land, usually with few trees **2 KNITTING STYLE OR STITCH** the simplest knitting style or stitch ■ **plains** *npl* **TREELESS LEVEL EXPANSES** large expanses of level, almost treeless country in some central states of the United States [13C. Via Old French < Latin *planus* 'flat'.] —**plainly** *adv* —**plainness** *n*

SPELLCHECK Do not confuse ***plain*** with ***plane***, which has a similar sound. Beware: your spellchecker will not catch this error.

plainchant /pláyn chaant/ *n* MUSIC = **plainsong** *n*.

plain chocolate *n* **1** chocolate that is darker and less sweet than milk chocolate, with no milk added **2** a sweet coated with plain chocolate

plain clothes *npl* ordinary civilian clothes when worn by a police officer on duty —**plain-clothes** *adj*

plain dealing *n* open and honest behaviour or business

plain flour *n* flour that has had no baking powder added to it

plain Jane /-jáyn/ *n* a woman who is not pretty or striking in looks (*informal; often considered offensive*)

plain knitting *n* HANDICRAFT = **garter stitch**

plain loaf *n Scotland* a white loaf baked in a batch, so the sides are flat and there is a dark crust on its top and bottom only

plain sailing *n* something that is straightforward and easy to do

Plains Indian /pláynz-/ *n* a member of any of the Native American peoples that formerly lived on the Great Plains of North America

plainsman /pláynzmən/ (*plural* **-men** /-mən/) *n* a man who lives on a plain, especially somebody who settled or lives on the Great Plains of North America

plainsong /pláyn song/ *n* church music intended to be sung in unison and unaccompanied by instruments that is particularly associated with services held in monasteries [15C. Translation of Latin *cantus planus*.]

plain-spoken *adj* saying or tending to say precisely what is thought without concealing anything or sparing other people's feelings —**plain-spokenness** *n*

plainswoman /pláynz wòomən/ (*plural* **-en** /-wimin/) *n* a woman who lives on a plain, especially one who settled or lives on the Great Plains of North America

plaint /playnt/ *n* **1** a statement in writing to a court of law showing the grounds on which a complainant is bringing an action and asking for the grievance to be redressed **2** an expression of grief or sadness (*archaic literary*) [12C. Via French < Latin *planctus* 'a beating of the breast' < *plangere* 'to beat' (see PLANGENT).]

plain text *n* a form of a message that is in ordinary readable language rather than in code

plaintiff /pláyntif/ *n* a person who begins a lawsuit against somebody else (**defendant**) in a civil court [14C. < French (see PLAINTIVE).]

plaintive /pláyntiv/ *adj* expressing sadness or sounding sad [14C. < French *plaintive, plaintif* < *plaint* (see PLAINT).] —**plaintively** *adv* —**plaintiveness** *n*

plain weave *n* a weave in which the weft passes alternately under and over the warp, the threads forming a simple crisscross pattern

plait /plat/ *n* **1 WOVEN STRANDS** something made by weaving strands together, especially a length of hair with strands woven together like rope or a loaf made by weaving strands of dough together **2 PLEAT** a pleat ■ *vt* **1 WEAVE STRANDS TOGETHER** to weave three or more strands of something over and under each other, usually to form them either into something that looks like a rope or into a flat band **2 MAKE SOMETHING BY PLAITING** to make something by plaiting **3 PLEAT** to pleat something [15C. Via Old French *pleit* < Latin *plicit-*, past participle of *plicare* 'to fold'.]

plan /plan/ *n* **1 SCHEME FOR ACHIEVING OBJECTIVE** a method of doing something that is worked out usually in some detail before it is begun and that may be written down in some form or simply retained in the memory **2 INTENTION** something that somebody intends or has arranged to do (*often plural*) **3 DIAGRAM OF LAYOUT** a drawing or diagram showing the layout, arrangement, or structure of something **4 LIST OR OUTLINE** a list, summary, or diagram that shows how the items that make up something such as a piece of writing or an organized meeting are to be arranged **5 HORIZONTAL SECTION OF BUILDING** a scale diagram showing a horizontal view of the arrangement of rooms and fixtures in a building on a particular level ■ *v* (**plans, planning, planned**) **1** *vti* **WORK OUT HOW TO DO** to work out in advance and in some detail how something is to be done or organized **2** *vt* **INTEND TO DO** to intend or to make arrangements to do something **3** *vt* **MAKE A SCALE DRAWING** to make a scale drawing of something, especially a building [Late 17C. < French, 'ground plan', an alteration (influenced by *plan* 'flat') of *plant* < Latin *plantare* 'push in with the sole of the foot' (see PLANT).]

PLANETS

	Mercury	Venus	Earth	Mars	Jupiter	Saturn	Uranus	Neptune	Pluto
mean distance from Sun (AU*)	0.39	0.72	1	1.52	5.2	9.54	19.18	30.06	39.33
period of revolution around Sun	88 days	226 days	1 year	1.88 yrs	11.86 yrs	29.46 yrs	84 yrs	164.79 yrs	247.7 yrs
period of rotation	58.6 days	243 days	24 hrs	24.6 hrs	9.9 hrs	10.7 hrs	17.2 hrs	16 hrs	6.4 days
mass (relative to Earth)	0.06	0.82	1	0.11	317.8	95.1	14.5	17.2	0.004
radius (relative to Earth)	0.38	0.95	1	0.53	11.2	9.42	4.01	3.88	0.18
known satellites	0	0	1	2	16	18	18	8	1

*1 AU is equivalent to 150 million km (93 million miles)

plan ahead vi to make preparations or arrangements for the future

plan for vt to make preparations and arrangements for something based on what is expected to happen

plan on vt to intend to do something (informal)

plan out vt to make a detailed plan for something to be done or organized

plan- prefix = **plano-**

planar /pláynər/ adj flat or lying in a single geometric plane —**planarity** /play nárrəti/ n

planarian /plə náiri ən/ n a small flatworm that mainly lives in fresh water, is not a parasite, and has a three-branched intestine. Order: Tricladida. [Mid-19C. Via modern Latin Planaria < Latin planarius 'on level ground' < planus 'flat' (see PLAIN).]

planation /play náysh'n/ n the levelling out of natural surfaces on land or under water by erosion or the depositing of new material [Late 19C. < PLANE².]

planchet /plaánchit/ n 1 a flat disc of metal ready to be stamped as a coin or medal 2 US a small metal container used to measure a radioactive substance [Early 17C. Literally 'little plank' < obsolete English planch 'wooden plank, metal plate' < French planche (see PLANK).]

planchette /plaan shét/ n a small heart-shaped or triangular wooden board on two castors and with a pencil attached that spells out messages supposed to be from the spirit world when people touch it lightly [Mid-19C. < French, 'little plank' < planche 'plank' (see PLANK).]

Planck /plangk/, **Max** (1858–1947) German physicist

Planck's constant /plángks-/, **Planck constant** n (symbol *h*) a basic physical constant that is equal to the energy of a photon divided by its frequency, with an approximate value of 6.6261×10^{-34} joule-seconds [Early 20C. After Max PLANCK.]

plane¹ /playn/ n an aeroplane ■ vi (**planes, planing, planed**) to travel by aeroplane [Late 20C. Shortening.]

SPELLCHECK See **plain**.

plane² /playn/ n 1 FLAT SURFACE a flat or level material surface 2 LEVEL OF REALITY a level or category of existence, mental activity, or achievement 3 TWO-DIMENSIONAL SURFACE a two-dimensional surface in which a straight line between any two points will lie wholly on that surface 4 WING OR HYDROFOIL a flat surface such as a wing or a hydrofoil that provides lift for an aircraft or hydroplane ■ adj 1 FLAT completely flat and level 2 TWO-DIMENSIONAL lying within a particular plane ■ vi (**planes, planing, planed**) 1 SKIM OVER WATER'S SURFACE to rise partly out of water and skim along the surface, in the way that a hydroplane does 2 SOAR to glide through the air without propulsion, in the way that a bird does without flapping its wings or an aeroplane does with its engine off [Early 17C. < Latin planus 'flat' (see PLAIN).] —**planeness** n

plane³ /playn/ n 1 TOOL FOR SMOOTHING WOOD a hand tool for smoothing or shaping wood consisting of a wooden or metal body with a flat base in which an adjustable metal blade is held at an angle 2 SMOOTHING TROWEL a hand tool with a flat metal blade used for smoothing the surface of clay or of plaster in a mould ■ vt (**planes, planing, planed**) SMOOTH WOOD to use a plane to smooth or shape the surface of wood, to reduce it to the required size, or to remove material from it [14C. Via French < late Latin plana < Latin planare 'make level' < planus 'flat' (see PLANE².)]

plane⁴ /playn/ n a tall deciduous tree that has leaves with pointed lobes, ball-shaped clusters of flowers and fruit, and bark that peels off in patches. Genus: Platanus. [14C. Via French plane and Latin platanus <Greek platanos < platus 'broad', from the shape of its leaf.]

plane angle n an angle formed by two straight lines meeting in the same geometric plane

plane geometry n a branch of geometry dealing with the study of curves and figures

planer /pláynər/ n 1 a person or machine that planes, especially a machine used to plane wood or to cut flat surfaces into metal 2 a flat block of wood used to hold type level in a chase [15C. < PLANE².]

plane sailing n sailing using a form of navigation that treats the earth's surface as if it were flat for the purposes of calculating a ship's position and course

planet /plánnit/ n 1 ASTRONOMICAL BODY ORBITING STAR an astronomical body that orbits a star and does not shine with its own light, especially one of the nine such bodies orbiting the Sun in the solar system 2 ASTROLOGICAL INFLUENCE in astrology, the Sun, the Moon, and the planets of the solar system, except Earth, that are considered to influence events on Earth and the fate or character of individuals 3 EARTH the Earth ○ save the planet [12C. Via French planète < Latin planeta 'planet, wandering star' < Greek planētēs 'wanderer'.]

plane table n a surveying instrument for use in the field, consisting of a drawing board mounted on adjustable legs with a sighting telescope and ruler

planetarium /plánnə táiri əm/ n (plural **-ums** or **-a** /-ri ə/) n 1 a building with a domed ceiling onto which movable images of the stars, planets, and other objects seen in the night sky are projected for an audience 2 the special projector used to project images of the night sky for an audience in a planetarium [Mid-18C. Via modern Latin < late Latin planetarius 'astrologer' < planeta 'planet' (see PLANET).]

planetary /plánnitəri/ adj 1 relating to, belonging to, involving, or typical of planets 2 involving or relating to the whole Earth, all the people or countries of the world, or a large proportion of them ■ n (plural **-taries**) ENG = **planetary gear**

planetary gear n a gearwheel especially in an epicyclic train that travels around another usually central gearwheel

planetary nebula n a glowing ring-shaped nebula of expanding gases surrounding a small very hot white star

planetesimal /plánni téssim'l/ n a small rocky astronomical object thought to have orbited the Sun in the early stages of the solar system before coalescing with others to form the planets [Early 20C. < PLANET + -esimal (as in 'infinitesimal').]

planetoid /plánni toyd/ n ASTRON = **asteroid** n. 1 —**planetoidal** /plánni tóyd'l/ adj

planetology /plánni tólləji/ n a branch of astronomy that studies the origin and composition of the planets and other solid bodies in the solar system such as comets and meteors —**planetological** /plánnitə lójjik'l/ adj —**planetologist** /plánni tólləjist/ n

plane tree, plane n a tall deciduous tree that has leaves with pointed lobes, globular fruit clusters, and flaking bark. Native to: temperate N hemisphere. Genus: Platanus. [14C. 'Plane' via French < Greek platanos < platus 'broad'; from the shape of its leaf.]

planet wheel n a wheel in an epicyclic gear system that rotates around the wheel with which it meshes

plangent /plánjant/ adj 1 expressing or suggesting grief or sadness, or resonating with a mournful sound (literary) 2 making a loud and resonant sound [Early 19C. < Latin plangent-, present participle of plangere 'to beat'.] —**plangency** n —**plangently** adv

plani- prefix = **plano-**

planimeter /pla nímmitər/ n a mechanical instrument that measures the area of a plane figure as a pointer is moved around the figure's edge [Mid-19C. < French planimètre.] —**planimetric** /plánni méttrik/ adj —**planimetrically** /-méttrikli/ adv

planish /plánnish/ vt to toughen and smooth the surface of a metal by hammering or rolling it [Late 16C. < Old French planiss-, the stem form of planir 'to smooth' < plain 'flat' (see PLAIN).] —**planisher** n

planisphere /plánni sfeer/ n a representation on a flat surface of all or part of a sphere, especially a map of the night sky as seen at a particular time and place [< medieval Latin planisphaerium < Latin planus 'flat, plane' (see PLAIN) + sphaera 'sphere' < Greek sphaira) —**planispheric** /plánni sférrik/ adj

plank /plangk/ n 1 LONG FLAT PIECE OF WOOD a piece of wood that has been sawn into a long flat fairly narrow rectangular shape, for use especially in building floors, shelves, and boats 2 POLICY OF POLITICAL PARTY a policy that is part of a political party's platform ■ vt COVER SOMETHING WITH PLANKS to cover something with planks [13C. Via Old Northern French planke, a variation of Old French planche < late Latin planca 'slab' < the feminine of Latin plancus 'flat'.]

planking /plángking/ n 1 a number of planks especially when they are used as building material or as part of a boat 2 the work of covering something with planks or fixing planks to something

plank spanker n a guitarist (slang)

plankter /plángktər/ n one of the tiny organisms that make up plankton [Mid-20C. Via German < Greek plagktēr 'wanderer' < plazein 'wander' (see PLANKTON).]

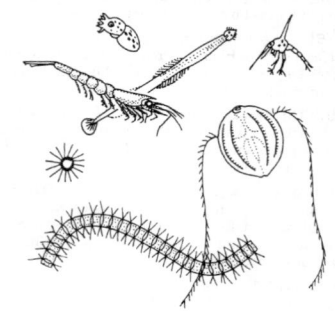

Plankton

plankton /plángktən/ n a mass of tiny animals and plants floating in the sea or in lakes usually near the surface and eaten by fish and other aquatic animals [Late 19C. Via German < Greek, 'wandering thing' < plazein 'wander, lead astray'.] —**planktonic** /plangk tónnik/ adj

planned obsolescence *n* a policy of designing and making products so that they will quickly become outdated or wear out, so that people will have to buy a replacement

planner /plánnər/ *n* 1 a person who plans something, especially the development of an area 2 a chart or notebook in which future events can be indicated or noted

planning permission *n* the authorization for which people must apply to a local authority before they can build a new building or structure or alter an existing one

plano- *prefix* flat ○ *planosol* ○ *plano-concave* [< Latin *planus* (see PLANE²)]

plano-concave /pláynō kón kayv/ *adj* flat on one side and concave on the other

plano-convex /pláynō kón veks/ *adj* flat on one side and convex on the other

planogamete /plánnəgə meet, plánnō gámmeet/ *n* a gamete such as a spermatozoon that is capable of moving

planosol /pláynə sol/ *n* a soil formation found on flat uplands that have high to moderate rainfall, in which a strongly leached upper layer overlies a layer of compacted clay or silt

plant /plaant/ *n* 1 VEGETABLE ORGANISM a photosynthetic organism that has cellulose cell walls, cannot move of its own accord, grows on the earth or in water, and usually has green leaves. Kingdom: *Plantae.* 2 SMALLER VEGETABLE ORGANISM a vegetable organism that does not have a permanent woody stem, e.g. a flower or herb rather than a bush or tree 3 SEEDLING a cutting or seedling that is ready to be planted out 4 FACTORY a factory, power station, or other large industrial complex where something is manufactured or produced 5 INDUSTRIAL EQUIPMENT equipment together with the buildings and land necessary for carrying on an industrial process or running a business 6 ACTION OR REMARK THAT BECOMES SIGNIFICANT an action or remark seemingly casually introduced into a narrative or play that turns out later to have great significance (*informal*) 7 SOMETHING HIDDEN TO INCRIMINATE something secretly put somewhere it can be discovered later, e.g. by the police, in order to incriminate somebody (*informal*) 8 SOMEBODY SECRETLY INTRODUCED INTO GROUP a person who has been placed secretly in an organization in order to spy on it or to influence its behaviour (*informal*) ■ *v* 1 *vti* PUT SOMETHING INTO THE GROUND TO GROW to put something such as a seed, plant, or tuber into the ground to enable it to grow ○ *plant a tree* 2 *vti* PLACE PLANTS SOMEWHERE to place young plants or sow seeds in an area of ground ○ *wanted to plant that bed with pansies* 3 *vt* PUT DOWN FIRMLY to put something down or take a position firmly or decisively ○ *planted the stakes about five feet apart* 4 *vt* PUT AN IDEA IN SOMEBODY'S MIND to introduce an idea into another person's mind ○ *She planted the notion in my head that we should move.* 5 *vt* PLACE IN A CONCEALED POSITION to place something such as an explosive or listening device where it will not be easily found by others 6 *vt* HIDE SOMETHING TO INCRIMINATE to put something secretly where it can be discovered later, e.g. by the police, to incriminate somebody (*informal*) ○ *plant evidence* 7 *vt* INTRODUCE A SPY INTO GROUP to introduce somebody into an organization in order to spy on it or to influence the behaviour of its members (*informal*) ○ *planted an informer in the group* 8 *vt* STRIKE to land a blow on somebody (*informal*) 9 *vt* STOCK WITH FISH to place spawn, young fish, or shellfish into an area of water so that they will develop there ○ *plant oysters* 10 *vt* ESTABLISH A COLONY to establish a colony or settlement in a place, or send people to a place as colonists or settlers [Pre-12C. < late Latin *plantare* 'to plant'.] —**plantable** *adj* —**plantlike** *adj*

plant out *vt* to transplant a seedling that has been grown in a pot or in a sheltered place to open ground

Plantagenet /plan tájjənət/ *adj* belonging or relating to the English royal family that ruled between 1154 and 1485, or to this period of English history. The period is spanned by the reigns of Kings Henry II, Richard I, John, Henry III, Edward I, Edward II, Edward III, Richard II, Henry IV, Henry V, Henry VI, Edward IV, Edward V and Richard III. ■ *n* a member of the Plantagenet royal family [< Latin *planta* 'sprig' + *genista* 'broom', after the sprig of broom worn by Geoffrey IV, father of Henry II, in his cap]

plantain¹ /plántin, -tayn/ *n* a small wild plant with leaves that grow mainly from the plant's base. Flowers: tiny, greenish, in spikes. Native to: northern temperate regions. Family: Plantaginaceae. [14C. Via French < Latin *plantago* < *planta* 'sole of the foot' (see PLANT).]

plantain² /plántin, -tayn/ *n* 1 a green fruit resembling a banana, eaten cooked as a staple food in many tropical countries 2 a large tropical plant of the banana family that produces plantains. *Musa paradisiaca.* [16C. Via Spanish *plátano* 'plane tree' < Latin *platanus* (see PLANE⁴).]

plantain lily *n* PLANTS = **hosta**

plantar /plántər/ *adj* relating to, affecting, or occurring on the sole of the foot [Early 18C. < Latin *plantaris* < *planta* 'sole of the foot' (see PLANT).]

plantar wart *n* MED = **verruca** *n.* 1

plantation /plaan táysh'n, plan-/ *n* 1 LARGE ESTATE OR FARM a large estate or farm especially in a hot country where crops such as cotton, coffee, tea, or rubber trees are grown, usually worked by resident labourers 2 AREA OF PLANTED LAND an area of land on which trees or crops are planted 3 GROUP OF CULTIVATED PLANTS a large group of plants, especially trees, that are being cultivated 4 *US* ESTATE IN S UNITED STATES a large landed estate in the S United States 5 COLONY a colony or settlement 6 COLONIZATION the act of colonizing a place (*archaic*)

planter /plaantər/ *n* 1 HEAD OF PLANTATION an owner or manager of a plantation 2 LARGE CONTAINER a large decorative container for houseplants or small trees 3 PLANTING MACHINE a machine for planting seeds, tubers, or other plant parts 4 SCOTS OR ENGLISH SETTLER IN ULSTER one of the Scots or English settlers who arrived in Ulster in the 17th century under official patronage

planter's punch *n* a drink made with rum, lime or lemon juice, sugar, water, or soda, and sometimes bitters

plant hormone *n* a hormone produced naturally by plants that activates or regulates their growth, or a synthetic equivalent used to promote growth in cultivated plants

plantigrade /plánti grayd/ *adj* describes an animal such as a bear or a human being that walks on the soles of its feet with the heel touching the ground ■ *n* an animal that walks on the soles of its feet [Mid-19C. Via French < modern Latin *plantigradus* < Latin *planta* 'sole of the foot' (see PLANT) + *-gradus* 'stepping' (see GRADE).]

plantilla /plan tíllə/ *n* *Philippines* the academic staff employed in a university faculty or department [< Spanish]

plantlet /plaantlət/ *n* a young or very small plant

plant louse *n* INSECTS = **aphid**

plantocracy /plaan tókrəssi/ (*plural* **-racies**) *n* a ruling class made up of the owners and managers of large plantations, or a society they rule

plant science *n* the scientific study of plants

plantsman /plaantsmən/ (*plural* **-men** /-mən/) *n* a man who has expert knowledge of garden plants and gardening

plantswoman /plaants wŏŏmən/ (*plural* **-men** /-wimmin/) *n* a woman who has expert knowledge of garden plants and gardening

planula /plánnyŏŏlə/ (*plural* **-lae** /-lī/) *n* a free-swimming larva of a coelenterate such as a hydra that has cilia and usually a flattened oval body [Late 19C. < modern Latin, 'little flat one' < Latin *planus* 'flat' (see PLAIN).] —**planular** *adj*

plaque /plak, plaak/ *n* 1 INSCRIBED METAL OR STONE a small flat piece of metal, stone, or other hard material with an inscription or decoration on it that is fixed onto a surface, often to commemorate somebody or something 2 DEPOSIT ON SURFACE OF TEETH a film of saliva, mucus, bacteria, and food residues that builds up on the surface of teeth and can cause gum disease 3 SMALL PATCH a small flattened patch or deposit, e.g. on the skin in psoriasis or on the inner wall of an artery in arteriosclerosis 4 CLEAR PATCH IN CULTURE a clear patch in a bacterial or cell culture caused by a virus destroying the cells 5 SMALL BADGE OR BROOCH a small badge or brooch worn to show membership of or rank in an organization [Mid-19C. Via French < Dutch *plak* 'tablet' < *plakken* < Middle Dutch *placken* 'flatten, patch'.]

plash¹ /plash/ *n* LIGHT SPLASH a light splash or splashing sound (*literary*) ■ *v* (*literary*) 1 *vi* SPLASH IN OR THROUGH LIQUID to move in or through something liquid, scattering drops of it and making a light splashing sound 2 *vt* SPLASH to splash or spatter something liquid [Early 16C. An imitation of the sound.]

plash² /plash/ *vt* = **pleach**

plashy /pláshi/ (**-ier, -iest**) *adj* (*literary*) 1 liable to splash or be splashed 2 wet and marshy

-plasia *suffix* growth, formation ○ *hyperplasia* [Via modern Latin < Greek *plassein* 'to form, mould']

plasm /plazəm/ *n* 1 BIOL = **plasma** 2 protoplasm of a specified type [Early 17C. < late Latin *plasma* 'image, creation' (see PLASMA).] —**plasmic** *adj*

plasm- *prefix* = **plasmo-** (*before vowels*)

-plasm *suffix* material that forms or is formed ○ *protoplasm* ○ *neoplasm* [Shortening of PROTOPLASM]

plasma /plázmə/, **plasm** /plazəm/ *n* 1 FLUID COMPONENT OF BLOOD the clear yellowish fluid component of blood, lymph, or milk, excluding the suspended corpuscles and cells 2 BLOOD SUBSTITUTE a blood substitute prepared by removing the cells and corpuscles from donated sterile blood and freezing the resulting fluid until it is needed 3 IONIZED GAS a hot ionized gas made up of ions and electrons that is found in the Sun, stars, and fusion reactors 4 GREEN CHALCEDONY a green variety of chalcedony. Use: gems, decorative ware. [Early 18C. Via late Latin, 'image, creation' < Greek, 'something moulded' < *plassein* 'to mould' (see PLASTIC).] —**plasmatic** /plaz máttik/ *adj*

plasma cell, plasmacyte /plázmə sīt/ *n* a lymphocyte that produces antibodies and is derived from a B cell

plasmagel /plázmə jel/ *n* a form of cytoplasm, often forming an outer layer in cells, that resembles jelly

plasmagene /plázmə jeen/ *n* a particle in the cytoplasm of organisms that can replicate itself and is thought to be able to pass on hereditary characteristics in the same way as a chromosomal gene —**plasmagenic** /plázmə jénnik/ *adj*

plasmalemma /plázmə lémmə/ *n* BIOL = **cell membrane**

plasma membrane *n* BIOL = **cell membrane**

plasmapheresis /plázmə férrəssiss/ *n* a process in which blood taken from a patient is treated to extract the cells and corpuscles, which are then added to another fluid and returned to the patient's body

plasmasol /plázmə sol/ *n* a form of cytoplasm that is more fluid than plasmagel, often forming an inner layer in cells

plasmid /plázmid/ *n* a small circle of DNA that replicates itself independently of chromosomal DNA, especially in the cells of bacteria

plasmin /plázmin/ *n* a plasma enzyme that helps break down fibrin [Mid-19C. < French < *plasma* 'plasma'.]

plasminogen /plaz mínnəjən/ *n* the inactive precursor of plasmin

plasmo- *prefix* plasma ○ *plasmogamy* [< PLASMA]

plasmodesma /plázmō dézmə/ (*plural* **-mata** /-mətə/) *n* a very fine thread of cytoplasm that in some plants passes through openings in the walls of adjacent cells and forms a living bridge between them [Early 20C. < German < *Plasma* 'plasma' + Greek *desma* 'bond'.]

plasmodium /plaz mṓdi əm/ (*plural* **-a** /plazmṓdi ə/) *n* 1 a mass of protoplasm containing many nuclei that is a stage in the life cycle of some organisms, especially slime moulds 2 a parasitic protozoan, especially one that causes malaria. Genus: *Plasmodium.* [Late 19C. < PLASMA + modern Latin *-odium* 'resembling' < Greek *-ōdēs* (see -OID).] —**plasmodial** *adj*

plasmogamy /plaz móggəmi/ *n* fusion between cells in certain fungi in which the cytoplasm merges but the nuclei remain distinct

plasmolysis /plaz mólləssiss/ *n* the shrinking of the protoplasm in a plant or bacterial cell away from the cell wall, caused by loss of water through osmosis —**plasmolytic** /plázmə líttik/ *adj* —**plasmolytically** /-líttikli/ *adv*

plasmon /pláz mon/ *n* the sum total of the genetic material in the cytoplasm, as opposed to the nucleus or nuclei, of a cell or an organism

-plast *suffix* living cell, small body ○ *spheroplast* [< Greek *plastos*, a past participle of *plassein* (see -PLASIA)]

plaster /plaastər/ *n* 1 LIME MIXTURE FOR WALLS a mixture of lime, sand, and water that is applied as a liquid paste to the ceilings and internal walls of a building and dries to a hard surface 2 STICKY BANDAGE a strip of adhesive material, usually with a dressing attached, for sticking over a cut or wound 3 PIECE OF IMPREGNATED MUSLIN a piece of muslin spread with a curative preparation formerly used for placing over a wound or sore. ◊ **mustard plaster** 4 ARTS, MED = **plaster of Paris** ■ *vt* 1 **COVER WALLS WITH PLASTER** to apply plaster to the interior walls and ceilings of a building 2 **APPLY SOMETHING THICKLY** to apply a thick layer of something to a surface (*informal*) 3 **STICK A MASS OF THINGS OVER A SURFACE** to stick or spread objects in great profusion over a surface 4 **MAKE SOMETHING APPEAR IN MANY LOCATIONS** to cause a name, story, or image to appear in many conspicuous places ○ *woke up to find her name plastered over every front page* 5 **BOMBARD** to hit somebody or something repeatedly and effectively with blows or weapons (*informal*) 6 **APPLY MEDICINAL PLASTER** to apply a medicinal plaster to a wound or sore [Old English *plaster* 'medical dressing' and Old French *plastre* 'wall plaster', both via medieval Latin *plastrum* < Greek *emplastron* < *emplassein* 'plaster up' < *plassein* (see -PLASIA)] —**plasterer** *n* —**plastery** *adj*

plasterboard /plaástər bawrd/ *n* reinforced gypsum plaster sandwiched between two layers of strong paper in large sheets, used chiefly for interior walls

plaster cast *n* 1 a rigid covering of plaster of Paris moulded round a broken limb to immobilize the fracture site during healing 2 a copy or mould of an object, such as a statue or footprint in plaster of Paris

plastered /plaástərd/ *adj* very drunk (*informal*) [Early 20C. < PLASTER in the sense 'hit hard'.]

plaster of Paris *n* a white powder, calcium sulphate, mixed with water to form a quick-hardening paste, used in the arts for sculpting and making casts and in medicine for moulding casts round broken limbs [After PARIS[2], where it originated]

plasterwork /plaástər wurk/ *n* objects in plaster, especially the layer of plaster applied to interior wall surfaces or decorative plaster mouldings on ceilings or walls

plastic /plástik/ *n* 1 **SYNTHETIC MATERIAL** an extremely versatile mouldable synthetic material made from the polymerization of organic compounds 2 **CREDIT CARDS** debit or credit cards as a form of payment as distinct from cash or a cheque (*informal*) ■ *adj* 1 **MADE OF PLASTIC** made of or consisting of plastic 2 **ABLE TO BE MOULDED** able to be shaped, moulded, or modelled 3 **OF MOULDING, MODELLING, OR SCULPTING** relating to or involving moulding, modelling, or sculpting 4 **ABLE TO HAVE SHAPE PERMANENTLY CHANGED** able to be bent, stretched, squeezed, or pulled out so that the resulting change of shape is permanent 5 **ADAPTING TO CONDITIONS** capable of adapting to conditions during growth or development 6 **ARTIFICIAL** seeming artificial and unnatural ○ *a plastic smile* 7 **ADAPTING EASILY** adapting easily and readily to change 8 **OF PLASTIC SURGERY** relating to or involving plastic surgery [16C. Via French *plastique* and Latin *plasticus* < Greek *plastikos* 'mouldable' < *plastos*, past participle of *plassein* 'to form, mould' (see -PLASIA).] —**plastically** *adv*

plastic art *n* 1 a three-dimensional art such as sculpture, modelling or bas-relief work, pottery, or ceramics 2 an art that represents subjects for visual appreciation, such as painting, sculpture, or architecture

plastic bomb *n* a bomb that employs a plastic explosive for its destructive force

plastic bullet *n* a large bullet made of PVC, sometimes used by the police for riot control in place of metal bullets

plastic explosive *n* an explosive with the consistency of putty that allows it to be easily moulded

Plasticine /plásti seen/ *tdmk* a trademark for a soft coloured modelling material used especially by children

plasticise *vti* INDUST = **plasticize**

plasticiser *n* INDUST = **plasticizer**

plasticity /pla stíssəti/ *n* 1 **ABILITY TO BE MOULDED** the condition of being soft and capable of being moulded 2 **ABILITY TO KEEP SHAPE AFTER CHANGE** the quality that will allow a substance to retain its change in shape after being bent, stretched, or squeezed 3 **THREE-DIMENSIONAL QUALITY** the three-dimensional quality of an image

plasticize /plásti sīz/ (**-cizes, -cizing, -cized**), **plasticise** (**-cises, -cising, -cised**) *v* 1 *vti* to give plastic or mouldable qualities to something, or become plastic or mouldable 2 *vt* to impregnate or coat something with plastic, usually to make it waterproof —**plasticization** /plásti sī záysh'n/ *n*

plasticizer /plásti sīzər/, **plasticiser** *n* an industrial compound that affects the physical properties of a substance to which it is added

plastic money *n* debit and credit cards as distinct from cash or cheques

plastic surgeon *n* a physician who performs or specializes in plastic surgery

plastic surgery *n* the branch of surgery that is concerned with repairing damage, relieving impairments, or improving appearance

plastid /plástid/ *n* a specialized organ or part (**organelle**) in a photosynthetic plant cell that contains pigment, ribosomes, and DNA, and serves specific physiological purposes such as food synthesis and storage [Late 19C. Via the Greek stem *plastid-* < *plastos* 'moulded' (see PLASTIC).]

plastique /pla steék/ *n* 1 plastic explosive 2 graceful poses or slow movements in dance [Late 19C. < French (see PLASTIC).]

plastisol /plásti sol/ *n* a suspension of synthetic resin particles convertible by heat into solid plastic [Mid-20C. < PLASTIC + SOL[2].]

plastoquinone /plástō kwínnōn/ *n* a compound found in plants that plays a role in photosynthesis [Mid-20C. < (CHLORO)PLAST + QUINONE.]

plastron /plástrən/ *n* 1 **UNDER PART OF TORTOISE SHELL** the under portion of the shell of a turtle or tortoise that is made up of several, often hinged bony plates joined to the carapace by bridges located between the animal's legs 2 **WATER-REPELLENT GILL IN AQUATIC INSECTS** a tuft of water-repellent hairs on the bodies of some aquatic insects that traps air bubbles and acts as an external gill 3 **STEEL BREASTPLATE** a steel breastplate worn as part of medieval armour beneath a chain-mail tunic (**hauberk**) 4 **CHEST PAD FOR FENCERS** a leather-covered pad for protecting the chest, worn by professional fencers [Early 16C. Via French < Italian *piastrone* 'large breastplate' < *piastra* 'metal plate'.] —**plastral** *adj*

-plasty *suffix* surgical repair, plastic surgery ○ *angioplasty* ○ *rhinoplasty* [Via modern Latin < Greek *plastos* (see PLASTIC)]

plat[1] /plat/ *n* 1 US **PLAN OR MAP** a plan or map showing property boundaries and geographical features 2 **PLOT OF LAND** a small plot or area of land (*archaic*) ■ *vt* (**plats, platting, platted**) US **MAP AREA OF LAND** to map an area of land to show boundaries and features [Early 16C. Probably alteration of PLOT.]

plat[2] /plat/ *n* a plait (*archaic*) ■ *vt* (**plats, platting, platted**) to plait something (*archaic*) [14C. Alteration of PLAIT.]

Plata, Río de la /plaátə/ marine inlet in SE South America, an estuary of the Paraná and Uruguay rivers, lying between Uruguay and Argentina. Length: 300 km/190 mi.

plat du jour /plaà doo zhoór/ (*plural* **plats du jour** /plaà doo zhoór/) *n* the featured dish on the menu of a restaurant for a particular day [Early 20C. < French, 'dish of the day'.]

plate /playt/ *n* 1 **DISH FROM WHICH FOOD IS EATEN** a flat or shallow dish, usually round and made of earthenware, china, glass, or sometimes plastic or metal, from which food is eaten 2 **CONTENTS OF PLATE** a portion of food consisting of the amount served on a plate 3 US **SERVED FOOD** a specified variety of prepared and served food ○ *a low-calorie plate* 4 **COLLECTION DISH FOR MONEY** a shallow metal or wooden container passed round a church for members of the congregation to put money in 5 **DISH FOR GROWING CULTURES** a small flat glass or plastic dish with a vertical rim, used in laboratories for growing cultures of microorganisms 6 **THIN SHEET** a thin flat rigid sheet or slice of some material, usually of uniform thickness and with a smooth surface 7 **FLAT ANATOMICAL STRUCTURE** a thin flat bony or horny anatomical part or formation 8 **THINLY BEATEN METAL** metal produced in thin sheets of uniform thickness by beating, rolling, or casting 9 **SHEET OF ARMOUR PLATING** a sheet of metal used as part of the cladding of a warship or tank 10 **SECTION OF SUIT OF ARMOUR** a thin piece of steel or iron used to make up a suit of armour (*often in combination*) 11 **COATING OF METAL** a thin coating of metal, typically silver or gold, applied by electrolysis to copper or another base metal 12 **PRIZE OF GOLD OR SILVER CUP** a prize, especially in horse-racing, consisting of a silver or gold cup 13 **RACE WITH CUP AS PRIZE** a race, especially a horserace, in which the prize is a silver or gold cup 14 **ENGRAVED PLAQUE** a metal plaque that bears an engraved or printed legend, name, number, or other inscription (*often in combination*) 15 **NUMBER PLATE** a vehicle's number plate 16 **SECTION OF EARTH'S CRUST** any segment of the Earth's crust that moves in relation to other segments as defined by the theory of plate tectonics 17 **FLAT CONSTITUENT PART OR FITTING** a flat slab of metal or other material that constitutes part of a machine or mechanism 18 **ARTIFICIAL PALATE FITTED WITH FALSE TEETH** a piece of plastic moulded to fit the mouth and holding false teeth or an orthodontic device such as a brace 19 **SENSITIZED SHEET OF GLASS** a sheet of glass or other material coated with a light-sensitive film to receive a photographic image 20 **SURFACE FROM WHICH TO PRINT** a template for printing, either an engraved metal sheet or a phototypeset page 21 **PRINT TAKEN FROM ENGRAVED SURFACE** a print made from a printing plate, especially one inserted into a book on paper different from that on which the text is printed 22 **ILLUSTRATION IN BOOK** a full-page illustration or photograph in a book, especially on glossy or coated paper 23 **ELECTRODE** a thin flat piece of metal acting as an electrode in a rechargeable battery 24 BASEBALL = **home plate** 25 **SHOE WORN BY RACEHORSE** a light shoe with which racehorses are shod in preparation for racing 26 **HORIZONTAL SUPPORTING TIMBER** a horizontal timber laid along the top of a wall of a building to support the ends of timbers laid at right angles to the wall 27 US **CUT OF BEEF** a thin cut of beef from the breast or ribs ■ *vt* (**plates, plating, plated**) 1 **COVER WITH GOLD OR SILVER** to cover something with a thin coating or film of metal, especially to overlay something made of a baser metal with gold or silver 2 **COVER WITH METAL SHEETS** to cover something, especially a ship or tank, with sheets of metal for protection and strength 3 **SET UP TYPE IN PAGE FORM** to set up movable type into page form ready for printing 4 **STRENGTHEN BROKEN BONE WITH PLATE** to hold a fractured bone in position once it has been set by screwing it, on either side of the fracture, to a metal plate [13C. Via Old French < Greek *platus* 'flat'.] —**plateful** *n* ◇ **have something handed to you on a plate** to obtain something without having to put any effort into obtaining it (*informal*) ◇ **have something on your plate** to have something that requires your attention (*informal*)

plate armour *n* body armour made up of metal plates, as distinct from the chain mail that it superseded

plateau /pláttō/ *n* (*plural* **-teaus** *or* **-teaux** /pláttōz/) 1 **RAISED AREA WITH LEVEL TOP** a hill or mountain with a level top 2 **STABLE PHASE** a period or phase in something when there is little increase or decrease 3 **PHASE OF STAGNATION** a phase in mental or physical development during which little headway is made ■ *vi* (**-teaus, -teauing, -teaued**) **LEVEL OUT** to reach a stable phase after a period of movement or development [Late 18C. Via French < Old French *platel* 'small flat thing' < *plate* (see PLATE).]

plate boundary *n* an area on the margins of tectonic plates where seismic, volcanic, and tectonic activity takes place as a consequence of the relative motion of the plates

plated /pláytid/ *adj* 1 **OVERLAID WITH GOLD OR SILVER** covered with a thin layer of gold or silver 2 **COVERED WITH PLATES** protected and strengthened by a covering of plates 3 **KNITTED WITH TWO YARNS** knitted with two kinds of yarn, one appearing on the front and one on the back of the fabric

plate glass *n* strong thick glass in large sheets used for windows and as a construction material for larger buildings (*hyphenated before nouns*)

platelayer /pláyt layər/ *n* somebody whose job is to lay and maintain railway lines. US term **trackman** ['Plate' < PLATE RAIL]

platelet /pláytlət/ *n* a tiny colourless disc-shaped particle found in large quantities in the blood that plays an important part in the clotting process

platemaker /pláyt maykər/ *n* a person or machine that prepares plates for printing

platen /plátt'n/ *n* 1 **METAL PLATE IN PRINTING PRESS** a flat metal plate in a printing press that holds the paper against the inked type 2 **TYPEWRITER ROLLER** the cylindrical roller against which the paper is held in a typewriter, and against which the type strikes 3 **WORKTABLE** the movable worktable of a machine tool [Mid-16C. < Old French *platine* 'metal plate' < *plat* 'flat', via assumed Vulgar Latin *plattus* < Greek *platus* (see PLATE).]

plater /pláytər/ *n* 1 **SOMEBODY OR SOMETHING THAT PLATES** a person or machine that plates things 2 **RACEHORSE IN MINOR RACES** a racehorse of average quality that is entered for minor races 3 **BLACKSMITH** a blacksmith who specializes in shoeing racehorses

plateresque /pláttə résk/ *adj* relating to a heavily decorated architectural style fashionable in 16th-century Spain, reminiscent of elaborate silverware [Late 19C. < Spanish *plateresco* < *platero* 'silversmith' < *plata* 'silver' (see PLATINA).]

plate tectonics *n* a theory that ascribes continental drift, volcanic and seismic activity, and the formation of mountain belts to moving plates of the Earth's crust supported on less rigid mantle rocks (*+ singular verb*)

~~**plateu**~~ incorrect spelling of **plateau**

ϟ **platform** /plát fawrm/ *n* **1 STAGE FOR PERFORMERS** a raised level area of flooring for speakers, performers, or participants in a ceremony, making them easily visible to the audience **2 FLAT RAISED STRUCTURE** a simple structure, especially one composed of wooden planks, serving as a base for keeping things clear of the ground **3 RAISED AREA PROVIDING ACCESS TO TRAINS** a raised structure beside the line at a railway station that makes it easier to get on or off and load or unload a train **4 REAR STEP ON BUS OR TRAM** an open step at the rear of a bus or tram for passengers to stand on as they get into or out of the vehicle **5 STATED POLICY OF PARTY SEEKING ELECTION** the publicly announced policies and promises of a party seeking election, understood as the basis of its actions should it come to power **6 OPPORTUNITY FOR DOING** a position of authority or prominence that provides a good opportunity for doing something **7 OFFSHORE DRILLING STRUCTURE** an anchored offshore structure with living and working accommodation above water level, from which oil or gas wells can be drilled or maintained **8 RAISED AREA OF GROUND** a flat raised area of ground **9 THICKENED SOLE OF SHOE** a thick layer of leather or other material between the sole and upper of a shoe **10 SHOE WITH PLATFORM SOLE** a shoe or boot with a platform sole **11 COMPUTER OPERATING SYSTEM** a standard configuration of computer hardware or a particular operating system ○ *Some software will only run on a particular platform.* [Mid-16C. < French *plateforme* 'diagram' < *plat* 'flat' + *forme* 'form'.]

platform scale *n* a scale with a flat surface that supports the object to be weighed

platform ticket *n* a ticket allowing access to a station platform, formerly purchased by nontravellers so that they could meet or see off passengers

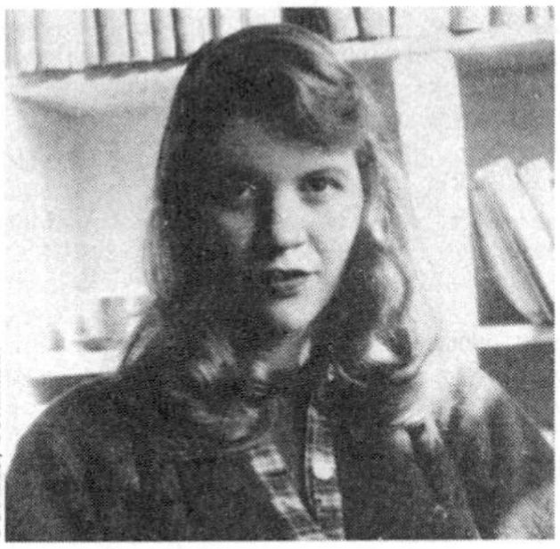

CORBIS/Bettmann

Sylvia Plath

Plath /plath/, **Sylvia** (1932–63) US poet

platin- *prefix* platinum ○ *platinic* [< PLATINUM]

platina /plátinə, plə teénə/ *n* a naturally occurring platinum alloy [Mid-18C. < Spanish < *plata* 'silver' (because of its silvery colour), from assumed Vulgar Latin *plattus*.]

plating /pláyting/ *n* **1 THIN COVERING CONSISTING OF VALUABLE METAL** a thin covering of a valuable metal applied to a surface of base metal ○ *gold plating* **2 COVERING OF METAL PLATES** a covering or armour of metal plates applied to the surface of something, especially a ship or tank **3 APPLICATION OF A COVERING OF METAL** the process of applying a covering of metal or metal plates to the surface of something

platinic /plə tínnik/ *adj* relating to, containing, or consisting of platinum, especially in a valency state of four

platinize /plátti nīz/ (**-nizes, -nizing, -nized**), **platinise** (**-nises, -nising, -nised**) *vt* to coat, combine, or treat something with platinum or a platinum compound —**platinization** /plátti nī záysh'n/ *n*

platinoid /plátti noyd/ *adj* **RESEMBLING PLATINUM** resembling or containing platinum ■ *n* **1 METAL CHEMICALLY SIMILAR TO PLATINUM** a metal that is chemically similar to platinum, specifically iridium, osmium, palladium, rhodium, or ruthenium **2 ALLOY SIMILAR TO PLATINUM** an alloy of copper, zinc, nickel, and tungsten that resembles platinum in not tarnishing readily and in having a strong resistance to the passage of an electric current

platinous /pláttinəss/ *adj* relating to, containing, or consisting of platinum, especially in a valency state of two

platinum /pláttinəm/ *n* (*symbol* **Pt**) a precious silvery-white metallic element, highly malleable and ductile and highly resistant to chemicals and heat. Source: copper, nickel ores. Use: jewellery, catalyst, electroplating. ■ *adj* having sold 300,000 copies of a single or an album [Early 19C. < PLATINA, after the names of other metals ending in *-um*.]

platinum black *n* platinum in the form of a fine black powder. Use: catalyst in organic synthesis.

platinum blonde, platinum blond *adj* describes hair that is pale silvery-blonde in colour (*hyphenated before nouns*)

platinum metal *n* platinum or any of the metals in its group, specifically iridium, osmium, palladium, rhodium, or ruthenium

platitude /plátti tyood/ *n* **1** a pointless, unoriginal, or empty comment or statement made as though it was significant or helpful **2** the making of platitudes [Early 19C. < French, 'flatness' < *plat* 'flat' (see PLATE).] —**platitudinal** *adj* —**platitudinous** /plátti tyoódinəss/ *adj*

platitudinize /plátti tyoódi nīz/ (**-nizes, -nizing, -nized**), **platitudinise** (**-nises, -nising, -nised**) *vi* to produce or talk in platitudes —**platitudinizer** /plátti tyoódi nīzər/ *n*

Plato /pláytō/ lunar crater visible in the NW quadrant of the Moon, approximately 100 km/60 mi. in diameter

Plato (428?–347 BC) Greek philosopher

platonic /plə tónnik/ *adj* **1** involving friendship, affection, or love without sexual relations between people who might be expected to be sexually attracted to each other **2** perfect in form or conception but not found in reality [Mid-16C. Via Latin < Greek *Platōnikos* < *Platōn*.] —**platonically** *adv*

Platonic *adj* relating to Plato or his philosophy

Platonism /pláytənizəm/ *n* the philosophy or teachings of Plato, especially the theory that both physical objects and instances of qualities are recognizable because of their common relationship to an abstract form or idea [Late 16C. < modern Latin *Platonismus* < Greek *Platōn* (see PLATO).] —**Platonist** *n*

platoon /plə toón/ *n* **1** a subdivision of a company of soldiers, usually led by a lieutenant and consisting of two to three sections or squads of ten to twelve people **2** a body of people or things with a common purpose or goal [Mid-17C. < French *peloton* 'small ball' < *pelote* 'ball' (see PELLET).]

platoon sergeant *n* a noncommissioned officer in the US army who assists a lieutenant in leading a platoon

Plattdeutsch /plát doych/ *n, adj* LANG = **Low German** [Mid-19C. Via German < Dutch *Platduitsch* 'low German'; from the flat landscape of the North German lowlands where it is spoken.]

platteland /plát land/ *n* remote rural areas in South Africa [Mid-20C. Via Afrikaans < Middle Dutch, 'flat country'.]

ϟ **platter** /pláttər/ *n* **1 LARGE FLAT DISH** a large flat dish for serving food **2 SERVED FOOD** a particular variety of prepared and served food (*often in combination*) ○ *seafood platter* **3 RECORD** a gramophone record (*dated informal*) **4 RECORDING SURFACE OF A HARD DISK** the recording surface of a hard disk [14C. Via Anglo-Norman *plater* < Old French *plat* (see PLATE).]

platy[1] /pláyti/ (**-ier, -iest**) *adj* describes minerals that crystallize in thin sheets and tend to flake along cleavage planes

platy[2] /plátti/ (*plural* **-ys** *or* **-ies** *or* **-y**) *n* a brightly coloured fish that bears live young, not eggs, often kept as an aquarium fish. Native to: Central America. Genus: *Xiphophorus*. [Early 20C. Shortening of modern Latin *Platypoecilus* < Greek *platus* 'flat' + *poikilos* 'spotted'.]

platyhelminth /plátti hélminth/ *n* a flatworm (*technical*) [Late 19C. < modern Latin *Platyhelminthes* < Greek *platus* 'flat' + *helminth-* 'worm'.] —**platyhelminthic** /-hel mínthik/ *adj*

platypus /pláttipəss/ (*plural* **-puses** *or* **-pi** /-pī/) *n* ZOOL = **duck-billed platypus** [Late 18C. Via modern Latin *Platypus* < Greek *platupous* 'flat-footed' < *platus* 'flat' + *pous* 'foot'.]

platyrrhine /plátti rīn/ *adj* describes animals, especially New World monkeys, whose nostrils are well separated and point to either side ■ *n* a platyrrhine animal, especially a monkey [Mid-19C. Via modern Latin *Platyrrhini* < Greek *platurrhis* 'broad-nosed'.]

plaudit /pláwdit/ *n* an expression of praise or approval ○ *won plaudits for her skilful handling of the crisis* [Early 17C. < Latin *plaudite* 'applaud!' < *plaudere*; from the customary appeal made by Roman actors at the end of a play.]

~~**plausable**~~ incorrect spelling of **plausible**

plausible /pláwzəb'l/ *adj* **1** believable and appearing likely to be true, usually in the absence of proof **2** having a persuasive manner in speech or writing, often combined with an intention to deceive [Mid-16C. < Latin *plausibilis* 'deserving applause' < *plaus-*, past participle of *plaudere*.] —**plausibility** /pláwzə bílləti/ *n* —**plausibleness** /pláwzəb'lnəss/ *n* —**plausibly** /-əbli/ *adv*

Plautus /pláwtəss/, **Titus Maccius** (254?–184 BC) Roman comic dramatist

play /play/ *v* **1** *vi* **ENGAGE IN ENJOYABLE ACTIVITY** to take part in enjoyable activity for the sake of amusement **2** *vi* **ACT IN JEST** to do something for fun, not in earnest **3** *vti* **TAKE PART IN A GAME OR SPORT** to take part in a game or a sporting activity ○ *likes to play football* **4** *vt* **COMPETE AGAINST** to compete against somebody in a game or sporting event ○ *They play their biggest rival tomorrow.* **5** *vti* **ASSIGN OR HAVE A POSITION ON FIELD** to assign a player to a particular position on the field, or be assigned such a position **6** *vt* **HIT BALL** to hit or kick a ball, puck, or shuttlecock in a specific direction ○ *playing the ball straight down the line* **7** *vt* **HIT A SHOT** to make a specific shot or stroke in a sporting event **8** *vt* **USE A PIECE OR CARD IN A GAME** to use a card from a hand in a card game or a piece in a board game **9** *vti* **ACT IN A PARTICULAR MANNER** to deal with a situation in a specific way to achieve a desired result ○ *Whether you get what you want depends on how you play it.* **10** *vti* **GAMBLE** to gamble on a game of chance such as roulette or on horse races **11** *vt* **SPECULATE IN A MARKET** to speculate with securities or commodities in a market **12** *vti* **ACT A PART IN A PLAY** to portray a character in a theatrical or film production ○ *played Macbeth on stage* ○ *'He that plays the king shall be welcome'.* (Shakespeare, *Hamlet*; 1602) **13** *vti* **PERFORM OR BE PERFORMED SOMEWHERE** to perform a play or show a film at a particular theatre or cinema, or be performed or shown there ○ *What's playing at the Luxor?* **14** *vt* **PERFORM A DRAMATIC WORK BY** to perform the work of a specific dramatist **15** *vt* **PERFORM IN PARTICULAR PLACES** to perform in specific places or types of places ○ *playing the northern industrial towns* **16** *vt* **PRETEND TO BE** to pretend to be a specific type of person ○ *Don't play the innocent with me.* **17** *vti* **PERFORM ON A MUSICAL INSTRUMENT** to use a musical instrument or the voice to produce music ○ *plays the trombone* **18** *vt* **PERFORM A COMPOSER** to perform the music of a particular composer ○ *Chopin is notoriously difficult to play well.* **19** *vti* **REPRODUCE RECORDED MUSIC** to reproduce recorded music for listening, or be reproduced for listening ○ *played my favourite CD* **20** *vti* **DIRECT LIGHT OR WATER** to direct light or water over a surface or in a particular way, or be directed in this manner **21** *vti* **MOVE IRREGULARLY OVER A SURFACE** to move or cause something to move unsteadily or irregularly over a surface, usually in a pleasing way ○ *sunlight playing on her brown hair* **22** *vt* **LET A FISH PULL ON A LINE** to tire an already hooked fish by letting it pull on the line as it tries to escape **23** *vi* **MAKE A PARTICULAR IMPRESSION ON** to be received in a particular way by somebody, or make a specific impression on that person ○ *a policy that is likely to play well with middle-class voters* ■ *n* **1 DRAMATIC COMPOSITION** a dramatic work written to be performed by actors on the stage, television, or radio **2 PLOY** a ploy or deceptive act intended to achieve a specific end ○ *The defendant's tears were just a play for your sympathy.* **3 ENJOYABLE ACTIVITIES** activities bringing amusement or enjoyment, especially the spontaneous activity of young children or young animals ○ *young cubs at play* **4 PUN** a pun on a word **5 ACTION DURING A GAME** the action during a game or series of games ○ *Bad light eventually stopped play.* ○ *The play was skilled during the first half but then the team began to tire.* **6** US **ACTION OR MOVE IN A GAME** a specific action or move in a game ○ *drilled the team in several new offensive plays* **7 TURN IN A GAME** somebody's turn to move in a game **8 HANDLING OF A SHOT OR MOVE** a player's handling of a shot or move or use of a piece or card **9 GAMBLING** participation in betting or gambling **10 FLICKERING MOVEMENT** flickering or shimmering movement, especially of light through or on something **11 LOOSENESS** the amount of looseness in something, such as a rope, or between moving parts [Old English *pleg(i)an* < Germanic, 'risk, exercise'] —**playability** /pláyə bílləti/ *n* —**playable** /pláyəb'l/ *adj* ◇ **make a play for somebody** *or* **something** to try openly to gain something ◇ **play fair** to act in an honest and reasonable way ◇ **play fast and loose** to act irresponsibly or recklessly without regard to facts or others' feelings ◇ **play hard to get** to avoid agreeing to a suggestion, invitation, or proposal, with the intention of appearing to be desirable or in demand ◇ **play safe** to exercise caution and take few risks

play about *vi* = **play around** *v.* 2

play along *vi* to pretend to agree with somebody or something in order to gain an advantage or avoid conflict

play around *vi* 1 to engage in sexual activity with somebody other than a spouse or long-term partner 2 to behave in an irresponsible or childish way

play at *v* 1 *vt* to pretend to do or be something, usually without conviction or commitment ○ *I was tired of playing at being an entrepreneur.* 2 *vi* to engage in a game that involves role-playing (*refers typically to children*) ○ *playing at doctors and nurses*

play back *vti* to reproduce recorded sound or video material

play down *vt* to represent something as being less important or significant than it is ○ *While some patients exaggerate their symptoms, others play them down.* ○ *The spin doctors are playing down the significance of the charge.*

play off *v* 1 *vi* TAKE PART IN DECIDING GAME to take part in a deciding game to find the winner of a tied contest 2 *vt* BRING INTO CONFLICT to set one person or group against another in order to gain an advantage ○ *children playing their parents off against each other* 3 *vt* REACT to interact with or react to somebody or something ○ *The women are distantly related and the subplot plays off that coincidence.*

play on, play upon *v* 1 *vt* TAKE ADVANTAGE OF to use somebody's hope, fear, or insecurity as a way of manipulating that person 2 *vt* MAKE A PUN to make a pun on a word 3 *vi* HIT BALL INTO OWN WICKET in cricket, to hit the ball into your own wicket, putting yourself out of the game

play out *v* 1 *vt* ACT OUT to act out a scene or situation that has been rehearsed or envisaged previously 2 *vt* FINISH PLAYING to continue to play something to the finish or end ○ *We'll play out this hand, then go home.* 3 *vt* LET SOMETHING OUT GRADUALLY to release something such as a rope bit by bit 4 *vti* US END to bring something to an end, or come to an end ○ *The calamity has yet to play out.*

play up *v* 1 *vt* EMPHASIZE to emphasize or exaggerate something ○ *She played up her commercial know-how for all she was worth.* 2 *vi* BEHAVE BADLY to be uncooperative or disruptive ○ *The children are playing up again.* 3 *vi* MALFUNCTION to fail to function properly ○ *My printer's playing up.* 4 *vti* HURT to cause pain to somebody (*refers to parts of the body*)

play up to *vt* 1 to attempt to please somebody by flattery and obsequiousness 2 to support another actor in a play

play with *vt* 1 THINK ABOUT to consider a plan or idea without doing very much to make it happen 2 TREAT CARELESSLY to treat somebody or somebody's feelings carelessly or irresponsibly 3 DEAL WITH SOMETHING HALF-HEARTEDLY to deal with something unenthusiastically or haphazardly, e.g. by pushing food around a plate without eating 4 MASTURBATE to masturbate

playa /plī́ ə/ *n* the lower part of an inland desert drainage basin that is periodically filled with alkaline and briny salts washed down by rainwater from surrounding highlands [Mid-19C. Via Spanish, 'beach' < late Latin *plagia* 'plain, shore' < ?]

play-act *v* 1 *vi* BEHAVE INSINCERELY to behave in an insincere and excessively dramatic fashion, usually in order to get attention (*informal*) 2 *vti* PRETEND TO BE ACTING to pretend to be acting a part, usually for fun 3 *vi* ACT IN A PLAY to take part in drama, especially as an amateur —**play-acting** *n* —**play-actor** *n*

playback /pláy bak/ *n* 1 the replay of a sound or video recording after it has been made, often as a check for quality or accuracy 2 the device or facility in a recording apparatus for replaying recordings

playback singer *n S Asia* a singer who sings songs mimed to by film actors

playbill /pláy bil/ *n* 1 a poster advertising a play or other theatrical performance (*dated*) 2 *US* the printed programme accompanying a theatrical performance or concert, sold to theatregoers before the performance ○ *We had barely two minutes to study the playbill before the lights went down.*

playboy /pláy boy/ *n* a rich man who does not work and devotes himself to a life of pleasure without commitments or responsibilities

LITERARY LINK ***The Playboy of the Western World***, a play (1907) by J. M. Synge. It is the story of Christy Mahon, who flees from his domineering father to a village in Mayo. There he impresses the inhabitants, particularly the women, with his exaggerated tales, claiming to have killed his father with a single blow. His period of glory is cut short, however, by the arrival in the village of his alleged victim, who suffered no more than a blow on the head from his son.

play-by-play *adj US* consisting of a description of each event as it happens, especially in a sports contest ■ *n US* SPORTS = **commentary** *n.* 1

Play-Doh /pláy dō/ *tdmk* a trademark for a soft coloured modelling material used especially by children

played out *adj* 1 drained of energy or inspiration as a result of excessive or prolonged effort or of being too long in the public eye 2 having lost all usefulness or relevance through overuse or overexposure (*hyphenated before nouns*) [Originally describing a fish that has fought until it is exhausted]

player /pláyər/ *n* 1 SOMEBODY TAKING PART IN GAME somebody taking part in a sport or game, e.g. a member of a team (*often in combination*) ○ *a hockey player* 2 MUSICIAN a person who plays a musical instrument (*usually in combination*) ○ *a trumpet player* 3 PARTICIPANT IN AN ACTIVITY a person, group, or business that has an influential role in a particular political or commercial activity ○ *a major player in the direct banking sector* 4 STAGE ACTOR an actor, especially a member of a theatrical company 5 DEVICE FOR PLAYING RECORDED SOUND a device for playing recorded sound (*usually in combination*) ○ *a CD player*

player piano *n* a piano with a mechanism for playing music automatically, usually by means of a perforated metal disc or roll of paper

playfellow /pláy felō/ *n* a friend with whom a child plays (*archaic*)

playful /pláyf'l/ *adj* 1 fond of having fun and playing games with others 2 said or done in a teasing way or in fun ○ *a playful poke in the ribs* —**playfully** *adv* —**playfulness** *n*

playgirl /pláy gurl/ *n* a rich woman who does not work and devotes herself to a life of pleasure without commitments or responsibilities

playgoer /pláygō ər/ *n* a frequent attender of plays at a theatre —**playgoing** *adj, n*

playground /pláy grownd/ *n* 1 ENCLOSED PLAY AREA an outdoor recreation area for children, usually equipped with swings, slides, seesaws, and other play equipment 2 SCHOOL PLAY AREA the yard attached to a school, for children to play in during break times. US term **schoolyard** 3 RESORT a resort or other place used for a recreation by a particular group of people ○ *The coast has become a playground for millionaires.*

playgroup /pláy groop/ *n* an organized meeting for preschool children to play together under supervision

playhouse /pláy howss/ (*plural* **-houses** /-howziz/) *n* 1 a theatre, especially the main theatre in a town or city (*often used in placenames*) ○ *appearing at the Nottingham Playhouse* 2 LEISURE = **Wendy house**

playing card *n* any of a set of cards printed with an identical design on the back and symbols on the face representing the numbers in different suits, used for playing various games

playing field *n* an area of level ground used for organized sporting activities ◇ **a level playing field** a situation in which all those involved have an equal chance of being successful

playlet /pláylət/ *n* a short play, often one with a rather slight plot

playlist /pláy list/ *n* a list of musical recordings that are to be played on a radio programme or by a radio station —**playlist** *vt*

playmaker /pláy maykər/ *n* in team games, a player who initiates moves that create scoring opportunities

playmate /pláy mayt/ *n* somebody, especially a child, who plays with another

play-off *n* 1 an additional match, game, or round to decide the winner in the case of a tie 2 *US, Can* one of a series of matches that decides a championship competition ○ *One more win should guarantee a spot in the play-offs.*

play on words *n* a pun

playpen /pláy pen/ *n* a portable structure that forms a small enclosure for a baby to play in safely

playroom /pláy room, -rōōm/ *n* a room reserved, designed, or equipped for children to play in

playschool /pláy skool/ *n* a place where preschool children can be taken for supervised play and learning, usually for half-day sessions

playsuit /pláy soot, -syoot/ *n* an outfit for a child or woman to wear when relaxing, either consisting of shorts and a top or made in one piece

plaything /pláy thing/ *n* 1 a toy or other object with which to play 2 somebody or something used for amusement rather than being treated with respect or taken seriously

playtime /pláy tīm/ *n* a time set aside for play, especially as a break for children at school

playwright /pláy rīt/ *n* a writer of plays

~~**playwrite**~~ incorrect spelling of **playwright**

plaza /plaázə/ *n* 1 an open square or marketplace in a Spanish-speaking country or somewhere influenced by Hispanic culture 2 *US* a mall or shopping centre [Late 17C. Via Spanish < Latin *platea* 'broad street' (see PLACE).]

PLC *abbr* 1 product life cycle 2 **PLC, plc** public limited company

plea /plee/ *n* 1 URGENT REQUEST an urgent, often emotional, request ○ *a plea for understanding* 2 DEFENDANT'S ANSWER TO CHARGE the defendant's answer to a charge in a court of law, especially one stating that he or she is guilty or not guilty 3 STATEMENT SUPPORTING DEFENDANT'S OR CLAIMANT'S CASE a statement or argument made in a court of law in support of a defendant's or claimant's case 4 COURT CASE in Scotland, a legal case conducted through the courts 5 EXCUSE an excuse or pretext [13C. Via Anglo-Norman *plai* 'lawsuit, agreement' < Latin *placitum* 'decree' < past participle of *placere* (see PLEASE).]

plea bargaining *n* the practice of arranging with the prosecution, and sometimes a judge, for a defendant to plead guilty to a less serious charge rather than be tried for a more serious one —**plea bargain** *n* —**plea-bargain** *vi*

pleach /pleech/, **plash** /plash/ *vt* to form or reinforce a hedge or arch by intertwining shoots or branches [14C. < Old French dialect *plechier*, a variant of Old French *plassier* < Latin *plectere* 'to plait' (see PLEXUS).]

plead /pleed/ (**pleads, pleading, pleaded** *or* **pled** *US, Can, Scotland* /pled/) *v* 1 *vi* BEG EARNESTLY to make an earnest or urgent entreaty, often in emotional terms ○ *I pleaded with her to stay.* 2 *vt* OFFER AS AN EXCUSE to use a particular reason or circumstance to excuse or justify behaviour ○ *It's no good pleading ignorance.* 3 *vt* DECLARE GUILT OR INNOCENCE to answer 'guilty' or 'not guilty' in response to a charge in a court of law 4 *vti* OFFER AN ARGUMENT IN SUPPORT to argue a case in support of somebody or something, especially in a court of law [13C. Via Anglo-Norman *pleder* < medieval Latin *placitare* 'to appeal' < *placitum* 'decree' (see PLEA).] —**pleadable** *adj* —**pleader** *n* —**pleadingly** *adv*

pleadings /pleédingz/ *npl* the formal written statements made by the plaintiff and the defendant in a lawsuit

pleasance /plézz'nss/ *n* a quiet tree-planted area laid out with walks and often statues and fountains [14C. < French *plaisance* < *plaisant* (see PLEASANT).]

pleasant /plézz'nt/ *adj* 1 bringing feelings of pleasure, enjoyment, or satisfaction ○ *We spent a very pleasant evening together.* 2 friendly, kind, or good-natured [14C. < Old French *plaisant*, present participle of Old French *plaisir* (see PLEASE).] —**pleasantly** *adv* —**pleasantness** *n*

Pleasant Island /plézz'nt-/ former name for **Nauru**

pleasantry /plézz'ntri/ (*plural* **-ries**) *n* 1 POLITE REMARK a conventionally polite remark or enquiry 2 WITTY REMARK a humorous or witty remark 3 AGREEABLE CONVERSATION pleasing light conversation

please /pleez/ *adv, interj* USED IN REQUESTS used to add politeness or urgency to requests, commands, and published rules and regulations ○ *Please be quiet.* ■ *interj* USED TO EXPRESS INDIGNATION used to express astonishment or indignation, often facetiously ○ *Please! Do you expect me to believe that?* ■ *v* (**pleases, pleasing, pleased**) 1 *vti* GIVE PLEASURE to give pleasure or satisfaction to somebody 2 *vt* BE WHAT SOMEBODY WANTS to be the wish or will of somebody (*formal or literary*) 3 *vi* LIKE to like or wish to do something ○ *You can do as you please.* [14C. Via Old French *plaisir* < Latin *placere.*] —**pleaser** *n* ◇ **if you please** 1 used to make a polite request or command (*dated formal*) 2 used to indicate mild annoyance, indignation, or amazement (*dated*)

pleased /pleezed/ *adj* **1** feeling or expressing satisfaction or pleasure ○ *I'm really pleased with their progress.* ○ *Pleased to meet you.* **2** willing to do something ○ *We would be pleased to answer any further requests you have.*

~~**pleasent**~~ incorrect spelling of **pleasant**

pleasing /pleézing/ *adj* **1** pleasant or gratifying ○ *a pleasing contrast* **2** welcome or satisfying —**pleasingly** *adv* —**pleasingness** *n*

pleasurable /plézhərəb'l/ *adj* giving pleasure or enjoyment —**pleasurability** /plézhərə bíllәti/ *n* —**pleasurably** /plézhərəbli/ *adv*

pleasure /plézhər/ *n* **1 HAPPINESS OR SATISFACTION** a feeling of happiness, delight, or satisfaction ○ *I took great pleasure in pointing out his mistake to him.* **2 SENSUAL GRATIFICATION** gratification of the senses, especially sexual gratification **3 RECREATION** recreation, relaxation, or amusement, especially as distinct from work or everyday routine ○ *travelling for pleasure* **4 SOMETHING SATISFYING** a source of happiness, joy, or satisfaction **5 SOMEBODY'S DESIRE** somebody's desire, wish, or preference (*formal or literary*) ■ *v* (**-ures, -uring, -ured**) **1** *vt* **GIVE SOMEBODY PLEASURE** to give somebody pleasure, especially through sensual or sexual stimulation or gratification **2** *vi* **ENJOY** to derive satisfaction or happiness from something (*archaic*) [14C. < Old French *plaisir* 'please', used as a noun (see PLEASE).] —**pleasureful** *adj* —**pleasureless** *adj*

pleasure principle *n* in Freudian psychology, the principle that guides instinctive behaviour, directing the subject towards gratifying immediate needs and avoiding pain

pleat /pleet/ *n* a vertical fold in cloth or other material, usually one of a number, sewn into position or pressed flat ■ *vt* to put pleats into cloth or a piece of clothing [14C. < an early variant of PLAIT.] —**pleater** *n*

pleb /pleb/ *n* **1** an offensive term for an ill-educated and unrefined person, especially somebody from a lower social class (*insult*) **2** HIST = **plebeian** *n.* 1 **3** *US* MIL = **plebe** [Mid-17C. Originally a back-formation < PLEBS, misunderstood as a plural, later also shortening of PLEBEIAN.] —**plebby** *adj*

plebe /pleeb/ *n US* a first-year student at the US Military Academy or the US Naval Academy [Mid-19C. Probably shortening of PLEBEIAN.]

plebeian /plə beé ən/ *n* **1 MEMBER OF THE ROMAN PLEBS** one of the ordinary citizens of ancient Rome as distinct from the patricians **2 SOMEBODY REGARDED AS ILL-EDUCATED** somebody thought to behave in a coarse or crude manner, and to have common or vulgar tastes, especially somebody from a lower social class (*insult*) ■ *adj* **1 OF THE ROMAN PLEBS** relating or belonging to the ordinary people in a society, especially the plebs of ancient Rome **2 COMMON OR VULGAR** regarded as coarse, vulgar, or tasteless (*insult*) [Mid-16C. < Latin *plebeius* < *plebs* (see PLEBS).] —**plebeianism** *n*

~~**plebian**~~ incorrect spelling of **plebeian**

plebiscite /plébbi sīt/ *n* **1 VOTE OF ALL CITIZENS** a vote by a whole electorate to decide a question of importance. ◊ **referendum** **2 EXPRESSION OF PUBLIC WILL** a public expression of the will or opinion of a whole community **3 COMMON PEOPLE'S LAW** a law enacted by the plebs or ordinary citizens of ancient Rome gathered in assembly [Mid-16C. Via French < Latin *plebiscitum* 'decree of the common people'.] —**plebiscitary** /plə bíssitəri/ *adj*

plebs /plebz/ *npl* the ordinary citizens of ancient Rome, as distinct from the patricians [Mid-19C. < Latin.]

plecopteran /plə kóptərən/ *n* INSECTS = **stonefly** ■ *adj* relating or belonging to the stoneflies. Order: Plecoptera. [Late 19C. < modern Latin *Plecoptera* < Greek *plekos* 'wickerwork' + *pteron* 'wing'.]

plectrum /pléktrəm/ (*plural* **-tra** /-trə/ *or* **-trums**) *n* a small flat pointed piece of plastic or other material, used for plucking or strumming the strings of a guitar or similar instrument. US term **pick**[2] *n.* 4 [Early 17C. Via Latin < Greek.]

pled /pled/ *US, Can, Scotland* past participle, past tense of **plead**

pledge /plej/ *n* **1 SOLEMN UNDERTAKING** a solemn promise or vow ○ *stood by her election pledges* **2 SOMETHING GIVEN AS SECURITY** something delivered as security for the keeping of a promise or the payment of a debt or as a guarantee of good faith **3** a promise to donate money, e.g. to a charity or a political cause ○ *They have raised over $10,000 in donations and pledges.* **4 BEING HELD AS SECURITY** the state of being held as security ○ *goods in pledge* **5 TOKEN OF** something given or received as a token of something such as love or friendship **6 TOAST** a toast drunk to somebody or something as a gesture of goodwill or support **7** *US* **RECRUIT TO A UNIVERSITY SOCIETY** a student who has been invited, and has promised, to join a fraternity or sorority in a university in the United States ■ *v* (**pledges, pledging, pledged**) **1** *vt* **PROMISE** to promise something solemnly, or promise solemnly to do something **2** *vt* **BIND** to submit somebody to a binding pledge **3** *vt* **GIVE SOMETHING AS SECURITY** to hand over something as security for the payment of a debt, repayment of a loan, or the carrying out of some obligation (*dated*) **4** *vti* **DRINK TO** to drink a toast to somebody (*archaic*) ○ *'Drink to me, only with thine eyes, And I will pledge with mine'* (Ben Jonson *'To Celia'*; 1616) **5** *vti US* **PROMISE TO JOIN A UNIVERSITY SOCIETY** to promise to join a society, fraternity, or sorority in a university in the United States [14C. Via Old French *plege* < late Latin *plebium* < *plebire* 'to pledge' < Germanic.] —**pledgable** *adj* ◇ **sign** *or* **take the pledge** to undertake solemnly to abstain forever from alcoholic drink (*dated*)

pledgee /ple jeé/ *n* somebody with whom a pledge or pawned object is deposited

Pledge of Allegiance *n* a formula recited by citizens of the United States when saluting the US flag as a promise of loyalty to the country

pledger /pléjjər/, **pledgor, pledgeor** *n* **1** a person who pledges or pawns something **2** a taker of a pledge or vow

pledget /pléjjit/ *n* a small tuft of cotton wool or other material used on forceps to cleanse or apply medication to a confined space such as the ear passage [Mid-16C. < ?]

pledgor *n* = **pledger**

-plegia *suffix* inability to move ○ *quadriplegia* [< *plēgē* 'a blow, stroke' < *plēg-*, stem of *plēssein* 'to strike' (see PLECTRUM)]

Pleiades /plī́ ə deez/ *npl* **1** in Greek mythology, the seven daughters of Atlas and Pleione who were pursued by Orion and were turned into a constellation to escape him **2** a cluster of more than 300 stars in the constellation Taurus, several of which are blue-white giants visible to the naked eye [14C. Via Latin < Greek (singular *Pleias*).]

plein-air /pláyn áir/ *adj* relating to or in the style of the French impressionist painters who sought to capture effects of light and atmosphere by completing their work out of doors [Late 19C. < French *(en) plein air* '(in) the open air'.] —**plein-airist** *n*

pleio- *prefix* = **pleo-**

pleiotropism /plī́ óttrəpizəm/, **pleiotropy** /plī́ óttrəpi/ (*plural* **-pies**) *n* the phenomenon in which a single gene determines two or more apparently unrelated characteristics of the same organism, or an instance of this —**pleotropic** /plī́ ə tróppik/ *adj* —**pleiotropically** /-tróppikli/ *adv*

Pleistocene /plī́stō seen/ *adj* relating to or used to describe the earlier epoch of the Quaternary Period in the Cenozoic Era, characterized by the disappearance of continental ice sheets and the appearance of humans ■ *n* the Pleistocene epoch [Mid-19C. < Greek *pleistos* 'most' + *kainos* 'recent'.]

plenary /pleénəri/ *adj* **1 FULL OR UNLIMITED** full and complete and not limited in any respect (*formal*) **2 ATTENDED BY EVERYONE** attended or meant to be attended by every member or delegate ○ *a plenary session* ■ *n* (*plural* **-ries**) **1 PLENARY MEETING** a plenary meeting, session, or lecture, e.g. at a conference **2 BOOK OF GOSPELS OR EPISTLES** a book containing all the gospels or all the epistles and accompanying homilies or sermons [Early 16C. < late Latin *plenarius* < Latin *plenus* 'full' (see PLENTY).] —**plenarily** *adv*

plenary indulgence *n* in the Roman Catholic Church, a complete remission of temporal punishment

plenipotentiary /plénnipə ténshəri/ *adj* **1 HAVING FULL POWER** invested with complete authority to act independently **2 CONFERRING FULL POWER** giving the holder complete authority to act independently ■ *n* (*plural* **-ies**) **OFFICIAL WITH FULL POWERS** an ambassador, envoy, or delegate invested with full authority to act or negotiate independently on behalf of a government or sovereign [Mid-17C. Via medieval Latin *plenipotentiarius* < late Latin *plenipotent-* 'having full power' < *plenus* 'full' + *potens* 'powerful'.] —**plenipotent** /plə nípp̄ətənt/ *adj*

plenitude /plénni tyood/ *n* (*literary*) **1** an abundance or plentiful supply of something **2** the state of being full or complete [15C. Via Old French < late Latin *plenitudo* < *plenus* 'full' (see PLENTY).]

plenteous /plénti əss/ *adj* (*literary*) **1** being in plentiful supply **2** giving an abundant yield [13C. Via Old French *plentivous* < *plentet* (see PLENTY).] —**plenteously** *adv* —**plenteousness** *n*

plentiful /pléntif'l/ *adj* **1** present or existing in good supply ○ *Water is plentiful on the island.* **2** supplying a large amount or number —**plentifully** *adv* —**plentifulness** *n*

plenty /plénti/ *n* **1 LOTS** an adequate or more than adequate amount or quantity ○ *There's plenty for the kids to do there.* ○ *Get plenty of rest.* **2 PROSPERITY** a situation in which there is a more than adequate supply of food, money, and other necessities ○ *had grown up in a time of plenty* ■ *adj* **AMPLY SUFFICIENT** ample or more than sufficient (*informal*) ■ *adv US* **SUFFICIENTLY** used to emphasize the degree to which something is the case (*informal*) ○ *It should be plenty big enough.* [13C. Via Old French *plentet* < Latin *plenitas* < *plenus* 'full'.]

Plenty, Bay of /plénti/ region in NE North Island, New Zealand. Population: 230,465 (1996). Area: 21,576 sq. km/8,330 sq. mi.

plenum /pleénəm/ (*plural* **-nums** *or* **-na** /pleénə/) *n* **1 ENCLOSURE CONTAINING GAS AT A HIGHER PRESSURE** an enclosure or chamber containing gas that is at a higher pressure than the surrounding atmosphere **2 GENERAL ATTENDANCE AT A MEETING** a full or general assembly, e.g. of all the branches of a legislature **3 MATTER-FILLED SPACE** space entirely filled with matter [Late 17C. < Latin *plenum spatium* 'full space'.]

pleo- *prefix* more ○ *pleomorphism* [< Greek *pleīon*. Ultimately < Indo-European 'full, to fill'.]

pleochroism /plee ókrō izəm/ *n* the property in some crystals of transmitting different colours when viewed along different axes [Mid-19C. < PLEO- + Greek *khrōs* 'skin, colour'.] —**pleochroic** /pleé ə krṓ ik/ *adj*

pleomorphism /pleé ə máwrfizəm/, **pleomorphy** /pleé ə mawrfi/ *n* the characteristic in some organisms of taking on at least two different forms during the life cycle, or the ability to do this under certain conditions —**pleomorphic** /-máwrfik/ *adj*

pleonasm /pleé ə nazəm/ *n* **1** the use of more words than are necessary to express a meaning **2** an example of using more words than are necessary to express a meaning, such as 'free gift' or 'sufficient enough' [Mid-16C. Via late Latin < Greek *pleonasmos* < *pleonazein* 'be in excess' < *pleōn* 'more' (see PLEO-).] —**pleonastic** /pleé ə nástik/ *adj* —**pleonastically** /-nástikli/ *adv*

pleotropic /pleé ə tróppik/ *adj* describes a gene that affects more than one characteristic of the phenotype

~~**plesant**~~ incorrect spelling of **pleasant**

plesiosaur /pleéssi ə sawr/ *n* an extinct marine reptile of the Mesozoic era with limbs like paddles, a large flattened body, and a short tail. Suborder: Sauropterygia. [Mid-19C. < modern Latin *Plesiosaurus* < Greek *plēsios* 'near' + *sauros* 'lizard', because it was similar to the saurians.]

plethora /pléthərə/ *n* **1** a very large amount or number of something, especially an excessive amount ○ *a plethora of new TV channels* **2** an excess of blood in part of the body, especially in the facial veins, causing a ruddy complexion [Mid-16C. Via late Latin < Greek *plēthorē* < *plēthein* 'be full'.] —**plethoric** /ple thórrik/ *adj* —**plethorically** /-thórrikli/ *adv*

pleur- *prefix* = **pleuro-** (*before vowels*)

pleura /plóorə/ *n* (*plural* **-rae** /plóoree/ *or* **-ras**) the thin transparent membrane that lines the chest wall and doubles back to cover the lungs, thereby forming a continuous sac enclosing the narrow pleural cavity ■ plural of **pleuron** [15C. Via medieval Latin < Greek, 'side, rib'.] —**pleural** *adj*

pleural cavity *n* the cavity formed between the pleural layer surrounding the lungs and the other layer lining the chest wall

pleurisy /plóorəssi/ *n* inflammation of the membrane (**pleura**) surrounding the lungs, usually involving painful breathing, coughing, and the buildup of fluid in the pleural cavity [14C. Via Old French < Greek *pleuritis* < *pleura* 'side, rib'.] —**pleuritic** /ploo ríttik/ *adj*

pleuro- *prefix* **1** side, lateral ○ *pleurodont* **2** pleura, pleural ○ *pleuropneumonia* [< Greek *pleura* 'side, rib']

pleurocentesis *n* MED = **thoracentesis**

pleurodont /ploórə dont/ *adj* **1** describes teeth, e.g. those found in some reptiles, that are not rooted in the jawbone but fused to its inner side **2** describes reptiles that have teeth not rooted in the jawbone but fused to its inner side

pleurodynia /plooərə dínni ə/ *n* **1** pain in the pleura, between the ribs or in the chest wall area **2** an illness caused by a Coxsackie virus (*not technical*) [Early 19C. < PLEURO- + Greek *odunē* 'pain'.]

pleuron /ploór on/ (*plural* **-ra** /ploórə/) *n* a membrane that encases the lung. ◆ **pleura** [Early 18C. Via modern Latin < Greek, 'rib, side'.]

pleuropneumonia /ploórō nyoo mṓni ə/ *n* inflammation of the membrane (**pleura**) surrounding the lungs and of the lungs themselves at the same time

pleuston /ploóstən/ *n* small animals and plants such as algae that float on the surface of a pool of fresh water [Mid-20C. < Greek *pleusis* 'sailing', after PLANKTON.] —**pleustonic** /ploo stónnik/ *adj*

Pleven /plév en/ city in N Bulgaria. Population: 125,000 (1996).

plexiform /pléksi fawrm/ *adj* resembling or in the form of a plexus or network [Early 19C. < PLEXUS + -FORM.]

plexor /pléksər/ *n* a small rubber-headed hammer formerly used to tap the body in a medical examination by percussion and in testing reflexes, e.g. by tapping the knee [Mid-19C. < Greek *plēxis* 'percussion' < *plēssein* 'to strike'.]

plexus /pléksəss/ (*plural* **-uses** *or* **-us**) *n* **1** a network of nerves, blood vessels, or other vessels in the body **2** any complex network or interwoven structure [Late 17C. < Latin, past participle of *plectere* 'to plait'.]

pliable /plī́ əb'l/ *adj* **1 FLEXIBLE** flexible and easily bent **2 EASILY INFLUENCED** easily persuaded or influenced **3 ADAPTABLE** adaptable to change [15C. < Old French, < *plier* 'to bend' (see PLY²).] —**pliability** /plī́ ə bíllәti/ *n* —**pliableness** /plī́ əb'lnəss/ *n* —**pliably** /plī́ əbli/ *adv*

SYNONYMS ***pliable, ductile, malleable, elastic, pliant***
CORE MEANING: able to be bent or moulded
pliable flexible and easily bent or moulded; **ductile** describes metals that can be easily drawn out into a long continuous wire or hammered into thin sheets; **malleable** describes metals that can be hammered or pressed into various shapes without breaking or cracking; **elastic** describes substances or materials that can be stretched without breaking and then return to their original shape; **pliant** supple and springy and therefore easily bent.

pliant /plī́ ənt/ *adj* **1 SUPPLE** supple and bending easily ○ *a pliant tree branch* **2 ADAPTABLE** easily adapted or modified **3 EASILY INFLUENCED** easily persuaded or influenced [14C. < Old French, present participle of *plier* 'to fold, bend' (see PLY²).] —**pliancy** *n* —**pliantly** *adv* —**pliantness** *n*

SYNONYMS See ***pliable***.

plica /plī́kə/ (*plural* **-cae** /-see/) *n* a fold or folded part, e.g. of skin [Early 18C. Via medieval Latin, 'fold' < Latin *plicare* 'to fold' (see PLY²).] —**plical** *adj*

plicate /plī́ kayt/, **plicated** /plī́ kaytid/ *adj* **1** arranged in folds like a fan **2** describes rock with a folded wrinkled texture [Late 17C. < Latin *plicat-*, past participle of *plicare* 'to fold' (see PLY²).] —**plicately** *adv* —**plicateness** *n*

plication /plī káysh'n/, **plicature** /plíkəchər/ *n* **1 STITCHING THE SIDES OF A BODY ORGAN** the pleating and stitching of the walls of a body organ in order to reduce its size **2 FOLDING** the action of folding or the condition of being folded **3 A FOLD** a fold in something

plié /pleé ay/ *n* a ballet movement in which the knees are bent and the back is kept straight [Late 19C. < French, past participle of *plier* 'to bend' (see PLY²).]

pliers /plī́ ərz/ *npl* a hand tool with two hinged arms ending in jaws that are closed by hand pressure to grip something [Mid-16C. < PLY¹.]

plight¹ /plīt/ *n* a difficult or dangerous situation, especially a sad or desperate predicament [14C. Via Anglo-Norman *plit* 'wrinkle, situation' (influenced by PLIGHT²) < Latin *plicitum* < past participle of *plicare* 'to fold' (see PLY²).]

plight² /plīt/ *vt* (**plights, plighting, plighted** *or* **plight**) to make a formal pledge, especially when promising to marry ■ *n* a formal promise or pledge (*archaic*) [Old English *plihtan* 'endanger' < *pliht* 'risk, danger' < Germanic, 'risk, pledge yourself'] —**plighter** *n*

plimsoll /plíms'l/, **plimsole** *n UK* a light canvas shoe with a rubber sole [Late 19C. Probably < PLIMSOLL LINE, because the line around the shoe resembles it.]

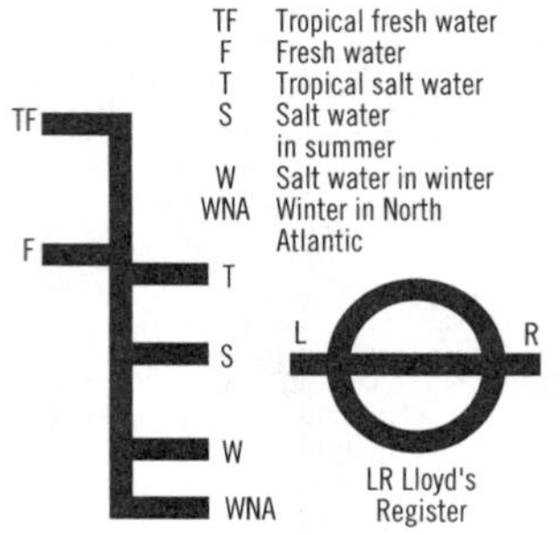

TF Tropical fresh water
F Fresh water
T Tropical salt water
S Salt water in summer
W Salt water in winter
WNA Winter in North Atlantic
TF
F
T
S
W
WNA
L
R
LR Lloyd's Register

Plimsoll line

Plimsoll line, Plimsoll mark *n* a mark on the side of a merchant ship indicating the limit to which it can legally be submerged when loaded [After Samuel *Plimsoll* (1824–98), British politician and reformer]

plink /plingk/ *n* **HIGH-PITCHED SOUND** a short high-pitched metallic sound such as that caused by the plucked string of a musical instrument ■ *vti* **1 MAKE HIGH-PITCHED SOUND** to create a short high-pitched metallic sound **2 SHOOT AT A TARGET** to shoot at or hit targets for fun, especially targets that make a short high-pitched metallic sound when hit [Mid-20C. An imitation of the sound.] —**plinker** *n*

plinth /plinth/ *n* **1 SUPPORTING BLOCK** a square block beneath a column, pedestal, or statue **2 SUPPORTING PART OF A WALL** the part of the wall of a building immediately above the ground, usually a course of stones or bricks **3 PART OF A DOORFRAME** the square block at the base on each side of a doorframe **4 FLAT BASE** any flat block used as a base for something, e.g. underneath a heavy machine [Late 16C. Via French < Greek *plinthos* 'tile, squared building stone'.]

Pliny (the Elder) /plínni/ (AD 23–79) Roman scholar

Pliny (the Younger) (62–113) Roman politician and writer

plio- *prefix* = **pleo-**

Pliocene /plī́ ō seen/, **Pleiocene** *adj* belonging to or typical of the last epoch of the Tertiary period, 5.4 to 1.6 million years ago, during which time a hominid species (**Homo erectus**) first appeared ■ *n* the Pliocene epoch, or rocks formed during that period [Mid-19C. < Greek *pleiōn* 'more' (see PLEO-) + *kainos* 'recent' (see -CENE), because it is later than the Miocene.]

plissé /pleé say/, **plisse** *n* **1** a permanently wrinkled finish given to a fabric by treating it chemically **2** fabric with a plissé finish [Late 19C. < French, past participle of *plisser* 'to pleat' < *pli* 'fold' < *plier* (see PLY²).]

PLO *abbr* Palestine Liberation Organization

plod /plod/ *vi* (**plods, plodding, plodded**) **1 WALK HEAVILY** to walk with a slow heavy tread **2 WORK SLOWLY BUT STEADILY** to work slowly but steadily, especially on something uninteresting or laborious ■ *n* **1 SLOW HEAVY STEPS** a walk with slow heavy steps **2 SOUND OF SOMEBODY PLODDING** the sound of slow heavy steps **3 LABORIOUS TASK** a task involving long and laborious work **4 POLICE OFFICER** a police officer, especially one of lower rank (*informal insult*) [Mid-16C. Thought to suggest the motion.] —**plodder** *n* —**plodding** *adj* —**ploddingly** *adv* —**ploddingness** *n*

-ploid *suffix* having a chromosome number in a particular relationship to the basic number of chromosomes in a group ○ *tetraploid* [< DIPLOID and HAPLOID]

ploidy /plóydi/ *n* the multiple of the number of chromosome sets in a cell [Mid-20C. < -PLOID.]

Ploieşti /plaw yéshtyə/ city in SE Romania. Population: 253,623 (1997 estimate).

plonk¹ /plongk/ *v* **1** *vi* **DROP HEAVILY OR SUDDENLY** to drop, be dropped, or sit down heavily or suddenly (*informal*) **2** *vt* **ABRUPTLY LAY DOWN** to drop or lay something down heavily or suddenly, often with deliberate emphasis ○ *She plonked the book down in front of me.* **3** *vi* **PLAY MUSIC INEXPRESSIVELY** to play a musical instrument without much expression or skill ■ *n* **ACTION OR SOUND OF SUDDEN FALL** the thudding action or sound of a sudden heavy fall (*informal*) ■ *adv* **WITH PLONKING SOUND** with a plonking sound or action (*informal*) ○ *It landed plonk in my lap.* [Late 19C. An imitation of the sound.]

plonk² /plongk/ *n* cheap inferior wine (*informal*) [Mid-20C. Shortening of *plink-plonk* < ?]

plonker /plóngkər/ *n* **1** an offensive term for a person who is regarded as stupid or foolish (*slang insult*) **2** an offensive term for a man's penis (*slang*) [Mid-19C. < PLONK¹.]

plop /plop/ *n* **1 SOUND OF SOMETHING DROPPING INTO WATER** the sound made by something dropping into water without making a large splash **2 DEFECATION OF FAECES** a human stool or animal dropping (*informal; usually used by or to children*) ■ *v* (**plops, plopping, plopped**) **1** *vti* **FALL WITH A PLOP** to fall or drop something into water without making a large splash **2** *vi* **DROP DOWN QUICKLY AND HEAVILY** to drop or sit down quickly and heavily ○ *He plopped down on the nearest chair.* ■ *adv* **WITH A PLOP** with a plopping sound or action ■ *interj* **IMITATION OF THE SOUND OF DROPPING INTO WATER** used to imitate the sound of something dropping into water without splashing [Early 19C. An imitation of the sound.]

plosion /plṓzh'n/ *n* the sound made by a sudden release of breath in pronouncing certain sounds, especially a stop consonant [Early 20C. Back-formation < EXPLOSION.]

plosive /plṓssiv/ *adj* describes a consonant such as the 'p' in 'pear' that is pronounced by completely closing the breath passage and then releasing air ■ *n* a consonant pronounced with a sudden release of breath [Late 19C. Back-formation < EXPLOSIVE.]

plot /plot/ *n* **1 SECRET HOSTILE PLAN** a plan decided on in secret, especially to bring about an illegal or subversive act **2 STORY LINE** the story or sequence of events in a narrated or presented work such as a novel, play, or film **3 PIECE OF GROUND** a small piece of ground **4** *US* **PLAN OF A BUILDING OR ESTATE** an architectural plan of a building or estate **5** *US* **A CHART** a graph, chart, or diagram ■ *v* (**plots, plotting, plotted**) **1** *vti* **MAKE SECRET PLANS** to make secret plans, especially to do something illegal or subversive with others **2** *vt* **MARK SOMETHING ON A CHART** to mark something on a chart, especially the course of a ship or aircraft **3** *vt US* **MAKE A PLAN** to make a plan or map of something, e.g. a building or estate **4** *vti* **MARK ON A GRAPH** to mark points on a graph or diagram using coordinates, or to be located on a graph by coordinates **5** *vt* **DRAW ON A GRAPH** to draw a line or curve through points marked on a graph or diagram **6** *vt* **PLAN EPISODES OF A STORY** to devise the sequence of events in a story or script [< Old English, 'area of ground', and Old French *complot* 'secret scheme']

ϟ **plotter** /plóttər/ *n* **1** a person who plans secretly, especially to do something illegal or subversive **2** a computer output device that draws graphs and other pictorial images on paper, sometimes using attached pens

plough /plow/ *n* **1 FARM IMPLEMENT** a heavy farming tool with a sharp blade or series of blades for breaking up soil and making furrows, usually pulled by a tractor or draught animal **2 HEAVY TOOL** any heavy tool or machine used like a plough to cut a cleared route or channel, e.g. a snowplough **3 NARROW-BLADED PLANE THAT CUTS GROOVES** a plane with a narrow blade used to cut grooves in wood **4 PLOUGHED LAND** land that has been ploughed ■ *v* **1** *vti* **MAKE FURROWS IN THE EARTH** to break up earth and turn it over into furrows ○ *ploughing a field* **2** *vti* **CUT THROUGH** to cut or force a way through something ○ *I ploughed my way through the crowd.* **3** *vt* **MAKE A CLEARING IN** to make a channel or cleared route in something **4** *vt* **PUT UNDER SOIL** to put something such as fertilizer or a crop under the surface of the soil, using a plough **5** *vti* **FAIL** to fail at an examination (*informal*) **6** *vti* **WORK METHODICALLY** to work at something and progress slowly and steadily ○ *We ploughed through the backlog of applications.* ○ *ploughing my way through pages of job ads* **7** *vti* to sail through a stretch of water (*literary*) ○ *a ship in full sail, ploughing an azure sea* **8** *vt US* **HAVE SEX** to have sexual intercourse with somebody (*slang*) [Old English *ploh*, via Germanic from a N Italic word] —**plougher** *n*

plough back *vt* to invest profits from a business back into the business

plough in *vt* to contribute or devote something, especially money, to a project or place

plough into *v* **1** *vt* to crash into or hit with a great deal of force ○ *We lost control and ploughed into the car in front.* **2** *vi* to start a job or undertaking, especially with energy and determination

plough on *vi* to persist determinedly in spite of obstacles, opposition, or warnings

plough under *vt* **1** to bury something so that it disappears ○ *Large tracts of forest had been ploughed under by the bulldozers.* **2** to overwhelm somebody with too many responsibilities or jobs, or to overwhelm something with too heavy a burden ○ *I was ploughed under for the whole weekend trying to fix the mess in the computer files.*

Plough /plow/ *n* a group of the seven brightest stars in the constellation Ursa Major. US term **Big Dipper**

ploughboy /plów boy/ *n* a boy who leads one or more animals while they pull a plough

ploughman /plówmən/ (*plural* **-men** /-mən/) *n* an operator of a plough, especially a plough drawn by animals — **ploughmanship** *n*

ploughman's lunch, plowman's lunch *n* a cold lunch, typically served in a pub, consisting of a plate of bread, cheese, pickle or chutney, and a pickled onion [Probably from the belief that bread and cheese were the staple lunch of the ploughman in former times]

ploughshare /plów shair/ *n* the part of a plough that cuts the soil for the furrow

Plovdiv /plóv dif/ city in S Bulgaria. Population: 344,326 (1996 estimate).

plover /plúvvər/ *n* **1** a wading bird that lives on the shoreline and has a short bill and tail and long pointed wings. Family: Charadriidae. **2** a bird that resembles the plover but is in a different taxonomic family, e.g. the Egyptian plover or upland plover [14C. Via Anglo-Norman < assumed Vulgar Latin *pluviarius* < Latin *pluvia* 'rain' (see PLUVIAL); from the fact that it lives near water.]

plow /plow/ *n, vti* US = **plough**

ploy /ploy/ *n* **1** DECEPTIVE TACTIC a tactic or manoeuvre, especially one calculated to deceive or frustrate an opponent **2** ACTIVITY something somebody does as a job, amusement, or pastime **3** *Scotland* PIECE OF FUN a light-hearted or carefree piece of fun [Late 17C. < ?]

PLP *abbr* Parliamentary Labour Party

PLR *abbr* Public Lending Right

⚡**PLS, PLZ** *abbr* please (*in e-mails*)

pluck /pluk/ *v* **1** *vt* TAKE SOMETHING AWAY QUICKLY to take something away swiftly, often by means of skill or strength **2** *vt* QUICKLY REMOVE SOMETHING ROOTED to pull out by the roots some or all of the feathers or hair from something **3** *vt* PULL OFF to pull something off or out of something else, e.g. fruit from a tree **4** *vt* TAKE SOMETHING CASUALLY to select something randomly or with no obvious reason **5** *vti* TUG AT to tug quickly at something ○ *felt someone plucking at my sleeve* **6** *vt* PULL AND RELEASE STRINGS to play a stringed musical instrument by quickly pulling and releasing strings with a finger or plectrum ■ *n* **1** BRAVERY courage and determination in meeting danger or difficulty **2** ACT OF PLUCKING one act or instance of plucking something **3** ANIMAL'S HEART, LIVER, AND LUNGS the heart, liver, and lungs of an animal used as meat [Old English *pluccian* < Germanic < ?] —**plucker** *n*

SYNONYMS See ***courage***.

pluck up *vt* to muster courage or audacity

plucky /plúki/ (**-ier, -iest**) *adj* showing courage and determination, especially in the face of difficulties or superior odds —**pluckily** *adv* —**pluckiness** *n*

plug /plug/ *n* **1** FILLER FOR A HOLE something used to fill and tightly close up a hole **2** STOPPER FOR A SINK a rubber or plastic stopper for the drainage hole in a sink or bath **3** ELECTRICAL CONNECTION the connection at the end of the wire leading from an electrical device, with prongs or pins that allow it to fit into the socket of a power supply **4** SOCKET an electrical socket, e.g. on a wall (*informal*) **5** PUBLICIZING MENTION a favourable mention of something to publicize it, e.g. during a broadcast about something else (*informal*) **6** WEDGE FOR A SCREW a hollow piece of plastic pushed inside a hole to act as a holder for a screw that, when inserted, makes the plug expand and completely fill the hole **7** SPARK PLUG a spark plug **8** CAKE OF CHEWING TOBACCO a cake of compressed or twisted tobacco or a piece of it used for chewing **9** SEISMOL = **volcanic plug 10** OLD HORSE an old and worn-out horse (*slang*) **11** WEIGHTED LURE an artificial weighted lure that has hooks attached to it **12** SMALL PIECE CUT FROM SOMETHING a small wedge cut away from something, especially as a test sample ■ *v* (**plugs, plugging, plugged**) **1** *vt* CLOSE UP to close up a hole or gap **2** *vt* GIVE SOMETHING A FAVOURABLE MENTION to make a favourable mention of something to publicize it, e.g. during a broadcast about something else (*informal*) ○ *a chance to plug her latest novel* **3** *vt* US SHOOT to shoot somebody with a gun (*slang*) **4** *vt* PUNCH to punch somebody (*slang*) **5** *vi* WORK STEADILY to work at something steadily and persistently (*informal*) ○ *He is still plugging away in the insurance business.* [Early 17C. Via Dutch < Middle Dutch *plugge* < ?] —**plugger** *n* ◇ **pull the plug on something** to bring something abruptly to an end, especially by cutting off funds

plug in *vti* to connect an electrical appliance to a power source or to another electrical appliance, or to function when connected in this way

plug into *vti* to connect or become connected to an electrical power source by means of a plug

⚡**plug and play** *n* **1** a technical standard that allows a peripheral device such as a printer or DVD drive to be connected to a computer and to function immediately without alteration of the system's configuration files **2** a new recruit who is able to take up a job without requiring further training (*slang*) —**plug-and-play** *adj*

plugged-in *adj* US closely involved with or well-informed about something (*informal*)

plughole /plúg hōl/ *n* an opening in something, such as a basin or bath, where liquid can drain away when a plug is removed

⚡**plug-in** *adj* CONNECTIBLE BY MEANS OF A PLUG capable of being connected by a plug to an electrical power source ○ *a plug-in hand drill* ■ *n* **1** SOMETHING CONNECTED BY PLUG a device or appliance that may be connected by a plug to an electrical power source **2** DATA FILE ALTERING APPLICATION a data file that alters or extends the operation of an application

plug-ugly *adj* regarded as extremely unattractive (*insult*) ■ *n* (*plural* **plug-uglies**) US a tough and intimidating person, especially a gangster (*slang*) [< the *Plug Uglies*, a gang of hoodlums in several US cities in the 1850s]

plum /plum/ *n* **1** DARK RED FRUIT a round or oval smooth-skinned fruit, usually red or purple, containing a flattened stone **2** FRUIT TREE a tree that bears plums. Genus: *Prunus.* **3** DARK REDDISH-PURPLE a dark reddish-purple colour **4** SOMETHING CHOICE something that is highly desirable or enviable, especially a job or contract (*informal*) ■ *adj* **1** DESIRABLE highly desirable or profitable (*informal*) ○ *a plum job* **2** DARK REDDISH-PURPLE of a dark reddish-purple colour [12C. Alteration of Middle Low German, and Middle Dutch *prūme* and Old High German *pfrūma* < Latin *prunum*, (see PRUNE[2]).]

SPELLCHECK Do not confuse ***plum*** with ***plumb***, which has a similar sound. Beware: your spellchecker will not catch this error.

plumage /plóomij/ *n* the feathers that cover a bird's body, considered collectively [14C. Via Old French < Latin *pluma* 'feather, plume' (see PLUME).]

plumate /plóo mayt/ *adj* resembling, having, or producing feathers [Early 19C. < Latin *plumatus* 'feathered' < *pluma* 'feather' (see PLUME).]

plumb /plum/ *n* **1** WEIGHT ATTACHED TO A LINE a weight, usually made of lead, attached to a line and used to find the depth of water or to verify a true vertical alignment **2** TRUE VERTICAL POSITION a true vertical position or alignment ■ *adv* **1** IN TRUE VERTICAL OR PERPENDICULAR POSITION in perfect alignment or a true vertical position **2** EXACTLY precisely or exactly (*informal*) ○ *plumb in the middle* **3** US COMPLETELY utterly or totally (*informal*) ○ *plumb lazy* ■ *vt* **1** FULLY COMPREHEND to succeed in fully understanding something, especially something mysterious **2** to experience something, especially something unpleasant, to an extreme degree ○ *had plumbed the depths of despair* **3** FIND THE DEPTH OR VERTICAL ALIGNMENT OF to find the depth of water or a vertical alignment with a plumb **4** MAKE VERTICAL to make something properly vertical **5** INSTALL PLUMBING to equip with plumbing [13C. Via Old French *plomb* 'lead weight' < Latin *plumbum* 'lead'.]

SPELLCHECK See ***plum***.

plumb in *vt* to attach a device such as a washing machine to a system of inlet and drainage pipes

plumbago /plum báygō/ (*plural* **-gos**) *n* **1** an evergreen Mediterranean or tropical plant of the leadwort family. Flowers: blue, white, or red, in clusters. Genus: *Plumbago.* **2** MINERALS = **graphite** [Early 17C. < Latin, 'lead ore, plumbago' < *plumbum* 'lead', translation of Greek *molubdaina* 'lead ore', hence 'flowering plant'; from the flower's colour.]

plumbate /plúm bayt/ *n* a weakly acidic compound formed by reaction of an lead oxide with an alkali [Mid-19C. < Latin *plumbum* 'lead'.]

plumb bob *n* the weight, usually a conical metal one, at the end of a plumb line

plumbeous /plúmbi əss/ *adj* made of, concerning, or like lead [Late 16C. < Latin *plumbeus* 'of lead' < *plumbum* 'lead' (see PLUMB).]

plumber /plúmmər/ *n* an installer and repairer of water, drainage, or heating pipes and fixtures in a building [14C. Via Old French *plommier* 'lead worker' < Latin *plumbum* 'lead'.]

plumber's snake *n* CONSTR = **snake** *n.* 3

plumbic /plúmbik/ *adj* containing or relating to lead, especially in a valency state of four [Late 18C. < Latin *plumbum* 'lead' (see PLUMB).]

plumbing /plúmming/ *n* **1** PLUMBER'S WORK the work that a plumber does **2** PIPES AND FIXTURES the pipes and fixtures that carry or use water or gas in a building **3** USE OF A PLUMB LINE the use of a plumb line to test depth or show a vertical alignment

plumbism /plúmbizəm/ *n* long-term lead poisoning (*technical*) [Late 19C. < Latin *plumbum* 'lead' (see PLUMB).]

plumb line *n* a line with a weight attached, used to find the depth of water or to verify a true vertical alignment

plumbous /plúmbəss/ *adj* containing or relating to lead, especially in a valency state of two [Mid-19C. < Latin *plumbum* 'lead' (see PLUMB).]

plumb rule *n* a plumb line attached to a board, used to check whether something is truly vertical

plume /ploom/ *n* **1** FEATHER a feather, especially a large or ornamental one **2** FEATHERS USED AS A CREST a feather or bunch of feathers used as a decoration, especially on a hat or helmet **3** COLUMN a rising column of something, e.g. smoke, dust, or water **4** MOLTEN ROCK COLUMN a column of molten rock rising through the Earth's mantle **5** PART RESEMBLING A FEATHER any plant part or formation that looks like a feather, e.g. the part of some seeds that allows them to be blown about by the wind **6** TOKEN OF HONOUR a prize, awarded decoration, or token of honour ■ *v* (**plumes, pluming, plumed**) **1** *vt* PREEN FEATHERS to preen, smooth, or clean the feathers **2** *vr* BE PROUD to take pride in or congratulate yourself on something **3** *vt* DECORATE WITH FEATHERS to decorate something with feathers [14C. Via Old French < Latin *pluma* 'down, feather'.] — **plumed** *adj*

plummet /plúmmit/ *vi* **1** DROP DOWNWARDS to drop steeply and suddenly downwards ○ *temperatures have plummeted* **2** SUDDENLY FALL IN VALUE to take a sudden unexpected drop in value or price **3** SUDDENLY BECOME PESSIMISTIC to decline or drop suddenly, particularly from a state of optimism to one of pessimism ■ *n* **1** SUDDEN DECLINE a sudden sharp fall in value or amount **2** CONSTR = **plumb bob** [14C. Via Old French *plomet* 'small lead ball' < Latin *plumbum* 'lead' (see PLUMB).]

plummy /plúmmi/ (**-mier, -miest**) *adj* **1** LIKE PLUMS resembling, full of, or tasting like plums **2** RICH AND RESONANT with a voice or tone that is rich, resonant, and mellow, and is thought to be typical of the British upper classes **3** DESIRABLE highly desirable or of superior quality (*informal*)

plumose /plóomōss/ *adj* ZOOL = **plumate** [Mid-18C. < Latin *plumosus* < *pluma* 'feather' (see PLUME).] —**plumosely** *adv* —**plumosity** /ploo mόssəti/ *n*

plump[1] /plump/ *adj* **1** SLIGHTLY OVERWEIGHT rounded and somewhat overweight (*sometimes offensive*) **2** WELL-FLESHED having a pleasing amount of flesh ○ *a plump chicken* **3** FILLED WITH rounded and filled with something ○ *a plump cushion* ■ *vti* FATTEN OR ROUND to become or make something fatter, rounder, or softer ○ *plump up the cushions* [15C. < Middle Dutch or Middle Low German *plomp* 'blunt, thick'.] —**plumply** *adv* —**plumpness** *n*

plump[2] /plump/ *vti* DROP ABRUPTLY OR HEAVILY to fall or come down heavily or suddenly, or to cause somebody or something to do so ○ *plumped down into an armchair* ■ *n* **1** ABRUPT FALL OR ITS SOUND a heavy or abrupt fall, or its sound **2** *Scotland* a sudden rainstorm (*nonstandard*) ○ *a thunder plump* ■ *adv* **1** HEAVILY in a sudden or heavy way **2** DIRECTLY directly or in a direct line **3** BLUNTLY in a blunt and direct way ■ *adj* DIRECT blunt, direct, and forceful [13C. Probably < Dutch *plompen* or Low German *plumpen* 'fall into water', an imitation of the sound.]

plump for *vt* to choose somebody or something, often after careful thought

plumper /plúmpər/ *n* a pad worn by an actor between the teeth and the inside of the cheeks to make the face seem fatter

plum pudding *n* a rich steamed pudding made from flour, suet, dried fruit, and spices that is often flavoured with brandy or rum [*Plum* from the use of PLUM to mean 'raisin']

plum tomato *n* an elongated firm-textured tomato that is often used in cooking and is the usual variety used for tinned tomatoes [*Plum* from its shape]

plumule /plŏŏ myool/ *n* 1 the rudimentary primary shoot of a plant embryo 2 one of a young bird's soft down feathers [Early 18C. < Latin *plumula* 'small feather' < *pluma* 'feather' (see PLUME).]

plumy /plŏŏmi/ (-ier, -iest) *adj* 1 like a feather or plume 2 made of, covered with, or decorated with feathers or plumes

plunder /plúndər/ *v* 1 *vti* **ROB A PLACE OR STEAL GOODS** to rob a place or the people living there or steal goods using violence and often causing damage, especially in wartime or during civil unrest ○ *gangs of looters plundering the electrical stores* 2 *vt* **ROB OR STEAL BY FRAUD** to rob a place or steal goods or money by fraudulent means ○ *a military government that had steadily plundered the country's wealth* 3 *vt* **GET BY SUPERIOR STRENGTH** to gain or acquire by superior strength or skill ○ *They plundered five goals in a one-sided game.* ■ *n* 1 **STOLEN GOODS** something stolen by force, especially during wartime or civil unrest 2 **ROBBERY** the theft of goods by force or fraud [Mid-17C. Via German *plündern* or Low German *plünderen* < Middle Low German *plunder* 'household goods' < ?] —**plunderable** *adj* —**plunderer** *n* —**plunderous** *adj*

plunderage /plúndərij/ *n* 1 the embezzlement of goods aboard a ship 2 goods embezzled aboard a ship

plunge /plunj/ *v* (**plunges, plunging, plunged**) 1 *vti* **MOVE OR BE THROWN SUDDENLY** to move, rush, dive, or be thrown suddenly downwards or forwards ○ *plunged into the undergrowth and disappeared* 2 *vt* **PUT SUDDENLY IN AN UNPLEASANT CONDITION** to bring or force somebody or something suddenly into an unpleasant or undesirable situation 3 *vt* **THRUST QUICKLY OR FIRMLY** to put or push something firmly into something such as a liquid or container ○ *Drain the beans and plunge them into cold water.* 4 *vi* **BECOME INVOLVED ENTHUSIASTICALLY** to become involved in something with great enthusiasm ○ *She plunged into student life.* 5 **EMBARK ON RECKLESSLY** to begin a course of action suddenly and in a reckless or impetuous way ○ *warned against plunging into full monetary union* 6 *vi* **GO DOWN SUDDENLY** to go or drop downwards suddenly or steeply 7 *vi* **DROP SUDDENLY IN VALUE** to drop suddenly and unexpectedly in value or price ○ *Prices plunged.* 8 *vi* **GAMBLE RECKLESSLY** to gamble, speculate, or take risks in a reckless way (*informal*) ■ *n* 1 **LEAP INTO WATER** a dive or leap into water ○ *a headlong plunge into the sea* 2 **SUDDEN SHARP FALL** a sudden sharp fall in value or amount ○ *a 38% plunge in PC sales* 3 **SUDDEN RUSH** a sudden or violent rush ○ *The dog made a plunge for the open door.* 4 **GAMBLE** a reckless gamble or speculation (*informal*) [14C. Via Old French *plongier* < assumed Vulgar Latin *plumbicare* 'heave a sounding lead' < Latin *plumbum* 'lead' (see PLUMB).] ◇ **take the plunge** 1 to commit suddenly to doing something new, difficult, or irrevocable 2 to get married or decide to get married (*informal humorous*)

plunge bath *n* a bath large enough for the whole body to be immersed

plunge pool *n* a small deep swimming pool used for cooling the body

plunger /plúnjər/ *n* 1 **TOOL FOR CLEARING DRAINS** a tool for clearing clogged drains consisting of a rubber suction cup attached to a long handle 2 **THRUSTING MACHINE PART** a part of a machine that thrusts or drops downwards, e.g. a piston 3 *US* **GAMBLER** a frequent gambler (*informal*)

plunging /plúnjing/ *adj* in a direction or at an angle that plunges downwards

plunk /plungk/ *vti* 1 **TWANG STRINGS** to twang the strings of a stringed instrument, especially in an inexpert or unexpressive way 2 *US* **DROP DOWN** to fall or cause something to drop heavily or suddenly ○ *He plunked down on the nearest chair.* ■ *n* 1 **TWANGING SOUND** a twanging sound, e.g. of a string on a stringed instrument being plucked 2 *US* **HARD BLOW** a hard blow (*informal*) 3 *US* **SUDDEN HEAVY FALL** the action or sound of a sudden heavy fall ○ *A stone hit the tin roof with a plunk.* ■ *adv US* 1 **EXACTLY** precisely or exactly (*informal*) ○ *plunk in the middle* 2 **WITH A PLUNK** with a plunking sound or action [Early 19C. An imitation of the sound.]

pluperfect /ploo púrfikt/ *adj, n* GRAM = **past perfect** [15C. < Latin *plus quam perfectum* 'more than perfect'.]

plural /plŏŏrəl/ *adj* 1 **REFERRING TO MORE THAN ONE** having a grammatical form that refers to more than one person or thing 2 **CONCERNING MORE THAN ONE** concerning, involving, or made up of more than one, or more than one kind of, person or thing ■ *n* 1 **PLURAL CATEGORY** the plural number category 2 **PLURAL FORM OF A WORD** the plural form of a word ○ *What's the plural of mouse in the computer sense?* [14C. Via Old French < Latin *pluralis* < *plus* 'more'.] —**plurally** *adv*

pluralise *vti* = **pluralize**

pluralism /plŏŏrəlizəm/ *n* 1 **SOCIETY WITH DIFFERENT INTERNAL GROUPS** the existence of groups with different ethnic, religious, or political backgrounds within one society 2 **SOCIAL POLICY AND THEORY** a policy or theory that minority groups within a society should maintain cultural differences but share overall political and economic power 3 **HOLDING OF MULTIPLE OFFICES** the holding of more than one office or position by an individual, especially in a church 4 **THEORY OF VARIED BEING OR SUBSTANCE** the philosophical theory that reality is made up of many kinds of being or substance 5 **STATE OF BEING PLURAL** state or condition of being plural —**pluralist** *n* —**pluralistic** /plŏŏrə lístik/ *adj* —**pluralistically** /-lístikli/ *adv*

plurality /ploor rálləti/ (*plural* **-ties**) *n* 1 **CONDITION OF BEING PLURAL** the condition of being plural or numerous 2 **GREAT NUMBER OR PART OF** a great number or part of something, particularly when this represents more than half of the whole 3 *US, Can* **MARGIN GAINED BY AN ELECTION CANDIDATE** the number of votes an election winner gets, or the number exceeding the nearest rival, when no one has more than fifty per cent of the total votes cast 4 CHR = **pluralism** *n.* 3

pluralize /plŏŏrə līz/ (**-izes, -izing, -ized**), **pluralise** (**-ises, -ising, -ised**) *v* 1 *vti* to make something plural or to become plural 2 *vi* to hold more than one office, especially ecclesiastical ones, at the same time —**pluralization** /plŏŏrə lī záysh'n/ *n* —**pluralizer** /plŏŏrə līzər/ *n*

plural marriage *n* = **polygamy** *n.* 1

plural voting *n* a system of voting that formerly permitted some voters to vote more than once in an election or to vote in different constituencies

plus /pluss/ *prep* **USED FOR ADDING** used to show that one number or amount is added to another ○ *The flight cost £180, plus £20 airport tax.* ■ *adj* 1 **INVOLVING ADDITION** showing or involving addition 2 **ON POSITIVE SIDE** with a figure or value on the positive side of a scale or axis (*often written as '+'*) 3 **ON ELECTRICAL POSITIVE SIDE** on or involving the positive side of an electrical circuit 4 **ADVANTAGEOUS** favourable, desirable, or advantageous ○ *On the plus side, there's a big garden.* ○ *one of its plus points* 5 **SOMEWHAT MORE THAN STATED GRADE** somewhat higher than a stated grade for academic work (*often written as '+'*) 6 **REPRODUCING ONLY WITH OPPOSITE STRAIN** reproducing as an alga or fungus only with an opposite strain ■ *n* (*plural* **pluses** *or* **plusses**) 1 MATH = **plus sign** 2 **POSITIVE QUANTITY** a positive quantity 3 **ADVANTAGEOUS FACTOR** something beneficial or advantageous (*informal*) ○ *Having her in the team is a real plus.* 4 **SURPLUS** a surplus ■ *conj* (*informal*) See Usage Note below 1 **AND** and also ○ *Exports have been affected by transport problems plus the effect of a strong pound.* 2 **FURTHERMORE** and also or furthermore ○ *I'm too busy to come, plus I'm short of cash.* [Mid-16C. < Latin *plus* 'more'.]

USAGE Avoid using ***plus*** to introduce an independent clause: *He is the head of the electrical engineering department, plus he has his own consulting firm.* Use instead: *As well as being the head of the electrical engineering department, he has his own consulting firm.* ***Plus which*** should not be used to introduce any sentence or clause. Avoid: *She is the head of a large college. Plus which, she is a TV personality.* Use instead: *In addition to being the head of a large college, she is a TV personality.* In formal writing avoid using ***plus*** in place of *and* as a conjunction joining two subjects in a sentence: *Lack of practice and* [not *plus*] *a knee injury have caused her to drop out.* This usage of ***plus*** as a conjunction is also contested syntactically. Some writers regard it as a preposition, in which case the verb *have caused* in the last sentence would switch from plural to the singular *has caused* with the single subject being *lack*.

plus fours *npl* baggy trousers gathered and fastened just below the knee, worn mainly for sports or hunting ○ *golfers in their plus fours* [Because they were four inches longer in the leg than standard knickerbockers]

plush /plush/ *n* a rich smooth fabric with a long soft nap ■ *adj* **plush, plushy** luxurious, expensive, or lavish (*informal*) [Late 16C. Via French *pluche* < assumed Vulgar Latin *piluccare* 'pluck' (see PLUCK).] —**plushness** *n*

plus sign *n* the symbol '+', used to show addition or a positive quantity

plus-size *adj* larger than average ○ *our new range of plus-size fashions*

Plutarch /plŏŏ taark/ (AD 46–120) Greek historian, biographer, and philosopher

Pluto /plŏŏtō/ *n* 1 in Roman mythology, the god of the underworld and husband of Proserpine. Greek equivalent **Hades** *n.* 2 2 the planet in the solar system that is the smallest in diameter and is, on average, the furthest away from the Sun. See table at **planet** [Via Latin < Greek *Ploutōn* < *ploutos* 'wealth'] —**Plutonian** /ploo tṓni ən/ *adj*

plutocracy /ploo tókrəssi/ (*plural* **-cies**) *n* 1 **RULE BY THE WEALTHY** the rule of a society by its wealthiest people 2 **SOCIETY RULED BY THE WEALTHY** a society that is ruled by its wealthiest members 3 **WEALTHY RULING CLASS** any wealthy social class that controls or greatly influences the government of a society [Mid-17C. < Greek *ploutokratia* < *ploutos* 'wealth'.] —**plutocrat** /plŏŏtə krat/ *n* —**plutocratic** /plŏŏtə kráttik/ *adj* —**plutocratically** *adv*

pluton /plŏŏ ton/ *n* a mass of intrusive igneous rock that solidified underground by the crystallization of magma [Mid-20C. < German, back-formation < *plutonisch* 'plutonic' < Latin *Pluto* (see PLUTO).] —**plutonic** /ploo tónnik/ *adj*

plutonium /ploo tṓni əm/ *n* (*symbol* **Pu**) a highly toxic silvery radioactive metallic element. Source: uranium ore. Use: as plutonium-239, production of atomic energy and weapons. [Mid-20C. After the planet PLUTO, because it follows uranium and neptunium in the periodic table.]

pluvial /plŏŏvi əl/ *adj* 1 **RELATING TO RAIN** concerning, involving, or caused by rain 2 **RAINY** involving a lot of rain ■ *n* **WET PERIOD** a period of increased rainfall [Mid-17C. < Latin *pluvialis* < *pluvia* 'rain' < *pluere* 'to rain'.]

pluvious /plŏŏvi əss/, **pluviose** /plŏŏvi ōss/ *adj* concerning, involving, or typical of rain, especially heavy rainfall [15C. Via Old French < Latin *pluviosus* < *pluvia* 'rain' (see PLUVIAL).]

ply[1] /plī/ (**plies, plying, plied**) *v* 1 *vti* **WORK HARD AT** to work at a trade or occupation, especially with diligence 2 *vt* **USE SOMETHING DILIGENTLY** to use something such as a tool or weapon in a diligent or skilful way ○ *the dexterity with which she plied her needle* 3 *vt* **OFFER SOMETHING FOR SALE** to offer goods or services for sale, especially regularly or as an occupation 4 *vt* **SUPPLY SOMEBODY WITH** to keep supplying somebody with something, especially in an insistent way ○ *kept plying us with offers of food* 5 *vt* **SUBJECT TO URGENTLY AND INSISTENTLY** to keep subjecting somebody to something in an urgent and insistent way ○ *We were plied with questions.* 6 *vti* **TRAVEL A ROUTE REGULARLY** to travel a route regularly, especially on water 7 *vi* **SAIL AGAINST THE WIND** to sail a boat on a zigzag course against the wind [14C. Shortening of APPLY.]

ply[2] /plī/ *n* (*plural* **plies**) (*often in combination*) 1 **TWISTED STRAND** a twisted single strand, especially in a yarn or rope 2 **THIN LAYER OF** a layer, sheet, or thickness of something such as wood or a tyre ■ *vti* (**plies, plying, plied**) **TWIST TOGETHER** to twist or fold things together [14C. < Old French *pli* < *plier* 'to fold' < Latin *plicare*.]

Plymouth /plímməth/ 1 port in SW England. Population: 260,000 (1996). 2 town in SE Massachusetts, settled by the Pilgrim Fathers. Population: 7,258 (1996 estimate).

Plymouth Brethren *n* a strict Protestant group founded in the United Kingdom in the late 1820s that has no organized ministry or formal creed, and accepts the Bible as its sole guide [After PLYMOUTH]

Plymouth Rock *n* a US breed of domestic hen with white or grey barred plumage, raised for its eggs and meat

plywood /plī wŏŏd/ *n* board made by gluing and compressing thin layers of wood together with the grain of each layer at right angles to the layer next to it [Early 20C. *Ply* < PLY².]

Plzeň /p'l zénnyə/ city in W Czech Republic. Population: 171,908 (1994).

pm[1], **PM, P.M.** between twelve noon and midnight. Full form **post meridiem**

⚡**pm**[2] *abbr* 1 phase modulation 2 postmortem 3 premium 4 St.-Pierre and Miquelon (*in Internet addresses*)

Pm *symbol* promethium

PM *abbr* **1** Past Master *(of a fraternity)* **2** Postmaster **3 PM, p.m., P.M.** postmortem **4** Prime Minister **5** Provost Marshal

P-mail /pee mayl/, **pmail** *n* mail sent through the postal service

PMG *abbr* **1** Postmaster General **2** Provost Marshal General **3** Paymaster General

PMS *abbr* premenstrual syndrome

PMT *abbr* premenstrual tension

⚡ pn *abbr* Pitcairn Island *(in Internet addresses)*

PNdB *abbr* perceived noise decibel

pneum- *prefix* = **pneumo-** *(before vowels)*

pneuma /nyóomə/ *n* in Stoicism, the vital spirit or soul [Late 19C. < Greek, 'breath, spirit' < *pnein* 'breathe'.]

pneumatic /nyoo máttik/ *adj* **1 USING COMPRESSED AIR** operated by compressed air in a tool or machine **2 FILLED WITH AIR** filled with air, especially compressed air **3 INVOLVING COMPRESSED GASES** relating to, involving, operated by, or typical of the pressure of compressed gases, especially air pressure or compressed air **4 OF GASES OR WIND** concerning, involving, or typical of air, gases, or wind **5 OF THE SOUL** concerning or involving the soul or spirit **6 WITH AIR-FILLED CAVITIES IN THE BONES** describes birds that have air-filled cavities in the bones **7 FULL-BREASTED** having large breasts *(informal; offensive in some contexts)* [Mid-17C. Via French and Latin < Greek *pneumatikos* < *pneuma* (see PNEUMA).] —**pneumatically** *adv*

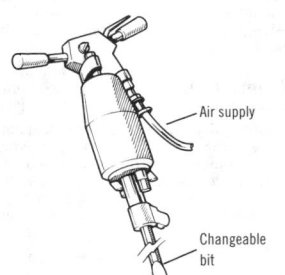

Air supply

Changeable bit

Pneumatic drill

pneumatic drill *n* a heavy powerful drill operated by compressed air and used especially for breaking up the surface of roads or pavements. ◊ **jackhammer**

pneumatics /nyoo máttiks/ *n* the branch of physics dealing with the mechanical properties of air and other gases *(+ singular verb)*

pneumatic tube *n* a tube through which letters and packets are propelled by compressed air

pneumato- *prefix* **1** air, gas, vapour ○ *pneumatolysis* **2** respiration, breathing ○ *pneumatometer* **3** spirits, spiritual ○ *pneumatology* [< Greek *pneumat-*, stem of *pneuma* (see PNEUMA)]

pneumatology /nyóomə tólləji/ *n* **1** the branch of Christian theology that deals with the Holy Spirit **2** the study of spirits or spiritual beings —**pneumatological** /-tə lójjik'l/ *adj* —**pneumatologist** /-tólləjist/ *n*

pneumatolysis /nyóomə tólləssiss/ *n* the alteration caused in rocks by hot gases escaping from solidifying magma —**pneumatolytic** /nyóo mátto líttik/ *adj*

pneumatophore /nyoo mátto fawr, nyóomətta fawr/ *n* **1** a branch in swamp plants such as the mangrove or bald cypress that grows upwards from the roots and carries out respiration **2** a gas-filled sac that acts as a float in coelenterates such as the Portuguese man-of-war

pneumo- *prefix* **1** air, gas ○ *pneumoencephalogram* **2** lung, pulmonary ○ *pneumocystis* **3** pneumonia ○ *pneumobacillus* **4** respiration ○ *pneumograph* [< Greek *pneuma* 'air, breath' (see PNEUMA)]

pneumobacillus /nyóombo síllǝss/ *(plural* **-li** /-síllee/*) n* a gram-negative bacterium that occurs in the respiratory tract and is one cause of pneumonia. *Klebsiella pneumoniae.*

pneumococcus /nyóomo kókǝss/ *(plural* **-ci** /-kók sī/*) n* a gram-positive bacterium that occurs in the respiratory

tract and is one cause of pneumonia. *Streptococcus pneumoniae.* —**pneumococcal** *adj*

pneumoconiosis /nyóomo kóni óssiss/, **pneumono-coniosis** /nyóomǝno kóni óssiss/ *n* a disease of the lungs, such as silicosis, caused by inhaling mineral or metallic dust over a long period [Late 19C. < PNEUMO- + Greek *konis* 'dust'.]

pneumocystis /nyóomo sístiss/, **pneumocystis pneumonia** *n* a form of pneumonia that mainly affects people with weakened immune systems. It is caused by the microorganism *Pneumocystis carinii.*

pneumonectomy /nyóomǝ néktǝmi/ *(plural* **-mies***) n* the surgical removal of a lung [Late 19C. < Greek *pneumōn* 'lung' (see PNEUMONIA) + -ECTOMY.]

pneumonia /nyoo móni ǝ/ *n* an inflammation of one or both lungs, usually caused by infection from a bacterium or virus or, less commonly, by a chemical or physical irritant [Early 17C. Via modern Latin < Greek *pneumōn* 'lung', alteration (influenced by *pneuma* 'breath') of *pleumōn*.]

pneumonic /nyoo mónnik/ *adj* **1** relating to or affecting the lungs **2** relating to, involving, or affected by pneumonia [Late 17C. Via French < Greek *pneumōn* 'lung' (see PNEUMONIA).]

pneumonitis /nyóomǝ nítiss/ *n* any inflammation of the air sacs in the lungs, usually caused by a virus [Early 19C. Via modern Latin < Greek *pneumōn* 'lung' (see PNEUMONIA).]

pneumonoconiosis /n MED = **pneumoconiosis** [Mid-19C. < Greek *pneumōn* 'lung' + *konis* 'dust'.]

pneumothorax /nyóomō tháwr aks/ *n* the presence of air or gas in a pleural cavity surrounding the lungs, causing pain and difficulty in breathing

PNG *abbr* Papua New Guinea

p-n junction *n* the boundary between an n-type semiconductor and a p-type semiconductor having rectifying characteristics and used in diodes

~~pnuematic~~ incorrect spelling of **pneumatic**

~~pnuemonia~~ incorrect spelling of **pneumonia**

po /pō/ *(plural* **pos***) n* a chamber pot *(informal)* [Late 19C. Shortening of French *pot de chambre* 'chamber pot'.]

Po[1] *symbol* polonium

Po[2] /pō/ *river in N Italy, flowing eastwards into the Adriatic Sea. Length: 652 km/405 mi.

PO *abbr* **1** Petty Officer **2** Pilot Officer **3 PO, p.o.** postal order **4** Post Office

POA *abbr* Prison Officers' Association

poach[1] /póch/ *v* **1** *vti* **CATCH GAME ILLEGALLY** to catch wild animals or fish illegally on public land or while trespassing on private land **2** *vti* **ENCROACH ON** to encroach on other people's rights, territory, or sphere of operation in order to appropriate or remove somebody or something ○ *A rival company was poaching our customers.* **3** *vti* **PLAY SOMEBODY ELSE'S SHOT** to play a shot that properly should be handled by a partner in badminton, tennis, squash, or handball **4** *vti* **SCORE SNEAK GOAL** to score a goal at close range by lingering inside the opposing penalty area while unobserved by defenders ○ *Their striker is an expert at poaching.* **5** *vti* **MAKE GROUND MUDDY** to become muddy or make ground muddy by trampling it **6** *vi* **SINK INTO MUD** to sink into soft earth or mud while walking across it [Early 17C. < Old French *pocher* 'trample, trespass', probably < Germanic.] —**poachable** *adj*

poach[2] /póch/ *vt* to cook something by simmering it in or over water or another liquid [15C. < Old French *pochier*, originally 'enclose in a bag' < *poche* 'bag' (see POCKET).]

poacher[1] /póchǝr/ *n* **1** an illegal hunter, fisher, or trapper, usually while trespassing **2** a player in football who scores a goal while lingering around the opposition's penalty area, unobserved by defenders

poacher[2] /póchǝr/ *n* a pan for poaching eggs that has a tightly fitting lid and small metal cups

POB *abbr* Post Office Box

PO Box *abbr* Post Office Box

Pocahontas: Posthumous portrait (1666)

AKG London

Pocahontas /pókǝ hóntǝss/ *(1595?–1617?)* Native American princess. Born **Matoaka**

pochard /póchǝrd/ *n* a heavy-bodied diving duck with a reddish head and a blue-and-black bill. Native to: coastal waters of Europe and Asia. Subfamily: Aythyini. [Mid-16C]

pochette /po shét/ *n* a small handbag shaped like an envelope [Late 19C. < French, 'small pouch' < *poche* (see POCKET).]

pock /pok/ *n* = **pockmark** *n*. 1 ■ *vt* to cover with pockmarks or disfiguring marks *(often passive)* [Old English *poc*] —**pocky** *adj*

pocket /pókit/ *n* **1 SMALL POUCH IN CLOTHES** a shaped piece of material forming part of an item of clothing and used to hold small items, e.g. inside trousers or on the outside of a shirt **2 SMALL FITTED POUCH** a small fitted pouch, e.g. a pouch-shaped compartment on the inside of a bag ○ *The suitcase has several inside pockets.* **3 SMALL POUCH** any small pouch, bag, or purse **4 PERSONAL MONEY** somebody's personal financial resources ○ *a holiday paid for out of his own pocket* **5 SMALL DIFFERENTIATED AREA** a small area differentiated from neighbouring areas by some feature ○ *pockets of wealth* **6 CAVITY** any type of cavity or opening **7 ORE IN CAVITY** the quantity of petroleum, natural gas, or mineral found in an underground cavity, or the cavity that contains this substance **8 POSITION IN RACE** a position in a race in which a competitor is blocked by others **9 POUCH ON PLAYING TABLE** a pouch or net at each corner and side of a billiard, snooker, or pool table ○ *He sank the red in the side pocket.* **10 SAC ON ANIMAL** any pouch-shaped sac on an animal's body **11** *Aus* **PLAYER IN SIDE POSITION** in Australian Rules football, a player in one of two side positions at the ends of the ground **12 AIR POCKET** an air pocket ■ *vt* **1 PUT IN POCKET** to put something into a pocket ○ *She pocketed the change.* **2 TAKE SOMETHING DISHONESTLY** to appropriate something, often dishonestly ○ *They buy tickets cheaply, sell them for high prices, and pocket the difference.* **3 HIT BALL INTO POCKET** to hit a ball into one of the pockets on a billiard, snooker, or pool table ○ *pocket the black* **4 PUT UP WITH** to tolerate something unpleasant, especially an insult, without protesting or retaliating **5 SUPPRESS FEELINGS** to hide or suppress feelings **6 ENCLOSE OR SURROUND** to enclose or hem in somebody or something **7** *US* **RETAIN PIECE OF LEGISLATION** to retain a legislative bill without signing it, especially as a US president, in order to stop it becoming approved by Congress ■ *adj* **1 SMALL ENOUGH TO CARRY IN POCKET** designed for carrying in a pocket ○ *a pocket torch* **2 SMALL** small, especially smaller than something larger of the same type ○ *a pocket trumpet* **3 CONTAINED** isolated and contained in small areas [15C. < Anglo-Norman *pokete* 'small bag' < *poke* 'bag'.] —**pocketability** /pókita bíllǝti/ *n* —**pocketable** /pókitab'l/ *adj* ◇ **have deep pockets** to have large financial resources ○ *a price-cutting war which will be won by whoever has the deepest pockets* ◇ **in pocket** making a profit from something ◇ **in somebody's pocket 1** fully under somebody's control **2** almost certain to be won by somebody ○ *We thought she had the race in her pocket.* ◇ **line your pocket(s)** to profit at the expense of others ◇ **out of pocket** having lost money on something or spent money without benefit ◇ **pick somebody's pocket** to steal something from somebody's pocket without the person feeling or noticing

pocket battleship *n* a small but powerful and heavily armed battleship, especially one built by Germany in the 1930s to conform to limitations that were placed by treaty on size and armament

pocketbook /pókit bòòk/ *n* **1** *US, Can* **SMALL CASE CARRIED IN THE POCKET** a small case or folder for money and documents, suitable for carrying in a pocket **2** *US, Can* **HANDBAG** a purse or handbag **3** *US, Can* **MONEY** somebody's financial resources **4** *US* PUBL = **pocket edition**

pocket borough *n* a political constituency in Britain before the Reform Act of 1832, whose representative in Parliament was determined by one landowner or landowning family [*Pocket* from the idea that the landowner had the borough 'in his pocket']

pocket edition *n* a book small enough to be carried in a pocket. US term **pocketbook** *n.* 4

pocketful /pókitfòòl/ *n* **1** the amount of something that would fit in a pocket **2** a large amount of something, especially money (*informal*)

pocket gopher *n* ZOOL = **gopher** *n.* 1

pocketknife /pókit nīf/ (*plural* **-knives** /-nīvz/) *n* US term **penknife**

pocket money *n* **1** a small sum of money paid regularly by parents to a child so that the child can make his or her own purchases. US term **allowance** *n.* 2 **2** a small amount of personal money, sufficient only for making minor purchases or to cover incidental expenses

pocket mouse *n* a small nocturnal rodent of the deserts of the W United States and Mexico, with long hind legs, a long tail, and fur-lined cheek pouches for carrying food. Genus: *Perognathus.*

pocket veto *n US* in the United States, a US presidential failure to return a bill passed by Congress during its last days in session, to prevent its being enacted [< the notion of the executive's holding the bill in a coat pocket]

pocket watch *n* a watch designed to be carried in a pocket, rather than worn on the wrist

pockmark /pók maark/ *n* (*often plural*) **1** **SCAR ON THE SKIN** a scar on the skin, especially one left by smallpox, chickenpox, or acne **2** **SMALL HOLLOW MARK** a small hollow mark disfiguring a surface ■ *vt* **1** **COVER THE SKIN WITH POCKMARKS** to disfigure the skin with pockmarks **2** **MAKE POCKMARKS IN** to make many small indentations or marks in the surface of something

pockmarked /pók maarkt/ *adj* covered in or disfigured by pockmarks

poco /pṓkō/ *adv* a little or slightly (*in musical directions*) [Early 18C. < Italian, 'little'.]

poco a poco *adv* little by little (*in musical directions*) [< Italian, 'little by little']

pococurante /pṓkō kyoo ránti/ *adj* uninterested, indifferent, or nonchalantly detached (*literary*) ■ *n* an unworried and indifferent person (*literary*) [Mid-18C. < Italian < *poco* 'little' + *curare* 'to care'.] —**pococuranteism** /-ránti izəm/ *n* —**pococurantism** /-rántizəm/ *n*

Pocono Mountains /pṓkə no-/ mountain range in NE Pennsylvania, rising to about 640 m/2,100 ft

pod[1] /pod/ *n* **1** **SEED CASE** the long narrow outer case holding the seeds of a plant such as the pea, bean, or vanilla **2** **DETACHABLE COMPARTMENT OF A SPACECRAFT** a specialized detachable compartment on a spacecraft, usually for carrying personnel or instruments **3** **STREAMLINED HOUSING FOR EQUIPMENT** a streamlined housing attached to the wing or fuselage of an aircraft, or to the hull of a submarine, to carry fuel, an engine, weaponry, or other equipment **4** **PROTECTIVE EGG CASE** a protective case surrounding the eggs of some fishes and insects, e.g. the grasshopper ■ *v* (**pods, podding, podded**) **1** *vt* **TAKE PEAS FROM POD** to strip peas out of their pod so that they can be eaten or cooked **2** *vi* **PRODUCE PODS** to produce fruit in the form of pods [Late 17C. < ?]

pod[2] /pod/ *n* a small group of marine animals, especially seals, whales, or dolphins [Mid-19C. < ?]

pod[3] /pod/ *n* **1** a socket holding the bit in a boring tool **2** a lengthwise channel in the barrel of a boring tool [Late 16C. < ?]

PO'd /pée ōd/, **p.o.'d** *adj* quite annoyed (*slang*) [Shortening of pissed off]

POD *abbr* pay on delivery

-pod *suffix* foot, part like a foot ○ *stomatopod* [< Greek *pod-*, stem of *pous* < Indo-European] —**-podous** *suffix*

podagra /po dággrə/ *n* gout in the foot or the big toe [13C. Via Latin < Greek, 'foot-trap' < *pod-* (stem of *pous* 'foot') + *agra* 'trap'.] —**podagral** *adj* —**podagric** *adj* —**podagrical** *adj* —**podagrous** *adj*

Podborski /pod báwrski/, **Steve** (*b.* 1957) Canadian skier

-pode *suffix* = **-pod**

podge /poj/ *n* US term **pudge** **1** excess weight on a person (*informal insult; sometimes considered offensive*) **2** an offensive term for somebody considered to be carrying more body weight than is desirable or advisable (*insult*) [Mid-19C. Probably a back-formation < PODGY.]

Podgorica /pód go reetsə/ capital of Montenegro, S Yugoslavia. Population: 118,059 (1991).

podgy /pójji/ (**-ier, -iest**) *adj* short and carrying more body weight than is desirable or advisable (*sometimes considered offensive*) US term **pudgy** [Mid-19C. Variant of PUDGY.] —**podgily** *adv* —**podginess** *n*

podia plural of **podium**

podiatry /po dī ətri/ *n US* MED = **chiropody** [Early 20C. < Greek *pod-*, stem of *pous* 'foot' + -IATRY.] —**podiatric** /pṓdi áttrik/ *adj* —**podiatrist** /po dī ətrist/ *n*

podium /pṓdi əm/ (*plural* **-ums** *or* **-a** /pṓdi ə/) *n* **1** **SMALL RAISED PLATFORM** a small raised platform that the conductor of an orchestra, a lecturer, or somebody giving a speech can stand on **2** **FOUNDATION WALL** a low wall forming a foundation or base, e.g. for a colonnade **3** **WALL AROUND AN AMPHITHEATRE'S ARENA** a low wall encircling the arena of an ancient amphitheatre [Mid-18C. Via Latin < Greek *podion* 'small foot' < *pous* 'foot'.]

-podium *suffix* foot, part like a foot ○ *pseudopodium* [Via modern Latin < Greek *podion* (see PODIUM)]

podophyllin /póddə fíllin/, **podophyllin resin** *n* a greenish or brownish bitter resin. Source: root of the May apple. Use: removal of warts. [Mid-19C. < modern Latin *Podophyllum* < the Greek stem *pod-* 'foot' + *phullon* 'leaf'.]

podsol *n* GEOG = **podzol**

podsolization, podsolisation *n* GEOG = **podzolization**

podzol /pód zol/, **podsol** /pód sol/ *n* a basically infertile type of soil that forms in cool moist climates, usually under coniferous or mixed forests [Early 20C. < Russian < *pod-* 'under' + *zol* 'ash'.] —**podzolic** /pod zóllik/ *adj*

podzolization /pód zo lī záysh'n/, **podzolisation, podsolization, podsolisation** *n* the process whereby minerals are leached from the upper into the lower layers of a soil, leaving the topsoil acidic and infertile and forming a podzol —**podzolize** /pódzə līz/ *vti*

Poe /pō/, **Edgar Allan** (1809–49) US writer and critic

POE *abbr* **1** port of embarkation **2** port of entry

poem /pṓ im/ *n* **1** **PIECE WRITTEN IN VERSE** a complete and self-contained piece of writing in verse that is set out in lines of a particular length and uses rhythm, imagery, and often rhyme to achieve its effect **2** **WRITING WITH POETIC EFFECT** a piece of writing that is not in verse but that has the imaginative, rhythmic, or metaphorical qualities and the intensity usually associated with a poem **3** **BEAUTIFUL OR DELIGHTFUL THING** something particularly lovely, beautiful, or delightful [15C. Via French *poème* < Greek *poiēma* 'making' < *poiein* 'to make'.]

poesy /pṓ əzi/ *n* poetry or poetic compositions in general, or a particular piece of poetry (*archaic or literary*) [14C. Via French *poésie* < Greek *poiēsis* 'making' (see -POIESIS).]

poet /pṓ it/ *n* **1** a writer of poems, especially as a vocation **2** an imaginative, creative, or artistic person [13C. Via French *poète* and Latin *poeta* < Greek *poiētēs* 'maker, author' < *poiein* 'make'.]

poet. *abbr* **1** poetic **2** poetical **3** poetry

poetaster /pṓ i tástər/ *n* a writer of inept poetry [Late 16C. < modern Latin < Latin *poeta* (see POET).]

poetic /pō éttik/, **poetical** /-ik'l/ *adj* **1** **RELATING TO POETRY** relating to, typical of, or in the form of poetry **2** **RESEMBLING POETRY** having qualities usually associated with poetry, especially in being gracefully expressive, romantically beautiful, or elevated and uplifting **3** **SENSITIVE OR INSIGHTFUL** characteristic of a poet, especially in possessing unusual sensitivity or insight or in being able to express things in a beautiful or romantic way —**poeticality** /pō étti kálləti/ *n* —**poetically** *adv* —**poeticalness** /pō éttik'lnəss/ *n*

poeticize /pō étti sīz/, **poeticise, poetize** /pṓ i tīz/ (**-izes, -izing, -ized**), **poetise** (**-ises, -ising, -ised**) *vti* to express or describe something in a poetic style or in poetry

poetic justice *n* a situation in which somebody meets a fate that seems a fitting punishment or, less often, a fitting reward for their past actions

poetic licence *n* liberties with the normal rules of fact, style, or grammar taken by a writer or speaker in order to achieve a particular effect

poetics /pō éttiks/ *n* **1** **BASIC PRINCIPLES OF POETRY** the literary or philosophical study of the basic principles, forms, and techniques of poetry or of imaginative writing in general (+ *singular verb*) **2** **TREATISE ON POETRY** a treatise on the nature or principles of poetry **3** **WAY OF COMPOSING A POEM** the art or technique of writing poetry (+ *plural verb*)

poetize, poetise *vti* = **poeticize**

poet laureate (*plural* **poets laureate**) *n* **1** a poet who is appointed a member of the royal household for life by a British monarch and is expected to write poems celebrating great national or royal events **2** any poet who is specially honoured for his or her work, or who is considered to be the most eminent poet in a particular country, state, or group

poetry /pṓ itri/ *n* **1** **LITERATURE IN VERSE** a literary work written in verse, in particular verse writing of high quality, great beauty, emotional sincerity or intensity, or profound insight **2** **POEMS COLLECTIVELY** all the poems written by a particular poet, in a particular language or form, or on a particular subject ○ *a collection of love poetry* **3** **WRITING OF POEMS** the art or skill of writing poems **4** **PROSE LIKE POETRY** writing in prose that has a poetic quality **5** **BEAUTY OR GRACE** something that resembles poetry in its beauty, rhythmic grace, or imaginative, elevated, or decorative style **6** **POETIC QUALITY** a poetic or particularly beautiful or graceful quality in something [14C. Via Old French < Latin *poeta* (see POET).]

po-faced *adj* **1** inappropriately solemn or disapproving **2** remaining expressionless or wearing a stern expression, especially when others are laughing or responding in some way [< ?]

pogo /pṓgō/ (**-gos, -going, -goed**) *vi* to dance in a punk style of the 1970s by jumping up and down on the spot [Late 20C. < POGO STICK.] —**pogo** *n* —**pogoer** *n*

pogonophoran /póggə nóffərən/, **pogonophore** /póggənə fawr/ *n* a marine animal resembling a worm that has tentacles around the head area, lacks a digestive tract, and lives in vertical tubes in deep water. Phylum: Pogonophora. [Late 20C. < modern Latin *Pogonophora* < Greek *pōgōn* 'beard' + *-phoros* '-bearing'.] —**pogonophoran** *adj*

pogo stick *n* a strong metal pole with a spring at the bottom and two footrests to stand on, used to jump up and down or hop along on for play or exercise [Early 20C. Formerly a trademark; < ?]

pogrom /póggrəm/ *n* a planned campaign of persecution or extermination sanctioned by a government and directed against an ethnic group, especially against the Jewish people in tsarist Russia [Early 20C. < Russian, 'devastation' < *gromit* 'wreak havoc' < *grom* 'thunder'.]

poi[1] /poy/ *n* a Hawaiian dish made from the root of the taro, cooked, pounded to a paste, and fermented [Early 19C. < Hawaiian.]

poi[2] /poy/ *n* a light ball on a string, rhythmically swung to accompany Maori dance and song

-poiesis *suffix* creation, formation, production ○ *erythropoiesis* [< Greek *poiēsis* < *poiein* 'to make']

poignant /póynyənt/ *adj* **1** **CAUSING SADNESS OR PITY** causing a sharp sense of sadness, pity, or regret **2** **SHARPLY PERCEPTIVE** particularly penetrating and effective or relevant (*literary*) **3** **SHARPLY PAINFUL** causing acute physical pain (*literary*) **4** **STRONG SMELLING OR TASTING** having an often pleasurably strong sharp smell or taste (*archaic*) [14C. < French, present participle of *poindre* 'to prick' < Latin *pungere* 'to prick, sting'.] —**poignance** *n* —**poignancy** /póynyənssee/ *n* —**poignantly** *adv*

poikilocyte /póykilō sīt/ *n* an abnormally shaped red blood cell [Late 19C. < Greek *poikilos* 'spotted, irregular' + -CYTE.]

poikilotherm /póykilō thurm/ *n* an organism such as a reptile, amphibian, insect, or fish that has a body temperature that varies according to the temperature of the local atmosphere. ◊ **ectotherm**

poikilothermic /póykilō thúrmik/, **poikilothermal** /póykilō thúrm'l/, **poikilothermous** /póykilō thúrməss/ *adj* having a body temperature that varies according to the temperature of the local atmosphere [Late 19C. < Greek *poikilos* 'spotted, varied' + -THERMIC.] —**poikilothermism** *n* —**poikilothermy** *n*

poilu /pwáaloo/ *n* a soldier in the French infantry, especially during World War I [Early 20C. Via French, 'hairy' < Latin *pilus* 'hair' (see PILE[3]).]

poinciana /póynssi áanə/ (*plural* **-as** *or* **-a**) *n* a tropical tree grown for its large reddish-orange flowers. Genera: *Caesalpinia* and *Delonix*. [Mid-18C. < modern Latin, after M. de *Poinci*, a 17C governor of the Antilles.]

poind /poynd/ *vt Scotland* **1** to seize the goods of a debtor so that they can be sold to pay a debt **2** to impound stray animals [Old English *gepyndan* 'impound' < *pund* 'enclosure' (see POUND[3])]

poinsettia /poyn sétti ə/ (*plural* **-as** *or* **-a**) *n* a shrub with bright red bracts resembling petals, popular as a house plant. Native to: Central America. *Euphorbia pulcherrima*. [Mid-19C. After Joel R. *Poinsett* (1775–1851), US botanist.]

ϟ**point** /poynt/ *n* **1 OPINION, IDEA, OR FACT** an opinion, idea, or fact put forward in the course of, or forming a main element of, a discussion or argument ○ *She made many valid points in her report.* **2 UNDERLYING ESSENTIAL IDEA** the essential idea conveyed or intended in something ○ *He seems to have missed the point entirely.* **3 PURPOSE** the purpose or usefulness of something ○ *Is there really any point in continuing?* **4 ITEM IN LIST OR PLAN** an individual item or detail in something such as a plan, a contract, or a list ○ *a four-point plan to revive the coal industry* ○ *a point-by-point examination of the contract* **5 CONVINCING ARGUMENT OR VIEWPOINT** a cogent or persuasive argument or observation ○ *You have to admit that she has a point there.* **6 QUALITY OR FEATURE** a distinguishing quality, feature, or item ○ *Generosity is one of her good points.* **7 PHYSICAL FEATURE OF LIVESTOCK ANIMAL** an external feature such as the face or fetlock that is assessed when judging the overall shape of a livestock animal **8 LOCATION** a specific place or position ○ *a point six miles east of here* **9 MOMENT** an individual moment in time ○ *At that point, the door opened and the teacher walked in.* **10 PARTICULAR STAGE IN PROCESS** a specific moment or stage in a process, especially at which a significant change or development occurs or a condition is reached ○ *We have reached the point at which a decision will have to be made.* **11 LEVEL OR DEGREE** a specific level or degree of a quality ○ *He was confident to the point of almost being arrogant* **12 TIME JUST BEFORE SOMETHING HAPPENS** the moment or period of time just before something happens ○ *at the point of death* **13 SHARP END** the sharp narrowed end of something such as a needle, pencil, or weapon **14 END OR TIP** the end or tip of something such as a finger or the projecting angle of something such as the elbow or chin **15 SMALL PROJECTION** a small sharp or perceptible projection such as that in a piece of writing in Braille **16 TIP OF A BOW** the tip of the bow of a stringed instrument. ◊ **heel**[1] *n.* 9 **17 ANTLER PRONG** one of the prongs on a deer's antlers **18 HEADLAND** a prominent headland on the coast that juts out into the sea, often the projecting tip of a peninsula (*often in placenames*) **19 ACT OF POINTING** the act of pointing, e.g. with a finger **20 DOT** a small dot or source of something such as colour or light **21 DECIMAL POINT** the dot separating the whole number and fraction in a decimal number ○ *five point nine* **22 DIMENSIONLESS GEOMETRIC ELEMENT** a dimensionless geometric element whose location in space is defined solely by its coordinates **23 PUNCTUATION MARK** in printing or writing, a punctuation mark, especially a full stop **24** PHON = **vowel point** **25 UNIT USED IN SCORING** a unit used in scoring a sport, game, or competition, or as a means of making a quantitative evaluation of something **26 UNIT ON SCALE** a single unit on a scale of measurement ○ *The earthquake measured 6 points on the Richter scale.* ○ *opened up a 10-point lead over her rivals in the polls* **27 INVESTMENT PRICE UNIT** a unit used to measure change in the value of an investment, e.g. on a stock exchange ○ *The FTSE index is up 5 points.* **28** *US* **PERCENTAGE OF LOAN** an amount equivalent to one per cent of the value of a loan, used to calculate the sum the borrower pays at once to the lender as a service charge **29 MOTORISTS' PENALTY UNIT** a penalty unit given for a driving offence recorded on somebody's driving licence. Receiving a certain number of points leads automatically to a penalty. **30** *US* **STUDENT'S UNIT OF CREDIT** a unit of academic credit for a student that is equivalent to one hour of class work per week over a period of one term **31 UNIT OF WINNING POTENTIAL** a unit used in assessing the strength of a hand in bridge **32 PRINTING UNIT OF MEASUREMENT** a unit of measurement in printing equal to one twelfth of a pica or approximately 0.03515 cm/0.01384 in **33 DIAMOND WEIGHT UNIT** a unit of weight for a diamond equivalent to one-hundredth of a metric carat **34 MARK ON COMPASS** any of the 32 individual bearings or directions marked on a compass, e.g. west, west by north, west-northwest, or northwest **35 ANGLE BETWEEN ADJACENT BEARINGS** the angle between any two adjacent bearings marked on a compass, measuring 11° 15′ **36 UNIT AHEAD OF FORMATION** an individual or unit that moves ahead of a larger formation, acting as a scout and advance guard **37 ADVANCE MILITARY POSITION** the position ahead of a larger formation taken by an individual or unit acting as point **38 OFFENSIVE BASKETBALL POSITION** in basketball, the position in front court taken by the guard who directs the offensive **39 OFF-SIDE FIELDING POSITION** a fielding position on the off side, level with the batsman's wicket and at a distance from it that varies between three or four yards (*silly point*) and about thirty yards (*deep point*) **40 FIELDER FIELDING AT POINT** a fielder fielding at point **41 DIVISION OF HERALDIC SHIELD** any position on or division of a heraldic shield in which a charge can be placed ■ **points** *npl* **1 JUNCTION OF TWO CONVERGING RAILWAY TRACKS** the mechanical arrangement by which one railway track diverges or converges with another, allowing trains to change to another line or route **2 ELECTRICAL CONTACTS IN DISTRIBUTOR** the two electrical contacts that act as circuit breakers in the distributor of an internal-combustion engine as current is passed in turn to the cylinders **3 BALLERINA'S TIPTOES** the ends of the toes on which a ballerina wearing special shoes raises herself up for certain moves and positions while performing **4 EXTREMITIES OF DOMESTIC ANIMAL** the ears, feet, and tail of a domestic animal ■ *v* **1** *vi* **INDICATE WITH AN EXTENDED FINGER** to extend the finger or a long and thin object in the direction of something in order to draw attention to it ○ *I pointed to one of the shrubs and asked its cost.* **2** *vt* **AIM AT** to hold an object so that its end is aimed at somebody or something ○ *pointed the hose at the flowers* **3** *vi* **BE TURNED TOWARDS** to be turned towards or aimed in a direction ○ *The arrow on the signpost was pointing to the right.* **4** *vt* **DIRECT SOMEBODY TOWARDS** to indicate the direction in which somebody should go ○ *If you can just point me in the right direction I expect I'll find it.* **5** *vti* **AIM MOUSE OR JOYSTICK** to move a mouse, joystick, or other device so that the cursor on a computer screen is positioned over or touching something ○ *Point at the icon, then double click on it.* **6** *vi* **SUGGEST SOMETHING IS THE CASE** to be strong evidence of something or lead the mind to believe or conclude something ○ *It all points to one conclusion.* **7** *vi* **CALL ATTENTION TO** to call attention to a fact or situation as being important **8** *vt* **GIVE FORCE TO REMARK** to give additional force, emphasis, or incisiveness to something said or written **9** *vt* **REPAIR WITH MORTAR** to repair or finish a wall, chimney, or other structural component by putting mortar or cement between the bricks or stones **10** *vt* **SHARPEN** to sharpen something so that it has a point at the end **11** *vt* **STRETCH FOOT DOWNWARDS** to stretch out the foot or toes so that leg and foot make one comparatively straight line, especially in ballet **12** *vti* **SAIL CLOSE TO WIND** to sail a boat close to the wind **13** *vti* **POINT MUZZLE AT GAME** to stand still with muzzle and tail outstretched indicating the whereabouts of game (*refers to a gun dog*) **14** *vt* **MARK PSALM FOR CHANTING** to mark a psalm to indicate how it is to be chanted **15** *vt* **ADD MARKS OVER LETTERS** to place diacritics or vowel points over the relevant letters in a text **16** *vt* **PUNCTUATE** to put punctuation marks into a text **17** *vi* **COME TO A HEAD** to reach the stage of spontaneous rupture or surgical opening, allowing pus to drain (*refers to boils and abscesses*) [13C. Via French < Latin *punctum* 'prick-mark, dot, particle', from the past participle of Latin *pungere* 'prick, pierce' (see PUNGENT).] ◇ **a sore point** a cause of annoyance ◇ **be on the point of doing something** to be just about to do something ○ *I was just on the point of leaving.* ◇ **beside the point** irrelevant or unimportant ◇ **in point of fact** used, often when correcting something said before, to emphasize that what is now being stated represents the truth ◇ **make a point of doing something** to be careful to do something and, often, to be seen by others to do it ◇ **not to put too fine a point on it** used to indicate that somebody is being or is about to be frank or blunt ◇ **stretch a point 1** to allow something as an exception to the rule **2** to exaggerate ◇ **stretch the point** to exaggerate ◇ **to the point** relevant or worth paying attention to ◇ **(up) to a point** to a certain extent, but not completely

point out *vt* **1** to point at or otherwise indicate something so that somebody will look at it ○ *Our guide pointed out the most interesting architectural features of the building.* **2** to tell somebody about or draw somebody's attention to something ○ *She did point out some of the difficulties we might expect to face.*

point up *vt* to emphasize something or an aspect of something

ϟ**point-and-click** *adj* describes an interface that allows a user to interact with a computer by using a mouse pointer to move a cursor on the computer screen and clicking the mouse button ■ *vi* to operate a mouse using a point-and-click interface

point-and-shoot *adj* describes cameras that require no adjustment by the user before taking a photograph because the focus and exposure are adjusted automatically or are fixed

point bar *n* a sand or gravel ridge found in groups formed by the flowing water of a meandering stream

point-blank *adv* **1 AT CLOSE RANGE** at or from very close range **2 OUTRIGHT** directly or bluntly and without further explanation ○ *told them point-blank what I thought of them* ■ *adj* **1 FIRED AT CLOSE RANGE** fired straight and from so close to the target that no adjustment to the aim is necessary for the drop in the bullet's trajectory ○ *point-blank shot* **2 CLOSE TO THE TARGET** very close to the target when shooting ○ *at point-blank range* **3 OUTRIGHT** direct and blunt ○ *a point-blank refusal* [< ?]

point defect *n* an imperfection in the lattice structure of a crystal

point duty *n* the task, usually undertaken by a police officer or traffic warden, of standing at a road junction in order to direct traffic

pointe /pwaaNt/ *n* the ends of the toes, a position on which a ballerina wearing special shoes raises herself up for certain moves and positions while performing [Mid-19C. < French, 'point'.]

pointed /póyntid/ *adj* **1 ENDING IN A POINT** ending in a point or sharp angle **2 MADE WITH EMPHASIS** made with emphasis and carrying an unmistakable message, often a criticism **3 CONSPICUOUS** made studiedly obvious or noticeable —**pointedness** *n*

pointed arch *n* ARCHIT = **lancet arch**

pointedly /póyntidli/ *adv* in a deliberate or emphatic way and with no attempt at tact or subtlety ○ *They pointedly ignored me.*

Pointe-Noire /pwáaNt nwaár/ port in SW Republic of Congo. Population: 576,206 (1992).

ϟ**pointer** /póyntər/ *n* **1 CANE USED FOR POINTING** a stick or cane used, especially by a teacher or lecturer, to point something out, e.g. on a chart or large map **2 INDICATOR ON MEASURING DEVICE** a needle that moves around on a measuring instrument to point to part of a dial **3 HELPFUL ADVICE OR INFORMATION** a piece of advice or information given to help somebody achieve something or do something the right way ○ *My coach gave me a few pointers on how to hold the racket.* **4 SIGN INDICATING SITUATION** a sign of what is happening or what might happen in the future **5 GUN DOG THAT INDICATES POSITION OF GAME** a gun dog, usually with a shorthaired white coat with coloured patches, belonging to a breed trained to indicate the whereabouts of shot game by standing still with the muzzle and tail outstretched **6 ARROW ON COMPUTER SCREEN** an arrow or other symbol on a computer screen that shows the current position of the mouse or other pointing device **7 COMPUTER MEMORY ADDRESS** an address, stored as data in a computer's memory, that is the location where desired data is stored ■ **pointers, Pointers** *npl* **GUIDE STARS IN PLOUGH** the two bright stars in the Plough constellation forming the side of the quadrilateral farthest from the handle, and used as a guide to find the Pole Star

pointillism /póyntilizəm/ *n* **1** a late 19th-century style of painting in which a picture is constructed from dots of pure colour that blend, at a distance, into recognizable shapes and various colour tones **2** a technique of musical composition using sparse isolated notes in widely varying registers rather than traditional closely connected melodies [Early 20C. < French *pointillisme*, via *pointiller* 'mark with dots' < Latin *punctum* 'dot'.] —**pointillist** *n, adj* —**pointillistic** /póynti lístik/ *adj*

pointing /póynting/ *n* the cement or mortar between the bricks of a wall

ϟ**pointing device** *n* an input device such as a mouse, trackball, or joystick used to manipulate a pointer on a computer display

point lace *n* lace made with a needle instead of bobbins [< POINT in the sense 'prick, stitch']

pointless /póyntləss/ *adj* **1** having no purpose, use, or sense, or any positive or beneficial effect ○ *It's pointless even attempting to make sense of it.* **2** in sports, having or scoring no points —**pointlessly** *adv* —**pointlessness** *n*

point man *n* **1** the lead soldier in a military formation or patrol **2** *US* a person who is in the forefront of an activity or endeavour

point mutation *n* a mutation that involves a change in a single base or base pair of the nucleotides in a gene, occurring as a result of addition, deletion, or substitution

point of departure *n* a starting point

point of honour *n* something that a sense of honour, self-respect, or pride obliges somebody to do

point of inflection *n* a point on a curve at which the arc changes from convex to concave or vice versa. US term **inflection point**

point of no return *n* **1** the time or stage in a process beyond which it becomes impossible to stop or discontinue it **2** the point in an aircraft's flight after which there will be insufficient fuel left to enable it to return to its starting point

point of order *n* a question raised by one of the participants in a formal debate or meeting that relates to the rules of procedure governing it, in particular as to whether those rules are being breached

ϟ**point of presence** *n* a location where a user can connect to a network, e.g. a place where subscribers can dial in to an Internet service provider

point of reference *n* something to which somebody can refer in order to check direction or progress, as a guide to action or conduct, or as an aid to understanding or communication

point-of-sale *adj* located, used, or occurring at the place where a product is sold ○ *point-of-sale display* —**point of sale** *n*

point of view *n* **1 PERSPECTIVE SOMEBODY BRINGS** somebody's particular way of thinking about or approaching a subject, as shaped by his or her own character, experience, mindset, and history **2 OPINION** somebody's personal opinion on a subject **3 PARTICULAR PERSPECTIVE ON SUBJECT** any aspect from which a subject may be considered or judged **4 ANGLE OF NARRATOR** the perspective on events of the narrator or a particular character in a story **5 POSITION OF OBSERVER** the position or angle from which somebody observes an event or a scene

point source *n* a source of something such as radiant energy or pollution that is or appears to be very small

point-to-point *n* a horse race for amateurs in which horses regularly used in hunting are raced over a marked cross-country course that includes various jumps and obstacles ■ *adj* from one particular place to another —**point-to-pointer** *n* —**point-to-pointing** *n*

ϟ**Point-to-Point Protocol** *n* a protocol for dial-up access to the Internet using a modem

point woman *n US* a woman who is in the forefront of any activity or endeavour, playing a crucial and possibly hazardous role in it

pointy /póynti/ (**-ier, -iest**) *adj* ending in a point (*informal*)

pointy-headed *adj US* intelligent or intellectual in an arrogant or impractical way (*slang*)

poise[1] /poyz/ *n* **1 COMPOSURE** calm self-assured dignity, especially in dealing with social situations **2 CONTROLLED GRACE IN MOVEMENT** a graceful controlled way of standing, moving, or performing an action **3 EQUILIBRIUM** a stable state of balance **4 SUSPENDED STATE** a state of hovering or being in suspension (*literary*) ■ *vti* **BALANCE OR SUSPEND** to be balanced or suspended, or to place or hold something in balance or suspension [14C. The noun is via Old French *pois* 'weight, balance'; the verb via *peser* 'weigh', both ultimately < Latin *pensare* (see PENSIVE).]

poise[2] /poyz/ *n* the centimetre-gram-second unit of viscosity equal to one dyne-second per square centimetre [Early 20C. After J. L. M. *Poiseuille* (1799–1868), French physiologist.]

poised /poyzd/ *adj* **1 READY TO ACT** fully prepared or in position and about to do something ○ *We are now poised to take over the company.* **2 READY TO MOVE** motionless and balanced, or motionless and suspended in the air, often just before or in the midst of an action ○ *a bird poised on a branch* **3 WITH COMPOSURE** calm, self-assured, and dignified **4 IN DANGER OF** teetering on the edge of a sudden change ○ *stock prices seemingly poised to rise*

~~**poisen**~~ incorrect spelling of **poison**

poisha /póy shə/ see table at **currency**

poison /póyz'n/ *n* **1 TOXIC SUBSTANCE** a substance that causes illness, injury, or death if taken into the body or produced within the body **2 SOMETHING EXERCISING AN INSIDIOUS INFLUENCE** something that exercises a powerful destructive or corrupting force, especially in an insidious way **3 REACTION-INHIBITING SUBSTANCE** a substance that inhibits a chemical reaction or diminishes the activity of a catalyst **4 SUBSTANCE SLOWING A NUCLEAR REACTION** any substance in a nuclear reactor that can absorb neutrons without undergoing fission and that therefore slows down the reaction ■ *vt* **1 GIVE POISON TO** to administer poison to a person or animal, especially with malicious intention **2 HARM WITH A TOXIC SUBSTANCE** to cause illness, injury, or death to somebody with a poison or other harmful chemical substance **3 ADD POISON TO** to put poison into or onto something so as to harm or kill somebody ○ *poisoned bait used to kill rats* **4 POLLUTE THE ENVIRONMENT** to pollute water, land, or air severely with harmful substances **5 CORRUPT OR UNDERMINE** to have an evil or corrupting influence on somebody or something, especially by planting hostility or suspicion in somebody's mind against another person **6 SPOIL A SITUATION** to have a harmful spoiling effect on something that should be pleasant, enjoyable, or friendly **7 INHIBIT A CHEMICAL REACTION** to inhibit a chemical reaction or activity **8 SLOW DOWN A NUCLEAR REACTION** to slow down or stop a nuclear reaction by the addition of a substance that can absorb neutrons without undergoing fission [13C. Via Old French < Latin *potion-* < *potare* 'to drink'.] —**poisoner** *n* ◇ **what's your poison?** *or* **name your poison** used to ask what somebody would like to drink (*informal*)

poisoned chalice *n* a task or decision that will almost inevitably bring harm or unpopularity upon the person who is forced to undertake it

poison gas *n* a lethal or incapacitating gas used as a weapon in warfare

poison ivy *n* **1 VINE CAUSING ITCHING RASH** a climbing vine of the cashew family that has three-part leaves and white berries. Contact with the plant produces an itching rash. Flowers: small, green. Native to: North America. Genus: *Rhus.* **2 RELATED PLANT** any plant related to poison ivy, such as poison oak **3 RASH** the rash produced by poison ivy

poison oak *n* a plant similar or related to poison ivy that produces a skin rash as a result of being touched. Native to: North America. Genus: *Rhus.*

poisonous /póyz'nəss/ *adj* **1** containing, producing, or acting as a poison **2** filled with or creating malice, distrust, or hostility —**poisonously** *adv* —**poisonousness** *n*

poison-pen letter *n* a letter sent anonymously to somebody that contains unpleasant or abusive comments

poison pill *n* a strategic move adopted by a company designed to make an unwelcome takeover by another firm less attractive to that firm

poison sumac, poison sumach *n* a shrub with greenish flowers and greenish-white berries that is poisonous to touch. Native to: swamps of SE United States. *Toxicodendron vernix.*

Poisson /pwáass on, pwáss-/, **Siméon-Denis** (1781–1840) French mathematician and physicist

Poisson distribution /pwáass on-/ *n* a probability distribution that represents the number of random events occurring over a fixed period of time [Early 20C. After Siméon POISSON.]

Poisson's ratio *n* the ratio of the decrease in width to the increase in length of a material when it is stretched [Early 20C. After Siméon-Denis POISSON.]

Poitier /pwáati ay/, **Sidney** (*b.* 1924) US actor and director

Poitiers /pwáati ay/ city in west-central France. Population: 83,448 (1999).

poke[1] /pōk/ *v* **1** *vti* **PROD WITH** to push the point of something such as an outstretched finger, elbow, or stick against somebody or something else **2** *vt* **MAKE HOLE IN** to make a hole or opening in something by pushing at it with a finger or a sharp object **3** *vt* **PUSH INTO HOLE** to push a finger or a long thin object into a hole, space, or opening **4** *vti* **PROTRUDE FROM** to stick, or stick something, out of or through an opening, surface, or covering in such a way that part of the object is visible ○ *One foot was poking out from under the covers.* **5** *vi* **SEARCH HAPHAZARDLY** to search or investigate in a haphazard or aimless manner ○ *poking around in a second-hand bookshop* **6** *vi* **MEDDLE** to pry or intrude into something, or meddle with something ○ *Stop poking around in my affairs.* **7** *vt* **STIR FIRE** to stir a fire with a poker or similar object to make it burn better **8** *vt* **OFFENSIVE TERM** an offensive term meaning to have penetrative sex (*slang*) **9** *vt* **PUNCH** to hit somebody with one of the fists (*informal*) **10** *vi* **GO SLOWLY** to move around or do things in a slow unhurried way ■ *n* **1 PROD** a push or prod with a finger, elbow, stick, or similar pointed object **2 LOOK OR SEARCH** the activity of haphazard or casual browsing or investigating **3 PROD** a short prod with the fist (*informal*) **4 OFFENSIVE TERM** an offensive term for a penetrative sex act (*slang*) **5** *US* = **slowpoke** (*informal*) [13C]

poke[2] /pōk/ *n* **1** a small bag or sack (*regional*) **2** *Scotland* a paper bag especially to hold groceries (*informal*) [13C. < Old French dialect, a variant of *poche* (see POUCH).]

poke[3] /pōk/ *n* PLANTS = **pokeweed** [Mid-17C. < Virginia Algonquian *poughkone.*]

pokeberry /pókbəri/ *n* **1** (*plural* **-ries**) the juicy blackish berry that grows on a pokeweed plant **2** (*plural* **-ry** *or* **-ries**) PLANTS = **pokeweed**

poke bonnet *n* a woman's bonnet with a deep projecting rim, fashionable in the first half of the 19th century [< POKE[2]]

poker[1] /pókər/ *n* a card game in which players attempt to acquire a winning combination of cards that involves betting at every deal [Mid-19C. < ?]

poker[2] /pókər/ *n* **1** a metal rod for stirring a fire to make it burn better **2** somebody or something that pokes, or something used for poking [Mid-16C. < POKE[1].]

poker face *n* a face showing no expression and revealing nothing about what somebody is thinking or feeling [< POKER[1]] —**poker-faced** *adj*

pokerwork /pókər wurk/ *n* CRAFT = **pyrography** *n.* 1

pokeweed /pók weed/ (*plural* **-weed** *or* **-weeds**) *n* a tall plant with blackish berries in elongated clusters, edible shoots, and a poisonous root. Flowers: white. Native to: North America. *Phytolacca americana.* [Mid-18C. < POKE[3].]

poky /póki/ (**-ier, -iest**), **pokey** (**-ier, -iest**) *adj* (*informal*) **1 CRAMPED** uncomfortably small and cramped **2** *US* **SLOW** annoyingly slow **3** *US* **FRUMPY** shabby and old-fashioned [Mid-19C. < POKE[1].] —**pokily** *adv* —**pokiness** *n*

pol. *abbr* **1** political **2** politics

Polack /pól ak/ *n US* a highly offensive term for a Polish person (*taboo*) [Late 16C. Directly or via French *Polaque* < Polish *Polak.*]

Poland /pólənd/ republic in E Europe, bordering on the Baltic Sea. Capital: Warsaw. Population: 38,612,000 (1996). Area: 312,684 sq. km/120,728 sq. mi.

Poland

polar /pólər/ *adj* **1 OF OR NEAR THE EARTH'S POLES** relating to, located at, or found in the regions surrounding the North or South Pole **2 OF A POLE OR POLES** relating to a pole or poles of a rotating body, a magnet, or an electrically charged object **3 PASSING OVER A PLANET'S POLES** passing over, or travelling in an orbit that passes over, a planet's poles ○ *polar orbit* **4 UTTERLY OPPOSITE** completely opposite to each other, or at the other extreme from something else **5 PIVOTAL** of pivotal or central importance **6 GUIDING** serving as a guide or giving direction (*literary*) **7 HAVING A DIPOLE** having a permanent dipole, or having molecules with permanent dipoles ○ *polar molecule* **8 HAVING AN IONIC BOND** having an ionic bond, or having crystals with ionic bonds ○ *polar crystal* **9 IN A POLAR COORDINATE SYSTEM**

relating to or measured with reference to a system of polar coordinates

polar axis *n* the fixed horizontal line in a system of polar coordinates from which the angle made by the radius vector is measured

polar bear *n* a large white mainly meat-eating bear that lives in the Arctic on coasts and ice floes

polar body *n* a cell with a nucleus but little cytoplasm that is produced along with an oocyte, and later discarded, in the process of cell division that leads to an ovum

polar cap *n* **1** the area around either the North or South Pole that is permanently covered in ice **2** either of the two polar regions on Mars that are permanently covered with frozen carbon dioxide and water

polar circle *n* the lines of latitude that define the Arctic and Antarctic regions, 66°33' N and 66°33' S

polar coordinates *npl* the two coordinates that locate a point in a plane by specifying the length of a radius vector and the angle it makes with a horizontal line (**polar axis**)

polar front *n* a weather front separating cold polar air and warmer air

polarimeter /pṓlə rímmitər/ *n* an instrument used to measure the rotation of the plane of polarization of light as it passes through a substance, especially a liquid or solution [Mid-19C. < modern Latin *polaris* 'polar'.] —**polarimetric** /pṓləri méttrik/ *adj* —**polarimetry** /pṓlə rímmətri/ *n*

Polaris /pō láariss/ *n* **1** the brightest star of the constellation Ursa Minor, near the celestial north pole. See illustration at **constellation 2** a US intermediate-range ballistic missile that usually carries a nuclear warhead and is launched from a submarine

polariscope /pō lárriskōp/ *n* an instrument used to study either a substance exposed to polarized light or the effects of a substance on polarized light [Early 19C. < modern Latin *polaris* 'polar'.]

polarise *vti* = **polarize**

polarity /pō lárrəti/ (*plural* **-ties**) *n* **1** a situation in which two individuals or groups have qualities, ideas, or principles that are diametrically opposed to each other **2** the condition, in a system, of having opposite characteristics at different points, especially with respect to electric charge or magnetic properties

polarize /pṓlə rīz/ (**-izes, -izing, -ized**), **polarise** (**-ises, -ising, -ised**) *vti* **1** CAUSE DIVISION OF OPINION to make the differences between groups or ideas ever more clear-cut and extreme and harden the opposition between them, or to become ever more sharply divided and opposed **2** ACQUIRE POLARITY to acquire, or cause something to acquire, polarity **3** RESTRICT LIGHT VIBRATION to cause light to vibrate within certain planes, or to be restricted to vibration within certain planes —**polarizable** *adj* —**polarization** /pṓlə rī záysh'n/ *n* —**polarizer** *n*

polarizing microscope *n* a microscope in which polarized light is used to examine specimens

polarography /pṓlə róggrəfi/ *n* an analytic technique used to study ions in a solution that compares the strength of electric currents passing through the solution during electrolysis and the voltages needed to produce them [Mid-20C. < *polarization*.] —**polarographic** /pṓlərə gráffik/ *adj*

Polaroid /pṓlə royd/ *tdmk* **1** a trademark for a camera that produces pictures that develop within seconds of being taken, or the film used in such a camera **2** a trademark for a specially treated transparent plastic that allows polarized light through and is used to reduce glare in sunglasses

polar star *n* ASTRON = **Polaris** *n.* 1

polder /pṓldər/ *n* an area of land reclaimed from the sea and protected by dykes, especially in the Netherlands [Early 17C. < Dutch.]

pole[1] /pōl/ *n* **1** NORTH OR SOUTH POLE either of the two points on the Earth, the North and South Poles, that are the endpoints of its axis of rotation, are farthest from the equator, and are surrounded by icecaps **2** AXIS ENDPOINTS OF SPHERE either of the two endpoints of the axis of rotation of a sphere or a planet or other astronomical object **3** ASTRON = **celestial pole 4** EITHER OF TWO OPPOSITES one of two completely opposed or contrasted positions, states, or views ○ *They're at opposite poles as far as their taste in music is concerned.* **5** END OF MAGNET either of the two ends of a magnet or magnetized body where the lines of force are most concentrated **6** ELECTRIC TERMINAL either of two terminals in something such as a battery, generator, or motor that have opposite electric charges **7** DISTINCT REGION IN CELL either of two opposite regions that are physiologically or functionally distinct in an organism, cell, or structure, e.g. the opposite ends of the spindle structure formed in the nucleus of a cell during cell division **8** ORIGIN OF POLAR COORDINATES the origin in a polar coordinate system **9** REFERENCE POINT a fixed point of reference (*literary*) [14C. Via Latin < Greek *polos* 'axis'.] ◇ **be poles apart** to be as different or as opposed as it is possible to be

SPELLCHECK Do not confuse ***pole*** with ***poll***, which has a similar sound. Beware: your spellchecker will not catch this error.

pole[2] /pōl/ *n* **1** LONG STRAIGHT OBJECT a long straight strong piece of wood, metal, or other material, usually with a round cross-section and thin enough to hold in the hands or arms **2** POLE-VAULTER'S POLE the long flexible shaft made of wood, metal, or fibreglass used by competitors in the pole vault **3** MOTOR SPORTS = **pole position** *n.* 1 **4** SHAFT ON HORSE-DRAWN VEHICLE a single shaft projecting forward from the front of a vehicle between the animals that draw it and to which those animals are hitched **5** MEASURE = **perch**[1] *n.* 4 **6** MEASURE = **perch**[1] *n.* 5 ■ *v* **1** *vti* PROPEL BOAT WITH POLE to move a boat along by pushing with a pole against a firm surface **2** *vt* SUPPORT PLANT WITH POLE to use a pole to provide support for a plant **3** *vti* USE SKI POLES to make forward progress on skis by pushing with ski poles [Old English *pāl* < Germanic, < Latin *palus* 'stake']

Pole *n* **1** somebody who comes from Poland **2** a person who is of Polish descent [Late 16C. Via German < Old Polish *Polanie* 'field-dwellers' < *pole* 'field' < Slavic.]

poleax *vt, n* US = **poleaxe**

poleaxe /pṓl aks/ *n* **1** BUTCHER'S AXE a specialized axe with a hammer face opposite the blade, used, especially formerly, for slaughtering animals **2** BATTLE-AXE a battle-axe with a long or short handle, especially one with a hammer or spike opposite the axe blade **3** AXE FOR CUTTING RIGGING a short-handled axe used to cut rigging or ropes on sailing ships, especially during combat ■ *vt* (**-axes, -axing, -axed**) **1** AMAZE AND STUPEFY to leave somebody stupefied and speechless with astonishment **2** HIT SOMEBODY VERY HARD to hit somebody hard enough to cause unconsciousness **3** HIT WITH A POLEAXE to hit somebody or something with a poleaxe [14C. Alteration of *pollax* 'head-axe' < POLL.]

polecat /pṓl kat/ *n* an animal related to but larger than the weasel that lives in woodlands in Europe, Asia, and North Africa, has brown fur, and emits a foul smell when disturbed. Genus: *Mustela* and *Vormela.* [14C]

poleis plural of **polis**[1] *n.* 1

polemic /pə lémmik/ *n* **1** PASSIONATE ARGUMENT a passionate, strongly worded, and often controversial argument against or, less often, in favour of something or somebody **2** PASSIONATE CRITIC a passionate disputer or arguer against something or somebody (*literary*) ■ *adj* **polemic, polemical** CONTAINING PASSIONATE ARGUMENT containing or expressing passionate and strongly worded argument against or in favour of something or somebody [Mid-17C. Via medieval Latin < Greek *polemikos* < *polemos* 'war' < ?] —**polemically** *adv*

polemics /pə lémmiks/ *n* the art or practice of arguing powerfully and effectively for or against something and engaging in controversy (+ *singular verb*)

polenta /pō léntə/ *n* in Italian cooking, fine yellow maize meal cooked to a mush with water or stock, sometimes set, sliced, and served baked or fried [Mid-16C. Via Italian < Latin, 'barley meal'.]

pole piece *n* a shaped piece of ferromagnetic material, usually soft iron, that concentrates and directs the magnetic field of a magnet to maximize the efficiency of devices such as loudspeakers and generators

pole position *n* **1** the best position on the starting grid of a motor race, usually on the inside of the front row and taken by the driver with the fastest prerace practice time **2** a very good or advantageous position at the beginning of something

pole star *n* something considered as a guiding light and giver of direction (*literary*)

Pole Star *n* ASTRON = **Polaris** *n.* 1

Poles'ye /pṓ lez yə/ = **Pripet Marshes**

pole vault *n* **1** a field event in which the competitors use a long flexible pole to swing themselves up and over a very high crossbar **2** a jump in the pole vault, or any jump made with the help of a pole —**pole-vault** *vti* —**pole-vaulter** *n*

police /pə leéss/ *n* **1** ORGANIZATION FOR MAINTAINING LAW AND ORDER a civil organization whose members are given special legal powers by the government and whose task is to maintain public order and to solve and prevent crimes ○ *a police car* **2** POLICE OFFICERS police officers considered as a group (+ *plural verb*) **3** SPECIALIZED FORCE an organized group of people whose job is maintaining order, ensuring that regulations are obeyed, and preventing crime within a particular area or sphere of activity ■ *vt* **1** ENSURE LAW AND ORDER to ensure that law and order are maintained in a particular area or at a particular event, using the police or a military force **2** ENSURE RULES ARE FOLLOWED to ensure that rules and procedures are followed correctly in something, or that something is implemented as agreed [15C. Via French < Greek *politeia* 'civil organization, the state' < *politēs* 'citizen' (see POLITIC).]

police action *n* a relatively small-scale military action undertaken without a declaration of war, e.g. to prevent violation of an international agreement

police constable *n* LAW = **constable**

police dog *n* a dog trained to work with the police in tracking or searching for people, or in detecting illegal substances by smell

police force *n* an organized body of police with jurisdiction within a particular geographical area or over a particular group of people

policeman /pə leéssmən/ (*plural* **-men** /-mən/) *n* a man who is a police officer

Police Motu /pə leéss mō too/ *n* LANG = **Hiri Motu**

police officer *n* a member of a police force

police procedural *n* a crime novel or drama in which the crime is investigated by police officers

police state *n* a country in which the government uses police, especially secret police, to exercise strict or repressive control over the population and deny them full civil liberties

police station *n* the local headquarters of a police force

policewallah /pə leéss wolə/ *n* S Asia a policeman

policewoman /pə leéss wòomən/ (*plural* **-en** /-wimin/) *n* a woman who is a police officer, especially a constable

policy[1] /pólləssi/ *n* (*plural* **-cies**) **1** COURSE OF ACTION a programme of actions adopted by an individual, group, or government, or the set of principles on which they are based **2** PRUDENCE shrewdness or prudence, especially in the pursuit of a particular course of action ■ *npl Scotland* ESTATE GROUNDS the grounds attached to a large country house [14C. < Old French *policie* 'government, civil organization' (see POLICE).]

policy[2] /pólləssi/ (*plural* **-cies**) *n* a contract that exists between an insurance company and an individual or organization buying insurance services, or the document that lists the contract terms [Mid-16C. < French *police* < ?]

policyholder /pólləssi hōldər/ *n* a named person or organization responsible for an insurance policy

polio /póli ō/ *n* MED = **poliomyelitis** [Mid-20C. Shortening.]

poliomyelitis /póli ō mī ə lítiss/ *n* a severe infectious viral disease, usually affecting children or young adults, that inflames the brain stem and spinal cord, sometimes leading to loss of voluntary movement and muscular wasting [Late 19C. < modern Latin < Greek *polios* 'grey' (because the motor neurons it affects are known as 'grey matter') + MYELITIS.] —**poliomyelitic** /-mī ə líttik/ *adj*

poliovirus /póli ō vīrəss/ *n* any of three forms of an enterovirus that causes poliomyelitis

polis[1] /pólliss/ (*plural* **-leis** /pó līss/) *n* **1** a city-state in ancient Greece, typical of Greek political organization from 800 to 400 BC **2** the city-state form of government [Late 19C. < Greek, 'city'.]

polis[2] /póliss/ (*plural* **-lis**) *n Scotland* the police as a force, or an individual police officer (*nonstandard*) [Late 19C. Alteration of POLICE.]

polish /póllish/ *v* **1** *vti* MAKE SMOOTH OR GLOSSY to make something smooth or shiny, or become smooth or shiny, by rubbing with something **2** *vt* REMOVE THE OUTER LAYER OF to remove the outer layers of brown rice to make white rice by rotating the grain in a drum **3** *vti* **IMPROVE** to make something more refined, elegant, or complete, or to become so ■ *n* **1 SUBSTANCE USED FOR POLISHING** a substance used to make something smooth or shiny ○ *furniture polish* **2 SMOOTHNESS** the smoothness or glossiness of something that has been polished ○ *car paintwork with a high polish* **3 RUB GIVEN TO** a rubbing of something designed to make it smooth or glossy **4 REFINEMENT** refinement, especially of style, that is the mark of expertise or experience [13C. Via the Old French stem *poliss-* < Latin *polire.*] —**polisher** *n*

polish off *vt* **1** to finish something, especially food or a task, quickly and completely **2** to kill or eliminate somebody (*informal*) [< the idea of putting the finishing touches to something]

polish up *vt* **1** to make something smooth or shiny by rubbing it **2** to improve or refine something, e.g. a prepared speech or knowledge of a foreign language

polish up on *vt* to improve knowledge or skill in a particular area

Polish /pólish/ *npl* **PEOPLE OF POLAND** the people of Poland ■ *n* **OFFICIAL LANGUAGE OF POLAND** the official language of Poland, also spoken in North America and Europe, especially Germany, belonging to the Balto-Slavic branch of Indo-European. Native speakers: 44 million. ■ *adj* **1 OF POLAND** relating to Poland, or its people or culture **2 OF POLISH** relating to the Polish language

Polish notation *n* a notation for symbolic logic where the logical operators are placed as prefixes in front of formulas instead of between them, allowing parentheses to be dispensed with [Because it was developed by mathematicians in Poland]

Politburo /póllit byoorō, pə lít-/ *n* the executive and policy-making committee of a governing Communist Party, especially the committee consisting of twenty members in the former Soviet Union [Early 20C. < Russian *politbyuro* 'political bureau'.]

polite /pə lít/ (**-liter, -litest**) *adj* **1** showing or possessing good manners or common courtesy **2** socially superior to ordinary people and considered refined or cultivated [15C. < Latin *politus*, past participle of *polire* 'to polish' (see POLISH).] —**politely** *adv* —**politeness** *n*

politesse /pólli téss/ *n* politeness of a very formal or genteel kind [Early 18C. < French, 'politeness'.]

politic /póllətik/ *adj* possessing or displaying shrewdness, tact or cunning [15C. Via Old French < Greek *politēs* 'citizen' < *polis* 'city' (see POLIS[1]).] —**politicly** *adv*

political /pə líttik'l/ *adj* **1 CONCERNED WITH PARTY POLITICS** relating to politics, especially party politics **2 CONCERNED WITH GOVERNMENT** relating to civil administration or government **3 RESULTING FROM UNACCEPTABLE BELIEFS** arising from somebody's voiced opposition to a government or from voiced support for policies and principles regarded by the authorities as unacceptable **4 PRAGMATIC** carried out for reasons that best serve a desired outcome rather than for reasons that are, e.g. morally justifiable ○ *denies that this was a political decision* —**politically** *adv*

political economy *n* the study of ways in which economics and government policies interact (*dated*) —**political economist** *n*

politically correct *adj* marked by language or conduct that deliberately avoids giving offence, e.g. on the basis of ethnic origin or sexual orientation —**political correctness** *n*

politically incorrect *adj* containing language or conduct that could give offence, e.g. on the basis of ethnic origin or sexual orientation

political prisoner *n* a person who is imprisoned because of his or her political actions or beliefs

political science *n* the study of political organizations and institutions, especially governments —**political scientist** *n*

political theatre *n* dramatic performances designed to advance or promote a political cause

politician /póllə tísh'n/ *n* **1 SOMEBODY ACTIVE IN POLITICS** a person who actively or professionally engages in politics **2 GOVERNMENT MEMBER** a member of a branch of government **3** *US* **SOMEBODY SEEKING PERSONAL POWER** somebody whose main political motive is self-advancement (*disapproving*) **4 SCHEMER** a manipulator of relationships, especially in a workplace [Late 16C. < POLITIC.]

politicize /pə lítti sīz/ (**-cizes, -cizing, -cized**), **politicise** (**-cises, -cising, -cised**) *v* **1** *vti* to bring something such as an issue of public interest into the political arena **2** *vt* to make somebody politically aware or active, or introduce a political element to something —**politicization** /pə lítti sī záysh'n/ *n*

politicking /póllə tiking/ *n* political activity, especially campaigning or speech-making, often when disapproved of as insincere or self-serving

politico /pə líttikō/ (*plural* **-cos**) *n* a politician, especially one whose words are dismissed as trite or whose motives are disapproved of as self-serving (*informal*) [Mid-17C. < Italian or Spanish, 'politician'.]

politics /póllətiks/ *n* **1 THEORY AND PRACTICE OF GOVERNMENT** the theory and practice of forming and running organizations connected with government (+ *singular verb*) **2 POLICYMAKING ACTIVITY** activity within a political party or organization that is concerned with debate and the creation and carrying out of distinctive policies rather than merely the administration of the state (+ *singular or plural verb*) **3 INTERRELATIONSHIPS IN A SPECIFIC FIELD** the totality of interrelationships in a particular area of life involving power, authority, or influence, and capable of manipulation (+ *singular or plural verb*) ○ *the politics of education* **4 CALCULATED ADVANCEMENT** the use of tactics and strategy to gain power in a group or organization (+ *singular or plural verb*) **5 POLITICAL LIFE** political life as a profession (+ *singular verb*) ■ *npl* **1 POLITICAL ACTIVITY** political activity at any level **2 POLITICAL BELIEFS** political persuasions or beliefs

polity /pólləti/ (*plural* **-ties**) *n* **1 PARTICULAR FORM OF GOVERNMENT** a particular form of government that exists within a state or an institution **2 POLITICS AND GOVERNMENT WITHIN SOCIETY** that aspect of society that is oriented to politics and government **3 POLITICAL ENTITY** a state, society, or institution regarded as a political entity [Mid-16C. Via Latin < Greek *politeia* (see POLICE).]

polje /pólyə/ *n* a large steep-walled plain in a limestone region, containing a marsh or small lake [Late 19C. < Serbo-Croat, 'field'.]

Polk /pōk/, **James Knox** (1795–1849) US statesman and 11th president of the United States (1845–49)

polka /pólkə, pṓl-/ *n* **1 LIVELY DANCE** a lively dance for couples consisting of three quick steps and a hop and originating in Central Europe **2 MUSIC FOR POLKA** the music for a polka ■ *vi* **DANCE POLKA** to dance a polka [Mid-19C. Probably via Czech < Polish, feminine form of *Polak* 'Pole' < a Slavic word meaning 'field'.]

polka dot *n* a round spot repeated to form a regular pattern in a contrasting colour on fabric

ϟ**poll** /pōl/ *n* **1 ELECTION** a political election in its entirety, including the casting, recording, and counting of votes **2 SURVEY OF PUBLIC** a questioning of the population or of a representative sample to tally opinions or gather other information. ◊ **opinion poll 3 NUMBER OF VOTES** the total number of votes cast in an election **4 STRIKING SURFACE OF HAMMER** the broad hitting part of a hammer ■ **polls** *npl* **PLACE FOR VOTING IN ELECTION** a place where votes are recorded during an election ■ *v* **1** *vt* **SAMPLE OPINION METHODICALLY** to sample the opinions or attitudes of a group of people systematically **2** *vt* **RECEIVE CERTAIN NUMBER OF VOTES** to receive a particular number of votes in an election **3** *vti* **CAST VOTE IN ELECTION** to cast a vote in an election **4** *vt* **CHECK AVAILABILITY OF COMPUTER COMMUNICATION LINES** to check communication lines in a computer or computer network to determine if they can receive or transmit data **5** *vt* **SHEAR ANIMAL** to clip or shear an animal **6** *vt* **REMOVE ANIMAL'S HORNS** to cut an animal's horns short or cut them off [13C. Probably < Middle Dutch or Middle Low German.]

SPELLCHECK See ***pole***.

pollack /pólløk/ (*plural* **-lacks** *or* **-lack**), **pollock** (*plural* **-locks** *or* **-lock**) *n* **1** a marine fish of the cod family, with a protruding lower jaw. Native to: North Atlantic. Genus: *Pollachius*. **2** the flesh of a pollack used as food [Early 16C. Alteration of Scots *podlok* < ?]

pollard /póllərd, -aard/ *n* **1 TREE WITH BRANCHES CUT** a tree whose branches are cut back extensively to encourage denser growth **2 ANIMAL WITH HORNS REMOVED OR SHED** an animal that has shed its horns or antlers or has had its horns removed ■ *vt* **CUT BRANCHES OR HORNS** to cut back the branches of a tree, or remove the horns of an animal [Mid-17C. < POLL.]

pollen /póllən/ *n* a powdery substance produced by flowering plants that contains male reproductive cells. It is carried by wind and insects to other plants, which it fertilizes. [Mid-18C. < Latin, 'fine flour, dust'.]

Pollen /póllən/, **Daniel** (1813–96) New Zealand statesman

pollen basket *n* the hollow part of a bee's hind leg, used to transport pollen

pollen count *n* a scientific measure of the amount of pollen in a specific volume of air during a 24-hour period

pollen mother cell *n* a cell in a flowering plant that produces four pollen grains after cell division

pollen sac *n* a cavity in the anther of a flower, where pollen is produced

pollen tube *n* a hollow tube that develops from a pollen grain and conveys male reproductive cells to the egg cell

pollex /pólleks/ (*plural* **-lices** /-seez/) *n* the first digit of the forelimb in birds and animals, or the thumb in humans (*technical*) [Mid-19C. < Latin < ?]

pollie /pólli/, **polly** (*plural* **-lies**) *n Aus* a politician (*informal*)

pollinate /póllə nayt/ (**-nates, -nating, -nated**) *vt* to transfer pollen grains from the male structure of a plant, e.g. the anther, to the female structure of a plant, e.g. the stigma, and fertilize it [Late 19C. < Latin *pollin-*, stem of *pollen* (see POLLEN).] —**pollination** /póllə náysh'n/ *n* —**pollinator** /-naytər/ *n*

polling booth *n* a booth in which an individual voter marks a ballot paper during an election. US term **voting booth**

polling place *n US* POL = **polling station**

polling station *n* a building officially designated for casting votes during an election. US term **polling place**

pollinia plural of **pollinium**

pollinium /pə línni əm/ (*plural* **-a** /-ə/) *n* a cohering mass of pollen grains transported as a whole during pollination, typical of orchids and milkweeds [Mid-19C. < modern Latin < Latin *pollin-* (see POLLINATE).]

pollinosis /pólli nṓssiss/ *n* hay fever (*technical*) [Early 20C. < Latin *pollin-* (see POLLINATE).]

polliwog /pólliwog/, **pollywog** *n* ZOOL = **tadpole** [15C. Alteration of earlier *polwygle* < *poll* 'head' (see POLL) + WIGGLE.]

pollock *n* ZOOL = **pollack**

Pollock /póllək/, **Jackson** (1912–56) US artist

pollster /pṓlstər/ *n* a conductor of public opinion polls

poll tax *n* **1** any flat-rate tax levied on all the individuals in a population, often as a prerequisite to voting **2** a community charge (*informal*)

pollucite /póllyoo sīt, pə lóoss īt/ *n* a rare colourless feldspathoid mineral that contains caesium [Mid-19C. Alteration of *pollux*; because it is associated with the mineral CASTOR[2] (in allusion to Castor and Pollux, sons of Zeus in Greek mythology).]

pollutant /pə lóot'nt/ *n* something that pollutes, e.g. chemicals or waste products that contaminate the air, soil, or water

pollute /pə lóot/ (**-lutes, -luting, -luted**) *vt* **1 CONTAMINATE** to cause harm to an area of the natural environment, e.g. the air, soil, or water, usually by introducing damaging substances such as chemicals or waste products **2 CORRUPT OR DEFILE** to make somebody morally or spiritually impure **3 DESECRATE** to violate the sacred nature of a holy place [14C. < Latin *pollut-*, past participle of *polluere.*] —**polluter** *n*

pollution /pə lóosh'n/ *n* **1** the act of polluting something, especially the natural environment **2** the state or condition of being polluted, or the presence of pollutants ○ *Pollution will destroy fish in the rivers.*

Pollux *n* ♦ **Castor and Pollux**

polly *n Aus* POL = **pollie**

Pollyanna /pólli ánnə/ *n* an unrealistically optimistic person [Early 20C. After the heroine of children's stories written by US author Eleanor Hodgman Porter (1868–1920).]

pollywog *n* ZOOL = **polliwog**

polo /pṓlō/ *n* **1 TEAM GAME PLAYED ON HORSEBACK** a game played by teams on horseback, with players using long-handled mallets to drive a wooden ball into a goal **2 TEAM GAME PLAYED WITH BALL** any of several team games whose object is to drive a ball into a goal, e.g. water polo (*usually in combination*) **3** (*plural* **-los**) **POLO SHIRT** a polo shirt (*informal*) **4 POLO NECK** a polo neck (*informal*) [Late 19C. < Tibetan *pholo* 'ball game'.]

Polo /pṓlō/, **Marco** (1254–1324) Venetian merchant and traveller

polo coat *n* a double-breasted overcoat, usually made of camel hair

polonaise /póllə náyz/ *n* **1 SLOW FORMAL DANCE FOR COUPLES** a slow dance of Polish origin in 3/4 time, for couples **2 MUSIC FOR POLONAISE** the music for a polonaise **3 CUTAWAY DRESS WITH UNDERSKIRT** a dress with a tight bodice, cut away at the waist to reveal an inner skirt [Mid-18C. < French, 'Polish'.]

polo neck *n* **1** high rollover collar that fits closely to the neck. US term **turtleneck** *n.* 1 **2** a sweater with a high rollover collar that fits closely to the neck. US term **turtleneck** *n.* 2 —**polo-necked** *adj*

polonium /pə lṓni əm/ *n* (*symbol* **Po**) a very rare radioactive metallic element. Source: uranium ores. Use: removal of static electricity. [Late 19C. < medieval Latin *Polonia* 'Poland', the home of Marie CURIE.]

polony /pə lṓni/ (*plural* **-ny** *or* **-nies**) *n* a large smoked sausage made with a variety of finely ground seasoned meats, usually including beef and pork [Mid-18C. Probably alteration of BOLOGNA.]

polo pony *n* a horse ridden in the game of polo

polo shirt *n* **1** a lightweight casual shirt, usually made of knitted cotton, with a small square collar and a buttoned opening at the neck **2** a shirt with a polo neck [Because it is traditionally worn by polo players]

Pol Pot /pól pót/ (1928–98) Cambodian leader of the Khmer Rouge (1975–79). Born **Saloth Sar**

poltergeist /póltərgīst/ *n* a supposed supernatural spirit that reveals its presence by creating disturbances, e.g. by knocking over objects [Mid-19C. < German, 'noisy ghost'.]

poltroon /pol trṓon/ *n* an offensive term for somebody regarded as a contemptible coward (*archaic*) [Early 16C. Via French < Italian *poltrone* 'coward, lazy person' < ?]

poly[1] /pólli/ (*plural* **-ys**) *n* (*informal*) **1 POLYMORPHONUCLEAR LEUCOCYTE** a polymorphonuclear leucocyte **2 POLYETHYLENE** polyethylene **3 POLYTECHNIC** a polytechnic [Late 20C. Shortening.]

poly[2] /pólli/ (*plural* **-lies**) *n* an aromatic plant of the mint family. Native to: S Europe. *Teucrium polium*. [Early 16C. Via Latin *polium* < Greek *polion*.]

poly- *prefix* **1** more than one ○ *polyandry* **2** more than normal ○ *polyphagia* **3** polymer ○ *polyethylene* [< Greek *polus* 'much' < Indo-European, 'to fill']

polyA /pólí áy/ *n* BIOCHEM = **polyadenylic acid**

polyacrylamide /pólli ə krílla mīd/ *n* a white solid polymer of acrylamide. Use: thickening, clouding, and absorbent agent.

polyacrylonitrile /pólli ə krillō nī trīl/ *n* a polymer used in the manufacture of artificial fibres

polyadenylic acid /pólli áddə níllik-/ *n* a segment of RNA made up of multiple units of adenylic acid

polyalcohol /pólli álkə hol/ *n* CHEM = **polyol**

polyamide /pólli ámmīd, -mid/ *n* a synthetic polymer that has recurring amide groups, e.g. nylon

polyamine /pólli ámm een, -ə meen/ *n* any organic compound containing more than one amino group

polyandry /pólli andri/ *n* **1 HAVING MULTIPLE HUSBANDS** the custom of having more than one husband **2 HAVING MULTIPLE MATES** animal mating in which a female mates with more than one male during any single breeding season **3 HAVING MANY STAMENS** possession by a plant of a large number of stamens [Late 17C. < Greek *poluandria* 'many husbands' < *andr-* 'man, husband'.] —**polyandrous** /pólli ándrəss/ *adj*

polyanthus /pólli ánthəss/ *n* a hybrid primrose with bright flowers in a variety of colours. *Primula polyantha*. [Early 18C. Via modern Latin < Greek *poluanthos* 'having many flowers'.]

polyatomic /pólli ə tómmik/ *adj* describes a molecule that has more than two atoms

polybasic /pólli báyssik/ *adj* describes a molecule or compound that has two or more atoms of replaceable hydrogen

polybasite /pólli báy sīt/ *n* a rare grey to black crystalline mineral containing silver [Mid-19C. < German *Polybasit* < Greek *polus* 'much' + German *Basis* 'base'; from its chemical composition.]

polycarbonate /pólli kaárbə nayt, -bənət/ *n* a strong synthetic resin. Use: moulded products, unbreakable windows, optical components.

polycarboxylic acid /pólli kaar bok síllik-/ *n* carboxylic acid that contains more than one carboxyl group

polycarpic /pólli kaárpik/, **polycarpous** /-kaárpəss/ *adj* describes a plant that is capable of producing flowers and fruit several times in succession —**polycarpy** /pólli kaarpi/ *n*

polychaete /pólli keet/, **polychete** *n* a marine worm with a segmented body and bristled fleshy appendages used in swimming. Class: Polychaeta. [Late 19C. < modern Latin *Polychaeta* < Greek *polukhaitēs* 'having much hair' < *khaitē* 'long hair'.] —**polychaetous** /pólli keétəss/ *adj*

polychete /pólli keet/ *n* US = **polychaete**

polychlorinated biphenyl /pólli kláwrə naytid bī feén'l/ *n* full form of **PCB**

polychromatic /pólli krō máttik/ *adj* **1** having, showing, or consisting of many colours, either at the same time or in sequence **2** describes electromagnetic radiation that has multiple wavelengths

polychrome /póllikrōm/ *adj* **1** decorated with many or varied colours **2** PHYS = **polychromatic** *adj.* 1 ■ *n* a polychrome object or artefact

polychromy /pólli krōmi/ *n* the practice of using several different colours in painting, sculpture, or decoration

polyclinic /pólli klínnik/ *n* a clinic, often independent of a hospital, in which medical care is provided by a range of specialists

polyclone /pólliklōn/ *n* a clone derived from groups of cells of different ancestry or genetic constitution —**polyclonal** /pólli klṓn'l/ *adj* —**polyclonally** /-klṓn'li/ *adv*

polyconic projection /pólli kónnik-/ *n* a conic map projection in which all meridians, except the central, are curved and the parallels are nonconcentric arcs

polycotton /pólli kot'n/ *n* a fabric that is made from a mixture of polyester and cotton [Late 20C. Blend of POLYESTER + COTTON.]

polycotyledon /pólli kótti leéd'n/ *n* a plant with more than two cotyledons —**polycotyledonous** *adj*

polycrystal /pólli kríst'l/ *n* a crystalline structure whose crystals were formed rapidly and randomly

polycrystalline /pólli krístə līn/ *adj* describes a metal or other solid that consists of randomly oriented crystals

polycyclic /pólli sīklik/ *adj* **1** describes a shell that has two or more whorls **2** describes a compound having two or more closed rings of atoms —**polycyclic** *n*

polycystic /pólli sístik/ *adj* describes an organ, e.g. a kidney or ovary, that has developed multiple cysts

polycythaemia /póllisī theémi ə/ *n* an abnormal increase in red blood cells, occurring on its own or in conjunction with other diseases, especially of the respiratory or circulatory systems [Mid-19C. < POLY- + -CYTE + HAEMO- + -IA, literally 'many-blood-cell disease'.]

polycythemia *n* US = **polycythaemia**

polydactyl /pólli dáktil/ *adj* describes vertebrates, including human beings, that have more than the normal number of fingers or toes —**polydactyl** *n*

polydipsia /pólli dípsi ə/ *n* abnormally excessive thirst [Mid-17C. < POLY- + Greek *dipsa* 'thirst' + -IA.] —**polydipsic** *adj*

polyelectrolyte /pólli i léktrə līt/ *n* an electrolyte that has a high molecular weight, e.g. a protein

polyembryony /pólli émbri əni/ *n* the production of more than one embryo from a single egg —**polyembryonic** /-émbri ónnik/ *adj*

polyene /pólli een/ *n* a hydrocarbon that has many alternating single and double carbon-carbon bonds

polyester /pólli éstər/ *n* **1** a synthetic polymer in which the monomers are linked together by the chemical group -COO-. Use: resins, plastics, textile fibres. **2** a strong hard-wearing synthetic fabric with low moisture absorbency, made from a polyester

polyethylene /pólli éthə leen/ *n* US INDUST = **polythene**

polyethylene glycol *n* any of several polymers of ethylene compounds. Use: emulsifiers and lubricants in ointments and cosmetics.

Polyfilla /póllifillə/ *tdmk* a trademark for a multipurpose filling plaster

polygamy /pə líggəmi/ *n* **1** the custom of having more than one spouse at the same time **2** animal mating in which an individual mates with more than one animal during any single breeding season [Late 16C. Via French < ecclesiastical Greek *polugamos* 'often married' < Greek *gamos* 'marriage'.] —**polygamist** *n* —**polygamous** *adj* —**polygamously** *adv*

polygene /pólli jeen/ *n* any in a group of genes where the number of those genes present collectively determines the extent of a characteristic, e.g. height —**polygenic** /pólli jénnik/ *adj* —**polygenically** /-jénnikli/ *adv*

polygenesis /pólli jénnəsiss/ *n* origin from more than one species, line of ancestors, or source —**polygenetic** /póllijə néttik/ *adj* —**polygenetically** /-néttikli/ *adv*

polyglot /pólli glot/ *adj* **1 COMPETENT IN MANY LANGUAGES** capable of reading, writing, or speaking many languages **2 IN MANY LANGUAGES** written or communicated in many languages ■ *n* **1 MULTILINGUAL PERSON** a speaker of many languages **2 BOOK CONTAINING TEXT IN MANY LANGUAGES** a book, especially a Bible, that gives the text in several languages **3 MIX OF LANGUAGES** a confused mixture of languages [Mid-17C. Via French < Greek *poluglōttos* < *glōtta* 'tongue, language'.] —**polyglotism** /pólli glotizəm/ *n*

polygon /pólligən, -gon/ *n* a geometrical plane figure with three or more straight sides [Late 16C. Via late Latin < Greek *polugōnos* 'many-angled' < *-gōnos* '-angled'.] —**polygonal** /pə líggən'l/ *adj* —**polygonally** *adv*

polygonum /pə líggənəm/ *n* a plant with bulbous stem joints and spikes of small flowers. Genus: *Polygonum*. [Early 18C. Via modern Latin < Greek *polugonon* 'knotgrass', literally 'many-jointed' < *gonu* 'knee, joint'.]

polygraph /pólli graaf, -graf/ *n* **1 DEVICE RECORDING INVOLUNTARY RESPONSES** an electrical device that registers involuntary physical activities, such as pulse rate and perspiration that is often used as a lie detector **2 TEST USING POLYGRAPH** a test using a polygraph, or a result of this test ■ *vt* **TEST SOMEBODY USING POLYGRAPH** to test somebody, usually somebody suspected of committing a crime, using a polygraph —**polygraphic** /pólli gráffik/ *adj* —**polygraphically** *adv*

polygyny /pə líjjəni/ *n* **1 HAVING MULTIPLE WIVES** the custom of being married to more than one wife at the same time. ◊ **polygamy 2 HAVING MULTIPLE MATES** animal mating in which a male mates with more than one female during any single breeding season **3 HAVING MANY PISTILS OR STYLES** the possession by a plant of many pistils or styles [Late 18C. < Greek *gunē* 'woman'.] —**polygynist** *n* —**polygynous** *adj*

polyhedra *n* plural of **polyhedron**

polyhedral angle *n* a geometrical angle formed by the intersection of three or more planes meeting at a point, e.g. the peak of a pyramid

polyhedron /pólli heédrən/ (*plural* **-drons** *or* **-dra** /-drə/) *n* a solid geometrical figure that has many faces [Late 16C. < Greek *poluedron* 'many-based figure' < *hedra* 'base'.] —**polyhedral** *adj*

polyhydroxy /pólli hī dróksi/, **polyhydric** /-hīdrik/ *adj* describes a compound that has two or more hydroxyl groups in each molecule

Polyhymnia /pólli hímni ə/ *n* in Greek mythology, the Muse responsible for songs and dances dedicated to the deities

polyimide /pólli ímmīd/ *n* a tough durable polymer that contains an imide group. Use: heat-resistant coatings.

polyisoprene /pólli īssə preen/ *n* a polymeric form of isoprene. Source: natural or synthetic rubber.

polymath /pólli math/ *n* a person with knowledge of many subjects [Early 17C. < Greek *polumathēs* 'somebody with much learning' < *manthanein* 'learn'.] —**polymathic** /pólli máthik/ *adj* —**polymathy** /pə límməthi/ *n*

polymer /póllimər/ *n* a natural or synthetic compound that consists of large molecules made of many chemically bonded smaller identical molecules, e.g. starch and nylon [Mid-19C. < Greek *polumerēs* 'having many parts' < *meros* 'part'.] —**polymeric** /pólli mérrik/ *adj*

polymerase /póllimə rayz, pə límmə-/ *n* an enzyme that catalyses the elongation of a polymer, especially in DNA or RNA

polymerase chain reaction *n* a technique used to replicate a fragment of DNA and produce a large amount of that sequence

polymerization /pə límmə rī záysh'n, póllimə rī-/, **polymerisation** *n* the chemical reaction in which a compound is made into a polymer by the addition or condensation of smaller molecules —**polymerize** /póllimə rīz, pə límmə rīz/ vti

polymerous /pə límmərəss/ adj 1 describes an organism that consists of many parts or segments 2 describes a flower that has its petals or sepals arranged in many whorls

polymethyl methacrylate /pólli mee thīl-/ n a clear thermoplastic polymer of methyl methacrylate, used in making Perspex™ and in fibre optics

polymorph /pólli mawrf/ n 1 ANIMAL OR PLANT WITH MANY FORMS an animal or plant that has several different adult forms 2 CHEMICAL COMPOUND WITH DIFFERENT FORMS a chemical compound that has several crystalline forms 3 WHITE BLOOD CELL WITH SEGMENTED NUCLEUS a white blood cell whose nucleus is segmented into lobes —**polymorphic** /pólli máwrfik/ adj —**polymorphism** /-máwrfizəm/ n

polymorphonuclear leucocyte /pólli máwrfō nyoōkli ər-/ n = **polymorph** n. 3

polymyxin /pólli míksin/ n a peptide antibiotic. Source: a soil bacterium [Bacillus polymyxa]. Use: treatment of meningitis, inner ear infections. [Mid-20C. < modern Latin Polymyxa < POLY- + Greek muxa 'slime'.]

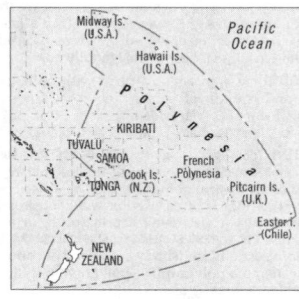

Polynesia

Polynesia /pólli neèzi ə/ ethnographic grouping of Pacific islands, encompassing a number of scattered islands in the central and S Pacific Ocean

Polynesian /pólli neèzi ən/ n 1 somebody who comes from an island of the central and S Pacific 2 a group of Austronesian languages, including Fijian, Hawaiian, and Maori, spoken on islands of the central and S Pacific. Native speakers: 800,000. —**Polynesian** adj

polyneuritis /pólli nyoor rítiss/ n simultaneous inflammation of several nerves at once

polynomial /pólli nōmi əl/ adj WITH MORE THAN TWO TERMS describes a mathematical expression that has more than two terms, or a system of taxonomic nomenclature that uses more than two names ■ n 1 MATHEMATICAL EXPRESSION a mathematical expression consisting of the sum of a number of terms, each of which contains a constant and variables raised to a positive integral power 2 MULTITERM TAXONOMIC NAME a taxonomic name of a plant or animal that has more than two terms, e.g. one giving a genus, species, and subspecies [Late 17C. Modelled on BINOMIAL.]

polynucleotide /pólli nyoōkli ə tīd/ n a chain of nucleotides, as in DNA and RNA

polyol /pólli ol/ n an alcohol that contains more than two hydroxyl groups, e.g. glycerol

polyoma /pólli ōmə/, **polyoma virus** n a virus in rodents that can produce tumours

polyp /póllip/ n 1 a single-cavity marine invertebrate (**coelenterate**) in its sedentary state 2 a small stalk-shaped growth sticking out from the skin or from a mucous membrane. Polyps are usually benign, but some become malignant. [14C. Via French polipe and Latin polypus < Greek polupous 'octopus', literally 'many-footed' < pous 'foot'.] —**polypoid** /pólli poyd/ adj —**polypous** adj

polypeptide /pólli pép tīd/ n a chain of amino acids, as in proteins

polypetalous /pólli péttələss/ adj describes flowers with many separate petals, e.g. roses and carnations

polyphagia /pólli fáyjə/ n 1 an abnormally insatiable appetite for food 2 the habit on the part of certain animals of feeding on many different types of food —**polyphagous** /pə líffəgəss/ adj

polyphase /pólli fayz/ adj producing two or more phases of alternating current, or two or more alternating voltages of the same frequency

Polyphemus /pólli feèməss/ n in Greek mythology, a cyclops who imprisoned Odysseus, who put out Polyphemus's one eye

polyphone /pólli fōn/ n a letter or character that has more than one way of being pronounced

polyphonic /pólli fónnik/ adj 1 consisting of two or more largely independent melodic lines, parts, or voices that sound simultaneously 2 describes a letter or character that may be pronounced in several different ways —**polyphonically** adv

polyphony /pə líffəni/ n 1 musical composition that uses simultaneous, largely independent, melodic parts, lines, or voices 2 the representation of different sounds by the same letter in a writing system [Early 19C. < Greek poluphōnia 'multiplicity of sounds' < phōnē 'voice, sound' (see -PHONE).] —**polyphonous** adj —**polyphonously** adv

polyphyletic /pólli fī léttik/ adj derived or descended from several groups of ancestors —**polyphyletically** adv

polyploid /pólli ployd/ adj having more than twice the basic number of chromosomes —**polyploid** n —**polyploidy** n

polypod /pólli pod/ adj describes an insect larva with a large number of legs and feet, or this larval stage in the development of some insects [Mid-18C. Via French < the Greek stem polupod- 'many-footed' < pous 'foot'.] —**polypod** n

polypody /póllipōdi/ (plural -dies) n a fern with evergreen pinnate leaves and a creeping rootstock. Genus: Polypodium. [15C. Via Latin polypodium < Greek polupodion 'many-footed one'.]

polyposis /pólli pṓssiss/ n a condition in which numerous polyps develop in a hollow organ, e.g. the bowel

polypropylene /pólli prōpə leen/, **polypropene** /pólli prōpeen/ n a thermoplastic substance that is a synthetic polymer of propylene. Use: pipes, industrial fibres, moulded objects.

polyptych /pólliptik/ n an arrangement of three or more panels with a painting or carving on each, usually hinged together and used as an altarpiece in a church [Mid-19C. Modelled on DIPTYCH.]

polypus /póllipəss/ (plural -pi /-pī/) n a polyp (archaic) [14C. < Latin (see POLYP).]

polyrhythm /póllirith'm/ n musical composition that employs several simultaneous, contrasting rhythms —**polyrhythmic** /pólli ríthmik/ adj —**polyrhythmically** /-ríthmikli/ adv

polyribosome /pólli ríbəsōm/ n a cluster of ribosomes linked by a strand of messenger RNA and functioning as a site of protein synthesis

polysaccharide /pólli sákə rīd/, **polysaccharose** /pólli sákərōss/ n a complex carbohydrate, e.g. starch or cellulose, made up of sugar molecules linked into a branched or chain structure

polysemy /pə líssimi, pólli seemi, pólli seèmi/ n the existence of several meanings for a single word or phrase [Early 20C. Via modern Latin polysemia < Greek polusēmos 'having many meanings' < sēma 'sign' (see SEMANTIC).] —**polysemous** /pə líssiməss, pólli seèməss/ adj

polysepalous /pólli séppələss/ adj describes flowers that have distinctly separate sepals

polysome /póllisōm/ n BIOCHEM = **polyribosome** [Mid-20C. Contraction.]

polysomic /pólli sṓmik/ adj describes a diploid cell or organism in which some of the chromosomes occur more than twice

polysorbate /pólli sáwr bayt/ n an emulsifier used in preparing some foods and drugs [Mid-20C. < POLY- + SORBITOL + -ATE.]

polyspermy /pólli spurmi/ n the fertilization of an egg by several spermatozoa

polystichous /pə lístikəss, pólli stíkəss/ adj describes parts of a plant that are arranged in two or more series of rows [Late 19C. Modelled on DISTICHOUS.]

polystyrene /pólli stī reen/ n a synthetic polymer of styrene that is stable in various physical forms. As a white rigid foam (**expanded polystyrene**) it is used for packing and insulation.

polysulphide /pólli súlfīd/ n a sulphide whose molecules have two or more atoms of sulphur

polysyllabic /pólli si lábbik/ adj 1 having more than two syllables 2 using or containing long words, often where shorter words would be adequate or better —**polysyllabically** adv

polysyllable /pólli siləb'l, pólli silləb'l/ n a word that has more than one or two syllables

polysynaptic /pólli si náptik/ adj describes a reflex in the central nervous system that uses two or more synapses

polysynthetic /pólli sin théttik/ adj describes a language in which the syntax is conveyed by means of multiple affixes to single words —**polysynthesis** /pólli sínthəssiss/ n —**polysynthetically** /pólli sin théttikli/ adv

polytechnic /pólli téknik/ n a college offering a range of courses, some of them vocational or technical, at or below the bachelor's degree level. In 1992 all polytechnics in England and Wales became universities. [Early 19C. Via French < Greek polutekhnos 'multi-skilled' < tekhnē 'skill'.]

polytene /pólli teen/ adj with multistranded chromosomes in contact with corresponding chromosomes —**polytenic** /pólli teènik/ adj —**polyteny** /pólli teeni/ n

polytetrafluoroethylene /pólli téttrə floōrō éthə leen/ n a durable, chemically resistant, nonflammable thermoplastic substance widely used to coat metal surfaces, especially the surfaces of cooking pots to make them nonstick

polytheism /pólli thi izam, pólli theè izəm/ n worshipping of or believing in more than one deity, especially several deities [Early 17C. Via French < Greek polutheos 'of many deities' < theos 'deity' (see THEO-).] —**polytheist** n —**polytheistic** /pólli thi ístik/ adj —**polytheistically** /-ístikli/ adv

polythene /pólli theen/ n a malleable thermoplastic used to make containers, packaging, and electrical insulation materials. It is a polymer of ethylene. US term **polyethylene** [Mid-20C. Contraction of POLYETHYLENE.]

polytonality /pólli tō nálləti/ n music composed in such a way that several keys are used at once —**polytonal** /pólli tōn'l/ adj —**polytonally** /-tōn'li/ adv

polytrophic /pólli trṓfik/ adj describes bacteria that derive food from several different sources

polytypic /pólli típpik/, **polytypical** /-típpik'l/ adj describes a taxonomic subset, especially a species, that has more than two subdivisions

polyunsaturated /pólli un sáchə raytid/ adj belonging to a class of fats, especially plant oils, that are less likely to be converted into cholesterol in the body

polyurethane /pólli yoōrə thayn/ n a thermoplastic polymer that contains an NHCOO chemical group. Use: resins, coatings, insulation, adhesives, foams, fibres.

polyuria /pólli yoòri ə/ n the passing of abnormally large amounts of urine, e.g. in untreated diabetes

polyvalent /pólli váylənt, pə lívvələnt/ adj 1 describes a chemical element that has more than one valency or a valency of more than two 2 describes a vaccine that is effective against more than one strain of microorganism, toxin, antigen, or antibody —**polyvalency** /pólli váylənssi/ n

polyvinyl /pólli vín'l/ adj describes plastics and resins produced by the polymerization of vinyls

polyvinyl acetate n full form of **PVA**

polyvinyl chloride n full form of **PVC**

polyzoan /pólli zō ən/ n MARINE BIOL = **bryozoan** [Mid-19C. < modern Latin Polyzoa < POLY- + -ZOON.]

pom /pom/ n ANZ a British person (informal humorous or disapproving) [Early 20C. Shortening of POMMY.]

pomace /púmmiss, pómmiss/ n 1 the pulpy mass that remains after apples or other fruits have been crushed and pressed to extract the juice, e.g. to make cider 2 the pulpy mass that remains after nuts, fish, or other foods have been crushed and pressed to extract oil or another liquid [Mid-16C. Via medieval Latin pomacium 'cider' < Latin pomum 'apple, fruit'.]

pomaceous /po máyshəss/ adj describes a fruit in the form of a large fleshy receptacle with a central seed-bearing core (**pome**), e.g. the apple and the pear [Early 18C. < Latin pomum 'apple'.]

pomade /pə máyd, -maàd/ n a perfumed oil or ointment used to make hair look smooth and shiny ■ vt (-mades, -mading, -maded) to dress hair with pomade [Mid-16C. Via French pommade < Latin pomum 'apple'.]

pomander /pə mándər/ *n* **1 AROMATIC MIXTURE** a mixture of aromatic substances enclosed in a sachet, ball, or other container, kept near stored clothes or in a room to impart a pleasant smell **2 POMANDER CONTAINER** a container for a pomander, usually a lidded pottery bowl with holes **3 CLOVE-STUDDED ORANGE** an orange or apple studded with cloves, used to scent clothes or a room [15C. < Old French *pome d'ambre* 'apple of amber'.]

Pomare /po maári/, **Sir Maui Wiremu Pita Naera** (1876–1930) New Zealand Maori leader and politician

pome /pōm/ *n* a fleshy fruit that has a central core typically containing five seeds, e.g. an apple or pear [14C. Via Old French < Latin *pomum* 'apple'.]

pomegranate /pómmi granit/ *n* **1** a round reddish fruit with a tough rind enclosing numerous seeds within a tart juicy red pulp **2** the tree that produces pomegranates. Native to: tropical Asia. *Punica granatum*. [14C. < Old French *pome grenate* 'seedy apple'.]

~~**pomegranite**~~ incorrect spelling of **pomegranate**

pomelo /pómmәlō/ (*plural* **-los**) *n* **1** a yellowy-orange citrus fruit similar to a large grapefruit **2** (*plural* **-los** *or* **-lo**) the citrus tree that produces pomelos. Native to: SE Asia. *Citrus maxima*. [Mid-19C. < ?]

Pomerania /pómmə ráyni ə/ historic region in present-day Poland and NE Germany

Pomeranian /pómmə ráyni ən/ *n* **1 SMALL DOG** a breed of small dog with a long silky coat, pointed ears, a pointed muzzle, and a long curling tail **2 SOMEBODY FROM POMERANIA** somebody who comes from Pomerania ■ *adj* **OF POMERANIA** relating to Pomerania, or its people or culture

pomfret[1] /póm frit/, **pomfret-cake** /póm frit-/ *n* FOOD = **Pontefract cake** [Mid-19C. After *Pomfret* (now *Pontefract*), West Yorkshire.]

pomfret[2] /póm frit/ (*plural* **-frets** *or* **-fret**) *n* **1** a tropical marine fish of open seas. *Stromateoides argentteus*. **2** the white flesh of a pomfret used as food, especially in Southeast Asian, Chinese, and Indian cooking [Early 18C. Probably literally 'little pampo' < Portuguese *pampo*.]

pomfret-cake *n* FOOD = **pomfret**[1]

pomiculture /pómmi kulchər/ *n* the cultivation of fruit [Late 19C. < Latin *pomum* 'apple, fruit' + CULTURE.]

pommel /pómm'l, púmm'l/ *n* **1 FRONT OF SADDLE** the front part of a saddle that curves upwards **2 PART OF SWORD HANDLE** the knob at the hilt of a sword **3 HANDLE ON POMMEL HORSE** each of the two curved handles on the top of a pommel horse ■ *vt* = **pummel** [14C. Via Old French *pomel* 'little fruit' < Latin *pomum* 'fruit'.]

pommel horse *n* **1** a padded oblong piece of gymnastics apparatus that is raised off the floor and has two curved handles on the top **2** the men's gymnastics event that involves balancing and manoeuvring on a pommel horse

pommy /pómmi/ *adj* ANZ British (*informal humorous or disapproving*) ■ *n* (*plural* **-mies**) *ANZ* = **pom** (*informal humorous or disapproving*) [Early 20C. Probably shortening of *pomegranate*, alteration of *Jimmy Grant* or *Pummy Grant*, rhyming slang for *immigrant*.]

pomo /pṓmō/, **po-mo** *adj* postmodern (*informal*) ○ *'beat-generation, counterculture, and pomo literature'* (Hawkeye, *FutureCulture FAQ parts 1 & 2*; 1992)

Pomo (*plural* **-mo** *or* **-mos**) *n* **1** a member of a group of Native North American peoples living in N California **2** any of several closely related Native North American languages spoken in parts of N California and belonging to the Hokan branch of Hokan-Siouan languages [Late 19C. < Northern Pomo *pʰóˑmoˑ* 'at the red earth hole'.] —**Pomo** *adj*

pomology /po móllәji/ *n* the study or practice of cultivating fruit [Early 19C. < Latin *pomum* 'fruit' + -LOGY.] —**pomological** /pómmə lójjik'l/ *adj* —**pomologically** /-lójjikli/ *adv* —**pomologist** /po mólləjist/ *n*

Pomona /pə mṓnə/ *n* the Roman goddess of fruit [Mid-17C. < Latin < *pomum* 'fruit'.]

pomp /pomp/ *n* **1** a display of great splendour and magnificence **2** an ostentatious and vain display of importance [14C. Via Old French < Greek *pompē* 'solemn procession, send-off, escort' < *pempein* 'send' < ?]

pompadour /pómpə door/ *n* a woman's hairstyle, popular in the 18th century, in which the hair is swept back high off the face over a pad [Mid-18C. After Jeanne-Antoinette Poisson, Marquise de *Pompadour* (1721–64).]

pompano /pómpənō/ (*plural* **-nos** *or* **-no**) *n* **1** a marine fish with a deep flat body and forked tail. Native to: S Atlantic and Gulf coasts of North America. *Trachinotus carolinus*. **2** ZOOL = **butterfish 3** the flesh of a pompano as food [Late 18C. < Spanish *pámpano* < ?]

Pompeii /pom páy i/ ancient Roman city in present-day S Italy, buried by volcanic ash during the eruption of Mount Vesuvius in AD 79

Pompey /pómpi/ (106–48 BC) Roman general and statesman. Full name **Gnaeus Pompeius Magnus**. Known as **Pompey the Great**

Pompidou /pómpi doo/, **Georges** (1911–74) French statesman

pompom /póm pom/ *n* **1** a small tufted ball made from wool, silk, or other material, attached as a decoration to hats, shoes, and other articles of clothing **2** a cheerleader's accessory in the form of a large white or brightly coloured ball-shaped mass of thin paper or plastic strips connected to a handle **3** PLANT SCI = **pompon** *n.* 2 [Mid-18C. < French < ?]

pom-pom /póm pom/ *n* a rapid-firing automatic weapon, especially a cannon used in the Boer War or a double-barrelled antiaircraft gun used in World War II (*slang*) [An imitation of the sound]

pompon /póm pon/ *n* **1** CLOTHING = **pompom** *n.* 1 **2** a small round flower of some chrysanthemum or dahlia varieties, or a variety that has this kind of flower [Mid-18C. < French < ?]

pomposity /pom póssəti/ (*plural* **-ties**) *n* **1** an excessive sense of self-importance, usually displayed through exaggerated seriousness or stateliness in speech and manner **2** an act, remark, or gesture that is exaggerated in its seriousness or stateliness and conveys an excessive sense of self-importance

pompous /pómpəss/ *adj* **1 SELF-IMPORTANT** having an excessive sense of self-importance, usually displayed through exaggerated seriousness or stateliness in speech or manner **2 REVEALING SELF-IMPORTANCE** displaying exaggerated seriousness or stateliness ○ *a pompous gesture* **3 CEREMONIALLY GRAND** full of splendour and magnificence [14C. Via Old French *pompeux* < Greek *pompē* (see POMP).] —**pompously** *adv* —**pompousness** *n*

'pon /pon/ *prep* upon (*archaic or literary*) [Mid-16C. Shortening.]

Ponca /póngkə/ (*plural* **-ca** *or* **-cas**) *n* a Native American language spoken in parts of Oklahoma and Nebraska. It belongs to the Siouan branch of Hokan-Siouan languages and is closely related to Omaha. [Late 18C. < Ponka *ppákka*.] —**Ponca** *adj*

ponce /ponss/ *n* (*slang*) **1** an offensive term that deliberately insults a man for being homosexual or for behaving in a way considered to be more characteristic of a woman **2** a pimp [Late 19C. < ?] —**poncy** *adj*

ponce about, ponce around *vi* (*slang*) **1** to behave in an affected way with the intention of impressing others (*offensive in some contexts*) **2** to spend time doing or achieving nothing at all

Ponce (de León) /pónss də lay ón, pónth ay də lee ón/, **Juan** (1460–1521) Spanish explorer

poncho /pónchō/ (*plural* **-chos**) *n* a simple outer garment for the upper body in the form of a single piece of heavy cloth, often wool, with a slit in it for the head [Early 18C. < American Spanish < ?]

pond /pond/ *n* a small still body of water formed naturally or created artificially, e.g. as a feature in a garden ■ *vi* to collect into shallow pools (*refers to water*) [13C. Alteration of POUND³, in the sense 'enclosure for fish'.]

ponder /póndər/ *vti* to think over something carefully over a period of time [14C. Via Old French *ponderer* < Latin *ponderare* 'weigh, consider' < *pondus* 'weight' (see PONDEROUS).] —**ponderability** *n* —**ponderable** *adj, n* —**ponderably** *adv*

ponderosa pine /póndə rṓzə-/ *n* a tall pine with yellowish bark and needles grouped in twos or threes, that yields valuable timber. Native to: W North America. *Pinus ponderosa*. [*Ponderosa* < modern Latin, < Latin *ponderosus* 'heavy' (see PONDEROUS), because of its dense wood]

ponderous /póndərəss/ *adj* **1 MOVING HEAVILY** lumbering and laborious in movement **2 DULL** without liveliness or wit **3 HEAVY-LOOKING** disproportionately thick and heavy [14C. Via Old French *pondereux* < Latin *ponderosus* < *ponder-*, stem of *pondus* 'weight'.] —**ponderously** *adv* —**ponderousness** *n*

pond lily *n* PLANTS = **water lily**

pondokkie /pon dóki/ *n S Africa* a roughly made house, especially one improvised from available materials (*informal*) [Early 19C. < Afrikaans < ?]

pond scum *n* green freshwater algae that form a layer on the surface of stagnant water

pond-skater *n* any of several types of long-legged insects that have slender hairy bodies and travel about on the surface of water. Family: Gerridae. US term **water strider**

pondweed /pónd weed/ (*plural* **-weed** *or* **-weeds**) *n* **1** an aquatic plant that grows in ponds and slow streams and has jointed stems, floating or submerged leaves, and greenish flowers. Genus: *Potamogeton*. **2** any of several aquatic plants such as mare's-tail unrelated to but resembling pondweed proper. US term **waterweed**

pone[1] /pōn/ *n* FOOD = **corn pone** *n.* [Early 17C. < Virginia Algonquian *poan*.]

pone[2] /pōn, pṓni/ *n* in card games, the person who does not deal in two-handed games, or the person sitting to the right of the dealer [Early 19C. < Latin *pone* 'put', imperative of *ponere* 'to place' (see POSITION).]

pong /pong/ *n* an unpleasant smell (*informal*) ■ *vi* to give off an unpleasant smell (*informal*) [Early 20C. < ?] —**pongy** *adj*

ponga /pónga/ (*plural* **-gas** *or* **-ga**) *n* a tall evergreen tree fern. Native to: New Zealand. *Cyathea dealbata*. [Mid-19C. < Maori.]

pongee /pon jeé, pón jee/ *n* a soft, usually unbleached, silk fabric from China or India, or a similar cotton or rayon imitation [Early 18C. Probably < Chinese *běnjī* 'own loom', or *běnzhì* 'home-woven'.]

pongid /pónjid, póng gid/ *n* any ape of the family that includes the gibbon and the great apes. Family: Pongidae. [Mid-20C. Via modern Latin *Pongidae* < Congolese *mpongo* 'ape'.]

pongo /póng gō/ (*plural* **-gos**) *n* **1** an orang-utan **2** a soldier (*slang; used by navy personnel*) [Early 17C. < Congolese *mpongo* 'ape'.]

poniard /pónnyərd, -yaard/ *n* a small dagger with a slim blade that is triangular or square in its cross section (*literary*) ■ *vt* to stab somebody with a poniard (*literary*) [Mid-16C. Via French *poignard* < Latin *pugnus* 'fist' (see PUGNACIOUS).]

Ponka *n, adj* PEOPLES, LANG = **Ponca**

pons /ponz/ (*plural* **pontes** /pón teez/) *n* a whitish band of nerve fibres on the surface of the brain stem between the medulla oblongata and midbrain [Late 17C. < Latin, 'bridge'.]

pons asinorum /pónz ássi náwrəm/ *n* a proposition or problem that is especially difficult for an inexperienced person to understand [< Latin, 'bridge of asses']

pons Varolii /pónz və rṓli ī/ *n* ANAT = **pons** [Late 17C. < Latin, 'bridge of Varolius', after C. *Varoli* (1543–75), Italian anatomist.]

pont /pont/ *n S Africa* a flat-bottomed ferryboat [Mid-17C. Via Dutch < Middle Dutch *ponte* 'ferryboat'.]

Ponta Delgada /póntə del gaádə/ capital of the Azores, on W São Miguel Island, Portugal. Population: 21,091 (1991).

Pontchartrain, Lake /pónchər trayn/ lake in SE Louisiana, north of New Orleans. Area: 1,632 sq. km/630 sq. mi.

Pontefract cake /pónti frakt-/ *n* a small flat round liquorice sweet [See POMFRET[1]]

pontes plural of **pons**

pontifex /pónti feks/ (*plural* **-tifices** /pon tíffi seez/) *n* a member of the highest council of priests in ancient Rome [Late 16C. < Latin, 'way-maker' < *pont-*, stem of *pons* 'bridge, way' (see PONS).]

Pontifex Maximus /pónti feks máksiməss/ (*plural* **Pontifices Maximi** /pon tíffi seez máksi mī/) *n* the chief priest who presided over the highest council of priests in ancient Rome

pontiff /póntif/ *n* **1** the head of the Roman Catholic Church and bishop of Rome **2** HIST = **pontifex** [Late 16C. Via Old French < Latin *pontifex* (see PONTIFEX).]

pontifical /pon tíffik'l/ *adj* **1 OF A PONTIFF** belonging to, befitting, or involving a pope, bishop, or pontifex **2 POMPOUS** displaying an exaggerated sense of self-importance ■ *n* **BISHOP'S BOOK** a book containing the rites that may be performed only by a bishop ■ **pontificals** *npl* **PONTIFF'S VESTMENTS** the vestments and insignia of a pope or bishop [15C. < Latin *pontificalis* < *pontifex* (see PONTIFEX).] —**pontifically** *adv*

Pontifical Mass *n* a High Mass that is celebrated by a bishop, especially in the Roman Catholic Church

pontificate *vi* /pon tíffi kayt/ (**-cates, -cating, -cated**) **1 SPEAK POMPOUSLY** to speak about something in a knowing and self-important way, especially when not qualified to do so **2 SERVE AS BISHOP** to officiate as a bishop, especially in celebrating Mass ■ *n* /pon tíffikət, -kayt/ **TERM OF OFFICE** the office or term of office of a pope or bishop [Early 19C. < medieval Latin *pontificat-*, past participle of *pontificare* < Latin *pontifex* (see PONTIFEX).] —**pontification** /pon tíffi káysh'n/ *n* —**pontificator** /pon tíffi kaytər/ *n*

pontil /póntil/ *n* GLASS = **punty** [Mid-19C. < French < ?]

pontine /pón tīn/ *adj* relating to or situated in the whitish band of nerve fibres (**pons**) on the surface of the brain stem between the medulla oblongata and midbrain [Late 19C. < Latin *pont-*, stem of *pons* 'bridge, way' (see PONS).]

pontoon[1] /pon to͞on/ *n* **1 FLOATING SUPPORT FOR BRIDGE** a floating structure used as a support for a bridge across a river, especially one put in place temporarily **2 FLOAT ON AN AIRCRAFT** a float on an aircraft providing buoyancy or stability when on water **3 FLOATING DOCK** a floating structure used as a dock [Late 17C. Via French *ponton* < Latin *ponton-* 'floating bridge' < *pont-*, stem of *pons* 'bridge' (see PONS).]

pontoon[2] /pon to͞on/ *n* **1** a gambling card game in which the aim is to accumulate cards that add up to an exact value of 21. US term **blackjack** *n*. 1 **2** a hand that contains exactly 21 points in the first deal in pontoon. US term **blackjack** *n*. 2 [Early 20C. Probably alteration of French *vingt-et-un* 'twenty-one'.]

pontoon bridge *n* a temporary bridge built across a river, supported by floating structures

Pontormo /pon tórmō/, **Jacopo da** (1494–1557) Italian painter

Pontypool /póntə po͞ol/ town in SE Wales. Population: 35,564 (1991).

Pontypridd /póntə pree͟th/ town in SE Wales. Population: 28,487 (1991).

pony /pṓni/ (*plural* **-nies**) *n* **1 SMALL HORSE** any breed of small horse **2 ANY HORSE** a horse of any kind, especially a racehorse (*informal*) **3 POLO HORSE** a horse used in polo **4 SMALL GLASS** a small drinking glass, especially one used for liqueurs **5 £25** the sum of £25 (*slang*) [Mid-17C. < ?]
pony up *vti US* to pay somebody the money that is owed to him or her (*informal*)

pony express *n* a system of carrying mail using relays of horses and riders that operated in the American West from St Joseph, Missouri, to Sacramento, California, from 1860 to 1861

ponytail /pṓni tayl/ *n* a hairstyle in which long hair is pulled back and tied behind the head so that it hangs down the back like a pony's tail —**ponytailed** *adj*

pony-trekking *n* a leisure activity that involves riding across open countryside on a pony, usually in organized groups

Ponzi scheme /pónzi-/ *n* an investment swindle in which high returns, which are supposedly profits, are made to early investors using funds from later investors [Early 20C. After Charles *Ponzi* (d. 1949).]

poo /poo/ *n* excrement, or an act of defecating (*informal; usually by or to children*) ■ *vti* to excrete faeces (*informal; usually by or to children*) [Variant of POOH]

pooch /pooch/ *n* a dog (*informal*) [Early 20C. < ?]

poodle /po͞od'l/ *n* a dog with a thick curly coat, usually clipped short, belonging either to a small breed (**toy poodle**), or a large breed (**standard poodle**) originally developed in Europe for hunting [Early 19C. < German *Pudel*, shortening of *Pudelhund* < Low German *pudeln* 'splash in water' + German *Hund* 'dog'.]

poodle-faker *n* a man who seeks out the company of women, especially a genteel young man who flatters older women, often for selfish reasons (*dated informal disapproving*) [< the idea that the man resembles a fawning lap dog]

poof[1] /po͝of, poof/, **pouf** *n* an offensive term that deliberately insults a man for being homosexual or for behaving in a way considered to be more characteristic of a woman (*slang*) [Mid-19C. Probably an alteration (influenced by French *pouf* 'women's hairstyle') of PUFF 'powder puff'.]

poof[2] /po͝of, poof/ *interj* (*informal*) **1** used to indicate that something happens suddenly **2** used to express disdain for or dismissal of something

poofter /po͝oftər, po͝oftər/ *n* = **poof**[1] (*slang offensive*) [Early 20C. Alteration of POOF[1].]

poofy /po͝offi, po͝offi/ (**-ier, -iest**) *adj* an offensive term that deliberately insults a man for being homosexual or for being perceived as behaving in a way considered to be more characteristic of a woman (*slang*) [Mid-20C. < POOF[1].]

pooh /poo/ *interj* (*informal*) **1** used to indicate that there is an unpleasant smell **2** used to express disdain or dismissal [Late 16C. An imitation of the sound made by blowing something away with the lips.]

Pooh-Bah /po͞o baa/, **pooh-bah** *n* **1** a pompous self-important official, especially one who holds more than one office but is ineffectual in all of them **2** a leader, high official, or important person [Late 19C. After a character in *The Mikado*, an operetta by W. S. Gilbert and Sir Arthur Sullivan.]

pooh-pooh *vt* to dismiss or express disdain for something [Late 18C. Doubled form of POOH.]

pooka /po͞okə/ *n Ireland* a mischievous spirit in Irish folklore, especially one who takes on the form of an animal [Early 19C. Via Irish *púca* < Old English *pūca* 'puck' (see PUCK).]

pool[1] /pool/ *n* **1 WATER** a small body of still water, usually one that occurs naturally **2 PUDDLE** a small amount of any liquid lying on a surface **3 SWIMMING POOL** a swimming pool or paddling pool **4 DEEP PART OF WATER** a deep place in a river or stream where the water runs more slowly **5 WATER BEHIND DAM** a body of water collected behind a dam **6 PATTERN RESEMBLING A POOL** a pattern or arrangement of something, e.g. light, that resembles a pool of liquid **7 UNDERGROUND OIL OR GAS** an accumulation of oil or gas in a region of porous sedimentary rock ■ *vi* **1 FORM A POOL** to collect in or form a pool **2 ACCUMULATE IN A BODY PART** to collect in a body part or organ (*refers to blood*) [Old English *pōl* < Germanic]

pool[2] /pool/ *n* **1 BALL AND CUE GAME** a game played with a cue ball and 15 balls on a felt-covered table with six pockets **2 FORM OF GAMBLING** a form of gambling in which the participants contribute an amount to a common fund that is divided among the winners **3 TOTAL AMOUNT STAKED** the collective amount that the players in a gambling game have staked **4 COLLECTIVE RESOURCE** a joint supply of vehicles, commodities, or workers that is shared and used by members of a group **5 GROUP OF REPORTERS** a selected group of reporters who cover an event and make their reports available to all participating news organizations **6 INVESTMENT FUND** a collection of investments, e.g. properties in an investment trust, that are managed as a group for a common purpose or group of owners **7 BUSINESS TRUST** an agreement between competing businesses to control production and sales in order to guarantee profits ■ *vt* **SHARE RESOURCES** to combine something to form a supply that can be shared by a group of people or companies [Late 17C. Via French *poule* 'hen, gambling stakes' (hens were used as game prizes) < Latin *pullus* 'young animal' (see PULLET).]

Poole /pool/ port in S England. Population: 140,000 (1995).

pool hall *n US* a commercial establishment where pool is played

poolroom /po͞ol room, -ro͝om/ *n* a room or commercial establishment where pool or billiards is played

pools /poolz/ *npl* an organized form of gambling, conducted mainly by post, that involves predicting the outcome of football matches

poolside /po͞ol sīd/ *n* the area around the sides of a swimming pool (*often before nouns*)

poon /poon/ (*plural* **poons** *or* **poon**) *n* a tree with leathery leaves and strong light wood. Native to: S Asia. Genus: *Calophyllum*. [Late 17C. Via Sinhalese *pūna* < Malayalam *punna* or Tamil *punnai*.]

Poons /poonz/, **Larry** (*b.* 1937) US painter

poop[1] /poop/ *n* **1 RAISED AREA AT SHIP'S REAR** the raised cabins at the stern of an old sailing ship, or the raised area at the stern of a modern ship, lying above the level of the main deck **2** SAILING = **poop deck** ■ *v* **1** *vt* **BREAK OVER STERN** to break over a ship at the stern **2** *vi* **HAVE WAVES BREAKING OVER STERN** to have waves break over its stern, especially repeatedly (*refers to ships*) [15C. Via Old French *pupe* < Latin *puppis* < ?]

poop out *vi* (*slang*) **1** to stop doing something, usually because of exhaustion or fear **2** to stop operating, e.g. because of mechanical failure

poop[2] /poop/ *vt* to make somebody feel exhausted (*informal; usually passive*) ○ *pooped by the long hike* [Mid-20C] —**pooped** *adj*

poop[3] /poop/ *n US* facts or information about something (*slang*) [Mid-20C. < ?]

poop[4] /poop/ *n* excrement, or a stool (*informal; often used by or to children*) ■ *vi* to defecate (*informal; often used by or to children*) [Mid-16C. Originally in the meaning of 'make a short blast of sound'.]

poop deck *n* a raised open deck at the stern of a ship, with cabins below it

pooper-scooper /po͞opər skoopər/ *n* a small shovel used to clean up dog excrement, used especially by a dog owner whose dog defecates in a public place (*informal*)

poo-poo *n* excrement, or the act of defecating (*babytalk*) ■ *vi* to defecate (*babytalk*) [Doubled form of POO]

poor /pawr, poor/ *adj* **1 NOT RICH** lacking money or material possessions **2 AFFECTED BY POVERTY** characterized by widespread, or evident poverty **3 INFERIOR** less than adequate, or below average in quality or condition **4 LACKING SKILL** below average in skill or ability **5 LOW OR INADEQUATE** lower than expected or needed in quantity, number, or amount **6 WEAK** lacking strength, power, stamina, or resilience **7 DEFICIENT** lacking or deficient in something (*often in combination*) **8 LACKING PRODUCTIVE POTENTIAL** lacking fertility or nutrients **9 LOW IN VALUATION** low in a scale of value ○ *has a poor opinion of himself* **10 DESERVING PITY** deserving pity or compassion, especially because of something that has just happened ■ *npl* **PEOPLE WHO ARE POOR** people who lack money or material possessions (+ *plural verb*) ○ *The poor are always with us.* [12C. Via Old French *povre* < Latin *pauper* (see PAUPER).] —**poorness** *n*

poor box *n* a box, especially one kept in a church, that is used to collect money for the poor

poor boy *n US* a sandwich made from a long roll cut horizontally [So called because the sandwich was originally made from discarded scraps and ends, and given to poor people]

poorhouse /páwr howss, po͝or-/ (*plural* **-houses** /-howziz/) *n* a publicly funded institution that formerly existed to house people who were too poor to provide for themselves

Poor Knights Islands /páwr nīts-/ uninhabited island group in the SW Pacific Ocean, lying northeast of New Zealand. Area: 2.7 sq. km/1 sq. mi.

poor law *n* a law or system of laws relating to the provision of support for poor people

poorly /páwrli, po͝orli/ *adv* **1 INADEQUATELY** in an inferior or inadequate way **2 UNFAVOURABLY** with an unfavourable opinion or attitude ■ *adj* **PHYSICALLY UNWELL** feeling physically unwell or in poor physical health (*informal*)

poor mouth *n US, Ireland* complaints about being poor, regarded as made to win sympathy, sometimes when the complainer is not truly poor (*disapproving*)

poor-mouth *vi US, Ireland* to complain of a lack of money, especially when feigning or exaggerating poverty, often in order to win sympathy (*informal disapproving*)

poor rate *n* a tax formerly levied from parishes to raise money for housing and feeding people in need of financial support

poor relation *n* a person or thing that is inferior compared to another

poor white *n US* an offensive term for an uneducated lower-class white person who has an income considerably lower than average (*informal*)

Pooterish /po͞otərish/ *adj* self-importantly genteel or middle-class, especially amusingly so [Mid-20C. After Charles *Pooter*, a character in *Diary of a Nobody* (1892), by George and Weedon Grossmith.]

pootle /po͞ot'l/ (**-tles, -tling, -tled**) *vi* to move at a leisurely pace (*informal*) [Late 20C. Blend of *poodle* 'move at a leisurely pace' and TOOTLE.]

pop[1] /pop/ *n* **1 SUDDEN BURSTING SOUND** a sudden explosive sound, like the sound produced when a balloon bursts or a cork comes out of a bottle **2 FIZZY DRINK** a carbonated drink, usually sweet and flavoured with fruit (*informal*) **3 GUNSHOT** a shot with a firearm **4 ATTEMPT** a try at doing something (*informal*) ■ *v* (**pops, popping, popped**) **1** *vti* **MAKE A BURSTING SOUND** to make, or cause something to make, a sudden explosive sound, like the sound of a cork coming out of a bottle or a balloon bursting **2** *vti* **BURST** to burst, or make something burst, with a sudden explosive sound **3** *vi* **BULGE** to become wide open and seem to bulge out of the sockets (*refers to somebody's eyes*) **4** *vi* **GO BRIEFLY** to go, come, or visit for a brief time (*informal*) ○ *I might pop in later for a chat.* **5** *vt* **OPEN OR CLOSE** to move something quickly and suddenly into an open or closed position (*informal*) **6** *vt* **PUT QUICKLY** to put or place something somewhere with a sudden rapid movement (*informal*) **7** *vt* **TAKE BY SWALLOWING** to take a drug orally (*informal*) **8** *vt* **PAWN** to pawn something (*informal*) ■ *adv* **1 WITH BURSTING NOISE** with a sudden bursting sound **2 UNEXPECTEDLY** suddenly or abruptly ■ *interj* **INDICATING BURSTING NOISE** used to indicate a sudden bursting noise [14C. An imitation of the sound.] ◇ **a pop** for each one (*slang*) ○ *It'll cost you £10 a pop.*

pop off *vi* to die suddenly (*informal*)

pop up *vi* to appear unexpectedly and suddenly

pop[2] /pop/ *n* **1 pop, Pop** a word used to refer to or address your father (*informal*) **2** a word used to address a much older man (*dated slang*) [Mid-19C. Shortening of POPPA.]

pop[3] /pop/ *n* **1** MUSIC = **pop music 2** ARTS = **pop art** ■ *adj* **1** musically commercial, especially by being tuneful, uptempo, and repetitive, and targeted at the general public and the youth market in particular ○ *a pop song* **2** intended for or appreciated by a wide public, and often regarded as oversimplified for the sake of greater accessibility (*informal*) ○ *magazines full of pop psychology* [Late 19C. Shortening of POPULAR.]

POP *abbr* **1** Post Office Preferred (*describes the size of envelopes and packages*) **2** proof of purchase

pop. *abbr* **1** persistent organic pollutant **2** popular **3** population

pop art *n* an art movement of the 1950s to 1970s that incorporated elements of modern popular culture and the mass media

QUICK FACTS ON... **POP ART**

Key dates: mid-1950s–early1970s
Key locations: United Kingdom, United States
Key elements: satire, social criticism; use and reproduction of everyday objects and images from mass media; wide range of materials and forms including collages, photomontages, assemblages
Key figures: Robert Rauschenberg, Jasper Johns, Andy Warhol, Roy Lichtenstein, Claes Oldenburg, Richard Hamilton, Peter Blake, David Hockney
Key works: *Three Flags* (Johns) 1954–55, *Just What Is It That Makes Today's Home So Different, So Appealing?* (Hamilton) 1956, *Monogram* (Rauschenberg) 1955–59, *Campbell's Soup Can* (Warhol) 1962, *Whaam!* (Lichtenstein) 1963
Key developments: op art, kinetic art; photorealism; conceptual art

popcorn /póp kawrn/ *n* **1** the kernels of a variety of maize, heated until they become puffy, then usually flavoured with butter and sugar and eaten as a snack **2** a variety of maize with hard kernels that pop open to form white puffs when heated. *Zea mays praecox.*

pope /pōp/ *n* **1 pope, Pope ROMAN CATHOLIC CHURCH HEAD** the head of the Roman Catholic Church and bishop of Rome **2 pope, Pope COPTIC CHURCH HEAD** the head of the Coptic Church **3 pope, Pope ORTHODOX PRIEST** a priest in the Eastern Orthodox Church **4 POWERFUL PERSON** a person who has great authority or status [Pre-12C. Via Latin < Greek *pappas* 'father'.] —**popedom** *n*

Pope /pōp/, **Alexander** (1688–1744) English poet

popery /pṓpəri/ *n* an offensive term for the Roman Catholic Church, its doctrines, or its practices

pope's nose *n* FOOD = **parson's nose**

popeyed /póp īd/ *adj* **1** with the eyes bulging out **2** with eyes wide open in surprise or disbelief

pop group *n* a small number of musicians who play pop music together as a unit

popgun /póp gun/ *n* **1** a toy gun that uses compressed air to shoot pellets, balls, or a cork tied to a string **2** a useless or unimpressive firearm (*informal*)

popinjay /póppin jay/ *n* a vain and conceited person (*archaic*) [13C. Via Old French *papegay* 'parrot' < Arabic *babbaġā*.]

popish /pṓpish/ *adj* an offensive term meaning associated with the Roman Catholic Church, its doctrines, or its practices —**popishly** *adv*

poplar /pópplər/ *n* **1** a slender tree of the willow family with triangular leaves, flowers in catkins, and soft wood. Native to: northern temperate regions. Genus: *Populus.* **2** TREES = **tulip tree 3** the light-coloured wood of a poplar (*often before nouns*) [14C. Via Anglo-Norman *popler* < Latin *populus.*]

poplin /pópplin/ *n* a plain strong cotton fabric with fine ribbing. Use: clothes, upholstery. (*often before nouns*) [Early 18C. Via obsolete French *papeline* < medieval Latin *papalis* 'papal' (because it was made at the papal town of Avignon) < Latin *papa* (see POPE).]

popliteal /póppli tée əl, po plítti əl/ *adj* relating to or located in the part of the leg behind the knee joint [Late 18C. < modern Latin *popliteus* < Latin *poples* 'ham, back of the knee'.]

pop music *n* modern commercial music, usually tuneful, uptempo and repetitive, that is aimed at the general public and the youth market in particular

Popocatepetl /póppə káttə pet'l/ volcano in south-central Mexico. Height: 5,452 m/17,887 ft.

popover /póp ōvər/ *n* **1** *US* a light hollow muffin-shaped quick bread made from eggs, flour, and milk **2** a simple garment for women or girls that can be slipped over the head

Popover /pop ṓvər/, **Liubov** (1889–1924) Russian painter

poppa /póppə/ *n US* = **papa** *n.* 1 (*informal*) [Late 19C. Alteration.]

poppadom /póppədəm, -dom/, **poppadum** *n* a thin crisp circular Indian bread made from gram flour or flour from pulses and flavoured with spices. Poppadoms are dried and fried in hot fat. [Early 19C. < Tamil *pappaṭam*]

popper /póppər/ *n* **1** CLOTHING = **press stud 2** a small capsule of amyl nitrate or butyl nitrate, prepared as an illicit drug (*slang*)

poppet /póppit/ *n* **1** used to address a sweet and dear person, especially a child (*informal*) **2** ENG = **poppet valve 3** a steel beam or timber that is used to support the front and back ends of a ship when it is launched [14C. < ?]

poppet head *n* the framework at the top of a mineshaft that supports the pulleys for the winding mechanism

poppet valve *n* a valve that is raised and lowered by a vertical guide, e.g. the intake and exhaust valves of the cylinders in an internal-combustion engine

popping crease /pópping-/ *n* the line at which a cricket batsman stands when facing the bowler. It runs parallel to the wicket and lies 1.2 metres/four feet in front of it. [Probably because it originally marked the line that the ball had to cross before it could be struck]

popple[1] /pópp'l/ (**-ples, -pling, -pled**) *vi* to move in an irregular tumbling or bubbling manner, like water does when it boils [14C. Probably < Middle Dutch *popelen* 'to babble, murmur', originally an imitation of the sound.]

popple[2] /pópp'l/ *n* a poplar tree (*informal*) [14C. < Latin *populus.*]

poppy /póppi/ (*plural* **-pies**) *n* **1 PLANT WITH RED FLOWERS** an annual or perennial plant that has cup-shaped seed pods and milky sap. Flowers: large, red, orange, or white. Genus: *Papaver.* **2 PLANT EXTRACT** an extract from the poppy that is used as a narcotic or medicine **3 PLANT LIKE TRUE POPPY** any flowering plant that is similar or related to the poppy, e.g. the California poppy and Welsh poppy **4 ORANGE-RED COLOUR** a bright red colour tinged with orange [Pre-12C. Via assumed Vulgar Latin *papavum* < Latin *papaver.*] —**poppy** *adj*

poppycock /póppi kok/ *n* absurd speech or writing (*dated informal*) [Mid-19C. < Dutch dialect *pappekak* < *pap* 'soft, pap' + *kak* 'dung'.]

Poppy Day *n* = **Remembrance Sunday**

poppyhead /póppi hed/ *n* an ornamental carved top on the end of a pew in a Gothic church

poppy seed *n* the small black seed of the poppy, used in cooking and in baking

pop shop *n* a pawn shop (*informal*) [*Pop* < POP[1] in the sense 'to pawn']

Popsicle /pópsik'l/ *tdmk US* a trademark for a coloured fruit-flavoured ice on one or two sticks

popsock /póp sok/ *n* a woman's short stocking, reaching up to the knee. Popsocks are usually sheer and are often worn under trousers. (*usually plural*)

pop-top *n* **1** *US, Can* **CAN TOP** the top or portion of the top of a can that can be removed by pulling an attached ring **2 VAN ROOF** a van roof that can be raised to create extra headroom while the van is stationary **3** *US, Can* **CAN** a can whose top is opened by pulling an attached ring or tab **4 VAN** a van with a pop-top

populace /póppyŏŏləss/ *n* **1** the inhabitants of a town, region, or other area **2** ordinary people, as distinct from the political elite or the aristocracy [Late 16C. Via French < Italian *popolaccio* 'rabble' < *popolo* 'people' < Latin *populus* (see POPULAR).]

SPELLCHECK Do not confuse ***populace*** with ***populous***, which has a similar sound. Beware: your spellchecker will not catch this error.

popular /póppyŏŏlər/ *adj* **1 APPEALING TO THE GENERAL PUBLIC** appealing to or appreciated by a wide range of people ○ *the most popular name for babies this year* **2 WELL-LIKED** liked by a particular person or group of people ○ *popular with young audiences* **3 OF THE GENERAL PUBLIC** relating to the general public ○ *popular appeal* **4 AIMED AT NONSPECIALISTS** designed to appeal to or be comprehensible to the nonspecialist ○ *a popular gardening magazine* **5 BELIEVED BY PEOPLE IN GENERAL** believed, embraced, or perpetuated by ordinary people ○ *popular myths* **6 INEXPENSIVE** designed to be affordable to people on average incomes ○ *a new popular car* [15C. Via Anglo-Norman *populer* < Latin *popularis* 'of the people' < *populus* 'people' < ?]

popular etymology *n* = **folk etymology** *n.* 2

popular front *n* a broad-based coalition of left-wing political parties, formed to oppose fascism or institute social reforms, especially in Europe in the mid-1930s

popularise *vt* = **popularize**

popularity /póppyŏŏ lárrəti/ *n* **1** admiration, approval, or acceptance of somebody or something by people in general or by a particular group of people **2** desire or demand for something, e.g. a manufactured product

popularize /póppyŏŏlə rīz/ (**-izes, -izing, -ized**), **popularise** (**-ises, -ising, -ised**) *vt* **1** to make something widely liked or appreciated **2** to make something accessible and comprehensible to a wide audience —**popularization** /póppyŏŏlə rī záysh'n/ *n* —**popularizer** *n*

popularly /póppyŏŏlərli/ *adv* **1** by most people or in most situations **2** by the general public, as distinct from specialists

popular music *n* = **pop music**

popular sovereignty *n* the doctrine in the United States that the people are sovereign and a government is subject to the will of the people

populate /póppyŏŏ layt/ (**-lates, -lating, -lated**) *vt* **1** to live in an area, region, or country (*often passive*) **2** to supply an area with inhabitants [Late 16C. < medieval Latin *populat-*, past participle of *populare* < Latin *populus* 'people' (see POPULAR).] —**populated** *adj*

population /póppyŏŏ láysh'n/ *n* **1 PEOPLE IN PLACE** all of the people who inhabit an area, region, or country **2 ALL PEOPLE OF GROUP** all of the people of a particular nationality, ethnic group, religion, or class who live in an area **3 NUMBER OF PEOPLE** the total number of people who inhabit an area, region, or country, or the number of people in a particular group who inhabit an area **4 SUPPLYING WITH INHABITANTS** the populating of an area with inhabitants **5 GROUP STATISTICALLY SAMPLED** the entire group of individuals or items from which a sample may be selected for statistical measurement **6 INDIVIDUALS OF SAME SPECIES** all the plants or animals of a particular species present in a place

populism /póppyŏŏlizəm/ *n* **1** politics or political ideology based on the perceived interests of ordinary people, as opposed to those of a privileged elite **2** focus or emphasis on the lives of ordinary people, e.g. in the arts and in politics [Late 19C. < Latin *populus* 'people' (see POPULAR).]

Populism *n* the political philosophy and programme of the Populist Party of the United States

populist /póppyŏŏlist/ *n* an advocate of the rights and interests of ordinary people, e.g. in politics or the arts ■ *adj* emphasizing or promoting ordinary people, their lives, or their interests [Late 19C. < Latin *populus* 'people' (see POPULAR).]

Populist /póppyŏŏlist/ *n* a political supporter of the Populist Party of the United States ■ *adj* belonging or relating to the Populist Party of the United States

populous /póppyŏŏləss/ *adj* with a large number of inhabitants [15C. < late Latin *populosus* < Latin *populus* 'people' (see POPULAR).] —**populously** *adv* —**populousness** *n*

SPELLCHECK See ***populace***.

ϟ **pop-up** *adj* **1 UPWARD-LIFTING** with a mechanism that makes it or something in it move quickly upwards ○ *pop-up headlights* **2 PRESENTED ON SCREEN TEMPORARILY** appearing quickly and temporarily on a computer screen when a special key is pressed or a button is clicked with a mouse ○ *a pop-up menu* **3 WITH RISING CUT-OUT FIGURES** containing cut-out figures that rise up as a page is opened ○ *a pop-up book* ■ *n* **ITEM WITH POP-UP FIGURES** a book or card that contains pop-up figures, or a pop-up figure

porbeagle /páwr beeg'l/ (*plural* **-gles** *or* **-gle**) *n* a large and voracious shark with a crescent-shaped tail. Native to: North Atlantic. *Lamna nasus*. [Mid-18C. < Cornish *porbugel*.]

porcelain /páwrssəlin, -layn/ *n* **1 CERAMIC MATERIAL** a hard translucent ceramic material used for making plates, cups, and other items (*often before nouns*) **2 ITEMS MADE OF PORCELAIN** objects made of porcelain, e.g. expensive crockery or decorative figurines **3 DECORATIVE OBJECT** a single object made from porcelain, especially a decorative object [Mid-16C. Via French < Italian *porcellana* 'cowrie shell, porcelain' (from its texture), literally 'like a young sow' (from its shape), via *porca* 'sow' < Latin *porcus* 'pig'.] —**porcellaneous** /páwrssə láyni əss/ *adj*

porcelain clay *n* INDUST = **kaolin**

porcelain enamel *n* a glass coating that is fused to a metal by firing

porch /pawrch/ *n* **1** a covered shelter at the entrance to a building **2** *US, Can* a raised platform with a roof that runs along the side of a house, partly enclosed with low walls or fully enclosed with screens or windows [13C. Via Old French < Latin *porticus* 'covered entry' < *porta* 'gate' (see PORT²).]

porcine /páwr sīn/ *adj* relating to or resembling pigs [Mid-17C. Via French < Latin *porcinus* < *porcus* 'pig' (see PORK).]

porcino /pawr seénō/ (*plural* **-ni** /-seéni/), **porcini mushroom** *n* FOOD = **cep** [Late 20C. < Italian, shortening of *fungo porcino* 'porcine mushroom'.]

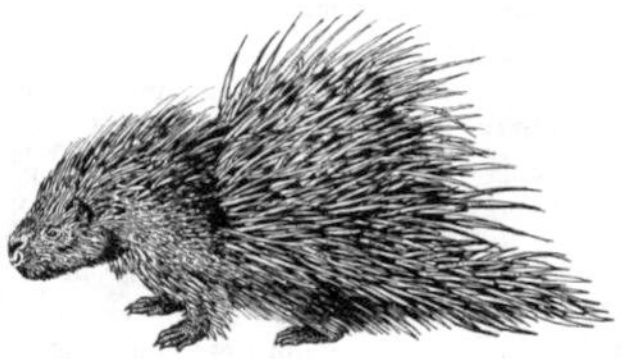

Porcupine

porcupine /páwrkyoo pīn/ *n* a large rodent whose body is covered with long protective quills that it can erect in defence against predators. Families: Hystricidae and Erethizontidae. [14C. < Old French *porc espin* 'spiny pig'.]

Porcupine /páwrkyoo pīn/ river in N Yukon Territory, Canada, and NE Alaska. Length: 721 km/448 mi.

porcupine fish *n* a marine fish with has strong sharp spines covering its body. Native to: tropics. Family: Diodontidae.

porcupine provisions *npl* measures taken by a company to discourage an unwanted takeover

pore[1] /pawr/ *n* **1 TINY OPENING IN SKIN** a tiny opening in human skin, or in the skin or other outer covering of an animal, through which substances can pass **2 TINY OPENING IN PLANT** a tiny opening in a leaf or stem of a plant used to absorb or release substances, e.g. in photosynthesis or respiration **3 SMALL SPACE IN ROCK** a small space that is surrounded by rock or soil [14C. Via Old French and Latin < Greek *poros* 'passage'.]

pore[2] /pawr/ (**pores, poring, pored**) *vi* **1** to study something carefully and thoughtfully ○ *poring over a book* **2** to meditate on or think carefully about something [13C. < ?]

USAGE See ***pour***.

pore fungus *n* any fungus that has spores in tiny tubules that lead to outside pores. Families: Boletaceae and Polyporaceae.

porgy /páwrgi/ (*plural* **-gy** *or* **-gies**) *n* **1 SEA FOOD FISH** a sea food fish that has a deep flat body with large scales. Native to: Mediterranean Sea, Atlantic Ocean. *Pagrus pagrus*. **2 FISH RELATED TO PORGY** a sea fish related to the porgy, with a similarly deep flat body. Family: Sparidae. **3 UNRELATED FISH LIKE PORGY** a fish that is similar to the porgy but unrelated, e.g. the menhaden [Mid-17C. Via Spanish or Portuguese *pargo* < Greek *phagros* 'sea bream'.]

poriferan /paw ríffərən/ *n* MARINE BIOL = **sponge** *n.* 1 (*technical*) ■ *adj* belonging or relating to the sponges [Mid-19C. < modern Latin *Porifera* 'passage-bearing' < Latin *porus* (see PORE¹).]

porin /páwrin/ *n* a ring-shaped protein that spans a membrane in living cells to create a channel for the passage of small molecules [Late 20C. < PORE¹ + -IN.]

pork /pawrk/ *n* **1** the flesh of a pig eaten as food, usually cooked fresh (*often before nouns*) **2** *US* government money and jobs awarded by politicians to their supporters or constituents to win their favour, especially when awarded wastefully (*informal*) [13C. Via Old French < Latin *porcus* 'pig'.]

pork barrel *n US* government-funded projects that bring jobs and other benefits to an area and give its political representative the opportunity to award favours and reap the ensuing prestige (*informal; hyphenated before nouns*)

pork belly *n* a side of fresh pork, commonly traded on the commodities markets, or a cut of meat from this

porker /páwrkər/ *n* **1** a young fattened pig, especially one raised for its meat. ◊ **baconer 2** an overweight person or animal (*informal insult*)

pork pie *n* **1** a round raised pie filled with minced pork and usually eaten cold **2** FOOD = **porky** *n.* (*slang*)

porkpie hat /páwrk pī-/, **porkpie** *n* **1** a man's hat with a flat crown and small brim that can be turned up, first popular in the 1850s **2** a woman's round hat without a brim, first popular in the 1860s [*Porkpie* from its shape]

pork rinds *npl US* = **pork scratchings**

pork scratchings *npl* small pieces of fried pork rind and fat that are eaten as a snack. US term **pork rinds**

porky /páwrki/ *adj* (**porkier, porkiest**) **1 RELATING TO PORK** relating to or resembling pork **2 OVERWEIGHT** overweight (*informal insult*) ■ *n* (*plural* **porkies**) **LIE** a lie (*slang; often plural*) ○ *Who's been telling porkies, then?* [In noun sense < 'pork pie', rhyming slang]

porn /pawrn/, **porno** /páwrnō/ *n* pornography (*informal; often before nouns*) [Mid-20C. Shortening.]

pornographic /páwrnə gráffik/ *adj* **1** sexually explicit and intended to cause sexual arousal **2** producing or selling sexually explicit magazines, films, or other materials —**pornographically** *adv*

pornography /pawr nóggrəfi/ *n* **1** films, magazines, writings, photographs, or other materials that are sexually explicit and intended to cause sexual arousal **2** the production or sale of sexually explicit films, magazines, or other materials [Mid-19C. Via French < Greek *pornographos* 'writing about prostitutes' < *pornē* 'prostitute'.] —**pornographer** *n*

porosity /paw róssəti/ (*plural* **-ties**) *n* **1 POROUS QUALITY** the porous nature of something, or the extent to which something is porous **2 PERCENTAGE OF PORE SPACE** the ratio of the space taken up by the pores in a soil, rock, or other material to its total volume **3 PORE** a pore in soil, rock, or other material (*technical*) [14C. Via French < medieval Latin *porosus* (see POROUS).]

porous /páwrəss/ *adj* **1 WITH PORES** with a surface that contains pores or a body that contains cavities **2 PERMEABLE** permitting the movement of fluids or gases through it by way of pores or other passages **3 BREACHABLE** easy to cross, infiltrate, or penetrate [14C. Via Old French *poreux* < medieval Latin *porosus* < Latin *porus* 'passage' (see PORE¹).] —**porously** *adv* —**porousness** *n*

porphyria /pawr fírri ə/ *n* a medical condition caused by the body's failure to metabolize porphyrins [Early 20C. < PORPHYRIN.]

porphyrin /páwrfərin/ *n* a metal-containing pigment in animal and plant tissue, consisting of four pyrrole rings linked by methylene groups, e.g. haemoglobin [Early 20C. < Greek *porphura* 'purple', from their colour.]

porphyritic /páwrfə ríttik/ *adj* **1** relating to or containing porphyry **2** containing isolated large and distinct crystals in a mainly fine-grained rock

porphyry /páwrfəri/ (*plural* **-ries**) *n* **1** a reddish-purple rock containing large distinct feldspar crystals embedded in a fine-grained groundmass **2** any predominantly fine-grained igneous rock that contains isolated large crystals [14C. Via Old French *porfire* < Greek *porphuritēs* < *porphura* 'purple' (see PURPLE), from its colour.]

porpoise /páwrpəss/ (*plural* **-poise** *or* **-poises**) *n* **1** a toothed sea mammal, related to the whales and dolphins, that has a blunt snout and a triangular dorsal fin. Family: Phocaenidae. **2** a popular but technically inaccurate term for a dolphin [14C. < Old French *porpeis* 'pig-fish' < Latin *porcus* 'pig' (see PORK) + *piscis* 'fish'.]

porridge /pórrij/ *n* **1** a dish made from oatmeal or another cereal cooked with milk or water to form a thick liquid, often eaten at breakfast. US term **oatmeal** *n.* 2 **2** a term of imprisonment (*slang*) [Mid-16C. Alteration of POTTAGE. In the meaning of 'imprisonment' < the idea that porridge is a common prison food, with a punning allusion to *stir* 'prison'.]

porringer /pórrinjər/ *n* a small bowl, usually with a handle, used for soup, stew, or porridge [Early 16C. Alteration of *potinger*, via Old French *potager* < *potage* 'pottage' (see POTTAGE).]

port[1] /pawrt/ *n* **1 HARBOUR** a place by the sea, or by a river or other waterway, where ships and boats can dock, load, and unload **2 TOWN WITH A HARBOUR** a town or city built around a port **3 WATERFRONT** the waterfront area of a port **4 COVE** a sheltered place along a coast, where boats are protected from storms and rough seas **5** GEOG = **port of entry** [Pre-12C. < Latin *portus*.]

ϟ **port**[2] /pawrt/ *n* **1 OPENING IN BOAT** a watertight opening in the side of a boat, used for loading and unloading and as a means of general access to the holds **2** NAUT = **porthole** *n.* 1 **3 GUN HOLE** a small opening in an armoured vehicle, military aircraft, naval vessel, or fortification through which a gun can be fired **4 VALVE-OPERATED OPENING** an opening controlled by a valve, e.g. any of the openings in the cylinder of an internal combustion engine **5 EXTERNAL COMPUTER CONNECTION** an external socket on a computer's main unit (**CPU**) where a peripheral device such as a printer, keyboard, or network cable is plugged in **6** *Scotland* **CITY GATE** a city gate, or the original site of a gate that is no longer there (*often in placenames*) [13C. Via Old French, 'gate' < Latin *porta*.]

port[3] /pawrt/ *n* **LEFT SIDE ON SHIP OR PLANE** the left-hand side of a boat or aeroplane when facing forwards ■ *adj, adv* **ON LEFT** on or to the left-hand side of boat or aeroplane when facing forwards ■ *vti* **TURN TO PORT** to turn towards the port side, or make a ship do this [Mid-16C. Shortening of *port side* < PORT¹, because it was the side that faced the pier and over which cargo was loaded.]

port[4] /pawrt/ *n* a strong sweet fortified wine usually drunk after dinner. It is usually a deep red colour, but some kinds are brownish (**tawny port**) and some white. [Late 17C. After the city of *Oporto* in Portugal.]

port[5] /pawrt/ *vt* to carry a weapon positioned diagonally across the body with the muzzle or blade in front of the left shoulder ■ *n* the position of a rifle or sword when ported [Mid-16C. Via French *porter* 'to carry' < Latin *portare*; see PORT¹.]

ϟ **port**[6] /pawrt/ *vt* to convert software to run on different computer operating systems [Mid-20C. < PORT².]

ϟ **portable** /páwrtəb'l/ *adj* **1 EASILY MOVED ABOUT** designed to be light or compact enough to carry or move easily from place to place **2 EASY TO CONVERT** easily converted to run on different computer operating systems ■ *n* **EASILY TRANSPORTED OBJECT** a device or an appliance that is designed to be easily carried or moved from place to place [14C. Via Old French < late Latin *portabilis* < *portare* 'to carry'.] —**portability** /páwrtə bílləti/ *n* —**portably** *adv*

ϟ **portable document format** *n* full form of **pdf**

Portadown /pàwrtə dówn/ town in central Northern Ireland. Population: 21,299 (1991).

portage /páwrtij, pawr taázh/ *n* **1 ACT OF CARRYING** the carrying or transporting of something **2 CHARGE FOR CARRYING** a charge made for carrying or transporting something **3 CARRYING OF BOATS OVERLAND** the carrying of boats or cargo across land from one waterway to another or around an unnavigable section of a waterway **4 OVERLAND ROUTE TO WATERWAY** an overland route used when transporting a boat or its cargo from one waterway to another ■ *vti* (**-ages, -aging, -aged**) **CARRY SOMETHING OVERLAND TO**

WATERWAY to carry boats or cargo across land from one waterway to another or around an unnavigable portion of a waterway [13C. Via Old French < Latin *portare* 'to carry'.]

Portakabin /páwrtə kabin/ *tdmk* a trademark for a portable building that can be assembled quickly and used for a variety of purposes, e.g. as an office or a schoolroom

portal /páwrt'l/ *n* **1** LARGE GATE a large or elaborate gate or entrance (*literary*) **2** ENTRANCE any entrance to a place, or any means of access to something (*literary*) **3** **portal, portal site** HOME SITE FOR WEB BROWSER a website that provides links to information and other websites ■ *adj* OF PORTAL VEIN OR SYSTEM relating to the portal vein, portal system, or the opening in the liver (**porta**) through which the portal vein passes [14C. Via Old French < Latin *porta* 'gate' (see PORT[1]).]

portal system *n* a network of blood vessels that begin in the capillaries of one organ and end in the capillaries of another, especially the portal veins connecting the liver and intestines

portal vein *n* a vein that carries blood from the digestive organs, gall bladder, and spleen to the liver, especially the vein from the intestines carrying nutrient-rich blood

portamento /páwrtə méntō/ (*plural* **-ti** /-ti/) *n* a smooth glide from one note to another when singing or playing a stringed instrument [Late 18C. < Italian, 'carrying', because the player slides the same finger from one note to the next.]

Port Arthur /-áarthər/ **1** town in S Tasmania, Australia, a former penal colony. Population: 190 (1994). **2** city in SE Texas. Population: 56,827 (1998 estimate). **3** former name for **Lushun**

portative organ /páwrtətiv-/ *n* a small portable organ operated by bellows, used in medieval and Renaissance music

Port Augusta city in SE South Australia. Population: 13,914 (1996).

Port-au-Prince /-ō prínss/ capital of Haiti, in the southwest of the country. Population: 743,000 (1994 estimate).

portcullis /pawrt kúlliss/ *n* a heavy iron or wooden grating that is set in vertical grooves and lowered to block the gateway to a castle or fortification [14C. < Old French *porte coleïce* < *porte* 'door' < Latin *porta* 'gate', + *col(e)ïce*, a form of *couleïs* 'sliding' < Latin *colare* 'to filter'.]

port de bras /páwr də bráa/ *n* the proper movement of the arms in ballet, or exercises for developing this [< French, 'carriage of the arms']

Port du Salut *n* FOOD = **Port-Salut** *n.*

Porte /pawrt/ *n* the court or government of the Ottoman Empire [Early 17C. < French *(la Sublime) Porte* '(the exalted) Gate', translation of the Turkish title of the central office; from the palace gate where justice was administered.]

porte-cochere *n* **1** a large covered entrance for vehicles in a wall or building leading to a courtyard **2** a large roof or awning extending from the entrance of a building to the driveway [Late 17C. < French *porte cochère* 'door for coaches'.]

Port Elizabeth /-i lízzəbəth/ city in SE South Africa. Population: 853,205 (1991).

portend /pawr ténd/ *vt* **1** to be an indication that something, especially something unpleasant, is going to happen (*formal*) **2** to indicate or signify something [15C. < Latin *portendere* 'to stretch forward' < *tendere* (see TENDER[2]).]

portent /páwr tent/ *n* **1** OMEN an indication that something, often something unpleasant, is going to happen **2** SIGNIFICANCE ominous or prophetic significance **3** MARVEL a wonderful or marvellous thing (*formal*) [Late 16C. < Latin *portentum* < *portendere* (see PORTEND).]

portentous /pawr téntəss/ *adj* **1** SIGNIFICANT very serious and significant, especially in terms of future events **2** POMPOUS excessively serious or pompous **3** AMAZING inspiring wonder and amazement —**portentously** *adv* —**portentousness** *n*

porter[1] /páwrtər/ *n* **1** LUGGAGE CARRIER a worker who carries people's luggage, e.g. at an airport or railway station, or in a hotel **2** HOSPITAL EMPLOYEE an employee who moves patients between departments or wards in a hospital **3** *US, Can* TRAIN ATTENDANT an attendant in a train [14C. Via French *porteur* < medieval Latin *portator* 'carrier' < *portare* (see PORT[1]).]

porter[2] /páwrtər/ *n* **1** GATEKEEPER somebody who is in charge of the door or gate of a building or institution **2** COLLEGE RECEPTION PERSON an employee who supervises the main entrance at a university or college, answering inquiries and doing other tasks **3** CARETAKER the caretaker of a building, especially a block of flats, who is responsible for the general maintenance of the building. US term **superintendent** *n.* 3 [13C. Via French *portier* < late Latin *portarius* < Latin *porta* 'gate' (see PORT[1]).]

porter[3] /páwrtər/ *n* a dark sweet beer, similar to light stout, made from malt that has been browned or charred [Early 18C. Shortening of *porter's ale* < PORTER[1]; probably because the beer was drunk mainly by porters.]

Porter /páwrtər/, **Cole** (1891–1964) US composer and lyricist

Porter, Peter (*b.* 1929) Australian-born British poet and critic

Porter, Rodney (1917–85) British biochemist

porterage /páwrtərij/ *n* **1** the work of carrying that is performed by porters **2** a fee charged by porters for carrying things

porterhouse /páwrtər howss/ (*plural* **-houses** /-howziz/) *n* an establishment that sold porter and sometimes also served meals (*archaic*)

porterhouse steak *n* a beef steak from the thick end of the sirloin

portfire /páwrt fīr/ *n* a slow fuse. Use: formerly, explosives in mining and for rockets and fireworks. [Mid-17C. Anglicization of French *porte-feu* 'fire-carrier'.]

portfolio /pawrt fṓli ō/ (*plural* **-os**) *n* **1** FLAT CASE a large flat case for carrying documents, e.g. maps, photographs, or drawings **2** PORTFOLIO CONTENTS the contents of a portfolio, especially as representing somebody's creative work **3** MINISTERIAL RESPONSIBILITIES the post or responsibilities of a cabinet minister, or minister of state **4** GROUP OF INVESTMENTS all the investments held by an individual or organization **5** RANGE OF PRODUCTS the complete range of products or designs offered by a company (*formal*) [Early 18C. < Italian *portafoglio* < *portare* 'to carry' + *foglio* 'sheet, page'.]

portfolio worker *n* an employee who acquires skills and experience in a number of different areas

Port-Gentil /pawr zhaaN teé/ city in W Gabon. Population: 125,000 (1993 estimate).

Port Harcourt /-háarkərt/ city in S Nigeria. Population: 39,970 (1995 estimate).

Porthcawl /pawrth káwl/ town in S Wales. Population: 15,922 (1991).

Port Hedland /-hédlənd/ town in NW Western Australia. Population: 12,846 (1996).

porthole /páwrt hōl/ *n* **1** a small round window with a metal frame in the side of a ship **2** a small opening in a fortified wall through which weapons can be fired

Portia /páwrshə/ *n* a small inner natural satellite of Uranus, discovered in 1986 by the Voyager 2 planetary probe. It is approximately 110 km/68 mi. in diameter.

portico /páwrtikō/ (*plural* **-coes** *or* **-cos**) *n* **1** a covered entrance to a large building **2** a covered walkway, often leading to the main entrance of a building, that consists of a roof supported by pillars [Early 17C. Via Italian < Latin *porticus* < *porta* 'gate' (see PORT[2]).]

portière /páwrti áir/ *n* a heavy curtain hung across a doorway [Mid-19C. < French < *porte* 'door' < Latin *porta* (see PORT[2]).]

portion /páwrsh'n/ *n* **1** FRACTION a part or section of a larger whole **2** HELPING OF FOOD an amount of food for one person **3** INHERITANCE a part of an estate that has been bequeathed to an heir **4** LAW = **dowry** *n.* 1 **5** FATE an unavoidable event or part of somebody's life (*literary*) ■ *vt* **1** DIVIDE to divide something into parts for use **2** ENDOW to give a dowry to a woman (*archaic*) [14C. Via French < Latin *portion-* < ?] —**portionable** *adj* —**portioner** *n*

Port Jackson /-jáks'n/ inlet of the South Pacific Ocean in SE Australia, the harbour of Sydney. Area: 54 sq. km/20 sq. mi.

Portland /páwrtlənd/ **1** city in SW Maine. Population: 62,786 (1998 estimate). **2** city in NW Oregon. Population: 503,891 (1998 estimate).

Portland, Isle of peninsula in S England. Area: 11.5 sq. km/4.5 sq. mi.

Portland cement *n* a cement that hardens under water, made by burning limestone and clay [After *Portland stone*, a stone of a similar colour quarried on the Isle of PORTLAND]

Port Laoise /-leésh/ county town of Laois, central Republic of Ireland. Population: 8,360 (1991).

Port Lincoln town in S South Australia. Population: 11,809 (1991).

Port Louis /-lóō iss, -lóō i/ capital of Mauritius, on the NE coast of the island. Population: 142,850 (1992).

portly /páwrtli/ (**-lier, -liest**) *adj* **1** slightly overweight but dignified **2** having an air of grandeur (*archaic*) [15C. < PORT[5] in the sense 'bearing, manner'.] —**portliness** *n*

Port Macquarie /-mə kwórri/ town in SE New South Wales, Australia. Population: 26,797 (1991).

portmanteau /pawrt mántō/ *n* (*plural* **-teaus** *or* **-teaux** /páwrt mán tōz/) an old type of large leather suitcase, especially one that opened out into two compartments ■ *adj* combining several uses or qualities [Mid-16C. < French *portemanteau* < *porter* 'to carry' + *manteau* 'cloak'.]

portmanteau word *n* a word that combines the sound and meaning of two words, e.g. 'smog', a combination of 'smoke' and 'fog' [< Humpty Dumpty's description (in Lewis Carroll's *Through the Looking Glass*) of the word 'slithy' as a *portmanteau* because 'there are two meanings packed up into one word']

Port Moresby /-máwrzbi/ capital of Papua New Guinea, in S New Guinea. Population: 193,242 (1990).

Porto /páwrt ō/, **Oporto** /ō páwrt ō/ port in NW Portugal. Population: 309,485 (1991).

Porto Alegre /páwrtōō ə légri/ capital of Rio Grande do Sul State, SE Brazil. Population: 1,286,251 (1996).

port of call *n* **1** any port, other than the home port, that a vessel visits on a journey **2** a place visited during a holiday, trip, or excursion (*informal*)

port of entry *n* a place, e.g. a port or an airport, where passengers and goods may enter a country under the supervision of customs officials

Port-of-Spain, Port of Spain capital of Trinidad and Tobago, in NW Trinidad. Population: 63,900 (1993 estimate).

Porto-Novo /páwrt o nṓv ō/ capital of Benin, in the south of the country. Population: 179,000 (1994).

Port Phillip Bay inlet of Bass Strait in SE Australia, the harbour of Melbourne. Area: 2,000 sq. km/800 sq. mi.

Port Pirie /-peéri/ city in SE South Australia. Population: 13,633 (1996).

portrait /páwrtrit, páwr trayt/ *n* **1** PICTURE OF PERSON a painting, photograph, or drawing of somebody, somebody's face, or a related group **2** DESCRIPTION a description of something, e.g. a person, place, or period ■ *adj* TALLER THAN WIDE describes a piece of paper, illustration, book, or page that is taller than it is wide. ◊ **landscape** [Mid-16C. < French < past participle of Old French *portraire* (see PORTRAY).]

LITERARY LINK ***Portrait of a Lady***, a novel (1881) by US writer Henry James. Through the story of Isabel Archer, a young American woman who travels to Europe and is duped into marrying an urbane but materialistic fellow expatriate, the author explores the contrasting characteristics of the Old World (sophisticated but corrupt) and the New (idealistic but naive).

portraitist /páwrtrətist, páwrtritist/ *n* somebody such as a photographer or painter who specializes in portraits

portraiture /páwrtrichər/ *n* **1** MAKING OF PORTRAITS the art or practice of making portraits **2** PORTRAITS portraits considered collectively **3** PORTRAIT a portrait painting, drawing, or photography (*formal*)

portray /pawr tráy/ *vt* **1** DEPICT VISUALLY to depict something, e.g. a person or a scene, in a painting, photograph, drawing, or sculpture **2** DEPICT VERBALLY to represent somebody or something in words **3** PLAY ROLE IN DRAMA to play a character in drama [13C. < Old French *portraire* 'to draw forth' < *traire* 'to draw' < Latin *trahere* (see TRACTION).] —**portrayable** *adj* —**portrayal** *n* —**portrayer** *n*

Port Said /-sīd/ city in NE Egypt. Population: 460,000 (1992).

Port-Salut /páwr sa lóō/, **Port du Salut** /páwr doo sa lóō/ *n* a flat round mild French cheese with an orange rind [Late 19C. After Notre Dame de *Port-du-Salut*, a Trappist monastery in NW France.]

Portsmouth /páwrtsməth/ **1** city in S England. Population: 192,000 (1996). **2** city in SE New Hampshire. Population: 25,388 (1998 estimate).

Port Stanley = **Stanley**

Port Sudan city in NE Sudan. Population: 305,385 (1993).

Port Sunlight village in NW England, created in 1888 to provide accommodation for the workers of the Sunlight soap factory

Port Talbot /-táwlbət, pawr táwlbət/ town in S Wales. Population: 37,647 (1991).

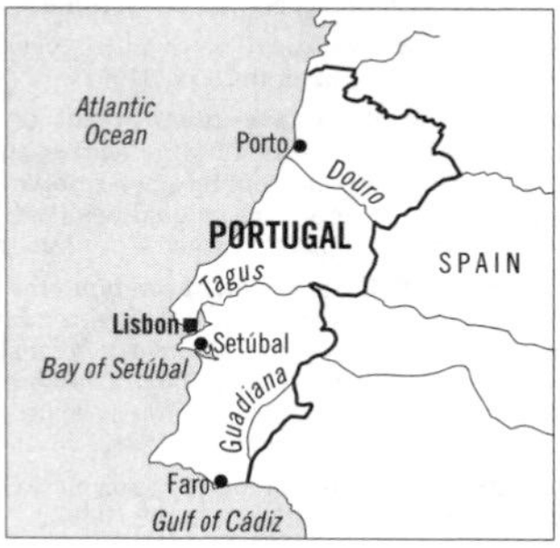

Portugal

Portugal /páwrchoōg'l/ republic in SW Europe, in the W Iberian Peninsula. Capital: Lisbon. Population: 9,865,114 (1996). Area: 92,345 sq. km/35,655 sq. mi.

~~**Portugese**~~ incorrect spelling of **Portuguese**

Portuguese /páwrchoō géez/ *n* **1** the Romance official language of Portugal and Brazil, also an official language in some African countries. Native speakers: 150 million. Other speakers: 30 million. **2** somebody who comes from Portugal [Late 16C. Via Portuguese *português* < medieval Latin *Portus Cale*, the port of Gaya (Oporto).] —**Portuguese** *adj*

Portuguese India territories in western peninsular India formerly ruled by Portugal, including Goa

Portuguese man-of-war *n* a sea organism (**hydrozoan**) resembling a jellyfish, that lives in warm waters, has a transparent gas-filled float, and long stinging, often poisonous, tentacles. Genus: *Physalia*. [< its crest, resembling a sail]

portulaca /pawrtyoō lákə/ *n* a widely cultivated fleshy-leaved plant. Flowers: brightly coloured. Native to: tropical and subtropical America. Genus: *Portulaca*. [Mid-16C. Via Latin, 'purslane' < *portula* 'little gate' < *porta* (see PORT²); from the covering of the seed capsule, that resembles a gate.]

port-wine stain *n* a conspicuous purplish birthmark, especially on the face or neck

POS *abbr* point of sale

posada /pō saádə/ *n* a hotel, pension, or hostel in a Spanish-speaking country [Mid-18C. < Spanish < *posar* 'to stay, lodge', via late Latin *pausare* < Latin *pausa* 'rest' (see PAUSE).]

pose¹ /pōz/ *v* (**poses, posing, posed**) **1** *vti* **ADOPT POSTURE** to adopt a particular physical posture for a photograph or painting, or position somebody or something for this purpose **2** *vi* **IMPERSONATE** to pretend to be somebody or something else ○ *got past the security guards by posing as a journalist* **3** *vt* **PRESENT** to be the cause of something, e.g. a problem, threat, danger, or challenge ○ *a breakdown of negotiations that poses a threat to peace* **4** *vt* **ASK** to ask a question, often one that requires some consideration **5** *vi* **BE PRETENTIOUS** to behave, dress, or assume a mental attitude intended to impress others (*disapproving*) ■ *n* **1 POSTURE** a particular physical posture, e.g. one adopted for a painting or photograph **2 PRETENCE** a way of behaving or dressing calculated to impress others (*disapproving*) ○ *His sudden interest in opera is just a pose.* [14C. Via Old French *poser* < late Latin *pausare* 'to rest, cease' < *pausa* (see PAUSE).]

pose² /pōz/ (**poses, posing, posed**) *vt* to confuse or baffle somebody (*archaic*) [Early 16C. Partly shortening of *appose* (variant of OPPOSE), and partly < Old French *poser* 'to assume'.]

Poseidon¹ /pə sīd'n/ *n* in Greek mythology, the god of the sea, water, earthquakes, and horses, the son of Cronus and brother of Zeus. Roman equivalent **Neptune**

Poseidon² *n* a US ballistic missile capable of being launched from a submarine and carrying a nuclear warhead

poser¹ /pózər/ *n* **1** a person who poses for a photograph or work of art **2** a poseur (*informal disapproving*) [Late 19C. < POSE¹.]

poser² /pózər/ *n* a difficult question or problem [Late 16C. < POSE².]

~~**posess**~~ incorrect spelling of **possess**

~~**posession**~~ incorrect spelling of **possession**

poseur /pō zúr/ *n* a person who tries to impress others in an affected or assumed way (*disapproving*) [Late 19C. < French < *poser* 'pose' (see POSE¹).]

posey /pózi/ (**-ier, -iest**) *adj* trying to impress others in an affected and insincere way (*disapproving informal*)

posh /posh/ *adj* (*informal*) **1 FOR THE WELL-OFF** elegant, fashionable, and expensive **2 UPPER-CLASS** from, imitative of, or characteristic of the upper classes ■ *adv* **LIKE AN UPPER CLASS PERSON** like somebody from the upper classes (*informal*) ○ *She talks posh on the phone to try to impress people.* [Early 20C. < ?] —**poshly** *adv* —**poshness** *n*

posit /pózzit/ *vt* (*formal*) **1 PUT SOMETHING FORWARD** to put something forward for consideration, e.g. a suggestion, assumption, or fact **2 POSITION** to place something firmly in position ■ *n* **SOMETHING PUT FORWARD** a fact, assumption, or suggestion for consideration (*formal*) [Mid-17C. < Latin *posit-*, past participle of *ponere* 'to place' (see POSITION).]

positif /póssitif/ *n* a manual that controls the softer stops on a church organ [Via Old French, 'positive organ' < Latin *positivus* (see POSITIVE)]

position /pə zísh'n/ *n* **1 LOCATION** the place where somebody or something is, especially in relation to other things ○ *confirm their position and direction by radio* **2 POSTURE** the posture that somebody's body is in ○ *The accident victim had been placed in the recovery position.* **3 ARRANGEMENT** the way or direction in which an object is placed or arranged ○ *the position of the hour hand* **4 SITUATION** a particular set of circumstances ○ *I wouldn't sell just yet if I were in your position.* **5 RANK** somebody's standing or level of importance in society or an organization ○ *In her position she should set an example for others.* **6 POST** a job or post in a company or organization ○ *the position of marketing manager* **7 VIEW** a policy, view, or opinion, especially an official one ○ *What's your position on the euro?* **8 CORRECT PLACE** the correct or usual place or arrangement of an object or person ○ *Once the dignitaries are in position, the ceremony can start.* **9 STRATEGIC PLACE** a strategic area or point that is occupied by military personnel or where weapons are placed ○ *The enemy took up positions on a hill overlooking the fort.* **10 PLACE IN ORDER** the place a person, team, or organization occupies in a race, contest, or list ○ *The liberals were squeezed into third position by the two main parties.* **11 ROLE IN TEAM** the part of a playing area where a player is based and usually plays ○ *The substitute took up a midfield position.* **12 ARRANGEMENT OF PIECES** the arrangement of the pieces or counters in a board game, e.g. chess or backgammon, at a given time **13 SEXUAL POSTURE** the posture used by a couple in sexual intercourse **14 DEALER'S RESPONSIBILITY** a dealer's commitment to buy or sell a particular number of securities or commodities **15 INVESTOR'S VULNERABILITY** an investor's status based on holdings with regard to market trends **16 HAND PLACEMENT** the placement of the fingers on a keyboard or string instrument **17 DEGREE OF EXTENSION OF TROMBONE SLIDE** the extent to which a trombone slide is pushed out **18 ARRANGEMENT OF NOTES IN CHORD** the arrangement of individual notes within a chord **19 VOWEL TYPE IN CLASSICAL POETRY** a short vowel counting as a long vowel in classical poetry because it comes before two or more consonants ■ *vt* **1 PUT SOMETHING IN PLACE** to put something in a particular or suitable place ○ *Position the two pieces so that they are at right angles.* **2 PLACE** to place somebody or yourself in a particular or suitable area, place, or situation ○ *This strategy will position us advantageously in the market.* **3 LOCATE** to determine the site or location of something ○ *Air traffic controllers have positioned the unknown aircraft at 50 miles north of the airport.* [14C. Via French < Latin *posit-*, past participle of *ponere* 'to place'.] —**positional** *adj* —**positionally** *adv* —**positioner** *n*

position audit *n* an assessment of a company's or organization's commercial standing carried out to help future planning

position effect *n* a change in a gene's expression depending on its location on the chromosome relative to other genes

position paper *n* an in-depth report on a particular matter that gives the official view and recommendations of a government or organization

positive /pózzətiv/ *adj* **1 OPTIMISTIC** confident, optimistic, and focusing on the good things rather than bad ○ *a positive attitude about work* **2 SURE** certain and not in doubt ○ *'Are you sure that's what you want to do?' 'Yes, I'm positive'.* **3 IRREFUTABLE** conclusive and beyond doubt or question ○ *positive identification of the suspect* **4 BENEFICIAL** producing good results because of having an innately beneficial character ○ *It was a positive experience.* **5 AFFIRMATIVE** indicating agreement or affirmation ○ *got some positive feedback from the survey* **6 QUANTIFIABLE** capable of being measured, detected, or perceived ○ *a positive correlation between investment in telecommunications and economic development* **7 INDICATING PRESENCE OF SOMETHING IN TEST** indicating the presence or existence of a particular organism, illness, or condition in the results of a test or examination ○ *a positive test for diabetes* **8** MED = **Rh positive** **9 ENCOURAGING GOOD BEHAVIOUR** encouraging behaviour, especially in the young, that is considered morally good ○ *a positive role model* **10 ADDING EMPHASIS** used to emphasize the degree to which something is true, striking, or impressive (*informal*) ○ *Hiring her is a positive triumph for the department.* **11 MORE THAN ZERO** (*symbol* +) with a value higher than zero **12 NOT NEGATIVE** measured in a direction or designated as a quantity equal in magnitude but opposite to that regarded as negative **13 EMPIRICAL** relating to the theory that knowledge can be acquired only through direct observation and experimentation rather than metaphysics and theology **14 SHOWING RESPONSE** indicating growth, response, or movement towards a stimulus, e.g. light **15 WITH ELECTRICAL CHARGE LIKE A PROTON** with an electrical charge of an opposite polarity to an electron's and the same polarity as a proton's **16 WITH POSITIVE CHARGE** with an overall positive electrical charge, sometimes caused by the loss of one or more electrons **17 WITH HIGHER ELECTRICAL POTENTIAL** with a higher electrical potential than the earth or the defined neutral point ○ *a positive electrode* **18** ELEC = **electropositive** *adj.* 1 **19 LIKE THE SUBJECT** describes photographic images that have colours or values of dark and light corresponding to the subject **20 MAKING LIGHT CONVERGE** making a parallel beam of light converge **21 NOT COMPARATIVE OR SUPERLATIVE** relating to the basic form of an adjective or adverb, rather than its comparative or superlative forms **22 MECHANICAL ACTION WITH NO SLACK** describes a mechanical action or device having little or no play **23 OF CERTAIN ZODIAC SIGNS** relating to the air and fire signs of the zodiac ■ *n* **1 POSITIVE THING** something that shows agreement, support, or affirmation (*informal*) ○ *Not a bad situation when we weigh up all the positives.* **2 SOMETHING GREATER THAN ZERO** a value or number higher than zero **3 IMAGE LIKE THE SUBJECT** a photographic image in which the light and dark tones and colours correspond to those of the original subject **4 SOMETHING WITH POSITIVE CHARGE** something that carries a positive electrical charge **5 CELL PLATE OR TERMINAL** a positively charged plate or terminal in a cell **6 BASIC FORM OF MODIFIER** an adjective or adverb in its basic form rather than the comparative or superlative **7 MEDIEVAL ORGAN** a small medieval organ with just one manual and no pedals **8** MUSIC = **positif** [14C. Via French < Latin *positivus* < *posit-*, past participle of *ponere* (see POSITION); the underlying meaning is 'firmly set down'.] —**positiveness** *n* —**positivity** /pózzə tívvəti/ *n*

positive discrimination *n* the practice of setting aside training or employment resources or positions for members of disadvantaged groups such as racial minorities, people with disabilities, or women. US term **affirmative action**

positively /pózzətivli/ *adv* **1 ENCOURAGINGLY** in an encouraging, supportive, or optimistic way **2 FOR ADDING EMPHASIS** used to emphasize an often already emphatic quality, characteristic, or action ○ *looking positively radiant* **3 DEFINITELY** used to emphasize the finality or extremity of a statement or response

positive prescription *n* LAW = **prescription** *n.* 7

positive vetting *n* the practice of investigating somebody's background and personal life in order to determine suitability for sensitive or confidential work, especially work involving matters of national security

positivism /pózzətivizəm/ *n* **1** the theory that knowledge can be acquired only through direct observation and experimentation rather than through metaphysics and theology **2** the state or quality of being positive — **positivist** *n, adj* —**positivistic** /pózzəti vístik/ *adj* —**positivistically** /-vístikli/ *adv*

positron /pózzi tron/ *n* an elementary particle of antimatter that has the same mass as an electron but the opposite electrical charge [Mid-20C. < POSITIVE + ELECTRON.]

positron emission tomography *n* a method of medical imaging capable of displaying the metabolic activity of organs in the body, and useful in diagnosing cancer, locating brain tumours, and investigating other brain disorders

positronium /pózzi trṓni əm/ *n* a combination of a positron and an electron that rapidly decays to produce two or three photons

posology /pə sólləji/ *n* the study of the dosage of medicines [Early 19C. < French *posologie* < Greek *posos* 'how much'.] —**posological** /póssə lójjik'l/ *adj*

posse /póssi/ *n* **1** *US* **SHERIFF'S HELPERS** a group of able-bodied citizens that a sheriff can call upon to assist in maintaining law and order **2 ASSEMBLED GROUP** a group of people assembled for a common purpose (*informal*) **3 STREET GANG** a group of youths who hang around together and have a leader (*slang*) [Mid-17C. Shortening of *posse comitatus* < medieval Latin, 'force of the county'.]

possess /pə zéss/ *vt* **1 OWN** to have or own something **2 HAVE AS AN ABILITY** to have a particular ability, quality, or characteristic **3 HAVE KNOWLEDGE OF** to have or acquire skill or knowledge of something **4 TAKE CONTROL** to take control of or influence somebody, affecting the person's behaviour or thinking ○ *possessed by fear and unable to speak* **5 INFLUENCE** to cause somebody to be influenced or controlled by something, especially an emotion ○ *The news possessed us with foreboding.* **6 CONTROL FEELING** to control yourself or a feeling in a particular situation (*formal*) **7 HAVE SEX** to have sex with somebody (*dated; sometimes offensive*) **8 SEIZE** to gain or seize something (*archaic*) [14C. Via Old French *possesser* < Latin *possess-*, past participle of *possidere* 'to sit on as head of' < *sedere*.] — **possessor** *n*

possessed /pə zést/ *adj* **1 OWNING** being the owner of something ○ *an only child possessed of a great fortune* **2 HAVING QUALITY** having as a quality, characteristic, or belief (*literary*) **3 CONTROLLED** controlled or strongly influenced, especially by a supposed evil supernatural force or a strong emotion ○ *screaming and shouting like a man possessed* **4** = **self-possessed**

possession /pə zésh'n/ *n* **1 OWNERSHIP** the act or state of owning or holding something ○ *You can take possession of the house on Friday.* **2 SOMETHING OWNED** something owned or held **3 COLONY** a country or region controlled or governed by another country (*often plural*) **4 STATE OF BEING CONTROLLED** the condition of being controlled by or appearing to be controlled by a supernatural force or strong emotion **5 OCCUPANCY** the physical occupancy of something, e.g. a house, whether or not accompanied by ownership **6 HAVING SOMETHING ILLEGAL** the crime of having or owning something illegal, e.g. a weapon, contraband, stolen property, or illegal drugs **7 CONTROL OF A BALL** control of the ball or puck in various sports ■ **possessions** *npl* **PERSONAL PROPERTY** personal property and wealth —**possessional** *adj*

possession order *n* a court order authorizing somebody to take possession of or recover property

possessive /pə zéssiv/ *adj* **1 DEMANDING EXCLUSIVITY** wishing to control somebody exclusively or to be the sole object of somebody's love **2 SELFISH** tending not to share possessions with others **3 OF OWNERSHIP** relating to ownership ○ *possessive pride* **4 SHOWING OWNERSHIP IN GRAMMATICAL TERMS** indicating grammatical ownership, e.g. in pronouns such as 'his' or 'her' ■ *n* **1 WORD SHOWING OWNERSHIP** a noun, pronoun, determiner, or form of a word that indicates ownership or association **2 POSSESSIVE CASE** the possessive or genitive case —**possessively** *adv* —**possessiveness** *n*

USAGE Possessives The possessive case indicates ownership. In English, the possessive form of singular nouns is indicated by adding an apostrophe + *s* to the end of the nouns: *my sister's car.* This rule applies even when the noun ends in an *s*: *the boss's desk*, although an apostrophe without an *s* is also possible, especially after names: *Charles' birthday.* For plural nouns ending in an *s*, the possessive is formed by adding an apostrophe after the *s*: *our soldiers' duty.* Plural nouns not ending in an *s* are treated like singular nouns: *the children's toys*; *men's socks.* The other main way of expressing possession in English is to use the preposition *of*: *the restaurants of Paris.* With people (including groups of people) and animals, it is standard to use the possessive form of the noun: *Bob's socks*; *the team's recent record*; *the elephant's trunk.* For things, it is standard to use *of*: *the door of the church.* With places, we can use either the apostrophe + *s* or *of*: *London's historic buildings* or *the historic buildings of London.* These are only general guidelines though, and many fixed phrases behave differently: *for pity's sake* and *the sins of the fathers.* In the so-called *double genitive* (known technically as the *post-genitive*), the apostrophe + *s* (or a possessive pronoun like *yours*) and the *of* construction are combined: *a friend of John's.* It can only be used with nouns, or pronouns, referring to people: *a song of Gershwin's*; *that brother of yours.* English has possessive adjectives and possessive pronouns. The adjectives come in front of a noun: *our country*; *his friends.* The pronouns are generally the subject, object, or complement of a verb: *That pen is mine. Yours is on the desk.* Note that possessive pronouns do not contain an apostrophe: *It is hers/theirs* [not *her's/their's*]. Remember that *it's* means 'it is': *The car will not run because its* [not *it's*] *battery is dead.*

PUNCTUATION See ***apostrophe***.

USAGE See ***its***.

possessory /pə zéssəri/ *adj* **1** relating to possession or a possessor (*formal*) **2** arising from or depending on possession

posset /póssit/ *n* a drink made from hot milk curdled with beer or wine and flavoured with spices, formerly drunk as a remedy for colds ■ *vi* to regurgitate milk (*refers to babies*) [15C. < ?]

possibility /póssə bílləti/ *n* (*plural* **-ties**) **1 SOMETHING POSSIBLE** something that is possible **2 STATE OF BEING POSSIBLE** the condition or quality of being possible **3 CONTENDER** a possible winner, choice, or candidate ■ **possibilities** *npl* **POTENTIAL** the potential for successful future development ○ *The house needs a lot of work, but it's got possibilities*

possible /póssəb'l/ *adj* **1 LIKELY TO HAPPEN** capable of happening or likely to happen in the future **2 MAYBE REAL OR TRUE** capable of being real, present, or true **3 CAPABLE OF HAPPENING BUT UNLIKELY** theoretically capable of being done, of happening, or of existing, although difficult or unlikely in practice **4 POTENTIAL** having potential as a particular thing or for a particular purpose **5 PROPER** in keeping with convention, decorum, or tradition ■ *n* **POSSIBILITY** a person or thing that is a possibility [14C. Via French < Latin *possibilis* < *posse* 'to be able' (see POTENT[1]).]

possibly /póssəbli/ *adv* **1 PERHAPS** likely, or maybe so, but not known for certain **2 AS A POSSIBILITY** as something that is possible or may be realized **3 ADDING EMPHASIS** used to express shock, disbelief, or amazement ○ *How could you possibly have believed that?* **4 SUGGESTING EFFORT** used to indicate the magnitude of effort or difficulty **5 SUGGESTING IMPOSSIBILITY** used in negative sentences and phrases to emphasize that something cannot be done or cannot happen **6 USED AS REQUEST MODIFIER** used with requests to suggest the speaker's awareness of an imposition ○ *Could you possibly post this letter for me on your way to the station?*

POSSLQ *abbr* person of the opposite sex sharing living quarters (*informal*)

possum /póssəm/ *n* **1** *US* an opossum (*informal*) **2** *ANZ* ZOOL = **phalanger** [Early 17C. Shortening.] ◇ **play possum** to feign death, illness, or sleep, or pretend to be uninvolved in something, in order to protect yourself

⚡**post**[1] /pōst/ *n* **1 UPRIGHT POLE** a pole of wood or metal fixed in the ground in an upright position, serving as a support, marker, or place for attaching things **2 UPRIGHT FRAME PART** a vertical piece in a building frame that supports a beam **3 RACECOURSE INDICATOR** either of two upright poles marking the starting point and finishing line on a racecourse **4 GOALPOST** a goalpost (*informal*) **5 FURNITURE SUPPORT** any of the upright supports of a piece of furniture such as a chair or a four-poster bed **6 EARRING PART** a metal stem on a pierced earring that passes through the ear, and fits into a cap at the back **7** ONLINE = **posting**[1] *n.* 1 ■ *vt* **1 DISPLAY** to display something, e.g. an announcement, name, or result, in a public place **2 PUBLISH ELECTRONICALLY** to make text appear online or at an Internet location **3 GIVE NOTICE OF MARRIAGE** to announce a forthcoming marriage in a church ○ *post the banns* **4 NAME SHIP** to publish the name of a ship presumed lost or sunk [Pre-12C. < Latin *postis* 'something that stands in front' < Indo-European, 'to stand'.] ◇ **pip somebody at the post** to beat somebody in the very final stages of something

⚡**post**[2] /pōst/ *n* **1 POSTAL SERVICE** the official system for collecting, delivering, and sending letters and parcels from one place to another ○ *I'll send the contract to you by post.* **2 LETTERS AND PARCELS** letters and parcels that have been sent or are to be sent through the postal system ○ *Is there any post for me today?* **3 LETTER COLLECTION TIME** the time when letters and parcels are collected from a post box or delivered ○ *If you rush you'll catch the last post.* **4 STATION ON ROUTE** any of a series of stations along a route where mounted messengers or couriers rest and change horses **5 MAIL DELIVERER** a rider who, in the past, covered the distance from one post to the next in a delivery system ■ *v* **1** *vi* **KEEP RHYTHM WITH HORSE** to bob up and down in the saddle in time with a horse's trot **2** *vt* **UPDATE DATABASE** to update a database record by entering or transferring information **3** *vti* **SEND MESSAGE ELECTRONICALLY** to place or send a message on a newsgroup or bulletin board on the Internet or some other electronic network **4** *vi* **TRAVEL BY POST** to travel using relays of horses **5** *vi* **TRAVEL FAST** to travel in haste (*archaic*) **6** *vt* **SEND LETTER** to send a letter or parcel through the postal system. ◊ **mail**[1] *v.* **7** *vt* **WRITE IN LEDGER** to enter a transaction in a ledger ■ *adv* **QUICKLY** quickly (*archaic*) [Early 16C. Via French, 'relay station' < Latin *posita*, feminine past participle of *ponere* (see POSITION).] ◇ **keep somebody posted** to keep somebody informed by supplying new information regularly

post[3] /pōst/ *n* **1 EMPLOYMENT SITUATION** a position of employment **2 WORKPLACE OR STATION** a place where somebody has particular responsibilities **3 MILITARY BASE** a place where a military operation is carried out **4 BUGLE CALL** in the British army, either of two evening bugle calls given as a signal for army personnel to retire to their quarters **5** COMM = **trading post** *n.* 1 ■ *vt* **1 SEND SOMEBODY TO WORK** to assign somebody to a particular position for a period of duty ○ *post a security guard at the exit* **2 SEND SOMEBODY AWAY TO WORK** to send somebody somewhere, often abroad, to do a particular job for a specific period of time ○ *After she qualified, she was posted to South America for two years.* **3 TRANSFER SOLDIER** to send somebody to a new military assignment or unit **4** *US* **PAY TO SET FREE** to pay somebody's bond or bail [Mid-16C. Via French *poste* < Latin *positum* < past participle of *ponere* 'to place' (see POSITION).]

post[4] /pōst/ *n* a postmortem examination of a corpse (*informal*)

⚡**POST** /pōst/ *abbr* **1** point-of-sale terminal **2** Power On Self-Test

post- *prefix* **1** after, later ○ *postwar* **2** behind ○ *postorbital* [< Latin *post* < Indo-European, 'off, away']

postage /pṓstij/ *n* the amount of money paid for the delivery of a piece of mail

postage due stamp *n* a stamp on a letter indicating that the postage charge has not been fully paid

postage meter *n US* MAIL = **franking machine**

postage stamp *n* **1 GUMMED POSTAGE MARKER** an illustrated paper stamp affixed to letters and parcels to show payment of postage **2 PRINTED MARK** a printed mark or impression on an envelope indicating that the postage charge has been paid ■ *adj* **TINY** unusually small (*hyphenated before nouns*)

postal /pṓst'l/ *adj* relating to a post office or the delivery of post —**postally** *adv*

postal card *n US* a plain postcard with prepaid postage, sold by post offices

postal code *n UK, Can* = **postcode**

postal money order *n US* = **postal order**

postal order *n* a voucher for a sum of money, payable to a named person, that can be bought at the Post Office.

postal vote *n* a vote that is posted instead of made in person, usually because the voter cannot get to the polling station. US term **absentee ballot**

post-and-rail fence *n* a fence of horizontal timbers threaded between upright posts

postbag /pṓst bag/ *n* **1** a bag or satchel used to carry mail by the person who delivers it. US term **mailbag** *n.* 2 **2** the mail received by an MP, a famous person, or television or radio programme on a particular subject. US term **mailbag** *n.* 3

post-bellum /pṓst bélləm/, **postbellum** *adj* relating to or during the period after a war, especially the American Civil War [< Latin *post bellum* 'after the war']

post-boost phase *n* the last phase of a multistage missile's flight, when it releases its payload

postbox /pōst boks/ *n UK* a box in a public place where letters can be posted for collection. US term **mailbox** *n.* 1

postcard /pōst kaard/, **post card** *n* a card used to carry a message, usually with a picture or a photograph on one side, that can be sent through the postal system without an envelope. ◊ **picture postcard**

post chaise *n* a closed horse-drawn carriage with four wheels that was used in the 18th and 19th centuries as a fast means of transporting mail and passengers [< POST2]

postclassical /pōst klássik'l/ *adj* relating to or occurring after what is regarded as the classical period in a civilization, art, or language, especially after the classical period in ancient Greek and Roman culture

postcode /pōst kōd/ *n* a group of letters and numbers added at the end of an address that helps to speed delivery. US term **ZIP code**

postcode lottery *n* an unequal or inconsistent distribution of a public service such as health care across different areas of the United Kingdom

postdate /pōst dáyt/ (**-dates, -dating, -dated**) *vt* **1 DATE A CHEQUE LATER** to put a date on a cheque later than the current day's date in order to delay payment **2 HAPPEN LATER** to happen or be at a later date than something **3 ASSIGN LATER DATE** to assign a date to something, e.g. an event in history, that is later than the one previously assigned

postdoc /pōst dok/ *n* a postdoctoral grant, fellowship, or scholar (*slang*) ■ *adj* relating to postdoctoral work or students (*slang*) [Late 20C. Shortening.]

postdoctoral /pōst dóktərəl/ *adj* relating to academic work or research done after a doctorate has been awarded

ϟ **poster** /pōstər/ *n* **1 PRINTED PICTURE** a printed picture, often a reproduction of a photograph or artwork, used for decoration **2 ADVERTISEMENT** a bill or placard in a public place advertising something **3 SENDER** a sender of a message to an online or Internet address

poster child *n* **1** a person or thing appearing as a representative or illustrative example of something (*sometimes offensive*) **2** *US* somebody, especially a child, chosen to represent a charitable or other cause by appearing in promotional material

poste restante /pōst ri stánt/ *n* **1** a department of a post office where mail is held for people until they collect it. US term **general delivery** *n.* 1 **2** an address on an item of mail indicating that it should be held at a post office until collection by the addressee. US term **general delivery** *n.* 2 [< French, 'mail remaining' (at the post office)]

posterior /po stéeri ər/ *adj* **1 BEHIND** situated at the rear or behind something **2 NEAR THE BACK** situated near or towards the back of a human being's or animal's body **3 NEAREST THE STEM** nearest the main stem or axis of a plant ○ *the posterior flower* **4 COMING AFTER** coming after something in an order or series (*formal*) **5 SUBSEQUENT** following something in time (*formal*) ■ *n* **BUTTOCKS** the buttocks (*humorous*) [Early 16C. < Latin, 'coming farther after' < *posterus* 'coming after' < *post* (see POST-).] —**posteriorly** *adv*

posterity /po stérrəti/ *n* (*formal*) **1** all future generations **2** all of somebody's descendants [14C. Via French *postérité* < Latin *posteritas* < *posterus* (see POSTERIOR).]

postern /póstərn/ *n* a small gate or entrance at the back of a building, especially a castle or a fort [13C. Via Old French *posterne* < late Latin *posterula* 'small back door' < Latin *posterus* (see POSTERIOR).]

poster paint *n* paint made from pigment mixed with water-soluble gum that is often used for painting posters and by children

post exchange *n US* a shop on a US military camp selling food, clothes, and other things

postfeminist /pōst fémminist/ *adj* **1 REFLECTING FEMINISM** developing out of or including the principles of feminism **2 GOING BEYOND FEMINISM** differing from or showing a re-evaluation of the principles of feminism **3 AFTER FEMINISM** occurring or having developed after the feminist movement of the 1970s (*offensive in some contexts*) ■ *n* **SUPPORTER OF POSTFEMINIST IDEAS** a supporter of or believer in postfeminist ideas —**postfeminism** *n*

postfix *vt* /pōst fíks/ to add a letter or group of letters to the end of a word (*formal*) ■ *n* /pōst fiks/ a suffix [Late 20C. After PREFIX.] —**postfixal** /pōst fíks'l/ *adj*

post-free *adj* = **postpaid**

post-genitive /pōst jénnətiv/ *n* a double possessive construction in which 'of' and an apostrophe + 's' are both used, e.g. a letter of Sam's

postglacial /pōst gláyssi əl/ *adj* occurring after a glacial period, especially one during the Quaternary Period

postgraduate /pōst gráddyoo ət/, **postgrad** *informal adj* relating to academic study after graduation from a university or college or to students who have graduated. US term **graduate** *adj.* ■ *n* somebody who has graduated from a university or college with a first degree, especially one who is doing further study

Postgraduate Certificate of Education *n* full form of **PGCE**

post-haste /pōst háyst/ *adv* as quickly as possible [Mid-16C. < *haste, post, haste*, an instruction on letters.]

post hoc /-hók/ *n* the fallacy of arguing that since one event happened before a second, the first caused the second [Mid-19C. < Latin, 'after this', referring to the fallacy *post hoc, ergo propter hoc* 'after this, therefore because of this'.]

post horn *n* a simple, usually valveless horn, formerly used to announce the arrival of a mailcoach [< POST2]

post horse *n* a horse that used to be kept at inns or post houses for use by postriders or for hire by travellers

post house *n* an inn where post horses were formerly kept

posthumous /póstyoōməss/ *adj* **1 AFTER SOMEBODY'S DEATH** occurring after somebody's death **2 PUBLISHED AFTER DEATH** published or printed after the author's death **3 BORN AFTER FATHER'S DEATH** born after the death of the father ○ *a posthumous heir* [Early 17C. < late Latin *posthumus*, alteration of Latin *postumus* 'last' (from *posterus*; see POSTERIOR), under the influence of *humare* 'to bury'.] —**posthumously** *adv* —**posthumousness** *n*

posthypnotic suggestion /pōst hip nóttik-/ *n* a suggestion made to somebody under hypnosis that is to be acted upon at a later time after the period of hypnosis is over

postie /pósti/ *n* a postman or postwoman (*informal*) [Late 19C. < POST2.]

postilion /po stílli ən/, **postillion** *n* somebody riding the near front horse in a team of horses drawing a carriage [Early 17C. Via French *postillon* 'postrider' < Italian *postiglione* < *posta* < Latin *posita* (see POST2).]

postimpressionism /pōst im présh'nizəm/ *n* a school of painting in late 19th century France that rejected the naturalism of impressionism but adapted its use of colour and form to a more subjective style —**post-impressionist** *n, adj* —**postimpressionistic** /pōst im préshə nístik/ *adj*

QUICK FACTS ON... **POSTIMPRESSIONISM**

Key dates: 1880–1906
Key locations: France, Tahiti
Key elements: observation of nature and contemporary life; withdrawal to countryside and to pre-technological settings; plein-air painting; formal composition; use of strong lines, distorted forms, and bright colours to express emotions; symbolism
Key figures: Paul Cézanne, Vincent van Gogh, Paul Gauguin, Pierre Bonnard, Henri Matisse, Édouard Vuillard
Key works: *Starry Night* (van Gogh) 1889, *Where Do We Come From? What Are We? Where Are We Going?* (Gauguin) 1897, *Mont-Ste-Victoire* (Cézanne) 1904
Key developments: neoimpressionism, fauvism, expressionism, cubism, primitivism, neoexpressionism

postindustrial /pōst in dústri əl/ *adj* relating to or characteristic of the decline of heavy industry in the western nations as an economic base and the rise of service industries, information technology, and research

ϟ **posting1** /pōsting/ *n* **1 MESSAGE** an online message sent to and displayed on, e.g. an Internet newsgroup or bulletin board **2 BOOKKEEPING ACTIVITY** the activity of making entries in a ledger **3 LEDGER ENTRY** an entry made in a ledger

posting2 /pōsting/ *n* an appointment to a job, position, or unit, usually overseas

posting3 /pōsting/ *adj* relating to sending and collecting post [Late 16C. < POST2.]

Post-it *tdmk* a trademark for self-sticking slips of paper sold in pad form

postlude /pōst lood/ *n* **1** a piece of organ music played at the end of a church service **2** a final or concluding phase, chapter, or development (*literary*) [Mid-19C. After PRELUDE.]

postman /pōstmən/ (*plural* **-men** /-mən/) *n* a man whose job it is to collect and deliver letters and parcels that have been sent by post. US term **mailman**

postman's knock *n* a children's game in which one player gives another a pretend letter and is given a kiss in return. US term **post office** *n.* 2

postmark /pōst maark/ *n* an official mark, usually covering a postage stamp, that indicates when and where a piece of mail was posted ■ *vt* to stamp a postmark on an item of mail

postmaster /pōst maastər/ *n* the person in charge of a post office or postal district

postmaster general (*plural* **postmasters general**) *n* the executive head of the postal service in some countries, e.g. the United Kingdom

postmenopausal /pōst mennə páwz'l/ *adj* relating to or occurring in the time following the menopause

post meridiem /-mə ríddi əm/ *adv* full form of **pm** [< Latin, 'after midday']

post mill *n* a windmill with its machinery assembled around an upright spindle and with a blade at the back that makes the sails turn to face the direction of the wind

postmillennial /pōst mi lénni əl/ *adj* occurring or existing after the millennium

postmistress /pōst mistrəss/ *n* a woman who has charge of a post office (*dated*)

postmodern /pōst módd'rn/ *adj* relating to art, architecture, literature, or thinking developed after and usually in reaction to modernism, returning to more classical or traditional elements and techniques —**postmodernist** *n*

postmodernism /pōst móddərnizəm/ *n* a style or tendency in architecture, art, literature and criticism developed after and often in reaction to modernism, characterized by the inclusion of elements that refer to other periods or styles in a self-conscious way and a rejection of the notion of high art

QUICK FACTS ON... **POSTMODERNISM**

Key dates: late 20th century and early 21st century
Key locations: North America, Europe
Key elements: eclecticism, irony, revivalism, self-consciousness
Key figures: Robert Venturi, Michael Graves, Richard Rogers, James Stirling (architecture); Joseph Beuys, Robert Smithson, Barbara Kruger, Jeff Koons (art); Jorge Luis Borges, Thomas Pynchon, Italo Calvino, Salman Rushdie (literature); Jacques Derrida (philosophy)
Key works: Pompidou Centre, Paris (Rogers and Piano) 1977, Staatsgalerie, Stuttgart (Stirling) 1977–84; *Spiral Jetty* (Smithson) 1970, *New Shelton Wet/Dry Triple Decker* (Koons) 1981; *Gravity's Rainbow* (Pynchon) 1973, *If on a Winter's Night a Traveller* (Calvino) 1979
Key developments: minimalism, conceptual art, earth art, nouveau roman, magic realism, deconstruction

postmortem /pōst máwrtəm/ *n* **1** MED = **autopsy** *n.* 1 **2** an analysis carried out shortly after the conclusion of an event, especially an unsuccessful one ○ *the usual media postmortems the day after the election* ■ *adj* occurring after death [Mid-18C. < Latin *post mortem* 'after death'.]

postnasal drip /pōst náyz'l-/ *n* a continual dripping of mucus from the rear of the nose into the throat, often caused by allergy or a cold

postnatal /pōst náyt'l/ *adj* occurring immediately or soon after childbirth —**postnatally** *adv*

postnatal depression *n* a state of severe, even suicidal depression that can affect a woman soon after giving birth to a baby. US term **postpartum depression**

postnuptial /pōst núpsh'l/ *adj* occurring in the period after a marriage —**postnuptially** *adv*

post-obit *n* a bond that pays after the death of a particular person (*dated*) ■ *adj* coming into effect after somebody's death (*formal*) ○ *post-obit payments* [Mid-18C. < Latin *post obitum* 'after death'.]

post office *n* **1** an office or building where the public has access to services of the postal system **2** *US* GAME = **postman's knock** **3** the national organization or government department that is responsible for a country's postal service

post office box *n* a private numbered box in a post office where letters are held until collected by the addressee

postop /pṓst óp/, **post-op** *adj* postoperative (*informal*) [Late 20C. Shortening.]

postoperative /pṓst ópprətiv/ *adj* occurring after a surgical operation —**postoperatively** *adv*

postorbital /pṓst áwrbit'l/ *adj* situated behind the eye or the eye socket

postpaid /pṓst páyd/ *adj* with the postage paid in advance

postpartum /pṓst paártəm/ *adj* occurring in or relating to the period immediately after childbirth [Mid-19C. < Latin *post partum* 'after childbirth'.]

postpartum depression *n US* MED = **postnatal depression**

postpone /pōst pṓn/ (**-pones, -poning, -poned**) *vt* **1** to put something off until a later time or date **2** to treat something with less importance (*formal*) [15C. < Latin *postponere* 'to place later' < *ponere* (see POSITION).] —**postponable** *adj* —**postponement** *n* —**postponer** *n*

postpose /pōst pṓz/ (**-poses, -posing, -posed**) *vti* to place a word or phrase after another or at the end of a sentence or construction [Late 19C. Back-formation < POSTPOSITION.]

postposition /pṓstpə zísh'n/ *n* **1** the placing of a word or phrase after the word or phrase it qualifies, e.g. the placing of 'bold and free' in the phrase 'poets bold and free' **2** = **postpositive** *n.* [Mid-17C. After 'preposition'.] —**postpositional** *adj* —**postpositionally** *adv*

postpositive /pṓst pózzətiv/ *adj* describes an adjective or modifier that is placed after the word or phrase it qualifies ■ *n* an adjective or modifier that is placed after the word it qualifies [Late 18C. Via late Latin *postpositivus* < Latin *postponere* (see POSTPONE).] —**postpositively** *adv*

postprandial /pṓst prándi əl/ *adj* occurring after a meal, especially an evening meal (*formal or humorous*) —**postprandially** *adv*

ϟ **post-print** *adj* belonging to the era of electronic communication rather than printing ○ *the post-print revolution*

postproduction /pṓst prə dúksh'n/ *n* the final stage of making a recording, film, or television programme that includes editing, sound dubbing, and adding special effects

postscript /pṓst skript/ *n* **1** a short message added on to the end of a letter, after the signature **2** an addition to the end of something such as a book, story, or document [Mid-16C. < Latin *postscriptum* < past participle of *postscribere* 'to write after' < *scribere* (see SCRIBE).]

post-structuralism *n* an intellectual movement derived from structuralism but questioning the basis upon which the structures of society, language, and mores have been conceptualized

QUICK FACTS ON... **POSTSTRUCTURALISM**

Key dates: late 20th century
Key locations: France
Key elements: use of concepts from linguistics and the social sciences in writing about literature and art; the self not stable and autonomous but a socially constructed product of language
Key figures: Roland Barthes; Jacques Derrida; Michel Foucault; Jacques Lacan; Julia Kristeva
Key works: *Madness and Civilization* (Foucault) 1966, *Écrits* (Lacan) 1966, *Of Grammatology* (Derrida) 1967, *The Empire of Signs* (Barthes) 1970, *The Revolution in Poetic Language* (Kristeva) 1974

postsynaptic /pṓst si náptik/ *adj* describes a nerve cell, muscle cell, or a region of cell membrane that receives signals transmitted across a synapse from another nerve cell

postsynch /pṓst síngk/ *vt* to add sound or music to a film at a later time

post transaction *n* submission by a retailer of a previously authorized transaction to the acquirer for payment

posttranscriptional /pṓst tran skrípsh'nəl/ *adj* describes processes or components involved in carrying out the genetic instructions of a living cell that participate only after the stage of transcription of a gene or genes

posttranslational /pṓst trans láysh'nəl/ *adj* describes processes or components involved in carrying out the genetic instructions of living cells that participate only after translation of RNA to protein

post-traumatic stress disorder *n* a psychological condition that may affect people who have suffered severe emotional trauma as a result of, e.g. combat, crime, or natural disaster, and may cause sleep disturbances, flashbacks, anxiety, tiredness, and depression

postulant /póstyŏŏlənt/ *n* somebody who applies to join a religious order (*formal*) [Mid-18C. Directly or via French < Latin *postulant-*, present participle of *postulare* (see POSTULATE).] —**postulancy** *n*

postulate *vt* /póst yŏŏ layt/ (**-lates, -lating, -lated**) **1 ASSUME** to assume or suggest that something is true or exists, especially as the basis of an argument **2 CLAIM** to demand or claim something **3 NOMINATE** to put forward a candidate for a post or office pending approval from a higher authority (*formal*) ■ *n* /póstyŏŏlət/ **1 SOMETHING ASSUMED TRUE** something that is assumed or believed to be true and that is used as the basis of an argument or theory **2 PRINCIPLE** a basic principle **3 PRECONDITION** an essential precondition or requirement **4 STATEMENT UNDERPINNING THEORY** a statement that is assumed to be true but has not been proved and that is taken as the basis for a theory, line of reasoning, or hypothesis [Mid-16C. < medieval Latin *postulare* 'to nominate', originally 'to demand'.] —**postulation** /póstyŏŏ láysh'n/ *n* —**postulational** /-láysh'nəl/ *adj*

postulator /póstyŏŏ laytər/ *n* **1** in the Roman Catholic Church, an official, usually a priest, who presents a request for a deceased person to be beatified or canonized **2** a person who postulates something

posture /póschər/ *n* **1 BODY POSITION** a position the body can assume, e.g. standing, sitting, kneeling, or lying down **2 CARRIAGE** the way in which somebody carries his or her body, especially when standing ○ *had poor posture as a child* **3 POSE CONVEYING ATTITUDE** a physical pose that conveys a mental or emotional attitude ○ *a posture of defiance* **4 DECEPTIVE STANCE** a position, attitude, or stance that is intended to deceive **5 CULTIVATED POSITION** a practised or cultivated arrangement of the body, e.g. a position used in yoga **6 ATTITUDE** a frame of mind or attitude towards a particular subject ○ *a conciliatory posture* **7 ARRANGEMENT OF PARTS** the way that components of an object or situation are arranged in relation to one another ■ *v* (**-tures, -turing, -tured**) **1** *vi* **ASSUME STANCE** to assume an affected or exaggerated pose or attitude **2** *vti* **MAKE A POSTURE** to arrange somebody in, or adopt, a particular posture [Late 16C. Via French < Latin *positura* < *posit-*, past participle of *ponere* (see POSITION).] —**postural** *adj* —**posturer** *n*

postviral syndrome /pṓst vīrəl-/ *n* MED = **chronic fatigue syndrome**

postvocalic /pṓst vō kállik/ *adj* coming after a vowel

postwar /pṓst wáwr/ *adj* occurring or existing after a war, especially World War II

postwoman /pṓst wŏŏmən/ (*plural* **-en** /-wimən/) *n* a woman whose job it is to collect and deliver letters and parcels that have been sent by post

posy /pṓzi/ (*plural* **-sies**) *n* **1** a small bunch of flowers **2** a short verse or inscription, especially on a trinket or ring (*archaic*) [Mid-16C. Alteration of POESY.]

pot[1] /pot/ *n* **1 WATERTIGHT CONTAINER FOR COOKING OR STORAGE** a container made of metal, pottery, or glass that is usually cylindrical and watertight with an open top and sometimes a lid, used especially for cooking or storage **2 SOMETHING RESEMBLING POT IN SHAPE** something similar to a pot in shape or function e.g. a flowerpot or teapot **3 CONTENTS OF POT** the contents of a pot, or the amount that it will hold ○ *made a pot of coffee* **4 OBJECT MADE FROM CLAY** a dish or container that is made from clay, especially one of artistic or historical interest **5** = **potty**[2] *n.* **6 LARGE AMOUNT OF MONEY** a large amount of money (*informal*) **7 MONEY BET IN CARD GAME** all the money that is bet in a game of cards, especially poker, and that is taken by the winning player **8** *US* **COMMON FUND** a common fund of money that is contributed to by the members of a group, usually for a particular purpose, e.g. a party or trip (*informal*) **9 DRINKING VESSEL** a large drinking vessel, usually glass or pewter, for beer **10 HIT OF BALL INTO POCKET** in billiards or snooker, a hit of a ball that sends it into any of the pockets at the edge of the table **11 CUP WON IN COMPETITION** a vessel, especially a silver cup, that is won in a competition, especially a sports contest (*informal*) **12 FISH OR LOBSTER TRAP** a basket or cage used for catching lobsters, eels, or fish **13 POTBELLY** a round bulging stomach or abdomen (*informal*) **14** SPORTS = **potshot** *n.* 1 ■ *v* (**pots, potting, potted**) **1** *vt* **PUT PLANT IN POT** to put a plant into a pot with soil or compost **2** *vti* **SHOOT ANIMAL FOR FOOD** to shoot or shoot at a bird or animal, especially for food **3** *vti* **SHOOT AT SOMETHING WITHIN EASY REACH** to shoot or shoot at an easy target, especially casually **4** *vt* **PRESERVE FOOD IN POT** to preserve food in a pot **5** *vti* **HIT BALL INTO POCKET** in billiards or snooker, to hit a ball into any of the pockets at the edge of the table **6** *vti* **SHAPE SOMETHING WITH CLAY** to shape a pot or other item from clay **7** *vt* to encapsulate electronic components in an insulating resin to protect them and hold them in place **8** *vt* **PUT CHILD ON POTTY** to put a young child on a potty [Pre-12C. < assumed Vulgar Latin *pottus* < ?] ◇ **go to pot** to get much worse or become useless, worthless, or extremely unsatisfactory (*informal*)

pot on *vt* to transfer a growing plant from a smaller to a larger pot

pot up *vt* to plant a seedling or cutting in a pot, separating it from others with which it originally grew

pot[2] /pot/ *n* the plant or drug cannabis (*slang*) [Mid-20C. Probably shortening of Mexican Spanish *potiguaya* 'marijuana leaves'.]

pot[3] /pot/ *n* a potentiometer (*informal*) [Mid-20C. Shortening.]

potable /pṓtəb'l/ *adj* suitable for drinking because it contains no harmful elements ■ *n* a liquid that is suitable for drinking, especially an alcoholic drink [15C. Directly or via French < late Latin *potabilis* < Latin *potare* 'drink' < *potus* 'to drink'.] —**potability** /pṓtə bílləti/ *n* —**potableness** /pṓtəb'lnəss/ *n*

potage /po taázh, pó taazh/ *n* a thick soup [Mid-16C. < French (see POTTAGE).]

potash /pót ash/ *n* **1** a potassium compound, especially potassium chloride, sulphate, or oxide. Use: in fertilizers. **2** CHEM = **potassium carbonate 3** CHEM = **potassium hydroxide** [Early 17C. < obsolete Dutch *potasschen*, plural of *potasch* 'pot ash'.]

potash alum *n* CHEM = **alum**

potassium /pə tássi əm/ *n* (*symbol* **K**) a soft silvery-white highly reactive element of the alkali metal group. Source: carnallite, sylvite. Use: coolant in nuclear reactors, in fertilizers. [Early 19C. < modern Latin < *potassa* 'potash' (see POTASH).]

potassium-argon dating *n* a technique for estimating the age of rocks older than 250,000 years, based on the time taken for the radioactive decay of the potassium-40 isotope into a stable argon isotope

potassium bitartrate /-bī taár trayt/ *n* $KHC_4H_4O_6$ a white powder or crystalline compound. Use: in baking powder, medicine, food preparation.

potassium bromide *n* KBr a white crystalline compound. Use: in lithography, medicine, photography, soap.

potassium carbonate *n* K_2CO_3 a white salt. Use: in brewing, ceramics, explosives, fertilizers, glass, soap.

potassium chlorate *n* $KClO_3$ a white salt that detonates with heat. Use: fireworks, matches, explosives, textile printing, paper manufacture, as a bleach and disinfectant.

potassium chloride *n* KCl a colourless crystalline salt. Use: as fertilizer, in photography, medicine.

potassium cyanide *n* KCN a very poisonous white crystalline chemical salt. Use: extraction of gold and silver from their ores, electroplating, photography, insecticide.

potassium dichromate *n* $K_2Cr_2O_7$ a yellow-red poisonous crystalline compound. Use: manufacture of explosives, safety matches, dyes.

potassium ferricyanide *n* $K_3Fe(CN)_6$ a bright red poisonous crystalline compound that decomposes when heated. Use: textile printing, wool dyeing, blueprint paper, fertilizer.

potassium ferrocyanide *n* $K_4Fe(CN)_6$ a yellow crystalline compound. Use: in medicine, explosives.

potassium hydrogen carbonate *n* $KHCO_3$ a white powder or granular compound. Use: in baking powder, as antacid.

potassium hydrogen tartrate *n* CHEM = **potassium bitartrate**

potassium hydroxide *n* KOH a caustic toxic white solid. Use: manufacture of soap, detergents, liquid shampoos, matches.

potassium iodide *n* KI a white crystalline compound with a salty taste. Use: in medicine and photography, additive in table salt.

potassium nitrate *n* KNO_3 a white crystalline salt. Use: in fireworks, explosives, matches, as fertilizer, meat preservative.

potassium permanganate *n* $KMnO_4$ a dark purple toxic odourless crystalline compound. Use: bleach, disinfectant, antiseptic, in deodorizers and dyes.

potassium sodium tartrate *n* Rochelle salt (*technical*)

potassium sulphate *n* K_2SO_4 a colourless crystalline compound. Use: in aluminium, glass, cement, fertilizers, medicine.

potation /pō táysh'n/ *n* (*literary*) **1** the act or an instance of drinking **2** a drink, especially an alcoholic drink [15C. Directly or via Old French < Latin *potation-* < *potare* 'to drink' (see POTABLE).]

potato /pə táytō/ (*plural* **-toes**) *n* **1 ROOT VEGETABLE** a rounded white tuber cooked in a variety of ways as a vegetable. Use: industrial source of starch. **2 POTATO PLANT** a perennial plant that produces potatoes underground. Native to: South America. *Solanum tuberosum*. **3 SWEET POTATO** a sweet potato [Mid-16C. < Spanish *patata*, alteration of Taino *batata* 'sweet potato'.]

potato beetle *n* INSECTS = **Colorado beetle**

potato blight *n* a highly destructive disease of the potato caused by the fungus *Phytophthora infestans*

potato cake *n* a flat round mass of seasoned potato, either cooked and mashed or raw and grated, that has been fried or sautéed

potato chip *n* US, ANZ a very thin slice of potato that has usually been deep-fried in oil, salted, sometimes flavoured, and packaged and sold to be eaten cold as a snack

potato crisp *n* UK = **crisp** *n.* 1

potato pancake *n* a pancake made from a mixture of coarsely grated potato with egg, flour, and seasonings

potato scone *n* a pancake of dough containing mashed potato and flour, fried and served hot

potato skin *n* a piece of skin from a hollowed-out baked potato that is then baked further, or a piece of deep-fried skin of a raw potato, served as an appetizer (*often plural*)

pot-au-feu /pót ō fö/ (*plural* **pot-au-feu** /pót ō fö/) *n* **1** a French stew of slowly boiled meat and vegetables, the meat usually being eaten separately from the vegetables and stock, which are served first as a soup **2** a large earthenware pot in which pot-au-feu is traditionally cooked [< French, 'pot on the fire']

Potawatomi /póttə wóttəmi/ (*plural* **-mi** *or* **-mis**) *n* the Algonquian language of the Potawatomi people—**Potawatomi** *adj*

potbellied stove *n* US = **potbelly stove**

potbelly /pót beli/ (*plural* **-lies**) *n* **1** a round bulging stomach or abdomen **2** a person with a potbelly —**potbellied** *adj*

potbelly stove, potbellied stove *n* US a wood- or coal-burning stove that has a rounded bulbous body

potboiler /pót boylər/ *n* a book, film, or other work that is produced quickly to make money and has little literary or artistic quality (*informal*) [< its purpose of 'boiling the pot', that is, providing a livelihood so that somebody can eat]

pot-bound *adj* describes a pot plant whose roots have grown very dense and have filled its pot so that its growth is restricted

poteen /po teén, po cheén/ *n* in Ireland, a spirit that has been distilled illegally, especially from potatoes [Early 19C. < Irish *(fuisce) poitín* 'small pot (whiskey)' < *pota* 'pot' < POT[1].]

potency /pṓt'nssi/ (*plural* **-cies**) *n* **1 STRENGTH OF MEDICINE** the strength of something such as a drug , medicine, or alcoholic drink **2 STATE OF BEING POTENT** the state or quality of being potent **3 ABILITY TO DEVELOP** a capacity to grow or develop in the future

potent[1] /pṓt'nt/ *adj* **1 STRONG AND EFFECTIVE** very strong, effective, or powerful **2 PERSUASIVE** exerting persuasion, influence, or force **3 WITH STRONG CHEMICAL EFFECT** with a strong or concentrated chemical or medicinal effect **4 HAVING POWER** having or using power, control, or authority **5 CAPABLE OF SEXUAL INTERCOURSE** capable of having an erection, sexual intercourse, or an ejaculation [15C. < Latin *potent-*, present participle of *posse* 'to be powerful', contraction of *potis esse* < *potis* 'able' + *esse* 'to be'.] —**potently** *adv* —**potentness** *n*

potent[2] /pṓt'nt/ *adj* describes a heraldic cross that has four arms with a bar across the end of each arm [14C. Alteration of obsolete English *potence* 'crutch' or its Old French source < Latin *potentia* 'power' < *potent-* (see POTENT[1]).]

potentate /pṓt'n tayt/ *n* a powerful, authoritative, and influential person, especially a monarch or other ruler

potential /pə ténsh'l/ *adj* **1 POSSIBLE BUT NOT YET REALIZED** with a possibility or likelihood of occurring, or of doing or becoming something in the future **2 EXPRESSING POSSIBILITY** describes a verb or verb form that expresses possibility, e.g. 'may' or 'might' in English ■ *n* **1 CAPACITY TO DEVELOP** the capacity or ability for future development or achievement **2 POTENTIAL VERB FORM** a verb or verb form that expresses possibility, e.g. 'may' or 'might' in English **3** PHYS = **electric potential** [14C. Directly or via Old French *potenciel* < late Latin *potentialis* < Latin *potent-* (see POTENT[1]).] —**potentially** *adv*

potential difference *n* (*symbol* ΔV *or* ΔU) the work done in moving a unit electric charge between two points in an electric field

potential divider *n* ELEC ENG = **voltage divider**

potential energy *n* (*symbol* V *or* E_p) the energy that a body or system has stored because of its position in an electric, magnetic, or gravitational field, or because of its configuration

potentiality /pə ténshi álləti/ (*plural* **-ties**) *n* **1** the capacity or ability for future development or for a future achievement or action **2** a person or thing capable of future development

potential well *n* a region in an electric, magnetic, or gravitational field in which an object has a lower potential energy than it would have in all adjacent regions

potentiate /pə ténshi ayt/ (**-ates, -ating, -ated**) *vt* to improve the effectiveness of a drug or treatment, especially by adding another drug or agent —**potentiator** *n*

potentilla /pṓt'n tíllə/ (*plural* **-las** *or* **-la**) *n* a cultivated flowering plant or small bush. Flowers: small, yellow, white, or red, five-petalled. Genus: *Potentilla*. [Mid-16C. < medieval Latin, 'powerful little (plant)' (from its use in medicine) < Latin *potent-* (see POTENT[1]).]

potentiometer /pə ténshi ómmitər/ *n* **1** a device for measuring an unknown potential difference or electromotive force by balancing part of it against a known standard **2** a three-terminal component, typically used as a volume or brightness control, that gives a variable electric potential by rotating a shaft or moving a slider [Late 19C. < POTENTIAL + -METER.] —**potentiometry** *n*

potentiometric /pə ténshi ə méttrik/ *adj* indicating the completion of a chemical reaction by a change in potential at an electrode immersed in the solution where the reaction is taking place [Early 20C. < POTENTIAL.]

pothead /pót hed/ *n* a regular or heavy smoker of cannabis (*slang disapproving*)

pother /pót̲hər/ *n* **1 NERVOUS STATE** a state of emotional agitation, especially over something trivial **2 COMMOTION** a great deal of frenzied activity or conversation, especially over something trivial **3 CHOKING CLOUD** a cloud of smoke or dust that chokes ■ *vti* **CONFUSE SOMEBODY OR BE CONFUSED** to confuse or worry somebody or to become confused or worried [Late 16C. < ?]

potherb /pót hurb/ *n* a herb or vegetable used to add flavour in cooking

potholder /pót hōldər/ *n* a pad of fabric used to protect the hands from hot pots and cooking utensils

pothole /pót hōl/ *n* **1 HOLE IN ROAD SURFACE** a hole that has formed in the surface of a road and that can be hazardous to motorists **2 VERTICAL HOLE IN LIMESTONE AREA** a vertical deep hole or shaft formed naturally in limestone regions by the erosive action of running water **3 HOLE IN RIVER BED** a bowl-shaped hole in the bed of a river or stream, formed by the abrasive action of stone, gravel, or ice being churned in an eddy

pothole lake *n* a small lake formed in a limestone pothole depression

potholing /pót hōling/ *n* the activity of exploring potholes and underground caves connected by them, especially as a hobby or sport —**potholer** *n*

pothook /pót hòòk/ *n* **1** an S-shaped hook fixed above an open fire, from which a pot or kettle is hung **2** a handwriting mark beginning or ending in a curve

pothunter /pót huntər/ *n* **1 HUNTER OF GAME FOR PROFIT** a person who hunts game, often indiscriminately and disregardful of rules **2 PRIZE-SEEKER** a participant in competitions and races with more interest in the prizes than the sport (*informal disapproving*) **3 AMATEUR ARCHAEOLOGIST** a digger of ancient pots and other objects who is not a professional archaeologist —**pothunting** *n*

potion /pṓsh'n/ *n* a liquid to be drunk that is medicinal, supposedly magical, or poisonous [13C. Via Old French < Latin *potion-* < *potare* 'to drink'.]

Potiphar /póttifər/ *n* in the Bible, the Egyptian who bought Joseph as a slave and later imprisoned him when he was falsely accused of attempting to have sexual relations with his wife. (Genesis 37).

potlatch /pót lach/ *n* among Native American peoples of the coast of NW North America, a ceremony of feasting in which the host gains prestige by giving gifts or, sometimes, destroying wealth [Mid-19C. < Chinook Jargon.]

potluck /pot lúk/ *n* **1 WHATEVER IS AVAILABLE** whatever happens to be available to satisfy a need **2 FOOD AVAILABLE TO UNEXPECTED GUEST** whatever food happens to be available to give to an unexpected guest **3** US **MEAL TO WHICH EVERYONE BRINGS** a meal to which each participant brings one dish that is shared with everyone else [Late 16C. < POT[1] + LUCK.]

potman /pótmən/ (*plural* **-men** /-mən/) *n* a man employed in a public house, especially to collect empty glasses (*dated*)

pot marigold *n* a garden plant of the daisy family. Flowers: large, bright yellow or orange. Native to: Europe. *Calendula officinalis*. US term **calendula** ['Pot' < its being grown for decoration]

Potomac /pə tṓm ak/ river of the E United States, flowing eastwards from West Virginia into Chesapeake Bay. Length: 460 km/285 mi.

potometer /pə tómmitər/ *n* an instrument used to determine the rate of a plant's transpiration by measuring water uptake [Late 19C. < Greek *poton* 'drink' + -METER.]

potoroo /póttə ròò/ (*plural* **-roos**) *n* a rabbit-sized member of the kangaroo family that looks like a rat and has powerful hind legs that it uses for jumping. *Potorous tridactylus*. [Late 18C. < Aboriginal.]

pot plant *n* a plant that is growing in a flowerpot and is kept in a house or office for display and decoration. US term **potted plant**

potpourri /pō pòòri, pṓpə reé/ (*plural* **-ris**) *n* **1** a collection of dried flower petals, leaves, herbs, and spices, sometimes coloured and scented, that are used to scent the air **2** a miscellaneous mixture of things [Early 17C. < French, 'mixed stew', literally 'rotten pot' (translation of Spanish *olla podrida*); *pourri*, past participle of *pourrir* 'to rot' < Latin *putris* 'rotten'.]

pot roast *n* a dish consisting of a piece of beef cooked slowly in the oven in a closed pot in its own juices, often on a bed of vegetables —**pot-roast** *vti*

Potsdam /póts dam/ city in NE Germany. Population: 138,268 (1997).

potsherd /pót shurd/, **potshard** /pót shard/ *n* a fragment of pottery, especially one found at an archaeological site [14C. < POT[1] + SHERD.]

potshot /pót shot/ *n* **1** a shot taken quickly, carelessly, or on a chance opportunity at something such as game, especially when within easy reach **2** a criticism made without careful consideration and aimed at an easy target ○ *journalists taking potshots at the government* [Mid-19C. < the purpose of the shot originally being to get food for the cooking 'pot'.]

pot still *n* an apparatus for distilling whisky that applies heat directly to the container holding the wash

pottage /póttij/ *n* a thick vegetable, or meat and vegetable, soup [12C. Originally *potage* < Old French, 'what is put in a pot' < *pot* (see POT[1]).]

potted /póttid/ *adj* **1 GROWING IN POT** planted in a pot **2 PRESERVED IN POT** cooked or preserved in a vessel such as a pot or jar **3 SUPERFICIALLY SUMMARIZED** reproduced in a brief and often superficial form (*informal*)

potted plant *n* = **pot plant**

potter[1] /póttər/ *n* a maker of pottery [Pre-12C]

potter[2] /póttər/ *vi* **1** to do relatively unimportant things in a relaxed and unhurried way ○ *pottering about in the greenhouse.* US term **putter**[2] *v.* **2** to move about slowly and without any particular goal [Mid-16C. < obsolete *pote* 'push' < Old English *potian* < ?] —**potterer** *n*

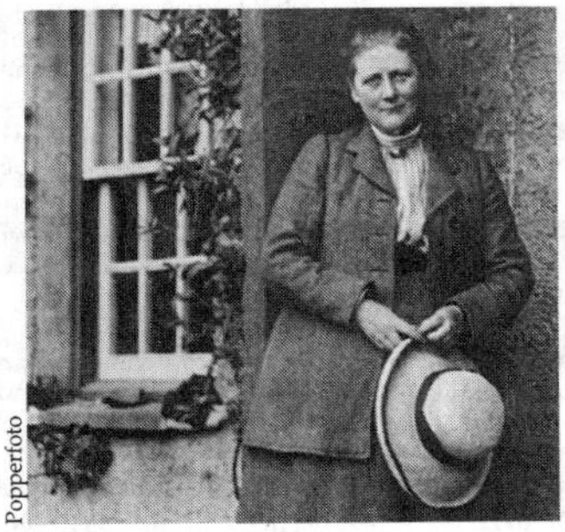

Popperfoto

Beatrix Potter

Potter /póttər/, **Beatrix** (1866–1943) British children's writer and illustrator

Potteries /póttəriz/ region of Staffordshire, west-central England, famous for its ceramics factories

potter's clay *n* clay that does not contain any iron and is suitable for making pottery

potter's field *n* in the Bible, an area of land near Jerusalem bought as a burial ground for strangers with the money that was given to Judas for betraying Jesus Christ

potter's wheel *n* a device for moulding clay into pottery by hand, consisting of a horizontal disc that holds the clay and is rotated manually or by electricity

potter wasp *n* a small solitary wasp that constructs elaborate clay pots in which it lays its eggs and puts caterpillars to serve as food for the young. Genus: *Eumenes.*

pottery /póttəri/ (*plural* **-ies**) *n* **1 OBJECTS MADE OF BAKED CLAY** objects such as vases, pots, plates, or sculptured articles that are made by moulding or shaping moist clay and hardening it by heating in a kiln **2 MAKING OF POTTERY** the art, craft, or occupation of making pottery **3 PLACE WHERE POTTERY IS MADE** a workshop, factory, or other place where pottery is made

potting compost *n* any mixture, e.g. based on soil or peat, with a balance of nutrients used for growing plants in pots

potting shed *n* a small shed in a garden for storing flowerpots, compost, and other gardening materials

potto /póttō/ (*plural* **-tos**) *n* a small primate of West and Central African rain forests that has small ears, large eyes, and a short bushy tail and lives in the lower branches of trees. *Perodicticus potto.* [Early 18C. Probably from a West African source.]

Pott's disease /póts-/ *n* a tubercular disease of the spine, marked by the destruction of the bone and discs and curvature of the spine [Mid-19C. After Sir Percivall *Pott* (1713–88), English surgeon.]

potty[1] /pótti/ (**-tier, -tiest**) *adj* (*informal*) **1 IRRATIONAL** slightly irrational **2 KEEN OR ENTHUSIASTIC** very enthusiastic about or obsessed by somebody or something **3 TRIVIAL** trivial and unimportant [Mid-19C. < ?] —**pottiness** *n*

potty[2] /pótti/ (*plural* **-ties**) *n* a bowl, used especially by young children who cannot yet use a toilet, to eliminate body waste (*informal*) [Mid-20C. < POT[1].]

potty-chair *n* a small chair with a pot in the seat, used by young children who are being trained to use a toilet

potty-train *vti* to train a young child to use a potty instead of a nappy (*informal*)

⚡**POTUS** /pṓtəss/ *n US* used as shorthand by White House staff in memos and internal documents to refer to the US president. Full form **President of the United States** ■ *abbr* President of the United States (*in e-mails*)

pouch /powch/ *n* **1 SMALL SOFT BAG** a small bag or container made of a soft material such as fabric or leather **2 SOMETHING RESEMBLING POUCH** something that looks like a pouch, especially a small baggy fold of skin **3 POCKET OF SKIN IN ANIMAL** a structure in an animal resembling a pouch, especially one on the abdomen of a marsupial for carrying young, or in the cheek of a rodent for carrying food **4 BODY CAVITY RESEMBLING POCKET** a pocket-shaped space or structure in the body **5 PLANT CAVITY** a cavity in a plant shaped like a pocket **6** *Scotland* **POCKET** a pocket **7 BAG FOR MAIL** a lockable bag or sack for carrying mail, especially diplomatic correspondence ■ *v* **1** *vt* **PUT IN POUCH** to put something into a pouch **2** *vt* **POCKET** to take something by putting it into your pocket **3** *vti* **FORM POUCH** to make something, or be made, into a shape resembling a pouch [13C. Via Anglo-Norman *puche*, Old Northern French *pouche*, and Old French *poche* < Germanic, 'bag'.] —**pouchy** *adj*

pouf[1] /poof/, **pouffe** *n* **1 PADDED STOOL** a round or square piece of padded furniture with an upholstered cover, used as a seat or footrest. US term **hassock** *n.* 3 **2 PUFFED-OUT HAIRSTYLE** a puffed-out hairstyle, similar to a bouffant, fashionable especially in the 18th century **3 PAD IN HAIR** a pad worn in the hair to help shape a pouf **4 BUNCHED-UP PART OF DRESS** a part of a dress or skirt gathered up to form a soft projecting shape [Early 19C. Via French < an imitation of the sound of a puff.]

pouf[2] /pŏŏf, poof/, **pouffe** *n* = **poof**[1] (*slang offensive*)

Pouilly-Fuissé /pŏŏ yee fwée say/ *n* a dry white wine produced from the Chardonnay grape in the area around Pouilly and Fuissé in the Burgundy region of France

Pouilly-Fumé /pŏŏ yee fyŏŏ may/ *n* a dry white wine produced from the Sauvignon Blanc grape in the area around Pouilly-sur-Loire in the Loire valley of France [Mid-20C. < French *fumé*, past participle of *fumer* 'smoke' < Latin *fumus* 'to smoke'.]

Poujadism /pŏŏ zhaadizəm/ *n* a right-wing political movement in France in the 1950s, with mainly middle-class support [Mid-20C. < French *Poujadisme*, after the French publisher and politician Pierre *Poujade* (born 1920).] —**Poujadist** *n, adj*

poulard /pŏŏ laard/, **poularde** *n* a young domestic hen (**pullet**) that has been spayed to encourage fattening [Mid-18C. < French *poularde* < *poule* 'hen' < Latin *pulla*, feminine of *pullus* 'chicken'.]

Poulenc /pŏŏl angk, pŏŏl aNk/, **Francis** (1899–1963) French composer and pianist

poult /pōlt/ *n* a young fowl, especially a turkey or pheasant [15C. Contraction of PULLET.]

poulterer /pṓltərər/ *n* a buyer, preparer, and seller of poultry [Late 16C. Alteration of archaic *poulter* < Old French *pouletier* < *poulet* 'young fowl'.]

poultice /pṓltiss/ *n* a warm moist preparation placed on an aching or inflamed part of the body to ease pain, improve circulation, or hasten the expression of pus [14C. Originally *pultes* < Latin, plural of *puls* 'pottage, thick gruel'.]

poultry /pṓltri/ *n* **1** domestic fowl in general, e.g. chickens, turkeys, ducks, or geese, raised for meat or eggs **2** the meat of domestic fowl such as chickens and ducks [14C. < Old French *pouletrie* < *pouletier* 'poulterer' < *poulet* 'young fowl'.]

pounce[1] /pownss/ *v* (**pounces, pouncing, pounced**) **1** *vi* **JUMP SUDDENLY ON** to jump or swoop suddenly towards or onto somebody or something, especially onto prey **2** *vi* **ATTACK OR TAKE QUICKLY** to move very quickly and suddenly in attacking somebody or obtaining something ○ *He pounced on the book and carried it off to his room.* **3** *vt* **REACT SWIFTLY TO** to be quick to notice and make use of something ○ *She immediately pounced on his admission that he'd known all about it.* ■ *n* **ACT OF SUDDENLY JUMPING ON** an act of suddenly jumping or swooping towards or onto somebody or something, especially onto prey [14C. Either a shortening of PUNCHEON[2], or < Old French *poinson* 'pointed tool' < Latin *punct-* (see PUNCTURE).] —**pouncer** *n*

pounce[2] /pownss/ *n* **1 POWDER USED FOR PRODUCING IMAGE** powdered charcoal or other fine powder sprinkled over a stencil to reproduce the main lines of a pattern or design on the surface beneath the stencil **2 POWDER TO STOP INK FROM RUNNING** a very fine powder formerly used to stop ink from spreading on unglazed paper ■ *vt* (**pounces, pouncing, pounced**) **1 REPRODUCE SOMETHING WITH POUNCE** to reproduce a pattern or design on something by sprinkling pounce over a stencil **2 SPRINKLE PAPER WITH POUNCE** to sprinkle paper with pounce [Late 16C. Via Old French *ponce* (noun) and *poncer* (verb) < Latin *pumic-*, stem of *pumex* 'pumice'.]

pouncet box /pównssət-/ *n* a small box with a perforated lid, used to hold a perfumed substance [Late 16C. *Pouncet* < ?]

pound[1] /pownd/ *n* **1** see table at **currency 2** = **pound scots 3 AVOIRDUPOIS UNIT OF WEIGHT** a unit of weight in the avoirdupois system, divided into 16 oz and equivalent to 0.45 kg **4 TROY UNIT OF WEIGHT** a unit of weight in the troy system that is divided into 12 oz and is equivalent to 0.37 kg **5 UNIT OF FORCE** a unit of force, equal to the gravitational force experienced by a pound mass accelerating at 9.80665 m/32.174 ft per second per second [Old English *pund*, via Germanic < Latin *pondo* 'weight of a pound' < *(libra) pondo* '(pound) by weight', a form of assumed *pondos* 'weight'] ◇ **get** *or* **have your pound of flesh** to get what is due to you, even if it causes difficulties or hardship to others

pound out *vt* **1** to produce something by working in a diligent continuous way ○ *pound out an essay* **2** to produce something with heavy blows or loud thumping noises ○ *pound out a tune on the piano*

pound[2] /pownd/ *v* **1** *vti* **STRIKE HARD AND REPEATEDLY** to strike somebody or something repeatedly and heavily **2** *vt* **BEAT SOMETHING TO PULP OR POWDER** to beat something into very fine pieces or to a mass, with repeated heavy blows **3** *vi* **THROB** to beat or throb heavily ○ *My heart was pounding.* **4** *vt* **ATTACK CONTINUOUSLY** to attack a place continuously with bombs or large guns ○ *pounding the city for a few weeks* **5** *vi* **RUN HEAVILY** to run with heavy steps **6** *vt* **TEACH BY REPETITION** to ensure that somebody learns or understands something by using constant repetition and drilling ■ *n* **ACT OF POUNDING** the act or sound of pounding [15C. Alteration of *pounen* < Old English *pūnian* < Germanic.] —**pounder** *n*

pound[3] /pownd/ *n* **1 ENCLOSURE FOR STRAY ANIMALS** a fenced-off area where stray animals, especially dogs, are kept **2 ENCLOSURE FOR VEHICLES OR OTHER GOODS** a fenced-off area where vehicles or other goods that have been taken by the police or another authority are kept until a debt or fine has been paid **3 PLACE FOR ANIMALS OR FISH** an area in which animals or fish are trapped or kept **4 PRISON AREA** a place where people are held prisoner ■ *vt* **PUT SOMETHING IN POUND** to confine somebody or something in a pound [< the Old English stem *pund-*]

Pound /pownd/, **Ezra** (1885–1972) US writer

poundage[1] /pówndij/ *n* **1 PAYMENT PER POUND OF WEIGHT** a tax, charge, commission, or other payment for something calculated per pound of weight **2 PAYMENT PER POUND STERLING** a tax, charge, commission, or other payment for something calculated per pound sterling **3 WEIGHT IN POUNDS** the weight of somebody or something expressed in pounds

poundage[2] /pówndij/ *n* **1** the confinement of animals in an enclosed area or pound **2** the fee that must be paid for the return of an impounded vehicle, animal, or other goods

poundal /pównd'l/ *n* a British unit of force, equal to the force that will impart an acceleration of one foot per second per second to a mass of one pound [Late 19C. < POUND[1].]

pound cake *n US* a rich dense yellow cake that is traditionally made with a pound each of butter, sugar, flour, and eggs, or with equal weights of each of these ingredients

pound cost averaging *n* the periodic purchase of the same amount in pounds sterling of the same security at regular time intervals regardless of the price of the security

pound-foolish *adj* unwise when dealing with large sums of money [< the phrase *penny-wise and pound-foolish*]

pound scots (*plural* **pounds scots**) *n* a former unit of currency in Scotland

⚡**pound sign** *n* **1** the symbol (£) which indicates pound sterling **2** *US* COMPUT = **hash**[1] *n.* 1

pound sterling (*plural* **pounds sterling**) *n* the official name for the unit of currency used in the United Kingdom

pour /pawr/ *v* **1** *vt* **MAKE SOMETHING FLOW** to make a substance flow in a stream ○ *poured the sugar into the bowl* **2** *vti* **SERVE DRINK** to serve a drink from a container such as a pot or jug into a cup, mug, or glass ○ *Let me pour you some tea.* **3** *vi* **FUNCTION AS CONTAINER FOR POURING** to function as a container from which liquid is poured ○ *This teapot doesn't pour very well.* **4** *vi* **FLOW IN LARGE QUANTITIES** to flow down or out, especially in large quantities ○ *Smoke poured from the burning building.* **5** *vi* **RAIN HEAVILY** to rain very heavily ○ *It poured for hours.* **6** *vi* **COME IN LARGE QUANTITIES** to come or go quickly and in large quantities ○ *Letters of complaint came pouring in.* **7** *vt* **EXPRESS FEELING** to express a feeling at length and without restraint ○ *poured his heart out to me* **8** *vt* **GIVE LARGE AMOUNT OF** to give a large amount of something such as effort or support to something ○ *poured a lot of blood, sweat, and tears into that project* [13C. Probably via Old French dialect *purer* 'to sift, pour out' < Latin *purare* 'to purify' < *purus* 'pure'.]

USAGE pour or **pore**? 'To study something carefully and thoughtfully' (***pore***) might seem to have more in common with 'to make a substance flow' (***pour***) than with 'a tiny opening' (***pore***). Perhaps it has, but all three words have been derived separately, despite the fact that one of the verbs has the same spelling as the noun. You ***pour*** from the pot into a teacup, ***pore*** over a text, and have ***pores*** in your skin.

pourboire /pŏor bwaar/ *n* a sum of money given for services rendered or anticipated [Early 19C. < French, 'for drinking'.]

pour point *n* the lowest temperature at which a liquid will continue to flow

pousse-café /pŏoss ka fáy/ *n* **1** a drink consisting of different-coloured liqueurs poured in one glass and forming layers because each liqueur has a different density **2** a liqueur served after dinner, with or after coffee [< French, 'push coffee']

poussin /pŏo saN/ *n* a chicken reared to be eaten when very young and tender [Mid-20C. Via French < late Latin *pullicenus* 'small young fowl' < Latin *pullus* 'young fowl'.]

Poussin /pŏo saN/, **Nicolas** (1594–1665) French-born Italian painter

pout[1] /powt/ *v* **1** *vti* **PUSH LIPS OUTWARDS** to move the lower lip or both lips outwards to form an expression of bad temper or sulkiness, or in order to look sexually provoking **2** *vi* **SULK** to show disappointment, anger, or resentment, usually in silence ○ *still pouting because he missed the game* **3** *vt* **SAY SOMETHING SULKILY** to say something with a pout ○ *pouted that the whole thing wasn't fair* ■ *n* **1 EXPRESSION WITH LIPS PUSHED OUT** an expression of the face with the lower lip or both lips pushed out **2 SULKY MOOD** a period or fit of sulking [14C. < ?] —**poutingly** *adv* —**pouty** *adj*

pout[2] /powt/ (*plural* **pout** *or* **pouts**) *n* **1** FISH = **bib** *n.* 3 **2** FISH = **hornpout** [Old English stem *-pūte* < ?]

pouter /pówtər/ *n* **1** a person who pouts **2 pouter, pouter pigeon** a domesticated pigeon belonging to a breed with a crop that can be greatly inflated [Early 18C. < POUT[1].]

poutine /poo teen/ *n Can* a dish originating in Quebec that consists of chips and curd cheese, covered with tomato sauce or gravy

poverty /póvvərti/ *n* **1 STATE OF BEING POOR** the state of not having enough money to take care of basic needs such as food, clothing, and housing **2 LACK** a deficiency or lack of something ○ *poverty of emotion* **3 INFERTILITY OF SOIL** lack of soil fertility or nutrients [12C. Via Old French *poverte* < Latin *paupertas* < *pauper* 'poor'.]

Poverty Bay /póvvərti-/ inlet of the S Pacific Ocean on east-central North Island, New Zealand

poverty line, poverty level *n* a level of income below which somebody is considered to be living in poverty

poverty-stricken *adj* extremely poor and with intense problems as a result

poverty trap *n* a situation in which an unemployed person will lose money by working because more will be lost in state benefits than is gained in income

pow /pow/ *interj* used to imitate the sound of an explosion or gun, or of a sudden impact, e.g. when somebody is hit (*informal*) [Late 19C. An imitation of the sound.]

POW *abbr* prisoner of war

powder /pówdər/ *n* **1 TINY LOOSE PARTICLES** a substance in the form of a loose grouping of many tiny dry grains **2 POWDER FOR PARTICULAR PURPOSE** a substance in the form of powder that is produced for a particular purpose by crushing or drying a solid or by mixing various powders ○ *face powder* **3 GUNPOWDER** gunpowder **4 DRY SNOW** light dry snow ■ *v* **1** *vt* **PUT POWDER ON** to cover something with powder, or to sprinkle powder on something **2** *vti* **TURN INTO POWDER** to turn a solid into powder or to become a powder [13C. Via French *poudrer* (verb) and *poudre* (noun, alteration of *poldre*) < Latin *pulver-*, stem of *pulvis* 'dust'.] —**powderer** *n* —**powdery** *adj*

powder blue *adj* of a very pale purplish-blue colour (*hyphenated before nouns*) —**powder blue** *n*

powder burn *n* a minor skin burn caused by being very close to a brief intense explosion, especially gunfire, sometimes used as evidence in a court of law

powder flask *n* a small flask for keeping gunpowder for loading a firearm

powder horn *n* a small container consisting of the hollow horn of an ox or cow for keeping gunpowder for loading a firearm

powder keg *n* **1** a small barrel used to hold gunpowder or blasting powder **2** a tense situation that may easily erupt into violence

powder metallurgy *n* the technology of working powdered metals or some carbides by compressing or heating without melting, or by compressing and heating without melting, to produce solid objects such as self-lubricating bearings

powder monkey *n* **1** a person who deals with explosives, e.g. in mining or construction (*slang*) **2** a boy formerly employed on a warship to carry gunpowder from the store to the guns (*dated*)

powder puff *n* a soft or fluffy pad used for putting powder on the face or skin

powder room *n* a toilet for women

powdery mildew *n* a fungal disease that produces a white powdery covering on plant leaves caused by various fungi

Powell /pṓ əl/, **Sir Anthony** (1906–2000) British novelist

Powell /pów əl/, **Cecil Frank** (1903–69) British physicist

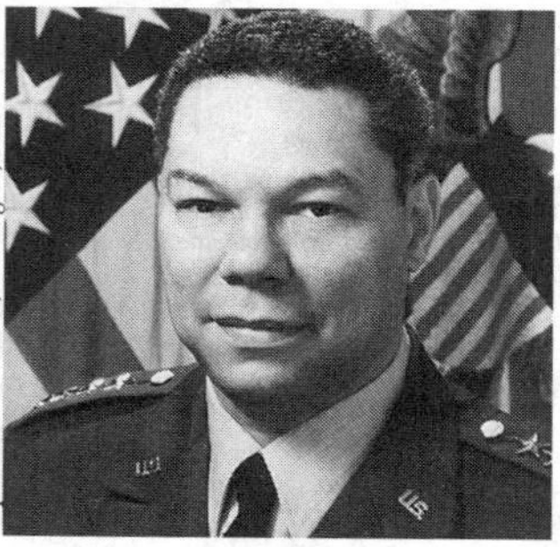

Department of Defense, Washington, D.C.

Colin Powell

Powell, Colin (*b.* 1937) US general and politician

Powell, Michael (1905–90) British film director

power /pówər/ *n* **1 ABILITY OR CAPACITY TO DO** the ability, skill, or capacity to do something **2 CONTROL AND INFLUENCE** control and influence over other people and their actions **3 AUTHORITY TO ACT** the authority to act or do something according to a law or rule **4 POLITICAL CONTROL** the political control of a country, exercised by its government or leader **5 SOMEBODY WITH POWER** a politically, financially, or socially powerful person **6 IMPORTANT COUNTRY** a country that has military or economic resources and is considered to have political influence over other countries **7 STRENGTH** physical force or strength **8 PERSUASIVENESS** the ability to influence people's judgment or emotions **9 SKILL** a faculty, skill, or ability ○ *musical powers* **10 ENERGY TO DRIVE MACHINERY** energy or force used to drive machinery or produce electricity **11 ELECTRICITY** electricity made available for use **12 MEASURE OF RATE OF DOING WORK** (*symbol P*) a measure of the rate of doing work or transferring energy, usually expressed in terms of wattage or horsepower **13 NUMBER OF MULTIPLICATIONS** the number of times a quantity is to be successively multiplied by itself, usually written as a small number to the right of and above the quantity **14 MAGNIFYING ABILITY** a measure of the ability of a lens, mirror, or prism to magnify an image **15 PROBABILITY OF REJECTING NULL HYPOTHESIS** the probability of rejecting the null hypothesis as false when a particular alternative hypothesis is true ■ *adj* **1 RUN BY ELECTRICITY OR FUEL** receiving power from a motor using electrical energy or fuel such as petrol, instead of relying on manual labour ○ *power tools* **2 INTENDED FOR BUSINESS SUCCESS** designed or believed to improve somebody's status, influence, or effectiveness in business ○ *power dressing* ■ *v* **1** *vt* **PROVIDE ENERGY TO OPERATE** to supply something such as a machine or tool with energy **2** *vi* **MOVE ENERGETICALLY** to move fast and with great determination and energy [13C. Via Anglo-Norman *poer* and Old French *poeir* < assumed Vulgar Latin *potere* 'to be powerful' < *potis* 'powerful'.] ◇ **do a** *or* **the power of good** to benefit somebody or something greatly (*informal*) ◇ **the powers that be** the people in authority

power down *vti* to switch a computer off in the correct way, bringing an orderly end to system operation

power up *v* **1** *vti* to switch on a computer, printer, or other peripheral device **2** *vt* to give somebody or something increased energy or capability

power base *n* a position, area, or group of voters providing the foundation of somebody's political power or support

powerboat /pówər bōt/ *n* a small motorboat with a powerful outboard or inboard motor, used especially for racing —**powerboating** *n*

power broker *n* a person or country that has great influence, especially in politics or commerce, and is able to use this influence to affect the policies and decisions of others

power cut *n* a temporary loss of electricity supply to a building or to an area of a town. US term **power outage**

power dive *n* a steep dive made by an aircraft with its engines at high power to increase the speed —**power-dive** *vti*

powerful /pówərf'l/ *adj* **1 INFLUENTIAL** able to exert a lot of influence and control over people and events ○ *a powerful nation* **2 STRONG** with great physical or mental strength or force **3 EFFECTIVE** with the strength or qualities to be effective in producing a result ○ *a powerful antibiotic* **4 PERSUASIVE** able to produce a strong effect on people's ideas or emotions ○ *a powerful film* —**powerfully** *adv* —**powerfulness** *n*

powerhouse /pówər howss/ (*plural* **-houses** /pówər howziz/) *n* somebody or something that is full of energy and very productive, especially of new ideas (*informal*)

powerless /pówərləss/ *adj* lacking power, strength, or effectiveness —**powerlessly** *adv* —**powerlessness** *n*

power line *n* a cable that carries electricity from a power station to the users of the electricity or between electric utilities in a network

power nap *n* a short sleep taken by a businessperson in the office in order to feel revitalized

power of appointment *n* the authority given to somebody to select beneficiaries and to allocate money and other property from a person's estate to those beneficiaries

power of attorney *n* the legal authority to act for another person in legal and business matters

power outage *n US* = **power cut**

power pack *n* a device for converting electrical supply to direct or alternating current at the correct voltage for a piece of electrical or electronic equipment

power plant *n* **1** INDUST = **power station 2** a unit that supplies the power to move a self-propelled object, e.g. a diesel-electric engine in a locomotive or an internal-combustion engine in an automobile

power play *n* **1 BID FOR ADVANTAGE** an attempt to gain an advantage by a display of strength or superiority, e.g. in a negotiation or relationship **2 TACTIC OF CONCENTRATING RESOURCES** a tactic in business, commerce, or politics of concentrating resources and effort on one particular area **3 TACTIC OF CONCENTRATING PLAYERS** a tactic used in sport consisting of concentrating players in a particular area **4 NUMERICAL ADVANTAGE IN ICE HOCKEY** a situation or period of time in ice hockey during which one team has a numerical advantage because the other team has one or more players in the penalty box

power point *n* ELEC = **socket** *n.* 2

power politics *n* political relations and actions based on an implied threat of use of political, economic, or military power by a participant (*takes a singular verb*)

power series *n* an infinite series in which the terms contain regularly increasing integral powers of a variable

power shovel *n* a mobile machine for excavating and removing debris, with a movable lever arm ending in a hinged digging bucket

power station *n* an industrial complex where power, especially electricity, is generated from another source of energy such as burning coal, nuclear reactions, or flowing water. US term **power plant** *n*. 1

power steering *n* a system of steering for a motor vehicle in which turning the steering wheel is made easier by supplementary power from the vehicle's engine

power takeoff *n* 1 the transfer of power from a vehicle's engine to another piece of machinery such as a winch or hydraulic pump 2 a device for transferring power from a vehicle's engine to another piece of machinery

power train *n* the portion of a vehicle's drive mechanism that transmits power from the engine to the wheels, tracks, or propellers. A car's power train includes the clutch, transmission, driveshaft, and differential.

⚡ **power user** *n* a computer user who is expert in one or more software applications (*informal*)

power walking *n* a form of exercise involving energetic walking in which the arms are swung backwards and forwards, sometimes using weights, in order to increase the heart rate —**power walker** *n*

powwow /pów wow/ *n* 1 **MEETING** a meeting or gathering to discuss something (*informal*) 2 **NATIVE AMERICAN CEREMONY** a traditional Native American ceremony featuring dance, feasting, and a blessing by a shaman for an event such as a marriage, a major hunt, or a gathering of nations ■ *vi* **HAVE POWWOW** to hold a powwow (*informal*) [Early 19C. < Narragansett *powah, powwaw* 'shaman'.]

Powys /pów iss/ county in central Wales. Area: 5,205 sq. km/2,009 sq. mi.

pox /poks/ *n* 1 a venereal disease, especially syphilis (*informal*) 2 a viral disease such as smallpox or chickenpox that causes pus-filled blisters (**pustules**) to form on the skin, and often leaves scars (**pockmarks**) [Alteration of the plural of POCK] ◇ **a pox on somebody** *or* **something** expresses a wish that misfortune will come to somebody *or* something (*archaic*)

poxvirus /póks vìrəss/ *n* an oval-shaped DNA-containing virus responsible for diseases that cause pus-filled blisters (**pustules**) to form on the skin

poxy /póksi/ (**-ier, -iest**) *adj* so contemptible or unpleasant as to be worthless (*informal*) [Early 20C. The literal sense is 'infected with pox'.]

Poznań /pőz nan/ city in west-central Poland. Population: 581,800 (1995).

pozzuolana /pótswə laánə/, **pozzolana** /pótsə-/ *n* a porous volcanic ash that when mixed with cement hardens either in air or under water [Early 18C. < Italian *pozz(u)olana (terra)* '(earth) of Pozzuoli (town near Naples in Italy)'.]

Pozzuoli /pot swáwli/ city in S Italy. Population: 75,706 (1991).

pp *abbr* 1 by proxy (*used when signing documents on behalf of somebody else*) 2 past participle 3 pianissimo 4 privately printed

PP *abbr* 1 after a meal (*in prescriptions*) 2 parcel post 3 parish priest 4 past president 5 postpaid 6 prepaid 7 prepositional phrase

ppb *abbr* parts per billion

PPV *abbr* pay-per-view

⚡ **pr** *abbr* Puerto Rico (*in Internet addresses*)

PR *abbr* Puerto Rico

pr. *abbr* pronoun

praam *n* NAUT = **pram**²

practicable /práktikəb'l/ *adj* 1 capable of being carried out or put into effect 2 capable of being used [Mid-17C. Via medieval Latin *practicabilis* < Greek *praktikē*, the feminine of *praktikos* 'practical' (see PRACTISE).]

practical /práktik'l/ *adj* 1 **CONCERNED WITH MATTERS OF FACT** concerned with actual facts and experience, not theory ○ *the practical applications of this research* 2 **USEFUL** sensible or useful, and likely to be effective ○ *practical advice* 3 **GOOD AT SOLVING PROBLEMS** good at managing matters and dealing with problems and difficulties 4 **SUITABLE FOR EVERYDAY USE** plain, functional, and suitable for everyday use 5 **VIRTUAL** resembling a particular thing in almost every way (*informal*) ○ *The campaign was a practical disaster.* ■ *n* **LESSON WITH HANDS-ON ACTIVITIES** a lesson or examination that requires actually doing something such as an experiment or a medical procedure ○ *a physics practical* [Via medieval Latin *practicalis* < Greek *praktikos* (see PRACTICE)] —**practicality** /prákti kálləti/ *n*

practical joke *n* a trick that is carried out on somebody to make him or her look silly and to amuse others —**practical joker** *n*

practically /práktikli/ *adv* 1 very nearly but not quite 2 in a way that is useful, sensible, or practical

practical nurse *n* US a nurse who has completed a level of training lower than that of a registered nurse

practice /práktiss/ *vti* US = **practise** ■ *n* 1 **REPETITION IN ORDER TO IMPROVE** the process of repeating something such as an exercise many times in order to improve performance 2 **PERFORMANCE OF RELIGION, PROFESSION, OR CUSTOMS** the performance of a religion, profession, set of customs, or established habit 3 **PROCESS OF CARRYING OUT IDEA** the process of carrying out an idea, plan, or theory ○ *It's more difficult to put these ideas into practice.* 4 **WORK OF PROFESSIONAL PERSON** the business of a lawyer, doctor, dentist, or other professional 5 **HABIT** a habit, custom, or usual way of doing something ○ *good business practices* [15C. < PRACTISE.] ◇ **practice what you preach** to do or act in the manner that you want others to do or act

SYNONYMS See *habit*.

practiced *adj* US = **practised**

practice teaching *n* US = **teaching practice**

practicing *adj* US = **practising**

~~**practicle**~~ incorrect spelling of **practical**

~~**practicly**~~ incorrect spelling of **practically**

practicum /práktikəm/ *n* US = **placement** *n*. 3 [Early 20C. < late Latin, the neuter of *practicus* 'active, practical' < Greek *praktikos* (see PRACTISE).]

practise /práktiss/ (**-tises, -tising, -tised**) *v* 1 *vti* **REPEAT IN ORDER TO IMPROVE** to do something, especially exercises, repeatedly in order to improve performance 2 *vt* **DO SOMETHING AS CUSTOM** to do something as an established custom or habit 3 *vti* **WORK IN LAW OR MEDICINE** to work in a particular job or profession, especially law or medicine 4 *vt* **FOLLOW RELIGION** to act according to the beliefs and customs of a religion 5 *vt* **PERPETRATE** to perpetrate something morally bad, e.g. deceit or cruelty 6 *vi* **TAKE ADVANTAGE OF** to take advantage of somebody, especially somebody who is gullible [14C. Directly or via obsolete French *practiser* < medieval Latin *practizare*, alteration of *practicare* < Greek *praktikos* 'practical' < *prattein* 'to do'.]

practised /práktist/ *adj* expert in doing something because of long experience

practising *adj* actively involved in a particular activity, e.g. a profession, religion, or way of life

practitioner /prak tísh'nər/ *n* a person who practises a profession, especially medicine [Mid-16C. < obsolete *practician* < Old French *practicien* < *practiser* 'practise' (see PRACTISE).]

Prado /praádō/ *n* a museum in Madrid that contains the Spanish national collection of paintings, sculptures, and drawings

praemunire /preé myoo nīri, -neéri/ *n* the offence under English law of accepting the authority of some other power over that of the English crown, or an accusation to that effect [< medieval Latin *praemunire facias* 'that you warn' (< the writ); *praemunire* 'to warn' < Latin, 'to fortify in front' < *munire* 'to fortify, defend' (see MUNITION)]

praenomen /pree nṓmən/ (*plural* **-nomens** *or* **-nomina** /-nómminə/) *n* in ancient Rome, somebody's first name [Early 17C. < Latin, 'forename' < *nomen* 'name'.] —**praenominal** /pree nómmin'l/ *adj* —**praenominally** /pree nómmin'li/ *adv*

praesidium *n* = **presidium**

praetor /preétər, -tawr/, **pretor** *n* in ancient Rome, any of several magistrates ranking immediately below the consuls and acting as the chief law officers of the state [15C. < Latin] —**praetorial** /pree táwri əl/ *adj* —**praetorship** *n*

praetorian /pree táwri ən/, **pretorian** *adj* 1 **RELATING TO PRAETORS** relating to praetors or to the office of praetor 2 **CORRUPT** corrupt and venal (*formal*) ■ *n* **ANCIENT ROMAN OF PRAETOR RANK** in ancient Rome, a holder or former holder of the office of praetor, e.g. an ex-praetor who became governor of a province

Praetorian, Pretorian *adj* belonging or relating to the Praetorian Guard ■ *n* a member of the Praetorian Guard

Praetorian Guard *n* 1 the emperor's bodyguard in ancient Rome 2 a soldier of the emperor's bodyguard in ancient Rome

pragmatic /prag máttik/ *adj* 1 **CONCERNED WITH PRACTICAL RESULTS** more concerned with practical results than with theories and principles 2 **RELATING TO PHILOSOPHICAL PRAGMATISM** relating to or characteristic of philosophical pragmatism 3 **POLITICAL** relating to the political affairs of a country (*formal*) 4 **LEARNING LESSONS FROM HISTORY** dealing with or looking at the facts of history with particular regard to the lessons that can be learned from them 5 **RELATING TO PRAGMATICS** relating or belonging to pragmatics [Late 16C. Via late Latin *pragmaticus* < Greek *pragma* 'deed, action'.] —**pragmaticality** /prag mátti kálləti/ *n* —**pragmatically** /prag máttikli/ *adv*

pragmatics /prag máttiks/ *n* the branch of linguistics that studies language use rather than language structure (+ *singular verb*)

pragmatic sanction *n* a special decree issued by a sovereign that has the force of law

pragmatism /prágmətizəm/ *n* 1 a straightforward practical way of thinking about things or dealing with problems, concerned with results rather than with theories and principles 2 a philosophical view that a theory or concept should be evaluated in terms of how it works and its consequences as the standard for action and thought. ◊ **instrumentalism** —**pragmatist** *n* —**pragmatistic** /prágmə tístik/ *adj*

Prague /praag/ capital of the Czech Republic, in the west of the country. Population: 1,213,000 (1995).

Praia /prī ə/ capital of the Republic of Cape Verde, in SE São Tiago island. Population: 95,000 (1998 estimate).

prairie /práiri/ *n* a treeless grass-covered plain in the United States and Canada, especially in the Midwest and the West ■ **prairies** *npl Can* the Prairie Provinces of Manitoba, Alberta, and Saskatchewan in Canada [Late 18C. Via French < assumed Vulgar Latin *prataria* < Latin *pratum* 'meadow' < ?]

prairie chicken *n* a game bird of the grouse family, having mottled brownish plumage, the male of which has inflatable air sacs on its throat, used in courtship. Native to: grasslands of North America. *Tympanuchus cupido* and *Tympanuchus pallidicinctus*.

prairie dog *n* a burrowing rodent of the squirrel family with light brown fur that lives in large underground colonies. Native to: grasslands of North America. Genus: *Cynomys*.

prairie oyster *n* 1 a drink consisting of a raw egg, Worcestershire sauce, salt, and pepper, taken as a cure for a hangover or hiccups 2 US the fried testicle of a calf or pig, eaten as a delicacy in the Midwestern United States (*usually plural*)

prairie schooner *n* a large covered wagon pulled by horses or oxen that was used by pioneers crossing the North American prairies in the 19th century [< the imagined resemblance of their canvas tops, seen from a distance, to a ship's sails]

praise /prayz/ *n* 1 **EXPRESSION OF ADMIRATION** words that express great approval or admiration, e.g. for somebody's ability or achievements or for something's good qualities 2 **WORSHIP** worship and thanks to God or a deity (*often plural*) ■ *vt* (**praises, praising, praised**) 1 **EXPRESS ADMIRATION FOR** to express great approval or admiration, e.g. for somebody's ability or achievements or for something's good qualities 2 **WORSHIP GOD** to give worship and thanks to God or a deity [13C. Via Old French *preisier* < late Latin *pretiare* 'to prize' < *pretium* 'price'.] —**praiser** *n* ◇ **sing somebody's or something's praises** to praise somebody or something enthusiastically ○ *She's not one to sing her own praises.*

praiseworthy /práyz wurthi/ *adj* deserving praise —**praiseworthily** *adv* —**praiseworthiness** *n*

prajna /prújnə, prúzhnə/ *n* in Buddhist teaching, direct awareness and understanding of truth not achieved by intellectual or rational means [Early 19C. < Sanskrit *prajñā* 'to know directly'.]

Prakrit /praákrit/ *n* an Indic language belonging to a group spoken in N India from approximately 400 BC to AD 1000 [Mid-18C. < Sanskrit *prākṛta* 'natural, vernacular' < *pra-* 'forward' + *kṛta-*, past participle of *karoti* 'it makes' (see SANSKRIT).] —**Prakrit** *adj*

praline /praá leen/ *n* 1 a nut caramelized in boiling sugar syrup that hardens when cold, or a substance made from crushed caramelized nuts and used as a dessert topping or chocolate filling 2 a chocolate with a soft filling made from crushed caramelized nuts, usually almonds [Early 18C. After Marshal de Plessis-*Praslin* (1598–1675), French officer.]

pralltriller /praál trilər/ *n* a musical embellishment made by the quick alternation of a particular note with the note immediately above it [Mid-19C. < German, 'bouncing trill'.]

pram[1] /pram/ *n* a cot on four wheels with a handle at one end and a hood at the other, in which a baby can be transported out of doors. US term **baby carriage** [Late 19C. Contraction of PERAMBULATOR.]

pram[2] /praam/, **praam** *n* **1** a small fishing boat with a flat bottom and a square front **2** a flat-bottomed barge used in Baltic ports [Mid-16C. Via Dutch *praam* < Czech *prám* 'raft'.]

prana /praánə/ *n* **1** in yoga, the use of inhalation, holding the breath, and exhalation according to particular patterns and time periods **2** in Hinduism, breath or breathing [Mid-19C. < Sanskrit *prāṇa* 'breathing out'.]

prance /praanss/ *v* (**prances, prancing, pranced**) **1** *vi* **MOVE IN LIVELY WAY** to move about in a lively and carefree, but often exaggerated way **2** *vi* **SWAGGER** to walk in a way that displays excessive pride, arrogance, or a desire to be noticed and admired **3** *vti* **JUMP FORWARD ON BACK LEGS** to raise the front legs and jump forward on the back legs, as a horse does, or to make a horse perform this step **4** *vti* **WALK WITH LIVELY STEPS** to walk with lively springing steps, or to make a horse walk this way ■ *n* **PRANCING MOVEMENT** a lively, springing, or carefree movement [14C] —**prancer** *n* —**prancing** *adj* —**prancingly** *adv*

prandial /prándi əl/ *adj* relating to a meal, especially lunch or dinner (*formal or humorous*) [Early 19C. < Latin *prandium* 'late breakfast'.] —**prandially** *adv*

prang /prang/ *vt* **1 CRASH** to crash or damage a vehicle or aircraft (*informal*) **2 BOMB** to bomb a target (*dated slang*) ■ *n* **1 CRASH** a crash in a vehicle or aircraft (*informal*) **2 BOMBING RAID** a bombing raid (*dated slang*) [Mid-20C. < ?]

prank[1] /prangk/ *n* a mischievous trick or silly stunt done for amusement [Late 16C. < ?] —**prankish** *adj*

prank[2] /prangk/ *vti* to embellish or display something in an ostentatious manner (*formal*) ○ *Don't prank yourself up, it's only a family dinner.* [Mid-16C. Probably < Middle Dutch *pronken* or Middle Low German *prunken* 'to show off'.]

prankster /prángkstər/ *n* somebody who enjoys playing mischievous tricks on people

Prasad /prə saád/, **Rajendra** (1884–1963) Indian statesman

prase /práyz/ *n* a green form of quartz [Late 18C. Via French < Greek *prasios* 'leek-coloured' < *prason* 'leek'.]

praseodymium /práyzi ō dímmi əm/ *n* (*symbol* **Pr**) a soft ductile silvery metallic element belonging to the rare-earth group. Use: alloys, colouring for glass. [Late 19C. < Greek *prasios* 'leek-coloured' (see PRASE) + DIDYMIUM.]

prat /prat/ *n* **1 prat, pratt FOOL** somebody regarded as unintelligent (*slang insult*) **2 BUTTOCKS** the buttocks (*slang*) ■ *vi* (**prats, pratting, pratted**) **BEHAVE THOUGHTLESSLY OR EXASPERATINGLY** to behave in an unintelligent way, especially when this causes exasperation or leads to time-wasting (*insult*) [Mid-16C. < ?]

prate /prayt/ *vi* (**prates, prating, prated**) to talk in a silly way and at length about nothing important ■ *n* silly or idle talk [15C. < Middle Dutch *praten*.] —**prater** *n* —**pratingly** *adv*

pratfall /prát fawl/ *n US* (*slang*) **1** a backward fall onto the buttocks, especially one executed deliberately for comic effect **2** an embarrassing or humiliating mistake or failure

pratie /práyti/ *n Ireland* a potato (*informal*) [Late 18C. < Irish *prátai*, plural of *práta*.]

pratincole /prátting kōl/ *n* a brown or grey bird with long pointed wings, a forked tail, and a short bill. Native to: Europe. Family: Glareolidae. [Late 18C. < modern Latin *pratincola* < Latin *pratum* 'meadow' + *incola* 'dweller'.]

pratique /pra teék/ *n* permission granted to a ship or boat to use a port on satisfying the local quarantine regulations or on producing a clean bill of health [Early 17C. < French, 'practice'.]

prattle /prátt'l/ *vi* (**-tles, -tling, -tled**) to talk in a silly, idle, or childish way ■ *n* silly, idle, or childish talk [Mid-16C. < ?] —**prattler** *n* —**prattlingly** *adv*

prau *n* = **proa**

pravastatin /právvə státtin/ *n* a drug used to reduce abnormally high levels of blood cholesterol

prawn /prawn/ *n* an edible sea animal resembling a shrimp, with a slender body, a long tail, five pairs of legs, and two pairs of pincers. Genera: *Palaemon* and *Penaeus*. ■ *vi* to fish for prawns [15C] —**prawner** *n* ◇ **come the raw prawn** *Aus* to try to deceive or mislead someone, usually by acting or pleading innocent (*informal*)

prawn cocktail *n* cooked and shelled prawns in a seafood dressing, usually served in a small bowl or glass with salad garnish and eaten cold as a starter

prawn cracker *n* a light and puffy prawn-flavoured snack food resembling a crisp, made from rice flour and often served with a Chinese meal as an appetizer

praxis /práksiss/ *n* (*formal*) **1** the practical side and application of something such as a professional skill, as opposed to its theory **2** an established custom or habitual practice [Late 16C. Via medieval Latin < Greek, < *prattein* 'to do'.]

Praxiteles /prak sittə leez/ (390?–330? BC) Greek sculptor

pray /pray/ *v* **1** *vti* **SPEAK TO GOD OR OTHER BEING** to speak to God, a deity, or a saint, e.g. in order to give thanks, express regret, or ask for help **2** *vti* **HOPE STRONGLY** to hope strongly for something ○ *I'm just praying that it won't rain on Saturday.* **3** *vti* **MAKE EARNEST REQUEST** to ask somebody for something, especially earnestly or with passion ○ *He prayed to be allowed to go back home to his family.* **4** *vt* to attempt to achieve something by prayer ○ *The villagers tried to pray the drought away.* ■ *interj* **EMPHASIZING QUESTION OR COMMAND** emphasizes a question or a command, either politely or sarcastically ○ *And what, pray, do you think you're doing?* [13C. Via Old French *preier* < Latin *precari* 'to entreat' < *prec-*, stem of prex 'prayer'.]

SPELLCHECK Do not confuse ***pray*** with ***prey***, which has a similar sound. Beware: your spellchecker will not catch this error.

prayer /prair/ *n* **1 COMMUNICATION WITH GOD OR OTHER BEING** a spoken or unspoken communication with God, a deity, or a saint **2 COMMUNICATING WITH GOD OR OTHER BEING** the act or practice of making spoken or unspoken communication with God, a deity, or a saint **3 RELIGIOUS SERVICE WITH PRAYERS** a religious service at which prayers are said (*often plural*) **4 EARNEST REQUEST** an earnest request for something **5 SOMETHING WISHED FOR** something that is wanted or hoped for very much ○ *My only prayer is to see grandchildren before I die.* **6 REQUEST IN PETITION** a request contained in a petition **7 SLIGHT CHANCE** a slight chance or hope ○ *I don't have a prayer of getting the manager's job.* [13C. Via Old French *preiere* < Latin *precarius* 'obtained by entreaty' < *precari* 'to entreat' (see PRAY).]

prayer beads *npl* a string of beads such as a rosary used to keep count of prayers being recited

prayer book *n* a book containing the prayers regularly used in religious services

prayerful /práirf'l/ *adj* **1 PRAYING FREQUENTLY** liking to pray or praying frequently **2 INFLUENCED BY PRAYER** strongly influenced by prayer, or in which prayer plays an important part **3 EARNEST** earnest or sincere —**prayerfully** *adv* —**prayerfulness** *n*

Prayer over the Gifts *n* a variable prayer said at the conclusion of the Preparation of the Gifts and before the Preface in the Roman Catholic Mass

prayer rug, prayer mat *n* a rug on which a Muslim kneels to pray

prayer shawl *n* JUDAISM = **tallith**

prayer wheel *n* in Tibetan Buddhism and some other religions, a hollow cylinder that contains prayers written on a scroll

praying mantis *n* a large greenish-brown predatory insect with long forelegs that are raised and folded at rest, as if in prayer. Native to: Europe. *Mantis religiosis.*

PRB *abbr* Pre-Raphaelite Brotherhood (*after the name of a painter*)

pre- *prefix* **1** before, earlier ○ *preschool* **2** in advance, preparatory ○ *presell* ○ *prerelease* **3** in front of ○ *premolar* [< Latin *prae* 'in front, before'. Ultimately < Indo-European.]

preach /preech/ *v* **1** *vti* **GIVE SERMON** to give a talk on a religious or moral subject, especially in church **2** *vi* **GIVE ADVICE IN IRRITATING WAY** to give people advice on their morals or behaviour in an irritatingly tedious or overbearing way **3** *vt* **URGE PEOPLE TO ACCEPT** to make an opinion or attitude known to others and urge others to share it [13C. Via Old French *prechier* < Latin *praedicare* (see PREDICATE).] —**preachable** *adj*

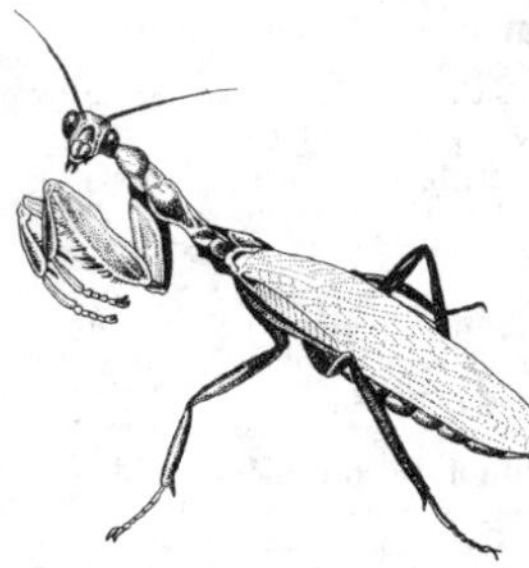

Praying mantis

preacher /preéchər/ *n* (*informal*) **1** a person whose occupation is to give sermons, preach the gospel, or conduct religious services, especially a minister of a Protestant church **2** a tedious or overbearing adviser or advocate of something

preachify /preéchi fī/ *vi* to preach or give advice on morals or behaviour in an irritatingly tedious or overbearing way (*informal*) —**preachifying** *n*

preachment /preéchmənt/ *n* (*informal*) **1** a sermon or talk on a moral or religious subject **2** tedious or overbearing advice on morals or behaviour

preachy /preéchi/ *adj* giving, or in the habit of giving, advice on morals or behaviour in an irritatingly tedious or overbearing way (*informal*) —**preachiness** *n*

preadaptation /pree áddap táysh'n/ *n* anatomical or behavioural feature of an organism that is highly suited to an adjacent habitat, thus allowing for migration and increased survival rate in response to environmental change —**preadapt** /preé ə dápt/ *vti* —**preadapted** *adj* —**preadaptive** /-dáptiv/ *adj*

preadolescence /pree áddə léssənss/ *n* the period of two or three years before adolescence —**preadolescent** *n, adj*

preagricultural /pree ággri kúlchərəl/ *adj* having not yet developed agriculture as a means of providing food. ◊ **hunter-gatherer**

preamble /pree ámb'l/ *n* **1** a section at the beginning of a speech, report, or formal document that explains the purpose of what follows **2** something that precedes, introduces, or leads up to something else [14C. Via French *préambule* < Latin *praeambulus* 'going in front' < *ambulare* 'to walk'.]

preamplifier /pree ámpli fīər/ *n* an amplifying circuit, e.g. in a radio or television, that is designed to strengthen very weak signals and then transmit them to a more powerful amplifier

prearrange /preé ə ráynj/ (**-ranges, -ranging, -ranged**) *vt* to arrange, plan, or agree on something beforehand —**prearrangement** *n*

preassemble /preé ə sémb'l/ (**-bles, -bling, -bled**) *vt* to fit components together before they are put into their final position or put to their final use ○ *Some of the mosaic pieces were preassembled before the floor was laid.*

prebend /prébbənd/ *n* **1** an allowance paid by a cathedral or collegiate church to a member of its clergy, or the property or tithe that is the source of this allowance **2** CHR = **prebendary 3** the position of prebendary in the Church of England [15C. Via French < late Latin *praebenda* 'things to be supplied' < Latin *praebere* 'to offer', literally 'to hold in front'.] —**prebendal** *adj*

prebendary /prébbəndəri/ *n* a member of the clergy of a cathedral or collegiate church, either one who receives an allowance from it or an honorary member who receives no payment —**prebendaryship** *n*

Precambrian /pree kámbri ən/ *n* the period of geological time when the Earth's crust consolidated and primitive life first appeared, 4,650 to 700 million years ago —**Precambrian** *adj*

precancel /pree kánss'l/ *vt* (**-cels, -celling, -celled**) to cancel the postage stamp on an envelope before posting it ■ *n* a stamp that has been cancelled before posting, or an item bearing such a stamp —**precancellation** /pree kánssə láysh'n/ *n*

precancerous /pree kánssərəss/ *adj* describes conditions or tissue abnormalities that are capable of becoming cancerous if left untreated

precarious /pri káiri əss/ *adj* **1** dangerously unstable, unsteady, uncertain, or insecure **2** based on uncertain premises or unwarranted assumptions (*formal*) [Mid-17C. < Latin *precarius* 'depending on entreaty, uncertain'.] —**precariously** *adv* —**precariousness** *n*

precast /prée kaast/ *adj* poured into a cast of the required shape and allowed to harden before being taken out and put into position ○ *buildings made entirely of precast concrete* —**precast** *vt*

precatory /prékətəri/ *adj* expressing a wish, a request, an entreaty, or a recommendation (*formal*) [Mid-17C. < late Latin *precatorius* < Latin *precari* 'to entreat' (see PRAY).]

precaution /pri káwsh'n/ *n* **1** an action taken to protect against possible harm or trouble or to limit the damage if something goes wrong ○ *wearing a hat as a precaution against sunstroke* **2** the foresight to protect against possible harm or trouble [Late 16C. Via French < Latin *praecaut-*, past participle of *praecavere* 'to take care before' < *cavere* 'to take heed' (see CAUTION).] —**precautional** *adj* —**precautionary** *adj* —**precautious** *adj*

precede /pri séed/ (**-cedes, -ceding, -ceded**) *vt* **1** to come, go, be, or happen before somebody or something else in time, position, or importance **2** to say or do something before something else [14C. Via French < Latin *praecedere* 'to go in front' < *cedere* 'to give way'.]

SPELLCHECK Do not confuse ***precede*** with ***proceed*** which has a similar sound. Beware: your spellchecker will not catch this error.

precedence /préssidənss/, **precedency** /préssidənssi/ *n* **1 PRIORITY** the right or need to be dealt with before somebody or something else or to be treated as more important than somebody or something else ○ *The interests of the rest of the group take precedence over their personal wishes.* **2 RELATIVE IMPORTANCE** relative importance in rank and status that determines something, e.g. the order in which participants are placed in a formal situation **3 GREATER IMPORTANCE** the fact of being more important than others (*formal*)

precedent *n* /préssidənt/ **1 EXAMPLE FOR LATER ACTION OR DECISION** an action or decision that can be subsequently used as an example for a similar decision or to justify a similar action **2 ESTABLISHED PRACTICE** an established custom or practice **3 REQUIREMENT TO FOLLOW EARLIER COURT DECISIONS** the doctrine that requires a court to follow decisions of superior or previous courts ■ *adj* /préssidənt, pri séed'nt/ **PRECEDING** coming, going, existing, or happening before somebody or something else (*formal*) —**precedently** *adv*

preceding /pri séeding/ *adj* coming, going, existing, or happening immediately before somebody or something else

~~preceed~~ incorrect spelling of **precede**

precentor /pri séntər/ *n* **1 LEADER OF CHURCH SINGING** a leader of the congregation or choir in a church **2 LEADER OF CATHEDRAL MUSIC** a member of the clergy of a cathedral who is nominally in charge of the music in the cathedral **3** *Scotland* **OFFICIAL SINGER IN SOME PRESBYTERIAN CHURCHES** in small Presbyterian denominations that disapprove of instrumental music in church, an official appointed by the Kirk Session to lead the singing by singing lines for the congregation to repeat [Early 17C. < Latin *praecentor* < *praecinere* 'to sing before' < *canere* 'to sing'.] —**precentorship** *n*

precept /prée sept/ *n* **1 PRINCIPLE** a rule, instruction, or principle that guides somebody's actions, especially one that guides moral behaviour (*formal*) **2 WARRANT OR WRIT** a warrant or writ that is issued by a legal authority **3 ORDER FOR PAYMENT** an order for the payment of money [14C. < Latin *praeceptum* 'something taught', past participle of *praecipere* 'to teach', literally 'to take before' < *capere* 'to take'.]

preceptive /pri séptiv/ *adj* giving instructions or orders, or setting out principles (*formal*) —**preceptively** *adv*

preceptor /pri séptər/ *n* **1 TEACHER** a teacher or instructor (*formal*) **2 SPECIALIZED TUTOR** a specialist in a profession, especially medicine, who gives practical training to a student **3 HEAD OF PRECEPTORY** the head of a community of Knights Templars —**preceptoral** *adj* —**preceptorate** *n* —**preceptorship** *n*

precess /pri séss/ *vti* to spin or make something spin with a motion in which the axis of rotation sweeps out a cone [Late 19C. Back-formation < PRECESSION.]

precession /pri sésh'n/ *n* the regular motion of a spinning body such as a spinning top or a planet, in which the axis of rotation sweeps out a cone [Late 16C. < late Latin *praecession-* < *praecess-*, past participle of *praecedere* 'to go before' (see PRECEDE).] —**precessional** *adj*

precession of the equinoxes *n* the slow westward movement of the equinoxes, resulting from the Earth's precessional motion, making them occur slightly earlier each year

pre-Christian *adj* existing or occurring before Jesus Christ or Christianity

precinct /prée singkt/ *n* **1 SPECIAL PART OF TOWN** a part of a town designated for a particular use, especially an area accessible only to pedestrians or a purpose-built area containing many shops ○ *a shopping precinct* **2** *US* **CITY AREA PATROLLED BY POLICE UNIT** a district of a city or town under a particular unit of the police force **3** *US* **POLICE UNIT OR STATION** the police unit or police station of a city or town district **4** *US* **ELECTORAL DISTRICT** a small electoral district of a city or town, part of a ward **5 BOUNDARY** a boundary marking out an area ■ **precincts** *npl* **AREA AROUND** the area surrounding a building or institution such as a cathedral or college [15C. < medieval Latin *praecinctum* 'something encircled', past participle of Latin *praecingere*, literally 'to gird about' < *cingere* 'to gird'.]

preciosity /préshi óssəti/ (*plural* **-ties**) *n* ridiculous over-refinement in language and manners, or an example of this ○ *It might be quite a good poem if all the preciosities were removed.* [14C. Via French < Latin *pretiosus* 'precious' (see PRECIOUS).]

precious /préshəss/ *adj* **1 VALUABLE** worth a great deal of money **2 VALUED** highly valued, much loved, or considered to be of great importance ○ *Your friendship is very precious to me.* **3 NOT TO BE WASTED** rare or unique and therefore to be used wisely or sparingly or treated with care **4 USED FOR EMPHASIS** used for emphasis to express irritation, dislike, contempt, bemusement, or some other strong emotion (*informal*) ○ *I'm tempted to tell them what they can do with their precious training course!* **5 FASTIDIOUS OR AFFECTED** too carefully refined in language, dress, and manners ■ *adv* **VERY** very ○ *And precious little thanks I got!* ■ *n* **TERM OF ENDEARMENT** used as term of affection in talking to somebody ○ *Good morning, my precious.* [13C. Via Old French *precios* < Latin *pretiosus* < *pretium* 'price'.] —**preciously** *adv* —**preciousness** *n*

precious coral *n* MARINE BIOL = **red coral**

precious metal *n* the metals gold, silver, or platinum, usually when found in the native state

precious stone *n* any relatively rare and valuable mineral used in jewellery

precipice /préssəpiss/ *n* **1** a high, vertical, or very steep rock face **2** a very dangerous situation [Late 16C. Directly or via French < Latin *praecipitium* < *praecipit-* 'headlong' (see PRECIPITATE).] —**precipiced** *adj*

precipitant /pri síppitənt/ *adj* **1 TOO HASTY** done too quickly and impulsively, often resulting in mistakes **2 SUDDEN OR UNEXPECTED** happening suddenly or unexpectedly **3 RUSHING** acting too quickly ■ *n* **SOMETHING CAUSING PRECIPITATION** a substance that causes precipitation [Early 17C. < French *précipitant*, present participle of *précipiter* (see PRECIPITATE).] —**precipitancy** *n* —**precipitantly** *adv*

precipitate *adj* /pri síppi tayt, -síppitət/ **1 DONE OR ACTING RASHLY** done or acting too quickly and without enough thought ○ *I may have been precipitate in accepting their offer.* **2 HURRIED** very hurried **3 SUDDEN** sudden and unexpected ■ *v* /pri síppi tayt/ (**-tates, -tating, -tated**) **1** *vt* **MAKE SOMETHING HAPPEN QUICKLY** to make something happen suddenly and quickly **2** *vt* **SEND SOMEBODY OR SOMETHING RAPIDLY** to send somebody or something suddenly and rapidly into some state or condition ○ *A minor border skirmish precipitated the two countries into war.* **3** *vti* **THROW OR FALL FROM ABOVE** to throw somebody or something or fall from a great height (*formal*) **4** *vti* **MAKE RAIN OR SNOW FALL** to cause liquid or solid forms of water, condensed in the atmosphere, to fall to the ground as rain, snow, or hail, or to fall in such a form **5** *vti* **SEPARATE SOLID OUT OF SOLUTION** to cause a solid to separate out from a solution as a result of a chemical reaction, or to separate out in this way ■ *n* /pri síppi tət, pri síppi tayt/ **SUSPENSION OF SMALL PARTICLES** a suspension of small solid particles that are formed in a solution as a result of a chemical reaction and usually settle out of the solution [Early 16C. < Latin *praecipitat-*, past participle of *praecipitare* 'to throw down' < *praeceps* 'headlong' < *caput* 'head'.] —**precipitability** /pri síppitə bílləti/ *n* —**precipitable** /-síppitəb'l/ *adj* —**precipitately** /-tətli/ *adv* —**precipitateness** *n* —**precipitative** *adj* —**precipitator** *n*

precipitation /pri síppi táysh'n/ *n* **1 RAIN OR SNOW OR HAIL** rain, snow, or hail, all of which are formed by condensation of moisture in the atmosphere and fall to the ground **2 FORMATION OF RAIN OR SNOW OR HAIL** the formation of rain, snow, or hail from moisture in the air **3 FORMATION OF SUSPENSION IN SOLUTION** the formation of a suspension of an insoluble compound by mixing two solutions **4 HASTE** great or excessive haste (*formal*) ○ *He deeply regretted the precipitation of his elopement.* **5 A QUICKENING OF** a bringing about of something earlier or more suddenly than expected (*formal*) ○ *circumstances that led to the precipitation of my divorce* **6 PROPULSION** the propelling or throwing of somebody or something (*formal*)

precipitin /pri síppitin/ *n* an antibody that, when combined with its antigen, forms a substance that separates out of solution and can be detected visually [Early 20C. < PRECIPITATE + -IN.]

precipitinogen /pri síppi tinnəjən/ *n* an antigen that causes the formation of a specific precipitin [Early 20C. < PRECIPITIN + -GEN.]

precipitous /pri síppitəss/ *adj* **1 DONE RASHLY** done or acting too quickly and without enough thought **2 LIKE A PRECIPICE** very high and steep **3 WITH A PRECIPICE** having several precipices [Mid-17C. Via French *précipiteux* < Latin *praecipitium* (see PRECIPICE).] —**precipitously** *adv* —**precipitousness** *n*

précis /práy see/ *n* (*plural* **-cis**) a shortened version of a speech or written text, containing the main points and omitting minor details ■ *vt* to make a précis of something [Mid-18C. < French, 'abridged'.]

precise /pri síss/ *adj* **1 EXACT OR DETAILED** exact and accurate, or detailed and specific ○ *The train leaves an hour from now, or 57 minutes, to be precise.* **2 HANDLING SMALL DETAILS** able to assimilate details or wanting to be given details **3 INDICATING SOMETHING SPECIFIC** indicating that something is the exact one that is being referred to ○ *At that precise moment, in he came.* **4 CAREFUL ABOUT DETAILS** very careful about small details, especially of correct behaviour **5 CLEAR** distinct and correct [Early 16C. Via French < Latin *praecisus*, past participle of *praecidere* 'to cut off in front' < *caedere* 'to cut'.] —**preciseness** *n*

precisely /pri síssli/ *adv* **1 EXACTLY** exactly ○ *That is precisely what I mean.* **2 IN DETAIL** in complete and accurate detail ○ *Tell me precisely what happened.* **3 ACCURATELY** with absolute accuracy ○ *instruments that must be adjusted precisely before use* **4 CLEARLY** clearly and distinctly ○ *She speaks very precisely.* **5 USED FOR EMPHASIS** used to add emphasis when specifying something ○ *It was precisely because you didn't ask that she thought you didn't need her help.* **6 EXPRESSING AGREEMENT** used to indicate complete agreement with what has been said ○ *'But I don't think they can be relied on'.'Precisely'.*

precisian /pri sízh'n/ *n* a person who is concerned about correct rules and behaviour, especially in moral and religious matters —**precisianism** *n*

precision /pri sízh'n/ *n* **1 EXACTNESS** exactness or accuracy **2 MATHEMATICAL ACCURACY** the accuracy to which a calculation is performed, specifying the number of significant digits with which the result is expressed ■ *adj* **RELATING TO EXACTNESS OR ACCURACY** allowing for, made with, or requiring great exactness or accuracy [Late 16C. Via French < Latin *praecis-*, past participle of *praecidere* (see PRECISE).]

preclassical /pree klássik'l/ *adj* relating to or occurring before what is regarded as the classical period in a civilization, art, or language, especially before the classical period in ancient Greek and Roman culture

preclinical /pree klínnik'l/ *adj* relating to or characteristic of a disease before the symptoms become evident —**preclinically** *adv*

preclude /pri klóod/ (**-cludes, -cluding, -cluded**) *vt* **1** to prevent something or make it impossible, or to prevent somebody from doing something (*formal*) ○ *That shouldn't preclude a satisfactory outcome.* **2** to exclude somebody or something, especially in advance ○ *Having a relative in the company precludes me from entering the contest.* [Early 17C. < Latin *praecludere* 'to close off ahead' < *claudere* 'to close'.] —**preclusion** /pri klóozh'n/ *n* —**preclusive** /-klóossiv/ *adj* —**preclusively** *adv*

precocial /pri kṓsh'l/ *adj* describes some animals that display independent activity at birth, especially young birds that are hatched covered with down and with open eyes [Late 19C. < modern Latin *praecoces* 'precocial birds', the plural of Latin *praecox* 'precocious' (see PRECOCIOUS).]

precocious /pri kṓshəss/ *adj* **1** more developed, especially mentally, than is usual or expected at a particular age, or showing such advanced development **2** describes a plant or tree that blossoms before its leaves appear, e.g. the magnolia, or one whose fruits ripen early [Mid-17C. < Latin *praecox* 'ripening early', literally 'cooked ahead' < *coquere* 'to cook'.] —**precociously** *adv* —**precociousness** *n* —**precocity** /pri kóssəti/ *n*

precognition /prée kog nísh'n/ *n* **1** the ability to know what is going to happen in the future, especially if based on extrasensory perception **2** in Scotland, an official investigation of the facts of a case by interrogating witnesses in preparation for a trial, to make it possible to prepare a relevant charge in defence —**precognitive** /pree kógnitiv/ *adj*

preconceived /prée kən séevd/ *adj* formed in the mind in advance, especially if based on little or no information or experience and reflecting personal prejudices —**preconceive** *vt*

preconception /prée kən sépsh'n/ *n* an idea or opinion formed in advance, especially if it is based on little or no information or experience and reflects personal prejudices

precondition /prée kən dísh'n/ *n* something that must be done or agreed before something else will happen ○ *They made a total ceasefire a precondition of the talks.* ■ *vt* to prepare somebody or something for a process or put somebody into a desired mental state

preconize /préekə nīz/, **preconise** (**-ises, -ising, -ised**) *vt* **1 PROCLAIM** to proclaim or announce something (*formal*) **2 SUMMON** to summon somebody publicly (*formal*) **3 GIVE PAPAL APPROVAL TO BISHOP** in the Roman Catholic Church, to make a public announcement of papal approval of the appointment of a bishop [15C. < medieval Latin *praeconizare* < Latin *praecon-*, stem of *praeco* 'public crier'.] —**preconization** /préekə nī záysh'n/ *n*

preconscious /pree kónshəss/ *n* in Freudian theory, the part of the mind lying between the conscious and the unconscious ■ *adj* relating to or contained in the preconscious —**preconsciously** *adv* —**preconsciousness** *n*

precontract *n* /pree kón trakt/ **CONTRACT MADE IN ADVANCE** a contract made in advance to prevent a subsequent contract, especially a betrothal ■ *vti* /pree kən trákt/ **1 MAKE AGREEMENT IN ADVANCE** to make a contract or enter into an agreement in advance **2 MAKE CONTRACT FOR ARRANGED MARRIAGE** in former times, to pledge somebody to marriage by an earlier agreement or to become pledged in this way

precook /pree kóok/ *vt* to cook food completely or partially in advance, especially before it is sold, so that only minimal cooking or merely reheating is required —**precooked** *adj*

precool /pree kóol/ *vt* to cool a substance or object in advance, ready for use

precritical /pree kríttik'l/ *adj* relating to the time or state before a crisis or before something such as a disease reaches a critical condition

precursor /pri kúrssər/ *n* **1 SOMEBODY OR SOMETHING THAT COMES EARLIER** somebody or something that comes before, and is often considered to lead to the development of, another person or thing **2 PREVIOUS HOLDER OF JOB** a previous holder of a specific position **3 CHEMICAL COMPOUND PRECEDING ANOTHER** a chemical compound that leads to another, usually more stable, product in a series of connected reactions [Early 16C. < Latin *praecursor* < *praecurs-*, stem of *praecurrere* 'to run before' < *currere* 'to run'.]

precursory /pree kúrssri, pri-/, **precursive** /-kúrssiv/ *adj* **1** at an initial or preparatory stage **2** serving as an indication of something to come (*formal*)

precut /pree kút/ *adj* cut or cut out before being used or sold

predacious /pri dáyshəss/, **predaceous** *adj* **1** describes animals that hunt, kill, and eat other animals **2** attacking and stealing from other people (*formal*) [Early 18C. < Latin *praedari* 'to seize as plunder' (see PREDATORY).] —**predaciousness** *n* —**predacity** /pri dássəti/ *n*

predate /prée dáyt/ (**-dates, -dating, -dated**) *vt* **1** to come before something or somebody in time **2** to put a date on something that is earlier than the actual date, or to say that something occurred at an earlier date than it actually did

predation /pri dáysh'n/ *n* **1** the relationship between two groups of animals in which one species hunts, kills, and eats the other **2** the act of plundering, stealing, or destroying [15C. < Latin *praedation-* < *praedari* 'to seize as plunder' (see PREDATORY).]

predator /préddətər/ *n* **1 CARNIVOROUS ANIMAL OR DESTRUCTIVE ORGANISM** a carnivorous animal that hunts, kills, and eats other animals in order to survive, or any other organism that behaves in a similar manner **2 SOMEBODY WHO PLUNDERS OR DESTROYS** a person, group, company, or state that steals from others or destroys others for gain **3 RUTHLESSLY AGGRESSIVE PERSON** an aggressive, determined, or persistent person (*disapproving*) [Early 20C. < Latin *praedator* < *praedari* 'to seize as plunder' (see PREDATORY).]

predatory /préddətəri/ *adj* **1 RELATING TO PREDATORS** relating to or characteristic of animals that survive by preying on others **2 GREEDILY DESTRUCTIVE** greedily eager to steal from or destroy others for gain **3 RUTHLESSLY AGGRESSIVE** extremely aggressive, determined, or persistent (*disapproving*) [Late 16C. < Latin *praedatorius* < *praedari* 'to seize as plunder' < *praeda* 'booty'.] —**predatorily** *adv* —**predatoriness** *n*

predatory pricing *n* the act of setting prices at very low levels in order to force other companies out of the market

predecease /préedi seéss/ (**-ceases, -ceasing, -ceased**) *vt* to die before somebody else ○ *His eldest son predeceased him.* —**predecease** *n*

predecessor /préedi sessər/ *n* **1 PREVIOUS HOLDER OF JOB** a person who previously held a specific position **2 ONE THING REPLACED BY SOMETHING ELSE** a thing previously in use or existence that has been replaced or succeeded by another ○ *I hope my new car will be more reliable than its predecessor.* **3 ANCESTOR** an ancestor [14C. Via French < late Latin *praedecessor* 'one who has departed before' < *decedere* 'to depart'.]

predefined /prée di fínd/ *adj* having been defined or established in advance

predella /pri déllə/ *n* **1** the platform for an altar, or the step on which an altar rests **2** the decorative base of an altarpiece, embellished with small paintings or sculptures [Mid-19C. < Italian, 'stool'.]

predestinarian /prée desti náiri ən/ *n* a believer in predestination ■ *adj* relating to predestination or to people who believe in it —**predestinarianism** *n*

predestinate /pree désti nayt/ *vt* (**-nates, -nating, -nated**) **PREDESTINE** to predestine something or somebody ■ *adj* **1 FOREORDAINED** decided in advance **2 FOREORDAINED BY GOD OR A DEITY** decided and decreed in advance by God, a deity, or fate [14C. < ecclesiastical Latin *praedestinatus*, past participle of *praedestinare* (see PREDESTINE).]

predestination /pree désti náysh'n/ *n* **1 ADVANCE DECISION BY GOD ABOUT EVENTS** the doctrine holding that God, a deity, or fate has established in advance everything that is going to happen and that nothing can change this course of events **2 GOD'S DECISION WHO GOES TO HEAVEN** the doctrine that God decided at the beginning of time who would go to Heaven after death and who would not **3 FOREORDAINING** the divine or human act of deciding the fate of people or things beforehand

predestine /pree déstin/ (**-tines, -tining, -tined**) *vt* **1** to decide in advance what is going to happen **2** to select in advance who will go to Heaven after death and who will not [14C. Directly or via French < ecclesiastical Latin *praedestinare* 'to foreordain' < Latin *destinare* 'to decree'.] —**predestinable** *adj*

predetermine /prée di túrmin/ (**-mines, -mining, -mined**) *vt* **1** to decide, agree, or arrange something in advance ○ *at a predetermined place* **2** to ordain something in advance (*usually passive*) ○ *Are our lives predetermined?* —**predeterminate** *adj* —**predeterminately** *adv* —**predetermination** /prée di túrmi náysh'n/ *n* —**predeterminative** *adj*

predeterminer /prée di túrminər/ *n* a word that precedes and qualifies another determiner, as 'both' does in 'both my hands'

predial *adj* AGRIC = **praedial**

predicable /préddikəb'l/ *adj* able to be stated, or able to be said about somebody or something (*formal*) ■ *n* a quality or attribute by which somebody or something can be described (*formal*) [Mid-16C. < medieval Latin *praedicabilis* < Latin *praedicare* (see PREDICATE).] —**predicability** /préddikə bílləti/ *n* —**predicableness** *n*

predicament /pri díkəmənt/ *n* **1** a difficult, unpleasant, or embarrassing situation from which there is no clear or easy way out **2** any category or class that can be assigned to something [14C. < late Latin *praedicamentum* 'class, category' (translation of Greek *katēgoria*) < Latin *praedicare* 'to proclaim' (see PREDICATE).]

predicant /préddikənt/ *adj* relating to or involved in preaching (*formal*) ■ *n* **1** a member of a religious order, especially the Dominicans, that has a particular commitment to preaching **2** *S Africa* = **predikant** [Late 16C. < Latin *praedicant-*, present participle of *praedicare* 'to preach' (see PREDICATE).]

predicate *n* /préddikət/ **1 PART OF SENTENCE EXCLUDING SUBJECT** a word or combination of words, including the verb, objects, or phrases governed by the verb that make up one of the two main parts of a sentence **2 EVERYTHING IN SENTENCE EXCLUDING NAMES** everything in a simple sentence other than names, e.g. 'runs' in 'Fred runs' and 'is taller than' in 'Fred is taller than Ginger' **3 SOMETHING AFFIRMED OR DENIED** that which is affirmed or denied about something ■ *vt* /préddi kayt/ (**-cates, -cating, -cated**) **1 BASE SOMETHING ON** to base an opinion, an action, or a result on something (*formal*) ○ *predicated on reason* **2 STATE** to state or assert something (*formal*) **3 IMPLY** to imply something (*formal*) **4 ASSERT SOMETHING ABOUT SUBJECT OF STATEMENT** to assert or affirm something about the subject of a statement **5 MAKE EXPRESSION PREDICATE OF STATEMENT** to make an expression or term the predicate of a statement [Mid-16C. < late Latin *praedicatum* < past participle of Latin *praedicare* 'to declare publicly', literally 'to declare before' < *dicare* 'to state'.] —**predication** /préddi káysh'n/ *n* —**predicative** /pri díkətiv/ *adj*

predicate calculus *n* the branch of symbolic logic that uses symbols to explore relationships between and within propositions

predict /pri díkt/ *vti* to say what is going to happen in the future, often on the basis of present indications or past experience [Mid-16C. < Latin *praedict-*, past participle of *praedicere* 'to say in advance' < *dicere* 'to say'.] —**predictor** *n*

predictable /pri díktəb'l/ *adj* **1** happening or turning out in the way that might have been expected or predicted **2** rarely or never being or doing anything unusual or unexpected —**predictability** /pri díktə bílləti/ *n* —**predictableness** /-díktəb'lnəss/ *n* —**predictably** /-díktəbli/ *adv*

prediction /pri díksh'n/ *n* **1** a statement of what someone thinks will happen in the future **2** the making of a statement or forming of an opinion about what will happen in the future —**predictive** *adj* —**predictively** *adv* —**predictiveness** *n*

predigest /prée dī jést, -di-/ *vt* **1** to treat food with chemicals or enzymes so that it is more easily digested, especially for people with digestion problems **2** to produce information in a simplified form so that it is easy to understand —**predigestion** /-jésch'n/ *n*

predikant /préddikənt/, **predicant** *n S Africa* a minister of the Dutch Reformed Church [Early 19C. < Dutch, 'predicant'.]

predilection /préedi léksh'n/ *n* a particular liking or preference for something [Mid-18C. Via French < medieval Latin *praediligere* 'to love first' < Latin *diligere* 'to love'.]

predispose /préedi spṓz/ (**-poses, -posing, -posed**) *vt* (*formal*) **1** to make somebody feel favourably about somebody or something in advance **2** to make somebody liable or inclined to do something, e.g. catch an illness or behave in a particular way ○ *Her fair skin predisposes her to sunburn.* —**predisposal** *n*

predisposition /prée dispə zísh'n/ *n* **1 FAVOURABLE ATTITUDE OR INCLINATION** a favourable attitude towards somebody or something or an inclination to do something **2 LIABILITY TO** a liability or tendency to do something, e.g. behave in a particular way **3 TENDENCY TO DEVELOP DISEASE** a susceptibility to a disease, arising from a hereditary or another factor

prednisolone /pred níssə lōn/ *n* a synthetic steroid hormone, similar to cortisone, used to treat allergies and suppress inflammatory diseases such as rheumatoid arthritis [Mid-20C. Blend of PREDNISONE + -OL.]

prednisone /préddni sōn/ *n* a synthetic steroid hormone produced from cortisone and used to treat allergies and autoimmune diseases [Mid-20C. < *pregnane* + DIENE + CORTISONE.]

predoctoral /pree dóktərəl/ *adj* relating to or involving research or studies that will lead to a doctoral degree

predominant /pri dómminənt/ *adj* **1** commonest or greatest in number or amount **2** most important, powerful, or influential —**predominance** *n*

predominantly /pri dómminəntli/ *adv* in the greatest number or amount

predominate (**-nating, -nated**) *v* /pri dómmi nayt/ **1** *vi* BE IN MAJORITY to be the most common or greatest in number or amount **2** *vi* BE MORE IMPORTANT to have greater importance, power, or influence than others **3** *vt* DOMINATE to dominate or control somebody or something [Late 16C. < medieval Latin *predominat-*, past participle of *predominari* 'to rule over' < Latin *dominari* 'to rule'.] —**predominately** /pri dóminətli/ *adv* —**predomination** /-dómmi náysh'n/ *n* —**predominator** *n*

~~**predominately**~~ incorrect spelling of **predominantly**

predyed /pree díd/ *adj* dyed in advance, ready for use

pre-eclampsia /prée i klámpsi ə/ *n* a potentially dangerous condition that may develop in late pregnancy and may lead to convulsions if not treated. Symptoms are high blood pressure, fluid retention, abnormal weight gain, and the presence of protein in the urine. [Early 20C. < PRE- + ECLAMPSIA.]

pre-embryo /pree émbri ō/ *n* a fertilized ovum before implantation in the womb and before differentiation of embryonic tissue —**pre-embryonic** /prée embri ónnik/ *adj*

pre-eminent /pri émminənt/ *adj* standing out among all others because of superiority in a particular field or activity [< Latin *praeeminent-*, present participle of *praeeminere* 'to stand out in front' < *eminere* 'to stand out'] —**pre-eminence** *n* —**pre-eminently** *adv*

pre-empt /pri émpt/ *v* **1** *vt* ACT TO PREVENT to do something that makes it pointless or impossible for somebody else to do what he or she intended **2** *vt US* OCCUPY to occupy land in order to have the right to buy it later **3** *vt* REPLACE to take the place of something, especially of something less important **4** *vi* MAKE BRIDGE BID THAT BLOCKS OTHERS to make a bid intended to prevent further bidding [Back-formation < PRE-EMPTION] —**preemptor** *n* —**preemptory** *adj*

pre-emption /pri émpsh'n/ *n* **1** ACTION PREVENTING action that makes it pointless or impossible for somebody else to do what he or she intended **2** *US* OCCUPATION OF PUBLIC LAND the occupation of public land in order to have the right to buy it later, or the right to buy that is gained in this way **3** OPTION TO BUY PROPERTY an option to purchase property if and when it is put up for sale **4** STRATEGY OF FIRST ATTACK the strategy of attacking an enemy in order to prevent that enemy from attacking first [< medieval Latin *praeemption-* < *praeemere* 'to buy first' < Latin *emere* 'to buy']

pre-emptive /pri émptiv/ *adj* **1** DONE BEFORE OTHERS CAN ACT done before somebody else has had an opportunity to act so making his or her planned action pointless or impossible **2** INTENDED TO PREVENT ATTACK intended to eliminate or lessen an enemy's capacity to attack ○ *a pre-emptive strike* **3** PREVENTING FURTHER BIDDING intended to prevent further bidding —**preemptively** *adv*

pre-emptive right *n* a right to be offered first refusal in selling or buying an asset

preen[1] /preen/ *vti* **1** GROOM FEATHERS WITH BEAK to clean, smooth, or arrange the feathers with the beak ○ *swans preening their feathers* **2** GROOM FUR WITH TONGUE to clean and smooth the fur by licking it ○ *The cat was quietly preening on the windowsill.* **3** CARE FOR PERSONAL APPEARANCE to spend a long or excessive time attending to personal appearance, especially making small finishing touches to the hair, the face, or clothes ○ *busy preening in front of the mirror* **4** SHOW SELF-SATISFACTION to feel excessively self-satisfied and display that feeling by gloating (*disapproving*) ○ *He preens himself on his ability to deflect criticism.* [15C. Probably < Old French *proignier* 'to prune'.] —**preener** *n*

preen[2] /preen/ *n* **1** *Scotland* a pin **2** a decorative pin or brooch [Old English *prēon* < Germanic]

pre-engineered /prée enji néerd/ *adj* constructed using prefabricated parts

pre-establish /prée i stáblish/ *vt* to set up, decide, or arrange something in advance

pre-exist /prée ig zíst/ *vti* to exist before another person, group, thing, or event —**pre-existence** *n* —**pre-existent** *adj*

pref. *abbr* **1** preface **2** prefatory **3** preference **4** preferred **5** prefix

prefab /prée fab/ *adj* relating to or constructed from prefabricated parts (*informal*) ■ *n* a prefabricated house or building (*informal*) [Mid-20C. Shortening.]

prefabricate /pree fábbri kayt/ (**-cates, -cating, -cated**) *vt* **1** to manufacture sections of something, especially a building, that can be transported to a site and easily assembled there **2** to produce something in an unoriginal or standardized way —**prefabrication** /pree fábbri káysh'n/ *n* —**prefabricator** /pree fábbri kaytər/ *n*

preface /préffəss/ *n* **1** INTRODUCTORY PART OF TEXT an introductory section at the beginning of a book or speech that comments on aspects of the text such as the writer's intentions ○ *in the preface to the second edition* **2** PRELIMINARY ACTION an action or thing that precedes something more important **3** **preface, Preface** PRAYER DURING MASS a prayer said by a priest during Mass, especially the prayer that begins 'Lift up your hearts' **4** **preface, Preface** PRAYER FOR PARTICULAR PURPOSE in the Roman Catholic Church, any one of a number of prayers used for particular purposes ■ *vt* (**-aces, -acing, -aced**) **1** INTRODUCE WITH PREFACE to introduce an action, speech, or piece of writing with something ○ *He prefaced his remarks with an apology.* **2** SERVE AS INTRODUCTION TO to act as a preface to an action, speech, or piece of writing [14C. Via French < Latin *praefatus*, past participle of *praefari* 'to say before' < *fari* 'to speak'.] —**prefacer** *n*

prefatory /préffətəri/ *adj* serving to introduce something else such as a main body of text or a speech ○ *prefatory remarks introducing the Prime Minister* [Late 17C. < Latin *praefatus*, past participle of *praefari* (see PREFACE).] —**prefatorily** *adv*

prefect /prée fekt/ *n* **1** PUPIL ASSISTING WITH DISCIPLINE a senior pupil who is given some authority over other pupils in matters of discipline **2** HIGH-RANKING ADMINISTRATIVE OFFICIAL the highest official in an administrative district (**department**) or former territorial possession of France or in an administrative region of Italy **3** FRENCH CHIEF OF POLICE the head of a French police force, especially in Paris **4** ROMAN MAGISTRATE OR COMMANDER a senior administrative or military official in ancient Rome **5** SENIOR MASTER AT JESUIT SCHOOL a senior master or administrator with special responsibilities at a Jesuit school or college [14C. Via Old French < Latin *praefectus* 'overseer', past participle of *praeficere* 'to set over' < *facere* 'to make'.] —**prefectorial** /prée fek táwri əl/ *adj*

prefecture /prée fekchər/ *n* **1** PREFECT'S JURISDICTION the district over which a prefect has jurisdiction **2** OFFICE OF PREFECT the office or authority of a prefect **3** PREFECT'S RESIDENCE the official residence of a prefect in countries such as France or Italy —**prefectural** /prée fékchərəl/ *adj*

prefer /pri fúr/ (**-fers, -ferring, -ferred**) *vt* **1** LIKE BETTER THAN SOMETHING ELSE to like or want one thing more than another ○ *I prefer tea to coffee.* **2** LAY BEFORE COURT to make a charge against somebody by submitting details of the alleged offence to a court, magistrate, or judge for examination, or prosecute such a charge ○ *prefer charges* **3** GIVE PRIORITY TO to give priority to one person, especially a creditor, over others **4** PROMOTE to promote somebody to a higher position or rank (*archaic*) [14C. Via French *préferer* < Latin *praeferre* < *prae-* 'before, in front' (see PRE-) + *ferre* 'to carry, bear'.] —**preferrer** *n*

preferable /préffərəb'l/ *adj* more likely to be enjoyable, useful, or desired than something else —**preferability** /préffərə bílləti/ *n* —**preferableness** /préffərəb'lnəss/ *n*

preferably /préffərəb'li/ *adv* used to specify more exactly what is required or desired ○ *Plan to arrive early, preferably before the rush hour.*

~~**preferance**~~ incorrect spelling of **preference**

~~**prefered**~~ incorrect spelling of **preferred**

preference /préffərənss/ *n* **1** SELECTION OF the view that a particular person, object, or course of action is more desirable than another, or a choice based on such a view ○ *The judges showed a marked preference for representational art.* **2** SOMEBODY OR SOMETHING PREFERRED a person, object, or course of action that is more desirable than another, or the state of being that desirable choice ○ *State your preferences clearly.* **3** RIGHT TO EXPRESS CHOICE the right or opportunity to choose a person, object, or course of action that is considered more desirable than another ○ *We exercised our preference.* **4** PRIORITY OF ONE CREDITOR OVER OTHERS priority given to a particular creditor, e.g. when a debtor goes bankrupt, or the right of a particular creditor to receive payment before others **5** FAVOURITISM IN INTERNATIONAL TRADE priority given to a particular country or group of countries in international trade ■ **preferences** *npl* VOTES UNDER PREFERENTIAL VOTING SYSTEM votes assigned to second or third choice candidates, and so on, under the preferential voting system, e.g. in Australia

preference shares *npl* shares whose holders are the first to receive dividends from available profit. Preference shares are redeemed before ordinary shares when a company is liquidated. US term **preferred stock**

preferential /préffə rénsh'l/ *adj* **1** giving advantage or priority to a particular person or group ○ *preferential treatment* **2** giving advantage or priority to a particular country or group of countries in international trade —**preferentialism** *n* —**preferentialist** *adj* —**preferentially** *adv*

preferential voting *n* an electoral system used in some countries, e.g. Australia, in which voters indicate their chosen candidates in order of preference

preferment /pri fúrmənt/ *n* (*formal*) **1** appointment to a higher position or rank, especially in the church **2** an office, appointment, or position of high rank or honour, especially one that brings social advancement or financial reward

preferred stock *n US FIN* = **preference shares**

prefiguration /prée figə ráysh'n/ *n* (*formal*) a representation, often in form or likeness, of a person, thing, or event that is to come

prefigure /pree fíggər/ (**-ures, -uring, -ured**) *vt* **1** to represent or suggest, often in form or likeness, a person, thing, or event that will come later ○ *designs that prefigured modern architecture* **2** to think about or imagine a person, thing, or event in advance [15C. < ecclesiastical Latin *praefigurare* 'to depict beforehand' < Latin *figura* 'figure'.] —**prefigurative** /pree fíggərətiv/ *adj* —**prefiguratively** *adv* —**prefigurativeness** *n* —**prefigurement** /prée fíggərmənt/ *n*

prefix /préefiks/ *n* **1** WORD ELEMENT BEGINNING VARIOUS WORDS a linguistic element that is not an independent word but is attached to the beginning of words to modify their meaning **2** TITLE a title before somebody's name, e.g. the prefix 'The Honourable' before an MP's full name **3** SOMETHING PRECEDING SOMETHING ELSE something that comes before something else, e.g. a fixed group of digits at the beginning of a telephone number ■ *vt* **1** PUT BEFORE to place something in front of something else ○ *You must prefix the number with the area code.* **2** INTRODUCE WITH to say or do something by way of introduction ○ *His requests for money were usually prefixed by an apology.* **3** ADD PREFIX TO to attach a prefix at the beginning of a word to alter its meaning **4** ARRANGE IN ADVANCE to decide on something such as a price, date, or meeting place beforehand ○ *They duly arrived at the prefixed hour.* [15C. Via French < Latin *praefixus*, *praefixum*, past participle of Latin *praefigere* 'to fix in front' < *figere* 'to fasten'.] —**prefixal** /prée fiks'l, prée fíks'l/ *adj* —**prefixally** *adv* —**prefixation** /prée fik sáysh'n/ *n* —**prefixion** /prée fíksh'n/ *n*

preflight /prée flīt/ *adj* CARRIED OUT BEFORE TAKEOFF occurring before an aircraft takes off ○ *The fault was discovered during a preflight check.* ■ *vt* CHECK TO DETERMINE AIRWORTHINESS to carry out a technical inspection of an aircraft before it takes off to ensure that it is airworthy ■ *n* PREFLIGHT CHECK the set of procedures and checks that pilots and ground crew are required to carry out before an aircraft's takeoff ○ *During the preflight, the pilot discovered a problem in the landing gear.*

preform /pree fáwm/ *vt* **1** to shape or form something beforehand **2** to give something a preliminary shape [Early 17C. < Latin *praeformare*.] —**preformation** /prée fawr máysh'n/ *n*

prefrontal /pree frúnt'l/ *adj* **1** relating to or situated in the foremost part of the brain **2** located in front of the frontal bone

prefrontal lobotomy *n* a surgical operation in which the nerves connecting the front part of the brain (**prefrontal lobe**) to the thalamus are severed

preggers /préggərz/ *adj* pregnant (*informal*) [Mid-20C. Alteration of PREGNANT.]

preglacial /pree gláysh'l/ *adj* formed or occurring before a glacial period, especially the period that began about a million years ago (**Pleistocene epoch**), when the surface of the earth was covered with ice

pregnable /prégnəb'l/ *adj* able to be captured or attacked [15C. Via Old French < Latin *prehendere* (see PREHENSION).] —**pregnability** /prégnə bílləti/ *n*

pregnancy /prégnənssi/ (*plural* **-cies**) *n* 1 **CONDITION OF BEING PREGNANT** the physical condition of a woman or female animal carrying unborn offspring inside her body, from fertilization to birth 2 **INSTANCE OF BEING PREGNANT** an individual occurrence or experience of being pregnant 3 **TIME OF CARRYING UNBORN OFFSPRING** the period during which a woman or female animal carries an unborn offspring inside her body, from fertilization to birth 4 **SIGNIFICANCE** importance or fullness of meaning ○ *the pregnancy of his words*

pregnant /prégnənt/ *adj* 1 **CARRYING OFFSPRING WITHIN THE BODY** carrying unborn offspring inside the body 2 **SIGNIFICANT** full of meaning or importance ○ *After a pregnant pause, the general began briefing the media on the surprise attack.* 3 **FULL OF** pervaded by something, usually something intangible 4 **CREATIVE** full of creative power ○ *the child's pregnant imagination* 5 **PRODUCTIVE** producing a lot of useful results ○ *It was a pregnant endeavour, yielding much experience, information, and help.* [15C. Via Old French *preigne* < Latin *praegnas* 'before birth' < *prae-* 'before' + *gnatus* 'born'.] —**pregnantly** *adv*

pregnant chad *n* US POL = **dimpled chad**

preheat /prée héet/ *vt* to heat an oven, dish, or other item before using it ○ *Preheat the oven to gas mark 7.*

prehensile /pri hén sīl/ *adj* 1 **ABLE TO GRASP** able to take hold of things, especially by wrapping around them ○ *The monkey has a prehensile tail.* 2 **QUICK TO UNDERSTAND** skilled at grasping ideas and concepts 3 **AGGRESSIVELY EAGER** excessively eager for gain or profit [Late 18C. Via French < Latin *prehendere* (see PREHENSION).] —**prehensility** /prée hen síllati/ *n*

prehension /pri hénsh'n/ *n* (*formal*) 1 **ACT OF FIRMLY GRASPING** the act of firmly taking hold of something 2 **PERCEIVING OF SOMETHING THROUGH SENSES** the perception by the senses of a sight, sound, smell, taste, or texture 3 **COMPREHENSION** the process of understanding [Mid-16C. < Latin *prehensionem* < *prehendere* 'to seize'.]

prehistoric /prée hi stórrik/, **prehistorical** /-stórrik'l/ *adj* 1 **BEFORE RECORDED HISTORY** relating to the period before history was first recorded in writing 2 **RELATING TO LANGUAGE BEFORE WRITING** relating or belonging to a language before it was recorded in writing 3 **VERY OLD AND OLD-FASHIONED** relating to or being an object, idea, or attitude that is very old or out of date ○ *prehistoric views about nutrition* —**prehistorically** *adv*

prehistory /prée hístəri/ *n* 1 **HISTORY BEFORE WRITTEN WORD** the period before history was first recorded in writing 2 **STUDY OF PREHISTORIC PERIOD** the study of the prehistoric period using archaeological evidence 3 **EVENTS LEADING UP TO** the events and circumstances preceding a current event or situation —**prehistorian** /prée hi stáwri ən/ *n*

preignition /prée ig nísh'n/ *n* ignition of fuel in an internal-combustion engine before the spark has been generated, causing inefficient operation —**preignite** *vti*

preindustrial /prée in dústri əl/ *adj* relating to a society, country, or economic system in which industry has not yet developed on an extensive scale

prejudge /prée júj/ (**-judges**, **-judging**, **-judged**) *vt* to judge a person, issue, or case before sufficient evidence is available [Late 16C. Via French *préjuger* < Latin *praejudicare*.] —**prejudgment** *n*

prejudice /préjjŏodiss/ *n* 1 **OPINION FORMED BEFOREHAND** a preformed opinion, usually an unfavourable one, based on insufficient knowledge, irrational feelings, or inaccurate stereotypes 2 **HOLDING OF ILL-INFORMED OPINIONS** the holding of opinions that are formed beforehand on the basis of insufficient knowledge 3 **IRRATIONAL DISLIKE OF** an unfounded hatred, fear, or mistrust of a person or group, especially one of a particular religion, ethnicity, nationality, or social status 4 **DISADVANTAGE OR HARM** disadvantage or harm caused to somebody or something ■ *vt* (**-dices**, **-dicing**, **-diced**) 1 **CAUSE TO PREJUDICE** to make somebody form an opinion about somebody or something in advance, especially an irrational one, based on insufficient knowledge 2 **AFFECT ADVERSELY** to cause harm or disadvantage to somebody or something [13C. Via French < Latin *praejudicium* 'judgment in advance' < *judicium* 'judgment'.] —**prejudiced** *adj* ◇ **without prejudice** without doing any harm to somebody's legal rights or any claim that somebody has (*formal*)

prejudicial /préjjŏo dísh'l/ *adj* 1 causing disadvantage or harm to somebody or something 2 leading to the formation of prejudiced ideas or opinions —**prejudicially** *adv*

prelacy /prélassi/ (*plural* **-cies**) *n* 1 the office or position of a prelate 2 prelates considered as a group 3 CHR = **prelatism** [14C. Via Anglo-Norman < medieval Latin *prelatia* < *praelatus* (see PRELATE).]

prelapsarian /prée lap sáiri ən/ *adj* relating or belonging to the biblical time before Adam and Eve lost their innocence in the Garden of Eden [Late 19C. < PRE- + Latin *lapsus* 'sin, fall'.]

prelate /préllat/ *n* a high-ranking member of the clergy, e.g. an abbot, bishop, or cardinal [13C. Via Old French < medieval Latin *praelatus*, past participle of Latin *praeferre* 'to prefer'.] —**prelatic** /pri láttik/ *adj*

prelature /préllachər/ *n* CHR = **prelacy** n. 1, **prelacy** n. 2

prelim /préelim/ *n* 1 **PRELIMINARY CONTEST** a preliminary contest or event (*informal*) 2 *Scotland* **SCOTTISH SCHOOL EXAMINATION** in Scotland, a school examination taken to prepare students for a public examination (*informal*) 3 **UNIVERSITY EXAM** the first public examination in some universities ■ *npl* **BOOK FRONT MATTER** the initial pages of a book, including the title page and table of contents, that precede the main text (*informal*) [Late 19C. Shortening of PRELIMINARY.]

preliminary /pri límminəri/ *adj* **COMING BEFORE** occurring before and leading up to something, especially an event of greater size and importance ■ *n* (*plural* **-ies**) 1 **INTRODUCTORY OR PREPARATORY ACTIVITY** something said or done before something else, often by way of introduction to or preparation for something of greater size and importance (*often plural*) 2 **INTRODUCTORY CONTEST** a sporting contest held before the main event, especially in boxing and wrestling 3 **ELIMINATORY CONTEST** an eliminatory contest to select the finalists in a sporting competition 4 **PREPARATORY EXAMINATION** a test that prepares students for a subsequent examination of greater difficulty and importance [Mid-17C. Directly or via French < modern Latin *praeliminaris* < Latin *prae-* 'before' + *limen* 'threshold'.] —**preliminarily** /pri límminərəli/ *adv*

preliterate /prée líttərət/ *adj* describes a society that has no written language ■ *n* a member of a society with no written language —**preliteracy** /prée líttərəssi/ *n*

prelude /prélyood/ *n* 1 **INTRODUCTORY PIECE OF MUSIC** a piece of music that introduces or precedes another one 2 **FREE-STANDING PIECE OF MUSIC** a short musical composition, often one for piano, and often forming part of a set of such works 3 **INTRODUCTORY EVENT OR OCCURRENCE** an event or action that introduces or precedes something else, especially something longer and more important ■ *v* (**-udes**, **-uding**, **-uded**) 1 *vti* **ACT AS PRELUDE TO** to act as an introduction to something else, especially something that is longer and more important 2 *vt* **INTRODUCE WITH PRELUDE** to precede something, especially a piece of music, with a prelude [Mid-16C. Via French < Latin *praeludere* 'to play before' < *ludere* 'to play'.] —**prelusive** /pri lóossiv/ —**prelusively** /-lóossivli/ *adv* —**prelusorily** /-lóossərəli/ *adv* —**prelusory** /-lóossəri/ *adj*

LITERARY LINK *The Prelude*, a poem (1805) by William Wordsworth. This autobiographical account of the poet's intellectual and spiritual development was published posthumously (1850) in a revised form. Rejecting contemporary rationalist philosophies, it proclaims Wordsworth's faith in the redeeming power of poetry and the imagination.

prem /prem/ *n* a premature baby (*informal*) [Mid-20C. Shortening of PREMATURE.]

premarital /prée márrit'l/ *adj* occurring or existing before marriage

premature /prémmachər/ *adj* 1 occurring, existing, or developing earlier than is expected, normal, or advisable ○ *It would be premature to suggest that there is a link between these events.* 2 born before completing the normal gestation period, or, for a human infant, weighing less than 2.5 kg/5 lb 8 oz at birth [Early 16C. < Latin *praematurus* 'ripening too early' < *maturus* 'ripe'.] —**prematurely** *adv* —**prematureness** *n* —**prematurity** /prémmə chŏorəti/ *n*

premaxilla /prée mak síllə/ (*plural* **-lae**) *n* either of two bones that form the front part of the upper jaw in vertebrates and that bear the incisors —**premaxillary** *adj*

premed /prée méd/ *n* (*informal*) 1 **PREMEDICATION** drugs administered to a patient before a general anaesthetic, e.g. to relieve anxiety before a surgical operation 2 US **PREMEDICAL STUDENT** a student in a premedical programme ○ *The premeds will be taking their exams soon.* 3 US **PREMEDICAL COURSEWORK** a premedical course of study ○ *majoring in premed* ■ *adj* **PREMEDICAL** premedical (*informal*) [Mid-20C. Shortening.]

premedical /prée méddik'l/ *adj* relating to or engaged in the course of studies that somebody must complete before entering medical school —**premedically** *adv*

premedication /prée medi káysh'n/ *n* the practice of giving drugs to a patient before a general anaesthetic, or the drugs given, to relieve anxiety, diminish body reactions to pain, or improve postoperative comfort

premeditate /pri méddi tayt/ (**-tates**, **-tating**, **-tated**) *v* 1 *vt* to plan or devise something, especially a crime, in advance 2 *vti* to consider or think carefully about something beforehand [Mid-16C. < Latin *praemeditatus*, past participle of *praemeditari* 'to think about beforehand' < *meditare* (see MEDITATE).] —**premeditatedly** *adv* —**premeditative** /-tətiv/ *adj* —**premeditator** /-taytər/ *n*

premeditation /pri méddi táysh'n/ *n* 1 thinking about and planning a crime beforehand, rather than acting on impulse in a moment of passion or mindlessness 2 thinking about something before doing it [15C. Directly or via French < Latin *praemeditationem* < *praemeditari* (see PREMEDITATE).]

premenopausal /prée menō páwz'l/ *adj* describes the stage in a woman's life just before the onset of the menopause, or a woman at this stage. Such a woman is still menstruating, but may show some signs of the menopause, e.g. irregular menstrual periods.

premenstrual /prée ménstrual/ *adj* relating to or occurring in the days immediately before the start of a woman's menstrual period

premenstrual syndrome *n* a group of symptoms, e.g. nervous tension, irritability, tenderness of the breasts, and headache, experienced by some women in the days preceding menstruation and caused by hormonal changes

premier /prémmi ər/ *adj* 1 **BEST OR MOST IMPORTANT** first in importance, size, or quality 2 **COMING FIRST** happening or existing first ■ *n* 1 **PRIME MINISTER** a prime minister or head of government 2 **LEADER OF AUSTRALIAN STATE GOVERNMENT** the head of government of an Australian state or territory 3 **LEADER OF CANADIAN PROVINCE** the governmental head of a Canadian province [15C. Via French < Latin *primarius* 'foremost'.]

premier danseur /prémm yay daaN súr/ (*plural* **premiers danseurs** /prémm yay daaN súr/) *n* the principal man dancer in a ballet company [Early 19C. < French, 'first (male) dancer'.]

premiere /prémmi air/ *n* 1 **FIRST PUBLIC PERFORMANCE** the first public performance or showing of something such as a play or film 2 **LEADING WOMAN ACTOR** the principal woman performer in a theatre company ■ *v* (**-mieres**, **-miering**, **-miered**) 1 *vti* **PRESENT OR BE PRESENTED AS PREMIERE** to be publicly performed, shown, or broadcast for the first time, or present the first performance of something such as a play or film ○ *The film premiered in Britain.* 2 *vi* **GIVE FIRST PUBLIC PERFORMANCE** to appear on stage or screen for the first time, especially in a leading role ○ *Not many young performers get to premiere on Broadway.* ■ *adj* **BEST OR MOST IMPORTANT** first in importance, quality, or size [Mid-20C. < French, feminine form of *premier* 'first' (see PREMIER).]

première danseuse /prémm yair daaN sōz/ (*plural* **premières danseuses** /prémm yair daaN sōz/) *n* the principal female dancer in a ballet company [Early 19C. < French, 'first (female) dancer'.]

premiership /prémmi ərship/ *n* 1 the office or position of premier 2 a championship in some sports, e.g. football and rugby, or the competition to decide this

premillennial /prée mi lénni əl/ *adj* relating to or occurring in the period immediately before a millennium —**premillennially** *adv*

premillennialism /prée mi lénni əlizəm/ *n* the belief that Jesus Christ will return to earth for the Last Judgment just before the one-thousand-year reign of peace (**millennium**) mentioned in the Bible —**premillenarian** /prée milə náiri ən/ *adj*, *n* —**premillennarianism** *n* —**premillennialist** *n*

Preminger /prémminjər/, **Otto** (1906–86) Austrian-born US film director, producer, and actor

premise /prémmiss/ *n* 1 **EVIDENCE FOR CONCLUSION** a statement given as the evidence for a conclusion 2 **BASIS OF ARGUMENT** a proposition that forms the basis of an argument or from which a conclusion is drawn ○ *I question the premise on which your whole theory is based.* ■ *v* (**-ises**,

-ising, -ised) 1 *vt* SAY BY WAY OF INTRODUCTION to state something in advance to introduce or explain what follows (*formal*) 2 *vti* PROPOSE AS PREMISE to put forward a proposition as a premise in an argument [14C. Via French < medieval Latin *praemissa (propositio)* '(the proposition) set before' < past participle of *praemittere* 'to set in front' < *mittere* 'to send'.]

premises /prémmissiz/ *npl* 1 LAND AND BUILDINGS a piece of land and the buildings on it 2 PART OR ALL OF BUILDING a building or part of a building, especially when used for commercial purposes 3 MATTERS PREVIOUSLY MENTIONED matters previously stated or referred to in a legal document such as a deed 4 PRELIMINARY EXPLANATORY SECTION the introductory part of a legal document, e.g. the part giving the names and other details of those concerned [15C. < medieval Latin *praemissa* 'things stated at the beginning' (see PREMISE).]

premiss /prémmiss/ *n* LOGIC = **premise** *n.* 1, **premise** *n.* 2

premium /préemi əm/ *n* 1 COST OF INSURANCE the sum of money paid, usually at regular intervals, for an insurance policy ○ *My insurance premium went up as a result of the accident.* 2 ADDITIONAL SUM a sum of money paid in addition to a normal wage, rate, price, or other amount 3 PRIZE an award or prize given, e.g. to the winner of a competition 4 INDUCEMENT TO BUY a gift or reduced price offered as an incentive to purchase another product or service ○ *The manufacturer offered premiums, in the form of free merchandise and trips, for every purchase of a new car.* 5 AMOUNT ABOVE PAR VALUE the amount above its nominal value at which something such as a security sells 6 *US* EXTRA CHARGE FOR BORROWING MONEY an amount charged in addition to interest on a loan 7 COST OF SECURITIES OPTION the sum or cost at which a securities option is bought or sold 8 FEE FOR INSTRUCTION a fee paid for training or apprenticeship in a profession or trade ■ *adj* 1 HIGH-QUALITY of very high quality 2 UNUSUALLY HIGH higher than normal, especially in price ○ *premium petrol prices* [Early 17C. < Latin *praemium* 'reward' < *prae-* 'pre-' + *emere* 'to take, buy'.] ◇ **at a premium** 1 much in demand and therefore difficult to obtain 2 selling for a high price, or for a higher price than usual, because of scarcity ◇ **put a premium on** to place a high value on somebody or something

Premium Bond, Premium Savings Bond *n* a savings bond issued by the Treasury and purchased by the public, on which no interest is paid. Instead, there are monthly draws for cash prizes.

premix *n* /pree miks/ a product consisting of previously mixed ingredients or elements ■ *vt* /pree míks/ to mix something beforehand

premolar /pree mólər/ *n* either of two teeth on each side of both jaws that lie immediately behind the canines and in front of the molars and are used for grinding and chewing —**premolar** *adj*

premonition /prémmə nísh'n/ *n* 1 a strong feeling, without a rational basis, that a particular thing is going to happen 2 an advance warning about a future event [Mid-16C. Via French < Latin *praemonere* 'to forewarn' < *monere* 'to warn'.] —**premonitorily** /pri mónnitərəli/ *adv* —**premonitory** /-mónnitəri/ *adj*

prenatal /pree náyt'l/ *adj* MED = **antenatal** —**prenatally** *adv*

prenominal /pree nómmin'l/ *adj* 1 occurring before a noun, or used only before a noun 2 relating to an ancient Roman's first name (**praenomen**)

prenuptial /pree núpsh'l/ *adj* occurring or existing before a marriage

prenuptial agreement *n* an agreement made between a couple before marriage relating to the arrangement of financial matters and division of property in the event of their divorce

preoccupation /pri ókyoo páysh'n/, **preoccupancy** (*plural* **-cies**) *n* 1 constant thought about or persistent interest in something ○ *a preoccupation with fame and fortune* 2 a particular subject or activity that constantly occupies somebody's thoughts ○ *His children are his main preoccupation at the moment.* [Early 17C. Via Latin *praeoccupationem* 'action' < *praeoccupare.*]

preoccupied /pri ókyoo pīd/ *adj* 1 HAVING ATTENTION TAKEN UP WITH completely absorbed in doing or thinking about something, sometimes excessively ○ *She was too preoccupied to notice what was going on.* 2 OCCUPIED already occupied by somebody or something else ○ *a preoccupied airline seat* 3 ALREADY IN USE describes a scientific name that has already been used to designate a species, genus, or other taxonomic group and therefore cannot be used again

preoccupy /pri ókyoo pī/ (**-pies, -pying, -pied**) *vt* 1 to fill somebody's thoughts completely, sometimes excessively 2 to occupy something in advance or before somebody else

preop /pree óp/ *adj* preoperative (*informal*) [Mid-20C. Shortening.]

preoperative /pree óppərətiv/ *adj* occurring or done before a surgical operation

preordain /preé awr dáyn/ *vt* 1 to decide in advance that something will happen, or determine somebody's future, usually by fate or divine decree 2 to decide, determine, or arrange something beforehand —**preordainment** *n* —**preordination** /preé awrdi náysh'n/ *n*

preovulatory /preé ovyoo laytəri/ *adj* relating to the stage of the menstrual cycle between menstruation and ovulation, lasting from 6 to 13 days

preowned /pree ōnd/ *adj US, ANZ* previously owned and now for sale

prep /prep/ *n* (*informal*) 1 HOMEWORK at a boarding school or private school, work to be done by pupils outside normal school hours 2 STUDY TIME at a boarding school, the time during which pupils do homework or prepare for lessons ○ *No talking was allowed during prep.* 3 PREPARATION preparation for activity 4 *US* PRIVATE SECONDARY SCHOOL a preparatory school in the United States, preparing students for college 5 *US* EDUC = **preppy** *n.* 2 ■ *v* (**preps, prepping, prepped**) 1 *vi US* PREPARE FOR to study or train for a particular examination, sporting event, or other activity (*informal*) 2 *vt* PREPARE SOMEBODY FOR SURGERY to make a patient ready for an operation or other hospital procedure (*informal*) 3 *vt* PREPARE SOMETHING FOR PAINTING to prime a surface for painting ■ *adj* PREPARATORY serving as preparation (*informal*) [Mid-19C. Shortening of PREPARATION.]

prep. *abbr* 1 preparation 2 preparatory 3 preposition

prepackage /pree pákij/ (**-ages, -aging, -aged**) *vt* 1 to package goods before selling them 2 to arrange all the elements of something in advance, allowing no individual variation ○ *a prepackaged holiday*

prepacked /pree pákt/ *adj* already packaged before being sold

preparation /préppə ráysh'n/ *n* 1 PREPARING SOMETHING OR SOMEBODY the work or planning involved in making something or somebody ready or in putting something together in advance (*often before nouns*) ○ *a preparation time of about 45 minutes* 2 READINESS a state of readiness ○ *Twenty place settings lay carefully arranged in preparation for the guests.* 3 PREPARATORY MEASURE something done in advance in order to be ready for a future event (*often plural*) ○ *Preparations for the next Olympic Games are already under way.* 4 MIXTURE a substance, e.g. a medicine, that is made for a particular purpose by combining various ingredients ○ *a cough preparation* 5 HOMEWORK at a boarding school or private school, work to be done by pupils outside normal school hours 6 STUDY TIME at a boarding school, the time during which pupils do homework or prepare for lessons 7 SOFTENING APPROACH TO DISSONANCE in traditional composition, a lessening of the effect of a dissonant chord by using the discordant note harmonically in a preceding chord [14C. Via French < Latin *praeparationem* < *praeparare* 'to prepare'.]

preparative /pri párrətiv/ *adj* having the purpose of making something ready or of introducing something (*formal*) ○ *a series of preparative lectures* [15C. Via French *préparatif* < medieval Latin *praeparativus* < *praeparare* 'to prepare'.] —**preparatively** *adv*

preparatory /pri párrətəri/ *adj* 1 serving to make something ready ○ *preparatory design work* 2 acting as an introduction ○ *preparatory remarks before a news conference* [15C. < medieval Latin *praeparatorius* < *praeparator* 'preparer' (see PREPARE).] —**preparatorily** *adv* ◇ **preparatory to** before or in preparation for

preparatory school *n* 1 in the United Kingdom, a private, usually single-sex school that prepares students between the ages of 6 and 13 for entrance into a private boarding school 2 *US* in the United States, a private secondary school that prepares students for college, often with academic requirements for entry

prepare /pri páir/ (**-pares, -paring, -pared**) *v* 1 *vti* MAKE READY to make something ready for use or action, or for a particular event or purpose ○ *preparing the aircraft for takeoff* 2 *vti* MAKE SOMEBODY READY to get ready or make somebody ready for something ○ *They prepared to go.* ○ *Prepare yourselves for a shock.* 3 *vt* MAKE BY PUTTING THINGS TOGETHER to make something by combining various elements or ingredients ○ *meals that can be prepared in less than half an hour* 4 *vt* PREPLAN to plan something in advance 5 *vt* EQUIP to provide a person or group with necessary equipment, e.g. for a ship or an expedition 6 *vt* LESSEN EFFECT OF DISSONANCE to lessen the effect of a dissonant chord by using the discordant note harmonically in a preceding chord [15C. Directly or via French < Latin *praeparare* 'to make ready beforehand' < *parare* 'to make ready'.] —**preparer** *n*

prepared /pri páird/ *adj* 1 ABLE AND WILLING willing and able to do something ○ *Are you prepared to testify in court?* 2 READY AND ABLE TO DEAL WITH ready and able to cope with something, often something hard or bad ○ *The students were prepared for the last exam.* 3 MADE, OR MADE READY, BEFOREHAND made ready or put together in advance ○ *a specially prepared surface* ○ *a prepared statement* —**preparedly** /pri páiridli/ *adv*

preparedness /pri páiridnəss/ *n* readiness for action, especially military action

prepared piano *n* a piano that has been modified to produce special effects, usually by placing objects on or between its strings

prepay /pree páy/ (**-pays, -paying, -paid** /-páyd/) *vt* to pay in advance for something, e.g. the postage on a letter or parcel —**prepayable** *adj* —**prepayment** *n*

prepense /pri pénss/ *adj* planned or contemplated in advance (*archaic*) ○ *acted with malice prepense* [Early 18C. Alteration of *purpensed* 'premeditated', via Anglo-Norman *purpenser* 'premeditate' < Latin *pensare* 'to think'.]

~~**preperation**~~ incorrect spelling of **preparation**

preplan /pree plán/ (**-plans, -planning, -planned**) *vt* to plan a project, trip, or other event in advance

preponderance /pri póndərənss/, **preponderancy** /-rənssi/ *n* (*formal*) 1 a large number or the majority (+ *singular or plural verb*) ○ *A preponderance of the settlers in this area were French.* 2 dominance or superiority in force, importance, or influence ○ *The preponderance of the evidence is in support of this theory.*

preponderant /pri póndərənt/ *adj* greater in number, power, or importance than something else of the same nature or class [Mid-17C. Via Latin *praeponderantem* < *praeponderare* 'to outweigh'.] —**preponderantly** *adv*

preponderate (**-ates, -ating, -ated**) *vi* /pri póndə rayt/ to be greater in weight, strength, number, or importance than something else [Early 17C. < Latin *praeponderat-*, past participle of *praeponderare* 'to weigh more' < *ponderare* 'to weigh'.] —**preponderately** /-póndərətli/ *adv* —**preponderation** /-póndə ráysh'n/ *n*

preposition /préppə zísh'n/ *n* a member of a set of words used in close connection with, and usually before, nouns and pronouns to show their relation to another part of a clause [14C. < Latin *praeposition-* 'putting before' < *praeponere* 'to put before' < *ponere* 'to put' (see POSITION).] —**prepositional** *adj* —**prepositionally** *adv*

USAGE A ***preposition*** usually goes in front of the noun or pronoun with which it is used (***under*** *the bed*; ***during*** *the performance*; ***by*** *myself*). But in certain circumstances it is quite normal for a preposition to go at the end of a sentence; for instance, in the case of the phrasal verbs *attend to* and *put up with*, where else could you put the prepositions in *Are you being attended to?* and *This noise is hard to put up with.* Some questions and clauses opening with *wh-* (*what, which, who*, etc.) typically have the preposition at the end, as in *What on earth were they thinking about?* Some infinitive clauses also have prepositions at their ends, as in *I would love to go to the dance, but I need someone to go with* as do informal or slang expressions such as *to die for*, as in *This is a dress to die for.* These examples notwithstanding, avoid nonstandard constructions such as *Where's Elaine at?*, in which *where* plus *at* are redundant. Say instead *Where's Elaine?* or *Where is Elaine?*

prepositional phrase /préppə zísh'nəl-/ *n* a phrase made up of a preposition followed by a noun or pronoun, e.g. 'over the hill'. Prepositional phrases can be used adverbially or adjectivally.

prepositive /pree pózzətiv/ *adj* describes a word that is placed before the word it modifies ■ *n* a prepositive word or element [Late 16C. < Latin *praepositivus*, past participle of *praeponere* (see PREPOSITION).] —**prepositively** *adv*

prepossessing /preé pə zéssing/ *adj* creating a pleasing impression —**prepossessingly** *adv* —**prepossessingness** *n*

prepossession /preè pə zésh'n/ *n* **1** prejudice or bias towards or against a particular person or thing **2** the occupation of the mind by particular thoughts

preposterous /pri póstərəss/ *adj* going very much against what is thought to be sensible or reasonable [Mid-16C. < Latin *praeposterus* 'inverted', literally 'having the first thing last'.] —**preposterously** *adv* —**preposterousness** *n*

prepotent /pri pṓt'nt/ *adj* **1** greater in power, force, or influence **2** having or exhibiting prepotency in conferring genetic traits or in fertilization [15C. Via Latin *praepotentem* < *praeposse* 'to be more powerful' < *posse* 'to be able'.] —**prepotency** *n* —**prepotently** *adv*

preppy /préppi/, **preppie** *adj US* **RELATING TO YOUNG WELL-EDUCATED AFFLUENT PEOPLE** relating to or characteristic of well-educated, fairly affluent young people who are known for their neat, traditional, often expensive clothing style (*informal*) ■ *n* (*plural* **-pies**) *US* (*informal*) **1 WELL-EDUCATED AFFLUENT YOUNG PERSON** a young person who dresses with preppy style or behaves in a preppy manner **2 PREPARATORY SCHOOL STUDENT** a young person who is studying or has studied at a preparatory school —**preppily** *adv* —**preppiness** *n*

preprandial /pree prándi əl/ *adj* taking place before a meal, especially an evening meal (*formal or humorous*)

preprint /pree prínt/ *n* **1 DRAFT CIRCULATED BEFORE PUBLICATION** a piece of writing, especially a contribution to an academic journal, that is printed and often distributed in a preliminary form before official publication **2 SOMETHING PRINTED IN ADVANCE** a part of a publication, e.g. an individual advertisement, printed in advance ■ *v* **1** *vt* **PRINT SOMETHING BEFORE OFFICIAL PUBLICATION** to print something in advance, especially an article or other piece of writing in draft form before its official publication **2** *vti* **PRINT SOMETHING IN ADVANCE** to print something in advance of its being used or prior to full printing ■ *n* **SOMETHING PRINTED IN ADVANCE** something that is printed in advance, especially before publication in full

ϟ **preprocess** /pree prṓssess/ *vt* to analyse computer data, e.g. control statements embedded in a program, and take appropriate action before processing the data

preproduction /preè prə dúksh'n/ *n* **PRELIMINARY WORK** the plans and activities, e.g. those relating to finance, equipment, and personnel, that precede the production phase of a project, especially in the entertainment and manufacturing industries ■ *adj* **1 HAPPENING BEFORE PRODUCTION** preceding a production phase **2 PROTOTYPIC** produced as a trial or prototype

preprogram /pree prṓ gram/ (**-grams, -gramming, -grammed**) *vt* **1** to program a computer or other device in advance **2** to prepare somebody in such a way that a later response in a particular desired manner is assured

prep school *n* a preparatory school (*informal*)

prepuberty /pree pyoóbərti/ *n* the phase of physical and emotional development that immediately precedes puberty —**prepubertal** *adj*

prepubescent /preèpyoō béss'nt/ *adj* at or characteristic of the stage of life just before puberty ■ *n* a child at the stage of development just before puberty

prepuce /preè pyooss/ *n* (*technical*) **1** the foreskin **2** the loose fold of skin that covers the tip of the clitoris [14C. Via French < Latin *praeputium*.] —**preputial** /pri pyoósh'l/ *adj*

prequel /preèkwəl/ *n* a film or novel set at a time preceding the action of an existing work, especially one that has achieved commercial success [Late 20C. Blend of PRE- + SEQUEL.]

Pre-Raphaelite /preè ráffə līt, -ráffi ə-/ *n* a member of a group of painters and writers (**the Pre-Raphaelite Brotherhood**) founded in 1848 with the aim of reviving the realistic style of Italian painting before Raphael ■ *adj* relating or belonging to the Pre-Raphaelites, or characteristic of their style of painting or writing —**Pre-Raphaelitism** *n*

QUICK FACTS ON... **PRE-RAPHAELITE BROTHERHOOD**

Key dates:
Key dates: 1848–54
Key locations: England
Key elements: rejection of academic conventions and materialism; realism; medievalism; religious, moral, and literary themes; vivid colour, intensely bright lighting, and rich detail
Key figures: Dante Gabriel Rossetti (poetry and painting); Holman Hunt, Sir John Everett Millais (painting); William Michael Rossetti, Frederick George Stephens (theory); Thomas Woolner (sculpture and poetry)
Key works: *Ecce Ancilla Domini [The Annunciation]* (Rossetti) 1850, *Ophelia* (Millais) 1851, *The Light of the World* (Hunt) 1854
Key developments: Arts and Crafts movement, symbolism

prerecord /preè ri káwrd/ *vt* to record something such as a message or television or radio programme for later use or broadcasting

preregister /preè réjjistər/ *vti* to register for something before the official registration period begins —**preregistration** /preè reji stráysh'n/ *n*

prerelease /peè ri leèss/ *n* a publication, recording, or product that is released before the appointed or official time ○ *The single is a prerelease from their forthcoming album.* ■ *adj* relating to or occurring during the period before the appointed or official time of release ○ *prerelease publicity*

prerequisite /pre rékwəzit/ *n* an object, quality, or condition that is required in order for something else to happen ○ *A degree is a prerequisite for entry into this profession.* ■ *adj* required in order for something else to happen ○ *A good command of Spanish is prerequisite for the Spanish literature course.*

prerogative /pri róggətiv/ *n* **1 PRIVILEGE RESTRICTED TO PEOPLE OF RANK** an exclusive privilege or right enjoyed by a person or group occupying a particular rank or position ○ *Being the leader, it was her prerogative to choose a successor.* **2 INDIVIDUAL RIGHT OR PRIVILEGE** a privilege or right that allows a particular person or group to give orders or make decisions or judgments ○ *It's not his prerogative to say who can come.* **3 PRIVILEGE RESULTING FROM NATURAL ADVANTAGE** the right conferred by a natural advantage that places somebody in a position of superiority ○ *the prerogatives conferred by age* **4 SOVEREIGN POWER, PRIVILEGE, OR IMMUNITY** the power or right of a monarch or government to do something or be exempt from something **5 SUPERIORITY** superiority in rank or nature [14C. Via Old French < Latin *praerogare* 'to ask first' < *rogare* 'to ask'.]

pres. *abbr* **1** present **2** presidential

Pres. *abbr* President

presage /préssij/ *n* **1 PORTENT OR OMEN** a sign or warning of a future event **2 SENSE OF SOMETHING TO COME** a feeling that a particular thing, often something unpleasant, is about to happen **3 FUTURE IMPORT** significance with regard to future events ○ *a moment of great presage* ■ *v* (**presages, presaging, presaged**) **1** *vt* **FORETELL** to be or give a sign or warning of a future event ○ *Clear skies that night presaged fine weather for the picnic.* **2** *vt* **HAVE PRESENTIMENT OF** to know intuitively that a particular thing is going to happen **3** *vti* **PREDICT** to predict a future event [14C. Directly or via French < Latin *praesagire* 'to forebode' < *sagire* 'to perceive'.] —**presager** *n*

presale /pree sáyl/ *n* a private sale of products, objects, or works of art that takes place before a public sale

presbyopia /prézbi ṓpi ə/ *n* progressive reduction in the eye's ability to focus, with consequent difficulty in reading at the normal distance, associated with ageing [Late 18C. < Greek *presbus* 'old man' (see PRESBYTER) + -OPIA.] —**presbyope** /prézbi ōp/ *n* —**presbyopic** /prézbi óppik/ *adj*

presbyter /prézbitər/ *n* **1 MEMBER OF EARLY CHURCH ADMINISTRATION** in early Christianity, an administrative official of a local church **2 MEMBER OF CLERGY** an ordained member of the clergy in many Christian churches **3 LAY OFFICIAL IN PRESBYTERIAN CHURCH** any lay person chosen by the congregation to govern a Presbyterian or other Reformed church [Late 16C. Via ecclesiastical Latin < Greek *presbuteros* 'elder' < *presbus* 'old man'.]

presbyterate /prez bíttərət/ *n* **1** the office or position of a presbyter **2** an order or group of presbyters

presbyterial /prézbi teèri əl/ *adj* relating to a presbyter or presbytery

presbyterian /prézbi teèri ən/ *adj* characterized by or relating to the government of a church by democratically elected lay officials ■ *n* a supporter and advocate of church government by democratically elected lay officials

Presbyterian /prézbi teèriən/ *adj* relating or belonging to one of the Reformed churches or any of the presbyterian churches ■ *n* a member of a presbyterian church —**Presbyterianism** *n*

presbytery /prézbitəri/ (*plural* **-ies**) *n* **1 GROUP OF PRESBYTERS** a group of presbyters in the early Christian church or in a modern Presbyterian church **2 COURT OF PRESBYTERIAN CHURCH** a court composed of ministers and lay officials in a Presbyterian Church, or the churches under the jurisdiction of such a court **3 GOVERNMENT BY PRESBYTERS** the government of a church by democratically elected lay officials **4 PART OF CHURCH FOR CLERGY** part of a church or cathedral, or a separate building, for the use of clergy only **5 HOME OF ROMAN CATHOLIC PARISH PRIEST** the home of a Roman Catholic parish priest

preschool /preè skool/ *adj* **1** below the age at which compulsory schooling begins **2** relating to or provided for children below the age at which compulsory schooling begins —**preschooler** *n* —**preschooling** *n*

prescience /préssi ənss/ *n* knowledge of actions or events before they happen [14C. Via French < late Latin *praescientia* 'foreknowledge' (see PRESCIENT).]

prescient /préssi ənt/ *adj* having or showing knowledge of actions or events before they take place [Early 17C. Via Latin *praescientem* < *praescire* 'to know beforehand' < *scire* 'to know'.] —**presciently** *adv*

prescientific /preè sī ən tíffik/ *adj* relating to or happening during the time before the development of modern science and the application of modern scientific methods

prescind /pri sínd/ *vi* to detach the mind from something, typically a concept, notion, or fixed idea (*formal*) ○ *if we can, for a moment, prescind from a focus on motive per se and consider instead opportunity and means* [Mid-17C. < Latin *praescindere* 'to cut off in front' < *scindere* 'to cut off'.]

prescribe /pri skrīb/ (**-scribes, -scribing, -scribed**) *v* **1** *vti* **ORDER USE OF MEDICATION** to direct a patient to follow a particular course of treatment, specifically to use a particular drug at set times and in specified dosages ○ *arguments that nurses should be allowed to prescribe as well as doctors* **2** *vt* **RECOMMEND REMEDY** to recommend a particular course of action or treatment as a remedy for something ○ *I prescribe lots of tender loving care.* **3** *vt* **LAY DOWN RULE** to say with authority that a certain course of action should be taken ○ *the penalties prescribed by law* **4** *vi* **SET DOWN REGULATIONS** to lay down rules or laws **5** *vti* **CLAIM PROPERTY RIGHT** to claim a right to something on the grounds of possession over a long period of time [15C. < Latin *praescribere* 'to write before' < *scribere* 'to write'.] —**prescribable** *adj* —**prescriber** *n*

prescribed illness *n* an illness arising from chemical hazards in the workplace, e.g. mercury poisoning, or from dangerous circumstances, e.g. decompression sickness

prescript /preèskript/ *n* a rule or regulation that has been laid down (*formal*) ■ *adj* laid down as a rule or regulation (*formal*) [Mid-16C. < Latin *praescriptum* 'something prescribed', past participle of *praescribere* 'to prescribe'.]

prescription /pri skrípsh'n/ *n* **1 WRITTEN ORDER FOR MEDICINE** a written order issued by a doctor or other qualified practitioner that authorizes a chemist to supply a particular medication for a particular patient, with instructions on its use (*often before nouns*) **2 PRESCRIBED MEDICINE** a drug or other medication prescribed by a doctor or other qualified practitioner ○ *I've got to pick up my son's prescription.* **3 ORDER FOR LENS TO CORRECT EYESIGHT** a written order from an optometrist or ophthalmologist for glasses or contact lenses of a particular type and strength to correct the eyesight of a particular person (*often before nouns*) ○ *prescription sunglasses* **4 PROVEN FORMULA FOR** a proven formula for causing something else to happen ○ *Caring about others' feelings is a prescription for a fulfilling life.* **5 ESTABLISHING OF REGULATIONS** laying down of laws, rules, and regulations **6 SOMETHING PRESCRIBED AS RULE** a practice or course of action laid down as a regulation **7 prescription, positive prescription PRESUMPTION OF RIGHT OF POSSESSION** a presumption of the right of possession of property, based on long-term exercise of property rights [14C. Via French < Latin *praescription-* < *praescribere* (see PRESCRIBE).]

prescription drug *n* a drug that can be dispensed only upon presentation of a legally valid prescription

prescriptive /pri skríptiv/ *adj* **1 MAKING OR ADHERING TO REGULATIONS** establishing or adhering to rules and regulations ○ *prescriptive grammarians* **2 GROUNDED IN LEGAL PRESCRIPTION** based on legal prescription **3 CUSTOMARY** based on or authorized by long-standing custom (*dated*) —**prescriptively** *adv* —**prescriptiveness** *n*

preseason /prée seez'n/ *n* the period just before the start of a new sporting season, during which players train intensively and play matches that are not part of a competition (*often before nouns*) ○ *a preseason game*

preselect /préesi lékt/ *vt* to select a person, object, place, or course of action in advance, usually on the basis of specific requirements

presell /pree sél/ (**-sells, -selling, -sold** /-sṓld/) *vt* **1 POPULARIZE SOMETHING BEFOREHAND** to promote a product or entertainment before it is generally available to the public, by means of advertising and publicity **2 SELL BOOK EARLY** to sell a book before its official publication date **3 ARRANGE SALE OF SOMETHING BEFOREHAND** to agree to sell a house, car, or other item before it is actually available

presence /prézz'nss/ *n* **1 BEING PRESENT** the physical existence of somebody or something in a particular place ○ *Our presence is requested at the board meeting.* **2 AREA WITHIN SIGHT OR EARSHOT** the immediate vicinity of somebody or something ○ *How dare you use that kind of language in my presence!* **3 PERSONAL DIGNITY** dignified appearance and bearing ○ *has a certain presence about her that garners respect* **4 IMPRESSIVE PERSON** a greatly respected or awe-inspiring person **5 INVISIBLE SUPPOSED SUPERNATURAL BEING** a supernatural spirit that is felt to be nearby ○ *a malevolent presence filled the room* **6 PERSON PRESENT** a person who is notably present ○ *the venerable scholar, a dignified presence in the academic procession* **7 ABILITY TO CAPTIVATE AUDIENCE** a quality of certain performers that enables them to achieve a rapport with and hold the attention of their audiences **8 STATIONING OF PERSONNEL** the existence of official personnel in a place, especially police, military, or diplomatic personnel ○ *maintained a heavy military, diplomatic, and intelligence presence in the capital* [14C. Via French < Latin *praesentia* < *praesent-* (see PRESENT²).]

presence chamber *n* the room in which a monarch or ruler or other important person receives guests and holds assemblies

presence of mind *n* the ability to remain calm and act decisively and effectively in a crisis ○ *At least she had the presence of mind to call the fire brigade.*

present¹ *v* /pri zént/ **1** *vt* **GIVE** to give something to somebody, often in a formal manner ○ *Then she presented me with the bill!* **2** *vt* **MAKE AWARD TO** to make a gift or award of something to somebody **3** *vt* **OFFER SOMETHING FORMALLY** to offer formally something such as compliments or apologies to somebody (*formal*) ○ *May I present my warmest congratulations?* **4** *vt* **MAKE SOMETHING EVIDENT** to show or display something in a particular way ○ *taking care to present his best side to the camera* **5** *vt* **HAND SOMETHING OVER OFFICIALLY** to put something forward for inspection or consideration, typically in a formal or official manner or capacity ○ *proposals to be presented at the next meeting* **6** *vt* **POSE PROBLEM** to pose a problem or difficulty to somebody ○ *presenting a direct threat to national security* **7** *vt* **PUT SOMETHING BEFORE COURT** to submit a criminal charge to a court for consideration and judgment **8** *vt* **BRING CHARGE** to put a charge before a court of law so that it can be considered or tried **9** *vt* **INTRODUCE WOMAN INTO SOCIETY** to introduce a young woman formally into fashionable society ○ *Her family planned to present her at the Christmas debutante ball in New York.* **10** *vt* **INTRODUCE SOMEBODY FORMALLY** to introduce somebody formally, especially to somebody of higher rank ○ *They were presented to the Queen.* **11** *vt* **HOST PROGRAMME** to introduce, or act as the host of, a television or radio programme or an infomercial ○ *He used to present a game show on ITV.* **12** *vt* **OFFER PUBLIC ENTERTAINMENT** to bring a film, play, or other form of entertainment to the public **13** *vt* **PORTRAY SOMETHING ARTISTICALLY** to represent something or somebody in a particular way in the arts ○ *In the film, Romeo and Juliet are presented as modern teenagers.* **14** *vr* **BE IN APPOINTED PLACE** to appear, especially at an appointed time and place ○ *Present yourselves at the gate at eight o'clock.* **15** *vr* **ARISE** to come into being or happen ○ *when an opportunity presents itself* **16** *vi* **HAVE PARTICULAR SYMPTOMS** to exhibit the specified symptom or symptoms on examination ○ *Monday, July 5th: The patient presents with arrhythmia and complains of arthralgia.* **17** *vi* **EXIT BIRTH CANAL IN POSITION** to appear during the process of being born (*refers to a foetus*) ○ *In most births, the first part to present is the back of the head.* **18** *vi* **PRODUCE SPECIFIED IMPRESSION** to produce a particular impression, especially a favourable one (*formal*) ○ *She presents as a pleasant young woman.* ■ *n* /prézz'nt/ **GIFT** something that is given to somebody out of kindness or to celebrate an occasion such as a birthday [13C. Via French < Latin *praesentare* 'make present' < *praesent-* (see PRESENT²).] —**presentee** /prézz'n tée/ *n* —**presenter** *n* ◇ **present arms** to perform a drill movement in which a salute is given by bringing a rifle vertically in front of the body

SYNONYMS See *give*.

present² /prézz'nt/ *adj* **1 CURRENTLY HAPPENING** taking place or existing now ○ *in our present circumstances* ○ *up to the present day* **2 IN A PLACE** in a particular place ○ *There were over a hundred people present at the reception* **3 NOW UNDER DISCUSSION** being considered or talked about at this time **4 RELATING TO CURRENT TIME** describes a verb form or tense that expresses the current time ■ *n* **1 THE HERE AND NOW** the current time or moment ○ *The story takes place in the present.* **2 CURRENT-TIME VERB TENSE** the verb tense that expresses current time **3 CURRENT-TIME VERB** a verb in the present tense, indicating that the action is happening now [13C. Via French < Latin *praesent-*, present participle of *praeesse* 'be in front of' < *esse* 'be'.] ◇ **at present** just now ◇ **for the present** as far as the present time is concerned

presentable /pri zéntəb'l/ *adj* **1** looking or being good enough to be introduced to other people ○ *Make sure you look presentable.* **2** good enough to be offered, shown, or given to other people ○ *still a presentable gift* —**presentability** /pri zéntə bílləti/ *n* —**presentableness** /-zéntəb'lnəss/ *n* —**presentably** /-zéntəbli/ *adv*

present arms *n* a drill movement in which a salute is given by bringing a rifle vertically in front of the body, or the command to give such a salute

presentation /prézz'n táysh'n/ *n* **1 ACT OF PRESENTING** an act of presenting something or the state of being presented **2 WAY SOMETHING APPEARS WHEN OFFERED** the manner in which something is shown, expressed, or laid out for other people to see ○ *Presentation is an important part of the chef's job.* **3 PREPARED REPORT READ BEFORE AUDIENCE** a formal talk made to a group of people, e.g. on somebody's recent work or some aspect of business, often with handouts, diagrams, or other visual aids ○ *He gave a presentation on modern irrigation methods.* **4 PREPARED PERFORMANCE FOR AUDIENCE** a performance, exhibition, or demonstration put on before an audience **5 FORMAL HANDING-OVER OF GIFT** the action of presenting somebody with an award or a token of appreciation in front of other people, or an occasion when this is done ○ *the presentation of the trophy* **6 PART OF BABY APPEARING FIRST** the part of a baby that appears first at birth, normally the crown of the head ○ *a breech presentation* **7 SOMEBODY'S INTRODUCTION INTO SPECIAL SOCIAL GROUP** an occasion when somebody is first presented at court or into society, or the official or recognized process of first presenting somebody in this way **8 ACT OF NOMINATING CLERGY MEMBER** the act or power of nominating a member of the clergy to a particular paid office in a church **9 OBJECT OF PERCEPTION** something that is perceived, remembered, or acquired as knowledge **10** FIN = **presentment** *n.* **2** —**presentational** *adj*

Presentation of the Virgin Mary *n* a festival celebrated by the Roman Catholic and Eastern Orthodox churches marking the Virgin Mary's presentation at the temple. Date: 21 November.

presentative /pri zéntətiv/ *adj* able to be known directly without any reflective or cognitive process being necessary —**presentativeness** *n*

present-day *adj* found or existing in modern times ○ *out of touch with present-day society and the Internet culture*

Present Era *n* the Christian era, especially as used in reckoning dates

presentiment /pri zéntimənt/ *n* an awareness of some event, especially an unpleasant event, before it takes place and before there is any reason to suspect it or know about it ○ *She had a presentiment that something terrible would happen.* [Early 18C. < obsolete French *pressentiment* < Latin *praesentire*.] —**presentimental** /pri zénti mént'l/ *adj*

presently /prézz'ntli/ *adv* **1** not at this exact moment but in a short while ○ *I'll be there presently.* **2** now, or during the current period (*some people object to this usage*) ○ *Yes, he's presently engaged in a research job for the company.*

presentment /pri zéntmənt/ *n* **1** the act of presenting something, or the way in which something is presented **2** the presenting of a negotiable document for payment

present participle *n* the form of a verb that suggests a progressive or active sense and that ends in '-ing' in English, e.g. 'flying'

present perfect *n* the form of a verb that suggests something completed, in English by preceding the verb with 'have' or 'has' and usually putting '-ed' after it, e.g. 'have departed' —**present perfect** *adj*

presents /prézz'nts/ *npl* this legal or formal document (*formal*) ○ *terms discussed in these presents*

present tense *n* the tense of a verb that suggests actions or the situation at the time of speaking or writing

present value *n* the value now of a sum of money expected to be received in the future, calculated by subtracting the interest and other value that will accrue in the intervening period

preservation /préssər váysh'n/ *n* **1 PROTECTION FROM HARM** the guarding of something from danger, harm, or injury **2 A KEEPING OF SOMETHING UNCHANGED** maintenance of something, especially something of historic value, in an unchanged condition **3 UPHOLDING** the keeping of something intangible intact ○ *preservation of freedom of speech*

preservationist /prézzər váysh'nist/ *n* a person who tries to prevent things from being damaged, destroyed, or altered, particularly things of natural or historical interest —**preservationism** *n*

preservative /pri zúrvətiv/ *adj* having the ability to protect something from decay or spoilage ■ *n* something that provides protection from decay or spoilage, e.g. a food additive

preserve /pri zúrv/ *vt* (**-serves, -serving, -served**) **1 MAKE SURE SOMETHING LASTS** to keep something protected from anything that would cause its current quality or condition to change or deteriorate or fall out of use ○ *They are anxious to preserve the area's rural character.* ○ *We need to preserve professional standards of conduct.* **2 MAINTAIN SOMETHING** to keep up or maintain something ○ *She preserved a cool and composed manner throughout the interrogation.* **3 STOP FOOD GOING BAD** to treat or store food in such a way as to protect it from decay, e.g. by pickling, drying, salting, freezing, or canning **4 MAKE JAM** to make jam or marmalade **5 PROTECT** to protect somebody or something from danger, especially the danger of being killed or damaged (*formal or literary*) ○ *'The Lord shall preserve thee from all evil'* (*Psalm 121*) **6 KEEP ANIMALS IN SECURE AREA** to rear wild animals, especially fish and birds, in a protected area of water or land, so that they can be fished or shot for sport in the hunting season ■ *n* **1 EXCLUSIVE AREA OF ACTIVITY** work, sport, or interest that one particular person or group retains exclusive use of, or a place kept for one person or group to enjoy exclusively ○ *The children considered the tree house their own preserve.* **2 FRUIT JAM** a sweet thick foodstuff made by boiling fruit in sugar and water, eaten on bread or in desserts and cakes (*often plural*) **3** *US* = **reserve** *n.* **2** **4 AREA FOR PRIVATE HUNTING** an area where game is kept for private hunting [14C. Via French *préserver* < medieval Latin *praeservare* 'to guard beforehand' < Latin *servare* 'keep'.] —**preservability** /pri zúə bílləti/ *n* —**preservable** *adj*

preserver /pri zúrvər/ *n* something used to keep somebody or something safe, undamaged, or unchanged

preset /pree sét/ *vt* (**-sets, -setting, -set**) to arrange the settings of a timing device controlling or built into an electrical appliance so that the appliance is automatically switched on at a specified time ○ *The central heating is preset to come on in the morning and evening.* ■ *n* an electronic timing device or system that is used to make an appliance operate at a later time

preside /pri zíd/ (**-sides, -siding, -sided**) *vi* **1 BE OFFICIALLY IN CHARGE** to be the chairperson or hold a similar position of authority at a formal gathering of people **2 HAVE CONTROL** to be the most powerful person or the one everyone else obeys, usually in a specified place or situation ○ *the question of who will preside over the business once their mother retires* **3 PERFORM AS INSTRUMENTALIST** to be the featured instrumentalist in a performance ○ *preside at the organ* [Early 17C. Via French *présider* < Latin *praesidere* 'sit in front of' < *sedere* 'sit'.] —**presider** *n*

presidency /prézzidənssi/ (*plural* **-cies**) *n* **1 POSITION OF PRESIDENT OF NATION** the job or function of president of a republic, or a president's term of office **2 JOB OF PRESIDENT** the status, post, or function of being president of a company, society, institution, or similar body ○ *The presidency of the club turned out to be a thankless task.* **3 LATTER-DAY SAINTS COUNCIL** a three-person executive council in the Church of Jesus Christ of Latter-Day Saints **4 LATTER-DAY SAINTS GOVERNING COUNCIL** the governing body of the Church of Jesus Christ of Latter-Day Saints

PRESIDENTS OF THE UNITED STATES

Term of office	President	Political party		Term of office	President	Political party
1789–1797	George Washington			1889–1893	Benjamin Harrison	*Republican*
1797–1801	John Adams	*Federalist*		1893–1897	Grover Cleveland	*Democrat*
1801–1809	Thomas Jefferson	*Democratic-Republican*		1897–1901	William McKinley	*Republican*
1809–1817	James Madison	*Democratic-Republican*		1901–1909	Theodore Roosevelt	*Republican*
1817–1825	James Monroe	*Democratic-Republican*		1909–1913	William Howard Taft	*Republican*
1825–1829	John Quincy Adams	*Democratic-Republican*		1913–1921	Woodrow Wilson	*Democrat*
1829–1837	Andrew Jackson	*Democrat*		1921–1923	Warren G. Harding	*Republican*
1837–1841	Martin Van Buren	*Democrat*		1923–1929	Calvin Coolidge	*Republican*
1841	William Henry Harrison	*Whig*		1929–1933	Herbert Hoover	*Republican*
1841–1845	John Tyler	*Whig*		1933–1945	Franklin Delano Roosevelt	*Democrat*
1845–1849	James Polk	*Democrat*		1945–1953	Harry S. Truman	*Democrat*
1849–1850	Zachary Taylor	*Whig*		1953–1961	Dwight D. Eisenhower	*Republican*
1850–1853	Millard Fillmore	*Whig*		1961–1963	John F. Kennedy	*Democrat*
1853–1857	Franklin Pierce	*Democrat*		1963–1969	Lyndon Johnson	*Democrat*
1857–1861	James Buchanan	*Democrat*		1969–1974	Richard Nixon	*Republican*
1861–1865	Abraham Lincoln	*Republican*		1974–1977	Gerald Ford	*Republican*
1865–1869	Andrew Johnson	*Democrat*		1977–1981	Jimmy Carter	*Democrat*
1869–1877	Ulysses S. Grant	*Republican*		1981–1989	Ronald Reagan	*Republican*
1877–1881	Rutherford B. Hayes	*Republican*		1989–1993	George Bush	*Republican*
1881	James Garfield	*Republican*		1993–2001	Bill Clinton	*Democrat*
1881–1885	Chester A. Arthur	*Republican*		2001–	George W. Bush	*Republican*
1885–1889	Grover Cleveland	*Democrat*				

president /prézzidənt/, **President** *n* **1** HEAD OF STATE OF A REPUBLIC the chief politician of a republic, e.g. the United States of America **2** HIGHEST-RANKING MEMBER OF AN ASSOCIATION the highest-ranking member of an organization or institution **3** *US* HEAD OF COMPANY the highest-ranking executive officer of a business or corporation **4** HEAD OF EDUCATIONAL ESTABLISHMENT the highest-ranking executive officer of certain universities and colleges **5** SOMEBODY IN CHARGE OF MEETING a person who is appointed or elected to oversee a meeting **6** LATTER-DAY SAINTS LEADER in the Church of Jesus Christ of Latter-Day Saints, a man who is a member of the church's governing board [14C. Via French *président* < Latin *praesidere* (see PRESIDE).] — **presidentship** *n*

president-elect (*plural* **presidents-elect**) *n* an elected or appointed president who has not yet been officially installed

presidential /prézzi dénsh'l/ *adj* **1** relating to the post of president, or used or owned by a president ○ *The presidential elections dominated the news.* **2** presided over by a president, or presiding like one — **presidentially** *adv*

Presidents' Day *n* an official holiday in the United States commemorating the birthdays of George Washington and Abraham Lincoln. Date: 3rd Monday in February.

presidio /pri síddi ō, pri zíddi ō/ (*plural* **-os**) *n* a fortified settlement, especially of the type established by Spanish colonizers in the southwestern part of what is now the United States [Mid-18C. Via Spanish < Latin *praesidium* 'garrison, fortification' < *praesidere* (see PRESIDE).]

presidium /pri síddi əm, -zíddi-/ (*plural* **-ums** *or* **-a** /-di ə/), **praesidium** (*plural* **-ums** *or* **-a**) *n* a permanent executive committee that acted for a larger legislature in the former Soviet Union and other Communist countries [Early 20C. Via Russian < Latin *praesidium* (see PRESIDIO).]

Presley /prézzli/, **Elvis** (1935–77) US singer and actor. Known as **The King**

press[1] /press/ *v* **1** *vti* PUSH AGAINST to use a steady and significant force to put weight on something, sometimes to make it move or start working ○ *I got into the lift and pressed the down button but nothing happened.* **2** *vt* SQUEEZE JUICE OUT OF to squeeze the juice or oil out of something using force or weight to compress it ○ *pressing grapes* **3** *vt* SMOOTH OUT to push a flat object, especially a hot iron, onto a garment or piece of cloth so as to smooth out unwanted creases or make a crease where desired ○ *pressed a shirt and put it on* **4** *vt* CHANGE SHAPE BY SQUEEZING to change the shape of something by squeezing it or putting a steady weight on it, especially in order to make it more compact ○ *pressed the clay into a ball* **5** *vt* HOLD TIGHTLY to grip or clasp somebody or something firmly but not roughly with the hands or arms, especially to show affection or moral support ○ *She pressed his hand in sympathy.* **6** *vt* FORCE SOMEBODY to force somebody into doing something he or she did not want or intend to do ○ *They pressed her into standing for the election.* **7** *vt* TRY TO OBTAIN SOMETHING FROM to ask somebody persistently or forcefully to supply, accept, or do a specific thing ○ *They pressed him for an immediate*

response. **8** *vt* EMPHASIZE to make sure that something is fully recognized and understood or stress its importance ○ *It is vital that you press the main items of the manifesto in your speech.* **9** *vt* DEMAND to plead or demand something insistently **10** *vti* PESTER to pester or worry somebody continually (*dated or literary*) ○ *They pressed her every day until she agreed to go with them.* **11** *vi* MOVE AS CROWD to crowd around or together (*literary*) ○ *The crowd pressed forward as the gates opened.* **12** *vi* REQUIRE ATTENTION to need to be dealt with urgently (*dated or formal*) ○ *I'd like to help now, but business presses.* **13** *vt* FLATTEN TO PRESERVE to flatten and dry a natural object such as a flower so that it does not decompose and can be kept or used decoratively ○ *pressed flowers as a hobby* **14** *vt* MAKE USING MOULD to form something in a mould, especially to make gramophone records ○ *went down to the studio to press a record* **15** *vti* HARASS BASKETBALL OPPONENT to use a harassing and aggressive defence against an opponent in basketball ■ *n* **1** ACT OF PRESSING an act of pressing something ○ *I gave the doorbell a few presses but nobody answered.* **2** CROWD a tightly-packed crowd of people **3** POWERFUL MOVEMENT the crowding and pressing together of a lot of people or things at the same time (*literary*) ○ *He could not move because of the press of people.* **4** DEVICE FOR SQUEEZING a piece of equipment designed to crush something to release the juices or create a pulp ○ *a garlic press* **5** DEVICE FOR FLATTENING a piece of equipment used to keep or make something smooth and uncreased **6** LINEN CUPBOARD a shelved cupboard, usually of a large size, for storing bed or table linens or clothes **7** MACHINE THAT APPLIES MECHANICAL PRESSURE a machine that, by applying pressure to a piece of metal or other material, can shape, form, cut, stamp, or otherwise cause a physical change to occur **8** NEWSPAPERS OR REPORTERS the news-gathering business generally, or all the people involved in gathering and reporting on the news, especially journalists working on newspapers ○ *She agreed to appear on television but refused to talk to the press.* **9** COMMENTS BY JOURNALISTS the opinions expressed in articles or reviews in the newspapers or magazines ○ *His new musical had a lot of good press.* **10** PRINTING = **printing press 11** PUBLISHING COMPANY a company that publishes books (*in names*) **12** PROCESS OR SKILL OF PRINTING the technical or physical process used by a printer and the skills a printer requires **13** CLAMP FOR RACKETS a clamp for holding a tennis or other racket to prevent it from warping when it is not in use **14** DEFENCE IN SPORT an aggressive defence, especially in basketball **15** LIFTING OF WEIGHT ABOVE HEAD in weightlifting, a lift in which the weight is raised to shoulder height and then to above the head without moving the legs [14C. Via French *presser* < Latin *pressare* 'keep on pressing' < *press-*, past participle of *premere* 'to press'.] — **pressed** *n* ▷ **be pressed for something** to be short of something, usually time

press for *vt* to seek or demand something with great urgency ○ *They pressed for an immediate review of the situation.*

press on *vi* to continue in an urgent or persistent manner ○ *Night was falling but they pressed on despite their weariness.*

press[2] /press/ *vt* **1** FORCE SOMEBODY INTO MILITARY SERVICE to forcibly recruit somebody into military service **2** USE SOMETHING FOR NEW PURPOSE to take something out of its intended place or function and make use of it in a different way (*literary*) ■ *n* FORCING OF SOMEBODY INTO MILITARY SERVICE the act of recruiting people into military service by force [Late 16C. Alteration (influenced by PRESS[1]) of obsolete *prest* 'enlist by paying in advance', via Old French *prester* < Latin *praestare* < *stare* 'stand'.]

press agent *n* a promoter who contacts, liaises with, and gives information to the press on behalf of a client

Press Association *n* the national news agency for the United Kingdom and Ireland

pressboard /préss bawrd/ *n* *US* **1** a heavy cardboard or pasteboard with a glazed finish **2** a small ironing board used especially for pressing the sleeves of garments

press box *n* a section in a sports stadium or similar venue kept exclusively for journalists to work in

Pressburger /préss burgər/, **Emeric** (1902–88) Hungarian-born British film director. Born **Imre Pressburger**

press conference *n* an invited meeting for members of the press to enable them to hear a prepared statement by somebody in the news, and usually to ask questions about that statement

pressed /prest/ *adj* **1** made compact and firm by being forced mechanically into cans or containers ○ *pressed meat* **2** having urgent or worrying things to deal with

Elvis Presley

○ *She is particularly pressed today, so I won't ask her to help if I can avoid it.*

press gallery *n* a raised gallery with seating at the back of a courtroom or legislative assembly room, where newspaper reporters and other members of the press can sit

press gang *n* formerly, a group of military personnel whose job was to find people to force into military service

press-gang *vti* to force people into military service or into doing anything that they are reluctant to do ○ *I never wanted to go to camp – my parents press-ganged me into it.*

pressie *n* = **prezzie**

pressing /préssing/ *adj* **1 URGENT** needing to be attended to without delay ○ *He had a pressing engagement and had to leave immediately.* **2 VERY PERSISTENT** persistent and demanding, and therefore difficult to ignore or refuse ○ *Her invitations were so pressing that we eventually had to accept.* ■ *n* **GRAMOPHONE RECORDS MADE AT ONE TIME** all the gramophone records produced at one time from a master mould —**pressingly** *adv* —**pressingness** *n*

press kit *n* a package of background and promotional material relating to a product, distributed to the media by a press agent or publicity department

pressman /préss man, -mən/ (*plural* **-men** /-men, -mən/) *n* **1** a man working as a newspaper reporter (*dated*) **2** an operator of a printing press

pressmark /préss maark/ *n* LIBRARIES = **shelf mark**

press officer *n* somebody employed by an organization or government department to provide the news media with information about the organization or department

press of sail, press of canvas *n* the largest amount of sail that a ship can safely carry

pressor /préssər/ *adj* relating to or bringing about an increase in blood pressure

press release *n* an official statement or account of a news story that is specially prepared and issued to newspapers and other news media for them to make known to the public

pressrun /préss run/ *n* **1** the continuous running of a printing press until a specified number of copies is printed **2** the number of copies run off in a continuous printing operation

press stud *n* a manufactured device with two halves that push tightly into each other, generally used instead of a button to keep a piece of clothing fastened. US term **snap** *n.* 7

press-up *n UK, NZ* any one of a series of identical exercise movements performed with the body straight and facing the floor. ◊ **pushup**

pressure /préshər/ *n* **1 PROCESS OF PRESSING STEADILY** the applying of a firm regular weight or force against something or somebody ○ *The pressure of her hand on his was comforting.* **2 CONSTANT STATE OF WORRY AND URGENCY** powerful and stressful demands on somebody's time, attention, and energy, or one of many demands of this sort ○ *They were under constant pressure to achieve near impossible output targets.* **3 FORCE THAT PUSHES OR URGES** something that affects thoughts and behaviour in a powerful way, usually in the form of several outside influences working together persuasively **4 FORCE PER UNIT AREA** (*symbol p*) the force acting on a surface divided by the area over which it acts **5** METEOROL = **atmospheric pressure** ■ *vt* (**-sures, -suring, -sured**) **MAKE SOMEBODY DO** to apply great persuasion or a strong influence on somebody to force him or her to do something [14C. < Latin *pressura* < *press-* (see PRESS[1]).] —**pressureless** *adj*

pressure cooker *n* a specially-designed pan used to steam food at high pressure, at a higher temperature and in a shorter time than by boiling —**pressure-cook** *vt*

pressure group *n* a number of people who work together to make their particular concerns known to those in government, and to influence the passage of legislation

pressure point *n* any point at which an artery can be compressed against a bone using a finger, so stemming blood flow to the part of the body that the artery supplies

pressure sore *n* MED = **bedsore**

pressure suit *n* an inflatable airtight suit, similar to that worn by deep sea divers, used to protect against the effects of low pressure at very high altitude or in space

pressure vessel *n* a cylindrical or spherically shaped container designed to withstand bursting pressures

pressurize /préshə rīz/ (**-izes, -izing, -ized**), **pressurise** (**-ises, -ising, -ised**) *vt* **1 INCREASE AIR PRESSURE IN ENCLOSED SPACE** to increase the air pressure in an enclosed space, e.g. inside an aircraft, to maintain air at close to normal atmospheric pressure when the external pressure falls **2 INCREASE AIR PRESSURE IN CONTAINER** to increase the air pressure in a container beyond normal levels **3 MAKE SOMEBODY DO SOMETHING** to apply great persuasion or a strong influence on people to force them, or try to force them, to do something they would not otherwise have done ○ *colleagues who had pressurized me to apply for membership* **4 PUT FLUID UNDER PRESSURE** to apply increased pressure to a fluid —**pressurization** /préshə rī záysh'n/ *n* —**pressurizer** /préshə rīzər/ *n*

presswoman /préss wòomən/ *n* a woman working as a newspaper reporter (*dated*)

presswork /préss wurk/ *n* the operation, management, or work done by a printing press

Prester John /préstər jón/ *n* a Christian priest-king who was believed to rule over a vast kingdom of great wealth in Asia or Africa during the Middle Ages [< Old French *prestre Jehan* and medieval Latin *presbyter Johannes* 'John the priest']

prestidigitation /présti dìjji táysh'n/ *n* sleight of hand used in performing magic tricks (*formal or humorous*) [Mid-19C. < French, < *prestidigitateur* 'person practising sleight of hand' < *preste* 'nimble' + Latin *digitus* 'finger'.] —**prestidigitator** /présti díjji taytər/ *n*

prestige /pre stéezh, -stéej/ *n* **1** honour, awe, or high opinion that is inspired by a high-ranking, influential, or successful person or product **2** attractiveness and importance that is very obvious or enviable, associated with wealthy or successful people ○ *It's a prestige car and its price reflects that.* [Mid-17C. Via French < Latin *praestigiae* 'illusions, juggler's tricks'.] —**prestigious** /pre stíjjəss/ *adj* —**prestigiously** *adv* —**prestigiousness** *n*

prestissimo /pre stíssi mō/ *adv* played or to be played as fast as possible (*musical direction*) ■ *n* (*plural* **-mos**) a musical composition or passage that is meant to be played as fast as possible [Early 18C. < Italian, superlative of *presto* 'presto'.] —**prestissimo** *adj*

presto /préstō/ *adv* **1 VERY FAST** played or to be played very fast (*musical direction*) **2 SUDDENLY** instantly, as if magically (*informal*) ■ *n* (*plural* **-tos**) **VERY FAST MUSICAL PIECE** a musical composition or passage that is meant to be played very fast [Late 16C. Via Italian, 'quick' < Latin *praesto* 'at hand'.] —**presto** *adj*

Preston /préstən/ town in NW England. Population: 134,300 (1995).

Preston /prést'n/, **Margaret Rose** (1875–1963) Australian artist

prestress /pree stréss/ *vt* to apply stress to something such as a cable or beam so that it will bear a load better when in use

prestressed concrete /prée strest-/ *n* concrete that is cast over cables that are under tension, so as to increase its strength

Prestwich /préstwich/ town in NW England. Population: 31,801 (1991).

Prestwick /préstwik/ town in SW Scotland. Population: 13,705 (1991).

presumably /pri zyóoməbli/ *adv* used to show that you expect that a specified thing is the case or will happen or has happened ○ *Presumably that man is her father.*

presume /pri zyóom/ (**-sumes, -suming, -sumed**) *v* **1** *vti* **BELIEVE SOMETHING TO BE TRUE** to accept that something is virtually certain to be correct even though there is no proof of it, on the grounds that it is extremely likely ○ *After several days of searching, they presumed that there were no survivors.* **2** *vi* **BEHAVE ARROGANTLY OR OVERCONFIDENTLY** to behave so inconsiderately, disrespectfully, or overconfidently as to do something without being entitled or qualified to do it (*usually in negative statements*) ○ *I would never presume to tell you how to run your business.* **3** *vt* **REGARD AS TRUE WITHOUT PROOF** to assume that something is true in the absence of proof that will confirm or contradict it **4** *vt* **SEEM TO PROVE** to indicate the existence or truth of something (*formal*) ○ *Your line of reasoning presumes his being at home the whole evening.* **5** *vi* **TAKE ADVANTAGE** to exploit or take advantage of somebody unscrupulously ○ *would not want to presume on the generosity of a stranger* [14C. Via French *présumer* < Latin *praesumere* 'take before, anticipate' < *sumere* 'take'.] —**presumable** *adj* —**presumer** *n* —**presuming** *adj* —**presumingly** *adv*

presumption /pri zúmpsh'n/ *n* **1 SOMETHING BELIEVED WITHOUT ACTUAL EVIDENCE** a belief based on the fact that something is considered to be extremely reasonable or likely ○ *I acted on the presumption that their IDs were genuine.* **2 RUDENESS OR ARROGANCE** behaviour that is inconsiderate, disrespectful, or overconfident **3 LEGAL INFERENCE** an inference that something is the case, in the absence of evidence rebutting that assumption and on the basis of other known facts ○ *a presumption of innocence* **4 BELIEF IN SOMETHING THAT SEEMS REASONABLE** the acceptance that something is correct, without having proof of it, on the grounds that it is extremely likely (*formal*) ○ *a decision based on presumption rather than on the facts* **5 SOMETHING THAT COULD BE PROOF** an indication that something exists or is true (*formal*) [12C. < Old French *presumpcion* < Latin *praesumere* (see PRESUME).]

presumptive /pri zúmptiv/ *adj* **1 PROBABLE** based on what is thought most likely or reasonable (*formal*) **2 CAUSING PEOPLE TO PRESUME** forming a reasonable basis for the acceptance that something exists or is true (*formal*) **3 POTENTIALLY ABLE TO DIFFERENTIATE** describes cells or tissue of an early embryo that, in the normal course of development, will differentiate to form a particular organ or tissue in the mature embryo [Mid-16C. < French *presomptif* < Latin *praesumere* (see PRESUME).] —**presumptively** *adv* —**presumptiveness** *n*

presumptuous /pri zúmptyoo əss, -zúmpshəss/ *adj* inconsiderate, disrespectful, or overconfident, especially in doing something when not entitled or qualified to do it [14C. < Old French *presumptueux* < Latin *praesumere* (see PRESUME).] —**presumptuously** *adv* —**presumptuousness** *n*

presuppose /prée sə pṓz/ (**-poses, -posing, -posed**) *vt* **1** to believe that a particular thing is true before there is any proof of it ○ *the tendency to presuppose that everybody will understand English* **2** to make something necessary if a particular thing is to be shown to be true or false. The sentence 'Fred loves his daughter' presupposes that Fred has a daughter. —**presupposition** /prée supə zísh'n/ *n*

prêt-à-porter /prét aa páwr tay/ *adj* manufactured in standard sizes ready to be bought off the peg in shops [Mid-20C. < French, 'ready to wear'.]

pretax /prée táks/ *adj* before tax is or was deducted ○ *the firm's pretax profits*

preteen /prée téen/, **preteenager** /-téen ayjər/ *n* a girl or boy in the few years before becoming a teenager

pretence /pri ténss/ *n* **1 INSINCERE OR FEIGNED BEHAVIOUR** something done or a way of behaving that is not genuine but is meant to deceive other people ○ *His display of affection was certainly a pretence.* **2 UNWARRANTED CLAIM** a claim, especially one with few facts to support it (*often in the negative*) ○ *He makes no pretence to being an expert.* **3 MAKE-BELIEVE** make-believe or things imagined **4** = **pretension**[1] *n.* 2 [14C. Via Anglo-Norman < medieval Latin *pretensus* 'alleged' < past participle of Latin *praetendere* (see PRETEND).]

pretend /pri ténd/ *v* **1** *vti* **ACT AS IF SOMETHING WERE TRUE** to make believe, e.g. by using the imagination or acting skills ○ *The little girl liked to pretend that she was an astronaut.* ○ *We pretended to be interested in what she was saying.* **2** *vt* **MAKE INSINCERE CLAIM ABOUT** to claim untruthfully or exaggeratedly to be or to have a particular thing, or imply something in this way ○ *I won't pretend to be an expert on the subject, but I can't believe those figures are correct.* **3** *vt* **MAKE SOMETHING SEEM TO BE TRUE** to act in a way intended to make people believe something untrue or misleading about somebody or something ○ *She pretended to be an orphan just to get our sympathy.* **4** *vi* **CLAIM TO OWN** to make an untruthful or dubious claim of ownership or the right to something, especially something valuable, admirable, or prestigious (*formal*) ○ *pretends to the throne* ■ *adj* **IMAGINARY** existing only in the imagination, not real (*informal; usually by or to children*) ○ *I made a pretend house where my pretend horse lives.* [14C. Directly or via French *prétendre* < Latin *praetendere* 'extend in front' < *tendere* 'stretch'.] —**pretended** *adj*

pretender /pri téndər/ *n* **1** a person who claims a disputed right to a special rank, title, or privilege, especially a royal title 2 a person who intentionally gives a false impression to somebody else

pretense *n* US = **pretence**

pretension[1] /pree ténsh'n/ *n* 1 **QUESTIONABLE CLAIM** an untruthful or dubious assertion of a right to something, especially something valuable, admirable, or prestigious (*often plural and with negatives*) ○ *His pretensions to aristocratic birth were unconvincing.* 2 **AFFECTED BEHAVIOUR** behaviour that is artificial, especially that which is given to display and grandeur 3 **MAKING OF CLAIM** the formal act of putting forward a claim (*formal*) [15C. < medieval Latin *praetension-* < the past participle of Latin *praetendere* (see PRETEND).]

pretension[2] /pree ténsh'n/ *vt* to strengthen reinforced concrete by applying tension to the reinforcing steel before the concrete has set

pretentious /pri ténshəss/ *adj* 1 **SELF-IMPORTANT AND AFFECTED** acting as though more important, valuable, or special than is warranted, or appearing to have an unrealistically high self-image 2 **MADE TO LOOK OR SOUND IMPORTANT** presenting itself unjustifiably as having a special quality or significance, and often seeming forced or too clever ○ *dismissed it as yet another pretentious film* 3 **OSTENTATIOUS** extravagantly and consciously showy or glamourous [Mid-19C. < French *prétentieux* < medieval Latin *praetension-* (see PRETENSION).] —**pretentiously** *adv* —**pretentiousness** *n*

preter- *prefix* beyond ○ *preterhuman* [< Latin *praeter* < *prae* 'before' (see PRE-)]

preterite /préttərit/ *n* the past tense [Via Old French < Latin (*tempus*) *praeteritum* 'past (tense)' < past participle of *praeterire* (see PRETERITION)] —**preterite** *adj*

preterition /prétta rísh'n/ *n* 1 the act of passing over something or leaving something out (*formal*) 2 the Calvinist doctrine that those people who were not predestined to be saved were passed over by God [Late 16C. < late Latin *praeterition-* 'a passing by' < Latin *praeterire* 'go by' < *ire* 'go'.]

preterm /preé túrm/ *adj* born before completion of a pregnancy of normal length

pretermit /preétər mít/ (**-mits, -mitting, -mitted**) *vt* (*formal*) 1 to overlook or ignore something deliberately 2 to leave something out or undone [15C. < Latin *praetermittere* 'let go by' < *mittere* 'let go'.] —**pretermission** /-mísh'n/ *n* —**pretermitter** /-míttər/ *n*

preternatural /preétər náchərəl/ *adj* 1 exceeding what is normal in nature (*formal or literary*) 2 supernatural or uncanny (*literary*) [Late 16C. < medieval Latin *praeternaturalis* < Latin *praeter naturam* 'beyond nature'.] —**preternaturalism** *n* —**preternaturality** /preétər náchə rálləti/ *n* —**preternaturally** *adv* —**preternaturalness** *n*

pretext /preé tekst/ *n* a misleading or untrue reason given for doing something in an attempt to conceal the real reason [Early 16C. < Latin *praetextus* 'show, display' < *praetext*, past participle of *praetexere* 'weave before, adorn' < *texere* 'weave'.]

pretor *n* HIST = **praetor**

Pretoria /pri táwri ə/ administrative capital of South Africa, in the NE of the country. Population: 525,583 (1991).

pretorian /pri táwri ən/ *adj, n* HIST = **praetorian**

Pretorian *adj* HIST = **Praetorian**

Pretorius /pri táwri əss/, **Andries** (1798–1853) South African soldier and statesman

Pretorius, Marthinus Wessels (1819–1901) South African statesman

pretrial /pree trī əl/ *adj* existing or occurring before a trial in a court of law takes place

prettify /prítti fī/ (**-fies, -fying, -fied**) *vt* to give a person, place, or thing some added decoration, especially of a rather superficial or fussy kind —**prettification** /prítti fi káysh'n/ *n* —**prettifier** /prítti fī ər/ *n*

pretty /prítti/ *adj* (**-tier, -tiest**) 1 **HAVING PLEASANT FACE** with an attractive, pleasant face that is graceful and appealing rather than outstandingly beautiful 2 **NICE TO LOOK AT** pleasing or charming in appearance in a delicate, gentle, or decorative way ○ *The garden looks so pretty at this time of year.* 3 **NICE TO LISTEN TO** with a pleasant, gentle, or delicate sound quality ○ *operas with pretty music* 4 **LARGE** large in size, extent or value (*dated informal*) ○ *a pretty sum* 5 **GRACEFUL** having, as a boy or man, the pleasing looks and graceful manner often associated with a woman (*offensive in some contexts*) 6 **UNSATISFACTORY** very bad or unsatisfactory (*dated informal*) ○ *That's a pretty mess you've got yourself into.* 7 **WEAK AND SUPERFICIAL** appealing or charming to hear or look at, but without any deep meaning or sincerity ○ *He knows how to paint pretty pictures but he's not an artist.* ■ *adv* **FAIRLY** to quite a large, noticeable, or reasonable extent (*informal*) ○ *I'm pretty sure I left my keys on the kitchen table.* ■ *n* (*plural* **-ties**) **SOMEBODY WHO IS PRETTY** a pretty person, thing, or animal (*archaic informal*) ■ *vt* (**-ties, -tying, -tied**) **MAKE PRETTY** to make somebody or something pretty to look at [Old English, *prættig* < Germanic, 'trick'] ◇ **pretty well** nearly completely (*informal*)

pretty up *vt* = **pretty** *v.*

⚡**Pretty Good Privacy** full form of **PGP**

pretty-pretty *adj* so pretty that it looks contrived or ridiculous (*informal*) ○ *a pretty-pretty hat covered in flowers and ribbons*

pretzel /préts'l/ *n* a crisp knot-shaped or stick-shaped biscuit with a golden-brown glaze (*used especially in the plural*) [Mid-19C. < German.]

prevail /pri váyl/ *v* 1 *vi* **BE UNBEATEN AND IN CONTROL** to prove to be stronger and in the position of greater influence and power ○ *He prevailed over his enemies.* 2 **WIN THROUGH** to prove to be effective ○ *Justice will prevail.* 3 *vi* **BE THE NORMAL THING** to predominate or be the most common or frequent ○ *Middle-class families prevail in this street.* 4 *vi* **BE CURRENT** to remain in general use or effect (*formal*) ○ *Witchcraft still prevails in some parts of the country.* [14C. < Latin *praevalere* 'be stronger' < *valere* 'be strong'.] —**prevailer** *n*

prevail on, prevail upon *vt* to persuade somebody to do something ○ *They prevailed on her to take part.*

prevailing /pri váyling/ *adj* 1 found most commonly or having the most power or effect in a particular area ○ *prevailing winds* 2 found, existing, or in force currently ○ *the prevailing view among modern scientists* —**prevailingly** *adv*

prevalent /prévvələnt/ *adj* occurring, or accepted and practised, commonly or widely ○ *Roman Catholicism is the prevalent religion in most of southern Europe.* [Late 16C. < Latin *praevalere* (see PREVAIL).] —**prevalence** *n* —**prevalently** *adv*

SYNONYMS See ***widespread***.

prevaricate /pri várri kayt/ (**-cates, -cating, -cated**) *vi* to avoid giving a direct and honest answer or opinion, or a clear and truthful account of a situation, especially by quibbling or being deliberately ambiguous or misleading [Mid-16C. < Latin *praevaricari* 'walk crookedly' < *varus* 'crooked, knock-kneed'.] —**prevarication** /pri várri káysh'n/ *n* —**prevaricator** *n*

~~**prevelant**~~ incorrect spelling of **prevalent**

~~**prevelent**~~ incorrect spelling of **prevalent**

prevenient /pri veéni ənt/ *adj* (*formal*) 1 coming or occurring in advance of another thing 2 producing a sense of anticipation [Early 17C. < Latin *praevenient-*, present participle of *praevenire* 'come before' (see PREVENT).]

prevent /pri vént/ *v* 1 *vt* **STOP SOMETHING FROM TAKING PLACE** to cause something not to happen or not to be done ○ *Rain prevented them from playing the match.* 2 *vt* **STOP SOMEBODY FROM DOING** to be the reason why somebody does not or cannot do a particular thing ○ *a sense of duty that prevented him from abandoning the project* 3 *vi* **STAND IN THE WAY** to be the reason that something is impossible or very difficult ○ *Modesty prevents that I reveal the true reason.* [15C. < Latin *prevent-*, past participle of *praevenire* 'come before, prevent' < *venire* 'come'.] —**preventability** /pri véntə bílləti/ *n* —**preventable** *adj* —**preventably** *adv* —**preventer** *n*

preventative /pri véntətiv/ *adj, n* = **preventive** —**preventatively** *adv* —**preventativeness** *n*

prevention /pri vénsh'n/ *n* 1 an action or actions taken to stop somebody from doing something or to prevent something from taking place ○ *the prevention of crime* 2 an action or measure that makes it impossible or very difficult for somebody to do a certain thing or for something to happen

preventive /pri véntiv/ *adj* used or devised to stop something undesirable from happening, or to stop people from doing something undesirable ○ *preventive dentistry* ■ *n* something that stops something undesirable from happening, especially something that protects against illness ○ *A good preventive against heart disease is a healthy lifestyle.* —**preventively** *adv* —**preventiveness** *n*

preventive detention *n* 1 imprisonment for a term of up to 14 years for criminals over the age of 30 2 the pretrial jailing without bail of somebody accused of a crime who is thought likely to attempt to flee, commit additional crimes, or intimidate witnesses or prosecutors, or an instance of such jailing

preverbal /preé vúrbal/ *adj* 1 at the stage of development when a child is not yet able to use speech 2 coming before a verb

preview /preé vyoo/ *n* 1 **OPPORTUNITY TO SEE SOMETHING IN ADVANCE** a showing of something, especially a film, play, exhibition, or work of art, to a select audience before the general public sees it 2 **DESCRIPTION OF A FORTHCOMING SHOW** a piece printed in a paper or magazine or broadcast on radio or TV describing and commenting on something that is soon to be broadcast or presented to the public 3 **PROMOTIONAL FILM** a short film shown on TV or at the cinema promoting an upcoming film or programme ■ *vt* 1 **SHOW SOMETHING IN ADVANCE** to put on a performance or showing of something for a select audience before the general public has the opportunity to see it 2 **DESCRIBE A SHOW IN ADVANCE** to write, print, or broadcast a short piece that describes and comments on something that is soon to be broadcast or presented to the public

previous /preévi əss/ *adj* 1 **COMING BEFORE** occurring before something or somebody of the same kind ○ *his previous girlfriend* ○ *the previous edition* 2 **ALREADY ARRANGED** existing, made, or settled before the one being referred to now ○ *She was unable to come because of a previous engagement.* 3 **ACTING TOO HASTILY** saying or doing something earlier than is appropriate (*informal*) [Early 17C. < Latin *praevius* 'going before' < *prae* 'before'.] —**previousness** *n* ◇ **previous to something** before a particular thing took place

previously /preévi əsli/ *adv* at an earlier time or on an earlier occasion

previous question *n* 1 in the House of Commons, a motion to stop a question being debated, so that a vote cannot be held on it 2 in the House of Lords and US legislative bodies, a motion to put a question that will end a debate so that a vote on a bill can be taken without delay

prevision /pri vízh'n/ *n* (*formal or literary*) 1 the ability to predict or foresee things 2 a prediction or premonition

prevocalic /preé vō kállik/ *adj* describes a consonant that comes immediately before a vowel —**prevocalically** *adv*

prewar /preé wáwr/ *adj* dating from or belonging to the period before a particular war, especially World War II or World War I ○ *prewar fashions*

prewashed /preé wósht/ *adj* washed before being packaged and sold in the shops

prey /pray/ (*plural* **prey** *or* **preys**) *n* 1 **ANIMALS HUNTED BY OTHER ANIMALS** an animal or animals caught, killed, and eaten by another animal as food ○ *The common shrew's prey consists largely of earthworms and woodlice.* 2 **SOMEBODY TREATED UNKINDLY BY OTHERS** a victim or recipient of cruel or unfair treatment from somebody else ○ *a young heiress who was the prey of fortune hunters* 3 **LIKELY PERSON TO SUFFER FROM** a person who is or seems prone to illness, worry, or upset ○ *He was tense, nervous, and prey to headaches.* 4 **PLUNDER** items stolen or plundered (*archaic or literary*) [13C. Via Old French *preie* < Latin *praeda* 'booty'.] —**preyer** *n*

SPELLCHECK See *pray*.

prey on, prey upon *vt* 1 **HUNT AND KILL OTHER ANIMALS** to hunt and kill other animals for food ○ *Owls prey on mice and rabbits.* 2 **VICTIMIZE** to victimize or exploit somebody 3 **WORRY** to cause somebody constant anxiety or distress ○ *ever-increasing debt that preyed on his mind*

prezzie /prézzi/, **pressie** *n* a gift or present (*informal*) ○ *Did you get lots of prezzies on your birthday?* [Mid-20C. Shortening and alteration of PRESENT[1].]

Priam /prī əm/ *n* in Greek mythology, the king of Troy, husband of Hecuba, and father of Hector, Paris, and Cassandra

priapic /prī áppik/ *adj* 1 **RELATING TO PHALLUS** relating to or resembling a phallus (*dated or literary*) 2 **WITH PENIS PERMANENTLY ERECT** having a permanently erect penis 3 **FASCINATED BY MALE SEXUAL ACTIVITY** showing a preoccupation with male sexual activity [Late 18C. < Latin *Priapus*, Greek *Priapos* 'Priapus', symbolized by the erect phallus <.]

priapism /prī́ əpizəm/ *n* a medical disorder in which there is persistent, often painful erection of the penis in the absence of sexual interest [Early 17C. < Latin *Priapus* (see PRIAPIC).]

Priapus /prī áypəss/ *n* in Greek mythology, the god of fertility

Pribilof Islands /príbbi lof-/ group of islands off SW Alaska, in the SE Bering Sea. Population: 901 (1990). Area: 161 sq. km/62 sq. mi.

price /prīss/ *n* **1 COST OF SOMETHING BOUGHT OR SOLD** the particular amount, usually of money, that is offered or asked for when something is bought or sold ○ *The price of food continued to soar.* **2 SOMETHING SACRIFICED TO GET SOMETHING ELSE** something lost or given in order to achieve a particular position or condition ○ *Unwanted media attention is the price of fame.* **3 SUFFICIENT BRIBE** the sum of money or other payment for which somebody is willing to do something or to refrain from doing something ○ *The price of her cooperation was an invitation to the gala dinner.* **4 REWARD MONEY** a sum of money offered as a reward for the capture or killing of a particular criminal or outlaw (*dated or literary*) ○ *an outlaw with a price on his head* **5 MEASURE OF SOMETHING'S VALUE** an estimate of what somebody or something is worth, e.g. how important, useful, or irreplaceable it is (*dated or literary*) **6 BETTING ODDS** betting or gambling odds ■ *vt* (**prices, pricing, priced**) **1 DECIDE HOW MUCH SOMETHING COSTS** to state or fix the exact price that a customer or consumer must pay for something ○ *He priced the antique clock at £500.* **2 MARK SOMETHING WITH PRICE** to show how much something costs, especially by writing on the article itself or by attaching a label or price tag ○ *spent the morning pricing merchandise* **3 FIND OUT WHAT SOMETHING COSTS** to check the price that has been set for a certain product, or compare the different prices charged at a variety of shops or from different companies ○ *priced a few computers before deciding which one to buy* [13C. Via Old French *pris* < Latin *pretium* 'price, money'.] —**pricer** *n* ◇ **at any price** no matter how much it costs (*often with a negative*) ◇ **at a price** for a lot of money ◇ **beyond price** priceless ◇ **what price something?** used to suggest that something such as an ideal or a promise has no value ○ *'What Price Glory?'* (Maxwell Anderson, *What Price Glory?*; 1924)

Price /prīss/, **Leontyne** (*b.* 1927) US soprano

price control *n* government control over prices of goods and services, usually introduced as an emergency measure

price-cutting *n* the reduction of prices below their usual level in order to sell more than competitors

price discrimination *n* the charging of different prices for the same product or service in different markets

price-dividend ratio *n* on a stock exchange, the ratio of a share's price to the dividends paid in the previous year

price-earnings ratio *n* on the stock exchange, the ratio of a share's price to its earnings, providing an indication of its value

price fixing *n* the setting of prices by government or following an agreement between producers, rather than by free market operation

price index *n* a mathematical quantity that is used to measure movements in price levels over different periods of time

price leadership *n* the setting of a price by the market leader at a level that competitors can match in order to avoid price-cutting

priceless /prīssləss/ *adj* **1** worth more than can be calculated in terms of money ○ *the priceless treasures of the pharaohs' tombs* **2** extremely comic and amusing (*informal*) ○ *You should have seen his face when I walked in – it was priceless!* —**pricelessly** *adv* —**pricelessness** *n*

price ring *n* a group of traders who cooperate, usually illegally, to maintain the price of the goods they sell, thus preventing competition

price support *n* government maintenance of price levels by means such as subsidy

price tag *n* **1** a small label attached to an article that is for sale, with the price written or printed on it **2** the amount something costs, whether in money or in something else, e.g. emotional outlay or loss of life or health (*informal*) ○ *The price tag for involvement in the war was more than the country could stand.*

pricey /prīssi/ (**-ier, -iest**), **pricy** (**-ier, -iest**) *adj* charging high prices or costing a great deal (*informal*) ○ *a pricey restaurant* —**priceyness** *n*

Prichard /prích aard/, **Katherine Susannah** (1883–1969) Australian writer

prick /prik/ *v* **1** *vt* **MAKE SMALL HOLE THROUGH SURFACE** to puncture the surface of something, especially the skin, by piercing it lightly with something sharp and finely pointed ○ *pricked her finger on a cactus needle* **2** *vti* **HURT IN A STINGING WAY** to feel a slight, stinging sensation, or to cause something such as the eyes or the skin to hurt in this way ○ *felt his eyes prick with tears* **3** *vt* **SUDDENLY CAUSE DISCOMFORT TO** to make somebody feel a sudden strong unease, e.g. because of guilt or shame ○ *His conscience began to prick him.* **4** *vt* **MARK OUT SHAPE USING TINY HOLES** to make a number of small holes in or through the surface of a board, piece of card, or fabric so as to form the outline of something **5** *vti* **RAISE EARS** to stick up straight or cause an animal's ears to stick up straight ○ *The dog pricked its ears at the sound of its master's voice.* **6** *vt* **PUSH SOMEBODY INTO ACTIVITY** to force or encourage somebody to speed up with some task or project or to get started on some definite course of action ○ *If only we could prick him into action on this.* **7** *vt* **MAKE ANIMAL MOVE FASTER** to urge an animal, especially a horse, to gallop or move more quickly by digging the spurs or heels into its flank (*archaic or literary*) ■ *n* **1 QUICK SHARP PAIN** a sudden twinge of pain caused by a fine point being pushed into the skin **2 SMALL PUNCTURE** a small puncture, hole, or indented mark, or an act of piercing that causes such a puncture **3 TABOO TERM** a highly offensive term for a penis (*taboo*) **4 TABOO TERM** a highly offensive term for a man regarded as pathetically inadequate or unpleasant (*taboo insult*) **5 PAINFUL THOUGHT** a sudden, unpleasant thought or feeling, often one related to some past action or event **6 POINTED IMPLEMENT** a pointed implement or weapon such as a goad (*archaic*) **7 HARE'S FOOTPRINT** the footprint of a hare [Old English *prica* < Germanic] ◇ **kick against the pricks** to show opposition to authority, rules, or circumstances that you have no power to influence

prick out *vt* to make a series of small holes in an area of earth and put young seedlings into these holes to grow

pricker /príkər/ *n* a tool used to prick or pierce small holes in something

pricket /príkit/ *n* **1** a male deer in its second year, typically one with unbranched antlers **2** a metal spike for sticking a candle on

prickle /prík'l/ *n* **1 PROJECTION ON PLANT** a sharp pointed projection on the outer surface of a leaf or plant **2 TINGLING FEELING** a tingling or stinging sensation ■ *vti* (**-les, -ling, -led**) **HURT IN A STINGING WAY** to feel a sharp, stinging pain, or cause something such as the eyes or the skin to hurt in this way [Old English *pricel* 'small prick' < Germanic, 'prick']

prickly /príkli/ (**-lier, -liest**) *adj* **1 WITH SMALL SHARP SPIKES** having a surface or skin with prickles on it **2 UNCOMFORTABLE** irritating to the skin, especially because of fibres or prickles that are rough to the touch **3 OVERSENSITIVE** easily angered, offended, or upset (*informal*) ○ *He's very prickly on that subject.* **4 TRICKY TO HANDLE OR SOLVE** especially difficult and likely to upset people (*informal*) ○ *They tried to keep off prickly subjects like politics and religion.* —**prickliness** *n*

prickly ash *n* **1** an aromatic bush or small tree with prickly branches and clusters of small greenish flowers. Native to: E North America. *Zanthoxylum americanum.* **2** a spiny bush or tree with pinnately compound leaves. Native to: S United States. *Zanthoxylum clavaherculis.*

prickly heat *n* a rash of tiny raised spots, accompanied by redness and itching, appearing in hot or humid conditions. Technical name **miliaria**

prickly pear *n* a cactus with flattened, jointed, spiny stems and pear-shaped fruits that are edible in some species. Flowers: large, yellow or orange. Native to: tropical America. Genus: *Opuntia.*

prickly poppy *n* a poppy plant with bristly stems and leaves. Flowers: yellow, lavender, or white. Use: formerly, in herbal medicine. Genus: *Argemone.*

prick-teaser, prick-tease *n* a highly offensive term for somebody who makes sexual advances towards a man without intending to have sex with him (*taboo*)

pricy *adj* = **pricey** (*informal*)

pride /prīd/ *n* **1 FEELING OF SUPERIORITY** a haughty attitude shown by people who consider, often unjustifiably, that they are better than others ○ *Her pride prevented her from mixing with those she considered her social inferiors.* **2 PROPER SENSE OF OWN VALUE** the correct level of respect for the importance and value of your personal character, life, efforts, or achievements ○ *He had lost all his confidence and pride.* **3 SATISFACTION WITH SELF** the happy satisfied feeling somebody experiences when having or achieving something special that other people admire ○ *She felt a sense of pride when she looked at her finished work.* **4 SOURCE OF PERSONAL SATISFACTION** something that somebody feels especially pleased and satisfied to own or to have achieved ○ *His grandchildren were his pride and joy.* **5 BEST TIME** the best condition or period of something (*literary*) **6 GROUP OF LIONS** a group of lions, typically consisting of up to a dozen related adult females, their cubs and juveniles, plus from one to six adult males ■ *vr* (**prides, priding, prided**) **BE PROUD** to obtain personal satisfaction and pleasure from a particular source, especially something accomplished or a quality possessed ○ *He prides himself on his meticulous timekeeping.* [Pre-12C. < PROUD.] —**prideful** *adj* —**pridefully** *adv* ◇ **take pride in something** to have a sense of personal satisfaction because of a particular achievement or effort that you or somebody connected with you has made ◇ **pride of place** the most important or prominent position

LITERARY LINK ***Pride and Prejudice***, a novel (1813) by Jane Austen. Through the story of the relationship between Elizabeth Bennet, the fiercely independent daughter of minor gentry, and Mr Darcy, a wealthy and haughty nobleman, Austen reveals how both pride and prejudices create barriers to mutual understanding.

prie-dieu /prée dyṓ/ (*plural* **prie-dieux** /-dyṓ/) *n* a shelved wooden desk for use when praying, usually with a low surface for kneeling on and a higher surface for resting the elbows or a book on [Mid-18C. < French, 'pray God'.]

prier /prī́ ər/, **pryer** *n* a person who pries

priest /preest/ *n* **1 ORDAINED PERSON** an ordained minister, especially in the Roman Catholic, Anglican, and Eastern Orthodox churches, responsible for administering the sacraments, preaching, and ministering to the needs of the congregation **2 MINISTER OF NON-CHRISTIAN RELIGION** a spiritual leader or teacher of a non-Christian religion **3 DESCENDANT OF FAMILY OF AARON** somebody descended from the family of Aaron of the tribe of Levi, appointed as priests in the Hebrew Scriptures ■ *vt* **ORDAIN** to perform the necessary ceremonies to make somebody into a priest (*archaic*) [Old English *prēost*, via Germanic < ecclesiastical Latin *presbyter* (see PRESBYTER)]

priestess /pree stéss, préest ess, préestiss/ *n* a woman who is a spiritual leader in a pagan religion

priest-hole, priest's hole *n* a small hidden room or space in an English house, created as a hiding-place for Roman Catholic priests and others trying to escape persecution after the English Reformation

priesthood /préest hòod/ *n* **1** the official role, position, or office of a priest **2** all Roman Catholic priests considered together, or all the priests of another religion

Priestley /préestli/, **Joseph** (1733–1804) British chemist and religous radical

priestly /préestli/ *adj* used, worn, or performed exclusively by priests, or in some way typical of or suitable for a priest (*literary*) ○ *priestly garments* —**priestliness** *n*

priest-ridden *adj* influenced or controlled by priests or religious dogma to what the speaker or writer regards as an unacceptable degree (*literary*)

prig /prig/ *n* somebody who is thought to take pride in behaving in a very correct and proper way, and in feeling morally superior to others (*disapproving*) [Late 17C. < ?] —**priggery** *n* —**priggish** *adj* —**priggishly** *adv* —**priggishness** *n*

prill /pril/ *vt* to make a solid into granules or pellets that flow freely and do not clump together ■ *n* a granule or pellet made by prilling [Late 18C. < ?]

prim /prim/ *adj* (**primmer, primmest**) **1 PRUDISH** easily shocked by vulgar or obscene language or behaviour **2 FORMAL AND PROPER** excessively formal and proper in manner or appearance ■ *v* (**prims, primming, primmed**) **1** *vti* **ASSUME PROPER EXPRESSION** to take on an affectedly proper expression **2** *vt* **MAKE SOMEBODY LOOK VERY PROPER** to make somebody look excessively proper [Early 18C. < ?] —**primly** *adv* —**primness** *n*

prima ballerina /préemə-/ *n* the principal woman dancer in a ballet company [< Italian, 'first ballerina']

primacy /prīməssi/ (*plural* **-cies**) *n* **1** the state of being the first or most important part or aspect of something ○ *Speech is regarded as having primacy over writing.* **2** the position or office of a primate in a Christian church

prima donna /preemə dònnə/ (*plural* **prima donnas**) *n* **1** the principal woman soloist in an opera production **2** a person who is regarded as demanding and difficult to please (*insult*) [< Italian, 'first lady']

primaeval *adj* = **primeval**

prima facie /prīmə fáyshi/ *adv* **AT FIRST GLANCE** on initial examination or consideration ○ *Prima facie, this lawsuit seems spurious.* ■ *adj* **1 APPARENT** clear from a first impression ○ *a prima facie counterexample to your hypothesis* **2 LEGALLY SUFFICIENT** sufficient in law to establish a case or fact, unless disproved [< Latin, 'at first appearance']

primage /prīmij/ *n NZ* a tax payable in addition to customs duty [15C. < Anglo-Latin *primagium* < ?]

primal /prīm'l/ *adj* **1** first or earliest, and often basic ○ *the primal instinct for survival* **2** most significant and primary ○ *our primal need for a new fuel source* [Mid-16C. < medieval Latin *primalis* < Latin *primus* 'first'.] —**primality** /prī mállәti/ *n*

primal scream *n* a cry of extreme anger that a client undergoing primal therapy is encouraged to use

primal therapy *n* a style of psychotherapy in which clients relive past traumas and unleash repressed anger and frustration through screams, tantrums, or beating inanimate objects

primaquine /prīmə kween/, **primaquine phosphate** *n* $C_{15}H_{21}N_3O$ a synthetic drug derived from quinoline. Use: treatment of malaria. [Mid-20C. < ?]

primarily /prīmərəli, prī márrəli/ *adv* **1** mainly or mostly ○ *Baldness is primarily found among adult men.* **2** originally or at first

primary /prīməri/ *adj* **1 FIRST IN SEQUENCE** first or earliest in a sequence ○ *the primary stage of development* **2 MOST IMPORTANT** ranked as most important **3 BASIC** essential or basic to something **4 ORIGINAL** being the first form of something **5 RELATING TO EARLY EDUCATION** relating to the early years of formal education, usually for children between the ages of 5 and 12 **6 RELATING TO NATURAL RESOURCE INDUSTRY** relating to or produced by an industry such as forestry, mining, or agriculture, that collects and processes a natural resource **7 PRODUCING ELECTRICITY** describes a cell that uses an irreversible chemical reaction to generate electricity and, as a result, cannot be recharged **8 OF CURRENT-INDUCING COMPONENT** describes a circuit component such as a coil that induces a current in a neighbouring circuit **9 SUBSTITUTING ATOMS** relating to or resulting from the replacement of one or more atoms in a molecule **10 OF ATTACHED CARBON ATOM** describes a carbon atom in a molecule that is bonded to one other carbon atom only **11 OF AMINO ACID SEQUENCE** the basic type, number, or sequence of amino acids in a polypeptide **12 OF MAIN WING FEATHERS** describes any of the main flight feathers on the outer edge of a bird's wing **13 GROWN FROM EMBRYONIC TISSUE** describes growth from embryonic tissue in the tip of a root or shoot ■ *n* (*plural* **-ies**) **1 FIRST THING** something that is first in time or order **2 MOST IMPORTANT THING** a part or aspect of something that is the most important **3 BASIC PART OR ASPECT** something that is essential or basic to something **4 ORIGINAL FORM** the earliest form of something **5 ELECTION OF CANDIDATES FOR GOVERNMENTAL POSITION** in the United States, an election in which members of a party choose candidates for a governmental position **6 ELECTION OF DELEGATES TO CHOOSE CANDIDATES** in the United States, an election to choose delegates who will choose the party's candidates at a political convention **7 PRIMARY SCHOOL** a primary school (*in school names*) **8** COLOURS = **primary colour 9** ELEC = **primary coil 10 BRIGHTER STAR OF DOUBLE STAR** the brighter or larger of two stars in a double star **11** ASTRON = **primary planet 12** BIRDS = **primary feather** [15C. < Latin *primarius* < *primus* 'first'.]

primary care *n* the level of health care at which a patient is assessed and treated by a general practitioner or nurse, or, if necessary, is referred to a specialist

primary cell *n* an electrical cell that uses an irreversible chemical reaction to generate electricity and, as a result, cannot be recharged

primary coil *n* a coil forming part of a machine or circuit in which the current flow sets up the magnetic flux necessary for the operation of the machine or circuit

primary colour *n* **1** any one of the three basic colours of the spectrum, red, green, or blue, from which all other colours can be blended **2** any one of the three basic colours cyan, magenta, or yellow, which when subtracted from white can produce all other colours

primary consumer *n* an animal that eats plants, in terms of its position in a food chain

primary feather *n* any one of the main flight feathers on the outer edge of a bird's wing

primary planet *n* a planet in direct orbit around a sun

primary process *n* in Freudian terminology, a basic process that is involved in the functioning of the id and is ruled by the pleasure principle

primary production *n* the total chemical energy produced by photosynthesis

primary qualities *npl* properties, e.g. spatial location, that are independent of the mind and are inseparable from the objects studied by sciences such as physics

primary school *n* **1** in the United Kingdom, a school in which children usually aged between 5 and 11 or 12 are taught **2** in the United States, a school in which the first three, or sometimes four, grades are taught, often including kindergarten as well

⚡**primary storage** *n* the main memory in a computer, including the random-access memory, and the read-only memory, directly accessible by the processor

primary stress *n* the strongest force used in pronouncing one of the syllables of a multisyllabic word or the mark, usually ', used to indicate this. US term **primary accent**

primary syphilis *n* the first of the three stages of syphilis, in which a painless growth (**chancre**) grows at the site of infection and the infecting bacterium (**spirochaete**) spreads throughout the body

primary wave *n* a seismic wave that creates vibrations parallel to its direction

primate /prī mayt/ *n* **1** a member of an order of mammals with a large brain and complex hands and feet, including humans, apes, and monkeys. Order: Primates. **2 primate, Primate** an archbishop or high-ranking bishop [12C. < Latin *primat-*, stem of *primas* 'of the first rank' < *primus* 'first'.] —**primatial** /prī máysh'l/ *adj*

~~**primative**~~ incorrect spelling of **primitive**

primatology /prīmə tóllәji/ *n* the scientific study of primates, especially nonhuman primates —**primatological** /prīmәtә lójjik'l/ *adj* —**primatologist** /prīmə tóllәjist/ *n*

primavera[1] /preemə váirə/ (*plural* **-ras** *or* **-ra**) *n* **1** the light coloured wood of a Central American tree. Use: furniture-making. **2** a tree that has yellow flowers and palmate leaves and yields primavera. Native to: Central America. *Cybistax donnellsmithii.* [Late 19C. Via Spanish, 'springtime' (because the tree flowers in spring) < late Latin *prima vera* (see PRIMAVERA[2]).]

primavera[2] /preemə váirə/ *adj* made with an assortment of fresh spring vegetables, especially sliced as an accompaniment to pasta, meat, or seafood [Late 20C. < Italian *(alla) primavera* '(in the) spring (style)' < late Latin *prima vera* 'early spring' < Latin *primum ver* 'first spring'.]

prime[1] /prīm/ *adj* **1 BEST** of the highest quality ○ *prime grade beef* **2 FIRST IN IMPORTANCE** of the greatest importance or the highest rank **3 EARLIEST** earliest in time or sequence **4 NOT DIVISIBLE WITHOUT REMAINDER** describes a number that can be divided without a remainder only by one and itself **5 BEING WITHOUT COMMON FACTORS** describes a number that has no common factors with another number ○ *15 is prime to 8.* ■ *n* **1 BEST STAGE** the best state or stage of something, especially the most active and enjoyable period in adult life ○ *In his prime, he was one of the country's best tennis players.* **2 EARLIEST PERIOD** the earliest part of something, e.g. the early hours of daylight or the first season of the year **3 DISTINGUISHING MARK** a mark (') added to a number, character, or expression in order to distinguish it from another, or as the symbol for measurement in feet **4 FIRST PARRYING POSITION** the first of the eight parrying positions in fencing **5 FIRST NOTE IN MUSICAL SCALE** the first note of a musical scale **6 SECOND CANONICAL HOUR** the second of the seven canonical hours assigned to morning prayer at the first hour of the day **7** MATH = **prime number 8** FIN = **prime rate** [Pre-12C. Via Old French < Latin *primus* 'first'.] —**primely** *adv* —**primeness** *n*

LITERARY LINK ***The Prime of Miss Jean Brodie***, a novel (1961) by Muriel Spark. It is set in an Edinburgh girls' school and describes the powerful and lasting influence of an unconventional schoolteacher, Miss Jean Brodie, on a group of promising but impressionable pupils.

prime[2] /prīm/ *v* **1** *vti* **MAKE OR BECOME READY** to make something ready for use or become ready for use **2** *vt* **PREPARE SURFACE FOR PAINTING** to prepare a surface for painting or a similar process by treating it with a sealant or an undercoat of paint **3** *vt* **PUT CHARGE IN GUN** to make a firearm ready for use by putting a charge in it **4** *vt* **PROVIDE EXPLOSIVE WITH FUSE** to make an explosive ready for use by inserting a fuse **5** *vt* **PREPARE PUMP** to put liquid in a pump in order to get it started **6** *vt* **PUT FUEL INTO CARBURETTOR** to put fuel into a carburettor in order to start an internal-combustion engine **7** *vt* **BRIEF** to give somebody, especially a witness in a court case, information or instructions on how to behave or answer questions **8** *vt* **PLY WITH DRINK** to provide somebody with large quantities of alcohol in order to prepare him or her for doing something [Early 16C. < ?]

prime cost *n* the cost of the material and labour necessary to make a product

prime meridian *n* the 0° longitude meridian passing through Greenwich, England, from which other longitudes are calculated

prime minister *n* **1** in a parliamentary system, the head of the cabinet and, usually, chief executive **2** the chief minister appointed by the ruler of a country —**prime ministerial** *adj* —**prime ministership** *n*

prime mover *n* **1 MOST IMPORTANT CAUSE** somebody or something that initiates a process or activity and is usually the most important factor in its continuation **2 GOD** God, considered to be the first cause or origin of everything **3 SOURCE OF ALL MOTION** in Aristotelian philosophy, the initial source of all movement **4 NATURAL OR PHYSICAL ENERGY SOURCE** a natural or physical source of energy such as wind or electricity that can be harnessed to power a machine **5 ENERGY CONVERTER** a machine that converts energy from a natural or physical source in order to power equipment such as a windmill or turbine

prime number *n* a whole number that can only be divided without a remainder by itself and one

primer[1] /prīmər/ *n* **1** a book used to teach young children to read, typically containing simple stories **2** a book that provides an introduction to a topic [14C. Via Anglo-Norman < Latin *primarius* (see PRIMARY).]

primer[2] /prīmər/ *n* **1 PRIMING AGENT** a person or device that primes something **2 UNDERCOAT** a paint or sealant used to prepare a surface for painting or a similar process, or a coat of this material **3 EXPLOSIVE IGNITER** a small container or wafer of explosive material such as gunpowder, used to ignite the main explosive charge of a firearm or explosive **4 GENETIC MATERIAL** a short sequence of RNA that is made before DNA formation can proceed [15C. < PRIME[2].]

prime time *n* the hours when television audiences are usually largest, typically from 7:00 pm to 11:00 pm —**primetime** *adj*

primeval /prī meév'l/, **primaeval** *adj* at or from the ancient, original stages in the development of something [Mid-17C. < Latin *primaevus* < *primus* 'first' + *aevum* 'age'.] —**primevally** *adv*

prime vertical *n* the imaginary circle around the Earth that goes through the highest point of the celestial sphere directly above an observer and meets the horizon at east and west

primigravida /prīmi grávvidə/ (*plural* **-das** *or* **-dae** /-dee/) *n* a woman experiencing her first pregnancy [Late 19C. < modern Latin, < *gravida* 'pregnant', after PRIMIPARA.]

priming /prīming/ *n* a small container or wafer of explosive material such as gunpowder, used to ignite the main explosive charge of a firearm or explosive

primipara /prī míppərə/ (*plural* **-ras** *or* **-rae** /prī míppəree/) *n* a woman who has given birth only once, whether it was a single or a multiple birth, and whether the baby was alive or stillborn [Mid-19C. < modern Latin < Latin *primus* 'first' + *-para* 'bearing', feminine form of *-parus* (see -PAROUS).] —**primiparity** /prīmi párrəti/ *n* —**primiparous** *adj*

⚡**primitive** /prímmətiv/ *adj* **1 FIRST** at or relating to the first stages or form of something **2 DEVELOPMENTALLY EARLY** relating to or appearing in an earlier stage of biological development, particularly of an embryo or species **3 VERY SIMPLE IN DESIGN** crudely simple in design or construction ○ *built a primitive shelter from palm leaves*

PRIME MINISTERS OF AUSTRALIA, CANADA, NEW ZEALAND, AND THE UNITED KINGDOM AFTER 1900

Prime Ministers of Australia

Term of Office	Prime Minister
1901–1903	Edmund Barton
1903–1904	Alfred Deakin
1904	John Christian Watson
1904–1905	George Houston Reid
1905–1908	Alfred Deakin
1908–1909	Andrew Fisher
1909–1910	Alfred Deakin
1910–1913	Andrew Fisher
1913–1914	Joseph Cook
1914–1915	Andrew Fisher
1915–1923	William Morris Hughes
1923–1929	Stanley Melbourne Bruce
1929–1932	James Henry Scullin
1932–1939	Joseph Aloysius Lyons
1939	Earle Page
1939–1941	Robert Menzies
1941	Arthur William Fadden
1941–1945	John Curtin
1945	Francis Michael Forde
1945–1949	Joseph Benedict Chifley
1949–1966	Robert Menzies
1966–1967	Harold Holt
1967–1968	John McEwen
1968–1971	John Gorton
1971–1972	William McMahon

Australia . . .

Term of Office	Prime Minister
1972–1975	Gough Whitlam
1975–1983	Malcolm Fraser
1983–1991	Bob Hawke
1991–1996	Paul Keating
1996–	John Howard

Prime Ministers of Canada

Term of Office	Prime Minister
1896–1911	Wilfred Laurier
1911–1920	Robert Laird Borden
1920–1921	Arthur Meighen
1921–1926	W.L. Mackenzie King
1926	Arthur Meighen
1926–1930	W.L. Mackenzie King
1930–1935	Richard Bedford Bennett
1935–1948	W.L. Mackenzie King
1948–1957	Louis St. Laurent
1957–1963	John G. Diefenbaker
1963–1968	Lester B. Pearson
1968–1979	Pierre Trudeau
1979–1980	Joseph Clark
1980–1984	Pierre Trudeau
1984	John M. Turner
1984–1993	Brian Mulroney
1993	Kim Campbell
1993–	Jean Chrétien

Prime Ministers of New Zealand

Term of Office	Prime Minister
1893–1906	Richard John Seddon
1906	William Hall-Jones
1906–1912	Joseph George Ward
1912	Thomas Mackenzie
1912–1925	William Ferguson Masey
1925	Francis Henry Dillon Bell
1925–1928	Joseph Gordon Coates
1928–1930	Joseph George Ward
1930–1935	George William Forbes
1935–1940	Michael Joseph Savage
1940–1949	Peter Fraser
1949–1957	Sydney George Holland
1957	Keith Jacka Holyoake
1957–1960	Walter Nash
1960–1972	Keith Jacka Holyoake
1972	John Ross Marshall
1972–1974	Norman Eric Kirk
1974–1975	Wallace Edward Rowling
1975–1984	Robert David Muldoon
1984–1989	David Russell Lange
1989–1990	Geoffrey Palmer
1990	Michael Moore
1990–1997	James Bolger
1997–1999	Jenny Shipley
1999–	Helen Clark

Prime Ministers of the United Kingdom

Term of Office	Prime Minister
1902–1905	Arthur James Balfour
1905–1908	Henry Campbell-Bannerman
1908–1916	Herbert Henry Asquith
1916–1922	David Lloyd George
1922–1923	Andrew Bonar Law
1923–1924	Stanley Baldwin
1924	Ramsay MacDonald
1924–1929	Stanley Baldwin
1929–1935	Ramsay MacDonald
1935–1937	Stanley Baldwin
1937–1940	Neville Chamberlain
1940–1945	Winston Churchill
1945–1951	Clement Attlee
1951–1955	Winston Churchill
1955–1957	Anthony Eden
1957–1963	Harold Macmillan
1963–1964	Alec Douglas-Home
1964–1970	Harold Wilson
1970–1974	Edward Heath
1974–1976	Harold Wilson
1976–1979	James Callaghan
1979–1990	Margaret Thatcher
1990–1997	John Major
1997–	Tony Blair

4 ORIGINAL not derived from other things **5 WITH SIMPLE TECHNOLOGICAL DEVELOPMENT** not using or relying on complex modern technologies to provide comfort and efficiency ○ *Facilities on the island were fairly primitive.* **6 BEING BASIS** acting as a basis from which something else is derived **7 NATURAL** arising from an inherent characteristic **8 ARTISTICALLY UNTRAINED** created by an artist with no formal training, especially using a simple style **9 EARLY MEDIEVAL** created by an early medieval European artist or a folk artist **10 FROM WHICH OTHER FORM DERIVES** having a word form from which another word is derived ○ *The primitive root in 'children' is 'child'.* **11 EARLIER IN LINGUISTIC DEVELOPMENT** being or belonging to an earlier form of a language ■ *n* **1 SOMEBODY OR SOMETHING FROM ORIGINAL STAGE** a person or thing from the first stage or form of something **2 SOMEBODY FROM CULTURE WITH SIMPLE TECHNOLOGIES** a member of a people who do not use or rely on complex modern technologies (*often considered offensive*) **3 UNTRAINED ARTIST** an artist without formal training, especially one using a simple style **4 EARLY MEDIEVAL ARTIST** an artist or folk artist, especially a painter, whose work was typical of the style of early medieval Europe **5 EARLY MEDIEVAL WORK OF ART** a painting or other work by an early medieval artist or a folk artist **6 DERIVATION** something such as a concept, feature, or formula from which something else is derived **7 BASIC GEOMETRIC FORM OR FUNCTION** a geometric form or function from which another is derived **8 BASIC ELEMENT OF COMPUTER PROGRAM** a simple element of a computer program or graphic design from which larger programs or images can be constructed **9 WORD ROOT** a word root (*dated technical*) [14C. Directly or via French < Latin *primitus* 'in the first place' < *primus* < *primitivus* 'first'.] —**primitively** *adv* —**primitiveness** *n*

primitivism /prímmətivizəm/ *n* **1 STATE OF BEING PRIMITIVE** the state of being primitive, or the qualities associated with being primitive **2 SIMPLICITY OF STYLE** simplicity or naivety of artistic style **3 OPPOSITION TO MODERN LIFE** the belief that less technologically dependent cultures and ways of living are inherently better than more technologically dependent ones —**primitivist** *n, adj* —**primitivistic** /prímməti vístik/ *adj*

primo /preé̀mō/ *n* (*plural* **-mos** *or* **-mi** /-mi/) the lead musical part in a duet, trio, or ensemble composition ■ *adj* first in a sequence or series (*formal*) [Mid-18C. Via Italian and Spanish, 'first, prime' < Latin *primus*.]

primogenitor /prímō jénnitər, preé̀mō-/ *n* (*formal*) **1** the first ancestor of a people or other group **2** any ancestor [Mid-17C. Alteration of PROGENITOR, after *primogeniture*.]

primogeniture /prímō jénnichər, preémō-/ *n* (*formal*) **1** the state of being the first-born child of a set of parents **2** the right of the first-born child, usually the eldest son, to inherit the parents' entire estate [Early 17C. < medieval Latin *primogenitura* < Latin *primus* 'first' + *genitura* 'birth'.] —**primogenital** *adj* —**primogenitary** /-jénnitəri/ *adj*

primordial /prī máwrdi əl/ *adj* **1** EXISTING FIRST existing at the beginning of time or the development of something **2** BASIC essential or basic to something **3** OF EARLIEST STAGE OF DEVELOPMENT relating to cells, tissues, organs, or individuals at the earliest stage of development [14C. < late Latin *primordialis* < Latin *primordium* 'origin' < *primus* 'first' + *ordiri* 'begin'.] —**primordiality** /prī máwrdi álləti/ *n* —**primordially** *adv*

primordium /prī máwrdi əm/ (*plural* **-a** /-di ə/) *n* a tissue or organ in the earliest stage of embryonic development, found when the dividing cells in the fertilized ovum first differentiate [Late 16C. < Latin (see PRIMORDIAL).]

primp /primp/ *vti* to groom yourself, somebody, or something in a fussy way ○ *spending all day primping in front of the mirror* [Late 16C. < ?]

primrose /prím rōz/ *n* **1** PLANTS a flowering plant from the family that includes the cowslip, cyclamen, and pimpernel. Native to: northern temperate regions. Family: Primulaceae. = **primula 2** a small perennial plant with pale yellow flowers that appear in early spring in northern temperate regions. Native to: Europe. *Primula vulgaris*. [14C. Via Old French *primerose* < medieval Latin *prima rosa* 'first rose', from its early flowering.]

primrose path *n* an easy or pleasurable way of life, especially one that leads to disaster (*literary*) [< 'the primrose path of dalliance' in Shakespeare's *Hamlet*]

primula /prímmyōōlə/ (*plural* **-las** *or* **-la**) *n* a small perennial plant with colourful flowers. Genus: *Primula*. US = **primrose** *n*. 1 [Mid-18C. Via modern Latin < medieval Latin *primula (veris)* 'first fruit (of spring)' < Latin *primulus* < *primus* 'first'.] —**primulaceous** /prímmyōō láyshəss/ *adj*

primum mobile /prīməm mṓbili/ *n* **1** in Ptolemaic astronomy, the outermost sphere of the universe, thought to revolve every 24 hours, moving the inner spheres with it **2** PHILOS = **prime mover** *n*. 3 [15C. < medieval Latin, 'first moving thing'.]

primus /prīməss/, **Primus** *n Scotland* the highest ranking bishop in the Scottish Episcopal Church [Late 16C. < Latin, 'first' (see PRIME).]

primus inter pares /prīməss intər paá reez, preé-/ *n* the representative or leader of a group of equals [< Latin, 'first among equals']

Primus stove /prīməss-/ *tdmk* a trademark for a portable paraffin cooking stove

prince /prinss/ *n* **1** SON OF MONARCH a man or boy in a royal family, especially a son of a reigning king or queen **2** MAN RULER a man who rules a principality **3** EUROPEAN NOBLEMAN a nobleman in some European countries, usually of a rank below duke **4** HIGHLY REGARDED MAN a man or boy who is ranked highly in his field ○ *Robin Hood was the prince of thieves.* **5** *US* GENEROUS, KIND MAN a man who is outstanding, especially because of his generous or chivalrous nature (*informal*) [12C. Via French < Latin *princeps* 'somebody who takes first place'.] —**princedom** *n*

Prince Albert *n* in body piercing, a ring put through the tip of the penis [Late 19C. After Prince ALBERT.]

Prince Charles Island island in E Nunavut, Canada, in Foxe Basin. Area: 9,521 sq. km/3,676 sq. mi.

prince charming, Prince Charming *n* **1** a man who fulfils the romantic ideal of the perfect lover (*informal*) **2** a man who actively seeks to charm people, especially women, and gain their liking [Mid-19C. After the hero of the fairy tale *Cinderella*.]

prince consort *n* a prince who is married to a reigning queen

Prince Edward Island island province in SE Canada in the S Gulf of St Lawrence. Capital: Charlottetown. Population: 134,557 (1996). Area: 5,660 sq. km/2,185 sq. mi. —**Prince Edward Islander** *n*

Prince Edward Island National Park national park in SE Canada. Area: 22 sq. km/8.5 sq. mi.

princeling /prínssling/, **princelet** /prínsslət/ *n* a prince of low rank, age, or importance

princely /prínssli/ (**-lier, -liest**) *adj* **1** relating to, belonging to, or suitable for a prince **2** generous as an amount of money, or requiring the expenditure of large sums of money ○ *a princely manor in the country* —**princeliness** *n*

Prince of Wales Island 1 island in SE Alaska, in the Alexander Archipelago. Population: 6,278 (1990). Area: 5,778 sq. km/2,231 sq. mi. **2** uninhabited island in central Nunavut, Canada, between Victoria and Somerset islands. Area: 33,339 sq. km/12,872 sq. mi. **3** island in N Queensland, Australia, one of the Torres Strait Islands. Population: 90 (1971). Area: 180 sq. km/69 sq. mi.

prince regent (*plural* **prince regents** *or* **princes regent**) *n* a prince who rules in the monarch's place, e.g. when the monarch is abroad, ill, or still a child

prince royal (*plural* **princes royal**) *n* the eldest son of a reigning monarch

prince's-feather (*plural* **prince's-feathers** *or* **prince's-feather**) *n* a tall annual plant with reddish leaves. Flowers: red, in spikes. Family: Amaranthus.

princess /prin séss, prínsess/ (*plural* **-cesses**) *n* **1** DAUGHTER OF MONARCH a woman or girl in a royal family, especially a daughter of the reigning king or queen **2** PRINCE'S WIFE the wife or widow of a prince **3** DAUGHTER OF MONARCH'S SON a daughter of a son of the sovereign **4** WOMAN RULER a woman who rules a principality **5** EUROPEAN NOBLEWOMAN a noblewoman in some European countries, usually of a rank below duchess **6** HIGHLY REGARDED WOMAN a woman who is ranked highly in her field, or who has other outstanding qualities (*dated*) **7** SPOILED YOUNG WOMAN a rich young woman considered to be spoiled or arrogant (*disapproving*)

princess royal (*plural* **princesses royal**) *n* the eldest daughter of a reigning monarch, especially of a British monarch, who confers the title on her as a special honour

Princeton /prínstən/ town in west-central New Jersey. Population: 11,814 (1998 estimate).

principal /prínssip'l/ *adj* **1** PRIMARY first or among the first in importance or rank **2** INITIALLY INVESTED relating to the initial amount of money that was invested or borrowed ■ *n* **1** MOST IMPORTANT PERSON the leading or most highly ranked person **2** SIGNIFICANT PARTICIPANT any one of the most significant participants in an event or a situation ○ *the principals to the property transaction* **3** HEAD OF SCHOOL the head administrator of a school, college, or university **4 principal, principal teacher** HEAD OF SCHOOL DEPARTMENT the head of a department in a Scottish school ○ *She was promoted to principal of English.* **5** SENIOR CIVIL SERVANT a civil servant of a rank below a Secretary **6** LEAD PERFORMER a lead actor, singer, or dancer in a theatrical or musical performance **7** LEAD MUSICIAN the lead musician in a section of an orchestra, or the part played by that musician **8** ORIGINAL AMOUNT INVESTED the initial sum of money invested or borrowed, before interest or other revenue is added, or the remainder of that sum after payments have been made **9** REPRESENTED PERSON somebody for whom a representative or proxy acts in a legal matter **10** RESPONSIBLE PARTY a person who is directly responsible for something **11** CRIMINAL the perpetrator of a crime **12** MAIN SUPPORT BEAM the main support beam, girder, or truss in a roof, bridge, or other construction [13C. Via French < Latin *principalis* < *princip-* 'somebody who takes first place'.] —**principally** *adv* —**principalship** *n*

USAGE principal or **principle**? These two words, though pronounced alike, have different meanings and functions. ***Principle*** is a noun only, meaning 'a basic assumption', 'an ethical standard', and 'a way of operating or working', as in *the principles of a democratic system; a woman of principle;* and *studied the principles of the internal-combustion engine.* By contrast, ***principal***, as a noun, means 'a head teacher', 'an important participant', 'a lead performer', and 'a monetary amount invested', as in *was sent to the principal's office; a principal in an accounting firm;* and *a principal of £500,000.* As an adjective it means 'primary': *our principal* [not *principle*] *reason for an appeal.*

principal axis *n* the line that passes through the centre of curvature of a lens

principal boy *n* a woman who plays the leading man's part in a pantomime

principal diagonal *n* in a square matrix, the diagonal line that extends from the upper left corner to the lower right corner

principality /prínssə pálləti/ *n* (*plural* **-ties**) **1** PRINCE'S OR PRINCESS'S COUNTRY a territory ruled by a prince or princess **2** POSITION OF PRINCE the position or jurisdiction of a prince ■ **principalities** *npl* ORDER OF ANGELS one of the nine orders of angels in the traditional Christian hierarchy

principal parts *npl* **1** the basic forms of a verb, from which other forms are derived, in an inflected language such as Latin **2** the infinitive, past tense, and participial forms of an English verb

Príncipe /prínssi pay/ island in São Tomé and Príncipe, in the Gulf of Guinea. Population: 5,900 (1995). Area: 109 sq. km/42 sq. mi.

principle /prínssip'l/ *n* **1** BASIC ASSUMPTION an important underlying law or assumption required in a system of thought **2** ETHICAL STANDARD a standard of moral or ethical decision-making ○ *I buy recyclable products as a matter of principle.* **3** WAY OF WORKING the basic way in which something works **4** SOURCE the primary source of something **5** CHARACTERISTIC INGREDIENT an ingredient of a substance that gives the substance a particular quality [14C. Anglo-Norman, alteration of French *principe* < Latin *principium* < *princip-* 'somebody who takes first place'.] —**principled** *adj* ◇ **in principle** in theory, or in the essentials ◇ **on principle** because of a particular ethical standard that somebody believes in

USAGE See ***principal***.

Principle /prínssip'l/ *n* a term used in Christian Science for God

prink /pringk/ *vti* to dress or groom somebody or yourself in a fancy or fussy way [Late 16C. < ?] —**prinker** *n*

print /print/ *n* **1** PRESSED MARK a mark made by pressing something onto a surface **2** WRITING ON A SURFACE words, figures, or symbols on a surface, especially when produced by a machine ○ *books available in large print* **3** PUBLISHED TEXT the state of being in a printed form or being published ○ *We don't want these typographical errors to make it into print.* **4** ARTWORK MADE BY PRESSING DESIGN a work of art made by inking a surface with a raised design and pressing it onto paper or another surface **5** FABRIC WITH INKED DESIGN a fabric with an ink or paint design on its surface, or the design itself (*often before nouns*) ○ *She was wearing a new print dress.* **6** PHOTOGRAPH a photograph, usually on paper, made from a negative **7** FILM COPY a copy of a film **8** STAMP OR DIE a stamp or die used to make marks on a surface **9** FINGERPRINT a fingerprint (*informal*) ■ *v* **1** *vti* MAKE SOMETHING WITH PRINTING MACHINE to make a copy, document, or publication using a printing press or a computer printer ○ *These books were printed in Canada.* **2** *vti* PUBLISH to publish information or a publication ○ *The company prints several news magazines in addition to books.* **3** *vti* MARK SOMETHING USING PRESSURE to produce a mark, design, or lettering on a surface by pressing something on it ○ *A machine prints the corporate logo onto pencils.* **4** *vti* PRESS DESIGNS ONTO to press a mark, design, or lettering onto something ○ *We printed enough T-shirts for the whole team.* **5** *vti* WRITE SEPARATED LETTERS to write something by hand, using separated letters rather than script ○ *Print your name under your signature.* **6** *vti* MAKE A COPY FROM A NEGATIVE to make a positive image or copy of a photograph or film from a negative **7** *vi* WORK AS PRINTER to do the work of a printer ■ *adj* RELATING TO PUBLISHED MEDIA produced by or relating to the published media [13C. < Old French *preinte*, feminine past participle of *preindre* 'to press' < Latin *premere*.] ◇ **in print 1** currently available from a publisher **2** printed in a book, newspaper, or magazine ◇ **out of print** not currently available from a publisher

print out *vt* to produce a printed copy of data from a computer

printable /príntəb'l/ *adj* **1** sufficiently inoffensive, correct, or well-written as to be fit to be printed in a publication ○ *Some of the player's comments weren't printable.* **2** capable of being printed or printed on ○ *This paper's too glossy to be printable.* —**printability** /príntə bílləti/ *n*

printed circuit *n* an electronic circuit in which some components and the connections between them are formed by etching a metallic coating on one or both sides of an insulating board

printed matter *n* published material such as books, newspapers, magazines, or catalogues

printer /príntər/ *n* **1** PERSON OR COMPANY IN PRINTING TRADE a person or company in the business of printing books, newspapers, or magazines **2** MACHINE FOR PRINTING BOOKS OR NEWSPAPERS a machine that prints books, newspapers, or magazines **3** MACHINE FOR PRINTING COMPUTER DATA a peripheral output device producing computer-generated text or graphics on paper, transparencies, or similar media **4 MACHINE FOR MAKING COPIES OF FILM** a machine that makes duplicates of film, normally a positive from a negative

⚡**printer driver** *n* a software routine that converts data for interpretation by a printer

printer's devil *n* an apprentice or young assistant to a printer [< DEVIL 'apprentice']

⚡**printhead** /prínt hed/ *n* a part of a computer printer that prints out the characters on paper

printing /prínting/ *n* **1 PRODUCTION OF COPIES** the process or business of producing copies of documents, publications, or images **2 PRINTED CHARACTERS** typographical characters as they appear on paper or another surface ○ *The printing has washed off this bottle.* **3 LETTERS WRITTEN SEPARATELY** letters written separately or the act of writing letters separately, in contrast to script characters ○ *Her printing is easier to read than her handwriting.* **4 PRINT RUN** the process or output of one print run of a publication ○ *This book is in its eighth printing.*

printing press *n* a machine that presses inked set type or etched plates onto paper or textiles that are fed through it

printmaker /prínt maykər/ *n* an artist who designs and makes prints —**printmaking** *n*

⚡**printout** /prínt owt/ *n* a paper copy of data from a computer

print run *n* the process or output of one printing of a publication, document, or artwork ○ *an initial print run of 30,000 copies*

prion[1] /prí ən, prée ən/ *n* an infectious particle of protein that, unlike a virus, contains no nucleic acid, does not trigger an immune response, and is not destroyed by extreme heat or cold [Late 20C. < *proteinaceous* + IN-FECTIOUS + -ON[1].]

prion[2] /prí ən/ *n* a small seabird with blue-grey markings like a pigeon and a flattened serrated bill. Native to: southern oceans. Genus: *Pachyptila.* [Mid-19C. Via modern Latin < Greek *priōn* 'saw'.]

prior[1] /prí ər/ *adj* **1 EARLIER** earlier in time or sequence ○ *a prior engagement* **2 MORE IMPORTANT** more important or basic ■ *n US* **EARLIER CONVICTION** an earlier conviction for a criminal act (*informal*) ○ *Check to see whether the suspect has any priors.* [Early 18C. < Latin, 'former, elder, superior', literally 'more before'.] ◇ **prior to somebody** *or* **something** before somebody or something in time

prior[2] /prí ər/ *n* **1 ABBOT'S DEPUTY** an officer in a monastery of a rank below abbot **2 MALE RELIGIOUS SUPERIOR** a man who is superior in some religious communities **3 SENIOR MEDIEVAL MAGISTRATE** a senior magistrate in some medieval Italian republics, especially Florence [Pre-12C. Via medieval Latin < Latin, 'elder, superior'.]

priorate /prí ərət/ *n* the position or term of office of a prior or prioress

prioress /prí ə réss/ *n* **1** a woman officer in a convent of a rank below abbess **2** a woman superior in some religious communities

prioritize /prī órri tīz/ (**-tizes, -tizing, -tized**), **prioritise** (**-tises, -tising, -tised**) *vti* **1** to order things according to their importance or urgency ○ *I must prioritize my list of things to do.* **2** to regard something as most important or urgent ○ *I have to prioritize finding a job.* —**prioritization** /prī órri tī záysh'n/ *n*

priority /prī órriti/ (*plural* **-ties**) *n* **1 GREATEST IMPORTANCE** the state of having most importance or urgency ○ *Give this case priority treatment.* **2 SOMEBODY OR SOMETHING IMPORTANT** somebody or something that is ranked highly in terms of importance or urgency ○ *You've got to get your priorities right.* **3 EARLIER OCCURRENCE** the state of having preceded something else **4 RIGHT OF PRECEDENCE** the right to be ranked above others

priory /prí əri/ (*plural* **-ies**) *n* a religious community or home such as a monastery or convent, headed by a prior or prioress

Pripet Marshes /príp ət-/, **Pripyat' Marshes** /préepyət-/, **Poles'ye** /pō les yə/ swamp region of S Belarus and NW Ukraine. Area: 270,000 sq. km/104,000 sq. mi.

prise /prīz/ (**prises, prising, prised**) *vt* **1** to open or part something by levering ○ *I used a screwdriver to prise the lid off the paint.* **2** to get something, especially information, from somebody or something with difficulty [14C. Probably < Old French *prise* (see PRIZE[2]).]

prism /prízzəm/ *n* **1 POLYGONAL SOLID FOR DISPERSING LIGHT** a transparent polygonal solid object with flat faces and a usually triangular cross-section, used for separating white light into a spectrum of colours **2 SOMETHING MADE OF CUT GLASS** a cut-glass object, especially one that can separate white light into a spectrum **3 CRYSTAL TYPE** a crystal form with faces that are parallel to a single axis **4 PARALLELOGRAM-SIDED SOLID** a solid figure with ends that are identical polygons and with sides that are parallelograms [Late 16C. Via late Latin < Greek *prisma* 'something sawn' (because of its shape) < *prizein* 'to saw'.]

prismatic /priz máttik/ *adj* **1 RELATING TO PRISM** resembling or relating to a prism **2 SEPARATED BY PRISM** describes light that shows the colours of the spectrum, as refracted by a prism **3 COLOURFUL** brightly coloured, like a rainbow [Early 18C. < French *prismatique* < Greek *prismat-*, stem of *prisma* (see PRISM).] —**prismatically** *adv*

prismoid /príz moyd/ *n* a prismatoid with sides that are parallelograms or trapezoids and equal-sided polygons as bases [Early 18C. < PRISM, after *rhomboid.*] —**prismoidal** /priz móyd'l/ *adj*

prison /prízz'n/ *n* **1 PLACE WHERE CRIMINALS ARE CONFINED** a secure place where somebody is confined as punishment for a crime or while waiting to stand trial **2 CONFINEMENT** a place or condition of captivity or unwanted restraint ○ *His fears are a prison that he cannot escape.* ■ *vt* **IMPRISON** to put somebody in prison (*archaic or literary*) [12C. Via Old French < Latin *prension-* 'seizing' < *prehendere* 'seize'.]

prison camp *n* a camp where prisoners of war are confined

prisoner /prízz'nər/ *n* **1 SOMEBODY HELD IN PRISON** somebody confined in a prison as a punishment for a crime or while waiting to stand trial **2 SOMEBODY HELD AGAINST WILL** a person who is confined in a place ○ *He's been taken prisoner by a group of rebel soldiers.* **3 SOMEBODY WHO IS OR FEELS TRAPPED** a person who cannot escape a situation or condition

prisoner of conscience *n* somebody held in a prison by a state, especially an oppressive regime, because of his or her political or religious beliefs

prisoner of war *n* a person who has been captured and imprisoned by an enemy during a war

prisoner's base *n* a children's game in which two teams try to tag each other's members, thereby adding them to their team at their base [Alteration of earlier *prison-bars*]

prissy /príssi/ (**-sier, -siest**) *adj* behaving in a very prudish and proper way [Late 19C. Probably blend of PRIM + SISSY.] —**prissily** *adv* —**prissiness** *n*

Priština /préeshtinə/ city in central Kosovo, Federal Republic of Yugoslavia. Population: 108,083 (1991).

pristine /prís teen/ *adj* **1 IMMACULATE** so clean and neat as to look as good as new ○ *The house is in pristine condition.* **2 UNSPOILT** not yet ruined by human encroachment ○ *acres of pristine forest* **3 IN OR OF ORIGINAL STATE** in or belonging to an original state or condition [Mid-16C. < Latin *pristinus* 'former'.]

prithee /príthi/ *interj* used to introduce a request to somebody (*archaic*) [Late 16C. Contraction of *(I) pray thee.*]

privacy /prívvəssi, prívəssi/ *n* **1 SECLUSION** the state of being apart from other people and not seen, heard, or disturbed by them ○ *Shut the door so we can have some privacy.* **2 FREEDOM FROM ATTENTION OF OTHERS** freedom from the observation, intrusion, or attention of others ○ *If you seek celebrity, you must sacrifice privacy.* **3 HIDDEN CONDITION** the state of being kept secret

private /prívət/ *adj* **1 KEPT SECRET OR RESTRICTED** not for other people to see or know about **2 SECLUDED** sufficiently secluded for people to be alone and not watched, heard, or disturbed by others ○ *Let's find a private corner where we can talk.* **3 PERSONAL** belonging to, restricted to, or intended for a specified person **4 NOT PUBLIC** not open to the public **5 ACTING IN PERSONAL CAPACITY** holding no official position in government ○ *a private citizen* **6 NON-GOVERNMENTAL** not supported by government funding ○ *private enterprise* **7 RESERVED** preferring not to disclose personal information or to discuss personal feelings with others ○ *She's a very private person.* **8 NOT UNDERSTANDABLE BY EVERYONE** excluding people who do not share the knowledge required to understand **9 LOWEST-RANKING** relating to the lowest rank of soldier ■ *n* **LOWEST-RANKING SOLDIER** a soldier of the lowest rank ■ **privates** *npl* **GENITALS** the genitals (*informal*) [14C. < Latin *privatus* 'isolated, not in public life', past participle of *privare* (see PRIVATION).] —**privately** *adv* —**privateness** *n*

private bank *n US* the department of a bank, or an entire bank, that offers individual financial management services to wealthy customers —**private banking** *n*

private bill *n* a legislative bill presented in Parliament or Congress that affects only an individual, corporation, or specific part of the nation

private company *n* a company that is not listed on the stock market and does not issue its shares to the public

private detective *n* a detective who is not a member of the police, but who is hired by individuals or companies

private enterprise *n* **1** business activities that are not regulated or owned by the government **2** a company that is owned by a private individual or individuals and not by the government

privateer /prívə téer/ *n* **1** a ship that belongs to and is run by a person or company but is authorized by the government to engage in battle during war **2** the commander or a crew member of a privateer [Mid-17C. After VOLUNTEER.]

private eye *n* a private detective (*informal*) [*Eye*, spelling of *I.*, abbreviation of *investigator.*]

private first class (*plural* **privates first class**) *n US* a soldier in the US Army or Marine Corps of a rank above private

private hotel *n* **1** a privately run hotel that has the right to refuse potential guests **2** *ANZ* a hotel that cannot sell alcoholic beverages legally because it lacks a liquor licence

private income *n* income from sources other than employment, e.g. from investments or allowances

private investigator *n* CRIME = **private detective**

⚡**private key cryptography** *n* an encryption method using a single key for encoding and decoding an Internet message

⚡**private label card** *n* a retailer credit card that is issued and managed by a third party (*in e-commerce*)

private language *n* an exclusive language devised and spoken by a restricted group of people, especially twins

private law *n* the branch of law concerned with the rights and responsibilities of individuals. ◊ **public law**

private life *n* the part of somebody's life that relates to his or her personal activities and relationships and not to his or her job or public duties

private means *npl* FIN = **private income**

private member *n* a member of the UK, Australian, New Zealand, and Canadian parliaments who does not hold a ministerial position

private member's bill *n* a bill introduced in a parliament by a private member

private parts *npl* the genitals

private patient *n* a patient who chooses to pay for medical treatment outside the National Health Service, usually to obtain advantages such as the avoidance of a long wait for surgery

private pay bed *n* a hospital bed reserved for a paying patient rather than a National Health Service patient

private practice *n* **1** a professional business owned and managed by an individual professional such as a lawyer, rather than by an organization **2** a doctor's practice that is not part of the National Health Service

private school *n* a primary or secondary school that is not run by the government and therefore charges fees for tuition

private secretary *n* a secretary employed to manage somebody's personal or confidential affairs, especially those of a business executive or public figure

private sector *n* the part of a free market economy that is made up of companies and organizations that are not owned or controlled by the government

private treaty *n* sale of property according to terms negotiated by the buyer and seller

private view, private viewing *n* a preview of a film or an exhibition that is open only to invited guests

privation /prī váysh'n/ *n* **1** lack of the basic necessities of life such as food, housing, and heating **2** the act of depriving somebody of something [14C. < Latin *privare* 'deprive, isolate' < *privus* 'single, isolated'.]

privatisation *n* = **privatization**

privatise *vt* = **privatize**

privatism /prívətizəm/ *n* an attitude or lifestyle in which somebody ignores all but his or her own interests —**privatist** *n, adj* —**privatistic** /prívə tístik/ *adj*

privative /prívvətiv/ *adj* 1 **RELATING TO LACK OR NEGATION** indicating the absence or negation of some quality ○ *a privative term* 2 **CAUSING DEPRIVATION** causing or experiencing deprivation ■ *n* **AFFIX DENOTING LACK OR NEGATION** an affix, word, or expression that denotes the absence or negation of some quality, e.g. English 'non-' or Greek 'a-' [Late 16C. Directly or via French < Latin *privativus* < *privare* (see PRIVATION).] —**privatively** *adv*

privatize /prívə tīz/ (**-tizes, -tizing, -tized**), **privatise** (**-tises, -tising, -tised**) *vt* to transfer to private ownership an economic enterprise or public utility that has been under state ownership —**privatization** /prívə tī záysh'n/ *n*

~~**privelage**~~ incorrect spelling of **privilege**

privet /prívvit/ *n* an evergreen bush commonly used for hedging. Flowers: white, in clusters. *Ligustrum vulgare* and *Ligustrum ovalifolium*. [Mid-16C. < ?]

~~**privilage**~~ incorrect spelling of **privilege**

~~**priviledge**~~ incorrect spelling of **privilege**

privilege /prívvəlij/ *n* 1 **RESTRICTED RIGHT OR BENEFIT** an advantage, right, or benefit that is not available to everyone 2 **RIGHTS AND ADVANTAGES ENJOYED BY ELITE** the rights and advantages enjoyed by a relatively small group of people, usually as a result of wealth or social status ○ *a system founded on privilege* 3 **SPECIAL HONOUR** a special treat or honour ○ *It was a privilege to work with you.* 4 **LAWMAKER'S RIGHT TO SPECIAL TREATMENT** the right to, or granting of, special treatment or benefits to members of a legislative body, e.g. freedom from prosecution ■ *vt* (**-leges, -leging, -leged**) 1 **GIVE SPECIAL RIGHTS TO** to grant special rights or benefits to somebody or something 2 **GRANT EXEMPTION TO** to exempt or release somebody or something from something [12C. Via Old French < Latin *privilegium* 'private law' < *privus* 'single, isolated' + *leg-* 'law'.]

privileged /prívvəlijd/ *adj* 1 **ENJOYING SPECIAL ADVANTAGES** enjoying privileges, especially the resources and advantages associated with the upper classes or the rich 2 **HONOURED OR FORTUNATE** fortunate in having a special advantage or opportunity to do something ○ *I feel privileged to be here today.* ■ *npl* **PEOPLE ENJOYING SPECIAL ADVANTAGES** a class of people, especially the rich or the upper classes, that benefits from special rights or resources (*+ plural verb*)

privileged communication *n* 1 a confidential conversation or correspondence that does not have to be disclosed in a court of law 2 speech or writing that is not subject to libel or slander laws

privity /prívvəti/ (*plural* **-ties**) *n* 1 **SHARED KNOWLEDGE OF SECRET** the state of sharing knowledge of, or colluding in, something secret 2 **LEGALLY RECOGNIZED RELATIONSHIP** a legally recognized relationship between two parties, e.g. between members of a family, between an employer and employees, or between others who have entered into a contract together 3 **RELATIONSHIP TO PROPERTY** a successive or mutual relationship to some property [12C. Via Old French < medieval Latin *privitas* < Latin *privus* 'single, isolated'.]

privy /prívvi/ *adj* 1 **SHARING SECRET KNOWLEDGE** sharing knowledge of something secret or private ○ *I was privy to their plans to elope.* 2 **RELATING TO SOMEBODY IN PRIVATE CAPACITY** relating to somebody, especially a British monarch, as a private individual, not as an official personage 3 **SECRET** done or spoken secretly or privately (*archaic*) ■ *n* (*plural* **-ies**) 1 **OUTSIDE TOILET** an outside toilet or latrine 2 **SOMEBODY ELSE INVOLVED** an individual who has an interest or agency in something that involves another party [12C. Via French *privé* < Latin *privatus* (see PRIVATE).]

privy chamber *n* an apartment reserved for private use in a royal residence

privy council *n* a committee that advises a ruler —**privy counsellor** *n*

Privy Council *n* the committee that advises a British king or queen —**Privy Counsellor** *n*

Privy Purse *n* 1 the allowance from public funds given to the British monarch to cover personal expenses 2 the official who manages the personal finances of the British monarch

Privy Seal *n* 1 a seal that used to be attached to documents authorized by the British king or queen 2 POL = **Lord Privy Seal**

prix fixe /prée féeks/ (*plural* **prix fixes**) *n* 1 a meal with several courses that is offered by a restaurant at a set price 2 a set price for a restaurant meal with several courses [< French, 'fixed price']

prize[1] /prīz/ *n* 1 **AWARD FOR WINNER** something that is given to the winner of a contest or competition 2 **SOMETHING HIGHLY VALUED** something that somebody values highly, especially because it takes great skill, effort, or luck to get ■ *vt* (**prizes, prizing, prized**) **TREASURE** to value something highly ○ *This award is something I'll always prize.* ■ *adj* **COMPLETE** perfect as an example of something, especially something undesirable (*dated informal*) ○ *I made a prize fool of myself.* [Late 16C. < earlier *prise* 'value, reward' < Old French, < *prendre* (see PRIZE²).]

SPELLCHECK See *prise*.

prize[2] /prīz/ *n* something captured and kept, especially a ship or its contents taken by another ship in wartime [13C. < Old French *prise* 'something seized', feminine past participle of *prendre* 'take, seize' < Latin *prehendere*.]

prize[3] *vt, n* US = **prise**

prizefight /príz fīt/ *n* a boxing match in which the winner receives a cash prize —**prizefighter** *n* —**prizefighting** *n*

prize-giving *n* a ceremony at which prizes are awarded, especially for schoolwork

prize ring *n* 1 a boxing ring where prizefights are held 2 the sport or business of professional boxing

prizewinner /príz winər/ *n* somebody or something that wins a prize in a competition, or that habitually wins prizes —**prizewinning** *adj*

prn *abbr* as required (*in prescriptions*) [< Latin *pro re nata*]

pro[1] /prō/ *n* (*plural* **pros**) 1 **SUPPORTING ARGUMENT** an argument in favour of a proposal or position 2 **SIDE ARGUING FOR SOMETHING** a person or side in a debate, argument, or campaign that is in favour of a proposal or proposition ■ *prep* **FOR** in favour of ■ *adv* **IN SUPPORT** on the side that favours one side of an issue [14C. < Latin, 'for' (see PRO-¹).]

pro[2] /prō/ *n* (*plural* **pros**) 1 **PROFESSIONAL PERSON** a professional, especially in sports (*informal*) 2 **SKILLED PERSON** an experienced and skilled person 3 **PROSTITUTE** a prostitute (*slang*) ■ *adj* **PROFESSIONAL** relating to or typical of an activity, especially a sport, from which somebody earns a living ■ *adv* **PROFESSIONALLY** as a professional [Mid-20C. Shortening.]

⚡**pro**[3] *abbr* professional (*in e-mails*)

PRO *abbr* 1 Public Record Office 2 public relations officer

pro-[1] *prefix* 1 substituting for, acting in place of ○ *proconsul* 2 in favour of ○ *pronuclear* [Via Old French < Latin *pro* 'for' < Indo-European, 'forward, before']

pro-[2] *prefix* 1 rudimentary, precursor ○ *promycelium* 2 before, earlier than ○ *procambium* 3 in front of ○ *procephalic* [Via Old French < Greek *pro* 'in front, before' < Indo-European 'forward, before']

proa /prṓ ə/ (*plural* **-as**), **prau** /prow/ (*plural* **praus**), **prahu** /praá oo/ (*plural* **-us**) *n* a Malayan boat with a triangular sail and a single outrigger [Late 16C. < Malay *pārāhū* 'boat'.]

proactive /prō áktiv/ *adj* taking the initiative by acting rather than reacting to events [Mid-20C. After RETROACTIVE.] —**proactively** *adv*

USAGE When people name words they dislike as jargon, ***proactive*** is often on the list. ***Proactive*** does meet a need, serving as the opposite of *reactive* more naturally than, for example, *anticipatory* or *assertive* is able to. Nonetheless, it should be used sparingly.

pro-am /prṓ ám/ *adj* involving or composed of professional and amateur sports players ■ *n* a competition in which professional players compete against amateurs, or in which professionals and amateurs compete together [Mid-20C. < PRO² + *am* shortening of AMATEUR.]

probabilism /próbbəbəlizəm/ *n* 1 the belief that certainty is impossible, and that therefore decisions must be based on probabilities 2 the principle whereby, in moral questions in which nothing is certain, somebody may follow the probability favourable to him or her rather than a more probable, but less favourable view —**probabilist** *n, adj* —**probabilistic** /próbbəbə lístik/ *adj* —**probabilistically** /-lístikli/ *adv*

probability /próbbə bílləti/ (*plural* **-ties**) *n* 1 **STATE OF BEING PROBABLE** the state of being probable, or the extent to which something is probable ○ *We must take into account the probability of another earthquake.* 2 **SOMETHING LIKELY TO HAPPEN** something that is likely to happen or exist ○ *We must prepare for all probabilities.* 3 **MATHEMATICAL LIKELIHOOD OF EVENT** the likelihood that an event will occur expressed as the ratio of the number of favourable outcomes in the set of outcomes divided by the total number of possible outcomes ◇ **in all probability** used to suggest that something is highly probable

probability density function *n* 1 = **probability function** 2 a function of a continuous variable such that the integral of the function over a specific region yields the probability that its value will fall within the region

probability function *n* a function of a discrete random variable that yields the probability of occurrence of distinct outcomes

probability theory *n* the branch of mathematics that deals with quantities having random distributions, with the aim of predicting how defined systems will behave

probable /próbbəb'l/ *adj* likely to exist, occur, or be true, although evidence is insufficient to prove or predict it ■ *n* somebody or something that is likely to be chosen for something or likely to do something ○ *a probable for the team* [14C. Directly or via French < Latin *probabilis* 'provable, plausible' < *probare* (see PROVE).]

probable cause *n* sufficient reason to believe that an arrest or search of a suspect is warranted

probable error *n* the amount by which a statistic may vary from fact, based on chance factors

probably /próbbəbli/ *adv* as is likely or to be expected ○ *I'll probably come tonight.*

proband /prṓ band/ *n* MED = **propositus** *n.* 3 [Early 20C. < Latin *probandus-* 'for testing, to be tested' < *probare* (see PROVE).]

probate /prṓ bayt/ *n* 1 the legal certification of the validity of a will 2 an official copy of a will that is legally certified as genuine and given to the executors [14C. < Latin *probatum* 'thing proved' < *probare* (see PROVE).]

probate court *n* a court that deals with the legal certification of wills and the administration of estates of the deceased

probation /prə báysh'n/ *n* 1 **SUPERVISION BY PROBATION OFFICER** the supervision of the behaviour of a young or first-time criminal offender by a probation officer 2 **PERIOD OF TESTING SOMEBODY'S SUITABILITY** a period during which somebody's suitability for a job or other role is being tested 3 **TESTING** the testing or proving of something (*formal*) —**probational** *adj* —**probationally** *adv* —**probationary** *adj*

probationer /prə báysh'nər/ *n* 1 a person on probation, especially one under supervision because he or she is new to a job or has just been released from prison 2 a student Scottish Presbyterian minister who has received a licence but has not yet been ordained

probation officer *n* an official who supervises criminal offenders on probation

probative /prṓbətiv/, **probatory** /prṓbətəri/ *adj* 1 supplying proof or evidence 2 designed to test or prove somebody or something [15C. < Old French *probatif* < Latin *probare* (see PROVE).]

probe /prōb/ *n* 1 **INVESTIGATION** a thorough investigation, often into illegal or suspicious activities 2 **CIRCUIT-TESTING DEVICE** a device with a metal tip used to test the behaviour of electrical circuits 3 **SURGICAL INSTRUMENT FOR EXPLORING** a long thin instrument used by doctors and dentists for exploring or examining 4 AEROSP = **space probe** ■ *vti* (**probes, probing, probed**) 1 **INVESTIGATE COMPLETELY** to conduct a thorough investigation into something 2 **CHECK USING PROBE** to examine something with a probe 3 **EXAMINE AREA** to search or explore a place [Mid-16C. < medieval Latin *proba* 'examination' < Latin *probare* 'to test' (see PROVE).] —**probeable** *adj* —**prober** *n* —**probingly** *adv*

probenecid /prō bénnəssid/ *n* a drug that promotes the excretion of uric acid. Use: treatment of gout. [Mid-20C. < PROPYL + BENZENE + ACID.]

probity /prṓbəti/ *n* absolute moral correctness [Early 16C. Via Old French < Latin *probitas* < *probus* 'good'.]

problem /próbbləm/ *n* **1 DIFFICULTY** a difficult situation, matter, or person **2 PUZZLE TO BE SOLVED** a question or puzzle that needs to be solved **3 STATEMENT REQUIRING MATHEMATICAL SOLUTION** a statement or proposition requiring an algebraic, geometric, or other mathematical solution ■ *adj* **HARD TO DEAL WITH** difficult to discipline or deal with [14C. Via Old French and Latin < Greek *problēma, problēmat-* 'projection, obstacle', literally 'thing thrown in front', < *ballein* 'to throw'.] ◇ **no problem** used to indicate that something will not cause any difficulty or inconvenience (*informal*)

problematic /próbblə máttik/, **problematical** /-máttik'l/ *adj* involving difficulties or problems ■ *n* a matter or issue that is problematic —**problematically** *adv*

~~**probly**~~ incorrect spelling of **probably**

pro bono /prō bṓnō/ *adj, adv* done or undertaken for the public good without any payment or compensation [Shortening of Latin *pro bono publico* 'for the public good']

proboscidean /próbbə síddi ən/, **proboscidian** *n* a very large mammal that has a trunk and tusks, e.g. an elephant, mammoth, or mastodon. Order: Proboscidea. [Mid-19C. < modern Latin *Proboscidea* < Latin *proboscid-*, stem of *proboscis* (see PROBOSCIS).] —**proboscidean** *adj*

proboscis /prō bóssiss/ (*plural* **-cises** *or* **-ces** /-eez/ *or* **-cides** /-bóssi deez/) *n* **1 ELEPHANT'S TRUNK** the trunk of an elephant or related extinct mammal **2 LONG FLEXIBLE SNOUT** the long flexible snout of some mammals such as the tapir, the elephant seal, or the proboscis monkey **3 LONG MOUTHPARTS OF INVERTEBRATE** the long or tubular mouthparts of certain insects, worms, and spiders, used for feeding, sucking, and other purposes **4 LARGE NOSE** a human nose, especially a large one (*humorous*) [Late 16C. Via Latin < Greek *proboskis* 'elephant's trunk' < *boskein* 'to feed'.]

proboscis monkey *n* a large monkey with reddish fur and a protruding bulbous nose that in older males becomes pendulous. Native to: Borneo. *Nasalis larvatus.*

procaine /prṓ kayn, -káyn/, **procain** *n* $C_{13}H_{20}N_2O_2$ a white or colourless crystalline ester. Use: local anaesthetic, in the form of its hydrochloride.

procaryote *n* BIOL = **prokaryote**

~~**procede**~~ incorrect spelling of **proceed**

⚡**procedure** /prə séejər/ *n* **1** an established or correct method of doing something **2** any means of doing or accomplishing something ○ *an extremely unorthodox procedure* **3** COMPUT = **routine** *n.* 5 **4** COMPUT = **subroutine** [Early 17C. < French *procédure* < *procéder* < (see PROCEED).] —**procedural** *adj, n* —**proceduralist** *n* —**procedurally** *adv*

proceed /prə séed/ *vi* **1 BEGIN ACTION** to go on to do something **2 CONTINUE WITH ACTION** to continue with a course of action **3 PROGRESS** to progress in a steady or particular manner **4 GO IN SOME DIRECTION** to go in a particular direction, especially forward **5 SUE** to bring legal action against somebody **6 DEVELOP** to come from or arise from something [14C. Via French < Latin *procedere* 'go forward' < *cedere* 'go'.] —**proceeder** *n*

SPELLCHECK See ***precede***.

proceeding /prə séeding/ *n* **PROCEDURE** an action or course of action ■ **proceedings** *npl* **1 LEGAL ACTION** legal action brought against somebody **2 SERIES OF EVENTS** a series of related events occurring at one time or in one place **3 PUBLISHED RECORDS** published records of a meeting or conference

proceeds /prṓ seedz/ *npl* the money derived from a sale or other commercial transaction

~~**proceedure**~~ incorrect spelling of **procedure**

⚡**process**[1] /prṓ sess/ *n* **1 SERIES OF ACTIONS** a series of actions directed towards a particular aim **2 SERIES OF NATURAL OCCURRENCES** a series of natural occurrences that produce change or development **3 SUMMONS TO APPEAR IN COURT** a summons or writ ordering somebody to appear in court **4 LEGAL PROCEEDINGS** the entire proceedings in a lawsuit **5 NATURAL OUTGROWTH** a part that naturally grows on or sticks out on an organism ■ *v* **1** *vt* **PREPARE USING PROCESS** to treat or prepare something in a series of steps or actions, e.g. using chemicals or industrial machinery **2** *vt* **TREAT WITH PHOTOGRAPHIC CHEMICALS** to treat light-sensitive film or paper with chemicals in order to make a latent image visible **3** *vt* **FOLLOW PROCEDURES** to deal with somebody or something according to an established procedure **4** *vti* **PREPARE FOOD IN FOOD PROCESSOR** to chop, mix, or otherwise prepare food in a food processor or blender **5** *vt* **USE PROGRAM ON DATA** to use a computer program to work on data in some way, e.g. to sort a database or recalculate a spreadsheet **6** *vt* **SERVE SUMMONS ON** to serve a summons or writ on somebody **7** *vt* **BRING LEGAL ACTION** to bring a legal action against somebody **8** *vt US* **STRAIGHTEN HAIR USING LYE** to straighten curly hair using lye [14C. Directly and via Old French *proces* < Latin *processus*, past participle of *procedere* (see PROCEED).]

process[2] /prə séss/ *vi* to move forwards in a procession [Early 19C. Back-formation < PROCESSION.]

processed cheese *n* a blend of several types of cheese with emulsifiers added, sometimes sold in individually wrapped thin slices

process engineering *n* the branch of engineering that determines the sequence of operations and the selection of tools required to manufacture a product

process industry *n* an industry in which raw materials are treated or prepared in a series of stages, e.g. using chemical processes. Process industries include oil refining, petrochemicals, water and sewage treatment, food manufacture, and pharmaceuticals.

procession /prə sésh'n/ *n* **1 GROUP OF PEOPLE MOVING FORWARDS** a group of people or vehicles moving forwards in a line as part of a celebration, commemoration, or demonstration **2 FORWARD MOVEMENT** the movement forwards of a group of people or vehicles as part of a celebration, commemoration, or demonstration **3 SUCCESSION** a series of people or things coming one after the other [12C. Directly or via Old French < Latin *procession-*, *processus* (see PROCESS[1]).]

processional /prə sésh'nəl/ *adj* **1 FOR PROCESSION** used for or in a procession **2 FORMING PROCESSION** taking the form of a procession ■ *n* **1 MUSIC FOR PROCESSION** a piece of music suitable for accompanying a procession **2 MUSIC FOR ENTRY OF CLERGY** a hymn or other piece of music that accompanies the entry of the clergy into a church **3 BOOK OF HYMNS AND PRAYERS** a book of hymns and prayers for use during a religious procession —**processionally** *adv*

process-server *n* a server of a writ or summons ordering somebody to appear in court

procès-verbal /próssay vur baál/ (*plural* **procès-verbaux** /próssay vur bṓ/) *n* a written account of official proceedings [Mid-17C. < French, 'oral proceedings', originally evidence from police officers who could not write.]

pro-choice *adj* advocating open legal access to voluntary abortion

proclaim /prə kláym/ *vt* **1 DECLARE SOMETHING PUBLICLY** to announce something publicly or formally **2 DECLARE SOMEBODY TO BE** to declare publicly that somebody is something **3 SHOW WHAT SOMETHING IS** to show or reveal clearly what something is **4 MAKE SOMETHING CLEAR** to state something emphatically or openly [14C. Via Old French *proclamer* < Latin *proclamare* 'to cry forth' < *clamare* 'to cry'.] —**proclaimer** *n* —**proclamatory** /prə klámmətəri/ *adj*

proclamation /próklə máysh'n/ *n* **1** a public or formal announcement **2** the act of announcing something publicly or formally [14C. Directly or via Old French < Latin *proclamation-*, *proclamare* (see PROCLAIM).]

proclitic /prō klíttik/ *adj* describes a reduced form of a word that is closely attached in pronunciation to the word following it and has no accent of its own, e.g. 'd'' in 'd'you' [Mid-19C. < modern Latin *procliticus-* < PRO-[2] after ENCLITIC.] —**proclitic** *n*

proclivity /prə klívvəti/ (*plural* **-ties**) *n* a natural tendency to behave in a particular way [Late 16C. < Latin *proclivitas* < *proclivis* 'inclined' < *clivus* 'slope'.]

Procne /prókni/ *n* in Greek mythology, an Athenian princess whose husband, Tereus, raped her sister, Philomela

proconsul /prō kónss'l/ *n* **1** a governor of an ancient Roman province, usually a former consul **2** a governor or administrator of a colony or other dependency [14C. < Latin '(person acting) for the consul' < *consul* (see CONSUL).] —**proconsular** /prō kónssyŏŏlər/ *adj* —**proconsulate** /-kónssyŏŏlət/ *n* —**proconsulship** *n*

Procopius /prə kṓpi əss/ (500?–565?) Byzantine historian

procrastinate /prō krásti nayt/ (**-nates, -nating, -nated**) *vti* to postpone doing something, especially as a regular practice [Late 16C. < Latin *procrastinare* 'put off until tomorrow' < *crastinus* 'of tomorrow' < *cras* 'tomorrow'.] —**procrastination** /prō krásti náysh'n/ *n* —**procrastinator** /prō krásti naytər/ *n*

procreate /prṓkri ayt, -áyt/ (**-ates, -ating, -ated**) *v* **1** *vti* to produce offspring by reproduction **2** *vt* to create or produce something [Mid-16C. < Latin *procreare* 'bring forth' < *creare* 'bring forth, produce'.] —**procreant** /prṓkri ənt/ *adj* —**procreation** /-áysh'n/ *n* —**procreative** /-ayti v/ *adj* —**procreator** /prṓkri aytər, -áytər/ *n*

Procrustean /prō krústi ən/ *adj* trying to establish conformity by using any and all means, including violence [Mid-19C. < PROCRUSTES.]

Procrustes /prō krús teez/ *n* in Greek mythology, a robber who abducted strangers and forced them to fit perfectly into a bed by either cutting off or stretching their limbs

proct- *prefix* = **procto-** (*before vowels*)

proctitis /prok títiss/ *n* inflammation of the rectum [Early 19C. < Greek *prōktos* 'anus'.]

procto- *prefix* anus, anal, rectum, rectal ○ *proctoscope* [< Greek *prōktos*]

proctodaeum /proktə dée əm/ (*plural* **-a** /-dée ə/ *or* **-ums**) *n* the exterior section of an embryo that develops into part of the anal canal [Late 19C. < modern Latin, < PROCTO- + Greek *hodaios* 'on the way' < *hodos* 'way'.]

proctology /prok tólləji/ *n* the branch of medicine concerned with disorders of the colon, rectum, and anus —**proctological** /próktə lójjik'l/ *adj* —**proctologist** /prok tólləjist/ *n*

proctor /próktər/ *n* **1 UNIVERSITY OFFICER IN CHARGE OF DISCIPLINE** either of two officers at certain universities elected annually and assigned to supervise undergraduate discipline **2** *US* EDUC = **invigilator** **3 REPRESENTATIVE** a conductor of somebody else's case in court (*dated*) **4 CLERGY REPRESENTATIVE** any one of the representatives of the clergy in the Church of England convocation ■ *vt US* EDUC = **invigilate** [14C. Contraction of PROCURATOR.] —**proctorial** /prok táwri əl/ *adj* —**proctorship** *n*

proctoscope /próktə skōp/ *n* a tubular medical instrument with an integral light source, used for examining the anal canal and rectum —**proctoscopic** /próktə skóppik/ *adj* —**proctoscopy** /prok tóskəpi/ *n*

procumbent /prō kúmbənt/ *adj* **1** lying down with the face to the ground **2** describes a plant stem that grows along the ground without taking root [Mid-17C. < Latin *procumbent-*, present participle of *procumbere* 'fall forward' < *cumbere* 'lie down'.]

procuration /prókyŏŏ ráysh'n/ *n* **1 ACQUIRING** the obtaining of something, especially by effort (*formal*) **2 PROVIDING OF PROSTITUTE** the crime of providing somebody for prostitution **3 ENGAGING OF PROCURATOR** the engaging of an agent to manage somebody's affairs **4 AUTHORIZING OF PROCURATOR** the authorization given to somebody who acts as an agent to manage somebody else's affairs [15C. Directly or via French < Latin *procuration-* < *procurat-* (see PROCURATOR).]

procurator /prókyŏŏ raytər/ *n* **1** an agent engaged to manage somebody else's affairs **2** in ancient Rome, an administrative official with legal or fiscal powers [13C. Directly or via French < Latin, 'agent, manager, tax-collector' < *procurat-*, past participle of *procurare* (see PROCURE).] —**procuratorial** /prókyŏŏrə táwri əl/ *adj* —**procuratorship** *n*

procurator fiscal (*plural* **procurators fiscal** *or* **procurator fiscals**) *n* a public prosecutor and coroner in Scotland

procure /prə kyŏŏr/ (**-cures, -curing, -cured**) *v* **1** *vt* to obtain something, especially by effort **2** *vti* to provide somebody for prostitution [13C. Via Old French < Latin *procurare* 'to take care of, manage' < *curare* 'to care for'.] —**procurable** *adj* —**procural** *n* —**procurance** *n* —**procurement** *n* —**procurer** *n*

SYNONYMS See ***get***.

procuress /prə kyŏŏr ess/ (*plural* **-esses**) *n* a woman who provides people for prostitution

prod /prod/ *vti* (**prods, prodding, prodded**) **1 POKE** to poke somebody or something with a finger, elbow, or pointed object **2 INCITE TO ACTION** to incite or encourage somebody to take action ■ *n* **1 A POKE** a poke with a finger, elbow, or pointed object **2 INCITEMENT TO ACTION** an incitement or encouragement to do something **3 POKING INSTRUMENT** an instrument used for poking a person or animal [Mid-16C. < ?] —**prodder** *n*

Prod, Proddie /próddi/ *n Scotland, Ireland* an offensive term for a Protestant (*slang*)

prodigal /próddig'l/ *adj* **1 WASTEFUL** tending to spend money wastefully **2 PRODUCING GENEROUS AMOUNTS** giving or producing something in large amounts ■ *n* **1 SPEND-**

THRIFT somebody who spends money wastefully **2** REPENTANT WASTREL a person who, after leaving home, behaves wastefully and disgracefully, but repents and is forgiven and warmly welcomed on returning (*literary*) [Early 16C. Via French < late Latin *prodigalis* < Latin *prodigus* 'wasteful' < *prodigere* 'drive away, squander' < *agere* 'to drive'.] —**prodigality** /próddi gálləti/ *n* —**prodigally** *adv*

prodigious /prə díjjəss/ *adj* **1** great in amount, size, or extent **2** very impressive or amazing [Mid-16C. < Latin *prodigiosus* 'marvellous' < *prodigium* 'prophetic sign, portent'.] —**prodigiously** *adv* —**prodigiousness** *n*

prodigy /próddiji/ (*plural* **-gies**) *n* **1** a person who shows an exceptional talent at an early age **2** something very impressive or amazing [15C. < Latin *prodigium* 'prophetic sign, portent'.]

prodrome /prṓdrōm/ *n* a symptom indicating the start of a disease [Mid-17C. Via French < Greek *prodromos* 'a running before' < *dromos* 'running'.] —**prodromal** /prō drṓm'l/ *adj* —**prodromic** /-drómmik/ *adj*

produce *v* /prə dyoóss/ (**-duces, -ducing, -duced**) **1** *vti* MAKE to make or create something **2** *vti* MANUFACTURE to manufacture goods for sale **3** *vt* CAUSE to cause something to happen or arise **4** *vti* YIELD to bring forth or bear something **5** *vt* OFFER to present or show something **6** *vt* ORGANIZE MAKING OF to organize and supervise the making of something **7** *vt* EXTEND SOMETHING IN SPACE to extend the length of a line ■ *n* /próddyooss/ FARM OR GARDEN PRODUCTS products of farms or gardens, especially fruits and vegetables [15C. < Latin *producere* 'lead or bring forth' < *ducere* 'to lead'.] —**producibility** /prə dyoóssə bílləti/ *n* —**producible** *adj*

producer /prə dyoóssər/ *n* **1** SOMETHING THAT PRODUCES somebody or something that produces something **2** SOMETHING GENERATING ITEMS FOR SALE a person, company, or country that produces goods or services for sale **3** ORGANIZER OF FILM OR RECORDING an organizer and administrator of the making of a film, play, broadcast, or recording **4** APPARATUS FOR PRODUCER GAS a furnace used for making producer gas **5** ORGANISM THAT MAKES ITS FOOD an organism such as a green plant that manufactures its own food from simple inorganic substances

producer gas *n* a fuel consisting of carbon monoxide, nitrogen, and hydrogen, made by passing air and steam over hot coke in a furnace

producer goods, producer's goods *npl* raw materials, equipment, and other goods that are used to manufacture consumer goods

product /próddukt/ *n* **1** COMMODITY PRODUCED FOR SALE a commodity that is produced by manufacture or by a natural process and is offered for sale **2** COMPANY'S GOODS OR SERVICES the goods or services produced by a company **3** RESULT something that arises as a consequence of something else **4** RESULT OF MULTIPLYING the result of the multiplication of two or more quantities **5** CHEMICAL SUBSTANCE a substance produced in a chemical reaction [15C. < Latin *productus*, past participle of *producere* (see PRODUCE).]

production /prə dúksh'n/ *n* **1** MAKING the making or creation of something **2** SOMETHING PRODUCED something that has been made or created **3** PRODUCING OF GOODS the process of manufacturing a product for sale **4** COMPANY'S PRODUCT the goods or services produced by a company **5** SUPERVISION OF RECORDING OR FILMING the organization and supervision of the making of a film, play, broadcast, or recording **6** FILM OR RECORDING a film, play, broadcast, or recording that has been produced for the public **7** SHOWING the showing or presenting of something such as evidence —**productional** *adj*

production line *n* a sequence of machines or processes in a factory through which the products pass until they are fully assembled

production number *n* a piece of music in a musical that is sung and danced by featured actors supported by the chorus

productive /prə dúktiv/ *adj* **1** PRODUCING producing or able to produce something **2** PRODUCING MUCH producing something abundantly and efficiently **3** WORTHWHILE producing satisfactory or useful results **4** PRODUCING GOODS producing goods and services of exchangeable value **5** PRODUCING MUCUS describes a cough that produces mucus **6** USED TO FORM WORDS describes a prefix or suffix that is used in forming new words —**productively** *adv* —**productiveness** *n*

productivity /próddduk tívvəti/ *n* **1** the ability to be productive **2** the rate at which a company produces goods or services, in relation to the amount of materials and number of employees needed

product liability *n* the liability of manufacturers and traders for damage or injury caused to purchasers or bystanders by their products

product line *n* **1** the whole range of products marketed by a company **2** a group of related products marketed by the same company that differ only in size or style

proem /prṓ em/ *n* an introduction to a literary work or a speech [14C. Via Old French *pro(h)eme* < Greek *prooimion* 'song before' < *oimē* 'song'.] —**proemial** /prō émmi əl/ *adj*

proenzyme /prō én zīm/ *n* the inactive precursor of an enzyme

proestrus *n* US = **pro-oestrus**

prof /prof/ *n* a college or university professor (*informal*) [Mid-19C. Shortening.]

Prof. *abbr* professor

profane /prə fáyn/ *adj* **1** IRREVERENT showing disrespect for God, any deity, or religion **2** SECULAR not connected with or used for religious matters **3** UNINITIATED not initiated into sacred or secret rites ■ *vt* (**-fanes, -faning, -faned**) TREAT SOMETHING IRREVERENTLY to treat something sacred with disrespect [14C. Via Old French *prophane* < Latin *profanus* 'outside the temple, not sacred' < *fanum* 'temple'.] —**profanation** /próffə náysh'n/ *n* —**profanatory** /prə fánnətəri/ *adj* —**profanely** *adv* —**profaneness** *n* —**profaner** *n*

profanity /prə fánnəti/ (*plural* **-ties**) *n* **1** language or behaviour that shows disrespect for God, any deity, or religion **2** a word or phrase that shows disrespect for God, any deity, or religion

profess /prə féss/ (**-fesses, -fessing, -fessed**) *v* **1** *vti* DECLARE SOMETHING OPENLY to acknowledge something publicly **2** *vt* DECLARE SOMETHING FALSELY to make a false claim about something **3** *vt* BELIEVE A RELIGION to follow a particular religion **4** *vti* BECOME PRIEST OR NUN to admit somebody, or be admitted, into a religious order [15C. < Old French *profes* 'having taken religious vows' < Latin *profess-*, past participle of *profiteri* 'declare publicly' < *fateri* 'acknowledge'.] —**professed** *adj* —**professedly** /prə féssidli/ *adv*

profession /prə fésh'n/ *n* **1** OCCUPATION REQUIRING EXTENSIVE EDUCATION an occupation that requires extensive education or specialized training **2** PEOPLE IN PROFESSION the members of a particular profession **3** DECLARATION a public acknowledgment or declaration of something **4** DECLARATION OF RELIGIOUS BELIEF a declaration of belief in a religion or faith [13C. Directly or via Old French < Latin *profession-* < *profess-* (see PROFESS).]

professional /prə fésh'nəl/ *adj* **1** OF PROFESSION relating to or belonging to a profession **2** FOLLOWING OCCUPATION AS PAID JOB engaged in an occupation as a paid job rather than as a hobby **3** VERY COMPETENT showing a high degree of skill or competence **4** DOING SOMETHING HABITUALLY habitually, and usually annoyingly, indulging in a particular activity ○ *a professional complainer* ■ *n* **1** MEMBER OF PROFESSION somebody whose occupation requires extensive education or specialized training **2** SOMEBODY IN SKILLED JOB a worker in a paid occupation that usually requires a high degree of training and skill **3** SOMEBODY VERY COMPETENT a person with a high degree of skill or competence **4** TEACHER AT SPORTS CLUB an expert player of a sport who is paid to teach other players in a club —**professionally** *adv*

professional association *n* a society of members of a profession that regulates entry to, and sets and maintains standards for, the profession

professional foul *n* a deliberate foul in football, usually committed in order to prevent the opposing team gaining a potentially crucial advantage in field position or goal-scoring opportunity

professionalise *vt* = **professionalize**

professionalism /prə fésh'nəlizəm/ *n* **1** the skill, competence, or character expected of a member of a highly trained profession **2** the following of an activity for financial gain rather than as an amateur

professionalize /prə fésh'nə līz/ (**-izes, -izing, -ized**), **professionalise** (**-ises, -ising, -ised**) *vt* to make an occupation professional, especially by paying the people who engage in it or improving the conditions or standards of their work

professor /prə féssər/ *n* **1** MOST SENIOR LECTURER the most senior lecturer in a university department **2** TEACHER OF SKILL a senior teacher of a nonacademic discipline in an institution other than a university such as a music or drama school **3** SOMEBODY PROFESSING BELIEF a person who professes a religious or other belief (*formal*) [14C. Directly or via Old French < Latin, < *profess-* (see PROFESS).] —**professorial** /próffə sáwri əl/ *adj* —**professorially** *adv* —**professorship** *n*

professoriate /próffə sáwri ət/, **professorate** /prə féssərət/ *n* **1** professors as a group **2** the status or position of professor

proffer /próffər/ *vt* **1** to hold something out to somebody so that he or she can take or grasp it **2** to offer something for consideration to somebody ○ *proffer a suggestion* [13C. < Old French *proffrir* 'offer forth' < *offrir* 'offer'.] —**profferer** *n*

~~**proffesor**~~ incorrect spelling of **professor**

~~**profffessor**~~ incorrect spelling of **professor**

proficient /prə físh'nt/ *adj* having a high degree of skill in something [Late 16C. Via Old French < Latin *proficient-*, present participle of *proficere* 'make progress' < *facere* 'make'.] —**proficiency** *n* —**proficiently** *adv*

profile /prṓ fīl/ *n* **1** SIDE VIEW OF FACE the outline of somebody's face as seen from the side **2** ARTWORK OF SOMEBODY'S PROFILE a visual representation of the outline of somebody's face as seen from the side **3** SHORT BIOGRAPHY a short biographical account of somebody **4** DESCRIPTIVE DATA a set of data, usually in graph or table form, that indicates the extent to which something matches tested or standard characteristics **5** VISIBILITY a level or degree of noticeability ○ *Though he had become famous, he still tried to keep a low profile.* **6** VERTICAL SECTION OF PHYSICAL FEATURE a vertical section through a physical feature, e.g. through soil, showing its development from bedrock, or through a river, showing its height above sea level along its course **7** PUPIL ASSESSMENT an assessment of the range of qualities, attitudes, and behaviour of a pupil, providing a fuller picture of the pupil than that given by traditional school reports ■ *vt* (**-files, -filing, -filed**) **1** DO SHORT BIOGRAPHY OF to write or present a short biographical account of somebody **2** DRAW PROFILE OF to draw or paint the outline of somebody's face as seen from the side [Mid-17C. < Italian *profilo* < *profilare* 'draw in outline' < *filo* 'thread' < Latin *filum*.] —**profiler** *n*

profit /próffit/ *n* **1** EXCESS OF INCOME OVER EXPENDITURE the excess of income over expenditure during a particular period of time **2** INCOME income from an investment or transaction **3** MONEY FROM BUSINESS ACTIVITY money made or to be made from business activity **4** ADVANTAGE an advantage or benefit derived from an activity ■ *v* **1** *vi* MAKE MONEY to gain financial profit from something **2** *vti* BENEFIT FROM to gain an advantage or benefit from something, or provide an advantage or benefit (*formal*) [13C. Via Old French < Latin *profectus* 'advance', past participle of *proficere* (see PROFICIENT).] —**profiter** *n* —**profitless** *adj* —**profitlessly** *adv*

SPELLCHECK Do not confuse ***profit*** with ***prophet***, which has a similar sound. Beware: your spellchecker will not catch this error.

---

profitable /próffitəb'l/ *adj* **1** yielding a financial profit **2** of some use, benefit, or advantage to somebody —**profitability** /próffitə bílləti/ *n* —**profitableness** *n* —**profitably** *adv*

profit and loss *n* an account showing income and expenditure over a given period and indicating net profit or loss

profit centre *n* a section or activity of a company that is independently profitable

profiteer /próffi téer/ *vi* to make excessive profits by charging high prices for scarce, necessary, or rationed goods —**profiteering** *n*

profiterole /prə fíttərōl/ *n* a small ball of choux pastry filled with cream and usually served with chocolate sauce [Early 16C. < French, 'small gain' < *profit* (see PROFIT).]

profitmaking /próffit mayking/ *adj* operated with the primary aim of making a profit

profit margin *n* the amount by which income exceeds related expenditure

profit sharing *n* a system by which the employees of a company receive a prearranged share of the company's profits (*hyphenated before nouns*)

profit taking *n* the selling of commodities, securities, or shares at a time when their current market value is greater than the price at which they were purchased

profligate /prófflіgət/ *adj* **1 WASTEFUL** extremely extravagant or wasteful **2 WITH LOW MORALS** having or showing extremely low moral standards ■ *n* **1 SOMEBODY WASTEFUL** an extremely extravagant or wasteful person **2 SOMEBODY WITH LOW MORALS** somebody with extremely low moral standards [Mid-16C. < Latin *profligatus*, past participle of *profligare* 'strike down, ruin' < *fligere* 'strike'.] —**profligacy** *n* —**profligately** *adv*

profluent /prófflooənt/ *adj* flowing smoothly or freely [15C. < Latin *profluere* 'flow forth' < *fluere* 'flow'.]

pro-form *n* a word that replaces a previously mentioned word or phrase and assumes its meaning, e.g. 'does' in the sentence 'You look tired and so does John'. US term **substitute**

pro forma /prō fáwrmə/ *adj* **1 FORMAL OR CONVENTIONAL** done or existing only as a formality **2 PROVIDED IN ADVANCE** provided in advance in order to supply descriptions of something or to serve as a model, e.g. of a later version of a document ■ *adv* **FOR CONVENTION'S SAKE** for the sake of or in accordance with convention [< Latin, 'for form's sake']

profound /prə fównd/ *adj* **1 GREAT** very great, strong, or intense **2 SHOWING GREAT UNDERSTANDING** showing great perception, understanding, or knowledge **3 REQUIRING GREAT UNDERSTANDING** requiring great perception, understanding, or knowledge **4 VERY DEEP** extending to or situated at a great depth [13C. Via Old French *profond* < Latin *profundus* 'bottom forward or downward' < *fundus* 'bottom'.] —**profoundly** *adv* —**profoundness** *n*

profundity /prə fúndəti/ (*plural* **-ties**) *n* **1 GREAT UNDERSTANDING** great perceptiveness, understanding, or knowledge **2 SOMETHING REQUIRING GREAT UNDERSTANDING** something requiring great understanding, perceptiveness, or knowledge **3 INTELLECTUAL COMPLEXITY** the intellectual complexity or abstruseness of something **4 GREATNESS** the greatness, strength, or intensity of something **5 GREAT DEPTH** extension to, or location at, a great depth [15C. Via Old French *profundite* < late Latin *profunditas* < *profundus* (see PROFOUND).]

profuse /prə fyóoss/ *adj* **1 GENEROUSLY PROVIDED** given freely and extravagantly ○ *profuse apologies* **2 GENEROUS IN GIVING** giving something freely and extravagantly **3 COPIOUS** being or appearing in large amounts [15C. < Latin *profusus*, past participle of *profundere* 'pour out' < *fundere* 'pour'.] —**profusely** *adv* —**profuseness** *n*

profusion /prə fyóozh'n/ *n* **1** a large quantity of something **2** the quality of being profuse

prog /prog/ *n* a television or radio programme (*informal*) [Late 20C. Shortening.]

prog. *abbr* **1** program **2** programme **3** progress **4** progressive

progenitor /prō jénnitər/ *n* **1** a direct ancestor of somebody or something **2** the originator of, or original model for, something [14C. < Latin, 'begetter' < *progenit-*, past participle of *progignere* < *gignere* 'beget'.]

progeny /prójjəni/ (*plural* **-nies**) *n* **1** the offspring of a person, animal, or plant **2** things that develop or result from something [13C. Via Old French *progenie* < Latin *progenies* 'offspring' < *progignere* (see PROGENITOR).]

progeria /prō jéeri ə/ *n* a rare condition of premature ageing that begins in childhood or early adult life and leads to death within a few years [Early 20C. < modern Latin, < Greek *progērōs* 'aged forward' < *gēras* 'old age'.]

progestational /prṓ je stáysh'nəl/ *adj* **1** relating to the stage of the menstrual cycle after ovulation when progesterone is produced **2** relating to or resembling progesterone or its effects

progesterone /prō jéstərōn/ *n* $C_{21}H_{30}O_2$ a sex hormone produced in women, first by the corpus luteum of the ovary to prepare the womb for the fertilized ovum, and later by the placenta to maintain pregnancy [Mid-20C. < PRO-[1] + GESTATION + STEROL + -ONE.]

progestin /prə jéstin/ *n* a progestogen, especially progesterone [Early 20C. < PRO-[1] + GESTATION + -IN.]

progestogen /prə jéstəjən/ *n* a steroid hormone or agent having effects similar to those of progesterone, or progesterone itself [Mid-20C. < PRO-[1] + GESTATION + -IN.]

proglottid /prō glóttid/, **proglottis** /-glóttiss/ (*plural* **-tides** /-deez/) *n* a segment of a tapeworm's body [Late 19C. < Greek *proglōttid* 'tip of the tongue'.] —**proglottic** *adj*

prognathous /prógnəthəss, prog náythəss/, **prognathic** /prog náthik/ *adj* describes an animal with a jaw that sticks out markedly [Mid-19C. < PRO-[2] + Greek *gnathos* 'jaw'.] —**prognathism** /prógnəthizəm/ *n*

prognosis /prog nóssiss/ (*plural* **-ses** /-seez/) *n* **1** a medical opinion as to the likely course and outcome of a disease **2** a prediction about how a given situation will develop [Mid-17C. Via late Latin < Greek *prognōsis* 'knowledge beforehand' < *gignōskein* 'know'.]

prognostic /prog nóstik/ *adj* **1 OF DISEASE PROGNOSIS** relating to or acting as a prognosis of a disease **2 OF PREDICTION** relating to or acting as a prediction ■ *n* **1 INDICATION OF COURSE OF DISEASE** an indicator used in making a prognosis concerning a disease **2 PREDICTION** a prediction as to how a given situation will develop [15C. Via Old French < Greek *prognōstikos* 'of knowledge beforehand' < *prognōsis* (see PROGNOSIS).]

prognosticate /prog nósti kayt/ (**-cates, -cating, -cated**) *v* **1** *vti* to predict or foretell future events **2** *vt* to be an indication of the likely future course of something —**prognostication** /prog nósti káysh'n/ *n* —**prognosticative** *adj* —**prognosticator** *n*

prograde /prṓ grayd/ *adj* moving in the same orbital or rotational direction as another astronomical body

⚡**program** /prṓ gram/ *n* **1** *US* = **programme** *n.* 1 **2** *US* BROADCAST = **programme** *n.* 2 **3** *US* ARTS = **programme** *n.* 3 **4** *US* EDUC = **programme** *n.* 4 **5** *US* **SET OF ACTIVITIES WITH SPECIFIC GOAL** a system of procedures or activities that has a specific purpose, e.g. to train an athletic team or provide certain social services ○ *an overseas aid program* **6 INSTRUCTIONS OBEYED BY COMPUTER** a list of instructions in a programming language that tells a computer to perform a certain task **7 OPERATING INSTRUCTIONS FOR MACHINE** a set of coded operating instructions used to run a machine automatically ■ *v* (**-grams, -gramming** *or* **-graming, -grammed** *or* **-gramed**) **1** *vt US* = **programme** *v.* 1 **2** *vti* **WRITE COMPUTER PROGRAM** to write or load a program for a computer **3** *vt* **INSERT OPERATING INSTRUCTIONS INTO MACHINE** to insert coded operating instructions into a machine **4** *vt US* = **programme** *v.* 2 [Mid-17C. Via French < Greek *programma* 'public notice', literally 'something written publicly' < *graphein* 'write'.]

program director *n US* BROADCAST = **head of programming**

⚡**programer** *n US* COMPUT = **programmer**

⚡**program evaluation and review technique** *n* full form of **PERT**

⚡**programing** *n US* COMPUT, BROADCAST = **programming**

⚡**programmatic** /prṓgrə máttik/ *adj* **1 RELATING TO PROGRAMME** relating to or consisting of a programme **2 SYSTEMATIC** following a plan or programme **3 OF PROGRAMME MUSIC** relating to or composed as programme music —**programmatically** *adv*

programme /prṓ gram/ *n* **1 PLAN** a plan of action. US term **program** *n.* 1 **2 BROADCAST** a television or radio broadcast. US term **program** *n.* 2 **3 BOOKLET GIVING DETAILS OF A PERFORMANCE** a booklet or leaflet giving details of a theatrical or musical performance. US term **program** *n.* 3 **4 SERIES OF CLASSES** a series of classes or lectures. US term **program** *n.* 4 ■ *vt* (**-grammes, -gramming, -grammed**) **1 SCHEDULE SOMETHING** to schedule something as part of a programme. US term **program** *v.* 1 **2 TRAIN SOMEBODY TO DO SOMETHING AUTOMATICALLY** to train a person or an animal to do a particular thing automatically. US term **program** *v.* 4 [Mid-17C. Via French < Greek *programma* 'written public notice', literally 'written publicly' < *graphein* 'write'.] —**programmability** /prṓ gramə bílləti/ *n* —**programmable** /prō grámməb'l, prṓ gramәb'l/ *adj*

programmed learning, programmed instruction *n* a learning method based on self-instructional materials that are designed to allow pupils to progress at their own pace, step by step, through structured sequences

programme music *n* music that depicts or is inspired by a specific story, object, or scene

programme of study *n* the subjects and skills taught to pupils of different abilities and maturities during each key stage of the National Curriculum in England and Wales

⚡**programmer** /prṓ gramər/ *n* a writer of computer programs

⚡**programming** /prṓ graming/ *n* **1** the designing or writing of computer programs **2** the selection and scheduling of television or radio programmes, or the programmes themselves

⚡**programming language** *n* a unique vocabulary and set of rules for writing computer programs

QUICK FACTS ON... **PROGRAMMING LANGUAGES**

Key elements: increasing programming productivity, allowing programs to be written and tested more rapidly; reducing the number of bugs that remain unrecognized when the program is made available for use.

First-generation (machine) languages were strings of binary – and later octal, decimal, hexadecimal – numbers that were recognized by only one type of computer, making the programs long and tedious to write. Second-generation (symbolic) languages used simple mnemonics – such as 'A' for 'add' – that were translated into machine language by a program called an assembler. Third-generation (algorithmic or procedural) languages, designed for solving a particular class of problem, are translated into machine language by a program called a compiler or interpreter. Fourth-generation (nonprocedural) languages specify what is to be accomplished without describing how. Fifth-generation languages, which are being developed for artificial intelligence applications, are still in their infancy

Key dates: 1957 FORTRAN, the first high-level language; 1959 COBOL, the first business-oriented language; 1966 BASIC, a teaching tool for undergraduates, later became the most popular language for personal computers; 1970 FORTH, used in scientific and industrial control applications; 1971 Pascal, a more sophisticated tool for teaching and personal computers; 1973 C, a high-level procedural language with the efficiency of a machine language; 1985 C++, a superset of C that became the language of choice for professional programmers; 1995 Java, a subset of C++, introduced specifically to write programs for the Internet

Key publications: *Programming Language Concepts* (Carlo Ghezzi and Mehdi Jazayeri) 1997, *Concepts of Programming Languages* (Robert W. Sebasta, 4th ed.) 1998

⚡**program trading** *n* the automatic buying and selling of large quantities of shares using computer programs that monitor price changes —**program trade** *n* —**program trader** *n*

progress /prṓ gress/ *n* **1 IMPROVEMENT** gradual development or improvement of something ○ *They've made no progress in the talks.* **2 MOTION TOWARDS** movement forwards or onwards ■ *v* **1** *vi* **IMPROVE** to develop or advance continuously **2** *vi* **MOVE ALONG** to move forwards or onwards **3** *vt* **HELP COMPLETE** to bring something towards completion [15C. < Latin *progressus*, past participle of *progredi* 'go forward' < *gradi* 'to walk'.]

progress chaser *n* somebody employed to check the progress of a piece of manufacturing or other work and ensure its prompt delivery

progression /prə grésh'n/ *n* **1 GRADUAL ADVANCEMENT** a gradual change or advancement from one state to another **2 FORWARD MOVEMENT** movement forwards or onwards **3 SERIES OF RELATED THINGS** a series or succession of related things **4 SEQUENCE OF RELATED NUMBERS** a sequence of numbers or terms in which each can be derived from its predecessor using a constant formula **5 SERIES OF NOTES OR CHORDS** a movement from one musical note or chord to another [14C. Directly or via French < Latin *progression-* < *progressus* (see PROGRESS).] —**progressional** *adj* —**progressionally** *adv*

progressive /prə gréssiv/ *adj* **1 PROGRESSING GRADUALLY** progressing gradually over a period of time ○ *a progressive decline in popularity over several years* **2 FAVOURING REFORM** advocating social, economic, or political reform **3 INFORMAL AND LESS STRUCTURED EDUCATIONALLY** relating to or using a more informal, less structured approach to the education of children **4 WITH HIGHER RATES FOR HIGHER INCOMES** describes a form of taxation in which the tax rate increases in proportion to the taxable income **5 HAVING CHANGES OF PARTNER** changing a partner at stages of a card game or dance **6 EXPRESSING CONTINUOUS ACTION** describes an aspect or form of a verb, expressing continuous action ■ *n* **1 ADVOCATE OF REFORM** a supporter or advocate of social, political, or economic reforms **2 PROGRESSIVE FORM OF VERB** the progressive aspect of a verb, or a verb in the progressive aspect [Early 17C. Directly or via French < medieval Latin *progressivus* < Latin *progressus* (see PROGRESS).] —**progressively** *adv* —**progressiveness** *n*

LANGUAGE NOTE ***Progressive*** (also called continuous) tenses express the idea of continuing, unfinished action, or condition. In English they are formed with the verb *to be* and the present participle of another verb. Progressives can refer to things going on at the present: *I'm cleaning my shoes*; or to things that were going on in the past: *We were living in*

Japan then; or to things that will be going on in the future: *He'll be sitting there till the restaurant closes.* In Standard English, not all verbs can be used in a progressive tense. For example, verbs connoting a permanent condition or state of affairs cannot: you would not say *Are you having any brothers or sisters?*

Progressive *adj* **1 OF PROGRESSIVE POLITICAL PARTY** belonging to or associated with any of various progressive political parties **2 OF NONORTHODOX JEWISH RELIGIOUS MOVEMENT** relating to a Jewish religious movement whose members do not believe that the Torah was given literally and directly by God to Moses ■ *n* **MEMBER OF PROGRESSIVE PARTY** a member of a progressive political party

Progressive Conservative *n* in Canada, a member or supporter of the Progressive Conservative Party

Progressive Conservative Party *n* a Canadian federal and provincial political party founded in the 1850s and taking its present name in 1942

progressive education *n* a 20th-century theory of education that stresses children's self-expression, an informal classroom atmosphere, and individual attention

Progressive Federal Party *n* a South African political party formed in 1977 by a merger between the Progressive Party and members of the United Party

progressive jazz *n* a form of experimental, free-flowing, and improvisational jazz that uses dissonance and complex rhythms

Progressive Party *n* **1** in the United States, any of three related political parties that favoured social reform and were active in the presidential elections of 1912, 1924, and 1948 **2** a Canadian national political party formed in 1920 from members of farmers' movements and dissident Liberals that was dissolved in 1942

Progressive Rock *n* rock music originating in the early 1970s and characterized by technically elaborate and sometimes experimental arrangements

progressivism /prə gréssivizəm/ *n* **1** the beliefs and practices of progressives **2** the theories and practices of progressive education —**progessivist** *n*

progress payment *n* a part of a larger payment made to a contractor when a stage of a job is completed

prohibit /prə híbbit/ *vt* **1** to forbid somebody to do something by a law or rule **2** to prevent somebody from doing something [15C. < Latin *prohibit-*, past participle of *prohibere* 'hold back' < *hibere* 'to hold'.] —**prohibiter** *n*

prohibition /prṓ i bísh'n/ *n* **1 FORBIDDING** the act or process of forbidding something **2 ORDER THAT FORBIDS** an act or order that forbids something **3 COURT ORDER** an order from a superior court that forbids an inferior court to decide on a matter beyond its jurisdiction **4 OUTLAWING OF TRADE IN ALCOHOLIC BEVERAGES** a policy that forbids by law the manufacture, sale, and transport of alcoholic beverages [14C. Directly or via French < Latin *prohibition-* < *prohibere* (see PROHIBIT).] —**prohibitionary** *adj*

Prohibitionism /prṓ i bísh'nizəm/, **prohibitionism** *n* the policy or belief that the manufacture and sale of alcoholic beverages should not be allowed by law —**Prohibitionist** *n*

Prohibition Party *n* a political party in the United States founded in 1869 that advocated the banning of alcoholic beverages

prohibitive /prə híbbitiv/ *adj* **1** too expensive or costly for most people to buy **2** prohibiting or forbidding something —**prohibitively** *adv* —**prohibitiveness** *n*

prohibitory /prə híbbitəri/ *adj* (*formal*) **1** likely to prevent or forbid something **2** preventing or forbidding something

proinsulin /prō ínssyŏŏlin/ *n* the inactive precursor of insulin produced in the pancreas

project *n* /prójjekt/ **1 TASK OR SCHEME** a task or scheme that requires a large amount of time, effort, and planning to complete **2 UNIT OF WORK** an organized unit of work ○ *a school project* **3 PUBLIC WORK** an extensive organized public undertaking ○ *a construction project* **4** *US* PUBLIC ADMIN = **housing project** (*often plural*) ■ *v* /prə jékt/ **1** *vt* **ESTIMATE** to estimate something by extrapolating data ○ *They projected 3% annual growth.* **2** *vti* **STICK OUT** to jut out beyond or farther than something ○ *The balcony projected several metres.* **3** *vt* **COMMUNICATE** to communicate something effectively ○ *He projects himself as a confident man.* **4** *vt* **BELIEVE OTHERS SHARE MENTAL LIFE** to make a thought or feeling seem to have an external and objective reality, especially to ascribe something personal to others ○ *He had projected his fear of heights onto her.* **5** *vt* **THROW** to throw or cast something (*formal; usually passive*) ○ *The ball was projected several metres upwards.* **6** *vt* **PROPOSE PLAN** to propose a plan of action (*often passive*) ○ *The tour was projected for the following summer.* **7** *vt* **DIRECT IMAGE ONTO SURFACE** to make an image appear on a surface ○ *projected the photograph onto the screen* **8** *vt* **IMAGINE** to use the imagination to see or remember something ○ *She projected herself back into the past.* **9** *vti* **MAKE VOICE AUDIBLE** to make the voice heard clearly and at a distance, or be effective in making the voice heard ○ *She projected her voice to the back of the auditorium.* **10** *vt* **DRAW PROJECTION OF FIGURE** to transform a geometric figure into another by drawing straight lines through every point of the figure to another plane [14C. < Latin *projectum* 'something thrown forwards' < *proicere* 'throw forwards' < *jacere* 'to throw'.]

projectile /prō jék tīl/ *n* **MISSILE OR SHELL** an object that can be fired or launched, e.g. an artillery shell or a rocket ■ *adj* **1 CAPABLE OF BEING THRUST FORWARDS** describes a part of an animal's body that can be thrust forwards, e.g. the jaws in some types of fish **2 IMPELLED FORWARDS** hurled or impelled forwards

projection /prə jéksh'n/ *n* **1 ESTIMATE** an estimate of the rate or amount of something **2 SOMETHING THAT STICKS OUT** something that juts out or overhangs **3 PROTRUSION** the act or process of protruding **4 CASTING OF SOMETHING ON SURFACE** the projecting of an image or picture on a surface **5 SOMETHING CAST ON SURFACE** an image or picture projected on a surface **6 UNCONSCIOUS TRANSFER OF INNER MENTAL LIFE** the unconscious ascription of a personal thought, feeling, or impulse to somebody else, especially a thought or feeling considered undesirable **7 REPRESENTATION ON SURFACE** a means of representing lines, figures, or solids on a flat surface such as a map that conforms to the viewing direction or follows particular rules **8 DRAWN REPRESENTATION** the representation of a line, figure, or solid on a flat surface **9 MIXING BY ALCHEMISTS** in alchemy, the mixing of powdered philosopher's stone with base metals in order to supposedly transmute them into gold or silver —**projectional** *adj*

projection booth *n US* CINEMA, THEATRE = **projection room**

projectionist /prə jéksh'nist/ *n* somebody whose job is to operate the projector and screen the film in a cinema and take responsibility for the quality of the image and sound

projection room *n* an enclosed compartment in a theatre from where films, slides, or lights are projected onto a screen or a stage. US term **projection booth**

projection television, projection TV *n* a television picture display system in which an enlarged picture is projected onto a screen

projective /prə jéktiv/ *adj* **1** relating to or made by projection **2** relating to or involving a psychological test in which something mentally hidden is revealed by a personal response to an image or group of images —**projectively** *adv*

projective geometry *n* the study of those properties of plane geometric figures that do not vary when they are projected onto another plane and of the transformations of size and perspective that accompany this

projective test *n* a psychological test that uses images in order to evoke responses from a subject and reveal hidden elements of the subject's mental life

projector /prə jéktər/ *n* a piece of equipment for projecting the image from film onto a screen and for playing back recorded sound from tracks on the film

projet /prózhay/ *n* a plan or outline, especially of a draft law or treaty [Early 19C. Via French < Latin *projectum* (see PROJECT).]

prokaryon /prō kárri on/ *n* the nucleus of a cell or organism with no membrane separating the area containing DNA from the rest of it [Mid-20C. < Greek *pro-* 'before' + *karuon* 'nut'.]

prokaryote /prō kárri ot/, **procaryote** *n* an organism such as a bacterium, whose DNA is not contained within a nucleus [Mid-20C. French < Greek *karuōtos* 'having nuts' < *karuon* 'nut'.] —**prokaryotic** /prō kárri óttik/ *adj*

Prokofiev /prə kóffi ef/, **Sergey Sergeyevich** (1891–1953) Russian composer

prolactin /prō láktin/ *n* a pituitary hormone that stimulates lactation after childbirth

prolamine /prṓlə meen, -min/ *n* a simple protein found in grains [Early 20C. < PROLINE + AMMONIA.]

prolapse /prṓ laps, prō láps/ *n* **prolapse, prolapsus** a slippage or sinking of a body organ or part such as a valve of the heart from its usual position ■ *vi* (**-lapses, -lapsing, -lapsed**) to slip or fall out of its proper place in the body [Late 16C. < Latin *prolaps-*, past participle of *prolabi* 'fall forwards' < *labi* 'to fall'.] —**prolapsed** *adj*

prole /prōl/ *n* a proletarian (*informal insult*) ■ *adj* proletarian (*informal*) [Late 19C. Shortening.]

proleg /prṓ leg/ *n* a leg on the abdomen of a caterpillar or other insect larva

prolegomenon /prṓ le gómminən/ (*plural* **-na** /-gómminə/) *n* a preliminary discussion or introductory essay, especially to a book or treatise [Mid-17C. < Greek, < *prolegein* 'say before' < *legein* 'say'.] —**prolegomenal** *adj*

prolepsis /prō lépsiss/ (*plural* **-ses** /-seez/) *n* **1** a preface intended to anticipate and answer an objection to an argument **2** the use after a verb of an adjective that anticipates the result of the verb's action, e.g. 'to iron a shirt smooth' [Late 16C. Via Latin < Greek *prolambanein* 'take before' < *lambanein* 'to take'.] —**proleptic** /prō léptik/ *adj*

proletarian /prṓlə táiri ən/ *adj* **OF WORKING CLASS** relating to the working class ■ *n* **1 WORKER** a member of the working class **2 INDUSTRIAL WAGE-EARNER** in Marxist theory, a member of the industrial working class whose only asset is labour sold to an employer **3 IMPOVERISHED ANCIENT ROMAN** a member of an impoverished social class of ancient Rome that had the lowest status and possessed no property [Mid-17C. < Latin *proletarius* 'low-status Roman who serves the state only by producing offspring' < *proles* 'offspring'.] —**proletarianism** *n*

proletariat /prṓlə táiri ət/ *n* **1 WORKING CLASS** the class of wage-earning workers in society (*takes a singular or plural verb*) **2 CLASS OF INDUSTRIAL WAGE-EARNERS** in Marxist theory, the class of industrial workers whose only asset is the labour they sell to an employer **3 ANCIENT ROMAN SOCIAL CLASS** a social class of ancient Rome that had the lowest status and possessed no property [Mid-19C. < French *prolétariat* < Latin *proletarius* (see PROLETARIAN).]

pro-life *adj* in favour of bringing the human foetus to full term, especially by campaigning against abortion and experimentation on embryos —**pro-lifer** *n*

proliferate /prə líffə rayt/ (**-ates, -ating, -ated**) *v* **1** *vi* to increase greatly in number **2** *vti* to multiply or be multiplied in the process of reproducing new cells, offspring, or parts, as in the budding of plants [Late 19C. Back-formation < *proliferation* < French *prolifération* < medieval Latin *prolifer* (see PROLIFEROUS).] —**proliferation** /prə líffə ráysh'n/ *n* —**proliferative** /-ərətiv/ *adj*

proliferous /prə líffərəss/ *adj* producing or growing many cells, buds, or shoots [Mid-17C. < medieval Latin *prolifer* 'bearing offspring' < *proles* 'offspring'.]

prolific /prə líffik/ *adj* **1 PRODUCTIVE** highly productive **2 FRUITFUL** abounding or fruitful (*formal*) **3 PRODUCING FRUIT OR OFFSPRING** producing a lot of fruit or many offspring [Mid-17C. < medieval Latin *prolificus* < *proles* 'offspring'.] —**prolificacy** *n* —**prolifically** *adv*

proline /prṓ leen/ *n* an amino acid found in many proteins, particularly in collagen [Early 20C. Contraction of *pyrrolidine*-2-carboxylic acid.]

prolix /prṓliks, prō líks/ *adj* tiresomely wordy [15C. Directly or via French < Latin *prolixus* 'that has flowed out' < the past participle of *liquere* 'to flow'.] —**prolixity** *n* —**prolixly** *adv*

SYNONYMS See ***wordy***.

prolocutor /prō lókyŏŏtər/ *n* a person who chairs an ecclesiastical convocation in the Anglican Church [15C. Latin, 'pleader, advocate' < *proloqui* 'speak out' < *loqui* 'speak'.] —**prolocutorship** *n*

prolog *n US* = **prologue**

ϟ **Prolog** /prṓ log/, **PROLOG** *n* a high-level programming language based on logical rather than mathematical relationships

prologue /prṓ log/ *n* **1 INTRODUCTORY STATEMENT** an introductory passage or speech before the main action of a novel, play, or long poem **2 ACTOR INTRODUCING ACTION OF PLAY** an actor who speaks introductory lines to a dramatic performance before the main action begins **3 PRELIMINARY EVENT** an event or act that leads to something more important ■ *vt* (**-logues, -loguing, -logued**) **PREFACE WITH PROLOGUE** to preface something such as a novel or play with a prologue [14C. Via French and Latin < Greek *prologos* 'speech before' < *logos* 'speech'.]

prolong /prə lóng/ *vt* to make something go on longer [15C. Directly or via French *prolonger* < late Latin *prolongare* 'lengthen out' < Latin *longus* 'long'.] —**prolongation** /prō long gáysh'n/ *n* —**prolonger** *n* —**prolongment** *n*

prolonge /prə lónj/ *n* a rope with a hook and a toggle used to tow something heavy, especially a gun carriage [Mid-19C. < French *prolonger* (see PROLONG).]

prom /prom/ *n* **1** = **promenade** *n.* 1 (*informal*) **2** a promenade concert (*informal*) **3** *US* a formal high-school or college dance for students, usually held at the end of the school year [Late 19C. Shortening of PROMENADE.]

ϟ**PROM** /prom/ *abbr* programmable read-only memory

prom. *abbr* promontory

promenade /prómmə naád/ *n* **1 SEAFRONT PATH** a paved path or terrace along a seafront **2 WALK FOR PLEASURE** a leisurely walk or stroll, usually in a public place, that is taken for pleasure or to be seen (*formal*) **3 MARCHING DANCE MOVEMENT** a marching movement in country dancing ■ *v* (**-nades, -nading, -naded**) **1** *vti* **STROLL IN PUBLIC PLACE** to walk in a slow and leisurely way, especially up and down a street or in a public place **2** *vi* **MARCH DURING DANCE** to perform a marching movement in country dancing [Mid-16C. < French, < *se promener* 'go for a walk' < late Latin *prominare* 'drive forwards' < *minare* 'to drive'.]

promenade concert *n* a concert, usually of classical music, at which part of the audience stands in an area without seating

promenade deck *n* a covered upper deck on a passenger ship on which passengers can walk

promethazine /prō méthə zeen/ *n* $C_{17}H_{20}N_2S$ an antihistamine drug. Use: treatment of allergies, motion sickness. [Mid-20C. < PROPYL + METHYL + AZINE.]

Promethean /prə meéthi ən/ *adj* **1** relating to Prometheus **2** creative and imaginatively original

Prometheus[1] /prə meéthi əss/ *n* in Greek mythology, a Titan who became a hero to humankind because he stole fire from the gods and gave it to them [Late 16C. Via Latin < Greek.]

Prometheus[2] /prə meéthi əss/ *n* a small inner natural satellite of Saturn

promethium /prə meéthi əm/ *n* (*symbol* **Pm**) a radioactive metallic element. Source: fission of uranium, thorium, or plutonium. Use: phosphorescent paints, X-ray source. [Mid-20C. After PROMETHEUS[1].]

prominence /prómminənss/, **prominency** /-nənssi/ (*plural* **-cies**) *n* **1 CONSPICUOUS IMPORTANCE** the condition or quality of being significantly important or well-known **2 SOMETHING THAT STICKS OUT** something that projects or protrudes, especially a geographic feature or a body part **3 GAS STREAM FROM SUN** a visible stream of glowing gas that shoots out from the Sun, seen in the upper chromosphere and lower corona

prominent /prómminənt/ *adj* **1 STICKING OUT** large and projecting **2 NOTICEABLE** noticeable or conspicuous **3 WELL-KNOWN** distinguished, eminent, or well-known [15C. < Latin *prominere* 'project forwards' < *minere* 'to project'.] —**prominently** *adv* —**prominentness** *n*

~~promiscous~~ incorrect spelling of **promiscuous**

promiscuity /prómmi skyoó əti/ *n* **1** behaviour characterized by casual and indiscriminate sexual intercourse, often with many people (*disapproving*) **2** a confused or indiscriminate mixing of elements (*formal*)

promiscuous /prə mískyoo əss/ *adj* **1 SEXUALLY INDISCRIMINATE** having many indiscriminate or casual sexual relationships (*disapproving*) **2 CONFUSEDLY MIXED** mixed in an indiscriminate or disorderly way (*formal*) **3 CHOOSING WITHOUT DISCRIMINATING** choosing carelessly or without discrimination (*disapproving*) **4 RANDOM** occurring without any set or specific pattern or time (*literary*) ○ *a sail caught by a promiscuous wind* [Early 17C. < Latin *promiscuus* 'mixed forwards' < *miscere* 'to mix'.] —**promiscuously** *adv* —**promiscuousness** *n*

promise /prómmiss/ *v* (**-ises, -ising, -ised**) **1** *vti* **VOW** to assure somebody that something will certainly happen or be done ○ *Promise that you'll be home on time.* **2** *vt* **PLEDGE** to pledge to somebody to provide or do something ○ *He promised the children a kitten.* **3** *vti* **MAKE SOMEBODY EXPECT** to cause somebody to expect something ○ *The overcast sky promised rain.* **4** *vt* **ASSURE OR WARN** to assure or warn somebody that something is true or inevitable ○ *Things will be fine, I promise you.* **5** *vt* **AFFIANCE** to engage somebody to be married (*dated*) ○ *She told him that she was promised to someone else.* ■ *n* **1 ASSURANCE OR UNDERTAKING** an assurance that something will be done or not done ○ *He never keeps his promises.* **2 GOOD INDICATION** an indication that somebody or something will turn out well or successfully ○ *She showed great promise as an athlete.* [14C. Directly or via French *promesse* < Latin *promissum* < *promittere* 'send forward' < *mittere* 'send'.] —**promisee** /prómmi seé/ *n* —**promiser** *n* —**promisor** /prómmi sáwr/ *n*

promising /prómmissing/ *adj* likely to be successful or to turn out well —**promisingly** *adv*

promissory /prómmissəri/ *adj* **1** concerning, containing, or implying a promise **2** stating how the terms of an insurance contract will be fulfilled [15C. < medieval Latin *promissorius* < Latin *promittere* (see PROMISE).]

promissory note *n* a signed agreement promising payment of a sum of money on demand or at a particular time

promo /prṓmō/ *n* (*plural* **-mos**) something that promotes or advertises a product, e.g. a recorded announcement, commercial, or video (*informal*) ■ *adj* involved or engaged in the promotion or advertising of something [Mid-20C. Shortening of PROMOTION or *promotional*.]

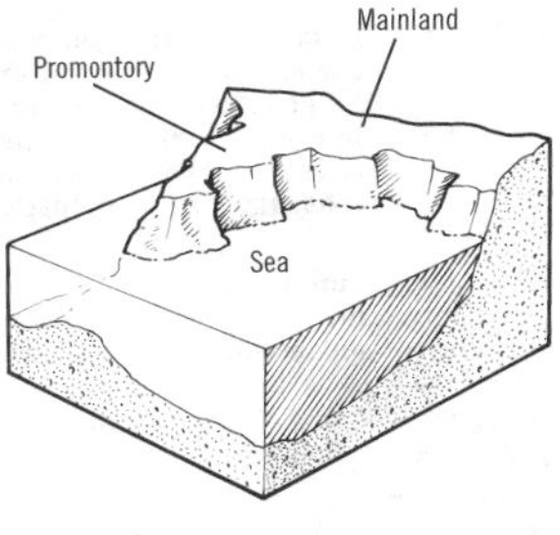

Promontory

promontory /prómməntəri/ (*plural* **-ries**) *n* **1** a point of land that juts out into the sea **2** a prominent or protruding part of the body [Mid-16C. < medieval Latin *promontorium*, alteration of Latin *promunturium*.]

promote /prə mṓt/ (**-motes, -moting, -moted**) *vt* **1 ADVANCE IN POSITION** to raise somebody to a more senior job or a higher position or rank **2 SUPPORT OR ENCOURAGE** to encourage the growth and development of something **3 ADVERTISE** to publicize a product so that people will buy or hire it **4 ADVANCE** to further something by helping to arrange or introduce it **5 EXCHANGE PAWN FOR MORE POWERFUL PIECE** in chess, to exchange a pawn for a more powerful piece, especially a queen, when it reaches an opponent's end of the board [14C. < Latin *promot-*, past participle of *promovere* 'move forwards' < *movere* 'to move'.] —**promotable** *adj*

promoter /prə mṓtər/ *n* **1 ARRANGER OF PUBLIC EVENT** a person or organization that stages entertainment, a sporting contest, or other public event **2 ACQUIRER OF CAPITAL FOR VENTURE** a person who raises money for a financial or commercial undertaking **3 BINDING SITE IN DNA CHAIN** in a DNA chain, a sequence to which the enzyme RNA polymerase binds so as to start transcription **4 SUBSTANCE ADDED TO CATALYST** a chemical additive that increases the efficiency of a catalyst **5 SOMETHING THAT ENCOURAGES TUMOUR CELLS** a substance that when given after a carcinogen encourages tumour cells to form or grow

promoter gene *n* GENETICS = **promoter** *n.* 3

promotion /prə mṓsh'n/ *n* **1 ADVANCEMENT IN POSITION** an advancement to a more senior job or a higher rank, grade, or position **2 SOMETHING THAT PROMOTES** something that is designed to promote or advertise a product, cause, or organization **3 ENCOURAGEMENT FOR ACTIVITY** encouragement for the growth or development of something **4 ADVANCE INTO HIGHER DIVISION** advance by a sports team into a higher division of a league **5 EXCHANGE OF PAWN FOR SUPERIOR PIECE** in chess, the act of exchanging a pawn for a more powerful piece, usually a queen, when it reaches an opponent's end of the board —**promotional** *adj*

promotive /prə mṓtiv/ *adj* tending to further or encourage something —**promotiveness** *n*

ϟ**prompt** /prompt/ *adj* **1 DONE IMMEDIATELY** done at once and without delay **2 QUICK TO ACT** ready, punctual, or quick to act ■ *adv* **PUNCTUALLY** in a punctual way (*informal*) ■ *v* **1** *vt* **URGE INTO ACTION** to incite or urge somebody to do something **2** *vt* **BRING ABOUT** to give rise to something **3** *vti* **PROVIDE ACTOR WITH LINES** to provide actors or performers with the words or lines they have forgotten **4** *vt* **REMIND OR SUGGEST** to suggest something or give a reminder to a speaker ■ *n* **1 REMINDER OF WORDS TO PERFORMER** words or lines supplied to a performer who has forgotten them **2 OCCURRENCE OF PROMPT** the act or occasion of words being supplied to a performer who has forgotten them **3 SOMETHING CUEING RESPONSE** a symbol or message displayed on a computer monitor or an audio signal informing a computer user that some input is required **4 TIME LIMIT FOR PAYMENT** the time limit of payment for goods or services, as stated on a prompt note [14C. < Latin *promptus* 'ready', past participle of *promere*, literally 'take forward' < *emere* 'to take'.] —**promptly** *adv* —**promptness** *n*

promptbook /prómpt bŏŏk/ *n* a copy of a script for a prompter to use

prompt box *n* a box situated beneath the stage in a theatre in which the prompter sits

prompter /prómptər/ *n* somebody in a theatre whose job is to prompt actors who have forgotten their words or lines

promptitude /prómpti tyood/ *n* punctuality or quickness to act

prompt note *n* a written reminder sent to the purchaser of something, stating when payment is due

prompt side *n* the side of the stage in a theatre where the prompter sits

promulgate /prómm'l gayt/ (**-gates, -gating, -gated**) *vt* (*formal*) **1** to proclaim or declare something officially, especially to publicize formally that a law or decree is in effect **2** to make something widely known [Mid-16C. < Latin *promulgare* 'milk forward' < *mulgere* 'to milk'.] —**promulgation** /-gáysh'n/ *n* —**promulgator** /-gaytər/ *n*

pron. *abbr* **1** pronominal **2** pronoun **3** pronounced **4** pronunciation

pronate /prṓ nayt/ (**-nates, -nating, -nated**) *v* **1** *vt* to turn the hand or forearm so that the palm faces downwards **2** *vti* to rotate the bones of the foot so that the weight is borne mainly on the inside of the foot [Mid-19C. Back-formation < *pronation* < PRONE or Latin *pronus* (see PRONE).] —**pronation** /prō náysh'n/ *n*

pronator /prṓ naytər/ *n* a muscle that turns a part of the body so that it faces downwards, e.g. one of the muscles in the forearm that rotates the hand into the palm-down position [Early 18C. < modern Latin, < Latin *pronus* (see PRONE), after SUPINATOR.]

prone /prōn/ *adj* **1 DISPOSED** inclined to do or be affected by something **2 FACE DOWN** lying face down **3 IN DOWNWARD DIRECTION** sloping, leaning, or moving downwards [15C. < Latin *pronus* 'bent forwards' < *pro* 'forwards'.] —**pronely** *adv* —**proneness** *n*

pronephros /prō néff ross/ (*plural* **-roi** /-roy/ *or* **-ra** /-rə/) *n* the first of three segments of the kidney, functional in some vertebrate embryos but not in adults [Late 19C. < PRO[2] + Greek *nephros* 'kidney'.] —**pronephric** *adj*

prong /prong/ *n* a thin sharp point at the end of something ■ *vt* to prick or stab something with a sharp pointed end [15C. < Anglo-Latin *pronga*.] —**pronged** *adj*

pronghorn /próng hawrn/, **pronghorn antelope** *n* an animal similar to an antelope that is the fastest North American mammal. Native to: Mexico, W United States. *Antilocapra americana*.

pronominal /prō nómmin'l/ *adj* like or functioning as a pronoun ■ *n* a word that functions like a pronoun [Late 17C. < late Latin *pronominalis* 'belonging to a pronoun' < Latin *pronomen* (see PRONOUN).] —**pronominally** *adv*

pronominalize /prō nómminə līz/ (**-izes, -izing, -ized**), **pronominalise** (**-ises, -ising, -ised**) *vt* in transformational grammars, to replace a noun or noun phrase in a sentence with a pronoun —**pronominalization** *n*

pronoun /prṓ nown/ *n* a word that substitutes for a noun or a noun phrase, e.g. 'I', 'you', 'them', 'it', 'ours', 'who', 'which', 'myself', and 'anybody' [15C. < NOUN after French *pronom* and Latin *pronomen* 'in place of a name' < *nomen* 'name'.]

pronounce /prə nównss/ (**-nounces, -nouncing, -nounced**) *v* **1** *vti* UTTER SOUNDS OR WORDS to articulate sounds or words, especially in a way acceptable to the person to whom they are spoken or by most speakers of a language **2** *vti* FORMALLY DECLARE to declare something officially to be the case **3** *vt* GIVE JUDGMENT to render an opinion or judgment **4** *vt* SYMBOLIZE SOUND OF WORD to indicate with symbols how a word should be spoken [14C. Via Old French *pronuncier* < Latin *pronuntiare* 'announce before' < *nuntiare* 'announce'.] —**pronounceable** *adj* —**pronouncement** *n* —**pronouncer** *n*

pronounced /prə nównst/ *adj* **1** noticeable or obvious **2** voiced or spoken —**pronouncedly** /prə nównssidli/ *adv*

~~**pronounciation**~~ incorrect spelling of **pronunciation**

pronto /próntō/ *adv* in a prompt or rapid way (*informal*) [Mid-19C. Via Spanish < Latin *promptus* (see PROMPT).]

pronuclear /prō nyóokli ər/ *adj* **1** in favour of using nuclear power in weapons or as a source of energy **2** relating to a pronucleus —**pronuclearist** *n, adj*

pronucleus /prō nyóokli əss/ (*plural* **-i** /-ī/ *or* **-uses**) *n* the nucleus of a fully matured ovum or spermatozoan before the nuclei are fused during fertilization

pronunciamento /prə núnssi ə méntō/ (*plural* **-tos**) *n* an announcement, proclamation, or manifesto, especially one issued by a revolutionary group [Mid-19C. < Spanish, < Latin *pronuntiare* (see PRONOUNCE).]

pronunciation /prə núnssi áysh'n/ *n* **1** MAKING SOUNDS OF SPEECH the way in which a sound, word, or language is articulated, especially in conforming to an accepted standard **2** ACT OF SPEECH the act of articulating a sound or word **3** TRANSCRIPTION OF SOUNDS a phonetic transcription of sounds [15C. Directly or via French < Latin *pronuntiation-* < *pronuntiare* (see PRONOUNCE).]

pro-oestrus /prō éestrəss/ *n* the period in the oestrus cycle immediately preceding oestrus

proof /proof/ *n* **1** CONCLUSIVE EVIDENCE evidence or an argument that serves to establish a fact or the truth of something **2** TEST a test or trial of something to establish whether it is true **3** STATE OF HAVING BEEN PROVED the quality or condition of having been proved **4** TRIAL EVIDENCE the evidence in a trial that helps to determine the court's decision **5** SCOTTISH LEGAL PROCESS OR TRIAL in Scottish law, a process by which evidence in a civil case is heard prior to a trial, or a civil trial before a judge and without a jury to determine the issues on which the trial will take place **6** STRENGTH OF ALCOHOLIC CONTENT the relative strength of an alcoholic beverage measured against a standard and expressed by a number that is twice the percentage of the alcohol present in the liquid **7** PRINTING IMPRESSION an impression used for checking corrections before the final printing of an image or text **8** SEQUENCE OF STEPS TO VALIDATE SOLUTION the sequence of steps or stages used in establishing the validity of a mathematical or philosophical proposition **9** ARTIST'S IMPRESSION an impression taken from an engraved plate before it is printed **10** PRINT FROM NEGATIVE a photographic print made from a negative and checked for quality prior to further reproduction **11** COIN IMPRESSION a preliminary impression of a coin, intended as a specimen for display ■ *adj* **1** IMPERVIOUS capable of resisting something that may have a harmful or unwanted effect **2** HAVING RELATIVE ALCOHOLIC STRENGTH having a specific alcoholic strength that is expressed by a number that is twice the percentage of alcohol present in the liquid (*often in combination*) **3** RESISTANT capable of resisting or withstanding something ■ *vt* **1** MAKE RESISTANT to make something capable of resisting harm, injury, or damage **2** PRINT PROOF to make a trial impression of something printed or engraved **3** INSPECT FOR ERRORS to proofread a text, or inspect a printed impression for errors **4** *US* ACTIVATE YEAST to cause yeast to become active by adding water and often sugar [13C. Alteration of *pref* (influenced by PROVE), via Old French *preve* < Latin *proba* < *probare* 'to prove, test'.]

proof of purchase *n* evidence such as a receipt that shows that something has been paid for

proofread /proof reed/ (**-reads, -reading, -read** /-red/) *vti* to read the proofs of a text in order to correct them —**proofreader** *n*

proof sheet *n* a sheet of paper that has a printer's proof on it, usually with wide margins so that corrections can be marked up easily

proof spirit *n* an alcoholic beverage or a mixture of alcohol and water formerly used as a standard for measuring alcoholic strength

proof theory *n* the part of the theory of logic concerned with the exact nature of deriving propositions and conclusions

prop[1] /prop/ *n* **1** RIGID SUPPORT a rigid object such as a beam, stake, or pole that supports something or holds it in place **2** COMFORTING PERSON OR THING somebody or something that provides comfort or assistance **3** RUGBY FORWARD in rugby, a forward at either end of the front row of a scrum **4** *Aus* SUDDEN STOP a sudden or unexpected stop, especially of a horse ■ *v* (**props, propping, propped**) **1** *vt* SUPPORT WITH PROP to use a rigid object to support something or hold it in place **2** *vi Aus* STOP ABRUPTLY to come to a sudden and unexpected stop (*refers to a horse*) [15C. < Middle Dutch *proppe* 'vine prop, support'.]

prop up *vt* to give support or help to somebody or something

prop[2] /prop/ *n* an object used during the performance of a play or film [Mid-19C. Shortening of PROPERTY.]

prop[3] /prop/ *n* an aircraft propeller (*informal*) [Early 20C. Shortening.]

prop. *abbr* **1** proper **2** properly **3** property **4** proposition **5** proprietor

propaedeutic /prō pee dyóotik/ *adj* providing preparatory instruction (*formal*) ■ *n* a preliminary course of study that introduces more advanced instruction (*often plural*) [Late 18C. < PRO[2] + *paedeutics* 'teaching', after Greek *propaideuein* 'teach beforehand'.]

propaganda /próppə gándə/ *n* **1** information or publicity put out by an organization or government to spread and promote a policy, idea, doctrine, or cause **2** deceptive or distorted information that is systematically spread [Early 18C. < modern Latin *Propaganda Fide* 'propagating the faith'.] —**propagandism** *n* —**propagandist** *n, adj*

Propaganda *n* a committee of Roman Catholic cardinals, the Congregation for the Propagation of the Faith, in charge of supervising foreign missions and educating priests to serve in them

propagandize /próppə gán dīz/ (**-dizes, -dizing, -dized**), **propagandise** (**-dises, -dising, -dised**) *vti* to organize or spread propaganda

propagate /próppə gayt/ (**-gates, -gating, -gated**) *v* **1** *vti* REPRODUCE ORGANISM to reproduce a plant or animal, or cause one to reproduce **2** *vti* CREATE NEW PLANTS to multiply plants by the use of seeds or cuttings **3** *vt* SPREAD SOMETHING WIDELY to spread ideas or customs to many people **4** *vti* IMPEL SOMETHING FORWARDS to move or transmit something forwards in space, especially as a light or sound wave [Late 16C. < Latin *propagare* 'breed plants in layers (of vines)' < *propago* 'layer'.] —**propagability** /próppəgə bílləti/ *n* —**propagable** *adj* —**propagableness** *n* —**propagation** /próppə gáysh'n/ *n* —**propagational** *adj* —**propagative** *adj*

propagator /próppə gaytər/ *n* **1** a disseminator of ideas or beliefs **2** a shallow box with a transparent cover used for germinating seeds or allowing cuttings to take root, especially one that can be heated

propagule /próppə gyool/, **propagulum** /prō pággyoolәm/ *n* a part of a plant or fungus such as a bud or a spore that becomes detached from the rest and forms a new organism [Mid-19C. < modern Latin *propagulum* 'little shoot' < *propago* 'layer'.]

propane /prō payn/ *n* C_3H_8 a flammable colourless hydrocarbon gas. Use: fuel, propellant, refrigerant. [Mid-19C. < PROPIONIC.]

propanoic acid /prōpə nō ik-/ *n* CHEM = **propionic acid** [< PROPANE]

propanol /prōpə nol/ *n* CHEM = **propyl alcohol**

propanone /prōpə nōn/ *n* acetone (*technical*)

proparoxytone /prōpə róksitōn/ *n* in classical Greek grammar, a word that has an acute accent on the third syllable from the end, or a heavy stress on this syllable ■ *adj* with or using a proparoxytone [Mid-18C. < Greek *proparoxutonos* 'having an accent before the last syllable' < *oxutonos* 'having an acute accent'.]

propel /prə pél/ (**-pels, -pelling, -pelled**) *vt* **1** to move or push something or somebody forwards **2** to impel or cause a course of action [15C. < Latin *propellere* 'drive forwards' < *pellere* 'to drive'.]

propellant /prə péllənt/, **propellent** *n* **1** EXPLOSIVE SUBSTANCE a substance that is burned to give upward thrust to a rocket **2** EXPLOSIVE CHARGE FOR GUN an explosive charge that projects a bullet from a gun **3** GAS IN AEROSOLS a compressed inert gas used to dispense the contents of an aerosol container when pressure is applied and released

propellent /prə péllənt/ *adj* tending to drive or move something forwards

propeller /prə péllər/ *n* a revolving shaft with spiral blades that causes a ship or an aircraft to move by the backward thrust of water or air

propeller shaft *n* **1** the shaft in a ship or aircraft that transmits power from the engine to the propeller **2** MECH ENG = **drive shaft** *n.* 1

propelling pencil *n* a pencil with a replaceable lead that can be extended as it gets worn down. US term **mechanical pencil**

~~**propellor**~~ incorrect spelling of **propeller**

propene /prō peen/ *n* CHEM = **propylene** [Mid-19C. < PROPYL + -ENE.]

propenoic acid /prōpə nō ik-/ *n* CHEM = **acrylic acid**

propensity /prə pénssəti/ (*plural* **-ties**) *n* a tendency to demonstrate particular behaviour [Late 16C. < obsolete *propense* 'inclined, prone' < Latin *propendere* 'hang forward' < *pendere* 'hang'.]

proper /próppər/ *adj* **1** CORRECT appropriate or correct ○ *need to put the issue in its proper perspective* **2** NEEDED AND APPROPRIATE fulfilling all expectations or criteria ○ *He needs proper medical care.* **3** WITH CORRECT MANNERS behaving in a respectable or socially acceptable way **4** CHARACTERISTIC characteristic of or belonging exclusively to somebody or something **5** NARROWLY IDENTIFIED strictly identified and distinguished from something else ○ *stayed in the suburbs, not the city proper* **6** *UK, Can* COMPLETE thorough and complete ○ *regards him as a proper nuisance* **7** SHOWING NATURAL COLOURS showing the natural colours in the design or device of a heraldic object **8** USED ON HOLY OCCASION reserved as a prayer, lesson, or rite for a holy day or festival **9** NON-IDENTICAL SET WITHIN SECOND SET included as a mathematical set in a second set but not being the same ■ *adv* **1** TOTALLY exceedingly or completely (*regional*) **2** PROPERLY in a correct or proper way (*nonstandard*) ■ *n* **proper, Proper** SERVICE FOR HOLY OCCASION a Christian church service that is used for a holy day or festival [13C. Directly or via Old French *propre* < Latin *proprius* 'your own, particular, special'.] —**properness** *n*

proper adjective *n* an adjective that is formed from a proper noun, as 'Canadian' is from 'Canada'

proper fraction *n* a fraction in which the value of the numerator is less than the value of the denominator, e.g. $\frac{6}{8}$

properly /próppərli/ *adv* **1** APPROPRIATELY in a suitable or appropriate way ○ *properly dressed for the occasion* **2** CORRECTLY in a correct or well-mannered way ○ *If you can't behave properly, we'll have to go home.* **3** IN REALITY in a correct and appropriate situation ○ *The chair properly belongs in the corner.* **4** TOTALLY to the fullest degree or extent ○ *By the end of the day she was properly tired.*

proper noun, proper name *n* the name of something particular, normally beginning with a capital letter and not used with the indefinite article or a modifier, e.g. 'York', 'Sally', or 'Henderson'

property /próppərti/ (*plural* **-ties**) *n* **1** SOMETHING OWNED something of value such as land or a patent that is owned **2** OWNED LAND OR REAL ESTATE a piece of land or real estate that is owned by somebody ○ *a property owner* **3** RIGHT TO OWN the right to own, possess, or use something **4** TRAIT OR ATTRIBUTE a characteristic quality or distinctive feature of something (*often plural*) **5** SOMETHING AT SOMEBODY'S DISPOSAL something at the disposal of a person, a group, or the public ○ *community property* **6** PROP a stage prop (*formal*) **7** DISTINCTIVE BUT NOT ESSENTIAL QUALITY in the thought of Aristotle, an attribute or quality that is peculiar to a whole class or species but not essential to it [13C. Via Anglo-Norman *proprete* and French *propriété* < Latin *proprietas* 'ownership' < *proprius* 'your own, particular'.]

property centre *n* a place where property is advertised for sale or purchase and where conveyancing is offered by a group of solicitors

property tax *n* a tax that is based on the value of a house or other property

prop forward *n* RUGBY = **prop**[1] *n.* 3

prophage /prō fayj/ *n* a stable form of virus that infects bacteria, with genetic material that is integrated into and replicated with that of its host without harming the host [Mid-20C. < PRO[2].]

prophase /prṓ fayz/ *n* the first phase in cell division, when chromosomes condense and can be seen as two chromatids. ◊ **anaphase, metaphase, telophase** [Late 19C. < PRO[2].]

prophecy /prόffəssi/ (*plural* **-cies**) *n* **1 DIVINE PREDICTION** a prediction of a future event that reveals the will of a deity **2 PREDICTION** a prediction that something will occur in the future **3 ABILITY TO PREDICT THE FUTURE** the ability to predict the future when inspired by a deity [13C. Via Old French *prophecie* and late Latin *prophetia* < Greek *prophētia* < prophetētes (see PROPHET).]

USAGE prophecy or **prophesy**? Though spelled almost alike, these two words are pronounced differently and have different grammatical functions. ***Prophecy***, a noun only, means 'a prediction or the ability to predict the future', as in *a dire economic prophecy.* ***Prophesy***, a verb, means 'to predict', as in *would not go so far as to prophesy a recession just yet.*

prophesy /prόffə sī/ (**-sies, -sying, -sied**) *v* **1** *vti* to predict what is going to happen **2** *vi* to reveal the will of a deity in predicting a future event [14C. < Old French *prophecier* < *prophecie* (see PROPHECY).] —**prophesiable** *adj* —**prophesier** *n*

USAGE See ***prophecy***.

prophet /prόffit/ *n* **1 SOMEBODY WHO INTERPRETS DIVINE WILL** an interpreter or transmitter of a deity's commands **2 SOMEBODY PREDICTING FUTURE** a foreteller of the future ○ *prophets of economic doom* **3 ADVOCATE** an advocate of a cause or idea **4 INSPIRED LEADER** somebody considered to be an inspired leader or teacher [12C. Via French *prophète* and Latin *propheta* < Greek *prophētēs* 'somebody who speaks beforehand' < *phētēs* 'speaker'.]

SPELLCHECK See ***profit***.

Prophet /prόffit/ *n* **1** Muhammad, the founder of Islam **2** Joseph Smith, the founder of the Church of Jesus Christ of Latter-Day Saints. ■ **Prophets** *npl* the prophetic books of the Bible

prophetess /prόffi téss/ *n* a woman prophet

prophetic /prə féttik/ *adj* **1** predicting or foreshadowing something that does eventually happen **2** relating to a prophet —**prophetical** *adj* —**prophetically** *adv*

Prophet's Birthday *n* ISLAM = **Mawlid al-Nabi**

prophylactic /prόffi láktik/ *adj* guarding against infection or disease ■ *n* **1** HEALTH = **condom** (*formal*) **2** a drug or agent that prevents the development of disease [Late 16C. Via French *prophylactique* < Greek *prophulassein* 'keep guard in front of' < *phulassein* 'to guard'.] —**prophylactically** *adv*

prophylaxis /prόffi láksiss/ (*plural* **-es** /-lák seez/) *n* **1** treatment such as vaccination that prevents disease or stops it spreading **2** a dental treatment to remove plaque and tartar from the teeth [Mid-19C. < modern Latin, 'guarding in front of' < Greek *pro* 'in front of' + *phulaxis* 'guarding'.]

propinquity /prə píngkwəti/ *n* nearness in space, time, or relationship (*formal*) [14C. Directly or via Old French *propinquité* < Latin *propinquitas* < *prope* 'near'.]

propionate /prṓpi ə nayt/ *n* a chemical compound that is a salt or ester of propionic acid [Late 19C. < PROPIONIC.]

propionic /prṓpi ónnik/ *adj* derived from propionic acid [Mid-19C. < Greek *pro* 'in front' + *piōn* 'fat', because it is first in order of the fatty acids.]

propionic acid *n* $C_3H_6O_2$ a colourless liquid fatty acid. Use: manufacture of artificial flavours, perfumes, and preservatives.

propitiate /prə píshi ayt/ (**-ates, -ating, -ated**) *vt* to appease or conciliate somebody or something [Late 16C. < Latin *propitiare* 'make favourable' < *propitius* 'favourable'.] —**propitiable** *adj* —**propitiation** /prə píshi áysh'n/ *n* —**propitiator** *n* —**propitiatorily** *adv* —**propitiatory** *adj*

propitious /prə píshəss/ *adj* **1** favourable and likely to lead to success **2** kindly disposed or gracious (*formal*) [15C. Directly or via Old French < Latin *propitius* 'favourable'.] —**propitiously** *adv* —**propitiousness** *n*

propjet /próp jet/ *n* **1** AIR = **turboprop** *n.* **1 2** MECH ENG = **turboprop** *n.* **2** [Mid-20C. < PROPELLER + JET[1].]

proplastid /prō plástid/ *n* a small membranous sac found in some plant tissues that develops into a food-producing or storage organ (**plastid**)

propolis /própp əliss/ *n* a waxy resinous substance that comes from buds, used by bees as a cement and caulking in making their hives [Early 17C. Via Latin < Greek, 'before a city' < *polis* 'city', because it originally referred to a structure around the opening of the hive.]

proponent /prə pṓnənt/ *n* **1 ADVOCATE** an advocate of something **2 PRESENTER OF WILL** a presenter of a will for probate **3 PROPOSER** a proposer of something [Late 16C. < Latin *proponent-*, present participle of *proponere* 'put forth' < *ponere* 'to place'.]

proportion /prə páwrsh'n/ *n* **1 PART OF WHOLE** a quantity of something that is part of the whole amount or number ○ *What proportion of their time is spent on administration?* **2 RELATIONSHIP BETWEEN QUANTITIES** the relationship between two or more amounts or numbers, or between the parts of a whole ○ *The proportion of lorries to cars on the road has remained the same.* **3 RELATIVE SIZE** the correct or desirable relationship of size, quantity, or degree between two or more things or parts of something ○ *An understanding of proportion is essential for an architect.* **4 RELATIVE IMPORTANCE** the importance of different aspects of a situation when compared with each other ○ *The media blew the incident all out of proportion.* **5 RATIO** a relationship or ratio between two variables that remains fixed **6 EQUALITY OF TWO RATIOS** a relationship of equality between two ratios, in which the first term divided by the second equals the third divided by the fourth, as in $1/2 = 3/6$ ■ **proportions** *npl* **1 SIZE** the size or shape of something **2 IMPORTANCE** the importance or seriousness of something ■ *vt* **1 MAINTAIN RELATIONSHIP** to create or maintain a relationship of size, quantity, or degree between two or more things **2 BALANCE** to give something a pleasing shape, appropriate dimensions, or a harmonious arrangement of parts (*usually passive*) ○ *a beautifully proportioned design* [14C. Directly or via Old French < Latin *proportion-* < *pro portione* 'according to (each) part' < *portion-* 'part, portion'.] —**proportionability** /prə páwsh'nə bílləti/ *n* —**proportionable** *adj* —**proportionably** *adv* —**proportionment** *n*

proportional /prə páwrsh'nəl/ *adj* **1 IN PROPORTION** in the correct relationship of size, quantity, or degree to something else, or remaining in the same relationship when things change ○ *The rate of pay is proportional to the complexity of the task.* **2 RELATED BY A RATIO** related by or possessing a constant ratio ■ *n* **TERM IN PAIR OF EQUIVALENT RATIOS** any one of the four terms in a relationship of proportion between two ratios, where the first term divided by the second equals the third divided by the fourth —**proportionality** /prə páwrsh'n álləti/ *n* —**proportionally** /-páwrsh'nəli/ *adv*

proportional representation *n* an electoral system in which each party's share of the seats in government is the same as its share of all the votes cast

proportional tax *n* a tax in which the proportion of income paid in tax is constant when income rises

proportionate *adj* /prə páwrsh'nət/ having the correct relationship of size, quantity, or degree to something else, or remaining in the same relationship when things change ○ *The fall in price led to a proportionate rise in sales.* ■ *vt* /prə páwshə nayt/ (**-ates, -ating, -ated**) to give two or more things the correct relationship of size, quantity, or degree —**proportionately** /prə páwsh'nətli/ *adv* —**proportionateness** *n*

proposal /prə pṓz'l/ *n* **1 IDEA OR PLAN** a suggestion or intention, especially one put forward formally or officially **2 ACT OF PROPOSING** the act of making a suggestion or stating an intention **3 REQUEST TO MARRY** a request for somebody to enter into marriage **4 DRAFT LAW FROM EC** a draft law proposed by the European Commission to the Council of Ministers

propose /prə pṓz/ (**-poses, -posing, -posed**) *v* **1** *vt* **MAKE SUGGESTION** to put something forward, often formally or officially, e.g. an idea or suggested course of action ○ *Harsher penalties have been proposed.* **2** *vt* **STATE INTENTION** to announce a plan or intended course of action ○ *What do you propose to do about it?* **3** *vt* **NOMINATE** to put forward somebody's name for an elected position or a promotion ○ *propose her for the new position* **4** *vti* **REQUEST MARRIAGE** to ask somebody to marry ○ *He proposed while we were on holiday.* **5** *vt* **SUGGEST TOAST OR VOTE OF THANKS** to ask others to join in something such as a toast or a vote of thanks ○ *I propose a toast to Chris and Sarah.* [14C. < Old French *proposer* 'put forward' < *poser* (see POSE[1]), after Latin *proponere* 'put forward'.] —**proposable** *adj* —**proposer** *n*

proposita /prō pózzitə/ (*plural* **-tae** /-tee/) *n* a woman who is involved in legal proceedings [< Latin, feminine of *propositus* (see PROPOSITUS)]

propositi plural of **propositus**

proposition /próppə zísh'n/ *n* **1 PROPOSAL** an idea, offer, or plan put forward for consideration or discussion **2 STATEMENT** a statement of opinion or judgment **3 SUGGESTION OF SEXUAL INTERCOURSE** an invitation to have sexual intercourse **4 PRIVATE AGREEMENT** a private deal or agreement **5 SOMETHING TO BE FACED** something or somebody to be dealt with (*informal*) ○ *The news that he would be there certainly made the party a more attractive proposition.* **6 THEOREM** a statement or theorem to be demonstrated **7 MEANING OF DECLARATIVE SENTENCE** the meaning of a declarative sentence and what is said to be true or false ■ *vt* **1 SUGGEST SEX** to invite somebody to have sexual intercourse **2 OFFER SOMEBODY A DEAL** to offer to make a private deal or agreement with somebody [14C. Directly or via French < Latin *proposition-* < *proposit-*, past participle of *proponere* 'put forth' < *ponere* 'to place'.] —**propositional** *adj* —**propositionally** *adv*

propositional attitude *n* in philosophy, an attitude taken by somebody towards a proposition, e.g. in believing it, knowing it, or desiring it

propositional calculus *n* the branch of deductive logic that deals with the relationships formed between propositions by connectives, e.g. 'and', 'but', 'if', or 'or'

propositional function *n* LOGIC = **open sentence**

propositus /prō pózzitəss/ (*plural* **-ti** /-tī/) *n* **1 ORIGINAL ANCESTOR** the original ancestor of a line of descent **2 MAN LITIGANT** a man who is involved in legal proceedings **3 FIRST PERSON INVESTIGATED IN FAMILY STUDY** the first person to be investigated in the genetic study of a family [Mid-18C. < Latin, past participle of *proponere*.]

propound /prə pównd/ *vt* **1** to put forward a suggestion or theory for others to consider **2** to present a document to a court or other authority in order that its validity can be established [Mid-16C. Alteration of obsolete *propone* < Latin *proponere* (see PROPONENT).] —**propounder** *n*

propoxyphene /prō póksi feen/ *n* a mild narcotic drug chemically similar to methadone. Use: analgesic. [Mid-20C. < PROPIONIC + OXY- + PHEN- + -ENE.]

propranolol /prō prànnə lol/ *n* $C_{16}H_{21}NO_2$ a drug that slows heart rate and heart output. Use: treatment of angina pectoris, abnormal heart rhythm, migraine, high blood pressure. [Mid-20C. < PROPYL + PROPANOL with repetition of *-ol*.]

proprietary /prə prí ətəri/ *adj* **1 USED WITH EXCLUSIVE LEGAL RIGHT** used, manufactured, or sold by a person or company with an exclusive property right, e.g. a patent or trademark ○ *a proprietary drug* **2 EXHIBITING CHARACTERISTICS OF OWNERSHIP** exhibiting characteristics that imply or assume ownership of somebody or something ○ *The child kept a proprietary hold on the toy.* **3 RELATING TO OWNERS OR OWNERSHIP** relating to, involving, or associated with an owner, ownership, or something owned **4 PRIVATELY OWNED** privately owned and run ■ *n* (*plural* **-ies**) **1 PROPRIETARY AGENT** a drug or other substance made and sold under the legal protection of a trademark or patent **2 OWNER** an owner or a group of owners **3 OWNERSHIP** the right of ownership, or something exclusively owned [15C. Directly or via French < medieval Latin *proprietarius*, < late Latin, 'of a property holder' < Latin *proprietas* (see PROPERTY).] —**proprietarily** *adv*

proprietary name *n* a product name that is registered as a trademark

proprietor /prə prí ətər/ *n* **1 BUSINESS OWNER** the owner of a commercial enterprise or business establishment such as a shop, hotel, or restaurant **2 LEGAL OWNER** the legal owner of something **3 FREEHOLDER OF PROPERTY** somebody identified on the Land Registry as the freeholder of a property [15C. < PROPRIETARY + -OR[1].] —**proprietorial** /prə prí ə táwri əl/ *adj* —**proprietorially** *adv* —**proprietorship** *n*

propriety /prə prí əti/ *n* (*plural* **-ties**) **1 SOCIALLY CORRECT OR APPROPRIATE BEHAVIOUR** conformity to the standards of politeness, respect, decency, or morality conventionally accepted by a society **2 QUALITY OF BEING SOCIALLY APPROPRIATE** the quality of displaying behaviour thought to be correct or appropriate ■ **proprieties** *npl* **RULES OF ETIQUETTE** the accepted standards of correct or appropriate social behaviour [15C. Via Old French < Latin *proprietas* 'appropriateness, ownership' < (see PROPERTY).]

proprioceptor /própri ə séptər/ *n* a sensory nerve ending in muscles, tendons, and joints that provides a sense of the body's position by responding to stimuli from within the body [Early 20C. < Latin *proprius* 'your own' + RECEPTOR.] —**proprioception** /própri ə sépsh'n/ *n* —**proprioceptive** *adj*

prop root *n* a root that grows from the stem of a plant above the ground and helps to support it

props master *n* a person in charge of stage props

proptosis /prop tṓsiss/ *n* the forward displacement or protrusion of an organ of the body, especially an eyeball [Late 17C. Via late Latin < Greek *proptōsis* 'a falling forward' < *propiptein* 'fall forward'.]

propulsion /prə púlsh'n/ *n* **1** the process by which an object such as a motor vehicle, ship, aircraft, or missile is moved forwards **2** the force by which something such as a motor vehicle, rocket, or ship is moved forwards [Early 17C. < obsolete *propulse* 'drive away' < Latin *propulsare* < *propuls-*, past participle of *propellere* (see PROPEL).] —**propulsive** *adj* —**propulsory** *adj*

propyl /prṓp il/ *n* C_3H_7 either of two isomeric chemical groups or radicals derived from propane [Mid-19C. < PROPIONIC + -YL.]

propylaeum /próppi lée əm/ (*plural* **-a** /próppi lée ə/) *n* a colonnaded gate or entrance to a building, especially a temple, or to a group of buildings [Early 18C. Via Latin < Greek *propulaion*, form of *propulaios* 'before the gate' < *pulē* 'gate'.]

propyl alcohol *n* C_3H_8O a colourless alcohol. Use: solvent, antiseptic.

propylene /prṓpi leen/ *n* C_3H_6 a flammable gaseous hydrocarbon. Source: petroleum. Use: organic synthesis.

propylene glycol *n* $C_3H_8O_2$ a colourless thick sweet-tasting liquid. Source: propylene. Use: antifreeze in brake fluid, solvent, lubricant.

propylon /prṓpi lon/ *n* ARCHIT = **propylaeum** [Mid-19C. Via Latin < Greek *propulon* 'before the gate' < *pulē* 'gate'.]

pro rata /prō ráatə/ *adv, adj* in accordance with a fixed proportion [< Latin, 'according to the rate']

prorate /prō ráyt/ (**-rates, -rating, -rated**) *vti US, Can* to calculate, divide, or distribute something on a pro rata basis [Mid-19C. < PRO RATA.] —**proratable** *adj* —**proration** /-ráysh'n/ *n*

prorogue /prō rṓg/ (**-rogues, -roguing, -rogued**) *v* **1** *vti* to discontinue the meetings of a parliament or other body without formally ending the session **2** *vt* to defer something to a later date or to a subsequent meeting [15C. Via French *proroguer* < Latin *prorogare* 'prolong' *rogare* 'ask'.] —**prorogation** /prṓrō gáysh'n/ *n*

prosaic /prō záy ik/ *adj* **1** not having any features that are interesting or imaginative **2** characteristic of, resembling, or consisting of prose [Late 16C. Directly and via French < late Latin *prosaicus* < Latin *prosa* (see PROSE).] —**prosaically** *adv* —**prosaicness** *n*

prosaism /prō záy izəm/, **prosaicism** /prō záy i sizəm/ *n* **1** a dull or unimaginative expression or style of writing **2** a word, phrase, or style of writing used in prose —**prosaist** *n*

pros and cons *npl* the arguments for and against something

prosauropod /prō sáwrə pod/ *n* a primitive dinosaur of the Triassic period that ate plants and walked partly on its hind legs, partly on all four legs. Suborder: Prosauropoda. [Mid-20C. < modern Latin *Prosauropoda* < Greek *pro* 'in front, before' + *sauros* 'lizard' + *-pod* 'foot'.]

proscenium /prə séeni əm/ (*plural* **-a** /-ə/ *or* **-ums**) *n* **1** the part of a theatre stage that is in front of the curtain **2** the stage of a theatre in ancient Greece or Rome [Early 17C. Via Latin < Greek *proskēnion* 'forestage' < *skēnē* 'stage, scenes'.]

prosciutto /prō shóotō/ *n* Italian cured ham, usually served cold and uncooked in thin slices [Mid-20C. Via Italian < Latin *exsuctus* 'lacking juice', past participle of *exsugere* 'suck out' < *sugere* 'suck'.]

proscribe /prō skríb/ (**-scribes, -scribing, -scribed**) *vt* **1** CONDEMN OR BAN to prohibit something that is considered undesirable by those in authority **2** CONDEMN to denounce or condemn something **3** BANISH to banish or exile somebody **4** OUTLAW SOMEBODY PUBLICLY to state publicly that somebody is no longer protected by the law, especially in ancient Rome (*archaic*) [15C. < Latin *proscribere* 'publish in writing, publish somebody's name as outlawed' < *pro-* 'in front of' + *scribere* 'write'.] —**proscriber** *n*

proscription /prō skrípsh'n/ *n* (*formal*) **1** CONDEMNATION an act of condemning or forbidding something **2** CONDITION OF BEING BANNED the condition of having been denounced or exiled **3** BANISHING OR BEING BANISHED the act of banishment or exile, or the state of being banished or exiled —**proscriptive** *adj* —**proscriptively** /-skríptivli/ *adv* —**proscriptiveness** *n*

prose /prōz/ *n* **1** LANGUAGE THAT IS NOT POETRY writing or speech in its normal continuous form, without the rhythmic or visual line structure of poetry **2** ORDINARY STYLE OF EXPRESSION writing or speech that is ordinary or matter-of-fact, without embellishment **3** PASSAGE FOR TRANSLATION a piece of text to be translated into another language as an exercise for students **4** CHR = **sequence** *n*. 6 ■ *v* (**proses, prosing, prosed**) **1** *vti* WRITE IN PROSE to write something in prose, as opposed to poetry **2** *vt* REWRITE AS PROSE to turn poetry into prose **3** *vi* SPEAK OR WRITE PROSAICALLY to speak or write in an ordinary, matter-of-fact, or unimaginative style [13C. Via Old French < Latin *prosa (oratio)* 'straightforward (discourse)' < *provertere* 'turn forward' < *vertere* 'turn'.]

prosector /prō séktər/ *n* a preparer or dissector of cadavers for anatomy demonstrations [Mid-19C. Directly or via French < late Latin, 'in place of the cutter' < Latin *sector* (see SECTOR).]

prosecute /próssi kyoot/ (**-cutes, -cuting, -cuted**) *v* **1** *vti* TAKE LEGAL ACTION AGAINST to have somebody tried in a court of law for a civil or criminal offence ○ *Trespassers will be prosecuted.* **2** *vti* TRY TO PROVE SOMEBODY IS GUILTY to represent the person or people who are taking legal action against somebody in a court of law **3** *vt* PERFORM ACTIVITY OR OCCUPATION to engage in or carry on some activity or occupation (*formal*) ○ *prosecute a trade* **4** *vt* CONTINUE TO COMPLETION to carry on doing something, usually until it is finished or accomplished (*formal*) ○ *prosecute an investigation* [15C. < Latin *prosecut-*, past participle of *prosequi* 'follow forward' < *sequi* 'follow'.] —**prosecutable** *adj*

~~**prosecuter**~~ incorrect spelling of **prosecutor**

prosecuting attorney *n US* a lawyer representing the state or the people in a criminal trial

prosecution /próssi kyóosh'n/ *n* **1** PURSUIT OF LEGAL ACTION the trial of somebody in a court of law for a criminal offence **2** LAWYERS TRYING TO PROVE SOMEBODY'S GUILT the lawyers representing the person or people who are taking legal action against somebody in a court of law, especially the Crown or the people in a criminal trial ○ *a witness for the prosecution* **3** PERFORMANCE OF ACTIVITY OR OCCUPATION the carrying on of an activity or occupation (*formal*) ○ *the prosecution of your duty* **4** CONTINUATION TO COMPLETION the continuation of or perseverance in some task or pursuit, usually until it is finished or accomplished (*formal*)

prosecutor /próssi kyootər/ *n* **1** *US* LAW = **prosecuting attorney** **2** an initiator of a legal prosecution ■ a person, group, state, or nation engaged in the initiation or continuation of an act, e.g. a military action ○ *a group of allied nations that were the prosecutors of the invasion*

proselyte /próssə lít/ *n* a new convert to a religious faith or political doctrine [14C. Via late Latin *proselytus* < Greek *prosēluthos* 'person who comes to a place' < *proserkhesthai* 'come to'.] —**proselytic** /próssə líttik/ *adj* —**proselytism** /próssələ tizəm/ *n*

proselytize /próssələ tíz/ (**-tizes, -tizing, -tized**), **proselytise** (**-tises, -tising, -tised**) *vti* to try to convert somebody to a religious faith or political doctrine —**proselytization** /-tī záysh'n/ *n* —**proselytiser** *n*

prose poem *n* a piece of creative writing that has the structure of prose but the style and language of poetry

Proserpina /prə súrpinə/, **Proserpine** /próssər pīn/ *n* the Roman goddess of the earth

prosimian /prō símmi ən/ *n* a nocturnal lower primate with large eyes and ears, e.g. a lemur or bush baby. Suborder: Prosimii.

prosit /prṓzit/ *interj* used as a drinking toast, to wish somebody good health or good fortune [Mid-19C. Via German < Latin, 'may it benefit', 3rd person present subjunctive singular of *prodesse* (see PROUD).]

prosody /próssədi/ (*plural* **-dies**) *n* **1** STUDY OF POETIC STRUCTURE the study of the structure of poetry and the conventions or techniques involved in writing it, including rhyme, metre, and the patterns of verse forms **2** SYSTEM OR THEORY OF WRITING VERSE a particular system or theory of writing poetry **3** RHYTHM OF SPEECH the rhythm of spoken language, including stress and intonation, or the study of these patterns [15C. Via Latin *prosodia* < Greek *prosōidiā* 'song with an instrumental accompaniment' < *pros* 'in addition to' + *ōidē* 'song'.] —**prosodic** /prə sóddik/ *adj* —**prosodically** /-sóddikli/ *adv* —**prosodist** /próssədist/ *n*

prosoma /prō sṓmə/ (*plural* **-mas** *or* **-mata** /-sṓmətə/) *n* the region near the head of spiders and some related arthropods, composed of fused segments of head and thorax [Late 19C. < PRO-[2] 'in front of' + Greek *sōma* 'body'.]

prosopography /próssə póggrəfi/ (*plural* **-phies**) *n* a collection of biographical sketches used by social and political historians to convey larger patterns in a historical period [Mid-16C. < modern Latin *prosopographia* 'writing about somebody' < Greek *prosōpon* 'face, person'.] —**prosopographer** *n* —**prosopographical** /próssəpə gráffik'l/ *adj*

prosopopoeia /próssəpə pée ə/, **prosopopeia** *n* **1** a figure of speech that presents an imaginary or dead person as speaking **2** a figure of speech in which human qualities are attributed to objects or abstract notions [Mid-16C. Via Latin < Greek *prosōpopoiia* 'representation in human form' < *prosōpon* 'face, person' + *poiein* 'make'.]

prospect *n* /prós pekt/ **1** POSSIBILITY OF SOMETHING HAPPENING SOON a chance or the likelihood that something will happen in the near future, especially something desirable **2** VISION OF FUTURE something that is expected or certain to happen in the future, or a mental picture of this ○ *I don't relish the prospect of spending five months at sea.* **3** EXTENSIVE OUTLOOK OR SCENE a view, especially one from a high position over a large expanse of land or water ○ *a pleasant prospect* **4** DIRECTION FACED the direction in which something faces ○ *a northerly prospect* **5** LIKELY CUSTOMER a customer who may be interested in buying something **6** SOMEBODY OR SOMETHING WITH POTENTIAL somebody or something that is likely to succeed ○ *She's our brightest prospect.* **7** SURVEY an act of making a survey, examination, or observation **8** MINERAL LOCATION location of a mineral deposit, or an area believed to have mineral deposits **9** MINERAL DEPOSIT a probable mineral deposit or one that definitely exists **10** MINERAL SAMPLE TO BE ANALYZED a sample of a mineral to be analyzed for its components **11** MINERAL YIELD the yield that can be obtained by mining a mineral ■ **prospects** *npl* EXPECTATIONS OF SUCCESS the likelihood of being successful or prosperous in the future, especially in a job or career ○ *eager to improve her career prospects* ■ *v* /prə spékt, prós pekt/ **1** *vti* SEARCH FOR MINERAL DEPOSITS to explore an area in search of oil or valuable minerals, especially gold **2** *vt* WORK MINE to work a mine to see how profitable it is **3** *vi* LOOK FOR to search or watch for something ○ *prospect for business* [15C. < Latin *prospectus* 'view' < past participle of *prospicere* 'look forward' < *specere* (see SPECTACLE).] —**prospectless** /prós pektləss/ *adj*

prospective /prə spéktiv/ *adj* **1** expected or hoping to do or become something ○ *his prospective mother-in-law* **2** likely or expected to happen ○ *prospective changes* —**prospectively** *adv*

prospector /prə spéktər, prós pektər/ *n* an explorer in search of oil, gold, or other mineral deposits

prospectus /prə spéktəss/ *n* **1** a brochure or pamphlet that advertises or describes the activities, staff, and facilities of an organization or an institution such as a school, college, or university. US term **catalog** *n*. **2** an official document giving details about something that is going to happen, e.g. an issue of shares, a forthcoming publication, a new business, or a proposed project [Mid-18C. < Latin (see PROSPECT).]

prosper /próspər/ *v* **1** *vi* to be successful, especially in financial or economic terms, through effort or good fortune **2** *vt* to make something or somebody successful or profitable (*archaic*) [14C. Directly or via Old French < Latin *prosperare* < *prosperus* 'doing well'.]

prosperity /pro spérrəti/ *n* the condition of enjoying great wealth, success, or good fortune

prosperous /prósperəss/ *adj* **1** FINANCIALLY SUCCESSFUL successful and flourishing, especially earning or producing great wealth **2** WEALTHY having great wealth, or associated with wealthy people **3** FULL OF GOOD FORTUNE characterized by success or good fortune ○ *wishing you a prosperous New Year* **4** PROMISING likely to be successful or bring a good result —**prosperously** *adv* —**prosperousness** *n*

pross /pross/, **prossie** /próssi/ *n* a prostitute (*slang*) [Early 20C. Shortening.]

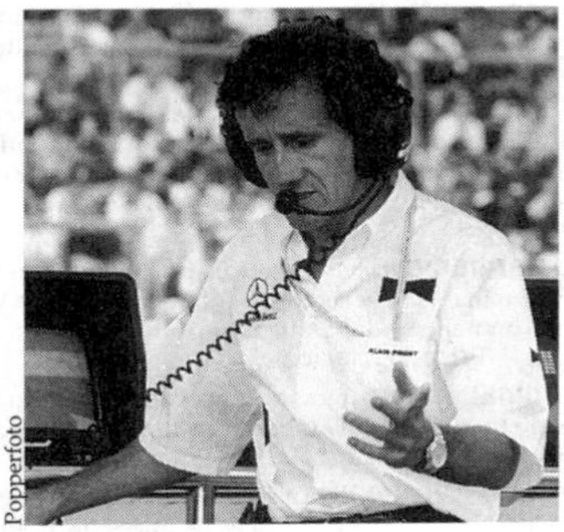

Alain Prost

Prost /prost/, **Alain** (*b.* 1955) French racing driver and team owner

prostacyclin /próstə sīklin/ *n* an unsaturated fatty acid (**prostaglandin**) that dilates blood vessels and inhibits the formation of blood clots [Late 20C. < PROSTATE + CYCLIC + -IN.]

prostaglandin /próstə glándin/ *n* an unsaturated fatty acid found in all mammals that resembles hormones in its activity, e.g. controlling smooth muscle contraction, blood pressure, inflammation, and body temperature [Mid-20C. < PROSTATE + GLAND[1] + -IN.]

prostate /pró stayt/ *n* ANAT = **prostate gland** [Mid-17C. Ultimately via modern Latin *prostata* < Greek *prostatēs* 'guardian' (of the bladder) < *proïstanai* 'set before' < *histanai* 'cause to stand'.] —**prostatic** /pro státtik/ *adj*

prostatectomy /próstə téktəmi/ (*plural* **-mies**) *n* surgical removal of the whole or part of the prostate gland

prostate gland *n* an O-shaped gland in males that surrounds the urethra below the bladder, secreting a fluid into the semen that acts to improve the movement and viability of sperm

prostatism /próstə tizəm/ *n* a disorder of the prostate gland, especially enlargement that blocks or inhibits urine flow

prostatitis /próstə tītiss/ *n* inflammation of the prostate gland

prosthesis /pros theéssiss/ (*plural* **-ses** /-seez/) *n* **1** an artificial body part, e.g. an artificial limb or eye **2** the branch of surgery concerned with replacing missing body parts with artificial devices **3** LING = **prothesis** *n.* 1 [Mid-16C. Via late Latin < Greek, 'addition' < *prostithenai* 'to add to' < *tithenai* 'place'.] —**prosthetic** /pros théttik/ *adj* —**prosthetically** /-théttikli/ *adv*

prosthetic group *n* the part of a conjugated protein that is not an amino acid, e.g. the lipid group in lipoprotein

prosthetics /pros théttiks/ *n* a branch of medicine dealing with the design, production, and use of artificial body parts (+ *singular verb*) —**prosthetist** /prósthətist/ *n*

prosthodontics /prósstha dóntiks/ *n* a branch of dentistry dealing with the replacement of teeth and parts of the jaw (+ *singular verb*) [Mid-20C. < PROSTHESIS + -ODONTIA after ORTHODONTICS.] —**prosthodontic** *adj* —**prosthodontist** *n*

prostitute /prósti tyoot/ *n* **1** SOMEBODY PAID FOR SEXUAL INTERCOURSE a person who is paid to provide sexual intercourse or other sex acts **2** SOMEBODY WHO DEGRADES TALENT FOR MONEY somebody who uses a skill or ability in an unworthy way, usually for financial gain ■ *vt* (**-tutes, -tuting, -tuted**) **1** MISUSE SOMETHING FOR GAIN to use a skill or ability in a way that is considered unworthy, usually for financial gain ○ *He has been accused of prostituting his talent by appearing in TV commercials.* **2** WORK OR OFFER SOMEBODY AS PROSTITUTE to work as a prostitute or offer somebody else for sexual intercourse or other sex acts in exchange for money [Mid-16C. < the past participle of Latin *prostituere* 'expose publicly, offer for sale' < *statuere* 'to set, place'.] —**prostitutor** *n*

prostitution /prósti tyoósh'n/ *n* **1** the act of engaging in sexual intercourse or performing other sex acts in exchange for money, or of offering another person for such purposes **2** the use of a skill or ability in a way that is considered unworthy, usually for financial gain

prostomium /prō stṓmi əm/ (*plural* **-a** /-ə/) *n* the part of the head of certain worms, including the earthworm, that is in front of the mouth [Late 19C. Via modern Latin < Greek *prostomion* 'something in front of the mouth' < *stoma* 'mouth'.] —**prostomial** *adj*

prostrate *v* /pro stráyt/ (**-trates, -trating, -trated**) **1** *vr* LIE FACE DOWNWARDS to lie flat on the face or bow very low, e.g. in worship or humility ○ *He prostrated himself before the soprano.* **2** *vt* LAY SOMEBODY OR SOMETHING ON GROUND to lay or throw somebody or something flat on the ground ○ *prostrated by a blow on the head* **3** *vt* INCAPACITATE to make somebody physically or emotionally weak or helpless ○ *prostrated by illness* ■ *adj* /pró strayt/ **1** LYING FLAT ON FACE lying prone or stretched out with the face downwards, e.g. in worship or submission **2** LYING DOWN stretched out in a horizontal position, often because of illness or injury **3** DRAINED OF ENERGY drained of physical strength or incapacitated by overexertion or powerful emotion ○ *prostrate with grief* **4** GROWING ALONG THE GROUND describes a plant that grows or trails along the ground ○ *a prostrate shrub* [14C. < Latin *prostratus*, past participle of *prosternere* 'throw in front of' < *sternere* 'spread out, lay down'.] —**prostration** /pro stráysh'n/ *n*

prostyle /prṓ stīl/ *adj* describes a building, e.g. a Greek temple, with a row of columns at the front [Late 17C. < Latin *prostylos* 'having pillars in front' < *stilus* 'pointed writing instrument, stake'.]

prosy /prṓzi/ (**-ier, -iest**) *adj* dull and commonplace, with no interesting, imaginative, or eloquent features —**prosily** *adv* —**prosiness** *n*

Prot. *abbr* **1** Protestant **2** Protectorate

prot- *prefix* = **proto-** (*before vowels*)

protactinium /prṓ tak tínni əm/ *n* (*symbol* **Pa**) a toxic radioactive metallic element. Source: uranium ores. [Early 20C. < PROTO- + ACTINIUM, because the most common isotope decays to give actinium.]

protagonist /prō tággənist/ *n* **1** MAIN CHARACTER the most important character in a novel, play, story, or other literary work **2** MAIN CHARACTER IN ANCIENT GREEK DRAMA the first actor who interacted with the chorus in ancient Greek drama **3** LEADING FIGURE a main participant in an event, e.g. a contest or dispute ○ *two protagonists in a long-running dispute* **4** SUPPORTER an important or influential supporter or advocate of something such as a political or social issue ○ *an early protagonist of educational reform* [Late 17C. < Greek *protagōnistēs* 'actor who plays the chief part' < *agōnistes* 'actor, competitor' < *agōn* 'contest' (see AGONY).] —**protagonism** *n*

protamine /prṓtə meen/ *n* a small arginine-rich protein found in chromosomes

protanopia /prṓtə nṓpi ə/ *n* a form of colour blindness in which the retina fails to distinguish between red and green [Early 20C. < PROTO- (red being regarded as the first of the primary colours) + AN- + -OPIA.] —**protanopic** /prṓtə nóppik/ *adj*

protasis /próttəssiss/ (*plural* **-ses** /-seez/) *n* the part of a conditional sentence that contains the condition, e.g. 'if he asks' in 'if he asks, I'll tell him' [Mid-16C. Via Latin < Greek < *proteinein* 'put forward, propose' < *teinein* 'stretch'.] —**protatic** /pro táttik/ *adj*

prote- *prefix* = **proteo-**

protea /prṓti ə/ (*plural* **-as** *or* **-a**) *n* an evergreen or tree, grown for its colourful bracts and dense flower heads. Native to: South Africa. Genus: *Protea*. [Mid-18C. < modern Latin, after PROTEUS, from the variety of form in the genus.]

protean /prō teé ən, prṓti ən/ *adj* **1** variable or continually changing in nature, appearance, or behaviour **2** showing great variety, diversity, or versatility

protease /prṓti ayz, -ayss/ *n* an enzyme that breaks down proteins and peptides by catalysing the hydrolysis of peptide bonds

protease inhibitor *n* a compound that breaks down protease, inhibiting the replication of viruses and development of certain cancers. Use: treatment of Aids.

protect /prə tékt/ *vt* **1** KEEP SOMETHING OR SOMEBODY SAFE to prevent somebody or something from being harmed or damaged **2** HELP HOME INDUSTRIES BY TAXING IMPORTS to help the industries in a country by imposing customs duties on imports from other countries **3** GUARANTEE PAYMENT OF DRAFT to put up money in advance to guarantee that a draft or note is paid [15C. < Latin *protect-*, past participle of *protegere* 'cover in front' < *tegere* 'to cover'.]

SYNONYMS See ***safeguard***.

protectant /prə téktənt/ *n* a substance that prevents something from being damaged, e.g. a coating used to stop metal going rusty

protected /prə téktid/ *adj* **1** ENDANGERED legally classified as a species in danger of extinction **2** SHELTERED sheltered from the elements **3** LOCKED AGAINST UNAUTHORIZED CHANGES locked against changes by unauthorized users of a computer program

protection /prə téksh'n/ *n* **1** SAFEGUARDING the act of preventing somebody or something from being harmed or damaged, or the state of being kept safe **2** SOMETHING THAT PROTECTS something that prevents somebody or something from being harmed or damaged **3** INSURANCE COVER an insurance company's agreement to pay compensation or costs if some specified undesirable event occurs **4** PROMISE OF SAFETY FROM CRIMINAL ATTACK a promise made by a gangster that somebody or something will not be harmed if money is paid, or the payment extorted in return for such a promise (*informal*) **5** *US* CONDOM a form of contraception, usually a condom, used during sexual intercourse to prevent sperm or disease-causing organisms from entering the body **6** GUARANTEE OF FREEDOM AND SAFETY a document that enables somebody to travel around in freedom and safety, especially in another country or in enemy territory **7** ECON = **protectionism** **8** MOUNTAIN CLIMBERS' SAFETY EQUIPMENT the safety equipment used by mountain climbers to keep them from falling, e.g. pitons, harnesses, and ropes

protectionism /prə téksh'nizəm/ *n* the system of imposing duties on imports into a country in order to protect domestic industries —**protectionist** *n, adj*

protection money *n* money paid to a gangster or other person who threatens to damage something or harm somebody unless the money is paid

protective /prə téktiv/ *adj* **1** GIVING PROTECTION preventing something or somebody from being harmed or damaged, or designed or intended for this purpose ○ *a protective covering* **2** TAKING GREAT CARE OF very anxious to protect or defend somebody or something, often excessively so ○ *She had always felt protective towards her younger brother.* **3** INTENDED TO HELP DOMESTIC INDUSTRIES intended to give an advantage to a country's domestic industries ■ *n* **1** SOMETHING THAT PROTECTS something that prevents somebody or something from being harmed or damaged **2** CONDOM a condom (*formal*) —**protectively** *adv* —**protectiveness** *n*

protective custody *n* detention in a particular place by the police in order to give protection from harm by other people

protector /prə téktər/ *n* **1** SOMETHING THAT PROTECTS something that prevents a person or thing from being harmed or damaged **2** SOMEBODY WHO PROTECTS a person who protects or defends somebody or something **3** **protector, Protector** SOMEBODY RULING IN PLACE OF MONARCH somebody in charge of a country while the monarch is absent or too young or unfit to rule —**protectoral** *adj* —**protectorship** *n*

Protector *n* the title given to the head of the Commonwealth of England, Scotland, and Ireland during the period without a monarch from 1653 to 1659

protectorate /prə téktərət/ *n* **1** STATE DEPENDENT ON ANOTHER a country or region that is defended and controlled by a more powerful state, or the relationship between the two **2** PLACE THAT IS DEPENDENT ON ANOTHER an area or country that is dependent on another more powerful nation **3** OFFICE OF PROTECTOR the position or term of office of a protector

protégé /prótti zhay, prṓti-/ *n* a young person who receives help, guidance, training, and support from an older person with more experience and influence [Late 18C. < French < the past participle of *protéger* 'protect' < Latin *protegere* (see PROTECT).]

protégée /próti zhay, prṓti-/ *n* a young woman who receives help, guidance, training, and support from somebody who is older and has more experience or influence [Late 18C. < French, feminine of *protégé* (see PROTÉGÉ).]

protei plural of **proteus**

proteid /prṓti id/ *n* a salamander such as an olm or a mudpuppy that retains its larval form. Family: Proteidae. [Late 19C. < modern Latin *Proteus*, after PROTEUS.]

protein /prṓ teen/ *n* **1** a complex natural substance that has a globular or fibrous structure composed of linked amino acids **2** a food source that is rich in protein ○ *a balanced diet of fresh vegetables, fruit, and protein* [Mid-19C.

Via French < Greek *prōteios* 'primary' < *prōtos* 'first'; from its importance to the proper functioning of the body.] —**proteinaceous** /prṓti náyshəss/ *adj* —**proteinic** /prō teénik/ *adj* —**proteinous** /prō teénəss/ *adj*

proteinase /prṓti nayz, -nayss/ *n* any enzyme that splits the peptide bonds of proteins

protein engineering *n* the process of making changes in the sequence of a gene coding for a protein, resulting in desirable changes in function

proteinoid /prṓti noyd/ *n* a protein-like polypeptide that is obtained by polymerization of mixtures of amino acids

proteinuria /prṓti nyoóri ə/ *n* the presence of protein in the urine, usually indicating disease

pro tem /prō tém/ *adv, adj* at the present time but not permanently [Shortening of Latin *pro tempore* 'for the time being']

proteo-, prote- *prefix* protein ○ *proteolysis* [< PROTEIN]

proteolysis /prṓti óllәssiss/ *n* the breakdown of proteins or peptides into amino acids —**proteolytic** /prṓti ə líttik/ *adj* —**proteolytically** /-líttikli/ *adv*

proteome /prṓtee ōm/ *n* the set of proteins expressed by genes within an organism [Late 20C. Blend of PROTEIN + GENOME.]

proteomics /prōtee ṓmiks/ *n* the study of proteins expressed by genes within an organism, with applications in the understanding of disease and in drug development [Late 20C. Blend of PROTEIN + GENOMICS.]

proteose /prṓti ōz/ *n* a water-soluble protein derivative formed during hydrolytic processes such as digestion

Proterozoic /prṓtərō zṓ ik/ *n* the latter half of the Precambrian era, during which sea plants and animals first appeared [Early 20C. < *protero-* + Greek *zōē* 'life' + -IC.] —**Proterozoic** *adj*

protest *v* /prə tést/ **1** *vti* **COMPLAIN OR OBJECT STRONGLY** to express strong disapproval of or disagreement with something, or to refuse to obey or accept something, often by making a formal statement or taking action in public **2** *vti* **SAY FIRMLY THAT SOMETHING IS TRUE** to state or affirm something in strong or formal terms ○ *He continued to protest his innocence.* **3** *vt* **DECLARE FINANCIAL NOTE DISHONOURED** to state formally that a note or bill has been dishonoured ■ *n* /prṓ test/ **1 STRONG COMPLAINT OR OBJECTION** an expression or display of strong disapproval of or disagreement with something, or a refusal to obey or accept something, often in the form of a public statement **2 DEMONSTRATION OF PUBLIC OPPOSITION OR DISAPPROVAL** an expression of strong opposition to or disapproval of something in the form of a public demonstration or other action ○ *student protests* ○ *went on a protest march* **3 CREDITOR'S FORMAL STATEMENT** a formal statement drawn up by a notary on behalf of a creditor, declaring that somebody has refused to honour a bill **4 CAPTAIN'S STATEMENT ABOUT DAMAGE TO SHIP** a statement made by the master of a damaged vessel, declaring when and how a ship was damaged [14C. Via French < Latin *protestari* 'declare publicly' < *testari* 'declare'.] —**protestant** /próttistənt/ *n, adj* —**protester** /prə téstər/ *n* —**protestingly** *adv*

SYNONYMS See ***complain***. See ***object***.

Protestant /próttistənt/ *n* a member or adherent of any denomination of the Western Christian church that rejects papal authority and some fundamental Roman Catholic doctrines, and believes in justification by faith —**Protestant** *adj*

Protestant ethic *n* CHR = **Protestant work ethic**

Protestantism /próttistəntizəm/ *n* **1 BELIEF IN PROTESTANT DOCTRINES** adherence to Protestant beliefs **2 RELIGIOUS MOVEMENT OPPOSING ROMAN CATHOLICISM** a Christian religious movement originating in the 16th century from Martin Luther's attack on Roman Catholic doctrine

Protestant work ethic *n* a belief in the moral value of work, thrift, and the responsibility of the individual for his or her actions

protestation /prótti stáysh'n/ *n* **1 FORMAL AFFIRMATION** a strong or firm declaration that something is true or false (*often plural*) ○ *protestations of loyalty* **2 ACT OF COMPLAINING OR OBJECTING** the expression of strong disapproval of or disagreement with something **3 COMPLAINT OR OBJECTION** an individual expression of strong disapproval of or disagreement with something

protest vote *n* the casting of a vote for a candidate or party as a means of showing dissatisfaction with another candidate or party

proteus /prṓti əss/ (*plural* **-i** /-ī/) *n* a rod-shaped bacterium associated with enteritis and urinary tract infections. Genus: *Proteus.* [Early 19C. < modern Latin, after PROTEUS.]

Proteus /prṓti əss/ *n* **1** in Greek mythology, a prophetic sea god who could change his shape at will **2** the second-largest natural satellite of Neptune, discovered in 1989 by Voyager 2. It is irregular in shape, having a maximum dimension of approximately 440 km.

prothalamion /prṓthə láymi ən/ (*plural* **-a** /-ə/), **prothalamium** /-mi əm/ (*plural* **-a** /-ə/) *n* a song or poem written or performed in celebration of a marriage (*literary*) [Late 16C. < *'Prothalamion'*, a poem by Spenser (1597), after *epithalamion*, a variant of EPITHALAMIUM.]

prothallus /prō thálləss/ (*plural* **-li** /-lī/), **prothallium** /prō thálli əm/ (*plural* **-a** /-ə/) *n* a flat green organ bearing the reproductive organs (**gametophytes**) of ferns and related plants [Mid-19C. < modern Latin < *pro-* 'before' + Greek *thallos* 'green shoot'.] —**prothallial** /prō thálli əl/ *adj* —**prothallic** *adj*

prothesis /próthəssiss/ (*plural* **-ses** /próthə seez/) *n* **1** the addition of a sound or sounds at the beginning of a word to make the word easier to pronounce **2** the preparations for the offering of the Eucharist in the Eastern Orthodox Church [Late 16C. < Greek, 'a placing before or in public' < *thesis* 'placing'.] —**prothetic** /prō théttik/ *adj* —**prothetically** /-théttikli/ *adv*

prothonotary /próthə nṓtəri, prō thónnətəri/ (*plural* **-ies**), **protonotary** /prṓtə nṓtəri, prō tónnətəri/ (*plural* **-ies**) *n* **1** the chief clerk in some courts of law **2 prothonotary, prothonotary apostolic** (*plural* **prothonotaries apostolic**) in the Roman Catholic Church, any one of twelve officials who can act as a notary to authenticate papal proceedings, documents, and acts [15C. Via medieval Latin < Greek *prōto* + Latin *notarios* 'first notary' < *notarios* (see NOTARY).] —**prothonotarial** /prō thónnə táiri əl/ *adj*

prothoracic gland /prōthə rássik glánd/ *n* a gland in insects that secretes the steroid hormone ecdysone, responsible for controlling moulting and metamorphosis

prothrombin /prō thrómbin/ *n* a plasma protein that is converted to thrombin during blood clotting

protist /prṓtist/ *n* an organism belonging, in an older classification system, to the kingdom that includes protozoans, bacteria, and single-celled algae and fungi. Kingdom: *Protista.* [Late 19C. < modern Latin *Protista* < Greek *prōtistos* 'very first' < *prōtos* 'first'.] —**protistan** /prō tístən/ *adj* —**protistology** /prṓti stólləji/ *n*

protium /prṓti əm/ *n* the most common and lightest isotope of hydrogen, with atomic mass 1 [Mid-20C. < Greek *prōtos* 'first' + -IUM.]

proto- *prefix* **1** first in time, earliest ○ *protolithic* ○ *protomartyr* **2** original, ancestral ○ *protostar* ○ *Proto-Norse* **3** first in a series, having the least amount of a particular element or radical ○ *protactinium* [< Greek *prōtos*]

protoceratops /prṓtō sérrə tops/ (*plural* **-tops**) *n* a plant-eating dinosaur that walked on all four legs and had a large head, bony neck frill, and a beak like a parrot's with sharp, shearing teeth. Genus: *Protoceratops.* [Mid-20C. < modern Latin *Protoceratops* < Greek *prōtos* (see PROTO-) + *kerat-* stem of *keras* 'horn'.]

⚡**protocol** /prṓtə kol/ *n* **1 ETIQUETTE OF STATE OCCASIONS** the rules or conventions of correct behaviour on official or ceremonial occasions **2 CODE OF CONDUCT** the rules of correct or appropriate behaviour for a particular group of people or in a particular situation **3 INTERNATIONAL AGREEMENT** a formal agreement between states or nations **4 AMENDMENT** something that amends a treaty or other formal document **5 SOMETHING ADDED TO TREATY** something added to a treaty that deals with minor details or that makes it easier to understand **6 RECORD OR DRAFT OF AGREEMENT** a written record or preliminary draft of a treaty or other agreement **7 RULES FOR EXCHANGING INFORMATION BETWEEN COMPUTERS** a set of technical rules about how information should be transmitted and received using computers **8** PHILOSOPHY = **protocol statement 9** *US* **RESEARCH PLAN** the detailed plan of a scientific experiment, medical trial, or other piece of research [15C. Directly and via Old French < medieval Latin < Greek *prōtokollon* 'first leaf of a book'.]

protocol statement *n* a statement that can be immediately verified by experience

protocontinent /prṓtō kóntinənt/ *n* **1** a large, unbroken mass of land capable of becoming a major continent **2** GEOL = **supercontinent**

protogalaxy /prṓtō gálləksi/ (*plural* **-ies**) *n* a hypothetical cloud of gas believed to have been formed about 14 billion years ago from dark matter, neutral hydrogen, and helium, from which all the galaxies and stars evolved

Proto-Germanic /prṓtō-/ *n* a reconstructed hypothetical language that is believed to be the ancestor of the Germanic branch of the Indo-European family of languages —**Proto-Germanic** *adj*

protohuman /prṓtō hyoómən/ *n* an extinct hominid or primate that has some of the characteristics of modern people —**protohuman** *adj*

Proto-Indo-European *n* a reconstructed hypothetical language that is believed to be the ancestor of all the Indo-European languages —**Proto-Indo-European** *adj*

protolanguage /prṓtō lang gwij/ *n* a recorded or reconstructed language that is the ancestor of another language or family of languages

protolithic /prṓtō líthik/ *adj* relating to the earliest part of the Stone Age [Late 19C. < PROTO- + -LITHIC after NEOLITHIC.]

protomartyr /prṓtō maártər/ *n* **1** St Stephen, the first Christian martyr **2** the first person to die for a particular cause

protomorphic /prṓtō máwrfik/ *adj* having a primitive structure

proton /prṓ ton/ *n* (*symbol* **p**) a stable elementary particle of the baryon family that is a component of all atomic nuclei and carries a positive charge equal to that of the electron's negative charge [Late 19C. < Greek *prōton*, a form of *prōtos* 'first, elementary'.] —**protonic** /prō tónnik/ *adj*

protonema /prṓtə neémə/ (*plural* **-mata** /-mətə/) *n* the primary thread-shaped structure of mosses and certain liverworts that results from the germination of a spore and gives rise to a new plant [Mid-19C. < PROTO- + Greek *nēma* 'thread'.] —**protonemal** *adj*

proton number *n* PHYS = **atomic number**

protonotary *n* LAW, CHR = **prothonotary**

proton synchrotron *n* a circular very high-energy particle accelerator that accelerates protons through the action of magnetic fields and a high-frequency electric field

proto-oncogene *n* a normal gene that can mutate or be activated by a cancer-causing virus to form a cancer-producing gene

protoplanet /prṓtō plannit/ *n* **1** a theoretical mass of gas in the clouds of gas and dust around a star that is believed to develop into a planet **2** a planet in the early stages of formation

protoplasm /prṓtō plazəm/ *n* the colourless liquid or colloidal contents of a living cell, composed of proteins, fats, and other organic substances in water, and including the nucleus and cytoplasm [Mid-19C. < German *Protoplasma* 'first created thing' < Greek *plasma* (see PLASMA).] —**protoplasmic** /prṓtō plázmik/ *adj*

protoplast /prṓtō plast/ *n* the living substance of a plant or bacterial cell, excluding the cell wall [Mid-16C. Directly or via French < late Latin *protoplastus* 'first created being' < Greek *prōtoplastos* < *plastos* 'formed' < *plassein* 'to form'.] —**protoplastic** /prṓt ō plástik/ *adj*

protoporphyrin /prṓtō páwrfirin/ *n* $C_{34}H_{34}N_4O_4$ a purple porphyrin acid that combines with iron to form the deep red of iron-containing proteins, e.g. haemoglobin and cytochrome

Proto-Romance *n* the language that developed from Vulgar Latin and gave rise to the Romance languages —**Proto-Romance** *adj*

protostar /prṓtō staar/ *n* an interstellar cloud of gas and dust thought to develop into a star when it has collapsed sufficiently for nuclear reactions to begin

protostome /prṓtə stōm/ *n* an invertebrate animal such as a mollusc or arthropod in which the mouth forms directly from the blastopore

prototherian /prṓtō theéri ən/ *n* an echidna, platypus, or any of the many extinct related mammals. Subclass: Prototheria. [Late 19C. < PROTO- + Greek *therion* 'wild animal'.]

prototroph /prṓtə trōf/ *n* an organism such as a bacterium or fungus that can grow without having to find nutrients in its surrounding environment. ◊ **auxotroph**

prototrophic /prṓtə trṓfik, -trṓffik/ *adj* having the same nutritional needs and metabolic characteristics as the wild parent strain

prototype /prṓtə tīp/ *n* **1 ORIGINAL USED AS MODEL** something having the essential features of a subsequent type, on which later forms are modelled **2 STANDARD EXAMPLE** a standard example of a particular kind, class, or group **3 FULL-SIZE FUNCTIONAL MODEL** a first full-size functional model to be manufactured, e.g. of a car or a machine ○ *A prototype of the new convertible will be on display next month.* **4 PRIMITIVE FORM** a primitive form believed to be the original type of a species or group, exhibiting the essential features of the later type ■ *vti* (**-types, -typing, -typed**) **CREATE PROTOTYPE** to create a prototype of something [Early 17C. Via French < late Latin *prototypus* 'original, primitive' and Greek *prototypon* 'primitive form' < *proto* 'first' + *typos* 'impression'.] —**prototypal** /prṓtə tīp'l/ *adj* —**prototypic** /-típpik/ *adj* —**prototypical** /-típpik'l/ *adj* —**prototypically** *adv*

protoxide /prō tók sīd/ *n* an oxide of an element that has the lowest proportion of oxygen of all the oxides of that element

protozoan /prṓtə zṓ ən/ (*plural* **-ans** *or* **-a** /-ə/), **protozoon** /-on/ (*plural* **-ons** *or* **-a** /-ə/) *n* a single-celled organism such as an amoeba that can move and feeds on organic compounds of nitrogen and carbon. Kingdom: *Protoctista*. [Mid-19C. < modern Latin *Protozoa* 'first animals' < Greek *zōia*, plural of *zōion* 'animal'.] —**protozoal** *adj* —**protozoan** *adj* —**protozoic** *adj*

protozoology /prṓtō zō ólləji, -zoo-/ *n* the branch of zoology that studies protozoans [Early 20C. < modern Latin *Protozoa* (see PROTOZOAN).] —**protozoological** /prṓtō zṓ ə lójjik'l, -zoo-/ *adj* —**protozoologist** /prṓtō zō ólləjist, -zoo-/ *n*

protozoon *n* BIOL = **protozoan**

protract /prə trákt/ *vt* **1 MAKE SOMETHING LAST** to make something last longer **2 EXTEND A BODY PART** to extend or lengthen a body part **3 PLOT AND DRAW LINES** to plot lines and draw them using a scale and protractor [Mid-16C. Back-formation < PROTRACTION.] —**protractive** *adj*

protracted /prə tráktid/ *adj* lasting or drawn out for a long time —**protractedly** *adv* —**protractedness** *n*

protractile /prə trák tīl/ *adj* **1** capable of being thrust out **2** ZOOL = **protrusile**

protraction /prə tráksh'n/ *n* **1** the act of protracting something **2** the act of drawing something such as a building or an area of land to scale, or a drawing of this kind

protractor /prə tráktər/ *n* **1 INSTRUMENT FOR MEASURING ANGLES** an instrument shaped like a semicircle marked with the degrees of a circle, used to measure or mark out angles **2 LENGTHENER** somebody or something that extends or lengthens something else **3 MUSCLE THAT EXTENDS BODY PART** a muscle with the function of extending a body part

protrude /prə tróod/ (**-trudes, -truding, -truded**) *vti* to stick out from the surroundings, or make something stick out [Early 17C. < Latin *protrudere* 'thrust forward' < *trudere* 'to thrust'.] —**protrudable** *adj* —**protrudent** *adj*

protrusile /prə tróo sīl/, **protrusible** /prə tróozəb'l/ *adj* describes an organ or appendage that can be quickly extended, as can the mouth of many fishes or the proboscis of nemertine worms [Mid-19C. < Latin *protrus-* (see PROTRUSION).]

protrusion /prə tróozh'n/ *n* **1** the act of protruding, or the state of being protruded **2** something that sticks out from its surroundings [Mid-17C. < medieval Latin *protrusion-* < Latin *protrus-*, past participle of *protrudere* (see PROTRUDE).]

protrusive /prə tróossiv/ *adj* **1** jutting or sticking out **2** having a brash forward manner [Late 17C. < Latin *protrus-* (see PROTRUSION).] —**protrusively** *adv* —**protrusiveness** *n*

protuberance /prə tyóobərənss/, **protuberancy** /-ssi/ (*plural* **-cies**) *n* **1** something, or a part of something, that sticks out from its surroundings ○ *the small fleshy protuberance that dangles down from the soft palate* **2** the fact or condition of sticking out or being swollen or bulging [Mid-17C. < *protuberant* 'bulging out' < late Latin *protuberare* 'swell in front' < *tuber* 'lump'.]

protuberant /prə tyóobərənt/ *adj* projecting out from the surroundings in a bulging, rounded manner [Mid-17C. < late Latin *protuberant-*, present participle of *protuberare* 'swell forward' < *tuber* 'lump'.] —**protuberantly** *adv*

protuberate /prə tyóobə rayt/ (**-ates, -ating, -ated**) *vi* to swell out from surroundings [Late 16C. < Latin *protuberat-*, past participle of *protuberare* (see PROTUBERANT).]

protyle /prṓ tīl/ *n* an imaginary substance from which the chemical elements were supposed to have been formed [Late 19C. < PROTO- + Greek *hulē* 'matter, hyle'.]

proud /prowd/ *adj* **1 PLEASED AND SATISFIED** feeling pleased and satisfied, e.g. about having done something or about owning something ○ *I am very proud to be here today to give you this award.* **2 HAVING SELF-RESPECT** having a proper amount of self-respect **3 FOSTERING FEELINGS OF PRIDE** characterized by feelings of pride ○ *the proudest moment in your life* **4 ARROGANT** having an exaggerated opinion of personal worth or abilities **5 IMPRESSIVE** looking magnificent and impressive, or behaving in an impressive way ○ *the proud spires of Oxford* **6 HIGH-SPIRITED** high-spirited and strong ○ *a proud horse* **7 PROJECTING** projecting slightly from a surrounding surface [Pre-12C. Via Old French *prud* < Latin *prodesse* 'be beneficial', literally 'be for' < *esse* 'be'.] —**proudly** *adv* —**proudness** *n* ◇ **do somebody proud 1** to treat somebody well and generously **2** to bring honour or distinction to somebody

SYNONYMS ***proud, arrogant, conceited, egotistic, vain***

CORE MEANING: describing somebody who is pleased with himself or herself

proud justifiably pleased and satisfied about a situation, or self-satisfied and having an exaggerated opinion of self-worth; **arrogant** feeling or showing self-importance and contempt for others; **conceited** showing excessive satisfaction with one's personal qualities or abilities; **egotistic** having an inflated sense of self-importance, especially when this is shown through constantly talking or thinking about oneself; **vain** excessively self-satisfied, especially suggesting that somebody is overly concerned with and admires his or her own personal appearance.

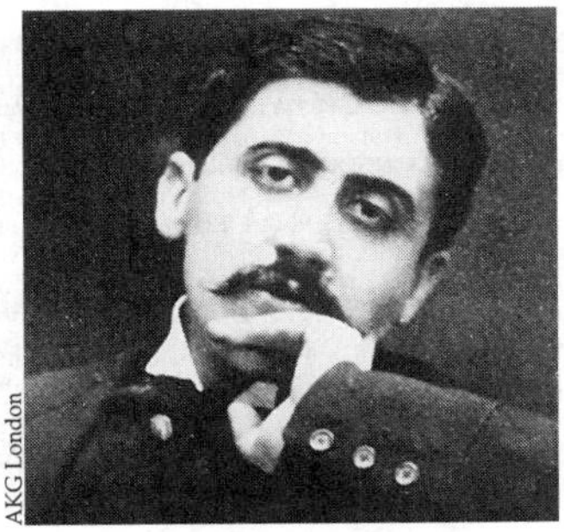

AKG London

Marcel Proust

Proust /proost/, **Marcel** (1871–1922) French novelist —**Proustian** /próosti ən/ *adj*

proustite /próost īt/ *n* a deep red mineral consisting of silver arsenic sulphide. Use: source of silver. [Mid-19C. After the French chemist Joseph L. *Proust* (1754–1826).]

prov. *abbr* **1** province **2** provincial **3** provisional

Prov. *abbr* **1** Provost **2** Proverbs **3** Provençal

prove /proov/ (**proves, proving, proved, proved** *or* **proven** /prṓv'n, próov'n/) *v* **1** *vt* **ESTABLISH TRUTH** to establish the truth or existence of something by providing evidence or argument **2** *vt* **TEST TO DETERMINE CHARACTERISTICS** to subject something to scientific analysis to determine its worth or characteristics **3** *vr* **DEMONSTRATE COMPETENCE** to show yourself to be competent and worthy **4** *vt* **CHECK MATHEMATICAL RESULT** to verify that a mathematical result is correct **5** *vt* **DEMONSTRATE TRUTH OF HYPOTHESIS** to demonstrate that a hypothesis or proposition is true **6** *vt* **DEMONSTRATE THAT A WILL IS GENUINE** to establish that a will is genuine or valid **7** *vt* **MAKE IMPRESSION** to make a test impression of a negative, etching, or type **8** *vi* **RISE IN WARM PLACE** to rise in a warm place before being baked (*refers to dough*) **9** *vti* **TURN OUT TO BE** to turn out to be a particular thing or a thing of a particular character after time or testing [12C. Via Old French *prover* < Latin *probare* 'prove to be good' < *probus* 'good'.] —**provability** /proovə bílləti/ *n* —**provable** /próovəb'l/ *adj* —**provably** /próovəbli/ *adv*

USAGE proved or **proven**? The past participles ***proved*** and ***proven*** are both often used as verbs, with auxiliaries, and also as predicative adjectives (after *be*). Whether to say, for example, *We have proved our case* or *We have proven our case*, and *The case is proved* or *The case is proven* is a matter of choice. ***Proved*** is not, however, ordinarily employed as an adjective preceding a noun: *proven case* is the standard form.

proven /prṓv'n, próov'n/ *adj* **1** done or used before and known to work or be satisfactory **2** having been demonstrated beyond a doubt to be true —**provenly** *adv*

provenance /prṓvənənss/ *n* **1** the place of origin of something **2** the source and ownership history of a work of art or literature or of an archaeological find [Late 18C. Via French < Latin *provenire* 'arise', literally 'come forth' < *venire* 'come'.]

SYNONYMS See ***origin***.

Provençal /próvvon saál/ *adj* **OF PROVENCE** relating to Provence or its people or culture ■ *n* **1 LANGUAGE OF SE FRANCE** a Romance language spoken in SE France, closely related to French, Italian, and Catalan. Native speakers: 4 million. **2 SOMEBODY FROM PROVENCE** somebody who comes from Provence [Late 16C. Via French < Latin *provincialis* 'provincial' < *provincia* 'province', a colloquial name for S Gaul during Roman rule.]

Provençale /próvvon saál/ *adj* prepared with olive oil, garlic, herbs, and tomatoes [Mid-19C. < French *à la provençale* 'in the Provençal manner'.]

Provence /pro vóNss/ region of SE France, bordering the Mediterranean Sea

provender /próvvindər/ *n* **1** food for livestock, especially hay or other dry fodder (*archaic*) **2** food (*literary or humorous*) [14C. < Old French *provendre*, variant of *provende*, alteration (influenced by Latin *providere* 'to supply') of *praebenda* 'things to be given'.]

provenience /prō véeni ənss/ *n* US = **provenance** [Late 19C. < Latin *provenient-*, present participle of *provenire* (see PROVENANCE).]

proventriculus /prṓ ven tríkyŏŏləss/ (*plural* **-li** /-lī/) *n* **1 PART OF BIRD'S STOMACH** the first part of a bird's stomach, where digestive enzymes are mixed with food before it goes to the gizzard **2 PART OF INVERTEBRATE'S STOMACH** the thin-walled section of the stomach of some invertebrates **3 PART OF INSECT'S STOMACH** the part of the foregut in some insects that has teeth or plates for grinding food —**proventricular** *adj*

proverb /próvvurb/ *n* a short well-known saying that expresses an obvious truth and often offers advice [14C. Via Old French *proverbe* < Latin *proverbium* 'saying, saw' < *pro* 'forth' + *verbum* 'word'.]

proverbial /prə vúrbi əl/ *adj* **1** expressed as a proverb, or resembling a proverb either in form or because of being widely known or referred to **2** often referred to metaphorically or as another descriptive device ○ *She was behaving like the proverbial cat on hot bricks.* —**proverbially** *adv*

Proverbs /próvvurbz/ *n* a book of the Bible made up of the proverbs of wise men, including Solomon

provide /prə víd/ (**-vides, -viding, -vided**) *v* **1** *vt* **SUPPLY SOMEBODY WITH** to supply somebody with or be a source of something needed or wanted **2** *vt* **MAKE SOMETHING AVAILABLE** to make something available to somebody **3** *vt* **REQUIRE SOMETHING AS A CONDITION** to require something in advance as a condition or as part of a contract **4** *vi* **TAKE PRECAUTIONS** to take precautions to prevent harm or bring about good **5** *vi* **SUPPLY MEANS OF SUPPORT** to supply the material means of support for somebody ○ *provides for his children* [15C. < Latin *providere* 'prepare in advance, supply', literally 'see ahead' < *videre* 'see'.]

provided /prə vídid/, **provided that** *conj* on the understanding that another thing will also occur or be done ○ *He can play provided that he has no injuries.*

providence /próvvid'nss/ *n* **1 providence, Providence GOD'S GUIDANCE** the wisdom, care, and guidance believed to be provided by God **2 providence, Providence GOD** God perceived as a caring force guiding humankind **3 GOOD JUDGMENT AND MANAGEMENT** good judgment and foresight in the management of affairs or resources [14C. Directly and via Old French < Latin *providentia* 'foresight' < *provident-*, present participle of *providere* 'provide'.]

Providence /próvvid'nss/ capital of Rhode Island, in the northeast of the state. Population: 150,890 (1998 estimate).

provident /próvvid'nt/ *adj* **1** carefully preparing for future needs **2** economical in the use of resources [15C. <

Latin *provident-*, present participle of *providere* 'prepare in advance, supply'.]

providential /próvvi dénsh'l/ *adj* **1** relating to or believed to be determined by providence **2** so lucky that it seems determined by providence

provident society *n* FINANCE = **friendly society**

ϟ **provider** /prə vídər/ *n* **1** a person who provides material support for somebody or something, especially a family **2** an organization or company that provides access to a service or system, e.g. a cellular phone, cable, or computer network ○ *a health care provider*

providing /prə víding/, **providing that** *conj* on the understanding that another thing will also occur or be done ○ *We can save these people providing we get the equipment we need.*

province /próvvinss/ *n* **1 ADMINISTRATIVE DIVISION OF NATION** an administrative region or division of a country **2 AREA OF KNOWLEDGE** a sphere of knowledge or activity **3 ECCLESIASTICAL TERRITORY** an ecclesiastical territory of more than two dioceses, under the jurisdiction of an archbishop or metropolitan **4 REGION OF ROMAN EMPIRE** a country or region controlled by the ancient Roman Empire through an appointed governor **5 CATEGORY FOR RANKING VEGETATION** a category superior to a subregion and subordinate to a subkingdom, used in certain biogeographical systems for ranking global vegetation types ■ **provinces** *npl* **NONMETROPOLITAN PARTS OF NATION** the parts of a country exclusive of the capital and larger cities [14C. Directly and via Old French < Latin *provincia* 'Roman territory' < *pro* 'before' + *vincere* 'conquer'.]

Provincetown /próvvins town/ town in SE Massachusetts, on the tip of Cape Cod. Population: 3,374 (1996 estimate).

provincial /prə vínsh'l/ *adj* **1 OF A PROVINCE** belonging to or coming from a province **2 UNSOPHISTICATED AND NARROW-MINDED** unsophisticated and unwilling to accept new ideas or ways of thinking (*disapproving*) **3 SIMPLE AND PLAIN** in a simple and plain decorative style ■ *n* **1 SOMEBODY FROM PROVINCES** somebody from the provinces, as opposed to somebody from a city or the capital **2 UNSOPHISTICATED PERSON** an unsophisticated or narrow-minded person (*disapproving*) **3 HEAD OF A PROVINCE** the head of an ecclesiastical province or of a religious order in a province [14C. Directly and via Old French < Latin *provincialis* < *provincia* (see PROVINCE).] —**provinciality** /prə vínshi állәti/ *n* —**provincially** /prə vínsh'li/ *adv*

Provincial Council *n* a council that formerly administered a New Zealand province

provincial court *n* a Canadian court that deals with less serious offences and whose judges are appointed and paid by the province

provincialism /prə vínshəlizəm/ *n* **1** narrowness in outlook and lack of sophistication (*disapproving*) **2** something such as a word, phrase, trait, or custom that originates in a province

provincial police *n* a Canadian police force that has jurisdiction within a province but not in urban areas that have their own municipal police

proving ground *n* a place or situation in which somebody or something new is tried out or tested

provirus /prṓ vīrəss/ *n* a form of a virus that is integrated into the genetic material of the host and passed on from one cell generation to the next

provision /prə vízh'n/ *n* **1 SUPPLYING** the act of providing or supplying something ○ *the provision of after-school clubs* **2 ACTION TAKEN TO PREPARE** a preparatory step taken to meet a possible or expected need ○ *No provision has been made for people with disabilities.* **3 LEGAL CLAUSE STATING CONDITION** a clause in a law or contract stating that a particular condition must be met **4 SOMETHING PROVIDED** something provided or supplied **5 ESTIMATE OF LIABILITY** an estimate of a known liability, e.g. depreciation, the value of which cannot be explicitly determined ■ **provisions** *npl* **FOOD AND OTHER SUPPLIES** supplies of food and other things required, especially for a journey ■ *vt* **PROVIDE SOMEBODY WITH SUPPLIES** to provide somebody with supplies, especially for a journey [14C. Via French < Latin *provision-* 'foresight, preparation' < *provis-*, past participle of *providere* (see PROVIDE).] —**provisioner** *n*

provisional /prə vízh'nəl/ *adj* **TEMPORARY OR CONDITIONAL** temporary or conditional, pending confirmation or validation ○ *a provisional government* ■ *n* **1** *US* **SOMEBODY HIRED TEMPORARILY** somebody hired temporarily for a job, especially before being qualified to do it permanently **2 TEMPORARY POSTAGE STAMP** a postage stamp used temporarily until an official permanent stamp is issued —**provisionally** *adv*

Provisional *n* a member of an unofficial faction of the Irish Republican Army that was originally set up to strive for an independent Ireland by force of arms ■ *adj* relating to the faction of the Irish Republican Army that strives to achieve its goals through using force

provisional licence *n* a driving licence for people who have not yet passed a driving test and are subject to various restrictions. US term **learner's permit**

proviso /prə vīzō/ (*plural* **-sos** *or* **-soes**) *n* **1** a condition asked as part of an agreement **2** a clause introducing a condition in a contract [15C. < medieval Latin *proviso quod* 'provided that' < Latin *proviso*, a form of *provisus*, past participle of *providere* 'prepare in advance, supply'.]

provisory /prə vīzəri/ *adj* **1** stating a condition **2** = **provisional** *adj*. [Early 17C. < medieval Latin *provisorius* 'of papal provision' < *provisus* (see PROVISO).] —**provisorily** *adv*

provitamin /prō víttəmin/ *n* a precursor that is converted to a vitamin during normal biochemical processes

Provo /prṓvō/ (*plural* **-vos**) *n* a Provisional (*informal*) [Late 20C. Shortening.]

provocation /próvvə káysh'n/ *n* **1 ACT OF PROVOKING** the act of provoking somebody or something **2 CAUSE OF ANGER** something that makes somebody angry or indignant **3 REASON FOR ATTACKING** something that incites somebody to attack somebody else [14C. Directly or via French < Latin *provocation-* < *provocare* (see PROVOKE).]

provocative /prə vókətiv/ *adj* **1** deliberately aimed at exciting or annoying people ○ *a provocative remark* **2** intended to arouse other people sexually [15C. Directly and via Old French *provocatif* < late Latin *provocativus* < *provocare* (see PROVOKE).] —**provocatively** *adv* —**provocativeness** *n*

provoke /prə vṓk/ (**-vokes, -voking, -voked**) *vt* **1 MAKE SOMEBODY FEEL ANGRY** to make somebody feel angry or exasperated **2 ELICIT RESPONSE** to be the cause or occasion of an emotion or response ○ *Her bravery provoked a lot of sympathy.* **3 STIR SOMEBODY TO EMOTION** to stir somebody to an emotion or response **4 INCITE** to act in a way intended to bring a desired result about **5 CAUSE ACTIVITY** to serve as the stimulating factor for an activity [14C. Directly or via Old French *provoker* < Latin *provocare* 'summon' < *vocare* 'to call' < *vox* 'voice'.] —**provoker** *n* —**provokingly** *adv*

provolone /prṓvə lṓni/ *n* **1** a smoked cheese originally made in Italy that has a mild flavour and is light in colour **2** a semisoft Italian cheese originally made from water buffalo's milk and now from cow's milk, often smoked and used widely in cooking [Mid-20C. < Italian < *provola* 'buffalo's milk cheese'.]

provost /próvvəst/ *n* **1 HEAD OF EDUCATIONAL ESTABLISHMENT** the head of some educational establishments, especially Oxford or Cambridge colleges **2 SENIOR DIGNITARY OF CATHEDRAL** the senior dignitary of a cathedral or collegiate church **3 HEAD OF SCOTTISH CITY GOVERNMENT** until 1975, the person elected to be head of government in a city, town, or borough in Scotland. ◊ **Lord Provost** [Pre-12C. < medieval Latin *propositus*, alteration of Latin *praepositus* 'somebody placed in front' < *ponere* 'to place'.]

provost court /prə vṓ-/ *n* a military court set up in an occupied hostile territory for the trial of minor offences

provost guard /prə vṓ-/ *n US* a detail of soldiers having police duties under the authority of the provost marshal

provost marshal /prə vṓ-/ *n* the army officer in charge of a unit of military police

prow /prow/ *n* **1** the forward part of a ship **2** the projecting front part of something other than a ship [Mid-16C. Via French *proue* < Latin *prora* < Greek *prōra* 'front of a ship' < *pro* 'forward'.]

prowess /prów ess/ *n* **1** exceptional ability or skill **2** extraordinary valour and ability in combat [13C. < Old French *proesce* 'bravery' < *prou* 'brave', variant of *prud* (see PROUD).]

prowl /prowl/ *vti* to roam around an area stealthily in search of prey, food, or opportunity ■ *n* the act of roaming stealthily for prey [14C. < ?] ◇ **on the prowl** moving around stealthily looking for something or somebody

prowl car *n US* a police patrol car

prowler /prówlər/ *n* **1** a person who goes about stealthily while waiting for the chance to commit criminal acts **2** an animal that or person who prowls

prox. *abbr* proximo

proxemics /prok séemiks/ *n* the study of the distance individuals maintain between each other in social interaction and how this separation is significant [Mid-20C. < PROXIMITY after PHONEMICS.]

proximal /próksim'l/ *adj* **1** nearer to the point of reference or to the centre of the body. ◊ **distal 2** describes the surface of a tooth nearest to either the one behind it or the one in front of it **3** = **proximate** [Early 18C. < Latin *proximus* (see PROXIMITY).] —**proximally** *adv*

proximate /próksimət/, **proximal** /próksiməl/ *adj* **1 NEAREST** nearest in order, time, or place **2 VERY CLOSE** very close in space or time **3 ABOUT TO HAPPEN** soon to appear or take place **4 APPROXIMATE** almost accurate [Late 16C. < Latin *proximat-*, past participle of *proximare* 'come near' < *proximus* (see PROXIMITY).] —**proximately** *adv* —**proximateness** *n* —**proximation** /próksi máysh'n/ *n*

proxime accessit /próksimi ak séssit, próksi may ək-/ *n* the person who comes immediately after the winner in a competitive examination (*formal*) [< Latin, 'he or she came very close']

proximity /prok símməti/ *n* closeness in space or time [15C. < Latin *proximitas* 'nearness' < *proximus* 'nearest', the superlative form of *prope* 'near'.]

proximity card *n* a plastic card carrying electronically coded information accessed by holding the card near a reading device

proximity fuse *n* a fuse, typically part of a warhead, that will activate and cause detonation when the warhead is at a specified distance from the target

ϟ **proximity operator** *n* a Boolean operator separating words or phrases in a text search that directs the search engine to locate pages in which the words are near one another in any direction, the acceptable distance varying among search engines

proximo /próksimō/ *adv* occurring during the next month (*archaic*) [Mid-19C. < Latin *proximo (mense)* 'in the next (month)'.]

proxy /próksi/ (*plural* **-ies**) *n* **1 FUNCTION OR POWER OF SUBSTITUTE** the function, power, or capacity to act of a deputy authorized to substitute for another **2 SOMEBODY ACTING AS SUBSTITUTE** somebody authorized to substitute for somebody else **3 AUTHORIZATION DOCUMENT FOR STAND-IN** a document authorizing somebody to act for another person **4 DOCUMENT AUTHORIZING VOTE ON ANOTHER'S STOCK** a document authorizing somebody to vote on matters of corporate stock on behalf of somebody else [15C. < medieval Latin *procuratia*, alteration of Latin *procuratio* 'care, management' < *procurare* 'take care of'.]

PRP *abbr* **1** profit-related pay **2** performance-related pay

prude /prood/ *n* a person who is easily offended by matters relating to sex or nudity [Early 18C. < French, back-formation < Old French *prudefemme* (misunderstood as 'virtuous woman'), feminine of *prud'homme* < assumed *pro de ome* 'fine (thing) of a man'.] —**prudery** *n* —**prudish** *adj* —**prudishly** *adv* —**prudishness** *n*

prudent /próod'nt/ *adj* **1 HAVING GOOD SENSE** having good sense in dealing with practical matters **2 CAREFULLY CONSIDERING CONSEQUENCES** using good judgment to consider consequences and to act accordingly **3 CAREFUL IN MANAGING RESOURCES** careful in managing resources so as to provide for the future [14C. Directly or via French < Latin *prudent-*, contraction of *provident-* (see PROVIDENT).] —**prudence** *n* —**prudently** *adv*

SYNONYMS See ***cautious***.

prudential /proo dénsh'l/ *adj* **1** resulting from, depending on, or marked by prudence **2** using prudence, especially in business matters —**prudentially** *adv*

pruinose /próo i nōss, -nōz/ *adj* having a white powdery coating, e.g. on a fruit or leaf [Early 19C. < Latin *pruinosus* < *pruina* 'hoarfrost'.]

prune[1] /proon/ (**prunes, pruning, pruned**) *v* **1** *vti* **CUT BRANCHES** to cut branches away from a plant to encourage fuller growth **2** *vt* **REDUCE SOMETHING BY REMOVING UNWANTED MATERIAL** to reduce something by removing whatever is unnecessary or unwanted **3** *vt* **REMOVE SOMETHING UNNECESSARY** to remove something considered unnecessary or unwanted [14C. < Old French *proignier* 'cut in a rounded shape in front' < Latin *rotundus* 'round'.] —**prunable** *adj* —**pruner** *n*

prune[2] /proon/ *n* **1 DRIED PLUM** a plum that has been preserved by drying **2** *US* **PLUM TO BE DRIED** a plum suitable for drying (*informal*) **3 OFFENSIVE TERM** an offensive term that deliberately insults somebody's intelligence, competence, or ability to interest others (*insult*) [14C. < French < Latin *prunum* < Greek *prounon*, variant of *proumnon* 'plum'.]

prunella /pro͝o néllə/ *n* a wool fabric with a twill weave. Use: academic gowns, clerical robes, shoe uppers. [Mid-17C. < French *prunelle* 'sloe', a diminutive of *prune* 'plum'.]

prunelle /pro͝o nél/ *n* **1** a sweet French liqueur flavoured with sloes **2** TEXTILES = **prunella** [15C. < French (see PRUNELLA).]

pruning hook *n* a tool with a hooked blade and sometimes a long handle, used to prune trees and bushes

prurient /pro͝ori ənt/ *adj* having or intended to arouse an unwholesome interest in sexual matters [Mid-17C. < Latin *prurient-*, present participle of *prurire* 'itch, long for' < ?] —**prurience** *n* —**pruriently** *adv*

prurigo /proor rígō/ *n* a chronic inflammatory skin disease causing small itchy swellings [Mid-17C. < Latin, 'itching' < *prurire* (see PRURIENT).] —**pruriginous** /proor ríjjinəss/ *adj*

pruritus /proor rītəss/ *n* an intense feeling of itchiness [Mid-17C. < Latin, past participle of *prurire* (see PRURIENT).]

prusik /prússik/ *n* **1 prusik, Prusik, prusik knot** KNOT ATTACHING SLING TO ROPE a knot used to tie a small sling to a climbing rope, forming a loop that holds fast when weighted but can be slid along the rope when unweighted **2 prusik, Prusik** SLING ATTACHED TO ROPE a small sling attached to a climbing rope using a prusik knot ■ *vi* ASCEND OR DESCEND ROPE to ascend or descend a climbing rope using a prusik sling [Mid-20C. After the Austrian mountaineer, Karl *Prusik*.]

Prussia /prúshə/ historical region of Germany and former kingdom in north-central Europe —**Prussian** *adj, n*

Prussian blue *n* **1 Prussian blue, prussian blue** a water-insoluble blue iron pigment **2** a rich dark blue colour tinged with green [*Prussian* because discovered in 1704 by a Prussian dyer called Diesbach] —**Prussian-blue** *adj*

prussiate /prúshi ət/ *n* **1** a chemical compound that is ferrocyanide or ferricyanide **2** a chemical compound that is a salt of hydrocyanic acid [Late 18C. < *prussic* (see PRUSSIC ACID).]

prussic acid /prússik-/ *n* CHEM = **hydrocyanic acid** [*Prussic* < *Prussian*, because it was first obtained from Prussian blue]

pry[1] /prī/ *vi* (**pries, prying, pried**) INQUIRE NOSILY to look inquisitively or inquire nosily about somebody's private affairs ■ *n* (*plural* **pries**) **1** ACT OF PRYING the act of prying into somebody's private affairs **2** SOMEBODY WHO PRIES a person who enquires and delves into other people's business [14C] —**pryingly** *adv*

pry[2] /prī/ (**pries, prying, pried**) *vt US* to open or part something by using leverage [Early 19C. Back-formation < PRISE, misunderstood as 3rd person present singular.]

pryer *n* = **prier**

Przewalski's horse /pəzhə válskiz-, shə-/ *n* a wild horse with a stocky body, a chestnut coat, and an erect dark mane. Native to: Asia. *Equus caballus przevalskii*. [Late 19C. Translation of Latin *equus przewalskii*, after the Russian explorer N. M. *Przheval'skiĭ* (1839–88).]

PS *abbr* **1** phrase structure **2** Police Sergeant **3 PS, ps** postscript **4** Permanent Secretary **5** private secretary **6** prompt side **7** Passenger Steamer

Ps. *abbr* (Book of) Psalms

Psa. *abbr* (Book of) Psalms

psalm /saam/, **Psalm** *n* a sacred song or poem of praise, especially one in the Book of Psalms in the Bible [12C. Via late Latin *psalmus* < Greek *psalmos* 'harpsong' < *psallein* 'to pluck'.] —**psalmic** *adj*

psalmist /saámist/ *n* the author of a psalm

psalmody /saámədi, sálm-/ (*plural* **-dies**) *n* **1** PSALM SINGING the singing of psalms in divine worship **2** MUSICAL ARRANGEMENTS FOR PSALMS the prescribed arrangements for singing individual psalms from the Book of Psalms **3** SET OF PSALMS a collection of psalms [14C. Via late Latin *psalmodia* < Greek *psalmōidia* < *psalmos* (see PSALM) + *ōidē* 'song'.] —**psalmodic** /saa móddik, sal-/ *adj* —**psalmodist** /saámədist, sálm-/ *n*

Psalms /saamz/ *n* a book of the Bible made up of 150 poems and hymns to God, traditionally believed to have been written by King David

Psalter /sáwltər, sóltər/, **psalter** *n* a book containing psalms, or the Book of Psalms, used in worship [Pre-12C. < Latin *psalterium* 'book of psalms' in ecclesiastical Latin (see PSALTERY); reinforced by Old French *sautier*.]

psalterium /sawl teéri əm, sol-/ (*plural* **-a** /-ə/) *n* ZOOL = **omasum** [Mid-19C. < Latin, 'stringed instrument' (see PSALTERY).]

psaltery /sáwltəri, sóltəri/ (*plural* **-ies**) *n* an ancient musical instrument with numerous strings, plucked with the fingers or with a plectrum [13C. Via Old French *sauterie* < Latin *psalterium* 'stringed instrument' < Greek *psaltērion* 'stringed instrument played by plucking' < *psallein* 'to pluck'.]

psammite /sámmīt/ *n* **1** rock formed principally of sand **2** a metamorphosed sandstone containing large amounts of quartz [Mid-19C. < Greek *psammos* 'sand'.] —**psammitic** /sa míttik/ *adj*

p's and q's /peéz ən kyoóz/ *npl* the polite manners and behaviour that somebody adopts, e.g., when eager to make a good impression ○ *We'd better mind our p's and q's.* [< *mind one's p's and q's* < ?]

PSBR *abbr* public sector borrowing requirement

PSE *n* the study of social, especially health-related, issues as a school subject. Full form **Personal and Social Education**

psephology /si fólləji/ *n* the statistical study of elections [Mid-20C. < Greek *psephos* 'pebble, vote'; from the Greek practice of using pebbles to vote.] —**psephological** /séffə lójjik'l/ *adj* —**psephologically** /-lójjikli/ *adv* —**psephologist** /si fólləjist/ *n*

pseud /syood/ *n* a person who pretends to know much about art and culture [Mid-20C. Shortening of PSEUDO.]

pseud. *abbr* pseudonym

pseud- *prefix* = **pseudo-** (*sometimes used before vowels*)

pseudepigrapha /syoódi píggrəfə/ *npl* certain anonymous or pseudonymous writings professing to be biblical but not included in any biblical canon [Late 17C. < Greek, a form of *pseudepigraphos* 'with false title' < PSEUDO- + *epigraphein* 'write on' (see EPIGRAPH).] —**pseudepigraphic** /syoód epi gráffik/ *adj* —**pseudepigraphical** /-gráffik'l/ *adj* —**pseudepigraphous** *adj*

pseudo /syoódō/ *adj* not authentic or sincere, in spite of appearances [14C. < Greek *pseudo-* < *pseudēs* (see PSEUDO-).]

pseudo- *prefix* **1** similar ○ *pseudobulb* **2** false, spurious ○ *pseudoscience* [< Greek *pseudēs* < *pseudein* 'lie' < ?]

pseudobulb /syoódō bulb/ *n* a thickened part of a stem that lies above the ground, e.g. in many orchids

pseudocarp /syoódō kaarp/ *n* a fruit formed by combining the ripened ovary with another structure, often the receptacle, as, e.g., in strawberries [Mid-19C. < PSEUDO- + Greek *karpos* 'fruit'.] —**pseudocarpous** /syoódō kaárpəss/ *adj*

pseudoclassic /syoódō klássik/ *adj* posing as or mistakenly believed to be classic

pseudoclassicism /syoódō klássissizəm/ *n* the use in art and literature of ancient Greek and Roman styles —**pseudoclassical** *adj*

pseudocoelomate /syoódō seéləmət, syoódō seélə mayt/ *n* an invertebrate such as a nematode or rotifer that has a fluid-filled body cavity not lined with mesoderm tissue —**pseudocoelomate** *adj*

pseudocyesis /syoódō sī eéssiss/ (*plural* **-ses** /-seez/) *n* a phantom pregnancy (*technical*) [Mid-19C. < Greek *kuesis* 'conception'.]

pseudogene /syoódō jeen/ *n* a nonfunctional DNA sequence that is very similar to the sequence of a functional gene

pseudohermaphroditism /syoódō hur máffrə dītizəm/ *n* a condition in which somebody has either ovaries (**female pseudohermaphroditism**) or testes (**male pseudohermaphroditism**) but has external genitalia of ambiguous appearance

pseudo-intransitive *adj* describes a normally transitive verb used when its direct object is not explicitly stated or when its direct object becomes the subject of the sentence

pseudomonad /syoódō mō nad/ *n* a rod-shaped bacterium that lives in soil or decomposing organic material, some of which are pathogenic to plants and animals. Genus: *Pseudomonas*. [Early 20C. < modern Latin *Pseudomonad-*, stem of *Pseudomonas* 'false monad' < *monad-* 'monad'.]

pseudomorph /syoódō mawrf/ *n* **1** a mineral that has replaced another and taken its shape **2** an irregular or deceptive form —**pseudomorphic** /syoódō máwrfik/ *adj* —**pseudomorphism** *n* —**pseudomorphous** /-máwrfəss/ *adj*

pseudonym /syoódənim/ *n* a name that is not somebody's original name, especially one used by an author in publications [Mid-19C. Via French *pseudonyme* < Greek *pseudōnumon* 'false name' < *onuma*, variant of *onoma* 'name'.] —**pseudonymity** /syoódə nímməti/ *n* —**pseudonymous** /syoo dónniməss/ *adj* —**pseudonymously** *adv* —**pseudonymousness** *n*

pseudopodium /syoódō pṓdi əm/ (*plural* **-a** /-ə/), **pseudopod** /syoódō pod/ *n* a temporary cytoplasmic protrusion in amoeba and other protozoa used for locomotion and to take up food

pseudopregnancy /syoódō prégnənssi/ (*plural* **-cies**) *n* MED = **phantom pregnancy**

ϟ **pseudorandom** /syoódō rándəm/ *adj* relating to random numbers generated by a computational process

pseudoscience /syoódō sī ənss/ *n* a theory or method doubtfully or mistakenly held to be scientific —**pseudoscientist** *n*

pseudoscorpion /syoódō skáwrpi ən/ *n* a minute eight-legged organism (**arthropod**) that lives beneath bark and in leaf litter catching larvae and other invertebrates, using long mouthparts that resemble pincers. Order: Pseudoscorpiones.

pseudosophistication /syoódō sə físti káysh'n/ *n* false or pretended sophistication

pseudotuberculosis /syoódō tyoō búrkyoō lṓssiss/ *n* a disease marked by the formation of nodules of inflamed tissue similar to those in tuberculosis but not caused by the tubercle bacillus

psf, p.s.f. *abbr* pounds per square foot

Psge *abbr* Passage (*in addresses*)

pshaw /pshaw/ *interj* used to express disbelief, impatience, or contempt [Late 17C. An imitation of the sound made.]

PSHE *n* the study of social, especially health-related, issues as a school subject. Full form **Personal, Social, and Health Education**

psi[1] /psī/ *n* the 23rd letter of the Greek alphabet [15C. < Greek *psei*.]

psi[2], **p.s.i.** *abbr* pounds per square inch

psilocin /sīləssin, síll-/ *n* $C_{12}H_{16}N_2O$ a hallucinogenic compound produced in the body after eating a particular mushroom [Mid-20C. < Greek *psilos* 'smooth'.]

psilocybin /sīlə sībin, síllə-/ *n* $C_{13}HN_2O_3P_2$ a crystalline hallucinogen obtained from a particular mushroom [Mid-20C. < Greek *psilos* 'smooth' + *kubē* 'head'.]

psilomelane /si lómmi layn/ *n* a mixed hydrated manganese oxide mineral occurring in dark-coloured rounded masses [Mid-19C. < Greek *psilos* 'smooth' + *melas* 'black'.]

psilophyte /sīlə fīt/ *n* **1** a primitive leafless vascular plant of the Silurian period with a horizontal stalk that grew beneath the ground sending up short vertical stems **2** PLANTS = **whisk fern** [Early 20C. < Greek *psilos* 'smooth' + *phyton* 'plant'.]

psi particle *n* SCI = **J/psi particle**

psittacine /síttə sīn, -ssin/ *adj* belonging to the parrot family, or affecting, resembling, or relating to parrots or related birds ■ *n* a bird that belongs to the parrot family [Late 19C. Via Latin *psittacinus* < *psittacus* < Greek *psittakos* 'parrot'.]

psittacosis /síttə kṓssiss/ *n* a contagious disease of parrots and related birds that can be transmitted to humans, sometimes causing serious lung infection. It is caused by the bacterium *Chlamydia psittaci*. [Late 19C. Via Latin *psittacus* < Greek *psittakos* 'parrot'.]

PSL *abbr* private sector liquidity

psoas /sṓ əss/ (*plural* **-ai** /-ī/ *or* **-ae** /-ee/) *n* either of two pairs of muscles that are located in the groin and help to flex the hip joint [Late 17C. < Greek, a plural of *psoa* 'muscle of the loins'.]

psocid /sṓkid, sóssid/ (*plural* **-cids** *or* **-cid**) *n* a tiny winged insect with reduced veins in the wings and unusual rasping mouthparts. Family: Psocidae. [Late 19C. Via modern Latin *Psocus* < Greek *psōkhein* 'to grind'.]

psoralen /sáwrələn/ *n* a toxic substance. Source: plants, e.g. celery, carrots, parsley. Use: in conjunction with ultraviolet light in treatment of severe acne and psoriasis. [Mid-20C. Via modern Latin *Psoralea* < Greek *psoraleos* 'itchy' < *psora* 'itch, mange'.]

psoriasis /sə rī əssiss/ *n* a skin disease marked by red scaly patches [Late 17C. Via Latin, 'scurvy, mange' < Greek

psōriasis 'being itchy' < *psōra* 'itch, mange'.] —**psoriatic** /sáwri áttik/ adj

PSS, pss abbr postscripts

psst /pst/ interj used to get the attention of one person without alerting others [Early 20C. An imitation of the sound.]

PST abbr Pacific Standard Time

PSTN abbr Public Switched Telephone Network

psuedonym incorrect spelling of **pseudonym**

PSV n, abbr public service vehicle

psych /sīk/ v US 1 vt = psych out v. 1 2 vr = psych up [Early 20C. < ?]
psych out v (informal) 1 vt INTIMIDATE to intimidate or undermine the confidence of somebody 2 vt PUZZLE SOMETHING OUT to analyse, solve, or understand something such as a problem 3 vt GUESS SOMEBODY'S THOUGHT PROCESSES to guess or anticipate correctly the intentions or thoughts of another person 4 vi COLLAPSE EMOTIONALLY to break down psychologically ○ The prisoner psyched out completely.
psych up vr to prepare yourself mentally for a task or action (informal) ○ She's been psyching herself up for this interview all week.

psych. abbr 1 psychological 2 psychology

psych- prefix = psycho- (before vowels)

psyche /sīki/ n 1 the human spirit or soul 2 the human mind as the centre of thought and behaviour [Mid-17C. Via Latin < Greek psukhē 'breath, soul, mind' < psukhein 'breathe'.]

Psyche /sīki/ n in Roman mythology, a beautiful young woman loved by Cupid

psyched /sīkt/ adj US extremely excited about and psychologically prepared for something (slang)

psychedelia /sīkə deeli ə/ n the subculture of artefacts, phenomena, writings, or art associated with psychedelic drugs [Mid-20C. Back-formation < PSYCHEDELIC.]

psychedelic /sīkə déllik/ adj 1 RELATING TO HALLUCINOGENIC DRUGS describes, relating to, or caused by, drugs that generate hallucinations, abnormal psychic states, or states that resemble psychiatric disorders 2 OVERLOADING THE SENSES weird, distorted, wildly colourful, or otherwise resembling images or sounds experienced by somebody under the influence of a psychedelic drug ■ n DRUG a psychedelic drug [Mid-20C. < Greek psukhē 'mind' < dēloun 'reveal, make visible' < dēlos 'clear'.] —**psychedelically** adv

psychiatric /sīki áttrik/ adj relating to psychiatry or its patients

psychiatric hospital n a hospital dedicated to the treatment, care, and protection of people with serious psychiatric disorders who are judged to be unfit or unsafe to be at large

psychiatric social worker n a social worker specializing in psychiatric cases

psychiatrist /sī kī́ ətrist/ n a doctor trained in the treatment of people with mental illnesses

psychiatry /sī kī́ atri/ n a medical specialization concerned with the diagnosis and treatment of disorders that have primarily mental or behavioural symptoms and with the care of people having such disorders [Mid-19C. < French psychiatrie < Greek psukhē (see PSYCHE) + iatreia 'cure'.]

psychic /sīkik/ adj 1 OF MIND relating to the human mind 2 OUTSIDE SCIENTIFIC KNOWLEDGE outside the sphere of scientific knowledge 3 SUPPOSEDLY SENSITIVE TO SUPERNATURAL FORCES claiming or believed to have extraordinary perception and sensitivity to nonphysical or supernatural forces ■ n SOMEBODY SUPPOSEDLY SENSITIVE TO SUPERNATURAL FORCES a person who is or is believed to be sensitive to nonphysical or supernatural forces [Late 18C. < Greek psukhikos 'pertaining to the soul or spirit' < psukhē (see PSYCHE).] —**psychical** adj —**psychically** adv

psycho /sīko/ n (plural -chos) an offensive term for somebody who has a psychiatric or personality disorder (slang) ■ adj an offensive term meaning behaving in an uncontrolled and unpredictable way (slang) [Mid-20C. Shortening of PSYCHOPATH.]

psycho- prefix 1 mind, mental ○ psychoactive 2 psychology, psychological ○ psychobabble [< Greek psukhē (see PSYCHE).]

psychoacoustics /sīkō ə koóstiks/ n the scientific study of the psychological and physiological principles of sound perception (+ singular verb)

psychoactive /sīkō áktiv/ adj describes drugs or medication having a significant effect on mood or behaviour

psychoanalyse /sīkō ánnə līz/ vt to apply the methods of psychoanalysis in a psychotherapeutic setting —**psychoanalyser** n

psychoanalysis /sīkō ə nálləssiss/ n 1 a psychological theory and therapeutic method developed by Sigmund Freud, based on the ideas that mental life functions on both conscious and unconscious levels and that childhood events have a powerful psychological influence throughout life 2 treatment by psychoanalysis, interpreting material presented by a patient in order to bring the processes of the unconscious into conscious awareness —**psychoanalyst** /sīkō ánnəlist/ n —**psychoanalytic** /sīkō ánnə líttik/ adj —**psychoanalytical** /-ánnə líttik'l/ —**psychoanalytically** /-ánnə líttikli/ adv

psychoanalyze vt US = psychoanalyse

psychobabble /sīkō babb'l/ n psychological jargon used inaccurately to talk about personal problems

psychobiography /sīkō bī óggrəfi/ (plural -phies) n a biography that focuses on the psychological profile of the subject

psychobiology /sīkō bī ólləji/ n the study of the biological bases of behaviour —**psychobiological** /sīkō bī ə lójjik'l/ —**psychobiologically** /-lójjikli/ adv —**psychobiologist** /sīkō bī ólləjist/ n

psychochemical /sīkō kémmik'l/ n a drug that affects mood or behaviour ■ adj relating to or acting like a psychoactive drug

psychodrama /sīkō draamə/ n a form of psychotherapy pioneered by Jacob Moreno in which patients are required to perform roles in dramas illustrating their own particular problems before an audience of other patients —**psychodramatic** /sīkō drə máttik/ adj

psychodynamics /sīkō dī́ námmiks/ n 1 the interaction of the emotional and motivational forces that affect behaviour and mental states, especially on a subconscious level (+ singular or plural verb) 2 the study of the emotional and motivational forces that affect behaviour and mental states (+ singular verb) —**psychodynamic** adj —**psychodynamically** adv

psychogenesis /sīkō jénnəssiss/ n the psychological rather than physical cause of a psychological disorder —**psychogenetic** /-jə néttik/ adj —**psychogenetically** adv

psychogenic /sīkō jénnik/ adj originating in mental or emotional rather than in physiological processes —**psychogenically** adv

psychogeriatric /sīkō jérri áttrik/ adj relating to psychiatric disorders experienced by senior citizens, or to senior citizens with such disorders

psychogeriatrics /sīkō jérri áttriks/ n the branch of medicine concerned with the psychology and psychiatric disorders experienced by senior citizens (+ singular verb)

psychohistory /sīkō hístəri/ (plural -ries) n psychological analysis of somebody's life or of historical events —**psychohistorian** /-hi stáwri ən/ n —**psychohistorical** /-stórrik'l/ adj

psychokinesis /sīkō ki neéssiss, -kī neéssiss/ n the supposed ability to use mental powers to make objects move or to otherwise affect them —**psychokinetic** /-ki néttik, -kī-/ adj

psychol. abbr 1 psychological 2 psychologist 3 psychology

psycholinguistics /sīkō ling gwístiks/ n the study of language acquisition and use in relation to the psychological factors controlling its use and recognition (+ singular verb) —**psycholinguist** /sīkō líng gwist/ n —**psycholinguistic** /-gwístik/ adj

psychological /sīkə lójjik'l/ adj 1 OF PSYCHOLOGY relating to psychology 2 OF THE MIND relating to the mind or mental processes 3 AFFECTING THE MIND affecting or intended to affect the mind or mental processes 4 EXISTING ONLY IN THE MIND existing only in the mind, without having a physical basis ○ His health problem is psychological. —**psychologically** adv

psychological dependence n strong desire for something without being physically addicted to it

psychological moment n the time at which the mental state of a person or group of people is most receptive or appropriate

psychological warfare n 1 tactics that use propaganda to try to demoralize an enemy in war, usually including the civilian population 2 the use of psychological tactics to disconcert and disadvantage an opponent in an everyday or a business context, e.g. causing fear or anxiety

psychologise vti = psychologize

psychologism /sī kólləjizəm/ n a belief in or emphasis on the importance of psychology in other fields, e.g. history or philosophy —**psychologistic** /sī kóllə jístik/ adj

psychologist /sī kólləjist/ n 1 a professional who studies behaviour and experience, and who is licensed to provide therapeutic services or work in an academic setting 2 a student of psychology, especially as a main subject at university or college

psychologize /sī kóllə jīz/ (-gizes, -gizing, -gized), psychologise (-gises, -gising, -gised) v 1 vt to interpret behaviour in psychological terms or concepts 2 vi to think, analyse, or reason psychologically

psychology /sī kólləji/ (plural -gies) n 1 STUDY OF MIND the scientific study of the human mind and mental states, and of human and animal behaviour 2 CHARACTERISTIC MENTAL MAKEUP the characteristic temperament and associated behaviour of an individual or group, or that exhibited by those engaged in a particular activity 3 SUBTLE MANIPULATIVE BEHAVIOUR subtle clever actions and words used to influence a person or group

psychomachia /sīkō máki ə/, **psychomachy** /sī kómaki/ n conflict of the soul between the spirit and the flesh (literary) [Early 17C. < late Latin < Greek psukhē 'soul' + makhē 'battle'.]

psychometrics /sīkō méttriks/ n a branch of psychology dealing with the measurement of mental traits, capacities, and processes (+ singular verb)

psychometry /sī kómmətri/ n 1 PSYCHOL = psychometrics 2 the alleged ability to obtain information about a person or event by touching an object related to that person or event —**psychometric** /sīkə méttrik/ adj —**psychometrical** adj —**psychometrically** adv —**psychometrician** /sīkō mə trísh'n/ n —**psychometrist** /sī kómmətrist/ n

psychomotor /sīkō mṓtər/ adj relating to bodily movement triggered by mental activity, especially voluntary muscle action

psychoneuroimmunology /sīkō nyooōrō ímmyoō nólləji/ n a branch of medicine concerned with how emotions affect the immune system

psychoneurosis /sīkō nyoō róssiss/ (plural -roses /-seez/) n PSYCHIAT = neurosis —**psychoneurotic** /-róttik/ adj

psychopath /sīkō path/ n an offensive term for somebody with a personality disorder marked by antisocial thought and behaviour —**psychopathic** /-páthik/ adj —**psychopathically** adv

psychopathology /sīkō pə thólləji/ n the study of the causes and development of psychiatric disorders —**psychopathological** /-páthə lójjik'l/ adj —**psychopathologist** n

psychopathy /sī kóppathi/ (plural -thies) n 1 a severe personality disorder marked by antisocial thought and behaviour (informal) 2 any psychiatric illness (dated)

psychopharmacology /sīkō faárma kólləji/ n the scientific study of the effects of drugs on thought and behaviour —**psychopharmacological** /-kə lójjik'l/ adj —**psychopharmacologist** n

psychophysics /síkō fízziks/ *n* a branch of psychology dealing with the effects of physical stimuli on sensory perceptions and mental states (*+ singular verb*) —**psychophysical** *adj*

psychophysiology /síkō fízzi óllәji/ *n* PSYCHOL = **physiological psychology**

psychosexual /síkō sékshoo әl/ *adj* relating to the mental and emotional aspects of sexuality and sexual development —**psychosexuality** /-állәti/ *n* —**psychosexually** *adv*

psychosis /sī kóssiss/ (*plural* **-ses** /-seez/) *n* a psychiatric disorder such as schizophrenia or mania that is marked by delusions, hallucinations, incoherency, and distorted perceptions of reality —**psychotic** /sī kóttik/ *adj* —**psychotically** *adv*

psychosocial /síkō sṓsh'l/ *adj* relating to both the psychological and the social aspects of something, or relating to something that has both of these aspects

psychosomatic /síkō sә máttik/ *adj* **1** describes a physical illness that is caused by mental factors such as stress, or the effects related to such illnesses **2** involving both the mind and body [Mid-19C. < PSYCHO- + SOMATIC.] —**psychosomatically** *adv*

psychosurgery /síkō súrjәri/ (*plural* **-ies**) *n* surgery now performed only in rare cases to relieve severe psychotic disorder or to prevent some forms of epileptic seizure —**psychosurgeon** /-surjәn/ *n*

psychosynthesis /síkō sínthәssiss/ *n* **1** a psychotherapeutic movement, opposed to psychoanalysis, that attempts to restore useful inhibitions and control **2** a holistic form of psychotherapy involving clients in an exploration of the emotional, intellectual, physical, and spiritual elements of the self

psychotherapy /síkō thérrәpi/ *n* the treatment of mental disorders by psychological methods —**psychotherapeutic** /-thérrә pyoótik/ *adj* —**psychotherapeutically** *adv* —**psychotherapist** /-thérrәpist/ *n*

psychothriller /síkō thrilәr/ *n* an exciting book or film in which tension is generated by the psychological pressures on the characters rather than by action

psychotomimetic /sī kóttō mi méttik/ *adj* describes a drug or other factor that produces a condition resembling psychosis ■ *n* a drug or other factor that produces a condition resembling psychosis [Mid-20C. < PSYCHOSIS + MIMETIC after *psychotic*.]

psychotropic /síkō trṓpik, -tróppik/ *adj* describes drugs that are capable of affecting the mind, e.g. those used to treat psychiatric disorders ■ *n* a drug capable of affecting the mind, e.g. one used to treat psychiatric disorders

psychro- *prefix* cold ○ *psychrophilic* [< Greek *psukhros* < ?]

psychrometer /sī krómmitәr/ *n* an instrument consisting of two thermometers, used to measure atmospheric humidity

psychrophilic /síkrō fíllik/ *adj* thriving at low temperatures ○ *psychrophilic bacteria*

psyllium /sílli әm/ *n* an annual plant of the plantain family with edible seeds. Use: dietary source of fibre, mild laxative. Native to: Europe, Asia. *Plantago psyllium*. [Mid-16C. Via Latin < Greek *psullion* 'little flea' < *psulla* 'flea'; because the seeds resemble fleas.]

pt^1 *abbr* **1** part **2** patient **3** payment **4** pint **5** point **6** port

ϟ **pt**^{2} *abbr* Portugal (*in Internet addresses*)

Pt^1 *abbr* (*in placenames*) **1** Point **2** Port

Pt^2 *symbol* platinum

PT^1 *abbr* **1** Pacific Time **2** *US* physical therapy **3** postal telegraph

PT^2 *n* gymnastics, athletics, team sports, and other forms of physical exercise taught to children at school. Full form **physical training**

pt. *abbr* preterite

p.t. *abbr* **1** past tense **2** part-time **3** pro tem

pta *symbol* peseta

PTA *abbr* **1** Parent Teacher Association **2** Passenger Transport Authority

ptarmigan /taármigәn/ (*plural* **-gan** *or* **-gans**) *n* a wild grouse of mountainous regions, having feet covered with feathers and white plumage in the winter. Genus: *Lagopus*. [Late 16C. Alteration (influenced by Greek *pt-* as in *pteron* 'wing') of Gaelic *tarmachan*, literally 'little ptarmigan' < *tarmach* 'ptarmigan'.]

ϟ **PTB** *abbr* powers that be (*in e-mails*)

PT boat *n US* NAVY = **motor torpedo boat**

PTC *abbr* phenylthiocarbamide

Pte *abbr* Private

PTE *abbr* Passenger Transport Executive

pteranodon /tә ránnә don/ *n* an extinct toothless flying reptile with a bony crest. Genus: *Pteranodon*.

pteridology /térri dóllәji/ *n* a branch of botany dealing with ferns [Mid-19C. < Greek *pterid-*, stem of *pteris* 'fern' + -LOGY.] —**pteridological** /térridә lójjik'l/ *adj* —**pteridologist** *n*

pteridophyte /térridә fīt/ *n* a plant that has no flowers or seeds and reproduces by means of spores. Ferns and some mosses are pteridophytes. Division: *Pteridophyta*. [Late 19C. < Greek *pterid-* (see PTERIDOLOGY) + -PHYTE.] —**pteridophytic** /-fíttik/ *adj* —**pteridophytous** /térri dóffitәss/ *adj*

pteridosperm /térridә spurm/ *n* an extinct plant resembling a fern that bore seeds [Early 20C. < Greek *pterid-* (see PTERIDOLOGY) + SPERM^1.]

pterodactyl /térrә dáktil/ *n* an extinct flying reptile (**pterosaur**) of the Jurassic and Cretaceous Periods with membranous wings and a rudimentary tail and beak. Genus: *Pterodactylus*. [Early 19C. < modern Latin *Pterodactylus*, literally 'wing finger' < Greek *pteron* 'wing' + *daktulos* 'finger'.]

pteropod /térrә pod/ *n* a marine gastropod mollusc that has a foot with wing-shaped lobes that are used as swimming organs. Group: *Pteropoda*. [Mid-19C. < modern Latin *Pteropoda* < Greek *pteron* 'wing' + modern Latin *-poda* '-pod'.]

pterosaur /térrә sawr/ *n* an extinct flying reptile of the Triassic, Jurassic, and Cretaceous Periods that had membranous wings supported by an elongated fourth digit. Order: Pterosauria. [Mid-19C. < modern Latin *Pterosauria* 'lizard with wings' < Greek *pteron* 'wing'.]

-pterous *suffix* having wings of a particular kind or number ○ *orthopterous* ○ *dipterous* [< Greek *pteron* 'wing, feather' < Indo-European, 'to fly, fall']

pteroylglutamic acid /térrō īl gloo támmik-/ *n* folic acid (*technical*) [*Pteroylglutamic* < PTEROIC + -YL + GLUTAMIC]

pterygium /tә ríjji әm/ (*plural* **-ums** *or* **-a** /-ә/) *n* a triangular patch of tissue that obstructs vision by growing over usually the inner side of the eye [Mid-17C. Via modern Latin < Greek *pterugion* 'little wing' < *pterux* 'wing'.]

pterygoid process /térri goyd-/ *n* either of two bony plates extending downwards from the sphenoid bone of the skull [*Pterygoid* via modern Latin *pterygoides* 'like a wing' < Greek *pterux* 'wing']

PTFE *abbr* polytetrafluoroethylene

PTH *abbr* parathyroid hormone

PTN *abbr* public telephone network

PTO, pto *abbr* please turn over

Ptolemaeus /tóllә máyәss/ hexagonal lunar crater visible in the northwestern quadrant of the Moon, approximately 140 km/85 mi. in diameter

Ptolemaic /tóllә máy ik/ *adj* **1** relating to the geographer and astronomer Ptolemy or to his system of planetary motion **2** relating to the Ptolemies, Pharaohs of ancient Egypt, or to Egypt during their rule

Ptolemaic system *n* a theory of planetary motion developed by Ptolemy that held that the Earth was at the centre of the universe with the Sun, Moon, and planets revolving around it

Ptolemaist /tóllә máy ist/ *n* a believer in the Ptolemaic system of planetary motion

Ptolemy /tóllәmi/ (AD 100?–170) Greek astronomer, mathematician, and geographer

Ptolemy I /tóllәmi/ (367?–283? BC) Macedonian king of Egypt (305BC–283? BC). Known as **Ptolemy Soter**

ptomaine /tṓ mayn/ *n* an organic base belonging to a foul-smelling group containing nitrogen. Source: bacteria during the decay of proteins. [Late 19C. Via French < Italian *ptomaina* < Greek *ptōma* 'fallen body, corpse' < *piptein* 'to fall'.]

ptomaine poisoning *n* food poisoning caused by bacteria, but formerly believed to be caused by ptomaines

ptosis /tṓssiss/ (*plural* **-ses** /-seez/) *n* a drooping of the upper eyelid, resulting from muscle weakness or inability to move muscles [Mid-18C. < Greek *ptōsis* 'a falling' < *piptein* (see PTOMAINE).]

pts *abbr* **1** parts **2** payments **3** pints **4** points **5** ports

PTSD *abbr* post-traumatic stress disorder

PTV *abbr* pay television

Pty *abbr* proprietary (*in 'Pty Ltd' to indicate a private limited company*)

ptyalin /tī әlin/ *n* an enzyme in saliva that catalyses the digestion of starches [Mid-19C. < Greek *ptualon* 'saliva' + -IN.]

ptyalism /tī әlizәm/ *n* excessive production of saliva [Late 17C. < Greek *ptualismos* 'salivation' < *ptualon* 'spittle' < *ptuein* 'to spit'.]

Pu *symbol* plutonium

pub /pub/ *n* **1** a building where drinks, especially alcoholic ones, can be bought and consumed. Food, and sometimes accommodation, may also be available. **2** hotel (*informal*) [Mid-19C. Shortening of PUBLIC HOUSE.]

pub. *abbr* **1** public **2** publication **3** published **4** publisher **5** publishing

pubbing /púbbing/ *n* the social activity of going to a pub or pubs (*informal*)

pub-crawl *n* a session of drinking at several pubs in succession (*informal*) ■ *vi* to go drinking at several pubs in succession (*informal*)

puberty /pyoóbәrti/ *n* the stage of becoming physiologically capable of sexual reproduction, marked by genital maturation, development of secondary sex characteristics, and, in girls, the first occurrence of menstruation [14C. Directly or via French *puberté* < Latin *pubertas* < *pubes* 'adult'.] —**pubertal** *adj*

puberulent /pyoo bérr yoōlәnt/ *adj* covered with fine down or hairs [Mid-19C. < *puber-*, stem of *pubes* 'adult'.]

pubes^1 *n* /pyoó beez/ (*plural* **-bes** /pyoó beez/) the part of the abdomen immediately above the external genitalia that is covered with hair from puberty onwards ■ *npl* /pyoobz/ the hair growing on the lower abdomen from puberty onwards (*informal; + plural verb*) [Late 16C. < Latin *pubes* 'adult males, genitals'.]

pubes^2 plural of **pubis**

pubescent /pyoo béss'nt/ *adj* **1** reaching or having attained puberty **2** covered with down or fine hair [Mid-17C. Directly or via French < Latin *pubescent-*, present participle of *pubescere* 'reach puberty' < *pubes* 'adult'.] —**pubescence** *n*

pub grub *n* food, usually of a relatively simple and inexpensive type, served in a pub (*informal*)

pubic /pyoóbik/ *adj* relating to or located near or on the pubes or pubis ○ *pubic hair*

pubic bone *n* ANAT = **pubis**

pubic louse *n* INSECTS = **crab**^{1} *n.* **4**

pubis /pyoóbiss/ (*plural* **-bes** /-beez/) *n* the joined pair of bones comprising the lower front of the hipbone in humans [Late 16C. < the Latin phrase *os pubis* 'bone of the genital region'.]

publ. *abbr* **1** publication **2** published **3** publisher

public /públik/ *adj* **1 CONCERNING ALL MEMBERS OF THE COMMUNITY** relating to or concerning people as a whole or all members of a community ○ *public health* **2 FOR COMMUNITY USE** provided for the use of a community **3 OPEN TO ALL** open to everyone, and typically frequented by large numbers of people **4 OF THE STATE** relating to or involving government and governmental agencies rather than private corporations or industry ○ *working in the public sector* ○ *a public servant* **5 WELL KNOWN** known to large numbers of the community because of being involved in activities such as politics or entertainment ○ *a public figure* **6 DONE OPENLY** made, done, or happening openly, for all to see ○ *a public debate* **7 KNOWN BY ALL MEMBERS OF COMMUNITY** known or potentially known by all members of a community ○ *make the information public* ○ *a public disgrace* **8 BELONGING TO THE COMMUNITY** belonging to the community as a whole and administered through its representatives in government ○ *public land* **9 HAVING OPENLY PURCHASABLE SHARES** describes companies whose shares are available, or are made available, for anyone to buy ■ *n* **1 EVERYONE** the community as a whole **2 PARTICULAR PART OF COMMUNITY** a part of a community sharing a particular interest ○ *the reading public* **3 FANS OR FOLLOWERS** the fans or followers of a performer or author **4** LEISURE = **public bar** [15C. Directly or via French < Latin *publicus*, alteration of *poplicus* (apparently under the influence of *pubes* 'adult') < *populus* 'people'.] —**publicness** *n*

public access *n* in US law, the availability of cable broadcasting facilities for the transmission of programmes produced by members of the public (*hyphenated before a noun*)

public-address system *n* full form of **PA**

public affairs *npl* issues that affect people generally, especially politics, or issues arising from the relationship of the public to an organization such as a government body or a financial institution

publican /públikən/ *n* **1** the owner or manager of a pub **2** a collector of taxes in ancient Rome [12C. Via French *publicain* < Latin *publicus* (see PUBLIC).]

public assistance *n US* aid consisting of money, food, food stamps, or other benefits, given by government agencies to people on low incomes, dependent children, and others in financial distress

publication /públi káysh'n/ *n* **1 PUBLISHING OF SOMETHING** the publishing of something, especially printed material for sale **2 PUBLISHED ITEM** an item that has been published, especially in printed form **3 PUBLIC COMMUNICATION OF SOMETHING** the communication of information to the public [14C. Via French < *publicare* (see PUBLISH).]

public bar *n* a bar in a pub that is furnished basically and in which drinks are sold more cheaply than in a lounge bar

public bill *n* a bill presented in a parliament or in Congress by a government, dealing with public policy

public company *n* a limited company whose shares can be bought and sold on the stock market. US term **public corporation** *n.* **2**

public convenience *n* a toilet in a public place, e.g. a town centre, for use by members of the public

public corporation *n* **1** in the United Kingdom, an organization set up by the government that runs a state-owned enterprise such as the BBC. Its chairman and governors are appointed by a government minister. **2** *US* COMM = **public company**

public defender *n* in the United States, an attorney who represents defendants who cannot afford their own lawyer

public domain *n* **1 NOT IN COPYRIGHT** in US law, the condition of not being protected by patent or copyright and so freely available for use ○ *public domain software* **2 REVEALED CONDITION** the condition of being openly known or revealed as opposed to being kept a secret ○ *The information is now in the public domain.* **3** *US* **GOVERNMENT LAND** land that is owned and administered by a government

public enemy *n* a threat to the public, especially a violent criminal

public enterprise *n* economic activity by government departments and quangos

public expenditure *n* spending by the government or government-owned bodies

public eye ◇ **in the public eye** regularly receiving attention from the media

public figure *n* a person known to the public, and whose lifestyle is the subject of great scrutiny

public health *n* the general health of a community and the practice and study of ways to preserve and improve this. It includes health education, sanitation, control of diseases, and regulation of pollution.

public house *n* a pub (*formal*)

public interest *n* **1** the general benefit of the public ○ *a law that would be contrary to the public interest* **2** the general level of interest shown by people towards an issue or event

publicise *vt* = **publicize**

publicist /púbblissist/ *n* **1** a promoter who seeks to obtain media publicity for a client **2** a journalist (*dated*) [Late 18C. Via French *publiciste* (after *canoniste* 'canon lawyer') < Latin *publicus* (see PUBLIC).]

publicity /pu blíssəti/ *n* **1 SOMETHING STIMULATING PUBLIC INTEREST** something such as advertising designed to increase public interest or awareness in something or somebody (*often before nouns*) ○ *The event was dismissed as a mere publicity stunt.* **2 INTEREST CREATED BY PUBLICITY** public interest or awareness created by publicity **3 ATTENTION-GETTING INFORMATION** information used to attract public attention, or the business of disseminating this ○ *She works in publicity.* ○ *the company's publicity campaign for their new product* **4 CONDITION OF BEING PUBLIC** the condition of being known or available to the public [Late 18C. < French *publicité* < *public* (see PUBLIC).]

publicize /púbbli sīz/ (**-cizes, -cizing, -cized**), **publicise** (**-cises, -cising, -cised**) *vt* to make something generally known or known to members of a particular group, typically by advertising

⚡**public key cryptography** *n* in computing, an encryption method that uses two mathematically related keys for encrypting and decrypting a message

⚡**public key encryption** *n* in computing, a message encryption technique in which encoding is done using a generally available public key but decoding is done using a private key available only to the receiver

public law *n* **1** the branch of law that deals with a state and its relationships with its citizens. ◊ **private law 2** a law that applies to the public

Public Lending Right *n* the right for authors to receive a small fee every time their books are borrowed from public libraries in the United Kingdom

public-liability insurance *n* insurance that compensates individuals if they experience injury or damage resulting from lack of reasonable care by an insured business or organization

public life *n* **1** a lifestyle that attracts a lot of publicity and public scrutiny, especially that of a politician **2** public service, especially by a politician

public limited company *n* a company whose shares can be bought and sold on the stock market and whose shareholders are subject to restricted liability for any debts or losses

publicly /púbblikli/ *adv* **1** in a public or open manner **2** by or in the name of the public

public nuisance *n* **1** an action or a thing that harms the community in general **2** an irritating or offensive person (*insult*)

public opinion *n* the general attitude or feeling of the public concerning an issue, especially when this has an effect on political decision-making

public ownership *n* ownership by the state of something regarded as a national asset, e.g. coal, water, or the telecommunications industry

public prosecutor *n* a government law official prosecuting criminal offences on behalf of the community or the state

Public Record Office *n* a British institution in which official documents, historical and modern, are stored after they are released under the thirty-year rule

public relations *n* **1 PROMOTION OF A FAVOURABLE IMAGE** the practice or profession of establishing, maintaining, or improving a favourable relationship between an institution or person and the public (+ *singular verb*) **2 PUBLIC IMAGE** how well or badly something such as an institution or person is regarded by the public (+ *singular or plural verb*) ○ *Such projects provide good public relations for the government.* **3 DEPARTMENT MANAGING PUBLIC RELATIONS** the department in an organization that is responsible for public relations (+ *singular verb*)

public room *n* **1** *Scotland* any room in a private house into which strangers may traditionally be invited, e.g. a sitting room, dining room, or study **2** *US* a room, e.g. the lobby in a hotel, into which the public is admitted without discrimination

public school *n* **1** in England and Wales, an independent fee-paying secondary school, typically a single-sex boarding school **2** in the United States, a state-funded elementary or secondary school providing education free for all local children and young people

public sector *n* the part of the economy that is controlled by government spending and employment (*hyphenated before nouns*)

public-sector borrowing requirement *n* the amount that the government needs to borrow in any fiscal year in order to be able to meet its budgeted costs

public servant *n* **1** an appointed or elected holder of a government position or office **2** *ANZ* a civil servant

public service *n* **1 GOVERNMENT EMPLOYMENT** government employment, especially within the civil service **2 PROVISION OF ESSENTIAL SERVICES** the business or activity of providing the public with essential goods or services such as electric power **3** *ANZ* **DEPARTMENTS IMPLEMENTING GOVERNMENT POLICY** the range of departments and organizations responsible for implementing government policy **4 SERVICE BENEFITING THE GENERAL PUBLIC** a service that is run for the benefit of the general public, e.g. the utilities, the emergency services, transport, and broadcasting (*hyphenated when used before a noun*)

public-service broadcasting *n* noncommercial broadcasting, specifically programmes broadcast by the BBC

public speaking *n* the skill, practice, or process of making speeches to large groups of people —**public speaker** *n*

public spending *n* spending by government and government bodies (*hyphenated when used before a noun*)

public-spirited *adj* motivated by or showing genuine concern for others in the community

public transport *n* a network of passenger vehicles for use by the public running on set routes, usually at set times and charging set fares (*hyphenated when used before a noun*)

public utility *n* a government-regulated company that provides an essential public service such as water, gas, or electricity (*hyphenated before a noun*)

public works *npl* civil-engineering projects that are government owned or financed, and undertaken specifically for the benefit of the public

publish /púbblish/ *v* **1** *vti* **PREPARE AND PRODUCE TEXT OR SOFTWARE** to prepare and produce material in printed or electronic form for distribution and, usually, sale **2** *vt* **PUBLISH THE WORK OF AN AUTHOR** to publish the work of a particular author **3** *vt* **MAKE SOMETHING PUBLIC KNOWLEDGE** to announce something publicly [14C. Via Old French *publiss-*, stem of *publier* < Latin *publicus* 'public'.] —**publishable** *adj*

publisher /púbblishər/ *n* **1** a company or person that publishes products such as books, journals, or software **2** the owner or representative of the owner of a newspaper, periodical, or publishing house

publishing /púbblishing/ *n* the trade, profession, or activity of preparing and producing material in printed or electronic form for distribution to the public

publishing house *n* an established publishing company that prepares and produces material in printed or electronic form for distribution and, usually, sale

PUC *n S Asia* a preuniversity junior college

Puccini /poo cheéni/, **Giacomo** (1858–1924) Italian composer

puccoon /pə kóon/ (*plural* **-coons** *or* **-coon**) *n* a plant such as gromwell or bloodroot whose roots yield a reddish dye, or the dye itself. Native to: North America. *Lithospermum canescens* and *Sanguinaria canadensis.* [Early 17C. < Algonquian *poughkone.*]

puce /pyooss/ *adj* of a brilliant purplish-red colour [Late 18C. Via French, 'flea' (in the phrase *couleur puce* 'flea-coloured') < Latin *pulex.*] —**puce** *n*

Pucelle /poo sél/, **Jean** (1300–55) French painter

puck /puk/ *n* **1 DISC IN ICEHOCKEY** a small disc of hard rubber that the players hit in icehockey **2 STROKE AT THE BALL** a player's stroke at the ball in the Irish sport of hurling ■ *vt* **1 STRIKE A BALL** to strike the ball in the Irish sport of hurling **2** *Ireland* **HIT SOMETHING HARD** to hit something with great force (*slang*) [Late 19C. < ?]

Puck[1] /puk/, **puck** *n* a mischievous or malevolent spirit in English folklore [Old English *pūca*]

Puck[2] *n* a small natural satellite of Uranus

pucka *adj* = **pukka**

pucker /púkər/ *vti* to gather something such as cloth or the skin around the lips in such a way that wrinkles or small creases are formed, or to become gathered in this way ■ *n* a small wrinkle, fold, or crease [Late 16C. Probably < POCKET.]

puckish /púkish/ *adj* mischievous or naughty in a playful way [Late 19C. < PUCK[1].] —**puckishly** *adv* —**puckishness** *n*

pud /pŏŏd/ *n* pudding (*informal*)

pudding /pŏŏdding/ *n* **1 SWEET COOKED DESSERT** a sweet cooked dessert containing flour or a cereal product and other ingredients such as sugar, fruit, or eggs (*often in combination*) **2 DESSERT** the dessert course of a meal ○ *What's for pudding?* **3 COOKED SAVOURY DISH** a substantial savoury cooked dish usually covered with, or encased in, suet pastry or sometimes breadcrumbs (*often in combination*) **4 TYPE OF SAUSAGE** a sausage made with ingredients such as minced meat, seasonings, and oatmeal packed into a skin or bag and usually boiled (*usually in combination*) ○ *black pudding* [13C. Via French *boudin* 'black pudding' < Latin *botellus* 'sausage', the original sense in English.] —**puddingy** *adj* ◇ **in the pudding club** pregnant (*slang; sometimes offensive*)

pudding basin *n* a deep bowl used for making puddings, especially steamed puddings (*hyphenated before nouns*)

pudding-basin haircut *n* a haircut with the hair cut in a continuous straight line all the way round the head

pudding stone *n* a conglomerate rock in which the pebbles have a different colour and texture from the material binding them together (**matrix**)

puddle /púdd'l/ *n* 1 SHALLOW POOL OF WATER a shallow pool of water, e.g. one formed by rainwater in a hollow on a road 2 POOL OF LIQUID a small pool of liquid 3 WATERPROOF LINING MATERIAL nonporous material made from thoroughly mixed wet clay and sand and used as a waterproof lining, e.g. in constructing a canal 4 EDDY FROM OAR STROKE the swirling surface of the water after the blade of an oar has completed a stroke ■ *v* (**-dles, -dling, -dled**) 1 *vi* MESS ABOUT to potter or mess about 2 *vi* SPLASH IN SHALLOW WATER to wade, dabble, or splash in shallow water or puddles 3 *vt* WATERPROOF SOMETHING WITH PUDDLE to make a canal or pool waterproof by lining it with puddle 4 *vt* MIX CLAY AND SAND to work clay and sand to make puddle 5 *vt* PROCESS PIG IRON to convert pig iron to wrought iron by heating it in a furnace in the presence of an oxidizing agent such as ferric oxide to remove carbon [14C. < Old English *pudd* 'ditch', with the literal sense 'small ditch'.] —**puddler** *n* —**puddly** *adj*

pudendum /pyoo déndəm/ (*plural* **-da** /-déndə/) *n* human external genital organs [Mid-17C. < Latin < *pudere* 'to make or feel ashamed'.] —**pudendal** *adj*

pudge /puj/ *n US* = **podge** (*informal insult*) [Mid-19C. Probably a back-formation < PUDGY.]

pudgy /pújji/ (**-ier, -iest**) *adj US* = **podgy** (*informal*) —**pudgily** *adv* —**pudginess** *n*

Pudsey /púdsi/ town in N England. Population: 31,636 (1991).

pudu /póo doo/ (*plural* **-dus** *or* **-du**) *n* a very small deer with tiny straight antlers. Native to: forests of Central and South America. Genus: *Pudu.* [Late 19C. < Araucanian.]

Puebla /pwéblə/ capital of Puebla State, central Mexico. Population: 1,057,454 (1990).

pueblo /pwébblō/ (*plural* **-los**) *n* 1 a village built by Native North or Central Americans in the SW United States and Central America, containing at least one, but typically a cluster of multi-storey stone or adobe houses 2 a town or village in a Spanish-speaking country [Early 19C. Via Spanish < Latin *populus* (see PUBLIC).]

Pueblo /pwébblō/ (*plural* **-lo** *or* **-los**) *n* a member of a Native North or Central American people who live or lived in pueblos —**Pueblo** *adj*

puerile /pyóor īl/ *adj* 1 silly or immature, especially in a childish way 2 relating to or characteristic of childhood [Late 16C. Directly or via French *puéril* < Latin *puerilis* < *puer* 'child, boy'.] —**puerilely** *adv* —**puerility** /pyoor rílləti/ *n*

puerilism /pyóorilizəm/ *n* childish or immature behaviour by an adult

puerperal /pyoo úrpərəl/ *adj* relating to childbirth or the time immediately following childbirth [Mid-18C. < Latin *puerperus* 'bringing forth children' < *puer* 'child' + *-parus* 'bringing forth'.]

puerperal fever *n* MED = **puerperal sepsis**

puerperal psychosis *n* a psychiatric disorder that may affect women in the first two weeks after giving birth

puerperal sepsis *n* blood poisoning following childbirth, caused by infection of the placental site

puerperium /pyóor péeri əm/ *n* the period immediately after childbirth when the womb is returning to its normal size, lasting approximately six weeks [Early 17C. < Latin, < *puerperus* (see PUERPERAL).]

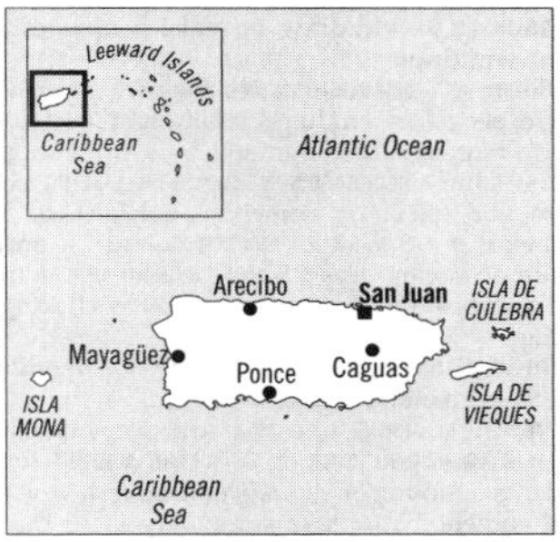

Puerto Rico

Puerto Rico /puərtə réekō/ island in the N Caribbean Sea, east of Hispaniola, a self-governing commonwealth of the United States. Capital: San Juan. Population: 3,522,037 (1990). Area: 8,959 sq. km/3,459 sq. mi. —**Puerto Rican** *n, adj*

puff /puf/ *n* 1 SHORT SUDDEN RUSH OF AIR a short sudden rush of air, wind, gas, or smoke 2 SOUND OF PUFF the short sound made by a puff 3 AMOUNT IN A PUFF the amount of substance contained in a puff 4 SHORT EXHALATION a short blowing out of breath 5 INHALING FOLLOWED BY EXHALING an inhalation followed by an exhalation, especially when smoking 6 LIGHT PASTRY SNACK a snack or cake consisting of puff pastry with a sweet or sometimes a savoury filling (*often in combination*) ○ *a cream puff* 7 EXAGGERATED PRAISE OR PUBLICITY an exaggerated or flattering expression of praise, especially in publicizing something or somebody 8 COSMETICS = **powder puff** 9 SWELLING a rounded swelling or projection on something 10 GATHERED SECTION OF FABRIC a piece of fabric gathered around the edges and bulging in the middle 11 *US* QUILTED BEDSPREAD a quilted and padded covering for a bed (*dated*) 12 VOLUMINOUS HAIRSTYLE hair arranged in an enlarged mass by combing, rolling, or padding it 13 ENLARGED REGION ON A CHROMOSOME an enlarged region on a chromosome resulting from active RNA synthesis ■ *v* 1 *vt* MAKE SOMEBODY BREATHLESS to make somebody breathless, e.g. after heavy exercise (*informal*) ○ *Phew! I'm puffed!* 2 *vi* BREATHE QUICKLY to breathe quickly in short blasts 3 *vti* EMIT GAS IN SHORT BLASTS to emit or blow steam, gas, or smoke in short blasts 4 *vti* INHALE AND EXHALE SMOKE to inhale and exhale smoke from a cigarette, cigar, or pipe 5 *vi* MOVE EMITTING SMOKE PUFFS to move in a particular direction or way emitting puffs of smoke or steam 6 *vi* MOVE WHILE PANTING to move in a particular direction or way while panting ○ *He puffed up the hill.* 7 *vti* SWELL to swell or make something swell, e.g. with air or pride ○ *puffed out his cheeks* ○ *puffing up balloons* 8 *vt* SPEAK HIGHLY OF to praise somebody or something extravagantly, especially in publicity material [12C. < ?] ◇ **out of puff** out of breath (*informal*) ◇ **puffed out** out of breath because of exertion (*informal*)

puff adder *n* 1 an African viper that inflates its body and hisses when alarmed. Genus: *Bitis.* 2 ZOOL = **hognose snake**

puffball /púf bawl/ *n* a round fungus that produces a cloud of dark spores when disturbed. Many species are edible when immature. Genus: *Lycoperdon* and *Calvatia.*

puffed-up *adj* self-important or pompous

puffer /púffər/ *n* 1 PUFFING PERSON OR THING something or somebody that puffs, especially a steam-driven train or cargo vessel 2 **puffer, pufferfish** INFLATING MARINE FISH a tropical marine fish, poisonous in some species, that can inflate its body with water to appear larger to predators. Family: Tetraodontidae. 3 **puffer, pufferfish** PUFFER AS FOOD the flesh of a puffer as food

puffery /púffəri/ *n* exaggerated or excessively flattering praise, especially in publicity (*informal*)

puffin /púffin/ (*plural* **-fins** *or* **-fin**) *n* a black-and-white diving bird of the auk family with a short neck and a triangular brightly coloured bill. Genus: *Fratercula.* [14C. < ?]

puff pastry *n* a light flaky multi-layered pastry made by repeated rolling and folding of extremely rich buttery pastry dough, which then rises during baking

puffy /púffi/ (**-ier, -iest**) *adj* 1 SWOLLEN swollen, especially because of tiredness, injury, crying, or poor health 2 SHORT OF BREATH with a tendency to puff and pant 3 POMPOUS pompous or self-important —**puffily** *adv* —**puffiness** *n*

pug[1] /pug/ *n* a short compact dog with a wrinkled face, short coat, and curled tail, belonging to a breed of Asian origin [Mid-18C. < ?]

pug[2] /pug/ *vt* (**pugs, pugging, pugged**) 1 KNEAD CLAY WITH WATER to mix clay with water to make it pliable enough to form bricks or pottery 2 FILL A GAP WITH CLAY to fill in a gap with clay or mortar ■ *n* CLAY SUITABLE FOR MOULDING clay mixed with water until it is pliable enough to form bricks or pottery [Early 19C. < ?] —**puggy** *adj*

pug[3] /pug/ *n* a boxer (*slang*) [Mid-19C. Shortening of PUGILISM.]

pugaree *n S Asia* CLOTHING = **puggree**

Puget Sound /pyóojit-/ arm of the Pacific Ocean, in NW Washington State. Area: 561 sq. km/217 sq. mi.

puggled /púgg'ld/, **puggled out** *adj Scotland* in a state of extreme tiredness, usually from working hard at something (*informal*) [Early 20C. < Earlier *puggle* 'psychiatrically disordered' < Hindi *pāgal, paglā* 'mentally disabled person'.]

puggree /púggri/, **pugree, pugaree** /púggəri/ *n S Asia* a turban [Mid-17C. < Hindi *pagṛī.*]

pugilism /pyóojilizəm/ *n* the practice, sport, or profession of boxing [Late 18C. < Latin *pugil* 'boxer'.] —**pugilist** *n* —**pugilistic** /pyóoji lístik/ *adj* —**pugilistically** /-lístikli/ *adv*

pugil-stick /pyóojil-/ *n* a long stick with padded ends used in game shows involving mock combats [*Pugil* probably a shortening of PUGILISM]

Pugin /pyóojin/, **Augustus** (1812–52) British architect and designer

pug mill *n* a machine in which materials are ground and mixed, e.g. clay with water for building or pottery-making, or cement for building [< PUG[2]]

pugnacious /pug náyshəss/ *adj* inclined to fight or be aggressive [Mid-17C. < Latin *pugnax* < *pugnus* 'fist'.] —**pugnaciously** *adv* —**pugnaciousness** *n* —**pugnacity** /pug nássəti/ *n*

pug nose *n* a short stubby nose with a turned-up or flattened end [< PUG[1]] —**pug-nosed** *adj*

puh-leeze /pə léez/, **puh-lease** *interj* used facetiously to express astonishment, disbelief, or indignation (*informal*) [Late 20C. Alteration of PLEASE.]

puisne /pyóoni/ *adj* 1 describes a justice of the High Court of England and Wales 2 *US* describes an associate justice of a higher court [Late 16C. < Old French, 'born after' < *puis* 'after' + *né* 'born'.]

puissance /pwée soNs, pyóo iss'nss/ *n* 1 a competition in showjumping in which horses attempt to clear an obstacle that is raised higher for each round, until all but the winner are eliminated 2 power or might (*literary*) [15C. Via French < Latin *potis* (see PUISSANT).]

puissant /pyóo iss'nt/ *adj* powerful or mighty (*literary*) [15C. Via French < Latin *potis* 'able'.] —**puissantly** *adv*

puja /póojə/ *n* daily devotion in Hinduism, consisting of a ritual offering of food, drink, and ritual actions and prayers, most commonly to an image of a deity [Late 17C. < Sanskrit *pūjā* 'worship'.]

puke /pyook/ *vti* (**pukes, puking, puked**) BE SICK to vomit, or vomit something up (*slang*) ■ *n* (*slang*) 1 SOMETHING VOMITED vomited food or other matter 2 VOMITING the vomiting up of something 3 DESPICABLE PERSON a contemptible or annoying person [Late 16C. Probably an imitation of the sound of vomiting.]

pukeko /póokəkō/ (*plural* **-kos** *or* **-ko**) *n* a wading bird with glossy black-and-blue plumage and a bright red bill and beak. Native to: New Zealand. *Porphyrio porphyrio.* [Mid-19C. < Maori.]

pukka /púkə/, **pucka** *adj* 1 *S Asia* WELL DONE OR MADE properly done or made, or of superior quality 2 GENUINE genuine or authentic (*informal*) 3 RESPECTABLE of high social status (*informal*) 4 EXCELLENT of the highest quality or standard (*informal*) [Late 17C. < Hindi *pakkā* 'cooked, ripe'.]

pul /pool/ (*plural* **puls** *or* **puli** /póoli/) *n* see table at **currency** [Mid-19C. < Pashto.]

pula /póolə/ (*plural* **-la**) *n* see table at **currency**

pulchritude /púlkri tyood/ *n* physical beauty (*literary or humorous*) [14C. < Latin *pulchritudo* < *pulcher* 'beautiful'.] —**pulchritudinous** /púlkri tyóodinəss/ *adj*

pule /pyool/ (**pules, puling, puled**) *vi* to whine, whimper, or cry plaintively (*archaic*) [Early 16C. Probably an imitation of the sound of whimpering.] —**puler** *n* —**pulingly** *adv*

puli /póoli/ (*plural* **-lik** /póolik/ *or* **-lis**) *n* a medium-sized Hungarian sheepdog with long hair that can be combed out or left corded [Mid-20C. < Hungarian.]

Pulitzer prize /póolitsər-/ *n* any of several prizes awarded annually for excellence in American journalism, literature, and music [Early 20C. After Joseph *Pulitzer* (1847–1911), Hungarian-born US journalist.]

pull /pool/ *v* **1** *vti* **DRAW A PHYSICAL OBJECT NEARER** to apply force to a physical object so as to draw or tend to draw it towards the force's origin **2** *vt* **REMOVE SOMETHING FORCIBLY** to remove or extract something by exerting force **3** *vt* **DRAW A LOAD** to draw a load, e.g. a trailer or plough **4** *vti* **TUG** to tug at or jerk something or somebody **5** *vt* **STRAIN AND DAMAGE A MUSCLE** to strain and damage a muscle, ligament, or tendon **6** *vt* **ATTRACT CROWD** to draw a large number of people (*informal*) **7** *vt* **TAKE OUT A WEAPON** to take out a weapon in readiness to attack somebody (*informal*) **8** *vt* **APPLY FORCE TO A TRIGGER** to apply force to a trigger, lever, or switch so as to operate a weapon or machine **9** *vt* **OPEN OR CLOSE CURTAINS** to open or close curtains or window coverings **10** *vti* **TEAR** to tear or rip something **11** *vt* **STRETCH** to stretch something elastic **12** *vt* **DO SOMETHING UNDERHANDEDLY** to do something undesirable or despicable in an underhand way (*informal*) ○ *I just know they're trying to pull something, but I don't know what.* **13** *vti* **MANOEUVRE A VEHICLE** to manoeuvre a vehicle in a particular direction **14** *vi* **DRIFT TO ONE SIDE BECAUSE FAULTY** to drift to one side or the other, usually because of a fault (*refers to motor vehicles or their steering*) ○ *My car pulls to the left.* **15** *vi* **PRODUCE SUFFICIENT DRIVING POWER** to produce sufficient driving power to move a vehicle **16** *vi* **INTAKE DEEPLY** to inhale deeply when smoking, or take a deep gulp at a drink **17** *vt* **POUR DRINK FROM CASK** to extract beer or a similar drink from a cask by operating a handle attached to a pump **18** *vt* **REMOVE SOMETHING FROM CIRCULATION** to remove something from circulation, or prevent it from ever getting into circulation (*informal*) **19** *vti* **ATTRACT SEXUAL PARTNER** to meet and succeed in attracting somebody, often so as to have a casual and usually brief sexual relationship (*slang*) ○ *Did you pull at the party?* **20** *vt* **MAKE A PRINTING PROOF** to make a proof from type **21** *vt* **REIN A HORSE BACK** to rein in a horse, especially so as to prevent it from winning a race **22** *vt* **HIT A BALL TOO FAR TO THE SIDE** to hit a ball farther left for a right-handed player or right for a left-handed player than intended ■ *n* **1 PULLING OR BEING PULLED** the pulling of somebody or something, or an instance of being pulled **2 PULLING FORCE** the physical force involved in the action of pulling **3 SUSTAINED EFFORT** a sustained effort, especially under difficult circumstances **4 INFLUENCE** special influence, typically because of personal position within an organization or society, or personal connection with an individual (*informal*) **5 POWER TO ATTRACT** the ability or power to attract an audience or supporters (*informal*) **6 SOMETHING USED FOR PULLING** something such as a knob, handle, or tab used for pulling (*often in combination*) **7 DEEP INHALING OR GULP** the inhaling or drinking of something deeply **8 PRINTING PROOF** a proof made from type **9 RESTRAINT OF A HORSE** the restraining of a horse by its rider, especially to keep it from winning **10 PULLING OF A BALL** the pulling of a ball, or a ball that is pulled **11 RESISTANCE IN A FIRING MECHANISM** the amount of resistance in a firing mechanism such as a trigger or bowstring [Old English *pullian*, originally 'to pluck'] —**puller** *n*

SYNONYMS ***pull, drag, draw, haul, tow, tug, yank***

CORE MEANING: to move something towards you or in the same direction as you

pull to move something towards you or in the same direction as you; **drag** to move something large or heavy with effort across a surface; **draw** to pull something with a smooth movement; **haul** to pull something with a steady strong movement, often involving strenuous effort; **tow** to pull something along behind by means of a rope or chain; **tug** to pull at something with a sharp forceful movement, without necessarily moving the object; **yank** to pull something suddenly and sharply with a single strong movement.

pull about *vt* to treat somebody or something roughly or brutally

pull ahead *vi* to move in front of or gain a lead over somebody or something moving in the same direction

pull away *vi* **1** to move away from somebody or something **2** to draw back from somebody or something, either physically or emotionally

pull back *vti* to withdraw, or make people, especially troops, withdraw

pull down *vt* **1 DEMOLISH** to destroy or demolish something, especially a building **2 REDUCE SOMETHING TO A LOWER LEVEL** to reduce something such as a price to a lower level or value **3 DECREASE SOMEBODY'S WELL-BEING** to have a detrimental effect on somebody's health or mental well-being **4** *US* **EARN AN AMOUNT** to earn a particular amount of money (*slang*) **5 MAKE A MENU APPEAR** to make a menu appear on a computer screen by clicking on its heading

pull for *vt US* to hope that somebody or something will succeed in an endeavour

pull in *v* **1** *vi* **ARRIVE** to arrive and stop, usually at a station **2** *vti* = **pull over** *v.* **3** *vi* **EARN AMOUNT** to earn a particular amount of money (*informal*) **4** *vt* **ARREST** to arrest somebody, or take somebody in to the police station for questioning (*slang*)

pull off *vt* to accomplish or arrange something despite difficulties (*informal*)

SYNONYMS See ***accomplish***.

pull on *vt* to put on clothing or an item of clothing, especially in haste

pull out *v* **1** *vti* **MANOEUVRE INTO THE TRAFFIC FLOW** to drive a vehicle away from the side of a road, e.g. to join a flow of traffic **2** *vi* **MANOEUVRE A VEHICLE BEFORE OVERTAKING** to drive a vehicle out from behind another vehicle so as to overtake **3** *vi* **DEPART** to depart from a station or stopping place **4** *vti* **RETREAT** to retreat or cause somebody to retreat ○ *the army is pulling out* **5** *vi* **WITHDRAW** to withdraw from an obligation or commitment ○ *they are threatening to pull out of the deal* **6** *vti* **LEVEL OUT AN AIRCRAFT** to level out or make an aircraft level out from a dive

pull over *vti* to drive a vehicle to the side of a road and stop, or force the driver of a vehicle to do this

pull through *vti* to recover or help somebody recover from a period of illness or difficulties

pull together *v* **1** *vi* to cooperate, collaborate, or otherwise work together **2** *vr* to recover your composure or self-control (*informal*) ○ *Just pull yourself together!*

pull up *v* **1** *vi* **STOP SOMEWHERE** to arrive and stop at a place **2** *vt* **TELL SOMEBODY OFF** to scold or reprimand somebody sharply **3** *vi* **CATCH UP IN A RACE** to move into a closer or level position with somebody, e.g. in a race

pullback /pool bak/ *n* **1** an act or the process of pulling back, especially a withdrawal of troops **2** a device for holding, restraining, or drawing something back

ϟ**pull-down** *adj* describes a menu or other screen item that can be made to appear on a computer screen by clicking on its heading ■ *n* a pull-down feature on a computer screen

pulled threadwork *n* an embroidery technique in which tight stitches are used to draw some threads together and separate others, thereby forming lacy patterns

pullet /póollit/ *n* a young female chicken, especially one that has not started to lay eggs [14C. Via French *poulet* 'little hen' < *poule* 'hen' < Latin *pullus* 'young animal'.]

pulley /póolli/ (*plural* **-leys**) *n* **1 WHEEL WITH A GROOVED RIM** a mounted rotating wheel with a grooved rim over which a belt or chain can move to change the direction of a pulling force **2 SYSTEM OF PULLEYS** a system of pulleys along with a mounting block and tackle, used to improve leverage in lifting heavy weights **3** *Scotland* **CLOTHES AIRER ON PULLEYS** in Scotland, a clothes airer that is raised to the ceiling by means of pulleys [14C. Via Old French *polie* < Greek *polos* 'pole'.]

pull-in *n* (*dated*) **1** an area at the side of a road where drivers can pull over and stop their vehicles **2** a café catering for drivers, situated beside a road

Pullman /póolmən/ *n* a comfortable train-carriage for sitting or sleeping in [Mid-19C. After George M. PULLMAN.]

Pullman /póolmən/, **George Mortimer** (1831–97) US inventor and manufacturer

pullorum disease /poo láwrəm-/ *n* a highly infectious disease of young poultry caused by the bacterium *Salmonella pullorum*, and marked by diarrhoea [*Pullorum* < modern Latin, 'of chickens']

pullout /pool owt/ *n* **1 OBJECT FOR PULLING OUT** an object intended to be pulled out of a publication, e.g. a removable section of a magazine or a part of a book that folds out **2 WITHDRAWAL** a withdrawal from an obligation or other demanding situation **3 RETREAT** a retreat from a place or military involvement **4 LEVELLING-OUT MANOEUVRE OF AIRCRAFT** an aircraft manoeuvre in which a dive changes to level flight

pullover /póollōvər/ *n* a garment, especially a jumper, put on by being pulled over the head

pull-tab *n US* BEVERAGES = **ring-pull**

pull-through *n* a weighted cord with a rag at one end, pulled through a wind instrument or the barrel of a rifle to clean the inside of it

pullulate /púllyoo layt/ (**-lates, -lating, -lated**) *vi* **1 GERMINATE** to germinate or sprout (*technical*) **2 BREED** to breed freely or rapidly (*technical*) **3 TEEM** to teem or swarm with something (*literary*) [Early 17C. < Latin *pullulare* < *pullus* (see PULLET).] —**pullulation** /púllyoo láysh'n/ *n*

pull-up *n* **1** a physical exercise in which the hands are placed on an overhead horizontal bar, and the body is lifted by pulling upwards with the arms **2** = **pull in** *v.* **1**, **pull in** *v.* **2** (*dated*)

pulmonary /púlmənəri, pool-/ *adj* **1** concerning, affecting, or associated with the lungs **2** ZOOL = **pulmonate** *adj.* **1** [Early 18C. < Latin *pulmonarius* < *pulmo* 'lung'.]

pulmonary artery *n* either of the two arteries that carry blood in need of oxygen from the right side of the heart to the lungs

pulmonary vein *n* any of the four veins that carry oxygen-rich blood from the lungs to the left side of the heart

pulmonate /púlmənət, pool-/ *adj* **1 WITH LUNGS** with lungs or organs that function as lungs **2 WITH SAC LIKE LUNG** describes a mollusc that has a sac functioning as a lung ■ *n* **MOLLUSC WITH LUNG SAC** a mollusc with a sac functioning as a lung, e.g. land snails, slugs, and many freshwater snails. Subclass: Pulmonata. [Mid-19C. < modern Latin *pulmonatus* < Latin *pulmo* (see PULMONARY).]

pulmonic /pul mónnik, pool-/ *adj* ANAT = **pulmonary** *adj.* **1** [Mid-17C. Directly or via French < modern Latin *pulmonicus* < Latin *pulmo* (see PULMONARY).]

pulp /pulp/ *n* **1 SOFT FLESHY PLANT TISSUE** soft or fleshy plant tissue such as the inner part of a fruit or vegetable **2 STEM PITH** the pith inside a plant stem **3 SOFT MATERIAL** a soft or soggy mass **4 CRUSHED WOOD FOR PAPER** crushed wood or other materials that are used to make paper **5 CHEAP BOOKS AND MAGAZINES** thrilling novels and magazines produced on cheap paper, especially crime, horror, or science fiction stories (*often before nouns*) ○ *a prize collection of classic pulp fiction* **6 INSIDE OF TOOTH** the sensitive tissue at the centre of a tooth, consisting of nerves and blood vessels **7 PULVERIZED ORE** ore that has been mined and pulverized, especially when mixed with water ■ *v* **1** *vti* **CRUSH** to crush something, or to be crushed, into pulp **2** *vt* **REMOVE PULP FROM FRUIT** to remove the soft fleshy tissue from fruit or vegetables [14C. < Latin *pulpa* < ?] —**pulpiness** *n* —**pulpy** *adj*

pulpit /póolpit/ *n* **1** a raised platform or stand in a church that is used by the priest or minister for preaching or leading a service **2** the clergy considered as a group [14C. Via late Latin < Latin *pulpitum* 'platform, scaffold' < ?]

pulpwood /púlp wood/ *n* a soft wood such as aspen, pine, or spruce that is used to make paper

pulque /póolki, pool kay/ *n* a thick alcoholic drink made in Mexico from the sap of the agave plant [Late 17C. Via Mexican Spanish < Nahuatl *puliúhki* 'decomposed'.]

pulsar /púl saar/ *n* a small dense star that emits brief, intense bursts of visible radiation, radio waves, and X-rays, and is generally believed to be a rapidly rotating neutron star [Mid-20C. Contraction of *pulsating star*, after 'quasar'.]

pulsate /pul sáyt/ (**-sates, -sating, -sated**) *vi* **1 THROB** to expand and contract with a strong regular beat **2 VIBRATE** to vibrate or quiver **3 BE FULL OF ENERGY** to be full of energy, bustling activity, and excitement ○ *The whole city is pulsating with excitement at this time of year.* **4 VARY REPEATEDLY IN INTENSITY OR MAGNITUDE** to vary in intensity or magnitude, especially in a repeated way [Late 18C. < Latin *pulsare* 'to beat repeatedly' < *pellere* (see PULSE[1]).] —**pulsatory** /púlssətəri, pul sáytəri/ *adj*

pulsatile /púlssə tīl/ *adj* pulsating or vibrating rhythmically —**pulsatility** /púlssə tílləti/ *n*

pulsation /pul sáysh'n/ *n* **1 PULSATING** the action of pulsating **2 BEATING OF HEART** the rhythmic change in volume that takes place in the heart or an artery **3 ONE BEAT** a single beat or pulse

pulsator /pul sáytər/ *n* **1** a device or machine that pulsates **2** a device that stimulates or maintains a rhythmic motion

pulse[1] /puls/ *n* **1 REGULAR BEAT OF BLOOD FLOW** the regular expansion and contraction of an artery, caused by the heart pumping blood through the body **2 SINGLE BEAT OF BLOOD FLOW** a single expansion and contraction of an artery, caused by a beat of the heart **3 RHYTHMICAL BEAT** a beat or throb, e.g. of a drum, or a series of rhythmical beats or throbs **4 CHANGE OR REPEATING CHANGE IN MAGNITUDE** a brief temporary change in a normally constant quantity, e.g. in a voltage, or a series of intermittent disturbances that are regular in form and frequency of occurrence **5 CURRENT ATTITUDES** the sentiments, opinions, or attitudes current among the public or a particular group ○ *a journalist who really has a finger on the pulse of society* **6 VITALITY** energy and excitement ○ *I love the pulse of city life.* ■ *vi* (**pulses, pulsing, pulsed**) **1 BEAT RHYTHMICALLY** to move or throb with a strong regular rhythm **2 UNDERGO BRIEF SUDDEN CHANGES** to undergo a series of brief sudden changes in quantity, e.g. in voltage **3 BE ENERGETIC** to be full of energy and excitement ○ *an area pulsing with creative energy* [14C. Via Old French < Latin *puls-*, past participle of *pellere* 'to beat'.]

pulse[2] /puls/ *n* **1** an edible seed from a pod, e.g. a pea or bean, eaten fresh or dried **2** a plant such as the pea, the bean, alfalfa, or clover that has pods as fruits and roots that bear nodules containing nitrogen-fixing bacteria [13C. Via Old French < Latin *puls* 'porridge' < ?]

pulse code modulation *n* a technique for electronic transmission of voice signals by sampling the amplitude of the signal and converting it to a coded digital form for transmission

pulsejet /púlss jet/ *n* a ramjet engine in which air, admitted through moveable vanes, mixes with fuel in the combustion chamber. The resulting explosion forces the vanes shut, causing a pulsating thrust.

pulseless /púlsləss/ *adj* without a pulse, especially an arterial pulse

pulse modulation *n* a way of transmitting information using a series of electrical pulses, with the duration, amplitude, or frequency of the pulses modified to carry the information

pulsometer /pul sómmitər/ *n* a lightweight pistonless pump that works using the partial vacuum created by pulses of condensing steam being forced between two chambers [Mid-19C. < PULSE[1] + -METER.]

pulverize /púlvə rīz/ (**-izes, -izing, -ized**), **pulverise** (**-ises, -ising, -ised**) *v* **1** *vti* to crush or grind something, or become crushed or ground, into a powder or dust **2** *vt* to subject an opponent to a crushing defeat (*informal*) ○ *We completely pulverized the opposition.* [15C. < late Latin *pulverizare* < Latin *pulver-*, stem of *pulvis* 'powder, dust'.] —**pulverizable** *adj* —**pulverization** /púlvər ī záysh'n/ *n* —**pulverizer** /púlvə rīzər/ *n*

pulvinate /púlvi nayt/ *adj* **1** shaped like a cushion **2** with a swelling at the base

pulvinus /pul vīnəss/ (*plural* **-ni** /-nī/) *n* a swelling at the base of a leafstalk that causes changes in the position of the leaf as it swells and shrinks [Mid-19C. < Latin, 'cushion, pillow' < ?]

puma /pyóomə/ (*plural* **-mas** *or* **-ma**) *n* a large tawny wild cat. Native to: mountains of Canada to the forests of South America. *Felis concolor.* US term **mountain lion** [Late 18C. Via Spanish < Quechua *púma*.]

pumice /púmmiss/, **pumicite** /púmmi sīt/ *n* a very light porous rock formed from solidified lava, used in solid form as an abrasive and in powdered form as a polish [15C. Via Old French < Latin *pumic-*, stem of *pumex* 'foam', because of the stone's spongy appearance.] —**pumiceous** /pyoo míshəss/ *adj*

pummel /púmm'l/ (**-mels, -melling, -melled**), **pommel** (**-mels, -melling, -melled**) *vt* to hit somebody or something with repeated blows, especially using the fists [Mid-16C. Alteration of POMMEL.]

pump[1] /pump/ *v* **1** *vti* **SHIFT LIQUID OR GAS** to force a liquid or gas to flow in a particular direction **2** *vt* **MAKE SOMETHING MOVE UP AND DOWN** to work a handle, lever, or other device energetically **3** *vt* **ASK SOMEBODY QUESTIONS** to try to get information from somebody by asking questions repeatedly and forcefully **4** *vt* **FLUSH OUT SOMEBODY'S STOMACH** to flush out the contents of somebody's stomach, usually to remove poison, drugs, or alcohol ■ *n* **1 DEVICE FOR SHIFTING LIQUID OR GAS** a device that is used to raise, compress, or transfer liquids or gases and is operated by a piston or similar mechanism **2 WAY OF MOVING IONS OR MOLECULES** a mechanism for the active movement of ions or molecules across a cell membrane [15C]

pump out *vt* **1** to produce something continually and in large quantities ○ *a new radio station pumping out dance music 24 hours a day* **2** to remove fluid from something using a pump ○ *We had to pump out the boat again because it was leaking so badly.*

pump up *vt* **1 INFLATE** to inflate something such as a tyre or ball using a pump **2 TURN SOMETHING UP** to turn up the sound, especially of music, produced by amplifiers or speakers (*informal*) **3** *US* **BUILD BODY MUSCLE** to increase the mass of a muscle by bodybuilding techniques (*informal*)

pump[2] /pump/ *n* **1 CANVAS SHOE WITH RUBBER SOLE** a low flat canvas shoe with a rubber sole, worn especially by children for gym **2** *US* CLOTHING = **court shoe 3** *US* **MAN'S FORMAL SHOE** a man's patent leather slip-on shoe worn with formal attire **4 SOFT SHOE FOR DANCING** a light, soft shoe for dancing [Mid-16C. < ?]

pump-and-dump, pump-'n-dump *adj US* describes a situation in which unscrupulous stock market commentators highly recommend a share that they themselves have bought in order to drive up the price then sell their own holdings quickly, usually bringing the price down again (*slang*)

pumped storage *n* in hydroelectric systems, a way of generating power during peak periods that involves pumping water up to a reservoir during periods of low demand and releasing it during peak periods

pumpernickel /púmpər nik'l, pŏŏm-/ *n* a dark, dense, slightly sour bread that originated in Germany and is made from coarse rye flour [Mid-18C. < German dialect, earlier 'lout' < *pumpern* 'to break wind' + *Nickel* 'goblin'.]

pumpkin /púmpkin/ *n* **1** a round large fruit with a thick orange-skinned rind, pulpy flesh, and many seeds, cooked and eaten as a vegetable or in sweet dishes **2** the trailing or climbing plant that produces pumpkins. Genus: *Cucurbita*. [Late 17C. Alteration of earlier *pumpion*, via obsolete French *pompon* < Latin *pepo* (see PEPO).]

pumpkinseed /púmpkin seed/ *n* a common freshwater sunfish that has an olive-coloured upper body shading to yellow or orange on its belly, with one red spot on each gill cover. Native to: North America. *Lepomis gibbosus*. [Early 19C. < its shape and its orange colour.]

pump priming *n* **1** the use of investment to stimulate the economy in depressed regions and bring about self-sustaining growth **2** the process or act of making a pump work more effectively by pouring fluid into it as it starts up

pump room *n* a building or room at a spa where mineral water can be drunk

pun /pun/ *n* a humorous use of words that involves a word or phrase that has more than one possible meaning ■ *vi* (**puns, punning, punned**) to make a pun or use puns [Mid-17C. < ?] —**punner** *n* —**punny** *adj*

puna /pŏŏnə/ *n* **1** MED = **altitude sickness 2** a cold dry flat treeless area at a high altitude in the Andes [Early 17C. Via American Spanish < Quechua.]

Puncak Jaya /pŏŏn chaak jáa yaa/ highest mountain in Indonesia, in the Surdiman Range, in W New Guinea. Height: 5,030 m/16,502 ft.

punch[1] /punch/ *vt* **1 HIT SOMEBODY WITH FIST** to hit somebody or something with the fist **2 PRESS BUTTON** to press a key or button on a computer keyboard or some other device with a quick thrusting movement of the finger ○ *Punch the return key.* **3** *US* **POKE** to poke or prod something ○ *He punched the pile of debris with a stick to see what was under it.* **4** *US, Can* **HERD CATTLE** to herd cattle on horseback ■ *n* **1 BLOW WITH FIST** a blow with the fist **2 VIGOUR** drive, energy, or power that livens or invigorates something ○ *performance lacked that punch* [14C. < Old French *poinsonner* 'to prick' < *poinson, poinchon* (see PUNCHEON[2]).] ◇ **pack a punch** to be very powerful or strong (*informal*) ◇ **not pull any** *or* **your punches, pull no punches** to use as much force and energy as necessary or possible to attain a goal or convey a message ◇ **roll with the punches** to adapt easily to a difficult situation (*informal*)

punch in *v* **1** *vi US* to arrive for work, or record the time of arrival by inserting a personalized card into a time clock **2** *vt* to enter information into a computer using the keyboard

punch out *vi US* to leave work, or record the time of departure from work by inserting a personalized card into a time clock

punch[2] /punch/ *n* **1 TOOL FOR MAKING HOLES** a tool used to make holes in a material or an object **2 STAMPING TOOL** a tool that is hit to stamp a design on something or to cut something to a particular shape **3 STAMPING OR CUTTING PART OF PUNCH** the die or solid part of a punch, containing the stamping or cutting tool **4 TOOL FOR DRIVING BOLTS OUT** a tool used to knock a bolt or rivet out of a hole ■ *vt* **1 MAKE HOLE USING PUNCH** to make a hole using a punch **2 STAMP SOMETHING USING PUNCH** to stamp or cut something using a punch [Early 16C. < ?]

punch[3] /punch/ *n* a drink made with a mixture of fruit juice, spices, and often wine or spirits, usually served hot [Mid-17C. < ?]

Punch /punch/ *n* a character from traditional children's puppet shows. He is a red-cheeked, hook-nosed clown who behaves in a quarrelsome or aggressive manner. [Late 17C. Shortening of PUNCHINELLO.] ◇ **pleased as Punch** extremely pleased (*informal*)

Punch and Judy, Punch-and-Judy, Punch-and-Judy show *n* a comic children's puppet show featuring Punch and Judy, a quarrelsome couple, together with a number of other standard characters

punchbag /púnch bag/ *n* a large heavy bag, usually suspended from a rope, used by boxers to improve their punching skills. US term **punching bag**

punchball /púnch bawl/ *n* a large heavy ball on a stand, used for training or exercise, especially by boxers

punchboard /púnch bawrd/ *n* a board with small holes, each containing a slip of paper

punchbowl /púnch bōl/ *n* **1** a large bowl for serving punch, often with a matching ladle and cups **2** a bowl-shaped hollow found on hills or mountains

⚡**punch card, punched card** *n* a card with patterns of holes punched in it, used to store information in early computers and telex machines

punch-drunk *adj* **1** dazed or confused by something such as a bad experience (*informal*) **2** showing signs of confusion and disorientation as a result of brain damage caused by blows to the head

⚡**punched card** *n* COMPUT = **punch card**

⚡**punched tape** *n* a strip of paper tape with patterns of holes punched in it, used to store information in early computers and telex machines

puncheon[1] /púnchən, púnshən/ *n* **1** a large cask containing between 70 and 100 gallons **2** a unit of capacity, equal to between 70 and 100 gallons [15C. < Old French *poinçon, poinchon* < ?]

puncheon[2] /púnchən, púnshən/ *n* a short upright piece of wood used for structural framing [15C. Via Old French *poinchon* < Latin *punct-*, past participle of *pungere* (see PUNGENT).]

Punchinello /púnchi néllō/ (*plural* **-los**) *n* **1** a short character who appears in Italian puppet and clown shows and is probably the source of Punch **2** somebody who is considered a buffoon [Mid-17C. < Italian dialect *Pollecinella* < ?]

punching bag *n US* BOXING = **punchbag**

punchline /púnch līn/ *n* the last part of a joke or funny story that delivers the meaning and the bulk of the humour [< PUNCH[1]]

punch-up *n* a fist-fight or brawl (*informal*)

punchy /púnchi/ (**-ier, -iest**) *adj* (*informal*) **1** forceful and concise ○ *What we need is a good punchy slogan.* **2** punch-drunk [Early 20C. < PUNCH[1].] —**punchily** *adv* —**punchiness** *n*

punctate /púngk tayt/ *adj* with tiny spots, holes, or dents ○ *a punctate leaf* [Mid-17C. < Latin *punctum* (see POINT).] —**punctation** /pungk táysh'n/ *n*

punctilio /pungk tílli ō/ (*plural* **-os**) *n* (*formal*) **1** strict adherence to even the finest points of etiquette **2** a very fine point of etiquette [Late 16C. Via obsolete Italian *puntiglio* and Spanish *puntillo* 'small point' < Latin *punctum* (see POINT).]

punctilious /pungk tílli əss/ *adj* **1** very careful about the conventions of correct behaviour and etiquette ○ *a courteous, punctilious manner* **2** showing great care in small details ○ *a punctilious execution of a complex design* [Mid-17C. < French *pointilleux* < *pointille* 'small point' < *pointe*.] —**punctiliously** *adv* —**punctiliousness** *n*

SYNONYMS See ***careful***.

punctual /púngkchoo əl/ *adj* **1** arriving or taking place at the arranged time ○ *a punctual start to a meeting* **2** relating to or with the properties of a point in space [14C. < medieval Latin *punctualis* < Latin *punctum* (see POINT).] —**punctuality** /púngkchoo állәti/ *n* —**punctually** /púngchoo əli/ *adv*

punctuate /púngktyoo ayt/ (**-ates, -ating, -ated**) *v* **1** *vti* **ADD PUNCTUATION TO TEXT** to put punctuation marks in written work **2** *vt* **INTERRUPT SOMETHING OFTEN** to interrupt a situation or activity frequently (*often passive*) ○ *a meeting punctuated by humorous anecdotes* **3** *vt* **EMPHASIZE** to do or say something in order to add emphasis [Mid-17C. < medieval Latin *punctuare* 'to mark with points' < Latin *punctum* (see POINT).] —**punctuator** *n*

punctuated equilibrium *n* a theory of evolution holding that evolutionary change tends to be characterized by long periods of stability or equilibrium punctuated by episodes of very fast development

punctuation /púngkchoo áysh'n/ *n* **1 MARKS USED TO ORGANIZE WRITING** the standardized nonalphabetical symbols or marks that are used to organize writing into clauses, phrases, and sentences **2 USE OF PUNCTUATION** the use of punctuation marks **3 ACT OF PUNCTUATING WRITING** the act of punctuating writing

punctuation mark *n* a symbol, e.g. a comma, full stop, or question mark, that is used to organize writing

puncture /púngkchər/ *n* **SMALL HOLE** a small hole or wound made by a sharp object ■ *v* (**-tures, -turing, -tured**) **1** *vti* **MAKE OR GET HOLE** to sustain or cause a small hole or wound in something such as a tyre or the skin **2** *vt* **RUIN SOMEBODY'S CONFIDENCE** to rapidly reduce or destroy somebody's confidence, arrogance, or conviction ○ *The interview punctured his self-esteem.* [14C. < Latin *punctura* < *punct-*, past participle of *pungere* 'prick' (see PUNGENT).] —**puncturable** *adj* —**puncturer** *n*

pundit /púndit/ *n* **1** a critic or authority on a specific subject, especially in the media ○ *The election results threw the political pundits into confusion.* **2** RELIG = **pandit** **3** somebody with knowledge and wisdom [Late 17C. Via Hindi *paṇḍit* < Sanskrit *paṇḍita-* 'learned' < ?]

Pune /poónə/ city in west-central India. Population: 1,566,651 (1991).

pungent /púnjənt/ *adj* **1 STRONG-SMELLING OR STRONG-TASTING** with a strong smell or powerfully sharp or bitter taste **2 CAUSTIC AND POINTED** expressed in or showing a witty and biting manner ○ *pungent observations about government corruption* **3 SHARP AND POINTED** describes a plant or animal part that ends in a sharp point ○ *a plant with elongated pungent leaves* [Late 16C. < Latin *pungent-*, present participle of *pungere* 'to prick, sting'.] —**pungency** *n* —**pungently** *adv*

Punic /pyoónik/ *adj* relating to the ancient Carthaginians, Carthage, or the Carthaginian language ■ *n* a Semitic language of ancient Carthage, related to Phoenician [15C. Via Latin *Punicus* < Greek *Phoinix* 'Phoenician'.]

punish /púnnish/ *v* **1** *vti* **MAKE SOMEBODY UNDERGO A PENALTY** to subject somebody to a penalty for wrongdoing **2** *vt* **IMPOSE CRIMINAL PENALTY** to respond to a crime or other wrong act by imposing a penalty (*often passive*) ○ *Any infringement of the rules will be punished by a fine.* **3** *vt* **TREAT SOMEBODY OR SOMETHING HARSHLY** to treat somebody or something harshly, causing damage or pain ○ *Lopez punished the champ with some powerful blows to the body.* **4** *vt* **TREAT SOMEBODY UNFAIRLY** to treat somebody unfairly or discriminate against somebody **5** *vt* **EAT OR DRINK** to eat or drink something quickly and enthusiastically (*informal*) ○ *The guests were really punishing the hors d'oeuvres.* [14C. Via Old French *puniss-*, stem of *punir* < Latin *punire* < *poena* (see PENAL).] —**punishability** *n* —**punishable** *adj* —**punisher** *n*

punishing /púnnishing/ *adj* very demanding, either physically or mentally —**punishingly** *adv*

punishment /púnnishmənt/ *n* **1 ACT OF PUNISHING** the act or an instance of punishing **2 PENALTY FOR DOING SOMETHING WRONG** a penalty that is imposed on somebody for wrongdoing **3 ROUGH USE** rough treatment or heavy use ○ *a sturdy car that can take a lot of punishment*

punitive /pyoónətiv/, **punitory** /pyoónitəri/ *adj* **1** relating to, done as, or imposed as a punishment ○ *punitive air strikes* **2** causing great difficulty or hardship [Early 17C. < medieval Latin *punitivus* < Latin *punit-*, past participle of *punire* (see PUNISH).] —**punitively** *adv* —**punitiveness** *n*

punitive damages *npl* damages that are awarded by a court to punish the defendant rather than to compensate the victim

punitory *adj* = **punitive**

Punjab /pun jaáb/ **1** state in NW India, bordering the province of Punjab in Pakistan. Capital: Chandigarh. Population: 21,695,000 (1994). Area: 50,362 sq. km/19,445 sq. mi. **2** province of NE Pakistan, bordering the Indian state of Punjab. Capital: Lahore. Population: 50,460,000 (1983). Area: 206,014 sq. km/79,542 sq. mi.

Punjabi /pun jaábi/, **Panjabi** *adj* **OF PUNJAB** relating to the state or province Punjab, or their people or culture ■ *n* **1 SOMEBODY FROM PUNJAB** somebody who comes from the Punjab **2 LANGUAGE OF PUNJAB** the official language of Punjab, belonging to the Indo-Iranian language family. Native speakers: 70 million. [Early 19C. < Urdu *Panjābī* < *Panjāb* 'Punjab' < Sanskrit *pañca āpas* 'five rivers'.]

punk /pungk/ *n* **1 YOUTH MOVEMENT** a youth movement of the late 1970s, characterized by loud aggressive rock music, confrontational attitudes, body piercing, and unconventional hairstyles, make-up, and clothing **2 SOMEBODY BELONGING TO PUNK MOVEMENT** a member of the punk movement **3** MUSIC = **punk rock** **4** *US* **OFFENSIVE TERM** an offensive term for a young man regarded as worthless, lazy, or arrogant (*insult*) **5 DRIED WOOD** dried or decayed wood used as tinder (*archaic*) ■ *adj* **NO GOOD** inferior in quality or condition (*informal*) [Late 17C. Originally 'rotten wood used as tinder' < ?]

punka /púngkə/, **punkah** *n* a large fan used in S Asia, consisting of palm leaves or a large cloth-covered frame suspended from the ceiling and operated by a servant [Early 17C. Via Hindi *paṅkhā* < Sanskrit *pakṣakaḥ* < *pakṣaḥ* 'wing'.]

punk rock *n* fast loud rock music often with confrontational lyrics that characterized the punk movement —**punk rocker** *n*

punnet /púnnit/ *n* a small light rectangular basket or container in which fruits such as strawberries or raspberries are sold [Early 19C. < ?]

punster /púnstər/ *n* somebody who frequently makes puns

punt[1] /punt/ *n* **FLAT-BOTTOMED BOAT** a narrow, open boat with square ends that has a flat bottom and is propelled using a long pole ■ *v* **1** *vi* **GO IN PUNT** to travel in a punt **2** *vti* **POLE PUNT** to propel a punt using a long pole [Pre-12C. < Latin *ponto* 'punt'.] —**punter** *n*

punt[2] /punt/ *vti* to drop a ball and then kick it before it hits the ground ■ *n* a kick in which somebody drops a ball and kicks it before it hits the ground [Mid-19C. < ?] —**punter** *n*

punt[3] /punt/ *n* a bet or gamble, especially one placed with a bookmaker (*informal*) ■ *vti* to bet or gamble, especially with a bookmaker [Early 18C. < French *ponter* < ?]

punt[4] /punt/ *n* see table at **currency** [Late 20C. < Irish *púnt*.]

punt[5] /punt/ *n* the indentation in the bottom of a champagne or wine bottle [Mid-19C. < ?]

Punta Arenas /poóntə ə ráynəss/ city in S Chile, on the Strait of Magellan, the southernmost city in the world. Population: 109,110 (1992).

punter /púntər/ *n* **1 CUSTOMER** an ordinary member of the public, especially a customer or a member of an audience (*slang*) ○ *Give the punters what they want, that's my motto.* **2 GAMBLER** a gambler (*informal*) **3 PROSTITUTE'S CLIENT** a prostitute's client (*informal*) [Early 18C. < PUNT[3].]

punty /púnti/ (*plural* **-ties**) *n* a long metal rod on which molten glass is turned and worked during the glass blowing process [Mid-17C. < French *pontil* (see PONTIL).]

puny /pyoóni/ *adj* **1** very small or thin and weak **2** less than is required to be effective ○ *a puny attempt at an apology* [Late 16C. Anglicization of *puisne*.] —**punily** *adv* —**puniness** *n*

pup /pup/ *n* **1 YOUNG DOG** a dog under a year old **2 YOUNG ANIMAL** a young animal of various species including mice, rats, and seals **3 CONCEITED YOUTH** an inexperienced or arrogant young person, especially a boy or young man ■ *vi* (**pups, pupping, pupped**) **BEAR PUPS** to give birth to pups [Late 16C. Shortening of PUPPY.] ◇ **be sold a pup** to buy something worthless or useless (*informal*)

pupa /pyoópə/ (*plural* **-pae** /-pee/ *or* **-pas**) *n* an insect at the stage between a larva and an adult in complete metamorphosis, during which the insect is in a cocoon or case, stops feeding, and undergoes internal changes [Late 18C. < Latin, 'girl, doll', feminine of *pupus* 'boy'.] —**pupal** *adj*

puparium /pyoo páiri əm/ (*plural* **-a** /-ri ə/) *n* the hard case that encloses the pupa of the housefly and various other insects while they develop into adults [Early 19C. < modern Latin < Latin *pupa* (see PUPA).]

pupate /pyoo páyt/ (**-pates, -pating, -pated**) *vi* to develop from a larva into a pupa —**pupation** /-páysh'n/ *n*

pupfish /púp fish/ (*plural* **pupfish** *or* **pupfishes**) *n* a tiny killifish. Native to: streams and springs in the SW United States and Mexico. Genus: *Cyprinodon*.

pupil[1] /pyoóp'l/ *n* **1 STUDENT** a young student, taught at school or by a private teacher **2 FOLLOWER OR STUDENT OF** a student who learns from a mentor or other person who is skilled, knowledgable, or experienced ○ *a pupil of Jung* **3 TRAINEE BARRISTER** a person who trains to become a barrister **4 CHILD IN CARE OF LEGAL GUARDIAN** in Scottish law, a girl under 12 or a boy under 14 who is in the care of a legal guardian [14C. < Latin *pupillus* 'little boy' < *pupus* 'boy'.]

pupil[2] /pyoóp'l/ *n* the dark circular opening at the centre of the iris in the eye, where light enters the eye [14C. Via French *pupille* < Latin *pupilla* 'little doll' < *pupa* (see PUPA); so called from the tiny image that you see when looking into another person's eye.]

pupillage /pyoópəlij/ *n* **1** the state of being a pupil, or the period during which somebody is a pupil **2** in English law, the period of time that a trainee barrister spends working in the chambers of a member of the bar immediately before qualifying

pupillary[1] /pyoópələri/ *adj* relating to a pupil or a legal ward of a guardian

pupillary[2] /pyoópələri/ *adj* relating to or affecting the pupil of the eye

puppet /púppit/ *n* **1** a doll or figure representing a person or animal that is moved using the hands inside the figure or by moving rods, strings, or wires attached to it **2** a person, government, or organization whose actions are controlled by others [Mid-16C. Variant of earlier *poppet* < ?]

puppeteer /púppi teér/ *n* an operator of puppets or producer of puppet shows

puppetry /púppitri/ *n* the art of making or operating puppets

Puppis /púppiss/ *n* a constellation of the southern hemisphere. See illustration at **constellation**

puppy /púppi/ (*plural* **-pies**) *n* **1** a dog under a year old **2** an inexperienced or arrogant young person, especially a boy or young man (*informal*) [15C. < ?] —**puppyhood** *n* —**puppyish** *adj*

puppy fat *n* the plumpness that some children develop when they are young but that disappears as they mature (*informal*)

puppy love *n* the love or infatuation felt by adolescents

pup tent *n* CAMPING = **shelter tent**

Purana /poo raánə/ (*plural* **-nas**) *n* one of a group of sacred Hindu texts written in Sanskrit that recount the lives of deities and the creation, destruction, and recreation of the universe [Late 17C. < Sanskrit *purāṇaḥ* < *purāṇa-* 'belonging to former times' < *purā* 'formerly'.] —**Puranic** /poo raánik/ *adj*

Purbach /púr bak/ hexagonal lunar crater visible in the southwestern quadrant of the Moon, approximately 120 km/75 mi. in diameter

purblind /púr blīnd/ *adj* **1** an offensive term meaning partly or completely unable to see **2** slow or unwilling to understand (*formal*) [13C. < PURE + BLIND.]

Purcell /pər séll/, **Henry** (1659–95) English composer

purchase /púrchəss/ *v* (**-chases, -chasing, -chased**) **1** *vti* **GET SOMETHING BY PAYING MONEY** to buy something using money or its equivalent **2** *vt* **OBTAIN SOMETHING THROUGH EFFORT** to obtain something by hard work or sacrifice ○ *a victory purchased with great effort* **3** *vt* **MOVE SOMETHING USING A LEVER** to move, lift, or hold on to something using a device such as a lever ■ *n* **1 ACT OF BUYING** the act of buying something **2 SOMETHING BOUGHT** an item that somebody has bought **3 HOLD** a firm grip or hold on something ○ *hands too slippery to get a purchase on the rock* **4 ADVANTAGE** influence, power, or another advantage that can be exercised ○ *an attempt to gain some purchase over his rivals* **5 POWER GIVEN BY A LEVER** a measure of the mechanical advantage given by a pulley or lever [13C. < Anglo-Norman *purchacer* 'pursue', literally 'chase eagerly' < Old French *chacier* (see CHASE[1]).] —**purchasability** *n* —**purchasable** *adj* —**purchaser** *n*

purchase ledger *n* a record kept by a business of

its accounts with other businesses from which it buys goods on credit

purchase tax *n* a former UK tax on nonessential consumer goods

purchasing power *n* **1** the ability to make purchases based on income and savings **2** the value of a particular currency, measured in terms of the goods and services it can buy ○ *the purchasing power of the yen*

purdah /púrdə/ *n* **1 KEEPING WOMEN FROM PUBLIC VIEW** the Hindu and Islamic custom of keeping women fully covered with clothing and apart from the rest of society **2 SCREEN** a screen or curtain used in Hindu communities to keep women out of view **3 VEIL** a veil worn by Hindu and Muslim women as part of purdah [Early 19C. Via Urdu *pardah* 'veil' < Middle Persian *pardak*.]

pure /pyoor, pyawr/ (**purer, purest**) *adj* **1 WITHOUT ANOTHER SUBSTANCE** not mixed with any other substance ○ *This jacket is pure wool.* **2 FREE FROM CONTAMINATION** clean and free from impurities ○ *The water from the spring is completely pure.* **3 COMPLETE** sheer or complete ○ *a look of pure terror* **4 CHASTE** virtuous and chaste (*literary*) **5 CLEAR** pleasingly clear and vivid (*refers to colour, sound, or light*) **6 RELATING TO THEORY** relating to theory rather than practical applications ○ *Opportunities for pure research are increasingly rare nowadays.* ◊ **applied 7 OF UNMIXED ANCESTRY** with unmixed parentage or ancestry **8 PRODUCED BY CONSTANT INBREEDING** produced by continual inbreeding or self-fertilization **9 COMPOSED OF SINGLE FREQUENCY** consisting of a single frequency without any overtones (*refers to sound*) ○ *a pure middle C* **10 WITHOUT DISCORD** free of discord and in tune (*refers to a musical tone*) **11 PRONOUNCED WITH ONE UNCHANGING SOUND** describes a vowel that is pronounced with a single unchanging sound **12 PRONOUNCED WITHOUT ANOTHER CONSONANT** describes a consonant that is pronounced unaccompanied by any other consonant [13C. Via French < Latin *purus*.] —**pureness** *n*

pureblood /pyŏŏr blud, pyáwr-/, **pureblooded** /pyŏŏr bludid, pyáwr-/ *adj* with an ancestry that is exclusively of a particular type —**pureblood** *n*

purebred /pyŏŏr bred, pyáwr-/ *adj* having ancestors that belong to the same breed or variety as a result of controlled breeding ○ *a purebred Arabian stallion* ■ *n* a purebred plant or animal

pure democracy *n* a form of democracy in which the people exercise direct power rather than electing representatives to govern on their behalf

purée /pyŏŏr ay, pyáwr-/, **puree** *n* food that has been made into a thick moist paste by rubbing it through a sieve, mashing it, or blending it ■ *vti* (**-rées, -réeing, -réed; -rees, -reeing, -reed**) to become a purée, or sieve, mash, or blend food into a purée ○ *Purée the vegetables and add them to the stock.* [Early 18C. < French *purée* < feminine past participle of *purer* 'squeeze out', literally 'make pure' < Latin *purare* < *purus* 'pure'.]

Pure Land Buddhism *n* groups of Mahayana Buddhism that venerate the Buddha Amitabha, or Amida, as a compassionate saviour and promise rebirth in paradise, known as the Pure Land, as a reward for faith [*Pure Land* is a translation of Chinese *Qingtu*]

purely /pyŏŏrli, pyáwrli/ *adv* **1 ENTIRELY** in a complete, entire, or total way ○ *It was a purely financial decision.* **2 MERELY** for the sole reason of ○ *surgery for purely cosmetic purposes* **3 WITH NOTHING ADDED** in a way that is free of any added substances or elements or of contaminants ○ *sheep that have been purely bred from the original stock* **4 INNOCENTLY** in a way that is innocent, pure, or chaste

purfle /púrf'l/ *n* an ornamental border on clothes or furniture, consisting of a ruffled or curved band ■ *vt* (**-fles, -fling, -fled**) to decorate clothes or furniture with a purfle [14C. Via Old French *porfil* < assumed Vulgar Latin *profilare* 'spin forward' < Latin *filum* 'thread' (see FILUM).]

purgation /pur gáysh'n/ *n* the act of purging or being purged, especially when freeing somebody or being freed from guilt or sin (*formal*)

purgative /púrgətiv/ *n* a drug or other substance that causes evacuation of the bowels (*formal*) ■ *adj* acting as a purgative (*formal*) —**purgatively** *adv*

purgatorial /púrgə táwri əl/ *adj* (*literary*) **1** relating to or similar to purgatory **2** serving to rid somebody of sin —**purgatorially** *adv*

purgatory /púrgətəri/ *n* **1 purgatory, Purgatory** in Roman Catholic doctrine, the place where souls remain until they have expiated their sins and can go to heaven **2** an extremely uncomfortable, painful, or unpleasant situation or experience ○ *the purgatory of lost love* [12C. Via Old French *purgatoire* < Latin *purgare* 'purify' (see PURGE).]

ϟ**purge** /purj/ *v* (**purges, purging, purged**) **1** *vt* **GET RID OF OPPONENTS** to remove opponents or people considered undesirable from a state or organization **2** *vt* **REMOVE SOMETHING UNDESIRABLE** to get rid of something undesirable, impure, or imperfect **3** *vt* **FREE SOMEBODY FROM GUILT OR SIN** to make somebody or something pure and free from guilt, sin, or defilement (*formal*) ○ *purge a soul of its sins* **4** *vt* **DELETE DATA** to delete unwanted or unneeded data from disk storage in a systematic fashion so as to remove all references to the data **5** *vi* **VOMIT OR USE LAXATIVES** to rid the body of food by using laxatives or inducing vomiting **6** *vti* **EMPTY THE BOWELS** to empty the bowels or cause somebody to empty the bowels ■ *n* **1 GETTING RID OF OPPONENTS** the removal of opponents or people considered undesirable from a state or organization **2 GETTING RID OF SOMETHING UNDESIRABLE** the removal of something unwanted, unneeded, imperfect, or impure **3 LAXATIVE SUBSTANCE** something that acts as a laxative (*archaic*) [13C. Via Old French *purgier* < Latin *purgare* 'purify'.] —**purger** *n*

puri /pŏŏri/ (*plural* **-ri** *or* **-ris**), **poori** (*plural* **-ri** *or* **-ris**) *n* a small piece of light, flat, unleavened Indian bread that is fried and served hot [Mid-20C. Via Hindi *pūrī* < Sanskrit *pūrikā*.]

purificator /pyŏŏrifi kaytər, pyáwr-/ *n* a linen cloth used in some Christian churches to wipe the chalice after the celebration of Communion —**purificatory** /pyŏŏrifi kaytəri, pyáwr-/ *adj*

purify /pyŏŏri fī, pyáwr-/ (**-fies, -fying, -fied**) *v* **1** *vti* to rid something or become rid of something harmful, inferior, or unwanted ○ *We use special filters to purify the water.* **2** *vt* to free somebody of sin, guilt, or uncleanness, e.g. in a ceremony or a ritual cleansing —**purifier** *n* —**purification** /-fi káysh'n/ *n*

Purim /pŏŏrim, pyŏŏrim, poo réem/ *n* a Jewish festival marking the Jewish people's deliverance from a plot to massacre them. Date: 14th day of Adar. [14C. < Hebrew *pū'rīm* 'lots' < *pūr* 'lot'.]

purine /pyŏŏr een, pyáwr-/ *n* **1** a nitrogen-containing substance derived from uric acid that is the precursor of several biologically important compounds **2** a derivative of purine, especially either of the bases adenine and guanine, which are found in RNA and DNA [Late 19C. < German *Purin* < blend of Latin *purus* 'pure' and modern Latin *uricum* 'uric acid'.]

purism /pyŏŏrizəm, pyáwr-/ *n* insistence on the maintenance or observance of traditional standards in a field, especially in the use of language

purist /pyŏŏrist, pyáwr-/ *n* a person who seeks to maintain the pure form of something —**puristic** /pyoor ístik, pyawr-/ *adj* —**puristically** *adv*

puritan /pyŏŏrit'n, pyáwrit'n/ *n* a person who lives by a strict moral or religious code, especially somebody who is suspicious of pleasure ■ *adj* = **puritanical** —**puritanism** *n*

Puritan /pyŏŏrit'n, pyáwr-/ *n* a member of a group of Protestants in 16th- and 17th-century England and 17th-century America who believed in strict religious discipline and called for the simplification of acts of worship ■ *adj* relating to Puritans, their beliefs, or movement ○ *a Puritan form of worship* [Late 16C. < Latin *puritas* 'purity' < *purus* 'pure'.] —**Puritanism** *n*

puritanical /pyŏŏri tánnik'l, pyáwr-/, **puritanic** /-itánnik/ *adj* adhering to strict moral or religious principles —**puritanically** *adv* —**puritanicalness** *n*

purity /pyŏŏrəti, pyáwrəti/ (*plural* **-ties**) *n* **1 FREEDOM FROM ADDED ELEMENTS** the absence, or degree of absence, of anything harmful, inferior, unwanted, or of a different type ○ *tests to establish the purity of the water in the river* **2 INNOCENCE** virtue and innocence ○ *the purity of young children* **3 CORRECTNESS** the observance of traditional standards of correctness in speech and writing **4 COLOUR SATURATION** the degree of saturation or lack of white in a colour **5 CLARITY** clarity of tone or sound

Purkinje cell /pur kínjee-/ *n* one of the many densely-branching neurons found in the middle layer of the brain's cerebellar cortex [Late 19C. After J. E. *Purkinje* (1787–1869), Bohemian physiologist.]

purl[1] /purl/ *n* **1 STITCH IN KNITTING** a reverse plain knitting stitch, often combined with a plain stitch to create a ribbed effect. ◊ **knit** *n.* 3 **2 purl, pearl GOLD OR SILVER THREAD** sewing thread that is made from gold or silver wire **3 purl, pearl BORDER ON LACE OR BRAID** a decorative looped border sewn on lace or braid ■ *vti* **KNIT WITH PURL** to knit something using a purl stitch [14C. < ?]

purl[2] /purl/ *vi* to flow with a soft murmuring sound, producing gentle ripples (*literary; refers to rivers and streams*) ■ *n* the soft sound and gentle movement of a river or stream (*literary*) [15C. Probably < N Germanic.]

purler /púrlər/ *n* a headlong fall (*informal*) [Mid-20C. < ?]

purlieu /púr lyoo/ *n* **1 OUTLYING DISTRICT** a district on the outskirts of a city or town **2 SHABBY AREA** an area or district, especially one that is old and poor (*formal*) ○ *the lowest slums and purlieus of our great towns* **3 FREQUENTED PLACE** a place that somebody often visits (*formal*) **4 LAND ON EDGE OF ROYAL FOREST** land that once lay within the boundary of a royal forest and was later separated from it, but remained subject to royal laws on hunting ■ **purlieus** *npl* **ENVIRONS** the outer regions or boundaries of a place (*formal*) ○ *the purlieus of the city* [15C. Probably an alteration (influenced by LIEU) of Anglo-Norman *puralee* 'king's trip around the borders' < *pur-* 'forth' + *aller* 'to go'.]

purlin /púrlin/ *n* a horizontal roof beam that supports the rafters [15C. < ?]

purloin /pur lóyn/ *vt* to steal something (*formal or humorous*) ○ *He purloined several small items, including a silk scarf.* [14C. < Anglo-Norman *purloigner* 'move far away' < Old French *loing* 'far' < Latin *longus* 'long' (see LONGITUDE).] —**purloiner** *n*

SYNONYMS See ***steal***.

puromycin /pyŏŏrō místin, pyáwrə-/ *n* an antibiotic. Source: the bacterium *Streptomyces alboniger*. Use: inhibits protein synthesis in experimental biology. [Mid-20C. < PURINE + -MYCIN.]

purple /púrp'l/ *n* **1 COLOUR COMBINING RED AND BLUE** a dark colour that is formed as a pigment by combining red and blue **2 PURPLE OBJECT** an object, substance, or fabric that is purple in colour **3 ROBE IN COLOUR PURPLE** a cloth or robe in the colour purple that was formerly worn as a symbol of imperial, royal, or other high rank **4 IMPERIAL RANK** imperial power or high rank **5 RANK OF CARDINAL OR BISHOP** the rank or office of a cardinal or a bishop **6 BISHOPS** bishops regarded as a group ■ *adj* **1 OF A DARK RED-BLUE** of a dark red-blue colour **2 ELABORATE OR EXAGGERATED** elaborate in style and containing too many literary effects ○ *purple prose* ■ *vti* (**-ples, -pling, -pled**) **TURN SOMETHING PURPLE** to become or make something become purple ○ *His eyes narrowed and his cheeks purpled.* [Pre-12C. Alteration of Latin *purpura* < Greek *porphura* 'shellfish yielding purple dye'.] —**purpleness** *n* —**purplish** *adj* —**purply** *adj*

LITERARY LINK ***The Color Purple***, a novel (1982) by US writer Alice Walker. In it Celie, an uneducated young African American woman growing up in the American South after the Civil War, confides the story of her life in a series of letters to her sister, a missionary in Africa, and to God. She tells of abuse and suffering, and her gradual empowerment through friendship and love. The novel is celebrated for the emotional power of its Black vernacular language.

purple gallinule /-gálli nyool/ *n* a water bird with dark bluish-purple plumage and red legs. Native to: Mediterranean, North and South America. Genus: *Porphyrio*.

purpleheart /púrp'l haart/, **purple heart** *n* a tree with hard brownish wood that turns purple when exposed to air, or the decorative wood of this tree. Native to: tropical South America. Genus: *Peltogyne*.

purple heart *n* a purple, heart-shaped amphetamine tablet (*slang dated*)

Purple Heart *n* a decoration awarded to members of the US armed forces who have been wounded in action [< the silver heart and the purple ribbon from which it is suspended]

purple loosestrife *n* a marsh plant with lance-shaped leaves. Flowers: purple, in spikes. *Lystrum salicaria*.

purple passage *n* a section in a piece of writing that is very elaborate or contains too much imagery [Translation of Latin *purpureus pannus*, a phrase coined by the poet HORACE in his *Ars Poetica* ('The Art of Poetry'); from the qualities of brilliance and ornateness ascribed to the colour purple]

purple patch *n* **1** a period of good luck or success (*informal*) **2** LITERAT = **purple passage**

purport *vti* /pur páwrt/ 1 **CLAIM TO BE** to claim, seem, or profess to be something specified ○ *The book purports to be a series of predictions.* 2 **INTEND** to intend to do something (*formal*) ○ *While this new measure provided money for research, it also purported to cut spending overall.* ■ *n* /pər páwrt, púr pawrt/ (*formal*) 1 **SENSE** the meaning or significance of something ○ *The purport of the remarks was difficult to discern.* 2 **INTENT** intention or purpose of something ○ *The principal purport of his letter was to inform them that he would soon be leaving the country.* [15C. Via Anglo-Norman *purporter* 'carry forward' < Latin *portare* 'carry' (see PORT[1]).] —**purported** *adj* —**purportedly** *adv*

purpose /púrpəss/ *n* 1 **REASON FOR EXISTENCE** the reason for which something exists or for which it has been done or made ○ *the purpose of life* 2 **DESIRED EFFECT** the goal or intended outcome of something ○ *The purpose of the law is to control pollution.* 3 **DETERMINATION** the desire or the resolve necessary to accomplish a goal ○ *You need to act with purpose.* ■ *vt* (**-poses, -posing, -posed**) **SET SOMETHING AS GOAL** to intend or determine to do something [13C. < Old French *purpos* < *purposer* 'intend', literally 'put forth', an alteration (influenced by *poser* 'put') of Latin *proponere* (see PROPOSE).] —**purposeless** *adj* —**purposelessly** *adv* —**purposelessness** *n* ◇ **at cross purposes** 1 to be talking about different things and so be involved in a misunderstanding 2 to have intentions that conflict with somebody else's, when you should both be working together ◇ **on purpose** deliberately ◇ **to good purpose** successfully, or with good results (*formal*) ◇ **to no purpose** without success or achieving useful results (*formal*) ◇ **to the purpose** relevant

purpose-built *adj* designed for a specific use or to meet specific needs ○ *a purpose-built swimming pool*

purposeful /púrpəssf'l/ *adj* 1 showing a clear determination ○ *She set off with a purposeful stride.* 2 having a definite purpose or aim ○ *purposeful activity* —**purposefully** *adv* —**purposefulness** *n*

purposely /púrpəssli/ *adv* deliberately or with an express purpose in mind ○ *They purposely humiliated me at the meeting.*

purposive /púrpəssiv/ *adj* 1 having a use or purpose ○ *Most human activity is purposive.* 2 showing determination ○ *She had a purposive air about her that morning.* —**purposively** *adv* —**purposiveness** *n*

purpura /púrpyŏŏrə/ *n* a condition in which bleeding under the skin causes purplish blotches to appear on the skin [Mid-18C. < Latin, 'purple' (see PURPLE).] —**purpuric** /pur pyŏŏrik/ *adj*

purpure /púrpyoor/ *n* in heraldry, the colour purple [Pre-12C. < Latin *purpura* 'purple', strengthened by Old French *purpre* (see PURPLE).]

purpurin /púrpyŏŏrin/ *n* $C_{14}H_8O_5$ a reddish-orange crystalline compound. Use: manufacture of dyes, biological stain, reagent for the detection of boron.

purr /pur/ *n* 1 **CAT'S LOW MURMURING NOISE** the characteristic soft low murmuring noise that a cat makes when it seems to be contented 2 **PURRING SOUND** a sound similar to the purr of a cat ○ *the purr of the engine* ■ *v* 1 *vi* **EMIT PURR** to emit a purr 2 *vti* **SPEAK IN SOFT THROATY VOICE** to speak, or say something, in a soft throaty voice that suggests pleasure, contentment, or sensuality 3 *vi* **MAKE LOW REGULAR MECHANICAL SOUND** to make the soft low vibrating noise that a machine, especially an engine, makes when it is perfectly tuned and is running well [Early 17C. An imitation of the sound of a cat.] —**purringly** *adv*

purse /purss/ *n* 1 **SMALL BAG FOR CARRYING PERSONAL MONEY** a small bag holding personal money, often with separate compartments for coins and notes, carried in the pocket or kept inside a handbag or other bag. US term **change purse** 2 *US* = **handbag** *n*. 1 3 **PRIZE MONEY** a sum of money offered as a prize, especially the total sum of money offered in prizes ○ *with a purse of over £20,000* 4 **AVAILABLE FUNDS** an amount of money available to spend ○ *The legislators overestimated the size of the public purse.* ■ *vt* (**purses, pursing, pursed**) **DRAW LIPS TOGETHER AT SIDES** to draw the lips together at the sides so that they wrinkle and form a circle, usually when deep in thought or to express disapproval [13C. Alteration of late Latin *bursa*, variant of *byrsa* < Greek *byrsa* 'hide' (see BURSA).] ◇ **you can't make a silk purse out of a sow's ear** used to emphasize the impossibility of making something of superior quality from inferior materials or beginnings

purser /púrssər/ *n* the officer on a merchant ship or commercial aircraft who is responsible for managing the money and who, on a passenger ship, is responsible for the well-being of the passengers

purse seine *n* a large commercial fishing net pulled by two boats, with ends that are pulled together round a shoal of fish so that the net forms a pouch

purse strings *npl* control over the money that is available to spend

purslane /púrsslən/ (*plural* **-lanes** *or* **-lane**) *n* a trailing weed sometimes used in salad or cooked and served as a vegetable. Native to: Asia. Genus: *Portulaca*. [14C. Via Old French (influenced by *porcelaine* 'porcelain') < Latin *porcilaca* < *portulaca*.]

pursuance /pər syŏŏ ənss/ *n* the process of doing something or carrying it out in the way that is expected or required (*formal*) ○ *in pursuance of our agreement*

pursuant /pər syŏŏ ənt/ *adj* following in order to catch [Mid-16C. < Old French *poursuiant*, present participle of *poursuir* (see PURSUE).] —**pursuantly** *adv* ◇ **pursuant to** in accordance with (*formal*)

pursue /pər syŏŏ/ (**-sues, -suing, -sued**) *v* 1 *vti* **CHASE** to follow or chase somebody in order to catch, overtake, or attack him or her 2 *vt* **BE EVER-PRESENT PROBLEM FOR** to be an ongoing, persistent problem for a person or organization ○ *Poor investment decisions pursued the company.* 3 *vt* **STRIVE FOR** to try hard to achieve or obtain something over a period of time 4 *vt* **CONTINUE WITH** to continue with something or follow it up ○ *pursuing a number of lines of inquiry* 5 *vt* **CARRY SOMETHING OUT** to work at something or carry it out ○ *pursuing his studies* 6 *vt* **SEEK SOMEBODY PERSISTENTLY FOR SEXUAL PARTNER** to make persistent attempts to start a sexual relationship with somebody 7 *vt* **FOLLOW ROUTE** to go along a specified route or direction [14C. Via Anglo-Norse *pursuer* and Old French *poursuir* < *pursivre* < Latin *prosequi* 'follow forward' (see PROSECUTE).] —**pursuable** *adj* —**pursuer** *n*

pursuit /pər syŏŏt/ *n* 1 **ACT OF CHASING AFTER** the act of chasing after somebody or something in order to catch, attack, or overtake that person or thing 2 **ACT OF STRIVING FOR** the effort made to try to achieve or obtain something over a period of time ○ *the pursuit of happiness* 3 **HOBBY** a pastime, hobby, or leisure activity 4 **CYCLE RACE WITH OBJECT OF OVERTAKING** a cycle race in which the riders start from points on opposite sides of a ring-shaped track and race to overtake each other rather than reach a set finish line first [14C. < Anglo-Norse *purseute* and Old French *poursuite* < *poursuir* (see PURSUE).]

pursuit plane *n* a fighter plane before World War II

pursy /púrssi/ (**-sier, -siest**) *adj* (*archaic*) 1 getting out of breath easily 2 weighing more than is healthy [15C. < Anglo-Norman *porsif*, variant of Old French *polsif* < *polser* 'to pant' < Latin *pulsare* 'agitate, drive' (see PUSH).] —**pursiness** *n*

purty /púrti/ (**-tier, -tiest**) *adj US* pretty (*regional*) [Early 19C. < a variant pronunciation of PRETTY.]

purulent /pyŏŏrŏŏlənt/ *adj* relating to, containing, or consisting of pus [15C. < French, < Latin *purulentus* 'full of pus' < *pur-* 'pus'.] —**purulence** *n* —**purulently** *adv*

purvey /pər váy/ *vt* 1 **SUPPLY GOODS** to be a commercial supplier of goods, especially foods (*formal*) 2 **CIRCULATE GOSSIP** to publish or pass on news or information, especially gossip, scandal, or other kinds of information that people generally feel should not be circulated ■ *n Scotland* **FOOD LAID ON** the food and drink that is provided at a party or other gathering (*dated*) [12C. Via Anglo-Norman *purveier* < Latin *providere* 'provide' (see PROVIDE).]

purveyance /pər váyənss/ *n* the supplying of something, especially food

purveyor /pər váyər/ *n* 1 a person or company supplying goods, especially foods (*formal*) 2 a supplier, seller, or circulator of something, especially something that is disapproved of or ridiculed ○ *a purveyor of cheap gossip*

purview /púr vyoo/ *n* 1 the scope or range of something, e.g. a court's jurisdiction or somebody's knowledge 2 the main body of a written piece of legislation that follows the introductory section or preamble and contains the clauses that state what the law requires [15C. < Anglo-Norman *purveii* and Old French *porveii*, past participle of *porve(i)er* (see PURVEY).]

pus /puss/ *n* the yellowish or greenish fluid that forms at sites of infection, consisting of dead white blood cells, dead tissue, bacteria, and blood serum [14C. < Latin (stem *pur-*) 'pus' (see PURULENT).] —**pussy** *adj*

Pusan /poo sán/ city and port in SE South Korea. Population: 3,813,814 (1995).

Pusey /pyŏŏzi/, **Edward** (1800–82) British clergyman and theologian

Puseyism /pyŏŏzi izəm/ *n* the teachings of Edward Pusey, leader of the Oxford Movement, who advocated a renewal of Catholic practices in the Church of England

⚡**push** /pŏŏsh/ *v* 1 *vti* **PRESS AGAINST TO MOVE** to press against somebody or something in order to move that person or object 2 *vti* **ADVANCE BY USING PRESSURE OR FORCE** to advance or make somebody or something advance by using pressure or force ○ *She pushed to the front.* 3 *vt* **ENCOURAGE SOMEBODY STRONGLY** to urge somebody strongly to take an action or move in a certain direction ○ *pushed their children to succeed* 4 *vt* **DEPEND ON OR EXPLOIT** to depend on or exploit something to the limits of what is wise or acceptable ○ *Don't push your luck.* 5 *vt* **USE ENERGY TO ACCOMPLISH** to use effort or energy to promote or accomplish something ○ *push a bill through the legislative process* 6 *vti* **EXTEND BEYOND LIMITS** to extend something beyond the usual limits ○ *pushing the boundaries of knowledge in this field* 7 *vt* **FORCE SOMETHING TO CHANGE** to force something, especially a financial system, to change in a particular way ○ *a fear that increased competition will push prices down* 8 *vt* **TRY TO SELL** to promote the sale or use of something, or the acceptance of an idea 9 *vt* **SELL DRUGS** to engage in the sale of illegal drugs (*slang*) 10 *vi* **ADVANCE AGAINST ENEMY** to make a sustained military advance 11 *vt* **ADD DATA TO PUSHDOWN LIST** to add an item at the top of a pushdown list ■ *n* 1 **APPLICATION OF PRESSURE** the act of applying pressure in order to move a person or object 2 **ACT OF ADVANCING** an act of advancing by using pressure or force 3 **ENERGETIC EFFORT** an energetic effort used to promote or accomplish something ○ *make a push to reform the tax code* 4 **DETERMINATION** vigorous energy or will to succeed ○ *dynamic graduates with plenty of push* 5 **MILITARY ADVANCE** a sustained military advance ○ *a push into enemy territory* 6 **STIMULUS** a stimulus or encouragement that helps the process of starting, finishing, or changing something 7 **CONTINUOUS NUDGING SHOT WITH STICK** in hockey, a shot in which the ball is moved forwards along the ground to another player by the application of continuous pressure with the stick, instead of being hit 8 **NETWORK SERVICE TRANSMITTING DATA** a network service in which the source of the data initiates the transmission. ◊ **pull** [14C. Via French *pousser* < Latin *pulsare* 'drive repeatedly' < *pellere* 'to drive, thrust'.] ◇ **at a push** if really necessary (*informal*) ◇ **be pushing...** to be approaching a particular age (*informal*) ○ *He must be pushing 40.* ◇ **give somebody the push** to dismiss somebody (*informal*) ◇ **when** *or* **if push comes to shove** at the point when something must be done or a decision must be made

push about, push around *vt* to treat somebody in a domineering way, especially by making unfair demands or giving repeated orders, and generally showing no respect (*informal*)

push along *vi* to leave or go away (*informal*) ○ *It's time I was pushing along.*

push in *vi* to force yourself unfairly into a queue of people, ahead of others who arrived before you

push off *v* 1 *vti* to move a boat out into open water, away from the place where it has been tied up 2 *vi* to leave or go away (*informal*)

push on *vi* to continue on a journey, or carry on with an activity with renewed determination or effort

push through *vt* to get something accepted or agreed quickly, especially by using persuasion or force

pushback /pŏŏsh bak/ *n* 1 a mechanism that forces something backwards, e.g. a device fitted to a door that forces it back into its closed position after somebody has opened it 2 a stick stroke used in hockey to start a game or to restart it after a goal has been scored

push-bike *n* a bicycle that is propelled by being pedalled (*informal*)

push broom *n* a very wide brush designed to sweep large areas of flooring by pushing

push button *n* a button that, when pushed, mechanically opens or closes an electrical circuit, e.g. a doorbell ○ *a row of levers and push buttons*

push-button *adj* 1 **OPERATED BY PUSHING BUTTON** operated by pushing a button or buttons to open or close an electrical circuit 2 **EQUIPPED WITH AUTOMATIC DEVICES** equipped with modern devices that perform tasks more or less automatically ○ *the push-button kitchen* 3 **INSTANTLY PROVIDED** obtained, provided, or produced easily and instantly

pushcart /pŏŏsh kaart/ *n US* a cart or barrow light enough to be pushed by hand, e.g. one from which goods are sold

pushchair /pŏŏsh chair/ *n* a lightweight wheeled chair for pushing a baby or young child around in, especially one that can be folded or collapsed for easy storage. ◊ **stroller**

⚡**pushdown** /pŏŏsh down/ *n* a technique for organizing a list or storage of data in which the item most recently added to the list or storage becomes the next item to be retrieved ○ *a pushdown stack*

pushed /pŏŏsht/ *adj* (*informal*) **1** lacking in something, usually time or money ○ *We're pushed for time now.* **2** able to do something only with difficulty or effort

pusher /pŏŏshər/ *n* **1** a dealer in illegal drugs (*slang*) **2** somebody ambitious who is always trying aggressively to outdo other people (*informal*)

push fit *n* a join that enables two pieces to be pushed together rather than fixed in some other way

pushing /pŏŏshing/ *adj* **1** showing energy, initiative, and ambition **2** aggressively self-confident or assertive —**pushingly** *adv* —**pushingness** *n*

Pushkin /pŏŏshkin/, **Aleksandr Sergeyevich** (1799–1837) Russian writer

push money *n* a cash reward that a manufacturing company pays to a retailer who sells large quantities of its products or sells off old or unwanted stock

pushover /pŏŏsh ōvər/ *n* (*informal*) **1** something that is very easy to do, deal with, or accomplish with success **2** an easily persuaded, deceived, or defeated person

pushpin /pŏŏsh pin/ *n US, Can* a drawing pin with a cylindrical head, used to fix paper or other lightweight materials to a wall or bulletin board

push-pull *adj* describes an electronic circuit in which two components are arranged so that an alternating input makes them transmit a current alternately

push rod *n* a metal rod operated by a cam to open and close a valve in an internal combustion engine

push-start *vt* to start a motor vehicle's engine by pushing the vehicle with the gear engaged and the clutch pressed down until it picks up speed, then releasing the clutch ■ *n* an act of push-starting a vehicle's engine

⚡**push technology** *n* Internet technology that allows subscribers to receive customized information directly

Pushto, Pushtu *n* PEOPLES, LANG = **Pashto**

⚡**push-up** *n* **1** *Aus, Can, US* a physical exercise in which, from a position of lying flat on the front with the hands under the shoulders, the body is pushed off the floor until the arms are straight **2** *US* a set of stored data in which the first item to be retrieved is the one stored earliest

pushy /pŏŏshi/ (**-ier, -iest**) *adj* excessively aggressive or forceful in competing or dealing with others (*informal*) ○ *pushy sales techniques* —**pushily** *adv* —**pushiness** *n*

pusillanimous /pyŏŏssi lánniməss/ *adj* showing a lack of courage or determination [15C. < late Latin *pusillanimis* < *pusillis* 'very small' + *animus* 'mind'.] —**pusillanimity** /pyŏŏssilə nímmәti/ *n* —**pusillanimously** /-lánniməssli/ *adv*

SYNONYMS See ***cowardly***.

puss[1] /pŏŏss/ *n* an affectionate word used for or to address a cat (*informal; often used by or to children*) [Early 16C. Probably < Middle Low German *pūs* < ?]

puss[2] /pŏŏss/ *n* somebody's face or mouth (*slang*) ○ *a familiar puss* [Late 19C. < Irish *pus* 'lip, mouth'.]

pussy[1] /pŏŏssi/ (*plural* **-ies**) *n* **1** an affectionate word used for or to address a cat (*informal; often used by or to children*) **2** a furry hanging flower (**catkin**) of the pussy willow or other tree [Late 16C. < PUSS[1].]

pussy[2] /pŏŏssi/ (*plural* **-ies**) *n* **1** a highly offensive term for the vulva (*taboo*) **2** an offensive term for sexual intercourse with a woman (*slang*) **3** an offensive term for women regarded as a source of sexual pleasure (*slang*) [See PUSSY[1]]

pussycat /pŏŏssi kat/ *n* **1** an affectionate word for a cat (*often used by or to children*) **2** a gentle and easy-going person (*informal*)

pussyfoot /pŏŏssi fŏŏt/ *vi* (*informal*) **1** to behave hesitantly or indecisively, or avoid speaking frankly or openly **2** to move quietly and usually secretively

pussy willow *n* **1** a willow with fluffy grey flowers (**catkins**) along its branches. Native to: North America. *Salix discolor.* **2** any of several willows similar to the pussy willow. Genus: *Salix.*

pustulant /pústyŏŏlənt/ *adj* causing pustules to form on the skin ■ *n* a substance that causes pustules to form on the skin

pustulate *vti* /pústyŏŏ layt/ (**-lates, -lating, -lated**) to become covered with pustules, or cause pustules to form on the skin ■ *adj* /pústyŏŏlət/ covered with pustules —**pustulation** /pústyŏŏ láysh'n/ *n*

pustule /pús tyool/ *n* **1** a small round raised area of inflamed skin filled with pus **2** a small raised discoloured area, especially on a plant [14C. < Latin *pustula*.] —**pustular** /pústyŏŏlər/ *adj*

put /pŏŏt/ *v* (**puts, putting, put**) **1** *vt* PLACE to move something into a particular place or position ○ *I put my arms around her.* ○ *They put the child's money into a trust fund.* **2** *vt* CAUSE SOMEBODY TO GO to cause somebody to go to a place and stay there for a period of time **3** *vt* PLACE SOMEBODY IN SITUATION to place somebody or something in a particular state or situation **4** *vt* MAKE SOMEBODY DO to make somebody do something ○ *She was put to work in the garden.* **5** *vt* MAKE SOMEBODY HAVE to make somebody or something have or be affected by something ○ *They put pressure on him to accept the offer.* **6** *vt* EXPRESS JUDGMENT OF to express or experience a feeling about somebody or something ○ *Most people put a high value on educational qualifications.* **7** *vt* USE to use or apply something for a particular purpose ○ *Put your mind to it.* **8** *vt* INVEST to invest money, time, or effort in something ○ *We offered to put some money into the scheme.* **9** *vt* EXPRESS to express or state something in a particular way ○ *How can I put this without offending you?* **10** *vt* CREATE SPECIFIED DISTANCE to create a particular distance of time or space between the self and something or somebody else **11** *vt* BRING SOMETHING UP to bring something up as a question, vote, or proposal for somebody **12** *vt* SET WORDS TO MUSIC to provide words with a musical form ○ *put the words to music* **13** *vt* ESTIMATE to make an estimate of something, e.g. the time ○ *I put the time at about 11 o'clock.* **14** *vt* SET RESTRICTION to set a limit or a restriction ○ *We must put a stop to this at once!* **15** *vt* WRITE OR PRINT to change or translate information from one kind of language to another **16** *vt* PLACE BET to bet an amount of money on a race or contest **17** *vt* THROW HEAVY METAL BALL to throw the heavy metal ball in the shot put **18** *vi* SET COURSE to take a particular course ○ *lifted anchor and put to sea* ■ *n* **1** THROW OF HEAVY METAL BALL in the shot put, a throw of the heavy metal ball **2** **put, put option** OPTION TO SELL an option giving the owner of an underlying asset the right to sell a set quantity at a set price during a specific time period [Assumed Old English *putian* 'to urge']

put about *v* **1** *vt* CIRCULATE INFORMATION to circulate something such as news or gossip **2** *vr* MAKE YOURSELF KNOWN TO MANY PEOPLE to make yourself known to many different people, e.g. in order to start friendships or establish business contacts (*informal*) **3** *vti* CHANGE COURSE to make a ship change course, or to change course

put across *vt* to make something understood or accepted by expressing it clearly ◇ **put one across (on) somebody** to deceive or trick somebody (*informal*)

put aside *vt* **1** SEPARATE SOMETHING FOR DISCARDING OR SAVING to separate something from something else and discard it or save it for later use **2** IGNORE to disregard something ○ *They agreed to put aside their differences.* **3** SET SOMETHING DOWN to stop holding, looking at, or concentrating on something and set it to one side

put away *vt* **1** PUT SOMETHING IN USUAL STORAGE PLACE to put something in the place where it is normally stored or kept ready for use **2** SAVE SOMETHING FOR THE FUTURE to save something, especially money, for future use **3** EAT FOOD QUICKLY to eat food, especially quickly, greedily, or in large quantities (*informal*) **4** CONFINE to put somebody in prison or another form of confinement (*informal*) **5** = **put down** *v.* 7

put back *vt* **1** RETURN SOMETHING TO WHERE IT BELONGS to return something to the place it was taken from or to the place where it is normally kept **2** PAY SOMETHING BACK to give something back to a person or group in exchange for help or benefits received **3** RESTORE SOMETHING TO OPERATION to restore a machine to operation **4** RESTORE PIECES TO WHOLE to restore pieces or fragments to a unified whole ○ *putting the engine back together again.* **5** DELAY OR POSTPONE to delay somebody or something, or postpone something **6** MAKE CLOCK SHOW EARLIER TIME to change the time on a clock so that it shows an earlier time **7** DRINK ALCOHOL QUICKLY to drink alcoholic drinks, especially quickly

put by *vt* to save something, especially money, for future use

put down *v* **1** RELEASE HOLD ON to release a hold or grip on something and put it on a lower surface, or restore somebody who has been lifted up to the ground **2** *vt* WRITE to write something on paper **3** *vt* SUPPRESS REBELLION to use force to bring a rebellion to an end **4** *vt* DISPARAGE OR BELITTLE to make somebody or something appear ridiculous or unimportant by being critical or scornful (*informal*) **5** *vt* SUBMIT FOR FORMAL DISCUSSION to submit something formally so that it can be discussed or debated **6** *vt* PAY DEPOSIT ON to pay part of the cost of a purchase as a deposit **7** *vt* ATTRIBUTE SOMETHING TO to give something as or understand something to be a cause or reason for something else ○ *I put his unfriendliness down to shyness.* **8** *vt* KILL ANIMAL HUMANELY to kill an animal in a humane way, usually because it is old, injured, or terminally ill **9** *vt* DEPOSIT PASSENGER to let a passenger get off or get out of a commercial transport vessel, aircraft, or vehicle **10** *vti* LAND AEROPLANE to land an aircraft somewhere **11** *vt* PUT CHILD TO BED to put a baby or small child to bed

put forth *vt* (*formal*) **1** MAKE SOMETHING KNOWN to make something known, e.g. by stating it, publishing it, or formally submitting it for discussion **2** GROW LEAVES OR OTHER PARTS to send out new leaves or new growth **3** EXERT EFFORT to exert strength or make an effort in an attempt to accomplish something **4** START JOURNEY to begin a journey or voyage

put forward *vt* **1** MAKE SOMETHING KNOWN to make something known, e.g. by stating it, publishing it, or formally submitting it for discussion **2** OFFER SOMEBODY AS CANDIDATE to suggest somebody as a candidate for something **3** MAKE CLOCK SHOW LATER TIME to change the time on a clock so that it shows a later time

put in *v* **1** *vt* GIVE TIME OR ENERGY to devote time or effort **2** *vt* INSTALL to install something, especially equipment or fittings in a house **3** *vt* MAKE CLAIM to make a claim or application for something **4** *vt* SAY to make a remark, especially to add something to a conversation **5** *vi* BRING SHIP INTO PORT to bring a ship into a port, especially for a short stay **6** *vt* MAKE OPPOSING CRICKET TEAM BAT in cricket, to decide that the opposing team should bat first

put off *v* **1** *vt* POSTPONE to delay or postpone something **2** *vt* DELAY OR HINDER to delay somebody or stop somebody from acting or proceeding **3** *vt* MAKE SOMEBODY DISGUSTED to disgust or repel somebody **4** *vt* DISCOURAGE to make somebody lose interest in or enthusiasm for something **5** *vt* DISTRACT to disturb somebody's concentration or divert somebody's attention **6** *vi* START BOAT JOURNEY to start a journey in a boat or ship ◇ **put somebody off his** *or* **her stride** *or* **stroke** to distract somebody from what he or she is doing and make that person do it less well

put on *vt* **1** START SOMETHING OPERATING to make something electrical or mechanical start operating, e.g. by turning a knob or pressing a switch **2** COVER WITH CLOTHING to cover the body or a part of the body with clothing, headgear, footwear, or other accessories **3** APPLY SOMETHING TO SKIN to apply something, e.g. make-up or lotion, to the skin **4** ORGANIZE to organize and present an event, e.g. a theatrical entertainment **5** GAIN OR ADD to gain something that is additional or extra ○ *He's been putting on weight.* **6** PRESCRIBE SOMETHING FOR to prescribe something for somebody, e.g. medication or a special diet **7** ADD to add something to a cost or value **8** ADOPT FALSE BEHAVIOUR to adopt an attitude or way of behaving that is false or insincere **9** PROVIDE to provide something as a service or facility **10** MAKE SOMETHING SUBJECT TO IMPOSITION to impose something such as a tax or a restriction **11** PLACE BET to make a bet, or offer money as a stake for a bet **12** HAND TELEPHONE TO to hand a telephone to somebody so that he or she can speak to somebody on the other end **13** TEASE to make fun of somebody, especially by pretending something (*informal*) ○ *You're putting me on.*

put on to *vt* **1** INFORM SOMEBODY ABOUT to tell a person about something previously unknown to him or her **2** ALLOW PEOPLE TO SPEAK BY TELEPHONE to allow one person to speak to another person by telephone, e.g. by handing over the telephone or making a connection via a switchboard **3** REVEAL TRUTH ABOUT to make one person suspect, or realize the truth about, somebody else (*informal*)

put out *v* **1** *vt* EXTINGUISH LIGHT OR FIRE to switch off a light or extinguish a fire **2** *vt* ANNOY to annoy, upset, or offend somebody ○ *He was very put out with me.* **3** *vt* MAKE SOMETHING KNOWN to make something widely known, e.g. by announcing or broadcasting it **4** *vt* CAUSE INCONVENIENCE to cause somebody inconvenience **5** *vt* TO CAUSE INJURY TO to cause injury to a part of the body ○ *I* *put my back out* **6** *vt* PRODUCE to manufacture or produce something **7** *vi US* AGREE TO SEX of a woman, to agree to have sex (*slang; often considered offensive*) **8** *vt* ELIMINATE PLAYER to eliminate a player from a game or competition **9** *vi* SET OFF IN BOAT to start sailing in a boat after a period spent at rest in harbour or on shore

put over *vt* to make something understood by expressing it clearly ◇ **put one over (on somebody)** to make somebody believe or accept something by using deceit (*informal*)

put through *vt* **1** MAKE SOMEBODY UNDERGO to make somebody experience something difficult or unpleasant **2** MAKE TELEPHONE CALL to make a telephone call to somebody **3** CONNECT BY TELEPHONE to connect somebody by telephone to somebody else **4** CARRY SOMETHING OUT to process something or take it to a successful conclusion

put to *vi* to tie up a boat in a sheltered spot or harbour

put up *v* **1** *vt* INCREASE to raise or increase something **2** *vt* BUILD to build or erect something **3** *vt* FASTEN SOMETHING TO WALL to fasten something to a wall, fence, or other upright surface **4** *vti* GIVE OR FIND SHELTER AND FOOD to give somebody accommodation, or find accommodation somewhere ○ *put us up for the night* **5** *vt* ENGAGE IN to engage in or carry on something ○ *put up a fight* **6** *vt* PROVIDE MONEY to offer or provide something, especially money **7** *vt* OFFER FOR SALE to offer something for sale ○ *The house contents were put up for auction.* **8** *vt* PILE HAIR ON TOP OF HEAD to fix long hair in a style that is coiled or piled on the top of the head and then secured, usually with hairpins **9** *vti* OFFER SOMEBODY AS CANDIDATE to offer somebody as a candidate **10** *vt* RETURN WEAPON TO HOLDER to return a weapon taken out for use to its holder (*archaic*) **11** *vt* SCARE GAME BIRD INTO AIR to scare a game bird out from its hiding place and up into the air ◇ **put up or shut up** used to indicate that somebody should either do something about something or else stop talking about it (*informal*)

put upon *vt* to treat somebody badly or take advantage of somebody

put up to *vt* to encourage or persuade somebody to do something unpleasant or destructive

put up with *vt* to tolerate or accept somebody or something calmly

putamen /pyoo táy men/ (*plural* **-tamina** /-támminə/) *n* the stone inside a peach, plum, apricot, or other similar fruit (*technical*) [Mid-19C. < Latin, 'shell, peel' < *putare* 'to prune' (see PUTATIVE).]

putative /pyóotətiv/ *adj* **1** generally believed to be or regarded as being something ○ *the putative father of the child* **2** believed to exist now or to have existed at some time [15C. < French *putatif* or late Latin *putativus* < *putare* 'prune, think over'.] —**putatively** *adv*

putdown /póot down/ *n* a critical or scornful remark intended to make somebody appear ridiculous or unimportant (*informal*)

Putin /póotin/, **Vladimir** (*b.* 1952) Russian president (2000–)

put-in *n* in rugby, an act of using the hands to send the ball into a scrum to restart play

putlog /póot log/ *n* a short horizontal bar or beam that helps to support the planks forming the floor of a scaffold [Mid-17C. < ?]

put-on *adj* FALSE assumed or adopted for effect or in order to deceive ○ *a put-on accent* ■ *n* (*informal*) **1** ACT OF TEASING the act of intentionally deceiving or giving somebody the wrong impression, especially for humorous effect **2** PRANK an instance of teasing somebody, especially as a joke

Putonghua /póo tóong hwaá/ *n* LANG = **Chinese** *n.* 2

put option *n* FIN = **put** *n.* 2

put out *adj* having been inconvenienced, upset, annoyed, or offended by somebody or something ○ *I do feel a little put out not to have been invited.*

putout /póot òwt/ *n* a play in which a batter or base runner is retired

put-put /pút put/ *n* (*informal*) **1** SOUND OF SMALL ENGINE the sound made by a small petrol engine, especially an old or broken one **2** PETROL ENGINE a small petrol engine **3** VEHICLE WITH PETROL ENGINE a vehicle, especially a boat, fitted with a small petrol engine ■ *vi* (**put-puts, put-putting, put-putted**) MOVE SLOWLY UNDER LITTLE POWER to move slowly or hesistantly under the power of a small petrol engine (*informal*) [An imitation of the sound]

putrefy /pyóotri fī/ (**-fies, -fying, -fied**) *vti* to decay or make something decay with a foul smell [15C. < Latin *putrefacere* < *putr-*, stem of *puter* 'putrid' (see PUTRID) + *facere* 'make'.] —**putrefaction** /-fáksh'n/ *n* —**putrefactive** /-fáktiv/ *adj* —**putrefiable** *adj* —**putrefier** *n*

putrescent /pyoo tréss'nt/ *adj* **1** decaying or rotting **2** relating to the process of decay [Mid-18C. < Latin *putrescent-*, present participle of *putrescere* 'begin to rot' < *putr-*, stem of *puter* 'rotten'.] —**putrescence** *n*

putrescible /pyoo tréssəb'l/ *adj* capable of decaying or rotting [Late 18C. < Latin *putrescere* 'become rotten' < *putr* (see PUTRID).]

putrescine /pyoo trésseen, -tréssin/ *n* $C_4H_{12}N_2$ a colourless crystalline compound (**ptomaine**). Source: decaying animal tissue. [Late 19C. < Latin *putrescere* 'become rotten' < *putr-* (see PUTRID).]

putrid /pyóotrid/ *adj* **1** DECAYING WITH DISGUSTING SMELL rotting and giving off a foul smell **2** DISGUSTING physically or morally disgusting **3** WORTHLESS worthless or contemptible (*informal*) [15C. < Latin *putridus* 'rotten' < *putr-*, stem of *puter*.] —**putridity** /pyoo tríddəti/ *n* —**putridly** /pyóotridli/ *adv* —**putridness** /pyóotridnəss/ *n*

putsch /pooch/ *n* a sudden planned attempt to overthrow a government using military force [Early 20C. < Swiss German, 'thrust, blow'.] —**putschist** *n*

putt /put/ *vti* to hit a golf ball with a gentle tapping stroke along the ground on a green, aiming for the hole ■ *n* a gentle tapping stroke that hits a golf ball along the ground on a green, aiming for the hole [Mid-18C. Variant of PUT.]

puttee /pútti/ *n* **1** a strip of cloth wrapped round the lower leg from the ankle to the knee, especially one worn as part of a military uniform **2** a leather legging or gaiter that covers the lower leg [Late 19C. < Hindi *patti* < Sanskrit *pattika* 'bandage, strip of cloth'.]

putter[1] /púttər/ *n* **1** a golf club with a flat-faced metal head, for hitting a golf ball with a gentle tapping stroke on a green **2** a golfer who is in the process of putting

putter[2] /púttər/ *vi US* = **potter**[2] *v.* 1 [Late 19C. Variant of POTTER[2].]

putting green /pútting-/ *n* **1** GOLF = **green** *n.* 8 **2** a lawn with holes for practising putting strokes

Puttnam /pútnəm/, **David, Baron Puttnam of Queensgate** (*b.* 1941) British film producer

putto /póottō/ (*plural* **-ti** /póotti/) *n* in art especially of the baroque period, an infant boy or cherub, often portrayed with wings [Mid-17C. Via Italian < Latin *putus* 'boy'.]

putty /pútti/ *n* **1** PASTE USED IN GLAZING WINDOWS a paste with the consistency of dough made from linseed oil and powdered chalk, used to fix glass into wooden window frames and to fill holes in wood **2** PASTE FORMING TOP COAT ON PLASTER a thin paste of lime, water, and sand or plaster of Paris, used as a finishing coat on plaster **3** LIGHT GREY COLOUR a light yellowish-grey colour ■ *adj* LIGHT GREY of a light grey colour with a tinge of yellow ■ *vt* (**-ties, -tying, -tied**) FIX OR REPAIR SOMETHING WITH PUTTY to fix windows into wooden frames, or fill holes in wood, using putty [Mid-17C. < French *potée*, originally 'potful' < *pot* 'pot' (see POT[1]).] ◇ **be putty in somebody's hands** to be easily influenced and controlled by somebody else

putty knife *n* a tool similar to a knife with a blunt wide flexible blade, especially one used by glaziers to spread putty onto wooden window frames

putty powder *n* a powder consisting of tin oxide or a mixture of tin and lead oxides that is used for polishing metal and glass

puttyroot /pútti root/ *n* an orchid with only one leaf. Flowers: brown or purplish-brown. Native to: N America. *Aplectrum hyemale.* [Mid-19C. So called because the substance found in the plant's corm resembles cement.]

put-up *adj* fraudulently, dishonestly, or deviously planned or organized (*informal*) ○ *Was the fire a put-up job?*

put-upon *adj* treated badly, especially by being taken advantage of or being asked to do an excessive amount of work

putz /puts/ *n* **1** *US, Can* somebody regarded as very unintelligent and unpleasant (*informal insult*) **2** *US* an offensive term for a penis (*slang*) [Early 20C. < Yiddish *potz* 'fool, penis'.]

Puvis de Chavannes /poo veé də sha ván/, **Pierre** (1824–98) French painter

Puy de Sancy /pwee də saaN seé/ highest peak in the Massif Central, central France. Height: 1,886 m/6,188 ft.

puzzle /púzz'l/ *vt* (**-zles, -zling, -zled**) CONFUSE to confuse somebody by being difficult or impossible to understand ■ *n* **1** DIFFICULT PROBLEM OR SITUATION a problem that is difficult or impossible to solve or a situation that is difficult to resolve **2** SOMEBODY MYSTERIOUS somebody whose behaviour or motives are difficult to understand **3** GAME OF SKILL OR INTELLIGENCE a game or toy designed to test skill or intelligence [Late 16C. < ?] —**puzzlement** *n*

puzzle out *vt* to use logic or reasoning to reach an understanding of something confusing or complicated

puzzle over *vt* to spend time thinking about and trying to understand something confusing or complicated

puzzler /púzzlər/ *n* **1** something confusing, mystifying, or testing skill or intelligence **2** a person who likes to solve puzzles

PVA *n* a colourless resin used in adhesives and paints. Full form **polyvinyl acetate**

PVC *n* a hard-wearing synthetic resin made by polymerizing vinyl chloride. Use: flooring, piping, clothing. Full form **polyvinyl chloride**

PVS *abbr* **1** persistent vegetative state **2** postviral syndrome

Pvt. *abbr* private

⚡ **pw** *abbr* Palau (*in Internet addresses*)

PW *abbr* Policewoman

p.w. *abbr* per week

PWA *abbr* person with Aids

PWR *abbr* pressurized-water reactor

PX *n* a store in a United States military base selling goods to military personnel and their families, as well as to some authorized civilians. Full form **Post Exchange**

⚡ **py** *abbr* Paraguay (*in Internet addresses*)

py- *prefix* = **pyo-** (*before vowels*)

pya /pyaa/ *n* see table at **currency** [Mid-20C. < Burmese.]

pyaemia /pī eémiə/ *n* a disease caused by pus-forming microorganisms in the bloodstream [Mid-19C. < Greek *puon* 'pus' + -AEMIA.]

pycnidium /pik níddi əm/ (*plural* **-a** /-di ə/) *n* an asexual flask-shaped structure in some fungi [Mid-19C. < modern Latin, < Greek *puknos* 'dense'.]

pycno- *prefix* dense, density ○ *pycnometer* [< Greek *puknos* 'strong, thick, dense']

pycnogonid /pik nóggənid/ *n* MARINE BIOL = **sea spider** [Late 19C. < modern Latin *Pycnogonida* < *pycnogonum* < *pycno-* + Greek *gonu* 'knee'.]

pycnometer /pik nómmitər/ *n* a standard container of accurately defined volume used to determine the relative density of liquids and solids —**pycnometric** /píknō méttrik/ *adj*

pye-dog /pī-/ *n* a stray, half-wild dog found in villages in Asia [Mid-19C. *Pye* < ?]

pyel- *prefix* = **pyelo-** (*before vowels*)

pyelitis /pī ə lítiss/ *n* inflammation of the part of the kidney (**pelvis**) from which urine drains into the tube leading to the bladder, sometimes caused by a bacterial infection that may occur during pregnancy —**pyelitic** /-líttik/ *adj*

pyelo- *prefix* kidney, pelvis of the kidney ○ *pyelonephritis* [< Greek *puelos* 'basin, trough']

pyelogram /pī əlō gram/ *n* an X-ray of the urine-collecting part of the kidney

pyelography /pī ə lóggrəfi/ *n* the branch of radiography dealing with the kidneys and surrounding tissue, usually involving introduction of a contrast medium to highlight the internal structures —**pyelographic** /-əlō gráffik/ *adj*

pyelonephritis /pī əlō ni frítiss/ *n* inflammation of the kidney, including both the urine-forming and urine-collecting parts [Mid-19C. < PYELITIS + NEPHRITIS.]

pyemia *n* US = **pyaemia**

pygidium /pī jíddiəm/ (*plural* **-a** /pī jíddiə/) *n* **1** the hindmost part of the body in some insects, worms, and other invertebrates **2** a protective covering of the anal portion of the abdomen of some invertebrates [Mid-19C. < Greek *puge* 'rump' + *-idium*.] —**pygidial** /pī jíddi əl/ *adj*

Pygmalion /pig máyli ən/ *n* a king of Cyprus in Greek mythology who fell in love with the goddess Aphrodite and made a statue of her that she brought to life as Galatea

pygmy /pígmi/, **pigmy** n (plural -mies) 1 OFFENSIVE TERM an offensive term for somebody who is of shorter than average height 2 OFFENSIVE TERM an offensive term that insults somebody's importance, especially in a particular field ■ adj OF SMALL BREED belonging to a small breed (offensive in some contexts) ○ a pygmy hippopotamus [14C. Via Latin pygmaei (plural) < Greek pugmaios (singular) 'dwarfish' < pugmē 'distance from the elbow to the knuckles'.]

Pygmy /pígmi/ (plural -mies), **Pigmy** (plural -mies) n 1 = Negrillo 2 = Negrito

pygmy chimpanzee n a species of chimpanzee that is smaller than other chimpanzees, with a lighter build and darker colour. Native to: West Africa. Pan paniscus.

pyinkado /pyíngka dō/ (plural -dos) n a tree that yields a valuable reddish-brown hardwood. Use: construction, flooring. Native to: SE Asia. Xylia xylocarpa. [Mid-19C. < Burmese.]

pyjama cricket n ANZ one-day cricket that takes place partly or wholly at night, on floodlit pitches, with players in brightly coloured outfits rather than in the traditional whites (informal humorous)

pyjama party n a party at which the guests wear pyjamas for fun or, especially in the case of children, bring their pyjamas so that they can stay the night

pyjamas /pə jàamz/ npl 1 SLEEPING CLOTHES a light loose pair of trousers and a matching loose-fitting shirt for wearing in bed 2 LOOSE TROUSERS WORN IN EASTERN COUNTRIES loose-fitting trousers made of silk or lightweight cotton tied at the waist, worn by both men and women in India, Turkey, and other Eastern countries 3 WOMAN'S LOOSE-FITTING TROUSER SUIT a woman's suit consisting of a loose blouse and flared trousers [Early 19C. Plural of pajama < Persian and Urdu pāy-jāmah 'leg garment'.]

pylon /pílən/ n 1 METAL TOWER SUPPORTING HIGH-VOLTAGE CABLES a tall metal tower typically made of criss-crossing steel bars that supports high-voltage cables across a long span 2 AIRFIELD TOWER TO GUIDE PILOT a tower erected at an airfield to mark a course for pilots, e.g. in a race 3 BRACKET FIXING SOMETHING TO AIRCRAFT BODY a rigid metal bracket that attaches an external aircraft part such as an engine, fuel tank, or armament to the main body of the aircraft 4 TALL VERTICAL PART OF STRUCTURE a tall vertical structure on or forming part of a building or other construction, especially an ancient structure, e.g. a decorative gateway or a monumental pillar [Mid-19C. < Greek pulōn 'gateway' < pulē 'gate'.]

pylorectomy /pílaw réktəmi/ (plural -mies) n the surgical removal of all or part of the pylorus, sometimes including the removal of part of the stomach [Late 19C. < PYLORUS + -ECTOMY.]

pylorus /pí láwrəss/ (plural -ri /-rī/) n the thick muscular ring (sphincter) surrounding the outlet of the stomach into the duodenum [Early 17C. Via late Latin < Greek puloros 'gatekeeper' < pulē 'gate'.] —**pyloric** /pī lórrik/ adj

Pym /pim/, **John** (1583?–1643) English Parliamentary leader

Pynchon /pínchən/, **Thomas** (b. 1937) US novelist

PYO abbr pick your own

pyo-, py- prefix pus ○ pyoderma [< Greek puon < Indo-European, 'to rot']

pyoderma /pí ō dúrma/ n a skin infection causing the development of pus or pustules

pyogenesis /pí ō jénnəssiss/ n the formation or production of pus —**pyogenic** adj

Pyongyang /pyóng yang/, **P'yŏngyang** capital of North Korea, in the west of the country. Population: 2,000,000 (1994).

pyorrhea n US = pyorrhoea

pyorrhoea /pí ə rée ə/ n inflammation of the gums with a loosening of the teeth and a discharge of pus from the tooth sockets [Early 19C. < modern Latin, 'flowing of pus' < Greek puon 'pus' (see PYO-).] —**pyorrhoeal** adj —**pyorrhoeic** adj

pyr- prefix = pyro- (before vowels or h)

pyracantha /pírə kántha/ n an evergreen bush of the rose family with spiky branches and leaves, and red or yellow berries. Flowers: white in clusters. Native to: Europe, Asia. Pyracantha coccinea. US term **fire thorn** [Early 17C. Via modern Latin < Greek purakantha, an unidentified plant < pur 'fire' + akantha 'thorn'.]

Pyramid: Chephren Pyramid, Giza, Egypt

pyramid /pírrəmid/ n 1 EGYPTIAN STONE TOMB a huge stone tomb of ancient Egyptian royalty with a square base and triangular walls that slope to meet in a point at the top 2 SOLID SHAPE WITH SLOPING TRIANGULAR SIDES a solid shape or structure that has triangular sides that slope to meet in a point and a base that is often, but not necessarily, a square 3 SYSTEM WITH GRADUALLY EXPANDING STRUCTURE an arrangement or system that has a small number of elements at one point and expands gradually to have a large number of elements at the opposite point 4 POINTED BODY PART a pointed or cone-shaped body part, e.g. either of two bundles of fibres located in the brain 5 INVESTMENT METHOD SPREADING RISK a financial risk structure that spreads investments between high, medium, and low risk 6 CRYSTALLINE FORM WITH MULTIPLE NONPARALLEL FACES a crystalline form in which three or more nonparallel faces intersect all three axes of the crystal ■ vi TAKE ON PYRAMID SHAPE to take on the shape of a pyramid, with few elements at one point or level and gradually increasing numbers of elements towards the opposite point or level [Mid-16C. Via Latin pyramid- < Greek puramis < ?] —**pyramidal** /pi rámmid'l/ adj —**pyramidally** adv —**pyramidic** /pírra míddik/ adj —**pyramidical** adj —**pyramidically** adv

pyramidal peak n a high mountain peak formed by the walls of three or more adjacent steep-sided glacial basins, e.g. the Matterhorn

pyramidal tract n either of two bundles of nerve fibres, shaped like inverted pyramids, running from either hemisphere of the cerebral cortex down the spinal cord to all voluntary muscles of the body

pyramid scheme n a fraudulent illegal scheme to make money, in which the perpetrators recruit people to pay money to those above them in a hierarchy, on the expectation that they will get similar payments from those below them in the hierarchy

pyramid selling n a method of distributing goods in bulk to a number of distributors, who in turn sell the goods in batches to a number of subdistributors, and so on

Pyramus and Thisbe /pírəməs and thízbi/ n two young Babylonian lovers in an ancient love story who were forbidden to marry

pyran /pí ran/ n C_5H_6O either of two isomers of a crystalline cyclic compound with a ring consisting of five carbon atoms and an oxygen atom with two double bonds [Early 20C. < PYRONE + -AN[1].]

pyranose /pírə nōz/ n a sugar whose structural formula consists of a ring with five carbon atoms and one oxygen atom

pyrargyrite /pī raárjə rīt/ n a deep-red to black lustrous mineral consisting of silver antimony sulphide, that is a source of silver [Mid-19C. < PYRO- + Greek arguros 'silver' + -ITE[1].]

pyrazole /pírəzōl/ n $C_3H_4N_2$ a crystalline cyclic compound with a ring consisting of three carbon atoms and two nitrogen atoms with two double bonds [Late 19C. < PYRROLE + AZO-.]

pyre /pīr/ n a pile of burning material, especially a pile of wood on which a dead body is ceremonially cremated [Mid-17C. Via Latin pyra < Greek pura < pur 'fire'.]

pyrene[1] /pí reen/ n the stone inside some types of fruit such as cherries (technical) [Mid-19C. < modern Latin pyrena < Greek purēn.]

pyrene[2] /pí reen/ n $C_{16}H_{10}$ a solid, crystalline, colourless to yellow, multiple-ringed hydrocarbon compound that has been shown to be carcinogenic. Source: coal tar. [Mid-19C. < Greek pur 'fire' + -ENE.]

Pyrenean mountain dog /pírrəneeən-/ n a large bulky dog with a thick shaggy white coat, originally bred to protect sheep from wild animals in mountain areas [After the PYRENEES]

Pyrenees /pírrə neèz/ mountain range forming a natural boundary between France and Spain, extending from the Bay of Biscay to the Mediterranean Sea. Area: 55,374 sq. km/21,380 sq. mi. Highest peak: Pic d'Aneto 3,404 m/11,168 ft.

pyrethrin /pī reèthrin/ n $C_{21}H_{28}O_3$ or $C_{22}H_{28}O_5$ either of two oily liquid complex organic compounds. Source: pyrethrum flowers. Use: insecticide. [Early 20C. < PYRETHRUM + -IN.] —**pyrethroid** adj

pyrethrum /pī reèthrəm/ n 1 a chrysanthemum cultivated for its ornamental flowers. Genus: Chrysanthemum. 2 a mixture of pyrethrins. Use: insecticide. [Mid-16C. Via Latin < Greek purethron 'feverfew' < ?]

pyretic /pī réttik/ adj relating to, producing, or having a fever ■ n an agent that causes fever [Mid-19C. < modern Latin pyreticos < Greek puretos 'fever'.]

Pyrex /pír eks/ tdmk a trademark for a type of borosilicate glass that is resistant to heat and chemicals and is used in household kitchenware and laboratory apparatus

pyrexia /pī réksi ə/ n fever (technical) [Mid-18C. Via modern Latin < Greek purexis < puressein 'be feverish' < pur 'fire'.] —**pyrexial** adj —**pyrexic** adj

pyrheliometer /pīr heèli ómmitər/ n an instrument that measures the intensity of the Sun's radiation received at the Earth's surface [Mid-19C. < Greek pur 'fire' + helios 'sun' + -METER.] —**pyrheliometric** /pīr heèli ə méttrik/ adj

pyric /pírik/ adj relating to burning, or produced as a result of burning [Mid-20C. < French pyrique < Greek pur 'fire'.]

pyridine /pírri deen/ n C_5H_5N a toxic flammable liquid with a noxious smell. Source: bone oil, coal tar. Use: manufacture of chemicals, pharmaceuticals, and paints, textile dyeing. [Mid-19C. < Greek pur 'fire' + -IDINE.]

pyridoxal /pírri dóks'l/ n a coenzyme derived from vitamin B_6 that is involved in the synthesis of amino acids [Mid-20C. < PYRIDOXINE.]

pyridoxamine /pírri dóksə meen/ n an amine form of vitamin B_6 derived from pyridoxine that acts as a coenzyme in protein metabolism [Mid-20C. < PYRIDINE + OXY- + -AMINE.]

pyridoxine /pírri dók seen/ n a form of vitamin B_6 derived from pyrimidine, found in cereals, yeast, liver, and fish [Mid-20C. < PYRIDINE + OXY-.]

pyriform /pírri fawrm/ adj shaped like a pear [Mid-18C. < modern Latin pyriformis < Latin pyrum 'pear'.]

pyrimethamine /pírə métha meen/ n a synthetic drug derived from pyrimidine. Use: treatment of malaria, toxoplasmosis. [Mid-20C. < PYRIMIDINE + ETHYLAMINE.]

pyrimidine /pī rímmi deen/ n 1 a nitrogenous base with a six-sided ring structure 2 a biologically significant derivative of pyrimidine, especially the bases cytosine, thymine, and uracil found in RNA and DNA [Late 19C. < PYRIDINE + IMIDE.]

pyrite /pír īt/ n a common iron sulphide mineral with a brassy metallic lustre. Use: source of iron and sulphur. [Mid-19C. < French or Latin (see PYRITES).] —**pyritic** /pī ríttik/ adj

pyrites /pī í teez/ (plural -tes) n MINERALS = pyrite [Mid-16C. Via Latin < Greek purites (lithos) 'fire (stone), flint' < pur 'fire'.]

pyro- prefix 1 fire, heat ○ pyromania 2 produced by fire or heat ○ pyroligneous 3 fever ○ pyrogenic 4 derived from an acid by loss of a molecule of water ○ pyrophosphate [< Greek pur 'fire' < Indo-European]

pyrocatechol /pírō kátti chol, -kol/ n CHEM = catechol

pyrocellulose /pírō séllyoōlōss/ n a highly nitrated cellulose. Use: manufacture of explosives, particularly smokeless powder.

pyrochemical /pírō kémmik'l/ adj relating to or resulting from chemical changes that take place at very high temperatures —**pyrochemically** adv

pyroclastic /pírō klástik/ adj describes sedimentary rock that is composed of fragments of volcanic rock produced by the explosion of a volcanic eruption

pyroconductivity /pírō kon duk tívvəti/ *n* the capacity to conduct electricity created in a solid substance by heating it to a high temperature

pyroelectricity /pírō i lek tríssəti, -əllek-/ *n* the production of electric charges on opposite faces of some crystals by a change in temperature —**pyroelectric** /-lék trik/ *adj*

pyrogallol /pírō gállol/, **pyrogallic acid** /pírō galik-/ *n* $C_6H_6H_3$ a lustrous white crystalline organic compound that is bitter and toxic. Use: photographic developer, absorbent for oxygen in gas analysis. [Late 19C. < PYROGALL(IC ACID) + -OL.] —**pyrogallic** *adj*

pyrogen /pírō jen/ *n* a substance that causes fever, especially a substance introduced into somebody's bloodstream

pyrogenic /pírō jénnik/ *adj* causing fever or produced as a result of fever

pyrography /pī rógrəfi/ (*plural* **-phies**) *n* 1 the art or technique of creating designs on wood and leather using heated tools that burn away some of the surface 2 a design burned into wood or leather using a heated tool —**pyrographer** *n* —**pyrographic** /pírō gráffik/ *adj*

pyroligneous acid /pírō lígni əss-/ *n* a reddish-brown liquid of which the primary constituent is acetic acid, produced by the destructive distillation of wood

pyrolusite /pírō loŏ sīt/ *n* a black or grey powdery metallic manganese oxide mineral. Source: deep-sea nodules. Use: source of manganese. [Early 19C. < PYRO- + Greek *lousis* 'washing' (from its use in decolourizing glass) + -ITE¹.]

pyrolysate /pírō lī sayt/ *n* a product of a chemical change caused by heating

pyrolyse /pírō līz/ (**-yses, -ysing, -ysed**) *vt* to make a complex chemical substance decompose into simpler substances by heating it [Early 20C. < *pyrolysis* by analogy with *analyse*.] —**pyrolyser** *n*

pyrolysis /pī róllassiss/ *n* the use of heat to break down complex chemical substances into simpler substances —**pyrolytic** /pírō líttik/ *adj*

pyrolyze /pírō līz/ *vt* US = **pyrolyse**

pyromancy /pírō manssi/ *n* attempting to tell the future by using fire or flames [14C. Via Old French *pyromancie* < late Latin *pyromantia* < Greek *puromanteia* < *pur* 'fire'.] —**pyromancer** *n* —**pyromantic** /pírō mántik/ *adj*

pyromania /pírō máyni ə/ *n* the uncontrollable urge to set fire to things —**pyromaniac** *n* —**pyromaniacal** /pírōmə nī ək'l/ *adj*

pyrometallurgy /pírō me tállərji/ *n* the treatment of ores and metals using high-temperature processes, or the study of these processes, which include alloying, casting, distilling, roasting, refining, sintering, smelting, and heat treating

pyrometer /pī rómmitər/ *n* an instrument that measures high temperatures, typically by converting brightness, radiation, or electric current measurements into temperature readings —**pyrometric** /pírō méttrik/ *adj* —**pyrometrical** *adj* —**pyrometrically** *adv* —**pyrometry** /pī rómmətri/ *n*

pyromorphite /pírō máwr fīt/ *n* a rare brown, green, grey, white, or yellow mineral consisting of lead chlorophosphate

pyrone /pírōn/ *n* $C_5H_4O_2$ either of two six-membered organic ring compounds containing five carbon atoms and an oxygen atom, with a second oxygen atom attached to one of the carbon atoms

pyronine /pírə neen/ *n* a red dye used in biological tests, especially a test to detect the presence of RNA [Late 19C. < German < ?]

pyrope /pírōp/ *n* a deep red garnet containing magnesium and aluminium. Use: gems. [Early 19C. Via Old French *pirope* < Latin *pyropus* < Greek *puropos* 'fiery-eyed' < *pur* 'fire'.]

pyrophobia /pírō fóbi ə/ *n* an irrational fear of fire

pyrophoric /pírō fórrik/ *adj* 1 bursting into flames spontaneously when exposed to air 2 giving off sparks when struck or scraped [Mid-19C. < Greek *purophoros* 'fire-bearing' < *pur* 'fire'.]

pyrophosphate /pírō fós fayt/ *n* a salt or ester produced when pyrophosphoric acid reacts with some metals or metallic compounds [Mid-19C. < *pyrophosphic* + -ATE.]

pyrophosphoric acid /pírō fosfórrik-/ *n* $H_4P_2O_7$ a viscous liquid, formed when phosphoric acid is heated and loses a water molecule. Use: catalyst.

pyrophotometer /pírō fō tómmitər/ *n* an instrument that determines the temperature of an incandescent body as a function of the light it emits

pyrophyllite /pírō fíllīt/ *n* a talc-like silvery-white or greenish hydrous aluminium silicate mineral. Source: metamorphic rocks. [Early 19C. < German *Pyrophyllit* < Greek *pur* 'fire' + *phullon* 'leaf'; so called because it exfoliates when exposed to flame.]

pyrosis /pī róssiss/ *n* heartburn (*technical*) [Late 18C. Via Greek *purōsis* 'burning' < *pur* 'fire' (see PYRO-).]

pyrostat /pírō stat/ *n* a thermostat that is suitable for use at very high temperatures [< PYRO- after 'thermostat'] —**pyrostatic** /pírō státtik/ *adj*

pyrotechnic /pírō téknik/, **pyrotechnical** /-téknik'l/ *adj* 1 relating to, used in, or involving fireworks 2 showing brilliance, e.g. in style or technique [Early 19C. < modern Latin *pyrotechnia* < Greek *pur* 'fire' + *tekhnē* 'craft'.] —**pyrotechnically** *adv* —**pyrotechnist** *n*

pyrotechnics /pírō tékniks/ *n* CRAFT OF MAKING FIREWORKS the craft or skill of making and using fireworks (+ *singular verb*) ■ *npl* (+ *singular or plural verb*) 1 FIREWORK DISPLAY a display of fireworks 2 SHOWY DISPLAY an extravagant display of brilliance, virtuosity, or strong emotion

pyroxene /pī rók seen/ *n* a mineral belonging to a group of dark green, brown, or black silicate minerals containing varying amounts of calcium, aluminium, iron, magnesium, and sodium. Source: igneous and metamorphic rocks. [Early 19C. < French *pyroxène* < Greek *pur* 'fire' + *xenos* 'stranger'; so called because it was originally thought to be a foreign substance in igneous rock.] —**pyroxenic** /pī rok sénnik/ *adj*

pyroxenite /pī róksə nīt/ *n* an igneous rock consisting mainly of pyroxene and olivine

pyroxylin /pī róksəlin/ *n* a form of cellulose nitrate. Use: manufacture of plastics and lacquers. [Mid-19C. < PYRO- + XYLO- + -IN.]

pyrrhic /pírrik/ *n* a unit of poetic rhythm that has two short or unaccented syllables ■ *adj* relating to or written in pyrrhics [Early 17C. Via Latin < Greek *purríkhē*, named after the chorist *Pyrrhikhos*, who is supposed to have invented it.]

Pyrrhic victory *n* a victory won at such great cost to the victor that it is tantamount to a defeat [Late 19C. After PYRRHUS.]

Pyrrhonism /pírrōnizəm/ *n* 1 the doctrine of the ancient Greek philosopher Pyrrho, who believed that it was impossible to be certain about anything and therefore suspended judgment on everything 2 scepticism to an

extreme or excessive degree [Late 17C. < Greek *Purrhōn* 'Pyrrho'.] —**Pyrrhonist** *n*, *adj*

pyrrhotite /pírō tīt/, **pyrrhotine** /-teen/ *n* a common yellow-brown lustrous iron sulphide mineral. Source: igneous rocks. Use: source of iron. [Mid-19C. Alteration of German *Pyrrhotin* < Greek *purrotēs* 'fiery redness' < *pur* 'fire' (see PYRO-).]

Pyrrhus /pírrəss/ (318?–272 BC) king of Epirus (307–272 BC)

pyrrole /pírrōl/ *n* C_4H_5N a colourless toxic liquid compound containing carbon, hydrogen, and nitrogen. Source: biological substances, e.g. chlorophyll, haemoglobin, and bile pigments. [Mid-19C. < Greek *purros* 'fiery red' (from *pur* 'fire') + -OLE.] —**pyrrolic** /pi róllik/ *adj*

pyruvate /pī roŏ vayt/ *n* a chemical compound derived from pyruvic acid [Mid-19C. < PYRUVIC ACID.]

pyruvic acid /pī roŏvik-/ *n* $C_3H_4O_3$ a colourless acid that is formed as an intermediate compound during the metabolism of carbohydrates and proteins [Mid-19C. < PYRO- + Latin *uva* 'grape'; so called because it was obtained by dry distillation from racemic acid.]

Pythagoras /pī tthággərəss/ (582?–500? BC) Greek philosopher and mathematician —**Pythagorean** /pī tthággə reè ən/ *adj*, *n*

Pythagoras' theorem *n* a proved geometric proposition stating that the square of the longest side (**hypotenuse**) of a right-angled triangle is equal to the sum of the squares of the other two sides [After *Pythagoras*]

Pythagoreanism /pī tthággə reè ənizəm/ *n* the theories and teachings of Pythagoras, especially those that apply mathematics to the workings of the universe

Pytheas /píthi əss/ (*fl.* 300 BC) Greek mathematician, astronomer, and explorer

python /píth'n/ *n* a nonvenomous constricting snake that kills its prey through suffocation and can reach lengths of over 6 m/19 ft. Native to: Asia, Africa, Australia. Family: Pythonidae. [Mid-19C. Directly or via French < Latin, a mythical serpent killed by Apollo < Greek *Puthōn*.]

Pythonesque /píthə nésk/ *adj* absurdly or surreally comical in a way that is reminiscent of the 1970s British TV comedy show *Monty Python's Flying Circus* [Late 20C]

pythoness /píthə ness/ *n* in Greek mythology, a woman believed to be possessed by the spirit of an oracle, especially Apollo's priestess at Delphi [14C. < late Latin *pythonissa*, feminine of *python* < Greek *Puthōn*, after the serpent that Apollo killed near Delphi.]

pyuria /pī yoŏri ə/ *n* the presence of pus in the urine [Early 19C. < PYO- + -URIA.]

pyx /piks/, **pix** *n* 1 a container in which the consecrated wafers for Communion are placed so that they can be taken to those who cannot leave home 2 a chest in which newly minted coins are placed before being tested [14C. Via Latin < Greek *puxis* 'box' (see PYXIS).]

pyxidium /pik síddi əm/ (*plural* **-a** /-di ə/) *n* PLANT SCI = **pyxis** *n*. [Mid-19C. Via modern Latin < Greek *puxídion* 'small box' < *puxis* (see PYXIS).]

pyxis /píksiss/ (*plural* **-ides** /-si dez/) *n* a seed capsule with a cap that falls off to release the seeds [Late 17C. Via Latin < Greek *puxis* 'box' < *puxos* 'boxwood' < ?]

Pyxis /píksiss/ *n* a small constellation of the southern hemisphere. See illustration at **constellation**

pzazz *n* = **pizzazz**

Qq

q¹ /kyoo/ (*plural* **q's**), **Q** (*plural* **Q's** *or* **Qs**) *n* the 17th letter of the English alphabet, representing a consonant sound

q² *symbol* electric charge

q³ *abbr* **1** quart **2** quarter **3** quarterly **4** quarto **5** query **6** question **7** quintal **8** quire

Q¹ /kyoo/ (*plural* **Q's** *or* **Qs**) *n* something shaped like a letter 'Q'

Q² *abbr* **1** quartermaster **2** quarto **3** Quebec **4** queen **5** quetzal

Q³ *symbol* heat

⚡ **qa** *abbr* Qatar (*in Internet addresses*)

Qadaffi /kə dáffi/ = **Muammar al-Gadaffi**

Qaddafi /gə daáfi/, **Gadaffi** = **Muammar al-Gadaffi**

qadi *n* ISLAM = **cadi**

Q & A *abbr* question and answer

Qaro /kaárō/ = **Caro**

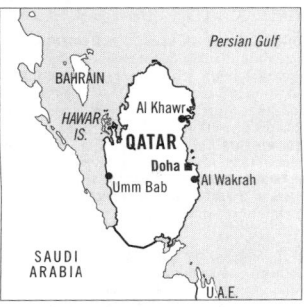

Qatar

Qatar /kataár, káttaar, kúttar/ emirate in E Arabia, on a peninsula in the SW Persian Gulf. Capital: Doha. Population: 125,665 (1991). Area: 11,437 sq. km/4,416 sq. mi. —**Qatari** *adj, n*

Qattara Depression /kə taára-/ desert basin in NW Egypt. Its lowest point is 133 m/435 ft below sea level. Area: 18,000 sq. km/6,950 sq. mi.

Qayrawan, Al- /kírə waàn/ ♦ **Kairouan**

QB¹ *abbr* queen's bishop

QB² *abbr* Queen's Bench

Q-boat *n* = **Q-ship**

QBP *abbr* queen's bishop's pawn

QC *abbr* **1** Quebec **2** Queen's Counsel

QCD *abbr* quantum chromodynamics

QED *abbr* **1** quantum electrodynamics **2** quod erat demonstrandum

Q fever *n* an infectious disease caused by rickettsial bacteria and characterized by fever, chills, and muscle pain [Mid-20C. Probably shortening of QUEENSLAND.]

qi, Qi *n* PHILOSOPHY = **chi²** *n*.

qibla *n* ISLAM = **kiblah**

Qin /chin/, **Ch'in** *n* a dynasty in ancient China that ruled from 221 until 206 BC, during which the first unified Chinese empire emerged and much of the Great Wall of China was built [Late 18C. < Chinese *Qín*.]

qindar /kin daar/ (*plural* **-dars** *or* **-darka** /kin daàrkə/), **qintar** /kín taar/ *n* see table at **currency**

Qing /ching/, **Ch'ing** *n* the last of the Chinese dynasties, founded by the conquering Manchu who ruled from 1644 until 1912, when the nationalist revolutionaries overthrew it [Late 18C. < Chinese *Qīng*.]

Qingdao /chíng dów/ city in E China, on the Yellow Sea. Population: 2,638,919 (1991).

Qinghai /chíng hí/ province of W China, on the Tibetan Plateau. Capital: Xining. Population: 4,740,000 (1994). Area: 720,999 sq. km/278,379 sq. mi.

Qinghai Hu /chíng hí hoo/ saline lake in west-central China, the largest lake in the country

qintar *n* MONEY = **qindar**

Qiqihar /chee chee haàr/ port in NE China. Population: 1,260,000 (1986).

qiviut /keévi ət/ *n* the soft wool that grows beneath the long outer coat of a musk ox. Use: yarn. [Mid-20C. < Inuit.]

QKt *abbr* queen's knight

QKtP *abbr* queen's knight's pawn

⚡ **QL** *abbr* query language

Qld *abbr* Queensland

QM *abbr* quartermaster

QMG *abbr* Quartermaster General

QMS *abbr* Quartermaster Sergeant

qof /kof/ *n* the 19th letter of the Hebrew alphabet [< Hebrew *qōph* < Semitic, 'eye of a needle']

Qom /koöm/ city in west-central Iran. Population: 777,677 (1996).

qorma *n* FOOD = **korma**

QP *abbr* queen's pawn

qqv *abbr* which (things) see (*used as cross reference to more than one item*) [Latin *quae vide*]

QR *abbr* queen's rook

qr. *abbr* **1** quarter **2** quarterly **3** quire

QRP *abbr* queen's rook's pawn

Q-ship *n* an armed ship disguised as a merchant ship, used to decoy or destroy enemy vessels [< the naval designation for this type of vessel]

QSO *abbr* quasi-stellar object

qt *abbr* **1** quart **2** quantity

q.t. *abbr* quiet (*informal*) ◇ **on the q.t.** quietly and secretly (*informal*)

qto *abbr* quarto

qty *abbr* quantity

qu. *abbr* **1** queen **2** query **3** question

qua /kway, kwaa/ *prep* in the capacity or function of ◇ '*Restrictions on trade, or on production for purposes of trade, are indeed restraints; and all restraint, qua restraint, is an evil*'. (John Stuart Mill, *On Liberty*; 1859) [Mid-17C. < Latin *qua*, a form of *qui* 'who'.]

quack¹ /kwak/ *n* SOUND MADE BY A DUCK the harsh sound typically made by a duck ■ *vi* **1** MAKE THE SOUND OF A DUCK to make the harsh sound that is characteristic of a duck **2** SPEAK IRRITATINGLY to speak loudly and endlessly in an

irritating manner (*slang*) [Early 17C. An imitation of the sound.]

quack² /kwak/ *n* **1** FAKE DOCTOR somebody who practises medicine without training or qualifications (*often used before a noun*) **2** DOCTOR a doctor (*dated informal*) **3** A FRAUD anyone who falsely claims skills and qualifications [Early 17C. Shortening of QUACKSALVER.] —**quack** *vi* —**quackery** *n* —**quackish** /kwákish/ *adj*

quack grass *n* PLANTS = **couch grass**

quacksalver /kwák salvər/ *n* a person who falsely claims to have medical or other skills or qualifications (*archaic*) [Late 16C. < obsolete Dutch, 'salve-hawker' < Dutch *kwaken* 'quack, prattle' + *zalf* 'salve'.]

quad¹ /kwod/ *n* a quadruplet (*informal*) [Late 19C. Shortening.]

quad² /kwod/ *n* a quadrangle (*informal*) [Early 19C. Shortening.]

quad³ /kwod/ *adj* quadraphonic (*informal*) [Late 20C. Shortening.]

quad⁴ /kwod/ *n* a piece of blank type metal used for spacing [Late 19C. Shortening of QUADRAT.]

quad⁵ /kwod/ *n* a quadriceps (*informal*) [Mid-20C. Shortening.]

quad⁶ /kwod/ *abbr* **1** quadrant **2** quadrilateral

quadr- *prefix* = **quadri-** (*before vowels*)

quadra- *prefix* = **quadri-** (*before consonants*)

quadragenarian /kwóddrəjə náiri ən/ *n* somebody between the ages of 40 and 49 (*formal*) ■ *adj* between the ages of 40 and 49 (*formal*) [Mid-19C. < late Latin *quadragenarius* < *quadraginta* 'forty']

Quadragesima /kwóddrə jéssimə/ *n* in the Christian liturgical calendar, the first Sunday in Lent [14C. < late Latin *quadragesima* (*dies*) 'fortieth (day)' (before Easter) < *quadrginta* 'forty']

quadragesimal /kwóddrə jéssim'l/ *adj* relating to Lent

quadrangle /kwód rang g'l/ *n* **1** FOUR-SIDED SHAPE a two-dimensional figure that consists of four points connected by straight lines, especially a rectangle **2** OPEN AREA SURROUNDED BY BUILDINGS an open rectangular yard that is surrounded on all four sides by buildings **3** BUILDINGS SURROUNDING YARD the buildings that surround an open rectangular yard [15C. Via Old French < Latin *quadrangulus* 'having four corners'.] —**quadrangular** /kwod ráng gyoôlər/ *adj*

quadrant /kwóddrənt/ *n* **1** QUARTER OF CIRCUMFERENCE OF CIRCLE a 90-degree arc representing one fourth of the circumference of a circle **2** QUARTER OF AREA OF CIRCLE the area bounded by a quadrant and the two perpendicular lines that connect it to the centre of the circle **3** QUARTER OF PLANE SURFACE any of the four sections into which the perpendicular axes of a coordinate system divide a two-dimensional surface **4** QUARTER OF AREA OR SURFACE any of the four approximately equal parts into which an area or a surface is divided by two real or imaginary perpendicular lines **5** DEVICE FOR MEASURING ANGLE OF STAR an instrument with a movable sighting mechanism attached to a 90-degree arc, formerly used in astronomy and navigation to measure the angles and altitudes of stars **6** DEVICE SHAPED LIKE QUARTER CIRCLE a mechanical device or machine part in the shape of a quarter of a circle [14C. < Latin *quadrant-*, stem of *quadrans* 'fourth part, quarter'.]

quadraphonic /kwóddrə fónnik/, **quadrophonic** *adj* using a four-channel system to record and reproduce sound —**quadraphonics** *n* —**quadraphony** /kwo dróffəni/ *n*

quadrat /kwódrət/ *n* 1 PRINTING = **quad**[4] 2 a small plot of land set aside for plant and animal population studies [Late 17C. Variant of QUADRATE.]

quadrate *n* /kwód rayt/ 1 **SQUARE OR CUBE** a square or cube, or a square or cubic area, space, or thing 2 **JAW JOINT OF SOME VERTEBRATES** in birds, fish, reptiles, and amphibians, a bony or cartilaginous part of the upper jaw that articulates with the lower jaw at the side of the skull ■ *adj* 1 **OF THE VERTEBRATE QUADRATE** relating to the quadrate in vertebrates 2 **SQUARE OR RECTANGULAR** with four sides and four right angles ■ *v* /kwo dráyt/ (**-rates, -rating, -rated**) 1 *vt* to make something square or rectangular 2 *vti* **CONFORM OR CORRESPOND WITH** to conform or correspond with something or to make one thing conform or correspond with another [14C. < Latin *quadratum* < *quadrum* 'square'.]

quadratic /kwo dráttik/ *adj* relating to or containing terms with powers no higher than the power of two ■ *n* MATH = **quadratic equation** [Mid-17C. < QUADRATE.] —**quadratically** *adv*

quadratic equation *n* an equation containing one or more terms raised to the power of two but no higher

quadratics /kwo dráttiks/ *n* the branch of algebra that deals with quadratic equations (*+ singular verb*)

quadrature /kwódrəchər/ *n* 1 **MAKING SOMETHING SQUARE** making something square or dividing something into squares 2 **MATHEMATICAL TECHNIQUE FOR EQUATING AREAS** the construction of a square with an area equal to that of a specified surface 3 **90-DEGREE SEPARATION OF ASTRONOMICAL OBJECTS** the relative position of two astronomical objects with a separation of 90 degrees as seen from a third, especially the Sun and Moon as seen from the Earth

quadrennia plural of **quadrennium**

quadrennial /kwo drénni əl/ *adj* 1 **HAPPENING EVERY FOUR YEARS** occurring every fourth year 2 **LASTING FOUR YEARS** lasting for four years ■ *n* **FOUR-YEAR PERIOD** a period of four years —**quadrennially** *adv*

quadrennium /kwo drénni əm/ (*plural* **-ums** *or* **-a** /-ni ə/) *n* a period of four years [Mid-19C. < Latin < *quadri-* 'four' + *annus* 'year'.]

quadri- *prefix* 1 four, fourth ○ *quadripartite* ○ *quadricentennial* 2 square ○ *quadric* [< Latin < Indo-European 'four']

quadric /kwóddrik/ *adj* MATH = **quadratic** *adj.* ■ *n* a surface or curve specified by a second degree equation [Mid-19C. < Latin *quadra*, feminine of *quadrum* 'square'.]

quadricentennial /kwóddri sen ténni əl/ *n* a 400th anniversary or a celebration of it ■ *adj* marking or relating to a 400th anniversary

quadriceps /kwódri seps/ (*plural* **-ceps** *or* **-cepses**) *n* a large four-part muscle at the front of the thigh that acts to extend the leg [Mid-19C. < Latin, 'four-headed'.] —**quadricipital** /kwóddri síppit'l/ *adj*

quadriga /kwo dreégə/ (*plural* **-gae** /-dreéjee/) *n* a two-wheeled chariot in ancient Greece or Rome that was drawn by four horses harnessed alongside each other [Early 18C. < Latin, < *quadrijuga* 'team of four' < *quadri-* 'four' + *jugum* 'yoke'.]

quadrilateral /kwóddri láttərəl/ *n* a two-dimensional geometric figure with four sides ■ *adj* with four sides

quadrille[1] /kwə dríl/ *n* 1 a French square dance in a lively duple time, popular in the 18th and 19th centuries, danced by four or more couples 2 the music for a quadrille [Mid-18C. Via French < Spanish *cuadrilla* 'troop, company' < *cuadro* 'square' < Latin *quadrum* (see QUADRATE).]

quadrille[2] /kwə dríl/ *n* a card game for four players that uses a deck of 40 cards [Early 18C. < French.]

quadrillion /kwo drílli ən/ (*plural* **-lions** *or* **-lion**) *n* 1 the number equal to 10^{15}, written as 1 followed by 15 zeros 2 the number equal to 10^{24}, written as 1 followed by 24 zeros (*dated*) [Late 17C. < QUADRI-, after BILLION.] —**quadrillion** *adj, pron* —**quadrillionth** *adj, n*

quadripartite /kwóddri paár tīt/ *adj* 1 made up of four parts or divided into four 2 involving the participation of four individuals or groups

quadriplegia /kwóddri pleéji ə/ *n* the inability to move all four limbs or the entire body below the neck. ◊ **hemiplegia, paraplegia** —**quadriplegic** *n, adj*

quadrivalent /kwóddri váylənt/ *adj* 1 CHEM = **tetravalent** 2 with four different valencies —**quadrivalency** *n*

quadrivial /kwo drívvi əl/ *adj* with four roads or ways going in different directions and meeting at the same point

quadrivium /kwo drívvi əm/ *n* four of the seven liberal arts taught in medieval universities, consisting of arithmetic, geometry, music, and astronomy. The three lower arts (**trivium**) were grammar, rhetoric, and logic. [Early 19C. Via late Latin < Latin, 'crossroads' < *quadri-* 'four' + *via* 'road'.]

quadroon /kwo dro͞on/ *n* an offensive term for somebody with one Black and three white grandparents [Mid-17C. < Spanish *cuarterón* < Latin *quartus* 'quarter' (see QUART[1]).]

quadrophonic *adj* RECORDING = **quadraphonic**

quadru- *prefix* = **quadri-** (*before consonants*)

quadrumvirate /kwo drúmvərət/ *n* a group of four people sharing power, especially forming a government [Mid-18C. < QUADRI-, after TRIUMVIRATE.]

quadruped /kwóddro͝o ped/ *n* an animal such as a lion or lizard with four limbs and feet, all of which are used for walking ■ *adj* with four feet —**quadrupedal** /kwo dro͞opid'l/ *adj*

quadruple /kwóddro͝op'l, kwo dro͞op'l/ *vti* (**-ples, -pling, -pled**) **INCREASE FOURFOLD** to multiply something by four or become four times as great ■ *adj* 1 **MULTIPLIED BY FOUR** four times as great 2 **WITH FOUR PARTS** made up of four parts 3 **WITH FOUR BEATS PER BAR** describes a time or metre consisting of four beats to a bar ■ *n* **QUANTITY FOUR TIMES AS GREAT** a number or amount that is four times as great as another [14C. Via French < Latin *quadruplus* 'fourfold' < *quadri-* 'four'.] —**quadruply** *adv*

quadruplet /kwóddro͝oplət/ *n* 1 **ONE OF FOUR BABIES** any of four babies born to the same mother from one pregnancy 2 **FOUR SIMILAR THINGS** a set of four identical or very similar things 3 **FOUR NOTES PLAYED FASTER THAN NORMAL** a group of four notes performed in the time usually occupied by three

quadruplicate *vti* /kwo dro͞opli kayt/ (**-cates, -cating, -cated**) **INCREASE FOURFOLD** to multiply something by four or to be multiplied by four ■ *adj* /kwo dro͞oplikət/ **WITH FOUR PARTS** consisting of four identical or corresponding parts ■ *n* /kwo dro͞oplikət/ **ONE OF FOUR** any of a set of four identical things or copies [Mid-17C. < Latin *quadri-* 'four', after DUPLICATE.] —**quadruplication** /kwo dro͞opli káysh'n/ *n*

quaere /kweéri/ *interj* used to introduce a query (*formal*) [Mid-16C. < Latin (see QUERY).]

quaestor /kweéstər/ *n* in ancient Rome, a magistrate responsible chiefly for financial administration [14C. < Latin < *quaest-*, past participle of *quaerere* 'inquire'.] —**quaestorial** /kwee stáwri əl/ *adj* —**quaestorship** /kweéstər ship/ *n*

quaff /kwof/ *vti* to drink something in large gulps or with great enjoyment (*literary or humorous*) ■ *n* a long deep drink (*literary or humorous*) [Early 16C. < ?] —**quaffer** *n*

quag /kwag, kwog/ *n* GEOG = **quagmire** *n.* 1 [Late 16C. < ?]

quagga /kwággə/ (*plural* **-gas** *or* **-ga**) *n* an extinct mammal of the horse family, related to the zebra, with yellowish-brown colouring and stripes on the head, neck, and shoulders. Native to: South Africa. *Equus quagga*. [Late 18C. < Afrikaans, < Nguni, imitation of the animal's call.]

quaggy /kwággi/ (**-gier, -giest**) *adj* 1 soft and wet like a marsh or bog 2 lacking in firmness —**quagginess** *n*

quagmire /kwág mīr, kwóg-/ *n* 1 a soft marshy area of land that gives way when walked on 2 an awkward, complicated, or dangerous situation from which it is difficult to escape

quahog /kwaá hog/, **quahaug** *n* a thick-shelled edible clam, the shells of which were formerly used as money by Native North Americans. Native to: North Atlantic coast of the United States. *Mercenaria mercenaria*. [Mid-18C. < Narraganset *poqua hock*.]

quaich /kwaykh/, **quaigh** *n Scotland* a shallow drinking vessel with two handles, usually made from wood or metal [Mid-17C. Via Scottish Gaelic < Old Irish *cúach* < medieval Latin *caucus* 'drinking cup'.]

Quai d'Orsay /káy dáw say/ *n* 1 the street along the south bank of the Seine in Paris on which the French foreign office is located 2 the French foreign office itself ○ *The Quai d'Orsay chose to make no immediate comment on the crisis.*

quaigh *n Scotland* = **quaich**

quail[1] /kwayl/ (*plural* **quails** *or* **quail**) *n* 1 a small game bird with a rounded body, mottled brown plumage, and a short tail. Native to: Europe, Asia, Africa. Genus: *Coturnix*. 2 any small game bird related to the quail, including the bobwhite. Native to: North America. [14C. Via Old French < medieval Latin *coacula* < Germanic, an imitation of its call.]

quail[2] /kwayl/ *vi* to tremble or shrink with fear or apprehension [Early 19C. Probably < Middle Dutch *qualen* 'suffer'.]

SYNONYMS See ***recoil***.

quaint /kwaynt/ *adj* 1 **ATTRACTIVELY OLD-FASHIONED** with a charming old-fashioned quality ○ *a quaint little shop* 2 **PLEASANTLY STRANGE** strange or unusual, especially in a pleasing or interesting way 3 **ECCENTRICALLY OUTDATED** amusingly or irritatingly inappropriate to modern circumstances [12C. Via Old French *cointe*, *queinte* 'clever' < Latin *cognit-*, past participle of *cognoscere* 'learn' (see COGNITION).] —**quaintly** *adv* —**quaintness** *n*

quake /kwayk/ *vi* (**quakes, quaking, quaked**) 1 **TREMBLE WITH FEAR** to shake or tremble, especially with fear 2 **SHAKE** to shake or rock, e.g. from instability or a geological disturbance ■ *n* 1 **EARTHQUAKE** an earthquake (*informal*) 2 **SHAKING** a tremor or shake [Old English *cwacian* < ?] —**quaky** *adj*

Quaker /kwáykər/ *n* a member of the Society of Friends, a Christian denomination founded in England in the 17th century that rejects formal sacraments, ministry, and creed, and is committed to pacifism [Late 17C. < QUAKE, probably because founder George Fox (1624–91) admonished that they should 'tremble at the word of the Lord'.] —**Quakerism** *n* —**Quakerly** *adj*

Quaker gun *n* a dummy gun or cannon, usually made of wood, used in military training or to deceive an enemy [< the Quakers' refusal to fight in wars]

quale /kwáyli/ (*plural* **-lia** /kwáyli ə/) *n* a property of something, e.g. its feel or appearance, rather than the thing itself [Mid-17C. < Latin, neuter of *qualis* 'of what kind'.]

qualification /kwóllifi káysh'n/ *n* 1 **ESSENTIAL ATTRIBUTE** a skill, quality, or attribute that makes somebody suitable for a particular job, activity, or task 2 **OFFICIAL REQUIREMENT** a condition or requirement, e.g. passing an examination, that must be met by somebody who is to be eligible for a position or privilege (*often plural*) 3 **MEETING OF REQUIREMENTS** the meeting of a condition or requirement to become eligible for a position or privilege 4 **SOMETHING RESTRICTIVE** something that modifies, limits, or restricts 5 **RESTRICTING OR CHANGING** the modification or limitation of something, e.g. in meaning, scope, or strength

qualifier /kwólli fī ər/ *n* 1 **QUALIFYING PERSON OR TEAM** an individual or team that is successful in the preliminary part of a competition and earns the right to take part in the next stage 2 **EARLY ROUND** a preliminary round of a competition 3 **SOMEBODY WITH A RIGHT OR SKILLS** somebody who has the appropriate qualifications for something 4 **MODIFIER** a word or phrase that restricts or modifies the meaning of another word or phrase, e.g. the word 'fairly'

qualify /kwólli fī/ (**-fies, -fying, -fied**) *v* 1 *vti* **BE OR MAKE SOMEBODY SUITABLE** to have or give somebody a skill or attribute necessary for a particular activity 2 *vti* **HAVE OR GIVE SOMEBODY ELIGIBILITY** to become legally eligible or make somebody legally eligible for a position or privilege 3 *vi* **WIN FIRST ROUND OF COMPETITION** to complete the preliminary part of a competition successfully and earn the right to go on to the next stage 4 *vt* **RESTRICT OR CHANGE** to modify or limit something in meaning, scope, or strength 5 *vt* **MODERATE** to make something less strong or extreme 6 *vt* **DESCRIBE AS SOMETHING** to attribute a particular quality or characteristic to something 7 *vt* **MODIFY OR RESTRICT MEANING** to modify or restrict the meaning of a word [Mid-16C. Via French *qualifier* < medieval Latin *qualificare* 'attribute a quality to' < Latin *qualis* 'of what kind'.] —**qualifiable** *adj* —**qualificatory** /kwóllifi kaytəri/ *adj* —**qualified** *adj* —**qualifiedly** *adv*

qualitative /kwóllitətiv/ *adj* relating to or based on the quality or character of something, often as opposed to its size or quantity [Early 17C. < late Latin *qualitativus* < Latin *qualitat-* (see QUALITY).] —**qualitatively** *adv*

qualitative analysis *n* identification of the chemical components of a substance

quality /kwólləti/ *n* **1 DISTINGUISHING CHARACTERISTIC** a distinctive characteristic of somebody or something **2 ESSENTIAL PROPERTY** an essential identifying nature or character of somebody or something **3 STANDARD** the general standard or grade of something ○ *the poor quality of the air* ○ *poor-quality work* ○ *goods of the highest quality* **4 EXCELLENCE** the highest or finest standard (*often before nouns*) ○ *quality products* **5 UPPER SOCIAL CLASS** high social position or aristocratic breeding (*dated informal*) ○ *a family of quality* **6 PEOPLE OF UPPER SOCIAL CLASS** people of high social position or aristocratic breeding (*dated informal*) ○ *mixing with the quality* **7 CHARACTER OF VOWEL SOUND** the character of a vowel sound that depends on such factors as the shape of the mouth and position of the tongue when it is uttered **8 TONE OF NOTE** the distinctive tone of a musical note **9 AFFIRMATIVE OR NEGATIVE CHARACTERISTIC** the positive or negative nature of a logical proposition [13C. Via French *qualité* < Latin *qualitat-* < *qualis* 'of what kind'.]

quality circle *n* a group of employees from different levels of a company who meet regularly to discuss ways of improving quality and to resolve any problems related to production

quality control *n* a system for achieving or maintaining the desired level of quality in a manufactured product by inspecting samples and assessing what changes may be needed in the manufacturing process

quality factor *n* a number by which a given dose of absorbed radiation is multiplied to determine the radiation's biological effect

quality of life *n* the degree of enjoyment and satisfaction experienced in everyday life as opposed to financial or material well-being

quality time *n* time spent with friends or family in enjoyable activities that enhance the relationship ○ *working parents determined to spend quality time with their kids*

qualm /kwaam/ *n* **1** a sudden feeling of uncertainty or apprehension, especially a misgiving about an action or conduct **2** a sudden pang of nausea [Early 16C. < ?] —**qualmish** *adj* —**qualmishly** *adv* —**qualmishness** *n*

quamash /kwə́ə mash, kwə másh/ (*plural* **-ashes** *or* **-ash**) *n* PLANTS = **camas** *n.* 1

quandary /kwóndəri/ *n* a state of uncertainty or indecision as to what to do in a particular situation [Late 16C. < ?]

quandong /kwón dong/ (*plural* **-dongs** *or* **-dong**) *n* **1 FRUIT OF QUANDONG** a large red fruit, or its edible kernel. Use: jam. **2 SMALL AUSTRALIAN TREE** a small tree that produces quandongs. Native to: Australia. *Santalum acuminatum*. **3 LARGE AUSTRALIAN TREE** a large timber tree with a buttressed trunk and shiny blue fruits containing edible seeds. Native to: Australia. *Elaeocarpus grandis*. [Mid-19C. < Wiradhuri *guwandhāng*.]

quango /kwáng gō/ (*plural* **-gos**) *n* an organization that is able to act independently of the government that finances it [Late 20C. Acronym < *quasiautonomous nongovernmental organization*.]

quant[1] /kwont/ *n* a long pole for pushing against the bottom of a river or lake to propel a boat ■ *vti* to move a punt or other boat along with a quant [15C. < ?]

⚡ **quant**[2] /kwont/, **quant jock** *n* somebody skilled in computing and the analysis of quantitative data, employed by a company to make financial predictions (*slang*) [Late 20C. Shortening of QUANTITATIVE.]

Quant /kwont/, **Mary** (*b.* 1934) British fashion designer

quanta plural of **quantum**

quantic /kwóntik/ *n* a mathematical expression with more than one variable that contains terms raised to the same power with respect to all the variables [Mid-19C. < Latin *quantus* 'how much'.]

quantifier /kwónti fī ər/ *n* a word such as 'all', 'some', or 'most', or a logical symbol with this meaning, that indicates the range of individuals or items referred to

quantify /kwónti fī/ (**-fies, -fying, -fied**) *vt* **1** to calculate or express the number, degree, or amount of something **2** to use a quantifier to limit the range of individuals or items referred to in a sentence or proposition [Mid-19C. < medieval Latin *quantificare* < Latin *quantus* 'how much'.] —**quantifiable** /kwónti fī əb'l/ *adj* —**quantification** /kwóntifi káysh'n/ *n*

quantise *vt* = **quantize**

quantitate /kwónti tayt/ (**-tates, -tating, -tated**) *vt* to estimate or determine precisely the number, degree, or amount of something [Mid-20C. Back-formation < QUANTITATIVE.] —**quantitation** /kwónti táysh'n/ *n*

quantitative /kwóntitətiv/ *adj* **1 RELATING TO QUANTITY** relating to, concerning, or based on the amount or number of something **2 MEASURABLE** capable of being measured or expressed in numerical terms **3 BASED ON LENGTH OF SYLLABLES** relating or belonging to a metrical system based on the length of syllables rather than on stress. Classical Latin and Greek verse uses a quantitative system. [Late 16C. < medieval Latin *quantitativus* < Latin *quantit-* (see QUANTITY).] —**quantitatively** *adv* —**quantitativeness** *n*

quantitative analysis *n* determination of the relative amounts of the components of a substance

quantitative digital radiography *n* a method of detecting thinning of the bones (**osteoporosis**) by assessing the levels of calcium present, usually in the spine and hip

quantity /kwóntəti/ *n* **1 AMOUNT** an amount or number of something **2 MEASURABLE PROPERTY** the measurable property of something **3 LARGE AMOUNTS** a large amount or number ○ *Foodstuffs were imported in quantity.* **4 MATHEMATICAL ENTITY WITH NUMERICAL VALUE** a mathematical entity that has a numerical value or magnitude **5 PARTICULAR MAGNITUDE** the product of a measurable phenomenon such as electric current or radiation intensity and the time during which the phenomenon is measured **6 UNIVERSAL OR PARTICULAR NATURE OF PROPOSITION** the characteristic of a logical proposition that distinguishes it as universal or particular **7 RELATIVE DURATION OF SOUND** the length of a vowel sound or syllable [13C. Via French *quantité* < Latin *quantitat-* < *quantus* 'how much'.]

USAGE See ***number***.

quantity surveyor *n* an assessor of the cost of a construction job based on the amount of labour and materials required to complete it

quantity theory *n* the theory that prices vary with the amount of money in circulation and the rate at which it circulates

quantize /kwón tīz/ (**-tizes, -tizing, -tized**), **quantise** (**-tises, -tising, -tised**) *vt* **1 EXPRESS IN QUANTUM NUMBERS** to express something in terms of quantum numbers **2 APPLY QUANTUM MECHANICS TO** to divide something into tiny discrete increments applying the rules of quantum mechanics **3** to separate a continuously variable signal into defined levels **4 QUOTE IN DIFFERENT CURRENCY** to express an asset or liability in a different currency from that normally used [Early 20C. < QUANTUM.] —**quantization** /kwón tī záysh'n/ *n* —**quantizer** *n*

Quantock Hills /kwóntək hílz/ ridge of hills in SW England, an Area of Outstanding Natural Beauty. Highest peak: Will's Neck 385 m/1,262 ft.

quantum /kwóntəm/ *n* (*plural* **-ta** /kwóntə/) **1 SMALLEST QUANTITY OF ENERGY** the smallest discrete quantity of a physical property such as electromagnetic radiation or angular momentum **2 QUANTITY** a required quantity or amount, especially an amount of money paid in recompense **3 PARTICULAR AMOUNT** a portion or allotment ■ *adj* **MAJOR** sudden, dramatic, and significant [Early 17C. Via Latin < *quantus* 'how much'.] —**quantal** *adj* —**quantally** *adv*

quantum chromodynamics *n* a quantum field theory of elementary particles that states that the colour properties of quarks are bound together by gluons

quantum electrodynamics *n* a quantum field theory that describes the properties of electromagnetic radiation and its interaction with electrically charged particles

quantum field theory *n* a theory developed from quantum mechanics based on the assumption that elementary particles interact through the influence of fields around them and the exchange of energy

quantum jump *n* **1** the sudden transition of an atom or particle from one energy state to another **2** = **quantum leap**

quantum leap *n* a sudden, dramatic, and significant change or advance ○ *a quantum leap in our understanding of molecular science*

quantum mechanics *n* the study and analysis of the interactions of atoms and elementary particles based on quantum theory (+ *singular verb*) —**quantum mechanical** *adj*

quantum number *n* any of the set of integers or half integers that characterize the properties and energy states of an elementary particle or system

quantum statistics *n* the statistical description of systems of particles that are subject to the laws of quantum physics rather than classical physics (+ *singular verb*)

quantum theory *n* a theory describing the behaviour and interactions of elementary particles or energy states based on the assumptions that energy is subdivided into discrete amounts and that matter possesses wave properties

QUICK FACTS ON... **QUANTUM THEORY**

Key elements: Experiments at the turn of the century created the need to replace the classical theory of matter. The Bohr theory, with its model of orbits or shells in which electrons circle the nucleus of an atom, proved to have limited success. Schrödinger and Heisenberg contributed significantly to the modern theory, which was extended by Dirac to include relativistic effects.

Key dates: 1900 Planck determines that there is a relationship between the frequency of an electromagnetic wave and its energy, an equation containing Planck's constant; 1905 Einstein proposes that radiation consists of photons that behave like particles; 1911 Rutherford proposes an atom with a positively charged nucleus surrounded by negatively charged electrons in orbit; 1913 Bohr incorporates quantum theory to explain both atomic structure and atomic spectra; 1923 de Broglie proposes that all matter and radiations have characteristics of both particles and waves; 1926 Schrödinger develops his theory of wave mechanics; 1927 Heisenberg proposes the uncertainty principle; 1933 Schrödinger and Dirac receive the Nobel Prize for the formulation of the wave equation

Key developments: quantum electrodynamics, gauge theory, particle physics, nuclear physics

Qu'Appelle /kwə pél, kə pél/ river in S Saskatchewan, Canada. Length: 435 km/270 mi.

quar. *abbr* **1** quarter **2** quarterly

quarantine /kwórrən teen/ *n* **1 ISOLATION TO PREVENT SPREAD OF DISEASE** enforced isolation of people or animals that may have been exposed to a contagious or infectious disease, e.g. when entering a country (*often used before a noun*) **2 PLACE OF ISOLATION** a place in which people or animals spend a period of isolation to prevent the spread of disease **3 TIME OF ENFORCED ISOLATION** the period of time during which people or animals are kept in isolation to prevent the spread of disease **4 CONDITION OR PERIOD OF ISOLATION** enforced isolation, e.g. for social or political reasons, or a period of such isolation ■ *vt* (**-tines, -tining, -tined**) **1 ISOLATE TO AVOID SPREAD OF DISEASE** to isolate a person or animal that may have been exposed to a contagious or infectious disease in order to prevent the possible spread of that disease **2 DETAIN** to isolate or detain somebody, e.g. for social or political reasons [Early 17C. Via Italian *quarantina* < Latin *quadraginta* 'forty'; because ships suspected of carrying disease were refused entrance to port for 40 days.] —**quarantinable** *adj*

quarantine flag *n* a yellow flag flown by a ship or boat arriving from distant waters to indicate that there is no disease aboard

quark[1] /kwaark/ *n* any elementary particle with an electric charge equal to one-third or two-thirds that of the electron. Quarks are believed to be the constituents of baryons and mesons. [Mid-20C. Alluding to 'three quarks for Mr. Mark' in James Joyce's *Finnegans Wake*; because originally there were thought to be three quarks.]

quark[2] /kwaark/ *n* a soft cheese of German origin made from skimmed milk [Mid-20C. Via German < Slavic.]

quarrel[1] /kwórrəl/ *n* **1 ARGUMENT BETWEEN PEOPLE** an angry dispute between two or more people **2 REASON TO ARGUE** a reason for a disagreement or dispute between people ○ *I have no quarrel with their proposals.* ■ *vi* (**-rels, -relling, -relled**) **1 ARGUE VEHEMENTLY** to engage in an angry dispute **2 DISAGREE WITH** to dispute or disagree with something such as a decision [14C. Via Old French < Latin *querela* 'complaint' < *queri* 'complain'.] —**quarreller** *n*

quarrel[2] /kwórrəl/ *n* **1** a short square-headed bolt or arrow used in a crossbow **2** any small square or diamond-shaped pane of glass in a window [12C. Via Old French < Latin *quadrellus* 'small square' < Latin *quadrum* 'square'.]

quarrelsome /kwórrəlsəm/ *adj* having a tendency to argue with people —**quarrelsomely** *adv* —**quarrelsomeness** *n*

quarrier /kwórri ər/ *n* a worker in a stone quarry

quarry[1] /kwórri/ *n* (*plural* **-ries**) **1 OPEN AREA FOR MINING** an open excavation from which stone or other material is extracted by blasting, cutting, or drilling **2 SOURCE** a rich source of something ■ *v* (**-ries, -rying, -ried**) **1** *vti* **OBTAIN SOMETHING FROM QUARRY** to extract stone or other material from a quarry **2** *vt* **USE PLACE FOR EXTRACTING STONE** to make a quarry in a particular place such as a hillside and remove material from it ○ *The area was extensively quarried last century.* **3** *vti* **EXTRACT LABORIOUSLY** to obtain something, such as facts or information, by searching laboriously and carefully [14C. < medieval Latin *quarreia* < Old French *quarriere* < *quarre* 'square-cut stone' < Latin *quadrum* 'square'.]

quarry[2] /kwórri/ (*plural* **-ries**) *n* **1** an animal or bird that is hunted by something or somebody **2** somebody or something that is chased or hunted by another [15C. Via Anglo-Norman *coure* 'entrails of an animal given to the hounds' < Latin *corata* < Latin *cor* 'heart'.]

quarry[3] /kwórri/ (*plural* **-ries**) *n* **1** a square or diamond shape **2** something with a square or diamond shape, e.g. a pane of glass in a latticed window [Mid-16C. Alteration of QUARREL[2].]

quarry tile *n* a tile with a square or diamond shape, especially a hard-wearing unglazed clay tile used for flooring [< QUARRY[3]]

quart[1] /kwawrt/ *n* **1 QUARTER OF GALLON** a unit of measurement for liquids equal to two pints **2 ONE-EIGHTH OF PECK** a unit of measurement for dry substances equal to two pints **3 CONTAINER OR CONTENTS** a container that holds one quart or its contents [13C. Via Old French *quarte* < Latin *quartus* 'fourth'.]

quart[2] /kwawrt/ *n* **1** a sequence of four cards in piquet and some other card games **2** FENCING = **quarte** [Mid-17C. Via French, 'fourth' < Latin *quartus*.]

quartan /kwáwrt'n/ *adj* describes a fever that recurs every fourth day, e.g. in some types of malaria [13C. < Old French *quartaine* < Latin *quartus* 'fourth'.]

quarte /kaart/, **quart, carte** *n* the fourth of the eight parrying or attacking positions in fencing [Mid-17C. Via French, 'fourth' < Latin *quartus*.]

quarter /kwáwrtər/ *n* **1 ONE OF FOUR PARTS** any of four equal or approximately equal parts into which something is divided **2 ONE-FOURTH** a number that is equal to one divided by four, represented by the symbol $\frac{1}{4}$ **3 PERIOD OF THREE MONTHS** any of the three-month periods into which the year is divided, especially for accounting purposes **4 25 CENTS** in the United States and Canada, the sum of 25 cents **5 COIN WORTH 25 CENTS** in the United States and Canada, a coin worth 25 cents or one quarter of a dollar **6 15 MINUTES BEFORE OR AFTER HOUR** either of the points in time 15 minutes before or after the hour, marked on a traditional clock face at 3 and 9 **7 28 LB IN WEIGHT** in the United Kingdom, a unit of weight equal to 12.71 kg/28 lb or one quarter of a hundredweight **8 25 LB IN WEIGHT** in the United States, a unit of weight equal to 11.35 kg/25 lb or one quarter of a hundredweight **9 8 BUSHELS** a unit of capacity for grain and similar substances equal to approximately 8 bushels **10 4 OZ** an amount of something weighing 113.4 g/4 oz or a quarter of a pound (*informal*) **11 QUARTER OF SQUARE MILE** one quarter of a square mile of rural land **12 quarter, Quarter DISTRICT OF TOWN** an area in a town of a particular type or inhabited by a particular group of people ○ *We visited the French Quarter while we were in New Orleans.* **13 UNSPECIFIED PERSON OR GROUP** an unspecified person or group of people ○ *They're looking for help from any quarter.* **14 MERCY** mercy offered to a defeated enemy **15 MOON PHASE** either of the two phases of the Moon in which half of its illuminated surface can be seen from the Earth **16 QUARTER OF MOON'S ORBIT** one fourth of the Moon's orbital period around the Earth **17 PART OF SPORTING CONTEST** one of the four equal parts into which games are divided in some sports **18 SIDE OF REAR HALF OF VESSEL** either side of the rear half of a boat or ship, usually behind the rearmost mast **19 NORTHEAST, SOUTHEAST, SOUTHWEST, OR NORTHWEST** any one of the four compass points that lie midway between north, east, south, and west **20 ANY SECTION OF HERALDIC SHIELD** any one of the four sections into which a heraldic shield may be divided **21 PART OF ANIMAL OR BIRD** any one of the four parts into which the body of an animal or bird may be divided, with a leg or wing forming part of each quarter **22 SIDE OF HOOF** the side of a horse's hoof **23 SHOE PART** the part of a shoe between the heel and the front part of the upper ■ **quarters** *npl* **ACCOMMODATION** living or sleeping accommodation provided for somebody, e.g. military personnel and their families, household employees, or members of a ship's crew ■ *adj* **DIVIDED BY FOUR** describes one fourth part of something ■ *v* **1** *vt* **DIVIDE SOMETHING INTO FOUR** to divide something into four equal or approximately equal parts **2** *vt* **CUT BODY INTO FOUR** to cut a human body into four parts following an execution **3** *vt* **GIVE SOMEBODY LODGINGS** to assign accommodation to somebody ○ *The soldiers were quartered in an old barn.* **4** *vt* **DIVIDE SHIELD INTO FOUR SECTIONS** to divide a heraldic shield into four sections **5** *vi* **CROSS IN ZIGZAG COURSE** to cover all parts of an area of land, sea, or air by ranging from side to side while moving forwards, e.g. while searching for somebody or something **6** *vi* **COME FROM REAR PART OF SIDE** to come from a direction at approximately 45 degrees to the stern of a boat or ship **7** *vt* **POSITION SOMETHING AT 90 DEGREES** to locate or position a machine part at right angles to another [13C. Via Old French *quartier* < Latin *quartus* 'fourth'.]

quarterage /kwáwrtərij/ *n* a sum of money paid or received every three months

quarterback /kwáwrtər bak/ *n* in American football, a player positioned behind the centre who directs the play by calling signals

quarter-bound *adj* describes a book that is bound in one material, usually leather, on the spine and another on the covers

quarter day *n* one of four days in a year regarded as the beginning or end of a quarter, when particular payments are due

quarterdeck /kwáwrtər dek/ *n* the rear part of the upper deck of a ship, where official ceremonies traditionally take place on a vessel

quarterfinal /kwáwrtər fīn'l/ *n* any one of four contests in a tournament or competition, the winners of which go on to play each other in the semifinals [Early 20C. After SEMIFINAL.] —**quarterfinalist** *n*

quarter horse *n* a strong horse formerly bred to run short races in the United States [< *quarter-race*, a race over a quarter mile]

quarter hour *n* **1** a period of 15 minutes **2** either of the points on a clock face that indicate a time 15 minutes before or after the hour ○ *The clock chimes on the quarter hour.*

quarterlight /kwáwrtər līt/ *n* a small triangular window in the side of some cars and other vehicles that can be pivoted open for ventilation

quarterly /kwáwrtərli/ *adj* **1 HAPPENING EVERY THREE MONTHS** happening, produced, or published four times a year, at three-month intervals **2 DIVIDED INTO FOUR SECTIONS** describes a heraldic shield that is divided into four sections ■ *adv* **EVERY THREE MONTHS** once every three months ■ *n* **JOURNAL PUBLISHED EVERY THREE MONTHS** a magazine or journal published four times a year, at three-month intervals

quartermaster /kwáwrtər maastər/ *n* **1** an army officer responsible for providing soldiers with food, clothing, equipment, and living quarters **2** in the navy, a petty officer or ship's mate with some responsibilities for navigation and signals

quartern /kwáwrtərn/ *n* **1 ONE FOURTH** a fourth part of something, especially of some old weights and measures **2 quartern, quartern loaf** (*plural* **quartern loaves**) **SMALL LOAF** a loaf of bread 10 cm/4 in square, used especially for making sandwiches **3 quartern, quartern loaf** (*plural* **quartern loaves**) **LARGE LOAF** a loaf of bread weighing 1.6 kg/4 lb [13C. < Anglo-Norman *quartrun*.]

quarter note *n* US MUSIC = **crotchet** *n.* 1

quarter-phase *adj* ELEC ENG = **two-phase** [Because the two currents are 90 degrees out of phase]

quarter round *n* a moulding that, in cross-section, is the shape of a quarter of a circle

quarters /kwáwrtərz/ *npl* a building or set of rooms where people live, especially military personnel or servants ◇ **at close quarters** from very near

quartersawn /kwáwrtər sawn/ *adj* describes wooden boards sawn from a log cut into quarters lengthwise so as to show off the grain of the wood

quarter section *n US, Can* a tract of land measuring 800 m/0.5 mi. on each side, equal to 65 hectares/160 acres or one fourth of a section

quarter sessions *npl* formerly in England and Wales, a local court sitting quarterly with limited authority to try civil and criminal cases

quarterstaff /kwáwrtər staaf/ (*plural* **-staves** /-stayvz/ or **-staffs**) *n* a long heavy wooden stick tipped with iron, formerly used in hand-to-hand fighting [Mid-16C. < ?]

quarter tone *n* a difference in pitch between two tones (**interval**) that is equal to half a semitone

quartet /kwawr tét/, **quartette** *n* **1 MUSICAL GROUP** a group of four singers or musicians (*takes a singular or plural verb*) **2 PIECE OF MUSIC** a piece of music written for four voices or instruments **3 GROUP OF FOUR** a group or set of four people or things (*takes a singular or plural verb*) [Late 18C. Via French *quartette* < Italian *quartetto* < *quarto* 'fourth' < Latin *quartus*.]

quartic /kwáwrtik/ *adj* of or relating to the fourth degree. A quartic equation has the general form $ax^4 + bx^3 + cx^2 + dx + e = 0$. [Mid-19C. < Latin *quartus* 'fourth'.]

quartier /kaarti ay/ *n* a district of a city or town in France [Early 19C. < French, 'quarter'.]

quartile /kwáwr tīl/ *n* **1 STATISTICAL DIVISION** any one of the four equal groups into which a statistical sample can be divided **2 STATISTICAL VALUE** in statistics, any one of the three values that divide a frequency distribution into four parts, each containing a quarter of the sample population **3 DISTANCE BETWEEN PLANETS** the astrological aspect of planets that are distant from each other by 90 degrees or one fourth of the zodiac [Early 16C. Via Old French *quartil* < Latin *quartus* 'fourth'.]

quarto /kwáwrtō/ (*plural* **-tos**) *n* **1** the page size created by folding a single sheet of standard-sized printing paper in half twice to create four leaves or eight pages **2** a book with quarto pages [Late 16C. < Latin *(in) quarto* 'in a fourth' < *quartus* 'fourth'.]

quartz /kwawrts/ *n* a common, hard, usually colourless, transparent crystalline mineral with coloured varieties. Use: electronics, gems. [Mid-18C. < German *Quarz* < W Slavic 'hard'.]

quartz clock *n* a clock in which the time-keeping mechanism is accurately controlled by a quartz crystal that vibrates at a fixed frequency in an oscillating electric circuit

quartz crystal *n* a small piece of quartz cut so that it vibrates at a known frequency

quartz glass *n* a clear glass made from melted silica that can withstand high or rapidly changing temperatures and is unusually transparent to ultraviolet radiation

quartz heater *n* a portable electric heater with heating elements sealed in quartz glass tubes

quartziferous /kwawrt síffərəss/ *adj* containing or consisting of quartz

quartz-iodine lamp *n* a very bright lamp with a bulb made of quartz glass that has a tungsten filament and usually contains iodine vapour. Use: car headlights, film projectors.

quartzite /kwáwrts īt/ *n* a pale metamorphic rock composed mainly of quartz, formed by the action of heat and pressure on sandstone. Use: building materials. —**quartzitic** /kwawrt síttik/ *adj*

quartz lamp *n* a mercury vapour lamp with a bulb made from quartz glass that produces light rich in ultraviolet radiation and is used for street lighting and sun lamps

quartz watch *n* a watch in which the time-keeping mechanism is accurately controlled by a quartz crystal that vibrates at a fixed frequency in an oscillating electric circuit

quasar /kwáy zaar, -saar/ *n* a compact object in space, usually with a large red shift indicating extreme remoteness, that emits huge amounts of energy, sometimes equal to the energy output of an entire galaxy [Mid-20C. Contraction of *quasi-stellar object*.]

quash[1] /kwosh/ *vt* **1** to put a stop to something forcibly **2** to prevent feelings from developing or being expressed [14C. Via Old French < medieval Latin *quassare* 'shake to pieces' < *quatere* 'shake'.]

quash[2] *vt* to declare formally that something such as a law or a court's verdict is not valid [13C. Via Old French < Latin *cassare* < *cassus* 'empty, void'.]

quasi /kwáy zī, kwáy sī, kwaazi/ *adj* resembling somebody or something in some ways, but not exactly the same

○ *a quasi colony of the US* [15C. Via Old French < Latin, 'as if' < *quam* 'as' + *si* 'if'.]

quasi- /kwáy zī/ *prefix* as if, resembling ○ *quasi-official* [Via Old French < Latin *quasi* 'as if' < *quam* 'as' + *si* 'if']

quasijudicial /kwáy zī joo díshl/ *adj* describes decision-making powers that are similar to those of a court judge, or to describe any arbitrator or inquiry with such powers —**quasijudicially** *adv*

quasilegislative /kwáy zī léj islàtiv/ *adj* describes regulations that are not regarded as laws proper but have the force of law, or to describe bodies that have the right to make such regulations

quasi-stellar object *n* ASTRON = **quasar**

quass *n* BEVERAGES = **kvass**

quassia /kwósha/ *n* **1** TREE YIELDING FINE-GRAINED TIMBER a shrub or small tree with scarlet flowers. Native to: tropical America. Genus: *Quassia*. **2** WOOD OF QUASSIA TREE the fine-grained pale wood of the quassia tree. Use: furniture-making. **3** INSECTICIDE DERIVED FROM QUASSIA WOOD a bitter substance obtained from the bark and wood of the quassia tree. Use: insecticide. [Mid-18C. < ?]

quatercentenary /kwátter sen téenəri/ *n* a four hundredth anniversary [Late 19C. < Latin, 'four times'.]

quaternary /kwə túrnəri/ *adj* **1** OCCURRING IN FOURS consisting of four parts, or occurring in sets of four **2** HAVING FOUR-ATOM BONDS bonded to four other nonhydrogen atoms or groups of atoms, or containing atoms bonded in this way ■ *n* (*plural* **-ies**) **quaternary, quaternion** SET OF FOUR OR FOURTH MEMBER a set of four, or the fourth member of a set [15C. < Latin *quaternarius* < *quaterni* 'by fours' < *quater* 'four times'.]

Quaternary /kwə túrnəri/ *adj* belonging to or dating from the most recent geological period, spanning the last 2 million years ■ *n* the current period of geological time and the second period of the Cenozoic era

quaternary ammonium compound *n* a nitrogen compound regarded as a derivative of ammonium. Use: solvents, disinfectants.

quaternion /kwə túrni ən/ *n* **1** = **quaternary** *n*. **2** a generalized complex number that contains four terms, one real and three imaginary, and is the sum of a real number and a vector [14C. < late Latin *quaternion-* < Latin *quaterni* (see QUATERNARY).]

quaternity /kwə túrnəti/ (*plural* **-ties**) *n* a set of four, especially the four beings that, in some religions, are unified in God [Early 16C. < late Latin *quaternitas* < Latin *quaterni* (see QUATERNARY).]

quatrain /kwó trayn/ *n* a verse of poetry consisting of four lines, especially one with lines that rhyme alternately [Late 16C. < French < *quatre* 'four' < Latin *quattuor*.]

quatrefoil /káttrə foyl/ *n* **1** a design or symbol in the shape of a flower with four petals or a leaf with four parts, often used in heraldry **2** an architectural decoration consisting of four arcs radiating from a centre like flower petals [14C. < Anglo-Norman, 'four-leaf'.]

quattrocento /kwáttró chéntó/ *n* the 15th century in Italy, especially with reference to art and literature [Late 19C. < Italian, shortening of *mil quattrocento* 'one thousand four hundred'.]

quaver /kwáyvər/ *v* **1** *vi* TREMBLE SLIGHTLY to tremble because of nervousness or fear **2** *vti* SAY TREMBLINGLY to say something or speak in a trembling voice because of nervousness or fear **3** *vi* SING WITH TRILL to sing in a trilling voice ■ *n* **1** TREMBLING SOUND a tremble in the voice caused by nervousness or fear **2** LENGTH OF NOTE a musical note equal in length to one eighth of a semibreve. US term **eighth note 3** TRILL an alternation of a musical tone with the tone just above it [15C. < obsolete *quave* 'tremble' < Germanic.] —**quaveringly** *adv* —**quavery** *adj*

quaver rest *n* a rest equal in length to an eighth note. US term **eighth rest**

quay /kee/ *n* a platform that runs along the edge of a port or harbour, where boats are loaded and unloaded [14C. Via Old N French *cai* < Gaulish *caio* 'rampart'.]

quayage /kée ij/ *n* **1** FEE FOR USING QUAY a charge that ship owners must pay to dock at a quay in order to load and unload there **2** QUAY SPACE the space available on a quay for ships to load and unload **3** QUAY SYSTEM a system of quays

Quayle /kwayl/, **Sir Anthony** (1913–89) British actor and director

quayside /kée sīd/ *n* the edge of a quay, where it meets the water

Que. *abbr* Quebec

quean /kween/ *n* an offensive term that deliberately insults a woman's morality (*archaic*) [Old English *cwene* 'woman', related to QUEEN]

queasy /kwéezi/ (**-sier, -siest**) *adj* **1** NAUSEOUS feeling ill in the stomach, as if on the point of vomiting **2** CAUSING NAUSEA causing a feeling of nausea **3** EASILY MADE NAUSEOUS easily made to feel nauseous **4** CAUSING UNEASINESS causing a feeling of uneasiness [15C. < ?] —**queasily** *adv* —**queasiness** *n*

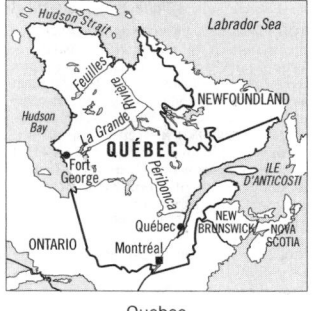

Quebec

Quebec[1] /kwi bék, ki-/, **Québec** /kay-/ **1** Québec, Quebec City capital of Quebec Province, Canada, on the St Lawrence River. Population: 167,264 (1996). **2** province in E Canada. Capital: Quebec. Population: 7,138,795 (1996). Area: 1,542,056 sq. km/595,391 sq. mi. —**Quebecer** /kwi békər, ki-/ *n*

Quebec[2] /kwi bék, ki-/ *n* a code word for the letter 'Q', used in international radio communications

Québécois /kwi békwaa, kay-/, **Québecois, Quebecois** *adj* relating to Quebec, especially its French-speaking inhabitants or their culture ■ *n* (*plural* **-cois**) somebody who comes from Quebec, especially somebody who is French-speaking [Late 19C. < French, 'from Quebec'.]

quebracho /kay braachó/ (*plural* **-chos**) *n* **1** TREE WITH MEDICINAL BARK a tree whose bark yields a respiratory stimulant. Native to: Chile, Argentina. *Aspidosperma quebracho-blanco*. **2** TREE WITH TANNIN-RICH WOOD a tree with hard tannin-rich wood. Native to: S South America. Genus: *Schinopsis*. **3** BARK OF QUEBRACHO TREE the bark of the quebracho tree. Use: treatment of respiratory ailments. **4** WOOD OF QUEBRACHO TREE the hard tannin-rich wood of the quebracho tree. Use: in the leather industry. [Late 19C. Spanish, alteration of *quiebrahacha* 'axe-breaker' < *quebrar* 'to break' + *hacha* 'axe'.]

Quechua /kéchwa/ (*plural* **-ua** *or* **-uas**), **Kechua** (*plural* **-ua** *or* **-uas**), **Quichua** /kíchwa/ (*plural* **-ua** *or* **-uas**) *n* **1** a member of a Native South American people, e.g. the Incas, living in the Andes **2** a group of Native South American peoples, e.g. the Incas, living in the Andes [Mid-19C. < Spanish.] —**Quechua** *adj* —**Quechuan** *adj, n*

queen /kween/ *n* **1** FEMALE RULER a woman who rules over a country, usually by right of birth **2** KING'S WIFE the wife or widow of a king **3** ADMIRED WOMAN, PLACE, OR THING a greatly admired woman who stands out above all others, or a place or thing considered the best of its kind and personified as a woman **4** MOST POWERFUL CHESS PIECE the most powerful piece in chess, able to move over any number of squares forwards, backwards, sideways, and diagonally **5** FACE CARD a playing card with a picture of a queen on it, ranking above a jack and below a king **6** EGG-LAYING BEE, ANT, OR TERMITE a large, fully developed female that lays eggs in a colony of social insects, such as bees or ants **7** OFFENSIVE TERM an offensive term for a homosexual man, especially one regarded as behaving in a flamboyant and stereotypically effeminate way ■ *vti* MAKE PAWN INTO QUEEN to promote a pawn to the rank of queen by managing to take it to the opponent's end of the board, or to become promoted from pawn to queen [Old English *cwēn* < Indo-European] —**queenship** *n* ◊ **queen it** to behave in a domineering, arrogant way (*informal*)

Queen Anne *n* a style of furniture popular in the early 18th century, characterized by the use of simple curves and cabriole legs [Early 19C. After Queen ANNE.]

Queen Anne's lace *n* PLANT SCI = **cow parsley** [Late 19C. After Queen ANNE.]

queen bee *n* **1** a large, fully developed female bee that lays eggs continually **2** a woman who is treated as the most important member of her group, or who behaves as if she is (*informal*)

queencake /kwéen kayk/ *n* a small currant cake, usually heart-shaped

Queen Charlotte Islands /-shaárlət-/ island group in British Columbia, Canada, northwest of Vancouver Island in the Pacific Ocean. Area: 9,596 sq. km/3,705 sq. mi. Population: 3,368 (1986).

queen consort (*plural* **queens consort**) *n* a woman married to a reigning king

queen cup *n* a stemless plant that produces a single white flower and a blue berry. Native to: W North America. *Clintonia uniflora*.

queen dowager *n* a widow of a king

Queen Elizabeth Islands /-i lízzəbəth-/ island group in the Arctic Archipelago, N Canada, in the Arctic Ocean, west of Greenland. Area: 425,000 sq. km/164,000 sq. mi.

queenly /kwéenli/ *adj* **1** REGAL having the qualities typical of a queen, especially grace and dignity **2** RELATING TO QUEEN relating to a queen or suitable for a queen ■ *adv* REGALLY in a way thought fitting for or typical of a queen, especially with grace and dignity —**queenliness** *n*

Queen Maud Gulf /-máwd/ gulf in the Arctic Ocean, between SE Victoria Island and the mainland of Nunavut, Canada

queen mother *n* the mother of a reigning king or queen and the widow of a former king

queen of puddings *n* a pudding made of breadcrumbs and milk, often with a layer of meringue on top

Queen of the May *n* = **May queen**

queen-of-the-prairie *n* a plant that grows in grasslands. Flowers: small, pink. Native to: central and E United States. *Filipendula rubra*.

queen olive *n* a large edible olive with a long flat stone

queen post *n* either of two vertical posts forming part of the triangular framework that supports a roof. ◊ **king post** [After KING POST]

queen regent (*plural* **queens regent**) *n* a queen reigning on behalf of another person, especially one too young to take the throne

queen regnant (*plural* **queens regnant**) *n* a queen who reigns in her own right, as distinct from the wife of a king

Queens /kweenz/ borough of New York City, on W Long Island. Population: 1,951,598 (1990). Area: 282 sq. km/109 sq. mi.

Queen's Bench *n* a division of the High Court of Justice in England. ◊ **King's Bench**

Queensberry rules /kwéenzbəri-/ *npl* **1** the rules that govern boxing, drawn up in 1867 under the supervision of the Marquess of Queensberry **2** accepted standards of fairness or courteousness in any situation (*informal*)

Queen's Counsel *n* a senior barrister in England, entitled to wear a silk gown and sit inside the bar of the court

Queen's English *n* standard written or spoken British English, regarded as the most correct form of the language

Queen's evidence *n* in English law, evidence for the prosecution given by somebody who took part in a crime, usually in exchange for leniency

Queen's Highway *n* a public road, regarded as belonging ultimately to the monarch (*formal; used when the reigning monarch is a woman or girl*)

queenside /kwéen sīd/ *n* the side of a chessboard on which the queen is located at the beginning of a game

queen-size *adj* US describes beds and bedclothes that are larger than the standard size but smaller than king-size ○ *a queen-size bed* [After KING-SIZE]

Queensland /kwéenzland, kwéenz lənd/ state in NE Australia. Capital: Brisbane. Population: 3,339,000 (1996). Area: 1,727,200 sq. km/666,880 sq. mi. —**Queenslander** *n*

Queen's proctor *n* in the United Kingdom, an official of the High Court of Justice who has the right to intervene in certain cases, including those involving divorces and wills, when there are charges of collusion among the people involved or suppression of facts (*used when the reigning monarch is a woman or girl*)

Queen's Regulations *n* regulations that govern the armed forces of the United Kingdom and certain commonwealth countries (*used when the reigning monarch is a woman or girl*)

Queen's speech *n* (*used when the reigning monarch is a woman or girl*) **1** a speech given by the monarch at the opening of Parliament each year, setting out the government's proposed legislation **2** in the United Kingdom, a speech by the monarch to the nation and the Commonwealth broadcast on Christmas Day

Queenstown /kweénz tawn/ town in SW South Island, New Zealand. Population: 3,500 (1996).

queen substance *n* a pheromone secreted by a queen bee and consumed by worker bees in the same hive that prevents the worker bees from becoming fully developed and reproducing

queer /kweer/ *adj* **1 NOT USUAL** not usual or expected (*dated*) **2 ECCENTRIC** eccentric or unconventional (*dated informal*) **3 SUSPICIOUS** arousing suspicion (*dated informal*) **4 NAUSEOUS** slightly unwell, especially nauseous or faint (*dated*) **5 OFFENSIVE TERM** an offensive term meaning homosexual ■ *n* **OFFENSIVE TERM** an offensive term for somebody who is homosexual, especially a man ■ *vt* **1 THWART** to spoil or thwart something, especially somebody's plans (*dated informal*) **2 COMPROMISE** to put somebody in an awkward situation [Early 16C. Probably < Low German *quer* 'oblique, crooked'.] —**queerish** *adj* —**queerly** *adv* —**queerness** *n*

USAGE See ***insult***.

queer bashing *n* an offensive term for the practice or an instance of committing unprovoked acts of violence against homosexual men and lesbians (*slang*) —**queer basher** *n*

queercore /kweér kawr/ *n* (*slang*) **1** a homosexual youth movement that rejects the stereotype of the homosexual person as a persecuted victim by confidently and assertively proclaiming homosexuality, especially in punk-style music **2** a style of music similar to punk rock with lyrics that proclaim homosexuality confidently and assertively [Late 20C. < QUEER + HARDCORE.]

queer fish *n* somebody with unusual habits or beliefs (*dated informal*)

quell /kwel/ *vt* **1** to bring something to an end, usually by means of force **2** to suppress or allay a feeling [Old English *cwellan* 'kill' < Indo-European, 'stab, kill']

quench /kwench/ *vt* **1 SATISFY THIRST** to satisfy a thirst by drinking something **2 EXTINGUISH FIRE** to put out a fire or light **3 SUBDUE FEELING** to subdue a feeling, especially enthusiasm or desire **4 COOL METAL** to cool hot metal by plunging it into cold water or other liquid [Old English *ācwencan* < Germanic] —**quenchable** *adj* —**quencher** *n* —**quenchless** *adj*

quenelle /kə nél/ *n* a seasoned meat or fish dumpling poached in water and served with a sauce [Mid-19C. Via French < German *Knödel* 'dumpling'.]

quercetin /kwúrssitin/ *n* $C_{15}H_{10}O_7$ a yellow compound. Source: rind and bark of many plants, especially of oak and Douglas fir. Use: treatment of abnormally fragile capillaries. [Mid-19C. < Latin *quercetum* 'oak-forest' < *quercus* 'oak'.]

quercitron /kwúrssitrən/ *n* **1** the bright orange inner bark of the black oak tree. Use: tanning, dyeing. **2** yellow dye made from quercitron [Late 18C. Blend of Latin *quercus* 'oak' + CITRON (from the colour of its bark).]

querida /ke reédə/ (*plural* **-das**) *n* *Philippines* a mistress [Mid-19C. < Spanish *querida* 'darling, beloved', 'desired one' < *querer* 'desire' < Latin *quaerere* 'seek'.]

querist /kweérist/ *n* a questioner (*archaic*) [Mid-17C. < *quere* (see QUERY).]

quern /kwurn/ *n* a simple stone mill used for grinding grain by hand [Old English *cweorn* < Indo-European, 'heavy']

querulous /kwérrōōləss, -ryōō-/ *adj* **1** inclined to complain or find fault **2** whining or complaining in tone [15C. < late Latin *querulosus* < Latin *queri* 'complain'.] —**querulously** *adv* —**querulousness** *n*

query /kweéri/ *n* (*plural* **-ries**) **1 QUESTION** a request for information **2 DOUBT** a doubt or criticism **3** GRAM = **question mark** ■ *vt* (**-ries, -rying, -ried**) **1 QUESTION** to express doubts about, or objections to, something **2 INQUIRE** to ask a question [Mid-17C. < obsolete *quere* < Latin *quaere* 'ask' < *quaerere* 'seek'.] —**querier** *n*

quest /kwest/ *n* **1 SEARCH** a search for something, especially a long or difficult one **2 ADVENTUROUS EXPEDITION** a journey in search of something, especially one made by knights in medieval tales **3 SOMETHING SOUGHT** the object or goal of a quest (*literary*) ■ *v* **1** *vti* **SEEK** to seek or go in search of something (*literary*) **2** *vi* **TRACK ANIMALS** to follow the track of a bird or animal that is being hunted (*refers to hunting dogs*) [14C. Via Old French *queste* < Latin *quaesta*, form of *quaerere* 'seek'.] —**quester** *n* —**questingly** *adv*

question /kwéschən/ *n* **1 WRITTEN OR SPOKEN INQUIRY** a request for information or for a reply, which usually ends with a question mark if written or on a rising intonation if spoken ○ *Does anyone have any questions?* **2 DOUBT** a doubt or uncertainty about somebody or something **3 ISSUE** a matter that is the subject of discussion, debate, or negotiation **4 EXAMINATION PROBLEM** a problem to be discussed or solved in an examination ■ *v* **1** *vti* **INTERROGATE** to ask somebody questions, especially formally or officially, about a particular topic **2** *vt* **DOUBT** to raise doubts about something, especially about its truth, genuineness, or usefulness [13C. Via French < Latin *quaestion-* 'inquiry' < *quaest-*, past participle of *quaerere* 'seek'.] —**questioner** *n* ◇ **beg the question 1** to take for granted the very point that needs to be proved, and so fail to address an issue properly **2** to give rise to something else that should be answered or explained ◇ **be out of the question** to be impossible or unacceptable ◇ **call something into question** to raise doubts about something ◇ **in question** used to indicate the person or thing under discussion ◇ **pop the question** to propose marriage to somebody (*informal*)

USAGE To ***beg the question*** is often used to mean 'to raise the question' or 'to avoid a direct answer', since both meanings are consistent with the form of the idiom. The basic meaning of this idiom relates to the validity of a proposition that is used as a basis of argument. For example, in an argument about the effect on the environment of gas emissions from road traffic, the proposition that a higher tax on vehicles would contribute to cleaner air ***begs the question*** because it needs to be proved that raising taxes would result in fewer road users. The fallacy implied by the notion of ***begging the question*** usually involves the omission of one stage in an argument or a questionable assumption of its validity.

questionable /kwéschənəb'l/ *adj* **1** open to doubt or disagreement **2** not respectable or morally proper ○ *questionable motives* —**questionability** /kwéschənə bílləti/ *n* —**questionably** /kwéschənəbli/ *adv*

~~**questionaire**~~ incorrect spelling of **questionnaire**

questioning /kwéschəning/ *n* a situation in which somebody is asked a lot of questions, especially formally or officially, or an instance of this ■ *adj* expressing a question without using words ○ *a questioning glance* —**questioningly** *adv*

questionless /kwéschənləss/ *adj* **1** = **unquestionable 2** = **unquestioning**

question mark *n* the punctuation mark (?) placed at the end of a sentence or phrase intended as a direct question ◇ **a question mark over something** an area of doubt and uncertainty concerning something

PUNCTUATION The ***question mark*** is used after a direct question: *'Where are you going?' 'What for?'* It is not used in indirect questions: *He asked her where she was going.* It may also be used in other contexts, e.g. in creative writing, to indicate that somebody is wondering about something: *He assumed she had gone to visit her mother. But why had she taken her passport?* or in journalism to anticipate a reader's question: *How is the tax calculated? It is based on the current market value of the property.* The question mark may also indicate uncertainty, especially when placed before or after a date: *François Rabelais (1493?-1553).* The question mark may mark a sentence that has the function but not the structure of a question: *You're from Liverpool then?* It may be omitted from a sentence that has the structure of a question, but is not intended as such: *Will you keep quiet for a minute.*

question master *n* somebody who asks questions on a broadcast quiz show

questionnaire /kwéschə náir, késchə náir/ *n* a set of questions used to gather information in a survey, or the printed paper that contains the questions [Late 19C. < French < *questionner* 'ask' < *question* 'inquiry'.]

question tag *n* a short phrase at the end of a statement that changes it into a question

question time *n* in Parliament, a period of time every day during which members of parliament may address questions to government ministers

Quetta /kwéttə/ capital of Baluchistan Province, west-central Pakistan. Population: 560,307 (1998).

Quetzal

quetzal /kéts'l/ (*plural* **-zals** *or* **-zales** /ket saá layss/) *n* **1** a bird with brilliant green and red plumage and, in the male, long streaming tail feathers. Native to: Central America. *Pharomachrus mocino.* **2** see table at **currency** [Early 19C. Via American Spanish < Nahuatl *quetzalli* 'brilliantly coloured tail feather'.]

Quetzalcoatl /kéts'l kō átt'l/ *n* a Toltec and Aztec god and the legendary ruler of Mexico, represented as a feathered serpent [Via Spanish < Nahuatl *Quetzalcōātl* < *quetzal(li)* 'brightly coloured tail feather' + *cōātl* 'snake']

ϟ **queue** /kyoo/ *n* **1 LINE OF PEOPLE WAITING** a line of people or vehicles waiting for something. US term **line**[1] *n.* **35 2 SET OF COMPUTER TASKS** a series of messages or jobs waiting to be processed automatically one after the other by a computer system **3 LIST OF DATA ELEMENTS** a list of computer data constructed and maintained in first in, first out fashion **4 MAN'S PIGTAIL IN FORMER TIMES** a short plait of hair worn at the back of the neck by soldiers and sailors in the late 18th and early 19th centuries ■ *v* (**queues, queueing** *or* **queuing, queued**) **1** *vt* **ADD TO COMPUTER'S TASKS** to add a job or message to the list of tasks being held in storage by a computer, awaiting automatic dispatching **2** *vi* **FORM WAITING LINE** to form a line while waiting for something **3** *vi* **WAIT IN LARGE NUMBERS** to be waiting for or eagerly anticipating something along with a lot of other people (*informal*) ○ *the most eminent critics queueing up to review her latest book* [Late 16C. Via French < Latin *cauda* 'tail'.] ◇ **jump the queue** to push in or move ahead of others unfairly in a queue

SPELLCHECK See ***cue***.

queue-jump *vt* to push in or move ahead of others unfairly in a queue or in a situation where people should wait their turn —**queue-jumper** *n*

Quezon City /káy son sítti/ city in central Luzon, Philippines. Population: 2,112,722 (1999 estimate).

Quezón y Molina /káyz on ee mo leénə, ke thón-/, **Manuel Luis** (1878–1944) Philippine statesman

quibble /kwíbb'l/ *vi* (**-bles, -bling, -bled**) **MAKE TRIVIAL OBJECTIONS** to argue over unimportant things and make petty objections ■ *n* **1 PETTY OBJECTION** an unimportant distinction or petty objection **2 PUN** a pun (*archaic*) [Early 17C. Probably < obsolete *quib* 'pun, equivocation' < Latin *quibus* 'whom, for whom', often used in legal documents.] —**quibbler** *n* —**quibblingly** *adv*

quiche /keesh/ *n* a savoury tart filled with an egg-and-cream mixture and various meat or vegetable ingredients [Mid-20C. Via French < German dialect *Küche* 'small cake' < German *Kuchen* 'cake'.]

quiche Lorraine /-lə ráyn/ *n* a quiche made with cheese and bacon [Mid-20C. After LORRAINE.]

Quichua /kíchwə/ *n, adj* PEOPLES, LANGUAGE = **Quechua**

quick /kwik/ *adj* **1 DOING SOMETHING FAST** moving or doing something fast **2 ALERT** demonstrating alertness or sharp perception ○ *She has a very quick mind.* **3 NIMBLE** moving swiftly and with skill ○ *quick fingers* **4 DONE WITHOUT DELAY** doing something without delay ○ *They promised a quick delivery.* **5 EASILY ANGERED** describes a temper that is easily roused **6 BRIEF** taking or lasting only a short time ○ *We stopped to have a quick chat.* **7 HASTY** tending to be hasty ○ *Don't be too quick to blame others.* ■ *n* **1 FLESH UNDER NAIL** the sensitive flesh under a fingernail or toenail **2 SENSITIVE AREA** somebody's deepest feelings or most private emotions ○ *criticisms that cut him to the quick* ■ *adv* **FAST** in a speedy manner (*informal*) ○ *Come quick!* [Old English *cwic(u)* 'alive, lively' < Indo-European, 'to live'] —**quickly** *adv* —**quickness** *n* ◇ **quick and dirty** produced to meet an immediate or pressing need, rather than in accordance with high standards of research or design (*informal*)

SYNONYMS See ***intelligent***.

quick assets *npl* cash along with other assets that can readily be converted into cash

quick bread *n* bread leavened with baking powder or soda, as opposed to yeast, and ready to bake as soon as it is mixed

quick-change artist *n* a performer or somebody else who is skilled at changing quickly from one costume or character to the next

quicken /kwíkən/ *v* **1** *vti* **BECOME OR MAKE SOMETHING FASTER** to become faster or make something faster **2** *vti* **STIMULATE OR BE STIMULATED** to stimulate something, e.g. interest or enthusiasm, or to be stimulated **3** *vi* **BEGIN TO COME TO LIFE** to begin a period of development **4** *vi* **MOVE IN WOMB** to begin to move and be felt moving in the womb (*refers to a foetus*)

quick-fire /kwík fīr/ *adj* **1** designed to fire shots in quick succession. US term **rapid-fire** *adj.* 1 **2** coming one after another in rapid succession (*informal*) ○ *a round of quick-fire questions.* US term **rapid-fire** *adj.* 2

quick fix *n* a speedily or hastily contrived solution to a problem, often one that fails to resolve long-term issues (*informal*)

quick-freeze (**quick-freezes, quick-freezing, quick-froze, quick-frozen**) *vt* to freeze food rapidly in an effort to keep its full flavour and nutritional value

quickie /kwíki/ *n* something that is done hurriedly, especially a hurried act of sex or a speedily consumed alcoholic drink (*informal*)

quicklime /kwík līm/ *n* CHEM = **lime**[1] *n.* 1 [14C. Translation of Latin *calx viva* 'living lime'.]

quick march *n* a march at the standard military pace known as quick time ■ *interj* used to order troops or a band to march in quick time

quicksand /kwík sand/ *n* **1** a deep mass of loose wet sand that sucks down any heavy object falling onto its surface **2** a hidden trap from which escape is difficult or impossible

quickset /kwík set/ *n* **1** a plant cutting, especially a cutting of hawthorn, planted with others to make a hedge **2** a hedge, especially of hawthorn, grown from cuttings

quicksilver /kwík silvər/ *n* mercury (*archaic or literary*) ■ *adj* tending to change rapidly and unpredictably [Pre-12C. Translation of Latin *argentum vivum* 'living silver' from the way it moves in its fluid state.]

quickstep /kwík step/ *n* **1 FAST BALLROOM DANCE** a ballroom dance with fast steps **2 DANCE MUSIC** the music for a quickstep **3 MARCHING STEP** the marching step used in the fastest marching pace (**quick time**)

quick study *n US* a fast learner of something

quick-tempered *adj* having a short temper —**quick-temperedness** *n*

quickthorn /kwík thawrn/ *n* a thorny plant, especially hawthorn, planted and cut to form a hedge [Early 17C. < its rapid growth.]

quick time *n* a fast military marching pace, approximately 120 paces per minute

quick trick *n* in bridge, a high-ranking card, or a combination of high-ranking cards, that make it possible to win a trick on the first or second round of the suit

quick-witted *adj* able to think quickly and inventively —**quick-wittedly** *adv* —**quick-wittedness** *n*

quid[1] /kwid/ (*plural* **quid**) *n* a pound sterling (*informal*) [Late 17C. < ?] ◇ **be quids in** to have made a profit or be in a financially advantageous position (*informal*) ◇ **not the full quid** *Aus* an offensive term meaning unintelligent (*slang insult*)

quid[2] /kwid/ *n* a piece of chewing tobacco [Early 18C. Alteration of CUD.]

quidditch /kwíddich/ *n* a fictional game played on broomsticks [Late 20C. Coined by J. K. ROWLING in her novel, *Harry Potter and the Philosopher's Stone* (1997).]

quiddity /kwíddəti/ (*plural* **-ties**) *n* (*formal*) **1** the real nature or essential character of something **2** an unimportant or trifling distinction [Mid-16C. < medieval Latin *quidditas* < Latin *quid* 'what'.]

quidnunc /kwíd nungk/ *n* a nosy or gossipy person (*formal*) [Early 18C. < Latin, 'what now'.]

quid pro quo /kwíd prō kwṓ/ (*plural* **quid pro quos**) *n* **1** something given or done in exchange for something else **2** the giving of something in return for something else, often in a spirit of cooperation [Mid-16C. < Latin, 'something for something'.]

quiescent /kwi éss'nt/ *adj* inactive or at rest [Early 17C. < Latin *quiescere* 'come to rest' (see QUIET).] —**quiescence** *n* —**quiescently** *adv*

quiet /kwī ət/ *adj* **1 MAKING LITTLE NOISE** making little or no noise **2 PEACEFUL** free from noise or commotion ○ *in a quiet corner of the room* **3 DONE IN PRIVATE** carried out in private, with voices not raised, so as not to be overheard ○ *I'd like a quiet word with you.* **4 FREE FROM TROUBLE** free from trouble or disturbance ○ *a quiet life* **5 RELAXING** relaxing, peaceful, and free from excitement ○ *a quiet evening at home* **6 NOT SHOWY** not grand, showy, or pretentious ○ *a quiet wedding* **7 DISPLAYING CALMNESS** displaying calmness and self-control **8 NOT EXPRESSED IN WORDS** not expressed in words ○ *a sense of quiet optimism* **9 NOT FLOURISHING** not busy, active, or flourishing ○ *Business is a little too quiet.* **10 CALM OR MOTIONLESS** marked by very little motion ○ *a quiet sea* ■ *n* **ABSENCE OF NOISE** the absence of noise or disturbance ○ *the quiet of the forest* ■ *v* **1** *vti US* = **quieten** *v.* 1 **2** *vt US* = **quieten** *v.* 2 **3** *vt* **SECURE LEGAL CLAIM** to make a legal claim secure by resolving all possible challenges to it [14C. Via Old French < Latin *quietus*, past participle of *quiescere* 'come to rest' < *quies* 'rest, quiet'.] —**quietly** *adv* —**quietness** *n* ◇ **on the quiet** secretly

SPELLCHECK Do not confuse ***quiet*** with ***quite***, which has a similar sound. Beware: your spellchecker will not catch this error.

SYNONYMS See ***silent***.

quieten /kwī ət'n/ *v* **1** *vti* to become calm and quiet, or make somebody calm and quiet ○ *Will you all just quieten down, please?* US term **quiet** *v.* 1 **2** *vt* to calm somebody's feelings, such as doubts or fears. US term **quiet** *v.* 2

quietism /kwī ətizəm/ *n* **1** a system of Christian mysticism that requires a withdrawal from the world, a renunciation of the individual will, and passive contemplation of God and divine things **2** a state of calmness, especially one arising from noninvolvement in something (*literary*) [Late 17C. < Italian *quietismo* < *quieto* < Latin *quietus* (see QUIET).] —**quietist** *adj, n* —**quietistic** /kwī ə tístik/ *adj*

quietude /kwī ə tyood/ *n* the state of being quiet, peaceful, or tranquil (*literary*) [Late 16C. Directly or via French *quiétude* < medieval Latin *quietudo* < Latin *quietus* (see QUIET).]

quietus /kwī éetəss, -áy-/ *n* (*literary*) **1 DEATH** death, especially when viewed as a welcome release from life **2 RELEASE** a release from a debt or duty **3 CHECK** something that brings an activity to an end [Mid-16C. < medieval Latin *quietus (est)* '(it is) at rest', acknowledging receipt or discharge of an obligation.]

quiff /kwif/ *n* part of a man's hairstyle in which the hair at the front is brushed upwards and backwards [Late 19C. < ?]

quill /kwil/ *n* **1 LARGE FEATHER** a large stiff feather from a bird's wing or tail, or the hollow shaft of one of these feathers **2 PEN MADE FROM FEATHER SHAFT** an old-fashioned pen made from the shaft of a feather **3 SPINE** a sharp hollow spine on the body of a porcupine or hedgehog **4 SPINDLE OR BOBBIN** a spindle or bobbin onto which thread or yarn is wound **5 HOLLOW SHAFT** in a mechanical device, a hollow shaft in which a second independently rotating shaft is enclosed ■ *vt* **1 WIND THREAD** to wind thread or yarn onto a spindle or bobbin **2 MAKE FOLDS IN** to make small rounded folds in fabric, e.g. to make a ruff [15C. < ?]

quillai bark *n* INDUST = **soapbark** *n.* 1

quillback /kwíl bak/ (*plural* **-backs** *or* **-back**), **quillback carpsucker** /kwíl bak kaárp sukər/ *n* a freshwater fish of the sucker family with a long ray projecting from its dorsal fin. Native to: North America. *Carpiodes cyprinus.*

Quiller Couch /kwíllər kóoch/, **Sir Arthur** (1863–1944) British author

quill pen *n* = **quill** *n.* 2

quillwort /kwíl wurt/ *n* a nonflowering water plant that produces a rosette of tubular leaves, at the bases of which are spore-forming organs. Genus: *Isoetes.*

quilt /kwilt/ *n* **1 BED COVER** a bed cover made of two layers of fabric stitched together with padding held in place by decorative intersecting seams **2 DUVET** a duvet (*informal*) **3 SOMETHING SIMILAR TO QUILT** something that resembles a quilt or is quilted ■ *vt* **MAKE FABRIC ARTICLE** to make a fabric article, by sewing two layers of fabric together with a filling, especially using decorative stitching [13C. Via Anglo-Norman < Latin *culcita* 'cushion, mattress'.] —**quilter** *n*

quilting /kwílting/ *n* **1** the sewing of quilted bed covers or other quilted work **2** material that has been quilted or that is used to make quilts

Quimper /kaN pér/ city in NW France. Population: 62,540 (1990).

quin /kwin/ *n* a quintuplet (*informal*) US term **quint** *n.* 2 [Mid-20C. Shortening.]

quin- *prefix* = **quino-** (*before vowels*)

quinacrine hydrochloride /kwínnə kreen-/ *n* a synthetic drug. Use: treatment of malaria and worm infections. [Blend of QUININE + ACRIDINE]

quinalizarin /kwínnə lízzərin/ *n* $C_{14}H_8O_6$ a red crystalline organic compound with a green metallic lustre. Use: cotton dye. [< QUINO-]

quinary /kwínəri/ *adj* consisting of five parts, or occurring in sets of five (*formal*) ■ *n* (*plural* **-ies**) a set of five, or the fifth member of a set (*formal*) [Early 17C. < Latin *quinarius* < *quini* 'five each' < *quinque* 'five'.]

quince /kwinss/ *n* **1** an aromatic pear-shaped yellow or orange fruit that is edible only when cooked. Use: preserves. **2** a small tree that bears quinces. Native to: W Asia. *Cydonia oblonga.* [14C. Via Old French *cooin* < Latin *(malum) cotoneum* < Greek *(mēlon) kudōnion* 'apple of Cydonia' (Canea).]

quincentenary /kwín sen téenəri, -ténnəri/ (*plural* **-ries**), **quincentennial** /-ténni əl/ *n* a 500th anniversary [Late 19C. *Quin* < Latin *quinque* 'five'.] —**quincentary** *adj*

quincunx /kwín kungks/ *n* an arrangement of five objects in a square, with four at the corners and one in the centre [Mid-17C. < Latin, 'five-twelfths' (from the use of this pattern on a Roman coin worth five-twelfths of an as) < *quinque* 'five' + *uncia* 'a twelfth' (see OUNCE[1]).] —**quincuncial** /kwin kúnsh'l/ *adj*

Quincy **1** port in W Illinois. Population: 39,918 (1998 estimate). **2** city in E Massachusetts. Population: 85,752 (1998 estimate).

quindecagon /kwin dékəgən/ *n* a flat geometric shape with 15 angles and 15 sides [Late 16C. < Latin *quindecim* 'fifteen'.]

quindecennial /kwíndi sénni əl/ *adj* **1 HAPPENING EVERY 15 YEARS** happening once every 15 years **2 LASTING 15 YEARS** lasting for 15 years ■ *n* **15TH ANNIVERSARY** a 15th anniversary [20C. < Latin *quindecim* 'fifteen', after CENTENNIAL.]

Quine /kwīn/, **W. V.** (*b.* 1908) US philosopher. Full name **Willard Van Orman Quine**

quinella /kwi néllə/ *n* a bet in which the punter picks the first two finishers in a race but does not have to place them [Early 20C. < American Spanish *quiniela* < Spanish *quina* 'keno' < French *quine* (see KENO).]

quinic acid /kwínnik-/ *n* $C_6H_7(OH)_4COOH$ a white crystalline organic compound. Source: cinchona bark, coffee beans, leaves of many plants. Use: in medicine. [< Spanish *quina* 'cinchona bark' (see QUINO-)]

quinidine /kwínni deen/ *n* $C_{20}H_{24}N_2O_2$ a colourless crystalline organic compound related to quinine. Source: cinchona bark. Use: treatment of malaria and heart disorders. [Mid-19C. < QUINO- + -IDINE.]

quinine /kwi néen, kwínneen/ *n* a bitter-tasting drug made from cinchona bark. Use: treatment of chloroquine-resistant malaria. [Early 19C. < Spanish *quina* 'cinchona bark'.]

quinine water *n US* BEVERAGES = **tonic water**

quinnat salmon /kwínnat-/ *n* ZOOL = **Chinook salmon** [< Chinook *ikwanat*]

quino- *prefix* quinone ○ *quinonoid* [Via Spanish *quina* 'cinchona bark' < Quechua *kina*]

quinoa /kwi nṓ ə/ *n* a plant of the goosefoot family that is cultivated for its seeds, which are ground and eaten. Native to: Andes. *Chenopodium quinoa*. [Early 17C. Via Spanish < Quechua *kinoa*.]

quinoline /kwínnə leen, -lin/ *n* C_9H_7N an oily colourless substance. Source: coal tar. Use: manufacture of antiseptics and dyes.

quinone /kwi nṓn, kwínnōn/ *n* **1** CHEM = **benzoquinone 2** an organic yellow, orange, or red compound. Source: pigments in plants, fungi, and bacteria and vitamins in animals. —**quinonoid** /kwínnə noyd, kwi nṓ noyd/ *adj, n*

quinquagenarian /kwíngkwəjə náiri ən/ *adj* 50 years old, or between the ages of 50 and 59 (*formal*) ■ *n* somebody between 50 and 59 years of age (*formal*) [Early 19C. < Latin *quinquagenarius* < *quinquaginta* 'fifty'.]

Quinquagesima /kwíngkwə jéssimə/ *n* in the Christian liturgical calendar, the Sunday before Lent, seven weeks or the fiftieth day before Easter [14C. Via medieval Latin, 'fiftieth (day)' < Latin *quinquagesimus* < *quinquaginta* 'fifty'.]

quinque- *prefix* five ○ *quinquepartite* [< Latin *quinque* 'five' < Indo-European]

quinquennium /kwing kwénni əm/ (*plural* **-a** /-ni ə/) *n* a period of five years [Early 17C. < Latin < *quinque* 'five' + *annus* 'year'.] —**quinquennial** *adj* —**quinquennially** *adv*

quinquereme /kwíngkwi reem/ *n* an ancient Greek or Roman galley ship propelled by five banks of oars on each side [Mid-16C. < Latin *quinqueremis* < *quinque* 'five' + *remus* 'oar'.]

quinquevalent /kwíngkwi váylənt/ *adj* CHEM = **pentavalent**

quinsy /kwínzi/ *n* a severe inflammation of the throat near a tonsil that sometimes leads to the formation of an abscess that may require surgery [14C. Directly or via Old French < medieval Latin *quinancia* < Greek *kunagkhē* 'dog-strangling' < *kuōn* 'dog' + *ankhein* 'squeeze'.]

quint /kwint/ *n* **1** in the card game piquet, a sequence of five cards of the same suit **2** *US* = **quin** (*informal*) [Late 17C. Via French, 'fifth' < Latin *quintus*.]

quintain /kwíntin/ *n* a medieval knight's target for jousting practice [15C. Via Old French < Latin *quintana (via)* 'fifth (street)' (in a Roman camp).]

quintal /kwínt'l/ *n* **1** in the metric system, a unit of weight equal to 100 kg **2** a hundredweight (*archaic*) [15C. Directly or via Old French < medieval Latin *quintale* < Arabic *ḳinṭār* < Latin *centenarius* 'containing one hundred' (see CENTENARY).]

quintan /kwíntən/ *adj* flaring up every fifth day ■ *n* a fever that flares up every fifth day [Mid-17C. < medieval Latin *quintana* < Latin *quintus* 'fifth'.]

quinte /kwint, kaNt/ *n* the fifth in the series of eight standard positions used to teach fencing [Early 18C. < French, feminine of *quint* (see QUINT).]

quintessence /kwin téss'nss/ *n* **1** EMBODIMENT the purest or most perfect example of something **2** EXTRACT the purest extract or essence of a substance, containing the substance's properties in their most concentrated form **3** FIFTH ELEMENT in ancient and medieval philosophy, the fifth element after earth, air, fire, and water [15C. Via French < medieval Latin *quinta essentia* 'fifth essence'.] —**quintessential** /kwínti sénsh'l/ *adj* —**quintessentially** /-sénsh'li/ *adv*

quintet /kwin tét/, **quintette** *n* **1** MUSICIANS a group of five singers or musicians (*takes a singular or plural verb*) **2** MUSIC a piece of music written for five voices or instruments **3** GROUP OF FIVE a group or set of five people or things [Late 18C. Via French *quintette* < Italian *quintetto* < *quinto* 'fifth' < Latin *quintus*.]

quintic /kwíntik/ *adj* relating to the fifth power in a mathematical expression or equation [Mid-19C. < Latin *quintus* 'fifth'.]

quintile /kwín tīl/ *n* **1** STATISTICAL DIVISION any one of the five equal populations into which a statistical sample can be divided **2** STATISTICAL VALUE in statistics, any one of the values that divide a frequency distribution into five parts, each containing a fifth of the sample population **3** DISTANCE BETWEEN PLANETS the astrological aspect of planets that are distant from each other by 72 degrees or one fifth of the zodiac [Early 17C. < Latin *quintilis* < *quintus* 'fifth'.]

quintillion /kwin tíllyən/ *n* **1** the number equal to 10^{18}, written as 1 followed by 18 zeros **2** the number equal to 10^{30}, written as 1 followed by 30 zeros (*dated*) —**quintillion** *adj, pron* —**quintillionth** *adj, n, pron*

quintuple /kwíntyŏŏp'l, kwin tyŏŏp'l/ *adj* **1** BEING FIVE TIMES AS MUCH being five times as much or as many **2** CONSISTING OF FIVE PARTS made up of five parts **3** HAVING FIVE BEATS TO BAR having five musical beats to the bar ■ *vti* (**-ples, -pling, -pled**) MULTIPLY BY FIVE to multiply something by five or to be multiplied by five [Late 16C. Via French < medieval Latin *quintuplus* 'fivefold' < *quintus* 'fifth'.]

quintuplet /kwín tyŏŏplət, kwin tyŏŏp-/ *n* **1** ONE OF FIVE OFFSPRING one of five offspring born to one mother from a single pregnancy **2** GROUP OF FIVE a group of five things, especially five of the same kind **3** GROUP OF FIVE MUSICAL NOTES a group of five musical notes to be played in the time usually occupied by three or four notes

quintuplicate *adj* /kwin tyŏŏplikit/ MULTIPLIED BY FIVE multiplied by five ■ *n* /kwin tyŏŏplikit/ **1** ONE OF FIVE one of a set of five identical things **2** GROUP OF FIVE a group of five usually identical things ■ *vt* /kwin tyŏŏpli kayt/ (**-cates, -cating, -cated**) MAKE FIVE COPIES to make five copies of something [Mid-17C. < Latin *quintus* 'fifth' after DUPLICATE.] —**quintuplication** /kwin tyŏŏpli káysh'n/ *n*

quip /kwip/ *n* a witty remark, especially one made on the spur of the moment ■ *vti* (**quips, quipping, quipped**) to make a witty remark [Mid-16C. < ?]

quipster /kwípstər/ *n* somebody who makes witty remarks

quipu /keé poo/ (*plural* **-pus**) *n* a device consisting of a set of coloured and knotted cords used by the Incas for conveying messages and for record-keeping [Early 18C. Via Spanish < Quechua *kipu* 'knot'.]

quire /kwīr/ *n* **1** a set of 24 or 25 sheets of paper of the same size and quality, equalling one twentieth of a ream **2** a bundle of sheets of paper folded together for binding into a book, especially a four-sheet bundle, folded once to make eight leaves or sixteen pages [15C. Via Old French *qua(i)er* 'copybook', 'set of four (sheets)' < Latin *quaterni* (see QUATERNARY).]

quirk /qwurk/ *n* **1** ODD EVENT a strange and unexpected turn of events ○ *a strange quirk of fate* **2** ODD MANNERISM a peculiar habit, mannerism, or aspect of somebody's character **3** CURVED SHAPE a curved shape, pattern, or decoration, e.g. a flourish in handwriting **4** GROOVE a continuous groove running along a moulding or separating a moulding from adjoining members [Mid-16C. < ?] —**quirkily** *adv* —**quirkiness** *n* —**quirky** *adj*

quirt /kwurt/ *n US* a riding whip with a short handle and a braided leather lash [Mid-19C. < Mexican Spanish *cuarta* 'whip'.]

quisling /kwízzling/ *n* a traitor, especially somebody who collaborates with an occupying force [Mid-20C. After Vidkun *Quisling*, puppet premier of Norway during Nazi occupation.] —**quislingism** *n*

ϟ **quit** /kwit/ *v* (**quits, quitting, quitted** *or* **quit**) **1** *vti* RESIGN to give up, leave, or resign from a position or organization **2** *vti* STOP DOING SOMETHING to stop doing something, especially something bad or irritating ○ *Quit moaning.* **3** *vt* LEAVE to depart from a place (*archaic*) ○ *'No, he would sooner quit Kellynch Hall at once, than remain in it on such disgraceful terms.'* (Jane Austen, *Persuasion*; 1818) **4** *vti* EXIT FROM PROGRAM to exit from a computer program using the required exit procedure, so that the data and program configuration are saved **5** *vti* MOVE OUT to move out of rented property ○ *He gave his tenants notice to quit.* ■ *adj* UNBURDENED no longer troubled with a problem or difficult situation (*formal*) ○ *'it would be easier to die than to live, and so be quit of all the trouble'* (Bram Stoker, *Dracula*; 1897) [13C. < Old French *quiter* 'release, set free' < Latin *quietus* (see QUIET).]

quitch grass /kwítch-/, **quitch** *n* PLANTS = **couch grass** [Old English *cwice*]

quitclaim /kwít klaym/ *n* RENUNCIATION OF CLAIM a formal statement renouncing a legal claim previously made ■ *vt* **1** RENOUNCE CLAIM to withdraw formally a legal claim previously made **2** FREE SOMEBODY OF LIABILITY to declare formally somebody to be no longer legally liable for something [13C. < Anglo-Norman *quiteclamer* 'proclaim (somebody) free' < *quite* 'free' + *clamer* 'proclaim'.]

quite /kwīt/ *adv* **1** SOMEWHAT to some degree, but not to a great degree ○ *The film was quite good, but I wouldn't bother seeing it again.* **2** ENTIRELY in the highest degree, or to the fullest extent ○ *I was quite sure I'd met him before.* **3** NEARLY used with a negative to indicate that something is almost in a particular state or condition ○ *The dress is not quite finished.* **4** EMPHASIZING EXTENT used with expressions of quantity to emphasize the great extent of something ○ *They spent quite some time considering the problem.* **5** EMPHASIZING EXCEPTIONAL QUALITY used to emphasize the exceptional or impressive nature of somebody or something ○ *That was quite a celebration we had yesterday.* **6** EXPRESSING AGREEMENT used on its own or with 'so' to express agreement or understanding [14C. Variant of QUIT (adj).] ◇ **be quite something** to be remarkably good, fine, attractive, or otherwise admirable or impressive (*informal*)

SPELLCHECK See *quiet*.

Quito /keétō/ capital of Ecuador, in the north-central part of the country. Population: 1,100,847 (1990).

quitrent /kwít rent/ *n* in the feudal system, a rent paid by a tenant to a feudal lord in exchange for being released from certain feudal obligations [15C. < QUIT (adj).]

quits /kwits/ *adj* on even terms, especially following the repayment of a debt (*informal*) [Mid-17C. Probably < QUIT (adj), influenced by medieval Latin *quittus* 'freed'.] ◇ **call it quits 1** to agree with somebody that neither owes the other money, a favour, or an act of vengeance **2** to agree or decide to stop doing work or an activity (*informal*) **3** to agree that an argument or dispute is over and that both parties are equal (*informal*)

quittance /kwítt'nss/ *n* **1** release from a debt or obligation **2** a document or statement that releases somebody from a debt or obligation [13C. < Old French *quitance* < *quiter* (see QUIT).]

quitter /kwíttər/ *n* somebody who gives up easily (*informal*)

quittor /kwíttər/ *n* an infectious disease that affects the feet of horses and donkeys, causing inflammation [13C. < ?]

quiver[1] /kwívvər/ *vi* to shake rapidly with small movements ■ *n* a repeated light and fast shaking movement [15C. Probably < assumed Old English *cwifer* 'active, nimble'.] —**quiverer** *n* —**quivery** *adj*

quiver[2] /kwívvər/ *n* **1** a long narrow case for holding arrows **2** the arrows contained in a quiver [14C. Via Anglo-Norman *quiveir* < medieval Latin *cucurum*.]

quiverful /kwívvərfŏŏl/ (*plural* **-erfuls** *or* **-ersful**) *n* **1** the full number of arrows held in a quiver **2** a large number of things or people, especially the full number of children in a large family (*literary*)

qui vive /keé veév/ [< French, 'long live who?', used by sentries] ◇ **on the qui vive** alert and vigilant

quixotic /kwik sóttik/ *adj* **1** ROMANTIC tending to take a romanticized view of life **2** IMPRACTICAL motivated by an idealism that overlooks practical considerations **3** IMPULSIVE tending to act on whims or impulses [Late 18C. < Don *Quixote*, hero of a novel by Miguel de CERVANTES.] —**quixotically** *adv* —**quixotism** /kwíksətizəm/ *n*

quiz /kwiz/ *n* (*plural* **quizzes**) **1** TEST OF KNOWLEDGE a test of knowledge in the form of a short or rapid series of questions (*often used after a noun*) **2** TRICK a hoax, joke, or other trick (*archaic*) **3** ODD PERSON an eccentric (*archaic*) ○ *'I could make out that he was at once the quiz of the wardroom'* (Robert Louis Stevenson, *The Wrecker*; 1896) ■ *vt* (**quizzes, quizzing, quizzed**) **1** INTERROGATE to subject somebody to a round of sustained close questioning ○ *She was quizzed about the disappearance of the money.* **2** RIDICULE to make fun of somebody (*archaic*) **3** PEER AT to look intently at somebody (*archaic*) [Late 18C. < ?] —**quizzer** *n*

quizmaster /kwíz maastər/ *n* the presenter of a quiz show, who puts the questions to the contestants

quiz show *n* a television or radio programme in the form of a game in which contestants compete against each other for prizes by answering questions that test their general or specialist knowledge

quizzical /kwízzik'l/ *adj* expressing an amused or mocking question or puzzlement or doubt, especially in a mocking or amused way ○ *a quizzical glance* —**quizzicality** /kwízzi kálləti/ *n* —**quizzically** /kwízzikli/ *adv*

quod /kwod/ *n* a prison (*slang*) [Late 17C]

quod erat demonstrandum /kwód érrat démmən strándəm/ *adv* used in a formal conclusion to indicate that a particular fact is proof of the theory that has just been been advanced. Full form of **QED** [< Latin, 'which was to be shown']

quodlibet /kwóddli bet/ *n* **1** a theological question put forth as an exercise for discussion **2** a musical performance composed largely of familiar tunes [14C. Via medieval Latin *quodlibetum* < Latin *quodlibet* 'whatever pleases'.]

quo-he /kwó hee/ *npl Ireland* an offensive term that disparages country people as unintelligent or uninformed (*insult*)

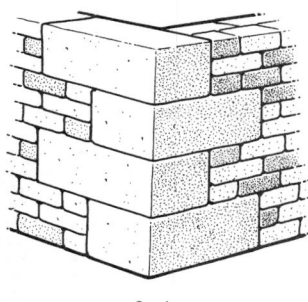

Quoin

quoin /koyn, kwoyn/, **coign, coigne** *n* **1** OUTER CORNER the outer corner of a wall **2** BLOCK FORMING CORNER a stone block used to form a quoin, especially when it is different, e.g. in size or material, from the other blocks or bricks in the wall **3** ARCHIT = **keystone** *n.* **1** ■ *vt* BUILD CORNER WITH DISTINCTIVE BLOCKS to build an outer corner of a wall using blocks that are different, e.g. in size or texture, from the other blocks or bricks used to build the wall [Mid-16C. Variant of COIN.]

quoit /koyt, kwoyt/ *n* a ring used in the game of quoits [14C. Probably via Old French *coite* 'flat stone, quoit' < Latin *culcita* 'cushion'.]

quoits /koyts, kwoyts/ *n* a game in which players attempt to throw rings over or near a small post (+ *singular verb*)

quokka /kwókə/ *n* a small short-tailed wallaby that lives in large colonies. Native to: islands off the coast of Western Australia. *Setonix brachyurus.* [Mid-19C. < Nyungar *kwaka*.]

quondam /kwón dam, -dəm/ *adj* of an earlier time (*archaic or literary*) ○ '… *now torn and rent by their quondam allies*' (Jack London, *The Iron Heel*; 1907) [Mid-16C. < Latin, < *quom* 'when'.]

quorate /kwáw rayt/ *adj* describes a meeting attended by at least the minimum number of members that the rules state are needed in order for business to be conducted

Quorn /kwawrn/ *tdmk* a trademark for a vegetable protein used in cooking as a meat substitute

quorum /kwáwrəm/ *n* a fixed minimum number of members of a legislative assembly, a committee, or other organization who must be present before the members can conduct valid business [15C. < Latin, 'of whom', used in requests for people to serve on committees.]

quota /kwótə/ *n* **1** a proportional share of something that somebody should contribute or receive ○ *You haven't done your quota of night shifts.* **2** a maximum number or quantity that is permitted or needed ○ *European fishing quotas* [15C. Via medieval Latin *quota (pars)* 'how large (a part)?', feminine of *quotus* (see QUOTE).]

quotable /kwótəb'l/ *adj* **1** worthy of being quoted **2** able to be quoted in a publication such as a newspaper because the person speaking or writing has given permission —**quotability** /kwótə bílləti/ *n*

quotation /kwō táysh'n/ *n* **1** SOMETHING QUOTED a piece of speech or writing quoted somewhere, e.g. in a book or magazine ○ *a quotation from Henry James* **2** QUOTING OF WHAT SOMEBODY HAS SAID the quoting of what somebody else has said or written **3** ESTIMATE FOR WORK an estimated price for a job or service. US term **quote** *n.* **3 4** SHARE PRICE the prevailing price at which a stock, bond, or commodity may be purchased or sold **5** QUOTING OF PRICES the quoting of prevailing stock, bond, or commodity market prices **6** RE-USE OF ARTISTIC MATERIAL the use in an artistic work, especially music, of material taken from or alluding to somebody else's work —**quotational** *adj* —**quotationally** *adv*

quotation mark *n* = inverted comma

quote /kwōt/ *v* (**quotes, quoting, quoted**) **1** *vti* REPEAT SOMEBODY'S EXACT WORDS to repeat or copy the exact words spoken or written by somebody **2** *vti* REFER TO SOMETHING FOR PROOF to refer to something as an example in support of an argument ○ *He quoted some recently published statistics.* **3** *vti* PUT PUNCTUATION AROUND QUOTATION to place quotation marks around a passage of speech or writing that is being quoted **4** *vti* GIVE ESTIMATE FOR COST to give an estimate of the price of providing somebody with a product or service **5** *vt* GIVE CURRENT MARKET PRICE to state the current market price of a share, bond, or commodity **6** *vt* GIVE BETTING ODDS to give somebody or something, e.g. a racehorse, particular betting odds (*usually passive*)

7 *vt* REPEAT FROM ARTISTIC WORK to repeat an excerpt from an artistic work created by somebody else, especially a piece of music ■ *n* **1** QUOTATION something that is repeated exactly (*informal*) **2** QUOTATION MARK one of a pair of quotation marks (*often plural*) **3** *US* BUSINESS = **quotation** *n.* **3** ■ *interj* INTRODUCING QUOTATION used to show that the following words are a quotation (*often used with* '*unquote*') ○ *She told me she is, quote, 'too good for him', unquote.* [14C. Via medieval Latin *quotare* 'to number chapters' < Latin *quotus* 'of what number or amount' < *quot* 'how many?'.] —**quoter** *n*

quoth /kwóth/ *vt* said, when used with direct speech (*archaic or literary*) ○ *quoth he* [Old English *cwað*, past tense of *cweþan* 'say' < Germanic]

quotidian /kwō tíddi ən/ *adj* **1** COMMONPLACE of the most ordinary everyday kind (*formal*) **2** DAILY done or experienced on a daily basis (*formal*) **3** RECURRING DAILY recurring or flaring up every day ■ *n* **quotidian, quotidian fever** FEVER RECURRING DAILY a fever, especially malaria, in which attacks of the illness recur daily [14C. Via Old French < Latin *quotidianus* < *cotidie* 'every day'.]

quotient /kwósh'nt/ *n* **1** RESULT OF DIVISION the number that results from the division of one number by another **2** RATIO a ratio of two numbers or quantities **3** WHOLE NUMBER RESULT OF DIVISION the whole number element of the result of dividing one number by another **4** AMOUNT OF PARTICULAR QUALITY a scale, or a point on a scale indicating the amount, degree, or level of something (*informal*) [15C. < Latin *quotiens* 'how many times?' < *quot* 'how many'.]

quo warranto /kwó wə rántō/ (*plural* **quo warrantos**) *n* a document issued by a court of law formally requiring somebody to state by what authority he or she has acted or has held a position [< legal Latin, 'by what warrant?', words in the writ]

Qüqon /koò kón/ *city in E Uzbekistan. Population: 175,000 (1991).

Qur'an *n* RELIG = **Koran**

Quttinirpaaq National Park /khoòt tee neelk paak-/ national park in N Nunavut, Canada. Area: 37,775 sq. km/14,585 sq. mi.

qv *abbr* which see (*indicates a cross reference to sth within the same book or article*) [Latin *quod vide*]

Q value *n* the energy released or absorbed during a particle or nuclear reaction

Qwaqwa /kwaʹákwə/ former homeland in east-central South Africa

✦ **qwerty** /kwúrti/, **QWERTY** *adj* describes a typewriter or computer keyboard with keys for the Roman alphabet, the top row of alphabetic characters being the letters q,w, e, r, t, and y. ◊ **azerty**

Rr

r[1] /aar/ (*plural* **r's**), **R** (*plural* **R's** *or* **Rs**) *n* the 18th letter of the English alphabet, representing a consonant sound

r[2] *symbol* **1** radius **2** resistance

r[3] *abbr* **1** railway **2** rare **3** recto **4** right **5** river **6** road **7** rod **8** rouble **9** run(s) **10** rupee

⚡R[1] /aar/, **r** a written form of 'are' (*informal; in e-mails*) [Because the letter *R* and *are* are pronounced the same]

R[2] /aar/ (*plural* **R's** *or* **Rs**) *n* **1 'R'-SHAPED OBJECT** something shaped like a letter 'R' **2 US CENSORSHIP CLASSIFICATION** in the United States, a censorship classification indicating that a film or video can be seen by children under the age of 17 only if accompanied by an adult. Full form **restricted 3 AUSTRALIAN CENSORSHIP CLASSIFICATION** in Australia, a censorship classification indicating that a film or video can only be seen by people over the age of 18 years of age. Full form **restricted** ◇ **the three R's** the basic skills of reading, writing, and arithmetic

R[3] *symbol* **1** gas constant **2** radical **3** Réaumur scale **4** resistance

R[4] *abbr* **1** rabbi **2** radius **3** railway **4** rand **5** range **6** rector **7** Regina (*after the name of a queen*) **8** republican **9** response (*in Christian liturgy*) **10** Rex (*after the name of a king*) **11** right **12** river **13** road **14** royal **15** rouble **16** rupee

Ra[1] /raa/, **Re** /ray/ *n* in ancient Egyptian mythology, the sun god, creator and controller of the universe, represented as having a human body and a hawk's head [< Egyptian *r*']

Ra[2] *symbol* radium

RA *abbr* **1** Rear Admiral **2** right ascension **3** Royal Academician **4** Royal Artillery

R.A. *abbr* right ascension

RAA *abbr* Royal Academy of Arts

RAAF /raf/ *abbr Aus* Royal Australian Air Force

raag *n MUSIC* = **raga**

Rabat /rə baàt/ capital of Morocco, in the NW of the country. Population: 1,385,872 (1994).

rabbet /rábbit/ *n CONSTR* = **rebate**[2] *n.* ■ *vt* **1** = **rebate**[2] *v.* 1 **2** = **rebate**[2] *v.* 2 [15C. < Old French *rab(b)at* 'recess' < *rabattre* (see REBATE[1]).]

rabbi /rábbī/ *n* **1** the leader of a Jewish congregation, or the chief religious official of a synagogue **2** a scholar qualified to teach or interpret Jewish law [Pre-12C. Via Late Latin and Greek < Hebrew *rabbī* 'my master'.]

rabbinate /rábbinət/ *n* **1** the post or term of office of a rabbi **2** rabbis considered as a group

rabbinic /rə bínnik/, **rabbinical** /-nik'l/ *adj* relating to rabbis or to their beliefs, language, teachings, or writings —**rabbinically** *adv*

Rabbinic Hebrew *n* the form of Hebrew used by rabbis between the 5th and 16th centuries

rabbinism /rábbinizəm/ *n* the teachings of Jewish scholars, especially the scholars of the Talmudic period —**rabbinist** *n, adj* —**rabbinistic** /rábbi nístik/ *adj*

rabbit /rábbit/ *n* (*plural* **-bits** *or* **-bit**) **1 SMALL FURRY MAMMAL** a small burrowing mammal with long ears, soft fur, and a short tail. Family: Leporidae. **2 RABBIT'S FUR** the fur of a rabbit **3 RABBIT'S FLESH** the meat of a rabbit ◇ *rabbit pie* **4 NOVICE** a beginner or an unskilful player of a game or sport (*dated informal*) ■ *vi* **1 HUNT RABBITS** to go hunting for wild rabbits **2 CHATTER** to talk for a long time about unimportant things (*informal*) ○ *He spent over an hour rabbiting to his mother on the phone.* [14C. Probably via Old French < Middle Dutch or Low German *robbe*.] —**rabbiter** *n*

rabbit ears *npl US* a V-shaped antenna made up of two metal rods on a base, designed to sit on top of a television set

rabbit fever *n VET* = tularaemia

rabbit food *n* an offensive term that deliberately dismisses a vegetarian diet, especially as providing insufficient nutrition for a human being (*informal*)

rabbiting /rábbiting/ *n* the activity of hunting for wild rabbits

rabbit punch *n* a short sharp blow to the back of the neck —**rabbit-punch** *vt*

rabbit warren *n* = **warren** *n.* 1

rabble[1] /rább'l/ *n* **1 UNRULY CROWD** a noisy and unruly crowd of people **2 OFFENSIVE TERM** an offensive term that deliberately insults people lacking in wealth and status (*insult; + singular or plural verb*) **3 OFFENSIVE TERM** an offensive term that deliberately insults the abilities or significance of a group of people (*insult*) [14C. < ?]

rabble[2] /rább'l/ *n* a device for stirring or skimming molten metal in a furnace ■ *vt* (**-bles, -bling, -bled**) to stir or skim molten metal with a rabble [Mid-19C. Via French *râble* 'fire rake' < Latin *rutabulum* < *ruere* 'rake up'.] —**rabbler** *n*

rabble-rouser *n* an agitator who stirs up anger, violence, or other strong feelings in a crowd (*disapproving*) —**rabble-rousing** *n, adj*

Rabelais /rábbə lay/, **François** (1493?–1553) French humanist and writer —**Rabelaisian** /rábbə láyziən, rábbə láyzh'n/ *adj*

Rabi /raàbi/, **Rabia** /rə beè ə/ *n* in the Islamic calendar, either the third month or the fourth month of the year, made up of 30 or 29 days [Mid-18C. < Arabic *rabī'*.]

Rabi /raàbi/, **Isidor Isaac** (1898–1988) Austrian-born US physicist

rabid /rábbid/ *adj* **1 HAVING RABIES** infected with rabies **2 FANATICAL** having extremist views, especially about politics (*disapproving*) **3 FURIOUS** extremely angry or violent **4 INTENSE** extremely intense and unceasing ○ *a rabid lust for power* [Early 17C. < Latin *rabidus* < *rabere* 'rave, be mad'.] —**rabidity** /rə bíddəti/ *n* —**rabidly** /rábbidli/ *adv* —**rabidness** *n*

rabies /ráy beez/ *n* an often fatal viral disease that affects the central nervous systems of most warm-blooded animals and is transmitted in the saliva of an infected animal [Late 16C. < Latin, 'fury' < *rabere* 'rave, be mad'.] —**rabic** *adj* —**rabietic** /ráybi éttik/ *adj*

Rabin /rə beèn/, **Yitzhak** (1922–95) Israeli statesman and prime minister (1974–77 and 1992–95)

RAC *abbr* **1** Royal Armoured Corps **2** Royal Automobile Club

raccoon /rə koòn, ra-/ (*plural* **-coons** *or* **-coon**), **racoon** (*plural* **-coons** *or* **-coon**) *n* **1** a small mammal with greyish-black fur, black patches around the eyes, and a long bushy ringed tail. Native to: forests of North and Central America. Genus: *Procyon.* **2** the fur of a raccoon [Early 17C. < Virginia Algonquian *aroughcun*.]

raccoon dog *n* a small wild dog with facial markings similar to a raccoon's and a thick yellow-brown coat.

Native to: woodland areas of E Asia. *Nyctereutes procyonoides.*

race[1] /rayss/ *n* **1 CONTEST OF SPEED** a contest, e.g. between or among runners or horseriders, to decide who is the fastest **2 CONTEST BETWEEN RIVALS** a contest between two or more people seeking to do or reach the same thing, or do or reach it first **3 WATER CURRENT** a strong localized current in the sea or a river **4 WATER CHANNEL** a channel that carries water from one place to another, especially from a stream to a millwheel **5 GROOVE GUIDING SLIDING OBJECT** a groove along which something, e.g. a ball bearing, slides **6 NARROW PASSAGE** any narrow track or passage, e.g. one leading sheep from their enclosure to a dip **7 REGULAR COURSE** the fixed course regularly followed or travelled by something, especially the Sun or the Moon (*archaic or literary*) ■ **races** *npl* **HORSE RACES OR HORSERACING** horse races, the racetrack at which they are run, or horseracing as a spectator sport ○ *We spent the day at the races.* ■ *v* (**races, racing, raced**) **1** *vti* **COMPETE AGAINST IN RACE** to compete with somebody in a contest of speed **2** *vt* **ENTER SOMETHING IN RACE** to enter, ride, or drive something, e.g. a horse or car, in a race **3** *vti* **MOVE VERY FAST** to move somewhere with great speed or haste, or make somebody or something move or be transported in this way **4** *vi* **BEAT FAST** to beat much faster than usual, e.g. out of nervousness or excitement (*refers to the heart*) **5** *vti* **IDLE FAST** to run or make an engine or motor run at a high speed [13C. < Old Norse *rás* 'rush, running' < Indo-European, 'be in motion'.]

race off *vt Aus* an offensive term meaning to take somebody away with the intention of having sex with him or her (*slang*)

race[2] /rayss/ *n* **1 GROUP OF HUMANS** any one of the groups into which the world's population can be divided on the basis of physical characteristics such as skin or hair colour **2 FACT OF BELONGING TO A GROUP** the fact of belonging to a group of humans who share the same physical features such as skin colour ○ *discrimination on grounds of race* **3 HUMANKIND** humanity considered as a whole ○ *the fate of the race* **4 STRAIN OF ORGANISM** a genetically distinct population within a species that may also be geographically isolated **5 WINE'S DISTINCTIVE TASTE** the distinctive taste of a particular wine, by which its grape variety or region of origin can be identified [Early 16C. Via French < Italian *razza*.]

racecar /rayss kaar/ *n US* = **racing car**

racecard /rayss kaard/ *n* the programme of events at a race meeting

race card ◇ **play the race card** to use the issue of race, e.g. in legal argumentation or in a debate, to win an advantage or make a point (*informal*)

racecourse /rayss kawrss/ *n* **1** a track around which horses race, or the grounds in which the track is sited. US term **racetrack** *n.* **2 2** *US SPORTS* = **racetrack**

racegoer /rayss gō ər/ *n* somebody attending a race meeting or who regularly goes to race meetings

racehorse /rayss hawrss/ *n* a horse bred and trained to run in races

racemate /rássə mayt/ *n* a chemical compound that does not deflect or absorb any of the light passing through it [Mid-19C. < RACEMIC.]

raceme /rásseem/ *n* a flower cluster (**inflorescence**) in which the flowers are borne on short stalks along a long main stem, as they are in the lily of the valley [Late 18C. < Latin *racemus* 'bunch of grapes'.]

race meeting *n* a series of horse races held on the same course on a single day or over consecutive days

racemic /rə seémik, -sémmik/ *adj* describes a chemical compound that does not deflect or absorb any of the light passing through it [Late 19C. < Latin *racemus* 'bunch of grapes', because the compound was originally derived from grapes.]

racemic acid *n* a form of tartaric acid that does not deflect or absorb any of the light passing through it. Source: grape juice.

racemization /rássi mī záysh'n/, **racemisation** *n* the process of converting from an optically active compound or mixture to one that is racemic —**racemize** /rássə mīz/ *vt*

racemose /rássimōss, -mōz/ *adj* describes glands that resemble a bunch of grapes in their structure —**racemosely** *adv* —**racemously** *adv*

racer /ráyssər/ *n* **1 SOMEBODY OR SOMETHING THAT RACES** a person, animal, or vehicle competing in a race **2 TRACK FOR MOVABLE ARTILLERY GUN** a circular rail on which the travelling platform of a heavy artillery gun is mounted **3 THIN FAST-MOVING SNAKE** a slender fast-moving non-venomous snake. Native to: North America. Genus: *Coluber*.

racerunner /ráyss runnər/ *n* a fast-moving lizard. Native to: North and Central America. Genus: *Cnemidophorus*.

racetrack /ráyss trak/ *n* **1** a track around which cars or runners race, or the grounds in which such a track is sited. US term **racecourse** *n*. **2 2** US HORSERACING = **racecourse** *n*. 1

race-walk *vi* to compete in the sport of race walking

race walking *n* the sport of racing at a fast walking pace, with rules that require walkers to keep at least one foot on the ground at all times —**race walker** *n*

raceway /ráyss way/ *n US* **1** CIV ENG = **race**[1] *n*. 4 **2** US a track on which races, especially harness races, are held, or the grounds in which the track is sited

Rachel /ráchəl/ *n* in the Bible, the daughter of Laban, wife of Jacob, and mother of Joseph and Benjamin (Genesis 29–35)

rachilla /rə kíllə/ (*plural* **-lae** /-lee/), **rhachilla** (*plural* **-lae**) *n* a side branch of a compound leaf, e.g. on a fern, that bears the individual leaflets [Mid-19C. < modern Latin, 'little rachis' < *rachis* (see RACHIS).]

rachio- *prefix* spine ○ *rachiotomy* [Via modern Latin < Greek *rhakhis* 'spine']

rachis /ráykiss/ (*plural* **rachises** *or* **rachides** /ráyki deez/), **rhachis** (*plural* **rhachises** *or* **rhachides**) *n* **1 PLANT STEM** the main stem of a flower cluster or a compound leaf **2 FEATHER SHAFT** the main shaft of a feather **3 SPINE** the spine of a vertebrate animal (*technical*) [Late 18C. Via modern Latin < Greek *rhakhis* 'spine, ridge'.] —**rachial** /ráyki əl/ *adj* —**rachidial** /rə kíddi əl/ *adj*

rachitis /rə kītiss/ *n* the disease rickets (*technical*) [Early 18C. < Greek *rhakhitis* 'disease of the spine' < *rhakhis* 'spine'.] —**rachitic** /rə kíttik/ *adj*

Sergey Rachmaninoff

Rachmaninoff /rak mánni nof/, **Sergey** (1873–1943) Russian-born composer and pianist

Rachmanism /rákmənizəm/, **rachmanism** *n* exploitation or intimidation by a landlord of tenants living in slum property [Mid-20C. After Peter *Rachman* (1919–62), a notoriously unscrupulous London landlord, in the 1950s.]

racial /ráysh'l/ *adj* **1** existing or taking place between different races ○ *racial harmony* **2** relating to or characteristic of races or a particular race of people —**racially** *adv*

racialism /ráysh'lizəm/ *n* racism (*dated*) —**racialist** *n*, *adj* —**racialistic** /ráyshə lístik/ *adj*

racial profiling *n* the alleged tendency of some police to attribute criminal intentions to members of particular ethnic groups and to stop and question them in disproportionate numbers without proper cause

Racine /ra seén/, **Jean Baptiste** (1639–99) French playwright

racing /ráyssing/ *n* the sport of taking part in races, e.g. as a runner, on a horse, or in a sports car

racing bike *n* a bicycle or motorcycle used, designed, or adapted for racing (*informal*)

racing car *n* a car used, designed, or adapted for racing. US term **racecar**

racism /ráyssizəm/ *n* **1** prejudice or animosity against people who belong to other races ○ *'I am a Muslim and ... my religion makes me against all forms of racism.'* (Malcolm X, *Speech, Prospects for Freedom*; 1965) **2** the belief that people of different races have different qualities and abilities, and that some races are inherently superior or inferior

racist /ráyssist/ *adj* **1 BASED ON RACISM** based on notions and stereotypes related to race **2 PREJUDICED AGAINST OTHER RACES** prejudiced against all people who belong to other races ○ *'Black power ... a call to reject the racist institutions and values of this society'* (Stokely Carmichael [Kwame Ture] and Charles Vernon Hamilton, *Black Power!*; 1967) ■ *n* **RACIST PERSON** a person who hates others who are not of his or her own race

rack[1] /rak/ *n* **1 FRAMEWORK FOR HOLDING THINGS** a framework or stand for carrying, holding, or storing things ○ *a wine rack* **2 FEED-HOLDING FRAMEWORK** a framework containing hay or other fodder for livestock **3 BOMB-HOLDING FRAMEWORK** a bomb- or rocket-carrying framework attached to an aircraft **4 TOOTHED BAR** a bar with notches, designed to engage the teeth of a pinion or worm gear and convert rotary motion to linear motion, e.g. in a vehicle's steering system **5 INSTRUMENT OF TORTURE** a torture device used to stretch the body of a victim strapped horizontally onto it **6** *US, Can* CUE GAMES = **frame** *n*. 16 **7** *US, Can* CUE GAMES = **frame** *n*. 17 **8** *US, Can* CUE GAMES = **frame** *n*. 15 ■ *vt* **1 CAUSE SOMEBODY PAIN** to cause somebody great pain or stress ○ *The coughing spasms that racked his body* **2 SHAKE** to shake or strain something with violent force ○ *The high winds racked villages all along the coast.* **3 STRAIN** to stretch something with extreme force or mental effort ○ *I racked my memory trying to think where I'd seen him before.* **4 TORTURE SOMEBODY ON RACK** to torture somebody on a rack **5 PUT SOMETHING IN RACK** to place something in or on a rack **6 MOVE SOMETHING WITH RACK** to move a device or part using a rack-and-pinion system [14C. < Dutch *rak* < Middle Dutch *rec* 'framework'.] —**racker** *n* ◇ **on the rack** experiencing great mental anguish (*informal*)

rack off *vi Aus* an offensive term often used as a command to tell somebody to go away (*slang*)

rack up *vt* to accumulate something, usually points (*informal*) ○ *The company racked up sales of $8 million in its first year of trading.*

rack[2] /rak/ *n* a joint of meat, usually lamb, consisting of one or both sides of the front ribs prepared for roasting, often joined end to end in a circle [Late 16C. < ?]

rack[3] /rak/ *vt* to siphon clear wine or beer out of a barrel, leaving the sediment behind [15C. < Provençal *arracar* < *raca* 'dregs'.]

rack[4] /rak/ *n* in dressage, a fast walking pace for a horse in which each foot is lifted off the ground in turn ■ *vi* to walk at a fast pace, lifting each foot off the ground in turn (*refers to horses*) [Late 16C. < ?]

rack[5] /rak/ *n* a mass of broken cloud blown fast by the wind (*literary*) ■ *vi* to be blown fast by the wind (*literary*; *refers to clouds*) [14C. < ?]

rack[6] /rak/, **wrack** [Late 16C. Variant of WRACK[2].] ◇ **go to rack and ruin** to deteriorate into a state of neglect or ruin

rack-and-pinion *adj* using or relating to a mechanical system in which a toothed wheel (**pinion**) engages a notched bar (**rack**) to convert rotary motion into linear motion

racket[1] /rákit/, **racquet** *n* **1** a lightweight bat with a network of strings, used in badminton, squash, tennis, and similar games **2** a snowshoe in the shape of a racket [Early 16C. Via French *raquette* < Arabic *ráhat* 'palm of the hand'.]

racket[2] /rákit/ *n* **1 NOISE** a loud noise, especially when it disturbs people (*informal*) **2 ILLEGAL SCHEME** an illegal or dishonest money-making scheme, involving activities such as bribery, fraud, or intimidation (*informal*) **3 BUSINESS** a business, job, or activity of any kind (*informal*) ○ *He's in the advertising racket.* **4 EASY LIVING** an easy and very profitable way of earning a living (*informal*) ○ *'We had a fine old racket in the commandant's office'.* (John Buchan, *Greenmantle*) **5 PARTY** an uproarious party (*dated*) ○ *'We had a riotous party'* (*dated*) **6 FORMER WOODWIND INSTRUMENT** a woodwind instrument of the renaissance and baroque periods, consisting of a long tube coiled and enclosed in a cylinder **7 ORGAN STOP** an organ stop that imitates the sound of the racket ■ *vi* **1 MOVE AROUND NOISILY** to make a lot of noise while moving around (*informal*) ○ *We could still hear them racketing around downstairs.* **2 LIVE DEBAUCHED LIFE** to lead a riotous life devoted to pleasure (*dated*) [Mid-16C. < ?]

racketeer /ráki teér/ *n* a criminal who profits from illegal activities such as bribery, fraud, or intimidation ■ *vi* to make money from illegal activities, or operate a racket —**racketeering** *n*

rackets *n* = racquets

rackety /rákiti/ *adj* **1** leading a lively but sometimes rather dissipated social life **2** noisy and boisterous (*dated*)

Rackham /rákəm/, **Arthur** (1867–1939) British illustrator and watercolour painter

rack railway *n* a mountain railway that has locomotives with a central cogwheel that engages with a toothed rack between the rails in order to pull the train up steep slopes. US term **cog railway**

rack-rent *n* an unreasonably high rent ■ *vti* to charge tenants an unreasonably high rent [< RACK[1], in the sense 'torture'] —**rack-renter** *n*

raclette /ra klét/ *n* **1** a Swiss dish consisting of slices of melted cheese served on boiled potatoes or bread **2** a hard-crusted type of Swiss cheese that melts easily, traditionally used for raclette [Mid-20C. < French, < *racler* 'scrape', because the cheese is melted and scraped onto a plate.]

racon /ráy kon/ *n* ELECTRONICS = **radar beacon** [Mid-20C. Blend of RADAR + BEACON.]

raconteur /rá kon túr/ *n* somebody who tells stories or anecdotes [Early 19C. < French, < Old French *raconter* 'recount, retell']

racoon *n* ZOOL = **raccoon**

racquet *n* SPORTS = **racket**[1]

racquetball /rákit bawl/ *n* a game played on a four-walled indoor court by two, three, or four players using short-handled rackets and a ball larger than the ball used in squash or rackets

racquets /rákits/, **rackets** *n* a fast game similar to squash played by two to four people on a four-walled indoor court using long-handled rackets and a small hard ball [Mid-18C. < French *raquette* (see RACKET[1]).]

racy /ráyssi/ (**-ier, -iest**) *adj* **1 MILDLY INDECENT** mildly shocking because of references to or descriptions of sex **2 LIVELY** full of energy or spirit ○ *'the peculiar mixture of accurate knowledge and of racy imagination which gave them their fascination'* (Arthur Conan Doyle, *The Lost World*; 1912) **3 DISTINCTIVE** with a distinctive quality or flavour **4 PUNGENT** sharp or piquant in taste or smell [Mid-17C. < RACE[1].] —**racily** *adv* —**raciness** *n*

rad[1] /rad/ *n* the unit formerly used to measure the level of ionizing radiation absorbed by something, equal to 0.01 joule per kilogram of irradiated material [Early 20C. Acronym < *radiation absorbed dose*.]

rad[2] /rad/ (**radder, raddest**) *adj US* very good, desirable, admirable, or fashionable (*slang*) ○ *a totally rad idea* [Early 19C. Shortening of RADICAL.]

rad[3] /rad/ *symbol* radian

rad. *abbr* **1** radiator **2** radical **3** radio **4** radius **5** radix

RADA /ráadə/ *abbr* Royal Academy of Dramatic Art

radar /ráy daar/ *n* **1** the use of reflected radio waves to determine the presence, location, and speed of distant objects **2** the electronic equipment that transmits and receives high-frequency radio waves to detect, locate, and track distant objects [Mid-20C. Acronym < *radio de-*

tection and ranging.] ◇ **be on somebody's radar screen** *US* to be a focal point of interest to somebody (*informal*) ○ *This issue of bank fraud has been on the district attorney's radar screen for at least six months.*

radar astronomy *n* the use of radar techniques to study and map astronomical objects in the solar system

radar beacon *n* a ground-based, fixed-position radar receiver-transmitter whose signals can be received by an aircraft or ship's navigator to determine bearing and range

radar gun *n* a small hand-held radar device used to determine the speed of nearby objects

radarscope /ráy daar skōp/ *n* the display screen on radar equipment, displaying the reflected radio signal as a dot of light

radar trap *n* TRANSP = **speed trap**

raddle[1] /rádd'l/ (**-dles, -dling, -dled**) *vt* to twist or weave things together [Late 17C. Via Anglo-Norman *reidele* 'wooden pole' < Old French *reddalle*.]

raddle[2] /rádd'l/ *n, vt* MINERALS, AGRIC = **ruddle**

raddled /rádd'ld/ *adj* with a worn-out appearance that suggests long life or a life of indulgence [Late 17C. < ?]

radial /ráydi əl/ *adj* **1 RUNNING FROM CENTRE OUTWARDS** spreading out from a common centre like the spokes of a wheel ○ *petals in a radial arrangement* **2 OF RADIUS** relating to a radius, especially moving along a radius **3 WITH BODY PARTS IN CIRCULAR ARRANGEMENT** describes the arrangement of the bodies of invertebrate marine animals such as the starfish and sea anemone that have parts spreading out from a single centre **4 OF FOREARM BONE** relating to the radius bone of the forearm ■ *n* CARS = **radial tyre** —**radially** *adv*

radial drilling machine *n* a machine with a drilling head mounted on an arm that can be freely rotated to allow a given workpiece to be drilled at any point

radial engine *n* an internal-combustion engine that has its cylinders arranged around a central crankshaft like the spokes of a wheel, instead of in one or two straight rows. ◊ **rotary engine**

radial keratotomy *n* a surgical procedure for correcting short-sightedness, using a series of small radial incisions to change the shape of the cornea

radial-ply *adj* describes a tyre in which the fabric cords that make up the foundation of the tyre run at right angles to the circumference of the tyre

radial symmetry *n* symmetry in which something can be divided into two identical halves by a line or plane passing through a central point or axis at any angle —**radially symmetrical** *adj*

radial tyre *n* a tyre in which the fabric cords that make up the foundation of the tyre run at right angles to the circumference of the tyre

radial velocity *n* the velocity of a star or other astronomical object measured along the observer's line of sight

radian /ráydi ən/ *n* (*symbol* **rad**) a unit of angular measurement equivalent to the angle between two radii that enclose a section of a circle's circumference (**arc**) equal in length to the length of a radius [Late 19C. < RADIUS.]

radiance /ráydi ənss/ *n* **1 HAPPINESS OR ENERGY** joy, energy, or good health discernible in somebody's face or demeanour **2 LIGHT** bright or glowing light **3 MEASURE OF RADIANT ENERGY** (*symbol* L_e) a measure of the amount of radiant energy emitted or received per unit area of a surface over a specified time

radiant /ráydi ənt/ *adj* **1 SHOWING HAPPINESS** expressing joy, energy, or good health in a pleasing way **2 SHINING** lit with a bright or glowing light **3 IN RAY FORM** describes light, heat, or other energy emitted in the form of waves or rays ○ *radiant heat* **4 EMITTING RADIANT ENERGY** emitting light, heat, or other energy in the form of waves or rays ■ *n* **1 HEATING ELEMENT** an element in a heater that gives out radiant heat **2 METEOR SHOWER'S POINT OF ORIGIN** a point in space from which a meteor shower appears to originate [15C. < Latin *radiant-*, present participle of *radiare* 'emit rays'.] —**radiantly** *adv*

radiant energy *n* (*symbol* Q_e) energy emitted as waves, usually electromagnetic waves, through space or some other medium

radiant flux *n* (*symbol* ϕ_e) the rate of flow of radiant energy

radiant heat *n* heat transmitted by infrared radiation from a heat source, as distinct from heat transmitted by conduction or convection

radiant heating *n* heating by means of heaters such as radiators, baseboard heaters, and electric coils rather than by forced hot air

radiate *v* /ráydi ayt/ (**-ates, -ating, -ated**) **1** *vti* **SEND OR BE SENT IN RAYS** to send out energy, e.g. heat or light, in the form of rays or waves, or be sent out in this form **2** *vti* **SHOW A FEELING OR QUALITY** to show a feeling or quality clearly through looks, speech, behaviour, or content ○ *a popular speech that radiated goodwill and commitment* **3** *vti* **SPREAD FROM CENTRE** to spread out, or cause something to spread out, from a central point like rays **4** *vi* **DEVELOP AND SPREAD** to develop into several different forms capable of exploiting different resources or of living in different environments (*refers to animal and plant species*) ■ *adj* /ráydi ət, -ayt/ **1 WITH RADIATING PARTS** with, or in the form of, parts spreading out from a common centre **2 WITH PETALS RADIATING FROM CENTRE** describes a flower head that has petals radiating from a centre, e.g. that of a daisy **3 WITH RADIALLY SYMMETRICAL BODY** describes the bodies of starfish and other vertebrate marine organisms with body parts radiating from a common centre **4 WITH RAYS** surrounded or decorated with rays [Early 17C. < Latin *radiat-*, past participle of *radiare* 'emit rays' < *radius* 'ray'.] —**radiately** /ráydi ətli/ *adv* —**radiative** /-ətiv/ *adj*

radiation /ráydi áysh'n/ *n* **1 PARTICLES EMITTED BY RADIOACTIVE SUBSTANCES** energy emitted in the form of particles by substances, e.g. uranium and plutonium, whose atoms are not stable and are spontaneously decaying **2 ENERGY EMITTED IN RAYS OR WAVES** any kind of energy that is emitted from a source in the form of rays or waves, e.g. heat, light, or sound **3 RADIATING OF ENERGY** the emission of energy in the form of waves **4 EFFECT OF RADIATING** the feeling of something being radiated, e.g. heat from a hot oven **5** MED = **radiotherapy** **6** ECOL = **adaptive radiation** —**radiational** *adj*

radiational cooling *n* loss of heat from the Earth's surface and from air near the Earth's surface, occurring mainly at night

radiation biology *n* = **radiobiology**

radiation chemistry *n* the branch of chemistry concerned with chemical changes caused by the impact of radiation

radiation sickness *n* a medical condition caused by overexposure to X-rays or to emissions from radioactive material. Symptoms include fatigue, headache, vomiting, diarrhoea, loss of hair and teeth, and in severe cases, haemorrhaging.

radiation therapy *n* PHYSIOL = **radiotherapy**

radiator /ráydi aytər/ *n* **1 ROOM HEATER WITH PIPES** a room-heating device that emits heat from pipes through which hot water, steam, or hot oil circulates, especially one connected to a central boiler-fed system **2 ENGINE-COOLING DEVICE** a device that prevents a vehicle's engine from overheating, consisting of tubes through which heated water from the engine circulates to be cooled **3** *ANZ* **ELECTRIC HEATER** an electric fire or heater **4 DEVICE EMITTING RADIANT ENERGY** a device that emits radiant energy, e.g. a light bulb or a television transmitter

radical /ráddik'l/ *adj* **1 BASIC** relating to or affecting the basic nature or most important features of something ○ *a radical difference between the two* **2 PERVASIVE** far-reaching, searching, or thoroughgoing ○ *a radical reorganization of the company* **3 FAVOURING MAJOR CHANGES** favouring or making economic, political, or social changes of a sweeping or extreme nature **4 REMOVING DISEASE'S SOURCE** describes medical treatment that is intended to remove the source of a disease, rather than simply treat the symptoms **5 GROWING FROM ROOT** growing from a root of a plant or from the base of a stem **6 OF A MATHEMATICAL ROOT** relating to the roots of numbers **7 OF WORD ROOTS** relating to the roots of words **8** *US* **EXCELLENT** very good, desirable, admirable, or fashionable (*slang*) ■ *n* **1 SOMEBODY WITH RADICAL VIEWS** somebody with radical views on political, economic, or social issues ○ *the radicals in the party* **2 MATHEMATICAL ROOT** a mathematical root of another number or quantity **3** CHEM = **free radical** **4 CHEMICAL GROUP** a chemical group that behaves as a single entity in reactions (*dated*) **5** LING = **root**[1] *n.* 10 [14C. < late Latin *radicalis* 'of roots' < *radix* 'root'.] —**radically** *adv* —**radicalness** *n*

radical chic *n* the fashionable adoption of radical left-wing views by rich or famous people (*disapproving*) ○ *'Radical chic invariably favors radicals who seem primitive, exotic, and romantic'.* (Tom Wolfe, *Radical Chic*; 1970)

radicalise *vti* = **radicalize**

radicalism /ráddik'lizəm/ *n* **1 POLITICS ADVOCATING MAJOR CHANGES** political policies that advocate more sweeping political, economic, or social change than that traditionally supported by the mainstream political parties **2 POLITICALLY RADICAL ATTITUDES** support for radical political policies **3 SIGNIFICANT CHANGE** sweeping change in any context, or the attitudes of people who favour sweeping change —**radicalistic** /ráddikə lístik/ *adj* —**radicalistically** *adv*

radicalize /ráddikə līz/ (**-izes, -izing, -ized**), **radicalise** (**-ises, -ising, -ised**) *vti* **1** to undergo fundamental change, or introduce sweeping change in something **2** to adopt, or cause somebody to adopt, politically radical views ○ *The experience of war radicalized the younger generation.* —**radicalization** /ráddikə lī záysh'n/ *n*

radical sign *n* the sign √ placed before a mathematical expression to denote the extraction of a square root or higher root

radicand /ráddi kand/ *n* a mathematical quantity from which a square root or higher root is to be extracted [Late 19C. < Latin *radicandus* < *radicare* 'take root'.]

radicchio /ra díki ō/ (*plural* **-os**), **radichio** (*plural* **-os**) *n* a variety of chicory with reddish-purple and white leaves, usually eaten raw in salads. Native to: Italy. [Late 20C. Via Italian, 'chicory' < Latin *radicula* (see RADICLE).]

radices plural of **radix**

radicle /ráddik'l/ *n* **1** the part of a plant embryo that forms the root of the young plant **2** a small body part such as a branch of a nerve that superficially resembles the root of a plant [Late 17C. < Latin *radicula* 'little root' < *radix* 'root'.] —**radicular** /ra díkyōōlər/ *adj*

radio /ráydi ō/ *n* (*plural* **-os**) **1 USE OF ELECTROMAGNETIC WAVES FOR COMMUNICATION** the use of electromagnetic waves to transmit and receive information, as in sound broadcasts or two-way communication, without the need for connecting wires **2 COMMUNICATION USING RADIO WAVES** communication that takes place by means of radio waves **3 DEVICE RECEIVING SOUND BROADCASTS** an electronic device for receiving sound broadcasts transmitted via radio signals **4 TWO-WAY COMMUNICATION DEVICE** an electronic device used to send and receive radio signals, used for two-way communication **5 RADIO BROADCASTS** sound broadcasts transmitted by means of radio waves **6 BROADCASTING OF PROGRAMMES BY RADIO** the broadcasting by radio of programmes for the public **7 RADIO BROADCASTING STATION OR ORGANIZATION** a station for transmitting radio broadcasts or an organization involved in radio broadcasting ○ *Radio 1* **8 SOUND BROADCASTING** radio broadcasting as an industry or profession ○ *She works in radio.* ■ *vti* (**-os, -oing, -oed**) **COMMUNICATE BY RADIO** to communicate by radio or send somebody a message by radio ■ *adj* **OF ELECTROMAGNETIC WAVES** relating to electromagnetic waves or electromagnetic phenomena with frequencies between 10 kHz and 300,000 MHz [Early 20C. Shortening of *radiotelegraph*.]

radio- *prefix* **1** radiation ○ *radiocarbon* **2** radio ○ *radiolocation* [Shortening of words such as RADIATION and RADIOACTIVE]

radioactive /ráydi ō áktiv/ *adj* **1** describes a substance such as uranium or plutonium that emits energy in the form of streams of particles, owing to the decaying of its unstable atoms **2** relating to or making use of radioactive substances or the radiation they emit —**radioactively** *adv*

radioactive dating *n* SCI = **radiometric dating**

radioactive decay *n* PHYS = **decay** *n.* 4

radioactive series *n* a series of related atom types (**nuclides**) of radioactive isotopes, each of which is transformed into the next by the emission of an elementary particle until a stable nuclide results

radioactive tracer *n* a substance with a radioactive isotope that can be introduced into and tracked within the body to study disease and biochemical processes

radioactivity /ráydi ō ak tívvəti/ *n* **1** the radioactive nature of a substance such as uranium or plutonium **2** the high-energy particles emitted by radioactive substances

radio alarm *n* an electronic device that combines a radio with the functions of an alarm clock

radio astronomy *n* a branch of astronomy that deals

with the detection and analysis of radio waves received from space —**radio astronomer** *n*

radio beacon *n* a fixed ground-based radio transmitter that sends out a distinctive signal to help aircraft and shipping to identify their position

radio beam *n* a beam of radio signals transmitted by a radio beacon for navigation purposes

radiobiology /ráydi ō bī óllәji/ *n* a branch of biology that deals with the effects of radiation on living tissues and organisms —**radiobiologic** /ráydi ō bī ә lójjik/ *adj* — **radiobiological** /ráydi ō bī ә lójjik'l/ *adj* —**radiobiologically** *adv* —**radiobiologist** /ráydi ō bī óllәjist/ *n*

⚡**radio button** *n* in a computer dialogue box, any of several circles or rectangles, each with text next to it, representing a fixed set of choices, one of which must be selected

radio car *n* **1** a car, especially a police car, equipped with a two-way radio **2** a vehicle from which radio broadcasts are made, especially interviews

radiocarbon /ráydi ō kaárbәn/ *n* a radioactive form of carbon, especially the isotope of carbon that has a mass number of 14

radiocarbon dating *n* GEOL = **carbon dating**

radio cassette, radio-cassette player *n* a radio and a cassette player combined in a single, usually portable machine

radiochemistry /ráydi ō kémmistri/ *n* a branch of chemistry that deals with radioactive elements and their applications —**radiochemical** *adj* —**radiochemically** *adv* —**radiochemist** *n*

radio compass *n* a navigation device that uses incoming radio signals from radio beacons to determine a ship's or aircraft's position

radio-controlled *adj* describes a device whose operation or movement is controlled from a distance using a transmitter, often hand-held, that sends radio signals to the device

radioelement /ráydi ō éllimәnt/ *n* a chemical element that is radioactive

radio frequency *n* **1** any of the frequencies of electromagnetic radiation in the range between 10 Khz and 300 MHz, including those used for radio and television transmission **2** a frequency on which a radio station broadcasts its programmes

radio galaxy *n* a galaxy that is a strong source of radio-frequency waves

radiogenic /ráydi ō jénnik/ *adj* **1** describes a substance created as a result of the spontaneous decaying of the unstable atoms of another substance ○ *a radiogenic isotope* **2** emitted as a result of radioactive decay ○ *radiogenic heat*

radiogram /ráydi ō gram/ *n* **1** a telegram sent by radio **2** MED = **radiograph** *n.* **3** a radio and a record player combined in a single unit (*dated*)

radiograph /ráydi ō graaf, -graf/ *n* an image produced on film or another sensitive surface by radiation, e.g. X-rays or gamma rays, passing through an object ■ *vt* to make a radiograph of something, especially a part of the body —**radiographer** /ráydi óggrәfәr/ *n* —**radiographic** /ráydi ō gráffik/ *adj* —**radiographically** *adv* —**radiography** /ráydi óggrәfi/ *n*

radioimmunoassay /ráydi ō ímmyŏonō ássay/ *n* the technique of measuring the levels of antibodies in the blood by introducing into the bloodstream a substance that has a radioactive tracer attached to it —**radioimmunoassayable** /ráydi ō ímmyәnō ássay әb'l/ *adj*

radioiodine /ráydi ō ī ә deen/ *n* a radioactive form of iodine, often used in medicine as a tracer

radioisotope /ráydi ō íssәtōp/ *n* a particular form of a chemical element (**isotope**) that is radioactive —**radioisotopic** /ráydi ō íssә tóppik/ *adj*

radiolabel /ráydi ō láyb'l/ *n* a radioactive substance attached to another substance as a means of tracing the location or tracking the movement of that substance ■ *vt* (**-labels, -labelling, -labelled**) to attach a radiolabel to a substance —**radiolabelled** *adj* —**radiolabelling** *n*

radiolarian /ráydi ō láiri әn/ *n* a single-celled marine organism with a round silica-containing shell that has the organs of movement radiating around it [Late 19C. < modern Latin *Radiolaria* < *radiolus* 'little staff, stick' < *radius* 'staff, spoke, ray'.]

radiolocation /ráydi ō lō káysh'n/ *n* the use of radar to detect distant objects

radiology /ráydi óllәji/ *n* **1** a branch of medicine dealing with the use of X-rays and radioactive substances, such as radium, in the diagnosis and treatment of diseases **2** the science of radiation and radioactive substances and their applications, such as in structural analysis — **radiologic** /ráydi ә lójjik/ *adj* —**radiological** /-lójjik'l/ *adj* —**radiologically** /-lójjikli/ *adv* —**radiologist** /ráydi óllәjist/ *n*

radiolucent /ráydi ō lŏoss'nt/ *adj* interfering very little or not at all with the passage of X-rays and other forms of electromagnetic radiation —**radiolucency** /ráydi ō lŏoss'nsi/ *n*

radiolysis /ráydi óllississ/ *n* the breakdown of something into its chemical components by means of X-rays or other radiation —**radiolytic** /ráydi ō líttik/ *adj*

radiometer /ráydi ómmitәr/ *n* a device used to detect and measure radiant energy, especially an instrument used to demonstrate the conversion of such energy into mechanical work —**radiometric** /ráydi ә méttrik/ *adj* — **radiometrically** /-méttrikli/ *adv* —**radiometry** /ráydi ómmitri/ *n*

radiometric dating *n* any method of determining the age of objects or material using the decay rates of radioactive components, such as potassium-argon

radiomimetic /rádi әmi méttik/ *adj* exerting effects similar to those of ionizing radiation ○ *the radiomimetic effects of certain chemicals, such as urethane*

radionuclide /ráydi ә nyŏoklīd/ *n* a radioactive nuclide

radiopaque /ráydi ō páyk/ *adj* blocking the passage of X-rays and other forms of electromagnetic radiation — **radiopacity** /-ō pássәti/ *n*

radiopharmaceutical /ráydi ō faarmә syŏotik'l/ *n* a radioactive drug or substance. Use: diagnosis and treatment of disease. —**radiopharmaceutical** *adj*

radiophotograph /ráydi ō fōtә graaf, -graf/, **radiophoto** *n* a photograph or another image that is sent from one location to another by means of radio waves

radioprotective /ráydi ō prә téktiv/ *adj* protecting or helping to protect against the harmful effects of X-rays and other radiation —**radioprotection** /ráydi ō prә téksh'n/ *n*

radioscopy /ráydi óskәpi/ *n* the use of X-rays or some other form of electromagnetic radiation to study the internal structure of something —**radioscopic** /ráydi ә skóppik/ *adj* —**radioscopical** /-skóppik'l/ *adj*

radiosensitive /ráydi ō sénsitiv/ sensitive to the biological effects of radiant energy such as X-rays — **radiosensitivity** /ráydi ō sénssә tívvәti/ *n*

radiosonde /ráydi ō sond/ *n* an instrument carried aloft by a balloon and used to measure and transmit meteorological data by radio

radio source *n* an astronomical object naturally producing radio emissions

radio spectrum *n* the range of radio frequencies used for radio, television, and other electromagnetic communications, between 10 Khz and 300 Mhz

radiostrontium /ráydi ō strónti әm, -shi әm/ *n* an isotope of strontium that is present in radioactive fallout and collects in bone

radiotelephone /ráydi ō téllә fōn/ *n* a telephone that transmits sound signals by radio waves rather than through wires —**radiotelephony** /ráydi ō tә léffәni/ *n*

radio telescope *n* an astronomical instrument used to detect and analyse radio waves from astronomical objects

radioteletype /ráydi ō téllitīp/ *n* **1** a teleprinter that transmits and receives by radio rather than along a cable **2** a receiving and transmitting system that uses radioteletypes

radiotherapy /ráydi ō thérrәpi/ *n* the treatment of disease using radiation X-rays or beta rays directed at the body from an external source or emitted by radioactive materials placed within the body —**radiotherapeutic** /ráydi ō therә pyŏotik/ *adj* —**radiotherapist** /ráydi ō thérrәpist/ *n*

radiothorium /ráydi ō tháwri әm/ *n* a radioactive isotope of the element thorium, with a mass number of 228

radiotoxic /ráydi ō tóksik/ *adj* relating to the toxic effects of radiation or radioactive substances

radiotracer /ráydi ō tráyssәr/ *n* a radioactive substance introduced into the body as a tracer, e.g. to observe the steps in a chemical or biochemical process or locate diseased cells or tissue

radio wave *n* an electromagnetic wave whose frequency falls within the radio spectrum

radish /ráddish/ *n* **1** a crisp pungent round or bloated root, with a red or white skin, eaten raw **2** a plant of the mustard family that produces radishes. Native to: Europe, Asia. *Raphanus sativus.* [Pre-12C. < Latin *radic-*, stem of *radix* (see RADIX).]

radium /ráydi әm/ *n* (*symbol* **Ra**) a white highly radioactive metallic element. Source: pitchblende, carnotite. Use: luminous coatings, treatment of cancer. [Late 19C. < Latin *radius* (see RADIUS), from the rays emitted by radium, which penetrate certain opaque materials.]

radium therapy *n* the medical use of radium to treat cancer and other diseases with radiation

radius /ráydi әss/ (*plural* **-i** /-di ī/ *or* **-uses**) *n* **1** LINE FROM CENTRE (*symbol* **r**) a straight line extending from the centre of a circle to its edge or from the centre of a sphere to its surface **2** LENGTH OF RADIUS (*symbol* **r**) the length of a radius **3** CIRCULAR AREA an area enclosed by a circle that has a radius of a specified length ○ *all the houses within a radius of 2 miles of the explosion* **4** RANGE OF EFFECTIVENESS OR INFLUENCE the area or range within which somebody or something can act, work, or exert influence effectively ○ *beyond the radius of the UN's influence* **5** BONE IN ARM OR FORELIMB the shorter and thicker of the two bones in the human forearm, the one on the thumb side, or the equivalent bone in the lower forelimbs of animals **6** RADIATING PART a radiating line, part, or structure [Late 16C. < Latin, 'staff, spoke, ray, beam of light'.]

radius of action *n* **1** a broadly circular area in which a military unit can operate or bring force to bear on an enemy **2** the distance a vehicle, ship, or aircraft can go out to and return safely to base without refuelling

radius of curvature *n* the radius of the circle whose curvature matches that of a curve at a particular point

radius vector *n* **1** a line connecting a fixed point or origin and a variable point, or the length of such a line **2** a line connecting the centre of an astronomical object and the centre of another in orbit around it

radix /ráydiks/ (*plural* **radices** /ráydi seez/ *or* **radixes**) *n* **1** the base of a number system or system of logarithms **2** a root part or point where a plant or animal part begins [Late 16C. < Latin, 'root, radish, foundation' < Indo-European.]

radome /ráy dōm/ *n* a dome-shaped protective enclosure for a radar antenna, made from materials that do not interfere with the transmission and reception of radio waves [Mid-20C. Blend of RADAR + DOME.]

radon /ráy don/ *n* (*symbol* **Rn**) a heavy gaseous radioactive element. Source: radioactive decay of radium, in small quantities in rock and soil. Use: radiotherapy. [Early 20C. < RADIUM + -ON.]

radula /ráddyŏolә/ (*plural* **-lae** /-lee/) *n* a band of tissue in the mouth of some molluscs (**gastropods**) containing rows of small teeth, used in scraping off particles of food and bringing them into the mouth [Mid-18C. < Latin, 'scraper' < *radere* 'scrape'.] —**radular** *adj*

radwaste /rád wayst/ *n* radioactive waste (*informal*) [Late 20C. Contraction of *radioactive waste*.]

Raeburn /ráybәrn/, **Sir Henry** (1756–1823) Scottish painter

RAF *abbr* Royal Air Force

Rafferty /ráffәrti/, **Chips** (1909–71) Australian actor. Born **John William Pilbean Goffage**

raffia /ráffi ә/, **raphia** *n* **1** fibre in the form of flexible straw-coloured ribbons. Source: leaves of the raffia palm. Use: mats, baskets. **2** TREES = **raffia palm** [Late 19C. < Malagasy *rafia*.]

raffia palm *n* a palm tree with large leaves that yield a strong fibre. Native to: Madagascar. *Raphia ruffia.*

raffinate /ráffi nayt/ *n* the remaining or refined part of a liquid mixture, left after other substances dissolved in it have been extracted [Early 20C. < French *raffinat* < *raffiner* 'refine'.]

raffinose /ráffi nōz, -nōss/ *n* $C_{18}H_{32}O_{16}$ a white crystalline slightly sweet sugar. Source: cottonseed meal, sugar beet, and molasses. [Late 19C. < French *raffiner* 'refine'.]

raffish /ráffish/ *adj* **1** displaying a charming, free-spirited disregard for the conventions of society or for approved behaviour ○ *a raffish politician whose engaging antics never alienated the voters* **2** displaying an exaggerated or obtrusive showiness ○ *a raffish hotel* [Early 19C. < obsolete *raff* 'common people'.] —**raffishly** *adv* —**raffishness** *n*

raffle[1] /ráff'l/ *n* an event in which numbered tickets are sold, some of which are drawn at random to win prizes ○ *I won this vase in a raffle.* ■ *vt* (**-fles, -fling, -fled**) to offer or give away something as a prize in a raffle [14C. < Old French, 'act of plundering'.] —**raffler** *n*

raffle[2] /ráff'l/ *n* **1** unwanted items or debris **2** tangled ropes or other bits and pieces on a ship [Late 18C. < ?]

Raffles /ráff'lz/, **Sir Stamford** (1781–1826) British colonial administrator

rafflesia /ra fleézi ə/ *n* a leafless tropical plant that is a parasite of other plants. Flowers: large, foul-smelling, pollinated by carrion flies. Native to: Asia. Genus: *Rafflesia.* [Early 19C. < modern Latin, after Sir Stamford RAFFLES.]

raft[1] /raaft/ *n* **1 FLAT BOAT** a flat floating structure made of wooden planks, logs, barrels, or similar materials, used as a boat or anchored in the water as a dock or diving platform **2 INFLATABLE BOAT OR MAT** an inflatable flat-bottomed rubber or plastic boat used for drifting along on a river, or an inflatable rectangular mat used for surfing or lounging in the water **3** *US* **COLLECTION OF FLOATING OBJECTS** a group of animals, especially wildfowl, or a mass of things floating or travelling together on water ○ *a raft of ducks* **4 BASE SLAB FOR BUILDING** a thick concrete slab laid down as a foundation for a building that is being constructed on soft ground ■ *v* **1** *vt* **MOVE SOMETHING BY RAFT** to transport something by raft **2** *vi* **SAIL ON A RAFT** to travel on a raft **3** *vt* **FORM A RAFT** to form something into a raft, or make something gather together into a raft ○ *The lumberjacks rafted the logs together before sending them downstream.* [13C. < Old Norse *raptr* 'log, beam'.]

raft[2] /raaft/ *n* a very large number or amount of something (*informal*) ○ *a whole raft of proposals* [Mid-19C. Alteration of *raff*, probably after RAFT[1].]

rafter[1] /raáftər/ *n* any sloping supporting timber, beam, or board that runs from the ridge beam of a roof to its edge [Old English *ræfter* < Germanic] —**raftered** *adj* —**raftering** *n*

rafter[2] /raáftər/ *n* **1** a traveller on a raft **2** a lumberjack who ties logs into a raft to transport them downstream

rafting /raáfting/ *n* the outdoor leisure pursuit of floating on a lake or sailing on a river in a raft

rafty /raáfti/ (**-ier, -iest**) *adj N England* rancid in taste or smell (*informal*)

rag[1] /rag/ *n* **1 SMALL PIECE OF CLOTH** a small piece or scrap of usually old or unwanted cloth used for cleaning, polishing, or applying liquid substances **2 SMALL TATTERED PIECE** a small, irregular, or tattered scrap or piece of something **3 PIECE OF CLOTHING** an item of clothing, thought of as being worn or tattered and not really fit to wear (*informal; often used ironically*) **4 INFERIOR NEWSPAPER** a newspaper with low journalistic standards, or any newspaper regarded with contempt (*informal*) **5 CLOTH FOR PAPERMAKING** cloth or cloth fibres that are used in making paper ■ **rags** *npl* **WORN-OUT CLOTHES** clothes that are tattered, frayed, or torn [14C. Probably < Old Norse *rogg* 'shaggy tuft'.] ◇ **be (like) a red rag to a bull (to somebody)** to be certain to make somebody angry ◇ **go from rags to riches** to start off in poverty and then become very wealthy ◇ **in rags** in a worn-out, tattered, and torn condition ◇ **lose your rag** to lose your temper (*informal*)

rag[2] /rag/ *v* (**rags, ragging, ragged**) **1** *vti* **TEASE OR TAUNT** to subject somebody to persistent teasing or taunting (*dated*) ○ *His friends ragged him about his new haircut.* **2** *vt* **PLAY PRANKS ON** to play pranks or jokes on somebody, often to the point of tormenting him or her (*dated*) **3** *vi* **BEHAVE BOISTEROUSLY** to take part in good-humoured, boisterous activity (*dated*) **4** *vt* **SCOLD** to scold somebody persistently or vehemently ■ *n* **1 CHARITY FUND-RAISING AT UNIVERSITY** an activity or a set of activities conducted by university students in order to raise money for charity while having a good time **2 PRACTICAL JOKE** a prank or practical joke, especially by a student on a fellow student (*dated*) [Mid-18C. < ?] —**ragging** *n*

rag[3] /rag/ *n* jazz in which a syncopated rhythm in the melody is accompanied by a steady beat, or a piece of music in this style ■ *vt* (**rags, ragging, ragged**) to compose or perform ragtime music [Late 19C. < ?]

rag[4] /rag/ *n* **1** = **ragstone 2** a roofing slate that has a rough surface on one side [13C. < ?]

rag[5] *n* = **raga**

raga /raágə/, **rag** /raag/, **raag** *n* any of the scales, melodies, or rhythmic patterns that form the basis of the classical music of the Indian subcontinent [Late 18C. < Sanskrit *rāga* 'colour, musical colour, harmony'.]

ragamuffin /rággə mufin/ *n* **1** a child dressed in worn or tattered clothes, often one allowed to roam the streets (*dated*) **2** *Carib* = **ragga** [14C. < ?]

rag-and-bone man *n* somebody who travels the streets buying and selling unwanted clothes and household items, and other discarded things

ragbag /rág bag/ *n* **1** a collection of miscellaneous things (*informal*) **2** a bag in which unwanted clothes and bits of cloth are kept for use as rags

rag doll *n* a floppy stuffed cloth doll

rage /rayj/ *n* **1 EXTREME ANGER** sudden and extreme anger, or an outburst of strong anger **2 FORCE OR INTENSITY** extreme or unrelenting intensity **3 OBJECT OF FAD** something that is the object of a short-lived fascination, fashion, or enthusiasm shared by many people ○ *Those toys are all the rage for kids at the moment.* **4** *ANZ* **PARTY** a party or celebration ○ *The kids are planning a bit of a rage this weekend to celebrate the end of term.* **5 STRONG PASSION OR ENTHUSIASM** a strong and sometimes overpowering desire or enthusiasm ■ *vi* (**rages, raging, raged**) **1 ACT WITH OR FEEL RAGE** to speak or do something with sudden, extreme anger, or feel such strong anger ○ *She was raging against the injustice of the situation.* **2 OCCUR WITH VIOLENCE** to occur, continue, move, or spread with great force and violence ○ *The battle raged for three days.* **3** *ANZ* **HOLD PARTY** to have a party to celebrate something or to socialize ○ *We were out raging all weekend.* [13C. Via Old French < Vulgar Latin *rabia*, alteration of Latin *rabies* (see RABIES).]

SYNONYMS See ***anger***.

ragee *n* PLANTS, FOOD = **ragi**

ragfish /rágfish/ (*plural* **-fishes** *or* **-fish**) *n* a scaleless deep-sea fish with a cartilaginous skeleton so flexible that it flops when taken out of the water. *Icosteus aenigmaticus.*

ragga /rággə/ *n* a style of reggae characterized by long rap monologues and repetitive beats

ragged /rággid/ *adj* **1 TATTERED** frayed or torn into irregular shapes or pieces, especially along the edge **2 WEARING RAGS** dressed in torn, tattered, or frayed clothes **3 WITH UNEVEN EDGE OR SURFACE** with a surface, edge, or outline that is rough, uneven, or jagged **4 UNKEMPT** rough and irregular in appearance and suggesting neglect and a lack of grooming ○ *a ragged beard* **5 NOT FIRM OR REGULAR** done in an uncoordinated, hesitant, or irregular way, especially by a group who do not manage to do something all together or in unison **6 OF VARYING QUALITY** of unequal quality, some parts being less good than others ○ *He gave a rather ragged performance as Othello.* **7 EXHAUSTED** extremely tired or anxious ○ *speaking with a ragged voice* [13C. < RAG[1].] —**raggedly** *adv* —**raggedness** *n*

ragged robin *n* a perennial plant of the pink family. Flowers: pink or white, with ragged petals. *Lychnis floscuculi.*

raggedy /rággidi/ *adj* (*informal*) **1 TATTERED** having been torn and worn excessively **2 BADLY DRESSED** wearing worn-out torn clothes **3 ROUGH OR UNEVEN** having rough untidy ends or edges

raggee *n* PLANTS, FOOD = **ragi**

raggle-taggle /rágg'l tágg'l/ *adj* consisting of a mixture of strange or very different things, often with an element of untidiness or scruffiness ○ *a raggle-taggle collection of animals in a small zoo* [Early 20C. Alteration of RAGTAG.]

ragi /rággi/, **ragee, raggee** *n* **1** a cereal grass cultivated for its edible grain in S Asia and parts of Africa. *Eleusine coracana.* **2** the grain of ragi used as food [Late 18C. < Hindi *rāgī*.]

raging /ráyjing/ *adj* **1 VERY ANGRY** out of control or angry **2 VERY STRONG** done or happening with great force or intensity **3 VERY SEVERE OR PAINFUL** very severe and causing great pain or distress ○ *a raging toothache* **4 VERY GOOD** very good or great ○ *The play was a raging success.*

raglan /rágglən/ *adj* **1 EXTENDING TO COLLAR** describes a sleeve extending to the collar of a garment instead of ending at the shoulder, attached with slanting seams running from under the arm to the neck **2 HAVING RAGLAN SLEEVES** made with raglan sleeves ■ *n* **GARMENT WITH RAGLAN SLEEVES** an overcoat, jumper, or other garment that has raglan sleeves [Mid-19C. After Field Marshal Lord *Raglan* (1788–1855), who favoured overcoats in this style.]

ragman /rág man/ (*plural* **-men** /-men/) *n* a dealer in old cloth and clothes

ragnail /rág nayl/ *n Scotland* a hangnail

Ragnarök /raágnə rok/ *n* in Norse mythology, the final destruction of the gods in a great battle against the forces of evil, after which a new world will arise [Mid-18C. < Old Norse *ragnarök* 'fate of the gods' < *regin* 'gods' + *rok* 'fate'.]

ragout /ra goó/ *n* a rich, slow-cooked stew of meat and vegetables [Mid-17C. < French, < *ragoûter* 'renew the appetite' < *goût* 'taste' < Latin *gustus*.]

ragpicker /rág pikər/ *n* a gatherer and seller of old clothes and other discarded items

rag-rolling *n* the decorative technique of using a crumpled cloth to dab paint that has been applied to a wall or other surface, in order to produce an irregularly patterned effect

rag rug *n* a rug made by knotting or hooking short strips of waste fabric through an openweave base to form a shaggy pile

ragstone /rág stōn/ *n* a hard sandstone or limestone that tends to break up into slabs and is used as a building material

ragtag /rág tag/ *adj* **1** made up of a wide-ranging mix of people or things, often ones that are of questionable quality ○ *a ragtag team made up of friends and acquaintances* **2** untidy, unkempt, or ragged in appearance [Late 19C. < RAG[1].]

ragtag and bobtail *n* people who are members of the lowest social classes, especially when considered as dissatisfied with their lives and likely to be disorderly or rebellious (*dated insult*)

ragtime /rág tīm/ *n* a style of US popular music of the late 19th and early 20th centuries characterized by distinctive syncopated right-hand rhythms against a regularly accented left-hand beat

ragtop /rág top/ *n* CARS = **soft top** (*slang*)

rag trade *n* the clothing industry and the various professions involved in the design, manufacture, and sale of clothing (*informal*)

ragweed /rág weed/ *n* **1** a weedy plant with small green flower heads producing large amounts of pollen that causes hay fever in many people. Native to: North America. Genus: *Ambrosia.* **2** PLANTS = **ragwort** [< the raggedness of the leaves]

ragworm /rág wurm/ *n* a marine worm often used as fishing bait. Genus: *Nereis.* [< the ragged appearance of its appendages]

ragwort /rág wurt/ *n* a plant that has clusters of small yellow flowers with radiating petals like those of daisies. Genus: *Senecio.* [< the raggedness of the leaves]

rah /raa/ *interj* used to express approval or encouragement (*informal*) [Mid-19C. Shortening of HURRAH.]

Rahman /rəmaán/, **Sheikh Mujibur** (1920–75) Bangladeshi statesman

Rahman, Ziaur (1935–81) Bangladeshi statesman

rah-rah /raá raa/ *adj US* spiritedly and often unthinkingly enthusiastic (*slang*) ○ *the rah-rah attitude of the project's supporters*

rah-rah skirt /raá raa skurt/, **ra-ra skirt** *n* a short full skirt usually layered or with rows of frills, popular in the 1980s and inspired by the costumes of US cheerleaders [Because originally worn by cheerleaders]

rai /rī/ *n* a form of music popular in Algeria that combines elements of Algerian traditional music with Western rock [Late 20C. < Arabic.]

raid /rayd/ *n* **1 SUDDEN ATTACK** a sudden attack made by soldiers, aircraft, police, bandits, or any other force in an attempt to seize or destroy something **2 ATTEMPT TO BUY CONTROL** the buying of a large number of shares in a company in an attempt to gain control of it ○ *The company beat off the raid but took on debt to buy its own shares.* **3 ILLEGAL ATTEMPT TO LOWER STOCK PRICE** the illegal coordinated selling of shares in a company's stock by a group of speculators in an attempt to make the stock price fall **4** *US* **LURING PEOPLE AWAY** in the business world, an attempt by an organization to lure away a competitor's employees, members, or clients ○ *a raid by one advertising agency on another's clients* ■ *v* **1** *vti* **MAKE SURPRISE ATTACK** to make or participate in a raid on somebody or something **2** *vt* **STEAL SOMETHING FROM SOMEWHERE**

to take something secretly or stealthily because it is illegal or forbidden ○ *The bank's funds had been raided by its former president.* **3** *vt US* **LURE SOMEBODY AWAY** to lure somebody away from another organization, usually from a competitor ○ *The new league began to raid players from its rival.* [15C. Scots dialect form of Old English *rād* 'expedition, riding, road'.] —**raider** *n*

rail[1] /rayl/ *n* **1 LONG PIECE OF WOOD OR METAL** a long horizontal or sloping piece of wood, metal, or other material that is used as a barrier, support, or place to hang things **2 FENCE OR RAILING** a structure made of a rail or rails and their supports, e.g. a fence or railing (*often plural*) **3 STEEL BAR OF RAILWAY TRACK** a narrow steel bar, or a series of connected bars laid in two parallel lines, supporting and guiding the wheels of railway engines and carriages or anything similar. ◊ **third rail** **4 RAILWAY** the railway as a means or form of transport ○ *rail travel* ■ *vt* **PUT RAIL ON OR ROUND** to put a rail or railing on or around something to provide a guard, barrier, or support ○ *They ought to rail off the children's play area.* [13C. Via Old French *reille* 'bar' < Latin *regula* 'straight stick, rod'.] —**railless** *adj* ◇ **go off the rails 1** to begin to behave in an unacceptable, irresponsible, or illegal way **2** to begin to go wrong and lose direction

rail[2] /rayl/ *vi* to denounce, protest against, or attack somebody or something in bitter or harsh language ○ *Some people rail against the injustice of the system.* [15C. Via French *railler* 'mock, tease' < Old Provençal *ralhar* 'chat, joke' < late Latin *ragere* 'neigh, roar'.] —**railer** *n*

rail[3] /rayl/ (*plural* **rails** *or* **rail**) *n* a small or medium-sized wading bird with a short tail, short wings, and long toes. Family: Rallidae. [15C. Via Old French *raale* < Latin *ras-*, past participle of *radere* 'to scrape'.]

railcar /ráyl kaar/ *n* **1** a self-propelled, usually diesel-powered passenger railway coach for use on branch lines **2** *US* a railway carriage

railcard /ráyl kaard/ *n* an identity card allowing the holder, e.g. a student, senior citizen, or family group, to buy rail tickets at reduced rates, usually restricted to off-peak travel times

railhead /ráyl hed/ *n* **1** the farthest point to which the track of a railway line runs **2** a place where supplies, often military materials, are unloaded from railway wagons for distribution to other points

railing /ráyling/ *n* **1 STRUCTURE WITH RAILS AND POSTS** a structure consisting of one or more rails and their supports, used to provide a barrier or support in walking or climbing, or the upper rail of such a structure **2 METAL FENCE** an often ornamental fence of vertical metal poles held in position by one or more narrow horizontal bars, providing a barrier round something such as a park (*usually plural*) ○ *ivy growing up the railings* **3 RAILS** rails for making a railing

raillery /ráyləri/ (*plural* **-ies**) *n* **1** humorous, playful, or friendly ridiculing of somebody or something **2** a remark that ridicules somebody or something jokingly and with good humour

raillink /ráyl lingk/ *n* a short connecting railway line, usually between a city centre and an airport

railroad /ráyl rōd/ *n US* **1** = **railway** *n.* 1 **2** = **railway** *n.* 2 ■ *v* **1** *vt* **FORCE SOMETHING THROUGH QUICKLY WITHOUT DISCUSSION** to push something through a legislature, committee, or other decision-making body quickly so that there is not enough time for objections to be considered ○ *The changes to the proposal were railroaded through the subcommittee.* **2** *vt* **FORCE SOMEBODY TO ACT HASTILY** to force a person or group to make a decision or take action quickly, without time for consideration or discussion (*informal*) **3** *vt* **CONVICT SOMEBODY TOO QUICKLY** to convict somebody on the basis of flimsy or false evidence (*informal*) **4** *vt US* **TRANSPORT SOMETHING BY RAIL** to transport or send something by rail **5** *vi US* **WORK ON RAILWAY** to work on a railway ○ *She used to railroad for the Southern Pacific.*

railslide /ráyl slīd/ (**-slides, -sliding, -slid**) *vi* in skateboarding, to slide along the top or upper edge of a ramp or obstacle using the bottom of the board rather than the wheels

railtour /ráyl toor/ *n* an excursion on a chartered or special train intended for railway enthusiasts

Railtrack /ráyl trak/ *n* a statutory company that owns and operates the track, stations, signals, and other plant in the UK railway system, but does not run trains

railway /ráyl way/ *n* **1** a track consisting of steel rails usually fastened to wood or concrete sleepers, designed to carry the engine and carriages of a train or anything similar. US term **railroad** *n.* 1 **2** a network of railway lines, together with the trains, buildings, equipment, and staff needed to operate a rail transport system, or the organization or company that owns or runs this. US term **railroad** *n.* 2 —**railwayman** *n*

raiment /ráymənt/ *n* clothing (*archaic or literary*) [14C. Shortening of *arrayment.*]

rain /rayn/ *n* **1 WATER FALLING FROM CLOUDS** water condensed from vapour in the atmosphere and falling in drops from clouds **2 PERIOD OF WET WEATHER** any storm, shower, or other quantity of water falling from the sky **3 RAINY WEATHER** weather marked by heavy or persistent rainfall **4 GREAT NUMBER OR FLOW** a great number of small individual things coming in a steady flow or anything else flowing or falling like rain ○ *A rain of dust fell from the crumbling ceiling.* ■ **rains** *npl* **RAINY SEASON** in some countries, a season of the year when a lot of rain falls ■ *v* **1** *vi* **DROP RAIN** to fall from the sky or release water in the form of rain ○ *It's raining again.* **2** *vti* **COME IN A GREAT NUMBER** to come or fall, or drop or deliver something, in the form of a great number of units arriving separately but in very quick succession, or in a continuous stream ○ *They rained blows on the poor man's head.* ○ *Missiles rained down on us from the defenders on the battlements.* **3** *vt* **GIVE SOMETHING GENEROUSLY** to give somebody something in large quantities, continuously, and over a considerable period of time ○ *Generous to a fault, they positively rained gifts on all their friends.* [Old English *regn, rēn* < Germanic] —**rainless** *adj* ◇ **(as) right as rain** perfectly all right (*informal*) ◇ **(come) rain or shine** whatever the weather or the circumstances ○ *The picnic will be held, rain or shine.*

SPELLCHECK Do not confuse ***rain*** with ***reign*** or ***rein***, which sound similar. Beware: your spellchecker will not catch this error.

rain off *vt* to cause an event such as a sporting fixture to be cancelled or postponed because of rain (*usually passive*) US term **rain out**

rain out *vt US* = **rain off**

rainbird /ráyn burd/ *n* a bird, e.g. the green woodpecker or certain members of the cuckoo family, thought to call before rainstorms

rainbow /ráynbō/ *n* **1 MULTICOLOURED ARC IN SKY** an arc of light separated into bands of colour that appears when the sun's rays are refracted and reflected by drops of mist or rain. The colours of the rainbow are conventionally said to be red, orange, yellow, green, blue, indigo, and violet. **2 ARC OF BANDS OF COLOUR** multicoloured arc similar to a rainbow **3 BRIGHT MULTICOLOURED SIGHT** an arrangement, display, or sight containing many bright colours or bright multicoloured objects ○ *Her makeup box was a rainbow of colours.* **4 FALSE HOPE** a goal, hope, or ideal that is unlikely to be achieved or realized **5 VARIED ASSORTMENT** a wide range or varied assortment of things, usually coexisting without clashing ■ *adj* **1 WITH VARIED COLOURS** having the colours of the rainbow or colours as varied as those of a rainbow **2 WITH MANY DIFFERENT THINGS** comprising a wide variety of types or elements, especially made up of people of different ethnic groups or from a variety of minority groups ○ *a rainbow coalition*

LITERARY LINK ***The Rainbow***, a novel (1915) by D. H. Lawrence. Set in the English Midlands between 1840 and 1905, it describes the impact of contemporary social developments on the lifestyles and attitudes of succeeding generations of a provincial family, the Brangwens. The latter part of the book focuses on Ursula, the family's first independent woman, whose story is continued in a subsequent novel *Women in Love* (1920).

rainbow lorikeet *n* a colourful bird of the parrot family with a blue head, orange breast, and green wings and back. Native to: Australia. *Trichoglossus haematodus.*

rainbow runner *n* a large colourful tropical fish. Native to: Indian and Pacific Oceans. *Elagatis bipinnulatus.*

rainbow trout *n* **1** a freshwater game fish with a reddish or pinkish band along either side of its body and numerous black spots. Native to: N America. *Salmo gairdneri.* **2** the flesh of a rainbow trout used as food

rain check *n US* **1** a ticket or ticket stub entitling somebody to attend an event cancelled because of rain at a later rescheduled time **2** a promise or voucher guaranteeing that an offer that cannot be fulfilled or accepted at present will be fulfilled or accepted at a later time ◇ **take a rain check (on something)** *US* to delay doing something until a later date or time (*informal*)

raincoat /ráyn kōt/ *n* a coat designed to keep the wearer dry when worn in the rain, with a water-resistant or waterproof surface or coating

rain date *n US* a date that an event will be rescheduled to if rainy weather forces cancellation on the intended date

rainfall /ráyn fawl/ *n* **1** the amount of rain that falls in a particular location over a particular period of time ○ *the annual rainfall in a city* **2** a rain shower or rainstorm

rainforest /ráyn forist/ *n* a thick evergreen tropical forest found in areas of heavy rainfall and containing trees with broad leaves that form a continuous canopy

rain gauge *n* a device used to measure the amount of rain that falls in a particular location

rain hat *n* a hat that provides protection from rain for the wearer's head

Rainier III /ráyni ay/ (*b.* 1923) prince of Monaco (1949–)

rainmaker /ráyn maykər/ *n* **1** a person who causes, or is believed to cause, rain to fall **2** *US* an achiever of outstanding results in business or politics (*informal*) —**rainmaking** *n*

rainout /ráyn owt/ *n* **1** atmospheric pollution such as radioactive fallout that is carried down to earth in rain **2** *US* an event that is cancelled or postponed because of rainy weather, or the cancellation or postponement of an event because of rain ○ *There was a rainout at the ballpark today.*

rainproof /ráyn proof/ *adj* designed or treated to prevent rain from soaking into it or passing through it ■ *vt* to treat something such as an item of clothing so that it becomes rainproof

rain shadow *n* an area on the side of a mountain barrier that is sheltered from prevailing winds and rain-bearing clouds, resulting in relatively dry conditions

rainstorm /ráyn stawrm/ *n* a storm with heavy or steady rain

rainwash /ráyn wosh/ *n* rock and soil washed away and deposited elsewhere by rainwater, or the process of erosion by rainwater

rainwater /ráyn wawtər/ *n* water that has fallen as rain, which usually has relatively small amounts of minerals dissolved in it

rainwear /ráyn wair/ *n* clothing, mainly outerwear, that is waterproof and is designed to keep the wearer dry in rainy weather

rainy /ráyni/ (**-ier, -iest**) *adj* characterized by or bringing rain, especially long or frequently recurring periods of rainfall —**rainily** *adv* —**raininess** *n*

rainy day *n* a possible time of need in the future

Rais /rayss/, **Gilles de, Baron** (1404–40) French politician

raise /rayz/ *v* (**raises, raising, raised**) **1** *vt* **MOVE SOMETHING HIGHER** to cause somebody or something to move upwards or to a higher level or position ○ *She was too weak to raise her head from the pillow.* **2** *vt* **STAND OR SIT UP** to move yourself or somebody else to a standing or sitting position ○ *I raised myself with difficulty and staggered to the door.* **3** *vt* **DIRECT SOMETHING AT HIGHER ANGLE** to direct something upwards, or make something point at a higher angle ○ *She answered without raising her eyes from the book.* **4** *vt* **PUT SOMETHING UP** to set up, erect, or build something **5** *vt* **STRETCH SOMETHING OUT** to make something such as a crest or frill stretch out and become more visible **6** *vt* **CAUSE SOMETHING TO SWELL UP** to make something rise up or swell up, e.g. on somebody's skin **7** *vt* **MAKE SOMETHING LARGER OR GREATER** to increase something in size, amount, value, or scope ○ *They've raised the ticket prices yet again.* **8** *vt* **INTENSIFY** to increase something in degree, strength, or pitch ○ *raised voices* **9** *vt* **IMPROVE** to make something better in some way ○ *Their visit raised his spirits.* ○ *You can't raise educational standards unless you train and motivate the teachers better.* **10** *vt* **IMPROVE SOMEBODY'S CONDITION** to improve somebody's situation or condition, or move somebody to a higher rank or status ○ *helping the downtrodden to raise themselves* **11** *vt* **GROW OR BREED** to grow vegetables or breed and care for animals, usually for profit or personal satisfaction **12** *vt* **ACT AS PARENT OR GUARDIAN TO** to look after somebody as or like a parent, while he or she is growing up (*often passive*) ○ *After my parents died, I was raised by my grandfather.* **13** *vt* **OFFER SOMETHING FOR CONSIDERATION** to put something forward for consideration or discussion ○ *I'd like to raise a number of points that I think need* *clarification.* **14** *vt* **COLLECT SOMETHING TOGETHER** to gather something together, collect something, or ask for something and be given it ○ *raising money for the local orphanage* **15** *vt* **CAUSE** to cause something to appear, arise, form, or occur ○ *The strict new rules raised a storm of protest.* **16** *vt* **GIVE SIGN OF FEELING** to produce a response such as a smile or cheer, or cause somebody else to produce one ○ *She obviously felt awful, but still managed to raise a faint smile.* **17** *vt* **START SOMETHING NOISY** to start something that involves a lot of loud noise or boisterous activity ○ *Raise the alarm!* **18** *vt* **ROUSE** to rouse somebody from sleep, or bring a dead person back to life ○ *They were shouting loud enough to raise the dead.* **19** *vt* **CALL SOMETHING UP** to attempt to cause a supernatural being to appear, e.g. by special ceremonies or magic **20** *vt* **PUT SOMEBODY IN AUTHORITY** to place somebody in a position of power or authority (*literary*) **21** *vt* **CONTACT SOMEBODY BY RADIO** to get into contact with somebody by radio ○ *Air traffic control was still trying to raise the missing plane.* **22** *vt* **MULTIPLY NUMBER** to multiply a term or number by itself a specified number of times ○ *2 raised by the power of 4 is 16.* **23** *vti* **INCREASE BET OR BID** in poker and other games, to increase a bet or bet more than another player, often specifying the amount of the increase **24** *vt* **INCREASE PARTNER'S BID** in bridge, to make a higher bid in the suit bid by your partner **25** *vt* **END SIEGE** to end a siege by withdrawing the besieging force or forcing it to withdraw **26** *vt* **END** to bring a ban or restriction imposed on somebody to an end ○ *finally raised the arms embargo* **27** *vt* **SEE LAND APPEAR ON HORIZON** to have approached near enough to land after a sea voyage for it to make its first appearance on the horizon ○ *The ship raised Bermuda two days after leaving New York.* **28** *vt US* **FRAUDULENTLY INCREASE SOMETHING'S VALUE** to increase the face value of something, especially a cheque, in an attempt to defraud somebody ○ *The embezzler was caught raising cheques.* **29** *vt* **MAKE DOUGH RISE** to make dough rise and swell by using yeast or a similar agent **30** *vt* **REPLACE VOWEL BY HIGHER VOWEL** to replace a vowel by one formed with the tongue higher in the mouth **31** *vi US* **RISE** to rise (*nonstandard*) ○ *'Jimmy gazed at her in such consternation that he felt his hair begin to raise!'* (George Randolph Chester, *The Jingo*; 1912) ■ *n* **1** *Aus, Can, US* **PAY INCREASE** a pay increase **2 ACT OF INCREASING** the raising of somebody or something, or the amount by which somebody or something is raised, e.g. in cards [12C. < Old Norse *reisa* < Germanic.] —**raisable** *adj* —**raiser** *n*

raised beach *n* a former beach found above the present shoreline of a sea or lake following a fall in water level or a rise in land level

raised point *n US* **1** = **gros point** *n.* 1 **2** = **gros point** *n.* 2

raised work *n* embroidery stitches that produce a raised surface on the fabric or that are worked over a piece of padding

raisin /ráyz'n/ *n* a sweet grape that has been dried in the sun or by being processed with heat, usually to prevent spoiling and permit long-term storage [14C. Via French, 'grape' < Latin *racemus* 'bunch, cluster'.]

raison d'état /ráy zoN day taá/ (*plural* **raisons d'état** /ráy zoN-/) *n* an overriding concern, usually the interests of the country concerned, that justifies political or diplomatic action that might otherwise be considered reprehensible [< French, 'reason of state']

raison d'être /ráy zoN déttrə/ (*plural* **raisons d'être** /ráy zoN-/) *n* something that gives meaning or purpose to somebody's life, or the justification for something's existence [< French, 'reason for being']

raita /rítə/ *n* an Indian dish served with curries, consisting of yoghurt usually mixed with finely chopped cucumber, mint, or garlic [Mid-20C. < Hindi *rāytā*.]

Raj /raaj/ *n* the British rule of the Indian subcontinent, now the countries of India, Pakistan, and Bangladesh, from 1757 to 1947 [Late 18C. Via Hindi *rāj* < Sanskrit *rājya* 'kingdom, rule'.]

raja *n* POL = **rajah**

Rajab /rə jáb/ *n* in the Islamic calendar, the seventh month of the year, made up of 30 days [Late 18C. < Arabic.]

rajah /raájə/, **raja** *n* a king, prince, or chief in India or among the Malay, Javanese, and other peoples of Southeast Asia [Mid-16C. Via Hindi *rājā* < Sanskrit *rājan* 'king'.]

Rajasthan /raájə staan/, **Rājasthān** state in NW India. Capital: Jaipur. Population: 48,040,000 (1994). Area: 342,239 sq. km/132,139 sq. mi.

Rajasthani /raájə staáni/ *n* **1** an Indic group of languages spoken in NW India and neighbouring parts of Pakistan. Native speakers: 25 million. **2** somebody who comes from Rajasthan [Early 20C. < Hindi, < RAJASTHAN] —**Rajasthani** *adj*

Rajkot /raáj kōt/ city in west-central India. Population: 556,137 (1991).

Rajneesh /raaj néesh/, **Bhaghwan Shree** (1931–90) Indian spiritual teacher. Born **Rajneesh Chandra Mohan**

Rajput /raáj pòot/ *n* a Hindu belonging to a warrior caste, the second-highest caste after the Brahmins [Late 16C. < Hindi *rājpūt* 'king's son' < Sanskrit *rājan* 'king' + *putra* 'son'.]

Rajya Sabha /raájyə súbbə/ *n* the upper house of India's national parliament. ◊ **Lok Sabha** [< Sanskrit, 'state assembly']

Rakaia /rə kí ə/ river in the east-central part of the South Island, New Zealand. Length: 145 km/90 mi.

rake[1] /rayk/ *n* **1 LONG-HANDLED TOOTHED GARDENING TOOL** a tool with a long handle and a head with long teeth, used for gathering leaves or cut grass, or for smoothing or loosening the surface of the soil **2 TOOL RESEMBLING A GARDEN RAKE** any tool that is broadly similar to a garden rake but is used for a different purpose, e.g. digging clams or gathering money at a gambling table **3 CLEARING, GATHERING, OR SMOOTHING** an act of clearing, gathering, or smoothing something with a rake or similar implement **4 SEARCH** a search through something ■ *v* (**rakes, raking, raked**) **1** *vti* **MOVE WITH A RAKE** to gather something together, or remove or clear something using a rake or similar implement ○ *raked up the dead leaves* **2** *vti* **WORK WITH A RAKE** to make something neat, smooth it out, or loosen it using a rake or similar tool **3** *vti* **SEARCH** to search through or examine something thoroughly, or to make a search for something **4** *vt* **USE SOMETHING LIKE A RAKE** to draw or move something through or across something else like a rake ○ *She raked her fingers through her hair.* **5** *vti* **SCRAPE OR SCRATCH** to claw, scrape, or scratch somebody or something with a dragging movement like the action of somebody using a rake **6** *vti* **PASS ACROSS** to pass across the whole length or extent of something in a continuous sweeping movement, or cause something to do this ○ *The spotlight raked around the perimeter fence.* **7** *vti* **SHOOT ALONG THE LENGTH OF** to aim shots from a gun or guns in quick succession over the whole length or extent of something ○ *The ship's cannon raked the land battery.* [Old English *raca, racu*]

rake in *vt* to take in large quantities of something, especially money gained or earned with relatively little effort (*informal*)

rake over *vt* = **rake up** *v.* 1 (*informal*)

rake together *vt* to gather people or things together with difficulty (*informal*)

rake up *vt* (*informal*) **1** to mention or bring up for discussion something unfortunate or undesirable that happened in the past **2** = **rake together**

rake[2] /rayk/ *n* **1 SLANT OR SLOPE** a slant away from an upright or perpendicular position, or an incline upwards from a flat or horizontal position such as that on a ship or a stage **2 ANGLE OF WING OR PROPELLER** the angle that a wing or propeller blade of an aircraft makes with a perpendicular or line of symmetry ■ *vti* (**rakes, raking, raked, raked**) **ANGLE** to design or build something, or be designed or built, with a slant or slope away from the vertical or horizontal ○ *a jet with wings that rake sharply back* [Early 17C. < ?]

rake[3] /rayk/ *n* an unrestrained indulger in pleasures and vices such as drinking and gambling [Mid-17C. Shortening of *rakehell*, by folk etymology < *rakel* 'hasty, rash'.]

rake[4] /rayk/ *n* a distinct break or shallow gully that slants obliquely across a rock face [14C. < Old Norse *rák* 'stripe, streak'.]

rakee *n* = **raki**

rake-off *n* a portion or share of a profit, fee, or something similar, especially as a bribe or other illegal or morally dubious payment (*informal*)

raki /ráki, raa kée/, **rakee** *n* any aniseed-flavoured alcoholic drink from the E Mediterranean, especially a brandy made in Turkey and the Balkans from grapes, plums, or grain [Late 17C. Via Turkish *rāqī* < Arabic *araḳī*.]

rakish[1] /ráykish/ *adj* **1** stylish in a dashing or sporty way ○ *a hat worn at a rakish angle* **2** having a streamlined look that suggests rapid movement through the water ○ *a rakish yacht* [Early 19C. < RAKE[2].] —**rakishly** *adv* —**rakishness** *n*

rakish[2] /ráykish/ *adj* having or showing a strong concern for presenting a stylish self-confident appearance [Early 18C. < RAKE[3].] —**rakishly** *adv* —**rakishness** *adv*

raku /raákoo/ *n* a pottery technique in which pots are raw-glazed at a low temperature then taken red-hot from the kiln and plunged in water or sawdust for reduction or carbonizing [Late 19C. < Japanese, 'ease, enjoyment'.]

rale /raal/, **râle** *n* an intermittent crackling or bubbling sound produced by fluid in the lungs and heard via a stethoscope [Early 19C. < French *râle* < *râler* 'make a rattling sound in the throat'.]

Raleigh /raáli, ráwli/ capital of North Carolina, in the central part of the state. Population: 236,707 (1994).

Raleigh, Sir Walter (1554–1618) English navigator and writer

rall. *abbr* rallentando

rallentando /rállən tándō/ *adv* with a gradual slowing of pace (*musical direction*) [Early 19C. < Italian, present participle of *rallentare* 'slow down'.]

rally[1] /rálli/ *v* (**-lies, -lying, -lied**) **1** *vti* **GATHER TOGETHER FOR** to come together, uniting for a common purpose or in a common cause, or to call on people to come together and unite ○ *The instinct of the party faithful was to rally behind the leader in a crisis.* **2** *vti* **FORM TOGETHER AGAIN** to reorganize, or reorganize forces, after a setback and restore order and morale, especially to stop troops retreating further ○ *The captain rallied his retreating troops and formed a defensive line.* **3** *vti* **REVIVE OR RECOVER** to recover or improve after a setback, crisis, or period of illness, inactivity, or deterioration, or to bring about a recovery or improvement in something ○ *Our spirits rallied once we had our first success.* **4** *vi* **INCREASE IN VALUE** to increase sharply in value or price owing to renewed buying by investors **5** *vi* **BEGIN BUYING STOCKS AGAIN** to be involved in renewed buying of stocks after a period of selling **6** *vi* **EXCHANGE SHOTS** to exchange a series of shots before scoring a point ■ *n* (*plural* **-lies**) **1 GATHERING** a large meeting or gathering of people, usually organized by a movement or political party and intended to inspire and generate enthusiasm among those present **2 RECOVERY OR IMPROVEMENT** a sudden recovery or improvement after a setback, crisis, or period of illness, inactivity, or deterioration **3 REASSEMBLY OF TROOPS** a regrouping of a disorganized military force and the reestablishment of command over it, or the signal calling for this ○ *The retreating hussars made a rally and drove the attackers back.* **4 RENEWED BUYING OF STOCKS** a renewed buying of stocks after a period of selling, leading to a rise in stock prices ○ *a rally in the industrial sector of the stock market* **5 EXCHANGE OF SHOTS** an exchange of several shots between two opponents or sides before a point is scored **6 CAR RACE** a car race that is held on public roads using a route not known in advance by the drivers and having special rules for speed or time [Late 16C. < French *rallier* 'reunite' < *alier* 'join, ally'.] —**rallier** *n*

rally round *vi* to come to the aid of somebody in difficulty or need, offering either practical or moral support

rally[2] /rálli/ (**-lies, -lying, -lied**) *vt* to tease or ridicule somebody in a friendly or good-humoured way ○ *She rallied him about his cooking skills.* [Mid-17C. < French *railler* (see RAIL[2]).]

rallycross /rálli kross/ *n* motor racing on a circuit partly on roads and partly across country [Mid-20C. Blend of RALLY[1] + AUTOCROSS.]

rallying /rálli ing/ *n* car racing on public roads using a route not known in advance by the drivers and with special rules for speed or time

ralph /ralf/ *vi US* to vomit (*slang*) [Late 20C. Probably from the male first name *Ralph*, chosen for a supposed resemblance to the sound of vomiting.]

ram /ram/ *n* **1 MALE SHEEP** a male sheep **2 BATTERING OR CRUSHING DEVICE** a device designed to batter, crush, press, or push something, e.g. a projecting underwater part of a boat's prow or the weight dropped by a pile driver **3 HYDRAULIC RAM** a hydraulic ram **4 WARSHIP WITH A RAM** a former type of warship equipped with a projecting underwater part on the prow that was designed to make a hole in the hull of an enemy warship ■ *v* (**rams, ramming, rammed**) **1** *vti* **STRIKE SOMETHING WITH GREAT FORCE** to hit or collide with something, or make something hit something else, with great force or violence ○ *She swerved, almost ramming into a wall.* **2** *vt* **COLLIDE WITH SOMETHING DELIBERATELY** to collide with another ship or vehicle deliberately in order to sink, disable, or damage it ○ *The police car rammed the getaway vehicle and pushed* *it off the road.* 3 *vt* FORCE SOMETHING INTO PLACE to press, force, or push something into place ○ *He quickly rammed another charge down the barrel and took aim* 4 *vt US* FORCE ACCEPTANCE OF to force the passage of a bill or acceptance of a suggestion, usually despite strong objection ○ *rammed the legislation through Congress.* 5 *vt* PRESENT SOMETHING VERY FORCEFULLY to present something forcefully in order to impress and convince people ○ *In a series of high-profile interviews she rammed home her message.* [Old English *ram(m)*] —**rammer** *n*

Ram /ram/ *n* ZODIAC = **Aries** *n.* 1

RAM /ram/ *abbr* 1 random-access memory 2 relative atomic mass 3 rocket-assisted motor 4 Royal Academy of Music

Rama /raáma/ *n* an incarnation (**avatar**) of the god Vishnu

Rama IX /raáma/ (*b.* 1927) king of Thailand (1950–)

Ramadan /rámmə daán, rámmə dan/ *n* in the Islamic calendar, the ninth month of the year, made up of 30 days [Late 16C. < Arabic, 'the hot month' < *ramaḍ* 'dryness'.]

Ramakrishna /raamə kríshnə/, **Sri** (1834–86) Indian religious teacher. Born **Gadadhar Chatterji**

Raman /raámən/, **Sir Chandrasekhara Venkata** (1888–1970) Indian physicist

Raman effect *n* the change in wavelength and phase exhibited by monochromatic light passing through a transparent medium [Early 20C. After Sir Chandrasekhara Venkata RAMAN.]

ramate *adj* BIOL = **ramose**

Ramayana /raa mí́ ənə/ *n* a great epic of the Hindu religion and of classical Sanskrit literature that tells of the adventures of Rama, an incarnation (**avatar**) of the god Vishnu

Dame Marie Rambert

Rambert /raam báir/, **Dame Marie** (1888–1982) Polish-born British ballet dancer and teacher. Born **Miriam Rambach**

ramble /rámb'l/ *vi* (**-bles, -bling, -bled**) 1 WALK FOR PLEASURE to go for a walk for pleasure, usually in the countryside and sometimes without a fixed route in mind ○ *He had spent a week rambling about among the villages of the Apennines.* 2 FOLLOW A CHANGING COURSE to have, follow, or proceed along a winding or often changing course ○ *The path rambled though the fields down to the river.* 3 GROW IN RANDOM WAY to grow in random directions, usually covering a sizable area in the process ○ *Vines rambled all over the low stone wall.* 4 TALK OR WRITE AIMLESSLY to talk, write, or continue for a long time, not always keeping to the intended subject or tending to change the subject ○ *The speaker rambled on for over an hour.* ■ *n* WALK a walk for pleasure, usually in the countryside and less strenuous than a hike ○ *a ramble through the woods on a spring holiday* [15C. < ?]

rambler /rámblər/ *n* 1 WALKER a person who walks in the countryside for pleasure 2 CLIMBING ROSE a hybrid climbing rose with long flexible canes and clusters of small double flowers 3 SOMEBODY WHO TALKS TOO MUCH a talker or writer who aimlessly rambles at length on a topic

rambling /rámbling/ *adj* 1 NOT TO THE POINT continuing for too long and with many changes of subject ○ *a long, rambling story* 2 SPREAD OUT built or spread over a large area and not clearly organized or regular in shape ○ *a rambling old house* 3 GROWING AS RAMBLER growing with long straggling shoots 4 MEANDERING not following a direct course ○ *a narrow rambling path through the hills* 5 PREFERRING TO ROAM preferring to move from place to place rather than stay in one place or settle down —**ramblingly** *adv*

SYNONYMS See ***wordy***.

Rambo /rámbō/ (*plural* **-bos**) *n* an aggressive or violent person who breaks rules or laws to achieve what he or she believes to be right (*slang*) [Late 20C. After John *Rambo*, the aggressive protagonist in the film *First Blood* (1982).] —**Ramboesque** /rámbō ésk/ *adj* —**Ramboism** /rámbō izəm/ *n*

Rambouillet /rámbooyay/ town in north-central France. Population: 24,343 (1990).

rambunctious /ram búngkshəss/ *adj* noisy, very active, and hard to control, usually as a result of excitement or youthful energy [Mid-19C. < ?] —**rambunctiously** *adv* —**rambunctiousness** *n*

rambutan /ram boót'n/ *n* 1 an oval red spiny fruit with a mildly acidic taste 2 a tree that produces rambutans. Native to: Malaysia. *Nephelium lappaceum.* [Early 18C. < Malay, < *rambut* 'hair'; from the hairy skin of the fruit.]

ramekin /rámmikin/, **ramequin** *n* 1 a small ovenproof dish with vertical fluted sides designed to hold a single serving of a prepared food, especially one that is baked 2 a portion of food cooked and served in a ramekin [Early 18C. Via French *ramequin* < Middle Dutch *rameken* 'little cream' < *ram* 'cream'.]

ramen /ráymən/ *n* a Japanese dish of thin white noodles in small dried cakes, served in a thin well-flavoured soup or stock [Late 20C. Via Japanese *rāmen* < Chinese *lāmiàn* 'pulled noodles'.]

ramequin *n* COOK, FOOD = **ramekin**

Rameses II /rámmə seez/, **Ramses II** (*fl.* 13th century BC) Egyptian pharaoh. Known as **Rameses the Great**

Rameses III, Ramses III (*fl.* 12th century BC) Egyptian pharaoh

ramet /ráymət/ *n* any individual in a clone [Early 20C. < Latin *ramus* 'branch'.]

rami plural of **ramus**

ramie /rámmi/ *n* 1 STRONG FIBRE a lustrous soft durable fibre obtained from the bark of a shrub. Use: fabric, rope. 2 ASIAN SHRUB a perennial shrub whose bark yields ramie. Native to: Asia. *Boehmeria nivea.* 3 CLOTH fabric made from ramie fibre [Early 19C. < Malay *rami.*]

ramification /rámmifi káysh'n/ *n* 1 COMPLICATING RESULT a usually unintended consequence of an action, decision, or judgment that may complicate the situation or make the intended result more difficult to achieve ○ *an unexpected ramification of a new law* 2 BRANCHING DIVISION the process of dividing or spreading out into branches 3 BRANCH a branch or arrangement of branches

ramiform /rámmi fawrm/ *adj* spreading out like branches or having the form of a branch or branches [Mid-19C. < Latin *ramus* 'branch'.]

ramify /rámmi fī/ (**-fies, -fying, -fied**) *vi* 1 to divide into branches or similar parts 2 to have unforeseen results or effects that will cause complications or interfere with the purpose intended ○ *Their difficulties ramified after they made the suggested changes.* [Mid-16C. Via Old French *ramifier* < medieval Latin *ramificare* < Latin *ramus* 'branch'.]

ramjet /rám jet/ *n* a jet engine in which fuel is burned in a duct with air compressed by the forward motion of the aircraft

rammies /rámmiz/ *npl Aus, S Africa* trousers (*informal*) [Early 20C. Probably alteration of *roundme's* < *round the houses*, rhyming slang for 'trousers'.]

rammy /rámmi/ (*plural* **-mies**) *n Scotland* a noisy argument or fight (*informal*) [Mid-20C. < ?]

ramose /ráy mōss, ra mṓss/, **ramous** /ráy məss/, **ramate** /ráy mayt/ *adj* having many branches or divided into many branches [Late 17C. < Latin *ramosus* 'having many branches' < *ramus* 'branch'.] —**ramosely** *adv*

ramp[1] /ramp/ *n* 1 SLOPING PATH OR ACCESS a sloping surface used, e.g., to allow access from one level to a higher or lower level, or to raise something up above floor or ground level ○ *The ship slid slowly down the ramp into the water.* 2 MOVABLE STAIRS a movable set of stairs used for boarding or disembarking from an aircraft 3 CURVED BEND IN A HANDRAIL a curved bend or slope in a handrail or coping where it changes direction, e.g. on a stair landing 4 ROAD RIDGE a raised part of a road constructed to make traffic slow down ■ *vt* BUILD SOMETHING WITH A SLOPE to build something with a sloped surface, or provide something with a ramp ○ *The entrance must be ramped for wheelchair access.* [Late 18C. < French *rampe* < *ramper* 'crawl, creep, rear up'.] —**ramped** *adj*

ramp up *vt* to cause the level or intensity of something to increase sharply ○ *'As business ramps up to manage greater responsibility for its social and environmental impacts...'* (*Marketing Week*; December 1998)

ramp[2] /ramp/ *vi* 1 ACT THREATENINGLY to act in a threatening manner or assume a threatening stance, e.g. rearing with the forelegs ready to strike 2 MOVE VIOLENTLY OR THREATENINGLY to move or rush violently, threateningly, or furiously 3 BE SHOWN REARED UP IN PROFILE to be in the rampant position ○ *an old seal marked with a ramping lion on a shield* [14C. < French *ramper* 'crawl, creep, rear up'.]

rampage *vi* /ram páyj/ (**-pages, -paging, -paged**) to engage in uncontrolled violent or riotous behaviour, or to commit a series of violent or riotous acts ○ *This weather system has rampaged up the coast, with blizzards and howling winds causing severe damage.* ■ *n* /rám payj, ram páyj/ an outburst of uncontrolled violent or riotous behaviour or a series of violent or riotous actions [Early 18C. Probably < RAMP[2].] —**rampageous** *adj* —**rampageously** *adv* —**rampageousness** *n* —**rampager** *n* —**rampaging** *adj* ◇ **on the rampage** behaving in a wild and uncontrolled manner

rampant /rámpənt/ *adj* 1 OCCURRING UNCHECKED happening in an unrestrained manner, usually so as to be regarded as a menace ○ *rampant inflation* 2 GROWING WILDLY growing strongly and to a very large size, or spreading uncontrollably 3 FIERCE exhibiting ferocious behaviour or fierceness of spirit 4 ON HIND LEGS describes a heraldic beast depicted reared up, in profile, and with its forelegs raised, the right one above the left 5 WITH UNEQUAL SUPPORTS having a support or an abutment that is higher on one side than the other [14C. < French, present participle of *ramper* 'rear up'.] —**rampancy** *n* —**rampantly** *adv*

rampart /rám paart/ *n* a defensive fortification made of an earthen embankment, often topped by a low protective wall ■ *vt* to protect somebody or something with ramparts or something similar ○ *walls ramparting a town* [Late 16C. < French *rempart* < *remparer* 'defend again' < Old French *emparer* 'defend'.]

rampike /rám pīk/ *n* a dead tree that is still standing, especially one reduced by fire to little more than a trunk [Late 16C. < ?]

rampion /rámpi ən/ *n* 1 a plant with a white edible root used in salads. Flowers: bluish, in clusters. Native to: Europe, Asia. *Campanula rapunculus.* 2 any plant related to the rampion, typically with blue flowers. Genus: *Phyteuma.* [Late 16C. Probably alteration of Old French *raiponce* < Old Italian *raponzo* < Latin *rapum* 'turnip'.]

Rampur /rám poór/ city in north-central India. Population: 243,000 (1991).

ram-raid *n* a theft carried out by driving a stolen car through a shop window and stealing the goods inside ■ *vti* to carry out a ram-raid on a shop —**ram-raider** *n* —**ram-raiding** *n*

ramrod /rám rod/ *n* 1 ROD FOR LOADING GUNS a rod for loading a charge into a muzzle-loading musket, cannon, or other gun 2 CLEANING ROD a rod for cleaning the barrel of a firearm 3 *US* STERN OR STRICT OVERSEER a stern or strict boss, commander, or other person in a position of authority ■ *vt* (**-rods, -rodding, -rodded**) *US* 1 PUSH SOMETHING THROUGH BY FORCE to push through or achieve something by force or threat ○ *tried to ramrod the bill through the legislature* 2 CONTROL SOMEBODY STRICTLY to exert strict control over somebody or enforce strict discipline on somebody

Ramsay /rámzi/, **Sir Alf** (1922–99) British footballer and manager. Full name **Alfred Ramsay**

Ramses II = **Rameses II**

Ramses III = **Rameses III**

Ramsey Island /rámzi-/ islet off the tip of SW Wales. Area: 2.6 sq. km/1 sq. mi.

Ramsgate /rámz gayt, rámzgit/ coastal town in SE England. Population: 37,895 (1991).

ramshackle /rám shak'l/ *adj* poorly maintained or constructed and seeming likely to fall apart or collapse [Mid-19C. Back-formation < *ramshackled* < *ransack.*]

ram's horn *n* JUDAISM = **shofar**

ramulose /rámmyoo lōss/ *adj* having many small branches [Mid-18C. < Latin *ramulosus* 'full of branching veins' < *ramus* 'branch'.]

ramus /ráyməss/ (*plural* **-mi** /-mī/) *n* a small branching body part such as a stem, bone, or nerve [Early 18C. < Latin, 'branch'.]

ran past tense of **run**

Ran /ran/ *n* in Norse mythology, the goddess of the sea

RAN *abbr* **1** *Aus* Royal Australian Navy **2** request for authority to negotiate

Rance /raaNss/ river in NW France. Length: 100 km/62 mi.

ranch /raanch/ *n* **1** LIVESTOCK FARM ON OPEN LAND a farm where cattle, sheep, horses, or other livestock are raised on large tracts of open land, especially in North and South America and Australia **2** SPECIALIZED FARM a large farm devoted to keeping a particular type of animal or growing a single type of crop **3** BUILDING = **ranch house** *n.* **1**, **ranch house** *n.* **2** **4** FOOD = **ranch dressing** ■ *v* **1** *vi* WORK ON A RANCH to own, manage, or work on a ranch ○ *ranching animals in western Texas* **2** *vt* RAISE ON A RANCH to breed, raise, or tend animals on a ranch [Early 19C. Via American Spanish *rancho* < Spanish, 'group of people who eat together' < French *ranger* 'arrange in position' < *rang* 'row, line'.] —**ranching** *n*

ranch dressing *n US* a creamy salad dressing that has a mixture of mayonnaise and buttermilk or milk as its base

rancher /ráanchər/ *n* **1** an owner or manager of a ranch **2** *US* ARCHIT = **ranch house** *n.* **2**

ranchero /raan cháirō/ (*plural* **-ros**) *n Southwest US* an owner or a manager of a ranch, especially a Hispanic rancher in the SW United States and in Latin America [Early 19C. < American Spanish, < *rancho* (see RANCH).]

ranch house *n US* **1** the building on a ranch where the owner or a manager lives, typically having one storey, a spread-out floor plan, and a roof that is not steeply pitched **2** a single-storey house built in a style similar to a traditional ranch house, especially one located in a suburban housing development

Ranchi /ránchi/ city in NE India. Population: 599,306 (1991).

rancho /ráanchō/ (*plural* **-chos**) *n Southwest US* **1** a ranch **2** a hut where a ranch worker lives, or a group of such huts [Early 19C. < American Spanish (see RANCH).]

Rancho Cucamonga /ránchō kóokə móng gə/ city in SW California. Population: 120,047 (1998 estimate).

rancid /ránssid/ *adj* **1** having the strong disagreeable smell or taste of decomposing fats or oils **2** causing disgust or greatly offensive [Mid-17C. < Latin *rancidus* 'stinking, rank' < *rancere* 'to stink'.] —**rancidity** /ran síddəti/ *n* —**rancidness** /ránssidnəss/ *n*

rancor *n* US = **rancour**

rancour /rángkər/ *n* bitter, deeply held, and long-lasting ill will or resentment [12C. Via Old French < Latin *rancor* 'stinking smell or offensive flavour, bitterness' < *rancere* 'to stink'.] —**rancorous** *adj* —**rancorously** *adv* —**rancorousness** *n*

rand /rand/ (*plural* **rand**) *n* see table at **currency** [Mid-20C. After the *Rand*, gold-mining district in the Transvaal < Afrikaans *rand* 'ridge of ground' < Dutch, 'edge'.]

randan[1] /ran dán, rán dan/ *n* a noisy and boisterous celebration (*informal*) [Early 18C. < ?]

randan[2] /ran dán, rán dan/ *n* **1** a boat designed to be rowed by three people **2** the method of rowing a randan, with one person using two oars and the other two one oar each [Early 19C. < ?]

R & B *abbr* rhythm and blues

R & D *abbr* research and development

randem /rándəm/ *adv* with a team of three horses harnessed one behind another ■ *n* a team of three horses harnessed one behind another, or a carriage pulled by such a team [Late 19C. Probably alteration of RANDOM, after TANDEM.]

random /rándəm/ *adj* **1** WITHOUT A PATTERN done, chosen, or occurring without a specific pattern, plan, or connection ○ *random testing for drugs* **2** LACKING REGULARITY with a pattern or in sizes that are not uniform or regular ○ *a wall constructed of random stones* **3** EQUALLY LIKELY relating or belonging to a set in which all the members have the same probability of occurrence ○ *a random sampling* **4** HAVING DEFINITE PROBABILITY relating to or involving variables that have undetermined value but definite probability [Mid-17C. < Old French *randon* 'impetuosity, rush' < *randir* 'run' < Germanic.] —**randomly** *adv* —**randomness** *n* ◇ **at random** with no set plan, system, or connection

⚡**random-access** *adj* relating to the capability of a computer to obtain information from any memory location without having to begin its search at the memory's starting-point ○ *random-access input/output*

⚡**random-access memory** *n* the primary working memory in a computer, used for the temporary storage of programs and data and in which the data can be accessed directly and modified

randomize /rándə mīz/ (**-ized, -izing, -izes**), **randomise** (**-ises, -ising, -ised**) *vti* to arrange or select items so that no specific pattern or order determines the resulting arrangement or the selection process —**randomization** /rándə mī záysh'n/ *n* —**randomizer** /rándə mīzər/ *n*

random number *n* any of a series of numbers that have no pattern in their progression

random sample *n* a sample of subjects that is randomly selected from a group and is therefore assumed to be representative of that group

random variable *n* a variable that can have any of a range of values that occur randomly but can be described probabilistically

random walk *n* a model applicable to various processes such as diffusion in which the direction and sometimes the magnitude of successive steps are determined by chance

R and R, R & R *abbr* **1** rest and recreation **2** rest and relaxation

randy /rándi/ (**-dier, -diest**) *adj* having a strong desire for sex (*informal*) [Late 17C. < *rand* 'rant', earlier Scots variant of RANT.] —**randily** *adv* —**randiness** *n*

ranee *n* POL = **rani**

rang past tense of **ring**[2]

rangatira /rángə téerə/ *n NZ* a Maori chief or noble [Early 19C. < Maori.]

range /raynj/ *n* **1** VARIEDNESS the number and variety of different things that something includes or can deal with **2** NUMBER OF SIMILAR THINGS a number or set of different things belonging to the same general category **3** PRODUCTS PRODUCED OR SOLD all the products produced or sold by somebody considered as a set, often ranked according to price and degree of sophistication ○ *the best-selling product in its range* **4** CATEGORY DEFINED BY LIMITS a category defined by an upper and a lower limit ○ *the age range 25 to 45* **5** AREA OF EFFECTIVE OPERATION the area within which, or the distance over which, something can operate effectively ○ *out of range of the radar* **6** FARTHEST DISTANCE FOR AN EFFECTIVE OPERATION the farthest distance at which something can operate effectively, e.g. the farthest distance to which a gun can shoot a bullet or shell **7** DISTANCE BETWEEN WEAPON AND TARGET the distance between two things, especially a gun or a tracking device and the object it is aimed at **8** PRACTICE AREA a place where an activity is practised or performed **9** DISTANCE TRAVELLED WITHOUT REFUELLING the farthest distance that a vehicle or aircraft can travel without refuelling **10** PRODUCIBLE NOTES the notes, from highest to lowest, that somebody's voice or a musical instrument can produce **11** REGISTER OF MUSICAL PASSAGE the register of a musical passage, from its highest to lowest note **12** ROW OF MOUNTAINS a number of mountains or hills forming a connected row or group **13** *US, Can* OPEN LAND FOR GRAZING FARM ANIMALS a large area of open land on which farm animals can graze **14** AREA WHERE ORGANISM IS NORMALLY FOUND a geographical area in which a species of organism normally lives or grows **15** MOVEMENT OVER AREA movement over or within an area **16** STOVE a cooking stove with one or more ovens and with hot plates or burners on top, especially a large old-fashioned one heated with solid fuel and often kept constantly burning **17** SET OF VALUES the set of values that can be taken by a function or a variable **18** EXTENT OF FREQUENCY DISTRIBUTION the difference between the smallest and the largest value in a frequency distribution **19** TWO-SIDED BOOKCASE a large free-standing bookcase in a library that is built to hold books on both sides **20** *US* NORTH-SOUTH STRIP OF TOWNSHIPS a north-south strip of townships six miles square and numbered east and west from a meridian in a US public land survey ■ *v* **1** *vi* VARY BETWEEN LIMITS to vary between a particular upper and lower limit ○ *prices ranging from £1.50 to £10.00* **2** *vi* DEAL WITH A NUMBER OF THINGS to include, cover, or deal with a number of different things, usually within a particular context ○ *Her interests range from parapsychology to parachuting.* **3** *vt* ARRANGE THINGS IN LINE to arrange things in a particular way, especially in a line or row (*usually passive*) ○ *Jars of pickles were ranged along the kitchen shelf.* **4** *vt* ALIGN OR CLASSIFY to put something or somebody into a particular group or category **5** *vr* GIVE PERSONAL SUPPORT to support or side with somebody **6** *vti* TRAVEL FREELY AND EXTENSIVELY to move freely across, through, or back and forth within a particular area ○ *She allowed her thoughts to range freely over the events of the previous week.* **7** *vt* TRAVEL CERTAIN DISTANCE to be able to travel a particular distance (*refers to bullets or missiles*) **8** *vti* POINT OR AIM SOMETHING to point or aim something such as a gun, missile, or telescope at a specific object, or to be pointed at a specific object **9** *vi* LIVE OR GROW to live or grow in a particular geographical area (*refers to animals or plants*) ○ *Buffalo once ranged over the plains.* **10** *vt* PUT LIVESTOCK OUT TO GRAZE to put livestock out to graze on a large open area [13C. < Old French *rangier* 'put in order' < *ranc* 'row'.]

rangefinder *n* an instrument used to estimate the distance between the user and an object, especially one that is to be shot at or photographed

rangeland /ráynj land/ *n* AGRIC = **range** *n.* **13**

range pole *n* CONSTR = **ranging pole**

ranger /ráynjər/ *n* **1** WANDERER a wanderer **2** OFFICIAL OVERSEEING COUNTRYSIDE AREA somebody whose job is to oversee, protect, and patrol a forest or an area of natural beauty **3** *US* MEMBER OF RURAL POLICE UNIT a member of an armed law-enforcement unit in certain parts of the United States, especially Texas

Ranger /ráynjər/ *n* **1** a member of the senior branch of the Guides for girls between 14 and 19 years old **2** a member of a military unit of the United States Army specially trained for commando raids

ranging pole, ranging rod, range pole *n* a pole, usually held vertically, used to mark a specific position when surveying a plot of land

rangiora /rúngi awrə/ *n* an evergreen tree with large oval leaves and small greenish-white flowers. Native to: New Zealand. *Brachyglottis repanda.* [Mid-19C. < Maori.]

Rangitaiki /rúngi tī ki/ river in central North Island, New Zealand. Length: 193 km/120 sq. mi.

Rangitata /rúngi taa taa/ river in E South Island, New Zealand. Length: 121 km/75 mi.

Rangitikei /rúngi tī kay/ river in central North Island, New Zealand. Length: 241 km/150 mi.

Rangitoto Island /ráng gə tṓtō-/ uninhabited volcanic island in Hauraki Gulf, N New Zealand. Area: 23 sq. km/9 sq. mi.

Rangoon /rang góon/ former name for **Yangon**

rangy /ráynji/ (**-ier, -iest**) *adj* tall and lean with long legs —**ranginess** *n*

rani /raáni, raa née/, **ranee** *n* a queen or princess, or the wife or widow of a rajah in India or a neighbouring country [Late 17C. Via Hindi < Sanskrit *rājñī* < *rājan* 'king'.]

Ranjit Singh /ránjit síng/ (1780–1839) Indian warrior

rank[1] /rangk/ *n* **1** OFFICIAL STATUS WITHIN ORGANIZATION an official title or category that shows the holder's relative importance or seniority within an organization, especially a military force **2** STATUS RELATIVE TO OTHERS the degree of importance or excellence of somebody or something relative to other members of a group ○ *a political journalist of the first rank* **3** HIGH STATUS high status or importance, especially in the military or among the wealthy **4** LINE OF PEOPLE OR THINGS a line of people, especially soldiers, or things standing side by side **5** PLACE FOR TAXIS TO WAIT a place where taxis wait for passengers **6** HORIZONTAL LINE OF SQUARES ON A CHESSBOARD any horizontal line of squares on a chessboard **7** LINEARLY INDEPENDENT ROWS in mathematics, the largest number of linearly independent rows in a matrix **8** SET OF ORGAN PIPES a set of organ pipes linked to a particular stop ■ **ranks** *npl* **1** ORDINARY SOLDIERS members of the armed forces who are not officers, or the ordinary members of any organization who do not hold high office **2** PEOPLE IN A GROUP OR CATEGORY people belonging to a particular group or category, considered collectively and usually with the understanding that there are large numbers of them ○ *among the ranks of her supporters* ■ *v* **1** *vti* HAVE OR GIVE A RATING to have, or to give somebody or something, a particular rating, position, or importance relative to other people or things in a group ○ *This ranks fairly high on my list of desirable improvements.* **2** *vti* POSITION OR STAND IN ROWS to place people or things in a row or rows, or to stand or form in rows (*usually passive*) **3** *vt US* OUTRANK to have a higher rank than and take precedence over somebody or something else in a group, especially in a hierarchy ○ *A colonel ranks a major.* [14C. < Old French *ranc* 'row' < Germanic.] ◇ **break ranks 1** to fall out of an ordered line of soldiers, especially when being attacked **2** to stop supporting the policy of a group of which you are a member ◇ **close ranks 1** to form into tight disciplined lines in preparation for an expected attack (*refers to soldiers*) **2** to unite closely, especially when taking some kind of defensive action ◇ **pull rank (on somebody)** to assert authority over other people in a hierarchy, especially in order to obtain personal advantage ◇ **rise (up) through the ranks** to reach a senior position in an organization by gradual promotions from an originally low position

rank[2] *adj* **1 SHOWING VIGOROUS GROWTH** growing and spreading in a particularly vigorous way (*refers to vegetation*) ○ *'the rank ailanthus of the April dooryard'* (T.S. Eliot, *The Dry Salvages*; 1941) **2 UTTER** of the most extreme and obvious kind ○ *a rank amateur* **3 FOUL** foul-smelling or foul-tasting (*literary*) ○ *'O, my offence is rank! It smells to heaven.'* (Shakespeare, *Hamlet* 3.ii; 1604) [Old English *ranc* 'haughty, full-grown'] —**rankly** *adv* —**rankness** *n*

Rank /rangk/, **J. Arthur, 1st Baron** (1888–1972) British film magnate

Rank, Otto (1884–1939) Austrian psychologist and psychotherapist

rank and file *n* **1** enlisted troops in a military organization, excluding officers **2** the majority of a group or organization, especially all of the members who have no power or influence —**rank-and-file** *adj* —**rank and filer** *n*

rank correlation *n* an assessment of the extent to which different ways of ranking the members of a set correlate with one another

ranker /rángkər/ *n* **1** a private in the army **2** a commissioned army officer who has previously served as a private

Rankine scale /rángkin-/ *n* an absolute temperature scale in which each degree equals one degree on the Fahrenheit scale, with the freezing point of water being 491.67°, and its boiling point 671.67° [Mid-19C. After the British physicist and engineer W. J. M. *Rankine* (1820–72).]

ranking /rángking/ *n* **POSITION RELATIVE TO OTHERS** the position or status held by or allocated to somebody or something relative to others in a particular group ■ *adj US* **1 FOREMOST** considered to be the most eminent or important of the members of a particular group ○ *the ranking diplomat at the reception* **2 HOLDING HIGH RANK** holding a high rank in a military or other organization

rankle /rángk'l/ *vi* to cause persistent feelings of bitterness, resentment, or anger ○ *It still rankles after all these years.* [14C. < Old French *rancler* < *raoncle* 'festering sore', literally 'little snake (bite)' < Latin *dracunculus* < *draco* (see DRAGON).]

ransack /rán sak/ *vt* **1** to go through a place stealing some things and usually destroying or spoiling everything else **2** to search something very thoroughly but handling things carelessly ○ *I ransacked the drawers but couldn't find my keys.* [13C. < Old Norse *rannsaka* < *rann* 'house' + *-saka* 'search'.] —**ransacker** *n*

ransom /ránsəm/ *n* **1 MONEY DEMANDED FOR RELEASING CAPTIVE** a sum of money demanded or paid for the release of somebody who is being held prisoner **2 RELEASE OF PRISONER** the release of a prisoner in return for the payment of money **3 DELIVERANCE** the act of saving somebody from an oppressed condition or dangerous situation through self-sacrifice (*literary*) ■ *vt* **1 PAY MONEY FOR SOMEBODY'S RELEASE** to release somebody from captivity by paying money to the captors **2 RELEASE CAPTIVE ON RECEIPT OF MONEY** to set a captive free or release something being held on the receipt of money **3 RESCUE OR REDEEM** to rescue or redeem somebody, especially by a self-sacrificing act, and especially from sin or its punishment (*literary*) [13C. Via Old French *ransoun* < Latin *redemption-* (see REDEMPTION).] —**ransomer** *n* ◇ **a king's or queen's ransom** a very large amount of money ◇ **hold somebody to ransom 1** to use threats to try to make somebody do what you want **2** to hold somebody captive until a sum of money is paid for his or her release

rant /rant/ *vti* to speak in a very loud, aggressive, or bombastic way, usually at length and repetitively ○ *He ranted for hours about how ungrateful we were.* ■ *n* speech or language that is very loud and threatening but also monotonous or unconvincing [Late 16C. < Dutch *ranten*.] —**ranter** *n* —**ranting** *adj, n* —**rantingly** *adv*

ranula /rányŏŏlə/ *n* a cyst that forms on the underside of the tongue when the duct of a salivary or mucous gland is blocked [Mid-17C. < Latin, 'little frog' < *rana* 'frog'.]

ranunculus /rə núngkyŏŏləss/ (*plural* **-luses** *or* **-li** /-lī/) *n* a plant that has divided leaves and flowers with five petals such as the buttercup, clematis, and columbine. Genus: *Ranunculus*. [Late 16C. < modern Latin, < Latin, 'little frog' < *rana* 'frog'.] —**ranunculaceous** /rə núngkyŏŏ láyshəss/ *adj*

RAOC *abbr* Royal Army Ordnance Corps

rap[1] /rap/ *v* (**raps, rapping, rapped**) **1** *vti* **HIT SOMETHING SHARPLY** to strike something with a quick sharp blow ○ *The teacher rapped on the desk to get the students' attention* **2** *vt* **SAY SOMETHING QUICKLY** to say something in a quick sharp way ○ *The sergeant rapped out an order.* **3** *vt* **REBUKE** to criticize or reproach somebody harshly ■ *n* **1 SHARP BLOW** a sharp quick blow **2 SOUND OF KNOCKING** a quick sharp knocking sound **3 REBUKE** a harsh rebuke or criticism (*slang*) [13C. < ?] —**rapper** *n* ◇ **not give a rap** *US* to not care at all (*informal*) ◇ **take the rap (for something)** to take the blame or punishment for something, whether or not it was your fault (*slang*)

rap[2] /rap/ *n* **1** *US* **INFORMAL TALK** an informal talk or discussion (*slang*) **2 POPULAR MUSIC WITH RHYMING VERSES** popular music characterized by spoken rhyming vocals and often featuring a looped electronic beat in the background ■ *v* (**raps, rapping, rapped**) **1** *vt US* **TALK INFORMALLY** to talk or discuss something informally (*slang*) ○ *We rapped till dawn.* **2** *vi* **PLAY RAP** to perform rap music —**rapper** *n*

rapacious /rə páyshəss/ *adj* **1 GRASPING** greedy and grasping, especially for money, and sometimes willing to use unscrupulous means to obtain what is desired **2 DESTRUCTIVE AND VICIOUS** engaging in violent pillaging and likely to harm or destroy things **3 PREDATORY** living by eating live prey [Mid-17C. < Latin *rapac-*, stem of *rapax* 'tearing, grasping' < *rapere* 'seize'.] —**rapaciously** *adv* —**rapaciousness** *n*

rape[1] /rayp/ *n* **1 FORCING OF SOMEBODY INTO SEX** the crime of forcing somebody to have sex **2 INSTANCE OF RAPE** an instance of the crime of rape **3 VIOLENT DESTRUCTIVE TREATMENT** violent, destructive, or abusive treatment of something ○ *the rape of a beautiful stretch of countryside* **4 ABDUCTION** an act of seizing somebody and carrying him or her away by force (*archaic*) ■ *vt* (**rapes, raping, raped**) **1 FORCE SOMEBODY TO HAVE SEX** to force somebody to have sex **2 VIOLATE** to treat something in a violent, destructive, or abusive way ○ *rape the land for its resources* [14C. Via Anglo-Norman *raper* < Latin *rapere* 'seize'.]

rape[2] /rayp/ *n* a commercially grown annual plant of the cabbage family. Flowers: bright yellow. Use: oil, fodder. *Brassica napus*. [14C. < Latin *rapa* 'turnip'.]

rape[3] /rayp/ *n* the skins and stalks of grapes after their juice has been extracted for use in winemaking [Early 17C. < French *râpe* 'grape stalk' < Old French *rasper* 'scrape'.]

rape oil *n* oil extracted from the seeds of the rape plant. Use: lubricant, making soap, cooking.

rapeseed /ráyp seed/ *n* the seeds of the rape plant

rapeseed oil *n* INDUST, FOOD = **rape oil**

rape shield law *n* a law that prohibits the defence in a rape trial from questioning the victim about her or his previous sexual experiences

Raphael /ráffay əl/ *n* in Hebrew tradition, one of the seven archangels, and the angel of healing

Raphael /ráffay əl/ (1483–1520) Italian artist. Born **Raffaello Sanzio**

raphe /ráyfi/ (*plural* **-phae** /-fee/) *n* **1 CONNECTING RIDGE** a connecting ridge or seam between two similar parts of an organ of the body, e.g. between the two halves of the medulla oblongata or along the scrotum **2 RIDGE ALONG SOME SEED COATS** a ridge along the coat of some seeds formed by fusion of the connecting stalk (**funiculus**) with the outer layer of the developing ovule **3 LONGITUDINAL GROOVE** a longitudinal groove on the valve of a diatom [Mid-18C. Via modern Latin < Greek *rhaphē* 'seam' < *rhaptein* 'sew'.]

raphia *n* INDUST = **raffia** *n*. 1

raphide /ráy fīd/, **raphis** /ráyfiss/ (*plural* **raphides** /ráffi deez/) *n* a crystal of calcium oxalate found in some plant cells as a by-product of their metabolism [Mid-19C. Via French < Greek *raphid-* 'needle' < *rhaptein* 'sew'.]

rapid /ráppid/ *adj* acting, moving, or happening very quickly ○ *a rapid increase in turnover* ■ **rapids** *npl* a part of a riverbed where the water moves very fast, usually over rocks or round boulders ○ *crossed the rapids in a small canoe* [Mid-17C. < Latin *rapidus* 'seizing' < *rapere* 'seize'.] —**rapidly** *adv* —**rapidness** *n*

rapid eye movement *n* jerky movements of the eyeballs while the eyes are closed, characteristic of somebody who is dreaming while asleep, especially during REM sleep

rapid eye movement sleep *n* PHYSIOL = **REM sleep**

rapid-fire *adj* **1** = **quick-fire** *adj*. 1 **2** = **quick-fire** *adj*. 2

rapid prototyping *n* a method of quickly creating mechanical components, especially those with complex shapes, from a computer-based drawing that can be used to check the validity of a design

rapid transit *n US* high-speed urban public-transport system using underground or elevated railways, or a combination of both

rapier /ráypi ər/ *n* a sword with a cup-shaped hilt and a long slender blade that can have two cutting edges, or only a sharply pointed tip for thrusting [Early 16C. Probably via Dutch or Low German *rappir* < French (*espee*) *rapière* 'rapier (sword)'.]

rapine /ráppīn, -ppin/ *n* the use of force to seize somebody else's property (*literary*) [14C. Directly or via French < Latin *rapina*.]

rapini /ra peéni/ *npl* the leaves of immature turnip plants, used especially in Italian and Chinese cooking [Late 20C. < Italian.]

rapist /ráypist/ *n* a man who forces somebody to have sex with him

rappee /ra peé/ *n* a moist, strongly flavoured snuff made from dark coarse tobacco [Mid-18C. < French *tabac râpé* 'rasped tobacco' < *râper* 'rasp' < Old French *rasper* 'to scrape' < Germanic.]

rappel /ra pél/ *vi US* CLIMBING = **abseil** *v*. ■ *n US* CLIMBING = **abseil** *n*. [Mid-20C. < French, < Old French *rapeler* 'to recall' < *apeler* 'to call'.]

rappen /rápp'n/ (*plural* **-pen**) *n* a Swiss centime [Mid-19C. < German, < Middle High German *rappe* 'raven', referring to the depiction of a bird on a coin of the Middle Ages.]

rapport /ra páwr/ *n* an emotional bond or friendly relationship between people based on mutual liking, trust, and a sense that they understand and share each other's concerns ○ *She manages to strike up a rapport with audiences as soon as she steps onto the platform.* [Mid-17C. < French, < Old French *raporter* 'bring back' < *aporter* 'bring' < Latin *portare* 'carry'.]

rapporteur /ráppawr túr/ *n* an appointed investigator of a subject who delivers a report on it [Late 15C. < French, < Old French *raporter* 'bring back'.]

rapprochement /ra próshmoN/ *n* the establishment or renewal of friendly relations between people or nations that were previously hostile or unsympathetic towards each other [Early 19C. < French, < *rapprocher* 'bring together' < *approcher* (see APPROACH).]

rapscallion /rap skálli ən/ *n* a mischievous and annoying child or a disreputable and dishonest person (*archaic or humorous*) [Late 17C. Alteration of earlier *rascallion*, probably < RASCAL.]

rap sheet *n US* a list of somebody's past arrests and convictions (*slang*)

rapt /rapt/ *adj* **1 COMPLETELY ENGROSSED** involved in, fascinated by, or concentrating on something to the exclusion of everything else ○ *staring with rapt attention at the speaker* **2 BLISSFULLY HAPPY** showing or suggesting deep emotions of joy or ecstasy **3 rapt, wrapped** *Aus* **PLEASED** extremely pleased (*informal*) [14C. < Latin *raptus* 'seized', past participle of *rapere* 'seize'.] —**raptly** *adv* —**raptness** *n*

raptor /ráptər/ *n* a bird of prey [14C. < Latin, 'robber' < *rapere* 'seize'.]

raptorial /rap táwri əl/ *adj* **1 LIVING BY PREDATION** able to live by catching prey **2 ADAPTED FOR CATCHING PREY** specially adapted for seizing prey, as are the feet of birds of prey with their sharp talons **3 OF PREDATORY BIRDS** typical of or relating to birds of prey

rapture /rápchər/ *n* **1 OVERWHELMING HAPPINESS** a euphoric transcendent state in which somebody is overwhelmed by happiness or delight and unaware of anything else **2 MYSTICAL TRANSPORTATION** a mystical experience of being transported into the spiritual realm, sometimes applied to the second coming of Jesus Christ when true believers are expected to rise up to join him in heaven ■ **raptures** *npl* **STATE OF GREAT HAPPINESS OR ENTHUSIASM** a state of great happiness or enthusiasm about something, or words and gestures that express this ○ *went into raptures about the meal they'd had* [Late 16C. Directly or via French < medieval Latin *raptura* 'seizure' < Latin *raptus* 'seized'.] —**rapturous** /rápchərəss/ *adj* —**rapturously** *adv* —**rapturousness** *n*

rapture of the deep *n* MED = **nitrogen narcosis**

rara avis /ráirə áyviss/ (*plural* **rarae aves** /ráir ee áy veez/) *n* somebody or something that is rarely encountered [< Latin, 'rare bird']

ra-ra skirt *n* = **rah-rah skirt**

rare[1] /rair/ (**rarer, rarest**) *adj* **1 NOT OFTEN HAPPENING** not often happening or found ○ *It's rare for them to miss a meeting.* **2 VALUABLE** particularly interesting or valuable, especially to collectors or scholars, because only a few exist ○ *a collection of rare 18th-century porcelain* **3 GREAT** unusually great or excellent ○ *a rare gift for languages* **4 CONTAINING LITTLE OXYGEN** thin in density and containing so little oxygen that breathing is difficult [15C. < Latin *rarus* 'having a loose texture, scarce'.] —**rareness** *n*

rare[2] /rair/ (**rarer, rarest**) *adj* describes meat that is cooked quickly and lightly so as to remain raw and juicy inside [Mid-17C. Alteration of dialect *rear* 'underdone' (of eggs) < Old English *hrēr*.]

rarebit /ráir bit/ *n* FOOD = **Welsh rarebit**

rare earth *n* an oxide of a rare-earth element

rare-earth element *n* a member of the lanthanide series, which contains 15 elements that have atomic numbers from 57 to 71 and share closely related chemical properties

raree show /ráiri-/ *n* a peepshow (*archaic*) [Alteration of *rare show*]

rarefaction /ráiri fáksh'n/, **rarefication** /ráirifi káysh'n/ *n* the process of becoming or of making something such as a gas less dense [Early 17C. < medieval Latin *rarefaction-* < Latin *rarefacere* 'make rare'.] —**rarefactional** *adj*

rarefied /ráiri fīd/ *adj* **1 WITH LOW DENSITY** having a low density, especially owing to a low oxygen content **2 ESOTERIC OR ELITE** seemingly distinct or remote from ordinary reality and common people, and often purged of elements perceived as coarse or tasteless **3 ABOVE THE ORDINARY** showing very high quality in character or style (*literary*) ○ *Milton's rarefied prose*

rarefy /ráiri fī/ (**-fies, -fying, -fied**) *v* **1** *vti* to make something, especially a gas, less dense, or to become less dense **2** *vt* to make something less connected with or typical of the ordinary [14C. Directly or via French *raréfier* < medieval Latin *rareficare* < Latin *rarefacere* 'make rare' < *rarus* 'scarce' + *facere* 'do'.] —**rarefiable** *adj*

rare gas *n* CHEM = **noble gas**

rarely /ráirli/ *adv* **1** almost never or not very often **2** exceptionally well

rareripe /ráir rīp/ *adj US* that ripens early ■ *n US* a fruit or vegetable that ripens early [Early 18C. *Rare* 'early' is a variant of *rathe* < Old English *hræþ* 'quick' < Germanic.]

raring /ráiring/ *adj* very enthusiastic and eager to start doing something ○ *They were raring to go.* [Early 20C. Present participle of *rare*, variant of REAR[1].]

rarity /ráirəti/ (*plural* **-ties**) *n* **1** the fact of happening very seldom or of being very unusual **2** something that happens rarely or that is particularly interesting or valuable because it is so unusual

RAS *abbr* **1** Royal Agricultural Society **2** Royal Astronomical Society

~~**rasberry**~~ incorrect spelling of **raspberry**

rasbora /raz báwrə/ *n* a tropical freshwater fish, several species of which are brightly coloured and often kept in aquariums. Native to: East Africa, Asia. Genus: *Rasbora*. [Mid-20C. < modern Latin, < ?]

rascal /raásk'l/ *n* **1** a mischievous teaser, especially a child (*humorous*) **2** somebody, especially a man, who is dishonest or otherwise unethical [14C. < Old French *rascaille* 'mob, rabble'.] —**rascally** *adj*

rase *vt* = **raze** (*literary*)

rash[1] /rash/ *adj* acting with, resulting from, or typical of thoughtless impetuous behaviour [14C. Probably via assumed Old English *ræsc* < Germanic 'quick'.] —**rashly** *adv* —**rashness** *n*

rash[2] /rash/ *n* **1** an outbreak on the skin's surface that is often reddish and itchy **2** a series of events that happen in a brief period and are considered to be unusual or rare ○ *a rash of burglaries* [Early 18C. < ?]

rasher /ráshər/ *n* **1** a slice of bacon or ham, cooked or uncooked **2** *US* an order or portion of slices of cooked bacon or ham [Late 16C. < ?]

Rashîd /ra shéed/ town in N Egypt, in the River Nile delta. The Rosetta Stone was discovered there. Population: 52,014 (1986).

rasp[1] /raasp/ *n* **1 TYPE OF FILE** a tool used for scraping or smoothing wood or metal, similar to a file but with larger teeth on its cutting surface **2 ACT OF SMOOTHING** the act of smoothing the surface of something such as wood or metal with a rasp **3 HARSH GRATING SOUND** a harsh grating sound, similar to that of a rasp or saw cutting into wood ■ *v* **1** *vt* **SAY SOMETHING IN HARSH VOICE** to say something, especially to give an order, in a harsh voice **2** *vti* **FILE OR SCRAPE** to use a rasp to file or scrape a surface in order to remove unevenness **3** *vt* **IRRITATE** to irritate or annoy somebody [13C. < Old French *rasper* 'scrape' < Germanic.] —**rasper** *n* —**rasping** *adj* —**raspingly** *adv* —**raspy** *adj*

rasp[2] /raasp/ *n Scotland* a raspberry [Mid-16C. Shortening of obsolete *raspis* 'raspberry'.]

raspatory /raáspətəri/ (*plural* **-ries**) *n* a surgical instrument similar to a rasp, used to smooth the ends of a bone [15C. < medieval Latin *raspatorium* < *raspare* 'scrape' < Germanic.]

raspberry /raázbəri/ (*plural* **-ries**) *n* **1 SMALL CUP-SHAPED FRUIT** a small red or black cup-shaped fruit with a sweet taste that grows round a pithy stalk and is made up of many tiny juicy globes (**drupelets**) **2 BUSH** a shrubby plant that produces raspberries. Genus: *Rubus*. **3 RUDE NOISE** a rude noise meant to imitate the sound of breaking wind, made by blowing air through pursed lips and intended as an insult or a gesture of disapproval or defiance (*informal*) US term **Bronx cheer 4 RED COLOUR** a deep purplish-pink colour [Early 17C. < RASP[2].]

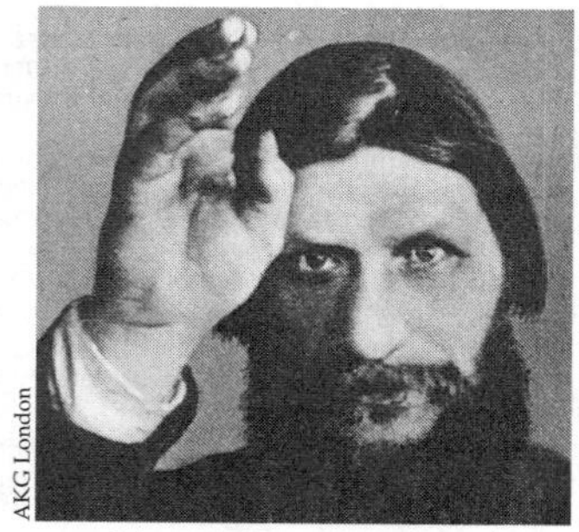

Grigory Yefimovich Rasputin

Rasputin /ra spyóotin/, **Grigory Yefimovich** (1872–1916) Russian peasant and self-proclaimed holy man

rasse /rássi, ráss/ *n* a small carnivorous mammal similar to a cat in appearance and having anal scent glands. Native to: South and Southeast Asia. *Viverricula indica*. [Early 19C. < Javanese.]

Rasta /rástə/ *n* a Rastafarian (*informal*) ■ *adj* relating to Rastafarians or Rastafarianism (*informal*) [Mid-20C. Shortening.]

Rastafarian /rástə fáiri ən/ *n* a member of an Afro-Caribbean religious group that venerates the former emperor of Ethiopia, Haile Selassie, forbids the cutting of hair, and stresses Black culture and identity [Mid-20C. < Amharic *Ras Tafari*, the name by which Haile Selassie was known prior to his coming to power, literally 'prince to be feared'.] —**Rastafarianism** *n*

ϟ **raster** /rástər/ *n* the pattern of horizontal scanning lines made by an electron beam on the surface of a cathode-ray tube that create the image on a television or computer screen [Mid-20C. Via German, 'screen' < Latin *rastrum* 'rake' < *radere* 'scrape, scratch'.]

ϟ **raster burn** *n* eyestrain caused by staring at a computer screen (*slang*)

ϟ **raster font** *n* a bitmapped font formed from pixels

ϟ **raster graphics** *npl* bitmapped graphics formed from pixels

ϟ **rasterize** /rástə rīz/ (**-izes, -izing, -ized**) *vt* to convert a digitized image into a format suitable for display on a computer monitor or printout

rat /rat/ *n* **1 LONG-TAILED RODENT** a long-tailed rodent, larger than a mouse. Genus: *Rattus*. **2 ANIMAL LIKE A RAT** an animal that resembles a rat **3 SOMEBODY UNTRUSTWORTHY** a mean sneaky deceitful person, especially somebody who betrays friends or confidences (*slang*) ■ *vt* (**rats, ratting, ratted**) **1 HUNT RATS** to hunt and kill rats **2** *US* **MAKE THE HAIR STAND HIGH ON THE HEAD** to use a comb to tease hair into knots with quick repeated movements, which makes it stand up high from the scalp ■ *interj* **rats EXPRESSION OF ANNOYANCE** used to express annoyance or contempt [Old English *ræt*] ◇ **smell a rat** be suspicious that something is not right (*informal*)

rat on *vt* (*informal*) **1** to betray somebody's trust, especially by revealing something told in confidence **2** to abandon somebody or something or fail to do something

rata /raátə/ *n* a tree of the myrtle family with hard red wood and crimson flowers. Native to: New Zealand. Genus: *Metrosideros*. [Late 18C. < Maori.]

ratable /ráytəb'l/, **rateable** *adj* **1 ABLE TO BE RATED** able to be estimated or have a value placed on it **2 TAXABLE** liable for a tax ■ **ratables, rateables** *npl US* **1 PROPERTY TAX INCOME** for a government, income from taxes on property **2 TAXABLE BUILDINGS OR OTHER PROPERTY** buildings or other property, especially those in commercial use, that supply local government with tax income —**ratability** /ráytə bíllәti/ *n* —**ratably** /ráytəbli/ *adv*

ratafia /ráttə fée ə/ *n* **1** a liqueur made from fruit juices or softened fruit in liquor, especially brandy, and often flavoured with almonds or with peach or apricot kernels **2 ratafia, ratafia biscuit** a small biscuit similar to a macaroon, flavoured with almond or ratafia. ◊ **macaroon** [Late 17C. Via French < Caribbean Creole.]

Ratana /raátənə/, **Tahupotiki Wiremu** (1870–1939) New Zealand religious leader

rataplan /ráttə plan/ *n* a noise like the rapid beating of a drum, the sound of horses' hooves striking the ground, or machine-gun fire, made up of a series of short repeated sounds [Mid-19C. < French, an imitation of the sound.]

rat-arsed /-aarst/ *adj* an offensive term meaning extremely drunk (*slang*)

ratatat-tat /ráttə tat tát/, **rat-a-tat** /ráttə tát/, **rat-tat, rat-tat-tat** *n* the distinctive rhythmic pattern of short loud sounds made by somebody knocking at a door ■ *interj* an imitation of the sound of somebody knocking on a door [Late 17C. An imitation of the sound.]

ratatouille /ráttə tóo i/ *n* a dish of stewed vegetables, originally from S France, usually consisting of tomatoes, onions, peppers, aubergines, and courgettes cooked slowly in olive oil [Late 19C. < French, alteration of *touiller* 'stir' < Old French *tooiller* 'drag around'.]

ratbag /rát bag/ *n* an offensive term for somebody whom the speaker dislikes, disapproves of, or feels angry with (*slang insult*)

ratbite fever /rát bīt-/ *n* an infectious disease in humans caused by the bite of a rat infected with either of two bacteria, *Streptobacillus moniliformis* or *Spirillum minus*

rat-catcher *n* somebody whose job is to rid buildings of rats and other vermin

rat cheese *n US* Cheddar cheese (*informal humorous*)

ratchet /ráchit/ *n* **1 TURNING DEVICE MOVING IN ONE DIRECTION** a mechanism, used especially in lifting devices and some hand tools, consisting of a metal wheel operating with a catch that permits motion in only one direction **2 RATCHET WHEEL OR PAWL** either of the main parts of a ratchet device, the toothed wheel or bar, or the pawl ■ *v* (**-ets, -etting, -etted**) *US* **1** *vti* **MOVE WITH RATCHET** to move, or to move something gradually up or down by means of a ratchet **2** *vt* **FORCE SOMETHING UP OR DOWN** to force something such as prices or political rhetoric to rise or fall in level or intensity by deliberately applying pressure in successive and irreversible stages [Mid-17C. < French *rochet* 'spool' < Germanic.]

ratchet effect *n* the failure of wages or prices that have risen or fallen because of temporary market pressure to return to their previous level once that pressure is removed

ratchet wheel *n* a toothed wheel in a ratchet mechanism

rate /rayt/ *n* **1 SPEED** the speed at which one measured quantity happens, runs, moves, or changes compared to another measured amount such as time ○ *We'll have to step up our work rate if we're going to finish on schedule.* **2 AMOUNT IN RELATION TO STANDARD FIGURE** the amount, frequency, or speed of something expressed as a proportion of a larger figure or in relation to a whole ○ *The drop-out rate at the end of the first year is around one in three.* **3 CHARGE** the amount of money charged per unit, e.g. per hour, per page, or per thousand, for a particular job, service, or commodity ○ *I'm charging you the going rate for the job.* ■ **rates** *npl* **FORMER LOCAL TAX** a tax formerly levied by local authorities in the United Kingdom on all properties in their areas of jurisdiction, based on a fixed ratable value for each property ■ *v* (**rates, rating, rated**) **1** *vt* **SET A VALUE ON** to calculate or appraise the value of something ○ *How would you rate this gem collection?* **2** *vti* **ASSESS** to have or to be regarded as having a particular value, position, or importance relative to other people or things ○ *This rates as undoubtedly the worst film I have ever seen.* **3** *vt* **DESERVE** to deserve or be worthy of something ○ *Her latest book didn't even rate a review.* **4** *vt* **CLASSIFY** to give a particular classification or rating to something such as a machine, that identifies its performance capabilities and limits **5** *vt* **VALUE SOMETHING FOR TAX PURPOSES** to value something, especially a property, for tax purposes **6** *vt* **THINK HIGHLY OF** to like, approve of, or regard somebody or something as good or excellent (*informal*) ○ *My friends really rate him, but I think his work is amateur.* [15C. Via Old French < medieval Latin *(pro) rata (parte)* '(according to a) fixed (part)' < Latin *ratus*, past participle of *reri* 'calculate'.] ◇ **at any rate** used to indicate that an important point is true, whatever other considerations there may be ◇ **at a rate of knots** very quickly

rateable *adj* = **ratable**

rate-cap (**rate-caps, rate-capping, rate-capped**) *vt* to set an upper limit on the amount of money that a local authority can raise by means of rates —**rate-capping** *n*

rate constant *n* the constant in a mathematical expression relating the concentrations of the reactants and the products for a given chemical reaction

ratel /ráyt'l/ *n* an aggressive carnivorous animal with short thick legs, a strong body with a thick furry coat, dark underneath and whitish on top, and a head similar to a badger's. Native to: Asia, Africa. *Mellivora capensis.* [Late 18C. < Afrikaans, < ?]

ratemaking /ráyt mayking/ *n US* the process or business of establishing rates of payment for such things as public transport or utilities

rate of change *n* the ratio of the difference in values of a variable during a time period to the length of that time period

rate of exchange *n* FIN = **exchange rate**

rate of return *n* the amount of income generated in a year by capital invested, expressed as a percentage of the total sum

ratepayer /ráyt payər/ *n* formerly, somebody who paid a tax to a local authority, based on the value of his or her dwelling

rater /ráytər/ *n US* **1** a person who establishes rates or ratings **2** a person with a specific rank or level of ability (*often in combination*) ○ *All of them are nothing but second-raters with delusions of grandeur.*

ratfink /rát fingk/ *n US* an offensive term for somebody regarded as objectionable or despicable (*insult*)

ratfish /rát fish/ (*plural* **-fish** *or* **-fishes**) *n* a cartilaginous deep-sea fish with a long narrow tail, found worldwide. Family: Chimaeridae.

rath /rath/ *n* a circular enclosure built in ancient Ireland, surrounded by an earth wall and used as a fort or dwelling place [14C. < Irish.]

ratha /rútə/ *n S Asia* a four-wheeled carriage, drawn by horses or oxen [< Sanskrit, 'wagon, chariot']

Rathenau /raátə noir/, **Walther** (1867–1922) German political economist and public servant

rather /raáthər/ *adv* **1 SOMEWHAT** to some extent or degree ○ *rather disappointing* **2 CONSIDERABLY** to a great extent or degree ○ *I think the irises are rather lovely.* **3 MORE WILLINGLY** more readily or willingly ○ *You go to the cinema; I'd rather stay in tonight.* **4 WITH MORE JUSTIFICATION** with more logic, evidence, precision, or justification ○ *You should praise rather than blame them.* **5 ON THE CONTRARY** in contrast or opposition to what has been stated or expected ○ *You think she's snobbish? Rather, I'd say she's shy.* ■ *interj UK* **MOST CERTAINLY** used to express complete or enthusiastic agreement with what has just been said (*dated*) [Old English *hræþor*, originally comparative of *hraeþ* 'quick' < Germanic]

Rathlin Island /ráthlin-/ island in N Northern Ireland. Area: 13 sq. km/5 sq. mi.

rat hole *n* the entrance to a rat's nest

rathskeller /raát skelər/ *n US* a beer hall or restaurant that serves German dishes, usually located below street level [Early 20C. < obsolete German, 'council cellar' (cellar of the town hall) < *Rat* 'council' + *Keller* 'cellar'.]

ratify /rátti fī/ (**-fies, -fying, -fied**) *vt* to give formal approval to something, usually an agreement negotiated by somebody else, in order that it can become valid or operative [14C. Via French *ratifier* < medieval Latin *ratificare* 'make fixed' < Latin *ratus* (see RATE).] —**ratifiable** *adj* —**ratification** /ráttifi káysh'n/ *n* —**ratifier** /rátti fī ər/ *n*

ratiné /rátti nay/, **ratine** /ra téen/ *n* a loosely woven cloth with a coarse knobbly texture [Early 20C. < French, past participle of *ratiner* 'raise a nap' < *ratine* 'nap'.]

rating /ráyting/ *n* **1 ASSESSMENT** an assessment or classification of something on a scale according to how much or how little of a particular quality it possesses ○ *On a scale of one to ten, their rating would be about six* **2 CREDIT STANDING** an assessment of the financial status and creditworthiness of a company or an individual **3 ORDINARY SEAMAN** a serving member of a navy, especially the Royal Navy, who is not an officer **4 HANDICAP IN YACHT RACING** a classification of a racing yacht, based on factors such as its size, weight, and area of sail **5 PERFORMANCE LIMIT OF A MACHINE** a stated performance limit of a machine or system, expressed as capacity, range, or working capability ■ **ratings** *npl* **LIST SHOWING SIZE OF AN AUDIENCE** a list or lists showing the estimated number of people who tuned in to a particular TV or radio programme, used as an indication of its relative popularity

ratio /ráyshi ō/ (*plural* **-tios**) *n* **1 PROPORTIONAL RELATIONSHIP** a proportional relationship between two different numbers or quantities **2 ONE NUMBER DIVIDED BY ANOTHER** a quotient of two numbers or expressions arrived at by dividing one by the other **3** *US* **RELATIVE VALUE OF GOLD AND SILVER** the relative value of gold and silver in a monetary system based on these two metals [Mid-17C. < Latin, 'calculation' < *ratus* (see RATE).]

ratiocinate /rátti óssi nayt/ (**-nates, -nating, -nated**) *vi* to think or put forward an argument about something in a strictly logical way (*formal*) [Mid-17C. < Latin *ratiocinat-*, past participle of *ratiocinari* 'compute' < *ratio* 'calculation'.] —**ratiocination** /rátti óssi náysh'n/ *n* —**ratiocinative** /rátti óssinətiv/ *adj* —**ratiocinator** /-naytər/ *n*

ration /rásh'n/ *n* **1 FIXED AMOUNT ALLOCATED TO AN INDIVIDUAL** a fixed and limited amount of something, especially food, given or allocated to somebody or a group from the stocks available, especially during a time of shortage or a war **2 ADEQUATE AMOUNT** the amount of anything that it seems normal or desirable for an individual to have ○ *rather more than your ration of good luck* ■ **rations** *npl* **AMOUNT OF FOOD OFFICIALLY ALLOCATED** food, especially an amount of food allocated to somebody, e.g. a soldier or hiker, from a limited stock ○ *The campers had to carry their own rations.* ■ *vt* **1 RESTRICT AVAILABLE AMOUNT OF** to restrict the amount of something, usually a commodity in short supply, that an individual is allowed to buy, consume, or use ○ *Petrol was rationed, so long journeys were out of the question.* **2 LIMIT QUANTITY AVAILABLE TO** to allow somebody only a limited quantity of something ○ *I'm trying to ration myself to one drink a day.* [Early 18C. Via French < Spanish *ración* < Latin *ratio* (see RATIO).]

ration out *vt* to distribute something, especially something that is in short supply, in fixed or strictly limited quantities

rational /rásh'nəl/ *adj* **1 REASONABLE AND SENSIBLE** governed by, or showing evidence of, clear and sensible thinking and judgment, based on reason rather than emotion or prejudice **2 IN ACCORDANCE WITH REASON AND LOGIC** presented or understandable in terms that accord with reason and logic or with scientific knowledge and are not based on appeals to emotion or prejudice **3 ABLE TO REASON** endowed with the ability to reason, as opposed to being governed solely by instinct and appetite **4 EXPRESSIBLE AS RATIO OF POLYNOMIALS** in mathematics, able to be expressed exactly as the quotient of two whole numbers or polynomials ○ *a rational function* ■ *n* **RATIONAL NUMBER** a rational number [14C. < Latin *rationalis* < *ratio* (see RATIO).] —**rationally** *adv* —**rationalness** *n*

USAGE rational, rationale, or rationalization? Each of these words has its own discrete meaning, and so they ought not be confused. ***Rational***, without an *-e* ending, is used chiefly as an adjective in the senses 'reasonable and sensible', 'thinking clearly', and 'in accordance with logic and reason': *took a rational approach to town planning; hard to remain rational after experiencing such a terrible accident; found a rational solution to the problem.* ***Rationale***, spelled with an *-e* ending, is a noun only, meaning 'an underlying set of reasons', as in *explained his rationale in assessing those auditioning for the play.* ***Rationalization*** is the process whereby someone attempts to justify or make logical something questionable or illogical: *Rationalization of his behaviour is impossible under the circumstances.*

rational choice theory *n* the hypothesis, derived from game theory, that there is a rational, definable, and calculable basis to human decision-making

rationale /ráshə naál/ *n* the reasoning or principle that underlies or explains a particular course of action, or a statement setting out these reasons or principles [Mid-17C. < modern Latin, < Latin *rationalis* (see RATIONAL).]

USAGE See ***rational***.

rational-emotive behaviour therapy, rational-emotive therapy *n* a form of cognitive-behavioural therapy in which the client is encouraged to examine and change irrational thought patterns and beliefs in order to reduce dysfunctional behaviour

rationalisation *n* = **rationalization**

rationalise *vti* = **rationalize**

rationalism /rásh'nəlizəm/ *n* **1** the belief that thought and action should be governed by reason **2** the belief that reason and logic are the primary sources of knowledge and truth and should be relied on in searching for and testing the truth of things —**rationalist** *n* —**rationalistic** /rásh'nə lístik/ *adj* —**rationalistically** *adv*

rationality /ráshə nálləti/ (*plural* **-ties**) *n* **1** thinking or behaving in a rational way, or having the ability to think rationally **2** a rational belief, opinion, or action (*often plural*)

rationalization /rásh'nə lī záysh'n/, **rationalisation** *n* **1** the process of rationalizing something, or an effect of rationalizing something **2** in psychoanalytic theory, a defence mechanism whereby people attempt to hide their true motivations and emotions by providing reasonable or self-justifying explanations for irrational or unacceptable behaviour

USAGE See ***rational***.

rationalize /rásh'nə līz/ (**-izes, -izing, -ized**), **rationalise** (**-ises, -ising, -ised**) *v* **1** *vt* **MAKE SOMETHING MORE LOGICAL OR RATIONAL** to make something rational, logical, or consistent **2** *vt* **INTERPRET SOMETHING LOGICALLY** to interpret something from a logical or rational perspective **3** *vti* **OFFER A REASONABLE EXPLANATION** to attempt to justify behaviour normally considered irrational or unacceptable by offering an apparently reasonable explanation **4** *vt* **ELIMINATE RADICALS** to eliminate irrational numbers from an expression or an equation **5** *vti* **MAKE SOMETHING MORE EFFICIENT AND PROFITABLE** to make something more efficient and profitable, especially by getting rid of staff, equipment, or parts of the business that are considered to be inefficient or unprofitable —**rationalizable** *adj* —**rationalizer** *n*

rational number *n* a whole number or the quotient of any whole numbers, excluding zero as a denominator

ratio scale *n* a scale for measuring data that makes it possible to compare different values and to state the difference between them in the form of a ratio

Rat Islands /rát-/ island group in the W Aleutian Islands, SW Alaska

ratite /ráttīt/ *n* a flightless bird such as the ostrich or emu that has a flat breastbone without the keel that flying birds have [Late 19C. < Latin *ratitus* 'having the figure of a raft' < *ratis* 'raft'.]

rat kangaroo *n* small kangaroo resembling a rat and having long hind legs for jumping. Native to: Australia, Tasmania. Genera: *Potorus* and *Bettongia*.

ratline /rάttlin/, **ratlin** *n* any small rope fastened horizontally between the shrouds in the rigging of a sailing ship to make a ladder for the crew going aloft [15C. < ?]

ratoon /ra tóon/, **rattoon** *n* **1 SHOOT AT THE BASE OF A CROP PLANT** a shoot growing up from the base of a crop plant such as sugar cane or bananas after the previous growth has been cut back **2 CROP PRODUCED ON RATOONS** a crop, e.g. sugar cane, bananas, or pineapple, that is produced on ratoons ■ *vti* **PRODUCE RATOONS** to propagate by inducing the formation of ratoons, or to send up ratoons [Mid-17C. Via Spanish *retoño* 'shoot' < Latin *autumnus* 'autumn'.]

rat pack *n* a group of people with close ties or common interests and aims, whose activities are sometimes regarded with suspicion or disapproval (*slang insult*)

rat race *n* the struggle of individuals to survive and make progress in the competitive environment of modern life, seen as a dehumanizing and ultimately futile activity (*informal*) ○ *I'd like to get out of this rat race and retire to an isolated farm.*

rat snake *n* a large nonvenomous snake that eats rodents. Native to: North America, Asia. Genera: *Elaphe* and *Ptyas*.

rattail /rát tayl/ *n* a hairless tail on a horse ■ *adj* **rattail, rat-tail** looking like or having a part that resembles a rat's tail ○ *a rat-tail comb*

rattan /ra tán/ *n* **1 STEMS OF A TROPICAL PLANT** the stems of a tropical plant. Use: wickerwork, furniture, canes. **2 TROPICAL ASIAN CLIMBING PALM** a climbing palm that is the source of rattan. Native to: tropical Asia. Genera: *Calamus* and *Daemonorops* and *Plectomia*. **3 WALKING STICK** a walking stick or cane made from rattan [Mid-17C. < Malay *rotan*.]

rat-tat, rat-tat-tat *n, interj* = **ratatat-tat**

ratted /ráttid/ *adj* **1** drunk (*slang*) **2** *US* having had a comb used repeatedly to make tangles in the hair, making the hair stand up higher from the scalp [Late 20C. < RAT, probably after RAT-ARSED.]

ratter /ráttər/ *n* an animal, especially a cat or dog, that is good at catching rats

rattle[1] /rátt'l/ *v* (**-tles, -tling, -tled**) **1** *vti* **MAKE SHORT SHARP KNOCKING SOUNDS** to make short sharp knocking or jangling sounds in quick succession, especially as a result of being moved or shaken, or to shake something so as to produce such sounds ○ *He picked up the box and rattled it.* ○ *The windows and doors rattled in the wind.* **2** *vi* **MOVE WITH RATTLING SOUND** to move while making a rattling sound ○ *The old car rattled noisily down the street.* **3** *vt* **DISCONCERT** to make somebody lose his or her composure and feel frightened, worried, confused, or annoyed ■ *n* **1 SHORT SHARP KNOCKING OR JANGLING SOUNDS** a succession of short sharp knocking or jangling sounds, usually caused by something shaking or being shaken **2 BABY'S TOY** a baby's toy consisting of a hollow shape with small objects inside, usually attached to a handle, that makes a rattling noise when shaken **3 NOISEMAKER** an object such as a musical instrument or a shaman's implement that produces a loud rattling sound **4 TIP OF RATTLESNAKE'S TAIL** a set of loosely attached horny segments at the end of a rattlesnake's tail that produce a buzzing or rattling sound when shaken **5 PLANT WITH RATTLING SEEDS** any European plant whose seeds make a rattling noise inside the seed capsule **6 RATTLING NOISE IN THE THROAT** a raspy or rattling noise made in the throat caused by obstructed breathing and heard especially near death [14C. Probably < Middle Low German *ratelen*, an imitation of the sound.]

rattle around *vi* to be in a room, house, or building that is bigger than it needs to be (*informal*) ○ *There's just the two of us rattling around in this place.*

rattle off *vt* to say, read aloud, or perform something very rapidly or with no apparent effort

rattle on *vi* to talk rapidly and at length about something that is of little interest or importance to the listener

rattle through *vt* to do something very quickly and often in a perfunctory way ○ *He rattled through the agenda, scarcely pausing for breath.*

rattle[2] /rátt'l/ (**-tles, -tling, -tled**) *vt* to attach ratlines to the shrouds in the rigging of a ship [Early 18C. Back-formation < *ratling*, a variant of RATLINE.]

Rattle /rátt'l/, **Sir Simon** (*b.* 1955) British conductor

rattlebrained /rátt'l braynd/ *adj US* regarded as showing a lack of intelligence or common sense, usually because of speaking rapidly and at length without much substance (*informal insult*)

rattler /rátt'lər/ *n* **1** = **rattlesnake 2** somebody or something that rattles **3** *US* a freight train (*informal*)

rattlesnake /rátt'l snayk/ *n* a large venomous snake of the pit viper family, whose tail has loosely attached horny segments that buzz or rattle when vibrated. Native to: North and South America. Genus: *Crotalis* and *Sistrurus*.

rattlesnake plantain *n* an orchid with striped or mottled leaves resembling a rattlesnake's skin. Flowers: white or yellow, in spikes. Genus: *Goodyera*.

rattletrap /rátt'l trap/ *n* an old noisy worn-out car or other vehicle (*informal*)

rattling /rátt'ling/ *adj* moving or talking at a very fast or lively pace ○ *a rattling TV debate* ■ *adv* extremely (*dated informal*) ○ *tells a rattling good story* —**rattlingly** *adv*

rattly /rátt'li/ (**-tlier, -tliest**) *adj* making a lot of noise, usually because of being in very bad condition or not firmly fixed ○ *a rattly air conditioner*

rattoon *n* PLANT SCI = **ratoon**

rat-trap *n* **1 TRAP FOR RATS** a trap designed to catch rats **2 TYPE OF BICYCLE PEDAL** a bicycle pedal with an all-metal footrest with serrated edges and a toe clip on the front (*informal*) **3** *US* **SQUALID DWELLING** a dilapidated dirty unsafe dwelling (*informal*) ○ *They bought a rat-trap and are fixing it up.*

ratty /rátti/ (**-tier, -tiest**) *adj* **1 IRRITABLE** irritable or annoyed (*informal*) ○ *Don't get ratty, it won't take very long.* **2 OF RATS** relating to or believed to be characteristic of rats **3 INFESTED WITH RATS** full of or overrun with rats **4 MESSY** having an appearance that is messy and generally unkempt (*informal*) **5** *US, Can* **DILAPIDATED** in an unsafe, rundown condition and unfit for human habitation (*informal*) —**rattily** *adv* —**rattiness** *n*

raucous /ráwkəss/ *adj* loud and hoarse or unpleasant-sounding, or characterized by loud noise, shouting, and ribald laughter [Mid-18C. < Latin *raucus* 'hoarse'.] —**raucity** /ráwssəti/ *n* —**raucously** *adv* —**raucousness** *n*

raunch /rawnch/ *n* (*slang*) **1 SEXUAL EXPLICITNESS** sexual explicitness or suggestiveness of an earthy or vulgar kind, especially as part of a performer's material or act **2 SEXUALLY EXPLICIT MATERIAL** sexually explicit or lewd material or language **3** *US* **MESSINESS** lack of cleanliness or neatness [Mid-20C. Back-formation < RAUNCHY.]

raunchy /ráwnchi/ (**-chier, -chiest**) *adj* **1** sexually explicit or obscene in a coarse vulgar way (*informal*) **2** *US* lacking neatness or cleanliness (*slang*) [Mid-20C. < ?] —**raunchily** *adv* —**raunchiness** *n*

Rauschenberg /rówsh'n burg/, **Robert** (*b.* 1925) US artist

rauwolfia /raw wóolfi ə, row-/ *n* **1** a tropical tree or shrub whose root has medicinal properties. Native to: SE Asia. *Rauwolfia serpentina*. **2** the dried root of. *Rauwolfia serpentina*. Use: sedatives. [Mid-18C. < modern Latin, after Leonhard *Rauwolf*.]

ravage /rávvij/ *v* (**-ages, -aging, -aged**) **1** *vti* **COMPLETELY WRECK OR DAMAGE** to wreck or utterly destroy something through a violent onslaught of some kind (*often passive*) ○ *a once-beautiful landscape ravaged by development* **2** *vt* **WRECK AND PLUNDER A PLACE** to plunder or sack a place or area ■ *n* **ACT OR HABIT OF DESTRUCTION** the act or habit of destroying or plundering something ■ **ravages** *npl* **DAMAGING EFFECTS** the damaging or disfiguring effects of something [Early 17C. < French *ravager*, alteration of *ravine* 'rushing of water' < Latin *rapere* 'seize'.] —**ravagement** *n* —**ravager** *n*

rave /rayv/ *v* (**raves, raving, raved**) **1** *vti* **SPEAK WILDLY AND INCOHERENTLY** to speak in a loud or angry way that suggests lack of rationality or loss of self-control **2** *vi* **GIVE HIGH PRAISE** to praise something in a very enthusiastic way (*informal*) ○ *All the critics raved about her performance.* **3** *vi* **STORM** to be very stormy and make a loud roaring noise (*literary*) **4 rave, rave it up** *vi* **HAVE A GOOD TIME** to have a good time, especially at a party, in a wild uninhibited way (*dated slang*) ■ *n* **1 ACT OF RAVING** an act or instance of raving **2 ENTHUSIASTIC PRAISE** something, especially a review, that expresses extremely enthusiastic praise (*informal; often before nouns*) ○ *gave the novel rave reviews* **3 LARGE-SCALE PARTY** a large-scale party or club event at which pop music is played, lasting sometimes all night **4 CRAZE** a craze or fad (*dated slang*) [14C. < Old French *raver*.]

ravel /rávv'l/ (**-els, -elling, -elled**) *v* **1** *vti* **TANGLE** to become tangled, or cause threads or fibres to tangle **2** *vti* **FRAY** to come, or cause threads to come, loose from a knitted or woven fabric **3** *vt* **RESOLVE** to clarify or resolve something complicated **4** *vt* **BREAK UP ROAD SURFACE** to break up a road surface or begin to break into fragments [Late 16C. Probably < Dutch *ravelen*.] —**raveler** *n* —**ravelment** *n*

Ravel /rə vél/, **Maurice** (1875–1937) French composer

ravelin /rávvlin/ *n* a small outwork in fortifications consisting of two embankments shaped like an arrowhead that point outwards in front of a larger defence work [Late 16C. Via French < Italian *ravellina*.]

raven[1] /ráyv'n/ *n* a large bird belonging to the crow family with glossy black plumage, a wedge-shaped tail, and a large beak. Native to: N hemisphere. *Corvus corax*. ■ *adj* of a deep lustrous black (*literary*) [Old English *hræfn* < Germanic, probably an imitation of its croaking]

LITERARY LINK ***The Raven***, a poem (1845) by US writer Edgar Allen Poe. This melancholy tale of lost love gained Poe national fame. As a young student mourns the death of his lover, a raven – a traditional symbol of doom – appears at his window. To every question that the student poses about his future and his lover, the bird responds 'Nevermore'.

raven[2] /rávv'n/ *vti* **1** to eat something voraciously or greedily **2** to take something away by force, especially prey or plunder [15C. Via Old French *raviner* 'seize' < Latin *rapere* 'seize'.] —**ravener** *n*

ravening /rávv'ning/ *adj* living by hunting prey, especially in a greedy voracious way —**raveningly** *adv*

Ravenna /rə vénnə/ city in NE Italy. Population: 134,000 (1994).

ravenous /rávv'nəss/ *adj* **1** extremely hungry **2** hungry or greedy for something, especially for the gratification of wants or desires —**ravenously** *adv* —**ravenousness** *n*

raver /ráyvər/ *n* (*informal*) **1** a person who has an active and uninhibited social life **2** a person who goes to raves

rave-up *n* a wild noisy party with music, drinking, and dancing (*dated slang*)

ravin /rávvin/ *n* the act of violently seizing something (*archaic or literary*) [14C. < Old French *ravine* (see RAVINE).]

ravine /rə véen/ *n* a deep narrow valley, especially one formed by running water [15C. < Old French *ravine* 'rapine, violent rush' < Latin *rapere* 'seize'.]

raving /ráyving/ *adj* **1 IRRATIONAL** wildly irrational, angry, or insulting **2 STUNNING** used to emphasize the sense of admiration and excitement felt for something (*informal*) ○ *a raving review of the play* ■ **ravings** *npl* **WILDLY IRRATIONAL SPEECH** wildly irrational, angry, or insulting utterances ○ *the ravings of a person cheated* —**ravingly** *adv*

ravioli /rávvi ōli/ *n* a food made from small squares of pasta sealed around a meat, cheese, or other filling [Mid-19C. < Italian, the plural of dialectal *raviolo* 'small turnip'.]

ravish /rávvish/ *vt* **1 OVERWHELM SOMEBODY EMOTIONALLY** to overwhelm somebody with deep and pleasurable feelings or emotions (*usually passive*) **2 RAPE** to force somebody to engage in sexual intercourse (*literary*) **3 CARRY SOMETHING OFF** to carry off something by violent force (*archaic or literary*) [13C. < French *raviss-* 'seize' < Latin *rapere*.] —**ravisher** *n* —**ravishment** *n*

ravishing /rávvishing/ *adj* extremely delightful or beautiful —**ravishingly** *adv*

raw /raw/ *adj* **1 UNCOOKED** not cooked **2 UNPROCESSED** not processed, refined, or treated in any way **3 HURT AND SORE** cut, scraped, or inflamed, often painfully so **4 INEXPERIENCED** lacking training for or experience with something **5 COLD** extremely cold and harsh **6 NOT SUBTLE** not subtle, restrained, or refined ○ *the raw power of the music* **7 BRUTALLY REALISTIC** factual and realistic, especially in connection with unpleasant matters ○ *a raw portrayal of a model's life* **8 NOT CHANGED OR INTERPRETED** in an original state and not yet subjected to correction or analysis [Old English *hrēaw* < Indo-European] —**rawly** *adv* —**rawness** *n* ◇ **touch somebody on the raw** to upset somebody or to make somebody uncomfortable by referring to something that he or she is very sensitive about ◇ **in the raw 1** not wearing clothes (*informal*) **2** in a natural state, without embellishment or refinement

Rawalpindi /ráwl píndi/, **Rāwalpindi** city in NE Pakistan. Population: 1,406,214 (1998).

rawboned /ráw bōnd/ *adj* having a lean body with prominent bones

raw deal *n* an arrangement, situation, or treatment that is unfair

rawhide /ráw hīd/ *n* **1** untanned animal hide **2** a whip or rope made of rawhide

rawhide hammer *n* a hammer designed to avoid damage to finished surfaces, with a head made from a tight roll of hide held in a metal tube

rawinsonde /ráywin sond/ n a balloon carrying meteorological instruments that has a trackable radar target and is used to observe the velocity and direction of upper-air winds [Mid-20C. Blend of RADAR + WIND[1], + radiosonde.]

Rawlings /ráwlingz/, **Jerry** (b. 1947) Ghanaian soldier and statesman

raw material n 1 a natural unprocessed material that is used in a manufacturing process 2 something or somebody considered to have potential for use or development

raw sienna n 1 a yellowish-brown colour 2 a natural brownish-yellow substance that is used as a pigment

raw silk n 1 silk fibres reeled from silkworm cocoons and left untreated 2 fabric or yarn made from raw silk

Rawsthorne /ráwss thawrn/, **Alan** (1905–71) British composer

rax /raks/ v Scotland 1 vti to stretch or reach out 2 vt to pass something with an outstretched hand [Old English raxan < Germanic]

ray[1] /ray/ n 1 BEAM OF LIGHT a narrow beam of light from the sun or an artificial light source 2 TRACE OF SOMETHING POSITIVE a slight indication of something positive in a difficult or worrying situation 3 BEAM OF ENERGY a thin beam of radiant energy or particles 4 LINE EXTENDING FROM POINT a straight line that extends from a point infinitely in one direction 5 ARM OF STARFISH an arm of a starfish or other animal with body parts radiating from the centre 6 BRIGHT STREAK FROM LUNAR CRATER any bright streak on the lunar surface that radiates from a crater 7 RADIAL STRAND OF PLANT PITH a distinct strand of tissue running radially through the conducting tissues in the stem of a plant ■ **rays** npl SUNSHINE hot or warm sunshine, especially when thought of as a tanning agent (slang) ◇ catch some rays ■ v 1 vti EMIT LIGHT to shine or emit rays, e.g. of light or electromagnetic particles 2 vi EXTEND IN LINES to extend in radiating lines from a point [14C. Via French rai < Latin radius 'staff, spoke, ray, beam of light'.] —**rayed** adj

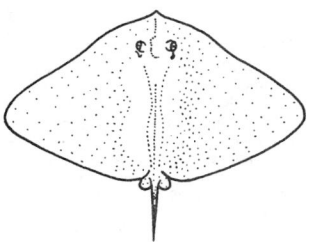

Ray

ray[2] /ray/ n a fish with a cartilaginous skeleton, a flat head and body, broad pectoral fins, and a tapering tail. Order: Rajiformes. ◊ **stingray** [14C. Via French raie < Latin raia.]

ray[3] /ray/ n a syllable that represents the second note in a scale, used for singing exercises (**solfeggio**). US term **re**[1] [15C. Alteration of RE[1].]

Ray /ray/, **Man** (1890–1976) US artist. Born Emanuel Rudnitsky

Ray, **Satyajit** (1921–92) Indian film director

ray flower, **ray floret** n any radiating part of the flower of a composite plant such as the dandelion or daisy, comprising either the whole flower head, as in a dandelion, or only its margin, as in a daisy

ray gun n in science fiction, a gun capable of firing rays of energy that stun or destroy

Rayleigh /ráyli/, **John William Strutt, 3rd Baron** (1842–1919) British physicist

Rayleigh scattering /ráyli-/ n the scattering of electromagnetic radiation into different wavelengths by very small particles of matter, responsible for red sunrises and sunsets as well as the blue of the daytime sky [Mid-20C. After John William Strutt RAYLEIGH.]

rayless /ráyless/ adj 1 dark, gloomy, or lacking light (literary) 2 lacking the ray flowers that typically form part of the flower heads of plants in the daisy family — **raylessly** adv —**raylessness** n

Satyajit Ray

Raymond Terrace /ráymənd-/ town in E New South Wales, Australia. Population: 11,151 (1991).

Raynaud's disease /ráy nóz-/ n a disorder of the blood vessels in which somebody is affected by Raynaud's phenomenon without any identifiable underlying cause [Late 19C. After the French physician Maurice Raynaud (1834–81).]

Raynaud's phenomenon n spasms of the arteries of the fingers and toes, typically brought on by cold, causing the hands and feet to become pale, cold, numb, and sometimes painful [Mid-20C. See RAYNAUD'S DISEASE.]

rayon /ráy on/ n 1 a synthetic textile fibre made from cellulose 2 a synthetic fabric or yarn made from rayon fibres [Early 20C. < RAY[1].]

raze /rayz/ (**razes, razing, razed**), **rase** (**rases, rasing, rased**) vt 1 to destroy or level a building or settlement completely 2 US to scrape or shave something off something else [Mid-16C. Via French raser 'shave off' < Latin radere 'scrape, scratch'.] —**razer** n

razoo /raa zóo, rə zóo/ (plural -**zoos**) n ANZ an imaginary coin that has little or no value (informal; in negatives) ◇ He didn't have a brass razoo. [Mid-20C. < ?]

razor /ráyzər/ n an instrument with a blade or powered cutting head that is used for shaving hair off the face or body ■ vt to shave or cut hair using a razor [13C. < Old French rasor < raser 'shave off'.]

razorback /ráyzər bak/ n 1 MARINE BIOL = **finback** 2 a feral pig of the SE United States that has a narrow body, ridged back, and long legs 3 US a hill that has a sharp ridge

razorbill /ráyzər bil/, **razor-billed auk** n a seabird of the auk family, with black-and-white plumage and a sharp hooked beak. Native to: North Atlantic coasts. Alca torda.

razor blade n a flat blade designed to be used in a safety razor

razor clam n US ZOOL = **razor-shell**

razor cut n a haircut that is done using a razor rather than scissors ■ vt to cut or style hair with a razor rather than scissors

razor-shell n any of various bivalve molluscs that have a long narrow tubular shell with squared ends. Native to: Atlantic and Pacific coasts. Family: Solenidae. US term **razor clam**

razor wire n wire with sharp pieces of metal fixed along its length, used for fences and barriers

razz /raz/ vt US to tease or make fun of somebody (informal) ■ n US, Can a raspberry noise (informal) [Early 20C. Shortening and alteration of RASPBERRY.]

razzle /rázz'l/ [Early 20C. Shortening.] ◇ **on the razzle, on the razzle-dazzle** enjoying a spell of unrestrained partying or heavy drinking (dated informal)

razzle-dazzle n 1 an often gaudy showiness that is designed to impress and excite people 2 = **razzle** [Late 19C. Rhyming compound < DAZZLE.]

razzmatazz /rázmə táz/ n showiness that is designed to impress and excite people, especially in the context of a stage show or other spectacle [Late 20C. < ?]

Rb symbol rubidium

rbc, RBC abbr red blood (cell) count

RBE abbr relative biological effectiveness

⚡**RBTL** abbr read between the lines (in e-mails)

rc abbr reinforced concrete

RC abbr 1 Red Cross 2 RC, R.C. Roman Catholic 3 Reserve Corps

RCA abbr Royal College of Art

RCM abbr Royal College of Music

RCMP abbr Royal Canadian Mounted Police

RCN abbr 1 Royal Canadian Navy 2 Royal College of Nursing

r-colour n in phonetics, the effect of an 'r' sound uttered simultaneously with a vowel by constricting the oral cavity with the tongue

RCP abbr Royal College of Physicians

RCS abbr 1 Royal College of Surgeons 2 Royal Corps of Signals 3 Royal College of Science

RCVS abbr Royal College of Veterinary Surgeons

rd abbr 1 rendered 2 rod 3 round

Rd abbr Road (in addresses)

RD abbr 1 refer to drawer (on cheques) 2 Rural Delivery

RDF abbr radio direction finder

RDS[1] n a system for tuning radio receivers automatically by sending digital signals with normal radio programmes [Abbreviation of radio data system]

RDS[2] abbr respiratory distress syndrome

re[1] /ray/ n MUSIC = **ray**[3] [15C. Shortening of medieval Latin resonare.]

re[2] /ree, ray/ prep with reference to [Early 18C. < Latin, 'on the matter of', a form of res 'thing, matter'.]

USAGE The use of **re** meaning 'with reference to' is largely restricted to the language of business, but it is also used informally as a convenient short form: Re your recent proposal – I fully agree.

⚡**re**[3] abbr Reunion (in Internet addresses)

're contr are ◇ They're planning to come.

Re[1] /ray/ n MYTHOL = **Ra**[1]

Re[2] symbol 1 rhenium 2 rupee 3 Reynolds number

RE abbr 1 Religious Education 2 Reformed Episcopal 3 Right Excellent 4 Royal Engineers

re- prefix 1 again, anew ◇ rebuild 2 back, backward ◇ recall [Via Old French < Latin]

reabsorption /ree ab záwrpsh'n, -záwrp-/ n the act or process of absorbing something again, especially a chemical or fluid

⚡**reach** /reech/ v 1 vti EXTEND to stretch out physically or extend as far as a particular place or point ◇ I can't reach the top shelf without a chair. 2 vi MOVE TOWARDS SOMETHING TO TOUCH IT to move towards something in order to touch or grasp it ◇ She reached for her coat. 3 vt ARRIVE AT PARTICULAR PLACE to arrive or come to a particular place or point 4 vti ARRIVE AT PARTICULAR STATE to get into a particular state or condition ◇ I had reached desperation point. 5 vti INFLUENCE PEOPLE to have an influence or impact on people or on a group ◇ This campaign will reach millions of people. 6 vt CONTACT to communicate with somebody ◇ I'll try to reach you at home. 7 vt PASS to pass or hand somebody something (informal) ◇ Just reach me down that file, would you. 8 vi STRIVE FOR to strive too much to achieve or acquire something, especially without success 9 vi SAIL WITH WIND TO THE SIDE to sail on a tack with the wind blowing from the side ■ n 1 ACT OF STRETCHING OUT the act of stretching out or extending 2 EXTENT OF REACHING the extent or range that somebody or something is able to reach ◇ The top shelf is just beyond his reach. 3 RANGE OF POWER the extent of the power or influence exercised by somebody or something ◇ beyond the reach of the law 4 STRETCH OF WATER a stretch of open water, e.g. on a river 5 TACK SAILED BY VESSEL a tack sailed by a vessel with the wind blowing from the side 6 NUMBER OF VIEWERS the number of viewers who visit a website or watch a particular television program (informal) ◇ Reach is one factor determining whether companies invest in the Web. ■ **reaches** npl AREA OR LEVEL an area or level of something ◇ the upper reaches of the Amazon [Old English rǣcan < Germanic] —**reachable** adj —**reacher** n ◇ **out of reach** 1 beyond the grasp of somebody's outstretched hand 2 not able to be achieved by somebody ◇ **within** or **in reach** 1 able to be grasped by somebody with outstretched hand 2 achievable or attainable

react /ri ákt/ *vi* 1 **RESPOND EMOTIONALLY** to respond to something by showing the feelings or thoughts it arouses 2 **RESPOND BY TAKING ACTION** to respond to something by taking action 3 **RESPOND PHYSICALLY** to respond to the physical effects of something, e.g. a medication or air pollutants 4 **CHANGE CHEMICALLY** to undergo a chemical reaction

reactance /ri áktənss/ *n* (*symbol X*) opposition to the flow of alternating current caused by the inductance and capacitance in a circuit, measured in ohms

reactant /ri áktənt/ *n* a substance that reacts with another in a chemical reaction

reaction /ri áksh'n/ *n* 1 **EMOTIONAL RESPONSE** an emotional or intellectual response that something arouses 2 **ACTIVE RESPONSE** a response to something that involves taking action, or an action taken in response to something 3 **PHYSICAL RESPONSE** a response to the physical effects of something such as heat, cold, or pollution 4 **BODILY RESPONSE TO SUBSTANCE** a response by the body to a foreign substance, especially to an infection, medication, food, or something that causes an allergy 5 **FORCES ACTING ON A BODY** an equal but opposite force exerted by a body when a force acts upon it 6 **STRONG CONSERVATISM** strong opposition to social or political changes that the speaker considers liberal or progressive (*disapproving*) 7 **NUCLEAR PROCESS** a nuclear process resulting in a change in structure of atomic nuclei ■ **reactions** *npl* **SOMEBODY'S ABILITY TO REACT QUICKLY** somebody's ability to respond quickly to an unexpected situation, especially one of danger ○ *His quick reactions saved us from certain death.* —**reactional** *adj*

reactionary /ri áksh'nəri/ *adj* opposed to social or political changes that the speaker considers liberal or progressive ■ *n* (*plural* **-ies**) an opponent of social and political changes that the speaker considers liberal or progressive

reaction engine *n* an engine that produces thrust by ejecting a stream of gas at high velocity, as do jet engines and rocket engines

reaction formation *n* in psychoanalysis, a defence mechanism in which somebody condemns something that has an unconscious appeal

⚡**reaction time** *n* 1 the interval of time between the application of a stimulus and the first indication of a response 2 COMPUT = **access time**

reactivate /ri ákti vayt/ (**-vates, -vating, -vated**) *vti* to make something active again, or to become active again —**reactivation** /ri ákti váysh'n/ *n*

reactive /ri áktiv/ *adj* 1 **REACTING TO EVENTS AND SITUATIONS** reacting to events, situations, and stimuli, especially when doing so spontaneously as they occur 2 **REACTING CHEMICALLY** taking part in chemical reactions 3 **CAUSED BY STIMULI OR EVENTS** describes a psychiatric condition caused by particular situations or stimuli, e.g. the behaviour of other people or the death of a loved one —**reactively** *adv* —**reactiveness** *n* —**reactivity** /rée ak tívvəti/ *n*

reactor /ri áktər/ *n* 1 **SOMETHING THAT REACTS** somebody or something that reacts or takes part in a reaction 2 **DEVICE IN WHICH NUCLEAR REACTION OCCURS** a device in which self-sustained controlled nuclear fission or experimental nuclear fusion takes place, producing heat energy 3 **CONTAINER IN WHICH CHEMICAL REACTION OCCURS** a vessel or other equipment in which an industrial chemical reaction takes place 4 **COMPONENT IN ELECTRICAL CIRCUIT** a component in an electrical circuit used to create reactance, e.g. a capacitor or an inductor 5 **SOMEBODY SENSITIVE TO MEDICATION** a person or animal that displays a reaction to a medication, vaccine, or other substance, especially one that shows a positive reaction to a skin test for latent infection

⚡**read** /reed/ *v* (**reads, reading, read** /red/) 1 *vti* **INTERPRET WRITTEN MATERIAL** to interpret the characters in written or printed material, understanding the sense of what is written 2 *vti* **UTTER WRITTEN WORDS** to say the words of written or printed material either internally or out loud 3 *vti* **LEARN SOMETHING BY READING** to find something out by studying written or printed material ○ *I read it in a book.* 4 *vt* **INTERPRET NONWRITTEN MATERIAL** to interpret the information conveyed by movements, signs, or signals ○ *We could no longer read the trail.* 5 *vti* **INTERPRET PRINTED SIGNS** to interpret the meaning of signs and symbols in printed material, some of which may not be in verbal form ○ *to learn to read music* 6 *vt* **BE ABLE TO READ IN FOREIGN LANGUAGE** to know a foreign language well enough to be able to read in it ○ *Can you read French?* 7 *vt* **TAKE UNIVERSITY COURSE** to pursue a particular course of study at a university 8 *vt* **UNDERSTAND SOMETHING INTUITIVELY** to have an understanding of something by experience or intuitive means ○ *claiming to be able to read the future* 9 *vti* **PROOFREAD** to read through something in order to find poor grammar, misprints, and other errors 10 *vti* **INTERPRET SOMETHING IN PARTICULAR WAY** to interpret or understand something, or be interpreted or understood, in a particular way ○ *I read this passage as being extremely optimistic.* 11 *vi* **HAVE QUALITIES THAT AFFECT UNDERSTANDING** to have particular characteristics that affect the way something is understood ○ *In the original it reads as poetry rather than prose.* 12 *vi* **HAVE PARTICULAR WORDS** to have a particular wording ○ *a sign that reads DANGER* 13 *vti* **HEAR SOMETHING ON TWO-WAY RADIO** to receive and understand a message sent by somebody on a two-way radio 14 *vt* **INDICATE DATA** to indicate or display data, e.g. a temperature ○ *What does the thermometer read?* 15 *vt* **SUBSTITUTE WORD** to substitute a word or words for others that were printed incorrectly ○ *For 'peasant' read 'pheasant'.* 16 *vti* **TRANSFER DATA INTO COMPUTER MEMORY** to transfer program instructions or data from a storage device into a computer's main memory ■ *n* 1 **READING MATERIAL** something that produces a particular reaction in the reader when read ○ *a thrilling read* 2 **TIME SPENT READING** a period devoted to reading ○ *She settled down for a long read.* [Old English *rǣdan* < Indo-European] ◇ **take something as read** to assume something to be the case

SPELLCHECK Do not confuse ***read*** with ***reed***, which has a similar sound. Beware: your spellchecker will not catch this error.

read into *vt* to detect meanings in speech or written text that were not necessarily intended by the speaker or writer

read out *vt* 1 **READ SOMETHING ALOUD** to read something out loud 2 **RETRIEVE INFORMATION FROM COMPUTER** to retrieve data from the memory or a disk or other storage device of a computer 3 *US* **EXPEL SOMEBODY FROM ORGANIZATION** to expel somebody formally from a political party, organization, or other group

read up *vti* to learn a lot about a subject by reading about it or researching it

Read /reed/, **Sir Herbert** (1893–1968) British art historian

readable /réedəb'l/ *adj* 1 able to be read easily 2 having a style that makes reading enjoyable and interesting —**readability** /réedə bílləti/ *n* —**readableness** *n* —**readably** *adv*

readdress /rée ə dréss/ *vt* 1 to put a new address on a letter, especially if the existing address is wrong or if the letter has to be forwarded 2 to return to a problem or issue, especially with the intention of resolving it

⚡**reader** /réedər/ *n* 1 **SOMEBODY WHO READS** a person who reads, especially one who reads a particular thing or who reads in a specific way 2 **READING DEVICE** a device that reads, especially one connected to a computer for reading media 3 **EDUCATIONAL BOOK** an educational book intended as an aid in learning to read or learning a foreign language 4 **ANTHOLOGY** a collection of literary works by a single author or by several authors linked, e.g. by their period or style 5 **SOMEBODY WHO READS FOR PUBLISHER** a person who reads manuscripts for a publisher to assess whether they are publishable 6 CHR = **lay reader** 7 JUDAISM = **cantor** *n.* 1 8 **LECTURER AT UNIVERSITY** a lecturer at university who ranks above a senior lecturer and below a professor

readership /réedər ship/ *n* 1 the group or number of people who read a particular newspaper, magazine, or journal 2 the position of reader in a British university, of a rank above senior lectureship

readily /réddili/ *adv* 1 promptly and without any hesitation 2 with little difficulty

reading /réeding/ *n* 1 **IDENTIFYING OF WRITTEN OR PRINTED WORDS** the identifying of combinations of written or printed letters or characters as words in a language and understanding their meaning 2 **MATERIAL THAT IS READ** printed or written material that can be read 3 **OCCASION OF READING** an occasion when somebody reads something, especially a poem or a piece of literature, to an audience 4 **TEXT READ TO AUDIENCE OR CONGREGATION** a piece of literature that is read to an audience, or a passage from a sacred text that is read to a congregation 5 **INTERPRETATION OF** an interpretation or understanding of a situation or of something that has been written or said 6 **INFORMATION TAKEN FROM EQUIPMENT** information or a measurement taken from a piece of equipment or with the help of equipment 7 **RECITAL OF PARLIAMENTARY BILL** the formal recital of a bill as part of the procedure in Parliament after which it has to pass through three other stages before it can become law 8 **ONE OF BILL'S THREE PARLIAMENTARY STAGES** one of the three stages that a bill passes through in parliament before it becomes law

Reading /rédding/ 1 city in S England. Population: 135,455 (1996). 2 city in NE Massachusetts. Population: 22,539 (1996 estimate). 3 city in SE Pennsylvania. Population: 74,762 (1998 estimate).

reading age *n* a child's competence in reading, measured against the average competence of children of the same age

reading frame *n* a sequence of three nucleotides on DNA or messenger RNA that indicates the starting point for translation to produce a polypeptide

readjust /rée ə júst/ *v* 1 *vi* to get used to something after a period of absence from it 2 *vt* to rearrange or make small changes to something —**readjustable** *adj* —**readjuster** *n* —**readjustment** *n*

⚡**README file** /réed mee-/ *n* a computer text file supplied with the software for a program and containing information that a user may need in order to install or operate the program

readmit /rée əd mít/ (**-mits, -mitting, -mitted**) *vt* to allow somebody to enter a building, have access to something, or join an organization again ○ *If you leave the theatre during the performance you cannot be readmitted.* ○ *After a relapse, she had to be readmitted to hospital.* —**readmission** /rée əd mísh'n/ *n*

⚡**read-only** *adj* describes computer files that can be retrieved and displayed but cannot be changed or deleted

⚡**read-only memory** *n* a small computer memory for storing permanently data that cannot subsequently be altered or added to

⚡**read-out** *n* 1 **DATA RETRIEVAL** the retrieving of data from a computer's memory, disk, or other storage device 2 **DATA RETRIEVED BY COMPUTER** the data retrieved from a computer's memory, disk, or other storage system 3 **DEVICE DISPLAYING INFORMATION** a part of a piece of equipment that displays information

readthrough /réed throo/ *n* a reading of a play without acting, allowing actors to familiarize themselves with the dialogue before full rehearsals begin

⚡**read-write head** *n* a magnetic device that can both read from and write data to a magnetic medium such as a computer floppy or hard disk

ready /réddi/ *adj* (**-ier, -iest**) 1 **PREPARED FOR** prepared for something that is going to happen ○ *Are you ready to leave?* 2 **FINISHED AND AVAILABLE FOR USE** finished or completed and so able to be used immediately ○ *When will dinner be ready?* 3 **ON THE POINT OF DOING** on the point of doing something or liable to do something ○ *This old roof is ready to cave in.* 4 **PREPARED IN ADVANCE** prepared or blended in advance, and able to be used with very little additional preparation (*often in combination*) ○ *available ready-sliced in small packets* 5 **WILLING TO DO** eager, willing, or prepared to do something ○ *Don't be so ready to give in!* 6 **QUICKLY PRODUCED** quickly and easily given, provided, or available ○ *a ready response to questions about wrongdoing* 7 **INTELLIGENT** intelligent, alert, and quick-witted ○ *a ready wit* ■ *vt* (**-ies, -ying, -ied**) **PREPARE** to prepare something, especially so that it is in a condition for something to happen to it ■ *n* **CASH** ready money (*informal*) [12C. < Old English *rǣde* 'prompt'.] —**readiness** *n* ◇ **at the ready** prepared for immediate use or action

ready cash *n* = **ready money**

ready-made *adj* 1 **ALREADY PREPARED** already prepared or made for convenience 2 **PRECONCEIVED** thought out in advance ■ *n* **READY-TO-WEAR GARMENT** an item of clothing that is offered for sale in a standard size and completely finished, as opposed to clothing that is made to the customer's specifications

ready-mix *n* a correct mixture of ingredients that is preblended and able to be used with very little additional preparation —**ready-mixed** *adj*

ready money *n* money that is available to be spent immediately, usually as notes and coins. US term **ready cash**

ready reckoner *n* a table that shows frequently used arithmetic calculations for easy reference

ready-to-wear *adj* already made in standard sizes, designs, and colours, rather than being specially made or designed for an individual ■ *n* an item of clothing that is already made in standard sizes and designs, rather than being specially designed or tailored for an individual

reaffirm /ree ə fúrm/ *vt* **1** to repeat a statement or promise and confirm that it is still true **2** to confirm that a situation is still right or proper —**reaffirmation** /rèe affər máysh'n/ *n*

reafforest *vt* = **reforest** —**reafforestation** /rèe ə fórri stáysh'n/ *n*

Reagan /ráygən/**, Ronald** (*b.* 1911) US statesman and 40th president of the United States (1981–89)

Reaganomics /ráygə nómmiks/ *n* the free-market economic approach espoused by US President Ronald Reagan, involving cuts in taxes and social spending together with deregulation of domestic markets [Late 20C. Blend of REAGAN + ECONOMICS.]

reagent /ri áyjənt/ *n* a substance taking part in a chemical reaction, especially one used to detect, measure, or prepare another substance

reagin /rèe əjin/ *n* an antibody involved in allergic reactions such as hay fever [Early 20C. < German, < *reagieren* 'react'.] —**reaginic** /rèe ə jínnik/ *adj*

real[1] /rèe əl, reel/ *adj* **1** PHYSICALLY EXISTING having actual physical existence **2** VERIFIABLE AS ACTUAL FACT verifiable as actual fact, e.g. legally or scientifically ○ *What is his real name?* **3** NOT IMAGINARY existing as fact, rather than as a product of dreams or the imagination ○ *In the real world things are somewhat different.* **4** NOT ARTIFICIAL genuine and original, and so not artificial or synthetic **5** TRADITIONAL AND AUTHENTIC prepared or made in a traditional or authentic way, rather than being mass-produced or artificial ○ *looking for some real food* **6** SINCERE honest or sincere, not feigned or affected ○ *express your real feelings* **7** EMPHASIZING TRUTH used to emphasize the accuracy or appropriateness of a particular thing ○ *He's a real professional.* **8** UNDISPUTED based on fact, observation, or experience and so undisputed ○ *The real success of the evening was the comedy act.* **9** ESSENTIAL of basic, essential, or critical importance **10** IN TERMS OF PURCHASING POWER regarded in terms of purchasing power rather than the actual amount **11** RELATING TO FIXED PROPERTY relating to land and the fixed property associated with it **12** INVOLVING ONLY REAL NUMBERS involving, relating to, or having elements of the set of rational or irrational numbers only **13** ABOUT EXISTENCE concerned with independent objective existence ■ *adv* US VERY very or extremely (*informal*) ○ *I'm real tired.* ■ *n* **1** MATH = **real number 2** REALITY everything that exists in the actual world [15C. Directly or via Old French < late Latin *realis* 'related to things (in law)' < Latin *res* 'thing, fact'.] —**realness** *n* ◇ **for real** *US* seriously, not as a joke or as a practice (*informal*) ◇ **get real** used to indicate strongly that what somebody said or thought is unrealistic, untrue, or out of date (*slang*) ◇ **(in) real life** in the course of normal life as opposed to imagined or fictional representations of life, e.g. in books and films

SPELLCHECK Do not confuse ***real*** with ***reel***, which has a similar sound. Beware: your spellchecker will not catch this error.

real[2] /ray áal/ (*plural* **-als** *or* **-ales** /ray áales/) *n* **1** see table at **currency 2** a former coin used in several Spanish-speaking countries [Late 16C. Via Spanish < Latin *regalis* (see ROYAL).]

real[3] /ray áal/ (*plural* **reals** *or* **reis** /rays/) *n* a former unit of Portuguese currency [Mid-20C. Via Portuguese < Latin *regalis* (see ROYAL).]

real ale *n* any beer that is allowed to ferment in the cask and does not have carbon dioxide added to it when it is served

real estate *n US, ANZ* land including all the property on it that cannot be moved and any attached rights

real-estate agent *n ANZ, US* a person who buys, sells, and leases property on behalf of somebody else. ◊ **estate agent** *n.* 1

real focus *n* a point from which light diverges or at which it converges

realgar /ri álgər/ *n* a soft orange-red arsenic sulphide mineral. Use: tanning, paints, fireworks. [14C. Via medieval Latin *realger* < Arabic *rahj al-ġār* 'powder of the cave'.]

realign /rèe ə lín/ *v* **1** *vt* STRAIGHTEN AGAIN to readjust or manipulate something so that it is in a straight line or is correctly oriented **2** *vti* CHANGE SOMETHING TO FIT SITUATION to alter or change something to fit particular circumstances **3** *vti* MAKE NEW ALLIANCES to form, or cause people or groups to form, new alliances or associations ○ *The party has realigned itself with several former ideological opponents.* —**realignment** *n*

real image *n* an optical image of something that is produced by reflection or refraction and can be transferred onto a surface such as the film inside a camera

realisation *n* = **realization**

realise *vti* = **realize**

realism /rèe əlizəm/ *n* **1** UNDERSTANDING OF NATURE OF REAL LIFE a practical understanding and acceptance of the actual nature of the world, rather than an idealized or romantic view of it **2** ACCURACY OF SIMULATION the simulation of something in a way that accurately resembles real things ○ *the increasing realism of computer graphics* **3** LIFELIKE ARTISTIC REPRESENTATION in artistic and literary works, lifelike representation of people and the world, without any idealization **4** THEORY THAT THINGS EXIST OBJECTIVELY the theory that things such as universals, moral facts, and theoretical scientific entities exist independently of people's thoughts and perceptions **5** THEORY THAT PEOPLE PERCEIVE INDEPENDENT WORLD the theory that there is an objectively existing world, not dependent on our minds, and that people are able to understand aspects of that world through perception **6** THEORY THAT STATEMENTS HAVE TRUTH VALUES the theory that every declarative statement is either true or false, regardless of whether this can be verified

realist /rèe əlist/ *n* **1** a person who only considers things as they are or appear to be, and avoids ideals and abstractions **2** a practitioner of realism in the arts or a believer in philosophical theories of realism

realistic /rèe ə lístik/ *adj* **1** PRACTICAL seeking what is achievable or possible, based on known facts ○ *set realistic goals when looking for a new job* **2** SIMULATING REALITY simulating real things or imaginary things in a way that seems real ○ *computer games with realistic graphics* **3** REASONABLE not priced or valued too low or high **4** REPRESENTING REAL LIFE in the arts and literature, representing life as it really is, rather than an idealized picture of it **5** RELATING TO PHILOSOPHICAL REALISM relating to philosophical theories of realism —**realistically** *adv*

reality /ri állәti/ (*plural* **-ties**) *n* **1** REAL EXISTENCE actual being or existence, as opposed to an imaginary, idealized, or false nature **2** ALL THAT ACTUALLY EXISTS OR HAPPENS everything that actually does or could exist or happen in real life **3** SOMETHING THAT EXIST OR HAPPENS something that has real existence and must be dealt with in real life ○ *a vision that ignores the realities of the business world* **4** TYPE OF EXISTENCE an existence or universe, either connected with or independent from other kinds ○ *fantastic notions of alternative realities* **5** TOTALITY OF REAL THINGS the totality of real things in the world, independent of people's knowledge or perception of them ◇ **in reality** in actual fact

reality check *n US* an action taken to reconcile somebody's ideas or desires with reality (*informal*)

reality principle *n* in Freudian theory, the ego's ability to postpone gratification to avoid unpleasant consequences or to gain greater reward

reality show *n* television or radio programme that deals with real people in real situations

reality TV *n* television programmes that present real people in live, though often deliberately manufactured, situations and monitor their emotions and behaviour

realize /rèe ə līz/ (**-izes, -izing, -ized**), **realise** (**-ises, -ising, -ised**) *v* **1** *vti* KNOW AND UNDERSTAND to know, understand, and accept something ○ *doesn't realize how lucky he is* **2** *vti* BE OR BECOME AWARE OF to be aware or conscious of something, or to become aware of something ○ *Do you realize the problems you've caused?* **3** *vt* ACHIEVE SOMETHING HOPED FOR to achieve in actuality something that has been hoped or worked for **4** *vt* TURN WORK INTO PERFORMANCE to turn something such as a play or novel into a stage or film performance **5** *vt* TRANSLATE SOMETHING INTO MONEY to translate something into a particular amount of money, usually by selling it **6** *vt* CONVERT GAIN OR LOSS INTO CASH to convert a paper gain or loss into a cash gain or loss by closing out the original transaction **7** *vt* INTERPRET PIECE OF MUSIC to interpret a musical composition, especially the figured bass of a baroque composition [Early 17C. < REAL[1] after French *réaliser*.] —**realizable** *adj* —**realization** /rèe ə lī záysh'n/ *n* —**realizer** *n*

SYNONYMS See ***accomplish***.

real-life *adj* actual or true, as opposed to fictional or imaginary

real-live *adj* not artificial, imagined, or invented ○ *face-to-face with a real-live gangster*

reallocate /ree állə kayt/ (**-cates, -cating, -cated**) *vt* to allocate something to a different person or for a different purpose or to a group of people in a different way ○ *Next year all these tasks will be reallocated.* —**reallocation** /rèe allə káysh'n/ *n*

really /rèe əli, rèeli/ *adv* **1** IN FACT in fact or in reality, especially as distinct from what has been believed until now ○ *She's really going to Paris, not Bangkok.* **2** GENUINELY used to emphasize the truthfulness or accuracy of what is being said ○ *She really is going to Paris next year.* **3** UNDOUBTEDLY truly and without any doubt ○ *That's really interesting.* **4** PROPERLY in order to act in the correct or proper manner ○ *You should really apply in writing.* ■ *interj* EXCLAMATION OF SURPRISE used to express surprise, doubt, or exasperation ○ *You're getting married? Really!* ○ *Well really, how rude!*

realm /relm/ *n* **1** SCOPE OF a particular or stated area, range, or domain ○ *Here the scenario enters the realms of fantasy.* **2** AREA OF INTEREST a defined area of interest or study ○ *the realm of pure mathematics* **3** KINGDOM a country ruled by a monarch [13C. Via Old French *realme* < Latin *regimen* 'government' < *regere* 'rule'.]

real number *n* a number that is either rational or irrational rather than imaginary. ◊ **imaginary number**

real part *n* the part of a complex number that does not have an imaginary factor, e.g. the number 3 in the complex number 3 + 5i

realpolitik /ray áal polli teek/ *n* politics based on pragmatism or practicality rather than on ethical or theoretical considerations [Early 20C. < German, 'real politics'.] —**realpolitiker** /ray áal polittikər/ *n*

real presence *n* the doctrine that the body and blood of Jesus Christ are actually present in the elements of Communion

real property *n* land together with all the property on it that cannot be moved, together with any attached rights

real tennis *n* a form of tennis played on an indoor court with a sloping roof against which the ball can be hit. US term **court tennis** [Because it was the original game of tennis]

ϟ **real time** *n* **1** the time in which certain computer systems process and update data as soon as it is received from some external source, e.g. an air-traffic control or anti-lock brake system **2** the actual time during which something happens —**real-time** *adj*

realty /rèe əlti/ *n* LAW = **real property**

real-world *adj* relevant or practical in terms of everyday life

~~**realy**~~ incorrect spelling of **really**

ream[1] /reem/ *n* a quantity of paper, formerly 480 sheets but now usually 500 sheets ■ **reams** *npl* a large quantity of material, especially written material [14C. Via Old French *raime* < Arabic *rizma* 'bundle'.]

ream[2] /reem/ *vt* **1** FORM HOLE WITH REAMER to form, enlarge, or shape a hole with a reamer **2** *US* SQUEEZE CITRUS JUICE to squeeze the juice from a citrus fruit with a reamer **3** *US* CHEAT to cheat or swindle somebody (*slang*) **4** *US* REPRIMAND to reprimand somebody severely (*slang*) **5** *US* TABOO TERM a highly offensive term meaning to have anal intercourse with somebody (*taboo*) [Mid-18C. < ?]

reamer /rèemər/ *n* **1** a tool that is used to form, enlarge, or shape holes **2** *US* COOK = **lemon-squeezer**

reap /reep/ *vt* **1** to cut and gather a crop, especially a grain crop, from the land where it is growing **2** to obtain something, especially as a consequence of previous effort or action [Old English *rīpan* < ?] —**reapable** *adj*

reaper /rèepər/ *n* **1** somebody or something that reaps, especially, formerly, a machine for harvesting grain crops **2 Reaper** = **Grim Reaper**

reappear /rèe ə péer/ *vi* to make another appearance or come into view once more —**reappearance** *n*

reapply /rèe ə plí/ (**-plies, -plying, -plied**) *v* **1** *vi* to make an application for a second or subsequent time ○ *Previous candidates need not reapply.* **2** *vt* to apply something for a second or subsequent time ○ *Reapply the paint after the first coat has dried.*

reappoint /ri ə póynt/ *vt* to designate or select somebody again to fill an official position or office —**re-appointment** *n*

reapportion /reē ə páwrsh'n/ *vt* to divide and allocate something again or in a different way

reapportionment /reē ə páwrsh'nmənt/ *n* in the United States, periodic redistribution of congressional or legislative seats based on changing census figures, as constitutionally required

reappraise /reē ə práyz/ (**-praises, -praising, -praised**) *vt* 1 to consider something again, often with a view to making changes 2 to assess again how useful, effective, or valuable a person or a thing is —**reappraisal** *n*

rear[1] /reer/ *v* 1 *vt* RAISE YOUNG ANIMALS OR CHILDREN to bring up and care for young animals or children until they are fully grown 2 *vt* GROW A PLANT to raise a plant to full growth 3 *vi* RISE ON HIND LEGS to rise up on the hind legs (*refers to animals*) 4 *vi* RISE HIGH to rise high into the air ○ *tall office buildings rearing into the night sky* [Old English *rǣran* < Indo-European] —**rearer** *n*

rear[2] /reer/ *n* 1 BACK OF the back of something, or the area near the back of something 2 PART OF ARMY FARTHEST FROM FRONT the part of an army or a procession that is farthest from the front 3 BUTTOCKS somebody's buttocks, or the similar part of an animal (*informal*) ■ *adj* BACK situated at the back ○ *Do not join the rear four carriages.* [Late 16C. Via Old French *rere* < Latin *retro* 'back, behind'.] ◇ **bring up the rear** to be at the back, particularly in a race or procession

rear admiral *n* an officer of a rank above commodore in the British or Canadian navies, or above captain in the US Navy or Coast Guard

rear end = **rear**[2] *n.* 1, **rear**[2] *n.* 3

rear-end *vt US* to collide with the back of another vehicle

rear-ender *n US* an accident in which one vehicle collides with the back of another (*informal*)

rearguard /reér gaard/ *n* 1 a body of troops designated to delay the enemy during a retreat or withdrawal 2 members of a political party or other organization who are strongly conservative and opposed to change and progress (*disapproving*)

rear lamp, rear light *n* a red light that is usually one of a pair at the back of a vehicle. US term **tail light**

rearm /ree áarm/ *vti* to equip people, an organization, or a nation with weapons and ammunition again, or to become so equipped —**rearmament** *n*

rearmost /reér mōst/ *adj* farthest towards the back

rearrange /reē ə ráynj/ (**-ranges, -ranging, -ranged**) *vt* 1 to change the order or position of something 2 to reschedule the time of something such as an event —**rearrangement** *n*

rearrest /reē ə rést/ *vt* to take somebody into custody for a second or subsequent time on suspicion of having committed a crime ○ *He was rearrested within an hour of his escape.*

rearview mirror /reér vyoo-/ *n* a mirror attached to the inside of the windscreen or the outside of a front door of a vehicle, allowing the driver to see behind the vehicle

rearward /reérwərd/ *adv* **rearward, rearwards** towards or in the rear or back ■ *adj* located in or near the rear or back

reason /reéz'n/ *n* 1 JUSTIFICATION an explanation or justification for something ○ *refused to give a reason for her behaviour* 2 MOTIVE a motive or cause for acting or thinking in a particular way ○ *His only reason for going was that she would be there.* 3 POWER OF ORDERLY THOUGHT the power of being able to think in a logical and rational manner ○ *use reason rather than force* 4 CAUSE THAT EXPLAINS a cause that explains a particular phenomenon ○ *What's the reason for grass being green?* 5 ABILITY TO THINK CLEARLY the ability to think clearly and coherently 6 INTELLECT AS BASIS FOR KNOWLEDGE the ability to think logically regarded as a basis for knowledge, as distinct from experience or emotions ■ *v* 1 *vi* THINK IN LOGICAL WAY to think logically or use rational faculties 2 *vi* USE RATIONAL ARGUMENT TO PERSUADE to try to persuade or influence somebody by means of rational argument ○ *I tried to reason with him but he insisted on going ahead.* 3 *vt* RESOLVE BY RATIONAL MEANS to formulate or resolve something using rational means ○ *reason out a maths problem* [13C. Via Old French *reisun* < Latin *ratio* 'calculation, thought' < *reri* 'think'.] —**reasoned** *adj* —**reasoner** *n* ◇ **it stands to reason** used to emphasize that something seems obvious or logical ◇ **within reason** within reasonable limits

SYNONYMS See ***deduce***.

USAGE the reason is that or **the reason is because**? Particularly in writing, ***reason*** is more correctly followed by *that* than by *because* in sentences of the type *The reason I left is that* [not *because*] *I was bored.* Alternatively, simply use: *I left because I was bored.* Informally, however, and especially in conversation, *the reason is because* does occur and *that* is sometimes omitted altogether: *The reason I left is I was bored.*

reasonable /reéz'nəb'l/ *adj* 1 RATIONAL sensible and capable of making rational judgments ○ *He did what any reasonable person would have done in that situation.* 2 IN ACCORD WITH COMMON SENSE acceptable and according to common sense ○ *hoping to arrive at a reasonable time* 3 NOT EXPECTING MORE THAN IS POSSIBLE not expecting or demanding more than is possible or achievable ○ *Come on, be reasonable!* 4 FAIRLY GOOD fairly good but not excellent ○ *The food was reasonable.* 5 FAIRLY LARGE large enough but not excessive ○ *He earns a reasonable amount of money.* 6 NOT EXORBITANT fairly priced and not too expensive ○ *Three bottles for £7.50 is very reasonable.* —**reasonableness** *n* —**reasonably** *adv*

SYNONYMS See ***valid***.

reasoning /reéz'ning/ *n* 1 the use of logical thinking in order to find results or draw conclusions 2 an argument or other example of logical thinking ○ *Her reasoning was based on the available facts.*

reassemble /reē ə sémb'l/ (**-bles, -bling, -bled**) *v* 1 *vt* to put something back together again by assembling its component parts ○ *She took it apart to check for breaks and then reassembled it.* 2 *vi* to gather together again as a group after being separated

ϟ**reassembly** /reē ə sémb'li/ *n* 1 the process of putting components back together again or coming together again after being separated 2 the reconstruction of a fragmented image processing or data packet after it has been transmitted over a network

reassert /reē ə súrt/ *vt* to assert something such as your rights or wishes again —**reassertion** *n*

reassess /reē ə séss/ *vt* to assess a situation again, especially on receipt of new information in a case where the situation has changed —**reassessment** *n*

reassign /reē ə sín/ *vt* 1 to give something a different value, designation, use, location, or owner ○ *The rankings have all been reassigned.* 2 to give somebody a different job to do, or send somebody to work in a different place or with a different group of people ○ *That team has been reassigned to another job.* —**reassignment** *n*

reassure /reē ə shoór, -sháwr/ (**-sures, -suring, -sured**) *vt* 1 to make a person feel less anxious or worried 2 INSUR = **reinsure** —**reassurance** *n* —**reassurer** *n*

reassuring /reē ə shoóring, -sháwring/ *adj* having the effect of making people feel less anxious or worried —**reassuringly** *adv*

Réaumur /ráy ə myoor/ *adj* using or measured on the Réaumur scale [Early 19C. After the French physicist René Antoine Ferchault de *Réaumur* (1683–1757).]

Réaumur scale *n* an obsolete temperature scale on which water freezes at 0 degrees and boils at 80 degrees under normal atmospheric conditions

reave /reev/ (**reaves, reaving, reaved** *or* **reft** /reft/, **reaved** *or* **reft**) *vt* (*archaic*) 1 to plunder something or carry something off by force 2 to rob somebody or deprive somebody of something [Old English *rēafian* < Germanic] —**reaver** *n*

reawaken /reē ə wáykən/ *v* 1 *vti* to wake another person up, or wake from sleep again 2 *vt* to stimulate or spur a person or group into a state of awareness or action again

reb /reb/, **Reb** *n US* MIL = **Johnny Reb** (*informal*) [Mid-19C. Shortening of REBEL.]

Reb /reb/ *n* a title of respect that is roughly equivalent to 'Mister' (*with a man's first name*) [Late 19C. < Yiddish, shortening of *rebbe* (see REBBE).]

rebadge /ree báj/ *vt* to change the name or other identifying marks of a product or business, e.g. a logo ○ *All hotels in the chain will be rebadged.*

rebarbative /ri báarbətiv/ *adj* unpleasant, annoying, or forbidding (*formal*) [Late 19C. < French *rébarbatif* < *rebarber* 'face beard to beard' < *barbe* 'beard'.] —**rebarbatively** *adv*

rebate[1] *n* /reē bayt/ money that is paid back, e.g. because somebody has overpaid tax or is entitled to a refund ■ *vt* /ri báyt/ (**-bates, -bating, -bated**) to give somebody a rebate [15C. < French *rabattre* 'beat down again' < *abattre* 'beat down' < Latin *battuere* 'beat'.] —**rebatable** /ri báytəb'l/ *adj* —**rebater** /ri báytər/ *n*

rebate[2] *n* /reē bayt/ GROOVE CUT FOR WOOD JOINT a groove or step cut along the length of the edge of a piece of wood that is to be joined to another with a corresponding tongue or ledge cut into it. US term **rabbet** *n.* ■ *vt* /ri báyt/ (**-bates, -bating, -bated**) 1 CUT REBATE IN SOMETHING to cut a rebate in a piece of wood. US term **rabbet** *v.* 1 2 JOIN PIECES WITH REBATE to join two pieces of wood at their edges by means of a rebate. US term **rabbet** *v.* 2 [Late 17C. Alteration of RABBET.]

rebbe /rébbə/, **Rebbe** *n* a rabbi or spiritual leader of a Hasidic Jewish community [Late 19C. Via Yiddish < Hebrew *rabbī* 'my teacher'.]

rebbetzin /rébbətsən/, **rebbitzin** *n* the wife of a rabbi [Late 19C. < Yiddish, < *rebbe* (see REBBE).]

rebec /reē bek/, **rebeck** *n* a two- or three-stringed medieval instrument that looks like a lute and is played with a bow [Early 16C. Via French < Arabic *rabāb*.]

Rebecca /ri békə/, **Rebekah** *n* in the Bible, the wife of Isaac, and mother of Jacob and Esau

rebeck *n* MUSIC = **rebec**

rebel *n* /rébb'l/ 1 PROTESTER a defiant protester against authority 2 UNCONVENTIONAL PERSON a person who rejects the codes and conventions of society 3 SOLDIER WHO OPPOSES GOVERNMENT IN POWER a soldier who belongs to a force seeking to overthrow a government or ruling power ■ *vi* /ri bél/ (**rebels, rebelling, rebelled**) 1 REVOLT AGAINST A GOVERNMENT to fight to overthrow a government or ruling power 2 PROTEST BY DEFYING AUTHORITY to protest by defying a government or other form of authority ○ *students rebelling against education funding cuts* 3 REFUSE TO CONFORM to refuse to conform to the usual codes and conventions of society 4 HAVE DISLIKE FOR SOMETHING to experience or express an intense dislike or distaste for something [13C. Via French *rebelle* < Latin *rebellis* < *bellum* 'war'.]

~~**rebelion**~~ incorrect spelling of **rebellion**

rebellion /ri béllyən/ *n* 1 an organized attempt to overthrow a government or other authority by the use of violence 2 opposition or defiance of authority, accepted moral codes, or social conventions

rebellious /ri béllyəss/ *adj* 1 opposing or defying authority, accepted moral codes, or social conventions 2 fighting to overthrow a government or other authority —**rebelliously** *adv* —**rebelliousness** *n*

rebel yell *n US* an exuberant high-pitched yell such as was used in battle by soldiers of the Confederacy during the American Civil War

rebid *n* /rí bid/ a further bid in an auction at bridge, especially one of the same suit as a previous one ■ *vi* /ri bíd/ (**-bids, -bidding, -bid** *or* **-bade** *or* **-bid, -bid**) to make a bid in an auction at bridge after previously bidding no trump or a suit, especially one in the same suit

rebirth /ree búrth/ *n* 1 REGENERATION OF SOMETHING DEAD OR DESTROYED the regeneration of something that has died or has been destroyed 2 REVIVAL OF IDEAS OR FORCES the revival of important ideas or forces, usually as part of broad and significant change 3 REINCARNATION the act or process of reincarnation

ϟ**reboot** *vti* /ree boót/ to restart a computer or an operating system, or to be restarted ■ *n* /ree boot/ a restart of a computer or an operating system ■ *vt* /ree boót/ COMPUT = **warmboot**

rebore *vt* /ree báwr/ (**-bores, -boring, -bored**) to enlarge the bore hole of a cylinder in a car's engine and fit it with new pistons ■ *n* /ree bawr/ the process of reboring a cylinder or all the cylinders in an engine

reborn /ree báwrn/ *adj* recreated or regenerated, especially in order to be more effective or modern, or renewed spiritually

rebound *vi* /ri bównd/ 1 SPRING BACK to spring back or recoil 2 MOVE BACK TO PREVIOUS LEVEL to recover from a setback and move back to a previous or higher level or position 3 HAVE UNDESIRABLE EFFECT to affect the person who does or creates something directly, especially in an unpleasant or unwelcome way ■ *n* /réé bownd/ **1 UPWARD MOVEMENT** an upward movement or a recovery, especially after a setback **2 BALL THAT BOUNCES** a ball that bounces back, particularly off a backboard or rim of the basket in basketball or off the goalkeeper or goalpost in hockey, football, or a similar sport —**rebounder** *n* ◇ **on the rebound** starting something new in the wake of a disappointment or setback, often the ending of a relationship, and therefore feeling uneasy or vulnerable

USAGE rebound or **redound**? In its figurative use, ***rebound on*** is a metaphor based on the image of an object bouncing and returning. Just as a ball that ***rebounds*** affects the person who threw it, so an action or statement ***rebounds*** on its creator when it affects him or her directly, usually in an unpleasant or unwelcome way: *The council's decision to cut library services rebounded on councillors when they were unable to get the information they needed.* ***Redound***, a much rarer word, is sometimes used in the same way as ***rebound***, but in its primary meaning it is followed by *to* and means 'to have a particular consequence', with something good or positive as the object (the opposite connotation to ***rebound***): *The individual performances redounded to the benefit of the team as a whole.* Note that only ***rebound*** can be used as a noun.

rebozo /ri bṓzō/ (*plural* **-zos**) *n* a long woollen or linen scarf worn over the head and shoulders, mainly by women in Mexico [Early 19C. Via Spanish < Latin *bucca* 'cheek, mouth'.]

rebroadcast *vti* /ree bráwd kaast/ (**-casts, -casting, -cast** *or* **-casted**) to broadcast something again, especially a radio or television programme ■ *n* /réé brawd kaast/ something that is broadcast again, especially a radio or television programme

rebuff /ri búf/ *vt* **1 REJECT OR SNUB** to reject or snub an offer, advance, or approach made by somebody **2 REPEL ATTACK** to beat back or repel an attack or an attacking force ■ *n* **1 REJECTION** a blunt rejection or snub of an offer, advance, or approach made by somebody else **2 SETBACK** a sudden severe setback to progress [Late 16C. Via obsolete French *rebuffer* and Italian *ribuffare* 'scold' < *buffo* 'puff', originally an imitation of the sound.]

USAGE rebuff/rebut/refute The core meaning of ***refute*** is 'to prove incorrect', though a more general sense 'to deny' has developed and is now widely established. In US English especially it is acceptable to use ***refute*** and ***rebut*** interchangeably in the sense 'to contradict or deny the truth of something', as in *a spokesperson who refuted/rebutted all allegations of impropriety.* Nonetheless, if you want to emphasize the idea of proving wrongness as opposed to mere denial or contradiction, then use ***refute***, as in *used unimpeachable facts to refute opposing counsel's allegations*, and use ***rebut*** to mean 'contradict', as in *rebutted opposing counsel's opening statement in my closing statement.* Do not confuse ***rebuff*** ('to reject; push away') with ***rebut*** (*I rebuffed his unwanted advances* and *I rebuffed* [not *rebutted*] *his protestations*).

rebuild /ree bíld/ (**-builds, -building, -built** /-bílt/, **-built**) *vt* **1 BUILD STRUCTURE AGAIN** to construct a building or other structure again because it has been damaged or destroyed **2 RESTORE** to work to restore something that has been weakened, damaged, or ruined **3 MAKE MAJOR CHANGES TO** to make major alterations or improvements to something ○ *to rebuild society for the information age* —**rebuilder** *n*

rebuke /ri byóók/ *vt* (**-bukes, -buking, -buked**) to criticize or reprimand somebody, usually sharply ■ *n* a reprimand or expression of criticism or disapproval [14C. < Anglo-Norman and Old N French *rebuker* 'chop wood' < Old French *busche* 'log' < Germanic.] —**rebuker** *n*

rebus /réébəss/ (*plural* **-buses**) *n* **1** a puzzle in which the syllables of words and names are represented either by pictures of things that sound the same or by letters **2** a heraldic emblem showing a picture that represents the name of the bearer, e.g. a picture of a lion for somebody named Lyon [Early 17C. Via French < Latin, 'by things' < *res* 'thing'.]

rebut /ri bút/ (**-buts, -butting, -butted**) *vti* to deny the truth of something, especially by presenting arguments that disprove it [13C. Via Anglo-Norman *rebuter* < Old French *reboter* < *boter* (see BUTT[1]).] —**rebuttable** *adj* —**rebuttal** *n*

USAGE See ***rebuff***.

rebutter /ri búttər/ *n* **1** the defendant's answer in the third round of pleading in a legal action (*archaic*) **2** a person who rebuts something

rec /rek/ *n* (*informal*) **1** recreation (*often before nouns*) ○ *rec room* **2** a recreation ground [Early 20C. Shortening.]

rec. *abbr* **1** receipt **2** received **3** recipe **4** recommended **5** recorded **6** recorder **7** recording **8** recreation

recalcitrant /ri kálssitrənt/ *adj* **1 RESISTING CONTROL** stubbornly resisting the authority or control of another **2 HARD TO DO OR HANDLE** difficult to deal with or operate ○ *struggling in front of the mirror with a recalcitrant tie* ■ *n* **STUBBORN OPPONENT** a person who stubbornly resists authority or control ○ *A few recalcitrants refused to submit.* [Mid-19C. Directly or via French < Latin *recalcitrant-* present participle of *recalcitrare* 'kick back' (used of horses) < *calcitrare* 'kick (with the heels)' < *calc-* 'heel'.] —**recalcitrance** *n* —**recalcitrantly** *adv*

SYNONYMS See ***unruly***.

recalculate /ree kálkyoo layt/ (**-lates, -lating, -lated**) *vti* to calculate something again in order to make sure it is correct, or to incorporate new information —**recalculation** /ree kálkyoo láysh'n/ *n*

recalesce /réékə léss/ (**-lesces, -lescing, -lesced**) *vi* to exhibit or undergo a sudden increase in temperature [Late 19C. Back-formation < RECALESCENCE.]

recalescence /réékə léss'nss/ *n* a sudden increase in the temperature and brightness of a cooling metal, caused by the release of latent heat as the metal undergoes a change in crystalline structure [Late 19C. < Latin *calescere* 'grow warm' < *calere* 'be warm'.] —**recalescent** *adj*

recall /ri káwl/ *v* **1** *vti* **REMEMBER** to remember something or bring something back to mind ○ *I don't recall what she was wearing.* **2** *vt* **ORDER SOMEBODY OR SOMETHING BACK** to order something or somebody to come back or be sent back **3** *vt* **REVOKE** to revoke or cancel a previous decision or instruction **4** *vt* **BRING ATTENTION BACK** to bring somebody's attention or thoughts back to an ongoing matter **5** *vt* **RESEMBLE** to remind another person of somebody or something familiar or previously seen ○ *Her face recalls that of her grandmother.* ■ *n* **1 RECALLING OF SOMETHING** the remembering of something or the calling back of somebody or something **2 MEMORY** somebody's memory or ability to remember ○ *a vague recall of the actual events* **3 REVOCATION** a revocation or cancellation of a previous decision or instruction **4 SIGNAL TO RETURN** a signal, especially a bugle call, ordering troops to return to their positions or to a rallying point **5 MANUFACTURER'S REQUEST TO RETURN PRODUCT** a request by a manufacturer to return a product because of a defect or contamination [Late 16C. < CALL after French *rappeler* or Latin *revocare*.] —**recallability** /ri káwlə bílləti/ *n* —**recallable** /ri káwləb'l/ *adj* —**recaller** *n*

recamier /ray kámmi ay/ *n* a couch with a high headrest and low footrest, often without a back [Early 20C. After Jeanne *Récamier*, French hostess, portrayed reclining on a couch in a painting.]

recanalization /ree kánnə lī záysh'n/, **recanalisation** *n* the surgical unblocking of an obstructed vessel within the body or the reconnection of a tube or duct

recant /ri kánt/ *vti* to deny believing in something or withdraw something previously said ○ *She stands by what she said and refuses to recant.* [Mid-16C. < Latin *recantare* 'sing back' (after Greek *palinōidein* 'recant') < *cantare* 'sing'.] —**recantation** /réé kan táysh'n/ *n* —**recanter** /ri kántər/ *n*

recap[1] /réé kap/ *vti* (**-caps, -capping, -capped**) to go over the main points of something such as an argument or a proposal again ■ *n* a summing-up of the main points of something previously put forward, e.g. a proposal [Mid-20C. Shortening of RECAPITULATE.]

recap[2] *n* /réé kap/ *ANZ, US* a retread ■ *vt* /ree káp/ *ANZ, US* to retread a tyre [Mid-20C. < CAP.] —**recappable** /ree káppəb'l/ *adj*

recapitalize /ree káppitə līz/ (**-izes, -izing, -ized**), **recapitalise** (**-ises, -ising, -ised**) *vt* to supply a business with new capital or change the way in which its capital is held —**recapitalization** /ree káppitə lī záysh'n/ *n*

recapitulate /réékə píchoo layt/ (**-lates, -lating, -lated**) *v* **1** *vti* to recap (*formal*) **2** *vt* to repeat stages from the evolution of the species during the embryonic period of an animal's life [Late 16C. Partly < Latin *recapitulat-*, past participle of *recapitulare* 'restate by chapters' < *capitulum* 'chapter'; partly a back-formation < RECAPITULATION.] —**recapitulative** /-píchoolətiv/ *adj* —**recapitulatory** /-píchələtəri/ *adj*

recapitulation /réékə píchoo láysh'n/ *n* **1 RECAP** a summing-up of the main points of something (*formal*) **2 REPEATING EVOLUTIONARY STAGES DURING EMBRYONIC PERIOD** the theoretical process of going through successive stages during the embryonic period of an animal's life that duplicate the evolutionary stages the species experienced **3 REPETITION OF THEMES** the repetition of earlier themes in a piece of music, especially in sonata form at the end of a movement [14C. Directly or via French < late Latin *recapitulation-* < Latin *recapitulat-* (see RECAPITULATE).]

recaption /ree kápsh'n/ *n* the taking back, by peaceful means, of property from somebody who has unlawfully taken it, or of a spouse or child from somebody who has unlawfully detained him or her [Early 17C. < Anglo-Latin *recaption-* 'capturing back' < Latin *caption-* 'capturing'.]

recapture /ree kápchər/ (**-tures, -turing, -tured**) *vt* **1** to capture again or take back somebody or something that has escaped or that has been taken away **2** to have, show, or experience again something that existed in the past or has been lost ○ *a failed attempt to recapture their youth* —**recapture** *n*

recast /ree kaast/ (**-casts, -casting, -cast**) *vt* **1 CAST OBJECT AGAIN** to repeat the casting process for an object formed in a mould **2 CHANGE** to change the form of something ○ *The experience led him to recast his philosophy of life.* **3 GIVE ROLES TO DIFFERENT ACTORS** to assign roles in something such as a play or film to different actors ○ *recast the play for a road tour*

recce /réki/ *n* a reconnaissance (*slang*) ○ *He's gone for a recce along the beach.* ■ *vt* (**-ces, -ceing, -ced**) to reconnoitre something (*slang*) [Mid-20C. Shortening and alteration.]

~~**reccommend**~~ incorrect spelling of **recommend**

recd, rec'd *abbr* received

recede /ri séed/ (**-cedes, -ceding, -ceded**) *vi* **1 GO BACK** to go back or down from a certain point or level ○ *waiting for the flood waters to recede* **2 GET FURTHER AWAY** to become more distant or unlikely ○ *As the ship gathered speed, the island receded in the distance.* **3 SLOPE** to slope backwards **4 GO BALD** to gradually go bald from the front of the head backwards **5 BECOME LESS** to become less in value or quality ○ *The value of her shares receded sharply.* **6 WITHDRAW** engage in a retreat [15C. Directly or via Old French *receder* < Latin *recedere* 'go back' < *cedere* 'give away'.]

~~**receeding**~~ incorrect spelling of **receding**

receipt /ri séet/ *n* **1 ACKNOWLEDGMENT OF RECEIVING** a written or printed acknowledgment that something such as money or goods has been given to the person who issues the acknowledgment ○ *The shop will exchange goods if you have a receipt.* **2 ACT OF RECEIVING** the receiving of something ○ *The balance is payable on receipt of the goods.* **3 RECIPE** a recipe (*archaic*) ■ **receipts** *npl* **AMOUNT RECEIVED** the amount of money or goods received, especially in business ○ *Receipts are down on last month.* ■ *v* **1** *vt* **ACKNOWLEDGE PAYMENT BY SIGNING** to acknowledge, with a signature, that a bill has been paid **2** *vti* **GIVE RECEIPT** to give a receipt for money or goods [14C. < Anglo-Norman or Old N French *receite* '(medicinal) recipe, receipt' < Latin *recipere* (see RECEIVE).]

receivable /ri séévəb'l/ *adj* **1 SUITABLE TO BE RECEIVED** suitable to be received, especially as payment ○ *receivable notes* **2 AWAITING PAYMENT** describes a bill or account that is due to be paid ■ **receivables** *npl* **MONEY OWED** business assets consisting of amounts of money that a company is owed

receive /ri séév/ (**-ceives, -ceiving, -ceived**) *v* **1** *vti* **GET** to take or accept something given ○ *It is better to give than to receive.* **2** *vti* **CONVERT ELECTRONIC SIGNALS** to pick up electronic signals and convert them into sound or pictures ○ *This radio is able to transmit and receive.* **3** *vt* **TAKE DELIVERY OF MESSAGE** to take delivery of a message, e.g. a letter or telephone call ○ *We've received a few complaints.* **4** *vt* **LEARN INFORMATION** to learn of something such as news or information **5** *vt* **MEET WITH** to meet with or experience something ○ *We received a warm reception from the crowd.* **6** *vt* **BEAR** to bear or sustain something such as a burden ○ *The bridge is reinforced to receive the weight of heavy traffic.* **7** *vt* **CATCH** to hold or take something ○ *A water butt receives the overflow from the guttering.* **8** *vt* **BE HURT BY** to be subjected to something such as an injury, blow, or pressure ○ *The parachutist received the full force of the* *earth's gravity upon landing.* **9** *vt* **ACQUIRE** to come to have something, e.g. through effort **10** *vti* **ENTERTAIN VISITORS** to be at home or available to entertain visitors ○ *Find out the hours during which patients can receive visitors.* **11** *vt* **GREET GUESTS** to greet and admit guests ○ *We were received by the duke himself.* **12** *vt* **ADMIT** to allow a person entry ○ *A knight had to prove himself worthy before being received into their fellowship.* **13** *vt* **REACT TO** to react to something in a specified way ○ *The proposals were not well received by the members.* **14** *vt* **HEAR AND ACKNOWLEDGE** to hear and acknowledge something formally ○ *The priest received her confession.* **15** *vti* **ACCEPT STOLEN GOODS** to accept or deal in stolen goods **16** *vi* **TAKE COMMUNION** to partake of Holy Communion **17** *vti* **PLAY BALL SENT BY OPPONENT** to catch, hit, or kick a ball played by an opponent [14C. Via Old French *receivre* < Latin *recipere* 'take back' < *capere* 'take'.]

received /ri seévd/ *adj* generally accepted as true ○ *The received wisdom in these matters is seldom wrong.*

Received Pronunciation *n* the accent of British English that educated people from the southern part of England traditionally use, widely regarded as the least regionally modified of all British accents

receiver /ri seévər/ *n* **1 SOMEBODY WHO RECEIVES** a person who receives or takes delivery of something **2 PART OF A PHONE** the part of a telephone that contains the earpiece and mouthpiece and receives and converts electronic signals into sound **3 DEVICE FOR PICKING UP SIGNALS** an electrical device that receives and converts electronic signals into sound or pictures **4 SOMEBODY COURT APPOINTS TO RUN BUSINESS** somebody appointed by a court to manage a business or property that is involved in a legal process such as bankruptcy **5 SOMEBODY DEALING IN STOLEN GOODS** a dealer in stolen goods **6 COLLECTING VESSEL IN CHEMISTRY** a vessel used during distillation to collect the distillate **7 PLAYER CATCHING FORWARD PASS** an American football player on the attacking side who is eligible to catch a forward pass **8 CATCHER** a catcher

receivership /ri seévərship/ *n* **1** the office or duties of somebody appointed by a court to manage a business or property that is involved in a legal process such as bankruptcy **2** management by a receiver of a business or property that is involved in a legal process such as bankruptcy ○ *The company is now in receivership.*

receiving end *n* the position of having to endure something ○ *We were on the receiving end of some harsh criticism.*

receiving line *n* a group of people who stand in a line to greet individually the guests at a formal occasion such as a wedding reception

receiving order *n* a court order that appoints a receiver to take charge of a business involved in a legal proceeding such as bankruptcy

recension /ri sénsh'n/ *n* **1** a critical revision carried out on a literary text **2** a literary text that has been given a critical revision [Mid-17C. < Latin *recension-* 'review' < *recensere* 'reassess' < *censere* 'appraise, assess'.]

recent /reéss'nt/ *adj* **1** having happened or appeared not long ago ○ *the recent birth of her child* **2** from current times or the very near past ○ *recent political trends* [15C. Directly or via French < Latin *recent-*, stem of *recens*.] — **recency** *n* —**recently** *adv* —**recentness** *n*

Recent /reéss'nt/ *adj, n* GEOL = **Holocene**

receptacle /ri séptək'l/ *n* **1 CONTAINER** a container that holds, contains, or receives a liquid or solid **2 FLOWER-BEARING PART OF PLANT** the end of a flower stalk, bearing the parts of a flower or the florets of a composite flower **3 PLANT PART BEARING REPRODUCTIVE ORGANS** in a plant that reproduces through spores, e.g. an alga or liverwort, the part that bears the reproductive organs [14C. Directly or via French < Latin *receptaculum* 'place in which to store something received' < *recipere* (see RECEIVE).]

reception /ri sépsh'n/ *n* **1 ACT OF RECEIVING** the receiving of something given or sent **2 WAY SOMEBODY OR SOMETHING IS RECEIVED** the way in which somebody or something is received or greeted ○ *The audience gave her a warm reception.* **3 FORMAL PARTY** a formal party to welcome somebody or celebrate an event, e.g. a wedding **4 PLACE WHERE VISITORS ARE RECEIVED** a place in a hotel, office, or public building where visitors are first received ○ *I'll be waiting for you in reception.* **5 CONVERSION OF ELECTRONIC SIGNALS** the receiving and conversion of electronic signals **6 QUALITY OF SIGNAL** the quality of the signal received by a radio or television set ○ *We don't get very good reception on this channel.* **7** = **reception room** *n.* **1**, **reception room** *n.* **2** **8 CATCHING OF FORWARD PASS** in American football, the catching of a pass made towards the opponent's goal **9 FIRST CLASS AT INFANT SCHOOL** the class of children beginning their first year of full-time education [14C. Directly or via French < Latin *reception-* < *recipere* (see RECEIVE).]

reception centre *n* **1** a place that accommodates people in need of shelter, e.g. homeless people, refugees, or survivors of natural disasters, until more permanent accommodation can be found **2** a children's home run by a local authority to house children whose families cannot look after them, either temporarily or for a longer period

receptionist /ri sépsh'nist/ *n* an employee who greets visitors, customers, or patients, answers the telephone, and makes appointments

reception room *n* **1** a room used for entertaining guests in a house ○ *The house has four bedrooms and two reception rooms.* **2** a room used for a party or reception in a hotel

receptive /ri séptiv/ *adj* **1 WILLING TO ACCEPT** ready and willing to accept something, e.g. new ideas ○ *The city's art collectors were highly receptive to the new wave in painting.* **2 ABLE TO RECEIVE** able to receive something ○ *countries that were not immediately receptive to the refugees* **3 QUICK TO LEARN** quick to take in new information **4 ABLE TO RECEIVE STIMULI** capable of transmitting and receiving stimuli (*refers to a sensory organ*) [15C. Directly or via French < medieval Latin *receptivus* < Latin *recipere* (see RECEIVE).] —**receptively** *adv* —**receptiveness** *n* —**receptivity** /reé sep tívvəti/ *n*

receptor /ri séptər/ *n* **1 SENSITIVE NERVE ENDING** a nerve ending that is sensitive to stimuli and can convert them into nerve impulses **2 RECEIVING DEVICE** a device designed to receive electronic signals **3 SPECIFIC CELL BINDING SITE OR MOLECULE** a molecule, group, or site that is in a cell or on a cell surface and binds with a specific molecule, antigen, hormone, or antibody **4 RECEIVER OF POLLUTION** somebody or something adversely affected by a pollutant [15C. Directly or via Old French *receptour* 'person who harbours criminals or stolen goods' < Latin *receptor* < *recipere* (see RECEIVE).]

recess /ri séss, reé sess/ *n* **1 INDENTED OR HOLLOWED-OUT SPACE** an area such as an alcove or niche, set into a wall or other flat surface ○ *a recess large enough to take a bed* **2 REMOTE PLACE** a remote or secluded place (*often plural*) ○ *A distant memory haunted the recesses of her mind.* **3 BREAK FROM BUSINESS** a time during which no work or business is done, specifically a long period in which a legislative body is not sitting **4** *US, Can* EDUC = **break** *n.* **4** **5 PERIOD WHEN COURT DOES NOT SIT** a period of time of varying length when a court of law does not sit ○ *The court will stand in recess until noon on Friday.* **6 BODY CAVITY** a concave area or cavity in a part of the body ■ *vt* **1 PUT SOMETHING IN ALCOVE** to put something in a recess, especially in a wall ○ *a chapel recessed in a transept of the cathedral* **2 MAKE INDENTATION IN** to make a recess in something, especially a wall ○ *The north wall of the chamber has been recessed to form an alcove.* [Mid-16C. Directly or via Old French *reces* < Latin *recessus* 'going back' < *recedere* 'go back'.]

recession /ri sésh'n/ *n* **1 DEPRESSION IN ECONOMIC ACTIVITY** a period, shorter than a depression, during which there is a decline in economic trade and prosperity **2 WITHDRAWAL OF SOMEBODY IN CEREMONY** the withdrawal of the participants in a ceremony, e.g. the clergy and choir after a church service **3 RECEDING** a going back or becoming more distant

recessional /ri sésh'nəl/ *adj* involving or typical of a recession ■ *n* a hymn sung as the clergy and choir withdraw from a church after a service

recessive /ri séssiv/ *adj* **1 RECEDING** tending to go backwards or to recede ○ *recessive flood waters* **2 PRODUCING EFFECT IN CERTAIN CONDITIONS ONLY** describes a gene that produces an effect in an organism only when its matching allele is identical **3 CONTROLLED BY RECESSIVE GENE** describes a characteristic or trait determined by a recessive gene **4 FALLING AT BEGINNING OF WORD** describes stress that is placed at or near the beginning of a word ■ *n* **1 RECESSIVE GENE OR TRAIT** a recessive gene or trait **2 ORGANISM WITH RECESSIVE GENE OR TRAIT** an organism that has a recessive gene or trait —**recessively** *adv* —**recessiveness** *n*

Rechabite /rékə bīt/ *n* an abstainer from alcoholic beverages, especially a member of the Independent Order of Rechabites [14C. < ecclesiastical Latin *Rechabita* 'descendants of Rechab', translation of Hebrew *rēkābīm* < *rēkāb* 'Rechab' (the Bible, Jeremiah 35:6), whose descendants refused to drink wine.]

recharge /ree chaárj/ (**-charges, -charging, -charged**) *vt* **1** to replenish the amount of electric power in something, especially a battery **2** to renew something, e.g. somebody's energy ○ *We felt recharged after the weekend.* —**rechargeable** *adj* —**recharger** *n*

réchauffé /ray shṓ fay/ *n* **1** a dish of reheated leftovers **2** a piece of work, e.g. a piece of writing, that is merely a reuse of old material [Early 19C. < French, past participle of *réchauffer* 'reheat'.]

recherché /rə sháir shay/ *adj* **1 RARE AND EXQUISITE** marked by such rare and exquisite quality that it is known only to connoisseurs **2 APPRECIATING FINE THINGS** having a deep appreciation of unusual or choice things ○ *a recherché taste in sculpture* **3 AFFECTED** marked by excessive refinement or exaggerated importance ○ *Some of his ideas are a little recherché for my taste.* [Late 17C. < French, past participle of *rechercher* 'seek thoroughly' < *chercher* 'seek'.]

rechristen /ree kríss'n/ *vt* to give a new name to something or somebody

recidivism /ri síddivizəm/ *n* the tendency to relapse into a previous undesirable type of behaviour, especially crime [Late 19C. < *recidivist*, < French *récidiviste* < Latin *recidivus* 'falling back' < *recidere* 'fall back' < *cadere* 'fall'.] —**recidivist** *n, adj* —**recidivistic** /ri síddi vístik/ *adj*

~~**reciept**~~ incorrect spelling of **receipt**

~~**recieve**~~ incorrect spelling of **receive**

Recife /re seéfə/ capital of Pernambuco State, NE Brazil. Population: 1,346,045 (1996 estimate).

recip. *abbr* **1** reciprocity **2** reciprocal

recipe /réssəpi/ *n* **1 INSTRUCTIONS FOR MAKING FOOD** a list of ingredients and instructions for making something, especially a food dish **2 METHOD** a method of doing something or a combination of circumstances likely to bring something about ○ *Hard work is the recipe for success.* **3 PRESCRIPTION** a prescription for a therapeutic preparation (*archaic*) [14C. Directly or via French < Latin, 'take!', a form of *recipere* (see RECEIVE).]

recipient /ri síppi ənt/ *n* somebody or something that receives something ■ *adj* tending or able to receive [Mid-16C. Directly or via French < Latin *recipient-*, present participle of *recipere* (see RECEIVE).] —**recipience** *n*

reciprocal /ri síprrək'l/ *adj* **1 GIVEN BY EACH SIDE** given or shown by each of two sides or individuals to the other ○ *reciprocal compliments* **2 IN RETURN** given or done in return for something else ○ *a reciprocal attack on the aggressor* **3 MULTIPLIED TO GIVE ONE** describes a number or quality that is related to another by the fact that when multiplied together the product is one **4 COMPLEMENTING** serving to complement one another ■ *n* **1 SOMETHING MUTUAL** something that is mutual or done in return **2 NUMBER MULTIPLIED TO GIVE ONE** a number or quantity that is related to another by the fact that when multiplied together the product is one ○ *4 and $\frac{1}{4}$ are reciprocals* [Late 16C. < Latin *reciprocus* 'that goes backwards and forwards' < *re-* 'backwards' + *pro-* 'forwards'.] —**reciprocality** /ri síprrə kálləti/ *n* —**reciprocally** /ri síprrəkli/ *adv* —**reciprocalness** *n*

reciprocal pronoun *n* a word or phrase such as 'each other' representing two or more things that mutually correspond to one another

reciprocate /ri síprrə kayt/ (**-cates, -cating, -cated**) *v* **1** *vti* **GIVE MUTUALLY** to give or feel something mutually or in return ○ *I couldn't accept such a generous gift without reciprocating.* **2** *vti* **MOVE BACKWARDS AND FORWARDS** to move backwards and forwards in an alternating motion, or move something in this way **3** *vi* **BE COMPLEMENTARY** to be the same or complementary [Late 16C. < Latin *reciprocat-*, past participle of *reciprocare* 'move back and forth, reciprocate' < *reciprocus* (see RECIPROCAL).] —**reciprocation** /ri síprrə káysh'n/ *n* —**reciprocative** /ri síprrəkətiv/ *adj* —**reciprocator** /-kaytər/ *n*

reciprocating engine *n* an engine with one or more cylinders in which pistons move backwards and forwards

reciprocity /réssi próssəti/ (*plural* **-ties**) *n* **1** something done mutually or in return **2** a relationship between people involving the exchange of goods, services, favours, or obligations, especially a mutual exchange of privileges between trading nations ○ *the long-standing tariff reciprocity between our two countries* [Mid-18C. < French *réciprocité* < Latin *reciprocus* (see RECIPROCAL).]

reciprocity failure *n* in photography, the failure of light intensity and exposure time to act reciprocally when their values are extremely high or low, sometimes affecting the colour characteristics of the resulting photograph

recision /ri sízh'n/ *n* the cancellation or rescinding of something [Early 17C. Via Latin *recision-* 'cutting back' < Latin *recidere* 'cut back' < *caedere* 'cut'.]

recit. *abbr* recitative

recital /ri sít'l/ *n* 1 SOLO PERFORMANCE a musical or dance performance given by a soloist or small group 2 PERFORMANCE BY MUSIC OR DANCE STUDENTS a performance given by music or dance students 3 RECITING the reading aloud or reciting from memory of something such as a poem 4 DETAILED ACCOUNT a detailed account or report of something ○ *his recital of the events of the day* 5 DETAILED PRESENTATION OF FACT a statement in a judgment laying out jurisdictional facts, or a deed's preliminary part laying out the circumstances leading to its existence (*often used in the plural*) —**recitalist** *n*

recitation /réssi táysh'n/ *n* 1 READING ALOUD the public reading aloud of something or reciting of something from memory, especially poetry 2 MATTER READ ALOUD material read aloud or recited from memory in public, especially poetry 3 REPORTING OF the listing or reporting of something

recitative[1] /réssitə teév/, **recitativo** /-teévō/ (*plural* **-vos**) *n* 1 a style of singing that is close to the rhythm of natural speech, used in opera for dialogue and narration 2 a passage in a musical composition that is sung in the form of recitative [Mid-17C. < Italian *recitativo* < Latin *recitat-*, past participle of *recitare* 'summon again'.]

recitative[2] /ri sítətiv/ *adj* relating to recital or recitation [Mid-17C. Via Italian *recitativo* < Latin *recitare* 'summon again'.]

recitativo *n* MUSIC = **recitative**[1]

recite /ri sít/ (**-cites, -citing, -cited**) *v* 1 *vti* REPEAT OR READ ALOUD to read something aloud or repeat something from memory, especially for an audience 2 *vt* REPEAT SOMETHING LEARNT to repeat aloud something learnt, e.g. a lesson in school 3 *vt* GIVE DETAILED ACCOUNT OF to give a detailed account of an occurrence or event ○ *There's no need to recite every detail of your weekend.* 4 *vt* LIST to give a list of something ○ *He then recited all my faults.* [15C. Directly or via French *réciter* < Latin *recitare* 'summon again' < *citare* 'summon repeatedly'.] —**reciter** *n*

reck /rek/ *vti* (*archaic*) 1 to care or mind about something 2 to matter, or matter to somebody [Old English *rēcan* (recorded only in the past tense), *reccan* 'care, take care of, be interested in' < Germanic]

reckless /rékləss/ *adj* marked by a lack of thought about danger or other possible undesirable consequences ○ *with a reckless disregard for the established safety procedures* [Old English *rec(c)elēas* < Germanic] —**recklessly** *adv* —**recklessness** *n*

reckon /rékən/ *v* 1 *vti* COUNT to count or calculate something 2 *vt* REGARD AS SOMETHING to consider somebody or something to be something (*often passive*) ○ *She's reckoned the best in her field.* 3 *vt* INCLUDE to include or class a person or thing as being part of a particular group ○ *I reckon him among my friends.* 4 *vt* THINK OR BELIEVE to suppose something to be true ○ *I reckon we're finished now.* 5 *vt* THINK HIGHLY OF to rate something or somebody highly (*informal*) ○ *This kid really reckons his chances of winning.* 6 *vi* DEPEND to expect with confident assurance (*informal*) ○ *You can reckon on my support.* [Old English *gerecenian* 'explain, recount, tell' < Germanic] —**reckonable** *adj*

reckon with *vt* 1 to deal or come to terms with somebody powerful ○ *If he lets you down he'll have me to reckon with.* 2 to take somebody or something into account ○ *We didn't reckon with the strength of the tide.*

reckon without *vt* to fail to take something into account ○ *The government reckoned without the strength of public feeling against the new measure.*

reckoner /rékənər/ *n* a book of tables of calculations that are already worked out and are used as an aid in calculation

reckoning /rékəning/ *n* 1 CALCULATION calculation of an aircraft's, a spacecraft's, or a vessel's position in the air, in space, or on the sea 2 SETTLEMENT OF AN ACCOUNT the settlement of an account 3 ACCOUNT OR BILL a statement of debts owed or repaid 4 TIME TO ACCOUNT FOR WRONGS a time to account for or be punished for wrongs ○ *day of reckoning*

reclaim /ri kláym/ *vt* 1 CLAIM SOMETHING BACK to claim back something that has been taken away or temporarily given to another 2 CONVERT WASTELAND to convert unusable land, e.g. desert or marsh, into land suitable for farming or other use 3 EXTRACT USEFUL SUBSTANCES to extract useful substances from waste or refuse 4 MAKE SOMEBODY REFORM cause somebody to return to a more moral way of life 5 TAME A BIRD to tame a hawk or falcon ■ *n* RECOVERY OR CONVERSION the reclaiming of something, or the state of being reclaimed ○ *polluted land beyond reclaim.* [14C. Via Old French *reclaim-* < Latin *reclamare* 'cry out against' < *clamare* 'cry out'.] —**reclaimable** *adj* —**reclaimant** *n* —**reclaimer** *n* —**reclamation** /réklə máysh'n/ *n*

réclame /ray klaám/ *n* 1 public attention or fame 2 the capacity or gift for attracting public attention or fame [Late 19C. < French, 'advertisement' < *réclamer* (see RECLAIM).]

reclassify /ree klássi fī/ (**-fies, -fying, -fied**) *vt* to assign somebody or something to a different class, category, or group —**reclassification** /reé klassifi káysh'n/ *n*

reclinate /rékli nayt/ *adj* describes a leaf or stem that is bent or curved backward or down

recline /ri klín/ (**-clines, -clining, -clined**) *v* 1 *vi* to lean back into a supported sloping or horizontal position, usually in order to rest or relax ○ *She was reclining on a chaise longue.* 2 *vti* to tilt back from an upright position, or make something tilt back ○ *These seats are more comfortable because they recline.* [15C. Directly or via Old French *recliner* < Latin *reclinare* 'bend back or against' < *clinare* 'bend'.] —**reclinable** *adj* —**reclination** /rékli náysh'n/ *n*

recliner /ri klínər/ *n* 1 a chair that tilts back to a sloping or almost horizontal position, often with a footrest that can be raised, allowing the person sitting in it to rest more comfortably 2 a person who reclines

reclosable /ree klṓzəb'l/ *adj* able to be closed and sealed again after being opened ○ *a reclosable package*

recluse /ri kloóss/ *n* 1 SOMEBODY LIVING APART FROM OTHERS a solitary person who avoids other people 2 SOMEBODY LIVING A LIFE OF PRAYER a person who lives a solitary life in prayer and meditation ■ *adj* RECLUSIVE reclusive (*archaic*) [12C. Via French *reclus*, past participle of Old French *reclure* 'shut up' < Latin *recludere* 'to shut again' < *claudere* 'shut'.] —**reclusion** /ri kloózh'n/ *n*

reclusive /ri kloóssiv/ *adj* solitary and withdrawn from the rest of the world ○ *lead a reclusive existence* [Late 16C. < obsolete *recluse* 'shut up' < Latin *reclus-*, past participle of *recludere* (see RECLUSE).] —**reclusively** *adv* —**reclusiveness** *n*

recognisance *n* = **recognizance**

recognise *vt* = **recognize**

recognised *adj* = **recognized**

ϟ**recognition** /rékəg nísh'n/ *n* 1 RECOGNIZING OF SOMETHING OR BEING RECOGNIZED the perception that somebody or something has been seen before or an identification based on such perception 2 APPRECIATION appreciation or fame earned by an achievement ○ *His pioneering work never got the recognition it deserved.* 3 ACKNOWLEDGMENT acknowledgment of validity ○ *They'll need recognition from the committee in order to proceed.* 4 ACCEPTANCE OF A COUNTRY'S EXISTENCE the formal acceptance by one country of the independent and legal status of another 5 TOKEN OF ACKNOWLEDGMENT something given or awarded as a token of acknowledgment or gratitude 6 SENSING OF DATA BY A COMPUTER the sensing and conversion of data into machine-readable form by a computer 7 COMPATIBILITY OF MOLECULES the ability of molecules with complementary shapes to attach to one another [15C. Directly or via Old French < Latin *recognition-* < *recognit-*, past participle of *recognoscere* (see RECOGNIZE).] —**recognitive** /ri kógnətiv/ *adj* —**recognitory** /-nətəri/ *adj*

recognizance /ri kógnizənss/, **recognisance** *n* 1 a formal agreement made by somebody before a judge or magistrate to do something, e.g. to appear in court at a set date ○ *He was released on his own recognizance.* 2 a sum of money pledged by somebody making a recognizance, to be forfeited if the agreed act is not carried out [14C. < Old French *recon(u)issance*, an alteration of *reconoissance* < stem of *reconoistre* (see RECOGNIZE).] —**recognizant** *adj*

recognize /rékəg nīz/ (**-nizes, -nizing, -nized**), **recognise** (**-nises, -nising, -nised**) *vt* 1 IDENTIFY SOMEBODY OR SOMETHING SEEN BEFORE to identify a thing or person because of having perceived him, her, or it before ○ *If you saw him again, would you recognize him?* 2 ACKNOWLEDGE SOMEBODY'S ACHIEVEMENT to show appreciation of or give credit to another's achievement ○ *I hope you recognize their contribution to the success of the campaign.* 3 ACCEPT to accept the validity or truth of something ○ *I recognize that I am at fault.* 4 ACCEPT STATE'S INDEPENDENCE to accept formally the independent and legal status of a country or regime ○ *refused to recognize the military government* 5 ALLOW SOMEBODY TO SPEAK to allow a person to speak to a meeting ○ *The chair recognizes the representative.* 6 SHOW ACKNOWLEDGEMENT to show in some way that somebody is personally known ○ *She recognized old friends in the crowd with a smile and a wave.* 7 REWARD to give or award something to a person as a token of acknowledgment or gratitude ○ *The government recognized his services to industry with a knighthood.* 8 BIND ANOTHER MOLECULE to bind another molecule that has a complementary structure [15C. Via Old French *recon(n)iss-*, stem of *reconnaistre* < Latin *recognoscere* 'know again' < *cognoscere* 'know'.] —**recognizability** /rékəg nīzə bílləti/ *n* —**recognizable** /rékəg nīzəb'l/ *adj* —**recognizably** *adv* —**recognized** *adj* —**recognizer** *n*

recoil *vi* /ri kóyl/ 1 MOVE BACK SUDDENLY to move back suddenly and violently, e.g. after impact 2 MOVE BACK IN HORROR to move back or away from something in horror or disgust 3 FAIL to go wrong and, as a consequence, hurt the perpetrator 4 CHANGE MOMENTUM to experience a change in momentum as a result of a nuclear collision or the emission of an elementary particle ■ *n* /ri kóyl, reé koyl/ 1 SUDDEN BACKWARD MOVEMENT a sudden and violent backward movement, especially that of a firearm when it is fired 2 MOVEMENT AWAY IN HORROR a movement back or away from something, especially in horror or disgust 3 CHANGE IN MOMENTUM a change in the momentum of an atom, nucleus, or elementary particle as a result of a nuclear collision or the emission of an elementary particle [12C. < French *reculer* < Latin *culus* 'backside'.] —**recoiler** /ri kóylər/ *n*

SYNONYMS ***recoil, flinch, quail, shrink, wince***

CORE MEANING: to draw back in fear or distaste

recoil to draw back suddenly or react mentally in fear, horror, disgust, or distaste; **flinch** to draw back physically because of fear or pain, or to avoid confronting something unpleasant; **quail** to tremble or cower with fear or apprehension; **shrink** to move away physically from something because of fear or disgust, or to feel reluctance to do something because of fear or apprehension; **wince** to make an involuntary movement away from something in response to a stimulus such as pain or embarrassment.

recoilless /ri kóyl ləss/ *adj* relating to a heavy firearm, e.g. an antitank gun, whose recoil is reduced by venting the blast to the rear

recoil-operated *adj* using the movement caused by the recoil of a firearm to operate part of its mechanism

recollect /rékə lékt/ *vti* to bring something back to mind ○ *Can you recollect what she was wearing?* [Early 16C. < Latin *recollect-*, past participle of *recolligere* 'gather again' (later 'recall') < *colligere* (see COLLECT[1]).] —**recollective** *adj* —**recollectively** *adv*

re-collect *vt* 1 to regain control, especially of the self 2 to collect again something that has been scattered or dispersed

recollection /rékə léksh'n/ *n* 1 the remembering of something, or the ability to remember ○ *That's not the way it happened, according to my recollection.* 2 something that a person remembers ○ *a recollection of having met him before*

recombinant /ri kómbinənt/ *adj* 1 OF GENETIC RECOMBINATION relating to or involved in genetic recombination ○ *a recombinant chromosome* 2 RELATING TO RECOMBINANT DNA relating to recombinant DNA or produced by recombinant DNA technology ■ *n* 1 RESULT OF GENETIC RECOMBINATION a cell or organism exhibiting genetic recombination 2 GENETIC MATERIAL FROM GENE-SPLICING genetic material resulting from the splicing of DNA fragments

recombinant DNA *n* DNA extracted from two or more different sources, e.g. genes from different organisms, and joined together to form a single molecule or fragment

recombination /reé kombi náysh'n/ *n* any process that gives rise to offspring that have combinations of genes different to those of either parent, such as crossing-over and independent assortment of chromosomes during gamete formation —**recombinational** *adj*

recombine /reékəm bín/ (**-bines, -bining, -bined**) *vti* 1 to become combined again or combine things again 2 to undergo or cause something to undergo genetic recombination

~~recomend~~ incorrect spelling of **recommend**

recommence /reèkə méns/ (**-mences, -mencing, -menced**) *vti* to start again or start something again [15C. < French *recommencer* 'commence again' < *commencer* (see COMMENCE).] —**recommencement** /reèkə ménsmənt/ *n*

recommend /rékə ménd/ *vt* **1 SUGGEST AS BEST IDEA** to suggest something as worthy of being accepted, used, or done **2 ENDORSE** to endorse a person or thing as being the most worthy or pleasing **3 MAKE APPEALING OR ATTRACTIVE** to make something worth doing or having because it is beneficial or pleasing ○ *The film has little to recommend it other than its special effects.* **4 ENTRUST TO ANOTHER** to entrust a person or thing to the care of another (*formal*) ○ *She was recommended to our care until her family returned.* [14C. < medieval Latin *recommendare* 'commit thoroughly' < Latin *commendare* 'entrust completely'.] —**recommendable** *adj* —**recommendatory** *adj* —**recommender** *n*

SYNONYMS ***recommend, advise, advocate, counsel, suggest***

CORE MEANING: to put foward ideas to somebody deciding on a course of action

recommend to put forward a course of action as being worthy of acceptance in the circumstances; **advise** to give advice in a relatively open and objective way; **advocate** to support or speak in favour of something; **counsel** (*formal or literary*) to advise somebody on a particular course of action; **suggest** to propose something in a tentative way as a possible course of action for somebody else to consider.

recommendation /rékə men dáysh'n/ *n* **1 RECOMMENDING OF** the suggestion or endorsement of something as the most worthy **2 SOMETHING THAT RECOMMENDS** a favourable reference about somebody or something or other endorsement of desirability ○ *You come to us with many recommendations.* **3 SOMETHING RECOMMENDED** the best course of action recommended ○ *My recommendation would be to leave on the next train.*

recommit /reèkə mít/ (**-mits, -mitting, -mitted**) *vt* **1** to return something, usually a bill, to a committee for more discussion **2** to commit something or somebody again —**recommittal** *n* —**recommitment** *n*

recompense /rékəm penss/ *vt* (**-penses, -pensing, -pensed**) **1 PAY OR REWARD** to pay another for doing work or for performing a service **2 GIVE COMPENSATION** to give compensation to another for an injury or loss ○ *The state will recompense you for the accidental destruction of your property.* ■ *n* **1 REMUNERATION** payment for services or work performed **2 COMPENSATION** compensation for a loss or injury [14C. Directly or via French *récompenser* < late Latin *recompensare* 'balance out again' < Latin *compensare* 'balance out'.]

recompose /reèkəm pṓz/ (**-poses, -posing, -posed**) *vt* **1** to return to a calm or composed state of mind **2** to change the arrangement or composition of a thing or group —**recomposition** /reèkompə zísh'n/ *n*

reconcile /rékən sīl/ (**-ciles, -ciling, -ciled**) *v* **1** *vt* **MAKE PEOPLE FRIENDLY** to bring about a friendly relationship between disputing people or groups (*often passive*) **2** *vt* **END CONFLICT** to solve a dispute or end a quarrel ○ *reconciled their differences* **3** *vt* **MAKE SOMEBODY ACCEPT** to make somebody accept that something undesirable cannot be changed ○ *He reconciled himself to the fact that his sporting career was over.* **4** *vti* **MAKE CONSISTENT OR COMPATIBLE** to make two or more apparently conflicting things consistent or compatible, or to become consistent or compatible ○ *trying to reconcile fitness with a penchant for fast food* [14C. Directly or via French *réconcilier* < Latin *reconciliare* 'make friendly again' < *conciliare* 'make friendly' < *concilium* 'meeting'.] —**reconcilability** /rékən sīlə bílləti/ *n* —**reconcilable** /rékən sīləb'l/ *adj* —**reconcilableness** *n* —**reconcilably** *adv* —**reconcilement** *n* —**reconciler** *n*

reconciliation /rékən sili áysh'n/ *n* **1 RECONCILING OF PEOPLE** the ending of conflict or renewing of a friendly relationship between disputing people or groups ○ *a series of quarrels and reconciliations* **2 ACHIEVEMENT OF CONSISTENCY OR COMPATIBILITY** the making of two or more apparently conflicting things consistent or compatible ○ *the reconciliation of such action with his pacifist principles* **3 SACRAMENT OF PENANCE** the sacrament in the Roman Catholic Church whereby an individual's sins are absolved through confession and penance [14C. Directly or via French < Latin *reconciliation-* < *reconciliare* (see RECONCILE).] —**reconciliatory** /rékən sílli ətəri/ *adj*

recondite /rékən dīt, ri kón-/ *adj* **1** requiring special detailed knowledge in order to be understood ○ *the recondite lore of the ancient Persians* **2** dealing with material that is too difficult to be understood by those without special knowledge ○ *recondite learning* [Mid-17C. < Latin *reconditus*, past participle of *recondere* 'store away' < *condere* 'store, hide'.] —**reconditely** *adv* —**reconditeness** *n*

SYNONYMS See ***obscure***.

recondition /reèkən dísh'n/ *vt* to bring something back into good condition, especially by repairing it and replacing worn-out parts

SYNONYMS See ***renew***.

reconfigure /reè kən fíggər/ (**-ures, -uring, -ured**) *vt* to configure something again or in a different way —**reconfiguration** /reè kən figgə ráysh'n/ *n*

reconfirm /reèkən fúrm/ *vt* **1** to confirm something such as an airline or hotel reservation again **2** to strengthen a commitment to or a belief in something ○ *reconfirmed their wedding vows* —**reconfirmation** /reè konfər máysh'n/ *n*

~~reconize~~ incorrect spelling of **recognize**

~~reconnaisance~~ incorrect spelling of **reconnaissance**

reconnaissance /ri kónniss'nss/ *n* **1** the exploration or examination of an area to gather information, especially about the strength and positioning of enemy forces **2** preliminary research or investigation of something [Early 19C. < French, < *reconnaiss-*, stem of *reconnaître* 'reconnoitre' < Latin *recognoscere* (see RECOGNIZE).]

reconnect /reèkə nékt/ *vt* to connect again something that has been disconnected or cut off, e.g. a telephone communication or an electricity supply —**reconnection** *n*

reconnoiter *n, vti* US = **reconnoitre**

reconnoitre /rékə nóytər/ *vti* (**-tres, -tring, -tred**) to explore an area in order to gather information, especially about the strength and positioning of enemy forces ○ *reconnoitre the drop zone* ■ *n* an exploration of an area in order to gather information [Early 18C. Via obsolete French *reconnoître* < Latin *recognoscere* (see RECOGNIZE).] —**reconnoitrer** *n*

reconquer /ree kóngkər/ *vt* to conquer territory, people, or your own emotions for a second or subsequent time —**reconquest** /ree kónkwest/ *n*

reconsider /reèkən síddər/ *vti* to think about something again, usually with the possibility or intention of changing a previous decision —**reconsideration** /reèkən sidə ráysh'n/ *n*

reconstitute /reè kónsti tyoot/ (**-tutes, -tuting, -tuted**) *vt* **1** to bring specified matter or a material back to its original state, usually by adding water to a concentrated, dried, or powdered form **2** to alter the form of something ○ *reconstitute the government* —**reconstituent** /reèkən stíttyoo ənt/ *adj, n* —**reconstitution** /reè konsti tyóosh'n/ *n*

reconstruct /reèkən strúkt/ *vt* **1** to put something back together from its component parts, pieces, or remains **2** to create a plausible scenario of the details of something based on the known evidence ○ *reconstruct the culture of an ancient society* —**reconstructible** *adj* —**reconstruction** *n* —**reconstructive** *adj* —**reconstructor** *n*

Reconstruction /reèkən strúksh'n/ *n* the period of US history from 1865 to 1877, during which the states that had seceded during the Civil War were reorganized under federal control and later restored to the Union

Reconstructionism /reèkən strúksh'nizəm/ *n* a movement in the United States, begun in the 1920s by Mordechai Kaplan, emphasizing the idea that Judaism is a worldwide religious civilization and advocating continuous adaptation to contemporary conditions

reconstructive surgery *n* the use of surgery to restore the appearance or use of a damaged body part

reconvene /reèkən veén/ (**-venes, -vening, -vened**) *vti* to convene something again or be convened again ○ *The hearing will reconvene tomorrow morning.*

reconvey /reèkən váy/ (**-veys, -veying, -veyed**) *vt* to transfer something, e.g. property, back to a former owner or location —**reconveyance** *n*

ϟ**record** *n* /ré kawrd/ **1 LASTING ACCOUNT** an account of something, preserved in a lasting form, e.g. in writing or on film ○ *Some people use a diary to keep a record of their daily lives.* **2 ACCOUNT OF PROCEEDINGS** a written account of the proceedings of something ○ *the records of the Pickwick Society* **3 WRITTEN ACCOUNT OF COURT PROCEEDINGS** an official written account of the proceedings of a court, available for use as evidence ○ *His remarks were struck from the record.* **4 DOCUMENT CONTAINING HISTORY** the document or book that bears the history of something ○ *The records are stored in the basement.* **5 BODY OF INFORMATION** a body of information or statistics, gathered over a period of time, about a particular subject (*often plural*) ○ *the hottest summer since records began* **6 EVIDENCE** something that acts as evidence or a memorial ○ *The Egyptian pyramids are a record of human engineering expertise.* **7 BEST ACCOMPLISHMENT** something that represents the greatest attainment so far, especially in sports ○ *a world record* **8 MUSIC DISC** something on which sound is copied, especially a plastic disc with a groove that can be played using a gramophone **9 COPY OF MUSIC** a piece of music in a format that can be listened to repeatedly (*informal*) ○ *Their new record is only available on CD.* **10 PAST PERFORMANCE** a person's accomplishments or performance to date **11 PAST CRIMES** a background of criminal convictions, or a list of the crimes committed by a person **12 COLLECTION OF DATA** a collection of related items of information treated as a unit by a computer, e.g. in a database ■ *v* /ri káwrd/ **1** *vt* **MAKE A LASTING ACCOUNT OF** to make a lasting account of something, e.g. in writing or on film ○ *Her journal records the last days of the Empire.* **2** *vt* **NOTE** to make a note of something, often for official purposes or for subsequent consultation ○ *The clerk recorded their names in the register.* **3** *vti* **INDICATE MEASUREMENT** to register or show something, usually on a scale of a measurement **4** *vti* **COPY SOUNDS OR IMAGES** to make a copy of sounds or pictures, e.g. on magnetic tape ○ *I recorded my grandmother reminiscing about the war.* ■ *adj* /ré kawrd/ **GREATEST YET** representing the greatest extreme yet accomplished ○ *A record crowd turned up for the game.* [12C. < French, < *recorder* 'bring to mind' < Latin *recordare, recordari* 'bring back to the heart' < stem of *cor* 'heart, (metaphorically) mind'.] —**recordable** /ri káwrdəb'l/ *adj* ◇ **off the record** said informally or privately and not intended to be recorded or made public ◇ **on the record** said formally or publicly with the knowledge that it may be recorded or disseminated ◇ **set the record straight** to put right a mistake or misunderstanding

recorded /ri káwrdid/ *adj* **1** copied to a record, tape, CD, or other form of permanent copy, rather than listened to or performed live ○ *recorded music* **2** sent through the mail by recorded delivery ○ *a recorded parcel*

recorded delivery *n* a method of postage in which an official record is kept of the sending and delivery of the item concerned. US term **certified mail**. ◊ **registered post**

recorder /ri káwrdər/ *n* **1 MACHINE FOR RECORDING** a machine that makes a permanent copy of sounds or pictures, e.g. a tape recorder or a video recorder **2 PERSON NOTING SOMETHING** a person who records something, especially official proceedings **3 MUSICAL INSTRUMENT** a wind instrument of the flute family that has finger holes and is blown through a whistle-shaped mouthpiece at one end **4 recorder, Recorder TYPE OF JUDGE** a barrister or solicitor in England and Wales who acts as a part-time judge in the crown court [15C. Partly < Anglo-Norman *recordour*, Old French *recordeur* 'person who records' < *recorder* (see RECORD); partly < RECORD.] —**recordership** *n*

recording /ri káwrding/ *n* **1 MAKING OF RECORD** the making of a record, especially a permanent copy of sounds or images **2 COPY OF MUSIC** a permanent copy of sounds or images, e.g. a tape, CD, or video ○ *She was eager to buy the band's latest recording.* **3 BROADCAST THAT IS NOT LIVE** a broadcast that is not live but has been recorded on an earlier occasion ○ *I watched a recording of the opera on TV.*

Recording Angel *n* an angel believed to keep an account of every person's good and bad deeds

recordist /ri káwrdist/ *n* somebody who records sound during the making of a film or broadcast

record of achievement *n* a document that details the personal and educational development of a school pupil

record player *n* a machine for reproducing the sounds recorded on records, consisting of a turntable on which the disc revolves and a needle that follows the groove to pick up sound

recount /ri kównt/ *vt* to tell the story or details of something ○ *a tale recounting the deeds of King Arthur* [15C. < Anglo-Norman, Old N French *reconter* 'relate again, count again' < *conter* (see COUNT[1]).] —**recountal** *n* —**recounter** *n*

re-count /rée kownt/ *n* a second counting of the votes cast in an election, usually done because the first counting indicated a very close result ■ *vti* to count something, especially the votes cast in an election, a second time

recoup /ri ko͞op/ *v* **1** *vt* **GET SOMETHING BACK** to regain something lost or an equivalent **2** *vt* **REIMBURSE ANOTHER** to give another party something to make up for that which has been lost ○ *We were adequately recouped for our losses.* **3** *vt* **DEDUCT** to deduct legally part of what is due to a claim **4** *vi* **MAKE UP FOR A LOSS** to make up for something lost ○ *It will take us years to recoup.* [Early 17C. < Old French *recouper* 'cut back' < *couper* 'cut' < *coup* 'blow'.] —**recoupable** *adj* —**recoupment** *n*

~~**recouperate**~~ incorrect spelling of **recuperate**

recourse /ri káwrss/ *n* **1 CHANCE TO SEEK ASSISTANCE** a turning to another for assistance ○ *Can we resolve our financial problems without recourse to further borrowing?* **2 SOURCE OF HELP OR SOLUTION** somebody, something, or a course of action to which a person turns for help or to solve a problem ○ *She felt she had no recourse but to sue.* **3 RIGHT TO DEMAND PAYMENT** the right to demand payment of a bill of exchange from the person who draws or endorses it, when the person who accepts it fails to pay [14C. Directly or via French *recours* < Latin *recursus* 'a running back' < *cursus* (see COURSE).]

recover /ri kúvvər/ *v* **1** *vt* **REGAIN** to get back something previously lost **2** *vi* **RETURN TO NORMAL** to return to a previous state of health, prosperity, or equanimity **3** *vr* **BRING SELF BACK TO NORMAL** to bring the self back to a normal condition ○ *He soon recovered himself enough to feign a friendly welcome.* **4** *vi* **RETURN TO THE RIGHT POSITION** to return to a suitable or correct state or position ○ *The goalkeeper stumbled, but recovered enough to save the goal.* **5** *vt* **COMPENSATE FOR** to make up for that which is lost ○ *They'll have to work hard in order to recover their losses.* **6** *vt* **OBTAIN SOMETHING THROUGH A COURT** to obtain something by the ruling of a court **7** *vt* **RECLAIM SOMETHING FROM WASTE** to extract useful substances from waste or refuse **8** *vi* **SUCCEED IN LITIGATION** to be successful in a lawsuit [13C. Via Anglo-Norman *recoverer*, Old French *recovrer* < Latin *recuperare* 'take back'.] —**recoverability** /ri kúvvərə bíllәti/ *n* —**recoverable** /ri kúvvərəb'l/ *adj* —**recoverer** *n*

re-cover /rée kúvvər/ *vt* **1** to put a new cover on something **2** to cover something again

recoverable error *n* a program error that can be corrected without causing a computer program to fail or data to be erased irretrievably

recovery /ri kúvvəri/ (*plural* **-ies**) *n* **1 RETURN TO HEALTH** the return to normal health of somebody who has been ill or injured **2 RETURN TO A NORMAL STATE** the return of something to a normal or improved state after a setback or loss ○ *an economic recovery* **3 GAINING BACK OF SOMETHING LOST** the regaining of something lost or taken away ○ *The arrests led to the recovery of large amounts of stolen property.* **4 RECLAMATION FROM WASTE** the extraction of useful substances from waste or refuse **5 OBTAINING SOMETHING THROUGH A COURT** the obtaining of something by the ruling of a court **6 SHOT OUT OF AN OBSTACLE** in golf, a shot played out of the rough or an obstacle onto the green or fairway **7 RETURN TO GUARD** in fencing, a return to the guard position after making an attack **8 BRINGING THE ARM FORWARD** in swimming or rowing, the bringing forward of the arm to make another stroke

recovery room *n* a hospital room equipped for the care of patients who have just undergone surgery and are recovering from anaesthesia

recreant /rékri ənt/ *adj* (*archaic*) **1** disloyal to a cause or duty **2** cowardly [13C. < Old French, present participle of *recroire* 'surrender' < Latin *credere* 'entrust'.] —**recreance** /-ənss/ *n* —**recreancy** /-ənssi/ *n* —**recreant** *n* —**recreantly** *adv*

recreate /rékri ayt/ (**-ates, -ating, -ated**) *vi* to take part in activities that are mentally or physically refreshing [15C. < Latin *recreat-*, past participle of *recreare* 'bring forth again' < *creare* 'bring forth, produce' also, later, a back-formation < RECREATION.] —**recreative** *adj* —**recreator** *n*

re-create /rée kri áyt/ (**re-creates, re-creating, re-created**) *vt* to create something again or reproduce it ○ *The decor aims to re-create a 19th-century interior.* —**re-creatable** *adj* —**re-creation** *n* —**re-creative** *adj*

SYNONYMS See ***copy***.

recreation /rékri áysh'n/ *n* **1** the refreshment of the mind and body after work, especially by engaging in enjoyable activities ○ *after-work recreation* **2** an activity that a person takes part in for pleasure or relaxation rather than as work ○ *She took up sketching as a recreation.*

recreational *adj* **1** done or used for pleasure or relaxation rather than work **2** describes controlled drugs taken illegally —**recreationally** *adv*

recreational vehicle *n US* a large motor vehicle, usually with facilities for sleeping and eating, used for recreational activities such as camping

recreation ground *n* a public area for sports and games, often incorporating a children's playground

recreation room *n* **1** a room set aside for games, social events, and other kinds of recreation in a public building **2** *US* a room used by the occupants of a house for relaxation and recreational activities ○ *a new TV for the recreation room*

recriminate /ri krímmi nayt/ (**-nates, -nating, -nated**) *vi* to accuse somebody who has already brought an accusation [Early 17C. < medieval Latin *recriminat-*, past participle of *recriminari* 'accuse back or again' < Latin *criminari, criminare* 'accuse'.] —**recriminative** /-nətiv/ *adj* —**recriminator** *n* —**recriminatory** /-nətəri/ *adj*

recrimination /ri krímmi náysh'n/ *n* **1** an accusation made against somebody who has brought a previous accusation ○ *It started out as a calm discussion and ended in tears and recriminations.* **2** an accusation that somebody accused of a crime makes against the accuser

rec room *n US* a recreation room (*informal*)

recross /ree króss/ *v* **1** *vt* **CROSS SOMETHING AGAIN** to pass across or over something again **2** *vt* **CROSS THINGS AGAIN** to place two things so that one lies across the other in a different direction from their previous position ○ *crossing and recrossing their legs* **3** *vi* **MEET AND PART AGAIN** to meet and then continue separately for a second or subsequent time ○ *Our paths recrossed several years later.*

recrudesce /rée kroo déss/ (**-desces, -descing, -desced**) *vi* to break out or become active again after a dormant period [Mid-17C. Back-formation < *recrudescence* < Latin *recrudescere* 'become raw again' < *crudus* 'raw, bloody'.] —**recrudescence** *n* —**recrudescent** *adj*

recruit /ri kro͞ot/ *v* **1** *vti* **ENLIST** to enlist somebody in a military force, or take part in enlisting people for a military force ○ *She was recruited by the Marines.* **2** *vti* **ENROL OR TAKE ON** to enrol somebody as a worker or member, or to take on people as workers or members ○ *The company has stopped recruiting.* **3** *vt* **RAISE AN ARMY** to put together a military force ■ *n* **1 NEW SOLDIER** a member of a military force who has joined recently **2 NEW MEMBER** a new member, worker, player, or supporter [Mid-17C. Via French *recruter* < French *recrue* 'new growth' < *recroître* 'increase again' < Latin *crescere* 'grow'.] —**recruiter** *n* —**recruiting** *n* —**recruitment** *n*

recrystallize /ree krístə līz/ (**-lizes, -lizing, -lized**), **recrystallise** (**-lises, -lising, -lised**) *vti* to crystallize something or become crystallized again —**recrystallization** /ree krístə lī záysh'n/ *n*

Rect. *abbr* **1** Rector **2** Rectory

recta plural of **rectum**

rectangle /rék tang g'l/ *n* a four-sided plane figure in which each angle is a right angle, especially one with adjacent sides of different length [Late 16C. Directly or via French < medieval Latin *rect(i)angulum*, < form of late Latin *rectiangulus* 'straight angle' < Latin *rectus* 'straight' + *angulus* 'angle'.]

rectangular /rek táng gyo͝olər/ *adj* **1** with four sides, usually with adjacent sides of different length, and four right angles ○ *The yard is rectangular rather than square.* **2** involving, having, or meeting at right angles [Early 17C. < ANGULAR after French *rectangulaire*.] —**rectangularity** /rek táng gyo͝o lárrəti/ *n* —**rectangularly** /rek táng gyo͝olərli/ *adv*

rectangular coordinate *n* a Cartesian coordinate used in a system of axes that meet at right angles

rectangular hyperbola *n* a hyperbola with asymptotes that are at right angles

recti plural of **rectus**

rectifier /rékti fī ər/ *n* **1 ELECTRONIC DEVICE** an electronic device that converts alternating current to direct current, e.g. a set of semiconductor diodes connected in a bridge circuit **2 CONDENSING APPARATUS** an apparatus that condenses vapour to liquid during distillation **3 SOMEBODY OR SOMETHING THAT RECTIFIES** somebody or something that puts something right

rectify /rékti fī/ (**-fies, -fying, -fied**) *vt* **1 CORRECT** to put something right **2 PURIFY** to purify a substance, especially by distillation **3 CONVERT A CURRENT** to convert alternating current to direct current **4 FIND THE LENGTH OF A CURVE** to find the length of a curve [14C. Directly or via French *rectifier* < medieval Latin *rectificare* 'make right' < *rectus* 'right'.] —**rectifiability** /rékti fī ə bílləti/ *n* —**rectifiable** /rékti fī əb'l/ *adj* —**rectification** /réktifi káysh'n/ *n*

rectilinear /rékti línni ər/, **rectilineal** /-ni əl/ *adj* **1** formed or consisting of straight lines **2** moving in a straight line [Mid-17C. < late Latin *rectilineus* < Latin *rectus* 'straight' + *linea* 'line'.] —**rectilinearly** *adv*

rectitude /rékti tyood/ *n* **1 RIGHTEOUSNESS** strong moral integrity in character or actions **2 CORRECTNESS** correctness in judgment (*formal*) ○ *the admirable rectitude of her assessments* **3 STRAIGHTNESS** straightness in form or shape (*formal*) [15C. Directly or via French < late Latin *rectitudo* < Latin *rectus* 'straight, correct'.] —**rectitudinous** /rékti tyo͞odinəss/ *adj*

recto /réktō/ (*plural* **-tos**) *n* **1** the front side of a printed sheet. ◊ **verso** *n.* 1 **2** the right-hand page of an open book. ◊ **verso** *n.* 2 [Early 19C. < modern Latin *(folio) recto* '(the page) being on the right', form of Latin *rectus* 'straight, correct'.]

rector /réktər/ *n* **1 CLERIC IN CHARGE OF AN ANGLICAN PARISH** a member of the clergy of the Church of England who is in charge of a parish **2 CLERIC IN CHARGE OF A CATHOLIC CONGREGATION** a member of the Roman Catholic clergy who is in charge of a congregation, a college, or a religious community **3 CLERIC IN CHARGE OF AN EPISCOPAL PARISH** a member of the Episcopal clergy who is in charge of a parish **4 HEAD OF A SCHOOL** the head of certain schools, colleges, or universities **5 OFFICER ELECTED BY STUDENTS** in certain Scottish universities, somebody elected by students to represent them on the University Court [14C. Directly or via Old French, 'captain (of a ship), head of a university' < Latin, 'ruler, governor' < *regere* 'rule'.] —**rectorate** *n* —**rectorial** /rek táwri əl/ *adj* —**rectorship** /réktər ship/ *n*

rectory /réktəri/ (*plural* **-ries**) *n* **1** the house that a rector lives in, provided by the church **2** the post of rector and the income that goes with it [Late 16C. Via Old French *rectorie* or medieval Latin *rectoria* < Latin *rector* (see RECTOR).]

rectrix /rék triks/ (*plural* **-trices** /-tri seez, -trī seez/) *n* any of a bird's long stiff tail feathers that help to control direction during flight [Mid-18C. < Latin, feminine of *rector* (see RECTOR).]

rectum /réktəm/ (*plural* **-tums** *or* **-ta** /-tə/) *n* the lower part of the large intestine, between the colon and the anal canal [15C. < Latin *(intestinum) rectum* 'straight (intestine)' < *rectus* 'straight'.] —**rectal** *adj* —**rectally** *adv*

rectus /réktəss/ (*plural* **-ti** /-tī/) *n* any straight muscle, e.g. any of the muscles in the abdomen or the thigh [Early 18C. < Latin, 'straight'.]

recumbent /ri kúmbənt/ *adj* **1 LYING** lying back or lying down (*literary*) ○ *a colossal recumbent statue* **2 RESTING OR LEANING** describes a plant or animal part that rests or leans against something else **3 HORIZONTAL** describes a fold whose axis is more or less horizontal [Early 18C. < Latin *recumbere* 'lie back' < *-cumbere* 'lie down'.] —**recumbence** *n* —**recumbently** *adv*

recuperate /ri ko͞opə rayt/ (**-ates, -ating, -ated**) *v* **1** *vi* to recover from an illness or injury **2** *vt* to recover something lost, especially a sum of money [Mid-16C. < Latin *recuperare* 'take back' < *capere*.] —**recuperation** /ri ko͞opə ráysh'n/ *n* —**recuperative** /ri ko͞opərətiv, -raytiv/ *adj* —**recuperatory** /-rətəri/ *adj*

USAGE ***Recuperate*** is normally used intransitively, that is, without an object, as in *She needed several weeks to recuperate.* When a noun such as *health* is the object, *recover* is a better choice: *She needed several weeks to recover her health.*

recuperator /ri ko͞opə raytər/ *n* **1** a device used to recover energy that would otherwise be lost, especially one that takes heat from exhaust gases and uses it to preheat incoming combustion air **2** a device in a gun that returns it to its firing position following recoil

recur /ri kúr/ (**-curs, -curring, -curred**) *vi* **1** ⚠ **OCCUR AGAIN** to happen or appear once again or repeatedly. **2 BE REPEATED INDEFINITELY** to occur as an infinitely repeated digit or series of digits at the end of a decimal fraction **3 RETURN** to return to a subject in speech, writing, or thought (*literary*) [Early 16C. < Latin *recurrere* 'run back' < *currere* 'run'.]

USAGE As the idea of *again* is an integral part of the meaning of ***recur***, it is unnecessary to say things like *The disease recurred again.* Simply say *recurred.*

recurrent /ri kúrrənt/ *adj* **1** happening or appearing again, especially repeatedly **2** describes a blood vessel or nerve that turns back on itself and runs in the opposite direction —**recurrence** /ri kúrrənss/ *n* —**recurrently** *adv*

recurrent fever *n* MED = **relapsing fever**

recurring decimal *n* a decimal number in which one or more digits repeat indefinitely after the decimal point, e.g. 3.77777…. or 8.691691691…. US term **repeating decimal**

⚡**recursion** /ri kúrsh'n/ *n* **1 RETURN OF** the return of something, often repeatedly **2 REPETITION OF STEPS TO GIVE RESULT** the use of repeated steps, each based on the result of the one before, to define a function or calculate a number **3 REPEATING OF COMPUTER PROCESS** a programming technique where a routine performs its task by delegating part of it to another instance of itself [Early 17C. Via late Latin *recursion-* 'a running back' < Latin *recurs-*, past participle of *recurrere* (see RECUR).]

recursive /ri kúrssiv/ *adj* **1** repeating itself, either indefinitely or until a specified point is reached **2** involving the repeated application of a function to its own values [Late 18C. < Latin *recurs-*, past participle of *recurrere* 'run back'.] —**recursively** *adv* —**recursiveness** *n*

recurvate /ri kúrvət, -vayt/ *adj* curved backwards, inwards, or downwards

recurve /ri kúrv/ (**-curves, -curving, -curved**) *vti* to curve backwards, inwards, or downwards, or cause something to curve in this way [Late 16C. < Latin *recurvare* 'curve back' < *curvus* 'curved, crooked'.] —**recurvation** /reè kur váysh'n/ *n* —**recurved** /ri kúrvd/ *adj*

recusant /rékyōoz'nt, ri kyóo-/ *n* **1 DISSENTING ROMAN CATHOLIC** a Roman Catholic who broke the law by refusing to attend Church of England services in England between the 16th and 18th centuries **2 SOMEBODY DISOBEYING AUTHORITY** somebody who refuses to obey authority ■ *adj* **DISOBEYING AUTHORITY** refusing to obey authority —**recusance** *n*

recuse /ri kyóoz/ (**-cuses, -cusing, -cused**) *vti* to disqualify somebody from judging or participating in something because of bias or personal interest, or withdraw for that reason [Early 19C. < Latin *recusare* 'refuse' < *re-* 'back' + *causa* 'cause, case'.] —**recusal** *n*

recut /ree kút/ *vt* to cut or shorten something again or in a different way

recycle /ree sík'l/ *v* (**-cles, -cling, -cled**) **1** *vti* **PROCESS FOR RE-USE** to process used or waste material so that it can be used again **2** *vti* **SAVE FOR RE-USE** to save or collect used or waste material for reprocessing into something useful **3** *vti* **USE AGAIN DIFFERENTLY** to adapt or convert something to a new use **4** *vt* **RE-USE** to use something again for the same purpose **5** *vt* **USE AGAIN UNIMAGINATIVELY** to use something abstract again in the same form, often at the expense of freshness or originality **6** *vti* **REPEAT A PROCESS** to repeat a process, or pass something through a process again ■ *n* **RECYCLING OF MATERIAL** the recycling of material, especially used or waste materials —**recyclable** *adj* —**recycler** *n*

recycled /ree sík'ld/ *adj* **1** manufactured from used or waste materials that have been reprocessed **2** used again or repeatedly, often at the expense of freshness or originality

recycling /ree síkling/ *n* **1** the processing of used or waste material so that it can be used again, instead of being wasted **2** the saving or collecting of used or waste material for reprocessing

red /red/ *adj* (**redder, reddest**) **1 OF THE COLOUR OF BLOOD** of or near the colour of blood, or a ripe tomato or strawberry **2 REDDISH-BROWN** describes hair or fur that is reddish-brown, orange, or golden-brown **3 BLOODSHOT** bloodshot or with red rims, e.g. from tiredness **4 WITH A TEMPORARILY RED FACE** blushing, e.g. from shame or embarrassment **5 MADE FROM BLACK GRAPES** describes wine made from black grapes **6 REPRESENTING DEBT** representing debt or financial loss **7 red, Red SOCIALIST** socialist or communist (*informal disapproving*) **8 red, Red SOVIET** relating or belonging to the former Soviet Union (*informal*) ■ *n* **1 COLOUR OF BLOOD** a colour such as that of blood, or of a ripe tomato or strawberry **2 RED COLOURING** a pigment or dye that is of or near to the colour of blood, or a ripe tomato or strawberry **3 RED FABRIC OR CLOTHES** fabric or clothing that is red in colour **4 SOMETHING RED** a red object **5 RED WINE** wine made from black grapes (*informal*) **6 SECTION OF GAMBLING TABLE** in roulette and other gambling games, one of the two coloured areas on the table on which players may place bets **7 RING ON ARCHERY TARGET** in archery, a red ring immediately outside the gold disc at the centre of a target **8 RED BALL** in billiards, snooker, and other cue games, a red ball **9 red, Red A SOCIALIST OR COMMUNIST** somebody with socialist or communist views (*informal disapproving*) [< Old English *rēad* < Indo-European] —**redly** *adv* —**redness** *n* ◇ **in the red** in debt, e.g. to a bank ◇ **see red** to suddenly become very angry (*informal*)

red. *abbr* **1** reduced **2** reduction **3** redeemable

redact /ri dákt/ *vt* **1** to compose or draft something for publication or for an announcement (*formal*) **2** to edit or revise something in preparation for publication ○ *formerly classified documents that were redacted before release to protect still confidential material* [Mid-19C. < Latin *redact-*, past participle of *redigere* 'reduce', literally 'bring down' < *agere* 'do'.] —**redaction** *n* —**redactional** *adj* —**redactor** *n*

red admiral *n* a brightly coloured butterfly with broad orange-red bands on its forewings. Native to: Europe, North America. *Vanessa atalanta.*

red alert *n* a warning or alarm that indicates a situation of the highest priority or greatest urgency, especially an imminent attack, or the state of readiness to deal with such a situation

red algae *npl* marine algae, e.g. dulse, laver, and carrageen, that contain a red pigment as well as chlorophyll. Family: Rhodophyceae.

redan /ri dán/ *n* a pair of parapets that form a V-shaped projection from the wall of a castle or other fortification [Late 17C. < French, variant of *redent* < *dent* 'tooth' < Latin *dens*.]

red ant *n* a reddish ant, especially the Pharaoh ant

Red Army *n* the military organization put into place by Leon Trotsky at the time of the Russian revolution

redback /réd bak/, **redback spider** *n* a small venomous dark brown or black spider, the female of which has a red stripe or patch on the back of the abdomen. Native to: Australia, New Zealand. *Latrodectus hasselti.*

redback spider *n* ZOOL = **redback**

red-bellied black snake *n* a large poisonous snake that is glossy black with an orange-red underside. Native to: E Australian woodlands. *Pseudechis porphyriacus.*

red biddy *n* a strong cheap alcoholic drink made by mixing red wine with methylated spirits (*dated informal*)

red blood cell *n* any red-coloured cell in blood that contains haemoglobin and carries oxygen to the tissues

red-blooded *adj* behaving in ways stereotypically associated with men, e.g. by showing strength or active sexual desire

redbreast /réd brest/ (*plural* **-breasts** *or* **-breast**) *n* **1** a bird with a reddish breast, especially a robin **2** a freshwater sunfish with a reddish belly. Native to: E United States. *Lepomis auritus.*

redbrick /rédbrik/ *adj* **1** relating to British universities that were founded in the late 19th and early 20th centuries, e.g. Manchester and Leeds **2** constructed of red bricks

Red Brigades *npl* a left-wing urban organization that was active in Italy during the 1970s and was responsible for the kidnapping and murder of the Italian statesman Aldo Moro in 1978 [Translation of Italian *brigate rosse*]

redbud /réd bud/ (*plural* **-buds** *or* **-bud**) *n* a tree with heart-shaped leaves and small pale pink flowers. Native to: North America. Genus: *Cercis.*

redcap /réd kap/ *n* **1** an officer in the military police (*slang*) **2** US in the United States, a porter at an airport or railway station (*informal*) [< the red caps traditionally worn by such personnel]

red card *n* **1** in soccer, a red card displayed by the referee when dismissing a player from the field for a serious infringement of the rules. ◊ **yellow card 2** any dismissal or rejection, e.g. from a job (*informal*) ○ *Even his girlfriend has threatened to give him the red card.*

red carpet *n* **1** a strip of red-coloured carpet laid on the ground for an important visitor to walk on when arriving or departing **2** attentive or deferential treatment given to a dignitary, celebrity, or other important person (*hyphenated before nouns*) ○ *Everywhere we went we got the red-carpet treatment.*

red cedar /-seédər/ *n* **1 TREE OF E NORTH AMERICA** an evergreen tree of the juniper family with reddish wood and fleshy cones. Native to: E North America. *Juniperus virginiana.* **2 TREE OF W NORTH AMERICA** an evergreen timber tree of the cypress family with reddish wood and small oval cones. Native to: W North America. *Thuja plicata.* **3 WOOD FROM RED CEDAR** the weather-resistant close-grained wood of either of the red cedar trees. Use: building material. **4 EVERGREEN CONIFEROUS TREE** an evergreen coniferous tree with reddish timber, e.g. the Japanese red cedar

red cell *n* BIOL = **red blood cell**

red cent *n* US the smallest amount of money (*informal*) [Because the one-cent coin is made of copper]

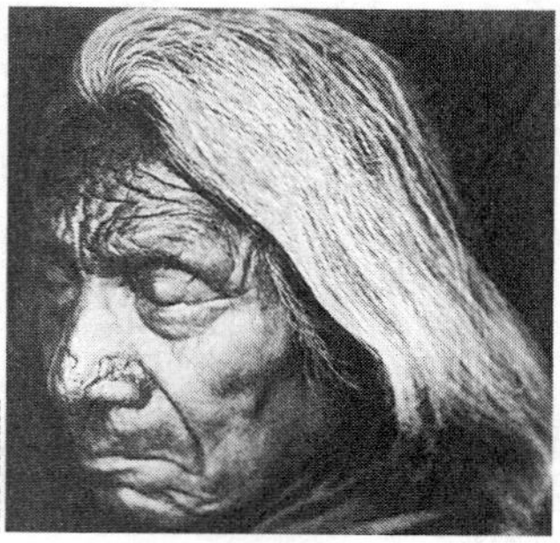
AKG London

Red Cloud

Red Cloud /red klówd/ (1822–1909) US Oglala Sioux leader

red clover *n* a clover often grown as a forage crop for horses or cattle. Flowers: fragrant, red. Native to: Europe, Asia, North America. *Trifolium pratense.*

redcoat /réd kōt/ *n* **1** a British soldier serving overseas in former times, especially during the American War of Independence **2** a uniformed attendant at a Butlin's holiday camp [< their bright-red uniform coats]

red coral *n* a coral with hard deep pink skeletons. Use: ornaments, jewellery. Genus: *Corallium.*

red corpuscle *n* BIOL = **red blood cell**

Red Crescent *n* the name under which any branch of the Red Cross functions in Islamic countries

Red Cross *n* an international organization founded in 1864 and dedicated to the medical care of the sick or wounded in wars and natural disasters

redcurrant /red kúrrənt/ *n* **1** a red berry with a tart flavour that grows in clusters. Use: jam or jelly. **2** a flowering shrub that produces redcurrants. Native to: northern temperate regions. *Ribes rubrum.*

redd[1] /red/ *vti* (**redds, redding, redd** *or* **redded**) to tidy something, or tidy things generally (*regional*) ■ *n* a spell of tidying (*regional*) [Early 16C. < Old Norse *ryðja* 'to clear land', with the sense 'rescue' < Old English *hreddan*.] —**redder** *n*

redd[2] /red/ *n* a hollow that is scooped out in the sand or gravel of a river bed for spawning by fish such as trout and salmon [Early 19C. < ?]

red deer *n* a large deer that has spreading antlers and a reddish-brown summer coat. Native to: Europe, Asia. *Cervus elaphus.*

redden /rédd'n/ *v* **1** *vti* to become red or redder, or make something red or redder **2** *vi* to go red in the face, e.g. with embarrassment, anger, or exertion

Redding /rédding/, **Otis** (1941–67) US singer and songwriter

reddish /réddish/ *adj* of a colour that is a shade of red or strongly tinged with red —**reddishness** *n*

Redditch /réddich/ town in W England. Population: 73,372 (1991).

reddle *n, vt* MINERALS, AGRIC = **ruddle**

red-dog *vt* in American football, to charge directly at the quarterback the moment the ball is put into play (*informal*)

rede /reed/ *n* ADVICE advice (*archaic*) ■ *vt* (**redes, reding, reded**) (*archaic*) **1** ADVISE to advise or counsel somebody **2** INTERPRET to explain, understand, or interpret something in a particular way [Old English *rǣd* (noun) < Old English *rǣdan*, (verb) < Germanic]

red earth *n* a clayey soil found in tropical grasslands, coloured red by the presence of iron compounds

redecorate /ree dékə rayt/ (**-rates, -rating, -rated**) *vti* to change or renew the interior decoration of a building or room —**redecoration** /reè dekə ráysh'n/ *n*

rededicate /ree déddi kayt/ (**-cates, -cating, -cated**) *v* **1** *vt* to dedicate something again or in a different way **2** *vr* to commit yourself to another person or to a mission or responsibility once more or in a different way —**rededication** /reè dedi káysh'n/ *n*

redeem /ri deém/ *vt* **1** MAKE SOMETHING ACCEPTABLE to make something acceptable or pleasant in spite of its negative qualities or aspects **2** RESTORE REPUTATION to do something that changes a negative opinion to a positive one **3** BUY SOMETHING BACK to buy back an item given, e.g. to a pawnbroker, as security for a loan **4** KEEP A PROMISE to fulfil a pledge or promise **5** EXCHANGE SOMETHING FOR MONEY to exchange or convert something such as a voucher for money or its equivalent **6** PAY SOMETHING OFF to pay off the outstanding portion of a debt **7** ATONE FOR HUMAN SIN to pay for the sins of humanity with death on the Cross (*refers to Jesus Christ*) [15C. Directly or via French *rédimer* < Latin *redimere* 'buy back' < *emere* 'buy'.] —**redeemability** *n* —**redeemable** *adj* —**redeemably** *adv*

redeemer /ri deémər/ *n* a person who redeems somebody or something, especially somebody who rescues another

Redeemer *n* Jesus Christ regarded as the saviour of humanity through his death on the Cross

redeeming /ri deéming/ *adj* compensating for faults or flaws

redefine /reèdi fín/ (**-fines, -fining, -fined**) *vt* to change the nature, appearance, or position of something consciously and sometimes arbitrarily —**redefinition** /-deffə nísh'n/ *n*

redemption /ri démpsh'n/ *n* **1** IMPROVING OF the saving or improving of something that has declined into a poor state **2** REDEEMED STATE the improved state of somebody or something saved from apparently irreversible decline **3** BUYING BACK OF the buying back of something given, e.g. to a pawnbroker, as security for a loan **4** ENDING OF FINANCIAL OBLIGATION the removal of a financial obligation, e.g. the repayment of a loan or promissory note **5** ATONEMENT FOR HUMAN SIN deliverance from the sins of humanity by the death of Jesus Christ on the Cross [14C. < French *rédemption* < Latin *redempt-*, past participle of *redimere* (see REDEEM).] —**redemptional** *adj*

redemptive /ri démptiv/ *adj* bringing about the redemption of somebody or something [15C. < Latin *redempt-*, past participle of *redimere* (see REDEEM).] —**redemptively** *adv*

Redemptorist /ri démptərist/ *n* a member of the Congregation of the Most Holy Redeemer, a Roman Catholic order specializing in preaching and missionary work, founded in Italy in 1732 [Mid-19C. < French *redemptoriste* < Latin *redemptor* 'redeemer' < *redempt-* (see REDEMPTIVE).]

red ensign *n* a red flag with the Union Jack in the upper corner of the vertical edge near the staff, it is flown by British merchant ships and pleasure craft

redeploy /reèdi plóy/ *vti* to move people or equipment from one area or activity to another —**redeployment** *n*

redesign /reèdi zín/ *vt* to change or revise the design of something ■ *n* a new or revised design

redetermine /reè di túrmin/ (**-mines, -mining, -mined**) *v* **1** *vt* DECIDE AGAIN to decide on or settle something again or in a different way **2** *vt* FIND OUT AGAIN to find out or ascertain something again or in a different way **3** *vti* ADOPT PURPOSE AGAIN to adopt, or cause somebody to adopt, a purpose again or in a different way —**redetermination** /reè di turmi náysh'n/ *n*

redevelop /reèdi vélləp/ *vt* to improve an area that has become run down by renovating buildings, making better use of wasteland, and encouraging inward investment —**redevelopment** *n*

redeye /rédī/ *n* **1** PHOTOGRAPHIC DEFECT red pupils in the eyes of a subject in flash photography, a common defect in photographs taken with simple cameras (*informal*) **2** *US* NIGHT FLIGHT a late night or overnight airline service (*informal*) **3** *US* CHEAP WHISKY cheap inferior whisky (*slang*)

red-faced *adj* blushing, especially with embarrassment

redfin (*plural* **-fins** *or* **-fin**), **redfin shiner** *n* a small freshwater fish with reddish fins, often kept in aquariums. Native to: central North America. Genus: *Notropis*.

red fire *n* a chemical mixture, especially one containing strontium salts, that burns with a vivid red flame and is used in fireworks and flares

redfish /réd fish/ (*plural* **-fishes** *or* **-fish**) *n* **1** REDDISH ROCKFISH a reddish rockfish. Native to: N Atlantic. **2** SALMON a male salmon that has recently spawned **3** REDFISH AS FOOD the flesh of a redfish used as food

red flag *n* **1** a plain red flag or banner used as an international symbol of communism or socialism **2** *US* = **red rag 3** a flag waved as a danger signal or a command to stop

Redford /rédfərd/, **Robert** (*b.* 1937) US actor, producer, and director

red fox *n* a common fox with sharply pointed ears, a reddish-orange to reddish-brown coat, and a white-tipped tail. Native to: fields and open woods of Europe, Asia, and North America. *Vulpes vulpes*.

red giant *n* a red-coloured star with a relatively low surface temperature and a diameter much greater than that of the sun

Redgrave /réd grayv/, **Sir Michael** (1908–85) British actor

Redgrave, Vanessa (*b.* 1937) British actor

red-green colourblindness *n* MED = **deuteranopia**

Red Guard *n* **1** the 1960s Chinese Communist youth movement that attempted to bring about the Cultural Revolution of Mao Zedong **2** a member of the Red Guard

red gum *n* **1** a eucalyptus tree with aromatic leaves and distinctive red wood. Native to: Australia. *Eucalyptus camaldulensis*. **2** TREES = **sweet gum**

red-handed *adj* in the act of committing a crime or doing something wrong ○ *caught red-handed* [< the notion of having blood on the hands]

red hat *n* **1** the broad-brimmed crimson hat that a Roman Catholic cardinal wears on ceremonial occasions **2** the rank or position of cardinal in the Roman Catholic Church

redhead /réd hed/ *n* **1** somebody, especially a woman, who has reddish-coloured hair **2** a diving duck, the male of which has a bright chestnut head. Native to: North America. *Aythya americana*.

redheaded /réd héddid/ *adj* **1** with reddish-coloured hair **2** describes an animal, especially a bird, with a red head

red heat *n* the temperature at which something is red-hot, or the state of being at such a temperature

red herring *n* **1** something introduced, e.g. into a crime or mystery story, in order to divert attention or mislead **2** a herring salted and smoked to a reddish-brown colour [< the practice of dragging smoked fish across a scent trail to teach hounds not to be distracted]

red-hot *adj* **1** GLOWING RED WITH HEAT heated to such a high temperature as to glow red **2** VERY HOT extremely hot **3** EXTREMELY POPULAR in great demand (*informal*) **4** VERY RECENT very recent and up to date (*informal*) **5** PASSIONATE feeling or expressing intense enthusiasm, passion, or anger (*informal*)

red-hot poker *n* a tall perennial ornamental plant. Flowers: erect spikes, red at the top and orange below. Native to: South Africa. Genus: *Kniphofia*.

redia /reèdi ə/ (*plural* **-ae** /-ee/) *n* one of the forms of the larvae of trematode worms [Late 19C. < modern Latin, after the Italian biologist Francesco *Redi* (1626–98).]

redial /ree dí əl/ *vti* (**-als, -alling, -alled**) to dial a particular telephone number again, e.g. because the line was engaged when the number was dialled earlier ■ *n* the function that permits automatic redialling of a telephone number

~~**rediculous**~~ incorrect spelling of **ridiculous**

redid past tense of **redo**

Red Indian *n* an offensive term for a Native North American (*dated*)

redingote /rédding gōt/ *n* **1** a belted woman's dress or coat of the 18th century that was open at the front to show a petticoat or dress **2** a man's double-breasted coat of the 18th century that had wide flat cuffs and flared out below the waist [Late 18C. < French, alteration of English *riding-coat*.]

redirect /reèdi rékt, -dī-/ *vt* **1** SEND SOMETHING ELSEWHERE to send something received to a different location, e.g. because the intended recipient has moved **2** REROUTE TRAFFIC to send traffic along a different route **3** CHANGE FOCUS to focus actions or activities on a different objective —**redirection** *n*

rediscover /reèdi skúvvər/ *vt* to experience something again, especially finding a new source of pleasure in it —**rediscovery** *n*

redistil (**-tils, -tilling, -tilled**) *vt* to distil a liquid or other substance for a second or subsequent time —**redistillation** /reè disti láysh'n/ *n*

redistribute /reèdi strí byoot/ (**-utes, -uting, -uted**) *vt* **1** to distribute more of something previously distributed **2** to divide something up or share something out in a different way, e.g. in more equal proportions or among a wider range of people —**redistribution** /reèdistri byoósh'n/ *n* —**redistributive** /reèdi strí byoōtiv/ *adj*

redivivus /réddi vívəss, -veè-/ *adj* revived, reborn, or brought back to life (*literary*) [Late 16C. < Latin, 'alive again' < *vivu* 'alive'.]

red kangaroo *n* a kangaroo of the largest species, varying in colour from brick red to grey. It is found in desert areas of Australia. *Megaleia rufa*.

red lead *n* Pb_3O_4 a bright red poisonous oxide of lead, used as a pigment in paints

redleg /réd leg/ *n* **1** RED-LEGGED BIRD a bird with red legs, e.g. the redshank **2** FROG DISEASE a bacterial disease of frogs that produces a red flush on the hind legs **3** *US* ARTILLERYMAN an artilleryman (*slang*)

red-letter day *n* a very special day or occasion [< the marking of feast days in red on church calendars]

red light *n* **1** a red warning signal, especially an instruction to drivers to stop **2** a sign of disapproval or rejection, e.g. an instruction not to proceed with something (*informal*)

red-light *adj* relating to the part of a town or city where brothels and other commercial sex-based activities are concentrated [< the red lights traditionally displayed in the doors and windows of brothels]

redline /réd līn/ (**-lines, -lining, -lined**) *v* **1** *vti* to refuse loans, insurance, or other financial services to individuals or businesses in a supposedly high-risk area **2** *vt* to select something such as an aircraft for removal from service [< the traditional use of red ink to cross out deleted items in a budget]

red marrow *n* the reddish bone marrow where red blood cells and some white blood cells are formed

red mass *n* a special Roman Catholic mass celebrated in red vestments for the opening of a court or congress

red meat *n* meat such as beef or lamb that is relatively dark red in colour when raw

Redmond /rédmənd/, **John** (1856–1918) Irish politician

red mullet *n* **1** a smallish orange-red marine fish. Native to: Europe. *Mullus surmuletus*. US term **goatfish 2** the flesh of a red mullet used as food

redneck /réd nek/ *n* **1** an offensive term for a white farmworker in the S United States, especially one regarded as uneducated or aggressively prejudiced **2** an offensive term for somebody who is opposed to liberal social changes, especially somebody regarded as prejudiced [< the sunburnt necks of those who work outdoors in sunny climates] —**rednecked** *adj*

redo /ree doó/ (**-does, -doing, -did** /-díd/, **-done** /-dún/) *vt* **1** to do something again, e.g. in order to correct mistakes in an earlier effort **2** to change the appearance of something such as a hairstyle or the interior decoration of a room

red oak *n* an oak tree with bristly lobed leaves that turn red in the autumn. Native to: E North America. Genus: *Quercus*.

red ochre *n* **1** a reddish earth that is rich in iron oxide and used as a red pigment in paints **2** a rich reddish-brown colour used in painting

redolent /rédd'lənt/ *adj* **1** SUGGESTING suggestive or reminiscent of something ○ *a report redolent of bias* **2** AROMATIC with a strong pleasant aroma (*literary*) **3** SMELLING with a particular scent or odour ○ *old oak furniture redolent of beeswax* [15C. < Old French, < Latin *redolere* 'smell strongly' < *olere* 'to smell'.] —**redolence** *n* —**redolently** *adv*

Redon /rə dón, rə doN/, **Odilon** (1840–1916) French painter and lithographer

redone past participle of **redo**

red osier *n* **1** a willow tree with reddish branches used in basketry **2 red osier, red osier dogwood** a shrub of the dogwood family with red twigs and clusters of white fruits. Native to: North America. *Cornus stolonifera*.

redouble /ridúbb'l/ *vti* (**-bles, -bling, -bled**) **1 INCREASE** to increase something considerably, especially the amount of effort expended on something, or to become much greater **2 ECHO** to echo or re-echo, or cause something to echo or re-echo **3 DOUBLE A DOUBLE BID** to double an opponent's double as a bid in bridge ■ *n* **DOUBLING OF A DOUBLE BID** a redoubling of a bid in bridge [15C. < French *redoubler* 'double again' < *double* 'double'.]

redoubt /ri dówt/ *n* **1** a castle, fortress, or other stronghold (*literary*) **2** a temporary fortification built to defend a position such as a hilltop [Early 17C. Alteration (influenced by *redoubtable*) of French *redoute*, via Italian *ridotto* < medieval Latin *reductus* 'refuge' < Latin, past participle of *reducere* (see REDUCE).]

redoubtable /ri dówtəb'l/ *adj* with personal qualities worthy of respect or fear [14C. < French *redoutable* < *douter* (see DOUBT).] —**redoubtably** *adv*

redound /ri dównd/ *vi* **1** to have a particular consequence, usually something good or positive ○ *All the effort can only redound to her credit.* **2** to return to affect somebody as a repercussion or consequence (*formal*) ○ *His attempts at revenge redounded upon his own head.* [14C. Via French *redonder* < Latin *redundare* 'overflow'.]

USAGE See ***rebound***.

redout /réd owt/ *n* sudden headache and reddening of the field of vision experienced by pilots or astronauts during rapid deceleration and other manoeuvres

redowa /réddəvə, -wə/ *n* a Bohemian folk dance similar to a waltz or a polka [Mid-19C. Via French or German < Czech *rejdovák* < *rejdovat* 'whirl around'.]

redox /rée doks/ *n* CHEM = **oxidation-reduction** [Early 20C. < REDUCTION + OXIDATION.]

red packet *n Hong Kong, Malaysia, Singapore* money enclosed in a red envelope and given for luck by married people to unmarried young people during the first 15 days of the Chinese New Year

red panda *n* a reddish-brown mammal that resembles a raccoon in appearance and lives in forests in the Himalayas and nearby areas of E Asia. *Ailurus fulgens*.

red-pencil *vt* to revise, correct, or censor written material

red pepper *n* **1** any red pod that belongs to the capsicum family of vegetables, especially a ripe sweet pepper. ◊ **green pepper 2** FOOD = **cayenne pepper**

red pine *n* **1** a pine tree with reddish bark and needles grouped in twos. Native to: NE North America. *Pinus resinosa*. **2** a coniferous tree with narrow pointed leaves. Native to: New Zealand. *Dacrydium cupressinum*.

red planet *n* the planet Mars (*informal*)

redpoll /réd pōl/ *n* a small bird of the finch family with a red crown and a pink breast. Native to: North America, Europe, Asia. Genus: *Carduelis*.

Red Poll *n* a hornless cow with short reddish hair belonging to a breed originating in England and bred for beef and milk

redraft /rée draaft/ *n* a second or further draft or rewriting ■ *vt* to rewrite something, making changes in it

red rag *n* something that provokes or infuriates somebody. US term **red flag** *n.* 2 [< the notion that bulls are enraged at the sight of red objects]

red rattle *n* a plant with a seed capsule that rattles. Native to: Europe. *Pedicularis palustris*.

redraw /ree dráw/ (**-draws, -drawing, -drew** /-dróo/, **-drawn** /-dráwn/) *vt* **1 DRAW SOMETHING AGAIN** to draw something another time, usually making changes **2 REPOSITION BOUNDARY** to change the position of the boundaries of a region **3 REDESIGN** to redesign something, changing its shape or the positions of its constituent parts

redress /ri dréss/ *n* **1 COMPENSATION** compensation or reparation for a loss or wrong somebody has experienced **2 ACT OF COMPENSATING** the compensating of somebody for a loss or wrong experienced ■ *vt* **1 MAKE UP FOR** to provide compensation or reparation for a loss or wrong experienced **2 IMPOSE FAIRNESS OR EQUALITY ON** to adjust a situation in order to make things fair or equal [14C. < Old French *redrecier* < *drecier* < Latin *directus* 'straight'.] —**redresser** *n*

redrew past tense of **redraw**

red ribbon *n US* a red-coloured ribbon, badge, or other decoration awarded to somebody who comes second in a competition

Red River /red/ **1** river in Southeast Asia, rising in S China and emptying into the Gulf of Tonkin. Length: 800 km/500 mi. **2** river in the north-central United States and south-central Canada, flowing northwards from Minnesota and emptying into Lake Winnipeg. Length: 877 km/545 mi.

redroot /réd root/ *n* **1** a perennial bog plant with red roots. Flowers: woolly, yellow. Native to: E North America. *Lachnanthes caroliana*. **2** a plant with red roots, e.g. a bloodroot or pigweed

red route *n* a major urban road where loading and parking is restricted by a system of red lines and signs at the kerb, enforced by patrols, in order to maintain traffic flows

red salmon *n* ZOOL = **sockeye**

Red Sea /réd-/ inland sea between Arabia and NE Africa. Area: 437,700 sq. km/169,000 sq. mi.

red setter *n* = **Irish setter**

redshank /réd shangk/ *n* a large wading bird of slender build with red legs and feet. Native to: Europe, Asia. Genus: *Tringa*.

red shank *n* an annual plant with red stems. Flowers: pink, in spikes. Native to: northern temperate regions. *Polygonum persicaria*.

red shift *n* a shift in the spectrum of an astronomical object towards longer wavelengths, or towards the red end of the spectrum, caused by its motion away from the Earth. ◊ **blueshift, Doppler effect** —**redshifted** *adj*

redshirt /réd shurt/ *n US* a college or university athlete who is kept out of competitions for one year in order to improve his or her skills and extend his or her period of eligibility [< the red jerseys that customarily distinguish these players at practices] —**redshirt** *vt*

red siskin *n* a bright red finch whose head, wings, and tail are black. Native to: N South America. *Carduelis cucullata*.

redskin /réd skin/ *n* a former offensive term for a Native North American (*dated offensive*)

red snapper *n* **1** a large reddish-coloured fish. Native to: Atlantic coasts of North, South, and Central America. Genus: *Lutjanus*. **2** the flesh of a red snapper used as food

red snow *n* fallen snow that is reddish in colour, either from the presence of airborne dust or from red algae growing in it

Red Spot *n* a large reddish oval and variable marking in the southern hemisphere of Jupiter

red spruce *n* a spruce tree with reddish-brown bark and cones, and light soft wood. Native to: E North America. *Picea rubens*.

Red Square *n* a large square in central Moscow, bordered by the Kremlin and Lenin's tomb

red squirrel *n* **1** a reddish-brown squirrel with tufted ears. Native to: Europe, Asia. *Sciurus vulgaris*. **2** a squirrel with reddish fur. Native to: coniferous forests of North America. *Tamiasciurus hudsonicus*.

redstart /réd staart/ *n* **1** a bird of the thrush family, the male of which has a black throat and a reddish-brown tail. Native to: Europe, Asia, Africa. Genus: *Phoenicurus*. **2** a flycatching warbler, the male of which has reddish-orange patches on black and white plumage. Native to: North and South America. *Setophaga ruticilla*. [*Start* < Old English *steort* 'a tail']

red tape *n* official procedure regarded as unnecessary, over-complicated, or obstructive (*informal*) [< the red tape once widely used to seal official documents]

red tide *n* a brownish-red discoloration in seawater, caused by the increased presence of plant-based plankton that sometimes leads to the poisoning of fish and, consequently, of those who eat fish

redtop /réd top/ *n* a grass plant that has clusters of red flowers and is used in North America for lawns and forage. Genus: *Agrostis*.

red-top, redtop *n* a tabloid newspaper (*informal*) ○ *'There is now a debate about whether the red-tops should "go up-market" to find their audiences'.* (*The Guardian*; November 1998) [< the red masthead of such a newspaper]

reduce /ri dyóoss/ (**-duces, -ducing, -duced**) *v* **1** *vti* **DECREASE** to become or make something smaller in size, number, extent, degree, or intensity **2** *vt* **WORSEN STATE** to bring somebody or something into a particular undesirable state ○ *The dreadful news reduced them all to tears.* ○ *Bombing had reduced the town to rubble.* **3** *vt* **MAKE SOMETHING CHEAPER** to lower the price or cost of an item for sale **4** *vt* **SIMPLIFY** to make something simpler, especially by extracting or summarizing essential elements **5** *vt* **ANALYSE SOMETHING SYSTEMATICALLY** to analyse something in terms of a system or rule, usually as an aid to explaining or understanding it **6** *vt* **DEMOTE** to place somebody officially in a lower rank or grade, e.g. as a punishment for breaking rules **7** *vt* **TAKE CONTROL OF PLACE OR PEOPLE** to bring a place or people under a particular authority using force **8** *vti* **THICKEN** to make a sauce or stock thicker by boiling off some of the liquid, or to become thicker in this way **9** *vt* **DECREASE THE DENSITY OF A NEGATIVE** to lessen the density of a photographic negative using a chemical substance **10** *vt* **REFINE ORE** to remove the impurities from an ore in order to obtain the pure metal **11** *vti* **UNDERGO CELL DIVISION** to undergo, or cause cells to undergo, the type of cell division (**meiosis**) that halves the number of chromosomes in the two resultant cells **12** *vti* **UNDERGO CHEMICAL REACTION** to undergo, or cause a substance to undergo, a chemical reaction in which there is a gain in hydrogen or a loss of oxygen **13** *vti* **GAIN ELECTRONS** to undergo, or cause a substance to undergo, a chemical reaction in which there is an increase in the number of electrons **14** *vt* **SIMPLIFY AN EQUATION** to simplify an expression or equation without changing its value [14C. < Latin *reducere* 'bring back' < *ducere* 'to lead'.] —**reducibility** /ri dyóossə bílləti/ *n* —**reducible** /ri dyóossəb'l/ *adj*

reducer /ri dyóossər/ *n* **1** a chemical solution that lessens the density of a photographic negative by oxidizing it **2** a pipe fitting that connects two pipes of different diameters

reducing agent, reductant /ri dúktənt/ *n* a chemical substance that reduces the amount of oxygen in another substance and becomes oxidized in the process

reductase /ri dúk tayz, -tayss/ *n* an enzyme that catalyses the chemical reduction of an organic compound [Early 20C. < REDUCTION.]

reductio ad absurdum /ri dúkti ō ad ab súrdəm/ (*plural* **reductiones ad absurdum** /-ő neez-/) *n* **1 TAKING SOMETHING TO ABSURD LENGTHS** the application of a rule or principle so strictly or literally that the result is ridiculous **2 LOGICAL DISPROOF** the disproving of a logical argument by showing that its ultimate conclusion is absurd **3 LOGICAL PROOF** the proving of a logical argument indirectly, by showing that the contradictory argument is absurd [Mid-18C. < Latin, 'reduction to the absurd'.]

reduction /ri dúksh'n/ *n* **1 REDUCING OF** the decreasing of something in size, number, extent, degree, or intensity **2 AMOUNT BY WHICH SOMETHING IS REDUCED** the amount by which something is made smaller or less **3 SIMPLIFICATION** a simplification or condensation of something **4 SMALLER COPY** a copy of something made on a smaller scale, e.g. a reduced photocopy **5 THICKENED SAUCE** a sauce or stock that has been thickened by boiling off some of the liquid **6 MAKING FRACTION SIMPLER** the cancelling of common factors in the numerator and denominator of a fraction **7 DECIMALIZATION OF FRACTION** the converting of a fraction into decimal form **8** BIOL = **meiosis** *n.* 1 **9 CHEMICAL REACTION** a chemical reaction that brings about a gain in hydrogen, a loss of oxygen, or an increase in electrons [15C. Via French < Latin *reduction-* < Latin *reducere* 'bring back'.] —**reductional** *adj*

reduction division *n* BIOL = **meiosis** *n.* 1

reduction firing *n* the firing of pottery in an oxygen-starved atmosphere in order to change the nature of the glaze applied

reduction gear *n* a set of gears in an engine used to reduce output speed relative to that of the engine while providing greater turning power when, e.g., climbing a hill

reductionism /ri dúksh'nizəm/ *n* **1** the analysis of something into simpler elements or organized systems, especially with a view to explaining or understanding it **2** the oversimplifying of something complex, or the misguided belief that everything can be explained in simple terms —**reductionist** *n, adj* —**reductionistic** /ri dúkshə nístik/ *adj*

reductive /ri dúktiv/ *adj* **1** seeking to explain complex things in terms of simple structures and systems **2** oversimplifying complex things and ignoring their subtleties or important details [Mid-16C. < medieval Latin *reductivus* < Latin *reducere* 'bring back'.] —**reductively** *adv* —**reductiveness** *n*

redundancy /ri dúndənssi/ (*plural* **-cies**) *n* **1 DISMISSAL FROM WORK** dismissal from employment because the job or the worker has been deemed no longer necessary ○ *There may be more redundancies if sales do not improve.* **2 SUPERFLUOUSNESS** the state or fact of not being or no longer being needed or wanted **3 DUPLICATION OF COMPONENTS** the fitting of duplicate electronic or mechanical components or backup systems that are designed to come into use to keep equipment working if their counterparts fail **4 DUPLICATION OF MESSAGE** duplication of information in telecommunications in order to reduce the risk of error **5 USE OF SUPERFLUOUS WORDS** the use of a word whose meaning is already conveyed elsewhere in a passage, without a rhetorical purpose

redundancy payment *n* an amount paid to an employee who has been made redundant, often calculated in relation to length of employment

redundant /ri dúndənt/ *adj* **1 DISMISSED FROM WORK** dismissed from employment because the job or the worker has been deemed no longer necessary ○ *The companies merged and half the workers were made redundant.* **2 SUPERFLUOUS** not needed or no longer needed **3 BACKUP** fitted as a backup component or system **4 REPEATING MEANING** with the same meaning as a word used elsewhere in a passage and without a rhetorical purpose [Late 16C. < Latin *redundare* 'overflow' < *undare* 'rise in waves' < *unda* 'wave'.] —**redundantly** *adv*

reduplicate /ri dyóopli kayt/ *v* (**-cates, -cating, -cated**) **1** *vti* **REPEAT OR DOUBLE** to repeat or double something, or be repeated or doubled **2** *vt* **REPEAT SPEECH SOUND** to repeat a vowel, syllable, or word in order to create a new word or linguistic element ■ *adj* **1 REPEATED** repeated in order to create a new word or other linguistic element **2 CURVING INWARDS** describes leaves or petals that have their edges curved inwards [Late 16C. < late Latin *reduplicare* < Latin *duplicare* (see DUPLICATE).] —**reduplication** /ri dyóopli káysh'n/ *n* —**reduplicative** /ri dyóoplikətiv/ *adj* —**reduplicatively** *adv*

reduviid /ri dyóovi id/ *n* INSECTS = **assassin bug** [Late 19C. < modern Latin *Reduviidae* < Latin *reduvia* 'hangnail'.]

redux /ree dúks/ *adj* brought back, especially in being restored to former importance or prominence (*literary*) [Late 19C. < Latin, < *reducere* 'bring back'.]

redware[1] /réd wair/ *n* MARINE BIOL = **kelp** *n.* 1 [< N dialect 'seaweed' (< Old English *wār*)]

redware[2] /réd wair/ *n* reddish earthenware pottery made from clay with a high iron oxide content

red water *n* a cattle disease characterized by the passage of reddish urine

redwing /réd wing/ *n* a bird of the thrush family that has reddish feathers under its wings and a spotted breast. Native to: Europe, Asia. *Turdus iliacus.*

redwood /réd wòod/ *n* a very tall sequoia with fibrous reddish bark. Native to: coastal California, SW China. *Sequoia sempervirens* and *Metasequoia glyptostroboides.*

reebok *n* ZOOL = **rhebok**

re-echo /ree ékō/ (**re-echoes, re-echoing, re-echoed**) *v* **1** *vi* to resound or echo back **2** *vt* to repeat again something that has already been repeated

reed /reed/ *n* **1 GRASS PLANT** a tall slender grass plant with jointed stalks that grows in marshes and other wet areas. Genus: *Phragmites.* **2 STALK OF REED** a reed stalk, or a bundle of reed stalks. Use: thatching, basketry, crafts. **3 VIBRATING PART OF MUSICAL INSTRUMENT** a thin piece of cane, metal, or plastic fitted inside a musical instrument that vibrates to produce sound, usually when the player blows into the instrument **4 MUSICAL INSTRUMENT** a wind instrument such as an oboe or a clarinet, fitted with a reed (*informal*) **5 WIRES ON A LOOM** a series of parallel wires on a loom that separate the threads of the warp evenly [Old English *hrēod* < Germanic]

SPELLCHECK See ***read***.

Reed /reed/, **Sir Carol** (1906–76) British film director

reedbuck /reéd buk/ *n* a tawny antelope with long horns that curve slightly forwards. Native to: sub-Saharan Africa. Genus: *Redunca.* [Mid-19C. Translation of Afrikaans *rietbok.*]

reed bunting *n* a small bird with brown streaked plumage, the male of which has a black head with a white moustache. Native to: Europe, Asia. *Emberiza schoeniclus.*

reed grass *n* a tall grass plant that grows in rivers and ponds in Europe, Asia, and North America. *Glyceria maxima.*

reeding /reéding/ *n* **1** a set of small convex decorative mouldings on a building **2** the narrow vertical grooves on the edge of a coin

re-edit *vt* to edit material again, or produce a new edition of pre-existing material

reedling /reédling/ *n* a small brownish-orange songbird with a long tail, the male of which has a black patch extending from the eye down the throat. Native to: Europe, Asia. *Panurus biarmicus.*

reed mace *n* a tall slender marsh plant. Flowers: brown, tube-shaped, in spikes. *Typha latifolia.*

reedman /reédmən/ (*plural* **-men** /-mən/) *n* a musician who plays a reed instrument, especially a jazz clarinettist or saxophonist (*informal*)

reed organ *n* a musical instrument such as a harmonica or accordion, in which air passing over a set of reeds produces sound

reed pipe *n* an organ pipe containing a reed that vibrates to make the pipe sound

reed stop *n* an organ stop that controls a set of reed pipes

re-educate *vt* **1** to teach somebody again, especially in order to change or update knowledge **2** to train or teach somebody again who has lost knowledge or a skill —**re-educative** *adj*

reed warbler *n* a small brown bird commonly found in marsh reeds and distinguished by its song. Native to: Europe. *Acrocephalus scirpaceus.*

reedy /reédi/ (**-ier, -iest**) *adj* **1 FULL OF REEDS** full of or thickly planted with reeds ○ *a reedy pond* **2 HIGH-PITCHED** thin and high-pitched, rather than deep or full-toned ○ *reedy voice* **3 THIN** long, thin, or flexible, like a reed —**reedily** *adv* —**reediness** *n*

reef[1] /reef/ *n* **1** a ridge of coral or rock in a body of water, with the top just below or just above the surface **2** a lode or vein of ore [Late 16C. < Dutch *rif.*] —**reefy** *adj*

reef[2] /reef/ *n* **PART OF SAIL** a section of a sail that can be gathered in and tied down to reduce the sail's surface ■ *vt* **1 MAKE SAIL SMALLER BY GATHERING** to reduce the area of a sail by gathering part of it in **2 SHORTEN RIGGING PIECE** to shorten or bring in one of the pieces that support rigging on a ship [14C. Via Dutch *reef* < Old Norse *rif* 'reef (of a sail)'.] —**reefable** *adj*

reefer[1] /reéfər/ *n* a person who reefs sails [Early 19C. < REEF[2].]

reefer[2] /reéfər/ *n* a marijuana cigarette (*slang*) [Mid-20C. < ?]

reefer[3] /reéfər/ *n US* a refrigerated railway wagon or truck trailer (*informal*) [Early 20C. < REFRIGERATOR.]

reefer jacket *n* a heavy double-breasted woollen jacket or coat, usually dark blue and hip-length, originally worn by sailors

reef knot *n* a symmetrical knot that will not slip after tying, made by passing one end of rope over and around another first in one direction, then again in the opposite direction. US term **square knot**

reek /reek/ *v* **1** *vti* **HAVE A VERY STRONG UNPLEASANT SMELL** to have a very strong and unpleasant smell, or give off such a smell ○ *The room reeked of smoke.* **2** *vti* **GIVE CLEAR EVIDENCE OF SOMETHING UNPLEASANT** to show very strong evidence of an unpleasant quality ○ *The whole document reeks of double standards.* **3** *vi* **GIVE OFF SMOKE** to give off smoke, steam, or fumes ○ *a reeking pile of burning tyres* **4** *vt US* **TREAT SOMETHING WITH SMOKE** to process or treat something with smoke ■ *n* **1 UNPLEASANT SMELL** a very strong and unpleasant smell ○ *a reek of disinfectant* **2 VISIBLE VAPOUR** smoke, steam, or other visible vapour (*regional*) [Old English *rēocan* < Indo-European] —**reeker** *n* —**reeky** *adj*

SPELLCHECK Do not confuse ***reek*** with ***wreak***, which has a similar sound. Beware: your spellchecker will not catch this error.

SYNONYMS See ***smell***.

reel[1] /reel/ *n* **1 REVOLVING STORAGE DEVICE** a usually revolving wheel-shaped device around which something such as thread, film, or wire can be wound for storage **2 A REELFUL** the amount of a material that a reel can hold **3 SECTION OF CINEMA FILM** the amount of cinema film stored on one reel **4 WINDER ON FISHING ROD** a winding device attached to a fishing rod that holds the fishing line and enables it to be cast and wound back ■ *vt* **WIND SOMETHING ONTO A REEL** to wind something such as thread or fishing line onto or off a reel [Old English *hrēol* 'spool (for winding thread)' < ?] —**reeler** *n* —**reelful** *n*

SPELLCHECK See ***real***.

reel in *vt* **1** to draw something, especially a fish, in by winding it in with a reel **2** to bring in or acquire somebody or something by using the appropriate skills or offering suitable inducements

reel off *vt* to list things in rapid succession and with no apparent effort

reel[2] /reel/ *vi* **1 STAGGER BACKWARDS** to move in a sudden and uncontrolled fashion, especially backwards as if struck by a blow ○ *reeled back in horror* **2 MOVE UNSTEADILY** to move about unsteadily, staggering or swaying from side to side **3 FEEL GIDDY OR CONFUSED** to feel giddy or shocked and confused ○ *still reeling from the shock of his resignation* **4 WHIRL ROUND AND ROUND** to move or whirl round in circles ■ *n* **STAGGERING MOTION** an unsteady or circling movement [14C. Probably < REEL[1].]

reel[3] /reel/ *n* **1** a lively Scottish folk dance for sets of two, three, or four couples **2** the music for a reel [Late 16C. Probably < REEL[2].]

re-elect *vt* to elect somebody to the same office for another term —**re-election** *n*

reel-to-reel *adj* describes magnetic tape that must be wound off a full source reel, threaded through the heads of the machine, and rewound on an empty take-up reel ■ *n* a tape recorder or player that uses reel-to-reel tape

re-emerge (**re-emerges, re-emerging, re-emerged**) *vi* **1** to come out again after being under or inside something **2** to reappear or return to prominence in a new role or guise —**re-emergence** *n* —**re-emergent** *adj*

re-enact *vt* to act out an event that took place in the past, sometimes using the same people who originally took part in it —**re-enactment** *n*

re-enforce *vt* = **reinforce**

re-engineering /reé enji neéring/ *n* a business management theory that advocates the reorganization of a business on the basis of the market value each department adds to the products produced by the business —**re-engineer** *vt*

ϟ **re-enter** *v* **1** *vti* **RETURN** to come back into a place again ○ *The rocket re-entered the atmosphere.* **2** *vt* **ENTER DATA AGAIN** to key or write something in again **3** *vti* **GO IN FOR AGAIN** to decide to take part in something again

re-entrant /ree éntrənt/ *n* MATH = **re-entrant angle** ■ *adj* pointing inwards into the interior of a polygon and thus greater than 180° when viewed or measured from inside the polygon

re-entrant angle, **re-entrant** *n* an inward-pointing angle in a polygon that is greater than 180° when viewed or measured from inside the polygon

re-entry *n* **1 ENTERING AGAIN** the act of entering again **2 RETURN TO EARTH'S ATMOSPHERE** the penetration of the earth's atmosphere by a spacecraft or missile returning from space (*often before nouns*) ○ *re-entry vehicle* **3 REPOSSESSION OF LAND** the repossession of land or other property under the terms of a previous agreement, e.g. where the terms of a lease have not been complied with **4 TAKING OF LEAD IN A CARD GAME** in some card games such as bridge, the regaining of control by taking a trick, or the card played to take the trick

re-equip /reé i kwíp/ (**re-equips, re-equipping, re-equipped**) *vt* to provide somebody or something with new or replacement equipment —**re-equipment** *n*

re-erect /reé i rékt/ *vt* to erect something such as a building again —**re-erection** *n*

Rees /reess/, **Lloyd Frederic** (1895–1988) Australian painter

re-escalation /reé eskə láysh'n/ *n* the action of escalating something again, especially a conflict, or the process of escalating again

re-establish /reé i stábblish/ *vt* to establish something or somebody again or in a different way ○ *She re-established her authority over the party.* —**re-establishment** *n*

re-evaluate *vt* to think again, or from a different point of view, about the nature, purpose, or value of something, especially after changes have taken place —**re-evaluation** *n*

reeve[1] /reev/ *n* 1 *US* **DISTRICT OFFICIAL** an administrative officer in a local district or parish who usually has the responsibility of enforcing the regulations connected with a particular area of activity 2 **CANADIAN TOWN COUNCIL PRESIDENT** in Ontario and some western provinces of Canada, the elected president of a town or village council 3 **REPRESENTATIVE OF THE KING** in Anglo-Saxon times, the representative of the monarch in a shire 4 **STEWARD OF A FEUDAL MANOR** in medieval times, a steward responsible for running the everyday affairs of a feudal manor [Old English *gerēfa* 'official over an assembly of soldiers']

reeve[2] /reev/ (**reeves, reeving, rove** /rōv/, **reeved**) *vt* 1 to thread a rope or rod through a ring or other opening 2 to fasten a line or rope by passing it around or through some solid object [Early 17C. < ?]

reeve[3] /reev/ *n* the female ruff sandpiper [Mid-17C. < ?]

Reeves /reevz/, **William Pember** (1857–1932) New Zealand politician and writer

re-examine *vt* 1 to subject somebody or something to careful further consideration, scrutiny, or checks 2 to question a witness in court again after he or she has been cross-examined by the other side —**re-examination** *n*

re-experience (**re-experiences, re-experiencing, re-experienced**) *vt* to experience something again or in a different way

re-export *vt* **EXPORT SOMETHING AFTER IMPORTING** to export goods that were previously imported from another country, especially after reprocessing them ■ *n* 1 **PROCESS OF RE-EXPORTING** the business or process of re-exporting imported goods 2 **SOMETHING RE-EXPORTED** something that is re-exported —**re-exportation** *n*

ref /ref/ *n* a sports referee (*informal*) ■ *vti* (**refs, reffing, reffed**) to referee a sport or game (*informal*) [Late 19C. Shortening of REFEREE.]

ref. *abbr* 1 reference 2 refining 3 reformed 4 refunding

reface /ree fáyss/ (**-faces, -facing, -faced**) *vt* 1 to restore or replace the exterior surface of a building or monument 2 to replace the facing of a garment

refashion /ree fásh'n/ (**-ions, -ioning, -ioned**) *vt* to fashion something again or in a different way ○ *They refashioned the restaurant into a more upmarket style.*

refection /ri féksh'n/ *n* (*literary*) 1 refreshment, especially in the form of food and drink 2 a portion of food or a light meal [14C. < Latin *refection-* 'restoration' < *reficere* (see REFECTORY).]

refectory /ri féktəri/ (*plural* **-ries**) *n* a dining hall, especially in a monastery, convent, or college [15C. < late Latin *refectorium* 'place where somebody is restored' < Latin *reficere* 'remake' < *facere* 'make'.]

refectory table *n* a long narrow dining table with straight heavy legs

refer /ri fúr/ (**-fers, -ferring, -ferred**) *v* 1 *vi* **MENTION** to make a comment in speech or writing that either specifically mentions somebody or something or is intended to bring somebody or something to mind ○ *referred to the subject only once in his speech* 2 *vi* **GIVE A DESCRIPTION** to describe somebody or something in a particular way ○ *tried to be respectful when referring to her colleague's thesis* 3 *vi* **BE RELATED** to relate to something or be connected with it ○ *This clause refers to your responsibilities as the homeowner.* 4 *vi* **CONSULT FOR INFORMATION** to consult a source in order to find information or assistance ○ *refer to the manual* 5 *vt* **DIRECT SOMEBODY TO SOURCE OF HELP** to direct somebody to something or somebody else for information, help, treatment, or judgment ○ *referred me to a specialist* 6 *vt* **ATTRIBUTE SOMETHING TO A CAUSE** to attribute the cause or source of something to something else ○ *They referred the high gains to the timing of their investment.* 7 *vt* **FAIL AN EXAM CANDIDATE** to fail an examination candidate or ask him or her to retake the exam 8 *vt* **RETURN THESIS FOR REVISION** to return a thesis to a student for further work or revision before it can be accepted [14C. Via French *référer* < Latin *referre* 'carry back' < *ferre* 'carry'.] —**referable** /ri fúrəb'l, réffərəb'l/ *adj* —**referrer** /ri fúrər/ *n*

USAGE Some people think that ***refer back*** is redundant, because one of the implicit meanings of *re-* is 'back'. But a person may ***refer*** a problem or request, for example ***on*** to a new authority for a decision, or ***refer*** it ***back*** to the original decision-maker for reconsideration. If ***refer*** directs people to something already mentioned, for example a text quoted, it would be better to say *In referring* [not referring *back*] *to page 321 of my book, I might add the following information not mentioned in Tuesday's lecture.*

USAGE See ***allude***.

~~**referal**~~ incorrect spelling of **referral**

~~**refered**~~ incorrect spelling of **referred**

referee /réffə reé/ *n* 1 **OFFICIAL OVERSEEING SPORT** an official who oversees the play in a sport or game, judges whether the rules are being followed, and penalizes fouls or infringements 2 **ARBITRATOR** somebody not directly involved in a matter who is called in to settle disputes, make decisions, or pass judgments concerning the matter 3 **PERSON WHO GIVES INFORMATION ABOUT SOMEBODY** somebody who is asked to comment on the character or qualifications of another person, especially when that person is applying for a job. US term **reference** *n.* 10 4 **SOMEBODY WHO REVIEWS CASE** somebody appointed by a court to review and make a report or judgment on a case ■ *vti* (**-rees, -reeing, -reed**) **ACT AS A REFEREE** to act as a referee in a sport, in a dispute, or for an applicant

reference /réffərənss/ *n* 1 **MENTION** a spoken or written comment that either specifically mentions or calls attention to somebody or something or is intended to bring somebody or something to mind 2 **PROCESS OF MENTIONING** the process of mentioning or alluding to somebody or something ○ *The document makes reference to three methods for filing a complaint.* 3 **APPLICABILITY** applicability or relevance to, or connection with, a particular subject or person ○ *Does what you're saying have any reference at all to the matter in hand?* 4 **SOURCE OF INFORMATION** a source of information such as a dictionary or an encyclopedia (*often before nouns*) ○ *the reference section of the library* 5 **SOURCE REFERRED TO** a source of information referred to by a footnote or citation 6 **FOOTNOTE OR BIBLIOGRAPHICAL CITATION** a note directing a reader's attention to a particular section of a work or to another source of information 7 PUBL = **reference mark** 8 **IDENTIFYING CODE** something, usually a set of letters or figures, that serves to identify somebody or something, e.g. a customer, client, business letter, or a spot on a map (*often before nouns*) ○ *asked for a customer reference number* 9 **STATEMENT OF CHARACTER AND QUALIFICATIONS** a statement concerning somebody's character or qualifications, given, e.g. to a potential employer 10 *US* COMM = **referee** *n.* 3 ■ *vt* (**-ences, -encing, -enced**) 1 **COMPILE REFERENCES FOR BOOK** to compile a list of references for a book, essay, or thesis 2 **USE SOMETHING AS A SOURCE** to use or refer to somebody or something as a source in the writing of something ○ *The author referenced some rather obscure works.* ■ *prep* **WITH REFERENCE TO** in connection with ○ *Reference our discussion of 5 June, I believe our prior decision stands.*

reference book *n* 1 a book that is intended to be used for looking up facts, definitions, or other information 2 POL = **passbook** *n.* 3

reference mark *n* a typographical symbol, such as an asterisk or number used to draw the attention of a reader to a note or bibliographic entry

referendum /réffə réndəm/ (*plural* **-dums** *or* **-da** /-də/) *n* a vote by the whole of an electorate on a specific question or questions put to it by a government or similar body [Mid-19C. < Latin, '(something) to be referred (to the Senate)', form of *referre* (see REFER).]

referent /réffərənt/ *n* the thing or idea that a symbol, word, or phrase denotes

referential /réffə rénsh'l/ *adj* 1 relating to references or in the form of a reference 2 describes a work of art that imitates other works or contains oblique references or homages to them, often at the expense of original content or style —**referentiality** /réffə renshi állәti/ *n* —**referentially** /réffə rénsh'li/ *adv*

~~**refering**~~ incorrect spelling of **referring**

referral /ri fúrəl/ *n* 1 the act or process of referring somebody or something to somebody else, especially of sending a patient to consult a medical specialist 2 somebody or something that has been referred, especially a patient who has been sent to a medical specialist

referred pain *n* pain that is felt not at its source but in another part of the body

~~**referrence**~~ incorrect spelling of **reference**

refill *vti* /ree fíl/ **FILL AGAIN** to fill a container again, or become filled again ■ *n* /reé fil/ 1 **SOMETHING THAT FILLS AGAIN** a sufficient amount of something to fill a container again after it has been emptied 2 **ANOTHER DRINK** another drink to refill an empty glass or cup 3 **REPLACEMENT FOR CONTENTS OF CONTAINER** an amount of a product packaged as a replacement for the used up contents of a previously purchased product 4 *US* **FURTHER AMOUNT OF A PRESCRIBED MEDICINE** a further amount of a medication prescribed on a previous occasion —**refillable** /ree fílləb'l/ *adj*

refinance /reé fī nánss, reéfi nánss, reé fī nanss/ (**-nances, -nancing, -nanced**) *vti* to obtain new financing for something on different terms, often involving the paying off of an existing high-interest loan by means of a new lower-interest one —**refinancer** *n*

refine /ri fīn/ (**-fines, -fining, -fined**) *vti* 1 **REMOVE IMPURITIES** to produce a purer form of something by removing the impurities from it, or to become pure through such a process 2 **MAKE OR BECOME MORE ELEGANT** to make somebody or something more cultured or elegant by eliminating less acceptable habits and tastes, or become more cultured in this way 3 **MAKE SOMETHING MORE EFFECTIVE** to improve something through small changes that make it more effective or more subtle —**refinable** *adj* —**refiner** *n*

refined /ri fīnd/ *adj* 1 **CULTURED AND POLITE** cultured and polite in habits, tastes, or appearance 2 **SOPHISTICATED AND EFFECTIVE** developed to or possessing a high degree of sophistication and effectiveness 3 **PURIFIED** made purer by an industrial refining process

refinement /ri fīnmənt/ *n* 1 **ELEGANCE** elegance, politeness, and good taste 2 **IMPROVEMENT** an addition or alteration that improves something by making it more sophisticated or effective 3 **PROCESS OF REFINING** the process of refining something 4 **SUBTLE, PRECISE POINT** a subtle or precise distinction in language or point in an argument

refinery /ri fīnəri/ (*plural* **-ies**) *n* an industrial site where substances such as oil or sugar are processed and purified

refit /ree fít/ *vti* (**-fits, -fitting, -fitted**) to make something, especially a ship, ready for further use by repairing and re-equipping it, or to undergo such a process ■ *n* a thorough overhaul of something, especially a ship, in which it is repaired and re-equipped

refl. *abbr* 1 reflection 2 reflective 3 reflex 4 reflexive

reflag /ree flág/ (**-flags, -flagging, -flagged**) *vt* to register a ship or plane with a different national authority

reflation /ree fláysh'n/ *n* the process of bringing an economy out of recession by increasing the amount of money in circulation within it [Mid-20C. After DEFLATION, INFLATION.] —**reflate** *vti*

reflect /ri flékt/ *v* 1 *vti* **SEND SOMETHING BACK** to redirect something that strikes a surface, especially light, sound, or heat, usually back towards its point of origin ○ *The Moon reflects light from the Sun towards the Earth.* 2 *vti* **SHOW A MIRROR IMAGE OF** to show a reverse image of somebody or something on a mirror or other reflective surface 3 *vt* **SHOW** to express or be an indicator of something ○ *The election results reflect discontent among voters.* 4 *vi* **THINK SERIOUSLY** to think seriously, carefully, and relatively calmly ○ *The retreat will give us time to reflect.* 5 *vi* **SAY TO SELF THOUGHTFULLY** to have a particular thought which may or may not be voiced ○ *That, he reflected, was the only positive thing one could say about the matter.* 6 *vti* **BRING CREDIT OR DISCREDIT** to bring credit, discredit, or another judgment on somebody or something ○ *His current success reflects real credit on the school.* [14C. Via Old French *reflecter* < Latin *reflectere* 'bend back' < *flectere* 'to bend'.]

reflectance /ri fléktənss/ *n* PHYS = **reflectivity**

reflecting telescope /ri flékting-/ *n* a telescope in which light from the object is initially focused by a concave mirror

reflection /ri fléksh'n/, **reflexion** n 1 ACT OF REFLECTING the process or act of reflecting something, especially light, sound, or heat 2 REFLECTED IMAGE the image of somebody or something that appears in a mirror or other reflecting surface 3 CAREFUL THOUGHT careful thought, especially the process of reconsidering previous actions, events, or decisions 4 CONSIDERED IDEA an idea or thought, especially one produced by careful consideration of something 5 INDICATION a clear indication or the result of something ○ *This award is a reflection of your hard work.* 6 CAUSE OF BLAME OR CREDIT a cause of blame or credit to somebody or something ○ *Of course, it's no reflection on you that the project failed.* 7 BENDING BACK OF A STRUCTURE the bending back upon itself of a membrane or other anatomical structure 8 SYMMETRICAL TRANSFORMATION a symmetrical transformation in which a figure is reversed along an axis so that the new figure produced is a mirror image of the original one —**reflectional** adj

reflective /ri fléktiv/ adj 1 THOUGHTFUL characterized by deep careful thought 2 ABLE TO REFLECT able to reflect light, sound, or other forms of energy 3 BY REFLECTION produced by reflection —**reflectively** adv —**reflectiveness** n

reflectivity /reè flek tívvəti/ (plural -ties) n (symbol **ρ**) the ratio of the energy of a wave reflected from a surface to the energy of the incident wave

reflectometer /reè flek tómmitər/ n an instrument used to measure the ratio of the energy of a wave after reflection to the energy of the wave before reflection

reflector /ri fléktər/ n 1 an object, usually glass, plastic, or metal, that reflects light 2 ASTRON = **reflecting telescope**

reflet /ri fláy/ n a shiny or iridescent effect, especially in ceramic finishes [Mid-19C. Via French *reflet*, earlier *reflès* < Italian *riflesso* 'reflection'.]

reflex adj /reè fleks/ 1 AUTOMATIC AND INVOLUNTARY occurring automatically and involuntarily as a result of the nervous system's reaction to a stimulus 2 EXTREMELY FAST very fast in reacting 3 PRODUCED AUTOMATICALLY produced automatically, unthinkingly, and totally predictably in response to events ○ *reflex opposition* 4 BETWEEN 180° AND 360° describes an angle of between 180° and 360° 5 **reflex, reflexed** BENT BACK bent or folded back ○ *reflex leaves* 6 REFLECTED involving a reflection of energy, e.g. of light or a stream of electrons ○ *reflex light* ■ n 1 INVOLUNTARY BODILY REACTION an involuntary physiological reaction such as a sneeze, triggered by a nerve impulse sent from a nerve centre in response to a nerve receptor's reaction to a stimulus 2 SOMETHING REFLECTED a reflected image, or a reflection of light, sound, or heat 3 WORD DEVELOPED FROM AN EARLIER FORM a later form of a word or other linguistic element that has developed from an earlier one ■ vti /rifléks/ BEND BACK to bend back, or cause something to bend back on itself [Early 16C. < Latin *reflexus* 'bent back', past participle of *reflectere* (see REFLECT).] —**reflexly** /reè fleksli, ri fléksli/ adv

reflex arc n a nerve pathway that is responsible for triggering a reflex action

reflex camera n a camera with an internal mirror that reflects the actual image from the lens into the viewfinder so that the photographer can check the composition and focus exactly. ◊ **single-lens reflex**

reflexion n = **reflection**

reflexive /ri fléksiv/ adj 1 REFERRING TO PREVIOUS NOUN referring to the same person or thing as another noun or pronoun in the same sentence. The reflexive pronouns in English end in '-self' or '-selves', e.g. 'myself', 'yourself', 'ourselves'. 2 DENOTING SELF-DIRECTED ACTION taking a reflexive pronoun as an object, thereby indicating an action that the subject does to or for itself ○ *a reflexive verb* 3 OF OR BY REFLEX relating to, or being the product of, a reflex 4 WITHOUT THINKING automatic and involuntary or unthinking 5 BEING THE SAME describes an association between pairs of logical objects or numbers (relation) that are the same or of the same size ■ n REFLEXIVE VERB OR PRONOUN a reflexive verb or pronoun —**reflexively** adv —**reflexiveness** n

reflexology /reè flek sóllaji/ n 1 MASSAGE THERAPY a form of massage in which pressure is applied to certain parts of the feet and hands in order to promote relaxation and healing elsewhere in the body 2 STUDY OF REFLEXES AND BEHAVIOUR the scientific study of physiological reflexes and their relation to behaviour 3 BEHAVIOURAL THEORY a theory that explains human behaviour as complex chains of conditioned and unconditioned reflexes —**reflexologist** n

refluent /réffloo ənt/ adj flowing back [Late 17C. < Latin *refluent-*, present participle of *refluere* 'flow back' < *fluere* 'flow'.]

reflux /reè fluks/ n 1 BACKWARD FLOW a returning flow of something 2 REGURGITATION OF STOMACH FLUID a backflow of liquid in the opposite direction to its normal movement such as the regurgitation of stomach and peptic juices associated with acid indigestion and hiatal hernia 3 HEATING WHILE CONDENSING VAPOUR a method of heating liquid so that escaping vapour is condensed and returned to the liquid ■ vt HEAT SOMETHING WHILE CONDENSING VAPOUR to heat a liquid in a container with a condenser that catches and returns escaping vapour

refocus /ree fókəss/ vti 1 to change or adjust the focus of something such as a camera or telescope 2 to concentrate attention or efforts on something different ○ *We need to refocus our marketing strategies.*

reforest /ree fórrist/, **reafforest** /ree ə fórrist/ vti to replant an area with trees after its original trees have been cut down —**reforestation** /reè forri stáysh'n/ n

reform /ri fáwrm/ v 1 IMPROVE SOMETHING BY REMOVING FAULTS to change and improve something by correcting faults, removing inconsistencies and abuses, and imposing modern methods or values 2 vti GET RID OF UNACCEPTABLE HABITS to adopt a more acceptable way of life and mode of behaviour or persuade or force somebody else to do so 3 vt CHANGE THE MOLECULAR STRUCTURE OF PETROLEUM to subject petroleum to a chemical process such as catalytic cracking, in order to convert it into petrol ■ n 1 REORGANIZATION AND IMPROVEMENT the reorganization and improvement of something, especially a political institution or system, that is considered to be faulty, ineffective, or unjust ○ *electoral reform* ○ *the reform candidate* 2 IMPROVING CHANGE a particular change and improvement, especially in the social or political sphere ○ *reforms designed to prevent fraud* 3 CHARACTER IMPROVEMENT the adoption by somebody of a more acceptable way of life [14C. Directly or via French *réformer* < Latin *reformare* 'form again' < *forma* 'form'.] —**reformability** /ri fáwrmə billəti/ n —**reformable** /ri fáwrmab'l/ adj —**reformation** /réffər máysh'n/ n —**reformational** adj —**reformative** /-fáwrmətiv/ adj

Reform adj relating or belonging to Reform Judaism ■ n JUDAISM = **Reform Judaism**

re-form /ree fáwrm/ vti to return to or cause something to return to a previous form —**re-formation** /reè fawr máysh'n/ n

Reform Act n any 19th-century act of Parliament in Britain, especially those of 1832 and 1867, that gave the vote to wider sections of society and redistributed parliamentary seats

⚡ **reformat** /ree fáwr mat/ (-mats, -matting, -matted) vt to format something in a different way, especially a floppy disk or computer hard disk or the text and graphic elements on a page when using a word processor

Reformation /réffər máysh'n/ n the 16th-century religious movement in Europe that set out to reform some of the doctrines and practices of the Roman Catholic Church and resulted in the development of Protestantism

QUICK FACTS ON... REFORMATION

Key dates: 16th century
Key locations: N Europe, especially Germany
Key elements: rebellion against papal corruption (especially the practice of selling indulgences); rejection of papal influence on salvation; belief in justification (salvation by faith alone)
Key figures: Martin Luther, Desiderius Erasmus, Huldreich Zwingli, John Calvin, John Knox, Menno Simons, Henry VIII of England, Thomas Cranmer
Key events: (possibly apocryphal) nailing of *95 Theses* to door of Wittenberg Church by Luther 1517, excommunication of Luther 1521, first use of term 'Protestant' at Diet of Speyer 1529, Act of Supremacy making Henry VIII head of Anglican Church 1534, Calvin takes control of church in Geneva 1541
Key works: *95 Theses* (Luther) 1517, 'A Prelude Concerning the Babylonian Captivity of the Church' (Luther) 1520, Luther's translation of the Bible 1534, *Institutes of the Christian Religion* (Calvin) 1536, *Book of Common Prayer* 1549
Key developments: Protestantism, Anabaptist movement, Mennonites, Calvinism; founding of Anglican Church, Presbyterianism; Huguenot churches; increase in nationalism; spread of education and use of vernacular languages; civil wars in France, England, Germany; Counter-Reformation

reformatory /ri fáwrmətəri/ n (plural -ries) formerly, a penal institution for young offenders ■ adj intended for the reform of somebody or something (formal)

reformed /ri fáwrmd/ adj 1 improved by the removal of outdated, ineffective, or unjust qualities 2 no longer behaving in an unacceptable way

Reformed adj relating or belonging to a Protestant Church, especially one based on the teachings of John Calvin rather than those of Martin Luther

reformer /ri fáwrmər/ n a person or movement that reforms or tries to reform others

Reformer n an active participant in the Reformation

reformism /ri fáwrmizəm/ n a philosophy or movement that advocates the reform of an existing institution

reformist /ri fáwrmist/ adj advocating reform to an existing institution ■ n somebody who advocates reform

Reform Judaism n the branch of Judaism that seeks to adapt religious practice to modern times and rejects the belief that Moses was literally given the Torah by God

refortify /ree fáwrti fī/ (-fies, -fying, -fied) vt to fortify a structure, place, or person again

refract /ri frákt/ vt 1 ALTER COURSE OF WAVE OF ENERGY to alter the course of a wave of energy that passes into something from another medium, as water does to light entering it from the air 2 MEASURE DEGREE OF REFRACTION IN to measure the degree of refraction in a lens or eye 3 SHOW SOMETHING THROUGH A DIFFERENT MEDIUM to alter the appearance of something by viewing or showing it through a different medium [Early 17C. < Latin *refractus*, past participle of *refringere* 'break off, break back' < *frangere* 'break'.]

refracting telescope n a telescope in which a lens receives and focuses light that is then viewed through a second, magnifying lens in the eyepiece

refraction /ri fráksh'n/ n 1 CHANGE OF DIRECTION OF A WAVE the change in direction that occurs when a wave of energy such as light passes from one medium to another of a different density, e.g. from air to water 2 DEGREE OF WAVE REDIRECTION the degree to which a wave of energy is refracted 3 DISTORTION OF AN ASTRONOMICAL OBJECT'S LOCATION the degree to which the apparent position of an astronomical object is distorted by the redirection of its light as it passes through the Earth's atmosphere 4 EYE'S ABILITY TO BEND LIGHT the ability of the eye to change the direction of light in order to focus it on the retina 5 MEASURING OF EYE'S REFRACTIVE CAPACITY the process of measuring the eye's ability to refract light —**refractional** adj

refractive /ri fráktiv/ adj relating to, involving, or capable of refraction —**refractively** adv —**refractiveness** n —**refractivity** /reè frak tívvəti/ n

refractive index n (symbol *n*) the ratio of the speed of refracted light in a vacuum or reference medium to its speed in the medium under examination. US term **index of refraction**

refractometer /reè frak tómmitər/ n an instrument that measures the refractive index of a medium —**refractometric** /ri fráktə méttrik/ adj —**refractometry** /reè frak tómmətri/ n

refractor /ri fráktər/ n 1 ASTRON = **refracting telescope** 2 a device that alters the direction of a beam of light by passing it between two transparent materials of different density

refractory /ri fráktəri/ adj 1 UNCONTROLLABLE stubborn, rebellious, and uncontrollable 2 HEAT-RESISTANT resistant to high temperatures, and therefore not easily melted or worked 3 UNRESPONSIVE TO TREATMENT unresponsive to medical treatment ○ *a refractory infection* 4 RESISTANT TO INFECTION resistant to infection or disease 5 UNRESPONSIVE TO STIMULUS not able to respond to a stimulus ■ n (plural -ries) HIGHLY HEAT-RESISTANT MATERIAL a material that is able to withstand high temperatures without melting, e.g. the fire clay used to line furnaces [Early 17C. Variant of *refractary* < Latin *refractarius* 'stubborn' < *refractus* (see REFRACT).] —**refractorily** adv —**refractoriness** n

refractory period n the time after receiving a stimulus during which a nerve or muscle cell cannot respond to further stimuli

refrain[1] /ri fráyn/ vi to avoid or hold yourself back from doing something [14C. Via Old French *refrener* < Latin *refrenare* 'hold back, curb' < *frenum* 'bridle'.] —**refrainment** n

refrain[2] /ri fráyn/ *n* **1** RECURRING PIECE OF VERSE a line or group of lines that recurs at regular intervals in a poem, especially at the ends of verses **2** CHORUS the chorus in a song, or the music that accompanies it **3** MELODY a melody or tune **4** SOMETHING REPEATED OFTEN something that is frequently repeated, such as a saying or an idea [14C. < Old French, past participle of *refraindre* 'repeat', alteration of Latin *refringere* 'break off, break back'.]

refrangible /ri fránjəb'l/ *adj* able to be refracted [Late 17C. < modern Latin *refrangibilis* < *refrangere*, alteration of Latin *refringere* 'break off, break back'.] —**refrangibility** /ri fránjə bílləti/ *n*

refreeze /ree fréez/ (**-freezes, -freezing, -froze** /-fróz/, **-frozen** /-fróz'n/) *vti* to freeze something once more after thawing, or become frozen once more after thawing

~~refrence~~ incorrect spelling of **reference**

⚡**refresh** /ri frésh/ *v* **1** *vt* RENEW SOMEBODY'S ENERGY to make somebody feel more energetic, especially with rest, food, or drink ○ *feel refreshed after a nap* **2** *vt* MAKE SOMEBODY FRESH AND COOL to make somebody feel fresh and cool or clean **3** *vt* REACTIVATE MEMORY to prompt or reactivate the memory with a piece of information ○ *Just refresh my memory.* **4** *vt* MAKE SOMETHING FRESH OR BRIGHT AGAIN to bring the freshness or the brightness and colour back to something that is stale, wilting, or faded ○ *Plunge the carrots in ice water to refresh them.* **5** *vt* REPLENISH to replenish the supplies of something ○ *Can I refresh your drink?* **6** *vt* UPDATE ELECTRONIC DEVICE WITH DATA to update an electronic device, especially a visual display unit or active memory chip, with data **7** *vti* UPDATE INFORMATION to update the information on a particular World Wide Web site, or to be updated ○ *This page refreshes every two minutes.* [14C. < Old French *refreschir* 'make fresh again' < *freis* 'fresh'.]

refresher /ri fréshər/ *n* **1** something that refreshes **2** an additional payment made to a lawyer during a lengthy case

refresher course *n* a course of instruction designed to bring somebody's knowledge and skills up to date

refreshing /ri fréshing/ *adj* **1** serving to restore energy and vitality **2** pleasingly different and exciting

refreshment /ri fréshmənt/ *n* **1** SOMETHING REFRESHING something that refreshes, especially food and drink **2** ACT OF REFRESHING the process of refreshing somebody or something, or a refreshing quality in something ■ **refreshments** *npl* SOMETHING TO EAT AND DRINK something to eat and drink, usually snacks or a light meal and drinks

⚡**refresh rate** *n* the number of times per second that an image displayed on a screen needs to be regenerated to prevent flicker when viewed by the human eye

~~refridgerator~~ incorrect spelling of **refrigerator**

refried beans /rée fríd-/ *npl* a Mexican dish of beans cooked with spices, mashed, then fried

refrigerant /ri fríjjərənt/ *n* **1** COOLING SUBSTANCE a substance used to cool or freeze, especially the liquid that circulates in a refrigerator **2** FEVER-REDUCING MEDICATION a medication that alleviates fever or reduces body heat ■ *adj* **1** COOLING having a cooling or freezing effect **2** REDUCING BODY HEAT reducing fever or body heat [Late 16C. < Latin *refrigerant-*, present participle of *refrigerare* (see REFRIGERATE).]

refrigerate /ri fríjjə rayt/ (**-ates, -ating, -ated**) *vt* to cool food or other heat-sensitive products to prevent deterioration in quality [Mid-16C. < Latin *refrigerare* 'chill again, cool' < *friger-*, old stem of *frigus* 'cold'.] —**refrigeration** /ri fríjjə ráysh'n/ *n* —**refrigerative** /ri fríjjərətiv/ *adj*

refrigerated /ri fríjjə raytid/ *adj* **1** describes a vehicle or container designed to keep its contents or cargo at a low temperature in order to preserve them, e.g. during a journey **2** kept or preserved at a low temperature in a refrigerator

refrigerator /ri fríjjə raytər/ *n* an electrical appliance in the form of an insulated cabinet that keeps items cool through artificial means, or an insulated walk-in chamber artificially cooled for this purpose

refringent /ri frínjənt/ *adj* refractive [Late 18C. < Latin *refringent-*, present participle of *refringere* 'break off, break back'.] —**refringence** *n*

refroze past tense of **refreeze**

refrozen past participle of **refreeze**

reft past tense, past participle of **reave**

refuel /ree fyóo əl, ree fyóol/ (**-els, -elling, -elled**) *vti* **1** to refill a vehicle's tank with fuel **2** to provide additional material for or give a renewed impetus to something

refuge /réff yooj/ *n* **1** SHELTER OR PROTECTION a sheltered or protected state safe from something threatening, harmful, or unpleasant **2** SHELTERING PLACE a place, or sometimes a person, offering protection or safe shelter from something **3** SAFE ACCOMMODATION FOR BATTERED WOMEN a place offering accommodation to women who are victims of violence, especially in the home **4** TRANSP = **traffic island** [14C. Via Old French < Latin *refugium* 'place to flee back to' < *fugere* 'flee'.]

refugee /réffyoo jée/ *n* a person who seeks or takes refuge in a foreign country, especially to avoid war or persecution (*often before nouns*)

refugium /ri fyóoji əm/ (*plural* **-a** /-ji ə/) *n* an area whose climate remains habitable for particular species, especially rare or endangered ones, when that of the surrounding areas has changed [Mid-20C. < Latin (see REFUGE).]

refulgent /ri fúljənt/ *adj* shining brilliantly or splendidly (*formal*) [Early 16C. < Latin *refulgent-*, present participle of *refulgere* 'shine back, reflect' < *fulgere* 'shine, flash'.] —**refulgence** *n* —**refulgently** *adv*

refund *vt* /ri fúnd/ RETURN MONEY TO to return money to somebody, usually because he or she paid too much or did not receive what was paid for ■ *n* /ree fúnd, rée fund/ **1** RETURNED MONEY an amount of money that is returned to somebody **2** PROCESS OF REPAYMENT the act or process of returning money [14C. Via Old French *refunder* < Latin *refundere* 'pour back' < *fundere* 'pour'.] —**refundable** /ri fúndəb'l/ *adj*

re-fund *vt* **1** FUND SOMETHING ANEW to fund something again **2** BORROW TO REPAY A DEBT to pay off a debt by new borrowing **3** REPLACE BOND ISSUE WITH NEW ISSUE to replace an existing issue of bonds with a new issue

refurbish /ree fúrbish/ *vt* to restore something to a cleaner, brighter, or more functional state —**refurbishment** *n*

refusal /ri fyóoz'l/ *n* **1** UNWILLINGNESS TO DO a declaration or an attitude of unwillingness to do or accept something **2** FIRST OFFER OF the chance to accept or reject something before it is offered to others **3** HORSE'S REFUSAL TO JUMP AN OBSTACLE a horse's stopping and not attempting to jump an obstacle in a race or competition

refuse[1] /ri fyóoz/ (**-fuses, -fusing, -fused**) *v* **1** *vti* INDICATE UNWILLINGNESS to declare or make known a decision or intention not to do something **2** *vt* NOT ACCEPT to decline to accept something offered ○ *refused the promotion* **3** *vt* DENY to be unwilling to give, allow, or agree to something asked for by somebody ○ *I refused them the use of my tools.* **4** *vti* BALK AT JUMP to stop and not jump over an obstacle (*refers to a horse*) [14C. < Old French *refuser*.] —**refusable** *adj*

refuse[2] /réffyooss/ *n* things thrown away as being of no value or use, especially household rubbish [14C. < Old French *refus* 'refusal' < *refuser*.]

refusenik /ri fyóoznik/ *n* **1** a citizen of the former Soviet Union, especially a Jewish person, who was not allowed by the government to emigrate **2** a person who refuses to agree to, take part in, or cooperate with something, especially out of principle (*informal*)

refute /ri fyóot/ (**-futes, -futing, -futed**) *vt* **1** to prove something to be false or somebody to be in error through logical argument or by providing evidence to the contrary **2** to deny an allegation or contradict a statement without disproving it [Early 16C. < Latin *refutare* 'drive back, rebut' < *-futare* 'to beat'.] —**refutability** /ri fyóotə bílləti, réffyootə-/ *n* —**refutable** /réffyootəb'l, ri-/ *adj* —**refutably** *adv* —**refutation** /réffyoo táysh'n/ *n*

USAGE See ***rebuff.***

reg[1] /rej/ *n* a vehicle's registration number, especially the first or last letter that indicates the vehicle's age (*informal*) ○ *an H-reg hatchback* [Late 20C. Shortening.]

reg[2] /reg/ *n* a regulation (*informal*) ○ *rules and regs* [Early 20C. Shortening.]

reg. *abbr* **1** region **2** registered **3** registrar **4** registry **5** regular **6** regularly **7** regulation **8** regulator **9** regulo

Reg. *abbr* **1** Regent **2** Regina

regain /ri gáyn/ *vt* **1** to recover something after losing it **2** to reach a place again ○ *She regained her seat and sat down.*

regal /réeg'l/ *adj* typical of or suitable for a king or queen, especially in splendour and magnificence [14C. Via Old French < Latin *regalis* < *reg-*, stem of *rex* 'king'.] —**regality** /ree gálləti/ *n* —**regally** /réeg'li/ *adv*

regale /ri gáyl/ (**-gales, -galing, -galed**) *vt* **1** to entertain or amuse somebody, especially by telling stories ○ *regaled us with stories from the early days* **2** to give somebody plenty of good things to eat and drink [Mid-17C. < French *régaler* 'entertain', literally 'give pleasure again' < Old French *gale* 'merriment, pleasure'.]

regalia /ri gáyli ə/ *n* ROYAL INSIGNIA the ceremonial and symbolic objects and clothing used and worn by royalty or other holders of high office on formal occasions (+ *singular or plural verb*) ■ *npl* (+ *singular or plural verb*) **1** DISTINCTIVE CLOTHING the distinctive clothing or trappings worn by a particular group of people, especially on formal occasions **2** SPLENDID ATTIRE splendid attire for a formal occasion ○ *The general appeared in full regalia.* [Mid-16C. < medieval Latin *regalia* 'royal privileges, royal residence', < form of Latin *regalis* (see REGAL).]

regard /ri gaard/ *vt* **1** CONSIDER to think of somebody or something as having a particular nature or quality or a particular role or function ○ *I regard his gift as an apology.* **2** HAVE FEELINGS IN RELATION TO to have a particular feeling towards somebody or something ○ *At first they regarded the idea of early retirement with horror.* **3** JUDGE to have an opinion as to the quality or worth of somebody or something ○ *I regard her highly.* **4** LOOK AT to look at something or somebody steadily or attentively ○ *regarded the photograph with interest* **5** BE ABOUT to be about or concerned with something ○ *This memo regards your performance review.* ■ *n* **1** ATTENTION attention to or concern for somebody or something ○ *with no regard for my feelings* **2** FAVOURABLE OPINION respect, often coupled with affection ○ *I hold her in the highest regard.* **3** GAZE a look, or somebody's gaze (*formal*) ■ **regards** *npl* FRIENDLY GREETINGS friendly good wishes and greetings ○ *Give my regards to your father.* [14C. < Old French *regarder* 'look at fully' < *garder* 'to look'.] ◇ **as regards** as far as somebody or something is concerned ◇ **in this** *or* **that regard** as far as this or that is concerned, or from this or that point of view (*formal*)

SYNONYMS ***regard, admiration, esteem, favour, respect, reverence, veneration***

CORE MEANING: appreciation of the worth of somebody or something

regard a mixture of liking and appreciation of somebody or something; **admiration** warm approval and appreciation of somebody or something, often suggesting a desire to copy or resemble somebody; **esteem** a high opinion and appreciation of somebody or something; **favour** a liking and preference for somebody or something; **respect** a strong acknowledgment and appreciation of somebody's abilities and achievements; **reverence** a feeling of deep respect and devotion combined with a slight sense of awe; **veneration** a profound feeling of respect and awe.

regardant /ri gaard'nt/ *adj* describes a heraldic figure that is looking backwards over its shoulder ○ *three lions regardant* [15C. < Old French, present participle of *regarder* (see REGARD).]

regardful /ri gaardf'l/ *adj* **1** paying due attention **2** full of esteem and often deferential respect for somebody —**regardfully** *adv* —**regardfulness** *n*

regarding /ri gaarding/ *prep* about or on the subject of ○ *I'd like a word with you regarding the schedule.*

regardless /ri gaardləss/ *adv* in spite of or ignoring setbacks, hindrances, or problems ■ *adj* paying no attention, especially failing to pay proper attention —**regardlessly** *adv*

USAGE See ***irregardless.***

regardless of *prep* **1** in spite of ○ *Regardless of what you were told, I cannot help you.* **2** no matter what or taking no account of ○ *We're going on holiday regardless of the weather.*

regatta /ri gáttə/ *n* a sports event consisting of a series of boat or yacht races [Mid-17C. < (Venetian) Italian, 'gondola race (on the Grand Canal)', originally 'contest for mastery' < *regattare* 'compete'.]

regd *abbr* registered

regelation /réeji láysh'n/ *n* **1** the process by which water, melted by pressure beneath a glacier, is refrozen **2** reduction of the freezing point of water by force of pressure

regency /reéjənssi/ (*plural* **-cies**) *n* **1** a group of people ruling on behalf of a monarch who is unable to rule because of youth, illness, or absence **2** the authority and responsibilities or period in office of a regent

Regency *n* **1 1811–20 IN GREAT BRITAIN** the period from 1811–20 in Great Britain during which George, Prince of Wales, ruled as regent for his father King George III **2 1715–23 IN FRANCE** the period from 1715–23 in France during which Philip, Duke of Orleans, ruled as regent on behalf of King Louis XV ■ *adj* **IN STYLE OF REGENCY** in the style prevalent and fashionable during either of the Regency periods

regenerate *v* /ri jénnə rayt/ (**-ates, -ating, -ated**) **1** *vti* **RECOVER FROM DECLINE** to return or bring something back from a state of decline to a revitalized state **2** *vti* **FORM AGAIN** to form or become formed again **3** *vti* **REPLACE BY NEW GROWTH** to replace lost tissue or a lost limb or organ with a new growth **4** *vt* **RESTORE SOMEBODY SPIRITUALLY** to restore and renew somebody morally or spiritually **5** *vt* **RESTORE SOMETHING TO ORIGINAL WAVE SHAPE** to restore digital electrical signals to their original wave shape after transmission over long distances ■ *n* /rə jénnə rayt/ **1 SOMEBODY SPIRITUALLY REFORMED** a person who is spiritually reborn or renewed **2 REPLACEMENT TISSUE** tissue that has grown to replace lost tissue, or a regenerated part, organ, or organism ■ *adj* /rə jénnə rayt/ **1 SPIRITUALLY REBORN OR RENEWED** spiritually reborn, renewed, or restored to health **2 NEWLY FORMED OR GROWN** newly formed or grown as a replacement for something lost —**regenerable** *adj* —**regeneracy** *n* —**regenerateness** *n* —**regeneration** /ri jénnə ráysh'n/ *n* —**regenerative** *adj* —**regenerator** *n*

Regensburg /ráygənss bòork/ city in SE Germany. Population: 126,000 (1995).

regent /reéjənt/ *n* a person who rules on behalf of a monarch who is unable to rule because of youth, illness, or absence ■ *adj* ruling as a regent ○ *the prince regent* [14C. Via Old French < Latin *regent-*, present participle of *regere* 'rule'.] —**regental** *adj*

reggae /rég gay/ *n* popular music, originally from Jamaica, that combines elements of rock, calypso, and soul and is characterized by heavy accentuation of the second and fourth beats of a four-beat bar (*often before nouns*) ○ *a reggae beat* [Mid-20C. < ?]

Reggio di Calabria /réji ō dee ka laábrya/ city in S Italy. Population: 180,371 (1997 estimate).

Reggio nell'Emilia /-nel ay meélya/ city in N Italy. Population: 133,191 (1992).

regicide /réjji sīd/ *n* **1** the killing of a king **2** a killer of a king [Mid-16C. < Latin *reg-*, stem of *rex* 'king'.] —**regicidal** /réjji sīd'l/ *adj*

regime /ray zheém, re-/, **régime** *n* **1 FORM OF GOVERNMENT** a system or style of government **2 OPPRESSIVE GOVERNMENT** a particular government, especially one that is considered to be oppressive **3 CONTROLLING GROUP** any controlling or managing group, or the system of control and management adopted by it **4 ESTABLISHED SYSTEM** an established system or way of doing things **5 CHARACTERISTIC CONDITIONS FOR A PROCESS** the characteristic conditions under which a natural, scientific, or industrial process occurs **6** MED = **regimen** *n.* 1 [15C. Via French < Latin *regimen* (see REGIMEN).]

regimen /réjjimən, -men/ *n* **1** a prescribed or recommended programme of medication, diet, exercise, or other measures intended to improve health or fitness, or stabilize a medical condition **2** a government or form of government (*archaic*) **3** INDUST, SCI = **regime** *n.* 5 [14C. < Latin, 'rule, government' < *regere* 'to rule'.]

regiment *n* /réjjimənt/ **1 ARMY UNIT** a permanent military unit usually consisting of two or three battalions of ground troops divided into smaller companies or troops and under the command of a colonel **2 LARGE NUMBER OF PEOPLE OR THINGS** a large number of people or things, especially an orderly group **3 GOVERNMENTAL RULE** governmental rule or administration (*archaic*) ■ *vt* /réjjiment/ **1 CONTROL SOMEBODY OR SOMETHING STRICTLY** to impose strict control or discipline on somebody or something, often to the extent of stifling flexibility, individuality, or imagination **2 GROUP SOMETHING SYSTEMATICALLY** to organize something systematically into groups **3 GROUP SOLDIERS INTO REGIMENTS** to form regiments out of a group of soldiers [14C. Via Old French < late Latin *regimentum* < Latin *regere* 'to rule'.] —**regimental** /réjji mént'l/ *adj* —**regimentally** *adv* —**regimented** /-mentid/ *adj*

regimentals /réjji mént'lz/ *npl* **1** the uniform and insignia worn by the members of a particular regiment **2** military dress and insignia, especially as worn for ceremonial occasions

regimentation /réjji men táysh'n/ *n* the act of placing somebody or something under strict and inflexible organization or control, or the condition of being very strictly organized and controlled ○ *They are individuals and do not respond well to regimentation.*

Regina[1] /ri jīnə/ *n* **1** the reigning queen **2** the Crown as the prosecuting authority in lawsuits when the ruling monarch is a queen ○ *the case of Regina versus Higgins* [Early 18C. < Latin, 'queen'.]

Regina[2] /ri jīnə/ capital of Saskatchewan, Canada. Population: 193,652 (1996).

regio-cop /reéjō kop/ *n* an area peacekeeping force, or a member of such a force [< REGION]

region /reéjən/ *n* **1 GEOGRAPHIC AREA** a large land area that has particular geographic, political, or cultural characteristics that distinguish it from others, whether existing within one country or extending over several **2 ADMINISTRATIVE UNIT** a large separate political or administrative unit within a country **3 ECOLOGICAL AREA** an area of the world with particular animal and plant life **4 LARGE INDEFINITE AREA** any large indefinite area of a surface **5 AREA OR ASPECT** an imprecisely defined area or part of something such as a sphere of activity **6 RANGE WITHIN WHICH FIGURE FALLS** the range within which something such as a figure, sum, or price might fall ○ *in the region of £1,000* **7 AREA OF THE BODY** an area of the body, usually an area surrounding a specific organ or part ■ **regions** *npl* **THE PROVINCES** the rest of a country outside its capital, or the rest of an area outside its main city [14C. Via Old French < Latin *region-* 'boundary, district' < *regere* 'to rule'.]

regional /reéjən'l/ *adj* **1 RELATING TO REGION** belonging to or typical of a particular geographical region **2 CONNECTED WITH ADMINISTRATIVE REGION** serving or connected with one of the administrative regions of a country ○ *a regional authority* **3 TYPICAL OF PARTICULAR AREA** typical of or limited to a particular area of a country, especially typical of the speech and usage of a particular area and different from standard speech and usage —**regionally** *adv*

regionalise *vt* = **regionalize**

regionalism /reéjənəlizəm/ *n* **1 DIVISION INTO ADMINISTRATIVE AREAS** the policy of dividing a political territory into areas with separate administrations, or support for such a policy **2 LOYALTY TO HOME REGION** loyalty to or prejudice in favour of a particular region **3 LINGUISTIC FEATURE RESTRICTED TO ONE AREA** a linguistic feature such as a word, pronunciation, or expression that is only found in a particular region —**regionalist** *n, adj*

regionalize /reéjənə līz/ (**-izes, -izing, -ized**), **regionalise** (**-ises, -ising, -ised**) *vt* **1** to divide an area into administrative regions **2** to allocate something to regional administrations —**regionalization** /reéjənə lī záysh'n/ *n*

régisseur /rézhi súr/ *n* a director who is responsible for staging a theatrical work, especially a ballet [Early 19C. < French, 'agent, manager' < *régir* 'manage, rule'.]

ϟ**register** /réjjistər/ *n* **1 OFFICIAL LIST** an official record, often in the form of a list **2 BOOK FOR OFFICIAL RECORDS** a book in which a register of names, attendance, or events is kept **3 ITEM IN OFFICIAL LIST** an item recorded in an official register **4 MEASURING DEVICE THAT RECORDS** a device that automatically records numbers, degrees, or quantities **5** COMM = **cash register** **6 CORRECT ALIGNMENT** correct alignment or positioning with respect to something else **7 HEATING GRATE** a closable grill or grate through which warm or cool air is forced in a household heating system **8 COMPUTER MEMORY LOCATION** a memory location in a processor or microprocessor that has a particular storage capacity, is usually intended for a particular purpose, and is accessible at very high speeds **9 MUSICAL RANGE** the range of a voice or instrument, or a part of this range **10 ORGAN STOP** one of a group of organ stops that are similar in tonal quality **11 SITUATION-SPECIFIC LANGUAGE VARIETY** language of a type that is used in particular social situations or when communicating with a particular set of people ■ *v* **1** *vti* **WRITE IN REGISTER** to enter something in a register, or to have something entered there by an official ○ *They registered at the hotel.* **2** *vti* **ENROL** to record a name with an organization in order, e.g. to enrol somebody for an academic course or fulfil a legal requirement ○ *register for the course in September* **3** *vt* **MAKE A RECORD OF** to make a record of something, or have something recorded ○ *I want to register a complaint with the manager.* **4** *vt* **SHOW SOMETHING AS MEASUREMENT** to indicate or record a measurement on a device or scale **5** *vti* **DISPLAY FEELING OR THOUGHT** to be visible in somebody's facial expression or body language, or to display something in this way ○ *Their expressions registered the relief they felt.* **6** *vt* **NOTE SOMETHING MENTALLY** to make a mental note of something ○ *I registered the time before moving on.* **7** *vi* **BE UNDERSTOOD** to be understood or remembered by somebody ○ *The implications finally registered with me.* **8** *vt* **ACHIEVE** to achieve or accomplish something (*formal*) ○ *The team registered several notable successes last season.* **9** *vt* **SEND SOMETHING BY REGISTERED POST** to send a letter or package by registered post **10** *vi* **BE ALIGNED** to be correctly aligned [14C. Via Old French *regestre* < medieval Latin *registrum*, alteration of late Latin *regesta* 'list', literally 'things collected or brought back' < *gerere* 'bring'.] —**registered** *adj* —**registrable** *adj* —**registrant** *n*

registered general nurse *n UK* a nurse who is qualified to practise, having undergone a three-year course of study and clinical training attached to a university. ◊ **registered nurse**

registered mail *n US* = **registered post**

registered nurse *n US, ANZ* a nurse who has passed a qualifying examination in order to be licensed to practice. ◊ **registered general nurse**

registered post *n* a service provided by post offices for an additional fee to ensure safe delivery of valuable items, providing certified delivery and compensation in case of loss. US term **registered mail**

registered trademark *n* LAW = **trademark** *n.* 1

register office *n* in the United Kingdom, an office where civil marriages are performed and births, marriages, and deaths are recorded (*used as the official name for 'registry office'*)

register ton *n* MEASURE = **ton**[1] *n.* 5

registrar /réjji straár, réjji straar/ *n* **1 SOMEBODY WHO KEEPS OFFICIAL RECORDS** a person who keeps official records **2 RECORDER OF BIRTHS, MARRIAGES, AND DEATHS** a public official who records births, marriages, and deaths **3 OFFICIAL RESPONSIBLE FOR STUDENT RECORDS** the most senior administrative officer in a university, or any university, college, or school official responsible for keeping records of such things as student enrolments and examination results **4 SENIOR HOSPITAL DOCTOR** a senior doctor in a hospital, of a rank lower than consultant, who specializes in a branch of medicine or surgery and may train junior doctors **5** *US* **OFFICIAL RESPONSIBLE FOR SHARE RECORDS** a company official who keeps records of shares issued **6 LAW COURT OFFICIAL** in the United Kingdom, an official who oversees the administration of justice in the High Court and other courts **7** *US* **HOSPITAL ADMINISTRATOR** an administrative officer in a hospital responsible for admitting patients —**registrarship** *n*

Registrar General (*plural* **Registrars General**) *n* in the United Kingdom, a senior civil servant responsible for population records and censuses

registration /réjji stráysh'n/ *n* **1 ACT OF REGISTERING OR BEING REGISTERED** the act or an instance of registering somebody or something, or the process of being registered **2 ENTRY IN REGISTER** an entry in a register, or somebody or something whose name or designation is entered in a register **3 TIME OF REGISTERING STUDENTS** the act of recording school students as present or absent at the beginning of the school day, or the time or session at which this takes place **4 ENROLMENT PROCESS** the process of enroling at a college or university, choosing courses, and paying fees at the beginning of an academic term **5 LETTER SHOWING VEHICLE'S AGE** a letter that identifies the year or part of a year in which a vehicle was registered and put on the road, forming part of its registration number **6** *US* **LEGAL PROOF FOR VEHICLE** a certificate showing that a motor vehicle has been properly registered with a state's department of motor vehicles **7 PEOPLE REGISTERING TOGETHER** the number of people who register for a particular thing or at a particular place at one time **8 COMBINATION OF ORGAN STOPS** a particular combination of organ stops used to play a piece of music **9 CHOICE OF COMBINATIONS OF ORGAN STOPS** the art of choosing combinations of organ stops appropriate for a particular piece or passage

registration document *n* an official document stating the name of the owner of a motor vehicle and giving details by which it can be identified

registration number *n* a sequence of letters and numbers by which a motor vehicle can be identified, printed on plates (**number plates**) fastened to the front and back of the vehicle

registration plate *n ANZ* a number plate

registry /réjjistri/ (*plural* **-tries**) *n* **1 RECORDS OFFICE** a place where registers and other records are kept **2 REGISTERING OF** the act of registering somebody or something **3 SHIP'S REGISTRATION IN PARTICULAR COUNTRY** the nationality of a ship, as defined by where it is registered not by the nationality of its owner or its usual place of operation

registry office *n* = **register office** (*not used in official contexts*)

regius professor /reéji əss-, reéjəss-/ *n* in the United Kingdom, a professor whose professorship was established by a king or queen, especially Henry VIII, and who is officially appointed by the current king or queen [< Latin, 'royal' < *rex* 'king']

reglet /régglit/ *n* **1** a flat narrow architectural moulding, or a narrow strip separating mouldings or panels **2** a piece of wood used to separate lines of type in traditional hot-metal printing [Late 16C. < Old French *régelet* 'small rule'.]

regnal /régn'l/ *adj* relating to a king or queen's reign, calculated from the date when he or she became the sovereign ○ *the third regnal year* [Early 17C. < Anglo-Latin *regnalis* < Latin *regnum* 'kingdom'.]

regnant /régnənt/ *adj* (*formal*) **1** actually reigning, usually as opposed to having a royal title by marriage ○ *queen regnant* **2** widespread, predominant, or especially fashionable at a particular time ○ *according to the regnant custom* [Early 17C. < Latin *regnant-*, present participle of *regnare* 'reign'.]

rego /réjjō/ (*plural* **-os**) *n Aus* the annual reregistration of a motor vehicle, usually including a roadworthiness check (*informal*) [Shortening]

Rego /ráygō/, **Paula** (*b.* 1935) Portuguese-born British painter

regolith /réggə lith/ *n* the layer of loose rock particles that covers the bedrock of most land on Earth and the Moon [Late 19C. < Greek *rhēgos* 'blanket'.]

regorge /ree gáwrj/ (**-gorges, -gorging, -gorged**) *v* **1** *vt* to bring up something that has been swallowed **2** *vi* to flow or gush back along a channel or out of a pit [Early 17C. Either < Old French *regorger* < *gorge* (see GORGE), or < RE- + GORGE.]

regress *v* /ri gréss/ **1** *vi* **RETURN TO EARLIER, WORSE CONDITION** to return to an earlier and less advanced, less healthy, or generally worse state from a more advanced, healthier, or generally better one **2** *vi* **GO BACK** to move backwards ○ *regress in time* **3** *vi* **TEND TOWARDS MEAN** to tend towards a statistical mean **4** *vti* **GO BACK TO EARLIER PERIOD PSYCHOLOGICALLY** to go back to or cause somebody to reenact an earlier emotional state and exhibit the type of behaviour associated with it **5** *vt* **SUPPOSEDLY MAKE SOMEBODY RECALL EARLIER LIVES** to cause somebody to think of and describe supposed earlier lifetimes while under hypnosis ■ *n* /reé gress/ **1 MOVEMENT BACKWARDS** a going backwards, especially from a more advanced or better state to a less advanced or worse one **2 REASONING FROM EFFECT TO CAUSE** a process of reasoning backwards from effects to their causes [Early 16C. < Latin *regress-*, past participle of *regredi* 'move backwards' < *gradi* 'walk'.] —**regressor** *n*

regression /ri grésh'n/ *n* **1 MOVEMENT BACKWARDS** a going backwards or a backward movement or progress, especially through the earlier stages or forms of something **2 REVERSION TO EARLIER STATE** a return to an earlier or less developed condition or way of behaving **3 REVERSION TO LESS MATURE STATE** reversion to an earlier, less mature, and less adaptive emotional or mental level, often involving the appearance of forms of behaviour associated with childhood **4 ASSOCIATION BETWEEN VARIABLES** a process for determining the statistical relationship between a random variable and one or more independent variables that is used to predict the value of the random variable **5 RETURN TO EARLIER PHYSICAL TYPE** the recurrence of an earlier, less complicated physical type among the later generations of a particular population **6 RETROGRADE MOTION** the apparent backward motion of an astronomical object, caused by the differing orbital periods of the Earth and the body being observed **7 MOVEMENT OF MOON'S ORBIT** the slow movement around the ecliptic of the two points where the Moon's orbit crosses it

regressive /ri gréssiv/ *adj* **1** reverting to an earlier, less developed condition or way of behaving **2** describes a tax system in which those with low incomes pay proportionally higher taxes than the wealthy —**regressively** *adv* —**regressiveness** *n*

regret /ri grét/ *vt* (**-grets, -gretting, -gretted**) **1 FEEL SORRY FOR** to feel sorry and sad about something previously done or said that now appears wrong, mistaken, or hurtful to others **2 USED POLITELY WHEN GIVING BAD NEWS** used as a polite expression of sorrow when making an apology or delivering a piece of bad or unwelcome news ○ *We regret to inform you that this service is no longer available.* **3 MOURN** to feel sadness about something, or feel a sense of loss and longing for somebody or something that is no longer there (*formal*) ■ *n* **1 SAD OR DISAPPOINTED FEELING** a feeling or expression of sorrow and guilt for a past action or event that you now wish had not happened or had happened differently **2 FEELING OF SADNESS** a feeling of sadness, disappointment, or of longing for somebody or something that is no longer there ○ *I let them go with regret, knowing that the visit would not be soon repeated.* ■ **regrets** *npl* **EXPRESSION OF SADNESS** a polite expression of real or pretended sadness, used especially when refusing something such as an invitation ○ *Do give them my regrets. I won't be able to come on Saturday.* [15C. < Old French *regreter*.] —**regretter** *n*

regretful /ri grétf'l/ *adj* feeling or showing regret for something —**regretfully** *adv* —**regretfulness** *n*

USAGE regretful or **regrettable**? ***Regrettable*** is used of something that is a cause for regret, whereas ***regretful*** describes somebody who has feelings of regret for something: *These mistakes are regrettable. They felt regretful at missing the opportunity.* The adverbs *regrettably* and *regretfully* are even more vulnerable to confusion, but again *regrettably* relates to the cause of regret and *regretfully* to the feeling itself: *The exam results are regrettably poor. She regretfully turned down the invitation.*

---

regrettable /ri gréttəb'l/ *adj* unfortunate or blameworthy, and causing feelings of regret, embarrassment, or even shame ○ *It was a regrettable lapse by a person of otherwise exemplary character.* —**regrettableness** *n* —**regrettably** *adv*

USAGE See ***regretful***.

---

regroup /ree gróop/ *v* **1** *vti* **FORM INTO ORGANIZED BODY AGAIN** to re-form, or re-form troops, into organized units or an effective fighting force, especially after their being dispersed or defeated **2** *vi* **REORGANIZE** to recover, reorganize, and prepare for a further effort after receiving a setback **3** *vt* **ARRANGE THINGS IN NEW GROUPS** to arrange people or things in new or different groups —**regroupment** *n*

regrow /ree grṓ/ (**-grows, -growing, -grew, -grown**) *vti* to grow again, or cause something, e.g. hair or a body part, to grow again —**regrowth** /reé grōth/ *n*

Regt *abbr* **1** Regent **2** Regiment

regular /réggyŏolər/ *adj* **1 HAVING EQUAL TIMES OR SPACES BETWEEN** occurring in a fixed, unvarying, or predictable pattern, with equal amounts of time or space between each one **2 HAPPENING FREQUENTLY** occurring or doing something frequently enough over a period of time to establish a pattern, though not necessarily a strict one **3 USUAL** normally expected, or most often used or done **4 FOLLOWING ROUTINE** carried out according to an established routine or schedule ○ *keep very regular hours* **5 PHYSICALLY PREDICTABLE AND CONSISTENT** having predictable physical processes, especially menstruating or having bowel movements at predictable times **6 STANDARD OR MEDIUM** of a standard or medium size or strength ○ *I'll have the regular fries.* **7 SYMMETRICAL** evenly and pleasingly shaped and symmetrical ○ *a regular facial profile* **8 PROPER** conforming to the normal or accepted rules or standards **9 QUALIFIED** officially or properly qualified to perform a specific job ○ *not a regular doctor* **10 FORMING PART OF PROFESSIONAL FORCE** belonging to or constituting a full-time professional military or police force ○ *an officer in the regular army* **11 COMPLETE AND UTTER** thoroughly deserving a particular description (*informal*) ○ *a regular tyrant in the office* **12** *US* **NICE** pleasant, reliable, and thoughtful (*informal*) ○ *a regular guy* **13 GRAMMATICALLY NORMAL** following the normal or common grammatical patterns of a language **14 OF RELIGIOUS ORDER** belonging to a religious or monastic order ○ *the regular clergy* **15** *US* **POLITICALLY LOYAL** connected with or loyal to a particular political party **16 HAVING EQUAL SIDES AND ANGLES** having both equal sides and equal angles ○ *a regular polygon* **17 COMPOSED OF IDENTICAL POLYGONS** having faces that are congruent identical polygons and that make equal angles with each other ○ *a regular polyhedron* **18 SYMMETRICAL** having flower parts that are similar in size and shape and are arranged symmetrically ■ *n* **1 FREQUENT VISITOR** a frequent visitor to a place (*informal*) **2 HABITUAL ORDER** something such as a drink that somebody usually asks for or buys (*informal*) **3 PROFESSIONAL SOLDIER** a full-time professional soldier (*often plural*) **4 SOMETHING STANDARD OR MEDIUM** something of a medium or standard size or strength, as opposed to something larger, smaller, stronger, or weaker **5 MEMBER OF RELIGIOUS ORDER** a member of a religious or monastic order **6** *US* **LOYAL PARTY SUPPORTER** a person who is loyal to a political party ■ *adv* **FREQUENTLY** most or all of the time (*informal*) ○ *We come here regular, don't we?* [14C. < Latin *rēgula* 'rule'.] —**regularity** /réggyŏo lárrəti/ *n* —**regularly** /réggyŏolərli/ *adv*

regularize /réggyŏolə rīz/ (**-izes, -izing, -ized**), **regularise** (**-ises, -ising, -ised**) *vt* to make something fit in with or conform to usual or accepted standards or practice —**regularization** /réggyŏolə rī záysh'n/ *n* —**regularizer** /réggyŏolə rīzər/ *n*

regulate /réggyŏo layt/ (**-lates, -lating, -lated**) *vt* **1 CONTROL** to control something and bring it to the desired level, e.g. by adjusting the output of a machine or by imposing restrictions on the flow of something **2 ADJUST MACHINERY OR SELECT OUTPUT** to adjust a piece of machinery or a control device on it so that the machinery works correctly **3 CONTROL SOMETHING BY RULES OR LAWS** to organize and control an activity or process by making it subject to rules or laws (*formal*) **4 MAKE SOMETHING REGULAR** to cause something to occur at predictable intervals or in a regular way [15C. < late Latin *regulat-*, past participle of *regulare* < Latin *regula* 'rule'.] —**regulative** /-lətiv/ *adj* —**regulatory** /réggyŏolətəri/ *adj*

regulation /réggyŏo láysh'n/ *n* **1 RULE OR ORDER** an official rule, law, or order stating what may or may not be done or how something must be done (*often plural*) **2 GOVERNMENT ORDER WITH FORCE OF LAW** an order issued by a government department or agency that has the force of law **3 REGULATING OF** the adjusting, organizing, or controlling of something, or the state of being adjusted, organized, or controlled **4 ABILITY OF EMBRYO TO GROW NORMALLY** the process or mechanism by which an embryo restores its ability to develop normally after being damaged or altered without creating new tissue **5 DIRECT EU LAW** a European Union law that automatically applies in all member states without the need for domestic legislation in the member states ■ *adj* **1 OFFICIALLY APPROVED FOR USE** officially approved for use, or conforming to the official guidelines for something **2 STANDARD AND UNADVENTUROUS** like everyone has or does, and completely standard and unadventurous

regulator /réggyŏo laytər/ *n* **1 CONTROL MECHANISM** a mechanism that controls something such as pressure, temperature, speed, or voltage (*often in combination*) **2 CONTROLLING OFFICIAL** an official who controls an activity and makes certain that regulations are complied with (*often in combination*) **3 VERY ACCURATE TIMEPIECE** a very accurate watch or clock, used as a standard by which others are set **4** GENETICS = **regulator gene**

regulator gene, regulatory gene *n* a gene that regulates the expression of one or more structural genes, thereby controlling the synthesis of their corresponding proteins

reguli plural of **regulus**

Regulo /réggyŏolō/ a trademark for a gas mark

regulus /réggyŏoləss/ (*plural* **-luses** *or* **-li** /-lī/) *n* **1** the semipurified mass of metal that forms beneath the slag in the smelting of ore **2** an impure intermediate metal product created by the smelting process [Late 16C. < Latin, diminutive of *rex* 'king'.] —**reguline** /-lin, -līn/ *adj*

Regulus *n* a bright double star in the constellation Leo

regurgitate /ri gúrji tayt/ (**-tates, -tating, -tated**) *v* **1** *vt* **BRING FOOD UP FROM STOMACH** to bring undigested or partially digested food up from the stomach to the mouth, as some birds and animals do to feed their young **2** *vt* **REPEAT INFORMATION MECHANICALLY** to repeat or reproduce what has been heard, read, or taught, in a purely mechanical way, with no evidence of personal thought or understanding **3** *vi* **FLOW OUT** to flow out or be ejected, especially from the mouth (*formal*) **4** *vi* **FLOW IN OPPOSITE DIRECTION TO NORMAL** to flow in the opposite direction to the normal or usual direction, especially through a defective heart valve [Late 16C. < medieval Latin *regurgitat-*, past participle of *regurgitare* 'flood back' < *gurges* 'whirlpool'.] —**regurgitant** /ri gúrjitənt/ *n, adj* —**regurgitation** /ri gúrji táysh'n/ *n* —**regurgitative** /ri gúrjitətiv/ *adj*

rehab /reé hab/ *n* (*informal*) **1** *US* **REHABILITATION** the period or process of rehabilitation, e.g. for somebody addicted to a chemical substance (*often before nouns*) ○ *a rehab clinic* **2 SOMETHING RECONSTRUCTED** something that has been rehabilitated, especially a rehabilitated building ■ *vt* (**-habs, -habbing, -habbed**) *US* **RESTORE BUILDING** to restore something, especially a building (*informal*) [Mid-20C. Shortening.] —**rehabber** *n*

rehabilitate /reé ə bílli tayt, reé hə-/ (**-tates, -tating, -tated**) *vt* **1 HELP SOMEBODY RETURN TO NORMAL LIFE** to help somebody to return to good health or a normal life by providing training or therapy **2 RESTORE SOMEBODY TO RANK OR RIGHTS** to restore somebody to a former position or rank and grant rights and privileges once more (*often passive*) **3 RESTORE SOMEBODY'S REPUTATION** to restore somebody's good reputation and standing after he or she has been disgraced or neglected **4 RESTORE PLACE TO GOOD CONDITION** to restore a building, or part of a town, to its former good condition [Late 16C. < medieval Latin *rehabilitat-*, past participle of *rehabilitare* 'habilitate again' < *habilitare* (see HABILITATE).] —**rehabilitatable** *adj* —**rehabilitation** /reé ə bílli táysh'n, reé hə-/ *n* —**rehabilitative** /-tətiv/ *adj* —**rehabilitator** /-taytər/ *n*

rehash *vt* /ree hásh/ to repeat something or reuse and rework old material, making some changes but without introducing anything new ■ *n* /reé hash/ a tiresome reuse of ideas or material to which nothing new or significant has been added

rehear /ree heér/ (**-hears, -hearing, -heard, -heard** /-húrd/) *vt* **1** to hear or, especially, listen to somebody or something again **2** to hear a case again in the same court —**rehearing** *n*

rehearsal /ri húrss'l/ *n* **1** a session or series of sessions in which something that is to be done later, especially a public performance, is practised **2** a detailed listing or repetition of something (*formal*)

rehearse /ri húrss/ (**-hearses, -hearsing, -hearsed**) *v* **1** *vti* **PRACTISE SOMETHING BEFORE PERFORMING** to practise something before doing it, especially to practise something such as a play, speech, or piece of music before performing it for the public **2** *vt* **TRAIN SOMEBODY FOR PERFORMANCE** to train or instruct somebody who is practising before doing something, especially before giving a public performance **3** *vt* **GO OVER LIST** to go over a list of items, often reasons, complaints, or troubles **4** *vti* **REPEAT** to tell or repeat something such as a story (*literary*) [13C. < Old French *rehercer* 'rake over' < *herce, herse* (see HEARSE).] —**rehearser** *n*

reheat /ree heét/ *v* **1** *vti* to heat something up again after cooling, or be heated up again **2** *vt* to inject fuel into the exhaust gases in the outlet pipe of a jet engine in order to obtain greater heat and thrust —**reheater** *n*

rehoboam /reé ə bő əm/ *n* a large wine bottle, six times the size of a normal bottle [Mid-19C. After *Rehoboam*, who 'fortified the strongholds, and put captains in them... and stores of oil and wine' (2 Chronicles 11:11).]

Rehoboam *n* in the Bible, the son of Solomon and king of ancient Judah (922? BC–915? BC). His reign was marked by conflict with the rival kingdom of the northern tribes of Israel (1 Kings 11–14).

rehouse /ree hówz/ (**-houses, -housing, -housed**) *vt* to provide a person or a group of people with a new or different place to live in, often one that is better than the previous dwelling

rehydrate /reé hī drayt, reé hī dráyt/ (**-drates, -drating, -drated**) *v* **1** *vt* **RETURN WATER TO** to add water to something that has been dried in order to return it to its natural state **2** *vt* **REPLENISH SOMEBODY'S BODY FLUID** to restore the body fluids of somebody to a normal or healthy level **3** *vi* **ABSORB WATER** to absorb water after dehydration —**rehydratable** *adj* —**rehydration** /reé hī dráysh'n/ *n*

Reibey /reé bee/, **Mary** (1777–1855) British-born Australian entrepreneur. Born **Molly Haydock**

Reich /rīk, rīkh/ *n* the German state or empire, especially the Holy Roman Empire (926–1806) or First Reich, the German Empire (1871–1919) or Second Reich, or the Nazi state (1933–45) or Third Reich [Early 20C. < German, 'empire, kingdom'.]

reichsmark /rīks maark, rīkhs-/ (*plural* **-mark** *or* **-marks**), **Reichsmark** (*plural* **-mark** *or* **-marks**) *n* the basic unit of German currency from 1923 to 1948 [Mid-20C. < German, < *Reich* 'empire, kingdom' + *Mark* 'mark' (currency).]

Reichstag /rīks taag, rīkhs-/ *n* **1 GERMAN LEGISLATIVE ASSEMBLY 1867–1919** the legislative assembly of both the North German Confederation, from 1867 to 1871, and the German Empire, from 1871 to 1919 **2 LEGISLATIVE ASSEMBLY OF WEIMAR REPUBLIC** the sovereign legislative assembly of the Weimar Republic, from 1919 to 1933 **3 PARLIAMENT BUILDING IN BERLIN** the building in Berlin in which the Reichstag formerly met, destroyed by fire in 1933, and now rebuilt to house the parliament of the reunified German federal state [Mid-19C. < German, < *Reich* 'empire, kingdom' + *Tag* 'diet, legislative assembly'.]

Reid /reed/, **Sir George Houston** (1845–1918) Scottish-born Australian statesman and prime minister (1904–05)

reify /reé i fī/ (**-fies, -fying, -fied**) *vt* to think of or treat something abstract as if it existed as a real and tangible object [Mid-19C. < Latin *re-* (stem of *res* 'thing').] —**reification** /reé ifi káysh'n/ *n* —**reificatory** /-káytəri/ *adj* —**reifier** /reé i fī ər/ *n*

Reigate /rīg ayt/ town in SE England. Population: 21,800 (1994).

reign /rayn/ *n* **1 PERIOD OF RULE** the period of time during which somebody, especially a king or queen, rules a nation **2 CONTROL OR INFLUENCE** the fact of being the dominant or controlling power or factor in something, or the period of time during which this dominance persists ■ *vi* **1 RULE A NATION** to exercise sovereign power or a controlling influence over something, especially to rule a country as its king or queen **2 BE TITULAR SOVEREIGN** to hold a royal title and be head of state while possessing only limited powers, as in a constitutional monarchy **3 BE MOST IMPORTANT FEATURE** to be the main or most noticeable feature of a situation, place, or period of time ○ *For a while, silence reigned.* [13C. Via Old French *reignier* < Latin *regnare* 'be king' < *regnum* 'kingship'.]

SPELLCHECK See ***rain***

reign of terror *n* a time when systematic violence is used by a government, individual, or group to intimidate other people and obtain or maintain dominance over them

Reign of Terror *n* the period of the French Revolution between September 1793 and July 1794, during which thousands of people were executed as enemies of the revolution

reiki /ráy ki/ *n* a treatment in alternative medicine in which healing energy is channelled from the practitioner to the patient to enhance energy and reduce stress, pain, and fatigue [Late 20C. < Japanese, 'universal life force energy'.]

reimagine /reé i májjin/ (**-ines, -ining, -ined**) *vt* **1** to recreate something, or plan to recreate something, in a fundamentally different way ○ *to reimagine the Shakespearean corpus for television* **2** to create a new and improved image or lifestyle for yourself

reimburse /reé im búrss/ (**-burses, -bursing, -bursed**) *vt* to pay somebody back money spent for an official or approved reason or taken as a loan, or give somebody money as compensation for loss or damage [Early 17C. < obsolete *imburse* 'pay, put in a purse' < Old French *borse* 'purse' < medieval Latin *bursa*.] —**reimbursable** *adj* —**reimbursement** *n* —**reimburser** *n*

reimport *vt* /reé im páwrt/ **IMPORT GOODS MADE FROM EXPORTED MATERIALS** to bring back into a country finished goods made from raw materials that were originally exported from that country ■ *n* /ree impawrt/ **1 IMPORTING OF GOODS USING EXPORTED MATERIALS** the business of bringing into a country goods made from raw materials originally exported from it **2 REIMPORTED ITEM** something that has been reimported —**reimportation** /reé im pawr táysh'n/ *n*

reimpression /reé im présh'n/ *n* a reprint of a book without any changes in the text

Reims /reemz/, **Rheims** city in NE France. Population: 187,206 (1999).

rein /rayn/ *n* (*often plural*) **1 STRAP FOR CONTROLLING HORSE** a strap, or either half of a strap, by which a horse is controlled by its rider or by the driver of a coach or cart it is pulling **2 EXERCISE OF POWER** any means of guiding, controlling, or restraining somebody or something ■ **reins** *npl* **STRAP FOR GUIDING CHILD** a harness that fits around the body of a very young child, with straps attached by means of which the child can be controlled and guided, especially when walking out ■ *vt* **CONTROL** to guide, control, or restrain somebody or something [13C. < Old French *rene, resne*.] —**reinless** *adj* ◇ **give (free) rein to somebody** *or* **something** to allow somebody or something complete freedom, imposing no restraints or limitations ◇ **have** *or* **keep a (tight) rein on somebody** *or* **something** to maintain strict control over somebody or something

SPELLCHECK See ***rain***

rein back *vt* to subject something or somebody to stricter control, often to reduce the amount of something or restrict somebody's freedom of action

rein in *v* **1** *vti* to make a horse stop or slow down by pulling on the reins **2** *vt* to bring somebody or something under control

reincarnate *vt* /ree ín kaar nayt, reé in kaár-/ (**-nates, -nating, -nated**) **1 GIVE NEW BIRTH** in some systems of belief, to return somebody to Earth to live another life in a different body (*often passive*) **2 PUT INTO NEW FORM** to present something again in a new form after it has been abandoned or discontinued ■ *adj* /reé in kaárnət, -nayt/ **1 REBORN** in some systems of belief, returned to Earth in a new body after death **2 REPACKAGED** embodied or presented in a new form

reincarnation /reé in kaar náysh'n/ *n* **1 REBIRTH OF SOUL** in some systems of belief, the cyclical return of a soul to live another life in a new body **2 BODY IN WHICH SOMEBODY IS REBORN** in some systems of belief, a person or animal in whose body somebody's soul is born again after he, she, or it has died **3 APPEARANCE IN NEW GUISE** a reappearance of something in a new form —**reincarnationism** *n* —**reincarnationist** *n*

reincorporate /reé in káwrpə rayt/ (**-rates, -rating, -rated**) *vt* **1 REJOIN ONE THING TO ANOTHER** to unite or combine one thing with another, or include one thing within something else, for a second or subsequent time **2 MERGE THINGS AGAIN** to merge or combine one thing with another so as to form a united whole, for a second or subsequent time **3 INCORPORATE FIRM AGAIN** to give a business the legal form of a corporation again —**reincorporation** /reé inkawrpə ráysh'n/ *n*

reindeer /ráyn deer/ (*plural* **-deer** *or* **-deers**) *n* a large deer with large branched antlers in both males and females. Native to: northern and Arctic regions of Europe, Asia, and North America. *Rangifer tarandus*. [14C. < Old Norse *hreinn* 'reindeer' + *dýr* 'animal'.]

Reindeer Lake /ráyn deer-/ lake in W Canada, on the Saskatchewan-Manitoba border. Area: 6,651 sq. km/2,568 sq. mi.

reindeer moss, reindeer lichen *n* a grey lichen that grows in large, erect, and branching tufts and provides food for reindeer and other animals. Native to: subarctic and Arctic regions. *Cladonia rangiferia*.

reindustrialize /reé in dústri ə līz/ (**-izes, -izing, -ized**), **reindustrialise** (**-ises, -ising, -ised**) *vti* to undergo a process of renewal, usually involving government help in the modernization of factories and equipment, or subject an industry or industrial society to such a process —**reindustrialization** /reé in dustri ə lī záysh'n/ *n*

reinfect /reé in fékt/ *vt* to cause somebody or something to become infected again —**reinfection** *n*

reinforce /reé in fáwrss/ (**-forces, -forcing, -forced**), **re-enforce** (**re-enforces, re-enforcing, re-enforced**) *vt* **1 STRENGTHEN** to make something stronger by providing additional external support or internal stiffening for it **2 GIVE SOMETHING SUPPORT** to give additional strength, force, or conviction to something such as an idea, opinion, or feeling, e.g. by providing further evidence to support it **3 STRENGTHEN MILITARY FORCE** to make a military force stronger by providing it with more troops or weapons **4 INFLUENCE BEHAVIOUR BY REWARD OR PUNISHMENT** to reward a particular action or type of behaviour to increase the probability that it will be repeated or punish an action in order to discourage it [15C. < ENFORCE, probably after Italian *rinforzare*.] —**reinforceable** *adj*

reinforced concrete *n* concrete made with metal wire or rods embedded in it to increase its strength

reinforced plastic *n* plastic with carbon or similar fibres embedded in it to make it stronger

reinforcement /reé in fáwrssmənt/ *n* **1 ADDED SUPPORT** the addition of strengthening or supporting material to make something stronger or more durable **2 SOMETHING ADDED TO INCREASE STRENGTH** something that is added to strengthen or support something else **3 REWARD OR PUN-**

ISHMENT the rewarding (**positive reinforcement**) or punishing (**negative reinforcement**) of particular actions, especially in an experimental situation, for the purpose of changing a subject's behaviour ■ **reinforcements** *npl* **ADDITIONAL TROOPS OR WEAPONS** additional troops, police, or weapons provided to make an existing force stronger

reinforcer /rée in fáwrssər/ *n* in behavioural psychology, a reward or stimulus used to encourage a particular action in order to increase the probability that it will be repeated

Reinga, Cape /ri ángə/ promontory at the northwestern tip of the North Island, New Zealand

Reinhardt /rín haart/, **Django** (1910–53) Belgian jazz musician. Born **Jean Baptiste Reinhardt**

Reinhardt, Max (1873–1943) Austrian-born US theatre director. Born **Max Goldmann**

reinsert /rée in súrt/ *vt* to put something back into the place where it had previously been inserted —**reinsertion** *n*

reinstall /rée in stáwl/ *vt* to install somebody or something again or in a different position —**reinstallation** /rée instə láysh'n/ *n*

reinstate /rée in stáyt/ (**-states, -stating, -stated**) *vt* **1** to give somebody back a job or position of influence that he or she once had and from which he or she was dismissed or deposed **2** to bring something back into use or force again after it has been out of use —**reinstatement** *n* —**reinstator** *n*

reinsure /rée in shoór, -sháwr/ (**-sures, -suring, -sured**) *vt* to insure something again, especially to obtain, as an insurer, additional cover from another insurer for a risk that a customer has been insured against —**reinsurance** *n* —**reinsurer** *n*

reintegrate /ree ínti grayt/ (**-grates, -grating, -grated**) *vt* **1** to bring somebody or something back into a group or a larger entity after a period of exclusion from it **2** to restore something to a state of wholeness or unity (*formal*) —**reintegration** /ree ínti gráysh'n/ *n*

reinterpret /rée in túrprit/ *vt* to interpret something again or in a different way, especially to find a new and different meaning in something —**reinterpretation** /rée in túrpri táysh'n/ *n*

reintroduce /rée intrə dyoóss/ (**-duces, -ducing, -duced**) *vt* **1 BRING OR TAKE BACK** to bring or take somebody or something back to a place where he, she, or it used to be common **2 BRING BACK FORMER SPECIES** to bring a species back into an area it had formerly inhabited ○ *They planned to reintroduce wild boar to the forests.* **3 BRING SOMETHING BACK INTO EFFECT** to bring something back into effect again ○ *They reintroduced tax relief on mortgages.* **4 INTRODUCE SOMETHING AGAIN** to reinstate something, e.g. a law or punishment **5 PUT ANIMAL BACK IN WILD** to introduce an animal or plant into its former habitat —**reintroduction** /rée intrə dúksh'n/ *n*

reinvent /rée in vént/ *vt* **1** to invent something again, or bring something back into existence, use, or popularity after a period of neglect or obscurity **2** to change radically the appearance, form, or presentation of something or somebody —**reinvention** *n*

reinvest /rée in vést/ *vti* **1** to invest money again, especially to buy more shares with the income made on a previous investment **2** to put income back into a business instead of distributing it as profit —**reinvestment** *n*

reinvestigate /rée in vésti gayt/ (**-gates, -gating, -gated**) *vti* to investigate something again or conduct an inquiry again —**reinvestigation** /rée in vesti gáysh'n/ *n*

reinvigorate /rée in víggə rayt/ (**-rates, -rating, -rated**) *vt* to imbue a person, organization, or idea with new strength, energy, dynamism or appeal —**reinvigoration** /rée in víggə ráysh'n/ *n* —**reinvigorator** *n*

reis plural of **real**[2]

reissue /ree íssyoo, -íshoo/ *vt* (**-sues, -suing, -sued**) to produce, distribute, or make something available again, especially something such as a book or recording, sometimes in a different form ■ *n* something, especially a book or recording, that is reissued

reiterate /ree ítti rayt/ (**-ates, -ating, -ated**) *vt* to say or do something again, once or several times, sometimes in a tiresome way —**reiterant** *adj* —**reiteration** /ree íttə ráysh'n/ *n* —**reiterative** /ree íttərativ, -raytiv/ *adj* —**reiteratively** *adv* —**reiterator** /ree íttə raytər/ *n*

USAGE The use of *again, once more, yet again,* and other such expressions with ***reiterate***, whose meaning includes the sense of 'again', is unnecessary and to be avoided.

Reiter's syndrome /rítərz-/, **Reiter's disease** *n* a disease that begins as an infection in genetically predisposed people and is characterized by recurring bouts of arthritis, conjunctivitis, and urethritis [Early 20C. After Hans *Reiter* (1881–1969), German bacteriologist.]

Reith /reeth/, **John, 1st Baron** (1889–1971) British broadcasting executive

reject *vt* /ri jékt/ **1 NOT ACCEPT** to refuse to accept, agree to, believe in, or make use of something e.g. because it is not good enough or not the right thing **2 TURN SOMEBODY DOWN** to decide not to give somebody something asked or applied for, e.g. a job or membership of an organization **3 BE UNKIND TO** to behave in an unkind and unfriendly way towards somebody who expects, or has a right to expect, love, kindness, and friendship **4 NOT KEEP** to put something aside or throw it away **5 BRING UP FOOD** to be unable to keep food down and vomit it up again **6 NOT ACCEPT TRANSPLANT** to fail to accept foreign tissue or an organ transplant because of immunological incompatibility ■ *n* /rée jekt/ **SOMETHING OR SOMEBODY NOT WANTED** somebody who or something that is refused as not meeting a required standard or is otherwise unsuitable [15C. < Latin *reject-*, past participle of *rejicere* 'throw back' < *jacere* 'to throw'.] —**rejectable** *adj* —**rejecter** *n* —**rejective** *adj* —**rejector** /ri jéktər/ *n*

rejection /ri jéksh'n/ *n* **1** the rejecting of something or somebody, or the fact of being rejected **2** the destruction by immune mechanisms of transplanted tissue or a transplanted organ from another individual

rejectionist /ri jéksh'nist/ *n* a person who refuses to accept a policy, proposal, or plan that others have agreed to

rejection slip *n* an official note stating that something has been rejected, e.g. a book submitted to a publisher or a painting submitted for exhibition

rejig /ree jíg/ (**-jigs, -jigging, -jigged**) *vt* **1** to alter, rearrange, or readjust something, or set it up differently, sometimes with the intention of deceiving a purchaser or user (*informal*) US term **rejigger 2** to re-equip a factory so that it can do a different kind of work

rejigger /ree jíggər/ *vt US* = **rejig** *v.* 1

rejoice /ri jóyss/ (**-joices, -joicing, -joiced**) *vi* to feel very happy or show great happiness about something (*literary*) [14C. < Old French *rejoir* 'be most joyful' < Latin *gaudere* 'rejoice'.] —**rejoicer** *n* —**rejoicing** *n* —**rejoicingly** *adv*

rejoice in *vt* to be lucky enough to have or own something (*often used ironically*)

rejoin[1] /ree jóyn/ *vti* **1 RETURN TO SOMEBODY AFTER BEING APART** to meet up again with somebody, or go back to somebody or something, after a usually brief period of being away or apart **2 BECOME MEMBER AGAIN** to become a member again of an organization or group you formerly belonged to **3 JOIN TOGETHER AGAIN** to join two things together again, or become joined together or merged with something again [< RE- + JOIN]

rejoin[2] /ri jóyn/ *v* **1** *vti* to say something in reply, especially to reply with a sharp, critical, angry, defensive, or clever remark (*formal*) **2** *vi* to respond to a plaintiff's reply or replication [15C. < French *rejoign-*, stem of *rejoindre* 'join again' < *joindre* 'to join'.]

rejoinder /ri jóyndər/ *n* **1** a reply to something said, especially one that is sharp, critical, angry, defensive, or clever (*formal*) **2** the answer that a defendant makes during pleading to the plaintiff's reply or replication [15C. Via Anglo-Norman < Old French.]

SYNONYMS See ***answer***.

rejuvenate /ri joóvi nayt/ (**-nates, -nating, -nated**) *vt* **1** to make somebody become, feel, or appear young again **2** to restore something to its condition when new, or make it more vigorous, dynamic, and effective [Early 19C. < RE- + Latin *juvenis* 'young'.] —**rejuvenation** /ri joóvi náysh'n/ *n* —**rejuvenative** /ri joóvinətiv, -aytiv/ *adj* —**rejuvenator** /ri joóvi naytər/ *n*

rejuvenesce /ri joóvə néss/ (**-nesces, -nescing, -nesced**) *vti* to become, or make somebody feel or look, young again (*formal*) [Late 19C. < late Latin *rejuvenescere* < Latin *juvenis* 'young'.] —**rejuvenescence** *n* —**rejuvenescent** *adj*

ϟ**rekey** /ree kée/ *vt* to re-enter lost text or data into a computer, or input text or data in a different form, using a keyboard

rekindle /ree kínd'l/ (**-dles, -dling, -dled**) *vt* **1** to set a fire burning again **2** to revive or renew something, e.g. a feeling or interest

rel. *abbr* **1** relating **2** relative **3** relatively **4** released **5** religion **6** religious

relapse *vi* /ri láps/ (**-lapses, -lapsing, -lapsed**) **1 GO INTO FORMER STATE** to fall back into a former mood, state, or way of life, especially a bad or undesirable one, after coming out of it for a while **2 BECOME ILL AFTER RECOVERY** to become ill again after seeming to have made a recovery ■ *n* /ri láps, rée laps/ **1 ACT OF RETURNING TO PREVIOUS CONDITION** a return to a former mood, state, or way of life, especially a bad or undesirable one, after coming out of it for a while **2 WORSENING OF HEALTH** a sudden worsening in the condition of a patient who was ill but who seemed to have made a recovery from the illness [15C. < Latin *relaps-*, past participle of *relabi* 'slip again' < *labi* 'to slip'.] —**relapser** *n*

relapsing fever *n* an infectious disease, characterized by chills and recurring fever, caused by a bacterium transmitted to people by ticks and lice

relate /ri láyt/ (**-lates, -lating, -lated**) *v* **1** *vi* **HAVE A CONNECTION WITH** to have a significant connection with or bearing on something ○ *How does this story relate to our conversation?* **2** *vt* **CONNECT PEOPLE OR THINGS** to find or show a connection between two or more people or things **3** *vi* **BE RELEVANT TO** to concern, involve, or apply to somebody or something specifically ○ *These regulations relate only to imported goods.* **4** ⚠ *vi* **FORM FRIENDLY ASSOCIATION** to have a friendly relationship with or friendly feelings towards somebody, based on an understanding of the person or on shared views or concerns. **5** *vi* **RESPOND TO** to understand and respond favourably to something, or feel that it has a personal meaning or relevance (*informal*) ○ *I just can't seem to relate to the cynicism of that generation.* **6** *vt* **TELL OR DESCRIBE** to tell a story or describe an event [15C. < French *relater* 'to report' < Latin *relatus*, past participle of *referre* 'carry back'.] —**relatable** *adj* —**relater** *n*

USAGE The use of ***relate*** without a prepositional phrase in the context of personal dealings between people is much used in the language of sociology but in general use is sometimes regarded as jargon, as in *Children who haven't learned to relate tend to be inadequately socialized.* A clearer way to express this would be *Children who haven't learned to relate to their peers....*

related /ri láytid/ *adj* **1 ASSOCIATED** connected by similarities or a common source **2 BELONGING TO THE SAME FAMILY** belonging to the same family by birth or through adoption or marriage **3 HAVING CLOSE HARMONIC CONNECTION** describes a musical key or chord that, harmonically speaking, is closely connected with another, e.g. by having particular notes in common with it —**relatedly** *adv* —**relatedness** *n*

relation /ri láysh'n/ *n* **1 CONNECTION BETWEEN THINGS** a meaningful connection or association between two or more things, e.g. one based on the similarity or relevance of one thing to another **2 MEMBER OF FAMILY** a member of the same family as somebody else, by birth or through adoption or marriage **3 CONNECTION BY FAMILY** connection by birth, adoption, or marriage **4 NARRATION** the narration of a story or description of something that has happened, or what is conveyed in the narration or description (*formal*) **5 TAKING OF SOMETHING AS DONE EARLIER** a procedure whereby an act done at a particular time is, for legal purposes, deemed to have been done at an earlier time **6 SHARED PROPERTY OF ASSOCIATION** a property of association, e.g. 'greater than' or 'less than', shared by ordered pairs of terms or objects ■ *npl* **1 relations CONTACTS BETWEEN GROUPS OR PEOPLE** contacts or dealings between two or more people or groups **2 SEXUAL ACTS** sexual activities carried out by people (*used euphemistically*) ◇ **in** *or* **with relation to** with reference or regard to, or in comparison with something

ϟ**relational** /ri láysh'nəl/ *adj* **1 INVOLVING A RELATIONSHIP** involving or expressing a relationship **2 CONVEYING SYNTACTIC RELATION** expressing or relating to a syntactic relation between elements in a phrase or sentence ○ *Prepositions are relational words.* **3 OF ORGANIZATION OF DATABASE** describes a way of organizing and presenting information in a database so that the user perceives it as a set of tables —**relationally** *adv*

relational grammar *n* a theory of descriptive grammar in which syntactic relationships, e.g. subject and object, are used to define grammatical processes rather than syntactic structures

relationship /ri láysh'nship/ *n* **1** CONNECTION a significant connection or similarity between two or more things, or the state of being related to something else **2** BEHAVIOUR OR FEELINGS TOWARDS SOMEBODY ELSE the connection between two or more people or groups and their involvement with each other, especially as regards how they behave and feel towards each other and communicate or cooperate **3** FRIENDSHIP an emotionally close friendship, especially one involving sexual relations **4** CONNECTION BY FAMILY the way in which two or more people are related by birth, adoption, or marriage, or the fact of being related by birth, adoption, or marriage **5** LOGIC, MATH = **relation** *n.* **6**

relative /réllətiv/ *adj* **1** COMPARATIVE measured or considered in comparison with each other or with something else ○ *discussing the relative merits of various methods of transport* **2** CHANGING WITH CIRCUMSTANCES not permanently fixed, but having a meaning or value that can only be established in relation to something else and will change according to circumstances or context ○ *'Big' and 'small' are relative terms.* **3** DEPENDENT ON depending on or in proportion to something else **4** CONNECTED WITH connected with or referring to something **5** REFERRING TO PREVIOUSLY USED WORD describes words, especially pronouns (**relative pronouns**) or clauses (**relative clauses**), that refer to another word previously used in the same sentence **6** HAVING IDENTICAL KEY SIGNATURES describes a musical key that has the same key signature as another, usually a minor key with the same sharps and flats as a major key, or vice versa ■ *n* **1** MEMBER OF FAMILY a member of the same family by birth, marriage, or adoption **2** THING RELATED TO SOMETHING ELSE one thing that is related to something else, especially a species that has developed from the same origin as another species **3** RELATIVE WORD a relative word, especially a pronoun, or a relative clause —**relativeness** *n*

relative atomic mass *n* (*symbol* A_r) the ratio of the average mass per atom of an element to one twelfth of the mass of a carbon-12 atom

relative clause *n* a clause that refers to and provides additional information about a preceding noun or pronoun, often beginning with a relative pronoun such as 'who','which', or 'that'

relative density (*plural* **relative densities**) *n* (*symbol* **d**) the ratio of the density of a substance to the density of a standard substance at the same temperature and pressure. For liquids and solids the standard substance is usually water, for gases, air.

relative humidity *n* the ratio of the amount of water vapour in the air at a given temperature to the maximum amount air can hold at the same temperature, expressed as a percentage

relatively /réllətivli/ *adv* in comparison with other things ○ *a relatively cool day, given the summer weather*

relative permittivity *n* (*symbol* ε_r) a measure of the resistance of a substance to an applied electric field equivalent to the ratio of the permittivity of a substance divided by that of free space

relative pitch *n* **1** the pitch of a tone, determined by its position in a scale with respect to other tones **2** the ability to identify or produce a tone by mentally comparing it to another tone recently heard

relative pronoun *n* a pronoun such as 'that','which', or 'who' that refers to a previously used noun and introduces a relative clause

relativise *vti* = **relativize**

relativism /réllətivizəm/ *n* the belief that concepts such as right and wrong, goodness and badness, or truth and falsehood are not absolute but change from culture to culture and situation to situation —**relativist** *n*

relativistic /rélləti vístik/ *adj* **1** MOVING CLOSE TO SPEED OF LIGHT moving at a velocity approaching the speed of light, the point at which certain properties such as mass act in accordance with the theory of relativity **2** RELATING TO RELATIVITY relating to or characterized by relativity **3** RELATING TO RELATIVISM involving or characterized by relativism —**relativistically** *adv*

relativity /rélla tívvəti/ (*plural* **-ties**) *n* **1** EQUIVALENCE OF MASS AND ENERGY the first of Einstein's two theories describing the relationship of matter, time, and space, showing that mass and energy are equivalent, and that mass, length, and time change with velocity **2** THEORY OF GRAVITATION AND ACCELERATION the principle put forward in the second of Einstein's two theories extending the principles of the first to gravitation and phenomena related to acceleration **3** DEPENDENCE ON CONTEXTUALLY VARIABLE FACTOR dependence on a factor that varies according to context **4** FACT OF BEING RELATIVE the fact or state of being relative to something else

QUICK FACTS ON... **RELATIVITY**

Key elements: development of theories that relate matter, energy, space, time, and gravity

Key dates: 1887 Michelson and Morley's experiment shows that light travels at a uniform speed and that 'ether' does not exist; 1889 Fitzgerald introduces the concept of space contraction, also independently developed by Lorentz; 1902 Lorentz and Zeeman win the Nobel Prize for the theory of electromagnetic radiation; 1905 Einstein proposes his special theory of relativity; 1915 Einstein expands his first theory to include gravitational and accelerative effects, also known as the general theory of relativity; 1916 Einstein proposes that the universe is curved due to the effects of gravitation; 1919 Eddington and colleagues confirm deflection of starlight passing near the Sun during a total solar eclipse; 1929 Hubble reports that the distant galaxies are receding from the Milky Way system, in which the Earth is located

Key developments: nuclear physics, string theory, black hole theory, big bang theory, gravitational waves

relativize /rélləti vīz/ (**-izes, -izing, -ized**), **relativise** (**-ises, -ising, -ised**) *vti* to make one thing relative to something else, or regard one thing as relative to something else

relator /ri láytər/ *n* **1** somebody who tells a story or gives an account of something **2** a provider of information used by the attorney general to bring a court action

relaunch *vt* /ree láwnch/ **1** INTRODUCE SOMETHING INTO MARKET AGAIN to introduce something such as a company, product, or service into the market again, sometimes in a new form **2** START SOMETHING GOING AGAIN to put something in motion or embark on something again ■ *n* /rée lawnch/ REINTRODUCTION OF the act or process of relaunching something

relax /ri láks/ *v* **1** *vti* BECOME OR MAKE SOMETHING LOOSER to slacken something that is tensed or tight, e.g. a muscle or a grip on something, or become looser, less tense, or less tight **2** *vi* SPEND TIME DOING SOMETHING ENJOYABLE to spend time resting or doing things for pleasure, especially in contrast to or as a relief from the effort and stress of everyday life **3** *vti* MAKE OR BECOME LESS TENSE to become, or make somebody or something, less anxious, hostile, defensive, or formal **4** *vti* MAKE OR BECOME LESS STRICT to make something such as a rule less strict or less severe, or become less strict **5** *vti* MAKE OR BECOME LESS INTENSE to become, or make something, less intense and concentrated **6** *vt* STRAIGHTEN HAIR to weaken or remove the curl from hair, usually by chemical means [14C. < Latin *relaxare* 'loosen' < *laxus* 'loose'.] —**relaxable** *adj* —**relaxer** *n* —**relaxing** *adj*

relaxant /ri láks'nt/ *n* a drug that reduces tension and strain, particularly in muscles ■ *adj* causing something such as a muscle to become less tense

relaxation /rée lak sáysh'n/ *n* **1** ENJOYABLE ACTIVITY a form of activity that provides a change and relief from effort, work, or tension, and gives pleasure **2** LOOSENING the process of becoming or of making something less firm, rigid, or tight **3** LESSENING OF SEVERITY a lessening of the strictness or severity of regulations, restrictions, or controls **4** REDUCTION IN INTENSITY a lessening or weakening of something that was previously concentrated or intense **5** RETURN OF SYSTEM TO EQUILIBRIUM the return of a system to equilibrium after it has been displaced or changed **6** WAY OF SOLVING EQUATIONS a way of solving equations using a series of approximate solutions, each of which reduces the number of errors contained in the previous one, until the errors fall within acceptable limits

relaxed /ri lákst/ *adj* **1** WITHOUT STRAIN OR TENSION under no strain or tension, and not exerting much strain or force on anything else **2** NOT FEELING ANXIOUS OR WORRIED feeling no anxiety, tension, pressure, or sense of threat **3** ENCOURAGING INFORMALITY encouraging informality and casual unhurried behaviour —**relaxedly** /ri láksidli/ *adv* —**relaxedness** *n*

relaxin /ri láksin/ *n* a polypeptide hormone that relaxes the pelvic ligaments of female mammals during pregnancy and is produced by the corpus luteum

relay *n* /rée lay/ **1** PASSING OF SOMETHING TO the passing on of something, especially a message or information received, to somebody else, or the process of being passed on **2** RELAY RACE a relay race (*informal*) **3** SECTION OF RELAY RACE a section or lap of a relay race, run or swum by an individual athlete **4** REPLACEMENT TEAM one of two or more teams of people or animals that relieve or replace each other in turn, e.g. as the previous team tires **5** DEVICE THAT REGULATES ANOTHER an electronic or electromechanical switching device, typically operated by a low voltage, that controls a higher-voltage circuit and switches it on or off **6** APPARATUS THAT RECEIVES AND TRANSMITS SIGNALS an apparatus consisting of a receiver and a transmitter, used to receive and retransmit signals **7** SIGNAL a message or broadcast passed on by an apparatus that receives and retransmits signals ■ *vt* /ri láy/ **1** PASS SOMETHING ON TO to pass information or a message on to somebody **2** RETRANSMIT SIGNAL to receive and retransmit a signal **3** REPLACE TEAM WITH FRESH PEOPLE to replace or relieve a team, squad, or crew with a new one **4** ARRANGE PEOPLE INTO TEAMS to organize somebody or something, especially workers, into relays [14C. < Old French *relayer* 'exchange tired horses' < Latin *relaxare* 'loosen'.]

re-lay /ree láy/ (**re-lays** /ree láyd/, **re-laying, re-laid**) *vt* to lay something such as a carpet again [< RE- + LAY[1]]

relay race *n* a race between teams of competitors in which each member of a team runs or swims only part of the total distance to be covered

release /ri léess/ *vt* (**-leases, -leasing, -leased**) **1** LET SOMEBODY OR SOMETHING GO to set free a person or animal who is imprisoned, trapped, or confined in some way **2** STOP CLUTCHING to stop gripping or holding something **3** LET SOMETHING OUT to let out something that has been contained or confined within something or pent up or latent inside somebody **4** FREE SOMEBODY FROM OBLIGATION to make somebody free of a debt, obligation, promise, or task **5** *US* FIRE EMPLOYEE to dismiss somebody from a job or position (*formal; used euphemistically*) **6** MAKE SOMETHING AVAILABLE to make something available, e.g. by putting it on sale, distributing it to the press or public, or allowing access to it **7** OPERATE CATCH TO LET MECHANISM WORK to take the tension off a mechanism such as a spring, brake, or catch and so allow something to move, open, or operate **8** RELINQUISH to relinquish something, e.g. a right or claim, to another party ■ *n* **1** LIBERATION the act of setting somebody or something free, or the fact of being freed, from imprisonment, restraint, an obligation, or anything burdensome and oppressive **2** AUTHORIZATION FOR FREEDOM a document or message stating that somebody is to be set free **3** ACT OF MAKING SOMETHING AVAILABLE the act of making something available for the first time, or the fact of being made available in this way ○ *His latest film is expected to be on general release in the autumn.* **4** SOMETHING MADE AVAILABLE TO PUBLIC something such as a film, recording, or item of information that is made available to the public, put on show, or put on sale **5** EMISSION the emission of something such as heat or radioactivity from the place where it is generated into the atmosphere or the environment **6** CONTROL MECHANISM a mechanism, catch, or handle that is moved or pressed so that something it controls can be used or allowed to operate **7** OPERATING OF DEVICE the moving or pressing of a mechanism so that what it controls can be used or allowed to operate **8** LEAVE OF ABSENCE leave of absence from a place, especially the workplace, or the granting of leave of absence, to enable somebody to do something else, e.g. attend an educational course **9** RELINQUISHING OF CLAIM the relinquishment of a right or claim to another party **10** DOCUMENT CONFIRMING SURRENDER OF a document stating that somebody has surrendered something, e.g. a claim or right [13C. Via Old French *relaisser* 'let go' < Latin *relaxare* 'loosen'.] —**releasability** /ri léessə bílləti/ *n* —**releasable** /ri léessəb'l/ *adj* —**releasably** *adv* —**releasee** /ri lee sée/ *n* —**releaser** *n*

re-lease /rée léess/ *vt* (**re-leases, re-leasing, re-leased, re-leased**) to lease something such as a flat again [< RE- + LEASE]

released time *n US* time given to somebody by an authority or manager to allow personal matters or interests to be attended to

release print *n* the version of a film released for distribution to commercial cinemas

releasing factor *n* a hormone produced by the hypothalamus that causes the pituitary gland to secrete other hormones

relegate /rélli gayt/ (**-gates, -gating, -gated**) *vt* 1 **DEMOTE** to move somebody or something to a less important position, category, or status 2 **TRANSFER TEAM TO LOWER DIVISION** to transfer a sports team from a higher to a lower division in a competition, usually as a result of its being one of the least successful teams in the higher division (*often passive*) 3 **HAND SOMETHING ON** to pass something on to somebody for the person to deal with it or provide information about it (*formal*) 4 **EXILE** to banish somebody from a country or community [15C. < Latin *relegat-*, past participle of *relegare* 'send away, refer' < *legare* 'send as an envoy, bequeath'.] —**relegation** /rélli gáysh'n/ *n*

~~releive~~ incorrect spelling of **relieve**

relent /ri lént/ *vi* 1 to become more sympathetic or amenable and do something previously ruled out or allow something previously forbidden 2 to slacken or become less intense ○ *At last my headache relented.* [14C. < RE- + Latin *lentare* 'bend, soften' < *lentus* 'flexible'.]

relentless /ri léntləss/ *adj* 1 never slackening, but continuing always at the same intense, demanding, or punishing level 2 pursuing, attacking, or opposing somebody or something persistently and without mercy —**relentlessly** *adv* —**relentlessness** *n*

relevant /rélləvənt/ *adj* 1 having some sensible or logical connection with something else, e.g. a matter being discussed or investigated 2 having some bearing on or importance for real-world issues, present-day events, or the current state of society 3 LING = **distinctive** *adj.* 2 [Early 16C. < medieval Latin *relevant-*, present participle of Latin *relevare* 'relieve', (later, 'take possession of').] —**relevantly** *adv* —**relevance** *n*

~~relevent~~ incorrect spelling of **relevant**

reliable /ri lī́ əb'l/ *adj* 1 able to be trusted to do what is expected or has been promised ○ *She is extremely reliable and a hard worker.* 2 able to be trusted to be accurate or correct or to provide a correct result ○ *I don't think that clock's very reliable.* —**reliability** /ri lī́ ə bílləti/ *n* —**reliableness** /ri lī́ əb'lnəss/ *n* —**reliably** *adv*

reliance /ri lī́ ənss/ *n* 1 **DEPENDENCE** dependence on another person or on, e.g. a service or a device, and the need for something that he, she, or it provides 2 **CONFIDENCE** trust or confidence in the eventual fulfilment of a promise or in the eventual success of a plan 3 **PRIMARY SUPPORT** somebody or something needed or depended on

reliant /ri lī́ ənt/ *adj* depending on or needing somebody or something —**reliantly** *adv*

relic /réllik/ *n* 1 **OLD THING SURVIVING FROM PAST** something that has survived from a long time ago, often a part of something old that has remained when the rest of it has decayed or been destroyed 2 **OLD CUSTOM** a tradition, practice, or rule that dates from some time in the past, especially one that is considered out of date or inappropriate at the present time 3 **KEEPSAKE** something that is kept for its interesting associations, e.g. with somebody famous or with a historic event 4 **SOMETHING FROM DEAD HOLY PERSON** something that is kept and venerated because it once belonged to a saint, martyr, or religious leader, especially a part of his or her body 5 **OFFENSIVE TERM** an offensive term that deliberately insults somebody's advanced age or somebody's or something's relevance to modern conditions (*insult*) [13C. Via Old French *relique* < Latin *reliquiae* 'remains' (particularly of a dead saint), plural of *reliquus* 'remaining'.]

relict /réllikt/ *n* 1 **SURVIVING SPECIES** a species of organism surviving long after the extinction of related species, or a once widespread natural population surviving only in isolated localities because of environmental changes 2 **REMNANT OF PRE-EXISTING FORMATION** a remnant of a pre-existing land or rock formation left behind after a destructive event has taken place 3 **MINERAL UNALTERED BY METAMORPHISM** a mineral that did not change when the host rock metamorphosed 4 **WIDOW** a widow (*archaic*) ■ *adj* **SURVIVING UNCHANGED** surviving in its original form when other related organisms have become extinct or its environment has changed completely [15C. < Latin *relictus* 'left behind' < *relinquere* 'relinquish'.]

reliction /ri líksh'n/ *n* the gradual withdrawal of water from land, leaving it permanently dry

relief /ri léef/ *n* 1 **FREEING OF SOMEBODY FROM ANXIETY** a release from anxiety or tension, or the feeling of release, lightness, and cheerfulness that accompanies this 2 **FACTOR THAT ENDS ANXIETY** a factor that ends a painful or stressful experience such as pain, hunger, or boredom 3 **AID TO THOSE IN NEED** public help in the form of money, food, clothing, shelter, or medicine, provided to people who are temporarily unable to care for themselves 4 **PAYMENT REDUCTION OR FINANCIAL HELP** a reduction somebody is entitled to in tax or other payments, or money given to him or her to help pay for something 5 **REPLACEMENT** a person who takes over a task or duty when a previous person completes his or her shift or spell of work, or one person who replaces another who is unable to work 6 **DIVERTING CONTRAST** a factor forming a contrast to the general character of something else, especially something that breaks the monotony or tension of a longer experience 7 **EXTRA TRANSPORT** a train, bus, or other public transport vehicle that is brought in to provide extra places for passengers when the regular, scheduled service is full 8 TRANSP = **bypass** *n.* 1 9 **FREEING FROM SIEGE** the freeing of a besieged town, castle, fort, or strategic position by soldiers belonging to the same side as those under siege 10 **PROMINENCE CAUSED BY CONTRAST** uniqueness or prominence caused by contrast ○ *to bring out the differences in clear relief* 11 **PROJECTION FROM SURFACE** the elevation of figures or shapes from a flat surface, as seen in sculpture, or their apparent elevation, as seen in painting 12 **WORK OF ART** a work of art with figures or shapes in relief 13 **ELEVATIONS OF LAND** the variations in height of a land surface and its being shaped into hills and valleys 14 **PRINTING PROCESS** a printing process such as engraving that uses raised surfaces to apply ink to the paper 15 **REDRESS AWARDED BY COURT** compensation or redress for a wrong or hardship, awarded to a party by a court 16 **PAYMENT TO LORD** a payment made to a feudal lord by the descendant of a tenant in order to inherit a fief [14C. < Old French, < *relever* (see RELIEVE).]

relief map *n* a map that shows variations in land height, usually by means of contour lines or different colours

relief road *n* TRANSP = **bypass** *n.* 1

relieve /ri léev/ (**-lieves, -lieving, -lieved**) *v* 1 *vti* **STOP SOMETHING UNPLEASANT** to end, lessen, or provide a temporary break from something unpleasant such as pain, hunger, tension, or boredom 2 *vt* **HELP** to provide help to people who are temporarily unable to care for themselves 3 *vt* **REPLACE** to replace somebody on a shift or at a job 4 *vt* **EASE SOMEBODY'S BURDEN** to remove something such as a burden or difficulty from the one on which it is imposed 5 *vt* **REMOVE SOMEBODY'S LOAD OR BURDEN** to take something from somebody, usually something that the person is carrying or wearing 6 *vt* **FIRE EMPLOYEE** to dismiss or suspend somebody from a job or position (*formal*) ○ *After the collision, the skipper was relieved of command.* 7 *vt* **SAVE SOMETHING FROM MILITARY SIEGE** to free a besieged town, castle, fort, or strategic field position 8 *vr* **URINATE** to empty the urinary bladder 9 *vt* **MAKE SOMETHING PROMINENT** to make something stand out by contrast (*formal*) [14C. < Old French *relever* < Latin *relevare* 'raise again, help', literally 'make light again' < *levis* 'light'.] —**relievable** *adj* —**reliever** *n*

relievo /ri lée vō/ (*plural* **-vos**), **rilievo** (*plural* **-vos**) *n* the elevation of figures or shapes from a flat surface, as seen in sculpture, or their apparent elevation, as seen in painting [Early 17C. < Italian *rilievo* < *rilevare* 'raise' < Latin *relevare* (see RELIEVE).]

relight /ree lī́t/ (**-lights, -lighting, -lighted** *or* **-lit** /-lít/) *vt* to light something such as a fire again

religion /ri líjjən/ *n* 1 **BELIEFS AND WORSHIP** people's beliefs and opinions concerning the existence, nature, and worship of God, a god, or gods, and divine involvement in the universe and human life 2 **PARTICULAR SYSTEM** a particular institutionalized or personal system of beliefs and practices relating to the divine 3 **PERSONAL BELIEFS OR VALUES** a set of strongly-held beliefs, values, and attitudes that somebody lives by 4 **OBSESSION** an object, practice, cause, or activity that somebody is completely devoted to or obsessed by ○ *The danger is that you start to make fitness a religion.* 5 **MONK'S OR NUN'S LIFE** life as a monk or a nun, especially in the Roman Catholic Church [12C. Via Anglo-Norman *religiun*, Old French *religion* < Latin *religion-* 'obligation, reverence'.] —**religionless** *adj* ◇ **get religion** 1 to become a believer or join a religious organization, and, usually, start to lead a life that follows its teachings (*informal*) 2 *US* to conform to the rules, regulations, customs, or expectations of somebody or something (*informal*)

religionism /ri líjjənizəm/ *n* excessive or affected religious enthusiasm —**religionist** *n*

religiose /ri líjji ōss/ *adj* excessively, sentimentally, or affectedly pious (*disapproving*) [Mid-19C. < Latin *religiosus*.] —**religiosely** *adv* —**religiosity** /-óssəti/ *n*

religious /ri líjjəss/ *adj* 1 **RELATING TO RELIGION** relating to belief in religion, the teaching of religion, or the practice of a religion ○ *religious freedom* 2 **BELIEVING IN HIGHER BEING** believing in, and showing devotion or reverence for, a deity or deities 3 **THOROUGH** very thorough or conscientious ○ *a religious attention to detail* 4 **BELONGING TO MONASTIC ORDER** describes Christians who have committed themselves to a monastic order ■ *n* (*plural* **-ious**) **MONK OR NUN** a member of a monastic order —**religiousness** *n*

religiously /ri líjjəssli/ *adv* 1 carefully and conscientiously 2 in a way that relates to religion or to a particular religion

~~religous~~ incorrect spelling of **religious**

relinquish /ri língkwish/ *vt* 1 **CEDE** to renounce or surrender something 2 **ABANDON** to give something up or put something aside 3 **LET SOMETHING GO** to let go of something physically [15C. < Old French *relinquiss-* < Latin *relinquere* 'leave behind' < *linquere* 'leave'.] —**relinquisher** *n* —**relinquishment** *n*

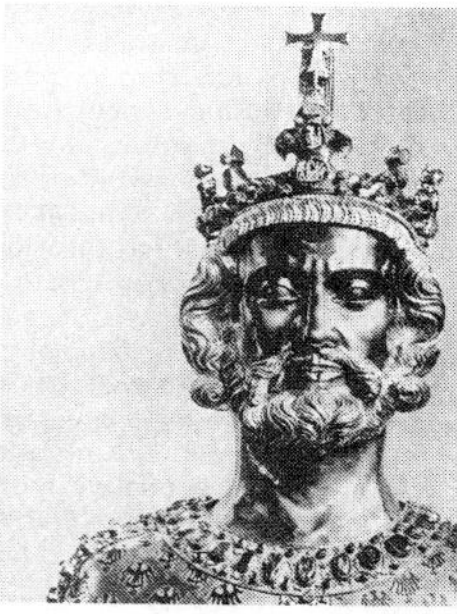

AKG London

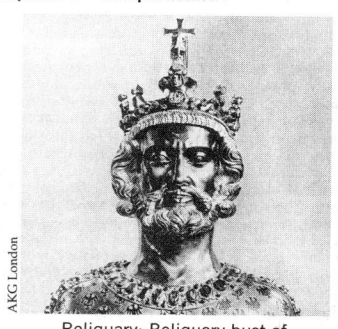

Reliquary: Reliquary bust of Charlemagne

reliquary /réllikwəri/ (*plural* **-ies**) *n* a container or shrine where relics, e.g. the remains of a saint, are kept

reliquiae /ri líkwi ee/ *npl* the remains of something, especially fossil remains of plants or animals [Mid-17C. < Latin (see RELIC).]

relish /réllish/ *vt* 1 **ENJOY** to enjoy or take great pleasure in an experience ○ *relished every minute of their trip* 2 **ENJOY EATING** to enjoy the taste of a particular food or drink ■ *n* 1 **ENJOYMENT** a liking or appreciation of food or of an experience ○ *a relish for Spanish food* 2 **SPICY SIDE DISH OR ACCOMPANIMENT** a spiced side dish or accompaniment to food, e.g. pickled or fresh vegetables with chilli 3 **STRONG TASTE** a pleasing sensation of strong taste or flavour 4 **INTEREST OR EXCITEMENT** interest or excitement, especially when it makes something more enjoyable ○ *The incident added relish to an otherwise dull weekend.* [Early 16C. < Old French *relais* 'remainder'.] —**relishable** *adj*

relit past tense, past participle of **relight**

relive /ree lív/ (**-lives, -living, -lived**) *vt* to experience something again, especially as a result of thinking about it

~~rellevant~~ incorrect spelling of **relevant**

rellies /rélliz/ *npl* somebody's relatives (*informal*) ○ *We'll be seeing all the rellies again at Christmas.* [Late 20C. Shortening.]

reload /ree lṓd/ *vti* to put a new load into something, e.g. film into a camera or fresh ammunition into a gun

relocate /rée lō káyt/ (**-cates, -cating, -cated**) *vti* to move or be moved to a new place on a long-term basis, especially to change the location of a business —**relocation** /réelōkáysh'n/ *n*

reluctance /ri lúktənss/ *n* 1 unwillingness or lack of enthusiasm 2 a measure of the resistance of a closed magnetic circuit to a magnetic flux

reluctant /ri lúktənt/ *adj* 1 feeling no willingness or enthusiasm to do something ○ *I am reluctant to drive in this weather.* 2 showing unwillingness to do something or cooperate ○ *a reluctant swimmer* [Mid-17C. < Latin *reluctant-*, present participle of *reluctari* 'struggle against' < *luctari* 'to struggle'.] —**reluctantly** *adv*

SYNONYMS See *unwilling*.

USAGE See *reticent*.

relume /ri lóom/ (**-lumes, -luming, -lumed**), **relumine** /ri lóomin/ (**-lumines, -lumining, -lumined**) *vt* to light or light something up again [Early 17C. < ILLUME.]

rely /ri lí/ (**-lies, -lying, -lied**) *vi* **1** to be dependent on somebody or something **2** to have faith or confidence in somebody or something [14C. < Old French *relier* < Latin *religare* 'tie back' < *ligare* 'bind'.]

rem /rem/ (*plural* **rem**) *n* a unit for measuring amounts of radiation, equal to the effect that one roentgen of X-rays or gamma-rays would produce in a human being. Full form **roentgen equivalent in man**

REM /rem, áar ee ém/ *abbr* rapid eye movement. ◊ **REM sleep**

remade past tense, past participle of **remake**

remain /ri máyn/ *v* **1** *vi* **STAY** to stay behind or wait somewhere **2** *vti* **CONTINUE IN A STATE** to continue in a particular state without changing **3** *vi* **BE LEFT** to be left after everything else has gone **4** *vi* **REQUIRE MORE WORK** to continue to need to be taken care of after everything else has been dealt with [14C. < Old French *remaindre*, *remanoir* < Latin *remanere* < *manere* 'to stay'.]

remainder /ri máyndər/ *n* **1 WHAT IS LEFT OF** the part of something that is left after other parts have gone or been used up **2 AMOUNT LEFT OVER AFTER DIVISION** the amount left over when a number or quantity cannot be divided exactly by another **3 UNSOLD BOOKS** the unsold copies of a book, sold by a publisher at a reduced price after demand has fallen off **4 INTEREST IN SOMEBODY ELSE'S ESTATE** an interest in an estate that passes to somebody only after a prior interest terminates, e.g. when the current holder of the estate dies ■ *vt* **SELL BOOK AT REDUCED PRICE** to sell copies of a book at a reduced price after demand has fallen off [14C. < Anglo-Norman variant of Old French *remaindre* (see REMAIN).]

remainderman /ri máyndər man/ (*plural* **-men** /-men/) *n* the person who is entitled to a particular estate once everything has been resolved

remaining /ri máyning/ *adj* still left or still existing

remains /ri máynz/ *npl* **1 WHAT IS LEFT** all that is left of something ○ *the remains of the barn after the fire* **2 CORPSE** a dead body, or what is left of a body **3 ANCIENT RUINS** the parts of something old that are still left ○ *the remains of ancient Roman baths* **4 DEAD AUTHOR'S UNPUBLISHED WRITINGS** all of an author's work that was still unpublished at the time of the author's death

remake *n* /rée mayk/ something that has been made again or differently, especially a new version of an old film ■ *vt* /ree máyk/ (**-makes, -making, -made** /-máyd/) to produce a remake of something

remand /ri máand/ *vt* **1 RETURN PRISONER TO CUSTODY** to return a prisoner or accused person to custody, or arrange for somebody to be released on bail when a court case is adjourned ○ *The judge ordered the prisoner to be remanded in custody.* **2 SEND SOMEBODY BACK** to send or order somebody back ■ *n* **RETURNING OF SOMEBODY UNTRIED TO PRISON** the return of a prisoner or accused person to custody, or the arrangement of bail for somebody, while waiting for trial [15C. < Old French *remander* < late Latin *remandare* 'send word back' < Latin *mandare* 'to command'.] —**remandment** *n*

remand centre *n* a place where accused people are detained while awaiting criminal trial

remand home *n* an institution to which juvenile offenders between the ages of 8 and 14 are remanded or sent for detention. US term **detention home**

remanence /rémmənənss/ *n* the magnetic inductance that remains in a substance after the magnetizing field has been removed [Mid-16C. < Latin *remanent-*, present participle of *remanere* (see REMAIN).] —**remanent** *adj*

remanent magnetism *n* magnetism shown by ferromagnetic minerals, which preserve the sense and direction of the Earth's magnetic field from the time of their formation

ϟ remark /ri máark/ *n* **1 CASUAL COMMENT** a casual or brief observation **2 ACT OF COMMENTING** the act of making a remark about something, or an occasion on which this takes place ○ *They consumed their meal without remark.* **3** COMPUT = **comment** *n.* 4 **4 ACT OF NOTICING** an act or instance of noticing something, especially something that deserves attention (*formal*) ○ *How could such a major change take place without remark?* ■ *v* **1** *vti* **COMMENT ON** to make a casual comment or observation about something **2** *vt* **OBSERVE** to notice or observe something (*formal*) [Late 16C. < French *remarquer* < *marquer* 'to mark'.] —**remarker** *n*

remarkable /ri máarkəb'l/ *adj* **1** worth noticing or commenting on **2** unusual or exceptional, and attracting attention because of this —**remarkableness** *n*

remarkably /ri máarkəbli/ *adv* **1** to an extent or degree that is remarkable **2** used to emphasize that something is worth noticing or commenting on ○ *Remarkably, no one was arrested.*

remarque /ri máark/ *n* **1** a mark in the margin of an engraved plate, made to indicate its stage of production and removed before final printing, or the plate with the mark itself **2** a proof of an engraving made from a plate with a remarque [Late 19C. < French, < *remarquer* (see REMARK).]

Remarque /ri máark/, **Erich Maria** (1898–1970) German-born US writer

remarry /ree márri/ (**-ries, -rying, -ried**) *vti* to marry somebody else after being widowed or divorced —**remarriage** /ree márrij/ *n*

remaster /ree máastər/ *vt* to make a new master copy of an earlier audio recording or film to improve its quality of reproduction

rematch /rée mach/ *n* a second or return contest between opponents ■ *vt* to arrange for opponents to meet in a second or return contest

Rembrandt van Rijn /rém brant von rín/ (1606–69) Dutch artist

REME /rée mee/ *abbr* Royal Electrical and Mechanical Engineers

remedial /ri méedi əl/ *adj* **1 ACTING AS REMEDY** acting as a remedy or solution to a particular problem **2 HELPING TO IMPROVE SKILLS** designed to help people with learning difficulties to improve their skills or knowledge, or relating to education designed to do this **3 INTENDED TO IMPROVE HEALTH** intended to cure or relieve the symptoms of somebody who is ill or has a physical disability ○ *remedial exercises* —**remedially** *adv*

remediation /ri méedi áysh'n/ *n* the use of remedial teaching or therapy to improve skills or health

remedy /rémmədi/ *n* (*plural* **-dies**) **1 TREATMENT FOR DISEASE** a medication or treatment that cures a disease or disorder or relieves its symptoms **2 HOMEOPATHIC TREATMENT** a substance prescribed by a homeopath, and taken in minute quantities **3 WAY OF PUTTING SOMETHING RIGHT** a means of setting something right or getting rid of something undesirable ○ *no easy remedy for society's ills* **4 LEGAL REDRESS** a legal means of enforcing a right or of providing redress **5 PERMITTED VARIATION IN COINS** the legally permitted variation from an established standard in the weight or quality of a coin ■ *vt* (**-dies, -dying, -died**) **1 CURE** to cure or relieve a disease or disorder **2 PUT RIGHT** to set something right, or get rid of something undesirable [13C. Via Anglo-Norman *remedie* < Latin *remedium* 'medicine'.] —**remediable** /ri méedi ab'l/ *adj* —**remediably** *adv*

remember /ri mémbər/ *v* **1** *vti* **RECALL SOMETHING FORGOTTEN** to recall something to mind or become aware of something that had been forgotten **2** *vti* **KEEP SOMETHING IN MEMORY** to retain an idea in the memory without forgetting it **3** *vt* **KEEP SOMEBODY IN MIND** to keep somebody in mind for attention or consideration **4** *vt* **GIVE SOMEBODY GIFT** to give somebody a gift, money, or a tip ○ *She always remembered him on his birthday.* **5** *vt* **SEND SOMEBODY'S GREETINGS** to mention somebody to somebody else as a greeting to yet another person ○ *Remember me to your Dad.* **6** *vr* **BECOME POLITE AGAIN** to resume behaving in a mannerly way after having briefly acted badly ○ *I was about to make a hurtful comment but I remembered myself just in time.* **7** *vt* **COMMEMORATE** to commemorate somebody or something, e.g. in a ceremony or funeral service [14C. Via Old French *remembrer* < late Latin *rememorari* < Latin *memor* 'mindful'.] —**rememberer** *n*

remembrance /ri mémbrənss/ *n* **1 REMEMBERING** the act or process of remembering people, things, or events **2 BEING REMEMBERED** the state of being remembered, or of remaining in people's minds ○ *We hold her name in fond remembrance.* **3 ACT OF HONOURING** the act of honouring the memory of a person or event ○ *a remembrance service* **4 SOMETHING REMEMBERED** something that is remembered **5 EXTENT OF MEMORY** the period of time over which memory extends **6 MEMENTO** something that reminds somebody of a thing, event, or another person **7 GREETING** a greeting, gift, or other expression of affection

LITERARY LINK ***Remembrance of Things Past***, a series of novels (1913–22) by French writer Marcel Proust. This remarkable meditation on time and memory describes the narrator's childhood encounters with his aristocratic neighbours and his subsequent introduction to Parisian society. A series of unconscious recollections triggers the realization that the past is not lost but can be retrieved by memory and preserved as art.

Remembrance Day *n* in Canada, a public holiday in remembrance of those who died in World Wars I and II and subsequent conflicts. Date: 11 November.

remembrancer /ri mémbrənssər/ *n* a person who reminds somebody else about something (*archaic*)

Remembrancer *n* **1** a British official of the Exchequer, the Queen's or King's Remembrancer, who collects debts owed to the Crown **2** the City Remembrancer, appointed by the Corporation of the City of London to represent its interests

Remembrance Sunday *n* the Sunday nearest to 11 November (**Armistice Day**), on which those who died in World Wars I and II and subsequent conflicts are remembered, especially in church

remex /rée meks/ (*plural* **remiges** /rémmi jeez/) *n* any flight feather of a bird's wing (*technical*) [Late 17C. < Latin, 'oarsman' < *remus* 'oar'.] —**remigial** /ri míjji əl/ *adj*

remind /ri mínd/ *vt* to cause a person to remember or think of something or somebody else ○ *Remind me to collect the dry-cleaning.* ○ *He reminds me of his grandfather.*

reminder /ri míndər/ *n* **1** something that is used to remind somebody about something, e.g. a letter or message ○ *If they don't settle the bill next week, send them a reminder.* **2** a person who or thing that reminds another of somebody or something else ○ *The monument is a reminder of their bravery.*

reminisce /rémmi níss/ (**-nisces, -niscing, -nisced**) *vi* to talk or write about events remembered from the past [Early 19C. Back-formation < REMINISCENCE.] —**reminiscer** *n*

reminiscence /rémmi níss'nss/ *n* **1 RECOLLECTION OF THE PAST** the recollection of past experiences or events in speech or writing, or the act of recalling the past **2 SOMETHING REMEMBERED** an experience or event remembered from the past **3 REMINDER** something that recalls or suggests something similar **4 IDEA FROM PLATO** the Platonic doctrine that anything we encounter is an imperfect recollection of an idea that our souls have encountered in a previous disembodied existence **5 ABILITY TO PERFORM TASK BETTER** the ability to perform a task or remember information better some time after it has been learnt than was possible immediately after it was learnt

reminiscent /rémmi níss'nt/ *adj* **1 LIKE SOMETHING OR SOMEBODY ELSE** suggesting similarities or comparisons with something or somebody else **2 SUGGESTING MEMORIES OF THE PAST** characterized by or containing recollections of the past ○ *scenes reminiscent of her childhood* **3 RECALLING THE PAST** given to reminiscing about the past [Mid-18C. < Latin, present participle of *reminisci* 'recollect'.] —**reminiscently** *adv*

remise /ri méez/ *n* in fencing, a further thrust made on the same lunge to follow up a first thrust that has missed ■ *vi* (**-mises, -mising, -mised**) to make a remise when a first thrust has missed [15C. < French, < Latin *remittere* 'send back'.]

remiss /ri míss/ *adj* careless or negligent about doing something that is expected [15C. < Latin *remissus*, past participle of *remittere* 'send back'.]

remissible /ri míssəb'l/ *adj* worthy of forgiveness —**remissibility** /ri míssə bíllәti/ *n*

remission /ri mísh'n/ *n* **1 SLOWING OF DISEASE** a lessening of the symptoms of a disease, or their temporary reduction or disappearance **2 REDUCTION IN A PRISON TERM** the reduction of somebody's prison sentence for good conduct **3 LESSENING OF** a lessening or a reduction in the severity of something ○ *The afternoon sun beat down without remission.* **4 RELEASE** a release from a debt, penalty, or obligation **5 FORGIVENESS** pardon or forgiveness **6 ACT OF REMITTING** an instance or the action of remitting something

remit *v* /ri mít/ (**-mits, -mitting, -mitted**) **1** *vti* **SEND PAYMENT** to send money to pay for goods or services, especially by post **2** *vt* **SEND CASE BACK TO LOWER COURT** to send a case back to a lower court for further action to be taken **3** *vt*

CANCEL to cancel or hold back from enforcing something **4** *vti* REDUCE INTENSITY to reduce or allow the reduction in the intensity of something **5** *vt* DEFER to postpone or defer something **6** *vt* PARDON to pardon or forgive something ■ *n* /reémit, ri mít/ **1** AREA OF RESPONSIBILITY the scope or area of responsibility belonging to a particular person, group, or investigation ○ *This matter is beyond the remit of the committee.* **2** TRANSFER OF LEGAL CASE the transfer of a legal case from a higher to a lower court for further action to be taken **3** SOMETHING REMITTED something sent to another person or authority for consideration [14C. < Latin *remittere* 'send back' < *mittere* 'send'.] —**remittable** *adj* —**remittal** *n* —**remitter** *n*

remittance /ri mítt'nss/ *n* **1** ACT OF PAYING the sending of money to pay for goods or services **2** MONEY money sent as payment for goods or services **3** REMITTING the act of remitting something

remittance man *n* a man living abroad, especially, in the past, somewhere in the British Empire, who is dependent on money sent from home (*dated*)

remittent /ri mítt'nt/ *adj* lessening and then intensifying again at intervals ○ *slowed down by a remittent fever* —**remittence** *n* —**remittency** *n* —**remittently** *adv*

remix *vt* /ree míks/ to produce a new version of a piece of music by altering the emphasis of the sound and, in pop music, often adding new tracks in place of existing ones ■ *n* /reémiks/ a recording that has been remixed

remnant /rémnənt/ *n* **1** SMALL PART STILL LEFT a small part of something that remains after the rest has gone **2** SMALL AMOUNT OF CLOTH OR CARPET a small amount of unsold cloth or flooring material left at the end of a roll, often sold at a reduced price **3** TRACE OF a small amount or trace of something such as a feeling or emotion **4** SMALL SURVIVING GROUP OF PEOPLE a small isolated group of people surviving from a particular culture or group [14C. < Old French *remanant*, present participle of *remanoir* (see REMAIN).]

remodel /ree módd'l/ (**-els, -elling, -elled**) *vt* to renovate or alter the structure or style of something, e.g. a building, room, or design

remonetize /ree múnni tīz/ (**-tizes, -tizing, -tized**), **remonetise** (**-tises, -tising, -tised**) *vt* to reinstate something as valid currency or legal tender —**remonetization** /ree múnni tī záysh'n/ *n*

remonstrance /ri mónstrənss/ *n* **1** a forceful argument in favour or against something, or the act of making such an argument **2** a formal protest, usually in the form of a document or petition

Remonstrance *n* **1** HIST = **Grand Remonstrance** **2** the statement expressing Arminian Protestant principles, drawn up in 1610 in Gouda, the Netherlands

remonstrant /ri mónstrənt/ *n* a person who remonstrates ■ *adj* involved in or used for a protest (*formal*) [Early 17C. < medieval Latin, present participle of *remonstrare* (see REMONSTRATE).]

Remonstrant *n* a Dutch dissenter and supporter of the Remonstrance of 1610

remonstrate /rémmən strayt/ (**-strates, -strating, -strated**) *vi* to reason or argue forcefully with somebody about something [Late 16C. < medieval Latin *remonstrat-*, past participle of *remonstrare* 'demonstrate' < *monstrare* 'to show'.] —**remonstration** /rémmən stráysh'n/ *n* —**remonstrative** /ri mónstrətiv/ *adj* —**remonstratively** *adv* —**remonstrator** /rémmən straytər/ *n*

SYNONYMS See ***object***.

remontant /ri móntənt/ *adj* blooming or bearing fruit more than once in a season ■ *n* a plant that blooms or bears fruit more than once a season [Late 19C. < French, present participle of *remonter* 'rise again'.]

remora /rémmərə/ *n* a bony salt water fish with a suction disc on the top of its head that it uses to attach itself to a larger fish or a ship's hull. Family: Echeneidae. [Mid-16C. < Latin, 'hindrance'; from the belief that it slowed ships down.]

remorse /ri máwrss/ *n* a strong feeling of guilt and regret [14C. < Old French *remors* < Latin *remordere* 'to torment' < *mordere* 'to bite'.] —**remorseful** *adj* —**remorsefully** *adv* —**remorsefulness** *n*

remorseless /ri máwrssləss/ *adj* **1** showing no pity or compassion **2** continuing without lessening in strength or intensity —**remorselessly** *adv* —**remorselessness** *n*

remortgage /ree máwrgij/ *vt* (**-gages, -gaging, -gaged**) **1** CHANGE MORTGAGE TERMS to revise the terms of a mortgage on a property **2** MORTGAGE SOMETHING AGAIN to mortgage something again after the original mortgage has been paid off ■ *n* NEW MORTGAGE a revised or second mortgage taken out on something

ϟ **remote** /ri mōt/ *adj* (**-moter, -motest**) **1** FAR AWAY situated a long way away **2** OUT-OF-THE-WAY far away from civilization, society, or any other populated area **3** DISTANTLY RELATED distantly related by blood, adoption, or marriage **4** LONG AGO distant in time **5** SLIGHT faint or slight ○ *not the remotest possibility of her coming here* **6** DISTANT distant in connection, relevance, or effect **7** ALOOF distant in manner or behaviour **8** SEPARATED operated or performed from a distance ○ *a remote camera* ○ *a remote shopping service* ■ *n* **1** REMOTE CONTROL a remote control for an electronic device (*informal*) **2** COMPUTER FAR FROM CENTRAL COMPUTER a device or computer system that is situated at a distance from a central computer and that can be accessed via a network **3** US BROADCAST = **outside broadcast** [15C. < Latin *remotus*, past participle of *removere* 'remove'.] —**remoteness** *n*

ϟ **remote access** *n* access that is gained to a computer by means of a separate terminal

remote control *n* **1** a hand-held device used to operate a television set, video cassette recorder, or other electronic device from a distance **2** the control of a device, system, or activity from a distance, usually by radio signals (*hyphenated before nouns*) ○ *a remote-control transmitter* —**remote-controlled** *adj*

remotely /ri mōtli/ *adv* **1** SLIGHTLY in a slight or tenuous way ○ *The two events were only remotely connected.* **2** IN THE LEAST in the least possible way or to the least possible extent ○ *I am not even remotely interested in what they say.* **3** BY REMOTE CONTROL using remote control **4** IN A DETACHED WAY in a distant or aloof manner **5** DISTANTLY far in the future or past ○ *looking to a remotely future epoch* **6** IN A DISTANT WAY distantly in terms of family or biological connection ○ *We are remotely related.* **7** FAR AWAY at a distance or far away

remote sensor *n* an instrument, e.g. a radar or photographic device, that gathers information about the Earth or another astronomical object from an airborne platform or from space

rémoulade /rémmoo laád, rémmə láyd/ *n* mayonnaise with herbs, mustard, capers, and gherkin added [Mid-19C. < French.]

remould *n* /reé mōld/ TYRE WITH NEW TREAD a second-hand tyre with a new tread bonded to it. US term **retread** *n.* 1 ■ *vt* /ree mōld/ **1** CHANGE to change or remodel something such as an idea or principle **2** FIT TYRE WITH NEW TREAD to bond a new tread onto an old tyre. US term **retread** *v.* 1

remount *v* /ree mównt/ **1** *vt* PUT SOMETHING ON AGAIN to mount something again or anew **2** *vti* GET BACK INTO SADDLE to get back on a horse or bicycle ■ *n* /reé mownt/ SUBSTITUTE HORSE a replacement horse to ride

removal /ri moóv'l/ *n* **1** REMOVING OF the taking away or getting rid of something **2** CHANGE OF LOCATION a change in location, or in the place where somebody lives **3** DISMISSAL dismissal from office or from a position

removalist /ri moóvəlist/ *n* ANZ a person or company that transports people's belongings from one house to another

removal van *n* a van that is used to transport somebody's furniture and personal effects from one house to another. US term **moving van**

remove /ri moóv/ *v* (**-moves, -moving, -moved**) **1** *vt* TAKE AWAY to take something away from somebody or from a place **2** *vti* RELOCATE to transfer somebody or something to another place, or change a place of residence **3** *vt* TAKE OFF to take off an article of clothing **4** *vt* GET RID OF to make something go away or disappear ○ *a detergent that can remove stains even more quickly* **5** *vt* DISMISS to dismiss somebody from office ■ *n* **1** DISTANCE the degree of distance or closeness between people or things ○ *He has only experienced war at one remove.* **2** CLASS a class or form in some British secondary schools, especially public schools (*dated*) **3** CHANGE OF LOCATION a change of residence or business (*formal*) **4** INDIVIDUAL DISH IN MEAL a dish that is taken away during a formal meal to make way for another (*dated formal*) —**removability** *n* —**removable** *adj* —**removableness** *n* —**removably** *adv*

removed /ri moóvd/ *adj* **1** separate or distant in space, time, or character from something or somebody else **2** separated from somebody to a specified degree by birth, adoption, or marriage ○ *a cousin twice removed* —**removedness** /ri moóvidnəss, ri moóvdnəss/ *n*

REM sleep *n* a stage of sleep that recurs several times during the night and is marked by dreaming, rapid eye movements under closed lids, and elevated pulse rate and brain activity

remunerate /ri myoónə rayt/ (**-ates, -ating, -ated**) *vt* to pay somebody for goods or services, or compensate somebody financially for losses sustained or inconvenience caused [Early 16C. < Latin *remunerat-*, past participle of *remunerari* 'reward' < *munus* 'gift'.] —**remunerability** /ri myoónərə bíllәti/ *n* —**remunerable** /ri myoónərəb'l/ *adj* —**remunerator** *n* —**remuneratory** *adj*

remuneration /ri myoónə ráysh'n/ *n* **1** a payment or reward for goods or services or for losses sustained or inconvenience caused **2** the paying or rewarding of somebody for goods or services or for losses sustained or inconvenience caused

SYNONYMS See ***wage***.

remunerative /ri myoónərətiv/ *adj* paying somebody or rewarding somebody with money —**remuneratively** *adv*

Remus /reéməss/ *n* in Roman mythology, the son of Mars and twin brother of Romulus, the founder of the city of Rome. ◊ **Romulus**

renaissance /ri náys'nss/, **renascence** *n* a rebirth or revival, e.g. of culture, skills, or learning forgotten or previously ignored [Late 19C. < French, < *renaître* 'be reborn' < Latin *renasci*.]

Renaissance *n* **1** END OF MIDDLE AGES the period in European history from about the 14th to 16th centuries regarded as marking the end of the Middle Ages and featuring major cultural and artistic change **2** CLASSICAL REVIVAL the cultural and religious spirit that characterized the Renaissance, including the decline of Gothic architecture, the revival of classical culture, the beginnings of modern science, and geographical exploration ■ *adj* **1** RELATING TO RENAISSANCE relating to the history and culture of the Renaissance **2** IN ARCHITECTURAL STYLE OF RENAISSANCE in the architectural style of classical revival that characterized the Renaissance

QUICK FACTS ON... **THE RENAISSANCE**

Key dates: 14th–16th centuries.
Key locations: W Europe, especially Italy
Key elements: rationalism, individualism, revival of classicism
Key developments: humanism; perspective in art; polyphony; exploration of the Americas; spread of printing; Protestantism
Key figures: Giotto, Leonardo da Vinci, Raphael, Titian, Michelangelo, Albrecht Dürer, Sandro Botticelli (art); Petrarch, Dante Alighieri (literature); Nicolaus Copernicus (science); Filippo Brunelleschi (architecture); Christopher Columbus, Ferdinand Magellan (exploration); Desiderius Erasmus (theology); Giovanni Pierluigi da Palestrina (music); Niccolò Machiavelli (politics)
Key works: dome of Florence Cathedral (Brunelleschi) 1420–61, *David* (Michelangelo) 1501–4, *The Birth of Venus* (Botticelli) 1482?, *Mona Lisa* (da Vinci) 1503–6, *The Prince* (Machiavelli) 1532, *Sistine Chapel* (Michelangelo) 1534–41

Renaissance man *n* a man who has a wide range of accomplishments and intellectual interests

Renaissance woman *n* a woman who has a wide range of accomplishments and intellectual interests

renal /reén'l/ *adj* relating to or affecting the kidneys [Mid-17C. Via French < Latin *renes* 'kidneys'.]

renal clearance *n* a measure of the removal of waste products from the blood by the kidneys, expressed as the volume of blood cleared of one particular substance in one minute

renal pelvis *n* the cavity in the kidney where urine collects before passing into the ureter

rename /ree náym/ (**-names, -naming, -named**) *vt* to give a new name to a person or to a thing such as a ship

renascence /ri náss'nss, -náy-/ *n* = **renaissance**

renascent /ri náss'nt, ri náyss'nt/ *adj* showing new life or activity [Early 18C. < Latin *renascent-*, present participle of *renasci* 'be reborn'.]

renature /ree náychər/ (**-tures, -turing, -tured**) *vt* to restore the physical and chemical properties of a denatured protein or nucleic acid

rencounter /ren kówntər/ *n* (*archaic*) **1** a hostile meeting between adversaries **2** an unexpected casual meeting [Early 16C. < French *rencontrer* 'have a (hostile) meeting' < *encontrer* 'confront'.]

rend /rend/ (**rends, rending, rent** /rent/, **rent**) *v* **1** *vti* **TEAR APART** to tear something apart violently, or be torn apart in this way ○ *The hurricane rent the flimsy houses in pieces.* **2** *vt* **TEAR CLOTHES** to tear or pull clothes or hair, out of rage, frustration, or grief **3** *vt* **TAKE AWAY FORCIBLY** to tear or wrest something or somebody away **4** *vt* **MAKE PIERCING SOUND** to disturb the silence or pierce the air with a loud sound ○ *a scream rent the air* **5** *vt* **DISTRESS** to cause pain or distress to the heart or emotions [Old English *rendan* < Germanic]

SYNONYMS See *tear*.

Rendell /réndʹl/, **Ruth** (*b.* 1930) British novelist

render /réndər/ *v* **1** *vt* **GIVE HELP** to give help or provide a service (*formal*) **2** *vt* **TRANSLATE** to translate something into another language (*formal*) ○ *fragments of poetry, hastily rendered into English* **3** *vt* **PORTRAY SOMETHING ARTISTICALLY** to portray something or somebody in art, literature, music, or acting (*formal*) ○ *a scene of utter desolation, skilfully rendered without sentiment* **4** *vt* **GIVE DECISION** to deliver a verdict or decision officially (*formal*) **5** *vt* **SUBMIT SOMETHING FOR ACTION** to submit something for consideration, approval, or payment (*formal*) ○ *render all passports for inspection* **6** *vt* **PAY RESPECT** to give what is due or appropriate to somebody who has authority or power (*formal*) ○ *'Render therefore unto Caesar the things which are Caesar's'* (Matthew 22:21, *The Bible*) **7** *vt* **PUT SOMEBODY OR SOMETHING IN PARTICULAR STATE** to make somebody or something be or become something (*formal*) ○ *His actions rendered her powerless.* **8** *vt* **PURIFY FAT** to purify or extract something by melting, especially to heat solid fat slowly until as much liquid fat as possible has been extracted from it, leaving small crisp remains **9** *vt* **COVER WALL WITH PLASTER** to cover masonry with a thin coat of plaster **10** *vti* **GIVE UP** to surrender something (*formal or literary*) **11** *vt* **TRADE** to give something in exchange for something else (*formal or literary*) **12** *vt* **RETURN** to give something back (*formal or literary*) ■ *n* **1 COAT OF PLASTER** the first thin coat of plaster applied to masonry **2 TENANT'S PAYMENT** a payment in goods, services, or money made by a tenant to a feudal lord [14C. Via Old French *rendre* < Latin *reddere* 'give back' < *dare* 'give'.] —**renderable** *adj* —**renderer** *n*

rendering /réndəring/ *n* **1 ARTISTIC PORTRAYAL** a portrayal of somebody or something in art, music, literature, or drama **2 TRANSLATION** a translation of a literary work **3 HEATING ANIMAL REMAINS TO EXTRACT FAT** the process or business of separating fat from meat or animal remains by slow heating **4 COAT OF PLASTER** a coat of plaster applied to masonry **5 ARCHITECT'S PERSPECTIVE DRAWING** an architect's representation of the inside and outside of a finished building, drawn in perspective

rendezvous /róndi voo, -day-/ *n* (*plural* **-vous** /-vooz/) **1 MEETING** a meeting arranged for a specified time and place **2 PLACE OF MEETING** the location of a prearranged meeting **3 PLACE WHERE PEOPLE MEET** a popular meeting place for people ■ *vti* (**-vouses, -vousing, -voused**) **MEET** to meet, or meet somebody, at a specified time and place, or cause this to happen [Late 16C. < French, 'present yourself'.]

rendition /ren dísh'n/ *n* **1 VERSION OF MUSICAL OR THEATRICAL PIECE** an interpretation or performance of a piece of music or drama **2 TRANSLATION** a translation of a literary work **3 TRANSLATING** the act of translating something into another language (*formal*) [Early 17C. < French, < *rendre* (see RENDER).]

rendzina /ren dzeénə/ *n* a dark rich soil that develops beneath grassland above a layer of limestone or chalk [Early 20C. < Polish *rędzina*.]

Rene /reen/, **Roy** (1892–1954) Australian actor. Born **Henry van der Sluys Rene**

renegade /rénni gayd/ *n* **1** a person who abandons previously held beliefs or loyalties **2** a person who chooses to live outside laws or conventions [15C. < Spanish *renegado* < medieval Latin *renegatus* < past participle of Latin *renegare* 'deny'.]

renege /ri neég, ri náyg/ (**-neges, -neging, -neged**) *vi* **1** to go back on a promise or commitment **2** in cards, to fail to follow suit when able and required to do so [Mid-16C. < medieval Latin *renegare* 'deny' < Latin *negare*.] —**reneger** *n*

renegotiate /reéni góshi ayt/ (**-ates, -ating, -ated**) *vti* to negotiate an agreement again in order to change the terms

renew /ri nyoó/ *v* **1** *vti* **RETURN TO DOING** to begin something again, or return to doing something **2** *vti* **EXTEND** to make something such as a contract, lease, or licence effective for a longer period ○ *You'll need to renew your lease at the end of the year.* **3** *vt* **REPLACE SOMETHING WORN** to replace something that is worn out or no longer suitable for use **4** *vt* **BORROW LIBRARY BOOK FOR LONGER** to extend the period of time a book or other item is borrowed from a library **5** *vt* **REPEAT PROMISE** to reaffirm or restate a promise or commitment ○ *renewed their marriage vows* **6** *vt* **GIVE NEW ENERGY** to give somebody or something new energy, strength, or enthusiasm ○ *I felt quite renewed after the weekend.* **7** *vt* **GET NEW SUPPLY** to get a new supply of something **8** *vt* **MAKE SOMETHING NEW AGAIN** to make something new or as if new again —**renewal** *n* —**renewer** *n*

SYNONYMS *renew, recondition, renovate, restore, revamp*

CORE MEANING: to improve the condition of something

renew to replace something worn or broken; **recondition** to bring something such as a machine or appliance back to a good condition or working state by means of repairs or replacement of parts; **renovate** to bring something such as a building back to a former better state by means of repairs, redecoration, or refurbishment; **restore** to bring something back to an original state after it has been damaged or fallen into a bad condition; **revamp** to improve the appearance or condition of something.

renewable /ri nyoó əb'l/ *adj* **1** capable of being renewed **2** able to be sustained or renewed indefinitely, either because of inexhaustible supplies or because of new growth ○ *renewable resources* —**renewability** /ri nyoó ə bíllәti/ *n* —**renewably** *adv*

renewable energy *n* INDUST = **alternative energy**

renewable resource *n* **1 RESOURCE THAT CAN BE SUSTAINED** a resource such as timber that can be renewed as quickly as it is used up so that it can, in theory, last indefinitely, unlike mineral resources **2 NATURAL RESOURCE THAT REPLACES ITSELF** a natural resource that replaces itself unless overused, e.g. animal or plant life or fresh water **3 RENEWABLE FORM OF ENERGY** a source of energy, e.g. sunlight, wind, or tidal power, that can be used indefinitely to generate electricity because it does not involve burning fuel or damaging the environment

Renfrew /rén froo/ town in SW Scotland. Population: 20,764 (1991).

Renfrewshire /rén frooshər/ council area in SW Scotland. Area: 309 sq. km/119 sq. mi.

reniform /rénni fawrm, reéni fawrm/ *adj* shaped like or suggestive of a kidney

renin /reénin/ *n* an enzyme released by the kidneys that breaks down proteins and plays an important role in regulating blood pressure

renitent /ri nít'nt, rénnitənt/ *adj* (*formal*) **1** resisting physical pressure, rather than being flexible or pliant **2** reluctant to have a change of mind or concede to others [Early 18C. < Latin *renitent-*, present participle of *reniti* 'struggle against'.] —**renitence** *n* —**renitency** *n*

renminbi /rén minbee/ (*plural* **-bi**) *n* **1** the national currency of the People's Republic of China, equivalent in value to the yuan [Mid-20C. < Chinese, < *rénmín* 'people' + *bì* 'currency'.]

Rennes /ren/ city in NW France. Population: 203,533 (1990).

rennet /rénnit/ *n* **1** the inner lining of the fourth stomach or abomasum of calves and other young ruminants **2** a preparation made from rennet that contains the enzyme rennin. Use: cheese making. **3** BIOCHEM = **rennin** [15C. Probably < assumed Old English.]

rennin /rénnin/ *n* a milk-curdling enzyme produced in the stomachs of young mammals [Late 19C. < RENNET.]

Reno /reénō/ city in W Nevada. Population: 163,334 (1998 estimate).

renogram /reénə gram/ *n* **1** a photographic record of kidney function, showing how quickly a radioactive substance injected into the bloodstream is removed when it passes through the kidneys **2** an X-ray image of a kidney [Early 20C. < Latin *ren* 'kidney'.]

Renoir /rén waar, rən waár/, **Jean** (1894–1979) French film director

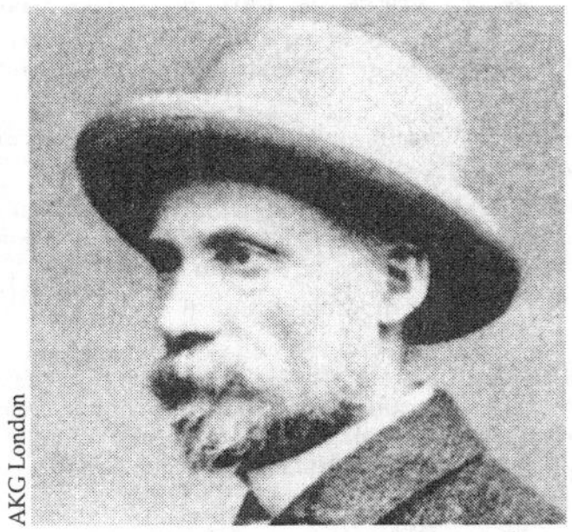

Pierre Auguste Renoir

Renoir, Pierre Auguste (1841–1919) French painter and sculptor

renormalization /reé nawrmə lī záysh'n/ *n* a mathematical technique used in quantum physics that eliminates infinite terms by carefully defining fundamental quantities such as mass and charge —**renormalize** /ree náwrmə līz/ *vt*

renounce /ri nównss/ *v* (**-nounces, -nouncing, -nounced**) **1** *vt* **GIVE UP CLAIM TO** formally to give up a claim, title, position, or right **2** *vt* **REJECT BELIEF** to reject or disavow a belief or theory **3** *vt* **GIVE SOMETHING UP** to give up a habit, pursuit, or practice **4** *vi* **NOT FOLLOW SUIT** in cards, to be unable to follow suit and be forced to play a card from a different suit ■ *n* **ACT OF NOT FOLLOWING SUIT** a failure to follow suit [14C. Via French *renoncer* < Latin *renuntiare* 'report' < *nuntiare* 'announce'.] —**renouncement** *n* —**renouncer** *n*

renovascular /reénō váskyóolər/ *adj* relating to the blood vessels of the kidneys [Mid-20C. < Latin *ren* 'kidney'.]

renovate /rénnə vayt/ (**-vates, -vating, -vated**) *vt* **1** to restore something to good condition **2** to give new vigour to somebody or something [15C. < Latin *renovare* < *novus* 'new'.] —**renovation** /rénnə váysh'n/ *n* —**renovative** *adj* —**renovator** *n*

SYNONYMS See *renew*.

renown /ri nówn/ *n* widespread fame or honour [14C. < Old French *renon* < *renomer* 'make famous' < *nomer* 'to name' < Latin *nominare*.]

renowned /ri nównd/ *adj* well known or famous, especially for a skill or expertise

rent[1] /rent/ *n* **1 PAYMENT BY TENANT** a regular payment made by a tenant to an owner or landlord for the right to occupy or use property **2 PAYMENT TO USE EQUIPMENT** a regular payment to the owner for the right to use equipment or personal property **3 PROFIT FROM CULTIVATED LAND** the financial return from cultivated land after production costs have been deducted **4 INCOME OF LANDOWNERS** the portion of the national income that is earned by landowners **5** ECON = **economic rent** *n.* 1 ■ *vti* **1 PAY TO USE SOMEBODY'S PROPERTY** to occupy somebody else's property or use somebody else's equipment in return for regular payments **2 ALLOW USE OF PROPERTY FOR PAYMENT** to allow somebody to occupy property or use equipment in return for regular payment [12C. < French *rente* < Latin *reddere* 'give back'.] —**rentable** *adj*

rent[2] /rent/ past tense, past participle of **rend** ■ *n* **1** an opening or hole made by tearing something **2** a rift in a relationship or breach in friendly relations

rental /rént'l/ *n* **1 RENT PAYMENT** the amount paid in rent **2 RENT INCOME** the amount received in rent **3 ACT OF RENTING** the renting of property or equipment **4** *US* **SOMETHING RENTABLE** something rented or available to rent **5** *US* **RENTING BUSINESS** a business that rents out property or equipment ■ *adj* **RELATING TO RENT** relating to property for rent or with rent payments

rent boy *n* an offensive term for a young man working as a prostitute (*slang*)

rent control *n* government regulation of the amount charged for housing rental and sometimes of eviction procedures —**rent-controlled** *adj*

renter /réntər/ *n* **1 SOMEBODY WHO RENTS FROM SOMEBODY** a person who rents property or equipment from somebody else **2 SOMEBODY WHO RENTS TO SOMEBODY** a person who rents property or equipment to somebody else **3 FILM DISTRIBUTOR** a film distributor renting films to cinemas

rent-free *adj* not subject to rent payments ■ *adv* without having to pay rent

rentier /ráaN tyay, rónti ay/ *n* somebody whose income is primarily from rent and securities [Mid-19C. < French, < *rente* (see RENT[1]).]

rent strike *n* an organized refusal by tenants to pay their rent

renunciation /ri núnssi áysh'n/ *n* **1** a denial or rejection of something, usually for moral or religious reasons **2** an official declaration giving up a title, office, claim, or privilege —**renunciatory** /ri núnsi ətəri/ *adj*

renvoi /ren vóy/ *n* the referral of a case or dispute from the country in which it arose to the laws of another [Late 19C. < French, < *renvoyer* 'send back'.]

reoccupy /ree ókyoo pī/ (**-pies, -pying, -pied**) *vti* to occupy a place or territory a second or subsequent time —**reoccupation** /reè okyoo páysh'n, ree ókyoo-/ *n*

reoccur /reè ə kúr/ (**-curs, -curring, -curred**) *vi* to occur a second or subsequent time —**reoccurrence** *n*

reoffend /reè ə fénd/ *vi* to commit a second or subsequent offence —**reoffender** *n*

reopen /ree ṓpən/ *vti* **1 OPEN AGAIN** to open again or cause something to be opened again ○ *I don't want to reopen old wounds.* ○ *The store will reopen in March.* **2 START SOMETHING AGAIN** to begin again something that was considered settled, or to be begun again **3 OPEN SOMETHING CLOSED** to open something that has been closed for a time, or to be opened after being closed for a long time

reorder /ree áwrdər/ *v* **1** *vti* **REQUEST NEW SUPPLY** to order the same goods again **2** *vt* **REARRANGE** to arrange something differently **3** *vt* **ARRANGE SOMETHING AGAIN** to put something in order again ■ *n* **ANOTHER ORDER** another order for the same goods from the same supplier

reorganisation *n* = **reorganization**

reorganise *vti* = **reorganize**

reorganization /ree áwrgə nī záysh'n/, **reorganisation** *n* **1** a change in the way something is organized, arranged, or done **2** the thorough physical or financial restructuring of a business or organization —**reorganizational** *adj*

reorganize /ree áwrgə nīz/ (**-izes, -izing, -ized**), **reorganise** (**-ises, -ising, -ised**) *vti* **1** to impose organization on something again after its being disturbed **2** to change the way that something is organized —**reorganizer** *n*

reorient /ree áwri ənt/, **reorientate** (**-tates, -tating, -tated**) *vti* **1** to change your behaviour or ideas to deal with a new situation **2** to find out where you are or where you are going after being lost —**reorientation** /ree áwri ən táysh'n/ *n*

reovirus /reè ō vīrəss/ *n* a virus that contains double-stranded RNA and is associated with various infections in plants and animals [Mid-20C. Acronym < *respiratory enteric orphan*.]

rep[1] /rep/, **repp** *n* a ribbed or corded silk, wool, rayon, or cotton fabric [Mid-19C. < French *reps*.]

rep[2] /rep/ *n* repertory theatre, or a repertory company (*informal*) [Early 20C. Shortening.]

rep[3] /rep/ *n* a sales representative (*informal*) ■ *vi* (**reps, repping, repped**) to work as a sales representative (*informal*) [Late 19C. Shortening.]

rep[4] /rep/ *n* a reputation (*informal*) [Early 18C. Shortening.]

rep[5] /rep/ *n* a repetition of a fitness exercise (*informal*)

rep. *abbr* **1** repair **2** report **3** reported **4** reporter **5** reprint

Rep. *abbr* **1** *US* Representative **2** Republic **3** *US* Republican

repack /ree pák/ *vti* to pack a container or items going into a container again or in a different way

repackage /ree pákij/ (**-ages, -aging, -aged**) *vt* **1** to package a product in a new and differently designed container or wrapping **2** to give somebody such as a political leader or celebrity a new public image

repaid past tense, past participle of **repay**

repaint /ree páynt/ *vti* to apply a fresh coat of paint to something, or paint it again differently ■ *n* an act of repainting something ○ *That could do with a repaint.*

repair[1] /ri páir/ *vt* **1 FIX OR MEND** to restore something broken or damaged to good condition ○ *repair a flat tyre* **2 RESTORE RELATIONSHIP** to restore a relationship or friendship by resolving a difficulty or disagreement **3 ATONE FOR** to make amends for something wrong ○ *How can I repair this wrong?* ■ *n* **1 JOB OF MENDING** the process of mending something, or the job that is done in order to achieve this ○ *carry out repairs* **2 REPAIRED ITEM** something that has been repaired **3 CONDITION OF** the condition of something with respect to whether it needs mending or fixing ○ *an air conditioner no longer in good repair* [14C. Via Old French *réparer* < Latin *reparare* < *parare* 'make ready'.] —**repairable** *adj* —**repairability** /ri páirə bílləti/ *n* —**repairer** *n*

repair[2] /ri páir/ *v* (*formal*) **1** *vi* **GO SOMEWHERE** to go to a particular place ○ *repaired to the library after dinner* **2** *vt* **CONSULT** to go to somebody for help or advice ■ *n* **1 ACT OF GOING SOMEWHERE** the act of going to a particular place, especially frequently (*archaic*) **2 HAUNT** a place where a person or animal is frequently found [14C. Via French *repairer* < late Latin *repatriare* 'go back home'.]

repairman /ri páir man/ (*plural* **-men** /-men/) *n* a man whose job is making repairs to equipment or machinery

repairperson /ri páir purss'n/ (*plural* **-people** /ri páir peep'l/ *or* **-persons**) *n* a person whose job is making repairs to equipment or machinery

repairwoman /ri páir woomən/ (*plural* **-en** /-wimin/) *n* a woman whose job is making repairs to equipment or machinery

repand /ri pánd/ *adj* with a wavy edge ○ *a repand leaf* [Mid-18C. < Latin *repandus* 'curving back' < *pandere* 'become curved'.]

repaper /ree páypər/ *vt* to cover a wall or room with new wallpaper

reparable /réppərəb'l/ *adj* able to be repaired, recovered, or put right —**reparability** /réppərə bílləti/ *n* —**reparably** *adv*

reparation /réppə ráysh'n/ *n* **1 AMENDS** compensation for a wrong, or something that is done to achieve this **2 REPAIR** restoration of something to good condition, or the process of doing this (*formal*) ■ **reparations** *npl* **COMPENSATION FOR WAR** compensation demanded of a defeated nation by the victor in a war, especially that demanded of Germany by the Treaty of Versailles after World War I —**reparative** /ri párrətiv/ *adj* —**reparatory** /-párrətəri/ *adj*

repartee /réppaar teé/ *n* **1 WITTY TALK** conversation consisting of witty remarks **2 WIT** skill in making witty remarks or conversation **3 WITTY REMARK** a witty remark or reply [Mid-17C. < French *repartie* < *repartir* 'set out again' < *partir* 'to leave'.]

repartition /reè paar tísh'n/ *n* **1 DISTRIBUTION** distribution or division of something **2 DIVIDING OF SOMETHING AGAIN** the act of dividing or distributing something again, either in the same way or differently ■ *vt* **DIVIDE SOMETHING UP AGAIN** to divide something up again, either in the same way or differently

repast /ri paást/ *n* a meal, or the food eaten at a meal (*literary*) [14C. < Old French, < *repaistre* 'feed' < Latin *pascere*.]

repatriate *v* /ree páttri ayt/ (**-ates, -ating, -ated**) **1** *vt* **SEND SOMEBODY BACK** to send somebody back to his or her country of birth, the country of which he or she is a citizen, or the country from which he or she arrived **2** *vt* **SEND BACK MONEY** to send money that has been earned or invested abroad back to its owner's country of origin **3 SEND BACK ARTEFACTS** to send cultural artefacts or works of art back to their country of origin ■ *n* /-ət/ **SOMEBODY REPATRIATED** a person who has been repatriated [Early 17C. < Latin *repatriare* 'go back home' < *patria* 'homeland'.] —**repatriation** /ree páttri áysh'n/ *n*

repay /ri páy/ (**-pays, -paying, -paid** /ri páyd/) *vt* **1 PAY BACK MONEY** to pay back money that is owed to somebody **2 RETURN FAVOUR** to reward somebody for his or her effort, aid, or success **3 RETURN IN KIND** to return something in kind —**repayable** *adj* —**repayment** *n*

repeal /ri peél/ *vt* to officially revoke or abolish something such as a law ■ *n* the act of repealing something such as a law [14C. < Anglo-Norman *repeler*, variant of Old French *rapeler* < *re-* 'again, back', + *apeler* (see APPEAL).] —**repealable** *adj* —**repealer** *n*

repeat /ri peét/ *v* **1** *vt* **SAY SOMETHING AGAIN** to say or write something again **2** *vti* **DO OR UNDERGO SOMETHING AGAIN** to do, produce, or experience something again or several times ○ *She repeated the exercises every day.* **3** *vti* **ECHO SOMEBODY'S WORDS** to say again what somebody else has said **4** *vt* **TELL WHAT HAS BEEN HEARD** to tell another person something that was told to you, especially when it was done in confidence ○ *I'll tell you, but you mustn't repeat it to anyone else.* **5** *vt* **SAY SOMETHING MEMORIZED** to recite something that has been learned **6** *vr* **SAY SAME THING OVER AGAIN** to do or say something again, especially more than once ○ *You get tired of repeating yourself after a while.* **7** *vr* **HAPPEN AGAIN AS BEFORE** to happen again in the same way as previously **8** *vti* **BROADCAST AGAIN** to broadcast a television or radio programme again, or be broadcast again **9** *vi* **BE TASTED AGAIN** to be tasted again after having been eaten, through wind or partial regurgitation (*informal*) ○ *Those spicy meatballs are repeating on me.* **10** *vi* **SIGNAL TIME** to make a sound signalling the latest hour, or sometimes quarter hour when somebody presses a spring (*refers to a clock or watch*) ■ *n* **1 RECURRING EVENT OR SITUATION** an event or situation that is the same as a previous one **2 SOMETHING SHOWN AGAIN** something that is broadcast, shown, or performed again **3 RECURRING MUSICAL PASSAGE** a passage of music played again within a single piece, or the notation indicating that this is to be done **4 UNIFORMLY REPRODUCED PATTERN** a pattern reproduced uniformly across a surface ○ *upholstery fabric with a large floral repeat* **5 ACT OF REORDERING** a reorder of the same goods or by the same customer [14C. Via French *répéter* < Latin *repetere* 'demand again' < *petere* 'demand'.] —**repeatability** /ri peétə bílləti/ *n* —**repeatable** *adj* —**repeated** *adj*

repeatedly /ri peétidli/ *adv* again and again, or on several occasions

repeater /ri peétər/ *n* **1 SOMEBODY OR SOMETHING REPEATING** a person who or something that repeats **2 GUN FIRING SEVERAL SHOTS WITHOUT RELOADING** a firearm such as a rifle with a magazine that can fire several shots before it has to be reloaded **3 TIMEPIECE THAT REPEATS CHIMES** a clock or watch that can be made to repeat its latest chime when somebody presses a spring **4 DEVICE FOR AMPLIFYING SIGNALS** an electrical device that boosts and amplifies incoming communications signals and retransmits them

repeating decimal *n* MATH = **recurring decimal**

repeating firearm *n* ARMS = **repeater** *n.* 2

repeat performance *n* an event that is the same as one that happened before

repeat prescription *n* *UK*, *Can* a prescription for a regularly needed medicine that has been prescribed before and can be renewed without the doctor having to see the patient

repechage /réppə shaazh/ *n* a heat within a competition such as a fencing, rowing, or cycling competition, during which runners-up in earlier heats have a final chance to qualify for the next round [Early 20C. < French, < *repêcher* 'fish out'.]

repel /ri pél/ (**-pels, -pelling, -pelled**) *v* **1** *vti* **CAUSE DISTASTE** to make somebody feel intense aversion, disgust, or revulsion **2** *vt* **RESIST ATTACK** to ward off or force back an attack or invasion **3** *vt* **KEEP SOMETHING AWAY** to ward something off or keep something away ○ *a cream that is effective in repelling mosquitoes* **4** *vti* **FAIL TO MIX** to fail to mix or blend with something else ○ *Oil and water repel each other.* **5** *vti* **EXERT OPPOSING FORCE** to exert a force that tends to push something away ○ *Particles of like charge repel each other.* **6** *vt* **SPURN** to reject or refuse to accept something or somebody [15C. Via Old French *repeler* < Latin *repellere* 'drive back' < *pellere* 'drive'.] —**repeller** *n*

~~**repellant**~~ incorrect spelling of **repellent**

repellent /ri péllənt/ *adj* **1 CAUSING DISGUST** making somebody feel intense dislike, disgust, or revulsion **2 RESISTANT** resistant or impervious to something (*often in combination*) ○ *water-repellent material* **3 PUSHING AWAY** pushing something away or driving something back ■ *n* **1 SOMETHING THAT REPELS INSECTS** a substance that drives away insects **2 SUBSTANCE THAT RESISTS SOMETHING HARMFUL** a substance that is applied to a surface of something to resist water, mould, or mildew —**repellence** *n* —**repellently** *adv*

USAGE repellent or **repulsive**? Both words mean 'causing disgust', but ***repulsive*** is rather stronger in effect than ***repellent***. ***Repellent*** is common in combinations such as *insect-repellent* and *water-repellent*, denoting substances that physically repel or resist the things specified. ***Repulsive*** does not have a literal meaning corresponding to this.

repent[1] /ri pént/ *vti* **1** to recognize the wrong in something you have done and be sorry about it **2** to feel regret about a sin or past actions and change your ways or habits [13C. < French *repentir* < *pentir* < Latin *paenitere*.] —**repentance** *n* —**repentant** *adj* —**repentantly** *adv* —**repenter** *n*

repent[2] /ri pént/ *adj* growing or lying along the ground [Mid-17C. < Latin *repent-*, present participle of *repere* 'creep'.]

~~**repentence**~~ incorrect spelling of **repentance**

repercussion /reépər kúsh'n/ *n* **1 RESULT OF ACTION** something, especially an unforeseen problem, that results from an action (*often plural*) **2 REBOUND** the rebounding of a force after impact **3 REFLECTION** the reflection of light or sound **4 POINT OF REAPPEARANCE IN FUGUE** in a fugue, the return of the theme after an episode [Mid-16C. Directly or via French < Latin *repercussion-*, < *repercutere* 'strike back through' < *percutere* 'strike through'.] —**repercussive** *adj*

repertoire /réppər twaar/ *n* **1 MATERIAL AVAILABLE FOR PERFORMANCE** a stock of musical or dramatic material that is known and can be performed **2 BODY OF ARTISTIC WORKS** the entire body of works in a specific area of the arts **3 RANGE OF RESOURCES THAT SOMEBODY HAS** the range of techniques, abilities, or skills that somebody or something has ○ *the surgeon's repertoire* [Mid-19C. Via French < late Latin *repertorium* (see REPERTORY).] ◇ **in repertoire** used to refer to performances of different plays or ballets given on different days

repertory /réppərtəri/ (*plural* **-ries**) *n* **1 SYSTEM OF PRESENTING PLAYS** a system by which a permanent theatre company presents a set of works during a season, usually in its own theatre. US term **stock** *n.* 31 **2 GROUP OR THEATRE USING REPERTORY SYSTEM** a theatre or company that uses the repertory system **3** ARTS = **repertoire** *n.* 1 **4** = **repertoire** *n.* 2 **5 COLLECTION OF AVAILABLE THINGS** a store or stock of available items ○ *a comedian with a large repertory of jokes* [Late 16C. < late Latin *repertorium* 'inventory' < Latin *reperire* 'get completely' < *parire* 'get'.] —**repertorial** /réppər táwri əl/ *adj*

repertory company *n* a theatre company that performs different plays on different days in the same theatre. US term **stock company** *n.* 2

repetend /réppi tend, réppi ténd/ *n* **1** the part of a repeating decimal that is repeated infinitely, e.g. '37' in '0.373737' **2** something that is repeated [Early 18C. < Latin *repetendum* 'thing to be repeated' < *repetere* 'demand again'.]

répétiteur /ray pétti túr, ri-/ *n* a musician in an opera company who coaches the singers and accompanies them on the piano in rehearsal [Mid-20C. < French, 'somebody who repeats'.]

repetition /réppə tísh'n/ *n* **1 REPEATING OF** an act of doing something again **2 SOMETHING THE SAME AS BEFORE** an event or situation that is the same as one that happened previously **3 PROCEDURE OF STATING SOMETHING AGAIN** the act or process of saying or writing something again **4 REPEATED WORDS** something that is repeated, especially unnecessary words [Early 16C. Via French < Latin *repetition-* < *repetere* 'demand again'.]

repetitious /réppə tíshəss/ *adj* full of things that are said or written over and over again, especially in an unnecessary or tiresome way —**repetitiously** *adv* —**repetitiousness** *n*

repetitive /ri péttətiv/ *adj* full of or involving things that are done over and over again ○ *a boring, repetitive task* —**repetitively** *adv* —**repetitiveness** *n*

repetitive strain injury, repetitive stress injury *n* full form of **RSI**

rephrase /ree fráyz/ (**-phrases, -phrasing, -phrased**) *vt* to say or write something again using different words as a clarification or for variety

repine /ri pín/ (**-pines, -pining, -pined**) *vi* to feel dissatisfied or fretful about something and complain or grumble about it (*literary*) [Early 16C. < PINE[2] 'fret', after *repent*.] —**repiner** *n*

~~**repitition**~~ incorrect spelling of **repetition**

replace /ri pláyss/ (**-places, -placing, -placed**) *vt* **1 SUBSTITUTE FOR** to take the place of or substitute for somebody or something ○ *The new ways rapidly replaced the old.* **2 SUPPLANT** to fill the place of something or somebody with something or somebody else ○ *You can be replaced.* **3 PUT SOMETHING IN ANOTHER'S PLACE** to provide or find a substitute for something ○ *can't afford to replace his car* **4 PUT SOMETHING BACK IN PLACE** to put an object back in its usual place ○ *She replaced the receiver slowly.* —**replaceable** *adj* —**replacer** *n*

USAGE replace or **substitute**? The constructions involving these two words are different, although the resulting meaning is usually the same. You ***replace*** item B *with* (or less often *by*) item A, but ***substitute*** item A *for* item B.

replacement /ri pláyssmənt/ *n* **1 SUBSTITUTION** the act or process of taking the place of or substituting for somebody or something **2 FILLING OF SOMEBODY'S OR SOMETHING'S PLACE** the filling of the place of somebody or something with somebody or something else **3 SUBSTITUTE** a person who or something that replaces another **4 CHANGE OF ONE MINERAL TO ANOTHER** the partial or complete transformation of one mineral into another in response to changing conditions such as the presence of water **5** *US* **SOMEBODY FILLING MILITARY VACANCY** a person who fills a vacancy in a military force

replant /ree plaánt/ *vt* **1 TRANSFER PLANT TO NEW PLACE** to transfer a plant or part of a plant into new soil or a new area **2 PROVIDE PLACE WITH NEW PLANTS** to put new plants in a place or container to replace previous plants ○ *replant the flower boxes every spring* **3 REATTACH OR REINSERT BODY PART** to reattach or reinsert a severed body part such as a limb or tooth —**replantation** /reé plaan táysh'n/ *n*

replay *vt* /ree pláy/ **1 PLAY MATCH AGAIN** to play a game, match, or contest again **2 PLAY RECORDING AGAIN** to play again something that has been recorded on tape, video, or film ■ *n* /reé play/ **1 CONTEST PLAYED AGAIN** a contest, match, or game that is played again **2 RECORDED MATERIAL REPLAYED** something recorded on tape, video, or film that is played again **3 REPEAT OF PREVIOUS EVENT** an event that repeats or appears to repeat something in the past ○ *The latest business failure was a replay of the previous one.*

replenish /ri plénnish/ *vt* **1 NOURISH** to fill somebody or something with needed energy or nourishment **2 REPLACE USED ITEMS** to restock depleted items or material ○ *time for the campers to replenish their supplies* **3 FURNISH NEW FUEL FOR FIRE** to resupply a fire with fuel [Early 17C. < Old French *repleniss-*, stem of *replenir* 'fill again' < *plenir* 'fill' < Latin *plenus* 'full'.] —**replenisher** *n* —**replenishment** *n*

replete /ri pleét/ *adj* **1** amply, completely, or fully supplied with something ○ *a kitchen replete with all the latest gadgets* **2** having eaten enough to be fully satisfied [14C. Directly or via French < Latin *repletus*, past participle of *replere* 'fill up' < *plere* 'fill'.] —**repleteness** *n*

repletion /ri pleésh'n/ *n* **1** a condition of being overfull after eating too much **2** the condition of being fully satisfied

replevin /ri plévvin/ *n* an act or writ to recover goods by somebody who claims to own them and who promises to have the claim later tested in court ■ *vt* LAW = **replevy** *v.* [14C. < Anglo-Norman, < *replevir* (see REPLEVY).]

replevy /ri plévvi/ *vt* (**-ies, -ying, -ied**) to seize goods on the grounds of ownership after promising to test the claim in court ■ *n* (*plural* **-ies**) a seizure of claimed goods after a promise that the claim will be tested in court later [Late 16C. < Anglo-Norman *replevir* 'recover thoroughly' < *plevir* 'recover'.] —**repleviable** *adj*

replica /réppliká/ *n* **1** an accurate reproduction of an object **2** a scrupulous copy of a work of art, especially one made, authorized, or supervised by the original artist [Early 19C. < Italian, 'repeat' < Latin *replicare* 'fold back'.]

replicant /répplikənt/ *n* an imaginary being, especially in science fiction, that has been constructed from organic and computerized components to look like a human being. ◊ **cyborg**

replicate *v* /réppli kayt/ (**-cates, -cating, -cated**) **1** *vt* **DO SOMETHING AGAIN** to do something again or copy something **2** *vi* **BE DONE AGAIN** to undergo a repetition or reproduction **3** *vt* **COPY CELLULAR OR GENETIC MATERIAL** to reproduce exactly an organism, genetic material, or a cell ■ *adj* /répplikət, réppli kayt/ **BENT BACK** folded back on itself [Mid-16C. < Latin *replicare* 'fold back' < *plicare* 'to fold'.] —**replicative** *adj*

SYNONYMS See ***copy***.

replication /réppli káysh'n/ *n* **1 PROCESS OF REPEATING** the process of repeating, duplicating, or reproducing something **2 MAKING OF CELLULAR OR GENETIC COPY** the production of exact copies of molecules, genetic material, or cells **3 REPLY OF PLAINTIFF** a plaintiff's reply to the plea of a defendant (*dated*) **4 FOLD** a fold or folding back

replicon /répli kon/ *n* a segment of DNA or RNA that replicates itself as a unit, distinct from adjacent segments in a chromosome or other genetic element [Mid-20C. < REPLICATION.]

reply /ri plí/ *v* (**-plies, -plying, -plied**) **1** *vti* **RESPOND TO WHAT SOMEBODY SAYS** to say or write something in response to what somebody else has said or written ○ *replied that she wouldn't be available to take the job* **2** *vi* **RESPOND WITH ACTION OR GESTURE** to respond to somebody's action with a countering action or gesture **3** *vi* **ANSWER DEFENDANT'S PLEA** to speak in response to the plea of a defendant **4** *vi* **ECHO** to echo or return a sound ■ *n* (*plural* **-plies**) **1 SPOKEN OR WRITTEN RESPONSE** something said or written as a response to something else **2 ACTION PERFORMED AS RESPONSE** something done as a response to somebody else's action ○ *Her only reply was to turn on her heel and leave.* **3 ANSWER TO DEFENDANT'S PLEA** a statement made in response to the plea of a defendant [14C. Via Old French *replier* < Latin *replicare* (see REPLICATE).] —**replier** *n*

SYNONYMS See ***answer***.

reply-paid *adj* COMMUNICATION = **postpaid**

repoint /ree póynt/ *vt* to repair a brick wall by putting new mortar or cement between the bricks

report /ri páwrt/ *v* **1** *vti* **TELL ABOUT WHAT HAPPENED** to give information about something that has happened ○ *reported that negotiations were proceeding slowly* **2** *vti* **TELL PEOPLE NEWS USING MEDIA** to find out facts and tell people about them in print or a broadcast **3** *vt* **INFORM AUTHORITIES ABOUT SOMETHING OR SOMEBODY** to inform somebody in authority about something that has happened, especially a crime or an accident, or about somebody who has done something wrong ○ *reported him missing two days ago* ○ *reported the break-in to the police* **4** *vti* **TELL ABOUT RESEARCH OR INVESTIGATION** to give detailed information about research or an investigation ○ *The committee will report their findings early next week.* **5** *vti* **MAKE FULL OFFICIAL STATEMENT** to make a formal statement regarding something **6** *vt* **RECORD COURT PROCEEDINGS** to record the proceedings of a court **7** *vi* **INFORM ABOUT ARRIVAL** to let somebody know you have arrived ○ *Guests should report to reception on arrival.* **8** *vi* **DECLARE STATE OF HEALTH** to declare that you are in a specified condition of health ○ *another worker reporting sick* **9** *vi* **BE UNDER SOMEBODY'S AUTHORITY** to be subordinate and responsible to somebody or something ○ *You'll be reporting to me from now on.* ■ *n* **1 ACCOUNT** an account of an event, situation, or episode **2 NEWS ITEM OR BROADCAST** an account of news presented by a journalist **3 DOCUMENT GIVING INFORMATION** a document that gives information about an investigation or a piece of research, often put together by a group of people working together **4 UNCONFIRMED ACCOUNT** a widely-known account of something that may be true but has not been confirmed ○ *Report had it that the company was approaching bankruptcy.* **5 PERIODIC STATEMENT OF COMPANY'S FINANCES** a detailed periodic account of a company's activities, financial condition, and prospects that is made available to shareholders and investors ○ *a quarterly report* **6 WRITTEN ACCOUNT OF CHILD'S SCHOOLWORK** a record of a child's academic performance at school over a specified period, prepared by teachers and given to the child's parents. US term **report card** **7 SHARP LOUD NOISE** a very sharp loud noise, especially that of an explosion or gunshot **8 REPUTATION** reputation or character ■ **reports** *npl* **ACCOUNTS OF CASE AT LAW** written accounts of a court's adjudication, summarizing arguments and findings [14C. Via Old French < Latin *reportare* 'carry back' < *portare* 'carry'.] —**reportable** *adj*

reportage /ri páwr tij, réppawr taázh/ *n* **1 PROCESS OF TELLING NEWS** the use of print and electronic media to inform people about news and current events **2 THINGS REPORTED** a body of reported news **3 WAY OF GIVING NEWS** a particular way of gathering and presenting news [Late 19C. < REPORT, after French *reportage*.]

report card *n US* EDUC = **report** *n.* 6

reportedly /ri páwrtidli/ *adv* according to an unconfirmed report ○ *Reportedly he lost all his money.*

reported speech *n* LING = **indirect speech**

reporter /ri páwrtər/ *n* **1 SOMEBODY WHO REPORTS NEWS** somebody whose job is to find out facts and use the print or broadcast media to tell people about them **2 SOMEBODY WHO REPORTS** a maker of a report **3 COMPILER OF COURT PROCEEDINGS** a compiler of summarized records of court proceedings 4 **COMPILER OF LEGISLATIVE PROCEEDINGS** an official who compiles the proceedings of a legislature —**reportorial** /réppawr táwri əl/ *adj* —**reportorially** *adv*

report stage *n* a phase in the passage of a piece of legislation in the British and Canadian parliaments, following the report of a committee and preceding a third reading

repose[1] /ri pṓz/ *n* 1 **REST** a state of rest or inactivity 2 **REST AFTER DEATH** eternal or heavenly rest 3 **TRANQUILLITY** a condition of peacefulness and tranquillity, e.g. in a place 4 **COMPOSURE** calmness and composure of manner ■ *v* (**-poses, -posing, -posed**) (*formal*) 1 *vti* **LIE RESTING** to lie or lay something at rest 2 *vi* **BE DEAD** to lie dead (*used euphemistically*) 3 *vi* **LIE RESTING ON TOP OF** to lie while resting on or supported by something 4 *vr* **SETTLE SELF AT REST** to settle yourself in a relaxed or restful position 5 *vi* **TAKE SUPPORT FROM** to be supported or based on something ○ *Your argument reposes on false analogies.* [15C. Via French *reposer* < Latin *repausare* 'rest completely' < *pausare* 'to rest'.] —**reposal** *n* —**reposer** *n*

repose[2] /ri pṓz/ (**-poses, -posing, -posed**) *vt* to place faith, confidence, or trust in somebody or something (*formal*) ○ *reposed a great deal of confidence in him* [Mid-16C. < Latin *repos-*, stem of *reponere* 'place again' < *ponere* 'to place'.]

reposeful /ri pṓzf'l/ *adj* showing or giving rise to restfulness or calm —**reposefully** *adv* —**reposefulness** *n*

reposition /reèpa zísh'n/ *vt* 1 to put something in a new position 2 to change the marketing strategy of a company or product so as to have a wider or different appeal

repository /ri pózzitəri/ (*plural* **-ries**) *n* 1 **PLACE OR RECEPTACLE FOR STORAGE** a place or container in which something is stored 2 **SOMEBODY WITH EXTENSIVE KNOWLEDGE** somebody with, or something such as a book that contains extensive detailed knowledge of something ○ *She was a repository of information about the history of the island.* 3 **CONFIDANT** somebody in whom something is confided 4 **WAREHOUSE FOR COMMODITIES** a place where goods are stored prior to sale 5 **TOMB** a burial vault or sepulchre

repossess /reè pə zéss/ *vt* to take back goods or property from a buyer who has failed to keep up payments on them —**repossession** *n* —**repossessor** *n*

repot /ree pót/ (**-pots, -potting, -potted**) *vt* to take a plant out of one pot and put it in another, usually larger one —**repotting** *n*

repoussé /rə poóssay/ *adj* 1 **FORMING PATTERN IN RELIEF** formed as a raised pattern on a thin piece of metal by having been hammered through from the reverse side 2 **DECORATED WITH HAMMERED PATTERN** decorated with a raised pattern that has been hammered through from the reverse side ■ *n* 1 **HAMMERED DESIGN ON METAL** a raised design on a piece of metal made by hammering the design through from the reverse side 2 **TECHNIQUE OF HAMMERING A DESIGN** the technique of producing a raised design on a thin piece of metal by hammering it through from the reverse side [Mid-19C. < French, past participle of *repousser* 'push back' < *pousser* 'push'.]

repp *n* TEXTILES = **rep**[1]

repr. *abbr* 1 representative 2 represented 3 representing 4 reprint

reprehend /réppri hénd/ *vt* to criticize or reprove somebody or something [14C. < Latin *reprehendere* 'seize again' < *prehendere* 'seize'.] —**reprehendable** *adj* —**reprehender** *n*

reprehensible /réppri hénssəb'l/ *adj* highly unacceptable and deserving censure [14C. < late Latin *reprehensibilis* < *reprehendere* (see REPREHEND).] —**reprehensibility** /-hénssə bílləti/ *n* —**reprehensibly** *adv*

reprehension /réppri hénsh'n/ *n* reproof or criticism for wrongdoing [14C. < Latin *reprehension-*, < *reprehendere* (see REPREHEND).] —**reprehensive** *adj* —**reprehensively** *adv*

represent /réppri zént/ *v* 1 *vt* **ACT OR SPEAK FOR ANOTHER** to act or speak on behalf of somebody or something 2 *vt* **GO SOMEWHERE ON BEHALF OF ANOTHER** to go or be present somewhere on behalf of somebody or something 3 *vt* **ACT FOR ANOTHER OFFICIALLY** to speak and act for somebody else in an official way ○ *Who will be representing France at the conference?* 4 *vt* **BE PRESENT** to be somewhere in large or small numbers 5 *vt* **BE EQUIVALENT OF** to be a sign or equivalent of something 6 *vt* **SYMBOLIZE** to symbolize something, especially as a sign on a map showing the position of something ○ *On the map a blue line represents a river.* 7 *vt* **DEPICT** to portray or present an image of somebody or something as being something in particular 8 *vr* **UNTRUTHFULLY CLAIM TO BE SOMETHING** to describe yourself as something you are not ○ *He was arrested at the airport despite trying to represent himself as a tourist.* 9 *vt* **DEPICT SOMEBODY ON STAGE** to portray or perform a character or role on stage [14C. Directly or via French < Latin *repraesentare* 'show back' < *praesentare* 'show'.] —**representability** /-zéntə bílləti/ *n* —**representable** /réppri zéntəb'l/ *adj* —**representer** *n*

USAGE See ***denote***.

---

re-present /reè pri zént/ *vt* to send, offer, or present something again

representation /réppri zen táysh'n/ *n* 1 **FACT OF BEING SERVED BY REPRESENTATIVE** the fact or right of being represented by somebody, especially of having a member in a legislature with power to vote or speak for an electorate 2 **VOTING SYSTEM OR BODY OF ELECTORS** the system by which electors vote for people to represent them as legislators, administrators, or judges, or the group of people so elected 3 **PICTURE** a visual depiction of somebody or something 4 **SOMETHING SPOKEN OR DONE FOR ANOTHER** action or speech on behalf of another, especially as an agent or deputy 5 **SOMETHING DESCRIBED OR STATED** a description, account, or statement of something real or alleged, especially one meant to induce a response from authority (*often plural*) 6 **STATEMENT INDUCING SOMEBODY TO MAKE CONTRACT** a statement, real or implied, that encourages somebody to make an agreement 7 **PERFORMANCE** a theatrical performance or production

representational /réppri zen táysh'nəl/ *adj* 1 relating to or characterized by representation 2 depicting something in a physically recognizable form, especially in art —**representationally** *adv*

representationalism /réppri zen táysh'nəlizəm/, **representationism** /-táysh'nizəm/ *n* 1 the theory that the mind directly apprehends external objects only through ideas or data provided by the senses 2 the practice or principle of depicting objects in recognizable form, especially in art —**representationalist** *n* —**representationalistic** /-táysh'nə lístik/ *adj*

representative /réppri zéntətiv/ *n* 1 **SOMEBODY WHO SPEAKS FOR OTHERS** a person who speaks, acts, or votes on behalf of others 2 **MEMBER OF LEGISLATURE** a member of a legislative assembly 3 **representative, Representative** *US* **MEMBER OF HOUSE OF REPRESENTATIVES** a member of the House of Representatives, the lower chamber in the US Congress, or of a state legislature 4 **COMMERCIAL AGENT OR SALESPERSON** an agent or salesperson for a company 5 **EXAMPLE** an example or type of something ■ *adj* 1 **TYPICAL** typical of something, especially of a class or kind 2 **MADE UP OF ELECTED PEOPLE** composed of elected or authorized people ○ *a representative assembly* 3 **LETTING PEOPLE ELECT** allowing people to vote for somebody to represent them in a legislative body such as the House of Commons in the United Kingdom or the Congress in the United States ○ *a representative form of government* 4 **MADE UP OF ALL TYPES** including a complete range of examples of something ○ *a representative sample* 5 **ACTING ON SOMEBODY'S BEHALF** acting as somebody's agent, deputy, or delegate —**representatively** *adv* —**representativeness** *n*

~~**representitive**~~ incorrect spelling of **representative**

repress /ri préss/ *vt* 1 **CURB ACTIONS THAT SHOW FEELINGS** to check or restrain an action that would reveal feelings ○ *He had to repress a smile.* 2 **USE AUTHORITY TO CONTROL PEOPLE'S FREEDOM** to control people's freedom by force or military means ○ *repress an uprising* 3 **BLOCK SOMETHING FROM MIND** to block unacceptable or painful impulses, desires, or memories from the conscious mind [14C. < Latin *repress-*, past participle of *reprimere* 'press back' < *premere* 'press'.] —**repressibility** /ri préssə bílləti/ *n* —**repressible** *adj*

re-press /ree préss/ *vt* to press something again, especially to manufacture another issue of a recording

repressed /ri prést/ *adj* 1 **WITH CURBED EMOTIONS** not acknowledging strong personal feelings, particularly of anger or sexual desire 2 **BLOCKED FROM CONSCIOUSNESS** in Freudian psychology, blocked from the conscious mind and relegated to the unconscious 3 **SUBDUED FORCIBLY** kept under control by force ○ *the repressed peoples of the invaded islands*

represser *n* = **repressor** *n.* 2

repression /ri présh'n/ *n* 1 in Freudian psychology, a mechanism by which individuals protect themselves from threatening thoughts by blocking them out of the conscious mind 2 the process of suppressing somebody or the condition of having political, social, or cultural freedom controlled by force

repressive /ri préssiv/ *adj* exerting strict control on the freedom of others —**repressively** *adv* —**repressiveness** *n*

repressor /ri préssər/ *n* 1 a protein that stops gene transcription 2 **repressor, represser** somebody who or something that represses

reprieve /ri preév/ *vt* (**-prieves, -prieving, -prieved**) 1 **STOP OR POSTPONE SOMEBODY'S PUNISHMENT** to halt or delay somebody's punishment, especially when the punishment is death (*often passive*) 2 **OFFER RESPITE TO** to provide somebody with temporary relief from something harmful, especially danger or pain ■ *n* 1 **STOPPING OR POSTPONEMENT OF PUNISHMENT** the halting or delay of somebody's punishment, especially when the punishment is death 2 **WARRANT HALTING OR POSTPONING PUNISHMENT** a warrant giving the authority to stop or postpone somebody's punishment, especially when the punishment is death 3 **RESPITE FROM SOMETHING HARMFUL** a relief from something harmful, especially danger or pain [Mid-17C. Alteration of obsolete *repry* 'take back to prison' (hence 'escape the death sentence'), < Old French *repris* 'taken back' < Latin *reprehendere* 'seize again'.] —**reprievable** *adj* —**repriever** *n*

reprimand /réppri maand/ *vt* to rebuke somebody for a wrongdoing ■ *n* a rebuke given for having done something wrong [Mid-17C. Via French *réprimande* < Latin *reprimenda* 'that is to be suppressed' < *reprimere* 'press back'.]

reprint *vt* /ree prínt/ **PRINT SOMETHING AGAIN** to print something again, especially with few or no changes ■ *n* /reè prínt/ 1 **COPY OF SOMETHING ALREADY PUBLISHED** a printed copy of something that has already been in print 2 PUBL = **offprint** 3 **REISSUE OF PRINTED WORK** a book or other printed work that is the same as, or has only minor changes from, one that was previously issued —**reprinter** /ree príntər/ *n*

reprisal /ri príz'l/ *n* 1 **RETALIATION IN WAR** a violent military action such as the killing of prisoners or civilians, carried out in retaliation for an enemy's action 2 **STRONG OR VIOLENT RETALIATION** a strong or violent retaliation for an action that somebody has taken 3 **RETALIATORY SEIZURE FROM ANOTHER COUNTRY** the forcible seizure of property or people from another country as retaliation for some injury [15C. < Anglo-Norman *reprisaille* < Latin *reprehendere* (see REPREHEND).]

reprise /ri preéz/ *n* 1 **REPEAT OF MUSICAL PASSAGE** a repeated passage of music, or a return to an earlier musical theme 2 MUSIC = **chorus** *n.* 1 3 **REPETITION** a repetition or recurrence of something ■ *vt* (**-prises, -prising, -prised**) 1 **REPEAT MUSIC** to repeat a passage of music or return to an earlier theme 2 **REPEAT ACTION** to repeat an action or performance ○ *reprised her role as Gertrude in the New York production* [Mid-20C. < French, past participle of *reprendre* 'take again', used as a noun < *prendre* 'take' < Latin *prehendere*.]

reprivatize /ree prívə tīz/ (**-tizes, -tizing, -tized**), **reprivatise** (**-tises, -tising, -tised**) *vt* to return something from public to private ownership —**reprivatization** /ree prívə tī záysh'n/ *n*

repro /reè prō/ *n* (*informal*) 1 a reproduction, especially of a painting or piece of furniture 2 a reproduction proof [Mid-20C. Shortening.]

reproach /ri prṓch/ *v* 1 *vt* **CRITICIZE** to criticize somebody for doing something wrong 2 *vr* **FEEL BLAMEWORTHY** to feel ashamed because you know you have done something wrong ○ *There's no reason to reproach yourself, because there was nothing you could do.* ■ *n* 1 **CRITICISM** criticism or disapproval for having done something wrong, or an expression of this 2 **SOMETHING DISGRACEFUL** something that reflects badly on somebody who has failed to improve or deal with it 3 **DISCREDIT** shame or disgrace that somebody or something incurs ○ *actions that brought reproach upon his family* [15C. < Old French *reprochier* < Latin *prope* 'near'.] —**reproachable** *adj* —**reproachableness** *n* —**reproachably** *adv* —**reproacher** *n* —**reproachingly** *adv* ◇ **above** *or* **beyond reproach** so good that no criticism can be made

reproachful /ri prṓchf'l/ *adj* expressing disapproval or blame —**reproachfully** *adv* —**reproachfulness** *n*

reprobate /répprō bayt/ *n* 1 **SOMEBODY IMMORAL** a disreputable or immoral person 2 **SOMEBODY DAMNED** somebody whose soul is believed to be damned ■ *adj* 1 **DISREPUTABLE** disreputable or immoral 2 **DAMNED** with a soul that is damned ■ *vt* (**-bates, -bating, -bated**) **1 CENSURE** to censure or condemn somebody (*formal*) **2 DENY SALVATION TO** to condemn somebody to supposed eternal damnation [Mid-16C. < late Latin *reprobatus* < Latin, past participle of *reprobare* 'prove to be unworthy'.] —**reprobacy** /-bəssi/ *n* —**reprobater** *n* —**reprobative** /-bətiv/ *adj*

reprobation /réppro̅ báysh'n/ *n* **1** strong condemnation or disapproval of somebody or something **2** the supposed condemnation of somebody's soul to eternal damnation [15C. Directly or via French < Latin *reprobation-* < *reprobare* 'prove to be unworthy'.] —**reprobationary** *adj*

reprocess /ree pro̅ séss/ *vt* to process something such as nuclear fuel again in order to reuse it

reproduce /reèprə dyóoss/ (**-duces, -ducing, -duced**) *v* **1** *vti* **MAKE DUPLICATE** to duplicate something, or be duplicated, by photographing, scanning, printing, or another process **2** *vt* **REPEAT** to do something in the same way as before **3** *vi* **PRODUCE OFFSPRING** to produce offspring or new individuals through a sexual or asexual process **4** *vt* **REMEMBER** to remember or imagine something again —**reproducer** *n* —**reproducibility** /reèprə dyóossə bílləti/ *n* —**reproducible** /reèprə dyóossəb'l/ *adj* —**reproducibly** *adv*

SYNONYMS See *copy*.

reproduction /reèprə dúksh'n/ *n* **1 COPY OF OBJECT** a copy of something in an earlier style, especially a painting or a piece of furniture **2 REPRODUCING OF** the act or process of reproducing something **3 PRINT, ELECTRONIC, OR PHOTOGRAPHIC DUPLICATE** a copy of something printed, scanned, photographed, or produced by other means **4 RECORDING OF SOUND** the recording of sound or the quality of recorded sound **5 PRODUCTION OF OFFSPRING** the production of young plants and animals of the same kind through a sexual or asexual process [Mid-17C. < REPRODUCE, after *production*.]

reproduction proof *n* a printed proof, usually on glossy paper, of such high quality that it can be photographed for making a printing plate

reproductive /reèprə dúktiv/ *adj* relating to, taking part in, or enabling the production of new offspring or individuals ○ *reproductive organs* [Mid-18C. < REPRODUCE, after *productive*.] —**reproductively** *adv* —**reproductiveness** *n*

reproductive system *n* the combination of bodily organs and tissues used in the process of producing offspring

ϟ**reprogram** /ree pro̅ gram/ (**-grams, -gramming** *or* **-graming, -grammed** *or* **-gramed**) *vt* to add new programs to a computer system, or program it in a different way —**reprogrammability** /ree pro̅ grammə bílləti/ *n* —**reprogrammable** *adj*

reprography /ri próggrəfi/ *n* the reproduction of something printed, e.g. by offset printing, microfilming, photography, or xerography [Mid-20C. < German *Reprographie*, blend of *Reproduktion* 'reproduction' + *Photographie* 'photography'.] —**reprographic** /répprə gráffik/ *adj*

reproof /ri próof/, **reproval** /ri próov'l/ *n* the act of criticizing somebody for having done something wrong, or something stated as a rebuke [14C. < Old French *reprove* < *reprover* (see REPROVE).]

reprove /ri próov/ (**-proves, -proving, -proved**) *vt* to speak to somebody in a way that shows disapproval of something he or she has done [14C. Via Old French *reprover* < Latin *reprobare* 'prove to be unworthy' < *probare* 'prove'.] —**reprovable** *adj* —**reprover** *n* —**reprovingly** *adv*

rept *abbr* **1** receipt **2** report

reptant /réptənt/ *adj* creeping or lying along the ground [Mid-17C. < Latin *reptare* 'keep creeping' < *repere* 'creep'.]

reptile /rép tīl/ *n* **1** an air-breathing, cold-blooded, egg-laying vertebrate such as the crocodile, tortoise, snake, or lizard, with an outer covering of scales or plates and a bony skeleton. Class: Reptilia. **2** an offensive term that deliberately insults somebody whose behaviour or character is regarded as suspicious, untrustworthy, or sickeningly ingratiating (*insult*) [14C. Via French < late Latin *reptilis* 'creeping' < Latin *rept-*, past participle of *repere* 'to creep'.] —**reptile** *adj* —**reptilian** /rep tílli ən/ *adj, n*

Repton /réptən/, **Humphry** (1752–1818) British landscape architect

Repub. *abbr* **1** Republic **2** Republican

republic /ri púbblik/ *n* **1 POLITICAL SYSTEM WITH POWERFUL ELECTORATE** a political system or form of government in which people elect representatives to exercise power for them **2 STATE WITH POWERFUL ELECTORATE** a state or other political unit with a form of government in which the supreme power is in the hands of representatives elected by the people **3 GROUP OF EQUALS WITH COLLECTIVE INTERESTS** a group of people who are considered to be equals and who have a collective interest, objective, or vocation (*formal*) ○ *the republic of letters* [Late 16C. Via French *république* < Latin *res publica* 'public matter'.]

republican /ri púbblikən/ *n* a believer that the best government is one in which supreme power is vested in an electorate ■ *adj* relating to, belonging to, or characteristic of a republic

Republican /ri púbblikən/ *adj* **1** supporting the idea that Northern Ireland should be united politically with the Republic of Ireland and should cease to form part of the United Kingdom **2** belonging to or supporting the Republican Party in the United States

republicanise *vt* POL = **republicanize**

republicanism /ri púbblikənizəm/ *n* **1** the belief that the supreme power of a country should be vested in an electorate **2** the theory and principles of republican government

Republicanism *n* **1** support for the idea of uniting Northern Ireland politically with the Republic of Ireland **2** support for the Republican Party in the United States

republicanize /ri púbblikə nīz/ (**-izes, -izing, -ized**), **republicanise** (**-ises, -ising, -ised**) *vt* to make a state or other political unit into a republic —**republicanization** /ri púbblikə nī záysh'n/ *n*

Republican Party *n* a political party at state and national level in the United States, founded in 1854

republication /reè púbbli káysh'n/ *n* **1** the act or process of publishing something again **2** something published again, especially in an unchanged form

republish /ree púbblish/ *vt* to reissue a publication, especially in an unchanged form —**republisher** *n*

repudiate /ri pyóodi ayt/ (**-ates, -ating, -ated**) *vt* **1 DISOWN** to disapprove of something formally and strongly and renounce any connection with it ○ *She repudiated the committee's actions.* **2 DENY** to state that something is untrue **3 REJECT** to reject something that is offered **4 DISOWN LOVED ONE** to disown a family member or lover **5 REJECT SOMETHING AS INVALID** to refuse to accept the validity of something **6 REFUSE TO PAY DEBT** to refuse to acknowledge or pay a debt [Mid-16C. < Latin *repudiare* 'to divorce' < *repudium* 'divorce'.] —**repudiable** *adj* —**repudiation** /ri pyóodi áysh'n/ *n* —**repudiationist** /ri pyóodi áysh'nist/ *n* —**repudiative** /ri pyóodi ətiv/ *adj* —**repudiator** /ri pyóodi aytər/ *n*

repugnant /ri púgnənt/ *adj* **1** offensive and completely unacceptable **2** making somebody feel physically repelled ○ *a repugnant odour* [Late 18C. Via Old French, 'contrary' < Latin *repugnant-*, present participle of *repugnare* 'fight back' < *pugnare* 'to fight'.] —**repugnance** *n* —**repugnantly** *adv*

repulse /ri púlss/ *vt* (**-pulses, -pulsing, -pulsed**) **1 FORCE BACK MILITARY ATTACK** to repel an attacking military force **2 SPURN** to reject or rebuff an approach from somebody ■ *n* **1 REJECTION** a refusal or rejection of somebody **2 ACT OF FORCING BACK ATTACK** the forcing back of an attacking military force [Mid-16C. < Latin *repuls-*, past participle of *repellere* 'drive back'.]

repulsion /ri púlsh'n/ *n* **1** a feeling of disgust or very strong dislike **2** a force between two bodies of like electric charge or magnetic polarity that tends to repel or separate them

repulsive /ri púlssiv/ *adj* **1** making somebody feel disgust or very strong dislike **2** tending to repel —**repulsively** *adv* —**repulsiveness** *n*

USAGE See *repellent*.

reputable /réppyòotəb'l/ *adj* known to be honest, reliable, or respectable [Late 17C. Directly or via French < medieval Latin *reputabilis* < Latin *reputare* (see REPUTE).] —**reputability** /réppyòotə bílləti/ *n* —**reputably** /réppyòotəbli/ *adv*

reputation /réppyoo táysh'n/ *n* **1** the views that are generally held about somebody or something **2** a high opinion that people hold about somebody or something [14C. < Latin *reputation-* 'consideration' < *reputare* (see REPUTE).]

repute /ri pyóot/ *n* (*formal*) **1** estimation or character according to what people in general think **2** good reputation or standing [Mid-16C. Directly or via French *reputer* < Latin *reputare* 'think repeatedly' < *putare* 'think'.]

reputed /ri pyóotid/ *adj* widely believed, although not necessarily established as fact [Late 16C. < REPUTE used as a verb.]

reputedly /ri pyóotidli/ *adv* according to popular belief

req. *abbr* **1** request **2** require **3** required **4** requirement **5** requisition

request /ri kwést/ *vt* **1 ASK POLITELY FOR** to ask formally or courteously for something to be given or done ○ *requested that he be excused* ○ *requested her favourite song* **2 ASK SOMEBODY FOR** to ask somebody to do something ○ *requested Father Peter to perform their marriage ceremony* ■ *n* **1 EXPRESSION OF A POLITE WISH OR DESIRE** an act of politely or formally asking that something be done or given **2 MUSIC THAT HAS BEEN ASKED FOR** a piece of music played on a radio programme, at a live performance, or at a disco because somebody asks for it ○ *We'll be taking several requests tonight.* **3 ACT OF EXPRESSING A WISH** the act of asking or petitioning for something to be done or given [14C. Via Old French < Latin *requisitus*, past participle of *requirere* (see REQUIRE).] —**requester** *n*

request stop *n* a bus stop at which the bus does not halt unless somebody at the stop signals for it to do so or if somebody wants to get off there

requiem /rékwi əm, -wi em/, **Requiem** *n* **1 ROMAN CATHOLIC SERVICE FOR THE DEAD** a Roman Catholic mass held to offer prayers for somebody who has died **2 MUSIC FOR A REQUIEM** a piece of music written to accompany a requiem mass **3 COMMEMORATIVE MUSIC** a piece of music written to commemorate somebody who has died [14C. < Latin, 'rest', in *Requiem aeternam dona eis Domine* 'Grant them eternal rest, O Lord'.]

requiem shark *n* a voracious shark of tropical waters. Hammerheads, tiger sharks, and soupfins are all requiem sharks. Family: Carcharhinidae. [By folk etymology < French *requin* 'shark']

requiescat /rékwi éss kat/ *n* a prayer asking that the soul of a dead person might be at rest [Early 19C. < Latin, 'may he or she rest'.]

require /ri kwír/ (**-quires, -quiring, -quired**) *vt* **1 NEED** to be in need of something or somebody for a particular purpose ○ *The recipe requires a cup of milk.* **2 MAKE NECESSARY** to have something as a necessary precondition ○ *A password is required for entry to the system.* **3 DEMAND BY LAW** to demand something by a law or regulation (*often passive*) ○ *Notification was required by law.* **4 INSIST ON** to insist that somebody do something ○ *All applicants are required to pass a medical exam.* [14C. < Old French *requ(i)er-*, stem of *requere* < Latin *requirere* 'seek in return' < Latin *quaerere* 'seek'.] —**requirable** *adj* —**required** *adj* —**requirement** *n* —**requirer** *n*

requisite /rékwizit/ *adj* necessary or indispensable for something (*formal*) ○ *the requisite skills for the job* ■ *n* something that is necessary or indispensable [15C. < Latin *requisitus*, past participle of *requirere* (see REQUIRE).] —**requisitely** *adv* —**requisiteness** *n*

SYNONYMS See *necessary*.

requisition /rékwi zísh'n/ *n* **1 DEMAND FOR** a demand for something that is required **2 OFFICIAL FORM** a written or printed request for something that is needed **3 FACT OF MAKING A FORMAL DEMAND** the act or process of making a formal demand for something **4 REQUEST FOR THE RETURN OF A FUGITIVE** a request by a government that another government return a fugitive from the law ■ *vt* **1 DEMAND AND TAKE SOMETHING OFFICIALLY** to demand and take something that is needed, especially for official or military use **2 REQUIRE AND OBTAIN SOMEBODY FOR A JOB** to require and obtain the services of somebody to do something ○ *requisitioned a few friends for the weekend to help paint the house* [Mid-16C. Directly or via French < Latin *requisitio-*, < past participle of *requirere* (see REQUIRE).] —**requisitionary** *adj*

requite /ri kwít/ (**-quites, -quiting, -quited**) *vt* **1** to return in kind a kindness or hurt that somebody has done **2** to pay somebody back for a service performed [Early 16C. < an earlier form of QUIT, 'pay up'.] —**requitable** *adj* —**requital** *n* —**requitement** *n* —**requiter** *n*

reradiate /ree ráydi ayt/ (**-ates, -ating, -ated**) *vt* to emit radiation after absorbing incident radiation —**reradiation** /reè raydi áysh'n/ *n*

reread /ree réed/ (**-reads, -reading, -read** /-réd/) *vt* to read something again

rerecord /rée ri káwrd/ *vt* to make a record or recording of something such as a musical performance that replaces or supersedes a previous one

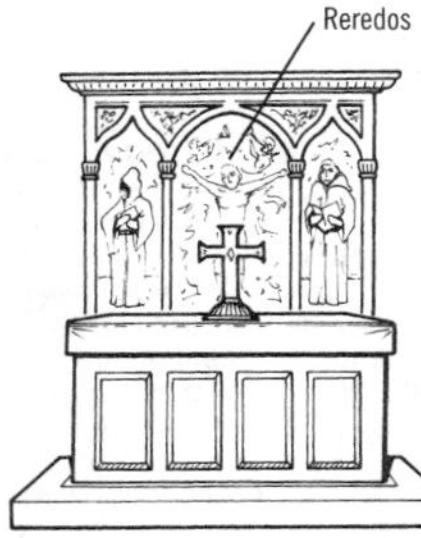

Reredos

reredos /réer doss/ *n* **1** an artistic decoration behind the altar in a church, e.g. a wood or stone screen or a wall-hanging **2** the back of an open fireplace [14C. Via Anglo-Norman < Old French *aredos* < *arere* 'behind' + *dos* 'back' (< Latin *dorsum*).]

reregulation /rée reg gyòo láysh'n/ *n US* the reintroduction of regulation to an industry that has previously been deregulated

rerelease /rée ri léess/ *vt* (**-leases, -leasing, -leased**) to release a music recording or a film again for distribution to the public ■ *n* a music recording or a film that has been released again to the public

reroute /ree ròot/ (**-routes, -routing, -routed**) *vt* to direct people or vehicles along an alternative route, e.g. because of an accident, road construction, or for security reasons

rerun *vt* /ree rún/ (**-runs, -running, -ran** /-rán/, **-run**) **1 SHOW RECORDED ENTERTAINMENT AGAIN** to show or broadcast a TV series, video, or film again **2 REPEAT A RACE** to run a race again, or cause a race to be run again, after the result on the first occasion has been disallowed because of an infringement ■ *n* /rée run/ (*plural* **-runs**) **1 REPEAT SHOWING OF RECORDED ENTERTAINMENT** a repeat showing of recorded entertainment, especially a TV series **2 REPEAT RUNNING OF RACE** the repeat running of a race after an infringement

res /rayz, rayss/ (*plural* **res**) *n* in law, a matter or thing [< Latin, 'thing, legal matter']

RES *abbr* **1** renewable energy source **2** renewable energy system **3** Royal Entomological Society

res. *abbr* **1** research **2** reservation **3** reserved **4** reservoir **5** residence **6** resident **7** resigned **8** resolution

res adjudicata *n* LAW = **res judicata**

resale /rée sayl, ree sáyl/ *n* **1** the selling of something again ○ *Not for resale.* **2** the selling of something secondhand —**resalable** /ree sáyləb'l/ *adj* —**resalability** /ree sáylə bílləti/ *n*

resale price maintenance *n* COMM = **retail price maintenance**

resat past tense, past participle of **resit**

rescale /ree skáyl/ (**-scales, -scaling, -scaled**) *vt* to modify the scale of something, especially to reduce it ○ *rescale a budget* ○ *rescale a drawing*

reschedule /ree shéddyool, -skédd-/ (**-ules, -uling, -uled**) *vt* **1** to arrange a new time slot for something **2** to extend the payment schedule of a loan

rescind /ri sínd/ *vt* **1 CANCEL** to remove the validity or authority of something **2 REVOKE CONTRACT** to revoke a contract and return the parties to their former positions before the contract **3 REPEAL A DECISION OR ENACTMENT** to declare a decision or enactment null and void [Mid-16C. < Latin *rescindere* 'cut back' < *scindere* 'to cut'.] —**rescindable** *adj* —**rescinder** *n* —**rescindment** *n*

rescission /ri sízh'n/ *n* the act of rescinding something [Early 17C. Via late Latin *rescission-* < Latin *rescindere* (see RESCIND).]

rescore /ree skáwr/ (**-scores, -scoring, -scored**) *vt* to write new instrumentation for a piece of music

rescript /rée skript/ *n* **1 ECCLESIASTICAL RULING** a formal reply by the pope or some other high dignitary of the Roman Catholic Church on a matter of doctrine or discipline **2 ROMAN EMPEROR'S LEGAL RULING** a formal reply by an ancient Roman or Holy Roman emperor on a point of law **3 REWRITE** an act of rewriting something [14C. < Latin *rescriptum*, neuter past participle of *rescribere* 'write back' < *scribere* 'write'.]

rescue /rés kyoo/ *v* (**-cues, -cuing, -cued**) **1** *vt* **REMOVE SOMEBODY OR SOMETHING FROM DANGER** to save somebody or something from a dangerous or harmful situation ○ *The boys had to be rescued from the rocks by helicopter* **2 SAVE** to prevent something from being discarded, rejected, or put out of operation ○ *At the last minute the factory was rescued from closure.* **3** *vt* **GET SOMEBODY OUT OF JAIL** to release somebody from legal custody by force **4** *vt* **TAKE FORCIBLE POSSESSION OF** to seize property or goods by force ■ *n* **1 REMOVAL FROM DANGER OR HARM** an act or instance of saving somebody or something from a dangerous or harmful situation (*often before nouns*) ○ *a daring rescue attempt* **2 PROVISION OF HELP** an instance of helping somebody in an awkward or difficult situation ○ *I couldn't think what to say, but luckily he came to my rescue.* **3 RELEASE FROM JAIL** the release of somebody from legal custody by force **4 SEIZURE OF GOODS** the seizure of property or goods by force [14C. < Old French *rescourre* 'shake loose' < *escourre* 'shake' < Latin *escutere* < *ex-* 'out'+ *quatere* 'to strike'.] —**rescuable** *adj* —**rescuer** *n*

research /ri súrch, rée surch/ *n* methodical investigation into a subject in order to discover facts, to establish or revise a theory, or to develop a plan of action based on the facts discovered ■ *vti* to carry out research into a subject [Late 16C. < obsolete French *recerche* < Old French *recercher* 'search closely' < *cerchier* 'explore'.] —**researchable** *adj* —**researcher** *n*

USAGE The traditional pronunciation is with the stress on the second syllable (ri súrch), both for the noun and the verb. More recently, a pronunciation with the stress on the first syllable (rée surch) has become common, especially in broadcasting.

research and development *n* the work in a company of investigating improved processes, products, and services and of developing new ones

reseat /ree séet/ *vt* **1 SEAT SOMEBODY ELSEWHERE** to seat somebody in another place **2 SEAT SOMEBODY AS BEFORE** to return somebody to the seat previously occupied **3 REPLACE THE SEATS IN BUILDING** to fit new seats in an auditorium or hall **4 PROVIDE A NEW SEAT FOR** to replace the material on a seat **5 REPLACE VALVE SEATING** to return the seating of a valve to good condition

reseau /rézzō/ (*plural* **-seaux** /rézzō, rézzōz/ *or* **-seaus**) *n* **1** a mesh foundation on which lace is made **2** a grid of lines photographed onto or cut into a glass plate and used as a reference for astronomical observations [Late 16C. Via French *réseau* 'network' < Old French *reseuil* 'little net' < *raiz* 'net' < Latin *rete*.]

resect /ri sékt/ *vt* to cut through and surgically remove part of an organ, bone, or other body part [Mid-17C. < Latin *resect-*, past participle of *resecare* 'cut back' < *secare* 'to cut'.]

resection /ri séksh'n/ *n* **1** the surgical removal of part of an organ, bone, or other body part **2** the establishment of the location of a point when surveying by sighting from that point to two other points whose locations are known

resectoscope /ri séktə skōp/ *n* a surgical instrument that allows a resection to be made without a bigger incision than that caused by the instrument itself

reseda /réssidə, ri séedə/ *n* (*plural* **-das** *or* **-da**) **1 MEDITERRANEAN PLANT** a plant that has small dense spikes of greyish-green flowers with divided petals. Native to: Mediterranean. Genus: *Reseda.* **2 GREYISH-GREEN** a greyish-green colour ■ *adj* **GREYISH-GREEN IN COLOUR** of a greyish-green colour [Mid-18C. Via modern Latin < Latin.]

reseed /ree séed/ *v* **1** *vt* to plant seeds on an area of land again **2** *vti* to grow a plant or to grow from seed dropped by the previous generation

reselect /rée si lékt/ *vt* to select somebody or something again, especially an existing office holder for re-election —**reselection** *n*

resell /ree sél/ (**-sells, -selling, -sold** /-sṓld/, **-sold**) *vt* to sell to another buyer an item that you yourself have bought

reseller /ree séllər, rée sellər/ *n* a wholesaler selling to other distributors or a retail organization that sells to end-users

resemblance /ri zémblənss/ *n* **1 SIMILARITY** similarity in appearance or quality to somebody or something else **2 DEGREE OF SIMILARITY** the extent to which somebody or something resembles somebody or something else ○ *the resemblance between them is striking* **3 POINT OF SIMILARITY** a respect in which somebody or something resembles somebody or something else **4 SOMETHING SIMILAR** something that resembles something else

resemble /ri zémb'əl/ (**-bles, -bling, -bled**) *vt* to be similar to somebody or something in appearance or behaviour [14C. < Old French *resembler* 'be very like' < *sembler* 'seem' < Latin *simulare* 'simulate'.] —**resembler** *n*

resend /ree sénd/ (**-sends, -sending, -sent, -sent** /-sént/) *vt* to send something again

resent /ri zént/ *vt* to feel aggrieved about something or towards somebody, often because of a perceived wrong or injustice [Late 16C. < obsolete French *ressentir* 'feel strongly' < *sentir* 'feel' < Latin *sentire*.]

resentful /ri zéntf'l/ *adj* **1** feeling aggrieved and ill-used **2** characterized by feelings of annoyance or ill-use ○ *a resentful silence* —**resentfully** *adv* —**resentfulness** *n*

resentment /ri zéntmənt/ *n* aggrieved feelings about something or towards somebody, usually as a result of ill-usage or insult, or an instance of these [Early 17C. < obsolete French *ressentiment* 'strong feeling' < *ressentir* (see RESENT).]

reserpine /réssər peen, ri súrp een/ *n* an alkaloid drug. Source: rauwolfia roots. Use: tranquillizer, treatment of high blood pressure. [Mid-20C. Shortening of modern Latin *Rauwolfia serpentina*.]

reservation /rézzər váysh'n/ *n* **1 ARRANGEMENT MADE BEFOREHAND** an advance booking, e.g. of a seat, hotel room, or ticket **2 PLACE ARRANGED BEFOREHAND** something such as a seat, hotel room, or ticket booked in advance **3 ARRANGING OF SOMETHING BEFOREHAND** the act of booking something in advance **4 LAND SET ASIDE** an area of land set aside for a particular purpose, especially in North America for the use of a Native North American people **5** TRANSP = **central reservation** **6 KEEPING SOMETHING BACK** the act of withholding something, or an instance of so doing **7 LIMITING CONDITION** a limiting condition to an agreement **8 RETAINED LEGAL INTEREST** a clause in a deed by which somebody retains an interest in something being granted or leased, or such an interest itself **9 PRESERVATION OF CONSECRATED ELEMENTS** the practice of retaining part of the consecrated bread and wine after celebrating Communion for later use, e.g. when visiting the sick ■ **reservations** *npl* **MISGIVINGS** doubts that prevent wholehearted agreement to or approval of something —**reservationist** *n*

reserve /ri zúrv/ (**-serves, -serving, -served**) *vt* **1 SET SOMETHING ASIDE** to keep something back for future use or for some specific purpose **2 BOOK A PLACE BEFOREHAND** to make arrangements in advance to secure a place such as a seat, ticket, table, or hotel room **3 RETAIN SOMETHING FOR YOUR OWN BENEFIT** to retain the option of future action on somebody's or your own behalf ○ *I reserve the right to change my mind.* **4 POSTPONE A DECISION** to defer making a decision until all the issues have been considered ○ *reserve judgement* ■ *n* **1 EMERGENCY SUPPLY** something kept back for later use, especially in an emergency **2 WILDLIFE CONSERVATION AREA** an area of land set aside for conserving wildlife. US term **preserve** *n.* 3 **3 COOLNESS OF MANNER** emotional restraint, resulting in a reticent or composed manner **4 SUBSTITUTE PLAYER** a team member called to play when a member of the original team withdraws, either before or during a game **5 INACTIVE PART OF THE ARMED SERVICES** the part of a country's armed services that is not on active service at a given time **6 REINFORCEMENT FORCE** the part of an armed force that is not initially committed during a military engagement but supplies reinforcements as necessary **7 MEMBER OF A RESERVE** a member of a military reserve **8 MONEY RETAINED FOR FUTURE USE** an amount of capital or revenue retained by a company or financial institution to meet future contingencies (*often plural*) **9 NATIONAL FUNDS** a country's supply of gold and foreign currency that is held by the central bank against future liabilities or to support the currency when the exchange rates fluctuate **10 UNEXPLOITED NATURAL RESOURCE** a supply of a natural resource such as a mineral or petrochemical that is estimated to exist from geological data but is not yet utilized **11** *ANZ* **LAND FOR PUBLIC RECREATION** an area of government-owned land set aside for public recreation **12** *Can* **LAND USED AS**

A RESERVATION an area of land set aside as a reservation for use by a Native North American people **13 NEXT RUNNER-UP** a competitor or exhibit such as an animal at an agricultural show that places immediately after the prizewinners and will receive a prize if a prizewinner is disqualified **14** COMM = **reserve price** ■ **reserves** *npl* **EXTRA STAMINA, USABLE IN AN EMERGENCY** additional personal resources of energy or strength that can be called upon in an emergency [14C. Directly and via French *réserver* < Latin *reservare* 'keep back' < *servare* 'keep'.] —**reservable** *adj* —**reserver** *n* ◇ **have** *or* **keep something in reserve** to use only part of something, keeping some of it back in case it is needed at a later time

reserve bank *n* **1** one of the 12 banks in the US Federal Reserve system **2** the central bank of Australia responsible for the issuing of currency, banking for federal and state governments, and regulating Australian financial systems

reserve clause *n* formerly, a clause in the contract of a professional sportsperson stating that the club, not the sportsperson, has the exclusive right to renew the contract

reserve currency *n* foreign currency that is acceptable for settling international transactions and that is held in reserve for that purpose by a central bank

reserved /ri zúrvd/ *adj* **1 BOOKED** booked in advance **2 EAR-MARKED FOR A SPECIFIC USE** kept or set aside for a particular purpose **3 HAVING A COOL MANNER** having a tendency to emotional restraint and so appearing reticent or composed —**reservedly** /ri zúrvidli/ *adv* —**reservedness** *n*

reserved list *n* a list of officers retired from the armed forces who are willing and available to be recalled to active service in an emergency

reserved occupation *n* an occupation of such national importance in wartime that those working in it are exempted from military service

reserve price *n* the lowest price that a seller is willing to accept for something being sold at auction. ◊ **upset price**

reservist /ri zúrvist/ *n* a member of a military force not on active service at a given time

reservoir /rézzər vwaar/ *n* **1 LAKE OR TANK FOR STORING WATER** a large tank or natural or artificial lake used for collecting and storing water for human consumption or agricultural use **2 LARGE BACKUP SUPPLY** a substantial reserve supply of something intangible **3 ORGANISM ACTING AS A PARASITE CARRIER** an organism in which a parasite lives and develops without damaging it, but from which the parasite passes to another species that is damaged by it **4** ANAT = **cisterna 5 LIQUID STORE IN A DEVICE** a part of a machine or device where liquid is stored for use by the machine or device **6 UNDERGROUND SUPPLY OF GAS OR OIL** a natural chamber in porous rock where a supply of natural gas or crude oil collects [Mid-17C. < French, < *réserver* (see RESERVE).]

reset[1] /ree sét/ (**-sets, -setting, -set**) *vt* **1** to set something again **2** to change the reading of a dial or counter to zero or a different number —**resettable** *adj* —**resetter** *n*

reset[2] /ree sét/ (**-sets, -setting, -set**) *vti Scotland* to receive stolen goods ■ /rée set/ *n Scotland* the crime of receiving stolen goods [14C. < Old French *recet(t)er* < Latin *receptare* < *recept-*, past participle of *recipere* 'take back'.] —**resetter** *n*

resettle /ree sétt'l/ (**-tles, -tling, -tled**) *vt* to provide a group or population with a new place to live and transfer it there —**resettlement** *n*

~~**resevoir**~~ incorrect spelling of **reservoir**

res gestae /-gést ɪ, ráyss jésti/ *npl* circumstances and facts that may be admitted as evidence in a lawsuit because they shed light on the matters in question [< Latin, 'things done']

resh /raysh/ *n* the 20th letter of the Hebrew alphabet [Early 19C. < Aramaic *rēš* 'head'.]

reshape /ree sháyp/ (**-shapes, -shaping, -shaped**) *vt* **1** to alter or restore the shape of something **2** to change the form or organization of something

reshow /ree shṓ/ (**-shows, -showing, -showed, -shown** /-shṓn/) *vti* to show something again, especially a film or television programme, or be shown again

reshuffle /rée shuff'l/ *n* **1 REDISTRIBUTION OF JOBS** a reorganization of the jobs of a group of people, especially a change by a prime minister or president of the posts or personnel of a cabinet **2 SHUFFLING OF CARDS AGAIN** an act of shuffling something, especially cards, again ■ *vt* /ree shúff'l/ (**-fles, -fling, -fled**) **1 REDISTRIBUTE JOBS** to carry out a reshuffle of jobs **2 SHUFFLE CARDS AGAIN** to shuffle something, especially cards, again

reside /ri zíd/ (**-sides, -siding, -sided**) *vi* **1 LIVE SOMEWHERE** to have a home in a particular place **2 BE PRESENT** to be present in or belong to somebody or something **3 BE VESTED** to be vested or placed in somebody or something [15C. Probably via French *résider* < Latin *residere* 'remain behind' < *sedere* 'sit'.]

residence /rézzidənss/ *n* **1 HOME** the house, flat, or other dwelling in which somebody lives **2 LARGE HOUSE** a grand and imposing dwelling **3 COLONIAL GOVERNOR'S HOUSE** the governor's official house in a colony or former colony **4 LIVING SOMEWHERE** the fact of living in a particular place **5 TIME LIVED IN PLACE** the period of time that somebody lives in a particular place **6** *US* MED = **residency** *n.* **4** ◇ **in residence 1** living in a place at a particular time **2** employed as a creative artist by an educational or other institution to foster interest in a subject

residency /rézzidənsi/ (*plural* **-cies**) *n* **1 PERFORMING AND TEACHING ENGAGEMENT** an engagement at a university or conservatory for a performer or group of performers, usually for at least a term, that involves performance, teaching, and master classes **2 OFFICIAL RESIDENCE OF AN INDIAN GOVERNOR** formerly, the official residence of a governor in India **3 TERRITORY ADMINISTERED BY RESIDENT AGENT** formerly, a territory such as the East Indies that was administered by the resident agent of a protecting state **4** *US* **MEDICAL TRAINING FOLLOWING INTERNSHIP** a period of specialized training in clinical medicine or surgery in a US hospital on completion of an internship **5** = **residence** *n.* **4, residence** *n.* **5**

ϟ**resident** /rézzidənt/ *n* **1 SOMEBODY LIVING IN PLACE** a permanent or long-term dweller in a particular place **2** *US* **DOCTOR COMPLETING RESIDENCY** a doctor or surgeon engaged in a residency **3 DOCTOR LIVING IN HOSPITAL** a junior doctor who lives in the hospital where he or she is working **4 SOMEBODY LIVING IN RESIDENTIAL SITUATION** a dweller in a nursing home, children's home, retirement home, or other communal housing **5 BRITISH COLONIAL OFFICIAL** a representative of the British government in a British colony or protectorate **6 DIPLOMAT** a diplomatic official based in a foreign country **7 NONMIGRATING BIRD OR OTHER ANIMAL** a bird or other animal that does not migrate seasonally ■ *adj* **1 LIVING IN PARTICULAR PLACE** living permanently or for a considerable period in a particular place **2 LIVE-IN** living somewhere as part of a particular job **3 BELONGING TO GROUP** forming part of a group of people **4 INHERENT** present or inherent in something **5 NONMIGRATING** not migrating seasonally **6 PERMANENTLY INSTALLED IN COMPUTER'S MEMORY** describes a computer program or data intentionally retained in random-access memory after being loaded so that it can be accessed quickly —**residentship** *n*

resident commissioner *n US* a representative from a dependency who is allowed to speak but not vote in the US House of Representatives

residential /rézzi dénsh'l/ *adj* **1 RELATING TO HOUSING** relating to or consisting of private housing rather than offices or factories **2 USED FOR LONG-TERM LIVING** used as a place to live for the long term **3 WITH LIVING ACCOMMODATION** providing living accommodation [Mid-17C. < RESIDENCE.] —**residentially** *adv*

residential care *n* a supervised home environment provided by a welfare agency for people unable to live alone, e.g. children in care or adults with severe learning disabilities

residential school *n* **1** a government-run school providing education and living accommodation for children with disabilities **2** *Can* formerly, a boarding school provided by the Canadian government and run by Christian organizations for the education and assimilation of Aboriginal children from thinly populated areas

residentiary /rézzi dénshəri/ *adj* **1** requiring the incumbent to live in an official residence **2** residing in official residence

residents' association *n* an association of people living in the same building or neighbourhood that deals with matters of common interest such as vandalism, traffic problems, or changes in local bylaws

residual /ri zíddyoo əl/ *adj* **1 LEFT OVER** remaining after the majority of something has been removed ○ *residual damp* **2 RELATING TO RESIDUE FROM ROCK WEATHERING** relating to the material left after the weathering of a rock has removed its soluble constituents ■ *n* **1 SOMETHING LEFT OVER** something that remains after part of something has been removed **2 DIFFERENCE BETWEEN ACTUAL AND THEORETICAL RESULTS** the difference between results obtained through theoretical calculation and those obtained through observation **3 REPEAT FEE** a payment to performers, directors, or writers when their filmed work is shown again, especially on television —**residually** *adv*

residual oil *n* the low-grade hydrocarbons that remain after the process of petroleum distillation. Use: in asphalt, furnace fuel.

residual unemployment *n* unemployment remaining during times of full employment, made up of people unable to work because of poor physical or mental health

residuary /ri zíddyoo əri/ *adj* **1** entitled to the residue of a deceased person's estate after debts have been paid and bequests distributed **2** remaining after a process has been gone through [Early 18C. < RESIDUUM.]

residue /rézzi dyoo/ *n* **1 SOMETHING LEFT OVER** something that remains after a process involving the removal of part of the original has been completed **2 REMAINDER OF AN ESTATE** the remainder of a deceased person's estate after debts have been paid and bequests distributed **3 REMAINDER AFTER PROCESSING** something remaining after a chemical or physical process such as combustion, distillation, evaporation, or filtration removes part of the original [14C. Via Old French < Latin *residuum* 'something remaining' < *residere* 'remain behind'.]

residuum /ri zíddyoo əm/ (*plural* **-a** /-ə/) *n* LAW = **residue** *n.* **2** [Late 17C. < Latin (see RESIDUE).]

resign /ri zín/ *v* **1** *vti* **LEAVE JOB** to give up a paid or unpaid post voluntarily **2** *vr* **ACCEPT SOMETHING RELUCTANTLY** to come to terms with something and acquiesce in it reluctantly ○ *He resigned himself to giving up work.* **3** *vt* **RELINQUISH CLAIM** to give up a right or claim to something [14C. < Old French *resigner* < Latin *resignare* 'unseal, cancel, give back' < *signare* 'to seal' < *signum* 'mark'.] —**resigned** *adj* —**resignedly** /ri zínədli/ *adv* —**resignedness** *n* —**resigner** *n*

re-sign *v* **1** *vti* to sign or cause a player to sign another contract **2** *vt* to sign a document again

resignation /rézzig náysh'n/ *n* **1 NOTIFICATION OF LEAVING A JOB** a formal notification of leaving a paid or unpaid post ○ *I've handed in my resignation.* **2 DEPARTURE FROM JOB** an instance of leaving a paid or unpaid post **3 UNPROTESTING ACCEPTANCE OF** agreement to something, usually given reluctantly but without protest

resile /ri zíl/ (**-siles, -siling, -siled**) *vi* (*formal*) **1** to spring back into the same shape or position **2** to jump or leap back [Early 16C. Directly or via obsolete French *resilir* < Latin *resilire* (see RESILIENT).]

resilient /ri zílli ənt/ *adj* **1** able to recover quickly from setbacks **2** able to spring back quickly into shape after being bent, stretched, or deformed [Mid-17C. < Latin *resilient-*, present participle of *resilire* 'jump back' < *salire* 'to jump'.] —**resilience** *n* —**resiliency** *n* —**resiliently** *adv*

resin /rézzin/ *n* **1 ORGANIC SUBSTANCE FROM PLANTS** a semisolid substance secreted in the sap of some plants and trees **2 SYNTHETIC COMPOUND RESEMBLING RESIN** a synthetic polymeric compound physically resembling natural resin, e.g. polyvinyl, polystyrene, or epoxy. Use: manufacture of petrochemicals and plastics. ■ *vt* **TREAT SOMETHING WITH RESIN** to coat or rub something with resin [14C. Via Old French *resine* and Latin *resina* < Greek *rhētinē*.] —**resinoid** *adj, n* —**resinous** *adj* —**resinously** *adv* —**resinousness** *n*

resinate /rézzi nayt/ (**-ates, -ating, -ated**) *vt* to impregnate, saturate, or flavour something with resin

res ipsa loquitur /-ípsə lókwitər/ *n* a rule of evidence that allows that mere proof that an accident occurred is enough to prove negligence on the part of the defendant [< Latin, 'the thing speaks for itself']

resist /ri zíst/ *v* **1** *vti* **FIGHT AGAINST** to oppose and stand firm against somebody or something **2** *vt* **REFUSE TO GIVE IN TO** to refuse to accept or comply with something ○ *resisted all attempts to force them out of their homes* **3** *vt* **BE UNHARMED** to remain unaltered by the damaging effect of something ○ *ability to resist infection* **4** *vti* **SAY NO TO SOMETHING TEMPTING** to refrain from something in spite of being tempted ○ *I couldn't resist having a peek.* ■ *n* **PROTECTIVE COATING** a protective coating used to prevent corrosion or oxidation, provide electrical insulation in a printed circuit, or prevent part of a fabric from accepting dye [14C. Directly and via French *résister* < Latin *resistere* 'stand against' < *sistere* 'make stand' < *stare* 'to stand'.] —

resister *n* —**resistibility** /ri zístə bílləti/ *n* —**resistible** *adj* —**resistibly** *adv*

resistance /ri zístənss/ *n* **1 OPPOSITION** opposition to somebody or something **2 REFUSAL TO GIVE IN** refusal to accept or comply with something **3 ABILITY TO WITHSTAND DAMAGING EFFECT** the ability to remain unaltered by the damaging effect of something, e.g. an organism's ability not to succumb to disease or infection **4 ABILITY TO SAY NO TO TEMPTATION** the ability to refrain from something in spite of being tempted **5 FORCE OPPOSING ANOTHER FORCE** (*symbol R*) a force that opposes or slows down another force **6 OPPOSITION TO AN ELECTRIC CURRENT** (*symbol R*) the opposition that a circuit, component, or substance presents to the flow of electricity **7 SOURCE OF RESISTANCE** (*symbol R*) something such as a resistor that is a source of opposition to the flow of electricity **8 REPRESSION OF THOUGHTS** in psychology, the process by which the ego keeps repressed thoughts and feelings from the conscious mind

Resistance *n* an illegal secret organization that fights for national freedom against an occupying power, especially one that fought in France, the Netherlands, Denmark, or Italy during World War II

resistant /ri zístənt/ *adj* **1 RESISTING** offering resistance to something ○ *resistant to change* **2 NOT DAMAGED BY** unaltered by or impervious to the damaging effect of something (*often in combination*) ○ *moisture-resistant* ■ *n* **SOMEBODY OR SOMETHING THAT RESISTS** somebody or something that offers resistance

~~**resistence**~~ incorrect spelling of **resistance**

resistin /ri zístin/ *n* a hormone that increases the resistance of cells to insulin, so causing levels of sugar in the bloodstream to rise [Early 21C. Blend of RESIST + INSULIN.]

resistive /ri zístiv/ *adj* **1** = **resistant** *adj.* 1, **resistant** *adj.* 2 **2** having the property of electrical resistance — **resistively** *adv* —**resistiveness** *n*

resistivity /réezi stívvəti/ *n* **1** (*symbol* ρ) the electrical resistance of a substance of a standard length and cross section **2** capacity to resist

resistless /ri zístləss/ *adj* (*archaic*) **1** not able to be resisted **2** not able to resist something

resistor /ri zístər/ *n* a component of an electrical circuit that has resistance and is used to control the flow of electric current

resit *vti* /ree sít/ (**-sits, -sitting, -sat**) to take an examination again after failing the first time ■ *n* /rée sit/ a later examination in the same subject for those who failed the first time

resize /ree síz/ (**-sizes, -sizing, -sized**) *vt* to make something a different size, e.g. a dress pattern or graphics on a computer screen

res judicata /-jóodi kaátə/, **res adjudicata** /-ə-/ *n* an issue already decided by a court [< Latin, 'judged matter']

reskill /ree skíl/ *vt* to teach somebody new skills, especially to find or change employment

Resnais /rénnay/, **Alain** (*b.* 1922) French film director

resold past tense, past participle of **resell**

resole /ree sṓl/ (**-soles, -soling, -soled**) *vt* to put a new sole on a shoe

resoluble /ri zóllyoob'l/ *adj* able to be resolved or analysed [Early 17C. Directly or via French < Latin *resolubilis* < *resolvere* (see RESOLVE).] —**resolubility** /ri zóllyoo bílləti/ *n* —**resolubleness** *n*

re-soluble /ree sóllyoob'l/ *adj* able to be dissolved again [15C. < RE- + SOLUBLE.] —**re-solubility** /ree sóllyoo bílləti/ *n* —**re-solubleness** *n* —**re-solubly** *adv*

resolute /rézzə loot/ *adj* **1** possessing determination and purposefulness **2** motivated by or displaying determination and purposefulness [15C. < Latin *resolutus*, past participle of *resolvere* (see RESOLVE).] —**resolutely** *adv* —**resoluteness** *n*

resolution /rézzə lóosh'n/ *n* **1 PROCESS OF RESOLVING** the process of resolving something such as a problem or dispute ○ *the resolution of a difficulty* **2 DECISION** a firm decision to do something **3 DETERMINATION** firmness of mind or purpose **4 SOLUTION** an answer to a problem **5 FORMAL EXPRESSION OF COLLECTIVE OPINION** a formal expression of the consensus at a meeting, arrived at after discussion and usually as the result of a vote **6 QUALITY OF DETAIL IN IMAGE** the quality of detail offered by a TV or computer screen or a photographic image **7 SEPARATION INTO CONSTITUENT PARTS** the process or act of separating something such as a chemical compound or a source of light into its constituent parts **8 SUBSIDING** the disappearance or coming to an end of a medical symptom or condition **9 HARMONIC PROGRESSION** the musical progression from a dissonant to a consonant chord or note **10 FINAL NOTE** the musical note or chord to which the harmony moves when progressing from dissonance to consonance **11 PART OF NARRATIVE WHEN CONFLICT IS RESOLVED** the point in a literary work when the conflict is resolved **12** PHYS = **resolving power** **13 SYLLABLE REPLACEMENT** the substitution of a long syllable for two short ones in the rhythm of a line of poetry [14C. Directly and via Old French < Latin *resolution-*, < past participle of *resolvere* (see RESOLVE).] —**resolutioner** *n*

resolve /ri zólv/ *v* (**-solves, -solving, -solved**) **1** *vti* **MAKE A DECISION** to come to or cause somebody to come to a firm decision about something ○ *He resolved to leave.* **2** *vt* **SOLVE A DIFFICULTY** to find a solution to a problem **3** *vt* **DISPEL DOUBTS** to dispel doubts or anxieties **4** *vt* **SETTLE AN ARGUMENT** to bring a disagreement to an end **5** *vr* **CHANGE** to change into something else **6** *vt* **EXPRESS A JOINT OPINION FORMALLY** to express the opinion of a meeting formally as a consensus, after discussion and usually as the result of a vote **7** *vti* **MAKE OR BECOME LESS SWOLLEN** to subside or to cause an inflammation, swelling, or tumour to subside **8** *vti* **SPLIT INTO CONSTITUENT PARTS** to cause something to separate into its constituent elements, or to become separated into constituent parts **9** *vt* **SEPARATE A RACEMIC MIXTURE** to separate a racemic compound or mixture into its two components **10** *vti* **MOVE FROM DISSONANT TO CONSONANT** to move, or cause a chord or note to move, from dissonant to consonant **11** *vt* **MAKE PARTS OF AN IMAGE DISTINCT** to make parts of an image distinct, e.g. in a microscope or telescope **12** *vt* **SPLIT A VECTOR INTO DIRECTIONAL COMPONENTS** to separate a vector into its directional components ■ *n* **1 DETERMINATION** firmness of purpose **2 DECISION** a firm decision to do something [14C. Directly and via Old French < Latin *resolvere* 'loosen up' < *solvere* 'loosen, dissolve'.] —**resolvability** /ri zólvə bílləti/ *n* —**resolvable** *adj* —**resolvableness** *n* —**resolver** *n*

resolved /ri zólvd/ *adj* determined in purpose —**resolvedly** /ri zólvidli/ *adv* —**resolvedness** *n*

resolvent /ri zólvənt/ *adj* **1 CAUSING SEPARATION INTO CONSTITUENT ELEMENTS** causing or capable of causing something to separate into its constituent elements **2 ANTI-INFLAMMATORY** able to cause reduction in inflammation or swelling ■ *n* **1 SOMETHING CAUSING SEPARATION INTO CONSTITUENT ELEMENTS** a substance that causes or is capable of causing something to separate into its constituent elements **2 ANTI-INFLAMMATORY MEDICINE** a medicine that reduces inflammation or swelling

resolving power *n* the ability of an optical system such as a telescope or microscope to distinguish objects separated by small angular distances

resonance /rézzənənss/ *n* **1 RESONANT QUALITY** the quality or state of being resonant **2 UNDERLYING MEANING** the effect of an event or work of art beyond its immediate or surface meaning **3 AMPLIFIED SOUND** an intense and prolonged sound produced by sympathetic vibration **4 RINGING QUALITY OF AN INSTRUMENT OR VOICE** an amplification of a sound, e.g. that of an instrument or the human voice, caused by sympathetic vibration in a chamber such as an auditorium or a singer's chest **5 LARGE OSCILLATION AT A NATURAL FREQUENCY** increased amplitude of oscillation of a mechanical system when it is subjected to vibration from another source at or near its own natural frequency **6 OSCILLATION IN AN ELECTRICAL CIRCUIT** a state of oscillation that occurs at a very specific frequency in an electrical circuit consisting of inductive and capacitive components **7 SOUND WHEN A BODY CAVITY IS TAPPED** the sound heard during tapping (**percussion**) of a healthy chest or abdomen **8 PROPERTY OF CERTAIN CHEMICAL COMPOUNDS** the property of some chemical compounds of having characteristics of two or more electronic structures simultaneously

resonant /rézzənənt/ *adj* **1 DEEP IN SOUND** deep and rich in sound **2 RESOUNDING** continuing to sound for some time **3 CAUSING ECHOES** producing or increasing amplification of sound or echoes, usually by sympathetic vibration [Late 16C. Directly or via French < Latin *resonant-*, present participle of *resonare* (see RESONATE).] —**resonantly** *adv*

resonate /rézzə nayt/ (**-nates, -nating, -nated**) *v* **1** *vti* **RESOUND** to resound or echo, or cause something to resound or echo **2 HAVE EXTENDED EFFECT** to have an effect or impact beyond that which is immediately apparent **3** *vti* **PRODUCE OR MAKE SOMETHING PRODUCE RESONANCE** to produce or exhibit chemical, mechanical, or electrical resonance, or to cause a chemical compound or a electrical system to produce or exhibit resonance **4** *vi* **BE FAMILIAR** to produce a response in somebody, especially by reminding that person of something [Late 19C. < Latin *resonare* 'resound' < *sonare* 'to sound' < *sonus* 'sound'.] —**resonation** /rézzə náysh'n/ *n*

resonator /rézzə naytər/ *n* **1** a device or part that resonates, especially one that produces sound or microwaves **2** a part of a musical instrument designed to produce resonance, e.g. the hollow body of a violin or the tubes in a vibraphone

resorb /ri-/ *vt* to absorb something again [Mid-17C. < Latin *resorbere* 'drink in again' < *sorbere* 'suck in'.] —**resorbent** *adj*

resorcinol /ri záwrssi nol/ *n* $C_6H_6O_2$ a colourless crystalline phenol. Use: manufacture of dyes, resins, drugs, in tanning. [Late 19C. < RESIN + *orcin*.]

resorption /ri sáwrpsh'n/ *n* **1** the process or state of resorbing or being resorbed **2** the partial fusion of a crystal in a magma in response to changing conditions of temperature and pressure [Early 19C. < RESORB, after *absorption*.] —**resorptive** *adj*

resort /ri záwrt/ *n* **1 HOLIDAY PLACE** a place that is popular for recreation and holidays and provides accommodation and entertainment **2 SOURCE OF HELP** a person, place, or course of action seen as a source of help in dealing with a problem ○ *As a last resort we could sell the car.* **3 ACT OF HAVING RECOURSE TO** the act of turning to somebody or something for help in dealing with a problem **4 FREQUENT VISITING** the act of going somewhere frequently or in large numbers **5 MUCH-VISITED PLACE** a place frequently visited [14C. < Old French *resortir* 'come back' < *sortir* 'go out'.]

resort to *vt* **1** to turn to something, sometimes something extreme, for help in dealing with a problem **2** to go somewhere that is frequently visited, or go somewhere in large numbers

re-sort *vt* to sort something again

resound /ri zównd/ *vi* **1 MAKE A REVERBERATING SOUND** to produce a long reverberating sound **2 SOUND CLEARLY** to sound loudly and clearly **3 BE FILLED WITH A REVERBERATING SOUND** to be filled with a long reverberating sound ○ *The hall resounded to the cheers of the audience.* **4 BE EXTREMELY WELL KNOWN** to be extremely well known, especially over a long period or a wide area [14C. Alteration of Old French *resoner* (influenced by SOUND[1]) < Latin *resonare* (see RESONATE).]

resounding /ri zównding/ *adj* **1** clear and unequivocal ○ *a resounding defeat* **2** making a loud noise that echoes — **resoundingly** *adv*

resource /ri záwrss, -sáwrss/ *n* **1 SOURCE OF HELP** a person or thing that is a source of help or information **2 BACKUP SUPPLY** a reserve supply of something such as money, personnel, or equipment **3 ABILITY TO FIND SOLUTIONS** adeptness at finding solutions to problems **4** = **natural resource** ■ **resources** *npl* **1 TALENT DRAWN ON WHEN NECESSARY** an inner ability or capacity that is drawn on in time of need **2 NATION'S NATURAL, ECONOMIC, OR MILITARY ASSET** a natural, economic, political, or military asset enjoyed by a nation, e.g. mineral wealth, labour, capital, or military personnel **3 CORPORATE ASSET** a source drawn on by a company for making profit, e.g. personnel, capital, machinery, or stock ■ *vt* (**-sources, -sourcing, -sourced**) **PROVIDE SOMETHING WITH RESOURCES** to provide something with monetary or other resources [Early 17C. < French *ressource* < Latin *resurgere* 'rise again, be replenished' < *surgere* 'rise up from below'.] —**resourceless** *adj*

resourceful /ri záwrsf'l, -sáwrs-/ *adj* full of initiative and good at problem-solving, especially in difficult situations —**resourcefully** *adv* —**resourcefulness** *n*

resp. *abbr* **1** respective **2** respectively **3** respiration **4** respondent

respect /ri spékt/ *n* **1 ESTEEM** a feeling or attitude of admiration and deference towards somebody or something ○ *won the respect of her colleagues* **2 STATE OF BEING ADMIRED** the state of being admired deferentially **3 THOUGHTFULNESS** consideration or thoughtfulness **4 CHARACTERISTIC** an individual characteristic or point ○ *satisfactory in all respects* ■ **respects** *npl* **REGARDS** polite greetings offered to somebody ■ *vt* **1 ESTEEM** to feel or show admiration and deference towards somebody or something **2 NOT VIOLATE** to pay due attention to and refrain from violating something ○ *respect the law* ○ *respect another's privacy* **3 BE CONSIDERATE TOWARDS** to show consideration or thoughtfulness in relation to somebody or something [14C. Via Old French < Latin *respectus*, past participle of *respicere* 'regard, look back at' < *specere* 'look at'.] —**respected** *adj* —**respecter** *n*

SYNONYMS See ***regard***.

respectable /ri spéktəb'l/ *adj* **1 MORALLY ABOVE REPROACH** in accordance with accepted standards of correctness or decency ○ *a respectable district* **2 SATISFACTORY** meeting an adequate standard ○ *a respectable salary* **3 WORTHY OF RESPECT** deserving or receiving respect **4 LARGE ENOUGH** sufficiently large **5 ACCEPTABLE IN APPEARANCE** tidy and fit to be seen in public (*informal*) —**respectability** /ri spéktə bílləti/ *n* —**respectableness** *n* —**respectably** *adv*

respectful /ri spéktf'l/ *adj* showing appropriate deference and respect —**respectfulness** *n*

respectfully /ri spéktfəli/ *adv* with respect or in a respectful manner

USAGE respectfully or **respectively**? ***Respectfully*** means 'with respect; with all due respect; in a respectful manner', as in the complimentary close of a letter (*Respectfully, Jane Smith*), and in *We respectfully* [not *respectively*] *reserve the right to disagree with the ruling*. ***Respectively*** matches one list with another in the order given for both, as in *The captain and the first officer have 20 and 15 years' experience, respectively* [not *respectfully*].

respecting /ri spékting/ *prep* regarding or concerning somebody or something

respective /ri spéktiv/ *adj* varying according to each of the people or things concerned ○ *They returned to their respective homes.* —**respectiveness** *n*

respectively *adv* matching one list with another in the order given for both ○ *Joe and his wife are aged 52 and 51, respectively.*

USAGE See ***respectfully***.

respell /ree spél/ (**-spells, -spelling, -spelt** *or* **-spelled**) *vt* to spell something again or in a different way —**respelling** *n*

respirable /résperəb'l, ri spírəb'l/ *adj* fit or able to be breathed —**respirability** /réspərə bílləti, ri spírə bílləti/ *n*

respiration /réspə ráysh'n/ *n* **1 BREATHING** the act of breathing air in and out **2 DISTRIBUTION OF OXYGEN** the complete chemical and physical process in which oxygen is delivered to tissues or cells of the body and carbon dioxide and water are given off **3 OXIDATION PROCESS IN CELLS** an energy-producing oxidation process in cells —**respirational** *adj*

respirator /réspə raytər/ *n* **1** a machine used in hospitals to maintain breathing **2** a device placed over the nose and mouth to filter out noxious particles and fumes from inhaled air or to warm chilled air before it is inhaled

respiratory /ri spírrətəri, réspərətəri/ *adj* relating to or used in breathing or the system in the body that takes in and distributes oxygen

respiratory distress syndrome *n* a respiratory disease of newborns, especially premature infants, caused by the inability of the lungs to take in oxygen and marked by cyanosis and difficult breathing

respiratory pigment *n* a protein such as haemoglobin that can bind with oxygen

respiratory quotient *n* the ratio of the volume of carbon dioxide released to the volume of oxygen absorbed by an organism, cell, or tissue over a given time period

respiratory system *n* the system of organs in the body responsible for the intake of oxygen and the expiration of carbon dioxide

respire /ri spír/ (**-spires, -spiring, -spired**) *v* **1** *vti* to breathe air in and out **2** *vi* to breathe again in a normal way after anxiety or exertion (*literary*) [14C. Directly or via French < Latin *respirare* 'breathe again' < *spirare* 'breathe'.]

respirometer /réspə rómmitər/ *n* an instrument for measuring and studying the process in which oxygen is taken into the body, delivered to tissues and cells, and used by them [Late 19C. < RESPIRATION.] —**respirometric** /réspərō méttrik/ *adj* —**respirometry** /réspə rómmətri/ *n*

respite /réspīt, réspit/ *n* **1 BRIEF INTERVAL OF REST** a brief period of rest and recovery between periods of exertion or after something disagreeable **2 DELAY** a temporary delay **3 REPRIEVE** a temporary stay of execution of a criminal [13C. Via Old French, 'refuge' < Latin *respectus*, past participle of *respicere* (see RESPECT).]

respite care *n* temporary residential care for patients that provides relief for the permanent care-givers

~~resplendant~~ incorrect spelling of **resplendent**

resplendent /ri spléndənt/ *adj* having a dazzlingly impressive appearance ○ *resplendent in his dress uniform* [15C. < Latin *resplendent-*, present participle of *resplendere* 'shine brightly' < *splendere* 'shine'.] —**resplendence** *n* —**resplendently** *adv*

respond /ri spónd/ *v* **1** *vti* **PROVIDE AN ANSWER** to reply something or to something in spoken or written words **2** *vi* **REACT** to act or do something in reaction to something else ○ *was unsure of how to respond to his moods* **3** *vi* **HAVE A POSITIVE MEDICAL REACTION** to react positively to medical treatment ■ *n* **1 PILASTER OR PILLAR SUPPORTING ARCH** a pilaster or pillar that supports an arch **2 CHORAL PART OF AN ANTHEM** the choral part in an anthem for priest and choir in a church service [Mid-16C. Via Old French *respondre* < Latin *respondere* 'promise in return' < *spondere* 'to pledge'.] —**respondence** *n*

~~respondant~~ incorrect spelling of **respondent**

respondent /ri spóndənt/ *n* **1 DEFENDANT** the person against whom a divorce petition or an appeal is brought **2 ANSWERER** a replier to something ■ *adj* **1 RESPONDING** giving a response **2 BEING RESPONDENT** being a defendant in a divorce petition or appeal

responsa plural of **responsum**

~~responsability~~ incorrect spelling of **responsibility**

response /ri spónss/ *n* **1 REPLY TO QUESTION** something said or written in reply to a statement or question from somebody else **2 REACTION** something done in reaction to something else **3 BID IN BRIDGE** a bid in bridge that is in reply to a partner's bid or double **4 REPLY MADE BY CHURCH CHOIR** a phrase sung or spoken by the choir or congregation in reply to the officiant during a church service **5 BODY'S REACTION TO STIMULUS** the reaction of an organism or any of its parts to a stimulus [14C. Directly or via Old French < Latin *responsum* < past participle of *respondere* (see RESPOND).] —**responseless** *adj*

SYNONYMS See ***answer***.

responsibility /ri spónssə bílləti/ (*plural* **-ties**) *n* **1 ACCOUNTABILITY** the state, fact, or position of being accountable to somebody or for something ○ *the responsibilities of parenthood* **2 SOMETHING TO BE RESPONSIBLE FOR** somebody or something for which a person or organization is responsible **3 BLAME** the blame for something that has happened ○ *took full responsibility for the mix-up* **4 AUTHORITY TO ACT** authority to take decisions independently

responsible /ri spónssəb'l/ *adj* **1 ANSWERABLE** accountable to somebody for an action or for the successful carrying out of a duty **2 IN CHARGE** expected to deal with something or take care of somebody **3 TO BLAME** being the cause of something, usually something wrong or disapproved of ○ *Who's responsible for this mess?* **4 IMPORTANT** conferring the authority to take decisions independently and requiring conscientiousness and trustworthiness ○ *in a responsible position* **5 RELIABLE** able to be counted on owing to qualities of conscientiousness and trustworthiness **6 RATIONAL AND ACCOUNTABLE** capable of taking rational or moral decisions, and therefore accountable for your actions **7 AUTHORIZED TO ACT** having the authority to take decisions independently **8 FINANCIALLY SOUND** having adequate means to meet financial obligations [Late 16C. < obsolete French, 'corresponding' < Latin *respons-*, past participle of *respondere* (see RESPOND).] —**responsibleness** *n* —**responsibly** *adv*

responsive /ri spónssiv/ *adj* **1 DONE IN RESPONSE** serving to respond to something **2 SHOWING A POSITIVE RESPONSE** reacting quickly, strongly, or favourably to something, especially a suggestion or proposal **3 REACTING TO STIMULUS** showing reaction to a stimulus **4 CONSISTING OF CHOIR'S OR CONGREGATION'S RESPONSES** consisting of responses by a choir or congregation in a church service —**responsively** *adv* —**responsiveness** *n*

responsory /ri spónssəri/ (*plural* **-ries**) *n* an anthem consisting of short verses sung or spoken by the officiant and responses sung or spoken by the choir, especially after the lesson in a church service —**responsorial** /ri spón sáwri əl/ *adj*

responsum /ri spónssəm/ (*plural* **-sa** /-sə/) *n* a definitive written reply by a rabbinic authority to a question on religion [Late 19C. < Latin (see RESPOND).]

res publica /-póbli kaa, -púbblikə/ *n* **1** the state, a republic, or the commonwealth as a concept **2** the public or common good [< Latin, 'public matter']

ressentiment /rə sóNti móN/ *n* a feeling of resentment and hostility characterized by an inability to act to change the situation [Mid-20C. Directly or via German < French, < *ressentir* 'feel strongly'.]

rest[1] /rest/ *n* **1 CESSATION OF LABOUR** a state or period of refreshing freedom from exertion ○ *a period of rest and recreation* **2 REFRESHING REPOSE OF SLEEP** the repose of sleep that is refreshing to body and mind and is marked by a reduction in metabolic activity **3 CESSATION OF MOVEMENT** the cessation of movement or action ○ *The boat lay at rest in the harbour.* **4 REPOSE OF DEATH** death perceived as freedom from earthly toil ○ *He is now at rest.* **5 FREEDOM FROM ANXIETY** freedom from mental or emotional anxiety ○ *I put her mind at rest.* **6 PAUSE IN MUSIC** a rhythmic pause between musical notes, or the mark indicating a musical pause **7** LITERAT = **caesura** *n.* 1 **8 PLACE TO STOP AND RELAX** a stopping place for shelter and relaxation **9 SUPPORT** something used for support, especially on a piece of furniture **10 SUPPORT TOOL IN POOL** a tool used to support the cue in pool ■ *v* **1** *vti* **SLEEP OR RELAX** to restore energy to somebody or something by means of relaxation or sleep ○ *rest the sled dogs* ○ *Put your feet up and rest.* **2** *vi* **BE TRANQUIL** to be in a state of tranquillity **3** *vi* **BE DEAD** to be dead, and so free from earthly concerns **4** *vti* **STOP MOVING** to cease activity, or cause something to cease activity **5** *vi* **BE LEFT ALONE** to be subject to no further discussion or attention ○ *Let the matter rest.* **6** *vi* **LIE FALLOW** to lie unfarmed **7** *vti* **SUPPORT OR BE SUPPORTED** to support something, or to be supported, on or against something ○ *The ornament was resting on a narrow ledge.* **8** *vi* **COME TO STOP** to allow the eyes to come to a stop on somebody or something **9** *vi* **BE VESTED** to be vested or placed in somebody or something **10** *vi* **DEPEND ON** to depend on somebody or something for action or as a burden or responsibility **11** *vi* **BE BASED ON** to rely on something for proof or explanation **12** *vti* **CONCLUDE LEGAL CASE** to conclude the presentation of evidence in a case ○ *I rest my case.* [(verb), Old English *ræstan*; (noun) *ræst*, < Germanic] —**rested** *adj* —**rester** *n*

rest[2] /rest/ *n* something left as a remainder (+ *singular or plural verb*) ■ *vi* to remain or continue to be (*usually a command*) ○ *Rest assured that we're doing everything possible.* [15C. < French *reste* 'remnant' < *rester* 'remain' < Latin *restare* 'stay behind' < *stare* 'to stand'.]

restage /ree stáyj/ (**-stages, -staging, -staged**) *vt* to organize a performance or an event again or in a different way

~~restaraunt~~ incorrect spelling of **restaurant**

rest area *n US, ANZ* an area at the side of a major road where motorists can rest

ϟ **restart** *v* /ree staárt/ **1** *vti* to begin doing something again after it was stopped or suspended **2** *vti* to start something or get it working again **3** *vt* COMPUT = **warmboot** —**restart** /reé staart/ *n* —**restartable** *adj*

restate /ree stáyt/ (**-states, -stating, -stated**) *vt* to say something again, especially in order to clarify or summarize what has already been said ○ *time to restate our goals* —**restatement** *n*

restaurant /réstə ront, -roN, -rənt/ *n* a place where meals and drinks are sold and served to customers [Early 19C. < French, < present participle of *restaurer* < Latin *restaurare* (see RESTORE).]

restaurant car *n* a railway carriage in which meals are served to passengers. US term **dining car**

~~restauranteur~~ incorrect spelling of **restaurateur**

restaurateur /réstərə túr/ *n* an owner or manager of a restaurant [Late 18C. < French, 'restorer' < *restaurer* (see RESTAURANT).]

rest cure *n* a treatment involving complete rest, e.g. as a remedy for stress

restenosis /reésta nóssiss/ *n* a return to a constricted or narrowed condition, e.g. in a coronary artery that has previously been widened by balloon angioplasty

restful /réstf'l/ *adj* **1** giving, promoting, or involving rest ○ *a restful holiday* **2** at rest or tranquil —**restfully** *adv* —**restfulness** *n*

restharrow /rést harō/ *n* a pod-bearing plant with three-lobed leaves and woody stems and roots. Flowers: white, purple, or pink, in clusters. Native to: Europe, Asia. *Ononis repens* and *Ononis spinosa*. [Because its tough roots can stop, or arrest, the progress of a harrow]

rest home *n* a place where infirm senior citizens and chronically ill people are housed and cared for

restiform /résti fawrm/ *adj* shaped like a rope or cord [Mid-19C. < modern Latin *restiformis* < Latin *restis* 'cord'.]

resting /résting/ *adj* **1 IMMOBILE** describes organisms that are not moving or active **2 NOT DIVIDING** not undergoing cell division **3 DORMANT** describes spores, seeds, and eggs that are dormant before germination **4 UNEMPLOYED** not currently employed as an actor (*informal; used euphemistically*)

restitution /résti tyóosh'n/ *n* **1 GIVING BACK** the return of something to its rightful owner **2 PAYING BACK** compensation for a loss, damage, or injury **3 RESTORATION** the return of something to the condition it was in before it was changed [13C. Directly or via French < Latin *restitution-* < *restituere* 'restore' < *statuere* 'set up'.] —**restitute** /résti tyoot/ *vt* —**restitutive** *adj* —**restitutory** *adj*

restive /réstiv/ *adj* **1 UNEASY** uneasy and on the verge of resisting control ○ *The people soon grew restive under the rule of the occupying force.* **2 IMPATIENT** having little patience and unwilling to tolerate annoyances **3 OBSTINATE OR AWKWARD** unwilling to be guided or controlled ○ *a restive horse* [Late 16C. Alteration of *restiff* < Old French *restif* < Latin *restare* 'to rest'.] —**restively** *adv* —**restiveness** *n*

restless /réstləss/ *adj* **1 CONSTANTLY MOVING** constantly moving, or unable to be still ○ *Some waited patiently but others were restless.* **2 DISCONTENTED** seeking a change because of discontent ○ *He began to feel restless after only a few weeks in the job.* **3 SLEEPLESS** lacking rest or sleep ○ *She spent a restless night worrying.* —**restlessly** *adv* —**restlessness** *n*

rest mass *n* the mass a body has when it is not moving, as opposed to the additional mass it gains as a result of its movement, according to the theory of relativity

restock /ree stók/ *vti* to replace or refill something after it has been used or its contents emptied

restoration /réstə ráysh'n/ *n* **1 RESTORING OF** the return of something that was removed, or the restoring of something to a former condition ○ *calls for the restoration of curfews* **2 THING RESTORED** something, especially a building, that has been brought back to an earlier and usually better condition **3 MODEL** a model made to resemble or represent something in its original condition ○ *a restoration of a Neandertal dwelling*

Restoration *n* the re-establishment of monarchy in Great Britain under Charles II in 1660, or the period of his reign

restorative /ri stáwrətiv/ *adj* tending or meant to give somebody new strength or vigour ○ *a restorative tonic* ■ *n* something that gives somebody new strength or vigour, especially an activity or medication —**restoratively** *adv* —**restorativeness** *n*

restore /ri stáwr/ (**-stores, -storing, -stored**) *vt* **1 GIVE BACK** to return something to its proper owner or place **2 RETURN TO PREVIOUS CONDITION** to bring something back to an earlier and better condition ○ *techniques used to restore old oil paintings* **3 ENERGIZE** to give somebody new strength or vigour ○ *I felt restored after my weekend away.* **4 RETURN TO PREVIOUS POSITION** to return somebody to a previously held rank, office, or position ○ *restore her to the throne* **5 PUT BACK** to re-establish or put back something that was once but is no longer there ○ *restore order in the capital* [13C. Via Old French *restorer* < Latin *restaurare* 'set upright again' < *-staurare.*] —**restorable** *adj* —**restorer** *n*

SYNONYMS See ***renew***.

restrain /ri stráyn/ *vt* **1 HOLD SOMEBODY BACK** to prevent somebody or yourself from doing something ○ *I couldn't restrain myself from calling out.* **2 CONTROL** to keep something under control or within limits ○ *trying to restrain his desire to flee* **3 CONTROL** to physically control the movements of a person or animal ○ *Restrain him before he hurts someone.* **4 IMPRISON** to put somebody in prison or otherwise take away his or her freedom [14C. Via Old French *restreindre* < Latin *restingere* 'bind fast, confine' < *stringere* 'draw tight'.] —**restrainable** *adj*

restrained /ri stráynd/ *adj* characterized by control, especially in not being excessively emotional or aggressive ○ *the artist's restrained use of colour* —**restrainedly** /-idli/ *adv*

restraining order *n US* a court order that commands somebody to stop doing something until the issuing court can determine its legality

restraint /ri stráynt/ *n* **1 HOLDING BACK** an act or the quality of holding back, limiting, or controlling something ○ *Although severely provoked, she showed admirable restraint in not retaliating.* **2 RESTRAINING THING** something that controls or limits somebody or something ○ *His poverty was no restraint on his ambition.* **3 HOLDING DEVICE** something that is fastened to limit somebody's freedom of movement [14C. < Old French *restreinte*, feminine past participle of *restreindre* (see RESTRAIN).]

restraint of trade *n* the limiting of commercial competition by means such as price-fixing or monopolistic practices

~~**restraunt**~~ incorrect spelling of **restaurant**

restrict /ri stríkt/ *vt* to keep something within fixed limits ○ *Entry is restricted to members only.* [15C. < Latin *restrict*, past participle of *restringere* (see RESTRAIN).]

restricted /ri stríktid/ *adj* **1 LIMITED** limited or made smaller or less than might be desired ○ *It's difficult to turn the vehicle in such a restricted space.* **2 SUBJECT TO CONTROLS** subject to controls or limits, e.g. of time or availability ○ *restricted use of the facilities* **3 REQUIRING AUTHORIZATION** intended only for authorized people ○ *You are entering a restricted area.* —**restrictedly** *adv* —**restrictedness** *n*

restriction /ri stríksh'n/ *n* **1** something that limits or controls something else ○ *There are restrictions on the use of the photocopier.* **2** a restricting of something, or the condition of being restricted ○ *the restriction of a person's freedom*

restriction digest *n* the product of using a restriction enzyme to cut DNA into fragments

restriction endonuclease *n* BIOCHEM = **restriction enzyme**

restriction enzyme *n* an enzyme that splits DNA into segments at precise locations. Use: genetic engineering.

restriction fragment *n* a specific portion of DNA produced by a restriction enzyme

restriction fragment length polymorphism *n* a variation between individuals in the length of the DNA fragments produced by a specific restriction enzyme

restrictive /ri stríktiv/ *adj* **1** acting as a limit or control on something **2** limiting the range of reference or application of a word, phrase, or clause —**restrictively** *adv* —**restrictiveness** *n*

restrictive covenant *n* a stipulation on a party buying or leasing land to refrain from uses or activities that would lessen its value

restrictive practice *n* **1** something done customarily by a group of workers, especially a trade union, that places limits on the work of others or the freedom of operation of employers **2** something done by companies in trade that is against the public interest, e.g. price-fixing

restrike /reé strīk/ *n* a coin struck at a later date from a die that has already been used to produce the original issue —**restrike** /ree strīk/ *vt*

restring /ree stríng/ (**-strings, -stringing, -strung** /ree strúng/) *vt* **1** to replace one or more strings of a stringed instrument **2** to renew the strings of a racket used in tennis or a similar sport —**restring** /reé string/ *n*

rest room *n US* = **cloakroom** *n.* 3

restructure /ree strúkchər/ (**-tures, -turing, -tured**) *v* **1** *vti* to change the way in which something is organized or arranged ○ *restructure the firm* **2** *vt* to alter the terms of a loan, especially to relieve its burden on the debtor

restructuring /ree strúkchəring/ *n* the process or an instance of changing the way in which something is organized or arranged

restrung past tense, past participle of **restring**

restyle /ree stīl/ (**-styles, -styling, -styled**) *vt* **1** to give something a new design or shape **2** to give somebody or something a new name or designation —**restyle** /reé stīl/ *n*

result /ri zúlt/ *n* **1 CONSEQUENCE** something that follows as a consequence of a particular action, condition, or event **2 SCORE** an outcome, especially the final score in a sporting competition or the grade awarded to somebody who has sat an examination ○ *The results were in Saturday's paper.* **3 NUMBER** a number arrived at by a calculation **4 SUCCESS** a successful outcome to something, especially a sporting competition (*informal*) ○ *If the lads play like this next week they'll definitely get a result.* ■ **results** *npl* **DESIRED OUTCOME** the desired outcome from an action ○ *The new policy is already showing results.* ■ *v* **1** *vi* **CAUSE AN OUTCOME** to produce a particular outcome ○ *Overgrazing results in soil erosion.* **2** *vi* **FOLLOW AS CONSEQUENCE** to follow as a consequence of a particular action, condition, or event ○ *This kind of error results from inattention.* **3** *vt* LAW = **revert** *v.* 5 [15C. < Latin *resultare* 'spring back, reverberate' ('result' in medieval Latin) < *saltare* 'to jump'.]

resultant /ri zúltənt/ *adj* happening as a consequence of something else ■ *n* a single vector that is equivalent to two or more other vectors

resultant tone *n* a tone that is created by the sounding together of two other tones but is different from both of them

resulting /ri zúlting/ *adj* happening as a consequence ○ *the heavy snowfall and the resulting chaos on the roads*

resume /ri zyóom/ (**-sumes, -suming, -sumed**) *v* **1** *vti* to continue with something after a temporary halt **2** *vt* to take, assume, or occupy a position again ○ *She came in and resumed her place at the head of the table.* [15C. Directly or via French *résumer* < Latin *resumere* 'take up again' < *sumere* 'take'.] —**resumable** *adj*

résumé /rézzyoo may, ráy-/ *n* **1** a summary of something such as events that have happened ○ *a résumé of the afternoon's activities* **2** *US, Can, ANZ* a curriculum vitae [Early 19C. < French, past participle of *résumer* (see RESUME).]

resumption /ri zúmpsh'n/ *n* the act or an instance of continuing with something that has been stopped for a while ○ *hoping for a resumption of negotiations* [15C. Directly or via French < Latin *resumption-*, < past participle of *resumere* (see RESUME).]

resupinate /ri syóopinit/ *adj* describes a plant part, especially the flower of an orchid, that grows upside down or appears to do so [Late 18C. < Latin *resupinatus*, past participle of *resupinare* 'bend back' < *supinus* 'turned upwards'.] —**resupination** /ri syóopi náysh'n/ *n*

resupply /reé sə plī/ *vt* (**-plies, -plying, -plied**) **PROVIDE NEW SUPPLY** to provide somebody with or acquire a fresh supply of something ■ *n* (*plural* **-plies**) **1 PROVISION OF NEW SUPPLY** the act of providing a new supply of something ○ *Resupply of the troops took two days.* **2 SOMETHING NEW SUPPLIED** a thing or a quantity of things supplied again ○ *We need a resupply of tinned goods.*

resurface /ree súrfiss/ (**-faces, -facing, -faced**) *v* **1** *vi* **COME TO SURFACE AGAIN** to come back to the surface of a body of water after having submerged **2** *vi* **APPEAR AGAIN** to appear again after having disappeared or been absent ○ *He resurfaced in Bangkok after the war.* **3** *vt* **PUT NEW SURFACE ON** to put a new surface on something, especially a road

resurfacing /ree súrfissing/ *n* the process of putting a new surface on something, especially a road ○ *The main road is closed for resurfacing.*

resurgence /ri súrjənss/ *n* the act or process of rising again or becoming stronger again ○ *a resurgence of patriotism*

resurgent /ri súrjənt/ *adj* rising or becoming stronger again [Late 18C. < Latin *resurgere* (see RESURGE).]

resurrect /rézzə rékt/ *v* **1** *vti* to come or bring somebody back to life after apparent death **2** *vt* to bring back into use something that had been stopped or discarded ○ *resurrect an old argument* [Late 18C. Back-formation < RESURRECTION.]

resurrection /rézzə réksh'n/ *n* **1** in some systems of belief, a rising from or raising of somebody from the dead, or the state of having risen from the dead **2** the revival of something old or long disused ○ *the resurrection of a youthful dream* [13C. < Old French *résurrection* < Latin *resurrect-*, past participle of *resurgere* (see RESURGE).] —**resurrectional** *adj*

Resurrection *n* **1** in Christian belief, the rising of Jesus Christ from the dead after his crucifixion and entombment **2** the rising of the dead on Judgment Day, as anticipated by Christians, Jews, and Muslims

resurrection plant *n* a plant that survives well in hot dry conditions e.g. the rose of Jericho

resuscitate /ri sússi tayt/ (**-tates, -tating, -tated**) *vti* to revive somebody or be revived from unconsciousness or apparent death [Early 16C. < Latin *resuscitare* < *suscitare* 'raise' < *citare* 'summon repeatedly'.] —**resuscitable** *adj* —**resuscitative** *adj* —**resuscitator** *n*

ret /ret/ (**rets, retting, retted**) *vti* to soak plant fibres such as flax or hemp so that they become easier to separate [15C. < Middle Dutch *reeten*.]

ret. *abbr* 1 retain 2 retired 3 return 4 returned

retable /ri táyb'l/ *n* a shelf or setting behind an altar for holding candles, flowers, or religious images [Early 19C. Via French *rétable* < Latin *retro-* 'back' + *tabula* 'table'.]

retail /reé tayl/ *n* SALE TO CONSUMERS the selling of goods directly to customers, e.g. in shops ○ *She works in retail.* ■ *adv* IN SMALL, NOT BULK, AMOUNTS from an ordinary shop or at the normal customer price and in small amounts rather than in bulk ○ *I bought it retail.* ■ *v* 1 *vti* SELL GOODS to sell goods, or be sold, to customers in small amounts and without a discount ○ *This item usually retails at a much higher price.* 2 *vt* REPEAT SOMETHING HEARD to regularly repeat what is heard, especially gossip [14C. < Old French *retaille* 'piece cut off' < *taillier* 'to cut'.]

retail price index *n* a list of the prices of essential consumer goods that is published each month by the government to show how much prices in general have risen or fallen

retail price maintenance *n* the setting by the manufacturer of a minimum price at which its goods are to be sold at retail

retain /ri táyn/ *vt* 1 KEEP to keep possession of something ○ *Despite losing the court case he retains all rights to the magazine article.* 2 REMEMBER THINGS to be able to keep ideas or information in mind or memory 3 KEEP SOMETHING IN POSITION to keep or hold something in a place or position ○ *water retained by a dam* 4 HOLD SOMETHING WITHIN to be able to hold or accumulate something, especially liquid 5 PAY SOMEBODY TO DO WORK to pay somebody regularly to do work 6 HIRE PROFESSIONAL PERSON to pay a preliminary fee to reserve the services of a barrister, accountant, or other professional person whenever needed [14C. Via Anglo-Norman *retaign-* < Latin *retinere* 'hold back' < *tenere* 'hold'.] —**retainability** /ri táynə bílləti/ *n* —**retainable** *adj* —**retainment** *n*

retained object *n* the direct or indirect object of a passive verb, e.g. 'letter' in 'She was sent a letter by her brother'

retained profits *npl* the part of the after-tax profits of a business that is not distributed to shareholders

retainer[1] /ri táynər/ *n* 1 HOLDER a device for holding something in place 2 DEVICE HOLDING TEETH IN POSITION a device for holding a tooth or teeth in position after orthodontic treatment 3 SERVANT a paid servant, especially one who has been employed for many years ○ *She gave the cottage to one of her old family retainers.* 4 FOLLOWER formerly, a soldier or other person who supported or was dependent on somebody of high rank

retainer[2] /ri táynər/ *n* 1 a fee paid to reserve the services of a professional person, especially a barrister or accountant, whenever needed 2 a fee paid by somebody who rents accommodation to reserve it while they are temporarily away ◇ **on (a) retainer** paid regularly in order to be consulted whenever necessary, rather than being paid for each job

retaining wall *n* a wall built to keep earth or water from moving

retake *vt* /ree táyk/ (**-takes, -taking, -took** /-to͝ok/, **-taken** /-táykən/) 1 RECAPTURE to recapture a place that has been captured by an enemy 2 FILM SOMETHING AGAIN to record, photograph, or film something again in order to get it right 3 TAKE SHOT AGAIN to take a shot in a game again because of some infringement during the first attempt ○ *The referee ordered him to retake the penalty.* ■ *n* /reé tayk/ ACT OF RECORDING SOMETHING AGAIN an instance of recording, photographing, or filming something again, or the product that results from this

retaliate /ri tálli ayt/ (**-ates, -ating, -ated**) *vi* to deliberately harm somebody in response or revenge for a harm he or she has done [Early 17C. < Latin *retaliare* 'pay back in kind' < *talio* 'punishment in kind'.] —**retaliative** /ri tálli ətiv/ *adj* —**retaliator** /ri tálli aytər/ *n* —**retaliatory** *adj*

retard *vt* /ri taárd/ to slow or delay the progress of something ■ *n* /reé taard/ *US* an offensive term that deliberately insults somebody with a learning disability or somebody regarded as unintelligent (*slang insult*) [15C. Via French *retarder* < Latin *retardare* < *tardus* 'slow'.] —**retardative** /ri taárdətiv/ *adj*—**retardatory** /-ətəri/ *adj*

retardant /ri taárd'nt/ *n* something designed to slow down a particular process or change, especially a chemical substance that inhibits change (*often in combination*) ■ *adj* capable of making something move or happen more slowly ○ *flame-retardant fabric*

retardation /reé taar dáysh'n/ *n* 1 SLOWING the process or fact of slowing down 2 *US* OFFENSIVE TERM an offensive term for the condition of having developmental disabilities (*dated*) 3 DELAY something that acts as a delay or obstacle to progress 4 DECELERATION deceleration, or the rate of deceleration

retarded /ri taárdid/ *adj* 1 not fully developed ○ *the retarded growth of the plant* 2 an offensive term meaning not intellectually or emotionally developed

retch /rech/ *v* 1 *vi* EXPERIENCE VOMITING SPASM to experience a spasm of vomiting without actually bringing anything up 2 *vti* VOMIT to vomit, or vomit something ■ *n* VOMITING SPASM a spasm of vomiting without bringing anything up [Mid-16C. Variant of obsolete *reach* 'spit, vomit' < Old English *hrǣcan* < Germanic, an imitation of the sound.]

SPELLCHECK Do not confuse ***retch*** with ***wretch***, which has a similar sound. Beware: your spellchecker will not catch this error.

retd *abbr* 1 retained 2 retired 3 returned

rete /reéti/ (*plural* **-tia** /reéshi ə, -ti ə/) *n* a network of veins, arteries, or nerve fibres in the body [14C. < Latin, 'net'.] —**retial** /reéshi əl/ *adj*

retell /ree tél/ (**-tells, -telling, -told** /-tṓld/) *vt* to tell something such as a story or joke again, especially in a different form or to somebody who has not heard it

retelling /ree télling/ *n* a repeating of an account or story that has been told before ○ *a modern retelling of an ancient fable*

retene /reé teen, ré-/ *n* $C_{18}H_{18}$ a yellow crystalline hydrocarbon. Source: pine tar, certain fossil resins. [Mid-19C. < Greek *rhētinē* 'resin' + -ENE.]

retention /ri ténsh'n/ *n* 1 HOLDING IN OF the act of retaining something or the condition of being retained 2 MEMORY the ability to remember things 3 ABNORMAL HOLDING OF WASTE the abnormal holding in the body of waste that is normally excreted 4 AMOUNT OF MONEY HELD BACK an amount of money that is part of a sum agreed to be paid to somebody but which is not paid until a condition has been satisfied ○ *a mortgage of £80,000 with a retention of £10,000 pending major repairs* [14C. Directly or via French < Latin *retention-* < *retinere* 'hold back'.]

retentive /ri téntiv/ *adj* 1 able to or tending to hold something ○ *a soil that is highly retentive of rainwater* 2 able to remember a great deal of information [14C. Directly or via Old French < medieval Latin *retentivus* < Latin *retent-*, past participle of *retinere* 'hold back'.] —**retentively** *adv*—**retentiveness** *n*

retentivity /reé ten tívvəti/ *n* 1 the power or condition of retaining something 2 the capacity of a material to remain magnetized after the force that magnetized it has been taken away

rethink /ree thíngk/ *vti* (**-thinks, -thinking, -thought** /-tháwrt/) to think about something again, especially using new information or in order to produce a better result ■ *n* an attempt to rethink something, or an occasion on which something is rethought ○ *Let's have a rethink before we proceed.*

retia plural of **rete**

retiarius /rétti aári əss, reéti áiri əss, reéshi-/ (*plural* **-i** /-aári ī, -áiri ī/) *n* an ancient Roman gladiator who fought using a net and a trident [Mid-17C. < Latin, < *rete* 'net'.]

reticent /réttis'nt/ *adj* 1 unwilling to communicate very much, talk freely, or reveal all the facts ○ *rather reticent on the subject of her finances* 2 ⚠ unwilling to do something. —**reticence** *n* —**reticently** *adv*

SYNONYMS See ***silent***.

USAGE In its traditional sense, ***reticent*** means unwilling to communicate. Thus it is more nearly a synonym for *silent* than it is for *reluctant*: *He was never reticent about wanting the job.* It is, however, increasingly seen in contexts in which it conveys other kinds of reluctance: *He was reticent to travel so much.* Many regard this as a misuse, and in fact such usages tend to convey nothing that *reluctant* would not convey better.

reticle /réttik'l/ *n* a grid of fine lines in the focus of an optical instrument, used for determining the scale or position of what is being looked at [Mid-17C. < Latin *reticulum* (see RETICULUM).]

reticula plural of **reticulum**

reticular /ri tíkyo͝olər/ *adj* relating to, involving, or structurally resembling a net or network [Late 16C. < modern Latin *reticularis* < Latin *reticulum* (see RETICULUM).]

reticular formation *n* a formation of neurons in the brain stem that regulates many body functions, including respiration, blood pressure, sleeping and waking, and transmission of stimuli

reticulate *adj* /ri tíkyo͝o lət, -layt/ = **reticular** *adj.* ■ *vti* /ri tíkyo͝o layt/ (**-lates, -lating, -lated**) to form a network, or be formed into a network [Mid-17C. < Latin *reticulatus* < *reticulum* (see RETICULUM).] —**reticulately** /ri tíkyo͝olətli/ *adv* —**reticulation** /ri tíkyo͝o láysh'n/ *n*

reticule /rétti kyool/ *n* 1 a small fabric handbag, usually closed with a drawstring, carried by women in the late 18th and early 19th centuries 2 OPTICS = **reticle** [Early 18C. Via French *réticule* < Latin *reticulum* (see RETICULUM).]

reticulocyte /ri tíkyo͝olə sīt/ *n* an immature red blood cell containing a network of fibres of ribosomal remains that show up with laboratory staining [Early 20C. < RETICULUM.] —**reticulocytic** /ri tíkyo͝olə síttik/ *adj*

reticulum /ri tíkyo͝oləm/ (*plural* **-la** /-y-lə/) *n* 1 a network or something resembling a network in structure 2 the second stomach or stomach compartment in cows, sheep, and other ruminants [Mid-17C. < Latin, 'little net' < *rete* 'net'.]

Reticulum /ri tíkyo͝oləm/ *n* a small constellation of the southern hemisphere

retin- *prefix* = **retino-** (*before vowels*)

retina /réttinə/ (*plural* **-nas** *or* **-nae** /-nee/) *n* a light-sensitive membrane in the back of the eye containing rods and cones that receive an image from the lens and send it to the brain through the optic nerve [14C. < medieval Latin < Latin *rete* 'net'; from the network of blood-vessels.] —**retinal** *adj*

retinae plural of **retina**

retinal /réttin'l/ *n* a derivative of vitamin A that forms part of the light-sensitive pigment in the eye

retinene /rétti neen/ *n* BIOCHEM = **retinal** *n.*

retinitis /rétti nītiss/ *n* inflammation of the retina

retinitis pigmentosa /-pígmən tṓzə/ *n* an inherited disorder of the eye involving progressive disintegration of the retina and optic nerve and leading eventually to tunnel vision or inability to see [< modern Latin, 'pigmented']

retino- *prefix* retina ○ *retinoblastoma* [< RETINA]

retinoblastoma /réttinō bla stṓmə/ (*plural* **-mata** /-mətə/ *or* **-mas**) *n* a malignant tumour of the eye, usually resulting from a genetic disorder and appearing in early childhood

retinoic acid /réttinō ik-/ *n* PHARM = **tretinoin** [< RETINOL]

retinoid /rétti noyd/ *n* a vitamin A-related compound that promotes DNA transcription. Use: treatment of acne, ageing skin, psoriasis, skin cancers. [Late 20C. < RETINOL.]

retinol /rétti nol/ *n* 1 BIOCHEM = **vitamin A** 2 CHEM = **rosin oil** [Mid-20C. < RETINA.]

retinopathy /rétti nóppəthi/ (*plural* **-thies**) *n* a disease of the retina, especially one that is noninflammatory and associated with damage to the blood vessels of the retina ○ *diabetic retinopathy* —**retinopathic** /réttinō páthik/ *adj*

retinoscope /réttinə skōp/ *n* an instrument for identifying refractive errors in the eye by measuring the angle of a beam of light reflected from the retina and back out through the pupil

retinoscopy /rétti nóskəpi/ (*plural* **-pies**) *n* a method of measuring refractive errors in the eye using a retinoscope —**retinoscopic** /réttinə skóppik/ *adj* —**retinoscopically** *adv* —**retinoscopist** /réttin óskəpist/ *n*

retinue /rétti nyoo/ *n* a group of people who travel with and attend an important person [14C. < Old French, 'retained (in service)' < past participle of *retenir* 'retain' < Latin *retinere* 'hold back'.]

retiral /ri tīrəl/ *n* *Scotland* retirement from a job or post ○ *He's due for retiral next year.*

retire /ri tīr/ (**-tires, -tiring, -tired**) *v* 1 *vi* STOP WORKING WILLINGLY to leave a job or career voluntarily, at or near the usual age for doing so 2 *vi* GO TO BED to stop engaging in daily activities and go to bed 3 *vi* WITHDRAW to leave a place, position, or way of life and go to a place of less activity ○ *retire from public life* 4 *vt* MAKE SOMEBODY STOP WORKING to stop a person or an animal performing some activity because of illness or an inability to continue ○ *injuries so extensive that the horse was retired* **5** *vt* WITHDRAW SOMETHING FROM SERVICE to take a machine or piece of equipment out of service **6** *vti* GO BACK OR MOVE TROOPS BACK to fall back, or move troops away from a position, action, or danger **7** *vti* WITHDRAW FROM SPORTS CONTEST to withdraw or withdraw somebody from a sports contest, because of an inability to continue **8** *vt* WITHDRAW SOMETHING FROM CIRCULATION to take a loan, stock, bond, or other financial instrument out of circulation by paying for it [Mid-16C. < French *retirer* 'retreat' < *tirer* 'draw'.] —**retirer** *n*

retired /ri tírd/ *adj* **1** having given up working, typically after having worked many years ○ *a retired bus driver* **2** having withdrawn from a busy way of life ○ *a retired lifestyle*

retiree /ri tī rée/ *n* a person who has retired from a job or career

retirement /ri tírmənt/ *n* **1** LEAVING OF JOB OR CAREER the act of leaving a job or career at or near the usual age for doing so **2** TIME AFTER HAVING STOPPED WORKING the time that follows the end of somebody's working life **3** BEING AWAY FROM BUSY LIFE a state of being withdrawn from the rest of the world or a former busy life ○ *He lives in retirement in the country.*

retirement pension *n* a pension paid to a retired person, usually by the state

retiring /ri tíring/ *adj* **1** avoiding social contact with other people **2** at, involving, or undergoing retirement from a job or career ○ *The retiring chairman made an emotional speech.* —**retiringly** *adv* —**retiringness** *n*

retitle /ree tít'l/ (**-tles, -tling, -tled**) *vt* to give a new or changed title to something, especially a literary, theatrical, or musical work

retool /ree tóol/ *v* **1** *vti* to replace the tools or machinery in a factory, or to obtain new tools or machinery **2** *vt US* to reorganize something in order to make it more efficient or powerful ○ *The company will have to retool if it's to remain competitive.*

retorsion /ri táwrsh'n/ *n* an act of retaliation by a government against citizens of another country for a similar offence committed by the other country [Mid-17C. < French *rétorsion* < Latin *retort-* (see RETORT).]

retort[1] /ri táwrt/ *vt* **1** RESPOND SHARPLY to say something sharp, angry, witty, or insulting in quick response to something somebody else has said **2** ARGUE IN REPLY to put forward something as an argument in reply to somebody else's argument ■ *n* SHARP ANSWER something sharp, angry, witty, or insulting said quickly in response to something somebody else has said [15C. < Latin *retort-*, past participle of *retorquere* 'twist again' < *torquere* 'twist'.] —**retorter** *n*

SYNONYMS See ***answer***.

retort[2] /ri táwrt/ *n* **1** GLASS VESSEL a glass vessel with a long downwards-pointing tapering spout, used for distilling by heat **2** CLOSED CONTAINER FOR HEATING SUBSTANCES a closed container in which large quantities of a substance are heated to extract something, e.g. metal from ore ■ *vt* HEAT SOMETHING IN RETORT to heat or distil something in a retort [Early 17C. Via French *retorte* < medieval Latin *retorta* < Latin *retorquere* 'twist back', from the shape of the neck.]

retortion *n* **1** an act or the process of saying something as a retort to somebody else **2** INTERNAT REL = **retorsion**

retouch *vt* /ree túch/ **1** IMPROVE to make small finishing, correcting, or improving changes to something **2** ALTER PHOTOGRAPH to alter a photographic negative or print by removing imperfections or adding details ■ *n* /rée tuch/ **1** ACTIVITY OF RETOUCHING the process of retouching something, or the occasion on which something is retouched **2** SOMETHING ALTERED something that has been retouched, especially a photograph **3** IMPROVING CHANGE a small, finishing, correcting, or improving change to something —**retoucher** *n*

retrace /ri tráyss/ (**-traces, -tracing, -traced**) *vt* **1** to go back over a path or route again **2** to review something in the mind, e.g. an argument, account, or series of events ○ *retraced the events leading up to the war* —**retraceable** *adj*

retract /ri trákt/ *v* **1** *vti* MOVE, OR MOVE SOMETHING, BACK INSIDE to draw something in from an extended position, or be able to be drawn in ○ *Cats can retract their claws but dogs can't.* **2** *vti* WITHDRAW STATEMENT to withdraw or deny something previously said, published, or promised ○ *She has since retracted her earlier statement.* **3** *vi* MOVE BACK to move back from something **4** *vt* CHANGE VOWEL SOUND to alter a vowel sound by drawing the tongue inwards from the lips [15C. < Latin *retract-*, past participle of *retrahere* 'draw back' < *trahere* 'pull'.] —**retractability** /ri tráktə bílləti/ *n* —**retractable** *adj* —**retractation** /rée trak táysh'n/ *n*

retractile /ri trák tīl/ *adj* capable of being retracted —**retractility** /rée trak tíllәti/ *n*

retraction /ri tráksh'n/ *n* **1** the act of retracting something or the condition of being retracted **2** a statement, sometimes formal, that withdraws or denies a previous statement

retractor /ri tráktər/ *n* **1** a surgical instrument used to hold back skin or tissue during surgery **2** a muscle that retracts a body part, e.g. one that closes the jaw

retrain /ree tráyn/ *vti* to teach somebody or learn new skills ○ *decided to retrain as a systems analyst*

retraining /ree tráyning/ *n* the process or activity of learning new skills or of updating existing skills

retransfusion /rée transs fyóozh'n/ *n* a new, different, or subsequent transfusion

retransmit /rée tranz mít, -transs-t, -traanz-, -traanss-/ (**-mits, -mitting, -mitted**) *v* **1** *vt* to transmit or broadcast something again, or transmit something onwards to another place **2** to transmit a television broadcast by cable —**retransmission** *n*

retread *n* /rée tred/ *US* **1** AUTOMOT = **remould** *n.* **2** REMAKE a revised or remade version of something **3** RETURNING WORKER a person who returns to a job previously given up (*informal*) ■ *vt* /ree tréd/ *US* **1** INDUST = **remould** *v.* **2** **2** REMAKE to make something over again, especially with minimal changes, and present it as a new version

re-tread /ree tréd/ (**re-treads, re-treading, re-trod** /ree tród/, **re-trodden** /ree tródd'n/) *vt* to walk again on a route that has already been walked over

retreat /ri tréet/ *n* **1** MOVEMENT BACK a movement away from danger or a confrontation, back along the original route ○ *The bear had the hunters in full retreat.* **2** TROOP WITHDRAWAL a withdrawal of military forces following a defeat or preceding a change of position **3** SIGNAL TO MOVE BACK a signal, usually a bugle call or drumbeat, telling soldiers to perform a retreat **4** WITHDRAWAL FROM POSITION a withdrawal from a particular position or point of view to one intended to lessen conflict ○ *their retreat from a previously inflexible position* **5** QUIET TIME a period of quiet rest and contemplation in a secluded place **6** QUIET PLACE a quiet, secluded place where people go for rest and privacy **7** SAFE PLACE a place where people or animals go to avoid danger or capture **8** PERIOD OF SECLUSION a period away from normal activities, devoted to prayer and meditation, often spent in a religious community **9** SPECIAL HOSPITAL a place for the long-term care and treatment of people who are incapable of caring for themselves (*dated*) **10** FLAG-LOWERING CEREMONY the ceremony of lowering the flag at a military institution, or the signal given to lower the flag ■ *v* **1** *vi* MOVE BACK to move back away from danger or a confrontation **2** *vi* MAKE MILITARY WITHDRAWAL to withdraw following a defeat or prior to a change of position **3** *vi* WITHDRAW FROM POSITION to withdraw from a particular position or point of view to one intended to lessen conflict **4** *vi* RECEDE to recede or fall back from a previous position **5** *vt* MOVE PIECE BACK to move a chesspiece back to an earlier position [13C. < Old French *retret*, < past participle of *retraire* < Latin *retrahere* (see RETRACT).] ◇ **beat a (hasty) retreat** to leave, especially in a hurry

retreatant /ri tréet'nt/ *n* a participant in a spiritual or religious retreat

retrench /ri trénch/ *v* **1** *vti* to reduce something such as costs **2** *vt* to cut out, cut back, or omit something [Late 16C. < French *retrancher* 'recut' < *trenchier* 'to cut'.] —**retrenchment** *n*

retrial /ree trī əl, rée trī əl/ *n* a second trial in a court of law replacing a prior one that was flawed or ended in a hung jury

retribution /réttri byóosh'n/ *n* something done or given to somebody as punishment or vengeance for something he or she has done ○ *a just retribution for their crime* [14C. < Latin *retribution-* < *retribuere* 'hand back, repay' < *tribuere* 'allot'.] —**retributive** /ri tríbbyòotiv/ *adj* —**retributively** *adv* —**retributory** *adj*

ϟ **retrieval** /ri tréev'l/ *n* **1** RECOVERY the act of getting something back, or a particular occasion on which this is done **2** POSSIBILITY OF BEING RESTORED the possibility of something being brought back, saved, or restored to an original condition ○ *Their business seemed beyond retrieval.* **3** DATA ACCESS the process of reading data from a storage device and returning it to the program or device that requested it

ϟ **retrieve** /ri tréev/ *v* (**-trieves, -trieving, -trieved**) **1** *vt* GET SOMETHING BACK to get something back **2** *vt* SAVE to save something from being lost, damaged, or destroyed **3** *vt* REMEDY to set something right or make it better ○ *attempt to retrieve the situation before it worsens* **4** *vt* RESTORE to revive or restore something to its original condition ○ *She quickly retrieved her sense of humour.* **5** *vt* REMEMBER to recall something from memory **6** *vt* GET DATA to read data from a storage device and return it to the program or device that requested it **7** *vti* RETURN SHOT to return a difficult shot in a game such as tennis or badminton **8** *vti* FETCH GAME to fetch small game that has been shot by a hunter ■ *n* RETRIEVING the act of retrieving something ○ *a successful retrieve* [15C. < Old French *retroev-*, stem of *retrover* 'find again' < *trover* 'find'.] —**retrievability** /ri tréevə bílləti/ *n* —**retrievable** *adj* —**retrievably** *adv*

retriever /ri tréevər/ *n* **1** a large strong-bodied dog originally bred to retrieve game for a hunter **2** a person who or thing that retrieves something

retro *adj* modelled on something from the past, e.g. a style of fashion or music ○ *retro clothing* ■ *n* (*plural* **-ros**) **1** the practice of modelling things such as clothes or music on styles from the past, or an example of such a practice ○ *The band is heavily into sixties retro.* **2** AEROSP = **retrorocket** [Late 20C. < French *rétro*, shortening of *rétrograde* 'retrograde' < Latin *retrogradus* (see RETROGRADE); influenced by RETRO-.]

retro- *prefix* **1** back, backward, after ○ *retrorocket* ○ *retrofit* **2** behind ○ *retrochoir* [< Latin *retro*]

retroact /réttrō ákt/ *vi* **1** to act in a way that opposes something else **2** to apply to things that have happened in the past

retroaction /réttrō áksh'n/ *n* **1** APPLICABILITY TO THE PAST the applicability of something to past circumstances or events **2** ACTION REACTING TO PAST SITUATION an action that responds or reacts to something in the past **3** COUNTERACTION an action that goes against or balances a previous action

retroactive /réttrō áktiv/ *adj* relating or applying to things that have happened in the past as well as the present ○ *a pay increase retroactive to the beginning of the year*

retroactive inhibition *n* the tendency of recently gained knowledge or skills to degenerate when new learning in a similar area is acquired

retrocede /réttrō séed/ (**-cedes, -ceding, -ceded**) *v* **1** *vi* to go back or return **2** *vt* to give back something such as land or a territory [Mid-17C. < French *rétrocéder* < *céder* 'give way'.] —**retrocedent** *adj* —**retrocession** *n* —**retrocessive** *adj*

retrochoir /réttrō kwīr/ *n* the area behind the high altar in a large church or cathedral [Mid-19C. < medieval Latin *retrochorus* 'back choir' < *chorus* (see CHOIR).]

re-trod past tense of **re-tread**

re-trodden past participle of **re-tread**

retro-engine *n* AEROSP = **retrorocket**

retrofire /réttrō fīr/ *vti* (**-fires, -firing, -fired**) to fire a retrorocket to decelerate ■ *n* the process of firing a retrorocket, or an occasion of doing this

retrofit /réttrō fit/ *vt* **1** MODIFY SOMETHING WITH NEW PARTS to modify something such as a machine or a building by adding parts or devices of types not originally included ○ *older cars retrofitted with catalytic converters* **2** INSTALL NEW PARTS to install new parts or devices of types not originally included in existing equipment, machinery, or buildings ○ *retrofit a microchip in the alarm system* ■ *n* **1** NEW PART OR SOMETHING WITH ONE something that has been equipped with a newly developed component, or such a component designed for something that is already in use **2** PROCESS OF ADDING NEW PART the process or an instance of modifying something such as a machine or a building by adding new parts or devices

retroflection *n* = **retroflexion**

retroflex /réttrō fleks/, **retroflexed** /-flekst/ *adj* **1** bent or curved backwards **2** describes speech sounds that are pronounced with the tip of the tongue raised and bent backwards [Late 18C. < Latin *retroflex-*, past participle of *retroflectere* 'bend back' < *flectere* 'bend'.]

retroflexion /réttrō fléksh'n/, **retroflection** *n* **1** BENT CON-

DITION the condition of bending or being bent backwards **2 PRONUNCIATION WITH TONGUE BENT BACK** the pronunciation of a letter or sound with the tongue raised and bent backwards **3 INABILITY TO EXTERNALIZE DIFFICULT EMOTION** in Gestalt therapy, the act of directing a difficult emotion such as anger at yourself rather than at somebody who has provoked the emotion [Early 19C. < RETRO- after REFLECTION.]

retrograde /réttrō grayd/ *adj* **1 MOVING BACKWARDS** moving backwards in space or time **2 INVERSE** in writing, inverse or reversed, especially in syntactic order **3 GETTING WORSE** worsening or returning to an earlier worse condition **4 HAVING A CONTRARY ORBIT** orbiting in a direction opposite to that of the Earth's orbit around the Sun, or of the Moon's orbit around the Earth **5 MOVING EAST TO WEST** moving or appearing to move from east to west in the sky, counter to the direction of most astronomical objects **6 REVERSING NOTES** reversing the sequence of notes of an earlier version of a musical composition ■ *vi* (**-grades, -grading, -graded**) **1 GO BACKWARDS** to go back or appear to be moving backwards in space or time **2** = **retrogress** *v.* 1 [14C. < Latin *retrogradus* 'going backwards' < *gradus* 'step'.] —**retrogradation** /réttrō gray dáysh'n/ *n* —**retrogradely** *adv*

retrogress /réttrō gréss/ *vi* **1 REVERT OR DEGENERATE** to return to an earlier and usually worse condition **2 GO BACKWARDS** to move or travel backwards **3 HAVE LESS COMPLEX FEATURES** to show or develop the less complex features of simpler organisms [Early 19C. < RETRO- after PROGRESS.] —**retrogressive** *adj* —**retrogressively** *adv*

retrogression /réttrō grésh'n/ *n* **1** the process of returning to an earlier and usually worse condition **2** the development of less complex features usually associated with simpler organisms

retrolental /réttrō lént'l/ *adj* located behind the lens of the eye or the lens of an optical instrument [Mid-20C. < RETRO- + modern Latin *lent-*, stem of *lens* 'lens'.]

retronym /réttrō nim/ *n US* a term that distinguishes a subclass from members of a superclass, e.g. 'snail mail' is a retronym coined by those for whom 'mail' is likely to mean 'e-mail' [Combination of RETRO- + SYNONYM]

retropack /réttrō pak/ *n* an array of retrorockets on a spacecraft, used for slowing down or for changing direction

retropulsion /réttrō púlsh'n/ *n* a tendency to walk backwards involuntarily, associated with Parkinson's disease [Late 18C. Blend of RETRO- + PROPULSION.]

retrorocket /réttrō rokit/ *n* a small rocket engine on a spacecraft or missile that produces thrust to act against the main engines and is used for decelerating

retrorse /ri tráwrss/ *adj* describes plant parts that are turned back or down [Early 19C. < Latin *retrorsus*, contraction of *retroversus* 'turning backwards' < *versus* 'turning'.] —**retrorsely** *adv*

retrospect /réttrō spekt/ *n* the remembering of past events [Early 17C. < RETRO- after PROSPECT.] ◇ **in retrospect** thinking about or reviewing the past, especially from a new perspective or with new information

retrospection /réttrō spéksh'n/ *n* the act of looking back over things in the past, especially personal memories

retrospective /réttrō spéktiv/ *adj* **1 REVIEWING THE PAST** looking back over things in the past **2 CONTAINING PAST WORKS** containing examples of work from many periods of an artist's life ○ *a retrospective exhibition* **3 APPLYING TO PAST EVENTS** applying to things that have happened in the past as well as the present ○ *a retrospective ruling* ■ *n* **EXHIBITION OF ARTIST'S PAST WORK** an exhibition of the work of a particular artist or artistic movement that shows examples from all periods or styles ○ *a Degas retrospective* —**retrospectively** *adv*

retrotransposon /réttrō transs pṓ zon/ *n* a segment of DNA (**transposon**) that duplicates itself by first making an RNA copy and then a DNA copy, which can reintegrate into the DNA of the cell

retroussé /rə tróo say/ *adj* turned up at the end ○ *a retroussé nose* [Early 19C. < French, 'turned up'.]

retroversion /réttrō vúrsh'n/ *n* **1** the act or condition of being turned backwards **2** the abnormal turning or tilting backwards of a body part, e.g. the uterus [Late 16C. < Latin *retroversus* 'turning backward'.] —**retroverse** *adj* —**retroverted** *adj*

retrovirus /réttrō vīrəss/ *n* a virus whose genetic information is contained in RNA rather than DNA —**retroviral** /-vīrəl/ *adj*

retry *v* /ree trī/ (**-tries, -trying, -tried**) **1** *vt* **TRY SOMEBODY AGAIN** to try a person or case again in a court of law **2** *vti* **ATTEMPT SOMETHING AGAIN** to try to do something again ■ *n* /rée trī/ (*plural* **-tries**) **SECOND ATTEMPT** another attempt to do something

retsina /ret séenə/ *n* a Greek wine flavoured with pine resin [Early 20C. < modern Greek < Greek *rhētinē* 'pine resin'.]

retune /ree tyóon/ (**-tunes, -tuning, -tuned**) *vt* **1 READJUST MUSICAL INSTRUMENT** to readjust a musical instrument so that a note is at a different pitch **2 READJUST ENGINE** to readjust an engine or machine to make it run better **3 READJUST ELECTRONIC DEVICE** to readjust an electronic device or instrument to a different frequency

ϟ**return** /ri túrn/ *v* **1** *vi* **COME OR GO BACK** to come or go back to a place after leaving it or to a former condition **2** *vi* **GO BACK** to go back to something that has already been mentioned or considered, especially in order to deal with it more thoroughly or conclusively ○ *Let's return to the matter in hand.* **3** *vi* **APPEAR AGAIN** to appear or happen again **4** *vt* **REPLY** to answer or reply to something somebody has said ○ *'Do it yourself!' she returned.* **5** *vt* **PUT BACK** to put, bring, send, or take something back to where it came from **6** *vt* **REPAY** to give back something of equivalent value ○ *I hope that some day I'll be able to return your kindness.* **7** *vt* **YIELD PROFIT** to yield something as a profit on an investment ○ *returns 6% per annum* **8** *vt* **RE-ELECT SOMEBODY TO OFFICE** to re-elect somebody to an office or position ○ *returned her to Parliament for a second term* **9** *vt* **REFLECT** to send back or reflect something such as an echo ○ *The cliff wall returned the sound of their laughter.* **10** *vt* **PRODUCE VERDICT** to give a particular verdict in a court of law ○ *return a guilty verdict* **11** *vt* **SUBMIT OFFICIAL REPORT** to give an official report, usually in response to a request or legal requirement **12** *vt* **GIVE RESPONSE** of a computer, to give a particular response to a command, routine, or subroutine ○ *returns zero if the condition is false* **13** *vt* **BUILD SOMETHING TO FACE OPPOSITE DIRECTION** to construct part of a building, e.g. a wall or decoration, so that it turns away from its original direction **14** *vti* **HIT BALL BACK** in sports such as tennis, to hit a ball, especially a service, back to an opponent **15** *vt* **LEAD SAME SUIT** to lead the same suit as a partner in a card game such as bridge or whist ■ *n* **1 GOING OR COMING BACK** a going or coming back to a place after having left it or to a former condition **2 REPLACEMENT** a putting, taking, sending, or bringing back of something to where it came from **3 SOMETHING GIVEN BACK** something that has come or been brought back, especially unsold merchandise ○ *Returns go in that bin over there* **4 REAPPEARANCE** a reappearance or recurrence of something **5 RECIPROCATION** a response to something done or given ○ *If you are kind to your puppy it will give you love in return* **6 ANSWER** something said in response to something else ○ *If you ask her an absurd question you can expect an angry return* **7 PROFIT** a profit made on an investment or business venture (*often plural*) **8** TRANSP = **return ticket 9 TAX RETURN** a tax return **10 FINANCIAL REPORT** a periodic financial report of an organization **11** COMPUT = **return key 12 ANGLED PART** part of a building, e.g. a wall or decoration, built so that it turns away from its original direction **13 BALL PLAYED BACK** an instance of hitting or playing the ball back to an opponent in a sport such as tennis **14 LEGAL REPORT** a report on a legal document previously issued, e.g. a subpoena or writ, by an officer of that court of law **15 LEAD OF SAME SUIT** an instance of leading the same suit as a partner in a card game such as bridge or pinochle **16** *Northern Ireland* **BUILDING EXTENSION** a rearward extension to a building ■ **returns** *npl* **ELECTION RESULTS** the results from an election or election district ○ *We sat up late waiting for the election returns.* ■ *adj* **1 CONNECTED WITH GOING BACK AGAIN** relating to an act of going or coming back to an earlier place or position ○ *I hope the return flight isn't delayed.* **2 GOING THERE AND BACK** involving a journey to somewhere and back again. US term **round-trip** *adj.* **3 HAPPENING AGAIN** given or done again or in order ○ *We enjoyed the resort so much that we decided to make a return visit the next year.* [14C. < Old French *reto(u)rner* 'turn again' < *to(u)rner* 'to turn' < Latin *tornare*.] —**returnable** *adj, n* —**returnee** /ri túr née/ *n* ◇ **by return (of post)** by the next post back to the sender ◇ **in return (for something)** as an exchange for something ◇ **many happy returns (of the day)** a conventional way of expressing good wishes to somebody whose birthday it is, often as an exclamation

returning officer *n UK, Aus, Can* a constituency official who is responsible for overseeing the count in an election and announcing the result

ϟ**return key** *n* the key on a computer or typewriter keyboard, usually marked with an angled arrow, that can be used to execute an instruction or create a new line

return ticket *n* a ticket that entitles a passenger to travel both to and back from a particular destination. US term **round-trip ticket**

Reuben /róobin/ *n* in the Bible, a Hebrew patriarch and the eldest son of Jacob and Leah

reunify /ree yóoni fī/ (**-fies, -fying, -fied**) *vti* to come together or bring people or factions together again, after they have been divided —**reunification** /ree yóonifi káysh'n/ *n*

reunion /ree yóonyən/ *n* **1** a gathering of old friends, relatives, or people who were colleagues at one time ○ *a high-school class reunion* **2** the coming together again of things or people that have been divided, or the condition of having come together in this way

reunionist /ree yóonyənist/ *n* a supporter of reunion between divided groups or parties, especially somebody who seeks reunion between the Anglican and Roman Catholic churches —**reunionism** *n* —**reunionistic** /-nístik/ *adj*

reunite /rée yoo nít/ (**-nites, -niting, -nited**) *vti* to bring people together, or come together, after a separation

reupholster /rée up hṓlstər/ *vt* to replace the worn or damaged upholstery on a chair or sofa

reuptake /ree úp tayk/ *n* the reabsorption of neurotransmitters by the nerve cells that produced them

reuse *vt* /ree yóoz/ (**-uses, -using, -used**) to use something again, often for a different purpose and usually as an alternative to throwing it away ■ *n* /ree yóoss/ the using of something again, often for a different purpose and usually as an alternative to throwing it away —**reusability** /-bílləti/ *n* —**reusable** *adj*

Reuter /róytər/, **Paul Julius, Baron von** (1816–99) German-born British journalist. Born **Israel Beer Josaphat**

Reuters /róytərz/ *n* a London news agency providing international news reports [Mid-19C. After Paul Julius, Baron von REUTER.]

reutilize /ree yóoti līz/ (**-izes, -izing, -ized**), **reutilise** (**-ises, -ising, -ised**) *vt* to make use of something for a second or subsequent time or for a different purpose —**reutilization** /rée yooti lī záysh'n/ *n*

rev /rev/ *vti* (**revs, revving, revved**) to increase a vehicle's engine speed by pressing down on the accelerator or advancing the throttle, especially while the vehicle is stationary ■ *n* a single revolution of a vehicle's engine (*informal; usually plural*) [Early 20C. Shortening of REVOLUTION.]

rev up *vt* (*informal*) **1** to increase the tempo, intensity, or amount of something ○ *We'd better rev up production if we're to meet our deadline.* **2** to stir up intense feelings in somebody, usually feelings of excitement, desire, or anger

rev. *abbr* **1** revenue **2** reverse **3** review **4** revised **5** revision **6** revolution **7** revolver **8** revolving

Rev. /rev/ *abbr* Reverend

revalue /rée vállyoo/ (**-ues, -uing, -ued**), **revaluate** /rée vállyoo ayt/ (**-ates, -ating, -ated**) *vt* **1** to increase the value of a nation's currency **2** to assign a new value to something such as assets

revamp *vt* /ree vámp/ to alter something in order to improve the way it looks or works ■ *n* /rée vamp/ a change made in something in order to improve its appearance or functioning [The word meant originally 'furnish a shoe with a new vamp']

SYNONYMS See ***renew***.

revanche /ri vánch/ *n* a nation's or an ethnic group's policy of regaining lost territory [Mid-19C. < French, < Old French *revancher* 'avenge' < *vengier*.] —**revanchism** *n* —**revanchist** *adj, n* —**revanchistic** /ri ván chístik/ *adj*

rev counter *n* a tachometer (*informal*)

Revd *abbr* Reverend

reveal[1] /ri véel/ *vt* **1 MAKE SOMETHING KNOWN** to disclose something that was unknown or secret **2 EXPOSE** to make something visible that had been hidden or covered **3 MAKE KNOWN DIVINE TRUTH** to make something known by divine or supernatural means [14C. Via French *révéler* < Latin *revelare* 'unveil' < *velum* 'sail'.] —**revealer** *n*

reveal[2] /ri véel/ *n* the vertical section of wall that lies between a doorframe or window frame and the outer wall [Late 17C. Alteration of obsolete *revale* 'lower' < Old French *revaler* < *val* 'valley'.]

revealed religion *n* a religion based on what its adherents believe to be the word of a supreme deity

revealing /ri veéling/ *adj* **1** exposing part of the body that would normally be kept covered **2** giving away new, surprising, or valuable information —**revealingly** *adv*

revegetate /ree véjji tayt/ (**-tates, -tating, -tated**) *vti* to provide eroded or otherwise barren land with new plant life —**revegetation** /-táysh'n/ *n*

reveille /ri válli/ (*plural* **-les**) *n* **1 WAKE-UP CALL** the sounding of a bugle to awaken and summon military personnel in a camp **2 TIME OF REVEILLE** the time of day at which reveille is sounded **3 EARLY-MORNING MILITARY FORMATION** the military formation that begins the day **4 SIGNAL TO AWAKE** any signal that it is time to get out of bed [Mid-17C. Alteration of French *réveillez* 'wake up!' < Old French *resveiller* 'awaken' < *esveiller* < Latin *vigil* 'awake, alert'.]

revel /révv'l/ *vi* (**-els, -elling, -elled**) **1 TAKE PLEASURE** to take great pleasure in something **2 ENJOY PARTY** to have an enjoyable time in the company of others, especially at a party ■ *n* **NOISY CELEBRATION** an uproarious party or celebration (*often plural*) [14C. Via Old French *reveler* 'rebel, carouse' < Latin *rebellare* 'to rebel' < *bellum* 'war'.] —**reveller** *n*

~~**revelant**~~ incorrect spelling of **relevant**

revelation /révvə láysh'n/ *n* **1 INFORMATION REVEALED** information that is newly disclosed, especially surprising, or valuable **2 SURPRISING THING** a surprisingly good or valuable experience **3 DISCLOSURE** the revealing of something previously hidden or secret **4 DEMONSTRATION OF DIVINE WILL** a showing or revealing of divine will or truth [14C. < French < Latin *revelare* 'unveil'.] —**revelational** *adj* —**revelatory** /révvə láytəri/ *adj*

Revelation, Revelations *n* a book of the Bible that includes a description of the end of the world

revelator /révvə laytər/ *n* somebody or something believed to reveal divine will or truth [15C. < late Latin < Latin *revelare* 'unveil'.]

revelry /révvəlri/ (*plural* **-ries**) *n* lively enjoyment or celebration, usually involving eating, drinking, dancing, and noise (*often plural*)

revenant /révvənənt/ *n* a dead person believed to have come back as a ghost (*formal*) [Early 19C. < French, < present participle of *revenir* 'return'.]

revenge /ri vénj/ *n* **1 PUNISHMENT** the punishing of somebody in retaliation for harm done **2 REVENGE** something done to get even with somebody else who has caused harm **3 DESIRE FOR REVENGE** the desire or urge to get even with somebody ■ *vt* (**-venges, -venging, -venged**) **1 PUNISH** to punish somebody in retaliation for harm or injury done **2 GET EVEN** to avenge yourself or somebody else who has been harmed [14C. < Old French *revengier* < *vengier* 'avenge' < late Latin *vindicare* 'claim, set free, avenge'.] —**revengeful** *adj* —**revengefully** *adv* —**revenger** *n*

revenue /révvə nyoo/ *n* **1 INCOME FROM BUSINESS** money that comes into a business from the sale of goods or services **2 GOVERNMENT INCOME** the income of a government from all sources, used to pay for a nation's expenses **3 PERSONAL INCOME** income or salary received from employment **4 YIELD ON INVESTMENT** the total return produced by an investment **5 TAX-COLLECTING DEPARTMENT** the department of a nation's government that is responsible for collecting taxes. ◊ **Inland Revenue** [15C. < French *revenu* < past participle of *revenir* 'return' < Latin *revenire* 'come back' < *venire* 'come'.]

revenue bond *n* a bond issued by a US government agency in order to build or improve a public property

revenue cutter *n* a small lightly armed boat used to patrol coastlines, enforce customs regulations, and prevent smuggling

revenuer /révvə nyoo ər/ *n* a US government agent who is in charge of stopping the illegal manufacture of alcoholic beverages (*informal*)

revenue tariff *n* a tax or duty imposed to produce public revenue, as distinct from one imposed to protect a domestic economy

reverb *n* /reé vurb/ **1 ECHO IN MUSIC** an echoing effect produced in live or recorded music by electronic means **2 ECHO-PRODUCING DEVICE** an electronic device used to produce an echoing effect in live or recorded music ■ *vi* /ri vúrb/ **PRODUCE ELECTRONIC ECHO** to produce an echoing effect in live or recorded music [Early 17C. Shortening of REVERBERATE.]

reverberate /ri vúrbə rayt/ (**-ates, -ating, -ated**) *v* **1** *vi* **ECHO** to echo repeatedly **2** *vi* **HAVE CONTINUING EFFECT** to have a far-reaching or lasting impact, especially as a result of being circulated widely **3** *vi* **BOUNCE BACK** to be reflected repeatedly off different surfaces (*refers to heat, light, or sound waves*) **4** *vt* **CAUSE SOUND TO ECHO** to cause sound to bounce back from a surface **5** *vt* **HEAT OR REFINE METAL** to treat metal in a furnace (**reverberatory furnace**) that reflects flame or heat [15C. < Latin *reverberare* 'beat again' < *verberare* 'beat' < *verber* 'scourge'.] —**reverberant** *adj* —**reverberantly** *adv* —**reverberation** /ri vúrbə ráysh'n/ *n* —**reverberative** /ri vúrbərətiv/ *adj* —**reverberator** *n*

reverberation time *n* the time it takes for a sound in a room to be reduced by 60 decibels

reverberatory /ri vúrbərətəri/ *adj* produced or functioning by the process of deflection of sound, light, or heat

reverberatory furnace *n* a furnace in which material is heated by heat reflected from above

revere /ri veér/ (**-veres, -vering, -vered**) *vt* to regard somebody with admiration and deep respect [Mid-17C. Via French *révérer* < Latin *revereri* < *vereri* 'be in awe of'.]

Revere, Paul (1735–1818) American silversmith and patriot

reverence /révvərənss/ *n* **1 RESPECT FELT** feelings of deep respect or devotion **2 RESPECT GAINED** the respect or devotion that others show somebody or something **3 reverence, Reverence USED TO ADDRESS CHRISTIAN CLERGY** used as a form of address for some members of the Christian clergy ■ *vt* (**-ences, -encing, -enced**) **RESPECT SOMEBODY OR SOMETHING DEEPLY** to regard somebody or something with deep respect (*formal*)

SYNONYMS See ***regard***.

reverend /révvrənd/ *adj* **1 OF CLERGY** relating or belonging to the Christian clergy. **2 RESPECTED** deserving to be shown respect (*formal*) ■ *n* **CHRISTIAN CLERIC** a member of the Christian clergy (*informal*) [15C. Directly or via French < Latin *reverendus* 'be revered' < *revereri* (see REVERE).]

USAGE reverend or **reverent**? Care should be taken in distinguishing between ***reverend***, which refers to a member of the clergy, and ***reverent***, which is a descriptive adjective, meaning 'feeling or expressing reverence', applicable to anyone who merits it.

Reverend *n* used as a title and form of address for some members of the clergy in many Christian churches

Reverend Mother *n* used as a title of respect to address the nun in charge of a convent

reverent /révvərənt/ *adj* feeling or expressing profound respect or awe. [14C. < Latin *reverent-*, present participle of *revereri* (see REVERE).] —**reverently** *adv*

USAGE See ***reverend***.

reverential /révvə rénsh'l/ *adj* **1** feeling or expressing deep respect or awe **2** worthy of deep respect or awe —**reverentially** *adv*

reverie /révvəri/ (*plural* **-ies**) *n* a state of idle and pleasant contemplation [Early 17C. < French, < *rêver* 'to dream'.]

revers /ri veér/ (*plural* **-vers**) *n* a part of a garment such as a lapel, turned back so that the reverse side shows [Mid-19C. < French (see REVERSE).]

reversal /ri vúrss'l/ *n* **1 CHANGE TO OPPOSITE DIRECTION** a change to an opposite direction or state **2 PROBLEM** an unfortunate experience or setback, particularly in business or financial affairs **3 REVERSING OF** the changing of something to an opposite direction or state **4 CHANGE OF JUDICIAL DECISION** a ruling made by a higher court that sets aside the decision of a lower court

reverse /ri vúrss/ *v* (**-verses, -versing, -versed**) **1** *vt* **CHANGE SOMETHING TO OPPOSITE** to change something to the opposite direction, order, or position ○ *reversing the trend of population growth* **2** *vti* **GO BACKWARDS** to go backwards, or move something in a backwards direction ○ *reverse the car* **3** *vt* **TURN SOMETHING INSIDE OUT** to change something so that the opposite side or part shows ○ *You can reverse the cloak and wear it with the lining on the outside.* **4** *vt* **REVOKE RULING** to overturn a previous ruling made by a lower court **5** *vt* **PRINT SOMETHING WHITE AGAINST DARK BACKGROUND** to print text or graphics in white against a dark or colour background **6** *vt* **TURN WEAPON UPSIDE DOWN** to turn a weapon upside down, especially as a sign of mourning ■ *n* **1 THE OPPOSITE** the contrary of something ○ *She always does the reverse of what I tell her.* **2 BACK SIDE** the rear or back side of something ○ *The names are written on the reverse of the photo.* **3 BACK SIDE OF COIN** the side of a coin, medal, or seal on which the primary design does not appear ○ *The reverse of some coins carries the national motto.* ◊ **obverse** *n.* 1 **4 CHANGE TO OPPOSITE DIRECTION** a change or turn to the opposite direction, position, or condition **5 SETBACK** a change for the worse ○ *a military reverse* **6 GEAR FOR BACKWARDS MOVEMENT** the gear in a vehicle or machine that makes it run backwards ○ *It's easier to get out of here in reverse.* **7 OFFENSIVE PLAY IN AMERICAN FOOTBALL** in American football, a move in which a back receives the hand off from the quarterback and then hands the ball to another back running in the opposite direction ■ *adj* **1 OPPOSITE TO USUAL OR PREVIOUS ARRANGEMENT** opposite to what is usual or what was previously said or arranged ○ *announce the results in reverse order* **2 ON BACK SIDE** on the other side or the back side of something **3 FOR BACKWARDS MOVEMENT** used to make a machine or vehicle go backwards ○ *reverse gear* [14C. Via Old French *revers* 'reversed' < Latin *reversus*, past participle of *revertere* 'turn back' < *vertere* 'turn'.] —**reversely** *adv* —**reverser** *n*

reverse-charge *adj* used to describe a telephone call paid for by the person receiving it. US term **collect**[1] *adj.*

reverse charges *adv* so as to be charged to the receiver of a call that is placed. US term **collect**[1] *adv.*

reverse commuting *n* the practice of travelling regularly between a home in a city and a job in the suburbs —**reverse commuter** *n*

reverse discrimination *n US* discrimination against a member of a social group generally regarded as dominant or privileged, e.g. in employment or admission to university

reverse engineering *n* the pirating of a competitor's technology by dismantling an existing product and reproducing its parts and construction to manufacture a replica —**reverse-engineer** *vt* —**reverse-engineered** *adj*

reverse mortgage *n* a financial document in the United States and Canada in which a residential mortgage is transferred to a bank, which then pays an annuity to the homeowner

reverse osmosis *n* a process of purifying water or other liquids such as fruit juices by passing them through a semipermeable membrane that filters out unwanted substances

reverse takeover *n* the sale of a company to another company in order to avoid takeover by an unwanted predatory company

reverse transcriptase *n* an enzyme, found naturally in retroviruses, that assists in the formation of DNA in genetic engineering, using RNA as a template

reverse video *n* the reversal of the usual character and background colour combination on a computer display, used in highlighting

reversi /ri vúrssi/ *n* a board game for two players, played on a draughtboard, in which captured pieces are turned upside down [Early 19C. < French, alteration of *reversin*, via Italian *rovescina* 'reversal' < Latin *reversus* (see REVERSE).]

reversible /ri vúrssəb'l/ *adj* **1 ABLE TO BE REVERSED** able to be changed or undone **2 USABLE INSIDE OUT** made so that either side can be used as the outer or upper side **3 UNDERGOING A REACTION AND REVERSING IT** capable of going through a stage such as a chemical reaction and then reversing the process —**reversibility** /ri vúrssə bíllәti/ *n* —**reversibleness** *n* —**reversibly** *adv*

reversing light *n* either one of the white lights on the rear of a vehicle that shine when the vehicle is being reversed

reversion /ri vúrsh'n/ *n* **1 RETURN TO FORMER CONDITION** a return to an earlier condition often perceived as less desirable or inferior **2 REVERSAL** a change to the opposite direction **3 RETURN TO ORIGINAL CHARACTERISTICS** the restoration of the normal genetic constitution in a mutant organism, e.g. by means of a second mutation that cancels out the effects of an earlier one **4 REVERTED ORGANISM** an organism that has reverted to ancestral genetic characteristics **5 RETURN TO FORMER OWNER** the return of property to its former owner or his or her heirs at the end of a specified period, usually when the present owner dies **6 PROPERTY RETURNED TO FORMER OWNER** property that has been returned to its former owner or his or her heirs **7 RIGHT TO INHERIT PROPERTY** the right to succeed to property, granted to somebody by the former owner —**reversional** *adj* —**reversionally** *adv* —**reversionary** *adj*

reversioner /ri vúrsh'nər/ *n* somebody to whom ownership of property will be returned after a specified period of time

revert /ri vúrt/ *vi* **1 GO BACK TO PREVIOUS STATE** to return to a former state, often one perceived as less desirable or inferior **2 RETURN IN DISCUSSION** to return to an earlier topic in the course of a discussion **3 REACQUIRE ORIGINAL FEATURES** to acquire or develop original genetic features again **4 RETURN TO OLD HABITS** to return to a former pattern of behaviour, usually something less acceptable **5 BE RETURNED TO OWNER** to become once again the property of the former owner or his or her heirs [14C. Via Old French *revertir* < Latin *revertere* (see REVERSE).] —**reverter** *n* —**revertible** *adj*

revertant /ri vúrt'nt/ *adj* describes an organism or part of an organism that has reacquired features that are original or simpler ■ *n* a revertant organism or part

revest /ree vést/ *vt* **1** to reinstate somebody in a position or office **2** to restore power or property to somebody

revet /ri vét/ (**-vets, -vetting, -vetted**) *vti* to give a structure additional support by adding a facing of bricks, stone, or concrete [Early 19C. Via French *revêtir* < late Latin *revestire* 'clothe again' < *vestire* 'clothe' < *vestis* 'clothing, garment'.]

revetment /ri vétmənt/ *n* **1** a facing added to a structure such as a wall or building that provides additional support **2** a barricade constructed to protect against damage or injury from explosives

review /ri vyoó/ *v* **1** *vt* **LOOK AT CRITICALLY** to examine something to make sure that it is adequate, accurate, or correct ○ *They need to review their sales strategy.* **2** *vt* **GIVE OPINION ON QUALITY** to write a journalistic report on the quality of a new play, book, film, concert, or other public performance ○ *He reviews films for a newspaper.* **3** *vt* **CONSIDER AGAIN** to consider, study, or check something again **4** *vi US* EDUC = **revise** *v.* 4 **5** *vt* **LOOK BACK** to discuss or examine something again ○ *She's writing an article reviewing the company's history.* **6** *vt* **RECONSIDER DECISION JUDICIALLY** to re-examine a judicial decision made in a lower court in order to consider whether it should be overturned **7** *vt* **SUBJECT TROOPS TO MILITARY INSPECTION** to make a formal inspection of a military force ■ *n* **1 SURVEY OF PAST** a report or survey of past actions, performance, or events ○ *a review of stock market performance during the past five years.* **2 JOURNALISTIC ARTICLE GIVING OPINION** a journalistic article giving an assessment of a book, play, film, concert, or other public performance ○ *The book got unexpectedly bad reviews.* **3 PUBLICATION FEATURING REVIEWS** a magazine or journal that publishes reviews ○ *the Literary Review* **4 RE-EXAMINATION** another look at or consideration of something **5** *US* **COVERING OF LEARNED MATERIAL AGAIN** a brief discussion of subject matter already learned, in preparation for a test **6 MILITARY INSPECTION** a formal military inspection **7 FORMAL MILITARY CEREMONY** a formal military ceremony staged to honour a person or an occasion **8 JUDICIAL RE-EXAMINATION** a critical examination by a higher court of a decision taken by a lower court **9** THEATRE = **revue** [15C. < obsolete French *reveue* 'inspection', < *revoir* 'inspect' < Latin *revidere* 'see again' < *videre* 'see'.] —**reviewable** *adj* —**reviewer** *n*

SPELLCHECK Do not confuse ***review*** with ***revue***, which has a similar sound. Beware: your spellchecker will not catch this error.

review copy *n* a copy of a new book that a publisher sends to potential critics and reviewers to encourage published reviews

revile /ri víl/ (**-viles, -viling, -viled**) *v* **1** *vt* to make a fierce or abusive verbal attack on somebody or something **2** *vi* to use insulting or abusive language [14C. < Old French *reviler* < *vil* (see VILE).] —**revilement** *n* —**reviler** *n*

revise /ri víz/ *v* (**-vises, -vising, -vised**) **1** *vt* **RETHINK** to come to different conclusions about somebody or something after thinking again **2** *vt* **GIVE UPDATED VERSION** to change a previous estimate in order to make it more accurate or realistic **3** *vt* **ALTER TEXT** to amend a text in order to correct, update, or improve it **4** *vti* **STUDY FOR EXAM** to study for a test by looking over notes and course materials. US term **review** *v.* 4 ■ *n* **1 SOMETHING REVISED** something that has been revised **2 LATE STAGE OF PRINTED PROOF** a late stage of a printed proof that incorporates corrections to earlier proofs (*often plural*) [Mid-16C. Via French *réviser* < Latin *revisere* 'look over again' < *visere* 'keep watching' < *videre* 'see'.] —**revisable** *adj* —**reviser** *n* —**revisory** *adj*

Revised Standard Version *n* a modern US revision of the American Standard Version of the Bible, published in full in 1953

Revised Version *n* a 19th-century British revision of the Authorized Version of the Bible

revision /ri vízh'n/ *n* **1 CHANGING OF TEXT** the amending of a text in order to correct, update, improve, or adapt it **2 CHANGING OF** the changing of a decision, estimate, statistic, or set of figures in order to correct it or make it more realistic **3 NEW EDITION** a revised and republished version of a text **4 STUDY FOR EXAM** study that involves looking over notes and course materials, in preparation for a test —**revisionary** *adj*

revisionism /ri vízh'nizəm/ *n* **1** the reconsidering of long-established practices, views, or beliefs **2** a socialist movement arguing against revolutionary Marxist theory and believing in the peaceful achievement of social progress through reforms —**revisionist** *adj, n*

revisit /ree vízzit/ *vt* **1 GO TO PLACE AGAIN** to visit a place again **2 RECONSIDER** to reconsider something such as an issue of public policy or a course of action, especially when additional facts indicate that an earlier decision was inappropriate ■ *n* **SUBSEQUENT VISIT** another visit to a place

revitalize /ree vítə līz/ (**-izes, -izing, -ized**), **revitalise** (**-ises, -ising, -ised**) *vt* to give new life or energy to somebody or something —**revitalization** /ree vítə lī záysh'n/ *n*

revival /ri vív'l/ *n* **1 RENEWAL OF INTEREST** a renewal of interest in something that results in its becoming popular once more **2 NEW PRODUCTION** a new production of a play or opera that has not been performed recently **3 REVIVING OF** the process of bringing somebody back to life, consciousness, or full strength **4 RECOVERY** the recovering of life, consciousness, or full strength **5 RENEWED RELIGIOUS INTEREST** a new interest in religion, or the reawakening of such interest **6 EVANGELICAL CHRISTIAN MEETING** a meeting or a series of meetings of evangelical Christians intended to awaken religious fervour in those who attend **7 RE-ESTABLISHING OF LEGAL VALIDITY** the renewal of the validity of a contract or the effect of a judicial decision

revivalism /ri vívəlizəm/ *n* **1** a desire or tendency to renew interest in something old, e.g. old customs or beliefs **2** the efforts of a religious movement, especially an evangelical Christian movement, to reawaken religious commitment

revivalist /ri vívəlist/ *n* **1 ADVOCATE OF PAST CUSTOMS OR INSTITUTIONS** a person who wishes to revive customs, ideas, or institutions **2 EVANGELIST** a promoter, organizer, or preacher at a religious revival meeting, especially one for evangelical Christians ■ *adj* **REAWAKENING RELIGIOUS FAITH** dedicated to reawakening or stimulating religious fervour in evangelical Christians —**revivalistic** /ri vívə lístik/ *adj*

revive /ri vív/ (**-vives, -viving, -vived**) *v* **1** *vti* **RECOVER CONSCIOUSNESS** to come, or bring somebody, back to life, consciousness, or full strength **2** *vti* **FLOURISH AGAIN** to become, or make something, active, accepted, or popular once more **3** *vt* **CAUSE EXPERIENCE TO RETURN** to cause something to be experienced again as a memory or feeling **4** *vt* **STAGE AGAIN** to stage a new production of an old play or opera [15C. Directly or via French *revivre* < late Latin *revivere* 'make live again' < Latin *vivere* 'live'.] —**revivable** *adj* —**reviver** *n*

revivify /ree vívvi fī/ (**-fies, -fying, -fied**) *vt* to impart new life, energy, or spirit to something or somebody —**revivification** /ree vívvifi káysh'n/ *n*

revocable /révvəkəb'l, ri vókə-/ *adj* able to be revoked or cancelled —**revocability** /révvəkə bílləti, ri vókə bílləti/ *n* —**revocably** *adv*

revoke /ri vók/ *v* (**-vokes, -voking, -voked**) **1** *vt* **FORMALLY CANCEL** to make something null and void by withdrawing, recalling, or reversing it **2** *vt* **SUMMON BACK** to call somebody back, e.g. from exile or from an overseas position **3** *vi* **NOT FOLLOW SUIT IN CARDS** in a card game, to fail to follow suit when able to do so ■ *n* **FAILURE TO FOLLOW SUIT IN CARDS** failure to follow suit in a card game when able to do so [14C. Via French *révoquer* < Latin *revocare* 'call back' < *vocare* 'call'.] —**revocation** /révvə káysh'n/ *n* —**revocatory** /révvəkə tawri/ *adj* —**revoker** *n*

revolt /ri vólt/ *v* **1** *vi* **REBEL AGAINST THE STATE** to try to overthrow an existing government **2** *vi* **DEFY AUTHORITY** to resist authority or rules **3** *vti* **FEEL DISGUST** to feel, or cause somebody to feel, disgust or repulsion ■ *n* **1 UPRISING AGAINST GOVERNMENT** an uprising that attempts to overthrow a government **2 DEFIANCE OF AUTHORITY** a protest against authority or rules [Mid-16C. < French *révolter* < Latin *revolvere* 'roll back'.] —**revolter** *n*

revolting /ri vólting/ *adj* **1** arousing feelings of disgust, nausea, or repulsion **2** unattractive or otherwise unpleasant (*informal*) —**revoltingly** *adv*

revolute /révvə loot/ *adj* describes leaves and other plant parts that are rolled backwards and downwards from the tip or edge [Mid-18C. < Latin *revolutus*, past participle of *revolvere* (see REVOLVE).]

revolution /révvə loósh'n/ *n* **1 OVERTHROW OF GOVERNMENT** the overthrow of a ruler or political system **2 MAJOR CHANGE** a dramatic change in ideas or practice **3 COMPLETE CIRCULAR TURN** one complete circular movement made by something round or cylindrical, e.g. a wheel, around a fixed point **4 CIRCLE ROUND** a complete circle made round something, e.g. the orbit made by a planet or satellite round another body [14C. Via French < Latin *revolut-*, past participle of *revolvere* (see REVOLVE).]

revolutionary /révvə loósh'nəri/ *adj* **1 OF A POLITICAL REVOLUTION** relating to or involving a political or social revolution **2 STIRRING REBELLION** causing, supporting, or advocating revolution **3 NEW AND DIFFERENT** so new and different as to cause a major change in something ■ *n* (*plural* **-ies**) **REBEL** somebody committed to a political or social revolution —**revolutionarily** *adv* —**revolutionariness** *n*

Revolutionary *adj* **1** *US* relating to the war with Great Britain fought by the American colonists **2** relating to a particular revolution that has taken place such as the Russian Revolution or the French Revolution

Revolutionary Calendar *n* HIST = **French Republican Calendar**

revolutionise *vt* = **revolutionize**

revolutionist /révvə loósh'nist/ *n* POL = **revolutionary** *n.*

revolutionize (**-izes, -izing, -ized**), **revolutionise** (**-ises, -ising, -ised**) *vt* **1 CHANGE SOMETHING RADICALLY** to cause a radical change in something such as a method or approach **2 INCITE PEOPLE TO REBELLION** to inspire people with revolutionary ideas **3 CAUSE REBELLION IN COUNTRY** to bring about a revolution in a country —**revolutionizer** *n*

revolve /ri vólv/ *v* (**-volves, -volving, -volved**) **1** *vti* **MOVE IN CIRCULAR FASHION** to move, or send something, in a circular movement, either around an object or on a central axis **2** *vi* **BE FOCUSED** to have something as a primary focus or theme **3** *vi* **RECUR** to happen in cycles or regular periodic intervals ■ *n* **TURNING STAGE** a circular part of a stage that can be turned mechanically in order to change a scene [14C. < Latin *revolvere* 'roll back' < *volvere* 'to roll'.] —**revolvable** *adj*

USAGE See ***centre***.

revolver /ri vólvər/ *n* a handgun with a revolving cylinder of chambers, allowing several shots to be fired without reloading

revolving credit *n* a credit scheme that imposes regular repayments and a predetermined spending limit

revolving door *n* **1** a door, usually in a large building, consisting of four panels that intersect at right angles and turn on a central pivot **2** any system in which people frequently enter and leave, e.g. a corporation that repeatedly hires and fires staff or a criminal justice system that returns offenders to society (*hyphenated before nouns*)

revolving fund *n* a fund that can be drawn upon and repaid as desired, established for a particular purpose

revue /ri vyoó/ (*plural* **-vues**) *n* a musical variety show consisting of skits, dance routines, and songs that often satirize current events and personalities [Late 19C. < French, < *revoir* 'inspect'.]

SPELLCHECK See ***review***.

revulsion /ri vúlsh'n/ *n* **1 FEELING OF DISGUST** a sudden and violent feeling of extreme loathing **2 WITHDRAWAL** a pulling or turning back (*formal*) **3 DIVERSION OF BLOOD** the diversion of blood or disease from one part of the body to another [Mid-16C. < French, < Latin *revuls-*, past participle of *revellere* 'pull back' < *vellere* 'tear, pull'.] —**revulsive** /-ssiv/ *adj*

reward /ri wáwrd/ *n* **1 THING GIVEN IN RETURN** something desirable given in return for what somebody has done **2 MONEY OFFERED IN RETURN** money offered for information about the whereabouts of a criminal or the return of something lost or stolen **3 BENEFIT RECEIVED** a benefit obtained as a result of an action taken or a job done **4 SOMETHING REINFORCING DESIRED BEHAVIOUR** something positive that follows a desired response and acts to encourage desired behaviour ■ *vt* **1 GIVE SOMEBODY SOMETHING AS REWARD** to give somebody something in return, especially in thanks for kindness or help **2 REPAY EFFORT** to be worth the effort or attention that is given [14C. < Anglo-Norman, variant of Old French *reguard* 'regard'.] —**rewardable** *adj* —**rewarder** *n*

rewarding /ri wáwrding/ *adj* **1** providing somebody with personal satisfaction or great pleasure **2** intended as a reward for something —**rewardingly** *adv*

reweave /ree wéev/ (**-weaves, -weaving, -wove** /-wóv/ *or* **-weaved, -woven** /-wóv'n/ *or* **-weaved**) *vt* to weave something again or in a different way

rewind *vt* /ree wínd/ (**-winds, -winding, -wound** /-wównd/) **WIND SOMETHING BACK** to wind something such as video or audio tape back onto its original spool or back to an earlier point ■ *n* /rée wīnd/ **1 REWINDING PROCESS** the process of rewinding something **2 REWINDING FUNCTION** a function, e.g. on a camera or video recorder, that rewinds film or tape

rewire /ree wír/ (**-wires, -wiring, -wired**) *vt* to install new electrical wiring in a building, vehicle, or electrical device

reword /ree wúrd/ *vt* to change the wording of something written or spoken

rework *vt* /ree wúrk/ **1** to alter or revise something in order to improve or update it **2** to alter something in order to reuse it in a different context ■ *n* /rée wurk/ = **reworking**

reworking /rée wúrking/ *n* a new version of something, especially a spoken or written text. US term **rework** *n.*

rewove past tense of **reweave**

rewoven past participle of **reweave**

ϟ**rewritable** /ree rítəb'l/ *adj* describes something, especially a magnetic disk, that can be written on repeatedly

rewrite *vt* /ree rít/ (**-writes, -writing, -wrote** /-rót/, **-written** /-rítt'n/) **1 AMEND WORDING OF TEXT** to redraft a text by changing the wording or structure **2 EDIT FOR PUBLICATION** to edit a reporter's copy for publication in a newspaper or magazine **3 ALTER INTERPRETATION** to change the way the past is perceived or known about ■ *n* /ree rīt, rée rīt/ **AMENDED TEXT** an amended version of a written document —**rewriter** /ree rítər/ *n*

Rex /reks/ *n* a word used in the formal title of a reigning king, especially on coins and official documents [Early 17C. < Latin, 'king'.]

Reye's syndrome /ríz-, ráyz-/ *n* a rare and serious childhood disease, usually following a respiratory infection, causing vomiting, fatty deposits in the liver, disorientation, and swelling of the kidneys and brain [After the Australian paediatrician Ralph Douglas *Reye* (1912–78)]

Reykjavik /ráykyə vik/ capital of Iceland, in the southwest of the country. Population: 108,351 (1998 estimate).

Reynolds /rénn'ldz/, **Sir Joshua** (1723–92) British painter

Reynold's number /rénn'ldz-/ *n* (*symbol* **Re**) a number used to indicate the flow of fluid through a pipe or around an obstruction [After the Irish physicist Osborne *Reynolds* (1842–1912)]

Rf[1] *symbol* rutherfordium

Rf[2] *abbr* rufiyaa

RF *abbr* **1** radio frequency **2** reconnaissance fighter **3** regular forces **4** releasing factor **5** representative fraction **6** République Française **7** Reserve Force **8** retention factor **9** right fielder **10** Royal Fusiliers

rf. *abbr* **1** reef **2** refund

r.f. *abbr* **1** radio frequency **2** rapid fire **3** reception fair **4** rough finish

R factor *n* a combination of genes that makes some bacteria resistant to antibiotics [*R* abbreviation of *resistance*]

RFC *abbr* **1** Royal Flying Corps **2** Rugby Football Club

RFD *abbr* **1** radio-frequency device **2** reporting for duty

RFLP *abbr* restriction fragment length polymorphism

ϟ**RGB** *abbr* red, green, blue (*describes a colour monitor or colour value*)

RGN *abbr* Registered General Nurse

RGS *abbr* Royal Geographical Society

rh *abbr* **1** relative humidity **2** right hand

Rh[1] *symbol* rhodium

Rh[2] *abbr* rhesus factor

RH *abbr* **1** relative humidity **2** right hand **3** Royal Highness

RHA *abbr* **1** Regional Health Authority **2** Royal Horse Artillery

rhabdom /rábdəm/ *n* a transparent rod-shaped part of the compound eye of insects, spiders, and other arthropods [Late 19C. < late Greek *rhabdōma* < *rhabdos* 'rod'.]

rhabdomancy /rábdō manssi/ *n* the use of a divining rod to locate underground water or mineral ores [Mid-17C. < Greek *rhabdomanteia* < *rhabdos* 'rod' + *-manteia* (see -MANCY).] —**rhabdomancer** *n* —**rhabdomantist** *n*

rhabdovirus /rábdō vīrəss/ *n* a rod-shaped virus that contains RNA such as the virus that causes rabies [Mid-20C. < Greek *rhabdos* 'rod'.]

rhachilla *n* PLANT SCI = **rachilla**

rhachis *n* PLANT SCI = **rachis**

Rhadamanthus /ráddə mánthəss/ *n* in Greek mythology, the son of Zeus and Europa, who became a judge of the underworld

Rhaetian /réesh'n/ *n* LANG = **Rhaeto-Romance** ■ *adj* **1** relating to Rhaeto-Romance **2** relating to Rhaetia, an Alpine province of ancient Rome, or the section of the Alps in this area [Late 16C. < *Rhaetia*, province of ancient Rome.]

Rhaeto-Romance /réetō rō mánss/ *n* a group of Romance dialects spoken in some Alpine regions of Switzerland and Italy, including Romansch, Ladin, and Friulian —**Rhaeto-Romance** *adj*

rhamnose /rámnōss, -nōz/ *n* a six-carbon sugar found in plant cells and bacteria [Late 19C. < modern Latin *rhamnus*, the buckthorn (in whose berries the substance is found) < Greek *rhamnos*.]

rhapsode /rápsōd/ *n* HIST = **rhapsodist** *n.* 2 [Mid-19C. < Greek *rhapsōidēs* < *rhapsōidein* 'recite' (see RHAPSODY).]

rhapsodic /rap sóddik/, **rhapsodical** /-ik'l/ *adj* **1** relating to a rhapsody, or with the emotional and improvisational qualities of a rhapsody **2** joyfully enthusiastic or ecstatic about something —**rhapsodically** *adv*

rhapsodise *vti* = **rhapsodize**

rhapsodist /rápsədist/ *n* **1** a person who is joyfully enthusiastic or ecstatic about something (*literary*) **2** an ancient Greek poet who recited epic poetry professionally

rhapsodize /rápsə dīz/ (**-dizes, -dizing, -dized**), **rhapsodise** (**-dises, -dising, -dised**) *v* **1** *vi* to speak or write in an enthusiastic or ecstatic manner **2** *vti* to write or recite a rhapsody

rhapsody /rápsədi/ (*plural* **-dies**) *n* **1 FREE-FORM MUSICAL COMPOSITION** a composition that is often irregular in form, emotional in effect, and improvisational in nature **2 ENTHUSIASTIC TALK** an expression of intense enthusiasm (*often plural*) **3 ANCIENT GREEK POEM** in ancient Greece, an epic poem recited by a professional reciter **4 EXALTED LITERARY COMPOSITION** any literary work written in an intense or exalted style [Mid-16C. Via Latin < Greek *rhapsōdia* < *rhapsōidein* 'recite poems' < *rhaptein* 'stitch together' + *ōidē* 'song'.]

rhatany /ráttəni/ (*plural* **-ny** *or* **-nies**) *n* **1** the dried root of a South American bush. Use: toothpaste, mouthwash. **2** a bush with spiny globular fruits and thick roots that produces rhatany. Native to: South America. Genus: *Krameria*. [Early 19C. Via modern Latin *rhatania* < Quechua *ratánya*.]

rhd *abbr* right-hand drive

rhea /rée ə/ (*plural* **-as** *or* **-a**) *n* a large, fast-running, flightless bird that looks like an ostrich but is slightly smaller. Native to: South America. Family: Rheidae. [Early 19C. < modern Latin.]

Rhea[1] /rée ə/ *n* in Greek mythology, a Titan who was the wife of Cronus and mother of the gods. Roman equivalent **Cybele**

Rhea[2] /rée ə/ *n* the second-largest natural satellite of Saturn, discovered in 1672. It is 1,528 km/949 mi. in diameter and occupies an intermediate orbit.

rhebok /rée bok/ (*plural* **-boks** *or* **-bok**), **reebok** (*plural* **-boks** *or* **-bok**) *n* a straight-horned antelope with brownish-grey woolly hair. Native to: South Africa. *Pelea capreolus*. [Late 18C. < Dutch *reebok* 'roebuck'.]

Rhee /ree/, **Syngman** (1875–1965) Korean statesman and president of South Korea (1948–60)

rheme /reem/ *n* the part of a sentence, often the predicate, that adds the greatest amount of new information to what is already available in the discourse [Late 19C. < Greek *rhēma* 'what is said'.]

Rhenish /rénnish, rée-/ *adj* coming from or relating to the Rhineland area of Germany [14C. < Anglo-Norman *reneis* < Latin *Rhenus* 'Rhine'.]

rhenium /reéni əm/ *n* (*symbol* **Re**) a rare heavy silvery-white metallic element with a high melting point. Source: molybdenite. Use: catalyst, with tungsten in thermocouples. [Early 20C. < German, < Latin *Rhenus* 'the Rhine'.]

rheo- *prefix* flow, current ○ *rheometer* [< Greek *rheos* 'stream, current' < *rhein* 'to flow' < Indo-European]

rheobase /rée ō bayss/ *n* the minimum electrical nerve impulse necessary to cause a twitch in a muscle

rheology /ri óllə ji/ *n* a branch of physics dealing with the way matter flows and changes shape —**rheological** /rée ə lójjik'l/ *adj* —**rheologically** *adv* —**rheologist** *n*

rheometer /ri ómmitər/ *n* an instrument that measures the flow of thick liquids such as blood —**rheometric** /rée ə méttrik/ *adj*

rheomorphism /rée ə máwrfizəm/ *n* the liquefying of rock

rheostat /rée ə stat/ *n* a resistor designed to allow variation in resistance without breaking the electrical circuit of which it is a part —**rheostatic** /rée ə státtik/ *adj*

rheotaxis /rée ə táksiss/ *n* the motion of an organism towards or away from a current of water or air —**rheotactic** /-táktik/ *adj*

rheotropism /rée ə trópizəm/ *n* growth of a plant, or of an immobile animal such as a coral, in the direction of a flow of water

Rhesus /réessəss/ *n* in Greek mythology, one of the kings of Thrace

rhesus baby *n* a baby born with a serious condition requiring blood transfusion because the baby's Rh-positive blood has been attacked by antibodies in the blood of its Rh-negative mother. ◆ **Rh factor** [See RHESUS FACTOR]

Rhesus factor *n* MED = **Rh factor** [Because the antigens were first discovered in the blood of rhesus monkeys]

rhesus monkey *n* a common brownish monkey of the macaque family. Native to: South Asia. *Macaca mulatta*. [< modern Latin, arbitrarily after RHESUS]

Rhesus negative *adj* MED = **Rh negative**

Rhesus positive *adj* MED = **Rh positive**

rhetoric /réttərik/ *n* **1 PERSUASIVE SPEECH OR WRITING** speech or writing that communicates its point persuasively **2 PRETENTIOUS WORDS** complex or elaborate language that only succeeds in sounding pretentious **3 SKILL WITH LANGUAGE** the ability to use language effectively, especially to persuade or influence people **4 STUDY OF WRITING OR SPEAKING EFFECTIVELY** the study of methods employed to write or speak effectively and persuasively [14C. Via Old French *rethorique* < Greek *rhētorikē (tekhnē)* '(art) of public speaking' < *rhētor* 'speaker'.]

rhetorical /ri tórrik'l/ *adj* **1** relating to or using language that is elaborate or fine-sounding but insincere **2** relating to the skill of using language effectively and persuasively —**rhetorically** *adv*

rhetorical question *n* a question asked for effect that neither expects nor requires an answer

rhetorician /réttə rísh'n/ *n* **1 RHETORIC TEACHER** a teacher of the effective and persuasive use of language **2 SKILLED SPEAKER OR WRITER** a skilled and effective speaker or writer **3 PRETENTIOUS SPEAKER OR WRITER** a speaker or writer of elaborate or fine-sounding but insincere language

rheum /room/ *n* watery discharge coming from the eyes, nose, or mouth [14C. Via Old French *reume* < Greek *rheuma* 'flow, bodily humour'.] —**rheumy** *adj*

rheumatic /roo máttik/ *adj* relating to or affected with rheumatism ■ *n* somebody who is affected with rheumatism —**rheumatically** *adv*

rheumatic fever *n* an acute infectious disease that causes fever and swelling in the joints, and often damage to the heart valves

rheumatic heart disease n damage to the valves or muscular tissue of the heart caused by rheumatic fever

rheumatics /roo máttiks/ n rheumatism (informal; + singular verb)

rheumatism /róomətizəm/ n 1 any painful condition of the joints or muscles that is not caused by infection or injury 2 a popular name for rheumatoid arthritis

rheumatoid /róomə toyd/ adj relating to or affected with rheumatism or rheumatoid arthritis —**rheumatoidally** /róomə tóyd'li/ adv

rheumatoid arthritis n a chronic disease of the joints that causes stiffness, swelling, weakness, loss of mobility, and eventual destruction and deformity of the joints

rheumatoid factor n an antibody found in the blood serum of many people who have rheumatoid arthritis

rheumatology /róomə tóllaji/ n a branch of medicine dealing with the study and treatment of rheumatic diseases —**rheumatologist** n

Rh factor n a group of antibody-producing substances (antigens) present in most people's red blood cells. ◊ **Rh negative, Rh positive** [< rhesus]

rhin- prefix = **rhino-** (before vowels)

rhinal /rín'l/ adj relating to the nose

Rhine n river in W Europe, flowing northwestwards from SE Switzerland through Germany and the Netherlands, emptying into the North Sea. Length: 1,320 km/820 mi.

rhinencephalon /rín en séffə lon/ (plural -**lons** or -**la** /-lə/) n the area of the forebrain that controls the sense of smell —**rhinencephalic** /rín enssə fállik/ adj

rhinestone /rín stōn/ n a small piece of paste or glass used as an imitation diamond [Late 19C. Translation of French caillou du Rhin, because the stones were first made in the city of Strasbourg, on the Rhine.]

rhinitis /rí nítiss/ n inflammation of the mucous membranes of the nose, usually accompanied by a discharge of mucus

rhino[1] /rínō/ (plural -**nos** or -**no**) n a rhinoceros (informal) [Late 19C. Shortening.]

rhino[2] /rínō/ n money (archaic slang) [Early 17C. < ?]

rhino- prefix nose, nasal ◊ rhinoplasty [< Greek rhin-, stem of rhis 'nose']

rhinoceros /rí nóssərass/ (plural -**oses** or -**os**) n a very large herbivorous mammal with very thick skin and one or two horns on its snout. Native to: Africa, Asia. Family: Rhinocerotidae. [13C. Via Latin < Greek rhinokerōs < rhin-, stem of rhis 'nose' + keras 'horn'.] —**rhinocerotic** /rínō sə róttik/ adj

rhinoceros beetle n any large tropical scarab beetle that has horns on its head and thorax

rhinoceros bird n BIRDS = **oxpecker**

~~rhinocerous~~ incorrect spelling of **rhinoceros**

rhinology /rí nólləji/ n the branch of medicine dealing with conditions and structures of the nose

rhinopharyngitis /rínō fárrən jítiss/ n inflammation of the mucous membranes in the nose and pharynx

rhinoplasty /rínō plasti/ (plural -**ties**) n plastic surgery performed on the nose, whether for medical or cosmetic reasons —**rhinoplastic** /rínō plástik/ adj

rhinoscope /rínō skōp/ n a device used by doctors to examine the nasal passages —**rhinoscopy** /rí nóskəpi/ n

rhinovirus /rínō vírəss/ n a virus containing RNA that causes infections of the upper respiratory system, including the common cold

rhiz- prefix = **rhizo-** (before vowels)

rhizo- prefix root ◊ rhizosphere [< Greek rhiza 'root'. Probably < Indo-European.]

rhizobium /rí zōbi əm/ (plural -**a** /-ə/) n a soil bacterium that forms nodules on the roots of legumes and takes up nitrogen from the atmosphere. Genus: Rhizobium. [Early 20C. < modern Latin < Greek rhiza 'root' + bios 'life']

rhizocarpous /rízō kaàrpəss/ adj describes plants that produce their fruit underground

rhizocephalan /rízō séffələn/ n a small crustacean that lives in water as a parasite on crabs. Order: Rhizocephala. [Late 19C. < modern Latin Rhizocephala < Greek rhiza 'root' + kephalē 'head'.] —**rhizocephalous** adj

rhizogenic /rízō jénnik/, **rhizogenetic** /rízōjə néttik/, **rhi-**

zogenous /rí zójjənəss/ adj describes plant cells and tissues from which roots develop

rhizoid /rí zoyd/ n a slender outgrowth on mosses, liverworts, and the reproductive cells of ferns that absorbs nourishment in much the same way as a root —**rhizoidal** /rí zóyd'l/ adj

rhizome /rízōm/ n a thick underground horizontal stem that produces roots and has shoots that develop into new plants [Mid-19C. Via Greek rhizōma 'mass of roots' < rhiza 'root'.] —**rhizomatous** /rí zómmətəss/ adj

rhizomorph /rízō mawrf/ n a structure in some pathogenic fungi that allows them to move from host to host —**rhizomorphous** /rízō máwrfəss/ adj

rhizophagous /rí zóffəgəss/ adj feeding on roots

rhizoplane /rízō playn/ n the part of a plant's root that lies at the surface of the soil, where many microorganisms adhere to it

rhizopod /rízō pod/ n a single-celled organism (protozoan) that moves and eats by means of filaments that it can extend temporarily. Subphylum: Rhizopoda. —**rhizopodous** /rí zóppədəss/ adj

rhizopus /rízōpəss/ n a mould that causes decay such as the common bread mould. Genus: Rhizopus. [Late 19C. < modern Latin < Greek rhiza 'root' + pous 'foot'; so called because of its shape.]

rhizosphere /rízō sfeer/ n the area of soil that immediately surrounds and is affected by a plant's roots

rhizotomy /rí zóttəmi/ (plural -**mies**) n surgery in which spinal nerves are cut in order to relieve pain or high blood pressure

Rh negative adj lacking the Rh factor in the blood. ◊ **Rh factor, Rh positive**

rho /rō/ (plural **rhos**) n the 17th letter of the Greek alphabet [14C. < Greek rhō, of Phoenician origin.]

rhod- prefix = **rhodo-** (before vowels)

rhodamine /rōdə meen/ n a red or pink fluorescent dye. Use: colouring wool and silk, as a biological stain. [Late 19C. < Greek rhodon 'rose' + -AMINE.]

Rhode Island /rōd-/ state in the NE United States, on the Atlantic Ocean. Capital: Providence. Population: 987,429 (1997). Area: 3,188 sq. km/1,231 sq. mi. —**Rhode Islander** n

Rhodes /rōdz/ **1** largest island of the Dodecanese, Greece. Population: 87,831 (1981). Area: 1,400 sq. km/540 sq. mi. **2** capital of Rhodes, Greece. Population: 40,656 (1981).

Rhodes, Cecil (1853–1902) British financier and colonial administrator

Rhodesia /rō déeshə, -zhə/ former name for **Zimbabwe** (1964–79) —**Rhodesian** adj, n

Rhodesian man n an early human being sharing features with the Neandertals and with modern human beings and living in Africa in the late Pleistocene period. Homo sapiens rhodesiensis. [Early 20C. After RHODESIA.]

Rhodesian ridgeback n a large dog with a ridge of hair growing down its back, belonging to a breed originally developed in Africa

Rhodes scholarship n a sum of money awarded annually to students from the United States, South Africa, and several Commonwealth countries to help pay for studies at Oxford University [Early 19C. After Cecil RHODES.] —**Rhodes scholar** n

rhodinal /rōdin'l/ n CHEM = **citronellal**

rhodium /rōdi əm/ n (symbol **Rh**) a hard, silvery-white, corrosion-resistant metallic element. Source: platinum and nickel ores. Use: alloys, in plating other metals. [Early 19C. < Greek rhodos 'rose' < the pink colour of its compounds.]

rhodo- prefix red, rosy ◊ rhodolite [< Greek rhodon 'rose']

rhodochrosite /rōdō krō sīt/ n a pink, red, brown, or grey manganese carbonate mineral. Use: source of manganese. [Mid-19C. < Greek rhodokhrōs 'rose-coloured'.]

rhododendron /rōdə déndrən/ n an evergreen shrub widely grown in temperate regions. Flowers: brightly coloured. Native to: South Asia. Genus: Rhododendron. [Early 17C. Via Latin, 'oleander' < Greek rhodon 'rose' + dendron 'tree'.]

rhodolite /rōddə līt/ n a pink to rose-red variety of garnet. Use: gems. [Late 19C. < RHODO- + -LITE.]

rhodonite /rōddə nīt/ n a pink to brown manganese silicate mineral. Source: metamorphic rock. Use: ornamental stone. [Early 19C. < Greek rhodon 'rose'.]

Rhodope Mountains /róddəpi-/ mountain range in SW Bulgaria and N Greece. Highest peak: Musala 2,925 m/9,596 ft.

rhodophyte /rōdə fīt/ n a marine alga, e.g. dulse, laver, or Irish moss, that contains a red pigment as well as chlorophyll. Phylum: Rhodophyta.

rhodopsin /rō dópsin/ n a reddish light-sensitive pigment found in the rod cells of the retina [Late 19C. < RHODO- + Greek opsis 'sight' + -IN.]

rhodora /rō dáwrə/ n a marshland shrub of the rhododendron family that blooms in spring before the leaves emerge. Flowers: deep pink. Native to: NE North America. Rhododendron canadense. [Late 18C. < modern Latin < ?]

rhomb /rom, romb/ n MATH = **rhombus**

rhombencephalon /rómb en séffə lon/ n ANAT = **hindbrain** [Late 19C. < RHOMBUS + ENCEPHALON.]

rhombi plural of **rhombus**

rhombohedral /rómbō heédral/ adj describes minerals that are shaped like a rhombohedron

rhombohedron /rómbō heédrən/ n a prism with six faces, each one a rhombus [Mid-19C. < RHOMBUS, after polyhedron.]

rhomboid /róm boyd/ n PARALLELOGRAM WITH UNEQUAL ADJACENT SIDES a parallelogram with adjacent sides that are not equal ■ adj 1 RHOMBOID-SHAPED shaped like a rhomboid 2 RELATING TO RHOMBUS relating to or characteristic of a rhombus [Late 16C. < Greek rhomboeidēs 'lozenge-shaped' < rhombos.]

rhombus /rómbass/ (plural -**buses** or **rhombi** /-bī/) n a parallelogram that has four equal sides and oblique angles [Mid-16C. Via Latin < Greek rhombos.] —**rhombic** adj

rhonchus /róngkass/ (plural -**chi** /-kī/) n a harsh rattling or whistling sound heard through a stethoscope on examination of the chest, caused by partial obstruction of the airways [Early 19C. Via Latin, 'snoring' < Greek rhegkhos < rhegkein 'snore'.] —**rhonchal** adj

Rhône /rōn/ river in Switzerland and France, flowing southwestwards from the Alps into the Mediterranean Sea. Length: 813 km/505 mi.

rhotacism /rōtəsizəm/ n unusual pronunciation of the letter 'r', or too much emphasis on this sound [Mid-19C. Via modern Latin rhotacismus < Greek rhōtakizein 'make wrong use of the letter r' < rhō.]

rhotic /rōtik/ adj pronouncing the letter 'r' when it occurs after a vowel or at the end of a syllable ◊ a rhotic accent [Mid-20C. < RHOTACISM.]

Rh positive adj containing the Rh factor in the blood or having blood that contains the Rh factor. ◊ **Rh factor, Rh negative**

RHS abbr Royal Horticultural Society

rhubarb /róo baarb/ n 1 STALKS COOKED AS FRUIT the pink stalks of a cultivated perennial plant, cooked as fruit 2 PLANT WITH EDIBLE STALKS a perennial plant with poisonous leaves that produces rhubarb. Genus: Rheum. 3 MEDICINAL ASIAN PLANT any medicinal rhubarb plant native to central and E Asia. Use: dried underground stems as laxative. 4 APPARENT CONVERSATION IN PLAY the word 'rhubarb' used repeatedly by several actors simultaneously to give the impression that they are talking to one another [14C. Via Old French reubarbe < Latin rha barbarum 'barbarian rhubarb' < Greek Rha, the river Volga, because rhubarb was once grown on its banks.]

rhumb /rum/ n 1 NAVIG = **rhumb line** n. 2 2 any of the 32 points of a compass

rhumba n DANCE, MUSIC = **rumba**

rhumb line n 1 an imaginary line on the surface of the Earth intersecting all meridians at the same angle 2 a steady course along one compass setting taken by a ship or aircraft

rhyme /rīm/ n 1 SIMILARITY IN SOUND similarity in the sound of word endings, especially in poetry 2 WORD SOUNDING SAME AS ANOTHER a word with an ending that sounds similar to the ending of another word 3 POEM a poem, or poetry generally, of a lighthearted kind with a pattern of similar sounds at the ends of the lines ■ v (**rhymes, rhyming, rhymed**) 1 vti SOUND SIMILAR to have an ending that sounds similar to the ending of another word or line of poetry ◊ 'Rough' rhymes with 'cuff'. 2 vt CHOOSE

RHYMING WORD to find or choose a word with an ending that sounds similar to another **3** *vti* **WRITE POETRY** to write rhyming poetry or express something in rhyme [12C. Alteration (influenced by RHYTHM) of earlier *rime* < Old French < Germanic.] ◇ **without rhyme or reason** without any rational explanation or apparent sense

rhymer *n* LITERAT = **rhymester**

rhyme royal *n* a form of poetry using verses with seven lines of iambic pentameter with a rhyme scheme ababbcc, or one of these verses [Mid-19C. < The use of the form by James I of Scotland.]

rhyme scheme *n* the pattern of rhyming lines in a poem or verse of a poem

rhymester /rímstər/ *n* a writer of poems with rhyming lines, especially popular or amateur verse

rhyming /ríming/ *adj* with lines that end in similar sounding words, forming a pattern

rhyming slang *n* a form of slang that replaces a word with an expression that rhymes with the word but has no meaningful connection with it, used especially in Cockney

rhynchocephalian /ríngkōssə fálli ən/ *adj* relating to an order of primitive reptiles resembling lizards with only one living representative, the tuatara of New Zealand. Order: Rhynchocephalia. ■ *n* a member of the rhynchocephalian order [Mid-19C. < modern Latin *Rhyncocephalia* < Greek *rhugkhos* 'snout' + *kephalē* 'head'.]

rhyolite /rí ə līt/ *n* a fine-grained acid rock that is the volcanic form of granite [Mid-19C. < Greek *rhuax* 'stream (of lava)' < *rhein* 'flow' + -LITE.] —**rhyolitic** /rí ə líttik/ *adj*

Rhys /reess/, **Jean** (1894–1979) Caribbean-born British writer. Pseudonym of **Ellen Gwendolen Rees Williams**

rhythm /ríthəm/ *n* **1 PATTERN OF BEATS IN MUSIC** the regular pattern of beats and emphasis in a piece of music ○ *The audience clapped in rhythm as we sang.* **2 PARTICULAR MUSIC PATTERN** a pattern of beats in a piece or kind of music **3 PATTERN OF STRESS IN POETRY** in poetry, the pattern formed by stressed and unstressed syllables **4 PARTICULAR POETRY PATTERN** a pattern of stress in a poem or kind of poetry **5 REGULAR PATTERN** a regularly recurring pattern of activity such as the cycle of the seasons, night and day, or repeated functions of the body **6 CHARACTERISTIC PATTERN** the characteristic pattern of an activity **7 PATTERN IN ART** a pattern of elements suggesting movement or pace in something such as a work of art **8 SOUND PATTERN** the pattern of sound that characterizes a language, dialect, or accent **9 PATTERN FROM REPEATED ELEMENTS** a mood or effect in a book, play, or film created from repeated elements [Mid-16C. Via Latin < Greek *rhuthmos*.]

rhythm and blues *n* a style of music combining elements of blues and jazz, originally developed by African American musicians

rhythm guitar *n* chordal accompaniment from a guitar that does not play the melody

rhythmic /ríthmik/, **rhythmical** /ríthmik'l/ *adj* **1** with a regularly recurring pattern or beat **2** relating to rhythm —**rhythmically** *adv* —**rhythmicity** /rith míssəti/ *n*

rhythmic gymnastics *n* gymnastics that combines dance movements with the use of apparatus such as ribbons and hoops

rhythmics /ríth miks/ *n* the study of rhythms and rhythmic forms (+ *singular verb*)

rhythm method *n* a method of contraception in which sexual intercourse is avoided at the times when a woman is most likely to conceive

rhythm section *n* the instruments in a band such as the drums, bass, piano, or guitar that provide the basic rhythm

rhythm stick *n* either of a pair of wooden sticks, often with notches, used as a simple percussion instrument

rhytidectomy /rìtidéktəmi/ (*plural* **-mies**) *n* a facelift (*technical*) [Mid-20C. < Greek *rhutid-*, stem of *rhutis* 'wrinkle' + -ECTOMY.]

rhyton /rí ton/ *n* a drinking vessel in ancient Greece with a hole in the bottom through which to drink [Mid-19C. < Greek *rhuton* < *rhutos* 'flowing'.]

RI *abbr* **1** religious instruction **2** Queen and Empress **3** King and Emperor **4** Royal Institution **5** Rhode Island

ria /rée ə/ *n* a narrow inlet running inland from the coastline, formed when a valley is permanently flooded as a result of a rise in sea-level [Late 19C. < Spanish *ría* 'estuary', feminine of *río* 'river' < Latin *rivus* 'stream'.]

RIA *abbr* **1** Royal Irish Academy **2** radioimmunoassay

rial /ri áal/ *n* see table at **currency** [Mid-20C. Via Persian and Arabic *riyāl* < Spanish *real* (see REAL[2]).]

rialto /ri ált ō/ (*plural* **rialtos**) *n* **1** a market or marketplace **2** a place where securities or commodities such as grain or raw materials are traded [Mid-16C. After *Rialto*, district of Venice in which the Exchange was located.]

riata /ri áatə/ *n* a lasso or lariat [Mid-19C. < Spanish *reata* < *reatar* 'retie' < *atar* 'tie', via Latin *aptare* 'join' < *apere* 'tie'.]

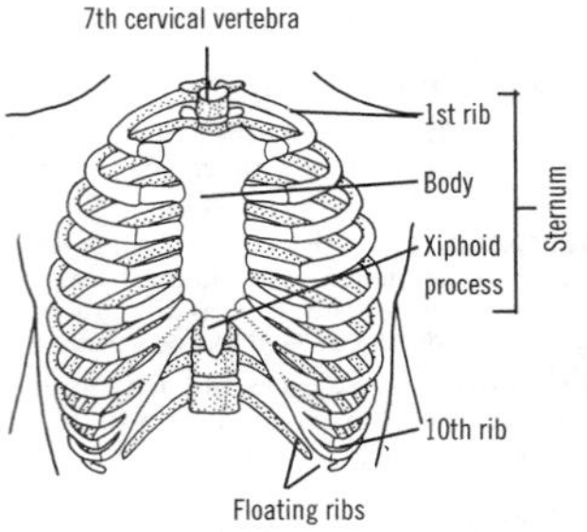
7th cervical vertebra
1st rib
Body
Xiphoid
process
Sternum
10th rib
Floating ribs

Rib

rib /rib/ *n* **1 CURVED BONE OF CHEST** any curved bone extending from the vertebrae and in some cases meeting the sternum, forming a cavity housing vital organs in many vertebrates **2 MEAT** a cut of meat that contains ribs **3 RIDGED KNITTING** a portion of knitted material with raised vertical lines of stitches, made by alternating purl stitches with plain stitches **4 LEAF VEIN** a raised vein on a leaf **5 MOULDING ON VAULT** a ridge or moulding on the underside of a vault or arched ceiling **6 PART OF SHIP'S HULL** a beam extending from the keel to the top of the hull of a ship, giving it its shape **7 PART OF AIRCRAFT WING** a part of an aircraft wing crossing from the leading to the trailing edge of the wing **8 PIECE RESEMBLING RIB** a bar, rod, or other supporting part that has the shape or function of a rib ○ *a broken rib on the umbrella* **9 TEASING COMMENT** a comment or action meant as a joke or to tease somebody (*informal*) ■ **ribs** *npl* **RIBS WITH LITTLE MEAT** ribs of an animal from which most of the meat has been removed, eaten as food ■ *v* (**ribs, ribbing, ribbed**) **1** *vti* **TEASE** to make playful teasing remarks to somebody about something (*informal*) ○ *They ribbed me about my haircut.* **2** *vti* **KNIT PLAIN AND PURL STITCHES** to knit plain stitches alternately with purl stitches to make raised lines in knitting **3** *vt* **PROVIDE WITH RIBS** to provide or strengthen something with ribs [Old English *ribb* < Germanic 'covering (of the chest cavity)'] ◇ **stick to your ribs** *US* to be substantial, nourishing, or hearty as a meal (*informal*)

RIBA /áar ī bee áy, rèebə/ *abbr* **1** Royal Institute of British Architects **2** Member of the Royal Institute of British Architects

ribald /ríbb'ld/ *adj* humorous but rude and vulgar, often involving jokes about sex [14C. < Old French *ribau(l)t* < *riber* 'sleep around' < Germanic.] —**ribaldly** *adv*

ribaldry /ríbb'ldri/ *n* language or behaviour that is humorous but rude and vulgar, often involving jokes about sex

riband /ríbbənd/, **ribband** *n* **1** a ribbon, especially one that is presented to somebody as an award or prize **2** a rail attached to the upright posts in a defensive fence (**palisade**) [14C. Variant of *riban* (see RIBBON).]

ribavirin /rìbə vírin/ *n* a synthetic antiviral agent that inhibits the synthesis of viral DNA and RNA. Use: treatment of viral diseases. [Late 20C. < *riba-*.]

ribband *n* = **riband**

ribbed /ribd/ *adj* **1 HAVING RIBS** with structural support or decoration in the form of ribs **2 KNITTED INTO PATTERN OF VERTICAL LINES** knitted to form a pattern of raised vertical lines, giving a stretchy fabric **3 STRIPED** with a surface marked by raised, roughly parallel bands

Ribbentrop /ríbbən trop/, **Joachim von** (1893–1946) German Nazi official

ribbing /ríbbing/ *n* **1 SECTION OF RIB IN KNITTING** a section of knitting in a pattern of raised vertical lines, making a stretchy fabric **2 RIB FRAMEWORK** a supporting structure or framework of ribs, e.g. in the hull of a boat **3 TEASING** playful or friendly teasing (*informal*)

Ribble /ríbb'l/ river in NW England. Length: 120 km/75 mi.

ribbon /ríbbən/ *n* **1 DECORATIVE STRIP OF FABRIC** a strip of fabric used to tie something or for decoration **2 STRIP OF INKED MATERIAL** a strip of material with ink on it, used in some printers and typewriters **3 FLAT CABLE** a flat cable in which all the wires are parallel to one another in a single plane **4 RIBBON AS AWARD OR BADGE** a decorative strip of fabric given to somebody as an award or worn as a sign of rank or membership **5 LONG NARROW STRIP** something that is long, narrow, and thin, in the shape of a ribbon **6** CONSTR = **ledger board** *n.* **2** ■ **ribbons** *npl* **BADLY DAMAGED STATE** a damaged state in which something is cut or torn very badly ○ *My shirt was in ribbons.* ■ *vt* **1 DECORATE WITH RIBBONS** to decorate something by attaching ribbons to it **2 TEAR INTO STRIPS** to tear something into strips [Early 16C. Variant of earlier *riban* < Old French, variant of *ruban*.] —**ribbony** *adj*

ribbon development *n* a planning scheme or development with houses built in a single row on each side of main roads leading out of a town or city centre

ribbonfish /ríbbən fish/ (*plural* **-fish** *or* **-fishes**) *n* a sea fish with a long tapering ribbon-shaped body and, typically, a dorsal fin extending from head to tail. Family: Trachypteridae.

ribbon grass *n* a grass that is grown as an ornamental in northern temperate regions for its drooping cream-striped leaves. *Phalaris arundinacea picta.*

ribbon snake *n* a nonvenomous snake with longitudinal reddish or yellow stripes that bears live young and feeds on frogs and worms. Native to: North America. *Thamnophis sauritus.*

ribbonwood /ríbbən wòod/ *n* an evergreen tree whose bark can be used to make cord. Native to: New Zealand. *Hoheria populnea.*

ribbon worm *n* ZOOL = **nemertean**

rib cage *n* the ribs as a whole, forming a protective bony enclosure surrounding the heart and lungs

ribo- *prefix* ribose ○ *riboflavin* [< RIBOSE]

riboflavin /rìbō fláyvin/, **riboflavine** *n* vitamin B_2, the yellow component of the B complex group, an important coenzyme in many biochemical processes

ribonuclease /rìbō nyóokli ayz, -ayss/ *n* any enzyme that splits or degrades RNA

ribonucleic acid /rìbō nyoo klée ik-/ *n* full form of **RNA**

ribonucleoprotein /rìbō nyóokli ō prṓ teen/ *n* a complex of RNA and a protein formed during the synthesis of RNA

ribonucleoside /rìbō nyóokli ō sīd/ *n* a nucleoside in which the sugar group is ribose

ribonucleotide /rìbō nyóokli ō tīd/ *n* a nucleotide that contains the sugar ribose, making up units in important molecules such as RNA and ATP

ribose /rìbōz/ *n* a five-carbon sugar found in all living cells as a constituent of RNA [Late 19C. Via German < ARABINOSE.]

ribosomal RNA /rìbə sṓm'l-/ *n* an RNA that is a structural and functional component of ribosomes

ribosome /rìbə sōm/ *n* a submicroscopic cluster of proteins and RNA, occurring in great numbers in the cytoplasm of living cells, that takes part in the manufacture of proteins [Mid-20C. < RIBONUCLEIC ACID + -SOME.] —**ribosomal** /rìbə sṓm'l/ *adj*

ribozyme /rìbō zīm/ *n* an RNA that can catalyse changes to its own structure [Late 20C. < RIBONUCLEIC ACID + ENZYME.]

rib-tickler *n* a very funny joke or story (*informal*) —**rib-tickling** *adj*

ribulose /rìbyoo lōz, -lōss/ *n* $C_5H_{10}O_5$ a sugar that occurs in plants and is used in photosynthesis [Mid-20C. < RIBOSE + -ULE.]

ribwort /ríb wurt/, **ribwort plantain** *n* a plant with long slender ribbed leaves. Flowers: small, white, in a dense rounded spike. Native to: Europe, Asia. *Plantago lanceolata.* [14C. Because the leaves resemble ribs.]

Riccio /rée chee ō/, **David** (1533?–66) Italian courtier

rice /rīss/ (*plural* **rices** *or* **rice**) *n* **1** an annual grass probably native to India but long cultivated for its grain in tropical and warm regions of the world. *Oryza sativa.* **2** the edible grains obtained from the rice plant, served hot or cold after cooking in water or other liquid [13C. Via Old French *ris* and Italian *riso* < Greek *oruza* < Iranian.]

Rice /rīss/, **Anne** (*b.* 1941) US writer. Born **Howard Allen O'Brien**

rice leafhopper *n* a small hopping insect that is a severe pest in India and other rice-growing regions. Genus: *Nephotettix*.

rice paper *n* **1** thin brittle edible paper made from plant sources, used to undercoat baked food that would otherwise stick to the tin during baking **2** thin paper made from the rice-paper plant

rice-paper plant *n* a bush grown for its fibre. Use: rice paper. Native to: China. *Tetrapanax papyriferus*.

ricer /rīssər/ *n* a kitchen utensil consisting of a perforated plate in one end of an open cylinder through which foods can be pressed to form long strings

rice rat *n* a rat that inhabits the marshes where rice fields are located. Native to: S United States, Central and South America. Genus: *Oryzomys*.

ricercare /reechər kaa ray/ (*plural* **ricercari** /-ree/) *n* a fugal composition for musical instruments [Late 18C. < Italian, 'seek out'.]

rice weevil *n* an insect of the weevil family that infests stored rice, wheat, and other grains. *Sitophilus oryzae*.

rich /rich/ *adj* **1 WEALTHY** owning a lot of money or expensive property **2 WORTH MUCH** worth a great deal **3 COSTLY AND FINE** made from or consisting of things of the highest quality ○ *rich fabrics* **4 WITH GOOD SUPPLY OF** with a good supply of a resource or substance ○ *an area rich in minerals* ○ *cotton-rich fabric* **5 PLENTIFUL** existing in large quantities in plentiful supply ○ *a rich supply of conscripts* **6 PRODUCTIVE** productive and so potentially very profitable **7 FERTILE** very fertile and able to produce strong healthy plants **8 WITH HIGH PROPORTION OF FATTY FOODS** containing a high proportion of foods such as cream, eggs, or butter, that are full of fat ○ *a very rich chocolate cake* **9 STRONG AND SMOOTH-FLAVOURED** with a pleasantly strong, smooth flavour ○ *rich coffee* **10 WITH STRONG PLEASANT SMELL** having a strong and pleasant smell **11 STRONGLY COLOURED** deep or fully saturated in colour ○ *a rich shade of brown* **12 WITH DEEP FULL SOUND** with a deep smooth full sound **13 WITH TOO MUCH FUEL IN MIXTURE** with a higher than normal proportion of fuel to air in the mixture supplied to an engine **14 UNLIKELY** hard to believe because ridiculous (*informal*) ○ *That's rich, coming from her!* ■ *npl* **WELL-OFF** wealthy people in general ○ *a playground for the rich and famous* [Old English *rīce* 'strong, powerful' and Old French *riche* < Germanic < Indo-European, 'king'] —**richness** *n*

Richard I /richərd/ (1157–99) king of England (1189–99). Known as **Richard the Lionheart**

Richard II (1367–99) king of England (1377–99)

Richard III (1452–85) king of England (1483–85)

Richards /richərdz/, **I. A.** (1893–1979) British critic, poet, and teacher. Full name **Ivor Armstrong Richards**

Richards, Mark (*b.* 1957) Australian surfer

Richards, Viv (*b.* 1952) Jamaican cricketer. Full name **Isaac Vivian Alexander Richards**

Richardson /richərdss'n/, **Henry Handel** (1870–1946) Australian novelist. Pseudonym of **Ethel Florence Robertson**. Born **Ethel Florence Lindsay Richardson**

Richardson, Sir Ralph (1902–83) British actor

Richardson, Samuel (1689–1761) British novelist

Richardson's ground squirrel /richərdsənz-/ *n* a ground squirrel that can be a pest of grain crops. Native to: NW United States and Canadian prairies. *Citellus richardsoni*. [Mid-20C. After Scottish naturalist Sir John *Richardson* (1787–1865).]

Richelieu /reesh lyö/, **Armand Jean du Plessis, Duc de** (1585–1642) French cardinal and statesman. Known as **Cardinal Richelieu**

ϟ **rich e-mail** *n* an e-mail that has a voice message attached to it

riches /richiz/ *npl* **1** great wealth or many valuable possessions **2** things occurring naturally in abundance ○ *enjoy the riches of the forest* [12C. Originally singular, misunderstood as plural; variant of *richesse* < Old French *richeise* < *riche* 'rich' < Germanic.]

Richler /richlər/, **Mordecai** (*b.* 1931) Canadian writer

richly /richli/ *adv* **1 ELABORATELY** beautifully and elaborately ○ *richly decorated* **2 WITH DEEP COLOUR** with a deep, fully saturated colour **3 COMPLETELY** completely and suitably ○ *a richly deserved award* **4 PLENTIFULLY** plentifully or very fully [Old English *riclice*]

Richmond /richmənd/ **1** town in NE England. Population: 7,862 (1991). **2** capital of Virginia, in the east of the state. Population: 194,173 (1998 estimate). **3** town in E New South Wales, Australia. Population: (including Windsor) 21,317 (1996).

Richmond-upon-Thames borough of SW London. Population: 160,732 (1991).

Richter /riktər, rikhtər/, **Johann Paul Friedrich** (1763–1825) German novelist and humorist. Pseudonym **Jean Paul**

Richter scale /riktər-, rikhtər-/ *n* a scale from 1 to 10 used to measure the severity of earthquakes according to the amount of energy released, with a higher number indicating stronger tremors. ◊ **Mercalli scale** [Mid-20C. After US seismologist Charles Francis *Richter* (1900–85).]

ϟ **rich text** *n* text that includes formatting codes, such as for bold or italic

Richthofen /rikt hōfən, rikht hōfən/, **Manfred, Baron von** (1882–1918) German aviator. Known as **the Red Baron**

ricin /rīssin/ *n* a toxic protein. Source: castor oil seeds. Use: to clump red blood cells. [Late 19C. < Latin *ricinus* 'castor oil plant'.]

ricinoleic acid /rissinō lee ik-/ *n* $C_{18}H_{34}O_3$ an unsaturated fatty acid that is the main constituent of castor oil. Use: soap, plastics, textile finishing. [< Latin *ricinus* 'castor oil plant' + OLEIC]

rick[1] /rik/ *n* a large quantity of hay or straw stacked into a rectangular shape for storage and covered at the top to protect it from the weather ■ *vt* to stack hay or straw to form a rick [Old English *hrēac*]

rick[2] /rik/, **wrick** *vt* to wrench or sprain a joint of the body slightly ■ *n* a slight injury to a joint caused by wrenching or spraining it [Late 18C. < ?]

rickets /rikits/ *n* a disease, especially of children, caused by a deficiency in vitamin D that makes the bones become soft and prone to bending and structural change. Technical name **rachitis** [Mid-17C. < ?]

rickettsia /ri ketsi ə/ (*plural* **-ettsiae** /ri ketsi ee/ *or* **-ettsias**) *n* a parasitic bacterium that typically lives inside ticks and can be transmitted to humans, causing Rocky Mountain spotted fever, certain forms of typhus, and other diseases. Order: Rickettsiales. [Early 20C. < modern Latin, after the US pathologist H. T. *Ricketts* (1871–1910).] —**rickettsial** *adj*

rickety /rikiti/ (**-ier, -iest**) *adj* **1 UNSTABLE** in bad condition, unstable, and likely to collapse ○ *a rickety chair* **2 INFIRM** weakened by the ageing process or illness **3 WITH RICKETS** affected by rickets **4 RELATING TO RICKETS** relating to or resembling rickets [Late 17C. < RICKETS, from the unsteadiness that the disease causes.] —**ricketiness** *n*

rickey /riki/ (*plural* **-eys**) *n* a cocktail made from soda water, lime or lemon juice, sugar, and gin or vodka [Late 19C. Probably from the name *Rickey*.]

rickrack /rik rak/, **ricrac** *n* a narrow decorative braid in a zigzag shape [Late 19C. Doubling of RACK[1].]

rickshaw /rik shaw/, **ricksha** *n* **1** a small vehicle with two wheels and a seat for passengers, pulled along by somebody walking in front of it, used especially in Asia **2** a small three-wheeled vehicle, like a tricycle with a seat at the back for passengers, that is driven by somebody sitting at the front and pedalling [Late 19C. Shortening of Japanese *jinrikisha* < *jin* 'man' + *riki* 'strength' + *sha* 'vehicle'.]

ricochet /rikə shay/ *vi* (**-chets, -cheting** *or* **ricochetting, ricochetted, -cheted** *or* **ricochetted**) to hit a surface and bounce, travelling away in a different direction ■ *n* the rebounding action of something that hits a surface and bounces off in a different direction [Mid-18C. < Old French, 'give-and-take, repetition'.]

ricotta /ri kottə/ *n* a soft white mild-tasting Italian cheese made from whey and used mostly in cooking, or a cheese made to resemble this [Late 19C. Via Italian, 're-cooked' < Latin *recocta*, feminine past participle of *recoquere* 'recook' < *coquere* 'cook'.]

ricrac *n* HANDICRAFT = **rickrack**

RICS *abbr* Royal Institution of Chartered Surveyors

rictus /riktəss/ (*plural* **-tus** *or* **-tuses**) *n* **1** a fixed open-mouthed grin or grimace, especially an expression of horror **2** the gape of a bird's beak [Mid-18C. < Latin, < past participle of *ringi* 'gape'.] —**rictal** *adj*

rid /rid/ (**rids, ridding, rid** *or* **ridded** *archaic*) *vt* **1** to free, relieve, or empty a place or thing of something, usually something undesirable ○ *an attempt to rid the town of crime* **2** to free somebody or yourself from something undesirable ○ *trying to rid myself of the habit* [12C. < Old Norse *ryðja* 'clear land' < *hrjóða* 'strip'.] —**ridder** *n* ◇ **be well rid of somebody** *or* **something** to be in a better position because you no longer have to deal with somebody or something burdensome, unpleasant, or unnecessary ◇ **get rid of somebody** *or* **something** to make somebody or something burdensome, unpleasant, or unnecessary go away

rid up *vti N England or Scotland* to tidy up a place (*informal*)

riddance /ridd'nss/ *n* the removal or destruction of something unwanted ◇ **good riddance (to somebody** *or* **something)** used to show that you are glad to be free of somebody or something

ridden past participle of **ride**

riddle[1] /ridd'l/ *n* **1 WORD PUZZLE** a puzzle in the form of a question or rhyme that contains clues to its answer **2 PUZZLING THING** something that is difficult to understand or presents a problem that needs to be solved ■ *v* (**-dles, -dling, -dled**) **1** *vti* **ANSWER RIDDLE** to find or explain the answer to a riddle **2** *vi* **TALK IN RIDDLES** to speak in an intentionally obscure way [Old English *rǣdels* < Indo-European] —**riddler** *n*

riddle[2] /ridd'l/ *vt* (**-dles, -dling, -dled**) **1 MAKE HOLES IN** to damage something by making a large number of small holes in it **2 AFFECT EVERY PART** to affect every part of something, e.g. by spreading throughout **3 SIEVE SOIL OR STONES** to put soil or stones through a sieve to separate the large pieces from the small ones **4 SHAKE ASHES FROM FIRE** to shake ashes from the bottom of a fire by poking it with a metal rod or moving a mechanism under the grate ■ *n* **SIEVE** a large flat shallow sieve for sifting soil or stones [Old English *hriddel* 'sieve', alteration of *hridder* < Indo-European, 'sort'] —**riddler** *n*

ride /rīd/ *v* (**rides, riding, ridden** /ridd'n/ *or* **rode** /rōd/) **1** *vti* **SIT ON AND CONTROL HORSE** to sit on a horse or other animal and control it as it moves along **2** *vti* **TRAVEL ON BIKE** to travel mounted on a bicycle or motorcycle **3** *vt* **USE SPORTS EQUIPMENT** to use any of various kinds of gliding or rolling sports equipment such as a skateboard or surfboard **4** *vti* **TRAVEL AS PASSENGER** to travel as a passenger in a vehicle **5** *vti US* **TRAVEL IN A LIFT** to travel in a lift **6** *vt* **TRAVEL OVER AREA** to travel across an area of land ○ *ride the range* **7** *vt* **BE IN RACE** to take part in a race or other event on a horse or bike **8** *vi US* **HANDLE WELL OR BADLY** to function in a particular way while moving ○ *a car that rides well over rough ground* **9** *vi S Africa* **DRIVE CAR** to drive a car **10** *vt* **TO CARRY SOMEBODY ALONG** to carry or take somebody along ○ *His mother rode him around on her bicycle.* **11** *vi* **APPEAR TO BE FLOATING** to appear to be floating in the sky or moving like a floating object ○ *Birds soared above our heads, riding the currents.* **12** *vi* **DO SOMETHING EFFORTLESSLY** to do something successfully and apparently effortlessly, as if carried along by a wave ○ *riding on a tide of sympathy* **13** *vi* **DEPEND ON** to depend on something for success ○ *Her future is riding on the outcome of the interview.* **14** *vi* **BE ALLOWED TO CONTINUE** to continue without intervention or alteration ○ *let it ride for a few days* **15** *vt* **DEAL WITH PROBLEM AND SURVIVE** to manage to deal with a difficult situation successfully and survive without too much harm ○ *to ride the storm* **16** *vt US* **TEASE OR TORMENT** to tease or torment somebody with criticism or mockery (*informal*) ○ *My sister always rides me about my hair.* **17** *vt* **RISE ON TOP OF WAVE** to rise up on a wave and move forward with it **18** *vti* **ANCHOR** to be moored with the anchor down, or to moor a ship by dropping its anchor ○ *a ship riding at anchor* **19** *vi* **BE SUPPORTED BY** to be supported by something such as a pivot or an axle ○ *Most of the weight rides on the central shaft.* **20** *vt* **PARTIALLY DEPRESS CLUTCH OR BRAKE** to put your foot on the clutch or brake, partially depressing it, while driving **21** *vt* **OVERLAP** to overlap or encroach on something such as another part **22** *vt* **YIELD TO BLOW** to move in the direction of something forceful such as a blow, in order to lessen the impact ■ *n* **1 JOURNEY BY VEHICLE OR ANIMAL** a journey or outing in a motor vehicle or on an animal ○ *to go for a ride* **2** *US* **MEANS OF TRANSPORT** transportation as a passenger in a vehicle, especially when this is offered to somebody who would otherwise have to walk or use public transport ○ *Do you want a ride?* **3 QUALITY OF TRAVEL** the quality of travel in a motor vehicle ○ *The new model offers a very smooth ride.* **4 FAIRGROUND ENTERTAINMENT** an entertainment such as a roller coaster at an amusement park or fairground, offering a thrilling experience **5 PATH FOR HORSES** a broad grassy path where horses can be ridden **6 JAZZ CYMBAL** one of the three cymbals in a drum set, used to keep time and mark rhythmic accents in jazz [Old English *rīdan* < Indo-European] —**ridable** *adj* ◇ **be riding high** to be enjoying a period or feeling of success ◇ **ride roughshod over somebody** to treat somebody very arrogantly without justice or consideration for his or her feelings ◇ **ride roughshod over something** to disregard a rule, law, or agreement ◇ **take somebody for a ride** to cheat or deceive somebody

ride down *vt* **1** to hit and knock down somebody while riding, especially on horseback **2** to catch up with or overtake somebody

ride out *vti* to manage to deal with a difficult situation successfully and survive without too much harm ○ *ride out the storm*

ride up *vi* to gradually move upward out of the correct position ○ *Her skirt was riding up.*

rider /rídər/ *n* **1 SOMEBODY ON HORSE OR BIKE** a person who rides on an animal or a vehicle **2 ADDITIONAL COMMENT** an extra comment or clause added to a document or statement **3 ADDITIONAL CLAUSE TO BILL** an extra clause added to a parliamentary or legislative bill, often not directly related to the main issue **4 ADDITIONAL STATEMENT BY JURY** a secondary statement made by a jury, giving a comment in addition to the verdict **5 STRENGTHENING ELEMENT** something that rests on or strengthens something else, e.g. the horizontal rail of a fence or additional timbers in the frame of a ship **6 SLIDING ADJUSTMENT** a small sliding weight on the arm of a chemical balance, used for adjusting the scales **7 MINERAL SEAM** a thin seam of a mineral lying above a thicker one

ridership /rídər ship/ *n* the number of passengers using a particular form of public transport

ridesharing /ríd shairing/ *n US* an arrangement in which commuters take turns using their cars for going to work, taking one another as passengers to cut down the number of cars on the roads

ridge /rij/ *n* **1 RAISED STRIP** a long narrow raised area of something **2 RAISED LAND FORMATION** a long narrow hilltop or range of hills **3 RIDGE ON OCEAN FLOOR** an elevation on the ocean floor resembling a ridge on land and resulting from volcanic eruption along the fissures between tectonic plates **4 AREA OF HIGH PRESSURE** a long area of high pressure in a weather system. ◊ **trough** *n.* 4 **5 RAISED BIT ON BONE** a long narrow protuberance or crest, e.g. on a bone **6 BACKBONE OF ANIMAL** the backbone of an animal, especially a whale **7 TOP OF ROOF** the line along the top of a roof or a tent where the two sloping sides meet ■ *vti* (**ridges, ridging, ridged**) **FORM RIDGES** to mark, form, or provide something with ridges, or make something into the shape of a ridge [Old English *hrycg* < Germanic, 'back, spine'] —**ridgy** *adj*

ridgeback /ríj bak/ *n* ZOOL = **Rhodesian ridgeback**

ridgeline /ríj līn/ *n* GEOG = **ridge** *n.* 2

ridgeling /ríjling/, **ridgling** *n* a male animal in which one or both testes fail to descend into the scrotum at the usual time [Mid-16C. < Earlier *ridgel*.]

ridgepole /ríj pōl/, **ridge tree** *n* **1** a long beam of wood that runs along the ridge of a roof, supporting the upper ends of the rafters **2** the horizontal pole supporting the top of a ridge tent

ridge tent *n* a tent with rectangular sides that stands chiefly by suspension from a supported ridgepole

ridgetree /ríj tree/ *n* BUILDING, CAMPING = **ridgepole**

ridgeway /ríj way/ *n* a track, usually of ancient origin, running along the top of a ridge of hills [Old English *hrycgweg*]

ridicule /ríddi kyool/ *vt* (**-cules, -culing, -culed**) to make fun of or mock somebody or something in a contemptuous way ■ *n* mocking laughter, mimicry, or comments intended to make fun of somebody in a contemptuous way [Late 17C. Directly or via French < Latin *ridiculum* 'joke' < *ridiculus* (see RIDICULOUS).] —**ridiculer** *n*

ridiculous /ri díkyŏŏləss/ *adj* **1** completely unreasonable and not at all sensible or acceptable **2** silly and funny [Mid-16C. < Latin *ridiculus* 'laughable' < *ridere* 'laugh'.] —**ridiculously** *adv* —**ridiculousness** *n*

riding[1] /ríding/ *n* **1 BEING ON A HORSE** the sport or hobby of sitting on a horse and controlling it as it moves along **2 TRAVELLING ON ANIMAL OR VEHICLE** the act of travelling on an animal or vehicle ■ *adj* **USED ON HORSEBACK** used while riding a horse ○ *riding breeches*

riding[2] /ríding/ *n* **1 riding, Riding DISTRICT OF YORKSHIRE** one of the three administrative districts into which Yorkshire was formerly split **2** *Can* **CANADIAN CONSTITUENCY** a constituency represented by either a federal member of parliament or a member of the provincial legislature **3** *NZ* **RURAL LOCAL GOVERNMENT ELECTORATE** a rural electorate for local government [Pre-12C. < Old Norse *þriðungr* 'third part' < *þriði* 'third'.]

riding coat *n* a coat with cutaway front and tails worn in the 19th century for riding

riding crop *n* a straight short riding whip with a loop at the end

riding habit *n* a jacket with a matching skirt worn by women for riding from the late 17th to the early 20th century

Riding Mountain National Park /ríding-/ national park in SW Manitoba, Canada. Area: 2,973 sq. km/1,148 sq. mi.

ridley /rídli/ (*plural* **-leys**) *n* a small turtle, especially the grey-shelled Kemp's ridley found in the Atlantic, or the larger greenish olive ridley found in the Pacific

ridotto /ri dóttō/ (*plural* **ridottos**) *n* a musical entertainment with dancing, popular in the 18th century [Early 18C. Via Italian, 'retreat, entertainment' < medieval Latin *reductus* < past participle of Latin *reducere* 'bring back'.]

riebeckite /reé bek īt/ *n* a blue-black silicate mineral of the amphibole group containing iron and sodium. Source: acidic igneous rocks, schists. [Late 19C. After German explorer Emil *Riebeck* (1853–85).]

Riefenstahl /reéf'n shtaal/, **Leni** (*b.* 1902) German film director and photographer. Born **Helena Bertha Amalie Riefenstahl**

riel /reé əl/ *n* see table at **currency** [Mid-20C. < Khmer.]

Riemann /reémən/, **Georg Friedrich Bernhard** (1826–66) German mathematician

Riemannian geometry /ree mánni ən-/ *n* a non-Euclidean geometry in which it is assumed that in a plane all pairs of straight lines intersect [Early 20C. After G. F. B. RIEMANN.]

~~**rien**~~ incorrect spelling of **rein**

riesling /reézling/, **Riesling** *n* **1** a fruity dry to sweet white wine produced from a white grape grown mainly in Germany, Austria, Alsace, and Australia **2** the grape used to make riesling [Mid-19C. < German, alteration of obsolete *Rüssling*.]

rifampicin /ri fámpissin/ *n* an antibiotic that works by interfering with RNA synthesis in the infecting bacteria. Source: derived from soil bacteria. Use: treatment of tuberculosis, leprosy, other bacterial infections. US term **rifampin** [Mid-20C. Blend of RIFAMYCIN + PIPERAZINE.]

rifampin /ri fámpin/ *n US* PHARM = **rifampicin** [Mid-20C. Blend of RIFAMYCIN + PIPERAZINE.]

rifamycin /reéfə míssin/ *n* any of a group of antibiotics. Source: soil bacterium *Streptomyces mediterranei*. Use: treatment of leprosy, tuberculosis, other bacterial infections. [Mid-20C. Probably < Italian *riformare* 'reform' < *formare* 'form' < Latin (see REFORM) + -MYCIN.]

rife /rīf/ *adj* **1** occurring everywhere in plentiful supply ○ *areas where poverty is rife* **2** full of or severely affected by something undesirable ○ *an organization rife with corruption* [Old English *rȳfe*] —**rifely** *adv* —**rifeness** *n*

SYNONYMS See ***widespread***.

riff /rif/ *n* a short, often repeated series of notes in pop music or jazz that forms a distinctive part of the accompaniment ■ *vi* to play riffs [Early 20C. Possibly shortening of RIFFLE, or perhaps alteration of REFRAIN[2].]

riffle /ríff'l/ *v* (**-fles, -fling, -fled**) **1** *vti* **FLICK THROUGH PAGES** to flick through the pages of a book, magazine, or newspaper, glancing casually at the contents **2** *vt* **SHUFFLE CARDS** to shuffle playing cards by halving the pack, lifting the corners, and flicking the cards so that they overlap as they fall **3** *vi* **BECOME CHOPPY** to become rough and choppy when passing over submerged rocks ○ *Water riffles over the rocks.* ■ *n* **1** *US* **SUBMERGED ROCKS OR SANDBAR** an area of rocks or a sandbar lying just below the surface of the water **2** *US* **ROUGH WATER** an area of rough water caused by submerged rocks or a sandbar **3 QUICK LOOK AT BOOK** a quick flick through the pages of a book, magazine, or newspaper **4 SHUFFLING** the shuffling of playing cards **5 GROOVED PART OF SLUICE** the bottom part of a sluice that has grooves for collecting gold or other mineral particles [Mid-18C. < ?]

riffler /ríffler/ *n* a curved file for smoothing concave surfaces [Late 18C. < French *rifloir* < *rifler* 'scratch'.]

riffraff /ríf raf/ *n* **1** an offensive term that deliberately insults somebody's social status, importance, and manners (*insult*) **2** rubbish or worthless objects (*informal*) [15C. < French *rif et raf* 'pieces of plunder of small value' < *rifler* 'plunder' and *raffler* 'snatch'.]

rifle[1] /rīf'l/ *n* **1 GUN** a gun with a long barrel that is fired from the shoulder **2 CANNON** a large cannon with spirals cut into the bore ■ **rifles, Rifles** *npl* **UNIT OF ARMED SOLDIERS** a unit of soldiers carrying rifles ■ *vt* (**-fles, -fling, -fled**) **1 CUT GUN BARREL** to cut the inside of a gun barrel with spiral grooves **2 THROW FAST BALL** to hit or throw a ball hard, making it travel very fast [Late 17C. < French *rifler* 'scratch'.]

rifle[2] /rīf'l/ (**-fles, -fling, -fled**) *v* **1** *vti* to search vigorously through something such as a drawer or room, often leaving things in disorder and sometimes with the intent to steal **2** *vt* to rob or plunder somebody or something [14C. < French *rifler* 'plunder, scratch'.] —**rifler** *n*

riflebird /rīf'l burd/ *n* a bird of paradise, the male of which performs an elaborate courtship dance. Native to: Australia, New Guinea. Genus: *Ptiloris*. [Mid-19C. *Rifle* < ?]

rifle green *n* a dark-green colour, similar to that of the uniform of a British army rifleman —**rifle-green** *adj*

rifle grenade *n* a grenade propelled to its target by a rifle-fired bullet, requiring special adapting hardware

rifleman /rīf'lmən/ (*plural* **riflemen** /-mən/) *n* **1 SOLDIER WITH RIFLE** a soldier who has been trained to use a rifle **2 RIFLE USER** somebody skilled in the use of a rifle **3 NEW ZEALAND WREN** a tiny wren found in bush areas, with a short tail, round wings, and a broad head. Native to: New Zealand. *Acanthisitta chloris*.

rifle range *n* an area with targets where people can practise shooting rifles

riflery /rīf'lri/ *n US* **1** the skill or practice of firing rifles **2** fire from rifles

riflescope /rīf'l skōp/ *n* a telescopic sight designed to be used on a rifle [Mid-20C. < RIFLE[1] + TELESCOPE.]

rifling /rífling/ *n* **1** the cutting of spiral grooves in the barrel of a gun **2** a series of spiral grooves cut in the barrel of a gun

rift /rift/ *n* **1 GAP OR BREAK** a gap or break in something where it has split apart **2 DISAGREEMENT** a serious disagreement that disrupts good relations **3** GEOL = **fault** *n.* 6 ■ *vti* **SPLIT** to split or make something split apart [14C. < Scandinavian.]

rift valley *n* a valley formed by geological faulting, where the land between two parallel faults drops down to give a broad central plain with steep sides

rift zone *n* an area of the earth's surface, often associated with the margins of continental plates, that is especially heavily faulted and may be subject to earth tremors

rig[1] /rig/ *vt* (**rigs, rigging, rigged**) **1 EQUIP VESSEL WITH RIGGING** to fit a boat or its mast with sails and rigging **2 EQUIP** to equip or fit out something so it is ready to use **3 MAKE** to make something temporary and serviceable, usually done in haste and lacking the proper materials ○ *rigged up a makeshift shelter* **4 PREPARE AIRCRAFT FOR USE** to make an aircraft ready for use by making sure that all the parts are correctly adjusted **5 DRESS** to dress or adorn something or somebody (*usually passive*) ○ *rigged in striped pyjamas* ■ *n* **1 DRILLING STRUCTURE FOR OIL** a structure and apparatus used for drilling for oil and gas **2 ARRANGEMENT OF SAILS AND MASTS** the arrangement of sails and masts on a boat **3 OUTFIT OF CLOTHING** an outfit that somebody is wearing (*informal*) **4 LORRY** an articulated lorry or lorry with a trailer (*informal*) **5** *US* **HORSE CARRIAGE** in former times, a carriage or cart pulled by one or more horses [15C. Probably < Scandinavian.]

rig out *vt* (*informal*) **1** to put a special kind of clothing on somebody ○ *rigged himself out for a heavyweight bout* **2** to fit a person, place, or object with proper or necessary equipment ○ *rigged out for a trekking expedition*

rig[2] /rig/ *vt* (**rigs, rigging, rigged**) to affect the outcome of something by intervening dishonestly or unfairly to gain an advantage ■ *n* a trick or swindle [Early 18C. < ?]

rig[3] /rig/ *n* a male animal in which one or both testes fail to descend into the scrotum at the usual time (*informal*) [15C. Variant of RIDGE.]

Riga /réegə/ capital of Latvia, in the east of the country, on the Baltic Sea. Population: 839,675 (1995).

rigadoon /ríggə do͞on/, **rigaudon** /ri gaw dáwN/ *n* **1** a French dance for couples in the 17th and 18th centuries in duple or quadruple time **2** the music for a rigadoon [Late 17C. < French *rigaudon*.]

rigatoni /ríggə tṓni/ *n* short rounded tubes of pasta with narrow ridges running along them [Mid-20C. < Italian, < *rigato* 'ridged', past participle of *rigare* 'draw a line' < *riga* 'line'.]

rigaudon *n* DANCE = **rigadoon**

Rigel /rīg'l/ *n* a blue-white double star in the constellation Orion [< Arabic *rijl* 'foot', because it appears at the base of the constellation]

rigger /ríggər/ *n* **1 BRACKET ON ROWING BOAT** a bracket supporting a rowlock on a rowing boat **2 SOMEBODY WHO RIGS BOATS** somebody whose job is to rig a boat **3 SHIP** a ship, especially one with a specific kind of rigging **4 SCAFFOLDING WORKER** somebody whose job is to erect and maintain scaffolding and lifting equipment **5 OIL-RIG WORKER** a worker on an oil or gas rig

rigging /rígging/ *n* **1 ROPES, WIRES, AND PULLEYS** the ropes, wires, and pulleys that support the masts and control the sails of a boat **2 THEATRE EQUIPMENT** the system of ropes, pulleys, and other equipment used to shift scenery on a stage **3 SUPPORTING EQUIPMENT** any system of ropes, pulleys, or other equipment used as a support for something, e.g. construction scaffolding **4 SPECIAL-PURPOSE CLOTHING** clothing, especially when designed for a special purpose

rigging loft *n* **1** a raised area or gallery in a boatyard where workers stand while fitting rigging **2** an area above a stage equipped with lifting gear for raising and lowering scenery

right /rīt/ *adj* **1 TRUE** consistent with facts or belief ○ *gave the right answer* **2 SOCIALLY APPROVED** adhering to or consistent with conventional ideas of morality, propriety, or decorum ○ *right conduct between nations* **3 USUAL** conforming to what is usual or expected ○ *Something didn't seem right when I walked in.* **4 PROPER** proper with regard to use, function, or operation ○ *You're not holding the thing by the right end.* **5 BEST** most suitable or desirable ○ *waiting for the right offer to come along* **6 SUPERIOR** holding a view or position that is superior, more proper, or more moral ○ *hard to tell who's right in this situation* **7 HEALTHY** in good physical and mental health ○ *hasn't felt right in weeks* **8 IN SATISFACTORY CONDITION** being in a satisfactory condition or proper state, or going into one ○ *You can't expect to put everything right overnight.* ○ *That should set things right.* **9 PROMINENT** prominent in business, society, or some other sphere ○ *knows all the right people* **10 EAST WHEN FACING NORTH** on the side of the body that is east when you face north **11 MAIN** main or most prominent ○ *has to be stored right side up* **12 PERPENDICULAR** being perpendicular or forming an angle of 90° ■ *adv* **1 PROPERLY** in the proper or conventional way, or a way that will be successful ○ *You didn't do it right.* **2 IMMEDIATELY OR EXACTLY** emphasizes immediacy or exactness ○ *right at that moment* **3 STRAIGHT** without deviating from a course ○ *went right to work from the hospital* **4 CORRECTLY** in conformity with fact or expectation ○ *If you'd answered right you would have won £100.* **5 MORALLY AND APPROPRIATELY** in conformity with conventional morality, propriety, or justice ○ *I want to do right by my children.* **6 DESIRABLY** desirably or advantageously ○ *afraid that it won't turn out right* **7 TOWARDS EAST WHEN FACING NORTH** in or towards the east when you are facing or moving north, and correspondingly for other directions ○ *turn right at the church* **8 VERY** very (*regional*) ○ *a right good deal* **9 INTENSELY** intensifies the meaning of another term ○ *He just kept right on going and didn't even think about anyone else.* **10 USED AS PART OF TITLE** used as part of a title of respect ○ *Right Reverend* ■ *n* **1 MORALLY APPROPRIATE THING** that which is conventionally moral or appropriate ○ *She's too young to know right from wrong.* **2 TRUTH** something that is correct, completely true, and accurate **3 ENTITLEMENT OR FREEDOM** an entitlement, freedom, or privilege (*often plural*) ○ *human rights* ○ *You're within your rights to complain.* **4 ENTITLEMENT UNDER LAW** an entitlement granted under law ○ *the right to an appeal* **5 CLAIM** somebody's interest in a property (*often plural*) **6 SECURITIES OPTION** an option to purchase or receive securities not offered for sale openly, or the certificate indicating this (*often plural*) **7 right, Right CONSERVATIVES** political conservatives considered as a group, or the opinions they hold **8 EAST WHEN FACING NORTH** the side of something that lies east when you are facing north **9 RIGHT-HAND TURN** a turn to the right **10 ONE OF PAIR** the member of a pair designed for the right hand or foot **11 BLOW MADE WITH RIGHT HAND** a blow delivered with the right hand ■ *v* **1** *vti* **MAKE OR BECOME UPRIGHT** to put something upright, or to return to an upright position ○ *I righted the vase and mopped up the water.* **2** *vt* **BRING JUSTICE** to bring justice or proper results to a situation **3** *vt* **CORRECT MISTAKE** to change something that is wrong so that it is correct **4** *vt* **MAKE AMENDS FOR WRONG** to redress an error or misdeed ■ *interj* **1 OK** indicates assent or understanding (*informal*) **2 CORRECT** solicits confirmation of a statement ○ *You just got here, right?* [Old English *riht* < Indo-European, 'to go straight'] —**rightable** *adj* —**righter** *n* —**rightness** *n* ◇ **have** *or* **catch somebody bang to rights** to catch a criminal in the act of committing a crime (*informal*) ◇ **in the right** correct in what you say or do ◇ **in your own right** because of your birth, ability, or other entitlement, without reference to anyone else ◇ **set** *or* **put something to rights** to put something into a correct or ordered state

rightabout /rītə bowt/ *n* a turn through 180° to face in the opposite direction ■ *adj, adv* facing in the opposite direction

right angle *n* an angle of 90° —**right-angled** *adj*

right-angled triangle *n* a triangle with one right angle. US term **right triangle**

right ascension *n* one of the two reference points in the equatorial coordinate system for specifying the position of an astronomical object on the celestial sphere

right atrioventricular valve *n* ANAT = **tricuspid valve**

right away *adv* immediately, without waiting or any delay

Right Bank district of central Paris, on the northern bank of the River Seine

right-brain *adj* relating to or involving emotions or creative ability that are believed to be associated with the right half of the cerebrum

right circular cone *n* MATH = **cone** *n.* **2**

⚡**right-click** *vi* to press and release the right-hand button of a computer mouse

righteous /rīchəss/ *adj* **1 STRICTLY OBSERVANT OF MORALITY** always behaving according to a religious or moral code **2 JUSTIFIABLE** considered to be correct or justifiable **3 RESPONDING TO INJUSTICE** arising from the perception of great injustice or wrongdoing ○ *righteous indignation* ■ *n* **MORALLY UPRIGHT GROUP** righteous people viewed as a group ○ *believing that the righteous will prevail* [Alteration of Old English *rihtwīs* < earlier forms of RIGHT + -WISE] —**righteously** *adv* —**righteousness** *n*

right field *n* **1** the right side of the outfield on a baseball field, when looking from home plate **2** the position covered by the right fielder in baseball —**right fielder** *n*

right-footed *adj* **1** having a natural tendency to lead with or use the right foot, especially in playing sports such as football **2** performed using the right foot ○ *a right-footed shot on goal*

rightful /rītf'l/ *adj* **1 HAVING CLAIM** with a legal or moral claim to something ○ *the rightful owner* **2 OWNED BY SOMEBODY WITH RIGHT** owned by somebody who has a right to it ○ *rightful property* **3 FAIR** considered to be right and fair ○ *a rightful objection* —**rightfully** *adv* —**rightfulness** *n*

right hand *n* **1** the side of something that lies east when you are facing north **2** somebody who is of invaluable help to another person

SYNONYMS See ***assistant***.

right-hand *adj* **1 ON OR TO THE RIGHT** on the right or bending to the right **2 FOR THE RIGHT HAND** designed for or done with the right hand **3 MOST IMPORTANT AND TRUSTED** most important and trusted, and relied upon to the greatest extent

right-handed *adj* **1 PREFERRING TO USE RIGHT HAND** using the right hand in preference to the left for writing, throwing, and other activities that require skill and careful control **2 DONE WITH RIGHT HAND** carried out with the right hand **3 DESIGNED FOR RIGHT HAND** designed to be done with or used by the right hand **4 TOWARDS THE RIGHT** turning towards the right in a clockwise direction ■ *adv* **1 WITH RIGHT HAND** using the right hand **2 TOWARDS THE LEFT** with a swing or direction towards the left ○ *hit a ball right-handed* —**right-handedly** *adv* —**right-handedness** *n*

right-hander *n* **1** a right-handed person, especially a sportsperson **2** a blow delivered with the right hand

Right Honourable *n* **1 USED WHEN REFERRING TO MP** a title used in the British House of Commons when referring to, but not talking directly to, a member of parliament **2 TITLE OF PRIVY COUNCILLOR OR JUDGE** a title used in Britain when referring to, but not talking directly to, a member of the Privy Council or a judge who presides over an appeal court **3 TITLE OF RESPECT** a title used in Britain when referring to, but not talking directly to, a baron, viscount, or earl, and to lord mayors and lord provosts of some cities **4** *Can* **CANADIAN TITLE OF RESPECT** a title of respect used to refer to the governor general, prime minister, or chief justice of Canada, and certain other eminent Canadians

rightio *interj* = **righto** (*dated informal*)

rightist /rītist/ *adj* favouring or relating to political conservatism ■ *n* somebody with politically conservative views —**rightism** *n*

rightly /rītli/ *adv* **1 CORRECTLY** correctly, properly, and appropriately **2 UNDERSTANDABLY** with very good reason **3 CERTAINLY** certainly or positively (*informal*)

right-minded *adj* with opinions and attitudes considered to be sensible and fair —**right-mindedly** *adv* —**right-mindedness** *n*

rightmost /rīt mōst/ *adj* in the position that is farthest to the right

righto /rī tṓ/, **right oh, rightio** /rīti ṓ/ *interj* used to say that you acknowledge what somebody has just said and will do what is suggested (*dated informal*) [Late 19C. < RIGHT + HO².]

right off *adv* immediately, without waiting or any delay

right of search *n* the right of a country at war to stop and search the merchant ships of neutral nations to determine if they are carrying forbidden goods that may be seized

right of way *n* **1 PERMISSION TO GO FIRST** the legal or accepted right of a vehicle or craft to proceed ahead of another **2 RIGHT TO CROSS PROPERTY** the right to cross somebody else's property by a specific route, e.g. as a means of accessing your own property **3 LAWFUL ROUTE ACROSS SOMEBODY'S PROPERTY** a lawful route that may be taken across somebody else's property **4** *US, Can* **LAND USED FOR ROAD OR LINE** a narrow length of land used for the route of a railway, electric power line, or public road

right on *interj US* used to show enthusiastic agreement with something said or done (*dated informal*)

right-on *adj* (*informal*) **1** socially and politically fashionable and forward-looking, particularly in a way that corresponds to the attitudes of the political left **2** *US* perfectly true

Right Reverend *n* a form of address for a Roman Catholic, Anglican, or Episcopal bishop, or for a Roman Catholic abbot or monsignor

right shoulder arms *n* the command or act of bringing a weapon to rest on the right shoulder during a military drill

rights issue *n* an instance of an organization offering shares to existing holders on favourable terms so that they can maintain their percentage share of ownership

right-size (**right-sizes, right-sizing, right-sized**) *vi* to achieve an optimal size appropriate to a particular company, usually an effort considered to require dismissal of employees

right stuff *n* exactly the psychological and physical characteristics called for by a task (*informal*)

right-thinking *adj* = **right-minded**

right-to-die *adj* having or concerned with the right to end one's own life by obliging others not to intervene and thereby let nature take its course ○ *the right-to-die question*

right-to-life *adj* = **pro-life**

right triangle *n US, Can* MATH = **right-angled triangle**

rightward /rītwərd/ *adj* moving towards or positioned on the right

rightwards /rītwərdz/, **rightward** *adv* towards the right

right whale *n* a large-headed whale with a deeply curved jawline and notched tail. Native to: North Atlantic, Pacific Ocean. Family: Balaenidae.

right wing *n* **1 CONSERVATIVE** the conservative membership of a group or political party **2 PLAYER OR POSITION**

AT RIGHT in certain team games, the player or position occupying the right-hand part of a playing area when facing an opponent **3 RIGHT-HAND MILITARY FORCE OR POSITION** the right-hand part or position of a military force while facing the enemy

right-wing *adj* **1 CONSERVATIVE** conservative in conviction or temperament **2 ON RIGHT WHILE FACING OPPONENT** in certain games, occupying the right-hand part of a playing area when facing an opponent **3 OCCUPYING RIGHT DURING MILITARY ENGAGEMENT** occupying the right-hand part or position of a military force when it is facing the enemy —**right-winger** *n*

rigid /ríjjid/ *adj* **1 FIRM AND STIFF** not bending or easily moved into a different shape or position ○ *lengths of rigid plastic pipe* **2 INFLEXIBLE** applied or carried out strictly, with no allowances or exceptions ○ *a rigid set of rules* **3 HELD INFLEXIBLY** inflexibly adhered to ○ *rigid opinions* **4 REFUSING TO CHANGE** unchanging in behaviour, opinions, or attitudes ○ *Despite arguments to the contrary, she remained rigid in her stand.* [15C. < Latin *rigidus* < *rigere* 'be stiff'.] —**rigidity** /ri jíddəti/ *n* —**rigidly** *adv* —**rigidness** *n*

rigid designator *n* in philosophy, a name that stands for the same thing in every possible world as opposed to a description that could stand for somebody or something else in some possible world

rigidify /ri jíddi fī/ (**-fies, -fying, -fied**) *vti* to become or cause something to become stiff and inflexible

rigmarole /rígmərōl/ *n* **1** a tediously long, complicated, or unhelpful explanation **2** an irritating, tedious, or confusing sequence of tasks, especially tasks that seem unnecessary or absurd [Mid-18C. Probably alteration of earlier *ragman roll*, a parchment scroll used in the gambling game of *ragman*.]

rigor *n* US = **rigour**

rigorism /ríggərìzəm/ *n* **1** great strictness or severity **2** in Roman Catholic philosophy, the theory that in matters of moral choice the stricter course should be taken —**rigoristic** /ríggə rístik/ *adj*

rigor mortis /ríggər máwrtiss/ *n* the progressive stiffening of the body that occurs several hours after death [< Latin, 'stiffness of death']

rigorous /ríggərəss/ *adj* **1 STRICT** harsh, strict, or difficult in nature ○ *a rigorous training programme* **2 EXACTING** extremely precise and exacting ○ *rigorous standards of cleanliness* **3 SEVERE** severe and extreme to experience ○ *climbing in rigorous conditions* **4 PRECISE** precise and formalized ○ *a rigorous proof* —**rigorously** *adv* —**rigorousness** *n*

rigour /ríggər/ *n* **1 LACK OF TOLERANCE** severity, strictness, or harshness in dealing with somebody **2 USE OF DEMANDING STANDARDS** the application of precise and exacting standards in the doing of something **3 SEVERE WEATHER** harshness of weather or climate **4 HARDSHIP** great hardship or difficulty **5 RIGIDITY OF BODY** stiffness and lack of response to stimuli in body organs or tissues **6 SUDDEN FEELING OF CHILLINESS** an abrupt attack of shivering and coldness, typically marking a rise in body temperature, e.g. at the onset of fever **7 INERTIA IN PLANTS** insensitivity of a plant due to unfavourable conditions [14C. Directly and via Old French < Latin *rigor* 'stiffness' < *rigere* 'be stiff'.]

rig-out *n* an outfit of clothes or set of equipment (*informal*)

Rig-Veda /ríg váydə/ *n* a large collection of Hindu hymns dating from 2,000 BC or earlier [Late 18C. < Sanskrit *ṛgvedaḥ* < *ṛc* 'verse' + *vedaḥ* 'knowledge' (see VEDA).]

Rijeka /ri ékə/ city in NW Croatia. Population: 167,964 (1991).

rijsttafel /rī́ss taaf'l/, **rijstafel** *n* a Dutch meal of Indonesian origin based on rice with many small side dishes [Late 19C. < Dutch, < *rijs* 'rice' + *tafel* 'table'.]

Riksdag /réeks dag/ *n* the parliament of Sweden [Late 19C. < Swedish, < *rike* 'realm' + *dag* 'day'.]

Riksmål /ríks mawl/ *n, adj* Bokmål (*dated*) [Early 20C. < Norwegian, 'state language'.]

rile /rīl/ (**riles, riling, riled**) *vt* **1** to irritate somebody enough that it provokes anger (*informal; often passive*) **2** *US, Can* to stir up water or other liquid violently [Early 19C. Variant of ROIL.]

Riley /rī́li/ [Early 20C. Probably from a popular late 19C song.] ◇ **the life of Riley** a comfortable well-off life with no worries

Riley /rī́li/, **Bridget** (*b.* 1931) British painter

rilievo *n* ARTS = **relievo**

rill /ril/ *n* **1 STREAM** a little stream or brook **2 GROOVE IN SOIL** a small channel cut in soil **3 TRENCH ON MOON** a long narrow valley on the Moon's surface ■ *vt* **FORM CHANNELS IN FIELD** to form small channels in a ploughed field as a result of the runoff of rainwater [Mid-16C. < Low German *rille* < Indo-European, 'run'.]

rillet /rí llit/ *n* **1** a little rill **2** a short narrow valley on the Moon's surface

rillettes /ri léts/ *n* seasoned pork or goose cooked in its own fat until very tender and potted as a type of soft spreadable pâté (+ *singular or plural verb*) [Late 19C. < French, 'small pieces of pork' < *rille* 'piece of pork', variant of *reille* 'board' < Latin *regula* (see RULE).]

rim /rim/ *n* **1 OUTER EDGE OF SOMETHING CIRCULAR** an outer edge, often slightly raised, that runs along the outside of something curved or circular **2 LIMIT** the farthest limit of something (*literary*) **3 PART AROUND WHEEL'S EDGE** the curved outer edge of a wheel of a motor vehicle or bicycle **4 PART OF GLASSES FRAME** a usually curved part that holds and forms an edge to lenses in a pair of glasses **5 HOOP FOR BASKETBALL NET** the metal hoop to which a basketball net is attached ■ *vt* (**rims, rimming, rimmed**) **FORM OUTER EDGE** to form an edge, usually a slightly raised edge, along the edge of something curved or circular [Old English *rima* 'border, coast'] —**rimless** *adj* —**rimmed** *adj*

rimaye /ri máy/ *n* GEOG = **bergschrund** [Early 20C. < French, 'group of fissures' < Latin *rima* (see RIMOSE).]

Rimbaud /rámb ō/, **Arthur** (1854–91) French poet

rim brake *n* a brake that acts on the rim of a wheel

rime[1] /rīm/ *n* a thin coating of frost formed on cold objects exposed to fog or cloud ■ *vt* (**rimes, riming, rimed**) to cover something with a thin frost or with something resembling it (*often passive*) [Old English *hrīm* < Germanic] —**rimy** *adj*

rime[2] /rīm/ *n* a rhyme (*archaic*) ■ *vti* (**rimes, riming, rimed**) to rhyme (*archaic*)

rimfire /rím fīr/ *adj* designed for or using a cartridge with its primer located in the rim of the base, rather than in the centre

Rimini /rímməni/ city in NE Italy. Population: 129,876 (1992).

rimose /rī mṓss/ *adj* covered with cracks, fissures, or crevices [Early 18C. < Latin *rimosus* < *rima* 'fissure' < Indo-European, 'scratch'.] —**rimosely** *adv* —**rimosity** /rī móssəti/ *n*

Rimouski /ri mo͝oski/ city in Quebec, Canada. Population: 48,104 (1996).

rimrock /rím rok/ *n* a layer of rock that forms a vertical boundary to a plateau, valley, or deposit of gravel

Rimsky-Korsakov /rímski káwssə kof/, **Nikolay** (1844–1908) Russian composer

rimu /rée moo/ *n* TREES = **red pine** *n.* 2 [Mid-19C. < Maori.]

rind /rīnd/ *n* **1 TOUGH OUTSIDE LAYER OF FRUIT** the thick tough outer skin of a fruit **2 HARD OUTER LAYER OF FOOD** a tough outer protective layer of a food product, e.g. a cheese **3 BARK** the bark of a tree or shrub [Old English *rind(e)* 'something torn off' < Indo-European, 'tear']

rinderpest /ríndər pest/ *n* a sometimes fatal viral disease mainly affecting cattle, sheep, and goats that occurs chiefly in central Africa and Asia [Mid-19C. < German < *Rinder* 'cattle' + *Pest* 'plague'.]

rinforzando /réen fawr tsándō/ *adj, adv* loud and with emphasis (*musical direction*) [Early 19C. < Italian, 'getting stronger'.]

ring[1] /ring/ *n* **1 BAND** a durable circular band of something, especially a small band made of a particular material or for some special use **2 CIRCULAR PIECE OF JEWELLERY** a band, usually made of precious metal and often engraved or mounted with gemstones, worn as an ornament, especially round a finger **3 ENCIRCLING MARK** an outline, mark, or figure in the shape of a circle (*often plural*) **4 CIRCLE** a circular arrangement of people or objects ○ *a ring of chairs* **5 CIRCULAR MOTION** a movement of steps, especially by people skipping or dancing, that goes round in a continuous circle ○ *dancing in a ring* **6 ROUND COOKING SURFACE** a circular device on a stove designed to stand a pan on so that heat may be turned on and adjusted for cooking **7 GROUP OF PEOPLE OPERATING DISHONESTLY** an organized group of people who work together in a dishonest or unethical way ○ *a gambling ring* **8 CIRCULAR AREA FOR PERFORMANCE** a round stage or piece of ground, usually surrounded by seating, on which a spectator event such as a circus or a theatrical performance takes place ○ *a three-ring circus* **9 PLATFORM FOR BOXING OR WRESTLING** a raised square roped platform on which a boxing or wrestling match takes place **10 BOXING** the sport of boxing ○ *choose the ring as a career* **11 BAND OF MATTER CIRCLING PLANET** a band of dust, particles, and small bodies revolving around a planet **12** TREES = **growth ring 13** SPORTS = **bullring 14 BETTING ENCLOSURE** an enclosed area in which bets are taken at a racecourse **15 CONTEST** a competition or contest, especially a political one **16 ENCLOSURE FOR LIVESTOCK AT FAIR** an enclosure at a market or agricultural show in which livestock are shown, paraded, or auctioned **17 TURN OF SPIRAL** a single turn of a spiral **18 SET OF MATHEMATICAL ELEMENTS** a set of elements that is associative under multiplication and distributive under addition **19 CLOSED LOOP OF ATOMS** a collection of bound atoms represented graphically in cyclic form **20 SPACE BETWEEN CIRCLES** a space between two concentric circles ■ **rings** *npl* **GYMNASTIC APPARATUS** a pair of metal rings that are suspended from a ceiling and used to perform gymnastic routines ■ *v* **1** *vt* **WRITE CIRCLE ROUND** to draw or mark a circle round something, e.g. a word or number **2** *vti* **ENCIRCLE** to encircle something, or be encircled by something ○ *We were ringed by the herd of cattle.* **3** *vt* **IDENTIFY AN ANIMAL WITH TAG** to attach a ring-shaped tag to an animal, especially to the leg of a bird, for subsequent identification **4** *vt* FORESTRY = **girdle**[1] *v.* 2 [Old English *hring* < Indo-European, 'to curl']

SPELLCHECK Do not confuse ***ring*** with ***wring***, which has a similar sound. Beware: your spellchecker will not catch this error.

ring off *vi UK* to finish speaking on the telephone and break the connection, usually by replacing the receiver

ring[2] /ring/ *v* (**rings, ringing, rang** /rang/, **rung** /rung/) **1** *vti* **MAKE THE SOUND OF A BELL** to make, or cause something such as a bell to make, a metallic sound when struck or played **2** *vti* **MAKE A SOUND TO ALERT** to produce or make something produce a continuous or regular high-pitched sound to alert somebody **3** *vti* **TELEPHONE** to telephone somebody ○ *He rang me to cancel the appointment.* **4** *vi* **ECHO LOUDLY** to be full of a loud, high-pitched, or reverberating sound, especially laughter or applause ○ *The hall rang with applause.* **5** *vi* **MAKE CALL FOR** to call for somebody or something by sounding a bell or buzzer **6** *vi* **IMPRESS SOMEBODY AS** to make a particular impression on somebody ○ *His excuse didn't ring true.* **7** *vi* **HAVE SENSATION OF HIGH-PITCHED SOUNDS** to have a sensation of a repeated or continuous high-pitched sound ○ *It made my ears ring.* ■ *n* **1 ACT OF SOUNDING BELL** the act of making a bell sound **2 BELL SOUND** the sound of a bell or something like a bell **3 PHONE CALL** a call on the telephone (*informal*) ○ *She gave us a ring about noon.* **4 GENERAL IMPRESSION** a general impression made by somebody or something ○ *It had a familiar ring to it.* **5 REPEATED SOUND** a loud continuous repeated or reverberating sound **6 SET OF BELLS IN TOWER** a set of bells in a tower or belfry [Old English *hringan*, probably < Germanic, 'make a noise']

ring back *vti* to make a return telephone call to somebody (*informal*) ○ *I left several messages but she never rang back.*

ring in *vt* **1** to make bells ring in celebration of the beginning of something **2** *Aus* to substitute something fraudulently, especially a horse in a race

ring out *v* **1** *vi* to be heard loudly and clearly **2** *vt* to make bells ring in celebration of the end of something

ring up *v* **1** *vti* to telephone somebody **2** *vt* to press keys on a cash register to record the amount of money being paid for something (*dated*)

ring-a-ring-a-roses /-rṓziz/ *n* a young children's game in which players sing while moving round in a circle and abruptly squat when the words 'all fall down' are sung [Late 19C. < ?, popularly thought to refer to the 'rosy' (rash) of the bubonic plague, but probably originally simply a singing game with a curtsy at the end.]

ringbark /ríng baark/ *vt* FORESTRY = **girdle**[1] *v.* 2

ring-bill *n* BIRDS = **ring-necked duck**

ring-billed gull *n* a white gull that nests by inland lakes and lives on the coast in winter, and has a black ring round its bill. Native to: North America. *Larus delawarensis.*

ring binder *n* a stiff cover with metal rings inside the spine that snap open for insertion or removal of punched loose-leaf paper

ring-bolt *n* a bolt with a ring fitted through the eye at its head

ringbone /ríng bōn/ *n* **1** a condition of a horse's pastern bone in which bony outgrowths develop, sometimes leading to pain and lameness. It is treated with rest, medication, or surgery. **2** a bony outgrowth characteristic of ringbone [Because the outgrowths encircle the bone]

ring buoy *n* a buoy in the shape of a ring

ring circuit *n* a wiring arrangement in which electrical power is distributed to sockets and appliances through a single loop of cable that begins and ends in a fuse box

ring dance *n* DANCE = **round dance** *n.* 1

ringdove /ríng duv/ *n* **1** BIRDS = **wood pigeon 2** a domesticated variety of collared dove that has a semicircular black collar. *Streptopelia risoria.*

ring-dyke *n* a system of volcanic outcrops of magma (**dykes**) that form a circular structure

ringed /ringd/ *adj* **1 WEARING RING** wearing one or more rings **2 ENCIRCLED** encircled by a ring **3 WITH MARKS THAT FORM RING** with markings that form a ring round the neck, bill, or other body part

ringed plover *n* a plover of sandy or shingle shores with a grey back and wings, white undersides, a black breast band, and a black-tipped orange bill. Native to: Europe, Asia, Africa. *Charadrius hiaticula.*

ringed seal *n* a seal of Arctic and subarctic regions that has a dark greyish coat with lighter markings that encircle the body. *Pusa hispida.*

ringer[1] /ríngər/ *n* **1 SOMETHING THROWN AT AND ENCIRCLING PEG** a quoit thrown skilfully so that it encircles a peg or stake **2** *Aus* **DROVER** a man who looks after the livestock on a farm, especially somebody whose job is to move herds or flocks of animals from one place to another **3** *Aus* **FASTEST SHEARER** the fastest shearer in a shed **4** *Aus* **FASTEST PERSON** the fastest or best person at something

ringer[2] /ríngər/ *n* **1** a person who rings a bell **2** *US* somebody or something fraudulently substituted in a competition (*informal*)

Ringer's solution /ríngərz-/, **Ringer solution** *n* a solution of inorganic salts used to sustain cells, tissues, or organs outside the body [Late 19C. After Sydney *Ringer* (1834–1910), British physician.]

ring-fence *vt* (**ring-fences, ring-fencing, ring-fenced**) **SPECIFY USE OF MONEY** to specify that money be used for a specific purpose ■ *n* **1 AGREEMENT RESTRICTING USE OF MONEY** an agreement in which money is reserved for a particular purpose **2 FENCE ENCLOSING AREA** a fence that encircles a large area or a whole estate within one enclosure

ring finger *n* the third finger of the hand, especially the left hand, on which an engagement or wedding ring is traditionally worn

ringgit /ríng git/ *n* see table at **currency** [Mid-20C. < Malay.]

ringhals /ríng halss/ (*plural* **-hals** *or* **-halses**) *n* a snake related to the cobra that has a small rough-skinned black or brown body and can spit jets of venom from its fangs at an aggressor. Native to: southern Africa. *Hemachatus hemachatus.* [Late 18C. < Afrikaans, 'ring-neck' < the one or two white rings across the snake's neck.]

ringing /rínging/ *n* a clear continuing usually high-pitched sound ■ *adj* expressed in a definite and unrestrained way —**ringingly** *adv*

ringing tone *n* a sequence of paired sounds heard in a telephone receiver when a number has been dialled successfully to a phone that is not already engaged

ringleader /ríng leedər/ *n* the member of a circle or gang who organizes and encourages others, especially in unlawful or rebellious activities [< The phrase *lead the ring* 'go first']

ringlet /rínglət/ *n* **1 CURLY LOCK OF HAIR** a spiral curl of hair **2 BROWN EUROPEAN BUTTERFLY** a brown butterfly with dark eyespots on the wings, found in hedges, wood margins, and other shady places. Native to: S Europe. Genus: *Erebia.* **3 SMALL RING** a small ring or circle —**ringleted** *adj*

ring main *n* a wiring circuit in which a number of outlet sockets are connected in parallel to a ring circuit which starts and finishes at a mains supply point

ringmaster /ríng maastər/ *n* a presider over a circus show who announces and comments on performances

Ring Nebula *n* a ring-shaped nebula in the constellation Lyra

ring-necked /ríng nékt/, **ringneck** /-nek/ *adj* with markings resembling a ring round the neck in a colour that contrasts with adjacent feathers, scales, or hair

ring-necked duck *n* a diving duck found on woodland ponds that has coppery ring neck markings and two white rings on the bill. Native to: North America. *Aythya collaris.*

ringneck snake /ríng nek-/, **ring-necked snake** *n* a small nonvenomous snake that has a yellowish or orange neck band. Native to: North America. Genus: *Diadophis.*

ring ouzel *n* BIRDS = **ouzel**

ring-pull *n* a ring or tab of metal on the top of a drinks can that is pulled in order to open it. US term **pull-tab**

ring road *n* a main road designed and built to take traffic round the edge of an urban area so that the urban centre can be kept free of traffic congestion. US term **belt highway, beltway**

ringside /ríng sīd/ *n* **1** the row of seats or area directly in front of a boxing, wrestling, or circus ring **2** a place or location offering a clear and close view of something (*informal*) —**ringsider** *n*

ring-spot *n* **1** a pale or yellowish ring-shaped discoloration occurring in plants infected with a virus disease **2** a fungus disease affecting members of the cabbage family, with brown spots appearing on the leaves

ringtail /ríng tayl/ *n* **1** a ring-tailed mammal, especially a member of the family that includes the cacomistle and raccoon. Family: Procyonidae. **2** ZOOL = **ringtail possum**

ring-tailed lemur *n* a lemur with a grey coat and a long tail with black and white bands. *Lemur catta.*

ringtail possum *n* a possum with a curly-tipped striped tail that it uses for grasping branches and carrying objects. Native to: Australasia, New Guinea. Family: Pseudocheiridae.

ringworm /ríng wurm/ *n* a fungal disease of the skin, scalp, or nails in which intensely itchy ring-shaped patches develop

rink /ringk/ *n* **1 AREA OF ICE USED FOR SPORTS** a smooth, enclosed, and often artificially prepared ice surface used for ice-skating, ice hockey, or curling **2 SURFACE USED FOR ROLLER-SKATING** a smooth, enclosed, usually wooden surface used for roller-skating **3 BUILDING FOR ICE SPORTS** a building or arena in which ice-skating, ice hockey, or curling takes place **4 PART OF BOWLING GREEN FOR MATCH** an area of a bowling green on which a single match takes place **5 PLAYING SIDE** a team of players in curling, bowls, or quoits [14C. < ?]

rinky-dink /ríngki dingk/ *adj US* (*informal*) **1 OUT-OF-DATE** broken down or no longer useful **2 OLD-FASHIONED** old-fashioned or outmoded **3 INSIGNIFICANT** small and insignificant [Late 19C. < ?]

rinse /rinss/ *vt* (**rinses, rinsing, rinsed**) **1 LIGHTLY CLEAN SOMETHING IN LIQUID** to wash something lightly by dipping it in a liquid, especially clean water, or by running liquid over it **2 FLUSH MOUTH WITH WATER** to flush the mouth or teeth with clean water **3 DIP SOMETHING INTO DYE** to dip fabrics or garments into a dye solution ■ *n* **1 GENTLE WASH** the act of washing something lightly by running a liquid, usually clean water, over or around it **2 COSMETIC TREATMENT FOR HAIR** a solution that is applied to somebody's wet hair to alter or enhance its colour or condition temporarily **3 CLEANSING LIQUID** a liquid, usually water or a water-based solution, used to wash away something lightly [13C. < Old French *reincier.*] —**rinsable** *adj* —**rinser** *n*

rinsing /rínssing/ *n* the process or action of washing something quickly, gently, or finally in clean water or a cleaning solution

Rio de Janeiro /reé ō də zhə neér ō, -day-, -di-/ city in SE Brazil, the capital of Rio de Janeiro State. Population: 5,551,538 (1996).

Rio Grande /reé ō gránd, -grándi/ river of SW North America, flowing from SW Colorado into the Gulf of Mexico and forming part of the Texas-Mexico border. Length: 3,034 km/1,885 mi.

Rioja /ri ṓhə, ri ókhə/ *n* a dry red or white wine with a distinctive flavour, produced in N Spain [Early 20C. After La *Rioja*, the district in northern Spain where the wine is produced.]

Río Muni /reé ō móoni/ mainland portion of Equatorial Guinea, on the western coast of central Africa. Area: 26,017 sq. km/10,045 sq. mi.

riot /rí ət/ *n* **1 VIOLENT DISTURBANCE** a public disturbance during which a group of angry people becomes noisy and out of control, often damaging property and acting violently **2 SOMETHING EXTREMELY ENJOYABLE** a social occasion, event, or experience that people enjoy in a wild, noisy, and energetic way (*informal*) **3 FUNNY PERSON** an extremely amusing person (*informal*) **4 GREAT DISPLAY** a spectacular visual display **5 UNCONTROLLED WAY OF LIFE** behaviour that shows complete lack of control, especially financially or sexually (*archaic*) ■ *vi* **1 TAKE PART IN PUBLIC DISTURBANCE** to act as part of a crowd in an unruly, violent, and unrestrained way **2 BE WILD AND SELF-INDULGENT** to behave without any personal control, especially financially or sexually (*archaic*) [12C. < Old French, 'quarrel' < *rioter* 'quarrel'.] —**rioter** *n* ◇ **read (somebody) the riot act** to reprimand somebody severely for doing something, often including a threat of punishment if the offending behaviour does not stop ◇ **run riot 1** to behave in a wild and uncontrolled way **2** to grow in profusion

Riot Act *n* an English law, passed in 1713, providing that persons making a public disturbance had to disperse within one hour of having had the act read to them by a magistrate

riot gun *n* a short-barrelled gun used to disperse crowds. It fires plastic or rubber bullets, or CS gas cartridges.

riotous /rí ətəss/ *adj* **1** loud, conspicuous, and unrestrained **2** involved in or taking part in serious public unrest (*formal*) —**riotously** *adv* —**riotousness** *n*

riot police *n* a police reserve specially equipped for controlling a rioting crowd

riot shield *n* a large oblong transparent shield used to protect the face and upper body of a police officer attempting to disperse a crowd

rip[1] /rip/ *v* (**rips, ripping, ripped**) **1** *vti* **TEAR OR BE TORN** to tear something or become torn, especially accidentally, with a sudden or rough splitting action, usually accompanied by a distinct tearing noise **2** *vt* **USE FORCE TO REMOVE** to remove something from a place where it has been firmly fixed, especially by tearing it out forcibly without taking time or care ○ *Most of the original features of the house were ripped out.* **3** *vi* **MOVE WITH EXTREME SPEED** to move with dangerous or violent speed ○ *The tornado ripped through northern Nebraska.* **4** *vt* **DIVIDE TIMBER LENGTHWAYS** to make a split along the grain of a piece of wood using a saw or chopping tool ■ *n* **1 ROUGHLY TORN PLACE** a rough tear or split, especially one that is caused suddenly and forcefully **2 RIPSAW** a ripsaw (*informal*) [14C. < ?] ◇ **let rip** to speak rapidly and without restraint, especially with a series of curses (*informal*)

SYNONYMS See ***tear.***

rip into *vt* to attack somebody or something, especially with a sudden and damaging criticism (*informal*)

rip off *vt* (*informal*) **1** to charge somebody an unfair price or cheat somebody financially **2** to rob somebody or steal something

rip up *vt* to tear something up with the hands into pieces or strips

rip[2] /rip/ *n* **1** an area of rough water caused by winds or opposing currents **2** OCEANOG = **rip current 3** OCEANOG = **riptide** [Late 18C. Probably < RIP[1].]

rip[3] /rip/ *n* (*archaic informal*) **1** somebody considered to be corrupt and dissolute **2** something, especially a horse, that is old and of no value [Late 18C. < ?]

RIP *abbr* rest in peace [Latin *requiescat in pace* or *requiescant in pace*]

riparian /rī páiri ən, ri-/ *adj* situated or taking place along or near the bank of a river [Mid-19C. < Latin *riparius* < *ripa* 'riverbank' < Indo-European, 'cut'.]

ripcord /ríp kawrd/ *n* **1** a cord that, when pulled, opens a parachute **2** a cord used to release gas from a hot air balloon during an emergency

rip current *n* a narrow current flowing strongly from the shore to the sea, visible as a band of agitated water [< RIP[2]]

ripe /rīp/ (**riper, ripest**) *adj* **1 READY AND PLEASANT TO EAT** ready to be picked and eaten because it is mature and has reached optimum flavour **2 READY TO HARVEST** having developed to the stage for harvesting and subsequent storage or sale **3 MATURE AND MELLOW** matured enough to have developed the best flavour and body ○ *ripe cheese* **4 IMPOLITE OR LEWD** full of rude words, swearwords, sexual references, or outrageous opinions (*informal*) **5 EXACTLY READY** at the most suitable stage of preparation or development ○ *The occasion was ripe for asking for a pay rise.* **6 ADVANCED IN YEARS** representing or constituting a long life **7 EXPERIENCED AND KNOWLEDGEABLE** showing plenty of experience and knowledge accumulated gradually over time **8 SMELLY** giving off a strong and unpleasant smell, especially caused by sweat from part of the body (*informal*) **9 FULL AND RED** full and ruddy, suggesting ripe fruit [Old English *rīpe* < Germanic] —**ripely** *adv* —**ripeness** *n*

ripen /rípən/ *vti* **1** to reach, or cause fruit or other food to reach, a ripe or mature condition **2** to become or make something fully developed, mature, or ready (*often passive*) —**ripener** *n* —**ripening** *adj, n*

ripieno /ríppi áyn ō/ *n* in a baroque concerto, the full ensemble, as contrasted with the soloist or group of soloists (**concertino**) [Mid-18C. < Italian, 'filled up' < *pieno* 'full'.]

rip-off *n* (*informal*) **1 UNFAIRLY PRICED ITEM** something that is not worth the price asked or paid **2 ACT OF BEING DISHONESTLY TREATED** an act or example of being cheated, tricked, or exploited **3 IMITATION OF** an imitation of something more inventive, successful, or famous, perpetrated in order to make a financial gain based on the other's reputation

Ripon /ríppən/ city in NE England. Population: 13,806 (1991).

riposte /ri póst/ *n* **1** something said or done quickly and effectively in response **2** a quick deft thrust made after parrying the lunge of a fencing opponent [Early 18C. Via French < Italian *risposta*, past participle of *rispondere* 'respond' < Latin *respondere* (see RESPOND).]

SYNONYMS See ***answer***.

ripper[1] /ríppər/ *n* (*informal*) **1 MURDERER USING KNIFE** a murderer who uses a knife to kill and mutilate people **2** *Aus* **EXCELLENT THING** something or somebody outstandingly good ○ *a ripper of a shot* ■ *interj Aus* **EXCLAMATION OF ENTHUSIASM** used to express enthusiasm or delight (*informal*)

⚡**ripper**[2] /ríppər/ *n* a program used to copy digital music from a compact disc onto a computer before converting it into a format storable as a computer file

ripping[1] /rípping/ *adj* wonderful or excellent (*dated informal*) —**rippingly** *adv*

⚡**ripping**[2] /rípping/ *n* the process of copying digitized music as a stored computer file

ripple[1] /ripp'l/ *v* (**-ples, -pling, -pled**) **1** *vti* **FLOW IN TINY GENTLE WAVES** to flow with, or be lightly disturbed by, a succession of tiny waves moving quickly and gently ○ *a breeze rippled the water* **2** *vti* **SHAPE SOMETHING INTO GENTLE WAVY PATTERN** to take on or give something an appearance of very small wavy shapes across its surface or length **3** *vi* **MAKE LAPPING SOUND** to make a gentle lapping sound **4** *vi* **BE HEARD BRIEFLY AMONG CROWD** to begin as a sound made by a few people, spreading and briefly becoming slightly louder before dying away ○ *Laughter rippled round the room.* ■ *n* **1 TINY WAVE OR SERIES OF WAVES** a small wave or series of gentle waves across a surface **2 GENTLE WAVY SHAPE OR MARK** something that resembles a ripple in its smooth undulating shape **3 GENTLE PATTERN OF SOUND** a sound that starts quietly and then spreads, becoming slightly louder for a few seconds before dying away ○ *a ripple of scorn* **4 SHALLOW BROKEN RIVER WATER** an area of shallow water in a river broken by rocks or sand bars **5 OSCILLATION OF CURRENT** a small oscillation of electrical current ■ **ripples** *npl* **CONSEQUENCES** a series of repercussions or consequences ○ *The ripples of the sector's downturn continue to be felt.* ■ *adj* **WITH SECOND FLAVOUR MIXED IN** with a second flavour partly combined or marbled through ○ *raspberry ripple ice cream* [Late 17C. < ?] —**rippler** *n* —**ripply** *adj*

ripple[2] /ripp'l/ *vt* (**-ples, -pling, -pled**) to remove seeds from a plant with a comb-shaped tool ■ *n* a comb-shaped tool used to remove seeds from a plant [Mid-17C. < ?]

ripple effect *n* a spreading series of effects or consequences caused by a single event [< the ripples that spread across the surface of a pool when something is dropped into the water]

ripple mark *n* a series of small wavy ridges created in sand or silt by wind or water —**ripple-marked** *adj*

rippling /rípp'ling/ *adj* **1 IN SMOOTH GENTLE WAVES** moving in or resembling the flow of small gentle waves **2 SOUNDING LIKE SOFTLY FLOWING WATER** moving with a gentle lapping or soothingly liquid sound ■ *n* **SOUND OF SOFTLY FLOWING WATER** the gentle lapping sound that shallow or lightly disturbed water makes as it flows

riprap /ríp rap/ *n* **1 BROKEN STONE USED IN CONSTRUCTION** broken stone used in making protective foundations and embankments for riverbeds and riverbanks **2 SOMETHING BUILT OF BROKEN STONE** a protective foundation or embankment made from broken stone loosely or irregularly combined ■ *vt* (**-raps, -rapping, -rapped**) **CONSTRUCT SOMETHING WITH BROKEN STONE** to build or strengthen a riverbed or riverbank with broken stone [Late 16C. Doubling of RAP[1].]

rip-roaring /-ráwring/ *adj* full of boisterous excitement or energy (*informal*) [Mid-19C. < RIP[1] + UPROARIOUS.] —**rip-roaringly** *adv*

ripsaw /ríp saw/ *n* a saw with coarse teeth used to cut along the grain of wood

ripsnorter /ríp snawrtər/ *n US* something or somebody exceptionally impressive (*informal*) [Mid-19C. < RIP[1] + SNORT 'something big and impressive'.]

ripstop /ríp stop/ *adj* woven with extra threads to make tearing less likely ○ *ripstop nylon*

riptide /ríp tīd/ *n* a strong narrow tide that opposes other currents and produces turbulence, especially sea water that rushes seawards after incoming waves mount up on the shore [< RIP[2]]

⚡**RISC** /risk/ *abbr* reduced-instruction-set computer

rise /rīz/ *vi* (**rises, rising, rose** /rōz/, **risen** /rízz'n/) **1 STAND UP** to assume a standing or nearly vertical position after sitting, kneeling, or lying **2 ASCEND** to go up to a higher position or location ○ *Disturbed by our footsteps, the birds rose above the trees.* **3 GET HIGHER** to gain a greater height or level ○ *After heavy rains the river rose dangerously.* **4 GROW LARGER** to increase in amount, degree, or quantity ○ *Prices are rising.* **5 ACHIEVE GREATER SOCIAL PROMINENCE** to achieve higher wealth, status, or importance ○ *He rose steadily through the ranks.* **6 EXTEND UPWARDS** to become elevated or extend upwards ○ *The church tower rose above the village.* **7 GROW LOUDER** to increase in volume or intensity of sound ○ *Their voices rose.* **8 INTENSIFY EMOTIONALLY** to become emotionally more intense or powerful ○ *Her temper rose.* **9 DEVELOP** to develop or intensify, especially until a particular state is reached ○ *When we woke, the wind had risen.* **10 SWELL** to swell and puff out, e.g. in the manner of dough containing yeast ○ *The bread is rising.* **11 REBEL OR REVOLT** to make an organized rebellion against something or somebody ○ *The entire region rose up against the authorities in protest.* **12 END MEETING** to adjourn after a meeting or assembly **13 BECOME ERECT** to become stiff and erect ○ *He felt the hair rise on the back of his neck.* **14 BECOME GREATER** to become stronger or more stimulated ○ *Her temper rose.* **15 ORIGINATE** to have an origin or beginning ○ *The stream rises a few miles back.* **16 GROW** to spring up or grow **17 BECOME APPARENT** to become visible or apparent ○ *After many days at sea, Africa rose before their astonished eyes.* **18 BE BUILT** to become larger during the process of building **19 APPEAR OVER HORIZON** to appear above the horizon ○ *The sun was rising when we went to bed.* **20 MOVE UP TO TAKE BAIT** to move up to the surface of water to take an angler's bait ○ *The trout rose to my fly.* **21 BE RESURRECTED** to become resurrected ○ *rise from the dead* ■ *n* **1 INCREASE** an increase in amount ○ *a rise in prices* **2 SALARY INCREASE** an increase in salary or wages **3 PROCESS OF BEING NOTICED** the process of becoming noticed and successful ○ *the rise of a new talent* **4 INCREASE IN STATUS** an increase in wealth, status, or importance ○ *the rise and fall of the empire* **5 UPWARD SLOPE** an upward slope or gradient ○ *a rise in the road* **6 HIGHER GROUND** a hill or piece of raised or rising ground **7 UPWARDS MOVEMENT** an ascent or upwards movement **8 INTENSIFICATION** an increase in degree, intensity, or force ○ *a rise in her fever* **9 INCREASE OF SOUND** an increase in loudness or pitch **10 HEIGHT** the vertical extent of something **11 APPEARANCE ABOVE HORIZON** the appearance of something above the horizon **12 ORIGIN** a beginning or origin of something **13 REBELLION** a rebellion against authority **14 APPEARANCE ON WATER SURFACE** the appearance of something, especially a number of feeding fish, at the surface of the water ○ *There was a good rise of trout this evening.* **15 DISTANCE BETWEEN CROTCH AND WAIST** the length between the crotch and the waist of a pair of trousers [Old English *rīsan* < Germanic] ◇ **give rise to something** to cause something ◇ **take** *or* **get a rise out of somebody** to produce a desired response, usually anger or annoyance, by teasing or taunting somebody (*informal*)

rise above *vt* to overcome something unpleasant by not letting it become too important

rise to *vt* (*informal*) **1** to behave well in response to a challenge or difficulty ○ *rose to the occasion* **2** to react to something angrily or excitedly

riser /rízər/ *n* **1 SOMEBODY WHO RISES FROM BED** a person who gets up in a specific way after sleeping ○ *We are late risers at the weekend.* **2 VERTICAL PART OF STEP** the vertical part of a step or stair **3 VERTICAL PIPE** a vertical pipe, duct, or conduit **4 SOMEBODY RISING** a person who or thing that rises

risible /rízzəb'l/ *adj* **1** causing or capable of causing laughter **2** able or inclined to laugh (*formal*) [Mid-16C. < late Latin *risibilis* < Latin *ris-*, past participle of *ridere* 'laugh'.] —**risibility** /rízzi bílləti/ *n* —**risibly** *adv*

rising /rízing/ *adj* **1 GETTING MORE IMPORTANT** becoming increasingly respected or significant in an occupation or activity **2 BECOMING POWERFUL** becoming more influential and powerful **3 GETTING HIGHER** going up or becoming higher ■ *adv* **CLOSE TO AGE** getting close to a particular age (*dated informal*) ○ *rising sixty* ■ *n* **1 REVOLT** a rebellion or revolt **2 SOMETHING GETTING HIGHER** something that rises in height **3 UPWARDS MOVEMENT** the action of something that moves upwards or to a higher level **4 ACTION OF STANDING UP** the action of assuming a standing or nearly vertical position after sitting, kneeling, or lying **5 LEAVENING PROCESS** the process of leavening bread

rising damp *n* moisture that is absorbed from the ground into walls, resulting in structural damage

rising diphthong *n* a diphthong in which the second of two sounds has more stress or sonority than the first

rising rhythm *n* a rhythmic pattern produced by a succession of metrical feet, each foot having an accented syllable preceded by one or more syllables that are unaccented

rising trot *n* a horse-riding technique used at the trot, in which the rider rises from the saddle every second beat. ◊ **sitting trot**

risk /risk/ *n* **1 CHANCE OF SOMETHING GOING WRONG** the danger that injury, damage, or loss will occur **2 HAZARD** somebody or something likely to cause injury, damage, or loss **3 CHANCE OF LOSS TO INSURER** the probability, amount, or type of possible loss incurred or covered by an insurer **4 POSSIBILITY OF INVESTMENT LOSS** the possibility of loss in an investment or speculation **5 STATISTICAL ODDS OF DANGER** the statistical chance of danger from something, especially from the failure of an engineered system ■ *vt* **1 ENDANGER** to place something valued in a position or situation where it could be damaged or lost or exposed to damage or loss **2 DO SOMETHING DESPITE DANGER** to incur the chance of harm or loss by taking an action [Mid-17C. Via French *risque* < Italian *rischo* < *rischiare* 'run into danger'.] —**risker** *n* —**riskily** *adv* —**riskiness** *n* —**risky** *adj* ◇ **at risk 1** in danger of injury, damage, or loss ○ *needlessly putting lives at risk* **2** in danger of being harmed or of harming others ◇ **run** *or* **take a risk** to do something that involves the possibility of injury, damage, or harm

risk arbitrage *n* the technique of using price discrepancies in a market in order to profit, e.g. by buying shares in a company being acquired while selling shares in the acquiring company —**risk arbitrageur** *n*

risk-benefit *adj* studying or testing whether the benefits of a procedure, process, or treatment outweigh the risks involved

risk capital *n* FIN = **venture capital**

risk factor *n* a feature of somebody's habits, genetic makeup, or personal history that increases the probability that disease or harm to health will occur

risk management *n* the profession or technique of determining, minimizing, and preventing accidental loss in a business, e.g. by taking safety measures and buying insurance

risk society *n* a society exposed to harm as a consequence of human activities, e.g. environmental damage or nuclear accidents, rather than naturally occurring events such as earthquakes or volcanic eruptions

Risorgimento /ri sáwrji méntō/ *n* the movement for, and period of, political unification in Italy beginning about 1750 and culminating in the occupation of Rome by Italian troops in 1870 [Late 19C. < Italian, 'resurgence'.]

risotto /ri zóttō/ (*plural* **-tos**) *n* a moist Italian dish of short-grained rice and other ingredients cooked gently in stock [Mid-19C. < Italian, < *riso*.]

risqué /rísk ay, ree skáy/ *adj* alluding to sexual conduct in a way that is close to being indecent or in bad taste [Mid-19C. < French, past participle of *risquer* 'risk' < *risque* (see RISK).]

Riss /riss/ *n* one of the four major glacial periods in Europe, at its peak 150,000 years ago [Early 20C. After the river *Riss*, a tributary of the Danube in Germany where signs of the glaciation were observed.]

rissole /ríssōl/ *n* a small fried cake of minced seasoned meat or poultry, often coated or mixed with bread-crumbs [Early 18C. Via French < Latin *russus* 'red'.]

Risso's dolphin /ríssōz-/ *n* ZOOL = **grampus** [Late 19C. After the Italian naturalist Giovanni Antonio *Risso* (1777–1845).]

risus sardonicus /rèessass saar dónnikass/ *n* a distorted grinning expression caused by involuntary prolonged contraction of the facial muscles, especially as a result of tetanus [< modern Latin, 'sardonic grin']

rit. *abbr* **1** ritardando **2** ritenuto

ritardando /ríttar dándō/ *adj, adv* becoming gradually slower (*musical direction*) [Early 19C. Italian, present participle of *ritardare* 'slow down' < Latin *retardare*.]

rite /rīt/ *n* **1** CEREMONIAL ACT a solemn and ceremonial act or procedure that follows the rule customary to a community, especially a religious group (*often plural*) ○ *the rite of baptism* **2** FORMAL PROCEDURE a formal, customary observance or procedure (*often plural*) ○ *rites of courtship* **3** CEREMONIAL WAY OF PROCEEDING a system of ceremonial procedure ○ *Roman rite* **4** rite, Rite LITURGICAL PROCEDURE a liturgy or version of a liturgy, especially of a Communion service **5** rite, Rite DIVISION OF CHURCHES a historical division of Christian churches based on their liturgies [14C. Directly or via French < Latin *ritus*.]

ritenuto /rítta nyoótō/ *adj, adv* played slightly slower than the rest of a piece of music (*musical direction*) [Early 19C. < Italian, 'held back'.]

rite of passage *n* **1** an event or act that marks a significant transition in a human life **2** a ceremony that marks somebody's passage from one stage of life to another, e.g. from childhood to puberty or from unmarried to married life [Translation of French *rite de passage*]

ritornello /rittar néllō/ *n* (*plural* **-los** *or* **-li** /-lee/) *n* **1** a short musical passage used as an orchestral refrain between verses of a song or aria **2** in a concerto grosso, the return of full orchestral music after a solo [Late 17C. < Italian, 'little return'.]

ritual /ríchoo əl/ *n* **1** ESTABLISHED FORMAL BEHAVIOUR an established and prescribed pattern of observance, e.g. in a religion **2** ACTIONS DONE FORMALLY AND REPEATEDLY the performance of actions or procedures in a set, ordered, and ceremonial way (*often before nouns*) ○ *a ritual dance* **3** UNCHANGING PATTERN a formalized pattern of actions or words followed regularly and precisely (*informal*) ○ *the weekend car-washing ritual* **4** SET FORM OF COMMUNICATION a set sequence of actions that an animal uses to communicate information or to reinforce social cohesion ○ *mating rituals* **5** REPETITIVE BEHAVIOUR an inflexible, stylized, and often repetitive sequence of actions, e.g. repeated hand-washing, that may indicate an obsession **6** BOOK OF CEREMONIES a book containing rites or ceremonial procedures, especially religious rites ■ *adj* CONCERNED WITH RITE concerned with or practising a rite ○ *ritual observance* [Late 16C. < Latin *ritualis* < *ritus* (see RITE).] —**ritually** *adv*

ritual abuse *n* the alleged physical abuse of children by adults taking part in supposed satanic rituals

ritualisation *n* = ritualization

ritualise *vt* = ritualize

ritualised *adj* = ritualized

ritualism /ríchoo əlizəm/ *n* a devotion or adherence to rituals

ritualistic /richoo ə listik/ *adj* forming part of or adhering to a ritual —**ritualistically** *adv*

ritualization /ríchoo ə lī záysh'n/, **ritualisation** *n* **1** the act of making something into a ritual **2** the process in which different forms of behaviour are modified and combined to form a ritual

ritualize /ríchoo ə līz/ (*-izes, -izing, -ized*), **ritualise** (*-ises, -ising, -ised*) *v* **1** *vt* to make a ritual of something **2** *vi* to promote the use of rituals —**ritualized** *adj*

ritual murder *n* **1** a human sacrifice, especially to appease a deity **2** a murder performed in a methodical, formalized, or ritualistic way

ritz /rits/ [Early 20C. Back-formation < RITZY.] ◇ **put on the ritz** to make a show of wealth and extravagance (*dated informal*)

ritzy /rítsi/ (*-ier, -iest*) *adj* expensively stylish and elegant (*informal*) [Early 20C. < *Ritz*, the luxurious hotels established by the Swiss-born entrepreneur César *Ritz* (1850–1918).] —**ritzily** /rítsili/ *adv* —**ritziness** *n*

rival /rív'l/ *n* **1** COMPETING PERSON OR GROUP a person or group competing with another for something or somebody **2** EQUAL OR BETTER COMPETITOR a person or thing that can equal or surpass another in a specific respect ■ *v* (*-vals, -valling, -valled*) **1** *vt* EQUAL OR SURPASS to equal or better somebody or something in a particular respect **2** *vti* COMPETE to compete with somebody **3** *vt* TRY TO EQUAL to try to equal or surpass somebody or something in a particular respect ■ *adj* COMPETING competing with somebody or something [Late 16C. < Latin *rivalis* 'using the same stream' < *rivus* 'stream'.] —**rivalrous** *adj*

LITERARY LINK *The Rivals*, a play (1775) by Irish dramatist Richard Brinsley Sheridan. This lively comedy of manners portrays the attempts of Captain Jack Absolute to woo Lydia Languish, the idealistic niece and ward of Mrs Malaprop. The latter's habit of misusing similar-sounding words gave rise to a new term: *malapropism*.

rivalry /rívalri/ (*plural* **-ries**) *n* **1** the condition or fact of competing with somebody or something **2** an act of competitiveness

rive /rīv/ (*rives, riving, rived* or *riven* /rívv'n/) *v* **1** *vti* to split a material such as wood by striking it, or to become split in this way (*archaic*) **2** *vt* to tear something apart (*literary*) [12C. < Old Norse *rífa* < Indo-European 'cut'.]

riven *adj* torn apart (*literary*) ○ *a political party riven by dissent* [Past participle of RIVE]

river /rívvər/ *n* **1** a natural formation in which fresh water forms a wide stream that runs across the land until it reaches the sea or another area of water **2** a large flow or stream of something (*often plural*) ○ *a river of mud* [13C. Via Anglo-Norman *rivere* < Latin *riparius* (see RIPARIAN).] ◇ **sell somebody down the river** to betray or desert somebody, usually for a selfish or mercenary motive (*informal*)

Rivera /ree vérraa/, **Diego** (1886–1957) Mexican artist

riverbank /rívvər bangk/ *n* a piece of sloping ground at the edge of a river

river basin *n* a large area of land that drains exclusively to a particular river

riverbed /rívvər bed/ *n* the ground or part of the ground covered by a river along its course and between its banks

river blindness *n* MED = **onchocerciasis**

riverboat /rívvər bōt/ *n* a boat built with a flat bottom or shallow draft, used for travelling on rivers

river catchment *n* GEOG = **river basin**

riverfront /rívvər frunt/ *n* the area of a town, property, or built-up area directly facing a river

riverhead /rívvər hed/ *n* the upstream source of a river or the area of land around it

Riverina /rívva reena/ region of south-central New South Wales, Australia. Area: 68,658 sq. km/26,509 sq. mi.

riverine /rívva rīn/ *adj* **1** relating to or produced by a river **2** located beside a river

river red gum *n* a large eucalyptus tree, widespread along inland waterways of Australia, that has pale smooth bark and durable dark-red timber. *Eucalyptus camaldulensis.*

riverside /rívvar sīd/ *n* the area of land beside a river ■ *adj* located beside a river

riverweed /rívvar weed/ *n* a small many-branched fresh-water plant that clings to rock with roots that function as suckers. Genus: *Podostema*.

rivet /rívvit/ *n* SHORT METAL FASTENER a fastener with a head attached to a metal shaft that is passed through a hole in a material and flattened on the other side ■ *vt* **1** FIRMLY FIX ATTENTION to fix or hold the attention completely (*informal; often passive*) **2** FASTEN WITH RIVET to fasten something using a rivet or rivets **3** PULL AND HOLD ONTO FIRMLY to draw and hold people's eyes or attention in a powerful absorbing way (*informal*) ○ *'Old Grannis dared not move, but sat rigid, his eyes riveted on his empty soup plate'.* (Frank Norris, *McTeague – A Story of San Francisco*; 1899) **4** FIX SOMETHING FIRMLY to fix or secure something firmly [14C. < Old French, < *river* 'fasten'.]

WORLD'S LONGEST RIVERS		
1	Nile	
Length	[4,160 mi. / 6,695 km]	
Location	Africa	
2	Amazon	
Length	[4,000 mi. / 6,400 km]	
Location	South America	
3	Yangtze (Chang Jiang)	
Length	[3,900 mi. / 6,300 km]	
Location	Asia	
4	Mississippi-Missouri	
Length	[3,710 mi. / 5,970 km]	
Location	North America	
5	Huang He (Yellow River)	
Length	[3,395 mi. /5,464 km]	
Location	Asia	
6	Ob'-Irtysh	
Length	[3,362 mi. /5,410 km]	
Location	Asia	
7	Congo	
Length	[2,710 mi. /4,374 km]	
Location	Africa	
8 =	Amur	
Length	[2,700 mi. /4,345 km]	
Location	Asia	
8 =	Lena	
Length	[2,700 mi. /4,300 km]	
Location	Asia	
10 =	Mekong	
Length	[2,600 mi. /4,200 km]	
Location	Asia	
10 =	Niger	
Length	[2,600 mi. /4,200 km]	
Location	Africa	

riveter /rívvitər/ *n* a worker or machine that joins metal plates together with rivets

riveting /rívviting/ *adj* completely fixing and holding the attention (*informal*) —**rivetingly** *adv*

Rivette /ri vét/, **Jacques** (*b.* 1928) French film director

~~**rivetting**~~ incorrect spelling of **riveting**

riviera /rívvi áirə/ *n* a stretch of coastland where the climate and beaches are good and there are fashionable resort towns

Riviera /rívvi áirə/ coastal region of SE France and NW Italy, bordering the Mediterranean Sea

rivière /rívvi áir/ *n* a necklace made of a string of gemstones that gradually increase in size up to a large centred gem [Mid-19C. Via French, 'river' < Latin *riparius* (see RIPARIAN).]

rivulet /rívvyōlət/ *n* **1** a small stream of flowing water (*literary*) **2** a small quick-flowing stream of something [Late 16C. < ?]

Riyadh /ree aád/ capital of Saudi Arabia, in the east-central part of the country. Population: 2,576,000 (1995 estimate).

riyal /ri aál/ *n* see table at **currency**

⚡ RL *abbr* **1** Rugby League **2** real life (*in e-mails*)

Rls *symbol* rials

rly *abbr* railway

rm *abbr* **1** ream **2** room

RM *abbr* **1** Royal Marines **2** Royal Mail **3** Registered Midwife

RMA abbr 1 Royal Marine Artillery 2 Royal Military Academy (Sandhurst)

rms abbr root mean square

RMS abbr 1 Royal Mail Ship 2 Royal Mail Service

RMT abbr National Union of Rail, Maritime, and Transport Workers

Rn symbol radon

⚡ **RN** abbr 1 right now (in e-mails) 2 Royal Navy

RNA n a nucleic acid containing ribose found in all living cells, essential for protein synthesis. Full form **ribonucleic acid**

RNA polymerase n a polymerase that catalyses the synthesis of RNA

RNAS abbr 1 Royal Naval Air Service(s) 2 Royal Naval Air Station

RNase /aar en ayz, -ayss/ abbr ribonuclease

RNA virus n a virus in which the core of nucleic acid consists of RNA

R'n'B, R & B abbr rhythm and blues

RNIB abbr Royal National Institute for the Blind

RNLI abbr Royal National Lifeboat Institution

RNZAF abbr NZ Royal New Zealand Air Force

RNZN abbr NZ Royal New Zealand Navy

⚡ **ro** abbr 1 recto 2 Romania (in Internet addresses)

roach[1] /rōch/ (plural **roach** or **roaches**) n 1 EUROPEAN FRESHWATER FISH a freshwater fish of the carp family with an olive-green or grey-green back and reddish fins, popular as a game fish. Native to: N Europe. *Rutilus rutilus*. 2 SMALL NORTH AMERICAN FISH a small sunfish resembling a European roach. Native to: E North America. *Hesperoleucus symmetricus*. 3 ROACH AS FOOD the flesh of a roach as food [12C. < Old French *roche*.]

roach[2] /rōch/ n 1 a cockroach (*informal*) 2 the end of a marijuana cigarette after the rest of it has been smoked (*slang*) [Mid-19C. Shortening of COCKROACH.]

roach[3] /rōch/ n the upward curve at the foot of a square sail ■ vt to cut a horse's mane short so that the hairs stand up [Late 18C. < ?]

road /rōd/ n 1 HARD TRACK FOR VEHICLES a long surfaced route broad enough for vehicles to be driven on it 2 COURSE OF ACTION a route or way that heads towards some predictable outcome ○ *the road to financial success* 3 MINE TUNNEL a tunnel used for hauling coal or ore in a mine 4 SHIPPING = **roadstead** (*often plural*) 5 N England, Scotland PATH the route to somewhere (*informal*) ○ *I went the wrong road.* ○ *Get out of my road!* [Old English *rād* 'a riding' < Indo-European, 'ride'.] ◇ **one for the road** an alcoholic drink taken just before leaving a place (*informal*) ◇ **on the road** travelling from place to place ○ *The band have been on the road all summer.*

LITERARY LINK *On the Road*, a novel (1957) by US writer Jack Kerouac. A thinly disguised memoir, it describes a series of cross-country journeys undertaken by a group of people united by their quest for new experiences and disregard for traditional values. It is both an engaging chronicle of the Beat generation and a lyrical evocation of the energy and passion of youth.

roadbed /rōd bed/ n a foundation of soil, cinders, or crushed rock that supports a road or railway

roadblock /rōd blok/ n 1 a temporary barrier used to prevent vehicles from continuing along a road so that they can be checked or their drivers questioned, usually by police or military personnel 2 a hindrance or obstacle to something

road book n a publication for road users showing maps and an index for all the routes in an area

road company n US a group of actors who tour with a show, usually performing a play that has been successful in a large city

road-fund licence n a disc affixed to a motor vehicle to show that its road tax has been paid (*formal*)

road hog n an inconsiderate and dominating motorist, especially one who refuses to let other drivers overtake or go first, or forces them to move out of the way (*informal*)

roadholding /rōd hōlding/ n the ability of a motor vehicle to remain controlled and safely positioned on the road, especially in bad conditions or on sharp corners

roadhouse /rōd howss/ (plural **-houses** /-howziz/) n a hotel or pub located beside a main road (*dated*)

road hump n TRANSP = **speed bump**

roadie /rōdi/ n a handler and setter-up of equipment used by a musical or theatrical group on tour, especially a rock band

roadkill /rōd kil/ n US a bird or animal that has been hit and killed by a motor vehicle on the road

road map n a motorists' map or atlas that shows routes, mileage, and often other features of interest to travellers

road metal n the cinders, crushed rock, and other materials used in the construction of roads

road movie n a film that depicts the adventures of a person or people who leave home and travel from place to place by road, often to find or escape from something

road pricing n a system for controlling road use in which drivers pay a charge to use their cars in specific situations, e.g. at peak periods

road race n a competitive event in which participants race on foot, bicycles, or in motorized vehicles on public roads instead of on a track —**road-race** v —**road racer** n

road racing n a race for motor vehicles or bicycles that takes place on a public road temporarily reserved for the purpose or on a racing course resembling a public road

road rage n feelings of anger experienced by people driving in difficult conditions, often leading to violent behaviour

roadroller /rōd rōlər/ n a machine with wide heavy wheels used to roll flat a new or repaired road

Roadrunner

roadrunner /rōd runnər/ n a swift-running bird of the cuckoo family with streaked brown-and-white plumage, a head crest, small round wings, and a long tail. Native to: deserts of W United States and Mexico. *Geococcyx californianus*.

road show n 1 TRAVELLING RADIO BROADCAST a live open-air radio show that travels to a series of locations, usually during the summer months 2 TRAVELLING PROMOTIONAL GROUP a group of people who travel from place to place in order to broadcast, publicize, or promote something, or to conduct a political campaign 3 PERFORMANCE BY TRAVELLING ACTORS a show staged by a touring company of entertainers, or the company performing such a show

roadside /rōd sīd/ n an area along or bordering a road

road sign n a sign by the side of the road giving directions or instructions

roadstead /rōd sted/ n a partly sheltered area for anchored vessels

roadster /rōdstər/ n 1 US a small open-topped car with a single seat in front and often with an additional folding seat (**rumble seat**) at the back (*dated*) 2 formerly, a sturdy horse for riding on a road

road test n 1 TEST OF VEHICLE OR TYRE PERFORMANCE a test of a motor vehicle or tyre under actual operating conditions 2 US PRACTICAL DRIVING TEST an official test on the road to determine whether a driver of a motor vehicle is competent to be issued a licence to drive 3 TEST OF HOW WELL SOMETHING WORKS a series of tests carried out on a new product or design to determine how well it performs during actual use —**road-test** vt

road-train n Aus a truck that pulls several large connected trailers, often to transport livestock or bulk goods over long distances

roadway /rōd way/ n the main part of a road area meant to be driven on

roadwork /rōd wurk/ n 1 US TRANSP = **roadworks** 2 a form of exercise consisting of long runs on roads, chiefly used as part of training for boxers

roadworks /rōd wurks/ n construction or repair work being carried out on a section of public road, or on the utilities located beneath it, creating a temporary obstruction for road users. US term **roadwork** n. 1

roadworthy /rōd wurthi/ adj in a safe condition to be driven on public roads [Early 19C. After 'seaworthy'.] —**roadworthiness** n

roam /rōm/ vti to move about a large area, especially without any particular purpose or definite destination ■ n an act of roaming [14C. < ?] —**roamer** n —**roaming** adj

roan /rōn/ adj WITH LIGHT SPECKLES IN DARK COAT having a reddish-brown, brown, or black coat speckled with white or grey ■ n 1 ROAN HORSE an animal, especially a horse, with a roan coat 2 ROAN COLOUR the colour of a roan animal 3 FINE-GRAINED LEATHER a soft pliable kind of sheepskin leather used in bookbinding [Early 16C. Via French < Old Spanish *roano*.]

Roanoke /rō ə nōk/ city in SW Virginia. Population: 96,397 (1990).

roar /rawr/ v 1 vi GROWL LOUDLY to make a loud natural growling noise, e.g. as a lion makes 2 vti SHOUT LOUDLY to make a loud shouting noise, or utter something with a loud shouting noise, especially in anger 3 vi LAUGH LOUDLY to give a loud, prolonged, and unrestrained laugh 4 vi BURN NOISILY to burn noisily while giving off a lot of heat ○ *a roaring fire* 5 vi CRASH LOUDLY to make a loud crashing or blowing noise, e.g. as wind, waves, and other natural phenomena do 6 vi BREATHE NOISILY to breathe with difficulty, making a rasping or wheezing noise, as some diseased horses do 7 vi MOVE NOISILY to move quickly and with a loud mechanical noise, especially a harsh or droning noise 8 vt BECOME BY ROARING to cause the voice to be in a particular condition through shouting, cheering, or making some other loud vocal noise ○ *roared themselves hoarse* ■ n 1 LOUD SHOUT a loud, often prolonged, shout or cry, especially one made by a person or crowd that is cheering, angry, or upset 2 LOUD LAUGH a loud, prolonged, and unrestrained laugh 3 LOUD GROWL a loud growling noise made by a large animal, especially a lion 4 NOISE OF SOMETHING BURNING a loud continuous noise made by something burning intensely 5 CRASHING NOISE a loud crashing or blowing noise made by waves, the wind, or some other natural phenomenon 6 LOUD MECHANICAL NOISE a loud, harsh or droning mechanical noise made by something as it moves or functions [Old English *rārian*] —**roarer** n

roaring /rawring/ adj VERY GREAT extreme, or extremely great or good ○ *a roaring success* ■ n BREATHING DIFFICULTIES IN HORSES noisy breathing in horses, especially when caused by loss of function of the recurrent laryngeal nerve ■ adv EXCEEDINGLY to an extreme degree ○ *roaring drunk* —**roaringly** adv ◇ **do a roaring trade** vi to sell a product easily and rapidly (*informal*) ○ *doing a roaring trade in computer games*

Roaring Forties npl the area of the ocean in the southern hemisphere lying between 40° and 50° latitude that is noted for its strong winds, storms, and difficult sailing conditions

Roaring Twenties npl the 1920s, especially when thought of as being a time of exuberance, hedonism, and prosperity in contrast to the hardship of World War I

roast /rōst/ v 1 vti COOK IN OVEN to cook something, especially meat or vegetables, by dry heat, usually in an oven or over an open fire, or be cooked in this way 2 vti PREPARE BY DRYING OR BROWNING to heat something until it is dry or brown, especially coffee beans or nuts, as part of a manufacturing process, or be heated in this way 3 vt HEAT ORE IN FURNACE to heat ore in a furnace without fusing in order to concentrate, dehydrate, or purify it or to cause a chemical change that will facilitate smelting 4 vti OVERHEAT to become too warm or make something or somebody too warm at a source of heat such as the sun or a fire ○ *roast in front of the log fire* 5 vt DISPARAGE to criticize somebody or something harshly (*informal*) 6 vt US MOCK to make fun of somebody (*informal*) ■ n 1 OVEN-COOKED MEAT something such as a piece of meat that is suitable for roasting, or that has been roasted 2 US OPEN-AIR MEAL an outside gathering or party with food cooked on open fires 3 US CELEBRATION a gathering, party, or other celebration where the guest of honour is the subject of speeches that alternate between praise and humorous criticism ■ *adj* **OVEN-COOKED** cooked by dry heat, usually in an oven or over an open fire [13C. < Old French *rostir* < Germanic.]

roaster /rṓstər/ *n* 1 **EQUIPMENT FOR ROASTING FOOD** a pan, dish, or oven for roasting food in 2 **SOMEBODY WHO ROASTS** a person who roasts something 3 **FOOD FOR ROASTING** an item of food, especially a chicken, that is suitable for roasting

roasting /rṓsting/ *adj* **VERY HOT** feeling or causing somebody to feel very hot (*informal*) ■ *n* **HARSH CRITICISM** a harsh criticism of somebody (*informal*) ■ *adv* **EXTREMELY** to a high degree of temperature (*informal*) ○ *roasting hot*

rob /rob/ (**robs, robbing, robbed**) *v* 1 *vt* **DEPRIVE SOMEBODY ILLEGALLY** to take something illegally from a person or place, especially by using force, threats, or violence 2 *vt* **DEPRIVE SOMEBODY UNFAIRLY** to deprive somebody of something unfairly or harmfully ○ *The wet weather robbed her of her holiday.* 3 *vi* **COMMIT ROBBERY** to commit robbery, especially habitually 4 *vt* **STEAL** to steal something (*nonstandard*) ○ *They broke in and robbed the TV and video.* [12C. < Old French *rober* < Germanic.]

robalo /róbbəlō, rṓ-/ (*plural* **-los** *or* **-lo**) *n* a fish belonging to a large diverse family that ranges from large ocean fish such as the snook to the tiny glass fish kept in aquariums. Family: Centropomidae. [Late 19C. < Spanish *robalo*, probably < *lobo* 'wolf' < Latin *lupus*.]

roband /róbbənd, rṓ-/, **robbin** /róbbin/ *n* a piece of rope used to attach a sail to a spar [15C. Probably < Dutch *raband* < *ra* 'sailyard' + *band* 'band'.]

Robbe-Grillet /rob greé ay/, **Alain** (*b.* 1922) French novelist and screenwriter

robber /róbbər/ *n* a committer of robbery

robber baron *n* 1 in the United States, a wealthy industrialist or businessman of the late 19th century who used unscrupulous business practices 2 a land-holding nobleman who, in feudal Europe, habitually stole from people travelling through his lands

robber fly *n* a predatory fly that catches other insects in its long bristly legs and pierces them with its sharp mouthparts. Family: Leptidae.

robbery /róbbəri/ (*plural* **-ies**) *n* the act or an instance of illegally taking something that belongs to somebody else, especially by using force, threats, or violence

robbin *n* SAILING = **roband**

robe /rōb/ *n* 1 **CEREMONIAL DRESS** a long loose garment worn on ceremonial occasions or as a symbol of authority, especially by the peerage, judiciary, academics, and members of the clergy (*often plural*) 2 **DRESSING GOWN OR BATHROBE** a loose garment for wear at home, especially a dressing gown or bathrobe 3 **WOMAN'S OUTER DRESS** in Europe in the 17th and 18th centuries, a woman's outer dress, especially a heavy brocade or ornately decorated one worn over a plainer one ■ *vti* (**robes, robing, robed**) **DRESS IN ROBE** to dress somebody in a robe, or be dressed in a robe [13C. < Old French, '(clothes taken as) booty, spoil' < Germanic.]

robe de chambre /rób də shaámbrə, rṓb-/ (*plural* **robes de chambre** /rób-, rṓb-/) *n* CLOTHING = **dressing gown** [Mid-18C. < French, 'chamber robe, dressing gown'.]

Robert I /róbbərt/ (1274–1329) king of Scotland (1306–29). Known as **Robert the Bruce**

Robert II (1316–90) king of Scotland (1371–90)

Robert III (1337–1406) king of Scotland (1390–1406)

Roberts /róbbərts/, **Tom** (1856–1931) British-born Australian painter. Full name **Thomas William Roberts**

Robertson /róbbərts'n/, **George** (1860–1933) British-born Australian publisher

Robeson /rṓbsən/, **Paul** (1898–1976) US singer and actor

Robespierre /rṓbz pyair/, **Maximilien** (1758–94) French lawyer and revolutionary

Robey /rṓbi/, **Sir George** (1869–1954) British comedian. Born **George Edward Wade**. Known as **the Prime Minister of Mirth**

robin /róbbin/ *n* 1 **EUROPEAN SONGBIRD** a small thrush, the adult male of which has a reddish-orange breast and head. Native to: Europe. *Erithacus rubercula.* 2 **LARGE NORTH AMERICAN THRUSH** a large thrush with a rust-coloured breast and dark grey or brown upper parts. Native to: North America. *Turdus migratorius.* 3 **BIRD WITH REDDISH BREAST LIKE ROBIN** a bird with a reddish breast that is similar to the European or North American robin, especially one of numerous Australian

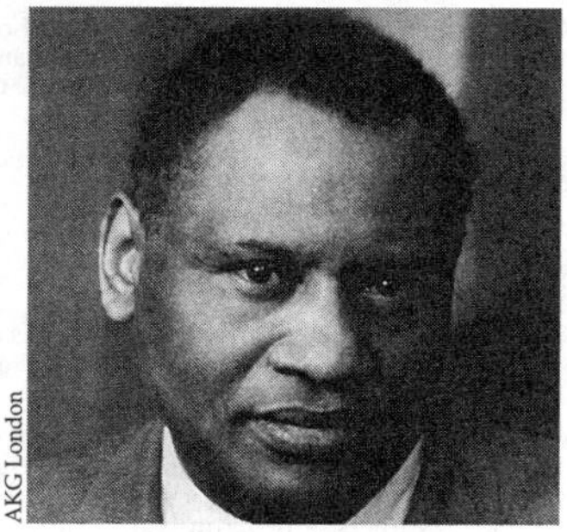

AKG London

Paul Robeson

species [Mid-16C. Shortening of ROBIN REDBREAST, after *Robin*, diminutive of *Robert*.]

Robin Goodfellow /róbbin go͝od fellō/ *n* MYTHOL = **Puck**[1]

robing room *n* a room set aside, e.g. in a court, church, parliament, or other building, for putting on ceremonial or official robes

robin redbreast *n* = **robin** *n.* 1, **robin** *n.* 2

robin's-egg blue *n* a pale greenish-blue colour — **robin's egg blue** *adj*

Robinson /róbbinss'n/, **Edward G.** (1893–1973) Romanian-born US actor. Born **Emmanuel Goldenberg**

Robinson, Jackie (1919–72) US baseball player and civil rights activist. Full name **Jack Roosevelt Robinson**

Robinson, Mary (*b.* 1944) Irish lawyer and stateswoman and president of Ireland (1990–97). Born **Mary Bourke**

Robinson, Sugar Ray (1921–89) US boxer. Born **Walker Smith**

Robinson, William Heath (1872–1944) British cartoonist

roble /rṓ blay/ *n* an oak with a short trunk, leathery leaves, and thin tapering acorns. Native to: California. *Quercus lobata.* [Mid-19C. Via Spanish and Portuguese < Latin *robur* 'oak tree, hardness, strength'.]

roborant /rṓbərənt, róbbə-/ *adj* describes medications or other remedies that have the effect of restoring somebody's strength or vigour ■ *n* a medication or other remedy that restores strength or vigour [Mid-17C. < Latin *roborant-*, present participle of *roborare* 'strengthen' < *robur* 'oak tree, hardness, strength'.]

robot /rṓ bot/ *n* 1 **MECHANICAL DEVICE PROGRAMMED TO PERFORM TASKS** any machine that can be programmed to carry out instructions and perform particular duties, especially one that can take over tasks normally done by people 2 **IMAGINARY MACHINE LIKE HUMAN** a machine that resembles a human in appearance and can function like a human, especially in science fiction 3 **PERSON LIKE MACHINE** a person who works or behaves mechanically and emotionlessly 4 *S Africa* **TRAFFIC LIGHT** a set of automatic traffic lights (*informal*) [Early 20C. Via German < Czech < *robota* 'forced labour'; coined by Karel Čapek in his play *R.U.R.* (Rossum's Universal Robots) (1920).] —**robotic** /rō bóttik/ *adj* —**robotically** /-tikli/ *adv* —**robotism** /rṓ botizəm/ *n* —**robotistic** /rṓ bo tístik/ *adj* —**robot-like** /rṓ bot līk/ *adj* —**robotry** /rṓ botri/ *n*

robot dancing, **robotic dancing** *n* a dance of the 1980s that has stiff jerky body movements

robotics /rō bóttiks/ *n* 1 the science and technology relating to computer-controlled mechanical devices, e.g. the automated tools commonly found on automobile assembly lines (+ *singular verb*) 2 DANCE = **robot dancing**

robotize /rṓ bo tīz/ (**-izes, -izing, -ized**), **robotise** (**-ises, -ising, -ised**) *vt* 1 to introduce automation into something, especially a factory or factory process 2 to make somebody act in an automated and unemotional or insensitive fashion —**robotization** /rṓ bo tī záysh'n, -bə-/ *n*

Rob Roy /rób róy/ (1671–1734) Scottish brigand. Born **Robert MacGregor**

Robson /róbss'n/, **Dame Flora** (1902–84) British actor

ϟ **robust** /rō búst/ *adj* 1 **STRONG AND HEALTHY** strong, healthy, and hardy in constitution 2 **STRONGLY CONSTRUCTED** built, constructed, or designed to be sturdy, durable, or hard-wearing 3 **NEEDING PHYSICAL STRENGTH** involving or requiring great physical strength and stamina ○ *Rugby is a robust sport.* 4 **FULL-FLAVOURED** rich, strong-tasting, and full-bodied 5 **DETERMINED** characterized by firmness and determination and a refusal to make concessions 6 **STRAIGHTFORWARD** showing clear thought and common sense 7 **BLUNT OR CRUDE** rough and direct or crude 8 **CAPABLE OF RECOVERY** describes a computer program or system that is able to recover from unexpected conditions during operation ○ *a robust operating system* [Mid-16C. < Latin *robustus* 'oaken, hard, strong' < *robur* 'oak tree, hardness, strength'.] —**robustly** *adv* —**robustness** *n*

robusta /rō bústə/ *n* 1 a widely cultivated species of coffee bush. Native to: west-central Africa. *Coffea canephora.* 2 beans from the robusta coffee plant, or coffee made from them [Early 20C. < Latin, feminine of *robustus* 'robust'.]

roc /rok/ *n* in Arabian legend, a large bird of prey strong enough to lift and fly with an elephant in its talons [Late 16C. Via Arabic *rukk* < Persian *ruk*.]

rocaille /ro kī́, rō kī́/ *n* decorative rococo stonework or shellwork, especially scrollwork [Mid-19C. < French, 'pebble work, rock work' < *roc* 'rock'.]

rocambole /rókəm bōl/ *n* a plant related to garlic sometimes used to flavour food. Native to: Europe, Asia. *Allium scorodoprasum.* [Late 17C. Via French < German *Rockenbolle* 'distaff bulb' (from its shape) < *Rocken* 'distaff' + *Bolle* 'bulb'.]

Rochdale /róch dayl/ town in NW England. Population: 207,100 (1994).

Roche /rōch/, **Tony** (*b.* 1945) Australian tennis player. Full name **Anthony Roche**

Roche limit /rósh-/ *n* the closest a satellite can come to the astronomical object it is orbiting before being destroyed by tidal forces generated by gravitational attraction [Late 19C. After Édouard *Roche* (1820–83), French astronomer.]

Rochelle salt /ro shél-/ *n* $KNaC_4H_4O_6$ a white powder. Use: mild laxative, food preservative, in electronics. [Mid-18C. After *La Rochelle*, France.]

roche moutonnée /rósh moo tónnay/ (*plural* **roches moutonnées** /rósh moo tónnay/) *n* an elongated mound of bare rock, modified by glacial erosion, that is smooth and striated on one side and shattered rubble on the other [Mid-19C. < French, 'fleecy rock' (that is, rounded like a sheep's back).]

Rochester /róchistər/ 1 city in SE England. Population: 145,000 (1994). 2 city in W New York State. Population: 216,887 (1998 estimate).

rochet /róchit/ *n* a white linen garment, similar to a surplice but with tight-fitting sleeves, worn on ceremonial occasions by bishops and other high-ranking members of the clergy [14C. < Old French, 'little mantle' < *roc* 'mantle' < Germanic.]

rock[1] /rok/ *n* 1 **HARD MINERAL AGGREGATE** any consolidated material, such as granite or limestone, consisting of more than one mineral and, sometimes, organic material 2 **rock, Rock PROJECTING MASS OF ROCK** a large mass of mineral material, especially an isolated or projecting one (*often in placenames*) ○ *Ayres Rock* 3 **BOULDER** a large stone or boulder 4 **SOMEBODY DEPENDABLE** a stable, dependable, or supportive person or thing, especially in times of trouble 5 **HARD SWEET** a hard, often brightly coloured, sweet made from boiled sugar, usually in the form of a long cylindrical stick and sometimes with the name of a seaside resort through it ○ *a stick of Blackpool rock* 6 **DIAMOND** a large gemstone, especially a diamond (*informal*) 7 **CRACK COCAINE** crack cocaine, or a small piece of crack cocaine (*slang*) 8 ZOOL = **rockfish** *n.* 2 ■ **rocks** *npl* 1 *US* **MONEY** money (*informal*) 2 **OFFENSIVE TERM** an offensive term for the testicles (*slang*) [14C. Via Old French *ro(c)que*.] ◇ **between a rock and a hard place** *US* faced with a choice between two equally unpleasant or undesirable alternatives ◇ **get your rocks off** 1 an offensive phrase meaning to have an orgasm (*slang; refers to men*) 2 an offensive phrase meaning to get a great deal of pleasure or excitement from some activity (*slang*) ◇ **on the rocks** 1 in great difficulties and heading for ruin or disaster, especially financially or emotionally (*informal*) 2 served with ice cubes

rock[2] /rok/ *v* 1 *vti* **SWAY TO AND FRO** to swing or sway, or cause something or somebody to swing or sway, backwards and forwards or from side to side, especially with a slow gentle rhythm 2 *vti* **SHAKE OR TREMBLE** to move or shake, or cause somebody or something to move or shake, violently ○ *An earth tremor rocked the city.* 3 *vt* **SHOCK** to disturb, upset, or shock somebody (*informal*) ○ *The ruling rocked the legal profession.* 4 *vi* **PLAY OR DANCE TO ROCK MUSIC** to sing, play, or dance to music, especially to rock music (*informal*) **5** *vi* **BE FILLED WITH ROCK MUSIC** to contain people performing or enjoying music, especially rock music (*informal*) ○ *The joint was really rocking.* **6** *vi* **HAVE STRONG BEAT** to have or play music with a strong solid beat (*informal*) **7** *vi* **TRAVEL** to advance steadily or quickly (*informal*) ○ *rocking along at 60 miles an hour* **8** *vti* **WASH ORE IN CRADLE** to wash gold-bearing or gem-bearing sands or gravel in a pivoting cradle (**rocker**) **9** *vt* **ROUGHEN COPPER PLATE** in engraving a mezzotint, to prepare a copper plate with a tool with a short, curved, jagged blade (**rocker**) ■ *n* **1 ACT OF ROCKING** an act or the process of rocking somebody or something **2 TYPE OF POP MUSIC** a style of pop music, derived from rock and roll, usually played on electric or electronic instruments and equipment [Old English *roccian*, probably < Germanic 'move']

Rock /rok/ *n* the Rock of Gibraltar (*informal*)

rockabilly /rókə billi/ *n* a style of pop music, originating in the late 1950s, that combines elements of rock and roll with elements of country music [Mid-20C. Blend of ROCK AND ROLL + HILLBILLY.]

rockabye /rókə bī/, **rockaby** *interj* used to encourage a baby or child to go to sleep [Early 19C. Blend of ROCK² + LULLABY.]

Rockall /rók awl/ rocky islet of disputed ownership in the N Atlantic Ocean, west of the Outer Hebrides. Area: 743 sq. m./8,000 sq. ft.

rock and roll /rókən rṓl/, **rock'n'roll** *n* **1** pop music derived from blues music that has heavily stressed beats and is played on electric instruments **2** dancing done to rock and roll music —**rock and roller** *n*

rock bass /rók bass/ *n* a sunfish with a dark olive back, white undersides, and red eyes. Native to: central and E North America. *Ambloplites rupestris.*

rock bottom *n* the lowest level or price possible —**rock-bottom** *adj*

rockbound /rók bownd/ *adj* **1** entirely, or almost entirely, surrounded by rocks **2** being so rocky as to be inaccessible

rock brake *n* a fern that has compound fronds and grows on rocky ground. Genus: *Crytogramma.*

rock cake, rock bun *n* a small individual cake containing dried fruit and sometimes spices and candied peel [< its lumpy, uneven, crusty surface]

rock candy *n US* a hard sweet consisting of dissolved sugar that is cooled to form large crystals

rock climb *n* **1** an act or instance of scaling a rock face, usually using ropes and other specialized equipment **2** the route followed on a rock climb

rock climbing *n* the activity of scaling rock faces, usually using ropes and other specialized equipment and often in a team —**rock-climb** *vi* —**rock-climber** *n*

rock crab *n* a fast-moving crab. Native to: rocky coastal areas of North America. Genus: *Cancer.*

rock crystal *n* a colourless transparent variety of quartz. Use: electronic and optical instruments.

rock dove *n* a bluish-grey dove from which domestic and wild pigeons are descended. Native to: Europe, Asia. *Columba livia.*

Rockefeller /rókə fellər/, **John D.** (1839–1937) US industrialist and philanthropist

rock elm *n* a deciduous tree with corky branches. Native to: E North America. *Ulmus thomasii.*

rocker /rókər/ *n* **1 ROCKING DEVICE** a device that functions by way of a rocking movement **2 FURNITURE STAND** an upwardly curved piece of wood or metal that allows something such as a rocking chair or baby's cradle to move backwards and forwards or from side to side **3** FURNITURE = **rocking chair 4** HOUSEHOLD = **rocker switch 5** MIN EXTRACT = **cradle** *n.* 8 **6 ENGRAVER'S TOOL** a tool with a short, curved, jagged blade used in the engraving of mezzotints for roughening the copper plates **7 TYPE OF ICE SKATE** an ice skate with a curved blade, or the curved blade itself (*often plural*) **8 ROCK MUSICIAN** a rock singer or musician (*informal*) **9 ROCK FAN** a fan of rock music or rock and roll (*informal*) **10 MEMBER OF 60S YOUTH GROUP** a follower of a youth group in 1960s Britain who rode motorcycles, liked rock and roll, wore leather jackets, and sometimes fought with smart youths on motor scooters (**mods**) ◇ **off one's rocker** an offensive term that deliberately insults somebody's state of mental balance

rocker arm *n* a pivoted lever, e.g. in an internal-combustion engine, that transmits motion from a cam or push rod at one end to open and close a valve at the other

rocker cam *n* a cam that oscillates or rocks but does not revolve

rocker panel *n* on a passenger vehicle, the exterior panel located below the doorsill of the passenger compartment

rocker switch *n* a switch on a central pivot, especially one that operates between an 'on' and 'off' position on an electrical appliance

rockery /rókəri/ (*plural* **-ies**) *n* a garden or area of a garden that has large stones in it with plants, especially low-growing colourful hardy ones such as edelweiss, gentian, and heathers growing in between them. US term **rock garden** *n.*

rocket¹ /rókit/ *n* **1 SPACE VEHICLE** a device or vehicle designed for space travel, propelled by a device that carries both fuel and oxidizer and produces thrust by expelling expanding hot gases (**rocket engine**) **2** AEROSP = **rocket engine 3 ROCKET-PROPELLED WEAPON** a weapon consisting of an explosive, nuclear, or other warhead that is propelled by a rocket engine **4 SELF-PROPELLED FIREWORK OR FLARE** a firework, flare, or similar device, usually cylindrical in shape, containing combustible propellants **5 TELLING OFF** a stern reprimand or rebuke (*informal*) ■ *v* **1** *vi* **MOVE FAST** to move or begin to move at great speed **2** *vti* **ATTAIN QUICKLY** to get to, or cause somebody or something to get to, a particular condition or position very quickly (*informal*) **3** *vi* **INCREASE QUICKLY** to increase very quickly and dramatically (*informal*) **4** *vt* **POWER USING ROCKET ENGINE** to send something, especially a spacecraft, warhead, or missile, into the air or atmosphere by means of a rocket engine or rocket engines **5** *vt* **BOMBARD WITH ROCKET** to fire a rocket at a target **6** *vi* **FLY UP QUICKLY** to fly up vertically at speed (*refers to game birds*) [Early 17C. < Italian *rocchetta* 'small distaff' (from its shape) < *rocca* 'distaff' < Germanic.]

rocket² /rókit/ *n* **1** a Mediterranean plant with peppery leaves that are eaten cooked or raw in salads. *Eruca vesicaria.* US term **arugula 2** a fast-growing plant with pale yellow flowers, typically growing on waste ground. Genus: *Sisymbrium.* **3** PLANTS = **dame's violet 4** PLANTS = **sea rocket** [Early 16C. Via French *roquette* < Italian *ruchetta* 'small ruca' (a cabbage) < Latin *eruca* 'caterpillar, cole'.]

rocketeer /róki teer/ *n* a scientist or engineer who designs space rockets

rocket engine *n* a device that carries both fuel and oxidizer that it burns in a combustion chamber, producing thrust by expelling the expanding hot gases through a nozzle

rocket plane *n* an aircraft that is designed to carry and launch rockets, missiles, or warheads

rocketry /rókitri/ *n* the science and technology of the design, construction, operation, flying, and maintenance of rockets

rocket science *n* a complex and intellectually demanding activity (*informal*) ○ *Using the Internet isn't exactly rocket science.* [Late 20C. < the idea that rocket science is the province of a few highly qualified specialists.]

rocket scientist *n* (*informal*) **1** an extremely intelligent person ○ *It doesn't take a rocket scientist to figure that one out!* **2** somebody highly skilled in quantitative analysis who studies the capital markets

rocket sled *n* a rocket-propelled vehicle that runs on a rail or rails and can be accelerated rapidly to high speeds, used in aeronautical applications such as crash and G-force tolerance testing

rocketsonde /rókit sond/ *n* an instrument transported by rocket to the upper atmosphere to carry out weather observations

rockfall /rók fawl/ *n* **1** a collection or mass of fallen rocks **2** an avalanche of falling rocks

rockfish /rók fish/ (*plural* **-fish** *or* **-fishes**) *n* **1** a fish that lives among rocks. Native to: Pacific Ocean. **2** the flesh of a dogfish or catfish as food

rock flour *n* fine powdery rock produced by grinding or abrasion, e.g. by the movement of a glacier

Rockford /rókfərd/ city in N Illinois. Population: 143,531 (1996).

rock garden *n US* GARDENING = **rockery**

Rockhampton /rok hámptən/ city in E Queensland, Australia. Population: 57,770 (1996).

rockhopper /rók hopər/ *n* a small penguin with a stout bill and a yellow crest. Native to: Antarctica, New Zealand, Falkland Islands. *Eudyptes crestatus.*

rock hound *n US* (*informal*) **1** a collector of rocks and minerals **2** a geologist —**rockhounding** *n*

Rockies /rókiz/ = **Rocky Mountains**

rocking chair *n* a chair that is set on a pair of curved pieces of wood so that somebody sitting in it can be rocked backwards and forwards

Rockingham /rókingəm/ town in SW Western Australia. Population: 49,917 (1996).

Rockingham, Charles Watson-Wentworth, 2nd Marquess (1730–82) British statesman

rocking horse *n* a small model horse fitted with reins and a saddle and set on a pair of rockers on which a child can sit and rock backwards and forwards

rocking stone *n* a large stone or boulder that is so finely balanced, e.g. on another stone or stones, that it can be made to rock backwards and forwards with little effort

rockling /rókling/ (*plural* **-lings** *or* **-ling**) *n* a small fish of the cod family. Native to: N Atlantic. Family: Gadidae.

rock lobster *n* MARINE BIOL = **spiny lobster**

rock mechanics *n* the study of the physical properties of rocks, e.g. density, elasticity, and strength, especially with relation to their behaviour in tunnels and mines and when subjected to environmental forces (+ *singular verb*)

rock'n'roll *n, vi* MUSIC, DANCE = **rock and roll**

rock oil *n* INDUST = **petroleum**

rock pigeon *n* BIRDS = **rock dove**

rock plant *n* a plant that has adapted to living on rocks or rocky ground

rockrose /rók rōz/ *n* a woody shrub or plant grown for its small light-yellow or reddish flowers that are shaped like roses. Genera: *Cistus* and *Helianthemum.*

rock salmon *n* ZOOL = **rockfish** *n.* 2

rock salt *n* MINERALS = **halite**

rockslide /rók slīd/ *n* **1** a collection or mass of rocks that have slipped downwards **2** an avalanche of rocks as a result of surface movement

rock snake *n* a large snake. Native to: Australia, Asia. Genus: *Liasis.*

rock-solid *adj* **1** firm and unshakable **2** extremely hard and unlikely to break

rock steady *n* Jamaican reggae of the early 1960s, popular as dance music

rock-steady *adj* firm, unshaking, and calm

rockumentary /rókyoo méntəri/ (*plural* **-ries**) *n* a film documentary about rock music in general or a particular rock band or musician, containing film footage of relevant performances (*informal*) [Late 20C. Blend of ROCK AND ROLL + DOCUMENTARY.]

Rockwell /rókwəl/, **Norman** (1894–1978) US illustrator

rock wool *n* INDUST = **mineral wool**

rockwork /rók wurk/ *n* artificial or decorative stonework designed to resemble the irregularity of natural rocks

rock wren *n* a grey wren commonly found in rocky areas. Native to: W North America. *Salpinctes obsoletus.*

rocky¹ /róki/ (**-ier, -iest**) *adj* **1 WITH ROCKS** consisting of or covered with rocks ○ *rocky terrain* **2 HARD** resembling rock in its hardness or firmness **3 UNEMOTIONAL** unyielding, unwavering, or lacking in human emotions —**rockiness** *n*

rocky² /róki/ (**-ier, -iest**) *adj* **1 DIFFICULT** characterized by difficulties, obstacles, or troubles ○ *a rocky start* ○ *a rocky reception* **2 UNSTEADY** wobbly and unsteady **3 UNWELL** unwell, especially feeling sick or dizzy (*informal*) —**rockily** *adv* —**rockiness** *n*

Rocky Mountain goat /róki mówntin-/ *n* ZOOL = **mountain goat**

Rocky Mountains major mountain system of W North America, extending more than 4,800 km/3,000 mi. from N Alaska to New Mexico. Highest peak: Mount Elbert 4,399 m/14,433 ft.

Rocky Mountain spotted fever *n* an acute infectious disease transmitted by the bite of ticks infected with the microorganism *Rickettsia rickettsi* [Because first reported in the area of the ROCKY MOUNTAINS]

~~**rococco**~~ incorrect spelling of **rococo**

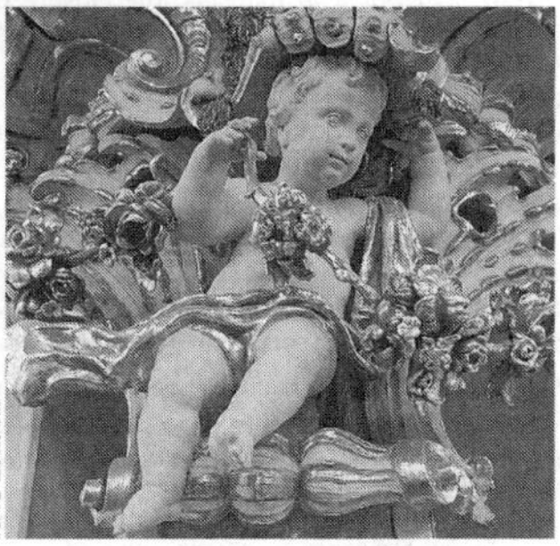

Rococo: Detail of stucco at Wies church, Bavaria, Germany (1745–54)

rococo /rə kṓkō/ *n* **1 rococo, Rococo ORNATE 18C ART STYLE** a style of architecture and the decorative arts characterized by intricate ornamentation that was popular throughout Europe in the early 18th century **2 rococo, Rococo ORNATE 18C MUSIC STYLE** a style of music characterized by the use of ornamentation and embellishment that was popular in Europe in the 18th century **3 ORNATE STYLE** any excessively ornate or fancy style ■ *adj* **1 rococo, Rococo IN STYLE OF ROCOCO** belonging to, relating to, or in the style of 18th-century rococo **2 ORNATE** excessively ornate or fancy [Mid-19C. < French, a fanciful alteration of ROCAILLE.]

QUICK FACTS ON... **ROCOCO**

Key dates: 1715–74
Key locations: France, Germany, Austria
Key elements: vitality, hedonism; depiction of pleasure, pastoral settings, pastel colours (painting); asymmetry, organic forms, arabesques and curves, tall windows, mirrors (architecture)
Key figures: Antoine Watteau, François Boucher, Jean-Honoré Fragonard, Giovanni Batista Tiepolo, Thomas Gainsborough (painting); Pierre Lepautre, François de Cuvilliés, Balthasar Neumann (architecture)
Key works: *The Embarkation for the Island of Cythera* (Watteau) 1717, *The Triumph of Venus* (Boucher) 1740, *The Swing* (Fragonard) 1766, Hôtel de Soubise, Paris (Gabriel Germain Boffrant, René Alexis Delamaire and others, begun 1732), Amalienburg, Munich (Cuvilliés, 1734–39)
Key developments: development of pastel colours; porcelain manufacturing; Regency style

rod /rod/ *n* **1 THIN STICK** a narrow, usually cylindrical, length of wood, metal, plastic, or other material **2** FISHING = **fishing rod 3 WHIPPING STICK** a stick, or bundle of sticks tied together, used for whipping somebody as a punishment **4 SURVEYING POLE** a graduated pole used by surveyors for sighting with a levelling instrument to determine elevation differences **5 STAFF OF OFFICE** a staff, especially one that indicates somebody's standing, office, authority, or power **6 POWER WIELDED** tyrannical or oppressive power **7 PLANT STEM** a straight stem or shoot that has been cut from, or that is growing on, a woody plant **8 BOARD MARKED WITH FULL-SCALE JOINERY PATTERN** a board on which the dimensions of a joinery assembly, e.g. a window or door frame, are marked in full scale **9 RECEPTOR CELL IN EYE** a rod-shaped receptor in the retina of the eye that is sensitive to dim light but not colour **10 BACTERIUM** a rod-shaped bacterium **11** *US* **METAL BAR SUPPORTING RAILWAY CARRIAGE** one of the metal bars that form the framework of the underside of a railway carriage, especially one on a goods carriage (*often plural*) **12 UNIT OF LENGTH** a unit of length equal to 5.03 m/$5\frac{1}{2}$ yd, now largely obsolete **13 UNIT OF AREA** a unit of area equal to 25.3 m^2/$30\frac{1}{4}$ sq. yd, now largely obsolete **14 OFFENSIVE TERM** an offensive term for a penis (*slang*) **15 PISTOL** a gun, especially a pistol (*slang*) ■ *vt* (**rods, rodding, rodded**) **CLEAR SOMETHING OUT USING ROD** to use a rod to clear an obstruction from something [Old English *rodd* 'pole, rod'] —**rodless** *adj* —**rodlike** *adj*

Rodchenko /rod chénkō/, **Aleksandr** (1891–1956) Russian painter, designer, and photographer

rode[1] past tense of **ride**

rode[2] /rōd/ *n* a rope or chain, especially one attached to an anchor [Early17C. < ?]

rode[3] /rōd/ (**rodes, roding, roded**) *vi* **1** to fly to roost at nightfall (*refers to wildfowl*) **2** to fly at nightfall as a mating display (*refers to male woodcock*) [Mid-18C. < ?] —**roding** *n*

rodent /rṓd'nt/ *n* a small mammal such as a mouse, rat, squirrel, or marmot with large gnawing incisor teeth that continue growing throughout the animal's life. Order: Rodentia. [Mid-19C. < modern Latin *Rodentia* < Latin *rodent-*, present participle of *rodere* 'gnaw'.]

rodenticide /rō dénti sīd/ *n* a substance designed to kill rodents, especially rats and mice

rodent ulcer *n* a persistent, usually cancerous ulcer of the skin, especially of the face [*Rodent* literally 'gnawing' (see RODENT)]

rodeo /rō dáy ō, rṓdi-/ (*plural* **-os**) *n* **1 COMPETITION IN COWBOY SKILLS** a competition or display of lassoing, riding unbroken horses, calf-roping, and cattle-wrestling **2 MOTORCYCLING COMPETITION** a competition or display of motorcycle riding that often includes stunts **3 CATTLE ROUND-UP** an occasion when cattle are rounded up, especially so that they can be branded, counted, or have their health checked **4 CATTLE PEN** a pen for rounded-up cattle [Mid-19C. < Spanish, 'cattle ring' < *rodear* 'go round, surround' < Latin *rotare* (see ROTATE).]

Rodgers /rójjərz/, **Richard** (1902–79) US composer

Rodin /rō dáN/, **Auguste** (1840–1917) French sculptor

rodman /ródmən, -man/ (*plural* **-men** /-mən, -men/) *n US* BUILDING = **staffman**

rodomontade /róddə mon táyd, -taád/ *n* **BOASTFULNESS** pretentious, self-important, or self-indulgent boasting, speech, or behaviour (*literary*) ■ *vi* (**-tades, -tading, -taded**) **BOAST** to boast, speak, or behave in a pretentious, self-important, or self-indulgent way (*literary*) ■ *adj* **BOASTFUL** boastful in a pretentious, self-important, or self-indulgent way (*literary*) [Early 17C. Via French < obsolete Italian *rodomontada* < *rodomonte* 'braggart' < *Rodomonte*, a boastful Saracen king in Boiardo's *Orlando Innamorato* and Ariosto's *Orlando Furioso*.]

roe[1] /rō/ *n* **1 FISH EGGS** a mass of mature fish eggs, especially when still inside the ovarian sac, sometimes eaten cooked **2 FISH SPERM** a mass of mature fish sperm, especially when it is still inside the testicular sac **3 CRUSTACEAN EGGS** a mass of mature eggs of certain crustaceans, e.g. lobsters, especially when still inside the ovarian sac [15C. < Middle Dutch or Middle Low German *roge*.]

roe[2] /rō/ (*plural* **roes** *or* **roe**) *n* ZOOL = **roe deer** [Old English *rā* < Germanic]

roebuck /rṓ buk/ (*plural* **-bucks** *or* **-buck**) *n* a male roe deer, especially an adult one

Roedean /rṓ deen/ *n* a public school for girls in S England

roe deer *n* a medium-sized reddish-brown deer. Native to: deciduous woodlands of Europe and Asia. *Capreolus capreolus*.

Roeg /rōg/, **Nicolas** (*b.* 1928) British film director

roentgen /róntgən/, **röntgen** *n* (*symbol* **R**) a unit of radiation, used to measure the exposure of somebody or something to X-rays and gamma rays, defined in terms of the ionization effect on air [Late 19C. After W. C. ROENTGEN.]

Roentgen /róntgən/, **Wilhelm Conrad** (1845–1923) German physicist

Roeslare /roōssə laarə/ city in W Belgium. Population: 53,706 (1996).

rogallo /rō gállō/ (*plural* **-los**), **rogallo wing** *n* a fabric-covered delta-shaped wing that can be folded compactly. Use: hang-gliders, microlight aircraft. [Mid-20C. After Francis M. *Rogallo*, US engineer who invented it in the 1940s.]

rogation /rō gáysh'n/ *n* **1** in the Christian Church, a solemn prayer or supplication, especially one made as part of the observation of the three days preceding Ascension Day (**Rogation Days**) (*often plural*) **2** in ancient Rome, the submission of a law by a consul or tribune to the people for their approval, or a law so submitted [14C. < Latin *rogation-* < *rogare* 'ask, beg'.]

Rogation Day *n* any of the three days preceding Ascension Day on which Christians are expected to pray (*often plural*)

Rogation Sunday *n* the Sunday before the Christian festival of Ascension Day. Date: five weeks after Easter.

rogatory /róggətəri, rṓgətəri/ *adj* requesting information, especially information that might be pertinent to a court case [Mid-19C. Via French *rogatoire* < medieval Latin *rogatorius* < Latin *rogare* 'ask, beg'.]

roger /rójjər/ *interj* **1 MESSAGE RECEIVED** indicates that the speaker has received and understood a transmitted message (*in telecommunications*) **2 OK** used to indicate the speaker's agreement to something (*informal*) ■ *vti* **OFFENSIVE TERM** an offensive term meaning to have sexual intercourse with somebody (*slang*) [Mid-20C. < the name *Roger*, used in radio communications for the letter *r* and meaning *received*.]

Roger II /rójjər/ (1095–1154) king of Sicily

Rogers /rójjərz/, **Ginger** (1911–95) US dancer and actor. Born **Virginia Katherine McMath**

Rogers, Sir Richard George, Baron Rogers of Riverside (*b.* 1933) British architect

Roget /rō zháy/, **Peter Mark** (1779–1869) British doctor and compiler of *Roget's Thesaurus of English Words and Phrases* (1852)

rogue /rōg/ *n* **1 SOMEBODY DISHONEST** an unscrupulous or dishonest person, especially somebody who is also likable **2 SOMEBODY MISCHIEVOUS** a mischievously playful person, especially a naughty child **3 BIOLOGICALLY INFERIOR VARIANT** a plant that is a biologically inferior variant of its type **4 DANGEROUS SOLITARY ANIMAL** a vicious or uncontrolled animal that lives apart from the rest of its herd or group, especially an elephant ■ *adj* **1 DANGEROUS AND SOLITARY** describes an animal that is vicious and uncontrolled and living apart from the rest of the herd or group ○ *a rogue male* **2 MAVERICK** acting independently and using unorthodox methods that are unpredictable and are likely to cause trouble ○ *a rogue trader* **3 STRAY** describes a plant that is inferior and unwanted ■ *vt* (**rogues, roguing, rogued**) **CLEAR PLANTS** to remove inferior plants from a crop or a group of plants [Mid-16C. Originally 'vagrant' < ?] —**roguery** /rṓgəri/ *n*

Rogue /rōg/ river in SW Oregon. Length: 320 km/200 mi.

rogues' gallery *n* a set of photographs of known criminals that the police show to witnesses to crimes for possible identification (*informal*)

⚡**rogue site** *n* a website that acquires visitors by having a domain name similar to that of a popular site

roguish /rṓgish/ *adj* **1** unscrupulous or dishonest in the manner of a rogue **2** mischievously playful —**roguishly** *adv* —**roguishness** *n*

Röhm /röm/, **Ernst** (1887–1934) German Nazi leader

Rohypnol /rō híp nol/ *tdmk* a trademark for flunitrazepam, a powerful sedative sometimes associated with date rape

ROI *abbr* **1** region of interest **2** return on investment

'roid /royd/ *n US* a steroid (*slang*) [Late 20C. Shortening.]

'roid rage *n* an outburst of violent or aggressive behaviour supposedly caused by taking too many anabolic steroids to improve athletic performance (*slang*)

roil /royl/ *v* **1** *vti* to stir up a liquid so that the sediment becomes dispersed through the liquid and makes it cloudy, or become cloudy with sediment by being stirred **2** *vt* to anger or annoy somebody [Late 16C. < ?] —**roily** *adj*

roister /róystər/ *vi* **1** to take part in loud rowdy partying or celebrations **2** to behave in a loud bragging manner [Mid-16C. Probably < Old French *ru(i)stre* 'boor, churl' < Latin *rusticus* 'rustic'.] —**roisterer** *n* —**roisterous** *adj* —**roisterously** *adv*

Roland /rṓlənd/ ◇ **a Roland for an Oliver** an equally good retort, response, or retaliation (*archaic*)

role /rōl/, **rôle** *n* **1 ACTING PART** an individual part in a play, film, opera, or other performance played by an actor, singer, or other performer **2 SPECIFIC FUNCTION** the usual or expected function of somebody or something, or the part somebody or something plays in a particular action or event **3 PART PLAYED IN SOCIAL CONTEXT** the part played by somebody in a given social context, with any characteristic or expected pattern of behaviour that it entails [Early 17C. < French *rôle* '(paper) roll on which an actor's part is written' < Old French *rol(l)e* (see ROLL).]

role model *n* a worthy person who is a good example for other people

role-play *n* role-playing, or an instance of it ■ *vti* to engage or act out a part in role-playing

role-playing *n* the acting out of a part, especially that of somebody with a particular social role, in order to understand the role or person better

Rolfing /rólfing/ a proprietary name for a type of therapy using vigorous massage to alleviate physical or psychological tension

roll /rōl/ *v* **1** *vti* **TURN OVER AND OVER** to move or cause something to move with repeated turning or rotating motions **2** *vti* **MOVE ON WHEELS** to move, or cause something to move, on wheels or rollers **3** *vti* **FORM INTO ROUND SHAPE** to form something, or be formed, into a ball, tube, cylinder, or other rounded shape, or form something with such a shape **4** *vt* **WRAP SOMETHING INTO CYLINDER** to make something into a cylinder shape, especially by wrapping something over and over on itself **5** *vt* **TURN BETWEEN OR ON** to revolve something between two surfaces or on a coating material **6** *vti* **MOVE WITH UNDULATIONS** to move, or cause something to move, in a steady flowing motion **7** *vi* **STRETCH OUT OR AWAY IN UNDULATIONS** to have or take the form of a succession of gentle slopes ○ *green hills rolling away into the distance* **8** *vi* **DRIVE IN VEHICLE** to move in a wheeled vehicle **9** *vi* **ELAPSE** to go by or elapse, especially uneventfully or imperceptibly (*refers especially to time*) **10** *vti* **ROTATE** to turn or cause something to turn in a complete or partial rotation **11** *vt* **FLATTEN SOMETHING WITH ROLLER** to flatten or spread something, especially by using a roller or rolling pin **12** *vi* **REVERBERATE LOUDLY** to make a low prolonged rumbling noise **13** *vi* **BEAT DRUM** to make a series of quick beats on a drum **14** *vt* **TRILL SOUND** to pronounce a sound, especially an 'r', with a trill **15** *vi* **WRITHE** to lie on the back and move about or from side to side, but without moving very far, often with a writhing motion (*refers to animals*) **16** *vti* **ROTATE AIRCRAFT** to cause an aircraft to perform a single complete rotation about its lengthwise axis while maintaining the same altitude and direction, or perform such a rotation **17** *vti* **ROCK FROM SIDE TO SIDE** to move with a sideways swaying or rocking motion on waves or a swell, or cause something, especially a ship, to move in this way **18** *vi* **MOVE AS CROWD** to move or arrive in large numbers or in a crowd **19** *vi* **ORBIT** to revolve in an orbit (*refers to astronomical objects*) **20** *vi* **WALK UNSTEADILY** to walk with an unsteady or staggering motion **21** *vi* **WALK WITH A SWAY** to sway rhythmically in walking **22** *vti* **OPERATE** to function or cause something, especially a movie camera or printing press, to function **23** *vti* **SEND OR GO UP ON SCREEN** to cause credits, titles, or other captions to move in a continuous upwards direction on a cinema or television screen, or move in this way **24** *vt* **INK SOMETHING WITH ROLLER** to apply ink to type or a plate with a roller **25** *vi* **TRAVEL AROUND** to travel from place to place **26** *vi* **CARRY ON** to proceed or continue successfully (*informal*) ○ *Now this project is finally rolling.* **27** *vti* **OVERTURN CAR** to overturn a motor vehicle, especially a car, or be overturned **28** *vti* **THROW DICE** to throw a die or dice **29** *vt* **SCORE NUMBER BY THROWING DICE** to achieve a specified number, position, or score by throwing a die or dice **30** *vi* **BE CARRIED BY RIVER** to be transported by river **31** *vt* **PLAY CHORD WITH SPREAD NOTES** to play a chord sounding its notes in rapid succession (**arpeggio**) rather than simultaneously **32** *vt* **ROB** to take money or belongings from somebody who cannot offer any resistance (*informal*) **33** *vti* **HAVE SEX** to have sexual intercourse or engage in sexual foreplay with somebody (*informal; offensive in some contexts*) ■ *n* **1 SOMETHING TUBE-SHAPED** a tube, cylinder, or coil of something, especially something that is wrapped around itself **2 INDIVIDUAL LOAF** a small individual-sized loaf of bread, usually round or long in shape, or a sandwich made from one **3 OFFICIAL LIST** an official register or list of names, especially of school pupils, members of a club, or people entitled to vote **4 TOTAL ON OFFICIAL LIST** the total number of people registered on a school, club, or electoral roll **5 ROUNDED LAYER** a thick rounded layer of something, especially of flesh **6 FILLED FOOD** a food made by wrapping pastry around a filling or by spreading a filling on something, e.g. sponge cake, and wrapping it around itself (*usually in combination*) **7 RUMBLING NOISE** a low prolonged rumbling noise **8 DRUM BEATS** a series of quick beats on a drum **9 SOMETHING UNDULATING** a gentle rounded hump on a surface, often one of a series **10 SINGLE TURN** a complete or partial rotation **11 REPEATED TURN** a repeated turning or rotating motion **12 ROTATION OF AIRCRAFT** a midair flight manoeuvre in which an aircraft maintains the same height and direction while doing a single complete rotation about its lengthwise axis **13 SOMERSAULT** a gentle somersault **14 ACT OF FLATTENING** an act of flattening or spreading something, especially by using a roller or rolling pin **15 MOVEMENT ON WHEELS** a movement on wheels or rollers **16 WRITHING MOTION** an action that involves writhing while turning backwards and forwards or from side to side, but without moving very far **17 MOVEMENT FROM SIDE TO SIDE** a swaying or rocking motion, especially by a ship **18 SWAYING WALK** a rhythmical sway in walking **19 UNDULATING MOVEMENT** a steady, flowing, undulating movement **20 RHYTHMICAL STREAM OF WORDS** a continuous stream of words with a rhythmical quality **21 EQUIPMENT HOLDER WITH POCKETS** a length of fabric or leather that has pockets to hold tools, medical instruments, or other equipment and can usually be wrapped around itself and tied up **22 ROLLER FOR METAL** a cylinder or roller used for pressing, shaping, or flattening something, especially one used for shaping metal in a rolling mill **23 BOOKBINDER'S TOOL** a bookbinder's tool for embossing decorative lines on book covers **24 TRILLING SOUND** a trilling noise, especially the sound of a trilled 'r' or the song of a canary **25 CHORD WITH SPREAD NOTES** a chord with its notes played in rapid succession (**arpeggio**) rather than simultaneously **26 SPIRAL SCROLL** in Greek architecture, a spiral scroll on an Ionic column **27 WAD OF MONEY** a cylindrical wad of banknotes formed by coiling the wad around itself (*informal*) **28 TOSS OF DICE** a throw of a die or dice **29 ACT OF ROBBERY** an act or the process of taking money or belongings from somebody who cannot offer any resistance (*informal*) **30 SEX ACT** an act of sexual intercourse or foreplay (*informal; offensive in some contexts*) [12C. Via Old French *rolle* 'scroll' < Latin *rotul-* 'little wheel' < Latin *rofa* 'wheel'.] ◇ **a roll in the hay** an instance of having sex with somebody (*informal*) ◇ **be rolling in it** to be very rich (*informal*) ◇ **on a roll** enjoying a period of good luck or of doing something well (*informal*) ◇ **rolled into one** forming a single unit consisting of a number of different aspects or qualities

roll back *vt* **1** *US* to cause something, especially prices or wages, to decrease **2** to reduce or nullify the influence or effectiveness of something

roll in *vi* **1** to come home or arrive at a destination, especially in a leisurely way, often later than expected **2** to arrive or attend in large numbers or quantities

roll off *vi* **1** to flow, especially with ease or in large numbers **2** to display a gradually decreasing response in the upper and lower portions of the amplitude-frequency range of an electronic system or transducer

roll on *vi* used in interjections to express a wish that a time or occasion may arrive soon (*informal*) ○ *Roll on summer!*

roll out *vt* **1 FLATTEN PASTRY** to flatten pastry, dough, or other uncooked food by shaping it with a rolling pin **2 UNCOIL** to unfold or uncoil something **3 SHOW TO PUBLIC** to put a new product on public display for the first time **4 LAUNCH PRODUCT GRADUALLY** to launch a new product or service by gradually increasing the number of outlets where it is available to the public

roll over *v* **1** *vi* **CAPSIZE** to capsize, tip over, or overturn **2** *vt* **EXTEND LOAN** to allow a loan to be paid at a later date **3** *vt* **NEGOTIATE NEW FINANCIAL TERMS FOR** to achieve new terms for a financial contract through discussion **4** *vt* **REINVEST FUNDS** to transfer funds from one investment to a similar investment **5** *vt* **ACCUMULATE PRIZE MONEY** to add the amount of prize money not won on one occasion to the prize money available on a subsequent occasion **6** *vt* **DEFEAT** to defeat a person or team overwhelmingly (*informal*)

roll up *v* **1** *vi* **ARRIVE** to come to a place or destination, often in a vehicle and especially when later than expected or when not expected at all **2** *vt* **PRODUCE CYLINDER SHAPE** to turn something into a cylindrical form **3** *vt US* **ACCUMULATE MONEY** to accumulate something, especially money

rollaway /rṓlə way/ *adj* fitted with wheels or castors so as to be easily moved or stored

rollback /rṓl bak/ *n* **1** a decrease in something, especially in something such as prices and wages involving money **2** a reduction or nullification of the influence or effectiveness of something

rollbar /rṓl baar/ *n* a reinforcing bar across the top of a vehicle, especially an open-top sports car or rally car, to protect the occupants if the vehicle overturns

roll bar *n* a reinforcing bar across the top of a vehicle, especially an open-top sports car or off-road vehicle, to protect the occupants if the vehicle overturns

roll cage *n* a reinforcing framework, usually built into the bodywork of a car, around and over the passenger cabin to protect the occupants if the vehicle turns over

roll call *n* **1** a check on attendance, especially in a school or military establishment, by calling out the names of those expected to be present, with each of those present responding **2** a time when a roll call is read out, especially one that is fixed at a regular time of day

roll down *n* in financial markets, the closure of one option position and the opening of another one of the same class, but with a lower strike price

rolled gold *n* a base metal, e.g. brass, that has been covered with a very thin layer of gold applied by a rolling method. US term **filled gold**

rolled paperwork *n* a decorative covering for boxes and other small objects that consists of curls of paper laid in a pattern

rolled steel *n* steel produced to a desired thickness by being passed through a set of rollers

rolled steel joist *n* a beam made of rolled steel with a cross-section shaped like the letter H

roller[1] /rṓlər/ *n* **1 DEVICE FOR APPLYING PAINT** a painting tool in the form of a revolving tube with a soft absorbent covering and a handle, used for applying paint to large surface areas **2 DEVICE FOR FLATTENING LAWNS** a large heavy revolving cylinder or pair of cylinders with a handle, used for flattening a lawn or green **3 HAIR CURLER** a short tube around which hair is wrapped in order to make it curly or wavy **4 HEAVY WAVE** a long heavy wave that does not break until it reaches the shoreline **5 SPOKELESS WHEEL** a small wheel without spokes, especially on a skate or a piece of heavy furniture **6 TUBE WRAPPED IN MATERIAL** a long tube with a particular material, e.g. a section of window blind or length of towel, wrapped around it **7 COILED BANDAGE** a long bandage that is rolled up tightly upon itself to form a dense cylinder **8 CYLINDER THAT TRANSMITS FORCE AND MOTION** a cylindrically shaped rotating device that transmits force and motion via its rotation, often used in sets or pairs and machine-operated **9 INKED TUBE** a hard tube, usually of compressed rubber, on which ink is spread and rolled over type or an engraved plate before printing **10 BELT FOR HORSE BLANKET** a strap around the belly of a horse to hold a blanket in place **11 SOMEBODY OR SOMETHING THAT ROLLS** a person who or thing that rolls **12** *US* **WEAKLY HIT BASEBALL** in baseball, a batted ball that rolls along the ground slowly

roller[2] /rṓlər/ *n* a brightly coloured bird with a hooked bill that flies erratically during the breeding season. Native to: Europe. Family: Coraciidae.

ϟ **rollerball** /rṓlər bawl/ *n* **1** a pen with a writing tip in the form of a small movable metal or plastic ball **2** a device containing a freely rotating ball that is moved by the fingers to control a cursor on a computer screen

roller bearing *n* a set of rotating cylindrically shaped parallel steel rollers contained within a closed track, used to prevent friction between machine parts

Rollerblade /rṓlər blayd/ *tdmk* a trademark for a type of roller skate on which the wheels are arranged in one straight line

roller blind *n* a blind consisting of a length of fabric rolled around a pole and fitted to the top of a window

roller chain *n* a power transmission chain consisting of freely rotating hollow cylindrical rollers mounted on pins that connect the plates that link adjacent rollers

roller coaster *n* **1** an amusement park ride consisting of a narrow rail track on a metal framework shaped into extreme peaks and troughs and sharp bends **2** a situation that is characterized by sudden, extreme, and often repeated, changes (*hyphenated before nouns*)

roller derby *n* competition between two teams of roller skaters

roller hockey *n* hockey played on a roller-skating rink or other hard surface by players wearing roller skates

roller rink *n US* a place where people can go to roller-skate

roller skate *n* **1** a metal or plastic frame with wheels attached, usually one pair at the front and another at the back, fastened onto a shoe and used for skating **2** a specially designed shoe or boot to which a roller skate is attached —**roller skater** *n* —**roller skating** *n*

roller-skate /rṓlər skáyt/ (**roller-skates, roller-skating, roller-skated**) *vi* to travel on roller skates

roller towel *n* a continuous roll of material housed inside a metal box and used for drying the hands

roll film *n* a length of film rolled around a spool and put inside a protective case ready to be loaded into a camera

roll forward *n* the closure of one option position and the opening of another one of the same class, but with a later expiry date

rollick /róllik/ *vi* to have fun, especially in a loud, rowdy way ■ *n* a loud, rowdy session of having fun [Early 19C. Probably blend of ROLL or ROMP and FROLIC.] —**rollick** *n* —**rollicksome** *adj* —**rollicky** *adj*

rollicking[1] /rólliking/ *adj* loud and rowdy —**rollickingly** *adv*

rollicking[2] /rólliking/ *n* a severe reprimand or scolding (*informal*)

rolling /rṓling/ *adj* **1 GRADUALLY DEVELOPING** proceeding in successive phases and usually gaining in momentum, intensity, or effectiveness **2 CONSTANTLY UPDATED** responsive to change and constantly updated **3 RICH** rich or very well-off (*informal*) **4 FOLDABLE UP OR DOWN** able to be turned up or down

rolling bearing *n* a bearing in which the rolling action of components such as balls or cylinders reduces friction

rolling blackout *n* a controlled series of power cuts imposed by an electricity company on selected areas in turn in order to conserve power supplies

rolling hitch *n* a knot used for joining two pieces of rope together or for attaching a rope to a spar

rolling launch *n* MARKETING = **roll-out** *n.* 2

rolling mill *n* 1 a factory, or part of a factory, where metal, usually in ingot form, is processed by being rolled into sheets or bars of the desired shape and size **2** a machine with rollers that press metal into sheets or bars of the desired shape and size

rolling paper *n* a small piece of fine paper used for rolling a handmade cigarette (*often plural*)

rolling pin *n* a cylinder, sometimes with small handles at either end, used for rolling out and flattening dough, pastry, or other uncooked food

rolling stock *n* **1** railway vehicles such as locomotives, passenger carriages, and goods wagons thought of collectively, especially those belonging to a particular company **2** *US* road vehicles thought of collectively, especially those belonging to a particular company

rolling stone *n* a person who is incapable of staying in the same job or place for very long [Originally in the proverb, *a rolling stone gathers no moss*]

Rolling Stones British rock group, formed in 1962.

rollmop /rṓl mop/ *n* a fillet of raw herring wrapped around a slice of onion or a pickle and left to marinate in spiced vinegar [Early 20C. < German < *rollen* 'roll' + *Mops* 'pug dog'.]

roll neck *n* **1** a garment neck that is loose-fitting and worn folded down (*hyphenated when used before a noun*) **2** a garment, especially a sweater, with a roll neck —**rollnecked** *adj*

Rollo /róllō/ (860?–932?) Viking leader

roll of honour *n* **1** a list of names of people who have all excelled in some way **2** a list of names of people who have died during a battle or war in the service of their country, especially people from one area

roll-on *adj* **WITH ROTATING-BALL APPLICATOR** applied to the skin by means of a rotating ball in the top of the container ■ *n* **1 DEODORANT WITH ROTATING-BALL APPLICATOR** a deodorant, cosmetic, or other product that comes in a container with a rotating ball in its top **2 WOMAN'S UNDERGARMENT** a woman's elasticated girdle that is pulled on rather than fastened down the front

roll-on roll-off *adj* describes a method of transport, especially a ferry, designed so that vehicles are driven on one end and, on arrival at their destination, are driven off the other end ■ *n* a roll-on roll-off vessel, especially a ferry

roll-out *n* **1** the first public display of a new product **2** a launch of a new product that involves gradually increasing the number of outlets where it is available to the public

rollover /rṓl ōvər/ *n* **1 TRANSFER OF FUNDS** a transfer of funds from one investment to another similar investment, often without taking possession of the funds **2 ACCUMULATION OF PRIZE MONEY** the addition of prize money not won on one occasion to the prize money available on a subsequent occasion **3 CAPSIZING INCIDENT** an act or the process of capsizing, tipping over, or overturning

roll-top desk, roll-top *n* a desk with a rounded cover consisting of connected parallel wooden slats that can be pulled down over the writing area and, usually, locked

roll-up *n* a hand-rolled cigarette made using a cigarette paper and loose tobacco (*informal*) US term **roll-your-own**

rollway /rṓl way/ *n* **1** a natural or artificial sloping area along which cylindrical objects are rolled, especially a slope used by lumberjacks to move felled timber to water for transportation **2** a series of parallel rollers used to facilitate the transportation of heavy loads

roll-your-own *n* = **roll-up** (*informal*)

Rolodex /rṓlə deks/ *tdmk* a trademark for a desktop card-index system in which cards containing names, addresses, and telephone numbers are attached to but removable from a central cylinder

roly-poly /rṓli pṓli/ *adj* of greater body weight than is considered desirable (*sometimes offensive*) ■ *n* **1 roly-poly, roly-poly pudding** a hot pudding made with suet pastry spread with jam or fruit, rolled to form a coil, and baked or steamed **2** *Aus* PLANTS = **tumbleweed** (*informal*) [Early 17C. Probably a rhyming compound of ROLL and POLL, originally meaning 'rascal', and the name of several games of rolling balls.] —**roly-poly** *n*

Rom /rom/ (*plural* **Roma** /rṓmmə/) *n* **1** a member of a nomadic people who migrated from India to Europe in the 15th century and now live throughout the world **2** a Romany man [Mid-19C. < Romany, 'married man'.] —**Roma** *adj*

⚡**ROM** /rom/ *abbr* read-only memory

rom., rom *abbr* roman

Rom. *abbr* **1** Romans **2** Romance **3** Romania

Roma plural of **Rom**

romaine /rō máyn/, **romaine lettuce** *n US, Can* PLANTS = **cos**[1] [Early 20C. < French, feminine of *romain* 'Roman'; perhaps because this lettuce was introduced into France during the 14C Avignon papacy.]

romaji /rṓ maaji/ *n* the Roman alphabet as used for transliterating Japanese [Late 19C. < Japanese, < *roma* 'Roman' + *ji* 'character'.]

roman[1] /rṓmən/ *adj* relating to a type with upright as opposed to slanting characters that is the standard type used in printing books, newspapers, and magazines ■ *n* roman type or characters [Early 16C. Because it imitates the style of Roman inscriptions.]

roman[2] /rō maaN, rōmaan/ *n* **1** a novel, especially a French one or one in a French genre (*literary*) **2** a medieval French narrative poem, especially one that has heroic exploits as its main theme [Mid-18C. < French, 'romance, novel'.]

Roman /rṓmən/ *adj* **1 OF MODERN ROME** relating to the modern city of Rome and its inhabitants **2 OF ANCIENT ROME** relating to the ancient city of Rome and its territories and inhabitants **3 IN ANCIENT ROMAN ARCHITECTURAL STYLE** relating to, or built in a style characteristic of the buildings of ancient Rome, especially in having rounded arches, vaults, and domes **4 OF ROMAN CATHOLIC CHURCH** belonging to or characteristic of the Roman Catholic Church ■ *n* **1 SOMEBODY FROM MODERN ROME** somebody who comes from the modern city of Rome **2 SOMEBODY FROM ANCIENT ROME** somebody who came from ancient Rome **3 OFFENSIVE TERM** an offensive term for a member of the Roman Catholic Church [Pre-12C. < Latin *Romanus* 'Roman, a Roman' < *Roma* 'Rome'; later reinforced by French *Romain*.]

roman à clef /rō maaN a kláy, rō maan aa-/ (*plural* **romans à clef** /rōmaaN a kláy, rōmaan aa-/) *n* a novel in which some or all of the characters are based on real people and that usually includes clues to the characters' true identities [< French, 'novel with a key']

Roman alphabet *n* the writing system that represents sounds by 26 letters from A to Z, used for most languages in Western Europe and many elsewhere

roman à thèse /rō maaN a téz, rō maan aa-/ (*plural* **romans à thèse** /rōmaaN a tēz, rōmaan aa-/) *n* a novel in which the author focuses on an injustice and suggests how it might be rectified, especially by putting forward a particular political message or social theory [< French, 'novel with a thesis']

Roman calendar *n* the lunar calendar, comprising 10 months and an intercalated month, that was used by the ancient Romans until the introduction of the Julian calendar in 46 BC. ◊ **Julian calendar, Gregorian calendar**

Roman candle *n* a short cylindrical firework that when placed on the ground and lit produces showers of sparks and occasional coloured balls or stars of fire

Roman Catholic *adj* relating to the Roman Catholic Church, its members, or its beliefs ■ *n* a member of the Roman Catholic Church

Roman Catholic Church *n* a Christian church that has a pope as the head of a hierarchy of bishops and priests and is administered from the Vatican City in Rome

Roman Catholicism *n* the system of beliefs, practices, and organization of the Roman Catholic Church

romance /rō mánss, rṓ manss/ *n* **1 LOVE AFFAIR** a love affair, especially a brief and intense one ○ *This is more than just a holiday romance.* **2 LOVE** sexual love, especially when the other person or the relationship is idealized or when it is exciting and intense ○ *The secret of a happy marriage is to keep the romance alive.* **3 SPIRIT OF ADVENTURE** a spirit or feeling of adventure, excitement, the potential for heroic achievement, and the exotic ○ *the romance of cruising down the Nile* **4 FASCINATION** a particular fascination or enthusiasm for something, especially of an uncritical or inexplicable kind ○ *his lifelong romance with football* **5 STORY OF LOVE** a novel, film, or play with a love story as its main theme ○ *a writer of cheap romances* **6 LOVE STORIES COLLECTIVELY** love stories considered as a genre **7 MEDIEVAL ADVENTURE STORY** a story of the adventures of chivalrous heroes written in verse or prose in a vernacular language in the Middle Ages **8 MEDIEVAL ADVENTURE STORIES COLLECTIVELY** the genre of medieval adventure stories ○ *Arthurian romance* **9 NARRATIVE OF ADVENTURES** a fictional narrative dealing with exciting and extravagant adventures ○ *a romance of piracy on the high seas* **10 FICTITIOUS ACCOUNT** an extravagant or absurd fictitious account of something **11 SHORT LYRICAL PIECE** a short lyrical song or instrumental composition, usually expressing or evoking tender emotions ■ *v* (**-mances, -mancing, -manced**) **1** *vi* **TELL ROMANTIC OR ADVENTUROUS STORIES** to tell or write extravagant or idealized fictitious accounts **2** *vi* **TELL LOVE STORIES** to tell or write stories about love **3** *vi* **THINK ROMANTICALLY** to think or behave in a romantic way **4** *vt* **TREAT SOMEBODY ROMANTICALLY** to treat somebody in a special way during a love relationship or with a view to entering on one **5** *vt* **HAVE AN AFFAIR WITH** to have a love affair with somebody [13C. < Old French *romanz* '(work composed) in French' < Latin *romanicus* 'Roman' < ROME.] —**romancer** *n*

Romance /rō mánss, rṓ manss/ *n* the Italic branch of the Indo-European group of languages that includes French, Italian, Portuguese, Romanian, and Spanish, all of which are descended from Latin. Native speakers: 500 million. —**Romance** *adj*

Roman collar *n* CLOTHING = **clerical collar**

Roman Empire *n* **1** the territories ruled by ancient Rome under its emperors, from 27 BC to AD 395. ◊ **Holy Roman Empire** **2** the rule or form of government of ancient Rome under its emperors

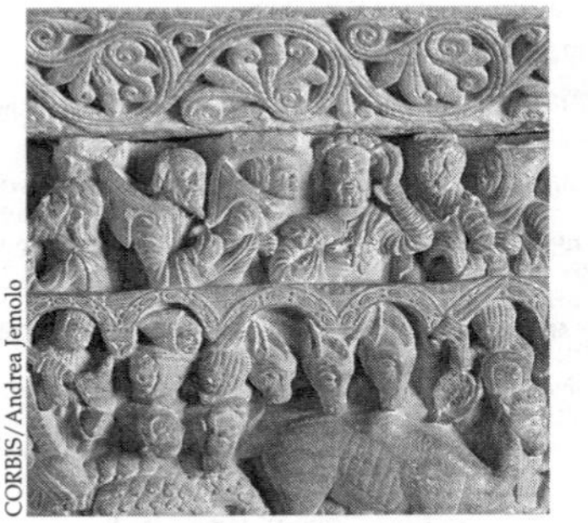
CORBIS/Andrea Jemolo

Romanesque: Carved stone capital (1127–45) from Pamplona Cathedral, Spain

Romanesque /rṓmə nésk/ *adj* **1 TYPICAL OF EARLY EUROPEAN ARCHITECTURAL STYLE** relating to or built in the style characteristic of European architecture from the 11th to the 12th centuries, especially in having rounded arches and barrel vaults **2 RELATING TO THE PERIOD OF ROMANESQUE ARCHITECTURE** characteristic of or relating to the style of European painting, sculpture, or decorative arts contemporary with Romanesque architecture ■ *n* **RO-MANESQUE STYLE** the Romanesque style in architecture or art

QUICK FACTS ON... **ROMANESQUE**

Key dates: 11th–12th century
Key locations: W Europe, especially France
Key elements: massiveness, solemnity; barrel, groined, and ribbed vaults, rounded arches, massive piers, heavy walls, increasingly elaborate sculptural reliefs (architecture); highly decorative metalwork, stained glass, and illuminated manuscripts
Key works: Durham Cathedral (1093?), Leaning Tower of Pisa, Italy (1173), Church of St Trophime, Arles, France (12th century), Church of Notre-Dame-la-Grande, Poitiers, France (12th century); Bayeux Tapestry, France (11th century)
Key developments: stone vaults, monumental sculpture, Gothic style, fortified castles; monastic cultural centres

roman-fleuve /rō maaN flōv, rō mán-/ (*plural* **romans-fleuves** /rō maaN flōv, rō mán-/) *n* a long novel or series of novels telling the stories of a linked group of people over many years [< French, 'river-novel']

Roman holiday *n* **1** an entertainment in which people are killed, e.g. a gladiatorial contest **2** a feeling of pleasure derived from watching other people be maimed or killed

Romani *n* PEOPLES, LANG = **Romany**

Romania

Romania /roō máyni ə, rō máyni ə/ republic in SE Europe, bordering the Black Sea. Capital: Bucharest. Population: 22,600,000 (1997). Area: 237,500 sq. km/91,700 sq. mi. —**Romanian** *n, adj*

Romanic /rō mánnik/ *adj* **1** OF ANCIENT ROME belonging or relating to ancient Rome or the ancient Romans **2** OF ROMANCE LANGUAGES relating to the Romance family of languages ■ *n* ROMANCE LANGUAGES COLLECTIVELY the Romance family of languages

Romanise *vti* CHR, LANG, HIST = **Romanize**

Romanism /rōmanizəm/ *n* an offensive term for Roman Catholicism, especially its rituals

Romanist /rōmanist/ *n* **1** SOMEBODY INFLUENCED BY CATHOLICISM a member of a church, especially the Church of England, who is sympathetic to or influenced by Roman Catholicism **2** OFFENSIVE TERM an offensive term for a member of the Roman Catholic Church **3** STUDENT OF ANCIENT ROME a student of or expert in ancient Roman history or law ■ *adj* **1** OFFENSIVE TERM an offensive term meaning belonging or relating to the Roman Catholic Church **2** OF ANCIENT ROMAN HISTORY relating to or involving ancient Roman history or law —**Romanistic** /rōma nístik/ *adj*

Romanize /rōmə nīz/ (**-izes, -izing, -ized**), **Romanise** (**-ises, -ising, -ised**) *v* **1** *vti* MAKE OR BECOME ROMAN to take on Roman characteristics, or make somebody or something take on Roman characteristics ○ *the Romanized Celts* **2** *vt* MAKE SOMETHING ROMAN CATHOLIC to make something take on a Roman Catholic character or influence **3** *vti* CONVERT TO ROMAN CATHOLICISM to become a Roman Catholic, or convert somebody to Roman Catholicism **4** **romanize, Romanize, romanise, Romanise** *vt* TRANSCRIBE INTO ROMAN ALPHABET to transcribe something such as a language or text into the characters of the Roman alphabet —**Romanization** /rōmə nī záysh'n/ *n*

Roman law *n* **1** the system of law established in ancient Rome, forming the basis of many modern legal systems **2** LAW = **civil law** *n*. **3**

Roman nose *n* a nose with a high and prominent bridge

ROMAN NUMERALS

Roman numerals are read from left to right. The symbols representing the largest quantities are placed at the left; immediately to the right of those are the symbols representing the next largest quantities, and so on. The symbols are usually added together

Arabic	Roman
0	
1	I
2	II
3	III
4	IV or IIII
5	V
6	VI
7	VII
8	VIII
9	IX or VIIII
10	X
11	XI
12	XII
13	XIII
14	XIV or XIIII
15	XV
16	XVI
17	XVII
18	XVIII
19	XIX or XVIIII
20	XX
21	XXI
30	XXX
40	XL or XXXX
50	L
60	LX
70	LXX
80	LXXX or XXC
90	XC or LXXXX
100	C
200	CC
400	CD or CCCC
500	D
600	DC
900	CM or DCCCC
1000	M
2000	MM

Roman numeral *n* any letter or sequence of letters used by the ancient Romans to represent cardinal numbers, including I for 1, V for 5, and X for 10

Romano /rō maanō/ *n* a hard and sharp-tasting Italian cheese, similar to Parmesan [Early 20C. Via Italian, 'Roman' < Latin *Romanus*.]

Romano /rō maanō/, **Giulio** (1499?–1546) Italian painter and architect

Romans /rōmənz/ *n* in the Bible, a letter from St Paul to the Church at Rome written in about AD 58, explaining his theory of religious thinking

Romansch /rō mánsh/, **Romansh** *n* a Romance language, an official language of Switzerland. Native speakers: 50,000. [Mid-17C. < Romansch, via medieval Latin *romanice* (see ROMANCE).] —**Romansch** *adj*

romans-fleuves plural of **roman-fleuve**

romantic /rō mántik/ *adj* **1** INVOLVING SEXUAL LOVE involving or characteristic of a love affair or sexual love, especially when the relationship is idealized or exciting and intense ○ *I don't think there's any romantic attachment between them.* **2** SUITABLE FOR LOVE characterized by or suitable for lovemaking or the expression of tender emotions ○ *a romantic candlelit dinner for two* **3** IDEALISTIC characterized by or arising from idealistic or impractical attitudes and expectations ○ *a romantic dreamer* **4** IMAGINARY imaginary or fictitious in an extravagant or glamorizing way ○ *a romantic version of the events of her life* **5** INVOLVING ADVENTURE relating to or characterized by adventure, excitement, the potential for heroic achievement, or the exotic ○ *a romantic tale about life in the outback* **6** ARTS = **Romantic** *adj*. ■ *n* **1** ROMANTIC PERSON a person who has a romantic personality or outlook **2** ARTS = **Romantic** *n*. [Mid-17C. < *romaunt* Mid-16C. < Old French, variant of *romanz* (see ROMANCE).] —**romantically** *adv*

Romantic /rō mántik/, **romantic** *adj* relating to the movement in late 18th- and early 19th-century music, literature, and art that departed from classicism and emphasized sensibility, the free expression of feelings, nature, and the exotic ■ *n* a writer, composer, or artist who was involved in the Romantic movement during the late 18th and early 19th centuries

romantic comedy *n* a humorous film, play, or novel about a love story that ends happily, or the genre itself

romanticise *vti* = **romanticize**

romanticism *n* the quality of being romantic or having romantic inclinations

Romanticism /rō mántissizəm/ *n* in the arts, the style and theories of the Romantic movement, or the movement itself —**Romanticist** *n*

QUICK FACTS ON... **ROMANTICISM**

Key dates: 1780–1840
Key locations: W Europe
Key elements: sensitivity, subjectivity, libertarianism, medievalism, melancholy, idealization of nature and childhood, interest in supernatural and other cultures
Key figures: Jean Jacques Rousseau, Johann Wolfgang von Goethe, William Wordsworth, Lord Byron, Percy Bysshe Shelley, Victor Hugo, Sir Walter Scott (literature); Henry Fuseli, Francisco de Goya, Théodore Géricault, Eugène Delacroix, Caspar David Friedrich, J. M. W. Turner (painting); Ludwig van Beethoven, Franz Schubert, Hector Berlioz, Franz Liszt (music)
Key works: *The Sorrows of Young Werther* (Goethe) 1774, *Confessions* (Rousseau) 1782–89, *Lyrical Ballads* (Wordsworth and Coleridge) 1798, *Childe Harold's Pilgrimage* (Byron) 1812–18; *The Raft of the Medusa* (Géricault) 1818–19, *Wanderer above the Sea of Fog* (Friedrich) 1818; *Eroica Symphony, Symphony no. 5* (Beethoven) 1803, 1808; *Symphony in B Minor, or Unfinished Symphony* (Schubert) 1822, *Symphonie Fantastique* (Berlioz) 1830
Key developments: free verse, historical novel, Gothic novel, symbolism, transcendentalism, aestheticism, Pre-Raphaelite Brotherhood, expressionism, symphonic poem, lieder, grand opera; nationalism, radicalism, democracy, progressive education

romanticize /rō mánti sīz/ (**-cizes, -cizing, -cized**), **romanticise** (**-cises, -cising, -cised**) *v* **1** *vt* to make something seem or believe something to be more glamorous or ideal than it really is ○ *The film tends to romanticize a rather sordid period in history.* **2** *vi* to think or express something in an amorous, idealistic, or sentimental way —**romanticization** /rō mánti sī záysh'n/ *n*

Romany /rōməni, rómməni/ (*plural* **-nies**), **Romani** *n* the Indic language of the Roma. Native speakers: 250,000. [Early 19C. < Romany *Romani*, a form of *Romano* 'Romany' (adjective) < *Rom* 'man'.] —**Romany** *adj*

Rome /rōm/ capital of Italy, in the west-central part of the country, on the River Tiber. Population: 2,651,503 (1997 estimate). ◇ **fiddle while Rome burns** to occupy yourself with unimportant things while extremely important things need to be done ◇ **when in Rome (do as the Romans do)** indicates the advisability of adopting the behaviour and customs of the place or circumstances in which you find yourself

Romeo /rōmi ō/ (*plural* **-os**) *n* **1** a man with a reputation for having or seeking romantic or sexual involvement with a large number of women ○ *the office Romeo* **2** a code word for the letter 'R', used in international radio communications [Mid-18C. After *Romeo*, lover of Juliet in William Shakespeare's play *Romeo and Juliet* (1594).]

Romish /rómish/ *adj* an offensive term meaning belonging to, characteristic of, or influenced by the Roman Catholic Church —**Romishly** *adv* —**Romishness** *n*

Rommel /rómməl/, **Erwin** (1891–1944) German general. Known as **the Desert Fox**

Romney /rómni, rúmni/, **George** (1734–1802) British painter

Romney Marsh[1] /rómni-/ *n* a sheep belonging to a breed that has long wool and produces mutton, originally from the Romney Marsh area in S England

Romney Marsh[2] /rómni-, rúmni-/ region in S Kent, England. It is protected from the sea by a sea wall. Area: 176 sq. km/68 sq. mi.

romp /romp/ *vi* **1 PLAY BOISTEROUSLY** to run around or play in a boisterous way ○ *kids romping in the playground* **2 WIN** to win a contest easily (*informal*) ○ *The horse romped home* **3 MAKE EASY PROGRESS** to progress swiftly and effortlessly ○ *romped through her final exam* ■ *n* **1 BOISTEROUS ACTIVITY** boisterous or playful activity ○ *The dogs had a romp in the park.* **2 LIGHTHEARTED WORK** a book, play or film that is lighthearted and lively as opposed to serious or weighty (*informal*) ○ *The novel is an exhilarating romp through the pages of recent history.* **3 CASUAL SEX** a casual or lighthearted sexual encounter (*informal*) **4 EASY VICTORY** a victory that is remarkably or unexpectedly easy (*informal*) [Early 18C. < ?]

Romulus /rómmyŏŏləss/ *n* in Roman mythology, the founder of the city of Rome. He was the son of Mars and twin brother of Remus, whom he is said to have killed. ◊ **Remus**

Romulus Augustulus /-aw gústyŏŏləss/ (461?–476) Roman emperor

ROMvelope /rómvəlōp/, **romvelope** (*plural* **ROMvelopes** or **romvelopes**) *n* a protective cardboard or similar cover for a CD [Blend of ROM + ENVELOPE]

rondavel /ron daávəl/ *n S Africa* a circular hut or other building, usually with a conical thatched roof [Late 19C. < Afrikaans *rondawel*.]

rondeau /róndō/ (*plural* **-deaux** /-dōz/) *n* **1** a poem of 13 or 10 lines in three stanzas, with two rhymes and with the opening phrase repeated twice as an unrhyming refrain **2** a medieval French song, especially a trouvère song with a two-part refrain [Early 16C. < French, later form of *rondel* (see RONDEL).]

rondel /rónd'l/, **rondelle** /ron dél/ *n* a poem, similar to a rondeau, that has 13 or 14 lines in 3 stanzas, with 2 rhymes and with the opening 2 lines repeated as a refrain [14C. < Old French, 'small round' (from the repetition of the opening two lines) < *rond* 'round' < Latin *rotundus*.]

rondelet /róndə let, -lay/ *n* a short form of rondeau, with five or seven lines and the first line repeated as a refrain

rondelle *n* LITERAT = **rondel**

rondo /róndō/ (*plural* **-dos**) *n* an instrumental piece or movement in which the principal theme is repeated between at least two sections that contrast with it, often forming the last movement of a sonata [Late 18C. Via Italian < French *rondeau* 'rondeau', a later form of Old French *rondel* (see RONDEL).]

rone /rōn/ *n Scotland* **1** a gutter at the edge of a roof, for channelling rain away **2** a drainpipe that channels rainwater down the side of a building away from a roof gutter [Late 16C. < ?]

ronepipe /rōn pīp/ *n Scotland* BUILDING = **rone** *n.* **2**

röntgen *n* = **roentgen**

roo /roo/ (*plural* **roos**) *n Aus* a kangaroo (*informal*) [Early 20C. Shortening.]

roo bar *n Aus* a metal bar on the front of a car or truck that prevents the vehicle from being damaged in the event of a collision with an animal

rood /rood/ *n* **1 CRUCIFIX** a crucifix, especially one mounted at the entrance to the choir or chancel of a church **2 JESUS CHRIST'S CROSS** the cross on which Jesus Christ was crucified (*archaic*) **3 QUARTER OF AN ACRE** a unit of area equal to 0.10117 hectares/0.25 acre [Old English *rōd* 'cross, pole']

rood screen *n* a partition separating the choir or chancel of a church from the nave or main part

roof /roof/ *n* **1 UPPER COVERING OF BUILDING** the outside covering of the top of a building, or the framework supporting this **2 TOP PART** the top part of something, forming a covering, e.g. the top of a vehicle ○ *a blue car with a black roof* **3 TOP OF INSIDE CAVITY** the top of the inside of a hollow structure ○ *the roof of the cave* **4 STRUCTURE COVERING BODY CAVITY** the upper covering structure of a body part, especially one with a vaulted structure such as the mouth **5 HIGHEST POINT** the highest point or upper limit of something ■ *vt* **FIX ROOF ON** to fix a top covering onto something, especially a building ○ *The house is roofed with slate tiles.* [Old English *hrōf* 'roof, ceiling, top' < Germanic] —**roofless** /róofləss/ *adj* —**rooflike** *adj* ◇ **hit the roof** to be extremely angry

LITERARY LINK ***Cat on a Hot Tin Roof***, a play (1955) by US dramatist Tennessee Williams. Set in the US South, it depicts the Pollitt family gathering to celebrate the 65th birthday of patriarch Big Daddy. The simmering conflicts between Daddy and sons Gooper and Buck and their wives reflect the lies and deceit that underpin many family relationships.

roofer /róofər/ *n* somebody whose job is to build or repair the roofs of buildings

roof garden *n* a garden on the flat roof of a building

roofing /róofing/ *n* **1 MATERIAL FOR A ROOF** material used to make a roof **2 TOP OF** something forming a top or roof **3 OCCUPATION OF MAKING OR REPAIRING ROOFS** the business or occupation of making or repairing roofs

roofline /róof līn/ *n* the outline of the roof of a building or a series of buildings

roof rack *n* a frame attached to the top of a motor vehicle, used for carrying things, especially luggage. US term **luggage rack** *n.* **1**

rooftop /róof top/ *n* the outer surface of the roof of a building

rooftree /róof tree/ *n* CONSTR = **ridgepole** *n.* **1**

rooinek /róo i nek, róy nek/ *n S Africa* an offensive term for a British person, or an English-speaking South African (*slang insult*) [Late 19C. < Afrikaans, 'red neck' < *rooi* 'red' + *nek* 'neck'.]

rook[1] /rŏŏk/ *n* **1 BIRD OF CROW FAMILY** a large bird of the crow family with black plumage and a pale area at the base of its bill, that nests in colonies in treetops. Native to: Europe, Asia. *Corvus frugilegus.* **2 SWINDLER** a swindler or cheat, especially at cards (*slang*) ■ *vt* **CHEAT** to overcharge, swindle, or cheat somebody (*slang*) ○ *If you paid that amount you've been rooked.* [Old English *hrōc* < Germanic] —**rooky** *adj*

rook[2] /rŏŏk/ *n* any one of four chess pieces that begin a game in the corner squares and that can move in a straight line in any direction over any number of unoccupied squares [13C. < Old French *rok* < Arabic *rukk*.]

rookery /rŏŏkəri/ (*plural* **-ies**) *n* **1 COLONY OF ROOKS** a colony of nesting rooks **2 ROOKS' BREEDING PLACE** a place, especially in the tops of trees, where rooks breed **3 ANIMALS' COLLECTIVE BREEDING PLACE** a breeding or living area for large numbers of animals, especially birds or mammals that come together in colonies to nest or breed **4 SLUM** a slum or overcrowded group of run-down houses, especially tenements (*archaic*)

rookie /rŏŏki/ *n US* a person who is new to an activity or job (*informal*) [Late 19C. < ?]

room /room, rŏŏm/ *n* **1 USABLE SPACE** space that may or may not be filled with something ○ *There's room for another passenger in my car.* **2 PART OF BUILDING** an area within a building that is enclosed by a floor, walls, and a ceiling ○ *a hotel room* **3 PEOPLE IN ROOM** the people in a room considered as a group ○ *Her entrance silenced the room.* **4 SCOPE** the scope, opportunity, or possibility for something to exist, happen, or be done ○ *there's room for improvement* ■ **rooms** *npl* **ACCOMMODATION** part of a house or hotel that may be rented as separate accommodation ○ *I managed to find myself rooms in town.* ■ *vi US* **SHARE LIVING QUARTERS** to occupy or share living quarters with one person or several people [Old English *rūm* < Germanic, 'spacious'] —**roomful** *n*

room and board *n* accommodation with all meals provided, given in return for work

roomer /róomər, rŏŏmər/ *n US* = **lodger** *n.*

roomette /roo mét, rŏŏ-/ *n US, Can* a private single compartment in a railway sleeping car

roommate /róom mayt, rŏŏm-/ *n* somebody with whom a person shares a room

room service *n* a service providing food and drinks served to hotel guests in their rooms ○ *Room service is available throughout the day.*

room temperature *n* the average normal temperature of a living room, usually thought of as around 68°F/20°C or slightly above ○ *This wine should be served at room temperature.*

roomy /róomi, rŏŏ-/ (**-ier, -iest**) *adj* having plenty of space in which to move around —**roomily** *adv* —**roominess** *n*

Roosevelt /rōzə velt/, **Eleanor** (1884–1962) US first lady, social activist, and writer. Born **Anna Eleanor Roosevelt**

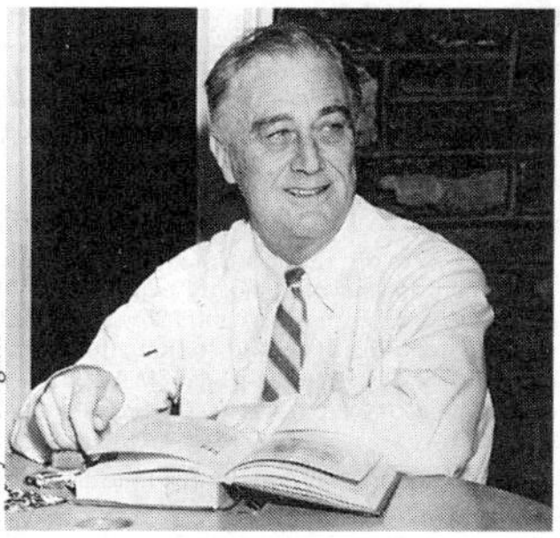

Library of Congress

Franklin D. Roosevelt

Roosevelt, Franklin D. (1882–1945) US statesman and 32nd president of the United States (1933–45). Full name **Franklin Delano Roosevelt**

Roosevelt, Theodore (1858–1919) US statesman and 26th president of the United States (1901–09). Known as **Teddy Roosevelt**

roost /roost/ *n* **1 PLACE WHERE BIRDS SLEEP** a place where a bird rests or sleeps such as a perch or a building with perches for domestic fowl **2 TEMPORARY ACCOMMODATION** a place where somebody may rest or sleep temporarily **3 BIRDS SHARING A ROOST** a group of birds sharing a roost ■ *vi* **GO TO SLEEP** to rest or sleep on or in a roost ○ *Starlings were roosting in the trees.* [Old English *hrōst*] ◇ **rule the roost** to be the person who is in charge and who must be obeyed

rooster /róostər/ *n US* an adult male bird, especially a domestic fowl

root[1] /root/ *n* **1 UNDERGROUND BASE OF PLANT** the part of a plant that has no leaves or buds and usually spreads underground, anchoring the plant and absorbing water and nutrients from the soil **2 UNDERGROUND EDIBLE PART OF PLANT** an underground plant part that is used as a vegetable, e.g. a carrot or turnip ○ *diced roots* ○ *root crops* **3 ATTACHMENT OF BODY PART** the portion of a body part such as a tooth or hair that is embedded in tissue, or the part by which something is attached to the body **4 BASE** the bottom or base of something ○ *the root of the tongue* **5 CAUSE** the fundamental cause, basis, or essence of something, or the source from which something derives ○ *the roots of discontent* **6 ANCESTOR** an ancestor or progenitor, especially one from whom many people are descended **7 NUMBER MULTIPLIED BY ITSELF** a number that when multiplied by itself a given number of times equals another number ○ *2 is the square root of 4.* **8 NUMBER SUBSTITUTABLE FOR VARIABLE** a number that can take the place of the variable in an equation and solve the equation **9 BASIC PART OF WORD** in linguistics, the basic meaningful part of a word that is left when any affixes are removed and that cannot be analysed further into other meaningful elements **10 ORIGINAL FORM OF WORD** in historical linguistics, the original reconstructed form from which a recorded word is derived, e.g. by phonetic change or the addition of affixes **11 FOUNDATION OF CHORD** the note that forms the foundation of a chord **12 END OF NERVE** the end of a nerve that is nearer to the centre of the body **13** *ANZ* **OFFENSIVE TERM** an offensive term for a sexual partner, especially of a man (*slang*) ■ **roots** *npl*

1 ORIGINS cultural or family origins, especially as the basis for a feeling of belonging in a particular place or environment ○ *I live in the city but my roots are in the country.* **2 SOMEBODY'S GENETIC ORIGIN** somebody's origins or ancestry ■ *v* **1** *vti* **GROW ROOTS** to develop a root or roots or cause a plant to grow roots **2** *vti* **BE FIXED** to become fixed, embedded, or immobile or to cause somebody or something to become fixed, embedded, or immobile ○ *news that rooted me to the spot* **3** *vi* **BE BASED** to have a basis or origin in something ○ *herbal remedies that are rooted in folk medicine* **4** *vti ANZ* **OFFENSIVE TERM** an offensive term meaning to have sexual intercourse with somebody (*slang*) [Pre-12C. < Old Norse *rót* < Indo-European, 'branch, root'.] —**rooter** *n* ◇ **root and branch** in every respect or to the fullest extent ○ *reformed the system root and branch* ◇ **take root** to become established and accepted

SPELLCHECK Do not confuse ***root*** with ***route***, which has a similar sound. Beware: your spellchecker will not catch this error.

SYNONYMS See ***origin***.

root out *vt* **1** to eradicate or remove somebody or something completely ○ *He ruthlessly rooted out all opposition.* **2** to find or remove something after rummaging for it ○ *I'll root out some old photos of him.*

root up *vt* root out to pull or dig up a whole plant, including its roots

root[2] /root/ *v* **1** *vti* to dig in the surface of the ground with the snout or nose out of curiosity or in search of food ○ *The pigs were rooting for beech nuts.* **2** *vi* to move things about unsystematically while looking for something ○ *rooting in the drawer for a pencil* [Mid-16C. Alteration (influenced by ROOT[1]) of *wroten* < Old English *wrōtan.*] —**rooter** *n*

root[3] /root/ *vi* **1** to cheer, shout, or applaud in support of a contestant or team **2** to provide support to or be actively in favour of somebody or something [Late 19C. < ?] —**rooter** *n*

rootage /ro͝otij/ *n* **1 PLANT ROOTS** a system of plant roots **2 GROWTH OF ROOTS** the developing of roots **3 ACT OR PROCESS OF BECOMING FIXED** the act or process of becoming rooted or established

root ball *n* the tightly packed mass of roots and soil produced by a plant, especially when grown in a container

root beer *n* a sweet fizzy soft drink made from the extracts of various roots and herbs

root canal *n* the cavity in the root of a tooth, containing pulp, nerves, and blood vessels

root cap *n* a thick protective mass of cells that covers the growing tip of the root of a plant

root climber *n* a vine such as an ivy that climbs up a structure by developing small roots on its stems that grip the structure

root crop *n* a crop grown for its edible underground parts, e.g. turnips, potatoes, or sugar beet

ϟ **root directory** *n* the top-level directory in a computer's filing system, usually called C:

rooted /ro͝otid/ *adj* **1 HAVING ROOTS** on which strong roots have developed ○ *a rooted plant* **2 WELL ESTABLISHED** arising from firmly held beliefs or long-standing traditions or practices ○ *a rooted conviction* **3** *US* **UNABLE TO MOVE** unable to move because of shock or fear **4 HAVING STRONG TIES** having strong emotional or cultural roots —**rootedness** *n*

root hair *n* a fine growth from the outer cells of a plant root that resembles a hair and absorbs nutrients

rootle /ro͝ot'l/ (**-tles, -tling, -tled**) *vi* to root about or around [Early 19C. < ROOT[2].]

rootless /ro͝otləss/ *adj* **1** with roots cut off or underdeveloped **2** lacking close ties to people or places —**rootlessly** *adv* —**rootlessness** *n*

rootlet /ro͝otlət/ *n* a small root or part of a root

root mean square *n* the square root of the mean of the squares of a set of numbers

root nodule *n* a swelling on the roots of leguminous plants such as alfalfa, soy beans, and peas, caused by symbiotic bacteria that can fix nitrogen in the soil

root pressure *n* the pressure that forces water upwards through the conducting tissues of a plant, caused by the water potential in the stem being lower than in the root

root run *n* the area of soil through which a plant extends its roots

rootstock /ro͝ot stok/ *n* **1** PLANTS = **rhizome** **2** a root or piece of root used as a stock in propagation by grafting **3** a source or origin of something

root vegetable *n* a vegetable such as a carrot, turnip, or beet that is grown for its fleshy edible underground parts

rootworm /ro͝ot wurm/ *n* a beetle whose larvae feed on the roots of crops, including corn. Genus: *Diabrotica.*

rooty /ro͝oti/ (**-ier, -iest**) *adj* **1** full of or having many roots **2** resembling a root or roots —**rootiness** *n*

ropable /rṓpəb'l/, **ropeable** *adj* **1** able to be caught or restrained using a rope **2** *ANZ* extremely angry (*informal*)

rope /rōp/ *n* **1 STRONG CORD** a strong cord made by twisting together strands of hemp or other fibres or wire **2 STRING OF THINGS** a row of things strung or twisted together ○ *a rope of pearls* **3 STRAND OF STICKY MATERIAL** a stringy strand of a sticky substance ○ *a rope of saliva* **4 CORD FOR HANGING** a cord with a noose at one end that is used for hanging people **5 DEATH BY HANGING** execution by hanging **6 FREEDOM** freedom or latitude to do something ■ **ropes** *npl* **1 CORDS OF RING USED FOR FIGHTING** the cords used to enclose a boxing or wrestling ring **2 USUAL PROCEDURES** the appropriate means and procedures for doing something or for functioning in an environment (*informal*) ○ *Her task was to show the new employee the ropes.* ■ *v* (**ropes, roping, roped**) **1** *vt* **SECURE SOMETHING WITH ROPE** to tie, link, or bind somebody or something with rope ○ *The two climbers were roped together for the ascent.* **2** *vt* **ENCLOSE AREA** to enclose or partition an area using ropes as barriers ○ *Museum staff had roped off the area.* **3** *vt* **LASSO ANIMAL** to catch an animal with a lasso ○ *rope a steer* **4** *vi* **FORM STRANDS** to form strands that resemble rope in shape or texture [Old English *rāp*] —**roper** *n* ◇ **give somebody enough rope to hang himself** *or* **herself** to give somebody enough freedom to make mistakes or reveal his or her shortcomings ◇ **on the ropes** in a desperate or hopeless position and likely to fail (*informal*)

rope in *vt* to involve somebody in an activity, especially if he or she was initially reluctant or unwilling ○ *We got roped in to help with the cleaning up.*

ropeable *adj* = **ropable**

ropedancer /rṓp daanssər/ *n* an acrobat who dances or performs feats on a rope, especially a tightrope, stretched above the ground —**ropedancing** *n*

Roper /rṓpər/ river in N Northern Territory, Australia. Length: 400 km/250 mi.

ropewalk /rṓp wawk/ *n* a long shed or covered walk where ropes are made

rope-walker *n* an acrobat who performs on a rope stretched above the ground, especially a tightrope walker

ropeway /rṓp way/ *n* a system of cables strung from high supports and used to carry heavy objects such as logs from one place to another through the air

ropy /rṓpi/ (**-ier, -iest**), **ropey** (**-ier, -iest**) *adj* **1 INFERIOR** not meeting an acceptable standard (*informal*) ○ *a rather ropy performance* **2 ILL** slightly unwell (*informal*) **3 FORMING STICKY THREADS** forming into sticky, stringy strands **4 SIMILAR TO ROPE** resembling a rope or ropes —**ropily** *adv* —**ropiness** *n*

roque /rōk/ *n* a US game developed from croquet and played on a hard court with a surrounding wall from which the ball can rebound and still be in play [Late 19C. Alteration of CROQUET.]

Roquefort /rók fawr/ *n* a moist, strongly flavoured, blue-veined cheese made from ewes' milk and matured in caves [Mid-19C. After ROQUEFORT-SUR-SOULZON.]

Roquefort-sur-Soulzon /rók fawr syoor so͞o zoN/ town in south-central France, famous for its blue cheese. Population: 880 (1998).

roquet /rṓkay, -ki/ *vti* in croquet, to strike another player's ball with your own ball ■ *n* in croquet, a stroke that makes the player's ball strike that of another player [Mid-19C. Probably alteration of CROQUET.]

roquette /ro két/ *n* PLANTS, FOOD = **rocket**[2] *n*. 1 [Early 20C. < French (see ROCKET[2]).]

ro-ro /rṓ rō/ *n* TRANSP = **roll-on roll-off**

rorqual /ráwrkwəl/ *n* any large streamlined baleen whale that has a small pointed dorsal fin and longitudinal grooves on the throat, e.g. the blue whale or the humpback whale. Genus: *Balaenoptera.* [Early 19C. Via French < Norwegian *røyrkval* < Old Norse *reyðarhvalr* < *reyðr* 'rorqual' < *rauðr* 'red' + *hvalr* 'whale'; from its reddish colour.]

Rorschach test /ráwr shaak-, -shaḵh-/ *n* a projective test of personality or mental state based on somebody's interpretation of a series of standard inkblots. ◊ **projective test** [Early 20C. After Hermann *Rorschach* (1884–1922), Swiss psychiatrist.]

rort /rawrt/ *n Aus* a dishonest scheme or practice (*informal*) ■ *vt Aus* to manipulate something to personal advantage dishonestly or fraudulently (*informal*) ○ *accused of rorting their travel expenses* [Mid-20C. Back-formation < *rorty* 'boisterous, rowdy' < ?] —**rorter** *n*

rosace /rṓz ayss/ *n* **1** a rose window **2** a rosette [Mid-19C. Via French < Latin *rosaceus* 'made of roses' < *rosa* (see ROSE[1]).]

rosacea /rō záyshə/ *n* a recurring inflammatory disorder of the skin of the nose, cheeks, and forehead that is characterized by swelling, dilation of capillaries, pimples, and a reddened appearance [Late 19C. Via modern Latin *(acne) rosacea* 'rose-coloured (acne)' < Latin *rosacea*, feminine of *rosaceus.*]

rosaceous /rō záyshəss/ *adj* **1** belonging or relating to the rose family (**Rosaceae**) of flowering plants **2** resembling a rose flower [Mid-18C. < Latin *rosaceus.*]

Rosalind /rózzə lind/ *n* a small inner natural satellite of Uranus

rosaniline /rō zánnə leen, -līn/, **rosanilin** /rō zánnə lin/ *n* $C_{20}H_{21}N_3O$ a brownish-red crystalline compound. Source: aniline. Use: dye, dye manufacture, antifungal drug, in Schiff's reagent. [Mid-19C. < ROSE[1] + ANILINE.]

rosarian /rō záiri ən/ *n* a cultivator of or expert in the growing of roses [Mid-19C. < Latin *rosarium* 'rose garden', a form of *rosarius* 'of roses' < *rosa* (see ROSE[1]).]

Rosario /rō sa̋ari ō/ city in east-central Argentina. Population: 894,645 (1991).

rosary /rṓzəri/ (*plural* **-ries**) *n* **1 SERIES OF PRAYERS** a series of Roman Catholic prayers, usually made up of five or 15 decades of Hail Marys, each decade beginning with an Our Father and ending with a Gloria **2 CATHOLIC PRAYER BEADS** a string of beads used in counting the prayers said in a rosary **3 rosary, rosary bead NON-CATHOLIC PRAYER BEADS** a string of beads used in praying by members of religions or denominations other than Roman Catholicism [15C. < Latin *rosarium* and Anglo-Latin *rosarius* 'rose garden' (see ROSARIAN).]

ROSCO /róskō/ (*plural* **ROSCOs**) *n* a company that leases trains to train-operating companies under the arrangements by which the UK national railway system was privatized [Late 20C. Acronym of *rolling stock operating company.*]

Roscommon /ross kómmən/ **1** county in west-central Republic of Ireland. Population: 51,897 (1997). Area: 2,463 sq. km/951 sq. mi. **2** town in west-central Ireland. Population: 1,363 (1986).

rose[1] /rōz/ *n* **1 PRICKLY BUSH WITH ORNAMENTAL FLOWERS** a prickly bush with compound leaves that is cultivated in many varieties and hybrids for its flowers. Genus: *Rosa.* **2 FLOWER OF ROSE SHRUB** a flower of the rose shrub **3 PLANT SIMILAR TO ROSE** a member of the family of flowering plants that includes the rose, or a plant that resembles it, especially in having similar flowers. Family: Rosaceae. **4 REDDISH COLOUR** a reddish-pink colour **5 ORNAMENT RESEMBLING ROSE** a representation of a rose flower as an emblem or decoration, or an ornament or design resembling a rose flower **6 FORM OF MINERAL** a mineral form that is round and resembles a rose **7 SPRINKLER NOZZLE** a perforated nozzle on a watering can or hose for producing a spray **8 CEILING FITMENT FOR WIRES** a circular fitting on a ceiling through which the lead of an electric light passes **9** CRAFT, INDUST = **rose cut** **10** CONSTR = **rose window** ■ **roses** *npl* **1 EASY CIRCUMSTANCES** favourable, comfortable, or easy circumstances **2 PINK COLOURING** pink colouration, especially in the cheeks ■ *adj* **1 REDDISH-PINK** of a reddish-pink colour **2 HAVING OR RESEMBLING ROSES** containing roses or resembling roses, especially in smell **3 RELATING TO ROSES** relating to or used for roses [Old English *rōse*, via Germanic < Latin *rosa*, probably < Greek *rhodon* < Iranian] ◇ **everything's coming up roses** everything is going very well

rose[2] /rōz/ past tense of **rise**

rosé /rṓ zay/ *n* a pink-coloured wine, especially one made by fermenting red grapes and removing the skins from the juice before all the colour has been extracted [Late 19C. < French, < *(vin) rosé* 'pink (wine)'.]

Rose /rōz/, **Murray** (*b*. 1939) British-born Australian swimmer

rose apple *n* **1** a rose-scented oval fruit. Use: jellies, confections. **2** an evergreen tree with decorative flowers, that produces rose apples. Native to: Southeast Asia. *Syzygium jambos.*

roseate /rōzi ət/ *adj* **1** of the reddish-pink colour of roses **2** optimistic or idealistic, especially to an absurd degree [15C. < Latin *roseus* 'rosy' < *rosa* 'rose' (see ROSE[1]).] —**roseately** *adv*

roseate spoonbill *n* a wading bird that has rosy plumage and a spoon-shaped bill. Native to: S North America, Central America. *Ajaia ajaja.*

rosebay /rōz bay/ *n* **1** = rosebay willowherb **2** = oleander

rosebay willowherb *n* a perennial plant of northern temperate regions. Flowers: pink spikes. *Chamaenerion angustifolium.* US term **fireweed**

rose beetle *n* INSECTS = rose chafer

Rosebery /rōz berri/ lake in the central part of the North Island, New Zealand. Area: 80 sq. km/31 sq. mi.

Rosebery, Archibald Philip Primrose, 5th Earl of (1847–1929) British statesman and prime minister (1894–95)

rose-breasted grosbeak *n* a woodland finch with a heavy bill, the male of which is black and white with a rose-red patch on its breast. Native to: North America. *Pheucticus ludovicianus.*

rosebud /rōz bud/ *n* the unopened flower of a rose

rose campion *n* a plant with white woolly down on its stems and leaves. Flowers: pink. Native to: Europe, Asia. *Lychnis coronaria.*

rose chafer *n* a greenish-gold beetle that feeds on the roots, leaves, and flowers of roses and other garden plants. *Cetonia aurata.*

rose-coloured *adj* **1** a reddish-pink colour **2** optimistic or idealistic, especially to an unjustifiable degree

rose cut *n* a way of cutting gemstones that gives them a flat base and a hemispherical crown with facets rising to a low point —**rose-cut** *adj*

rosefish /rōz fish/ (*plural* -**fish** *or* -**fishes**) *n* **1** a spiny-finned red fish. Native to: N Atlantic. *Sebastes marinus.* **2** ZOOL = redfish *n.* **1 3** the flesh of a rosefish as food

rose geranium *n* a pelargonium with scented leaves. Flowers: pink. Use: leaves: flavouring, perfumes. *Pelargonium graveolens.*

rosehip /rōz hip/ *n* the fleshy fruit of a rose, resembling a berry. Use: jelly, herbal tea, medicinal syrups. [Mid-19C]

rosella /rō zéllə/ *n* a parrot with bright colourful plumage and a long graduated tail, sometimes kept as a cage bird. Native to: Australia. Genus: *Platycercus.* [Early 19C. Probably alteration of *Rose Hiller*, after *Rose Hill*, Parramatta, near Sydney in Australia.]

rose mallow *n* **1** a tall plant that grows in marshy areas and has downy leaves. Flowers: pink or white. Native to: E North America. Genus: *Hibiscus.* **2** US PLANTS = hollyhock

rosemary /rōzməri/ (*plural* -**ies**) *n* **1** aromatic grey-green needle-shaped leaves. Use: food flavouring, perfume. **2** an aromatic shrub with grey-green needle-shaped leaves that produces rosemary. Native to: S Europe. *Rosmarinus officinalis.* [14C. By folk etymology < *rosmarine* < Latin *rosmarinus* < *ros* 'dew' + *marinus* 'of the sea' < its growth near seacoasts and its blossom's resemblance to dew.]

rose moss *n* a low-growing fleshy-leaved plant widely grown for its bright flowers. Native to: Brazil. *Portulaca grandiflora.*

Rosenberg /rōz'n burg/, **Julius** (1917–53) US Soviet spy

rose of Jericho *n* a plant that curls up into a ball in dry conditions and unfolds and grows in wet conditions. Native to: desert regions. *Anastatica hierochuntica* and *Selaginella lepidophylla.* [After JERICHO]

rose of Sharon /-shárən/ *n* **1** a creeping shrub, widely grown as ground cover. Flowers: large, yellow. Native to: S Europe. *Hypericum calycinum.* **2** a bush widely grown as an ornamental. Flowers: large, red, purple, or white. Native to: Syria. *Hibiscus syriacus.* [Early 17C. Translation of the Hebrew name in the *Song of Solomon*; *Sharon* refers to the fertile plain south of Mount Carmel in Israel.]

rose oil *n* an essential oil. Source: rose flowers. Use: in perfumes, flavourings, medicines.

roseola /rō zee ələ, rōzi ólə/ *n* a red rash on the skin, seen in diseases such as measles, scarlet fever, and syphilis [Early 19C. Formed after RUBEOLA < Latin *roseus* 'rosy' < *rosa* (see ROSE[1]).] —**roseolar** *adj*

roseola infantum /- in fántəm/ *n* a mild disease of young children, typically involving a three-day fever and the eruption of pink spots

rose periwinkle *n* PLANTS = Madagascar periwinkle

rose quartz *n* a pink translucent variety of quartz. Use: gems, ornaments.

roseroot /rōz root/ *n* a perennial mountain plant with fleshy leaves and a pinkish underground stem. Flowers: yellow. Native to: Europe, Asia. *Sedum rosea.* [Late 16C. *Rose* from its root, which smells of roses when bruised.]

rose topaz *n* a pink form of topaz made by applying heat to yellowish-brown topaz

Rosetta /rō zéttə/ = **Rashîd**

Rosetta stone /rō zéttə-/ *n* a stone tablet found in 1799 near Rashid in Egypt that contained the same text repeated three times: in Egyptian hieroglyphics, Egyptian demotic script, and Greek, thereby supplying the key to deciphering hieroglyphics

rosette /rō zét/ *n* **1** ROSE-SHAPED BADGE a circular badge made from gathered loops of ribbon or pleated material, worn to demonstrate support for a team or political party or to indicate having won a prize **2** ORNAMENT RESEMBLING A ROSE a carved or painted ornament resembling the open flower of a rose **3** MARKING RESEMBLING A ROSE a patch of colour or a marking resembling the open flower of a rose, especially a cluster of spots on the fur of a leopard **4** CLUSTER OF LEAVES a circular or spiral cluster of leaves at the base of the stem of a plant [Mid-18C. < French, 'small rose' < *rose* 'rose' < Latin *rosa* (see ROSE[1]).]

Rosewall /rōz wawl/, **Ken** (*b*. 1934) Australian tennis player. Full name **Kenneth Robert Rosewall**

rose water, rose-water *n* a fragrant liquid made by distilling or steeping rose petals in water, used as toilet water and in cooking

rose window, rose *n* a round window, often made of stained glass with tracery radiating from the centre in a pattern that resembles a rose

rosewood /rōz wŏŏd/ *n* **1** the dark heavy rose-scented wood of various tropical trees, especially blackwood. Use: furniture. Genus: *Dalbergia.* **2** a tree that yields rosewood

Rosh Chodesh /rósh khóddəsh/ *n* the first day of a new month in the Jewish religious calendar [< Hebrew *rō'š̌hodeš* 'head of the month']

Rosh Hashanah /rósh hə sháana/, **Rosh Hashana** *n* the festival that marks the Jewish New Year and the beginning of the Days of Awe. Date: 1st and 2nd of Tishri in the autumn. [Mid-18C. < Hebrew *rō'š̌ haššānāh* 'head of the year'.]

Rosicrucian /rōzi kroosh'n/ *n* a member of an international organization concerned with esoteric wisdom derived from ancient mystical and philosophical doctrines [Early 17C. < modern Latin *rosa crucis* 'rose of the cross', translation of German *Rosenkreuz*, after the organization's reputed founder, Christian Rosenkreuz.] —**Rosicrucianism** *n*

rosin /rózzin/ *n* a hard translucent resin ranging in colour from amber to dark brown that is derived from the sap, stumps, or other parts of pine trees ■ *vt* to treat something with rosin, in particular to rub rosin on the bow of a stringed instrument to increase friction [13C. Alteration of Old French *raisine*, variant of *resine* < Latin *resina*; also via Anglo-Latin *rosina* < Latin *resina*.] —**rosiny** *adj*

rosin oil *n* a thick yellowish sticky liquid distilled from rosin. Use: manufacture of varnishes, and inks.

Roskilde /róss killə/ city in E Denmark. Population: 49,080 (1990).

RoSPA /róspə/ *abbr* Royal Society for the Prevention of Accidents

Ross /ross/, **Diana** (*b*. 1944) US pop singer

Ross, Sir James Clark (1800–62) British explorer

Rossellini /róssə leéni/, **Roberto** (1906–77) Italian film director

AKG London

Christina Rossetti

Rossetti /rə zétti/, **Christina** (1830–94) British lyric poet

Rossetti, Dante Gabriel (1828–82) British painter and poet

Rossetti, William Michael (1829–1919) British art critic

Rossini /ro seéni/, **Gioacchino Antonio** (1792–1868) Italian composer

Rosslare /róss láir/ town and port in SE Ireland. Population: 1,386 (1996).

Ross River virus *n* an Australian virus transmitted by mosquitoes that causes recurring fever, headaches, lethargy, rashes, and muscle and joint pains [Mid-20C. After *Ross River*, a river near Townsville in northeastern Australia, near which the virus was first isolated.]

Ross Sea /róss-/ arm of the S Pacific Ocean, extending into E Antarctica between Victoria Land and Marie Byrd Land, and incorporating the Ross Ice Shelf. Area: 958,000 sq. km/370,000 sq. mi.

rostellum /ro stéllam/ (*plural* -**la** /-lə/) *n* a part of an animal or plant that resembles a beak, e.g. the hooked projection from the head of a tapeworm [Mid-18C. < Latin, 'small beak' < *rostrum* (see ROSTRUM).] —**rostellar** *adj* —**rostellate** *adj*

roster /róstər/ *n* **1** LIST OF NAMES a list, especially of employees, athletes, or members of the armed forces, often detailing their duties and the times when they are to be carried out **2** PEOPLE ON A LIST the people listed on a roster ■ *vt* PUT SOMEBODY ON A ROSTER to put somebody's name on a roster [Early 18C. < Dutch *rooster*, originally 'gridiron', hence (from the resemblance of its pattern to lines on paper) 'list' < *roosten* 'roast'.]

rösti /rósti/ *n* a Swiss fried potato cake made from thinly sliced or grated potatoes, sometimes with added onions and bacon [Mid-20C. < Swiss German.]

Rostock /róst ok/ city and port in NE Germany. Population: 236,100 (1994).

Rostov /róss tov/ city in SW European Russia, on the River Don. Population: 1,027,100 (1992).

rostra *plural of* **rostrum**

rostrum /róstrəm/ (*plural* -**trums** *or* -**tra** /-trə/) *n* **1** PLATFORM FOR PUBLIC SPEAKING a platform or raised area where somebody stands to address an audience **2** CONDUCTOR'S PLATFORM a platform on a stage or in front of an orchestra where the conductor stands **3** PLATFORM FOR CAMERA a platform, stand, or raised area supporting a film or television camera **4** PROW OF ROMAN SHIP the beak-shaped prow of an ancient Roman ship, especially a war galley **5** BEAK-SHAPED PART a beak or beak-shaped part of something [Mid-16C. < Latin, 'beak, ship's prow', in plural, 'platform' (because ships' prows decorated the orator's platform in the Forum) < *rodere* 'gnaw'.] —**rostral** *adj* —**rostrally** *adv* —**rostrate** *adj*

rosy /rōzi/ (-**ier**, -**iest**) *adj* **1** ROSE-COLOURED of the reddish-pink colour of roses ○ *the sunset turning the sky a rosy hue* **2** HAVING A PINKISH COMPLEXION having a pinkish complexion that is regarded as indicating good health in white people **3** PROMISING likely to be characterized by success or happiness ○ *predicts a rosy future for the business* **4** OPTIMISTIC optimistic, especially to an unreasonable degree ○ *takes a rosy view of things* **5** LIKE A ROSE resembling roses, characteristic of roses, or full of roses —**rosily** *adv* —**rosiness** *n*

rosy pastor *n* BIRDS = **pastor** *n.* 4

rot /rot/ *v* (**rots, rotting, rotted**) 1 *vti* **DECOMPOSE** to be broken down or to break something organic down by the action of bacteria or fungi ○ *The fruit rotted quickly in the heat.* 2 *vti* **CHANGE BY DECOMPOSITION** to be reduced, damaged, or broken by the action of bacteria or fungi, or to affect something organic in this way ○ *allow the compost to rot down* 3 *vi* **LANGUISH** to endure the effects of complete neglect ○ *thrown into prison and left to rot* ■ *n* 1 **PROCESS OF DECAYING** the process or condition of decaying or a decayed area 2 **NONSENSE** irrelevant or ridiculous talk (*informal*) 3 **FUNGAL DISEASE** disease caused by fungi, e.g. foot rot of sheep, dry rot of timber and plants, and wet rot of timber 4 **ANIMAL DISEASE** infestation with liver flukes 5 **BACTERIAL PLANT DISEASE** a plant disease in which the tissue is broken down by the action of bacteria ■ *interj* **EXPRESSION OF DISAGREEMENT** used to disagree with what somebody has said or to express annoyance or exasperation (*informal*) [Old English *rotian* (verb), perhaps < Indo-European. The noun perhaps came < Scandinavian.]

rota /rṓtə/ *n* a list of people's names and the order in which they are to carry out specified duties [Mid-17C. < Latin, 'wheel'.]

Rota *n* the supreme ecclesiastical tribunal of the Roman Catholic Church

rotary /rṓtəri/ (*plural* **-ries**) *n* a machine or part of a machine that rotates around an axis or a fixed point [Mid-18C. < medieval Latin *rotarius* < Latin *rota* 'wheel'.]

Rotary Club *n* a local club that is a member of an international organization of business and professional people that encourages service to the community [From the organization's early practice of holding meetings in rotation at members' business premises] —**Rotarian** /rō táiri ən/ *n* —**Rotarianism** *n*

rotary cultivator *n* AGRIC = **rotary plough**

rotary engine *n* 1 an internal-combustion engine with cylinders that rotate about a fixed crankshaft 2 an engine that produces torque or power entirely by a rotating mechanism rather than by a crankshaft and reciprocating piston arrangement. ◊ **radial engine**

Rotary International *n* an international organization of business and professional people formed in the United States in 1905 to encourage service to the community [See ROTARY CLUB]

rotary mower *n* a lawn mower with a single blade attached in the middle and sharpened at both ends that rotates as the mower is moved

rotary plough *n* a machine for breaking up and tilling soil, consisting of a series of blades mounted on a revolving power-driven shaft. US term **rototiller**

rotary press *n* a printing press that prints from curved plates mounted on a revolving cylinder, often onto a continuous roll of paper

rotary pump *n* a pump that imparts motion by internal sets of rotating vanes or screws, used to move water or other fluids

rotary tiller *n* AGRIC = **rotary plough**

rotary-wing aircraft *n* an aircraft, especially a helicopter, that is lifted or propelled by rotating aerofoils

rotate /rō táyt/ *v* (**-tates, -tating, -tated**) 1 *vti* **TURN AROUND AXIS** to turn like a wheel around an axis or a fixed point, or make something turn around an axis or a fixed point ○ *The earth rotates around the axis through its poles.* ○ *The windmill's sails are rotated by the wind.* 2 *vti* **VARY CROPS** to vary the crops grown on the same piece of ground so as not to exhaust the soil or make it susceptible to disease 3 *vti* **FOLLOW IN ORDER** to follow in a sequence, taking turns, or make things follow in such a sequence ○ *Rotate the plates in the pile so that they all get used.* 4 **REPLACE PERSONNEL** to be replaced by somebody else, or replace one person or group by another, e.g. in a sports team or military unit ○ *The manager rotates first-team players with promising newcomers in less important games.* ■ *adj* **WHEEL-SHAPED** having parts that radiate from a central point [Late 17C. Either < Latin *rotat-*, past participle of *rotare* < *rota* 'wheel'; or back-formation < ROTATION.] —**rotatable** *adj* —**rotative** *adj* —**rotatively** *adv* —**rotatory** /rō táytəri/ *adj*

rotation /rō táysh'n/ *n* 1 **TURNING MOTION** a turning motion like that of a wheel around an axis or a fixed point, or the act or process of turning in such a way ○ *the rotation of the earth* 2 **SINGLE REVOLUTION** a single turn of something around an axis or a fixed point ○ *one full rotation of the wheel* 3 **REGULAR VARIATION** a regular or planned recurrent sequence of events or changes of position ○ *The families use the holiday cottage by strict rotation.* 4 **CROP ROTATION** crop rotation 5 **MATHEMATICAL TRANSFORMATION** a mathematical transformation in which axes are rotated by a fixed angle while the origin remains unchanged —**rotational** *adj*

rotator /rō táytər/ *n* 1 a person who or thing that rotates or causes rotation 2 (*plural* **-tores**) a muscle that rotates part of the body on an axis

rotator cuff *n* the deep muscles of the shoulder and their tendons that connect the arm to the shoulder joint, encircle it, and provide strength and stability while permitting rotation of the arm

rotavate /rṓtə vayt/ (**-vates, -vating, -vated**), **rotovate** (**-vates, -vating, -vated**) *vt* to break up or till soil using a rotary plough

Rotavator /rṓtə vaytər/, **Rotovator** *tdmk* a trademark for a type of rotary plough

rotavirus /rṓtə vīrəss/ *n* a wheel-shaped RNA virus that causes gastroenteritis, especially in infants [Late 20C. < modern Latin, 'wheel-virus' < Latin *rota* 'wheel' + *virus* 'poison, virus'.]

rote[1] /rōt/ *n* mechanical repetition of something so that it is remembered, often without real understanding of its meaning or significance ○ *learned it by rote* [13C. < ?]

rote[2] /rōt/ *n* a medieval stringed instrument played by plucking [14C. < Old French, probably < late Latin *chrotta* 'British musical instrument', from Welsh *crwth* '(type of) Celtic stringed instrument' or Old Irish *crot* 'harp, cithara'.]

rotenone /rṓtə nōn/ *n* $C_{23}H_{22}O_6$ a white crystalline insecticide. Source: roots of derris. [Early 20C. < Japanese *roten* 'derris'.]

rotgut /rót gut/ *n* cheap and rough alcoholic drink (*informal*)

Roth /roth/, **Philip** (*b.* 1933) US writer

Rother /ró*th*ər/ river in SE England. Length: 50 km/31 mi.

Rotherham /ró*th*ərəm/ town in NE England. Population: 251,637 (1994).

Rothermere /ró*th*ər meer/, **Harold Sydney, 1st Viscount Harmsworth** (1868–1940) British newspaper magnate

Rothesay /róthsi, -say/ town in SW Scotland, on the island of Bute. Population: 5,264 (1991).

Rothko /róth kō/, **Mark** (1903–70) Russian-born US artist

Rothschild /róth chīld, róths-/, **Lionel Nathan** (1808–79) British financier

Rothschild, Mayer Amschel (1743–1812) German financier

Rothschild, Nathan Mayer (1777–1836) German-born British financier

roti /rṓti/ (*plural* **-tis**) *n* an unleavened bread originally from South Asia, also eaten in the Caribbean [Early 20C. < Hindi *roṭī*.]

rotifer /rṓtifər/ *n* a microscopic invertebrate that has a wheel-shaped crown of projecting threads (**cilia**) at the anterior end and lives mostly in freshwater habitats. Phylum: Rotifera. [Late 18C. < modern Latin, 'wheel-bearing, wheel-bearer' < Latin *rota* 'wheel'.] —**rotiferal** /rō tíffərəl/ *adj* —**rotiferous** *adj*

rotisserie /rō tíssəri/ *n* 1 a cooking appliance for roasting meat using a rotating spit 2 a shop or restaurant where meat is roasted and sold [Mid-19C. < French *rôtisserie* < *rôtir* 'roast' < Old French *rostir* < Germanic.]

rotl /rótt'l/ *n* a unit of weight used in many Islamic countries, varying from approximately 0.45 to 2.25 kg/1 to 5 lbs [Early 17C. < Arabic *raṭl* < ?]

⚡**ROTM** *abbr* right on the money (*in e-mails*)

rotogravure /rṓ tōgrə vyóor/ *n* 1 a printing process in which images are etched photomechanically onto copper cylinders mounted in a rotary press, from which they are printed onto a moving web of paper 2 something printed using rotogravure, e.g. a magazine or a photographic section of a newspaper [Early 20C. < German *Rotogravur*, company name.]

rotor /rṓtər/ *n* 1 **ROTATING AEROFOILS** an assembly of aerofoils that rotates about a hub to give lift to an aircraft, especially a helicopter 2 **ROTOR BLADE** a blade or aerofoil of a rotor (*informal*) 3 **ROTATING PART OF MACHINE** a rotating part of an electrical apparatus, e.g. the armature of a generator, or of a mechanical device [Late 19C. Contraction (perhaps after VECTOR) or ROTATOR.]

rotorcraft /rṓtər kraaft/ (*plural* **-craft**) *n* a helicopter or any similar aircraft that uses a rotor to gain lift

Rotorua /rṓtə roó ə/ city in the central part of the North Island, New Zealand. Population: 55,100 (1998 estimate).

Rotorua, Lake lake in the central part of the North Island, New Zealand. Area: 80 sq. km/31 sq. mi.

rototiller /rṓtə tillər/ *n* US AGRIC = **rotary plough** [Early 20C. < Latin *rota* 'wheel' + TILLER[2].]

rotovate *vt* AGRIC = **rotavate**

Rotovator *tdmk* AGRIC = **Rotavator**

rotten /rótt'n/ *adj* 1 **DECAYED** affected by rot or decay ○ *a rotten apple* 2 **FOUL** extremely unpleasant, unfortunate, or nasty (*informal*) ○ *rotten weather* 3 **INFERIOR** below the acceptable standard (*informal*) ○ *He's a rotten driver.* 4 **NOT FEELING WELL** feeling unwell, usually without a specific complaint (*informal*) 5 **UNHAPPY** feeling unhappy or uncomfortable, especially through guilt or embarrassment (*informal*) ○ *I feel rotten about letting you down.* 6 **UNETHICAL** lacking ethical principles in the treatment of other people or animals ■ *adv* **TO A GREAT DEGREE** to a great degree, especially so much as to be disapproved of (*informal*) ○ *The grandmother spoils those kids rotten.* ○ *She fancies you rotten.* [13C. < Old Norse *rotinn*.] —**rottenly** *adv* —**rottenness** *n*

rotten borough *n* formerly, a political constituency with few electors but the same right to elect a representative as a more populous constituency, especially any of various parliamentary constituencies in England before 1832

rottenstone /rótt'n stōn/ *n* a form of silica-rich limestone that has been decomposed by weathering and is used in powdered form for polishing metal

rotter /róttər/ *n* a nasty or unpleasant person (*dated informal*) [Early 17C. Originally in the sense 'causer of rotting'.]

Rotterdam /róttər dam/ port in SW Netherlands. Population: 593,321 (2000).

Rottweiler *n* a large powerful dog belonging to a breed that has a black smooth coat with tan markings

rotund /rō túnd/ *adj* 1 with a greater body weight than is advisable 2 having a full, rich sound [15C. Directly or via Italian *rotondo* < Latin *rotundus* 'round' < *rotare* 'rotate' < *rota* 'wheel'.] —**rotundity** *n* —**rotundly** *adv* —**rotundness** *n*

rotunda /rō túndə/ *n* 1 a round building, usually covered with a dome 2 a large round hall or room [Early 17C. Alteration (after Latin *rotundus* 'round') of Italian *rotonda* < Latin *rotunda*, feminine of *rotundus* 'round'.]

Rouault /roó ō/, **Georges Henri** (1871–1958) French painter and engraver

Roubaix /roo bé/ city in N France. Population: 96,984 (1999).

rouble /roób'l/, **ruble** *n* see table at **currency** [Mid-16C. Via French *rouble* < Russian *rubl'*.]

roué /roó ay/ *n* a man who regularly engages in drinking, gambling, and womanizing [Early 19C. < French, noun use of past participle of *rouer* 'break on the wheel' (a medieval instrument of torture) < Latin *rotare*.]

Rouen /roó aaN/ city in N France. Population: 105,470 (1990).

rouge /roo*zh*/ *n* 1 **REDDISH MAKEUP FOR CHEEKS** red or pink makeup in powder or cream form used to add colour to the cheeks or lips (*dated*) 2 **POLISH IN POWDER FORM** any polish in powder form containing metallic oxides, especially a polish for metal (**jeweller's rouge**) that contains ferric oxide ■ *vt* (**rouges, rouging, rouged**) **COLOUR SOMETHING WITH ROUGE** to put rouge on the cheeks or lips (*dated*) [Mid-18C. Via French < Latin *rubeus* 'red'.]

rouge et noir /-ay-/ *n* a card game in which gamblers place their stakes on a table marked with two red and two black diamonds and all betting is against the house at even money [< French, 'red and black']

rough /ruf/ *adj* 1 **NOT SMOOTH OR FLAT** having a bumpy, knobbly, or uneven surface rather than being smooth, flat, and regular 2 **NOT SOFT** not soft and smooth, but rather coarse in texture ○ *a dog with a rough bristly coat* 3 **WINDY OR TURBULENT** stormy, or unpleasantly turbulent as a result of stormy conditions ○ *The weather had been rough for days.* 4 **WILD AND UNCULTIVATED** not cleared, flattened, and cultivated, but in a natural state with wild vegetation, or else allowed to fall into a derelict, disused state ○ *marching over rough terrain* 5 **NOT GENTLE** done with or using a lot of force or violence ○ *toys that will stand up to rough handling* **6 BOORISH** not refined or polite in manner and behaviour ○ *rough talk* **7 HARSH** harsh on the ears or to the taste **8 GENERAL** not exact, precise, or detailed, but broadly correct ○ *a rough estimate* **9 THROWN TOGETHER** made quickly or without using proper or good-quality materials, or reaching only the most basic standard ○ *used branches to build a rough shelter* **10 CRUDE** hastily or incompletely made ○ *a rough wooden carving* **11 SEVERE OR UNPLEASANT** severe, unfair, or generally unpleasant (*informal*) ○ *received rough treatment at the hands of the judge* **12 SLIGHTLY ILL** rather ill, especially as a result of tiredness or overindulgence rather than because of illness (*informal*) ○ *She felt a bit rough the next morning.* **13 ROWDY** noisy, rowdy, or violent ○ *a rough crowd* **14 FREQUENTED BY UNSAVOURY PEOPLE** frequented or inhabited by people who tend to be noisy, rowdy, or violent (*informal*) ○ *a rough part of town* ■ *n* **1 UNMOWN PART OF GOLF COURSE** that area of a golf course on which grass and other vegetation is allowed to grow higher than on the fairway **2 PRELIMINARY OUTLINE** a preliminary version of something, e.g. a sketch giving the broad layout of an artwork **3 VIOLENT PERSON** a violent or brutal person, especially a hired thug **4 SIDE OF RACQUET** the side of a tennis or other racquet where the binding of the strings is not smooth ■ *vt* **ROUGHEN** to make something rough [Old English *rūh* < Germanic] —**roughish** *adj* —**roughness** *n* ◇ **in the rough** in a crude, unfinished, or uncultivated state ◇ **rough it** to live in a less comfortable or less sophisticated way than usual (*informal*) ◇ **rough or smooth** used as a call when spinning a racket in a game of tennis or squash to decide which player should serve first or choose the end to serve from ◇ **take the rough with the smooth** to accept the disadvantages of a situation as well as the advantages

SPELLCHECK Do not confuse ***rough*** with ***ruff***, which has a similar sound. Beware: your spellchecker will not catch this error.

rough out *vt* to prepare a rough model, plan, or sketch of something ○ *The scriptwriters meet to rough out a scene-by-scene narrative long before a word of dialogue is written.*

rough up *vt* **1** to subject somebody to a violent beating (*informal*) **2** to make something such as somebody's hair look untidy by rubbing it to make it stick up or stick out

roughage /rúffij/ *n* MED = **fibre** *n*. 7 [Late 19C. Originally in the sense 'rough grass, weeds'.]

rough-and-ready *adj* **1** not elegant or stylish but practical or usable ○ *rough-and-ready accommodation in a hostel* **2** not polite or well-mannered but friendly or kind-hearted

rough-and-tumble *n* a situation characterized by a lack of restraint and a ruthless disregard for rules and conventions —**rough-and-tumble** *adj*

rough breathing *n* in ancient Greek, a sound like that of the English 'h', occurring with an initial vowel or the letter ρ and indicated by the symbol ʽ. ◊ **smooth breathing**

roughcast /rúf kaast/ *n* **1 PEBBLED SURFACE ON WALLS** a surface of coarse plaster covered with pebbles on the outside walls of a building (*often before nouns*) ○ *roughcast walls* **2 ROUGH MODEL** a preliminary form or model of something ○ *made a roughcast in clay before starting to work the marble* ■ *vt* (**-casts, -casting, -cast**) **1 COVER A WALL WITH ROUGHCAST** to cover the surface of a wall or the walls of a building with roughcast **2 FORM SOMETHING ROUGHLY** to shape or form something in a crude fashion or as a preliminary to more polished work —**roughcaster** *n*

rough copy *n* a preliminary draft of a piece of writing, usually raw and unedited

rough cut *n* the preliminary version of a cinema film, with only basic editing done to put the scenes together in sequence

rough diamond *n* **1** a diamond in its natural state, before it has been cut into shape and polished **2** somebody who does not care about good manners or formality but is likeable or trustworthy. US term **diamond in the rough**

rough-dry *vt* to dry washed laundry but not iron it —**rough-dry** *adj*

roughen /rúff'n/ *vti* to make something rough, or become rough

rough endoplasmic reticulum *n* endoplasmic reticulum containing ribosomes that give its surface an uneven appearance, involved in the synthesis of proteins in plant and animal cells. ◊ **smooth endoplasmic reticulum**

rough fish *n* a species of fish that is neither caught for food nor fished for by anglers

rough-hew (**rough-hews, rough-hewing, rough-hewed, rough-hewed** *or* **rough-hewn**) *vt* **1** to cut or carve something roughly without smoothing the surface or edges ○ *He rough-hewed the wood to make a crude table.* **2** to shape or form something crudely

rough-hewn *adj* **1 NOT SMOOTHED** cut or shaped only roughly, with the surface and the edges not smoothed ○ *blocks of rough-hewn sandstone* **2 CRUDELY MADE** crudely shaped or formed **3 UNREFINED** uncouth and unrefined in character

roughhouse /rúf howss/ *n* rough behaviour or excessively boisterous play (*informal*) ○ *The party turned into a roughhouse.* ■ *vti* (**-houses, -housing, -housed**) to behave or treat somebody in a rough boisterous way (*informal*) [Late 19C. < the idea of an establishment such as a bar or brothel where disorderly behaviour occurs.]

rough-legged buzzard /-léggid-/ *n* a large hawk with a dark body, feathers covering its legs, and a white tail with a broad dark band at the end. Native to: Arctic. *Buteo lagopus.* US term **rough-legged hawk**

rough-legged hawk *n US* BIRDS = **rough-legged buzzard**

roughly /rúf li/ *adv* **1 CRUDELY** in a crude or incomplete way ○ *shape the minced beef roughly into balls* **2 VIOLENTLY OR RUDELY** in a violent way or a manner lacking in gentleness and politeness **3 APPROXIMATELY** as a guess without any claim to exactness ○ *Roughly one third of the funding comes from government.*

roughneck /rúf nek/ *n* **1 HIRED THUG** a violent person, especially a hired thug (*informal*) **2 COARSE PERSON** a rough, bad-mannered person (*informal*) **3 OIL-FIELD WORKER** an unskilled worker on an oil rig or at an oil well (*slang*) [Mid-19C. *Neck* used here for 'person'.]

roughrider /rúf rīdər/ *n* a breaker or trainer of wild or untrained horses

roughshod /rúf shod/ *adj* fitted with horseshoes that have short spikes to prevent slipping in wet weather

rough shooting *n* shooting prey on moorland without using beaters

rough stuff *n* violent behaviour or acts (*informal*)

rough trade *n* an offensive term for a man whose physicality and lack of refinement are found sexually attractive by a homosexual man from a higher social class (*slang*)

rouille /roo ée/ *n* a sauce made from chillies, garlic, and olive oil served as an accompaniment to Provençal foods such as bouillabaisse [Mid-20C. Via French, 'rust' (from its colour) < Latin *robigo*.]

roulade /roo láad/ *n* **1** a dish in which a piece of food is coated with a sauce or filling and rolled up before being cooked, so that each slice has a spiral appearance **2** a run of several musical notes sung rapidly to one syllable [Early 18C. < French, < *rouler* 'to roll' < Latin *rota* 'wheel'.]

rouleau /róolō/ (*plural* **-leaux** /-lō/ *or* **-leaus** /-lōz/) *n* **1** a stack of coins wrapped in a paper cylinder **2** rolled or folded ribbon used as decorative piping or trimming [Late 17C. Via French, 'small roll' < Latin *rotula* 'small wheel' < *rota* 'wheel'.]

roulette /roo lét/ *n* **1 GAMBLING GAME WITH A SPINNING WHEEL** a game in which a ball is rolled onto a spinning horizontal wheel divided into compartments, with players betting on which compartment the ball will come to rest in (*often before nouns*) **2 TOOL WITH A TOOTHED WHEEL** a tool with a toothed wheel used for making dots, e.g. in engraving, or for making perforations in paper, e.g. on a sheet of postage stamps **3 SLITS CUT IN PAPER** a line of slits or perforations made by a cutting tool on a sheet of paper ■ *vt* (**-lettes, -letting, -letted**) **MARK SOMETHING WITH DOTS OR PERFORATIONS** to use a roulette to mark a surface with a line of dots or make perforations in a sheet of paper [Mid-18C. < French, 'small wheel' < late Latin *rotella* < Latin *rota* 'wheel'.]

round¹ /rownd/ *adj* **1 CIRCULAR OR SPHERICAL** shaped like a circle or a ball ○ *a big, perfectly round bowl* **2 CURVED** curved rather than square or angular **3 IN CIRCULAR MOTION** done with or involving a circular motion **4 COMPLETE** not less or more than ○ *I'll have a round dozen of them.* **5 EXPRESSED BY INTEGER** expressed as an approximate value, especially to the nearest integer or power of ten ○ *use 1,500 as a round number* **6 CONSIDERABLE** large in amount or size ○ *a round sum* **7 FULLY DEVELOPED** fully developed in terms of personality, or fully depicted, as in a character in a book ○ *His heroes are always very round and colourful.* **8 PLUMP** full and plump, especially in facial features ○ *kindly eyes surrounded by a round face* **9 SONOROUS** mellow and rich in tone **10 BRISK** lively and rather fast ○ *We set off at a round pace.* **11 STRAIGHTFORWARD** plain and outspoken ○ *'I said in good round English 'I'm going to knock the stuffing out of you''.* (John Buchan, *Greenmantle*; 1916) **12 PRONOUNCED WITH ROUNDED LIPS** describes speech sounds articulated with the lips forming an oval opening ○ *a round vowel sound* [13C. Via Old French *ro(u)nd-*, stem of *ro(o)nt*, < Latin *rotundus* (see ROTUND).] —**roundish** *adj* —**roundness** *n*

round² /rownd/ *n* **1 ROUND SHAPE** a round shape or object ○ *little rounds of cheese* **2 SESSION** a session or instance of a particular event, usually in a series of similar or related events ○ *the Uruguay round of global talks* ○ *the dreary round of fruitless calls* **3 STAGE OF COMPETITION** a game or series of games in a competition ○ *the first round of the competition* **4 PERIOD OF BOXING OR WRESTLING** a time period, usually three minutes, during which boxers or wrestlers fight **5 GAME OF GOLF** a playing of all the holes on a golf course once **6 TURN OF PLAY** a single turn of play, as in a game of cards **7 ARROWS SHOT** a specified number of arrow shot from a specified distance **8 CHARGE OF AMMUNITION** a bullet, blank cartridge, or other charge of ammunition ○ *hundreds of mortar rounds* **9 GUN DISCHARGE** a single discharge by a gun or guns ○ *fired a few rounds* **10 SERIES OF VISITS** a series of visits made on a regular basis to different places or people (*often plural*) **11 SET OF DRINKS** a number of drinks bought, one for each person in a group **12 SLICE OF BREAD** a slice of bread or toast, or a sandwich made from two slices of bread **13 APPLAUSE** an outburst of applause or cheering ○ *She entered the hall to a huge round of applause.* **14 PART SONG** a song sung by several people in which each person sings a different part of the song at the same time **15 MOVEMENT IN CIRCLE** movement in a circle or around an axis **16 BELLS RUNG** a sequence of bells rung in order of treble to tenor **17 CIRCULAR DANCE** a dance with a sequence of movements in a circle **18 CUT OF BEEF** a cut of beef from between the rump and the shank [14C. < ROUND¹.] ◇ **in the round** **1** visible or viewed from all sides (*of a theatre*) **2** with full detail and perspective from all sides ◇ **make** *or* **do** *or* **go the rounds** **1** to circulate and become widespread ○ *a new rumour making the rounds* **2** to go from place to place in a regular pattern

round³ /rownd/ *v* **1** *vt* **MOVE PAST AN OBSTACLE** to move in a curve past the edge or corner of something ○ *as they rounded the corner* **2** *vti* **EXPRESS AS A ROUND NUMBER** to express a number containing several units as the nearest significant number above or below it, e.g. treating 5,753 as 6,000, or 6.375 as 6 ○ *The estimate was rounded to the nearest pound.* **3** *vt* **PRONOUNCE SOUNDS** to pronounce a sound with rounded lips ○ *Try to round your vowels.* **4** *vt* **PURSE LIPS** to purse the lips [15C. < ROUND¹.]

round down *vt* to express a number as a smaller and less exact number for ease of calculation

round off *vt* **1** to make the edges, sides, or corners of something less straight or angular and more rounded **2** to bring something to a pleasant or satisfactory end by doing or adding one last thing

round on *vt* to attack somebody suddenly, either physically or verbally, in a fit of anger

round out *vti* to achieve or cause something to achieve a more complete or satisfactory form

round up *vt* **1** to gather people or animals together in one place **2** to express a number as a larger and exact number for ease of calculation

round⁴ /rownd/ CORE MEANING: a grammatical word used to indicate that a circle of people, a place, or an object surrounds or encloses something ○ (prep) *She sat clasping her hands round her knees.* ○ (prep) *an area of green belt round the town* ○ (adv) *a crowd soon gathered round*

1 *prep, adv* **IN DIFFERENT PARTS OF** situated at various points in, or moving to various places in ○ (prep) *newspapers and books scattered round the room* ○ (adv) *We managed to find someone to show us round.* ○ (adv) *She keeps moving things round and I can't find anything!* **2** *prep, adv* **IN ALL DIRECTIONS** situated or moving in all directions from a central point of reference ○ (prep) *gazing round him at the strange sights of this new country* ○ (adv) *They could see nothing but green fields for 10 miles round.* ○ *driving round for hours looking for them* **3** *prep* **IN A PARTIAL CIRCUIT** so as to move to the other side of a corner or obstacle in a partial circuit, or be reached by such a movement ○ *The lorry came round the bend at breakneck speed.* **4** *prep,* *adv* **TURNING ON AN AXIS** revolving round a centre or axis ○ (prep) *the movement of the planets round the sun* ○ (adv) *cylinders going round at 1,000 revolutions per minute.* **5** *adv* **IN THE OPPOSITE DIRECTION** to turn so as to be facing in the opposite direction ○ *She turned round when he called her name.* **6** *prep, adv* **IN CIRCUMFERENCE** on or outside the circumference or perimeter ○ (prep) *I measure 25 inches round the waist.* ○ (adv) *The tower was 60 feet tall and 30 feet round.* **7** *prep, adv* **TO EVERYONE** to all members in a group, from person to person ○ (adv) *She handed round the drinks.* ○ (prep) *News of the closure was passed round the factory.* **8** *adv* **VISIT** to visit a particular place ○ *She went round to give them the news.* **9** *adv* **IN A CURVE** in a curved shape or by a circuitous route ○ *After the pedestrian crossing, the road bends round to the left.* **10** *prep* **HAVING A BASIS IN** used to indicate the thing that is the basis for something such as a concept or a story line ○ *The plot is centred round the relationship between two brothers.* [14C. Partly < ROUND¹; partly shortened < AROUND.] ◇ **round about 1** approximately ○ *round about midnight* **2** surrounding somebody or something on all sides

roundabout /równdə bowt/ *n* **1 REVOLVING RIDE IN PLAYGROUND** a piece of playground equipment in the form of a revolving structure for children to sit on and push or be pushed round and round. US term **merry-go-round** *n.* 2 **2 CIRCULAR ROAD JUNCTION** a road junction with a central island around which traffic moves in one direction. US term **traffic circle** ■ *adj* **INDIRECT** proceeding in a way that is not direct or straightforward ○ *went by a roundabout route* ○ *answered in a roundabout way* —**roundaboutness** *n*

round-arm *adj* **1** made with a near-horizontal swing of the arm **2** in cricket, with the bowler's arm coming over the shoulder at an angle nearer horizontal than vertical ○ *a round-arm action*

round clam *n* ZOOL = **quahog** [< its rounded shell]

round dance *n* **1 FOLK DANCE** a folk dance in which several dancers or couples form a circle **2 BALLROOM DANCE** a ballroom dance in which couples revolve as they move round the room, as in a waltz **3 BEE'S MOVEMENT** a more or less circular sequence of movements that a honeybee performs in or near the hive to show other bees that food is nearby

rounded /równdid/ *adj* **1** having curved, not straight or angular, surfaces or edges ○ *a rounded lawn* **2** having many different features or aspects that together form a whole that is complete and interestingly complex or diverse ○ *received a very rounded education* **3** PHON = **round**¹ *adj.* 12 —**roundedness** *n*

roundel /równd'l/ *n* **1 ROUND PART** a round part or piece such as a round section in a stained-glass window or a round panel in a section of wood panelling **2 IDENTIFYING DISC ON AIRCRAFT WING** a coloured disc on a military aircraft wing identifying the aircraft's country of origin **3 ROUND PIECE OF ARMOUR** a circular section of armour that protects the wearer's armpit **4 MODIFIED FORM OF RONDEAU** an English form of the rondeau that has eleven lines arranged in three stanzas of three lines and a one-line refrain after the first and third stanzas **5 TYPE OF RONDEL** a modified form of the rondel that has ten lines arranged in two stanzas of three lines and one of four lines, with the opening line repeated as a refrain **6** DANCE = **roundelay** *n.* 2 [13C. < Old French *rondel* 'small circle' < *ro(u)nd-* (see ROUND¹).]

roundelay /równdə lay/ *n* **1** a simple song in which one of the verses is repeated at intervals, or the music for such a song **2** a slow medieval dance performed by a group who form a circle [15C. Anglicization of French *rondelet* 'small roundel' < *rondel* 'small circle' < *ro(u)nd-*, (see ROUND¹).]

rounder /równdər/ *n* **1** a score in the game of rounders made when the batter runs round all four bases after a single hit of the ball **2** a tool that makes edges or surfaces round

rounders /równdərz/ *n* a ball game in which batters score a point, or rounder, if they run round all four marked fielding positions or bases after a single hit of the ball (+ *singular verb*)

round hand *n* handwriting with broad rounded letters as opposed to, e.g., copperplate

Roundhead /równd hed/ *n* a supporter of Oliver Cromwell and the Parliamentarians against King Charles I during the English Civil War. ◊ **Cavalier** [Mid-17C. < their close-cropped hair (contrasted with that of the Cavaliers).]

roundhouse /równd howss/ (*plural* **-houses** /-howziz/) *n* **1 BUILDING FOR RAILWAY ENGINES** a circular building in which railway engines are stored or serviced, consisting of a central turntable with several sections of track radiating from it **2 CABIN ON A SAILING SHIP** a large cabin or set of cabins at the rear of an old-fashioned sailing ship **3 PUNCH DELIVERED WITH A CIRCULAR SWING** a punch made with a wide circular swing of the arm (*slang*) **4 PINOCHLE MELD** a meld of four kings and four queens in all suits in the card game pinochle

roundlet /równdlət/ *n* a small circular or disc-shaped object (*formal*)

round lot *n* a regular number of stocks or bonds as a trading unit, usually 100 shares of stock or 5 bonds

roundly /równdli/ *adv* **1** forcefully and thoroughly ○ *They were roundly criticized for their failure.* **2** so as to form a circle or sphere (*dated*)

round robin *n* **1 TOURNAMENT WITH EVERYONE PLAYING ONE ANOTHER** a tournament in which each player or team plays against every other player or team in turn (*hyphenated before a noun*) ○ *a round-robin contest* **2 DOCUMENT EACH PERSON PASSES ON** a letter or other document circulated in turn to all members of a group, with each of them adding comments if they wish **3 PETITION WITH SIGNATURES IN CIRCLE** a letter, especially a petition or letter of protest, on which the signatures are arranged in a circle in order to hide the identity of the first person to sign [< the man's first name *Robin*]

round-shouldered *adj* with the shoulders hunched or drooping and the upper back bent forward slightly

roundsman /równdzmən/ (*plural* **-men** /-mən/) *n* **1 SOMEBODY DOING THE ROUNDS OF PLACES** a regular visitor to places on a route, e.g. to make deliveries or inspections **2** *US* **POLICE OFFICER SUPERVISING A PATROL** a police officer, especially a sergeant, in charge of all the officers patrolling a particular area **3** *ANZ* **REPORTER COVERING FIXED AREA OR SUBJECT** a journalist employed to cover stories on a particular topic or field of interest

round table *n* a discussion or negotiation between several parties or groups who all take part on equal terms (*hyphenated when used before a noun*) [< ROUND TABLE]

Round Table *n* **1 KING ARTHUR'S TABLE** the legendary table at which King Arthur and his knights sat, made round so that no one would appear to have precedence **2 KING ARTHUR'S KNIGHTS** the knights of King Arthur as a group **3 INTERNATIONAL ASSOCIATION UNDERTAKING CHARITABLE WORK** an international association of businessmen set up in 1927 to carry out charitable work in local communities worldwide, or a local branch of the association

round-the-clock *adj* lasting or operating throughout the day and night ○ *mounted round-the-clock surveillance on the house*

round trip *n* **1** a journey to a place and back again, usually returning by the same route (*hyphenated before a noun*) ○ *the round-trip fare* **2** CARDS = **roundhouse** *n.* 4

round-trip *adj US* TRANSP = **return** *adj.* 2

round-trip ticket *n US* = **return ticket**

round-up *n* **1** a gathering together of people or animals, e.g. suspects in a criminal investigation or livestock on a farm or ranch **2** a gathering together of things of any kind, especially information or news ○ *a news round-up on the hour*

roundworm /równd wurm/ *n* a parasitic round-bodied worm (**nematode**) that infests the intestine of people and some animals. *Ascaris lumbricoides.*

roup /roop/ *n* an infectious respiratory disease that affects poultry [14C. Probably < N Germanic.]

rouse /rowz/ (**rouses, rousing, roused**) *v* **1** *vti* **WAKE** to wake up, or wake somebody from sleep or unconsciousness **2** *vt* **SHAKE OUT OF APATHY** to stir somebody into action or a more active state, or become more active ○ *Anger roused her to write a letter of complaint.* **3** *vt* **PROVOKE FEELING IN** to cause somebody to feel a particular emotion ○ *the feelings of guilt that the whole affair roused in us* **4** *vt* **SCARE HUNTED ANIMAL INTO THE OPEN** to scare a hunted animal or bird out of its hiding place [15C. < ?] —**rouser** *n*

rouseabout /rówzə bowt/ *n ANZ* an unskilled worker who carries out menial tasks, especially on a sheep or cattle station (*dated*)

rousing /rówzing/ *adj* **1** filling people with passion, emotion, and enthusiasm ○ *a rousing speech* **2** suggesting energy and vigour, especially by its fast pace —**rousingly** *adv*

Rous sarcoma /rówss-/ *n* a cancerous tumour found in chickens, caused by a specific tumour-producing RNA virus [Early 20C. After Francis Peyton *Rous* (1879–1970), US physician.]

Rousseau /roos ṓ/, **Jean Jacques** (1712–78) French philosopher and writer

roust /rowst/ *vt* **1 FORCE TO GET UP** to make somebody get up, make a move, or take action, especially abruptly or roughly **2** *US* **HARASS** to bother, annoy, or jostle somebody (*slang*) ■ *n US* **HARASSING** a harassing of somebody (*slang*) [Mid-17C. Probably alteration of ROUSE.]

roustabout /rówstə bowt/ *n* **1** *US, Can* an unskilled labourer, especially on an oil rig, on a ship or wharf, or in a circus **2** *ANZ* AGRIC = **rouseabout** (*dated*)

rout¹ /rowt/ *n* **1 DEFEATED ARMY'S RETREAT** a swift and disorderly retreat by a defeated army **2 CRUSHING DEFEAT** any severe and humiliating defeat ○ *the rout suffered at the general election* **3 RABBLE** a noisy and disorganized group of people ■ *vt* **1 FORCE AN ARMY TO RETREAT** to defeat an army completely and force it to make a swift and disorderly retreat **2 DEFEAT SOMEBODY THOROUGHLY** to subject an opponent to a thorough and humiliating defeat [13C. < Anglo-Norman *rute*, Old French *route* 'dispersed group' < Latin *rumpere* 'break'.]

rout out *vt* **1** to drive a person or animal from a place, especially by the use of force **2** to reveal or uncover something, especially after a search ○ *routed out his true motives*

rout² /rowt/ *v* **1** *vt* to cut a groove in wood or metal, especially with a router **2** *vti* to search for something by poking about, as pigs do with their snouts [Mid-16C. Variant of ROOT².]

route /root/; *in military usage also* /rowt/ *n* **1 WAY TO TRAVEL** a way, path, or road for travelling from one place to another **2 PROGRESSION** the course that something follows, or the way it progresses or develops ○ *My career might have taken an entirely different route.* **3 REGULAR JOURNEY** a journey somebody regularly makes, especially a set sequence of calls or stops made, e.g. by somebody delivering something ○ *Their store wasn't on my usual route.* ■ *vt* (**routes, routeing, routed**) **SEND ALONG ROUTE** to direct or arrange for somebody or something to follow a particular course ○ *All phone calls were routed through my office.* [12C. < Old French *route* < feminine past participle of Latin *rumpere* 'break'.]

SPELLCHECK See ***root***.

routeman /rootmən/ (*plural* **-men** /-mən/) *n US* a person who regularly calls or stops in the course of a job, especially somebody selling or delivering something

route march *n* a long march over rough ground, often used as training in physical endurance for soldiers, in which discipline is often relaxed and route step is allowed —**route-march** *vti*

ϟ **router**¹ /rootər/ *n* a computer switching program that transfers incoming messages to outgoing links via the most efficient route possible, e.g. over the Internet [< ROUTE]

router² /rówtər/ *n* a tool that cuts shaped grooves and hollows in wood or metal, originally a hand tool but now usually driven by electricity [< ROUT²]

route step *n* a mode of marching in formation where there is no requirement to keep in step and talking and singing are allowed

ϟ **routine** /roo teén/ *n* **1 USUAL SEQUENCE OF ACTIVITIES** the usual way tasks or activities are arranged **2 SOMETHING REPETITIVE** something that is unvarying or boringly repetitive ○ *a life of mindless routine* **3 REGULAR PATTERN OF BEHAVIOUR** a typical pattern of behaviour that somebody adopts in particular circumstances, especially insincere or affected behaviour (*informal*) ○ *The salesman went into his routine about the car's unique reliability and performance.* **4 REHEARSED PERFORMANCE** a rehearsed set of movements, actions, or speeches that make up a performance ○ *her gymnastic routine on the parallel bars* **5 PART OF A COMPUTER PROGRAM** a part of computer program that performs a particular task ○ *a dump routine* ■ *adj* **1 USUAL OR STANDARD** regular or standard and nothing out of the ordinary ○ *carrying out routine inquiries* **2 REPETITIVE** boringly predictable, monotonous, and unchanging ○ *found the work pretty routine* [Late 17C. < French, < *route* (see ROUTE).] —**routinely** *adv*

SYNONYMS See ***habit***.

routinise *vt* = **routinize**

routinize /roo tēen īz, rōotin īz/ (**-izes, -izing, -ized**), **routinise** (**-ises, -ising, -ised**) *vt* to arrange or plan something so that it follows a regular or unchanging pattern —**routinization** /roo tēen ī zāysh'n, rōoti nī-/ *n*

roux /roo/ (*plural* **roux** /rooz/) *n* a mixture of flour and fat that is cooked briefly and used as the thickening base of a sauce or soup [Early 19C. Via French, 'browned' < Old French *rous* 'reddish brown' < Latin *russus* 'red'.]

rove[1] /rōv/ (**roves, roving, roved**) *v* **1** *vti* to wander or travel about with no definite purpose, often over a wide area **2** *vi* to move, especially to look, in changing directions ○ *The officer's trained gaze roved around the room, taking it all in.* [Early 16C. < ?]

rove[2] /rōv/ *vt* (**roves, roving, roved**) to twist fibres slightly before they are spun into yarn or thread ■ *n* wool, cotton, or other fibres twisted slightly in preparation for spinning [Late 18C. < ?]

rove[3] past tense, past participle of **reeve**[2]

rove beetle *n* a carnivorous or scavenging beetle with a long body and short wing covers. Family: Staphylinidae. [< ?]

rover[1] /rōvər/ *n* **1 WANDERER** a person who wanders from place to place, never settling anywhere for long **2 ARCHERY TARGET** a mark or object selected randomly as a target in archery **3 CROQUET BALL** a ball in croquet that has been through all the hoops but has not yet hit the final peg **4** *ANZ* **AUSTRALIAN RULES PLAYER** in Australian Rules football, a player, usually smaller than the others, who plays alongside the two ruckmen, and who gathers and clears the ball when it emerges from a ruck **5 VEHICLE FOR EXPLORING PLANET** a small vehicle launched from a lander and used to explore the surface of the moon or a planet

rover[2] /rōvər/ *n* a pirate or pirate ship (*archaic*) [14C. < Middle Low German or Middle Dutch *rōver* < *rōven* 'rob'.]

rover[3] /rōvər/ *n* a machine or attachment for twisting fibres slightly in preparation for spinning

Rover Scout *n* a Venture Scout

roving /rōving/ *adj* **1** moving or travelling from one place or thing to another ○ *a bulletin from our roving reporter* **2** tending to wander or waver rather than settle or concentrate on one thing

roving eye *n* a wide and often promiscuous sexual interest

row[1] /rō/ *n* **1 LINE OF THINGS** a group of things or people arranged in a line that is usually straight, or the line itself ○ *cabbages planted in a row* **2 LINE OF SEATS** a line of seats in a theatre, cinema, lecture hall, or similar public place ○ *the second row in the balcony* **3 NARROW STREET BETWEEN LINES OF HOUSES** a narrow street that is lined with houses or other buildings on both sides **4 STREET WITH A PARTICULAR CHARACTER** a street where a particular occupation or type of person predominates ○ *lawyer's row* **5** MUSIC = **tone row** [Old English *rāw* < Germanic] ◇ **in a row** one after the other in succession ◇ **a hard row to hoe** something difficult to do

row[2] /rō/ *v* **1** *vti* to propel a boat across water by using oars **2** *vi* to take part in the sport of rowing [Old English *rōwan* < Germanic, 'steer'] —**rower** *n*

row back *vi* to moderate or modify a previous assertion, claim, or opinion, or retreat from a previous position on an issue (*informal*)

row[3] /row/ *n* **1 LOUD FIGHT** a noisy quarrel or dispute **2 RACKET** an unpleasant or excessively loud noise ■ *vi* **ARGUE NOISILY** to have a noisy argument [Mid-18C. < ?]

rowan /rō ən, rów ən/ *n* **1** a deciduous tree with greyish compound leaves, clusters of white flowers, and bright red berries. Native to: Europe, W Asia, North Africa. *Sorbus aucuparia.* **2 rowan, rowanberry** (*plural* **-ries**) a red to orange berry from a rowan tree [Early 19C. < N Germanic, < Indo-European, 'red'.]

rowboat /rō bōt/ *n* *US* = **rowing boat**

rowdy /rówdi/ *adj* (**-dier, -diest**) noisy and disorderly ○ *The debate was a pretty rowdy affair.* ■ *n* (*plural* **-dies**) a rough and noisy person who often causes disturbances ○ *a bar full of local rowdies* [Early 19C. Probably < ROW[3].] —**rowdily** *adv* —**rowdiness** *n* —**rowdyism** *n*

rowel /rów əl/ *n* a small spiked revolving wheel on the end of a horse-rider's spur ■ *vt* (**-els, -elling, -elled**) to urge a horse on by digging rowels into its sides [14C. Via Old French *roel(e)* 'small wheel' < late Latin *rotella* < (see ROULETTE).]

rowen /rów ən/ *n* *New England* a second mowing of hay or grass in the same season [14C. < Old N French, variant of Old French *regain* 'till again' < *gaignier* 'till' < Germanic.]

row house *n* *US* = **terraced house**

rowing /rō ing/ *n* the propelling of a small boat through the water using oars, especially the sport of racing in specially designed lightweight boats (*often before nouns*) ○ *a member of the rowing team*

rowing boat *n* a small lightweight boat designed to be propelled through the water by one or more people rowing with oars. US term **rowboat**

rowing machine *n* a fitness machine that imitates the action of rowing a boat

Rowlandson /rōləndsʼn/, **Thomas** (1756–1827) British painter and caricaturist

Rowling /rōling/, **Bill** (1927–95) New Zealand statesman and prime minister of New Zealand (1974–75). Full name **Sir Wallace Edward Rowling**

Rowling, J. K. (*b.* 1965) British author. Full name **Joanne Kathleen Rowling**

rowlock /róllək, rúllək/ *n* a more or less U-shaped pivoting metal rest fitted to the side of a rowing boat, in which an oar rests. US term **oarlock** [Mid-18C. Alteration of OARLOCK after ROW[2].]

Rowntree /równ tree/, **Benjamin Seebohm** (1871–1954) British manufacturer and philanthropist

Roy /roy/, **Arundhati** (*b.* 1961) Indian writer

royal /róy əl/ *adj* **1 OF KINGS AND QUEENS** relating to, belonging to, or consisting of a king, queen, or other member of a monarch's family ○ *members of the royal household* **2 ENJOYING ROYAL PATRONAGE** a word used in the titles of organizations and societies established by a monarch or a member of a monarch's family, or given his or her formal approval and support **3 LARGEST OR BEST** of the largest size or of the highest standard **4 EXCELLENT** of the most excellent kind ○ *given a royal welcome* **5 EXTREMELY BAD** used to emphasize how extremely bad something is (*informal*) ○ *a right royal pain in the neck* **6 ABOVE THE TOPGALLANT** located in the area of a sailing ship's rigging that is above the topgallant ■ *n* **1 MONARCH OR MEMBER OF MONARCH'S FAMILY** a monarch, or a member of a monarch's family, especially his or her immediate family (*informal*) **2 STAG WITH LARGE ANTLERS** a stag with large antlers that have 12 or more points on them **3 SAIL ABOVE TOPGALLANT SAIL** the sail above the topgallant sail on a full-rigged ship **4 SIZE OF PAPER** a size of paper, especially a British size of writing paper 483 x 610 mm/19 x 24 in or a size of printing paper 508 x 635 mm/20 x 25 in [13C. Via Old French *roial* < Latin *regalis* < *reg-*, stem of *rex* 'king'.]

Royal Air Force *n* the air force of the United Kingdom, formed on 1 April, 1918 from the amalgamation of the Royal Flying Corps and the Royal Naval Air Service

Royal Assent, royal assent *n* the British monarch's formal signing of an act of Parliament, making it law

royal blue *adj* of a bright deep blue colour (*hyphenated before a noun*) —**royal blue** *n*

Royal British Legion *n* MIL = **British Legion**

Royal Canadian Mounted Police *n* a police force that operates throughout Canada except in cities and provinces with their own police forces

Royal Commission *n* in the United Kingdom, a committee set up by the monarch on the prime minister's advice to inquire into an issue ○ *set up a Royal Commission to investigate environmental pollution*

royal fern *n* a deep-rooted fern with branched stems, found throughout the world. *Osmunda regalis.*

royal flush *n* in poker, a hand that consists of a ten, jack, queen, king, and ace of the same suit

Royal Flying Doctor Service *n* a medical service operated in remote parts of Australia that involves doctors and emergency medical services travelling to patients by light aircraft

Royal Highness *n* a title used when speaking of or referring to a member of a royal family other than a king or queen

royal icing *n* a crisp icing made by mixing icing sugar with egg whites

royalist /róy əlist/ *n* a supporter of a monarch or the monarchical system of government (*often before nouns*) —**royalism** *n*

Royalist /róy əlist/ *n* **1** a Cavalier or supporter of Charles I during the English Civil War **2** HIST = **Tory** *n.* **5 3** in France, a supporter of the Bourbon dynasty after the Revolution

royal jelly *n* a protein-rich substance that worker bees secrete and feed to larvae in the early stages of their development and to the larvae of queen bees in all stages of their development

Royal Leamington Spa ♦ **Leamington Spa**

royally /róy əli/ *adv* with impressive generosity and hospitality ○ *royally entertained*

royal mast *n* the highest section of a sailing ship's mast that is immediately above the topgallant

royal palm *n* a palm tree with a tall naked trunk. Native to: tropical America. Genus: *Roystonea.*

royal purple *adj* of a deep vivid reddish-purple colour (*hyphenated before a noun*) —**royal purple** *n*

royal road *n* the route or method by which progress or a particular result is guaranteed, often by virtue of special privileges ○ *a young singer on the royal road to stardom*

royal standard *n* the flag of the British monarch, flown from the place he or she is staying in at the time

royalty /róy əlti/ (*plural* **-ties**) *n* **1 ROYAL PERSON OR PEOPLE** a king, queen, or other member of a monarch's family, or members of a royal family generally ○ *mixing with royalty at garden parties* **2 ROYAL PERSON'S STATUS** the status or authority of a king, queen, or other member of a monarch's family **3 KINGLY OR QUEENLY QUALITIES** the personal qualities conventionally ascribed to a king or queen, especially great dignity **4 MONARCH'S PERMISSION TO HAVE SOMETHING** the right to have or take something, especially minerals, granted by a king or queen to a person or company **5 PERCENTAGE OF INCOME PAID TO CREATOR** a percentage of the income from a book, piece of music, or invention that is paid to the author, composer, or inventor (*often plural*) ○ *still living on the royalties from her first novel* **6 MINING COMPANY'S PAYMENT TO LANDOWNER** money paid to a landowner by a company taking minerals, oil, or gas from his or her land (*often plural*)

royal warrant *n* a king's or queen's official authorization to a company to supply goods to a royal household

rozzer /rózzər/ *n* a member of a police force (*dated slang*) [Late 19C. < ?]

RP *abbr* **1** Received Pronunciation **2** Regius Professor **3** Republic of the Philippines

RPB *abbr* Recognized Professional Body

⚡**RPG**[1] *n* a high-level computer language used primarily for business reports. Full form **report program generator**

RPG[2] *n* a game in which the participants assume roles, often as fantasy characters such as heroes or elves, in a scenario that develops as the game progresses. Full form **role-playing game**

RPI *abbr* retail price index

rpm *abbr* revolutions per minute

RPM *abbr* resale price maintenance

RPO *abbr* Royal Philharmonic Orchestra

rpt *abbr* **1** repeat **2** report

RPV *abbr* remotely piloted vehicle

RR *abbr* **1** railroad **2** Right Reverend

-rrhagia *suffix* abnormal or excessive flow or discharge ○ *metrorrhagia* [< Greek < *rhag-*, stem of *rhēgnunai* 'burst forth']

-rrhoea, -rrhea *suffix* flow, discharge ○ *pyorrhoea* [< modern Latin, < Greek *rhein* 'flow']

rRNA *abbr* ribosomal RNA

RRP *abbr* recommended retail price

Rs *symbol* rupees

RS *abbr* **1** recording secretary **2** right side **3** Royal Society

RSA[1] *abbr* **1** Republic of South Africa **2** Returned Services Association (New Zealand) **3** Royal Scottish Academician **4** Royal Scottish Academy **5** Royal Society of Arts

⚡**RSA**[2] *n* in computing, a system of encryption based on the difficulty of factoring very large numbers [After *RSA* Security Inc., who devised it.]

RSC *abbr* **1** Royal Shakespeare Company **2** Royal Society of Chemistry

RSI *n* a painful condition affecting some people who overuse muscles as a result of activities such as regularly operating a computer keyboard and mouse or playing the piano. Full form **repetitive strain injury**. US term **cumulative trauma disorder**. ◊ **tenosynovitis**

RSJ *abbr* rolled steel joist

RSL *n* an organization established in Australia in 1916 to provide help for former members of the armed forces and their families. Full form **Returned Services League** ■ *abbr* Royal Society of Literature

RSM *abbr* **1** regimental sergeant major **2** Republic of San Marino **3** Royal Society of Medicine

RSPB *abbr* Royal Society for the Protection of Birds

RSPCA *abbr* Royal Society for the Prevention of Cruelty to Animals

RSV *abbr* Revised Standard Version

RSVP used on an invitation to request a response to it [French *répondez s'il vous plaît*]

rt *abbr* right

⚡**RT** *abbr* **1** radio telegraph **2** radio telegraphy **3** radio telephone **4** radio telephony **5** real time (*in e-mails*) **6** room temperature

⚡**RTDS** *abbr* real-time data system

Rte *abbr* route (*in addresses*)

RTE *abbr Ireland* Radio Telefís Éireann [Gaelic, 'Irish Radio and Television']

⚡**rtf** *abbr* used after the dot in a computer file name to show that the file contains rich text. Full form **rich text format**

Rt Hon. *abbr* Right Honourable

⚡**RTM** *abbr* read the manual (*in e-mails*)

Rt Rev. *abbr* Right Reverend

⚡**ru** *abbr* Russian Federation (*in Internet addresses*)

Ru *symbol* ruthenium

⚡**RU** *abbr* **1** Rugby Union **2** are you (*in e-mails*)

Ruahine Range /roō ə hee nay-/ mountain range in the S of the North Island, New Zealand. Highest peak: Mount Mangaweka 1,733 m/5,686 ft.

Ruanda-Urundi /roō ándə oō roōndi/ former name for **Burundi**

Ruapehu /roō ə páy hoo/ active volcano in the centre of the North Island, New Zealand. Height: 2,797 m/9,177 ft.

rub /rub/ *v* (**rubs, rubbing, rubbed**) **1** *vt* **PRESS AND MOVE HAND ON** to move the hand or an object over the surface of something, pressing down with a repeated circular or backwards and forwards motion ○ *rubbing ointment into his skin* **2** *vi* **TOUCH WITH DRAGGING PRESSURE** to make dragging contact with a surface ○ *metal parts rubbing against one another* **3** *vti* **CLEAN WITH REPEATED STROKES** to clean, dry, or polish something, or be able to be cleaned, dried, or polished, by moving a cloth, sponge, or other implement over the surface repeatedly ○ *Rub the flaking paint off with sandpaper.* **4** *vti* **CAUSE ABRASION ON SKIN** to cause discomfort or pain by repeatedly scraping the skin ○ *These shoes are rubbing my heels.* **5** *vt* **ANNOY** to cause annoyance to somebody (*informal*) ○ *Her brusqueness was beginning to rub me.* **6** *vi* **BE SLOWED DOWN IN BOWLS** in bowls, to be slowed by an uneven patch on the green ■ *n* **1 RUBBING ACTION** a rubbing motion, or a rubbing of something with or against something else **2 MASSAGE** a massaging of part of the body ○ *a soothing back rub* **3 DIFFICULTY** a problem or difficulty ○ *That's the rub: too little time.* **4 IRRITATING THING** something that somebody does or says that irritates or offends somebody else **5 UNEVEN PATCH IN BOWLS** in bowls, an uneven patch of grass in the green [14C. < ?]

rub along *vi* to have a friendly enough relationship or existence together (*informal*)

rub down *vt* **1 MAKE SURFACE SMOOTH FOR PAINTING** to prepare a surface for painting or varnishing by smoothing it or removing the old paint or varnish with sandpaper or some other abrasive **2 MASSAGE** to massage somebody or part of the body vigorously **3 DRY BODY WITH VIGOROUS RUBBING** to dry a person's or animal's body by vigorous rubbing with a towel

rub in *v* **1** to keep reminding somebody of something that person does not want to be reminded of, usually because it is embarrassing (*informal*) **2** *vt* to mix fat, usually butter, into flour in small pieces between the fingertips

rub off *vi* to be passed to somebody, or be an influence on somebody who is exposed to it

rub out *v* **1** *vti* to remove something written, or to be removed, with a rubber **2** *vt US, Can* to murder somebody (*slang*)

rub up *v* **1** *vt* to polish something by vigorous rubbing ○ *Let the polish soak into the leather before you rub them up.* **2** *vti* to refresh old knowledge of something, or bring a skill back up to its former standard ○ *rubbing up on his French* ◇ **rub somebody up the wrong way** to irritate or annoy somebody

Rub al-Khali /roōb al kaáli/ desert region in SE Arabia. Area: 2,300,000 sq. km/900,000 sq. mi.

rubasse /roō bass, roo báss/ *n* a ruby-red variety of quartz containing iron oxide [Late 19C. < French *rubace* < *rubis* 'ruby' < Latin *rubeus, ruber* 'red'.]

rubato /roo baátō/ *n* rhythmic freedom in musical performance, often against a steady accompaniment ■ *adj, adv* performed with rubato [Late 18C. < Italian *(tempo) rubato* 'robbed (time)', past participle of *rubare* 'rob'.]

rubber[1] /rúbbər/ *n* **1 NATURALLY OCCURRING ELASTIC SUBSTANCE** a strong elastic material made by drying the sap from various tropical trees, especially the rubber tree **2 ELASTIC SYNTHETIC SUBSTANCE** a strong elastic synthetic substance made either by improving the qualities of natural rubber or by an industrial process using petroleum and coal products **3** *US* **WATERPROOF OVERSHOE** a waterproof overshoe worn over normal shoes to protect them in wet weather (*usually plural*) **4 SPOT PITCHER STANDS ON** the rectangle of hard rubber on the mound that the pitcher stands on to throw the ball in baseball **5 RUBBING OR POLISHING CLOTH** a cloth or pad used for rubbing or polishing something, especially the pad that a cabinetmaker uses to apply varnish or French polish **6 DEVICE THAT RUBS** any machine or device that rubs a surface **7 DEVICE FOR ERASING** a piece of rubber used for erasing writing. US term **eraser** **8** *US* **CONDOM** a contraceptive sheath that fits over a man's penis (*slang; offensive in some contexts*) [Mid-16C. < RUB.] ◇ **burn rubber** to drive very fast (*informal*)

rubber[2] /rúbbər/ *n* **1 BRIDGE MATCH OF THREE GAMES** a match of three or five games in cards, especially bridge and whist **2 DECIDING GAME IN CARDS MATCH** in some card games, an extra game played to decide a tied match **3 SESSION OF PLAY IN CARD GAME** a match or session of playing in a card game (*informal*) **4 SET OF GAMES** a set or series of games in some sports (*informal*) [Late 16C. < ?]

rubber band *n* a loop of thin rubber that is wrapped round objects to hold them together

rubber bridge *n* a form of contract bridge in which a new hand is dealt for each round

rubber bullet *n* a cylindrical block of hard rubber fired by police officers or troops during crowd-control operations, designed as a deterrent but capable of inflicting serious injury

rubber cement *n* an adhesive made by dissolving rubber in an organic solvent

rubber cheque *n* a cheque that is returned by a bank because the person who wrote it has insufficient funds in his or her account to cover it (*informal humorous*) [Because it bounces]

rubber-chicken circuit *n US* a series of events that people feel obliged to attend, especially lunches or dinners for politicians or other public figures (*informal*) [Because the food served is usually unappetizing]

rubber goods *npl* condoms (*used euphemistically*)

rubberise *vt* = **rubberize**

rubberize /rúbbə rīz/ (**-izes, -izing, -ized**), **rubberise** (**-ises, -ising, -ised**) *vt* to coat or impregnate something, especially fabric, with rubber

rubberneck /rúbbər nek/ *n* somebody who stares in an over-inquisitive or insensitive way (*informal*) US term **rubbernecker** ■ *vi* to stare at somebody or something in an excessively inquisitive or insensitive way (*informal*) [Late 19C. < craning or turning the neck as if it were made of rubber. Originally a US word.] —**rubbernecking** *n*

SYNONYMS See ***gaze***.

rubbernecked /rúbbər nekt/ *adj* staring insensitively or in an excessively inquisitive way (*informal*) ○ *a crowd of rubbernecked onlookers*

rubbernecker /rúbbər nekər/ *n* = **rubberneck** (*informal*)

rubber plant *n* **1** a tropical plant with thick glossy leaves and a rubbery sap, widely grown as a houseplant but growing as a full-size tree in Southeast Asia. *Ficus elastica.* **2** any plant that produces a rubbery sap

rubber stamp *n* **1 STAMPING DEVICE** a device for stamping words or numbers on paper, consisting of an embossed flat rubber pad that is inked **2 AUTOMATIC AUTHORIZATION** authorization or approval that is given automatically **3 SOMEBODY GIVING APPROVAL AUTOMATICALLY** a person or group who gives authorization or approval automatically, without thinking, questioning, or dissenting

rubber-stamp *vt* **1** to authorize or approve something automatically, without thinking, questioning, or dissenting **2** to mark a document with an imprint from a rubber stamp

rubber tree *n* **1** a tree whose sap is the main source of natural rubber. Native to: tropical America. *Hevea brasiliensis.* **2** any tree whose sap is made into rubber

rubbery /rúbbəri/ *adj* with the elastic or tough texture of rubber

rubbing /rúbbing/ *n* an impression of a textured surface, e.g. a raised design on a tombstone, made by placing paper over the surface and rubbing with a drawing implement

rubbing alcohol *n* a liquid, usually consisting of 70% denatured ethanol or isopropanol, used for massaging and as an antiseptic

rubbish /rúbbish/ *n* **1 MATERIAL** things that are thrown away as unwanted, usually the remains of things that have been used or used up (*often before nouns*) **2 WORTHLESS THINGS** things that are worthless or of very poor quality **3 NONSENSE** foolish things said or written, or things dismissed as wrong or not to be believed ○ *Don't talk rubbish!* ■ *vt* **DISMISS SOMETHING OR CRITICIZE** to dismiss something as worthless or to criticize somebody severely (*informal*) ○ *The scheme has been rubbished in the national press.* [14C. < Anglo-Norman *rubbous.*] —**rubbishy** *adj*

rubbish bin *n* a large usually cylindrical container with a lid for household rubbish, kept outdoors

rubble /rúbb'l/ *n* **1 FRAGMENTS OF BROKEN BUILDINGS** broken stones, bricks, and other materials from buildings that have fallen down or been demolished **2 ROUGH STONES AS FILLER OR BULK** rough unfinished stones used to fill space between walls or to build the bulk of a wall that will have a finishing surface of dressed stone **3 rubble, rubblework MASONRY OF ROUGH STONES** masonry that is constructed using rough unfinished stones [14C. < ?] —**rubbly** *adj*

Rubbra /rúbbrə/, **Edmund** (1901–86) British composer

rubdown /rúb down/ *n* a brisk rubbing down, usually of a person's or animal's body after exercising

rube /roob/ *n US, Can* an offensive term for somebody who is regarded as naive or unsophisticated, especially somebody from the country who is not used to city ways (*slang*) [Late 19C. Shortening of the forename *Reuben*.]

rubefacient /roōbi fáysh'nt/ *adj* causing the skin to become red (*formal*) ■ *n* a substance that causes the skin to become red, especially a cream or ointment used as a counterirritant [Early 19C. < Latin *rubefacient-*, present participle of *rubefacere* 'make red' < *rubeus* 'red' + *facere* 'make'.] —**rubefaction** /-fáksh'n/ *n*

rubefy /roōbi fī/ (**-fies, -fying, -fied**) *vti* to use a rubefacient on skin [14C. < Old French *rubifier* 'make red' < Latin *rubeus* 'red'.]

rubel /roōb'l/ see table at **currency** [Late 20C. < Belarusian.]

rubella /roo béllə/ *n* MED German measles (*technical*) [Late 19C. < modern Latin, 'rash' < Latin *rubellus* 'reddish' < *rubeus* 'red'.]

rubellite /roōbi līt, roo béllīt/ *n* a red variety of tourmaline. Use: jewellery. [Late 18C. < Latin *rubellus* (see RUBELLA).]

Rubens /roōbənz/, **Peter Paul** (1577–1640) Flemish painter

rubeola /roō bee ələ, roōbi ṓlə/ *n* measles (*technical*) [Late 17C. < modern Latin, < Latin *rubeus* 'red'.] —**rubeolar** *adj*

rubescent /roo béss'nt/ *adj* turning red or reddish, e.g. by blushing (*literary*) [Mid-18C. < Latin *rubescent-*, present participle of *rubescere* 'redden' < *ruber* 'red'.]

Rubicon[1] /roōbikən, -kon/, **rubicon** *n* a point at which any action taken commits the person taking it to a further particular course of action that cannot be avoided [Early 17C. After the RUBICON, stream in N Italy that Julius Caesar crossed illegally with his army in 49 BC, making civil war inevitable.] ◇ **cross the Rubicon** to do something that commits you to a particular course of action

Rubicon[2] /ro͝obikən/ ancient name of a stream in NE Italy. Now called the 'Rubicone', it empties into the Adriatic Sea north of Rimini. Length: 24 km/15 mi.

rubicund /ro͝obikənd/ *adj* with the reddish skin colour that is widely regarded as a sign of good health in people with white skin (*literary*) [15C. < Latin *rubicundus* < *ruber* 'red'.] —**rubicundity** /ro͝obi kúndəti/ *n*

rubidium /roo bíddi əm/ *n* (*symbol* **Rb**) a soft silvery-white radioactive element of the alkali metal group that reacts strongly with water and bursts into flame when exposed to air. Source: lepidolite, carnallite. Use: photocells. [Mid-19C. < modern Latin, < Latin *rubidus* 'red' < *rubere* 'be red'; from the two red lines in its spectrum.]

Rubinstein /ro͝obin stīn/, **Artur** (1887–1982) Polish-born US pianist

ruble *n* MONEY = **rouble**

rubric /ro͝obrik/ *n* **1 TITLE OR HEADING** a printed title or heading, usually distinguished from the body of the text in some way, especially the heading of a section of a legal statute, originally underlined in red **2 SET OF PRINTED INSTRUCTIONS** a set of printed rules or instructions, e.g. the rules governing how Christian services are to be conducted, often printed in red in a prayer book **3 ESTABLISHED CUSTOM** a well-established custom or tradition that provides rules for conduct **4 CATEGORY** a class or category of things ■ *adj* **IN RED** printed or marked in red [13C. Directly or via Old French < Latin *rubrica* 'red ochre' < *rubeus, ruber* 'red'.] —**rubrical** *adj* —**rubrically** *adv*

rubricate /ro͝obri kayt/ (**-cates, -cating, -cated**) *vt* (*formal*) **1 ADD HEADINGS TO TEXT** to add titles or heading to a text, or print them in red **2 MARK IN RED** to print or mark something in red **3 REGULATE** to apply a set of rules to something —**rubrication** /ro͝obri káysh'n/ *n* —**rubricator** /ro͝obri kaytər/ *n*

rubrician /roo brísh'n/ *n* an expert in the way religious services should be conducted

ruby /ro͝obi/ *n* (*plural* **-bies**) **1 RED GEMSTONE** a red precious stone that is a form of corundum. Use: jewellerey, manufacture of watches, precision instruments. (*often before nouns*) ○ *a ruby ring* **2 DEEP RED** a deep glowing purplish-red colour like that of a ruby ■ *adj* **DEEP RED IN COLOUR** of a deep glowing red colour tinged with purple, like that of a ruby [14C. Via Old French < Latin *ruber, rubeus* 'red'.]

ruby port *n* a port that is matured for a minimal period in the barrel and then bottled for immediate drinking

ruby spinel *n* a red transparent form of the mineral spinel. Use: jewellery.

ruby wedding *n* the 40th anniversary of a couple's wedding

RUC *abbr* Royal Ulster Constabulary

ruche /roosh/ *n* a decorative strip of gathered, pleated, or frilled fabric on a garment ■ *vt* (**ruches, ruching, ruched**) to decorate the edges of a garment with ruches [Early 19C. Via French < medieval Latin *rusca* 'tree bark' < Celtic.]

ruching /ro͝oshing/ *n* decorative edges of gathered, pleated, or frilled fabric

ruck[1] /ruk/ *n* **1 LARGE NUMBER** a large number of people or things **2 ORDINARY PEOPLE OR THINGS** the great mass of unexceptional people or things **3 FOLLOWERS** the group of competitors behind the leader in a race **4 LOOSE SCRUM** in rugby, a loose scrum formed around the ball when it is on the ground **5 GROUP OF ROVING PLAYERS** in Australian Rules football, three players who have no fixed positions but follow play, trying to win possession of the ball for their team ■ *vi* **FORM A RUCK** in rugby, to form a loose scrum around the ball on the ground [13C. Probably < N Germanic, 'pile of combustible material'.]

ruck[2] /ruk/ *vti* to become creased, or cause something, especially fabric, to become creased ○ *The carpet is rucked up under your chair.* ■ *n* a crease, especially in a fabric [Late 18C. < Old Norse *hrukka* 'wrinkle'.]

rucksack /rúk sak, ro͝ok-/ *n* a large bag, usually with two straps and often with a supporting frame, carried on the back and used especially by walkers and climbers [Mid-19C. < German, 'back-sack'.]

ruckus /rúkəss/ *n* a noisy and unpleasant disturbance [Late 19C. < ?]

ruction /rúksh'n/ *n* a noisy, often violent, quarrel or fight ■ **ructions** *npl* angry reactions, protests, or arguments ○ *There'll be ructions if the boss finds out!* [Early 18C. < ?]

rudbeckia /rud béki ə/ (*plural* **-as** *or* **-a**) *n* a plant with alternate leaves and showy yellow flowers that have green or black centres. Native to: North America. Genus: *Rudbeckia*. [Mid-19C. < modern Latin, after Olof *Rudbeck* the elder (1630–1702) and the younger (1660–1740), Swedish botanists.]

rudd /rud/ (*plural* **rudds** *or* **rudd**) *n* a freshwater fish of the carp family with a thin greenish-brown body and red fins. Native to: Europe. *Scardinius erythrophthalmus*. [Early 16C. Variant of obsolete *rud* 'redness'.]

Rudd /rud/, **Steele** (1868–1935) Australian writer. Pseudonym of **Arthur Hoey Davis**

rudder /rúddər/ *n* **1 MEANS OF STEERING BOAT OR SHIP** a means of steering a boat or ship, usually in the form of a pivoting blade under the water, mounted at the stern and controlled by a wheel or handle (**tiller**) **2 AEROFOIL FOR STEERING AEROPLANE** an aerofoil, usually on the tail of an aeroplane, that pivots vertically and controls left-to-right movement **3 CONTROLLING FORCE** a guiding or controlling force or influence [Old English *rōþer* < Germanic] —**rudderless** *adj*

rudderfish /rúddər fish/ (*plural* **-fish** *or* **-fishes**) *n* a small-to-medium oval fish known for its habit of following oceangoing ships in schools. Family: Kyphosidae.

ruddle /rúdd'l/, **reddle** /rédd'l/, **raddle** /rádd'l/ *n* a red ochre. Use: dye, formerly to mark sheep. ■ *vt* (**-dles, -dling, -dled**) to dye or mark something such as a sheep with ruddle [Mid-16C. < obsolete *rud* 'redness'.]

ruddy /rúddi/ *adj* (**-dier, -diest**) **1 ROSY WITH HEALTH** with a healthy reddish glow ○ *ruddy cheeks* **2 REDDISH** red or reddish in colour ○ *ruddy sky* ■ *adj* (**-dier, -diest**), *adv* **SWEARWORD** used as a swearword to emphasize how good, bad, or severe something is (*slang; offensive in some contexts*) [Old English *rudig* < Germanic] —**ruddily** *adv* —**ruddiness** *n*

ruddy duck *n* a duck with a broad bill, upright tail, and white cheeks, the male of which is brownish-red with a black crown and blue bill during the mating season. Native to: North America. *Oxyura jamaicensis*.

rude /rood/ (**ruder, rudest**) *adj* **1 ILL-MANNERED** disagreeable or discourteous in manner or action ○ *Don't be rude!* **2 INDECENT** offensive to accepted standards of decency ○ *rude words* **3 UNREFINED** lacking refinement or social skills **4 SUDDEN AND UNPLEASANT** happening with unexpected suddenness and unpleasantness ○ *a rude awakening* **5 ROUGHLY MADE** in a rough or incomplete state ○ *a rude wooden bench* **6 UNSKILLED** showing a lack of skill or training ○ *rude paintings* **7 INEXPERIENCED** without schooling or experience ○ *a rude youth raised in the wilderness* **8 RAW** in a raw or unprocessed state ○ *rude fibres* **9 VAGUE** lacking precision ○ *a rude guess* **10 UNDEVELOPED** technologically or economically undeveloped **11 ROBUST** strong and energetic ○ *in rude health* [13C. Via French < Latin *rudis* 'raw, rough'.] —**rudely** *adv* —**rudeness** *n*

ruderal /ro͝odərəl/ *adj* describes a plant growing in wasteland, rubbish, or disturbed ground [Mid-19C. < Latin *ruder-* 'rubble'.] —**ruderal** *n*

rudiment /ro͝odimənt/ *n* **1 SOMETHING BASIC TO SUBJECT** a basic principle or skill, especially in a particular field or subject (*often plural*) ○ *the rudiments of computer programming* **2 BEGINNING** an early stage in the development of something such as a plan (*often plural*) **3 UNDEVELOPED BODY PART** a body part that does not develop fully and performs no useful function. The mammary gland in males is a rudiment. **4 EMBRYO OF ORGAN** an embryonic stage of an organ or body part [Mid-16C. Directly or via French < Latin *rudis* 'raw, rough'.]

rudimentary /ro͝odi méntəri/, **rudimental** /-mént'l/ *adj* **1 BASIC** existing at an elementary or basic level **2 DEVELOPING** in an early or partially developed stage **3 UNDEVELOPED** not fully developed ○ *a rudimentary tail* **4 IN FORM OF EMBRYO** in an embryonic state —**rudimentarily** *adv* —**rudimentariness** *n*

Rudolf /ro͝o dolf/ (1858–89) archduke and crown prince of Austria

Rudolf I (1218–91) king of Germany and Holy Roman Emperor (1273–91)

Rudolf, Lake former name for **Lake Turkana**

rue[1] /roo/ *vti* (**rues, ruing, rued**) to feel regret or sorrow for something in the past ○ *I rue the day I offered to help.* ■ *n* a feeling of regret or sorrow (*archaic*) [Old English *hrēowan* < Germanic]

rue[2] /roo/ (*plural* **rues** *or* **rue**) *n* a woody plant with bitter, strongly scented leaves that yield an oil formerly used in medicines. Flowers: small, yellow. Native to: Europe, Asia. *Ruta graveolens*. [14C. Via French and Latin *ruta* < Greek *rhutē*.]

rueful /ro͝of'l/ *adj* **1** feeling, showing, or causing regret **2** causing people to feel pity —**ruefully** *adv* —**ruefulness** *n*

ruff[1] /ruf/ *n* **1 FANCY PLEATED COLLAR** a separate collar of starched pleated linen or lace worn by men and women in the 16th and 17th centuries **2 NECK HAIR OR FEATHERS** a growth of long, colourful, or bushy hair or feathers on the neck of a bird or other animal **3** (*plural* **ruffs** *or* **ruff**) **BIRD WITH ELABORATE RUFF** a bird of the sandpiper family, the male of which has a ruff of feathers that are erected during courtship displays. Native to: Europe, Asia. *Philomachus pugnax*. [Early 16C. Probably variant of ROUGH.] —**ruffed** *adj*

SPELLCHECK See *rough*.

ruff[2] /ruf/ *n* **1 PLAYING OF TRUMP CARD** in bridge or whist, the act of playing a trump card **2 CARD GAME** an old card game similar to whist ■ *vti* **PLAY TRUMP ON DIFFERENT SUIT** in bridge or whist, to play a trump card on a card from a different suit [Late 16C. < Old French *roffle*, a card game.]

ruffe /ruf/ (*plural* **ruffes** *or* **ruffe**), **ruff** (*plural* **ruffs** *or* **ruff**) *n* a small freshwater fish of the perch family with a single spiny dorsal fin. Native to: Europe. *Acerina cernua*. [15C. Probably a variant of ROUGH (from its rough scales).]

ruffian /rúffi ən/ *n* a rough, bullying, or violent person, often a member of a gang of thugs (*dated*) ■ *adj* behaving in a rough, bullying, or violent way [15C. Via French < Italian *ruffiano* < Germanic.] —**ruffianism** *n* —**ruffianly** *adj*

ruffle[1] /rufl/ *v* (**-fles, -fling, -fled**) **1** *vti* **MAKE WAVES IN A SURFACE** to disturb or ripple something, especially a surface, or become disturbed or rippled **2** *vti* **ANNOY** to bother or fluster somebody, or become bothered or flustered ○ *gets ruffled so easily* **3** *vt* **MAKE FEATHERS ERECT** to erect feathers, e.g. in defence, as a display, or for warmth or grooming **4** *vt* **GLANCE QUICKLY THROUGH** to flick rapidly through the pages of a book or magazine (*dated*) **5** *vt* **GATHER OR PLEAT** to draw a strip of material into pleats or gathers to use as trim **6** *vt* **SHUFFLE CARDS** to shuffle playing cards (*dated*) ■ *n* **1 WAVE IN SURFACE** a disturbance or ripple in something, especially a surface **2 IRRITATING THING** a source of irritation or annoyance **3 TRIM OF PLEATED FABRIC** a strip of closely pleated or gathered material used as trim **4** ZOOL = **ruff**[1] *n.* **2** [14C. < ?] —**ruffled** *adj* —**ruffly** *adj*

ruffle[2] /rúff'l/ *n* a low continuous drumbeat ■ *vt* (**-fles, -fling, -fled**) to play a ruffle on a drum [Early 18C. Probably an imitation of the sound.]

rufiyaa /roo fée yaa/ (*plural* **-yaa**) *n* see table at **currency** [Late 20C. Via Maldivian < Hindi *rupiya* (see RUPEE).]

rug /rug/ *n* **1 FABRIC FLOOR COVERING** a thick heavy fabric covering for a floor, especially one that is smaller than a carpet **2 ANIMAL SKIN MAT** an animal skin used as a mat or small carpet **3 BLANKET** a thick blanket, especially one formerly used by car or carriage passengers to cover their legs and feet **4 HAIRPIECE** a toupee or wig (*informal*) [Mid-16C. Probably < N Germanic.]

ruga /ro͝ogə/ (*plural* **-gae** /ro͝o jee, ro͝o gī/) *n* a natural crease or ridge in a body part, especially in the internal organs (*often plural*) [Late 18C. < Latin, 'wrinkle'.] —**rugate** /ro͝o gayt/ *adj*

rugby /rúgbi/, **rugby football** *n* a team sport in which players run with an oval ball, pass it laterally from hand to hand, and kick it (*often before nouns*) [Mid-19C. After RUGBY School, where it was reputedly invented.]

Rugby /rúgbi/ town in central England. Population: 84,300 (1991).

rugby league *n* a form of rugby that has teams of 13 players

rugby union *n* a form of rugby that has teams of 15 players

rugged /rúggid/ *adj* **1 WITH IRREGULAR SURFACE** with a sharply rising and falling, rough, or jagged surface ○ *over rugged terrain* **2 STRONG-FEATURED** with furrowed facial features thought to suggest physical strength or strength of character, especially in men ○ *their rugged faces* **3 PHYSICALLY RESILIENT** physically strong enough to endure harsh conditions, or used to enduring them **4 SEVERE IN MANNER** harsh and forbidding in manner **5 STORMY** affected by violent and dangerous storms **6 LACKING REFINEMENT** coarse or unrefined in behaviour **7 TESTING** requiring strength, skill, or endurance **8 STRONGLY BUILT** designed and manufactured to withstand hard use or harsh environments [13C. Probably < N Germanic.] —**ruggedly** *adv* —**ruggedness** *n*

ϟ **ruggedize** /rúggi dīz/ (**-izes, -izing, -ized**), **ruggedise** (**-ises, -ising, -ised**) *vt* to make something such as a piece of computer equipment capable of withstanding rough treatment —**ruggedization** /rúggi dī záysh'n/ *n*

rugger /rúggər/ *n* rugby (*informal*) [Late 19C. Alteration of RUGBY.]

rugosa rose /roo gṓssə-/ *n* a common wild hedge rose. Flowers: fragrant, pink or white. Native to: E North America. *Rosa rugosa*. [< Latin, feminine form of *rugosus* (see RUGOSE)]

rugose /rŏŏ gōss, rŏŏ-, roo gṓss/, **rugous** /rŏŏgəss/ *adj* **1** with creases, wrinkles, or ridges **2** describes a leaf or other plant part that has a surface of alternating depressions and ridges [15C. < Latin *rugosus* < *ruga* 'wrinkle'.] —**rugosely** *adv* —**rugosity** /roo góssəti/ *n*

rug rat *n* a young child, especially an infant or toddler (*humorous informal*)

Ruhr /rŏŏr/ river in W Germany. Length: 235 km/146 mi.

ruin /rŏŏ in/ *n* **1 BROKEN REMAINS** the physical remains of something such as a building or city that has decayed or been destroyed (*often plural*) **2 COMPLETE DEVASTATION** a state of complete destruction, decay, collapse, or loss ○ *The buildings had gone to ruin.* **3 COMPLETE FAILURE** complete moral, social, or economic failure ○ *facing financial ruin* **4 SOMEBODY OR SOMETHING DESTROYED** somebody or something completely lost or destroyed **5 CAUSE OF DESTRUCTION** a cause of complete loss or destruction ○ *Alcohol was their ruin.* ■ **ruins** *npl* **COMPLETE DEVASTATION** a state of complete destruction, decay, collapse, or loss ○ *Her dreams lay in ruins.* ■ *v* **1** *vt* **DESTROY** to cause something to be destroyed or lost **2** *vt* **DESTROY SOMEBODY FINANCIALLY** to bring about somebody's financial demise **3** *vt* **DAMAGE SOMETHING BEYOND REPAIR** to spoil something so severely that it cannot be restored **4** *vi* **DECLINE** to fall into a state of complete destruction or loss (*literary*) [14C. Via French *ruine* < Latin *ruina* < *ruere* 'fall'.] —**ruined** *adj* —**ruiner** *n*

ruination /rŏŏ i náysh'n/ *n* **1** the destruction or loss of something **2** something that brings about destruction or loss

ruinous /rŏŏ inəss/ *adj* **1** causing severe damage or complete destruction or loss **2** decayed or deteriorated beyond repair —**ruinously** *adv* —**ruinousness** *n*

rule /rool/ *n* **1 PRINCIPLE GOVERNING CONDUCT** an authoritative principle set forth to guide behaviour or action ○ *the rules of the game* **2 NORM** something regarded as customary or normal **3 USUAL CONDITION** a prevailing condition or quality **4 GOVERNING POWER** a governing or reigning power ○ *under Communist rule* **5 REIGN OR GOVERNMENT** a period during which a person or group reigns or governs **6 RELIGIOUS PRINCIPLES** a body of principles governing a religious order or group ○ *the Benedictine rule* **7 METHOD OF CALCULATING** a mathematical procedure for performing an operation or solving a problem **8** = **ruler** *n.* **2 9 LINE BETWEEN PRINTED COLUMNS** a thin strip or design used for borders or for separating columns of type **10 LAW GOVERNING COURT PROCEDURE** a law made to govern procedure in court **11 COURT ORDER** an order issued by a court of law or by a judge ■ *v* (**rules, ruling, ruled**) **1** *vti* **GOVERN** to exercise controlling authority over somebody or something ○ *She ruled for almost 50 years.* **2** *vti* **DOMINATE** to prevail, or be the prevailing influence over something ○ *He let his heart rule his head.* **3** *vt* **MARK WITH LINES** to make a straight line or mark something with straight lines **4** *vt* **CONTROL** to subject something to control, or restrain something **5** *vti* **MAKE LEGAL DECISION** to issue a legal decision or order ○ *The judge ruled against the plaintiff.* [13C. Via French *riule* < Latin *regula* 'straight stick, standard'.] —**rulable** *adj* —**ruleless** *adj*

rule out *vt* **1** to exclude something, or take a decision not to consider something **2** to make something impossible

rulebook /rool bŏŏk/ *n* **1** a book or pamphlet containing the official rules of a game, sport, organization, or job **2** the strictly correct or orthodox way of doing something ○ *doing everything by the rulebook*

rule of thumb *n* **1** a way of proceeding based on experience or sound judgment **2** any practical, though not entirely accurate, method that can be relied on for an acceptable result [Probably < the practice of using the thumb as a rough measure] —**rule-of-thumb** *adj*

ruler /rŏŏlər/ *n* **1** somebody such as a sovereign who governs a state or nation **2** a strip of plastic, wood, or metal with at least one straight edge and units of length marked on it

Rules *Australian* informal name for Australian Rules football (*informal*)

ruling /rŏŏling/ *adj* **1 IN POWER** exercising controlling or governing authority ○ *the ruling party* ○ *joined the ruling body* **2 MOST POWERFUL** exerting the strongest influence ○ *a ruling passion* ■ *n* **DECISION BY AUTHORITY** an official or binding decision made, e.g., by a court or judge

rum[1] /rum/ *n* **1** an alcoholic spirit made from sugar cane or molasses. It can be clear but is usually coloured brownish-red by storage in oak casks or by the addition of caramel. **2** *US* any intoxicating liquor [Mid-17C. Shortening of obsolete *rumbullion* < ?]

rum[2] /rum/ (**rummer, rummest**) *adj* out of the ordinary (*dated informal*) [Late 18C. < ?] —**rumly** *adv* —**rumness** *n*

Rum /rum/ uninhabited island in the Inner Hebrides, W Scotland. Area: 109 sq. km/42 sq. mi.

Rumanian *n, adj* LANG, PEOPLES = **Romanian** (*dated*) [Variant]

rumba /rúmbə, rŏŏm-/, **rhumba** *n* **1 CUBAN DANCE** a rhythmically complex Cuban dance **2 RHYTHMIC BALLROOM DANCE** a ballroom dance based on the Cuban rumba, with exaggerated swinging of the hips **3 MUSIC FOR RUMBA** the music for a rumba ■ *vi* (**-bas, -baing, -baed**) **DANCE RUMBA** to dance a rumba [Early 20C. Via American Spanish and Spanish *rumbo* 'course, direction' < Latin *rhombus* 'rhombus'.]

rumble /rúmb'l/ *v* (**-bles, -bling, -bled**) **1** *vi* **MAKE DEEP SOUND** to make a deep rolling sound ○ *thunder rumbling in the distance* **2** *vi* **MOVE NOISILY** to travel, e.g. along a road, with a deep rolling sound ○ *Trucks rumbled past.* **3** *vt* **UTTER WITH RUMBLE** to say something with a deep rolling voice **4** *vt* **FIND OUT ABOUT** to discover the truth about somebody or something (*informal*) ○ *We've been rumbled!* **5** *vi* *US, NZ* **FIGHT** to be involved in a street fight, especially one between members of rival gangs (*slang*) **6** *vt* **CLEAN STONES OR METAL** to polish stones or metal in a rotating drum (**tumbler**) ■ *n* **1 DEEP SOUND** a deep rolling sound **2 MURMUR OF DISSATISFACTION** a feeling of dissatisfaction quietly expressed by several people (*informal*) **3** *US, NZ* **STREET FIGHT** a street fight, especially one fought by members of rival gangs (*slang*) **4** TECH = **tumbler** *n.* **7** [14C. Probably < obsolete Dutch *rommelen*, an imitation of the sound.] —**rumbler** *n* —**rumbly** *adj*

rumble strip *n* a strip of textured road surface that alerts drivers by vibration or tyre noise to an approaching junction, speed restriction, or hazard

rumbling /rúmbling/ *n* **1 DEEP SOUND** a deep rolling sound **2 FIRST INDICATION** an early sign of growing discontent, or an indication of an unpleasant event that is about to happen (*often plural*) ■ *adj* **MAKING DEEP SOUND** making a deep rolling sound ○ *rumbling stomach*

rumbustious /rum bússchəss/ *adj* full of noisy uncontrollable exuberance [Late 18C. Probably alteration of ROBUSTIOUS.] —**rumbustiously** *adv* —**rumbustiousness** *n*

rumen /rŏŏ men, rŏŏmən/ (*plural* **-mens** *or* **-mina** /rŏŏminə/) *n* the large first chamber of a ruminant animal's stomach in which microorganisms break down plant cellulose before the food is returned to the mouth as cud for additional chewing [Early 18C. < Latin.] —**ruminal** /rŏŏminəl/ *adj*

ruminant /rŏŏminənt/ *n* **HOOFED ANIMAL THAT CHEWS CUD** any cud-chewing hoofed mammal with an even number of toes and a stomach with multiple chambers, e.g. cattle, camels, and giraffes. Suborder: Ruminantia. ■ *adj* **1 OF RUMINANTS** relating or belonging to the suborder of animals that chew the cud **2 THOUGHTFUL** inclined to be thoughtful and reflective [Mid-17C. < Latin *ruminant-*, present participle of *ruminare* (see RUMINATE).] —**ruminantly** *adv*

ruminate /rŏŏmi nayt/ (**-nates, -nating, -nated**) *v* **1** *vi* to regurgitate partially digested food and chew it again (*refers to ruminants*) **2** *vti* to think carefully and at length about something [Mid-16C. < Latin *ruminat-*, past participle of *ruminare* < *rumen* 'rumen'.] —**rumination** /rŏŏmi náysh'n/ *n* —**ruminative** /rŏŏminətiv/ *adj* —**ruminatively** *adv*

rummage /rúmmij/ *v* (**-mages, -maging, -maged**) **1** *vti* **SEARCH THROUGH THINGS** to make a rapid search for or through something by carelessly moving and disarranging things **2** *vt* **FIND** to find something by searching ■ *n* **1 THOROUGH SEARCH** a thorough search for or through something **2** *US* = **jumble**[1] *n.* **2 3 GROUP OF THINGS** a miscellaneous collection of items [15C. Via Old French *arrumage* 'arrangement of cargo in a ship' < *run* 'ship's hold' < Dutch *ruim* 'space'.] —**rummager** *n*

rummage sale *n* *US* = **jumble sale**

rummer /rúmmər/ *n* a large drinking glass, especially one with a short stem [Mid-17C. Directly or via German *Römer* < Dutch *roemer* < *roemen* 'praise'.]

rummy[1] /rúmmi/ *n* a card game in which the players try to get three or more cards of the same rank or a sequence of three or more cards of the same suit [Early 20C. < ?]

rummy[2] /rúmmi/ *adj* tasting or smelling of rum, or similar to rum in smell or taste

rumor *n, vt* US = **rumour**

rumour /rŏŏmər/ *n* **1 UNVERIFIED REPORT** a generally circulated story, report, or statement without facts to confirm its truth **2 IDLE SPECULATION** general talk or opinion of uncertain reliability ■ *vt* **TO PASS ON RUMOURS** to pass along information by rumour (*usually passive*) ○ *It is rumoured that they are leaving the company.* [14C. Via Old French < Latin, 'noise, rumour'.]

rumour mill *n* the process by which rumours are started and spread

rumourmonger /rŏŏmər mung gər/ *n* a habitual spreader of rumours ■ *vi* to participate actively in spreading rumours

rump /rump/ *n* **1 ANIMAL'S HINDQUARTERS** the fleshy hindquarters of a four-legged mammal, not including its legs **2 BEEF FROM HINDQUARTERS** a cut of beef that is tender and contains some fat, taken from the animal's rump ○ *rump steak* **3 BUTTOCKS** somebody's buttocks (*informal*) **4 REMAINS OF LEGISLATURE** the remnant of a legislative body after the majority of its members have resigned or been expelled **5 BIRD'S TAIL END** the lower part of a bird's back nearest the tail that is sometimes coloured distinctively [15C. Probably < N Germanic.]

rumple /rúmp'l/ *vti* (**-ples, -pling, -pled**) to take on a dishevelled appearance, or make clothes or hair untidy, e.g. by creasing clothes or pulling hair out of style ■ *n* a wrinkle or crease [Early 16C. < ?]

rumpus /rúmpəss/ *n* an outcry or noisy disturbance [Mid-18C. < ?]

rumpus room *n* *Can, ANZ, US* a room in a house for recreational activities such as parties and children's play

run /run/ *v* (**runs, running, ran** /ran/, **run**) **1** *vi* **GO AT FAST PACE** to move rapidly on foot so that both feet are momentarily off the ground in each step **2** *vi* **GALLOP** to go at a fast pace in which all four feet are momentarily off the ground in each stride (*refers to four-footed animals*) **3** *vt* **TRAVEL DISTANCE BY RUNNING** to cover a particular distance while running **4** *vti* **PARTICIPATE IN RACE** to compete in a race on foot or on a horse or other animal **5** *vt* **ENTER ANIMAL IN RACE** to enter a horse or other animal in a race **6** *vti* *Can, US* **CAMPAIGN IN ELECTION** to be a candidate, or enter somebody as a candidate, in an election ○ *running for president* **7** *vi* **BE IN RELATIVE POSITION** to be or end in a particular position, e.g. in a race, election, or contest ○ *running behind until the last lap* **8** *vt* **PERFORM** to carry out or accomplish something ○ *run a test* **9** *vi* **LEAVE QUICKLY** to leave a place quickly or in a hurry, usually in order to escape notice or capture ○ *take the money and run* **10** *vi* **MOVE FREELY** to move around without restraint ○ *allow the cats to run* **11** *vt* **SPEED ACROSS** to travel quickly across, over, or through something ○ *running the rapids* **12** *vt* **TRANSPORT** to take or transport somebody or something, usually by motor vehicle ○ *ran me into town* **13** *vi* **GO FOR HELP** to turn to somebody for assistance, especially in desperation or as a dependant to a protector ○ *He always runs to his brother for money.* **14** *vi* **VISIT** to make a brief trip or visit somewhere ○ *ran out to the mountains for the weekend* **15** *vti* **MOVE SMOOTHLY** to pass, or cause something to pass, quickly or smoothly through or over something ○ *ropes running easily through the pulleys* **16** *vi* **ENTER CONDITION** to enter into a particular state or condition ○ *Supplies were running low.* **17** *vti* **OPERATE** to be functioning, or put or leave something in a functioning mode ○ *Let the engine run.* **18** *vt* **CONTROL** to direct the activities, affairs, or operation of something ○ *responsible for running the whole department* **19** *vti* **POUR OR FLOW** to flow, or cause water or another liquid to flow from or to something ○ *run a tap* **20** *vi* **RELEASE MUCUS** to discharge a fluid such as pus or mucus ○ *a nose that was constantly running* **21** *vti* **GO BACK AND FORTH** to travel, or cause somebody or something to travel, regularly over a set route ○ *running a shuttle between stations* **22** *vi* **ROLL**

FREELY to roll unhindered or unchecked ○ *could only stand and watch it run down the hill* **23** *vti* **GO OR TAKE OFF COURSE** to deviate, or allow something such as a ship or car to deviate, from the usual or proper course ○ *run a car off the road* **24** *vi* **SPREAD OR LEAK UNDESIRABLY** to spread as a result of unwanted dissolving or mixing ○ *The red stripes ran into the white.* **25** *vi* **RANGE** to range between particular limits ○ *The work ran from difficult to impossible.* **26** *vi* **KEEP COMPANY** to associate with a particular person or group **27** *vti* **EXTEND** to route something or be routed in a particular direction or for a particular distance ○ *They plan to run the cable under the road.* **28** *vi* **CONTINUE** to continue for a particular length or period ○ *a report running to ten pages* **29** *vti* **SHOW PUBLICLY** to print, broadcast, or exhibit something, or to be printed, broadcast, or exhibited ○ *run a news story* **30** *vt* **EXPERIENCE** to experience, undergo, or be subject to something ○ *a child running a high temperature* **31** *vti* **BE COVERED WITH** to be covered or flowing with something ○ *The valley ran lava.* **32** *vti* **TOTAL** to total a particular amount ○ *The bill runs to four figures.* **33** *vt* **BREACH** to break through a barrier of some kind ○ *run a checkpoint* **34** *vi* **BE WORDED** to be worded in a particular way ○ *in a statement that runs as follows* **35** *vi* **EXHIBIT TENDENCY** to tend or be inclined in a particular direction ○ *His tastes in art run towards abstractions.* **36** *vi* **RECUR** to appear recurrently as a feature or quality ○ *Stubbornness runs in the family.* **37** *vi* **BE COMMUNICATED** to be communicated from person to person ○ *a story running round the office* **38** *vti* **UNRAVEL** to come undone, causing damage to a garment (*refers to stitches*) **39** *vi* **REMAIN LEGALLY VALID** to continue to have force in law ○ *The contract has a year to run.* **40** *vt* **TRADE GOODS ILLEGALLY** to import or export goods illegally ○ *running guns to the rebels* **41** *vi* **GO UPSTREAM TO SPAWN** to migrate in large numbers, usually upstream, to spawn (*refers to fish*) **42** *vti* **CARRY FOOTBALL DOWNFIELD** to advance the ball in American football, while running as opposed to passing **43** *vt* **PRODUCE METAL BY CASTING** to cast or mould molten metal ■ *n* **1 FAST PACE** a rapid pace faster than a walk or jog **2 GALLOPING PACE** an animal's fastest pace **3 SPELL OF RUNNING** a spell of running, especially for pleasure or exercise **4 RACE** a race in which the competitors run **5 REGULAR TRIP** a regular or scheduled trip or route ○ *the run to work each day* **6 TRIP FOR PLEASURE** a trip in a vehicle, especially for pleasure ○ *went for a run along the coast road* **7 DISTANCE OR TIME COVERED** a distance or period covered while travelling or running **8 ERRAND** a brief trip made in order to get something **9 FREE USE OF PLACE** unrestricted access to, use of, and movement around a place ○ *given the run of the whole house* **10 UNINTERRUPTED PERIOD** an extended period during which a specified condition or circumstance prevails ○ *a run of bad luck* **11 QUANTITY MANUFACTURED** an amount of something produced in a period of continuous operation of a machine or factory ○ *an initial print run of five thousand copies* **12 OPERATING PERIOD** a period of continuous operation of a machine or factory **13 SEQUENCE OF CARDS** in card games, a sequence of playing cards in one suit **14 SUCCESSIVE SHOTS** a series of successful shots in some games such as billiards **15 SERIES OF PERFORMANCES** a series of continuous showings or performances **16 URGENT REQUIREMENT** a sudden large demand for something such as goods or payment ○ *Rumours of a shortage led to a run on coffee.* **17 FLOW** a flow of liquid **18 PIPE FOR LIQUID** a channel or pipe in which a liquid flows **19 PERIOD OF FLOW** a period during which a liquid flows **20 AMOUNT OF LIQUID** an amount of liquid in a flow **21 STEEP ROUTE** a sloping course or track for a particular activity ○ *a ski run* **22 PASSAGE DOWN TRACK** a single trip along a course or down a slope **23 DIRECTION OF PATTERN** the natural direction of a pattern in something, e.g. wood grain **24 TENDENCY** the general direction in which things or events are moving ○ *the usual run of things* **25 SOMETHING ORDINARY** an average or typical kind of person or thing ○ *the general run of merchandise* **26 UNRAVELLING OF STITCHES** a damaged section of a stocking or other knitted garment caused by unravelling stitches **27 ANIMAL ENCLOSURE** an outdoor enclosure for domestic animals, often one attached to or used as a temporary break from a standard enclosure that allows less freedom of movement **28 ANIMAL TRAIL** a trail followed regularly by a group or herd of animals **29 REPORTER'S TERRITORY** a media reporter's regular territory **30 RAPID MUSICAL PASSAGE** a rapid musical scale or melodic passage, especially one for the piano **31 POINT SCORED IN CRICKET** a point scored in cricket, usually when one or both batsmen run between the wickets **32 SCORE IN BASEBALL** a score in baseball made by travelling round all the bases to home plate **33 runs DIARRHOEA** an attack of diarrhoea (*informal; + singular or plural verb*) ○ *have the runs* ■ *adj* **1 MELTED** in a melted state **2 WORN OUT** exhausted or out of breath, especially from running [Old English *rinnan* < Germanic] ◇ **be on the run** to be fleeing from something, especially the law ◇ **give somebody a run for his** *or* **her money** to provide somebody with some serious, sometimes unexpected, competition ◇ **run yourself** *or* **somebody ragged** to work yourself *or* somebody else to the point of exhaustion

run about *vi* to move hurriedly from place to place

run across *vt* to meet somebody or find something unexpectedly

run after *vt* **1** to chase after somebody or something **2** to pursue somebody romantically or sexually (*informal*)

run along *vi* to go away (*usually a command*)

run around *vi* (*informal*) **1** to behave promiscuously **2** to spend a lot of time with somebody ○ *running around with a bad crowd*

run away *vi* to escape or flee from somebody or something

run away with *vt* **1 TAKE SOMETHING AND LEAVE** to steal something and escape with it **2 ELOPE WITH** to leave secretly with a lover, especially in order to marry **3 TAKE CONTROL OF** to cause somebody to lose self-control ○ *His excitement ran away with him.* **4 WIN EASILY** to win a competition, contest, or election easily

run down *v* **1** *vti* **STOP FUNCTIONING** to lose power and cease to function, or allow a device to lose its power **2** *vt* **HIT WITH A VEHICLE** to knock somebody or something to the ground with a vehicle **3** *vti* **REDUCE** to shrink in size or amount, or reduce the size or amount of something **4** *vt* **BELITTLE** to speak of somebody in a disparaging or critical manner **5** *vt* **CATCH SOMEBODY EVENTUALLY** to find or capture somebody after a long search or chase **6** *vt US* **TRACE** to find the source of something ○ *run down a lead* **7** *vt* **READ QUICKLY** to read or review something quickly **8** *vt* **CAUSE SHIP TO SINK** to collide with a ship and cause it to sink **9** *vt* **REMOVE BASEBALL PLAYER** in baseball, to chase and tag out a base runner trapped between two bases

run in *v* **1** *vt* **TREAT VEHICLE CAREFULLY WHILE STILL NEW** to operate a new vehicle or engine carefully until it is functioning efficiently **2** *vt* **ARREST** to take somebody into police custody (*informal*) **3** *vi US* **VISIT** to pay somebody a casual visit (*informal*) **4** *vt* **ADD SOMETHING AS TEXT** to insert additional text in printed matter

run into *v* **1** *vt* **MEET BY CHANCE** to meet somebody unexpectedly **2** *vti* **COLLIDE WITH** to have, cause, or allow a collision between people or things **3** *vt* **ENCOUNTER** to encounter something unanticipated, usually problems or trouble **4** *vt* **AMOUNT TO** to add up to something, or be approximately equal to something ○ *left debts running into millions*

run off *v* **1** *vi* **LEAVE IN HASTE** to leave quickly without notifying anyone **2** *vt* **MAKE COPIES** to produce or print copies, e.g. on a photocopier **3** *vt* **FORCE SOMEBODY TO LEAVE** to force trespassers off property **4** *vt* **SETTLE TIED CONTEST** to settle a tied competition or election by running a final deciding contest

run off with *vt* **1** to steal and escape with something **2** to leave secretly with a lover, especially in order to marry

run on *v* **1** *vi* **TALK AT LENGTH** to talk at length, especially about trivial things **2** *vi* **CONTINUE** to continue without interruption, often boringly or frustratingly **3** *vt* **PRINT TEXT WITHOUT PARAGRAPH BREAK** to print or typeset following text without a paragraph break

run out *v* **1** *vi* **COME TO AN END** to be consumed completely ○ *Time is running out.* **2** *vi* **EXHAUST SUPPLIES** to consume all of a supply of something ○ *We've run out of milk.* **3** *vi* **BECOME INVALID** to become invalid because of time restrictions **4** *vt US* **CHASE SOMEBODY AWAY** to expel somebody using force **5** *vt* **DISMISS RUNNING BATSMAN** in cricket, to dismiss a player who is trying to complete a run by breaking the wicket with the ball at the end he or she is running to

run out on *vt* to leave somebody or something in a helpless state or at a time when support is needed (*informal*)

run over *v* **1** *vt* **KNOCK DOWN WITH VEHICLE** to hit somebody or something with a vehicle while driving it **2** *vi* **OVERFLOW** to overflow the limits or capacity of a container **3** *vti* **TAKE LONGER THAN PLANNED** to go beyond a limit or time previously set **4** *vt* **REVIEW** to examine or consider something again, especially reviewing its main points

run past *vt* = **run by**

run through *vt* **1 USE UP** to exhaust a supply of something, especially money, quickly and without much consideration **2 REVIEW** to examine or consider something again, especially reviewing its main points **3 REHEARSE QUICKLY** to read or perform at speed the whole or part of a play, script, piece of music, lecture or other prepared text in order to rehearse it **4 STAB WITH SWORD** to push a sword all the way through somebody's body (*literary*)

run to *vt* **1** to be or have sufficient resources for something ○ *finances might run to two holidays this year* **2** to have the particular length

run up *vt* **1 INCUR AS EXPENSE** to amass or accumulate a large expense **2 SEW** to make something, usually a garment, by means of fast sewing **3 RAISE ON FLAGPOLE** to hoist a flag on a flagpole

run up against *vt* to suddenly encounter an unexpected problem

runabout /rúnnə bowt/ *n* **1** a small car, motorboat, or aircraft, especially one used for short trips **2** a wanderer from place to place

runaround /rún ə rownd/ *n* **1** inconvenience deliberately engineered in order to mislead or delay somebody (*informal*) ○ *They've been giving me the runaround.* **2** an arrangement of printed type in which lines are shortened to leave room for an illustration or symbol

runaway /rúnnə way/ *n* **SOMEBODY WHO ESCAPES** a person who escapes from something, e.g. confinement or harm (*often before nouns*) ■ *adj* **1 OUT OF CONTROL** moving too fast to be stopped or controlled **2 EASILY WON** won by an overwhelming margin (*informal*) ○ *a runaway success*

Runaway, Cape /rúnnə way/ promontory on the NE of the North Island, New Zealand

run by, run past *vt* to tell somebody about something in order to find out his or her opinions or ideas about it ○ *Could I run these figures by you before I send them out?*

runcible spoon /rúnssib'l-/ *n* a fork with three curved prongs, one of which is sharp [< nonsense word coined by Edward Lear in *The Owl and the Pussy Cat* (1871)]

Runcorn /rún kawrn/ town in NW England. Population: 64,154 (1991).

rundown /rún down/ *n* **1** a summary of the main points of a subject **2** a deliberate and controlled decrease in size, amount, or production (*often before nouns*)

run-down *adj* **1 EXHAUSTED** tired out, e.g. from overwork or poor health **2 SHABBY** in poor repair from neglect or hard use **3 OUT OF POWER** depleted of energy or power and unable to operate

Rundstedt /rúnt shtet, ro͝ont-/, **Karl Rudolf Gerd von** (1875–1953) German military commander

rune /roon/ *n* **1 OLD GERMANIC ALPHABET CHARACTER** a character in an ancient Germanic alphabet used from about the 3rd to the 13th centuries **2 MAGICAL SYMBOL OR SPELL** a mysterious symbol, inscription, or incantation, especially one with supposed magical power **3 POEM IN FINNISH** a Finnish poem or stanza [Old English *rūn* < Germanic] —**runic** *adj*

rung[1] /rung/ *n* **1 LADDER STEP** a step of a ladder **2 CROSSPIECE OF CHAIR** a horizontal bar used to strengthen the legs of a chair or stool **3 LEVEL IN HIERARCHY** a position in a hierarchy, e.g. of a profession **4 PART OF SHIP'S WHEEL** a spoke or handle on the wheel of a ship by which the wheel is turned [Old English *hrung* < Germanic]

rung[2] /rung/ past participle of **ring**[2]

run-in *n* **1** a heated argument or quarrel (*informal*) **2** a section of text added to a page that has already been typeset or printed

runnel /rúnn'l/ *n* **1** a small brook or stream **2** any narrow channel for water such as a gutter [Late 16C. Alteration of obsolete *rindle* < Germanic.]

runner /rúnnər/ *n* **1 RACER** somebody or something that runs, especially an athlete or a horse in a flat race **2 CANDIDATE** somebody entered as a candidate in an election **3 SLED BLADE** either of the long blades that a sledge or sleigh slides on **4 SKATE BLADE** the blade of an ice skate **5 CARPET STRIP** a long narrow piece of carpet **6 FABRIC STRIP** a strip of fabric, often linen or lace, used to protect or decorate the top of a piece of furniture **7 DOOR OR DRAWER SLIDE** a guide on which a drawer or door slides **8 MESSENGER** a messenger or undertaker of errands for a bank, brokerage firm, or other business **9 CREEPING STEM THAT GROWS ROOTS** a thin horizontal stem that grows roots from nodes at regular intervals **10 PLANT GROWING FROM STEM NODES** a plant such as a strawberry that has runners or grows by runners **11 CLIMBING PLANT** any plant that climbs and twists, e.g. a bean plant **12 SMUGGLER** somebody involved in smuggling (*often in combination*) ○ *gun runner* **13 SMUGGLER'S VESSEL** a boat or ship used for smuggling (*often in combination*) **14 OPERATOR** a manager or operator of something such as a business or a machine **15 FLEEING PERSON** a person who flees, e.g. an escaped prisoner (*informal*) **16** AMERICAN FOOTBALL = **ball carrier** **17 DEEP-WATER MARINE FISH** a swift streamlined deep-water sea fish of the jack family, especially either of two edible bluish species. *Caranx crysos* and *Elagatis bipinnulata*. **18 ANCHORING LOOP** in mountaineering, a continuous loop of webbing used to provide an anchor to a rock, tree, or other point

SYNONYMS See ***candidate***.

runner bean *n* **1** a long flat green seed pod, cooked and eaten as a vegetable **2** a climbing bean plant that produces runner beans. *Phaseolus coccineus*. US term **scarlet runner**

runner-up (*plural* **runners-up**) *n* **1** a contestant or competitor who comes second, e.g. in a sports event or an election **2** a contestant or competitor who comes near the winner in an event or race and often receives a small prize

running /rúnning/ *n* **1 FAST MOVEMENT** rapid movement on foot, with long strides and both feet momentarily off the ground **2 RUNNING AS EXERCISE** the sport or exercise of running **3 MANAGEMENT** the managing of a business or organization ■ *adj* **1 FLOWING** flowing continuously in a stream **2 FUNCTIONING** in operation or in working order **3 FOR USE OR WEAR BY RUNNERS** relating to or intended for the sport or exercise of running ○ *running shoes* **4 WHILE RUNNING** begun with a run, or performed during a run ○ *a running jump* **5 LONG-STANDING** begun long ago and still continuing ○ *a running joke* **6 MADE DURING AN EVENT** made while something is operating or happening ○ *a running commentary* **7 OPEN** open and discharging fluid or pus ○ *a running sore* **8 CREEPING** growing by means of horizontal stems that creep along the ground **9 GAINING YARDS WHILE RUNNING** advancing the ball while running rather than passing ■ *adv* **CONSECUTIVELY** in succession ○ *for five days running* ◇ **be in** *or* **out of the running** to have *or* not have a chance of success

running back *n* in American football, an offensive back who advances the ball in running plays

running board *n* a narrow step beneath the doors of some motor vehicles, typically vintage cars

running hand *n* handwriting done without lifting the pen or pencil from the writing surface

running head, running title *n* a heading printed on every page or every other page of a book

running light *n* a light displayed on a ship or aircraft at night to show its location and size

running mate *n* **1** *US* a candidate for the lesser of two associated political offices, e.g. a vice-presidential candidate **2** in horseracing, a horse that is entered in a race for the purpose of setting the pace for a stronger horse from the same stable

running stitch *n* a simple sewing stitch that goes down and up evenly through cloth without being looped

running title *n* PUBL = **running head**

runny /rúnni/ (**-nier, -niest**) *adj* **1 OF LIQUID CONSISTENCY** of a liquid or semiliquid consistency that pours or flows **2 WATERY** of a consistency that is too thin **3 RELEASING MUCUS** producing excessive flowing mucus ○ *a runny nose* —**runniness** *n*

Runnymede /rúnni meed/ meadow in Egham, S England, where King John accepted the Magna Carta in 1215

runoff /rún of/ *n* **1 WATER NOT ABSORBED BY SOIL** rainfall that does not soak into the soil but flows into surface waters **2 WATER POLLUTION** agricultural or industrial waste products that are carried by rainfall and melting snow into surface waters **3 SECOND CONTEST TO DETERMINE THE WINNER** an election, race, or other contest held after an earlier one that produced no clear winner

run-of-the-mill *adj* with no exceptional or distinguishing qualities

run-on *adj* **ON THE SAME LINE** added to a line of text without a line break ■ *n* **1 TEXT ADDED WITHOUT A LINE BREAK** an added section of text that continues a line, without a line break **2 WORD UNDERSTOOD BUT UNDEFINED** an undefined word appearing at the end of a dictionary entry, whose meaning can be understood from the previous defined senses

runrig /rúnnrig/ *n* formerly in Scotland, a system of land-sharing in which tenants each worked several separate strips (**rigs**) of land allocated by lot each year ■ *adv* using a runrig system [15C. < RUN + *rig*.]

runt /runt/ *n* **1 SMALLEST ANIMAL** an animal that is considerably smaller than others of the same kind, especially the smallest or weakest animal in a litter **2 OFFENSIVE TERM** an offensive term for somebody regarded as short in stature or lacking physical strength (*insult*) **3 PIGEON** a large domestic pigeon [Mid-16C. < ?] —**runtiness** *n* —**runtish** *adj* —**runty** *adj*

run-through *n* **1** a practice or rehearsal of something, especially a dramatic performance **2** a brief review of something such as an agenda or report

ϟ **run time** *n* **1** COMPUT = **execution time 2** the time during which a computer program runs **3** a version of a computer program that allows a user to perform some, but not all, of the program's functions (*hyphenated when used before a noun*) ○ *a run-time module*

run-up *n* **1** a run taken to gather momentum, e.g. for a jump or kick in an athletics or sports event **2** the period of time that leads up to an important event

runway /rún way/ *n* **1 STRIP FOR AIRCRAFT LANDINGS AND TAKEOFFS** a long wide level roadway or other strip of land on which aircraft land and take off **2 EXTENSION OF STAGE INTO AUDIENCE** a narrow ramp or platform that is part of a stage and extends into the auditorium of a theatre or nightclub **3** *US* **CHUTE FOR LOGS** a chute down which logs are slid **4 TRACK** a track, passageway, or channel along which something runs

Runyon /rúny'n/, **Damon** (1884–1946) US journalist and short-story writer

rupee /roo peé/ *n* see table at **currency** [Early 17C. Via Hindi *rūpiyā* < Sanskrit *rūpya* 'wrought silver' < *rūpa* 'shape'.]

Rupert (of the Rhine) /róopərt-/, **Prince** (1619–82) German prince

Rupes Recta /róopez rékta/ lunar fault visible in the southwest quadrant of the Moon. Length: 120 km/75 mi.

rupiah /roo peé ə/ (*plural* **-ahs** *or* **-ah**) *n* see table at **currency** [Mid-20C. Via Malay < Hindi *rūpiyā* (see RUPEE).]

rupicolous /roo píkələss/ *adj* describes organisms that live or grow on or among rocks [Mid-19C. < Latin *rupes* 'rock' + *-cola* 'inhabitant'.]

rupture /rúpchər/ *n* **1 BROKEN STATE OF** a break in or breaking apart of something ○ *a rupture in the fabric of the balloon* **2 TORN TISSUE** a tear in or tearing of bodily tissue ○ *the rupture of a blood vessel* **3** MED = **hernia 4 BREACH IN RELATIONS** a breakdown in a friendly or peaceful relationship ■ *vti* (**-tures, -turing, -tured**) **1 BREAK, BURST, OR TEAR** to break, burst, or tear something, or become broken, burst, or torn **2 CAUSE RIFT IN RELATIONSHIP** to cause or undergo a breakdown in a friendly or peaceful relationship **3 TEAR TISSUE** to cause or suffer a tearing of bodily tissue **4 PRODUCE OR HAVE HERNIA** to cause or suffer a hernia [15C. Via Old French < Latin *ruptura* < *rumpere* 'break'.] —**rupturable** *adj*

rural /róorəl/ *adj* **1 OUTSIDE THE CITY** found in or living in the country **2 TYPICAL OF COUNTRY** relating to or characteristic of the country or country living **3 AGRICULTURAL** relating to, characteristic of, or involving farming [15C. Via Old French < Latin *rural-* < *rur-*, stem of *rus* 'country, countryside'.] —**rurality** /roor rállәti/ *n* —**rurally** /róorəli/ *adv*

rural dean *n* somebody with authority over the clergy of a number of parishes

rural district *n* formerly, an administrative division of a county in England, Wales, and Northern Ireland, abolished in the 1970s

ruralise *vti* = **ruralize**

ruralist /róorəlist/ *n* **1** a person who lives in the countryside **2** a supporter or promoter of a rural lifestyle and rural interests

ruralize /róorə līz/ (**-izes, -izing, -ized**), **ruralise** (**-ises, -ising, -ised**) *v* **1** *vt* to make something rural in character or habit **2** *vi* to live or pass time in the country after having lived in a city or town —**ruralization** /róorə lī záysh'n/ *n*

Rurik /róorik/ *n* (*d.* AD 879) Scandinavian leader who established the first kingdom of Russia

Ruritania /róori táyni ə/ *n* a place of romance, adventure, and intrigue [Late 19C. After a fictional central European kingdom in novels by Anthony Hope (1863–1933).] —**Ruritanian** *adj, n*

rurp /rurp/ *n* a small piton used by mountain climbers [Mid-20C. Acronym < *realized ultimate reality piton*.]

ruse /rooz/ *n* a clever trick or plot used to deceive others [15C. Old French *ruser* 'repulse, retreat, dodge'.]

Ruse /róoss ay/ city in N Bulgaria. Population: 168,000 (1996).

Ruse /rooss/, **James** (1760–1837) British-born Australian farmer

rush[1] /rush/ *v* **1** *vi* **MOVE FAST** to move, act, or proceed quickly **2** *vt* **HURRY** to make somebody or something move, act, or proceed quickly ○ *Don't rush me*. **3** *vt* **TAKE URGENTLY** to take or send somebody or something to a place quickly and urgently ○ *We rushed him to the airport to catch his flight*. **4** *vt* **DO HASTILY** to do something in a hurry and without careful thought ○ *rush a job* **5** *vi* **GO RECKLESSLY** to proceed in a quick and reckless way ○ *We mustn't rush into things*. ○ *'For fools rush in where angels fear to tread'*. (Alexander Pope, *An Essay on Criticism*; 1711) **6** *vi* **FLOW FAST** to flow somewhere quickly **7** *vt* **CAPTURE ENEMY QUICKLY** to seize a position or overcome an enemy by a sudden quick attack **8** *vt* **CHEAT** cheat somebody, especially by overcharging for something (*slang*) ○ *How much did they rush you for that jacket?* **9** *vt* **PASS RUGBY BALL UP PITCH** in rugby, to move the ball up the field by giving it short kicks and running after it in a loose group ■ *n* **1 HURRY** a hurry, or a need for hurry ○ *Slow down; you're always in a rush!* ○ *There's no great rush for it*. **2 SUDDEN FAST MOVEMENT BY CROWD** a sudden and quick movement of a person or group of people towards a place or objective ○ *There was a rush to the door*. **3 BUSY TIME** a very busy period, e.g. a time when large numbers of people try to do something at the same time ○ *a rush during the store's sale* **4 GREAT DEMAND** a sudden and high demand for something **5 SUDDEN ATTACK** a sudden quick forward movement in an attack **6 SUDDEN FLOW** a sudden quick flow or movement of something **7 SUDDEN FEELING** a sudden powerful onset of an emotion **8 SUDDEN PLEASURABLE SENSATION** a sudden feeling of elation and pleasure (*informal*) **9 ACT OF RUSHING RUGBY BALL** in rugby, the act or an instance of rushing the ball ■ **rushes** *npl* **UNEDITED PRINTS OF FILM SCENES** the first unedited prints of a scene or scenes shot for a film ■ *adj* **1 DONE QUICKLY** done or needing to be done quickly ○ *a rush job* **2 VERY BUSY** very busy, especially with many people travelling at the same time [14C. < Old French *re(h)usser* 'repel'.] —**rushed** *adj* —**rusher** *n*

rush into *vt* to do or agree to something or cause somebody to do or agree to something quickly, with little consideration of the consequences

rush through *vt* **1** to get something approved or put in place hurriedly, often without allowing time for full consideration ○ *The government hoped to rush the bill through Parliament before the election*. ○ *The plans for the new building were rushed through*. **2** to do something quickly and with little thought or preparation

rush[2] /rush/ *n* **1 PLANT GROWING IN WET AREAS** a marsh plant with a cylindrical stem that is sometimes hollow and leaves that resemble blades of grass. Genus: *Juncus*. **2 STEM OF THE RUSH PLANT** the stem of a rush plant, used in weaving baskets and mats and in bottoming chairs (*often before nouns*) ○ *a rush mat* **3 SOMETHING UNIMPORTANT** something of very little importance or value (*archaic*) **4** HOUSEHOLD = **rush light** [Old English *rysc* < Germanic] —**rushy** *adj*

Rush /rush/, **Geoffrey** (*b.* 1951) Australian actor

rush candle *n* HOUSEHOLD = **rush light**

Rushdie /rúshdi/, **Salman** (*b.* 1947) Indian-born British novelist

rush hour *n* a period of heavy traffic in the morning and evening during which people are travelling to and from work (*hyphenated when used before a noun*)

rush light *n* a candle made from pith of the stem of a rush that has been dipped in tallow

Rushmore, Mount /rúsh mawr/ mountain in the Black Hills, SW South Dakota, carved with the heads of US presidents Washington, Jefferson, Lincoln, and Theodore Roosevelt, a national memorial. Height: 1,700 m/5,600 ft.

rusk /rusk/ *n* a sweet crisp golden-brown biscuit, often given to children and babies [Late 16C. Alteration of Portuguese or Spanish *rosca* 'screw, coil, bread twist'.]

Ruskin /rússkin/, **John** (1819–1900) British art and social critic

Russell /rúss'l/, **Bertrand, 3rd Earl Russell** (1872–1970) British philosopher and mathematician

Russell, Ken (*b.* 1927) British film director. Full name **Henry Kenneth Alfred Russell**

Russell's paradox *n* the contradiction in set theory resulting from assuming that it is possible to form any set whatsoever, contradicted by the set of all and only things that are not members of themselves [Early 20C. After Bertrand RUSSELL.]

Russell's viper *n* a venomous snake common in South Asia. *Vipera russelli*. [Early 20C. After Patrick *Russell* (1727–1805), Scottish naturalist and physician.]

russet /rússit/ *n* **1 REDDISH BROWN** a reddish-brown colour **2 russet, russet apple APPLE WITH ROUGH SKIN** an apple with a rough brownish skin, a deep sweet-sharp flavour, and a firm texture **3 HOMESPUN FABRIC** a coarse homespun fabric with a reddish-brown colour [13C. < Old French *rousset* 'small red' < *rous* 'red' < Latin *russus*.] —**russet** *adj*

Russia

Russia /rúshə/ republic in E Europe and N Asia, extending from the Baltic Sea to the Pacific Ocean, and from the Arctic Ocean to the Caucasus. Capital: Moscow. Population: 147,501,000 (1997). Area: 17,075,400 sq. km/6,592,850 sq. mi.

Russia leather *n* a smooth brownish-red leather impregnated with oil from birch bark. Use: binding books.

Russian /rúsh'n/ *n* **1 SOMEBODY FROM RUSSIA** somebody who comes from Russia **2 OFFICIAL LANGUAGE OF RUSSIA** the official Balto-Slavic language of Russia, also spoken elsewhere in the world. Native speakers: 160 million. Other speakers: 110 million. ■ *adj* **1 OF RUSSIA** relating to Russia, or its people, language, or culture **2 OF SOVIET UNION** relating to the former Soviet Union, or its peoples or cultures (*dated*)

Russian doll *n* a hollow painted wooden doll made in Russia. The top and bottom come apart to reveal a smaller, similar doll inside that similarly comes apart, and so on.

Russian dressing *n* a salad dressing with a mayonnaise or vinaigrette base and sometimes added chilli sauce or pickles

Russianize /rúshə nīz/ (-izes, -izing, -ized), **Russianise** (-ises, -ising, -ised) *vti* to become or make somebody or something become Russian in style, character, or appearance —**Russianization** /rúshə nī záysh'n/ *n*

Russian olive *n* PLANT SCI = oleaster *n*. 2

Russian Orthodox Church *n* the national church of Russia, an independent section of the Eastern Orthodox Church with the Patriarch of Moscow at its head

Russian roulette *n* **1** a deadly game in which people take turns to fire a revolver loaded with only one bullet at their own heads, after spinning the cylinder **2** a dangerous or reckless action or activity [Because reportedly played by Russian officers in Romania in 1917]

Russian salad *n* a mixed salad of cooked diced vegetables in a mayonnaise or Russian dressing

Russian tea *n* tea boiled with lemon and orange juice and spices such as cinnamon and cloves, and often served in a glass instead of a cup

Russian thistle, Russian tumbleweed *n* a saltwort with narrow spiny leaves that has become a troublesome weed in W North America. Native to: Europe. *Salsola kali*.

Russki /rúski/ (*plural* **-skis**), **Russky** (*plural* **-skies**) *US* an offensive term for a Russian (*slang*) [Mid-19C. < Russian *russkiĭ*.]

Russo- *prefix* Russia, Russian ○ *Russophile* [< RUSSIA]

Russo-Japanese War /rússō jáppə neez-/ *n* a war fought in 1904–05 between Russia and Japan, mainly over control of Korea, in which Russia was unexpectedly defeated

Russolo /ru ssólō/, **Luigi** (1885–1947) Italian painter

russula /rússyōōlə/ (*plural* **-lae** /-yōō lee/ *or* **-las**) *n* a common genus of mushroom found widely in Europe and North America. Genus: *Russula*. [Mid-20C. < modern Latin *Russula*.]

rust /rust/ *n* **1 REDDISH-BROWN COATING ON METAL** a reddish-brown coating of iron oxide on the surface of iron or steel that forms when the metal is exposed to air and moisture **2 SOMETHING RESEMBLING RUST** something that resembles rust, especially in colour, e.g. another type of corrosion or a stain **3 REDDISH BROWN** a reddish-brown colour **4 PLANT DISEASE** a disease of plants caused by rust fungus, in which reddish-brown spots form on the leaves and stems **5 PLANT SCI = rust fungus** ■ *v* **1** *vti* **CORRODE WITH RUST** to cause something to corrode with rust or to become corroded with rust **2** *vt* **DEVELOP A PLANT DISEASE** to become infected with a disease caused by rust fungus **3** *vi* **DETERIORATE** to deteriorate from neglect or lack of use ○ *His knowledge of German had rusted over the years.* [Old English *rūst* < Germanic] —**rust** *adj*

rust bucket *n* a car that is badly affected by rust (*informal humorous*)

rust fungus *n* a fungus that lives as a parasite on many plants, causing reddish-brown spots on the plant parts. Order: Uredinales.

rustic /rústik/ *adj* **1 RELATING TO COUNTRY LIFESTYLE** relating to, characteristic of, or appropriate to the country or country living **2 PLAIN AND SIMPLE** lacking excessive refinement or elegance **3 MADE OF ROUGH BRANCHES** made of rough wood, especially branches with the bark left on them **4 WITH ROUGH SURFACE** with a rough finish ○ *rustic bricks* ■ *n* **1 SOMEBODY LIVING IN COUNTRY** a person who lives in the country, especially somebody who is unsophisticated (*offensive in some contexts*) **2 BRICK WITH ROUGH FINISH** brick or stone with a rough finish [15C. < Latin *rusticus* < *rus* 'country'.] —**rustically** *adv* —**rusticity** /ru stíssəti/ *n*

rusticate /rústi kayt/ (-cates, -cating, -cated) *v* **1** *vi* **MOVE TO THE COUNTRY** to go to the country to live **2** *vt* **SEND TO THE COUNTRY** to send somebody to the country to live **3** *vt* **MAKE APPEAR RUSTIC** to become or cause somebody or something to become rustic in appearance or quality **4** *vt* **SUSPEND FROM UNIVERSITY** to suspend a student from university for a set time as a punishment **5** *vt* **FINISH WITH ROUGH MASONRY** to finish the outside of a wall with large blocks of masonry that are left with a rough surface, bevelled, and have deep joints between them —**rustication** /rústi káysh'n/ *n* —**rusticator** /rústi kaytər/ *n*

rusticwork /rústik wurk/ *n* BUILDING = rustic *n*. 2

rustle /rúss'l/ *v* (-tles, -tling, -tled) **1** *vti* **MAKE SWISHING SOUND** to make or cause something to make a swishing or soft crackling sound, e.g. that made by dry leaves rubbing together **2** *vi* **MOVE WITH RUSTLING SOUND** to move with a swishing or soft crackling sound ■ *n* **RUSTLING SOUND** a swishing or soft crackling sound ○ *the rustle of paper money* [14C. An imitation of the sound.] —**rustlingly** *adv*

rustle up *vt* (*informal*) **1** to prepare a meal or snack quickly using any food that is immediately available **2** to quickly find and bring together things or people

rustle[2] /rúss'l/ (-tles, -tling, -tled) *v* **1** *vti* *US, Can* to steal livestock, especially cattle or horses **2** *vi* *US* to move or work quickly and energetically [Early 20C. < RUSTLE[1].] —**rustler** *n*

rust mite *n* a gall mite that produces brown spots on leaves and fruit by burrowing into them

rustproof /rúst proof/ *adj* not susceptible to rust, or treated so as not to be susceptible to rust ■ *vt* to treat metal to prevent it rusting —**rustproofing** *n*

rusty /rústi/ (-ier, -iest) *adj* **1 CORRODED** covered with or corroded by rust **2 OUT OF PRACTICE** out of practice or impaired because of advanced age, neglect, or lack of use ○ *My German is very rusty.* **3 RUST-COLOURED** the colour of rust **4 INFECTED WITH RUST FUNGUS** affected by rust fungus **5 DISCOLOURED** faded and threadbare from wear and age **6 OLD** old or old-fashioned ○ *rusty ideas* **7 ROUGH-SOUNDING** croaking or rough-sounding ○ *a rusty voice* —**rustily** *adv* —**rustiness** *n*

rut[1] /rut/ *n* **1 NARROW GROOVE** a narrow channel or groove in something, especially one made by the wheels of vehicles **2 BORING SITUATION** a routine procedure, situation, or way of life that has become uninteresting and tiresome ○ *I felt I was in a rut.* ■ *vt* (**ruts, rutting, rutted**) **MAKE RUTS IN** to make ruts in a road, track, or other surface [Late 16C. Probably < Old French *rote* 'route'.]

rut[2] /rut/ *n* a period of sexual excitement that recurs annually in male ruminants, especially deer ■ *vi* (**ruts, rutting, rutted**) to be in a state of sexual excitement (*refers to male ruminants*) [12C. < Old French, 'bellowing, roaring (of a stag in rut)' < late Latin *rugitus* 'roaring' < Latin *rugire* 'to roar'.] —**ruttish** *adj*

rutabaga /rōōtə baygə, -báygə/ *n US* **1 FOOD = swede** *n*. **2 2 PLANTS = swede** *n*. **1** [Late 18C. Swedish dialect *rotabagge* < *rot* 'root' + *bagge* 'bag'.]

ruth /rooth/ *n* (*archaic*) **1** pity for another person's troubles **2** sorrow or remorse for having done something wrong [12C. < RUE[1] after words like TRUTH.]

Ruth /rooth/ *n* **1** in the Bible, a Moabite widow who left her own people to live with her mother-in-law Naomi, married Boaz, and was an ancestor of King David **2** the book of the Bible that tells the story of Ruth

Babe Ruth

Ruth /rooth/, **Babe** (1895–1948) US baseball player. Born George Herman Ruth

Ruthenia /roo théeni ə/ region of W Ukraine corresponding to present-day Zakarpats'ka, formerly part of Czechoslovakia —**Ruthenian** *n, adj*

ruthenic /roo thénnik/ *adj* relating to or containing ruthenium, especially with a high valency [Mid-19C. < RUTHENIUM.]

ruthenious /roo théeni əss/ *adj* relating to or containing ruthenium, especially with a low valency [Mid-19C. < RUTHENIUM.]

ruthenium /roo théeni əm/ *n* (*symbol* **Ru**) a brittle white metallic element. Source: platinum ores. Use: hardening of platinum and palladium alloys. [Mid-19C. After RUTHENIA.]

Rutherford /rúthər furd/, **Ernest, 1st Baron Rutherford of Nelson and Cambridge** (1871–1937) New Zealand-born British physicist

Rutherford, Dame Margaret (1892–1972) British actor

rutherfordium /rúthər fáwrdi əm/ *n US* (*symbol* **Rf**) a radioactive element. Source: produced artificially in high-energy atomic collisions.

ruthless /róothləss/ *adj* having or showing no pity or mercy —**ruthlessly** *adv* —**ruthlessness** *n*

rutilant /róotilənt/ *adj* shining or glowing with a red light (*archaic*) [15C. < Latin *rutilant-*, present participle of *rutilare* 'redden' < *rutilus* 'reddish'.]

rutile /roō tīl/ *n* a dark reddish-brown or lustrous black titanium dioxide mineral forming needle-shaped crystals. Source: igneous and metamorphic rocks. Use: source of titanium. [Early 19C. Via French and German < Latin *rutilus* 'reddish'.]

rutin /róotin/ *n* a bioflavonoid found mainly in buckwheat that can be taken as a dietary supplement for the treatment of varicose veins and other conditions [Mid-19C. < Latin *ruta* (see RUE[2]).]

Rutland /rútlənd/ county in central England. Area: 394 sq. km/152 sq. mi.

rutting /rútting/ *adj* describes male ruminants, especially deer, that are in a state of sexual excitement

Ruwenzori Range /roŏ ən záwri-/ mountain range in central Africa, along the Uganda-Democratic Republic of the Congo border, between lakes Edward and Albert. Highest peak: Margherita Peak 5,109 m/16,762 ft.

RV *abbr* **1** *US* recreational vehicle **2** re-entry vehicle **3 RV** Revised Version

R-value *n* a measure of the ability of a material such as insulation to retard heat flow [Mid-20C. *R* is the symbol for RESISTANCE.]

⚡ **rw** *abbr* Rwanda (*in Internet addresses*)

RW *abbr* **1** Right Worshipful **2** Right Worthy

Rwanda[1] /roŏ ándə/ *n* a Bantu official language of Rwanda, also spoken in other parts of east-central Africa. Native speakers: 15 million. [Early 20C. < Bantu.] —**Rwanda** *adj*

Rwanda[2] /roŏ ándə/ republic in east-central Africa. Capital: Kigali. Population: 6,727,000 (1996). Area: 26,338 sq. km/10,169 sq. mi. —**Rwandan** *n, adj* —**Rwandese** *n, adj*

Rwanda

RWD *abbr* rear-wheel drive

ry, Ry *abbr* railway

-ry *suffix* = **-ery**

rya /reè ə/ *n* **1** a handwoven Scandinavian rug with a deep pile and a colourful pattern **2** the weaving pattern or style used in making a rya [Mid-20C. After *Rya*, Sweden.]

rye[1] /rī/ *n* **1** the light brown grain of rye, an annual cereal grass. Use: to make flour and whisky, as fodder. **2** a tall hardy annual cereal grass that has bluish-green leaves and is widely cultivated. *Secale cereale.* **3** BEVERAGES = **rye whisky** [Old English *ryge* < Germanic]

LITERARY LINK *Catcher in the Rye*, a novel (1951) by US writer J. D. Salinger. A moving and realistic account of a young boy's attempt to come to terms with encroaching adulthood, it describes two days in the life of disaffected teenager Holden Caulfield. Holden absconds to New York, then resolves to leave home for good; his failure to accomplish this results in his mental collapse.

rye[2] /rī/ *n* used by Roma people to mean gentleman [Mid-19C. < Romany *rai* < Sanskrit *rājan* 'rajah'.]

Rye /rī/ *n* town in SE England, one of the Cinque Ports. Population: 3,708 (1991).

rye bread *n* a dark or light bread made using rye flour, often flavoured with caraway seed

rye-grass *n* a European grass that is widely cultivated as forage, as a cover crop, and for lawns. *Lolium perenne.*

rye whisky *n* whisky distilled from fermented rye

Ryle /rīl/, **Sir Martin** (1918–84) British astronomer

ryot /rī ət/ *n* in India, a subsistence farmer who owns or rents a small piece of land [Early 17C. Via Persian and Urdu *ra'īyat* < Arabic *ra'īyya(t)* 'subjects', literally 'herd, flock' < *ra'ā* 'pasture'.]

⚡ **RYS** *abbr* read your screen (*in e-mails*)

~~**rythm**~~ incorrect spelling of **rhythm**

~~**rythmn**~~ incorrect spelling of **rhythm**

Ryukyu Islands /ri oò koo-/ archipelago in SW Japan, in the W Pacific Ocean between Kyushu and Taiwan. Population: 1,222,458 (1990). Area: 2,260 sq. km/870 sq. mi.

S[1] /ess/ (*plural* **s's**), **S** (*plural* **S's** *or* **Ss**) *n* the 19th letter of the English alphabet, representing a consonant sound

s[2] *symbol* second

s[3] *abbr* **1** semi- **2** shilling **3** singular **4** sire **5** sister **6** solo **7** son **8** soprano **9** stere **10** stock **11** strange quark **12** substantive

S[1] (*plural* **S's** *or* **Ss**) *n* something shaped like a letter 'S'

S[2] *symbol* **1** entropy **2** siemens **3** sulphur

S[3] *abbr* **1** Sabbath **2** Saint **3** Samuel **4** satisfactory **5** Saturday **6** Saxon **7** schilling **8** Sea **9** September **10** small (*in clothes sizes*) **11** Socialist **12** South **13** strangeness **14** sucre **15** Sunday

-'s *suffix* forms the possessive of nouns ○ *school's* ○ *person's* [Old English *-es*]

-s, -es *suffix* forms the plural of many regular nouns ○ *dogs* ○ *bananas*. ◊ **-es** [Old English *-as*]

⚡**sa** *abbr* Saudi Arabia (*in Internet addresses*)

SA *abbr* **1** Salvation Army **2** South Africa **3** South America **4** South Australia **5** Sturmabteilung

s.a. *abbr* **1** semiannual **2** subject to approval **3** without date

⚡**SAA** *abbr* systems application architecture

Saadi = **Sadi**

Saadia ben Joseph /saádi ə ben jṓzif/ (882–942) Arabian philosopher and scholar

Saarbrücken /sá brṓkən, za brýkən/ capital of Saarland State, SW Germany. Population: 189,012 (1997).

Saarinen, Eero /saárinən/, **Eero** (1910–61) Finnish-born US architect

Saarinen, Eliel (1873–1950) Finnish-born US architect

sab /sab/ *vti* (**sabs, sabbing, sabbed**) to obstruct a fox hunt because of opposition to blood sports (*slang*) ■ *n* an obstructor of a fox hunt who opposes blood sports (*slang*) [Late 20C. Shortening of SABOTAGE.]

sabadilla /sábbə dílla/ (*plural* **-las** *or* **-la**) *n* **1** a plant of the lily family with bitter brown seeds. Flowers: long spikelets. Native to: Mexico. *Schoenocaulon officinale.* **2** the seeds of the sabadilla plant. Use: insecticides, source of veratrine. [Early 19C. < Spanish *cebadilla*, diminutive of *cebada* 'barley', ultimately < Latin *cibus* 'food'.]

Sabah /saá baa/ the second largest state in Malaysia, on the northeast of the island of Borneo. Capital: Kota Kinabalu. Population: 1,736,902 (1991). Area: 73,711 sq. km/28,800 sq. mi.

Sabatier, Paul /saa baa tyáy/, **Paul** (1854–1941) French chemist

sabbat /sábbət/ *n* PARANORMAL = **witches' Sabbath** [Via French < Latin *sabbatum* (see SABBATH)]

Sabbatarian /sábbə táiri ən/ *n* **1** STRICT OBSERVER OF SABBATH a believer in the strict observance of a designated day of worship and rest **2** OBSERVER OF SATURDAY AS SABBATH a person who observes the Sabbath on Saturday, e.g. in Judaism ■ *adj* OF SABBATH OR SABBATARIANS relating to the Sabbath or its observance, or to Sabbatarians [Early 17C. < Latin *sabbatarius*, < Latin *sabbatum* (see SABBATH).] —**Sabbatarianism** *n*

Sabbath /sábbəth/ *n* **1** Sunday, observed by most Christians as the day of worship and rest from work **2** Saturday, observed as a day of religious worship and rest from work in Judaism and some Christian denominations **3** = **witches' Sabbath** [Pre-12C. < Latin *sabbatum*, < Greek *sabbaton*, < Hebrew *šabbāt* 'rest' < *šābat* 'to rest'.]

sabbath school, Sabbath School *n* in the tradition of the Seventh-Day Adventists, a school for religious teaching held on Saturday

sabbatical, sabbatic *n* a period of leave from work for research, study, or travel, often with pay and usually granted to university lecturers every seven years ■ *adj* relating to a sabbatical [Late 16C. < Greek *sabbatikos* 'of the Sabbath' < *sabbaton*, (see SABBATH).]

Sabbatical, Sabbatic *adj* relating to or suitable for the Sabbath ■ *n* = **Sabbatical Year**

sabbatical year, sabbatical leave *n* = **sabbatical** *n*.

Sabbatical Year *n* every seventh year, during which the ancient Israelites allowed their land to lie fallow

SABC *abbr* S Africa South African Broadcasting Corporation

saber *n*, *vt* US = **sabre**

sabin /sáybin/ *n* a unit of sound absorption equal to the absorption of one square foot of a perfectly absorbing surface [Mid-20C. After Wallace Clement Ware *Sabine* (1868–1919), US physicist.]

Sabin, Albert (1906–93) Russian-born US microbiologist and immunologist

Sabine[1] /sábbīn/ *n* **1** a member of an ancient people who lived in central Italy **2** the Italic language of the Sabine people [14C. < Latin *Sabinus*.] —**Sabine** *adj*

Sabine[2] /sə beén/ river in E Texas, forming part of the Texas-Louisiana border and flowing into the Gulf of Mexico. Length: 612 km/380 mi.

Sabin vaccine /sáybin-/ *n* an oral vaccine used to immunize against poliomyelitis and containing live poliovirus [Mid-20C. After Albert SABIN.]

sabji /súbji/ *n* S Asia a raw or cooked vegetable dish [Early 19C. < Urdu *sabzī* 'greenness', < *sabz* 'green', < Persian *sebz*.]

sable /sáyb'l/ *n* (*plural* **-bles** *or* **-ble**) **1** N ASIAN MARTEN a marten of N Asia. *Martes zibellina.* **2** SABLE FUR the soft dark fur of a sable (*often before noun*) **3** SABLE GARMENT a garment made of sable **4** ARTIST'S BRUSH an artist's brush made with the hairs of a sable **5** BLACK COLOUR the black colour of sable fur (*literary*) **6** COLOUR BLACK IN HERALDRY in heraldry, the colour black ■ **sables** *npl* MOURNING CLOTHES black clothes worn in mourning (*archaic*) ■ *adj* **1** OF BLACK COLOUR of a black colour, like sable fur (*literary*) **2** DARK very dark or gloomy (*literary*) **3** OF HERALDIC BLACK in heraldry, black [15C. Via Old French < medieval Latin *sabelum*, probably < Lithuanian *sàbalas* or Russian *sobol'.*]

sable antelope *n* a large African antelope with long backwards-curving horns. The male has a black coat. *Hippotragus niger.*

sablefish /sáyb'l fish/ *n* (*plural* **-fish** *or* **-fishes**) a large dark-coloured fish that is important for commercial fisheries. Native to: North American Pacific coast. *Anaplopoma fimbria.*

sabot /sábbō/ *n* **1** a wooden shoe, or a shoe with a wooden sole, formerly worn in Belgium, France, the Netherlands, and Germany **2** a sleeve placed around a projectile so that it can be fired from a weapon with a larger bore [Early 17C. Via French < Old French *çabot.*]

sabotage /sábbə taazh/ *n* **1** DELIBERATE DESTRUCTION the deliberate damaging or destroying of property or equipment, e.g. by resistance fighters, enemy agents, or disgruntled workers **2** ACTION TO HINDER an action taken to undermine or destroy somebody's efforts or achievements ■ *vt* (**-tages, -taging, -taged**) **1** DAMAGE to damage, destroy, or disrupt something deliberately, especially in a war **2** HINDER to undermine or destroy somebody's efforts or achievements [Mid-19C. < French, < *saboter* 'clatter in clogs', hence 'act clumsily, work badly, ruin', < *sabot* (see SABOT).]

saboteur /sábbə túr/ *n* a committer of sabotage [Early 20C. < French, < *sabot* (see SABOTAGE).]

sabra /saábrə/ *n* a Jewish person who was born in Israel [Mid-20C. Directly or via colloquial modern Hebrew *ṣābrāh*, < Arabic *ṣabr* 'prickly pear'.]

sabre /sáybər/ *n* **1** HEAVY SWORD WITH CURVED BLADE a heavy cavalry sword with a slightly curved blade that is sharp on one edge **2** FENCING SWORD WITH TAPERING BLADE a light sword with a guard to cover the hand and a tapering flexible blade, used in fencing **3** FENCING WITH SABRE the sport or technique of fencing with a sabre **4** CAVALRY SOLDIER a soldier in a cavalry regiment ■ *vt* (**sabres, sabring, sabred**) INJURE SOMEBODY WITH SABRE to jab, injure, or kill somebody with a sabre [Late 17C. Via French *sabre* < obsolete German *Sabel.*]

sabre rattling *n* an aggressive display or threat of force, especially military force

sabretache /sábbər tash/ *n* a small leather case worn on a cavalryman's belt [Early 19C. < French, translation of German *Säbeltasche* 'sabre pocket'.]

sabre-toothed tiger, sabre-toothed cat *n* an extinct animal of the cat family that lived in the Oligocene and Pleistocene epochs and had long curving upper canine teeth. Genus: *Smilodon.*

sabulose /sábbyoŏ lṓss/, **sabulous** /-ləss/ *adj* **1** having a gritty texture like sand **2** growing in sand or sandy soil [Mid-19C. < Latin *sabulum* 'sand'.] —**sabulosity** /sábbyoŏ lóssəti/ *n*

sac /sak/ *n* a small bag or pouch, especially one that contains a fluid, formed by a membrane in an animal or plant ○ *amniotic sac* [Mid-18C. Via French < Latin *saccus* (see SACK[1]).] —**saccate** /sá kayt/ *adj*

SPELLCHECK Do not confuse *sac* with *sack*, which has a similar sound. Beware: your spellchecker will not catch this error.

---

sacaton /sáka tòn/ *n* a coarse perennial grass grown in the SW United States and Mexico and used for hay and pasture in dry alkaline areas. *Sporobolus wrightii.* [Mid-19C. < American Spanish *zacatón* 'large coarse grass', < *zacate* 'coarse grass', < Nahuatl *zacatl* 'straw'.]

saccade /sa kaàd, -káyd/ *n* **1** a rapid irregular movement of the eye as it changes focus moving from one point to another, e.g. while reading **2** a sudden brief pull by a rider on a horse's reins in order to check the horse [Early 18C. < French, 'twitch', ultimately < *sac* 'sack', < Latin *saccus* (see SACK[1]).] —**saccadic** *adj* —**saccadically** *adv*

facchar- *prefix* = **saccharo-** (*before vowels*)

saccharase /sáka rayss, -rayz/ *n* BIOCHEM = **invertase**

saccharate /sáka rayt/ *n* a compound that is a salt or ester of saccharic acid [Early 19C. < SACCHARIC ACID + -ATE.]

saccharic acid /sə kárrik-/ *n* COOH(CHOH)₄COOH a white soluble solid formed by the oxidation of sugar or starch

saccharide /sákə rīd/ *n* any sweet-tasting, water-soluble carbohydrate based on a ring of four or five carbon atoms and one oxygen atom

saccharify /sə kárri fī/ (**-fies, -fying, -fied**) *vt* to convert a starch into simple sugars —**saccharification** /sə kárrifi káysh'n/ *n*

saccharimeter /sákə rímmitər/ *n* an instrument, e.g. a polarimeter, used to measure the concentration of sugar in a solution —**saccharimetry** *n*

saccharin /sákərin/ *n* $C_7H_5NO_3S$ a white crystalline compound that is several hundred times sweeter than sugar. Use: sugar substitute.

saccharine /sákə reen, -rīn, -rin/ *adj* **1 OF OR LIKE SUGAR** relating to, resembling, or containing sugar **2 TOO SWEET** excessively sweet and ingratiating ○ *a saccharine smile* **3 TOO SENTIMENTAL** excessively sentimental and cloying —**saccharinely** *adv* —**saccharinity** /sákə rínnəti/ *n*

saccharo- *prefix* sugar ○ *saccharometer* [Via Latin and Greek < Sanskrit *śarkarā* 'sugar']

saccharoid /sákə royd/, **saccharoidal** /sákə róydl/ *adj* describes rocks and minerals that have a texture resembling loaf sugar

saccharometer /sákə rómmitər/ *n* a hydrometer used to determine the strength of a sugar solution by measuring its density

saccharomycete /sákərō mī seet/ (*plural* **-cetes**) *n* a single-celled yeast that has no mycelium, reproduces asexually, and ferments sugar. Genus: *Saccharomyces.* [Late 19C. < SACCHARO- + Greek *mukēs* 'mushroom, fungus'.]

saccharose /sákə rōss, -rōz/ *n* CHEM = **sucrose**

saccular /sákyŏolər/ *adj* resembling a sac or saccule [Mid-19C. < Latin *sacculus* (see SACCULE).]

saccule /sákyool/, **sacculus** /sákyŏoləss/ (*plural* **-li** /-yŏo lī/) *n* **1** a small membranous bag or pouch in an animal or plant **2** the smaller of two sacs in the vestibule of the inner ear [Mid-19C. < Latin *sacculus* 'little sack', < *saccus* (see SACK[1]).] —**sacculate** *adj* —**sacculated** *adj* —**sacculation** /sákyŏo láysh'n/ *n*

sacerdotal /sássər dṓt'l, sákər-/ *adj* relating to or characteristic of a priest or the priesthood [14C. Via Old French < Latin *sacerdotalis* 'priestly', < *sacerdot-*, stem of *sacerdos* 'priest'.] —**sacerdotally** *adv*

sacerdotalism /sássər dṓt'lizəm, sákər-/ *n* **1 PRINCIPLES OF PRIESTHOOD** the beliefs or methods of priests **2 BELIEF IN PRIEST'S POWER AS MEDIATOR** the belief that a priest is able to mediate between God and human beings **3 PRIEST'S POWER OVER ORDINARY PEOPLE** power that a priest has over ordinary people, especially when this is seen as excessive or dishonestly achieved —**sacerdotalist** *n*

sac fungus *n* FUNGI = **ascomycete**

sachem /sáychəm/ *n* **1** a chief of a Native North American people or confederation, especially of the Algonquian people **2** *US* a leader or official of the Tammany Society [Early 17C. < Algonquian.] —**sachemic** /say chémmik/ *adj*

sachertorte /sákər tawrt, zaákhər tawrtə/ *n* a dark rich chocolate cake covered with glossy chocolate icing [Early 20C. < German, after Franz *Sacher,* German pastry chef.]

sachet /sásh ay/ *n* **1** a small flat sealed packet that contains a powder, cream, or liquid **2** a small bag containing perfumed powder or potpourri, used to scent clothes in wardrobes or drawers [15C. < Old French, 'little sack', diminutive of *sac* 'bag', < Latin *saccus* (see SACK[1]).]

sack[1] /sak/ *n* **1 LARGE BAG** a large bag, especially one that is made from hessian, other coarse cloth, or thick heavy-duty paper **2 AMOUNT IN SACK** the amount that a sack will hold **3 JOB DISMISSAL** dismissal from a job (*informal*) ○ *to get the sack* **4 BED** bed (*informal*) **5 WOMAN'S DRESS** a woman's loose-fitting dress that narrows below the knee **6 18C WOMAN'S GOWN** a gown worn by women in the 18th century that had a bodice with loose pleats at the back ■ *vt* **1 FIRE SOMEBODY** to dismiss somebody from a job (*informal*) **2 PUT SOMETHING IN SACK** to put something into a sack, e.g. for storage or transport [Pre-12C. < Latin *saccus* 'bag, wallet', < Greek *sakkos* 'packing material', < Semitic.] —**sacker** *n* ◇ **hit the sack** to go to bed (*informal*)

SPELLCHECK See ***sac.***

sack out *vi US* to go to sleep or to bed (*informal*)

sack[2] /sak/ *vt* to destroy a captured town or city and plunder its goods and valuables ■ *n* the destruction of a captured town or city and the plundering of its goods and valuables [Mid-16C. < Old French *(a) sac,* call to plunder, literally '(to the) bag', < Latin *saccus* 'sack' (see SACK[1]).]

sack[3] /sak/ *n* dry white wine from Spain, Portugal, or the Canary Islands (*archaic*) [Mid-16C. Alteration of earlier *wine seck,* partial translation of French *(vin) sec* 'dry (wine)', < Latin *siccus* 'dry'.]

sackbut /sák but/ *n* a wind instrument with a long slide like a trombone, played in medieval times [Early 16C. < Old French *saqueb(o)ute* 'hooked lance for pulling riders from their horses', < ?]

sackcloth /sák kloth/ *n* **1** a coarse cloth made from goat or camel's hair or cotton, hemp, or flax. Use: sacks. **2** clothes made from sackcloth, formerly worn as a sign of mourning or penitence ◇ **sackcloth and ashes** a show of mourning or repentance

sacking /sáking/ *n* a coarse cloth woven from hemp or jute. Use: sacks.

sack race *n* a race in which each competitor stands in a sack and jumps towards the finish line while holding up the sack

Sackville /sákvil/, **Thomas, 1st Earl of Dorset** (1536–1608) English poet, playwright, and diplomat

Sackville-West /sák vil wést/, **Vita** (1892–1962) British writer

Saco /sáykō/ city in SW Maine, United States. Population: 15,681 (1996).

sacra plural of **sacrum**

~~**sacrafice**~~ incorrect spelling of **sacrifice**

sacral[1] /sáykrəl, sák-/ *adj* relating to or near the sacrum

sacral[2] /sáykrəl, sák-/ *adj* relating to or used in sacred rites [Late 19C. < Latin *sacr-,* stem of *sacer* 'sacred'.]

sacrament /sákrəmənt/ *n* **1 RELIGIOUS RITE OR CEREMONY** in Christianity, a rite that is considered to have been established by Jesus Christ to bring grace to those participating in or receiving it **2 sacrament, Sacrament CONSECRATED ELEMENTS OF COMMUNION** the bread and wine consecrated at Communion **3 SOMETHING SACRED** something considered to be sacred or have a special significance [12C. Via Old French < late Latin *sacramentum* 'rite, mystery, revelation', < Latin, 'soldier's oath, solemn obligation', < sacer 'sacred'.]

sacramental /sákrə mént'l/ *adj* **1 USED IN SACRAMENT** relating to or used in a sacrament **2 SACRED** bound by a sacrament or in a way considered inviolable ■ *n* **RITUAL ACTION OR SIGN** in the Roman Catholic Church, an object, act, or ritual such as the sign of the cross that is used to show religious devotion —**sacramentality** /sákrə men tálləti/ *n* —**sacramentally** *adv* —**sacramentalness** *n*

sacramentalism /sákrə mént'lizəm/ *n* in Christianity, the belief in the necessity of the sacraments to attain salvation and God's grace —**sacramentalist** *n*

Sacramentarian /sákrə men táiri ən/ *n* **1 BELIEVER IN SYMBOLIC NATURE OF COMMUNION** in Christianity, a believer that the consecrated bread and wine of the Communion merely symbolize the body and blood of Jesus Christ **2 SACRAMENTALIST** a believer in sacramentalism ■ *adj* **OF SACRAMENTARIANS** relating to or characteristic of Sacramentarians —**Sacramentarianism** *n*

Sacramento /sákrə méntō/ capital of California, in the north-central part of the state, on the Sacramento River. Population: 404,168 (1998 estimate).

sacrarium /sa kráiri əm/ (*plural* **-a** /-ri ə/) *n* **1** a Christian church's sanctuary or sacristy **2** CHR = **piscina** *n.* 1 [Early 18C. < Latin 'shrine', < *sacer* 'holy, sacred'.]

sacred /sáykrid/ *adj* **1 DEVOTED TO DEITY** dedicated to a deity or religious purpose **2 OF RELIGION** relating to or used in religious worship **3 WORTHY OF WORSHIP** worthy of or regarded with religious veneration, worship, and respect **4 DEDICATED TO SOMEBODY** dedicated to or in honour of somebody **5 INVIOLABLE** not to be challenged or disrespected [14C. < past participle of archaic *sacre* 'consecrate', via Old French *sacrer* < Latin *sacrare,* < *sacr-,* stem of *sacer* 'holy, sacred'.] —**sacredly** *adv* —**sacredness** *n*

sacred cow *n* somebody or something exempt from any criticism or interference [Early 20C. < the sacrosanctity of cattle for Hindus.]

Sacred Heart *n* **1** in the Roman Catholic Church, the heart of Jesus Christ, seen as a symbol of his love **2** an image representing the Sacred Heart, often shown as bleeding

sacred ibis *n* a large wading bird with bold black-and-white plumage, a large downwards-curving beak, and decorative plumes on its back. Native to: sub-Saharan Africa, Arabia. *Threskiornis aethiopica.* [Because it was held sacred by the ancient Egyptians]

sacred mushroom *n* a hallucinogenic American mushroom formerly eaten in Native American rituals. Genus: *Psilocybe.*

sacred thread *n* a cotton thread worn by Brahmin men to symbolize initiation into adulthood

~~**sacreligious**~~ incorrect spelling of **sacrilegious**

sacrifice /sákri fīss/ *n* **1 GIVING UP OF SOMETHING VALUED** a giving up of something valuable or important for somebody or something else considered to be of more value or importance **2 SOMETHING VALUED AND GIVEN UP** something valuable or important given up as a sacrifice **3 LOSS IN GIVING UP SOMETHING VALUED** a loss incurred by giving away or selling something below its value **4 STRATEGIC GIVING UP OF CHESS PIECE** in chess, an act or instance of allowing or forcing an opponent to take one of your pieces or pawns so that you can gain an advantage in position ■ *v* (**-fices, -ficing, -ficed**) **1** *vt* **GIVE UP SOMEBODY OR SOMETHING VALUED** to give up somebody or something important or valued in exchange for somebody or something else that is considered more important or valuable **2** *vt* **ABANDON SOMEBODY OR SOMETHING FOR ADVANTAGE** to allow somebody or something to be hurt, killed, or destroyed for your own advantage **3** *vti* **MAKE OFFERING TO A GOD** to make an offering of a ritually slaughtered animal or person to a god **4** *vt* **STRATEGICALLY GIVE UP CHESS PIECE** in chess, to allow or force one of your pieces or pawns to be taken by an opponent so that you can gain an advantage in position [13C. Via Old French < Latin *sacrificium* 'making sacred', < *sacr-,* stem of *sacer* 'sacred'.] —**sacrificeable** *adj* —**sacrificer** *n*

sacrifice bunt, sacrifice hit *n* in baseball, an act of bunting the ball, expecting to be put out, in order to advance a base runner

sacrifice fly *n* in baseball, a fly ball that is caught in the outfield and on which a runner scores

sacrifice hit *n* BASEBALL = **sacrifice bunt**

sacrificial /sákri físh'l/ *adj* relating to, used in, or offered as a sacrifice —**sacrificially** *adv*

sacrilege /sákrilij/ *n* **1** the violation, desecration, or theft of something considered holy or sacred **2** the disrespectful or irreverent treatment of something other people consider worthy of respect or reverence [14C. Via Old French < Latin *sacrilegium* 'temple robbery', < *sacrilegus* 'collector of sacred things', < *sacr-,* stem of *sacer* 'sacred' + *legere* 'collect'.] —**sacrilegious** /sákri líjjəss/ *adj* —**sacrilegiously** *adv* —**sacrilegiousness** *n* —**sacrilegist** /sákri léejist/ *n*

sacristan /sákristən/, **sacrist** /sákrist, sáy-/ *n* **1** a person in charge of the contents of a Christian church, especially objects kept in the sacristy **2** a sexton (*dated*) [14C. < medieval Latin *sacristanus,* < *sacrista* 'keeper of sacred things', < *sacer* 'sacred'.]

sacristy /sákristi/ (*plural* **-ties**) *n* a room in a Christian church in which sacred objects such as vessels and vestments are kept [15C. Via French < medieval Latin *sacristia,* < *sacrista* (see SACRISTAN).]

sacroiliac /sáykrō ílli ak, sák-/ *adj* relating to the sacrum and the upper portion of the hip bone (**ilium**), or to the joint between the sacrum and ilium ■ *n* the joint in the back where the sacrum and the ilium meet [Mid-19C. < SACRUM + ILIUM.]

sacrosanct /sákrō sangkt/ *adj* **1** very holy and sacred **2** not to be criticized or tampered with [Early 17C. < Latin *sacrosanctus,* < *sacro sanctus* 'made holy through religious rites', < *sacer* 'sacred'.] —**sacrosanctity** /sákrō sángktəti/ *n* —**sacrosanctness** *n*

sacrum /sáykrəm, sák-/ (*plural* **-crums** *or* **-cra** /-krə/) *n* a triangular bone at the base of the spine that joins to a hip bone on each side and forms part of the pelvis [Mid-18C. < Latin *(os) sacrum,* translation of Greek *hieron (osteon)* 'sacred (bone)' (from the belief that the soul resided there).]

sad /sad/ (**sadder, saddest**) *adj* **1 UNHAPPY** feeling or showing unhappiness, grief, or sorrow ○ *a sad expression* **2 CAUSING UNHAPPINESS** causing or containing unhappiness ○ *sad news* **3 REGRETTABLE** unfortunate or to be deplored ○ *The sad fact is that there are not enough funds available to support this project.* **4 PITIABLE OR CONTEMPTIBLE** uninteresting and pitiable or contemptible, especially because lacking taste and style (*slang informal*) ○ *wearing a really sad shirt* **5 DULL IN COLOUR** dull or dark in colour **6 NOT HAVING RISEN PROPERLY** doughy, or not having risen properly [Old English *sæd* 'weary, heavy, sated'. Ultimately < Indo-European.] —**sadly** *adv* —**sadness** *n*

SAD *abbr* seasonal affective disorder

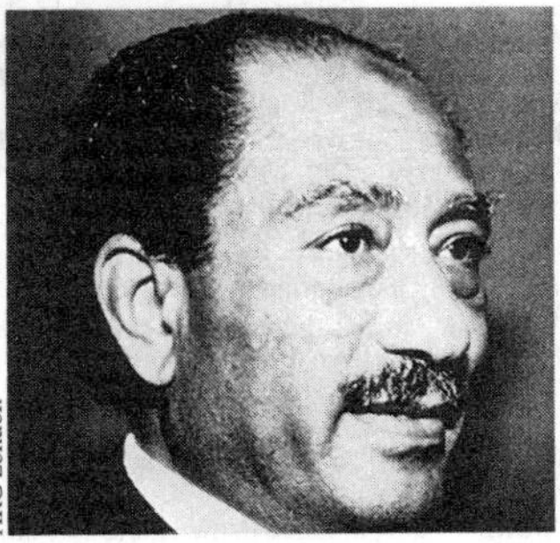
AKG London

Anwar al-Sadat

Sadat /sə dát/, **Anwar al-** (1918–81) Egyptian statesman and president of Egypt (1970–81)

sadden /sádd'n/ *vti* to become sad or to cause somebody to become sad (*often passive*)

saddhu *n* RELIG = **sadhu**

saddle /sádd'l/ *n* **1 SEAT FOR RIDING AN ANIMAL** a seat, usually made of leather, used by a rider on the back of an animal such as a horse or donkey **2 SEAT ON BICYCLE OR MOTORCYCLE** a padded seat for a rider on a vehicle such as a bicycle, motorcycle, or tractor **3 PART OF ANIMAL'S BACK** the part of an animal where a saddle is placed **4 PART OF HARNESS** a pad that forms part of a harness and fits across the back of an animal carrying or pulling something **5 SOMETHING RESEMBLING SADDLE** something that looks like or is used like a saddle **6 LOW POINT OF RIDGE** a low point of a ridge connecting two peaks **7 CUT OF MEAT** a cut of meat that includes part of the backbone and both loins **8 BACK PART OF CHICKEN** the back part of a chicken or other fowl nearest its tail ■ *v* (**-dles, -dling, -dled**) **1** *vt* **STRAP SADDLE ONTO ANIMAL** to put a saddle onto a horse or other animal **2** *vi* **MOUNT AN ANIMAL** to mount a horse, or other animal, that has a saddle on it [Old English *sadol*. Ultimately < Indo-European, 'sit'.] ◇ **in the saddle** in control of something

saddle up *vti* to put a saddle on a horse in readiness for riding it

saddle with *vt* to give somebody an unwelcome or unpleasant task or responsibility

saddleback /sádd'l bak/ *n* **1** an animal such as a bird, fish, or other vertebrate that has a saddle-shaped marking on its back **2** ARCHIT = **saddle roof 3** GEOG = **saddle** *n*. **6**

saddle-backed *adj* **1** with its back curved into a shape like a saddle **2** with a saddle-shaped marking on its back

saddlebag /sádd'l bag/ *n* a bag, sometimes one of a pair, carried near or attached to an animal's saddle or attached to a frame over a wheel of a bicycle or motorcycle

saddlebill /sádd'l bil/ (*plural* **-bills** *or* **-bill**) *n* a stork with black-and-white plumage, black legs with red joints, and a red bill with a black band. Native to: sub-Saharan Africa. *Ephippiorhynchus senegalensis*.

saddle blanket *n* a blanket or other pad placed under a saddle to prevent it from chafing the animal's back

saddlebow /sádd'l bō/ *n* the high arch or raised part (**pommel**) at the front of a horse's saddle [Old English]

saddlecloth /sádd'l kloth/ *n* **1** a cloth placed under a saddle to prevent it from chafing the horse's back **2** a cloth placed under or over a racehorse's saddle that shows the horse's number

saddle horn *n* a projection like a horn on the arch at the front of a horse's saddle

saddle horse *n* a horse that is used or trained for riding

saddler /sáddlər/ *n* a maker, repairer, or seller of saddlery

saddle roof *n* a roof that has two gables and a ridge

saddlery /sáddləri/ (*plural* **-ies**) *n* **1 EQUIPMENT FOR HORSES** saddles, harnesses, and other equipment for horses **2 JOB OF SADDLER** the work done by a saddler **3 SADDLER'S SHOP** a shop that sells equipment for horses **4 PLACE FOR STORING SADDLES** a room in or near a stable used for making, repairing, or storing equipment for horses

saddle soap *n* a mild soap containing neat's-foot oil, used for cleaning, softening, and preserving leather

saddle sore *n* **1** a sore on the buttocks, groin, or inner thighs of a rider, caused by the rubbing of the saddle **2** a sore on a horse's body, caused by the rubbing of an ill-fitting saddle

saddle-sore *adj* **1** sore from having ridden something with a saddle such as a horse or bicycle **2** sore, or affected by sores, from the wearing of a saddle

saddle stitch *n* **1** a long running stitch, usually made with a contrasting colour for ornamentation **2** in bookbinding, a method of binding the pages of a small book or magazine together by folding it in half and stitching along the line of the fold

saddle-stitch *vti* to sew something using a saddle stitch

saddletree /sádd'l tree/ *n* the frame of a saddle

saddo /sáddō/ *n* a person who is considered uninteresting and pitiable or contemptible, especially because of a lack of taste and style (*slang insult*) [Late 20C. < SAD.]

Sadducee /sáddyŏŏ see/ *n* a member of an ancient Jewish group of priests and aristocrats who accepted the literal interpretation of the Torah but rejected Oral Law and belief in the afterlife [Pre-12C. Via late Latin < late Greek *Saddoukaios* < post-Biblical Hebrew *Ṣĕḏūqī* 'follower of Zadok' < *Ṣāḏōq* 'Zadok' (the high priest who supposedly founded the group).] —**Sadducean** /sáddyŏŏ seé ən/ *adj* —**Sadduceeism** *n*

sade *n* = **sadhe**

Sade /saad/, **Marquis de** (1740–1814) French philosopher and novelist. Full name **Donatien Alphonse François, Comte de Sade**

sadhe /saádi/, **sade, tsade** *n* the 18th letter of the Hebrew alphabet [Late 19C. < Hebrew *ṣāḏhē*.]

sadhu /saá doo/, **saddhu** *n* a Hindu holy man who lives by begging [Mid-19C. < Sanskrit *sādhu-* 'good, holy'.]

Sadi /saa deé/, **Saadi, Mosharref al-Din ebn Mosleh al-Din** (1213?–92) Persian poet

sadiron /sád ī ərn/ *n* a heavy iron that curves to a point at both ends, has a removable handle, is heated on an external source, and is used for pressing clothes and linens [Mid-18C. < SAD in the obsolete sense 'solid, heavy' + IRON.]

sadism /sáydizəm/; *formerly also* /sáddizəm/ *n* **1 HURTING OTHERS FOR SEXUAL PLEASURE** the gaining of sexual gratification by causing physical or mental pain to other people, or the acts that produce such gratification **2 BEING CRUEL FOR FUN** the gaining of pleasure from causing physical or mental pain to people or animals **3 CRUELTY** great physical or mental cruelty [Late 19C. < French *sadisme*, after the Marquis de SADE.] —**sadist** *n* —**sadistic** /sə dístik/ *adj* —**sadistically** *adv*

sadomasochism /sáydō mássəkizəm/ *n* **1** the gaining of sexual gratification by alternately or simultaneously enduring pain and causing pain to somebody else, or the acts that produce such gratification **2** a combination of sadistic and masochistic sexual tendencies within an individual, who may derive sexual pleasure both from inflicting and from enduring pain and cruelty [Mid-20C. < SADISM + MASOCHISM.] —**sadomasochist** *n* —**sadomasochistic** /sáydō mássə kístik/ *adj*

sad sack *n US* somebody, especially a soldier, who means well but is hopelessly inept (*informal*) [Mid-20C. < a melancholy cartoon soldier created by US cartoonist George Baker.]

s.a.e., SAE *abbr* **1** self-addressed envelope **2** stamped addressed envelope

SAEF /sayf/ *abbr* Stock Exchange Automatic Execution Facility

Safar /sə faár/, **Saphar** *n* in the Islamic calendar, the second month of the year, made up of 29 days [Late 18C. < Arabic *safar*.]

safari /sə faári/ *n* **1** a journey across a stretch of land, especially in Africa, for the purpose of hunting or observing wild animals ○ *go on safari* **2** a group of people on a safari, together with the animals or vehicles that transport them [Late 19C. Via Swahili < Arabic *safar* 'journey'.]

safari jacket *n* a casual jacket with four large pockets and a belt

safari park *n* a large enclosed area of land where wild animals wander relatively freely and people pay to drive around and observe them

safari suit *n* a short-sleeved safari jacket with matching trousers, shorts, or skirt

Safavid dynasty /sa faávid-/ *n* a Persian dynasty that ruled from 1500 to 1722 and established the Shiite branch of Islam as the state religion [Early 20C. < Arabic *ṣafawī*, < *Ṣīī* al-Din Isḥaq, the dynasty's founder.]

safe /sayf/ *adj* (**safer, safest**) **1 NOT DANGEROUS** unlikely to cause or result in harm, injury, or damage ○ *Have a safe journey!* **2 NOT IN DANGER** in a position or situation that offers protection, so that harm, damage, loss, or unwanted tampering is unlikely ○ *You'll be safe with me.* ○ *It's hidden in a safe place.* **3 UNHARMED OR UNDAMAGED** in an unharmed, uninjured, or undamaged condition ○ *They're safe, but the car's a write-off* **4 SURE TO BE SUCCESSFUL** certain to be successful or profitable, and not at risk of failure or loss ○ *a safe investment* ○ *This investment is as safe as houses.* **5 UNLIKELY TO CAUSE TROUBLE** unlikely to cause trouble or controversy ○ *Is it safe to talk about politics with them?* **6 PROBABLY CORRECT** unlikely to be wrong ○ *It's safe to assume that the weather will be good.* **7 CAUTIOUS AND CONSERVATIVE** cautious with regard to risks or unforeseen problems, conservative with regard to estimates, or unadventurous with regard to choices and decisions ○ *The safe option is just to put the money in the bank.* **8 DEPENDABLE** able to be trusted or depended on ○ *Don't worry, your child's in safe hands.* **9 HAVING REACHED BASE SUCCESSFULLY** in baseball, having reached a base or home plate without being put out ■ *n* **1 CONTAINER FOR VALUABLES** a strong metal container, often with a complex locking system, for the storage of money and other valuables **2 STORAGE CONTAINER** a container for storage or protection, especially a ventilated box or small cupboard for keeping food cool or fresh (*dated*) **3** *US* **CONDOM** a condom (*slang*) [13C. Via Old French *sauf* < Latin *salvus*.] —**safely** *adv* —**safeness** *n*

safeblower /sáyf blō ər/ *n* somebody who uses explosives to open a safe in order to steal the contents

safebreaker /sáyf braykər/ *n* a person who breaks into a safe, with or without the use of force, in order to steal the contents. US term **safecracker** —**safebreaking** *n*

safe-conduct *n* **1** official protection from harm or immunity from arrest for somebody passing through a dangerous area, such as enemy territory in wartime **2** a document or escort providing safe-conduct

safecracker /sáyf krakər/ *n* = **safebreaker** —**safecracking** *n*

safe-deposit *n* a place where money and other valuables can be stored without risk of loss or damage by fire or theft, e.g. a bank vault or strongroom

safe-deposit box *n* a strong metal container for valuables, e.g. jewellery or documents, usually kept in a bank vault or strongroom

safeguard /sáyf gaard/ *n* **1 PROTECTIVE MEASURE** something intended to prevent undesirable consequences from happening, e.g. a safety device or measure, or a proviso in a legal document **2 SAFE-CONDUCT DOCUMENT** a document providing safe-conduct ■ *vt* **KEEP SOMETHING SAFE** to prevent something or somebody from being harmed, damaged, or lost [14C. < Anglo-Norman *salve garde* and French *sauve garde*, < *sauf* 'safe' (see SAFE) + *garde* (see GUARD).] —**safeguarder** *n*

SYNONYMS ***safeguard, protect, defend, guard, shield***

CORE MEANING: to keep safe from actual or potential damage or attack

safeguard to take steps to prevent somebody or something from being harmed or damaged; **protect** to keep somebody or something from any kind of harm or damage; **defend** to deter an actual or threatened attack; **guard** to work to prevent damage, loss, or attack by being vigilant and taking defensive measures; **shield** to prevent harm, damage, or attack by using a physical barrier or by intervening in a protective way.

safe house *n* a house or other place of refuge where people in danger can hide or meet in secret

safekeeping /sayf keéping/ *n* protection from harm, damage, loss, or theft ○ *I put the documents in my desk for safekeeping.*

safelight /sáyf līt/ *n* a light used in darkrooms to filter out the rays that are harmful to sensitive film and photographic paper

safe seat *n* a parliamentary seat that is likely to continue to be held by the same party after an election

safe sex *n* sexual activity in which precautions are taken to avoid spreading sexually transmitted diseases, e.g. by using a condom

safety /sáyfti/ (*plural* **-ties**) *n* **1 FREEDOM FROM DANGER** protection from or nonexposure to the risk of harm or injury ○ *a safety device* ○ *The captain is responsible for the safety of the crew.* **2 LACK OF DANGER** inability to cause or result in harm, injury, or damage ○ *People are beginning to question the safety of the medication.* **3 SAFE PLACE** a place or situation where harm, damage, or loss is unlikely ○ *She led the passengers to safety.* **4 BEING UNHARMED OR UNDAMAGED** the fact of being or remaining unharmed, uninjured, or undamaged ○ *There are fears for their safety.* **5 SAFETY DEVICE** a safety catch or other device intended to prevent harm, injury, or damage **6 DEFENSIVE BACK** in American football, a player defending the back of the field **7** *US* **CONDOM** a condom (*slang*) [14C. Via French *sauveté* < medieval Latin *salvitas* < Latin *salvus* 'safe'.]

safety belt *n* **1** = **seat belt 2** a strong strap attached to a fixed point, worn by a person in danger of falling, e.g. somebody working in a high place

safety catch *n* a device designed to prevent a mechanism from being operated unintentionally, e.g. one that stops a gun from being fired or a hoisting device from falling

safety curtain *n* a fireproof curtain that can be lowered at the front of the stage in a theatre to isolate the auditorium from the stage in the event of fire

safety film *n* nonflammable cinema film made with a cellulose acetate or polyester base

safety glass *n* **1** strong laminated glass designed not to shatter, made with a layer of clear plastic sandwiched between two glass sheets **2** glass that, if it breaks, forms rounded fragments rather than sharp splinters

safety lamp *n* a miner's lamp in which the flame is enclosed in fine wire gauze to prevent the combustion of flammable gases

safety match *n* a match that will only produce a flame if it is struck against a specially prepared surface

safety net *n* **1** a net installed below a high place, such as a circus tightrope or trapeze, from which somebody might fall or jump **2** something intended to help people in the event of hardship or misfortune, especially something providing financial security, such as insurance or benefit payments

safety pin *n* **1** a loop-shaped pin that fastens into itself with its point under a protective cover to prevent accidental opening or injury **2** a pin, e.g. in a grenade, that when properly seated prevents accidental or premature detonation

safety razor *n* a razor in which the blade is partially covered to minimize the risk of accidental injury

safety valve *n* **1** a valve that will automatically open and release a fluid when the pressure in a chamber, e.g. a steam engine or a boiler, approaches a dangerous level **2** something that enables people to get rid of strong feelings such as anger, grief, anxiety, or excitement without harming themselves or others

safflower /sá flow ər/ *n* **1 PLANT YIELDING OIL AND DYE** an annual composite plant. Flowers: orange or red. Use: dye, cooking oil, paints, medicines. Native to: South Asia. *Carthamus tinctorius.* **2 DRIED FLOWERS** the dried flowers of the safflower plant. Use: red dye. **3 RED DYE** a red dye made from the dried flowers of the safflower plant. Use: colourant for fabric, food, and cosmetics. [15C. Via Dutch or German < Old French *saffleur*, via obsolete Italian *asfiore*, < Arabic *asfar* 'yellow plant'.]

saffron /sáffrən/ (*plural* **-frons** *or* **-fron**) *n* **1 COOKING SPICE** the deep orange-coloured stigmas of the saffron flower, or an orange or yellow powder obtained from these. Use: food colourant or flavouring. **2 SPICE-PRODUCING CROCUS** a crocus introduced into Europe from Asia Minor whose flowers produce saffron. Flowers: showy, purple or white. *Crocus sativus.* **3 BRIGHT ORANGE-YELLOW COLOUR** a bright orange-yellow colour [Pre-12C. Via Old French *safran* and medieval Latin *safranum* < Arabic *za'farān*.] —**saffron** *adj*

Saffron Walden /sáffrən wáwld'n/ town in SE England. Population: 13,201 (1991).

Safi /saa fée/ capital of Safi Province, W Morocco, on the Atlantic Ocean. Population: 278,000 (1993).

safranine /sáffrə neen/, **safranin** /sáffrə nin/ *n* a red organic azine. Use: textile colour, biological stain. [Mid-19C. < French, < *safran* (see SAFFRON).]

safrole /sáffrōl/ *n* $C_{10}H_{10}O_2$ a colourless or yellow poisonous oily liquid. Source: sassafras, camphor oils. Use: manufacture of perfumes and soaps. [Mid-19C. < SASSAFRAS + -OLE.]

~~**saftey**~~ incorrect spelling of **safety**

~~**safty**~~ incorrect spelling of **safety**

sag /sag/ *v* (**sags, sagging, sagged**) **1** *vti* **BEND UNDER WEIGHT** to bend downwards in the middle, or to hang or droop instead of remaining firm or level, or to make something bend in this way, usually through having to support excessive weight ○ *My cakes always sag in the middle.* **2** *vi* **BECOME WEAKER OR LOSE INTENSITY** to become weaker or lose intensity or enthusiasm **3** *vi* **FALL IN VALUE** to decrease in value **4** *vi* **DRIFT LEEWARD** to drift to leeward ■ *n* **1 PLACE WHERE SOMETHING SAGS** a bend, depression, or slackness in something where it has sagged **2 DECLINE IN STRENGTH** a decline in strength, intensity, or value ○ *a sag in the stock market* **3 LEEWARD DRIFT** a tendency to drift to leeward [14C. Possibly < Scandinavian or < Middle Low German *sacken* 'to sink'.] —**saggy** *adj*

saga /saagə/ *n* **1 NORSE LITERARY GENRE** an epic tale in Old Norse literature, usually in prose, recounting events in the lives of historical and mythological figures from medieval Iceland and Norway **2 LONG NOVEL OR SERIES OF NOVELS** a long story or novel, or a series of stories or novels, often following the lives of a family or community over several generations **3 SERIES OF EVENTS** a complicated series of events or personal experiences stretching over a considerable period of time, or a detailed account of such a series of events or experiences (*informal*) ○ *Have you heard the saga of our house move?* [Early 18C. < Old Icelandic *saga*.]

LITERARY LINK ***The Forsyte Saga***, a series of novels (1906–22) by John Galsworthy. Set in early 20th-century England, it charts the decline of Victorian values in upper-middle-class society through the story of three generations of the Forsyte family.

sagacious /sə gáyshəss/ *adj* having or based on a profound knowledge and understanding of the world combined with intelligence and good judgment [Early 17C. < Latin *sagac-*, stem of *sagax* 'of quick perception'.] —**sagaciously** *adv* —**sagaciousness** *n*

sagacity /sə gássəti/ *n* profound knowledge and understanding, coupled with foresight and good judgment [15C. Via Old French *sagacite* < Latin *sagacitas*, < *sagac-* (see SAGACIOUS).]

sagamore /sággə mawr/ *n* among the Native North American Algonquian people, a subordinate chief [Early 17C. < Algonquian (Abenaki) *sangman* 'he overcomes' or 'chief'.]

Sagan /saa gaan/, **Françoise** (*b.* 1935) French writer. Pseudonym of **Françoise Quoirez**

saga novel *n* = **roman-fleuve**

sag bag *n* FURNITURE = **beanbag** *n.* **2**

sage[1] /sayj/ *n* somebody who is regarded as knowledgeable, wise, and experienced, especially a man of advanced years revered for his wisdom and good judgment (*literary*) ■ *adj* having or showing great wisdom, especially that gained from long experience of life (*literary*) [14C. Via Old French < Latin *sapere* 'be wise, have taste'.] —**sagely** *adv* —**sageness** *n*

sage[2] /sayj/ (*plural* **sages** *or* **sage**) *n* **1** a plant or shrub with aromatic greyish-green leaves. Use: flavouring food. *Salvia officinalis.* **2** PLANTS = **sagebrush 3** COLOURS = **sage green** [14C. Via Old French *sauge* < Latin *salvia* 'healing plant', < *salvus*.]

sagebrush /sáyj brush/ (*plural* **-brushes** *or* **-brush**) *n* a bush of dry regions with silvery wedge-shaped leaves and large flower clusters. Native to: W North America. Genus: *Artemisia.*

sage Derby *n* a hard British cheese that is flavoured with sage and marbled with a green colour

sage green *adj* of a greyish-green colour, like sage leaves —**sage green** *n*

sage grouse *n* a large grouse with mottled plumage, a black belly, and a long pointed tail that it spreads during courtship. Native to: W North America. *Centrocercus urophasianus.*

saggar /sággər/, **sagger** *n* a clay box into which delicate ceramic objects are placed to protect them in the kiln during firing [Mid-18C. Probably contraction of SAFEGUARD.]

Sagitta /sə gíttə/ *n* a small prominent constellation of the northern hemisphere. See illustration at **constellation**

sagittal /sájjit'l/ *adj* **1** relating to or situated on the imaginary plane that divides a human or animal body into right and left halves **2** resembling an arrow or an arrowhead in shape [Mid-16C. < medieval Latin *sagittalis* < Latin *sagitta* 'arrow'.] —**sagittally** *adv*

Sagittarius /sájji táiri əss/ *n* **1** a large zodiacal constellation of the southern hemisphere. See illustration at **constellation 2** the ninth sign of the zodiac, represented by an archer and lasting from approximately 22 November to 21 December [Pre-12C. < Latin, 'archer' < *sagitta* 'arrow'.] —**Sagittarian** *adj, n*

sagittate /sájji tayt/, **sagittiform** /sá jítti fawrm/ *adj* describes a leaf that is shaped like an arrowhead [Mid-18C. < Latin *sagitta* 'arrow'.]

sago /sáygō/ *n* a powdery substance obtained from the pith of the sago palm. Use: cookery, fabric stiffener. [Mid-16C. < Malay *sagu*.]

sago palm *n* a tall palm tree that yields sago. Native to: Asia. Genus: *Metroxylan.*

saguaro /sə gwaarō, sə waarō/ (*plural* **-ros** *or* **-ro**), **sahuaro** /sə waarō/ (*plural* **-ros** *or* **-ro**) *n* a large cactus growing up to 18 m/60 ft tall, with upwards-curving branches and edible red fruit. Flowers: white, nocturnal. Native to: SW United States, Mexico. *Carnegiea gigantea.* [Mid-19C. < Mexican Spanish.]

Sahaptin /sə háptin/ (*plural* **-tin** *or* **-tins**) *n* **1** a member of a group of Native North American peoples who once lived in a wide area around the Columbia River and who now mainly live in its basin **2** the language of the Sahaptin peoples, in some classifications belonging to the Penutian group of Native American languages. Native speakers: 4,000. [Mid-19C. < Salish.] —**Sahaptin** *adj*

Sahaptin-Chinook *n* in some language classifications, a northern branch of the Penutian family of Native American languages consisting of Sahaptin and Chinook —**Sahaptin-Chinook** *adj*

Sahara /sə haarə/ largest desert in the world, covering much of N Africa between the Atlantic Ocean and the Red Sea. Area: 9,100,000 sq. km/3,500,000 sq. mi. —**Saharan** *adj, n*

Sahel /sə hél/ semiarid zone in N Africa, extending from Sudan westwards to Senegal

sahib /saab, saa hib, saa ib/ (*plural* **-hibs** *or* **-hebs**) *n S Asia* a respectful form of address for men, formerly widely used to address white men during the colonial period [Late 17C. Via Hindi < Arabic, 'friend'.]

Sahitya Akademi /sə híttyə ə kaddəmi/ *n* an institute set up by the Indian government to promote literature in the Indian languages and in English

saice *n* = **syce**

said[1] *v* past tense, past participle of **say** ■ *adj* previously named or mentioned ○ *The said car was later found abandoned.*

said[2] *n* ISLAM = **sayyid**

saiga /sáygə/ (*plural* **-gas** *or* **-ga**) *n* an antelope of central Asia, with a thick tawny coat and enlarged snout, considered a genetic link between the antelope and the sheep. Genus: *Saiga.* [Early 19C. < Russian.]

Saigon /sī gón/ former name for **Ho Chi Minh City**

sail /sayl/ *n* **1 FABRIC CATCHING WIND ON BOAT** a large piece of strong fabric, usually triangular or rectangular in shape, fixed by rigging, masts, and booms to catch the wind and propel a vessel forward **2 JOURNEY IN VESSEL** a trip or voyage in a boat or ship, especially a sailing vessel ○ *a pleasant sail across the bay* **3** (*plural* **sail**) **VESSEL WITH SAILS** a boat or ship with sails, or such vessels considered collectively ○ *go by sail* **4 SAILS OF VESSEL** the sails of a boat or ship considered collectively ○ *a ship under full sail* **5 THING OR PART RESEMBLING SAIL** something that resembles a sail of a boat or ship in form, function, or position **6 BLADE OF WINDMILL** any of the long flat structures on the outside of a windmill that are turned by the wind **7 PART OF SUBMARINE** the conning tower of a submarine ■ *v* **1** *vti* **GO BY VESSEL ON WATER** to travel in a boat or ship across a stretch of water **2** *vti* **MOVE ON WATER** to move across the surface of water, or across a particular stretch of water, driven by wind or engine power ○ *pirate ships that sailed the high seas* **3** *vt* **DRIVE**

BOAT OR SHIP to control the movement of a boat or ship, especially one with sails ○ *She sailed the boat into the harbour.* **4** *vi* **BEGIN SEA JOURNEY** to depart in a boat or ship, or to leave a harbour, mooring, or anchorage ○ *The ferry sails at noon.* **5** *vi* **MOVE SMOOTHLY** to move smoothly or swiftly and usually in a graceful way ○ *The ball sailed over the fence.* [Old English *segl*, < Germanic] —**sailable** *adj* —**sailless** *adj* ◇ **set sail** to depart in a boat or ship, or to leave a harbour, mooring, or anchorage ◇ **under sail** with sails hoisted, and not propelled by an engine

SPELLCHECK Do not confuse *sail* with *sale*, which has a similar sound. Beware: your spellchecker will not catch this error.

sail into *vt* (*informal*) **1** to make a violent physical or verbal attack on somebody ○ *She sailed into me for forgetting to post the letter.* **2** to tackle something with vigour and enthusiasm ○ *He sailed into the task of re-designing the building.*

sail through *vti* to do something, especially to pass a test, with ease ○ *He sailed through the exam.*

sailboard /sáyl bawrd/ *n* a large surfboard with a keel and a mast and a sail mounted on it that is operated by one person standing up in the sport of windsurfing ■ *vi* to ride on a sailboard or take part in the sport of windsurfing —**sailboarder** *n*

sailboarding /sáyl bawrding/ *n* WINDSURFING = **windsurfing**

sailboat /sáyl bōt/ *n US* SAILING = **sailing boat**

sailcloth /sáyl kloth/ *n* **1** any strong fabric used to make sails **2** a lightweight cotton fabric with a texture like that of canvas. Use: clothes.

sailer /sáylər/ *n* a boat or ship, especially a sailing vessel, that has particular sailing characteristics

sailfish /sáyl fish/ (*plural* **-fish** *or* **-fishes**) *n* a warm-water marine fish with a large high dorsal fin resembling a sail and an elongated upper jaw that projects forward like a spear. Genus: *Istiophorus.*

sailing /sáyling/ *n* **1** TRAVELLING IN A VESSEL WITH SAILS the sport, leisure activity, or occupation of travelling in or operating a boat or ship propelled by sails **2** SKILL OF OPERATING VESSEL the art or a method of controlling a boat or ship, especially one with sails ○ *Expert sailing is required in such conditions.* **3** SHIP'S DEPARTURE OR DEPARTURE TIME the departure of a ship, or the time at which a ship is scheduled to leave port ○ *The next sailing is at noon.* [Old English *segling*]

sailing boat *n* a boat with one or more masts and sails that is propelled by the wind, chiefly used for sport and leisure. US term **sailboat**

sailing ship *n* a ship with masts and sails that is propelled by the wind, formerly used for transporting passengers and goods

sailor /sáylər/ *n* **1** somebody who works aboard a boat or ship, especially a low-ranking member of the crew of a merchant or naval ship **2** somebody who frequently sails or travels on a boat or ship, especially with reference to his or her susceptibility to seasickness ○ *I'm not a good sailor.*

sailor blouse *n* a pull-on top with a collar that is large and square at the back and comes to a V in the front, of the type often worn by sailors

sailor collar *n* a collar that is V-shaped in front and has a broad square shape at the back, traditionally worn by sailors

sailor hat *n* a hat with a flat top, a low crown, and wide brim that is either straight or rolled upwards all around

sailor suit *n* an outfit for children resembling the traditional sailor uniform, made up of a top with a sailor collar and trousers or a skirt, usually in dark blue and white

sailplane /sáyl playn/ *n* a light glider particularly well adapted to making use of rising air currents, used for soaring ■ *vi* (**-planes, -planing, -planed**) to travel in a sailplane —**sailplaner** *n*

Saimaa, Lake /sī́maa/ lake in SE Finland. Area: 1,300 sq. km/500 sq. mi.

sainfoin /sán foyn/ (*plural* **-foins** *or* **-foin**) *n* a forage plant. Flowers: pink, in clusters. Native to: Europe, Asia. *Onobrychis viciifolia.* [Early 17C. Via obsolete French, < modern Latin *sanctum foenum* 'holy hay', alteration of *sanum foenum* 'wholesome hay'.]

saint *stressed* /saynt/; *unstressed* /sənt, sən/; *in French names often* /saN/ *n* **1** SOMEBODY HONOURED BY CHURCH AFTER DEATH a member of a religion who after death is formally

designated as having led a life of exceptional holiness **2** MEMBER OF CHOSEN PEOPLE somebody chosen by God because of personal righteousness or the nature of his or her faith, sometimes used by particular religious groups to refer to their own members (*often plural*) **3** VIRTUOUS PERSON a particularly good or holy person, or one who is kind and patient in dealing with difficult people or situations ■ *vt* RECOGNIZE SOMEBODY AS SAINT to declare somebody officially to be a saint of a Christian church [Pre-12C. < Latin *sanctus* 'holy', literally 'consecrated', past participle of *sancire* 'confirm, consecrate'.] —**saintdom** *n*

St Agnes's Eve /-ágnəssəz-/ *n* the eve of St Agnes's Day, on which, according to British folklore, people dream of their future partners if they have performed particular rituals before going to sleep. Date: 20 January.

St Albans /-áwlbənz/ city in SE England. Population: 128,700 (1994).

St Andrews /-ándrooz/ town in E Scotland. Population: 69,181 (1991 estimate).

St Andrew's cross *n* a diagonal cross with arms of equal length, especially a white one on a blue background, as on the flags of St Andrew and Scotland

St Andrew's Day *n* the day commemorating St Andrew, the patron saint of Scotland. Date: 30 November.

St Anthony's cross /-sənt ántəneez-/ *n* = **tau cross**

St Anthony's fire *n* any acutely painful inflammatory skin disorder such as cellulitis, shingles, or erysipelas (*archaic*)

St Austell /-óst'l/ town in SW England. Population: 21,622 (1991).

St Bartholomew's Day Massacre /-baar thóllə myooz-/ *n* a massacre of Huguenots that began in Paris on St Bartholomew's Day, 24 August, 1572

St Bernard /-búrnərd/ *n* a very large working dog belonging to a breed developed in Switzerland to rescue lost mountain travellers [Mid-19C. After the Hospice of the Great ST BERNARD PASS.]

St Bernard Pass /-búrnərd-/ either of two mountain passes through the Alps between Italy and Switzerland

St-Brieuc /saN bri ő́/ city in NW France. Population: 44,752 (1990).

St Catharines /-káthərənz/ city in SE Ontario, Canada. Population: 129,300 (1996).

St Croix /-króy/ largest of the US Virgin Islands. Population: 50,139 (1990). Area: 218 sq. km/84 sq. mi.

St David's /-dáyvidz/ village in SW Wales with the status of city, noted for its cathedral. Population: 1,460 (1991).

St David's Day *n* the day commemorating St David, the patron saint of Wales. Date: 1 March.

St-Denis /saN də nee/ city in north-central France, on the River Seine. Population: 90,806 (1990).

sainted /sáyntid/ *adj* **1** RECOGNIZED AS SAINT officially declared to be a saint of a Christian church **2** IN HEAVEN dead and thought to be in heaven **3** VIRTUOUS good, virtuous, or holy (*literary*)

St Elias, Mount /-ə lí ass/ second highest mountain in Canada, on the Alaska-Yukon Territory border. Height: 5,489 m/18,008 ft.

St Elmo's fire /-élmōz-/ *n* a luminous region of electrical discharge that appears during stormy weather around a narrow pointed object such as a church spire or the mast of a ship [Early 19C. After *St Elmo* (died AD 303), patron saint of sailors.]

St-Émilion /sánt e meeli on/ *n* a red wine produced in the area around St-Émilion in the Bordeaux region of France

St-Étienne /sánt eti én/ city in east-central France. Population: 201,695 (1990).

St. Ex. *abbr* Stock Exchange

Saint-Exupéry /sánt eg zoópe ree/, **Antoine Marie Roger de** (1900–44) French aviator and writer

St Gallen /sənt gaálən/, **St Gall** /-gáll/ city in NE Switzerland. Population: 75,541 (1990).

St George's Channel /-jáwrjəz-/ sea passage between SE Ireland and SW Wales

St George's cross *n* a red cross on a white background, as on the flags of St George and England

St George's Day *n* the day commemorating St George, the patron saint of England. Date: 23 April.

St Gotthard Pass /-góthərd-/ pass through the St Gotthard Range of the Lepontine Alps, in south-central Switzerland. Length: 26 km/16 mi.

St Helena /-hə leénə/ British island in the S Atlantic Ocean, off the coast of W Africa, the site of Napoleon's death in exile in 1821. Population: 5,644 (1997). Area: 122 sq. km/47 sq. mi.

St Helens /-héllənz/ town in NW England. Population: 179,900 (1995).

St Helens, Mount active volcano in SW Washington State. Height: 2,550 m/8,365 ft.

St Helier /-hélli ər/ port on Jersey, in the Channel Islands. Population: 27,083 (1991).

sainthood /sáynt hood/ *n* **1** the condition or status of being a saint or saintly **2** saints regarded as a group

St Ives /-ī́vz/ town in SW England. Population: 9,700 (1994).

St John /-jón/ **1** river forming part of the border between Maine and New Brunswick, Canada. Length: 673 km/418 mi. **2** city in New Brunswick, Canada, on the Bay of Fundy. Population: 72,494 (1996).

St Johns /-jónz/ river in NE Florida. Length: 444 km/276 mi.

St John's /-jónz/ **1** capital of Newfoundland, Canada, in the southeast of the province. Population: 174,051 (1996). **2** capital of Antigua and Barbuda, on the NW coast of Antigua. Population: 21,514 (1991).

St John's day *n* CALENDAR = **Midsummer Day**

St John's wort *n* a herb or shrub with five-petalled yellow flowers. Genus: *Hypericum.* [Because it is said to flower on the feast of St John the Baptist.]

St Kilda /-kíldə/ uninhabited island group in the Outer Hebrides, W Scotland

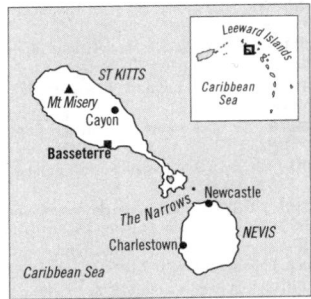

St Kitts and Nevis

St Kitts and Nevis /-kits and neéviss/ independent state in the Caribbean, comprising two islands that are part of the Leeward Islands group. Capital: Basseterre. Population: 39,400 (1996). Area: 269 sq. km/104 sq. mi.

St Laurent /sán lo rón/, **Louis Stephen** (1882–1973) Canadian lawyer and statesman

St Lawrence /-lórrənss/ river in SE Canada, flowing northeastwards from Lake Ontario into the Gulf of St Lawrence. Length: 1,300 km/800 mi.

St Lawrence, Gulf of deep inlet of the Atlantic Ocean between Newfoundland and the Canadian mainland. Area: 259,000 sq. km/100,000 sq. mi.

St Lawrence Seaway /-seé way/ waterway in SE Canada and the NE United States that permits ocean-going vessels to navigate between the Atlantic Ocean and the Great Lakes

St Leger /-léjjər/ *n* a horse race run annually since 1776 at Doncaster in England

St-Lô /saN lố/ city in NW France. Population: 22,819 (1990).

St Louis /-loó iss, -loó i/ city in E Missouri, on the Mississippi River. Population: 339,316 (1998 estimate).

St-Louis /sáN loo ee/ port in NW Senegal. Population: 132,444 (1994).

St Louis encephalitis *n* a viral inflammation of the brain, found in parts of North America and transmitted by mosquitoes [Mid-20C. After ST LOUIS, Missouri, US.]

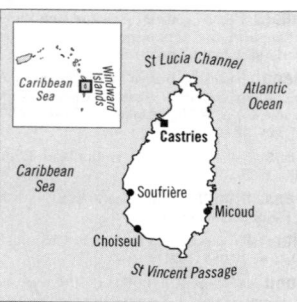

St Lucia

St Lucia /-loòsha/ independent island state in the Caribbean, one of the Windward Islands. Capital: Castries. Population: 143,000 (1995). Area: 617 sq. km/238 sq. mi.

St Luke's summer /-loòks-/ n a period of warm weather occurring in the autumn, around 18 October, the festival of St Luke (archaic)

saintly /sáyntli/ (**-lier, -liest**) adj **1** characteristic of or associated with a saint of a Christian church **2** very good, virtuous, or holy —**saintlily** adv —**saintliness** n

St Martin /-maàrtin/ one of the Leeward Islands, divided between a dependency of Guadeloupe in the north and part of the Netherlands Antilles in the south. Area: 52 sq. km/20 sq. mi. Population: 65,774 (1994).

St Martin's summer n a period of warm weather occurring in the autumn, around 11 November, the festival of St Martin (archaic)

St Matthews /-máth yooz/ city in N Kentucky. Population: 16,562 (1996).

St Michael's Mount /-mík'lz-/ small island off the coast of SW England. Population: 25 (1991).

St Moritz /sáN ma ríts/ town in SE Switzerland. Population: 5,600 (1996).

St-Nazaire /sáN na záir/ port in W France. Population: 66,087 (1990).

St Neots /-nèe əts/ town in east-central England. Population: 25,540 (1990).

St Patrick's Day /-páttriks-/ n the day commemorating St Patrick, the patron saint of Ireland. Date: 17 March.

St Paul /-páwl/ capital of Minnesota, in the southeast of the state. Population: 262,071 (1994).

saintpaulia /sənt páwli ə/ (plural **-lias** or **-lia**) n PLANTS = **African violet** [Late 19C. After the German explorer Baron Walter von Saint-Paul (1860–1910).]

St Paul's Cathedral n a large domed baroque cathedral in the City of London, designed by Christopher Wren and completed in 1710

St Peter Port /-pèetar-/ port in Guernsey, in the Channel Islands. Population: 15,587 (1981).

St Peter's /-pèetarz/ n a large baroque basilica in the Vatican City, Rome, that was completed in 1612. It is one of the largest churches in the world.

St Petersburg /-pèetarz burg/ second-largest city in Russia, in the northwest of the country. Population: 4.8 million (1996).

St-Pierre /-pyáir/ town on Martinique, in the French West Indies. Population: 5,007 (1990).

St-Pierre and Miquelon /-mèe kloN/ two small islands in the N Atlantic Ocean, off the coast of Newfoundland, Canada, an overseas territory of France. Capital: St Pierre. Population: 6,392 (1990). Area: 242 sq. km/93 sq. mi.

Saint-Saëns /sáN sóNss, -sóN/, **Camille** (1835–1921) French composer

saint's day n a day of the year on which a particular saint is remembered or honoured

St Swithin's Day /-swíthinz-/ n the day commemorating St Swithin. Date: 15 July.

St Thomas /-tómməss/ island of the US Virgin Islands. Population: 48,166 (1990). Area: 73 sq. km/28 sq. mi.

St-Tropez /sáN trò páy/ town in S France, on the Mediterranean coast. Population: 5,790 (1990).

St Valentine's Day n CALENDAR = **Valentine's Day**

St Vincent, Cape /-vínsənt/ cape at the south-westernmost point of Portugal

St Vincent, Gulf of gulf in S Australia, located between the Yorke and Fleurieu peninsulas

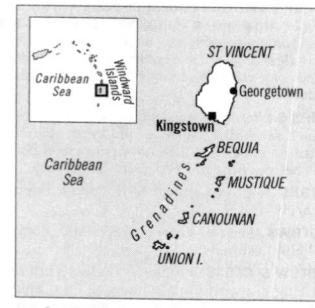

St Vincent and the Grenadines

St Vincent and the Grenadines /-grénnə deenz/ independent state in the Caribbean comprising the island of St Vincent and 32 of the islands of the Grenadine group. Capital: Kingstown. Population: 112,000 (1995). Area: 389 sq. km/150 sq. mi.

St Vitus's dance /sənt vítəssiz-/ n Sydenham's chorea (no longer in technical use) [Early 17C. After St Vitus (3C), patron saint of those affected by this condition.]

saith /seth/ 3rd person present singular of **say** (archaic)

Saiva /síva/ n a member of a Hindu religious group that worships Shiva [Late 18C. < Sanskrit śaiva- 'sacred to Shiva'.] —**Saiva** adj —**Saivism** n —**Saivite** n

Sakai /saa kí/ town on W Honshu Island, Japan. Population: 807,765 (1990).

sake[1] /sayk/ n **1** the good, benefit, or welfare of somebody or something ○ I hope you're right, for all our sakes! **2** the purpose of doing, obtaining, achieving, or maintaining something ○ It's not worth risking your life for the sake of getting there a few minutes earlier. [Old English sacu, < Germanic, 'seeking', hence 'accusation, cause']

sake[2] /saàki/, **saki, saké** n a Japanese alcoholic beverage made from fermented rice and usually served warm [Late 17C. < Japanese.]

saker /sáykər/ n a large falcon with brown body plumage and a pale-coloured head, used in falconry. Native to: central Asia, E Europe. Falco cherrug. [15C. Via (Old) French sacre < Arabic sakr 'hawk, falcon'.]

saketini /saàka teèni/ n US a martini consisting variously of vodka or gin, vermouth, and sake [Early 21C. Blend of SAKE + MARTINI.]

Sakhalin /sə̀khəl yín/ island off E Russia, in the Sea of Okhotsk. Area: 76,000 sq. km/29,300 sq. mi. Population: 660,000 (1983).

Sakkara /sə kaàra/ village near Cairo, Egypt, the site of a pyramid built in the third millennium BC

Sakta /shaàkta/, **Shakta** n a member of a Hindu religious group who particularly worship the female principle or the female gods

Sakti /sákti/, **Shakti** /shúkti/ n in Hinduism, the vital generative and creative principle at work in the universe, typically associated with the feminine component of the divine, often embodied as a goddess [Early 19C. < Sanskrit śaktih 'power' < śak- 'be strong'.]

Sakyamuni /saàkya moòni/ n one of the names of the Buddha, deriving from Sakya, the name of his clan

sal /sal/ n in pharmacology, salt (usually in combination) ○ sal ammoniac [14C. < Latin.]

salaam /sə laàm/ n **1** DEEP BOW WITH HAND ON FOREHEAD a deeply respectful or deferential gesture of greeting or acknowledgment, used especially in Islamic countries, made by bowing low with the palm of the right hand against the forehead **2** RESPECTFUL GREETING the word 'salaam', meaning 'peace', used as a respectful greeting ■ vti MAKE SALUTATION OF GREETING OR RESPECT to perform a salaam, or to greet somebody with a salaam [Early 17C. < Arabic salām 'peace'.]

salacious /sə láyshəss/ adj **1** intended to titillate or arouse people sexually, usually by having an explicit erotic content **2** having or showing crude or explicit sexual

---

desire or interest [Mid-17C. < Latin salac- < salire 'leap'.] —**salaciously** adv —**salaciousness** n —**salacity** /sə lássəti/ n

salad /sálləd/ n **1** MIXTURE OF RAW VEGETABLES a cold dish consisting mainly of a mixture of raw vegetables, whole, sliced, chopped, or in pieces, usually served with a dressing for moisture and flavour **2** DISH OF COLD INGREDIENTS a cold dish consisting of a particular type of food, e.g. a single vegetable or a selection of fruit, cut into pieces or slices, and served usually with a dressing ○ potato salad **3** COLD MEAL a dish consisting of cold meat, fish, cheese, or egg served with a salad of lettuce, tomato, cucumber, and other vegetables ○ chicken salad **4** LEAFY VEGETABLES any leafy vegetable commonly used to make a green salad, typically the many types of lettuce, watercress, chicory, endive, mustard, and cress **5** CONFUSED MIXTURE a confused or varied mixture ○ a salad of ideas [14C. Via French salade < Latin sal 'salt'.]

salad bar n a counter in a restaurant or shop where salads of various types are available, often set up as a buffet where customers can choose their own ingredients

salad cream n a ready-made creamy white dressing with a flowing consistency for eating with salad

salad days npl the period of a person's life when he or she is young, innocent, naive, and inexperienced (literary) [< the words of Cleopatra in Shakespeare's Antony and Cleopatra: 'My salad days, When I was green in judgement, cold in blood']

salad dressing n a well-seasoned sauce poured over or mixed with the ingredients of a salad, e.g. a vinaigrette made from oil and vinegar

salade niçoise /sálləd nee swaàz/ n a cold dish originally from the region around Nice in France, containing anchovies, tuna fillets, olives, green beans, and sometimes other ingredients, served with a dressing of olive oil and garlic [Early 20C. < French, after NICE.]

Saladin /sálladin/ (1137–93) sultan of Egypt and Syria (1174–93). Full name **Salah ed-din Yussuf ibn Ayub**

salal /sə lál/ (plural **salals** or **salal**) n an evergreen shrub with leathery leaves and edible purple berries. Flowers: pink or white, in clusters. Native to: coast of W North America. Gaultheria shallon. [Early 19C. < Chinook Jargon sallal.]

Salam /saa laàm/, **Abdus** (1926–96) Pakistani physicist

Salamanca /salə mángkə/ city in west-central Spain. Population: 167,316 (1995).

Salamander

salamander /sállə mandər/ n **1** SMALL ANIMAL RESEMBLING LIZARD an amphibian that resembles a lizard but has porous moist skin instead of scales, and that lives in water as a larva and on land as an adult. Order: Caudata. **2** MYTHICAL REPTILE LIVING IN FIRE a mythical reptile that can live in fire **3** HOT METAL PLATE FOR BROWNING FOOD a cooking utensil most often in the form of a metal plate with a handle, designed to be heated until very hot then held over food to produce a browned or caramelized surface **4** PORTABLE STOVE a stove that is used on construction projects to heat or dry out buildings or to thaw frozen water pipes [14C. Directly and via Old French < Latin and Greek salamandra.] —**salamandrine** /sállə mándrin/ adj

salami /sə laàmi/ n a large thick highly seasoned sausage, Italian in origin and very often cured, usually served cold in thin slices [Mid-19C. < Italian, plural of salame, < Latin sal 'salt'.]

Salamis /sálləmiss/ island of E Greece, in the Saronic Gulf. Population: 28,574 (1981). Area: 10 sq. km/39 sq. mi.

sal ammoniac /sál ə mṓni ak/ *n* = **ammonium chloride** [< Latin *sal ammoniacus* 'salt of Ammon' (see AMMONIA)]

salary /sálləri/ (*plural* **-ries**) *n* a set sum of money paid at regular intervals to an employee, especially for professional or clerical work [13C. Via Old French *salaire* and directly < Latin *salarium* 'money given to a Roman soldier to buy salt', < *sal* 'salt'.] —**salaried** *adj*

SYNONYMS See ***wage.***

salbutamol /sal byṓtə mol/ *n* $C_{13}H_{21}NO_3$ bronchodilator. Use: relief of asthma, emphysema, and chronic bronchitis. [Mid-20C. < *salicylic acid* + BUTYL + AMINE +-OL.]

salchow /sálkō/ *n* a jump in figure skating in which the skater takes off from one skate, does a complete rotation in the air, and lands on the opposite skate [Early 20C. After Ulrich *Salchow* (1877–1949), Swedish figure-skater.]

sale /sayl/ *n* **1 SELLING OF** the exchanging of goods or services for an agreed amount of money, or a single transaction of this nature **2 OPPORTUNITY TO BUY GOODS AT DISCOUNT** a period of time when a shop sells goods at reduced prices, often in order to clear stocks ○ *I never go shopping during the sales.* **3 OPPORTUNITY TO BUY SECOND-HAND GOODS** an event at which personal possessions or other second-hand items are sold, usually at low prices, sometimes to raise money for a charitable or other cause **4 AUCTION** an event at which goods are sold to the highest bidder **5 MARKET OR DEMAND** demand that creates an opportunity to sell something **6 AMOUNT SOLD OR RATE OF SELLING** a quantity of things sold, or the rate at which they are sold ■ **sales** *npl* **1 DEPARTMENT SELLING THINGS** the department of a company involved with selling its products or services **2 THINGS SOLD** the total number or value of items sold ○ *Sales fell by 10 per cent last month* [Pre-12C. < Old Norse *sala*, < Germanic.] ◇ **for sale** available for purchase ◇ **on sale** available for purchase, usually from a shop or other commercial organization

SPELLCHECK See ***sail.***

Sale /sayl/ town in NW England. Population: 56,052 (1991).

Salé /saa láy/ city in NW Morocco. Population: 521,000 (1993).

saleable, salable *adj* suitable for selling or capable of being sold

sale and leaseback *n* the sale of an asset that the vendor rents back from the buyer immediately after the sale, thereby raising cash and allowing a tax deduction

sale and return *n* = **sale or return**

Saleh /saa lékh/, **Ali Abdullah** (*b.* 1942) Yemeni soldier and statesman

Salem /sáyləm/ **1** city in NE Massachusetts. Population: 38,351 (1998 estimate). **2** capital of Oregon, in the northwest of the state. Population: 126,702 (1998 estimate).

sale of work *n* an event at which home-made goods are sold, usually to raise money for a church or other charitable cause

sale or return, sale and return *n* an agreement between a supplier and a purchaser or retailer whereby the latter returns any unused or unsold goods, paying only for those that have been used or sold

salep /sálləp/ *n* the dried ground tubers of various orchids. Use: food, formerly, medicine. [Mid-18C. Via French < Turkish *sālep*, < Arabic *ṯa'lab*, shortening of *ḵuṣa-ṯ-ṯa'lab* 'orchid', literally 'fox's testicles'.]

Salerno /sə lúrnō/ capital of Salerno Province, Italy. Population: 147,564 (1994).

saleroom /sáyl room, sáyl rŏŏm/ *n* a large room where goods are sold by auction. US term **salesroom** *n.* **2**

~~**salery**~~ incorrect spelling of **salary**

sales assistant *n* = **shop assistant**

salesclerk /sáylz klaark/ *n US* = **shop assistant**

sales force *n* the body of salespeople employed by a company to sell its goods and services

salesgirl /sáylz gurl/ *n* an offensive term for a young woman employed to sell goods to customers in a shop (*dated*)

Salesian /sə leézi ən, -leézh'n/ *n* a member of the Roman Catholic order of Saint Francis de Sales founded in Turin, Italy, in 1845 and dedicated to education and missionary work —**Salesian** *adj*

salesman /sáylzmən/ (*plural* **-men** /-mən/) *n* a man who sells goods or services, either in a shop or by contacting potential customers within a particular area

LITERARY LINK ***Death of a Salesman,*** a play (1949) by US dramatist Arthur Miller. The tragic story of Willi Loman, an ageing salesman tormented by an overwhelming sense of failure, highlights the false values of contemporary consumer society and questions traditional ideas of success and failure.

salesmanship /sáylzmən ship/ *n* the skills, techniques, and tactics involved in persuading people to buy goods or services

salesperson /sáylz purss'n/ (*plural* **-people** /-peep'l/ *or* **-persons**) *n* a seller of goods or services, usually in a shop or by telephone

sales pitch *n* the statements made, arguments used, and assurances given by somebody trying to sell something

sales rep *n* a sales representative (*informal*) [Shortening]

sales representative *n* somebody employed by a company to visit prospective customers with a view to selling them the company's products

sales resistance *n* reluctance or refusal to buy, especially when aggressive selling techniques are used

salesroom /sáylz room, -rŏŏm/ *n* **1** a large room where goods for sale are put on display **2** *US* COMM = **saleroom**

sales slip *n US* a record of a purchase or sale made in a store, usually given to the customer as a receipt

sales tax *n* a tax on retail merchandise that is levied by the government and collected at the point of sale by the retailer

sales team *n* = **sales force**

saleswoman /sáylz wŏŏmən/ (*plural* **-en** /-wimin/) *n* a woman who sells goods or services, usually in a shop or by contacting potential customers within a particular area

Salford /sáwlfərd, sólfərd/ city in NW England. Population: 230,700 (1994).

Salian /sáyli ən/ *n* a member of an ancient Frankish people who settled in the Rhine valley in the Netherlands during the 4th century AD [Early 17C. < late Latin *Salii* 'Salian Franks'.]

Salic /sáylik, sállik/, **Salique** *adj* **1** relating to Salic Law **2** relating to the Salian people or their culture [Mid-16C. Via French *salique* or medieval Latin *Salicus* < late Latin *Salii* 'Salian Franks'.]

salicaceous /sálli káyshəss/ *adj* describes trees or woody shrubs that have catkins, e.g. the willow and poplar. Family: Salicaceae. [Mid-19C. < modern Latin *salicaceus* < Latin *salic-*, stem of *salix* 'willow'.]

salicin /sállissin/, **salicine** *n* a colourless crystalline substance obtained from the bark of willow trees. Use: formerly, analgesic. [Mid-19C. Via French *salicine* < Latin *salic-*, stem of *salic* 'willow'.]

salicional /sə lish'nəl/ *n* a stop and pipes on an organ that produce a soft, gentle tone [Mid-19C. Via German < Latin *salic-*, stem of *salix* 'willow'.]

Salic law *n* a law excluding women from the right to succeed to the throne that formerly applied in France and some other European monarchies

salicylate /sə líssi layt/ *n* a salt or ester of salicylic acid [Mid-19C. < French *salicyle*, < Latin *salictum* < *salic-*, stem of *salix* 'willow'.]

salicylic acid /sálli síllik-/ *n* $C_7H_6O_3$ a white crystalline acid. Use: manufacture of aspirin and dyes, preservative. [< French *salicyle* (see SALICYLATE)]

salient *adj* **1 NOTICEABLE OR STRIKING** particularly noticeable, striking, or relevant **2 PROJECTING** sticking out from a surface **3 PROJECTING OUTWARDS** describes an angle that projects outwards from a polygon **4 JUMPING** in heraldry, represented as a jumping or leaping animal ■ *n* **1 PROJECTING PART OF DEFENSIVE ALIGNMENT** a part of a military front, line, or fortification that projects outwards into enemy-held territory or towards the enemy **2 SALIENT ANGLE** a salient angle [Mid-17C. < Latin *salient-*, present participle of *salire* 'jump'.] —**salience** *n* —**saliency** *n* —**saliently** *adv*

salientian /sáyli énshi ən/ *adj* = **anuran** [Mid-20C. < modern Latin *Salentia*, < Latin *salient-* (see SALIENT).]

Salieri /sálli áiri/, **Antonio** (1750–1825) Italian composer

salimeter /sa límmitər/ *n* CHEM = **salinometer** [Mid-19C. < Latin *sal* 'salt' + -METER.] —**salimetric** /sálli méttrik/ *adj* —**salimetry** *n*

salina /sə línə, sə leénə/ *n* a salt marsh, lake, pond, or spring [Late 16C. Via Spanish < medieval Latin, 'salt pit', < *sal* 'salt'.]

Salinas /sə leénəss/ river in W California. Length: 241 km/150 mi.

saline /sáy līn/ *adj* **1 CONTAINING SALT** containing or impregnated with salt **2 CONTAINING SALTS** relating to or containing alkali metal salts or magnesium salt ■ *n* **SOLUTION OF SALT AND DISTILLED WATER** a solution of common salt (**sodium chloride**) and distilled water, especially one having the same concentration as body fluids [15C. < Latin *salinum* 'saltcellar', < *sal* 'salt'.] —**salinity** /sə línnəti/ *n*

Salinger /sállinjər/, **J. D.** (*b.* 1919) US writer. Full name **Jerome David Salinger**

salinize /sálli nīz/ (**-nizes, -nizing, -nized**), **salinise** (**-nises, -nising, -nised**) *vt* to treat or contaminate something with salt —**salinization** /sálli nī záysh'n/ *n*

salinometer /sálli nómmitər/ *n* an instrument used to measure the concentration of salt in solutions —**salinometric** /sállinə méttrik/ *adj* —**salinometry** *n*

Salisbury /sáwlzbəri, -bri/ city in S England. Population: 39,700 (1994).

Salisbury Plain area of rolling, chalky downs in SW England, the site of Stonehenge. Area: 775 sq. km/300 sq. mi.

Salish /sáylish/ *n* **1** a small family of Native North American languages spoken in the NW United States and British Columbia. Native speakers: 2,000. **2** a member of a Salish-speaking Native North American people who live in British Columbia (+ *plural verb*) [Mid-19C. < Salish *séʔliš* 'Flatheads'.] —**Salishan** *adj, n*

saliva /sə līvə/ *n* the clear liquid secreted into the mouth by the salivary glands, consisting of water, mucin, protein, and enzymes [15C. < Latin, 'spittle'.]

salivary /sə līvəri, sállivəri/ *adj* relating to saliva or the salivary glands

salivary gland *n* any gland in mammals that produces and secretes saliva into the mouth

salivate /sálli vayt/ (**-vates, -vating, -vated**) *v* **1** *vi* **PRODUCE SALIVA** to produce saliva in the mouth, especially at an increased rate, e.g. when food is seen, smelled, or expected **2** *vt* **CAUSE ANIMAL TO SALIVATE** to cause something, e.g. an animal in an experiment, to produce large amounts of saliva **3** *vi* **LONG FOR** to feel or show an immense desire for or appreciation of something (*informal*) ○ *salivating over the magnificent range of fitted kitchens* [Mid-17C. Back-formation < *salivation*, < Latin *saliva* 'saliva'.] —**salivation** /sálli váysh'n/ *n*

Salk /sawk/, **Jonas** (1914–95) US physician and epidemiologist

Salk vaccine *n* a vaccine against poliomyelitis containing a form of the virus that causes it, which has been made inactive by treatment with a solution of formaldehyde. ◊ **Sabin vaccine** [Mid-20C. After Jonas SALK.]

sallet /sállit/ *n* a light helmet protecting the head and the back of the neck, worn in the late Middle Ages [15C. Via French *salade* < Latin *caelata* 'engraved (helmet)', < *caelum* 'chisel'.]

sallow[1] /sállō/ *adj* unnaturally pale and yellowish ○ *a sallow complexion* ■ *vt* to make something unnaturally pale and yellowish ○ *The illness had sallowed her skin.* [Old English *salo* 'dark, dusky', < Germanic] —**sallowish** *adj* —**sallowly** *adv* —**sallowness** *n*

sallow[2] /sállō/ (*plural* **-lows** *or* **-low**) *n* a willow tree with large catkins that yields a hard wood used to produce charcoal. Native to: Europe. *Salix caprea.* [Old English *salh.* Ultimately < Indo-European, 'willow'.] —**sallowy** *adj*

Sallust /sálləst/ (86–35? BC) Roman historian. Full name **Gaius Sallustius Crispus**

sally /sálli/ *n* (*plural* **-lies**) **1 ATTACK FROM DEFENSIVE POSITION** an offensive thrust from a defensive position, especially, formerly, a sudden attack by the defenders of a besieged position on the people besieging them **2 SUDDEN RUSH FORWARD** a sudden rush or spring forward **3 SUDDEN ACTION** a sudden burst of activity or springing into action **4 SUDDEN EXPRESSION** a sudden outburst of speech or expression of emotion **5 WITTY REMARK** a witty remark, reply, or retort **6** EXPEDITION an expedition or excursion ■ *vi* (**-lies, -lying, -lied**) **1** MAKE SALLY to make an offensive thrust from a defensive position **2** SET OUT to go out after being indoors or set out on a journey or excursion **3** RUSH OUT SUDDENLY to rush or spring out suddenly [Mid-16C. < French *saillie*, < past participle of *saillir* 'leap', < Latin *salire*.] —**sallier** *n*

Sally Army /sálli-/ *n* the Salvation Army (*informal*) [Shortening and alteration of *Salvation*]

Sally Lunn /sálli lún/ *n* a sweet bread leavened with yeast that is typically baked in a tin and served warm in slices with butter. It is particularly popular in the S United States. [Late 18C. < ?]

sallyport /sálli pawrt/ *n* an opening in a fortification from which the defenders can make sallies [Mid-17C]

salmagundi /sálmə gúndi/ *n* **1** a mixed salad of various ingredients, such as meat, poultry, fish, and vegetables, arranged in rows on a platter **2** a mixture or miscellany (*literary*) [Late 17C. < French *salmagondis*, originally 'seasoned salt meats'.]

Salmanazar /sálmə názzər/, **salmanazar** *n* a large wine bottle that holds the equivalent of 12 standard bottles, used especially for champagne [Mid-20C. < late Latin *Salmanasar*, a variant of *Shalmaneser*, a king of Assyria in the Bible.]

salmon /sámmən/ (*plural* **-on** *or* **-ons**) *n* **1** LARGE N ATLANTIC FOOD FISH a large fish that has soft fins and migrates up freshwater rivers to spawn. Native to: N Atlantic. Family: Salmonidae. **2** LARGE N PACIFIC FOOD FISH a fish of the salmon family, e.g. the Chinook, sockeye, coho, or chum. Native to: N Pacific. Genus: *Oncorhynchus*. **3** SALMON AS FOOD the red or pink flesh of salmon as food **4** COLOURS = **salmon pink** [13C. Via French *saumon* < Latin *salmon-*, stem of *salmo*.]

Salmon /sámmən/ river in central Idaho. Length: 676 km/420 mi.

salmonberry /sámmənbəri/ (*plural* **-ries** /sámmən beri/) *n* **1** a salmon-pink raspberry **2** a plant that produces salmonberries. Flowers: red. Native to: Pacific coast of North America. *Rubus spectabilis*.

salmonella /sálmə néllə/ (*plural* **-lae**) *n* a rod-shaped bacterium found in the intestine that can cause food poisoning, gastroenteritis, and typhoid fever. Genus: *Salmonella*. [Early 20C. < modern Latin, after Daniel Elmer *Salmon* (1850–1914), US veterinary surgeon.] —**salmonellosis** /sálmə ne lóssiss/ *n*

salmonid /sálmənid/ *n* a bony soft-finned fish of the family that includes salmon, trout, whitefish, and char. Family: Salmonidae.

salmon pink *n* a pale orange-pink colour, like salmon flesh —**salmon-pink** *adj*

Salome /sə lómi/ *n* in the Bible, the daughter of Herodias who demanded and received John the Baptist's head as reward for her dancing before her stepfather, Herod Antipas (Matthew 14:6–11 and Mark 6:21–28)

salometer /sa lómmitər/ *n* = **salinometer** [Mid-19C. < Latin *sal* 'salt' + -METER.]

salon /sáll on/ *n* **1** GRAND SITTING ROOM an elegantly furnished room in a large house where guests are received and entertained **2** SOCIAL GATHERING OF INTELLECTUALS a regular gathering of prominent people from the worlds of literature, art, music, or politics, especially one held at the home of a wealthy woman **3** PLACE FOR HAIRDRESSING OR BEAUTY TREATMENTS a commercial establishment where hairdressers or beauticians work, sometimes part of a larger shop or department store or a hotel **4** EXPENSIVE CLOTHES SHOP a shop selling elegant or fashionable women's clothes, especially expensive designer clothes **5** ART EXHIBITION OR GALLERY an art exhibition, especially one devoted to the work of living artists, or the hall in which the exhibits are displayed [Late 17C. Via French < Italian *salone* 'large hall', < *sala* 'hall', < Germanic.]

Salonika /sə lónnikə/ = **Thessaloníki**

salon music *n* light classical music for easy listening

saloon /sə lóon/ *n* **1** DRINKING PLACE in North America, a commercial establishment serving alcoholic drinks to the general public **2** LEISURE = **lounge bar 3** *UK* CLOSED CAR WITH BOOT a car with two or four doors, four to six seats, a fixed roof, and a separate boot. ◊ **sedan 4** PART OF SHIP OR TRAIN a large room on a ship or, formerly, a carriage on a train where passengers can sit and relax **5** LARGE PUBLIC ROOM a large public room used for any of various purposes, e.g. receptions, dances, entertainment, or sport **6** *S Asia* BARBER'S SHOP a men's barber's shop [Early 18C. Anglicization of SALON.]

saloon bar *n* LEISURE = **lounge bar** *n*.

salopettes /sállə péts/ *npl* a garment worn by skiers, comprising a pair of usually padded, water-resistant trousers that reach up to the chest with straps passing over the shoulders [Late 20C. < French.]

salp /salp/, **salpa** /sálpə/ (*plural* **-pae** /-pee/ *or* **-pas**) *n* a tiny free-swimming organism (**tunicate**) that has a transparent barrel-shaped body. Native to: warm seas. Genus: *Salpa*. [Mid-19C. Via French < modern Latin *salpa*, < Greek *salpē* 'fish'.] —**salpiform** /sálpi fawrm/ *adj*

salpiglossis /sálpi glóssiss/ (*plural* **-ses** /-seez/ *or* **-sis**) *n* a plant of the nightshade family. Flowers: large, funnel-shaped. Native to: Chile. Genus: *Salpiglossis*. [Early 19C. < modern Latin, < Greek *salpigx* 'trumpet' + *glossa* 'tongue', < the plant's shape.]

salpingectomy /sálpin jéktəmi/ (*plural* **-mies**) *n* the severing or surgical removal of a fallopian tube [Late 19C. < Greek *salpigg-*, stem of *salpigx* 'trumpet' + -ECTOMY.]

salpingitis /sálpin jítiss/ *n* inflammation of a fallopian tube [Mid-19C. < Greek *salpigg-* 'trumpet' + -ITIS.] —**salpingitic** /sálpin jíttik/ *adj*

salsa /sálssə/ *n* **1** a spicy sauce of finely-chopped vegetables, including tomatoes, onions, and chillis, eaten with tortilla chips and other Mexican foods **2** Latin American dance music combining jazz and rock elements with African-Cuban melodies [Late 20C. < Spanish, 'sauce', < Latin, 'salted', < past participle of *sallere* 'salt', < *sal* 'salt'.]

salsify /sálssəfi/ (*plural* **-fies** *or* **-fy**) *n* **1** a long pale edible root cooked as a vegetable **2** a plant with long thin leaves that produces salsify. Native to: Europe. *Tragopogon porrifolius*. [Early 18C. Via French *salsifis* < Italian *salsefica*.]

sal soda *n* CHEM = **washing soda**

salt /sawlt, solt/ *n* **1** WHITE CRYSTALS USED IN FOOD PREPARATION small white tangy-tasting crystals consisting largely of sodium chloride. Source: seawater, mineral deposits. Use: food seasoning and preservative. ◊ **sodium chloride 2** CRYSTALLINE CHEMICAL COMPOUND a crystalline compound formed from the neutralization of an acid by a base containing a metal or group acting like a metal **3** SOMETHING THAT ADDS ZEST something that adds zest, piquancy, liveliness, or vigour **4** DRY WIT sharp or dry wit **5** NAVY = **old salt 6** HOUSEHOLD = **saltcellar** *n*. 1 ■ **salts** *npl* SUBSTANCE RESEMBLING SALT a chemical or crystalline solution used for a particular purpose ○ *smelling salts* ■ *adj* **1** PRESERVED WITH SALT preserved with salt or a salt solution ○ *salt cod* **2** CONTAINING SALT containing or consisting of salt ○ *salt tears* **3** CONTAINING OR ASSOCIATED WITH SALT WATER containing, covered with, or growing near salt water **4** TASTING OF SALT tasting or smelling of salt ■ *vt* **1** SEASON FOOD WITH SALT to add salt to food, during or after preparation, to emphasize its flavour **2** PRESERVE FOOD WITH SALT to preserve food by treating it with salt or a salt solution **3** PUT SALT ON COLD GROUND to scatter salt over a road or pavement to melt ice or prevent it from forming **4** ADD ZEST TO to add a more lively or entertaining quality to something ○ *She salted her speech with jokes.* **5** ENRICH ORE SAMPLE to enrich a mining area or sample with a valuable ore artificially introduced in order to increase its apparent value [Old English *sealt*, < Indo-European] —**saltness** *n* ◇ **rub salt in the wound** to add to somebody's distress, embarrassment, or sense of shame, often deliberately ◇ **take something with a grain** *or* **pinch of salt** to listen to something without fully believing it ◇ **the salt of the earth** a very good, worthy person or group of people ◇ **worth your salt** efficient and doing the job well

salt away *vt* to hoard or save money for future use, often secretly or illegally [Probably from the practice of preserving food in salt]

salt out *vt* to separate a dissolved substance from a solution by adding a salt

SALT /sawlt, solt/ *abbr* Strategic Arms Limitation Talks (or Treaty)

salt-and-pepper *adj* = **pepper-and-salt**

saltarello /sáltə réllō/ (*plural* **-los** *or* **-li** /-rélli/) *n* **1** a dance in triple time originating in medieval times and especially popular in Spain and Italy **2** the music for a saltarello [Late 16C. Via Italian < Latin *saltare* 'dance' (see SALTATION).]

Saltash /sáwlt ash, sólt-/ town in SW England. Population: 14,139 (1991).

saltation /sal táysh'n, sawl-/ *n* **1** JUMPING OR JUMP leaping or jumping, or a sudden jump or leap (*formal*) **2** SUDDEN CHANGE development or transition that takes place in jumps or leaps (*formal*) **3** ABRUPT EVOLUTIONARY DEVELOPMENT the abrupt evolutionary development of a new species or property, especially as a result of genetic mutation **4** JUMPING MOTION OF PARTICLES the transportation of particles of soil or sand in the wind or in running water, characterized by bouncing movements [Early 17C. < Latin *saltation-*, < *saltare* 'keep leaping', < *salire* 'leap'.]

saltatorial /sáltə táwri əl, sáwltə-, sóltə-/, **saltatory** /sáltətəri, sáwltətəri/ *adj* **1** RELATING TO JUMPING relating to or adapted for jumping ○ *an insect with saltatorial legs* **2** ASSOCIATED WITH JUMPING OR DANCING associated with or involving jumping, leaping, or dancing **3** DEVELOPING IN JUMPS OR LEAPS involving or characterized by sudden change rather than gradual transition

saltbox /sáwlt boks, sólt-/ *n* **1** a box in which salt is stored, especially one with a sloping lid **2** *US* a wood-frame house that has two floors at the front but only one at the back, and with a long sloping roof on the rear side

saltbush /sáwlt bòosh, sólt-/ (*plural* **-bushes** *or* **-bush**) *n* = **orache**

salt cake *n* an impure form of sodium sulphate. Use: manufacture of glass, paper pulp, soap, and ceramic glazes.

saltcellar /sáwlt selər, sólt-/ *n* **1** a small container for salt, especially one used at the table to season food after it is served **2** one of two depressions above the collarbone, at either side of the neck, especially prominent in very slim people (*informal*)

salt dome *n* a dome-shaped structure formed in sedimentary rock when buried salt deposits move up through overlying rocks, owing to their low density and high buoyancy

salted /sáwltid, sóltid/ *adj* **1** with salt added for seasoning, preservation, or some other purpose **2** hardened or experienced, e.g. in a trade or profession

salter /sáwltər, sól-/ *n* **1** a producer or seller of salt **2** a preserver of food by using salt

saltern /sáwltərn, sól-/ *n* **1** a place where salt is produced commercially **2** a place where salt is produced naturally when pools of sea water evaporate [Old English < *sealt* 'salt' + *ærn* 'building']

saltfish /sáwlt fish, sólt fish/ *n* *Carib* cod or other fish preserved with salt

salt flat *n* a broad flat area in hot deserts encrusted with salt left after the evaporation of water from shallow saline lakes (*often plural*)

salt gland *n* a gland in some marine animals, e.g. birds or reptiles, used to excrete excess ingested salt

salt glaze *n* a glaze formed by throwing salt into a kiln during the firing process

salt grass *n* any grass native to salt marshes or alkaline regions

salt hay *n* hay produced from salt grass, used as fodder

Saltillo /sal tée̱l yō/ capital of Coahuila State, N Mexico. Population: 420,845 (1990).

saltimbocca /sáltim bókə/ *n* a dish consisting of thin slices of veal rolled up with prosciutto ham and fresh sage leaves, lightly fried and braised in white wine [Mid-20C. < Italian, < *saltare* 'leap' + *in* 'into' + *bocca* 'mouth'.]

saltine /sawl tée̱n, sol-/ *n* *US* a thin crisp cracker sprinkled with salt

salting /sáwlting, sól-/ *n* a low-lying area of land regularly flooded with salt water (*often plural*)

saltire /sáwl tīr, sál-/ *n* in heraldry, one of the basic designs used on coats of arms, consisting of a diagonal cross [15C. Via Old French *sau(l)toir* 'stirrup, style' < Latin *saltare* (see SALTATION).]

salt lake *n* a lake with no outlet and having a high salt content as a result of evaporation, e.g. the Dead Sea

Salt Lake City /sáwlt layk-, sólt-/ capital of Utah, in the north-central part of the state. Population: 174,348 (1998 estimate).

salt lick *n* **1** a place where animals go to lick salt deposits that occur naturally **2** a block of salt or other preparation that livestock lick in order to supplement their salt intake

salt marsh *n* a marshy grassland area regularly flooded with salt water

saltpan /sáwlt pan, sólt-/ *n* a basin in a semiarid region where salts are precipitated after saline floodwaters evaporate

saltpeter *n* US = **saltpetre**

saltpetre *n* 1 = **Chile saltpetre** 2 = **potassium nitrate** [14C. Alteration of earlier *salpetre*, < Latin *sal* 'salt' + *petra* 'rock' (from its appearance as a crust on rock).]

salt pork *n* a fat cut of pork from the belly, back, or sides, cured by salting

saltwater /sáwlt wawtər, sólt-/ *adj* 1 containing or involving salt water 2 living or growing in salt water

salt water *n* 1 water containing a lot of salt 2 the water of the sea and coastal inlets

saltwater crocodile *n* a large crocodile that inhabits coastal waterways and feeds on fish, birds, reptiles, and small mammals. Native to: N Australia, SE Asia. *Crocodylus porosus*.

saltworks /sáwlt wurks, sólt-/ *n* a place or factory where salt is produced commercially (*+ singular or plural verb*)

saltwort /sáwlt wurt, sólt-/ (*plural* **-worts** *or* **-wort**) *n* a prickly leaved seashore plant. Native to: Europe, Asia. Genus: *Salsoa*.

salty /sáwlti, sólti/ (**-ier, -iest**) *adj* 1 TASTING OF SALT containing or tasting of salt 2 OF SEA OR SAILORS associated with the sea or with nautical life 3 LIVELY AND AMUSING lively, amusing, and sometimes mildly indecent ○ *salty jokes* —**saltily** *adv* —**saltiness** *n*

salubrious /sə lóobri əss/ *adj* 1 beneficial to or promoting health or well-being 2 decent, respectable, or generally pleasant (*informal humorous*) ○ *advised to avoid the less salubrious parts of the old quarter* [Mid-16C. < Latin *salubris* < *salus* 'health'.] —**salubriously** *adv* —**salubriousness** *n* —**salubrity** *n*

Saluda /sə lóodə/ river in west-central South Carolina. Length: 322 km/200 mi.

saluki /sə lóoki/ *n* a tall slender dog belonging to a breed originally developed in Arabia and Egypt. It has a smooth coat and long fringes on the ears and tail. [Early 19C. < Arabic *salūḳī* < *Salūḳ*, a town in Yemen.]

salutary /sállyootəri/ *adj* 1 of value or benefit to somebody or something ○ *We asked if military service had been a salutary experience for him.* 2 promoting good health (*formal*) [15C. Via French *salutaire* < Latin *salutaris* < *salus* 'health'.] —**salutarily** *adv* —**salutariness** *n*

salutation /sállyoo táysh'n/ *n* 1 SIGN OF GREETING a gesture or phrase that is used to greet, welcome, or recognize somebody 2 ACT OF GREETING the expression of greetings, welcome, or recognition 3 OPENING GREETING the opening phrase of a letter or speech, used to address the recipient or audience, e.g. 'Dear Sir or Madam' or 'Ladies and Gentlemen' ■ *interj* **salutations** *npl* GREETINGS greetings or regards (*formal*) ○ *Salutations from us all!* —**salutational** *adj* —**salutatory** /sə lóotətəri/ *adj, n*

salutatorian /sə lóotə táwri ən/ *n* in the United States, a student in a graduating class who is second highest in academic ranking and is usually required to give a welcoming speech or salutatory at the graduation ceremony

salute /sə lóot/ *v* (**-lutes, -luting, -luted**) 1 *vti* GIVE FORMAL SIGN OF RESPECT to formally signal respect to another member of the armed forces or to a flag, usually by raising the right hand to the forehead or by presenting arms 2 *vt* GREET to greet, welcome, or acknowledge somebody, either with a gesture or in words 3 *vt* FORMALLY PRAISE OR HONOUR to praise or honour somebody for something, especially in a formal ceremony ○ *We salute you for your contribution.* ■ *n* 1 GESTURE OF RESPECT a gesture used by members of the armed forces and some other organized groups as a formal sign of respect 2 FIRING GUNS AS MILITARY HONOUR a military display of honour for a dignitary or on a special occasion, e.g. the firing of guns into the air at the funeral of an officer ○ *a 21-gun salute* 3 ACT OF SALUTING an act or an occasion of saluting [14C. < Latin *salutare* < *salut-*, stem of *salus* 'health'.] —**saluter** *n*

Salvador /sálvədawr/ capital of Bahia State, E Brazil. Population: 2,209,465 (1996).

Salvador, El ➧ **El Salvador**

salvage /sálvij/ *vt* (**-vages, -vaging, -vaged**) 1 SAVE SOMETHING FROM DESTRUCTION to save a ship, cargo, crew, or other property or goods from destruction or loss (*often passive*) ○ *They salvaged what they could from the wreckage.* 2 SAVE SOMETHING FOR FURTHER USE to save used, damaged, or rejected goods for recycling or further use ○ *Maybe we can salvage some spare parts from your old car.* 3 RESCUE SOMETHING FROM BAD SITUATION to save something of worth or merit from a situation or event that is otherwise a failure ■ *n* 1 RESCUE OF PROPERTY FROM DESTRUCTION the rescue of property or goods from destruction or loss, e.g. because of a flood or fire 2 RESCUE OF SHIP FROM SEA the rescue of a ship, its cargo, or crew from loss at sea 3 RESCUED GOODS something such as a ship or goods that have been saved from destruction or loss 4 SOMETHING REUSED something that would otherwise be destroyed or discarded but is recycled or put to further use 5 PAYMENT TO RESCUERS payment made to volunteers who help in the rescue of ships, property, or goods from destruction or loss 6 MONEY FROM SALE OF RESCUED GOODS money from the sale of property or goods that have been saved from destruction or loss [Mid-17C. Via French < late Latin *salvare* 'save', < Latin *salvus* 'safe'.] —**salvageability** /sálvijə bílləti/ *n* —**salvageable** *adj* —**salvager** *n*

salvation /sal váysh'n/ *n* 1 ACT OF SAVING FROM HARM the saving of somebody or something from harm, destruction, difficulty, or failure ○ *The business was clearly beyond salvation.* 2 MEANS OF SAVING somebody or something that protects or delivers somebody or something else from harm, destruction, difficulty, or failure ○ *Those long walks were my salvation.* 3 DELIVERANCE FROM SIN THROUGH JESUS CHRIST in the Christian religion, deliverance from sin or the consequences of sin through Jesus Christ's death on the cross 4 CHRISTIAN SCIENCE PHILOSOPHY OF LIFE in the Christian Science religion, belief in the supremacy of life, truth, and love, and in their destruction of such illusions as sin, illness, and death [13C. Via Old French *salvacion* < Latin *salvare* 'save' (see SALVAGE).] —**salvational** *adj*

Salvation Army *n* a worldwide evangelical Christian organization that provides aid to those in need. It was founded by William Booth in London in 1865.

salvationist /sal váysh'nist/ *n* a Christian who preaches the doctrine that Jesus Christ died on the cross to save people from sin or the consequences of sin —**salvationism** *n*

Salvationist *n* a member of the Salvation Army

salve[1] /salv/; *old fashioned* /saav/ *n* 1 SOOTHING OINTMENT a soothing healing ointment 2 SOMETHING THAT SOOTHES OR CALMS anything that eases pain or anxiety ○ *Her forgiveness was a salve to my conscience.* ■ *vt* (**salves, salving, salved**) EASE PAIN OR WORRY to soothe or ease pain or anxiety ○ *salve your wounded pride* [Old English *salf* < Germanic]

salve[2] /salv/ (**salves, salving, salved**) *vt* to save something from destruction or loss [Early 18C. Back-formation < SALVAGE.] —**salvor** *n*

salver /sálvər/ *n* a tray, especially a silver one, used to serve food or drinks, or to present things such as letters or visiting cards [Mid-17C. Via French *save* 'tray for presenting things to the king' < late Latin *salvare* 'save' (see SALVAGE).]

salvia /sálvi ə/ (*plural* **-as** *or* **-a**) *n* an ornamental plant with opposite leaves. Flowers: red, whorled, with two-lipped corolla. *Salvia splendens*. [Mid-19C. Via modern Latin *Salvia* < Latin *salvia* 'sage', < *salvus* 'safe'.]

salvo[1] /sálvō/ (*plural* **-vos** *or* **-voes**) *n* 1 SIMULTANEOUS DISCHARGE OF WEAPONS the firing of several weapons simultaneously, especially at a formal military ceremony 2 HEAVY BURST OF FIRING OR BOMBING a concentrated burst of firing or bombing from several different sources during a battle 3 NUMBER OF BOMBS RELEASED AT ONCE a number of bombs or projectiles released simultaneously 4 OUTBURST a sudden burst of applause or cheering ○ *a salvo of applause* 5 VERBAL ATTACK a vigorous written or spoken attack ○ *a blistering salvo* [Late 16C. Via French *salve* or Italian *salva* 'greeting' < Latin *salvus* 'safe'.]

salvo[2] /sálvō/ (*plural* **-vos**) *n* something that is used to save a reputation or soothe somebody's conscience or wounded pride [Early 17C. < Latin, a form of *salvus* 'safe'.]

Salvo /sálvō/ (*plural* **-vos**) *n Aus* a member of the Salvation Army (*informal*) [Late 19C. Shortening.]

sal volatile /sál və láttəli/ *n* 1 = **ammonium carbonate** 2 a solution of ammonium carbonate in alcohol and ammonia in water, often mixed with aromatic oils. Use: smelling salts. [Mid-17C. < modern Latin, 'volatile salt'.]

Salween /sálween/ river in Southeast Asia, flowing through SW China and Myanmar into the Gulf of Martaban. Length: 2,900 km/1,800 mi.

Salzburg /sáltsburg, zaáltsboorg/ capital of Salzburg Province, W Austria. Population: 143,978 (1991).

Salzgitter /zaálts gitər/ city in north-central Germany. Population: 117,700 (1994).

SAM /sam, éss ay ém/ *abbr* surface-to-air missile

Sam. *abbr* Samuel

samara /sə maárə, sámmərə/ *n* PLANT SCI = **key**[1] *n.* 25 [Late 16C. < Latin, 'elm seed'.]

Samaria /sə máiri ə/ city and state in ancient Palestine —**Samarian** *n, adj*

Samaritan /sə márritən/ *n* 1 SOMEBODY FROM SAMARIA somebody who came from ancient Samaria 2 = **Good Samaritan** 3 WORKER FOR SAMARITANS ORGANIZATION a volunteer who works for the Samaritans organization ■ **Samaritans** *npl* ORGANIZATION HELPING PEOPLE IN CRISIS a charitable organization that runs a telephone helpline for people in crisis [Pre-12C. < late Latin *Samaritanus* < Greek *Samareia* 'Samaria'.] —**Samaritanism** *n*

samarium /sə máiri əm/ *n* (*symbol* **Sm**) a silvery-grey metallic element. Source: monazite, bastnaesite. Use: strong magnets, carbon-arc lighting, laser materials, neutron absorber. [Late 19C. < SAMARSKITE + -IUM.]

Samarkand /sámmaar kánd, sámmər kand/, **Samarqand** city in S Uzbekistan. Population: 368,000 (1994).

samarskite /sə maár skīt/ *n* a black mineral containing uranium and rare-earth elements. Source: pegmatite. [Mid-19C. After V. E. *Samarskii*-Vykhovets (1803–70), Russian mining engineer.]

Sama-Veda /saámə váydə/ *n* one of the four collections of chants (**Vedas**) used during Hindu sacrifices, containing songs based on the Rig-Veda with instructions on their recitation [Late 18C. < Sanskrit < *sāman* 'chant' + *vedaḥ* 'knowledge'.]

samba *n* 1 a lively Brazilian ballroom dance with strong African influences 2 the music for a samba [Late 19C. < Portuguese, < ?]

sambal /sám bal/ *n* a spicy condiment or relish of Southeast Asia made of chilli, spices, tomato, and vegetables [Early 19C. < Malay.]

sambar /sámbər/ (*plural* **-bars** *or* **-bar**) *n* a large deer that has a reddish-brown coat and three-pronged antlers. Native to: SE Asia. *Cervus unicolor*. [Late 17C. Via Hindi *sāmbar* < Sanskrit *śambaraḥ*.]

sambo[1] /sámbō/ *n* a highly offensive term for a Black person (*dated taboo insult*)

sambo[2] /sámbō/, **sambo wrestling** *n* a form of wrestling based on judo that originated in the former Soviet Union and is now practised internationally [Mid-20C. Acronym < Russian *samozashchita bez oruzhiya* 'unarmed self-defence'.] —**sambo wrestler** *n*

sambo wrestling *n* WRESTLING = **sambo**[2]

Sam Browne belt /sám brówn-/, **Sam Browne** *n* a wide belt supported by a diagonal strap that passes from the left-hand side over the right shoulder, worn as part of military or police uniforms [After Sir *Samuel Browne* (1824–1901), British military commander]

sambuca /sam bóokə/ *n* an Italian liqueur made from elderberries and flavoured with liquorice or aniseed [Late 20C. Via Italian < Latin *sambucus* 'elder tree'.]

same /saym/ CORE MEANING: a word indicating that one thing or person is involved rather than two or more different things or people ○ (adj) *I can't drive and talk at the same time.* ○ (adj) *He lives in the same street as I do.*

1 *adj, pron* PREVIOUSLY MENTIONED previously mentioned, or as previously described (*used as pronoun without 'the' in business contexts; see usage note below*) ○ (adj) *She left because she was bored, and I left two months later for the same reason.* ○ (pron) *Wool should always be washed carefully. The same applies to silk.* 2 *adj, pron, adv* IDENTICAL resembling something exactly ○ (adj) *They turned up at the party wearing the same dress.* ○ (adj) *All the houses looked exactly the same.* ○ (adj) *Look – their curtains are the same as ours!* ○ (pron) *All the experts say the same.* 3 *adj* UNCHANGED unchanged or unchanging ○ *After the accident, he just wasn't the same person.* ○ *The house looked the same as always.* ○ *I want things to stay the same.* [12C. < Old Norse *samr* < Indo-European, 'one'.] —**sameness** *n*

◇ **same here** indicates that somebody does, feels, or thinks the same as the previous speaker ○ *'I feel tired'. – 'Same here!'* ◇ **the same as** in the identical way that (*informal*) ○ *He wants to win, the same as I do.*

USAGE The use of ***same*** as a pronoun as in *We have received your order and have pleasure in completing same* is characteristic of commercial language and is not normally suitable for general use, except for special or humorous effect: *She poured out a large glass of water and drank same.*

samekh /saá mek, -mekh/ *n* the 15th letter of the Hebrew alphabet [Early 19C. < Hebrew *sāmekh* 'a support'.]

same-sex *adj* homosexual or lesbian ○ *involved in a same-sex relationship*

samey /sáymi/ *adj* boringly repetitive or unchanging (*informal*)

Sami /saámi/ (*plural* **-mi** *or* **-mis**) *n* **1** a member of an indigenous people of Lapland **2** the Finno-Ugric language of the Sami people. Native speakers: 80,000. [Late 18C. < Sami.]

Samian /sáymi ən/ *n* somebody who comes from the Greek island of Samos —**Samian** *adj*

Samian ware *n* reddish-brown or black earthenware pottery found in large quantities at Roman archaeological sites

samisen /sámmi sen/ *n* a Japanese three-stringed musical instrument that has a long fretless neck and is plucked with a plectrum [Early 17C. Via Japanese < Chinese *sānxián* 'three strings'.]

samite /sámm īt, sáy-/ *n* a heavy silk fabric, often interwoven with gold or silver threads. Use: formerly, clothing. [12C. Via Old French *samit* < medieval Latin *examitum* < Greek *hexamiton* 'six threads'.]

samiti /súmmiti/, **samithi** *n* a committee in the Indian subcontinent, especially one that is formed to organize political activity [Mid-20C. < Sanskrit *samitiḥ* 'assembly'.]

samizdat /sámmiz dát/ *n* **1 UNDERGROUND PUBLISHING IN FORMER USSR** in the former Soviet Union, the printing and distribution of secret or banned literature **2 BANNED LITERATURE** literature produced by the samizdat system **3 SECRET PRINTING PRESS** a secret printing press, especially in the former Soviet Union [Mid-20C. < Russian, < *sam-* 'self' + *izdatel'stvo* 'publishing house'.]

Samnite /sám nīt/ *n* a member of an ancient people who lived in central and S Italy in the 4th and 3rd centuries BC ■ *adj* relating to the Samnite people, or their culture or empire ○ *the Samnite Wars* [14th C. < Latin *Samnites* 'the Samnites'.]

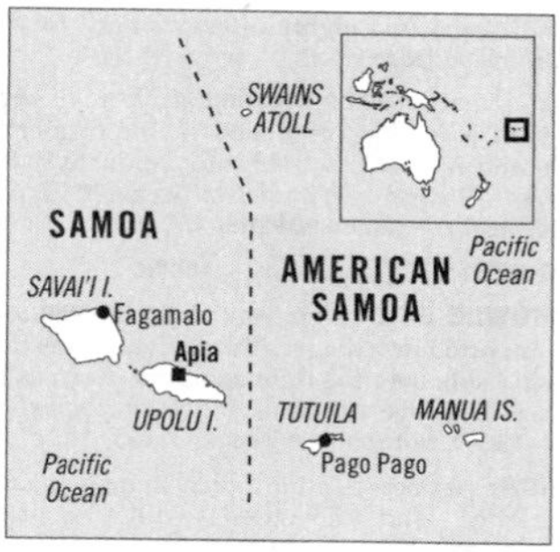

Samoa

Samoa /sə mṓ ə/ island country in the S Pacific Ocean, northeast of Fiji. Capital: Apia. Population: 167,400 (1996). Area: 2,831 sq. km/1,093 sq. mi. —**Samoan** *n, adj*

Samos /sámmoss/ island of E Greece, in the Aegean Sea. Population: 41,965 (1991). Area: 505 sq. km/195 sq. mi.

samosa /sə móssə, -mṓzə/ (*plural* **-sas** *or* **-sa**) *n* a savoury Indian snack consisting of a thin pastry case filled with spiced vegetables or meat and then deep-fried [Mid-20C. < Urdu.]

Samothrace /sámmə thrayss/ island of NE Greece, in the Aegean Sea. Population: 2,871 (1981). Area: 178 sq. km/69 sq. mi.

samovar /sámmə vaar/ *n* a large and often ornate Russian tea urn [Mid-19C. < Russian, < *samo-* 'self' + *varit'* 'boil'.]

Samoyed /sámmə yed/ *n* **1** (*plural* **-yeds** *or* **-yed**) **MEMBER OF SIBERIAN PEOPLE** a member of a people living in NE European Russia and W Siberia **2 SAMOYED LANGUAGE** the group of Uralic languages spoken by the Samoyed people, related to Finno-Ugric. Native speakers: 35,000. **3 SIBERIAN DOG** a dog belonging to a Siberian breed that has a thick creamy-white coat, distinctive ruff, and tightly-curled tail [Late 16C. < Russian.] —**Samoyed** *adj*

samp /samp/ *n S Africa* coarsely crushed maize, frequently cooked with dried beans as a staple food by black South Africans [Mid-17C. < Algonquian *nasàump*.]

sampan /sám pan/ *n* a small flat-bottomed boat (**skiff**) propelled by two oars or a single rear-mounted oar (**scull**) [Early 17C. < Chinese *sānbǎn* 'three-board (boat)'.]

samphire /sám fīr/ (*plural* **-phires** *or* **-phire**) *n* **1** a coastal plant with fleshy leaves that are used in pickles. Flowers: small, white. Native to: Europe. *Crithmum maritimum.* **2** = **glasswort** [Mid-16C. Contraction of French *herbe de Saint Pierre*.]

sample /saámp'l/ *n* **1 EXAMPLE OF SOMETHING** a small amount of something, used as an example of more general character, features, or quality ○ *a free sample of the new shampoo* **2 SPECIMEN FOR ANALYSIS** a small part or quantity of something, e.g. blood or soil, for scientific or medical examination or analysis ○ *took a blood sample* **3 PIECE OF RECORDED SOUND** a piece of recorded sound or a musical phrase taken from an existing recording, especially in digital form, used as part of a new recording ○ *a CD of drum samples* **4 GROUP SELECTED FOR TESTING** a representative selection of a population that is examined to gain statistical information about the whole ■ *vti* (**-ples, -pling, -pled**) **1 GET A SAMPLE OF SOMETHING** to take a sample of something, especially to determine its character, features, or quality ○ *sample the river water* **2 TAKE SAMPLE OF SOMETHING FOR RECORDING** to take a sample of recorded music, especially in order to use it in another recording ○ *sampled whatever albums happened to be lying around* **3 CONVERT SOUND INTO DIGITAL INFORMATION** to convert sound into digital information in order to store or manipulate it electronically [13C. Shortening of Norman French *assample* 'example'.]

⚡**sampler** /saámplər/ *n* **1 SOMEBODY WHO ANALYSES SAMPLES** a person who samples small quantities of something, especially to determine quality **2 DEVICE FOR TAKING SAMPLES** a machine or device used to take and analyse samples **3 REPRESENTATIVE SELECTION** a selection that is intended to represent what is available in a particular range **4 EMBROIDERED CLOTH** a piece of embroidered cloth containing rows of different stitches, either as a practice piece or, originally, as a demonstration of the embroiderer's skill **5 ELECTRONIC EQUIPMENT FOR SAMPLING MUSICAL PHRASES** an electronic device that can record sounds or take short musical phrases from an existing recording, and allow them to be manipulated digitally before being used to make a new recording **6 MACHINE CONVERTING SOUND TO DIGITAL INFORMATION** an electronic device that converts sound to digital information for electronic storage or manipulation

sample space *n* the set of all possible outcomes of a statistical experiment, represented by points

sampling /saámpling/ *n* **1 PROCESS OF SELECTING SAMPLE GROUP** the process of selecting a group of people or products to be used as a representative or random sample **2 SOMETHING USED AS A SAMPLE** a small part, number, or quantity of something that has been taken or selected as a sample **3 REUSE OF RECORDED MUSICAL PHRASES** the process of taking a short musical phrase from one recording and using it in another recording, often in repeated sequences and sometimes in an adapted or edited form ○ *recent advances in sampling technology*

sampling frame *n* a list of the people or items from which a statistical sample is taken

Sampras /sámprəss/, **Pete** (*b.* 1971) US tennis player. Known as **Pistol Pete**

samsara /səm saárə/ *n* **1** in Hinduism, the endless cycle of birth, life, death, and rebirth **2** in Buddhism, somebody's rebirth [Late 19C. < Sanskrit *saṃsāraḥ* < *sam* 'together' + *sarati* 'it flows'.]

samshu /sám shoo/ *n* a Chinese alcoholic drink made from fermented rice [Late 17C. < Pidgin English.]

Samson /sámss'n/ *n* **1** in the Bible, an Israelite judge and warrior. He used his enormous strength to fight the Philistines, to whom he was ultimately betrayed by his mistress, Delilah (Judges 13–16). **2** any very strong man —**Samsonian** /sam sṓni ən/ *adj*

Samuel *n* in the Bible, the leader of the Israelites in the 11th century BC. He was the first prophet after Moses.

samurai /sámmōō rī, sámmyōō-/ (*plural* **-rai** *or* **-rais**) *n* **1** the powerful class of Japanese warriors that dominated the military aristocracy from the 11th to the 19th centuries **2** an aristocratic Japanese warrior of a class that dominated the military aristocracy from the 11th to the 19th centuries [Early 18C. < Japanese.]

san /san/, **-san** *n* used in Japanese after somebody's first name, last name, or title, as a polite form of address [Late 19C. < Japanese, contraction of *sama*.]

San[1] /san/ *n* used as a title, usually in place names, before the name of a man who has been made a saint. ◊ **Santo, Santa**[1] [Via Spanish and Italian, 'Saint' < Latin *sanctus* 'sacred' (see SAINT)]

San[2] /saan/ (*plural* **San** *or* **Sans**) *n* **1** a member of a people living in southern Africa **2** the group of Khoisan languages spoken by the San people [Late 19C. < Nama *san*.]

San Andreas Fault /sán an dráyəss-/ *n* a geological fault zone between two tectonic plates that runs from San Francisco south to San Diego in California. Length: 970 km/600 mi. [Because it runs along the San Andreas valley]

San Antonio /-an tṓni ō/ city in south-central Texas. Population: 1,114,130 (1998 estimate).

sanative /sánnətiv/ *adj* able to restore health (*archaic formal*) [15C. Via Old French *sanatif* < late Latin *sanativus* < Latin *sanare* 'heal'.]

sanatorium /sánnə táwri əm/ (*plural* **-ums** *or* **-a** /-táwri ə/) *n* **1 MEDICAL FACILITY FOR LONG-TERM ILLNESS** a medical facility where people affected by long-term illnesses can receive treatment and those recovering from severe illnesses can recuperate **2 HEALTH RESORT** a resort for maintaining or improving health (*dated*) **3 MEDICAL ROOM IN BOARDING SCHOOL** a room or unit in a boarding school where pupils who are ill can receive treatment and recuperate [Mid-19C. Via modern Latin < Latin *sanat-*, past participle of *sanare* 'cure', < *sanus* 'healthy'.]

San Bernardino /sán bərnər deénō/ city in S California. Population: 181,718 (1994).

San Bernardino Mountains mountain range in S California. Highest peak: San Gorgonio Mountain 3,506 m/11,485 ft.

San Cristobal /san krístə baal/ one of the Galapagos Islands, off the coast of Ecuador. Area: 505 sq. km/195 sq. mi.

San Cristóbal /sang kri stṓ bal/ capital of Táchira State, W Venezuela. Population: 238,670 (1992).

sancta plural of **sanctum**

sancta sanctorum plural of **sanctum sanctorum**

sanctify /sángkti fī/ (**-fies, -fying, -fied**) *vt* **1 BLESS** to make something holy **2 FREE SOMEBODY FROM SIN** to free somebody from sin, e.g. by a ritual act of purification **3 BLESS SOMETHING THROUGH RELIGIOUS VOW** to give a religious blessing to something, e.g. a marriage, usually through an oath or vow **4 OFFICIALLY APPROVE** to give social, moral, or official approval to something **5 MAKE SOMETHING ROUTE TO HOLINESS** to make something a means of achieving holiness or a source of grace [14C. < Old French *saintifier* < Latin *sanctus* 'sacred' (see SAINT).] —**sanctifiable** *adj* —**sanctification** /sángktifi káysh'n/ *n* —**sanctifier** *n*

sanctimonious /sángkti mṓni əss/ *adj* making an exaggerated show of holiness or moral superiority (*disapproving*) [Early 17C. < Latin *sanctimonia* 'sanctity' < *sanctus* 'sacred' (see SAINT).] —**sanctimoniously** *adv* —**sanctimoniousness** *n* —**sanctimony** /sángktiməni/ *n*

sanction /sángksh'n/ *n* **1 AUTHORIZATION** official permission or approval for a course of action ○ *unable to proceed without the sanction of the board* **2 SUPPORT** something that serves as approval or encouragement, e.g. social acceptance or custom **3 LAW** a law or rule that leads to a penalty being imposed when it is disobeyed **4 PENALTY IMPOSED FOR BREAKING RULE** a punishment imposed as a result of breaking a law or rule **5 PUNITIVE MEASURE TO PRESSURE A COUNTRY** a measure taken by one or more nations to apply pressure on another nation to conform to international law or opinion (*often plural*) ○ *to impose trade sanctions* **6 PRINCIPLE DETERMINING BEHAVIOUR** an ethical principle or consideration that determines or influences somebody's conduct ■ *vt* **1 AUTHORIZE** to grant official approval or permission for something ○ *The town council refused to sanction the proposed design of the new building.* **2 APPROVE OF** to allow something to be tolerated or accepted ○ *The school's inaction further sanctions this behaviour.* [15C. Via Old French < Latin *sanctus* 'sacred' (see SAINT).] —**sanctionable** *adj* —**sanctioner** *n* —**sanctionless** *adj*

sanctity /sángktəti/ (*plural* **-ties**) *n* **1** the condition of being considered sacred or holy, and therefore entitled to respect and reverence **2** something considered holy or sacred (*formal*) [14C. Via Old French *saintcite* < Latin *sanctitas* < *sanctus* 'sacred' (see SAINT).]

sanctuary /sángkchoo ari/ (*plural* **-ies**) *n* **1 REFUGE** a safe place, especially for people being persecuted **2 SAFETY PROVIDED BY REFUGE** the safety and protection afforded by a place of refuge ○ *immigrants seeking sanctuary in the United States* **3 PLACE WHERE WILDLIFE IS PROTECTED** a place or area of land where wildlife is protected from predators and from being destroyed or hunted by human beings ○ *a bird sanctuary* **4 CHURCH PROTECTING FUGITIVES** in medieval times, a holy place, usually a church, that provided immunity from the law **5 CHURCH PROTECTION FOR FUGITIVES** the immunity from arrest, violence, or execution provided to fugitives under medieval church law **6 HOLY PLACE** a holy place such as a church, mosque, or temple **7 MOST SACRED PART OF HOLY BUILDING** the most sacred part of a consecrated building, e.g. the area around the altar in a Christian church **8 ISRAELITE HOLY OF HOLIES** the holy of holies in the Israelite temple at Jerusalem [14C. Via Anglo-Norman *sanctuarie* < Latin *sanctus* 'sacred' (see SAINT).]

sanctum /sángktəm/ (*plural* **-tums** *or* **-ta** /-tə/) *n* **1** a sacred place inside a church, temple, or mosque **2** a quiet private place where somebody is free from interference or interruption [Late 16C. Via late Latin < Latin *sanctus* 'sacred' (see SAINT).]

sanctum sanctorum /sángktəm saángk táwrəm/ (*plural* **sancta sanctorum** /sángktə-/ *or* **sanctum sanctorums**) *n* **1** JUDAISM = **holy of holies** *n.* 1 **2** a very private quiet place in which to be alone or relax [14C. < late Latin, 'holy of holies'.]

Sanctus /sángktəss, -tōoss/ *n* in some Christian churches, a musical setting that forms part of the Mass and praises the power and holiness of God [14C. Via late Latin < Latin *sanctus* 'sacred' (see SAINT), the first word of the hymn.]

Sanctus bell *n* in the Roman Catholic Church, a bell rung at the beginning of the Sanctus and at other times during Mass, e.g. at the elevation of the consecrated elements

sand /sand/ *n* **1 MATERIAL MADE OF TINY GRAINS** a substance consisting of fine loose grains of rock or minerals, found on beaches, in the desert, and in soil, sometimes used as a building material **2 AREA OF SAND** an area covered with or made up of sand, e.g. a beach or a desert ○ *playing on the sand and swimming in the sea* **3 BROWNISH YELLOW** a brownish-yellow colour like sand **4 PARTICLES IN HOURGLASS** the tiny grains in an hourglass ■ **sands** *npl* **TIME REMAINING** remaining or allotted portion of time (*literary*) ○ *the sands of time* ■ *v* **1** *vt* **SMOOTH SOMETHING USING SANDPAPER** to rub a surface with sandpaper or sand to make it smoother **2** *vt* **SPRINKLE SOMETHING WITH SAND** to cover or sprinkle something such as an icy road with sand **3** *vt* **ADD SAND TO** to add sand to something, e.g. to a mixture of materials when making mortar **4** *vti* **FILL WITH SAND** to become filled with sand, or fill something with sand [Old English, < Germanic] —**sand** *adj* —**sandlike** *adj* ◇ **kick sand in somebody's face** to show contempt for or dominance over somebody less strong or powerful, especially somebody already in a weak position

Sand /saan, saaN/, **George** (1804–76) French writer. Pseudonym of **Amandine Aurore Lucille, Baronne Dudevant**

sandal /sánd'l/ *n* **1** a light open shoe that is held on by straps across the instep or around the heel or ankle, usually worn during warm weather **2** a strap for going around the ankle or across the instep to keep a shoe on a foot [14C. < Latin *sandalium* < Greek *sandalon*.] —**sandalled** *adj*

sandalwood /sánd'l wŏŏd/ *n* **1 TROPICAL EVERGREEN TREE** a tropical evergreen tree that produces wood and oil. Native to: S Asia, Australia. Genus: *Santalum*. **2 WOOD OF SANDALWOOD TREE** the fragrant wood of the sandalwood tree. Use: furniture-making, incense. **3 AROMATIC OIL OF SANDALWOOD TREE** the aromatic oil extracted from the wood of the sandalwood tree. Use: perfumes, incense, aromatherapy oil. **4 TREE RESEMBLING SANDALWOOD TREE** any tree that resembles the sandalwood and is harvested for wood. Native to: South Asia, Australia. Genera: *Adenanthera* and *Myroporum* and *Pterocarpus*.

sandarac /sándə rak/, **sandarach** *n* **1 EVERGREEN TREE OF AFRICA AND SPAIN** a coniferous tree with flat branches and leaves with overlapping scales, that produces resin and wood. Native to: NW Africa, Spain. *Tetraclinis articulata*. **2 RESIN FROM SANDARAC TREE** a brittle yellowish translucent resin exuded by the sandarac. Use: varnishes, incense. **3 WOOD OF SANDARAC TREE** the hard dark aromatic wood of the sandarac. Use: building material. [Mid-17C. Via Latin *sandaraca* < Greek *sandarakē*.]

Sandawe /san daá way/ (*plural* **-we** *or* **-wes**) *n* **1** a member of a people who live in Tanzania **2** the Khoisan language of the Sandawe people. Native speakers: 70,000. [Early 20C. < Sandawe.] —**Sandawe** *adj*

sandbag /sánd bag/ *n* **1 SACK OF SAND** a sealed bag full of sand, used in building defences against gunfire or flooding, or as ballast in hot air balloons **2 BAG OF SAND USED AS WEAPON** a small bag filled with sand and used as a weapon in the same way as a cosh ■ *v* (**-bags, -bagging, -bagged**) **1** *vt* **PROTECT SOMETHING WITH SANDBAGS** to put sandbags in or around something as protection **2** *vt* **KNOCK SOMEBODY OR SOMETHING DOWN** to attack or hit somebody or something with a sandbag (*informal*) **3** *vti* **DELAY NEGOTIATIONS** to delay negotiations or a business deal in the hope of receiving a more favourable offer from somebody else (*slang*) —**sandbagger** *n*

sandbank /sánd bangk/ *n* a mound or bank of sand, especially one that is submerged at most states of the tide

sandbar /sánd baar/ *n* a long ridge of sand formed in a body of water by currents or tides

sandblast /sánd blaast/ *n* **1 JET OF SAND FIRED UNDER PRESSURE** a jet of pressurized air or steam mixed with sand or grit that is fired through a fine nozzle, used to clean, polish, or mark glass, metal, or stone surfaces **2 MACHINE FOR FIRING SANDBLAST** a machine that is used to fire a sandblast ■ *vti* **POLISH WITH SAND** to clean, polish, or mark glass, metal, or a stone surface with a sandblast —**sandblaster** *n*

sand-blind *adj* having reduced ability to see (*archaic or literary*) [15C. Alteration of Old English *samblind* < *sam-* 'half' + *blind* 'blind'.]

sandbox /sánd boks/ *n* **1** a container on a railway locomotive that releases sand onto the track to increase traction **2** *US* = **sandpit** *n.* 1

sandbox tree *n* a spiny tree with woody seed capsules that explode when ripe. Native to: tropical America. *Hura crepitans*. [Because the seed capsules formerly served as boxes for sand]

sandboy /sánd boy/ [Early 19C. Perhaps originally 'a boy selling sand'.] ◇ **(as) happy** *or* **jolly as a sandboy** extremely happy or cheerful

sand-cast *vt* to make a casting by pouring molten metal into a sand mould

sand casting *n* a casting made by pouring molten metal into a sand mould

sandcastle /sánd kaass'l/ *n* a small model of a castle that is made out of damp sand, usually by children on a beach

sand crack *n* a crack in a horse's hoof that starts at the top (**coronet**) and extends vertically towards the sole

sand dab *n* a small flatfish caught for food. Native to: North American Pacific coast. Genus: *Citharichthys*.

sand dollar *n* a flat circular animal (**echinoderm**) related to the starfish and sea urchin, with a white disc-shaped shell with an imprint that resembles a flower. Native to: shallow sandy North American coastal waters. Genus: *Citharichthys*.

sand eel *n* a small slender marine fish resembling an eel. Genus: *Ammodytes*.

sander /sándər/ *n* **1** an electric power tool that is used to smooth wooden or metal surfaces **2** a person who sands something or operates a sander

sanderling /sándərling/ (*plural* **-lings** *or* **-ling**) *n* a small bird with grey and white plumage. Native to: coastal regions worldwide. *Calidris alba*. [Early 17C]

Sanderson /saándərss'n/, **Tessa** (*b.* 1956) British athlete. Born **Teresa Ione Sanderson**

sand flea *n* **1** INSECTS = **chigoe** **2** MARINE BIOL = **sand hopper**

sandfly /sánd flī/ *n* a hairy fly that resembles a moth and lives in tropical regions. Bloodsucking females transmit several tropical diseases. Genus: *Phlebotomus*.

sandfly fever *n* a mild viral illness transmitted by the bite of a female sandfly. It causes fever, headaches, eye pain, and general discomfort.

sandglass /sánd glaass/ *n* TIME = **hourglass**

sandgrouse /sánd growss/ (*plural* **-grouses** *or* **-grouse**) *n* a bird related to the pigeon with long pointed tail and wings, and a short bill and feet. Native to: arid and semiarid Europe and Asia. Genus: *Pterocles*.

S & H *abbr* shipping and handling

sandhi /sándi/ *n* the modification of the sound or form of a word under the influence of a preceding or following sound [Early 19C. < Sanskrit *saṃdhiḥ* 'combination'.]

sandhill crane *n* a crane with grey drooping plumage and a bald red crown. Native to: North America, NE Siberia. *Grus canadensis*. [Because it is commonly found among sand dunes]

sandhog /sánd hog/ *n US, Can* a worker inside a caisson in underwater building projects such as tunnels (*slang*)

sand hopper *n* a tiny jumping crustacean that lives on sandy tidal beaches. Genus: *Orchestia*. US term **sand flea**

San Diego /-di áygō/ city in SW California, on San Diego Bay. Population: 1,220,666 (1998 estimate).

Sandinista /sándi neéstə/ *n* a member of a socialist movement in Nicaragua that successfully overthrew the government of President Anastasio Somoza in 1979 and fought a US-backed insurgent force in the 1980s [Early 20C. Spanish, after Augusto César *Sandino* (1893–1934), Nicaraguan revolutionary leader.]

S & L *abbr* savings and loan association

sand leek *n* a plant such as rocambole that has a bulb shaped like that of garlic. Flowers: reddish-pink. Native to: Europe, Asia. *Alium scorodoprasum*.

sand lizard *n* a small greyish-brown lizard that is found among sand dunes. Native to: Europe. *Lacerta agilis*.

sandlot /sánd lot/ *n US* a vacant lot or area of land used by children for playing games, especially baseball (*informal*) —**sandlotter** *n*

sandman /sánd man/ *n* a character from folklore and fairy tales, personifying drowsiness, who makes children go to sleep by sprinkling sand in their eyes

sand martin *n* a small songbird related to the swallow that nests in burrows in sand or river banks and is brown with a white underbelly. Native to: Europe. *Riparia riparia*.

sand painting *n* **1** a ceremonial practice of the Navajo and Pueblo peoples, in which different colours of sand are distributed over a flat surface to create symbolic pictures and designs **2** a picture or design made by sand painting

sandpaper /sánd paypər/ *n* strong paper coated on one side with sand or another abrasive, used for smoothing surfaces ■ *vt* to rub a surface, e.g. a piece of wood or a wall, with sandpaper —**sandpapery** *adj*

sandpiper /sánd pīpər/ (*plural* **-pers** *or* **-per**) *n* a wading shore bird with a long slender sensitive bill that it uses to catch insects, worms, and soft molluscs in sand and mud. Family: Scolopacidae. [Late 17C. *Piper* from its piping voice.]

sandpit /sánd pit/ *n* **1** an area of sand for children to play in, often contained in a box or frame. US term **sandbox** *n.* 2 **2** a large deep pit from which sand is excavated

sand shark *n* a shark of mainly shallow waters. Native to: central and S Atlantic and W Pacific coasts. Genus: *Carcharias*.

sandshoe /sánd shoo/ *n* a light low-cut canvas shoe with a rubber sole

sandsoap /sánd sōp/ *n* a gritty abrasive soap used for heavy cleaning

sandstone /sánd stōn/ *n* a sedimentary rock made up of particles of sand bound together with a mineral cement. Use: building material.

sandstorm /sánd stawrm/ *n* a strong windstorm, especially in the desert, that carries clouds of sand or dust, reducing visibility

sand table *n* a table covered with a layer of sand moulded to imitate the relief of a battleground terrain, used to plan military tactics

sand trap *n US* GOLF = **bunker** *n.* 4

sand viper *n* **1** ZOOL = **horned viper** **2** a viper with a yellowish-brown zigzag pattern along its back. Native to: S Europe. *Vipera ammodytes*.

sand wedge *n* a golf club with a face angle of more than 50° that is used for chipping the ball out of a bunker

sandwich /sánwij, -wich/ *n* **1 BREAD SLICES WITH FILLING IN BETWEEN** a snack or light meal usually made of two slices of bread or a split roll with a filling, or a single slice of bread with a topping. ◊ **club sandwich 2** FOOD = **sand-wich cake 3** SOMETHING LIKE A SANDWICH something resembling a sandwich, especially something in which various things are squashed together or arranged in layers ■ *vt* PLACE SOMEBODY OR SOMETHING BETWEEN THINGS to fit something or somebody tightly between two other things or people in space or time ○ *I'll see if I can sandwich you in on Tuesday.* [Mid-18C. After John Montague, fourth Earl of *Sandwich* (1718–92), said to have taken to eating meat between two slices of bread to avoid leaving the gaming-tables for meals.]

Sandwich /sán wich/ town in SE England, one of the Cinque Ports. Population: 4,164 (1991).

sandwich board *n* **1** a pair of boards, usually displaying advertisements or notices, joined by straps and hung from the shoulders with one displayed in front and one behind **2** either of the two boards that make up a sandwich board [Because the boards sandwich the person wearing them]

sandwich cake *n* a cake with two or more layers separated by a filling such as jam or cream

sandwich coin *n* a three-layered coin that has a middle layer made of a different metal from the outside layers

sandwich course *n* an educational course in which work experience or practical training alternates with periods of study

sandwich man *n* a man who carries a sandwich board

sandwich tern *n* a tern that nests in colonies on beaches and cliffs and has white plumage, a forked tail, and a black yellow-tipped bill. Native to: Europe. *Sterna sandvicensis*. [After SANDWICH, England]

~~sandwitch~~ incorrect spelling of **sandwich**

sandworm /sánd wurm/ *n* a segmented worm living in coastal sand or mud, often used as fishing bait. Genera: *Nereis* and *Anicola.*

sandwort /sánd wurt/ (*plural* **-worts** *or* **-wort**) *n* a plant that grows in thick tufts close to the ground on sandy soil. Flowers: single, white or pink. Genus: *Arenaria.*

sandy /sándi/ (**-ier, -iest**) *adj* **1** FULL OF SAND made up of, covered in, or full of sand **2** LIKE SAND having a grainy texture or consistency similar to that of sand **3** OF COLOUR OF SAND of a reddish- or brownish-yellow colour — **sandiness** *n*

sand yacht *n* a small light boat equipped with a sail and wheels that allow it to be propelled by the wind over flat land, especially beaches

sane /sayn/ (**saner, sanest**) *adj* **1** mentally healthy and able to make rational decisions **2** based on sensible, reasonable, or rational thinking ○ *a sane and practical solution to the problem* [Early 17C. < Latin *sanus* 'healthy'.] —**sanely** *adv* —**saneness** *n*

San Fernando Valley /sán fər nándō-/ residential and industrial region in S California. Population: 1,300,000 (1998).

San Francisco /-fran sískō/ city in W California, on San Francisco Bay. Population: 745,774 (1998 estimate). —**San Franciscan** *n, adj*

San Francisco Bay inlet of the Pacific Ocean in W California. Length: 80 km/50 mi.

sang past tense of **sing**

sangar /sángər/ *n* a small low temporary defensive work (**breastwork**), usually built of stone around an existing hollow in the ground [Mid-19C. < Persian and Pashto < ?]

sangaree /sáng gə reé/ *n* a chilled drink of wine mixed with fruit juice, nutmeg, and sometimes other spirits [Mid-18C. Alteration of Spanish *sangría* (see SANGRIA).]

Sanger /sángər/, **Frederick** (*b.* 1918) British biochemist

Sanger, Margaret (1883–1966) US social reformer. Born **Margaret Louise Higgins**

sang-froid /song frwaá, sang-/ *n* self-possession or calmness, especially in a dangerous or stressful situation [Mid-18C. < French, 'cold blood'.]

sangoma /sang gōma/ *n* S Africa in South Africa, a traditional healer (**shaman**) or herbalist [Late 19C. < Nguni.]

Sangrail /sang gráyl/, **Sangraal, Sangreal** /san grí al/ *n* CHR = **Grail** *n*. [15C. < Old French *saint graal* 'Holy Grail'.]

Sangre de Cristo Mountains /sáng gri də krístō-/ range of the Rocky Mountains in SE Colorado and N New Mexico. Highest peak: Blanca Peak 4,372 m/14,345 ft.

sangria /sang greè ə, sáng gri ə/ *n* a chilled Spanish drink of red wine, fruit juice, lemonade or soda water, and brandy or another spirit, usually served in a jug with pieces of fruit [Mid-20C. < Spanish *sangría* 'a bleeding', ultimately < Latin *sanguis* 'blood'.]

sanguinaria /sáng gwi náiri ə/ *n* the dried rhizome and roots of the bloodroot plant. Use: formerly, internally as medicine, now, antiplaque agent in toothpaste. [Early 19C. Via modern Latin *Sanguinaria* < Latin *sanguis* 'blood'.]

sanguinary /sáng gwinəri/ *adj* (*formal*) **1** INVOLVING BLOOD-SHED involving death or bloodshed **2** BLOODTHIRSTY bloodthirsty or eager to kill **3** BLOODIED consisting of or stained with blood —**sanguinarily** *adv* —**sanguinariness** *n*

sanguine /sáng gwin/ *adj* **1** CONFIDENT cheerfully optimistic **2** RUDDY flushed with a healthy rosy colour **3** BLOOD-RED of a blood-red colour **4** HAVING BLOOD AS DOMINANT HUMOUR in medieval physiology, having blood as the dominant humour and therefore characterized by a ruddy complexion and a courageous, optimistic, and romantic temperament ■ *n* RED CRAYON a red crayon that contains ferric oxide [14C. Via French < Latin *sanguis-*, stem of *sanguis* 'blood'.] —**sanguinely** *adv* —**sanguineness** *n* —**sanguinity** /sang gwínnəti/ *n*

sanguineous /sang gwínni əss/ *adj* **1** CONTAINING BLOOD relating to or containing blood, especially mixed with other fluids (*often in combination*) ○ *a sero-sanguineous discharge* **2** BLOOD-COLOURED of the colour of blood **3** BLOOD-THIRSTY involving or enjoying bloodshed (*literary*) [Early 16C. < Latin *sanguineus* < *sanguin-*, stem of *sanguis* 'blood'.] —**sanguineousness** *n*

Sanhedrin /sánnedrin/ *n* the supreme Jewish judicial, ecclesiastical, and administrative council in ancient Jerusalem before AD 70, having 71 members from the nobility and presided over by the high priest [Late 16C. Via Hebrew < Greek *sunedrion* 'council' < *sun* 'together' + *hedra* 'seat'.]

sanicle /sánnik'l/ *n* a widely distributed plant with oval fruits and hooked bristles. Flowers: small, variously coloured, in clusters. Use: formerly, astringent. Genus: *Sanicula*. [15C. Via Old French < medieval Latin *sanicula.*]

sanidine /sánnidin/ *n* a glassy high-temperature form of the mineral orthoclase. Source: lavas. [Early 19C. < Greek *sanid-*, stem of *sanis* 'board' < the shape of the mineral's crystals.]

sanitary /sánnitəri/ *adj* **1** relating to public health, especially general hygiene and the removal of human waste through the sewage system **2** clean and free from agents that cause disease or infection [Mid-19C. Via French *sanitaire* < Latin *sanus* 'healthy'.] —**sanitarian** /sánni táiri ən/ *adj, n* —**sanitarily** *adv* —**sanitariness** *n*

sanitary engineering *n* the branch of civil engineering concerned with the building, maintenance, and development of water and sewage systems and other public health services —**sanitary engineer** *n*

sanitary landfill *n* US ENVIRON = **landfill** (*dated*)

sanitary pad, sanitary napkin = **sanitary towel**

sanitary protection *n* sanitary towels and tampons, used to absorb the blood flow during menstruation

sanitary towel *n* a disposable cotton pad worn by women to absorb the blood flow during menstruation. US term **sanitary pad**

sanitation /sánni táysh'n/ *n* **1** the study and maintenance of public health and hygiene, especially the water supply and sewage systems ○ *sanitation laws* **2** con-

Margaret Sanger

ditions or procedures related to the collection and disposal of sewage and refuse [Mid-19C. < SANITARY.]

sanitize /sánni tīz/ (**-tizes, -tizing, -tized**), **sanitise** (**-tises, -tising, -tised**) *vt* **1** to clean something thoroughly by disinfecting or sterilizing it **2** to make something more likely to be acceptable by removing anything that might be considered offensive or controversial (*usually passive*) ○ *a sanitized version of the article* [Mid-19C. < SANITARY.] —**sanitization** /-tī záysh'n/ *n* —**sanitizer** /-tīzar/ *n*

~~sanitorium~~ incorrect spelling of **sanatorium**

sanity /sánnəti/ *n* **1** the condition of being mentally healthy and able to make rational decisions **2** common sense, reasonableness, and predictability ○ *to restore a little sanity to the situation* [Early 17C. Via Old French *sanite* < Latin *sanus* 'whole, sound'.]

San Jose /-hō sáy/ city in W California. Population: 861,284 (1998 estimate).

San José /-hō sáy/ capital of Costa Rica, in the centre of the country. Population: 324,011 (1996).

San Juan /-waán/ **1** river in S Colorado, NW New Mexico, and SE Utah. Length: 580 km/360 mi. **2** capital of Puerto Rico, on the NE coast of the island. Population: 433,705 (1996).

sank past tense of **sink**

USAGE See **sink**.

Sankhya /sángkya/ *n* one of six systems of orthodox Hindu philosophy, based on the perpetual interaction of spirit and matter [Late 18C. < Sanskrit *sāṁkhya-* 'relating to number'.]

San Marino

San Marino /-mə reénō/ republic in S Europe, an enclave in NE Italy. Capital: San Marino. Population: 24,521 (1996). Area: 61 sq. km/24 sq. mi. —**Sammarinese** /sa márri neéz/ *n, adj* —**San Marinese** /sán mari neéz/ *n, adj*

San Martín /sán maar teén/, **José Francisco de** (1778–1850) Argentinian statesman and soldier

San Miguel de Tucumán /-mi gél də too koo maàn/ capital of Tucumán Province, NW Argentina. Population: 626,143 (1990).

sannyasi /sun yaássi/, **sannyasin** /-yaàssin/ *n* in Hinduism, a Brahmin who has reached the fourth and final stage of life as a mendicant and will be absorbed into the Universal Soul instead of being reborn [Early 17C. < Sanskrit *saṁnyāsī* 'somebody who renounces'.]

S-A node *abbr* sinoatrial node

San Pedro Sula /-péddrō soò laa/ city in NW Honduras. Population: 353,800 (1993).

San Remo /-reémō/ town in NW Italy. Population: 59,600 (1990).

sans /sanz/ *prep* without (*archaic or literary or humorous*) ○ *looking forward to a well-earned break sans children* [13C. < Old French *sanz* < Latin *sine* 'without'.]

San Salvador /san sálvədawr/ **1** capital of El Salvador, in the central part of the country. Population: 422,520 (1992). **2** island of the central Bahamas. Population: 465 (1990). Area: 155 sq. km/60 sq. mi.

sans-culotte /sánz kyōó lót/ *n* **1** during the French Revolution, a revolutionary either from the poorer classes or with extreme republican sympathies **2** a revolutionary in any country who has extremist views (*formal*) [Late 18C. < French, 'without breeches'.] —**sans-culottic** *adj* —**sans-culottism** *n* —**sans-culottist** *n*

Library of Congress

San Sebastián /-sə básti ən/ city in N Spain. Population: 178,470 (1995).

sanserif n PRINTING = **sans serif**

sansevieria /sánssi veéri ə/ (plural **-as** or **-a**) n a common houseplant with thick variegated blade-shaped leaves. Use: bowstring hemp. Native to: Africa, Asia. Genus: *Sansevieria*. [Early 19C. After Raimondo de Sangro, Prince of *Sanseviero* (1710–70), Italian patron of horticulture.]

Sanskrit /sánskrit/ n the extinct Indo-European language of ancient India, which survives as the language of classical Indian literature and Hindu religious texts [Early 17C. < Sanskrit *saṃskṛta-* 'perfected'.] —**Sanskritic** /san skríttik/ n, adj —**Sanskritist** n

sans serif /sán sérrif/, **sanserif** n any style of typeface in which there are no fine lines (**serifs**) at the ends of the main strokes of the characters

Santa¹ /sántə/ n used as a title, usually in place names, before the name of a woman who has been made a saint. ◊ **San**¹, **Santo** [< Spanish and Italian, a form of *Santo* 'Saint']

Santa² /sántə/ n Santa Claus (*informal*) [Early 20C. Shortening.]

Santa Barbara Islands island group off S California, in the Pacific Ocean

Santa Claus /sántə klawz, -kláwz/ n LITERAT = **Father Christmas** [Late 18C. < Dutch dialect *Sante Klaas* 'St. Nicholas'.]

Santa Cruz /-króoz/ **1** river in S Argentina. Length: 400 km/250 mi. **2** city in central Bolivia. Population: 767,260 (1993 estimate). **3** city in W California. Population: 52,853 (1998 estimate).

Santa Cruz de Tenerife /sántə krooz də tenə reèf/ capital of Tenerife in the Canary Islands. Population: 211,930 (1998 estimate).

Santa Fe /-fáy/ **1** capital of Santa Fe Province, NE Argentina. Population: 353,063 (1991). **2** capital of New Mexico, in the north of the state. Population: 67,879 (1998 estimate).

Santa Gertrudis /-gər tròodiss/ (plural **Santa Gertrudises** or **Santa Gertrudis**) n a large red cow belonging to a breed developed in Texas from Brahman and shorthorn cattle and bred for beef [After a section of the King Ranch in Kingsville, Texas, where the breed was developed]

Santamaria /-mə reè ə/, **B. A.** (1915–98) Australian writer and political activist. Full name **Bartholomew Augustine Santamaria**

Santa Marta /-maártə/ city in N Colombia. Population: 309,372 (1995).

Santa Monica /-mónnikə/ city in SW California, on Santa Monica Bay. Population: 89,522 (1998 estimate).

Santander /sántən dáir/ port in N Spain. Population: 184,165 (1998 estimate).

Sant'Elia /san télyə/, **Antonio** (1888–1916) Italian architect

Santería /sántə reè ə/, **santería** n a religion that combines the West African Yoruba religion with Roman Catholicism [Mid-20C. Via Spanish *santería* 'holiness' < Latin *sanctus* 'sacred' (see SAINT).]

Santiago /sánti aàgò/ capital of Chile, in the centre of the country. Population: 4,295,593 (1992).

Santiago de Compostela /santi aàgò day kompo stáylə/ capital of Galicia, NW Spain, a major place of Christian pilgrimage. Population: 94,057 (1995).

Santiago de Cuba /-koòbə/ second-largest city in Cuba, in the SE of the country. Population: 440,084 (1993).

santim /sán teem/ n see table at **currency**

Santo /sántò/ (plural **-tos**) n used as a title, usually in place names, before the name of a man who has been made a saint. ◊ **San**¹, **Santa**¹ [Via Spanish and Italian < Latin *sanctus* (see SAINT)]

Santo Domingo /sántò də míng gò/ capital of the Dominican Republic, in the south of the country. Population: 2,100,000 (1993).

santolina /sántə leènə/ (plural **-nas** or **-na**) n an evergreen plant with distinctive silvery-grey velvety foliage. Native to: Mediterranean. *Santolina chamaecyparissus*. [Late 16C. < modern Latin, perhaps alteration of SANTONICA.]

santonica /san tónnikə/ (plural **-cas** or **-ca**) n **1** a wormwood plant with twin needle-shaped leaves and abundant flower heads. Native to: Europe, Asia. Genus: *Artemisia*. **2** the dried unopened flower heads of the santonica plant. Use: source of santonin. [Mid-17C. Via

modern Latin < Latin *santonicus* 'of the Santoni', a tribe of the Gauls.]

santonin /sántənin/ n $C_{15}H_{18}O_3$ a white crystalline compound. Source: extracted from santonica flower heads. Use: formerly, to eradicate parasitic worms. [Mid-19C. < SANTONICA.]

Santorini /sántò rí ni/ = **Thera**

Santos /sántooss/ city in SE Brazil. Population: 412,288 (1996).

Sanusi /se noòssi/ n a member of an Islamic Sufi religious group in Arabia and North Africa [Late 19C. After Sīdī Muhammad ibn 'Alī as-*Sanūsī* (d. 1859), the group's founder.]

San Yu /sán yoò/ (b. 1919) Burmese soldier and statesman

São Miguel /sow mi gél/ largest island of the Azores. Population: 126,388 (1991). Area: 746 sq. km/288 sq. mi.

Saône /sòn/ river in east-central France. Length: 431 km/268 mi.

São Paulo /-pówlò/ capital of São Paulo State, SE Brazil. Population: 9,811,776 (1996).

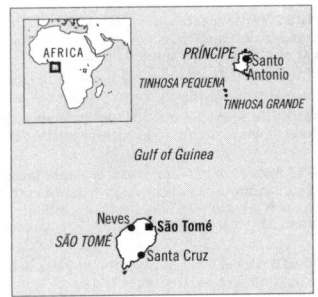

São Tomé and Príncipe

São Tomé and Príncipe /-tò máy ənd prínssi pay/ island republic off the coast of Gabon, in the Gulf of Guinea. Capital: São Tomé. Population: 134,000 (1996). Area: 964 sq. km/372 sq. mi.

sap¹ /sap/ n **1** PLANT FLUID a watery liquid containing mineral salts, sugars, and other nutrients that circulates through the conducting tissues of a plant **2** PLANT SCI = **sapwood 3** BODY FLUID any essential body fluid **4** ENERGY bodily strength or vitality ○ *feel the sap rising* **5** OFFENSIVE TERM an offensive term that deliberately insults somebody's intelligence and judgment (*slang insult*) **6** US COSH a weapon such as a cosh or blackjack ■ vt (**saps, sapping, sapped**) **1** DRAIN PLANT OF SAP to drain a plant of sap **2** US HIT SOMEBODY WITH SAP to hit or knock somebody out with a sap [Old English *sæp* < Germanic] —**sapless** adj

sap² /sap/ n COVERED TRENCH LEADING TO ENEMY TERRITORY a deep narrow covered trench, dug to approach or get inside enemy territory, especially during a siege ■ v (**saps, sapping, sapped**) **1** vti DIG SAP to dig a sap, or undermine the foundations of an enemy fortification by digging a tunnel **2** vt TAKE AWAY SOMEBODY'S ENERGY to gradually weaken or reduce something, especially somebody's strength or energy ○ *The long hours were sapping his strength.* [Late 16C. Via obsolete French *sappe* and Italian *zappa* < late Latin *sappa*.]

sapele /sə peéli/ (plural **-les** or **-le**) n **1** a tall rainforest tree. Native to: W Africa. Genus: *Entandrophragma*. **2** the wood of the sapele tree, which resembles mahogany. Use: furniture-making. [Early 20C. After *Sapele*, Nigeria.]

Saphar n CALENDAR = **Safar**

saphead /sáp hed/ n an offensive term that deliberately insults somebody's intelligence and judgment (*slang insult*) —**sapheaded** adj

saphenous vein /sə feènəss/ n either of two major veins in the leg that run from the foot to the thigh near the surface of the skin [< medieval Latin *saphena* 'vein']

saphire incorrect spelling of **sapphire**

sapid /sáppid/ adj (*formal*) **1** having a strong and pleasant taste **2** engaging or pleasant to think about [Early 17C. < Latin *sapidus* < *sapere* 'taste'.] —**sapidity** /sə píddəti/ n —**sapidness** n

sapient /sáypi ənt/ adj wise or learned [15C. Via Old French < Latin *sapient-*, present participle of *sapere* 'be wise'.] —**sapience** n —**sapiently** adv

sapindaceous /sáppin dáyshəss/ adj belonging to an order of trees and shrubs that includes the soapberry. Order: Sapindaceae. [19C. < modern Latin *Sapindaceae* < *Sapindus* 'Indian soap' < *sapo* 'soap' < Nahuatl 'India'.]

Sapir-Whorf hypothesis /sə peèr wáwrf-/ n the theory that the structure of a language helps determine how its native speakers perceive and categorize experience [Mid-20C. After Edward *Sapir* (1884–1939) and Benjamin Lee *Whorf* (1897–1941), US linguists.]

sapling /sáppling/ n **1** a young tree with a slender trunk **2** a young person (*literary*)

sapodilla /sáppə dillə/ n **1 sapodilla plum** a brown roughskinned fruit with sweet yellowish pulp **2** an evergreen tree that yields chicle and sapodillas. Native to: Mexico, Central America, Caribbean. *Manilkara zapota*. [Late 17C. Alteration of Spanish *zapotillo* < *zapote* < Nahuatl *tzapotl*.]

saponify /sə pónni fī/ (**-fies, -fying, -fied**) vti to be converted into soap or to convert a fat into soap, especially by reaction with an alkali [Early 19C. < French *saponifier* < Latin *sapon-*, form of *sapo* 'soap'.] —**saponifiable** adj —**saponifier** n

saponin /sáppənin/ n any glucoside extracted from plants that forms a soapy lather when mixed with water. Use: detergents. [Mid-19C. Via French *saponine* < Latin *sapon-* (see SAPONIFY).]

saponite /sáppə nīt/ n a soft soapy clay mineral. Source: veins and cavities of rocks altered by hot water. [Mid-19C. < Latin *sapon-* (see SAPONIFY).]

sapotaceous /sáppə táyshəss/ adj belonging to an order of trees that includes the balata tree. Order: Sapotaceae. [Mid-19C. < modern Latin *sapote* (see SAPOTE).]

sapote /sə pòtə/ n **1** an oval brown sweet fruit **2** a tree that produces sapotes. Native to: Mexico, Central America. *Poulteria sapota*. [Mid-16C. Via modern Latin < Spanish *zapote* < Nahuatl *tzapotl*.]

sappanwood /sáppən wòod/, **sapanwood** n **1** a leguminous tree that yields valuable timber. Native to: tropical Asia. *Caesalpina sappan*. **2** the wood of the sappanwood tree, which yields a red dye [Late 16C. Via Dutch < Malay *sapang*.]

sapper /sáppər/ n **1** SPECIALIST IN TRENCHES AND TUNNELS a military engineer who specializes in trenches, especially tunnels dug under enemy territory **2** SPECIALIST IN MINES a military engineer who lays, detects, and disarms mines **3** PRIVATE IN ROYAL ENGINEERS in the British Army, a private in the Royal Engineers [Early 17C. < SAP².]

Sapphic /sáffik/ adj **1** RELATING TO SAPPHO'S POETRY relating to the Greek poet Sappho or her poetry, largely written in 11-syllable lines, with stanzas of three such lines and a shorter fourth line **2** LESBIAN lesbian (*literary*) ■ n GREEK POEM a Sapphic line, stanza, or poem

sapphire /sáff īr/ n **1** a clear hard precious stone that is a variety of the mineral corundum and is usually deep blue in colour **2** a brilliant blue colour like that of a sapphire [13C. Via Old French *safir* and Latin *sapphirus* < Greek *sappheiros*.] —**sapphire** adj

sapphirine /sáffə reen/ adj resembling a sapphire, especially in being a brilliant blue colour ■ n a rare blue or green aluminium magnesium silicate mineral

sapphism /sáffizəm/ n lesbianism (*literary*) [Late 19C. After the Greek poet SAPPHO.]

Sappho /sáffò/ (fl. 7th century BC) Greek poet

Sapporo /sáppòrò, sə póρρò/ city on W Hokkaido Island, Japan. Population: 1,792,167 (1999).

sappy /sáppi/ (**-pier, -piest**) adj **1** full of sap **2** an offensive term meaning regarded as thoughtless or unintelligent (*slang insult*) —**sappily** adv

sapr- prefix = **sapro-** (before vowels)

sapro- prefix **1** death, decay, putrefaction ○ *saprozoic* **2** dead or decaying organic matter ○ *saprophagous* [< Greek *sapros* 'rotten']

saprobe /sáp pròb/ n an organism that gets its nourishment from inorganic or decaying organic matter [Mid-20C. < SAPRO-, after *microbe*.] —**saprobic** /sə pròbik/ adj

saprobiology /sápprò bī ólləji/ n the study of environments that support organisms (**saprobes**) that feed on decaying organic matter —**saprobiological** /-ə lójjik'l/ *adj* —**saprobiologist** *n*

saprogenic /sáprō jénnik/ *adj* causing or resulting from decay —**saprogenicity** /-jə níssəti/ *n*

sapropel /sáprrə pel/ *n* a soft black layer of decaying organic matter at the bottom of a body of water [Early 20C. < German, < Greek *sapros* 'rotten' + *pēlos* 'mud'.] —**sapropelic** /-péllik/ *adj*

saprophagous /sa próffəgəss/ *adj* feeding on or obtaining food from decaying organic matter

saprophyte /sáprō fīt/ *n* an organism, especially a fungus or bacterium, that obtains food from dead or decaying organic matter —**saprophytic** /-fíttik/ *adj* —**saprophytically** *adv*

saprophytism /sáprō fītizəm/ *n* the process of obtaining nourishment from dissolved decaying organic matter

saprotrophic /sáprō tróffik/ *adj* describes an organism that feeds by absorbing dead or decaying organic matter. Many fungi and bacteria are saprotrophic. —**saprotroph** /sáprō trōf/ *n*

saprozoic /sáp prō zṓ ik/ *adj* getting nourishment by absorbing dissolved organic matter and salts

sapsago /sápsəgō/ (*plural* **-gos** *or* **-go**) *n* a hard green Swiss cheese made with sour skimmed milk and flavoured with sweet clover [Mid-19C. Alteration of German *Schabzieger* < *schaben* 'scrape' + *zieger* 'curd cheese'.]

sapsucker /sáp sukər/ *n* a small woodpecker that drills holes in trees in order to drink the sap and eat insects attracted by the sap. Native to: North America. Genus: *Sphyrapicus*.

sapwood /sáp wòod/ *n* the soft wood of a tree between the inner bark and the heartwood

SAR *n* the rate at which a mass, especially human tissue, absorbs radiated electrical energy, e.g. when using a mobile phone, measured in watts or milliwatts per kilogram. Full form **specific absorption rate**

saraband /sárrə band/, **sarabande** *n* **1** a dignified Spanish dance of the 17th and 18th centuries in triple time **2** music for a saraband [Early 17C. Via French < Spanish *zarabanda*.]

Saracen /sárrəss'n/ *n* **1 MUSLIM OPPOSING CHRISTIAN CRUSADES** a Muslim who fought against the Christian Crusaders in the Middle Ages **2 MEMBER OF ANCIENT DESERT PEOPLE** a member of an ancient desert people of Syria and Arabia living on the fringes of the Roman Empire **3 ARAB** an Arab (*archaic*) ■ *adj* **RELATING TO SARACENS** relating to the ancient or medieval Saracens or their culture [Pre-12C. Via Old French *sarazin* < late Greek *sarakēnos*.] —**Saracenic** /sárrə sénnik/ *adj* —**Saracenical** *adj*

Saragossa /sárrə góssə/ = **Zaragoza**

Sarah /sáirə/ *n* in the Bible, the wife and half-sister of Abraham, and mother of Isaac (Genesis 17:15–22)

Sarajevo /sárrə yáyvō/ capital of Bosnia-Herzegovina, in the east-central part of the country. Population: 415,631 (1991).

saran /sə rán/ *n* a thermoplastic resin created from a vinyl compound. Use: fabrics, plastic wrap. [Mid-20C. Originally a trademark.]

sarangi /saa rúng gi/ (*plural* **-gis**) *n* a musical instrument of South Asia resembling a violin, with a rectangular soundbox and three strings that have sympathetic strings [Mid-19C. < Sanskrit *sāraṅgī*.]

sarape *n* CLOTHING = **serape**

Sarawak /sə ráawək/ state in Malaysia, occupying the northwest portion of the island of Borneo. Capital: Kuching. Population: 1,648,217 (1990). Area: 124,449 sq. km/48,050 sq. mi.

Sarazen /sárrəzən/, **Gene** (1902–99) US golfer. Born **Eugene Saraceni**

sarc- *prefix* = **sarco-** (*before vowels*)

sarcasm /sáar kazzəm/ *n* remarks that mean the opposite of what they seem to say and are intended to mock or deride [Mid-16C. < French, < Greek *sarkazein* 'tear flesh' < *sarx* 'flesh'.]

sarcastic /saar kástik/ *adj* **1** characterized by words that mean the opposite of what they seem to say and make fun of something or somebody or express irritation **2** fond of or habitually using sarcasm —**sarcastically** *adv*

SYNONYMS ***sarcastic, ironic, sardonic, satirical, caustic***

CORE MEANING: used to describe remarks that are designed to hurt or mock

sarcastic contemptuous, scornful, or mocking and intended to hurt or belittle; **ironic** deliberately stating the opposite of the truth, usually with the intention of being amusing; **sardonic** mocking and cynical or disdainful, though not deliberately hurtful; **satirical** using ridicule, especially in a work of art, to criticize somebody's or something's faults, especially in the arts; **caustic** harsh and bitter and intended to mock, offend, or belittle.

sarcenet /sáarssnət/, **sarsenet** *n* a soft delicate silk cloth. Use: formerly, veils, linings, ribbons. [15C. < Old French *sarzinet* < ?]

sarco- *prefix* **1** striated muscle ○ *sarcolemma* **2** flesh ○ *sarcoid* [< Greek *sark-*, stem of *sarx* 'flesh'. Ultimately < Indo-European, 'cut, tear'.]

sarcodinian /sáarkə dínni ən/ *adj* belonging to the class of protozoans that includes amoebas ■ *n* a protozoan that belongs to the same class as amoebas [< modern Latin *Sarcodina* < Greek *sarkōdēs* 'fleshy' < *sarx* 'flesh']

sarcoid /sáar koyd/ *n* a small area of chronic infection in the body of a person affected by sarcoidosis ■ *adj* relating to or resembling flesh

sarcoidosis /sáar koy dṓssiss/ *n* a disease in which lumps of fibrous tissue and collections of cells (**granulomas**) appear on the skin and internal organs

sarcolactic acid /sáarkō láktik-/ *n* a form of lactic acid produced by muscle tissue during anaerobic activity

sarcolemma /sáarkō lémmə/ (*plural* **-colemmas** *or* **-colemmata** /-mətə/) *n* a thin clear membrane that covers a striated muscle fibre

sarcoma /saar kṓmə/ (*plural* **-mas** *or* **-mata** /-mətə/) *n* a malignant tumour that begins growing in connective tissue such as muscle, bone, fat, or cartilage —**sarcomatoid** *adj* —**sarcomatosis** /-tṓssiss/ *n* —**sarcomatous** *adj*

sarcomere /sáarkō meer/ *n* any of the tiny segments that make up a fibril of striated muscle

sarcophagus /saar kóffəgəss/ (*plural* **-gi** /-gī/ *or* **-guses**) *n* an ancient stone or marble coffin, often decorated with sculpture and inscriptions [Early 17C. Via Latin < Greek *sarkophagos* 'flesh-eater'.]

sarcoplasm /sáarkō plazəm/ *n* the cytoplasm of a striated muscle fibre —**sarcoplasmic** /-plázmik/ *adj* —**sarcoplasmous** /-plázməss/ *adj*

sarcoplasmic reticulum *n* the endoplasmic reticulum of a striated muscle fibre that regulates the concentration of calcium ions in the cell cytoplasm

sarcoptic mange /saar kóptik-/ *n* a form of mange caused by a parasitic mite that burrows into the skin [< modern Latin *Sarcoptes*, genus of mites < Greek *sarx* 'flesh' + *koptein* 'cut']

sarcous /sáarkəss/ *adj* consisting of or relating to flesh or muscle tissue

sard /saard/ *n* a deep orange-red variety of chalcedony used in making jewellery [15C. < Latin *sarda* < Greek *sardios*.]

Sardanapalus /sáardə náppələss/ (*fl.* 7th century BC) legendary Assyrian monarch

sardar *n* = **sirdar** [Late 16C. < Persian, 'holding the position of chief'.]

sardine /saar déen/ *n* **1** a small marine fish related to the herring, especially the European pilchard. *Sardinia pilchardus*. **2** the flesh of a sardine as food, usually preserved in cans, packed tightly in oil [15C. Via French < Greek *Sardō* 'Sardinia'.] ◇ **be packed like sardines** to be crowded closely together

Sardinia /saar dínni ə/ Italian island in the W Mediterranean Sea. Capital: Cagliari. Population: 1,659,466 (1995). Area: 23,813 sq. km/9,194 sq. mi. —**Sardinian** *adj, n*

Sardis /sáardiss/ ancient city of W Asia Minor, near present-day Izmir, Turkey, the capital of the ancient kingdom of Lydia

sardius /sáardi əss/ *n* CRYSTALS = **sard** [15C. < Latin, < *sarda* (see SARD).]

sardonic /saar dónnik/ *adj* disdainfully or ironically mocking [Mid-17C. < French *sardonique* < Greek *sardanios* 'scornful'.] —**sardonically** *adv* —**sardonicism** /-sizəm/ *n*

SYNONYMS See ***sarcastic***.

sardonyx /sáardəniks/ *n* a variety of onyx with alternating bands of light orange-brown sard and white chalcedony, once widely used in making cameos [14C. Via Latin < Greek *sardonux* < *sardios* (see SARD) + *onux* (see ONYX).]

sargasso /saar gássō/ *n* = **gulfweed** [Late 16C. < Portuguese *sargaço*.]

Sargasso Sea /sar gássō-/ section of the North Atlantic Ocean between the Caribbean and the Azores, noted for its predominantly still waters. Area: 5,200,000 sq. km/2,000,000 sq. mi.

sargasso weed *n* = **gulfweed**

sargassum /saar gássəm/ *n* = **gulfweed** [Early 20C. < modern Latin < SARGASSO.]

sargassum fish *n* a brown and black fish that lives in floating gulfweed. Native to: Atlantic and W Pacific oceans. *Histrio histrio*.

sarge /saarj/ *n* a sergeant in the armed forces or police (*informal*) [Mid-19C. Shortening.]

Sargent /sáarjənt/, **John Singer** (1856–1925) Italian-born US artist

Sargeson /sáarjəss'n/, **Frank** (1903–82) New Zealand writer. Pseudonym of **Norris Frank Davey**

Sargodha /saar gṓdə/ city in NE Pakistan. Population: 291,361 (1981).

sari /sáari/, **saree** *n* a traditional garment worn by Asian women, consisting of a long rectangle of fabric reaching the feet, wrapped and pleated around the waist over an underskirt and choli, and draped over the shoulder [Late 18C. Via Hindi *sāṛī* < Sanskrit *śāṭī* 'garment'.]

sarin /sáarin, sárrin/ *n* $C_4H_{10}FO_2P$ an extremely toxic gas that attacks the central nervous system, causing convulsions and death [Mid-20C. < German, < ?]

Sark /saark/ one of the Channel Islands, a dependency of Guernsey, in the English Channel. Population: 575 (1991). Area: 5 sq. km/2 sq. mi.

sarking /sáarking/ *n Scotland, N England, NZ* planks of wood nailed to the rafters of a building to support a slate roof

sarky /sáarki/ (**sarkier, sarkiest**) *adj* sarcastic in tone or manner (*informal*) [Early 20C. Shortening of SARCASTIC.]

sarmentose /saar mént ōss/, **sarmentous** /-təss/ *adj* producing long slender stems that reach out and take root along the ground [Mid-18C. < Latin *sarmentosus* 'full of twigs' < *sarmentum* 'twig'.]

Sarnia /sáarni ə/ city in SE Ontario, Canada, at the southern tip of Lake Huron. Population: 72,738 (1996).

sarnie /sáarni/ *n* a sandwich (*informal*) [Mid-20C. Probably alteration of SANDWICH.]

sarod /sa rṓd/ *n* a stringed instrument of N India that resembles a lute with two resonating gourds but is played with a bow [Mid-19C. Via Urdu < Persian *sarūd*.]

sarong /sə róng/ *n* **1 TRADITIONAL MALAYSIAN GARMENT** a traditional Malayan and Javan garment for men or women, consisting of a length of fabric wrapped and tied around the body at the waist or under the arms **2 FASHION VERSION OF SARONG** a fashion version of the sarong worn by a woman as a wrapped skirt, often for the beach **3 CLOTH FOR MALAYSIAN GARMENTS** cloth for a sarong, often brightly coloured [Mid-19C. < Malay, 'covering'.]

Saronic Gulf /sə rónik-/ inlet of the Aegean Sea in central Greece, between the Attica peninsula south of Athens and the E Peloponnese

saros /sáir oss/ *n* the cycle of 6,585.32 days, or approximately 18 years 11 days, after which a sequence of eclipses of the sun and moon repeats itself [Early 19C. Via Greek < Babylonian *sāru* 'the number 3,600'.] —**saronic** /sə rónnik/ *adj*

sarpanch /sər púnch/ *n* the head of a village council (**panchayat**) in India [Mid-20C. < Urdu, < *sar* 'head' + *panch* 'five'.]

sarracenia /sárrə séeni ə/ (*plural* **-as** *or* **-a**) *n* a pitcher plant with hollow tubular leaves that trap insects. Native to: E North America. Genus: *Sarracenia*. [Mid-18C. < modern Latin, after D. *Sarrazin*, 17C Canadian botanist.]

sarrusophone /sə rṓozə fōn/ *n* a woodwind musical instrument resembling a bassoon but made of brass [Late 19C. After M. *Sarrus*, French bandmaster.]

sarsaparilla /sáarspə ríllə/ (*plural* **-las** *or* **-la**) *n* **1 MEDICINAL ROOT** the dried root of a tropical vine or temperate plant. Use: traditional or herbal medicine, soft drink.

2 TROPICAL VINE a tropical vine with aromatic roots and heart-shaped leaves. Native to: America. Genus: *Smilax*. **3 PLANT SIMILAR TO SARSAPARILLA VINE** a plant similar to the sarsaparilla vine, especially American sarsaparilla and Australian sarsaparilla **4 SOFT DRINK** a carbonated drink flavoured with sarsaparilla root [Late 16C. < Spanish *zarzaparrilla* < *zarza* 'bramble' + *parra* 'vine'.]

sarsen /sáarssn/ *n* any large sedimentary rock that has been broken into blocks by frost action and is found on the chalk downs of S England [Late 17C. Alteration of SARACEN.]

sarsenet *n* = sarcenet

sartor /saártər/ *n* a tailor (*archaic*) [Mid-17C. < Latin, < *sart-*, past participle of *sarcire* 'patch'.]

sartorial /saar táwri əl/ *adj* **1** relating to tailoring or clothing in general **2** relating to the sartorius muscle in the thigh

sartorius /saar táwri əss/ (*plural* **-i** /-ri ī/) *n* a flat narrow muscle that extends from the hip to the inner thigh and helps rotate the leg to a cross-legged position [Early 18C. < modern Latin *musculus sartorius* 'tailor's muscle' < *sartor* (see SARTOR).]

AKG London

Jean-Paul Sartre

Sartre /saártrə/, **Jean-Paul** (1905–80) French philosopher, playwright, and novelist

Sarum /sáirəm/ former name for **Salisbury, England**

Sarvodaya /saar vódəyə/ *n* the name that Mahatma Gandhi and his followers gave to the new social order that they sought to establish in India [Early 20C. < Sanskrit, 'prosperity for all'.]

SAS *n* a British military force that is specially trained to undertake dangerous clandestine operations. Full form **Special Air Service**

SASE *abbr* self-addressed stamped envelope

sash /sash/ *n* **1 FABRIC BELT** a strip of cloth tied around the waist, e.g. as part of ceremonial dress **2 WIDE RIBBON WORN ACROSS CHEST** a band of cloth draped over one shoulder and across the chest as a symbol of rank or office **3 FRAME FOR GLASS** a frame holding the glass panes of a window or door [Late 17C. < Arabic *šāš* 'muslin'.]

sashay /sásh ay/ *vi* **1 FLOUNCE GRACEFULLY** to walk in a way that is intended to attract attention, especially by swaying the hips or swinging the elbows (*humorous*) **2 PERFORM STEPS IN SQUARE DANCING** to dance a sequence of steps in square dancing ■ *n* **1 DANCE** = **chassé** *n*. **2 PATTERN IN SQUARE DANCING** a figure in square dancing in which partners circle each other using sideways steps [Mid-19C. < French *chassé* 'chasing, chase'.]

sashimi /sáshimi/ *n* a Japanese dish consisting of slices of raw fish, usually served with a dipping sauce such as a seasoned soy sauce [Late 19C. < Japanese.]

sashing /sáshing/ *n* strips of fabric used to separate blocks in a patchwork

sash saw *n* a small saw with a thin blade, used in making window sashes

sash window *n* a window that consists of two frames, one above the other in vertical grooves, allowing either to be opened or shut by sliding it up or down

Sask. *abbr* Saskatchewan

Saskatchewan /sa skáchəwən/ **1** river in central Canada, rising in central Saskatchewan and flowing into Lake Winnipeg in Manitoba. Length: 547 km/340 mi. **2** province in central Canada. Capital: Regina. Population: 990,237 (1996). Area: 652,330 sq. km/251,865 sq. mi. —**Saskatchewanian** /sə skácha wáyni ən/ *n, adj*

Saskatoon /sáskə toon/ second-largest city in Saskatchewan, Canada, in the central part of the province. Population: 193,647 (1996).

sasquatch /sásk wach/ *n* MYTHOL = **Bigfoot** [Early 20C. < Salish.]

sass /sass/ *n* US disrespectful or impudent remarks, especially in reply to an older person or somebody in authority (*informal*) ■ *vt* US to talk disrespectfully or impudently, especially to somebody who is older or in authority (*informal*) [Mid-19C. Back-formation < SASSY¹.]

sassaby /sássəbi/ (*plural* **-bies**) *n* ZOOL = **topi**¹ *n*. [Early 19C. Alteration of Tswana *tsessébi*.]

sassafras /sássə frass/ (*plural* **-fras**) *n* **1** a deciduous tree with aromatic bark, lobed leaves, and small bluish fruits. Native to: E North America. *Sassafras albidum*. **2** the dried root bark of the sassafras tree. Use: flavouring, perfumes, medicines. [Late 16C. < Spanish *sasafrás* < ?.]

~~sassafrass~~ incorrect spelling of **sassafras**

Sassanid /sássənid/ *n* a member of a Persian dynasty that ruled from AD 224–651 [Late 18C. After Persian monarch *Sasan*, grandfather of the first Sassanian king.] —**Sassanian** /sə sáyni ən/ *adj*

Sassari /sássəri/ capital of Sassari Province, NW Sardinia, Italy. Population: 121,961 (1992).

Sassenach /sássə nak, -nakh/ (*plural* **-nachs**) *n* Scotland, Ireland an offensive term for an English person [Early 18C. Via Gaelic *Sassunach* < Latin *Saxones* 'Saxons' < Germanic.]

Sassoon /sə soón/, **Siegfried** (1886–1967) British poet and novelist

sassy¹ /sássi/ (**-sier, -siest**) *adj* US **1 IMPUDENT** impudent or disrespectful **2 HIGH-SPIRITED** lively and high-spirited ○ *The show has refreshingly sassy hoedown-style choreography.* **3 STYLISH** stylish or fashionable ○ *a sassy look for spring* [Mid-19C. Alteration of SAUCY.] —**sassily** *adv* —**sassiness** *n*

sassy² /sássi/ (*plural* **-sies**) *n* a tree with poisonous bark and insect-resistant wood used for building. Native to: West Africa. *Erythrophleum suaveolens*. [Mid-19C. < ?]

sastra *n* RELIG = **shastra**

sastruga /sə stroógə/ *n* a long wave-shaped ridge of hard snow formed by the wind and common in polar regions [Mid-19C. Via German < Russian *zastruga*.]

sat past tense, past participle of **sit**

SAT /sat/ *abbr* **1** standard assessment task ■ **2** a trademark for a standardized test taken by applicants to colleges in the United States. Full form **Scholastic Aptitude Test**

Sat. *abbr* Saturday

~~satalite~~ incorrect spelling of **satellite**

Satan /sáyt'n/ *n* in Christianity, the enemy of God, the lord of evil, and the tempter of human beings. He is sometimes identified with Lucifer, the leader of the fallen angels. [Pre-12C. Via Latin < Hebrew *śāṭān* 'accuse'.]

satang /sa táng/ (*plural* **-tang**) *n* see table at **currency**

satanic /sə tánnik/ *adj* **1** relating to Satan or the worship of Satan **2** extremely evil or cruel —**satanically** *adv* —**satanicalness** *n*

Satanism /sáyt'nizəm/ *n* the worship of Satan, especially as a parody of Christian rites

satay /sáttay/ *n* a popular Indonesian and Malaysian dish consisting of marinated pieces of meat, chicken, or fish grilled on wooden skewers and served with peanut sauce [Mid-20C. < Malay.]

SATB *abbr* soprano, alto, tenor, bass

satchel /sáchəl/ *n* a small bag, often with a shoulder strap, used for carrying books and personal belongings [14C. Via Old French *sachel* < Latin *saccus* 'bag'.]

sate /sayt/ (**sates, sating, sated**) *vt* **1** to satisfy completely somebody's hunger or some other desire **2** to provide somebody with more than enough, to the point of exhaustion or disgust [Old English *sadian*. Ultimately < Indo-European.]

sateen /sə teén/ (*plural* **-teens** *or* **-teen**) *n* a cotton or polyester fabric with a shiny side intended to look like satin [Late 19C. Alteration of SATIN, after 'velveteen'.]

~~satelite~~ incorrect spelling of **satellite**

satellite /sáttə līt/ *n* **1 DEVICE THAT ORBITS PLANET** an object put into orbit around Earth or any other planet in order to relay communications signals or transmit scientific data **2 MOON ORBITING OTHER BODY** an astronomical object that orbits a larger one **3 COUNTRY DEPENDENT ON ANOTHER COUNTRY** a nation or political unit that is dependent economically and politically on another more powerful nation **4 SUBURB** a town or small city located near and dependent on a larger city **5 ATTENDANT** an attendant of an important person [Mid-16C. Via French < Latin *satelles* 'attendant'.]

satellite broadcasting *n* the global transmission of television programmes via satellite

satellite cell *n* one of the cells forming the capsule that encloses the nerve cells in many spinal ganglia

satellite dish *n* a dish-shaped device for receiving television signals broadcast via satellite

satellite DNA *n* a component of an animal's DNA that differs in density from surrounding DNA, consists of short repeating sequences of nucleotide pairs, and does not undergo transcription

satellite station *n* a radio or television station that receives programmes from another station and rebroadcasts them immediately on a different wavelength

satellite television *n* a television for which the signal is relayed via satellite and is broadcast to customers who have appropriate receiving equipment

satellitium /sáttə lítti əm/ *n* in astrology, a group of planets in one sign of the zodiac

satem /saátəm/ *adj* relating to Indo-European languages in which the consonant sounding like 'k' developed into the sound 's' and 'sh'. ◊ **centum** [Early 20C. < Avestan *satem* 'hundred'.]

sati *n* RELIG = **suttee**

satiate /sáyshi ayt/ *vt* (**-ates, -ating, -ated**) **1 GLUT** to provide somebody with too much of something desirable, to the point of overindulgence (*often passive*) **2 GRATIFY DESIRE** to satisfy hunger or another appetite completely ■ *adj* **HAVING TOO MUCH** having had enough or too much [15C. < Latin *satiat-*, past participle of *satiare* < *satis* 'enough'.] —**satiability** *n* —**satiable** *adj* —**satiably** *adv*

Satie /saáti/, **Erik** (1866–1925) French composer

satiety /sə tī́ əti/ *n* a state in which somebody has had enough or too much [Mid-16C. Via French *satiété* < Latin *satis* 'enough'.]

satin /sáttin/ *n* **1 GLOSSY SILK OR RAYON FABRIC** a fabric woven of silk or rayon, with a smooth glossy finish and a dull back ■ *adj* **1 OF SATIN** made of satin fabric **2 GLOSSY LIKE SATIN** smooth and glossy like satin [14C. Via Old French < Arabic *zaytūnī* 'of the town of Zaytun', probably the Chinese city of Tsinkiang.] —**satiny** *adj*

satinet /sátti nét/, **satinette** /-nét/ *n* **1** an imitation satin made from cotton and wool **2** thin or inferior satin

satin spar *n* a fibrous variety of gypsum. ◊ **gypsum**

satin stitch *n* an embroidery stitch that is worked in close parallel lines to fill in an area or form a solid line

satin walnut *n* the wood of the sweet gum tree, often used to make furniture. ◊ **sweet gum**

satin weave *n* a weave in which the face of the fabric is covered entirely with warp threads, producing a smooth finish

satinwood /sáttin wŏŏd/ *n* **1 WOOD FROM S ASIAN TREE** a smooth hard yellow-brown wood. Use: furniture making. **2 S ASIAN TREE** a deciduous tree with hard yellow-brown wood. Native to: India, Sri Lanka. *Chloroxylon swietenia*. **3 CARIBBEAN TREE** an evergreen tree with smooth lustrous wood. Native to: Caribbean. *Zanthoxylum flavum*.

satire /sáttīr/ *n* **1** the use of wit, especially irony, sarcasm, and ridicule, to attack the vices and follies of humankind **2** a literary work that uses satire, or the branch of literature made up of such works [Early 16C. Directly or via French < Latin *satira* 'poetic medley, satire'.]

satirical /sə tírrik'l/ *adj* relating to satire or the use of wit to attack the vices and follies of humankind —**satirically** *adv*

SYNONYMS See *sarcastic*.

satirise *vt* = satirize

satirist /sáttərist/ *n* a writer or performer of satires

satirize /sáttə rīz/ (**-rizes, -rizing, -rized**), **satirise** (**-rises, -rising, -rised**) *vt* to attack or criticize somebody or something by means of satire —**satirization** /-rī záysh'n/ *n* —**satirizer** *n*

satisfaction /sàttiss fáksh'n/ *n* **1 GRATIFICATION** the feeling of pleasure that comes when a need or desire is fulfilled ○ *job satisfaction* **2 FULFILMENT** the fulfilment of a need, claim, or desire **3 HAPPINESS WITH ARRANGEMENT** happiness with the way that something has been arranged or done ○ *organized to her satisfaction* **4 FREEDOM FROM DOUBT** the assurance that something has been fully explained or settled ○ *a solution that was never explained to my satisfaction* **5 COMPENSATION** compensation for an injury or loss ○ *demanded satisfaction for their mistreatment* [14C. Via French < Latin *satisfacere* (see SATISFY).]

satisfactory /sàttiss fáktəri/ *adj* good enough to meet a requirement or to be considered acceptable [15C. Via French *satisfactoire* < Latin *satisfacere* (see SATISFY).]

satisfy /sáttiss fī/ (**-fies, -fying, -fied**) *v* **1** *vt* **CONTENT SOMEBODY** to do or offer enough to make somebody feel pleased or content **2** *vti* **FULFIL NEED** to fulfil a need or gratify a desire **3** *vt* **RESOLVE DOUBTS** to convince somebody by resolving questions or doubts **4** *vt* **MEET CONDITION** to achieve or be of sufficient standard to meet a requirement or condition **5** *vt* **SOLVE MATHEMATICAL PROBLEM** to make both sides of an equation equal by finding the quantities of the unknown variables **6** *vt* **PAY DEBT** to pay a debt in full **7** *vt* **COMPENSATE** to compensate somebody for an injury or loss [15C. Via Old French *satisfier* < Latin *satisfacere* 'satisfy' < *satis* 'enough' + *facere* 'make'.] —**satisfied** *adj* —**satisfier** *n* —**satisfyingly** *adv*

Sato Eisaku /saàtō áyss akoo, -ay saákoo/ (1901–75) Japanese statesman and prime minister of Japan (1964–72)

satori /sə táwri/ *n* in Zen Buddhism, a state of spiritual enlightenment that is a spiritual objective [Early 18C. < Japanese, 'awakening'.]

satrap /sáttrap/ *n* **1** the governor of a province in ancient Persia **2** a subordinate official, especially a self-important one [15C. Via French and Latin < Old Persian *kšathrapāvā* 'protector of the country'.]

satrapy /sáttrəpi/ (*plural* **-pies**) *n* the province or territory ruled by a satrap

satsuma /sat sóomə/ *n* **1** a cultivated variety of mandarin orange, with a thin orange skin **2** a citrus tree that bears satsumas. Native to: Japan. *Citrus reticulata*. [Late 19C. After a province in Kyushu, Japan.]

Satsuma ware, Satsuma *n* cream-coloured Japanese pottery

~~**sattelite**~~ incorrect spelling of **satellite**

saturant /sáchərənt/ *n* a substance that is used to saturate another substance ■ *adj* causing saturation [Mid-18C. < Latin *saturant-*, present participle of *saturare* (see SATURATE).]

saturate *vt* /sáchə rayt/ (**-rates, -rating, -rated**) **1 MAKE SOMETHING WET** to soak something with liquid **2 FILL SOMETHING COMPLETELY** to fill something with so many people or things that no more can be added **3 SUPPLY MARKET FULLY** to supply a market fully, so that all existing demand for a product is met **4 FILL SOLUTION WITH ANOTHER SUBSTANCE** to add as much of a liquid, solid, or gas to a solution as it can absorb at a given temperature **5 BOMB ENEMY HEAVILY** to overwhelm an enemy with intensive bombing ■ *adj* /sáchərət/ **SATURATED** saturated with liquid (*archaic*) [Mid-16C. < Latin *saturare* < *satur* 'satiated'.] —**saturability** *n* —**saturable** *adj*

saturated /sáchə raytid/ *adj* **1 WET** soaked with liquid **2 CONTAINING MAXIMUM SOLUTE** containing the maximum amount of solute that can be absorbed at a given temperature **3 PACKED FULL** completely packed or full so that no more can be added **4 CONTAINING SINGLE BONDS BETWEEN CARBON ATOMS** containing only single bonds between carbon atoms, as in some fatty acids

saturated fat *n* a fat in which the carbon atoms are fully hydrogenated, found in animal products

saturation /sáchə ráysh'n/ *n* **1 STATE OF TOTAL WETNESS** a state in which something is completely soaked with liquid **2 STATE OF BEING PACKED FULL** a state in which something is so full or packed that no more can be added **3 HEAVY BOMBING** intensive bombing of a military target in order to overwhelm an enemy **4 FULL SUPPLYING OF MARKET** the full supplying of a market, to the point where all existing demand for a product is met **5 MAXIMUM ABSORPTION** the absorption of the greatest possible amount of a liquid, solid, or gas by a solution at a given temperature **6 STATE OF MAGNETIZATION** a state of complete magnetization **7 100 PER CENT HUMIDITY** the condition of the atmosphere when it contains as much water vapour as it can hold at a specific temperature **8 COLOUR INTENSITY** the intensity of a colour **9 CONDITION OF STABLE OUTPUT CURRENT** a condition where the output current of an electronic device is substantially constant and no longer increases as a function of increasing input ■ *adj* **COMPREHENSIVE** comprehensive in the use of outlets or other resources ○ *The event had saturation coverage in the press.*

saturation diving *n* a method of diving in which the diver's bloodstream is saturated with an inert gas so that the time required for decompression is unaffected by the duration of the dive

saturation point *n* **1** the point at which no more can be added **2** the point at which the greatest possible amount of a substance has been absorbed by a solution at a given temperature

saturation zone *n* the zone below the water table that is saturated with ground water

Saturday /sáttər day, -di/ *n* the day of the week after Friday and before Sunday [Pre-12C. Earlier *sæternesdæg*, translation of Latin *Saturni dies* 'day of Saturn'.]

Saturday night special *n US* a small cheap handgun that is easy to obtain and conceal [Because the guns are most often used in the types of crime that typically occur on a Saturday night]

Saturdays /sáttər dayz, -diz/ *adv* every Saturday

Saturn /sáttərn/ *n* **1** in Roman mythology, the god of agriculture and ruler of the universe during the Golden Age. Greek equivalent **Cronus 2** the second-largest planet in the solar system and the sixth planet from the sun. Saturn has bright rings made up of orbiting fragments of rock. See table at **planet** [Old English. < Latin *Saturnus*.] —**Saturnian** /sa túrni ən/ *adj*

saturnalia /sàttər náyli ə/ (*plural* **-as** *or* **-a**) *n* a wild celebration or orgy [Late 18C. Generalized use of SATURNALIA.]

Saturnalia *npl* an ancient Roman festival of feasting and revelry in celebration of the god Saturn and the winter solstice. Date: mid-December. [Late 16C. < Latin, < *Saturnus* 'Saturn'.]

saturniid /sa túrni id/ *n* a large brightly coloured moth that has a stout hairy body. Family: Saturniidae. [Late 19C. < modern Latin *Saturniidae* < Latin *Saturnus* 'Saturn'.]

saturnine /sáttər nīn/ *adj* gloomy and morose [15C. Directly or via French < medieval Latin *saturninus* < Latin *Saturnus* 'Saturn'.] —**saturninely** *adv*

satyagraha /sut yaágrəhə/ *n* the doctrine of nonviolent resistance originated by Mahatma Gandhi and used in the opposition to British rule in India [Early 20C. < Sanskrit *satyāgrahaḥ* 'force born out of truth'.]

satyr /sáttər/ *n* **1 HALF-MAN, HALF-GOAT** in Greek mythology, a wood-dwelling creature with the head and body of a man and the ears, horns, and legs of a goat. Roman equivalent **faun 2 MAN DISPLAYING INAPPROPRIATE SEXUAL BEHAVIOUR** a man who displays inappropriate or excessive sexual behaviour **3 BUTTERFLY** a brown or grey butterfly with spotted wings. Family: Satyridae. [14C. Via French < Latin *satyrus* < Greek *saturos*.] —**satyric** /sə tírrik/ *adj* —**satyrical** *adj*

satyriasis /sàttə rī́ əssiss/ *n* excessive and uncontrollable sexual desire in a man

satyrid /sə téerid/ *n* a small brown butterfly. Family: Satyridae.

satyr play *n* in ancient Greece, a comic play that mocked a mythological subject and included a chorus of satyrs

sauce /sawss/ *n* **1 FLAVOURING LIQUID FOR FOOD** a thick liquid that is served with food to add extra flavour **2 IMPUDENT REMARKS** impudent or disrespectful remarks (*informal*) **3** *US, Can* **STEWED FRUIT** stewed fruit served with a meal ○ *cranberry sauce* **4 ZEST** something that adds zest or excitement **5** *US* **LIQUOR** alcoholic liquor (*slang*) ■ *vt* (**sauces, saucing, sauced**) **1 SPEAK TO SOMEBODY DISRESPECTFULLY** to make impudent or disrespectful remarks to somebody (*informal*) **2 ADD SAUCE TO FOOD** to add flavour to food using a sauce **3 ENLIVEN** to add zest or interest to something [14C. Via Old French < Latin *salsus*, past participle of *sallere* 'to salt' < *sal* 'salt'.]

sauce boat *n* a low boat-shaped jug used for serving sauce or gravy

saucepan /sáwspən/ *n* a cooking pot with a handle, used on top of a cooker

saucer /sáwssər/ *n* **1** a small shallow dish designed to hold a matching cup **2** anything circular and shallow like a saucer

saucy /sáwssi/ (**-ier, -iest**) *adj* **1 CHEEKY** showing a lack of respect **2 PERT** cheerfully pert ○ *a hat at a saucy angle* **3 SEXUALLY EXPLICIT** intended to be amusingly vulgar, especially in sexual innuendo ○ *a range of saucy postcards* [Early 16C] —**saucily** *adv* —**sauciness** *n*

Saud /sowd, saa óod/ (1902–69) king of Saudi Arabia (1953–64)

Saudi /sówdi, sáwdi/ *n* somebody who comes from Saudi Arabia ■ *adj* relating to Saudi Arabia or its people or culture [Mid-20C. After the *Sa'ūd*, family of the ruling dynasty.]

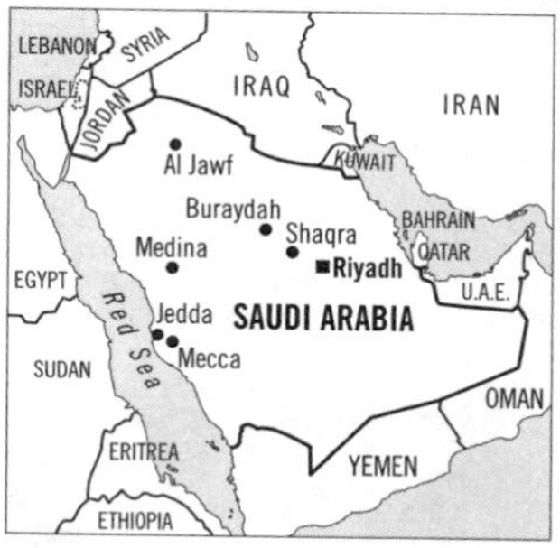

Saudi Arabia

Saudi Arabia /sówdi ə ráybi ə/ monarchy in the Middle East, on the Arabian Peninsula. Capital: Riyadh. Population: 18,426,000 (1996). Area: 2,240,000 sq. km/864,869 sq. mi. —**Saudi Arabian** *n, adj*

sauerbraten /sówər braat'n/ *n* a German dish of beef marinated and cooked in vinegar [Late 19C. < German, 'sour roast meat'.]

sauerkraut /sówər krowt/ *n* a German dish of shredded cabbage fermented in its own juice with salt [Mid-17C. < German, 'sour cabbage'.]

sauger /sáwgər/ *n* a freshwater fish similar to but smaller than a walleyed pike and valued in sport fishing. Native to: North America. *Stizostedion canadense*. [Late 19C. < ?]

Sauk /sawk/ (*plural* **Sauk** *or* **Sauks**), **Sac** /sak/ (*plural* **Sac** *or* **Sacs**) *n* **1** a member of a Native North American people that lived in Wisconsin, Illinois, and Iowa and who now live mainly in Oklahoma **2** the Algonquian language of the Sauk people, related to Fox [Early 18C. < Canadian French *Saki* < Ojibwa *osāki*.]

Saul /sawl/ (*fl.* 11th century BC) first king of ancient Israel (about 1020–00 BC)

Sault Sainte Marie /soo sənt mə rée/ **1** city in S Ontario, Canada, between Lakes Superior and Huron. Population: 80,054 (1996). **2** city in N Michigan, opposite Sault Sainte Marie, Ontario. Population: 15,385 (1998 estimate).

sauna /sáwnə/ *n* **1** a bath involving a spell in a hot steamy room followed by a plunge into cold water or a light brushing with birch or cedar boughs **2** a room designed or prepared for having a sauna [Late 19C. < Finnish.]

saunter /sáwntər/ *vi* **STROLL** to walk at an easy unhurried pace ■ *n* **1 EASY PACE** an easy unhurried pace ○ *walk at a saunter* **2 SLOW WALK** a slow leisurely walk ○ *go for a saunter round the grounds* [Mid-17C. < ?] —**saunterer** *n*

saurian /sáwri ən/ *n* any of a former suborder of reptiles that included all lizards. Suborder: Sauria. ■ *adj* relating to or resembling a lizard [Early 19C. < modern Latin *Sauria* < Latin *saurus* 'lizard' < Greek *sauros*.]

saurischian /saw ríski ən/ *n* a dinosaur that had a pelvis like that of a modern lizard. Order: Saurischia. ■ *adj* relating to the saurischians [Late 19C. < modern Latin *Saurischia* 'lizard hip-joint'.]

~~**saurkraut**~~ incorrect spelling of **sauerkraut**

sauropod /sáwrō pod/ *n* a gigantic plant-eating dinosaur that had a long neck and tail and a small head. Suborder: Sauropoda. ■ *adj* relating to the sauropods [Late 19C. < modern Latin *Sauropoda* 'lizard foot'.] —**sauropodous** /saw róppədəss/ *adj*

saury /sáwri/ (*plural* **-ries**) *n* a small offshore tropical or temperate marine fish resembling a needlefish but with shorter jaws and a series of finlets behind the dorsal and anal fins. Family: Scomberosocidae. [Late 18C. < modern Latin *saurus* 'lizard' < Greek *sauros*.]

sausage /sóssij/ *n* **1** seasoned pork or other meat chopped fine and stuffed into a tube of animal intestine or another tube-shaped skin **2** FOOD = **sausagemeat** [15C. Via Old French *saussiche* < medieval Latin *salsicius* 'made by salting' < Latin *salsus* (see SAUCE).] ◇ **not a sausage** nothing at all (*informal*)

sausage dog *n* ZOOL = **dachshund** (*informal*)

sausagemeat /sóssij meet/ *n* seasoned minced pork, usually mixed with fat and bread or cereal

sausage roll *n* a short length of sausagemeat wrapped in pastry and baked

sausage tree *n* a tree with clusters of scarlet flowers and long hard-shelled fruits. Native to: tropical Africa. *Kigelia pinnata*.

Saussure /sō syóor, -sóor/, **Ferdinand de** (1857–1913) Swiss linguist

sauté /sō tay/ *vt* **FRY SOMETHING LIGHTLY** to cook food quickly and lightly in a little butter, oil, or fat ■ *n* **SAUTÉED DISH** a dish consisting of food, usually meat, that has been sautéed and prepared with a sauce ■ *adj* **BEING COOKED LIGHTLY** cooked by being sautéed [Early 19C. < French, past participle of *sauter* 'leap' < Latin *salire*.]

Sauternes /sō túrn/ *n* a sweet white wine made from grapes grown in the Sauternes region of France [Early 18C. After the French region of *Sauternes*.]

sauve qui peut /sōv kee pő/ *n* a disordered or panicked escape [< French, 'save who can']

Sauvignon blanc /sō veen yon-/ *n* a variety of grape from which white wine is made [< French, 'white Sauvignon']

savage /sávvij/ *adj* **1 VIOLENT** unrestrained, violent, or vicious **2 BRUTAL** brutal and severe ○ *savage cuts in funding* **3 UNDOMESTICATED** living wild, beyond the control of people ○ *savage beasts* **4 OFFENSIVE TERM** an offensive term meaning belonging or relating to a culture perceived as inferior to your own ■ *n* **1 VICIOUS OR VIOLENT PERSON** a person who enjoys treating people and animals cruelly and violently **2 OFFENSIVE TERM** an offensive term for a member of a people considered inferior to or not as advanced as your own group ■ *vt* (**-ages, -aging, -aged**) **1 ATTACK SOMEBODY OR SOMETHING VIOLENTLY** to attack somebody or something violently, viciously, and without restraint **2 CRITICIZE SOMEBODY OR SOMETHING CRUELLY** to criticize somebody or something cruelly and unrestrainedly ○ *The same critics who praised her first book savaged her second.* [13C. Via French *sauvage* < Latin *silvaticus* 'wild' < *silva* 'forest'.] —**savagely** *adv* —**savageness** *n*

USAGE The use of ***savage*** to refer to peoples not using complex modern technologies and with an unfamiliar culture was a feature of 19th-century and earlier English (*Vouchsafe to show the sunshine of your face, that we, like savages, may worship it*, Shakespeare, *Love's Labour's Lost* Act 5, scene 2) but is regarded as inappropriate and offensive in current use.

Savage /sávvij/, **Michael Joseph** (1872–1940) Australian-born New Zealand statesman

savagery /sávvijəri/ *n* **1** barbarity or violent cruelty **2** an offensive term for a culture perceived to be inferior to or less advanced than your own

savanna /sə vánnə/, **savannah** *n* a flat grassland, sometimes with scattered trees, in a tropical or subtropical region [Mid-16C. Via Spanish *zavana* < Taino.]

Savannah /sə vánnə/ **1** river rising in NW South Carolina and flowing along the South Carolina-Georgia border into the Atlantic Ocean. Length: 505 km/314 mi. **2** city in SE Georgia, United States, at the mouth of the Savannah River. Population: 140,597 (1994).

savant /sávvənt/ *n* a wise or scholarly person [Early 18C. < French, present participle of *savoir* 'know' < Latin *sapere* 'be wise'.]

savate /sə vát/ *n* a form of boxing in which kicking as well as hitting is allowed [Mid-19C. < French, originally a kind of shoe.]

ϟ **save**[1] /sayv/ *v* (**saves, saving, saved**) **1** *vt* **RESCUE** to rescue somebody or something from harm or danger ○ *The entire crew were saved.* **2** *vti* **ACCUMULATE MONEY** to set aside money for later use, often adding to the sum periodically ○ *She's saving for a new computer.* **3** *vt* **CONSERVE** to avoid wasting something or using it unnecessarily ○ *take a short-cut to save time* **4** *vt* **KEEP SOMETHING BACK FOR LATER** to set something aside, keep something back, or protect something so that it can be used later ○ *Save some of the pie for tomorrow.* **5** *vti* **REDUCE EXPENSE** to reduce or limit the expense of something ○ *Extra insulation helps us to save on fuel.* **6** *vt* **COLLECT ITEMS FOR LATER** to collect as many items of a particular kind as possible, usually in order to do something with them later ○ *She saves old jam jars for when she makes marmalade.* **7** *vt* **SPARE SOMEBODY FROM** to make it possible for somebody to be spared from a situation or activity ○ *It will save me from having to decide.* **8** *vt* **PRESERVE** to treat something carefully or stop using it in order to keep it from being used up or worn out ○ *Switch the radio off to save the batteries.* **9** *vt* **PREVENT GOAL** to prevent an opponent from scoring a goal **10** *vti* **COPY DATA FOR STORAGE** to store a copy of a data file on a storage medium such as a hard drive or disk **11** *vt* **REDEEM** to free somebody from the consequences of sin ■ *n* **BLOCK** an action that keeps an opponent from scoring [13C. < Old French *salver* < late Latin *salvare* < Latin *salvus* 'safe'.]

save[2] /sayv/ *prep, conj* except ○ *Everyone agreed save one.*

save-all *n* **1** a receptacle for catching waste products so that they can be reused **2** something that prevents waste or loss

save as you earn *n* a savings plan in the United Kingdom in which monthly deposits are made over a five-year period

saveloy /sávvə loy/ *n* a spicy smoked pork sausage [Mid-19C. < French *cervelas* < Italian *cervellata* 'sausage'.]

saver /sáyvər/ *n* **1 SOMEBODY WHO SAVES MONEY** a person who saves money, especially in a bank or building society account ○ *The fall in interest rates is not such good news for savers.* **2 SOMETHING THAT CONSERVES RESOURCES** something that avoids wasting resources or using them unnecessarily (*in combinations*) ○ *E-mail is a great time-saver.* **3 CHEAP TRAVEL TICKET** an airline, coach, or train ticket that is cheaper than the normal price and usually places a number of restrictions on the date and time of travel ○ *A weekend saver to Leeds, please.*

Savernake Forest /sávvər nayk-/ ancient beech forest in SW England, formerly a royal hunting ground. Area: 18 sq. km/7 sq. mi.

Savery /sáyvəri/, **Thomas** (1650?–1715) English engineer and inventor

Save the Children Fund *n* an organization that provides international aid directed towards children's well-being

Savimbi /sa vímbi/, **Jonas** (*b.* 1934) Angolan soldier and revolutionary

savin /sávvin/, **savine** *n* an evergreen shrub that yields an oil formerly used medicinally and in perfumes. Native to: Europe, N Asia, North America. *Juniperus sabina*. [Pre-12C. Via Old French *savine* < Latin *herba Sabina* 'Sabine plant'.]

saving /sáyving/ *n* **1 SOMETHING KEPT FROM BEING WASTED** an amount of time or money that is reduced or not spent or used **2 RESCUE FROM DANGER** rescue of somebody or something from harm or danger **3 LEGAL EXCEPTION** an exception or reservation in law ■ **savings** *npl* **MONEY SET ASIDE** money set aside for future use ■ *prep, conj* **EXCEPT** except (*literary*)

USAGE ***Saving*** or ***savings***? ***Savings*** is 'money saved', as in *Strong savings are essential to a secure retirement.* In this sense it takes a plural verb. In US English, ***savings*** is commonly used with a singular verb to mean 'a specific amount of money not spent', as in *A savings of $3,000 was gained during the transaction.* This usage undoubtedly has its origins in the well-established expressions *a savings and loan association, a savings bank*, and *a savings account.*

saving grace *n* a quality or feature that redeems a person or situation

savings account /sáyvingz-/ *n* a bank or building society account that earns interest on money saved

savings and loan association *n US* a financial institution that issues shares to members who deposit savings and invests the money mainly in home mortgage loans

savings bank *n* a bank that invests the savings of individual depositors and pays interest on the deposits

savings bond *n* **1** a registered bond issued by the US government in denominations of $50 to $10,000 **2** *Can* a bond issued by the Canadian government in denominations of $100 to $100,000

savings method *n US* a method of testing memory by assessing how much faster somebody can learn information already previously learned, seen, or read

savings ratio *n* the ratio of national disposable income to consumer spending, used as a measure of national saving

savior *n* US = **saviour**

Savior *n* US = **Saviour**

saviour /sáyvyər/ *n* a rescuer of somebody or something from harm or danger [13C. Via Old French *sauveour* < late Latin *salvare* (see SAVE[1]).]

Saviour /sáyvyər/ *n* a name used by Christians for Jesus Christ

savoir-faire /sáv waar fáir/ *n* the ability to act appropriately and adroitly in any situation [Early 19C. < French, 'know how to do'.]

savoir-vivre /-veévrə/ *n* a combination of worldly wisdom, self-confidence, and refinement in a person [Mid-18C. < French, 'know how to live'.]

savor *n, vti* US = **savour**

savory[1] *adj, n* (*plural* **-ies**) US = **savoury**

savory[2] /sáyvəri/ *n* a herb with aromatic leaves. Use: flavouring food. *Satureja hortensis*. [14C. < Old French *sarree* < Latin *satureia*.]

savour /sáyvər/ *v* **1** *vt* **ENJOY SOMETHING UNHURRIEDLY** to enjoy something with unhurried appreciation ○ *savour the moment* **2** *vi* **SHOW TRACES** to show traces of something ○ *something in his manner that savoured of deceit* **3** *vt* **RELISH** to enjoy the taste or smell of something ■ *n* **1 ENJOYMENT** enjoyment and relish **2 TASTE OR SMELL SOMETHING HAS** the way that something tastes or smells **3 DISTINCTIVE QUALITY** a quality that identifies or distinguishes something [12C. Via Old French < Latin *sapor* 'taste' < *sapere* 'have a taste'.] —**savourless** *adj* —**savorous** *adj*

savoury /sáyvəri/ *adj* **1 NOT SWEET** salty or sharp-tasting rather than sweet **2 APPETIZING** having an appetizing taste or smell **3 RESPECTABLE** respectable or morally acceptable ○ *not a very savoury character* ■ *n* (*plural* **savouries**) **DISH THAT ADDS RELISH** a light salty or spicy dish served before or at the end of a meal [13C. < Old French *savoure*, past participle of *savourer* 'taste' < Latin *sapor* (see SAVOUR).] —**savourily** /sáyvərili/ *adv* —**savouriness** *n*

savoy /sə vóy/, **savoy cabbage** *n* a winter cabbage with crinkled leaves [16C. After the *Savoy* region of SE France.]

Savoyard /sə vóy aard, sávvoy àard/ *n* **1** a person who comes from the French region of Savoy **2** a performer, producer, or admirer of the operettas of W. S. Gilbert and Arthur Sullivan. [Early 17C. < French, < *Savoie* 'Savoy'; in sense 2, < the Savoy Theatre in London.]

Savoy opera *n* an operetta by Gilbert and Sullivan or a work composed in the same style

savvy /sávvi/ *n* **SHREWDNESS** shrewdness and practical knowledge (*informal*) ■ *adj* **SHREWD** shrewd and well informed (*informal*) ■ *vti* (**-vies, -vying, -vied**) **COMPREHEND** to understand something, especially what somebody has said (*informal*) [Late 18C. < Spanish *sabe (usted)?* 'you know?'.]

saw[1] /saw/ *n* **TOOL FOR CUTTING WOOD** a hand-operated or power-driven tool with a toothed metal blade, used to cut wood or other hard materials ■ *v* (**saws, sawing, sawed, sawed** *or* **sawn** /sawn/) **1** *vti* **CUT SOMETHING USING SAW** to cut something using a saw **2** *vt* **MOVE FORWARD AND BACK** to make back-and-forth motions, as if using a handsaw [Old English *saga*. Ultimately < Indo-European.]

SPELLCHECK Do not confuse ***saw*** with ***soar*** or ***sore***, which may sound similar. Beware: your spellchecker will not catch this error.

saw[2] /saw/ *n* an old saying, especially a cliché [Old English *sagu*. Ultimately < Germanic.]

saw[3] /saw/ past tense of **see**[1]

SAW *abbr* surface acoustic wave

sawbones /sáw bōnz/ (*plural* **-bones** *or* **-boneses**) *n* a surgeon or physician (*slang*) [Mid-19C. < early surgeons' role as amputators.]

sawbuck /sáw buk/ *n US* **1** BUILDING = **sawhorse** **2** a ten-dollar bill (*slang*) [Mid-19C. < Dutch *zaagbok*; in sense 2, < the resemblance between the X-shaped end of a sawhorse and the Roman numeral for 'ten'.]

saw doctor *n* **1** a machine that gives a saw a serrated edge **2** *NZ* somebody employed to sharpen the blades in a sawmill

sawdust /sáw dust/ *n* tiny particles of wood produced when wood is sawn

sawed-off *adj* US = **sawn-off**

sawfish /sáw fish/ (*plural* **-fish** *or* **-fishes**) *n* a tropical ray having a long snout with projections resembling teeth that it uses as a weapon. Family: Pristidae.

sawfly /sáw flī/ (*plural* **-flies**) *n* an insect in which the female has a prominent, often serrated appendage at the tip of its abdomen, for boring holes and laying eggs in wood and plants. Family: Tenthredinidae.

saw grass *n* any of various sedges that have serrated leaves. Genus: *Cladium*.

sawhorse /sáw hawrss/ *n* a support for wood during sawing

saw log *n* **1 LOG BIG ENOUGH TO SAW** a log of sufficient size to be suitable for sawing **2 TREE TRUNK USED FOR TIMBER** a trunk of a tree that has been felled and can be cut up into timber **3** *US* **HARVESTABLE LOG** a log that meets the minimum commercial requirements of diameter, length, and quality for harvesting

Saw Maung /sow maa óong/ (*b.* 1928) Myanmar general

sawmill /sáw mil/ *n* **1** a factory in which wood is sawn into planks or boards by machine **2** a powerful sawing machine

sawn past participle of **saw**[1]

sawn-off *adj* **1** describes a firearm that has the barrel cut short so that it is less cumbersome or obtrusive and its field of fire is increased ○ *a sawn-off shotgun* **2** an offensive term meaning of small stature (*slang*)

saw palmetto *n* a palm tree with spiny-toothed leafstalks. Native to: SE United States. *Serenoa repens*.

saw-scaled viper *n* a small venomous snake that lives in dry areas and is believed to have the most powerful venom of all the vipers. Native to: North Africa, Central Asia. *Echis carinaus*.

saw set *n* an instrument that bends alternating teeth of a saw in opposite directions

Sawtell /saw tél/ coastal town in NE New South Wales, Australia. Population: 10,810 (1991).

sawtooth /sáw tooth/ *n* (*plural* **-teeth** /-teeth/) any one of the teeth of a saw ■ *adj* **sawtooth, sawtoothed** in a zigzag shape, like the teeth of a saw

saw-toothed *adj* **1** having notched teeth like a saw **2** = **sawtooth** *adj*.

saw-whet owl *n* a small owl with a call that is a long series of short whistles. Native to: North America. *Aegolius acadicus*. [*Saw-whet* because its call was considered to resemble the sound of a saw being sharpened]

saw-wort *n* a plant of the daisy family with serrated leaves that yield a yellow dye. Native to: Europe. *Serratula tinctoria*.

sawyer /sáw yər/ *n* **1 SOMEBODY WHO SAWS WOOD** a person who saws wood for a living **2 HORNED BEETLE** a horned beetle whose larvae bore into coniferous trees. Genus: *Monochamus*. **3** *NZ* **HORNED GRASSHOPPER** a wingless horned grasshopper whose larvae bore into trees [13C. < SAW + *-yer*, variant of -IER.]

sax /saks/ *n* a saxophone (*informal*) [Early 20C. Shortening.]

saxatile /sáksə tīl/ *adj* growing on or living in rocks [Mid-17C. < Latin *saxatilis* < *saxum* 'rock'.]

saxe blue /sáks-/ *adj* of a light greyish-blue colour [*Saxe* via French < German *Sachsen* 'Saxony'] —**saxe blue** *n*

saxhorn /sáks hawrn/ *n* a valved brass wind instrument, often used in military brass bands [Mid-19C. After Charles Joseph *Sax* (1791–1865) and his son Antoine Joseph *Sax* (1814–94) (known as 'Adolphe'), Belgian instrument makers.]

saxicolous /sak síkələss/, **saxicoline** /-līn/ *adj* BIOL = **saxatile** [Mid-19C. < modern Latin *saxicola* < Latin *saxum* 'rock' + *colere* 'inhabit'.]

saxifrage /sáksi frayj/ (*plural* **-frages** *or* **-frage**) *n* a plant growing on rocky ground. Flowers: small, white, yellow, purple, or red. Genus: *Saxifraga*. [14C. Via French < Latin *saxifraga* 'rock-breaking' < *saxum* 'rock, stone'.]

Saxon /sáks'n/ *n* **1 MEMBER OF ANCIENT GERMANIC PEOPLE** a member of a West Germanic people who started to spread west during Roman times, establishing kingdoms in S Britain in the 7th century AD **2 LANGUAGE OF ANCIENT SAXONS** the group of West Germanic dialects spoken by the ancient Saxons **3 SOMEBODY FROM SAXONY** a person who comes from Saxony [12C. Via French < Latin *Saxones* 'Saxons' < Germanic.] —**Saxon** *adj*

Saxon blue *n* a dye made from a solution of indigo in sulphuric acid

Saxonism /sáks'nizəm/ *n* a word, phrase, or idiom in English supposedly from an Anglo-Saxon rather than Latin source

saxony /sáksəni/ *n* **1** a fine three-ply knitting yarn **2** a fine woollen fabric. Use: coats. [Mid-19C. Originally 'fine wool', after SAXONY.]

Saxony /sáksəni/ state in east-central Germany. Capital: Dresden. Population: 5,000,000 (1990). Area: 18,337 sq. km/7,078 sq. mi.

saxophone /sáksə fōn/ *n* a metal wind instrument with keys and a reed that comes in several sizes and registers, the alto and tenor saxophones being the most popular [Mid-19C. After Antoine Joseph *Sax* (1814–94) (known as 'Adolphe'), Belgian instrument maker.] —**saxophonic** /-fónnik/ *adj* —**saxophonist** /sak sóffənist/ *n*

saxtuba /sáks tyoobə/ *n* a large bass saxhorn [Mid-19C. Blend of SAXHORN + TUBA.]

say /say/ *v* (**says, saying, said** /sed/) **1** *vt* **UTTER** to utter something in a normal voice, not singing, shouting, or whispering **2** *vti* **EXPRESS VERBALLY** to convey information or express feelings in spoken words **3** *vt* **STATE** to utter something as a matter of fact, belief, or prediction ○ *said to be the largest in captivity* **4** *vt* **INDICATE** to convey information in written or printed words, numbers, or symbols ○ *The clock said midnight.* ○ *The rules say that you should not kick your opponent.* **5** *vt* **MAKE CASE FOR OR AGAINST** to utter something by way of argument, explanation, or excuse ○ *There's much to be said for being rich.* **6** *vt* **COMMAND** to utter something as an instruction ○ *She said to buy some wine for tonight.* **7** *vt* **SUPPOSE** to assume something for the sake of argument, or take something as a suitable example ○ *Let's say that it will cost you £500.* **8** *vt* **RECITE** to utter something that has a formula or set form of words ○ *says his prayers* **9** *vt* **CONVEY SOMETHING INDIRECTLY** to convey something over and above the immediate words or superficial sound or appearance ○ *The finale says that we can all triumph in the end.* **10** *vt* **CONVEY SOMETHING IMPORTANT** to convey something substantial or significant in what is said or written ○ *We talked for hours but didn't really say anything.* ■ *n* **1 CHANCE TO SPEAK** a chance or turn to say something, especially to give an opinion ○ *You've already had your say.* **2 RIGHT TO GIVE OPINION** the right to express an opinion and have it considered by others ○ *The junior staff appeared to have no say in the way things were done.* ■ *interj US, Can* (*informal*) **1 EXPRESSING SURPRISE** used to express surprise, admiration, or protest **2 ATTRACTING ATTENTION** used to attract somebody's attention [Old English *secgan* < Germanic] —**sayer** *n* ◇ **enough said** used to indicate that nothing more need be said for a situation to be understood ◇ **I say 1** used to express surprise, admiration, or protest (*dated*) **2** used to attract somebody's attention (*dated*) ◇ **it goes without saying** used to emphasize that there should be no doubt concerning something ◇ **say when** used to ask somebody to indicate when enough drink has been poured or food served (*informal*) ◇ **that is to say** used to indicate that you are repeating something more clearly or in other words ◇ **you can say that again** used to indicate complete agreement with what has just been said (*informal*)

SAYE *abbr* save as you earn

Sayers /sáy ərz/, **Dorothy L.** (1893–1957) British writer

sayest /sáy əst/ 2nd person present singular of **say** (*archaic*)

saying /sáy ing/ *n* a frequently offered piece of advice or information, or a frequently heard reflection on the way things are

sayonara /sī ə naárə/ *n* goodbye [Late 19C. < Japanese, 'if it be so'.]

say-so *n* (*informal*) **1** permission or authorization from somebody **2** a mere assertion by somebody that something is so

sayst 2nd person present singular of **say** (*archaic*)

sayyid /sī yid/, **said** *n* **1** a Muslim who claims to be descended from Muhammad's grandson Husain **2** an Islamic title of respect for a man [Mid-17C. < Arabic, 'prince'.]

⚡**sb** *abbr* Solomon Islands (*in Internet addresses*)

Sb *symbol* antimony [Shortening of Latin *stibium*]

SBA *n* a system of radio navigation that provides an aircraft with lateral guidance and marker beam indicators at set points during its landing approach. Full form **standard beam approach**

S-bend *n* an S-shaped bend in a road or a pipe

SBS *abbr* **1** sick building syndrome **2** Special Boat Service

SBU *abbr* strategic business unit

⚡**sc**[1] *abbr* Seychelles (*in Internet addresses*)

sc[2], **s.c.** *abbr* small capital

Sc *symbol* scandium

SC *abbr* **1** Security Council **2** Signal Corps **3** South Carolina

sc. *abbr* **1** scilicet **2** scene **3** scruple

s/c *abbr* self-contained (*in advertisements*)

scab /skab/ *n* **1 CRUST OVER HEALING WOUND** a hard crust of dried blood, serum, or pus that forms over a wound during healing **2 STRIKEBREAKER** a person who continues to work or replaces a worker during a strike (*disapproving*) **3 SKIN DISEASE OF SHEEP** a skin disease of sheep and other animals that resembles mange **4 PLANT DISEASE CAUSING CRUSTY SPOTS** a fungal plant disease causing crusty spots on the affected parts **5 CRUSTY SPOT ON A PLANT** a crusty spot on a plant caused by a fungal disease **6 DISLIKABLE PERSON** somebody regarded as despicable or dislikable (*slang insult*) ■ *vi* (**scabs, scabbing, scabbed**) **1 BECOME COVERED WITH SCAB** to become covered with a scab during healing **2 WORK DURING STRIKE** to continue to work during a strike, or do a striker's job during a strike (*disapproving*) [13C. < Old Norse *skabb* < Indo-European, 'to scrape'.]

scabbard /skábbərd/ *n* a sheath, hanging from a belt, for a sword, dagger, or bayonet ■ *vt* to put a sword, dagger, or bayonet into a sheath [13C. < Anglo-Norman *escauberge* < ?]

scabbard fish *n* a marine fish with an elongated body and long sharp teeth. Family: Trichiuridae.

scabble /skább'l/ (**-bles, -bling, -bled**) *vt* to give a rough shape to stone [Early 17C. Alteration of Middle English *scapple* < Old French *escapeler* 'shape timber', < *capler* 'cut'.]

scabby /skábbi/ (**-bier, -biest**) *adj* **1** having or covered in scabs **2** despicable or dislikable (*slang*) —**scabbily** *adv* —**scabbiness** *n*

scabies /skáy beez/ *n* a contagious skin disease marked by intense itching, inflammation, and red papules [14C. < Latin, < *scabere* 'scratch'.] —**scabietic** /skáybi éttik/ *adj*

scabious /skáybi əss/ *n* (*plural* **-ouses** *or* **-ous**) a plant with blue, pink, or white dome-shaped flowers. Genera: *Scabiosa* and *Knautia*. ■ *adj* having scabs or scabies [14C. Directly and via French *scabieux* < Latin *scabiosus* < *scabies* (see SCABIES).]

scablands /skábblәndz/ *npl* tracts of elevated land with bare rock, thin soil, and sparse vegetation, crossed by dry channels formed by glacial floodwaters

scabrous /skáybrəss, skább-/ *adj* **1 WITH A ROUGH SURFACE** having a rough surface because of scales or short stiff hairs **2 REQUIRING TACT** having to be handled with tact and care **3 OBSCENE** dealing with sex or referring to sex in an obscene way (*literary*) [Late 16C. < late Latin *scabrosus* < Latin *scaber* 'scurfy, scaly'.] —**scabrously** *adv* —**scabrousness** *n*

scad /skad/ (*plural* **scad** *or* **scads**) *n* **1** a fish with a long body and sharp bony plates on either side of the narrow point of the tail. Native to: tropical and subtropical seas. Family: Caringidae. **2** FISH = **horse mackerel** [Early 17C. < ?]

scads /skadz/ *npl* large numbers or quantities (*informal*) ○ *scads of money* [Mid-19C. < ?]

Scafell Pike /skáw fel-/ highest mountain in the Lake District, NW England. Height: 978 m/3,209 ft.

scaffold /skáffōld, -f'ld/ *n* **1 FRAMEWORK TO SUPPORT WORKERS** a temporary framework of poles and planks that is used to support workers and materials during the erection, repair, or decoration of a building **2 PLATFORM FOR EXECUTIONS** a raised platform on which somebody is executed by hanging or beheading **3 DEATH BY HANGING** death by hanging or beheading as a form of punishment **4 SUPPORT** any supporting framework ■ *vt* **ERECT SCAFFOLD AROUND BUILDING** to put up a scaffold around or against a building [13C. Via Old French *(e)schaffaut* < Vulgar Latin *catafalcum*.] —**scaffolder** *n*

scaffolding /skáffōlding, -f'lding/ *n* **1** a scaffold or a system of scaffolds **2** the poles and planks used to build a scaffold

scag /skag/, **skag** *n* = **heroin** (*slang*) [Early 20C. < ?]

scagliola /skal yṓlə/ *n* imitation marble made of gypsum mixed with glue, with a polished surface of marble or granite dust [Late 16C. < Italian, 'tiny scale, chip of marble' < Germanic.]

⚡**scalable** /skáyləb'l/ *adj* **1 CLIMBABLE** able to be climbed up or over **2 VARIABLE** describes computer graphics fonts generated by an algorithm that permits the size to vary proportionately over a wide range **3 EXPANDABLE** describes a computer, component, or network that can be expanded to meet future needs —**scalability** /skáylə bílləti/ *n* —**scalableness** *n* —**scalably** *adv*

⚡**scalable font** *n* a computer font in which vector graphics are used to make characters available to display or print in any size

scalage /skáylij/ *n US* **1** an allowance in the form of a percentage deducted from the cost of goods to reflect loss in amount or size during storage or shipping **2** the estimated yield of lumber from a log

scalar /skáylər/ *n* a quantity, e.g. mass or time, that has magnitude but no direction ■ *adj* describes a quantity that has magnitude but no direction [Mid-17C. < Latin *scalaris* < *scala* (see SCALE²).]

scalariform /skə láari fawrm/ *adj* describes the walls of a cell that have parallel structural formations resembling the rungs of a ladder [Mid-19C. < Latin *scalaris* 'of a ladder' < *scala* (see SCALE²).]

scalar product *n* a number (**scalar**) equal to the product of the magnitudes of any two vectors and the cosine of the angle formed between them

scalawag *n* = **scallywag**

scald /skawld/ *v* **1** *vt* **BURN SOMEBODY WITH HOT LIQUID** to burn somebody or a part of the body with hot liquid or steam **2** *vt* **STERILIZE SOMETHING WITH BOILING LIQUID** to subject something to the action of boiling liquid or steam in order to clean or sterilize it **3** *vt* **HEAT LIQUID TO NEAR BOILING POINT** to heat a liquid to just below the boiling point **4** *vt* **TREAT FRUIT WITH BOILING WATER** to plunge a fruit or vegetable into boiling water or pour boiling water over it and leave it briefly before draining to prevent cooking **5 BREW TEA** to pour boiling water on tea and leave it to brew (*informal*) ■ *n* **1 BURN CAUSED BY LIQUID** a burn caused by hot liquid or steam **2 PLANT DISEASE** a plant disease or condition that produces brownish discoloration of leaves and fruit [12C. Via Anglo-Norman *escalder* < late Latin *excaldere* 'bathe in hot water' < Latin *calidus* 'hot'.]

scalding /skáwlding/ *adj* **1** extremely hot, especially hot enough to scald somebody **2** severely critical

scale¹ /skayl/ *n* **1 BONY PLATE ON FISH** any of the small flat bony or horny overlapping plates that cover the bodies of fish and some reptiles and mammals **2 FLAKE** a thin flat piece or flake of something such as dead skin **3 COVERING OF BUTTERFLY WING** any of the small overlapping structures that cover the wings of butterflies and moths **4 BLACK OXIDE ON HEATED IRON** a flaky oxide that forms on the surface of some metals undergoing heat treatment, especially the black oxide that forms on iron or steel at high temperatures **5 DEPOSIT INSIDE KETTLE OR BOILER** a white deposit sometimes formed on the inside of a kettle or boiler by the action of heat on the water **6** DENT = **tartar** *n.* 1 **7** PLANT SCI = **scale leaf 8** INSECTS = **scale insect 9 PLANT DISEASE** the diseased condition of plants caused by scale insects ■ *v* (**scales, scaling, scaled**) **1** *vt* **CLEAN SCALES OR SCALE FROM** to remove the scales or scale from something **2** *vi* **FLAKE OFF** to come off in scales **3** *vi* **SHED SCALES** to shed scales **4** *vi Aus* **DODGE FARE** to travel by public transport without paying (*informal*) [13C. < Old French *escale* < Germanic, 'husk'.] —**scaleless** *adj*

scale² /skayl/ *n* **1 MEASURING SYSTEM** a system of measurement based on a series of marks laid down at regular intervals and representing numerical values **2 CLASSIFICATION SYSTEM** a system of classification based on differing quantity or value, e.g. one used in paying employees **3 LEVEL** the extent or relative size of something **4 SIZE RATIO** a ratio representing the size of an illustration or reproduction, especially a map or a model, in relation to the object it represents ○ *The scale of the map is 1:50,000.* **5 MEASURING INSTRUMENT** an instrument or apparatus with graduated markings for measuring something **6 SERIES OF MUSICAL NOTES** a series of musical notes, usually sequential, arranged in ascending or descending order of pitch ■ *v* (**scales, scaling, scaled**) **1** *vt* **CLIMB** to climb up something, especially a steep incline, often using a ladder **2** *vt* **MAKE SOMETHING TO SCALE** to make a model or draw a map in a regular proportion to the size of the original **3** *vi* **RISE IN STAGES** to go upward in stages or steps [14C. < Latin *scala* 'staircase, ladder'.] ◇ **to scale** with the same proportion of reduction or enlargement throughout, e.g. in a map or model

scale down *vt* to reduce something in size, amount, or extent

scale up *vt* to increase something in size, amount, or extent

scale³ /skayl/ *n* **1 WEIGHING MACHINE** a device on which something or somebody can be weighed (*often used in the plural*) **2 PAN OF BALANCE** either of the dishes or pans of a balance ■ *vt* (**scales, scaling, scaled**) **1 WEIGH SOMETHING OR** to weigh something or somebody with a scale **2 WEIGH SO MUCH** to have a particular weight when put on a scale [12C. < Old Norse *skál* 'bowl, scales' < Germanic, 'shell'.] ◇ **tip the scales at something** to weigh a particular amount

scaleboard /skáyl bawrd/ *n* **1** very thin board used to back a picture or mirror **2** a thin strip of wood used to justify hand-set type

scale insect, scale *n* any plant-sucking insect that covers itself with a waxy secretion resembling scales. Superfamily: Coccoidea.

scale leaf, scale *n* a leaf that protects a plant bud before the bud expands

scale moss *n* a liverwort with leaves resembling scales. Order: Jungermanniales.

scalene /skáyl een/ *adj* describes a triangle in which each side is a different length [Mid-17C. < Latin *scalenus* < Greek *skalenos* 'unequal'.]

scaler /skáylər/ *n* an electronic circuit that produces an output pulse for every specified number of input pulses received

Scales /skaylz/ *npl* ZODIAC = **Libra** *n.* 2

scaling /skáyling/ *n* in social research, the creation of a measurement system for such qualities as attitudes and strength of feeling, where there is no existing scale

scaling ladder *n* a ladder used to climb high walls, especially those of a besieged fortress

scallion /skálli ən/ *n* any onion with a small bulb and long green leaves, e.g. spring onions and shallots [13C. < Anglo-Norman *scal(o)un* < Old French *escalo(i)gne* < Latin *Ascalonia (caepa)* '(onion) of Ascalon' < *Ascalon*, port in ancient Palestine.]

scallop /skólləp, skáll-/, **scollop** *n* **1 MARINE MOLLUSC** a marine bivalve mollusc that has a fan-shaped shell with radial ribs and wavy edges. Family: Pectinidae. **2 SCALLOP AS FOOD** the round white edible muscle of a scallop, often with bright red roe around one side **3** MARINE BIOL = **scallop shell** *n.* **4 DISH SHAPED LIKE SCALLOP SHELL** a dish shaped like a scallop shell, used for cooking and serving food in **5 PILGRIM'S BADGE** a representation of a scallop shell worn as a badge by pilgrims in the Middle Ages **6 FABRIC EDGING** an ornamental undulating edging in fabric **7** *US* FOOD = **escalope 8** *Aus* **FRIED POTATO CAKE** a slice of potato deep-fried in batter ■ *v* **1** *vt* **MAKE EDGE WAVY** to decorate the edge of a fabric or object with an undulating pattern **2** *vt* **COOK FOOD IN SCALLOP SHELL** to cook food in a scallop shell or in a dish shaped like a scallop shell **3** *vi* **COLLECT SCALLOPS** to gather or dredge for scallops [14C. < Old French *escalope* < ?] —**scalloped** *adj* —**scalloper** *n* —**scalloping** *n*

scallop shell *n* either of the fan-shaped shell valves of the scallop, with radial ribs and a wavy edge

scally /skálli/ (*plural* **-lies**) *n N England* a mischievous or naughty person (*informal*) [Late 20C. Shortening of SCALLYWAG.]

scallywag /skálli wag/, **scalawag** /skállə wag/ *n* **1** a rascal or scamp (*dated informal*) **2** in the United States, a white person in the South who worked with the federal government during the Reconstruction period after the Civil War [Mid-19C]

scalogram /skáylə gram/ *n* a test of attitudes or opinions in which the questions are ranked so that the answer to one implies the same answer to all questions lower on the scale [Mid-20C. < SCALE², probably after CARDIOGRAM.]

scalp /skalp/ *n* **1 SKIN ON TOP OF HEAD** the skin and underlying tissues covering the dome of the skull **2 SCALP CUT OFF AS TROPHY** the scalp of an enemy cut off as a trophy **3 TROPHY** a trophy or achievement belonging to somebody that somebody else wants to win or take away ■ *vt* **1 CUT OFF SOMEBODY'S SCALP** to cut off the scalp of an enemy as a trophy **2** *US* **RESELL SOMETHING FOR QUICK PROFIT** to resell something quickly or at an inflated price in order to make a quick profit [14C. Probably < Scandinavian.] —**scalper** *n*

scalpel /skálp'l/ *n* a surgical knife with a short, very sharp blade [Mid-18C. Directly or via French < Latin *scalpellum* 'small cutting tool'.]

scalp lock *n* a tuft or plait of hair left on the otherwise shaven scalp by the men among some Native North American peoples

scaly /skáyli/ (**-ier, -iest**) *adj* covered in scales or flakes —**scaliness** *n*

scaly anteater *n* = **pangolin**

scam /skam/ *n* a scheme for making money by dishonest means (*slang*) ■ *vt* (**scams, scamming, scammed**) to obtain money from somebody by dishonest means (*slang*) [Mid-20C. < ?] —**scammer** *n*

scammony /skámməni/ (*plural* **-nies** *or* **-ny**) *n* **1** a twining plant with arrow-shaped leaves. Flowers: white, pink, or purple, funnel-shaped. Native to: Asia. *Convulvulus scammonia.* **2** a resin obtained from the roots of the scammony or similar plants. Use: purgative. [Pre-12C. Via Old French *escamonie* and Latin *scammonia* < Greek *skammōnia.*]

scamp¹ /skamp/ *n* **1** a mischievous person, especially a child who misbehaves in harmless or humorous ways (*informal*) **2** a rascally or dishonest person (*dated informal*) [Mid-18C. Possibly < Middle Dutch *schampen* (see SCAMPER).] —**scampish** *adj*

scamp² /skamp/ *vt* to do something hastily, carelessly, or in a perfunctory manner [Mid-19C. < ?]

scamper /skámpər/ *vi* to run quickly or playfully ■ *n* a quick or playful run [Late 17C. Probably < Middle Dutch *schampen* 'slip away, decamp' < Old French *esc(h)amper* < Latin *campus* 'field'.] —**scamperer** *n*

scampi /skámpi/ *npl* pieces of tail meat from Dublin Bay prawns, usually fried in batter or breadcrumbs (+ *singular or plural verb*) [Mid-20C. < Italian, plural of *scampo*, a kind of lobster < Greek *kampē* 'bending'; from its shape.]

⚡**scan** /skan/ *v* (**scans, scanning, scanned**) **1** *vt* **EXAMINE SOMETHING IN DETAIL** to subject something to a thorough examination **2** *vt* **LOOK THROUGH SOMETHING QUICKLY** to look through or read something quickly **3** *vt* **LOOK AT SOMETHING INTENTLY** to look over and around something intently **4** *vi* **CONFORM TO VERSE RULES** to conform to the rules of metre **5** *vt* **ANALYSE VERSE** to analyse verse according to the rules of metre **6** *vt* **EXAMINE SOMETHING WITH BEAM OF LIGHT** to direct a light-sensitive device over a surface in order to convert an image into digital or electronic form for further storage, retrieval, and transmission **7** *vt* **EXAMINE STORED DATA** to make an automatic search of a computer storage medium such as a magnetic disk or tape for data in anticipation of retrieving that data **8** *vt* **OBTAIN IMAGE OF BODY** to obtain an image of internal organs with any of various devices, especially in order to make a diagnosis without the need for exploratory surgery. ◊ **CT scan, MRI 9** *vti* **SEARCH AREA USING RADAR** to search a region for specific objects, such as aircraft, by systematically sweeping a radar or sonar beam across it ■ *n* **1 BRIEF PERUSAL** a quick look at or through something **2 IMAGE OF BODY** an image of an internal body part taken using a scanner, or the process involved in obtaining one [14C. < late Latin *scandere* 'scan a verse' < Latin, 'climb'.] —**scannable** *adj*

scandal /skánd'l/ *n* **1 SOMETHING CAUSING PUBLIC OUTRAGE** a situation or event that causes public outrage or censure **2 PUBLIC OUTRAGE** an outburst of public outrage or censure as a consequence of some event **3 MALICIOUS TALK** malicious talk, especially about other people's private lives [12C. Via French *scandale* < Latin *scandalum* 'trap, temptation' < Greek *skandalon.*]

LITERARY LINK ***School for Scandal***, a play (1777) by Irish dramatist Richard Brinsley Sheridan. In this satire on contemporary middle-class mores, Sir Oliver Surface attempts to spy on his nephews Charles and Joseph in order to discover their true characters. Among the play's many targets are the hypocrisy and vindictiveness of gossipmongers, personified by the characters of Lady Sneerwell, Sir Benjamin Backbite, and Mrs Candour.

scandalize /skándə līz/ (**-izes, -izing, -ized**), **scandalise** (**-ises, -ising, -ised**) *vt* to shock people by outrageous or improper behaviour —**scandalization** /skándə lī záysh'n/ *n* —**scandalizer** /-līzər/ *n*

scandalmonger /skánd'l mung gər/ *n* a spreader of malicious talk about other people's private lives —**scandalmongering** *n*

scandalous /skándələss/ *adj* **1** causing or deserving to cause public outrage or censure **2** causing or having the potential to cause damage to somebody's reputation —**scandalously** *adv* —**scandalousness** *n*

scandal sheet *n* a periodical publication that features scandalous stories about people's private lives (*disapproving*)

scandent /skándənt/ *adj* describes a plant that climbs as it grows [Late 17C. < Latin *scandent-*, present participle of *scandere* 'climb'.]

scandic /skándik/ *adj* relating to or containing the element scandium

Scandinavia /skán di náyvi ə/ region in N Europe comprising Norway, Sweden, Denmark, Finland, Iceland, and the Faroe Islands —**Scandinavian** *n, adj*

scandium /skándi əm/ *n* (*symbol* **Sc**) a rare silvery-white metallic element. Source: wolframite. Use: tracer. [Late 19C. < Latin *Scandia*, shortening of SCANDINAVIA, because it is found in various minerals there.]

scanner /skánnər/ *n* **1 BODY-SCANNING DEVICE** a device used to obtain information about the internal parts of the body without the need for surgery, or the contents of something without the need for opening it. ◊ **CT scanner 2 DATA-SCANNING DEVICE** a device for examining written or recorded data, e.g. for reading a product bar code for inventory and pricing purposes **3 DEVICE PUTTING SOMETHING INTO DIGITAL FORM** an input device used to convert an image or text into digital form for storage or display **4 RADAR SEARCHING DEVICE** a rotating directional radar antenna that emits a beam to search for or locate objects **5 SOMEBODY WHO SCANS TEXTS** a person who scans texts, e.g. for errors or in poetic analysis

scanning electron microscope *n* a microscope that uses a beam of electrons to scan an object and produce an enlarged image of it on a cathode-ray tube —**scanning electron microscopy** *n*

scansion /skánsh'n/ *n* **1** analysis of verse according to the rules of metre **2** the way that a line, verse, or poem scans [Late 17C. < late Latin *scansion-* < Latin *scansio* 'climbing' < *scandere* 'climb'.]

scant /skant/ *adj* **1** not sufficient **2** only just at or just below the amount stated ○ *a scant twenty votes* [14C. < Old Norse *skamt*, neuter form of *skammr* 'short'.] —**scantly** *adv* —**scantness** *n*

scantling /skántling/ *n* **1 THIN PIECE OF TIMBER** a piece of timber with a small cross-section, e.g. a rafter **2 SIZE** the dimension of a building material or a structural part of a ship **3 SMALL AMOUNT** a small amount or quantity [Early 16C. Alteration of obsolete *scantillon* 'gauge' < late Latin *scandaculum* 'ladder' < Latin *scandere* 'climb'.]

scanty /skánti/ (**-ier, -iest**) *adj* **1 INADEQUATE** not much and less than is needed **2 MEAGRE** only just enough **3 REVEALING** not covering much of the part of the body that it is worn on —**scantily** *adv* —**scantiness** *n*

Scapa Flow /skaápə-/ anchorage in the Orkney Islands, off N Scotland. It was used as a base for Britain's Home Fleet during both world wars. Area: 310 sq. km/120 sq. mi.

scape[1] /skayp/ *n* **1 LEAFLESS FLOWER STALK** a leafless flower stalk rising directly from the root **2 PART OF FEATHER OR ANTENNA** a shaft of a feather or other animal part, or a segment of an antenna **3 ARCHITECTURAL COLUMN** the shaft of an architectural column [Early 17C. < Latin *scapus* < Greek *skapos* 'rod'.] —**scapose** /skáppōss/ *adj*

scape[2] /skayp/ (**scapes, scaping, scaped**) *vti* to escape (*archaic*) [13C. Shortening of ESCAPE.]

-scape *suffix* a scene or view ○ *seascape* ○ *lunarscape* [< LANDSCAPE]

scapegoat /skáyp gōt/ *n* **1 SOMEBODY MADE TO TAKE BLAME** a person who is made to take the blame for others **2 SOMEBODY WRONGLY BLAMED** a person who is unjustly blamed for another's misdeeds **3 GOAT GIVEN SINS IN JEWISH RITUAL** on the Jewish Day of Atonement, a goat on which the high priest symbolically loaded all the sins of the community before sending the animal out into the wilderness ■ *v* **1** *vt* **MAKE SOMEBODY TAKE BLAME** to force somebody to take the blame for others **2 BLAME SOMEBODY TO AVOID TAKING RESPONSIBILITY** to blame another person unjustly for causing upset or distress as a way of avoiding taking personal responsibility [Mid-16C. *Scape* < SCAPE[2], because in Jewish ritual the goat, having had the sins of the people symbolically laid on it, was allowed to 'escape' into the desert.]

scapegrace /skáyp grayss/ *n* a lazy, mischievous, or irresponsible person, especially a child (*archaic*) [Early 19C. < SCAPE[2] + GRACE.]

scaphoid /skáffoyd/ *adj* navicular [Mid-18C. < modern Latin *scaphoides* < Greek *skaphoeidēs* < *skaphē* 'boat'.]

scapolite /skáppō līt/ *n* a variously coloured aluminosilicate mineral. Source: metamorphic rocks, weathered basic igneous rocks. Use: semiprecious gems. [Early 19C. < Greek *skapos* 'rod' + -LITE.]

scapula /skáppyŏŏlə/ (*plural* **-lae** /-lī/ *or* **-las**) *n* **1** either of two large flat triangular bones that form the back of the shoulder in humans **2** a bone in vertebrates that corresponds to the human shoulder blade [Late 16C. Via late Latin < Latin *scapulae* 'shoulder blades'.]

scapular[1] /skáppyŏŏlər/ *n* any one of the feathers on a bird's shoulder ■ *adj* relating to or associated with the shoulder blade

scapular[2] /skáppyŏŏlər/, **scapulary** /-ləri/ (*plural* **-ies**) *n* **1** a loose sleeveless garment worn by monks **2** two pieces of cloth joined together and worn over the shoulder and back underneath other garments to signify membership in a particular religious order or some other devotional purpose [15C. < late Latin *scapulare* < *scapula* (see SCAPULA).]

scar[1] /skaar/ *n* **1 MARK ON SKIN AFTER WOUND HEALS** a mark left on the skin after a wound, burn, or sore has healed over **2 MENTAL EFFECT OF DISTRESSING EXPERIENCE** a lasting effect left on somebody's mind by a personal misfortune or unpleasant experience **3 MARK ON SURFACE** a mark on a surface caused by damage **4 MARK OF FORMER ATTACHMENT ON PLANT** the mark on a plant indicating the place where a part such as a leaf was formerly attached ■ *v* (**scars, scarring, scarred**) **1** *vt* **MARK SOMEBODY OR SOMETHING WITH SCARS** to leave somebody or something with a physical or emotional scar **2** *vi* **FORM SCAR** to form or become marked by a scar [14C. Via Old French *escharre* 'scar, scab' < Greek *eskhara* 'brazier, scab formed after a burn'.]

scar[2] /skaar/ *n* **1** a steep bare rocky cliff, typically in the limestones of the Yorkshire Dales **2** a rock submerged or partly submerged in the ocean [14C. < Old Norse *sker* 'low reef' < Germanic, 'something cut off'.]

scarab /skárrəb/ *n* **1** a beetle regarded as sacred by the ancient Egyptians. Family: Scarabaeidae. **2** a representation of a beetle used on amulets and signets by the ancient Egyptians [Late 16C. < Latin *scarabaeus* < Greek *karabos* 'crab, beetle'.]

scarabaeid /skárrə beé id/, **scarabaean** /-ən/ *n* INSECTS = **scarab** *n.* 1 [Mid-19C. < modern Latin *Scarabaeidae* < Latin *scarabaeus* (see SCARAB).]

Scaramouch /skárrə mooch, -moosh, -mowch/, **Scaramouche** *n* a boastful and cowardly man (*literary*) [Mid-17C. Via French *Scaramouche* < Italian *Scaramuccia*, character in the commedia dell'arte.]

Scarborough /skaárbərə/ town in NE England, on the North Sea. Population: 53,600 (1994 estimate).

scarce /skairss/ *adj* (**scarcer, scarcest**) **1 INSUFFICIENT** being in insufficient supply **2 RARE** rarely found or rarely occurring ■ *adv* **SCARCELY** scarcely (*archaic or literary*) [13C. Via Anglo-Norman *(e)scars* < Latin *excerpere* 'pick out' < *carpere* 'pluck'.] —**scarceness** *n* ◇ **make yourself scarce** to go or stay away, often in order to avoid trouble or difficulty (*informal*)

scarcely /skáirssli/ *adv* **1** only to the slightest degree ○ *I scarcely slept all night.* **2** surely or almost certainly not ○ *That is scarcely a good reason for taking the day off.*

USAGE See ***hardly***.

scarcement /skáirssmənt/ *n* a ledge in a wall [Early 16C. < obsolete *scarce* 'make scarce'.]

scarcity /skáirssəti/ (*plural* **-ties**) *n* **1** an insufficient supply of something **2** an infrequency of occurrence of something

scare /skair/ *v* (**scares, scaring, scared**) **1** *vt* **FRIGHTEN** to make somebody afraid or alarmed **2** *vi* **BE FRIGHTENED** to be or become frightened ■ *n* **1 FRIGHT** a sudden fright or feeling of fear **2 SOMETHING THAT FRIGHTENS** a situation causing general fear or alarm [12C. < Old Norse *skirra* 'frighten' < *skjarr* 'timid'.] —**scarer** *n*

scare off, scare away *vt* to frighten a person or an animal into going away

scare up *vt US, Can* to manage to find something or put something together from whatever is available (*informal*)

scarecrow /skáirkrō/ *n* **1 OBJECT FOR SCARING BIRDS AWAY** an object in the shape of a person dressed in old clothes, set up in a field to scare birds away from the crops **2 POORLY DRESSED PERSON** a wearer of ragged clothes (*informal*) **3 SOMETHING FRIGHTENING BUT NOT DANGEROUS** somebody or something that may have a frightening effect but is not dangerous

scared /skaird/ *adj* feeling full of worry or fear —**scaredly** *adv* —**scaredness** *n*

scaredy-cat /skáirdi-/ *n* somebody who is unusually timid and frightened (*informal; usually used by or to children*) US term **fraidy-cat**

scaremonger /skáir mung gər/ *n* a spreader of alarming rumours —**scaremongering** *n*

scarf[1] /skaarf/ *n* (*plural* **scarfs** *or* **scarves** /skaarvz/) **1 CLOTH WORN ROUND NECK** a piece of cloth of various shapes, worn round the neck or on the head for warmth, decoration, or concealment **2 MILITARY SASH** an official sash, usually indicating military rank ■ *vt* **WRAP SOMETHING IN SCARF** to wrap a scarf round something (*literary*) [Mid-16C. Via Old Northern French *escarpe* < Old French *escherpe* 'bag hung around the neck' < Frankish *skirpja* 'bag woven from rushes' < Latin *scirpus* 'rush'.]

scarf[2] /skaarf/ *n* **1 scarf, scarf joint JOINT MADE BETWEEN NOTCHED ENDS** a joint made by joining two notched boards together **2 NOTCHED END** either of the notched ends of a scarf joint ■ *vt* **JOIN BOARDS USING NOTCHES** to join boards together by means of a scarf joint [13C. Probably via Old French < Scandinavian.]

scarf[3] /skaarf-/, **scarf down** *vt US* to eat or drink something greedily or noisily (*slang*) [Mid-20C. Variant of SCOFF[2].]

scarf joint *n* = **scarf**[2] *n.* 2

scarfskin /skaárf skin/ *n* the outermost layer of skin, especially the cuticle of a nail [Early 16C. Probably < SCARF[1].]

scarify[1] /skárri fī/ (**-fies, -fying, -fied**) *vt* **1 MAKE SCRATCHES ON SKIN** to make scratches on or superficial incisions in the skin, done in the past, e.g. to promote an improved blood supply in the underlying tissues **2 LOOSEN SOIL** to break up and loosen the surface of soil **3 SCRATCH SEEDS** to break the outer cover of hard seeds to aid germination [14C. Via French *scarifier* < Greek *skariphasthai* 'scratch an outline' < *skariphos* 'stylus'.] —**scarification** /skárrifi káysh'n, skáiri-/ *n* —**scarificator** /-fi kaytər/ *n* —**scarifier** *n*

scarify[2] (**-fies, -fying, -fied**) *vt* to make somebody afraid or alarmed (*informal*) [Late 18C. < SCARE, perhaps after TERRIFY.] —**scarifyingly** *adv*

scarious /skáiri əss/, **scariose** /-ōss/ *adj* describes parts of plants that have a thin dry membranous appearance [Late 18C. Via French *scarieux* < modern Latin *scariosus*.]

scarlatina /skaárlə teénə/ *n* = **scarlet fever** (*technical*) [Early 19C. Via modern Latin < Italian *scarlattina* 'little scarlet things' < *scarlatto* 'scarlet' < Arabic *siqillāt* (see SCARLET).] —**scarlatinal** *adj*

Scarlatti /skaar látti/, **Alessandro** (1659–1725) Italian composer

Scarlatti, Domenico (1685–1757) Italian composer

scarlet /skaárlət/ *n* **1** a bright orange-tinged red colour **2** scarlet clothing or cloth, especially the traditional red uniforms of the British army [13C. Via Old French *escarlate* < Arabic *siqillāt*, a rich red cloth < Latin *sigillatus* 'decorated with raised figures' < *signum* 'sign'.] —**scarlet** *adj*

scarlet fever *n* a contagious bacterial infection marked by fever, a sore throat, and a red rash, mainly affecting children

scarlet pimpernel *n* a common pimpernel whose flowers close in cloudy weather. Flowers: small, scarlet, purple, or white. *Anagallis arvensis*.

scarlet runner *n* PLANTS = **runner bean**

scarlet woman *n* an offensive term for a woman believed to be an adulterer or prostitute or to engage excessively in sexual activity (*literary*) [< Revelations 17:1–6 in the Bible, in which a sinful woman appears 'in purple and scarlet colour']

scarp /skaarp/ *n* **1** a steep slope or cliff, formed by erosion or faulting **2** a steep slope, e.g. the inner wall of a ditch, in front of a fortification [Late 16C. < Italian *scarpa* < ?]

scarper /skaárpər/ *vi* to leave a place quickly (*slang*) [Mid-19C. Probably < Italian *scappare* 'escape'.]

scart /skaart/ *vti Scotland* to scratch something or the skin (*nonstandard*) [14C. Alteration of dialect *scrat* < ?]

Scart /skaart/, **SCART** *n* an electrical device for connecting video equipment that has a socket and plug with 21 pins ○ *a Scart lead* [Late 20C. < French, acronym < *Syndicat des Constructeurs des Appareils Radiorécepteurs et Téléviseurs*, the committee that designed the connector.]

scar tissue *n* dense fibrous tissue that forms the scar over a healed wound

scarves plural of **scarf**[1]

scary /skáiri/ (**-ier, -iest**) *adj* (*informal*) **1** causing fear or alarm **2** easily frightened —**scarily** *adv* —**scariness** *n*

scat[1] /skat/ (**scats, scatting, scatted**) *vi* to leave immediately and quickly (*informal; usually a command*) [Mid-19C. < ?]

scat[2] /skat/ *n* a style of jazz singing that uses nonsense syllables to approximate the sound of a solo instrument ■ *vi* (**scats, scatting, scatted**) to sing in scat style [Early 20C. Probably an imitation of the sound.]

scat[3] /skat/ (*plural* **scats** *or* **scat**) *n* a small tropical marine fish, popular for aquariums because of its bright colour. Native to: Indian or Pacific oceans. Family: Scatophagidae. [Mid-20C. Shortening of modern Latin *Scatophagidae* < Greek *scatophagos* 'dung-eating', because it frequents sewage outlets.]

scat[4] /skat/ *n* a faecal dropping of an animal [Mid-20C. < Greek *skat-* (see SCATO-).]

scathe /skayth/ *vt* (**scathes, scathing, scathed**) **1 CRITICIZE** to subject somebody to severe criticism (*literary*) **2 DAMAGE SOMETHING BY BLASTING** to damage something by blasting or scorching it (*archaic*) ■ *n* **HARM** injury or harm (*archaic*) [12C. < Old Norse *skaða* 'harm, damage'.] —**scatheless** *adj*

scathing /skáything/ *adj* severely critical and scornful —**scathingly** *adv*

scato- *prefix* excrement ○ *scatology* [< Greek *skat-*, stem of *skōr* 'excrement'. Ultimately < Indo-European, 'cut off'.]

scatology /ska tóllәji/ *n* **1** preoccupation with excrement or obscenity **2** the scientific study of excrement, especially for diagnostic purposes —**scatological** /skáttә lójjik'l/ *adj* —**scatologist** *n*

scatter /skáttәr/ *v* **1** *vt* **THROW THINGS ABOUT** to throw things about so that they land with an irregular distribution over a relatively wide area ○ *scatter seed* **2** *vt* **SCATTER AREA** to cover an area by throwing things about over it **3** *vti* **DISPERSE** to separate and move suddenly in different directions, or cause people or animals to move in this way **4** *vti* **DEVIATE** to cause waves or a beam of particles to be irregularly deflected, dispersed, or reflected, or to be turned aside in such a fashion ■ *n* **THINGS SCATTERED ABOUT** a number of things spread untidily about an area (*literary*) [12C. Probably variant of SHATTER.] —**scatterable** *adj* —**scatterer** *n*

SYNONYMS ***scatter, broadcast, distribute, disseminate***
CORE MEANING: to spread around
scatter to spread things around physically, especially in a random widespread manner; **broadcast** to spread or transmit information, especially by means of radio or television, or to scatter seeds over the ground; **distribute** to allocate, share, or give out something in a structured or organized way, or to spread something over a particular surface or area; **disseminate** to spread ideas, information, or attitudes such as goodwill.

scatterbrain /skáttәr brayn/ *n* a person who cannot think seriously or systematically or cannot remember important things —**scatterbrained** *adj*

scatter cushion *n* a small moveable cushion placed on a sofa or armchair (*often used in the plural*) US term **throw pillow**

scatter diagram *n* a graph that represents the joint relationship of two variables by depicting the data as points along two axes at right angles to each other

scattered /skáttәrd/ *adj* **1** in a number of different places far away from each other ○ *scattered communities* **2** few in number and far apart in distance or time ○ *scattered showers*

scattergood /skáttәr good/ *n* a wasteful spender of money

scatter-gun *n US* a shotgun

scattering /skáttәring/ *n* **1** a small amount or number of things irregularly spread over a large area **2** the deflection of a wave or beam of particles caused by collisions with other particles

scattering layer *n* an undersea zone where there is a high concentration of plankton that causes sound waves to become scattered

scatter pin *n* a small decorative pin typically worn as part of a cluster on clothing

scatter rug *n* a small decorative rug

scattershot /skáttәr shot/ *adj* indiscriminate and lacking in focus ○ *a scattershot approach to the operation*

scatty /skátti/ (**-tier, -tiest**) *adj UK, Can* (*informal*) **1** lacking in serious or organized thought, forgetful, and often eccentric in behaviour **2** extremely muddled, irritated, or angry ○ *These children are driving me scatty.* [Early 20C. Probably < shortening of *scatterbrained*.] —**scattily** *adv* —**scattiness** *n*

scaup /skawp/ (*plural* **scaups** *or* **scaup**), **scaup duck** *n* a diving duck, the male of which has a black-and-white body. Native to: Europe, North America. Genus: *Aythya*. [Late 17C. Variant of *scalp* 'shellfish-bed' < ?]

scauper /skáwpәr/ *n* an engraving tool used to clear away lines or other unwanted areas on wood [Mid-19C. Variant of *scalper* < SCALP.]

scaur /skawr/ *n Scotland* a steep eroded hill or precipice (*often in placenames*) [Early 18C. Variant of SCAR[2].]

scavenge /skávvinj/ (**-enges, -enging, -enged**) *vti* **1 LOOK FOR SOMETHING USABLE** to search for or through discarded material in order to find something usable **2 FEED ON CARRION OR SCRAPS** to feed on dead and rotting flesh or discarded food scraps **3 CLEAN UP** to remove waste material and dirt from an area **4 GET RID OF IMPURITIES** to neutralize or remove impurities in a chemical reaction or mixture [Mid-17C. Back-formation < SCAVENGER.]

scavenger /skávvinjәr/ *n* **1 ANIMAL FEEDING ON CARRION OR SCRAPS** an animal, bird, or other organism that feeds on dead and rotting flesh or discarded food scraps **2 SOMEBODY LOOKING FOR SOMETHING USABLE** a person who seeks or looks through discarded items in the hope of finding something usable **3 SUBSTANCE REMOVING IMPURITIES** something that is added to a chemical reaction or mixture to neutralize or remove impurities **4 STREET CLEANER** a paid street cleaner or refuse collector (*archaic*) [Mid-16C. Alteration of *scavager* 'tax collector' < Anglo-Norman *scawager* < Flemish *scauwen* 'look at'.] —**scavengery** *n*

scavenger beetle *n* a dark oval-shaped beetle that lives in water and feeds on decaying vegetation. Family: Hydrophilidae.

scavenger hunt *n* a game in which people must obtain items on a list within a time limit and without buying them

ScD *abbr* Doctor of Science [Latin, *Scientiae Doctor*]

SCE *n* in Scotland, any of three levels of examinations in a wide range of subjects taken in the last three years of secondary school. Full form **Scottish Certificate of Education**

~~**scedule**~~ incorrect spelling of **schedule**

~~**sceince**~~ incorrect spelling of **science**

~~**sceme**~~ incorrect spelling of **scheme**

scena /sháynә/ (*plural* **-ne** /sháynay/) *n* **1** a division of an opera that is equivalent in length or structure to a scene in a play **2** a dramatic concert piece written and performed in the style of an operatic scena [Early 19C. Via Italian < Latin *scaena* (see SCENE[1]).]

scenario /si naári ō/ (*plural* **-os**) *n* **1 POSSIBLE SITUATION** an imagined sequence of possible events ○ *the worst-case scenario* **2 PLOT OUTLINE** an outline of the plot of a play or opera **3 SCREENPLAY** a screenplay [Late 19C. < Italian < *scena* 'scene' < Latin *scaena* (see SCENE[1]).]

USAGE The use of **scenario** in a generalized way to denote an imagined sequence of possible events or set of circumstances (*an alternative scenario if the vote goes the other way*) is widely deprecated in dictionaries and books on usage, although it is hard to see why this figurative use of a word is to be rejected when so many others (for example *scene*) are accepted without comment. It is a useful word when the imagined events or circumstances can be regarded as a whole and are therefore directly comparable to the elements of a film or theatre plot.

scenarist /seénәrist, sә naárist, si-/ *n* a writer of film scripts

scend /skend/, **send** *n* the upward movement of a ship that is pitching in heavy seas ■ *vi* to rise up high under the force of a strong wave (*refers to ships*) [15C. Probably alteration of DESCEND or ASCEND.]

scene[1] /seen/ *n* **1 DIVISION OF ACT OF PLAY** a division of an act of a play or opera, presenting continuous action in one place **2 SHORT SECTION OF PLAY OR FILM** a short section of a play, film, opera, or work of literature that presents a single event ○ *the love scene* **3 SETTING IN DRAMATIC WORK** a setting for the whole or a part of a play, film, opera, or work of literature **4 PLACE WHERE SOMETHING HAPPENS** a location at which an event or action happens ○ *the scene of many battles* **5 SCENERY FOR DRAMATIC WORK** the backgrounds, sets, or props for a play, film, or opera (*often before nouns*) ○ *a couple of quick scene changes* **6 VIEW OR PICTURE** a view of a place or an activity, especially one presented in a painting or photograph **7 EMBARRASSING PUBLIC DISPLAY** an embarrassing or disconcerting public display of emotion ○ *Don't make a scene, but I think they've lost your coat.* **8 MILIEU** the characteristic environment in which an activity or pursuit is carried out ○ *new to the fashion scene* **9** *US* **SITUATION** a set of circumstances of any kind (*informal*) ○ *We seem to have stumbled into a bad scene.* [Mid-16C. Via Latin *scaena* < Greek *skēnē* 'tent, stage'.] ◇ **behind the scenes 1** out of sight of the audience at a performance or spectacle **2** in private and away from public view ◇ **it's not somebody's scene** it is not the kind of thing that somebody likes to do or takes an interest in ◇ **set the scene 1** to describe a situation or the background to an event **2** to create the circumstances in which something can or does happen

scene[2] plural of **scena**

scenery /seénәri/ *n* **1** the set or decorated background for a play, film, or opera **2** landscape or natural surroundings, especially when regarded as picturesque ○ *admired the scenery from the hotel balcony* [Mid-18C. Alteration of *scenary* < Italian *scenario* (see SCENARIO).]

sceneshifter /seén shiftәr/ *n* somebody employed to move sets or props in a theatre or opera house

scene-stealer *n* a performer who, by his or her performance or personal qualities, takes the audience's attention away from another performer who is supposedly the focus of the scene

scenic /seénik/ *adj* **1 PICTURESQUE** with attractive or impressive natural scenery **2 OF NATURAL SCENERY** relating to the natural scenery of an area ○ *famous for its scenic beauty* **3 OF DRAMATIC SCENES** relating to scenes in a play, film, or opera **4 OF STAGE SCENERY** relating to stage scenery —**scenically** *adv*

scenic railway *n* **1** a miniature railway that carries customers past artificial scenery in a theme park or other place of entertainment **2** a roller coaster (*dated*)

scenography /see nóggrәfi/ *n* **1** the artistic representation of objects according to the rules of perspective **2** the painting of theatrical scenery —**scenographer** *n* —**scenographic** /seénә gráffik/ *adj* —**scenographical** *adj* —**scenographically** *adv*

scent /sent/ *n* **1 CHARACTERISTIC PLEASANT SMELL** a distinctive odour, especially a pleasant one ○ *the scent of jasmine* **2 SMELL USED AS TRAIL** a smell left behind by a person or animal and used especially for tracking ○ *They followed the scent deep into the forest.* **3 PERFUME** cosmetic fragrances, especially women's perfume **4 SMELLING SENSE** the sense of smell **5 ABILITY TO SENSE** an ability to sense or detect something as likely to happen **6 HINT** a faint indication that something is likely to happen ○ *There was the scent of danger in the air.* ■ *v* **1** *vti* **SMELL** to perceive somebody or something by smelling **2** *vt* **DETECT SOMETHING AS IMMINENT** to sense that something is likely to happen ○ *They could scent victory.* **3** *vt* **IMBUE SOMETHING WITH PLEASANT SMELL** to fill something with a distinctive odour, especially a pleasant one ○ *Roses scented the room.* [14C. < French *sentir* 'to sense' < Latin *sentire* 'feel'.] ◇ **put** *or* **throw somebody off the scent** to divert somebody from finding or discovering something

SYNONYMS See ***smell***.

scent gland *n* a specialized skin gland that enables an animal to secrete a scent designed to send social or sexual signals or serve as a deterrent

scent strip *n* a strip of perfumed paper used to advertise a commercially available perfume to potential customers

scepter *n, vt* US = **sceptre**

sceptic /sképtik/ *n* **1** a doubter of accepted beliefs **2** a doubter of religious doctrines and principles [Late 16C. < Latin *scepticus* 'follower of the Greek philosopher Pyrrho' < Greek *skeptikos* < *skeptesthai* 'look about'.]

Sceptic *n* a member of an ancient Greek school of philosophy holding the doctrine that real knowledge is impossible, or a later follower of this doctrine —**Sceptic** *adj* —**Scepticism** /sképtisizəm/ *n*

sceptical /sképtik'l/ *adj* **1** tending not to believe things but to question them **2** marked by a doubting attitude —**scepticalness** *n* —**sceptically** *adv*

SYNONYMS See ***doubtful***.

scepticism /sképtisizəm/ *n* **1** an attitude marked by a tendency to doubt what others accept to be true **2** a doubting attitude toward religious beliefs [Mid-17C]

sceptre /séptər/ *n* **1 STAFF USED AS ROYAL EMBLEM** a ceremonial staff, rod, or wand used as an emblem of a monarch's authority. ◊ **orb** *n.* 1 **2 ROYAL AUTHORITY** royal or imperial power or authority ■ *vt* (**-tres, -tring, -tred**) **GIVE SOMEBODY ROYAL AUTHORITY** to endow somebody with royal power or authority [13C. Via Old French < Greek *skēptron* 'staff' < *skēptein* 'lean on'.] —**sceptred** *adj*

SCF *abbr* Save the Children Fund

schadenfreude /shaád'n froydə/, **Schadenfreude** *n* malicious or smug pleasure taken in somebody else's misfortune [Late 19C. < German < *Schaden* 'harm' + *Freude* 'joy'.]

Schaffhausen /shaaf hówzən/ town in north-central Switzerland, on the River Rhine. Population: 34,396 (1983).

schappe /sháppə/ *n* yarn or fabric made from the waste products of silk [Late 19C. < German.]

schedule /shéddyool, skéd-/ *n* **1 WORK PLAN** a plan of work to be done in a specified order and by specified times ○ *The project was completed ahead of schedule.* ○ *We're behind schedule on the delivery dates.* **2 LIST OF MEETINGS, COMMITMENTS, OR APPOINTMENTS** an outline description of the things somebody is to do and the times at which they are to be done ○ *Her schedule was full from daylight to dark.* **3** = **timetable** *n.* **4** *US* **STUDENT'S TIMETABLE** a list of the classes that are the responsibility of a student or a teacher in a given period **5 LIST OF ITEMS** a table of items of information ○ *a schedule of tariffs* **6 SUPPLEMENTARY LIST** a list of details, often in the form of an appendix to a legal or legislative document ■ *vt* (**-ules, -uling, -uled**) **1 PLAN SOMETHING FOR PARTICULAR TIME** to plan something to happen at a particular time ○ *They are scheduled to arrive at midday.* **2 MAKE LIST OF THINGS** to put together a table of items of information, or place an item in the table **3 PROTECT BUILDING BY LAW** to put a building on a list of officially protected buildings [14C. Via Old French *cedule* < late Latin *schedula* 'small piece of paper' < Greek *skhedē* 'page'.] —**schedular** *adj* —**scheduler** *n*

Scheduled Castes *npl* castes in India that are officially considered disadvantaged and granted special treatment

scheduled territories *npl* FIN = **sterling area**

scheelite /sheé līt/ *n* a variously coloured calcium tungstate mineral. Use: source of tungsten. [Mid-19C. After Karl Wilhelm *Scheele* (1742–86), German-born Swedish chemist.]

schefflera /shéfflərə/ (*plural* **-ras** *or* **-ra**) *n* a tropical tree or shrub with glossy leaves, often cultivated as a house plant. Genus: *Schefflera*. [Mid-20C. < modern Latin, after J. C. *Scheffler* (1742–86), German botanist.]

Schelling /shélling/, **Friedrich Wilhelm Joseph von** (1775–1854) German philosopher

Schelte /skéltə/ river rising in N France and flowing through W Belgium and the SW Netherlands into the North Sea. Length: 435 km/270 mi.

schema /skeémə/ (*plural* **-mata** /skeémətə/) *n* **1 DIAGRAM** a diagram or plan showing the basic outline of something **2 MENTAL PATTERN** an organizational or conceptual pattern in the mind **3 KANTIAN PHILOSOPHICAL PRINCIPLE** in the philosophy of Kant, a method that allows the understanding to apply concepts to the evidence of the senses **4 DUMMY EXPRESSION IN LOGIC** in logic, a dummy expression indicating where certain words should appear, e.g. in 'S and R', 'S' and 'R' are schemata for sentences [Late 18C. Via German < Greek *skhēma*.]

schematic /skee máttik, ski-/ *adj* showing the basic form or layout of something ○ *a schematic drawing* ■ *n* a diagram, especially of electrical circuits

schematise *vt* = **schematize**

schematism /skeémətizəm/ *n* the basic arrangement or layout of parts in a complex object or system

schematize /skeémə tīz/ (**-tizes, -tizing, -tized**), **schematise** (**-tises, -tising, -tised**) *vt* to arrange or organize something according to a system —**schematization** /skeémə tī záysh'n/ *n*

scheme /skeem/ *n* **1 SECRET PLOT** a secret and cunning plan, especially one designed to cause damage or harm **2 PLAN** a systematic plan of action **3 SYSTEM** a systematic and coherent arrangement of parts **4 DIAGRAM** a diagram, chart, or map **5 GOVERNMENT OR BUSINESS PROGRAMME** a plan, policy, or programme carried out by a government or business ○ *training scheme* ○ *pension scheme* **6 ASTROLOGER'S CHART** an astrological chart of the sky **7** *Scotland* = **housing scheme** ■ *v* (**schemes, scheming, schemed**) **1** *vi* **MAKE SECRET PLAN** to devise a secret and cunning plan, especially one intended to cause damage or harm **2** *vt* **PLAN SOMETHING SYSTEMATICALLY** to devise a systematic plan for something [Mid-16C. Via Latin *schema* 'form' < Greek *skhēma*.]

scheming /skeéming/ *adj* making secret and cunning plans, especially to do damage or cause harm —**schemingly** *adv*

Schenectady /skə néktədi/ city in E New York State. Population: 61,698 (1998 estimate).

Schengen Agreement /shéngən-/ *n* an agreement between some countries in the European Union and associated states, abolishing internal border controls over the movement of people and goods between member countries [After Schengen, village on the borders of Luxembourg, France, and Germany where agreement was signed]

Schepisi /sképsi/, **Fred** (*b.* 1939) Australian filmmaker

scherzando /skairt sándō/ *adj, adv* performed in a playful musical style and tempo (*musical direction*) ■ *n* (*plural* **-di** /-di/ *or* **-dos**) a scherzando piece or passage of music [Early 19C. < Italian < *scherzare* (see SCHERZO).]

scherzo /skáirtsō/ (*plural* **-zos** *or* **-zi** /-si/) *n* **1** a rapid, playful, or humorous movement, usually the third of four, in a musical work **2** an independent musical work in a rapid, playful, or humorous style [Mid-19C. < Italian < *scherzare* 'to joke'.]

Scheveningen /skáyvən ingən/ district of The Hague, SW Netherlands, on the North Sea

Schiaparelli /skee aápə rélli, skáppə-/, **Elsa** (1896–1973) Italian fashion designer

Schick test /shík-/ *n* an injection of nontoxic diphtheria under the skin, used to determine whether a patient is immune to diphtheria [Early 20C. After Bela *Schick* (1877–1967), Hungarian-born US paediatrician.]

Schiele /sheélə/, **Egon** (1890–1918) Austrian painter

Schiff's reagent /shífs-/, **Schiff reagent** *n* an acid solution of fuchsine. Use: test for aldehydes. [Late 19C. After Hugo *Schiff* (1834–1915), German chemist.]

schiller /shíllər/ *n* an iridescent lustre in some minerals [Early 19C. < German, 'iridescence'.]

Schiller /shíllər/, **Friedrich von** (1759–1805) German poet, dramatist, historian, and philosopher

schilling /shílling/ *n* see table at **currency** [Mid-18C. < German.]

schipperke /shíppərki, skíp-/ (*plural* **-kes** *or* **-ke**) *n* a small black tailless dog of a breed with pointed ears and a thick coat [Late 19C. < Dutch dialect, diminutive of Dutch *schipper* (see SKIPPER[1]).]

schism /skízzəm, sízzəm/ *n* **1 SPLITTING INTO FACTIONS** the division of a group into mutually antagonistic factions **2 FACTION** a faction formed as a result of a schism **3 DIVISION IN OR FROM A RELIGIOUS DENOMINATION** a division within a religious denomination or a breaking away from it, usually on the grounds of differing beliefs or practices [14C. Via Old French *scisme* < late Latin *schisma* < Greek *skhizein* (see SCHIZO-).]

schismatic /skiz máttik, siz-/, **schismatical** /-máttik'l/ *adj* relating to, involved in, or causing schism ■ *n* a participant in or cause of a schism —**schismatically** *adv* —**schismaticalness** *n*

schist /shist/ *n* any rock whose minerals have aligned themselves in one direction in response to deformation stresses, with the result that the rock can be split in parallel layers [Late 18C. Via French *schiste* < Latin *(lapis) schistos* 'fissile (stone)' < Greek *skhistos* < *skhizein* (see SCHIZO-).] —**schistose** /shístōss, -tōz/ *adj* —**schistosity** /shiss tóssəti/ *n*

schistocyte /shístō sīt/ *n* a red blood cell undergoing fragmentation, or any of the fragments that are formed as a result

schistosome /shístō sōm/ *n* a tiny flatworm that often lives as a parasite in the blood of birds and mammals. In humans, it causes the disease schistosomiasis.

schistosomiasis /shístō sō mī́ əssiss/ *n* an often chronic illness that results from infection of the blood with a parasitic flatworm (**schistosome**)

schiz- *prefix* = **schizo-** (*before vowels*)

schizanthus /skit sánthəss, ski zánth-/ (*plural* **-thus**) *n* a plant with small flowers that resemble orchids. Native to: Chile. Genus: *Schizanthus*. [Early 19C. < modern Latin, < Greek *skhizein* 'split' + *anthos* 'flower'.]

schizo /skítsō/ *n* (*plural* **-os**) an offensive term for somebody who has schizophrenia (*slang*) ■ *adj* an offensive term meaning having characteristics often erroneously thought of as symptomatic of schizophrenia (*slang*) [Mid-20C. Shortening of SCHIZOPHRENIC.]

schizo- *prefix* **1** split, cleft ○ *schizocarp* **2** cleavage, fission ○ *schizogenesis* **3** schizophrenia ○ *schizoaffective* [Via modern Latin < Greek *skhizein* 'split' < Indo-European]

schizocarp /skítsō kaarp, shī́zō-/ *n* a dry fruit that splits into individually seeded parts (**carpels**) when ripe —**schizocarpic** /skítsō kaárpik, shī́zō-/ *adj* —**schizocarpous** /-kaárpəss/ *adj*

schizogony /skit zóggəni, shī-/ *n* a form of asexual reproduction that occurs in some single-celled organisms (**protozoans**), in which the nucleus of an individual divides many times before the cytoplasm divides to form the daughter cells

schizoid /skít soyd/ *adj* **1** showing some of the symptoms of schizophrenia, e.g. withdrawal into the self and a tendency to fantasize ○ *exhibits a schizoid personality* **2** an offensive term describing a personality that suggests inner conflicts and exhibits outer contradictions

schizont /skítsont, shī́z-/ *n* a cell formed during the asexual phase of the life cycle of some single-celled organisms (**protozoans**)

schizophrenia /skítsō freéni ə/ *n* **1** a severe psychiatric disorder with symptoms of emotional instability, detachment from reality, and withdrawal into the self **2** an offensive term for contradictory or conflicting attitudes, behaviour, or qualities [Early 20C. < SCHIZO- + Greek *phrēn* 'mind'.]

schizophrenic /skítsō frénnik/ *adj* **1** relating to or resulting from schizophrenia **2** an offensive term meaning characterized by conflicts and contradictions —**schizophrenic** *n*

schizophyte /skítsə fīt, shī́zə-/ *n* a microorganism that reproduces by fission. Bacteria and bluish-green algae are schizophytes. —**schizophytic** /skítsə fíttik, shī́zə-/ *adj*

schizopod /skítsə pod, shī́zə-/ (*plural* **-pods** *or* **-pod**) *n* any crustacean that resembles shrimp, including krill. Order: Mysidacea and Euphausiacea.

schizothymia /skítsō thī́mi ə/ *n* an introverted psychiatric condition that resembles a mild form of schizophrenia [Mid-20C. < Greek *skhizein* 'split' + *thumos* 'soul, mind'.] —**schizothymic** *adj*

schizy /skítsi/ (**-ier, -iest**) *adj* an offensive term meaning emotionally sensitive or moody to a degree that makes others feel uneasy (*slang*) [Mid-20C. Shortening of SCHIZOPHRENIC or SCHIZOID with alteration.]

schlemiel /shlə meél/, **schlemihl** *n US* an offensive term for somebody regarded as bungling, inept, or unlucky (*slang insult*) [Late 19C. < Yiddish *shlemiel* < ?]

schlep /shlep/, **shlep** *v* (**schleps, schlepping, schlepped; shleps, shlepping, shlepped**) (*informal*) **1** *vt* **MOVE SOMETHING WITH DIFFICULTY** to lug or haul something from one place to another **2** *vi* **GO WITH DIFFICULTY** to move slowly, clumsily, or tediously ■ *n* **1 TEDIOUS JOURNEY** a long, tedious, or difficult journey (*informal*) ○ *It's such a schlep all the way across town.* **2 OFFENSIVE TERM** an offensive term for somebody who is regarded as unintelligent or clumsy (*slang insult*) [Early 20C. Via Yiddish *shlepn* < German *schleppen* 'drag'.] —**schlepper** *n*

Schleswig-Holstein /shléz vig hólstīn/ state in N Germany, occupying the S Jutland peninsula. Capital: Kiel. Population: 2,708,000 (1994). Area: 15,710 sq. km/6,066 sq. mi.

schlieren /shléerən/ *npl* zones of different density and refraction in a transparent fluid, visible as streaks and caused by pressure or temperature variations [Late 19C. Via German, 'streaks' < Middle High German *slier* 'mud'.]

schlieren photography *n* a form of flash photography that records schlieren present in a fluid

schlock /shlok/ *n US* something that has no value and is shoddily made (*slang*) ■ *adj US* cheap and lacking any redeeming quality (*slang*) ○ *a schlock horror film* [Early 20C. Possibly < Yiddish *shlak* 'evil blow' < Middle High German *slag*.] —**schlocky** *adj*

schmaltz /shmawlts, shmolts/, **schmalz, shmaltz** *n* cloying or exaggerated sentimentality (*informal*) [Mid-20C. Via Yiddish *shmalts* 'melted fat' < German *Schmalz*.] —**schmaltzily** *adv* —**schmaltziness** *n* —**schmaltzy** *adj*

schmatte /shmáttə/, **shmatte** *n US* a rag or worthless thing (*informal*) [Late 20C. Via Yiddish < Polish *szmata* 'rag'.]

Schmeling /shmáyling/, **Max** (*b.* 1905) German boxer

Schmidt /shmit/, **Helmut** (*b.* 1918) German statesman and chancellor of West Germany (1974–82)

Schmidt camera *n* = **Schmidt telescope**

Schmidt system *n* an optical system that uses a special concave spherical mirror to correct optical aberrations [Mid-20C. After Bernhard Voldemar *Schmidt* (1879–1935), Estonian-born German specialist in optics.]

Schmidt telescope *n* a wide-angle photographic telescope used in astronomy [Mid-20C. Because it uses a SCHMIDT SYSTEM.]

Schmitt trigger /shmít-/ *n* an electronic circuit that produces an output when the input exceeds a predetermined turn-on or threshold level [Mid-20C. After Otto H. *Schmitt* (b. 1913), US electronics engineer.]

schmo /shmō/ (*plural* **schmoes**), **shmo** (*plural* **shmoes**) *n US* an offensive term for somebody regarded as boring, easily deceived, or having otherwise objectionable qualities (*slang insult*) [Mid-20C. Alteration of SCHMUCK.]

schmooze /shmooz/ *v* (**schmoozes, schmoozing, schmoozed**) **1** *vi* **CHAT INFORMALLY** to chat socially and agreeably (*slang*) **2** *vt* **BE INGRATIATING TOWARDS** to talk persuasively to somebody, often to gain personal advantage ■ *n* **A CHAT** an informal chat about trivial matters (*slang*) [Late 19C. Via Yiddish *schmuesn* 'talk' < Hebrew *šĕmūʿāh* 'rumour'.] —**schmoozer** *n*

schmuck /shmuk/, **shmuck** *n US* an offensive term for somebody who is regarded as being unworthy of respect (*slang insult*) [Late 19C. < Yiddish *shmok* 'penis' < ?]

Schnabel /shnaáb'l/, **Artur** (1882–1951) Austrian pianist and composer

schnapps /shnaps/ (*plural* **schnapps**), **schnaps** (*plural* **schnaps**) *n* **1** a strong alcoholic spirit made in Germany and the Netherlands **2** a glass or measure of schnapps [Early 19C. Via German < Low German or Dutch *snaps* 'mouthful'.]

~~**schnaps**~~ incorrect spelling of **schnapps**

schnauzer /shnówtsər/ *n* a wiry-coated dog with bushy eyebrows and whiskers that grow like a beard, belonging to any of three breeds that originated in Germany [Early 20C. < German, < *Schnauze* 'snout'.]

schnitzel /shníts'l/ *n* a piece of meat, typically veal, beaten flat and served fried, usually coated in egg and breadcrumbs [Mid-19C. < German < Old High German *snidan* 'cut'.]

Schnitzler /shnítslər/, **Arthur** (1862–1931) Austrian doctor, playwright, and novelist

schnozzle /shnózz'l/, **schnoz** /shnoz/ (*plural* **schnozes**) *n US* a nose, especially a large one (*slang*) [Mid-20C. < Yiddish *shnoytsl*, diminutive of *shnoyts* 'snout' < German *Schnauze*.]

Schoenberg /shúrn burg, shōn bòork/, **Arnold** (1874–1951) Austrian composer

schola cantorum /skṓlə kan táwrəm/ (*plural* **scholae cantorum** /skṓlee-/) *n* a choir or choir school housed in a church or cathedral [< medieval Latin, 'school of singers']

scholar /skóllər/ *n* **1** **LEARNED PERSON** a learned person, especially an academic specialist in one area of knowledge **2** **SCHOLARSHIP STUDENT** a student who receives a scholarship **3** **PUPIL** a school pupil (*formal*) [Pre-12C. < late Latin *scholaris* < Latin *schola* (see SCHOOL[1]).]

scholarly /skóllərli/ *adj* **1** **LEARNED** with a great deal of knowledge, especially knowledge of an academic subject **2** **OF SCHOLARS** relating to scholars or to formal study ○ *scholarly journals* **3** **ACCORDING TO PRINCIPLES OF FORMAL STUDY** in keeping with a rigorous and systematic approach to acquiring knowledge or to setting out the results of formal study —**scholarliness** *n*

scholarship /skóllər ship/ *n* **1** **FINANCIAL HELP FOR A STUDENT** a sum of money awarded to a student on the basis of academic merit, to help with living expenses, study, or travel **2** **FORMAL STUDY** academic learning or achievement **3** **ACADEMIC WORKS** a body of learning on an academic subject ○ *a review of German scholarship on the topic*

scholastic /skə lástik/ *adj* **1** **OF SCHOOLS OR STUDYING** relating to students, schools, or studying **2** **PEDANTIC** too concerned with details or fine distinctions and too ready to criticize minor errors **3** **OF SCHOLASTICISM** relating to the medieval movement of religious and philosophical learning known as scholasticism ■ *n* **1** **STUDENT OR TEACHER UNDER SCHOLASTICISM** a student or teacher in the medieval intellectual movement known as scholasticism **2** **PEDANT** a quibbling or pedantic person **3** **SOMEBODY UNDERGOING ROMAN CATHOLIC SCHOLASTICATE** a probationer in a scholasticate at a Roman Catholic seminary [Late 16C. < Latin *scholasticus* < Greek *skholastikos* 'learned' < *skholē* (see SCHOOL[1]).] —**scholastically** *adv*

scholasticate /skə lástikət/ *n* **1** a probationary period of study for a Jesuit student at a Roman Catholic seminary **2** a seminary where a scholasticate is undertaken

scholasticism /skə lástissizəm/ *n* **1** a medieval theological and philosophical system of learning based on the authority of St Augustine and other leaders of the early Christian Church, and on the works of Aristotle **2** narrowly traditional learning, or adherence to traditional educational methods

scholia plural of **scholium**

scholiast /skṓli ast/ *n* a medieval scholar who wrote commentaries on ancient Greek and Latin texts [Late 16C. < medieval Greek *skholiastēs* < *skholion* (see SCHOLIUM).] —**scholiastic** /skṓli ástik/ *adj*

scholium /skṓli əm/ (*plural* **-a** /-li ə/) *n* a medieval annotation or commentary written on an ancient Greek or Latin text [Mid-16C. < Greek *skholion* 'interpretation' < *skholē* (see SCHOOL[1]).]

school[1] /skool/ *n* **1** **BUILDING FOR TEACHING CHILDREN** a building or institution in which children and teenagers are taught, usually up to the age of 16 or 18 (*often before nouns*) **2** *US* **COLLEGE OR UNIVERSITY** any college or university **3** **DEPARTMENT SPECIALIZING IN ACADEMIC SUBJECT** a faculty, department, or institution that offers specialized instruction in an academic subject ○ *medical school* **4** **INSTITUTION TEACHING NONACADEMIC SKILL** an institution that specializes in teaching a specific skill, especially a practical or sports skill ○ *tennis school* **5** **STAFF AND STUDENTS** all the staff and students of an educational institution (*often before nouns*) **6** **DAY AT SCHOOL** the part of a day spent teaching or being taught in a school ○ *School was over for another day.* **7** **YEARS SPENT AT SCHOOL** the part of somebody's life spent being taught in a school ○ *After school, he went abroad for two years.* **8** **INSTRUCTIVE PLACE OR PERIOD** any place or period of activity regarded as providing knowledge or experience ○ *the school of life* **9** **ARTISTS OR WRITERS SHARING SAME APPROACH** a group of people, especially artists, writers, or philosophers, who share the same principles, methods, ideals, or style ○ *the Impressionist school* ○ *the Aristotelian school* ■ *vt* **1** **INSTRUCT** to train or instruct somebody in a specific skill ○ *schooled in the art of debate* **2** **EDUCATE** to educate a child or teenager formally in a school **3** **DISCIPLINE** to exert control or discipline over somebody or yourself **4** **TRAIN HORSE** to train a horse, especially for riding and dressage [Pre-12C. Via Latin *schola* < Greek *skholē* 'learned discussion, school'.]

SYNONYMS See ***teach***.

school[2] /skool/ *n* a group of fish, whales, porpoises, or other aquatic animals of a single type ■ *vi* to congregate in a school or swim in a school [14C. < Middle Dutch *schole* < West Germanic.]

school age *n* the age at which a child is required legally to attend school —**school-age** *adj*

school board *n* in Britain, between 1870 and 1902, an elected committee that supervised local elementary schools

schoolbook /skóol bòok/ *n* a textbook or other book used at school

schoolboy /skóol boy/ *n* a boy who attends school ■ *adj* at a level of maturity typical of, or designed to appeal to, boys of school age ○ *schoolboy humour*

school bus *n* a large motor vehicle that takes children to and from school or on school-related trips

school captain *n Aus, Scotland* a boy or girl appointed or elected to be the senior representative of a school's pupils

School Certificate *n* in New Zealand, and from 1917 to 1951 in England and Wales, a public examination taken by 16-year-olds

schoolchild /skóol chīld/ (*plural* **-children** /-childrən/) *n* a child who attends school

school crossing patrol *n* somebody employed to stop traffic to allow schoolchildren to cross a road. ◊ **lollipop man, lollipop lady**

school day *n* any day on which school is conducted, or the hours of instruction in that day ■ **school days** *npl* the period of time in somebody's life spent attending school

schoolfellow /skóol fellō/ *n* a schoolmate (*formal*)

school figure *n* any one of a number of basic movements in figure-skating that are performed in competition (*often plural*)

schoolgirl /skóol gurl/ *n* a girl who attends school

schoolhouse /skóol howss/ (*plural* **-houses** /-howziz/) *n* **1** a building that houses a school, especially a rural primary school **2** a house attached to a school where a teacher lives, often the head teacher

schooling /skóoling/ *n* **1** **EDUCATION AT SCHOOL** the education or instruction that is acquired at school **2** **INSTRUCTION** instruction or training in anything, carried out systematically and in a disciplined way **3** **TRAINING OF A HORSE** the training of a horse, especially for riding and dressage

school inspector *n* in the United Kingdom, an official appointed by the government to check on the standards of education in state-funded schools

schoolkid /skóol kid/ *n* a child or teenager who attends school (*informal*)

school-leaver *n* a pupil who has left school or is about to do so, especially one who leaves at the minimum age and does not go on to further or higher education

Schoolman /skóolman/ (*plural* **-men**) *n* a teacher or student who participated in scholasticism

schoolmarm /skóol maarm/ *n* **1** an offensive term for a woman schoolteacher, especially one considered too proper and old-fashioned (*dated insult*) **2** an offensive term for a woman thought to live in a way regarded as old-fashioned (*insult*) —**schoolmarmish** *adj*

schoolmaster /skóol maastər/ *n* **1** **MAN SCHOOLTEACHER** a man who teaches school, especially in a private school **2** (*plural* **-ters** *or* **-ter**) **TROPICAL FISH** a fish of the snapper family that has yellow fins. Native to: Caribbean, tropical Atlantic. *Lutjanus apodus.* ■ *vi* **BE A SCHOOLMASTER** to be a schoolmaster by profession (*dated*) —**schoolmasterish** *adj* —**schoolmasterly** *adj* —**schoolmastership** *n*

schoolmate /skóol mayt/ *n* a friend or companion at school

school milk *n* a third of a pint of milk formerly provided free to British schoolchildren

schoolmistress /skóol mistrəss/ *n* a woman schoolteacher, especially in a private school —**schoolmistressy** *adj*

school of hard knocks *n* difficult or challenging experiences that are considered to be instructive

school of thought *n* a way of thinking about something, or a group of people who share the same attitude or opinion

school psychologist *n* a psychologist who visits a group of schools to give teachers and parents advice on the psychological and developmental problems of individual schoolchildren

schoolroom /skóol room, -ròom/ *n* a classroom in a school

Schools /skoolz/ *n* (+ *singular or plural verb*) **1** at Oxford University, the university building in which examinations are held **2** at Oxford University, the final examinations for the degree of BA that are held in the Examination Schools

schoolteacher /skóol teechər/ *n* a teacher in a school —**schoolteaching** *n*

schoolwork /skoŏl wurk/ *n* the work that a pupil does in or after school

schoolyard /skoŏl yaard/ *n US* EDUC = **playground** *n*. 2

school year *n* 1 a period of twelve months, beginning usually in late August or early September, throughout which pupils are assigned to the same class 2 the months during which instruction is given at a school

schooner /skoŏnər/ *n* 1 SAILING VESSEL a fast sailing ship with at least two masts and with sails set lengthways (**fore and aft**) 2 SHERRY GLASS a large glass for sherry 3 *US, Aus* BEER GLASS a tall slim glass for beer 4 HIST = **prairie schooner** [Early 18C]

schooner rig *n* an arrangement of masts and sails (**rig**) in which the mainmast is taller than the foremast — **schooner-rigged** *adj*

Schopenhauer /shópən hówər/, **Arthur** (1788–1860) German philosopher

schorl /shawrl/ *n* a black opaque form of the mineral tourmaline, often occurring in needle-shaped radiating crystals [Late 18C. < German *Schörl* < ?] —**schorlaceous** /shawr láyshəss/ *adj*

schottische /sho teésh/ *n* 1 a round dance of German origin, resembling a slow polka 2 the music for a schottische [Mid-19C. < German *schottische (Tanz)* 'Scottish dance'.]

Schottky effect /shótki-/ *n* a reduction in the energy needed to remove an electron from a solid surface caused by the application of an electric field [Mid-20C. After Walter *Schottky* (1886–1976), German physicist.]

Schrödinger /shrúrdingər, shród-, shród-/, **Erwin** (1887–1961) Austrian physicist

schtetl *n* JUDAISM = **shtetl**

schtick *n* = **shtick**

schtoom *adj* = **shtoom**

Schubert /shoŏbərt/, **Franz** (1797–1828) Austrian composer

schul *n* JUDAISM = **shul**

Schulz /shoŏlts/, **Charles** (1922–2000) US cartoonist

Schumacher /shoŏ makər/, **E. F.** (1911–77) German-born British economist and conservationist. Full name **Ernst Friederich Schumacher**

Schumacher /shoŏ maakər, -maàkher/, **Michael** (*b.* 1969) German racing driver

Schumann /shoŏmən/, **Robert** (1810–56) German composer

Schumpeter /shoŏm paytər/, **Joseph Alois** (1883–1950) Austrian-born US economist

schuss /shoŏss/ *vi* to ski straight downhill at high speed ■ *n* a straight fast downhill run on skis [Mid-20C. < German, 'shot'.]

schussboomer /shoŏss boomər/ *n* a skier adept at making fast straight downhill runs (*informal*)

schwa /shwaa/, **shwa** *n* an unstressed vowel, e.g. 'a' in 'above' or 'e' in 'sicken', It is represented in the International Phonetic Alphabet by the symbol ə [Late 19C. Via German < Hebrew *šĕwâ*.]

Schwann cell /shwón-, shván-/ *n* a cell of the peripheral nervous system that wraps around a nerve fibre and forms the myelin sheath [Early 20C. After Theodor *Schwann* (1810–82), German physiologist.]

Schwarzenegger /shvaártsə negər, swáwrtsə-/, **Arnold** (*b.* 1947) Austrian-born US body builder and film actor

Schwarzkopf /shváarts kopf, sváwrts kopf/, **Dame Elisabeth** (*b.* 1915) German soprano

Schwarzschild radius /shwáwrts shild-/ *n* the critical radius within which the gravitational force of a gravitationally collapsing astronomical object becomes so great that neither matter nor energy can escape, creating a black hole [Mid-20C. After Karl *Schwarzschild* (1873–1916), German astronomer.]

Albert Schweitzer

Schweitzer /shwítsər/, **Albert** (1875–1965) German-born theologian, musicologist, and missionary

Schwitters /shvíttərz/, **Kurt** (1887–1948) German artist

sciamachy /sī ámməki/ (*plural* -**chies**), **skiamachy** /skī ámməki/ (*plural* -**chies**) *n* (*literary*) 1 practice fighting with a shadow or with an imaginary opponent 2 fighting with an imagined foe or against a foe who cannot be defeated, or an instance of this [Early 17C. < Greek *skiamakhia* < *skia* 'shadow' + *makhē* 'fight'.]

sciatic /sī áttik/ *adj* 1 relating to or affecting the back of the hip or the sciatic nerve 2 causing sciatica or caused by sciatica [Early 16C. Via French *sciatique* < medieval Latin *sciaticus* < Greek *iskhion* 'hip joint'.]

sciatica /sī áttikə/ *n* pain and tenderness extending from the back of the hip down to the calf, usually caused by a protrusion of vertebral disc substance pressing on the roots of the sciatic nerve [15C. < medieval Latin *sciaticus*, feminine of *sciaticus* (see SCIATIC).]

sciatic nerve *n* either of two nerves that run from the back of the hip down the thigh to the calf

SCID *abbr* severe combined immunodeficiency

science /sī ənss/ *n* 1 STUDY OF PHYSICAL WORLD the study of the physical world and its manifestations, especially by using systematic observation and experiment (*often before nouns*) 2 BRANCH OF SCIENCE a branch of science of a particular area of study ○ *the life sciences* 3 KNOWLEDGE GAINED FROM SCIENCE the knowledge gained by the study of the physical world 4 SYSTEMATIC BODY OF KNOWLEDGE any systematically organized body of knowledge about a specific subject ○ *the social sciences* 5 SOMETHING STUDIED OR PERFORMED METHODICALLY any activity that is the object of careful study or that is carried out according to a developed method ○ *the science of dressing for success* [14C. Via Old French < Latin *scientia* < *scient-*, present participle of *scire* 'know, discern' < Indo-European, 'cut'.] ◊ **blind somebody with science** to confuse or overwhelm somebody by giving an impenetrable explanation using technical terms and concepts

science fiction *n* a form of fiction, usually set in the future, that deals with imaginary scientific and technological developments and contact with other worlds (*often before nouns*)

science park *n* an area, usually associated with a university, where scientific research is carried out by commercial companies

scienter /sī éntər/ *adv* with full knowledge or awareness [Early 19C. < Latin, 'knowingly' < *scient-* (see SCIENCE).]

sciential /sī énsh'l/ *adj* 1 relating to science or knowledge 2 possessing considerable knowledge or skill (*formal*)

scientific /sī ən tíffik/ *adj* 1 relating to, using, or conforming to science or its principles 2 proceeding in a systematic and methodical way —**scientifically** *adv*

scientific method *n* the system of advancing knowledge by formulating a question, collecting data about it through observation and experiment, and testing a hypothetical answer

scientific notation *n* a way of expressing a given number as a number between 1 and 10 multiplied by 10 to the appropriate power. 5,743.6 expressed in scientific notation is 5.7436×10^3.

scientism /sī əntizəm/ *n* 1 the use of the scientific method of acquiring knowledge, whether in the traditional sciences or in other fields of inquiry 2 the belief that science alone can explain phenomena, or the ap-

plication of scientific methods to fields unsuitable for it (*disapproving*) ○ *'We feel that the attitude that predominates in science at present is arrogance, which has fostered dogmatism and scientism'.* (Brian D. Josephson, Beverly A. Rubik, *The Challenge of Consciousness Research*; 1992) —**scientistic** /sī ən tístik/ *adj*

scientist /sī əntist/ *n* a person with scientific training or who works in one of the sciences ○ *a social scientist*

Scientist /sī əntist/ *n* 1 in Christian Science belief, Jesus Christ as the paramount spiritual healer 2 a Christian Scientist

sci-fi /sī fī/ *n* science fiction (*informal*) [Mid-20C. Shortening.]

scilicet /sílli set, síli-, sílla-, skeéli ket/ *adv* used to introduce a word or phrase of clarification, or a missing word or phrase [14C. < Latin, contraction of *scire licet* 'it is permitted to know'.]

scilla /síllə/ (*plural* -**las** *or* -**la**) *n* a plant with flowers shaped like small bells. Native to: Europe, Asia. Genus: *Scilla*. [Early 19C. Via Latin < Greek *skilla* 'squill'.]

Scilly Isles /sílli-/ group of about 150 islands off the coast of SW England, in the Atlantic Ocean. Population: 2,000 (1994). Area: 16 sq. km/6 sq. mi.

scimitar /símmitər, -taar/ *n* an Arab or Turkish sword with a curved blade that broadens out as it nears the point [Mid-16C. < French *cimeterre* or Italian *scimitarra* < ?]

scindapsus /skin dápsəss/ (*plural* -**suses** *or* -**sus**) *n* a climbing plant with heart-shaped, often variegated leaves that is popular as a house plant. Native to: Asia. Genus: *Scindapsus*. [Mid-20C. Via modern Latin < Greek *skindapsos*, an ivy-like plant.]

scintigram /sínti gram/ *n* a two-dimensional image of the distribution of a radioactive tracer in a body organ such as the brain or a kidney, obtained using a special scanner (**scintiscanner**) [Mid-20C. < SCINTILLATION + -GRAM.]

scintilla /sin tíllə/ *n* a tiny amount of something ○ *There's not a scintilla of truth in what he said.* [Late 17C. < Latin, 'spark'.]

scintillate /sínti layt/ (-**lates**, -**lating**, -**lated**) *v* 1 *vi* SPARKLE to give off or reflect light in sparks or flashes 2 *vi* BE VERY DAZZLINGLY CLEVER to be dazzlingly lively, clever, or witty 3 *vt* EMIT LIGHT FLASHES to produce sparks of light when hit by particles or photons [Early 17C. < Latin *scintillare* < *scintilla* 'spark'.] —**scintillant** *adj* —**scintillantly** *adv* —**scintillator** *n*

scintillating /sínti layting/ *adj* possessing or displaying dazzling liveliness, cleverness, or wit —**scintillatingly** *adv*

scintillation /sínti láysh'n/ *n* 1 TWINKLING OF STARS the twinkling of stars, caused by refraction of light rays from the stars because of different densities in the Earth's atmosphere 2 FLASH OF LIGHT a flash of light caused by the impact of particles or photons 3 LIVELINESS dazzling liveliness, cleverness, or wit (*literary*)

scintillation counter *n* a device that detects and measures high-energy radiation through flashes of light produced when ionizing radiation impacts on a phosphorescent substance

scintiscan /sínti skan/ *n* MED = **scintigram** [Mid-20C. < SCINTILLATION + SCAN.]

scintiscanner /sínti skanər/ *n* an apparatus used in diagnosing certain diseases that produces an image (**scintigram**) of the distribution in the body of a radioactive tracer that has been administered to the patient

sciolism /sī əlizəm/ *n* displays of sham learning intended to deceive or impress [Early 19C. < late Latin *sciolus*, diminutive of *scius* 'having knowledge' < *scire* 'know'.] —**sciolist** *n* —**sciolistic** /sī ə lístik/ *adj*

scion /sī ən/ *n* 1 a living shoot or twig of a plant used for grafting to a stock 2 a child or descendant of a family, especially a rich, famous, or important family [13C. < Old French *ciun* < ?]

Scipio /skíppi ō, síppi ō/, **Publius Cornelius** (*d.* 211 BC) Roman general

Scipio Africanus (the Elder) /-áffri kaànəss/ (234?–183 BC) Roman general. Full name **Publius Cornelius Scipio**

Scipio Africanus (the Younger) (185?–129 BC) Roman general. Full name **Publius Cornelius Scipio Aemilianus**

scire facias /sīri fáyshi ass/ a writ that requires the defendant to appear in court and show why the plaintiff should not be permitted to take a specified legal step ■ *n* the judicial proceeding that produces a writ of scire facias [< Latin, 'you should cause (him) to know']

scirocco *n* METEOROL = **sirocco**

scirrhous /sírrəss, skírrəss/ *adj* describes a cancerous tumour (**carcinoma**) that is hard and fibrous [Mid-16C. < modern Latin *scirrhosus* < *scirrhus* 'hard growth' < Greek *skirros* 'hard'.] —**scirrhosity** /si róssəti, ski-/ *n*

scissel /skíss'l/ *n* metal clippings left over after discs, especially coins, have been punched out of sheets of metal [Early 17C. < French *cisaille* < *cisailler* 'clip with shears'.]

scissile /síssīl/ *adj* capable of being easily and smoothly cut, separated, or divided [Early 17C. < Latin *scissilis* < *sciss-* (see SCISSION).]

scission /sízh'n, sísh'n/ *n* the act or process of cutting, separating, or dividing [15C. Via French < Latin *scission-* < *sciss-*, past participle of *scindere* 'cut'.]

scissor /sízzər/ *vti* **1** to use scissors to cut something **2** to move the legs, arms, or body in the way that the blades of a pair of scissors open and shut ○ *The swimmer scissored through the water.* [Early 17C. < SCISSORS.]

scissors /sízzərz/ *npl* **INSTRUMENT FOR CUTTING** a hand-held cutting instrument made up of two crossed connected blades, each with a ring-shaped handle, that cut as they slide and pivot ■ *n* (*plural* **-sors**) **1 GYMNASTICS MOVEMENT** in gymnastics, a movement of the legs that resembles the opening and closing of scissors **2 TECHNIQUE IN HIGH-JUMPING** in the high jump, a simple technique of clearing the bar sideways on with each leg separately in a fast scissors movement **3** WRESTLING = **scissors hold** [14C. Via French *cisoires* < late Latin *cisoria* 'cutting tool' < Latin *cis-*, past participle stem of *caedere* 'cut'.]

scissors-and-paste *adj* crudely or hastily put together

scissors hold *n* a wrestling hold in which the legs are wrapped and the feet locked around an opponent's head or body

scissors kick *n* **1** in swimming, a kicking motion that resembles the opening and closing of scissors, used especially when doing the sidestroke **2** in soccer, a mid-air kick of the ball with the legs moving in a way that resembles the movement of scissor blades

scissortail /sízzər tayl/ (*plural* **-tails** *or* **-tail**) *n* a bird with a long forked tail, especially a scissor-tailed flycatcher

sciurine /sī yŏŏrīn/, **sciurid** /sī yŏŏrid/ *n* any rodent belonging to the family that includes squirrels, marmots, and chipmunks. Family: Sciuridae. ■ *adj* relating to or belonging to the squirrel family of rodents [Mid-19C. < Latin *sciurus* (see SQUIRREL).]

sclaff /sklaf/ *vti* in golf, to play a faulty stroke in which the club head scrapes the ground before coming into contact with the ball ■ *n* a golf stroke that is sclaffed [Early 19C. Probably an imitation of the sound.] —**sclaffer** *n*

scler- *prefix* = **sclero-** (*before vowels*)

sclera /skléerə/ *n* the dense outer coating of the eyeball that forms the white of the eye [Late 19C. Via modern Latin < Greek *sklēros* 'hard'.]

sclerenchyma /skleer éngkimə/ *n* strengthening or supporting walls of plant tissue made up of long cells or fibres and short cells (**sclereids**) [Mid-19C. < SCLERO- after *parenchyma*.] —**sclerenchymatous** /skleer eng kímmətəss/ *adj*

scleriasis /skleer ī əssiss/ *n* = **scleroderma**

sclerite /skléer īt/ *n* a hard plate or layer of chitin or calcium on the outer skeleton of an arthropod —**scleritic** /skleer íttik/ *adj*

scleritis /skleer ītiss/ *n* inflammation of the tough outer coat of the eyeball that forms the white of the eye (**sclera**) [Mid-19C. < SCLERA + -ITIS.]

sclero- *prefix* **1** hard ○ *scleroderma* **2** hardness ○ *sclerometer* **3** sclera ○ *scleritis* [< Greek *sklēros* 'hard'. Ultimately < Indo-European, 'dried up'.]

scleroderma /skléerō dúrmə/ *n* a disease in which the skin becomes progressively hard and thickened

sclerodermatous /skléerō dúrmətəss/ *adj* **1** with a hard external covering of scales or plates **2** relating to or characteristic of the skin disease scleroderma

sclerometer /sklə rómmətər, skli-, skleer rómmitər/ *n* an instrument that determines the hardness of a metal or mineral by measuring the force required to scratch or pierce it —**sclerometric** /sklérrə méttrik, skléerō-/ *adj*

sclerophyll /skléerəfil, sklérrəfil/ *n* any woody plant of dry areas with thick leathery evergreen foliage that retains water —**sclerophyllous** /sklə róffiləss, skleer-/ *adj*

scleroprotein /skléerō prṓ teen, sklerrō-/ *n* any one of a group of fibrous insoluble proteins, such as keratin, elastin, and collagen that are found in body tissue

sclerosis /sklə rṓssiss, skli-, skleer-/ (*plural* **-ses**) *n* **1** the hardening and thickening of body tissue as a result of unwarranted growth, degeneration of nerve fibres, or deposition of minerals, especially calcium **2** the hardening and thickening of a plant cell wall that occurs as lignin is deposited, turning young green growth woody —**scleroid** /skléeroyd/ *adj* —**sclerosal** *adj* —**sclerosed** *adj*

sclerotia plural of **sclerotium**

sclerotic /sklə róttik, skleer-/ *adj* **1 OF PLANT CELL WALL HARDENING** relating to the hardening and thickening of plant cell walls that turns young green growth woody **2 OF WHITE OF EYE** relating to the dense outer coating of the eyeball that forms the white of the eye (**sclera**) **3 OF SCLEROSIS OF BODY TISSUE** relating to or suffering from sclerosis of body tissue **4 INFLEXIBLE** having become unresponsively rigid, especially from longevity ○ *a political party grown sclerotic from too many years in power* ■ *n* BIOL = **sclera** [Mid-16C. < Greek *sklēros* 'hard'; + -OTIC.]

sclerotin /skléerōtin, sklérrō-/ *n* an insoluble protein that hardens and darkens the chitin on the outer skeleton of arthropods [Mid-20C. < SCLERO- after words such as *keratin*.]

sclerotise *vt* = **sclerotize**

sclerotium /sklə rṓti əm/ (*plural* **-a** /-ə/) *n* in fungi, a compact hard mass that contains stored food [Mid-19C. < modern Latin, genus of fungi < Greek *sklērotēs* 'hardness' < *sklēros* 'hard'.] —**sclerotial** *adj* —**sclerotioid** *adj*

sclerotize /skléerō tīz, sklérrō-/ (**-tizes, -tizing, -tized**), **sclerotise** (**-tises, -tising, -tised**) *vt* to harden and darken an arthropod's outer skeleton [Mid-20C. < SCLEROTIC.] —**sclerotization** /skléerō tī záysh'n, sklérrō tī-/ *n*

sclerotomy /sklə róttəmi, skleer-/ (*plural* **-mies**) *n* a surgical operation in which the outer coat (**sclera**) of the eyeball is cut, e.g. in order to remove an underlying tumour

sclerous /skléerəss, sklérrəss/ *adj* **1** describes animal parts that are bony or scaly **2** describes body tissue or body parts that have become especially hardened, as a result of the deposition of minerals

SCM *abbr* **1** State Certified Midwife **2** Student Christian Movement

Sc.M. *abbr* Master of Science

scoff[1] /skof/ *vi* **BE DERISIVE OR SCORNFUL** to express derision or scorn about somebody or something ○ *She scoffed at all our suggestions.* ■ *n* **1 EXPRESSION OF SCORN** an expression of derision or scorn **2 OBJECT OF SCORN** somebody or something that is derided or scorned [14C. Probably < Scandinavian.] —**scoffer** *n* —**scoffing** *adj* —**scoffingly** *adv*

scoff[2] /skof/ *vti* to eat food quickly and hungrily or greedily (*informal*) ■ *n* food (*slang*) [Late 18C. Variant of dialect *scaff* < ?]

Scofield /skṓ feeld/, **Sir Paul** (*b.* 1922) British actor

scold /skōld/ *v* **1** *vt* **TELL OFF** to rebuke somebody angrily **2** *vi* **SPEAK HARSHLY** to use harsh language, especially when complaining or finding fault ■ *n* **1 REBUKING PERSON** an insistent rebuker of others **2 OFFENSIVE TERM** an offensive term for a woman regarded as making a habit of using abusive language, especially when constantly reminding a man to do something (*archaic*) [13C. Possibly < Old Norse *skáld* 'poet' < the poet's role of satirizing people.] —**scolder** *n* —**scoldingly** *adv*

scolecite /skólli sīt, skṓli sīt/ *n* a white zeolite mineral consisting of hydrated calcium aluminium silicate [Early 19C. < Greek *skōlēk-*, stem of *skōlēx* 'worm'.]

scolex /skṓ leks/ (*plural* **-leces** /-li seez/ *or* **-lices**) *n* the head of a tapeworm, with suckers or hooks that enable the parasitic worm to attach itself to its host [Mid-19C. Via modern Latin < Greek *skōlēx* 'worm'.]

scoliosis /skṓli ṓssiss/ *n* an excessive sideways curvature of the spine [Early 18C. Via modern Latin < Greek *skoliōsis* < *skolios* 'bent, curved'.] —**scoliotic** /-óttik/ *adj*

scollop *n* MARINE BIOL = **scallop**

sconce[1] /skonss/ *n* a wall bracket for holding candles or, sometimes, electric light bulbs [14C. Via Old French *esconse* < medieval Latin *absconsa laterna* 'hidden lantern' < *abscondere* (see ABSCOND).]

sconce[2] /skonss/ *n* a small defensive fort or earthwork [Late 16C. < Dutch *schans* 'brushwood, earthwork' < ?]

scone /skon, skōn/ *n* **1** an individual baked product similar to a sweet or savoury unyeasted cake, usually served split and buttered **2** *ANZ* the human head (*informal humorous*) [Early 16C]

Scone /skoon/ village in central Scotland, famous for the Stone of Destiny, on which Scottish kings were crowned, which was originally located there. Population: 4,533.

scoop /skoop/ *n* **1 SHOVEL** a utensil with a short handle and deep rounded sides, used for shovelling or ladling grain, flour, or other dry or semisolid substances **2 LADLE** a utensil with a long handle and round bowl, used for transferring liquids **3 UTENSIL WITH BOWL-SHAPED HEAD** a utensil with a long handle and a small hemispherical bowl, used for serving such things as ice cream and mashed potato or making melon balls **4 DIGGING PART** the part of a dredge or digging machine that is used for excavating **5 QUANTITY LIFTED BY A SCOOP** the quantity that is taken by a scoop ○ *three scoops of ice cream* **6 DIGGING MOTION** a curving digging movement of a scoop or the hand **7 CAVITY** a shallow cavity, hole, or other hollow area in something **8 EXCLUSIVE** a news story that is published by a newspaper, magazine, or news programme before its rivals (*informal*) ○ *scoop of the year* **9 NEWS** the latest news or gossip (*informal*) ○ *What's the scoop?* **10 SLIDING UP TO PITCH** in vocal and instrumental music, a sliding up to a pitch **11 QUICK PROFIT** a large amount of money made quickly (*informal*) ■ *v* **1** *vt* **HOLLOW OUT** to create a shallow hole in something with a scoop or similar object, or a curved hand ○ *He scooped out a hole in the earth.* **2** *vt* **REMOVE** to remove an amount of a liquid or solid substance with a scoop or similar object, or a curved hand ○ *scooping up water with a ladle* **3** *vt* **LIFT SWIFTLY** to pick somebody or something up swiftly and without ceremony ○ *She scooped him up in her arms.* **4** *vt* **PUBLISH OR BROADCAST FIRST** to publish or broadcast an item of news before any other newspaper, magazine, or news programme ○ *The newspaper scooped its rivals for the second time in a week.* ○ *scooping the hottest story of the year* **5** *vt* **GET MONEY** to win or otherwise obtain a large amount of money **6** *vti* **HIT BALL UPWARDS** to hit a ball upwards from underneath so that it rises into the air [14C. < Middle Low German and Middle Dutch *schōpe* 'bucket for bailing, bucket of a waterwheel'.] —**scooper** *n*

scoop neck *n* a low curved neckline on an article of women's clothing

scoosh /skŏŏsh/ *vti Scotland* **SQUIRT** to squirt a liquid, or be squirted (*informal*) ■ *n Scotland* (*informal*) **1 SQUIRTING** an act of squirting **2 FIZZY DRINK** a sweet fizzy drink, especially lemonade [19C. An imitation of the sound.]

scoot /skoot/ *v* **1** *vi* **LEAVE** to go away quickly (*informal; usually used as a command*) **2** *vi* **MOVE QUICKLY** to move, run, or go somewhere quickly (*informal*) **3** *vt US* **SEND QUICKLY** to move or send something quickly (*informal*) ○ *Scoot that file to me as soon as you can.* **4** *vti Scotland* **SQUIRT LIQUID** to squirt a liquid, or be squirted ■ *n* (*informal*) **1 SWIFT MOVEMENT** a swift movement or trip ○ *a quick scoot to the supermarket* **2** *Scotland* **A SQUIRT** a gush of liquid [Mid-18C. < ?]

scooter /skŏŏtər/ *n* **1** a child's toy consisting of a handlebar attached by a long rod to a footboard on two wheels **2** AUTOMOT = **motor scooter** [Early 19C. < SCOOT.]

scope[1] /skōp/ *n* **1 ROOM TO ACT** freedom, space, or capacity to act ○ *not much scope for originality* **2 RANGE COVERED** the range covered by an activity, subject, or topic ○ *a question that is beyond the scope of this lecture* **3 MENTAL CAPACITY** the extent of somebody's mental capacity **4 MOORING CABLE** the length of a ship's mooring cable **5 RANGE OF A LOGICAL OPERATOR** the range of application or boundaries of a logical operator, usually indicated by parentheses. The scope of 'and' in '(p and q) or r' is limited to 'p' and 'q'. [Mid-16C. Via Italian *scopo* 'aim, purpose' < Greek *skopos* 'target'.]

scope[2] /skōp/ *n* any optical device or tool whose name ends in '-scope' such as a telescope, microscope, endoscope, or oscilloscope (*informal*) [Early 17C. Shortening.]

scope[3] /skōp/ (**scopes, scoping, scoped**) *vt* to look at or examine something (*informal*) [Mid-17C. < SCOPE[1].]

scope out *vt US* to investigate or study something (*informal*)

-scope *suffix* an instrument for viewing or observing ○ *nephroscope* [Via modern Latin *-scopium* < Greek *skopein* 'look, see'. Ultimately < Indo-European.] —**-scopic** *suffix* —**-scopy** *suffix*

scopolamine /skə póllə meen, -min/ *n* $C_{17}H_{21}NO_4$ a colourless thick liquid poisonous alkaloid found in some plants of the nightshade family and used as a truth serum, to prevent motion sickness, and as a sedative [Late 19C. < modern Latin *Scopolia japonica*, the Japanese belladonna, after G. A. Scopoli (1723–88), Italian naturalist.]

scopula /skóppyŏŏlə/ (*plural* **-las** *or* **-lae** /-lee/) *n* a tuft of dense hairs on the back of the legs of some insects or spiders [Early 19C. < late Latin, 'little broom'.]

scorbutic /skawr byŏŏtik/ *adj* relating to, affected with, or causing scurvy [Mid-17C. Via modern Latin *scorbuticus* < medieval Latin *scorbutus* 'scurvy'.] —**scorbutically** *adv*

scorch /skawrch/ *v* **1** *vti* **BURN SURFACE** to burn the surface of something, or to be burnt so as to cause pain, injury, or discolouring ○ *scorched the handkerchief with the iron* **2** *vti* **DRY OUT** to dry or parch something with intense heat, or to become dried out or parched because of intense heat ○ *The plains had been scorched by the sun.* **3** *vt* **CRITICIZE** to subject somebody to severe criticism (*informal*) **4** *vi* **DRIVE FAST** to drive or travel extremely fast (*informal*) ○ *scorching down the motorway in a Porsche* ■ *n* **1 SURFACE BURN** a burn, or burn mark on the surface of something ○ *The iron left a slight scorch on the blouse.* **2 DISCOLORATION ON PLANTS** a brown marking on plants or vegetables caused by disease, insecticide, or heat [12C. Probably < Scandinavian.]

scorched earth policy *n* **1** a policy of destroying crops or buildings, especially by burning, or of removing anything that might be useful to an advancing enemy in wartime **2** a strategy adopted by a company facing a hostile takeover whereby it makes itself appear a financially less attractive acquisition until the threat has gone

scorcher /skáwrchər/ *n* **1 SOMETHING THAT BURNS** somebody or something that scorches **2 HOT DAY** an extremely hot day (*informal*) ○ *Yesterday was fairly warm but today is a scorcher!* **3 CRITICAL REMARK** a severely critical remark **4 SOMETHING VERY GOOD** something extraordinary or excellent (*informal*)

scorching /skáwrching/ *adj* extremely hot (*informal*)

score /skawr/ *n* **1 POINTS GAINED** the total number of points gained by a player or team at the end of or during a match or game **2 TALLY OF POINTS GAINED** a record of the number of points gained by a player or team in a match or game ○ *Who's keeping the score?* **3 GAINING OF POINT** the gaining of a point or points in a match or game **4** (*plural* **score** *or* **scores**) **GROUP OF 20** a group of twenty things or people ○ *A score or more people showed up.* **5 PRINTED MUSIC** a written or printed copy of a musical composition ○ *distributed copies of the score to the chorus* **6 MUSIC COMPOSED** the music that has been composed for a film, play, or musical ○ *a film with a breathtaking score* **7 COPY OF CHOREOGRAPHIC NOTATION** a written record of the choreography for a dance **8 NOTCH** a notch or incision cut into the surface of something **9 PARTIAL CUT** a crease or superficial cut made in something, such as a piece of paper to enable it to be folded or separated easily **10 GRUDGE** a grievance that is not resolved and incurs resentment **11 RECORD OF MONEY OWED** a record of an amount of money due for payment **12 MONEY OWED** an amount of money due for payment **13 PRESENT SITUATION** the present state or actual facts of a situation (*informal*) ○ *What's the score, are you coming or not?* **14 SUCCESS** a successful result or achievement, especially one that is significant (*informal*) **15 DRUG DEAL** a purchase of illegal drugs (*slang*) **16 ROBBERY** the successful theft of something (*informal*) **17 SEXUAL CONQUEST** a successful seduction of somebody or the sexual encounter itself (*informal*) **18 GROOVE FOR ROPE** a groove cut in wood to hold a rope ■ **scores** *npl* **MANY** a great many ○ *Scores of members protested at the decision.* ■ *v* (**scores, scoring, scored**) **1** *vti* **GAIN POINTS** to gain a point or points in a match or game ○ *scored twice in the second half* **2** *vt* **GAIN TOTAL OF POINTS IN GAME** to gain a total number of points in a match, game, or other competition **3** *vti* **RECORD POINTS** to keep a record of the number of points gained in a match, game, or other competition ○ *Who's scoring?* **4** *vt* **ASSIGN SOMEBODY POINTS** to award a particular number of points to somebody in a match, game, or other competition ○ *Three of the judges scored her a perfect 10.* **5** *vt* **BE WORTH CERTAIN POINTS IN GAME** to count for a particular number of points in a match, game, or other competition ○ *Hitting the red area scores ten.* **6** *vt* **CUT LINES IN** to make notches, cuts, or lines in a surface **7** *vt* **CUT SUPERFICIALLY** to make a superficial cut or crease in something, such as a piece of paper in order to fold, tear, or break it easily **8** *vt* **WRITE SOMETHING BY MAKING INCISIONS** to write something by means of notches, incisions, or lines cut into a surface ○ *names scored on the back of the bench with a penknife* **9** *vti* **CROSS OUT** to draw a line through something in order to mark it as cancelled or deleted **10** *vt* **RECORD MONEY OWED** to keep a record of an amount of money owed by somebody by making a series of marks next to his or her name **11** *vi* **DO WELL** to secure an advantage in a particular field or area of activity ○ *She scores because she can communicate.* **12** *vt* **ORCHESTRATE** to orchestrate or arrange a piece of music **13** *vt* **COMPOSE MUSIC FOR** to write the music for a film, play, or musical **14** *vt* **WRITE CHOREOGRAPHY FOR** to write out the choreography for a dance **15** *vt* **GET** to succeed in getting something (*informal*) ○ *scored front-row tickets for the concert* **16** *vti* **BUY DRUGS** to buy illegal drugs (*slang*) **17** *vi* **HAVE SEX** to succeed in having sex with somebody, especially a new sexual partner (*slang*) **18** *vt US* to get to see or experience something (*slang*) [Pre-12C. < Old Norse *skor* 'notch, tally, 20'.] ◇ **on this** *or* **that score** as far as this or that is concerned ○ *Her health is fine, so there's no need to worry on that score.*

scoreboard /skáwr bawrd/ *n* a board at a sporting venue on which the score of a game, match, or other competition in progress is displayed

scorecard /skáwr kaard/ *n* **1** a small card used by a player to keep a record of his or her own score, e.g. in golf **2** a card listing the players in a game or match that enables a spectator to identify who is who and to keep a record of the progress of play

score draw *n* a result in a match, especially a football match, in which both sides have scored the same number of goals

scorekeeper /skáwr keepər/ *n* a keeper of the score in a game, match, or other competition —**scorekeeping** *n*

scoreless /skáwrləss/ *adj* having no points or goals scored

scoreline /skáwr līn/ *n* the total number of points gained by players or teams in a match or game

scorer /skáwrər/ *n* **1** a person who scores a point or goal in a game or match **2** SPORTS = **scorekeeper 3** a device for cutting a notch or incision into something

Scoresby Sound /skáwrzbi-/ arm of the Norwegian Sea in E Greenland. Length: 451 km/280 mi.

scoresheet /skáwr sheet/ *n* a record of who has scored a point or goal in a game or match, especially in soccer or rugby

scoria /skáwri ə/ (*plural* **-ae** /-ri ee/) *n* **1** loose rubbly porous solidified lava that is ejected from a volcano and builds up round the crater **2** METALL = **slag** *n.* 1 [14C. Via Latin < Greek *skōria* 'refuse, dross' < *skōr* 'dung'.] —**scoriaceous** /skáwri áyshəss/ *adj*

scorify /skáwri fī/ (**-fies, -fying, -fied**) *vt* to purify ore by separating it out into metal and slag —**scorification** /skáwrifi káysh'n/ *n* —**scorifier** *n*

scorn /skawrn/ *n* **1 DISDAIN** a strong feeling of contempt ○ *poured scorn on my attempts at writing* **2 OBJECT OF CONTEMPT** somebody or something that is held in contempt ○ *Their behaviour made them the scorn of the entire community.* ■ *v* **1** *vt* **DISDAIN** to hold somebody or something in contempt **2** *vti* **REJECT CONTEMPTUOUSLY** to reject something with contempt ○ *They had scorned our attempts at peace.* [12C. < Old French *escarn* < *escharnir* 'mock, despise' < Germanic.] —**scorner** *n*

scornful /skáwrnf'l/ *adj* feeling or expressing great contempt for somebody or something —**scornfully** *adv* —**scornfulness** *n*

Scorpio /skáwrpi ō/ *n* **1** ASTRON = **Scorpius 2** the eighth sign of the zodiac, represented by a scorpion and lasting from approximately 23 October to 21 November **3 Scorpio** (*plural* **-os**), **Scorpian** somebody whose birthday falls between 23 October and 21 November [14C. < Latin (see SCORPION).] —**Scorpio** *adj*

scorpioid /skáwrpi oyd/ *adj* **1** having the main stem curled at the end ○ *a scorpioid cyme* **2** relating to or resembling a scorpion [Mid-19C. < Greek *skorpioeidēs* < *skorpios* 'scorpion'.]

scorpion /skáwrpi ən/ *n* **1** a nocturnal arachnid of warm dry regions that has a long body with pincers in front and a thin segmented upturned tail tipped with a venomous sting. Order: Scorpionida. **2** in the Bible, a whip with metal barbs [12C. Via French < Latin *scorpion-*, stem of *scorpio*, alteration of *scorpius* < Greek *skorpios* 'scorpion, scorpion fish'.]

Scorpion /skáwrpi ən/ *n* **1** ASTRON = **Scorpius 2** ZODIAC = **Scorpio** *n.* 2

scorpion fish *n* a small brightly coloured fish with venomous spines in its fins. Family: Scorpaenidae.

scorpion fly *n* a nonvenomous insect that has downward-pointing mouthparts and a reproductive organ in the male resembling the sting of a scorpion. Order: Mecoptera.

Scorpius /skáwrpi əss/ *n* a bright zodiacal constellation containing the red star Antares. See illustration at **constellation** [15C. < Latin *scorpius* (see SCORPION).]

Scorsese /skawr sáyzi/, **Martin** (*b.* 1942) US film director

scot /skot/ *n* formerly, a type of tax (*archaic*) [Pre-12C. Partly < Old Norse *skot* 'shot', partly < Old French *escot* < Germanic.]

Scot /skot/ *n* **1** a person who comes from Scotland, or is of Scottish descent. **2** a member of a people who lived in Ireland and who after making invasions of W Britain from the 3rd century AD, settled in N Britain during the 6th century [Pre-12C. Via medieval Latin < late Latin *Scottus*.]

USAGE Scot, Scotch, Scots, or **Scottish**? All these words make a direct connection to Scotland, but they are used in different ways. ***Scottish*** is the most generally used adjective to describe the country and people of Scotland (*Scottish history*; *a Scottish poet*; *Scottish Gaelic*; *a Scottish accent*), whereas ***Scots*** is normally applied to people or to a form of English spoken in lowland Scotland (*Scots Guard*; *a Scots speaker*). A ***Scot*** is a person from Scotland; more specific words are *Scotsman* and *Scotswoman*. ***Scotch*** as an adjective is a literary word more closely associated with the writing of Robert Burns and Sir Walter Scott and has fallen out of general use, usually being considered offensive except in fixed expressions such as *Scotch pine* and *Scotch mist*.

scot and lot *n* formerly, a municipal tax that entitled those who paid it to receive the vote [*Lot* in an earlier sense 'tax or due']

scotch[1] /skoch/ *vt* **1 STOP** to put a stop to something such as a rumour **2 GASH** to make a gash or score in something (*archaic*) ■ *n* **SCORE IN SOMETHING** a cut or score in something (*archaic*) [15C. < ?]

scotch[2] /skoch/ *n* a wedge used to prevent something from moving ■ *vt* to wedge something in order to prevent it from moving [Early 17C. < ?]

Scotch /skoch/ *n* **1 Scotch, Scotch whisky WHISKY** whisky produced in Scotland **2** LANG = **Scots** *n.* ■ ⚠ *npl* **OFFENSIVE TERM** an offensive term for people who come from Scotland or who are of Scottish descent ■ ⚠ *adj* **1 OFFENSIVE TERM** an offensive term meaning relating to Scotland, its people, or its culture **2 FROM SCOTLAND** made in Scotland, or typical of a style prevalent in Scotland ○ *Scotch broth* [Late 16C. Contraction of SCOTTISH.]

Scotch broth *n* a traditional Scottish soup made with lamb or beef, mixed root vegetables, and pearl barley

Scotch catch *n* MUSIC = **Scotch snap**

Scotch egg *n* a hard-boiled egg wrapped in sausagemeat, coated with breadcrumbs, and deep fried. It is served cut in half, either hot or cold.

Scotch-Irish *npl US* = **Scottish-Irish** —**Scotch-Irish** *adj*

Scotchman /skóchmən/ (*plural* **-men** /-mən/) *n* an offensive term for a Scotsman (*archaic*)

Scotch mist *n* **1** a fine, damp mist **2** a figment of somebody's imagination (*humorous*)

Scotch pine *n US* **1** TREES = **Scots pine** *n.* 1 **2** INDUST = **Scots pine** *n.* 2

Scotch snap *n* in music, a rhythmic figure consisting of a dotted note preceded by a note the value of the dot

Scotch terrier *n* = **Scottish terrier**

Scotch whisky *n* BEVERAGES = **Scotch** *n.* 1

Scotchwoman /skóch wŏŏmmən/ (*plural* **-en** /-wimmin/) *n* an offensive term for a Scotswoman (*archaic*)

scoter /skṓtər/ (*plural* **-ters** *or* **-ter**) *n* a large sea duck, the male of which has black plumage with white spots on its head. Native to: northern coasts of North

America, Asia, and Europe. Genus: *Melanitta*. [Late 17C]

scot-free *adv* without punishment being exacted or payment being made

scotia /skṓshə/ *n* a deep concave moulding, especially on the base of a column [Mid-16C. Via Latin < Greek *skotia* < *skotos* 'darkness' (from the shadow inside the moulding).]

Scotia /skṓshə/ *n* a former name for Scotland, still sometimes used in literary contexts (*archaic or literary*) [Early 17C. < medieval Latin.] —**Scotian** *adj*

Scotism /skṓtizəm/ *n* the philosophical tenets of, or school of scholastic philosophy founded by, Duns Scotus, the 13th-century Scottish philosopher and theologian —**Scotist** *adj* —**Scotistic** /skō tístik/ *adj*

Scotland /skótlənd/ country forming the northernmost part of Great Britain and of the United Kingdom. Capital: Edinburgh. Population: 5,132,400 (1994). Area: 77,080 sq. km/29,750 sq. mi.

Scotland Yard *n* the headquarters of the Metropolitan Police in London, from which national criminal investigations are coordinated [Because it was originally located in *Great Scotland Yard*, where the palace used by visiting kings of Scotland once stood]

Scot Nat /-nát/ *n* a Scottish Nationalist (*informal*) [Shortening]

scotoma /skə tṓmə/ (*plural* **-mas** *or* **-mata** /-mətə/) *n* a permanent or temporary area of diminished sight in the field of vision [Mid-16C. Via late Latin < Greek *skotōma* 'dizziness' < *skotos* 'darkness'.] —**scotomatous** *adj*

scotopia /skə tṓpi ə, skō-/ *n* the ability to see in poor light or in the dark [Early 20C. < Greek *skotos* 'darkness' + -OPIA.] —**scotopic** /-tóppik, -/ *adj*

Scots /skots/ *adj* relating to Scotland or its people or culture ■ *n* a Germanic language spoken in Scotland, closely related to English [14C. Contraction of SCOTTISH.]

Scots Guards *npl* one of the regiments of the Household Division in the British Army (+ *singular or plural verb*)

Scots-Irish *npl, adj* = **Scottish-Irish**

Scots law *n* the Scottish legal system, different from that of England and based on Roman Law

Scotsman /skótsmən/ (*plural* **-men** /-mən/) *n* a man who comes from Scotland or who has Scottish ancestry

USAGE See ***Scot***.

Scots pine *n* **1** a pine with a reddish trunk, twisted needles, and hard yellow wood. Native to: Europe, Asia. *Pinus sylvestris*. US term **Scotch pine** *n*. 1 **2** the wood of the Scots pine, valuable as timber. US term **Scotch pine** *n*. 2

Scotswoman /skóts wŏŏmən/ (*plural* **-en** /-wimin/) *n* a woman who comes from Scotland or who has Scottish ancestry

USAGE See ***Scot***.

Scott /skot/, **Sir Peter** (1909–89) British ornithologist and painter

Scott, Robert Falcon (1868–1912) British naval officer and explorer. Known as **Scott of the Antarctic**

Scott, Sir Walter (1771–1832) Scottish novelist and poet

Scotticism /skóttissizəm/ *n* a word, phrase, or idiom that is characteristic of the Scots language or the English spoken in Scotland

Scottie /skótti/ *n* (*informal*) **1** a Scottish terrier **2** an offensive term for somebody, especially a man, who is Scottish

Scottish /skóttish/ *adj* relating to Scotland or its people or culture ■ *npl* people who come from Scotland ■ *n* LANG = **Scots** *n*. [12C. < SCOT.] —**Scottishness** *n*

USAGE See ***Scot***.

Scottish Blackface /-blák fayss/ *n* a mountain sheep with horns and a black face, belonging to a breed mainly bred in Scotland

Scottish Certificate of Education *n* full form of **SCE**

Scottish English *n* a variety of English spoken in Scotland

Scottish Gaelic *n* the Celtic language spoken in parts of the Highlands and Western Isles of Scotland

Scottish-Irish, Scots-Irish *npl* Irish people of Scottish descent or Americans descended from these people. US term **Scotch-Irish** —**Scottish-Irish** *adj*

Scottish Land Court *n* a Scottish court whose jurisdiction covers the various forms of agricultural tenancy

Scottish Nationalist *n* a member or supporter of the Scottish National Party ■ *adj* relating to or belonging to the Scottish National Party

Scottish National Party *n* a Scottish political party founded in 1934 that advocates full political independence for Scotland

Scottish terrier, Scotch terrier *n* a terrier of a breed with short sturdy legs, pointed ears, and thick wiry, usually black hair

scoundrel /skówndrəl/ *n* a dishonourable or unprincipled person [Late 16C. < ?] —**scoundrelly** *adj*

scour[1] /skowr/ *v* **1** *vti* CLEAN BY RUBBING to clean or brighten something by rubbing it with an abrasive substance or material **2** *vti* REMOVE SOMETHING BY RUBBING to remove something by rubbing with an abrasive substance or material **3** *vt* FREE SOMETHING FROM DIRT OR IMPURITIES to remove dirt or impurities from something by washing **4** *vt* FLUSH SOMETHING OUT to clear something out by using water **5** *vi* HAVE DIARRHOEA to be affected by diarrhoea (*refers to cattle*) ■ *n* **1** SCOURING a scouring of something **2** CLEANING SUBSTANCE a substance or tool that can be used for cleaning **3** PLACE SCOURED a place that has been scoured, especially by water **4** DIARRHOEA diarrhoea affecting cattle and pigs (*often used in the plural with a singular or plural verb*) [12C. Via Middle Low German or Middle Dutch < late Latin *excurare* 'clean out, take care of' < Latin *cura* 'care'.] —**scourer** *n*

scour[2] /skowr/ *vti* **1** to search something thoroughly and quickly for somebody or something ○ *They scoured the countryside for him, but to no avail.* **2** to move quickly over or through an area [15C. Probably < N Germanic.] —**scourer** *n*

scourge /skurj/ *n* **1** TORMENTOR somebody or something that is perceived as an agent of punishment, destruction, or severe criticism ○ *the scourge of my childhood* **2** WHIP a whip that is used for inflicting punishment ■ *vt* (**scourges, scourging, scourged**) **1** PUNISH to punish or criticize somebody severely **2** WHIP to whip somebody severely [12C. < Old French *escorgier* 'to whip' < Latin *corrigia* 'thong, whip'.] —**scourger** *n*

scouring rush *n* a horsetail with a rough stem, especially the Dutch rush. Use: formerly, scouring. Genus: *Equisetum*.

scourings /skówringz/ *npl* the material removed or left after scouring something, especially that left after scouring grain

scouse /skowss/ *n* a stew made from leftover meat with potatoes and vegetables (*regional*) [Mid-19C. Shortening of LOBSCOUSE.]

Scouse /skowss/ *n* (*informal*) **1** **Scouse, Scouser** /skówssər/ SOMEBODY FROM LIVERPOOL somebody who comes from Liverpool **2** LIVERPOOL DIALECT the dialect spoken in Liverpool ■ *adj* OF LIVERPOOL relating to Liverpool or its people or English dialect (*informal*) [Mid-19C. Shortening of LOBSCOUSE.]

scout /skowt/ *n* **1** SOLDIER SENT TO GATHER INFORMATION somebody, especially a soldier, who is sent to gather information about an enemy's position or movements **2** SPORTS, ARTS = **talent scout** **3** RECONNAISSANCE CRAFT OR VEHICLE a ship, aircraft, or vehicle designed and used for reconnaissance purposes **4** RECONNOITRING a gathering of information concerning an enemy's position or movements **5** PERSON a person, usually a boy or man (*dated informal*) ○ *Be a good scout and give me a hand here.* **6** OXFORD COLLEGE SERVANT somebody employed to clean students' rooms at Oxford University ■ *v* **1** *vti* SEARCH AREA to make a search of an area for somebody or something ○ *scouting around for a place to camp* **2** *vi* GATHER INFORMATION to seek out information about somebody or something, especially about an enemy's position or movements **3** *vti* SEEK OUT NEW TALENT to look for talented players for a sports team, or for talented performers for a show or group [14C. < Old French *escouter* 'to listen' < Latin *auscultare*.] —**scouter** *n*

Scout, scout *n* a member of the Scout Association, an international youth organization founded for boys in 1908 by Lord Baden-Powell [Early 20C. < SCOUT.]

Scouter /skówtər/ *n* an adult who is a troop leader in the Scout Association

Scouting /skówting/ *n* the activities of the Scout Association

scoutmaster /skówt maastər/ *n* a man who is in charge of a troop of Scouts

scow /skow/ *n* **1** a barge for transporting freight **2** a flat-bottomed sailing boat [Mid-17C. < Dutch *schouw*.]

scowl /skowl/ *n* an expression of anger, displeasure, or menace made by drawing the eyebrows together towards the middle of the forehead ■ *vi* to draw the eyebrows together towards the middle of the forehead in an expression of anger, displeasure, or menace [14C. Probably < N Germanic.] —**scowler** *n*

SCPO *abbr* Senior Chief Petty Officer

SCR *abbr* senior common room

scrabble /skrább'l/ *v* (**-bles, -bling, -bled**) **1** *vi* SCRATCH AT to scrape or scratch at something with small, hurried movements of the fingers, toes, or claws ○ *The cat was scrabbling at the door.* **2** *vi* FEEL WITH FINGERS to grope about frantically in an effort to find something ○ *She scrabbled around trying to find the torch.* **3** *vi* CLIMB OVER to climb hastily or clumsily up or over something **4** *vi* STRUGGLE TO GET SOMETHING to struggle desperately to get something **5** *vt* PRODUCE SOMETHING WITH DIFFICULTY to produce something hastily and with difficulty from scarce resources **6** *vti* SCRIBBLE to scribble something ■ *n* **1** A SCRATCHING AT a scraping or scratching at something with short hurried movements of the fingers, toes, or claws **2** A SEARCH WITH FINGERS a frantic groping about in an effort to find something **3** A CLIMB OVER SOMETHING a climb up or over something, performed hastily or clumsily **4** A STRUGGLE TO GET SOMETHING a desperate struggle to acquire or gain something **5** A SCRIBBLING a scribbling of something **6** SOMETHING SCRIBBLED something that somebody has scribbled [Mid-16C. < Middle Dutch *schrabbelen* 'scratch repeatedly' < *schrabben* 'scratch or scrape'.] —**scrabbler** *n*

Scrabble /skrább'l/ *tdmk* a trademark for a board game in which the players try to form words by placing tiles, each with a single letter on it, on the squares of a board

scrabbly /skrábbli/ (**-blier, -bliest**) *adj* characterized by a scratching sound

scrag /skrag/ *n* **1** THIN PERSON OR ANIMAL an unattractively thin person or animal **2** NECK somebody's neck (*informal*) ■ *vt* (**scrags, scragging, scragged**) STRANGLE to throttle or strangle somebody (*informal*) [Mid-16C. Probably < dialect *crag* 'neck' < Middle Dutch *crāghe* 'throat'.]

scraggly /skrággli/ (**-glier, -gliest**) *adj* untidy in appearance or shape [Mid-19C. < SCRAG.] —**scraggliness** *n*

scraggy /skrággi/ (**-gier, -giest**) *adj* bony and thin ○ *a scraggy little cat* [Early 17C. < SCRAG.] —**scraggily** *adv* —**scragginess** *n*

SYNONYMS See ***thin***.

scram /skram/ *v* (**scrams, scramming, scrammed**) **1** *vi* LEAVE QUICKLY to get out or leave quickly (*informal; usually used as a command*) **2** *vti* SHUT DOWN NUCLEAR REACTOR to shut down a nuclear reactor rapidly in an emergency, or be shut down rapidly ■ *n* REACTOR SHUTDOWN a rapid shutting-down of a nuclear reactor in an emergency [Early 20C. < ?]

scramble /skrámb'l/ *v* (**-bles, -bling, -bled**) **1** *vi* CLAMBER to climb or advance over something using both hands and feet ○ *We managed to scramble over the fence.* **2** *vi* HURRY to move in haste and with a sense of urgency **3** *vi* COMPETE FRANTICALLY to struggle or compete frantically in order to get something ○ *Everyone was scrambling for the best seats.* **4** *vt* JUMBLE THINGS TOGETHER to mix or gather two or more things together haphazardly **5** *vt* BEAT AND COOK EGGS to beat together and cook eggs, butter, and milk **6** *vt* ENCODE TRANSMITTED SIGNALS to render a telecommunications or broadcast signal unintelligible by means of an electronic device **7** *vti* LAUNCH AIRCRAFT AGAINST ATTACK to launch a large number of aircraft in a short space of time in response to an impending attack, or to be launched in these circumstances ■ *n* **1** HARD CLIMB a difficult climb or walk that involves using the hands as well as the feet but no ropes **2** DASH OR STRUGGLE a hasty, undignified, or disorganized struggle for something or in order to do something **3** MOTORCYCLE RACE a motorcycle race over rough terrain **4** LAUNCH OF AIRCRAFT the scrambling of military aircraft **5** CONFUSED MASS a jumbled mass of people or things [Late 16C. Thought to suggest the action.]

scrambled eggs *n* a dish made by beating eggs, milk, and butter together and cooking them in a pan ■ *npl* gold braid attached to the peak of the cap of a senior military officer (*slang*)

scrambler /skrámblər/ *n* **1 STRAGGLING PLANT** a plant with long straggling shoots that are held up by adjacent plants **2 DEVICE TO ENCODE TRANSMITTED SIGNALS** an electronic device that renders telecommunications or broadcast signals unintelligible without a special receiver **3 ROUGH-TERRAIN MOTORCYCLE** a motorcycle designed for racing across rough terrain

scramjet /skrám jet/ *n* a ramjet aircraft in which fuel is burned in air that is moving at supersonic speeds [Mid-20C. < The initial letters of SUPERSONIC and COMBUSTION + RAMJET.]

scran /skran/ *n* food (*regional*) [Early 19C. < ?]

scrap[1] /skrap/ *n* **1 FRAGMENT** a small piece or remnant that has been detached or torn off from a larger piece **2 WASTE MATERIAL** waste material, especially metal awaiting reprocessing **3 SMALL PIECE** a very small piece of something ○ *There's not a scrap of evidence to prove it.* **4 BIT OF WRITTEN OR PRINTED MATERIAL** a short piece of writing, or a cutting from something printed ■ **scraps** *npl* **LEFTOVERS** pieces of leftover food ○ *table scraps* ■ *vt* (**scraps, scrapping, scrapped**) **1 GET RID OF SOMETHING** to discard or discontinue something because it is considered useless or ineffective **2 CONVERT SOMETHING TO SCRAP** to convert something into scrap material ○ *scrapping old warships* [14C. < Old Norse *skrap* 'scraps, trifles'.]

scrap[2] /skrap/ *n* a minor fight or disagreement (*informal*) ■ *vi* (**scraps, scrapping, scrapped**) to have a minor fight or disagreement with somebody [Late 17C. < ?]

scrapbook /skráp bòòk/ *n* a blank book or album for pasting in photos, pictures, cuttings, or other material

scrape /skrayp/ *v* (**scrapes, scraping, scraped**) **1** *vti* **RUB SURFACE** to move something hard, sharp, or rough across a surface, especially in order to clean it ○ *scraping the wall to remove the paint* **2** *vt* **TAKE OFF** to remove something by applying a hard or sharp edge to it and rubbing with it ○ *My efforts to scrape the paint off failed.* ○ *scraped out the burnt contents of the pot* **3** *vt* **SCRATCH** to scratch, cut, or damage something by bringing it into contact with a rough or abrasive surface ○ *fell and scraped my knees* **4** *vti* **MAKE GRATING NOISE** to make a harsh grating sound or cause something to make such a sound ○ *scraping his chair along the floor* **5** *vi* **SCRIMP** to live economically in an effort to save money ○ *scraping by on a single income* **6** *vti* **ONLY JUST DO SOMETHING** to manage only just to do or achieve something ○ *He just scraped through law school.* **7** *vt* **DRAW HAIR BACK** to draw something, especially the hair, back tightly ○ *She wore her hair scraped back in a bun.* ■ *n* **1 SCRAPING** a scraping of something ○ *I'll give the paint a quick scrape.* **2 LIGHT SCRATCH** a light cut, graze, or area of damage caused by contact with a rough or abrasive surface **3 GRATING SOUND** a sharp, grating sound ○ *the scrape of chairs on the bare floor* **4 DANGEROUS SITUATION** a dangerous, difficult, or awkward situation (*informal*) **5 MINOR FIGHT** a minor fight or disagreement (*informal*) [Old English *scrapian* 'scratch' < Germanic] — **scraper** *n*

scrape together, scrape up *vt* to manage with difficulty to collect together an amount of something, especially money, or a number of people or things

scraperboard /skráypər bawrd/ *n* **1** a drawing board that is covered with a layer of white clay on top of which is a layer of black that can be scraped away to make white-line drawings. US term **scratchboard 2** a drawing produced on a scraperboard

scrapheap /skráp heep/ *n* **1** a large pile of unwanted or discarded items, especially those being used as scrap material **2** an imagined place to which people and things discarded as worn out and useless are consigned (*informal*) ○ *workers who are relegated to the scrapheap at 50*

scrapie /skráypi/ *n* a usually fatal disease affecting the nervous system of sheep and goats that is marked by intense itching and loss of muscular control [Early 20C. < SCRAPE, because the animals rub against objects to alleviate itching.]

scrapper /skráppər/ *n* an enthusiastic, determined fighter, especially a boxer (*slang*) [Late 19C. < SCRAP[2].]

scrapple /skrápp'l/ *n US* scraps of pork cooked with cornmeal and seasonings, formed into a loaf, and cooled [Mid-19C. < SCRAP[1].]

scrappy[1] /skráppi/ (**-pier, -piest**) *adj* **1** consisting of scraps or fragments **2** poorly held together or structured — **scrappily** *adv* —**scrappiness** *n*

scrappy[2] /skráppi/ (**-pier, -piest**) *adj* (*informal*) **1** fighting with enthusiasm and determination **2** too ready to fight or quarrel —**scrappily** *adv* —**scrappiness** *n*

scrapyard /skráp yaard/ *n* a place where scrap is brought and kept before being reprocessed or discarded

scratch /skrach/ *v* **1** *vt* **MAKE MARK** to scrape or make a slight mark in the surface of something ○ *He scratched the table top with the knife.* **2** *vti* **TEAR SKIN** to make a thin tear in the surface of the skin of a person or animal ○ *The cat scratched me.* **3** *vti* **MAKE SCRAPING MOVEMENT** to rub or scrape a surface, e.g. with claws or a scraping instrument ○ *The cat was scratching at the door.* **4** *vi* **MAKE HARSH NOISE** to make a scraping sound **5** *vti* **PRODUCE SCRAPING SOUND FROM RECORD** to run a record backwards and forwards on a turntable in order to repeat and distort the original sound **6** *vt* **DRAG ALONG SURFACE** to drag something along a rough surface so that the object is scraped **7** *vti* **RELIEVE ITCHING** to rub the skin with nails or claws, especially to relieve itching or discomfort **8** *vti* **CAUSE ITCHING** to irritate the surface of the skin by being rough or prickly **9** *vt* **WRITE WITH SHARP INSTRUMENT** to write or draw something by marking a surface with a pointed or sharp instrument ○ *names scratched on the tree* **10** *vti* **PEN QUICKLY** to write or draw something hastily **11** *vt* **DELETE** to delete or erase something by scraping it off, crossing it out, or rendering it illegible **12** *vt* **CANCEL** to cancel or abandon a project, plan, or proposal completely **13** *vi* **SEARCH AIMLESSLY** to search for something in an unsystematic way by picking through things or looking on the ground ○ *scratching around for evidence* **14** *vti* **WITHDRAW FROM COMPETITION** to withdraw an individual or team from a race or competition **15** *vi* **INCUR PENALTY** to make a billiard shot that incurs a penalty, e.g. by hitting the cue ball into a pocket **16** *vi* **MAKE FLUKE SHOT** in billiards, to make a mishit that produces a score **17** *vti* **JUST GET BY** to make a barely adequate living ○ *scratching out a living* ■ *n* **1 MARK ON SURFACE** a slight cut or mark on a surface **2 TEAR IN SKIN** a thin cut or tear in the surface of the skin of a person or animal **3 SCRAPING SOUND** a scraping sound, especially one made with the claws or nails **4 ACTION TO RELIEVE ITCHING** a rubbing of the skin with the nails or claws, especially to relieve itching or discomfort **5 SCRIBBLY WRITING** something written hastily or illegibly **6 WITHDRAWN COMPETITOR** an individual or team withdrawn from a race or competition **7 HANDICAP OF ZERO** in golf, a zero handicap **8 SHOT INCURRING PENALTY** a billiard shot that incurs a penalty **9 FLUKE SHOT** in billiards, a mishit that produces a score **10 TYPE OF POP MUSIC** music produced by running a record backwards and forwards on a turntable, repeating and distorting the original sound **11 MONEY** money or cash (*slang*) ■ *adj* **1 DONE RANDOMLY** done randomly or by chance **2 FOR JOTTED NOTES** used for making quick or preliminary notes ○ *scratch paper* **3 ASSEMBLED HASTILY** assembled hastily from available resources ○ *a scratch team* **4 WITH NO HANDICAP** playing golf with a handicap of zero [14C. Probably blend of *scrat* + *cratch*, both meaning 'scratch'.] ◇ **from scratch** right from the beginning, or with nothing having been done previously (*informal*) ◇ **up to scratch** of or up to a satisfactory standard (*informal*) ○ *exam results that aren't really up to scratch*

scratch together, scratch up *vt* = **scrape together**

scratch-and-sniff *adj* designed to release a smell when scratched, especially as a complement to a visual experience

scratchboard /skrách bawrd/ *n US* ART = **scraperboard** *n.* 1

scratch card *n* a card containing one or more sections covered in an overlay that can be scratched off to reveal a possible prize printed beneath

⚡**scratch file** *n* a temporary computer file created in a memory device as a work area or for use when executing a program

scratchie /skráchi/ *n* a scratch card (*informal*)

scratch line *n* **1 scratch line, scratch** a starting line in a race **2** a line that a competitor may not step over without committing a foul

⚡**scratchpad** /skrách pad/ *n* **1** *US* a pad of paper for making rough notes **2** a high-speed temporary storage area in a computer memory

scratchproof /skrách proof/ *adj* resistant to being scratched

scratch test *n* a test to discover if somebody is allergic to a substance (**allergen**), in which a small amount of the substance is rubbed into a lightly scratched area of skin

scratchy /skráchi/ (**-ier, -iest**) *adj* **1 ITCHY** causing or feeling itchiness on the skin ○ *a scratchy sweater* **2 SOUNDING LIKE SCRATCHES** making a scratching or scraping sound ○ *a scratchy recording* **3 PENNED QUICKLY** written or drawn hastily or illegibly —**scratchily** *adv* —**scratchiness** *n*

scrawl /skrawl/ *vti* to write or draw something untidily or hastily, especially in large letters that are difficult to read ■ *n* untidy or hurried-looking handwriting or drawing [Early 17C. < ?] —**scrawler** *n* —**scrawly** *adj*

scrawny /skráwni/ (**-nier, -niest**) *adj* unpleasantly or unhealthily thin and bony [Mid-19C. Variant of dialect *scranny* < ?] —**scrawnily** *adv* —**scrawniness** *n*

SYNONYMS See ***thin***.

screak /skreek/ *vi US* **1 TO SCREECH** to produce a screech **2 TO CREAK** to produce a creak ■ *n US* **1 SCREECH** a screeching sound **2 CREAK** a creaking sound [15C. < Old Norse *skrækja*, an imitation of the sound.] —**screaky** *adj*

scream /skreem/ *n* **1 PIERCING CRY** a loud, piercing, high-pitched cry, uttered especially in fear, pain, excitement, or amusement **2 HIGH-PITCHED NOISE** a very loud, high-pitched sound such as that of a siren or jet engine **3 SOMEBODY OR SOMETHING HIGHLY AMUSING** an extremely funny or entertaining person, event, or activity (*informal*) ■ *v* **1** *vi* **CRY** to utter a loud, piercing, high-pitched cry, especially in fear, pain, or excitement ○ *He screamed for help.* **2** *vt* **SHOUT IN PIERCING VOICE** to utter something in a loud, piercing, high-pitched voice, especially in fear, panic, desperation, or excitement ○ *'Get out'! he screamed.* **3** *vi* **LAUGH LOUDLY** to laugh shrilly and loudly **4** *vi* **MAKE HIGH-PITCHED SOUND** to make a loud high-pitched sound ○ *The ambulance went by, sirens screaming.* **5** *vi* **MOVE AT SPEED** to move extremely quickly while producing a loud high-pitched sound ○ *The police car screamed by.* **6** *vi* **BE OBVIOUS** to be extremely obvious or noticeable ○ *The mistakes just scream out at you.* [13C. < ?] —**screamingly** *adv*

screamer /skreémər/ *n* **1 SOMETHING THAT SCREAMS** somebody or something that screams **2 BIRD RESEMBLING GOOSE** a water bird that resembles a goose, but with a smaller bill, and a harsh call. Native to: South America. Family: Anhimidae. **3 EXCLAMATION MARK** in printing, an exclamation mark (*slang*) **4 HILARIOUS PERSON OR THING** somebody or something that is extremely funny or entertaining (*informal*)

screaming abdabs /skreéming áb dabz/, **screaming habdabs** /-háb dabz/ *npl* an attack of nervous anxiety (*informal*) US term **screaming meemies** [*Abdabs* < ?]

screaming meemies /-meémiz/ *npl US* = **screaming abdabs** (*informal; + singular or plural verb*) [*Meemies* < ?]

scree /skree/ *n* **1** an accumulation of rock debris at the base of a cliff, hill, or mountain slope, often forming a heap **2** a slope covered with a layer of scree [Early 18C. < Old Norse *skriða* 'landslip'.]

screech /skreech/ *n* **1 SHRILL SCREAM** a high-pitched grating cry or scream, uttered especially in fear, pain, excitement, or amusement ○ *the screech of an owl* **2 HIGH-PITCHED SOUND** a loud high-pitched grating sound ○ *a screech of brakes* ■ *v* **1** *vi* **UTTER SHRILL SCREAM** to utter a high-pitched grating cry or scream, especially in fear, pain, excitement, or amusement **2** *vt* **SHRIEK** to utter something in a high-pitched and grating tone of voice **3** *vi* **MAKE SCREECHING SOUND** to make a loud high-pitched grating sound **4** *vi* **PRODUCE SCREECHING SOUND BY MOVING FAST** to move, usually extremely fast, while producing a screeching sound ○ *The car screeched to a stop.* [Mid-16C. Alteration of archaic *scritch*, ultimately an imitation of the sound.] —**screecher** *n* —**screechiness** *n* —**screechy** *adj*

screech owl *n* any owl that has a characteristic screeching cry. Native to: Europe.

screed /skreed/ *n* **1 LENGTHY PIECE OF WRITING** a long and often tedious piece of writing or speech (*often used in the plural*) **2 GUIDE FOR PLASTERING** a strip of plaster, wood, or other material placed on a surface as a guide to the correct thickness of plaster or concrete to be applied there **3 BOARD FOR LEVELLING** a board or tool used to level a layer of concrete, sand, or other loose material **4 TOP LAYER** a smooth top layer on a concrete floor or other surface **5** *Scotland* **A TEAR** a tear or tearing sound [14C. Variant of SHRED, in the sense 'torn strip'.]

⚡**screen** /skreen/ *n* **1 PARTITION OR SHELTER** a fixed or movable partition or frame that is used to conceal, divide, separate, or provide shelter ○ *You may get changed behind the screen.* **2 SOMETHING THAT CONCEALS** anything that serves to conceal, divide, separate, or provide shelter ○ *A screen of leaves protected her from the sun.* **3 DECORATIVE**

FRAME a decorative frame or partition, e.g. in a church choir ○ *a rood screen* **4 ELECTRONIC DISPLAY SURFACE** the broad flat end of a cathode-ray tube or liquid crystal display on which images are displayed, e.g. in a television set or computer monitor **5 DATA DISPLAYED ON MONITOR** the data displayed on the screen of a computer monitor ○ *to print the screen* **6 SURFACE FOR PROJECTING FILM ONTO** a large flat white or silver surface onto which a film or slide is projected **7 FILM** the film industry **8 MESH FRAME OR MESH** a frame with a fine wire or plastic mesh designed to prevent the entry of mosquitoes or other insects, or the mesh itself **9 WINDSCREEN** a windscreen **10 CONCEALMENT** a measure taken to conceal something ○ *This report is just a screen for the government's inaction.* **11 SELECTION SYSTEM** a system for selecting suitable people, e.g. for a post, membership of an organization, or tenancy of property **12 SIEVE** a sieve used to filter out fine particles, e.g. of sand or gravel **13 ADVANCE DETACHMENT** a military detachment sent in advance of a main force to protect it from the enemy or give warning of enemy approach **14 CAMERA PLATE FOR FOCUSING** a ground-glass plate in a camera that is used for getting an image properly focused before it is photographed **15 GLASS PLATE FOR HALF-TONE REPRODUCTIONS** a glass plate marked with very fine lines and used in producing half-tone reproductions **16 EMOTIONAL BLOCK** something that prevents somebody from understanding his or her real feelings ■ *v* **1** *vt* **CONCEAL OR SHELTER** to provide shelter, protection, or concealment from somebody or something **2** *vt* **PARTITION OFF** to partition, separate, or divide something off from something else ○ *They had screened the area into cubicles.* **3** *vt* **FIT WITH SCREEN** to provide something with a screen **4** *vt* **PROTECT** to protect somebody from something unpleasant or dangerous **5** *vti* **SHOW IN CINEMA** to project a film onto a screen in a cinema **6** *vti* **SHOW ON TELEVISION** to broadcast a film, programme, or other item on television **7** *vti* **TEST FOR DISEASE** to test somebody or something for a particular illness or disease **8** *vti* **SELECT BY WEEDING OUT** to select somebody as being suitable for something, e.g. a post, membership of an organization, or tenancy of property **9** *vt* **SIEVE** to filter something through a sieve **10** *vt* **PHOTOGRAPH FOR HALF-TONE REPRODUCTION** to photograph something through a glass plate to make a half-tone reproduction [14C. < Old Northern French *escren*.] —**screenable** *adj* —**screener** *n* —**screenful** *n*

screenager /skréen ayjər/ *n* a young person who has grown up watching TV and playing with computers and is knowledgeable about and skilled in operating electronic devices (*informal*)

⚡**screen dump** *n* the process of printing or saving the contents of a computer display screen

⚡**screen font** *n* a font used to display text on a computer screen

screening /skréening/ *n* **1 A SHOWING IN A CINEMA** a projection of a film on a screen in a cinema **2 A SHOWING ON TELEVISION** a showing of a film, programme, or other item on television **3 TEST FOR DISEASE** a test or testing carried out routinely on supposedly healthy people in order to establish, as early as possible, whether or not an illness or disease is present **4 PROTECTING SCREENS** screens for providing shelter, protection, or concealment, or for separating or dividing **5 WIRE MESH** fine wire or plastic mesh used on a door or window to prevent the entry of mosquitoes or other insects ■ **screenings** *npl* **SIEVED MATERIAL** waste material that has been screened from something

screen memory *n* an early childhood memory that is used subconsciously to mask another related, often distressful, memory

screenplay /skréen play/ *n* a script or scenario for a film

screen-print *n* a print produced by silk-screen printing —**screen-printing** *n* —**screen-print** *vti*

⚡**screen saver** *n* a computer utility that automatically makes the screen go blank or display a particular image after a given period of time

screen test *n* an audition for a film role in which an actor is filmed, or the film made of the audition —**screen-test** *vti*

screenwriter /skréen rītər/ *n* the writer of a script that is intended to be filmed —**screenwriting** *n*

screw /skroo/ *n* **1 THREADED FASTENER INSERTED INTO MATERIAL** a piece of metal with a tapering threaded body and grooved head by which it is turned into something in order to fasten things together **2 SCREW FOR NUT** a screw with a blunt end onto which a nut is fitted to hold two objects together **3 DEVICE SIMILAR TO SCREW** anything that

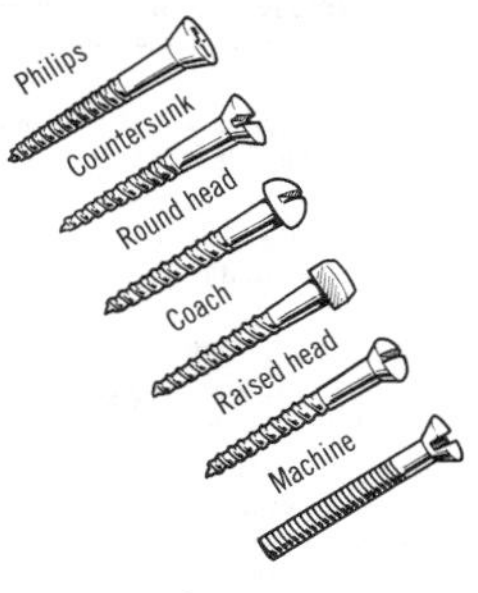
Philips
Countersunk
Round head
Coach
Raised head
Machine

Screw

has a form similar to a tapering metal screw, e.g. a corkscrew **4 TWISTING ACTION** a turn of a screw or of a device like a screw **5** ENG = **propeller 6 SHOT IN WHICH CUE BALL REBOUNDS** a shot in billiards or snooker in which the cue ball returns towards the player after hitting the ball it was aimed at **7 OFFENSIVE TERM** an offensive term for an act or instance of sexual intercourse (*slang*) **8 OFFENSIVE TERM** an offensive term for a sexual partner considered with regard to his or her sexual performance (*slang*) **9 WARDER** a prison warder (*slang*) **10 PAPER TWIST** a small twist of paper, especially one containing tobacco (*dated informal*) **11 SALARY** a salary or wages earned by somebody (*dated informal*) **12 MISER** a miser (*informal*) **13 OLD HORSE** a decrepit old horse (*informal*) ■ *v* **1** *vti* **FASTEN WITH SCREWS** to fasten or tighten something with a screw or screws ○ *He screwed the shelf to the wall.* **2** *vti* **FASTEN BY ROTATING** to rotate something along a thread in order to fasten or tighten it ○ *screwed the bulb in carefully* **3** *vt* **CRUSH** to crumple or crush something into a tight ball **4** *vti* **CONTORT** to contort or crumple a part of or all of the face, or to be contorted or crumpled ○ *She screwed her eyes up against the glare.* **5** *vt* **CAUSE CUE BALL TO REBOUND** in billiards or snooker, to hit the cue ball below its centre of gravity so that, when it strikes a ball it is aimed at, it rolls back on itself **6** *vti* **OFFENSIVE TERM** an offensive term meaning to have sexual intercourse with somebody (*slang*) **7** *vt* **CHEAT** to cheat or swindle somebody (*informal*) **8** *vt* **EXTORT** to get something out of somebody with great difficulty (*informal*) ○ *We managed to screw some money out of him in the end.* **9** *vt* **OFFENSIVE TERM** an offensive term expressive of anger or frustration (*slang*) [15C. < Old French *escroue*, directly or via Germanic < Latin *scrofa* 'sow' (from its curly tail).] —**screwable** *adj* —**screwer** *n* ◇ **have a screw loose** to be irrational or lack common sense or good judgment (*informal*) ◇ **put the screws on somebody** to use force or pressure on somebody (*slang*)

screw around *vi* (*slang*) **1** an offensive term meaning to have sex with a number of different people, especially when married or in an established relationship **2** an offensive term meaning to waste time in trivial or pointless activities

screw up *v* **1** *vti* **OFFENSIVE TERM** an offensive term meaning to mismanage, disrupt, or make a mess of something (*slang*) **2** *vt* **OFFENSIVE TERM** an offensive term meaning to disturb somebody psychologically or emotionally (*slang*) **3 MUSTER** to gather courage or nerve before doing something

screwball /skroó bawl/ *n* an offensive term for somebody who is regarded as behaving in an unconventional, irrational, or strange way (*slang insult*) ■ *adj* an offensive term meaning regarded as unconventional, irrational, or strange (*slang*)

screwball comedy *n* a film, especially a Hollywood comedy of the 1930s, featuring the amusing antics of appealing characters in a glamorous world

screw bean *n* **1** a shrub of the legume family that produces twisted pods. Native to: SW United States, Mexico. *Prosopis pubescens.* **2** a pod of the screw bean plant. Use: fodder.

screwdriver /skroó drīvər/ *n* **1** a tool for driving screws that consists of a handle with a metal rod shaped at the tip to fit into the head of a screw **2** a cocktail made from vodka and orange juice

screwed /skrood/ *adj* **1 FASTENED WITH SCREW** fastened or tightened with a screw or screws **2 WITH SCREW THREAD** having a screw thread **3 CONTORTED** misshapen or contorted **4 OFFENSIVE TERM** an offensive term meaning in serious difficulties (*slang*) **5 DRUNK** drunk (*dated slang*)

screwed up *adj* (*slang; hyphenated before nouns*) **1** an offensive term meaning affected by or displaying symptoms of psychological or emotional disorder **2** an offensive term meaning mismanaged, disrupted, or made a mess of

screw eye *n* a screw with a looped instead of a flat head

screw jack *n* a jack used for lifting heavy items such as vehicles, operated by a screw mechanism

screw pine *n* TREES = **pandanus**

screw propeller *n* ENG, INSUR = **propeller**

screw tap *n* = **tap**² *n.* 7

screw thread *n* **1** the continuous helical outer surface of a screw or the inner surface of a nut **2** a full turn of a screw thread

screw top *n* a lid or cap that screws onto a container (*hyphenated before nouns*) ○ *a screw-top jar*

screwup /skroó up/ *n* an offensive term for a mess, muddle, or bungled event (*slang*)

screwworm /skroó wurm/ *n* the larva of the screwworm fly that grows under the skin of livestock and other mammals, causing injury and death [Late 19C. *Screw* from the spiny hairs of the larva, which encircle each segment.]

screwy /skroó i/ (**-ier, -iest**) *adj* an offensive term meaning regarded as irrational, unconventional, or strange (*slang*) —**screwily** *adv* —**screwiness** *n*

scribble¹ /skríbb'l/ *v* (**-bles, -bling, -bled**) **1** *vti* **WRITE MESSILY** to write something hastily or untidily, often in smallish letters **2** *vti* **MAKE MEANINGLESS MARKINGS** to write or draw meaningless or undecipherable marks on something ○ *Don't scribble on the wall!* **3** *vi* **BE WRITER** to be a writer, especially one of little merit (*humorous*) ■ *n* **1 MESSY HANDWRITING** untidy or careless handwriting **2 HASTY NOTE** something written untidily or hastily **3 DOODLES** meaningless marks written or drawn on something [15C. Ultimately < Latin *scribere* 'write'.] —**scribbler** *n* —**scribbly** *adj*

scribble² /skríbb'l/ (**-bles, -bling, -bled**) *vt* to card wool roughly [Late 17C. < ?]

scribbly gum /skríbbli-/ *n* a eucalyptus tree whose bark has patterns resembling scribbles that are created by burrowing insect larvae. Genus: *Eucalyptus.*

scribe /skrīb/ *n* **1 BOOK COPIER** a copier or transcriber of documents, especially somebody who copied manuscripts in medieval times **2 COPIER OF JEWISH RELIGIOUS DOCUMENTS** a copier of the Sefer Torah and other religious documents using a quill pen on parchment **3 CLERK** an official public clerk **4 JOURNALIST** a writer, especially a journalist (*humorous*) **5** TECH = **scriber** ■ *vti* (**scribes, scribing, scribed**) **MARK LINES ON** to mark something such as wood or metal with a line using a pointed instrument, especially as a guide for cutting [12C. < Latin *scriba* 'official or public writer' < *scribere* 'write'.] —**scribal** *adj*

scriber /skrībər/ *n* a sharp instrument for marking lines on wood or other material

scrim /skrim/ *n* **1** a drop curtain in the theatre that appears opaque to the audience when lit from the front but transparent when lit from behind **2** a durable open-weave cotton or linen fabric. Use: curtains, clothing, upholstery lining. [Late 18C]

scrimmage /skrímmij/ *n* **1 FIGHT** a skirmish or minor battle **2 STRUGGLE** a rough or confused struggle ■ *vti* (**-mages, -maging, -maged**) **TAKE PART IN SCRIMMAGE** to engage in a scrimmage against somebody [15C. Alteration of SKIRMISH.]

scrimp /skrimp/ *v* **1** *vi* **ECONOMIZE** to economize drastically or be extremely frugal ○ *scrimp on food* **2** *vt* **BE STINGY** to treat somebody meanly or limit provision to somebody severely **3** *vt* **MAKE SOMETHING TOO SMALL** to make something too small or scanty [Mid-18C. < obsolete *scrimp* 'scant, meagre' < ?] —**scrimpily** *adv* —**scrimpiness** *n* —**scrimpy** *adj*

scrimshank /skrím shangk/ *vi* to shirk work or obligations (*dated slang*) [Late 19C. < ?] —**scrimshanker** *n*

scrimshaw /skrím shaw/ *n* **1 CARVED WHALE IVORY** a carved or engraved article made originally by North American whalers from the teeth and bones of whales, or such articles collectively **2 MAKING OF SCRIMSHAW** the skill or pastime of making scrimshaw ■ *v* **1** *vi* **MAKE SCRIMSHAW** to make scrimshaw **2** *vt* **CARVE OR ENGRAVE** to carve or engrave something into scrimshaw [Mid-19C. < earlier *scrimshonting* 'carving whale ivory' < ?]

scrip[1] /skrip/ *n* **1** a list, receipt, or other short piece of writing **2** *US* paper currency issued for temporary emergency use, e.g. by an occupying force [Late 16C. Alteration of SCRIPT, influenced by SCRAP[1].]

scrip[2] /skrip/ *n* a document or certificate representing a fraction of a share or stock [Mid-18C. Shortening of *subscription receipt*.]

scrip issue *n* FIN = **bonus issue**

script /skript/ *n* **1 TEXT OF PLAY OR BROADCAST** the printed version of a stage play, film screenplay, or radio or television broadcast, including the words to be spoken and often also technical directions **2 MANUSCRIPT** an original document or manuscript **3 SYSTEM OF WRITING** any system of characters used in writing **4 HANDWRITING** characters written by hand, especially in cursive form **5 PRINTED TYPE RESEMBLING WRITING** printed type designed to imitate handwriting **6** a sequence of automated computer commands embedded in a program that tells the program to execute a specific procedure when a Web page is opened or a hypertext link is clicked **7 ANSWER PAPER** an answer paper in an examination ■ *vt* **WRITE SCRIPT FOR** to write or prepare a script for something [14C. Via Old French *escri(p)t* < Latin *scriptus* < *scribere* 'write'.]

script kiddie *n US* a computer hacker, often relatively young or unsophisticated, who scans the Internet using prewritten software tools to search for weaknesses in computer systems that he or she can exploit (*slang*) [*Script* in the computing sense, 'automated set of instructions']

scriptorium /skrip táwri əm/ (*plural* **-ums** *or* **-a** /-ri ə/) *n* a room in a monastery for storing, copying, illustrating, or reading manuscripts [Late 18C. Via medieval Latin < Latin *scribere* 'write'.]

scripture /skrípchər/, **Scripture** *n* **1 BIBLICAL WRITINGS** the sacred writings of the Bible **2 BIBLICAL TEXT** a passage from the Bible **3 SACRED WRITING** any sacred writing or book ○ *Buddhist scripture* **4 AUTHORITATIVE STATEMENT** a statement regarded as authoritative [14C. < Latin *scriptura* 'what is written' < *script-*, past participle of *scribere* 'write'.] —**scriptural** *adj* —**scripturally** *adv*

scriptwriter /skrípt rītər/ *n* a writer of scripts for material to be broadcast

scrivener /skrívvənər/ *n* **1** in former times, somebody whose job involved writing or making handwritten copies of documents, books, or other texts **2** a notary public (*archaic*) [14C. < Old French *escrivein* < Latin *scriba* (see SCRIBE).]

scrobiculate /skrō bíkyōōlət, -layt/ *adj* with a grooved or pitted surface [Early 19C. < late Latin *scrobiculus* 'groove' < Latin *scrobis* 'trench'.]

scrofula /skróffyōōlə/ *n* tuberculosis of the lymph glands, especially of the neck [14C. < medieval Latin, 'swelling of glands' < *scrofa* 'breeding sow'.]

scrofulous /skróffyōōləss/ *adj* **1 HAVING OR RESEMBLING SCROFULA** affected with or characteristic of scrofula **2 SHABBY IN APPEARANCE** run-down, diseased, or shabby in appearance **3 MORALLY CORRUPT** morally corrupt and degenerate —**scrofulously** *adv* —**scrofulousness** *n*

scroggin /skróggin/ *n NZ* a mixture of dried fruit, nuts, chocolate, and other high-energy foods eaten as a snack by hikers [Mid-20C. < ?]

scroll /skrōl/ *n* **1 ROLL OF PARCHMENT** a roll of paper, parchment, leather, or other material for writing a document **2 LIST** a list, roll, or roster **3 ORNAMENTAL DESIGN RESEMBLING ROLL OF PAPER** an ornamental design shaped like a rolled or partially rolled piece of paper **4 CURVED HEAD OF STRINGED INSTRUMENT** the curved head of a stringed musical instrument where the tuning pegs are set **5 HERALDIC RIBBON WITH MOTTO** in heraldry, a ribbon with rolled ends inscribed with a motto ■ *vti* **MOVE TEXT OR GRAPHICS** to move text or graphics smoothly up, down, or across a computer display screen, or to be moved in this way [15C. Alteration of *scrowe*, influenced by ROLL, via Old French *escroe* 'strip of parchment' < medieval Latin *scroda* 'strip' < Germanic, 'something cut'.]

scroll bar *n* for a computer with a graphical interface, a narrow horizontal or vertical bar on the screen containing a box used to make text or graphics move up, down, or across the screen

scroll saw *n* a saw with a narrow blade used for cutting curved ornamental designs

scrollwork /skrōl wurk/ *n* ornamental designs characterized by scrolls, especially in wood

scrooge /skrooj/, **Scrooge** *n* a miser (*informal*) [Mid-19C. < Ebenezer *Scrooge*, a character in *A Christmas Carol* (1843), by Charles Dickens.]

scroop /skroop/ *n* a rasping sound like that of rustling silk ■ *vi* to make a rustling or rasping noise [Late 18C. An imitation of the sound.]

scrote /skrōt/ *n* an offensive term for a man who is seen as unpleasant or malicious (*slang*) [Probably back-formation < SCROTUM]

scrotum /skrṓtəm/ (*plural* **-tums** *or* **-ta** /-tə/) *n* the external pouch of skin and muscle containing the testes in mammals [Late 16C. < Latin.] —**scrotal** *adj*

scrounge /skrownj/ *vti* (*informal*) **1** to acquire something from somebody by begging or borrowing without intending to make repayment or return **2** to seek and acquire something from any available source, e.g. by foraging [Early 20C. Alteration of *scringe* 'prowl around' < CRINGE.] —**scrounger** *n*

scrub[1] /skrub/ *v* (**scrubs, scrubbing, scrubbed**) **1** *vti* **CLEAN BY RUBBING** to clean something by rubbing hard **2** *vt* **REMOVE DIRT BY RUBBING** to remove dirt by rubbing hard, usually with a brush **3** *vt* **REMOVE IMPURITIES FROM GAS** to remove impurities from a gas by passing it over or through a liquid **4** *vi* **CLEANSE FOR SURGERY** to cleanse the arms and hands in preparation for surgery **5** *vt* **CANCEL** to cancel or postpone something (*informal*) ■ *n* **ACT OF SCRUBBING** the act of cleaning something by rubbing hard ■ **scrubs** *npl US* **CLOTHING WORN WHILE PERFORMING SURGERY** the clothing, usually a matching green shirt and trousers, worn by surgeons and nurses in an operating theatre (*informal*) [13C. Probably < Middle Low German or Middle Dutch *schrubben*.]

scrub round *vt* to dispense with, cancel, or ignore something (*informal*) ○ *We'll scrub round the formalities and get straight down to business.*

scrub[2] /skrub/ *n* **1 AREA OF LOW VEGETATION** low, stunted, or straggly vegetation or an area of such vegetation **2 STUNTED TREE** a stunted tree or bush **3 MONGREL** a domestic animal of mixed breeding **4 OFFENSIVE TERM** an offensive term for somebody regarded as small or insignificant (*slang*) **5** *US* **PLAYER NOT IN FIRST TEAM** a player not in the first team or a team made up of such players **6** *Aus* **REMOTE PLACE** a remote part of the countryside (*informal*) [14C. Alteration of SHRUB[1].]

scrubber /skrúbbər/ *n* **1** *UK, Aus* **OFFENSIVE TERM** an offensive term for a prostitute or a woman who is considered to be sexually promiscuous, coarse, or slovenly (*slang*) **2 SOMEBODY OR SOMETHING THAT SCRUBS** somebody or something that cleans by rubbing hard, often with a brush **3 APPARATUS FOR PURIFYING GAS** a device for removing impurities from a gas [Mid-19C. < SCRUB[1] in the sense 'promiscuous woman', or < SCRUB[2] in the sense 'mongrel'.]

scrubby /skrúbbi/ (**-bier, -biest**) *adj* **1 STUNTED OR STRAGGLY** inferior in size or quality **2 COVERED WITH LOW TREES** covered with or consisting of low or undersized shrubs or trees **3 SHABBY** shabby, untidy, or wretched in appearance —**scrubbiness** *n*

scrubland /skrúb land/ *n* land covered with low trees and shrubs

scrub nurse *n* a nurse who helps a surgeon in an operating theatre

scrub oak *n* a small oak of scrubland. Native to: North America. *Quercus ilicifolia.*

scrub typhus *n* a common infectious disease in Asia that is caused by the microorganism *Rickettsia tsutsugamushi* and spread by a biting mite

scruff[1] /skruf/ *n* the back of the neck, especially when used to seize, drag, or lift a person or animal [Late 18C. Alteration of earlier *scuff* < Old Norse *skoft* 'hair of the head'.]

scruff[2] /skruf/ *n* an untidy or disreputable person (*informal*) [Old English *scruf*, variant of SCURF]

scruffy /skrúffi/ (**-ier, -iest**) *adj* untidy, shabby, or rundown in appearance [Mid-17C. < SCRUFF[2].] —**scruffily** *adv* —**scruffiness** *n*

scrum /skrum/ *n* **1 RUGBY FORMATION DECIDING POSSESSION OF BALL** a part of a rugby match in which the two sets of forwards gather around the ball with heads down and arms linked and try to obtain possession of it **2 CONFUSED JOSTLE OR STRUGGLE** a crowd of people jostling or struggling for something ■ *vi* (**scrums, scrumming, scrummed**) **FORM RUGBY SCRUM** to form a scrum in rugby [Late 19C. Shortening of SCRUMMAGE.]

scrum half *n* in rugby, the halfback who places the ball in the scrum, or the position of this player

scrummage /skrúmmij/ *n* RUGBY = **scrum** *n.* 1 [Early 19C. Variant of SCRIMMAGE.] —**scrummager** *n*

scrummy /skrúmmi/ *adj* very attractive, delicious, or excellent (*informal*) [Early 20C. < shortening of SCRUMPTIOUS.]

scrump /skrump/ *vti* to steal fruit, especially apples, from a garden or orchard (*informal*) [Mid-19C. < Dialect *scrump* 'withered apple' < ?]

scrumptious /skrúmpshəss/ *adj* very pleasing, especially to the taste (*informal*) [Mid-19C. Probably alteration of SUMPTUOUS.] —**scrumptiously** *adv* —**scrumptiousness** *n*

scrumpy /skrúmpi/ (*plural* **-pies**) *n S W England* a rough strong dry cider, traditionally made in the southwest of England (*informal*) [Early 20C. < Dialect *scrump* (see SCRUMP).]

scrunch /skrunch/ *v* **1** *vt* to crumple, crush, or squeeze something together tightly **2** *vi* to move with or make a crunching sound [Late 18C. An imitation of the sound.]

scrunch up *vt* = **scrunch** *v.* 1

scrunch-dry (**scrunch-dries, scrunch-drying, scrunch-dried**) *vt* to dry hair while squeezing it together tightly in your hand to add volume and create a natural curly style

scrunchie /skrúnchi/ *n* a thick elasticated band loosely covered with fabric. Use: hair fastener. [Late 20C. < SCRUNCH, because of its crumpled appearance.]

scruple /skrōōp'l/ *n* **1 MORAL OR ETHICAL CONSIDERATION** a moral or ethical consideration that tends to restrain action or behaviour **2 UNIT OF WEIGHT** a unit of apothecaries' weight equal to or about 1.3 g/20 grains **3 VERY SMALL AMOUNT** a minute amount or portion of something (*archaic*) ■ *vi* (**-ples, -pling, -pled**) **HESITATE BECAUSE OF MORAL CONSIDERATIONS** to hesitate because of moral or ethical considerations ○ *She wouldn't scruple to cheat.* [15C. Via Old French *scrupule* < Latin *scrupulus* 'small sharp stone, uneasiness' < *scrupus* 'sharp stone'.]

scrupulous /skrōōpyōōləss/ *adj* **1** having or showing careful regard for what is morally right **2** rigorously precise and exact —**scrupulosity** /skrōōpyōō lóssəti/ *n* —**scrupulously** *adv* —**scrupulousness** *n*

SYNONYMS See ***careful***.

scrutineer /skrōōti néer/ *n* an inspector or examiner of something, e.g. votes at an election or vehicles participating in motor sport [Mid-16C. < SCRUTINY + -EER.]

scrutinize /skrōōti nīz/ (**-nizes, -nizing, -nized**) *vt* to examine somebody or something closely and carefully [Late 17C. < SCRUTINY.] —**scrutinizer** *n*

scrutiny /skrōōti ni/ (*plural* **-nies**) *n* **1 CAREFUL INSPECTION** close, careful, searching examination or inspection **2 OBSERVATION** careful study or surveillance **3 GAZE** a searching look [15C. < Latin *scrutinium* 'inquiry' < *scrutinari* 'examine' < *scruta* 'rubbish'.]

scry /skrī/ (**scries, scrying, scried**) *vi* to predict the future using a crystal ball [Early 16C. Shortening of DESCRY.]

SCSI /skúzzi/ *n* a specification for a high-speed computer interface used to connect peripheral devices to a computer. Full form **small computer systems interface**

scuba /skōōbə/ *n* an apparatus for breathing underwater consisting of a portable canister of compressed air and a mouthpiece [Mid-20C. Acronym < *Self-Contained Underwater Breathing Apparatus*.]

scuba diver *n* an underwater swimmer using scuba equipment —**scuba diving** *n*

scud /skud/ *vi* (**scuds, scudding, scudded**) **1 MOVE SWIFTLY** to move swiftly and smoothly **2 SAIL BEFORE GALE** to sail with a gale or strong wind blowing from behind ■ *n* **1 SWIFT MOVEMENT** a swift smooth movement **2 CLOUDS DRIVEN BY WIND** low clouds that are driven swiftly by the wind **3 SUDDEN SHOWER OR GUST** a sudden shower of rain or gust of wind [Mid-16C. < ?]

Scudamore /skyōōdə mawr, skōōdə-/, **Peter** (*b.* 1958) British jockey

Scud missile /skud-/ *n* a surface-to-surface missile that can take a nuclear, conventional, or chemical warhead [< a NATO codename < SCUD]

scudo /skōōdō/ (*plural* **-di** /-dee/) *n* a former gold or silver coin in various Italian states, or a modern commemorative coin issued occasionally by the republic of San Marino [Mid-17C. Via Italian < Latin *scutum* 'shield'.]

scuff /skuf/ *vti* **1 SCRAPE OR RUB** to scrape, rub, or wear away the surface of something, or to become scraped, rubbed, or worn with use **2 SCRAPE FEET WHILE WALKING** to scrape the feet on the ground while standing or walking or to walk in a manner that makes the feet scrape ■ *n* **1 ACT OF SCUFFING** a scraping or shuffling movement or sound **2 MARK FROM SCRAPING OR RUBBING** a mark or scratch made by scuffing **3 FLAT SHOE** a flat-soled shoe with no strap or back [Late 16C. Possibly < N Germanic.]

scuffle[1] /skúff'l/ *n* **DISORDERLY FIGHT** a disorderly confused fight or struggle at close quarters ■ *v* (**-fles, -fling, -fled**) **1** *vti* **FIGHT IN CONFUSION** to struggle or fight at close quarters and in confusion **2** *vi* **SHUFFLE QUICKLY** to shuffle along hurriedly [Late 16C. Probably < SCUFF, in the meaning 'dodge repeatedly'.] —**scuffler** *n*

scuffle[2] /skúff'l/, **scuffle hoe** *n US* a hoe that is used by pushing it back and forth [Late 18C. < Dutch *schoffel*.]

scull /skul/ *n* **1 SINGLE OAR AT BACK OF BOAT** a single oar that is moved from side to side at the stern of a boat to propel the boat forwards **2 EITHER OF A PAIR OF OARS** either of a pair of relatively short oars used by a single rower **3 LIGHT RACING BOAT** a light narrow racing boat propelled by one, two, or four rowers using sculls ■ *vti* **PROPEL BOAT WITH SCULLS** to propel a boat using a scull or sculls [14C. < ?] —**sculler** *n*

scullery /skúlləri/ (*plural* **-ies**) *n* a small room for washing and storing dishes and utensils and doing other kitchen chores such as preparing vegetables [15C. < French *escuelerie* 'duty of servant in charge of plates' < *escuelle* 'dish' < Latin *scutella* 'serving platter'.]

Scullin /skúllin/, **James Henry** (1876–1953) Australian statesman

scullion /skúlli ən/ *n* a servant employed to perform menial kitchen chores [15C. Via Middle French *escouillon* 'swab, wash-cloth' < *escouve* 'broom' < Latin *scopae*.]

sculpin /skúlpin/ (*plural* **-pin** *or* **-pins**) *n* **1** a fish, mostly bottom-dwelling, with a large flat head, large pectoral fins, and spines. Native to: North American coasts. Family: Cottidae. **2** a scorpion fish with venomous spines, caught for food and for sport. Native to: S California coast. *Scorpaena guttata*. [Late 17C]

sculpt /skulpt/ *v* **1** *vti* **MAKE SCULPTURE** to carve, model, cast, or otherwise create a three-dimensional representation of something as a work of art **2** *vti* **CARVE OR MODEL MATERIAL** to use a material to create a three-dimensional work of art **3** *vi* **BE SCULPTOR** to create three-dimensional works of art as a profession or pastime **4** *vt* **CHANGE SHAPE OF SOMETHING NATURALLY** to change the shape or contours of something by natural processes such as erosion [Mid-19C. Via French *sculpter* < Latin *sculpere* 'carve, scratch', variant of *scalpere*.]

~~**sculpter**~~ incorrect spelling of **sculptor**

sculptor /skúlptər/ *n* an artist who creates three-dimensional works of art, especially by carving, modelling, or casting [Mid-17C. < Latin < *sculpere* 'carve'.]

Sculptor /skúlptor/ *n* a faint constellation of the southern hemisphere. See illustration at **constellation**

~~**sculptur**~~ incorrect spelling of **sculpture**

sculpture /skúlpchər/ *n* **1 CREATION OF THREE-DIMENSIONAL ART** the creation of a three-dimensional work of art, especially by carving, modelling, or casting **2 THREE-DIMENSIONAL WORK OF ART** a work of art created by sculpture, or such works collectively **3 NATURAL MARKING ON PLANT OR ANIMAL** a natural indentation or other marking on a plant or animal, e.g. a ridge on a seashell ■ *vti* (**-tures, -turing, -tured**) **1** = **sculpt** *v.* 1 **2** = **sculpt** *v.* 2 [14C. < Latin *sculptura* < *sculpere* (see SCULPT).] —**sculptural** *adj* —**sculpturally** *adv*

sculpturesque /skúlpchə résk/ *adj* resembling sculpture —**sculpturesquely** *adv* —**sculpturesqueness** *n*

scum /skum/ *n* **1 FILMY LAYER ON SURFACE OF LIQUID** a filmy layer of extraneous matter or impurities that rises to or is formed on the surface of a liquid **2 OFFENSIVE TERM** an offensive term for a person or group of people regarded as contemptible or worthless (*insult*) **3 REFUSE** refuse or worthless items **4 REFUSE FROM MOLTEN METAL** dross or refuse from molten metals ■ *v* (**scums, scumming, scummed**) **1** *vi* **HAVE SCUM** to become covered with scum **2** *vt* **CLEAR SOMETHING OF SCUM** to remove scum from something [14C. < Middle Dutch *schūme* 'foam, froth' < Germanic.] —**scummer** *n* —**scummy** *adj*

scumbag /skúm bag/ *n* an offensive term for somebody who is seen as unpleasant or malicious (*slang insult*) [Mid-20C. < its original US slang meaning '(used) condom'.]

scumble /skúmb'l/ *vt* **1 SOFTEN SOMETHING WITH OPAQUE COLOUR** to soften the colours or outlines of a painting or drawing by covering it with a film of opaque or semiopaque colour **2 SOFTEN COLOURS BY RUBBING** to soften the colours or outlines of a painting or drawing by rubbing ■ *n* **1 TECHNIQUE OF SCUMBLING** the technique or effect of scumbling **2 SCUMBLING MATERIAL** a material used for scumbling [Late 17C. < ?]

scunge /skunj/ *vti ANZ* **SCROUNGE** to scrounge something (*slang*) ■ *n ANZ* **1 SLOVENLY PERSON** somebody considered to be slovenly and messy (*slang insult*) **2 DIRTY MESS** a sticky and dirty mess (*slang*) [Early 19C. < ?]

scungy /skúnji/ (**-gier, -giest**) *adj ANZ* messy, shabby, and unattractive (*slang*)

scunner /skúnnər/ *n* **1 AVERSION** an unreasonable or extreme dislike (*regional*) **2** *Scotland* **SOMEBODY OR SOMETHING DISLIKED** a person or thing that provokes an unreasonable or extreme dislike (*informal*) ■ *vti Scotland* **FEEL OR INSPIRE DISGUST** to feel or show, or to cause somebody to feel or show disgusted aversion (*informal*) [14C. < ?]

Scunthorpe /skún thawrp/ town in east-central England. Population: 60,700 (1994).

scup /skup/ (*plural* **scups** *or* **scup**) *n* a fish of the porgy family. Native to: E Atlantic coast of the United States. *Stenotomus chrysops*. [19C. < Narraganset *mishcup* 'big and close together', because of the shape of the fish's scales.]

scupper[1] /skúppər/ *n* **1** an opening in the bulwarks of a ship that allows water on the deck to drain overboard **2** an opening allowing water to drain from the roof or floor of a building [15C. < ?]

scupper[2] /skúppər/ *vt* **1** to sink a ship, especially to sink your own vessel intentionally **2** to wreck, defeat, or ruin something [Late 19C. < ?]

scuppernong /skúppər nong/ *n* **1** a cultivated variety of the muscadine grape that has sweet yellowish-green fruit **2** a sweet amber-coloured wine made from scuppernong grapes [Early 19C. After the *Scuppernong* River in North Carolina.]

scurf /skurf/ *n* **1 DANDRUFF** thin dry flaking scales of skin, usually as a result of a particular skin condition such as dandruff **2 FLAKY INCRUSTATION** a flaky or scaly incrustation on a surface **3 SCALY DEPOSIT ON PLANT** a scaly deposit or covering on a plant **4 PLANT DISEASE** a plant disease characterized by a scaly deposit or covering [Old English]

scurrility /skə ríllәti/ (*plural* **-ties**) *n* **1** coarseness, vulgarity, or a lack of refinement **2** language that is coarse and vulgar, or a remark made in coarse vulgar language

scurrilous /skúrrilәss/ *adj* **1 ABUSIVE OR DEFAMATORY** containing abusive language or defamatory allegations **2 FOUL-MOUTHED OR VULGAR** using or containing coarse, vulgar, or obscene language **3 WICKED** behaving in ways thought to be evil or immoral [Late 16C. < *scurrile*, via French < Latin *scurrilis* < *scurra* 'buffoon'.] —**scurrilously** *adv* —**scurrilousness** *n*

scurry /skúrri/ *vi* (**-ries, -rying, -ried**) **1 MOVE BRISKLY** to move at a hurried pace, usually with small fast steps **2 MOVE ABOUT AGITATEDLY** to move about in an agitated manner or with a swirling motion ■ *n* (*plural* **-ries**) **SCURRYING MOVEMENT** a hurried, agitated, or swirling movement [Early 19C. < ?]

Scurry /skúrri/, **Briana** (*b.* 1971) US soccer player

scurvy /skúrvi/ *n* a disease caused by insufficient vitamin C, the symptoms of which include spongy gums, loosening of the teeth, and bleeding into the skin and mucous membranes ■ *adj* (**-vier, -viest**) behaving in ways thought to be mean or contemptible [15C. < SCURF + -Y[1].] —**scurvily** *adv* —**scurviness** *n*

scut /skut/ *n* a short erect tail such as that of a rabbit [15C. < ?]

scuta plural of **scutum**

scutage /skyóotij/ *n* in feudal times, a tax paid by a knight or vassal to his lord that freed him from military service [15C. < medieval Latin *scutagium* 'shield tax' < Latin *scutum* 'shield'.]

scutate /skyóo tayt/ *adj* **1** shaped like a shield ○ *a scutate leaf* **2** covered or protected by external bony or horny plates or scales [Early 19C. < SCUTUM + -ATE.] —**scutation** /skyoo táysh'n/ *n*

scutch /skuch/ *vt* to beat flax in order to separate the valuable fibres from the woody parts ■ *n* a tool or machine for scutching flax or cotton [Late 17C. Via Old French *escoucher* < Latin *excutere* 'shake'.]

scutch grass *n* **1** PLANTS = **Bermuda grass 2** couch grass (*regional*)

scute /skyoot/ *n* an external bony or horny plate or scale in some animals, especially snakes and other reptiles [14C. < Latin *scutum* 'shield'.]

scutellum /skyoo téllәm/ (*plural* **-la** /-téllә/) *n* **1** a hard plate or scale, e.g. on the thorax of an insect or a toe of a bird **2** the shield-shaped embryonic leaf (**cotyledon**) of a grass seed [Mid-18C. Via modern Latin < Latin *scutella* 'platter'; mistaken as 'small shield' < Latin *scutum* 'shield'.] —**scutellar** *adj* —**scutellate** /skyóotәlәt, -layt/ *adj* —**scutellation** /skyóotә láysh'n/ *n*

scutter /skúttәr/ *vi* to move hastily in a scurrying manner [Late 18C. Alteration of *scuttle* 'scamper about' < ?]

scuttle[1] /skútt'l/ *n* **1 SMALL HATCH** a small hatchway with a cover in the deck or hull of a ship **2 SCUTTLE COVER ON SHIP** the cover for a scuttle on a ship ■ *vt* (**-tles, -tling, -tled**) **1 SINK SHIP BY LETTING WATER IN** to sink a ship by making or opening holes in the bottom **2 DESTROY** to destroy or bring something to an end ○ *had effectively scuttled his plans* [15C. Via French *escoutille* < Spanish *escotilla* 'hatchway' < *escotar* 'cut out' < Germanic.]

scuttle[2] /skútt'l/ *n* **1 COAL CONTAINER** a metal container shaped like a wide-rimmed bucket with a lip and a handle, used to carry or store coal indoors **2 SHALLOW BASKET** an open shallow basket used to carry foods or small items **3 TOP PART OF CAR BODY** the part of a motor car behind the bonnet where the windscreen and instrument panel are fixed [15C. Via Old English *scutel* and Old Norse *skutill* < Latin *scutella* 'dish, tray'.]

scuttle[3] /skútt'l/ *vi* (**-tles, -tling, -tled**) to run or move quickly with short steps ■ *n* a hurried pace or scuttling movement

scuttlebutt /skútt'l but/ *n* **1** a drinking fountain on a ship **2** *US* rumours about somebody's activities, often of an intimate and scandalous nature (*slang*) [Early 19C. < SCUTTLE[2] + BUTT[5].]

scutum /skyóotәm/ (*plural* **-ta** /-tә/) *n* **1** ZOOL = **scute 2** a large shield used by legionaries in ancient Rome [Late 18C. < Latin, 'shield'.]

Scutum *n* a small faint constellation of the southern hemisphere

scuzz /skuz/ *n* **1** something dirty, disgusting, or disreputable (*slang*) **2 scuzz, scuzzball** /skúz bawl/, **scuzzbucket** /skúz búkәt/, **scuzzbag** /skúz bag/ an offensive term for somebody regarded as unpleasant and contemptible (*slang insult*) [Mid-20C. < ?] —**scuzzily** *adv* —**scuzziness** *n* —**scuzzy** *adj*

scuzzbag /skúz bag/ *n* = **scuzz** *n.* 2

scuzzball /skúz bawl/ *n* = **scuzz** *n.* 2

scuzzbucket /skúz búkәt/ *n* = **scuzz** *n.* 2

Scylla /síllә/ *n* in Greek mythology, a sea monster who attacked sailors. In later times, Scylla was thought to be a rock on the Italian side of the Straits of Messina. ◇ **be between Scylla and Charybdis** to be faced with the necessity of choosing between two equally undesirable or unpleasant things

scyphozoan /sífә zō әn/ *n* a marine invertebrate animal such as a jellyfish that is free-swimming and does not have a significant sedentary stage [Early 20C. < modern Latin < Greek *skuphos* 'cup' + *zōa* 'animals'.]

scythe /sīth/ *n* an implement with a long handle and a long curved single-edged blade, used to cut grass, crops, or similar plants by swinging the blade horizontally close to the ground ■ *vti* (**scythes, scything, scythed**) to cut or reap something with a scythe [Old English *siþe*. Ultimately < Indo-European, 'cut'.]

Scythia /síthi ә, síthi ә/ ancient region in what is now Moldova, Ukraine, and E Russia

Scythian /síthi әn, síthi әn/ *n* a member of an ancient people who lived in Scythia ■ *adj* relating to ancient Scythia or its people or culture

sd[1] *abbr* **1** sine die **2** standard deviation

ϟ **sd**[2] *abbr* Sudan (*in Internet addresses*)

SD *abbr* **1 SD** South Dakota **2** standard deviation

S. Dak. *abbr* South Dakota

SDI *abbr* Strategic Defense Initiative

SDLP *abbr* Social Democratic and Labour Party

SDP *abbr* Social Democratic Party

SDR, SDRs *abbr* special drawing rights

ϟ **se** *abbr* Sweden (*in Internet addresses*)

Se *symbol* selenium

SE *abbr* 1 southeast 2 southeastern 3 stock exchange

sea /see/ *n* 1 SALT WATERS OF EARTH the great body of salt water that covers a large portion of the Earth ○ *swimming in the sea* ○ *sea air* ○ *a sea fish* 2 BODY OF SALT WATER a body of salt water that is surrounded by land on all or most sides, or that is part of one of the oceans ○ *the Caribbean Sea* 3 LARGE LAKE a large inland body of fresh water 4 ASTRON = **mare**² *n.* 5 TURBULENCE OF OCEAN the motion and disturbance of a large body of water such as the ocean, or the waves themselves 6 SEAFARER'S JOB OR LIFE the occupation or way of life of a sailor 7 VAST BODY a large area or great number of something [Old English *sæ* < Germanic] ◇ **at sea** 1 travelling on the ocean 2 bewildered and confused

SPELLCHECK Do not confuse ***sea*** with ***see***, which has a similar sound. Beware: your spellchecker will not catch this error.

sea anchor *n* a device such as a conical canvas bag that is thrown overboard and dragged behind a ship to control its speed or heading

sea anemone *n* a solitary and often colourful sea animal with a squat cylindrical body that bears a ring of tentacles and is attached to rock or other nonliving material. Order: Actiniaria.

sea aster *n* a biennial or perennial plant with narrow fleshy leaves. Flowers: purple-and-yellow. Native to: salt marshes throughout Europe. *Aster tripolium.*

sea bass /-bass/ *n* 1 a bony marine fish that has a long body, large mouth, and spiny dorsal fin and is a popular game fish. Native to: Atlantic coast of North America. *Centropristis striata.* 2 the flesh of a sea bass as food

seabed /seé bed/ *n* the surface of the Earth at the bottom of the sea

Seabee /seé bee/ *n* a member of one of the construction battalions of the US Navy that build naval shore facilities in combat zones [Mid-20C. < *CB*, abbreviation of 'Construction Battalion'.]

sea beet *n* a wild beet with leathery leaves. Flowers: inconspicuous, green, in long spikes. Native to: European seashores. *Beta vulgaris.*

seabird /seé burd/ *n* a bird such as a gull, albatross, or petrel that frequents the open sea

sea biscuit *n* FOOD = **hardtack**

seablite /seé blīt/ *n* an annual plant that grows in salt marshes. *Suaeda maritima.* [Mid-18C. *Blite* via Latin < Greek *bliton.*]

seaboard /seé bawrd/ *n* land that borders the sea

seaborgium /see báwrgi əm/ *n* a very unstable chemical element produced by high-energy collisions [Late 20C. After Glenn T. *Seaborg* (1912–99), US nuclear chemist.]

seaborne /seé bawrn/ *adj* 1 carried on or in the sea 2 transported by ship across the sea

sea bream *n* 1 a marine fish. Native to: European waters. Family: Sparidae. 2 the flesh of a sea bream as food

sea breeze *n* a cooling breeze that blows inland from the sea during the daytime when the land is warmer than the surface of the water

sea buckthorn *n* a shrub with silvery leaves and orange-red berries found on seashores. Flowers: greenish. Use: yellow dye. Native to: Europe, Asia. *Hippophaë rhamnoides.*

sea captain *n* the person in charge of a ship, especially a merchant ship

sea change *n* a substantial transformation

sea chest *n* a large box or trunk in which a sailor's personal belongings are stored

seacoast /seé kōst/ *n* the land that borders the sea

seacock /seé kok/ *n* a valve in the hull of a ship used to let water in or out

sea cow *n* ZOOL = **sirenian**

sea crayfish *n* ZOOL = **spiny lobster**

sea cucumber *n* a marine invertebrate (**echinoderm**) that has a long tough muscular body and a mouth encircled by tentacles, and lives on the seabed. Class: Holothuroidea.

sea dog *n* a sailor of long experience

seadog /seé dog/ *n* METEOROL = **fogbow** [Mid-16C. Originally 'animal like a seal'.]

sea eagle *n* a fish-eating eagle that lives near the sea

sea-ear (*plural* **sea-ears** *or* **sea-ear**) *n* MARINE BIOL = **abalone**

sea elephant *n* ZOOL = **elephant seal**

sea fan *n* a coral with a fan-shaped skeleton. Native to: Florida, Caribbean. Genus: *Gorgonia.*

seafarer /seé fairər/ *n* a traveller by sea

seafaring /seé fairing/ *adj* 1 REGULARLY GOING TO SEA regularly travelling by sea or working at sea 2 OF SEA TRAVEL OR TRANSPORT relating to travel or transport by sea ■ *n* SAILOR'S WAY OF LIFE the work and way of life of a sailor

sea fire *n* light that is produced by marine organisms

seafloor /seé flawr/ *n* the surface of the Earth at the bottom of the sea

seafloor spreading *n* a process in which molten material from the Earth's mantle rises up at ocean ridges, causing volcanic and seismic activity, spreads out, and creates a new seafloor

seafood /seé food/ *n* fish and shellfish from the sea eaten as food

seafowl /seé fowl/ (*plural* **-fowl** *or* **-fowls**) *n* BIRDS = **seabird**

seafront /seé frunt/ *n* the part of a town that faces the edge of the sea

sea-girt *adj* encircled by the sea (*literary*)

seagoing /seé gō ing/ *adj* 1 made or fit for sailing on the open sea 2 INSUR = **seafaring** *adj.* 1

sea gooseberry *n* a marine invertebrate (**ctenophore**) that resembles a gooseberry in having a round body and fine tentacles like hairs. Genus: *Pleurobrachia.*

sea grape *n* a tree with large rounded leaves and clusters of purple-to-whitish berries. Native to: sandy shores from Florida to South America. *Coccoloba uvifera.*

sea green *n* a blue-green colour —**sea-green** *adj*

seagull /seé gul/ *n* BIRDS = **gull**¹

LITERARY LINK ***The Seagull***, a play (1896) by the Russian writer Anton Chekhov. The plot centres on the young writer Triplev's love for the aspiring actress Nina, who, to Triplev's dismay, allows herself to be seduced by an older, more famous writer, Trigorin.

sea hare *n* a large marine mollusc that has an arched back, a reduced or absent external shell, and two tentacles resembling rabbit ears. Genus: *Aplysia.*

sea holly *n* a spiny-leaved perennial plant of the carrot family. Flowers: blue. Use: formerly, aphrodisiac. Native to: European seashores. *Eryngium maritimum.*

sea horse *n* 1 a small bony fish with a head shaped like that of a horse, a vertical swimming position, and a prehensile tail that it uses to cling to seaweed. Genus: *Hippocampus.* 2 a mythological creature with the head and forelegs of a horse and the body of a fish

sea-island cotton *n* a cotton with long silky fibres, grown chiefly in the Caribbean. *Gossypium barbadense.* [After the Sea Islands]

Sea Islands chain of several hundred low islands off the coast of South Carolina, Georgia, and N Florida, in the Atlantic Ocean

sea kale *n* a seashore plant related to the cabbage, with edible leaves and shoots. Native to: Europe, Asia. *Crambe maritima.*

sea king *n* a Norse pirate chief of the early Middle Ages

seal¹ /seel/ *n* 1 TIGHT OR PERFECT CLOSURE a closure that prevents the entrance or escape of something such as air or water, or a substance or device that forms such a closure 2 SPECIAL CLOSURE THAT REVEALS TAMPERING a closure for something such as a package or container that must be broken to open it and can thereby reveal tampering 3 AUTHENTICATING STAMP a ring or stamp with a raised or engraved symbol or emblem that is pressed into wax in order to certify a signature or authenticate a document 4 WAX MARKED WITH SEAL a piece of wax bearing the mark of a seal 5 SYMBOL OF OFFICE a device, emblem, or symbol that is a mark of office 6 ORNAMENTAL ADHESIVE STAMP an ornamental adhesive stamp used to close a letter or package 7 SOMETHING GIVING CONFIRMATION something that gives confirmation or assurance ○ *Mother gave our plans for the party her seal of approval.* ■ *vt* 1 CLOSE FIRMLY to close something tightly or securely with a seal, e.g. to prevent tampering 2 MAKE WATERTIGHT OR AIRTIGHT to make something watertight, airtight, or nonporous, e.g. by filling gaps or applying a special substance to the surface 3 ATTACH AUTHENTICATING SEAL to affix a marked piece of wax to something in order to authenticate or certify it 4 CONFIRM to confirm a decision or come to an agreement on something 5 SETTLE to determine something irrevocably ○ *His fate was sealed when his lies were discovered.* 6 SOLEMNIZE MARRIAGE OR ADOPTION to solemnize a marriage or adoption in the Church of Jesus Christ of Latter-Day Saints [12C. Via Anglo-Norman < Latin *sigillum* 'little mark' < *signum* 'sign, token'.] —**sealable** *adj*

seal off *vt* to prevent people or things from entering or leaving a place, e.g. by surrounding it or closing it securely ○ *Police sealed off the area.*

seal² /seel/ *n* 1 FISH-EATING MARINE MAMMAL a carnivorous marine mammal with a sleek body adapted for swimming and living in cold regions and webbed feet modified as flippers. Families: Otariidae and Phocidae. 2 SEAL'S PELT the pelt or fur of a seal 3 LEATHER FROM SEAL'S SKIN leather made from the skin of a seal ■ *vi* HUNT SEALS to hunt seals, usually for their skins or blubber [Old English *seolh*]

sea lace *n* a seaweed with long thin blackish fronds. *Chorda filum.*

sea lamprey *n* a large eel-shaped jawless marine fish that swims up rivers to spawn and lives as a parasite on other fish. Native to: Atlantic coast of North America. *Petromyzon marinus.*

sea lane *n* an established and commonly used sea route for large ships

sealant /seélənt/ *n* a substance used to seal something, e.g. by filling gaps or making a surface nonporous

sea lavender *n* a perennial plant of the thrift family with a rosette of slender leaves at the base. Flowers: bluish-purple, in branching spikes. Native to: temperate salt marshes. Genus: *Limonium.*

sea lawyer *n* an argumentative sailor, or any contentious person (*informal*)

sealed-beam headlight *n* a vehicle headlight with a prefocused reflector and lens sealed in one unit

sealed orders *npl* written instructions not to be opened or read before a particular time, e.g. instructions to the captain of a ship whose destination is not revealed before it leaves harbour

sea legs *npl* the ability to move with ease on a ship and not feel seasick despite its pitching and rolling motion (*informal*)

sealer¹ /seélər/ *n* 1 a person, substance, or device that seals something, e.g. a substance used to make a surface nonporous 2 an official who inspects and certifies weights and measures

sealer² /seélər/ *n* a hunter of seals or a boat used by such hunters

sealery /seéləri/ (*plural* **-ies**) *n* 1 REARING OR BREEDING PLACE FOR SEALS a place where seals are reared or where seals congregate and breed 2 PLACE WHERE SEALS ARE HUNTED a place where seals are hunted 3 HUNTING OF SEALS the occupation or practice of hunting seals

sea letter *n* a passport issued to a neutral ship in wartime that entitles the ship to sail under the flag of the nation to which it belongs

sea lettuce *n* a seaweed sometimes used as food in salads. Genus: *Ulva.*

sea level *n* the level of the surface of the sea relative to the land, halfway between high and low tide, used as a standard in calculating elevation

sealift /seé lift/ *n* SYSTEM FOR SHIPPING CARGO BY SEA a system for transporting people and cargo by ship in an emergency ■ *vt* TRANSPORT CARGO BY SHIP to transport people or cargo by ship, especially at short notice ■ *n* TRANSPORTATION OF TROOPS BY SEA an act or the operation of transporting troops or equipment by sea

sea lily *n* a marine invertebrate that has a stalk anchored to the seabed and a flower-shaped body. Class: Crinoidea.

sealing wax *n* a resinous substance that is soft when heated and used for sealing letters, documents, batteries, or jars

sea lion *n* a large gregarious seal that has external ears and coarse hair with no underfur. Family: Otariidae.

sea loch *n Scotland* GEOG = **loch** *n.* 2

Sea Lord *n* either one of the two most senior serving naval officers on the Admiralty Board of the British Ministry of Defence

seal point *n* a Siamese cat with a cream or fawn body and a dark brown face, paws, and tail

seal ring *n* = **signet ring**

sealskin /seél skin/ *n* the pelt or fur of a seal, or a garment made from this

Sealyham terrier /seéli əm-/ *n* a dog with short legs, a long head, powerful jaws, and a wiry, mostly white coat, belonging to a breed developed in Wales for catching rabbits and similar animals [Late 19C. After the South Welsh village of *Sealyham*.]

seam /seem/ *n* **1 PLACE WHERE PIECES JOIN** the line along which pieces of cloth or leather are joined by sewing **2 STITCHES FORMING SEAM** the stitches used to form a seam **3 LINE FORMED BY ADJACENT SECTIONS** any line, groove, or ridge formed by joining or fitting together two sections along their edges **4 LINEAR INDENTATION** a scar, wrinkle, or other linear indentation **5 THIN LAYER OF ROCK** a thin layer of a rock or mineral such as a coal deposit occurring between different strata of bedrock ■ *v* **1** *vt* **JOIN THINGS ALONG EDGES** to join two parts or pieces along their edges, e.g. by sewing them together **2** *vti* **MARK WITH LINES** to mark something with wrinkles, scars, furrows, or other lines, or to become marked in this way [Old English *sēam* < Germanic, 'sew'] ◇ **bulging** *or* **bursting at the seams** extremely full ◇ **come** *or* **fall apart at the seams** to enter into a state of collapse

SPELLCHECK Do not confuse ***seam*** with ***seem***, which has a similar sound. Beware: your spellchecker will not catch this error.

seaman /seémən/ (*plural* **-men** /-mən/) *n* **1** NAUT = **sailor** *n.* 1 **2** an enlisted person in the US Navy or Coast Guard of a rank above seaman apprentice [Old English] —**seamanship** *n*

seamark /seé maark/ *n* an object on land easily visible from the sea that serves as an aid to navigation

sea mat *n* MARINE BIOL = **bryozoan**

seam bowler *n* a fast bowler in cricket who makes the ball bounce on its seam and so deviate from a straight line —**seam bowling** *n*

seamer /seémər/ *n* **1** a person or machine that makes seams or the operator of such a machine **2** CRICKET = **seam bowler 3** a ball that bounces on its seam and so deviates from a straight line

sea mew *n* a seagull, especially the common gull

sea mile *n* MEASURE = **nautical mile** *n.* 2

sea milkwort *n* a plant of the primula family. Flowers: small, pink. Native to: northern temperate coasts. *Glaux maritima.*

seamless /seémləss/ *adj* **1** having no seams **2** free from awkward transitions and creating perfectly smooth continuity —**seamlessly** *adv* —**seamlessness** *n*

seamount /seé mownt/ *n* an isolated undersea mountain of volcanic origin that rises from the seabed to a height of up to 1,000 m/3,300 ft, usually 1,000 m/3,300 ft to 2,000 m/6,500 ft below the surface of the sea

sea mouse *n* a large marine worm with a broad flat body covered in bristles resembling hair. Genus: *Aphrodite.*

seamstress /sémstrəss, seém-/ *n* a woman who sews or whose occupation is sewing [Late 16C. < *seamster* 'tailor, person who sews' < SEAM.]

seamy /seémi/ (**-ier, -iest**) *adj* having unpleasant qualities associated with a degraded or degenerate way of living —**seaminess** *n*

Seanad Éireann /shánnəth áirən, -nəd-/ *n* the upper chamber of parliament in the Republic of Ireland [Early 20C. < Irish, 'Senate of Ireland'.]

seance /sáy oNss, -onss, -aanss/ *n* **1** a meeting at which a spiritualist attempts to receive communications from the spirits of the dead **2** a sitting, session, or meeting, e.g. of a society or a legislative body [Late 18C. Via French, 'sitting' < Old French *seoir* 'sit' < Latin *sedere.*]

sea nettle *n* a stinging jellyfish. Native to: Atlantic estuaries from Cape Cod to the Caribbean.

sea otter *n* a marine animal of the weasel family with a thick brown coat that feeds mainly on shellfish. Native to: N Pacific coasts. *Enhydra lutris.*

sea pea *n* a plant of the pea family that grows wild along sandy shores of the northern hemisphere. Flowers: purple. *Lathyrus japonicus.*

sea pen *n* a marine organism related to coral that forms feathery colonies in warm seas. Genus: *Pennatula.*

sea pink *n* PLANTS = **thrift** *n.* 2

seaplane /seé playn/ *n* a plane designed in such a way that it can take off from and land on water

seaport /seé pawrt/ *n* a port, town, or harbour that can accommodate seagoing ships

sea power *n* **1** a nation that has formidable naval strength **2** the military power that a nation can deploy to fight on water

⚡**SEAQ** /seé ak/ *n* a computerized system for displaying prices and transactions in securities on the UK Stock Exchange. Full form **Stock Exchange Automated Quotation**

seaquake /seé kwayk/ *n* an earthquake occurring under the sea

sear[1] /seer/ *v* **1** *vt* **BURN** to burn or scorch something with an application of intense heat **2** *vt* **HAVE UNPLEASANT EFFECT** to have a sudden painful or unpleasant effect on somebody or something **3** *vti* **WITHER** to wither, shrivel, or dry up, or to cause something to wither, shrivel, or dry up ■ *n* **BURN OR SCORCH MARK** a mark or scar made by searing [Old English *sēarian* 'wither away' < Germanic]

sear[2] /seer/ *n* the catch that holds a gunlock cocked or at half-cock [Mid-16C. < French *serre* 'grasp, lock' < *serrer* 'grasp' < Latin *sera* 'bar for a door'.]

sear[3] /seer/ *adj* = **sere**[1] (*archaic or literary*)

Sea Ranger *n* a senior Guide aged between 14 and 20 who specializes in activities at sea

sea raven *n* a large fish that swallows air and blows up like a balloon when removed from the water. Native to: Atlantic coast of North America. *Hemitripterus americanus.*

⚡**search** /surch/ *v* **1** *vti* **EXAMINE THOROUGHLY** to look into, over, or through something carefully in order to find somebody or something ○ *searched his pockets for some change* ○ *searching through the pile of papers on the desk* **2** *vt* **EXAMINE FOR CONCEALED ITEMS** to examine the clothing, personal effects, or body of somebody in order to discover something such as weapons or illegal drugs that have been deliberately concealed **3** *vt* **EXAMINE PUBLIC RECORD** to examine a public record to find information about something **4** *vt* **DISCOVER SOMETHING BY EXAMINATION** to discover, come to know, or find something by examination ○ *searched out the relevant file* **5** *vt* **EXAMINE COMPUTER FILE** to examine a computer file, disk, database, or network for particular information ■ *n* **1 THOROUGH EXAMINATION** a careful and thorough examination in order to find somebody or something **2 EXAMINATION OF COMPUTER FILE** the examination of a computer file, disk, database, or network in order to find particular information **3 BOARDING OF SHIP TO SEARCH IT** the boarding of a ship in accordance with international law in order to search it, especially during wartime [14C. Via Anglo-Norman *sercher* and Old French *cerchier* 'explore' < Latin *circare* 'go around in circles' < *circus* 'circle'.] —**searchable** *adj* —**searcher** *n* ◇ **search me** emphasizes your lack of knowledge about something (*informal*)

⚡**search engine** *n* a computer program that searches for particular keywords and returns a list of documents in which they were found, especially a commercial Internet service

searching /súrching/ *adj* observing acutely or examining thoroughly —**searchingly** *adv* —**searchingness** *n*

searchlight /súrch līt/ *n* **1** an apparatus for projecting a high-intensity beam of light in any direction **2** the light from a searchlight

search party *n* a group of volunteers or professionals organized to search for a missing person

search warrant *n* a court order authorizing entry to somebody's property to look for unlawful possessions

sea rocket *n* a plant of the mustard family that grows along seashores and has sharp-tasting leaves. Flowers: white or lavender. Genus: *Cakile.*

searoom /seé room, -rŏŏm/ *n* open space at sea in which to turn or manoeuvre a ship

sea rover *n* a pirate or a pirate ship (*literary*)

sea salt *n* coarse salt obtained from the evaporation of seawater

seascape /seé skayp/ *n* a painting or picture of the sea, or a view of the sea [Late 18C. < SEA, after 'landscape'.]

Sea Scout *n* a member of a scouting organization who learns sailing, boating, canoeing, and other water activities

sea serpent *n* **1** a giant creature resembling a snake often reported to have been seen at sea, but never proved to exist **2** ZOOL = **sea snake** *n.* 1

seashell /seé shel/ *n* the empty shell of a sea creature, especially a mollusc

seashore /seé shawr/ *n* **1** the land lying next to the sea, especially a beach **2** the land lying between the usual high and low water marks

seasick /seé sik/ *adj* feeling sick or dizzy as a result of the rocking movement of a vessel on water —**seasickness** *n*

seaside /seé sīd/ *n* the area of land bordering the sea, especially as a place for holidays and leisure activities ■ *adj* situated or taking place at the seaside ○ *a seaside cottage*

sea slater *n* a small marine organism that resembles a large woodlouse, lives in cracks in the rocks around the high-water mark, and is active mainly at night. *Ligea oceanica.*

sea slug *n* a marine mollusc without gills that resembles a sea snail with no shell and is often brightly coloured. Order: Nudibranchia.

sea snail *n* **1** a small sea creature such as a whelk or periwinkle with a spiral shell resembling that of a snail. Class: Gastropoda. **2** ZOOL = **snailfish**

sea snake *n* **1** a venomous snake that swims by means of an oar-shaped tail and bears live young. Native to: tropical waters. Family: Hydrophidae. **2** MYTHOL = **sea serpent** *n.* 1

season /seéz'n/ *n* **1 TRADITIONAL DIVISION OF YEAR** any one of the periods marked by particular weather conditions into which the year is traditionally divided **2 PERIOD FOR PARTICULAR ACTIVITY** a time or period of the year during which a particular activity usually takes place in the human world or among plants and animals ○ *planting season* ○ *mating season* **3 PERIOD SET ASIDE FOR ACTIVITY** a fixed period of every year during which particular activities, especially sports, take place or are permitted ○ *cricket season* **4 PLAYER'S OR TEAM'S PERFORMANCE** the performance of a player or team during a sporting season in relation to others ○ *had his best season ever* **5 TIME FOR FOOD** the time of year when something, especially a kind of food, is abundant and at its best ○ *asparagus season* **6 CONNECTED SERIES OF PERFORMANCES** a period of time during which works that are all by or featuring the same person, or are connected by theme or period, are shown or performed **7 HIGH SEASON AT RESORTS** the time of year at which resorts receive most visitors and charge their highest rates **8 SOCIAL SEASON** the time during which the important social events of the year involving members of high society take place **9 TIME AROUND HOLIDAY** the period of time just before, after, and including a holiday ○ *the Christmas season* **10 SEXUAL RECEPTIVENESS** the period during which a female animal is sexually receptive and ready to be mated **11 PERIOD OF TIME** a period of time of unspecified length ○ *a brief season* **12 SUITABLE TIME** a fit or appropriate time for something or to do something (*literary*) **13 SEASON TICKET** a season ticket (*informal*) ■ *v* **1** *vti* **ADD FLAVOURINGS** to add flavourings such as salt, spices, or herbs to food **2** *vt* **ENLIVEN** to liven up something such as a speech or piece of writing by inserting exciting or amusing material ○ *a speech seasoned with wit* **3** *vti* **DRY OUT BEFORE USE** to allow wood to dry out fully before use, or to become fully dried out before being used **4** *vt* **PREPARE NEW PAN FOR USE** to prepare a new frying pan or wok for use by rubbing vegetable oil into the heated cooking surface **5** *vt* **CAUSE SOMEBODY TO GAIN EXPERIENCE** to cause or enable somebody to gain experience and become more skilled, or to gain toughness and strength ○ *seasoned troops* **6** *vt* **MODERATE** to temper something such as a strong emotion (*literary*) [14C. Via Old French < Latin *sation-* 'sowing' < *sat-*, past participle of *serere* 'sow'.] —**seasoner** *n* ◇ **in season 1** plentifully available and at a peak of quality ○ *Strawberries are in season now.* **2** allowed to be hunted, caught, or killed **3** sexually receptive to males **4** at an appropriate time (*literary*) ◇ **out of season 1** not widely available or not of good quality because of the time of year ○ *Tulips are out of season at this time of year.* **2** not allowed to be hunted, caught, or killed because of the time of year **3** at an inappropriate time (*literary*)

seasonable /seéz'nəb'l/ *adj* 1 typical of or appropriate for a particular season of the year 2 done, given, or occurring at a time when needed or appropriate —**seasonableness** *n* —**seasonably** *adv*

seasonal /seéz'nəl/ *adj* 1 dependent on or determined by the time of year 2 available or employed only during a particular time or at particular times of the year —**seasonally** *adv* —**seasonalness** *n*

seasonal affective disorder, seasonal affective disorder syndrome *n* medical depression associated with the onset of winter and thought to be caused by decreasing amounts of daylight

seasoning /seéz'ning/ *n* 1 salt, pepper, or any herb or spice used to give additional flavour to food 2 the process of treating timber to reduce its moisture sufficiently so that it is suitable for the function for which it will be used

season ticket, season pass *n* a ticket or pass valid for a season or particular period of time for travel on public transport, use of sport or leisure facilities, or attendance at sporting or cultural events

sea spider *n* a marine organism resembling a spider, with a fairly small body and four to six pairs of long jointed legs. Class: Pycnogonida.

sea squill *n* a plant that has an onion-shaped bulb with medicinal properties. Flowers: small, white, in dense spikes. Native to: Mediterranean. *Urginea maritima*.

sea squirt *n* a marine organism that has a transparent sac-shaped body with openings through which water passes in and out. It squirts out a stream of water when disturbed. Class: Ascidiacea.

sea star *n* ZOOL = **starfish**

sea steps *npl* a set of metal bars fixed to the side of a ship to allow people to climb on or off

sea swallow *n* a tern, especially the common tern. *Sterna hirundo*.

seat /seet/ *n* 1 **PLACE TO SIT** something for sitting on, especially something designed for this such as a chair or bench 2 **PART OF CHAIR SAT ON** the usually horizontal part of a chair or other seat that takes most of the weight of the person sitting on it 3 **VIEWER'S OR TRAVELLER'S SITTING PLACE** a place to sit and watch an event or travel in a vehicle, for which a ticket is usually required ○ *We don't really want seats in the front row.* 4 **PART OF GARMENT COVERING BUTTOCKS** the part of a garment that covers the buttocks 5 **MEMBERSHIP IN OFFICIAL GROUP** a position as a member of an official body or group, especially in an elected legislature ○ *won a seat in the legislature* 6 **CONSTITUENCY** the constituency represented by a member of parliament 7 **BASE** a place where something is located or based (*formal*) ○ *the seat of consciousness* 8 **RESIDENCE** a residence, especially a large house associated with a particular family 9 **OBJECT ON WHICH SOMETHING RESTS** an object, part, or space on which something such as a part of a machine or device rests or into which it fits 10 **RIDER'S POSITION** the position in which a rider sits on a horse ■ *v* 1 *vt* **PLACE SOMEBODY IN SEAT** to place somebody or yourself in a chair or other seat 2 *vt* **PROVIDE SEATS FOR PEOPLE** to have or provide seats for a particular number of people ○ *The hall seats five hundred.* 3 *vti* **REST OR FIT SECURELY** to rest something securely on or fit something firmly into something else, or to be firmly resting on or fitted into something ○ *The valve isn't seating properly.* 4 *vt* **INSTALL SOMEBODY IN POWERFUL POSITION** to establish somebody in a position of power or authority (*literary*) 5 *vt* **FIT SEAT ON SOMETHING** to put or refurbish a seat in or on something such as a chair or garment [12C. < Old Icelandic *sæti* < Germanic, 'sit'.] ◇ **by the seat of your pants** 1 using intuition and guesswork rather than theory or specialized knowledge 2 without the help of any instruments or technical aids

seatback /seét bak/ *n* the part of a seat against which the back rests

seat belt *n* a strong strap or harness designed to keep the wearer securely in a seat, especially in a vehicle or aircraft

-seater *suffix* indicates how many people a venue, vehicle, or piece of furniture can seat ○ *a three-seater sofa* ○ *drove up in a two-seater*

seating /seéting/ *n* 1 **SEATS** the places provided for people to sit, especially in a public building or a vehicle 2 **ARRANGEMENT OF SEATS OR SITTERS** the way in which seats or people sitting are arranged ○ *a seating plan* 3 **SOMETHING OBJECT RESTS ON** something on which an object rests or into which it fits 4 **UPHOLSTERING MATERIAL** material for upholstering the seat of a chair

seat-of-the-pants *adj* relying on intuition or guesswork rather than mechanical aids, rules and procedures, or planning (*informal*) [Because pilots claim to feel an aircraft's motion through the seat]

sea trout *n* 1 a large silvery-coloured trout living mainly in the sea but returning to fresh water to spawn. Native to: Europe, North Africa. *Salmo trutta*. 2 a marine fish of the croaker family resembling a trout. Native to: Atlantic coast of North America. *Cynoscion regalis*.

SEATS /seets/ *abbr* Stock Exchange Alternative Trading Service

Seattle /si átt'l/ city in west-central Washington State. Population: 536,978 (1998 estimate).

sea turtle *n* ZOOL = **turtle** *n.* 1

sea urchin *n* a small sea animal with a soft body enclosed in a spiny spherical shell. Class: Echinoidea.

sea wall *n* a wall built to prevent flooding or coastal erosion by the sea

seaward /seéwərd/, **seawards** /seéwərdz/ *adv* **TOWARDS THE SEA** in a direction towards the sea ■ *adj* 1 **SITUATED TOWARDS THE SEA** situated towards the sea 2 **BLOWING FROM SEA** describes wind that blows in towards the shore from the sea

seaware /seé wair/ *n* seaweed collected from the shore and used as fertilizer

sea wasp *n* a jellyfish that has a cube-shaped body with tentacles hanging from the lower corners. Its sting is very venomous and sometimes fatal. Order: Cubomedusae.

seawater /seé wawtər/ *n* salt water in or from the sea

seaway /seé way/ *n* 1 **INLAND CHANNEL FOR SHIPS** an inland canal, passage, or channel large enough for seagoing ships to navigate ○ *the St Lawrence Seaway* 2 **ROUTE ACROSS SEA** a shipping route across a sea 3 **SHIP'S PROGRESS** the progress of a ship through the sea 4 **ROUGH SEAS** seas that are moderate to rough [Old English]

seaweed /seé weed/ *n* plants such as kelp that grow in the sea

sea whip *n* a coral that forms long flexible structures with few or no branches and is common on Atlantic reefs

seaworthy /seé wurthi/ *adj* suitable or in a fit state to sail safely on the sea —**seaworthiness** *n*

sea wrack *n* seaweed, especially clumps of the larger varieties, found cast up on the shore

sebaceous /sə báyshəss/ *adj* relating to or producing a waxy yellowish body secretion (**sebum**) [Early 18C. < Latin *sebaceus* < *sebum* (see SEBUM).]

sebaceous gland *n* a gland that secretes sebum into hair follicles to lubricate the hair and skin

sebacic acid /sə bássik-, -báyssik-/ *n* $COOH(CH_2)_8COOH$ a white crystalline acid. Use: manufacture of synthetic resins, rubbers, plasticizers. [< SEBACEOUS]

Sebastian /sə básti ən/, **St** (*fl.* 3rd century) Roman Christian martyr

Sebastopol /sə bástə pol/, **Sevastopol** city in S Ukraine, on the southern coast of the Crimean Peninsula. Population: 366,200 (1991).

seborrhea *n* US = **seborrhoea**

seborrhoea /sébbə reé ə/ *n* excessively oily skin caused by heavy discharge from the sebaceous glands [Late 19C. < SEBUM + -RRHOEA.] —**seborrhoeal** *adj* —**seborrhoeic** *adj*

sebum /seébəm/ *n* an oily substance secreted by the sebaceous glands that lubricates the hair and skin and gives some protection against bacteria [Late 19C. < Latin, 'grease, tallow'.]

sec[1] /sek/ *n* a second (*informal*) [Late 19C. Shortening.]

sec[2] /sek/ *adj* describes a wine, especially champagne, that is dry in taste [Mid-19C. Via French < Latin *siccus* 'dry'.]

sec[3] *abbr* secant

SEC *abbr* Securities and Exchange Commission

SECAM /seé kam/ *n* a broadcasting system for colour television used in France, Russia, and a number of other countries. Full form **séquentiel couleur à mémoire**

secant /seékənt/ *n* 1 a straight line that intersects with a curve in two or more places 2 the ratio of the hypotenuse to the side adjacent to a given angle in a right-angled triangle [Late 16C. < Latin *secant-*, present participle of *secare* (see SECTION).]

secateurs /sékə turz, -túrz/ *npl* a gardening tool used for pruning that has two short heavy blades with a spring mechanism [Mid-19C. < French, < Latin *secare* (see SECTION).]

secco /sékō/ *n* (*plural* **-cos**) 1 **WALL PAINTING TECHNIQUE** the technique of wall painting on dry plaster using tempera or pigments ground in limewater 2 **PICTURE PAINTED ON WALL** a painting on a wall made by the secco method 3 **RECITATIVE STYLE** a style of vocal recitative in which the natural stress of the words is paramount and, if accompanied at all, is supported only by occasional chords of continuo instruments ■ *adj* 1 **ACCOMPANIED ONLY BY CONTINUO INSTRUMENTS** used to refer to vocal recitatives that are unaccompanied or accompanied only by occasional chords of continuo instruments 2 **STACCATO** played and released quickly and lacking resonance (*musical direction*) ■ *adv* **IN STACCATO MANNER** with the notes played and released quickly and without resonance (*musical direction*) [Mid-19C. Via Italian < Latin *siccus* 'dry'.]

secede /si seéd/ (**-cedes, -ceding, -ceded**) *vi* to make a formal withdrawal of membership from an organization, state, or alliance [Early 18C. < Latin *secedere* 'go apart' < *cedere* (see CEDE).] —**seceder** *n*

secession /si sésh'n/ *n* a formal withdrawal from an organization, state, or alliance [Mid-16C. Directly or via French < Latin *secedere* (see SECEDE).] —**secessional** *adj*

Secession *n* the withdrawal from the Union of 11 Southern States in 1860–61 that led to the formation of the Confederacy and the beginning of the American Civil War

secessionism /si sésh'n izəm/ *n* a belief or policy in favour of withdrawal from a nation, state, organization, or alliance —**secessionist** *n, adj*

seclude /si klood/ (**-cludes, -cluding, -cluded**) *vt* 1 to remove somebody from contact with others 2 to make a place private and quiet by screening or isolating it [15C. < Latin *secludere* 'shut out' < *claudere* 'shut'.]

secluded /si kloodid/ *adj* 1 cut off from other places and therefore private and quiet 2 having or involving little or no contact with others —**secludedly** *adv* —**secludedness** *n*

seclusion /si kloozh'n/ *n* 1 **CONDITION OF BEING SECLUDED** the condition of being cut off from others, or from other places 2 **ACT OF SECLUDING** an act of setting somebody or something apart from others 3 **SECLUDED PLACE** a quiet place removed from activity and people [Early 17C. < Latin *seclusion-* < *secludere* (see SECLUDE).]

seclusive /si kloossiv/ *adj* disposed to be solitary [Mid-19C. < SECLUDE, after INCLUSIVE.] —**seclusively** *adv* —**seclusiveness** *n*

second[1] /sékənd/ *adj* 1 **COMING AFTER FIRST** coming after the first in a series 2 **ANOTHER** additional to, repeating, or following one that came before or was previously mentioned ○ *I need a second look at those figures.* 3 **ADDITIONAL AND LESS IMPORTANT** additional to and less important than the first or main one ○ *a second home* 4 **SIMILAR TO PREDECESSOR** similar or comparable in many respects to a particular renowned personality or event ○ *a second Watergate* 5 **INFERIOR TO** inferior to or less important than somebody or something else ○ *second only to the president* 6 **PERFORMING LOWER OR LESS IMPORTANT PART** singing or playing a lower or less important part ■ *n* 1 see table at **number** 2 **ANOTHER PERSON OR THING** another person or thing of the same kind as one previously mentioned 3 **COMPETITOR'S OR DUELLIST'S ASSISTANT** an official assistant to a contestant in a boxing match or a participant in a duel 4 **SECONDER** a seconder for a proposal, a motion, or nomination in a debate 5 **ARTICLE WITH FAULT** an imperfectly manufactured article that is sold at a discount 6 **FORWARD GEAR** a forward gear of a transmission that is higher than first gear and lower than third gear 7 BASEBALL = **second base** *n.* 1 8 **SECOND CLASS DEGREE** a second class degree from a university or college 9 **INTERVAL OF TWO NOTES** in a standard musical scale, the interval between one note and another that lies one note above or below it 10 **NOTE A SECOND AWAY FROM ANOTHER** in a standard musical scale, a note that is a second away from another note 11 BALLET = **second position** ■ **seconds** *npl* (*informal*) 1 **ANOTHER HELPING OR SERVING** another helping or serving of a dish or type of food 2 **SECOND COURSE OF A MEAL** the second course of a meal, usually the dessert ■ *vt* 1 **ACT AS SECONDER** to state support officially for a proposal, motion, or nomination introduced by somebody else, so that discussion or voting can take place **2 EXPRESS AGREEMENT AND SUPPORT** to express agreement and support for something that somebody has just said (*informal*) ○ *I second that.* **3 ACT AS COMPETITOR'S OR DUELLIST'S SECOND** to act as second to a contestant in a boxing match or duel **4 ASSIST OR SUPPORT** to assist or support somebody or something (*formal*) ○ *seconded her efforts* ■ *adv* **1 EXCEPT FOR ONE** the one that exceeds all the rest, except for one, in a particular way (*qualifies a superlative*) ○ *the second-highest mountain in the world* **2** = **secondly** [14C. Via Old French < Latin *secundus* 'following' < *sequi* 'follow'.] ◇ **second to none** better than anyone or anything else

second[2] /sékənd/ *n* **1 60TH OF MINUTE** (*symbol* **s**) a unit of time that is equal to 1/60th of a minute **2 UNIT OF MEASUREMENT OF ANGLES** (*symbol* **″**) a unit of measurement of angles equal to 1/60th of a minute or 1/360th of a degree **3 VERY SHORT TIME** a very short period of time [14C. Via French < medieval Latin *secunda* < *secunda pars minuta* 'second diminished part'.]

second[3] /si kónd/ *vt* to transfer an employee, official, or soldier temporarily to other duties [Early 19C. < French *en second* 'in the second rank'.] —**secondment** *n*

Second Advent *n* = **Second Coming**

secondary /sékəndəri/ *adj* **1 NOT PRIMARY OR MAJOR** less important than or subordinate to something else ○ *matters of secondary importance* **2 DERIVED FROM SOMETHING ORIGINAL** derived from or reliant on something original ○ *a secondary source* **3 HAPPENING AS RESULT OF PRIMARY DISORDER** happening as a result of something else, e.g. an infection starting after a primary illness ○ *secondary tumours* **4 OCCURRING AFTER PRIMARY SCHOOL** intended for students who have completed their primary education, usually for children aged between eleven and eighteen **5 GROWING ALONG INNER EDGE OF WING** describes feathers that grow along the trailing edge of the inner segment of a bird's wing **6 ELECTRICALLY INDUCED** describes a circuit or coil that has an electric current produced by induction **7 INVOLVED IN MANUFACTURING** involved in the manufacture of goods from raw materials **8 ORGANIC CARBON COMPOUND** describes an organic compound having a carbon atom attached to three organic groups, at least one of which is chemically active **9 RELATING TO ORGANIC NITROGEN COMPOUND** describes an amine having two alkyl groups and one hydrogen atom attached to a nitrogen atom **10 OF RAPIDLY DIVIDING TISSUE** relating to or derived from rapidly dividing tissue (**cambium**) that gives rise to increased girth, not increased length ■ *n* (*plural* **-ies**) **1 SOMEBODY OR SOMETHING SECONDARY** somebody or something that is secondary or subordinate **2 SECONDARY TUMOUR** a cancerous growth at a site remote from that of the original malignant tumour **3 SECONDARY FEATHER** a secondary feather **4 INDUCED COIL OR CIRCUIT** a coil or circuit in which an induced current flows [14C. < SECOND[1].] —**secondarily** *adv* —**secondariness** *n*

secondary accent *n* **1** *US* PHON = **secondary stress 2** a mark used to indicate where the secondary accent is placed

secondary cell *n* an electric cell in which electricity is produced by a reversible chemical reaction

secondary colour *n* a colour such as orange, green, or purple produced by mixing two primary colours in roughly equal quantities

secondary electron *n* an electron released by secondary emission

secondary emission *n* the emission of electrons from the surface of a substance bombarded with electrons or ions

secondary infection *n* an infection that is acquired during the course of a separate initial infection

secondary modern school, secondary modern *n* formerly, a secondary school offering a more practical and less academic education than a grammar school and attended by students who did not pass the eleven-plus exam

secondary picketing *n* the picketing by strikers of premises other than those of the company with which they are in dispute, often those of the suppliers or distributors of their company's products

secondary school *n* a school for students who have completed their primary education, usually attended by children aged between eleven and eighteen

secondary sexual characteristic *n* a characteristic that develops at puberty but is not directly concerned with reproduction, e.g. a woman's breasts or a man's facial hair

secondary stress *n* an accentuation on a syllable that is weaker than that on the syllable receiving the main accent. US term **secondary accent**

secondary syphilis *n* the second, highly infectious stage of syphilis that appears several weeks or months after primary infection and is marked by a faint skin rash, fever, and muscular pain

second ballot *n* a second round of voting in an election in which no candidate obtained a winning majority in the first round

second base *n* **1** the base opposite home plate in the baseball diamond, or the position of the infielder playing nearest to second base on the first-base side **2** BASEBALL = **second baseman**

second baseman *n* in baseball, the player positioned closest to second base, on the first-base side of it

second best *adj* (*hyphenated before nouns*) **1 NEXT IN QUALITY TO BEST** next in quality to, or surpassed only by, the best **2 INFERIOR TO BEST** inferior to the best or the favourite ○ *had to make do with a second-best alternative* ■ *n* **1 SOMEBODY OR SOMETHING NEXT TO BEST** somebody or something that is next in quality to, or surpassed only by, the best **2 SOMEBODY OR SOMETHING INFERIOR TO BEST** somebody or something inferior to the best or the favourite

second chamber *n* the upper house in a two-chamber legislative assembly, e.g. the British House of Lords

second childhood *n* an offensive term for a condition associated with ageing that manifests itself in behaviour regarded as resembling that of a child

second class *n* **1 CATEGORY AFTER BEST** the category or standard of something, especially of accommodation or travel, that comes immediately below the best **2 MAIL DELIVERY SERVICE** a mail delivery service for letters and packets that is slower but less expensive than first class **3 SECOND HIGHEST DEGREE** the second highest division on the classification of university results, or a degree awarded for a result in this division ■ *adj* (*hyphenated before nouns*) **1 BELONGING TO SECOND CLASS** belonging to or meeting the standards of second class, especially regarding mail service or travel accommodation ○ *second-class accommodation* **2 INFERIOR** inferior to, or less important than, somebody or something else ■ *adv* **second-class BY SECOND-CLASS MEANS OF TRAVEL** by second-class mail delivery service or travel accommodation ○ *travelled second-class*

second-class citizen *n* a person who does not have the same rights, privileges, or opportunities as a full citizen

Second Coming *n* in Christian belief, the anticipated and prophesied return of Jesus Christ to judge humanity at the end of the world

second cousin *n* a child of a first cousin of either of your parents

second-degree burn *n* a burn that causes blistering on the skin, but does not damage the deeper layers of the skin or require grafting

seconde /sə kóNd/ *n* the second of the eight classic parrying positions in fencing [Early 18C. < French, 'second'.]

Second Empire *n* **1** the reign or the government of the Emperor Napoleon III of France, lasting from 1852 until 1870 **2** the weighty, grandiose, and highly ornamented style of architecture, furnishing, and decoration typical of the Second Empire

seconder /sékəndər/ *n* a person who states support for a proposal, motion, or nomination introduced by somebody else, so that discussion or voting can take place

second estate *n* the nobility, as one of the three broad traditional classes of people within a monarchical state

second fiddle *n* a less important or less prominent role or somebody or something in such a role

second generation *n* **1** the children of immigrants to a particular country **2** a later stage in the development of something that benefits from what was learned from the first stage of development —**second-generation** *adj*

second growth *n* the trees and plants that grow back naturally in an area of forest after the original trees have been removed by cutting or fire

second-guess *vti* **1** to predict a course of events, outcome, or what someone will do, from a position of relative ignorance ○ *no point in trying to second-guess what they'll do* **2** *US* to criticize, assess, or correct somebody or something after an event is over and the outcome is known —**second-guesser** *n*

second hand *n* the hand of a clock or watch that shows time passing second by second and rotates once around the dial in the space of a minute

second-hand *adj* **1 PREVIOUSLY OWNED** previously owned or used **2 SELLING USED GOODS** selling or dealing in used goods **3 NOT ORIGINAL** received from or reliant on somebody or something other than the original source ○ *second-hand accounts of the incident* ■ *adv* **1 IN USED CONDITION** after being owned or used by somebody else ○ *bought it second-hand* **2 THROUGH INTERMEDIARY** from or through somebody or something else and not by direct experience or personal effort ○ *acquires the information second-hand* ◇ **at second-hand** from or through somebody or something else

secondi plural of **secondo**

second-in-command *n* a person ranking next below somebody in command

Second International *n* an international socialist association established in 1889 in Paris and lasting until World War I

second language *n* (*hyphenated before nouns*) **1** a language learned by somebody after the first language he or she learns at home **2** a language in widespread use in a country, sometimes having official status

second lieutenant *n* **1** in the US and Canadian army and air force, the US Marine Corps, and the Royal Marines, a commissioned officer of the lowest rank above chief warrant officer **2** in many military forces, the lowest commissioned rank

secondly /sékəndli/ *adv* used to introduce the second point in an argument or discussion

second man *n* a crew member who assists the driver of a railway train

second mate *n* the officer on a merchant ship next in the line of command after the first mate, usually the third-highest-ranking officer on board

second mortgage *n* an additional mortgage on a property that has been mortgaged once already and secondary to the main lien for settlement

second name *n* **1** somebody's surname **2** somebody's second forename

second nature *n* a habit or tendency so well-developed and long-practised that it seems to be done unconsciously

secondo /se kóndō/ (*plural* **-di** /-di/) *n* the second or lower part in a piece of music for two players, especially a piano duet [Late 18C. < Italian, 'second'.]

second opinion *n* an opinion, especially one of a professional nature, from somebody other than the usual or first person consulted

second person *n* **1** the form of a verb or pronoun used when addressing somebody. In English, the second-person singular and plural pronoun is 'you'. **2** the grammatical set containing the forms indicating the second person

second position *n* a position in ballet in which the feet are turned outwards with the feet slightly apart

second-rate *adj* inadequate in quality or performance ○ *a second-rate pianist* —**second-rater** *n*

second reading *n* the second presentation of a bill to a legislature as part of the process of turning the bill into law

Second Republic *n* the period of the Republican government in France from 1848 to 1852

~~**secondry**~~ incorrect spelling of **secondary**

second sight *n* the supposed ability to see things that the physical eye cannot see, especially events taking place in the future or elsewhere —**second-sighted** *adj* —**second-sightedness** *n*

second-strike *adj* relating to, involving, or intended for use in, a retaliatory nuclear attack with weapons designed to survive a first nuclear strike by an enemy ○ *second-strike capabilities*

second string, second team *n* a fallback plan of action —**second-string** *adj*

second thought *n* a reconsideration of something tentatively decided, e.g. in light of new developments or something not previously taken into account (*often plural*) ○ *having second thoughts about getting married* ◇ **on second thoughts** after reconsideration

second wind /-wínd/ *n* a renewal of energy following a period of effort and exertion

Second World War *n* = **World War II**

~~**seceratary**~~ incorrect spelling of **secretary**

secrecy /séekrəssi/ *n* **1 STATE OF CONCEALMENT** the state of being concealed or secret ○ *talks held in secrecy* **2 KEEPING OF SECRETS** the keeping of a secret or secrets ○ *sworn to secrecy* **3 SECRETIVENESS** a tendency to keep things secret [Late 16C. < SECRET.]

secret /séekrət/ *adj* **1 NOT WIDELY KNOWN** known by only a few people and intentionally withheld from general knowledge **2 UNDERCOVER** working or operating without the knowledge of the general public **3 UNADMITTED** acting or feeling in a particular way without admitting to it ○ *a secret admirer* **4 PRIVATE AND SECLUDED** known to very few people and consequently quiet and secluded **5 SECRETIVE** tending by nature to keep things secret (*informal*) **6 MYSTERIOUS** mysterious and often beyond common understanding ■ *n* **1 INFORMATION NOT WIDELY KNOWN** a piece of information that is known only to a few people and is intentionally withheld from general knowledge **2 MYSTERY** something that is unknown, hidden, or not understood **3 SOMETHING ENSURING SUCCESS** a little-known technique, approach, or piece of information that is the key to success in a particular endeavour [14C. Via French < Latin *secretus* 'separate, hidden' < *secernere* 'separate apart'.] —**secretly** *adv* ◇ **in secret** without anyone else's knowledge ○ *meet in secret*

SYNONYMS ***secret, clandestine, covert, furtive, stealthy, surreptitious***

CORE MEANING: conveying a desire or need for concealment

secret intentionally withheld from general knowledge; **clandestine** describes an activity that needs to be concealed, usually because it is illegal or unauthorized; **covert** not intended to be known, seen, or found out, suggesting a lack of honesty or openness; **furtive** cautious and careful in order to escape notice; **stealthy** quiet, slow, and cautious in order to escape notice; **surreptitious** done in a concealed or underhand way to escape notice.

Secret, secret *n* formerly, the Prayer over the Gifts in the Roman Catholic Mass (*dated*) [14C. < ecclesiastical Latin *secreta oratio* 'concealed speech' < the low voice used.]

secret agent *n* somebody engaged in espionage for a government or organization

secretagogue /si kréetə gog/ *n* a substance such as a hormone that causes or stimulates secretion [Early 20C. < SECRETE[1] + -AGOGUE.] —**secretagogic** /si kréetə gójjik/ *adj*

secretaire /sékrə táir/ *n* a large cabinet with a fold-down desktop, usually with drawers below and an enclosed bookcase above. US term **secretary** [Late 18C. Via French < late Latin *secretarius* (see SECRETARY).]

secretariat /sékrə táiri ət/ *n* **1 ADMINISTRATIVE DEPARTMENT** a department that carries out the administrative and clerical work of an organization or legislature **2 SECRETARIAL STAFF** the secretarial staff under the direction of a secretary-general **3 BUILDING HOUSING SECRETARIAT** the headquarters or offices of a secretariat [Early 19C. Via French < medieval Latin *secretariatus* < late Latin *secretarius* (see SECRETARY).]

secretary /sékritəri/ (*plural* **-ies**) *n* **1 CLERICAL WORKER** an employee who does clerical and administrative work in an office for somebody or an organization **2 OFFICER OF ORGANIZATION** somebody elected or appointed to keep the records of the meetings of an organization such as a club, society, or committee, and to write or answer letters on its behalf **3** POL = **secretary of state** *n.* **4 SENIOR CIVIL SERVANT** a senior civil servant who advises a government minister **5** FURNITURE = **secretaire** [14C. < late Latin *secretarius* 'confidential officer' < *secretus* (see SECRET).] —**secretarial** /sékri táiri əl/ *adj* —**secretaryship** *n*

secretary bird *n* a large long-legged bird of prey that has grey-and-black plumage and a crest projecting from the back of its head and feeds mainly on snakes. Native to: Africa. *Sagittarius serpentarius.* [*Secretary* from the resemblance of the bird's crest to quill pens stuck behind a secretary's ear]

secretary-general (*plural* **secretaries-general**) *n* the chief executive officer of an organization such as the United Nations, who oversees a secretariat

secretary of state *n* a member of the British government and cabinet who is in charge of a major department such as Education or Defence

Secretary of State *n* the US government official and cabinet member who is in charge of foreign affairs

secret ballot *n* a situation in which people cast votes secretly in order to determine the outcome of an election or some other decision

secrete[1] /si kréet/ (**-cretes, -creting, -creted**) *vti* to produce and discharge a secretion [Early 18C. < Latin *secret-*, past participle of *secernere* (see SECRET).] —**secretor** *n* —**secretory** *adj*

secrete[2] /si kréet/ (**-cretes, -creting, -creted**) *vt* to conceal somebody or something [Mid-18C. Alteration of obsolete *secret* 'hide' < SECRET.]

secretin /si kréetin/ *n* a hormone secreted in the duodenum that stimulates the pancreas and the bowel to produce digestive enzymes and the liver to produce bile [Early 20C. < SECRETION.]

secretion /si kréesh'n/ *n* **1** the process of producing a substance from the cells and fluids within a gland or organ and discharging it **2** a substance formed and discharged by a cell, tissue, gland, or organ [Mid-17C. Via French < Latin *secret-*, past participle of *secernere* (see SECRET).] —**secretionary** *adj*

secretive /séekrətiv/ *adj* tending to keep information secret —**secretively** *adv* —**secretiveness** *n*

secret partner *n* a partner whose involvement in a business is kept secret

secret police *n* a police force that operates in secret and whose function is to prevent subversion or suppress political opposition to a regime (*takes a plural verb*)

secret service *n* a government department that carries out secret investigations and covert operations

Secret Service *n* a branch of the US Treasury Department whose main function is the protection of the president and vice president and their families

secret society *n* an organization that requires its members to keep all or some of its activities secret from nonmembers

sect /sekt/ *n* **1 NONMAINSTREAM RELIGIOUS GROUP** a religious group with beliefs and practices at variance with those of a more established main group **2 RELIGIOUS DENOMINATION** a denomination of a larger religious group **3 CLOSE-KNIT GROUP** a small close-knit group with strongly held views that are sometimes regarded as extreme by the majority [14C. Via French < Latin *secta* 'school of thought' < *sequi* 'follow'.]

-sect *suffix* **1** to cut or divide ○ *quadrisect* **2** cut, divided ○ *pinnatisect* [< Latin *sectus*, past participle of *secare* 'cut']

sectarian /sek táiri ən/ *adj* **1 OF RELIGIOUS GROUP** relating to or involving relations between religious groups or denominations **2 OF SINGLE RELIGIOUS GROUP** relating to, involved with, or devoted to a particular religious group or denomination **3 DOGMATIC AND INTOLERANT** rigidly adhering to a particular set of doctrines and intolerant of other views ■ *n* **1 MEMBER OF RELIGIOUS GROUP** a member of a religious group or denomination **2 SOMEBODY DOGMATIC AND INTOLERANT** somebody who rigidly adheres to a particular set of doctrines and is intolerant of other views —**sectarianism** *n*

sectarianize /sek táiri ə nīz/ (**-izes, -izing, -ized**), **sectarianise** (**-ises, -ising, -ised**) *vt* to cause somebody or something to become sectarian

sectary /séktəri/ (*plural* **-ries**) *n* a member of a religious group or denomination (*archaic*)

sectile /sék tīl/ *adj* describes minerals that can be cut so as to leave a smooth surface [Early 18C. < Latin *sectilis* < *sect-* (see SECTION).] —**sectility** /sek tílləti/ *n*

section /séksh'n/ *n* **1 DISTINCT PART** a distinct part that can be separated or considered separately from the whole of something **2 UNIT OF PEOPLE** a group of people forming a unit within a larger group, e.g. a subdivision of a military unit, or the musicians playing a particular kind of instrument in an orchestra **3 SUBDIVISION OF DOCUMENT** a major subdivision of a written work such as a book or newspaper, or of an official or legal document, often numbered **4 VIEW OF SOMETHING CUT THROUGH** a view or representation of something cut through to show its internal structure or workings **5 VERY THIN SLICE** a very thin slice of something removed for examination under a microscope ○ *a tissue section* **6 SURGICAL CUT** a surgical incision **7 CAESAREAN SECTION** a caesarean section (*informal*) **8 LENGTH OF RAIL TRACK** a length of railway track maintained by a single crew or controlled from a single signal box **9 SEGMENT OF CITRUS FRUIT** a segment of an orange, grapefruit, or other citrus fruit **10** PRINTING = **section mark** **11** *US* **AREA OF ONE SQUARE MILE** an area of land, for purposes of land surveying, equal to one square mile, 2.59 square kilometres, or one thirty-sixth of a township ■ *vt* **1 DIVIDE** to divide something up into separate parts **2 CUT SOMETHING SURGICALLY** to make a surgical incision in something **3 CONFINE SOMEBODY TO PSYCHIATRIC HOSPITAL** to order somebody who is mentally ill to be confined in a psychiatric hospital under the appropriate section of the Mental Health Act [14C. Via French < Latin *section-* < *sect-*, past participle of *secare* 'cut'.]

sectional /séksh'nəl/ *adj* **1 OF SECTION** relating to a particular group or section **2 INVOLVING DIFFERENT SECTIONS** involving different groups or sections **3 CONSISTING OF SECTIONS** divided into or made up of sections —**sectionally** *adv*

sectionalise *vt* = **sectionalize**

sectionalism /séksh'nəlizəm/ *n* excessive concern for the interests of a particular group or area to the detriment of the whole —**sectionalist** *n, adj*

sectionalize /séksh'nə līz/ (**-izes, -izing, -ized**), **sectionalise** (**-ises, -ising, -ised**) *vt* to divide something, especially a geographical area, into sections —**sectionalization** /séksh'nə lī záysh'n/ *n*

section mark *n* a symbol (§) sometimes used in printing to mark the beginning of a section of a book or one of a series of footnotes, and for various other purposes

ϟ**sector** /séktər/ *n* **1 COMPONENT PART** a component of an integrated system such as an economy or a society **2 PART OF AREA OF MILITARY OPERATIONS** a part of an area where military forces are operating or in control **3 PART OF CIRCLE** a part of a circle bounded by two radii and the part of the circumference that lies between them **4 MEASURING INSTRUMENT** a measuring instrument consisting of two arms marked with graduations, hinged together at one end **5 UNIT OF MAGNETIC STORAGE DEVICE** the smallest addressable unit of a magnetic storage device ■ *vt* **DIVIDE** to divide something into sectors [Late 16C. < late Latin, 'something that cuts' < *sect-* (see SECTION).] —**sectoral** *adj*

sectorial /sek táwri əl/ *adj* **1** relating to a sector or consisting of sectors **2** adapted or specialized for cutting ○ *sectorial teeth*

secular /sékyŏŏlər/ *adj* **1 NOT CONCERNED WITH RELIGION** not controlled by a religious body or concerned with religious or spiritual matters **2 NOT RELIGIOUS** not religious or spiritual in nature ○ *secular music* **3 NOT MONASTIC** not belonging to a monastic order **4 OCCURRING ONCE IN CENTURY** occurring only once in the course of an age or century **5 OCCURRING OVER LONG PERIOD** taking place over an extremely or indefinitely long period of time ■ *n* **1 MEMBER OF SECULAR CLERGY** a member of the secular clergy **2 LAY PERSON** a member of the laity [14C. < Old French *seculer* < Latin *saecularis* < *saeculum* 'world, generation'.] —**secularity** /sékyŏŏ lárrəti/ *n* —**secularly** *adv*

secular humanism *n* a philosophy or world view that stresses human values without reference to religion or spirituality

secularise *vt* = **secularize**

secularism /sékyŏŏlərizəm/ *n* **1** the belief that religion and religious bodies should have no part in political or civic affairs or in running public institutions, especially schools **2** the rejection of religion or its exclusion from a philosophical or moral system —**secularist** *n* —**secularistic** /sékyŏŏlə rístik/ *adj*

secularize /sékyŏŏlə rīz/ (**-izes, -izing, -ized**), **secularise** (**-ises, -ising, -ised**) *vt* **1** to transfer something from a religious to a nonreligious use, or from control by a religious body to control by the state or a lay body or person **2** to remove the religious dimension or element from something, or otherwise make it secular —**secularization** /sékyŏŏlə rī záysh'n/ *n* —**secularizer** *n*

secund /si kúnd/ *adj* arranged on or curving towards only one side of an axis [Late 18C. < Latin *secundus* (see SECOND[1]).] —**secundly** *adv*

secure /si kyŏŏr, -kyáwr/ *adj* **1 NOT WORRIED** untroubled by feelings of fear, doubt, or vulnerability **2 FIRMLY FIXED** firmly fixed or placed in position and unlikely to come loose or give way ○ *made the rope secure* **3 RELIABLE** reliable and unlikely to fail or be lost ○ *a secure investment* **4 WELL GUARDED AND FORTIFIED** well guarded and strongly fortified or protected **5 SAFE** safe, especially against attack or theft **6 SAFE FOR SECRET COMMUNICATIONS** safe to use for secret or confidential communication ○ *a secure line* **7 ASSURED** certain to be achieved or gained ○ *Just when victory seemed secure, we let it slip from our grasp.* ■ *v* (**-cures, -curing, -cured**) **1** *vt* **FIX FIRMLY** to fix something firmly in position **2** *vti* **MAKE SAFE** to make a building or area safe to occupy, usually by ensuring that all internal sources of danger are removed or that it is defended against attack **3** *vt* **ACQUIRE** to obtain something, especially after using considerable effort to persuade somebody to grant or allow it ○ *secure an agreement* **4** *vt* **ENSURE PAYMENT FOR** to provide security for something or otherwise guarantee payment ○ *a loan secured against your house* **5** *vti* **GUARANTEE** to guarantee or ensure something **6** *vt* **PREVENT FROM ESCAPING** to ensure that somebody cannot escape ○ *secure a prisoner* **7** *vt* **MAKE SAFE FOR SECRET COMMUNICATIONS** to ensure that a means of communication can be safely used for secret or confidential messages ○ *secure a telephone line* **8** *vt* **MAKE SAFE ON SHIP** to make sure that everything on board a ship is safely stowed and that openings are covered ○ *secure a ship* ○ *secure the cargo* [Mid-16C. < Latin *securus* 'without care' < *cura* 'care'.] —**securable** *adj* —**securely** *adv* —**securement** *n* —**secureness** *n* —**securer** *n*

SYNONYMS See ***get***.

ϟ**secure server** *n* an Internet server that allows for the encryption of data and thus is suitable for use in e-commerce (*in e-commerce*)

secure tenancy *n* a form of tenancy with a landlord such as a local authority or housing association in which the tenant has security of tenure

Securities and Exchange Commission *n* an agency of the US government set up to regulate transactions in securities and protect investors against malpractice

Securities and Investment Board *n* a regulatory body set up in 1986 to oversee financial markets in the City of London

securitization /si kyo͝ori tī záysh'n, -kyáwri-/, **securitisation** *n* the preparation of readily marketable securities representing an ownership interest in some asset such as credit card loans or forestry land that is not otherwise conveniently traded

security /si kyo͝orəti, -kyáwr-/ (*plural* **-ties**) *n* **1 STATE OR FEELING OF SAFETY** the state or feeling of being safe and protected **2 FREEDOM FROM WORRY ABOUT POSSIBLE LOSS** the assurance that something of value will not be taken away **3 SOMETHING GIVING ASSURANCE** something that provides a sense of protection against loss, attack, or harm **4 SAFETY** protection against attack from without or subversion from within ○ *a matter of national security* **5 PRECAUTIONS TO MAINTAIN SAFETY** precautions taken to keep somebody or something safe from crime, attack, or danger ○ *security measures* **6 GUARDS** people or an organization entrusted with the job of protecting somebody or something, especially a building or institution, against crime **7 ASSET DEPOSITED TO GUARANTEE REPAYMENT** something pledged to guarantee fulfilment of an obligation, especially an asset guaranteeing repayment of a loan that becomes the property of the creditor if the loan is not repaid **8 GUARANTOR** a person who pledges to fulfil somebody else's obligation should that person fail to do so **9 FINANCIAL INSTRUMENT** a tradable document such as a share certificate or bond that shows evidence of debt or ownership

security blanket *n* **1** a familiar blanket, toy, or other object that a child carries around for the feeling of security it gives, or any object that fulfils the same function for an adult **2** a policy of withholding information in the interests of security adopted as a temporary measure by the police or any other official body

Security Council *n* the permanent committee of the United Nations that oversees its peacekeeping operations throughout the world

security guard *n* somebody employed by a private organization to guard and protect a building or other property

security of tenure *n* the right of a tenant to continue occupying a property unless or until the landlord obtains a court order to regain possession of the property or terminate the tenancy

security risk *n* somebody or something considered a threat to security, especially somebody whose behaviour is thought likely to compromise the security of a country

securocrat /sə kyo͝orə krat, -kyáwrə-/ *n S Africa* a military or police officer with power to influence government policy, often from behind the scenes [Blend of SECURITY + BUREAUCRAT]

SED *abbr Scotland* Scottish Education Department

sedan[1] /si dán/ *n US, Can, ANZ* a car with a fully enclosed passenger compartment, a permanent roof, two or four doors, front and rear seats, and a separate boot [Mid-17C. < ?]

sedan[2], **sedan chair** *n* in the 17th and 18th centuries, an enclosed chair carried by porters at the front and rear on two long poles passed through handles on the sides of the box

Sedan /sə dán, sə doN/ town in NE France. Population: 22,407 (1990).

sedan chair *n* = **sedan**

sedate[1] /si dáyt/ *adj* dignified, subdued, and lacking any sense of hurry or urgency [Mid-17C. < Latin *sedatus*, past participle of *sedare* 'to calm' < *sedere* 'sit'.] —**sedately** *adv* —**sedateness** *n*

sedate[2] /si dáyt/ (**-dates, -dating, -dated**) *vt* to administer a sedative to somebody [Mid-20C. Back-formation < SEDATIVE.]

sedation /si dáysh'n/ *n* **1** a state of calm, restfulness, or drowsiness, especially as induced by a sedative or tranquillizing drug **2** the use of a sedative or tranquillizing drug to induce a state of calm, restfulness, or drowsiness

sedative /séddətiv/ *n* a drug or other agent that induces sedation ■ *adj* inducing sedation, especially by means of a tranquillizing drug ○ *a sedative effect*

Seddon /sédd'n/, **Richard John** (1845–1906) British-born New Zealand statesman. Known as **King Dick**

sedentary /sédd'ntəri/ *adj* **1 INVOLVING SITTING** involving a lot of sitting and correspondingly little exercise ○ *sedentary work* **2 USUALLY SITTING** tending to sit most of the time and taking little exercise ○ *a sedentary person* **3 NOT MOVING** describes shellfish that remain in one place, usually attached to a rock, for most of their lives **4 NON-MIGRATORY** remaining in the same area throughout the year and not migrating [Late 16C. Via French *sédentaire* < Latin *sedentarius* < *sedere* 'sit'.] —**sedentarily** *adv* —**sedentariness** *n*

Seder /sáydər/ (*plural* **-ders** *or* **-derim** /sə deérim/) *n* in Judaism, a ceremonial meal eaten on either of the first two nights of Passover, commemorating the exodus of the Jews from Egypt [Mid-19C. < Hebrew, 'order, procedure'.]

sederunt /si deérənt/ *n Scotland* **1** a formula used to introduce the list of those present at a sitting of a body such as an ecclesiastical assembly or a court, or the list itself **2** a sitting of a body such as an ecclesiastical assembly or a court [Early 17C. < Latin, 'they sat' < *sedere* 'sit'.]

sedge /sej/ *n* a wetland plant that resembles grass and has a triangular stem, leaves growing in three vertical rows, and inconspicuous spikes of flowers. Genus: *Carex*. [Old English *secg*. Ultimately < Indo-European, 'cut'.] —**sedgy** *adj*

Sedgemoor /séj moor, -mawr/ former marshland in SW England, where the Duke of Monmouth's rebellion was defeated in 1685

sedge warbler *n* a songbird with streaked brownish plumage and a white strip around its eye. Native to: marshes of Europe and Central Asia. *Acrocephalus schoenobaenus*.

sedge wren *n* a wren that lives in grassy meadows and sedge marshes. Native to: E North America. *Cistothorus platensis*.

Sedgwick /séjjwik/, **Adam** (1785–1873) British geologist

sedilia /si dílli ə/ *npl* a set of three seats placed near the altar of a church and often recessed into the wall used by priests celebrating Mass or Holy Communion [Late 18C. < Latin, plural of *sedile* 'seat' < *sedere* 'sit'.]

sediment /séddimənt/ *n* **1** material, originally suspended in a liquid, that settles at the bottom of the liquid when it is left standing for a long time **2** material eroded from preexisting rocks that is transported by water, wind, or ice and deposited elsewhere [Mid-16C. < Latin *sedimentum* 'settling' < *sedere* 'sit'.] —**sedimentous** /séddi méntəss/ *adj*

sedimentary /séddi méntəri/ *adj* **1** forming at the bottom of a liquid **2** describes rocks formed from material, including debris of organic origin, deposited as sediment by water, wind, or ice and then consolidated by pressure —**sedimentarily** *adv*

sedimentation /séddi men táysh'n/ *n* **1** the process by which rocks are formed by the accumulation of sediment **2** the process by which particles in suspension in a liquid form sediment

sedimentation tank *n* a tank in which sewage is left in order to allow its solid constituents to separate out

sedimentology /séddi men tólləji/ *n* the branch of geology concerned with the nature and formation of sedimentary rocks —**sedimentologic** /séddi mentə lójjik/ *adj* —**sedimentologist** *n*

sedition /si dísh'n/ *n* actions or words intended to provoke or incite rebellion against government authority, or such a rebellion [14C. Via Old French < Latin *seditio* 'coming apart' < *ire* 'go'.]

seditious /si díshəss/ *adj* **1** involving or encouraging rebellion against a government or other authority **2** taking part in activities that are directed against a government or other authority [15C. Via French *seditieux* < Latin *seditio* (see SEDITION).] —**seditiously** *adv* —**seditiousness** *n*

seduce /si dyo͞oss/ (**-duces, -ducing, -duced**) *vt* **1 INDUCE SOMEBODY TO HAVE SEX** to persuade somebody to have sex, especially by using a romantic or deceptive approach **2 LEAD SOMEBODY ASTRAY** to persuade somebody into doing something wrong **3 WIN SOMEBODY OVER** to persuade somebody into giving support or agreement [15C. < Latin *seducere* 'lead astray' < *ducere* 'lead'.] —**seducer** *n* —**seducible** *adj*

seducement /si dyo͞ossmənt/ *n* something that tempts or persuades ○ *'ere any flattering seducement, or vain principle seize them'* (John Milton, *Civil War Polemic, part I*)

seduction /si dúksh'n/ *n* **1 LEADING ASTRAY OF SOMEBODY** the act of persuading somebody to do something wrong ○ *their easy seduction into a life of crime* **2 LURING OF SOMEBODY INTO SEX** the act of persuading somebody to have sex, especially by using a romantic or deceptive approach **3 TEMPTING THING** something that tempts, persuades, or attracts

seductive /si dúktiv/ *adj* **1** aiming to be or regarded as being sexually inviting ○ *his seductive smile* **2** serving to tempt, persuade, or attract ○ *made me a very seductive offer* —**seductively** *adv* —**seductiveness** *n*

seductress /si dúktrəss/ *n* a woman who seduces other people [Early 19C. < obsolete *seductor* 'seducer' + -ESS.]

sedulous /séddyo͝oləss/ *adj* (*literary*) **1** working with great zeal and persistence **2** carried out with great care, concentration, and commitment ○ *sedulous attention to detail* [Mid-16C. < Latin *sedulus* < *se* 'without' + *dolus* 'deception'.] —**sedulity** /si dyo͞oləti/ *n* —**sedulously** *adv* —**sedulousness** *n*

sedum /seédəm/ *n* any of a genus of low-growing herbaceous plants that grow naturally in rocky places and have fleshy leaves. Flowers: white, yellow, or pink, in clusters. Genus: *Sedum*. [Mid-16C. < Latin, 'houseleek'.]

see[1] /see/ (**sees, seeing, saw** /saw/, **seen** /seen/) *v* **1** *vti* **PERCEIVE WITH EYES** to perceive, or perceive something, with the eyes **2** *vi* **HAVE VISION** to be able to perceive things with the eyes ○ *sees fine without his glasses* **3** *vti* **VIEW OR WATCH** to examine, look at, or watch somebody or something using the eyes ○ *He asked to see my passport.* **4** *vti* **COMPREHEND** to have a clear understanding of something ○ *I'm not sure I see what you mean.* **5** *vti* **REALIZE BY SEEING** to realize that something is true or exists by using the eyes, e.g. by reading about it ○ *I see from his letter that he's worked here before.* **6** *vt* **PERCEIVE AS PLEASING OR GOOD** to perceive or find a trait in somebody, especially one that is interesting or pleasing ○ *I don't understand what she sees in him.* **7** *vt* **MEET OR CONSULT** to meet somebody or spend time with somebody, either socially or professionally ○ *I'm seeing an old friend for lunch.* **8** *vt* **HAVE A RELATIONSHIP** to meet with somebody in a romantic context or have a romantic or sexual relationship with somebody ○ *Is he seeing anyone at the moment?* **9** *vt* **HAVE INTERVIEW** to meet somebody in order to raise or discuss an issue such as a complaint ○ *She asked to see the customer care manager.* **10** *vt* **RECEIVE FOR INTERVIEW** to admit or receive somebody who has come for a visit or an interview ○ *The doctor can't see you until next week.* **11** *vt* **IMAGINE** to picture something in the mind ○ *I couldn't see someone like him in a jacket and tie.* **12** *vt* **BELIEVE** to regard it as likely that somebody will do something ○ *We couldn't see them agreeing to that.* **13** *vt* **CONSIDER** to regard somebody or something in a particular way ○ *We don't really see them as good friends.* **14** *vt* **UNDERGO** to experience something firsthand ○ *They've seen a lot of unhappiness in their short lives.* **15** *vt* **ESCORT** to go somewhere with somebody, usually as a guide, for company, or for protection ○ *Would you see me to my car?* **16** *vt* **REMEMBER** to be sure to do something or make sure that someone does something ○ *See that they wipe their feet before they come in.* **17** *vt* **REFER TO** to consult something or refer to something ○ *See our main advertisement on page 25.* **18** *vti* **ASCERTAIN** to find something out ○ *See if you can get this book locally.* **19** *vi* **WAIT UNTIL LATER TO DECIDE** to allow time to elapse, either in order to be better able to judge what the outcome will be or in order to delay making a decision ○ *I don't know; we'll have to see.* **20** *vt* **MATCH BET** to match an opponent's bet by staking the same amount [Old English *sēon* < Germanic] —**seeable** *adj* ◇ **what you see is what you get** used to emphasize that nothing is disguised, hidden, or insincere. ◊ **WYSIWYG**

SPELLCHECK See ***sea***.

see about *vt* to take care of a particular matter
see into *vt* **1** to discern the true nature or content of something hidden, e.g. somebody's thoughts **2** to be able to predict future events
see off *vt* **1 ATTEND SOMEBODY'S DEPARTURE** to accompany somebody to a place of departure and say goodbye **2 FORCE SOMEBODY TO GO** to make somebody leave a place, especially by force (*informal*) ○ *The dogs soon saw them off.* **3 DEFEAT** to withstand a challenge, e.g. by beating an opponent in a sporting contest ○ *There's no question that the Brazilians will see off the others in their group.*
see out *vt* **1 ESCORT SOMEBODY OUT** to accompany somebody who is leaving a room, building, or other place **2 STAY UNTIL THE END OF** to stay in a place or stay committed to something until the end **3 OUTLIVE** to last until the end of somebody's life and beyond (*informal*) ○ *I reckon this old car will see me out.*
see over, see round *vt* to make a tour of a place, especially a building, in order to inspect it ○ *We can arrange for you to see over the property.*
see through *vt* **1 HELP SOMEBODY THROUGH DIFFICULTY** to provide somebody with help, advice, and support, especially in times of trouble ○ *He's seen me through some bad times.* **2 FINISH** to continue with something until it is completed ○ *a professional who sees every job through personally* **3 PERCEIVE TRUTH BENEATH EXTERIOR** to discern the true nature of somebody or something beneath a façade or disguise ○ *I saw through all his bravado.*
see to *vt* to do what is required in order to deal with something or take care of somebody successfully ○ *We need an usher to see to guests as they arrive.* ○ *I'll see to it immediately.*

see[2] /see/ *n* **1** the area that is under the jurisdiction of a bishop or archbishop **2** the position or authority of a bishop or archbishop [13C Via Old French *se* < Latin *sedes* 'seat' < *sedere* 'sit']

Seebeck effect /sée bek-/ *n* the production of an electric current in a circuit containing junctions between different metals or semiconductors kept at different temperatures [Early 20C. After Thomas *Seebeck* (1770–1831), Russian-born German physicist.]

seed /seed/ *n* **1 PLANT PART CONTAINING EMBRYO** the body produced by reproduction in most plants that contains the embryo and gives rise to a new individual. In flowering plants it is enclosed within the fruit. **2 FRUIT OF GRASS PLANT** the small dry hard fruit produced by cereal plants or grasses **3 PROPAGATIVE PART OF PLANT** any compact part of a plant such as a bulb, tuber, or spore that is used for propagation **4 PROPAGATIVE PLANT PARTS COLLECTIVELY** propagative plant parts as a whole, including seeds, tubers, rhizomes, spores, and bulbs ○ *a dry place to store seed* **5 SOURCE** something that is the source of a significant change in outlook or action ○ *sowing the seeds of doubt in her mind* **6 SOMETHING RESEMBLING SEED** something that resembles a seed in shape, size, or function **7 CRYSTAL** a small crystal added to a supersaturated or supercooled solution to induce crystallization **8 DESCENDANTS** descendants (*literary*) ○ *the seed of Abraham* **9 GRADED COMPETITOR** a competitor who is graded according to the perceived likelihood of his or her winning a particular tournament **10 SPERM** sperm or semen as a vehicle of reproduction (*literary*) **11** MARINE BIOL = **seed oyster** ■ *v* **1** *vt* **PLANT SEEDS** to plant seeds in soil or plant something by sowing seeds ○ *The lower field was seeded with barley.* **2** *vi* **DROP SEEDS** to shed seeds that develop into new plants (*refers to plants*) ○ *Those poppies have seeded themselves everywhere.* **3** *vt* **REMOVE SEEDS** to take the seeds out of a fruit or vegetable before eating or cooking **4** *vt* **ADD CRYSTAL TO SOLUTION** to add a small crystal to a supersaturated or supercooled solution to induce crystallization **5** *vt* **SPRINKLE CLOUD WITH CRYSTALS** to release silver iodide into clouds to encourage precipitation **6** *vt* **STRUCTURE TOURNAMENT** to arrange the draw of a tournament so that the best players meet in the later rounds **7** *vt* **RANK PLAYER** to rank a player according to the perceived likelihood of his or her winning a tournament **8** *vt US* **ENCOURAGE ENTERPRISE** to give financial or other assistance to something such as a business during the early stages of its development ○ *'Big venture capital funds have helped seed a start-up culture…'* (*Newsweek*; November 1998) ■ *adj* **RESERVED FOR USE AS SEED** reserved for planting to grow the next crop ○ *seed potatoes* [Old English *sǣd* < Germanic, 'sow'] —**seedless** *adj* ◇ **go** *or* **run to seed 1** to reach the stage of producing seeds **2** to become shabby or unhealthy from lack of proper care or attention

SPELLCHECK See ***cede***.

seedbed /séed bed/ *n* **1** a plot of ground in which seeds and seedlings are cultivated before being transplanted **2** a place where conditions encourage the development of a significant change in outlook or action

seedcake /séed kayk/ *n* a cake flavoured with seeds, usually caraway seeds

seed capital *n* money provided to enable a business venture to be developed. US term **seed money**

seed corn *n* **1** cereal grain that is reserved for use as seed **2** investments that are expected to yield good profits in the future

seeder /séedər/ *n* **1** a mechanical device designed to scatter seed on the surface of the ground, usually either one pulled by a tractor or one with wheels and a handle that is pushed **2** a kitchen device used to remove the seeds from fruit and vegetables

seed fern *n* PLANTS = **pteridosperm**

seedhead /séed hed/ *n* a fertilized flower or flower cluster that contains numerous seeds

seed leaf *n* PLANT SCI = **cotyledon** *n.* 1

seedling /séedling/ *n* a young developing plant that is grown from a seed

seed money *n US* FIN = **seed capital**

seed oyster *n* a small young oyster, especially one that is transplanted to a commercial oyster bed

seed pearl *n* a very small round pearl, natural or cultured, weighing less than one quarter of a grain

seed pod *n* PLANT SCI = **pod**[1] *n.* 1

seedsman /séedzmən/ (*plural* **-men** /-mən/) *n* a commercial producer or seller of seeds

seed stock *n* **1** a supply of seed for planting **2** a supply of animals kept or provided for breeding purposes, capable of founding a new population or sustaining an existing population (*hyphenated when used before a noun*)

seed tick *n* the tiny larva of a tick

seedtime /séed tīm/ *n* **1** the time of the year when seeds are sown **2** a period of new development or growth

seed weevil *n* any one of several species of insect of the weevil family that lays its eggs in seeds, where the larvae then develop

seedy /séedi/ (**-ier, -iest**) *adj* **1 UNWELL** somewhat ill, especially with a stomach complaint (*informal*) **2 DINGY** shabby, dirty-looking, and often disreputable ○ *He discovered her singing in some seedy bar.* **3 HAVING SEEDS** containing many seeds ○ *seedy raspberry jam* —**seedily** *adv* —**seediness** *n*

Seeger /séegər/, **Pete** (*b.* 1919) US singer and songwriter

seeing /sée ing/ *n* **1 VISION** vision or perception with the eyes ○ *My seeing isn't too good.* **2 ATMOSPHERIC CONDITIONS** the clarity of the Earth's atmosphere for astronomical observations using an optical telescope, or the quality of the images obtained ■ *conj* ⚠ **IN VIEW OF** used to introduce a statement that takes into account something mentioned before or after ○ *Seeing that you're an old friend, I can give you a special price.*

USAGE The use of ***seeing that*** as a conjunction not grammatically attached to a particular subject is established in current English and conforms to a pattern used also in *given that, granted that*, and others, as in the sentence: *Perhaps a bonus on my wages might be an idea, seeing that I shall be doing this out of hours* (Paula Marshall, *An American Princess*). On the other hand, ***seeing as***, used in the same way, is informal only: *I'll leave now seeing as you look tired.* To avoid using *seeing that*, substitute *since*.

seek /seek/ (**seeks, seeking, sought** /sawt/, **sought**) *v* **1** *vti* **SEARCH FOR** to try to find a particular thing or place ○ *journeyed to America to seek their fortune* **2** *vt* **STRIVE FOR** to try to achieve or obtain something ○ *candidates seeking election* **3** *vt* **HEAD FOR** to go to or towards a place or thing ○ *As the water rose, they sought higher ground.* **4** *vt* **ASK FOR** to consult somebody in order to obtain something such as help or advice ○ *His advice was regularly sought on such matters.* **5** *vt* **ATTEMPT** to try to do something ○ *seeking to exploit the rift between them* [Old English *sēcan*. Ultimately < Indo-European, 'seek out'.] —**seeker** *n*
seek out *vt* to find somebody or something as a result of active searching

seel /seel/ *vt* to sew up the eyelids of a hawk or falcon in order to make it tame [15C. Via Old French *siller* < medieval Latin *ciliare* < Latin *cilium* 'eyelid'.]

seem /seem/ *v* **1** *vti* to give a particular impression, either of a quality or of something happening ○ *It's not as difficult as it seems.* **2** *vt* to appear to exist or be true, used especially to lessen the force of a following statement, usually by suggesting uncertainty or mitigating criticism, often for the sake of politeness ○ *We seem to have a misunderstanding.* [12C. < Old Norse *sœma* 'conform to' < *sœmr* 'fitting'.]

SPELLCHECK See ***seam***.

seeming /séeming/ *adj* apparent to the senses or to the mind, but not necessarily true or real ○ *her seeming joy at his return* —**seemingly** *adv* —**seemingness** *n*

seemly /séemli/ (**-lier, -liest**) *adj* in keeping with accepted standards and appropriate to the circumstances [12C. < Old Norse *sœmiligr* < *sœmr* 'fitting'.] —**seemliness** *n*

seen past participle of **see**[1]

seep /seep/ *vi* **1 PASS THROUGH** to pass or escape through an opening very slowly and in small quantities (*refers to liquids or gases*) ○ *water seeping out of the cracks* **2 DISAPPEAR** to diminish slowly but steadily ○ *with her resistance gradually seeping away* **3 GO SLOWLY** to enter or escape slowly but inexorably ○ *new sensations seeping into his consciousness* ■ *n* **1 PLACE WHERE LIQUID ESCAPES** a small pool or spring where liquid escapes from the ground **2** = **seepage** [Late 18C. Variant of dialect *sipe* < ?]

seepage /séepij/ *n* the escape of liquid or the amount of liquid that escapes

seer[1] /seer, sée ər/ *n* **1** a predictor of future events **2** a person with supernatural powers

seer[2] /seer/ (*plural* **seers** *or* **seer**) *n* a unit of weight in India approximately equal to 0.9 kg/2 lbs [Early 17C. Via Hindi *ser* < Greek *statēr*, a unit of weight.]

seersucker /séer sukər/ *n* a lightweight cotton, linen, or synthetic fabric with a pattern of alternate puckered and smooth stripes [Early 18C. Via Hindi *śīrśakar* < Persian *shīr o shakar* 'milk and sugar'.]

seesaw /sée saw/ *n* **1 PLAYGROUND TOY** a playground toy in which two people sit at either end of a bar balanced in the middle and take turns at riding up into the air **2 SEESAW RIDING** the game of riding a seesaw **3 UP-AND-DOWN MOVEMENT** an up-and-down, back-and-forth, or otherwise alternating movement, e.g. in the popularity of one political party over another ■ *vi* **1 RIDE SEESAW** to ride up and down on a seesaw **2 MOVE LIKE SEESAW** to move in an alternating fashion, especially back and forth or up and down **3 ALTERNATE** to change regularly and repeatedly from one thing to another, e.g. one state of mind to another ○ *seesawing between one plan and another* [Mid-17C. Thought to suggest the repetitive action of a two-handled saw.]

seethe /seeth/ *v* (**seethes, seething, seethed**) **1** *vi* **MAKE BOILING MOVEMENTS** to boil or to churn or foam as if boiling **2** *vi* **BE ANGRY** to be in a state of extreme emotion, especially unexpressed anger ○ *I sat in my office quietly seething.* **3** *vi* **BE BUSY** to be full of bustling activity, especially with crowds of people moving in many different directions **4** *vt* **BOIL** to cook food by boiling it or boil something to extract its essence (*archaic*) ■ *n* **SEETHING MOVEMENT OR ACTION** an act of seething [Old English *sēothan*]

seething /séething/ *adj* **1 ANGRY** full of anger, especially pent-up anger **2 BOILING** boiling and bubbling or foaming **3 BUSTLING** moving in all directions, busily or frantically ○ *'the seething crowd of Paris'* (Baroness Orczy, *The Scarlet Pimpernel*; 1905) —**seethingly** *adv*

see-through *adj* made of transparent material, especially so as to reveal clothes or skin underneath

Sefer Torah /séyffər táwrə/ (*plural* **Sefer Torahs** *or* **Sifrei Torah** /sí fray-/) *n* a parchment scroll on which the Pentateuch is handwritten [Mid-17C. < Hebrew *sēpēr tōrāh* 'book of (the) Law'.]

segment *n* /ségmənt/ **1 COMPONENT PART** any one of the parts or sections into which an object or group is divided **2 ORGANISM'S BODY PART** any one of the individual units that make up an animal's body or part of its body **3 PART OF GEOMETRIC FIGURE** the portion of a line or curve between any two of its points or the portion of a solid cut by a plane **4 SPEECH SOUND** any one of the individual speech sounds that make up a longer string of sounds ■ *vt* /seg mént/ **SPLIT SOMETHING INTO SEGMENTS** to divide an object or group into segments [Late 16C. < Latin *segmentum* < *secare* 'cut'.] —**segmental** /seg mént'l/ *adj* —**segmentally** *adv* —**segmentary** *adj*

segmentation /ség men táysh'n/ *n* **1 SPLITTING INTO SEGMENTS** the dividing of something into segments **2 SEGMENTED STRUCTURE** the structure of something that is made up of a series of similar segments **3 BODY STRUCTURE** the structure of the body of an organism such as a worm or centipede that consists of a linear series of similar subunits

segmentation cavity *n* BIOL = **blastocoel**

segno /sénnyō/ (*plural* **segni** *or* **segnos** /-yi/) *n* a symbol used on sheet music to mark the beginning or end of a repeated section [Early 20C. Via Italian <Latin *signum* 'sign'.]

Ségou /sáy goo/ capital of Ségou Region, SW Mali. Population: 88,877 (1987).

Segovia /sə gṓvi ə/ capital of Segovia Province, central Spain. Population: 54,750 (1989).

Segovia /si gṓvi ə/, **Andrés** (1893–1987) Spanish guitarist

segregant /séggrigənt/ *adj* having a genetic makeup that differs from that of either parent because of genetic segregation ■ *n* an organism having a genetic makeup that differs from that of either parent because of genetic segregation

segregate /séggri gayt/ *v* (**-gates, -gating, -gated**) **1** *vt* **SEPARATE PEOPLE OR THINGS** to separate one person or group from the rest or to keep different people or groups separate **2** *vti* **KEEP GROUPS SEPARATE** to enforce a policy of keeping different groups within a population separate, especially different ethnic, racial, religious, or gender groups **3** *vti* **UNDERGO GENETIC SEGREGATION** to undergo or cause cells to undergo genetic segregation ■ *n* GENETICS = **segregant** *n.* [Mid-16C. < Latin *segregare* 'separate from the flock' < *grex* 'flock'.] —**segregable** *adj* —**segregative** *adj* —**segregator** *n*

segregation /séggri gáysh'n/ *n* **1 ENFORCED SEPARATION OF RACIAL GROUPS** the practice of keeping ethnic, racial, or religious groups separate, especially by enforcing the use of separate schools, transport, housing, and other facilities, and usually discriminating against a minority group **2 ACT OF SEGREGATING** the separating of one person, group, or thing from others or the dividing of people or things into separate groups kept apart from each other **3 SEGREGATED STATE** the state or position of somebody or something kept separate from others **4 GENE SEPARATION** the separation of the two versions (**alleles**) of each gene and their distribution to separate sex cells during the formation (**meiosis**) of these cells in organisms with paired chromosomes —**segregational** *adj*

segregationist /séggri gáysh'nist/ *n* an advocate or enforcer of segregation, especially racial or religious segregation —**segregationist** *adj*

segue /sé gway/ *vi* (**-gues, -gueing, -gued**) **1 CONTINUE PLAYING** to continue by playing the following piece or passage of music without a pause **2 MOVE SMOOTHLY** to make a smooth, almost imperceptible transition from one state, situation, or subject to another ○ *segued into a discussion of the playoffs without skipping a beat* ■ *n* **1 CONTINUATION OF MUSIC** the act of moving without a pause from one musical piece or passage into another **2 INSTRUCTION TO CONTINUE** an instruction to a musician to begin playing a following piece or passage without a pause **3 SMOOTH TRANSITION** the act of making a smooth transition from one state or situation to another [Mid-18C. < Italian, < *seguire* 'follow' < Latin *sequi*.]

seguidilla /séggi deélyə/ *n* **1 SPANISH DANCE** a Spanish dance in triple time, usually accompanied by castanets and guitars **2 DANCE MUSIC FOR SEGUIDILLA** the music for a seguidilla **3 SPANISH VERSE FORM** a poem with either four or seven very short verses that makes use of assonance rather than rhyme [Mid-18C. < Spanish, < *seguida* 'sequence' < *seguir* 'follow' < Latin *sequi*.]

seicento /say chéntō/ *n* the 17th century, with reference to Italian art and literature [Early 20C. < Italian, shortening of *milseicento* 'one thousand six hundred'.]

seiche /saysh/ *n* a movement on the surface of an enclosed body of water such as a lake, usually caused by intense storm activity [Mid-19C. < Swiss French, < ?]

seidel /sīd'l, zīd'l/ *n* a large beer glass [Early 20C. < German, < Latin *situla* 'bucket'.]

Seidler /zīdlər/, **Harry** (*b.* 1923) Austrian-born Australian architect

Seidlitz powder /séddlits-/ *n* a powdered preparation containing sodium bicarbonate, tartaric acid, and potassium sodium tartrate (**Rochelle salt**), taken dissolved in water. Use: laxative. [Late 18C. After the village of *Seidlitz* in Bohemia, which had a mineral spring noted for its laxative properties.]

seif dune /sáyf-, seéf-/ *n* a sand dune with curved edges, found in hot deserts in a series of parallel ridges and often several miles long and up to 100 m/300 ft in height [Early 20C. < Arabic *sayf* 'sword'.]

~~**seige**~~ incorrect spelling of **siege**

seigneur /say nyúr/, **Seigneur** *n* **1** HIST = **seignior 2** in French Canada until 1854, the owner of an estate originally granted by the king of France and farmed by tenants holding a form of feudal tenure over the land [Late 16C. Via French < Latin *senior* 'older'.]

seigneury /sáynyəri/ (*plural* **-ies**) *n* **1** the estate of a seigneur **2** the rank or authority of a seigneur

seignior /sáynyər/ *n* a feudal lord, especially in England [13C. Via Old French < Latin *senior* 'older'.] —**seigniorial** /say nyáwri əl/ *adj*

seigniorage /sáynyərij/ *n* **1 MONARCH'S PERCENTAGE OF BULLION** a monarch's right to a percentage of the bullion brought to a mint for the minting of coins **2 COINING PROFIT** the profit represented by the difference between the value of bullion and the face value of the coins minted from it **3 ARISTOCRAT'S PRIVILEGE** a right or privilege claimed by a sovereign or other person of high rank

seigniory /sáynyəri/ (*plural* **-ies**), **signiory** (*plural* **-ies**), **signory** (*plural* **-ies**) *n* **1 SEIGNIOR'S LAND** the estate of a seignior **2 SEIGNIOR'S RANK** the rank or authority of a seignior **3 LORDS COLLECTIVELY** lords considered as a group, especially English lords under the feudal system

seine /sayn/ *n* a large commercial fishing net that is weighted so that it hangs vertically in the water ■ *vti* (**seines, seining, seined**) to catch fish with a seine [Pre-12C. < Latin *sagena* < Greek *sagēnē* 'net'.] —**seiner** *n*

Seine /sayn, sen/ river rising in E France and flowing northwestwards through Paris into the English Channel. Length: 776 km/482 mi.

seise *vt* LAW = **seize** *v.* 11 [Early 17C. Variant of SEIZE.]

seisin /seézin/, **seizin** *n* **1** the legal possession of land, or the act of taking possession of it **2** land that is wholly and legally owned, especially land taken possession of legally [13C. Via Anglo-Norman *sesine* < Old French *saisir* (see SEIZE).]

seism- *prefix* = **seismo-** (*before vowels*)

seismic /sīzmik/, **seismical** /-mik'l/ *adj* **1** relating to or caused by an earthquake or earth tremor **2** extremely large or great (*informal*) ○ *This had a seismic impact on the music world.* —**seismically** *adv*

seismic array *n* a network of seismometers positioned so as to maximize the sensitivity of each of them and best monitor seismic activity in a particular region of the world

seismicity /sīz míssəti/ *n* the distribution and frequency of seismic events

seismic wave *n* a shock wave travelling through the Earth from the epicentre of an earthquake

seismo- *prefix* earthquake [Late 19C. < Greek *seismos* 'earthquake' < *seiein* 'shake'.]

seismogram /sīzmə gram/ *n* a record of an earthquake made by a seismograph

seismograph /sīzmə graaf, -graf/ *n* an instrument that detects the presence of an earthquake and measures and records its magnitude —**seismographer** /sīz móggrəfər/ *n* —**seismographic** /sīzmə gráffik/ *adj* —**seismography** /sīz móggrəfi/ *n*

seismology /sīz mólləji/ *n* the scientific study of earthquakes —**seismological** /sīzmə lójjik'l/ *adj* —**seismologically** *adv* —**seismologist** *n*

seismometer /sīz mómmitər/ *n* an instrument used to measure vibrations caused by an earthquake —**seismometric** /sīzmə méttrik/ *adj*

~~**seive**~~ incorrect spelling of **sieve**

sei whale /sáy-/ *n* a dark bluish-grey whale similar to the blue whale but smaller and more streamlined. *Balaenoptera borealis.* [Early 20C. < Norwegian *sejhval* < *sei* 'coalfish' + *hval* 'whale'.]

seize /seez/ (**seizes, seizing, seized**) *v* **1** *vt* **TAKE HOLD OF** to take hold of an object quickly and firmly ○ *seized the letter from his hand* **2** *vt* **EXPLOIT IMMEDIATELY** to take advantage of something such as a chance eagerly and immediately ○ *seize an opportunity* **3** *vt* **AFFECT SUDDENLY** to overwhelm the mind or emotions suddenly ○ *seized by panic* **4** *vt* **AFFECT PHYSICALLY** to overwhelm somebody physically ○ *Yet another spasm seized him.* **5** *vt* **APPROPRIATE** to take official or legal possession of something, often something held illegally such as arms, drugs, or stolen goods ○ *The shipment was seized by customs officials.* **6** *vt* **ARREST** to take somebody into custody ○ *Attempts to seize the attackers have so far failed.* **7** *vti* **COMPREHEND** to understand an idea or concept, especially quickly **8** *vi* **STOP WORKING** to become jammed, especially as a result of great heat, pressure, or friction, often arising from lack of lubrication ○ *The clutch has seized up.* **9** *vi* **STIFFEN UP** to become painfully stiff and immobile ○ *My leg's just seized up.* **10** *vi* **STOP** to come to a sudden and sometimes permanent halt ○ *The negotiations seized up after the most recent incident.* **11** *vt* **GIVE LEGAL POSSESSION** to make somebody the legal owner of property or goods ○ *The families were seized of all the relevant documentation.* **12** *vt* **LASH** to tie or secure something by lashing it using several turns of thin rope or wire [13C. < Old French *saisir* < medieval Latin *sacire* 'claim' < Germanic.] —**seizable** *adj* —**seizer** *n*

seizin *n* LAW = **seisin**

seizing /seézing/ *n* a knot or lashing made using thin rope or wire, e.g. to join two ropes or to secure an item of ship's gear

seizure /seézhər/ *n* **1 ACT OF SEIZING** the seizing of something, especially the taking of something by force or the official or legal appropriation of something **2 FACT OF BEING SEIZED** capture or appropriation **3 DISEASE ATTACK** a sudden attack of an illness or of particular symptoms, especially of the kind experienced by people with epilepsy **4 EMOTIONAL FIT** a sudden and intense rush of emotion ○ *a seizure of panic*

sejant /seéjənt/, **sejeant** *adj* in heraldry, describes a figure on a coat of arms that is in a sitting position [15C. < French *séant* < Latin *sedere* 'sit'.]

Sejm /saym/ *n* the national parliament of Poland [Late 19C. < Polish, 'Assembly'.]

Sekondi-Takoradi /sekən deé takə raádi/ capital of Western Region, SW Ghana. Population: 116,500 (1990).

sekuhara /sékoo haárə/ *n* sexual harassment [Early 21C. < Japanese.]

selachian /si láyki ən/ *n* a fish of the order that includes all sharks, rays, and skates. Order: Selachii. [Mid-19C. < modern Latin *selachii* < Greek *selakhē* 'shark'.]

selaginella /si lájji néllə, sélləji néllə/ *n* a mossy plant with branching stems and small leaves bearing spores. Genus: *Selaginella.* [Mid-19C. Via modern Latin < Latin *selago*, a herb similar to savin.]

selah /seélə, seé laa/ *interj* an ancient Hebrew word of unknown meaning and uncertain grammatical status that appears in some books of the Bible and is therefore, when included in English translations, left untranslated [Mid-16C. < Hebrew *selāh*.]

Selby /sélbi/ port in N England, on the River Ouse. Population: 15,292 (1991).

seldom /séldəm/ *adv* not often [Old English *seldum*, variant of *seldan* < Germanic] —**seldomness** *n*

select /si lékt/ *vti* **CHOOSE FROM OTHERS** to choose somebody or something from among several ○ *select a coffee cream from the box* ■ *adj* **1 OF GOOD QUALITY** chosen on grounds of particularly high quality **2 HAVING LIMITED MEMBERSHIP** admitting only a few carefully chosen members ○ *one of the more select gentlemen's clubs* **3 SPECIALLY CHOSEN** chosen from several others and given special treatment or a special privilege ○ *advance copies sent to a select few* **4 DISCRIMINATING** showing care and discernment when choosing ○ *'foreign films which generally attract a select audience'* (James Berardinelli, *Review: Deception*; 1993) [Mid-16C. < Latin *select-*, past participle of *seligere*

< *legere* 'pick out'.] —**selectee** /si lék teé/ *n* —**selectness** *n* —**selector** *n*

select committee *n* a small group of members of parliament instructed by either the House of Commons or the House of Lords to investigate and report on a particular matter

selection /si léksh'n/ *n* **1 SOMEBODY OR SOMETHING CHOSEN** somebody or something chosen from among others **2 AVAILABLE CHOICE** the range from which somebody or something can be selected ○ *a fantastic selection of carpets* **3 ACT OF CHOOSING** an act of choosing somebody or something from a wide variety of others **4 CHOSEN STATE** the status of somebody or something chosen from among others **5 SURVIVAL OF FITTEST** the production of more offspring by organisms with particular desirable characteristics, resulting in a better gene pool for the species **6 GAMBLER'S CHOICE** a competitor on whom a bet is placed, especially in horse-racing ○ *always a popular selection here at Goodwood*

selection box *n* a selection of chocolate bars and other sweets made by a particular manufacturer, packaged in a seasonally decorated box to be used as a gift to a child at Christmas

selectionist /si léksh'nist/ *n* a believer or promoter of the theory that natural selection is the chief or only force governing biological development

selection rule *n* a rule derived from quantum mechanics that governs whether changes may or may not occur in quantized systems such as molecules, atoms, or nuclei

selective /si léktiv/ *adj* **1 NOT UNIVERSAL** applying to some but not others **2 DISCERNING** tending to make careful choices **3 RECEIVING ON SOME FREQUENCIES ONLY** capable of selecting certain frequencies or frequency bands and blocking out all others, and therefore eliminating interference in reception —**selectively** *adv* —**selectiveness** *n*

selective attention *n* the ability to pay attention to those things that are considered important and to ignore those that are not

selective serotonin reuptake inhibitor /-ree úp tayk-/ *n* a drug such as Prozac™ that increases serotonin levels in synapses, resulting in elevation of mood. Use: antidepressant.

selective service *n* a system for calling up men for US military service

selectivity /si lék tívvəti/ *n* **1 CHOOSING ONLY SOME** the choosing of only some, not all, and the exercising of judgment in making the choice **2 ABILITY TO DISTINGUISH FREQUENCIES** the degree to which an electronic device or circuit can distinguish a desired frequency from others **3 WELFARE PRINCIPLE** the principle that government aid should be given only to those shown to be in greatest need

selen- *prefix* = **seleno-** (*before vowels*)

selenate /séllə nayt/ *n* a salt or ester of selenic acid [Early 19C. < SELENIUM + -ATE.]

Selene /sə leé ni/ *n* in Greek mythology, the goddess of the Moon. Roman equivalent **Luna**

selenic /si leénik/ *adj* relating to or containing selenium, especially with a valency of six [Early 19C. < SELENIUM + -IC.]

selenic acid *n* H_2SeO_4 a highly corrosive acid usually found in the form of a whitish solid

seleniferous /séllə níffərəss/ *adj* containing or producing selenium [Early 19C. < SELENIUM + -FEROUS.]

selenious /si leéni əss/ *adj* relating to or containing selenium, especially with a valency of two or four [Early 19C. < SELENIUM + -OUS.]

selenite /sélli nīt/ *n* a transparent colourless variety of gypsum that cleaves to reveal lustrous crystal faces [Mid-16C. Via Latin < Greek *selēnitēs lithos* 'moon stone' < *selēnē* (see SELENIUM).]

selenium /si leéni əm/ *n* (*symbol* **Se**) a nonmetallic element that occurs in several forms ranging from a red powder to grey-black crystals that is an essential trace element, although toxic in excess. Source: copper refining. Use: photocells, photocopiers. [Early 19C. Via modern Latin < Greek *selēnē* 'moon' < *selas* 'light'.]

selenium cell *n* a photoelectric cell based on the light-sensitive properties of selenium and containing a strip of selenium mounted between two metal electrodes

seleno- *prefix* **1** the moon ○ *selenography* **2** selenium ○ *selenite* [< Greek *selēnē* 'moon' (see SELENIUM)]

selenography /seélə nóggrəfi/ *n* the branch of astronomy that is concerned with mapping the surface features of the Moon —**selenographic** /si leénə gráffik/ *adj* —**selenographically** *adv*—**selenographist** /seélə nóggrəfist/ *n*

selenology /seélə nólləji/ *n* the branch of astronomy concerned with the origin and physical characteristics of the Moon —**selenological** /si leénə lójjik'l/ *adj* —**selenologist** *n*

Seles /sél ez, sél esh/, **Monica** (*b.* 1973) Yugoslavian-born US tennis player

Seleucid /si lóossid/ (*plural* **-cids** *or* **-cidae** /-sidee/) *n* any of a dynasty of rulers who ruled Asia Minor from 312 to 64 BC, after the death of Alexander the Great [Mid-19C. < Latin *Seleucides* < Greek *Seleukidēs* < *Seleukos*, the dynasty's founder.] —**Seleucid** *adj*

Seleucus I /si lóokəss/ (358?–280 BC) Macedonian general. Known as **Seleucus Nicator**

Seleucus II (265?–226? BC) Syrian monarch

self /self/ *n* (*plural* **selves** /selvz/) **1 PERCEIVED PERSONALITY** somebody's personality or an aspect of it, especially as perceived by others ○ *He's not his usual cheery self this morning.* **2 COMPLETE PERSONALITY** a complete and individual personality, especially one that somebody recognizes as his or her own and with which there is a sense of ease ○ *A person needs to develop a sense of self.* **3 SELF-INTEREST** somebody's own individual interests and welfare, especially when placed before those of other people **4 OWN BODY PARTS** the set of organs and tissues that the body recognizes as its own and does not attack with antibodies **5 SELF-COLOURED ANIMAL** an animal that is one colour all over, especially a pigeon ■ *pron* **ONESELF** myself, yourself, himself, or herself (*informal*) ○ *not enough to sustain self and family* ■ *adj* **1 SELF-COLOURED** having the same colour all over **2 OF SAME FABRIC** made of the same material as the garment it is worn with [Old English. Ultimately < Indo-European.]

USAGE The two main uses of ***-self*** compounds such as *himself*, *herself*, and *myself* are, first, to serve as a reflexive pronoun when the object of the verb is the same as the subject (*He saw himself in the mirror*) and, second, to reinforce or emphasize a noun (*Jane herself had wanted to go with them*). In formal contexts, compounds with ***-self*** should not be used simply as alternatives for other pronouns, such as *him*, *her*, *me*, and *I*: *It was up to her* [not *herself*] *whether she came or not. This is between him and me* [not *myself*]. The plural of ***-self*** is *-selves*; thus you should use *themselves* not themself.

self- *prefix* **1** of, by, for, or in itself ○ *self-assured* **2** automatic ○ *self-winding* [< SELF]

self-abandoned *adj* showing little self-control and tending to give in to impulse —**self-abandonment** *n*

self-abasement *n* the humbling of yourself in response to feelings of guilt or shame

self-abnegation *n* the setting aside of personal welfare and interests in favour of those of others or for the sake of a cherished belief or principle

self-absorbed *adj* excessively concerned with your own life and interests

self-absorption *n* **1** excessive concern with your own life and interests **2** a radioactive material's absorption of part of the radiation that it emits

self-abuse *n* **1** somebody's deprecation or deliberate misuse of his or her talents and abilities **2** masturbation when viewed as being detrimental to character (*disapproving or humorous*) —**self-abuser** *n*

self-acting *adj* operating itself —**self-action** *n*

self-actualization *n* the successful development and use of personal talents and abilities

self-addressed *adj* **1** addressed to the sender for return by post **2** directed by somebody towards himself or herself

self-adhesive *adj* having adhesive on one side and able to be stuck in position without needing to be moistened or to have adhesive applied

self-administer *vt* to administer something, especially medical treatment, to yourself —**self-administered** *adj*

self-advocacy *n* **1** the principle and practice of allowing people with psychiatric disorders to assume legal and practical responsibility for their own lives, rather than making them dependent on others **2** somebody's legal representation of himself or herself, especially in court

self-aggrandizement *n* the ambitious or ruthless pursuit of increased personal importance, wealth, reputation, or power —**self-aggrandizer** *n* —**self-aggrandizing** *adj*

self-analysis *n* a systematic attempt to try and gain insight into your own personality and emotions

self-annihilation *n* **1** loss of awareness of being an individual, achieved through meditation or other mystical means **2** an act or instance of suicide

self-appointed *adj* assuming a role personally, rather than being given it or being regarded as worthy of it by others ○ *a self-appointed arbiter of good taste*

self-assembly *n* the construction by the purchaser of something such as a piece of furniture sold in kit form

self-assertive *adj* tending to be aggressively confident in making your views heard and your presence felt —**self-assertively** *adv* —**self-assertiveness** *n*

self-assurance *n* relaxed confidence that your views and abilities are of value

self-assured *adj* behaving in a relaxed manner that displays confidence that your views and abilities are of value —**self-assuredly** *adv* —**self-assuredness** *n*

self-aware *adj* having a balanced and honest view of your own personality, and often an ability to interact with others frankly and confidently —**self-awareness** *n*

self-basting *adj* commercially prepared with added fat to prevent drying out when cooked in an oven ○ *a self-basting turkey*

self-catering *adj* describes accommodation, especially for holidaymakers or students, in which meals are not provided but cooking facilities are ■ *n* holidaying in self-catering accommodation ○ *decided on two weeks self-catering in Corfu*

self-centred *adj* tending to concentrate selfishly on your own needs and affairs and to show little or no interest in those of others —**self-centredly** *adv* —**self-centredness** *n*

self-certification *n* the system in the United Kingdom under which employees claim sick pay by making their own formal statement to their employer declaring they have been unfit for work, rather than by submitting a doctor's statement

self-cleaning *adj* designed to stay clean when being used, usually by virtue of being coated with materials that shed dirt ○ *a self-cleaning oven*

self-closing *adj* describes a door, gate, or window fitted with a mechanism that returns it to a closed position after it has been opened

self-coloured *adj* **1 UNIFORM IN COLOUR** of the same colour all over or throughout **2 RETAINING NATURAL COLOUR** describes a flower whose colour has not been artificially changed by hybridization **3 UNDYED** describes cloth that has not been dyed and so retains its natural colour

self-concept *n* the whole inner picture that somebody has of himself or herself, including a complete evaluation of such traits as competence, worth, and attractiveness

self-confessed *adj* admitting freely to possessing a particular quality or to behaving in a certain way —**self-confessedly** *adv*

self-confidence *n* confidence in yourself and your own abilities —**self-confident** *adj* —**self-confidently** *adv*

self-congratulation *n* the frequent mentioning of personal achievements and the displaying of the smug satisfaction taken in them —**self-congratulatory** *adj*

self-conscious *adj* **1** feeling acutely and uncomfortably aware of your failings and shortcomings when in the company of others and believing that others are noticing them too ○ *too self-conscious to speak in public* **2** highly conscious of the impression made on others and tending to act in a way that reinforces this impression ○ *swinging his car keys in a self-conscious manner* —**self-consciously** *adv* —**self-consciousness** *n*

self-contained *adj* **1 HAVING OWN FACILITIES AND ENTRANCE** describes accommodation that has its own kitchen, bathroom, and entrance ○ *self-contained two-bed flat near tube* **2 HAVING EVERYTHING REQUIRED** possessing all the features and facilities required to function independently

○ *a number of self-contained holiday villages* 3 **KEEPING FEELINGS PRIVATE** able or tending to keep feelings and opinions private or to control feelings and reactions in front of others 4 **INDEPENDENT** not needing the company or support of other people to be a complete and fulfilled person —**self-containedly** *adv* —**self-containment** *n*

self-contented *adj* feeling contented with personal achievements and good fortune —**self-contentedly** *adv* —**self-contentedness** *n*

self-contradiction *n* 1 speech, thoughts, or actions that contradict what their author previously said, thought, or did 2 a statement, idea, or theory that contradicts itself —**self-contradicting** *adj* —**self-contradictory** *adj*

self-control *n* the ability to control your own behaviour, especially in terms of reactions and impulses —**self-controlled** *adj*

self-correcting *adj* 1 describes a word processor that automatically corrects typing errors as they occur 2 able or tending to notice personal mistakes and correct them

self-critical *adj* tending to notice and dwell on your own shortcomings —**self-criticism** *n*

self-dealing *n* the benefiting or attempting to benefit from a financial transaction carried out on behalf of somebody else

self-deceiving *adj* 1 refusing to recognize the truth, usually because to do so would be painful or difficult 2 cherishing self-indulgent beliefs about yourself —**self-deception** *n*

self-defeating *adj* defeating the very aim or purpose it is designed to fulfil

self-defence *n* 1 **LEGAL RIGHT TO DEFEND SELF** the use of reasonable force to defend yourself, your family, and your property against physical attack, or the right to do this 2 **FIGHTING TECHNIQUES** fighting techniques used to defend yourself against physical attack, especially unarmed combat techniques such as any of the martial arts 3 **JUSTIFYING OF SELF** the defending of your own ideas, principles, or actions —**self-defensive** *adj*

self-delusion *n* misguided belief in something that is unreal or untrue

self-denial *n* the setting aside of your own wishes, needs, or interests, whether voluntary, altruistic, or enforced by circumstances —**self-denying** *adj* —**self-denyingly** *adv*

self-deprecating, self-deprecatory *adj* tending to belittle yourself or your achievements

self-destruct *vi* 1 **DESTROY ITSELF AUTOMATICALLY** to destroy itself by means of a built-in mechanism 2 **RUIN OWN LIFE** to behave in a way that destroys any chance of your success, credibility, or effectiveness ■ *adj* **CAUSING DESTRUCTION OF ITSELF** causing a device or machine to destroy itself if certain conditions are met

self-destruction *n* 1 **RUINING OF OWN LIFE** the ruining of your own life or an aspect of it such as your health, happiness, or career 2 **AUTOMATIC DESTRUCTION OF DEVICE** the automatic destruction of a device fitted with a self-destruct mechanism 3 **SUICIDE** an act or instance of suicide

self-destructive *adj* causing or tending to cause harm to yourself

self-determination *n* 1 the right of a people to determine their own form of government without interference from outside 2 the ability or right to make your own decisions without interference from others —**self-determining** *adj*

self-directed *adj* 1 able to undertake something without outside supervision or control, or undertaken in this way 2 directed at yourself

self-discipline *n* the ability to do what is necessary or sensible without needing to be urged by somebody else —**self-disciplined** *adj*

self-discovery *n* the process of learning about your true personality and motives

self-disgust *n* a feeling of disgust at your own physical or mental attributes

self-doubt *n* feelings of doubt about your own worth and abilities

self-drive *adj* describes a hired car that is driven by the hirer

self-effacing *adj* tending to be modest about your achievements and to avoid drawing attention to yourself in company —**self-effacement** *n* —**self-effacingly** *adv*

self-employed *adj* earning a living by working independently of an employer, either freelance or by running a business —**self-employment** *n*

self-esteem *n* confidence in your own merit as an individual

self-evaluation *n* the process of evaluating your own character, work, achievements, or goals

self-evident *adj* obvious without explanation or proof —**self-evidence** *n* —**self-evidently** *adv*

self-examination *n* 1 careful reflection on your own thoughts, beliefs, behaviour, and circumstances 2 the regular examination of parts of your own body for signs of disease —**self-examining** *adj*

self-excited *adj* describes an electrical device with a field system that is excited by a current the device generates for itself

self-executing *adj* legally effective without intervention ○ *self-executing clauses in the contract*

self-explanatory *adj* clear and easy to understand with no need for explanation

self-expression *n* the expressing of your own ideas, emotions, or individuality through behaviour or an activity such as painting, music, or writing

self-feeder *n* a machine or device that automatically supplies or replaces materials as they are needed, e.g. a device for feeding animals

self-fertilization *n* fertilization of a plant or animal ovum using pollen or sperm from the same individual —**self-fertilized** *adj* —**self-fertilizing** *adj*

self-financing *adj* paid for or run without outside financial support

self-flagellation *n* 1 very strong or harsh self-criticism 2 severe self-administered physical punishment, formerly used as an act of penance, often in the form of beatings or floggings

self-flattery *n* the exaggerating of positive personal traits while overlooking negative traits

self-focusing *adj* focusing automatically rather than manually

self-fulfilling *adj* 1 brought about or proved true because of having been expected or predicted 2 providing satisfaction or pleasure through personal labour, initiative, or talent

self-fulfilment *n* contentment or happiness as a result of personal work, initiative, or talent

self-glorification *n* promotion of your own qualities and abilities, especially beyond what is true or appropriate

self-governed *adj* run by the people who live or work in a particular area or place rather than by external government

self-governing *adj* run by its own members, employees, or citizens, rather than being run from outside

self-government *n* 1 the ability or right of the citizens of a region to choose their own government rather than having it imposed from outside 2 the ability to exercise self-control (*archaic*)

self-gratification *n* the satisfying of your own desires for the sake of pleasure

self-hardening *adj* becoming harder without special treatment after being heated above a certain temperature

self-harming *n* the practice of causing physical harm to yourself, usually as a symptom of a psychiatric disorder

self-hatred, self-hate *n* hatred or contempt for your own weaknesses

selfheal /sélf heel/ *n* a low-growing creeping mint that grows as a weed in North America. Flowers: purple-blue, in small spikes. Native to: Europe, Asia. *Prunella vulgaris*. [14C. Because it is believed to have medicinal properties.]

self-help *n* 1 the practice of meeting or working with others who share a common problem rather than relying on professional or government help 2 the practice of dealing with your own problems and challenges without seeking outside help

selfhood /sélf hòod/ *n* 1 **INDIVIDUALITY** the possession of a unique identity, distinct from others 2 **COMPLETE SENSE OF SELF** the possession of a fully developed personality and sense of identity 3 **SOMEBODY'S CHARACTER OR PERSONALITY** all the qualities and characteristics that make up somebody's character or personality

self-hypnosis *n* PSYCHOL = **autohypnosis**

self-identity *n* 1 the awareness that an individual or group has of being unique 2 the quality that something has of being one with itself

self-ignite *vi* to begin to burn or to explode spontaneously as, e.g., the fuel mixture in a compression-ignition engine does —**self-ignition** *n*

self-image *n* the opinion that you have of your own worth, attractiveness, or intelligence

self-immolation *n* suicide, usually by burning, as an act of sacrifice or protest

self-importance *n* an unrealistically high evaluation of your own importance or worth —**self-important** *adj* —**self-importantly** *adv*

self-imposed *adj* chosen willingly as a burden or limit ○ *a self-imposed deadline*

self-improvement *n* improvement of yourself or advancement in career or status as a result of your own effort

self-incrimination *n* speech or action that suggests your own guilt, especially during court testimony —**self-incriminating** *adj* —**self-incriminatory** *adj*

self-induced *adj* 1 brought on by your own actions 2 produced by the process of self-induction

self-induction *n* induction of an electromotive force in a circuit by means of a changing current in that circuit —**self-inductive** *adj*

self-indulgence *n* 1 lack of self-control in pursuing your own pleasure or satisfaction 2 something that reveals lack of self-restraint —**self-indulgent** *adj* —**self-indulgently** *adv*

self-inflicted *adj* caused or done by your own actions

self-insurance *n* the saving of money to protect against a loss instead of buying an insurance policy

self-interest *n* 1 the placing of your own needs or desires before those of others 2 your own needs and desires —**self-interested** *adj* —**self-interestedness** *n*

self-involved *adj* = **self-absorbed**

selfish /sélfish/ *adj* 1 concerned with your own interests, needs, and wishes while ignoring those of others 2 showing that personal needs and wishes are thought to be more important than those of other people —**selfishly** *adv* —**selfishness** *n*

selfish DNA *n* a segment of DNA that increases itself, e.g. as repeated sequences, within the total genetic material of a population over successive generations without apparent benefit to the organisms concerned

selfish gene *n* a gene that exploits the organism in which it occurs as a vehicle for its self-perpetuation

self-justification *n* 1 an attempt to explain your own behaviour or actions by making excuses 2 something that somebody does or says in an attempt to explain personal behaviour or actions

self-justifying *adj* 1 **ATTEMPTING TO EXPLAIN** making excuses in an attempt to explain your own behaviour or actions 2 **AUTOMATICALLY MAKING TEXT UNIFORM ON MARGIN** automatically providing an even right or left margin for text printed on a page 3 **LOGICALLY COMPLETE** describes an argument or rule that justifies or explains itself without referring to something else because of being regarded as completely logical or obvious

self-knowledge *n* knowledge or understanding of your own motives and behaviour

selfless /sélfləss/ *adj* putting other people's needs first —**selflessly** *adv* —**selflessness** *n*

self-limited, self-limiting *adj* 1 limited by internal or personal characteristics rather than by outside influences 2 describes a disease that lasts for a particular length of time time whether or not it is treated

self-liquidating *adj* 1 describes a loan to fund a transaction that is expected to make money before the loan is due to be repaid 2 describes a business transaction that makes enough money to cover its costs

self-loading *adj* describes a firearm that automatically ejects a spent cartridge and puts a new round into the chamber each time it is fired —**self-loader** *n*

self-locking *adj* describes a window or door that locks automatically when closed

self-love *n* concern with only your own wishes and desires —**self-loving** *adj*

self-lubricating *adj* not requiring external application of lubrication to parts that experience friction

self-made *adj* **1** successful or wealthy through your own efforts, rather than through birth or from the work of others **2** made without the help of others

self-mastery *adj* control over your own emotions, needs, or desires and their expression

self-medication *n* the practice of treating illnesses and medical complaints without consulting a doctor, e.g. by buying treatments from a chemist —**self-medicator** *n*

self-mortification *n* self-administered punishment, often as prescribed by religious precepts, because of some perceived fault or flaw

self-motivated *adj* energetic and ambitious, and so able to make plans and get things done without being directed by others —**self-motivation** *n*

self-mutilation *n* self-inflicted injury, especially with a sharp object

self-obsessed *adj* interested only in yourself and your own problems

self-opinion *n* a very high opinion of your own abilities or worth

self-opinionated, self-opinioned *adj* **1** confident of holding the correct opinions **2** very conceited

self-parody *n* unintentional exaggeration or over-emphasis by somebody of his or her worst characteristics

self-perpetuating *adj* continuing because of having the power to preserve or renew itself indefinitely

self-pity *n* the self-indulgent belief that your life is harder and sadder than everyone else's —**self-pitying** *adj* —**self-pityingly** *adv*

self-pollination *n* pollination that takes place within a flower through the transfer of pollen from its anthers to its stigmas —**self-pollinate** *vi* —**self-pollinating** *adj*

self-portrait *n* a visual image, sculpture, or written description of somebody, produced by that person —**self-portraiture** *n*

self-possessed *adj* confident and in control of your own emotions —**self-possessedly** *adv*

self-possession *n* the ability to remain calm and confident, especially in difficult or emotional circumstances

self-preservation *n* the instinctive need to do what is necessary to survive danger

self-proclaimed *adj* claiming to be something, often without justification

self-promotion *n* behaviour shown or action taken by somebody in order to attract attention, especially in relation to work or business

self-propelled *adj* **1** able to move or travel using its own power source such as a motor or batteries, rather than needing power from an external source **2** relating to a piece of heavy military equipment that is mounted on a vehicle rather than needing to be towed —**self-propelling** *adj* —**self-propulsion** *n*

self-protection *n* action taken to protect against attack on or injury to yourself —**self-protecting** *adj* —**self-protective** *adj*

self-published *adj* published without a publisher, and therefore at the author's own expense

self-punishment *n* punishment for supposed failings that you inflict upon yourself

self-raising *adj* having a leavening agent added, so that baking powder need not be added when baking ○ *self-raising flour.* US term **self-rising**

self-realization *n* fulfilment of personal potential

self-referential *adj* describes an art form that employs references to the art itself or to personal experience or character —**self-reference** *n* —**self-referentially** *adv*

self-reflection *n* = **self-examination** *n.* 1

self-regard *n* **1** self-interest rather than concern for the well-being of others **2** belief in your own worth and dignity —**self-regarding** *adj*

self-regulating, self-regulatory *adj* **1** regulating its own affairs rather than being regulated by an outside organization or by law **2** capable of regulating its functions automatically —**self-regulation** *n*

self-reliance *n* the ability to make your own decisions confidently and independently —**self-reliant** *adj* —**self-reliantly** *adv*

self-replicating *adj* describes a molecule or bacterium that reproduces on its own by making copies of itself —**self-replication** *n*

self-reproach *n* self-criticism or blame —**self-reproachful** *adj* —**self-reproachfully** *adv*

self-respect *n* belief in your own worth and dignity —**self-respecting** *adj*

self-restraint *n* self-control over speech, behaviour, or action

self-righteous *adj* sure of the moral superiority of your own beliefs and actions (*disapproving*) —**self-righteously** *adv* —**self-righteousness** *n*

self-righting *adj* able to right itself after being capsized

self-rising *adj US* COOK = **self-raising**

self-rule *n* POL = **self-government** *n.* 1

self-sacrifice *n* the giving up of personal wants and needs, either from a sense of duty or in order to benefit others —**self-sacrificing** *adj* —**self-sacrificingly** *adv*

selfsame /sélf saym/ *adj* being the very same

self-satisfaction *n* a feeling of satisfaction in personal achievements and good fortune —**self-satisfied** *adj*

self-scanner *n* a hand-held electronic device that supermarket customers can use to scan the prices of goods they intend to buy and add up their total bill in order to save time at the checkout

self-sealing *adj* **1** describes an envelope that has a flap coated with adhesive that can be closed without being moistened **2** describes a tyre that can seal itself after being punctured

self-seeking *adj* interested only in gaining an advantage over others, rather than in sharing or co-operating ■ *n* behaviour intended to secure an advantage over others —**self-seeker** *n*

self-selection *n* **1** COMM = **self-service** **2** choice of, by, or for yourself —**self-selected** *adj* —**self-selective** *adj*

self-service *adj* describes a retail outlet or device used by customers or users helping themselves ○ *a self-service petrol station* ○ *a self-service drinks machine* —**self-service** *n*

self-serving *adj* putting personal concerns and interests before those of others

self-starter *n* **1** somebody with the initiative and motivation to work without needing help or supervision **2** an electrically operated device for starting an internal-combustion engine —**self-starting** *adj*

self-sterile *adj* describes an organism, e.g. a flowering plant, that is unable to fertilize its female sex cells using its own male sex cells —**self-sterility** *n*

self-stick, self-sticking *adj US* = **self-adhesive**

self-storage *n* a property divided into storage units of varying sizes that are rented to individuals who store their personal property there

self-styled *adj* using a particular name or title or professing knowledge of a subject without having training or independent proof

self-sufficient, self-sufficing *adj* **1** able to provide what is needed, e.g. by making enough money or growing enough food, without having to borrow or buy from others **2** able to live independently of others —**self-sufficiency** *n* —**self-sufficiently** *adv*

self-suggestion *n* PSYCHOL = **autosuggestion**

self-supporting *adj* **1** earning enough money to live or operate without external financial support **2** able to stand or stay upright without being supported —**self-support** *n* —**self-supported** *adj*

self-sustaining *adj* able to live or continue existing without outside support

self-talk *n* the things that an individual says to himself or herself mentally

self-tanner *n* an ointment or lotion that can be applied to the skin in order to produce the effect of a suntan

self-tapping *adj* describes a screw that cuts a thread for itself when it is screwed into a hole in metal

self-taught *adj* having learned a skill, job, or subject without formal instruction

self-tender *n* an offer made by a company to buy back shares from its shareholders, e.g. to avoid a hostile takeover bid

self-test *n* **1** SELF-ADMINISTERED TEST a diagnostic test, e.g. for blood pressure, that you give yourself to determine your health **2** TEST OF KNOWLEDGE a test you give yourself to find out how well you know a particular subject ■ *v* **1** *vti* TEST YOUR HEALTH to perform a diagnostic test on yourself in order to determine your health **2** *vr* TEST YOURSELF ON KNOWLEDGE to test yourself on a particular subject to find out how well you know it

self-treatment *n* an individual's treating of his or her own illnesses or injuries rather than seeking the advice of a doctor

self-will *n* stubborn determination to hold to personal views and behaviour —**self-willed** *adj*

self-winding *adj* not needing to be wound ○ *a self-winding watch*

self-worth *n* confidence in personal value and worth as an individual

Seljuk /séll jook/ *n* a member of one of the Turkish dynasties that ruled large areas of Asia during the 11th to 13th centuries before the Ottoman Empire [Mid-19C. < Turkish *Selčük*, the dynasty's reputed founder.] —**Seljuk** *adj*

selkie /sélki/ *n Scotland* **1** a seal **2** a mythical creature which assumes human form on land and that of a seal in water [Variant of SEAL²]

Selkirk /sél kurk/, **Alexander** (1676–1721) Scottish sailor

Selkirk Mountains /sél kurk-/ mountain range in SE British Columbia, Canada. Highest peak: Mount Sandford 3,522m/11,555 ft.

sell /sel/ *v* (**sells, selling, sold** /sōld/, **sold**) **1** *vti* EXCHANGE FOR MONEY to exchange a product or service for money **2** *vt* OFFER FOR SALE to offer a particular product or range of products for sale **3** *vi* BE BOUGHT IN QUANTITY to be bought in large numbers ○ *The book is selling well.* **4** *vt* MAKE PEOPLE WANT TO BUY to increase the sale of or the demand for a particular product ○ *Advertising sells products.* **5** *vt* PERSUADE to persuade somebody to accept an idea or proposal ○ *You've convinced me but now you have to sell it to the shareholders.* **6** *vt* GIVE SOMETHING UP FOR MONEY to sacrifice an important personal quality in order to obtain wealth or success ○ *He's sold his integrity for a long-term contract.* **7** *vt* CHEAT to cheat or trick somebody (*informal*) ■ *n* **1** PROCESS OF SELLING the activity or process of persuading people to buy a product or service (*informal*) ○ *use an aggressive sell* **2** TRICK a trick or deception (*informal*) **3** *Ireland* DISAPPOINTMENT a big disappointment [Old English *sellan* 'hand over' < Germanic] —**sellable** *adj* ◇ **sell somebody** *or* **something short 1** to make an estimate of the quality and worth of somebody or something that is too low **2** to sell goods or securities without owning them, expecting to buy them at a price lower than the selling price ◇ **sell yourself 1** to work hard to persuade others that you are talented, pleasant, well-qualified, or suitable for a particular job **2** to abandon your principles in order to get something you want or need, e.g. money or success ◇ **sold on something** enthusiastic about something (*informal*)

sell off *vt* to sell something, especially at a low price, in order to get rid of it

sell out *v* **1** *vi* SELL ALL OF SOMETHING to sell the entire stock of a particular product or range **2** *vti* SELL ALL TICKETS to sell all the tickets for a show, concert, or sports event **3** *vti* BETRAY PRINCIPLES to be disloyal to your own personal principles or another person for reasons of short-term advantage (*informal*)

sellback /séll bak/ *n US* the act of selling something back to the person it was bought from

sell-by date *n* a date displayed on food and pharmaceutical products, after which they should not be sold ◇ **past its** *or* **your sell-by date** thought to be too advanced in years or old-fashioned to be taken seriously any longer (*informal; offensive in some contexts*)

seller /séllər/ *n* **1** a person, shop, or company that offers something for sale **2** a product that sells in a specified way, especially well or badly **3** HORSERACING = **selling race**

Sellers /séllərz/, **Peter** (1925–80) British comic actor

seller's market *n* a situation or market in which the demand for something is greater than the supply, so that its price can be forced up. ◊ **buyer's market**

selling climax *n* a large volume of trading at the end of a downturn in the stock markets (*informal*)

selling plate *n* HORSERACING = **selling race**

selling-plater *n* **1** a horse that races in, or is only good enough to race in, a selling race **2** somebody or something that is not very good, important, or valuable

selling point *n* a feature of something such as a product or an idea that makes people more likely to want to buy or support it

selling race, selling plate *n* a horse race in which the winner is auctioned and sold

sell-off *n* the quick sale of a large amount of goods, especially at low prices

Sellotape /séllō tayp/ *tdmk* a trademark for a type of transparent adhesive tape

sellout /séll owt/ *n* **1** a show, concert, or sports event for which all the tickets are sold **2** betrayal of personal principles or another person (*informal*)

selsyn /sél sin/ *n* a system used to transmit angular rotation or position in a generator to a motor [Early 20C. Blend of SELF + SYNCHRONOUS.]

Seltzer /séltsər/, **Seltzer water** *n* **1** mineral water that contains naturally occurring dissolved gases that make it slightly fizzy, often used for medicinal purposes **2** soda water (*dated*) [Mid-18C. Alteration of German *Selterser* 'from Selters', alluding to mineral springs in the village of Nieder- *Selters* near Wiesbaden.]

selva /sélvə/ *n* a dense tropical rain forest, especially in the Amazon Basin [Mid-19C. Via Spanish or Portuguese < Latin *silva* 'wood'.]

selvage /sél vij/, **selvedge** *n* **1** NON-FRAYING EDGE OF FABRIC an edge of a piece of fabric that is woven so that it will not fray **2** STRIP OF MATERIAL an edge or strip of material included when manufacturing something such as a metal or plastic article or a sheet of postage stamps that allows it to be handled **3** LOCK PLATE a slotted plate or surface through which the bolt of a lock passes **4** RUG FRINGE a decorative fringe on the ends of an oriental rug [15C. Alteration of 'self-edge' (because it 'edges' itself and does not need hemming).] —**selvaged** *adj*

selves plural of **self**

Selznick /sélznik/, **David O.** (1902–65) US film producer

SEM *abbr* scanning electron microscope

semanteme /sə mán teem/ *n* the smallest possible unit of meaning in language [Early 20C. < French *sémantème* < Greek *semantikos* (see SEMANTIC), after *morphème* (see MORPHEME).]

semantic /sə mántik/ *adj* **1** RELATING TO WORDS' MEANINGS relating to meaning or the differences between meanings of words or symbols **2** OF SEMANTICS relating to semantics **3** RELATING TO TRUTH relating to the conditions in which a system or theory can be said to be true [Mid-17C. Via French *sémantique* < Greek *sēmantikos* 'significant' < *sēmainein* 'signify' < *sēma* 'sign, mark'.] —**semantically** *adv*

semantics /sə mántiks/ *n* **1** STUDY OF MEANING IN LANGUAGE the study of how meaning in language is created by the use and interrelationships of words, phrases, and sentences **2** STUDY OF SYMBOLS the study of the relationship between symbols and what they represent **3** STUDY OF LOGIC the study of ways of interpreting and analysing theories of logic —**semanticist** *n*

semaphore /sémmə fawr/ *n* **1** SYSTEM OF SIGNALLING a system for sending messages using hand-held flags that are moved to represent alphabetical letters **2** MECHANICAL SIGNALLING DEVICE a signalling device for sending information over distances using mechanically operated arms or flags mounted on a post, especially on a railway ■ *vti* (**-phores, -phoring, -phored**) USE SEMAPHORE TO SIGNAL to send messages using semaphore [Early 19C. Via French *sémaphore* 'sign-bearer' < Greek *sēma* 'mark, sign'.] —**semaphoric** /sémmə fórrik/ *adj* —**semaphorically** *adv*

Semarang /sémmə ráng/ port on the island of Java, Indonesia. Population: 1,250,971 (1990).

semasiology /sə máyzi óllәji/ *n* LING, LOGIC = **semantics** *n.* **1, semantics** *n.* **2** [Mid-19C. < German *Semasiologie* 'science of meaning' < Greek *sēmasia* 'meaning' < *sēmainein* (see SEMANTIC).] —**semasiological** /sə máyzi ə lójjik'l/ *adj* —**semasiologically** *adv* —**semasiologist** /sə máyzi óllәjist/ *n*

sematic /sə máttik/ *adj* describes bright colourings on particular animals that act as a warning to predators, e.g. because the animals are poisonous [Late 19C. < Greek *sēmat-*, stem of *sēma* 'mark, sign'.]

semblable /sémbləb'l/ *adj* resembling or similar to something or somebody else (*formal*) [13C. < Old French, < *sembler* (see SEMBLANCE).] —**semblably** *adv*

semblance /sémbləns/ *n* **1** TRACE a small amount of something ○ *a semblance of dignity* **2** LOOK OF BEING an outward appearance or imitation of something ○ *a semblance of competence* **3** COPY a representation, likeness, or copy (*literary*) [14C. < Old French, < *sembler* 'seem' < Latin *simulare* (see SIMULATE).]

semé /sémmay/ *adj* covered with many small dots or delicate designs [15C. < French, past participle of *semer* 'sow' < Latin *semere*.]

sememe /sée meem/ *n* the meaning that a morpheme has in a linguistic system [Early 20C. < Greek *sēma* 'sign', after MORPHEME.]

semen /séemən/ *n* the thick white fluid containing sperm that a male ejaculates [14C. < Latin, 'seed'.]

semester /sə méstər/ *n* **1** either one of two periods of 15 to 18 weeks into which the academic year is often divided in the United States **2** in German universities, an academic session lasting six months [Early 19C. Via German < Latin *semestris* 'of six months' < *sex* 'six' + *mensis* 'month'.] —**semestral** *adj*

semi /sémmi/ *n* **1** a house with a wall in common with the next house (*informal*) **2** a semifinal (*informal*) **3** *US* CARS = **tractor-trailer** [Early 20C. Shortening.]

semi- *prefix* **1** partial, partially, somewhat ○ *semisweet* ○ *semiterrestrial* **2** half ○ *semiround* **3** resembling, having some characteristics of something ○ *semitropical* ○ *semivowel* **4** occurring twice during a particular period ○ *semiweekly* [< Latin, 'half'. Ultimately < Indo-European.]

semiabstract /sémmi áb strakt/ *adj* describes art that has heavily stylized but still recognizable subject matter —**semiabstraction** /sémmi ab straksh'n/ *n*

semiannual /sémmi ánnyoo əl/ *adj* **1** HAPPENING TWICE A YEAR happening or issued every six months or twice a year **2** LASTING SIX MONTHS lasting for half a year ■ *n* SEMIANNUAL PLANT a semiannual plant or flower —**semiannually** *adv*

semiaquatic /sémmi ə kwáttik/ *adj* growing or living near water as well as in it

semiarboreal /sémmi aar báwri əl/ *adj* describes an animal that lives in trees for part of the time

semiarid /sémmi árrid/ *adj* with little rainfall and scrubby vegetation —**semiaridity** /sémmi ə ríddəti/ *n*

semiautobiographical /sémmi áwtə bī ə gráffik'l/ *adj* describes something such as a novel or film that is based in part on the life or experiences of its author

semiautomatic /sémmi áwtə máttik/ *adj* **1** RELOADING AUTOMATICALLY automatically ejecting a spent shell from a weapon's chamber and replacing it with another round each time the weapon is fired **2** PARTIALLY AUTOMATED operated partly automatically and partly manually ■ *n* SEMIAUTOMATIC WEAPON a weapon that is semiautomatic —**semiautomatically** *adv*

semiautonomous /sémmi aw tónnəməss/ *adj* **1** ruled partly by its own citizens or rulers and partly by another country or region **2** self-governing but remaining within a larger organization of which it is part —**semiautonomously** *adv* —**semiautonomy** *n*

semibold /sémmi bṓld/ *adj* darker than ordinary type but not as dark as bold type

semibreve /sémmi breev/ *n* the longest musical note in common use, written as an open note-head without a stem or tail, with a duration equivalent to four crotchets or two minims. US term **whole note**

semicentennial /sémmi sen ténni əl/ *adj* **1** MARKING 50TH ANNIVERSARY marking the date or year that is 50 years after a particular event **2** HAPPENING EVERY 50 YEARS happening every 50 years ■ *n* 50TH ANNIVERSARY OF EVENT the 50th anniversary of an important event

semicircle /sémmi surk'l/ *n* **1** half of the area or circumference of a circle **2** a curved or crescent-shaped line of things or people in the shape of a semicircle [Early 16C. < Latin *semicirculus* < *circulus* 'small circle'.] —**semicircular** /sémmi súrkyoolər/ *adj* —**semicircularly** *adv*

semicircular canal *n* any one of three tubes in the inner ear, semicircular in shape and set at right angles to one another, that help to maintain balance

semiclassical /sémmi klássik'l/ *adj* classical in musical style, pleasant, easy to listen to, and usually written relatively recently —**semiclassically** *adv*

semicolon /sémmi kṓlən, -lon/ *n* a punctuation mark (;) used to separate parts of a sentence or list

PUNCTUATION A ***semicolon*** is used to separate two parts of a sentence that have a relationship to each other in terms of meaning when each part could stand alone as a sentence in its own right: *The building is chiefly a tourist attraction; it is rarely used as a church these days. There is no proof that the disease is caused by agricultural use of this chemical; however, experts admit that there could be a link.* Semicolons may also separate parts of a complex list when it would be confusing to use commas for this purpose: *We invited Jack and Kate, who live next door; Maria, my sister-in-law; Tom, an old school friend of my husband's; and some of our colleagues from work.* Like commas, semicolons are sometimes used to break up a lengthy complicated sentence, but it is often better and clearer to split the sentence up into smaller units.

PUNCTUATION See ***colon***.

semicoma /sémmi kṓmə/ *n* a partial or light comatose state from which it is sometimes possible to rouse people by stimulating them

semiconductor /sémmi kən dúktər/ *n* a solid material that has electrical conductivity between that of a conductor and an insulator —**semiconducting** *adj* —**semiconduction** *n* —**semiconductive** *adj* —**semiconductivity** /sémmi kon duk tívvəti/ *n*

semiconscious /sémmi kónnshəss/ *adj* only partly conscious —**semiconsciously** *adv* —**semiconsciousness** *n*

semiconservative /sémmi kən súrvətiv/ *adj* relating to the replication of a nucleic acid molecule such as DNA in which a double stranded molecule separates into two templates for the formation of complementary strands —**semiconservatively** *adv*

semidarkness /sémmi daárknəss/ *n* a state in which it is neither fully dark nor fully light

semidesert /sémmi dézzərt/ *n* a region that is not completely arid, usually one lying between desert and a more heavily vegetated area

semidetached /sémmi di tácht/ *adj* joined to a neighbouring building by a shared wall ■ *n* a house with a wall in common with the next house

semidiameter /sémmi dī ámmitər/ *n* half of the angular diameter of the visible disc of an astronomical object as measured by an observer

semidiurnal /sémmi dī úrn'l/ *adj* **1** continuing or happening over half a day **2** happening approximately once every twelve hours

semidivine /sémmi di vī́n/ *adj* having some of the characteristics or powers of a deity, or existing on a higher spiritual plane than ordinary mortals but not wholly divine

semidocumentary /sémmi dokyoo méntəri/ (*plural* **-ries**) *n* a film or TV programme that is fictional but makes use of or is based on factual details or events

semidome /sémmi dōm/ *n* a half dome, especially one used as the roof for a semicircular space or recess

semidry /sémmi drī́/ *adj US* describes wine that is partially or moderately dry

semidwarf /sémmi dwáwrf/ *adj* in botany, growing to heights greater than a true dwarf plant but less than standard specimens

semielliptical /sémmi i lípptik'l/ *adj* resembling half an ellipse in shape, especially one that is divided along its major axis

semifinal /sémmi fī́n'l/ *n* either one of two matches or games, the winners of which will play each other in the final round of a competition —**semifinal** *adj* —**semifinalist** *n*

semifinished /sémmi fínnisht/ *adj* partially finished, treated, or processed

semifluid /sémmi floo id/ *adj* having properties between those of a fluid and a solid —**semifluid** *n* —**semifluidity** /sémmi floo íddəti/ *n*

semiformal /sémmi fáwrm'l/ *adj* designed to be worn on moderately formal occasions

semigloss /sémmi glóss/ *n* a paint or varnish with a finish that is midway between gloss and matt when it dries

semihard /sémmi haárd/ *adj* describes cheese that has a consistency firm enough to slice but that is moist and pliable

semi-infinite *adj* unbounded in one dimension or direction

semilegendary /sémmi léjjəndəri/ *adj* having some of the characteristics of a legend ○ *semilegendary figures such as El Cid*

semilethal /sémmi leéth'l/ *adj* lethal in more than 50 per cent but fewer than 100 per cent of cases

semiliquid /sémmi líkwid/ *adj* SCI = **semifluid** —**semiliquid** *n* —**semiliquidity** /sémmi li kwíddə ti/ *n*

semiliterate /sémmi líttərət/ *adj* **1** unable to read or write properly **2** *US* having only limited understanding of a particular subject, especially a technical one —**semiliteracy** *n*

Sémillon /sémmi yoN/ *n* a late-maturing French grape variety used to produce white wine [Mid-19C. Via French < Latin *semen* 'seed'.]

semilunar /sémmi loónər/ *adj* shaped like a crescent or a half moon

semilunar cartilage *n* either one of two crescent-shaped pieces of cartilage in the knee joint

semilunar valve *n* either one of two crescent-shaped valves in the heart that prevent blood from flowing back into the ventricles

semimetal /sémmi mét't'l/ *n* CHEM = **metalloid** *n.* —**semimetallic** /sémmi mə tállik/ *adj*

semimonthly /sémmi múnthli/ *adj* **HAPPENING TWICE IN MONTH** happening or published twice each month, usually at equal intervals ■ *adv* **TWICE DURING MONTH** twice each month, usually at equal intervals ■ *n* (*plural* **-lies**) **SEMIMONTHLY PUBLICATION** a publication that appears twice each month, usually at equal intervals

seminal /sémmin'l/ *adj* **1 INFLUENTIAL** highly original and influential **2 CAPABLE OF DEVELOPMENT** containing an idea or set of ideas that forms a basis for later developments **3 OF SEMEN OR SEEDS** relating to, containing, or carrying semen or seeds [14C. Via French < Latin *seminalis* < *semin-*, stem of *semen* 'seed'.] —**seminality** /sémmi nálləti/ *n* —**seminally** *adv*

seminal fluid *n* ZOOL = **semen**

seminal vesicle *n* either one of a pair of glands that secrete the fluid component of semen into the ejaculatory duct in males

seminar /sémmi naar/ *n* **1 MEETING ON SPECIALIZED SUBJECT** a single session or short, often one-day meeting devoted to presentations on and discussion of a particular topic, usually at an advanced or professional level ○ *a seminar on the industrial applications of biotechnology* **2 MEETING OF STUDENTS AND TUTOR** a meeting of university or college students for study or discussion with a tutor, or the group that participates in it **3 SPECIALIZED EDUCATIONAL CLASS** a course of specialized, especially postgraduate study under academic supervision, in which ideas, approaches, and advances are regularly shared among participants [Late 19C. Via German, 'advanced class' < Latin *seminarium* 'seed plot, breeding ground' < *semin-* (see SEMINAL).]

seminary /sémminəri/ (*plural* **-ies**) *n* a college for the training of priests, ministers, or rabbis [15C. < Latin *seminarium* 'seed plot, breeding ground' < *semin-* (see SEMINAL).] —**seminarian** /sémmi náiri ən/ *n*

seminiferous /sémmi nífførəss/ *adj* **1** carrying, containing, or producing semen **2** bearing or producing seeds [Late 17C. < Latin *semin-* (see SEMINAL) + -FEROUS.]

Seminole /sémmi nōl/ *n* (*plural* **-nole** *or* **-noles**) **1 NATIVE NORTH AMERICAN PEOPLE** a member of a Native North American people who lived to the east of the Mississippi River, and now live mainly in Oklahoma and Florida **2 SEMINOLE LANGUAGE** the Muskogean language of the Seminole people ■ *adj* **OF SEMINOLE** relating to the Seminole people or their languages or culture [Mid-18C. < Creek *simanó:li*, alteration of *simaló:ni*, alteration of American Spanish *cimarrón* 'wild, untamed'.]

seminoma /sémmi nṓmə/ (*plural* **-mas** *or* **-mata** /-mətə/) *n* a malignant tumour of the sperm-producing tissue in the testicle [Early 20C. Via modern Latin *seminoma* < Latin *semin-* (see SEMINAL).]

seminomadic /sémmi nō máddik/ *adj* belonging or relating to an ethnic group or people who migrate seasonally as well as cultivating crops during periods of settlement

seminude /sémmi nyoód/ *adj* only partly clothed, usually in underclothes or skimpy outer clothing —**seminudity** *n*

semiochemical /sémmi ō kémmik'l/ *n* an organic chemical such as pheromone that plays a role in animal communication [Late 20C. < Greek *sēmeion* 'sign' + CHEMICAL.]

semiofficial /sémmi ə físh'l/ *adj* with only some degree of authority or official status and therefore not completely reliable —**semiofficially** *adv*

semiology /sémmi óllәji, seém-/ *n* SOC SCI, MED = **semiotics** [Late 17C. < Greek *sēmeion* 'sign' + -LOGY.] — **semiologic** /sémmi ə lójik, seém-/ *adj* —**semiological** *adj* —**semiologically** *adv* —**semiologist** /sémmi óllәjist, seémi-/ *n*

semiotics /sémmi óttiks, seémi-/ *n* (+ *singular verb*) **1** the study of signs and symbols of all kinds, what they mean, and how they relate to the things or ideas they refer to **2** the study of identifying the ways that various symptoms indicate the diseases that underlie them —**semiotic** *adj* —**semiotician** /sémmi ə tísh'n, seémi-/ *n*

semipalmate /sémmi pál mayt/, **semipalmated** /sémmi pál máytid/ *adj* with feet or toes that are partially webbed. Some shore birds have semipalmate feet.

semipermanent /sémmi púrmənənt/ *adj* set up or arranged to last quite a long time but not indefinitely

semipermeable /sémmi púrmi əb'l/ *adj* describes a membrane or tissue that allows some types of particle to pass through, but not others —**semipermeability** /sémmi púrmi ə bílləti/ *n*

semipolar bond /sémmi pōlər-/ *n* CHEM = **coordinate bond**

semiporcelain /sémmi páwrssəlin, -layn/ *n* a durable glazed ceramic material widely used for tableware

semiprecious /sémmi préshəss/ *adj* describes stones, gems, and minerals that have commercial value but are not valued as highly as those called precious

semipro /sémmi prṓ/ *n* (*plural* **-pros**) a semiprofessional (*informal*) ■ *adj* relating to or being semiprofessional (*informal*)

semiprofessional /sémmi prə fésh'nəl/ *adj* **1 PAID BUT NOT FULL-TIME** participating in a sport or artistic activity for pay but not as a full-time professional **2 FOR SEMIPROFESSIONAL ATHLETES** played in or contested by semiprofessional athletes **3 LIKE A PROFESSIONAL** displaying some aspects of a professional ■ *n* **PART PROFESSIONAL** somebody, especially an athlete or performing artist, who is intermediate between an amateur and a professional —**semiprofessionally** *adv*

semiquaver /sémmi kwayvər/ *n* a musical note equivalent to one-sixteenth of a semibreve. US term **sixteenth note**

semiretired /sémmi ri tírd/ *adj* working only part-time following the end of a full-time career —**semiretirement** *n*

semirigid /sémmi ríjjid/ *adj* **1** partly rigid or rigid only in some parts **2** describes an airship with a rigid keel that maintains its shape

semirural /sémmi roórəl/ *adj* intermediate between rural and urban

semisecret /sémmi seékrət/ *adj* intended or supposedly intended to be secret but actually known about

semisedentary /sémmi sédd'ntəri/ *adj* partly but not entirely sedentary

semiskilled /sémmi skíld/ *adj* with or requiring relatively few skills or little training ○ *semiskilled workers* ○ *a semiskilled job*

semi-skimmed *adj* describes milk that has part of the cream removed, so that it contains less animal fat and fewer calories than full cream milk

semisoft /sémmi sóft/ *adj* softer than most things, especially foods, of its type

semisolid /sémmi sóllid/ *adj* not quite solid or liquid, but somewhere in between, like a gel ■ *n* a substance that has most of the qualities of a solid but can also flow, e.g. a gel

semisubmersible /sémmi səb múrssəb'l/, **semisubmersible rig** *n* a self-propelled oil-drilling platform resting on vertical pontoons that can be flooded for stability in deep water

semisweet /sémmi sweét/ *adj* slightly sweet, or having only a small amount of sugar or other sweetening ingredient added ○ *semisweet biscuits*

semisynthetic /sémmi sin théttik/ *adj* **1** chemically synthesized from natural ingredients **2** made up of some natural and some synthetic ingredients

Semite /seé mīt, sémm-/ *n* **1** a member of a Semitic-speaking people of the Middle East, including the Arab and Jewish peoples, and the ancient Assyrians, Babylonians, Carthaginians, Ethiopians, and Phoenicians **2** an offensive term for a Jewish person [Mid-19C. Via modern Latin *Semita* < Greek *Sēm* 'Shem', son of Noah < Hebrew *Šēm*.]

semiterrestrial /sémmi tə réstri əl/ *adj* living partly on land but requiring a watery environment

Semitic /sə míttik/ *n* **LANGUAGES SPOKEN BY SEMITES** a group of languages belonging to the Afro-Asiatic family and spoken in North Africa and SW Asia, including Hebrew, Arabic, Aramaic, Maltese, and Amharic ■ *adj* **1 OF SEMITIC** in or relating to Semitic **2 OF SEMITIC-SPEAKING PEOPLES** relating to the peoples who speak Semitic languages

Semitics /sə míttiks/ *n* the study of the Semitic peoples, languages, and culture (+ *singular verb*) —**Semiticist** /sə míttissist/ *n* —**Semitist** /sémmitist/ *n*

Semitism /sémmətizəm/ *n* **1** the customs, traditions, and characteristics of Semitic people, especially Jewish people **2** a word or other language feature of Semitic origin, especially one occurring in a non-Semitic language

semitone /sémmi tōn/ *n* the smallest interval of the diatonic scale, half of a whole tone [15C. Via Old French < medieval Latin *semitonus* < *tonus* (see TONE).] —**semitonal** /sémmi tṓ n'l/ *adj* —**semitonally** *adv* —**semitonic** /-tónnik/ *adj*

semitrailer /sémmi tráylər/ *n* **1** a large rectangular vehicle with wheels only at the rear and a hitch at the front that attaches to a tractor or other towing vehicle **2** a tractor with an attached semitrailer

semitransparent /sémmi tráns párrənt/ *adj* partly, but not completely, transparent

semitropical /sémmi tróppik'l/ *adj* ENVIRON = **subtropical** —**semitropics** *npl*

semivowel /sémmi vowəl/ *n* a sound that is like a vowel in involving no major obstruction of the airflow but that functions as a consonant in preceding vowels that form the nucleus of syllables

semiweekly /sémmi weékli/ *adj* happening or published twice each week ■ *adv* twice each week

semolina /sémmə leénə/ *n* gritty ground-up grains of wheat that are a by-product of flour milling. Use: pasta, couscous, other foods. [Late 18C. Alteration of Italian *semolino* 'small bran' < *semola* 'bran' < Latin *simila* 'fine wheat flour'.]

semper fidelis /sémpər fi dáyliss/ *adj* 'always faithful', the motto of the United States Marine Corps [< Latin]

sempervivum /sémpər veévəm/ *n* a widely grown ornamental garden plant that has rosettes of fleshy leaves. Flowers: pink, in clusters on stems. Genus: *Sempervivum*. [Late 16C. Via modern Latin < Latin *sempervivus* 'ever-living' < *semper* 'ever' + *vivus* (see VIVACIOUS).]

sempiternal /sémpi túrn'l/ *adj* lasting forever (*literary*) [15C. Via Old French < Latin *sempiternus* < *semper* 'always' + *-ternus*, suffix of time.] —**sempiternally** *adv* —**sempiternity** *n*

semplice /sémmplichi, -chay/ *adv* in a simple manner, without rubato (*in musical directions*) [Mid-18C. < Italian, 'simple'.]

sempre /sémpri, -pray/ *adv* to be played or sung throughout in the manner indicated (*in musical directions*) ○ *sempre largo* [Early 19C. < Italian, 'always'.]

sempstress /sémpstrəss/ *n* a seamstress (*archaic*) [Mid-17C. < *sempster*, variant of *seamster*.]

Semtex /sém teks/ *tdmk* a trademark for a type of plastic explosive of Czech origin

sen /sen/ (*plural* **sen**) *n* see table at **currency** [Early 18C. < Japanese, < Mandarin Chinese *qián* 'money, coin'.]

SEN *abbr* **1** special educational needs **2** State Enrolled Nurse (*dated*)

Sen. *abbr* **1** senate **2** senator **3** senior

Senanayake /sénnə nī yəkə/, **D. S.** (1884–1952) Sinhalese statesman. Full name **Don Stephen Senanayake**

Senanayake, Dudley (1911–73) Sinhalese statesman

senate *n* **1 US STATE LEGISLATURE** the higher of two elected legislative bodies in many states of the United States **2 LEGISLATIVE BODY** the sole or upper law-making chamber of government in many countries or states, past or present **3 ANCIENT ROMAN ASSEMBLY** the highest council of the ancient Roman Republic and of the Roman Empire **4 SENATE BUILDING** the building where a senate meets **5 UNIVERSITY BODY** the main faculty governing body in some universities and colleges [12C. Via Old French < Latin *senatus* 'assembly of elders' < *senex* 'male elder'.]

Senate *n* **1 US LEGISLATURE** the upper of the two elected legislative bodies of the United States government **2 UPPER HOUSE OF CANADIAN PARLIAMENT** the upper chamber of the federal parliament of Canada **3 UPPER HOUSE OF AUSTRALIAN PARLIAMENT** in Australia, the upper house of the federal parliament. It consists of 76 members, 12 from each state plus two each from the Northern Territory and Australian Capital Territory.

senator /sénnətər/ *n* an elected or appointed member of a senate, e.g. in the United States, Australia, or ancient Rome

senatorial /sénnə táwri əl/ *adj* **1** relating to or characteristic of a senate or the post of senator ○ *senatorial privileges* **2** made up of senators —**senatorially** *adv*

Senatus Academicus /sə naàtəss əkə démmikəss/ *n* in the older Scottish universities, the body, consisting of the principal, professors, and, more recently, readers and lecturers, that superintends and regulates the teaching and discipline of the university [< Latin, 'Academic Senate']

⚡**send**[1] /send/ *v* (**sends**, **sending**, **sent** /sent/, **sent**) **1** *vt* **CAUSE SOMEBODY OR SOMETHING TO GO** to cause somebody or something to be moved or taken to another place **2** *vt* **COMMUNICATE** to transmit information to somebody who is somewhere else **3** *vt* **COMMAND SOMEBODY TO GO** to ask or command somebody to come or go **4** *vt* **ENABLE SOMEBODY TO GO** to enable somebody to go somewhere special ○ *Let's send the children to camp this summer.* **5** *vt* **REFER SOMEBODY SOMEWHERE** to suggest that somebody go somewhere or see somebody, usually for a specific kind of information **6** *vt* **BRING ABOUT** to make something happen ○ *Our blessings were sent by a higher power.* **7** *vt* **PROPEL** to make something move or travel by pushing it or hitting it ○ *A gust of wind sent the papers swirling round the office.* **8** *vt* **DRIVE SOMEBODY INTO PARTICULAR STATE** to make somebody enter a particular condition ○ *The delay is sending her crazy.* **9** *vt* **EXCITE SOMEBODY GREATLY** to excite or thrill somebody intensely (*dated slang*) **10** *vi* **BE TRANSMITTED** to be transmitted or transmittable ○ *This e-mail won't send.* **11** *vi* **BROADCAST INFORMATION** to transmit information by telecommunication ○ *The operator was still sending when the power was cut off.* ■ *n* **COMMAND TO TRANSMIT COMPUTER DATA** a command, key, or icon on a computer monitor or keyboard that is used to start the transmission of data [Old English *sendan* < Germanic, 'cause to go'] ◇ **send flying** to make somebody or something fly through the air by force of impact ◇ **send somebody packing** to dismiss or send somebody away in a firm, not very polite way (*informal*)

send away for *vt* to order something by post or through a mail order catalogue

send down *vt* **1** to expel a student from a university, especially Oxford or Cambridge (*often passive*) ○ *He was sent down as a result of this escapade.* **2** to imprison somebody following conviction (*informal*) ○ *He got sent down for armed robbery.*

send for *vt* to request the delivery, dispatch, or appearance of somebody or something ○ *send for reinforcements*

send in *vt* to post something, e.g. an application form, for processing along with those sent by other people

send off *vt* **1 DISPATCH** to dispatch something in the post **2 SEND SOMEBODY AWAY** to send somebody away, either on an errand, or by way of dismissal ○ *We sent him off to buy some things.* **3 DISMISS SOMEBODY FROM GAME** to dismiss a player from a game or competition for breaking the rules, e.g. in football, rugby, or hockey (*often passive*) **4 BID SOMEBODY FAREWELL** to say goodbye or good luck to somebody who is leaving ○ *Who was there to send her off?*

send on *vt* **1** to send something such as mail or belongings to a second place for somebody or ahead of somebody or yourself **2** to send occurring in mail to a subsequent place or person

send out for *vt* to order food by telephone, to be delivered to a particular address and paid for when it arrives (*informal*) ○ *Let's send out for a pizza.*

send up *vt* **1 RAISE** to make something rise or climb, especially a scale or index such as on a thermometer or a listing of stock market values ○ *News of lower interest rates sent the stock market index up 60 points.* **2 MOCK BY IMITATION** to make fun of somebody or something by humorous imitation (*informal*) **3 US SEND TO PRISON** to

imprison somebody following conviction (*informal*) ○ *He was sent up for armed robbery.*

SYNONYMS See **ridicule**.

send[2] *vi*, *n* NAUT = **scend**

Sendai /sen dí/ city on NE Honshu Island, Japan. Population: 918,398 (1990).

sender /séndər/ *n* somebody or something that sends or transmits something

sendoff /sénnd of/ *n* an act of showing goodwill towards somebody who is leaving or something that is starting, especially in a group at a place such as an airport or at a farewell party ◇ **give somebody a good sendoff** to have a good party after somebody's funeral (*informal*)

sendup /sénnd up/ *n* a parody done as a joke (*informal*)

sene /seen/ (*plural* **-ne**) *n* see table at **currency** [Mid-20C. < Samoan, 'cent'.]

Seneca /sénnikə/ (*plural* **-ca** *or* **-cas**) *n* **1** a member of an Iroquois people who lived in W New York State and who now mainly live there and in S Ontario, Canada **2** the Iroquoian language of the Seneca people [Mid-17C. < Dutch *Sennecaas* 'the Upper Iroquois peoples'.] —**Senecan** *adj*

Seneca /sénnəkə/ (4? BC–AD 65) Spanish-born Roman statesman, philosopher, and dramatist. Known as **Seneca the Younger**

senecio /sə néeshi ō, -néessi ō/ (*plural* **-os**) *n* PLANTS = **ragwort** [Mid-16C. < Latin, 'groundsel' < *senex* 'male elder' (from the plant's white hairs).]

Senegal

Senegal /sénni gáwl, -gaàl/ republic in W Africa, on the Atlantic Ocean. Capital: Dakar. Population: 8,532,000 (1996). Area: 196,192 sq. km/75,750 sq. mi. —**Senegalese** /sénni gaw leéz/ *n*, *adj*

~~senery~~ incorrect spelling of **scenery**

senescent /si néss'nt/ *adj* approaching an advanced age [Mid-17C. < Latin *senescent-*, present participle of *senescere* < *senex* 'advanced in age'.] —**senescence** *n*

seneschal /sénnish'l/ *n* in medieval times, a steward who managed the retainers of a noble house [14C. Via Old French < medieval Latin *seniscalcus* < Germanic.]

Senghor /sáN gawr/, **Léopold Sédar** (*b*. 1906) Senegalese statesman and writer

senhor /se nyáw/ (*plural* **-hors** *or* **-hores** /-n yáw ress/) *n* a Portuguese title equivalent to English 'Mr' [Late 18C. Via Portuguese < medieval Latin *senior* 'lord, superior' < Latin, 'elder'.]

senhora /sényáwrə/ *n* a Portuguese title equivalent to English 'Mrs' [Early 19C. < Portuguese, < *senhor* (see SENHOR).]

senhorita /sénnyə reétə/ *n* a Portuguese title equivalent to English 'Miss' [Late 19C. < Portuguese, < *senhor* (see SENHOR).]

senile /seé nīl/ *adj* **1** forgetful, confused, or otherwise mentally less acute in later life **2** occurring in or believed to be characteristic of later life [Mid-17C. < Latin *senilis* 'advanced in age' < *senex* 'old'.] —**senilely** *adv* —**senility** /sə nilləti/ *n*

senile dementia *n* a form of brain disorder marked by progressive and irreversible mental deterioration, memory loss, and disorientation, known to affect some people in later life

senior /seéni ər/ *adj* **1 MORE ADVANCED IN AGE** of a more advanced age **2 HIGHER IN RANK** of higher rank or having

longer service or employment than another ○ *Everyone on the committee is senior to me* **3** *senior*, *Senior* **RELATING TO EARLIER GENERATION** used to distinguish the elder of two members of the same family with the same name from the younger person of that name ■ *n* **1 PERSON OF GREATER AGE** a person who is older than somebody else **2 HIGHER-RANKING PERSON** a person who ranks higher than somebody else or has worked in the same place longer ○ *She is my only senior in the department.* **3** *US* **FINAL-YEAR STUDENT** a student in the last year of high school or college **4** *Aus* **AUSTRALIAN BARRISTER** in Australia, a barrister who has qualified for a Queen's Counsel [14C. < Latin, 'elder, older' < *senex* 'old'.]

senior aircraftman *n* a person in the Royal Air Force of a rank above leading aircraftman

senior chief petty officer *n* a noncommissioned officer in the US Navy of a rank above chief petty officer

senior citizen *n* somebody of retirement age or beyond

senior common room *n* a common room for the use of academic staff in some colleges and universities

senior debt *n* an indebtedness with no claims ahead of it and the first in line to be paid off

senior executive officer *n* *US* **1** one of the most important managers in an organization **2** the most important manager in an organization

senior high school *n* *US* a school for the last three or four years of secondary education in the United States, grades 9 or 10 to 12

seniority /seéni órrəti/ (*plural* **-ties**) *n* **1** status accorded to greater age, higher rank, or longer service or employment ○ *Days off will be awarded on the basis of seniority.* **2** the state of being of greater age or higher rank than somebody else

senior lecturer *n* a university teacher of a rank above lecturer

senior master sergeant *n* an enlisted person in the US Air Force of a rank above master sergeant

senior service *n* the Royal Navy, especially as viewed in relation to the army

seniti /sénni ti/ (*plural* **-ti**) *n* see table at **currency**

senna /sénnə/ *n* **1** dried plant leaves or pods of the senna plant. Use: purgative, laxative. **2** a leguminous plant. Flowers: yellow, in clusters. Native to: temperate regions. Genus: *Cassia*. [Mid-16C. Via modern Latin *senna* < Arabic *sanā'*.]

Ayrton Senna

Senna /sénnə/, **Ayrton** (1960–94) Brazilian racing driver

Sennacherib /sen ákərib/ (*d*. 681 BC) king of Assyria (705–681 BC)

sennet /sénnit/ *n* a trumpet call that announced the exits and entrances of actors in Elizabethan drama [Late 16C]

Sennett /sénnit/, **Mack** (1880–1960) Canadian-born US film director. Born **Mikall (or Michael) Sinnott**

sennit /sénnit/ *n* **1** braided cord in flat strands, used on ships **2** braided straw, reeds, or leaves, used to make hats [Mid-18C. < ?]

señor /se nyáw/ (*plural* **-ñors** *or* **-ñores** /-nyáw ress/) *n* a Spanish title equivalent to English 'Mr' [Early 17C. Via Spanish < medieval Latin *senior* (see SENHOR).]

señora /se nyáwrə/ *n* a Spanish title equivalent to English 'Mrs' [Late 16C. < Spanish, < *señor* (see SEÑOR).]

señorita /sénnyaw reétə/ *n* a Spanish title equivalent to English 'Miss' [Early 19C. < Spanish, < *señora* (see SEÑOR).]

senryu /sénnri oo/ (*plural* **-u**) *n* a three-line ironic or satirical Japanese poem, similar in structure to a haiku [Mid-20C. After Karai *Senryu* (1718–90), Japanese poet.]

sensation /sen sáysh'n/ *n* **1 PHYSICAL FEELING** a physical feeling caused by having one or more of the sense organs stimulated ○ *a burning sensation in my mouth and throat* **2 POWER TO PERCEIVE** the capacity to receive impressions through the sense organs ○ *He has lost all sensation in his legs.* **3 MENTAL IMPRESSION** a vague or general feeling, especially one not attributable to an obvious cause ○ *a sensation of falling* **4 PUBLIC INTEREST** a state of avid public interest in a phenomenon ○ *Her speech caused a sensation.* **5 INTERESTING PHENOMENON** a phenomenon that creates avid public interest [Early 17C. Via French < medieval Latin *sensation-* 'perception' < Latin *sensus* (see SENSE).]

sensational /sen sáysh'nəl/ *adj* **1 EXTRAORDINARY** attracting a great deal of attention and interest ○ *a sensational defeat* **2 OUTSTANDING** exceptionally good (*informal*) ○ *sensational results* **3 EMPHASIZING LURID DETAILS** giving too much emphasis to the most shocking and lurid aspects of something ○ *sensational coverage of the murder trial* **4 SENSORY** connected with the senses or sense impressions —**sensationally** *adv*

sensationalise *vt* = **sensationalize**

sensationalism /sen sáysh'nəlizəm/ *n* **1** the practice of emphasizing the most lurid, shocking, and emotive aspects of anything under discussion or investigation, especially by the media **2** the belief that all knowledge is obtained only through the senses —**sensationalist** *n, adj* —**sensationalistic** /sen sáysh'nə lístik/ *adj*

sensationalize /sen sáysh'nə līz/ (**-izes, -izing, -ized**), **sensationalise** (**-ises, -ising, -ised**) *vt* to place excessive emphasis on the most shocking and emotive aspects of a subject —**sensationalization** /-lī záysh'n/ *n*

sense /senss/ *n* **1 PHYSICAL FACULTY** one of the faculties by which a person or animal obtains information about the physical world **2 FEELING DERIVED FROM SENSES** a feeling derived from multiple or subtle sense impressions ○ *Flying filled him with a sense of insecurity.* **3 ABILITY TO APPRECIATE** the faculty whereby somebody appreciates a particular quality ○ *She has no sense of humour.* **4 MORAL DISCERNMENT** an ability to perceive and be motivated by moral or ethical principles ○ *instil a sense of right and wrong in the children* **5 INTELLIGENCE** the ability to make intelligent decisions or sound judgments ○ *He's got no sense at all.* **6 POINT** useful purpose or good reason ○ *There's no sense in waiting any longer.* **7 REASONED OPINION** an opinion arrived at through reflection or perception, often as a consensus ○ *The sense of the meeting was clearly against the proposal.* **8 MAIN IDEA** the essence or gist of something ○ *What was the sense of her argument?* **9 MEANING** a single meaning of a word or phrase that may have many **10 TERM'S MEANING** the meaning as opposed to the reference of a term or sentence ■ **senses** *npl* **RATIONAL MIND** a sensible, rational state of mind ○ *I must be out of my senses.* ■ *vt* (**senses, sensing, sensed**) **1 PERCEIVE** to perceive somebody or something with a sense or the senses ○ *I sensed a movement behind me.* **2 INFER** to understand something intuitively ○ *He must have sensed that I was disappointed.* **3 DETECT AND IDENTIFY CHANGE** to detect and identify a change in something ○ *The device senses when the door is opened and sounds the alarm.* [14C. Via Old French < Latin *sensus* 'perception' < *sens-*, past participle of *sentire* 'feel'.] —**sensate** /sén sayt/ *adj* —**sensately** *adv* ◇ **in a sense 1** considered from a point of view that may not be the most obvious or the most popular **2** used when saying that something could be described in a particular way, but that the description is not complete or accurate ◇ **make sense** to be understandable and consistent with reason ◇ **make sense of something** to understand something well enough to be able to act on it or evaluate it

LITERARY LINK ***Sense and Sensibility***, a novel (1811) by Jane Austen. Set in Devonshire, Austen's first novel describes the emotional development of two sisters, Elinor and Marianne Dashwood, who live with their widowed mother in a modest cottage. Outwardly, Elinor appears dull and practical, Marianne sensitive and passionate, but the story of their involvement with two seemingly appropriate suitors warns against simplistic character judgments.

sense datum *n* in the doctrine of phenomenalism, a sensation

sensei /sen sáy/ (*plural* **-sei**) *n* **1** a teacher of a martial art such as karate or T'ai chi **2** used as a title to address somebody who is a teacher, especially in the martial arts [Late 19C. < Japanese.]

senseless /sénssləss/ *adj* **1 WITHOUT INTELLIGENCE** demonstrating a lack of reason and intelligence ○ *a senseless decision* **2 UNCONSCIOUS** unconscious, or unable to perceive anything ○ *was knocked senseless by the blow* **3 WITH NO APPARENT PURPOSE** apparently or really without purpose or meaning ○ *a senseless activity* —**senselessly** *adv* —**senselessness** *n*

sense organ *n* an organ such as an eye or ear that is specialized to receive stimuli from the physical world and transmit them via nerve impulses to the brain

sensibilia /sén sə bílli ə/ *npl* things that can be sensed, considered collectively [Mid-19C. < Latin, < *sensibilis* 'perceptible by the senses' < *sensus* (see SENSE).]

sensibility /sénn sə bíllәti/ *n* (*plural* **-ties**) the capacity to respond emotionally or aesthetically ○ *the sensibility of a child.* ■ **sensibilities** *npl* sensitivity about moral or ethical issues ○ *careful not to offend their sensibilities*

USAGE sensibility or **sensitivity**? ***Sensitivity*** is used in ways corresponding to the meanings of the adjective *sensitive*, and is mainly concerned with physical or emotional reactions of various kinds: *a sensitivity to bright light.* ***Sensibility*** is less closely related in meaning to *sensible* than ***sensitivity*** is to *sensitive*, and chiefly denotes somebody's capacity to respond emotionally or aesthetically as in *poetry that appealed to his sensibility.*

sensible /sénsəb'l/ *adj* **1 SHOWING GOOD SENSE** having or demonstrating sound reason and judgment ○ *a sensible decision* ○ *She's not very sensible.* **2 PRACTICAL** practical, usually comfortable and hard-wearing, and not worn as an adornment ○ *a pair of sensible shoes* **3 SUBJECT TO PERCEPTION** able to be perceived through the senses ○ *sensible objects in the world around us* **4 AWARE OF** aware or conscious of something (*formal*) ○ *not sensible of the tragic mistake he'd made.* **5 CONSCIOUS** awake or conscious, and having the capacity to understand [14C. Via French *sensible* < late Latin *sensibilis* 'perceptible by the senses, able to perceive' < *sens-* (see SENSE).] —**sensibleness** *n* —**sensibly** *adv*

SYNONYMS See ***aware***.

USAGE sensible or **sensitive**? The two words overlap in meaning to some extent in the sense illustrated by the sentence *I am sensible of your difficult situation* ('I can appreciate your difficult situation'). In this meaning, ***sensible*** is normally used to express emotional or intellectual awareness. In a comparable use, ***sensitive*** is followed by *to* and denotes a finely attuned feeling about or for something: *He was always sensitive to their needs.*

sensible horizon *n* ASTRON = **horizon** *n.* 2

sensillum /sen síllәm/ (*plural* **-la** /-sílla/) *n* a simple sense organ made up of one or a few cells connected by a nerve cell, often found in insects [Early 20C. < modern Latin, < Latin *sensus* (see SENSE).]

sensitise *vt* = **sensitize**

sensitive /sénssətiv/ *adj* **1 ACUTELY PERCEPTIVE** unusually responsive to stimuli from the physical world ○ *a sensitive nose* **2 DELICATE** easily damaged or irritated physically ○ *a toothpaste for people with sensitive teeth* **3 AFFECTED BY EXTERNAL STIMULUS** affected in some way by a particular external stimulus such as an allergen (*often in combination*) ○ *eyes sensitive to light* ○ *a touch-sensitive screen* ○ *a price-sensitive product* **4 SUBTLE IN ARTISTIC EXPRESSION** subtly expressive in one of the arts **5 THOUGHTFUL AND SYMPATHETIC** tactful and sympathetic in relation to the feelings of others **6 TOUCHY** easily offended or annoyed if something is spoken about ○ *He's very sensitive about his driving.* **7 REQUIRING TACTFULNESS** needing to be dealt with tactfully to avoid embarrassment ○ *a sensitive issue* **8 SECRET OR CONFIDENTIAL** not to be mentioned or divulged ○ *sensitive matters of national security* **9 ARTISTICALLY IMPRESSIONABLE** susceptible to artistic effects, e.g. in music, writing, or painting **10 ABLE TO SENSE** with the capacity to perceive via the sense organs **11 ABLE TO MEASURE SMALL DIFFERENCES** capable of detecting minute changes in levels, conditions, or amounts ○ *a sensitive scientific instrument* **12 FLUCTUATING** volatile and subject to fluctuation ○ *a sensitive market* **13 RESPONSIVE TO LIGHT** extremely responsive to radiation, especially to light of a specific wavelength **14 RESPONSIVE TO SIGNALS** able to respond to transmitted signals ■ *n* **PSYCHIC PERSON** a person with clairvoyant or psychic powers [14C. Via French < medieval Latin *sensitivus* < Latin *sens-* (see SENSE).] —**sensitively** *adv* —**sensitiveness** *n* —**sensitivity** /sénsə tívvəti/ *n*

USAGE See ***sensibility***.

USAGE See ***sensible***.

sensitive plant *n* **1** a tropical shrub that recoils when touched. Flowers: purplish. Native to: America. *Mimosa pudica.* **2** a person who is easily upset (*informal*)

sensitize /sénssə tīz/ (**-tizes, -tizing, -tized**), **sensitise** (**-tises, -tising, -tised**) *vt* **1 MAKE SOMEBODY SENSITIVE** to make somebody sensitive, especially to a situation **2 MAKE SOMEBODY ALLERGIC** to induce undue sensitivity in somebody to a particular substance such as a food ingredient or drug so that subsequent exposure to the substance triggers an allergic reaction **3 MAKE FILM SENSITIVE TO LIGHT** to make a film, plate, or other medium sensitive to light by coating it with an emulsion [Mid-19C. < SENSITIVE + -IZE.] —**sensitization** /-tī záysh'n/ *n* —**sensitizer** *n*

sensitometer /sénssə tómmitər/ *n* an instrument for measuring degrees of sensitivity, especially one used on photographic materials [Late 19C. < SENSITIVE + -METER.] —**sensitometry** *n*

sensor /sénssər/ *n* a device capable of detecting and responding to physical stimuli such as movement, light, or heat [Mid-20C. < SENSE or Latin *sens-* (see SENSE) + -OR[1].]

sensoria plural of **sensorium**

sensorial /sén sáwri əl/ *adj* relating to sensation and the sense organs [Mid-18C. < SENSORIUM + -AL[1].] —**sensorially** *adv*

sensorimotor /sénssəri mṓtər/ *adj* **1** relating to both the motor and sensory functions in the brain or the neurological structures underlying these functions **2** relating to motor functions arising from sensory stimuli

sensorimotor stage *n* the first major stage in Piaget's theory of cognitive development, from birth to approximately two years, in which children begin to understand their world through sensory and motor experience

sensorineural /sénssəri nyóorəl/ *adj* involving or relating to sensory nerves

sensorium /sen sáwri əm/ (*plural* **-a** /-ri ə/) *n* **1** the sensory components of the brain and nervous system that deal with the receiving and interpreting of external stimuli **2** all the sensory functions in the body, considered as a single unit [Mid-17C. < late Latin, 'organ of sensation' < *sens-* (see SENSE).]

sensory /sénssəri/ *adj* relating to sensation and the sense organs ○ *heightened sensory awareness* [Mid-18C. < SENSE or Latin *sens-* (see SENSE) + -ORY.]

sensory deprivation *n* the elimination of or a sharp reduction in sensory stimulation, usually as part of an experiment in psychology or as part of repressive interrogation procedures or brainwashing

sensual /sénssyoo əl, -shoo əl/ *adj* **1** relating to physical or, especially, sexual pleasure **2** relating to the body and the senses as opposed to the mind or the intellect [15C. < late Latin *sensualis* 'equipped with feeling or sensation' < Latin *sensus* (see SENSE).] —**sensually** *adv* —**sensualness** *n*

USAGE sensual or **sensuous**? Both words are connected with gratification of the human senses. ***Sensual*** is the older word, and in the 17th century it developed special meanings associated with the bodily appetites, especially eating and above all sexual satisfaction: *Her mouth looked sensual and inviting. They enjoyed the sensual pleasures of the table.* About this time the poet John Milton seems to have invented the word ***sensuous*** to refer more specifically to the aesthetic and spiritual senses (seeing, hearing, thinking), and it was taken up by Samuel Taylor Coleridge in the 19th century. In current use, it is almost impossible to keep the two sets of meanings apart, since the senses cannot readily be compartmentalized in this way, but it is prudent to have regard for the main distinction when using these words. ***Sensuous***, for example, is the word to use in connection with music or poetry: *The conductor relished the sensuous parts of Ravel's score.*

sensualism /sénssyoo əlizəm, -shoo əlizəm/ *n* **1** devotion to sensual gratification **2** PHILOS, ETHICS = **sensationalism** *n.* 2 —**sensualist** *n* —**sensualistic** *adj*

sensuality /sénssyoo álləti, -shoo álləti/ *n* **1** the capacity for enjoying the pleasures of the senses **2** the quality of being pleasing to the senses

sensuous /sénssyoo əss, -shoo əss/ *adj* **1 OF SENSE STIMULATION** relating to stimulation of the senses **2 APPRECIATING STIMULATION** enjoying or appreciating pleasurable stimulation of the senses ○ *a sensuous lover* **3 CAUSING STIMULATION** causing pleasurable stimulation of the senses ○ *a sensuous experience* [Mid-17C. < Latin *sensus* (see SENSE).] —**sensuously** *adv* —**sensuousness** *n*

USAGE See ***sensual***.

sent[1] past tense, past participle of **send**[1]

sent[2] /sent/ (*plural* **senti** /sénti/) *n* see table at **currency** [Via Estonian < CENT]

~~**sentance**~~ incorrect spelling of **sentence**

sente /sénti/ (*plural* **lisente** /li sénti/) *n* see table at **currency** [Late 20C. < Sesotho, 'cent'.]

sentence /séntənss/ *n* **1 MEANINGFUL LINGUISTIC UNIT** a group of words or a single word that expresses a complete thought, feeling, or idea **2 JUDGMENT** a judgment by a court specifying the punishment of somebody convicted of a crime, or the punishment itself ○ *a sentence of 15 years in prison* **3 WELL-FORMED EXPRESSION** a well-formed expression in a symbolic language ■ *vt* (**-tences, -tencing, -tenced**) **ALLOCATE SOMEBODY PUNISHMENT** to allocate a particular punishment to somebody convicted of a crime, usually stating its nature and its duration ○ *was sentenced to two years in prison* [13C. Via French < Latin *sententia* 'feeling, opinion' < *sentient-*, present participle of *sentire* 'feel'.] —**sentencer** *n*

sentence adverb *n* an adverb that modifies an entire sentence. 'Frankly' is a sentence adverb in 'Frankly, I don't care'.

LANGUAGE NOTE Sentence adverbs Many English adverbs can be used to qualify whole sentences; for example: *Obviously there must be some mistake. Regrettably I shall be away that week. Financially it was a disaster. I've never liked him, frankly.* They are known as sentence adverbs. Sentence adverbs are concise; they allow you to express in a single word what you might otherwise have to say in several words. Sentence adverbs form a completely standard aspect of English grammar, but there are a few, such as *ironically* and *hopefully*, that give rise to widespread criticism as they express the user's attitude to the sentence content rather than qualify the sentence as a whole. Others that may incur criticism in the same way are *mercifully, thankfully*, and *truthfully*. In formal contexts, writers are advised to avoid all these and simply recast their sentences accordingly.

sentence substitute *n* a single word that, when used in the proper context, meets all the semantic requirements of a sentence. Words such as 'yes' and 'no' are sentence substitutes.

sentencing /séntənssing/ *n* the phase of a court trial in which a sentence is arrived at and pronounced, or the act of making such a pronouncement

sentential /sen ténsh'l/ *adj* relating to sentences in natural language or logic —**sententially** *adv*

sentential calculus *n* LOGIC = **propositional calculus**

sententious /sen ténshəss/ *adj* **1 FULL OF APHORISMS** tending to use, or full of, maxims and aphorisms **2 OVER-MORALIZING** inclined to moralize more than is merited or appreciated **3 PITHY** expressing much in few words [15C. Via Old French *sententieux* < Latin *sententiosus* 'meaningful' < *sententia* (see SENTENCE).] —**sententiously** *adv*

sentient /sénsh'nt, -shi ənt/ *adj* **1** capable of feeling and perception ○ *a sentient being* **2** capable of responding emotionally rather than intellectually [Mid-17C. < Latin *sentient-*, present participle of *sentire* 'feel'.] —**sentience** *n* —**sentiently** *adv*

sentiment /séntimənt/ *n* **1 MENTAL FEELING** a thought or idea based on a feeling or emotion **2 GENERAL FEELING** a feeling or opinion prevailing among a group of people ○ *The sentiment emerged that we were acting too soon.* **3 UNDERLYING FEELING** an underlying feeling, as distinct from the action that it brings about ○ *His speech was awkward but the sentiment was right.* **4 APPEAL TO FEELING** a calculated appeal to feeling or emotion, especially one that is excessive and unreasoning ○ *The book ends on a note of cheap sentiment.* **5 DEEP FEELING, ESPECIALLY IN ART** refined or tender feeling, especially when expressed in a work of art (*formal*) ■ **sentiments** *npl* **OPINION** a point of view or judgment on something ○ *What are her sentiments on the matter?* [14C. Via French < medieval Latin *sentimentum* 'opinion, feeling' < Latin *sentire* 'feel'.]

sentimental /sénti mént'l/ *adj* **1 MAWKISH IN FEELING** affected acutely by emotional matters, often to the point of mawkishness **2 MAWKISH IN EXPRESSION** displaying too much uncontrolled or self-indulgent emotion **3 APPEALING TO TENDER FEELINGS** appealing to or expressing tender, often romantic, feelings ○ *a sentimental portrait of our town* **4 NOSTALGIC** expressing or experiencing tender sadness or nostalgia **5 EXPRESSING DEEP FEELING** expressing deep, refined feeling (*formal*) —**sentimentally** *adv*

LITERARY LINK *A Sentimental Journey*, a novel (1768) by Laurence Sterne. Sterne's second and last novel was intended as a riposte to Tobias Smollett's ill-tempered *Travels Through France and Italy* (1766). A rambling account of a journey through France from Calais to Lyons, it is transformed into an engaging work of art by the author's wit, sensitivity, and sharp social observation.

sentimentalise *vti* = **sentimentalize**

sentimentalism /sénti méntəlizəm/ *n* **1** a tendency to express or use obvious or powerful feelings or emotions without appealing to reason **2** something that expresses excessive emotion, especially something that is self-indulgent or nostalgic —**sentimentalist** *n*

sentimentality /sénti men tálləti/ *n* the tendency or practice of indulging in emotion or nostalgia

sentimentalize /sénti mént'l īz/ (**-izes, -izing, -ized**), **sentimentalise** (**-ises, -ising, -ised**) *v* **1** *vi* to indulge excessively in emotion or nostalgia **2** *vt* to treat somebody or something, or express something, with undue emphasis on feeling —**sentimentalization** /-ī záysh'n/ *n*

sentimental value *n* a value placed on something because of its emotional associations rather than its monetary worth

sentinel /séntinəl/ *n* **SENTRY** a guard ■ *vt* (**-nels, -nelling, -nelled**) **1 GUARD** to stand guard over something or a group of people **2 PROVIDE GUARD FOR** to provide a guard for something or for a group of people [16C. Via French *sentinelle* < Italian *sentinella*.]

sentry /séntri/ (*plural* **-tries**) *n* a member of the armed services who is assigned to keep watch to warn of danger and to guard entrances and exits [Early 17C. < ?]

sentry box *n* a covered shelter for a sentry, typically at an entrance or crossing

senza /séntsə, -zə/ *prep* without something indicated by a following Italian noun (*in musical directions*) ○ *senza ritenuto* [Early 18C. < Italian.]

Seoul /sōl/ capital and largest city of South Korea, in the northwest of the country. Population: 10,229,260 (1995).

Sep. *abbr* **1** September **2** Septuagint

sepal /sépp'l/ *n* a modified leaf in the outermost whorl (**calyx**) of a flower that encloses the petals and other parts [Early 19C. Via French < modern Latin *sepalum*, blend of Greek *skepē* 'covering' and Latin *petalum* 'petal'.] —**sepalled** *adj* —**sepalous** *adj*

-sepalous *suffix* having a particular number or kind of sepals ○ *trisepalous*

separable /séppərəb'l/ *adj* capable of being divided, taken apart, or removed, either from each other or from something else —**separability** /séppərə bílləti/ *n* —**separableness** *n* —**separably** *adv*

separate *adj* /séppərət/ **1 APART** not touching or connected, not together, or not in the same place ○ *They slept in separate rooms.* **2 UNRELATED** distinct from or unrelated to something else ○ *I think we should treat that as a separate issue.* **3 DIFFERENT** not shared with somebody or something else ○ *The book will be sent to you under separate cover.* ■ *v* /séppə rayt/ (**-rates, -rating, -rated**) **1** *vt* **MOVE OR KEEP SOMETHING APART** to move two or more people or things away from each other or prevent them from coming into contact with each other ○ *Somehow we got separated in the crowd.* **2** *vt* **BE BETWEEN THINGS** to stand or lie between one person or thing and another **3** *vt* **DISTINGUISH** to be the factor that makes two people or things different from one another ○ *There was something about her that separated her from the other interviewees.* **4** *vi* **COME APART** to come apart or stop being attached or connected **5** *vi* **PART COMPANY** to leave one another and go off in different directions ○ *A crowd had gathered but it separated as soon as the police arrived.* **6** *vi* **CEASE LIVING AS COUPLE** to stop living together as a couple **7** *vt* **CATEGORIZE** to put somebody or something into different categories or groups **8** *vt* **SHOW HOW THINGS DIFFER** to see or show that two or more things are different ○ *We must separate these two issues in the mind of the public.* **9** *vti* **DIVIDE** to split something, or to be split, into component parts **10** *vti* **MAKE OR BECOME INDEPENDENT** to leave a larger group and become independent, or to cause part of a larger group to leave and form an independent unit **11** *vt US* **RELEASE OR FIRE** to dismiss somebody from a job or release somebody from military service ■ **separates** *npl* **INDIVIDUAL ITEMS OF CLOTHING** articles of women's clothing such as blouses, skirts, jackets, and trousers that can be bought as individual items and worn in various combinations [15C. < Latin *separare* 'arrange apart' < *parare* 'make ready'.] —**separately** *adv* —**separateness** *n* —**separator** /-raytər/ *n*

separate off *vt* to divide somebody or something from a larger group or unity

separate out *vti* to come out of a mixture and form a distinct mass, or to make something do so

separated /séppə raytid/ *adj* no longer living together as a couple but still legally married

separating funnel *n* a large funnel that has a valve in its output tube. Use: separation of liquids that do not mix.

separation /séppə ráysh'n/ *n* **1 ACTION THAT SEPARATES OR SEPARATE CONDITION** the act of separating things or people **2 STATE OF BEING APART** the state of not being with somebody else, or the period of time spent apart **3 PLACE OF MEETING OR SPACE BETWEEN** a place, line, or mark that shows where two things meet, or the gap between them **4 AGREEMENT NOT TO LIVE TOGETHER** the act of stopping living together as husband and wife while remaining married, or a formal agreement to do so, especially one made in a court of law **5 DIVISION** splitting into component parts **6** *US* **DEPARTURE FROM GROUP** dismissal from a job or release from military service **7 DUMPING PART OF ROCKET** the act of detaching the rear section of a multistage rocket when it is burnt out, or the time when this happens

separation anxiety *n* a state of anxiety caused in somebody, especially a young child, by the thought or fact of being separated from his or her mother or primary caregiver

separationist /séppə ráysh'nist/ *n, adj* = **separatist**

separation of powers *n* in the United States, the constitutional requirement that each of the three branches of government, executive, judicial, and legislative, be autonomous and distinct from the others

separatist /séppərətist/ *n* **1** a person who breaks away from or who is in favour of breaking away from a group, organization, or country **2** a person who favours keeping members of racial, religious, sexual, or cultural groups separate —**separatism** *n* —**separatistic** /séppərə tístik/ *adj*

separative /séppərətiv/ *adj* tending to become separate or make something become separate —**separatively** *adv* —**separativeness** *n*

~~**seperate**~~ incorrect spelling of **separate**

Sephardi /se faárdi/ (*plural* **-dim** /si faár dim, sə-, se-/) *n* a Jewish person of Spanish or Portuguese origin, now used loosely to refer to any Jewish person who is not of German or eastern European descent. ◊ **Ashkenazi** [Mid-19C. < modern Hebrew, < *sĕpārad*, land of exile mentioned in the Bible.] —**Sephardic** *adj*

sepia /seé pi ə/ *n* **1 REDDISH-BROWN PIGMENT** a deep reddish-brown pigment made from the dark liquid in the ink sacs of various species of cuttlefish or an artificial form of it, used in painting **2 SEPIA DRAWING OR PHOTOGRAPH** a drawing done in sepia or a photograph with a brownish tone **3 DARK BROWN** a dark brown colour tinged with yellow or red **4 BROWNISH COLOUR IN PHOTOGRAPHS** a brownish tone produced, especially in early photographs, by some photographic processes [14C. Via Latin < Greek *sēpia* 'cuttlefish'.] —**sepia** *adj*

sepiolite /seépi ə līt/ *n* a clayey hydrated magnesium silicate mineral, formed by hydrothermal alteration of basic igneous rocks. US term **meerschaum** *n.* 1 [Mid-19C. < German *Sepiolith* < Greek *sēpion* 'cuttlefish bone'.]

sepoy /seé poy/ *n* an Indian soldier under British command, especially one who served in the British East India Company [Early 18C. < Persian and Urdu *sipāhī* 'horseman, soldier'.]

Sepoy Mutiny, Sepoy Rebellion *n* HIST = **Indian Mutiny**

seppuku /se pŏŏkoo/ *n* ETHNOL = **hara-kiri** [Late 19C. < Japanese, 'cut the abdomen'.]

sepsis /sépsiss/ *n* the condition or syndrome caused by the presence of microorganisms or their toxins in the tissue or the bloodstream [Late 19C. < Greek *sēpsis* < *sēpein* 'make rotten'.]

sept /sept/ *n* **1** a branch of a Scottish or Irish clan **2** a section of a people that believes itself to be descended from one particular ancestor [Early 16C. Probably alteration of SECT.]

Sept., Sept *abbr* **1** September **2** Septuagint

septa plural of **septum**

September /sep témbər, səp-/ *n* the ninth month of the year in the Gregorian calendar, made up of 30 days [Pre-12C. Via French *septembre* < Latin *September* < *septem* 'seven', because September was the seventh month of the Roman year.]

septenary /séptinəri, sep téenəri/ *adj* **1 RELATING TO 7** relating to the number seven **2 CONTAINING 7** made up of seven people or things **3** TIME = **septennial** *adj.* **1**, **septennial** *adj.* **2** ■ *n* (*plural* **-ries**) **1 NUMBER 7** the number seven **2 GROUP OF 7** a group of seven people or things **3 7 YEARS** a period of seven years **4 LINE OF VERSE CONTAINING 7 FEET** a line of verse that contains seven metrical feet [15C. < Latin *septenarius* < *septeni* 'seven each' < *septem* 'seven'.]

septennial /sep ténni əl/ *adj* **1 FOR 7 YEARS** lasting seven years **2 HAPPENING EVERY 7 YEARS** occurring once every seven years ■ *n* **SOMETHING HAPPENING EVERY 7 YEARS** something that happens every seven years [Mid-17C. < Latin *septennium* (see SEPTENNIUM).] —**septennially** *adv*

septennium /sep ténni əm/ (*plural* **-ums** *or* **-a** /-ni ə/) *n* a period of seven years [Mid-19C. < Latin, < *septem* 'seven' + *annus* 'year'.]

septet /sep tét/, **septette** *n* **1 7 MUSICAL PERFORMERS** a group of seven instrumentalists or singers **2 MUSIC FOR 7 PERFORMERS** a musical piece composed for seven instrumentalists or singers **3 GROUP OF 7** a group of seven people or things [Early 19C. Via German *Septett* < Latin *septem* 'seven'.]

septi- *prefix* seven ○ *septivalent* [< Latin *septem*]

septic /séptik/ *adj* **1** full of or generating pus **2** relating to, involving, or causing sepsis [Early 17C. < Latin *septicus* < Greek *sēptikos* < *sēpein* 'make rotten'.] —**septically** *adv* —**septicity** /sep tíssəti/ *n*

septicaemia /sépti séemi ə/ *n* a disease caused by toxic microorganisms in the bloodstream —**septicaemic** /sépti séemik/ *adj*

septicemia *n* US = **septicaemia**

septic tank *n* a tank, usually underground, in which human waste matter is decomposed by bacteria

Sept-Îles /se téel/ city in SE Quebec, Canada, on the St Lawrence River. Population: 28,005 (1996).

septillion /sep tíllyən/ (*plural* **-lions** *or* **-lion**) *n* **1** the number equal to 10^{42}, written as 1 followed by 42 zeros (*dated*) **2** *US* the number equal to 10^{24}, written as 1 followed by 24 zeros [Late 17C. < French, < *sept* 'seven' + *-illion* as in *million*.] —**septillion** *adj, pron* —**septillionth** *adj*

septime /sep téem/ *n* in fencing, the seventh of eight positions from which a parry or attack can be made [Late 19C. Via French < Latin *septimus* 'seventh' < *septem* 'seven'.]

septuagenarian /séptyoo əjə náiri ən/ *n* a person between 70 and 79 years of age ■ *adj* between 70 and 79 years old [Early 18C. < Latin *septuaginarius* < *septuaginta* 'seventy'.]

Septuagesima /séptyoo ə jéssimə/ *n* the third Sunday before Lent in the Christian calendar [14C. < Latin *septuagesima (dies)* 'seventieth (day)' < *septuaginta* 'seventy'.]

Septuagint /séptyoo əjint/ *n* a Greek translation of the Hebrew Bible made in the 3rd and 2nd centuries BC to meet the needs of Greek-speaking Jewish people outside Palestine [Mid-16C. < Latin *septuaginta* 'seventy' (because it is said that about seventy translators worked on it).]

septum /séptəm/ (*plural* **-ta** /-tə/) *n* **1** a thin partition or membrane dividing something into two or more cavities such as the tissue separating the nostrils or the internal dividing walls in the seed heads of poppies **2** a thin partition that separates components in a machine [Mid-17C. < Latin, 'partition' < *sepire* 'enclose' < *sepes* 'hedge'.] —**septal** *adj* —**septate** /sép tayt/ *adj*

septuple /séptyŏŏp'l, -tyŏŏp'l/ *adj* **1 7 TIMES AS MUCH** seven times as many or as much as something else **2 HAVING 7 PARTS** consisting of seven parts ■ *vti* (**-ples, -pling, -pled**) **INCREASE BY 7 TIMES** to multiply something by seven, or become seven times as much or as many (*formal*) [Early 17C. < late Latin *septuplus* < Latin *septem* 'seven'.]

septuplet /séptyŏŏplət, -tyŏŏplət/ *n* **1 ONE OF 7 BORN TOGETHER** any one of seven people or animals born to the same mother at one time **2 GROUP OF 7** a group of seven people or things **3 GROUP OF 7 NOTES** a group of seven notes to be played or sung in the time of four, six, or eight of the same notated value [Late 19C. < SEPTUPLE, after *triplet*.]

sepulcher *n, vt* US = **sepulchre**

sepulchral /si-/ *adj* **1** suggesting or possessing the characteristics associated with the grave, e.g. gloominess **2** relating to burial vaults or funerals and burials (*formal*) —**sepulchrally** *adv*

sepulchre /sépp'lkə/ *n* a vault in which a corpse is buried. US = **sepulcher** ■ *vt* (**sepulchres, sepulchring, sepulchred**) to put a corpse into a sepulchre (*literary*) [12C. Via Old French *sépulchre* < Latin *sepulc(h)rum* < *sepult-*, past participle of *sepelire* 'bury'.]

sequacious /si kwáyshəss/ *adj* argued, or developing an argument, in a logically consistent and coherent way (*formal*) [Early 17C. < Latin *sequax* 'inclined to follow' < *sequi* 'follow'.] —**sequaciously** *adv* —**sequaciousness** *n* —**sequacity** /si kwássəti/ *n*

sequel /séekwəl/ *n* **1** a film, novel, or play that continues a story begun in a previous film, novel, or play **2** something that happens after something else, especially as a consequence of it [15C. Via Old French < Latin *sequel(l)a* < *sequi* 'follow'.]

sequela /si kwéelə/ (*plural* **-ae** /-lee/) *n* a disease or disorder that is caused by a preceding disease or injury in the same individual [Late 18C. < Latin (see SEQUEL).]

sequence /séekwənss/ *n* **1 SERIES OF THINGS** a number of things arranged in a particular order or connected in some way, or a number of actions or events that happen one after another ○ *Can you recall the sequence of events?* **2 ORDER OF THINGS** the order in which things are arranged, actions are carried out, or events happen **3 SECTION OF FILM** a section of a film showing a single incident or set of related actions or events ○ *a chase sequence* **4 CARDS OF CONSECUTIVE VALUES** three or more consecutive playing cards, usually of the same suit **5 REPEATED MUSICAL PHRASE** a musical passage or chant consisting of three or more related short phrases repeated several times at successively higher or lower pitch levels **6 HYMN** in the Roman Catholic Church, a hymn sung or said between the gradual and the gospel **7 ORDERED SET OF ELEMENTS** in mathematics, an ordered set of elements that can be put into a one-to-one correspondence with the set of positive integers **8 ORDER OF MOLECULAR ELEMENTS** the order of the amino acids in a protein or the nucleotides in a nucleic acid ■ *vt* (**-quences, -quencing, -quenced**) **1 PUT OR DO THINGS IN ORDER** to arrange things or perform actions in a definite order **2 DETERMINE MOLECULE'S SEQUENCE** to determine the sequence of a protein or nucleic acid [14C. < late Latin *sequentia* 'what follows' < Latin *sequent-*, present participle of *sequi* 'follow'.]

sequence of tenses *n* the grammatical relationship that causes the tense of a verb in a subordinate clause to be influenced or dictated by the tense of the verb in the related main clause

USAGE Sequence of tenses English has various verb tenses that identify and differentiate degrees of past time. The past tense indicates past time: *She left.* The perfect tense indicates past time extending into the present: *She has left* (i.e. *She has just this minute, or quite recently, gone somewhere*). The past perfect tense indicates a past time extending back beyond the immediate past: *She had left* (i.e. *She had done this long ago*). The past progressive indicates an attenuated, or extended, period in the past when something was going on: *She was leaving.* Take care to use these tenses in such a way that you express correctly differences in past time. As an example, when the verb of a main clause is in the past (*left*) or the past perfect tense (*had left*), the verb in the subordinate clause is also in the past or past perfect, depending on the degree of time you mean: *The nation finally started to understand what its armed forces accomplished/had* [not *have*] *accomplished on the peacekeeping missions.* An exception to this occurs when we use the present infinitive after a verb in the past: *We would have liked to go* [not *to have gone*] *to the concert, but we could not get tickets.*

sequencer /séekwənssər/ *n* **1 DEVICE FOR SORTING DATA** an instrument for sorting information into the correct order for data processing **2 ELECTRONIC DEVICE FOR STORING MUSIC** an electronic device or software that digitally stores sequences of musical notes, chords, or rhythms that can be transmitted to an electronic musical instrument **3 DEVICE FOR DETERMINING SEQUENCES** an apparatus for automatically determining the sequence of a protein or nucleic acid

sequent /séekwənt/ *adj* **1 CONSEQUENT** following as a consequence or result (*formal*) **2 FOLLOWING** following one after another (*formal or archaic*) ■ *n* **1 CONSEQUENCE** a consequence or result (*formal*) **2 FORMAL LOGICAL REPRESENTATION** in logic, a formal representation of an argument showing that an element is a theorem [Mid-16C. < Latin *sequent-* (see SEQUENCE).] —**sequently** *adv*

sequential /si kwénsh'l/ *adj* **1** happening in a particular order or forming a particular sequence **2** being a consequence or result of something else [Early 19C. < SEQUENCE, after *consequence, consequential*.] —**sequentiality** /si kwénshi álləti/ *n* —**sequentially** *adv*

sequential access *n* a way of accessing and reading a computer file by starting at the beginning. ◊ **direct access**

sequential scanning *n* a system that scans a television picture using lines in a numerical sequence. ◊ **interlaced scanning**

sequester /si kwéstər/ *vt* **1 PUT SOMEBODY INTO ISOLATION** to put somebody in an isolated or lonely place away from other people, the pressures of everyday life, or possible disturbances (*formal*) **2 TAKE PROPERTY TO COVER OBLIGATION** to take legal possession of somebody's property temporarily until a debt that person owes is paid, a dispute is settled, or a court order obeyed **3 TAKE ENEMY'S PROPERTY** to demand or seize the property of an enemy [14C. Via French *séquestrer* < late Latin *sequestrare* 'place in safe keeping' < *sequester* 'follower, trustee'.] —**sequestrable** *adj*

sequestrant /si kwés-/ *n* a chemical that in effect removes ions from a solution. Use: soil treatment to correct mineral deficiencies.

sequestrate /séekwə strayt, si kwé-/ (**-trates, -trating, -trated**) *vt* **1 TAKE SOMEBODY'S PROPERTY TEMPORARILY** to take legal possession of somebody's property temporarily until a debt that person owes is paid, a dispute is settled, or a court order obeyed **2** *Scotland* **DECLARE SOMEBODY BANKRUPT** in Scottish law, to declare somebody bankrupt **3** *Scotland* **TAKE BANKRUPT'S PROPERTY** in Scottish law, to hand over the property of a bankrupt to a trustee so that it can be used to pay off the bankrupt's debts [15C. < late Latin *sequestrare* (see SEQUESTER).] —**sequestrator** /séekwi straytər/ *n*

sequestration /sée kwe stráysh'n, sék-/ *n* **1 CONFISCATING OR BEING CONFISCATED** the act or process of legally confiscating somebody's property temporarily until a debt that person owes is paid, a dispute is settled, or a court order obeyed **2 SEIZING OR BEING SEIZED** the seizing of an enemy's property, or the fact or process of being seized **3 GOING INTO OR BEING IN ISOLATION** the act of going into or putting somebody in an isolated place, away from people or everyday pressures, or the fact of being in such a place (*formal*) **4 ION-BINDING PROCESS** the chemical process of binding an ion, especially a metallic ion, in a coordination complex

sequestrum /si kwéstrəm/ (*plural* **-tra** /-trə/) *n* a fragment of dead tissue, usually bone, that separates from surrounding living tissue [Mid-19C. < medieval Latin *sequestrum* 'sequestration' < late Latin *sequester* (see SEQUESTER).] —**sequestral** *adj*

sequin /séekwin/ *n* **1** a small round flat piece of shiny metal or plastic that is sewn onto clothing as a decoration, usually in large numbers **2** a gold coin that was used in Venice and Turkey between the 16th and 18th centuries [Late 16C. Via French < Italian *zecchino* < *zecca* 'mint' < Arabic *sikka* 'coin, die for making coins'.] —**sequined** *adj*

sequoia /si kwóy ə/ (*plural* **-a** *or* **-as**) *n* a large coniferous tree of the redwood family. Native to: California. Genus: *Sequoia*. [Mid-19C. < modern Latin, after *Sequoya* (1766?–1843), US Cherokee leader.]

Sequoia National Park /si kwóy ə-/ national park in south-central California, noted for its giant sequoia trees. Area: 1,629 sq. km/629 sq. mi.

sera plural of **serum**

serac /sə rák/, **sérac** *n* a ridge, pinnacle, or block of ice in the crevasses or slope of a glacier [Mid-19C. < Swiss French *sérac*, originally 'kind of firm white cheese'.]

seraglio /sə ráali ō/ (*plural* **-glios**) *n* **1** the women's quarters in a Muslim house, or the women themselves **2** a Turkish palace, especially the Ottoman sultan's palace at Istanbul [Late 16C. < Italian *serraglio*, alteration of Turkish *saray* 'palace' < Persian *sarāī* 'inn'.]

serai /sə rī/ *n* BUILDING = **caravanserai** *n.* **1** [Early 17C. < Turkish *saray* (see SERAGLIO).]

serail /sə rī/ *n* = **seraglio** [Late 16C. Via French *sérail* < Italian *serraglio* (see SERAGLIO).]

serape /sə ráapi, -pay/, **sarape** *n* a usually brightly coloured woollen blanket worn as a cloak by men in Mexico and Central and South America [Early 19C. < Mexican Spanish *sarape*.]

seraph /sérrəf/ (*plural* **-aphs** *or* **-aphim** /sérrəfim/) *n* an angel of the highest rank in the traditional medieval hierarchy of nine categories of angels [Pre-12C. < late Latin *seraphim* (plural) < Hebrew *sĕrāpīm*.] —**seraphic** /sə ráffik/ *adj* —**seraphically** *adv*

Serb /surb/ *n* a member of a Slavic people living mainly in Serbia, as well as other parts of the Balkan region [Early 19C. < Serbo-Croat *Srb*.]

Serbia /súrbi ə/ republic in SE Europe that, together with Montenegro, makes up the Federal Republic of Yugoslavia. Capital: Belgrade. Population: 9,979,116 (1996). Area: 88,361 sq. km/34,116 sq. mi.

Serbian /súrbi ən/ *n* **1** SOMEBODY FROM SERBIA somebody who comes from Serbia **2** DIALECT OF SERBO-CROATIAN the Slavic language of Serbia, written in the Roman or Cyrillic alphabet and closely related to Bosnian and Croatian ■ *adj* OF SERBIA relating to Serbia or its language, people, or culture

Serbo-Croatian /súrbō krō áysh'n/, **Serbo-Croat** /-krṓ at/ *n* **1** SLAVIC LANGUAGE the Slavic language spoken by the Serbians and Croatians, now considered as Bosnian, Croatian, and Serbian **2** SPEAKER OF SERBO-CROATIAN somebody whose native language is Serbo-Croatian ■ *adj* OF SERBO-CROATIAN relating to the Serbo-Croatian language or speakers of languages derived from it

sere[1] /seer/, **sear** *adj* dry and withered (*archaic or literary*) [Old English *sēar* 'withered'. Ultimately < Indo-European.]

SYNONYMS See ***dry***.

sere[2] /seer/ *n* the series of different communities of plants and animals that occupy a given site and create a stable system during the process of ecological succession [Early 20C. < Latin *serere* 'join, connect'.] —**seral** *adj*

serein /se ráyn, sə ráN/ *n* in the tropics, a very fine rain that falls from a clear sky at dusk [Late 19C. Via French < Latin *serum* 'evening' < *serus* 'late'.]

serenade /sérrə náyd/ *n* **1** LOVE SONG a song or the performance of a song used to court somebody, traditionally sung by a man in the evening outside a woman's window **2** INSTRUMENTAL COMPOSITION FOR SMALL ENSEMBLE an instrumental work similar to a sonata, designed for evening outdoor performance by a small ensemble of musicians ■ *vti* (**-nades, -nading, -naded**) PERFORM LOVE SONG to sing or play a serenade ○ *A mockingbird serenades us every evening.* [Mid-17C. Via French *sérénade* < Italian *serenata* (see SERENATA).] —**serenader** *n*

serenata /sérrə naátə/ *n* **1** a choral work popular during the 18th century, often based on a religious text and having solos and duets **2** MUSIC = **serenade** *n.* **1**, **serenade** *n.* **2** [Mid-18C. < Italian, < *sereno* 'serene' < Latin *serenus*.]

serendipity /sérrən díppəti/ *n* a natural gift for making useful discoveries quite by accident [Mid-18C. < *The Three Princes of Serendip*, a Persian story about three princes who had this ability.] —**serendipitous** *adj* —**serendipitously** *adv*

USAGE The phrase *serendipitous discovery* manages to suggest that ***serendipity*** is nothing other than good luck. However, the idea of a discovery is necessary to the word, and ***serendipity*** and *serendipitous* are nonstandard in senses unrelated to making happy discoveries by chance.

serene /sə reén/ *adj* **1** without worry, stress, or disturbance **2** bright and without clouds [15C. < Latin *serenus* 'clear, calm'.] —**serenely** *adv* —**sereneness** *n* —**serenity** /sə rénnəti/ *n*

SYNONYMS See ***calm***.

Serene /sə reén/ *adj* a word used in the titles of members of some European royal families, e.g. that of Monaco

Serengeti National Park /sérrəng gétti-/ national park in W Tanzania. Area: 14,760 sq. km/5,700 sq. mi.

serf /surf/ *n* **1** an agricultural worker, especially in feudal Europe, who cultivated land belonging to a landowner, and who was bought and sold with the land **2** a labourer legally bound to and obliged to serve a lord [15C. Via French < Latin *servus* 'slave'.] —**serfdom** *n* —**serfhood** *n*

~~**sergant**~~ incorrect spelling of **sergeant**

serge /surj/ *n* a strong cloth, usually made of wool but sometimes of other fibres, used especially to make coats, jackets, and trousers [14C. Via Old French *sarge* < Latin *serica lana* 'silken wool' < *sericus* (see SILK).]

sergeant /saárjənt/ *n* **1** in the British or Canadian army and air force, in the Royal Marines, and in the US Army and Marine Corps a noncommissioned officer of a rank above corporal, and in the US Air Force of a rank above airman first class **2** a police officer of a rank above constable **3 sergeant, serjeant** LAW = **sergeant at arms** *n.* **1** [12C. Via Old French *sergent* 'servant' < Latin *servient-*, present participle of *servire* (see SERVE).] —**sergeancy** *n* —**sergeantship** *n*

sergeant at arms (*plural* **sergeants at arms**), **serjeant at arms** (*plural* **serjeants at arms**) *n* **1** somebody appointed to keep order within an organization, e.g. a parliament or court of law, and to perform certain other duties, e.g. making arrests **2** formerly, an armed attendant for a noble or monarch

sergeant at law *n* LAW = **serjeant at law**

sergeant first class (*plural* **sergeants first class**) *n* an enlisted person in the US Army of a rank above staff sergeant

sergeant fish *n* **1** = **cobia 2** = **snook**[1] [Because of the stripes on its body]

sergeant major (*plural* **sergeants major** *or* **sergeant majors**) *n* **1** ARMY RANK in the British Army a noncommissioned warrant officer of the highest rank, and in the US Army and Marine Corps a noncommissioned officer of a rank above master sergeant **2** *US* MILITARY ADMINISTRATIVE OFFICER the highest ranking noncommissioned officer at a US Army, Air Force, or Marine Corps headquarters **3** LARGE TROPICAL FISH a large tropical damselfish ranging from blue-green to yellow in colour with black vertical stripes. Native to: Atlantic waters. *Abudefduf saxatilis.*

Sergt *abbr* sergeant

ϟ **serial** /seéri əl/ *n* **1** STORY IN PARTS a story that is published or broadcast in parts, normally at regular intervals **2** REGULAR NEWSPAPER OR MAGAZINE a magazine or newspaper published at regular intervals, especially weekly or monthly ■ *adj* **1** IN SERIES in or forming a series, or done or doing something repeatedly in a series **2** PRODUCED IN PARTS published or broadcast in parts, usually at regular intervals **3** SENDING COMPUTER INFORMATION SEQUENTIALLY describes a form of data communication in which the individual bits that comprise each byte or character travel one after another through a single wire. ◊ **parallel** *adj.* **4 4** RELATING TO MUSICAL COMPOSITION describes a method of musical composition in which all 12 chromatic tones of the octave appear in strict order with no note repeated before the sequence is completed [Mid-19C. < SERIES.] —**serially** *adv*

SPELLCHECK See ***cereal***.

serialise *vt* = **serialize**

serialism /seéri əlizəm/ *n* a method of musical composition in which all 12 chromatic tones of the octave appear in strict order with no note repeated before the sequence is completed —**serialist** *n*

serialize /seéri ə līz/ (**-izes, -izing, -ized**), **serialise** (**-ises, -ising, -ised**) *vti* to publish or broadcast a story in parts at intervals, or to be divided into parts suitable for publishing or broadcasting —**serialization** /-lī záysh'n/ *n*

serial killer *n* a murderer who kills a number of people over a period of time, especially somebody who uses the same method each time —**serial killing** *n*

serial monogamy *n* the idea or practice of having only one sexual partner at a time and entering another relationship when one comes to an end

serial number *n* a set of numbers assigned to, and usually marked on, each of a series of identical products, e.g. television sets, cars, paper money, or computers

ϟ **serial port** *n* a computer socket used to connect peripherals such as mouse, keyboard, external modem, and monitor

serial rights *npl* the right to publish a story or book in parts as a serial

seriate /seéri it/ *adj* arranged in rows or a series —**seriately** *adv*

seriatim /seéri áytim, sérri-, -aátim/ *adv* one after another, or in a series [15C. < medieval Latin, < Latin *series* (see SERIES).]

sericeous /sə ríshəss/ *adj* **1** covered with small soft silky hairs **2** having the soft smooth feel of silk (*formal*) [Late 18C. < Latin *sericus* 'silken' < Greek *Sēres*, Asian people who originally made silk.]

sericin /sérris sin/ *n* a gelatinous protein that binds together the filaments of a silk fibre [Mid-19C. < Latin *sericum* 'silk', a form of *sericus* (see SERICEOUS).]

sericulture /sérri kulchər/ *n* the commercial breeding of silkworms for their silk [Mid-20C. Shortening of French *sériciculture* < Latin *sericum* 'silk', a form of *sericus* (see SERICEOUS).] —**sericultural** /-kúlchərəl/ *adj* —**sericulturist** *n*

seriema /sérri eémə/ (*plural* **-ma** *or* **-mas**) *n* either one of two large, crested, mainly ground-dwelling birds with long tails and legs. Native to: South America. Family: Cariamidae. [Mid-19C. Via Portuguese < Tupi *siriema*.]

series /seér eez/ (*plural* **-ries**) *n* **1** THINGS ONE AFTER ANOTHER a number of similar or related things coming one after another ○ *a series of lectures on modern philosophy* **2** SET OF BROADCAST PROGRAMMES a set of regularly broadcast programmes, each of which is complete in itself **3** SIMILAR PUBLICATIONS FROM ONE ORGANIZATION a number of books, pamphlets, or periodicals brought out by one company or organization on the same or related topics or in the same format **4** SET OF MATCHES BETWEEN SAME TEAMS in some sports, e.g. cricket and baseball, a set of matches between the same teams **5** RELATED ITEMS PRODUCED AT ONE TIME a number of related items, e.g. stamps or coins of different values, brought out at one time **6** RELATED CHEMICALS a group of related chemicals that are similar in structure or properties **7** SUM OF SEQUENCE OF TERMS in mathematics, the indicated sum of a finite or infinite sequence of terms, each term being added to those that precede it **8** ROCK LAYER a succession of rock strata deposited during a particular period of geological time **9** ARRANGEMENT OF ELECTRIC ELEMENTS a set of two or more electronic components through which current flows in sequence **10** SET OF 12 NOTES a set of 12 notes, the 12 chromatic pitches of an octave, in which no pitch is repeated **11** TWO OR MORE COORDINATE ELEMENTS a sequence of two or more elements in a sentence that have the same grammatical structure [Early 17C. < Latin, < *serere* 'join, connect'.] ◇ **in series** connected in a circuit so that the same current flows through each component in sequence

USAGE ***Series*** can be a singular or a plural noun, depending on its meaning. If you use it to mean 'a single set of things', use a singular verb even if ***series*** is followed by the preposition *of* and a plural noun: *A series of medical tests is planned for next week.* If you use ***series*** to mean 'two or more sets of things', use a plural verb: *Three series of medical tests are planned for next week.*

serif /sérrif/ *n* a short decorative line at the start or finish of a stroke in a letter [Mid-19C. < ?]

serigraph /sérri graaf, -graf/ *n* ART = **silk-screen** *n.* **2** [Late 19C. < Latin *sericum* 'silk', a form of *sericus* (see SERICEOUS).] —**serigrapher** /sə ríggrəfər/ *n* —**serigraphy** *n*

serin /sérrin/ (*plural* **-ins** *or* **-in**) *n* a yellowish or greyish finch such as a canary. Native to: North Africa, the Mediterranean. Genus: *Serinus*. [Mid-16C. < French, 'canary' < ?]

serine /seér een, sérreen/ *n* an amino acid produced in the hydrolysis of proteins that is a precursor of a number of biochemically important molecules [Late 19C. < German *Serin* < Latin *sericum* 'silk', a form of *sericus* (see SERICEOUS).]

seringa /sə ríng gə/ *n* a tree that yields rubber. Native to: Brazil. Genus: *Hevea*. [Mid-18C. Via French and Portuguese < Latin *syringa* (see SYRINGA).]

seriocomic /seèri ō kómmik/, **seriocomical** /-kómmik'l/ *adj* with both serious and comic elements —**serio-comically** *adv*

serious /seèri əss/ *adj* 1 VERY BAD OR GREAT very great, bad, dangerous, harmful, or difficult to handle 2 IMPORTANT important or grave enough to require thought and attention ○ *There are serious arguments against this proposal.* 3 LIKELY TO SUCCEED having a possibility of success or showing an intention to succeed ○ *Only two of the five applicants can be considered serious candidates for the post.* 4 THOUGHTFUL OR THOUGHT-PROVOKING discussing or dealing with matters in a thoughtful or thought-provoking way, as opposed to in a superficial or merely entertaining manner ○ *a serious discussion of the issues* 5 NEEDING CAREFUL THOUGHT OR ATTENTION needing careful thought, study, or attention ○ *a serious proposal* 6 NOT LIGHTHEARTED quiet, thoughtful, not laughing or making jokes very often, and always being sensible 7 MEANING SOMETHING LITERALLY not joking, pretending, or exaggerating about something ○ *Do you think she's serious about helping us out?* 8 SUBSTANTIAL substantial or sustained rather than trivial or insignificant (*informal*) ○ *I've invested serious money in this endeavour.* 9 DEDICATED TO SOMETHING showing great interest in or commitment to an endeavour, skill, or pastime ○ *a serious stamp collector* [15C. Via French *sérieux* < late Latin *seriosus* < Latin *serius*.] —**seriousness** *n*

seriously /seèri əssli/ *adv* 1 BADLY in a great, bad, dangerous, harmful, or problematic way ○ *seriously ill* 2 GRAVELY in a grave and thoughtful way, without being lighthearted or dismissive ○ *We have to take this threat seriously.* 3 TRULY in a true or literal way, without exaggeration or deceit ○ *Do you seriously expect me to go along with this?* 4 EXTREMELY to a great or remarkable extent (*informal*) ○ *I'm getting seriously fed up with her arrogance.*

serious-minded *adj* earnest and taking an interest in matters that are weighty and important

serjeant *n* 1 = serjeant at arms *n*. 1 2 = serjeant at law

serjeant at arms *n* = sergeant at arms

serjeant at law (*plural* **serjeants at law**), **sergeant at law** (*plural* **sergeants at law**) *n* a high-ranking English barrister (*archaic*)

Serkin /súrkin/, **Rudolf** (1903–91) Czechoslovakian-born US pianist

sermon /súrmən/ *n* 1 a talk on a religious or moral subject given by a member of the clergy as part of a religious service 2 a long and tedious talk, especially one telling somebody how or how not to behave [12C. Via Anglo-Norman *sermun* < Latin *sermo* 'talk, conversation'.] —**sermonic** /sur mónnik/ *adj*

sermonize /súrmə nīz/ (**-izes**, **-izing**, **-ized**), **sermonise** (**-ises**, **-ising**, **-ised**) *vti* to give somebody a long tedious talk about how or how not to behave —**sermonizer** *n*

Sermon on the Mount *n* a collection of Jesus Christ's religious and moral teachings recorded in Matthew's Gospel in the Bible, much of which Jesus Christ set out in a speech to his disciples from a hillside

sero- *prefix* serum ○ *serology* [< SERUM]

seroconvert /seèrō kən vúrt/ *vi* to produce specific antibodies in response to the presence of an antigen such as a bacterium or virus —**seroconversion** *n*

serology /seer róllǝji/ *n* the branch of medicine concerned with the study of blood serum and its constituents, especially its role in protecting the human body against disease —**serologic** /seèrə lójjik/ *adj* —**serologist** *n*

seronegative /seèrō néggətiv/ *adj* after a blood test, showing no immunological evidence of infection, either current or previous, with a particular bacterium, virus, or other infective agent

seropositive /seèrō pózzitiv/ *adj* after a blood test, showing immunological evidence of infection, either current or previous, with a particular bacterium, virus, or other agent

seropurulent /seèrō pyóoróolant/ *adj* consisting of a mixture of blood serum and pus

serosa /sə róssə/ (*plural* **-sae** /-səə/ *or* **-sas**) *n* ANAT = serous membrane [Late 19C. < modern Latin (*membrana*) *serosa* 'serous (membrane)'.]

serostatus /seèrō stáytəss/ *n* the condition of being either seropositive or seronegative

serotine /sérrō tīn, -tin/ *n* a small brown bat. Native to: Europe, Asia. Genus: *Eptesicus*. [Late 18C. Via French *sérotine* < a late Latin sense 'in or of the evening' of Latin *serotinus* 'belated, late flowering' < *serus* 'late'.]

serotonergic /sérrǝtō núrjik/, **serotoninergic** /sérrǝtōni-/ *adj* describes neurons or nerves that are capable of releasing serotonin as a neurotransmitter at their endings

serotonin /sérrə tōnin/ *n* $C_{10}H_{12}N_2O$ a chemical derived from the amino acid tryptophan, and widely distributed in tissues. It acts as a neurotransmitter, constricts blood vessels at injury sites, and may affect emotional states. [Mid-20C. < SERO- + TONIC + -IN.]

serotoninergic *adj* ANAT = serotonergic

serous /seèrəss/ *adj* relating to, resembling, or producing serum [15C. < French *séreux* or medieval Latin *serosus*, both < Latin *serum* 'whey, watery fluid'.]

serous fluid *n* any bodily fluid that resembles serum

serous membrane *n* a thin moist transparent membrane that lines the body cavities and surrounds the internal organs, e.g. the peritoneum that lines the abdomen

serow /sérrō/ (*plural* **serows** *or* **serow**) *n* a goat antelope. Native to: the mountains of tropical and subtropical E Asia. Genus: *Capricornus*. [Mid-19C. Probably < Lepcha *sä-ro*.]

Serpens /súr penz/ *n* a constellation near the celestial equator. See illustration at **constellation**

serpent /súrpənt/ *n* 1 SNAKE a snake (*literary*) 2 TREACHEROUS PERSON a sly or treacherous person 3 OLD WIND INSTRUMENT a woodwind instrument shaped like a curving snake, dating back to the medieval period [13C. Via French < Latin *serpent-*, present participle of *serpere* 'creep'.]

Serpent /súrpənt/ *n* 1 in the Bible, the reptile said to have tempted Eve 2 Satan (*literary*) 3 ASTRON = Serpens

serpentine /súrpən tīn/ *adj* 1 WINDING winding and twisting, with many bends and curves 2 RESEMBLING SNAKE like a snake in motion or shape (*literary*) 3 CUNNING untrustworthy and cunning, as a snake is conventionally thought to be (*literary*) 4 CURVING relating to or being a complex curve that is symmetric about the x-axis and the central part of which is convex ■ *n* GREEN OR BROWN MINERAL a dull green or brownish mineral consisting of hydrous magnesium silicate. Use: ornamental stone. [15C. In the noun sense < French *serpentin*; from its being mottled like a snake's skin.]

Serpentine Ridge /súrpən tīn-/ low ridge on the Moon running north to south across the eastern side of the Mare Serenitatis, or Sea of Tranquillity

SERPS /surps/, **Serps** *n* a pension paid by the government to people who have been employed during their lives. Full form **state earnings-related pension scheme**

serpulid /súr pyóollid/ *n* a round segmented marine worm with a flat, coiled, shell, from which it projects a crown of tentacles, typically found on rocks and seaweed. Family: Serpulidae. [Late 19C. < modern Latin *Serpulidae* < late Latin *serpula* 'small serpent'.]

serrate /sérrayt/ *adj* with notches or projections like the teeth of a saw ■ *vt* (**-rates** /sə ráyt/, **-rating**, **-rated**) to give something an edge that is notched like the teeth of a saw [14C. < late Latin *serratus*, past participle of *serrare* 'saw' < Latin *serra* 'saw'.] —**serrated** /sə ráytid/ *adj*

serration /sə ráysh'n/ *n* 1 NOTCHES LIKE SAW TEETH a row of notches like the teeth of a saw 2 TOOTH OR NOTCH a tooth or notch in a series or row that is like the teeth of a saw 3 STATE OF BEING NOTCHED the state of having a sharp notched edge like the teeth of a saw

serried /sérrid/ *adj* crowded together with little space between each (*literary*) [Mid-17C. Past participle of obsolete *serry* 'close ranks' < French *serrer* 'press close together' < Latin *sera* 'bolt'.]

serriform /sérri fawrm/ *adj* with notches like the teeth of a saw [Early 19C. < Latin *serra* 'saw' + -FORM.]

serrulate /sérrōō layt/, **serrulated** /sérrōō laytid/ *adj* having an edge with tiny notches like the teeth of a saw [Late 18C. < modern Latin *serrulatus* < Latin *serrulus* 'small saw' < *serra* 'saw'.] —**serrulation** /sérrōō láysh'n/ *n*

Sertoli cell /sur tóli-/ *n* a cell, found in large numbers lining the semen-producing tubules of the testis, that provides support and nourishment for developing sperm [Early 20C. After Enrico *Sertoli* (1842–1910), Italian histologist.]

Sertorius /sur táwri əss/, **Quintus** (121?–72 BC) Roman general and statesman

serum /seèrəm/ (*plural* **-rums** *or* **-ra** /seèrə/) *n* 1 the fluid that separates from clotted blood, similar to plasma but without clotting agents 2 MED = **antiserum** 3 any clear watery body fluid, especially that exuded by serous membranes [Late 17C. < Latin, 'whey, watery fluid'.] —**serumal** *adj*

serum albumin *n* an abundant protein in blood serum that helps regulate the osmotic pressure of blood

serum globulin *n* a globular protein or mixture of proteins in the blood that contains many antibodies

serum hepatitis *n* MED = **hepatitis B**

serum sickness *n* an adverse reaction to an injection of serum, with symptoms such as swelling, fever, or a rash

serval /súrv'l/ (*plural* **-vals** *or* **-val**) *n* a wild cat that has a reddish-brown coat with black spots, long legs, a long neck, and a relatively small head with large ears. Native to: sub-Saharan Africa. *Felis serval.* [Late 18C. Via French < Portuguese *lobo cerval* 'lynx' < Latin *cervus* 'deer'.]

servant /súrvant/ *n* 1 an employee who serves somebody, especially somebody employed to do household tasks 2 somebody in the public employ. ◊ **civil servant, public servant** [12C. < Old French, present participle of *servir* (see SERVE).]

serve /surv/ *v* (**serves, serving, served**) 1 *vti* PREPARE AND SUPPLY FOOD to prepare and supply food or drinks 2 *vti* GIVE SOMEBODY FOOD OR DRINK to bring food or drink to somebody 3 *vt* PROVIDE CUSTOMERS WITH GOODS to wait on customers in a shop, and provide them with goods, supplies, or services 4 *vti* BE OF USE to be useful or helpful for a particular purpose 5 *vti* HAVE PARTICULAR EFFECT to have a particular effect or result ○ *This letter will serve to remind you of our appointment.* 6 *vti* SPEND TIME IN PRISON to spend a certain length of time in a place, especially in prison 7 *vi* BE IN ARMED FORCE to be a member of an armed force, especially in wartime 8 *vti* PUT BALL OR SHUTTLECOCK IN PLAY to hit a ball or shuttlecock towards an opponent in a racket game as a way of beginning play 9 *vt* DELIVER LEGAL DOCUMENT TO to deliver to somebody a legal document such as a summons, writ, or warrant (*formal*) 10 *vti* WORK FOR to work, or work for somebody 11 *vti* WORK AS SERVANT to work, or work for somebody, as a servant 12 *vt* ASSIST DURING MASS to assist a Roman Catholic priest in the celebration of Mass 13 *vt* WORSHIP to worship or follow somebody or something (*formal*) 14 *vt* COPULATE WITH FEMALE of a male animal, to copulate with a female 15 *vt* BIND ROPE WITH WIRE OR CORD to bind a rope with something such as fine wire to keep it from wearing or fraying ■ *n* HIT THAT STARTS POINT in racket games, the shot used to begin every point [12C. Via Old French *servir* < Latin *servire* < *servus* 'slave'.] —**servable** *adj* ◇ **serve somebody right** to be a deserved punishment for doing something wrong

serve up *vt* to supply something, especially food

⚡**server** /súrvər/ *n* 1 SOMEBODY WHO SERVES a person who serves something, e.g. food at a meal 2 SOMEBODY WHO STARTS GAME the player who starts a game in a sport such as tennis or badminton by hitting the ball or shuttlecock across the net to an opponent 3 TRAY FOR SERVING a tray for serving food or drinks on 4 FOOD UTENSIL a utensil for serving food 5 ASSISTANT AT MASS an assistant to a Roman Catholic priest during a mass. ◊ **acolyte** 6 COMPUT = file server

serviceable incorrect spelling of **serviceable**

service[1] /súrviss/ *n* 1 WORK DONE FOR SOMEBODY ELSE work done by somebody for somebody else as a job, a duty, a punishment, or a favour 2 MEETING OF PUBLIC NEED the system or operation by which people are provided with something they need, e.g. public transport, or the organization that runs such a system 3 GOVERNMENT AGENCY an official organization, especially a government department, or the work performed for such an organization ○ *the diplomatic service* 4 DOMESTIC SERVANT'S WORK the work done as a servant in a private house 5 ONE OF THE ARMED FORCES one of a country's armed forces 6 SERVING SOMEBODY FOOD the act of bringing food to somebody or the way in which this is done 7 MAINTENANCE OF MACHINERY the act of cleaning, checking, adjusting, or making minor repairs to a piece of machinery, especially a motor vehicle, to make sure that it works properly 8 USE OR OPERATION current use or operation 9 PUBLIC WORSHIP CEREMONY a religious ceremony usually involving specific forms for worship and prayer 10 RELIGIOUS RITUAL a specific religious ritual that is performed according to a prescribed form **11 ACT OF SERVING BALL OR SHUTTLECOCK** the act or manner of serving in a racket game, or the right to do so **12 GAME** a game in which a player serves **13 SET OF DISHES** a set of dishes and cups for use in serving a particular meal ○ *dinner service* **14 SERVING OF LEGAL DOCUMENT TO** the delivery of a legal document such as a writ or summons **15 MATERIAL USED TO BIND ROPE** something such as fine wire or cord used to bind a rope to prevent it from fraying **16 COLLECTION OF RELIGIOUS MUSICAL SETTINGS** a collection of the musical arrangements prescribed for use in the Church of England ■ **services** *npl* **1 FACILITIES FOR TRAVELLERS** facilities such as shops, cafés, and toilets available at certain places along a motorway ○ *There are no services at the next exit.* **2 WORK THAT DOES NOT MAKE ANYTHING** jobs and businesses such as banking and insurance that provide something for other people but do not produce tangible goods **3 THINGS PROVIDED BY GOVERNMENT** things such as education, healthcare, and roads that are provided by national or local government and paid for by taxation **4 ARMED FORCES** the armed forces of a country ■ *vt* (**services, servicing, serviced**) **1 CLEAN AND ADJUST MACHINERY** to clean, check, adjust, and make minor repairs to a piece of machinery in order to make sure that it works properly ○ *It's time to have my car serviced.* **2 PROVIDE SOMETHING FOR COMMUNITY** to provide a community or organization with something that it needs ○ *The electric company services all nine counties.* **3 PAY INTEREST ON DEBT** to pay interest on a debt **4 COPULATE WITH FEMALE** of a male animal, to copulate with a female ■ *adj* **1 USED BY EMPLOYEES OR FOR DELIVERIES** intended for employees or deliveries rather than for members of the public (*often before nouns*) ○ *a service elevator* **2 PROVIDING A SERVICE NOT GOODS** relating to jobs or businesses such as banking and insurance that do something useful for people but that do not manufacture any goods **3 FOR MAINTENANCE AND REPAIR** providing maintenance and repair for manufactured products [Pre-12C. Via French < Latin *servitium* 'servitude' < *servus* 'slave'.] —**servicer** *n*

service[2] /súrviss/ *n* TREES = **service tree** [Mid-16C. Plural of obsolete 'serve' < Latin *sorbus* 'service tree'.]

serviceable /súrvissəb'l/ *adj* **1 MADE TO WEAR WELL** suitable for everyday use and hard wear **2 WORKING** in working condition **3 EFFECTIVE** useful or effective —**serviceableness** *n* —**serviceably** *adv*

service area *n* **1** a place beside a motorway where there are facilities for travellers such as a restaurant, toilets, and a service station **2** the area over which a radio or television broadcasting station can transmit a satisfactory signal for reception

serviceberry /súrviss berri/ (*plural* **-ries**) *n* **1 PLANT WITH SMALL EDIBLE BERRIES** a commonly cultivated small tree or shrub that produces small dark blue fruits. Flowers: white in clusters. Native to: North America. Genus: *Amelanchier.* **2 ROUND FRUIT** the round fruit of the serviceberry **3 FRUIT OF SERVICE TREE** the fruit of the service tree [< SERVICE[2]]

service book *n* a book containing the correct forms of worship authorized for use in a church

service break *n* a game won by a player in a racket game when an opponent was serving

service centre *n* **1** a garage that sells parts and carries out repairs on motor vehicles **2** a retail store that provides repairs and parts for the items it sells

service charge *n* **1 MONEY ADDED TO BILL FOR SERVICE** a sum of money, usually calculated as a percentage of a customer's bill, added to the bill in a restaurant or hotel to pay the staff for their service **2 CHARGE FOR CARRYING BALANCE** a fee added to the balance of a bill when it is paid in instalments rather than being paid in one lump sum **3 MONEY CHARGED FOR PERFORMING SERVICE** a sum of money charged by a business or bank for handling a transaction

service contract *n* **1** a contract between a company and a senior employee such as a director or senior executive **2** a contract with a company or manufacturer to maintain equipment in working order at an agreed price over a fixed period

service court *n* in racket games, the area within which a served ball or shuttlecock must land

service dog *n US* a dog that has been specially trained to assist people with disabilities

service flat *n* a flat in which some domestic services, e.g. cleaning and laundry, and sometimes also meals, are provided by the management

service industry *n* an industry that provides a service rather than goods, or such industries as a whole

service line *n* in racket games and volleyball, a line on a court that the server must not cross before serving

serviceman /súrvissmən/ (*plural* **-men** /-mən/) *n* **1** a man serving in the armed forces **2 serviceman, service man** a man whose job is repairing and servicing equipment

service mark *n* a sign or symbol used by people or companies who provide a particular service to identify themselves and set them apart from other companies

service module *n* the section of an Apollo spacecraft in which elements of the propulsion and navigation systems are kept until the unit has re-entered the Earth's atmosphere and is jettisoned. ◊ **lunar module, command module**

serviceperson /súrviss purss'n/ (*plural* **-people** /-peep'l/ *or* **-persons**) *n* **1** somebody serving in the armed forces **2 serviceperson, service person** somebody whose job is maintaining and servicing equipment

ϟ**service provider** *n* **1** a company that makes money by providing individuals and other businesses with access to the Internet, usually charging a monthly fee **2** a company that makes money by providing specific services, e.g. health or life insurance

service road *n* a minor road that runs alongside a main road, giving access to houses, shops, offices, and other businesses

service station *n* a place where petrol, oil, and other requirements for motor vehicles can be bought, and that usually also provides other facilities for motorists such as toilets and a shop

service tree, service *n* a tree that has leaves consisting of numerous toothed leaflets and produces fruits sometimes used for cider-making. Native to: central and S Europe. *Sorbus domestica.*

servicewoman /súrviss wŏŏmən/ (*plural* **-en** /-wimmin/) *n* **1** a woman serving in the armed forces **2 servicewoman, service woman** a woman whose job is repairing and servicing equipment

serviette /súrvi étt/ *n* DOMESTIC = **napkin** *n.* 1 [15C. < French, < *servir* 'serve' (see SERVE).]

servile /súr vīl/ *adj* **1 TOO OBEDIENT** too willing to agree with somebody or to do whatever demeaning thing somebody wants **2 MENIAL** relating to work that is considered menial or degrading ○ *servile tasks* **3 RELATING TO SLAVERY** relating to slaves or the condition of slavery [14C. < Latin *servilis* < *servus* 'slave'.] —**servilely** *adv* —**servileness** *n* —**servility** /sur víllәti/ *n*

serving /súrving/ *n* an amount of food served to one person

serving dish *n* a large dish used to serve food at table, especially vegetables or rice

serving hatch *n* an opening in the wall between a kitchen and a dining area, through which food and dishes may be passed. US term **pass-through** *n.*

servitor /súrvitər/ *n* a servant or attendant (*archaic*) [14C. Via Old French < late Latin, < Latin *servire* 'serve' (see SERVE).]

servitude /súrvi tyood/ *n* **1 STATE OF SLAVERY** the state of being a slave **2 SUBJECTION** the state of being ruled or dominated by somebody or something **3 WORK IMPOSED AS PUNISHMENT** work imposed as a punishment for a crime **4 RESTRICTION OR OBLIGATION ON PROPERTY** a restriction or obligation attached to a property that entitles somebody other than the owner to a specified use of it, e.g. the right to cross it [15C. Via Old French < Latin *servitudo* < *servus* 'slave'.]

servo /súrvō/ *adj* relating to, forming part of, or activated by a servomechanism ■ *n* (*plural* **-vos**) **1** MECH ENG = **servomechanism 2** = **servomotor** [Late 19C. Shortening of French *servo-moteur* 'auxiliary motor' < Latin *servus* 'slave'.]

servomechanism /súrvō mekənizəm/ *n* a closed-circuit device in which a small input power controls a much larger power, as in a radio telescope —**servomechanical** /súrvō mi kánnik'l/ *adj*

servomotor /súrvō mōtər/ *n* a motor that supplies the initial power in a servomechanism

sesame /séssəmi/ (*plural* **-mes** *or* **-me**) *n* **1** the small oval white seeds of the sesame plant. Use: cooking, oil extraction. **2** an annual plant cultivated for its oil-rich seeds. Native to: tropical and subtropical Asia. *Sesamum indicum.* [15C. < Latin *sesamum* < Greek *sēsamon.*]

sesame oil *n* a strongly flavoured oil from sesame seeds, widely used in Asian and Southeast Asian cooking

sesamoid /séssə moyd/ *n* a small, roughly spherical bone lying within a tendon to assist in its mechanical action or to bear pressure ■ *adj* relating to or being various small bones or cartilages in a tendon or joint such as the knee [Late 17C. < SESAME.]

Sesotho /si sóotoo/ *n* the dialect of Sotho spoken by the Basotho people in Lesotho [Mid-19C. < Sesotho.] —**Sesotho** *adj*

sesqui- *prefix* one and a half ○ *sesquicentennial* [< Latin, < *semis* 'half' + *-que* 'and']

sesquicentennial /séskwi sen ténni əl/, **sesquicentenary** /séskwi sen teénəri, -ténnəri/ *n* (*plural* **-ies**) **1 150TH ANNIVERSARY** a 150th anniversary or the celebration of one **2 150 YEARS** a period of 150 years ■ *adj* **OCCURRING EVERY 150 YEARS** relating to or happening after a period of 150 years —**sesquicentennially** *adv*

sesquipedalian /séskwi pi dáyli ən/, **sesquipedal** /se skwíppid'l/ *adj* (*literary*) **1 USING LONG WORDS** characterized by the use of long words **2 LONG** relating to a long word ■ *n* **LONG WORD** a word with many letters or syllables (*literary*) [Early 17C. < Latin *sesquipedalis* 'measuring one and one-half feet' < *ped-* 'foot'.] —**sesquipedalianism** *n*

sessile /séssīl/ *adj* **1** describes a leaf or flower that has no stalk but is attached directly to the stem **2** describes an animal that is permanently attached to something rather than free-moving, e.g. a barnacle [Early 18C. < Latin *sessilis* 'lying close to the ground' < *sess-*, past participle of *sedere* 'sit'.] —**sessility** /sə sílləti/ *n*

sessile oak *n* TREES = **durmast oak**

session /sésh'n/ *n* **1 MEETING** a meeting of an official body, especially a court or legislature **2 PERIOD OF MEETING** a period during which an official body meets or does business **3 SERIES OF MEETINGS** a series of meetings of an official body **4 TEACHING PERIOD** the time of year or the time of day during which a school or university holds classes **5 PERIOD OF DOING** a period of time during which people are involved in doing something together **6 PERIOD OF PLAYING MUSIC** a period during which musicians play together, especially in a recording studio **7 GOVERNING BODY OF PRESBYTERIAN CONGREGATION** the governing body of a Presbyterian congregation, consisting of the minister and elders ■ **sessions** *npl* **SITTINGS OF JUSTICE OF PEACE** the sittings of a justice of the peace in court ■ *adj* **1 RELATING TO FREELANCE MUSICIAN** relating to or being a musician paid to play or sing on recordings in a studio but not a permanent member of a band **2 RELATING TO FREELANCE MUSIC** relating to playing or singing done by a session musician [14C. Via Old French < Latin *session-* 'a sitting' < *sess-* (see SESSILE).] —**sessional** *adj*

sesterce /sést urss/, **sestertius** /se stúrti əss, -stúrshəss/ (*plural* **-i** /-ti ī, -hi ī/) *n* an ancient Roman coin, originally silver but later bronze, worth a quarter of a denarius [Late 16C. < Latin *sestertius* 'two and one-half times as great' < *semis* 'half' + *tertius* 'third'.]

sestet /se stét/ *n* a stanza or poem of six lines, especially the last six lines of a Petrarchan sonnet [Early 19C. < Italian *sestetto* < *sesto* 'sixth' < Latin *sextus* 'sixth'.]

sestina /se steénə/ *n* a poem of six six-line stanzas and a three-line envoy, with the last words of the first six lines repeated, in different order, at the ends of the other lines [Mid-19C. < Italian, < *sesto* (see SESTET).]

Seswati /se swaáti/ *n* LANG = **Swazi** *n.* 2

set[1] /set/ *v* (**sets, setting, set**) **1** *vt* **PLACE** to put somebody or something somewhere ○ *Set the books on the table.* **2** *vt* **PUT SOMEBODY INTO CONDITION** to get or put somebody or something into a particular condition ○ *set the hostages free* **3** *vt* **MAKE SOMETHING HAPPEN** to cause something to happen ○ *set an unfortunate train of events in motion* **4** *vt* **FOCUS ON** to focus on a goal or task ○ *Set your mind to the task.* **5** *vt* **ARRANGE FOR USE** to arrange, place, or prepare something to be used ○ *set a trap for them* **6** *vti* **BECOME OR MAKE SOLID** to form or cause something to be formed in a solid state ○ *Let the concrete set.* **7** *vt* **ADJUST MEASURING DEVICE** to adjust a device such as a clock to a desired time, level, or position ○ *Remember to set the alarm.* **8** *vt* **DECIDE ON OR IMPOSE** to decide on a particular time or impose a rule as a condition for something ○ *We've set a date for the wedding.* **9** *vt* **BE EXAMPLE** to be an example of a type of behaviour ○ *tried to set an example for her younger siblings* **10** *vt* **DETERMINE PRICE OF** to determine or state the price of something ○ *set the price at £20* **11** *vt*

CONSIDER AS HAVING VALUE to consider something as having a particular value ○ *set a high value on his own work* **12** *vt* **DETERMINE COURSE** to determine a direction or course to travel ○ *set a course for home* **13** *vt* **ESTABLISH RECORD** to establish a record ○ *set a new 100-metre record* **14** *vt* **ASSIGN SOMETHING FOR STUDY** to assign something such as a book or subject to be studied **15** *vt* **ARRANGE HAIR** to arrange hair in a particular style by using styling products or clips **16** *vt* **PUT GEM IN SETTING** to put a gem or stone in a metal setting **17** *vt* **PUT BROKEN BONE IN POSITION** to put a broken bone back in its normal position so it can heal properly **18** *vi* **HEAL** to heal up and become solid after being broken (*refers to a bone*) **19** *vt* **PROVIDE MUSIC FOR** to provide the music for something such as lyrics or a poem ○ *set his words to music* **20** *vt* **ADORN** to adorn something with decorations ○ *set a gown with sequins* **21** *vt* **PORTRAY IN PARTICULAR SETTING** to portray something as happening in a particular place or time period (*usually passive*) ○ *The play is set in the 19th century.* **22** *vt* **PLACE SCENERY ON** to place scenery on stage **23** *vt* **ARRANGE TYPE** to arrange type for printing **24** *vti* **POSITION SAIL** to rig a sail to catch the wind, or to be rigged in this way **25** *vi* **GO BELOW HORIZON** to go below the horizon ○ *watched the sun set* **26** *vi* **FIT WELL OR POORLY** to fit in a particular way (*refers to clothes*) ○ *The skirt sets well.* **27** *vi* **START** to begin something, especially work ○ *set to work with a will* **28** *vi* **GET READY TO START RACE** to get into a position ready to start a race ○ *Ready, get set, go!* **29** *vi* **BECOME PERMANENT** to become permanent (*refers to a dye or colour*) **30** *vt* **LET DOUGH RISE** to place dough aside to allow it to rise **31** *vt* **SHARPEN** to sharpen a blade **32** *vt* **DISPLACE TEETH ON SAW** to bend the teeth of a saw alternately to either side of the blade **33** *vt* **DRIVE NAIL HEAD BELOW SURFACE** to drive the head of a nail below the surface **34** *vti* **PRODUCE FRUIT OR SEEDS** to produce fruit or seeds after being pollinated, or be produced in this way **35** *vt* **PLANT** to plant something **36** *vti* **SIT OR MAKE SIT ON EGGS** to put a hen on eggs to keep them warm, or to sit on eggs **37** *vti* **INDICATE GAME** to indicate the presence of game by turning towards it and holding that position **38** *vt* **BEAT IN BRIDGE** to prevent an opponent meeting the contract in bridge **39** *vi* **BECOME BENT** to become bent from strain **40** *vi* **END** to come to an end (*literary*) ■ *n* **1 CONDITION OF SOLIDITY** the condition of being solid **2 POSTURE** the posture or bearing of somebody or an animal **3 FIT OF CLOTHES** the way something hangs when worn **4 THEATRICAL SCENERY** scenery for a play or film or the place where this has been put up **5 WIDTH OF PIECE OF TYPE** the width of a piece of type **6 WIDTH OF LINE OF TYPE** the width of a column or a page of type **7 ARRANGEMENT OF SAILS** the way the sails and other rigging are arranged on a sailing boat **8 DIRECTION** the direction of a wind, tide, or current **9 PREFERENCE** a preference for or increased ability in a particular activity **10 BIAS INFLUENCING REACTION TO STIMULUS** the psychological state that causes an organism to react to a stimulus in a particular way **11 SEEDLING READY FOR PLANTING** a plant such as a seedling that is ready to be planted **12 DISTORTION DUE TO STRESS** a distortion or bending that occurs in metal as a result of stress **13 HAIRSTYLE** a way of styling the hair **14 CLUTCH** the number of eggs that a hen lays at one time **15** CIV ENG, ZOOL, TEXTILES = **sett** ■ *adj* **1 ESTABLISHED** previously established such as by tradition, agreement, or authority **2 INFLEXIBLE** being rigid and unwilling to change, especially in the way of doing things ○ *Living alone he's become more set in his ways.* **3 READY** prepared for somebody or something, or to do something ○ *We're all set to go.* **4 STEREOTYPED** conforming to an established often conventional formula ○ *a set speech* **5 DETERMINED** determined to do something ○ *We're set on the idea and won't consider changing.* **6 ASSIGNED TO STUDY** assigned for students to study ○ *a set text* [Old English *settan* 'cause to sit' < Germanic, 'sit']

set about *vt* **1** to begin doing something **2** to attack somebody

set against *vt* **1** to consider one thing in relation to another, especially when the other thing is very important **2** to make people or groups start to fight with or be hostile to people they used to be friendly with

set apart *vt* **1** to keep something for a specific use or purpose **2** to make somebody conspicuous or different ○ *Her knowledge sets her apart.*

set aside *vt* **1 RESERVE** to keep something, especially time or money, for a particular purpose **2 PUT TO ONE SIDE** to put something to one side **3 REJECT PREVIOUS DECISION** to discard, reject, or annul a previous decision or judgment

set back *vt* **1** to block or delay the progress of something or somebody **2** to cost somebody a lot of money (*informal*)

set down *vt* **1 PUT DOWN** to put something down on a surface **2 WRITE DOWN** to write something down **3 JUDGE** to judge somebody or something as being something specified ○ *set the whole thing down as a failure* **4 ATTRIBUTE** to attribute an event or quality to something specified ○ *set his mistake down to inexperience* **5 LET SOMEBODY GET OFF** to allow a passenger in a vehicle to get off at a specific place **6 SCOLD** to snub or rebuke somebody **7 LAND AIRCRAFT** to land an aircraft

set forth *v* **1** *vi* to leave on a journey (*literary*) **2** *vt* to state or present an argument or a set of figures in speech or writing (*formal*)

set in *v* **1** *vi* **BEGIN** to begin and become established ○ *once the winter snows set in* **2** *vi* **MOVE SHOREWARDS** to move in a shorewards direction (*refers to a wind, tide, or current*) **3** *vt* **ADD ON** to add a separately made part to a garment

set off *v* **1** *vi* **START OUT ON TRIP** to start out on a journey **2** *vt* **MAKE SOMETHING WORK** to make something such as an alarm or fireworks operate or explode **3** *vt* **MAKE SOMEBODY START DOING SOMETHING** to make somebody start doing something such as laughing, crying, or talking about something ○ *When she started crying it set us all off too.* **4** *vt* **START** to make something start happening ○ *set off a chain of events that eventually led to war* **5** *vt* **MAKE SOMETHING LOOK ATTRACTIVE** to provide a contrast to something in a way that makes it look more attractive ○ *The new frame really sets off the painting.* **6** *vt* **COUNTERBALANCE CREDIT** to counterbalance a credit in the accounts of one person or organization against a debit in those of another

set on *vt* **1** to attack somebody or encourage a person or animal to attack somebody or something **2** to encourage somebody to do something

set out *v* **1** *vi* **BEGIN JOURNEY** to begin something, especially a journey **2** *vi* **INTENTIONALLY START DOING SOMETHING** intentionally to start doing something or planning to do something ○ *set out to ruin the performance* **3** *vt* **DISPLAY** to arrange, display, or decorate something ○ *merchants setting out their wares* **4** *vt* **LAY OUT** to lay out something in a planned way ○ *The gardens are beautifully set out.* **5** *vt* **PRESENT** to present or explain something, especially in a full way ○ *a book that clearly sets out the author's philosophy*

set to *vi* **1** to start doing something, especially work **2** to start fighting

set up *v* **1** *vt* **ERECT** to erect something or put something in an upright or usable position ○ *set up road blocks* **2** *vti* **PREPARE EQUIPMENT FOR EVENT** to prepare the equipment needed for an event ○ *The band is setting up on stage.* **3** *vt* **PUT IN POSITION OF POWER** to put a person or group in a position of power **4** *vt* **ORGANIZE** to arrange, establish, or bring about something ○ *I've set up a meeting for next week.* **5** *vti* **CLAIM TO BE** to claim to be something, especially an expert or authority on something ○ *set herself up as an expert* **6** *vti* **START BUSINESS** to start a business or give somebody everything needed to start a business ○ *His family set him up in business.* **7** *vt* **MAKE HEALTHY** to make somebody feel healthy or invigorated, especially after having been ill **8** *vt* **PRODUCE** to produce or create something ○ *The spectators set up a howl of protest.* **9** *vt* **CAUSE TO BE BLAMED** to cause somebody to be caught and blamed for something (*informal*) ○ *claims he was set up* **10** *vt* **GIVE DRINKS** to buy or provide an alcoholic beverage for somebody (*informal*) **11** *vt* **PLAN** to make necessary arrangements for something, e.g. a meeting or conference **12** *vt* **PROPOSE** to put an idea, theory, or proposal to a group for consideration

set upon *vt* to attack somebody violently

set[2] /set/ *n* **1 COLLECTION CONSIDERED AS UNIT** a collection of people or things considered together and usually having something in common **2 SOCIAL GROUP** a group of people who form a social group ○ *They were the first in our set to have kids.* **3 DEVICE RECEIVING SIGNALS** a device that receives radio or television signals **4 PART OF TENNIS MATCH** a part of a tennis match that is won when one player or couple wins a minimum of six games **5 PREFERENCE** a preference for or increased ability in a particular activity **6 SONGS PLAYED IN ONE SESSION** a number of songs or acts that an entertainer or band performs on a single occasion **7 NUMBER OF REPETITIONS OF EXERCISE** a number of repetitions of an exercise done at one time **8 COLLECTION OF ELEMENTS** a collection of elements in mathematics or logic, e.g. numbers or terms **9 COUPLES REQUIRED FOR DANCE** a number of couples required for certain dances ○ *We need another couple to complete our set.* ■ *vi* (**sets, setting, set**) **DANCE FACING PARTNER** to perform a series of moves while facing another dancer [14C. Via Old French *sette* < Latin *secta* (see SECT).]

seta /séetə/ (*plural* **-tae** /-tee/) *n* a slender, usually rigid bristle or hair [Late 18C. < Latin, 'bristle'.] —**setal** *adj*

setaceous /si táyshəss/ *adj* **1** having bristles or made up of bristles **2** having the appearance or feel of bristles (*formal*) [Mid-17C. < modern Latin *setaceus* < Latin *seta* 'bristle'.]

set-aside *n* a European Union scheme whereby farmers are paid not to produce crops on particular areas of land as a way of reducing surpluses or controlling prices

setback /sét bak/ *n* **1** something that reverses or delays the progress of somebody or something **2** a place in the wall of a building where there is a shelf or recess

se tenant /sə tə naáN/ *adj* describes two stamps that are joined together but have different values or designs ■ *n* a pair of stamps that are joined together but have different values or designs [Early 20C. < French, 'holding together'.]

SETI /sétti/ *n* a scientific attempt to detect or communicate with intelligent beings from beyond Earth, especially using radio signals. Full form **Search for Extraterrestrial Intelligence**

setiferous /sə tíffərəss/ *adj* describes a living organism that has bristles or projections that resemble bristles [Early 19C. < SETA + -FEROUS.]

set-in *adj* describes a part of a garment that is made separately and stitched in

setline /sét līn/ *n* a fishing line suspended over a stream or between buoys with shorter hooked and baited lines hanging down from it into the water

set-off *n* **1 COUNTERBALANCE** something that compensates for something else **2 SOMETHING IMPROVING APPEARANCE** something that contrasts with something else in a way that improves its appearance **3** ARCHIT = **setback** *n.* **2** **4** PRINTING = **offset** *n.* **6** **5 COUNTERBALANCING CLAIM** a claim brought by a debtor against a creditor that counterbalances the debt owed

Seton /séet'n/, **Ernest Thompson** (1860–1946) British-born US writer and illustrator. Born **Ernest Seton-Thompson**

setose /séetōss/ *adj* covered with bristles [Mid-17C. < Latin *setosus* < *seta* 'bristle'.]

set phrase *n* a phrase whose elements do not vary and whose meaning is different from the literal combination of its elements, e.g. 'the apple of somebody's eye' or 'make waves'

set piece *n* **1 PLANNED ACTION** a carefully planned and rehearsed performance or action, especially a military or diplomatic operation **2 FORMAL WORK OF ART** a work of art with a formal theme, undertaken to show the artist's skill **3 PLANNED MANOEUVRE** a planned manoeuvre used by a team in a game, e.g. the way a soccer team takes a corner or free kick (*hyphenated before nouns*) **4 PIECE OF SCENERY** a piece of stage scenery that can stand unsupported **5 FIXED FIREWORKS IN DISPLAY** a fixed arrangement of fireworks in a display

set point *n* **1** a time in a tennis match when a player can win a set by winning the next point, or the point itself **2** the natural weight that somebody's body will assume if provided with a balanced diet

setscrew /sét skroo/ *n* a screw that fixes one part of a mechanism to another and prevents it moving relative to the part to which it is fixed

set square *n* a flat metal or plastic instrument in the shape of a right-angled triangle, used in technical drawing. US term **triangle** *n.* **3**

Setswana /set swaánə/ *n* the Bantu language of the Tswana people of southern Africa, belonging to the Sotho group. Native speakers: 3 million. [Early 19C. < Setswana.] —**Setswana** *adj*

sett, set *n* **1 PAVING STONE** a rectangular stone paving block **2 BADGER'S BURROW** the burrow of a badger **3 TARTAN PATTERN** the precise pattern of squares and stripes in a tartan, with particular colours and numbers of threads **4 SQUARE OF TARTAN** an individual square in a tartan pattern [Variant of SET[1]]

settee /se teé, sə-/ *n* **1** a comfortable seat for two or more people, with a cushioned back and arms **2** *US* a long wooden bench with a back [Early 18C. < ?]

setter /séttər/ *n* **1** a long-haired gun dog belonging to various breeds that is trained to crouch in a set position when it finds game **2** somebody or something that sets something

set theory *n* **1** the branch of mathematics that deals with the properties and relationships of sets **2** the system of axioms for sets

setting /sétting/ *n* **1 SURROUNDINGS** the surroundings or environment in which something exists **2 PERIOD OR PLACE OF STORY** the period in time or the place in which the events of a story take place **3 SET FOR PERFORMANCE** the set, including props and scenery, where actors perform for a film or play **4 MUSIC FOR POEM** the music composed for a particular text, e.g. a poem or hymn **5 SURROUNDINGS OF JEWEL** the metal fixture into which a jewel is fixed **6 LEVEL ON SCALE** a chosen point or level in the operation of a machine **7 CUTLERY** the cutlery, napkin, table mat, and any other items placed on a table to be used by one person during a meal **8 CLUTCH OF EGGS** a batch of eggs in a bird's nest, especially a hen's

setting circle *n* a scale on the mounting of an equatorial telescope, used to show right ascension or declination

settle /sétt'l/ *v* (**-tles, -tling, -tled**) **1** *vti* **MAKE SOMEBODY COMFORTABLE** to make somebody feel comfortable in a particular position **2** *vt* **PUT IN PLACE** to put something in a place firmly or permanently **3** *vi* **STOP MOVING** to stop moving and come to rest somewhere **4** *vi* **MOVE DOWNWARDS** to move downwards and spread over something ○ *A blanket of mist settled over the field.* **5** *vi* **SINK INTO GROUND** to sink slowly to a lower level **6** *vti* **SOLVE** to solve a problem or end a dispute **7** *vti* **DECIDE ON** to decide on something so that other arrangements can be made ○ *That's settled then.* ○ *Can we settle on a date for the meeting first?* **8** *vti* **PAY** to pay a bill, debt, or claim ○ *We're waiting for a couple of major clients to settle up.* **9** *vt* **PUT IN ORDER** to put all the details of a piece of business in order or into a desired arrangement **10** *vti* **MAKE OR BECOME CALM** to become or cause somebody or something to become calm, quiet, or stable **11** *vti* **MAKE OR BECOME RESIDENT** to become or cause somebody to become a resident of a place **12** *vt* **COLONIZE** to populate an area with permanent residents **13** *vti* **ESTABLISH OR BECOME ESTABLISHED** to establish somebody or become established in a place, occupation, or way of life **14** *vti* **STOP FLOATING** to stop floating and sink to the bottom or the ground, or to cause something to do this ○ *waited for the dust to settle before opening their eyes* **15** *vti* **MAKE OR BECOME CLEAR** to cause a cloudy liquid to become clear after a sediment has sunk to the bottom, or to become clear in this way **16** *vti* **END LEGAL DISPUTE** to end a legal dispute by mutual agreement out of court **17** *vt* **ASSIGN PROPERTY** to give something, especially property or money, to somebody legally and formally ○ *settled her with a substantial inheritance* **18** *vti* **GET REVENGE** to get revenge on somebody for an injury or offence **19** *vi* **CONCEIVE** of an animal, to become pregnant ■ *n* **LONG WOODEN SEAT WITH HIGH BACK** a long wooden seat with a high back, and often with storage space inside the box-shaped seat [Old English *setlan* < *setl* 'chair, bench'. Ultimately < Indo-European, 'sit'.] —**settleable** *adj*

settle down *v* **1** *vti* **MAKE OR BECOME CALM** to become or cause somebody or something to become calm, quiet, or orderly **2** *vi* **LIVE ORDERLY LIFE** to begin a stable, orderly, and often conventional way of life **3** *vi* **DO SOMETHING DILIGENTLY** to begin doing something in a diligent and orderly way ○ *settled down to her morning's work*

settle for *vt* to accept or agree to something that is not ideal or exactly what was wanted

settle in *v* **1** *vti* to adapt or cause somebody to adapt to a new environment ○ *settling in at a new school* **2** *vi* to get comfortable in a place because the intention is to stay there for a long time ○ *decided to settle in for the night*

settlement /sétt'lmənt/ *n* **1 SETTLING** an act of settling or the state of being settled **2 AGREEMENT** an agreement reached after discussion or negotiation **3 AGREEMENT OUT OF COURT** an agreement reached without completing legal proceedings **4 PAYMENT** the payment of a bill, debt, or claim **5 COLONY** a place that has recently been populated with permanent residents **6 SMALL COMMUNITY** a small community **7 POPULATING** the act of populating a place with permanent residents **8 SUBSIDENCE** subsidence in a building **9 WELFARE SERVICES BUILDING** a public building in which social workers provide welfare services in a deprived area **10 SETTLING OF PROPERTY ON** a conveyance of property to a person or trustees for somebody **11 CONVEYANCE DOCUMENT** a document recording a conveyance of property

settler /séttlər/ *n* a new resident of a place, especially a place that is unpopulated or populated by people of a different race or civilization

settlings /séttlings/ *npl* solid material that has sunk to the bottom of a liquid

settlor /séttlər/ *n* a creator of a trust or settlement

set-to (*plural* **set-tos**) *n* a brief and hot-tempered argument or fight (*informal*)

set-top box *n* a device used with a traditional television set to enable the reception and decoding of satellite, cable, or digital signals

Setúbal /se tŏŏb'l/ port in W Portugal. Population: 83,550 (1991).

setup /sét up/ *n* **1 ORGANIZATION** the way that something is organized or arranged **2 SET OF PREPARED OBJECTS FOR TASK** an assembly of prepared tools or apparatus required for performing a task **3 DISHONEST PLAN OR TRICK** something that is planned to bring about a desired result dishonestly (*informal*) **4 POSITION OF CAMERA FOR SCENE** the position of a camera at the beginning of a film scene **5** *US* **TABLE SETTING** a table setting for a single person

set width *n* PRINTING = **set**[1] *n.* **5**, **set**[1] *n.* **6**

Seurat /súr aa, sör a/, **Georges** (1859–91) French painter

Seuss /syooss/, **Dr** (1904–91) US writer and illustrator. Pseudonym of **Theodor Seuss Geisel**

Sevan, Lake /se vaán/ largest lake in Armenia, in the north of the country. Area: 1,397 sq. km/540 sq. mi.

Sevastopol = **Sebastopol**

seven /sévv'n/ *n* **1** see table at **number 2** a fast and open form of rugby played by teams of seven players (+ *singular verb*) [Old English *seofon*. Ultimately < Indo-European, 'seven'.] —**seven** *adj, pron*

seven deadly sins *npl* CHR = **deadly sins**

sevenfold /sévv'n fōld/ *adj* **1 BEING SEVEN TIMES AS MUCH** relating to something that is seven times as much as something else **2 CONSISTING OF SEVEN PARTS** relating to something that is made up of seven parts ■ *adv* **BY SEVEN TIMES** by seven times as much or as many [Old English]

seven seas *npl* all the oceans of the world

Seven Sisters *n* ASTRON, MYTHOL = **Pleiades**

seventeen /sévv'n teén/ *n* see table at **number** [Old English *seofontīene* < *seofon* 'seven' + - *tīene* 'ten more than']

seventeenth /sévv'n teénth/ *n* see table at **number** [Old English] —**seventeenth** *adj, adv*

seventh /sévv'nth/ *n* **1** see table at **number 2** MUSIC = **seventh chord 3** in a standard musical scale, the interval between one note and another that lies six notes above or below it **4** in a standard musical scale, a note that is a seventh away from another note [Old English] —**seventh** *adj, adv* —**seventhly** *adv*

seventh chord *n* a chord with a seventh note above the base note

Seventh-Day Adventist *n* a member of a Protestant denomination that believes in the imminent Second Coming of Jesus Christ and observes Saturday as the Sabbath

seventh heaven *n* **1** a state of extreme happiness **2** the highest of the seven heavens in Islamic and Talmudic belief

seventieth /sévv'nti əth/ *n* see table at **number** —**seventieth** *adj, adv*

seventy /sévv'nti/ *n* (*plural* **-ties**) see table at **number** ■ **seventies** *npl* the years from 70 to 79 in a century or somebody's life [Old English *hundseofontig* < *hund* (< ?) + *seofon* 'seven' + *-tig* 'ten'] —**seventy** *adj, pron*

seventy-eight, 78 *n* a gramophone record designed to be played at 78 revolutions per minute, a former standard speed

seventy four *n* either of two large, colourfully striped sea fish related to the sea bream. Native to: South Africa. *Polysteganus undulosus*. [< ?]

seven-up *n* a card game in which the first person to reach seven points wins the game

seven-year itch *n* an inclination towards sexual infidelity, popularly believed to begin after seven years of marriage (*informal*)

Seven Years' War *n* a war fought from 1756 to 1763 by Prussia, assisted by British subsidies and Hanoverian troops, against France and Austria

sever /sévvər/ *vti* **1 CUT THROUGH OR OFF** to cut through something or cut off, or be cut through or off **2 SEPARATE** to separate or put things or people apart, or to become separated or put apart **3 BREAK OFF TIE** to break off a tie, or to become broken off ○ *severed her relationship with him* [14C. Via Anglo-Norman *severer* < Latin *separare* (see SEPARATE).] —**severability** *n* —**severable** *adj*

several /sévvərəl/ CORE MEANING: a grammatical word indicating a small number ○ (det) *I sent the cheque several days ago.* ○ (pron) *Several of the apples were bruised.* *adj* **1** various or separate ○ *They all went their several ways.* **2** relating to separate individuals ○ *joint and several liability* [15C. Via Anglo-Norman < medieval Latin *separalis*, < Latin *separare* (see SEPARATE).]

severalfold /sévvərəl fōld/ *adj* **1 BEING SEVERAL TIMES AS MUCH** relating to something that is several times as much as something else **2 CONSISTING OF SEVERAL PARTS** relating to something that is made up of several parts ■ *adv* **BY SEVERAL TIMES** by several times as much or as many

severally /sévvrəli/ *adv* (*formal or literary*) **1** in a separate or individual way **2** in turn or respectively

severance /sévvərənss/ *n* **1** an act of severing or the state of being severed **2** BUSINESS = **severance pay 3** the splitting into separate parts of something held jointly, e.g. an estate

severance pay, severance *n* money paid as compensation, on the basis of length of service, to an employee whose job ceases to exist

severe /si veér/ *adj* **1 HARSH** very harsh or strict **2 STERN** looking stern or serious **3 DANGEROUS** extremely bad or dangerous ○ *severe injuries* **4 EXTREMELY UNPLEASANT** causing great discomfort by being extreme ○ *a severe frost* **5 DIFFICULT TO ENDURE** difficult to do or endure ○ *severe hardship* **6 EXACTING** having standards or other criteria that are difficult to meet ○ *a severe test* **7 PLAIN** plain or austere in style, with little or no decoration ○ *severe clothing* [Mid-16C. < Latin *severus* 'serious' < ?] —**severely** *adv* —**severeness** *n*

Severini /sevə reéni/, **Gino** (1883–1966) Italian artist

severity /si vérrəti/ *n* **1 STATE OR EXTENT OF BADNESS** the state of being very bad, or the extent to which something is bad **2 STRICTNESS OR STERNNESS** the state of being very strict or stern **3 PLAINNESS** the plainness or austerity of something such as a building or style of dress **4** (*plural* **-ties**) **HARSH ACT OR CRITICISM** an instance of harsh treatment or censure

Severn /sévvurn/ **1** longest river in Britain, rising in Wales and flowing through W England to the Bristol Channel. Length: 354 km/220 mi. **2** river in NW Ontario, Canada, flowing northeastwards into Hudson Bay. Length: 982 km/610 mi.

Severus /si veérəss/, **Lucius Septimus** (146–211) North African-born Roman emperor (193–211)

Seveso /se váyssō/ town in N Italy, scene of an industrial accident in 1976 involving poisonous gas

seviche *n* FOOD = **ceviche**

Seville /sə víl/ capital of Sevilla Province and the autonomous region of Andalusia, SW Spain. Population: 719,590 (1995).

Seville orange *n* US term **bitter orange 1** a bitter orange often used to make marmalade **2** an orange tree cultivated to produce Seville oranges. Native to: tropical and subtropical regions. *Citrus aurantium*. [Late 16C. After SEVILLE.]

~~**sevral**~~ incorrect spelling of **several**

Sèvres /sévvrə/ *n* a highly decorated French porcelain

sew /sō/ (**sews, sewing, sewed, sewn** /sōn/ *or* **sewed**) *vti* to join things or repair or make something by using a needle to pass thread repeatedly through material [Old English *siowan*. Ultimately < Indo-European.] —**sewable** *adj*

SPELLCHECK Do not confuse ***sew*** with ***so*** or ***sow***, which may sound similar. Beware: your spellchecker will not catch this error.

sew up *vt* to finish a business or plan successfully

sewage /sŏŏ ij, syŏŏ-/ *n* human and domestic waste matter from buildings, especially houses, that is carried away through sewers [Mid-19C. < SEWER[1].]

sewage farm *n* a place where sewage is treated to make it nontoxic, and especially to make it into manure. US term **sewage plant**

sewage plant *n US* = **sewage farm**

Sewell /syŏŏ əl, sŏŏ-/, **Anna** (1820–78) British writer

Sewell /sŏŏ əl/, **Henry** (1807–79) British-born New Zealand statesman

sewellel /sə wéllel/ *n* ZOOL = **mountain beaver** [Early 19C. < Chinook *šwalál* 'robe made of sewellel skin'.]

sewer[1] /sŏŏ ər, syŏŏ-/ *n* a pipe or drain, usually underground, that carries away waste or rainwater ■ *vt* to provide a place with sewers [15C. Via Anglo-Norman *sever* < Vulgar Latin *exaquare* 'remove water' < Latin *ex-* 'out' + *aqua* 'water'.]

sewer[2] /sŏŏ ər, syŏŏ-/ *n* a medieval servant who served meals [14C. < Anglo-Norman *asseour* < French *asseoir* 'place a seat for' < Latin *sedere* 'sit'.]

sewer[3] /sō ər/ *n* somebody or something that sews

sewerage /sŏŏ ərij, syŏŏ-/ *n* **1** a system of sewers **2** the removal of waste by means of sewers **3** INDUST = **sewage**

sewin /syŏŏ in/ (*plural* **-ins** *or* **-in**), **sewen** (*plural* **-ens** *or* **-en**) *n Wales, Ireland* a sea trout [Mid-16C. < ?]

sewing /sō ing/ *n* **1** the act or work of using a needle and thread to join or repair material **2** a piece of material that somebody is sewing

sewing machine *n* a machine for sewing material

sewn past participle of **sew**

sex /seks/ *n* **1 MALE OR FEMALE GENDER** either of the two reproductive categories, male or female, of animals and plants **2 INTERCOURSE** sexual intercourse **3 SEXUAL BEHAVIOUR** sexual activity or behaviour leading to it **4 GENITALS** the genitals (*literary*) **5 REPRODUCTIVE CHARACTERISTICS** the set of characteristics that determine whether the reproductive role of an animal or plant is male or female ■ *adj* **OF SEX** relating to sexual matters or the sexes ■ *vt* **DETERMINE SEX OF** to determine the sex of an animal or plant [14C. Via French *sexe* or directly < Latin *sexus*.]

USAGE See *gender*.

sex- *prefix* six ○ *sexangular* [< Latin *sex* < Indo-European]

sexagenarian /séksəjə náiri ən/, **sexagenary** /sek sájjinəri/ *n* somebody aged between 60 and 69 —**sexagenarian** *adj*

Sexagesima /séksə jéssimə/ *n* in the Christian calendar, the second Sunday before Lent, eight weeks before Easter [14C. < ecclesiastical Latin, < Latin *sexagesimus* (see SEXAGESIMAL).]

sexagesimal /séksə jéssim'l/ *adj* relating to or based on the number 60 ■ *n* a fraction in which the denominator is a power of 60 [Late 17C. < Latin *sexagesimus* 'sixtieth' < *sexaginta* 'sixty'.]

sex appeal *n* the quality of being sexually attractive

sexavalent /séksə váylənt/ *adj* CHEM = **hexavalent**

sex cell *n* GENETICS = **gamete**

sexcentenary /sék sen teénəri/ *adj* **1 OF 600** relating to the number 600 or a period of 600 years **2 OF 600TH ANNIVERSARY** relating to a 600th anniversary ■ *n* (*plural* **-ies**) **600TH ANNIVERSARY** a 600th anniversary or the celebration of one

sex change *n* an operation with accompanying hormonal treatment that changes somebody's physical characteristics from those of one sex to the other

sex chromatin *n* GENETICS = **Barr body**

sex chromosome *n* a chromosome that determines the sex of an organism, such as the X and Y chromosomes in humans and other mammals

sexduction /seks dúksh'n/ *n* the transfer of a fragment of chromosome from one bacterial cell to another by its incorporation into a special DNA particle (**plasmid**) that initiates sexual conjugation between the cells [Mid-20C. Blend of SEX + TRANSDUCTION.]

sexed /sekst/ *adj* **1** having a particular degree of interest in sex ○ *highly sexed* **2** possessing sexual characteristics

sexennial /sek sénni əl/ *adj* happening every six years or over a period of six years ■ *n* something that happens every six years or over a period of six years [Mid-17C. < Latin *sexennium* 'period of six years' < *sex* 'six' + *annus* 'year'.] —**sexennially** *adv*

sex factor *n* a genetic element found in certain bacteria that enables the cell to put out a fine tube to another bacterial cell and transfer some of its genetic material

sex gland *n* ANAT = **gonad**

sex hormone *n* a hormone that affects the development of the reproductive organs and sexual characteristics

sexism /séksizəm/ *n* **1** discrimination against women or men because of their sex **2** the tendency to treat people as cultural stereotypes of their sex

sexist /séksist/ *adj* **1 BELIEVING ONE SEX IS INFERIOR** believing that one sex is inferior to the other in a variety of attributes **2 RESULTING FROM SEXIST BELIEF** resulting from or relating to the belief that one sex is inferior to the other in a variety of attributes ■ *n* **SOMEBODY WHO IS SEXIST** somebody who believes that one sex is weaker or inferior to another

sexivalent /séksi váylənt/ *adj* CHEM = **hexavalent**

sex kitten *n* an offensive term for a young woman perceived as sexually appealing

sexless /séksləss/ *adj* **1 NOT SEXY** sexually unattractive **2 WITHOUT SEXUAL ACTIVITY** living without sexual intercourse or interest in sex **3 WITHOUT SEXUAL CHARACTERISTICS** describes an animal or plant that has no, or no obvious, sexual characteristics —**sexlessly** *adv* —**sexlessness** *n*

sex-limited *adj* describes genetically inherited traits or conditions that appear in one sex only, although the genes themselves may be found in either sex

sex-linked *adj* relating to a gene located on a sex chromosome, typically the X chromosome, or inheritance determined by such a gene —**sex-linkage** *n*

sex object *n* somebody treated or seen as worthy of notice because of characteristics perceived as sexually appealing

sex offender *n* a committer of a crime involving a sexual act

sexology /sek sólləji/ *n* the study of human sexual behaviour —**sexological** /séksə lójjik'l/ *adj* —**sexologist** *n*

sexpartite /seks paár tīt/ *adj* **1** divided into or made up of six parts ○ *a sexpartite vault* **2** involving six participants [Mid-18C. < SEX- + PARTITE.]

sexploitation /séks ploy táysh'n/ *n* the deliberate use of sexual material to make a product, especially a film, commercially successful [Mid-20C. Blend of SEX + EXPLOITATION.]

sexpot /séks pot/ *n* an offensive term for a woman who appears to radiate sexuality

sex role *n* a set of behaviours characteristic of or expected of members of one sex or the other

sex-starved *adj* lacking sexual activity even though it is desired

sex symbol *n* somebody such as a film star whose fame is linked to a widely perceived sex appeal

sext /sekst/ *n* in Christianity, especially Roman Catholicism, the fourth of the seven canonical hours of the divine office, or the prayers said then [14C. < Latin *sexta (hora)* 'sixth (hour)'.]

Sextans /sékstənz/ *n* a faint constellation near the celestial equator. See illustration at **constellation**

sextant /sékstənt/ *n* a navigational instrument incorporating a telescope and an angular scale that is used to work out latitude and longitude [Late 16C. < Latin *sextant-* 'sixth part (of a circle)' (from the arc on which the scale is marked) < *sextus* 'sixth'.]

sextet /sek stét/, **sextette** *n* **1** a group of six musicians or singers, or a piece of music composed for them **2** any group of six people or things [Mid-19C. Alteration of SESTET under the influence of Latin *sex* 'six'.]

sex therapy *n* the treatment of sexual problems through counselling and psychotherapy —**sex therapist** *n*

sextile /séks tīl/ *n* **1 STATISTICAL DIVISION** any of the six equal groups into which a statistical sample can be divided **2 STATISTICAL VALUE** any of the five statistical values that divide a frequency distribution into six parts, with each containing a sixth of the sample population **3 ANGLE BETWEEN PLANETS** a position of two celestial bodies in which they are 60° apart as viewed from the Earth [Mid-16C. < Latin *sextilis* < *sextus* 'sixth'.] —**sextile** *adj*

sextillion /seks tílli ən/ (*plural* **-lions** *or* **-lion**) *n* **1** the number equal to 10^{21}, written as 1 followed by 21 zeros **2** the number equal to 10^{36}, written as 1 followed by 36 zeros (*dated*) [Late 17C. < French, < Latin *sex* 'six', after *million*.] —**sextillion** *adj, pron* —**sextillionth** *n, adj*

sextodecimo /séksto déssimō/ (*plural* **-mos**) *n* a size of book page obtained by folding a sheet of paper into 16 leaves, producing 32 pages [Mid-17C. < Latin *sexto decimo*, form of *sextus decimus* 'sixteenth'.]

sexton /sékstən/ *n* **1** the caretaker of a church and its graveyard whose duties often include ringing the bell and digging graves **2 sexton, sexton beetle** a beetle that buries the bodies of dead small animals such as mice by digging beneath them, using the bodies as food for itself and its larvae. Genus: *Necrophorus*. [14C. Via Anglo-Norman *segerstein* < medieval Latin *sacristanus* (see SACRISTAN).]

sextuple /sékstyŏŏp'l, sekstyŏŏp'l/ *n* **NUMBER SIX TIMES ANOTHER** a number or quantity that is six times another number or quantity ■ *adj* **1 BEING SIX TIMES ANOTHER** relating to or being a number or quantity that is six times another number or quantity **2 CONSISTING OF SIX PARTS** made up of six parts or members **3 HAVING SIX BEATS TO BAR** describes a time or rhythm in which there are six beats to the bar ■ *vti* (**-ples, -pling, -pled**) **MULTIPLY BY SIX** to multiply something by six or be multiplied by six [Early 17C. < medieval Latin *sextuplus* < Latin *sex* 'six'.]

sextuplet /sékstyŏŏplət, seks tyŏŏplət/ *n* **1 ONE OF SIX OFFSPRING BORN TOGETHER** one of six offspring born in a single birth **2 GROUP OF SIX** a group of six things **3 GROUP OF SIX NOTES** in music, a group of six notes played in a time normally given to four [Mid-19C. < SEXTUPLE, after *triplet*.]

sextuplicate *n* /seks tyŏŏplikət/ **SET OF SIX COPIES** a set of six things, especially identical copies ■ *adj* /seks tyŏŏplikət/ **BEING SIX TIMES ANOTHER** relating to or being a number or quantity that is six times another number or quantity ■ *v* /seks tyŏŏpli kayt/ (**-cates, -cating, -cated**) **1** *vti* **MULTIPLY BY SIX** to multiply something by six or be multiplied by six **2** *vt* **MAKE SIX COPIES** to make six copies of something [Mid-17C. < medieval Latin *sextuplicat-*, past participle of *sextuplicare* 'increase sixfold' < *sextuplus* (see SEXTUPLE).]

sex-typed *adj* intended for or conventionally perceived as appropriate for one sex and not the other —**sex-typing** *n*

sexual /sékshoo əl/ *adj* **1 OF SEX** relating to sex, sexuality, or the sexual organs **2 RELATING TO EITHER SEX** relating to the two sexes or to either of them **3 INVOLVING REPRODUCTIVE UNION** relating to the union of male and female gametes in reproduction [Mid-17C. < late Latin *sexualis* < Latin *sexus* 'sex'.] —**sexually** *adv*

sexual assault *n* an incident that involves sexual contact that is forced on somebody or to which somebody cannot consent

sexual dimorphism *n* the existence of differences in the appearance of the male and female of a species

sexual harassment *n* unwanted sex-related behaviour towards somebody, e.g. touching somebody or making suggestive remarks, especially by somebody with authority to a subordinate

sexual intercourse *n* an act carried out for reproduction or pleasure involving penetration, especially one in which a man inserts his erect penis into a woman's vagina

sexualise *vt* = **sexualize**

sexuality /sékshoo álləti/ *n* **1 SEXUAL APPEAL** sexual appeal or potency **2 STATE OF BEING SEXUAL** the state of being sexual **3 INVOLVEMENT IN SEXUAL ACTIVITY** involvement or interest in sexual activity

sexualize /sékshoo ə līz/ (**-izes, -izing, -ized**), **sexualise** (**-ises, -ising, -ised**) *vt* to impose a sexual interpretation or perception on something or somebody

sexually transmitted disease *n* a disease such as syphilis or genital herpes that is normally passed from one person to another through sexual activity

sexual orientation *n* the direction of somebody's sexual desire, towards people of the opposite sex or of the same sex, or of both sexes

sexual relations *npl* = **sexual intercourse**

sexual reproduction *n* reproduction that involves the union of male and female gametes, each contributing half of the genetic makeup of the resulting zygote

sexual selection *n* the choice by a female animal of a mate on the basis of a characteristic, e.g. a bird song or bright plumage

sexvalent /seks váylənt/ *adj* CHEM = **hexavalent**

sex work *n* the work of somebody in one of the sex industries such as pornography or prostitution —**sex worker** *n*

sexy /séksi/ (**-ier, -iest**) *adj* **1 AROUSING DESIRE** arousing or intended to arouse sexual desire **2 AROUSED** sexually aroused **3 APPEALING** appealing especially because of being new, interesting, or trendy (*informal*) —**sexily** *adv* —**sexiness** *n*

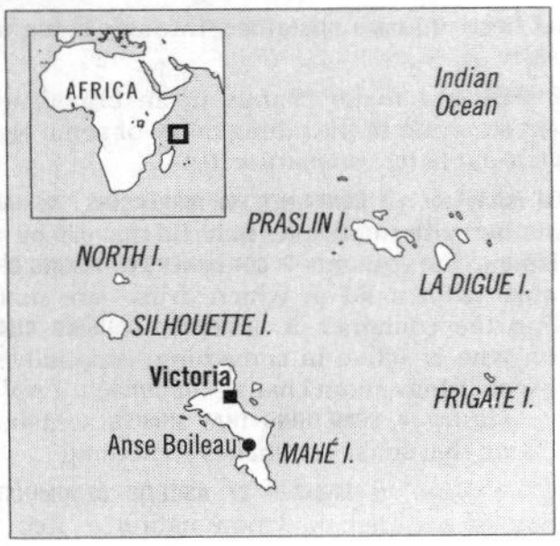

Seychelles

Seychelles /say shélz/ island republic in the W Indian Ocean. Capital: Victoria. Population: 76,100 (1996). Area: 455 sq. km/175 sq. mi. —**Seychellois** /sáy shel wáa/ *adj, n*

Seyfert galaxy /sífərt-/ *n* a small spiral galaxy that varies in brightness and emits radio waves and X-rays [Mid-20C. After Carl K. *Seyfert* (1911–60), US astronomer.]

Seymour /seém awr/, **Jane** (1509?–37) queen of England and Ireland

sf *abbr* **1** science fiction **2** sforzando

SF *abbr* **1** science fiction **2** sinking fund

SFA *abbr* **1** *Scotland* Scottish Football Association **2** Securities and Futures Authority Ltd

Sfax /sfaks/ port in east-central Tunisia. Population: 230,900 (1994).

sferics /sférriks/ *npl US* = **spherics**

SFO *abbr* **1** Superannuation Funds Office **2** Serious Fraud Office

sforzando /sfawrt sándō/, **sforzato** /zfawrt saátō/ *adv* with a sudden strong accent (*musical direction*) ■ *n* (*plural* **-dos** *or* **-di** /-di/; *plural* **-tos** *or* **-ti** /-ti/) a note or chord that is to be played with a sudden strong accent, or a symbol indicating this [Early 19C. < Italian, < *sforzare* 'use force' < Latin *fortis* 'strong'.] —**sforzando** *adj*

sfumato /sfoo maátō/ *n* the gradual blending of one area of colour into another without a sharp outline [Mid-19C. < Italian, past participle of *sfumare* 'tone down', < Latin *fumus* 'smoke'.]

sfz. *abbr* sforzando

ϟ **sg** *abbr* Singapore (*in Internet addresses*)

Sg *symbol* seaborgium

SG *abbr* **1** singular **2** solicitor general **3** specific gravity

sgian-dhu, **sgian-dubh** *n Scotland* ACCESSORIES = **skean-dhu**

SGM *abbr US* Sergeant Major

ϟ **SGML** *n* an international standard for the definition of system-independent methods of representing texts in electronic form by describing the relationship between a document's form and its structure. Full form **Standard Generalized Markup Language**

sgraffito /sgraa feétō/ (*plural* **-ti** /-ti/) *n* **1 DECORATION TECHNIQUE** a technique used to decorate ceramics or plaster walls, in which the top layer has patterns scratched into it, revealing the different-coloured layer beneath **2 DECORATION** a decoration made using the sgraffito technique **3 DECORATED OBJECT** an object decorated using the sgraffito technique [Mid-18C. < Italian, past participle of *sgraffire* 'scratch' < *sgraffio* 'scratch' < *sgraffiare* 'scratch' < Old Italian, 'scratch completely' < *graffiare* (see GRAFFITO).]

Sgt *abbr* Sergeant

sh[1], **shh** *interj* used to tell somebody to be silent or quieter [Mid-19C. Naturally produced interjection.]

ϟ **sh**[2] *abbr* St Helena (*in Internet addresses*)

Shaanxi /shaa aánshi/ province in east-central China. Capital: Xi'an. Population: 34,810,000 (1994). Area: 195,799 sq. km/75,598 sq. mi.

Sha'ban /shə baán, shaa-/, **Shaban** *n* in the Islamic calendar, the eighth month of the year, made up of 30 days [Mid-18C. < Arabic *ša'bān*.]

Shabbat /shaa baát/ (*plural* **-batot** /shaá baa tót/ *or* **-bes** /shaábəss/) *n* the Jewish Sabbath, celebrated on Saturday [Mid-19C. < Hebrew *šabbāṯ* 'day of rest'.]

shabby /shábbi/ (**-bier, -biest**) *adj* **1 WORN AND THREADBARE** worn out, frayed, or threadbare after long use **2 WEARING WORN CLOTHES** wearing worn-out clothing and perceived as being unappealing to the eye **3 INCONSIDERATE** inconsiderate and unfair ○ *won't put up with shabby treatment* **4 INFERIOR IN QUALITY** inferior in quality ○ *shabby goods* **5 RUN DOWN** poorly maintained and thus falling apart or dirty ○ *a shabby section of town* [Mid-17C. < obsolete *shab* 'disreputable person' < Old English *sceabb* 'scab'.] —**shabbily** *adv* —**shabbiness** *n*

shabby-genteel *adj* trying to keep up the appearances that a middle- or upper-middle-class lifestyle demands, despite not having enough money

Shacharis /shaákhəriss/ *n* the Jewish morning liturgy [< Hebrew *šaḥărīṯ* 'morning time']

shack /shak/ *n* a small crude building typically made of boards or sheets of material, usually without a foundation [Late 19C. < ?]
shack up *vi* to live with a lover without being married (*informal disapproving*) [< the practice of military personnel living with local women off base]

shackle /shák'l/ *n* **1 METAL BRACELET FOR HOLDING PRISONERS** a round metal band that can be opened or locked in order to hold the wrist or ankle of a captive, usually attached by chains in pairs or fours (*often plural*) **2 BINDER FOR ANIMAL LEGS** a device used to hold together the legs of horses and other animals **3 U-SHAPED FASTENER** a U-shaped bar that is fastened with a straight pin or bolt to hold something securely **4 RESTRAINT ON FREEDOM** an oppressive restraint on something or somebody (*often plural*) ○ *mental shackles* ■ *vt* (**-les, -ling, -led**) **1 RESTRICT FREEDOM** to restrict the freedom of somebody or something ○ *felt shackled by the inflexible rules* **2 RESTRAIN WITH SHACKLES** to restrain somebody or an animal using shackles **3 SECURE WITH SHACKLE** to connect or secure something with a shackle [Old English *sceacul*. Ultimately from Germanic, 'fastening'.] —**shackler** *n*

Shackleton /shák'ltən/, **Sir Ernest Henry** (1874–1922) Irish explorer

shad /shad/ (*plural* **shads** *or* **shad**) *n* **1** a fish similar to herring that spawns upstream in rivers. Native to: N Atlantic. Genus: *Alosa*. **2** the flesh of a shad as food [Old English *sceadd*]

shadberry /shádbəri/ (*plural* **-ries**) *n* TREES = **serviceberry** *n*. **2** [Mid-19C. Because it flowers when shad appear in the rivers to spawn.]

Shadbolt /shádbōlt/, **Maurice Francis Richard** (*b.* 1932) New Zealand writer

shadbush /shád boōsh/ *n US* TREES = **serviceberry** *n*. **1**

shadchan /shaad khaán, shaádkhən/ (*plural* **-chanim** /shaad khaánīm/ *or* **-chans**), **shadkhan** (*plural* **-kanim** *or* **-khans**) *n* a marriage broker for Jewish couples [Mid-19C. Via Yiddish *shadkhn* < medieval Hebrew *šaddĕkān* < *šiddēk* 'make marriage proposals'.]

shaddock /sháddək/ *n* TREES, FOOD = **pomelo** *n*. **1**, **pomelo** *n*. **2** [Late 17C. After a 17C English ship captain named *Shaddock*.]

shade /shayd/ *n* **1 AREA OUT OF DIRECT SUNLIGHT** an area of relative darkness where direct sunlight is blocked or obscured **2 SLIGHTLY DIFFERENT COLOUR** a colour that is a variation on a basic colour, e.g. by being more or less bright or dark ○ *a pretty shade of blue* **3 SOMETHING THAT BLOCKS LIGHT** something, e.g. a lampshade, used to block a direct light source **4** *US* **WINDOW DEVICE** a flexible piece of material mounted on a window that can be rolled down to block light or up to admit light **5 DARK PARTS OF PAINTING** the darker areas of a painting, drawing, or photograph **6 SMALL AMOUNT** a slight degree or amount ○ *a shade too close* **7 VARIATION** a slight variation on something similar ○ *different shades of opinion* **8 OBSCURITY** relative obscurity **9 GHOST** a ghost or phantom (*literary*) ■ **shades** *npl* **SUNGLASSES** sunglasses (*informal*) ■ *v* (**shades, shading, shaded**) **1** *vt* **PROTECT FROM SUNLIGHT** to protect something or block it off from direct light, particularly from direct sunlight ○ *The awning shades the porch well.* **2** *vt* **DARKEN PART OF PICTURE** to darken part of a drawing or picture using pencil, ink, or some other dark medium ○ *He shaded in the trees in the background.* **3** *vi* **CHANGE SLIGHTLY OR GRADUALLY** to change imperceptibly into something slightly different ○ *The cream gradually shades into gold.* **4** *vt* **DARKEN** to make a place or area darker **5** *vt* **REDUCE PRICE** to reduce a price slightly [Old English *sceadu*. Ultimately < Indo-European, 'darkness'.] ◇ **put somebody** *or* **something in the shade** to make somebody or something seem unimportant by appearing much more special or attractive ◇ **shades of somebody** *or* **something** used to say that somebody or something is reminiscent of somebody or something else, especially a time in the past or the work of a writer or other artist ○ *You can take tea on the terrace – shades of E. M. Forster – or ride on an elephant.*

Shades /shaydz/ *npl* the underworld (*literary*) [Late 16C. Originally in the meaning 'darkness' (as of the underworld).]

shade tree *n* a tree planted to provide shade

shading /sháyding/ *n* **1** an area of relatively dark tone or close lines, dots, or hatching that produces darkness or shadow in a drawing or picture **2** a subtle difference or variation

shadkhan *n* JUDAISM = **shadchan**

shadoof /shə doóf/, **shaduf** *n* a water-raising device used in ancient Egypt consisting of a suspended pivoting pole with a bucket on one end and a counterweight on the other [Mid-19C. < Egyptian Arabic *šādūf*.]

shadow /sháddō/ *n* **1 DARKENED SHAPE OF SOMETHING IN LIGHT** a darkened shape on a surface that falls behind somebody or something blocking the light **2 DARKNESS** relative darkness in a place that is being screened or blocked off from direct sunlight ○ *Part of the room was in shadow.* **3 HINT OF** a slight suggestion or hint of something ○ *beyond the shadow of a doubt* **4 OMINOUS GLOOM** a depressing or ominous gloom ○ *The news cast a shadow over the party.* **5 THREAT** an ever-present threat or blight ○ *living under the shadow of environmental disaster* **6 DARK AREA UNDER EYES** a darkened area of skin under the eyes usually caused by fatigue **7 OVERSHADOWED STATE** a state in which somebody is always overshadowed by another person ○ *grew up in his brother's shadow* **8 REGULAR COMPANION** a person who is the invariable companion of another **9 PERSON SECRETLY TRAILING ANOTHER** somebody, e.g. a detective or spy, who secretly follows somebody **10 OPPOSITION MINISTER WITH PARTICULAR JOB** a politician in an opposition party who speaks on a particular area of policy and would hold a ministerial job if the party were in government **11** ARTS = **shade** *n*. **5** **12** PARANORMAL = **shade** *n*. **9** **13 REFLECTION** a reflection of something in water ○ *the shadow of the stars in the dark lake* **14 COPY** an imitation or copy of something **15 INFERIOR REMNANT** a remnant of somebody or something formerly greater or more important ○ *now a shadow of her former self* **16 SOMEBODY LEARNING JOB BY OBSERVATION** somebody who learns a job by observing the person who regularly does the job **17 ABNORMAL AREA IN X-RAY** an abnormal area showing up on an X-ray **18 JUNGIAN ARCHETYPE** in Jungian psychology, the archetype that represents sexual and aggressive instincts inherited from a more primitive stage of humanity **19 SHELTER** something that provides protection ■ *vt* **1 PROTECT FROM LIGHT** to shade something from the light ○ *Her face was shadowed by a wide-brimmed straw hat.* **2 FOLLOW** to follow somebody secretly ○ *The police had been shadowing him for days.* **3 LEARN JOB BY FOLLOWING WORKER** to learn a job by following somebody who is actually doing the job **4 REPRESENT VAGUELY** to represent something vaguely or in outline ■ *adj* **IN CAPACITY OF OPPOSITION COUNTERPART** describes a member of the largest opposition party who speaks on a particular area of policy and would hold a ministerial job if that party were in government ○ *the shadow cabinet* [Old English *sceaduwe*, a form of *sceadu* 'shade'] —**shadower** *n*

shadow-box *vi* to practise boxing moves by sparring with an imaginary partner

shadow dance *n* a dance performance in which the dancers' shadows are seen on a screen

shadowgraph /sháddō graaf, -graf/ *n* **1** an image of a shape made by casting a shadow onto a surface, e.g. by shaping the hands so that their shadow resembles the silhouette of an animal **2** MED = **radiograph** *n*.

shadow mask *n* a perforated metal sheet mounted close to the rear of the phosphor dot faceplate of a three gun colour picture tube

shadow play *n* a theatrical performance where the audience views a screen on which the shadows of puppets or performers are cast by a light source behind them

shadow price *n* the estimated price of goods or a service for which no market price exists

shadow senator *n* a nonvoting representative of the District of Columbia in the US Senate

shadowy /sháddō i/ (**-ier, -iest**) *adj* **1 FULL OF SHADOWS** full of shadows or shade **2 NOT CLEARLY SEEN** not clearly or only vaguely seen **3 MYSTERIOUS** mysteriously little-known or obscure —**shadowiness** *n*

shaduf *n* AGRIC = **shadoof**

shady /sháydi/ (**-ier, -iest**) *adj* **1 HAVING SHADE** having little natural light, often giving shelter from harsh sunlight **2 DISHONEST** probably dishonest or illegal ○ *shady dealings with foreign investors* **3 PROVIDING SHADE** providing shade —**shadily** *adv* —**shadiness** *n*

SHAEF /shayf/ *abbr* Supreme Headquarters Allied Expeditionary Forces

shaft /shaaft/ *n* **1 LONG HANDLE** the long slender handle on various instruments and tools, e.g. golf clubs and hammers **2 VERTICAL PASSAGE** a vertical passage, especially one in which a lift travels or one that gives access to a mine **3 PASSAGE FOR VENTILATION IN BUILDING** a small passageway in a building, particularly in a wall, ceiling, or floor, to allow for air circulation **4 ROTATING ROD IN MACHINE** a rotating rod that provides motion or power for a machine **5 LIGHT BEAM** a beam of light ○ *a shaft of sunlight* **6 SHARP COMMENT** a sharp or barbed comment directed at somebody ○ *a shaft of wit* **7 POLE FOR HARNESSING HORSE** either of the two parallel bars by which an animal is harnessed to a cart or wagon **8** *US* **HARSH TREATMENT** unkind or harsh treatment or dismissal (*informal*) ○ *His girlfriend gave him the shaft.* **9 ARROW** an arrow (*literary*) **10 BODY OF PROJECTILE** a long narrow rod that forms the body of a spear, arrow, harpoon, or other projectile **11 MIDDLE OF LONG BONE** the middle part of a long bone **12 BODY OF PENIS** the cylindrical body of the penis **13 MAIN PART OF HAIR** the part of a hair that is visible above the skin **14 BODY OF COLUMN** the main body of a column, between the capital and base **15 COLUMN** a column, especially one of a pair supporting an arch **16 FEATHER RIB** the central rib of a feather **17 TREE TRUNK** the trunk of a tree **18 UPRIGHT PART OF CROSS** the upright bar in a cross ■ *vt* (*slang*) **1 TREAT UNFAIRLY** to cheat somebody or treat somebody unfairly ○ *She got shafted on her book contract.* **2 OFFENSIVE TERM** an offensive term meaning to have sexual intercourse with somebody [Old English *sceaft*]

Shaftesbury /shaáftsbəri/ town in SW England. Population: 6,203 (1991).

shag[1] /shag/ *n* **1 LONG PILE ON TEXTILE** a long rough nap or pile on a textile **2 LAYERED HAIRCUT** a hairstyle with layers that are cut progressively shorter from base to crown **3 SHREDDED TOBACCO** a strong, coarse tobacco that is finely shredded **4 MATTED TANGLE OF HAIR** a rough matted tangle of hair or wool ■ *v* (**shags, shagging, shagged**) **1** *vt* **MAKE ROUGH** to cause something to be rough-looking and shaggy **2** *vi* **HANG UNTIDILY** to hang in an untidy manner **3** *vt* **PROVIDE WITH SHAFT** to provide something such as a tool with a shaft [Old English *sceacga*]

shag[2] /shag/ *n* a small crested cormorant. Native to: Europe, North Africa. *Phalacrocorax aristotelis*. [Mid-16C. < ?]

shag[3] /shag/ *vti* (**shags, shagging, shagged**) an offensive term meaning to have sexual intercourse with somebody (*slang*) ■ *n* an offensive term for an act of sexual intercourse (*slang*) [Late 18C. < ?] —**shagger** *n*

shag[4] /shag/ *n* a 1930s dance step involving hopping alternately on each foot ■ *vi* (**shags, shagging, shagged**) to dance the shag [Early 20C. < ?]

shag[5] /shag/ (**shags, shagging, shagged**) *vt US* **1** to run and retrieve something **2** to chase somebody or something away [Early 20C. < ?]

shagbark /shág baark/, **shagbark hickory** *n* a hickory that has grey shaggy bark, hard wood, and bears edible nuts. Native to: E North America. *Carya ovata*.

shagged /shagd/, **shagged out** *adj* extremely tired (*slang*)

shaggy /shággi/ (**-gier, -giest**) *adj* **1 LONG AND UNTIDY** growing long and untidily **2 HAVING COARSE LONG FIBRES** covered with or resembling coarse, long, and usually uneven hair, wool, or similar fibres **3 ROUGH NAPPED** having a rough, relatively long nap or pile

shaggy cap *n* FUNGI = **shaggymane**

shaggy dog story *n* a long drawn-out absurd story or joke, often with an ending or punchline that is anti-climactic [< One such anecdote involving a shaggy dog]

shaggymane /shággi mayn/ *n* a common edible mushroom with shaggy scales on its cap that contain black spores. *Coprinus comatus*.

shagreen /shə greén/ *n* **1** the rough skin of some sharks and rays, used as an abrasive or as leather **2** rough untanned leather with a grainy surface, made from the hide of various animals and often dyed green [Late 17C. Via French *chagrin* 'untanned leather', < Turkish *sağri* 'back of a horse'.]

shah /shaa/ *n* formerly, the hereditary monarch of some Middle Eastern nations, especially Iran [Mid-16C. Via Persian *šāh* < Old Persian *xšāyathiya-* 'king'.] —**shahdom** *n*

Shah Jahan /shaá jə haán/ (1592–1666) Mughal emperor of India (1628–58)

shaikh *n* POL = **sheik**

shaikha *n* POL = **sheika**

shaitan /shī taán/ *n* in Islamic countries, an evil spirit or person [Mid-17C. Via Arabic *šayṭān*, < Hebrew *śāṭān*.]

Shaitan /shī taán/ *n* in Islamic belief, the Devil

Shaka /shaákə/ (1787?–1828) South African Zulu ruler

shake /shayk/ *v* (**shakes, shaking, shook** /shŏŏk/, **shaken** /sháykən/) **1** *vti* **MOVE BACK AND FORTH** to move or make something or somebody move back and forth or up and down in short quick movements ○ *I shook my coat to see if my keys were in the pockets.* **2** *vi* **TREMBLE** to tremble uncontrollably ○ *shaking with fright* **3** *vti* **BECOME BY SHAKING** to achieve a particular state by shaking, or shake something in order to achieve a particular state ○ *The door finally shook free of its hinges.* **4** *vt* **SHAKE TO DISLODGE** to shake something in order to make parts attached to it come off ○ *We shook the apples from the tree.* **5** *vi* **QUAVER WITH EMOTION** to sound uncertain, nervous, angry, or distressed ○ *Her voice was shaking.* **6** *vt* **SHOCK AND UPSET** to shock and upset or disturb somebody ○ *He was badly shaken by the accident.* **7** *vt* **MAKE SOMEBODY LESS CONFIDENT** to cause somebody to lose confidence or certainty ○ *Nothing could shake his faith.* **8** *vti* **CLASP HANDS AS GREETING** to grasp another person's hand and move it up and down as a greeting or sign of trust **9** *vt US* = **shake off** *v.* 1 **10** *vt* **MIX BY SHAKING** to mix ingredients together in a container by shaking the container **11** *vt* **MOVE HEAD TO EXPRESS 'NO'** to move the head from side to side in order to express disagreement, disbelief, commiseration, or sorrow **12** *vt* **WAVE SOMETHING THREATENINGLY** to wave something in the air in a threatening way ○ *She shook her fist at them.* **13** *vti* **RATTLE DICE BEFORE THROWING** to rattle a die or dice in the hand or in a dice cup before throwing **14** *vti* **TRILL** to trill a note ■ *n* **1 ACT OF SHAKING** a shaking of something ○ *She gave the bag a good shake.* **2 VIBRATION** a trembling motion or vibration ○ *The device moves smoothly along the track without shake.* **3 MOMENT** a brief moment (*informal*) ○ *I'll do it in two shakes.* **4** BEVERAGES = **milk shake** *n.* **5 SHAKEN BEVERAGE** a beverage made without milk or ice cream but blended or shaken like a milk shake ○ *a fruit and yogurt shake* **6 HANDSHAKE** an act of grasping somebody's hand as a greeting **7** *US* **REASONABLE CHANCE** reasonable treatment or a reasonable opportunity to succeed ○ *give everybody a fair shake* **8 FISSURE OR CRACK** a fissure or crack in a rock or timber **9 TRILL** a trilled note **10 EARTHQUAKE** an earthquake (*informal*) **11 WOODEN SHINGLE** a rough wooden shingle cut with a hatchet ■ **shakes** *npl* **UNCONTROLLABLE TREMBLING** uncontrollable trembling caused, e.g., by fear or illness [Old English *sceacan*] —**shakable** *adj* ◇ **no great shakes** not very good or not very important (*informal*)

shake down *v* **1** *vt US* **EXTORT MONEY FROM** to extort money from somebody (*slang*) **2** *vt US* **TAKE SOMETHING FOR TRIAL RUN** to subject a ship or aircraft to a trial run in order to look for defects or train the crew **3** *vi* **BECOME ACCUSTOMED** to become comfortable in a new setting (*informal*) **4** *vi* **SLEEP IN MAKESHIFT BED** to go to bed in a makeshift bed

shake off *vt* **1** to get rid of something unwanted. US term **shake** *v.* 9 **2** to get away from a following or pursuing person

shake out *vt* to open something, spread something, or dislodge things from something by holding it and shaking it

shake up *vt* **1 MAKE MAJOR CHANGES** to make major changes in an organization or institution, especially with the intention of improving or modernizing it **2 UPSET** to make somebody feel upset and disturbed **3 MIX BY SHAKING** to mix something by shaking it in a container

shakedown /sháyk down/ *n* **1** *US* **ACT OF EXTORTION** an act of extorting money from somebody using threats (*slang*) **2 TRIAL RUN OF VESSEL** a trial run of a ship or aircraft in order to locate and fix problems or to familiarize the crew with their duties **3 MAKESHIFT BED** a makeshift bed such as a pile of blankets on a floor

shaken past participle of **shake**

shaken baby syndrome, shaken infant syndrome *n* in young babies, a series of often life-threatening internal head injuries sustained through being shaken violently

shake-out *n* a major change in an organization or system resulting in the falling away of some elements ○ *a shake-out in the voluntary sector*

shaker /sháykər/ *n* **1 CONTAINER FOR DISPERSING FINE PARTICLES** a container with small holes in its lid that can be shaken to disperse the contents **2 CONTAINER FOR MIXING DRINKS** a container with a lid in which drinks are mixed by shaking the container **3 SOMEBODY CAUSING CHANGE** a person who is active in something, especially somebody who brings about change (*informal*) ○ *a real shaker in the industry* **4 SOMETHING THAT SHAKES** somebody or something that shakes or shakes something

Shaker /sháykər/ *n* **MEMBER OF ASCETIC DENOMINATION** a member of a Christian denomination related to the Quakers who live communally, simply, and celibately ■ *adj* **1 SIMPLE AND FUNCTIONAL** designed or made in the simple, functional style that originated with the Shakers **2 Shaker, shaker PARALLEL RIBBED** knitted in a large gauge in thin parallel ribs [Late 18C. < The shaking movements in their ritual dances.]

~~Shakespear~~ incorrect spelling of **Shakespeare**

Shakespeare /sháyks peer/, **William** (1564–1616) English poet and playwright —**Shakespearean** /shayk speéri ən/ *adj, n* —**Shakespearian** *adj, n*

Shakespeareana /shayk speéri aánə/, **Shakespeariana** *n* collectively, things relating to William Shakespeare

Shakespearean sonnet *n* a sonnet in iambic pentameter composed of three quatrains followed by a couplet. The rhyme pattern is abab cdcd efef gg.

Shakespeariana *n* LITERAT = **Shakespeareana**

shake-up, shakeup *n* a major reorganization or change

shaking palsy *n* Parkinson's disease (*informal dated*) [< its characteristic tremor]

shako /shákō, sháykō/ (*plural* **-os** *or* **-oes**) *n* a tall cylindrical military hat made of stiff material with a short visor and a plume at the front [Early 19C. Via French *schako* < Hungarian *csákós (süveg)* 'peaked (cap)'.]

~~Shakspeare~~ incorrect spelling of **Shakespeare**

Shakta /shúktə/, **Sakta** *n* a Hindu who worships Shakti, the female consort of Shiva [Early 19C. < Sanskrit *śāktaḥ* < *śaktiḥ* (see SHAKTI).] —**Shaktism** *n* —**Shaktist** *n*

Shakti *n* = **Sakti**

shakuhachi /sháchoo haáchi/ (*plural* **-chis**) *n* a Japanese bamboo flute [Late 19C. < Japanese.]

shaky /sháyki/ (**-ier, -iest**) *adj* **1 TREMBLING** trembling or unsteady **2 NOT STURDY** not sturdy or firm and likely to collapse **3 WEAK AND NOT LIKELY TO LAST** weak or wavering and unlikely to last long or to be successful ○ *a shaky financial venture* **4 UNRELIABLE** unreliable or uncertain ○ *made us a rather shaky promise* —**shakily** *adv* —**shakiness** *n*

shale /shayl/ *n* a dark fine-grained sedimentary rock composed of layers of compressed clay, silt, or mud [Mid-18C. Ultimately from Germanic, 'split'.] —**shaly** *adj*

shale oil *n* crude oil distilled from heated shale

shall *stressed* /shal/; *unstressed* /sh'l/ (*2nd person present singular* **shalt** *archaic*, *2nd person present plural* **shalt** *archaic*) CORE MEANING: will happen in the future, or intended to happen ○ *I shall as president promote measures that keep families whole.*
vi **1 MUST** used especially in formal speech and writing to indicate determination on the part of the speaker that something will happen or somebody will do something ○ *If you want to behave like that you shall certainly not do it here.* **2 RULES AND LAWS** indicating that something must happen or somebody is obliged to do something because of a rule or law ○ *The department shall issue an account number to the vehicle owner.* **3 OFFERS AND SUGGESTIONS** used to make offers and suggestions or to ask for advice (*in questions*) ○ *Shall I arrange it for you?* ○ *What shall I do next?* **4 CERTAINTY** indicating the certainty or inevitability of something happening in the future (*usually used with 'you'*) ○ *If you want a new outfit that badly then you shall have one.* [Old English *sceal* < Germanic, 'owe']

LANGUAGE NOTE shall or **will**? The traditional rule, often stated in grammars and usage books, is that to express a simple future tense ***shall*** is used after *I* and *we* and ***will*** in other cases, and to express intention or wish their roles are reversed; but it is unlikely that this rule has ever been regularly observed, and many examples of written English can be found that contradict it. (The distinction is often difficult to establish, especially in the first person when the speaker is also the performer of the future action, and intention must always be involved to some extent.) Although *will* and, occasionally, *shall* are used as auxiliary verbs with reference to future action or state, there are other ways of expressing this that are often preferred as more natural, such as *am going to*. When *shall* and *will* are used in conversation, they are normally contracted to '*ll*, so that the difference between the two words becomes irrelevant. In all parts of the English-speaking world other than England, *shall* has been more or less replaced by the contracted negative form *shan't*. In the English of England (not Britain as a whole), *shall* is still sometimes used in such cases as *Shall we go now? They shall apologize immediately* (a command) and *Shall you bring the children?* (an inquiry rather than a request), but the last two examples sound old-fashioned, and *will* is now more common, especially in speech.

SHAKESPEARE'S PLAYS

Although the precise dates for the writing and first performance of many of Shakespeare's plays are in doubt, his dramatic career is generally divided into four periods, as below. The dates shown are approximations based on available evidence.

First period	
1590–92	Henry VI Parts 1, 2, and 3
1592	The Comedy of Errors
1592–3	Richard III
1593	The Taming of the Shrew
1594	Titus Andronicus
	Love's Labour's Lost
	The Two Gentlemen of Verona

Second period	
1595	A Midsummer Night's Dream
	Richard II
	Romeo and Juliet
1596	King John
	The Merchant of Venice
1597	Henry IV Parts 1 and 2
1598	Henry V
1599	Much Ado About Nothing
	Julius Caesar
	The Merry Wives of Windsor
	As You Like It
1600	Twelfth Night

Third period	
1601	Hamlet
1602	Troilus and Cressida
	All's Well That Ends Well
1604	Othello
	Measure for Measure
1605	King Lear
1606	Macbeth
	Antony and Cleopatra
1608	Timon of Athens
	Coriolanus

Fourth period	
1608	Pericles, Prince of Tyre
1610	Cymbeline
	The Winter's Tale
1611	The Tempest
1613	Henry VIII

shalloon /sha loŏn/ *n* a light wool twill. Use: garment lining. [Mid-17C. < French *chalon* < ?]

shallop /shálləp/ *n* a light boat with oars, sails, or both, used in shallow waters [Late 16C. < French *chaloupe* < ?]

shallot /sha lót/ *n* 1 an edible bulb with a delicate onion flavour 2 a plant of the onion family that produces shallots. *Allium ascalonicum.* [Mid-17C. < French *échalotte*, alteration of Old French *esc(h)aloigne* < Vulgar Latin *escalonia* (see SCALLION).]

shallow /shállō/ *adj* 1 NOT DEEP with little space between the bottom and the surface or top 2 NOT THINKING OR FEELING DEEPLY having or displaying little intellectual or emotional complexity or value 3 TAKING IN LITTLE AIR characterized by the inhaling and exhaling of an abnormally small amount of air ■ **shallows** *npl* AREA OF SHALLOW WATER an area of shallow water ■ *vti* MAKE OR BECOME SHALLOW to become less deep or to make water less deep [15C. < ?] —**shallowly** *adv* —**shallowness** *n*

shallow water blackout *n* the sudden loss of consciousness by a diver upon resurfacing, caused by oxygen starvation

shalom /sha lóm/ *interj* used as a Jewish greeting or leave-taking [Late 19C. < Hebrew *šālôm* 'peace'.]

shalt /shalt/ 2nd person present singular, 2nd person present plural of **shall** (*archaic*)

sham /sham/ *n* 1 A FAKE something that is presented as genuine but that is not 2 IMPOSTER a person who pretends to be something that he or she is not ■ *adj* NOT GENUINE not genuine and used for deception ○ *sham credentials* ■ *vti* (**shams, shamming, shammed**) FEIGN to pretend to be experiencing a condition, e.g. illness or an emotion, in order to deceive [Late 17C. Probably variant of SHAME.] —**shammer** *n*

shaman /sháhmən, sháymən, shaámən/ *n* a spiritual leader who has special powers such as prophecy and healing [Late 17C. Via Russian < Tungus *šaman* < Sanskrit *śramanáḥ* 'Buddhist ascetic' < *śramas* 'religious exercise'.] —**shamanic** /sha mánnik/ *adj*

shamanism /shámmən izəm, sháy-, shaá-/ *n* 1 a religion of N Asia, in which shamans can intercede between humanity and powerful good and evil spirits 2 any animistic belief system involving shamans

shamash *n* JUDAISM = **shammash**

shamateur /shámmətər, shámmə choor/ *n* an athlete who is officially an amateur but who is secretly paid [Late 19C. Blend of SHAM + AMATEUR.]

shamble /shámb'l/ *vi* (**-bles, -bling, -bled**) to walk clumsily keeping the feet close to the ground ■ *n* a shuffling, awkward walking style [Late 16C. Probably from the obsolete expression *shamble legs* 'ungainly legs'.]

shambles /shámb'lz/ *n* 1 DISORGANIZED FAILURE a failure caused by inadequate planning or organization 2 MESSY DISORDER a state of messy disorder or chaos 3 PLACE OF CARNAGE a place of great destruction and carnage (*literary*) [15C. < obsolete *shamble* 'meat vendor's stall' < Latin *scamellum* 'small bench'.]

shambolic /sham bóllik/ *adj* poorly organized and in a messy or chaotic state (*informal*) [Late 20C. < SHAMBLES, perhaps after *symbolic*.]

shame /shaym/ *n* 1 NEGATIVE EMOTION a negative emotion that combines feelings of dishonour, unworthiness, and embarrassment 2 CAPACITY TO FEEL UNWORTHY the capacity or tendency to feel shame ○ *He has no shame.* 3 STATE OF DISGRACE a state of disgrace or dishonour ○ *bring shame on the family* 4 CAUSE FOR REGRET a cause for regret or disappointment ○ *It's a shame you couldn't stay for lunch.* 5 CAUSE OF SHAME somebody or something that causes somebody to feel shame ■ *vt* (**shames, shaming, shamed**) 1 MAKE SOMEBODY FEEL ASHAMED to make somebody feel ashamed ○ *It shamed her that she had cheated.* 2 FORCE SOMEBODY THROUGH SHAME to make somebody do something by exploiting the fact that he or she would be ashamed not to do it ○ *He shamed us into making higher donations to the ministry.* 3 MAKE SOMEBODY FEEL INFERIOR to be so much better or more successful than others as to expose their comparative inadequacy ○ *Their exam results shame other local schools.* ■ *interj* USED IN SYMPATHETIC REACTION used to react sympathetically to something disappointing ○ *Shame, man, we would have invited you if we'd known you were free.* [Old English *sceamu*] ◇ **put somebody *or* something to shame** to make somebody *or* something seem inferior or of inferior quality by comparison

shamefaced /sháym fáyst/ *adj* 1 showing a feeling of shame or embarrassment 2 timid or easily embarrassed [Mid-16C. Alteration of obsolete *shamefast* 'bashful' < Old English *sceamfæst*.] —**shamefacedly** /sháym fáysidli, -fáystli/ *adv* —**shamefacedness** /-fáyssidnəss, -fáystnəss/ *n*

shameful /sháymf'l/ *adj* bad enough to inspire shame in those responsible [Old English *sceamful*] —**shamefully** *adv* —**shamefulness** *n*

shameless /sháymləss/ *adj* 1 untroubled or unaffected by shame, especially in situations where others would be ashamed 2 done without shame, especially where others would feel shame [Old English *sceamlēas*] —**shamelessly** *adv* —**shamelessness** *n*

shamiana /shámmi aánə, sháymi-/ *n* S Asia a decorative circus-style tent used for outdoor entertaining or weddings [Early 17C. < Persian and Urdu *shāmiyāna*.]

Shamir /sha meér/, **Yitzhak** (*b.* 1914) Polish-born Israeli statesman. Born **Yitzhak Jazernicki**

shammash /sháməss/ (*plural* **-mashim** /sha móssim/), **shammes** (*plural* **-mosim**) *n* 1 the beadle of a synagogue 2 the candle used to light the candles in the Hanukkah candlestick [Mid-17C. Via Yiddish *shames* < Hebrew *šammāš* 'attendant' < *šimmēš* 'serve'.]

shammy /shámmi/ (*plural* **-mies**) *n* INDUST, HOUSEHOLD = **chamois** *n.* **2**, **chamois** *n.* **3**

shampoo /sham poó/ *n* 1 HAIR-CLEANING SOAP soap for cleaning the hair and scalp, usually in liquid or gel form 2 SUDSY DETERGENT sudsy detergent for cleaning upholstery and carpets 3 USE OF SHAMPOO a cleaning of the hair with shampoo ■ *vt* (**-poos, -pooing, -pooed**) CLEAN WITH SHAMPOO to clean something with shampoo [Mid-18C. Via Anglo-Indian < Hindi *cāpō* < *cāpnā* 'knead, massage'.]

shamrock /shám rok/ *n* a three-leafed clover or a plant similar to clover that serves as the national emblem of Ireland [Late 16C. < Irish *seamróg* 'small clover' < *seamar* 'clover'.]

shamus /sháyməss, shaáməss/ *n* US (*slang*) 1 a police officer 2 a private detective [Early 20C. Alteration of SHAMMASH, or < the Irish name *Séamus*.]

Shan /shaan, shan/ (*plural* **Shan** *or* **Shans**) *n* 1 a member of a group of people living mainly in NE Myanmar and also in neighbouring parts of China, Laos, and Thailand 2 the Tai language of the Shan people. Native speakers: 2.5 million. [Early 19C. < Burmese.] —**Shan** *adj*

Shandong /shan doóng/ province in east-central China, bordering on the Yellow Sea. Capital: Jinan. Population: 86,710,000 (1994). Area: 153,300 sq. km/59,200 sq. mi.

shandy /shándi/ (*plural* **-dies**) *n* a drink made of beer and lemonade [Late 19C. Shortening of SHANDYGAFF.]

shandygaff /shándi gaf/ *n* US a drink made of beer and ginger beer [Mid-19C. < ?]

Shang /shang/ *n* a Chinese dynasty that ruled from 1766? to 1027? BC, a period that coincided with the development of China's system of handwriting and bronzework (*often before nouns*) [Mid-17C. < Chinese *Shāng*.]

shanghai /sháng hī́/ (**-hais, -haiing, -haied**) *vt* 1 to recruit somebody forcibly into a navy 2 to trick or force somebody to do something or go somewhere [Late 19C. After SHANGHAI, a typical destination of ships crewed in this way.]

Shanghai /sháng hī́/ port in E China, on the River Huang-pu. Population: 8,760,000 (1993). —**Shanghainese** /sháng hī́ neéz/ *npl*

Shango /sháng gō/ *n* a religious group in the Caribbean characterized by a blend of West African religious practice and Christianity [Mid-20C. < Yoruba, the god of thunder.]

Shangri-la /sháng gri laá/ *n* an imaginary and remote paradise on earth [Mid-20C. < The name given to an imaginary land in the novel *Lost Horizon* (1933) by the English novelist James Hilton.]

shank /shangk/ *n* 1 LONG, NARROW PART the long narrowest part of something such as a key or pipe, especially when it connects two functional parts 2 CUT OF MEAT a cut of meat from the leg of cattle, pigs, or sheep 3 BOTTOM OF ANIMAL LEG the lower part of an animal's leg, between the bottom and middle joints 4 LOWER LEG the lower part of the human leg, from ankle to knee 5 LEG a human leg (*informal*) 6 BODY OF PIN OR NAIL the long, narrow part of a pin, nail, screw, or bolt, between the head and the pointed or threaded part 7 PART CONNECTING TOOL HEAD TO HANDLE a part sticking out from the head of a tool, by which it can be fitted into a handle 8 RING BAND the plain band part of a ring, not including the jewels and their settings **9 NARROW PART OF SOLE** the narrow part of the sole of a shoe, beneath the arch of the foot, or any fitting at this part of a shoe **10 ANCHOR'S STEM** the stem of an anchor **11 PART OF PRINTING TYPE** the body of a piece of type, between the foot and shoulder **12 BUTTON STEM** a loop or stem at the back of a button, by which it is sewn to the cloth **13 HOMEMADE DAGGER** a makeshift dagger, e.g. one made from a shard of glass, and especially one made by a prisoner (*slang*) ■ *v* **1** *vt* **MISHIT A GOLF BALL** to hit a golf ball with the heel of the club, sending it in the wrong direction **2** *vi* **SHOW DISEASE FROM BASE UP** of plants, to shrivel, or show other signs of disease spreading upwards from the base of the stem [Old English *sceanca* 'shinbone']

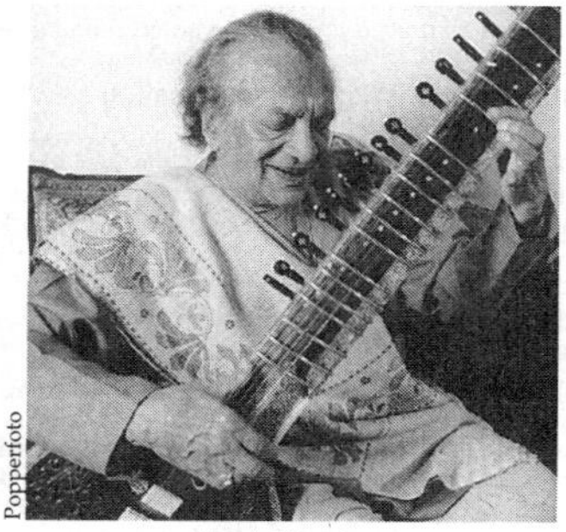

Popperfoto

Ravi Shankar

Shankar /shángk aar/, **Ravi** (*b.* 1920) Indian sitarist, composer, and teacher

shanking /shángking/ *n* a disease of plants marked by shrivelling and decay from the base of the stems

shank's mare *n US* = **shanks's pony** (*dated or informal*)

shanks's pony *n* the legs or feet, as a means of transportation (*dated informal humorous*) US term **shank's mare**

shannachie /shánna khée/ *n Ireland* a traditional Irish storyteller [< Irish *seanchaidhe*]

Shannon /shánnən/ longest river in the British Isles, rising in north-central Republic of Ireland and flowing southwestwards to the Atlantic Ocean. Length: 386 km/240 mi.

shanny /shánni/ (*plural* **-nies** *or* **-ny**) *n* a fish with a small tapering body and a long dorsal fin. Native to: rocky European coasts. *Blennius pholis*. [Mid-19C. < ?]

shan't /shaant/ *contr* contraction of 'shall not'

shantey /shánti/ *n* MUSIC = **shanty**²

shantung /shán túng/ *n* **1** heavy silk cloth with a nubby uneven weave **2** cotton or synthetic fabric made to resemble silk shantung [Late 19C. After the Chinese province of *Shantung* (Shandong).]

shanty¹ /shánti/ (*plural* **-ties**) *n* a crudely built shack or hut [Early 19C. Possibly < Canadian French *chantier* 'lumberjack's hut', via French, 'timberyard' < Latin *cant(h)erius* 'rafter'.]

shanty² /shánti/ (*plural* **-ties**), **shantey** (*plural* **-teys**), **chanty** (*plural* **chanties**) *n* a rhythmical song of a kind originally sung by sailors while they were working in groups

shantytown /shánti town/ *n* a settlement consisting of crudely built shacks

Shanxi /shánshi/ province of east-central China. Capital: Taiyuan. Population: 28,759,014 (1990). Area: 157,099 sq. km/60,656 sq. mi.

shape /shayp/ *n* **1 OUTLINE OF SOMETHING'S FORM** the outline of something's form ○ *His face has a square shape.* **2 SOMETHING NOT CLEARLY SEEN** something that has bulk but is not clearly seen in outline ○ *She could see a shape through the fog.* **3 GEOMETRIC FORM** a geometric form such as a square, triangle, cone, or cube **4 GENERAL CHARACTER OF** the broad character that something has ○ *the overall shape of the proposals* **5 ORIGINAL FORM** the original or optimal form of something ○ *The pleats lost their shape in the wash.* **6 HEALTH** the condition of somebody's health or fitness ○ *She exercises regularly and is in pretty good shape.* **7 CONDITION OF** the condition of something ○ *The lawn is in great shape.* **8 MOULD** a mould or pattern for making or giving something its form **9 GHOST** a ghostly form or phantom ■ *v* (**shapes, shaping, shaped**) **1** *vt* **INFLUENCE SOMETHING GREATLY** to have a profound or crucial influence over something ○ *His beliefs were shaped by his upbringing.* **2** *vt* **PLAN FOR NATURE OF** to plan or decide on what the character of something should be ○ *They are meeting to shape the nation's future.* **3** *vt* **GIVE SOMETHING PARTICULAR SHAPE** to mould something into a different shape ○ *She shapes the clay into little animals.* **4** *vi* **HAPPEN** to happen or occur **5** *vt* **TRAIN WITH REWARD AND PUNISHMENT** to change somebody's behaviour gradually using reward as the person comes closer to the desired behaviour, and punishment for moving away from it [Old English *gesceap* 'creation' < Germanic, 'cut out'] ◇ **knock** *or* **lick** *or* **whip somebody** *or* **something into shape** to bring somebody or something to a desired state quickly, roughly, or haphazardly (*informal*) ◇ **take shape** to take a definite form

shape up *vi* **1 IMPROVE** to improve or develop in the way that is wanted (*informal*) **2 REACH ACCEPTABLE STANDARD** to reach an acceptably high standard of behaviour, skill, or attitude **3 DEVELOP IN PARTICULAR WAY** to seem to be developing in the way specified ○ *It's shaping up to be an environmental disaster.*

SHAPE /shayp/ *abbr* Supreme Headquarters Allied Powers Europe

shapeless /sháypləss/ *adj* **1** with an indefinite or imprecise shape **2** put together in a very haphazard way —**shapelessly** *adv* —**shapelessness** *n*

shapely /sháypli/ (**-lier, -liest**) *adj* having a shape that is visually appealing —**shapeliness** *n*

shape-shifter *n* in fiction, somebody or something that is able to change form

shape-up, shapeup /sháyp up/ *n US* a method of hiring dock workers in which those seeking work arrive at the docks in the morning and employers select from among them

shard /shaard/, **sherd** /shurd/ *n* **1 BROKEN PIECE OF GLASS** a sharp broken piece of glass or metal **2** ARCHAEOL = **potsherd 3 SCALE OR SHELL** an animal's scales, shell, or other tough outer covering **4 BEETLE'S OUTER WING** the outer wing covering of a beetle [Old English *sceard* 'cut, notch'. Ultimately < Indo-European, 'cut'.]

share¹ /shair/ *v* (**shares, sharing, shared**) **1** *vti* **USE SOMETHING ALONG WITH OTHERS** to have or use something in common with other people ○ *We shared a flat.* **2** *vti* **TAKE RESPONSIBILITY TOGETHER** to take equal responsibility for something along with other people ○ *We shared the blame.* **3** *vti* **LET SOMEBODY USE** to allow somebody to use something or have part of something ○ *I shared my ice cream with him.* **4** *vt* **DIVIDE SOMETHING EQUALLY BETWEEN PEOPLE** to allocate equal parts of something to different people or groups ○ *She shared out the money between her six grandchildren.* **5** *vt* **HAVE SIMILAR FEELING OR EXPERIENCE** to have something the same as or in common with somebody else ○ *He shared my view that the plan would not work.* **6** *vt* **TELL SOMEBODY** to express something to another person rather than keeping silent ○ *Do you want to share your feelings?* ■ *n* **1 PART OF SOMETHING ALLOTTED** a part of something that is owned by, paid for by, done by, or set aside for each of several people ○ *He hasn't had his share of the cake.* **2 PART OF COMPANY'S STOCK** any of the equal, usually small, parts into which a company's capital stock is divided ○ *She owns shares in several companies* **3 REASONABLE OR APPROPRIATE PORTION** the portion that somebody deserves or should be responsible for ○ *She does more than her share of the work.* [Old English *scearu* 'division, portion'. Ultimately < Indo-European, 'cut'.] —**sharer** *n*

share² /shair/ *n* AGRIC = **ploughshare** [Old English *scear*. Ultimately < Indo-European, 'cut'.]

share certificate *n* a document certifying ownership of shares, issued by a company to an individual who holds shares in that company. US term **stock certificate**

sharecropper /sháir kroppər/ *n US* a tenant farmer who farms land for the owner and is paid a share of the value of the yielded crop —**sharecrop** (**-cropping, -cropped**) *vti*

shared ownership *n* a form of home ownership in which the resident buys part of the property and rents part of it from a housing association

shareholder /sháir hōldər/ *n* somebody who owns one or more shares of a company's stock. US term **stockholder**

share index *n* an index showing movement of share prices

share option *n* a benefit by which an employee of a company can buy its shares at a special price

⚡ **shareware** /sháir wair/ *n* software made available for free trial with the understanding that users will voluntarily pay a fee to the author or publisher for continued use

sharia /shə rée ə/, **shari'a, shari'ah** *n* Islamic religious law, based on the Koran (*often before nouns*) [Mid-19C. Via Arabic *šarī'ya* 'lawfulness' < *aš-šar'* 'Islamic law'.]

sharif /sha réef/, **sherif** /she réef/, **shereef** *n* **1 DESCENDANT OF MUHAMMAD** a descendant of the prophet Muhammad through his daughter Fatima **2 GOVERNOR OF MECCA** the governor or chief magistrate of Mecca during the years of Ottoman Turkish rule **3 ARAB RULER** an Arab prince or ruler [Late 16C. < Arabic *šarīf* 'illustrious'.] —**sharifian** /shə réefi ən/ *adj*

Sharjah /shaárjə/ member state of the United Arab Emirates. Capital: Sharjah. Population: 400,000 (1995). Area: 2,590 sq. kms/1,000 sq. mi.

shark /shaark/ *n* **1 CARNIVOROUS FISH** a carnivorous fish with a long body, two dorsal fins, sharp teeth, a cartilaginous skeleton, and thick, rough skin. Class: Chondrichthyes. **2 RUTHLESS PERSON** a ruthless greedy person (*informal*) **3 LOANSHARK** a loanshark (*informal*) ■ *vi* **CHEAT OTHERS PROFESSIONALLY** to make a living as a cheater or fraud [Mid-16C. < ?]

Shark Bay /shaárk-/ arm of the Indian Ocean on the coast of W Western Australia

sharkskin /shaárk skin/ *n* **1** a smooth glossy fabric made from a mixture of acetate and rayon **2** leather made from shark's skin

Sharman /shaármən/, **Helen** (*b.* 1963) British astronaut

Sharon, Plain of /shárrən/ plain in W Israel, extending southwards from Haifa to Tel Aviv

Sharon /sha rón/, **Ariel** (*b.* 1928) Israeli soldier, politician, and prime minister (2001–)

sharon fruit /shárrən-/ *n* FOOD = **persimmon** *n.* 1 [After the Plain of SHARON]

sharp /shaarp/ *adj* **1 ABLE TO CUT** with an edge or point that is very acute and able to cut or puncture things ○ *a sharp blade* **2 POINTED** ending in a point or sharp angle ○ *a sharp nose* **3 ABRUPT IN CHANGING DIRECTION** making a change in direction that forms an acute angle ○ *a sharp turn* **4 QUICK-WITTED** quick-witted and intelligent or quick to notice and understand **5 CRITICAL** critical and unsympathetic ○ *a sharp rebuke* **6 IRRITABLE** irritable or angry ○ *a sharp temper* **7 SUDDEN** sudden and significant ○ *a sharp rise in prices* **8 SURPRISED** abrupt or unexpected ○ *a sharp intake of breath* **9 DISTINCT** clearly and definitely distinct ○ *Her soft voice was in sharp contrast to her forbidding expression.* **10 CLEARLY DETAILED** with the detail clear and distinct ○ *a sharp image* **11 PIERCING** loud, piercing, and abrupt or unexpected ○ *a sharp cry* **12 STRONG IN TASTE** strong and slightly bitter in taste ○ *a sharp cheese* **13 INTENSE** penetrating and intense ○ *a sharp frost* **14 HIGHER BY SEMITONE** higher in pitch by a semitone ○ *F sharp* **15 TOO HIGH PITCHED** a little too high in pitch and therefore slightly out of tune **16 STYLISH** neat, stylish, and fashionable ○ *a sharp dresser* **17 FRAUDULENT** deceitful or fraudulent ○ *sharp practice* ■ *adv* **1 PRECISELY** exactly, and not before or after ○ *at 9 o'clock sharp* **2 AT SLIGHTLY TOO HIGH A PITCH** at higher than the usual pitch and therefore slightly out of tune ○ *She's singing sharp.* ■ *n* **1 NOTE HIGHER BY SEMITONE** (*symbol* ♯) a note or tone that is a semitone higher in pitch than the natural or unmodified pitch **2 SHARP SYMBOL** (*symbol* ♯) the symbol for a sharp note **3 LONG SEWING NEEDLE** a long thin needle for hand-sewing **4 SHARP MEDICAL INSTRUMENT** a sharp medical instrument such as a hypodermic or surgical blade that requires careful disposal (*usually plural*) ○ *a container labelled 'sharps only'* **5 SHARPER** a sharper (*informal*) **6 EXPERT** somebody expert at something (*informal*) [Old English *scearp*. Ultimately < Indo-European, 'cut'.] —**sharply** *adv* —**sharpness** *n*

Sharp /shaarp/, **Cecil** (1859–1924) British musicologist

shar-pei /shaar páy/, **Shar-Pei** *n* a medium-sized dog with a squarish snout, blue tongue, short hair, and loose skin that falls in folds over its body, especially when young [Late 20C. < Chinese *shā pí* 'sand skin'.]

sharpen /shaárpən/ *v* **1** *vti* **BECOME OR MAKE SHARPER** to become or make something sharp or sharper **2** *vt* **RAISE PITCH OF NOTE** to raise a note in pitch, especially by a semitone **3** *vt* **IMPROVE** to improve something so that it is more efficient or stylish than before —**sharpener** *n*

sharper /shaárpər/ *n* a skilful cheat, especially in gambling

Sharpeville /shaárp vil/ township near Vereeniging, NE South Africa. Population: 42,000 (1972).

sharp-eyed *adj* **1** alert and able to notice detail **2** with very keen eyesight

sharpie /shaárpi/, **sharpy** (*plural* **-ies**) *n US* a sharper (*informal*)

sharpish /shaárpish/ *adv* quickly or without delay (*informal*)

sharp-set *adj* eagerly wanting something, especially food

sharpshooter /shaárp shootər/ *n* a person who can shoot a firearm extremely accurately

sharp-sighted *adj* **1** with very good eyesight **2** quick to notice detail —**sharp-sightedly** *adv* —**sharp-sightedness** *n*

sharp-tongued *adj* critical or sarcastic and unsympathetic in speech

sharp-witted *adj* quick to think, understand, or react —**sharp-wittedly** *adv*

sharpy *n* GAMBLING = **sharpie**

shashlik /shásh lik, shaásh lik/, **shashlick** *n* FOOD = **shish kebab** [Early 20C. Via Russian *shashlyk* < Crimean Turkish *şişlik* 'small skewer' < *şiş* 'skewer'.]

Shasta /shástə/ (*plural* **-ta** *or* **-tas**) *n* **1** a member of a group of Native North American peoples of the highlands of N California **2** the Hokan language of the Shasta people, which is nearly extinct —**Shasta** *adj*

Shasta, Mount /shástə/ extinct volcano in N California. Height: 4,317 m/14,162 ft.

Shasta daisy *n* a chrysanthemum with large white flower heads. *Chrysanthemum maximum*. [Early 20C. After Mount SHASTA, or the SHASTA people of northern California.]

shastra /shaástrə/, **sastra** *n* in Hinduism, a sacred text [Mid-17C. < Sanskrit *śāstra* 'lesson' < *śās-* 'instruct'.]

shat past tense, past participle of **shit** (*taboo offensive*)

Shatt al-Arab /shát al árrəb/ river channel in SE Iraq, rising at the confluence of the Tigris and Euphrates rivers and emptying into the Persian Gulf. It forms part of the border between Iran and Iraq. Length: 193 km/120 mi.

Shatten /shátt'n/, **Gerald P.** (*b.* 1949) US developmental biologist

shatter /sháttər/ *v* **1** *vti* **SMASH INTO PIECES** to break or cause something to break suddenly into many small brittle pieces **2** *vt* **DESTROY HOPE OR BELIEF** to destroy something that somebody believed in or hoped for **3** *vt* **SHOCK** to shock and distress somebody badly ■ **shatters** *npl* **FRAGMENTS** fragments made by shattering something [Assumed Old English *sceaterian*. Ultimately < Indo-European, 'split apart'.] —**shatterer** *n*

shatter cone *n* a cone-shaped rock piece that has stripes running from its point, created by volcanic pressure or meteoric impact

shattered /sháttərd/ *adj* thoroughly tired out

shatterproof /sháttər proof/ *adj* made to resist shattering

shave /shayv/ *v* (**shaves, shaving, shaved, shaved** *or* **shaven** /sháyvən/) **1** *vti* **REMOVE HAIR WITH RAZOR** to remove hair from the body using a razor **2** *vt* **REDUCE AMOUNT SLIGHTLY** to reduce an amount, price, or time taken by a very slight amount ○ *shaved two seconds off her best time* **3** *vt* **BARELY TOUCH IN PASSING** barely to touch something when passing **4** *vt* **REMOVE A THIN LAYER** to remove a thin layer from something using a razor, rasp, or similar tool **5** *vt* **TRIM SOMETHING CLOSELY** to trim something closely ■ *n* **1 ACT OF SHAVING** the act, process, or result of shaving **2** = **shaving** *n.* 1 **3 SHAVING TOOL** any tool for shaving or scraping [Old English *sceafan* < Indo-European, 'scrape, scratch']

shaven /sháyvən/ *v* past participle of **shave** ■ *adj* (*often in combination*) **1** with the beard or the hair shaved off **2** trimmed or cropped

shaver /sháyvər/ *n* **1** a device that is used to shave the beard or hair, especially an electric razor (*often before nouns*) **2** a boy who is not old enough to shave (*dated informal*)

Shavian /sháyvi ən/ *adj* **1 BY OR LIKE G. B. SHAW** written by or in the style of the work of the playwright George Bernard Shaw **2 OF SHAW** relating to or studying Shaw or his works ■ *n* **ADMIRER OR STUDENT OF SHAW** an admirer or student of Shaw or his works [Early 20C. < *Shavius*, Latinized form of SHAW.]

shaving /sháyving/ *n* **1** a thin slice shaved off **2** the removing of hair or a beard with a razor (*often before nouns*)

Shavuoth /shə voó ōth/, **Shavuot** /-ōt/ *n* a Jewish festival marking the Law being given by God to Moses on Mount Sinai. Date: 6th of Sivan, in May or June. [Late 19C. < Hebrew *šāḇūʿōṯ* 'weeks' (between Passover and Pentecost).]

shaw /shaw/ *n UK, Midwest* a thicket of shrubs or small trees [Old English *sceaga* < Germanic, 'something sticking out']

Shaw /shaw/, **George Bernard** (1856–1950) Irish playwright

Shaw, Norman (1831–1912) British architect

Shawinigan /shə wínnigən/ city in S Quebec, Canada. Population: 18,678 (1996).

shawl /shawl/ *n* a fabric square worn by women over the shoulders or head and shoulders or used to wrap a baby in ■ *vt* to cover somebody or something with a shawl or with something performing a similar function [Early 17C. < Persian and Urdu *šāl*.]

shawm /shawm/ *n* a woodwind instrument of the Middle Ages and Renaissance that has a double reed and was the predecessor of the modern oboe [14C. Probably back-formation < *schalmys*, plural of *shalemie* < Old French *chalemie* < Latin *calamus* 'reed'.]

Shawnee /sháw neé/ (*plural* **-nee** *or* **-nees**), **Shawano** /shə waánō/ (*plural* **-no** *or* **-nos**) *n* **1** a member of an Algonquian people who lived along the Ohio, Cumberland, and Tennessee rivers, and now live mainly in Oklahoma **2** the Algonquian language of the Shawnee people, almost extinct [Late 17C. < Delaware *šaːwanoːwː*.] —**Shawnee** *adj*

Shawwal /shə wól/ *n* in the Islamic calendar, the tenth lunar month of the year [Late 18C. < Arabic *shawwāl*.]

she *stressed* /shee/; *unstressed* /shi/ *pron* (*used as the subject of a verb*) **1 PREVIOUSLY MENTIONED FEMALE PERSON OR ANIMAL** used to refer to a female person or animal who has been previously mentioned or whose identity is known ○ *Ms Jones continues to enjoy high approval ratings as she starts her third year in office.* **2 OBJECT PERCEIVED AS FEMALE** used to refer to something previously mentioned or known that has been traditionally thought of as female, e.g. a nation, a car, a machine, a boat, or a ship ○ *Iran stated that she is ready to start talks on the issue.* ○ *She'll have to go to the scrap yard; she can't be repaired any longer.* ■ *n* **SOMETHING FEMALE** a female animal or person, sometimes used of a new baby ○ *Is it a he or a she?* [12C. Probably variant of Old English *hēo*.]

s/he /sheé awr heé/ *pron* used in writing as a pronoun to mean 'she or he' (*intended to avoid sexism in writing*) ○ *If a student wishes to change courses s/he should consult me before the end of term.*

shea butter *n* a white fat obtained from the seeds of the shea tree. Use: food, soap and candle manufacture.

sheading /sheéding/ *n* any of the six administrative districts of the Isle of Man [Late 16C. Variant of *shedding* 'division', originally present participle of SHED[1] in the sense 'divide'.]

sheaf /sheef/ *n* (*plural* **sheaves** /sheevz/) **1** a bundle of the harvested stalks of a plant, especially wheat or another cereal, with the heads still containing their seeds **2** a bundle of objects gathered or tied together ■ *vt* = **sheave**[1] *v.* [Old English *sceaf* < Germanic]

shear /sheer/ *v* (**shears, shearing, sheared, sheared** *or* **shorn** /shawrn/) **1** *vti* **CUT OFF** to remove something with a sharp tool **2** *vti* **CUT HAIR, WOOL, OR FOLIAGE FROM** to cut hair, fleece, or foliage from the surface of something using a sharp tool **3** *vt* **DEPRIVE** to take something valuable or prized away from somebody ○ *sheared of all self-respect* **4** *vti* **MOVE CLEANLY THROUGH** to move quickly and cleanly through something **5** *vti* **DEFORM BY APPLYING TWISTING FORCE** to cause something to deform or break by applying a twisting force ■ *n* **1 REMOVAL OF FLEECE** a cutting off of a sheep's wool, often used as a measure of the age of a sheep **2 WOOL CUT OFF** a quantity of wool cut off **3** PHYS, ENG = **shear strain 4** PHYS, ENG = **shear stress** ■ **shears** *npl* **1 CUTTING TOOL** a tool like a large pair of scissors, used for cutting or trimming **2 SHEERLEGS** a sheerlegs [Old English *sceran*, < Indo-European, 'to cut']

SPELLCHECK Do not confuse ***shear*** with ***sheer***, which has a similar sound. Beware: your spellchecker will not catch this error.

shearer /sheérər/ *n* a farm worker who shears sheep for a living, especially in Australia and New Zealand

Shearer /sheérər/, **Alan** (*b.* 1970) English footballer

shear force *n* a force, or a component of a force, that acts parallel to a plane

shearling /sheérling/ *n* **1** a young sheep, usually between six and twelve months old, after its first shearing **2** the tanned skin of a recently sheared lamb or sheep, with the short wool that remains after shearing still attached

shear modulus *n* the ratio of the shear stress to the shear strain, taken as an indication of the strength of a material under shear forces

shear pin *n* a pin inserted in a machine as a safety device. If safe loads are exceeded, the pin breaks and the machine shuts down.

shear strain *n* the angular deformation of a body, quantitatively taken to be the sideways displacement of two adjacent planes divided by the distance between them

shear stress *n* the forces acting on a body that produce shear strain

shearwater /sheér waatər/ (*plural* **-ters** *or* **-ter**) *n* a long-winged dark-coloured seabird with a short hooked bill, that flies low over the water in search of food. Genus: *Puffinus*. [< the impression when the bird flies that its wings are shearing the water]

sheath /sheeth/ *n* (*plural* **sheaths**) **1 CASE FOR A BLADE** a case for the blade of a knife, sword, or other cutting implement **2 CLOSE-FITTING COVERING** a covering or case that fits closely around something in the way that a sheath covers a blade **3 CLOSELY FITTING DRESS** a woman's closely fitting dress, originally floor-length, but now also knee-length **4** HEALTH = **condom 5 PROTECTIVE TUBE** a tubular covering that protects some body parts and plant parts, e.g. certain nerves and blood vessels in animals or leaf stems in some grasses ■ *vt* ARMS = **sheathe** [Old English *scǣð* < Germanic, 'divide, split']

sheathbill /sheéth bil/ *n* a squat shore bird with a horny sheath on its face, around the bill. Native to: rocky Antarctic and subantarctic coasts. *Chionis alba* and *Chionis minor*.

sheathe /sheeth/ (**sheathes, sheathing, sheathed**), **sheath** /sheeth/ *vt* **1 PUT INTO A SHEATH** to put a knife, sword, or other cutting implement into a sheath **2 ENCLOSE WITH A COVERING OR CASE** to enclose something in a covering or case ○ *PVC-sheathed cable* ○ *sheathed in a tight silk dress* **3 RETRACT** to retract the claws, in the way a cat does **4 THRUST INTO FLESH** to thrust a knife or sword into somebody's flesh (*literary*) [14C. < SHEATH.]

sheathing /sheéthing/ *n* something that encloses and protects, e.g. a covering of boards on a building's framework or a protective material applied to the underwater surfaces of a boat's hull

sheath knife *n* a knife with a fixed blade that is carried in a sheath

sheave[1] /sheev/ (**sheaves, sheaving, sheaved**), **sheaf** /sheef/ *vt* to gather something, especially the cut stalks of a cereal crop, into a sheaf [Late 16C. Back-formation < SHEAVES.]

sheave[2] /sheev/ *n* a wheel with a grooved rim for a rope, cable, or belt, especially one used as a pulley [13C. < Germanic, 'disc, slice of bread'.]

sheaves plural of **sheaf**

Sheba /sheébə/ ancient kingdom of SW Arabia, in present-day Yemen

shebang /shi báng/ [Mid-19C. < ?] ◇ **the whole shebang** the whole of something (*informal*)

Shebat *n* CALENDAR, JUDAISM = **Shevat**

shebeen /shi beén/ *n* a small establishment that sells alcoholic beverages illegally or without a licence, traditionally operating in the poorer regions of Ireland, Scotland, and South Africa [Late 18C. < Irish *síbín* 'little mug' < *séibe* 'mug'.]

Shechina /shə kínə, -keénə/, **Shechinah, Shekhinah** *n* in Jewish theology, God's presence in and throughout the world [Mid-17C. < late Hebrew *šěḵīnāh* < *šāḵan* 'rest, dwell'.]

shechita /shə kheétə/, **schechita** *n* the prescribed method of slaughter of animals and birds under Jewish dietary laws [Late 19C. < Hebrew *šěḥīṭāh* 'slaughter' < *šāḥaṭ* 'slaughter'.]

shed[1] /shed/ *v* (**sheds, shedding, shed**) **1** *vt* CAUSE TO FLOW to cause tears or blood to pour out **2** *vt* RADIATE to radiate or disperse something, especially light **3** *vti* LOSE NATURALLY to cast off a growing part, e.g. hair or leaves, as a result of a natural process such as moulting **4** *vt* GET RID OF to get rid of somebody or something that is unwanted or unnecessary **5** *vti* REPEL OR BE REPELLED to flow off or drop off, or cause something, especially water, to flow off or drop off **6** *vt* LOSE ACCIDENTALLY to have a transported load accidentally fall off onto the road **7** *vt Scotland* PART HAIR to part the hair ■ *n Scotland* DIVISION IN HAIR a parting in the hair [Old English *scēadan* 'divide, separate' < Germanic]

shed[2] /shed/ *n* **1** a small structure, either free-standing or attached to a larger building, used especially for storage or shelter **2** a large building with an open interior, used for storage or shelter or as a work area [15C. Probably variant of SHADE.]

she'd /sheed/ *contr* a short form of 'she had' or 'she would'

shed dormer *n* a dormer window with a flat roof that slopes in the same direction as the main roof that surrounds it

she-devil *n* a woman who is perceived as treating people with cruelty or contempt

sheen /sheen/ *n* **1** a bright, softly shining surface or appearance **2** fine or brightly coloured clothing (*literary*) [14C. < earlier *sheen* 'beautiful' < Old English *scēne* < Germanic, 'see'.] —**sheeny** *adj*

Sheene /sheen/, **Barry** (*b.* 1950) British motorcyclist

sheeny /sheéni/ (*plural* **-nies**) *n* an offensive term for a Jewish person (*slang*)

sheep /sheep/ (*plural* **sheep**) *n* **1** a stocky hooved mammal, with ribbed horns in the male. Kept for: wool, meat. Genus: *Ovis.* **2** a timid person who submits readily to others or is easily led [Old English *scēap* < Germanic] ◇ **separate the sheep from the goats** to distinguish good or competent members of a group from the bad or incompetent

sheep-dip *n* **1** a disinfectant in which sheep are immersed to rid them of external parasites such as mites, ticks, and flies **2** a bath containing a disinfectant in which sheep are immersed to rid them of external parasites

sheepdog /sheép dog/ *n* a dog that is used to herd sheep, or belongs to a breed traditionally used to herd sheep

sheepfold /sheépfōld/ *n* an enclosure or shelter for sheep

sheepish /sheépish/ *adj* **1** showing embarrassment as a result of having done something awkward or wrong **2** showing the meekness popularly associated with sheep —**sheepishly** *adv* —**sheepishness** *n*

sheep ked /-ked/ *n* INSECTS = **sheep tick** [*Ked* 'sheep tick' < ?]

sheep laurel *n* a low-growing evergreen shrub with leaves that are poisonous to young grazing animals. Flowers: crimson or pink. Native to: E United States, Canada. *Kalmia angustifolia.*

sheep's eyes *npl* shy glances full of love and longing [< the large size and the docile appearance of the eyes of sheep]

sheepshank /sheép shangk/ *n* a knot used to shorten a rope in which the rope is doubled up upon itself

sheepshead /sheéps hed/ (*plural* **sheepshead** *or* **sheepsheads**) *n* **1** a sea fish with a deep body marked with dark vertical bands. Native to: Atlantic coastal waters of North America. *Archosargus rhomboidalis.* **2** a freshwater fish of the drum family. Native to: E North America. *Aplodinotus grunniens.* [Mid-16C. < a supposed resemblance of its head to that of a sheep.]

sheepskin /sheép skin/ *n* **1** SHEEP LEATHER WITH OR WITHOUT WOOL the skin of a sheep used as leather, with or without the wool still attached (*often before nouns*) **2** SHEEPSKIN GARMENT OR RUG a rug or a garment, especially a coat or jacket, made from sheepskin with the wool attached **3** PARCHMENT a parchment made from the skin of a sheep (*often before nouns*) **4** *US* DIPLOMA a diploma, traditionally made of sheepskin parchment (*informal*)

sheep tick *n* a wingless fly that lives as a bloodsucking parasite on sheep and can cause serious skin irritations. *Melophagus ovinus.*

sheer[1] /sheer/ *adj* **1** COMPLETE AND UTTER used to emphasize the unlimited extent or unmitigated quality of something ○ *That explanation is sheer nonsense.* **2** EXCLUSIVE OF ANYTHING ELSE considered by itself without reference to anything else, or acting by itself without help from anything else ○ *She won the race by sheer endurance.* **3** PURE OR UNADULTERATED free from any impurities, or not mixed with anything else **4** VERTICAL rising nearly straight up or falling nearly straight down over a long distance ○ *They looked over the edge and there was a sheer drop.* **5** THIN AND ALMOST TRANSPARENT so thin and fine as to be almost transparent ○ *a sheer summer blouse* ■ *adv* **1** VERTICALLY with an almost vertical rise or fall **2** COMPLETELY completely and utterly ■ *n* NEARLY TRANSPARENT FABRIC a fabric or piece of clothing that is very thin and fine and almost transparent [Mid-16C. < ?] —**sheerly** *adv* —**sheerness** *n*

SPELLCHECK See *shear.*

sheer[2] /sheer/ *vti* SWERVE FROM A COURSE to swerve from a course, or cause a vehicle or vessel to swerve from its course ■ *n* **1** CHANGE OF COURSE an abrupt or sudden change of course **2** POSITION OF SHIP AT ANCHOR the position of a ship in relation to its anchor [Early 17C. < ?]

sheer[3] /sheer/ *n* the upward curve of a boat's hull as seen from the side, or the degree to which the hull curves upwards [Late 17C. < ?]

sheerlegs /sheér legz/ *n* a lifting device consisting of two poles tied together at the top and spread apart at the bottom with a pulley suspended from the apex (+ *singular or plural verb*)

Sheerness /sheér néss/ river port on the Isle of Sheppey, SE England. Population: 11,653 (1991).

sheet[1] /sheet/ *n* **1** CLOTH USED ON BED a large rectangular piece of cloth that is used to cover the mattress of a bed or somebody sleeping on the mattress **2** FLAT THIN RECTANGULAR PIECE a broad flat thin piece of a material, especially a rectangular piece of paper, metal, or glass **3** BROAD THIN EXPANSE a broad flat thin expanse of a substance, especially ice or water **4** EXPANSE OF SOMETHING MOVING a broad expanse of something that is in motion, e.g. falling water **5** PAGE OF STAMPS an entire rectangular page of postage stamps that were printed as a unit **6** NEWSPAPER a newspaper or periodical, especially one dismissed as trivial ■ *v* **1** *vt* PUT A SHEET OVER to cover or wrap something in a sheet **2** *vt* COVER WITH THIN LAYER to cover something with a thin layer of a material **3** *vt* MAKE INTO FLAT THIN PIECES to form something, especially metal, into broad flat thin pieces **4** *vi* FALL OVER BROAD EXPANSE to fall, flow, or spread out over a broad area ■ *adj* **1** BROAD, FLAT, AND THIN made in broad, flat, thin, usually rectangular pieces **2** COVERING THINLY covering a broad area thinly [Old English *scēte* 'cloth' < Germanic, 'project']

sheet down *vi* to fall in torrents (*refers to rain*)

sheet[2] /sheet/ *n* a rope or line attached to a bottom corner of a sail and used to change the sail's position ■ **sheets** *npl* the spaces in the bow and stern of an open boat that are not occupied by the seats [Old English *scēata* 'corner; lower part of a sail']

sheet anchor *n* **1** a large anchor that is dropped only in emergencies **2** a personal source of help in a time of crisis or danger [*Sheet* of unknown origin: perhaps influenced by SHEET[2]]

sheeting /sheéting/ *n* **1** wide cotton or linen cloth. Use: sheets. **2** thin material for lining and covering surfaces

sheet lightning *n* lightning that appears in a broad sheet as a result of being diffused by cloud cover

sheet metal *n* metal that has been formed into a sheet by being pressed between rollers until it is thinner than plate but thicker than foil

sheet music *n* music printed on folded or unfolded sheets of paper that have not been bound into a book

sheet pile *n* a vertical column of steel, wood, or concrete driven into the ground alongside others to form an underground barrier impeding the movement of earth or water

Sheffield /shéffeeld/ city in N England. Population: 528,500 (1995).

shegetz /sháygits/ (*plural* **shkotzim** /shkótsim/) *n* an offensive Jewish term for a boy or man who is not Jewish (*insult*) [Early 20C. Via Yiddish *sheygets* < Hebrew *šeqeṣ* 'abomination, detested thing'.]

sheik /shayk, sheek/, **sheikh, shaikh** *n* **1** ARAB CHIEF the leader of an Arab family or village **2** ISLAMIC RELIGIOUS LEADER a senior official in an Islamic religious organization **3** PHYSICALLY APPEALING MAN a handsome and physically appealing man (*dated informal*) [Late 16C. < Arabic *šayḵ* 'old man' < *šāḵa* 'be old'.] —**shaikhdom** *n* —**sheikhdom** *n* —**sheikdom** *n*

sheika /sháy kaa/, **sheikha, shaikha** *n* the wife of a sheik [Mid-19C. < Arabic *šayka.*]

sheikh *n* = **sheik**

sheikha *n* = **sheika**

sheila /sheélə/ *n ANZ* a woman, especially a girl or young woman (*informal*) [Mid-19C. < ?]

~~**sheild**~~ incorrect spelling of **shield**

sheitel /sháyt'l/ *n* a wig worn by an Orthodox married Jewish woman to avoid showing her natural hair, which she is not supposed to do according to Orthodox belief [Late 19C. Via Yiddish *sheytl* < Middle High German *scheitel* 'crown of the head'.]

shekel /shék'l/ *n* **1** see table at **currency** **2** ANCIENT JEWISH UNIT OF WEIGHT an ancient Jewish unit of weight equivalent to approximately 16g/0.5 oz **3** ANCIENT JEWISH COIN an ancient Jewish coin ■ **shekels** *npl* MONEY money or cash (*slang*) [Mid-16C. < Hebrew *šeqel* < *šaqal* 'weigh'.]

Shelburne /shélbərn, shél burn/, **William Petty Fitzmaurice, 2nd Earl of** (1737–1805) British statesman

sheldrake /shél drayk/ (*plural* **-drakes** *or* **-drake**) *n* **1** a male shelduck **2** BIRDS = **merganser** [14C. < ?]

shelduck /shél duk/ (*plural* **-ducks** *or* **-duck**) *n* a large thick-set often brightly coloured or variegated duck with a thick bill. Native to: Europe. Genus: *Tadorna.* [Early 18C. < SHELDRAKE + DUCK.]

shelf /shelf/ (*plural* **shelves** /shelvz/) *n* **1** FLAT SURFACE FOR HOLDING OBJECTS a flat usually rectangular board on which things are stored or displayed **2** CONTENTS OF SHELF the contents of a shelf, or the quantity of something that a shelf holds **3** LEDGE ON THE LANDSCAPE a ledge of rock, ice, or sand **4** LAYER OF UNDERGROUND ROCK a layer of underground rock encountered when sinking a shaft **5** HEEL OF HAND the part of the heel of the hand on which the back end of an arrow is supported before being fired from a bow [14C. < Low German *schelf* < ?] —**shelfful** *n* ◇ **be (left) on the shelf 1** to be thought too old to have any chance of marrying (*sometimes offensive*) **2** to be no longer wanted, used, or taken account of

shelf fungus *n* FUNGI = **bracket fungus**

shelf ice *n* a large plate of floating ice that has broken off from an ice shelf

shelf life *n* **1** the length of time a product may be stored before it begins to lose its freshness or effectiveness **2** the length of time that somebody or something is popular or lasts (*informal*)

shelf mark *n* a series of numbers or letters on a book indicating its location in a library

ϟ**shell** /shel/ *n* **1** COVERING OF TURTLE OR CRAB the hard protective outer covering of turtles, crabs, and other molluscs and crustaceans, or the calcium-based material this covering is made of **2** COVERING OF INSECT'S BODY the hard outer covering (**exoskeleton**) of an insect's body **3** COVERING OF EGG the hard or tough protective outer covering of the eggs of birds, reptiles, and a few mammals **4** NUT'S OUTER COVERING the hard or fibrous protective outer covering of some seeds and fruits such as nuts **5** PROTECTIVE CASING any hard casing or covering that protects or holds its contents, or the material composing it **6** FRAMEWORK OF BUILDING the basic framework of a building, especially while under construction or after damage by fire **7** SHIP'S HULL the outer hull of a ship **8** PASTRY CASE a casing of pastry that has a filling put into it **9** HOLLOW OR EMPTY THING an external form that contains nothing ○ *a mere shell of her former self* **10** RESERVED MANNER a reserved manner behind which a shy person hides feelings or thoughts ○ *eventually came out of her shell and joined in* **11** LARGE EXPLOSIVE PROJECTILE an explosive projectile fired from a large-bore gun such as a field gun or tank gun **12** GUN CARTRIDGE a piece of ammunition fired by a gun, especially a shotgun cartridge, which holds the shot and explosive powder **13** FIREWORK CARTRIDGE the cartridge that forms the outside of a firework and contains the explosive powder **14** *US* SMALL GLASS a small beer glass **15** UNLINED JACKET an unlined usually lightweight jacket **16** *US* SLEEVELESS BLOUSE a sleeveless blouse or sweater for a woman **17** BUSINESS = **shell company** **18** NARROW RACING BOAT a narrow light boat used for racing, rowed by one or more people **19** GROUP OF ELECTRONS IN SIMILAR ORBITS a group of electrons orbiting the nucleus of an atom and having the same principal quantum number **20** COMMAND PROGRAM a computer program that simplifies the interface between a user and the operating system by allowing the user to pick from a set of menus instead of entering commands ■ *v* **1** *vti* TAKE SOMETHING OUT OF A

SHELL to take something out of a shell, or be taken out of a shell ○ *shell peas* **2** *vti* **SEPARATE KERNELS FROM A COB** to separate kernels from a cob, or be separated from a cob ○ *shell sweet corn* **3** *vti* **BOMBARD TARGET** to fire artillery shells at something **4** *vi* **FLAKE OFF** to fall off in thin scales **5** *vi US* **COLLECT SEASHELLS** to look for and gather shells at the seashore [Old English *scell*, originally 'something that splits off']

shell out *vti* to pay out money, especially a great deal of money (*informal*)

she'll /sheel/ *contr* a short form of 'she will' or 'she shall'

shellac /shə lák, shéllak/ *n* **1 PURIFIED RESIN** yellowish-orange flakes of a resin (**lac**) secreted by a tropical insect **2 VARNISH** a thin varnish made of purified lac dissolved in alcohol. Use: formerly, as a coating on wooden items. **3 78 RPM GRAMOPHONE RECORD** an old type of gramophone record originally made from a material containing purified lac, played at 78 rpm ■ *vt* (**-lacs, -lacking, -lacked**) **1 APPLY SHELLAC TO** to coat something with shellac varnish **2** *US* **HIT REPEATEDLY** to beat somebody repeatedly with hard blows (*slang*) **3** *US* **DEFEAT EASILY** to defeat somebody easily or decisively (*slang*) [Mid-17C. < SHELL + LAC[1], after French *laque en écailles* 'lac (melted) in thin plates'.]

shellacking /shə láking, shéllaking/ *n US* (*slang*) **1** a severe physical beating **2** an easy or decisive defeat

shellback /shél bak/ *n* **1** a sailor who has crossed the equator, especially one whose crossing was marked by a traditional initiation ceremony **2** an old or experienced sailor [< the idea that limpets and barnacles have grown on the sailor's back during the long time at sea]

shell company *n* a company that has no independent assets or operations of its own but is used by its owners to conduct certain business dealings or maintain control of other companies

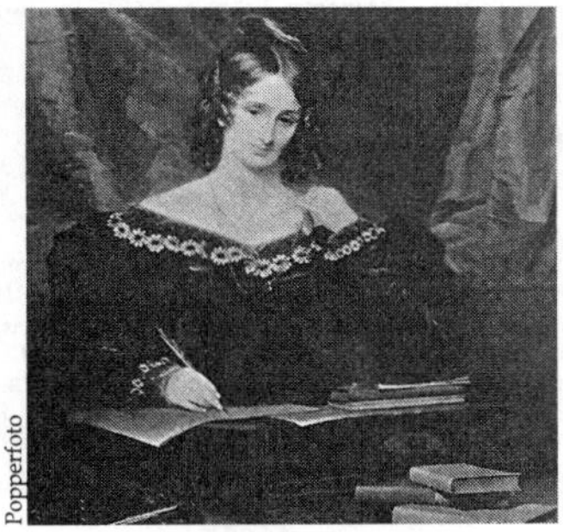

Mary Shelley

Shelley /shélli/, **Mary** (1797–1851) British writer. Born **Mary Wollstonecraft Godwin**

Shelley, Percy Bysshe (1792–1822) British poet

shellfire /shél fīr/ *n* **1** artillery shells or projectiles fired at a target **2** the firing or exploding of artillery shells or projectiles

shellfish /shél fish/ (*plural* **-fish** *or* **-fishes**) *n* an aquatic invertebrate animal with a shell, especially an edible mollusc or crustacean such as an oyster, shrimp, or lobster

shell game *n US* **1** a form of the game thimblerig in which spectators bet on the final location of an object hidden under one of three walnut shells or cups that have been shuffled **2** a scheme for defrauding or deceiving people

shell jacket *n* a tight-fitting military jacket that extends only to the waist and is worn on semiformal occasions

shell-like *n* somebody's ear (*slang humorous*)

shell pink *adj* of a pale pink colour (*hyphenated before nouns*) —**shell pink** *n*

shell shock *n* a psychiatric disorder caused by exposure to warfare, especially shellfire (*dated*)

shell-shocked *adj* **1** stunned, upset, or exhausted as a result of a stressful experience (*informal*) **2** experiencing severe psychological effects from exposure to warfare, especially shellfire

shell star *n* a star that is thought to have a surrounding shell of gas

shell suit *n* a lightweight shiny brightly coloured tracksuit worn casually or for sport

shellwork /shél wurk/ *n* seashells stuck on furniture and other items to give a decorative finish

Shelta /shéltə/ *n* an ancient secret language used by the Roma and other travelling people in Ireland and the United Kingdom, based on Gaelic [Late 19C. < ?]

shelter /shéltər/ *n* **1 STRUCTURE THAT PROTECTS OR COVERS** a structure or building that provides cover from weather or protection against danger **2 REFUGE** an establishment providing accommodation and food for people who need to leave a violent or otherwise dangerous situation **3 PROTECTION OR COVER** the protection, cover, refuge, or safety that a shelter provides **4 DWELLING OR HOUSING** a place to live, considered as one of life's necessities **5** *US* **REFUGE FOR ANIMALS** an establishment that takes in and looks after lost or unwanted animals ■ *v* **1** *vt* **PROVIDE WITH PROTECTION** to provide somebody or something with protection, cover, refuge, or safety **2** *vi* **FIND PROTECTION** to find protection, cover, refuge, or safety **3** *vt* **INVEST TO AVOID TAXES** to put money into an investment that is subject to a lower tax rate or is free from taxes [Late 16C. < ?]

sheltered /shéltərd/ *adj* **1** protected from the adverse effects of the weather, especially wind **2** protected from the unpleasant, upsetting, or testing experiences of life

sheltered housing, sheltered accommodation *n* accommodation specially designed for elderly or disabled people. It usually consists of self-contained self-catering units with some communal facilities and live-in staff to help when required.

sheltered workshop *n US* a workplace specially designed to provide a noncompetitive environment where people who have various limitations can acquire job skills and experience

shelter tent *n US* a small tent for two people usually made from two similar pieces of waterproof fabric

sheltie /shélti/, **shelty** (*plural* **-ties**) *n* a Shetland pony or a Shetland sheepdog (*informal*) [Early 16C. Probably via Orkney dialect < Old Norse *Hjalti* 'Shetlander'.]

shelve[1] /shelv/ (**shelves, shelving, shelved**) *vt* **1 PUT ON SHELF** to put or store something on a shelf **2 SET ASIDE** to put something off until later, or set something aside **3 DISMISS** to dismiss or withdraw somebody or something from active service [Late 16C. Back-formation < SHELVES.]

shelve[2] /shelv/ (**shelves, shelving, shelved**) *vi* to descend with a flat, usually gradual slope [Late 16C. < ?]

shelves plural of **shelf**

shelving /shélving/ *n* **1** the shelves in a place, or shelves in general **2** material used for making shelves

Shema /shə maá/ *n* the confession of faith made in Jewish religious practice [Early 18C. < Hebrew *šĕma* 'Hear!'.]

shemozzle /shə mózz'l/ *n* (*dated informal*) **1** a confused or muddled situation **2** a noisy quarrel or argument [Late 19C. Via Yiddish, 'crooked luck' < Middle High German *slim* 'crooked' + *mazzāl* 'luck'.]

Shenandoah National Park /shénnən dō ə-/ national park in N Virginia. Area: 802 sq. km/310 sq. mi.

shenanigan /shi nánnigən/ *n* (*informal*) **1** something that is deceitful, underhand, or otherwise questionable (*usually plural*) **2** a playful trick, mischievous prank, or other display of high spirits [Mid-19C. < ?]

Shenyang /shən yúng/ city in NE China. Population: 3,860,000 (1993).

Sheol /sheé ol, sheé ōl/ *n* in ancient Hebrew theology, the dwelling place of the dead [Late 16C. < Hebrew *šĕ'ōl*.]

~~shepard~~ incorrect spelling of **shepherd**

Shepard /shéppərd/, **Alan, Jr.** (1923–98) US astronaut

Shepard, Sam (*b.* 1943) US playwright and actor. Full name **Samuel Shepard Rogers, Jr.**

shepherd /shéppərd/ *n* **1 SOMEBODY TENDING SHEEP** a person who tends sheep **2 SOMEBODY PROVIDING GUIDANCE** a leader or guide of a group, especially a Christian minister ■ *v* **1** *vti* **TEND SHEEP** to look after sheep **2** *vt* **GUIDE** to guide a group of people somewhere **3** *vt* **TAKE CARE OF OTHERS** to look after the well-being of a group of people **4** *vti Aus* **SHIELD TEAM-MATE** in Australian Rules football, to shield a team-mate by blocking the approach of an opposing player [Old English *scēaphirde* < *scēap* 'sheep' + *hierde* 'herder']

shepherdess /shéppər déss/ *n* **1** a girl or woman who looks after sheep (*dated*) **2** in pastoral literature, a character who is an idealized representation of a country girl

shepherd's check *n* (*often before nouns*) **1** a pattern of small black-and-white squares **2** a fabric in a shepherd's check pattern

shepherd's pie *n* a baked dish made of cooked minced meat, traditionally lamb or mutton, in gravy with a topping of mashed potato

shepherd's purse *n* an annual plant that has heart-shaped seed pods and is a common garden weed. *Capsella bursa-pastoris.* [< the pod's resemblance to a bag used by shepherds to carry food]

~~sheppard~~ incorrect spelling of **shepherd**

Sheppard /shéppərd/, **Jack** (1702–24) English robber. Born **John Sheppard**

Sheppard, Kate (1848–1934) British-born New Zealand suffragist. Born **Catherine Wilson Malcolm**

Shepparton /shéppərtən/ city in N Victoria, Australia. Population: 30,510 (1991).

Sheppey, Isle of /shéppi/ island off the coast of SE England, at the mouth of the River Medway. Area: 91 sq. km/35 sq. mi.

Sheraton /shérrətən/ *adj* relating to furniture designed by or in the graceful simple style of Thomas Sheraton, who favoured straight lines, understated classical ornamentation, and light thin legs

Sheraton /shérrətən/, **Thomas** (1751–1806) British cabinetmaker

sherbet /shúrbət/ *n* **1 FIZZY POWDER** a fruit-flavoured sweet powder that fizzes when moistened on the tongue and is eaten as a confection or is stirred into water to make a fizzy drink (*often before nouns*) **2 FRUIT DRINK** a drink made from fruit juice, water, and sugar and served chilled **3 sherbet, sherbert** *US* **FROZEN DESSERT** a frozen dessert made with fruit syrup, milk and the white of an egg, whisked until smooth and opaque **4 sherbet, sherbert BEER** beer (*dated humorous slang*) [Early 17C. Via Turkish *şerbet* and Persian *šerbet* < Arabic *šarbat* 'drink' < *šariba* 'drink'.]

Sherborne /shúr bawrn/ market town in S England. Population: 7,606 (1991).

Sherbrooke /shúr bro͝ok/ city in S Quebec, Canada. Population: 76,429 (1991).

sherd *n* ARCHAEOL = **potsherd**

shereef *n* ISLAM, POL, HIST = **sharif**

Sheridan /shérridən/, **Richard Brinsley** (1751–1816) Irish-born British playwright

sherif /she reéf/ *n* ISLAM, POL, HIST = **sharif**

sheriff /shérrif/ *n* **1 SENIOR OFFICIAL OF ENGLISH COUNTY** in England and Wales, the senior representative of the monarch in a county, who performs ceremonial and some judicial duties **2 SCOTTISH JUDGE** in Scotland, a judge who presides over one of the lower courts for civil and criminal cases (**sheriff courts**) **3 US COUNTY LAW ENFORCEMENT OFFICER** in the United States, the chief law enforcement officer for a county, whose duties are sometimes restricted to the enforcement of the orders of the courts **4 CANADIAN COURT OFFICER** in Canada, an officer of the courts who assists with the administration of the justice system, e.g. by serving writs **5 AUSTRALIAN COURT OFFICIAL** in Australia, a court official charged with managing juries and implementing orders from the Supreme Court [Old English *scīrgerēfa* 'reeve of the shire' < *scīr* 'shire' + *gerēfa* 'reeve'] —**sheriffdom** *n*

sheriff court *n* in Scotland, the lower court for civil and criminal cases

sheriff officer *n* in Scotland, a court official who carries out warrants and serves writs

Sherlock Holmes /shúr lok hṓmz/ *n* **1** somebody with exceptional powers of deduction or perception (*humorous*) **2** a private detective (*informal*) [Early 20C. After the detective in the stories of Sir Arthur Conan Doyle (1859–1930).]

Sherman /shúrmən/, **Cindy** (*b.* 1954) US photographer

Sherman, William T. (1820–91) US Union general

sherpa /shúrpə/ *n* **1** fabric with a fleecy pile. Use: lining for winter outdoor wear. **2** CLIMBING = **Sherpa** *n.* **2 3** POL = **Sherpa** *n.* **3**

Sherpa (*plural* **-pas** *or* **-pa**) *n* **1 MEMBER OF HIMALAYAN PEOPLE** a member of a people originally from Tibet who live on the S Himalayan slopes in Nepal and Sikkim **2 HIMALAYAN GUIDE** a Sherpa who works as a guide for mountaineers in the Himalayas **3 EXPERT POLITICAL AIDE** an expert who helps a government leader prepare for a summit meeting [Mid-19C. < Tibetan *sharpa* 'inhabitant of an eastern country'.]

~~**sherrif**~~ incorrect spelling of **sheriff**

sherry /shérri/ (*plural* **-ries**) *n* a wine, especially one made near Jerez, Spain, that has a higher alcohol content as a result of adding brandy, and ranges from very sweet to very dry [Late 16C. Alteration of earlier *sherris*, interpreted as plural, after *Xeres* (now Jerez), Spain.]

Sherwood Forest /shúr wŏŏd-/ ancient forest in central England

she's /sheez/ *contr* a short form of 'she is' or 'she has'

Shetland /shétlənd/ *n* **1** ZOOL = **Shetland sheepdog 2** TEXTILES = **Shetland wool 3** an item of clothing made of Shetland wool, especially a sweater ■ *adj* made of Shetland wool

Shetland Islands group of about 150 islands north of mainland Scotland. Capital: Lerwick. Population: 23,232 (1996). Area: 1,438 sq. km/555 sq. mi. —**Shetlander** *n*

Shetland pony *n* a small sturdy pony with a long shaggy mane and tail, belonging to a breed that originated in the Shetland Islands

Shetland sheepdog *n* a small herding dog with a heavy coat that resembles a collie, belonging to a breed that originated in the Shetland Islands

Shetland wool *n* fine wool from sheep raised in the Shetland Islands, or a yarn spun from this wool

Shevardnadze /shévvərd naádzi/, **Eduard** (*b.* 1928) Georgian statesman

Shevat /shə vót/, **Shebat** /-bót, -vót/ *n* in the Jewish calendar, the fifth month of the civil year and the 11th month of the religious year [Mid-16C. < Hebrew *šĕbaṭ*.]

shew /shō/ (**shews, shewing, shewed, shewed** *or* **shewn** /shōn/) *vti* to show (*archaic*) [Variant spelling]

shewbread /shṓ bred/ *n* in the Bible, the twelve loaves of bread placed in the tabernacle every Sabbath by the Hebrew priests of ancient Israel (*archaic*)

SHF, shf *abbr* superhigh frequency

shh *interj* = **sh**

Shia, Shi'a, Shi'ah *n* (*plural* **-a** *or* **-as**; *plural* **-'a** *or* **-'as**; *plural* **-'ah** *or* **-'ahs**) **1** the branch of Islam that considers Ali, the cousin of Muhammad, and his descendants as Muhammad's true successors. ◊ **Sunni 2** ISLAM = **Shiite** *n*. ■ *adj* ISLAM = **Shiite** *adj*. [Early 17C. < Arabic *šīʿa* 'faction, party'.]

shiatsu /shi aát soo/, **shiatzu** *n* a form of healing massage in which the hands are used to apply pressure at acupuncture points on the body in order to stimulate and redistribute energy [Mid-20C. < Japanese, 'finger pressure'.]

shibboleth /shíbbə leth/ *n* **1** CATCHWORD OR SLOGAN a word or phrase frequently used, or a belief strongly held, by members of a group that is usually regarded by outsiders as meaningless, unimportant, or misguided **2** COMMON SAYING OR BELIEF a saying that is widely used or a belief that is widely held, especially one that interferes with somebody's ability to speak or think about things without preconception **3** IDENTIFYING WORD OR CUSTOM a unique pronunciation, word, behaviour, or practice used to distinguish one group of people from another and to identify individuals as either members of the group or outsiders [Mid-17C. < Hebrew *šibbōleṯ* 'stream'.]

shidduch /shí dak͟h/ (*plural* **-duchim** /shi dŏŏk͟him/) *n* a Jewish marriage, formerly usually arranged by a professional matchmaker (**shadchan**) [Late 19C. Via Yiddish < Hebrew *šiddūḵ* 'negotiation'.]

~~**shiek**~~ incorrect spelling of **sheik**

Shiel, Loch /sheel/ long narrow lake in W Scotland. It is a National Scenic Area. Length: 27 km/17 mi.

shield /sheeld/ *n* **1** PIECE OF ARMOUR CARRIED ON ARM a flat or convex piece of armour carried on the arm and used as a protection against weapon blows, arrows, bullets, or projectiles **2** PROTECTION OR DEFENCE somebody or something that serves as protection or acts as a defence **3** COAT OF ARMS a shield or a shield-shaped insignia that contains somebody's coat of arms **4** PRIZE OR TROPHY a prize or trophy, especially in a sports competition, that is made in the shape of a shield **5** DECORATIVE OFFICIAL EMBLEM a decorative device used as an official emblem by a government or organization, usually containing symbolic images associated with the government's territory or the organization's purpose **6** US POLICE OFFICER'S BADGE the official badge that a US police officer wears or carries **7** CLOTHING = **dress shield 8** PROTECTIVE PLATE ATTACHED TO ARTILLERY a steel plate attached to a piece of artillery to protect those operating the artillery from bullets and shrapnel **9** MACHINE'S SAFETY BARRIER a protective barrier such as a screen or housing around the moving parts of a piece of machinery **10** ANTISTATIC OR ANTIMAGNETIC SCREEN a screen used to protect equipment or people from unwanted electric or magnetic fields **11** WALL PROTECTING FROM RADIATION an encasing structure or wall, usually made of lead or concrete that is put around a nuclear reactor or other source of radiation to prevent the release of radiation **12** FLAT AREA OF ROCK a broad flat area of exposed Precambrian basement rock that lies at the centre of each continent **13** ANIMAL'S PROTECTIVE COVERING the protective covering of an animal, e.g. a shell, scale, or plate ■ *v* **1** *vt* PROTECT WITH SHIELD to defend or protect somebody or something with a shield or by using the body or another object as a shield **2** *vi* ACT AS SHIELD to serve or act as a protection or defence **3** *vt* HIDE to conceal or shelter somebody or something from view [Old English *scield* < Germanic] —**shielder** *n*

SYNONYMS See ***safeguard***.

shielding /sheélding/ *n* the use of material such as lead or concrete around a source of radiation to prevent the harmful release of radiation

Shield of David *n* JUDAISM = **Star of David**

shieling /sheéling/ *n Scotland* **1** a mountain hut used by a cowherd **2** a mountain pasture that is used by cattle in the summer [Mid-16C. < earlier *shiel* < ?]

ϟ **shift** /shift/ *v* **1** *vti* MOVE to move somebody or something to a different position, or be moved to a different position **2** *vti* EXCHANGE to change or exchange something for something else of the same group, set, or class ○ *I've shifted jobs three times in the last year.* **3** *vti* REMOVE STAIN to remove a mark or stain from a material or surface, especially with difficulty, or be removed from a material or surface **4** *vti* CHANGE GEARS to change gears in a motor vehicle **5** *vi* PROVIDE FOR OWN NEEDS to provide personal needs or manage personal affairs ○ *You need to learn to shift for yourself.* **6** *vi* GET BY WITH DECEIT to get by through the use of deceit, tricks, or underhand methods **7** *vi* MOVE FAST to move at great speed (*informal*) **8** *vt* EAT OR DRINK QUICKLY to eat or drink something quickly or in large amounts (*informal*) **9** *vt* SELL QUICKLY to sell something quickly or in large amounts, often when it is stolen or illegal or difficult to sell (*informal*) **10** *vi* PRESS SHIFT KEY to press the shift key on a computer or typewriter keyboard to produce capital letters and certain other characters **11** *vti* ALTER PHONETICALLY to alter a sound phonetically in the course of the development of a language, or be altered phonetically **12** *vi Malaysia, Singapore* MOVE HOUSE to move house ○ *We are going to shift to Penang.* ■ *n* **1** CHANGE MADE a change in position, direction, makeup, or circumstances **2** PERIOD OF TIME WORKED a period of working time, especially any of the fixed periods that the day is divided into in workplaces that operate 24 hours a day **3** PEOPLE WORKING DURING PERIOD the group of people who are working during a particular period of time **4** COMPUT = **shift key 5** DRESS a loose-fitting dress that hangs down from the shoulders **6** WOMAN'S UNDERGARMENT a woman's shirt-shaped undergarment of the 17th and 18th centuries **7** PLAN a tactic or plan required to accomplish something difficult **8** TRICK a deceitful or underhand scheme or plan **9** ROCK DISPLACEMENT a displacement of rocks on a fault line **10** CHANGE IN HAND POSITION a change in hand position in order to play a different set of notes in a different register on a keyboard or stringed instrument **11** CHANGE IN PRONUNCIATION a change in the pronunciation of a sound in the course of the development of a language **12** CHANGE IN FREQUENCY a change in the position of a spectral line representing a change of frequency, e.g. that caused by the Doppler effect [Old English *sciftan* 'divide, arrange' < Germanic] ◇ **shift base** to move one's headquarters or base for operations to another place

SYNONYMS See ***change***.

ϟ **shift key** *n* a key on a computer or typewriter keyboard that is pressed to produce capital letters or certain other characters

shiftless /shíftləss/ *adj* **1** unwilling to make the effort to be successful or do something properly **2** lacking the abilities or knowledge required to do something successfully or properly —**shiftlessly** *adv* —**shiftlessness** *n*

shiftwork /shíft wurk/ *n* a system of working in which people work one of a set of usually two 12-hour or three eight-hour shifts in a 24-hour period (*often before nouns*)

shifty /shífti/ (**-ier, -iest**) *adj* **1** UNTRUSTWORTHY likely to try to deceive or avoid responsibility **2** *US* CHANGING DIRECTION OR POSITION changing direction or position often or quickly, or able to do so **3** RESOURCEFUL with the abilities and knowledge needed to do something successfully —**shiftily** *adv* —**shiftiness** *n*

shigella /shi géllə/ (*plural* **-lae** /-li/ *or* **-las**) *n* a rod-shaped bacterium that lives in the intestinal tracts of human beings and animals and causes dysentery. Genus: *Shigella*. [Mid-20C. < modern Latin *Shigella*, after Kiyoshi *Shiga* (1870–1957), Japanese bacteriologist.]

shigellosis /shíggə lóssiss/ (*plural* **-ses** /-seez/) *n* a highly infectious form of dysentery caused by the shigella bacterium

shih tzu /sheé tsŏŏ/ (*plural* **shih tzus** *or* **shih tzu**) *n* a small short-legged dog with a short muzzle, long dense coat, and a tail that curls over its back, belonging to a breed developed in Tibet [Early 20C. < Chinese *shīzigǒu* 'lion dog'.]

Shiism /sheé izəm/, **Shi'ism** *n* the Shiite branch of the Islamic religion [Late 19C. < SHIA or SHIITE.]

shiitake /shi taáki/, **shiitake mushroom, shitake, shitake mushroom** *n* a dark-coloured mushroom with an edible fleshy cap. Native to: E Asia. *Lentinus edodes*. [Late 19C. < Japanese, 'oak-tree mushroom'.]

Shiite /sheé īt/, **Shi'ite** *n* a follower of the Shia branch of Islam. ◊ **Sunni** ■ *adj* relating to Shiites or to the Shia branch of Islam —**Shiitic** /shee íttik/ *adj*

Shijiazhuang /shəji ə jŏŏ ung/ capital of Hebei Province, east-central China. Population: 1,472,460 (1991).

shikari /shi kaári/, **shikaree** *n S Asia* a big-game hunter, especially a professional hunter who works as a guide [Early 19C. Via Urdu < Persian *šikārī* 'of hunting' < *šikār* 'hunting'.]

shiksa /shíksə/, **shikse** *n* an offensive Jewish term for a girl or woman who is not Jewish (*insult*) [Late 19C. < Yiddish *shikse*, feminine of *sheygets* (see SHEGETZ).]

shill /shil/ *n US* **1** PRETENDED CUSTOMER OR GAMBLER an accomplice who pretends to be an interested customer or gambler in order to lure others into buying or gambling **2** SELF-INTERESTED PROMOTER a promoter of somebody or something for reasons of self-interest ■ *v US* **1** *vi* BE SHILL to be or work as a shill **2** *vt* PROMOTE AS SHILL to promote or sell something using the tactics of a shill [Early 20C. < ?]

shillelagh /shi láylə, -li/, **shillalah** *n Ireland* a stick or club, traditionally made of oak or blackthorn wood [Late 18C. After *Shillelagh*, town in Co. Wicklow, Ireland, famous for oaks.]

shilling /shílling/ *n* **1** FORMER BRITISH COIN a former subunit of British currency **2** FORMER US COIN a former US coin **3** see table at **currency 4** *Malaysia, Singapore* COIN a coin (*informal*) [Old English *scilling*] ◇ **not the full shilling** an offensive phrase meaning extremely unintelligent or affected to some extent by mental illness (*informal*)

Shillong /shi lóng/ capital of Meghalaya State, NE India. Population: 131,719 (1991).

Shilluk /shi lŏŏk/ (*plural* **-luk** *or* **-luks**) *n* **1** a member of a people who live in NE Africa, mainly along the western bank of the Nile in S Sudan **2** the Nilo-Saharan language of the Shilluk people. Native speakers: 110,000. [Late 18C. < Shilluk.] —**Shilluk** *adj*

shilly-shally /shílli shali/ *vi* (**shilly-shallies, shilly-shallying, shilly-shallied**) **1** HESITATE OR VACILLATE to be unable to make a choice or decision when one is needed **2** WASTE TIME to waste time on unimportant things ■ *adv* IRRESOLUTELY with hesitation or a lack of decision ■ *adj* LACKING DECISIVENESS feeling or showing a lack of decisiveness ■ *n* (*plural* **shilly-shallies**) HESITATION a failure or inability to make a choice or decision [Early 18C. Alteration of 'shall I? shall I?'.] —**shilly-shallier** *n*

shim /shim/ *n* a thin usually wedge-shaped piece of wood, metal, plastic, or other material that is used to help position something properly, usually by adjusting a level or filling a gap ■ *vt* (**shims, shimming, shimmed**) to position or adjust something using a shim [Early 18C. < ?]

shimmer /shímmər/ *vti* **1** SHINE WITH A WAVERING LIGHT to shine softly with a wavering or flickering light, or cause something to shine in this way **2** BE VISIBLE AS WAVERING IMAGE to be visible as a wavering or flickering and sometimes distorted image, or make something visible in this way ■ *n* 1 **WAVERING LIGHT OR GLOW** a wavering or flickering soft light or glow 2 **WAVERING IMAGE OR APPEARANCE** a wavering or flickering and sometimes distorted image, e.g. that caused by hot air rising from the ground [Old English *scymrian* < Germanic, 'shine'] — **shimmery** *adj*

shimmy /shímmi/ *n* 1 **WOBBLING OF A VEHICLE** a wobbling motion or vibration, especially in the front wheels of a motor vehicle 2 **POPULAR 1920S DANCE** a 1920s jazz dance in which the body was held straight and shaken rhythmically and rapidly from the shoulders down 3 **CHEMISE** a chemise (*informal*) ■ *vi* (**-mies, -mying, -mied**) 1 **MOVE WITH A WOBBLE** to wobble or be shaken with a wobbling motion, especially in the front wheels (*refers to vehicles*) 2 **DANCE THE SHIMMY** to dance the shimmy 3 **MOVE WITH A SHAKE** to move the body in a shaking or swaying way [Early 20C. < ?]

Shimonoseki /shímmənō séeki/ port on SW Honshu Island, Japan. Population: 262,635 (1990).

shin[1] /shin/ *n* 1 **FRONT OF LOWER LEG** the front portion of the leg from below the knee to above the ankle, or the leg bone (**tibia**) located there 2 **CUT OF BEEF** the lower portion of the foreleg in cattle, used as a cut of beef in stews ■ *v* (**shins, shinning, shinned**) 1 *vti* **CLIMB USING ARMS AND LEGS** to climb a rope, tree, or pole with speed and agility by gripping with the arms and legs and then pulling up with the arms and sliding upwards 2 *vt* **HIT IN SHIN** to kick or hit somebody in the shin [Old English *scinu* < Germanic]

shin[2] /shin/, **sin** *n* the 22nd letter of the Hebrew alphabet [Early 19C. < Hebrew *shīn*.]

shinbone /shínbōn/ *n* the flat surface of the bone immediately under the skin on the front of the lower leg. Technical name **tibia** *n.* 1 [Old English *scinbān*]

shindig /shíndig/ *n* 1 a noisy and festive party or celebration (*informal*) 2 = **shindy** *n.* 1 [Late 19C. Probably alteration of SHINDY.]

shindy /shíndi/ (*plural* **-dies**) *n* 1 a disturbance or commotion (*informal*) 2 = **shindig** *n.* 1 [Early 19C. Probably a variant of SHINTY.]

shine /shīn/ *v* (**shines, shining, shone, shone** /shon/) 1 *vi* **EMIT LIGHT** to give out light 2 *vi* **BE BRIGHT** to be bright or reflect light 3 *vt* **DIRECT LIGHT** to direct the light emitted by something ○ *Shine the torch over here.* 4 *vi* **EXCEL** to be very good at or do very well in some form of activity 5 *vi* **APPEAR CLEARLY** to appear clearly 6 *vi* **HAVE RADIANT QUALITY** to appear to have a specially bright or radiant quality as a result of good health or a strong positive emotion ○ *Her face shone with happiness.* 7 *vt* **POLISH** to make something bright and gleaming by polishing it ■ *n* 1 **BRIGHTNESS FROM LIGHT SOURCE** brightness or radiance emitted by a source of light 2 **BRIGHT SURFACE** the bright or gleaming surface of something 3 **ACT OF POLISHING** an act of polishing something to make it shiny 4 *US* **MOONSHINE** moonshine (*informal*) [Old English *scīnan* < Indo-European, 'glimmer'] ◇ **take a shine to somebody** to develop a liking for somebody (*informal*)

shiner /shīnər/ *n* 1 **BLACK EYE** a black eye (*informal*) 2 **SHINY FRESHWATER FISH** a small silvery freshwater fish. Native to: North America. Genus: *Notropis.* 3 **SOMETHING SHINY** something that shines or makes something shine

shingle[1] /shíng g'l/ *n* 1 **ROOF OR WALL TILE** a small flat tile, especially one made of wood, used in overlapping rows to cover a roof or wall 2 **HAIRSTYLE** a short hairstyle for women, popular in the 1920s, in which the back hair was cut to taper at the nape of the neck 3 *US, Can* **SIGN OR NAMEPLATE** a nameplate or a small sign giving the name of a doctor, lawyer, or other professional person, fixed outside that person's office ■ *vt* (**-gles, -gling, -gled**) 1 **COVER SOMETHING WITH TILES** to cover something with small overlapping tiles 2 **TAPER HAIR AT BACK** to cut hair so that it is tapered at the nape of the neck [12C. Alteration of late Latin *scindula*, variant of Latin *scandula*.] — **shingler** *n* ◇ **hang out your shingle** *US, Can* to begin working as a professional from your own office (*informal*)

shingle[2] /shíng g'l/ *n* 1 small round pebbles on a beach 2 an area of beach covered in shingle [Mid-16C. < ?] — **shingly** *adj*

shingle[3] /shíng g'l/ (**-gles, -gling, -gled**) *vt* to remove the slag from iron by hammering or squeezing it in the process of making wrought iron [Late 17C. Via French *cingler* < German *zängeln* < *Zange* 'tongs'.]

shingles /shíng g'lz/ *n* a disease of adults caused by the reactivation of chickenpox viruses in a nerve ganglion and resulting in inflammation, pain, and a rash of small skin blisters. Technical name **herpes zoster, zoster** *n.* 1 [14C. Alteration of Latin *cingulum* 'girdle' < *cingere* 'gird'.]

shining /shīning/ *adj* 1 giving out or reflecting light, or having a bright or radiant quality 2 conspicuously excellent and admirable ○ *a shining example to all* —**shiningly** *adv*

shinleaf /shín leef/ (*plural* **-leaves** /-leevz/) *n US* a plant of the wintergreen family with a low cluster of evergreen leaves. Flowers: white or pink, on a long stem. Native to: Europe, Asia, North America. Family: Pyrolaceae. [Early 19C. Because it was used to treat shin soreness.]

shinny[1] /shínni/ (**-nies, -nying, -nied**) *vi* to climb up or down something using the hands and legs [Late 19C. < SHIN[1].]

shinny[2] /shínni/, **shinney** *n* (*plural* **-nies**) 1 **N AMERICAN GAME RESEMBLING HOCKEY** in the United States and Canada, an informal game similar to hockey, played with a small hard ball and curved wooden sticks 2 **STICK USED IN SHINNY** the stick that is used to play shinny ■ *vi* (**-nies, -nying, -nied; -neys, -neying, -neyed**) **PLAY SHINNY** to play the game of shinny [Late 17C. Variant of SHINTY.]

shinplaster /shín plaastər/ *n US* a piece of low-value paper money, especially one issued in the United States during the Civil War [Early 19C. < its resemblance to the plaster used for leg plasters.]

shin splints *n* a painful inflammation of the muscles surrounding the shinbone, often caused by running or jogging on hard roads (+ *singular or plural verb*)

shintaido /shin tīdō/ *n* a form of exercise based on the movements used in Japanese martial arts, performed by a group [< Japanese]

Shinto /shíntō/ *n* a Japanese religion in which devotees worship and make offerings to numerous gods and spirits associated with the natural world [Early 18C. < Japanese *shintō* 'way of the gods'.] —**Shintoism** *n* — **Shintoist** *n, adj*

shinty /shínti/ *n* (*plural* **-ties**) 1 **SCOTTISH GAME RESEMBLING HOCKEY** a game resembling hockey traditionally played in the Highlands of Scotland 2 **STICK USED IN SHINTY** the stick that is used to play shinty ■ *vi* (**-ties, -tying, -tied**) **PLAY SHINTY** to play the game of shinty [Late 17C. Probably from the phrase *shin (t')ye!*, uttered by players of the game.]

shiny /shīni/ (**-ier, -iest**) *adj* 1 bright and polished or with a glossy or glistening surface 2 smooth and glossy on the surface through too much wear ○ *a shiny patch on the seat of his trousers* —**shininess** *n*

ship /ship/ *n* 1 **LARGE BOAT** a large wind-driven or engine-powered vessel designed to carry passengers or cargo over water, especially across the sea 2 **LARGE SQUARE-RIGGED SAILING VESSEL** a large sailing vessel with three, four, or five square-rigged masts 3 **SHIP'S CREW** the crew of a ship 4 **AIRCRAFT OR SPACECRAFT** a large aircraft or spacecraft ■ *v* (**ships, shipping, shipped**) 1 *vti* **TRANSPORT OVER WATER** to transport something by ship 2 *vt* **TRANSPORT OVERLAND OR BY AIR** to send or transport something overland or by air, using a common carrier 3 *vt* **SEND** to send somebody to a place ○ *shipped the children off to their grandparents for the holidays* 4 *vti* **BE SENT TO SHOPS** to send a product to shops and make it available for purchase ○ *If all goes well, the new software will be shipping early next year.* 5 *vt* **TAKE IN WATER** to take in water over the sides of a ship or boat ○ *We're shipping water.* 6 *vt* **BRING OARS INSIDE BOAT** to bring oars inside a boat and lay them down 7 *vi* **GO ON SHIP** to travel on a ship 8 *vi* **WORK ON SHIP** to take a job aboard a ship [Old English *scip* < Germanic] — **shippable** *adj* ◇ **desert** *or* **leave a sinking ship** to leave an organization that is having difficulties ◇ **when your ship comes in** when you become rich

-ship *suffix* 1 condition, state, or quality ○ *companionship* 2 skill, art, craft ○ *musicianship* 3 office, title, position, profession ○ *governorship* 4 a group of people collectively ○ *membership* 5 person holding a particular title ○ *ladyship* 6 something showing a particular quality or condition ○ *township* [Old English *-scipe*]

ship biscuit *n* FOOD = **hardtack**

shipboard /shíp bawrd/ *adj* used, intended for, or occurring on board a ship ◇ **on shipboard** on board a ship

shipborne /shíp bawrn/ *adj* transported by ship

shipbreaking /shíp brayking/ *n* 1 the dismantling and breaking up of old ships for scrap 2 the crime of breaking into and entering a ship with the intent to do harm such as stealing —**shipbreaker** *n*

ship broker *n* an agent who acts on behalf of ship owners, organizing cargoes, passengers, and insurance for their ships

shipbuilder /shíp bildər/ *n* a person or business that constructs ships —**shipbuilding** *n*

ship canal *n* a canal that is wide and deep enough for ships to pass through

ship chandler *n* a person, shop, or company that sells supplies for ships —**ship chandlery** *n*

Shipley /shíppli/, **Jenny** (*b.* 1952) New Zealand stateswoman

shipload /shíp lōd/ *n* the quantity of cargo carried by a ship

shipmaster /shíp maastər/ *n* the captain or master of a ship

shipmate /shíp mayt/ *n* a fellow sailor in a ship's crew

shipment /shípmənt/ *n* 1 a quantity of goods that are shipped together as part of the same cargo 2 the act of shipping something

ship money *n* a tax formerly levied by English monarchs, especially by King Charles I, to raise money to provide ships for the navy

ship of the line *n* formerly, a sailing warship large enough to be in the line of battle

shipowner /shíp ōnər/ *n* a person or company owning one, several, or many ships

shipper /shíppər/ *n* a person or company that sends or receives goods by sea, land, or air

shipping /shípping/ *n* 1 the act or business of transporting goods 2 ships considered collectively, especially those belonging to a single port, country, or industry, and often referred to in terms of their tonnage

shipping agent *n* a person or company that prepares the documents required for cargoes to be transported, and deals with insurance and customs matters on behalf of ships

shipping clerk *n* an employee who prepares, sends, receives, and records shipments of goods

shipping forecast *n* a weather forecast for ships and sailors around the UK coast broadcast at particular times by the BBC

ship-rigged *adj* describes a sailing ship with three, four, or five masts and square sails set at right angles to the hull

ship's biscuit *n* FOOD = **hardtack**

shipshape /shíp shayp/ *adj* neat, tidy, and in good order ■ *adv* in a neat, tidy, and orderly way [Mid-17C. Shortening of obsolete *shipshapen* 'made appropriate for use aboard ship'.]

shipside /shíp sīd/ *n* the area, especially at a dock, beside a ship

ship's papers *npl* documents stating the ownership, nationality, cargo, and destination of a ship, required by international law to be carried by all ships

shipway /shíp way/ *n* 1 a structure on which a ship is built and down which it slides when it is launched 2 SHIPPING = **ship canal**

shipworm /shíp wurm/ *n* a burrowing marine mollusc that drills into wood, damaging wharves and ships. Family: Teredinidae.

shipwreck /shíp rek/ *n* 1 **SINKING OR DESTRUCTION OF SHIP** the sinking, destruction, or damaging of a ship while at sea 2 **SUNKEN SHIP** a ship that has been destroyed or sunk 3 **DESTRUCTION** the destruction or failure of something ■ *v* 1 *vti* **INVOLVE SOMEBODY IN SHIPWRECK** to experience the sinking or destruction of a ship or cause somebody to experience this (*usually passive*) ○ *shipwrecked on a desert island* 2 *vti* **DESTROY SHIP** to sink or destroy a ship, or to be sunk or destroyed, at sea (*usually passive*) 3 *vt* **RUIN** to ruin or destroy something utterly (*literary*) [Old English *scipwræc*]

shipwright /shíp rīt/ *n* a builder or repairer of ships [Old English *scipwyrhta*]

shipyard /shíp yaard/ *n* a place where ships are built or repaired

Shiraz /shi ráz/ *n* a black grape, grown mainly in Australia and South Africa, used for making red wine [Mid-17C. After the port of Shiraz, Iran.]

shire[1] /shīr/ *n* **1** a county in England or Wales **2 shire, Shire** ZOOL = **shire horse** [Old English *scīr* 'administrative office, district' < ?]

shire[2] /shīr/ (**shires, shiring, shired**) *vt Ireland* to clear the head by taking fresh air (*informal*) [Old English *scīr* 'bright, clear']

Shire /sheéray/ river flowing from S Malawi to the River Zambezi in central Mozambique. Length: 402 km/250 mi.

Shire Highlands plateau in S Malawi. Height: 900 m/2,953 ft.

shire horse, Shire horse *n* a large heavy carthorse with long hair growing from its fetlocks, belonging to a breed originating in the Midlands of England

Shires /shīrz/ *npl* a group of counties in the Midlands of England, especially Northamptonshire and Leicestershire, famous as fox-hunting country

shire town *n* the administrative capital of a British county, especially one whose name ends in '-shire'

shirk /shurk/ *v* **1** *vt* to avoid having to carry out something such as an obligation, task, or responsibility through lack of initiative, cowardice, or distaste for it **2** *vi* to lack initiative or deliberately avoid work or duty [Mid-17C. Possibly < German *Schurke* 'scoundrel'.] —**shirker** *n*

Shirley poppy /shúrli-/ *n* an annual poppy. Flowers: red, pink, or white, single or double. [Late 19C. After the district of *Shirley* in Croydon, Surrey.]

shirr /shur/ *v* **1** *vti* to gather fabric into two or more parallel rows for decoration on a garment such as a skirt, usually using elasticated thread **2** *vt US* to bake an egg without its shell, e.g. in a ramekin dish [Mid-19C. < ?]

shirt /shurt/ *n* **1 CLOTHING FOR UPPER BODY** an article of clothing for the upper part of the body, usually made of a fairly light material and having a collar, sleeves, and buttons down the front **2 MAN'S UNDERGARMENT** a usually loose linen garment for the upper body with sleeves that was worn by men as underwear until the early 20th century **3 NIGHTSHIRT** a nightshirt [Old English *scyrte* < Indo-European, 'cut'] ◇ **keep your shirt on** to keep your temper (*informal; usually a command*) ◇ **lose your shirt** to lose everything you have, especially as a result of losing a bet ◇ **put your shirt on something** to bet or risk everything you have on something (*informal*)

shirtdress /shúrt dress/ *n US* CLOTHING = **shirtwaister**

shirtfront /shúrt frunt/ *n* the front part of a shirt, especially the stiffened fabric on the front of a dress shirt

shirting /shúrting/ *n* plain or striped cotton fabric. Use: men's shirts.

shirtsleeve /shúrt sleev/ *n* the part of a shirt that covers all or part of the arm ◇ **in (your) shirtsleeves** not wearing a jacket

shirt-tail *n* the lower part of a shirt, usually cut in a curved shape, that extends below the waist at the back and is usually tucked into trousers

shirtwaist /shúrt wayst/ *n US* a woman's blouse styled like a man's shirt

shirtwaister /shúrt waystər/ *n* a woman's dress that is tailored to resemble a shirt, with buttons fastening down the front. US term **shirtdress**

shirty /shúrti/ (**-ier, -iest**) *adj* aggressive or bad-tempered because of being annoyed about something (*informal*) [Mid-19C. Probably from the expression 'get your shirt out, lose your temper'.] —**shirtily** *adv* —**shirtiness** *n*

shisha mirror /shíshə-/ *n* a small mirrored disc. Use: surface decoration on textiles. [Via Persian *šīša* or Urdu *šīšah* 'mirror']

shish kebab /shísh-/ *n* a dish of cubes of marinated meat and vegetables grilled and served on a skewer [Early 20C. Via Armenian < Turkish *şiş kebabiu* < *şiş* 'skewer' + *kebab* 'roast meat'.]

shit /shit/ *n* **1** a highly offensive term for human or animal excrement (*taboo*) **2** a highly offensive term for an act of defecating (*taboo*) **3** a highly offensive term for somebody regarded as unpleasant or malicious (*taboo insult*) **4** a highly offensive term for something that is unpleasant, of no value, or of inferior quality (*taboo*) **5** a highly offensive term for useless or unnecessary things (*taboo*) **6** a highly offensive term for nonsense or lies (*taboo*) **7** a highly offensive term for difficulty or trouble (*taboo*) **8** a highly offensive term for criticism perceived as unhelpful or mean-spirited (*taboo*) **9** a highly offensive term for illegal drugs, especially cannabis (*taboo*) ■ **shits** *npl* a highly offensive term for an attack of diarrhoea (*taboo*) ■ *interj* a highly offensive term used as a swearword (*taboo*) ■ *v* (**shits, shitting, shitted** *or* **shit** *or* **shat, shitted** *or* **shit** *or* **shat** /shat/) (*taboo*) **1** *vti* a highly offensive term meaning to eliminate waste from the body via the rectum **2** *vr* a highly offensive term meaning to be extremely scared **3** *vt US* a highly offensive term meaning to tease somebody or deceive somebody for amusement **4** *vi* a highly offensive term meaning to behave towards or criticize somebody with arrogant contempt and a total disregard for his or her feelings, especially from a position of power ■ *adj* a highly offensive term meaning very bad or inferior (*taboo*) [Old English *scitte* < Indo-European, 'cut, split'] ◇ **get your shit together** *US* a highly offensive phrase meaning to get organized (*taboo*) ◇ **in deep shit** a highly offensive phrase meaning in trouble or in a difficult situation (*taboo*) ◇ **knock** *or* **beat the shit out of somebody** a highly offensive phrase meaning to strike or kick somebody violently and repeatedly (*taboo*) ◇ **no shit** *US* a highly offensive term indicating surprise, disbelief, or sarcasm (*taboo*) ◇ **tough shit** a highly offensive phrase indicating in an unfriendly way that there is no alternative to a difficult or undesirable situation (*taboo*) ◇ **when the shit hits the fan** a highly offensive phrase meaning when trouble starts (*taboo*)

shitake, shitake mushroom *n* FUNGI = **shiitake**

shite /shīt/ *n* **1** a highly offensive term for human or animal excrement (*taboo regional*) **2** a highly offensive term somebody regarded as unpleasant or malicious (*taboo insult regional*) **3** a highly offensive term for something unpleasant, worthless, or of poor quality (*taboo regional*) **4** a highly offensive term for nonsense or lies (*taboo regional*) ■ *interj* a highly offensive term used as a swearword (*taboo regional*)

shitfaced /shít fayst/ *adj* a highly offensive term meaning completely drunk (*taboo*)

shithead /shít hed/ *n* a highly offensive term that deliberately insults somebody's intelligence or character (*taboo*)

shit hot *adj* a highly offensive term indicating emphatic approval (*taboo*)

shithouse /shít howss/ *n* a highly offensive term for a toilet (*taboo*)

shitless /shíttləss/ *adv* a highly offensive term expressing extreme fear (*taboo*) [Mid-20C. < the tendency to lose control of the bowels when terror-stricken.]

shitlist /shít list/ *n* a highly offensive term referring to a list of people who are out of favour, especially in the view of somebody in authority (*taboo*)

shitload /shít lōd/ *n US* a highly offensive term referring to an undesirably large amount or quantity of something (*taboo*)

shittah /shíttə/ (*plural* **-tim** /shíttim/ *or* **-tahs**) *n* the tree that yielded the shittim wood of the Bible, probably a species of acacia [Early 17C. < Hebrew *šiṭṭāh*.]

shittim wood /shíttim-/ *n* the wood of the shittah tree that according to the Bible was used to make the Ark of the Covenant

shitty /shítti/ *adj* (*taboo*) **1** a highly offensive term meaning regarded as inferior, unpleasant, or unenjoyable **2** a highly offensive term meaning wretched or miserable **3** a highly offensive term meaning of very poor quality **4** a highly offensive term meaning covered with excrement —**shittily** *adv* —**shittiness** *n*

shiv *n, vt* = **chiv** (*slang*) [Late 17C. Alteration of CHIV.]

shiva /sheévə/, **shivah** *n* seven days of formal mourning observed by close relatives of a deceased Jewish person during which they sit on low stools and do not go out, work, bathe, or shave [Late 19C. Via Yiddish *shive* < Hebrew *šiḇ'āh* 'seven'.]

Shiva /sheévə/, **Siva** /seévə/ *n* an important Hindu deity, worshipped as the god of destruction [Late 18C. < Sanskrit, 'the auspicious one'.]

shivah *n* JUDAISM = **shiva**

shivaree /shívvə reé, shívvəri/ *n US* = **charivari** [Mid-19C. Alteration of French *charivari* < ?]

shiver[1] /shívvər/ *v* **1** *vi* **TO TREMBLE** to tremble or shake slightly because of cold, fear, or illness **2** *vti* **FLAP OR MAKE SAIL FLAP** to flap, or make a sail flap, when a sailing vessel is too close to the wind ■ *n* **BODY TREMOR** a tremor or shudder in the body caused by fear, cold, or illness ■ **shivers** *npl* **ATTACK OF SHIVERING** an attack of shivering caused by fear, cold, or illness (*informal*) [13C. < ?] —**shiverer** *n* —**shiveringly** *adv*

shiver[2] /shívvər/ *n* a very small piece of something such as glass that has splintered off a larger piece ■ *vti* to splinter into fragments or cause something to splinter into fragments [12C. < assumed Old English *scifer* < Indo-European, 'to split'.]

shivery /shívvəri/ *adj* trembling from cold, fear, or illness

Shizuoka /shee zoo ṓkə/ city on SE Honshu Island, Japan. Population: 472,196 (1990).

Shkodër /shkṓdair/ city in NW Albania. Population: 83,700 (1991).

shkotzim plural of **shegetz**

shlemiel *n* JUDAISM = **schlemiel** (*informal*)

shlep *vti* = **schlep**

Shluh /shloo/ (*plural* **Shluh** *or* **Shluhs**) *n* the Berber dialect of the Shluh people [Early 18C. < Berber.]

SHM *abbr* simple harmonic motion

shmaltz *n* = **schmaltz**

shmatte *n* = **schmatte**

shmo (*plural* **shmoes**) *n US* = **schmo** (*informal*)

shmuck *n* JUDAISM = **schmuck**

Shoah /shṓ ə/ *n* a Hebrew word for the Holocaust [Mid-20C. < Hebrew *šōāh* 'catastrophe'.]

shoal[1] /shōl/ *n* **1 GROUP OF FISH** a large group of fish or other marine animals swimming together **2 GROUP OF PEOPLE** a large group of similar people or things ○ *a shoal of reporters* ■ *vi* **FORM SHOAL** to group together to form a shoal [Late 16C. < Middle Dutch *scōle* or Middle Low German *schōle* (see SCHOOL[2]).]

shoal[2] /shōl/ *n* **1 SHALLOW WATER** an area of shallow water in a larger body of water **2 UNDERWATER SANDBANK** an underwater sandbank or sandbar that is visible at low water ■ *v* **1** *vti* **MAKE OR BECOME SHALLOW** to become shallow or shallower, or to make something shallow **2** *vi* **ENTER SHALLOWER WATER** to enter a shallower area of water ■ *adj* **shoal, shoaly SHALLOW** shallow [Old English *sceald*]

shoat /shōt/, **shote** *n* a young pig that has just been weaned [15C. < ?]

shochet /shṓkhət/ (*plural* **-etim** /shṓkhətim/) *n* somebody licensed to perform the ritual kosher slaughter of animals for food (**shechita**) [Late 19C. < Hebrew *šōḥēṭ*, present participle of *šāḥaṭ* 'slaughter'.]

shock[1] /shok/ *n* **1 SOMETHING SURPRISING AND UPSETTING** an unexpected, intense, and distressing experience that has a sudden and powerful effect on somebody's emotions or physical reactions ○ *The news of her death came as a great shock to us all.* **2 DISTRESSING FEELINGS AFTER SHOCK** the feeling of distress or numbness experienced by somebody who has had a shock **3 PHYSIOLOGICAL COLLAPSE** a state of physiological collapse, marked by a weak pulse, coldness, sweating, and irregular breathing, and resulting from, e.g., blood loss, heart failure, allergic reaction, or emotional trauma ○ *in shock* **4 PHYSICAL IMPACT** a sudden and violent impact, collision, or blow **5 MOVEMENT AFTER IMPACT** the movement or violent shaking felt after a collision, explosion, or earthquake **6 SOMETHING THREATENING OR DAMAGING** an unexpected event that threatens or damages a system, organization, or conventional situation ○ *The economy cannot take any more shocks.* **7 ELECTRIC SHOCK** an electric shock **8** *US* MECH ENG = **shock absorber** ■ *v* **1** *vt* **UPSET** to make somebody feel suddenly and acutely distressed or upset **2** *vti* **OFFEND OR BE OFFENDED** to make somebody feel deeply offended or disgusted, or to be likely to feel offended or disgusted ○ *He shocks easily.* **3** *vt* **GIVE SOMEBODY ELECTRIC SHOCK** to give an electric shock to a person or animal **4** *vt* **PUT SOMEBODY INTO SHOCK** to cause a state of shock in somebody **5** *vti* **COLLIDE** to collide, or to cause people or things to collide (*archaic*) [Mid-16C. The noun is via French *choc*, the verb directly < French *choquer* 'strike'.] —**shockability** /shókə bílləti/ *n* —**shockable** *adj*

shock[2] /shok/ *n* a group of sheaves of corn set upright in a field for drying ■ *vt* to arrange sheaves of corn in a shock [14C. < ?]

shock[3] /shok/ *n* a large amount of thick shaggy hair [Early 19C. < ?]

shock absorber *n* a device on a vehicle designed to absorb jarring or jolting, e.g. that caused by wheels moving over a rough surface

shocker /shókər/ *n* (*informal*) **1** a highly unpleasant experience, thing, or person **2** a story, play, or film that is particularly lurid and intended to shock people

shockheaded /shók héddid/ *adj* having a large amount of thick shaggy hair that sticks up or is tousled

shock-horror *adj* lurid, sensational, and apparently intended to cause a shocked or horrified reaction (*informal; ironic*)

shocking /shóking/ *adj* 1 **OUTRAGEOUS** provoking a deeply offended or outraged response 2 **DISTRESSING** emotionally distressing or horrifying 3 **VERY BAD** very bad or unpleasant (*informal*) ■ *adj, adv* **VERY BRIGHT** very bright or glaring in shade of colour —**shockingly** *adv* —**shockingness** *n*

shocking pink *adj* of a garish pink colour —**shocking pink** *n*

shock jock *n* a disc jockey or radio host who uses provocative language and broadcasts his or her extreme views (*slang*)

shockproof /shók proof/ *adj* designed or able to withstand the effects of jarring or impact

shock tactics *npl* the use of methods that are likely to shock people in order to achieve something

shock therapy, shock treatment *n* a method of treating patients affected with psychiatric disorders that involves passing an electric current through the brain

shock troops *npl* soldiers who are specially trained and equipped to be in the forefront of an attack [Translation of German *Stosstruppen*]

shock wave *n* 1 a wave of increased temperature or pressure as a result of an explosion or earthquake or the movement of a supersonic body 2 a widespread reaction of shock or distress caused by an event or piece of news (*often plural*)

shod past participle, past tense of **shoe**

shoddy /shóddi/ (**-dier, -diest**) *adj* 1 **POORLY MADE** poorly or carelessly made or done 2 **OF INFERIOR MATERIAL** made from inferior material 3 **DISHONEST** dishonest or disgraceful ○ *shoddy treatment* ■ *n* (*plural* **-dies**) 1 **CLOTH MADE WITH OLD WOOL** cloth made using a mixture of old unravelled woollen cloth and new wool 2 **SOMETHING INFERIOR** something that is of inferior quality, especially if it is imitating something better [Mid-19C. < ?] —**shoddily** *adv* —**shoddiness** *n*

shoe /shoo/ *n* 1 **STIFF OUTER COVERING FOR THE FOOT** an outer covering for the foot, usually made of leather, fabric, or plastic, with a stiff sole and usually not reaching above the ankle 2 EQUESTRIAN = **horseshoe** *n.* 1 3 **PROTECTIVE PART IN AN ENGINE** a lining or part in an engine or machine that protects another part from being worn down 4 **PLAYING CARD DISPENSER** a special box that dispenses playing cards one at a time 5 **POWER COLLECTOR ON AN ELECTRIC TRAIN** the part of an electric train that connects with the electrified rail from which it draws power 6 **METAL STRIP ON SLEDGE** a strip of metal along the runner of a sledge 7 **PART OF A BRIDGE** a base that supports the upper part of a bridge ■ *vt* (**shoes, shoeing, shod** /shod/) 1 **PROVIDE WITH HORSESHOES** to fix a horseshoe on a horse 2 **SUPPLY WITH SHOES** to provide somebody with shoes (*usually passive*) 3 **PUT A PROTECTIVE COVERING ON** to cover something with a hard, especially metal, plate to protect against wear [Old English *scōh*] —**shoeless** *adj* ◇ **be in somebody's shoes** to be in somebody else's position (*informal*)

shoebill /shoóbil/ *n* a large tropical wading bird with shaggy grey plumage, a large head, black legs, and a broad hooked bill. Native to: East Africa. *Balaeniceps rex.*

shoebox /shoó boks/ *n* 1 a box, usually made of cardboard, in which shoes are packed for sale 2 a small and cramped living or working space (*informal*)

shoegazing /shoó gayzing/ *n* a style of early 1990s guitar music characterized by ambient sounds and static performances [Late 20C. < the typical stance of the performers and audience.]

shoehorn /shoó hawrn/ *n* a curved piece of plastic, metal, or horn used to help ease the heel into a tight-fitting shoe or boot ■ *vt* to squeeze somebody or something into a space that is barely large enough

shoelace /shoó layss/ *n* a thin cord of leather or fabric, used as a shoe fastener

shoemaker /shoó maykər/ *n* a maker or repairer of footwear —**shoemaking** *n*

shoepac /shoó pak/, **shoepack** *n US* a heavy laced waterproof boot [Mid-18C. Alteration of pidgin Delaware *seppock* 'shoes' < Unami Delaware *čipahko* 'moccasins'.]

shoeshine /shoó shīn/ *n* 1 the act of giving a clean or shiny finish to shoes by polishing them 2 a polished finish on shoes

shoestring /shoó string/ *adj* 1 consisting of or running on a very limited amount of money ○ *a shoestring allocation for new classrooms* 2 *US* cut or made long and narrow in shape ○ *shoestring licorice* ■ *n* ACCESSORIES = **shoelace** ◇ **on a shoestring** using very little money

shoetree /shoó tree/ *n* a wooden or metal block that is inserted into a boot or shoe to stretch it or help it to keep its shape when not being worn

shofar /shṓ faar/ (*plural* **-fars** *or* **-froth** /shṓ froth/) *n* a horn, usually a ram's horn, blown in a synagogue on Rosh Hashanah [Mid-19C. < Hebrew *šōpār* 'ram's horn'.]

shogi /shṓgi/ *n* a Japanese board game for two players that resembles chess [Mid-19C. < Japanese *shōgi*.]

shogun /shṓ gun/ *n* any one of the hereditary military commanders in feudal Japan who ruled the country under the nominal rule of an emperor between the years 1192 and 1867 [Mid-17C. Via Japanese *shōgun* < Chinese *jiāng jūn* 'general'.] —**shogunal** *adj*

shogunate /shṓgə nayt/ *n* the office, period in office, or rule of a shogun

shoji /shṓji/ (*plural* **-ji** *or* **-jis**) *n* a rice paper screen in a wooden frame used as a sliding partition or door in traditional Japanese houses [Late 19C. < Japanese *shōji*.]

Sholapur /shōlə poór/ city in west-central India. Population: 604,215 (1991).

~~**sholder**~~ incorrect spelling of **shoulder**

Shona /shṓnə/ (*plural* **-na** *or* **-nas**) *n* 1 a member of a people living in parts of southern central Africa, mainly in Zimbabwe and Mozambique 2 the Bantu language of the Shona people. Native speakers: 8 million. [Mid-20C. < Bantu.] —**Shona** *adj*

shone past tense, past participle of **shine**

shoneen /shṓ neen/ *n Ireland* an Irish person who, in order to seem of a higher social class, imitates an English person, especially in accent [Mid-19C. < Irish *seóinín* 'little John' < *Seón* 'John, John Bull'.]

shonky /shóngki/ (**-kier, -kiest**) *adj ANZ* unreliable, untrustworthy, or inferior (*informal*) [Late 20C. < *shonk* 'Jewish person', shortening of *shonicker*.]

shoo /shoo/ *interj* used to tell a child or animal to go away ■ *vti* (**shoos, shooing, shooed**) to say shoo and gesture to a child or animal to go away ○ *He shooed the pigeons away from the table.* [15C. A natural exclamation.]

shoofly pie /shoó flī-/ *n US* a pie made with a filling of crumbs, butter, and brown sugar or molasses [< its sweet filling, which is apt to attract flies]

shoogle /shoógg'l/ *vti* (**-gles, -gling, -gled**) *Scotland* to rock back and forth with small rapid movements, or to cause something to do this (*informal*) ■ *n Scotland* a small, rapid rocking movement (*informal*) [Late 16C. Variant of *shoggle* < *shog* 'shake'.]

shoogly /shoóggli/ *adj Scotland* wobbling or liable to wobble (*informal*)

shoo-in *n US, Can* a certain winner

shook[1] past tense of **shake**

shook[2] /shoók/ *n* 1 AGRIC = **shock**[2] *n.* 2 *US* a set of timber parts for assembling a barrel or box [Late 18C. < ?]

shook-up *adj US* disturbed and upset (*informal*)

shoon /shoon/ *Scotland* plural of **shoe** *n.* 1

shoot /shoot/ *v* (**shoots, shooting, shot**) 1 *vti* **FIRE A WEAPON OR PROJECTILE** to fire a projectile such as a bullet, missile, or arrow from a weapon, or make a weapon fire a projectile ○ *Don't shoot!* 2 *vt* **HIT SOMEBODY OR SOMETHING WITH A BULLET** to fire a weapon at and hit, injure, or kill a person or animal ○ *She shot herself.* 3 *vti* **HUNT ANIMALS WITH A GUN** to hunt animals or birds with a gun for sport 4 *vti* **MOVE FAST** to move or cause something to move quickly and suddenly ○ *She shot out her hand to catch the ball.* 5 *vi* **DASH** to go somewhere quickly and suddenly (*informal*) ○ *He shot off to his interview.* 6 *vt* **TRAVEL OVER SOMETHING FAST** to travel quickly over a stretch of water where the current is fast ○ *shoot the rapids* 7 *vi* **PROGRESS VERY RAPIDLY** to make extremely rapid progress or undergo a startlingly rapid change of state ○ *She shot to fame.* 8 *vi* **MOVE SWIFTLY THROUGH THE BODY** to seem to move very swiftly, and usually painfully, through the body ○ *Pain shot up her leg.* 9 *vti* **SEND SOMETHING OUT RAPIDLY** to send out something rapidly or forcefully or in a beam or ray 10 *vt* **DIRECT SOMETHING QUICKLY** to direct a look or glance at something briefly and rapidly ○ *He shot a glance at her.* 11 *vt* **ASK OR SAY SOMETHING RAPIDLY** to say something rapidly or ask a question rapidly 12 *vti* **RECORD SOMETHING ON FILM** to record a shot, scene, film, or programme on film with a camera 13 *vti* **KICK BALL TO GET POINT** to kick, hit, or throw a ball in a sport such as football or basketball in an attempt to score a goal or point 14 *vt US, Can* **SCORE A POINT IN A SPORT** to score a goal or point in a sport 15 *vi US* **STRIVE TO ACHIEVE** to try to achieve something difficult (*informal*) ○ *shooting for a five percent increase in productivity* 16 *vt* **MOVE A BOLT INTO PLACE** to move something such as a bolt into or out of a fastening 17 *vi* **GERMINATE** to germinate or begin to grow 18 *vt* DRUGS = **shoot up** *v.* 4 (*slang*) 19 *vt US* **PLAY CUE GAME** to play a game of pool or billiards 20 *vti* **THROW DICE** to throw a die or dice 21 *vt* **MEASURE THE DISTANCE TO ASTRONOMICAL OBJECT** to measure the altitude of a star or other astronomical object ■ *n* 1 **NEW PLANT GROWTH** a newly grown aerial part of a plant, e.g. a leaf bud or branch 2 **OCCASION FOR PHOTOGRAPHING OR FILMING** an occasion when a professional photographer or filmmaker is photographing or filming something 3 **ACT OF FIRING** an act of firing a weapon 4 **HUNTING EVENT** an occasion for hunting animals with guns for sport 5 **HUNTING PARTY** a party of people gathered together to hunt animals with guns for sport 6 **HUNTING AREA** an area where people shoot animals with guns for sport 7 **VEIN OF ORE** a narrow vein of ore ■ *interj* (*informal*) 1 **USED TO TELL SOMEBODY TO START** used to tell somebody to go ahead and start talking 2 *US* **USED TO EXPRESS ANNOYANCE** used as an exclamation of annoyance or disappointment [Old English *scēotan* < Germanic]

SPELLCHECK See ***chute***.

shoot down *vt* 1 **BRING DOWN AN AIRCRAFT** to bring down an aircraft while it is in the air by firing a weapon or missile 2 **KILL SOMEBODY OR SOMETHING BY SHOOTING** to fire a weapon at and hit, injure, or kill a person or animal 3 **DESTROY ARGUMENT** to destroy somebody's argument, theory, or idea by disproving, criticizing, or discrediting it

shoot up *v* 1 *vi* **INCREASE SUDDENLY** to increase suddenly by a large amount 2 *vi* **GET TALLER** to grow considerably taller in a short space of time 3 *vt* **HARM SOMEBODY OR SOMETHING BY GUNFIRE** to cause serious injuries to somebody or damage to something with gunfire 4 *vti* **INJECT A DRUG** to inject an illegal drug (*slang*)

⚡**shoot-'em-up** /shoótəm up/ *n* 1 *US* **FILM WITH SHOOTING** a film or television programme featuring a large amount of shooting and bloodshed (*dated*) 2 **COMPUTER GAME WITH SHOOTING** a video or computer game in which a player scores points by shooting at figures on the screen 3 **FAIRGROUND SHOOTING STALL** a stall in a fairground where a player shoots a rifle at a sequence of targets in order to win a prize

shooter /shoótər/ *n* 1 a pistol or other gun (*informal*) 2 somebody or something that shoots

shooting box *n* a cabin or small house in the country in which guests stay while on a shoot for game

shooting brake *n* an estate car (*dated*)

shooting gallery *n* 1 a place used for target practice using guns or rifles 2 a place such as an abandoned building where addicts inject drugs (*slang*)

shooting iron *n US* a handgun (*informal*)

shooting lodge *n* FIELD SPORTS = **shooting box**

shooting party *n* a group of people who gather together in the country to hunt game with guns for sport

shooting script *n* the final screenplay for a cinema or television film that includes directions for shooting and is broken down into scenes with the shots numbered consecutively

shooting star *n* 1 ASTRON = **meteor** *n.* 2 2 a plant with slender flower stems rising above the leaves. Flowers: drooping with backward-curving petals. Native to: North America.

shooting stick *n* a walking stick with handles at one end that fold out to form a small seat, often used by a spectator at an outdoor sporting event

shoot-out *n* 1 a fight to the finish with guns 2 a means of resolving a tie in a football match in which five players from each side take alternate penalty shots at the goal

shoot-to-kill *adj* relating to or involving the aiming of a gun to kill, not wound, somebody

shop /shop/ *n* 1 **RETAIL BUSINESS** a retail business that sells consumer merchandise and sometimes services 2 **ACT OF BUYING GOODS** the act of going out to buy goods, especially food and household supplies (*informal*) **3** WORKSHOP a place where goods are manufactured or repaired **4** *US* INDUSTRIAL ARTS SCHOOL SUBJECT a school subject in which students are taught to work with tools and machinery, especially on wood **5** *US* SCHOOLROOM FOR LEARNING INDUSTRIAL ARTS a schoolroom or building with tools and equipment for students to learn industrial arts ■ *v* (**shops, shopping, shopped**) **1** *vi* BUY GOODS to go to a shop or shops in order to buy things **2** *vt US* VISIT PARTICULAR SHOP to buy goods from a particular shop **3** *vt* INFORM ON to inform on somebody to the police or authorities (*slang*) **4** *vt US* TRY TO SELL to try to sell something such as a company or creative work by bringing it to the attention of potential buyers [Old English *sceoppa* 'booth, peddler's stall'] ◇ **all over the shop 1** scattered or spread out over a wide area, usually untidily (*informal*) **2** in a confused or disorganized state (*informal*) ◇ **shut up shop 1** to stop working or doing something **2** to close down a business ◇ **talk shop** to talk about your work or some other specialized activity

shop around *vi* **1** to look around for the best deal or bargain **2** to review a number of possibilities before making a choice

shopaholic /shóppə hóllik/ *n* a compulsive shopper (*informal*)

shop assistant *n* somebody who serves customers in a shop. US term **salesclerk**

shop-bought *adj* bought ready-made from a shop as opposed to being home-made. US term **store-bought**

shop floor *n* **1** the area in a factory where goods are manufactured **2** the manual workers in a factory

shopfront /shóp frunt/ *n* the front façade of a shop building, facing onto the street. US term **storefront** *n.* 1

shopkeeper /shóp keepər/ *n* somebody who owns or manages a shop. US term **storekeeper** *n.* 2

shoplift /shóplift/ *vti* to steal something from a shop or store while pretending to shop for goods —**shoplifter** *n* —**shoplifting** *n*

shoppe /shop/ *n* used in shop names in order to create a quaint old-fashioned impression [Early 20C. Alteration of SHOP.]

shopper /shóppər/ *n* **1** SOMEBODY DOING SHOPPING a person who searches for things to buy, especially in a shop **2** SHOPPING TROLLEY OR BAG a trolley or large bag for putting shopping in **3** *US* LOCAL NEWSPAPER a usually free newspaper that carries advertising and some local news

shopping /shópping/ *n* **1** the activity of visiting shops and stores to look at and buy things **2** goods bought in a shop or shops, especially food and household items

ϟ **shopping agent** *n* a computer program used to browse websites searching for a product or service (*in e-commerce*)

shopping bag *n* a large strong bag with handles used for carrying purchases when shopping

shopping cart *n US* COMM = **shopping trolley**

shopping centre *n* a large enclosed purpose-built area consisting of shops and other facilities, together with a large area for parking. US term **mall** *n.* 1

ϟ **shopping experience** *n* the virtual environment in which a buyer browses a retailer's website, places items in a virtual shopping cart, and sends the order to the merchant (*in e-commerce*)

shopping list *n* **1** a list of all the things somebody wants to buy when shopping **2** a list of demands, requirements, or things wanted

shopping mall *n* a pedestrianized shopping area with enclosed walkways in a town

shopping precinct *n UK* a pedestrianized area in a town where shops and other facilities are grouped together

shopping trolley *n* a small trolley consisting either of a square bag on a frame or a basket on wheels that is pushed or pulled along to carry shopping. US term **shopping cart**

shopsoiled /shóp soyld/ *adj* **1** faded, tarnished, or otherwise slightly spoiled from being on display in a shop. US term **shopworn 2** old, overused, and hackneyed

shop steward *n* a worker elected by fellow union members as their representative in dealings with the management

shoptalk /shóp tawk/ *n* **1** conversation about work or another specialized activity at a time when more light-hearted chat is the norm, especially outside working hours **2** *US* jargon used in a particular field, job, or profession

shopwalker /shóp wawkər/ *n* an employee in a department store who supervises sales staff and assists customers. US term **floorwalker**

shopworn /shóp wawrn/ *adj US* COMM = **shopsoiled** *adj.* 1

shoran /sháw ran/ *n* a short-range navigational system in which a ship's or aircraft's precise location is determined by the time taken for a signal to travel to two fixed stations and back [Mid-20C. Contraction of *short-range navigation*.]

shore[1] /shawr/ *n* **1** LAND AT EDGE OF WATER the land that runs along the edge of a sea or lake **2** DRY LAND dry land as opposed to water ○ *on shore* **3** COUNTRY a land or country (*literary; often plural*) ○ *having reached our native shores* **4** COAST BETWEEN LOW AND HIGH TIDES the area of land that lies between normal low and high tide marks [Old English *scora* < Indo-European, 'cut']

shore[2] /shawr/ *vt* (**shores, shoring, shored**) **1** PROP UP A STRUCTURE to stop something such as a wall from falling down or over by propping a support against it ○ *shored up the old wall* **2** HELP TO STOP SOMETHING FAILING to give support or help in order to stop something failing ■ *n* PROP TO SUPPORT a beam or other prop set at an angle to support something such as a wall or tree [14C. < Middle Low German or Middle Dutch *schōre* 'prop'.]

shore bird *n* a bird that lives and feeds near the shores of coastal or inland waters, e.g. the plover, sandpiper, avocet, or snipe. Suborder: Charadrii.

shore dinner *n US* a meal consisting mainly of fish and seafood

shorefront /sháwr frunt/ *n US* land situated immediately next to a body of water

shore leave *n* **1** permission for a member of a ship's crew to go ashore **2** a period of time spent ashore by a member of a ship's crew

shoreless /sháwrləss/ *adj* having no flat shore on which a boat can land

shoreline /sháwr līn/ *n* the edge of a body of water, especially a sea, where it meets the shore

shore patrol *n* the military police of the Royal Navy or the US Navy, Coast Guard, or Marine Corps while on shore

shoreward /sháwrwərd/ *adj* facing or near the shore ■ *adv* **shoreward, shorewards** towards the shore

shoring /sháwring/ *n* a structure or arrangement designed to shore something up

shorn /shawrn/ past participle of **shear** ■ *adj* **1** with hair cut short **2** having had something removed or taken away ○ *shorn of all the trappings of power*

short /shawrt/ *adj* **1** NOT LONG having little or relatively little length, or extending only a small distance ○ *short hair* **2** NOT TALL having little or relatively little height ○ *shorter than her sister* **3** NOT LASTING LONG lasting for only a small amount of time ○ *a short stay* **4** NOT SEEMING LONG IN DURATION seeming or imagined not to last very long ○ *in a few short weeks* **5** CONCISE expressed economically and briefly ○ *a short summary* **6** ABBREVIATED expressed in fewer words or using fewer letters or characters than the full form ○ *Typo is short for typographical error.* ○ *the short form of the word* **7** HAVING LESS THAN NEEDED having less than the amount needed, expected, or thought to be sufficient ○ *I'm rather short of cash at the moment.* **8** INSUFFICIENTLY LONG OR TALL not long or tall enough by a particular amount ○ *All the beams are six inches short.* **9** NOT REMEMBERING MORE DISTANT EVENTS unable or unwilling to recall events that happened before the comparatively recent past ○ *a short memory* **10** DISCOURTEOUS rude and abrupt when speaking to somebody ○ *She was very short with the cashier.* **11** FULL OF FAT made with lots of fat so as to be flaky or crumbly when baked ○ *short pastry* **12** SOLD WITHOUT POSSESSING THE SHARES SOLD involving a seller who, at the time of sale, does not possess the shares he or she is selling and has to borrow them before being able to deliver ○ *short sale* **13** MATURING SOON being due for payment or repayment within a comparatively short space of time ○ *short bill* **14** PRONOUNCED WITH A RELATIVELY BRIEF SOUND describes phonemes or syllables that, when spoken, are comparatively brief in duration or are categorized as being of this type **15** PITCHING CLOSE TO BOWLER describes a cricket ball pitching comparatively close to the bowler and likely to bounce higher than usual before reaching the batsman ○ *short ball* **16** NEAT not diluted with water or a mixer drink ■ *adv* **1** ABRUPTLY abruptly and unexpectedly ○ *stop short* **2** NOT REACHING THE TARGET before reaching a goal, target, or destination ○ *The pass fell 3 yards short.* **3** WITHOUT ACTUAL POSSESSION without actually possessing the things being sold when the sale is agreed on ○ *sell short* ■ *n* **1** FILM OF SHORT DURATION a film whose running time is approximately 30 minutes or less **2** ELEC ENG = **short circuit 3** BASEBALL = **shortstop 4** SMALL DRINK a drink consisting of a small measure of spirits in a small glass (*informal*) **5** GARMENT SIZE a size of garment for a short person ■ *npl* **shorts 1** SHORT TROUSERS trousers that end somewhere between the upper thigh and the knee **2** *US* UNDERPANTS men's underpants **3** MIXTURE OF BRAN AND COARSE FLOUR a mixture of bran and coarse flour left over from the milling of wheat **4** SHORT-DATED ITEMS bills or securities that are due to mature within a comparatively short space of time ■ *vti* ELEC = **short-circuit** *v.* 1 [Old English *sceort* < Indo-European, 'cut'] —**shortness** *n* ◇ **for short** as an abbreviation or shortened form ◇ **go short** to have insufficient money or food ◇ **in short** used to introduce a rephrasing of something in a more concise form ◇ **short and sweet** pleasant or bearable because brief ◇ **short of 1** not having something, or not having enough of something **2** less than **3** without actually doing something, usually something unpleasant or wrong

short-acting *adj* effective for a short period

shortage /sháwrtij/ *n* a lack of something that is needed or required

SYNONYMS See ***lack***.

short back and sides *n* a hairstyle in which the hair at the back and sides of the head is cut short

shortbread /sháwrt bred/ *n* a rich crumbly biscuit made with a high proportion of butter to flour and a comparatively small proportion of sugar

shortcake /sháwrt kayk/ *n* **1** = **shortbread 2** a dessert consisting of a shortbread base topped with fruit and cream

shortchange /sháwrt cháynj/ (**-changes, -changing, -changed**) *vt* **1** to give somebody less change than is due to him or her **2** to behave unfairly towards somebody by giving him or her less of something than he or she deserves or expects —**shortchanger** *n*

short circuit *n* a failure in an electrical circuit caused by an accidental connection of low resistance such as when there is a break in the insulation, across which an excessive current can flow

short-circuit *v* **1** *vti* HAVE OR CAUSE FAILURE IN A CIRCUIT to have or cause a failure in an electrical circuit by creating a connection of low resistance across which an excessive current flows **2** *vt* USE SHORT-CUT TO DO to use a much quicker or more direct method to achieve something **3** *vt US* FRUSTRATE OR HINDER PLANS to hinder a plan or project by erecting obstacles

shortcoming /sháwrt kumming/ *n* a defect or failure in somebody's character or in a system or organization (*often plural*)

shortcrust pastry /sháwrt krust-/ *n* pastry with a crisp crumbly texture made with one measure of fat to every two measures of flour

short cut *n* **1** a route that is shorter or more direct than the usual one **2** a way of saving time and effort in doing something —**short-cut** *vti*

short-day *adj* able to flower only upon exposure to relatively short periods of sunlight, e.g. during spring or autumn

short division *n* a method of dividing relatively simple numbers without writing down all the steps in the process

shorten /sháwrt'n/ *v* **1** *vti* BECOME OR MAKE SHORTER to make something shorter or become shorter **2** *vti* MAKE ODDS SHORTER to reduce the odds on a bet, or to be reduced in this way **3** *vt* REDUCE SAIL AREA to reduce the area of a sail **4** *vt* MAKE PASTRY SHORTER to make pastry more crumbly by adding more fat —**shortener** *n*

shortening /sháwrtning/ *n US* fat such as lard that is solid at room temperature, used for making pastry

shortfall /sháwrt fawl/ *n* an amount by which something falls short of what is required

short fuse *n* a tendency to get angry quickly and with little provocation (*informal*)

shorthair /sháwrt hair/ *n* a medium-sized muscular domestic cat with a short thick coat

shorthand /sháwrt hand/ *n* 1 a fast method of writing, using symbols to represent letters, words, or phrases 2 a shorter or quicker way of referring to something

short-handed *adj* having fewer than the usual or required number of staff, helpers, or players —**short-handedness** *n*

shorthand typist *n* somebody who takes notes in shorthand, especially from dictation, and types a full version of the text from the notes

short-haul *adj* travelling or used for travelling a short distance

short head *n* a distance shorter than the length of a horse's head, used in describing the relative finishing positions of horses in a race

shorthold tenancy /sháwrt hōld-/ *n* a tenancy that provided only limited security of tenure for the tenant, now made obsolete by legislation

shorthorn /sháwrt hawrn/ (*plural* **-horns** *or* **-horn**) *n* a reddish-brown or white breed of cattle with short curved horns developed in N England and kept for beef or milk

short-horned grasshopper *n* a winged grasshopper with short antennae belonging to the family that includes the locust and many other common crop pests. Family: Acrididae.

short hundredweight *n* MEASURE = **hundredweight** *n.* 2

shortie *n* = **shorty**

short interest *n* the number of shares in a particular security that have been borrowed and sold and must eventually be returned to the lender

short leg *n* 1 a fielding position in cricket close to and behind the batsman who is being bowled at 2 in cricket, a fielder in the short leg position

short list *n* a list of the best candidates for a position or award after all others have been eliminated

short-list *vt* to put somebody or something on a final list of candidates for a position or award

short-lived *adj* lasting or living for only a short period of time

shortly /sháwrtli/ *adv* 1 IN SHORT TIME soon or in a short time ○ *The guests will arrive shortly.* 2 CURTLY in a curt or discourteous manner ○ *'I wish you'd stop interrupting me', he said shortly.* 3 BRIEFLY using only a few words [Old English]

short odds *npl* a nearly even chance in betting

short order *n Can, US* food in a restaurant that is prepared and served quickly (*hyphenated before nouns*)

short position *n* an open position in a security in which the investor borrowed the security from somebody, sold it, and promised to replace the borrowed security at a later time

short radius *n* the perpendicular distance or line from the centre of a regular polygon to one of its sides

short-range *adj* 1 designed for or capable of travelling or operating only over a short distance 2 concerned with the near future ○ *short-range plans*

short ribs *npl US* a cut of beef consisting of tough fatty meat on rib ends from between the rib roast and plate

short sale *n* the sale of a borrowed security in anticipation that the security price will fall and can be paid back from the profits earned after repurchasing it at the lower price

short score *n* a condensed orchestra score omitting some of the less important instruments and often combining several parts on one staff

short shrift *n* 1 brief and inconsiderate or unsympathetic treatment 2 a short period of time before execution during which a condemned prisoner could confess (*archaic*) ◇ **make short shrift of something** to deal with a matter quickly, giving it little attention

short sight *n* an inability to see distant objects clearly

short-sighted *adj* 1 able to see things clearly only if they are very close. US term **nearsighted** 2 without taking the future into account —**short-sightedly** *adv* —**short-sightedness** *n*

short-spoken *adj* inclined to speak abruptly

short-staffed *adj* lacking the normal or required number of staff

shortstop /sháwrt stop/ *n* 1 the position of the infielder in baseball playing closest to second base on the side towards third base 2 the baseball player playing at shortstop

short story *n* a work of prose fiction that is shorter than a novel

short subject *n US* a short film of approximately 30 minutes or less, sometimes a documentary, shown before a full-length feature film (*dated*)

short-tempered *adj* easily made angry or impatient

short-term *adj* 1 NOT LASTING LONG lasting for or affecting a relatively short period of time 2 MATURING OR DUE SOON maturing or payable within a relatively short period of time 3 FROM ASSETS HELD BRIEFLY realized from assets held for a short time and then sold

short-termism /-túrmizəm/ *n* a tendency to disregard long-term consequences in favour of short-term benefits —**short-termist** *adj, n*

short-term memory *n* the part of the mind used for retaining temporary information over a short period

short time *n* a situation in which employees work fewer hours than normal for correspondingly reduced pay because of a work shortage

short ton *n* MEASURE = **ton**[1] *n.* 1

short-waisted *adj* unusually short between the shoulders and the waist

short wave *n* a radio wave with a wavelength between 10 and 100 metres (*hyphenated when used before a noun*) ○ *short-wave radio*

shortwave /sháwrt wayv/ *adj* transmitting or receiving wavelengths shorter than 100 m ■ *n US* a radio capable of transmitting or receiving short waves

short-winded *adj* 1 experiencing shortness of breath, especially after mild exertion 2 expressed in few words

shorty /sháwrti/ (*plural* **-ies**), **shortie** *n* somebody or something very short or shorter than average (*informal*)

Shoshone /shō shṓ ni/ (*plural* **-nes** *or* **-ne**), **Shoshoni** (*plural* **-nis** *or* **-ni**) *n* 1 a member of a Native North American people living mainly in Nevada, Idaho, Wyoming and Utah 2 the group of Uto-Aztecan languages spoken by the Shoshone people. Native speakers: 3,000. [Early 19C. < ?] —**Shoshonean** *n, adj*

Shostakovich /shóstə kṓvich/, **Dmitry** (1906–75) Russian composer

shot[1] /shot/ *n* 1 SHOOTING OF GUN a firing of a gun or other weapon 2 SOMEBODY WHO SHOOTS somebody who shoots in a particular way ○ *a good shot* 3 SHOOTING OF A PROJECTILE AT A TARGET an aimed discharge of a projectile, e.g. a bullet from a gun 4 BULLET OR CANNONBALL a single solid metal missile for a gun or cannon, e.g. a bullet or cannonball 5 SMALL METAL PELLETS small steel or lead pellets used in shotgun shells 6 ATTEMPT TO SCORE an attempt to score points in a sport by throwing, hitting, kicking, or shooting something ○ *Howells struck a superb shot from just outside the penalty area.* 7 ACT OF HITTING BALL an act of hitting the ball in sports such as golf, tennis, or snooker ○ *His shot from the fairway was perfectly placed.* 8 ATHLETICS = **shot put** 9 PARTICULAR VIEW ON FILM a particular view recorded on film with a camera ○ *The cameraman bent down to get a low shot of the damaged wheels.* 10 CONTINUOUS UNINTERRUPTED FILM SEQUENCE a continuous action or image on the screen that appears to be the result of a single uninterrupted operation of the camera 11 CAMERA VIEW the range of, or view from, a camera 12 ATTEMPT an opportunity to attempt something ○ *He had a shot at repairing the vacuum cleaner.* 13 GUESS a wild guess or speculation, usually based on little or no information (*informal*) 14 MED = **jab** *n.* 3 (*informal*) 15 SMALL AMOUNT OF ALCOHOL a small glass or drink of a strong alcoholic beverage (*informal*) 16 SHARP COMMENT an angry or critical remark 17 ROCKET LAUNCH the launching of a rocket or probe to a particular destination 18 BLASTING EXPLOSION a charge of explosives used in blasting 19 PROJECTILE FLIGHT PATH a flight or path of a projectile 20 CHANCE AT WINNING something such as a racehorse to bet on at particular odds (*informal*) ○ *The horse was a 3 to 1 shot.* 21 SMALL QUANTITY a small amount given or taken on one occasion (*informal*) ○ *You need a shot of energy.* 22 MONEY OWED an amount due for something such as a round of drinks (*archaic*) 23 MEASUREMENT IN FATHOMS a unit of chain length equal to 15 fathoms in the United States and 12.5 fathoms in the United Kingdom [Old English *sceot*, *gesceot* 'act of shooting' < Germanic, 'project'] ◇ **a shot in the arm** something that has a sudden good effect on somebody or something ◇ **a shot in the dark** 1 a guess made without any information 2 an attempt made in desperation but with little hope of success ◇ **deliver** *or* **fire a shot across somebody's bows** to give somebody a warning of what might happen ◇ **get shot of somebody** *or* **something** to get rid of somebody *or* something (*informal*) ◇ **like a shot** very eagerly and quickly

shot[2] /shot/ past tense, past participle of **shoot** ■ *adj* 1 TWO-TONE IN COLOUR woven of two colours in such a way that when the fabric is viewed from different angles the visible colours change 2 MARKED WITH VARYING COLOUR streaked or flecked with a different colour 3 FILLED WITH PARTICULAR QUALITY filled with or permeated by an emotion or quality 4 MADE USELESS brought to a state of ruin or exhaustion (*informal*) ○ *I've been so busy my nerves are shot.* 5 USED UP no longer full or operating properly (*informal*) ○ *This tube of toothpaste is shot.*

shot-blasting *n* the process of projecting metal shot, usually steel or cast iron, at a surface to remove scale or prepare the surface for further treatment

shote *n* AGRIC = **shoat**

shotgun /shót gun/ *n* 1 GUN THAT SHOOTS PELLET LOAD a short-range smoothbore gun that discharges a load of small pellets 2 FORMATION IN AMERICAN FOOTBALL an offensive formation in American football, usually used when passing, in which the quarterback receives the snap a few yards behind the line of scrimmage ■ *adj* INVOLVING INTIMIDATION brought about by pressure, threats, or force

shotgun wedding, **shotgun marriage** *n* a marriage that takes place at short notice, usually because the bride is pregnant [Because the parties are compelled as if at gunpoint]

shot hole *n* 1 a hole bored into rock in which an explosive charge is placed 2 a small hole made in wood or leaves by insects or parasites (*informal*)

shot put *n* 1 an athletic field event in which contestants compete to throw a heavy metal ball as far as possible 2 a heavy metal ball used in the shot put —**shot-putter** *n*

shotten /shótt'n/ *adj* having recently spawned and therefore less valuable as food ○ *a shotten fish* [15C. < SHOOT.]

shot tower *n* a tower formerly used for making lead shot, in which molten lead was dropped from the top into water at the bottom in which the drops solidified

should /(stressed) shŏŏd, (unstressed) shəd/ CORE MEANING: modal verb indicating that something is the right thing for somebody to do ○ *You should get more exercise.* ○ *I should have told her I was leaving.* ○ *The report recommended that children should be tested regularly.*
v 1 EXPRESSING LIKELIHOOD OR PROBABILITY to be scheduled or expected to be or do something ○ *I should be back by 12.* ○ *The scissors should be in the second drawer down.* ○ *They should have arrived at Grandma's by now.* 2 EXPRESSING CONDITIONS OR CONSEQUENCES used to express the conditionality of an occurrence and suggest it is not a given, or to indicate the consequence of something that might happen (*in conditional clauses*) ○ *If anything should happen to my car, I'd be heartbroken.* ○ *Should you have any questions, our staff will be available to help.* ○ *'If I should die, think only this of me...'* (Rupert Brooke, *The Soldier*; 1887–1915) 3 WOULD used to mean the same thing as the verb would (*with 'I' or 'we'*) ○ *If we spent that much every month, we should soon run out of money.* ○ *I should love to meet her.* 4 REPORTING PAST VIEWPOINT ABOUT FUTURE used when reporting something from a past perspective, e.g. somebody's words or thoughts, about a future event ○ *It was intended that the library should be for the use of everyone.* ○ *He was keen that I should meet his publisher friend.* 5 USED TO SOFTEN HARSH WORDS used to soften a blunt statement or make one more polite ○ *I should hope you're sorry now.* ◇ **I should** used to advise somebody to do something ○ *I should take him up on his offer, if I were you.*

USAGE should or **would**? The same general pattern is true here as for *shall* and *will*. As an auxiliary verb, ***would*** is more usual than ***should*** when stating a condition or proposition and is the only choice when asking a question (*They would like to come. I would think so. Would you like to go to the cinema?*). ***Should*** has the special role of denoting obligation, validity, or likelihood (*I should stay until they arrive. Should you be lifting that? That should be our visitors now*) and must be used in inverted constructions expressing a condition: *Should it rain, the party will be held indoors.* ***Would*** has to be used when referring to habitual action in the past: *On Wednesdays I would go to the library.* In conversational English, the contracted forms *I'd, you'd*, etc. are regularly used instead of the full forms in making simple statements (*They'd like to come*), but these are not available in place of ***should*** in its senses of obligation or likelihood.

shoulder /shṓldər/ *n* **1 PLACE WHERE AN ARM ATTACHES TO THE TRUNK** either one of the two parts of the human body immediately below and at each side of the neck, where the arm joins the trunk **2 JOINT ATTACHING A FORELIMB TO THE TRUNK** the part of the body of a vertebrate animal equivalent to the shoulder, where the forelimb joins the pectoral girdle **3 PART OF GARMENT FITTING SHOULDER** a part of a piece of clothing that covers the shoulder **4 MEAT FROM SHOULDER** a fairly fatty cut of meat consisting of the upper part of a foreleg of an animal **5 SOMETHING SLOPED LIKE SHOULDER** something resembling a shoulder in position or slope, e.g. the part of a stringed instrument between the neck and body or the slope near the top of a hill **6** *US* TRANSP = **hard shoulder 7 TYPE SURFACE THAT IS NOT LETTER** a flat surface of printers' type below the base of the raised letter or character **8 WIDER PORTION OF SHAFT** any portion of a shaft or other instrument for transmitting force that has an increase in diameter to withstand thrust **9 OFF-PEAK SEASON** a season preceding or following the peak season, often characterized by lower levels of use as well as lower travel fares and accommodation prices ■ **shoulders** *npl* **1 UPPER AREA OF BACK** the upper back, including both shoulders and the area between them **2 CAPACITY TO HANDLE RESPONSIBILITY** the capacity to carry responsibility for something, especially something unpleasant or worrying ○ *The blame rests on her shoulders.* ■ *v* **1** *vt* **CARRY OR PLACE SOMETHING ON SHOULDERS** to carry, lift, or place something on the shoulders **2** *vt* **ACCEPT RESPONSIBILITY** to accept and bear a burden or responsibility **3** *vti* **MOVE SOMETHING WITH SHOULDER** to push something or make way using a shoulder ○ *She successfully shouldered her way to the front of the crowd.* [Old English *sculdor* < Germanic] ◇ **put your shoulder to the wheel** to work hard ◇ **rub shoulders with somebody** to associate with somebody of a particular type or social class ◇ **shoulder to shoulder 1** side by side **2** in a cooperative effort ◇ **straight from the shoulder** in a frank or blunt way

shoulder bag *n* a bag carried by a long strap hung over the shoulder

shoulder blade *n* either one of two large flat triangular bones over the upper outer parts of the ribs at the top of the back that joins with the upper arm bone. Technical name **scapula** *n.* 1

shoulder board *n US* CLOTHING, MIL = **shoulder strap** *n.* 2

shoulder flash *n* CLOTHING = **shoulder patch**

shoulder girdle *n* an incomplete ring of bones formed by the two shoulder blades (**scapulas**), the two collar bones (**clavicles**), and the upper edge of the breastbone (**sternum**)

shoulder holster *n* a holster hung from a shoulder strap and worn under the arm, used to hide a gun under a coat or jacket

shoulder pad *n* a pad inserted into the shoulder of a piece of clothing to improve its shape, often making it appear larger

shoulder patch *n* a cloth patch with an identifying emblem on it, worn on the upper part of the sleeve of a uniform

shoulder strap *n* **1** a strap that goes over a shoulder for carrying a bag or holding up a garment **2** one of a pair of stiff cloth patches worn on the shoulders of a military uniform to indicate rank. US term **shoulder board**

shouldn't /shŏŏd'nt/ *contr* should not

shouldst /shoodst/ 2nd person present singular of **should** (*archaic*)

shout /showt/ *v* **1** *vt* **SAY LOUDLY** to say or utter something very loudly **2** *vi* **SPEAK LOUDLY** to speak in a loud or angry voice **3** *vti ANZ* **PAY FOR FOOD OR DRINK** to buy something for somebody else, especially a drink in a pub or a meal in a restaurant (*informal*) ■ *n* **1 LOUD CRY** a loud call or cry **2 TURN TO PAY** somebody's turn to buy something, especially a drink or meal (*informal*) ○ *'It's my shout. What would you like to drink?'* [14C. < ?] —**shouter** *n* ◇ **be all over bar the shouting** used to say that something is nearly over, and the outcome is clear ◇ **nothing to shout about** not good enough to speak of with pride (*informal*)

shout down *vt* to prevent somebody from being heard by shouting loudly

shove /shuv/ *vti* (**shoves, shoving, shoved**) **1 MOVE SOMETHING WITH FORCE** to push somebody or something along or forward with force **2 PUSH SOMEBODY OR SOMETHING ROUGHLY** to push somebody or something in a rude or careless way ■ *n* **PUSH** a strong push [Old English *scufan* 'push away' < Germanic] —**shover** *n*

shove off *vi* **1** to leave (*informal; sometimes used as a command*) **2** to move from shore or a mooring in a boat

shove-halfpenny *n* a game in which players use the side of the hand to knock coins or discs into ruled scoring areas on a wooden board

shovel /shúvv'l/ *n* **1 LONG-HANDLED SCOOP** a hand tool consisting of a broad, usually curved blade attached to a long handle, used for lifting and moving loose material **2 MACHINE FOR EARTH DIGGING** a power-driven machine that operates with a scooping motion, especially one used for digging or moving earth **3 AMOUNT HELD BY SHOVEL** the amount that a shovel is capable of holding ■ *v* (**-els, -elling** *or* **-elling, -elled** *or* **-elled**) **1** *vti* **DIG WITH SHOVEL** to lift, move, or clear something with a shovel **2** *vt* **THROW SOMETHING CARELESSLY** to move large amounts of something from one place to another in a careless or clumsy way [Old English *scoff*] —**shovelful** *n*

shoveler /shúvvələr/ *n* **1** *US* = **shoveller 2** a small freshwater duck with a broad spoon-shaped bill. Native to: marshes in the N hemisphere. *Anas clypeata.*

shovelhead /shóvv'l hed/ (*plural* **-heads** *or* **-head**) *n* a common hammerhead shark with a broad shovel-shaped head. Native to: shallow Atlantic and Pacific waters. *Sphyrna tiburo.*

shoveller /shúvvələr/ *n* somebody or something that uses a shovel to move or throw something. US term **shoveler** *n.* 1

shovel-nosed *adj* having a broad shovel-shaped head, snout, or bill

show /shō/ *v* (**shows, showing, showed, shown** *or* **showed**) **1** *vti* **MAKE VISIBLE** to cause or allow something to come into view ○ *Show me your hand.* **2** *vti* **BE VISIBLE** to be visible or allow something to be seen easily ○ *Does the spot on my shirt show?* **3** *vti* **EXHIBIT** to put on an exhibition or performance or to present something for the public to see ○ *She's showing her paintings all over the world now.* ○ *Several new films are showing this week.* **4** *vti* **DISPLAY FOR SALE** to present something for sale to the public ○ *His work was showing at the Museum of Modern Art.* **5** *vt* **GUIDE** to guide or accompany somebody ○ *Show them to the office.* **6** *vt* **POINT SOMETHING OUT TO** to call somebody's attention to something ○ *She showed him the mistake.* **7** *vt* **DEMONSTRATE QUALITIES** to make somebody's or something's fundamental qualities or characteristics evident ○ *He has shown that he is honest.* **8** *vt* **ESTABLISH SOMETHING USING REASON** to explain, demonstrate, or prove something in a logical way ○ *The teacher showed them the solution.* **9** *vt* **DEMONSTRATE SOMETHING FOR INSTRUCTION** to give a demonstration of something in order to teach others ○ *She showed us how to apply the glaze to the pot.* **10** *vt* **GIVE INFORMATION** to register information ○ *This chart shows the sudden increase in temperature.* **11** *vt* **DISPLAY ATTITUDE** to display a personal feeling or attitude ○ *She's never shown much interest in art.* **12** *vi* **APPEAR IN CERTAIN WAY** to have a particular appearance when being viewed ○ *The horse shows well.* **13** *vi* **ARRIVE** to put in an appearance at a place (*informal*) ○ *They never showed.* **14** *vi US* **COME IN THIRD** to finish at least third in a race, especially a horse race or a dog race **15** *vt* **PLEAD SOMETHING IN LAWSUIT** to allege or plead something in a legal document ■ *n* **1 DEMONSTRATION** an expression or demonstration of something ○ *a show of force* **2 PUBLIC PRESENTATION** a public entertainment such as a theatre performance, film, or radio or television programme ○ *Shall we go to a show tonight?* **3 EXHIBITION** an exhibition, e.g. of art, flowers, animals, or an industry's products ○ *a flower show* **4 EVENT WITH FARM COMPETITIONS AND AMUSEMENTS** an annual outdoor event, held especially for a county, with competitions for the best livestock, produce, and prepared foods and with entertainments, rides, and other amusements. US term **fair**[2] *n.* 5 **5 APPEARANCE** an appearance given, either as an outward display of an emotion or trait, or as a demonstration of falseness and pretence ○ *a show of diligence* **6 SIZABLE VENTURE** an undertaking or task, especially one of some size and complexity (*informal*) ○ *You decide – it's your show!* **7 IMPRESSIVE DISPLAY** an extravagant or impressive display **8 SPECTACLE** a display or exhibition designed to evoke laughter or ridicule **9** *ANZ, US* **OPPORTUNITY** a chance or opportunity (*informal*) ○ *no show of winning* **10 INDICATION** a trace of something indicating its presence, e.g. oil in the ground **11 BLOOD INDICATING START OF LABOUR** a bloody mucous discharge indicating the onset of labour in childbirth ■ **shows** *npl Scotland, N England* **FUNFAIR** a funfair (*informal*) [Old English *scēawian* 'look at' < West Germanic, 'look'] —**showable** *adj* ◇ **get the** *or* **this show on the road** to begin an activity or start an event (*informal*) ◇ **good show** used to express approval or to congratulate somebody on doing well (*dated*) ◇ **steal the show** to attract the most attention or admiration

show off *v* **1** *vi* **ATTRACT THE ATTENTION OF OTHERS** to try to impress others by behaving in a way that attracts attention **2** *vt* **PRESENT SOMETHING FOR APPROVAL** to display somebody or something proudly for others to admire **3** *vt* **PRESENT SOMETHING IN AN APPEALING WAY** to display something in a way that enhances it

show up *v* **1** *vi* **ARRIVE** to arrive or put in an appearance (*informal*) **2** *vt* **BRING SOMETHING TO LIGHT** to expose or reveal something, especially an error or personal shortcoming **3** *vi* **BE SEEN** to be easily seen **4** *vt* **EMBARRASS SOMEBODY BEFORE OTHERS** to embarrass or humiliate somebody publicly **5** *vt* **MAKE SOMEBODY LOOK BAD** to perform in a superior way and make somebody look inferior by comparison

show-and-tell, show and tell *n* a classroom activity for children in which each child brings an object to school and tells the other children about it

show bill *n* a poster advertising or publicizing something

show biz *n* show business (*informal*)

showboat /shṓ bōt/ *n* a river steamboat equipped with a theatre and carrying an acting company that performs for communities along the river

show business *n* the entertainment industry, including films, radio, television, theatre, and music recording

showcase /shṓ kayss/ *n* **1 GLASS CASE FOR DISPLAYING OBJECTS** a box or case, usually one made of glass, used to display objects, especially in a museum or shop **2 MOST FAVOURABLE SETTING** an event, setting, or medium in which something or somebody is presented to advantage ■ *vt* (**-cases, -casing, -cased**) **PRESENT SOMETHING TO ADVANTAGE** to present something or somebody in a way that is designed to attract attention and admiration

showdown /shṓ down/ *n* **1** a confrontation to settle a conflict or dispute **2** in poker, the moment at the end of a round when the players show their cards to see who has the best hand

shower[1] /shówər/ *n* **1 BATH UNDER SPRAY** a method of washing in which somebody stands upright under a spray of water from a nozzle **2 PLACE AND EQUIPMENT FOR SHOWER** an enclosure or the plumbing apparatus for a shower **3 PERIOD OF PRECIPITATION** a short period of rain, snow, hail, or sleet **4 SOMETHING LIKE RAIN** a sudden spray or fall of something, e.g. meteors, sparks, or bullets **5 LARGE AMOUNT OF** something that somebody receives all at once in quantity **6** *ANZ, Can, US* **PARTY WITH GIFTS** a party given by friends, especially in honour of a woman who is about to be married or is expecting a baby, at which gifts are given **7** *UK* **DISAGREEABLE GROUP** a group of people considered unpleasant, worthless, or inferior (*informal*) **8 IONIZING PARTICLES CAUSED BY COSMIC RAY** a large number of ionizing particles and photons caused by the collision of a cosmic-ray particle with the upper atmosphere ■ *v* **1** *vi* **WASH UNDER SHOWER** to wash using a shower **2** *vti* **RAIN DOWN ON** to fall or make things fall in a spray **3** *vt* **GIVE SOMEBODY SOMETHING PLENTIFULLY** to give somebody something in abundance ○ *They were showered with gifts.* [Old English *scūr* < West Germanic] —**showery** *adj*

shower[2] /shṓ ər/ *n* somebody or something that shows, especially an exhibitor at a public exhibition [Old English *scēawere* 'scout, watchman' < *scēawian* 'look at']

shower bath *n* = **shower**[1] *n.* 1

shower gel *n* a liquid soap with the consistency of a gel, used especially when in the shower and often scented

showerhead /shówər hed/ *n* a spray nozzle that is part of an overhead plumbing fixture used in a shower

showerproof /shówər proof/ *adj* resistant to light but not heavy rain —**showerproofing** *n*

showgirl /shṓ gurl/ *n* a young woman who performs in the chorus of a stage show, usually a musical, as a dancer or singer

showground /shṓ grownd/ *n* an area of land where an open-air event such as an agricultural show is held

show house *n* a house decorated and furnished for prospective buyers to view as an example of the type of house for sale on a newly built estate. US term **model home**

showing /shṓ ing/ *n* **1 DISPLAY** a presentation or exhibition, e.g. of a film or artwork **2 TYPE OF PERFORMANCE** the way a person, group, or team performs **3 PRESENTATION OF FACTS** a presentation of facts [Old English *scēawung*]

showjumping /shṓ jumping/ *n* a competitive sport in which riders on horseback take turns jumping over a series of obstacles on a set course and are judged on speed and ability —**showjump** *vi* —**showjumper** *n*

showman /shṓmən/ (*plural* **-men** /-mən/) *n* **1 GIFTED ENTERTAINER** a person who is naturally talented in dramatic presentation or entertainment **2 PRODUCER OF SHOW** a producer or promoter of commercial entertainment ventures, especially in musical theatre **3 CIRCUS MANAGER** manager or owner of a circus or fairground —**showmanship** *n*

shown past participle of **show**

show-off *n* a flamboyant person who seeks attention (*informal*)

show of hands *n* a form of voting that involves counting the hands raised by people to vote for or against a proposal

showpiece /shṓ peess/ *n* something considered or offered as a fine example of something

showplace /shṓ playss/ *n* **1** a place visited for its beauty or historical significance **2** a place that is considered or offered as an example of beauty

showroom /shṓ room, -rŏŏm/ *n* a room in which goods for sale, especially cars or electrical appliances, are displayed

showstopper /shṓ stoppər/ *n* **1** a performance receiving so much applause from an audience that the show is interrupted **2** somebody or something so spectacular as to attract and hold everyone's attention

showtime /shṓ tīm/ *n US* **1** the scheduled time for an entertainment such as a film or play to begin **2** the scheduled time for any event or activity to begin (*informal*)

show trial *n* a trial with a predetermined verdict held for propaganda purposes

showy /shṓ i/ (**-ier, -iest**) *adj* **1** making an attractive or impressive display **2** appearing tasteless and ostentatious —**showily** *adv* —**showiness** *n*

shoyu /shṓ yoo/ *n* a Japanese variety of soy sauce [Early 18C. < Japanese.]

shpilkes /shpílkəss/ *npl* a state of great nervousness or anxiety

shraddh *n* ETHNOL = **sraddhaa**

shrank past participle of **shrink**

shrapnel /shrápnəl/ *n* **1** metal balls or fragments that are scattered when a shell, bomb, or bullet explodes **2** an artillery shell designed to explode before impact producing a shower of metal balls and fragments [Early 19C. After General Henry *Shrapnel* (1761–1842), British artillery officer.]

shred /shred/ *n* **1 LONG TORN STRIP** a ragged scrap or strip cut or torn from something **2 SMALL PART** a very small amount or fragment of something ■ *v* (**shreds, shredding, shredded**) **1** *vt* **TEAR SOMETHING INTO SHREDS** to cut or tear something into shreds **2** *vt* **PUT SOMETHING THROUGH SHREDDER** to reduce a document to unreadable strips in a shredder **3** *vti Aus, US* **SURF OR SNOWBOARD EXPERTLY** to ride a wave on a surfboard or descend a slope on a snowboard with expert skill (*informal*) [Old English *scrēade* < West Germanic, 'cut']

shredded wheat *n* a breakfast cereal made from cooked dried whole wheat that has been shredded, shaped into cakes, and baked

shredder /shréddər/ *n* **1** an office machine used to destroy documents by cutting them into very small pieces so that they cannot be read **2** *Aus, US* an expert surfer or snowboarder (*informal*)

Shreveport /shreév pawrt/ city in NW Louisiana. Population: 188,319 (1998 estimate).

shrew /shroo/ *n* **1** a small nocturnal mammal that resembles a mouse but is an insectivore, with velvety fur, a long pointed snout, and small eyes and ears. Family: Soricidae. **2** an offensive term for a woman who is regarded as quarrelsome, nagging, or ill-tempered [Old English *scrēawa* < ?]

LITERARY LINK ***The Taming of the Shrew***, a play (1593–94?) by William Shakespeare. Set in Verona, it describes Petruchio's attempts to woo the wealthy but haughty and temperamental Katharina (the 'shrew' of the title). The rounded and convincing protagonists make this an intriguing character study as well as a boisterous farce.

shrewd /shrood/ *adj* **1 GOOD AT JUDGING PEOPLE OR SITUATIONS** showing or possessing intelligence, insight, and sound judgment, especially in business or politics **2 CLEVER AND PROBABLY ACCURATE** based on good judgment and probably correct ○ *a shrewd assessment of the situation* **3 CRAFTY** inclined to deal with others in a clever underhand way [13C. < SHREW in the obsolete sense 'wicked man'.] —**shrewdly** *adv* —**shrewdness** *n*

shrewish /shrŏŏ ish/ *adj* with a quarrelsome ill-tempered disposition —**shrewishly** *adv* —**shrewishness** *n*

Shrewsbury /shrṓzbəri, shrŏŏzbəri/ town in W England, on the River Severn. Population: 94,600 (1994).

shriek /shreek/ *v* **1** *vi* **MAKE SHRILL SOUND** to make a loud high-pitched piercing sound **2** *vt* **SAY SOMETHING IN LOUD SHRILL VOICE** to utter something in a loud high-pitched piercing voice ■ *n* **LOUD SHRILL CRY** a loud high-pitched piercing cry or sound [15C. < N Germanic.] —**shrieker** *n*

shrieval /shreév'l/ *adj* belonging or relating to a sheriff [Late 17C. < SHRIEVE[1].]

shrievalty /shreév'lti/ (*plural* **-ties**) *n* **1 SHERIFF'S OFFICE** the office or position of sheriff **2 SHERIFF'S TERM** the term of office of a sheriff **3 SHERIFF'S JURISDICTION** the jurisdiction of a sheriff [Early 16C. < SHRIEVE[1].]

shrieve[1] /shreev/ *n* a sheriff (*archaic*) [Alteration of SHERIFF]

shrieve[2] /shreev/ *vti* to shrive or shrive somebody (*archaic*) [Variant of SHRIVE]

shrift /shrift/ *n* (*archaic*) **1** confession to a priest **2** absolution granted by a priest [Old English *scrift* < *scrīfan* 'shrive']

shrike /shrīk/ (*plural* **shrikes** *or* **shrike**) *n* a brown or grey songbird with a screeching call and a hooked bill, that eats insects and small animals that it impales on sharp objects such as thorns. Family: Laniidae. [Mid-16C. < ?]

shrill /shril/ *adj* **1 PENETRATINGLY HIGH-PITCHED** with a high-pitched penetrating quality **2 MAKING A SHRILL SOUND** making a high-pitched penetrating sound **3 INSISTENT** with an obtrusive insistent quality ■ *v* **1** *vi* **MAKE A SHRILL SOUND** to make a high-pitched penetrating sound (*literary*) **2** *vt* **SAY SOMETHING IN A PIERCING VOICE** to utter something in a high-pitched penetrating voice [13C. < ?] —**shrillness** *n* —**shrilly** /shríl li/ *adv*

shrimp /shrimp/ *n* **1 SMALL MARINE CRUSTACEAN** a small mainly marine crustacean with ten legs of a suborder that includes several edible species. Suborder: Natantia. **2 SOMETHING UNDERSIZED** somebody or something very small or considered insignificant (*informal*) ■ *vi* **FISH FOR SHRIMPS** to fish for shrimps [14C. < ?] —**shrimper** *n*

shrimp plant *n* an ornamental plant with long curving flower spikes within overlapping pink bracts. Native to: tropical America. *Beloperone guttata.*

shrine /shrīn/ *n* **1 HOLY PLACE OF WORSHIP** a sacred place of worship associated with a holy person or event **2 CONTAINER FOR HOLY RELICS** a case or other container for sacred relics, e.g. the bones of a saint **3 TOMB OF HOLY PERSON** the tomb of a saint or other revered figure **4 NICHE FOR RELIGIOUS ICON** a ledge or alcove for a religious icon, e.g. in a church **5 SOMETHING REVERED** an object or place revered for its associations or history ■ *vt* (**shrines, shrining, shrined**) **ENSHRINE** to enshrine something (*literary*) [Pre-12C. < Latin *scrinium* 'case for books or papers'.]

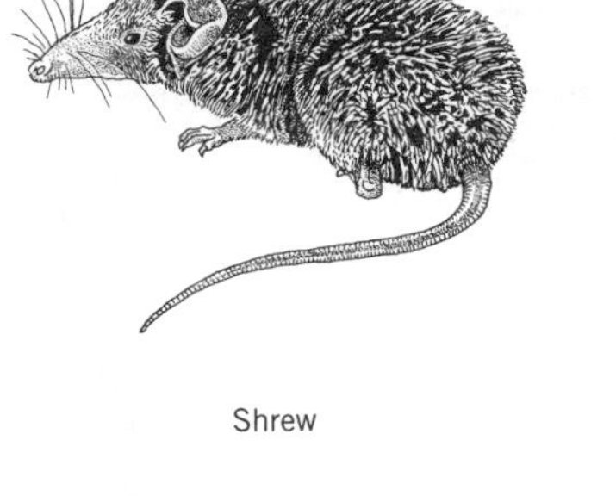

Shrew

shrink /shringk/ *v* (**shrinks, shrinking, shrank** /shrangk/ *or* **shrunk** /shrungk/, **shrunk** *or* **shrunken** /shrúngkən/) **1** *vti* **MAKE OR BECOME SMALLER** to become smaller or cause something to become smaller, e.g. when exposed to cold, heat, or damp **2** *vti* **REDUCE SIZE** to decrease or cause something to decrease in amount, extent, value, or weight **3** *vi* **DRAW AWAY FROM** to move back and away, especially out of disgust, fear, or horror ○ *shrinking back in revulsion* **4** *vi* **BE DISINCLINED TO DO** to be unwilling or reluctant to do something, especially something difficult or unpleasant ○ *She does not shrink from tackling tough problems.* ■ *n* **1 PSYCHIATRIST** a psychiatrist (*slang; considered offensive by some people*) **2 ACT OF SHRINKING AWAY** an act of shrinking away from something [Old English *scrincan* 'wither' < Indo-European, 'turn, bend'] —**shrinkable** *adj* —**shrinker** *n*

SYNONYMS See ***recoil***.

shrinkage /shríngkij/ *n* **1 DECREASE AFTER SHRINKING** the amount lost when something is decreased or reduced, or when it shrinks **2 ACT OF SHRINKING** the shrinking of something **3 MERCHANDISE STOLEN OR BROKEN** the loss of goods due to theft or breakage **4 LOSS OF VALUE** the decrease in value of something **5 WEIGHT REDUCTION IN CARCASSES** the loss in body weight of livestock carcasses during shipping, storage, and preparation for sale **6 REDUCED SIZE OF CLAY ITEM** the reduction in size of a clay object when it is fired in a kiln, caused by the moisture burning off

shrink fit *n* the fit of two interlocking parts in which the outer is heated and therefore expands before being put in position, the contraction during cooling ensuring that it is tight

shrinking violet *n* a shy or retiring person (*informal*)

shrink-wrap *n* a clear thermoplastic film that is wrapped around a product and shrunk to its original smaller size using heat, thereby forming a tightly sealed package ■ *vt* to wrap goods in shrink-wrap

shrive /shrīv/ (**shrives, shriving, shrove** /shrōv/ *or* **shrived, shriven** /shrívv'n/ *or* **shrived**) *v* **1** *vt* **ABSOLVE SOMEBODY OF SINS** in Christianity, to hear somebody's confession of sins and give the person absolution **2** *vt* **IMPOSE PENANCE** in Christianity, to impose a penance on a sinner **3** *vi* **CONFESS** to confess sins to a priest (*archaic*) [Pre-12C. < Latin *scribere* 'write'.] —**shriver** *n*

shrivel /shrívv'l/ (**-els, -elling, -elled**) *vti* **1 SHRINK** to become or cause somebody or something to become shrunken or wrinkled, especially from drying out or ageing **2 WEAKEN** to become or cause somebody to become useless or ineffectual **3 BECOME OR MAKE SMALLER** to become or cause something to become gradually smaller or less [Mid-16C. < ?]

SYNONYMS See ***dry***.

shriven past participle of **shrive**

Shrivijaya /shreévi jay ə/ *n* a trading empire centred on the Malacca Straits between Malaya and Sumatra with a Buddhist government that opened up Southeast Asia to Muslim conversion when it fell [Late 19C. < Hindi.]

shroff /shrof/ *n* **1 INDIAN BANKER** a banker or moneychanger in India **2 EXPERT IN COUNTERFEIT COINS** somebody employed in E Asia to separate counterfeit from real coins ■ *vt* **SEPARATE COUNTERFEIT COINS** to separate counterfeit from real coins [Early 17C. Alteration of Hindi *śarāf* < Arabic *ṣarrāf*.]

Shropshire /shrópshər/ county in W England, on the Welsh border. Area: 3,490 sq. km/1,348 sq. mi.

shroud /shrowd/ *n* **1 BURIAL CLOTH** a cloth in which a dead body is wrapped before burial **2 COVERING** something that covers or conceals something or somebody **3 PROTECTIVE COVERING** a protective covering such as a guard for a piece of machinery **4 PROTECTIVE COVERING FOR SPACECRAFT** a shield that protects a spacecraft from heat during launch **5 MAST STAY** any one of the supporting ropes or wires that extend down from the top of a mast **6 CABLE TO STOP SWAY** a supporting cable that extends from the top of a tall structure such as a smokestack to the ground **7 PART OF AEROFOIL SURFACE** a rearward extension of a fixed aerofoil surface covering the leading edge of a movable surface hinged to it **8 PARACHUTE LINE** any one of the lines by which the harness of a parachute is attached to the canopy ■ *vt* **1 WRAP CORPSE** to wrap a dead body in a cloth **2 COVER OR CONCEAL** to cover or conceal somebody or something [Old English *scrūd* 'garment' < West Germanic, 'cut']

shroud-laid *adj* describes a rope that is made up of four twisted strands

shrove past tense of **shrive**

Shrovetide /shrṓv tīd/ *n* in the Christian calendar, the three-day period preceding Ash Wednesday and the season of Lent

Shrove Tuesday *n* in the Christian calendar, the last day before the beginning of Lent [< SHRIVE, from the practice of going to confession at the beginning of Lent]

shrub¹ /shrub/ *n* any woody plant without a trunk but with several stems growing from the base [Old English *scrybb* 'shrubbery' < Indo-European, 'to cut']

shrub² /shrub/ *n* a drink made with fruit juice, sugar, spices, and rum or other alcohol [Early 18C. < Arabic *surb* 'a drink'.]

shrubbery /shrúbbəri/ (*plural* **-ies**) *n* **1** a part of a garden where shrubs grow **2** shrubs considered collectively

shrubby /shrúbbi/ (**-bier, -biest**) *adj* **1** having shrubs or covered with shrubs **2** resembling a shrub in size or in having little or no trunk —**shrubbiness** *n*

shrug /shrug/ *vti* (**shrugs, shrugging, shrugged**) to raise and drop the shoulders briefly, especially to indicate indifference or lack of knowledge ■ *n* a gesture of raising and dropping the shoulders briefly [14C. < ?]

shrug off *vt* **1** DISMISS to reject or disregard something as unimportant **2** GET FREE OF to become free of something such as a disease **3** REMOVE CLOTHING to get out of clothing by wriggling

shrunk past tense, past participle of **shrink**

shrunken past participle of **shrink**

shtetl /shtétt'l/ (*plural* **shtetls** *or* **shtetlach** /shtét laak/), **schtetl** (*plural* **schtetls** *or* **schtetlech** /shtétlak/) *n* formerly, a small Jewish town or village in Eastern Europe [Mid-20C. Via Yiddish, 'little town' < German *Stadt* 'town'.]

shtick /shtik/, **schtick, shtik** *n* **1** a comedian's or entertainer's act, routine, or gimmick (*informal*) **2** something, e.g. an interest, talent, trait, job, or hobby, that especially characterizes somebody (*slang*) [Mid-20C. Via Yiddish, 'piece, routine' < Old High German *stucki*.]

shtoom /shtōōm/, **schtoom, shtum, stumm** *adj* quiet or silent (*informal*) [Mid-20C. Via Yiddish < German *stumm*.]

shtuck /shtōōk/ *n* trouble resulting from a failing such as an error or misjudgment (*informal*) [Mid-20C. < ?]

shtum *adj* = **shtoom**

shuck /shuk/ *n* **1** *Can, US* OUTER COVERING OF GRAIN OR FRUIT the husk, pod, or shell of something such as a nut, pea, or ear of corn **2** OYSTER OR CLAM SHELL the shell of a clam or oyster ■ *vt* GET RID OF to get rid of or remove something or throw something off (*informal*) [Late 17C. < ?] —**shucker** *n*

shucks /shuks/ *interj Can, US* used to express disappointment, bashfulness, or irritation (*informal*) [Mid-19C. < *shuck* 'something worthless'.]

shudder /shúddər/ *vi* **1** SHIVER VIOLENTLY to shake or tremble uncontrollably from a reaction such as cold, fear, or disgust **2** VIBRATE to vibrate rapidly ■ *n* **1** VIOLENT SHAKING MOVEMENT an uncontrolled shaking or trembling movement **2** VIBRATION a rapid vibrating movement [12C. Probably < Middle Low German *schōderen* or Middle Dutch *shūderen* 'keep on shuddering'.] —**shuddery** *adj*

Shudra /shōōdrə/ (*plural* **-dra**) *n S Asia* an offensive term for a member of the lowest caste in the Hindu system of social stratification. ◊ **Dalit** [Mid-17C. < Sanskrit *śūdraḥ*.]

shuffle /shúff'l/ *v* (**-fles, -fling, -fled**) **1** *vi* WALK WITHOUT LIFTING FEET to walk slowly without picking up the feet **2** *vti* DRAG FEET to move the feet without picking them up **3** *vi* MOVE AWKWARDLY to move in an awkward clumsy way **4** *vi* DANCE BY SHUFFLING THE FEET to slide the feet in a dance step **5** *vt* CHANGE WHERE SOMETHING IS LOCATED to move things around from one place to another **6** *vt* MIX THINGS UP to mix things together carelessly **7** *vti* REARRANGE ORDER OF PLAYING CARDS to rearrange playing cards randomly so that the order is not known **8** *vt* AVOID OR HIDE to put something aside in order to avoid or hide it **9** *vi* BEHAVE EVASIVELY to be deliberately evasive or shifty in addressing an issue ■ *n* **1** FOOT-DRAGGING WALK a slow walk while dragging the feet **2** SLIDING DANCE STEP a dance or dance step in which the feet drag or slide **3** REORDERING OF CARDS a random reordering of playing cards **4** SOMEBODY'S CHANCE TO SHUFFLE a player's turn to shuffle playing cards **5** EVASION a deliberate evasion of an issue [Mid-16C. < ?] —**shuffler** *n*

shuffleboard /shúff'l bawrd/ *n* **1** a game in which players use a long pronged cue to push discs along a smooth hard surface into numbered scoring areas **2** the surface on which shuffleboard is played [Mid-19C. Alteration of *shovelboard*, alteration of obsolete *shove-board*, an earlier name for the game.]

shufti /shōōfti/ (*plural* **-ties**), **shufty** (*plural* **-ties**) *n* a quick look or glance (*informal*) [Mid-20C. < Colloquial Arabic *šuftī* 'have you seen?' < *šāfa* 'see'.]

shul /shool/, **schul** *n* a synagogue [Late 19C. Via Yiddish < German *Schule* 'school'.]

shun /shun/ (**shuns, shunning, shunned**) *vt* to avoid somebody or something intentionally [Old English *scunian* < ?] —**shunner** *n*

shunt /shunt/ *v* **1** *vt* MOVE SOMEBODY OR SOMETHING ELSEWHERE to move somebody or something to a different place, especially for convenience rather than fairness or kindness **2** *vti* CHANGE TRACKS to move rolling railway stock from one track to another, either by using an engine or by means of an automatic switch, especially when assembling trains **3** *vt* GET RID OF RESPONSIBILITY to avoid something by ignoring it or shifting responsibility for it to somebody else **4** *vt* CRASH CAR to crash a car (*informal*) **5** *vt* DIVERT CURRENT to use an electrical device to divert electrical current from an instrument **6** *vt* SURGICALLY DIVERT FLOW to use an artificially created passage to redirect the circulation of blood or cerebrospinal fluid ■ *n* **1** DIVERSION OF SOMETHING a turning aside or means of turning something aside **2** MINOR CAR CRASH a minor collision between road vehicles in which one runs into the back of another at a relatively low speed (*informal*) **3** SORTING OF RAILWAY VEHICLES the act of a locomotive pushing railway vehicles in the process of sorting them **4** DEVICE FOR DIVERTING ELECTRIC CURRENT a component in an electric circuit that is connected in parallel with an instrument and diverts the majority of current from the instrument **5** BYPASS FOR BODILY FLUID a passage in the body that diverts the flow of blood or other bodily fluid form one channel to another, created either as a result of disease or injury or artificially by surgery [13C. < ?]

shush /shōōsh, shush/ *interj* used to tell somebody to be quiet ■ *vti* to silence somebody or to become silent (*informal*) [Early 20C. A natural exclamation.]

Shuswap /shōōss wop/ (*plural* **-wap** *or* **-waps**) *n* **1** a member of a Native North American people of S British Columbia **2** the Salishan language of the Shuswap people. Native speakers: 500. [Mid-19C. < Shuswap.] —**Shuswap** *adj*

shut /shut/ *v* (**shuts, shutting, shut**) **1** *vti* CLOSE OPENING to move something or move into a position that blocks or covers an opening ○ *leaned over to shut the window* **2** *vt* STOP ACCESS OR EXIT to prevent entrance to or exit from something, e.g. by locking doors ○ *Rising water levels meant that they had to shut the tunnel.* **3** *vt* FOLD PARTS CLOSED to close something by bringing its covering or parts together ○ *had to shut her eyes against the light* **4** *vt* LOCK to secure something with a lock or latch ○ *The gate had not been shut properly.* **5** *vti* STOP OPERATION to discontinue or cause something to discontinue operation temporarily or permanently ○ *another factory shut because it was losing money* ■ *adj* SECURED closed or fastened against entrance or exit ■ *n* CONNECTION REGION BETWEEN WELDED METAL PIECES the region of connection between pieces of metal that are welded together [Old English *scyttan* < Germanic]

shut down *v* **1** *vti* to cease or cause something to cease operation or activity **2** *vt* to reduce the power output of a nuclear reactor by maintaining it at its lowest possible level

shut in *vt* to confine or enclose somebody or something

shut off *v* **1** *vti* STOP SOMETHING WORKING to stop operating or to cause something to stop operating **2** *vt* CUT OFF FLOW to stop the passage, flow, or supply of something **3** *vt* BLOCK SOMETHING OFF to impede the flow or progress of something **4** *vt* ISOLATE to put somebody or something into a state of isolation

shut out *vt* **1** EXCLUDE to exclude somebody or something **2** STOP SOMEBODY ENTERING to prevent somebody or something from entering a place **3** HIDE to hide something from sight **4** *Can, US* KEEP SOMEBODY FROM SCORING to prevent an opponent from scoring in a game

shut up *v* **1** *vi* STOP TALKING to be quiet or stop talking (*informal*) ○ *I shut up before saying something I would regret.* **2** *vt* SILENCE to cause somebody to be quiet or stop talking (*informal*) ○ *She shot me a look that shut me up instantly.* **3** *vt* CONFINE to confine or imprison somebody or something ○ *She shut the dog up in the pen.* **4** *vt* CLOSE to close or prevent entrance to something ○ *The building is all shut up.*

shutdown /shút down/ *n* **1** the cessation or suspension of activities at a business, factory, or plant **2** the reduction of power in a nuclear reactor by maintaining the core at the lowest level possible

Shute /shoot/, **Nevil** (1899–1960) British novelist and aeronautical engineer. Born **Nevil Shute Norway**

shuteye /shút ī/ *n* a short sleep (*informal*)

shut-in *n US* somebody who is rarely or never able to leave home, especially because of illness or lack of physical mobility (*informal*)

shut-off *n* **1** a device, usually a valve, that shuts something off **2** an interruption or stoppage, e.g. in flow or supply

shutout /shút owt/ *n* **1** MANAGEMT = **lockout** *n.* **2** *Can, US* a game in which one team does not score

shutter /shúttər/ *n* **1** DOOR OR WINDOW COVER a hinged cover for a door or window, often with louvres and usually fitted in pairs **2** CAMERA DEVICE a mechanical part of a camera that opens and closes the lens aperture to expose the film or plate to light ■ *vt* **1** CLOSE SOMETHING USING SHUTTERS to close or protect something by means of shutters **2** FIT SOMETHING WITH SHUTTERS to equip something with shutters

shuttering /shúttəring/ *n* BUILDING = **formwork**

shuttle /shútt'l/ *n* **1** WEAVING DEVICE a device in weaving that holds the weft thread and is used to pass it between the warp threads **2** SPINDLE OR BOBBIN HOLDING THREAD a thread holder, e.g. in tatting or netting or for the lower thread in a sewing machine **3** ROUTE TAKEN OR VEHICLE USED the route taken or the aircraft, bus, or train used to travel frequently between two places, often relatively near each other **4** AEROSP = **space shuttle** **5** GOING BACK AND FORTH frequent travel by vehicle between two places **6** RACKET GAMES = **shuttlecock** *n.* 1 ■ *vti* (**-tles, -tling, -tled**) **1** GO BACK AND FORTH to move or cause somebody or something to move between two places frequently **2** GO BY SHUTTLE to transport somebody or something or to be transported by a shuttle [Old English *scytel* 'arrow, dart' < Germanic, 'shoot']

shuttlecock /shútt'l kok/ *n* **1** OBJECT HIT IN BADMINTON a small rounded piece of cork or rubber attached to a cone of feathers that is hit back and forth in badminton and in the old game of battledore **2** SUBJECT OF ARGUMENT something that is continually argued about by two opposing sides ○ *The sovereignty of the island became a shuttlecock between the two countries.* ■ *vt* SEND SOMETHING BACK AND FORTH to toss or send something back and forth [Early 16C. *Shuttle* probably < its going back and forth, like the shuttle in a loom; *cock* < the feathers, like a bird's crest.]

shuttlecraft /shútt'l kraaft/ (*plural* **-craft**) *n* a reusable spacecraft for carrying astronauts or material between Earth and space or between objects in space

shuttle diplomacy *n* diplomatic negotiations carried on between countries by a mediator who travels back and forth between the countries

shwa *n* PHON = **schwa**

shy¹ /shī/ *adj* (**shier, shiest**) **1** UNCOMFORTABLE WITH OTHERS reserved, diffident, and uncomfortable in the company of others ○ *She was always shy at parties.* **2** TIMID easily frightened ○ *The deer were shy and ran when we tried to approach them.* **3** CAUTIOUS unwilling to trust or put confidence in somebody or something ○ *The children were shy of their new classmates.* **4** RELUCTANT fearful of making a commitment ○ *Don't be shy of speaking your mind.* **5** DISLIKING showing a disinclination for something (*usually in combination*) ○ *workshy* **6** SHORT OF short of the full or a particular amount ○ *We are £100 shy of the down payment.* **7** NOT REPRODUCING EASILY describes plants and animals that do not breed readily or freely ■ *vi* (**shies, shying, shied**) **1** MOVE SUDDENLY to move suddenly in fright or alarm ○ *That horse shies at anything in the path.* **2** STAY AWAY to avoid or evade something ○ *He always shies away from public speaking.* ■ *n* (*plural* **shies**) SUDDEN MOVE a sudden movement in fright or alarm [Old English *scēoh* < Germanic] —**shyer** *n* —**shyly** *adv* —**shyness** *n*

shy² /shī/ *vt* (**shies, shying, shied**) THROW to toss something quickly and suddenly ■ *n* (*plural* **shies**) **1** QUICK THROW a quick sudden throw of something **2** VERBAL ATTACK a rude or insulting remark **3** ATTEMPT an attempt made to do or get something (*informal*) ○ *We'll have a shy at it.* [Late 18C. < ?] —**shyer** *n*

shylock /shī lok/ *n* a ruthless and demanding money-lender or creditor [Late 18C. After *Shylock*, a moneylender in Shakespeare's play *The Merchant of Venice*.]

shyster /shístər/ *n US* an unscrupulous person, especially a lawyer or political representative (*slang insult*) [Mid-19C. < ?]

si[1] /see/ *n* MUSIC = **te** [Early 18C. < the initial letters of Latin *Sancte Iohannes* 'St John', the words sung to this note in the hymn for St John's day.]

si[2] *abbr* Slovenia (*in Internet addresses*)

Si *symbol* silicon

SI *abbr* **1** *NZ* South Island **2** International System of Units [< French *Système International (d'Unités)*]

sialagogue *n* a drug or agent that stimulates the flow of saliva —**sialagogic** /sī allə góggik/ *adj*

sialic acid /sī állik-/ *n* an amino sugar found in animal tissues

Sialkot /si álkot/ town in NE Pakistan. Population: 302,009 (1981).

sialoid /sī ə loyd/ *adj* resembling saliva

Siam /sī ám/ former name for **Thailand**

Siam, Gulf of former name for **Thailand, Gulf of**

siamang /seé ə mang/ *n* the largest species of gibbon, with a large throat sac that inflates during calls. Native to: Sumatra, Malaysia. *Hylobates syndactylus*. [Early 19C. < Malay.]

Siamese /sī ə meéz/ *adj* relating to Siam, now Thailand, or its people or culture (*dated*) ■ *n* (*plural* **-mese**) **1** a person who comes from Thailand (*dated*) **2** ZOOL = **Siamese cat**

Siamese cat *n* a short-haired domestic cat with blue eyes and a long cream-coloured body with dark ears, paws, face, and tail, belonging to a breed that originated in Thailand (formerly Siam)

Siamese fighting fish *n* a brightly coloured long-finned freshwater fish often kept in aquariums, the male of which is very aggressive. Native to: Thailand, Malaysia. *Betta splendens*.

Siamese twins *npl* twins born physically joined together [After twins, Chang and Eng (1811–74), born in Siam (Thailand)]

sib /sib/ *n* **1 BROTHER OR SISTER** a brother or sister **2 INDIVIDUAL WITH SAME PARENTS AS ANOTHER** an individual that has the same parents as another individual **3 GROUP WITH SINGLE COMMON ANCESTOR** a group of people who trace their descent lineally from a single real or presumed ancestor ■ **sibs** *npl* **WIDER FAMILY** members of an extended family considered as a group (+ *plural verb*) ■ *adj* **CLOSELY RELATED** with the same parents or closely related [Old English *sib(b)* < ?] —**sibship** *n*

SIB *abbr* Securities and Investments Board

Sibelius /si báyli əss/, **Jean** (1865–1957) Finnish composer

Siberia /sī beéri ə/ vast region of E Russia, extending from the Ural Mountains to the Pacific Ocean —**Siberian** *n, adj*

sibilant /síbbilənt/ *adj* **1 PRONOUNCED WITH HISSING SOUND** describes consonants that are pronounced with a hissing sound **2 PRODUCING HISSING SOUND** producing a hissing sound ○ *the sibilant sound of air escaping from a tyre* ■ *n* **SIBILANT CONSONANT** a sibilant consonant [Mid-17C. < the present participle of Latin *sibilare* 'hiss', thought to be imitative of the sound.] —**sibilance** *n* —**sibilantly** *adv*

sibilate /síbbi layt/ (**-lates, -lating, -lated**) *vti* to pronounce sounds with a hiss [Mid-17C. < Latin *sibilare* (see SIBILANT).]

sibling /síbbling/ *n* **1** a brother or sister (*often before nouns*) **2** a member of a group of people who trace their descent from a single real or presumed ancestor [Old English < *sib(b)* 'sib']

sibling species *n* a species that closely resembles another in appearance and other characteristics but cannot interbreed with it

sibyl /síbbil, síbb'l/ *n* **1** a woman of ancient Greece and Rome believed to be an oracle or a prophet **2** a woman prophet or fortune teller [13C. Via Old French *Sibile* < Latin *Sibylla* < Greek *Sibulla*.] —**sibyllic** /si bíllik/ *adj* —**sybilline** /síbbi līn, -leen/ *adj*

sic[1] /sik/ *adv* thus or so, used within brackets to indicate that what precedes it is written intentionally or is copied verbatim from the original, even if it appears to be a mistake [Late 19C. < Latin.] ◇ **sic passim** used to show that a particular word or term is used in the same form throughout a printed work ◇ **sic transit gloria mundi** 'thus passes the glory of the world', used, e.g. when a distinguished person dies or an important era comes to an end

sic[2] /sik/ (**sics, siccing** *or* **sicking, sicced** *or* **sicked**), **sick** *vt* **1** to attack somebody physically, usually used as a command to a dog **2** to urge a person or animal, especially a dog, to attack somebody physically [Mid-19C. Dialect variant of SEEK.]

siccar /síkər/, **sicker** *adj Scotland* free from doubt or uncertainty [Old English *sicor*. Via Germanic < Latin *securus* 'secure'.]

siccative /síkətiv/ *n* a substance added to liquids to speed drying ■ *adj* absorbing moisture to promote drying [15C. < late Latin *siccativus* < Latin *siccare* 'dry' < *siccus* 'dry'.]

sice *n* HIST = **syce**

Sichuan /si chwaán/ province of S China. Capital: Chengdu. Population: 112,140,000 (1994). Area: 569,000 sq. km/219,691 sq. mi.

siciliano /si sílli aánō/ (*plural* **-nos**), **siciliana** /-nə/ *n* **1** an old Sicilian folk dance **2** the music for a siciliano, in a minor key with six or twelve beats to the bar [Early 18C. < Italian, 'Sicilian'.]

Sicily /síssəli/ island of S Italy, the largest in the Mediterranean Sea. Population: 5,082,697 (1995). Area: 25,710 sq. km/9,927 sq. mi. —**Sicilian** /si sílli ən/ *n, adj*

sick[1] /sik/ *adj* **1 ILL** affected by an illness **2 RELATING TO ILLNESS** relating to illness or to people who are ill ○ *sick leave* **3 LIKELY TO VOMIT** feeling on the point of vomiting **4 OFFENSIVE TERM** an offensive term referring to somebody thought to have a mental illness that makes him or her dangerous to others **5 IN BAD TASTE** dealing with subjects regarded by most people as bizarre, gruesome, or otherwise unsuitable for lighthearted treatment (*informal*) **6 DISTRESSED** spiritually or emotionally distraught ○ *sick with anxiety* **7 VERY BORED WITH SOMETHING** utterly tired of something because of having had too much of it ○ *I am sick of watching television.* **8 YEARNING** feeling a deep or passionate longing for something or somebody **9 DISGUSTED** filled with disgust or repulsion ○ *His rudeness makes me sick.* **10 IMPAIRED** in need of repair ○ *a sick economy* **11 SUGGESTING ILLNESS** pale and unhealthy looking **12 UNPRODUCTIVE** unable to produce a profitable crop ○ *a sick field* **13 FORMING UNHEALTHY ENVIRONMENT** describes a building or other location that is seen as an unhealthy environment for people ○ *a sick office building* ■ *n* **1 ILL PEOPLE** people who are ill **2 VOMIT** vomited stomach contents (*informal*) [Old English *sēoc* < ?]

USAGE See Usage at ***ill***.

sick up *vti* to vomit (*informal*)

sick[2] *vt* = **sic**[2]

sickbag /sík bag/ *n* a bag made of stiff paper, used for vomiting into by somebody who is travel-sick, e.g. on an aircraft (*informal*)

sickbay /sík bay/ *n* **1** a hospital and dispensary on a ship **2** a place for treating the sick or injured

sickbed /sík bed/ *n* a bed on which a sick person lies

sick building syndrome *n* a group of symptoms typically including headaches and respiratory problems that affect workers in usually new or remodelled office buildings and are attributed to toxic building materials or poor ventilation

sick call *n US* MIL = **sick parade**

sicken /síkən/ *vti* **1 MAKE OR BECOME NAUSEOUS** to become ill or nauseous, or make somebody feel ill or nauseous ○ *I sicken at the sight of blood.* **2 MAKE OR FEEL DISGUSTED** to feel disgust for something or somebody, or inspire disgust in somebody **3 MAKE OR BECOME BORED** to grow weary of somebody or something, or make somebody weary ○ *We soon sickened of their chatter.*

sickener /síkənər/ *n* **1** a widely distributed poisonous mushroom with a fragile red cap. *Russula emetica* and *Russula fragilis*. **2** something that causes great disappointment or discouragement (*informal*)

sickening /síkəning/ *adj* **1 DISGUSTING** inspiring feelings of disgust or repulsion ○ *sickening cruelty* **2 VERY DISAPPOINTING** extremely disappointing or annoying (*informal*) **3 CAUSING ILLNESS** bringing on illness —**sickeningly** *adv*

sick headache *n* a headache accompanied by feelings of nausea

sickie /síki/ *n* **1** a day of sick leave, especially one taken for reasons other than genuine sickness (*informal*) **2** *US* = **sicko** (*offensive*)

sickle /sík'l/ *n* **1 TOOL FOR CUTTING GRASS** a short-handled implement with a curved blade used for cutting tall grass or grain **2 BLADES OF FARM IMPLEMENT** the cutting mechanism of a combine, reaper, or mower ■ *v* (**-les, -ling, -led**) **1** *vt* **CUT SOMETHING WITH SICKLE** to cut something using a sickle **2** *vti* **DEFORM RED BLOOD CELL** to change a red blood cell into a sickle cell, or become a sickle cell ■ *adj* **CURVED** curved in shape like a sickle (*literary*) [Old English *sicol*. Via Germanic < Latin *secula* < *secare* 'cut'.]

sick leave *n* absence from work for reasons of illness

sicklebill /sík'l bil/ *n* any of various birds with long curved bills, e.g. the curlew and the honeycreeper

sickle cell *n* an abnormal red blood cell that is crescent-shaped as a result of an inherited defect in the cell's haemoglobin

sickle-cell anaemia *n* a chronic hereditary form of anaemia that occurs mainly in people of African descent

sickle cell trait *n* a hereditary condition of the blood in which some red cells become sickle-shaped, but not enough cells to cause anaemia

sick list *n* a list of people who are sick, especially in the military

sickly /síkli/ *adj* (**-lier, -liest**) **1 OFTEN ILL** unhealthy, or tending to be frequently ill ○ *a sickly child* **2 FROM ILLNESS** produced by or related to illness ○ *a sickly complexion* **3 BRINGING ILLNESS** causing or conducive to illness ○ *a sickly climate* **4 CAUSING DISGUST** provoking feelings of disgust or nausea ○ *a sickly smell* **5 FEEBLE** lacking in strength or intensity **6 TOO SENTIMENTAL** sentimental to a degree that inspires disgust or scorn ○ *a sickly display of affection* ■ *adv* **FEEBLY** in a weak or feeble way —**sickliness** *n*

sickly-sweet *adj* excessively sweet or sentimental ○ *a sickly-sweet smile*

sickness /síknəss/ *n* **1 ILLNESS** an illness or a disease **2 NAUSEA** feelings of nausea **3 IMPAIRED CONDITION** an unsound or corrupt condition [Old English]

sickness benefit *n* **1** a weekly payment made by the government to somebody who is off work through illness for more than three days and less than six months **2** *NZ* a payment made by a government department to somebody who is unable to work owing to a medical condition

sick note *n* a certification given by an employee to an employer to state that an absence from work for more than four days is due to illness. US term **excuse** *n.* 4

sicko /síkō/ (*plural* **-os**) *n* an offensive term for somebody thought to have a mental illness that makes him or her dangerous to others

sick-out *n US, Carib* an organized absence from work by employees on the pretext of illness in an effort to force an employer to grant demands

sick parade *n* a daily lineup or formation for military personnel in need of medical attention, or the scheduled time at which they may receive medical attention. US term **sick call**

sick pay *n* wages paid to an employee who is absent from work owing to illness

sickroom /sík room, -rōōm/ *n* a room to which an ill person is confined

Siddons /sídd'nz/, **Sarah** (1755–1831) British actor. Born **Sarah Kemble**

siddur /síddər/ (*plural* **-durim** /si d ōōrim/ *or* **-durs**) *n* a Jewish daily and Sabbath prayer book [Mid-19C. < Hebrew *siddūr* 'arrangement, order'.]

side /sīd/ *n* **1 PERIMETER OF FIGURE** a line segment that forms the perimeter of a plane geometric figure ○ *A square has four sides.* **2 SURFACE OF FIGURE** a surface of a solid geometric figure ○ *A cube has six sides.* **3 SURFACE OF SOMETHING FLAT** either of the two surfaces of a flat object **4 LEFT OR RIGHT OF** the left or right of an object as opposed to the top, bottom, front, or back **5 EITHER DIVISION** either of two parts or areas into which something can be divided relative to the observer ○ *The playing field is on the far side of the park.* **6 PLACE RELATIVE TO CENTRE** a location, place, or direction relative to a central point ○ *We live on the east side of the city.* **7 PLACE SEPARATED BY BARRIER** a place or area on either side of a barrier or boundary ○ *We live on the south side of the river.* **8 VERTICAL SURFACE** a vertical surface of something ○ *the side of a building* **9 EDGE** the area at the edge of something ○ *the side of the road* **10 HALF OF BODY** either half of the body of an animal or person, especially the area of a person's body between the shoulder and the hip ○ *complaining of a pain in her side* **11 HALF OF CARCASS** half of a meat carcass ○ *a side of pork* **12 NEARBY POSITION** the place next to somebody or something ○ *Come and stand at my side.* **13 PARTY IN CONTEST** any one of two or more opposing individuals, teams, groups, or factions **14 OPINION IN A DISPUTE** any one of the positions or opinions held in a dispute **15 SUPPORTERS** the group of people who support a particular party in a dispute ○ *I'm on your side.* **16 ASPECT** an aspect or view of an issue or event ○ *the funny side of a situation* **17 PART OF FAMILY** a line of descent ○ *He gets his red hair from his father's side.* **18 TELEVISION CHANNEL** a television channel (*dated informal*) ○ *What's on the other side?* **19 ARROGANCE** an air of pretentiousness, arrogance, or superiority (*informal*) ○ *You wouldn't think he was a high court judge – there's no side to him.* **20 SPIN** spin put on a ball by striking it off-centre with the cue. US term **English** *n.* 5 ■ *adj* **1 AT THE SIDE** situated at or on a side ○ *The side door is open.* **2 FROM THE SIDE** directed to or from the side ○ *a side blow* ○ *a side view* **3 INCIDENTAL** having only minor or subsidiary importance ○ *a side issue* ■ *vi* (**sides, siding, sided**) **ALIGN WITH OR AGAINST** to align with or against one or other of the individuals, teams, groups, or factions in a contest or dispute ○ *We all sided with the home team.* [Old English *sīde* < Germanic] ◇ **be on the safe side** to take as few risks, or eliminate as many risks, as possible ◇ **from the wrong side of the tracks** from the less affluent and socially advantaged part of a town or area (*informal*) ◇ **get** *or* **keep on the right side of somebody** to get into or remain in somebody's favour ◇ **get on the wrong side of somebody** to make yourself disliked by somebody ◇ **let the side down** to disappoint associates or supporters by not doing as well as expected or by behaving in a way that causes them shame or embarrassment ◇ **look on the bright side** to make a deliberate attempt to see the positive aspects of a situation instead of the negative ones ◇ **on the side 1** illegally or secretly **2** in addition to a main job or activity ◇ **on** *or* **to one side** out of the focus of attention for the moment, to be dealt with later ◇ **side by side** close beside each other ◇ **take sides** to support one person or group against another ◇ **the other side of the coin** the contrasting or contrary aspect of something ◇ **this side of** almost or just short of

side arm *n* a weapon such as a pistol that is worn at the waist, usually on a belt

sidearm /sīd aarm/ *adj US* in baseball, describes a throw made by sweeping the arm out to the side while keeping it below shoulder height ○ *a sidearm pitch* — **sidearm** *adv*

sideband /sīd band/ *n* the band of frequencies on either side of the carrier frequency, produced by modulation of a carrier wave

sidebar /sīd baar/ *n US* **1** a short news story containing supplementary information that is printed alongside a featured story **2** a conversation among a judge and lawyers at a trial that those on the jury cannot hear

sideboard /sīd bawrd/ *n* a piece of dining room furniture with a flat top, drawers, and cupboards to store tableware and linens [14C. < BOARD in the meaning 'table'.]

sideboards /sīd bawrdz/ *npl* HAIR = **sideburns**

sideburns /sīd burnz/ *npl* hair grown down the side of a man's face in front of his ears [Late 19C. Alteration of *burnsides*, after Ambrose *Burnside* (1824–81), US general.]

sidecar /sīd kaar/ *n* **1** a one-wheeled passenger vehicle attached to the side of a motorcycle **2** a cocktail of brandy, orange liqueur, and lemon juice

side chain *n* a group of atoms attached to an atom in a principal chain or ring

side chair *n US* a straight-backed chair with no arms, especially a dining chair

side deal *n* a mutually beneficial agreement made between two people aside from an agreement negotiated by them on behalf of the parties or organizations they represent

side dish *n* accompanying food, e.g. vegetables or salad, served with the main dish of a meal

side-dress *vt* to fertilize plants by applying nutrients to the soil near the roots

side-dressing *n* **1** fertilizer that is put into the soil near the roots of a growing crop **2** the adding of fertilizer near the roots of growing crops

side drum *n* MUSIC = **snare drum** [< its place at the drummer's side]

side effect *n* **1** an undesirable secondary effect of a drug or other form of medical treatment **2** a usually undesirable secondary effect produced by something

sidefoot /sīd fo͝ot/ *vt* to kick a football with the side of the foot (*informal*) ○ *He coolly rounded the keeper and sidefooted the ball into the net.*

side-glance *n* **1** a glance directed sideways **2** a casual or indirect reference or allusion

side-impact *adj* describes features of vehicles that are designed to protect from an impact from the side

side issue *n* a matter that tends to distract from the important issue

sidekick /sīd kik/ *n* an associate or companion who is sometimes considered subordinate (*informal*) [Early 20C. < *side-kicker*.]

sidelevers /sīd leevərz/ *n Aus* = **sideburns**

sidelight /sīd līt/ *n* **1 LIGHT FROM SIDE** light coming from the side **2 SMALL LIGHT ON VEHICLE** either of two small or faint lights on a motor vehicle, used in poor light but not total darkness. US term **parking light 3 INCIDENTAL INFORMATION** incidental information, usually additional to what is known already **4 SIDE WINDOW** a window at the side of a door **5 SHIP'S LIGHT** either of a ship's two navigational running lights, red on the port bow and green on the starboard bow

sideline /sīd līn/ *n* **1 SPORTS FIELD'S SIDE BOUNDARY** either of two lines marking the side limits of a playing field **2 SUPPLEMENTARY SOURCE OF INCOME** a job or activity that supplements income from a primary job ○ *He does television repairs as a sideline.* **3 ADDITIONAL RANGE OF MERCHANDISE** a supplementary line of merchandise ■ **sidelines** *npl* **1 AREA OF A PLAYING FIELD** the area of a playing field outside the lines marking its limits **2 PLACE FOR UNINVOLVED PEOPLE** a place for people who are not involved in something, or the condition of being uninvolved ○ *I'm strictly on the sidelines in this affair.* ■ *vt* (**-lines, -lining, -lined**) **EXCLUDE** to keep somebody from participating in an activity

sidelong /sīd long/ *adj* **1 TO THE SIDE** directed to the side **2 SLOPING** slanting to one side **3 INDIRECT** not direct or straightforward ○ *a sidelong remark* ■ *adv* **OBLIQUELY** towards an area that lies at the side

sideman /sīdmən/ (*plural* **-men** /-mən/) *n* a member of a jazz or dance band who is neither the leader nor a soloist

side mirror *n* a mirror attached to the side of the windscreen or the outside of a front door of a vehicle, allowing the driver to see behind the vehicle

side order *n* a portion of food ordered as an accompaniment to the main dish in a restaurant or other food outlet

sidepiece /sīd pees/ *n* a part attached to or forming the side of something

sider- *prefix* = **sidero-** (*before vowels*)

side reaction *n* a chemical reaction that occurs as a secondary or subsequent reaction to the primary one

sidereal /sī déeri əl/ *adj* relating to the stars, especially measured with reference to the apparent motion of the stars [Mid-17C. < Latin *sidereus* < *sidus* 'star'.]

sidereal day *n* the time it takes for the Earth to make one complete revolution in relation to a given star, equal to 23 hours, 56 minutes, 4.1 seconds

sidereal hour *n* a 24th part of a sidereal day

sidereal month *n* the time it takes for the Moon to make one revolution around the Earth in relation to a given star, equal to 27 days, 7 hours, 43 minutes, 4.5 seconds

sidereal period the time it takes for an astronomical object to make one revolution in relation to a given star

sidereal time *n* time measured by the daily rotation of the Earth in relation to a given star, rather than to the Sun

sidereal year *n* the time it takes the Sun to make one revolution with reference to a given star, equal to 365 days, 6 hours, 9 minutes, 9.5 seconds

siderite /sīdə rīt/ *n* **1** a yellow-brown mineral consisting of iron carbonate. Source: sedimentary rocks. Use: source of iron. **2** a dense metallic meteorite, chiefly iron alloyed with nickel [Late 18C. < Greek *sidēros* 'iron'.] — **sideritic** /sīdə ríttik/ *adj*

sidero- *prefix* iron ○ *siderolite* [< Greek *sidēros* 'iron']

sideroad /sīd rōd/ *n* a secondary road off the main road

siderolite /síddərə līt/ *n* a meteorite that is made up of approximately equal amounts of iron and stone

siderophilin /síddə róffəlin/ *n* = **transferrin**

siderosis /síddə róssiss/ *n* **1** a chronic lung disease caused by inhaling dust particles of iron or other metals **2** an abnormal accumulation of iron in the blood and tissues —**siderotic** /-róttik/ *adj*

siderostat /síddərə stat/ *n* an astronomical instrument consisting of a plane mirror driven by a clock mechanism that keeps an astronomical object within the same field of view of a telescope [Mid-19C. < Latin *sider-*, stem of *sidus* 'star' + -STAT.] —**siderostatic** /síddərə státtik/ *adj*

sidesaddle /sīd sad'l/ *n* a saddle designed for women wearing long skirts so that the rider sits with both legs on the same side of the horse ■ *adv* seated with both legs on the same side of a horse

sideshow /sīd shō/ *n* **1** a minor attraction offered in addition to the main entertainment at a circus or fair **2** a subordinate event or spectacle

sideslip /sīd slip/ *vi* (**-slips, -slipping, -slipped**) **1 SLIDE SIDEWAYS** to skid or slide sideways **2 SLIP SIDEWAYS IN AEROPLANE** to move sideways and downwards while banking steeply in an aeroplane **3 SLIDE SIDEWAYS DOWN SLOPE** to slide at an angle down a slope ■ *n* **1 SIDEWAYS SKID** a skid sideways ○ *The car went into a sideslip.* **2 SIDEWAYS MOVEMENT OF AEROPLANE** a sideways and downward movement made by a steeply banking aircraft **3 ANGLED SLIDE DOWN SLOPE** a sideways slide at an angle down a slope

sidesman /sīdzmən/ (*plural* **-men** /-mən/), **sidesperson** /sīdz purss'n/ (*plural* **-people** /-peep'l/ *or* **-persons**) *n* in the Church of England, an assistant to the parish churchwarden [Mid-17C. < the idea of being at the side of the churchwarden.]

sidesplitting /sīd splitting/ *adj* extremely funny [< the idea of bursting with laughter] —**sidesplittingly** *adv*

sidestep /sīd step/ *vti* (**-steps, -stepping, -stepped**) **1 STEP ASIDE** to step aside or out of the way of somebody or something ○ *I sidestepped to avoid the running children.* **2 EVADE** to avoid saying or discussing something ○ *good at sidestepping awkward questions* ■ *n* **SIDEWAYS MOVEMENT** a movement to one side —**sidestepper** *n*

sidestream smoke /sīd streem-/ *n US* smoke from a cigarette or cigar that is exhaled into the surrounding air, rather than inhaled

side street *n* a secondary street, often off a main street

sidestroke /sīd strōk/ *n* a swimming stroke performed on the side by thrusting the arms alternately forward and downward while doing a scissors kick

sideswipe /sīd swīp/ *n* **1 GLANCING BLOW** a glancing blow from or on the side **2 JIBE** a critical or insulting remark made in passing (*informal*) ○ *They were all taking sideswipes at my golfing skills.* ■ *vt* (**-swipes, -swiping, -swiped**) **STRIKE SIDE OF** to strike a glancing blow to or from the side of something ○ *sideswiped a car in the car park* —**sideswiper** *n*

side tone *n* the reproduction of a speaker's voice in a telephone earpiece so that both the speaker's and the other person's voices can be heard in the earpiece

sidetrack /sīd trak/ *vt* to divert somebody from the original subject or activity ○ *They were sidetracked from their chores when their friends arrived.* ■ *n* something that causes a diversion from the original subject or activity [Mid-19C. Originally in the meaning 'moving trains off the main line'.]

sidewalk /sīd wawk/ *n US* TRANSP = **pavement** *n.* 1

sidewall /sīd wawl/ *n* the side surface of a vehicle's tyre, between the edge of the tread and the rim

sideward /sīdwərd/ *adj* towards one side or at one side ■ *adv* **sideward, sidewards** towards one side

sideways /sīd wayz/, **sidewise** /sīd wīz/ *adj, adv* **1 TO ONE SIDE** to or towards one side ○ *a sideways jump* **2 FROM SIDE** from one side ○ *a sideways approach* **3 WITH SIDE FACING FRONT** with or into a position with the side towards the front ○ *See if it will fit in sideways.* **4 INTO NEW BUT EQUAL POSITION** into a job or position with the same rank or status as previously held ○ *not a promotion but more of a sideways move into another department*

sidewheel /sīd weel/ *n* either of the paddle wheels on the sides of a sidewheeler ■ *adj* propelled by a paddle wheel on each side ○ *a sidewheel steamboat*

sidewheeler /sīd weelər/ *n* a steamboat driven by a paddle wheel on each side

side whiskers *npl* sideburns, especially long ones

sidewinder /sīd wīndər/ *n* **1** a small rattlesnake that moves forward with a diagonal looping motion. Native to: SW United States, N Mexico. *Crotalus cerastes.* **2** *US* a hard swinging punch from the side

sidewise *adj, adv* = **sideways**

Sidi-bel-Abbès /seédi belə béss/ capital of Sidi-bel-Abbès Province, NW Algeria. Population: 152,778 (1995).

siding /sīding/ *n* **1** a short stretch of railway track that connects with the main track **2** *US, Can* sheets of wood, vinyl, aluminium, or other material used to surface the outside of a building

sidle /sīd'l/ *v* (**-dles, -dling, -dled**) **1** *vi* **MOVE FURTIVELY** to edge along in a furtive way ○ *I sidled to the door in the hope that no one would notice me.* **2** *vti* **MOVE SIDEWAYS** to move, or move something, sideways ■ *n* **SIDLING MOVEMENT** a sideways or furtive movement [Late 17C. Probably back-formation < earlier *sideling* 'sideways'.]

Sidney /sídni/, **Sir Philip** (1554–86) English soldier, courtier, and poet

Sidon /sīd'n/ city in SW Lebanon, on the Mediterranean Sea. Population: 38,000 (1988).

Sidra, Gulf of /sídrə/ arm of the Mediterranean Sea off the coast of Libya, N Africa

SIDS /sidz/ *abbr* sudden infant death syndrome

siege /seej/ *n* **1 MILITARY OPERATION** a military or police operation in which troops or the police surround a place and cut off all outside access to force surrender (*often before nouns*) ○ *siege warfare* **2 PROLONGED EFFORT** a prolonged effort to gain or overcome something **3 TIRESOME PERIOD** a prolonged and tedious period ■ *vt* (**sieges, sieging, sieged**) **SUBJECT PLACE TO SIEGE** to assail or assault an enemy's fortifications militarily ○ *a town sieged with troops* [12C. Via Old French *sege* 'seat' < Latin *sedere* 'sit'.] ◇ **lay siege to something 1** to besiege a place **2** to make a persistent attempt to gain something

Siegfried /seég freed/ *n* in German legend, a prince who kills the dragon guarding the treasure of the Nibelungs, and wins Brunhild for Gunther

Siegfried line /seég freed-/ *n* the line of fortifications constructed by Germany before and during World War II on its western frontier, facing the Maginot line in France [Mid-20C.After SIEGFRIED.]

Sieg Heil /seég hīl/ *interj* 'hail to victory', a Nazi salute usually accompanied by the right arm raised with the palm facing downward [Mid-20C. < German.]

siemens /seémənz/ (*plural* **-mens**) *n* (*symbol* **S**) the SI unit of electrical conductance equal to one ampere per volt [Mid-20C. After Werner von *Siemens* (1816–92), German inventor.]

Siena /si énnə/ capital of Siena Province, Tuscany Region, in north-central Italy. Population: 58,300 (1990). —**Sienese** /seé ə neéz/ *n, adj*

~~**sience**~~ incorrect spelling of **science**

~~**siene**~~ incorrect spelling of **scene**

sienna /si énnə/ *n* **1** artists' paint made with iron-rich soil **2** an iron-rich soil. Use: paint pigment. [Late 18C. After SIENA.] —**sienna** *adj*

sierra /si érrə/ *n* a range of mountains with jagged peaks, or the country surrounding such a range [Mid-16C. Via Spanish < Latin *serra* 'saw'.] —**sierran** *adj*

Sierra *n* a code word for the letter 'S', used in international radio communications

Sierra Leone /si érrə li ṓn/ republic in W Africa, bordered by the Atlantic Ocean. Capital: Freetown. Population: 4,630,000 (1996). Area: 71,740 sq. km/27,699 sq. mi. —**Sierra Leonean** *n, adj*

Sierra Madre /si érrə maá dray/ mountain system in Mexico, extending from the US border in the north to the border with Guatemala in the south. Length: 2,500 km/1,500 mi. Highest peak: Orizaba 5,610 m/18,406 ft.

Sierra Nevada /si érrə nə vaádə/ **1** mountain range in SE Spain. Highest peak: Cerro de Mulhacén 3,480

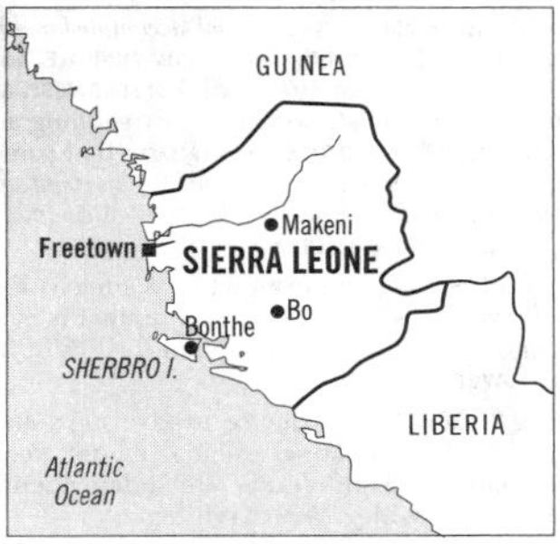

Sierra Leone

m/11,411 ft. **2** mountain range in E California. Highest peak: Mount Whitney 4,417 m/14,491 ft.

siesta /si éstə/ *n* an early afternoon rest or nap [Mid-17C. Via Spanish < Latin *sexta (hora)* 'sixth (hour of the day), noon'.]

sieve /siv/ *n* a utensil consisting of a round frame surrounding a mesh and used to separate solids from liquids, large particles from small particles, or to purée foods ■ *vt* (**sieves, sieving, sieved**) to pass something through a sieve [Old English *sife* < Germanic]

sieve element *n* PLANT SCI = **sieve tube element**

sieve plate *n* an area of perforations in the end walls of the cells that make up a sieve tube in plants

sievert /seévərt/ *n* (*symbol* **Sv**) the SI unit measuring the probability that a stated dose of a particular radiation type will cause a biological effect. 1 sievert is equal to 1 joule per kilogram. [Mid-20C. After R. M. *Sievert* (1896–1966), Swedish radiologist.]

sieve tube *n* a sap-conducting tube within the phloem tissue of a plant

sieve tube element, sieve element *n* any one of the numerous cells connected end to end and separated by porous sieve plates in a sieve tube

~~**sieze**~~ incorrect spelling of **seize**

sifaka /si faákə/ *n* a large rare tree-dwelling lemur of Madagascar. *Propithecus verreauxi* and *Propithecus diadema.* [Mid-19C. < Malagasy.]

sift /sift/ *v* **1** *vti* **SEPARATE PARTICLES** to pass a substance through a sieve to separate out or break up coarse particles **2** *vt* **TAKE SOMETHING OUT** to separate something out with a sieve, or by a process of selection or elimination ○ *sift the good from the bad* **3** *vt* **SCATTER** to scatter something with or as if with a sieve ○ *We sifted sugar onto the strawberries.* **4** *vti* **EXAMINE** to sort or examine something carefully ○ *sift evidence* **5** *vi* **PASS THROUGH** to pass or fall through or as if through a sieve [Old English *siftan* < Germanic] —**sifter** *n*

siftings /síftingz/ *npl* parts or elements separated out using a sieve or by a process of elimination

⚡**SIG** /sig/ *abbr* special interest group

sig. *abbr* **sig., Sig. 1** signor **2** signore

Sig. used on prescriptions before the instructions to appear on the label of the medicine given to a patient [< Latin *signa* 'mark or label it']

⚡**sig file** *n* a signature file (*informal*)

sigh /sī/ *v* **1** *vi* **BREATHE LONG AND LOUD** to take in and let out a deep audible breath in relief or weariness **2** *vi* **MAKE EXHALING SOUND** to make a sound like the exhalation of a deep breath ○ *The wind sighed in the trees.* **3** *vi* **YEARN** to long for somebody or something ○ *sigh for simpler times* **4** *vt* **EXPRESS FEELING IN SIGHS** to express an emotion by sighs ○ *She sighed her relief when she found us.* ■ *n* **1 EXHALATION** an audible exhalation of a deep breath **2 SOUND OF EXHALING** a sound like that of somebody exhaling a deep breath [13C. Probably back-formation from the past tense form of Old English *sīcan*.]

sight /sīt/ *n* **1 FACULTY OF SEEING** the ability to see using the eyes **2 SEEING** the perception of something using the visual sense **3 RANGE OF SEEING** the range or field of vision ○ *By now the coastline was out of sight.* **4 SOMETHING SEEN** something that somebody sees **5 SOMETHING WORTH SEEING** something that is worth seeing, especially the landmarks of a particular place (*often plural*) ○ *the sights of the city* **6 SOMETHING UNPLEASANT TO LOOK AT** something or somebody that has an unpleasant, distressing, or disarranged appearance (*informal*) ○ *He was a sight after the fight.* **7 ALIGNMENT DEVICE** an alignment device on a gun or surveying instrument used to guide the eye in aiming or determining direction **8 AIM** a determination of direction made with a gun or surveying instrument **9 OPPORTUNITY FOR OBSERVATION** an opportunity to observe or inspect **10 OPINION** a point of view ○ *In the sight of his followers he was infallible.* ■ *v* **1** *vt* **SEE** to see or notice somebody or something ○ *They sighted the plane in the distance.* **2** *vti* **OBSERVE USING OPTICAL DEVICE** to observe something, or take measurements of something, using an optical device **3** *vti* **AIM AT SOMETHING WITH GUN** to take aim at something with a firearm **4** *vt* **ADJUST GUN'S SIGHTS** to adjust the sights of a gun **5** *vi* **DIRECT THE EYES** to look carefully in a particular direction ○ *sight down a line* [Old English *(ge)sihþ*] —**sighted** *adj* —**sightedness** *n* ◇ **a sight** a great deal or quantity (*informal*) ○ *He's feeling a sight better today.* ◇ **a sight for sore eyes** a very welcome sight ◇ **at** *or* **on sight** as soon as something is able to be seen ◇ **in sight 1** able to be seen **2** likely to happen in the near future ◇ **know somebody by sight** to be able to recognize somebody whom you have never actually met or spoken to ◇ **out of sight 1** no longer able to be seen **2** used to express approval and surprise (*informal*) ◇ **set** *or* **have your sights on something** to decide to try to get something ◇ **sight unseen** without seeing or inspecting first ○ *buy something sight unseen*

USAGE See *cite*.

sighter /sītər/ *n* a practice shot allowed in a shooting or archery tournament, or a shot used to assess the setting of the sights of a gun

sight gag *n* a joke or comic episode that depends on it being seen to be funny (*informal*)

sighting /sīting/ *n* an occasion on which something is seen, usually something unusual or searched for ○ *sightings of UFOs*

sightless /sītləss/ *adj* **1** without the faculty of sight **2** invisible (*literary*) ○ *'heaven's cherubim, hors'd upon the sightless couriers of the air'* (William Shakespeare, *Macbeth*; 1623) —**sightlessly** *adv* —**sightlessness** *n*

sightline /sīt līn/ *n* a line of vision between a person and an object, especially between a member of an audience and the stage in a theatre

sightly /sītli/ (**-lier, -liest**) *adj* pleasing to look at

sight-read *vti* to read or perform something, e.g. music or a foreign language, without having practised or seen it beforehand —**sight reader** *n*

sight rhyme *n* LITERAT = **eye rhyme**

sightscreen /sīt skreen/ *n* a large white screen placed near the boundary of a cricket field behind the bowler to help the batsman see the ball

sightsee /sīt see/ (**-sees, -seeing, -saw** /-saw/, **-seen** /-seen/) *vi* to visit a place's interesting sights —**sightseer** *n*

sightseeing /sīt see ing/ *n* visiting places of interest (*often before nouns*) ○ *a sightseeing tour*

sigil /síjjəl/ *n* **1** a seal or signet **2** a sign or image that is supposed to have magical power [16C. Via late Latin < Latin *sigillum* 'small sign' < *signum* 'sign'.] —**sigillary** /si jíllәri/ *adj*

Sigismund /síggissmənd/ (1368–1437) king of Hungary (1387–1437) and Holy Roman Emperor (1411–37)

sigma /sígmə/ *n* **1** the 18th letter of the Greek alphabet **2** the symbol (σ) indicating the addition of the numbers or quantities indicated **3** PHYS = **sigma hyperon** [Early 17C. Via Latin < Greek.] —**sigmate** *adj* —**sigmation** *n*

sigma hyperon, sigma, sigma particle *n* any of three unstable elementary particles of the baryon group, with a mass of 2,328 to 2,343 times that of an electron, and a positive, negative, or neutral electric charge

sigmoid /síg moyd/ *adj* **1** shaped like the letter S **2** relating to the sigmoid colon of the large intestine

sigmoid colon *n* the final S-shaped portion of the large intestine leading to the rectum

sigmoid flexure *n* **1** ANAT = **sigmoid colon 2** an S-shaped curve or bend, e.g. in the neck of a bird or turtle

sigmoidoscope /sig móydə skōp/ *n* a fibre-optic tubular instrument inserted through the anus for examining the interior of the rectum and sigmoid colon —**sigmoidoscopic** /sig móydə skóppik/ *adj* —**sigmoidoscopy** /síg moy dóskəpi/ *n*

sign /sīn/ *n* **1 SOMETHING REPRESENTING SOMETHING ELSE** something that indicates or expresses the existence of something else not immediately apparent ○ *a sign of wealth* **2 SOMETHING CONVEYING IDEA** an action or gesture used to convey an idea, information, a wish, or a command ○ *His kick under the table was a sign that we should leave.* **3 ADVERTISING NOTICE** a publicly displayed structure, e.g. a painted board or neon lights, carrying lettering or designs intended to advertise a business or product **4 INFORMATION NOTICE** a publicly displayed notice or board bearing directions, instructions, or warnings ○ *a road sign* **5 INDICATION** something that indicates the presence of something or somebody ○ *no sign of life* **6 TRACE LEFT BY ANIMAL** a trace of a wild animal, e.g. spoor, scent, or footprints **7 OMEN** something interpreted as being an omen **8 DIVISION OF ZODIAC** any of the 12 equal parts into which the zodiac is divided, each represented by a symbol **9 EVIDENCE OF DISEASE** an indication of the presence of a disease or disorder, especially one observed by a doctor but not apparent to the patient ○ *Fever is a sign of an infection.* **10 SYMBOL USED IN MATHS OR LOGIC** a symbol indicating an operation or relation in mathematics or logic ○ *the plus sign* **11 MUSICAL NOTATION SYMBOL** a symbol used in musical notation **12** COMMUNICATION = **sign language** ■ *v* **1** *vti* **WRITE NAME** to write a signature on something **2** *vti* **APPROVE DOCUMENT** to affirm or approve a document formally by affixing a signature or seal **3** *vt* **EMPLOY** to engage somebody or somebody's services by written agreement ○ *The manager signed two promising young players.* **4** *vi* **AGREE TO TAKE JOB** to agree to be employed by writing the signature on a contract ○ *He signed for a year.* **5** *vti* **COMMUNICATE IN SIGN LANGUAGE** to use sign language to communicate a message ○ *She signed 'yes'.* **6** *vti* **SIGNAL INFORMATION** to convey information using a signal or signals **7** *vt* **PORTEND** to be an omen of something to come ○ *That signs danger.* **8** *vt* **GIVE BLESSING TO** to bless somebody or something by making the sign of the cross [13C. Via French *signe* < Latin *signum* 'mark'.] —**signer** *n*

SPELLCHECK Do not confuse ***sign*** with ***sine***, which has a similar sound. Beware: your spellchecker will not catch this error.

sign away *vt* to convey rights or property to somebody by signing a document ○ *He signed away his property to pay his debts.*

sign in *v* **1** *vi* to write a signature in a register, usually as a way of recording presence or attendance **2** *vt* to put your signature on a register, especially in a members-only club, so that your guest can be admitted

sign off *v* **1** *vi* **END SOME FORM OF COMMUNICATION** to bring a communication or transmission, e.g. a radio or TV programme, a letter, or an e-mail message, to an end by announcing its conclusion **2** *vt* **CERTIFY SOMEBODY AS UNFIT FOR WORK** to state that somebody is not fit to work because of illness or injury (*often passive*) **3** *vi* **STOP DOING** to stop doing something, especially work, or to record or announce the end of some activity

sign on *v* **1** *vi* **CONSENT BY SIGNING** to agree to do some activity, especially by signing a contract **2** *vi* **REGISTER AS UNEMPLOYED** to register as unemployed in order to receive state benefits **3** *vt* **EMPLOY** to take somebody on as an employee or to do a particular job

sign out *v* **1** *vi* to write a signature as a record of having left somewhere, especially a workplace **2** *vt* to sign your name as an acknowledgment of having received something, especially as being temporarily in possession of it

sign over *vt* to transfer possession of something to somebody else by writing a signature on a document

sign up *vti* **1** to agree, or get somebody to agree, to participate in something, especially by way of a signature **2** to enlist, or enlist somebody, for military service

signa., Signa. *abbr* signorina

Signac /sín yak/, **Paul** (1863–1935) French painter

signage /sínij/ *n* **1** signs collectively **2** the design and display of signs

signal /sígnəl/ *n* **1 MEANS OF COMMUNICATION** an action, gesture, or sign used as a means of communication ○ *Yellow is a signal for caution.* **2 COMMUNICATED INFORMATION** a piece of information communicated by an action, gesture, or sign **3 INCITEMENT** something that incites somebody to action ○ *The threat of a shortage was a signal to hoard.* **4 TRANSMITTED INFORMATION** information transmitted by means of a modulated current or an electromagnetic wave and received by telephone, telegraph, radio, television, or radar ■ *adj* **NOTABLE** of considerable importance ○ *a signal accomplishment* ■ *v* (**-nals, -nalling, -nalled**) **1** *vti* **COMMUNICATE** to communicate a message to somebody **2** *vt* **SEND MESSAGE USING SIGNAL** to communicate something by sending a signal of some kind **3** *vt* **INDICATE** to be a sign that something has happened or is about to happen ○ *This event signalled the end of the conflict.* [14C. Via Old French *seignal* < Latin *signum* 'sign'.] —**signaller** *n*

signal box *n* a building from which a stretch or system of railway track is controlled, either manually by means of levers, or electrically and semiautomatically. US term **signal tower**

signal generator *n* a device used to test electronic equipment by generating a signal whose frequency, wave shape, and amplitude are independently adjustable over a wide range of settings

signalize /sígnə līz/, (**-izes, -izing, -ized**), **signalise** (**-ises, -ising, -ised**) *vt* **1** to make something conspicuous or remarkable **2** to indicate something distinctly —**signalization** /sígnə lī záysh'n/ *n*

signally /sígnəli/ *adv* completely and unmistakably

signalman /sígnəlmən/ (*plural* **-men** /-mən/) *n* **1** a member of the armed forces who sends and receives signals **2** a railway employee who is in charge of operating signals

signal-to-noise ratio *n* the ratio of the strength of a signal carrying information to unwanted interference in an electronic circuit

signal tower *n* US RAIL = **signal box**

signatory /sígnətəri/ *n* (*plural* **-ries**) a person, government, or organization that has signed a treaty or contract and is bound by it ■ *adj* bound by the terms of a treaty or contract ○ *a signatory nation*

signature /sígnəchər/ *n* **1 SIGNED NAME** somebody's name signed by him or her or by somebody authorized by him or her to sign **2 SIGNING OF NAME** a signing of somebody's name **3 DISTINCTIVE CHARACTERISTIC** a distinctive mark, characteristic, or thing that identifies somebody (*often before nouns*) ○ *a signature song* **4 DIRECTIONS ON PRESCRIPTION** the part of a doctor's prescription that contains the directions for use **5** MUSIC = **key signature** **6** MUSIC = **time signature** **7 MARK INDICATING PAGE ORDER** a letter or mark printed on what will become the first page of a section of a book, indicating its order in binding **8 SHEET PRINTED WITH MULTIPLE PAGES** a sheet of paper printed with several pages that, when folded, will become a section of a book **9 SECTION OF BOOK** a section of a book consisting of a folded sheet with several pages printed on it [Mid-16C. Via French < medieval Latin *signatura* < Latin *signare* < *signum* 'sign'.]

⚡**signature file** *n* a short text file with information such as the user's name and address, serving as a signature at the end of e-mails and Usenet messages

signature tune *n* a piece of music used to introduce or identify a performer, group, or television or radio programme. US term **theme song**

signboard /sín bawrd/ *n* a board carrying a notice or advertisement

signed /sīnd/ *adj* **1** with a positive or negative value, as indicated by a plus or minus sign **2** bearing a signature, e.g. written to authenticate a document or as an autograph

signed-ranks test *n* STATS = **Wilcoxon test**

signet /sígnət/ *n* **1 SMALL SEAL** a small seal, e.g. one that is engraved on a ring **2 STAMP FOR DOCUMENTS** a seal used to stamp official documents **3 IMPRESSION MADE BY SEAL** the impression made on a document with a seal ■ *vt* **STAMP DOCUMENT WITH SEAL** to stamp a document with a seal [14C. Via French < medieval Latin *signetum* 'small seal' < Latin *signum* 'sign'.]

signet ring *n* a finger ring containing a small seal

significance /sig níffikənss/, **significancy** /-kənssi/ *n* **1 IMPORTANCE** the quality of having importance or being regarded as having great meaning **2 MEANING** implied or intended meaning **3 VALUE AS STATISTICAL POINTER** status as a statistical value that is not accidental or random (*often before nouns*)

significant /sig níffikənt/ *adj* **1 MEANINGFUL** having or expressing a meaning **2 COMMUNICATING SECRET MEANING** having a hidden or implied meaning ○ *a significant nod of the head* **3 MOMENTOUS AND INFLUENTIAL** having a major or important effect ○ *a significant idea* **4 SUBSTANTIAL** relatively large in amount ○ *Her work was a significant contribution to the project.* **5 OCCURRING NOT MERELY BY CHANCE** relating to the occurrence of events or outcomes that are too closely linked statistically to be mere chance [Late 16C. < Latin *significant-*, present participle of Latin *significare* (see SIGNIFY).]

significant figures *npl* the figures necessary in a decimal number to express accuracy, beginning with the first nonzero figure to the left and ending with the figure farthest to the right. US term **significant digits**

significantly /sig níffikəntli/ *adv* **1** to a large extent or degree ○ *significantly higher* **2** in an important or fundamental way ○ *Your ideas will contribute significantly.*

significant other *n* **1** a spouse or someone with whom somebody has a long-term sexual relationship **2** an influential or supportive person in somebody's life

signification /sìgnifi káysh'n/ *n* **1** the meaning of something, e.g. a word, event, or other phenomenon **2** the signifying or indicating of something [13C. Via Old French < Latin *signification-* 'indication, sign' < *significare* (see SIGNIFY).]

~~**significent**~~ incorrect spelling of **significant**

signify /sígni fī/ (**-fies, -fying, -fied**) *v* **1** *vt* **MEAN** to have something as a particular meaning **2** *vt* **BE SIGN OF** to be a sign or symbol of something **3** *vi* **BE IMPORTANT** to be important or significant [13C. Via French *signifier* < Latin *significare* < *signum* 'sign'.] —**signifiable** *adj* —**significative** /sig níffi kətiv/ *adj* —**significatively** *adv* —**significativeness** *n* —**signifier** *n*

signing *n* COMMUNICATION = **sign language**

signing bonus *n* US an extra amount paid to somebody when he or she signs a contract, especially in entertainment and sports

signior *n* = **signor**

signiory *n* HIST = **seigniory**

sign language *n* communication, or a system of communication, by gestures as opposed to written or spoken language, especially the highly developed system of hand signs used by or to people who are hearing-impaired

sign manual *n* somebody's signature, especially that of a king or queen on an official document [Translation of Anglo-Latin *signum manuale* 'sign made with the hand']

sign of the cross *n* in Christianity, a movement of the hand as if tracing a cross in the air or on the body, usually by touching the forehead, chest, and shoulders in turn

signor /seé nyawr/ (*plural* **-gnors** *or* **-gnori** /-nyáwri/), **signior** (*plural* **-gniors** *or* **-gniori**), **Signor** (*plural* **-gnors** *or* **-gnori**), **Signior** (*plural* **-gniors** *or* **-gniori**) *n* the usual Italian form of title or address for a man. ◊ **signora, signore, signorina** [Late 16C. < Italian, reduced form of *signore* (see SIGNORE).]

signora /see nyáwrə/ (*plural* **-ras** *or* **-re** /-nyáw ray/), **Signora** (*plural* **-ras** *or* **-re**) *n* the usual Italian form of title or address for a married or older woman. ◊ **signor, signore, signorina** [Mid-17C. < Italian, feminine form of *signore* (see SIGNORE).]

signore /see nyáw ray/ (*plural* **-ri** /-ri/) *n* the Italian form of title or address for a highly respected man or a man of advanced age. ◊ **signor, signora, signorina** [Late 16C. Via Italian < Latin *senior* 'elder' < *senex* 'old'.]

signorina /see nyaw reénə/ (*plural* **signorinas** *or* **signorine** /-reé nay/) *n* the usual Italian form of title or address for a young or unmarried woman. ◊ **signor, signora, signore** [Early 19C. < Italian, 'little signora' < *signora* (see SIGNORA).]

signory *n* HIST = **seigniory**

sign painting *n* US = **signwriting** —**sign painter** *n*

signpost /sín pōst/ *n* **1 INFORMATION SIGN** a pole with a sign on it, especially one that gives directions or other information **2 SOMETHING THAT INDICATES** something that gives a clue, indication, hint, or guide ■ *vt* **1 DIRECT SOMEBODY TO PLACE** to direct somebody or mark the way to a place with signposts or similar indications ○ *a series of notices signposting patients to the X-ray department* **2 GIVE INDICATION** to give a clear indication of something, especially some future action or decision

signwriting /sín rīting/ *n* the activity or profession of designing and painting signs, especially for shops, hotels, and other businesses. US term **sign painting** —**signwriter** *n*

sigra., Sigra. *abbr* signora

Sihanouk /seé ə nook/, **Norodom** (*b.* 1922) king of Cambodia (1993-)

sika /seéka/ *n* a small deer that has a brown, often spotted coat with a white patch on the rump. Native to: Japan, China. *Cervus nippon.* [Late 19C. < Japanese, 'deer'.]

sike /sīk/ *n N England, Scotland* **1** a small, usually slow-moving stream, especially one that tends to dry up in summer **2** a ditch [Old English *sīc*]

Sikh /seek/ *n* a member of a religious group that broke away from Hinduism during the 16th century and advocated a monotheistic doctrine, incorporating some aspects of Islam. ◊ **five Ks** ■ *adj* belonging or relating to the Sikhs or their religion, beliefs, customs, or history [Late 18C. Via Punjabi or Hindi < Sanskrit *śiṣya* 'disciple'.] —**Sikhism** *n*

Sikkim /síkim/ state in NE India. Capital: Gangtok. Population: 406,457 (1991). Area: 7,096 sq. km/2,740 sq. mi. —**Sikkimese** *n, adj*

Sikorski /si káwrski/, **Władysław** (1881–1943) Polish statesman and soldier

Sikorsky /si káwrski/, **Igor** (1889–1972) Russian-born US aeronautical engineer and corporate executive

sila /seéla/ *n* in Buddhism, morality, one of the three major divisions of the noble eightfold path, which consists of right speech, right action, and right livelihood [Mid-20C. < Pali.]

silage /sīlij/ *n* animal fodder that is made by storing green plant material in a silo where it is preserved by partial fermentation [Late 19C. Via French *ensilage* < Spanish *ensilar* 'store in a silo' < *silo* (see SILO).]

silane /sīlayn, síllayn/ *n* Si_nH_{2n+2} any of a group of silicon and hydrogen compounds analogous to the paraffin hydrocarbons [Early 20C. < SILICON.]

Silbury Hill /sílbəri-/ artificial mound near Avebury, S England, made about 2100 BC. Height: 40 m/130 ft.

sild /sild/ (*plural* **silds** *or* **sild**) *n* an immature herring, especially one that has been processed and canned [Early 20C. Via Danish and Norwegian < Old Norse *sīld* 'herring'.]

sildenafil citrate /sil dənnəfil sítràyt-/ *n* a drug used to treat impotence [Late 20C. *Sildenafil*, an invented name.]

silence /sīlənss/ *n* **1 QUIETNESS** the absence or lack of noise **2 NOT SPEAKING** a refusal, failure, or inability to speak **3 ABSENCE OF ACKNOWLEDGMENT OF** an absence of notice or acknowledgment of something ○ *Most remarkable was the statement's silence about the recent policy change.* ■ *vt* (**-lences, -lencing, -lenced**) **1 STOP SOMETHING OR SOMEBODY MAKING NOISE** to stop something or somebody from making a noise **2 SUPPRESS** to suppress the expression of something or stop a person or group from speaking out ○ *silence criticism* **3 END SOMEBODY'S HOSTILE BEHAVIOUR** to cause somebody to stop hostile or aggressive behaviour [13C. Via Old French < Latin *silentium* < *silent-* (see SILENT).]

silencer /sīlənssər/ *n* **1 PART OF EXHAUST SYSTEM** the drum-shaped part of a vehicle's exhaust system that is designed to lessen noise. ◊ **muffler** *n.* 2 **2 FIREARM MUFFLER** a device that muffles the noise of a gun **3 SOMEBODY OR SOMETHING IMPOSING SILENCE** somebody or something that causes silence or lessens noise

silene /sī leéni/ *n* a widespread perennial plant. Flowers: pink or red. Genus: *Silene.* [Late 18C. < modern Latin < Latin *Silenus* (see SILENUS).]

silent /sīlənt/ *adj* **1 UTTERLY QUIET** lacking any noise or sound ○ *a silent country lane* **2 NOT SPEAKING** not speaking or communicating, especially through choice ○ *The children all remained silent.* **3 SAYING LITTLE** not inclined to say much ○ *the strong silent type* **4 UNSPOKEN** not expressed or voiced, though felt or believed ○ *rolled her eyes in silent disbelief* **5 WITHOUT SOUNDTRACK** relating to films made without sound, typically those made before 1927 **6 UNABLE TO SPEAK** unable or not allowed to speak ○ *a silent order of monks* **7 INACTIVE** currently inactive or not operating ○ *a silent volcano* **8 QUIETLY EXPRESSED** drawing attention inconspicuously, without making noise ○ *a silent warning* **9 NOT PRONOUNCED** describes a letter that appears in a word but is not pronounced, e.g. the 'k' in 'knight' or the 'b' in 'debt' ■ *n* **SILENT FILM** a film made without sound [15C. < Latin *silent-*, present participle of *silere* 'be silent'.] —**silently** *adv* —**silentness** *n*

SYNONYMS *silent, quiet, reticent, taciturn, uncommunicative*

CORE MEANING: not speaking or not saying much

silent not speaking or communicating at any particular time, especially through choice, or not inclined to speak much; **quiet** not inclined to speak much, often because of shyness; **reticent** unwilling to communicate very much, talk freely, or reveal all the facts; **taciturn** habitually reserved in speech and manner; **uncommunicative** not willing to say much, especially not to reveal information, or tending not to say much.

silent auction *n* an auction that is conducted by submitting bids in sealed envelopes before the sale

silent majority *n* a significant number of a given population who choose not to express their views, often because of apathy or because they do not believe their views matter

silent partner *n US* BUSINESS = **sleeping partner**

silenus /sī leénəss/ (*plural* **-ni** /sī leénī/) *n* in Greek mythology, a woodland god resembling an elderly satyr [Early 18C. Via Latin < Greek *Silēnos.*]

Silenus *n* in Greek mythology, an old woodland god in charge of Dionysus' education

silesia /sī leézi ə, sī leéssi ə, sī leéshə/ *n* a hard-wearing cotton twill fabric. Use: pockets, linings. [Late 17C. After SILESIA.]

Silesia /sī leéshə/ historic region in east-central Europe, lying mostly within present-day SW Poland —**Silesian** *n, adj*

silex /sī leks/ *n* **1** powdered silica or tripoli, used as a filter material **2** a heat-resistant glass with high quartz content [Late 16C. < Latin, 'flint'.]

silhouette /sílloo ét/ *n* **1 SHADOWED CONTOUR** an outline of somebody or something filled in with black or a dark colour on a light background, especially when done as a likeness or work of art **2 SOMETHING DARK ON LIGHT BACKGROUND** something lit in such a way as to appear dark but surrounded by light, or the effect produced by such lighting ○ *silhouettes dancing in front of the bonfire* ■ *vt* (**-ettes, -etting, -etted**) **MAKE SOMETHING APPEAR AS A SILHOUETTE** to cause somebody or something to appear surrounded by light (*often passive*) ○ *The buildings were silhouetted against the rising sun.* [Late 18C. < French, after Etienne de *Silhouette* (1709–67), French finance minister.]

silic- *prefix* = **silici-**

silica /síllikə/ *n* silicon dioxide found naturally in various crystalline and amorphous forms, e.g. quartz, opal, sand, flint, and agate. Use: manufacture of glass, abrasives, concrete. [Early 19C. Via modern Latin < Latin *silic-*, stem of *silex* 'flint'.] —**siliceous** /si líshəss/ *adj*

silica gel *n* gelatinous silica in a form that readily absorbs water from the air, used as a drying agent, a carrier for catalysts, and an anticaking agent

silicate /sílliкət, sílli kayt/ *n* any of the most important and common of the rock-forming minerals, formed from silicon and oxygen combined with various elements, classified by their crystalline structures

silici- *prefix* **1** silica ○ *silicosis* **2** silicon ○ *silicate* [< SILICON and SILICA]

silicic /si líssik/ *adj* relating to or containing silica or silicon

silicic acid *n* a weak gelatinous acid obtained by adding an acid to sodium silicate

silicide /sílli sīd/ *n* a binary compound of silicon with another element

siliciferous /sílli síffərəss/ *adj* containing or yielding silica

silicify /si líssi fī/ (**-fies, -fying, -fied**) *vti* to convert something or become converted into silica —**silicification** /si líssifi káysh'n/ *n*

silicon /síllikən/ *n* (*symbol* **Si**) an abundant brittle nonmetallic element. Source: sand, granite, clay, many minerals. Use: alloys, semiconductors, building materials. [Early 19C. < SILICA + -ON[1].]

silicon carbide *n* SiC an extremely hard bluish-black crystalline compound. Use: abrasive, refractory, semiconductor.

silicon chip *n* a small wafer of silicon forming the base on which an integrated circuit is laid out, or such a wafer together with its integrated circuit

silicon dioxide *n* SiO_2 a colourless transparent solid that melts at a very high temperature. Use: manufacture of microchips.

silicone /sílli kōn/ *n* a heat-resistant silicon-based synthetic substance in the form of a grease, oil, or plastic. Use: lubricants, insulators, water-repellents, resins, adhesives, coatings, paints, prosthetics. ◊ **siloxane**

Silicon Valley /síllikən-/ region in W California, an important centre for the electronics and computer industries

silicosis /sílli kṓssiss/ *n* a lung disease caused by prolonged inhalation of dust containing silica, and marked by the development of fibrous tissue in the lungs resulting in chronic shortness of breath —**silicotic** /sílli kóttik/ *adj*

silicula /si líkyŏŏlə/ (*plural* **-lae** /-lee/ *or* **-las**), **silicule** /sílli kyool/, **silicle** /síllik'l/ *n* a dry fruit, e.g. that of honesty, consisting of a broad flat pod divided by a membrane into two seed chambers [Mid-18C. < Latin, 'little pod' < *siliqua* 'seed pod'.]

silique /si leék/, **siliqua** /síllikwə/ (*plural* **-quae** /-kwee/ *or* **-quas**) *n* a long dry seed capsule of plants of the mustard family that has two valves that open, leaving a central partition to which seeds are attached [Late 18C. Via French < Latin *siliqua* 'seed pod'.] —**siliquaceous** /sílli kwáyshəss/ *adj* —**siliquose** /síllikwōss/ *adj* —**siliquous** /-kwəss/ *adj*

silk /silk/ *n* **1 THREAD FROM SILKWORMS** the fine fibre that silkworms secrete to make their cocoons. Use: threads, fabrics. **2 SILK THREAD OR FABRIC** fabric woven from spun silk **3 THREAD FROM SPIDERS** a fine fibre that spiders secrete and use to make their webs, nests, and cocoons **4 KING'S OR QUEEN'S COUNSEL** a lawyer who has the right to practise as a King's or Queen's Counsel (*informal*) **5 HIGH BARRISTER'S GARMENT** the gown worn by a King's or Queen's Counsel ■ **silks** *npl* **JOCKEY'S SILK GARMENTS** distinctively coloured silk clothes worn by a jockey as a mark of identification [Old English *seoloc.* Probably via Slavic < Chinese.] ◇ **take silk** to become a King's or Queen's Counsel

silkaline /sílkə leen/, **silkalene** *n* a fine cotton fabric with a glossy finish [Late 19C. < SILK.]

silk cotton *n* INDUST = **kapok**

silk-cotton tree *n* TREES = **ceiba**

silken /sílkən/ *adj* **1 MADE OF SILK** made or consisting of silk **2 LIKE SILK IN TEXTURE OR APPEARANCE** resembling silk, especially in smoothness, softness, or shininess ○ *Spaniels have lovely silken ears.* **3 IN SILK CLOTHES** dressed in garments made of silk **4 SOFT OR GENTLE** pleasingly soft, gentle, or delicate ○ *silken phrases* **5 LUXURIOUS** luxurious or opulent (*dated*)

silk gland *n* a salivary gland of a cocoon-spinning insect or an abdominal gland of a web-spinning spider that produces a viscous liquid that is expelled in a thread and polymerizes into a filament

silk hat *n* a man's top hat with an outer covering made of silk or a similar fabric

silkie /sílki/ *n Scotland* ZOOL, MYTHOL = **selkie**

silk-screen *vti* to print a design on paper or fabric using the silk-screen printing technique ■ *n* **1** PRINTING = **silk-screen printing** **2** a print made using the silk-screen printing technique

silk-screen printing *n* a method of printing on paper or fabric in which ink is forced through areas of a silk screen that are not blocked out with an impermeable substance

silk tree *n* a widely cultivated tree of the mimosa family. Flowers: showy, pink, with silky filaments. Native to: Asia. *Albizia julibrissin.*

silkweed /sílk weed/ *n* = **milkweed**

silkworm /sílk wurm/ *n* **1** a yellowish caterpillar, the larva of an Asian moth, that feeds on mulberry leaves and is a commercial source of silk. *Bombyx mori.* **2** a moth larva that excretes a substance resembling silk. Family: Bombycidae.

silkworm moth *n* a moth with larvae that spin silk for cocoons. Family: Bombycidae.

silky /sílki/ (**-ier, -iest**) *adj* **1 LOOKING OR FEELING LIKE SILK** resembling silk, especially in smoothness, softness, or shininess ○ *silky hair* **2 MADE OF SILK** made of silk or a similar fibre or fabric ○ *a silky blouse* **3 SMOOTH IN MANNER** smooth, refined, elegant, or sophisticated, often to the extent of being unctuous ○ *a silky manner* **4 COVERED WITH FINE HAIRS** covered with delicate downy hairs or feathers —**silkily** *adv* —**silkiness** *n*

silky oak *n* an ornamental evergreen tree with feathery leaves and smooth silky wood. Flowers: orange. Native to: Australia. *Grevillea robusta.*

sill /sil/ *n* **1 WINDOW LEDGE** a ledge below a window, especially one on the inside of a building **2 BOTTOM OF FRAME** the horizontal part at the bottom of a window or door frame **3 LAYER OF IGNEOUS ROCK** a more or less horizontal layer of igneous rock forced between layers of sedimentary rock or older volcanic beds [Old English *syll* 'foundation of a wall']

sillimanite /síllimə nīt/ *n* a white or greenish-brown fibrous mineral consisting of aluminium silicate. Source: metamorphic rocks. [Mid-19C. After Benjamin *Silliman* (1779–1864), US geologist.]

Sillitoe /síllitō/, **Alan** (*b.* 1928) British novelist, short story writer, and poet

silly /sílli/ *adj* (**-lier, -liest**) **1 RIDICULOUS** lacking common sense **2 TRIVIAL** unworthy of serious concern **3 DAZED OR HELPLESS** in or into a stunned, dazed, or helpless condition ○ *be scared silly* **4 NEAR BATSMAN** describes a fielder or fielding position near the batsman in cricket ○ *silly mid-on* ■ *n* (*plural* **-lies**) **SILLY PERSON** a foolish person (*informal*) [Old English *sǣlig* 'happy' < W Germanic, 'luck, happiness'] —**sillily** *adv* —**silliness** *n*

silly billy *n* a silly or foolish person (*informal*)

silly season *n* a period in summer when newspapers print frivolous articles because there is a lack of political news

silo /sílō/ *n* (*plural* **-los**) **1 CONTAINER FOR GRAIN OR ANIMAL FEED** a tall cylindrical tower used for storing grain, animal feed, or other material or for making silage **2 MISSILE SAFETY CHAMBER** a reinforced, protective underground chamber where a missile or missiles can be stored and from which they can be launched ■ *vt* **STORE IN SILO** to store something in a silo [Mid-19C. Via Spanish < Latin *sirus* < Greek *siros* 'storage pit for corn'.]

~~**silouette**~~ incorrect spelling of **silhouette**

siloxane /si lók sayn/ *n* any compound containing alternating silicon and oxygen atoms in which the silicon atoms are attached to organic groups or hydrogen. ◊ **silicone** [Early 20C. < SILICON + OXYGEN + METHANE.]

silt /silt/ *n* fine-grained sediment, especially of mud or clay particles at the bottom of a river or lake ■ *vti* to become full or obstructed, or to fill or obstruct something, with silt [15C. Probably < N Germanic.] —**siltation** *n* —**silty** *adj*

siltstone /sílt stōn/ *n* a form of fine-grained sandstone consisting of compressed silt

Silurian /sī lyŏŏri ən/ *n* the period of geological time when fishes first appeared, 439 to 408.5 million years ago [Early 18C. < Latin *Silures*; from the discovery of rocks of this period in SE Wales, home of the ancient people the Silures.] —**Silurian** *adj*

silurid /sī lŏŏrid/ *n* a freshwater catfish with an elongated scaleless body, a short dorsal fin, and a long anal fin. Native to: Europe, Asia. Family: Siluridae. [Via modern Latin < Latin *silurus*, type of catfish < Greek *silouros*] —**silurid** *adj*

silva /sílvə/ (*plural* **silvas** *or* **silvae** /-vee/ *or* **sylvas** *or* **sylvae**) *n* **1** the forests or trees of a particular region **2** a book or treatise on the trees or forests of a particular region

silvan *adj* = **sylvan**

Silvanus /sil váynəss/, **Sylvanus** *n* in Roman mythology, the god of fields and forests, protector of flocks and cattle

silver /sílvər/ *n* **1 SHINY ELEMENT** (*symbol* **Ag**) a shiny greyish-white metallic element that has the highest thermal and electric conductivity of any substance. Use: coins, ornaments, jewellery, dental materials, solders, photographic chemicals, conductors. **2 SILVER ARTICLES** items of tableware or other household goods that are made of silver, coated with silver plate, or made of a silver-coloured metal **3 COINS** money, especially coins made of silver or a silver-coloured metal **4 LUSTROUS GREYISH-WHITE** a lustrous greyish-white colour **5 SILVER MEDAL** a silver medal (*informal*) **6 SILVER COMPOUND** a compound of silver used in photography, e.g. to make paper sensitive to light ■ *adj* **1 MADE OF SILVER** made of, plated with, or containing some silver ○ *a silver bracelet* **2 WITH COLOUR OF SILVER** of the colour silver **3 SHINY** shining like silver ○ *silver moonlight* **4 OF 25TH ANNIVERSARY** connected with or describing the 25th anniversary of something ○ *silver wedding anniversary* **5 RESONANT** pleasingly resonant and clear in tone **6 FLUENT** fluent or persuasively eloquent ○ *a silver tongue* ■ *v* **1** *vt* **COAT WITH SILVER** to coat something with a layer of silver or a similar shiny material **2** *vti* **MAKE OR BECOME LIKE SILVER** to become, or cause something to become, like silver in colour or sheen ○ *Frost silvered the trees.* [Old English *siolfor*] —**silverer** *n* —**silvering** *n*

Silver Age *n* in classical mythology, the epoch following the Golden Age that was characterized by a refusal to serve the gods and a love of luxury

silverback /sílvər bak/ *n* an older adult male gorilla with greyish-white hair on its back

silverbell /sílvər bel/, **silverbell tree** *n* a deciduous tree or shrub with toothed leaves. Flowers: drooping, white, bell-shaped. Native to: SE United States, Asia. Genus: *Halesia*.

silverberry /sílvər beri/ (*plural* **-ries**) *n* **1** a shrub with silvery leaves and berries. Native to: North America. *Elaeagnus commutata*. **2** PLANTS = **oleaster** *n.* **2**

silver birch *n* a deciduous tree with peeling silvery-white bark. Native to: Europe, Asia. *Betula pendula*.

silver bromide *n* **AgBr** a yellowish powder that darkens when exposed to light. Use: photographic emulsions.

silver chloride *n* **AgCl** a white powder that darkens when exposed to light. Use: photographic emulsions.

silver dollar *n* **1** a one-dollar coin with high silver content, minted from time to time in the United States **2** *Can* a commemorative Canadian dollar coin issued annually

silver dollar fish *n* a tropical freshwater fish with a flattened round silver body. Native to: Central and South America. Genera: *Metynnis* and *Myleus*.

silvereye /sílvər ī/ *n ANZ* BIRDS = **white-eye**

silver fern *n* **1** PLANTS = **ponga** **2** *NZ* a stylized depiction of a silver fern leaf on a dark background [< the colour of its foliage]

silver fir *n* a fir tree with leaves that have a white or silvery underside. Genus: *Abies*.

silverfish /sílvər fish/ (*plural* **-fish** *or* **-fishes**) *n* **1** a small silvery wingless insect with three long tail bristles and two long antennae that feeds on the starch of books, wallpaper, food, and other materials. *Lepisma saccharina*. **2** a silvery fish, e.g. a tarpon

silver fox *n* **1** a North American red fox in the colour phase in which the black fur is silver-tipped **2** the pelt of the silver fox, once valued for making fur coats and other articles

silver frost *n* METEOROL = **glaze ice**

silver-gilt *n* **1** silver that has been coated with a very thin layer of gold **2** a decorative coating of silver leaf

silver-grey *n* a pale lustrous grey colour —**silver-grey** *adj*

silver gull *n* a common seagull with a white head and breast, a grey back, black-tipped wing feathers, and red beak, legs, and eye-ring. Native to: Australia. *Larus novaehollandiae*.

silver hake *n* a fish resembling a cod with silvery scales. Native to: North American Atlantic coastal waters. *Merluccius bilinearis*.

silver iodide *n* **AgI** a yellow powder that darkens when exposed to light. Use: photographic emulsions, antiseptics, seeding of clouds to make rain.

silver lining *n* something that offers hope or benefit in a situation that is generally adverse [< the proverb 'Every dark cloud has a silver lining']

silver maple *n* **1** the hard wood of a maple tree **2** a common maple tree with deeply cut five-lobed leaves that are silvery-white underneath. Native to: North America. *Acer saccharinum*.

silver medal *n* an award for taking second place in a race or other competition, usually in the form of a silver disc on a ribbon —**silver medallist** *n*

silvern /sílvərn/ *adj* made of or resembling silver (*archaic or literary*) [Old English *silfren* < *siolfor* 'silver']

silver nitrate *n* $AgNO_3$ a white poisonous compound that turns black when it is exposed to light while in contact with organic matter. Use: photographic emulsions, reagent, antiseptic, astringent.

silver plate *n* **1** a thin layer of silver, especially one that is used to coat a base metal **2** items, especially of tableware, that are made from a base metal coated with a thin layer of silver

silver-plate (**silver-plates, silver-plating, silver-plated**) *vt* to coat something, especially a base metal, with a thin layer of silver, usually by electroplating

silverpoint /sílvər poynt/ *n* **1** a drawing technique that involves using a silver-tipped pencil on specially prepared paper or parchment **2** a drawing made using the silverpoint technique

silver screen *n* **1** films or the cinema industry in general **2** the screen that films are projected onto

silver service *n* **1** a method of serving food in restaurants that includes correct table settings, changing cutlery to suit dishes ordered, and serving vegetables and other side dishes to diners at table (*hyphenated before nouns*) **2** *US* a silver tray, coffee pot, teapot, sugar bowl, and cream jug used in formal entertaining

silverside /sílvər sīd/ *n* **1** a small bony fish with a broad silvery stripe along each side of its body. Family: Atherinidae. **2** a cut of beef taken from behind and below rump and topside, usually used for roasting or pot-roasting

silversmith /sílvər smith/ *n* a maker or repairer of silver or silver-plated objects [Old English *seolforsmiþ*] —**silversmithing** *n*

silver spoon *n* inherited wealth and high social status [< The expression 'be born with a silver spoon in your mouth']

silverspot /sílvər spot/ *n* a butterfly of northern temperate areas that has silver-coloured spots. Family: Nymphalidae.

silver standard *n* a basis for currency consisting of a reserve of silver for which issued bills are redeemable at a fixed rate

silver-tongued *adj* having the gift of persuading or complimenting people eloquently and with charm

silverware /sílvər wair/ *n* **1** items made of silver or silver plate, especially tableware **2** *US* metal knives, forks, and other items of tableware

silverweed /sílvər weed/ *n* a creeping plant of the rose family that has leaves with silvery undersides. Flowers: yellow. *Potentila anserina*.

silvery /sílvəri/ *adj* **1 LIKE SILVER** resembling silver, especially in colour or sheen **2 WITH SILVER** containing some silver or coated with a thin layer of silver **3 CLEAR AND RESONANT** clear and ringing in tone ○ *silvery peals of laughter* —**silveriness** *n*

silvicolous /sil víkələss/ *adj* describes plants and animals that grow or live in woods or forests [< Latin *silvicola* 'living in woods']

silviculture /sílvi kulchər/, **sylviculture** *n* the study, cultivation, and management of forest trees [Late 19C. Via French < Latin *silva* 'a wood' + French *culture* 'cultivation'.] —**silvicultural** /sílvi kúlchərəl/ *adj* —**silviculturist** *n*

sima /sīmə/ *n* an area consecrated for the ordination of Buddhist monks, and for other formal monastic activities

simarouba /símmə rŏŏbə/, **simaruba** *n* a tree of the quassia family whose bark has medicinal properties. Native to: tropical America. Genus: *Simaruba*. [Mid-18thC. Via French and Portugese < Galibi *simaruppa*.]

Simchat Torah /símchass-/, **Simchas Torah** /sím-as-/, **Simchath Torah** *n* a Jewish festival marking the end of the annual cycle of reading from the Torah. Date: end of Sukkoth. [Late 19C. < Hebrew *śimḥath tōrā* 'rejoicing of the Torah'.]

Simenon /seemə náwN/, **Georges** (1903–89) Belgian-born French writer

Simeon Stylites /símmi ən stī lī́t eez/, **St** (390?–459) Syrian ascetic

Simferopol /símfə ráwpəl/, **Simferopol'** city in S Ukraine, on the Crimean Peninsula. Population: 353,000 (1991).

simian /símmi ən/ *adj* belonging to or characteristic of monkeys or apes, or resembling such animals in appearance or behaviour ■ *n* a monkey or an ape [Early 17C. < Latin *simia* 'ape' < Greek *simos* 'snub-nosed'.]

similar /símmilər/ *adj* **1 ALIKE** sharing some qualities, but not identical. **2 THE SAME PROPORTIONALLY** describes geometric figures that differ in size or proportion but not in shape or angular measurements **3** *Malaysia, Singapore* **IDENTICAL** exactly the same [Late 16C. Via French *similaire* < medieval Latin *similaris* < Latin *similis* 'like'.]

USAGE similar to: In its meaning 'sharing some qualities', ***similar*** is followed by *to*: *My own experience has been similar to yours.* Use with *as*, though occasionally found, is incorrect: *I had a similar experience as yours.*

similarity /símmi lárrəti/ (*plural* **-ties**) *n* **1** the possession of one or more qualities in common **2** a quality or feature that two or more things or people have in common

similarly /símmilərli/ *adv* **1** so as to share some qualities but not exactly identical **2** used to indicate that something corresponds to or is similar to something else

simile /símmili/ *n* a figure of speech that draws a comparison between two different things, especially a phrase containing the word 'like' or 'as' [14C. < Latin, 'a like thing' < *similis* 'like'.]

~~**similer**~~ incorrect spelling of **similar**

similitude /si mílli tyood/ *n* **1 BEING SIMILAR** likeness or resemblance (*formal*) **2 SOMETHING OR SOMEBODY THAT RESEMBLES ANOTHER** something or somebody that is like something or somebody else **3 A SIMILARITY** a shared characteristic (*formal*) **4 FORM OR SEMBLANCE** a form or semblance of somebody or something (*formal or literary*) [14C. Via Old French < Latin *similitudo* 'likeness' < *similis* 'like'.]

Simla /símlə/ capital of Himachal Pradesh State, NW India. Population: 81,463 (1991).

~~**simlar**~~ incorrect spelling of **similar**

SIMM /sim/ *n* a module plugged in to the motherboard of a computer to add memory. Full form **single inline memory module**

Simmental /símmen taal/ (*plural* **-tals** *or* **-tal**), **Simmenthal** (*plural* **-thals** *or* **-thal**) *n* a large cow with a yellowish-brown or reddish coat, a white head, and white legs [Early 20C. After the *Simmental* valley, Switzerland.]

simmer /símmər/ *v* **1** *vti* **COOK JUST BELOW BOIL** to cook gently or cook something gently just below boiling point, usually with the occasional bubble breaking on the surface **2** *vti* **STAY OR KEEP SOMETHING BELOW BOIL** to stay just below boiling point, or to cause a liquid to stay just below boiling point **3** *vi* **BE GROWING ANGRY** to have anger, or some other strong emotion, building up inside ○ *simmering with rage* **4** *vi* **BUILD UP** to build up or ferment, often without being expressed ○ *'with grief and rage and laughter all simmering within me like a boiling pot'* (Arthur Conan Doyle, *The Lost World*; 1912) ■ *n* **GENTLE COOKING TEMPERATURE** a cooking temperature that cooks food or keeps liquid at just below boiling point [Mid-17C. Alteration of obsolete *simper*.]

simmer down *v* **1** *vi* to become calm, e.g. after an outburst of anger or a state of excitement **2** *vti* to condense something by simmering or boiling it gently, or to reduce the volume of something in this way

simnel cake /símnəl-/ *n* a fruitcake covered with marzipan or with a layer of marzipan baked in the middle, traditionally served during the Christian celebrations of Lent or Easter [13C. Via Old French *simenel* < Latin *simila* 'fine flour'.]

Simon /símən/ *n* in the New Testament, one of the 12 apostles, traditionally believed to have been martyred in Persia with St Jude. Known as **Simon the Zealot**

Simon /símən/, **Neil** (*b.* 1927) US playwright

Simone /si mṓn/, **Nina** (*b.* 1933) US jazz singer and composer. Born **Eunice Kathleen Waymon**

simoniac /si mṓni ak/ *n* a dealer in sacred objects ■ *adj* **simoniac, simoniacal** relating or belonging to the buying or selling of sacred or spiritual things [14C. < French *simoniaque* < late Latin *simonia* (see SIMONY).]

simon-pure /símən-/ *adj* completely genuine or authentic [Late 18C. After *Simon Pure*, a character in Susannah Centlivre's play *A Bold Stroke for a Wife* (1717).]

Simons /símənss/, **Menno** (1496–1591) Dutch religious reformer

Simon's Town /símənz-/ town and naval base in SW South Africa. Population: 6,500 (1997).

simony /símənì, símməni/ *n* in Christianity, the buying or selling of sacred or spiritual things [13C. Via French *simonie* < late Latin *simonia* < *Simon* Magus, a Samaritan who tried to buy the power of conferring the Holy Spirit.] —**simonist** *n*

simoom /si mo͞om/, **simoon** /si mo͞on/ *n* a hot dry wind that blows across N Africa and the Arabian Peninsula, carrying dust and sand particles [Late 18C. < Arabic *samūm* < *samma* 'poison'.]

simp /simp/ *n US* an offensive term for somebody who seems to lack intelligence or common sense (*slang*) [Early 20C. Shortening of *simpleton*.]

simpatico /sim páttikō/ *adj* sharing similar temperaments or interests and, therefore, able to get on well together [Mid-19C. Via Spanish or Italian 'sympathetic' < Latin *sympathia* 'sympathy'.]

simper /símpər/ *v* **1** *vi* **SMILE COYLY** to smile in an affected, coy, and usually irritating way **2** *vt* **SAY SOMETHING COYLY** to say something with a coy smile ■ *n* **AFFECTED SMILE** a coy and affected smile [Mid-16C. < ?] —**simperer** *n* —**simpering** *adj, n* —**simperingly** *adv*

simple /símp'l/ *adj* (**-pler, -plest**) **1 EASY** easy to do, understand, or work out ○ *a simple task* **2 NOT ELABORATE** lacking decoration or embellishment and therefore plain in appearance ○ *a simple black dress* **3 NOT COMPLEX** made up of or having only one part or element ○ *a simple organism* **4 WITHOUT COMPLICATIONS** with no complications, luxuries, or embellishments ○ *the simple life* **5 STRAIGHTFORWARD** ordinary or straightforward ○ *It's a simple case of the flu and I should be back to work in a couple of days.* **6 OFFENSIVE TERM** an offensive term meaning having an intellectual capacity that does not permit the performance of higher level cognitive processes **7 NAIVE** naive and lacking in depth and detail **8 HUMBLE** humble and unsophisticated ○ *simple folk* **9 GUILELESS** direct, sincere, or lacking any form of deceitfulness **10 CONTAINING ONE COMPOUND ONLY** consisting of a single chemical compound **11 NOT DIVIDED** not divided, either totally or partially, into separate segments ○ *a simple leaf.* ◊ **compound**[1] *adj.* **3** ■ *n* **HERBAL MEDICINE** a herbal medicine or a herb that yields medicine (*archaic*) [Pre-12C. Via French < Latin *simplus*.] —**simpleness** *n*

USAGE See ***simplistic***.

simple closed curve *n* a plane curve, e.g. a circle or ellipse, that is closed and does not intersect itself

simple equation *n* MATH = **linear equation**

simple fraction *n* a fraction that consists of two whole numbers separated by a horizontal or slanting line, as opposed to a decimal fraction

simple fracture *n* a fracture of a bone in which the fragments remain in their correct alignment, with little damage to the surrounding tissue

simple fruit *n* a fruit, e.g. a pea pod or a tomato, that forms from a single pistil

simple harmonic motion *n* a type of periodic motion in which a body experiences a force proportional to its distance from a fixed point and directed towards the fixed point. US term **harmonic motion**

simple-hearted *adj* honest, open, and lacking deceit or deviousness

simple interest *n* interest on an investment that is calculated once per period, usually annually, on the amount of the capital alone and not on any interest already earned

simple machine *n* any of the six devices formerly considered to be the elements from which all machines were composed. They were the inclined plane, lever, pulley, screw, wedge, and wheel and axle.

simple-minded *adj* **1 LACKING DUE THOUGHT** showing a lack of intelligent thinking or proper consideration **2 OFFENSIVE TERM** an offensive term for somebody who is regarded as having limited intellectual ability **3 UNSOPHISTICATED** without guile or complexity —**simple-mindedly** *adv* —**simple-mindedness** *n*

simple protein *n* a protein such as globulin that yields only amino acids on complete hydrolysis

simple sentence *n* a sentence that takes the form of a single main clause with no relative or subordinate clause, e.g. 'I read the book'. ◊ **complex sentence, compound sentence**

Simple Simon *n* an offensive term for somebody, especially a man or boy, who is perceived as lacking intelligence or sophistication (*insult*) [After a character in a nursery rhyme]

simple sugar *n* CHEM = **monosaccharide**

simple tense *n* a grammatical form of a verb that expresses a relationship of time without using any auxiliary or modal verbs

simple time *n* a musical tempo in which the main beats are divisible by two, e.g. 2/2 or 4/4 time

simpleton /símp'ltən/ *n* an offensive term for somebody who seems to lack intelligence or common sense (*insult*)

simplex /sím pleks/ *adj* **1 SIMPLE** containing, using, or designed for a single element or component **2 ALLOWING TRANSMISSION IN ONE DIRECTION** allowing transmission of signals or communication in only one direction at a time ■ *n* **1 ROOT FORM OF WORD** a word in its base form, without any inflections, prefixes, or suffixes, and not formed by putting two distinct words together **2 GEOMETRICAL FIGURE OR ELEMENT** a geometrical element in a Euclidean space that exhibits the minimum number of dimensions of the space, e.g. a line in one-dimensional space or a triangle in two-dimensional space **3** *US* **APARTMENT ON ONE FLOOR** an apartment with all rooms on one floor [Late 16C. < Latin, < *simplus* 'simple'.]

simplicity /sim plíssəti/ (*plural* **-ties**) *n* **1** lack of complexity, complication, embellishment, or difficulty **2** a simple quality or thing [14C. Via French *simplicité* < Latin *simplicitas* < *simplex* (see SIMPLEX).]

simplify /símpli fī/ (**-fies, -fying, -fied**) *vt* **1** to make something less complicated or easier to understand **2** to convert a mathematical expression, e.g. a fraction or equation, to a simpler form by removing common factors or regrouping elements [Mid-17C. Via French *simplifier* < medieval Latin *simplificare* < Latin *simplus* 'simple'.] —**simplification** /símplifi káysh'n/ *n* —**simplificative** /símplifikətiv/ *adj* —**simplifier** *n*

simplism /símplizəm/ *n* a tendency to avoid or ignore the complexities of something —**simplist** *n*

simplistic /sim plístik/ *adj* **1** characterized by naive simplicity **2** tending to oversimplify something, especially by avoiding or ignoring its complexities —**simplistically** *adv*

USAGE simple or **simplistic**? ***Simplistic*** is normally a derogatory word, implying that something is oversimplified rather than naturally simple: *He argued that it was simplistic to reject these methods as unscientific.* It should not be used as an alternative or supposedly stronger word for ***simple***: *A simple* [not *simplistic*] *approach would be helpful here.*

Simplon Pass /sím plon-/ mountain pass in the Alps between south central Switzerland and NW Italy. Height: 2,009 m/6,590 ft.

simply /símpli/ *adv* **1 NOTHING OTHER THAN** with nothing else involved ○ *It was simply a misunderstanding.* **2 PLAINLY** in an uncomplicated, straightforward, or plain way ○ *To put it simply, I can't afford it.* **3 AT ALL OR TOTALLY** to any or the fullest degree or extent ○ *simply astonishing* **4 FRANKLY** frankly and without embellishment ○ *It was, quite simply, the best they had in stock.* **5 NAIVELY** without full understanding

Simpson /símps'n/, **Sir James Young** (1811–70) British obstetrician

Simpson, O.J. (*b.* 1947) US American football player, sportscaster, and actor. Full name **Orenthal James Simpson**

Simpson Desert desert in central Australia, centred on the junction of the South Australia, Northern Territory, and Queensland borders. Area: 77,000 sq. km/29,723 sq. mi.

simulacrum /símmyo͝o láykrəm/ (*plural* **-cra** /-krə/) *n* **1** a representation or image of something **2** something that has a vague, tentative, or shadowy resemblance to something else [Late 16C. < Latin, < *simulare* (see SIMULATE).]

simulant /símmyo͝olənt/ *adj* serving to imitate or reproduce the essential features of something (*formal*) ■ *n* = **simulator** *n.* 1 [Mid-18C. < Latin *simulant-*, present participle of *simulare* (see SIMULATE).]

simulate /símmyo͝o layt/ (**-lates, -lating, -lated**) *vt* **1 REPRODUCE FEATURES OF SOMETHING** to reproduce an essential feature or features of something, e.g. as an aid to study or training ○ *a computer model simulating the process of continental drift* **2 FAKE** to feign something, or pretend to experience something ○ *simulating enjoyment* **3 MIMIC** to mimic or imitate somebody or something [15C. < Latin *simulare* < *similis* 'like'.] —**simulative** /-lətiv/ *adj* —**simulatively** *adv*

simulated /símmyoo laytid, símmyə-/ *adj* **1 REPRODUCED BY SIMULATION** reproduced or realized by simulation, especially computer simulation **2 NOT GENUINE** artificial, especially made in imitation of a genuine article, fabric, or other substance **3 FALSE** feigned or faked

simulation /símmyo͝o láysh'n/ *n* **1 REPRODUCTION OF FEATURES OF** the reproduction of the essential features of something, e.g. as an aid to study or training **2 FALSE APPEARANCE** the imitation or feigning of something **3 FAKE** an artificial or imitation object **4 CONSTRUCTION OF MATHEMATICAL MODEL** the construction of a mathematical model to reproduce the characteristics of a phenomenon, system, or process, often using a computer, in order to infer information or solve problems

simulator /símmyǒǒ laytər/ *n* **1** a device, instrument, or piece of equipment designed to reproduce the essential features of something, e.g. as an aid to study or training. ◊ **emulator** *n.* 2 **2** a person who feigns or imitates something —**simulatory** *adj*

simulcast /símm'l kaast/ *n* **1** SIMULTANEOUS TV AND RADIO BROADCAST a programme that is broadcast simultaneously on both television and radio, on multiple channels, or in multiple languages **2** LIVE BROADCAST a live broadcast of an event on closed-circuit television ■ *vt* (**-casts, -casting, -cast**) MAKE SIMULTANEOUS BROADCAST to broadcast a simulcast programme [Mid-20C. Blend of SIMULTANEOUS + BROADCAST.]

simultaneous /símm'l táyni əss/ *adj* **1** AT THE SAME TIME done, happening, or existing at the same time **2** TAKING SAME VARIABLES describes equations that are satisfied by the same values of the variables ■ *n* DISPLAY OF CHESS-PLAYING an exhibition of chess-playing skills in which one player is involved in several games at the same time, systematically moving from one board to the next [Mid-17C. < medieval Latin *simultaneus* < Latin *simul* 'at the same time', probably after *momentaneus* 'momentary'.] —**simultaneity** /símm'ltə née əti/ *n* —**simultaneously** *adv* —**simultaneousness** *n*

~~**simultanious**~~ incorrect spelling of **simultaneous**

sin[1] /sin/ *n* **1** TRANSGRESSION OF THEOLOGICAL PRINCIPLES an act, a thought, or behaviour that goes against the law or teachings of a particular religion, especially when the person who commits it is aware of this **2** ESTRANGEMENT FROM GOD in Christian theology, the condition of being denied God's grace because of a sin or sins committed **3** SHAMEFUL OFFENCE something that offends a moral or ethical principle ■ *vi* (**sins, sinning, sinned**) **1** KNOWINGLY DO WRONG to commit a sin, especially by knowingly violating a law or the teachings of a particular religion **2** COMMIT SHAMEFUL OFFENCE to commit serious moral or ethical offence [Old English *synn* < Indo-European] —**sinless** *adj* —**sinlessly** *adv* —**sinlessness** *n* ◊ **live in sin** to live together as husband and wife without being married (*dated or humorous*)

sin[2] *n* ALPH = **shin**[2]

sin[3] *abbr* sine

Sinai /sí nī/ peninsula of NE Egypt, bounded on the east by the Gulf of Aqaba and on the west by the Gulf of Suez. Area: 60,863 sq. km/23,500 sq. mi.

Sinai, Mount mountain in NE Egypt on the south-central Sinai Peninsula. Height: 2,888 m/7,500 ft.

sinamay /sínnə mī/ *n* a stiff open-weave fabric spun from the fibres of the banana plant. Use: hats. [Mid-20C. < Tagalog.]

Sinanthropus /sin ánthrəpəss/ *n* the original scientific name for Peking man [Early 20C. < modern Latin, < late Latin *Sinae* 'the Chinese' + Greek *anthrōpos* 'person'.]

Sinatra /si naátrə/, **Frank** (1915–98) US singer and actor

sin bin *n* an area with a bench beside an ice-hockey rink where penalized players must stay during the period they have to serve as a time penalty for an offence (*slang*)

since /sinss/ CORE MEANING: a grammatical word used to indicate that a situation has continued from a particular time or event in the past ○ (prep) *Karen has lived in London since 1988.* ○ (adv) *She left the firm in 1980 and has since been self-employed.* ○ (conj) *He has been on a high since he got married in January.*

1 *prep, conj* HAPPENING AFTER happening at some point or points after the stated period of time or event ○ *The rate of job growth is higher than under any administration since 1920.* ○ *Since Ryland became commissioner in 1994, all complaints are investigated fully.* **2** *adv* SUBSEQUENTLY at some point between then and now ○ *even when the department had an engineer, who has since retired* **3** *conj* BECAUSE because, seeing that ○ *Since it was still light, they were allowed to play in the park.* [15C. Contraction of earlier *sithence* < Old English *siððan* < *sīþ* 'after' + *þām* 'that'.]

USAGE See ***ago***.

USAGE See ***because***.

sincere /sin séer/ (**-cerer, -cerest**) *adj* **1** honest and unaffected in a way that shows what is said is really meant **2** based on what is truly and deeply felt [Mid-16C. < Latin *sincerus* 'pure, whole'.] —**sincereness** *n*

sincerely /sin séerli/ *adv* in an honest and straightforward way ○ *He sincerely told her everything that was in his heart.* ◇ **yours sincerely** used immediately before the signature to end a letter that is addressed to somebody by name ○ *Yours sincerely, John Smith*

sincerity /sin sérrəti/ *n* honesty in the expression of true or deep feelings ○ *We had no reason to doubt her sincerity.*

~~**sincerly**~~ incorrect spelling of **sincerely**

sinciput /sínssi put, -pət/ (*plural* **-ciputs** *or* **-cipita** /-síppətə/) *n* the part of the skull that includes the forehead and the area above it [Late 16C. < Latin, 'half head'.] —**sincipital** /sin síppit'l/ *adj*

Sinclair /síng klair/, **Sir Clive** (*b.* 1940) British engineer and inventor

Sinclair /síng klair, sing kláir/, **Upton** (1878–1968) US writer and reformer

Sind /sind/ region of SE Pakistan in the lower Indus valley. Capital: Karachi. Population: 25,000,000 (1991). Area: 140,914 sq. km/54,407 sq. mi.

Sindhi /síndi/ (*plural* **-dhi** *or* **-dhis**) *n* **1** a person who comes from Sind **2** the Indic language of the people of Sind. Native speakers: 14 million. [Early 19C. < Persian and Urdu *sindī* < *Sind* 'the Indus River' < Sanskrit *sindhu*.] —**Sindhi** *adj*

sine /sīn/ *n* **1** for a given angle in a right-angled triangle, a trigonometric function equal to the length of the side opposite the angle divided by the hypotenuse **2** a mathematical function equal to the vertical coordinate of a circumference point divided by the radius of a circle with its centre at the origin of a Cartesian coordinate system [Late 16C. < Latin *sinus* 'curve, fold'.]

SPELLCHECK See ***sign***.

sinecure /sínni kyoǒr, sīni-, -kyawr/ *n* **1** a job or position that provides a regular income but requires little or no work **2** a church office whose holder is paid but is not required to do pastoral work [Mid-17C. < medieval Latin *beneficium sine cura* 'benefice without care (of souls)'.]

sine curve *n* a graph of the sine equation 'y = a sin bx', with 'a' and 'b' being constants

sine die /sīni dī ee, sínni dée ay/ *adv* without a day being fixed for a further meeting ○ *The committee was adjourned sine die.* [< Latin, 'without a day']

sine prole /sīnee prṓ lee, sínnay prṓlay/ *adv* without offspring ○ *She died in 1985, aged 59, sine prole.* [< Latin, 'without offspring']

sine qua non /sī nee kway nón, sínnay kwaa nṓn, sīni kway nṓn, sínni kwaa nṓn/ *n* an essential condition or prerequisite ○ *The suspension of industrial activity is considered a sine qua non for talks to proceed.* [< Latin, 'without which (cause) not']

sinew /sínnyoo/ *n* **1** ANAT = **tendon** **2** STRENGTH strength, power, or resilience (*literary*) **3** SOURCE OF POWER a source of strength or power (*literary; often plural*) ■ *vt* STRENGTHEN to give added strength to somebody or something [Old English *sin(e)we* < Germanic] —**sinewless** *adj*

sine wave *n* a waveform with the shape of a sine curve, representing a single frequency indefinitely repeated in time

sinewy /sínnyoo i/ *adj* **1** THIN AND STRONG lean, tough, and muscular ○ *a sinewy 20-year-old.* **2** CONTAINING OR RESEMBLING TENDONS consisting of or containing tendons or stringy parts resembling tendons ○ *a rather sinewy steak* **3** FORCEFUL vigorous and forceful (*literary*) ○ *rich, sinewy prose* —**sinewiness** *n*

sinfonia /sínfə née ə, sin fṓni ə/ (*plural* **-as** *or* **-e** /-ay/) *n* **1** a piece of orchestral music used as an overture or interlude in an opera **2** a complex instrumental composition, usually for a group of stringed instruments or an orchestra [Late 18C. Via Italian < Latin *symphonia* 'sound of instruments, harmony'.]

sinfonietta /sínfōni éttə, sínfəni-/ *n* **1** an orchestral piece that resembles a symphony but is shorter or written for fewer instruments, often for strings only **2** a small symphony orchestra, often composed of stringed instruments only [Early 20C. < Italian, 'little sinfonia' < *sinfonia* (see SINFONIA).]

sinful /sínf'l/ *adj* **1** engaging in or characterized by behaviour that goes against the law or teachings of a particular religion **2** morally or ethically wrong ○ *a sinful waste of an expensive education* [Old English] —**sinfully** *adv* —**sinfulness** *n*

sing /sing/ *v* (**sings, singing, sang** /sang/, **sung** /sung/) **1** *vti* MAKE MUSIC WITH VOICE to use the voice to produce words or sounds in a musical way **2** *vti* PERFORM SONGS PROFESSIONALLY to perform songs as a trained or professional singer ○ *The last I heard she was singing with a group in Edinburgh.* **3** *vti* MAKE TUNEFUL ANIMAL SOUND to make a melodious sound that is typical of a species (*refers to animals*) **4** *vi* MAKE CONTINUOUS MUSICAL SOUND to make a continuous whistling, humming, or ringing sound ○ *a strong wind making the wires sing* **5** *vi* MAKE BRIEF SPEEDING SOUND to make a brief whistling or whizzing sound **6** *vi* EXPERIENCE RINGING OR HUMMING IN HEAD to experience a continuous ringing or humming sound in the head **7** *vt* INTONE to chant something, especially a religious text, on a single note or a small range of notes **8** *vt* SING FOR PARTICULAR PURPOSE to bring something to a particular condition by singing ○ *sing the baby to sleep* **9** *vi* CONFESS OR IMPLICATE to confess to or implicate others in a crime (*slang*) ○ *McGrath had a reputation for making even the toughest criminals sing.* **10** *vti* TELL ABOUT to praise somebody or proclaim something, especially in verse **11** *vi* BE HAPPY to rejoice in something ■ *n* PERFORMANCE OF SONGS a session of singing (*informal*) [Old English *singan* < Indo-European] —**singability** /síngə bílləti/ *n* —**singable** *adj* —**singingly** *adv* ◇ **sing from the same hymn-sheet** *or* **song-sheet** to express the same opinion or act in the same way (*informal*)

sing along *vi* to join in a song that somebody else is singing

sing out *vi* to call out in a loud voice, especially to warn somebody ○ *Sing out if you see any rocks ahead.*

sing-along *n US* = **singsong** *n.* 2

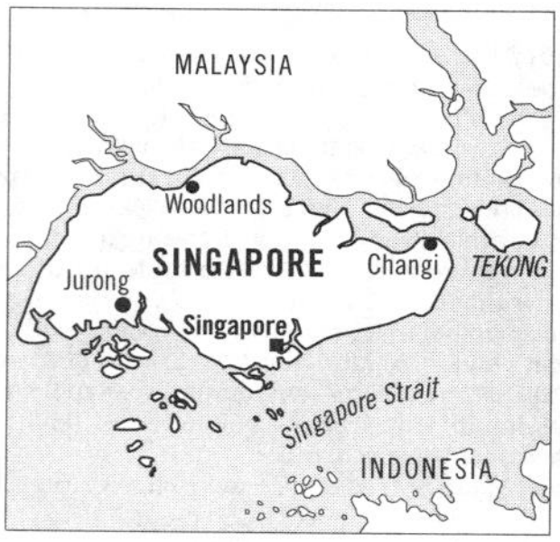

Singapore

Singapore /síngə páwr/ city-state in Southeast Asia, comprising one major island and several islets south of the Malay Peninsula. Capital: Singapore. Population: 2,986,500 (1995). Area: 640 sq. km/247 sq. mi. —**Singaporean** *n, adj*

Singapore English *n* a variety of English spoken in Singapore

singe /sinj/ *v* **1** *vti* SCORCH SOMETHING SLIGHTLY to burn or cause something to burn slightly so that only the surface, edge, or tip is affected ○ *The heat from the fire had singed his jacket.* **2** *vt* REMOVE FEATHERS OR HAIR WITH FLAME to expose the carcass of a bird or animal to a flame in order to remove unwanted feathers, bristles, or hair **3** *vt* BURN ENDS OF CLOTH FIBRES to burn the short fuzzy ends of fibres from cloth in the manufacturing process ■ *n* SCORCH a superficial burn [Old English *sencgan*]

singer /síngər/ *n* **1** PERFORMER OF SONGS a person who sings, especially professionally **2** SINGING BIRD a bird that sings **3** POET a poet (*literary*)

Singer /síngər/, **Isaac** (1811–75) US inventor and entrepreneur

Singer, Isaac Bashevis (1904–91) Polish-born US writer

Singh /sing/ *n* a title adopted as a surname by a Sikh boy when he is initiated at puberty into the fraternity of warriors [Early 17C. Via Punjabi *siṅgh* 'lion' < Sanskrit *siṃha*.]

Singh /sing/, **V. P.** (*b.* 1931) Indian statesman. Full name **Vishwanath Pratap Singh**

Singhalese *n, adj* PEOPLES, LANG = **Sinhalese**

singing /sínging/ *n* **1** USE OF VOICE TO PRODUCE SONGS the technique of producing musical sounds with the voice, or the performance of songs **2** MELODIC SOUNDS the melodic or other sounds made by somebody or something that sings ■ *adj* MAKING MUSICAL SOUND performing songs or making a melodic, whistling, humming, or ringing sound ◇ **all-singing, all-dancing** elaborate and inclusive (*informal*)

singing telegram *n* a message sung by a messenger paid to do so, or the service of providing sung messages

single /síng g'l/ *adj* 1 **ONE** only one ○ *We didn't get a single reply.* ○ *in the space of a single day* 2 **CONSIDERED INDIVIDUALLY** considered separately as something distinct or unique ○ *every single time* 3 **UNMARRIED** unmarried or characteristic of being unmarried 4 **FOR ONE PERSON** suitable or designed for one person ○ *He has a single room on the third floor.* ○ *a single bed* 5 **CONSISTING OF ONE THING** consisting of one part, element, or quality 6 **BETWEEN ONLY TWO PEOPLE** taking place as a contest or competition between two persons only, one on each side ○ *a single competition* 7 **FORMING ONE UNDIVIDED UNIT** forming a whole and left undivided or unbroken ○ *The sculpture had been carved from a single block of ice.* 8 **UNIFORM** sole and the same for all ○ *a single rate for the job* 9 **WITH ONE PETAL ROW** describes a flower that has only one whorl or row of petals ■ *n* 1 **ACCOMMODATION FOR ONE** a room, cabin, or bed for one person ○ *Do you have any singles left?* 2 **RECORDING OF ONE SONG** a recording of an individual song released for sale on its own, often with another song included 3 **OUTWARD-BOUND TICKET** a ticket that covers the outward-bound part of a journey to a destination but not the return 4 **BASEBALL HIT** a hit in baseball that allows the batter to reach first base 5 **CRICKET STROKE** a stroke in cricket that scores one run 6 **TWO-PLAYER MATCH** a match between two golfers 7 **ONE-POUND NOTE** a banknote of the value of one pound (*dated*) ■ *vti* **HIT BASEBALL SINGLE** to hit a single in baseball or advance a runner by hitting a single [13C. Via Old French < Latin *singulus* < *simplus* 'simple'.] —**singleness** *n*

single out *vt* to select an individual from a group for a particular reason

single-action *adj* requiring the hammer of a firearm to be cocked by hand before each shot can be fired ■ *n* a firearm that cannot be fired until the hammer is cocked by hand

single-blind *adj* describes an experiment or clinical trial in which the subjects are not told whether the tested substance or procedure they receive is active, in order to avoid subjective bias in the results

single bond *n* a covalent bond between two atoms formed through the sharing of a pair of electrons

single-breasted *adj* with a small overlap at the front and fastened with a single row of buttons

single-cell protein *n* a protein derived from one-celled organisms grown in various cultures

single cream *n UK* cream with a butterfat content of 18 per cent that cannot be whipped and is used for pouring over desserts or enriching savoury or sweet dishes

single cross *n* the first generation of offspring resulting from hybridization between two inbred lines

single currency *n* a monetary unit that is shared by several countries

single-cut file *n* a file that has all its teeth pointing in one direction

single-decker *n* a bus that has only one passenger deck

single-end *n Scotland* a flat with one room only

single-ended *adj* designed for use with an unbalanced electrical signal and having one input and one output permanently earthed

single entry *n* a system of bookkeeping in which the amounts owed or due are kept in a single account (*hyphenated before nouns*)

single file *n* a line of people, animals, or vehicles standing or moving one behind another ○ *We moved along the track in single file.* ■ *adv* moving in a line, one behind another

single-foot *n* RIDING = **rack**[4] *n.* ■ *vti* RIDING = **rack**[4] *v.*

single-handed *adj* 1 **UNAIDED** accomplished alone and unaided ○ *the first single-handed circumnavigation of the world* 2 **WITH ONE HAND ONLY** with only one hand or the use of one hand 3 **FOR ONE HAND ONLY** using or requiring only one hand ■ *adv* **WITHOUT HELP** without any help from anyone ○ *sailed round the world single-handed* —**single-handedly** *adv* —**single-handedness** *n*

single-hearted /-haártid/ *adj* sincere, faithful, and straightforward [*Single* in the obsolete sense of 'honest'] —**single-heartedly** *adv* —**single-heartedness** *n*

single-issue *adj* concerned with only a single public issue ○ *the multiplication of single-issue groups*

single-lens reflex *n* a camera in which the light passes through one lens to the film and, by means of a mirror and prism system, to the focusing screen. ◊ **reflex camera**

single-minded *adj* 1 with only one goal in mind 2 with the mind fixed on one task or preoccupation —**single-mindedly** *adv* —**single-mindedness** *n*

single nucleotide polymorphism *n* a commonly found change in a single nucleotide base in a DNA sequence, occurring about every 1,000 bases. It is of significance in biomedical research.

single parent *n* a parent who brings up a child or children alone, usually because he or she is unmarried, widowed, or divorced (*hyphenated before nouns*) —**single-parenting** *n*

single-phase *adj* with, generating, or powered by a single alternating voltage

single photon emission computed tomography *n* a technique used in diagnosing some diseases that generates a three-dimensional computer image of the distribution of a radioactive tracer in a particular organ

singles /síng g'lz/ *n* (*plural* **-gles**) a game of tennis or badminton between two people ○ *Our singles was pretty close.* ■ *npl* unmarried people considered as a group

singles bar *n* a bar frequented by men and women, usually unmarried, who are seeking romance, companionship, or sex

single-serve *adj* packaged in small amounts intended for one person ○ *available in single-serve sizes*

single-sex *adj* restricted to either men or to women

single-space *vt* to type or print text without a blank space between the lines

singlestick /síng g'l stik/ *n* 1 a stick fitted with a hand-guard, formerly used in fencing 2 the former sport or skill of fencing with a singlestick

singlet /síng glət/ *n* 1 a sleeveless undershirt 2 a sleeveless shirt worn with shorts in sports such as basketball or amateur boxing [Mid-18C. < SINGLE after DOUBLET, because it originally referred to an unlined, one-layered garment.]

singleton /síng g'ltən/ *n* 1 somebody or something that occurs singly and not as part of a group, e.g. the only child in a family 2 a playing card that is the only one of its suit in a hand

Singleton /síng g'ltən/ town in E New South Wales, Australia. Population: 12,519 (1996).

single-tongue *vti* to articulate notes on a wind instrument by raising the tip of the tongue against the palate, temporarily obstructing the flow of air

single-track *adj* 1 **FIXED ON SINGLE IDEA** fixed on one thought or idea only 2 **WITH ONE TRACK ONLY** with only one track and passing places for trains coming from opposite directions 3 **WIDE ENOUGH FOR ONE VEHICLE ONLY** not wide enough to allow motor vehicles to pass each other

single transferable vote *n* a system of voting in a multimember constituency in which voters list the candidates in order of preference and any candidate receiving the required number of votes is elected

singletree /síng g'l tree/ *n US* AGRIC = **swingletree** [Mid-19C. Alteration of SWINGLETREE, after DOUBLETREE 'crosspiece to which the whiffletree is attached'.]

singly /síng gli/ *adv* 1 **INDIVIDUALLY IN SEQUENCE** one at a time or one by one ○ *They drifted back into camp singly or in small groups.* 2 **WITHOUT HELP** alone and by unaided efforts 3 **SEPARATELY** solely and separately

singsong /síng song/ *n* 1 **WAY OF SPEAKING** a voice with an intonation that rises and falls regularly in pitch 2 **OCCASION WHEN PEOPLE SING TOGETHER** a meeting of a group of people to sing songs together for fun, or an impromptu session of singing ○ *After we've eaten we'll have a singsong.* US term **sing-along** *n.* 3 **SINGSONG VERSE RHYTHMS OR RHYMES** a singsong rhythm or rhyme in verse, or a verse marked by such monotony ■ *adj* **WITH REPEATEDLY RISING AND FALLING INTONATION** with an intonation that regularly rises and falls in pitch

singspiel /síng speel, zíng shpeel/, **Singspiel** *n* an 18th-century German comic opera consisting of folksongs or classical music performed in a popular or folk style interspersed with spoken dialogue [Late 19C. < German, 'singing play'.]

singular /síng gyoolər/ *adj* 1 **REFERRING TO ONE PERSON OR THING** describes a word or form that refers to one person or thing 2 **EXCEPTIONAL** remarkably good or admirable 3 **UNUSUAL** unusual, odd, or striking ○ *The room had a singular colour scheme.* 4 **STANDING FOR INDIVIDUAL THING** in logic, describes a term intended to stand for an individual thing, or a proposition containing such a term ■ *n* 1 **SINGULAR WORD OR FORM** the form of a word that is used when referring to one person or thing 2 **THING IN ISOLATION** something considered solely by itself [14C. Via Old French < Latin *singularis* 'alone of its kind' < *singulus* 'single'.] —**singularly** *adv* —**singularness** *n*

singularise *vti* = **singularize**

singularity /síng gyoo lárrəti/ (*plural* **-ties**) *n* 1 **SINGULAR QUALITY** singular, exceptional, or unusual quality 2 **SOMETHING UNIQUE OR UNUSUAL** something that is unique, distinctive, or remarkable 3 **CHARACTERISTIC** a distinguishing trait 4 **HYPOTHETICAL POINT IN SPACE** a hypothetical region in space in which gravitational forces cause matter to be infinitely compressed and space and time to become infinitely distorted 5 **FUNCTION THAT IS NOT DIFFERENTIABLE** in mathematics, a point at which a complex function is undefined because it is neither differentiable nor single-valued while the function is defined in every neighbourhood of the point [13C. Via Old French *singularite* < Latin *singularis* (see SINGULAR).]

singularize /síng gyoolə rīz/ (**-izes, -izing, -ized**), **singularise** (**-ises, -ising, -ised**) *v* 1 *vti* to make a word singular or to become singular 2 *vt* to distinguish somebody or something or make somebody or something stand out from the rest (*formal*) —**singularization** /síng gyoolə rī záysh'n/ *n*

singular point *n* MATH = **singularity** *n.* 5

Sinhalese /sínhə léez/ (*plural* **-leses** *or* **-lese**), **Singhalese** /síngə léez, síng gə-/ (*plural* **-leses** *or* **-lese**) *n* 1 a member of a people who live mainly in Sri Lanka 2 the Indic language of the Sinhalese people. Native speakers: 13 million. [Late 18C. Via Portuguese *Singhalez* < Sanskrit *Siṁhala*, a variant of *Siṁhala* 'Sri Lanka'.] —**Sinhalese** *adj*

Sinicize /síni sīz, sínni-/ (**-cizes, -cizing, -cized**), **Sinicise** (**-cises, -cising, -cised**) *vti* to acquire, or give somebody or something, a Chinese idiom, form, or cultural trait (*often passive*) [Late 16C. < obsolete *Sinic* 'Chinese'.]

sinister /sínnistər/ *adj* 1 threatening or suggesting malevolence, menace, or harm 2 on the left side of a heraldic shield as seen by the holder ○ *a bend sinister* [15C. Via Old French < Latin, 'left' < the superstition that the left side is unlucky.] —**sinisterly** *adv* —**sinisterness** *n*

sinistral /sínnistrəl/ *adj* 1 **OF OR ON LEFT SIDE** relating to or located on the left side, especially the left side of the body (*archaic*) 2 **LEFT-HANDED** left-handed (*archaic*) 3 **COILING CLOCKWISE** coiling in a clockwise direction from the apex to the aperture —**sinistrally** *adv*

sinistrorse /sínni strawrss/ *adj* growing upward in a clockwise spiral [Mid-19C. < Latin *sinistrorsus* < *sinister* 'left'.] —**sinistrorsely** *adv*

Sinitic /sī níttik, si-/ *n* the branch of the Sino-Tibetan language group that includes the Chinese languages [Late 19C. < late Latin *Sinæ* (see SINO-).] —**Sinitic** *adj*

sink /singk/ *v* (**sinks, sinking, sank** /sangk/ *or* **sunk** /sungk/, **sunk** *or* **sunken**) 1 *vti* **FALL BENEATH SURFACE OF LIQUID** to go beneath the surface of a liquid or a soft substance and become partly or wholly submerged ○ *The paper boat began to sink.* 2 *vi* **APPEAR TO FALL** to appear to descend towards or below the horizon ○ *We watched the sun sink in the sky.* 3 *vi* **FALL TO LOWER LEVEL** to become lower in height or depth ○ *The water level in the lake must have sunk six inches.* 4 *vi* **GO DOWN GRADUALLY** to slowly subside or settle at a lower level 5 *vi* **FALL GENTLY** to fall or collapse slowly ○ *He sank to his knees in exhaustion.* 6 *vt* **DRILL INTO GROUND** to drill a well, tunnel, or shaft in the ground 7 *vt* **DRIVE INTO GROUND** to force something into the ground ○ *We need to sink more piles.* 8 *vti* **PENETRATE OR MAKE PENETRATE** to penetrate something, or cause something to penetrate something 9 *vi* **BE ABSORBED** to become absorbed in something 10 *vi* **BECOME QUIETER** to sound quieter or weaker ○ *voice sank to a whisper* 11 *vi* **SUBSIDE** to diminish in degree, volume, or strength 12 *vi* **DECLINE PHYSICALLY** to deteriorate physically, usually because of fatigue, injury, or ill health ○ *There's a danger he'll sink into a coma.* 13 *vi* **FEEL DISCOURAGEMENT** to pass gradually into a condition of hopelessness, dejection, or despair 14 *vi* **LOSE SOCIAL STATUS** to gradually pass from a higher to a lower social status or position 15 *vt* **INVEST IN SOME-**

THING to invest or lose money in a business or project ○ *He must have sunk millions into these theatres.* **16** *vi* **DECLINE IN VALUE** to decline in value or amount ○ *The pound sank again yesterday.* **17** *vt* **BRING TO RUIN** to defeat, undo, or ruin somebody or something ○ *If they won't accept our offer, we're sunk.* **18** *vt* **DEFEAT IN CONTEST** to defeat an opponent easily in a game or contest (*informal*) **19** *vt* **SHOOT OR HIT SUCCESSFULLY** to take aim at something and make a successful shot or stroke (*informal*) ○ *sink a critical putt* ■ *n* **1 BASIN FOR WASHING** a basin that is fixed or mounted against a wall, and has a piped water supply and drainage ○ *Just put the pans in the sink.* **2 CESSPOOL** a cesspool, drain, or sewer **3 BAD OR CORRUPT PLACE** a place considered to be wicked and corrupt (*archaic*) **4 POORLY DRAINED LAND** an area of low-lying, poorly drained land in which water collects, sometimes in the form of a salt lake, and evaporates or sinks into the ground **5** GEOG = **sinkhole** *n.* 1 **6 DEVICE ABSORBING ENERGY** a device or component of a system at which a physical entity such as energy or neutrons is absorbed **7 MINE SHAFT** a shaft in a mine [Old English *sincan*] —**sinkable** *adj* ◇ **sink or swim** to have no alternative but to succeed or fail without help from anyone else

SPELLCHECK Do not confuse ***sink*** with ***sync***, which has a similar sound. Beware: your spellchecker will not catch this error.

USAGE sank, sunk, or **sunken**? The inflections of the verb ***sink*** have been variable over many centuries of use. In current usage, the preferred past tense is ***sank***, although ***sunk*** is also used and is not incorrect. For the past participle, ***sunk*** is used (*Six enemy ships were sunk on a single day*); ***sunken*** is now used only as an adjective: *a sunken garden.*

sink in *vi* to become fully understood ○ *I don't think the news of her death has sunk in yet.*

sinkage /síngkij/ *n* the process of sinking or the extent to which something sinks

sinker /síngkər/ *n* **1 WEIGHT USED IN FISHING** a weight used to take a fishing line or net to the bottom **2** *US* **DOUGHNUT** a doughnut (*informal*) **3 DOWNWARD CURVING BASEBALL THROW** in baseball, a pitched ball that curves sharply downward as it reaches the plate

sinkhole /síngk hōl/ *n* **1** a natural depression in the land surface, especially in limestone, where a stream flows underground into a passage or cave **2** a sunken area where waste collects

sinking fund *n* a fund created by setting aside regular sums for investment, usually in bonds, in order to repay a debt that will fall due at a future date

sinner /sínnər/ *n* somebody who commits a sin or who habitually does wrong

Sinn Féin /shín fáyn/ *n* a nationalist Irish republican party founded in 1905 [Early 20C. < Irish *sinn féin* 'we ourselves'.] —**Sinn Féiner** *n* —**Sinn Féinism** *n*

Sino- China or Chinese ○ *Sino-American* [< late Latin *Sinae* 'the Chinese' < Arabic *Sīn* 'China']

sinoatrial /sīnō áytri əl/ *adj* relating to the sinus venosus and the right atrium of the heart

sinoatrial node *n* a small mass of specialized cardiac muscle fibres in the wall of the right atrium of the heart which originates the regular electrical impulses that stimulate the heartbeat

Sinology /sī nólləji, si-/ *n* the study of Chinese civilization, literature, and language —**Sinological** /sīnə lójjik'l, sínnə-/ *adj* —**Sinologist** *n*

Sinope /si nṓpi/ *n* the outermost known natural satellite of Jupiter, discovered in 1914

Sino-Tibetan /sínoti bétt'n/ *n* a family of languages of East and Southeast Asia, including two main branches, Chinese (**Sinitic**) and Tibeto-Burman. Native speakers: 1,200 million. —**Sino-Tibetan** *adj*

sinsemilla /sínssə méelyə, -míllə/ *n* a very strong form of marijuana obtained from unpollinated female hemp plants [Late 20C. < American Spanish, 'seedless'.]

sin tax *n* a tax on something that is considered to have harmful personal and social effects, such as tobacco, alcoholic beverages, or gambling

sinter /síntər/ *vti* **BOND METAL PARTICLES** to use pressure and heat below the melting point to bond and partly fuse masses of metal particles, or to be bonded in this way ■ *n* **1 BONDED METAL PARTICLES** a mass of metal particles bonded and partly fused by the use of pressure and heat below the melting point **2 POROUS MINERAL SEDIMENT** a whitish chemical sediment consisting of porous silica or calcium carbonate deposited by a mineral spring [Late 18C. < German, 'cinder'.]

Sintra /síntrə/ resort town in W Portugal. Population: 20,000 (1981).

Sintu /sín too/ *n* **1** = **Bantu** *n.* 1 **2** *S Africa* the Bantu group of languages [Mid-20C. < Bantu *(i)si-* 'language, culture' + *-ntu* 'person'.] —**Sintu** *adj*

sinuate /sínnyoo ət, -ayt/ *adj* **sinuate, sinuated** describes a leaf with a wavy indented edge ■ *vi* (**-ates, -ating, -ated**) to wind in and out [Late 16C. < Latin *sinuare* 'to bend, curve' < *sinus* 'curve'.] —**sinuately** *adv* —**sinuation** /sínnyoo áysh'n/ *n*

sinuosity /sínnyoo óssəti/ (*plural* **-ties**) *n* **1** the condition of being winding or curving in shape or movement **2** a winding bend or curving movement

sinuous /sínnyoo əss/ *adj* **1 MOVING IN GRACEFUL CURVES** with graceful winding or curving movements ○ *the sinuous movements of the dancer's arm* **2 WINDING OR SERPENTINE** full of bends and curves ○ *the sinuous course of a hill stream* **3 DEVIOUS** indirect and devious **4** PLANT SCI = **sinuate** *adj.* [Late 16C. < Latin *sinuosus* < *sinus* 'curve'.] —**sinuously** *adv* —**sinuousness** *n*

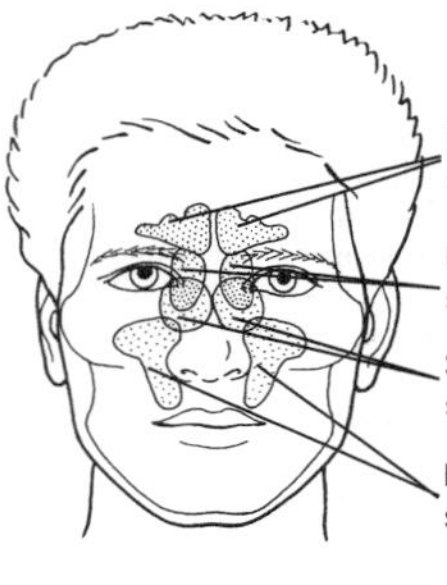

Sinus

sinus /sīnəss/ *n* **1 CAVITY IN BONE OF SKULL** a cavity filled with air in the bones of the face and skull, especially one opening into the nasal passages **2 CHANNEL FOR BLOOD** a widened channel containing blood, especially venous blood **3 CHANNEL LEADING FROM BODY CAVITY** an elongated tract leading from a pus-filled region of the body to the exterior or to the cavity of a hollow organ **4 NOTCH BETWEEN LEAVES** a cleft or indentation between the lobes of a leaf or the fused petals of a corolla [15C. < Latin, 'curve, fold, hollow'.]

Sinus Iridum /sīnəss írridəm/ *n* a large half-crater on the Moon adjoining the northwest side of Mare Imbrium. Its walled perimeter forms the Montes Jura and it is approximately 260 km/160 mi. in diameter.

sinusitis /sīnə sítiss/ *n* inflammation of the membrane lining a sinus of the skull

sinus node *n* ANAT = **sinoatrial node**

sinusoid /sīnə soyd/ *n* **1** a small blood vessel or cavity in the tissue of an organ such as the liver, heart, or pancreas **2** MATH = **sine curve** ■ *adj* resembling a sinus in shape or function —**sinusoidal** /sīnə sóyd'l/ *adj* —**sinusoidally** *adv*

sinusoidal projection *n* a map projection on which equal areas appear equal, the parallels of latitude are regularly spaced straight lines, and all the lines of longitude except the prime meridian are curved

sinus venosus /-vee nṓssəss/ (*plural* **sinus venosi** /-sī/) *n* an enlarged pouch attached to the heart of fish, amphibians, and reptiles through which blood from the veins is forced into the atrium [< modern Latin, 'veined sinus']

Siouan /sṓo ən/ *n* **1** a family of Native North American languages that includes Dakota, Omaha, and Choctaw. Native speakers: 30,000. **2** a speaker of a Siouan language —**Siouan** *adj*

Sioux /soo/ (*plural* **Sioux**) *n* a member of a group of Native North American peoples who lived throughout the Great Plains, and now live mainly in North and South Dakota [Early 18C. < North American French, shortening of *Nadouessioux* < Ojibwa (Ottawa dialect) *nātowēssiwak*.] —**Sioux** *adj*

Sioux City /sṓo-/ city in W Iowa. Population: 82,697 (1998 estimate).

Sioux Falls city in SE South Dakota. Population: 116,762 (1998 estimate).

sip /sip/ *vti* (**sips, sipping, sipped**) to drink something slowly, taking only a small amount at a time ■ *n* a very small amount of liquid taken into the mouth ○ *a few sips of champagne* [14C. Probably variant of SUP[1].] —**sipper** *n*

sipe /sīp/ *n* a groove in the tread of a vehicle tyre [Mid-20C. < ?]

siphon /sīf'n/, **syphon** *v* **1** *vt* **DRAW LIQUID THROUGH TUBE** to transfer liquid from one container to another through a tube using atmospheric pressure to make it flow ○ *Why not siphon some petrol from the tank?* **2** *vti* **ILLEGALLY TAP FUNDS OR RESOURCES** to convey or draw money or resources from something, especially illegally ○ *It looks as though they were siphoning money from the pension fund.* ■ *n* **1 BENT TUBE FOR DRAWING OFF LIQUID** a bent tube or pipe used to transfer liquid from one container to another using atmospheric pressure to make it flow **2** = **soda siphon** **3 TUBULAR ORGAN** a tubular organ, especially of arthropods and molluscs, by which water is taken in or expelled [14C. Via Latin *siphon-* < Greek *siphōn* 'pipe, tube'.] —**siphonage** *n* —**siphonal** /sīfənəl/ *adj* —**siphonic** /sī fónnik/ *adj*

siphon bottle *n US* = **soda siphon**

siphonophore /sīfənə fawr, sī fónnə-/ *n* a marine hydrozoan such as the Portuguese man-of-war that forms floating or swimming transparent or lightly-coloured colonies. Order: Siphonophora. —**siphonophorous** /sīfə nóffərəss/ *adj*

siphuncle /sī fungk'l/ *n* a cord of tissue that secretes gas into the buoyancy chambers of the external shell of a nautilus or similar mollusc [Early 19C. < Latin *siphunculus* 'small tube' < *siphon-* (see SIPHON).] —**siphuncular** /sī fúngkyŏŏlər/ *adj* —**siphunculate** /sī fúngkyŏŏlət/ *adj*

sipunculid /sī púngkyə lid/ *n* a burrowing or crevice-dwelling marine worm that gathers food particles using tentacles surrounding its mouth and can retract its front end into its trunk. Phylum: Sipuncula. [Late 19C. < modern Latin *Sipunculidae* < Latin *sipunculus*, variant of *siphunculus* (see SIPHUNCLE).]

sir (*stressed*) /sur/; (*unstressed*) /sər/ *n* **1** a form of address to a man often used in speech as a sign of respect or as a salutation in a letter ○ *Excuse me, sir, do you know what time it is?* **2** a form of address or way of referring to a male teacher, mainly used by his students ○ *Let's ask sir if we can leave early.* [13C. Variant of SIRE.]

Sir *n* a title of honour used before the name of a knight or baronet ○ *Have you met Sir Robin?*

Siraj-ud-Daula /sí raaj ŏŏd dówlə/ (1729?–57) Bengali ruler. Born **Mirza Muhammad**

sirdar /súr daar/ *n* **1 HIGH-RANKING LEADER** in India or Pakistan, a political or military leader of high rank **2 FORMER BRITISH COMMANDER OF EGYPTIAN ARMY** formerly, the title given to the British commander of the Egyptian army **3 TITLE FOR SIKH MAN** a title of respect for a Sikh man [Early 17C. Via Hindi *sardār* < Persian, 'head holder'.]

sire /sīr/ *n* **1 sire, Sire ADDRESS TO KING OR LORD** a respectful form of address for a king or lord (*archaic*) ○ *We are honoured by your presence, Sire.* **2 MALE PARENT OF FOUR-LEGGED ANIMAL** the male parent of a four-legged animal, especially a domesticated animal such as a stallion or bull ■ *vt* (**sires, siring, sired**) **FATHER OFFSPRING** to father young, especially animals ○ *A filly sired by the great Man o' War.* [12C. Via Old French < Latin *senior* (see SENIOR).]

siren /sīrən/ *n* **1 STATIONARY WARNING DEVICE** a warning device that produces a loud wailing sound when a current of compressed air or steam is forced through a rotating perforated disk ○ *The siren sounded the all clear.* **2 PORTABLE WARNING DEVICE** an electronic warning device, often mounted or placed on a moving vehicle, that produces a loud wailing sound **3 SEA NYMPH LURING SAILORS ONTO ROCKS** a sea nymph, half-woman half-bird, who was believed to sing beguilingly to passing sailors in order to lure them to their doom on the rocks she sat on **4 OFFENSIVE TERM** an offensive term for a woman who is considered to be desirable in a dangerous way **5 SALAMANDER RESEMBLING EEL** a salamander with a long thin body and tail, permanent external gills, lungs, small forelegs, and no hind limbs. Family: Sirenidae. [14C. Via Old French *sereine* 'sea nymph' and Latin *Siren* < Greek *Seirēn*.]

siren call *n* = **siren song**

sirenian /sī réeni ən/ *n* an aquatic herbivorous placental mammal that has forelimbs like paddles, no hind limbs, and a broad flat tail. Order: Sirenia. [Late 19C. < modern Latin *Sirenia* < Latin *Siren* (see SIREN).] —**sirenian** *adj*

siren song *n* an alluring appeal that something possesses, even though it may have unfortunate effects ○ *She yielded to the siren song of a higher salary.*

siren suit *n* a long-sleeved one-piece garment that covers the whole body [< its original use as an air-raid shelter garment]

Sirius /sírri əss/ *n* a binary star in the constellation Canis Major, the brightest star in the sky

sirloin /súr loyn/ *n* an expensive prime cut of beef used for roasting or steaks, taken from the lower part of the ribs or the upper loin [15C. < an Old French word meaning 'above the loin'.]

sirocco /si rókō/ (*plural* **-cos**), **scirocco** (*plural* **-cos**) *n* a hot dusty humid southeast wind in S Europe that begins in the Sahara and picks up moisture as it crosses the Mediterranean [Early 17C. Via French < Italian *scirocco* < Arabic *sharūq* 'east'.]

sirrah /sírrə/ *n* a form of address for a man or boy that was used to express contempt (*archaic*) [Early 16C. Alteration of SIRE.]

sirree /sur rée, sə rée/ [Early 19C. Alteration of SIR.] ◇ **yes** *or* **no sirree** *US* used to emphasize agreement *or* disagreement (*informal*)

Sir Roger de Coverley /-rójjər də kúvvərli/ *n* an English country dance performed to a traditional tune by two rows of dancers facing each other [Alteration of earlier *Roger of Coverley*, probably < *Roger*, the personal name + *Coverley*, a fictitious place name]

sis /siss/ *n* a form of address for a sister (*informal*) [Mid-17C. Shortening.]

sisal /sīss'l, síz'l/, **sisal hemp** *n* **1** a strong white fibre obtained from the leaves of an agave plant. Use: rope, rugs. ◊ **henequen 2** an agave plant that produces sisal. Native to: Mexico. *Agave sisalana*. [Mid-19C. After *Sisal*, a town in the Yucatán.]

siskin /sískin/ *n* a yellow-and-black finch related to the goldfinch. Native to: Europe, Asia, North Africa. *Carduelis spinus*. [Mid-16C. < Middle Dutch *siseken* and early Flemish *sijsken* 'little siskin'.]

Sisley /sízzli, síssli/, **Alfred** (1839–99) French painter

~~**sissors**~~ incorrect spelling of **scissors**

sissy /síssi/, **cissy** *n* (*plural* **-sies**) an offensive term for a boy or man who is considered not to exhibit stereotypical masculine behaviour, especially by other boys or men (*informal offensive insult*) ■ *adj* an offensive term referring to a boy, man, behaviour, or object that is considered not to exhibit or be characteristic of stereotypical masculinity (*informal*) [Mid-19C. < SIS.] —**sissyish** *adj* —**sissiness** *n*

sister /sístər/ *n* **1 FEMALE SIBLING** a girl or woman who has the same parents as another person **2 STEPSISTER OR HALF-SISTER** a girl or woman who has one parent in common with another person **3 NUN** a female member of a religious community, or a form of address to such a person ○ *Sister Brigit joined us a few weeks ago.* **4 WOMAN SENIOR NURSE** a woman who holds the most senior grade of hospital nurse, above staff nurse, often in charge of a ward. ◊ **charge nurse 5 WOMAN MEMBER OF SAME ORGANIZATION** a woman who belongs to the same organization as another **6 WOMAN SUPPORTER OF FEMINISM** a woman who advocates or supports feminist principles **7 AFRICAN AMERICAN WOMAN** a form of address or way of referring to an African American woman, used especially by other African Americans **8 CLOSE WOMAN FRIEND** a close woman friend, especially of another woman ■ *adj* **1 CLOSELY LINKED** belonging to or closely associated with something ○ *links with sister organizations in Europe* **2 WITH PAIRED CELL** describes either of an identical pair of cells or cell components formed by division of a parent cell or component [Old English *sweostor* < Indo-European]

LITERARY LINK ***The Three Sisters***, a play (1900) by the Russian dramatist Anton Chekhov. Set in rural Russia, this powerful and compassionate study of the quiet desperation of bourgeois life centres on the three Pozarov sisters. Stifled by the dreariness of local society, they look to the officers of the local garrison for romance and entertainment. But when the army departs, the sisters are left with only their dreams and each other.

sisterhood /sístər hŏŏd/ *n* **1 SOLIDARITY AMONG WOMEN** the empathy and loyalty that women feel for other women who have shared goals, experiences, or viewpoints **2 WOMEN'S GROUP** a group of women who have shared goals, experiences, or viewpoints (*takes a singular or plural verb*) **3 STATUS AS SISTER** the status of a sister or the relationship of sisters **4 COMMUNITY OF NUNS** a religious community of women

sister-in-law (*plural* **sisters-in-law**) *n* **1** the sister of somebody's husband or wife **2** the wife of somebody's brother

sisterly /sístərli/ *adj, adv* relating to, coming from, or characteristic of a sister, especially in an affectionate, kind, or caring way —**sisterliness** *n*

Sistine /sís teen, -tīn/ *adj* **1** relating to any of the popes named Sixtus, especially Sixtus IV who was pope 1471–84 **2** relating to the Sistine Chapel [Late 18C. < Italian *Sistino* 'of Sixtus'.]

sistrum /sístrəm/ (*plural* **-tra** /-trə/) *n* an ancient Egyptian percussion instrument consisting of a thin metal frame with rods or loops attached that jingle when shaken [14C. Via Latin < Greek *seistron* < *seiein* 'shake'.]

Sisulu /si sŏŏ loo/, **Walter** (*b.* 1912) South African political activist

siSwati /si swaáti/, **Siswati** *n S Africa* LANG = **Swazi** *n.* **2** —**siSwati** *adj*

Sisyphean /síssi fée ən/ *adj* involving endless but futile labour [Late 16C. < Latin *Sisypheius* < Greek *Sisuphos* (see SISYPHUS).]

Sisyphus /síssifəss/ *n* in Greek mythology, a cruel king of Corinth who was condemned for eternity to roll a boulder up a hill only to have it roll down again just before it reached the top

sit /sit/ *v* (**sits, sitting, sat, sat** /sat/) **1** *vi* **REST WITH WEIGHT ON BUTTOCKS** to assume a position of rest in which the weight is largely supported by the buttocks, usually with the body vertical and the thighs horizontal ○ *Where would you like to sit?* **2** *vt* **PLACE IN SEAT** to place somebody or yourself in a seat or a sitting position ○ *They sat us down to hear the whole story.* **3** *vi* **REST BODY ON HINDQUARTERS** to rest the body with the weight supported by the lowered hindquarters (*refers to four-legged animals*) ○ *The hound sat in the corner, looking strangely thoughtful* **4** *vi* **PERCH, ROOST, OR COVER EGGS** to perch, roost, or cover and warm eggs for hatching ○ *A falcon sat on the telephone wire, staring down at us.* **5** *vi* **EXERCISE AUTHORITY** to occupy a position of authority while deciding or legislating something ○ *The legislature sat through the night.* **6** *vi* **POSE FOR** to pose for a portrait or picture ○ *He sat for the country's best-known photographer.* **7** *vti* **TAKE EXAM** to take an examination for something ○ *She sat her finals last week.* **8** *vi* **BE IDLE** to be or remain idle ○ *They just sit around and do nothing.* **9** *vi* **BE PLACED OR SITUATED** to be located or positioned somewhere ○ *The dinner dishes were still sitting on the table.* **10** *vi* **FIT OR HANG** to fit or hang on somebody in a specified way ○ *The gown sat beautifully on the model.* **11** *vi* **BE IN SPECIFIED WAY** to rest, weigh, or lie as specified ○ *Authority sits lightly on his shoulders.* **12** *vi* **BE TAKEN AS SPECIFIED** to be accepted or considered in the way specified ○ *The news didn't sit well with me.* **13** *vi* **BABY-SIT** to baby-sit (*informal*) **14** *vt* **HAVE SEATING SPACE FOR** to have seats or seating space for a specified number of people ○ *We can sit 10 around the dining table.* **15** *vi* **BE DIGESTIBLE** to be digestible (*informal*) **16** *vt* **BE ASTRIDE** to keep astride of a horse or similar animal ○ *She sat her gelding with great poise.* ■ *n* **1 TIME SPENT BEING SEATED** a period of being seated, especially while waiting ○ *We had a long sit waiting for the dentist.* **2 WAY GARMENT FITS** the way a garment hangs on somebody **3 MOUNTED POSITION** a position astride a horse or similar animal [Old English *sittan* < Indo-European] ◇ **sit tight** refrain from moving or acting until the right time (*informal*) ◇ **sitting pretty** in a good or favourable position (*informal*)

sit back *vi* to take no action ○ *sat back and watched the crisis develop*

sit down *vti* to become seated, or make somebody become seated ○ *time to sit him down and tell him the truth*

sit in *vi* **1 ATTEND WITHOUT TAKING PART** to attend something but not take an active part in it ○ *Do you mind if I sit in on your meeting?* **2 TEMPORARILY REPLACE** to do a job for the person who normally does it ○ *sitting in for the regular announcer on the show* **3 OCCUPY BUILDING AS PROTEST** to take part in a sit-in

sit on *vt* **1** to be a member of a group that decides something **2** to suppress something or delay dealing with it ○ *The government sat on the information for weeks.*

sit out *v* **1** *vt* **STAY UNTIL END OF** to remain until the end of something, especially something unpleasant **2** *vt* **NOT PARTICIPATE IN** to remain seated during something and not join in ○ *I think I'll sit this one out.* **3** *vi* to lean backwards over the side of a sailing boat to counterbalance the wind in the sails and keep the boat flat in the water

sit up *vi* **1 SIT STRAIGHT** to sit upright or rise from lying down **2 STAY UP LATE** to stay up past the usual time of going to bed **3 BECOME ALERT** to become alert or interested

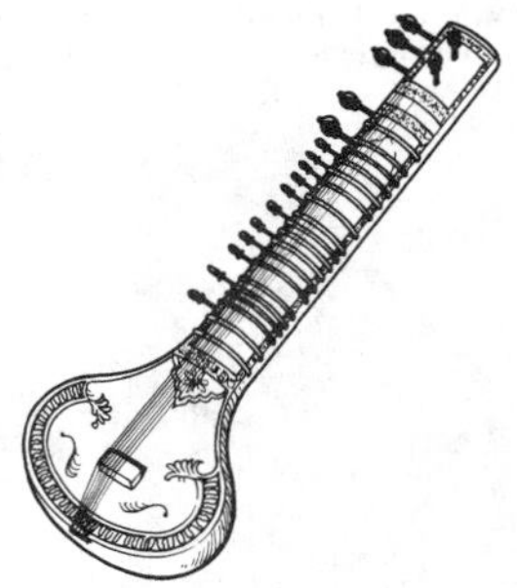

Sitar

sitar /si taár, síttaar/ *n* an Indian stringed instrument with a rounded resonating body and a long fretted neck [Mid-19C. Via Hindi < Persian, 'three-stringed'.] —**sitarist** *n*

sitcom /sít kom/ *n* a situation comedy (*informal*) [Mid-20C. Shortening.]

⚡**SITD** *abbr* still in the dark (*in e-mails*)

sit-down *n* **1** a short spell of sitting in order to relax (*informal*) ○ *After all that shopping I could do with a sit-down.* **2** POL = **sit-down strike 3** POL = **sit-in** ■ *adj* served to people sitting at a table ○ *There's a sit-down dinner before the dancing.*

sit-down strike *n* a form of protest in which people refuse to leave a place, often sitting or lying down, until their demands are granted or negotiated

⚡**site** /sīt/ *n* **1 PLACE WHERE SOMETHING STANDS** an area or piece of land where something was, is, or will be located ○ *The whole area has become one vast building site.* **2 PLACE OF SIGNIFICANT EVENT** a place where something important happened ○ *The field was the site of a terrible massacre.* **3** ONLINE = **website** ■ *vt* (**sites, siting, sited**) **POSITION** to locate something in a particular place or position ○ *The heavy artillery had been sited in the hills.* [14C. Via Anglo-Norman < Latin *situs* 'place, position' < *sinere* 'put'.]

USAGE See ***cite***.

site-specific *adj* designed, built, or intended for one particular site

Sithole /si tóli/, **Ndabaningi** (*b.* 1920) Zimbabwean clergyman and politician

sit-in *n* a form of protest in which people occupy a building or public place and refuse to leave until their demands have been met or negotiated

sitkamer /sít kaamər/ *n S Africa* a living room [Early 20C. < Afrikaans, 'sitting room'.]

sitka spruce /sítkə-/ *n* a spruce tree with reddish-brown bark and silvery-white needles, widely planted for timber. Native to: NW coast of North America. *Picea sitchensis*. [Late 19C. After Sitka, a town in Alaska.]

sitology /sī tólləji/ *n* the scientific study of food, diet, and nutrition as they relate to health [Mid-19C. < Greek *sitos* 'food, grain'.]

sit spin *n* a spin on one ice skate made in a squatting position with one leg stretched out in front of the body

sitter /síttər/ *n* **1 HIRED MINDER** somebody hired to look after something (*often in combination*) **2** = **babysitter 3 SOMEBODY HIRED TO WATCH PATIENTS** somebody hired to watch over patients in order to respond to urgent needs or to prevent them from harming themselves accidentally **4 ARTIST'S OR PHOTOGRAPHER'S MODEL** a poser for a portrait **5 BROODY HEN** a hen or other bird sitting on eggs to hatch them **6 EXTREMELY EASY TASK** something that is very easy to accomplish, e.g. an effortless catch in cricket (*informal*)

sitting /sítting/ *n* **1 TURN TO EAT** a period when a meal is served in a place where there is insufficient room for everyone to eat at the same time ○ *The first sitting is at 12 o'clock.* **2 TIME FOR POSING** a period of time during which somebody is posing for a portrait ○ *I'd like to get another sitting in this afternoon.* **3 SESSION OF PUBLIC BODY** a meeting or session of an official body such as a legislature or court **4 PERIOD OF BEING SEATED** a period of being seated while engaged in an activity ○ *It took him three sittings to read the book.* **5 SET OF EGGS** a clutch of eggs under a brooding bird **6 INCUBATION OF EGGS** the period of time during which a hen sits on eggs to hatch them ■ *adj* **1 SEATED** seated or for being seated ○ *a sitting area* **2 IN OFFICE** holding office at the present time ○ *the sitting MP for Southgate*

Sitting Bull

Sitting Bull /sítting bool/ (1831?–90) Sioux leader

sitting duck *n* somebody or something that is defenceless, exposed to danger, and easy to attack or exploit (*informal*) ○ *The company's competitors regarded it as a sitting duck for a takeover.*

sitting room *n* a room in a house or flat used for relaxing or entertaining guests in comfortable seats. ◊ **living room**

sitting target *n* = **sitting duck**

sitting tenant *n* a tenant who has a legal right to continue living in a property when it changes ownership

sitting trot *n* a slow trot during which the rider does not rise from the horse's saddle. ◊ **rising trot**

situate /síttyoo ayt/ *vt* to place something in a context or set of circumstances and show its connections ○ *I shall endeavour to situate these ideas in the early Gnostic tradition.* [15C. < late Latin *situare* 'to place' < Latin *situs* (see SITE).]

situated /síttyoo aytid/ *adj* (*often in combination*) **1** located in a place or position ○ *The hotel is situated within the medieval walls of the old town.* ○ *a conveniently situated building* **2** in a specified financial condition ○ *comfortably situated, living off their investments*

situation /síttyoo áysh'n/ *n* **1 EXISTING CONDITIONS** the general conditions that prevail in a place or society ○ *the current political situation in Ireland* **2 CIRCUMSTANCES OF SOMEBODY'S LIFE** the circumstances that somebody is in at a particular moment ○ *In your situation I'd sell my car.* **3 LOCATION** the location of a property ○ *The property is in an idyllic situation on the southern slope of a hill.* **4** US **COMBINATION OF DIFFICULT CIRCUMSTANCES** a difficult or problematic set of circumstances **5 JOB** a job or position of employment (*formal*) **6 SET OF CIRCUMSTANCES IN PLOT** a significant combination of circumstances in a drama, film, or work of literature —**situational** *adj*

situation comedy *n* a television or radio comedy series in which a regular cast of characters, usually working or living together, respond to everyday situations in a humorous way

situation ethics *n* a system of ethics in which moral judgments are thought to depend on the context in which they are to be made, rather than on general moral principles (+ *singular verb*)

sit-up *n* an exercise in which you lie flat on your back with your legs bent and then raise the upper part of your body to a sitting position without using your hands

situs /sítass/ (*plural* **-tus**) *n* the position of an organ or part of the body, especially the normal position [Early 18C. < Latin (see SITE).]

situs inversus /-in vúrtass/ *n* an uncommon reversal of organs in the body in which the apex of the heart points to the right and the liver and appendix are on the left side [< Latin, shortening of *situs inversus viscerum* 'inverted position of the internal organs']

Sitwell /sít wel, síttwal/, **Dame Edith** (1887–1964) British writer

Sitwell, Sir Osbert (1892–1969) British writer

Sitwell, Sir Sacheverell (1897–1988) British writer

sitz bath /síts-/ *n* **1** a bath shaped like a chair in which the bather sits immersed up to the waist in water, to which salts may be added for therapeutic purposes **2** an act of immersion in a sitz bath, especially for therapeutic purposes [Partial translation of German *Sitzbad* 'sitting bath']

sitzkrieg /síts kreeg/ *n* a period in a war during which there is little offensive activity or change in the positions of the combatants [Mid-20C. < German *sitzen* 'sit' after BLITZKRIEG.]

sitzmark /síts maark/ *n* a depression in the snow made by a skier who has fallen backwards [Mid-20C. Partial translation of German *Sitzmarke* 'sitting mark'.]

SI UNITS WITH SPECIAL DESIGNATIONS

Name of unit	Symbol	Physical quality
becquerel	Bq	Radioactivity
coulomb	C	Electric charge
degree Celsius	°C	Temperature
farad	F	Capacitance
gray	Gy	Absorbed dose of radiation
henry	H	Inductance
hertz	Hz	Frequency
joule	J	Energy
lumen	lm	Luminous flux
lux	lx	Illuminance
newton	N	Force
ohm	Ω	Electrical resistance
pascal	Pa	Pressure
siemens	S	Electrical conductance
sievert	Sv	Dose equivalent (biological effect of radiation)
tesla	T	Magnetic flux density
volt	V	Electric potential
watt	W	Power
weber	Wb	Magnetic flux

SI unit *n* a unit adopted for international use under the Système International d'Unités in science and technology

Siva *n* RELIG = **Shiva**

Sivan /sívv'n, see vaán/ *n* in the Jewish calendar, the ninth month of the civil year and the third month of the religious year [14C. < Hebrew *sīwān*.]

six /siks/ *n* **1** see table at **number 2** a division of a Cub Scout pack or Brownie Guide troop **3** a stroke in cricket that clears the boundary without bouncing, or the six runs scored by this stroke [Old English *si(e)x* < Indo-

European] —**six** *adj, pron* ◊ **at sixes and sevens 1** disorganized or in disarray (*informal*) **2** in disagreement (*informal*) ◊ **knock** *or* **hit somebody for six** to surprise somebody completely (*informal*) ◊ **six of one and half-a-dozen of the other** used when there is not much difference between two choices

sixain /síks ayn/ *n* a six-line stanza in poetry [Late 16C. French, < *six* 'six'.]

Six-Day War *n* a war between Israel and the states of Egypt, Jordan, and Syria that lasted six days in June 1967

sixer /síksar/ *n* a Cub Scout or Brownie who leads one of the divisions of the pack [Early 20C. < the six members of the division.]

sixfold /síks fōld/ *adj* **1 SIX TIMES GREATER** with six times as much or as many ○ *a sixfold increase in absenteeism* **2 WITH SIX PARTS** with six parts or elements ■ *adv* **MULTIPLIED BY SIX** by six times as much or as many ○ *The number of teenagers who enrolled increased sixfold.*

six-footer *n* a person who is six feet tall or taller (*informal*)

six-gun *n* US ARMS = **six-shooter**

Six Nations *n* a confederacy of six Iroquois peoples, the Cayuga, Mohawk, Oneida, Onondaga, Seneca, and Tuscarora, that was formed in 1722. ◊ **Five Nations**

six o'clock swill *n* Aus the period of heavy drinking that used to occur just before closing time in the days when public houses had to close at 6 pm (*informal dated*)

six-pack *n* **1** six cans or bottles, usually of beer, sold together in a pack **2** a well-developed block of abdominal muscles (*informal*)

sixpence /síkspanss/ *n* a small silver-coloured coin used in Britain between 1550 and 1980, worth 6 old pennies or 2.5 new pence

sixpenny nail /síkspani-/ *n* a nail that is 5 cm/2 in long [< the original price of a hundred such nails.]

six-shooter *n* a handgun whose bullets are loaded into a revolving cylinder containing six chambers (*informal*)

sixte /síkst/ *n* the sixth of the eight basic defensive positions in fencing [Late 19C. < French, 'sixth'.]

sixteen /síks téen/ *n* see table at **number** [Old English *si(e)xtiene* 'ten more than six' < -tiene 'ten more than'] —**sixteen** *adj, pron*

sixteenmo /síks téen mō/ (*plural* **-mos**) *n* PRINTING = **sextodecimo** [Mid-19C. English reading of the symbol *16mo*.]

sixteenth /síks téenth/ *n* see table at **number** —**sixteenth** *adj, adv*

sixteenth note *n* US, Can MUSIC = **semiquaver**

sixth /síksth/ *n* **1** see table at **number 2 INTERVAL OF SIX NOTES** in a standard musical scale, the interval between one note and another that lies five notes above or below it **3 NOTE A SIXTH AWAY FROM ANOTHER** in a standard musical scale, a note that is a sixth away from another note **4 HARMONY OF A SIXTH** the harmony created by playing two notes a sixth apart **5 ONE NOTE IN A SIXTH** one of the two notes in a sixth —**sixth** *adj, adv*

sixth chord *n* a musical chord made up of a note plus a note a third above and a note a sixth above

sixth form *n* the final optional stage of school education for students in England and Wales aged 16 to 18 in which they study for and sit A-level examinations (*hyphenated before nouns*) —**sixth-former** *n*

sixth-form college *n* a college for students in England and Wales between the ages of 16 and 18 that offers A-level courses

sixth sense *n* a supposed special ability to perceive something not using any of the five senses of sight, hearing, touch, smell, and taste

sixth year *n* Scotland the final optional year in Scottish secondary schools during which students can study for Highers and sixth-year studies (*hyphenated before nouns*) **2** a student in the sixth year

sixth-year studies *npl* Scotland a one-year course of study taken in the final year at Scottish secondary schools after the completion of Highers

sixtieth /síksti əth/ *n* see table at **number** —**sixtieth** *adj, adv*

Sixtus V /síkstass/ (1521–90) pope (1585–90)

sixty /síksti/ (*plural* **-ties**) see table at **number** ■ **sixties** *npl* **1** the numbers 60 to 69, particularly as a range of Fahrenheit temperatures ○ *in the low sixties* **2** the years from 60 to 69 in a century or somebody's life [Old English *sixtig*] —**sixty** *adj, pron*

⚡**64 bit key** *n* the industry standard encryption key length for e-commerce transactions (*in e-commerce*)

sixty-fourmo /-fáwrmō/ (*plural* **sixty-fourmos**) *n* **1** a book or paper size that results from a sheet of paper being folded 64 times **2** paper or a book that is sixty-fourmo in size [English reading of the symbol *64mo*]

sixty-fourth note *n US* MUSIC = **hemidemisemiquaver**

sixty-nine *n* an offensive term for a sexual activity in which two people simultaneously stimulate each other's genitals orally (*slang*) [< the position of the couple]

six-yard box *n* a rectangle of lines on the pitch in front of the goal in association football. It extends six yards from the goal line and goal kicks are taken within it.

sizable /sízəb'l/, **sizeable** *adj* fairly large —**sizableness** *n* —**sizably** *adv*

sizar /sízər/ *n* an undergraduate student at some universities who receives a grant for expenses from a college [Late 16C. < SIZE[1] in the obsolete sense 'quantity of bread or ale'.] —**sizarship** *n*

size[1] /sīz/ *n* **1** HOW MUCH SOMETHING MEASURES the amount, scope, or degree of something, in terms of how large or small it is **2** HOW BIG SOMETHING IS the large quality or extent of a particular thing **3** STANDARD MEASUREMENT OF MANUFACTURED ITEM a set of measurements used when making or classifying articles that are produced and sold, e.g., clothing or shoes ■ *vt* (**sizes, sizing, sized**) **1** SORT ACCORDING TO SIZE to put things into different groups according to their size **2** MAKE TO A PARTICULAR SIZE to cut, shape, or manufacture goods so that they have the necessary or chosen measurements **3** MEASURE to work out or find out the measurements of something [13C. < Old French *sise*, alteration of *assise*, < Latin *assidere* 'sit beside'.] —**sized** *adj* ◇ **cut somebody down to size** to make somebody be less self-important and arrogant ◇ **that's about the size of it** used to indicate that something describes a situation very well (*informal*) ◇ **try something (on) for size 1** to put something on to see whether it fits you or not **2** to find out how much you like something

size up *vt* to assess a person or situation and form a judgment

size[2] /sīz/ *n* a gelatinous mixture made from glue, starch, or varnish. Use: filling pores in the surface of paper, textiles, or plaster. ■ *vt* (**sizes, sizing, sized**) to coat a porous surface such as paper, textile, or plaster with size [15C. < ?]

sizeable /síz əbəl/ *adj* = **sizable**

sizeism /sízizəm/ *n* discrimination against somebody on the basis of the person's size, especially the person's unusual tallness, shortness, fatness or thinness —**sizeist** *adj*

sizing /sízing/ *n* **1** INDUST, ARTS = **size**[2] *n.* **2** the process of coating something with size

sizzle /sízz'l/ *v* (**-zles, -zling, -zled**) **1** *vti* MAKE THE NOISE OF FOOD FRYING to make the hissing and spattering sound typical of frying fat, or to cook food so that it makes a hissing sound **2** *vi* BE FURIOUS to show or feel great anger (*informal*) **3** *vi* BE HOT to be extremely hot (*informal*) **4** *vi* BE PHYSICALLY APPEALING to be physically appealing or very popular (*informal*) ■ *n* HISSING, FRYING NOISE the sound of something frying, or a sound resembling this [Early 17C. An imitation of the sound.]

sizzler /sízzlər/ *n* **1** something that sizzles **2** an extremely hot day (*informal*)

sizzling /sízzling/ *adj* (*informal*) **1** extremely hot **2** physically appealing or very popular —**sizzlingly** *adv*

⚡**sj** *abbr* Svalbard and Jan Mayen Islands (*in Internet addresses*)

SJ *abbr* Society of Jesus

Sjaelland /syélland/ main island of Denmark, on which Copenhagen, the country's capital, is situated. Population: 2,159,260 (1994). Area: 7,000 sq. km/2,700 sq. mi.

sjambok /shám bok/ *n S Africa* a sturdy whip or riding crop made from the hide of a rhinoceros or hippopotamus ■ *vt* (**-boks, -bokking, -bokked**) *S Africa* to whip somebody or something with a sjambok [Late 18C. Via Afrikaans < Malay *chambuk* < Persian *chābuk* 'whip'.]

SJD *abbr* Doctor of Juridical Science [Latin, *Scientiae Juridicae Doctor*]

⚡**sk** *abbr* Slovakia (*in Internet addresses*)

SK *abbr* Saskatchewan

ska /skaa/ *n* dance music in 4/4 time originating in Jamaica in the late 1950s, marked by emphasis on the second and fourth beats [Mid-20C. < ?]

skag *n* DRUGS = **scag** (*slang*)

Skagerrak /skággə rak/ arm of the North Sea between Norway and the Jutland Peninsula, Denmark. Length: 240 km/150 mi.

skald /skawld/, **scald** *n* a medieval Scandinavian poet or travelling minstrel (*archaic or literary*) [Mid-18C. < Old Norse *skáld*.] —**skaldic** *adj*

Skåne /skṓnə/ province of S Sweden. Population: 1,084,755 (1993). Area: 10,984 sq. km/4,241 sq. mi.

skank /skangk/ *vi* to dance to reggae music, especially in a jerky way [Late 20C. < ?]

skanky /skángki/ *adj* disgusting or unpleasant (*slang*) [Late 20C. < ?]

skat /skat/ *n* a card game for three players played with 32 cards and involving bids, contracts, and the taking of tricks [Mid-19C. Via German < Italian *scarto* 'discarded card' < Latin *charta* 'paper' (see CARD[1]).]

skate[1] /skayt/ *n* **1** ICE SKATE an ice skate **2** ROLLER SKATE a roller skate **3** METAL BLADE FOR AN ICE SKATE a steel runner that is fastened to the sole of a boot or shoe to make an ice skate **4** TIME SPENT SKATING a period of time spent skating ■ *vi* (**skates, skating, skated**) **1** MOVE AROUND ON SKATES to glide along a surface wearing ice skates or roller skates **2** SLIDE SMOOTHLY to slide along a slippery surface [Mid-17C. < Dutch *schaats* 'skate, stilt' < Old French *eschasse* 'stilt'.] ◇ **get your skates on** to hurry (*informal*)

skate over *vt* to mention or deal with something in a cursory way (*informal*)

skate[2] /skayt/ (*plural* **skate** *or* **skates**) *n* a bottom-dwelling marine cartilaginous fish with a flattened body, very large flat pectoral fins, two small dorsal fins, a long snout, and short slender tail. Family: Rajidae. [14C. < Old Norse *skata*.]

skateboard /skáyt bawrd/ *n* a short narrow board to which a set of small wheels is fitted on the underside, used to move rapidly or to perform jumps and stunts ■ *vi* to ride on a skateboard —**skateboarder** *n*

skateboarding /skáyt bawrding/ *n* the sport or pastime of riding a skateboard

skatepark /skáyt paark/ *n* an area specially designed and constructed for people practising and performing on skateboards and in-line skates

skater /skáytər/ *n* **1** an ice skater or roller skater **2** INSECTS = **pond-skater**

skating /skáyt ing/ *n* the pastime or sport of sliding on ice skates or rolling on roller skates

skatole /skáttōl/ *n* C_9H_9N an organic crystalline solid having a strong faecal odour. Source: faeces, beetroot, coal tar. Use: perfume fixative. [Late 19C. < Greek *skat-* (see SCATO-).]

skean /skeen/ *n Scotland* a dagger with a double-edged blade formerly used in Scotland and Ireland [Early 16C. Via Gaelic *scian* < Old Irish.]

skean-dhu /skeén dóo/, **sgian-dhu** *n Scotland* a small black-hilted dagger tucked into the top of a man's stocking in Highland dress [< Gaelic, 'black skean']

skedaddle /ski dádd'l/ *vi* (**-dles, -dling, -dled**) to run away quickly (*slang*) ■ *n* a very quick or agitated departure (*slang*) [Mid-19C. < ?] —**skedaddler** *n*

skeet /skeet/, **skeet shooting** *n* a form of clay-pigeon shooting in which clay targets are tossed into the air [Early 20C. Possibly < *skeet*, invented as a supposedly archaic form of SHOOT.]

skeet shooting *n* SPORTS = **skeet**

skeg /skeg/ *n* **1** a part of the keel of a ship, near the stern, that connects the keel with the rudderpost **2** the short stabilizing fin on the rear underside of a surfboard or sailboard [Early 17C. Via Dutch *scheg* < Old Norse *skegg* 'beard, point of a ship's stern'.]

Skegness /skeg néss/ seaside resort in E England. Population: 15,149 (1991).

skein /skayn/ *n* **1** TWISTED BUNDLE OF YARN a length of yarn or thread wound loosely and coiled together **2** GROUP OF GEESE IN FLIGHT a flock of geese flying across the sky in a line **3** TANGLE a tangled or complex mass of material [15C. < Old French *escaigne*.]

skeletal /skéllitəl/ *adj* **1** relating to a skeleton **2** extremely thin or emaciated —**skeletally** *adv*

skeleton /skéllitən/ *n* **1** BONES OF PERSON OR ANIMAL the rigid framework of interconnected bones and cartilage that protects and supports the internal organs and provides attachment for muscles in humans and other vertebrate animals **2** SUPPORTIVE PROTECTIVE STRUCTURE OF INVERTEBRATES something that provides support, gives protection, or maintains shape in an invertebrate animal, such as the shell of a snail or cuticle of a crab **3** BASIC FRAME SOMETHING IS BUILT AROUND a structure that is needed to support and hold something together as an internal framework, onto which the connecting or covering parts are attached **4** SOMETHING WITH ONLY ESSENTIAL PARTS LEFT a plan, organization, or structure that has been reduced so that only its most basic and necessary elements are still functioning or in place **5** OUTLINE OR LAYOUT OF a description that gives the main points but no details of something such as a book or plan **6** SOMEBODY VERY THIN an emaciated person or animal (*informal*) [Late 16C. Via modern Latin < Greek *skeleton (sōma)* 'dried up (body)' < *skellein* 'dry up'.] ◇ **a skeleton in the cupboard** a closely kept secret that is a source of shame or embarrassment

skeletonize /skéllitə nīz/ (**-izes, -izing, -ized**), **skeletonise** (**-ises, -ising, -ised**) *vt* **1** CUT BACK TO ABSOLUTE BASICS to reduce something until only its most basic structure or outline remains **2** CREATE OUTLINE OF SOMETHING to create something in basic outline **3** REDUCE TO A SKELETAL FORM to reduce something to a skeleton

skeleton key *n* a key with the usually serrated part that connects with the lever of a lock (**bit**) filed down so that it can open many different unsophisticated locks [< its basic cut-back shape]

skelf /skelf/ *n N England, Scotland* a thin splinter of wood, especially one that has gone into the skin [14C. Probably < Low German *schelf* (see SHELF).]

skell /skel/ *n US* a homeless or jobless person who lives on the street (*slang*) [Late 20C. < ?]

skelly /skélli/ *adj Scotland* with a squint or crossed eyes [Late 18C. < Old Norse *skjelga* < *skjálgr* 'wry, oblique'.]

Skelmersdale /skélmərz dayl/ town in NW England. Population: 42,104 (1991).

skelp /skelp/ *v N England, Scotland* **1** *vt* SMACK to slap somebody sharply with the hand or with something flat **2** *vi* MOVE AT GREAT SPEED to hustle along quickly and energetically ■ *n N England, Scotland* A SMACK a slap, usually with the hand [14C. Probably an imitation of the sound of a slap.]

skep /skep/ *n* a beehive made of straw or similar material [Pre-12C. < Old Norse *skeppa* 'basket, bushel'.]

skeptic *n* US = **sceptic**

Skeptic *n* US = **Sceptic**

skeptical *adj* US = **sceptical**

skerrick /skérrik/ *n Aus, NZ* a tiny scrap or trace of something (*informal*) [Early 19C. Originally a dialect form < ?]

skerry /skérri/ (*plural* **-ries**) *n Scotland* a rocky islet or reef [Early 17C. Via Scots dialect < Old Norse *sker* 'reef'.]

sketch /skech/ *n* **1** PICTURE DONE QUICKLY AND ROUGHLY a drawing or painting that is done quickly without concern for detail **2** ROUGH DESCRIPTION OR EXPLANATION a short written or spoken account that conveys just a general outline or idea, with little detail **3** SHORT PIECE OF WRITING a short, often descriptive, piece of writing **4** SHORT PERFORMANCE a quick comic routine or piece of acting that is part of a variety show or comedy revue **5** SHORT MUSICAL COMPOSITION a short piece of instrumental music, often for piano ■ *vti* MAKE A SKETCH to create a sketch of something [Mid-17C. Via Dutch *schets* or German *Skizze* < Italian *schizzo* < Vulgar Latin *schediare* 'do hastily' < Latin *schedius* < Greek *skhedios* 'on the spur of the moment'.] —**sketchable** *adj* —**sketcher** *n*

sketchbook /skéch bòòk/, **sketchpad** *n* **1** a book of plain paper for making sketches on **2** a book containing a collection of literary sketches

sketchy /skéchi/ (**-ier, -iest**) *adj* **1** giving only the main points with little detail **2** lacking in substance, clarity, or detail —**sketchily** *adv* —**sketchiness** *n*

skew /skyoo/ *v* **1** *vti* SLANT OR CAUSE TO SLANT to make something uneven, sloping, or unsymmetrical, or to be in this state **2** *vt* MAKE INCORRECT OR DISTORTED to misrepresent the true meaning or nature of something **3** *vi* SQUINT to look sideways at something ■ *adj* **1** IN A SLANTED POSITION OR LINE being in a slanted or unsymmetrical position **2** DISTORTING THE TRUTH giving an unfair or untrue account of something, especially statistics **3 NOT PARALLEL OR INTERSECTING** describes a line that is neither parallel nor intersecting ■ *n* **1 TILTED OR INACCURATE POSITION** a position that is not straight but that slants or twists out of correct alignment **2 SLANTING DIRECTION** a slanting movement, line, or direction [14C. Shortening of Old Northern French *eskiuer*, variant of Old French *eschiver* (see ESCHEW).]

skew arch *n* an arch, e.g. on a bridge or tunnel, with sides that are not at right angles to the span

skewback /skyoō bak/ *n* either of the sloping surfaces on which the sides of a segmental arch abut

skewbald /skyoō bawld/ *adj* describes a horse that has a spotted coat consisting of white and another colour other than black, generally brown ■ *n* a skewbald horse [Mid-17C. < obsolete *skewed* 'having mixed colours', after PIEBALD.]

skewer /skyoō ər/ *n* **1 THIN ROD TO COOK FOOD ON** a thin metal or wooden rod with a sharp end used to hold meat or meat and vegetables during cooking **2 SOMETHING SIMILAR TO SKEWER** a thin pointed object used to pierce something or hold it in place ■ *vt* **PIERCE WITH SKEWER** to pierce somebody or something with a skewer or with something else that is thin and sharp [15C. < ?]

skewness /skyoōnəss/ *n* **1** the way or amount that something is tilted or distorted from the true or straight position **2** a lack of symmetry, especially about the mean in a frequency distribution

skewwhiff /skyoō wíf/ *adj* not level or straight, but crooked, tilted, or lopsided (*informal*) [Mid-18C. Fanciful formation < SKEW.]

ski /skee/ *n* (*plural* **skis** *or* **ski**) **1 BOARD USED TO SLIDE ACROSS SNOW** either of a pair of long thin boards made of wood, metal, or other material that curve up at the front and are used to slide across snow **2** WATER SKIING = **water-ski** *n.* **3 RUNNER FOR VEHICLES TRAVELLING ON SNOW** a runner fitted to vehicles such as snowmobiles and aeroplanes for landing or travelling on snow and ice ■ *vti* (**skis, skiing, skied** *or* **ski'd**) **MOVE ALONG ON SKIS** to glide over the surface of snow or water wearing skis, as a means of travel or as a leisure pursuit or sport [Mid-18C. Via Norwegian < Old Norse *skíð* 'piece of split wood, snowshoe'.] —**skiable** *adj* —**skier** *n*

skibob /skeé bob/ *n* a vehicle similar to a bicycle that has skis instead of wheels and is used to travel over snow [Mid-20C. *Bob*, shortening of BOBSLED.] —**skibobber** *n* —**skibobbing** *n*

skid /skid/ *n* **1 UNCONTROLLED SLIDE** an uncontrolled slide across a surface in a wheeled vehicle **2 AIRCRAFT RUNNER** a runner on the underside of an aircraft, used as part of its landing gear **3 PALLET** a low pallet on which goods are loaded for handling or transport **4 BLOCK USED TO PREVENT WHEEL TURNING** a shoe or block used to prevent a wheel from turning, e.g. when a vehicle is descending a hill **5 SHIP'S FENDER** a wooden structure hung over the side of a ship to protect the ship in loading and unloading cargo ■ *v* (**skids, skidding, skidded**) **1** *vti* **SLIDE DANGEROUSLY ACROSS SURFACE** to slide or make a vehicle slide across a surface, usually unintentionally, so that the wheels lose their grip and control is lost **2** *vi* **SLIDE OVER SURFACE WITHOUT ROLLING** to slide across a surface without turning round and gripping it in the proper way **3** *vti* **SLIDE SIDEWAYS** to slide or make an aircraft slide sideways away from the centre of curvature when it is insufficiently banked in making a turn [Early 17C. < ?] —**skiddy** *adj* ◇ **on the skids** in difficulties and heading for failure (*informal*)

ski'd past tense, past participle of **ski**

skidlid /skídlid/ *n* a crash helmet (*dated informal*)

skidpan /skíd pan/ *n* an area with a surface that is deliberately made slippery so that drivers can practise dealing with a skidding vehicle

skidproof /skíd proof/ *adj* designed to prevent skidding

skid road *n* **1** *US* = **skid row** (*informal*) **2** *Can, US* a road with logs embedded in it, along which timber is hauled to a mill or loading area

skid row *n* an area of a city that has cheap bars and rundown hotels and is frequented by members of the city's underclass (*informal*) [Alteration of *skid road*, originally an area of a town frequented by loggers]

skied[1] /skeed/, **ski'd** past tense, past participle of **ski**

skied[2] /skīd/ past participle, past tense of **sky**

skies **1** plural of **sky** **2** 3rd person present singular of **sky**

skiff /skif/ *n* a small flatbottomed boat of shallow draft that is usually propelled with oars, a sail, or a motor [Late 15C. Via French *esquif* < Italian *schifo*, probably < Old High German *schif*.]

skiffle /skíff'l/ *n* music popular in the 1950s, usually played by a small group on guitars with improvised instruments such as a washboard used as percussion [Early 20C. < ?]

skiing /skeé ing/ *n* the activity, sport, or pastime of travelling on skis

skijoring /skeé jawring/ *n* a sport in which a skier is towed across a frozen surface by a horse or vehicle [Early 20C. < Norwegian *skikjøring* 'ski driving'.] —**skijorer** *n*

ski jump *n* **1** a steep artificial slope with a sharp upturn at the bottom **2** a jump made by a skier from a ski jump —**ski jumper** *n*

ski-jump *vi* to perform a ski jump

Skikda /skik daa/ port in NE Algeria. Population: 128,747 (1987).

skilful /skílf'l, skílfool/ *adj* **1** with a special ability and dexterity in a particular type of work or activity **2** requiring or done with specialized techniques and abilities developed over a period of time —**skilfully** *adv* —**skilfulness** *n*

~~**skilfull**~~ incorrect spelling of **skilful**

ski lift *n* a motor-driven apparatus consisting of a continuously moving cable with seats, gondolas, or tow bars suspended from it, built to transport skiers to the top of a ski run

skill /skil/ *n* **1** the ability to do something well, usually gained through experience and training **2** something such as an art or trade that requires training and experience to do well [12C. < Old Norse *skil* 'discernment'.] —**skilled** *adj* —**skill-less** *adj* —**skill-lessness** *n*

SYNONYMS See ***ability.***

skillet /skíllit/ *n* **1** *US* COOK = **frying pan** **2** a small shallow pan with a long handle, used for frying or braising food [15C. Probably < Old French *escuelete* 'small platter' < *escuele* 'platter' < Latin *scutella* 'flat dish'.]

skilly /skílli/ (*plural* **-lies**) *n* a watery type of soup, made from oatmeal or something similar [Mid-19C. Shortening of *skilligalee*, a nonsense word.]

skim /skim/ *v* (**skims, skimming, skimmed**) **1** *vt* **SCOOP FROM TOP OF LIQUID** to remove a substance such as fat forming a layer on the surface of a liquid, usually with a large shallow spoon **2** *vt* **RID LIQUID OF FLOATING MATERIAL** to rid a liquid of material accumulating on its surface **3** *vti* **PASS CLOSELY OVER SURFACE OF** to pass or make something pass quickly across and just above the surface of something, sometimes touching it lightly and briefly **4** *vt* **GLANCE THROUGH A BOOK OR PAPER** to read something very quickly looking only at occasional lines or words, to get a general idea of its contents **5** *vt* **SEND SOMETHING BOUNCING ALONG** to throw something so that it bounces lightly along the surface of water **6** *vt* **GIVE LITTLE OR NO ATTENTION TO** to deal with something in a superficial way **7** *vti* **COAT OR BECOME COATED WITH LAYER** to develop a thin surface layer of something, or coat an object so that its surface is covered in a thin layer of something **8** *vt* *US* **HIDE PROFITS TO AVOID TAXES** to hide earnings or profits in order to avoid paying taxes on them (*informal*) ■ *n* **1 THIN FILM** a layer coating a surface **2 CURSORY LOOK** a cursory look at or treatment of something ○ *a quick skim over the main topics on the agenda* **3 SUBSTANCE REMOVED FROM SURFACE** the matter that forms a layer on a surface and is skimmed off **4 SKIMMING PROCESS** the process of removing a substance from a surface [15C. < Old French *escumer* < *escume* 'scum'.]
skim off *vt* to cull the best people or items from a group

ski mask *n* a protective covering for the face and sometimes the head, worn by skiers and made of knitted or other material and often having openings for the eyes, nose, and mouth

skimmed milk *n* milk with most or all of its fat content removed

skimmer /skímmər/ *n* **1 SOMEBODY OR SOMETHING THAT SKIMS** a person, object, or device that skims **2 LONG-WINGED MARINE BIRD** a long-winged marine bird that has a bill with the lower half longer than the upper, used for skimming food from the surface of water while in flight. Genus: *Rynchops.* **3 UTENSIL USED FOR SKIMMING** a broad flat spoon with small perforations in it, used to skim something such as fat from the surface of a liquid

skim milk *n* US = **skimmed milk**

skimmings /skímmingz/ *npl* the floating fat or debris skimmed off the surface of a liquid

skimp /skimp/ *v* **1** *vti* **USE TOO LITTLE OF SOMETHING** to use or provide hardly enough of something **2** *vt* **DO SOMETHING IMPROPERLY** to carry out a piece of work poorly, without spending enough time, trouble, or materials on it **3** *vt* **NOT PROVIDE WITH ENOUGH** to give or allow yourself or another person only an inadequate amount of money, food, or other necessary items [Late 18C. < ?]

skimpy /skímpi/ (**-ier, -iest**) *adj* **1** made or done using barely enough of the necessary materials **2** not giving somebody enough of something through meanness —**skimpily** *adv* —**skimpiness** *n*

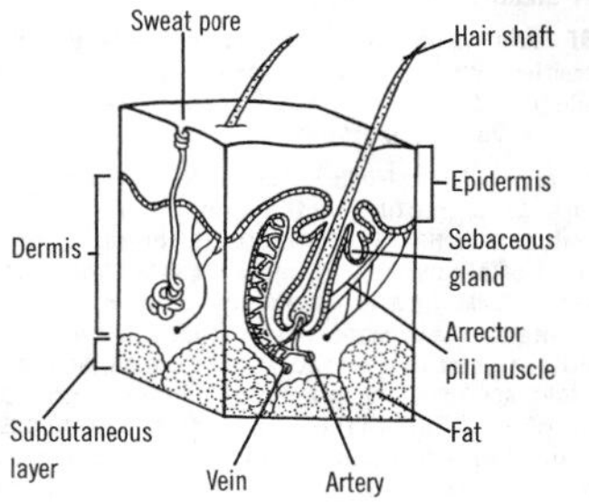

Sweat pore
Hair shaft
Epidermis
Dermis
Sebaceous gland
Arrector pili muscle
Fat
Subcutaneous layer
Vein
Artery

Skin: Cross-section of human skin

ϟ **skin** /skin/ *n* **1 NATURAL LAYER COVERING AN ANIMAL'S BODY** the external protective membrane or covering of an animal's body, consisting of the dermis and epidermis and often covered in hair, fur, scales, or feathers **2 SKIN ON FACE** somebody's skin, especially on the face, in terms of its colour and appearance ○ *Do you have oily, dry, or combination skin?* ○ *skin tone* **3 THIN NATURAL COVERING** a relatively thin but protective layer closely surrounding the flesh of a fruit or vegetable **4 FUR OR LEATHER FROM DEAD ANIMAL** skin or a piece of skin removed from an animal's body, especially once it has been cleaned and treated to use as fur or leather **5 SOLID SURFACE LAYER ON A LIQUID** a thin pliant surface that forms on the top of some liquids, e.g. on hot milk left to cool **6 TIGHT-FITTING COVERING** a thin tough casing or cover that fits closely round something such as a sausage to hold in, protect, or preserve the enclosed material **7 SKINHEAD** a skinhead (*slang informal*) **8 SMALL LEATHER SACK** a bag made from animal hide used to hold liquid such as wine or water **9 OUTER COVERING OF STRUCTURE** the outer protective covering of a structure such as an aircraft **10 SOFTWARE FOR EDITING IMAGES** a piece of software that enables the user to change the appearance of images produced by existing software without changing their function, or the changed image that results **11 CIGARETTE PAPER** a piece of paper used for making marijuana joints or other roll-up cigarettes (*slang*) ■ **skins** *npl* **JAZZ DRUMS** drums, especially in a jazz band (*informal*) ■ *v* (**skins, skinning, skinned**) **1** *vt* **TAKE THE SKIN OFF** to remove the skin from a fruit or vegetable, or from an animal or person, especially by cutting or ripping it **2** *vt* **SCRAPE THE SKIN** to make the skin on a part of the body red, sore, and broken, especially by falling on it or scraping it **3** *vt* **REMOVE OUTSIDE PART OF** to strip off an outer, covering layer that resembles a skin **4** *vti* **PUT SKIN ON** to grow or become covered with a skin, or cover somebody or something with a skin **5** *vt* **SWINDLE** to trick somebody out of money or property (*slang*) **6** *vti* **ALTER SOFTWARE IMAGES** to change the appearance of images produced by existing software, without changing their function ■ *adj* *US* **PORNOGRAPHIC** relating to or containing pornographic material (*informal*) [12C. < Old Norse *skinn*.] —**skinless** *adj* —**skinning** *n* ◇ **be no skin off somebody's nose** to be a matter that does not harm you at all and therefore may be of little interest (*informal*) ◇ **by the skin of your teeth** by a very narrow margin (*informal*) ◇ **get under somebody's skin** **1** to annoy or irritate somebody (*informal*) **2** to make somebody feel great interest or attraction (*informal*) ◇ **save somebody's skin** to prevent somebody from suffering hurt, loss, or punishment by giving vital help (*informal*)

skin-deep *adj* appearing to be important, meaningful, or valuable but having little deep or lasting importance ■ *adv* in a superficial way

skin diving *n* the sport of underwater diving using flippers, and a mask and snorkel —**skin-dive** *vi* —**skin diver** *n*

skin effect *n* the tendency of a high-frequency alternating current to flow near the surface of the conductor rather than in its interior

skin flick *n* a pornographic film (*slang*)

skinflint /skínflint/ *n* a miser [Late 17C. < the phrase 'skin a flint', used of somebody so miserly as to try to remove the skin from a piece of flint.]

skin friction *n* a frictional force, or drag, acting on the surface of an aerofoil or other object immersed in a large volume of fluid that is in motion relative to the object

skinful /skín fòol/ *n* **1** a large amount of alcoholic drink, especially as much as somebody can drink (*informal*) **2** the amount of liquid that a skin bag holds

~~**sking**~~ incorrect spelling of **skiing**

skin game *n* a confidence trick or scheme used to cheat people of their money (*slang*) [< SKIN 'swindle']

skin graft *n* a piece of skin taken from part of the body and used to replace lost or damaged skin

skinhead /skín hed/ *n* (*slang*) **1** somebody whose hair is very short or whose head is shaved **2** one of a group of young white men with closely-cropped or shaven hair who often have racist or fascist beliefs, are sometimes violent, and typically wear jeans, braces, and boots

skink /skingk/ *n* a small smooth insect-eating lizard with a long thin body and small limbs. Family: Scincidae. [Late 16C. < Latin *scincus* < Greek *skigkos*.]

skinner /skínnər/ *n* a person who skins animals, or deals in animal skins

Skinner /skínnər/, **B. F.** (1904–90) US behavioural psychologist. Full name **Burrhus Frederic Skinner** —**Skinnerian** /ski neéri ən/ *adj, n*

skinny /skínni/ (**-nier, -niest**) *adj* **1** thin, especially in an unappealing or unhealthy way **2** made with skimmed milk (*slang*) ○ *One skinny latte to go.* [Mid-16C. < SKIN.] —**skinniness** *n*

SYNONYMS See ***thin***.

skinny-dip *vi* (**skinny-dips, skinny-dipping, skinny-dipped**) to go swimming in the nude (*informal*) ■ *n* a swim in the nude (*informal*) [< SKINNY in its original sense 'pertaining to the skin'] —**skinny-dipper** *n* —**skinny-dipping** *n*

skin-pop (**skin-pops, skin-popping, skin-popped**) *vti* to take narcotic drugs by inserting the needle under the skin, not straight into a vein (*slang*)

skint /skint/ *adj* without any money (*informal*) [Early 20C. Variant of *skinned* (from SKIN).]

skin test *n* a test in which a substance is applied to the skin to determine somebody's allergic sensitivity or immunity to it

skintight /skín tīt/ *adj* fitting tightly to the body

skin up *vi* to roll a marijuana joint or cigarette (*slang*)

skip[1] /skip/ *v* (**skips, skipping, skipped**) **1** *vi* **MOVE WITH SMALL HOPPING STEPS** to move along by hopping from one foot to the other **2** *vti* **JUMP REPEATEDLY OVER CIRCLING ROPE** to jump repeatedly over a rope as it is swung round over the head and under the feet **3** *vt* **NIMBLY JUMP OVER** to jump nimbly over something **4** *vti* **OMIT** to pass over or leave something out that should properly follow as part of a sequence or a complete work **5** *vt* **DEAL WITH CURSORILY** to deal with or look at something in a cursory way **6** *vt* **NOT ATTEND OR BE AT** to choose or decide to miss an event or activity (*informal*) **7** *vi* **NOT PLAY CORRECTLY** to fail to play a CD or record properly by jumping from one place to another, or to undergo this kind of faulty playing **8** *vti* **LEAVE SOMEWHERE SECRETLY** to make a secret getaway, especially for some dishonest reason, e.g. to avoid being punished for something (*informal*) **9** *vti* **MOVE IN SERIES OF SMALL HOPS** to move lightly across a surface in a series of small hops, or make something move in this way ■ *n* **1** **SMALL HOPPING STEP** a small forwards hopping step **2** **ACT OF OMITTING** an act of omitting part of something [13C. Probably < Old Norse.] —**skippable** *adj*

skip off *vi* to make a secret getaway, especially for a dishonest reason, e.g. to avoid paying for something or being punished for something (*informal*)

skip[2] /skip/ *n* a large flat-bottomed metal container kept outdoors for putting unwanted materials, furniture, or any bulky refuse in, especially when a building is being renovated or constructed [Early 19C. Variant of SKEP.]

skip[3] /skip/ *n* a skipper (*slang*) ■ *vi* (**skips, skipping, skipped**) to be the skipper of a vessel (*slang*) [Early 19C. Shortening.]

ski pants *npl* **1** women's trousers made of stretchy fabric with elasticated straps that go under the feet. US term **stirrup pants** **2** lined, windproof, water-resistant trousers that are worn for skiing and other cold weather activities

skip distance *n* the shortest distance between a radio transmitter and receiver that permits waves of a particular frequency to be sent and received by reflection from the ionosphere

skipjack /skíp jak/ (*plural* **-jack** *or* **-jacks**) *n* **1** **LEAPING MARINE FISH** a marine fish that leaps out of the water, e.g. the bonito or bluefish **2** **skipjack, skipjack tuna** **MARINE FOOD FISH** a tropical marine fish of the tuna family that is blue and silver with dark stripes on its abdomen. *Euthynnus pelamus*. **3** **SKIPJACK AS FOOD** the flesh of a skipjack as food **4** = **click beetle** **5** *US* **SAILING BOAT** a sailing boat with straight sides and a V-shaped bottom

skiplane /skeé playn/ *n* an aircraft equipped with skis for taking off from and landing on snow

ski pole, ski stick *n* one of a pair of lightweight poles held by skiers for balance and control

skipper[1] /skíppər/ *n* **1** **SOMEBODY IN CHARGE OF SHIP** somebody in charge of a ship or boat **2** **LEADER OF A TEAM** somebody in charge of a squad or group of others, especially the captain or coach of a sports team (*informal*) ■ *vt* **BE SKIPPER OF** to be in charge of a ship, team or aircraft (*informal*) [14C. < Middle Dutch *schipper* < *schip* 'ship'.]

skipper[2] /skíppər/ *n* **1** somebody or something that skips **2** a quick-flying insect that has a stout hairy body and clubbed antennae with hooked tips, and is closely related to true butterflies. Families: Hesperiidae and Megathymidae. **3** ZOOL = **saury** [Mid-18C. < SKIP[1].]

skipping /skípping/ *n* the children's pastime or adult exercise in which you skip over a rope as it swings round over your head and under your feet

skipping rope *n* a piece of rope, often with handles at either end, for skipping over. US term **jump rope**

Skipton /skíptən/ market town in N England. Population: 13,583 (1991).

skirl /skurl/ *n Scotland* the high-pitched wailing sound that bagpipes typically make ■ *vti Scotland* to produce a high-pitched wailing sound on the bagpipes [14C. Probably < N Germanic.]

skirmish /skúrmish/ *n* **1** **SMALL RELATIVELY UNIMPORTANT BATTLE** an incident where fighting breaks out briefly between two small contingents away from the main battlefield in a war **2** **SHORT ARGUMENT** a brief fight or disagreement between people ■ *vi* **ENGAGE IN MINOR BATTLE** to become involved in a skirmish [14C. < Old French *eskermiss-* 'to fence' < Germanic, 'defend'.] —**skirmisher** *n*

SYNONYMS See ***fight***.

skirr /skur/ *vti* to rush along, or rush through an area ■ *n* a whirring sound [Mid-16C. < ?]

skirret /skírrət/ *n* a plant cultivated for its sweetish edible root. Native to: Europe. *Sium sisarum*. [14C. Earlier *skirwhit* < ?]

skirt /skurt/ *n* **1** **GARMENT THAT HANGS FROM THE WAIST** a piece of clothing that hangs from the waist and does not divide into two separate legs, usually worn by women and girls **2** **AREA OF FABRIC FALLING FROM WAISTLINE** the section from the waist to the hem on a dress, coat, or robe **3** **SOMETHING SIMILAR TO SKIRT** an attachment shaped like a skirt, or covering the lower part of something like a skirt **4** **FLAP AROUND BOTTOM OF HOVERCRAFT** the lower outer section of a rocket or the flap around the bottom of a hovercraft **5** **CUT OF BEEF** a stewing cut of beef taken from the flank, below the sirloin and rump, and cut from the inside of flank steak **6** **FLAP ON SADDLE** one of a pair of leather flaps that hang from a saddle **7** **OFFENSIVE TERM** an offensive term for a girl or woman, or women in general, suggesting that they are objects (*slang*) ■ *v* **1** *vti* **BE AROUND THE OUTSIDE OF** to form a border along the edge of an area or object **2** *vti* **MOVE AROUND THE OUTSIDE OF** to travel along the edge of something such as an area, structure, or geographical feature **3** *vt* **AVOID GIVING PROPER ATTENTION TO** to avoid dealing with a particular subject in any depth, usually because it is tricky or unpleasant **4** *vt* **GIVE AN EDGE TO** to provide something with an attachment shaped like a skirt or border [13C. < Old Norse *skyrta* 'shirt' < Germanic, 'cut'.] —**skirter** *n*

skirt-chaser *n* an offensive term for a man who is regarded as being excessively interested in pursuing women sexually (*slang*) —**skirt-chasing** *n*

skirting /skúrting/ *n* **1** CONSTR = **skirting board** **2** material used to make skirts

skirting board *n* a narrow board, attached to the base of an interior wall, that covers the joint between the wall and the floor. US term **baseboard** *n.* 2

ski stick *n* SKIING = **ski pole**

skit /skit/ *n* **1** a short, usually comic, dramatic sketch **2** a short piece of comic writing that satirizes somebody or something [Early 18C. < ?]

skite[1] /skīt/ *v* (**skites, skiting, skited**) *Scotland* **1** *vi* **SLIP** to slip on a slippery surface **2** *vti* **HIT SOMETHING SHARPLY** to hit something or somebody else with a sharp blow, or to hit something and bounce sharply from it ■ *n Scotland* **1** **ACT OF SKIDDING OR SLIPPING** an instance of something or somebody sliding suddenly across a slippery surface **2** **SHARP KNOCK OR SLAP** a sudden forceful glancing blow [Early 18C. < ?]

skite[2] /skīt/ *vi* (**skites, skiting, skited**) *Aus* **BOAST** to talk with excessive pride about yourself or your accomplishments (*informal*) ■ *n Aus* **1** **BOASTING TALK** talk that exaggerates your own importance and accomplishments **2** **BOASTER** an arrogant or boastful person [Mid-19C. < ?]

ski touring *n* travelling over long distances on skis, especially in wilderness areas

ski tow *n* an apparatus consisting of a motor-driven rope that skiers hang onto to be towed up a mountain

skitter /skíttər/ *v* **1** *vi* **RUN WITH TINY STEPS** to move about or run off quickly with small scampering steps **2** *vti* **SKID LIGHTLY ACROSS** to pass quickly across something, touching its surface very lightly and briefly, or to send something skidding rapidly over the surface of something ■ *n Ireland* **UNRELIABLE PERSON** somebody regarded as unreliable (*slang insult*) ■ **skitters** *npl Ireland, Scotland* **DIARRHOEA** an attack of diarrhoea (*slang*) [Mid-19C. < ?]

skittish /skíttish/ *adj* **1** **SILLY AND IRRESPONSIBLE** with moods or ideas that constantly change, in a frivolous and unreliable way **2** **NERVOUS** easily agitated or alarmed **3** **LIVELY** tending to dash about in an energetic or restless way [14C. < ?] —**skittishly** *adv* —**skittishness** *n*

skittle /skítt'l/ *n* one of the set of wooden or plastic bottle-shaped pins that are stood upright in a group for players to aim at in the game of skittles. US term **ninepin** [Mid-17C. < ?]

skittle out *vt* to put a batting side out quickly in cricket

skive[1] /skīv/ *vti* (**skives, skiving, skived**) to avoid doing work, studies, or duties (*informal*) ■ *n* time spent avoiding work, studies, or duties, or something that somebody uses to disguise doing this (*informal*) [Early 20C. < ?]

skive[2] /skīv/ (**skives, skiving, skived**) *vt* to scrape thin slices off leather in preparing it [Early 19C. < N Germanic.]

skiver[1] /skívər/ *n* an avoider of work (*informal*)

skiver[2] /skívər/ *n* **1** a thin soft tanned leather taken from the outer side of a skin **2** somebody or something that skives leather

skivvy /skívvi/ *n* (*plural* **-vies**) a domestic servant, usually a woman, who performs menial tasks (*informal insult*) ■ *vi* (**-vies, -vying, -vied**) to perform menial tasks for somebody else (*informal*) [Mid-20C. < ?]

skiwear /skeé wayr/ *n* clothing designed for skiers to wear

skol /skōl/, **skoal** *interj* used as a drinking toast [Early 17C. Via Danish *skaal* and Swedish and Norwegian *skål* < Old Norse *skál* 'bowl'.]

skollie /skólli/, **skolly** (*plural* **-lies**) *n S Africa* an offensive term for a young man, usually Black or of mixed race, who is involved in petty crime and violence and often belongs to a gang (*slang*) [Mid-20C. < Afrikaans, probably < Dutch *schoelje* 'scoundrel'.]

Skomer /skṓmər/ islet off the SW Wales, in St. George's Channel.

Skopje /skóp yi/ capital of the Former Yugoslav Republic of Macedonia, in the north-central part of the country. Population: 563,102 (1994).

SKU /éss kay yoō, skyoo/, **Sku** *n* a unique code, consisting of numbers or letters and numbers, assigned to a product by a retailer for identification and stock control. Full form **stockkeeping unit**

skua /skyoō ə/ *n* a large, brown, predatory seabird with slender wings that chases other birds to make them drop their prey. Genera: *Catharacta* and *Stercorarius.* ◊ **great skua** [Late 17C. Via modern Latin < a variant of Faeroese *skugvur* < Old Norse *skufr.*]

skulduggery /skul dúggəri/, **skullduggery** *n* unfair and dishonest practices carried out in a secretive way so as to trick other people (*humorous*) [Mid-19C. Alteration of *sculduddery* 'sexual impropriety, indecency' < ?]

skulk /skulk/ *vi* **1 MOVE FURTIVELY** to move about in a furtive way **2 HIDE FOR SINISTER PURPOSE** to hide, especially in order to do something sinister **3 SHIRK** to avoid work or responsibilities ■ *n* **1 SOMEBODY WHO SKULKS** a furtive person, or somebody who conceals a sinister purpose **2 GROUP OF FOXES** a pack of foxes [12C. < N Germanic.]

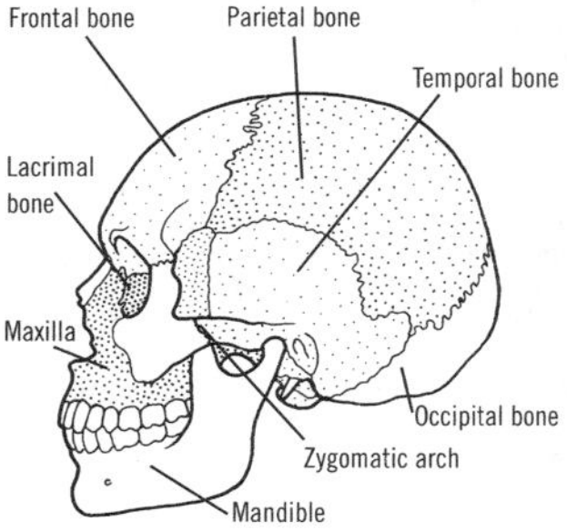

Skull

skull /skul/ *n* **1** the skeletal part of the head in humans and other vertebrates, consisting of the cranium, which encases the brain, and the bones of the face and jaws **2** a person's head or mind (*informal*) ○ *tried to din the principles of thermodynamics into his skull* [13C. Probably < N Germanic.]

skull and crossbones *n* **1** a representation of a human skull above two human thighbones crossed over each other, used as a symbol of danger or death **2** HIST = **Jolly Roger**

skullcap /skúl kap/ *n* **1 SMALL ROUND BRIMLESS HAT** a simple hat consisting of a small circle of fabric shaped to fit over the crown of the head **2 TOP OF SKULL** the top part of the skull **3 PERENNIAL MINT** a perennial plant of the mint family. Flowers: blue or pinkish, with helmet-shaped calyx. Genus: *Scutellaria.*

skunk /skungk/ *n* (*plural* **skunk** *or* **skunks**) **1 BLACK-AND-WHITE MAMMAL** a black-and-white mammal of the weasel family that ejects a foul-smelling liquid from an anal gland as a defensive action. Native to: North and South America. **2 OFFENSIVE TERM** an offensive term for a person considered to be despicable (*slang insult*) ■ *vt US, Can* **DEFEAT SOUNDLY** to defeat an opponent soundly, especially by not allowing him or her to score any points in a sporting competition (*slang*) [Mid-17C. < Massachusett.]

skunk cabbage, skunkweed /skúngk weed/ (*plural* **-weeds** *or* **-weed**) *n* **1** a foul-smelling broad-leaved perennial herb with small flowers enclosed in greenish spathe. Native to: swampy areas of E North America. *Symplocarpus foetidus.* **2** a plant similar to skunk cabbage and with a large yellow spathe. Native to: W North America. *Lysichitum americanum.*

skunkworks /skúngk wurks/ *n US* a department or laboratory involved in usually secret cutting-edge research and development (*informal; usually + singular verb*) [Mid-20C. < *Skonk Works*, a place in Al Capp's comic strip *L'il Abner.*]

sky /skī/ *n* (*plural* **skies**) **1 REGION ABOVE THE EARTH** the area high above the trees, buildings, landscape, or horizon **2 WAY SKY APPEARS** the way the sky looks in a particular part of the world (*often plural*) **3 sky, Sky HEAVEN** the plane, thought of as being high above the Earth, in which immortal powers or beings exist, e.g. God or immortal souls (*literary; often plural*) **4 HIGHEST LIMIT** the topmost limit or the best and most it is possible to achieve ■ *vti* (**skies, skying, skied**) **MAKE SOMETHING GO VERY HIGH** to kick, hit or throw a ball high up into the air [13C. < Old Norse *ský* 'cloud'.] ◇ **praise somebody** *or* **something to the skies** to praise somebody *or* something very highly ◇ **the sky's the limit** there is no upper limit on something (*informal*)

sky blue *n* a pale blue colour like that of the sky on a clear day —**sky blue** *adj*

skycap /skī kap/ *n US* a porter who works at an airport [Mid-20C. < SKY after REDCAP.]

skydive /skī dīv/ (**-dives, -diving, -dived**) *vi* to jump from an aeroplane and descend in free fall, sometimes performing acrobatic manoeuvres, before pulling the ripcord of a parachute —**sky diver** *n* —**skydiving** *n*

Skye /skī/ largest island in the Inner Hebrides, W Scotland. Population: 8,843 (1991). Area: 1,676 sq. km/647 sq. mi.

Skye terrier *n* a small terrier with short legs, a long body, and a long straight coat belonging to a breed originating in Scotland [Mid-19C. After the Isle of SKYE.]

sky-high *adv, adj* up to or at the highest level ■ *adv* high into the air or in all directions, forcefully and often in pieces

sky-hook *n* **1** an imaginary hook conceived as hanging from the sky **2** a helicopter that is specially configured with a hook-and-cable apparatus in its fuselage, used to lift, drop, and transport heavy objects

skyjack /skī jak/ *vt* to use force to take over control of an aircraft, especially a commercial aircraft, when it is in the air [Mid-20C. < SKY after HIJACK.] —**skyjacker** *n* —**skyjacking** *n*

skylark /skī laark/ *n* a lark with streaked brown-and-white plumage that is noted for singing melodiously while hovering high in the air. Native to: Europe, Asia. *Alauda arvensis.* ■ *vi* to take part in lively physical playful behaviour (*dated informal*) —**skylarker** *n*

skylight /skī līt/ *n* an opening in a roof or ceiling, fitted with glass to let in daylight

skylight filter *n* a photographic filter that is slightly pink and is used to filter out ultraviolet light and reduce blueness

skyline /skī līn/ *n* **1** the pattern of shapes made by the various features of a landscape such as hills or buildings against the sky **2** the apparent line where the Earth joins the sky

sky pilot *n* an offensive term for a priest or chaplain, associated especially with the armed forces (*slang*)

skyrocket /skī rokit/ *n* INDUST = **rocket**[1] *n.* 4 ■ *vti* to rise or make something rise suddenly to a very high level or value (*informal*)

Skyros /skeé ross/ largest of the Greek Sporades Islands, in the N Aegean Sea. Population: 2,757 (1981). Area: 205 sq. km/79 sq. mi.

skysail /skī sayl/ *n* a small light square sail that goes above the royal on a square-rigged sailing vessel

skyscape /skī skayp/ *n* a scene or picture showing chiefly sky, especially an artistic study of a section of sky

skyscraper /skī skraypər/ *n* a modern building that is extremely tall

skysurfing /skī surfing/ *n* **1** the sport of jumping from an aeroplane and performing a series of moves before descending by parachute **2** a version of skydiving in which participants carry out acrobatic manoeuvres on a surfboard while in free fall —**skysurf** *vi* —**skysurfer** *n*

skywalk /skī wawk/ *n US* a raised walkway, usually joining two buildings

skyward /skīwərd/ *adv* **skyward, skywards** in the direction of the sky ■ *adj* heading towards the sky

sky wave *n* a radio wave that is transmitted around the curved surface of the Earth by being reflected back to Earth by the ionosphere

skyway /skī way/ *n* **1** a route used by aircraft **2** *US* an elevated highway, supported by tall spans ○ *the Chicago Skyway*

skywriting /skī rīting/ *n* **1** the use of an aircraft releasing coloured smoke to form letters in the sky **2** letters or a message formed in the sky by coloured smoke released from an aircraft —**skywrite** *vti* —**skywriter** *n*

⚡**sl** *abbr* Sierra Leone (*in Internet addresses*)

slab /slab/ *n* **1 THICK PIECE** a thick flat broad piece of something, especially when cut or trimmed **2 STONE BASE** a flat rectangular base or foundation of concrete or stone **3 MORTUARY TABLE** a table on which a body is laid in a mortuary (*informal*) **4 OFFCUT FROM LOG** any large outer section of a log that is sawn off before it is made into planks **5** *Aus* **PACK OF BEER** a pack or box of 24 cans or bottles of beer (*informal*) ■ *adj ANZ* made of coarse wooden planks ■ *vt* (**slabs, slabbing, slabbed**) **1 MAKE INTO SLABS** to cut or make something into slabs **2 COVER WITH SLABS** to cover something by laying stone or concrete slabs on it **3 TRIM BY SAWING** to saw off the rough outer parts of a log [13C. < ?]

slabbing /slábbing/ *n* **1** the laying of stone or concrete slabs to form a surface such as a pathway **2** stone or concrete slabs, collectively

slab pottery *n* pottery made by hand using rolled-out sheets of clay

slack /slak/ *adj* **1 NOT TIGHT** not tight or stretched taut, but hanging loosely or having a good deal of give ○ *The reins are too slack.* **2 NOT SHOWING ENOUGH CARE** not showing enough care, attention, or rigour ○ *They've been rather slack about keeping to performance targets.* **3 NOT BUSY** not busy or active, or less busy than usual ○ *the slack period following the main tourist season* **4 MOVING SLOWLY** moving slowly or sluggishly **5** PHON = **lax** *adj.* 4 ■ *adv* **LOOSELY** in a loose or limp way ○ *His clothes hung slack on him.* ■ *n* **1 LOOSENESS** looseness or give in something such as a rope, or the extra length or fullness in it that needs to be taken in to make it taut **2 UNUSED POTENTIAL** productive potential in an organization or system that is not being fully made use of ○ *take in some of the slack in the administrative division* **3 QUIET TIME** a period of time that is not busy **4 STILL WATER** a stretch of water that is still or moving only slowly ■ *vti* **1 AVOID WORK** to be lazy, to avoid work, or to work with insufficient vigour or concentration **2** = **slacken** *v.* 1 **3** CHEM = **slake** *v.* 2 [Old English *slæc* < Indo-European, 'be loose']

slacken /slákən/ *vti* **1** to become or to make something become less intense, vigorous, or fast **2** to become or to make something become looser or more relaxed

slacker /slákər/ *n* **1** a shirker or somebody who avoids doing something, especially work or military service **2** an offensive term for a young educated person who is regarded as being disaffected or apathetic, and underachieving (*slang*)

slacks /slaks/ *npl* casual trousers, especially loose-fitting ones [Early 19C. < SLACK.]

slack water *n* the period of time during which the tide is turning and the water is still or slow-moving because of this

SLADE /slayd/ *abbr* Society of Lithographic Artists, Designers, Engravers, and Process Workers

slag /slag/ *n* **1 WASTE MATERIAL FROM SMELTING** fused glassy material that is produced when a metal is separated from its ore during smelting **2 COAL WASTE** the mixture of coal dust and mineral waste produced after coal has been mined **3** GEOL = **scoria** *n.* 1 **4 OFFENSIVE TERM** an offensive term for a woman who is considered to be sexually promiscuous or generally coarse and sluttish (*slang*) **5 SOMEBODY DESPISED** any individual, especially a man, regarded as despicable (*slang insult*) ■ *v* (**slags, slagging, slagged**) **1** *vti* **TURN SOMETHING INTO SLAG** to convert something into slag or become slag **2** *vt* **INSULT OR CRITICIZE** to make insulting, mocking, or critical comments about somebody or something (*slang*) ○ *Don't you dare slag off my team!* [Mid-16C. < Middle Low German *slagge* < Germanic, 'strike'.]

slagging /slágging/ *n* a series of insulting, mocking, or critical comments (*slang*) ○ *I took a right slagging over that haircut.*

slag heap *n* a large mound of waste material from a coal mine or factory

slain past participle of **slay**

slàinte /slaáanchə/, **slàinte mhath** /slaáanchə vaá/ *interj Scotland* used as a drinking toast, meaning 'good health!' [Early 19C. < Gaelic *slàinte (mhath)* '(good) health'.]

slake /slayk/ (**slakes, slaking, slaked**) *v* **1** *vt* to satisfy a desire for something, especially a drink **2** *vti* to treat lime with water to produce calcium hydroxide, or to undergo this process [Old English *slacian* 'relax' < *slæc* 'loose'] —**slakable** *adj*

slaked lime *n* CHEM = **calcium hydroxide**

slalom /slaáləm/ *n* **1 ZIGZAG SKI RACE** a downhill ski race in which competitors follow a winding course and zigzag through flags on poles or through other obstacles **2 ZIGZAG RACE** any race that involves following a zigzag course through obstacles, e.g. in canoes ■ *vi* **FOLLOW ZIGZAG COURSE** to follow a zigzag or winding course, especially in a race [Early 20C. < Norwegian *slalåm* 'sloping track'.]

slam[1] /slam/ *v* (**slams, slamming, slammed**) **1** *vti* **CLOSE FORCEFULLY** to close something forcefully and noisily **2** *vti* **PUT SOMETHING DOWN VIOLENTLY** to put something down violently and noisily **3** *vti* **HIT** to hit with sudden or violent force ○ *The waves slammed into the dock.* **4** *vt* **CRITICIZE** to criticize somebody or something forcefully (*informal*) ○ *The press slammed the government's performance.* **5** *vt US* to change the telephone service provider of a customer without his or her consent or authorization (*informal*) ■ *n* **1 IMPACT** a heavy, noisy, or violent blow or impact **2 CRITICISM** a forceful criticism [Late 17C. < ?]

slam[2] /slam/ *n* the winning of all, or all but one, of the tricks in a hand of bridge or whist [Mid-17C. < ?]

slam-bang *adv US* (*informal*) **1** = **slap-bang** *adv.* 1 **2 CARELESSLY** in a careless and reckless way **3 EXCITINGLY** in an exciting and vigorous way ○ *The novel ended slam-bang with a fight to the finish.* ■ *adj US* (*informal*) **1 SUDDEN AND NOISY** sudden, noisy, or violent ○ *a slam-bang fight* **2 CARELESS AND RECKLESS** careless and reckless ○ *a slam-bang approach to his work* **3 EXCITING** exciting and vigorous ○ *slam-bang action scenes*

slam dancing *n* boisterous dancing to rock music in which young people hurl their bodies against one another, more out of enthusiasm than aggression — **slam dance** *vi*

slam-dunk, slam dunk *n* **1 SHOT THROWN DOWN FORCEFULLY INTO BASKET** a shot in basketball in which a player jumps up and throws the ball forcefully down into the basket **2 SOMETHING EASILY DONE** something done without any effective opposition (*informal*) ■ *vt* **THROW FORCEFULLY INTO BASKET** in basketball, to jump up and throw the ball forcefully down into the basket ■ *adj US* **CERTAIN OF SUCCESS** without risk and sure to be successful ○ *a slam-dunk scenario*

slammer /slámmər/ *n* a jail or prison (*slang*) [Mid-20C. < the idea of the doors slamming shut.]

slamming /slámming/ *n US* the illegal practice of changing a telephone customer's service provider without informing the customer or obtaining his or her permission (*informal*)

slander /slaándər/ *n* **1 SAYING OF SOMETHING FALSE AND DAMAGING** the act of saying something false or malicious that damages somebody's reputation **2 FALSE AND DAMAGING STATEMENT** a false and malicious statement that damages somebody's reputation ■ *vt* **UTTER A SLANDER AGAINST** to make a false and malicious oral statement about somebody [13C. Via Old French *esclandre* < ecclesiastical Latin *scandalum* 'cause of offence' (see SCANDAL).] —**slanderer** *n* —**slanderous** *adj* —**slanderously** *adv* —**slanderousness** *n*

SYNONYMS See ***malign***.

slang /slang/ *n* **1 VERY CASUAL SPEECH OR WRITING** words, expressions, and usages that are casual, vivid, racy, or playful replacements for standard ones, are often short-lived, and are usually considered unsuitable for formal contexts **2 LANGUAGE OF AN EXCLUSIVE GROUP** a form of language used by a particular group of people, often deliberately created and used to exclude people outside the group ○ *a word that came from surfers' slang* ■ *adj* **IN SLANG** belonging to, expressed in, or containing slang ○ *a slang dictionary* ■ *vt* **ATTACK VERBALLY** to use abusive language, usually slang, to attack somebody verbally ○ *We'll get nowhere just slanging each other.* [Mid-18C. < ?] —**slangily** *adv* —**slanginess** *n* —**slangy** *adj*

slanging match *n UK, Can* a dispute in which people insult and accuse each other ○ *The level of political debate had deteriorated to a series of slanging matches.*

slant /slaant/ *v* **1** *vti* **BE OR SET SOMETHING AT AN ANGLE** to be at an angle, or set something at an angle **2** *vt* **CAUSE SOMETHING TO HAVE A PARTICULAR APPEAL** to make something appeal to a particular group of people ○ *a magazine slanted towards the youth market* **3** *vt* **PRESENT WITH BIAS** to present something in a way that is biased towards a particular person, group, or viewpoint ○ *The news report was slanted in favour of the nationalists.* ■ *n* **1 ANGLED POSITION** an angled position or a direction that is at an angle to something else ○ *the roof was built on a slant* **2 BIASED PERSPECTIVE** a particular bias, or a perspective on something that is likely to appeal to a particular group ○ *The news was given a progovernment slant.* **3 POINT OF VIEW** a point of view or way of looking at something ○ *Her diaries give us a new slant on the events of the time.* ■ *adj* **slant, slanting, slanty SLOPING** sloping, or at an angle (*informal*) [15C. Variant of earlier *slent* < ?] —**slanted** *adj* —**slantingly** *adv*

slantways /slaánt wayz/, **slantwise** /-wīz/ *adv* at an angle to something else

slap /slap/ *n* **1 BLOW MADE WITH THE OPEN HAND** a blow made with the open hand or a flat object **2 NOISE OF A SLAP** the noise made by a slap, or something that sounds like it ○ *the slap of a wave on the side of the boat* **3 REBUKE** something that rebukes, insults, or hurts **4 MAKE-UP** make-up, whether for personal everyday use or for the theatre (*slang*) ○ *She said she'd just put some slap on and meet us downstairs.* ■ *v* (**slaps, slapping, slapped**) **1** *vt* **HIT WITH THE OPEN HAND** to hit somebody or something with the open hand or a flat object **2** *vi* **STRIKE SHARPLY** to strike sharply and noisily, as if with a slap **3** *vt* **PUT DOWN SHARPLY** to put something down sharply or noisily on something else ○ *He slapped the money on the table and walked away.* **4** *vt* **APPLY CARELESSLY** to put something on or make something, quickly and carelessly ○ *I slapped on some makeup and ran for the car.* **5** *vt* **APPLY AS A PENALTY** to apply something as a punishment, penalty, or restriction to somebody or something (*informal*) ○ *The government slapped an embargo on the story.* ■ *adv* (*informal*) **1 FORCEFULLY** forcefully, and often with the sound or effect of a slap ○ *landed slap on the floor* **2 EXACTLY** exactly, and usually with suddenness and force ○ *slap in the middle of the target* [Mid-17C. An imitation of the sound.] ◇ **a slap in the face** a rebuke or rebuff (*informal*) ◇ **a slap on the back** congratulations (*informal*) ◇ **a slap on the wrist** a mild rebuke or punishment (*informal*) ◇ **slap and tickle** playful sexual behaviour (*informal*)

slap down *vt* (*informal*) **1** to rebuke somebody sharply or cruelly **2** to suppress or check something thought to be unacceptable ○ *Any disrespect is slapped down immediately.*

slap-bang *adv* (*informal*) **1** in a sudden, noisy, or violent way. US term **slam-bang** **2** exactly or directly, and usually with suddenness and force ○ *The ball landed slap-bang in the middle of the pond.* US term **smack-dab**

slapdash /sláp dash/ *adj* careless, hasty, and unskilful ■ *adv* in a careless, hasty, and unskilful way ■ *n* BUILDING = **roughcast** *n.* 1

slaphappy /sláp happi/ *adj* (*informal*) **1** irresponsible or careless in a cheerful way **2** dazed or disoriented, like a boxer who has been hit on the head too many times

slaphead /sláp hed/ *n* an offensive term for a bald person, especially a man who has gone bald naturally rather than a man who has shaved his head by fashion choice (*slang insult*)

slapper /sláppər/ *n* an offensive term for a woman who is considered sexually promiscuous or vulgar (*slang*) [Late 18C. < SLAP in an obsolete dialectal sense.]

slap shot *n* in ice hockey, a shot in which the player swings the stick with a fast powerful stroke [< the loud sound made when the stick hits the ice]

slapstick /sláp stik/ *n* comedy with the emphasis on fast physical action, farcical situations, and obvious jokes that do not depend on language (*often before nouns*) ○ *slapstick comedy* [Early 20C. < *slapstick*, a device made of two flat linked pieces of wood, formerly used in comic performances to simulate the sound of a blow.]

slap-up *adj* with lots of good food to eat and served in style (*informal*) ○ *First prize is a slap-up dinner at the restaurant of your choice.*

slash /slash/ *vt* **1 MAKE CUTS IN** to make long deep cuts in something **2 ATTACK WITH A SHARP OBJECT** to cut or attack somebody with the sharp sweeping strokes of a sword, knife, stick, or whip **3 REDUCE OR SHORTEN** to greatly reduce or shorten something ○ *All prices slashed!* **4 MAKE A SLIT IN** to make a slit in fabric or a garment to reveal the lining **5 CLEAR BY CUTTING** to cut bushes and undergrowth from a wooded area ■ *n* **1 SHARP SWEEPING STROKE** a sharp sweeping stroke of a sword, knife, stick, or whip **2 LONG AND DEEP CUT** a long deep cut or wound **3 SLIT IN FABRIC** a slit in fabric or a garment, made to reveal the lining **4** *US* **DEBRIS FROM CUT TREES** the debris left after trees have been cut down **5 PRINT CHARACTER** a punctuation mark, (/), that is used to separate optional items in a list or to express fractions or division, and that has various uses in computer programming. Technical name **solidus** *n.* 1 **6 URINATION** an act of urination, usually by a male (*slang*) ○ *Hang on a minute while I go for a quick slash.* [Late 16C. Possibly < French *esclachier* 'break', variant of Old French *esclater* < *esclat* 'splinter'.] —**slasher** *n*

PUNCTUATION A ***slash*** is used between optional or alternative elements: *He refused to work with children and/or animals. Please place unwanted clothes/toys/books in the box.* It may also mean 'to' or 'between': *the academic year 2001/2002; the parent/child relationship.* Slashes are used to separate numbers in fractions: *33/140 of the total weight;* dates: *your invoice of 9/12/00;* to stand for 'per': *at the rate of 2 mm/sec;* and in some abbreviations, such as *c/o* meaning 'care of'. They are also used to indicate line breaks when quoting poetry, when they are usually followed by a space *The weight of the world/ is love* (Allen Ginsberg). In computing the slash (/) is called a ***forward slash*** to distinguish it from the ***backslash*** (\), which is used for specific purposes, e.g. to show the location of a file or document: *c:\letters\surfclub.doc.* Internet locations usually have forward slashes.

slash-and-burn *adj* **1** describes a form of agriculture characterized by the cutting down and burning of trees and vegetation in order to plant crops **2** having or showing the intention to deal with somebody or something drastically and ruthlessly or to destroy somebody or something completely (*informal*) ○ *her slash-and-burn approach to budget cuts*

slasher movie *n* a horror film featuring gory effects such as people being slashed with blades (*slang*)

slashing /sláshing/ *adj* **1 CRITICAL** aggressively critical **2 REDUCING** severely reducing or shortening something ○ *make slashing cuts to the budget* ■ *n* **1 ILLEGAL ACT IN HOCKEY AND LACROSSE** the illegal striking or swinging of a stick at an opposing player in hockey or lacrosse **2 CUTTING ATTACK** an act of attacking and cutting somebody with a blade —**slashingly** *adv*

slash pine *n* **1** a pine of swampy regions that yields turpentine and timber. Native to: SE United States. *Pinus caribaea.* **2** the hard durable wood of a pine tree [< *slash* 'swamp' < ?]

slash pocket *n* a pocket in a garment fitted with a diagonal slit for easy access

slat /slat/ *n* **1 THIN STRIP** a light thin narrow strip of wood or metal **2 AEROFOIL ON AN AIRCRAFT WING** an auxiliary aerofoil fixed to the leading edge of a wing to give extra lift ■ *vt* (**slats, slatting, slatted**) **ADD SLATS TO** to put slats in something [Mid-18C. < Old French *esclat* 'splinter, piece broken off'.]

slate[1] /slayt/ *n* **1 LAYERED ROCK** a fine-grained metamorphic rock that splits easily into layers and is widely used as a roofing material **2 ROOFING TILE** a roofing tile made of slate **3 WRITING TABLET** a small square piece of slate formerly used for writing on, especially by school students **4 DARK GREY** a dark grey colour **5** *US, Can* **LIST OF CANDIDATES** a list of the candidates in an election **6 IDENTIFYING BOARD ON A FILM SET** an identifying board used on a film set showing information such as the shot number that is held in front of a camera at the beginning or end of a shot ■ *vt* (**slates, slating, slated**) **1 COVER WITH SLATE** to cover a roof with tiles made of slate **2** *US* **INCLUDE IN LIST OF CANDIDATES** to put somebody's name on a list of candidates for election [14C. < Old French *esclate*, feminine of *esclat* 'splinter, piece broken off'.] —**slate** *adj* —**slatiness** *n* —**slaty** *adj* ◇ **a clean slate** an imaginary record of somebody's past, with no transgressions recorded on it or with all previous transgressions forgotten (*informal*) ◇ **have a slate loose** *Scotland* an offensive phrase meaning to be irrational or very odd ◇ **on the slate** on credit (*informal*) ◇ **wipe the slate clean** to forget about what has happened and make a fresh start (*informal*)

slate[2] /slayt/ (**slates, slating, slated**) *vt* to criticize severely somebody or something (*informal*) ○ *His last play was slated by the critics.* [Early 19C. < SLATE[1].]

slate blue, slate grey *adj* of a dark bluish-grey colour — **slate blue** *n*

slater /sláytər/ *n* **1** somebody whose job is to lay roofing tiles made of slate **2** *Scotland, ANZ, US* a woodlouse

slather /sláthər/ *vt US, Can* **1 SPREAD SOMETHING THICKLY** to spread something thickly or excessively on something else **2 SQUANDER** to use something wastefully (*informal*) ■ **slathers** *npl US* **LARGE AMOUNT** a large or generous quantity (*informal*) [Mid-19C. < ?]

slating[1] /sláyting/ *n* the process of covering something with slates, or the slates themselves

slating[2] /sláyting/ *n* harsh criticism, or a severe reprimand (*informal*)

slattern /sláttərn/ *n* (*dated*) 1 an offensive term for a woman regarded as ignoring conventional standards of hygiene and grooming 2 an offensive term for a woman regarded as being sexually promiscuous [Mid-17C. Possibly from a dialect word meaning 'slop, be slovenly'.] —**slatternliness** *n* —**slatternly** *adj*

slaughter /sláwtər/ *n* 1 KILLING OF ANIMALS the killing of animals for their meat 2 KILLING OF PEOPLE the brutal killing of a person or large numbers of people 3 MAJOR DEFEAT an overwhelming defeat (*slang*) ■ *vt* 1 KILL AN ANIMAL FOR MEAT to kill an animal or animals, usually for their meat 2 KILL PEOPLE BRUTALLY to kill a person or large numbers of people brutally 3 DEFEAT SOMEBODY CONVINCINGLY to defeat a person or a group of people overwhelmingly (*slang*) [13C. < Old Norse *slátr* 'meat, butchery'.] —**slaughterer** *n* —**slaughterous** *adj*

slaughterhouse /sláwtər howss/ (*plural* **-houses** /-howziz/) *n* = **abattoir**

LITERARY LINK ***Slaughterhouse-Five***, a novel (1970) by US writer Kurt Vonnegut. In this highly original blend of realism and science fiction, World War II veteran Billy Pilgrim is kidnapped by aliens who enable him to revisit his past. He subsequently relives the Allied firebombing of Dresden in 1945, an event witnessed by Vonnegut himself and here presented as a symbol of the unending cruelty and suffering of humanity.

slaughterman /sláwtərmən/ (*plural* **-men** /-mən/) *n* a worker in a slaughterhouse

Slav /slaav/ *n* a member of a people of E Europe and NW Asia who speak a Slavonic language [14C. < medieval Latin *Sclavus* < medieval Greek *Sklabos*, ultimately < Slavic.] —**Slav** *adj*

slave /slayv/ *n* 1 PERSON FORCED TO WORK FOR ANOTHER in former times, a person who was forced to work for another person for no payment and was regarded as the property of the person he or she worked for 2 DOMINATED PERSON a person who is dominated by somebody or something 3 SOMEBODY ACCEPTING ANOTHER'S RULE a person who meekly accepts being ruled by somebody else 4 VERY HARD WORKER a person who works hard, in bad conditions, and for low pay 5 DEVICE CONTROLLED BY ANOTHER a device that is totally controlled by another (*often before nouns*) ■ *vi* (**slaves, slaving, slaved**) WORK VERY HARD to work very hard ○ *I've been slaving away over this manuscript all day.* ■ *adj* 1 USING ENSLAVED LABOURERS using or relating to enslaved labourers 2 HARSH very harsh and unfair ○ *slave conditions* [13C. Via Old French *esclave* < medieval Latin *sclavus* 'Slav, captive'.]

slave ant *n* an ant captured and forced to work for an ant colony of another species

slave cylinder *n* a small, piston-bearing cylinder in a hydraulic system [Because its action is linked to a master cylinder]

slave-driver *n* 1 a person who makes employees work unduly hard 2 in the past, somebody who was employed to make sure that enslaved people worked hard

slaveholder /sláyv hōldər/ *n* somebody owning slaves

slave labour *n* 1 a workforce consisting of people who are forced to work against their will ○ *The pyramids were built by slave labour.* 2 hard or demanding work, in poor conditions, that is not well paid (*informal*) ○ *It's nothing but slave labour in that department.*

slave-making ant, slave-maker ant *n* a species of ant that raids the colonies of other ant species, capturing larvae and pupae to be used in its own colony

slaver[1] /sláyvər/ *n* an owner of or dealer in slaves

slaver[2] /slávvər, sláyvər/ *vi* 1 DRIBBLE SALIVA to dribble saliva from the mouth 2 BEHAVE OBSEQUIOUSLY to fawn or behave obsequiously to somebody 3 LUST AFTER to desire or lust after something or somebody greatly ■ *n* DRIPPING SALIVA saliva that drips from somebody's mouth [14C. Probably < N Germanic.]

slavery /sláyvəri/ *n* 1 CONDITION OF BEING AN ENSLAVED LABOURER the condition of being forced to work for somebody else in past times 2 SYSTEM BASED ON ENSLAVED LABOUR a system based on using the enforced labour of other people 3 STATE OF BEING DOMINATED a state of being completely dominated by another 4 HARD WORK very hard work, especially for low pay and under bad conditions

Slave State *n* any of the 15 states in the United States where slavery was legal until the Civil War

slave trade *n* the business of capturing people and buying and selling them as enslaved labourers

Slavic /slaávik/ *n* a branch of the Indo-European family of languages that includes Bulgarian, Russian, and Polish —**Slavic** *adj*

slavish /sláyvish/ *adj* (*offensive in some contexts*) 1 behaving in an unquestioning way 2 showing a lack of originality or independence of thought —**slavishly** *adv* —**slavishness** *n*

Slavism /slaávizəm/ *n* a feature or characteristic of the Slavs or Slavonic languages

slavocracy /slay vókrəssi/ *n* slave owners considered collectively as a ruling group, or rule by slave owners

Slavonic *n, adj* LANG = **Slavic** [Early 17C. < medieval Latin *S(c)lavonicus* < *S(c)lavonia* 'country of the Slavs'.]

Slavophile /slaávō fīl/, **Slavophil** *n* an admirer of Slavonic culture or people (*often before nouns*) —**Slavophilism** /slaávōfilizəm/ *n*

slaw /slaw/ *n US, Can* FOOD = **coleslaw** [Late 18C. < Dutch *sla*, contraction of French *salade* (see SALAD).]

slay /slay/ (**slays, slaying, slew** /sloo/, **slain** /slayn/) *vt* 1 to kill somebody or something (*formal or literary*) 2 (*past* **slayed,** *past participle* **slayed** *or* **slain**) to amuse somebody very much (*informal*) [Old English *slēan* < Germanic, 'strike'] —**slayer** *n*

SPELLCHECK Do not confuse ***slay*** with ***sleigh***, which has a similar sound. Beware: your spellchecker will not catch this error.

slaying /sláy ing/ *n* a killing or murder

SLBM *abbr* submarine-launched ballistic missile

SLE *abbr* systemic lupus erythematosus

sleaze /sleez/ *n* 1 corruption, dishonesty, or scandal, especially among public figures such as politicians 2 = **sleazebag** (*slang insult*) [Mid-20C. Back-formation < SLEAZY.]

sleazebag /sleéz bag/, **sleazeball** /sleéz báwl/ *n* an offensive term for somebody whose behaviour is perceived as immoral, unethical, or despicable (*slang insult*)

sleazy /sleézi/ (**-zier, -ziest**) *adj* 1 dirty, disreputable, or sordid in character or appearance 2 dishonest or immoral ○ *You get some pretty sleazy types in here.* [Mid-17C. Originally 'flimsy in texture' < ?] —**sleazily** *adv* —**sleaziness** *n*

sled /sled/ *n, vti* TRANSP = **sledge**[1] [14C. < Middle Low German *sledde* < Germanic, 'slip, slide'.]

sledge[1] /slej/ *n* 1 SMALL VEHICLE SLIDING OVER SNOW a small, low vehicle on ski-style or other runners, designed to be pulled over snow or ice by people or dogs 2 CHILD'S TOY VEHICLE FOR SNOW a child's toy vehicle on runners, used for sliding down snowy hills ■ *vti* (**sledges, sledging, sledged; sleds, sledding, sledded**) MOVE USING SLEDGE to ride, travel, or transport something by sledge [Late 16C. < Dutch dialect *sleedse*.] —**sledger** *n*

sledge[2] /slej/ *n* = **sledgehammer** *n.* [Old English *slecg* < Germanic, 'strike']

sledgehammer /sléj hammər/ *n* LARGE HAMMER a large heavy hammer swung with both hands ■ *vt* STRIKE WITH A SLEDGEHAMMER to hit something with a sledgehammer or with the force of one ■ *adj* VERY FORCEFUL extremely forceful ○ *sledgehammer blows*

sledging /sléjjing/ *n* 1 the activity, sport, or pastime of sliding over snow or ice on a sledge 2 the attempt by a cricket fielder or bowler to undermine a batsman's confidence by verbal abuse (*informal*)

sleek /sleek/ *adj* 1 SMOOTH AND SHINY attractively smooth and shiny 2 WELL-GROOMED well-groomed and healthy looking 3 SUAVE smooth and polished in behaviour or speech, often insincerely or suspiciously so ○ *a sleek sales pitch* ■ *vt* MAKE SOMETHING SLEEK to make something appear smooth or shiny [Late 16C. Variant of SLICK.] —**sleekly** *adv* —**sleekness** *n*

sleekit /sleékit/ *adj Scotland* superficially charming but cunning and untrustworthy ○ *He's the kind of sleekit character that gets round people.* [14C. Variant of *sleeked*, past participle of SLEEK (verb).]

sleep /sleep/ *n* 1 STATE OF NOT BEING AWAKE a state of partial or full unconsciousness in people and animals, during which voluntary functions are suspended and the body rests and restores itself, or a period in this state 2 STATE RESEMBLING SLEEP any state that is inactive or dormant, like sleep 3 DEATH death (*literary; also used euphemistically*) 4 MUCUS IN EYES small amounts of dried mucus that often collect in the eyes during sleep (*informal*) 5 PLANT SCI = **nyctitropism** ■ *v* (**sleeps, sleeping, slept** /slept/) 1 *vi* BE IN A STATE OF SLEEP to go into or be in a state of sleep 2 *vi* BE INACTIVE to be in an inactive or dormant state ○ *a city that never sleeps* 3 *vi* CHANGE POSITION AT NIGHT in plants, to assume a position at night that is different from the daytime position 4 *vt* PROVIDE BEDS FOR PEOPLE to provide sleeping accommodation for a particular number of people ○ *The yacht sleeps eight.* 5 *vi* BE DEAD to be dead (*literary; also used euphemistically*) ○ *He sleeps in the bosom of Abraham.* 6 *vt* SPEND TIME IN SLEEP to spend a period of time sleeping ○ *We slept the night in a hotel.* [The noun is < Old English *slǣp*, the verb < Old English *slǣpan*, both < Germanic] ◇ **get** *or* **go to sleep** to begin sleeping ◇ **in your sleep** 1 while you are sleeping 2 with ease, as if not having to be fully awake (*informal*) ○ *I could find my way there in my sleep, I've been so often.* ◇ **not lose (any) sleep over something** not to worry about something because it is thought to be trivial or irrelevant ◇ **put something to sleep** to kill an animal in a humane way, especially because it is ill, injured, or in pain ◇ **sleep on it** to postpone a decision until at least the next day in order to give it more thought ◇ **sleep rough** to sleep outdoors, especially in the street and usually because of being homeless

sleep around *vi* to have a lot of casual sexual relationships with different people (*informal*)

sleep in *vi* to sleep longer than you usually do

sleep off *vt* to get rid of illness by sleeping until it is gone

sleep out *vi* sleep out of doors

sleep over *vi* to sleep at somebody else's house as part of a visit

sleep together *vi* to have sex (*used euphemistically*)

sleep with *vt* to have sex with somebody (*informal; used euphemistically*)

sleep apnoea *n* a temporary cessation of breathing that happens to some people while they are sleeping

sleeper /sleépər/ *n* 1 SOMEBODY SLEEPING a person who sleeps, or who sleeps in a specific way ○ *a light sleeper* 2 RAILWAY CARRIAGE WITH BEDS a railway carriage or compartment with beds for passengers 3 TRAIN WITH BEDS an overnight train with beds for passengers to sleep in ○ *Should I go down on the sleeper or get an early-morning flight?* 4 BEAM SUPPORTING RAILS any of the beams of wood or concrete on which the rails of a railway track are laid. US term **tie** 5 HEAVY BEAM a heavy beam used as a sill, footing, or support 6 SURPRISING SUCCESS somebody or something that is not immediately successful but, often surprisingly, becomes so after a while (*informal*) 7 SPY INACTIVE UNTIL CALLED INTO ACTION a spy or secret agent who lives an ordinary life until called into action (*informal*) 8 SMALL GOLD EARRING a small gold stud or ring worn to keep the hole of a pierced ear from closing 9 TROPICAL FISH a marine or freshwater tropical fish related to the goby that often lies immobile. Family: Eleotridae. ■ **sleepers** *npl US* CHILDREN'S PYJAMAS children's one-piece pyjamas with feet

sleeping bag *n* a long padded or lined fabric bag for sleeping in, especially when camping

sleeping car *n* a railway carriage that has bunks or compartments in which passengers can sleep

sleeping draught *n* a drink containing a drug that is meant to help somebody sleep

sleeping partner *n* a person who puts money into a business but does not play an active part in running it. US term **silent partner**

sleeping pill, sleeping tablet *n* a pill containing a drug that is meant to induce sleep

sleeping policeman *n* a speed bump

sleeping sickness *n* 1 a disease in tropical Africa caused by parasitic protozoans that are carried by tsetse flies 2 an epidemic form of encephalitis causing lethargy, muscular weakness, and impaired vision

sleeping tablet *n* MED = **sleeping pill**

sleep-learning *n* a method of learning something that involves the continuous playing of recordings of it to a sleeping learner

sleepless /sleépləss/ *adj* 1 without sleep, or unable to sleep ○ *a sleepless night* 2 always awake, active, or busy —**sleeplessly** *adv* —**sleeplessness** *n*

sleep-out *n ANZ* a part of a veranda or yard that has been turned into an outdoor sleeping area, usually partially or fully enclosed with glass or insect screens

sleepover /sleépōvər/ *n* an overnight stay for children at somebody else's house after a party (*informal*)

sleepsuit /sleep syoot/ *n* a one-piece sleeping garment for a baby or child, usually covering the feet

sleepwalk /sleep wawk/ *vi* **1** to walk while you are asleep **2** to do something in an inattentive or lethargic way (*informal*) —**sleepwalker** *n* —**sleepwalking** *n*

sleepwear /sleep wair/ *n* CLOTHING = **nightwear**

sleepy /sleepi/ (**-ier, -iest**) *adj* **1 DROWSY** feeling drowsy and wanting to sleep **2 QUIET AND WITHOUT MUCH ACTIVITY** quiet and not very lively or exciting ○ *a sleepy mining town* **3 CAUSING SLEEP** tending to make somebody fall asleep —**sleepily** *adv* —**sleepiness** *n*

sleepyhead /sleepi hed/ *n* a person who is drowsy and is nearly falling asleep or has just woken up (*informal*) —**sleepyheaded** *adj*

sleepy sickness *n* MED = **sleeping sickness** *n.* 2

sleet /sleet/ *n* **1 RAIN MIXED WITH SNOW** rainfall mixed with snow **2** *US* **THIN COATING OF ICE** the thin coating of ice formed when rain freezes on something ■ *vi* **FALL AS SLEET** to fall as sleet [13C. Probably < Old English.]

sleeve /sleev/ *n* **1 COVERING FOR THE ARM** either of the two parts of a garment that wholly or partially cover the arms **2 TUBULAR PIECE** a tubular piece designed to fit inside or over a cylinder **3 RECORD COVER** a decorated protective cover for a record or CD that usually lists the performers and contents. US term **jacket** *n.* 5 ■ *vt* (**sleeves, sleeving, sleeved**) **FIT WITH A SLEEVE** to provide something with a sleeve [Old English *slēfe* < Indo-European, 'slide, slip'] —**sleeveless** *adj* ◇ **roll up your sleeves** to get ready to do something vigorously (*informal*) ◇ **up your sleeve** kept hidden or secret but available for use

sleeve board *n* a small, narrow ironing board used for pressing sleeves

sleeveen /slee veen/ *n* *Ireland* a sly, plausible, and ingratiating person [Mid-19C. < Irish *slíbhín* 'sly person, trickster'.]

sleeve notes *npl* information about a record, printed on its cover. US term **liner notes**

sleeve valve *n* a valve for an internal-combustion engine, fitted and reciprocating inside a cylinder

sleeving /sleeving/ *n* flexible, tubular insulation inside which wires that carry electric current can be fitted. US term **spaghetti** *n.* 3

sleigh /slay/ *n* an open, usually horse-drawn vehicle on runners, used for travel on snow and ice ■ *vi* to move over snow or ice in a sleigh [Early 18C. Via Dutch *slee* < Middle Dutch *slēde*.]

SPELLCHECK See *slay*.

sleighbell /sláy bel/ *n* a small bell attached to a sleigh or to the harness of horses pulling it

sleight /slīt/ *n* (*archaic*) **1** dexterity or skill in doing something **2** cunning or trickery [13C. < Old Norse *slœgð* 'cunning' < *slœgr* 'crafty'.]

sleight of hand *n* **1** skill or dexterity with the hands in conjuring, card tricks, or juggling **2** any kind of skill by which something happens without it being obvious how it is done

slender /sléndər/ *adj* **1 SMALL IN WIDTH** small or slight in width in proportion to height or length ○ *a flower with a slender stem* **2 SLIM** thin in a graceful way **3 LIMITED** small or limited in degree, extent, or size ○ *The home team won by a slender margin.* [13C. < ?] —**slenderly** *adv* —**slenderness** *n*

SYNONYMS See *thin*.

slenderize /sléndə rīz/ (**-izes, -izing, -ized**), **slenderise** (**-ises, -ising, -ized, -ised**) *vti* *US* to become slender, or make somebody or something slender

slender loris *n* a small tailless slow-moving primate. Native to: rainforests of India and Sri Lanka. *Loris tardigradus.*

slept past tense, past participle of **sleep**

Slessor /sléssər/, **Kenneth** (1901–71) Australian poet

sleuth /slooth/ *n* **1 DETECTIVE** a detective (*informal*) **2** ZOOL = **sleuthhound** *n.* 1 ■ *v* **1** *vi* **INVESTIGATE** to investigate as or in a similar way to a detective **2** *vt* **TRACK** to track or find somebody or something [Early 19C. Shortening of SLEUTHHOUND.]

sleuthhound /slooth hownd/ *n* **1** a dog used for tracking people, especially a bloodhound (*dated*) **2** a detective (*informal dated*) [14C. *Sleuth* < *sleuth* 'track, trail' < Old Norse *slóð*.]

S level *n* an advanced qualification, above and in addition to A level, taken in a subject in England and Wales for the General Certificate of Education. Full form **special level**

slew[1] past tense of **slay**

slew[2] /sloo/ *vti* to turn or twist something around, or be turned or twisted around, especially suddenly, violently, or uncontrollably ○ *She jammed on the brakes and the car slewed to a halt.* US term **slue** *v.* ■ *n* a forceful or uncontrolled turn or twist around. US term **slue** *n.* [Mid-18C. < ?]

slew[3] /sloo/ *n* *US* a large quantity or number of something (*informal*) ○ *They hit us with a whole slew of complaints.* [Mid-19C. Via Irish *sluagh* 'multitude' < Old Irish *slúag* 'host, army'.]

slewed /slood/ *adj* drunk (*slang*) [Mid-19C. < SLEW[2].]

SLI *abbr* specific language impairment

slice /slīss/ *n* **1 PIECE CUT FROM SOMETHING** a thin broad piece cut from something larger ○ *a slice of ham* **2 SHARE** a part, portion, or share of something ○ *a slice of the profits* **3 SERVING UTENSIL** a utensil with a thin, flat, triangular blade, used for cutting and serving food, especially fish or cake **4 OBLIQUE STRIKE OF A BALL** a stroke in which the ball is hit off-centre so that it follows a curving path **5 FLIGHT OF A BALL** the flight of a ball that has been sliced **6 TENNIS SHOT** a tennis shot that makes the ball spin and stay low when it bounces in the opponent's court ■ *v* (**slices, slicing, sliced**) **1** *vti* **CUT INTO PORTIONS** to cut something, or to be cut, into slices or portions **2** *vti* **CUT CLEANLY** to cut something cleanly and effortlessly ○ *The sword sliced the rope in half.* **3** *vi* **MOVE SWIFTLY AND CLEANLY** to move swiftly and cleanly, especially through a medium such as air or water **4** *vti* **CUT OFF** to cut something off something else ○ *The spinning blade sliced off log after log.* **5** *vt* **SET ON A CURVING PATH** to hit a ball off-centre so that it follows a curving path, whether intentionally or as a result of a bad swing or stroke **6** *vti* **HIT WITH A CHOPPING ACTION** to hit a tennis shot with a chopping stroke so that the ball spins and stays low when it bounces in the opponent's court **7** *vt* **PUT IN THE WATER SLANTWISE** to put the blade of an oar into the water at an angle [15C. < Old French *esclice* 'splinter' < *esclicier* 'splinter' < Germanic.] —**sliceable** *adj* —**slicer** *n*

slice of life *n* a realistic portrayal of life, especially a harsh or unpleasant life, e.g. in a film (*hyphenated before a noun*) ○ *a slice-of-life drama* [< the idea of cutting into something to see inside]

slick /slik/ *adj* **1 POLISHED** done or able to do things with great skill and apparently effortlessly ○ *a slick presentation* **2 CRAFTY** clever and resourceful or suave and sophisticated but not entirely trustworthy (*informal*) **3 GLIB** superficially impressive or persuasive but lacking substance or sincerity ○ *a slick sales pitch* **4 SLIPPERY** having a smooth, glossy, or slippery surface ○ *a slick runway* ■ *n* **1 SLIPPERY PATCH** a thinly spread or slippery patch of something, especially a quantity of oil floating on top of water **2** *US* PUBL = **glossy magazine** **3 TREADLESS TYRE** a wide treadless tyre used in motor racing ■ *vt* **MAKE SMOOTH** to make something smooth, glossy, or presentable [14C. Ultimately < Indo-European, 'slippery'.] —**slickly** *adv* —**slickness** *n*

slickenside /slíkən sīd/ *n* a rock surface that is smooth and marked with fine scratches caused by friction with another rock surface [Early 19C. < a dialect variant of SLICK + SLIDE.]

slicker /slíkər/ *n* **1 SOPHISTICATED BUT UNTRUSTWORTHY PERSON** an apparently sophisticated, stylish, or clever person who is not honest or trustworthy (*informal*) ◊ **city slicker** **2** *US* **RAINCOAT** a shiny raincoat, often made of a plastic or rubber material **3 SMOOTHING TOOL** a tool used for smoothing something

slide /slīd/ *v* (**slides, sliding, slid** /slid/) **1** *vti* **MOVE SMOOTHLY** to move or make something move smoothly across a surface ○ *The car slid for 50 yards when the brakes locked.* **2** *vti* **MOVE UNOBTRUSIVELY** to move or move something unobtrusively ○ *He slid the letter into his pocket.* **3** *vi* **SLIP** to lose your grip or secure footing on a surface ○ *I slid on an icy patch and nearly ended up flat on my back.* **4** *vi* **TO CHANGE TO A DIFFERENT CONDITION** to change to a different, usually worse, state or condition ○ *unable to stop the economy from sliding into recession* **5** *vi* **PLAY A GLIDE BETWEEN NOTES** to make a gliding change from one note to another **6** *vti* **APPROACH A BASE HORIZONTALLY** to approach a base in baseball or softball while skidding feet first, low to the ground ■ *n* **1 SLIDING** a sliding movement **2 STRUCTURE THAT CHILDREN PLAY ON** a structure with a metal slope that children slide down for fun **3 SMALL POSITIVE PHOTOGRAPH** a positive photograph reproduced on a small piece of film, mounted in a frame or on a plate and viewed by projection on a screen or through a magnifying device **4 FALL OF ROCK, MUD, OR EARTH** a downhill displacement of rock, mud, or earth, often caused by rainfall or erosion **5 SPECIMEN HOLDER** a small glass plate on which a specimen is mounted for viewing under a microscope **6** = **hair slide** **7 SLIDING MACHINE PART** a machine part that slides, or the part on which it moves **8** ROWING = **sliding seat** **9 TROMBONE MECHANISM** the U-shaped tube of a trombone that is pushed in and out to allow for changes in pitch **10 MUSICAL FEATURE** a sliding change from one note to another [Old English *slīdan* < Germanic] ◇ **let things** *or* **something slide** to let a situation gradually deteriorate ◇ **on the slide** in the process of becoming worse (*informal*)

slide-action *adj* describes a shotgun or rifle with a lever that ejects the case of a spent round and loads a new one

slide rule *n* a manual calculating device, now largely obsolete, consisting of two rulers marked with graduated logarithmic scales, one sliding inside the other

slide show *n* a sequence of photographic slides projected on a screen or wall as education or entertainment

slide trombone *n* a trombone with a slide that is moved to select different pitches as distinct from a trombone fitted with valves

sliding /slīding/ *adj* **1** varying according to changing conditions **2** moved by sliding ○ *a sliding door*

sliding scale *n* any scale, e.g. of wages, costs, or fees, that varies according to changes in some other factor

sliding seat *n* a seat in a rowing boat that slides backwards and forwards, allowing a rower to lengthen the stroke of the oars

~~**slieght**~~ incorrect spelling of **sleight**

slier comparative of **sly**

sliest superlative of **sly**

Slieve Donard /sleev dónnərd/ highest peak in the Mourne Mountains, SE Northern Ireland. Height: 852 m/2,796 ft.

slight /slīt/ *adj* **1 VERY SMALL** very small in size, degree, amount, or importance ○ *a slight resemblance* **2 THIN** having a slim body that does not look very strong **3 INSUBSTANTIAL** not very substantial or convincing ○ *an assertion made without the slightest evidence* ■ *vt* **1 SNUB** to treat somebody rudely, e.g. by deliberately ignoring him or her **2 TREAT SOMETHING AS UNIMPORTANT** to think of or treat something as unimportant **3** *US* **DO SOMETHING CARELESSLY** to handle duties or responsibilities carelessly ■ *n* **IMPOLITE ACT** an action that shows contempt for somebody or something [14C. Possibly < N Germanic.] —**slightness** *n* ◇ **not in the slightest** not at all (*informal*)

slighting /slīting/ *adj* showing contempt or disrespect ○ *make slighting remarks about it* —**slightingly** *adv*

slightly /slītli/ *adv* **1** to a small extent or degree ○ *slightly injured* **2** slimly and rather delicately ○ *slightly built*

Sligo /slīgō/ county in Connacht Province, NW Ireland. Area: 1,796 sq. km/693 sq. mi.

slim /slim/ *adj* (**slimmer, slimmest**) **1 SMALLER IN WIDTH THAN HEIGHT** small in width, thickness, or girth and generally long and narrow in shape **2 PLEASINGLY THIN** slender and well-proportioned **3 SMALL** small in degree, quality, or extent ○ *Hopes of their survival were slim.* ■ *v* (**slims, slimming, slimmed**) **1** *vi* **LOSE WEIGHT** to lose weight, especially by dieting **2** *vt* **REDUCE** to reduce the size or scope of something ○ *slim down the bloated bureaucracy* [Mid-17C. Via Dutch, 'inferior, small' < Middle Dutch, 'crooked'.] —**slimly** *adv* —**slimmer** *n* —**slimness** *n*

SYNONYMS See *thin*.

Slim /slim/, **William Joseph, 1st Viscount** (1891–1970) British general

slime /slīm/ *n* **1 SLIPPERY LIQUID** a fluid that is thick and slippery, especially one that is unpleasant to touch **2 MUCOUS SECRETION OF SOME LIVING THINGS** a mucous substance secreted by some living things such as fish, snails, and fungi ■ *vt* (**slimes, sliming, slimed**) **1 COVER SOMETHING WITH SLIME** to cover or smear something with slime **2 REMOVE SLIME FROM** to remove slime from something such as a fish before preparing it for cooking [Old English *slīm* < Indo-European, 'slippery']

slimeball /slím bawl/ *n* an offensive term that deliberately insults somebody regarded as despicable or repellent (*slang insult*)

slime mould, slime fungus *n* a simple organism that forms a small slimy amoeboid mass, e.g. on fallen logs, and produces spore-bearing reproductive organs similar to those of a fungus

slimline /slím līn/ *adj* **1** thinner than the standard type or model ○ *a slimline pocket tape recorder* **2** designed to help with a weight-reducing diet ○ *slimline tonic*

slimming /slímming/ *n* **EFFORT TO LOSE WEIGHT** the process of trying to lose weight, especially by dieting ■ *adj* **1 USED IN LOSING WEIGHT** used for losing weight or intended to help with losing weight **2 GIVING SLIM APPEARANCE** tending to make somebody look slimmer (*informal*) ○ *That dress is very slimming on you.*

slimsy /slímzi/ (**-sier, -siest**), **slimpsy** *adj US* both slight and flimsy (*informal*) [Mid-19C. Blend of SLIM + FLIMSY.]

slimy /slími/ (**-ier, -iest**) *adj* **1 LIKE SLIME** covered with or resembling slime ○ *a slimy secretion* **2 DISGUSTING** having the semiliquid, sticky consistency of slime ○ *a slimy mess* **3 OFFENSIVE TERM** an offensive term meaning thought to behave in an excessively ingratiating way (*insult*) —**slimily** *adv* —**sliminess** *n*

sling[1] /sling/ *n* **1 SUPPORTING BANDAGE** a wide bandage suspended from somebody's neck to support an injured arm or hand **2 CARRYING STRAP** a carrying strap attached to something such as a rifle **3 LOOP FOR CARRYING SOMETHING HEAVY** a loop of rope, leather, chain, or net used to lift, lower, or carry something heavy **4 LOOP USED AS WEAPON** a weapon used for throwing a stone or other object, consisting of a loop of leather or other material in which the missile is twirled before being released **5 SUPPORT FOR A YARD** a rope or chain that supports a ship's beam ■ **slings** *npl* **ANCHORING LOOP** a fixed loop of webbing used to provide an anchor to a rock, tree, or other point ■ *v* (**slings, slinging, slung, slung** /slung/) **1** *vt* **THROW WITH FORCE** to throw something with a lot of force **2** *vt* **PASS OR PUT SOMETHING CASUALLY** to throw or pass something or to put or place something somewhere in a casual or careless way (*informal*) ○ *Sling me that newspaper, will you?* **3 USE A CARRYING LOOP ON** to attach something to, carry something with, or hang something from a carrying loop [13C. < ?] —**slinger** *n*

sling off *vi ANZ* to speak abusively, often while blaming or criticizing ○ *I'm sick of my boss slinging off at me.*

sling[2] /sling/ *n* a mixed alcoholic drink made with spirits, sugar, lemon or lime juice, and water [Mid-18C. < ?]

slingback /slíng bak/ *n* a woman's shoe that is open at the heel and is held on the foot by a strap (*often before nouns*)

slingshot /slíng shot/ *n US* MIL = **catapult** *n.* 2

slink /slingk/ *v* (**slinks, slinking, slunk, slunk** /slungk/) **1** *vi* **MOVE FURTIVELY** to move or behave quietly and secretively ○ *I could see her trying to slink away through the back door.* **2** *vi* **MOVE SEXILY** to walk in a sexually alluring way **3** *vt* **BEAR PREMATURELY** to give birth to young prematurely, especially to a calf ■ *n* **PREMATURE ANIMAL** a prematurely born animal, especially a calf ■ *adj* **BORN EARLY** describes an animal, especially a calf, that is born prematurely [Old English *slincan* < Germanic, 'slide, throw']

slinky /slíngki/ (**-ier, -iest**) *adj* **1** having a seductive appearance or way of moving **2** close-fitting and emphasizing the curves of the body ○ *a slinky outfit* —**slinkily** *adv* —**slinkiness** *n*

sliotar /slṓtər/ *n* the ball used in the sport of hurling [Early 19C. < Irish Gaelic.]

slip[1] /slip/ *v* (**slips, slipping, slipped**) **1** *vi* **LOSE YOUR FOOTING** to lose your footing or grip on a slippery surface ○ *I slipped and fell.* **2** *vi* **MOVE FROM ITS PROPER POSITION** to slide or move accidentally out of the proper or desired position ○ *This strap keeps slipping off my shoulder.* **3** *vti* **MOVE SMOOTHLY** to move or make something move smoothly and easily and usually with a sliding motion ○ *It slips easily in and out of its case.* **4** *vi* **GO QUIETLY** to go somewhere in a quiet, furtive, or unnoticed way ○ *He slipped out while nobody was looking.* **5** *vt* **PASS SOMETHING SECRETLY** to give somebody something furtively or secretly ○ *I saw the man slip her an envelope.* **6** *vti* **PUT ON OR TAKE OFF** to put on or take off something quickly and easily **7** *vti* **BE FORGOTTEN** to be forgotten or overlooked by somebody ○ *It slipped my mind.* **8** *vi* **ERR** to make a mistake or to do something wrong ○ *You must have slipped up when you were making a note of the number.* **9** *vi* **GET WORSE** to decline from a previous standard, e.g., of performance or awareness ○ *He's slipping – two years ago he would have spotted that mistake at once.* ○ *She's in danger of slipping back into her bad old ways.* **10** *vt* **DISLOCATE A BONE** to dislocate or displace a bone, especially in the spine **11** *vti* **DISENGAGE THE CLUTCH** to disengage the clutch of a motor vehicle or be disengaged **12** *vi* **FAIL TO ENGAGE** to fail to engage properly, usually because of wear (*refers to mechanical parts*) **13** *vt* **LET A RESTRAINING CABLE GO** to let a line or cable that is securing a vessel to a mooring or anchor fall over the side **14** *vti* **RELEASE** to release an animal from a restraint, or be released in this way ■ *n* **1 ACT OF SLIPPING** an act of slipping, especially a sudden slide on a slippery surface **2 ERROR** an error or oversight **3 LAPSE** a moral lapse or instance of misconduct **4 DECLINE** a fall from some previous standard or level **5 UNDERGARMENT** a light sleeveless woman's undergarment worn under a dress **6** NAUT = **slipway 7 DEFORMATION OF A CRYSTAL** the deformation of a metallic crystal by shearing along a plane **8 FIELDING POSITION** in cricket, the position of a fielder behind and near the wicketkeeper, especially on the off side, or the fielder who takes up this position **9 CLOTH COVERING** a cloth covering for something **10** GEOL = **landslide** *n.* 1 **11** AIR = **sideslip** *n.* 2 [13C. Probably < Middle Dutch or Middle Low German *slippen*.] ◇ **give somebody the slip** to get away from somebody who is chasing or pursuing you ◇ **let slip 1** to say something without meaning to, or reveal something that should be kept secret **2** to allow somebody or something to escape ◇ **slip one over on somebody** to trick or deceive somebody (*informal*)

SYNONYMS See ***mistake***.

slip up *vi* **1** to make a mistake (*informal*) ○ *Somebody slipped up and forgot to put your name on the guest list.* **2** to slip and fall while walking or running

slip[2] /slip/ *n* **1 NARROW PIECE** a narrow strip of something ○ *a slip of paper* **2 SMALL PIECE OF PAPER** a small piece of paper, especially a small form, document, or record of a transaction ○ *a paying-in slip* **3 CUTTING** a stem or branch of a plant broken off and used to start a new plant **4 DELICATE YOUNG PERSON** a young and slightly built person ○ *a slip of a lad* **5** *US* **NARROW CHURCH PEW** a church pew that is narrow ■ *vt* (**slips, slipping, slipped**) **REMOVE A SLIP** to remove a slip from a plant in order to grow a new plant

slip[3] /slip/ *n* a mixture of clay and water, used as a decorative layer on pottery or for casting in moulds to form an actual piece [17C. < Old English *slipa*, *slyppe* 'slime'.]

SLIP /slip/ *n* the older of two protocols for dial-up access to the Internet using a modem. It has now been largely replaced by a higher-level protocol (**PPP**). Full form **serial line Internet protocol**

slipcase /slíp kayss/ *n* a box for protecting a book or set of books, usually made of sturdy cardboard, with one or more open ends

slipcover /slíp kuvər/ *n US, Can* FURNITURE = **loose cover**

slipe /slīp/ *n Scotland, N England* a sledge or sledge runner used in a mine [15C. < Low German *slīpe*, variant of *slēpe* 'sledge, train'.]

slipknot /slíp not/, **slip knot** *n* a knot that slips easily along the rope or cord around which it is tied

slip-on *n* a shoe that does not have a fastening ■ *adj* used to describe a shoe that does not have a fastening

slipover /slípōvər/ *n* CLOTHING = **pullover**

slippage /slíppij/ *n* **1 SLIDE** the process or an instance of slipping, especially from a stable or desired position ○ *Recent thunderstorms have caused slippage in the banks along rivers.* **2 AMOUNT OF SLIPPING** an amount or extent that something slips **3 DECLINE** a decrease in the quality, performance, or production of something **4 LOSS OF POWER** a loss of power or forward motion caused by the slipping of a mechanical part

slipper /slíppər/ *n* a flat shoe of soft or lightweight material, usually worn indoors —**slippered** *adj*

slipper bath *n* **1** a bath that is covered at one end **2 slipper baths** a place where people can pay to have a bath (*dated*)

slipper flower *n US* PLANTS = **calceolaria**

slipperwort /slíppər wurt/ *n* PLANTS = **calceolaria**

slippery /slíppəri/ (**-ier, -iest**) *adj* **1 CAUSING SLIDING** likely to cause somebody or something to slip **2 HARD TO HOLD FIRMLY** sliding easily from the grasp or from a position **3 PRECARIOUS** unstable and liable to change ○ *We're in a slippery situation; things could go either way.* **4 UNTRUSTWORTHY** behaving in a devious or deceitful way ○ *a slippery character* —**slipperily** *adv* —**slipperiness** *n*

slippery elm *n* **1** the moist sticky inner bark of an elm. Use: natural remedy in alternative medicine to relieve inflammation in the digestive tract. **2** a deciduous hardwood tree that yields slippery elm. Native to: North America. *Ulmus rubra.*

slippery slope *n* a dangerous situation that can lead to ultimate downfall

slippy /slíppi/ (**-pier, -piest**) *adj* likely to cause somebody or something to slip, or sliding easily from the grasp or from a position (*informal*)

slip ring *n* a metal ring in a generator or motor to which current is delivered or from which it is removed by brushes

slip road *n* a short road for driving onto or off a motorway or fast road

slipsheet /slíp sheet/ *n* a sheet of blank paper placed between newly printed sheets to prevent wet ink on the printed sheets from rubbing off or smearing ■ *vt* to place a blank sheet of paper between newly printed papers on which the ink is still wet

slipshod /slíp shod/ *adj* **1** done in a sloppy way without attention to details **2** not neat in appearance [Late 16C. < SLIP[1] 'slide' + SHOD 'wearing shoes'.] —**slipshodly** *adv* —**slipshodness** *n*

slip step *n* a step in Scottish reels and jigs in which the left foot moves one step to the side and the right foot moves to the left

slip stitch *n* a hidden stitch used to connect two layers of fabric —**slip stitch** *vt*

slipstream /slíp streem/ *n* **1 AIR FROM PROPELLER** a stream of air driven backwards by an aircraft's propeller **2 AREA BEHIND FAST-MOVING VEHICLE** an area of reduced air pressure and forward suction that is directly behind and caused by a rapidly moving vehicle ■ *vi* **FOLLOW IN SLIPSTREAM** to follow in another vehicle's slipstream so as to take advantage of the decreased air resistance

slip-up *n* an accidental mistake or blunder (*informal*)

slipware /slíp wair/ *n* pottery that has been coated or decorated with slip

slipway /slíp way/ *n* a sloping surface used to build or repair boats before returning them to the water

slit /slit/ *vt* (**slits, slitting, slit**) **1 SLICE** to make a long straight cut in something ○ *She slit the bag open with a knife.* **2 CUT SOMETHING INTO STRIPS** to cut something into thin strips ■ *n* **NARROW CUT OR OPENING** a long narrow cut or opening [12C. < Old English *slitan* 'cut up' < Germanic.] —**slitter** *n*

SYNONYMS See ***tear***.

slither /slíthər/ *v* **1** *vti* **SLIDE OR CAUSE SOMETHING TO SLIDE** to move along a slippery or uneven surface, or make something slide along ○ *We slithered down the muddy river bank.* **2** *vi* **GLIDE** to slide along easily, using friction to move forward, as a snake does ■ *n* **GLIDING MOVEMENT** a gliding, effortless movement [12C. < Old English *slidrian* 'slide repeatedly' < *slidan* 'slide'.]

slit trench *n* a narrow trench dug as protection against shelling during a battle

sliver /slívvər/ *n* **1 SPLINTER** a thin piece of something that has been split, cut, or broken off **2 SMALL PIECE** a small narrow portion or piece of something **3 LOOSE FIBRE** a loose strand of wool, cotton, or some other material prepared for drawing and twisting by carding ■ *vti* **BREAK INTO SPLINTERS** to break something into splinters, or become splintered [14C. < Old English *slifan* 'cleave, split' < Germanic.]

slivovitz /slívvəvits/ *n* a dry colourless plum brandy made in E Europe [Late 19C. < Serbo-Croat *sljivovica* 'plum brandy' < *sljiva* 'plum'.]

Sloane Ranger /slṓn-/, **Sloane** *n* a fashionable and conventional upper-class young person, usually a woman, who lives in London and has a lively social life among people of the same kind (*informal*) [Late 20C. Pun on *Sloane* Square, London, and the fictional cowboy the Lone *Ranger*.]

slob /slob/ *n* an offensive term that deliberately insults somebody's personal habits, hygiene, and manners (*insult*) [Late 18C. Via Irish *slab* 'mud' < English *slab* 'bog' < N Germanic.] —**slobbish** *adj*

slob around *vi* to spend time being relaxing and doing

nothing much (*informal*) ○ *I spent the day slobbing around in my pyjamas.*

slobber /slóbbər/ *v* 1 *vti* **DRIBBLE SALIVA** to drool or allow saliva or a liquid to run from the mouth 2 *vi* **EXPRESS EXTREME EMOTION** to be overly sentimental or emotional 3 *vt* **SMEAR SOMETHING WITH SALIVA** to soak or cover something with saliva or liquid from the mouth ■ *n* 1 **SALIVA** saliva or liquid that has been drooled from the mouth 2 **SENTIMENTAL WRITING OR TALK** overemotional or sentimental talk or writing ○ *I can't stand to read such slobber.* [14C. Probably < Middle Dutch *slobberen* 'feed noisily, walk through mud'.] —**slobberer** *n* —**slobbery** *adj*

sloe /slō/ (*plural* **sloes** *or* **sloe**) *n* 1 **SOUR BLUE-BLACK FRUIT** a small sour blue-black fruit of the blackthorn 2 **DARK RED OR YELLOW FRUIT** a dark purple fruit, or a red or yellow fruit produced by different species of North American plum trees 3 TREES = **blackthorn** *n.* 1 4 **N AMERICAN PLUM TREE** a plum tree that bears sloes. Native to: E North America. *Prunus alleghaniensis* and *Prunus americana.* [Old English *slāh* < Indo-European, 'bluish']

sloe-eyed *adj* with dark almond-shaped eyes [Because of the blue-black colour of the fruit]

sloe gin *n* a liqueur made of gin flavoured with sloes

slog /slog/ *v* (**slogs, slogging, slogged**) 1 *vi* **PLOD** to walk slowly with great effort ○ *How long did it take us to slog up that mountain?* 2 *vi* **WORK LONG AND HARD** to work at something for a long time with little progress ○ *They've all been down at the office, slogging through endless reams of paperwork.* 3 *vt* **MAKE YOUR WAY** to make headway or progress through something with great difficulty ○ *We had to slog our way through several muddy fields.* 4 *vt* **HIT SOMEBODY OR SOMETHING HARD** to hit somebody or something with great force ○ *It was like being slogged by a heavyweight boxer.* ■ *n* 1 **LONG HARD WALK** a long difficult trip or walk ○ *It was quite a slog from the station to the hostel.* 2 **HARD WORK** a long period of hard work ○ *Hard slog is the only way you'll pass those exams.* 3 **HARD HIT** a hard blow or swipe [Early 19C. < ?] —**slogger** *n*

slogan /slṓgən/ *n* 1 **MOTTO** a short distinctive phrase used to identify a company or organization or its goals 2 **ADVERTISING PHRASE** a short catchy phrase used in advertising to promote something 3 *Scotland* **SCOTTISH BATTLE CRY** the battle cry of a Highland clan (*archaic*) [Early 16C. < Gaelic *sluagh-ghairm* < *sluagh* 'army' + *gairm* 'cry'.]

sloganeer /slṓgə neér/ *n* a creator or frequent user of slogans ○ *the kind of politician who is little more than a clever sloganeer* ■ *vi* to create or use slogans

sloganize /slṓgə nīz/ *vt* to express something in a slogan or make a slogan of something ○ *the sloganizing of political ideals* —**sloganizer** *n*

sloop /sloop/ *n* a single-masted sailing boat, rigged fore-and-aft, with one headsail extending from the foremast to the bowsprit [Early 17C. Via Dutch *sloep* < French *chaloupe* < Old French *chalupe* 'sloop-rigged boat'.]

sloop of war *n* a small armed sailing ship that is larger than a gunboat and carries guns on only one deck

slop[1] /slop/ *n* 1 **SOMETHING SPILLED** a liquid that has spilled or overflowed ○ *Look at all the slop on the floor!* 2 **MUD OR SLUSH** soft mud or slushy snow ○ *How far do we have to wade through this slop?* 3 **UNAPPEALING FOOD** poor-quality unappetizing or watery food (*often plural*) 4 **MASH** what remains of the mash after an alcoholic beverage has been distilled (*often plural*) 5 **HUMAN WASTE** human waste such as urine 6 **OVERLY SENTIMENTAL WRITING OR SPEECH** overly emotional or sentimental speech or writing without any literary value (*informal*) ○ *Not all romantic novels are slop.* ■ **slops** *npl* **PIG FOOD** leftover food, especially kitchen waste, that is fed to pigs ■ *v* (**slops, slopping, slopped**) 1 *vti* **SPILL LIQUID** to spill a liquid, or be spilled on or over somebody or something 2 *vi* **WALK THROUGH MUD OR WATER** to trudge or splash through water, mud, or slush 3 *vi* **WRITE GUSHILY** to write or speak about something in an overly emotional or sentimental way (*informal*) 4 *vt* **SERVE FOOD MESSILY** to serve food in a careless and unappetizing way 5 *vt* **FEED ANIMALS SLOPS** to feed kitchen waste to pigs and other livestock [14C. < Old English *sloppe* 'dung' < Germanic.]

slop out *vi* to empty a chamber pot as part of prison routine ○ *All prisoners must slop out every morning.*

slop[2] /slop/ *n* a loose smock or pair of overalls (*archaic*) ■ **slops** *npl* clothes and personal articles that are sold from a slop chest to sailors on a merchant ship (*archaic*) [14C. Probably < Middle Dutch.]

slop chest *n* a store of merchandise, e.g. tobacco or clothes, kept aboard merchant ships to be sold to the crew

slope /slōp/ *n* 1 **SLANTED GROUND** ground that inclines slightly 2 **SIDE OF A HILL OR MOUNTAIN** the part of a hill or mountain that is at an angle ○ *Let's hit the slopes and do some skiing!* 3 **SLANT** a slant upwards or downwards, or the degree of such a slant 4 **SOMETHING SLANTED** a line, surface, direction, or plane that is inclined 5 **TANGENT** the tangent of the angle between a straight line and the x-axis 6 **FIRST DERIVATIVE OF CURVE** the first derivative of a curve at a point ■ *v* (**slopes, sloping, sloped**) 1 *vti* **GO UP OR DOWN** to ascend or descend, or make something ascend or descend ○ *From here, the road slopes gently down to the valley.* 2 *vt* **TAKE SOMETHING UP OR DOWN** to make something rise or descend gradually ○ *We had a landscaper slope the path through our garden.* 3 *vi* **BE AT A SLANT** to be or have an angle that deviates from horizontal ○ *Does the floor in this room slope?* [Late 16C. < Old English *aslopen*, past participle of *aslupan* 'slip away' < *slupan* 'slip'.] —**sloper** *n* —**sloping** *adj*

slope off *vi* to leave unobtrusively or furtively (*informal*) ○ *I managed to slope off without anyone noticing.*

sloppy /slóppi/ (**-pier, -piest**) *adj* 1 **MESSY** lacking order or tidiness 2 **WET** slushy, muddy, or very wet 3 **NOT DONE WELL** carelessly or badly done (*informal*) 4 **GUSHY** excessively sentimental or emotional (*informal*) 5 **WATERY** cooked or prepared in a way that results in excessive wateriness 6 **BAGGY** loose-fitting so as to be casual and comfortable ○ *a big sloppy sweater* 7 **DIRTY** splashed or covered with liquid

sloppy joe *n* a long, baggy, loose-fitting sweater (*informal*)

slopwork /slóp wurk/ *n* 1 clothing or the manufacture of clothing that is cheap and of inferior quality (*dated*) 2 any kind of work that has been done quickly and carelessly —**slopworker** *n*

slosh /slosh/ *v* 1 *vt* **SPILL LIQUID CLUMSILY** to spill or splash a liquid on or over something 2 *vti* **STIR SOMETHING IN LIQUID** to move or splash something, or move or splash in a liquid (*informal*) ○ *Slosh the shirt in some warm water before the stain sets.* 3 *vi* **WADE IN LIQUID** to wade or splash around in water, mud, or slush (*informal*) 4 *vt* **HIT** to hit somebody very hard (*informal*) ■ *n* 1 **SLUSH** wet snow or mud 2 **LIQUID SPLASHING** liquid splashing, or its sound ○ *We could hear the slosh of water against the docks all night because of the storm.* 3 **HIT** a heavy blow (*informal*) [Early 19C. Probably blend of SLOP[1] 'bog' and SLUSH.] —**sloshy** *adj*

sloshed /slosht/ *adj* thoroughly intoxicated (*informal*)

slot[1] /slot/ *n* 1 **OPENING** a narrow vertical or horizontal opening into which something can be inserted ○ *Put the coin in the slot.* 2 **SCHEDULED TIME** an assigned place and time in a sequence or schedule ○ *The station is moving the new comedy to a prime-time slot next month.* 3 **JOB** a job or a position in a company or other organization 4 **AIR PASSAGE** an air passage in an aerofoil that directs air from the lower to the upper surface 5 ELEC ENG = **expansion slot** ■ *v* (**slots, slotting, slotted**) 1 *vti* **ASSIGN A PLACE TO** to put something in a specific place, position, or time ○ *Slot the shelves into the grooves.* 2 *vt* **MAKE SLOT IN** to cut a slot or slots in something [14C. < Old French *esclot* 'hollow of the breastbone' < ?]

slot in *vti* to find a suitable time or place for somebody or something in a plan, organization, or series of events ○ *The doctor is busy this morning but she could slot you in at 2 o'clock.*

slot[2] /slot/ *n* the track of an animal, especially a deer [Late 16C. < Old French *esclot* 'horse's hoof-print' < ?]

slot car *n US* an electric toy racing car that is operated by a rheostat and has a pin underneath that fits into a groove on a slotted track

sloth /slōth/ *n* 1 a slow-moving mammal that uses its long claws to hang upside down from tree branches. Native to: Central and South America. Genera: *Bradypus* and *Choloepus.* 2 a dislike of work or any kind of physical exertion [12C. < SLOW + *-th.*]

sloth bear *n* a bear with long shaggy fur and a long snout that enables it to feed on plants and insects. Native to: India, Sri Lanka. *Melursus ursinus.*

slothful /slṓthf'l/ *adj* disliking work or any form of physical exertion —**slothfully** *adv* —**slothfulness** *n*

slot machine *n* 1 a gambling machine in which a player inserts coins in a slot and pulls a lever that spins symbols in matching combinations that determine winnings 2 a coin-operated vending machine

slouch /slowch/ *vti* **WALK OR SIT IN A LAZY WAY** to stand, sit, or walk in a careless drooping way, or make a part of the body droop carelessly ○ *He slouched his back and shoulders and leaned against the wall.* ■ *n* 1 **EXTREMELY CASUAL POSTURE** an extremely relaxed or ungainly way of sitting, standing, or walking 2 **LAZY OR INEPT PERSON** a person who will not or cannot do something well (*informal; usually in negative statements*) ○ *very good with children and no slouch around the house, either* [Early 16C. Probably < N Germanic.] —**sloucher** *n* —**slouchily** *adv* —**slouchiness** *n* —**slouchy** *adj*

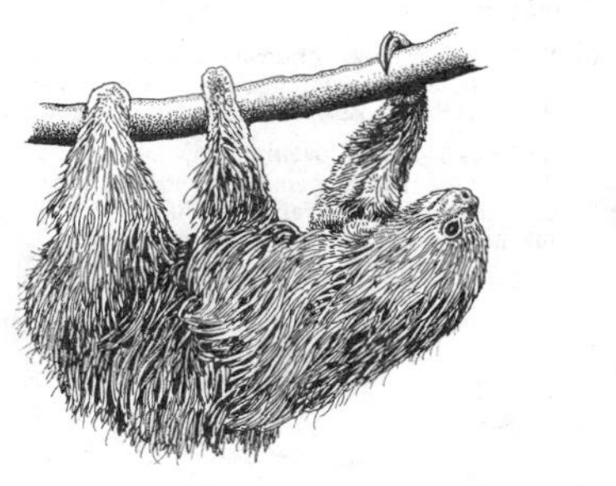

Sloth

slouch hat *n* a hat made of a soft material, e.g. felt, that has a broad drooping brim, especially an Australian army hat

slough[1] /slow/ *n* 1 **DEEP MUDDY HOLE** a hole or low area in the ground filled with mud or water 2 **slough, slue** *US* **SWAMPY AREA** a stagnant area of water connected to a larger body of water such as a marsh, inlet, bayou, or backwater 3 *US, Can* **ESTUARY** a saltwater estuary 4 *US, Can* **HOLE FILLED WITH WATER** on the prairies, a low area filled with water, especially from melting snow 5 **SPIRITUAL LOW POINT** deep despair or disgrace [Old English *slōh* < ?] —**sloughy** *adj*

slough[2] /sluf/ *n* 1 **DEAD OUTER COVERING** the dead outer skin shed by a reptile or an amphibian 2 **DEAD TISSUE LAYER** a layer of dead skin that separates from healthy skin after an infection or inflammation 3 **slough, sluff** **DISCARDED CARD** in card games, a card that has been discarded 4 **SOMETHING CAST OFF** something discarded or shed ■ *v* 1 *vti* **CAST SOMETHING OFF** to shed something, or be shed ○ *Snakes slough off their dead skins.* 2 *vi* **SEPARATE FROM HEALED TISSUE** to separate from surrounding healthy skin (*refers to dead skin*) 3 *vt* **DISCARD** to get rid of somebody or something that is no longer wanted or needed ○ *She sloughs off friends when she no longer has a use for them.* 4 *vt* **IGNORE** to pay no attention to something 5 **slough, sluff** *vti* **DISCARD CARD** to get rid of an unwanted card [14C. < ?]

Slough /slow/ town in south-central England. Population: 109,300 (1995).

slough of despond /slow-/ *n* a state of extreme despair and depression [After the deep bog in *Pilgrim's Progress, Part 1* (1678) by John Bunyan (1628–88)]

Slovak /slṓ vak/, **Slovakian** /slō vá ki ən/ *n* 1 a person who comes from Slovakia 2 the Slavic national language of Slovakia. Native speakers: 5 million. —**Slovak** *adj* —**Slovakian** *adj*

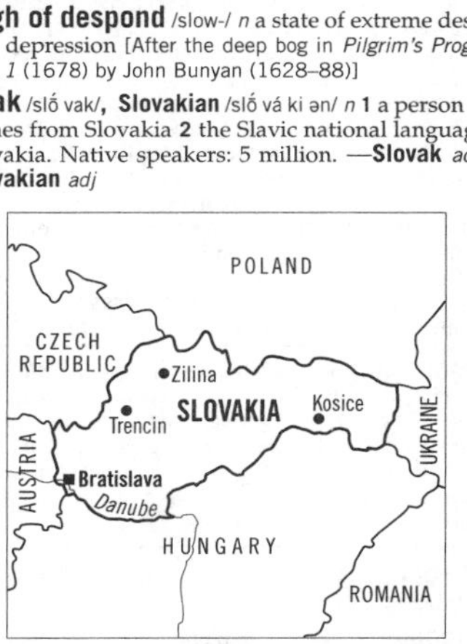

Slovakia

Slovakia /slō vaáki ə/ republic in east-central Europe. Capital: Bratislava. Population: 5,343,000 (1996). Area: 49,035 sq. km/18,932 sq. mi.

Slovakian *n, adj* PEOPLES, LANG = **Slovak**

sloven /slúvv'n/ *n* an offensive term that deliberately insults somebody's standards of personal hygiene and tidiness [15C. Probably < Middle Flemish *sloovin* 'a scold'.]

Slovene /slṓ veen/, **Slovenian** /slō veéni ən/ *n* **1** a person who comes from Slovenia **2** the Slavic national language of Slovenia. Native speakers: 2 million. —**Slovene** *adj*

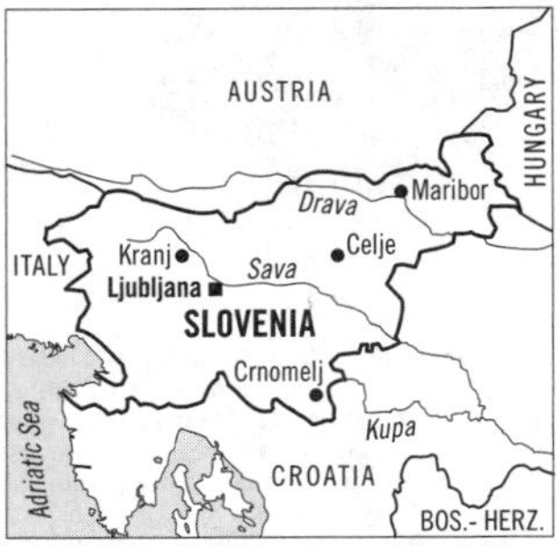

Slovenia

Slovenia /slō veéni ə/ republic in E Europe, on the Balkan Peninsula. Capital: Ljubljana. Population: 1,991,000 (1996). Area: 20,254 sq. km/7,820 sq. mi.

Slovenian *n, adj* PEOPLES, LANG = **Slovene**

slovenly /slúvv'nli/ (**-lier, -liest**) *adj* an offensive term meaning not concerned about conventional standards of personal hygiene and tidiness —**slovenliness** *n*

Slovo /slṓvō/, **Joe** (1926–95) Lithuanian-born South African political leader. Full name **Yossel Mashel Slovo**

slow /slō/ *adj* **1 NOT FAST** not moving quickly or at a fast pace **2 LENGTHY** taking a long time to do or create something ○ *Writing software is a slow process.* **3 TAKING TOO MUCH TIME** requiring more time than is usual or expected **4 NOT KEEPING ACCURATE TIME** showing a time that is earlier than the correct time ○ *I was late for my appointment because my watch was slow.* **5 HESITANT** doing something hesitantly or unwillingly ○ *Why were you so slow to answer my question?* **6 SLUGGISH** lacking the usual volume of sales or customers ○ *Business is usually slow during the summer months.* **7 UNINTELLIGENT** lacking in intelligence or mental sharpness (*informal insult*) **8 DULL** lacking in interest or activity ○ *The acting was good but the plot was terribly slow.* **9 WARM** operating at a low temperature that ensures thorough cooking throughout ○ *A turkey should be cooked in a slow oven.* **10 REDUCING SPEED OF BALL OR RUNNER** tending to reduce the speed or ability to travel of a ball, runner, or other competitor ○ *That horse usually wins on a slow track.* **11 DELIVERING A BALL SLOWLY** in cricket, delivering a ball slowly and with spin ○ *a slow bowler* ■ *adv* **1 BEHIND** behind the correct time or pace ○ *My watch seems to be running slow.* **2** ⚠ **AT A LOW SPEED** at a reduced speed or pace (*nonstandard*) ○ *The law requires motorists to drive slow through residential areas.* ■ *vti* **1 MAKE SOMETHING SLOW** to make somebody or something slow or slower, or become slow or slower ○ *Could you slow your speed a little on those sharp turns?* **2 DELAY OR BE DELAYED** to reduce the speed or progress of something, or become reduced in speed or progress ○ *slowed down the company's rate of expansion* [Old English *slaw* 'sluggish'] —**slowly** *adv* —**slowness** *n* ◇ **go slow** to officially work slower than usual as a form of protest

USAGE slowly or **slow**? The normal adverb is ***slowly***: *The car moved slowly up the hill.* ***Slow***, although usually an adjective, is used as an adverb of keeping time (*My watch is running slow*), and informally more generally (*Don't walk so slow*), though this is not regarded as standard. However, in some expressions, for example *go slow*, and *slow-moving*, ***slow*** is idiomatic and acceptable.

slow burn, slow boil *n* a steadily growing anger (*informal*) ○ *doing a slow burn*

slowcoach /slṓ kōch/ *n* somebody who moves or does something too slowly (*informal*) ○ *If you hadn't been such a slowcoach we'd have been on time.* US term **slowpoke**

slowdown /slṓ down/ *n US* = **go-slow** *n.*

slow-footed *adj* happening or proceeding at an extremely slow pace ○ *Congress has been slow-footed in passing the bill.* —**slow-footedness** *n*

slow handclap *n* a very slow, steady clapping, used by an audience to show its dislike of a performance ○ *The audience broke into a slow handclap.*

slow loris *n* a small slow-moving primate that has a rounded, almost tailless body. Native to: Indonesia. *Nycticebus coucang.*

slow match *n* a flameless match or fuse that burns very slowly or at a known rate, used to set off explosives

slow motion *n* a method of filming action at a rate faster than the normal projection rate, so that it appears on the screen at a slower than normal rate

slow-motion *adj* **1** photographed or shown in slow motion **2** taking place at a slower pace than normal ○ *her slow-motion reaction*

slow neutron *n* a relatively slow-moving neutron that possesses less than 100 electronvolts of kinetic energy and is capable of bringing about nuclear fission

slowpoke /slṓ pōk/ *n US* = **slowcoach** (*informal*) [Mid-19C. *Poke* < POKE[1] in the sense 'dawdling person'.]

slow time *n* a very slow marching step, used especially in funeral ceremonies

slow virus *n* any virus or agent resembling a virus that causes diseases with very long incubation periods. Technical name **lentivirus**

slow-witted *adj* an offensive term meaning slow to understand ideas, events, or situations

slowworm /slṓ wurm/ *n* a legless lizard with a smooth body resembling that of a snake. Native to: Europe, North Africa, W Asia. *Anguis fragilis.* [By folk-etymology < Old English *slāwyrm* < *slā* 'slowworm' + *wyrm* 'worm']

SLP *abbr* Scottish Labour Party

SLR *abbr* single-lens reflex

slub /slub/ *n* **1 KNOT IN YARN** a lump in yarn or fabric that is sometimes an imperfection, but is often made to provide a knobby effect **2 TWISTED THREAD** a loosely twisted roll of fibre, e.g. of silk or cotton, prepared for spinning ■ *vt* (**slubs, slubbing, slubbed**) **PREPARE FIBRE FOR SPINNING** to draw out and twist a strand of fibre to prepare it for spinning [Early 19C. < ?]

sludge /sluj/ *n* **1 SLUSH** wet material, especially watery mud or snow **2 SEDIMENT** a solid deposit found at the bottom of a liquid **3 BROKEN ICE** a layer of broken or half-formed ice on a body of water, especially the sea **4 SOLID WASTE** the solids in sewage that separate out during treatment **5 MASS OF BLOOD CELLS** a sticky grouping of blood cells that form a mass and hinder the circulation of blood [Mid-17C. Possibly from obsolete *slutch* 'mud, mire', or a variant of SLUSH.] —**sludgy** *adj*

slue /sloo/ *vti* (**slues, sluing, slued**) *US* = **slew**[2] *v.* ■ *n US* = **slew**[2] *n.* [Variant of SLOUGH[1] and SLEW[2] 'turn']

sluff *n* CARDS = **slough**[2] *n.* **3** ■ *vti* CARDS = **slough**[2] *v.* **5**

slug[1] /slug/ *n* **1 BULLET** a metal projectile that is fired from a gun or rifle **2 DRINK** a single shot of a strong alcoholic drink (*informal*) **3 TYPE-METAL** a strip of type-metal, less than type-high, used for spacing in traditional hot-metal printing **4 LINE OF TYPE** a strip of cast type in a single strip of metal in traditional hot-metal printing **5 TEMPORARY TYPE LINE** a temporary type line inserted in copy that carries identifying marks or a compositor's instructions **6 METAL OR GLASS BLANK FOR PROCESSING** a metal or glass blank that will receive further processing **7 UNIT OF MASS** a foot-pound-second unit of mass equal to 32.17 pounds that will acquire an acceleration of one foot per second per second when acted on by a one pound force ■ *vt* **1 DRINK SOMETHING QUICKLY** to gulp down a drink (*informal*) **2 ADD SLUGS** to add printers' slugs to copy in traditional hot-metal printing [Early 17C. < ?]

slug[2] /slug/ *n* **1 MOLLUSC WITHOUT A SHELL** a small slow-moving terrestrial mollusc that resembles a snail but has no shell, or only a rudimentary one. Order: Stylommatophora. **2 LARVA** a soft smooth larva of some insects, e.g. that of the sawfly **3 CELLS THAT DEVELOP INTO SPORE-BEARING STRUCTURE** a sticky mass of cells from which the sporophore of a slime mould develops **4 OFFENSIVE TERM** an offensive term that deliberately insults somebody's level of energy or activity [15C. Probably < N Germanic.]

slug[3] /slug/ *vt* (**slugs, slugging, slugged**) to strike somebody or something very hard with the fist or a bat ■ *n* a hard strike or blow [Mid-19C] ◇ **slug it out** *US* to fight to a conclusion (*informal*)

slugabed /slúggə bed/ *n* a person who likes to stay in bed late (*archaic*) [Late 16C. < SLUG[2] + ABED.]

slugfest /slúg fest/ *n US* **1 BRAWL** a long fight in which many heavy blows are exchanged (*slang*) **2 BASEBALL GAME WITH MANY HITS** a baseball game in which both teams make a large number of hits and score a large number of runs **3 HEATED ARGUMENT** an intense debate or dispute **4 BOXING MATCH** a vigorously contested boxing match (*informal*) [Early 20C. < SLUG[3] + FEST.]

sluggard /slúggərd/ *n* an avoider of work or physical exertion (*archaic*) ■ *adj* sluggishly lazy [14C. < SLUG[2].] —**sluggardliness** *n* —**sluggardly** *adj* —**sluggardness** *n*

slugger /slúggər/ *n* a fighter who delivers hard blows [< SLUG[3]]

sluggish /slúggish/ *adj* **1 NOT MOVING MUCH** inactive and moving slowly or very little **2 NOT VERY RESPONSIVE** slow to react or to respond to stimulation **3 LACKING ALERTNESS AND ENERGY** not alert and showing little energy or vitality —**sluggishly** *adv* —**sluggishness** *n*

sluice /slooss/ *n* **1 WATER CHANNEL** an artificial channel for a flow of water that is controlled by a valve or gate **2 FLOODGATE** a valve or floodgate that controls the water in a sluice **3 WATER BEHIND FLOODGATE** a body of water contained by a floodgate **4 DRAINAGE CHANNEL** a channel for carrying away excess water **5 TROUGH** a long inclined trough used to separate gold ore from sand or gravel **6 CHANNEL TO MOVE LOGS** an artificial stream or channel for floating logs ■ *v* (**sluices, sluicing, sluiced**) **1** *vt* **FLUSH SOMETHING WITH WATER** to flood or clean something with a sudden heavy flow of water **2** *vt* **WASH GOLD** to wash gold or other minerals in water flowing in a sluice **3** *vti* **RELEASE SOMETHING FROM A SLUICE** to flow from or let something out of a sluice **4** *vt* **MOVE SOMETHING IN SLUICE** to float something, especially logs, down a sluice **5** *vt* **WASH** to wash something in running water ○ *He sluiced his hands under the tap.* [14C. Via Old French *escluse* < Latin *exclus-*, past participle of *excludere* (see EXCLUDE).]

sluicegate /slóoss gayt/ *n* = **sluice** *n.* **2**

sluiceway /slóoss way/ *n* an artificial channel into which water flows from a sluice

slum /slum/ *n* **POOR AREA** an overcrowded area of a city in which the housing is typically in very bad condition (*often plural*) ■ *v* (**slums, slumming, slummed**) **1 ACCEPT LOWER STANDARDS THAN USUAL** to stay in or go to a place that you would usually consider unacceptable (*often used humorously*) ○ *We'll have to slum it and stay here until we can find a better place.* **2** *vi* **VISIT SLUMS** to go into a slum out of curiosity [Mid-19C. < the expression *back slum* 'street housing poor people' < *slum* 'room'.] —**slummer** *n*

slumber /slúmbər/ *vi* **1 SLEEP** to be asleep **2 BE IN QUIET STATE** to be in a state of inactivity or rest ■ *n* **1 SLEEPING** the state of being asleep, or a period of sleep ○ *A loud noise disturbed my slumber.* **2 INACTIVITY** a state of being dormant or quiet [14C. Alteration of obsolete *sloom* < Old English *slūma* 'light sleep' < Germanic.] —**slumberless** *adj*

slumberous /slúmbərəss/ *adj* **1 DROWSY** feeling sleepy **2 INACTIVE** characterized by inactivity or sluggishness ○ *A slumberous atmosphere seemed to stifle sound and motion in the town.* **3 CAUSING SLEEP** inducing lethargy or sleep ○ *She dozed in the slumberous heat of the afternoon.* —**slumberously** *adv* —**slumberousness** *n*

slumber party *n US* a party at which a group of girls, wearing nightgowns or pyjamas, talk, eat, and stay overnight at one of the girls' homes

slumlord /slúm lawrd/ *n US* an owner of housing in slum areas, especially a neglectful landlord who overcharges tenants [Mid-20C. Blend of SLUM + LANDLORD.]

slump /slump/ *vi* **1 COLLAPSE** to sink or fall suddenly and heavily **2 SLOUCH** to have a hunched drooping posture ○ *She was slumped over her desk.* **3 DECREASE** to decline suddenly and sharply in value ○ *share prices slumped* ■ *n* **1 SLOUCHED POSTURE** a drooping or hunched posture **2 ECONOMIC RECESSION** a sudden decline in business, stock prices, or productivity ○ *an economy fluctuating between boom and slump* [Mid-17C. < ?]

slumpflation /slump fláysh'n/ *n* an economic situation in which an economic depression is accompanied by increasing inflation [Late 20C. Blend of SLUMP + INFLATION.]

slung past tense, past participle of **sling**[1]

slungshot /slúng shot/ *n* a weight or weights attached to the end of a cord and used as a weapon

slunk past tense, past participle of **slink**

slur /slur/ *v* (**slurs, slurring, slurred**) **1** *vti* **SPEAK INDISTINCTLY** to pronounce sounds or words so that they cannot be distinguished **2** *vt* **DEMEAN** to speak of somebody in an insulting or demeaning way **3** *vt* **GLOSS OVER** to ignore something or treat it superficially ○ *The committee slurred over my protests.* **4** *vt* **PERFORM MUSIC SMOOTHLY** to play musical notes in a smooth, uninterrupted way **5** *vti* **SMEAR OR BE SMEARED** to blur or smear wet ink on a page, or be blurred or smeared ■ *n* **1 INSULT** an insulting or demeaning statement about somebody **2 SLURRED PRONUNCIATION** an indistinct pronunciation or sound **3 MUSIC SYMBOL** a curved line that connects two or more notes on a score, indicating that they are to be performed smoothly **4 BLURRED IMAGE** an image that has been smeared or blurred [Early 17C. < ?]

slurp /slurp/ *vti* **DRINK SOMETHING NOISILY** to make a loud sucking sound while drinking or eating something ○ *Would you stop slurping your milkshake?* ■ *n* **1 SUCKING SOUND** a loud sucking sound made while drinking or eating **2 LIQUID MOUTHFUL** a mouthful of a liquid (*informal*) ○ *Can I have a slurp of your lemonade?* [Mid-17C. < Dutch *slurpen*.] —**slurpingly** *adv*

slurry /slúrri/ (*plural* **-ries**) *n* a liquid mixture of water and an insoluble solid material, e.g. cement or clay [15C. < SLUR.]

slush /slush/ *n* **1 MELTING SNOW OR ICE** snow or ice that has begun to melt **2 SEMILIQUID SUBSTANCE** a solid substance such as mud that has become wet and sloppy **3 GREASE FROM SHIP'S GALLEY** the waste grease or fat produced by a ship's galley **4 GREASE** a greasy substance used to lubricate machine parts **5 OVERLY SENTIMENTAL EXPRESSION** extremely sentimental speech or writing **6 ICE DRINK** a drink made of finely crushed ice with a flavoured syrup poured over it ■ *v* **1** *vt* **GREASE MACHINERY** to lubricate the parts of a machine **2** *vt* **PUT MORTAR IN JOINTS** to fill masonry joints with mortar, or cover a surface with cement **3** *vt* **SOAK SOMETHING WITH SLUSH** to splash or cover something with mud or slush **4** *vi* **WALK THROUGH SLUSH** to walk through wet snow or mud ○ *It had been raining so hard we had to slush through mud to get there.* **5** *vi* **MAKE A SPLASHING SOUND** to make a splashing or squelching sound [Mid-17C. < ?]

slush fund *n* **1 MONEY FOR ILLEGAL ACTIVITIES** money set aside by a business or other organization for corrupt activities such as the bribery of public officials **2 MONEY FOR ENTERTAINMENT** money set aside to use for fun or entertainment expenses **3 LUXURY FUND FOR SHIP'S CREW** money raised by selling refuse and garbage from a ship to pay for small luxuries for the crew [< the money gained from selling a ship's *slush*, the grease collected in a ship's galley. 'Money used for bribes' comes from 'greasing' somebody's palm with money.]

slush pile *n* a pile of unsolicited manuscripts accumulated in a publisher's office (*informal*)

slushy /slúshi/ (**-ier, -iest**) *adj* **1 FULL OF SLUSH** covered with or full of melting snow and ice **2 RESEMBLING SLUSH** with the consistency of slush **3 OVERLY SENTIMENTAL** filled with or expressing excessive sentiment ○ *a slushy love story* —**slushiness** *n*

slut /slut/ *n* **1** an offensive term for a woman thought to be sexually promiscuous (*slang*) **2** an offensive term for a woman who is regarded as not concerned about conventional standards of domestic cleanliness (*dated*) [15C. < ?] —**sluttish** *adj* —**sluttishly** *adv* —**sluttishness** *n* —**slutty** *adj*

Sluter /slóotər/, **Claus** (1350?–1406) Dutch sculptor

SLV *abbr* standard launch vehicle *or* space launch vehicle

sly /slī/ (**slier, sliest**) *adj* **1 CRAFTY** cleverly skilful and cunning **2 EVASIVE** lacking honesty or straightforwardness **3 MISCHIEVOUS** full of playful mischief [13C. < Old Norse *slœgr* 'clever, crafty'.] —**slyly** *adv* —**slyness** *n* ◇ **on the sly** without the knowledge or permission of others

slyboots /slī boots/ *n* somebody considered to be cunning or devious (*insult; + singular verb*)

slype /slīp/ *n* a covered passage in a cathedral or church that joins the transept to a chapter house [Mid-19C. < ?]

sm *abbr* San Marino (*in Internet addresses*)

Sm *symbol* samarium

SM *abbr* sergeant major

S/M, S-M *abbr* sadomasochism

smack[1] /smak/ *v* **1** *vti* **SLAP** to hit somebody with a quick stinging and usually noisy blow with the palm of the hand **2** *vi* **HIT AGAINST SOMETHING NOISILY** to strike against, collide with, or land in something with a sharp loud noise **3** *vt* **PRESS LIPS TOGETHER** to press together and then open the lips with a short loud noise ■ *n* **1 SLAP** a sharp quick blow with the palm of the hand **2 NOISY SOUND** a sharp loud noise made when one thing strikes another **3 LOUD KISS** a brief noisy kiss ■ *adv* **1 WITH A LOUD NOISE** with a sharp loud noise or collision **2 DIRECTLY** directly or precisely ○ *I was smack in the middle of getting ready to leave when you called.* [Mid-16C. < Middle Low German *smacken* 'open the lips noisily', an imitation of the sound.]

smack[2] /smak/ *n* **1 DISTINCTIVE TASTE** a unique flavour or taste of something **2 HINT** a small amount or trace ■ *vi* **1 BE DISTINCTIVELY FLAVOURED** to have a unique flavour or taste **2 EXPRESS SOMETHING INDIRECTLY** to suggest or hint at something ○ *an editorial that smacked of snobbery* [Old English *smæc* 'taste' < Germanic]

smack[3] /smak/ *n* a sailing vessel used for fishing, usually for carrying the catch to market [Early 17C. < Dutch *smak* < ?]

smack[4] /smak/ *n* heroin (*slang*) [Mid-20C. Probably alteration of *schmeck* 'drug' < Yiddish, 'sniff' < Middle High German *smecken* 'smell'.]

smack-dab *adj US* = **slap-bang** *adv.* 2 (*informal*)

smacker /smákər/ *n* (*informal*) **1** a noisy smacking kiss **2** a pound

smacking /smáking/ *adj* very brisk or lively ○ *a smacking breeze*

small /smawl/ *adj* **1 LITTLE** of a relatively little size ○ *a small animal* **2 NOT MUCH** little in quantity or value ○ *a small sum of money* **3 INSIGNIFICANT** unimportant or trivial ○ *a small matter* **4 LIMITED** operating on a limited scale ○ *small businesses* **5 MINOR** lacking in power, influence, or status **6 NOT YET MATURE** young or not fully grown ○ *small children* **7 ORDINARY** humble or modest ○ *He came from small beginnings.* **8 MEAN** petty and mean-spirited **9 LOWER-CASE** in lower case rather than capitals ○ *small letters* **10 WITHOUT SELF-RESPECT** humiliated or feeling little self-worth ○ *Her criticisms and ridicule made me feel very small.* ■ *adv* **1 IN SMALL PIECES** in or into little pieces ○ *Cut it up small.* **2 IN A SMALL WAY** in a moderate or limited way ○ *start out small* **3 QUIETLY** quietly or softly (*archaic*) ■ *n* **1 NARROW PART** a part of something that is narrower or smaller than the rest of it ○ *the small of the back* **2 SIZE FOR SOMEBODY SMALL** a size or a garment in a size that fits somebody who is of less than average proportions ■ **smalls** *npl UK* **UNDERGARMENTS** items of underwear (*informal or humorous*) [Old English *smæl* 'slender, small' < Germanic, 'small animal'] —**smallish** *adj* —**smallness** *n*

small arms *n* firearms such as pistols and rifles that can be held in one or both hands while firing

small beer *n* **1** something of little or no importance (*informal*) ○ *A thousand pounds is small beer to people like him.* **2** weak or inferior beer (*dated*)

small-bore *adj* describes .22-calibre firearms or ammunition.

small calorie *n* MEASURE = **calorie** *n.* 1

small capital *n* a capital letter that is the same height as a lower-case letter

small change *n* **1** coins that have a low denomination **2** something that is considered to be insignificant, especially when compared with something else

small claims court *n* a local court that has jurisdiction to try civil actions involving claims worth only a small sum of money

small fry *npl* **1 TRIVIAL THINGS** people, events, or issues that are thought to be of little importance **2 YOUNG FISH** young, immature, or small fish **3 CHILDREN** young children (*informal*)

small game *n* small animals and birds that are hunted for sport

small goods *npl ANZ* processed meats such as sausages and salamis

smallholding /smáwl hōlding/ *n* a piece of farmland that is smaller than the average farm —**smallholder** *n*

small hours *n* the early morning hours after midnight

small intestine *n* the part of the intestine between the stomach and large intestine, consisting of the duodenum, jejunum, and ileum, where digestion of food and most absorption of nutrients takes place

small-minded *adj* petty and intolerant of the ideas and beliefs of others —**small-mindedly** *adv* —**small-mindedness** *n*

smallmouth bass /smáwl mowth báss/ *n* a greenish-brown freshwater bass found in clear streams and lakes that is a popular game fish. Native to: North America. *Micropterus dolomieu*.

smallpox /smáwl poks/ *n* a highly contagious disease caused by a poxvirus and marked by high fever and the formation of scar-producing pustules. Technical name **variola**

small print *n* the very fine, hard-to-read print in a contract or other legal document that often contains important information that could be overlooked. US term **fine print**

small-scale *adj* **1** limited in scope or size **2** made or constructed on a small scale ○ *She built a small-scale replica of the ship.*

small screen *n* the medium of television, especially as distinct from the cinema (*informal*)

small slam *n* CARDS = **little slam**

small stores *npl* small items such as clothing sold on a ship or at a naval base

small stuff *n* light twine or yarn used on a ship

smallsword /smáwl sawrd/ *n* a light sword used in the 17th and 18th centuries for duelling and fencing (*archaic*)

small talk *n* polite conversation about matters of little importance, especially between people who do not know each other well

small-time *adj* of minor importance or influence (*informal*) ○ *He's just a small-time crook.*

smalt /smawlt/ *n* **1** silica glass that has been coloured a deep blue by cobalt oxide **2** a deep blue pigment made by crushing smalt [Mid-16C. Via French < Italian *smalto* (see SMALTO).]

smaltite /smáwl tīt/ *n* a blue-grey cobalt nickel arsenide mineral. Use: source of cobalt.

smalto /smáaltō/ *n* small bits of pottery, glass, and tiles used in mosaics [Early 18C. < Italian, < Germanic.]

smaragdite /smə rág dīt/ *n* a fibrous green amphibole mineral [Early 19C. < Latin *smaragdus*, via Greek < Hebrew *bāreqet* 'emerald'.]

smarm /smaarm/ *n* (*informal*) **1 SELF-SERVING FLATTERY** ingratiating or servile flattery **2 INSINCERE CHARM** charm that is distastefully self-conscious or insincere ■ *v* (*informal*) **1** *vi* **FLATTER** to make a lot of fuss over somebody in order to ingratiate yourself **2** *vt* **GREASE THE HAIR** to flatten hair by smoothing it down with grease [Early 20C. < ?]

smarmy /smáarmi/ (**-ier, -iest**) *adj* excessively and unpleasantly polite and ingratiating (*informal*) [Early 20C. < SMARM.] —**smarmily** *adv* —**smarminess** *n*

smart /smaart/ *adj* **1 TIDY** with a neat and well-cared-for appearance **2 CLEVER** showing intelligence and mental alertness ○ *smart students* **3 INSOLENT** disrespectful or impertinent ○ *Whatever you say to him he has some smart answer.* **4 WITTY AND AMUSING** amusingly clever and possessing a quick wit **5 KEEN** shrewd and calculating in business and other dealings ○ *a smart dealer* **6 FASHIONABLE** fashionable and stylish ○ *smart restaurants* **7 LIVELY** vigorous and brisk ○ *a smart pace* **8 STINGING** causing a sharp stinging sensation ○ *a smart slap* **9 LASER- OR RADIO-GUIDED** describes a missile or weapon that is guided to its target by laser or radio beams **10 ELECTRONIC** with a built-in microprocessor ○ *smart traffic lights* ■ *vi* **1 CAUSE OR HAVE SHARP PAIN** to feel, cause, or be the site of a sharp stinging pain ○ *My hand smarts.* **2 BE EMBARRASSED** to feel acute embarrassment or distress ○ *She still smarted when she remembered his criticism.* **3 BE PUNISHED** to be punished severely ■ *adv* **SMARTLY** in a smart manner ■ *n* **1 PAIN** a sharp stinging localized pain **2 EMBARRASSMENT OR MENTAL DISCOMFORT** a feeling such as embarrassment, remorse, or shame [Old English *smeortan* 'be painful' < ?] —**smartly** *adv* —**smartness** *n*

SYNONYMS See ***intelligent***.

smart aleck /-alik/, **smart alec** *n* a person who makes a show of knowing something or being cleverer than others (*informal*) [Mid-19C. < ?]

smart-aleck, smart-alecky /smáart aliki/ *adj* pretentiously clever and annoyingly self-assertive (*informal*)

smartarse /smáart aarss/ *n* an offensive term for somebody who makes an annoying show of knowledge (*slang*) US term **smartass**

smartass /smaáart ass/, **smart-ass** *n US* = **smartarse** (*slang offensive*)

smart bomb *n* a missile that is guided to its target by laser or radio beams

ϟ **smart card** *n* a small plastic card containing a microchip that can store personal data and bank-account details, used for identification and payment for purchases (*in e-commerce*)

smarten /smaáart'n/ *vt* **1** to improve the appearance of somebody or something **2** to increase the speed of something
smarten up *vti* **1 IMPROVE APPEARANCE** to improve your appearance, or the appearance of somebody or something else **2 MAKE OR BECOME LIVELIER** to make somebody or something brighter or livelier, or become brighter or livelier **3** *US* **MAKE OR BECOME WISER** to make somebody wiser or more knowing, or become wiser or more knowing

smart growth *n* economic growth that consciously seeks to avoid wastefulness and damage to the environment and communities

smart money *n* **1 WISE INVESTMENT OR BET** money bet on or invested in something likely to yield a good profit **2 WISE INVESTORS** those with privileged information to make wise bets or investments **3** *US* **DAMAGES AWARDED TO PUNISH A DEFENDANT** damages awarded to a plaintiff in excess of the normal level of compensation to punish a defendant in cases of serious negligence or wilful misconduct

ϟ **smart terminal** *n* a network terminal that carries out processing but uses another computer for data and program storage

smarty-pants /smaárti-/ (*plural* **smarty-pants**), **smarty** (*plural* **smarties**) *n* an annoying person who is always trying to be clever (*informal; + singular verb*)

smash /smash/ *v* **1** *vti* **BREAK WITH FORCE** to break something, or break through something, with great force or violence **2** *vti* **BREAK INTO PIECES** to break, or break something, into many small pieces **3** *vti* **HIT AGAINST** to hit something, or make something hit something else, with great force **4** *vt* **DEFEAT OR DESTROY** to ruin, defeat, or put an end to somebody or something completely **5** *vt* **HIT WITH OVERHAND STROKE** in games such as tennis and badminton, to hit a ball or shuttlecock with great force, especially with an overhand stroke ■ *n* **1 LOUD NOISE** the loud sound of something hitting or being hit by something else and breaking into pieces ○ *The mirror hit the floor with a smash.* **2 BLOW** a heavy blow **3 COLLISION** a crash or collision ○ *There's been a bad smash on the motorway.* **4 OVERHAND STROKE** in games such as tennis and badminton, a strong overhand stroke hit downwards into the opponent's court **5 GREAT SUCCESS** an unqualified success ○ *The new show was a smash hit.* **6 BIG FAILURE** a major failure, especially one involving finances ■ *adv* **WITH A SMASH** with the sound of a smash [Late 17C. < ?] —**smashable** *adj*
smash up *v* **1** *vti* to damage something severely, or become badly damaged, because of a collision with something solid **2** *vt* to damage or destroy something by breaking

smash-and-grab *adj* relating to a robbery committed by breaking a shop window in order to steal the goods on display ■ *n* a smash-and-grab robbery

smashed /smasht/ *adj* very drunk or under the influence of drugs (*informal*)

smasher /smáshər/ *n* something impressive or a person who is physically attractive (*informal*)

smashing /smáshing/ *adj* extremely good or pleasing

smash-up *n* a road accident between vehicles in which all those involved are badly damaged

smatter /smáttər/ *n* = **smattering** *n.* 1, **smattering** *n.* 2 [15C. < ?]

smattering /smáttəring/ *n* **1** a slight knowledge of something such as a subject or language **2** a small amount or number ○ *a smattering of rain*

SMATV *abbr* satellite master antenna television

smear /smeer/ *v* **1** *vti* **SPREAD OVER** to spread over, or spread something liquid or greasy over something ○ *This lipstick is made not to smear.* **2** *vt* **SPREAD DAMAGING RUMOURS ABOUT** to deliberately spread damaging rumours about somebody **3** *vt US* **DEFEAT** to severely defeat a competitor or enemy (*informal; usually passive*) ○ *We got smeared.* ■ *n* **1 PATCH OF SMEARED SUBSTANCE** an act of smearing, or a smeared patch of something **2 SAMPLE OF CELLS** a sample of cells taken from body tissue or a bodily secretion or discharge and smeared on a microscope slide for examination **3 SMEAR TEST** a cervical smear test (*informal*) **4 HARMFUL RUMOUR** a harmful rumour or story about somebody [The verb is < Old English *smeirwan*, the noun < *smeoru*, both from Germanic] —**smearer** *n*

smear campaign *n* a concerted effort to diminish somebody's reputation by spreading harmful information about him or her

smear test *n* MED = **cervical smear**

smeary /smeéri/ (**-ier, -iest**) *adj* **1** smeared on, easily smeared, or likely to smear **2** having or covered with smears

smectic /sméktik/ *adj* describes materials whose liquid phase consists of elongated molecules arranged in layers and with their axes parallel to each other [Late 17C. Via Latin *smecticus* < Greek *smēktikos* < *smēkhein* 'rub, cleanse'.]

smectite /smék tīt/ *n* any of a group of clay minerals that swell in water. Use: ion exchange materials. [Early 19C. < Greek *smēktis* 'fuller's earth'.]

smeddum /sméddəm/ *n Scotland* **1** common sense and resourcefulness **2** fine dust, powder, or flour [Old English *smedena* 'fine flour' < ?]

smegma /smégmə/ *n* a cheesy secretion of the sebaceous glands that collects under the foreskin or around the clitoris [Early 19C. Via Latin < Greek *smēgma* 'soap' < *smēkhein* 'rub, cleanse'.]

smell /smel/ *v* (**smells, smelling, smelt** *or* **smelled** /smelt/) **1** *vti* **DETECT BY NOSE** to detect or recognize something by means of sensitive nerves in the nose **2** *vt* **USE NOSE** to use the sensitive nerves in the nose to assess something ○ *Smell that and see if it's still good.* **3** *vi* **BE DETECTED WHEN BREATHED IN** to seem to be in a particular condition, or give a particular impression, when judged by somebody breathing in through the nose ○ *Something smells good.* **4** *vi* **GIVE UNPLEASANT IMPRESSION** to be considered unpleasant when breathed in through the nose **5** *vi* **GIVE IMPRESSION** to give off a suggestion or impression of something ○ *It smells dangerous.* **6** *vt* **FEEL OR DETECT** to detect the presence or existence of something, usually something bad ■ *n* **1 SENSE BASED ON NERVES IN NOSE** the sense based on the sensitive nerves in the nose that distinguish odours **2 QUALITY DETECTED BY NOSE** the quality of something that can be detected by the sensitive nerves in the nose **3 ACT OF SMELLING** an act or instance of breathing something in through the nose in order to make a judgment about it **4 SUGGESTION OF** a suggestion or impression of something [12C. < ?] —**smeller** *n*

SYNONYMS ***smell, odour, aroma, bouquet, scent, perfume, fragrance, stink, stench, reek***
CORE MEANING: the way something smells
smell a neutral, pleasant, or unpleasant quality detected by the nerves of the nose; **odour** a neutral or unpleasant smell; **aroma** a distinctive pleasant smell, especially one related to cooking or food; **bouquet** a characteristic pleasant smell, usually associated with fine wines; **scent** a pleasant, sweet smell, for example the smell of flowers, or the characteristic smell given off by a particular animal; **perfume** a sweet, pleasant, and heady smell, especially the smell of flowers or plants; **fragrance** a sweet pleasant smell, especially a delicate or subtle one; **stink** a strong unpleasant smell; **stench** a strong unpleasant smell, especially one associated with burning or decay; **reek** a strong unpleasant smell.

smelling salts *npl* a mixture of ammonium carbonate and perfume. Use: formerly, to revive somebody who felt faint or had become unconscious.

smelly /smélli/ (**-ier, -iest**) *adj* giving off a strong or unpleasant smell —**smelliness** *n*

smelt¹ /smelt/ *v* **1** *vt* to melt ore in order to get metal from it, or produce metal in this way. The separation of the metal usually requires a chemical change. **2** *vi* to undergo fusing or melting in the process of smelting [Mid-16C. < Middle Low German *smelten*.]

smelt² /smelt/ (*plural* **smelts** *or* **smelt**) *n* **1** a small silvery marine or freshwater fish. Native to: northern waters. Family: Osmeridae. **2** the oily flesh of a smelt as food [Old English < ?]

smelt³ past tense, past participle of **smell**

smelter /sméltər/ *n* **1** a person who smelts ore or who owns a place where ore is smelted **2** a place where smelting is carried out, or an apparatus used for smelting

Smetana /sméttənə/, **Bedřich** (1824–84) Czech composer

smew /smyoo/ (*plural* **smews** *or* **smew**) *n* a duck related to the mergansers that has a hooked serrated bill, and the male of which has predominantly white plumage with black markings. Native to: Europe, Asia. *Mergus albellus*. [Late 17C. Probably ultimately < W Germanic.]

smidgen /smíjjən/, **smidgin, smidgeon, smidge** /smij/ *n* a small amount (*informal*) [Mid-19C. < ?]

smilax /smī laks/ *n* **1** a climbing plant with red or bluish-black berries and often prickly stems. Flowers: small, white or yellowish. Native to: temperate and tropical regions. Genus: *Smilax*. **2** a vine prized by florists for its glossy bright green leaves. Native to: southern Africa. *Asparagus asparagoides*. [Late 16C. Via Latin < Greek, 'bindweed'.]

smile /smīl/ *v* (**smiles, smiling, smiled**) **1** *vti* **HAVE OR MAKE PLEASANT EXPRESSION** to have or make an expression with the corners of the mouth raised, usually expressing amusement, pleasure, or approval **2** *vi* **HAVE PLEASANT APPEARANCE** to appear to be in a state of happiness or enjoying good fortune or pleasure **3** *vi* **FAVOUR** to be favourably disposed to somebody ○ *Fortune smiled on their journey* **4** *vt* **EXPRESS SOMETHING BY SMILING** to express something by or while smiling ■ *n* **1 PLEASANT EXPRESSION** a facial expression in which the corners of the mouth are raised, usually expressing amusement, pleasure, or approval **2 PLEASANT APPEARANCE** an appearance of pleasure or approval (*often plural*) **3 SIGN OF FAVOUR** an expression or sign of favour [13C. Probably < N Germanic.] —**smiler** *n* —**smilingly** *adv*

ϟ **smiley** /smīli/ *adj* (**-ier, -iest**) smiling or often smiling ■ *n* (*plural* **-eys**) a symbol (**emoticon**), often in the form :-), keyed to communicate feelings such as pleasure, approval, or humour

smilodon /smīlə don/ *n* a large sabre-toothed tiger existing during the Pleistocene epoch, between about 2 million and 10,000 years ago. Genus: *Smilodon*. [Mid-19C. < modern Latin, 'knife-toothed' < Greek *smilē* 'knife'.]

smir /smur/, **smirr** *n Scotland* drizzle or very fine rain ■ *vi* (**smirs, smirring, smirred**) *Scotland* to be raining very fine rain [Early 19C. < ?]

smirch /smurch/ *vt* **1 DAMAGE REPUTATION** to damage somebody's or something's reputation or good name **2 DIRTY** to make something dirty by smearing or staining it (*archaic or literary*) ■ *n* **1 DIRTY STAIN** a dirty stain or smear (*archaic or literary*) **2 SOMETHING DAMAGING** something that damages a reputation [15C. < ?]

smirk /smurk/ *n* **INSOLENT SMILE** an insolent smile expressing feelings such as superiority, self-satisfaction, or conceit ■ *v* **1** *vi* **SMILE INSOLENTLY** to smile in an insolent, smug, or contemptuous way **2** *vt* **EXPRESS WITH SMIRK** to express something with a smirk [Old English *smearcian* 'smile' < Germanic]

smirr *n, vi Scotland* METEOROL = **smir**

smit past tense of **smite** (*archaic or literary*)

smite /smīt/ (**smites, smiting, smote** /smōt/ *or* **smit** /smit/, **smitten** /smítt'n/) *v* **1** *vti* **HIT HARD** to hit somebody or something hard (*archaic or literary*) **2** *vt* **AFFECT OR AFFLICT** to affect somebody strongly or disastrously, or afflict somebody with something (*literary; often passive*) **3** *vt* **FILL WITH LOVE** to fill somebody with love or longing (*literary; usually passive*) [Old English *smītan* 'smear, pollute' < Germanic] —**smiter** *n*

smith /smith/ *n* **1** a maker or repairer of metal objects **2** OCCUPATIONS = **blacksmith** [Old English *smiþ* < Germanic, 'coppersmith']

Smith /smith/, **Adam** (1723–90) British philosopher and economist

Smith, Bernard William (*b.* 1916) Australian art historian

Smith, Bessie (1894–1937) US blues singer

Smith, Dick (*b.* 1944) Australian entrepreneur and aviator. Born **Richard Harold Smith**

Smith, Grace Cossington (1892–1985) Australian painter

Smith, Harvey (*b.* 1938) British showjumper

Smith, John (1580–1631) English-born North American colonist

Smith, Joseph (1805–44) US founder of the Church of Jesus Christ of Latter-Day Saints

Smith, Dame Maggie (*b.* 1934) British actor. Full name **Margaret Nathalie Smith**

Smith, Stevie (1902–71) British poet and novelist. Born **Florence Margaret Smith**

smithereens /smíthə reénz/ *npl* very small broken pieces (*informal*) [Early 19C. Probably < Irish *smidirín* 'small fragment' < *smiodar* 'fragment'.]

smithery /smíthəri/ (*plural* **-ies**) *n* **1** the work or craft of a smith **2** INDUST = **smithy** *n.*

Smithsonian Institution /smith sṓni ən-/, **Smithsonian** *n* a government trust founded in Washington, D.C., by an act of Congress in 1846 to promote research and education. It sponsors scientific research and publications and maintains the national collections. [Early 19C. After James L. M. *Smithson* (1765–1829), British mineralogist.]

smithsonite /smíthsə nīt/ *n* a white or yellow to brown zinc carbonate mineral. Use: source of zinc. [Mid-19C. After James L. M. *Smithson* (1765–1829), British mineralogist.]

smithy /smíthi/ (*plural* **-ies**) *n* the place where a blacksmith works

smitten past participle of **smite**

smock /smok/ *n* **1** LOOSE DRESS a loose dress for a child or woman with the cloth gathered at the chest **2** OVERSHIRT a loose garment worn to protect the clothes **3** UNDERGARMENT a woman's loose-fitting undergarment or chemise of a type used until the 18th century ■ *vt* SEW WITH GATHERING STITCHES to sew or decorate something with decorative gathering stitches [Old English *smoc* < Germanic, 'creep']

smocking /smóking/ *n* decorative stitching in a honeycomb or zigzag pattern, used to gather fabric evenly

smog /smog/ *n* a mixture of fog and smoke or other airborne pollutants such as exhaust fumes [Early 20C. Blend of SMOKE + FOG.] —**smoggy** *adj*

smoke /smōk/ *n* **1** CLOUD OF TINY PARTICLES a mass of tiny particles in the air that rises up from something burning **2** VAPOUR RESEMBLING SMOKE something that resembles smoke, usually consisting of minute particles suspended in a gas ○ *a white, stinging smoke of chemical fumes* **3** INHALING OF BURNING TOBACCO FUMES an act of smoking a cigarette, cigar, or pipe **4** CIGARETTE a cigarette or other tobacco product (*informal*) **5** SMOKABLE SUBSTANCE something that can be smoked (*informal*) **6** SOMETHING THAT OBSCURES something that obscures or obstructs information, understanding, or awareness **7** SOMETHING TRANSIENT something transient or illusory **8** GREY COLOUR a grey colour tinged with blue or brown ■ *v* (**smokes, smoking, smoked**) **1** *vti* USE TOBACCO to have the habit of inhaling the smoke of burning tobacco in cigarettes, cigars, or pipes **2** *vti* INHALE VAPOURS to inhale the smoke of any substance that can burn and be inhaled **3** *vi* GIVE OFF SMOKE to give off smoke, often in a way that indicates some malfunction **4** *vt* CURE FOOD WITH SMOKE to cure or treat food such as meat, fish, or cheese with wood smoke **5** *vt* FUMIGATE WITH SMOKE to fumigate, clean, or clear something with smoke **6** *vt* DARKEN to darken something to give it the colour of smoke **7** *vt* STUPEFY to stupefy something with smoke **8** *vt US* to defeat somebody heavily, or outclass a competitor (*informal*) [Old English *smoca* < Germanic] —**smokable** *adj* —**smoke** *adj*
◇ **go up in smoke 1** to be destroyed by burning **2** to fail completely to happen as planned or hoped
smoke out *vt* **1** to drive somebody or something from a hiding place by using smoke **2** to bring something to light by clever or assertive inquiry

smoke alarm *n* a device intended to give a warning of fire by triggering an alarm when it detects the presence of smoke. US term **smoke detector**

smoke and mirrors *n US, Can* something that is intended to draw people's attention away from something else that somebody would prefer remained unnoticed [< the use of smoke and mirrors in magic acts]

smoke bomb *n* a device that gives off dense clouds of irritating chemical smoke, used to drive people or animals out of a place

smoke detector *n US* HOUSEHOLD = **smoke alarm**

smoke-dried *adj* cured with or dried in smoke

smoked rubber *n* crude rubber prepared by drying coagulated latex sheets in smokehouses before they are packed into bales

smoke-filled room *n* a room where deals are negotiated in private, traditionally considered to be filled with the smoke of the negotiators' cigarettes, cigars, and pipes

smokehouse /smṓk howss/ (*plural* **-houses** /-howziz/) *n* a small building where meat, fish, or other materials are cured in smoke

smokeless /smṓkləss/ *adj* **1** producing little or no smoke **2** describes an area where smoke, e.g. from coal fires, is not permitted

smokeless powder *n* a nitrocellulose-based explosive or propellant that produces little smoke

smokeless zone *n* an area in which only smokeless fuels can be burned

smoker /smṓkər/ *n* **1** SOMEBODY WHO SMOKES a person who smokes something, especially tobacco products **2** RAILWAY CARRIAGE DESIGNATED FOR SMOKING a railway compartment where smoking is permitted **3** APPARATUS FOR SMOKING FOOD an apparatus for smoking food in **4** GATHERING OF MEN a social gathering of men

smoker's cough *n* a hacking cough, often accompanied by phlegm, caused by excessive smoking

smoke screen *n* **1** a mass of smoke produced to conceal the movements of ships, troops, or equipment **2** an action taken to mislead somebody or obscure something

smoke signal *n* **1** a signal made by creating or interrupting a column of smoke in order to convey a message **2** an unstated but clearly conveyed message (*informal*)

smokestack /smṓk stak/ *n* **1** *US* ENG = **chimney** *n.* **4 2** a tall, often cylindrical industrial chimney, often attached to a factory

smokestack industry *n* any industry characterized by large factories, heavy equipment, high energy consumption, and usually pollution of the environment

smoke tree *n* a shrub or small tree whose clusters of small flowers resemble puffs of smoke. Genus: *Cotinus.*

smoking gun *n* conclusive evidence or proof, especially of some wrongdoing [< the idea of finding a recently fired gun in a suspect's hand]

smoking room *n* a room designated for people to smoke in

smoky /smṓki/ (**-ier, -iest**) *adj* **1** FILLED WITH SMOKE filled with smoke, or smelling as if it had been filled with smoke **2** COLOURED LIKE SMOKE of a grey colour, like smoke **3** TASTING OF SMOKE having or suggesting a taste imparted by smoke or an open flame **4** GIVING OFF EXCESSIVE SMOKE giving off smoke, especially excessively **5** AFFECTED BY SMOKE discoloured or marked with smoke —**smokily** *adv* —**smokiness** *n*

smoky quartz *n* MINERALS = **cairngorm**

smolder *vi, n* US = **smoulder**

Smolensk /smo lénsk/ city in W Russia, on the River Dnieper. Population: 398,405 (1995).

smolt /smōlt/ *n* a young salmon before it has swum to the sea [15C. < ?]

smooch /smooch/ *v* (*informal*) **1** *vti* TO KISS to kiss and caress somebody **2** *vi* DANCE INTIMATELY to dance slowly and closely ■ *n* (*informal*) **1** KISS an instance of kissing and cuddling **2** SLOW DANCING a period of slow, intimate dancing in which a couple hold each other closely [Mid-20C. An imitation of the sound of kissing.] —**smoochy** *adj*

smooth /smooth/ *adj* **1** NOT ROUGH OR BUMPY not having a rough or uneven surface **2** WITHOUT LUMPS without lumps or pieces of solid matter ○ *Beat the mixture to a smooth paste.* **3** WITHOUT UPHEAVAL OR DIFFICULTIES proceeding without interruption, upheaval, or problems **4** WITHOUT JERKS OR JOLTS in a steady flowing motion, without jolts or interruptions **5** NOT HARSH without harshness **6** NOT SHARP OR SOUR not tasting sharp or sour **7** NOT EASILY UPSET not easily ruffled or upset ○ *a smooth and serene personality* **8** INSINCERELY CONVINCING using insincere flattery and pleasantness, especially in order to persuade somebody to do something ○ *his smooth talk* **9** HAIRLESS without a beard or moustache ○ *a smooth-faced young man* **10** FRICTIONLESS offering no apparent resistance to sliding **11** UNASPIRATED spoken without audible breath ■ *vt* **1** EVEN OUT ROUGHNESS to remove bumps, unevenness, or roughness **2** PRESS OUT CREASES to remove lines and creases **3** MAKE CREAMY to remove lumps from something **4** REMOVE DIFFICULTIES to remove obstacles and difficulties ○ *Influential allies smoothed his path to power.* **5** LESSEN BAD FEELINGS to remove or lessen bad feeling or disagreement between people ○ *I tried to smooth things over with her.* **6** REMOVE IRREGULARITIES FROM DATA to modify a sequential set of numerical data by reducing the differences in magnitude between adjacent numbers **7** REMOVE IRREGULARITIES IN CURRENT to remove the slight irregularities (**ripples**) in a rectified current ■ *adv* WITHOUT PROBLEMS without problems or difficulties ○ *The path of true love never runs smooth.* ■ *n* **1** ACT OF SMOOTHING the action of smoothing something **2** SOMETHING SMOOTH a smooth part of something [Old English *smōþ* < ?] —**smoothable** *adj* —**smoother** *n* —**smoothly** *adv* —**smoothness** *n*
smooth down *vti* to make something flat by a smoothing action, or become flat by being smoothed
smooth out *vti* **1** to make something smooth, or become smooth, by the removal of lines and creases **2** to make something easier or calmer, or become easier or calmer, after a period of difficulty
smooth over *vt* to remove or lessen difficulties or tensions

smoothbore /smóoth bawr/ *adj* having a barrel with no ridges or grooves in the bore ■ *n* a gun with a smooth surface inside its barrel

smooth breathing *n* a mark (') written over some initial Greek vowels to show that they are not aspirated. ◊ **rough breathing**

smoothen /smóoth'n/ *vti* to make something smooth, or become smooth

smooth endoplasmic reticulum *n* endoplasmic reticulum that stores key enzymes in plant and animal cells and is involved in various processes including the synthesis of fatty acids and the detoxification of chemicals such as drugs and alcohol. ◊ **rough endoplasmic reticulum**

smooth hound *n* a small shark. Genus: *Mustelus.*

smoothie /smóothi/ *n* **1** **smoothie, smoothy** (*plural* **-ies**) an attractive and charming man perceived as being insincere (*informal*) **2** a drink similar to a milk shake made with fruit, cream, or milk, and ice cream

smoothing circuit *n* a circuit used to remove the alternating current component from a direct current power source

smooth muscle *n* a muscle found in the viscera that functions involuntarily by slow contraction and is made up of layers of spindle-shaped cells lacking cross striations

smooth snake *n* a brownish snake with dark markings and small, smooth scales. Native to: Europe. *Coronella austriaca.*

smooth-spoken *adj* speaking in a gentle, quiet, and agreeable way

smooth-tongued *adj* speaking or spoken skilfully and persuasively

smoothy *n* = **smoothie** *n.* 1 (*informal*)

smorgasbord /smáwrgəss bawrd/ *n* **1** a meal served buffet-style, consisting of a large variety of hot and cold dishes **2** a wide variety (*informal*) [Late 19C. < Swedish *smörgåsbord.*]

smote past tense of **smite**

smother /smúthər/ *v* **1** *vti* ALLOW OR GET TOO LITTLE AIR to deprive somebody or something of air, or be deprived of air **2** *vti* SUFFOCATE to kill somebody or something, or die, by suffocation **3** *vt* OVERWHELM WITH AFFECTION to give somebody too much love or affection with the effect that he or she feels restricted **4** *vti* PUT OUT OR BE PUT OUT to extinguish something such as a fire, or go out from lack of oxygen **5** *vt* SUPPRESS OR HIDE to suppress or hide the expression of something **6** *vt* COVER THICKLY to cover something with a thick layer of something else ■ *n* **1** DENSE SMOKE dense smoke or gas **2** THICK COATING a thick coating of something [12C. < Old English *smorian* 'suffocate, choke (with smoke)'.] —**smotherer** *n* —**smotheringly** *adv* —**smothery** *adj*

smothered mate *n* checkmate resulting when a surrounded king is unable to move and thus escape a threatening knight

smoulder *vi* **1** BURN SLOWLY to burn slowly and gently, usually with some smoke but without a flame **2** HAVE SUPPRESSED EMOTION to have or show a strong emotion that is suppressed but liable to flare up at any time **3** EXIST IN BACKGROUND to exist in the background, liable to appear or reappear at any moment ■ *n* **1** THICK SMOKE thick smoke from a slow-burning fire **2** SMOKY FIRE a slow-burning fire [< Old English *smorian* 'smoke, suffocate']

smout /smowt/, **smowt** *n Scotland* a small person, especially a young child [Variant of SMOLT]

SMP *abbr* statutory maternity pay

smriti /smrítti/ *n* a group of Hindu scriptures giving instruction on social and domestic matters [< Sanskrit, 'what is remembered']

⚡**SMS** *n* a service that allows short textual messages to be sent, e.g. between mobile phones and pagers. Full form **short message service**

smudge /smuj/ *n* 1 **SMEARED INK OR PAINT** a patch of smeared ink or paint blurring what has been written or painted 2 **DIRTY MARK** a dirty or greasy mark 3 **INDISTINCT AREA** something visible but blurred or indistinct and not easily identifiable 4 *US, Can* **SMOKE OR FIRE** smoke produced to protect trees from frost or insect damage, or a fire that produces such smoke ■ *v* (**smudges, smudging, smudged**) 1 *vti* **SMEAR OR BE SMEARED** to smear or blur something by rubbing it, or become smeared or blurred by being rubbed 2 *vti* **MAKE OR BECOME DIRTY** to smear something, or become smeared, with dirt or grease 3 *vt US, Can* **PROTECT WITH SMOKE** to fill an orchard with smoke to protect the trees from frost or insects [15C. < ?] —**smudgily** *adv* —**smudginess** *n* —**smudgy** *adj*

smudge pot *n US, Can* a container in which material is burned to produce smoke for protecting trees from frost or insects

smug /smug/ (**smugger, smuggest**) *adj* conceited and self-satisfied [Mid-16C. < ?] —**smugly** *adv* —**smugness** *n*

smuggle /smúgg'l/ (**-gles, -gling, -gled**) *v* 1 *vti* to carry goods into a country secretly because they are illegal or in order to avoid paying duty on them 2 *vt* to take, bring, or carry somebody or something secretly into or out of a place [Late 17C. < Low German *smukkelen* or Dutch *smokkelen* < ?] —**smuggler** *n*

⚡**smurf** /smurf/ *vi* to route data to a computer or a network of computers in such a way as to flood the target's machine or system with messages, causing a crash (*slang*) [Late 20C. < *Smurf* a children's tiny blue toy which sold in millions.]

smut /smut/ *n* 1 **OBSCENE MATERIAL** obscene jokes, stories, or pictures 2 **SMALL PIECE OF SOOT** a speck of dirt or soot 3 **PLANT DISEASE** a plant disease, especially of cereals and other grasses, caused by fungi and characterized by sooty black masses of spores forming on leaves and other parts 4 **FUNGUS BEARING DISEASE** a parasitic fungus that causes smut. Order: Ustilaginales. ■ *v* (**smuts, smutting, smutted**) 1 *vt* **MAKE DIRTY** to mark or dirty something with smuts 2 *vi* **BECOME AFFECTED WITH SMUT** to become affected with smut [15C. Ultimately < Germanic.]

smutch /smuch/ *n* a smudge of something dirty or greasy ■ *vt* to mark something with a smudge of something dirty or greasy [Mid-16C. < ?] —**smutchy** *adj*

Smuts /smutss, smötss/, **Jan** (1870–1950) South African statesman and general

smutty /smútti/ (**-tier, -tiest**) *adj* 1 **OBSCENE** obscene or pornographic (*informal*) 2 **MARKED WITH SMUTS** covered with sooty marks of dirt 3 **AFFECTED BY SMUT** affected by the disease smut —**smuttily** *adv* —**smuttiness** *n*

Smyrna /smúrnə/ former name for **Izmir**

Smyth /smīth/, **Dame Ethel Mary** (1858–1944) British composer and social reformer

⚡**sn** *abbr* Senegal (*in Internet addresses*)

Sn *symbol* tin

SN *abbr US* seaman

⚡**SNA** *abbr* systems network architecture

snack /snak/ *n* 1 **SMALL MEAL** a small meal of prepared or easy-to-prepare food eaten in place of a regular meal or between regular meals 2 **FOOD FOR SNACK** any sort of food suitable for eating between meals or instead of a main meal ■ *vi* **EAT BETWEEN MEALS** to eat between the times that meals are usually served, or eat a snack instead of a main meal ○ *I've been snacking all afternoon.* [15C. < Middle Dutch *snac* 'bite'.]

snack bar *n* a small restaurant or food outlet that sells snacks

snaffle /snáff'l/ *n* **snaffle, snaffle bit BIT FOR HORSES** a bit for a horse that is jointed in the middle and has rings on either end where the reins are attached ■ *vt* (**-fles, -fling, -fled**) 1 **STEAL** to steal or take something, usually something relatively unimportant (*informal*) 2 **FIT WITH BIT** to fit a horse or pony with a snaffle bit [Mid-16C. < a Low Dutch word.]

snafu /sna fóo/ *n* a mishap or mistake generally caused by incompetence and resulting in delay or confusion (*informal*) ■ *vti* (**-fus, -fuing, -fued**) *US* to cause a situation or process to become confused or delayed, generally by incompetence, or become confused or delayed (*informal*) [Mid-20C. < 'situation normal all fouled up'.]

⚡**SNAFU** *abbr* situation normal all fouled up (*in e-mails*)

snag /snag/ *n* 1 **SMALL PROBLEM** a minor problem or obstacle to progress 2 **UNWANTED SHARP POINT** a sharp projection on which something may catch and tear 3 **HOLE IN FABRIC** a hole or loose thread in a fabric resulting from catching it on something sharp 4 **NAVIGATIONAL OBSTRUCTION** an object underwater, e.g. a tree stump, that may obstruct boats 5 *ANZ* **SAUSAGE** a sausage (*slang*) ■ *v* (**snags, snagging, snagged**) 1 *vti* **CATCH ON A SNAG** to catch on or collide with a sharp projection ○ *snagged my sleeve on a nail* 2 *vt US* **OBSTRUCT** to obstruct the progress of something 3 *vt US* **OBTAIN** to obtain by luck, skilful manoeuvring, or both 4 *vt US* **CLEAR OF OBSTRUCTIONS** to clear a river or lake of underwater obstructions 5 *vi US* **MEET A PROBLEM** to come up against a problem or obstacle that deters progress 6 *vi* **GET TANGLED** to become tangled or entangled [Late 16C. Probably < N Germanic.] —**snaggy** *adj*

snagging item *n* an outstanding minor unsatisfactory detail of workmanship detected during final inspection of a building project and listed for repair or completion (*usually plural*)

snaggletooth /snágg'l tooth/ (*plural* **-teeth** /-teeth/) *n* a broken, projecting, or crooked tooth [Early 19C. *Snaggle* 'snag repeatedly' < SNAG.] —**snaggletoothed** *adj*

snaggle-toothed fish /snágg'l tootht-/ *n* a long-bodied deep-sea fish with a long chin barbel, a large mouth with sharp projecting teeth, and a large stomach for digesting prey. Family: Astronesthidae.

snail /snayl/ *n* 1 a small organism with a coiled shell and a retractable muscular foot on which it crawls. Class: Gastropoda. 2 somebody or something that moves very slowly (*informal*) [Old English *snægel* < Germanic, 'to crawl']

snailfish /snáyl fish/ (*plural* **-fish** *or* **-fishes**) *n* a small elongated flabby bottom-dwelling marine fish, often with ventral fins modified to form a sucking disc. Native to: cold oceans, mostly the N Pacific. Family: Liparidae. [< ?]

⚡**snail mail** *n* mail sent through the postal service, as distinct from the faster electronic mail (*informal*) ■ *vti* to send mail through the postal service

snail's pace *n* a speed that is thought unbearably or unaccountably slow —**snail-paced** *adj*

snake /snayk/ *n* 1 **LEGLESS REPTILE** a legless reptile with a scaly tubular body tapering toward the tail, lidless eyes, and often venomous fangs. Suborder: Serpentes. 2 **OFFENSIVE TERM** an offensive term that deliberately insults somebody's reliability and honesty, especially in personal dealings (*insult*) 3 **PLUMBER'S TOOL** a plumber's tool consisting of a long flexible wire that can be inserted into and rotated inside drains to unblock them 4 **EC CURRENCY RESTRICTION** a former system restricting the amount by which the values of the currencies of EC countries were allowed to vary against each other ■ *v* (**snakes, snaking, snaked**) 1 *vi* **MOVE LIKE SNAKE** to move or lie like a snake, with many bends or twists 2 *vt US* **DRAG** to drag something by a rope or chain 3 *vt US* **TUG** to pull or jerk something suddenly [Old English *snaca* < Germanic, 'to crawl'] ◇ **a snake in the grass** an offensive term for somebody perceived as betraying or deceiving others

snakebird /snáyk burd/ *n* BIRDS = **darter** *n.* 2

snakebite /snáyk bīt/ *n* 1 the bite of a poisonous snake, or illness resulting from this 2 an alcoholic drink that is a mixture of cider and lager

snake charmer *n* an entertainer who elicits a swaying movement from snakes, especially cobras, by means of music and rhythmic body movements

snake dance *n* a ritual dance of some Native North American peoples in which live snakes are handled

snakefish /snáyk fish/ (*plural* **-fish** *or* **-fishes**) *n* a long-bodied predatory fish of the lizard fish family. Native to: E Pacific and W Atlantic inshore regions. *Trachinocephalus myops.*

snake fly *n* an insect with a small head and long prothorax. Family: Raphidiidae.

snakehead /snáyk hed/ *n* 1 a tropical freshwater fish that has a protruding lower jaw and is able to breathe air for long periods of time. Native to: Africa, Asia. Family: Channidae. 2 *Hong Kong* a smuggler of illegal immigrants from mainland China

snake lizard *n* a legless lizard, resembling a snake except that its tongue is flat and fleshy like a lizard's. Native to: Australia, New Guinea. Family: Pygopodidae.

snake oil *n* 1 any worthless liquid preparation sold as a medicine, especially in the past by travelling pedlars 2 something said or written with the intention of deceiving, pacifying, or persuading others

snake pit *n* 1 a place or situation of aggression and destruction (*informal*) 2 *US* an offensive term for a place used to house and care for people judged to have a psychiatric disorder

snakeroot /snáyk root/ *n* a plant with roots used in folk medicine to treat snakebite, or the root of any of these plants used as medicine

snakes and ladders *n* a game played on a board marked out with squares and with a number of snakes and ladders printed on it, in which players move counters towards the finishing point (+ *singular verb*)

snake's head *n* a plant that grows in damp areas. Flowers: drooping, purplish, chequered. Native to: Europe. *Fritillaria meleagris.*

snakeskin /snáyk skin/ *n* 1 the skin of a snake 2 the skin of a snake or snakes made into leather, e.g. for shoes

snakeweed /snáyk weed/ *n* a plant used in folk medicine to cure snakebite, especially bistort

snaky /snáyki/ (**-ier, -iest**) *adj* 1 resembling a snake in being long and narrow with bends or coils, or like a snake's twisting and turning movements 2 treacherous and deceitful —**snakily** *adv* —**snakiness** *n*

snap /snap/ *v* (**snaps, snapping, snapped**) 1 *vti* **BREAK WITH SHARP NOISE** to break or break something suddenly with a sharp cracking sound 2 *vti* **DO SOMETHING WITH A SHARP NOISE** to move, strike, or operate something in a way that makes a sharp noise 3 *vti* **BREAK** to break under force or pressure, or break something by excessive force or pressure 4 *vi* **LOSE CONTROL** to lose control or erupt in anger suddenly 5 *vti* **SPEAK ANGRILY** to say something or reply in anger or irritation 6 *vt* **TAKE A PHOTOGRAPH** to take a photograph of somebody or something, especially in a casual way (*informal*) 7 *vi* **BITE** to bite or try to bite somebody or something with a quick movement or movements 8 *vti US* **TAKE** to take or grasp something eagerly, or take something away from somebody suddenly 9 *vti* **MOVE SHARPLY** to move or be moved quickly and sharply 10 *vi* **APPEAR ANGRY** to flash, especially in anger (*refers to eyes*) 11 *vt US* **FLICK AWAY** to flick something away with a finger coming forward sharply from the thumb 12 *vt* **PLAY THE BALL** in American football, to put the ball into play by passing it back to the quarterback behind the line of scrimmage ■ *n* 1 **SHARP SOUND** a short sharp sound, e.g. of something brittle suddenly breaking or of something clicking shut 2 **SHORT TIME** a short period of time, especially one with cold weather ○ *a sudden cold snap* 3 **SWEET BISCUIT** a crisp thin sweet biscuit 4 **CARD GAME** a game where players lay cards face up in a pile and try to be the first to shout 'snap' when two identical cards are played one after the other 5 PHOTOGRAPHY = **snapshot** *n.* 1 6 **LIVELINESS** liveliness and vigour ○ *His campaign needs more snap.* 7 *US* CLOTHING = **press stud** 8 *US* **SOMETHING EASY** something easily done ○ *The test was a snap.* 9 *N England* **SNACK** a meal or snack, especially a packed lunch (*informal*) 10 **FOOTBALL PLAY** in American football, the action required to start play, when the ball is passed to the quarterback behind the line of scrimmage ■ *adj* 1 **DECIDED WITHOUT REFLECTION** arrived at quickly and without reflection ○ *a snap decision* 2 **COMING WITHOUT WARNING** coming suddenly and without warning 3 **OPERATING WITH A SHARP SOUND** operating with interlocking parts that snap when being shut 4 *US* **EASILY DONE** easily done with success ■ *adv* **WITH A SNAP** so as to make a sharp sound ■ *interj* **NOTING TWO IDENTICAL THINGS** used to acknowledge or draw attention to the simultaneous presence of two identical things or people, and also in the game of snap when attempting to win cards [15C. Partly an imitation of the sound, and partly < Middle Dutch *snappen* 'seize'.]

snap up *vt* to quickly buy or take up something offered or available

snap bean *n US* an edible bean with long tubular pods that are harvested and eaten when immature [*Snap* either from its crispness, or because the pods are broken into pieces before being cooked]

snapdragon /snáp dragən/ *n* a common perennial plant with spikes of flowers of various colours. Genus: *An-*

tirrhinum. [Late 16C. Because the flowers are said to be similar to a dragon's mouth.]

snap link *n* CLIMBING = **karabiner**

snapper /snáppər/ *n* **1** (*plural* **-pers** *or* **-per**) **CARNIVOROUS FISH** a carnivorous reddish sea fish. Native to: tropical waters. Family: Lutjanidae. **2** (*plural* **-pers** *or* **-per**) **AUSTRALIAN FOOD FISH** a fish with a reddish body and bright blue spots, popular as a game fish. Native to: Australian and New Zealand waters. *Chrysophrys auratus.* **3 SNAPPER AS FOOD** the flesh of a snapper as food **4** ZOOL = **snapping turtle 5 SOMETHING THAT SNAPS** a person who or thing that snaps

snapping beetle *n US* INSECTS = **click beetle**

snapping turtle *n* a freshwater turtle with a large head and powerful hooked jaws. Native to: North America. Family: Chelydridae.

snappish /snáppish/ *adj* **1** showing a sharpness or curtness caused by irritation or impatience **2** inclined to snap at things —**snappishly** *adv* —**snappishness** *n*

snappy /snáppi/ (**-pier, -piest**) *adj* **1 SHOWING IMPATIENCE** expressing or showing impatience or irritation **2 INTERESTING** interesting and to the point, or able to write something interesting and to the point (*informal*) **3 HASTY** done or produced without delay **4 STYLISH** fashionable and stylish (*informal*) ○ *a snappy dresser* —**snappily** *adv* —**snappiness** *n* ◇ **make it snappy** to do something quickly (*informal*)

snap ring *n* CLIMBING = **karabiner**

snap roll *n* an aerial manoeuvre in which an aeroplane turns a complete circle longitudinally while maintaining altitude and direction of flight

snapshot /snáp shot/ *n* **1** a photograph, especially one taken by an amateur with simple equipment **2** a record or view of a particular point in a sequence of events or continuing process [Early 19C. Originally 'quick shot from a gun'.]

snare[1] /snair/ *n* **1 ANIMAL TRAP** a trap for small animals that operates like a noose **2 TRAP FOR UNWARY** a situation that is both alluring and dangerous **3 SURGICAL DEVICE** a surgical instrument for removing small polyps and tumours by means of a noose that is tightened by being pulled into a narrow tube ■ *vt* (**snares, snaring, snared**) **1 CATCH IN TRAP** to catch somebody or something in a snare **2 ENTRAP** to entrap somebody by alluring deception [Pre-12C. < Old Norse *snara.*] —**snarer** *n*

snare[2] /snair/ *n* a gut or wire cord stretched across the bottom skin of a drum to create a rattling sound when the drum is hit (*often plural*) [Late 17C. Probably < Dutch *snaar* 'string'.]

snare drum *n* a drum fitted with snares to produce a rattling effect

Snares Islands /snáirz-/ group of uninhabited islands south of Stewart Island, New Zealand. Area: 39 sq. km/15 sq. mi.

snarl[1] /snaarl/ *v* **1** *vi* **GROWL** to growl threateningly **2** *vti* **SPEAK ANGRILY** to speak or say something angrily or threateningly ■ *n* **GROWLING NOISE** the sound of somebody or something snarling [Late 16C. 'Snar repeatedly' < obsolete *snar* 'to snarl'.] —**snarler** *n* —**snarlingly** *adv*

snarl[2] /snaarl/ *n* **1 TANGLE** a tangled mass of something such as hair or wool **2 KNOT IN WOOD** a knot in wood **3** *US* = **snarl-up** ■ *vti* **1 TANGLE** to tangle something or become tangled **2** *US* = **snarl up** [14C. Probably 'small snare' < SNARE[1].]

snarl up *vti* to become or make something become complicated, confused, or too congested to move (*often passive*) US term **snarl**[2] *v.* **2**

snarl-up *n* a tangle of objects, especially a traffic jam. US term **snarl**[2] *n.* **3**

snatch /snach/ *vt* **1 TAKE QUICKLY** to grab or grasp somebody or something hastily **2 MOVE SOMETHING QUICKLY** to move or remove something quickly **3 TAKE WHEN OPPORTUNITY ARISES** to take or get something while there is an opportunity ○ *snatched a few hours of sleep* **4** *US* **KIDNAP** to kidnap somebody (*informal*) ■ *n* **1 GRABBING** an instance of grabbing or grasping somebody or something **2 SMALL AMOUNT** a small, incomplete bit or short period of something **3 THEFT** an act of stealing (*informal*) **4** *US* **KIDNAPPING** an act of kidnapping (*informal*) **5 LIFTING FEAT** a weightlifting feat in which the barbell is raised from the floor to over the lifter's head in one motion **6** *US* **TABOO TERM** a highly offensive term for the outer sexual organs of a woman (*taboo*) [12C. < ?] —**snatcher** *n*

snatch block *n* a block that can be opened on one side to insert a rope, thereby avoiding the necessity of threading the rope through from one end

snatch squad *n* a group of soldiers or police officers trained to single out and seize the apparent ringleaders in situations of public disorder

snatchy /snáchi/ (**-ier, -iest**) *adj* occurring or done in short spells

snath /snath/, **snathe** /snayth/ *n* the handle of a scythe [Late 16C. Variant of *snead* < Old English *snǣd* < ?]

snazzy /snázzi/ (**-zier, -ziest**) *adj* attractively new, bright, or fashionable (*informal*) [Mid-20C. < ?] —**snazzily** *adv* —**snazziness** *n*

SNCF *n* Société Nationale des Chemins de Fer, the rail system in France

sneak /sneek/ *v* **1** *vi* **GO STEALTHILY** to go or act in a stealthy, secretive way **2** *vt* **DO FURTIVELY** to do something stealthily, furtively, and without being noticed ○ *He sneaked a look over the wall.* **3** *vt* **BRING STEALTHILY** to get or carry somebody or something secretly, furtively, and without being noticed ○ *sneak friends into the house for a surprise party* **4** *vi* **TELL TALES** to tell somebody about something wrong that somebody else has done ■ *n* **1 UNTRUSTWORTHY PERSON** a person considered to be cunning and deceitful (*insult*) **2 SOMEBODY WHO TELLS TALES** a person who informs somebody in authority about another's wrongdoing **3 STEALTHY DEPARTURE** a departure intended to be unobserved ■ *adj* **STEALTHILY DONE** done stealthily or furtively [Late 16C. < ?]

sneak up on *vt* **1** to approach stealthily, with the intention of surprising or frightening somebody or something **2** to arrive more quickly than expected ○ *The weekend sneaked up on me.*

sneaker /sneékər/ *n US, Can, ANZ* a shoe with a rubber sole and, usually, a cloth upper (*often plural*)

sneaking /sneéking/ *adj* **1 HIDDEN FROM OTHERS** unknown to or hidden from others **2 SLIGHT BUT PERSISTENT** slight but persistent ○ *a sneaking suspicion* **3 DECEPTIVE** deceptive or given to cunning and deception —**sneakingly** *adv*

sneak preview *n* **1** a public screening of a film prior to its general release, in order to test public reaction to it **2** a surreptitious or private preview

sneak thief *n* a thief who surreptitiously steals unguarded or unsecured articles when the opportunity arises

sneaky /sneéki/ (**-ier, -iest**) *adj* done, doing something, or in the habit of behaving, in an underhanded and unfair way —**sneakily** *adv* —**sneakiness** *n*

sneck /snek/ *n N England, Scotland* a latch on a door or a catch on a door lock that allows it to be left open or shut ■ *vt N England, Scotland* to operate or set the sneck on a door or lock [14C. < ?]

sneer /sneer/ *n* **EXPRESSION OF SCORN** a facial expression of scorn or hostility in which the upper lip may be raised ■ *v* **1** *vi* **FEEL OR SHOW SCORN** to feel or show scorn, contempt, or hostility, either in speech or facial expression **2** *vt* **SAY WITH SCORN** to speak or say something with scorn or contempt [14C. < ?] —**sneerer** *n* —**sneering** *adj* —**sneeringly** *adv*

sneeze /sneez/ *n* a sudden involuntary expulsion of air through the nose and mouth, caused by irritation of the nasal passages ■ *vi* (**sneezes, sneezing, sneezed**) to suddenly, forcefully, and involuntarily expel air through the nose and mouth because of irritation of the nasal passages [15C. Alteration of *fnesan*, < Old English *fneosan*, imitation of breathing.] —**sneezer** *n* —**sneezy** *adj*

sneezewood /sneéz wòòd/ *n* a tree whose peppery-smelling wood is used for posts and beams. Native to: southern Africa. *Ptaeroxylon utile.* [Mid-19C. Probably after Cape Dutch *nieshout.*]

sneezewort /sneéz wurt/ *n* a composite plant with silvery leaves that when powdered induce sneezing. Flowers: small, white, like daisies. Native to: Europe, Asia. *Achillea ptarmica.*

snell /snel/ *adj Scotland* bitingly cold [Old English, < Germanic]

Snell /snel/, **Peter George** (*b.* 1938) New Zealand runner

Snellen chart /snéllən-/ *n* a chart for vision testing on which are printed rows of letters and numbers in decreasing size from top to bottom [Mid-19C. After Herman *Snellen* (1834–1908), Dutch ophthalmologist.]

Snell's law /snélz-/ *n* the law stating that for a light ray passing between two media the ratio of the sines of the angle of incidence and the angle of refraction is a constant [Late 19C. After Willebrord Van Roijen *Snell* (1591–1626), Dutch astronomer and mathematician.]

snib /snib/ *n Ireland, Scotland* a bolt or catch on a door or a catch on a lock ■ *vt* (**snibs, snibbing, snibbed**) *Ireland, Scotland* to operate or fasten the snib on a door or lock [Early 19C. < ?]

snick /snik/ *n* **1 SMALL CUT** a small cut or notch **2 GLANCING BLOW** a glancing blow to the ball from a cricket bat ■ *vt* **1 CUT** to cut something slightly **2 HIT OBLIQUELY** to hit the ball with a glancing blow [Late 17C. Probably < obsolete *snick or snee* 'cut or thrust in knife-fighting'.]

snicker /sníkər/ *n, vti* US = **snigger** ■ *vi* to neigh or whinny ■ *n* a horse's neigh or whinny [Late 17C. < ?]

snide /snīd/ (**snider, snidest**) *adj* derisively sarcastic [Mid-19C. < ?] —**snidely** *adv*

sniff /snif/ *v* **1** *vti* **BREATHE IN THROUGH NOSE** to breathe in through the nose, e.g. to see how something smells **2** *vt* **SUSPECT** to have a suspicion of something, especially something bad ○ *sniff trouble* ■ *n* **1 ACT OR SOUND OF SNIFFING** an instance or the sound of inhaling through the nose **2 SUSPICION** a hint or suspicion, especially of something bad [14C. An imitation of the sound.]

sniff at *vt* to show contempt or disdain for somebody or something

sniff out *vt* to discover something, especially something bad, by investigation (*informal*)

⚡**sniffer** /sníffər/ *n* **1 SOMEBODY WHO SNIFFS** a person who sniffs, especially somebody who takes drugs by inhaling them **2 DEVICE MONITORING DATA TRANSMISSION** a device or program that monitors and analyzes network traffic, detecting bottlenecks and problems **3** a program on a computer system designed legitimately or illegitimately to capture data being transmitted on a network, often used by hackers to appropriate passwords and user names

sniffer dog *n* a dog trained to detect explosives, drugs, or other contraband by scent

sniffle /sníff'l/ *vi* (**-fles, -fling, -fled**) **1 INHALE MUCUS** to inhale through the nose to prevent mucus from dripping out of it **2 WEEP QUIETLY** to sniff repeatedly while gently weeping ■ *n* **ACT OR SOUND OF SNIFFLING** an instance or the sound of sniffling ■ **sniffles** *npl* **SLIGHT COLD** a slight cold that causes sniffling (*informal*) [Mid-17C. An imitation of the sound.] —**sniffler** *n*

sniffy /sníffi/ (**-ier, -iest**) *adj* (*informal*) **1** behaving in a haughty, disdainful way **2** tending to sniff a lot, e.g. because of a cold —**sniffily** *adv* —**sniffiness** *n*

snifter /sníftər/ *n* **1** a stemmed glass with a bowl that tapers upwards, typically used for brandy **2** a small amount of drink, especially of alcohol (*informal*) [Mid-18C. Originally 'strong breeze' < archaic *snifter* 'sniff, snuffle', an imitation of the sound.]

snigger *v* **1** *vi* **LAUGH DISRESPECTFULLY** to laugh disrespectfully in a covert way **2** *vt* **SAY DISRESPECTFULLY** to speak or say something while laughing disrespectfully ■ *n* **ACT OR SOUND OF SNIGGERING** an instance of or the sound of sniggering [Early 18C. Variant of SNICKER.]

sniggle /snígg'l/ *vti* (**-gles, -gling, -gled**) to fish for eels by putting a baited hook into crevices where they hide, or to catch eels using this method ■ *n* a baited hook used for catching eels [Mid-17C. < *snig* 'young eel' < ?] —**sniggler** *n*

snip /snip/ *vti* (**snips, snipping, snipped**) **CUT USING SMALL STROKES** to cut with scissors or shears, especially using small strokes, or cut something using small strokes ■ *n* **1 A CUT** a short quick cut, made with scissors **2 SMALL PIECE** a small piece of something that has been snipped off **3 BARGAIN** something costing less than its real value (*informal*) **4 EASY THING** something that is a certainty or is easily done (*informal*) **5 ACT OR SOUND OF SNIPPING** the act or sound of using scissors to snip something ■ *interj* **SOUND OF SNIPPING** used to represent the sound that scissors make [Mid-16C. < Dutch or Low German *snippen*, an imitation of the sound.]

snipe /snīp/ *n* (*plural* **snipes** *or* **snipe**) **1 WADING BIRD** a wading bird with a long straight bill. Native to: N hemisphere. *Gallinago gallinago.* **2 BIRD RELATED TO SNIPE** a bird related to the snipe, e.g. a sandpiper or curlew **3 SHOT FIRED FROM CONCEALMENT** a shot fired from a concealed place ■ *vi* (**snipes, sniping, sniped**) **SHOOT FROM CONCEALED PLACE** to shoot at people from a concealed position [14C. Probably < Old Norse *snípa.*] —**sniper** *n*

snipefish /snīp fish/ (*plural* **-fish** *or* **-fishes**) *n* a fish with a long snout and a spine extending from its dorsal fin to its tail. Native to: tropical and temperate seas. Family: Macrorhamphosidae.

snipe fly *n* a fly with a long body and long legs that eats other insects. Family: Leptidae.

snippet /snɪ́ppət/ *n* a small piece of something such as information or music [Mid-17C. < SNIP + -ET.]

snipping /snɪ́pping/ *n* = **snip** *n.* 2

snippy /snɪ́ppi/ (**-pier, -piest**) *adj* **1** behaving in a curt and irritable way (*informal*) **2** made up of scraps or fragments —**snippily** *adv* —**snippiness** *n*

snips *npl* shears used for cutting sheet metal (*+ singular or plural verb*)

snit /snit/ *n US* a state of mild irritation or bad temper [Mid-20C. < ?]

snitch /snich/ *v* (*slang*) **1** *vt* **PILFER** to steal something in a sneaky way, especially something of little value **2** *vi* **INFORM** to inform on somebody ○ *Friends don't snitch on each other.* ■ *n* **1 INFORMER** a person who informs on others (*slang*) **2 NOSE** a person's nose (*dated slang*) [Late 17C. < ?] —**snitcher** *n*

snivel /snɪ́vv'l/ *vi* (**-els, -elled, -elling** *or* **-eled**) **1 SNIFF** to sniff audibly **2 WHINE** to behave in a whining, tearful, or self-pitying way **3 SNIFFLE** to have a runny nose ■ *n* **WHINE OR SNIFF** an act of snivelling [Assumed Old English *snyflan*] —**sniveller** *n* —**snivelling** *n, adj* —**snivelly** *adj*

snob /snob/ *n* **1** an admirer and cultivator of people with high social status who disdains those considered inferior **2** a person who disdains people considered to have inferior knowledge or tastes [Late 18C. < ?] —**snobbery** *n* —**snobbism** *n* —**snobby** *adj*

snobbish /snóbbish/ *adj* displaying an offensively superior condescending manner —**snobbishly** *adv* —**snobbishness** *n*

ϟ**SNOBOL** /snṓ bawl/ *n* a high-level computer programming language designed for dealing with strings of symbols [Mid-20C. After COBOL.]

snob value *n* worth or desirability arising from being seen as superior (*informal*)

snoek /snook/ (*plural* **snoeks** *or* **snoek**) *n* a long predatory fish of the mackerel family. Native to: Australia, New Zealand, southern Africa. *Thyrsites atun.* [Late 18C. Via Afrikaans < Middle Dutch *snoec* 'pike'.]

snog /snog/ *vti* (**snogs, snogging, snogged**) *UK* to kiss and cuddle somebody, especially for a long time (*slang*) ■ *n UK* a long kiss or a prolonged kissing and cuddling session (*slang*) [Mid-20C. < ?]

snood /snood/ *n* **1 DECORATIVE HAIR NET** a net that holds a woman's hair at the back of her head **2 RIBBON WORN BY UNMARRIED SCOTTISH WOMEN** in the 17th and 18th centuries, a hairband or ribbon worn by unmarried women in Scotland ■ *vt* **WEAR A SNOOD OVER THE HAIR** to fasten the hair with a snood [Old English *snōd*, < Indo-European, 'to spin, sew']

snook[1] /snook/ (*plural* **snook** *or* **snooks**) *n* a large bony fish that lives in warm seas and rivers. *Centropomus undecimalis.* [Late 17C. Via Dutch *snoek* 'pike' < Middle Dutch *snoec.*]

snook[2] /snook, snŏŏk/ *n* a gesture made as a sign of contempt, by putting the thumb to the nose with the fingers outstretched [Late 18C. < ?]

snooker /snŏŏkər/ *n* **1 BALL AND CUE GAME** a game played on a table in which a white cue ball is used to hit fifteen red balls and six balls of different colours into any of six pockets **2 POSITION IN SNOOKER** a position in snooker in which a player is forced to play an indirect shot because another ball is between the cue ball and the target ball ■ *vt* **1 PUT SOMEBODY AT DISADVANTAGE IN SNOOKER** to put a snooker player in the position of being forced to play an indirect shot because another ball is between the cue ball and the target ball **2 THWART** to thwart somebody or put somebody in a position of being unable to proceed (*informal*) [Late 19C. < ?]

snoop /snoop/ *vi* **PRY** to pry into other people's business or affairs, especially in a furtive way (*informal*) ■ *n* (*informal*) **1 SOMEBODY WHO SNOOPS** a prier into other people's lives **2 SURREPTITIOUS INVESTIGATION** a furtive search or investigation of somebody's private property or affairs [Mid-19C. < Dutch *snoepen* 'eat on the sly'.] —**snooper** *n*

snooperscope /snŏŏpər skōp/ *n* a device that converts infrared radiation into a visual image and is used for seeing in the dark

snoopy /snŏŏpi/ (**-ier, -iest**) *adj* tending to pry into the affairs of others

snoot /snoot/ *n* a nose or snout (*informal*) [Mid-19C. Variant of SNOUT.]

snooty /snŏŏti/ (**-ier, -iest**) *adj* showing a haughty, condescending manner, especially to those considered socially inferior (*informal*) [Early 20C. < SNOOT.] —**snootily** *adv* —**snootiness** *n*

snooze /snooz/ *vi* (**snoozes, snoozing, snoozed**) to have a short sleep (*informal*) ■ *n* a short sleep (*informal*) [Late 18C. < ?] —**snoozer** *n* —**snoozy** *adj*

snore /snawr/ *vi* (**snores, snoring, snored**) to breathe noisily while asleep because of vibrations of the soft palate ■ *n* a snorting or whistling sound made while sleeping, or an act of snoring [14C. < ?] —**snorer** *n*

snorkel /snáwrk'l/ *n* **1 BREATHING APPARATUS** a device allowing somebody to swim just below water, consisting of a face mask and a breathing tube held in the mouth while the other end projects above the water **2 VENTILATOR ON SUBMARINE** a ventilation device on a submarine **3 DEVICE ON TANK** a device on a tank or other vehicle that functions like the snorkel on a submarine and enables the vehicle to go through shallow water ■ *vi* (**snorkels, snorkelling, snorkelled, snorkelled**) **SWIM WITH SNORKEL** to swim underwater breathing air through a snorkel [Mid-20C. < German dialect *Schnorchel* 'nose'.] —**snorkeller** *n*

snorkelling /snáwrkəling/ *n* the activity or pastime of swimming with a snorkel

snort /snawrt/ *v* **1** *vi* **FORCE AIR THROUGH NOSE** to make a harsh sound by forcing air out through the nostrils **2** *vi* **SHOW CONTEMPT** to express a feeling, especially of contempt or impatience, by snorting **3** *vti* **INHALE DRUG** to inhale a powdered drug through the nostrils (*informal*) ■ *n* **1 HARSH SOUND** a harsh sound made by snorting, or an instance of this **2 GULP OF ALCOHOL** a short drink, especially of alcohol, taken all at once (*informal*) **3 INHALATION OF DRUG** an act of inhaling a powdered drug through the nostrils (*informal*) **4 SUBMARINE SNORKEL** the snorkel of a submarine (*slang*) [14C. Probably a variant of SNORE.] —**snorter** *n* —**snorting** *n, adj*

snot /snot/ *n* **1** an offensive term for mucus produced in the nose (*slang*) **2** an offensive term for somebody whose behaviour is regarded as arrogant or condescending (*slang insult*) [Old English *gesnot* < Germanic]

snot-nosed *adj* an offensive term meaning regarded as being young and precocious but not to be taken seriously (*slang*)

snotter /snóttər/ *n Scotland* **NASAL MUCUS** a lump of mucus in or from somebody's nose ■ *vi Scotland* **1 SNUFFLE** to breathe through the nose while it is partially blocked up with mucus **2 SNIVEL** to cry in a way that produces nasal mucus [Early 18C. < SNOT.]

snotty /snótti/ (**-tier, -tiest**) *adj* **1** an offensive term meaning wet or dirty with nasal mucus (*slang*) **2** an offensive term meaning behaving in an arrogant and condescending manner (*slang insult*) **3** an offensive term describing actions that are regarded as malicious or rude (*slang*) —**snottily** *adv* —**snottiness** *n*

snout /snowt/ *n* **1 ANIMAL'S NOSE** the projecting part of a vertebrate's head, consisting of the nose and mouth **2 PROJECTING PART OF INSECT'S HEAD** the projecting part of the head of an insect or other invertebrate such as a weevil **3 LARGE NOSE** somebody's nose (*slang*) **4 PROJECTION** something that sticks out, e.g. the muzzle of a gun **5 SOMETHING TO SMOKE** tobacco, or a cigarette (*slang*) **6 INFORMER** a person who informs on somebody to the police (*slang*) **7 STEEP END OF GLACIER** the leading face of a glacier, usually heavily loaded with rock debris [13C] —**snouted** *adj*

snout beetle *n* INSECTS = **weevil** *n.* 1 [< the shape of its head]

snow /snō/ *n* **ICE CRYSTAL FLAKES** water vapour in the atmosphere that has frozen into ice crystals and then falls to the ground in the form of flakes ■ *npl* **FALL OF SNOW** an amount of snow that falls at one time ○ *had a heavy snow last night* ■ *n* **1 SNOW ON GROUND** a layer of snow on the ground **2 SUBSTANCE RESEMBLING SNOW** a substance that resembles snow in colour or texture **3 WHITE SPECKS ON TELEVISION SCREEN** random patterns of small white specks on a television or radar screen caused by electrical interference **4 NARCOTIC DRUG** cocaine or heroin in the form of a white powder (*slang*) ■ *v* **1** *vi* **TO FALL AS SNOW** to fall from the sky as snow (*refers to precipitation*) ○ *It's snowing!* **2** *vt* **COVER SOMETHING WITH SNOW** to cover, close in, or block with a fall of snow **3** *vti* **FALL LIKE SNOW** to fall or scatter like snow, or make something fall in this way **4** *vt US, Can* **PERSUADE SOMEBODY WITH GLIB TALK** to overwhelm or deceive somebody especially with flattery or charm (*slang*) ○ *She snowed us into buying worthless stock.* [Old English *snāw* < Indo-European]

snow under *vt US* to defeat an opposing team soundly

snowball /snṓ bawl/ *n* **1 BALL OF SNOW** a soft lump of snow for throwing at somebody or something, made from handfuls of snow pressed together **2 ALCOHOLIC DRINK** a drink made from advocaat mixed with lemonade ■ *v* **1** *vi* **INCREASE RAPIDLY** to grow or multiply rapidly or at an accelerating rate ○ *The event snowballed until hundreds of people were involved.* **2** *vti* **THROW SNOWBALLS** to throw snowballs at each other or at somebody else ◇ **not have a snowball's chance (in hell)** to have no chance at all (*informal*)

snowberry /snṓbəri/ (*plural* **-ries**) *n* an ornamental shrub with pink flowers and white berries. Native to: North America, naturalized in Great Britain. Genus: *Symphoricarpos.*

snowbird /snṓ burd/ *n* a bird that is seen chiefly in winter, e.g. a snow bunting

snow-blind *adj* affected by temporary blindness and pain in the eyes caused by bright light reflected from snow and ice

snow blindness *n* a condition of temporary blindness caused by the bright sunlight and intense radiation reflected from snow or ice, which causes swelling of parts of the eyeball and severe pain

snowblink /snṓ blingk/ *n* a white glow in the sky, especially in polar regions, caused by the reflection of light from distant snowfields

snowblower /snṓ blō ər/ *n* a machine that clears snow from roads by scooping it into a fast-rotating spiral blade and ejecting it to one side

snowboard /snṓ bawrd/ *n* a board that somebody stands on to slide down snow slopes ■ *vi* to slide down snow slopes using a snowboard —**snowboarder** *n* —**snowboarding** *n*

snowbound /snṓ bownd/ *adj* prevented from moving or leaving a place by heavy snow

snow bunting *n* a white finch with dark markings that nests on tundra and winters in coastal regions. *Plectrophenax nivalis.*

snowcap /snṓ kap/ *n* a covering of snow on a mountain peak —**snowcapped** *adj*

snow cone *n US, Can, Carib* a paper cupful of crushed ice with a fruit syrup

Snowdon, Mount /snṓd'n/ highest peak in Wales, in the NW of the country. Height: 1,085 m/3,560 ft.

Snowdonia National Park /snō dṓni ə-/ national park in NW Wales, incorporating Mount Snowdon. Area: 2,171 sq. km/840 sq. mi.

snowdrift /snṓ drift/ *n* a bank of snow piled up by the wind

snowdrop /snṓ drop/ *n* an early spring-flowering plant that grows from a bulb. Flowers: small, white, drooping. Native to: Europe, Asia. *Galanthus nivalis.*

snowfall /snṓ fawl/ *n* **1** a period during which snow falls or an instance of snow falling **2** the amount of snow that falls in a particular place or in a given period ○ *What is the average snowfall for the area?*

snow fence *n* a portable flexible fence made of upright slats, designed to stop snow from drifting onto roads or ski runs

snowfield /snṓ feeld/ *n* a large area permanently covered in snow

snowflake /snṓ flayk/ *n* **1** an individual mass of ice crystals that falls with others as snow **2** a garden plant grown from a bulb. Flowers: white, resembling a snowdrop but larger. Genus: *Leucojum.* **3** BIRDS = **snow bunting**

snow goose *n* a goose with white plumage and black wing tips. Native to: Arctic regions, migrating to coastal areas. *Anser caerulescens.*

snow grass *n* **1** a grey-green grass that grows in upland areas of Australia. Genus: *Poa.* **2** a grass that grows in the hills of New Zealand. Genus: *Danthonia.*

snow-in-summer *n* a perennial plant with woolly stems and notched silvery green leaves. Flowers: white. Native to: Europe. *Cerastium tomentosum.*

snow job *n US, Can* an attempt to mislead or persuade somebody by insincere talk or flattery (*slang*)

snow leopard *n* a large cat with a thick pale-grey or brown coat marked with dark splotches. Native to: mountainous regions of Central Asia. *Panthera uncia.*

snow line *n* the line of altitude above which there is permanent snow, or the line of latitude that marks the extent of permanent snow in the polar regions

snowman /snṓ man/ (*plural* **-men** /-men/) *n* a roughly human figure made by piling up and shaping snow

snowmelt /snṓ melt/ *n US, Can* **1** runoff produced when snow melts **2** the season when snow melts

snowmobile /snṓmə beel, -mō beel/ *n* a small vehicle used for travelling over snow

snowpack /snṓ pak/ *n* accumulated snow, usually in a mountainous area

snow pea *n US, Can, ANZ* a variety of garden pea with an edible thin flat pod. *Pisum sativum.*

snow pellet *n* a soft white round mass of ice that falls as precipitation (*often plural*)

snow plant *n* a plant with a fleshy reddish stalk that often flowers before the snow has melted. Flowers: scarlet. Native to: mountains of W North America. *Sarcodes sanguinea.*

snowplough /snṓ plow/ *n* **1 VEHICLE FOR CLEARING SNOW** a vehicle or an implement that can be fixed to a vehicle, used for clearing snow from roads or paths **2 CONTROL TECHNIQUE IN SKIING** a technique used in skiing in which the points of the skis are brought together to make a V, enabling the skier to turn or stop ■ *vi* **SKI IN SNOWPLOUGH POSITION** to use the snowplough position to turn or stop in skiing

snowplow /snṓ plow/ *n, vi* US = **snowplough**

snowshed /snṓ shed/ *n* a shelter over an open section of a railway track, especially on a mountainside, to prevent it getting covered in snow

snowshoe /snṓ shoo/ *n* a metal or wood framework with interwoven straps that is attached to a boot allowing the wearer to walk on snow without sinking ■ *vi* (**-shoes, -shoeing, -shoed**) to walk on snow wearing snowshoes

snowshoe hare, snowshoe rabbit *n* a hare with a white winter coat that turns brown in summer and large heavily furred hind feet that allow it to move quickly in snow. Native to: North America. *Lepus americanus.*

snowstorm /snṓ stawrm/ *n* a storm with heavy snow and sometimes strong winds

snow tyre *n* a tyre with a deep tread pattern or studs to provide extra traction for a vehicle driving in snowy conditions

snow-white *adj* as white as fresh snow

snowy *adj* **1** characterized by the presence of snow ○ *a snowy day* **2** resembling snow, especially in colour or purity ○ *a snowy beard* —**snowily** *adv* —**snowiness** *n*

Snowy /snṓ i/ river in SE Australia, rising in SE New South Wales and flowing through E Victoria to the Tasman Sea. Length: 435 km/270 mi.

LITERARY LINK ***The Man From Snowy River***, a long poem (1895) by Australian writer A. B. Paterson. Set in the high country of SE Australia, this verse sequence tells of the heroic exploits of a horseman as he rounds up a mob of wild and escaped horses. It is one of Australia's best-known poems.

snowy egret *n* a small egret with white feathers, black legs, and yellow feet. Native to: North and South America. *Egretta thula.*

Snowy Mountains mountain range in SE New South Wales, Australia. Highest peak: Mount Kosciusko 2,228 m/7,310 ft.

snowy owl *n* a large white owl that builds nests on the ground and feeds mainly on lemmings. Native to: Arctic. *Nyctea scandiaca.*

SNP[1] *abbr* Scottish National Party

SNP[2] /snip/ *abbr* single nucleotide polymorphism

Snr, snr *abbr* Senior

snub /snub/ *vt* (**snubs, snubbing, snubbed**) **1 TREAT SOMEBODY RUDELY** to treat somebody with deliberate coldness or contempt **2 BRING SOMETHING TO A STOP** to stop a line from paying out by wrapping it around something, or to stop something attached to a line such as a boat or horse from getting away by wrapping the line around something ■ *n* **HUMILIATING ACTION** a remark or act intended to humiliate or insult, e.g. ignoring somebody ■ *adj* **SMALL** short and flat or turned up at the end [14C. < Old Norse *snubba* < ?] —**snubber** *n*

snub-nosed *adj* **1** with a nose that is short and flat or turned up **2** having a very short barrel or a blunt end ○ *snub-nosed pliers*

snuff[1] /snuf/ *v* **1** *vt* **INHALE** to inhale something through the nose **2** *vti* **SNIFF** to sniff, especially noisily, or to examine something by sniffing it ○ *The hounds snuffed the ground searching for the trail.* ■ *n* **SNIFFING SOUND** a sound made by sniffing noisily [Early 16C. < Dutch *snuffen* 'snuffle' < Germanic, 'to do with the nose'.]

snuff[2] /snuf/ *vt* **1 EXTINGUISH FLAME** to extinguish a flame, e.g. that of a burning candle **2 TRIM CANDLEWICK** to remove the burnt end from the wick of a candle **3 DESTROY** to put an end to somebody or something (*informal*) ○ *snuff out enthusiasm* ■ *n* **SOOTY WICK** the sooty, charred end of a candlewick [14C. < ?] ◇ **snuff it** to die (*informal*)

snuff[3] /snuf/ *n* **1 POWDERED TOBACCO** tobacco in the form of powder, taken by sniffing it up the nostrils **2 AMOUNT OF SNUFF** a portion of snuff ■ *vi* **TAKE SNUFF** to inhale snuff [Late 17C. < Dutch *snuf*, shortening of *snuftabak* 'sniffing tobacco'.]

snuffbox /snúf boks/ *n* a small ornamental box for powdered tobacco

snuff-coloured *adj* of a dark yellowish-brown colour

snuffer /snúffər/ *n* **1** a device used to extinguish a candle, consisting of a long handle with a cone shape at one end **2 snuffers** an instrument resembling a pair of scissors, used for trimming wicks or extinguishing candles or oil lamps (+ *singular or plural verb*)

snuff film, snuff movie *n* a pornographic film or video that allegedly ends with the murder of one of the participants in a sex act (*slang*)

snuffle /snúff'l/ *v* (**-fles, -fling, -fled**) **1** *vi* **BREATHE NOISILY** to breathe noisily through a partially blocked nose **2** *vti* **SPEAK NASALLY** to speak or say something in a nasal or whining way **3** *vi* **SNIFF** to make repeated sniffing sounds ■ *n* **SOUND OF SNUFFLING** the act of snuffling, or the sound made by breathing noisily through the nose ■ **snuffles** *npl* **RUNNY NOSE** a cold or other condition in which somebody sniffs a lot [Late 16C. < ?] —**snuffler** *n* —**snuffly** *adj*

snuff movie *n* CINEMA = **snuff film**

snuffy /snúffi/ (**-ier, -iest**) *adj* **1 LIKE SNUFF** like snuff in colour or smell **2 COVERED WITH SNUFF** soiled or marked with snuff **3 DISAGREEABLE** in a bad temper and acting irritably —**snuffiness** *n*

snug /snug/ *adj* (**snugger, snuggest**) **1 COSY** warm and comfortable **2 SMALL BUT COMFORTABLE** small in size but offering a comfortable well-arranged space ○ *a snug cottage* **3 SHELTERED** protected from the weather ○ *The fishing boats were snug in the harbour.* **4 CLOSE-FITTING** fitting comfortably close or too close ○ *The sweater was perhaps a little too snug.* **5 CONCEALED** offering a safe and private hiding place ■ *n* **1 SMALL ROOM IN A PUB** a small room or enclosed area in a pub allowing a small number of people to sit in private **2 PEG FOR HOLDING A BOLT** a small peg used to hold the head of a bolt in place while a nut is tightened onto the end ■ *v* (**snugs, snugging, snugged**) **1** *vt* **MAKE SNUG** to make somebody or something comfortable and warm **2** *vti* **SECURE A BOAT** to make a boat secure to weather a storm [Late 16C. Probably < N Germanic or Low Dutch.]

snuggery /snúggəri/ (*plural* **-ies**) *n* **1** a place that is warm and comfortable **2** = **snug** *n.* 1 [Early 19C. < SNUG.]

snuggle /snúgg'l/ (**-gles, -gling, -gled**) *v* **1** *vi* to get into a comfortable, cosy position, especially close to another person **2** *vt* to draw close to somebody or something to offer or receive comfort and affection ○ *snuggled in front of the fireplace* [Late 17C. < SNUG.]

so[1] /sō/ CORE MEANING: a conjunction indicating the reason for an action or situation, or its result ○ *Let's go upstairs and talk, so as to get a bit of privacy.* ○ *Keep your password secret so that others cannot use your user name.* ○ *I had the flu, so I couldn't attend the meeting.*

1 *conj* **IN ORDER THAT** introduces the reason for doing what has just been mentioned ○ *The poles are joined together so as to enclose an area of about twenty feet in diameter.* ○ *He held her tight so that she wouldn't fall.* **2** *conj* **INTRODUCES RESULT** introduces the result of the situation that has just been mentioned ○ *Everything is done on a shoestring, so their prices are very low.* **3** *adv* **REFERS BACK** refers back to something that has just been mentioned ○ *Lunch may be purchased on the island, for those who desire to do so.* **4** *adv* **INDICATES IDENTITY** indicates that what is true of one person or thing is also true of another person or thing (*followed by auxiliary or modal, or by the main verb 'do', 'have', or 'be'*) ○ *If you can keep a secret, so can I.* **5** *adv* **AS IT IS** indicates that something is the way it has been described ○ *The city has the potential to be very important, and will soon be so, both politically and commercially.* **6** *adv* **TO SUCH AN EXTENT** emphasizes the degree of something by mentioning its result ○ *He is so busy working at Nathan's, he doesn't have time to study.* ○ *He's not so unobservant as to miss seeing the change.* **7** *adv* **EMPHASIZES A QUALITY** adds emphasis to the meaning of an adverb or adjective ○ *I was so scared.* ○ *He acts so stubbornly sometimes.* **8** *adv* **THEREFORE OR IN CONSEQUENCE** introduces an event in a sequence ○ *It's not working out so we'll have to go back to the beginning and start again.* ○ *She said she would like to see me again so I gave her my phone number.* **9** *adv* **INTRODUCES COMMENT** introduces a new topic, or a question or comment about something ○ *So what are we going to do about it?* ○ *So I see you've changed your mind.* **10** *adv* **INDICATES POSITION OR DIMENSIONS** indicates the position or dimensions of something, using actions or gestures ○ *Hold onto the boat like so, and hoist yourself up.* **11** *conj* **INDICATES SIMILARITY** indicates that two events or situations are alike in some way ○ *Just as my circumstances have changed, so too have my aims in life.* **12** *adv* **INDEED** used to contradict a negative statement (*nonstandard*) ○ *'You never explained what to do'.'I did so!'* [Old English *swā* < Indo-European] ◇ **and so on** *or* **forth** used at the end of a list to indicate that there are other things that could be mentioned ○ *These systems are traditionally used in industries such as insurance, banking, universities, and so on.* ○ *Remove any additional hardware from the system (mouse, network card, fax board, modem, and so forth.)* ◇ **so be it** expresses agreement or resignation ○ *I wish you'd think again, but never mind – so be it!* ◇ **so much, so many** a certain degree or amount ○ *The government can only do so much.* ○ *I can only take so many insults.* ◇ **so much for 1** indicates that there is nothing more that can be said or done about something (*informal*) ○ *So much for the morning. I still had the afternoon to get through.* **2** indicates that something has not been successful or helpful (*informal*) ○ *Well, so much for simple fairness!* ◇ **so there** used to express defiance, triumph, or finality ◇ **so what?** used to ask rather rudely why something is important, implying that it is not ○ *You amass all these facts, but the question is, 'so what?'*

SPELLCHECK See ***sew***

so[2] *n* MUSIC = **soh**

ϟ**so**[3] *abbr* Somalia (*in Internet addresses*)

SO *abbr* **1** significant other (*in e-mails*) **2** standing order **3** strike-out

soak /sōk/ *v* **1** *vti* **STEEP** to immerse something in liquid, or be immersed in liquid, for a period of time **2** *vt* **MAKE WET** to make something or somebody completely wet (*often passive*) ○ *We got soaked in the rain on the way home.* **3** *vti* **ABSORB** to draw something such as moisture in through the pores or other small holes ○ *This sponge soaks up moisture.* **4** *vti* **PERMEATE** to penetrate something by saturating it and passing into pores or small holes ○ *The water quickly soaked through her shoes.* **5** *vti* **REMOVE STAIN BY SOAKING** to remove something, especially a mark or a stain from an item of clothing, by leaving it in liquid for a time **6** *vti* **GET DRUNK** to drink too much alcohol, or make somebody drunk (*informal*) **7** *vt* **OVERCHARGE** to overcharge or tax somebody heavily (*slang*) ■ *n* **1 ACT OF SOAKING** an act or the process of immersing something in liquid ○ *had a long, leisurely soak in the bath* **2 SOAKING LIQUID** a solution or liquid for soaking something in **3 HARD DRINKER** a drunkard (*slang*) [Old English *socian*, < *sūcan*, an earlier form of SUCK] —**soaker** *n*

soakaway /sṓkə way/ *n* a hole where waste water can drain away by filtering down through the soil

soaking /sṓking/ *n* **1 STEEPING** an act or the process of steeping something in liquid **2 DRENCHING** an instance of being made very wet (*informal*) ■ *adj* **VERY WET** very wet, especially because of being rained on (*informal*)

so-and-so (*plural* **so-and-sos**) *n* **1** somebody or something not named or specified (*informal*) **2** somebody regarded as annoying or disagreeable (*informal insult*)

Soane /sōn/, **Sir John** (1753–1837) British architect

soap /sōp/ *n* **1 CLEANSING AGENT** a solid, liquid, or powdered preparation made by reacting potassium or sodium hydroxide with animal or vegetable oils. Use: cleaning. **2 METALLIC SALT COMBINED WITH FATTY ACID** a metallic salt of a fatty acid, often made with calcium, copper, aluminium, or lithium. Use: bases for waterproofing agents, ointments, greases. 3 **SOAP OPERA** a soap opera (*informal*) ■ *vt* **PUT SOAP ON** to put soap on something or somebody [Old English *sāpe* < Germanic, 'soap']

soapbark /sṓp baark/ *n* 1 a bark containing saponin. Use: formerly, as soap. 2 an evergreen tree that yields soapbark. Flowers: small, white. Native to: South America. *Quillaja saponaria.*

soapberry /sṓp beri/ (*plural* **-ries**) *n* 1 a pulpy fruit that is rich in saponins. Use: soap substitute. 2 a tree or shrub that bears soapberries. Native to: tropical America. Genus: *Sapindus.*

soapbox /sṓp boks/ *n* 1 a box in which soap is packed 2 something, such as a wooden box, used as a platform for making an impromptu speech

soap bubble *n* 1 a bubble formed with soapy water 2 something that is beautiful but that does not last

soap opera *n* a serial on television or radio that deals with the lives of a group of characters, especially in a melodramatic or sentimental way [Because often sponsored by soap manufacturers]

soap powder *n* a detergent in powdered form used in washing machines

soapstone /sṓp stōn/ *n* a dark grey or green soft soapy compact variety of talc. Use: decorative carving.

soapsuds /sṓp sudz/ *npl* = **suds** *npl.*

soapwort /sṓp wurt/ *n* a plant with roots and leaves that yield saponin. Flowers: pink and white. Native to: Europe. *Saponaria officinalis.* US term **bouncing Bet**

soapy /sṓpi/ (**-ier, -iest**) *adj* 1 **WITH SOAP** full of or covered with soap 2 **LIKE SOAP** with the look or feel of soap ○ *a soapy texture* 3 **INSINCERE** given to excessive insincere flattery (*slang*) —**soapiness** *adv*

soar /sawr/ *vi* 1 **FLY** to fly or rise high in the air 2 **GLIDE HIGH** to glide, on rising currents of air 3 **INCREASE RAPIDLY** to increase rapidly in number, volume, size, or amount ○ *soaring prices* 4 **BECOME MORE INTENSE** to rise to a higher, more intense, or exalted level ■ *n* **ACT OF SOARING** the act of soaring, or the height or range reached by soaring [14C. Via Old French *essorer* < Latin *ex-* 'out' + *aura* 'air'.] —**soarer** *n*

SPELLCHECK See ***saw***

Soares /swaáresh/, **Mário** (*b.* 1924) Portuguese statesman

Soave /sō aá vay, swaá vay/ *n* a dry white wine made in Italy [Mid-20C. After the village of *Soave*, Italy.]

Soay /sṓ ay, sóy/ *n* a small dark brown sheep. Native to: Outer Hebrides.

sob /sob/ *v* (**sobs, sobbing, sobbed**) 1 *vi* **GASP WHILE CRYING** to draw in breath while crying, making gasping sounds 2 *vt* **SPEAK WHILE SOBBING** to say something while sobbing 3 *vr* **BECOME BY SOBBING** to get into a particular state by sobbing ○ *to sob yourself to sleep* ■ *n* **SOUND OF SOBBING** a convulsive breath made while sobbing, or the sound of this breath ○ *stifled a sob* [12C] —**sobbingly** *adv*

soba /sṓbə/ *n* a Japanese dish of buckwheat noodles [Late 19C. < Japanese.]

sober /sṓbər/ *adj* 1 **NOT INTOXICATED** not under the influence of alcohol 2 **TENDING NOT TO DRINK** not in the habit of drinking much alcohol 3 **SERIOUS** serious and thoughtful in demeanour or quality ○ *a sober face* 4 **DULL** lacking vitality or brightness in appearance ○ *He always dresses in sober colours.* 5 **NOT FANCIFUL OR SPECULATIVE** based on facts and rational thinking rather than on speculation ○ *a sober assessment of the situation* ■ *vti* **LESSEN INTOXICATION** to become or make somebody become less drunk or completely sober [14C. Via Old French < Latin *sobrius*.] —**sobering** *adj* —**soberingly** *adv* —**soberly** *adv* —**soberness** *n*

sobersides /sṓbər sīdz/ *n* a solemn and serious person —**sobersided** *adj*

sobriety /sə brī́ əti/ *n* 1 abstinence from or moderation in the use of alcohol 2 the quality of being serious and thoughtful [15C. Via Old French < Latin *sobrius* 'sober' (see SOBER).]

sobriquet /sṓbri kay/, **soubriquet** *n* an unofficial name or nickname, especially a humorous one [Mid-17C. < French, 'a tap under the chin'.]

sob sister *n* a journalist who writes or edits sentimental stories or answers problems sent in by readers (*informal*)

sob story *n* a story told to gain somebody's sympathy or pity, especially when offered as an excuse (*informal*)

soca /sṓkə/ *n* a style of Caribbean music that combines calypso and soul and has a fast beat [Late 20C. Blend of SOUL + CALYPSO.]

socage /sókkij/, **soccage** *n* a feudal system of holding land in which the tenant either paid rent or performed a fixed service, usually agricultural and nonmilitary in nature [14C. < Anglo-Norman, < *soc*, variant of *soke* 'right of jurisdiction'.] —**socager** *n*

so-called *adj* 1 popularly known as, but not necessarily by the speaker or writer ○ *the so-called Information Superhighway* 2 incorrectly known as ○ *a so-called art expert*

USAGE Do not put quotation marks around expressions immediately following words like ***so-called*** and *self-styled*. These words already convey the ideas 'popularly called or known' and 'incorrectly or falsely called or known', respectively: *He is a so-called generalissimo of capitalism*, not *a so-called 'generalissimo of capitalism'*.

soccage *n* HIST = **socage**

soccer /sókər/ *n* = **football** *n.* 1 [Late 19C. < *Assoc.*, shortening of *Association football* (referring to the Football Association).]

~~**soceity**~~ incorrect spelling of **society**

sociable /sṓshəb'l/ *adj* 1 **GREGARIOUS** inclined to seek out the company of other people. 2 **FRIENDLY** friendly and pleasant to other people 3 **OFFERING OPPORTUNITY FOR SOCIAL INTERACTION** allowing people to mix in an informal way ○ *a sociable occasion* [Mid-16C. Directly or via French < Latin *sociabilis* < *socius* 'companion' (see SOCIAL).] —**sociability** /sṓshə bíləti/ *n* —**sociableness** *n* —**sociably** *adv*

USAGE sociable or **social**? ***Social*** is a neutral word that classifies a person or thing as being concerned in some way with society or its organization. A *social club* is a place provided for people to enjoy themselves, and a *social worker* is involved in work done for people's welfare. ***Sociable***, by contrast, refers to a person's capacity to deal in social ways with other people, so a *sociable worker* is a worker who enjoys the company of colleagues.

social /sṓsh'l/ *adj* 1 **RELATING TO SOCIETY** relating to human society and how it is organized 2 **RELATING TO INTERACTION OF PEOPLE** relating to the way people in groups behave and interact ○ *the social sciences* 3 **LIVING IN COMMUNITY** living or preferring to live as part of a community or colony, rather than alone ○ *social insects such as ants* 4 **OFFERING OPPORTUNITY FOR INTERACTION** allowing people to meet and interact with others in a friendly way ○ *a social club* 5 **RELATING TO HUMAN WELFARE** relating to human welfare and the organized welfare services that a community provides ○ *social services* 6 **TO DO WITH RANK** relating to or thought appropriate to a particular rank in society, especially the upper classes 7 **SOCIABLE** tending to seek out the company of others (*informal*) ○ *a very social person* 8 **GROWING IN CLUMPS** describes plants that grow in clumps or masses ■ *n* 1 **INFORMAL GET-TOGETHER** an informal gathering or party, usually of a particular group of people who meet regularly 2 **social, Social SOCIAL SECURITY** the Social Security services (*slang*) [Mid-17C. Via French < Latin *socialis* < *socius* 'companion'.] —**socially** *adv* —**socialness** *n*

USAGE See ***sociable***.

social anthropology *n* the scientific study of human society or a particular society, including study of kinship systems, traditional political and economic practices, rituals, and beliefs. ◊ **cultural anthropology**

social capital *n* the educational, social, and cultural advantages that somebody from the upper classes is believed to possess

Social Charter *n* a declaration that outlines the rights of workers in countries that are part of the European Community

social climber *n* a person who tries to rise in status by associating with people of a higher social class (*disapproving*) —**social climbing** *n*

social contract, social compact *n* an agreement among individuals in a society or between the people and their government that describes the rights and duties of each party

Social Credit *n* a Canadian conservative political party founded in 1935 —**Social Crediter** *n*

social Darwinism *n* a discredited social theory stating that the political and economic advantages in a developed society are derived from the biological advantages of its collective membership —**social Darwinist** *n*

social democracy, Social Democracy *n* the political belief that a change from capitalism to socialism can be achieved gradually and democratically —**social democrat** *n* —**social democratic** *adj*

Social Democratic and Labour Party *n* a political party in Northern Ireland, many of whose supporters want to unite Northern Ireland and the Republic of Ireland peacefully

Social Democratic Party *n* 1 a British political party existing from 1981 to 1990 2 a German political party advocating gradual reform to socialism

social disease *n* a sexually transmitted disease (*informal; used euphemistically*)

social drinker *n* a drinker of alcoholic beverages who only consumes them with other people

social engineering *n* the use of policies that are based on the findings of social science to deal with social problems

social insurance *n* state insurance that uses compulsory contributions to pay for benefits for unemployed and retired people

socialise *vti* = **socialize**

socialised medicine *n* = **socialized medicine**

socialism /sṓshəlizəm/ *n* 1 **POLITICAL SYSTEM OF COMMUNAL OWNERSHIP** a political theory or system in which the means of production and distribution are controlled by the people and operated according to equity and fairness rather than market principles 2 **MOVEMENT BASED ON SOCIALISM** any political movement or theory based on principles of socialism, typically advocating an end to private property and the exploitation of workers 3 **STAGE BETWEEN CAPITALISM AND COMMUNISM** in Marxist theory, the stage after the proletarian revolution when a society is changing from capitalism to communism, marked by pay distributed according to work done rather than need

socialist /sṓshəlist/, **Socialist** *n* **BELIEVER IN SOCIALISM** a believer in or supporter of socialism or a socialist party ■ *adj* 1 **ADVOCATING SOCIALISM** relating to, based on, or advocating socialism 2 **socialist, Socialist RELATING TO SOCIALISTS** relating to socialists or a socialist party —**socialistic** /sṓshə lístik/ *adj* —**socialistically** *adv*

socialist realism *n* an artistic doctrine officially sanctioned in many Communist countries, especially during the 1930s–50s, that proposed the idea that art and literature should serve to promote and glorify the ideals of a socialist state

socialite /sṓshə līt/ *n* a person who is well known in fashionable society

sociality /sṓshi áləti/ (*plural* **-ties**) *n* 1 the quality of being social, or an instance of it 2 the tendency to form social groups or live in a community

socialize /sṓshə līz/ (**-izes, -izing, -ized**), **socialise** (**-ises, -ising, -ised**) *v* 1 *vi* to take part in social activities or behave in a friendly way to others ○ *a group of friends who like to socialize after work* 2 *vt* to teach somebody to be a fit member of society ○ *socialize a child* —**socialization** /sṓshə lī záysh'n/ *n* —**socializer** *n*

socialized medicine, socialised medicine *n* a system of national health care that provides medical care to all and is regulated and subsidized by the government

social mobility *n* the capacity for individuals in a society to change their class or social status within their lifetimes

social psychology *n* the area of psychology that deals with how groups behave and how individuals are affected by the group —**social psychologist** *n*

social realism *n* the use of realistic portrayals of life in art or literature to make a social or political point

social science *n* 1 the study of people in society and how individuals relate to one another and to the group 2 a discipline that studies a particular area of human society, e.g. sociology, psychology, economics, political science, history, or anthropology —**social scientist** *n*

social secretary *n* somebody whose job is to arrange social activities and handle correspondence for a person or organization

social security *n* 1 **social security, Social Security** a government programme providing for the economic welfare of the individual, e.g. through payments to people who are retired, unemployed, or unable to work **2** money paid by a government to an individual through a Social Security programme

Social Security number *n* in the United States, a unique reference number assigned to each person within the Social Security system

social service *n* a service provided by a government agency for the welfare of an individual or community. Such services include housing, child protection, free school lunches, or health care. *(often plural)* ■ **social services** *npl* a government agency that provides social services to individuals or a community

social studies *n* an academic subject devoted to the study of society and including geography, economics, and history *(+ singular or plural verb)*

social welfare *n* the social services provided by a state or by a private organization

social work *n* the profession or work of providing people in need with social services —**social worker** *n*

society /sə sí əti/ *(plural* **-ties***)* *n* **1 RELATIONSHIPS AMONG GROUPS** the sum of social relationships among groups of humans or animals **2 STRUCTURED COMMUNITY OF PEOPLE** a structured community of people bound together by similar traditions, institutions, or nationality **3 CUSTOMS OF COMMUNITY** the customs of a community and the way it is organized, e.g. its class structure ○ *the role of women in society* **4 SUBSET OF SOCIETY** a particular section of a community that is distinguished by particular qualities ○ *In those days, the subject was never mentioned in polite society.* **5 PROMINENT PEOPLE** the prominent or fashionable people in a community, or their social life **6 COMPANIONSHIP** the state of being with other people **7 GROUP SHARING INTERESTS** an organized group of people who share an interest, aim, or profession [Mid-16C. Via French < Latin *societas* 'companionship' < *socius* 'companion' (see SOCIAL).] —**societal** *adj* —**societally** *adv*

Society of Friends *n* the Christian group also known as the Quakers

Society of Jesus *n* the Roman Catholic religious order also known as the Jesuits

Socinian /sō sínni ən/ *n* a follower of Laelius and Faustus Socinus, Italian theologians who preached belief in God but rejected other traditional Christian doctrines such as the Trinity and the divinity of Christ ■ *adj* relating to the Socinians and their beliefs —**Socinianism** *n*

socio- *prefix* society, social ○ *sociopath* ○ *sociopsychological* [Via French < Latin *socius* 'companion' (see SOCIAL)]

sociobiology /sṓssi ō bī óllәji/ *n* the study of the social behaviour of animals and humans and how this is related to genetics and the survival of species —**sociobiological** /-bī ə lójjik'l/ *adj*

sociocultural /sṓssi ō kúlchərəl, sṓshi ō-/ *adj* involving cultural and social factors —**socioculturally** *adv*

socioeconomic /sṓsi ō ékkə nómmik, sṓshi ō-, sṓssi ō éekə nómmik/ *adj* involving economic and social factors —**socioeconomically** *adv*

sociolinguistics /sṓssi ō ling gwístiks, sṓshi ō-/ *n* the study of the relationships between language and the social and cultural factors that affect it —**sociolinguist** /-líng gwist/ *n* —**sociolinguistic** *adj*

sociology /sṓssi ólləji, sṓshi-/ *n* **1** the study of the origin, development, and structure of human societies and the behaviour of individuals and groups in society **2** the study of a particular social institution and the part it plays in society [Mid-19C. < French *sociologie* 'science of companions' < Latin *socius* 'companion' (see SOCIAL).] —**sociologic** /sṓssi ə lójjik, sṓshi ə-/ *adj* —**sociological** *adj* —**sociologically** *adv* —**sociologist** *n*

sociometry /sṓssi ómmətri, sṓshi-/ *n* the statistical study of behaviour and relationships within social groups, especially expressed in terms of preferences —**sociometric** /sṓssi ō méttrik, sṓshi ō-/ *adj* —**sociometrist** /sṓssi ómmətrist, sṓshi-/ *n*

sociopath /sṓssi ō path, sṓshi ō-/ *n* PSYCHIAT = **psychopath** *(offensive)* [Mid-20C. After PSYCHOPATH.] —**sociopathic** /sṓssi ō páthik, sṓshi ō-/ *adj* —**sociopathy** /sṓssi óppəthi, sṓshi-/ *n*

sociopolitical /sṓssi ō pə líttik'l, sṓshi ō-/ *adj* relating to or involving both social and political factors

sock[1] /sok/ *n* **1** a soft, usually knitted covering for the foot and ankle that may reach as high as the knee **2** METEOROL = **windsock 3** a removable inner sole used for warmth or to make a shoe fit better [Old English *socc* 'light shoe, slipper', via Germanic < Latin *soccus* < Greek *sukkhos* '(kind of) shoe'] ◇ **pull your socks up** to make an effort to improve *(informal)* ◇ **put a sock in it** used to tell somebody to be quiet *(informal)*

sock away *vt US, Can, NZ* to save money for the future *(informal)* [< the practice of storing savings in a sock]

sock[2] /sok/ *vti* to hit somebody or something hard, usually with the fist *(informal)* ■ *n* a hard hit or blow, usually with the fist *(informal)* [Late 17C. < ?] ◇ **sock it to somebody** to speak or behave in a way that makes a strong impression upon somebody *(dated informal)*

socket /sókit/ *n* **1 SHAPED HOLE FOR CONNECTION** a hole or recess in something specially shaped to receive a particular object or part, e.g. the hole that receives a light bulb or one that receives a plug on an electrical device **2 CONNECTION WITH ELECTRICITY SUPPLY** a receptacle, usually mounted on a wall, into which an electric plug is inserted to make a connection to a source of electric power. US term **outlet** *n.* 5 **3 HOLLOW IN BODY** a bony hollow in the body into which another part fits ■ *vt* **PUT IN SOCKET** to insert something into a socket, or to provide something with a socket [13C. < Anglo-Norman *soket* 'small ploughshare' < Old French *sok* 'ploughshare' < ?]

socket spanner *n* TECH = **socket wrench**

socket wrench *n* a long-handled wrench with interchangeable heads that fit over various sized nuts and bolts and a ratchet that makes tightening nuts and bolts easier

sockeye /sók ī/ *(plural* **-eyes** *or* **-eye***)*, **sockeye salmon** *n* a food fish of the salmon family that has red flesh. Native to: Pacific waters. *Oncorhynchus nerka*. [Late 19C. By folk etymology < Salish *sukai* 'fish of fishes'.]

socle /sók'l/ *n* a base that sticks out from under the bottom of a wall, or the lowest part of the base of a column or pedestal [Early 18C. Via French < Latin *socculus* 'small light shoe' < *soccus* (see SOCK[1]).]

Socrates /sókrə teez/ (469–399 BC) Greek philosopher

Socratic /sə kráttik/ *adj* relating to Socrates, to his philosophy, or to his method of arriving at truth ■ *n* a student or follower of Socrates —**Socratically** *adv* —**Socraticism** /sə kráttisizəm/ *n* —**Socratist** /sókrətist/ *n*

Socratic irony *n* ignorance feigned in order to elicit explanations from somebody whose own ignorance can then be exposed through subsequent clever questioning

Socratic method *n* a means of arriving at truth by continually questioning, obtaining answers, and criticizing the answers

sod[1] /sod/ *n* **1 TURF** a surface section or strip of earth with growing grass and roots **2 GROUND** ground or soil *(literary)* ■ *vt* **(sods, sodding, sodded) COVER WITH TURF** to cover ground with sods [15C. < Middle Dutch or Low German *sode* 'turf', < ?]

sod[2] /sod/ *n* **1 OFFENSIVE TERM** an offensive term for somebody regarded as thoughtless, annoying, or objectionable *(slang insult)* **2 ANY PERSON** used, often humorously or affectionately, to refer to a person *(slang; offensive in some contexts)* ■ *vt* **OFFENSIVE TERM** an offensive term used as a swearword to express anger or defiance *(slang)* [Early 19C. Shortening of SODOMITE.]

sod off *vi* an offensive term meaning to go away *(slang)*

soda /sṓdə/ *n* **1** *US* **SOFT DRINK** a flavoured and carbonated drink, served cold **2** BEVERAGES = **soda water** *n.* 1 **3** *US* **ICE CREAM IN FLAVOURED CARBONATED WATER** a refreshment made with flavoured carbonated water and ice cream, usually served in a tall glass **4 SODIUM** sodium that is chemically combined with other elements **5** CHEM = **sodium bicarbonate 6** CHEM = **sodium carbonate** *n.* 1 **7** CHEM = **sodium hydroxide 8 CARD THAT STARTS FARO** the card from the top of the pack that is turned face up in the dealing box at the start of the card game faro [15C. Via Italian, 'saltwort' (from which sodium carbonate is obtained) < Arabic *suwwād*.]

soda ash *n* sodium carbonate when sold commercially. Use: manufacture of soap and paper.

soda biscuit *n* a biscuit leavened with bicarbonate of soda

soda bread *n* bread leavened with bicarbonate of soda rather than yeast, associated especially with Irish cooking

soda cracker *n US* a cracker leavened slightly with baking soda and cream of tartar

soda fountain *n US* a counter or stand where beverages, ice cream, and snacks are sold *(dated)*

soda lime *n* a mixture of sodium hydroxide and calcium hydroxide. Use: moisture and carbon dioxide absorbent.

sodalite /sṓdə līt/ *n* a blue, greyish, or yellow translucent aluminosilicate mineral containing sodium and chlorine. Source: alkaline igneous rocks.

sodality /sō dálləti/ *(plural* **-ties***)* *n* **1** a Roman Catholic lay society that is run as a charity or a religious fellowship **2** an association or fellowship of any kind [Early 17C. Directly or via French *sodalité* < Latin *sodalitas* 'fellowship' < *sodalis* 'fellow, companion'.]

soda nitre *n* MINERALS = **Chile saltpetre**

soda pop *n US* a flavoured and carbonated drink, served cold *(informal)*

soda siphon *n* a sealed bottle containing water and carbon dioxide gas under pressure, used to produce soda water. US term **siphon bottle**

soda water *n* **1** carbonated water drunk as a beverage or used as a mixer in alcoholic drinks **2** a weak solution of water, bicarbonate of soda, and acid, taken to aid digestion

sodbuster /sódbustər/ *n* **1** *US* **FARMER** a farmer **2 PLOUGH** a plough that is used to break the sod **3** *Can* **HOMESTEADER** a prairie homesteader, especially one who raised crops *(informal)*

sodden /sódd'n/ *adj* **1 THOROUGHLY WET** saturated with moisture **2 DRUNK** with dulled senses from excessive drinking ■ *vti* **MAKE OR BECOME SODDEN** to make something or somebody sodden or to become sodden [13C. The obsolete past participle of SEETHE.] —**soddenly** *adv* —**soddenness** *n*

sodium /sṓdi əm/ *n (symbol* **Na***)* a soft silver-white metallic element that reacts readily with other substances and is essential to the body's fluid balance. Source: common salt, calcium chloride. Use: catalyst, chemical processes, tracer. [Early 19C. < SODA (from its being isolated from caustic soda) + -IUM.]

sodium benzoate *n* $C_7H_5O_2Na$ a white crystalline powder. Use: food preservative, antiseptic, manufacture of pharmaceuticals.

sodium bicarbonate *n* $NaHCO_3$ a white crystalline slightly alkaline salt. Use: leavening agent, antacid, in effervescent drinks, fire extinguishers.

sodium carbonate *n* **1** Na_2CO_3 a white crystalline salt of carbonic acid. Use: water softener, manufacture of glass, ceramics, cleansing agents, paper. **2** CHEM = **washing soda**

sodium chlorate *n* $NaClO_3$ a colourless crystalline salt. Use: weedkiller, bleaching agent, manufacture of explosives.

sodium chloride *n* $NaCl$ a colourless crystalline compound. Source: sea water, halite deposits. Use: preservative, food seasoning. ◊ **salt** *n.* 1

sodium citrate *n* $Na_3C_6H_5O_7$ a white crystalline salt. Use: photography, buffering agent in foods, anticoagulant in stored blood.

sodium cyanide *n* $NaCN$ a poisonous white salt. Use: fumigant, gold and silver mining, manufacture of steel and dyes.

sodium cyclamate *n* CHEM = **cyclamate**

sodium dichromate *n* $Na_2Cr_2O_7$ a red or orange crystalline salt. Use: leather tanning, manufacture of dyes and inks, oxidizing agent, corrosion inhibitor.

sodium fluoride *n* NaF a poisonous colourless crystalline salt. Use: pesticide, in metallurgical processes, trace amounts for water fluoridation and tooth decay prevention.

sodium fluoroacetate *n* $C_2H_2FNaO_2$ a white poisonous powder. Use: rodenticide. [Mid-20C. 'Fluoroacetate' < FLUORO- + ACETATE.]

sodium glutamate *n* CHEM = **monosodium glutamate**

sodium hydroxide *n* $NaOH$ a brittle white alkaline solid. Use: manufacture of paper, rayon, soap, chemicals, pharmaceuticals.

sodium hypochlorite *n* $NaOCl$ a green crystalline unstable salt, usually kept in solution. Use: bleach, disinfectant, water purifier.

sodium hyposulphite *n* CHEM = **sodium thiosulphate**

sodium nitrate *n* $NaNO_3$ a white crystalline salt. Use: curing of meats, rocket propellant, fertilizer, manufacture of explosives, pottery, glass enamels.

sodium peroxide *n* Na_2O_2 a yellowish odourless powder. Use: bleaching agent, antiseptic, disinfectant.

sodium phosphate *n* a sodium salt of phosphoric acid. Use: medical preparations, cleaning agents.

sodium propionate *n* $C_3H_5NaO_2$ a colourless crystalline powder. Use: spoilage retardant in packaged foods.

sodium pump *n* the exchange of sodium ions for potassium ions across a cell membrane

sodium silicate *n* a compound of silicate glass. Use: preservatives, textile processing, cement.

sodium sulphate *n* Na_2SO_4 a bitter white salt. Use: manufacture of glass, wood pulp, rayon, dyes, detergents, ceramic glazes, cathartics.

sodium thiosulphate *n* $Na_2S_2O_3$ a white crystalline salt. Use: photographic fixer, bleach.

sodium-vapour lamp *n* an electric lamp containing neon gas and sodium vapour through which a current runs to produce an orange-yellow light used for street lighting

Sodom /sóddəm/ *n* **1** in the Bible, a city full of moral corruption and evil that was destroyed along with Gomorrah by God **2** a place that is regarded as corrupt

sodomise *vt* = **sodomize**

sodomite /sóddə mīt/ *n* an offensive term for somebody who practises anal intercourse [14C. Via French < Greek *Sodomitēs* 'inhabitant of Sodom' < *Sodoma* 'Sodom'.] —**sodomitic** /sóddə míttik/ *adj*

sodomize /sóddə mīz/ (**-izes, -izing, -ized**), **sodomise** (**-ises, -ising, -ised**) *vt* an offensive term meaning to practise anal intercourse

sodomy /sóddəmi/ *n* an offensive term for anal intercourse [13C. Directly or via French *sodomie* < medieval Latin *sodomia* < ecclesiastical Latin *peccatum Sodomiticum* 'sin of Sodom'.]

Sod's Law *n* the law or principle that if anything can go wrong, it will (*informal*) US term **Murphy's Law** [Late 20C. 'Sod's' < SOD[2].]

soever /sō évvər/ *adv* in any way or to any degree possible [13C. < SO[1] + EVER.]

sofa /sṓfə/ *n* a long upholstered seat that has a back and arms and is made to seat more than one person [Early 17C. Via French < Arabic *ṣuffa* 'long bench'.]

sofa bed *n* a sofa that can be temporarily converted into a bed as required, e.g. by unfolding its seat

sofar /sṓ faar/ *n* a way of locating survivors at sea by measuring the time it takes sound waves to reach three shore locations from an explosion set off underwater by the survivors [Mid-20C. Acronym < *sound fixing and ranging*.]

soffit /sóffit/ *n* the underside of a structural component of a building, e.g. the underside of a roof overhang or the inner curve of an arch [Early 17C. Via French *soffite* or Italian *soffitto* < Latin *suffixus* 'fixed under' (see SUFFIX).]

Sofia /sṓfi ə/ capital of Bulgaria, in the west-central part of the country. Population: 1,116,000 (1995).

soft /soft/ *adj* **1 MALLEABLE** easily shaped, bent, or cut **2 YIELDING** giving way to externally applied pressure or weight ○ *a soft cushion* **3 SMOOTH-TEXTURED** having a texture that is smooth to the touch ○ *soft fur* **4 WITH SMOOTH OUTLINE** with no sharp or jagged edges ○ *furniture designed with soft lines* **5 QUIET-SOUNDING** quiet and soothing in sound **6 EASY ON THE EYES** without glare or intensity of light or colour **7 MILD** not blowing strongly or falling heavily ○ *a soft rain* **8 AFFECTIONATE** conveying love and tenderness **9 EMOTIONAL** easily moved to tender emotions **10 COWARDLY** lacking determination or strength of character **11 LENIENT** lenient in treatment or punishment, often too lenient **12 UNDEMANDING** requiring little effort or attention (*informal*) ○ *a soft job* **13 NOT WELL TONED** out of good physical condition **14 INCAPABLE OF ENDURING HARDSHIP** unable or unwilling to put up with hardship or privation, especially from having lived a life of ease **15 LACKING GOOD SENSE** lacking intelligence or sound judgment (*informal*) **16 NOT EASILY VERIFIABLE** dealing with data that is not easily proved or disproved using scientific method **17** = **soft-core 18 VULNERABLE** unprotected against violent attack **19 UNARMOURED** describes military vehicles and sites with little or no protection against military attack **20 NOT POLITICALLY EXTREME** holding moderate rather than radical or hardline political views **21 RELATING TO PAPER MONEY** relating to currency or a monetary system that is not backed by gold, and is therefore not easily convertible to a foreign currency **22 DECLINING ECONOMICALLY** exhibiting a downward trend, e.g. in price, demand, or economic activity **23 SIBILANT OR FRICATIVE** describes the consonant sounds 'c' and 'g' when pronounced as a fricative, as in 'dance' and 'age', rather than as a stop, as in 'cat' and 'get'. ◊ **hard** *adj.* 27 **24 PALATALIZED** describes a consonant that is palatalized in a Slavic language **25 LOW-ENERGY** describes radiation that has low energy and lacks penetrating ability ■ *adv* **SOFTLY** in a quiet, tender, or lenient way ■ *n* **SOMETHING SOFT** a soft thing or part of something ■ *npl* **SOFTS** ECON = **soft commodities** [Old English *sōfte* (earlier *sēfte*) < Germanic] —**softly** *adv* —**softness** *n* ◇ **be soft on somebody** to be romantically attracted to somebody

softback /sóft bak/ *n, adj* PUBL = **paperback** *n.*, **paperback** *adj.*

softball /sóft báwl/ *n* **1** baseball played with a larger softer ball on a smaller field, between two teams of ten people **2** the ball used to play softball

soft-boiled *adj* **1** boiled so that the yolk is soft but the white is firm **2** with a sympathetic or sentimental nature

soft chancre *n* MED = **chancroid** *n.* 2

soft coal *n* INDUST = **bituminous coal**

soft commodities *npl* traded commodities that are not metals, e.g. cocoa, sugar, cotton, and cereals

ϟ **soft copy** *n* data stored on a computer disk, as distinct from data that is printed on paper

soft-core *adj* sexually suggestive or provocative without being explicit

softcover /sóft kuvvər/ *n, adj* PUBL = **paperback** *n.*, **paperback** *adj.*

soft drink *n* any still or carbonated nonalcoholic beverage

soft drug *n* any illicit drug that is thought by some to be less addictive and harmful than the narcotic drugs heroin and cocaine

soften /sóff'n/ *vti* **1 MAKE OR BECOME LESS HARD** to become soft or softer, or to make something soft or softer **2 BE KINDER** to become gentler or less harsh, or to make something gentler or less harsh **3 WEAR SOMEBODY DOWN** to make somebody's resolve less firm, or to become less firmly resolved **4 HARASS ENEMY** to weaken an enemy's resistance or morale by continuous bombardment, or to have resistance or morale weakened **5 REDUCE** to decline, e.g. in price, demand, or economic activity, or to cause something such as a market to decline

softener /sóff'nər/ *n* a substance added to something such as water or laundry to make it softer

soft focus *n* a deliberate slight blurring of a photograph or a filmed image giving it a hazy appearance, so as to achieve a special effect such as romance or nostalgia (*hyphenated before nouns*)

soft fruit *n* a small stoneless fruit, such as the raspberry, strawberry, or blackberry

soft furnishings *npl* furnishings made from fabric, such as curtains and rugs, that decorate a house and make it more comfortable

soft goods *npl* textiles and the items such as clothing and bedding that are made from them

soft hail *n* METEOROL = **graupel**

soft-hearted *adj* showing sympathy, kindness, or generosity —**soft-heartedly** *adv* —**soft-heartedness** *n*

softie *n* = **softy**

soft-kill *adj US* intended to disable rather than kill an enemy

soft landing *n* **1** a landing of a spacecraft, especially on the moon, without enough impact to cause damage **2** a resolution of a problem, especially an economic problem, found without undue effort

softly-softly *adj* characterized by caution or discretion

soft option *n* the easier or easiest course of action when given a choice

soft palate *n* the fleshy rear portion of the roof of the mouth, extending from the hard palate at the front and tapering to the hanging uvula at the rear

soft pedal *n* a pedal on a piano that reduces the usual volume

soft-pedal (**soft-pedals, soft-pedalling, soft-pedalled**) *vti* **1** to reduce the volume of music played on a piano by operating the soft pedal **2** to try to make something seem less important, noticeable, or objectionable (*informal*)

soft rock *n* rock music that tends to be slower and more melodic than hard rock, often influenced by folk or country and western music

soft rot *n* any bacterial or fungal plant disease that causes plant parts, especially fruits and vegetables, to decay into a pulpy mass

soft sell *n* a method of selling or advertising goods and services that uses subtlety and persuasion, rather than aggressive insistence (*informal; hyphenated before nouns*)

soft-shell *adj* describes an aquatic animal with a soft or thin and brittle shell, sometimes as a result of having recently moulted

soft-shelled turtle *n* a freshwater turtle with sharp claws, a pointed snout, and a soft flat shell covered with leathery skin. Family: Trionychidae.

soft-shoe *n* tap dancing for which soft-soled shoes without metal taps are worn (*often before nouns*)

soft soap *n* **1** a liquid or semiliquid soap, usually made with potassium hydroxide **2** flattery used for the purpose of persuading or distracting somebody (*informal*)

soft-soap *vt* to use flattery to persuade or distract somebody (*informal*)

softsore /sóft sawr/ *n* MED = **chancroid** *n.* 1

soft-spoken *adj* speaking or said with a quiet gentle voice

soft spot *n* a place, position, or area in which something is weak or vulnerable ◇ **have a soft spot for somebody** *or* **something** to have especially tender feelings or affection for somebody or something

soft top *n* a car that has a soft roof made of fabric that can be opened and folded back. US term **ragtop**

soft touch *n* somebody who can be easily persuaded to do something, e.g. to give a loan or handout

ϟ **software** /sóft wair/ *n* computer programs and applications, e.g. word processing or database packages, that can be run on a particular computer system (*often before nouns*)

ϟ **software engineering** *n* the application of mathematics and technology to the design, implementation, and testing of computer programs to optimize their production and support

soft water *n* naturally occurring or treated water in which soap lathers easily because of low levels of calcium and magnesium salts

soft wheat *n* wheat with soft kernels and weak gluten that is relatively low in protein. Use: cakes, biscuits, pastries, livestock feed.

softwood /sóft wŏŏd/ *n* **1** the open-grained wood of a pine, cedar, or other coniferous tree **2** a tree that yields softwood, e.g. a pine or cedar

softy /sófti/ (*plural* **-ies**), **softie** *n* a weak, timid, or sentimental person (*informal*)

Sogdian /sógdi ən/ *n* **1** a member of a people who lived in central Asia **2** the extinct Iranian language of the Sogdian people [Mid-16C. Via Latin < Greek *Sogdianos* < Old Persian *Suguda*.] —**Sogdian** *adj*

soggy /sóggi/ (**-gier, -giest**) *adj* **1 THOROUGHLY WET** soaked through with moisture **2 WITH TOO MUCH LIQUID** unpleasantly wet and heavy in texture **3 UNINTERESTING** lacking animation or vitality [Early 18C. < obsolete *sog* 'area of marshy ground'.] —**soggily** *adv* —**sogginess** *n*

Sogne Fjord /sóngnə-/ inlet of the North Sea in SW Norway. Length: 200 km/125 mi.

soh *n* the fifth note in the sol-fa musical scale. US term **sol**[1]

Soho /sṓhō/ *n* **1** an area of central London well known for its theatres, restaurants and clubs **2 Soho, SoHo** an area of the lower west side of Manhattan well known for its art studios and galleries [In sense 2, < SOUTH + *Houston Street*]

soi-disant /swaa deézaaN, swaádee zaáN/ *adj* self-styled or so-called [< French, 'saying oneself']

soigné /swaán yay/, **soignée** *adj* **1** neat and smart in dress and appearance **2** designed or furnished in an elegant style [Early 19C. < French, past participle of *soigner* 'care for' < Germanic.]

soil[1] /soyl/ *n* **1 TOP LAYER OF LAND** the top layer of most of the earth's land surface, consisting of the unconsolidated products of rock erosion and organic decay, along with bacteria and fungi (*often before nouns*) **2 KIND OF EARTH** earth or ground of a particular kind **3 COUNTRY** somebody's country or land (*literary*) 4 **FARMING** agricultural life and work (*literary*) 5 **NURTURING MEDIUM** any medium in which growth and development takes place (*literary*) [13C Via Anglo-Norman, 'piece of land' < Latin *solium* 'seat', by association with *solum* 'ground, soil']

soil[2] /soyl/ *vt* 1 **MAKE DIRTY** to make something dirty or stained 2 **BRING DISHONOUR ON** to damage somebody's reputation, character, or good name ■ *n* 1 **DIRT** dirt or dirty condition ○ *remove soil from linens* 2 **MORAL CORRUPTION** immoral behaviour or lack of moral standards (*literary*) [13C. < Old French *soill(i)er* 'to soil, wallow'.]

SYNONYMS See *dirty*.

soil[3] /soyl/ *n* excrement or sewage ○ *a soil pipe* [15C. < Old French *souille* 'muddy place' < *soill(i)er* (see SOIL[2]).]

soilure /sóylyər/ *n* the soiling or staining of something (*literary*) [14C. < Old French *soilleure* < *soillier* (see SOIL[2]).]

soiree /swaaray/, **soirée** *n* a party or gathering held in the evening, especially in somebody's home [Late 18C. < French, < *soir* 'evening' < Latin *sero* 'at a late hour' < *serus* 'late'.]

soixante-neuf /swássont núrf/ *n* = **sixty-nine** (*slang offensive*) [< French, 'sixty-nine']

sojourn /sójjurn, sójjərn/ *n* a short stay at a place (*literary*) ■ *vi* to stay at a place for a time (*literary*) [13C. Via Anglo-Norman *sujurn* or Old French *sojorn* (noun) < *sojourner* (verb) 'spend the day' < late Latin *diurnum* 'day'.] —**sojourner** *n*

Sokoto /sókətō/ capital of Sokoto State, NW Nigeria. Population: 207,000 (1995).

sol[1] /sol/ *n* MUSIC = **soh** [14C. < medieval Latin, < Latin *solve* 'purge!, release!', word sung to this note in a medieval hymn.]

sol[2] /sol/ *n* a liquid colloidal solution [Late 19C. Shortening of SOLUTION.]

sol[3] /sol/ (*plural* **soles** /solays/) *n* see table at **currency** [< Spanish, literally 'sun']

Sol /sol/ *n* 1 the personification of the sun (*literary*) 2 in Roman mythology, the god of the sun. Greek equivalent **Helios** [14C. < Latin, 'sun'.]

sola[1] /sólə/ *adj* used as a stage direction to indicate that a female character appears alone on stage

sola[2] plural of **solum**

solace /sólləss/ *n* 1 **RELIEF FROM EMOTIONAL DISTRESS** comfort at a time of sadness, grief, or disappointment 2 **SOURCE OF COMFORT** somebody or something that provides comfort in times of sadness, grief, or disappointment ■ *vt* (**-aces, -acing, -aced**) **PROVIDE WITH COMFORT** to comfort somebody at a time of sadness, grief, or disappointment [13C. Via Old French *solas* < Latin *solatium* < *solari* 'comfort'.] —**solacer** *n*

solan /sólən/, **solan goose** *n* a gannet. Native to: North Atlantic. *Morus bassanus*. [15C. Probably < Old Norse *súla* 'gannet' + *and-*, stem of *ōnd* 'duck'.]

solanaceous /sóllə náyshəss/ *adj* relating to or belonging to the nightshade family of plants, a family that includes the potato, tomato, and tobacco [Early 19C. < modern Latin *Solanaceae* < Latin *solanum* (see SOLANUM).]

solan goose *n* BIRDS = **solan**

solanine /sólə neen/ *n* $C_{45}H_{73}NO_{15}$ a bitter poisonous alkaloid found in several plants of the nightshade family. Use: formerly to treat epilepsy, bronchitis, asthma.

solanum /sō láynəm, sō láynəm/ (*plural* **-nums** *or* **-num**) *n* a plant of the nightshade family, e.g. the potato or aubergine. Genus: *Solanum*. [Late 16C. Via modern Latin < Latin < *sol* 'sun' (see SOLAR).]

solar /sólər/ *adj* 1 **FROM THE SUN** relating to or originating from the Sun 2 **OPERATING USING ENERGY FROM THE SUN** using the Sun's radiation as a source of energy 3 **MEASURED BY THE SUN'S POSITION** measured with reference to the Earth's movement in relation to the Sun [15C. < Latin *solaris* < *sol* 'sun'.]

solar apex *n* the point in space towards which the sun appears to be moving, located in the constellation Hercules

solar battery *n* an arrangement of several solar cells for converting solar radiation into electricity

solar cell *n* an electric cell that converts solar radiation directly into electricity

solar constant *n* the average amount of solar radiation received at the outer atmosphere at the Earth's mean distance from the Sun, equal to 0.140 watt per square centimetre

solar day *n* the time taken for the Earth to make a complete revolution on its axis, measured with respect to the Sun

solar eclipse *n* an eclipse in which the Moon blocks all or part of the Sun's light from reaching the Earth's surface, because it passes directly between the Earth and the Sun

solar energy *n* energy radiated from the Sun in the form of heat and light, used by green plants for photosynthesis, and harnessed as solar power

solar flare *n* a brief sudden eruption of high-energy hydrogen gas from the surface of the Sun, associated with sunspots

solar furnace *n* a furnace equipped with a series of concave mirrors that are motorized to follow the Sun and focus its radiation to obtain and maintain extremely high temperatures

solaria plural of **solarium**

solarimeter /sólə rímmitər/ *n* an instrument used to measure solar radiation [Early 20C. < SOLAR + -METER.]

solarise *vt* = **solarize**

solarium /sə láiri əm/ (*plural* **-a** /-ri ə/ *or* **-ums**) *n* 1 a room built for the purpose of enjoying sunlight, usually with large windows or glass walls, especially a room in a hospital or other healthcare establishment 2 a room or establishment equipped with sunlamps or sunbeds for acquiring a tan [Mid-19C. < Latin, 'sundial, terrace' < *sol* 'sun'.]

solarize /sólə rīz/ (**-izes, -izing, -ized**), **solarise** (**-ises, -ising, -ised**) *vt* 1 to affect or damage something with solar radiation 2 to overexpose photographic materials to light for deliberate effect, usually in order to exaggerate highlights —**solarization** /sólə rī záysh'n/ *n*

solar month *n* one-twelfth of a solar year, equal to 30 days, 10 hours, 29 minutes, 3.8 seconds

solar panel *n* a large panel containing solar cells or heat-absorbing plates that convert the Sun's radiation into electricity, for use, e.g. in heating buildings and powering satellites and spacecraft

solar plexus *n* 1 a mass of nerve cells in the upper abdomen behind the stomach, kidneys, and other internal organs 2 a point on the upper abdomen just below where the ribs separate [< its radial network of nerves]

solar system *n* the Sun and all the planets, satellites, asteroids, meteors, and comets that are subject to its gravitational pull

solar wind *n* the flow of high-speed ionized particles from the Sun's surface into interplanetary space. ◊ **stellar wind**

solar year *n* the time taken for the Earth to move around the Sun, equal to 365 days, 5 hours, 48 minutes, 45.51 seconds

solation /sō láysh'n/ *n* the process of changing from a gel to a liquid

solatium /sō láyshi əm/ (*plural* **-a** /-shi ə/) *n* damages awarded for emotional suffering, as opposed to financial loss or physical injury or suffering [Early 19C. < Latin (see SOLACE).]

sold past participle, past tense of **sell**

solder /sóldər/ *n* 1 **ALLOY FOR JOINING METAL** an alloy with a low melting point, typically a mixture of tin and lead, used to join electrical components to a circuit board or to join metal objects together 2 **SOMETHING THAT UNITES** something that forms a bond or union ■ *vti* 1 **JOIN THINGS WITH SOLDER** to work with solder or to join things using solder 2 **UNITE TO FORM WHOLE** to come together in unity, or to establish a bond of unity between people or things [Via Old French < Latin *solidare* 'fasten together' < *solidus* 'solid'] —**solderer** *n*

soldering iron *n* a tool with a point that is heated for melting and applying solder

soldier /sóljər/ *n* 1 **SOMEBODY SERVING IN ARMY** a person who serves in a military organization 2 **ARMY MEMBER BELOW OFFICER RANK** a member of an army of a rank below commissioned officer 3 **DEDICATED WORKER** a dedicated worker for a cause 4 **SKILLED WARRIOR** a skilled and experienced fighter or military strategist 5 **ANT THAT PROTECTS COLONY** a sterile member of an ant or termite colony with a large head and powerful jaws 6 **PIECE OF BREAD AND BUTTER** a thin strip of bread or toast, especially one for dipping into a soft-boiled egg or the yolk of a fried egg (*informal*) ■ *vi* 1 **SERVE IN ARMY** to serve as a soldier in an army 2 **PRETEND TO WORK** to give the appearance of working while really idling (*archaic slang*) [13C. < Old French, 'somebody having pay' < *soulde* '(soldier's) pay' < Latin *solidus (nummus)* 'Roman gold coin', literally 'solid (coin)' (see SOLID).] —**soldierly** *adj*

soldier on *vi* to persevere despite difficulties or setbacks

soldier crab *n* a small pale blue crab, often seen in large groups on rocky shores. Native to: Australia. *Mictyris longicarpus*. [Because it resembles a sentry in a sentry box]

soldierfish /sóljər fish/ (*plural* **-fishes** *or* **-fish**) *n* = **squirrelfish** [*Soldier* from its sharp spines and rough scales]

soldier of fortune *n* a soldier who enlists or serves in order to gain money or adventure

soldiers' home *n* US an institution funded by the US government for the care of war veterans

soldiery /sóljəri/ *n* 1 soldiers as a group 2 the profession or skill of a soldier

sold-out *adj* for which all available tickets have been sold

sole[1] /sōl/ *n* 1 **BOTTOM OF FOOT** the underside of the foot, stretching from the toes to the heel 2 **BOTTOM OF SHOE** the underside of a shoe, boot, or other piece of footwear, sometimes excluding the heel 3 **BOTTOM SURFACE OF GOLF CLUB** the underside of the head of a golf club ■ *vt* (**soles, soling, soled**) 1 **PUT SOLE ON SHOE** to put a sole on a shoe, boot, or other piece of footwear 2 **PLACE ON GROUND** to put the sole of a golf club on the ground in preparation for a stroke [14C. Via Old French < Latin *solea* 'sandal' < *solum* 'foot'.]

SPELLCHECK Do not confuse ***sole*** with ***soul***, which has a similar sound. Beware: your spellchecker will not catch this error.

sole[2] /sōl/ *adj* 1 **ONLY** of which there is only one ○ *the sole reason* 2 **EXCLUSIVE** belonging to one person or group ○ *has sole responsibility for the department* 3 **UNFETTERED** free from the interference of others 4 **UNMARRIED** without husband or wife [13C. Via Old French *soule* < Latin *sola*, the feminine of *solus*.] —**soleness** *n*

sole[3] /sōl/ (*plural* **soles** *or* **sole**) *n* 1 a brownish marine fish with a small mouth and both eyes on the upper side of its flat body. Family: Soleidae. 2 the flesh of a sole or a similar fish, as food [14C. Via French < Latin *solea* 'sandal'.]

solecism /sólləssizəm/ *n* 1 **GRAMMATICAL MISTAKE** a mistake in grammar or syntax 2 **ERROR** something incorrect, inappropriate, or inconsistent 3 **BREACH OF GOOD MANNERS** an action that breaks the rules of etiquette or good manners [Mid-16C. Ultimately via Latin *soloecismus* < Greek *soloikismos* < *soloikos* 'speaking incorrectly', literally 'inhabitant of Soloi' (in ancient Cilicia, E Turkey), whose Attic dialect was considered barbarous.] —**solecist** *n* —**solecistical** /sóllə sístik'l/ *adj* —**solecistically** *adv*

solely /sōl li/ *adv* 1 for nothing other than ○ *sold the company solely for commercial reasons* 2 to the exclusion of all else or others ○ *He is solely to blame.*

~~**solemly**~~ incorrect spelling of **solemnly**

solemn /sólləm/ *adj* 1 **EARNEST** demonstrating sincerity and gravity 2 **HUMOURLESS** without joy or humour 3 **FORMAL** characterized by ceremony or formality 4 **RELIGIOUS** observed with sacred or religious ceremony 5 **AWE-INSPIRING** inspiring wonder or reverence [14C. Via Old French *solemne* < Latin *sol(l)emnis* 'customary, religious', < *sollus* 'whole, entire' + an unknown element.] —**solemnly** *adv* —**solemnness** *n*

solemnify /sə lémni fī/ (**-fies, -fying, -fied**) *vt* to make something serious or solemn

solemnise *vt* = **solemnize**

solemnity /sə lémniti/ (*plural* **-ties**) *n* 1 **SOLEMN QUALITY** the solemn nature or quality of something 2 **SOLEMN CEREMONY** a formal or solemn ceremony held to observe an occasion or event (*often plural*) 3 **LEGAL FORMALITY** a formality that must be complied with before a contract or agreement can become effective

solemnize /sólləm nīz/ (**-nizes, -nizing, -nized**), **solemnise** (**-nises, -nising, -nised**) *v* 1 *vt* **CELEBRATE WITH CEREMONY** to observe an event or occasion with ceremony or formality 2 *vt* **PERFORM MARRIAGE CEREMONY** to celebrate a marriage with a religious ceremony 3 *vt* **MAKE DIGNIFIED** to bring dignity or formality to something 4 *vi* **SPEAK SOLEMNLY** to speak or reflect with great seriousness —**solemnization** /sólləm nī záysh'n/ *n*

solenodon /sə lénnə don/ *n* a rare nocturnal insect-eating mammal with a long snout and a long scaly tail. Native to: Caribbean. Family: Solenodontidae. [Mid-19C. < modern Latin, 'pipe-tooth' < Greek *sōlēn* 'pipe, channel'.]

solenoid /sóllə noyd/ *n* a device consisting of a cylindrical coil of wire surrounding a moveable iron core that moves along the length of the coil when an electric current is passed through it [Early 19C. < French *solénoïde* 'pipe-shaped' < Greek *sōlēn* 'pipe, channel'.] —**solenoidal** /sóllə nóyd'l/ *adj* —**solenoidally** *adv*

Solent /sṓlənt/ arm of the English Channel separating the Isle of Wight from mainland England. Length: 24 km/15 mi.

soleplate /sṓl playt/ *n* **1** the underside of an iron for pressing clothes **2** the plate that supports the bases of the studs used in framing a wall

soleus /sṓli əss/ (*plural* **-i** /-li ī/) *n* a broad flat muscle in the calf of the leg that helps to flex the ankle and depress the sole of the foot [Late 17C. Via modern Latin < Latin *solea* (see SOLE[1]).]

sol-fa *n* MUSIC = **tonic sol-fa** ■ *vti* (**sol-fas, sol-faing, sol-faed**) to sing a tune using the sol-fa syllables

solfatara /sólfə taárə/ *n* a vent in a volcano through which sulphur-rich gases and steam escape, leaving bright yellow sulphur deposits [Late 18C. < Italian, 'sulphurous volcano' < *solfo* 'sulphur' < Latin *sulfur*.] —**solfataric** *adj*

solfège *n* MUSIC = **solfeggio** [Early 20C. Via French < Italian *solfeggio* (see SOLFEGGIO).]

solfeggio /sol féjji ō/ (*plural* **-gi** /-féjji/ *or* **-gios**), **solfège** /sol fézh/ *n* an exercise in singing using the sol-fa syllables [Late 18C. < Italian, < *sol-fa* 'sol-fa'.]

solferino /sólfə reé nō/ *adj* of a purplish-red colour [Mid-19C. After *Solferino*, Italian town at which a dye of this colour was invented.] —**solferino** *n*

soli plural of **solo**

solicit /sə líssit/ *v* **1** *vti* PLEAD FOR to try to get something by making insistent requests or pleas **2** *vt* ASK SOMEBODY FOR to plead with or petition a person or group for something **3** *vti* OFFER SEX FOR MONEY to offer to participate in sexual activities in return for money **4** *vt* GET SOMEBODY TO DO SOMETHING WRONG to attempt to draw somebody into participating in illegal or immoral acts [15C. Via French *solliciter* < Latin *sollicitare* 'disturb' < *sollicitus* 'completely moved' < *sollus* 'whole' + *citus*, past participle of *ciere* 'move'.] —**solicitation** /sə líssi táysh'n/ *n*

solicitor /sə líssitər/ *n* a lawyer who gives legal advice, draws up legal documents, and does preparatory work for barristers —**solicitorship** *n*

Solicitor General (*plural* **Solicitors General**) *n* **1** LAW OFFICER OF CROWN in England and Wales, the second most senior law officer of the Crown, of a rank below Attorney General **2** *Scotland* LAW OFFICER OF CROWN IN SCOTLAND in Scotland, the second most senior law officer of the Crown, of a rank below Lord Advocate **3** *NZ* NEW ZEALAND'S TOP LEGAL OFFICER in New Zealand, the chief law officer and prosecutor for the Crown **4** *Can* a member of a federal or provincial cabinet responsible for law enforcement, prisons, and some forms of licensing

solicitous /sə líssitəss/ *adj* **1** CONCERNED expressing an attitude of concern and consideration **2** READY AND WILLING full of eagerness and anticipation to do something **3** METICULOUS paying very careful attention to details [Mid-16C. < Latin *sollicitus* (see SOLICIT).] —**solicitously** *adv* —**solicitousness** *n*

solicitude /sə líssi tyood/ *n* **1** concern and consideration, especially when expressed **2** a cause of concern or uneasiness (*often plural*)

solid /sóllid/ *adj* **1** NOT SOFT OR YIELDING consisting of compact unyielding material **2** NOT HOLLOW having no open interior spaces **3** UNADULTERATED OR UNMIXED made of the same material throughout **4** OF STRONG AND SECURE CONSTRUCTION built out of strong substantial material and not likely to break or collapse **5** UNANIMOUS in complete agreement ○ *Support for the amendment was solid.* **6** NOURISHING providing ample nourishment **7** UNINTERRUPTED continuing without breaks or openings ○ *It took a solid two hours to crack the code.* **8** RELIABLE able to be relied or depended upon **9** FINANCIALLY SECURE in sound financial condition **10** THREE-DIMENSIONAL with the three dimensions of length, breadth, and depth, or relating to geometric figures that have three dimensions **11** RETAINING ITS SHAPE with a shape that resists change, unlike a liquid or gas **12** AS SINGLE WORD written as one word without a space or hyphen **13** WITHOUT SPACES without spaces between lines of type in printing **14** *NZ* EXPENSIVE excessively high in price (*informal*) ■ *n* **1** SOLID THING something that is solid **2** SOLID FIGURE a three-dimensional geometric figure or object **3** SUBSTANCE THAT RETAINS SHAPE a substance that resists change in shape, unlike a liquid or gas [14C. Directly or via French *solide* < Latin *solidus* 'firm, whole'.] —**solidity** /sə líddəti/ *n* —**solidly** *adv* —**solidness** *n*

solid angle *n* a three-dimensional angle formed at the vertex of a cone or the intersection of three planes

solidarity /sólli dárrəti/ *n* harmony of interests and responsibilities among individuals in a group, especially as manifested in unanimous support and collective action for something

Solidarity /sólli dárrəti/ *n* a federation of trade unions in Poland, founded in 1980. Under the leadership of Lech Walesa it challenged the Soviet-backed government of the day. [Late 20C. Translation of Polish *Solidarność*.]

solid geometry *n* the branch of geometry dealing with three-dimensional figures

solidi plural of **solidus**

solidify /sə líddi fī/ (**-fies, -fying, -fied**) *vti* **1** to become compact or firm, or make something compact or firm **2** to become strong and united, or make something strong and united —**solidifiable** *adj* —**solidification** /sə líddifi káysh'n/ *n* —**solidifier** /sə líddi fī ər/ *n*

solid of revolution *n* a three-dimensional mathematical figure formed by rotating a plane figure about an axis in its plane

solid solution *n* a crystalline substance such as an alloy in which different kinds of atoms or molecules share the same structure

solid-state *adj* **1** working by means of the flow of electric current through solid material, as happens with semiconductors and transistors **2** relating to the electronic characteristics of solids, especially at the atomic or molecular level

solidus /sóllidəss/ (*plural* **-di** /-dī/) *n* **1** a line sloping from right to left, used to separate items of information, such as dates, as in '11/11/99', to write fractions, and to indicate alternatives, as in 'and/or' (*technical*) US term **virgule 2** a gold coin used in the Roman Empire from the fourth century BC [14C. < Latin (see SOLDIER).]

solifluction /sólli flúksh'n/ *n* the slow movement of soil downhill as a result of water saturation after rainfall or the melting of ice [Early 20C. < Latin *solum* 'ground' + *fluct-*, past participle of *fluere* 'flow'.]

Solihull /sṓli húl, sṓli hul/ town in central England. Population: 94,531 (1991).

soliloquize /sə líllə kwīz/ (**-quizes, -quizing, -quized**), **soliloquise** (**-quises, -quising, -quised**) *vi* to speak a soliloquy in the course of a play —**soliloquist** *n* —**soliloquizer** *n*

soliloquy /sə lílləkwi/ (*plural* **-quies**) *n* **1** the act of speaking while alone, especially when used as a theatrical device that allows a character's thoughts and ideas to be conveyed to the audience **2** a section of a play or other drama in which a soliloquy is spoken [14C. < late Latin *soliloquium* 'a speaking alone' < Latin *solus* 'alone' (see SOLE[2]) + *loqui* 'speak'.]

Solingen /zṓlingən/ city in west-central Germany. Population: 166,000 (1994).

solipsism /sóllipsizəm/ *n* the belief that the only thing somebody can be sure of is that he or she exists, and that true knowledge of anything else is impossible [Late 19C. < Latin *solus* 'alone' + *ipse* 'self'.] —**solipsist** *n* —**solipsistic** /sóllip sístik/ *adj* —**solipsistically** *adv*

solitaire /sólli tair, sólli táir/ *n* **1** BOARD GAME FOR ONE a board game for one person, in which pegs are eliminated from the board by being moved into empty spaces, the object being to end with one remaining centre peg **2** *US* CARDS = **patience** *n.* **3 3** SINGLE GEMSTONE a gem, especially a diamond, that is set alone in a ring **4** SONGBIRD a thrush. Native to: North and Central America. Genus: *Myadestes*. [14C. Via French, 'recluse' < Latin *solitarius* (see SOLITARY).]

solitary /sóllitəri/ *adj* **1** DONE ALONE done without the company of other people **2** SHUNNING COMPANY preferring to be or live alone **3** SECLUDED in a remote location, apart from others **4** SINGLE existing as the only one of its kind ○ *a solitary boat on the sea* **5** NOT LIVING IN SOCIAL GROUPS describes animals that live alone or in pairs rather than in colonies or social groups **6** GROWING SINGLY describes flowers that grow singly rather than as a cluster ■ *n* (*plural* **-ies**) **1** RECLUSE a person who lives or prefers to be alone **2** CRIME = **solitary confinement** [14C. Directly or via French *solitaire* < Latin *solitarius* < *solus* 'alone' (see SOLE[2]).] —**solitarily** *adv* —**solitariness** *n*

solitary confinement *n* confinement of a prisoner in an area or cell isolated from other prisoners, used as a punishment or for protection

soliton /sólli ton/ *n* an isolated wave that can travel without dissipating its energy. Its behaviour is similar to that of a particle under some conditions. [Mid-20C. < SOLITARY + ON.]

solitude /sólli tyood/ *n* **1** STATE OF BEING ALONE the state of being alone, separated from other people, whether considered as a welcome freedom from disturbance or as an unhappy loneliness **2** REMOTENESS a quality of quiet remoteness or seclusion in places from which human activity is generally absent **3** LONELY PLACE a remote or uninhabited place (*literary*) [14C. Directly or via Old French < Latin *solitudo* < *solus* 'alone'.] —**solitudinous** /sólli tyoód'nəss/ *adj*

LITERARY LINK ***One Hundred Years of Solitude***, a novel (1967) by Colombian writer Gabriel García Márquez. It recounts a hundred years in the lives of the Buendía family, founders of the town of Macondo in Colombia, a story that mirrors the history of the nation. Marquez's skilful use of fantasy and myth to convey the depth of his characters' experiences makes this a key work in the magic realism school of literature.

---

solitudinarian /sólli tyoodi náiri ən/ *n* a person who lives or prefers to be alone (*literary*)

solleret /sóllə ret/ *n* a shoe made of steel plates riveted together, forming part of a suit of armour [14C. Via the diminutive of Old French *soller* 'shoe' < late Latin *subtel* 'hollow of the foot' < *sub* 'under' + *talus* 'ankle'.]

solmization /sóllmi záysh'n/ *n* the assignment of separate syllables to different musical pitches for singing or training the ear, as, e.g. in solfeggio [Mid-18C. French *solmisation* < *solmiser* 'sing sol-fa'.]

solo /sṓlō/ *n* (*plural* **-los** *or* **-li** /-li/) **1** MUSICAL PIECE PERFORMED BY ONE PERSON a piece of music performed by one musician or singer, or a passage for a single player or singer within a longer piece for two or more, a choir, or an orchestra **2** PERFORMANCE BY ONE ARTIST a performance by a single artist such as a musician, singer, or dancer with or without accompaniment **3** ACT DONE BY SINGLE PERSON an action or feat carried out by one person alone, e.g. a flight in an aircraft or a climb up a mountain **4** MOTORCYCLE WITHOUT SIDECAR a motorcycle without a sidecar **5** CARD GAME FOR INDIVIDUAL PLAYERS a card game in which players play on their own, not in pairs or teams, especially solo whist ■ *adj* **1** FOR SINGLE PERFORMER intended for or executed by somebody performing singly, not as one of a group **2** DONE BY ONE PERSON carried out by one person unaccompanied by anyone else **3** *ANZ* HAVING NO PARTNER bringing up a child or children alone, without a partner ■ *adv* ALONE unaccompanied by anyone, or not performing or doing something as one of a group ■ *vi* (**-los, -loing, -loed**) DO SOMETHING WITHOUT HELP OR ACCOMPANIMENT to do something alone, without help or accompaniment, especially to fly an aircraft without an instructor or to perform an artistic solo [Late 17C. Via Italian < Latin *solus* 'alone'.]

soloist /sṓlō ist/ *n* a performer of a solo —**soloistic** /sṓlō ístik/ *adj*

Solo man /sṓlō-/ *n* an extinct variety of the human species Homo sapiens that lived 50,000 years ago during the late Pleistocene epoch and whose fossils were discovered near the River Solo in Java

Solomon /sólləmən/ *n* a wise person (*informal*)

Solomon /sólləmən/ king of Israel (*fl.* 10th century BC)

Solomon Islands /sólləmən-/ monarchy comprising over 35 islands and atolls in the South Pacific Ocean. Capital: Honiara. Population: 412,902 (1996). Area: 28,446 sq. km/10,980 sq. mi. —**Solomon Islander** *n*

Solomon's seal *n* **1** a perennial woodland plant. Native to: northern countries. Flowers: drooping, whitish, in pairs. *Polygonatum multiflorum.* **2** a six-pointed symbol resembling a star, made up of one triangle laid on top of another facing the other way

solon /sṓ lon/ *n* somebody wise, especially an experienced and wise legislator or politician (*literary*) [Early 17C. After *Solon* (638?–558? BC), Athenian statesman, legal reformer, and poet.]

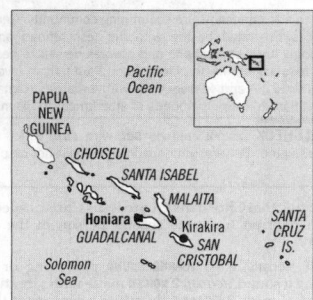

Solomon Islands

solonchak /sóllən chák/ n an intrazonal soil with a greyish crust that develops in semiarid and desert areas and contains large amounts of soluble salts [Early 20C. < Russian, 'salt marsh, salt lake' < sol 'salt'.]

solonetz /sólla néts/, **solonets** n an intrazonal soil with a blackish crust developed from solonchak soil by leaching of the salts [Early 20C. < Russian, 'salt marsh, salt lake' < sol 'salt'.]

so long interj used to say goodbye (informal)

solo stop n a stop on an organ with a penetrating tone, used in isolated passages of organ pieces to give the effect of a single instrument playing the melody

solo whist n a version of the card game whist in which each of the four players plays on his or her own, instead of in the usual pairs

solstice /sólstiss/ n 1 either of the times when the Sun is farthest from the equator, on or about 21 June or 21 December 2 either of the two points on the ecliptic when the Sun reaches its northernmost or southernmost point relative to the celestial equator [13C. Via Old French < Latin solstitium < sol 'sun' + past participle of sistere 'stand still'.] —**solstitial** /sol stísh'l/ adj

Solti /shólti/, **Sir Georg** (1912–97) Hungarian conductor

solubilise vti = **solubilize**

solubility /sóllyōō bíllati/ n (plural -ties) n 1 the extent to which one substance is able to dissolve in another 2 a measure of one substance's ability to dissolve in a specific amount of another substance at standard temperature and pressure

solubilize /sóllyōōbə līz/ (-lizes, -lizing, -lized), **solubilise** /sóllyōōbi līz, sóllyabi-/ (-lises, -lising, -lised) vti to make a substance soluble or more soluble, or become soluble or more soluble

soluble /sóllyōōb'l/ adj 1 DISSOLVING IN LIQUID able to be dissolved in another substance (often in combination) ◇ water-soluble 2 DESIGNED TO DISSOLVE designed to be dissolved in water 3 SOLVABLE able to be solved or answered [14C. Via Old French < late Latin solubilis < solvere 'loosen, dissolve'.] —**solubility** n (see SOLUBLE.)

soluble glass n CHEM = **sodium silicate**

soluble RNA n BIOCHEM = **transfer RNA**

solum /sóləm/ (plural -lums /-lə/ or -la) n the upper layers of a soil profile where the formation of new soil takes place and where most plant roots and soil animals are found [Mid-19C. Via Modern Latin < Latin solum 'ground, foundation'.]

solus /sóləss/ adj 1 ALONE ON STAGE used as a stage direction to indicate that a character appears alone on stage ◇ Enter Hector solus 2 FEATURED ON OWN in or on which an advertisement appears on its own, rather than alongside advertisements for different products or from competing companies 3 SELLING ONE COMPANY'S PRODUCTS selling the products of one company only [Late 16C. < Latin, 'alone'.] —**solus** adv

solute /so lyoot/ n a substance dissolved in another substance ■ adj dissolved in a solution [15C. < Latin solutus, past participle of solvere (see SOLUBLE.)]

solution /sə loōsh'n/ n 1 WAY OF RESOLVING DIFFICULTY a method of successfully dealing with a problem or difficulty 2 ANSWER TO PUZZLE the answer to a puzzle or question 3 FINDING OF SOLUTION the process of resolving a difficulty or finding the answer to a puzzle or question 4 FLUID WITH SUBSTANCE DISSOLVED IN IT a substance consisting of two or more substances mixed together and uniformly dispersed, most commonly the result of dissolving a solid, fluid, or gas in a liquid 5 PROCESS OF FORMING SOLUTION the process of forming a solution or dissolving one substance in another, or the state of being dissolved in another substance 6 VALUE SATISFYING EQUATION a value for a variable that satisfies an equation 7 TERMINATION OF A DISPUTE the termination of a dispute or payment of a debt 8 ENDING the act of ending, breaking, or separating something (literary) [14C. Via Old French < Latin solutionem < solvere (see SOLVE.)]

solution set n the set of values for a variable that satisfy an equation

Solutrean /sə lootri ən/ adj belonging to a prehistoric culture that existed in Europe between 40,000 BC and 12,000 BC, at the end of the Palaeolithic period, in which people worked with leaf-shaped flint blades [Late 19C. < French solutréen < Solutré, village in France.]

solvate /sól vayt/ vti (-vates, -vating, -vated) to enter into solution with a solvent, or cause a solute to dissolve in solution with a solvent ■ n a compound consisting of an ion or molecule of solute combined with one or more of solvent [Early 20C. < SOLVENT + -ATE.] —**solvation** /sol váysh'n/ n

Solvay process /sól vay-/ n an industrial process for producing sodium carbonate or washing soda from common salt [Late 19C. After Ernest Solvay (1838–1922), Belgian chemist.]

solve /solv/ (solves, solving, solved) vt 1 DEAL WITH PROBLEM SUCCESSFULLY to find a way of dealing successfully with a problem or difficulty 2 FIND ANSWER TO PUZZLE to find the answer to a question or puzzle 3 FIND ANSWER TO MATHS PROBLEM to work out the solution to an equation or other mathematical problem [15C. < Latin solvere 'loosen, dissolve'.] —**solvability** n —**solvable** adj —**solvableness** n —**solver** n

solvent /sólvənt/ adj 1 HAVING ENOUGH MONEY having enough money to cover expenses and debts 2 DISSOLVING able to dissolve substances ■ n SUBSTANCE THAT DISSOLVES THINGS a substance in which other substances are dissolved, often a liquid [Early 17C. Directly or via French < Latin solventem, present participle of solvere (see SOLVE.)] —**solvency** /sólvənssi/ n —**solvently** adv

solvent misuse, **solvent abuse** n the inhaling of fumes from solvents such as glues and petrol in order to produce a feeling of euphoria

solvolysis /sol vóllasiss/ n a chemical reaction in which a dissolved solute and its solvent combine to form a new compound

Solway Firth /sól way-/ arm of the Irish Sea on the border between NW England and SW Scotland. Length: 64 km/40 mi.

Solzhenitsyn /sólzhə neétsin, səlzhə nyeétsin/, **Aleksandr Isayevich** (b. 1918) Russian writer

som /sōm/ (plural som) n see table at **currency**

Som. abbr 1 Somalia 2 Somerset

soma[1] /sóma/ (plural -mata /-mətə/ or -mas) n 1 all the cells and tissues in the body considered collectively, with the exception of germ cells 2 the body considered separately from the mind or soul [Mid-19C. Via modern Latin < Greek sōma 'body'.]

soma[2] /sóma/ n 1 an intoxicating drink made from plant juice, mentioned in the Vedas, the most ancient sacred writings of Hinduism 2 the plant that soma is made from, thought to be ephedra, but not identified in the Vedas [Early 19C. < Sanskrit.]

Somali /sə maáli/ (plural -lis or -li), **Somalian** /sə maáli ən/ n 1 a member of an Islamic African people living mainly in Somalia 2 the Cushitic national language of Somalia, also spoken in E Ethiopia. Native speakers: 5 million. [Early 19C. < Somali.] —**Somali** adj

Somalia /sə maáli ə/ republic in NE Africa. Capital: Mogadishu. Population: 6,802,000 (1996). Area: 637,657 sq. km/246,201 sq. mi.

Somalian n, adj PEOPLES, LANG = **Somali**

Somaliland /sə maáli land/ region of NE Africa, comprising Somalia, Djibouti, and part of Ethiopia

somat- prefix = **somato-** (before vowels)

somatic /sə máttik/ adj 1 AFFECTING BODY relating to or affecting the body, especially the body as considered to be separate from the mind 2 RELATING TO OUTER WALLS OF BODY relating to the outer walls of the body, not the inner organs 3 OF SOMATIC CELL relating to a somatic cell [Late 18C. < Greek sōmatikos 'bodily' < sōma (see SOMA[1].)] —**somatically** adv

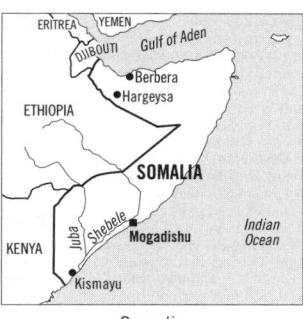

Somalia

somatic cell n any cell of the body with the exception of germ cells

somaticize /sə mátti sīz/ (-cizes, -cizing, -cized), **somaticise** (-cises, -cising, -cised) vti to believe mistakenly that an emotional pain is a physical symptom

somatic nervous system n the part of the nervous system that serves the sense organs and muscles of the body wall and limbs, and brings about voluntary muscle activity. ◊ **autonomic nervous system**

somato- prefix body ◇ somatoplasm [< Greek sōmat-, stem of sōma]

somatology /sōma tólləji/ n 1 the study of both the physiology and anatomy of the body 2 the branch of anthropology that studies human evolution through variation and development in physical characteristics —**somatologic** /sōmata lójjik/ adj —**somatological** adj —**somatologically** adv

somatomedin /sōmata meédin/ n a hormone produced in the liver that stimulates the growth of bone and muscle [Late 20C. < SOMATO- + INTERMEDIARY + -IN.]

somatoplasm /sōmata plazəm/ n the protoplasm of body cells as distinct from the protoplasm of germ cells —**somatoplastic** adj

somatopleure /sōmata ploor, -plur/ n a fold of embryonic tissue in vertebrates formed by the fusion of ectoderm and mesoderm that gives rise to an embryo's inner and outer membranes —**somatopleural** /sōmata plóōral, -plúral/ adj —**somatopleuric** adj

somatosensory /sōmata sénssari/ adj describes sensory stimuli coming from the skin and internal organs and the perception of these stimuli

somatostatin /sōmata státtin/ n a hormone produced in the hypothalamus that inhibits the release of growth hormone [Late 20C. < SOMATO- + stat- < Latin stare 'stand' + -IN.]

somatotrophin /sōmata trófin/, **somatotropin** /sōmata trópin/ n BIOL = **growth hormone** [Mid-20C. < SOMATO- + -TROPHIC + -IN.] —**somatotrophic** /sōmata tróffik/ adj

somatotype /sōmata tīp/ n the type of physical build that a person has

somber adj US = **sombre**

sombre /sómbər/ adj 1 DARK AND GLOOMY lacking light or brightness and producing a dull, dark, or melancholy atmosphere 2 DARK IN COLOUR having a colour or tone that is dark, dull, or suitable for a serious mood or occasion 3 SERIOUS AND MELANCHOLY marked by or conveying strict seriousness combined with sadness or a troubled state of mind [Mid-18C. Via French, 'gloomy' < late Latin subumbrare 'shadow' < sub 'under' + umbra 'shade'.] —**sombrely** adv —**sombreness** n

sombrero /som bráirō/ (plural -ros) n a straw or felt hat with a very wide upturned brim, originally worn by men in Mexico and some other Spanish-speaking countries [Late 16C. Via Spanish, 'hat' < sombra 'shade' < Vulgar Latin subumbrare (see SOMBRE.)]

some /(stressed) sum, (unstressed) səm/ CORE MEANING: a grammatical word used to indicate an unspecified or unknown quantity of people or things ◇ (det) There is always some risk in any project. ◇ (pron) There was plenty of food left over, so I took some.

1 det, pron A LITTLE used to indicate an unspecified number, quantity, or proportion of a total, generally a fairly small to average or reasonable one ◇ I agree with you to some extent. ◇ Some of you, I know, will disagree with me. 2 det QUITE A FEW used with a slight emphasis to

indicate an unspecified but fairly large number or quantity ○ *We have been debating this problem for some months now.* **3** *det* **PARTICULAR BUT UNSPECIFIED** used to indicate an unspecified single person or thing, often in a dismissive way ○ *He was reading some medical book.* **4** *det* **USED FOR EMPHASIS** used to emphasize that somebody or something is impressive or remarkable in a certain way (*informal*) ○ *That was some performance you put on for us!* **5** *adv* **APPROXIMATELY** used to indicate that a number is approximate ○ *for some 30 years* **6** *adv US* **TO A SMALL EXTENT** to a small extent or degree (*informal*) ○ *I do write some, but not as much as I'd like.* **7** *adv US* **A GREAT DEAL** a great deal, at a considerable rate, or vigorously (*informal*) ○ *I'm going to have to study some to get through this exam.* [Old English *sum* 'one, someone' < Indo-European, 'together with'] ◇ **and then some** *US* used to emphasize that more, often considerably more, has been done than was suggested in a previous statement (*informal*)

-some[1] *suffix* **1** characterized by a particular quality, condition, or thing ○ *troublesome* ○ *quarrelsome* **2** a group containing a particular number of members ○ *foursome* [Old English *-sum*]

-some[2] *suffix* **1** body ○ *cytosome* **2** chromosome ○ *autosome* [< Greek *sōma* 'body']

somebody /súmbədi/, **someone** /súm wun/ *pron* some unspecified person ■ *pron, n* (*plural* **-ies**) an important or well-known person in society or in a particular place

someday /súm day/ *adv* at some unknown, unspecified, and usually fairly distant time in the future

USAGE someday, someplace, sometime: In British English it is idiomatic to say ***someday*** (*Someday [or some day] I'll take you away from all this*) but it is often written as two words, while ***someplace*** is not used at all except as a conscious Americanism (*I must have left it someplace*). ***Sometime*** is written as one word as an adjective meaning 'former' (*a sometime president of the Rotary Club*), and as an adverb meaning 'at some time' (*I'll see you again sometime*).

somehow /súm how/ *adv* **1** in some unspecified or unknown way, often with great effort or difficulty ○ *He somehow managed to scramble back on board.* **2** for some unknown or inexplicable reason ○ *She somehow forgot to tell anyone where she was going.*

someone *pron, n* = **somebody**

someplace /súm playss/ *adv US, Can* somewhere (*informal*)

USAGE See ***someday***.

somersault /súmmər solt/, **summersault** /súmmər sawlt/ *n* **1 ACROBATIC ROLLING OVER OF BODY** an acrobatic movement in which the body is rolled over, feet over head, either forwards or backwards, on the ground or in midair, finally returning to an upright position **2 REVERSAL OF OPINION OR DECISION** a complete change of mind or reversal of policy (*informal*) ■ *vi* **PERFORM SOMERSAULT** to perform an acrobatic somersault [Early 16C. Via Middle French *sombresault*, a variant of *sobresault* < Latin *super* (see SUPER) + *saltus* 'leap'.]

Somerset /súmmər sət/ county in SW England. Area: 3,458 sq. km/1,335 sq. mi.

Somerset /súmmərssət/, **Edward Seymour, 1st Duke of** (1506?–52) English statesman. Known as **Protector Somerset**

Somerset House *n* a building in London that formerly housed the General Register Office

Somerset Island island in N Nunavut, Canada, north of the Boothia Peninsula. Area: 24,786 sq. km/9,570 sq. mi.

something /súm thing/ *pron* **1 UNSPECIFIED THING** an unspecified or unidentified object, phenomenon, action, utterance, or feeling ○ *Don't just stand there, do something!* ○ *I had a feeling that there was something wrong.* ○ *Would you like something to eat?* **2 A CERTAIN AMOUNT** an unspecified and approximate amount expressed in relation to a specific number or quantity ○ *something over 50* ○ *something between 20 and 30%* **3 SUGGESTING RESEMBLANCE** used to suggest that one thing or person resembles another to a certain extent or has some of the qualities of the other ○ *There's definitely something of the knight errant about him.* **4 RATHER** used to qualify a description of a thing or event and tone it down or make it sound more guarded ○ *It was something of a disappointment.* **5 SOMETHING IMPRESSIVE** an impressive or important person or thing ○ *He's really something!* ■ *adv* **1 SOMEWHAT** slightly or to some degree ○ *It sounds something like what she might have said.* **2 TO AN EXTREME DEGREE** used to intensify the effect of an adjective, especially a strong adjective used as an adverb (*informal*) ○ *It hurts something awful.* **3 AND A BIT MORE** used to indicate that a number is slightly higher than the one mentioned (*informal*) ○ *She's thirty something.* ◇ **something else** somebody or something really special, remarkable, or extreme (*informal*) ◇ **have something to do with somebody** *or* **something** to be connected with or involve somebody *or* something

sometime /súm tīm/ *adv* **1 AT SOME TIME** at some unspecified or unknown time ○ *They intend to marry sometime soon.* **2 FORMERLY** at one time in the past (*formal*) ○ *our speaker today, sometime a scholar of Lincoln College, Oxford* ■ *adj* **FORMER** who at one time in the past had the job, position, or status in question ○ *a sometime student of this university*

USAGE See ***someday***.

sometimes /súm tīmz/ *adv* from time to time, not continually or every time ○ *We go to the theatre sometimes.* [Early 16C. The *-s* is possessive (genitive) singular, not a plural.]

someway /súm way/ *adv* using some means or method that is not yet known or not stated ○ *We'll figure it out someway.*

somewhat /súm wot/ *adv* to a certain extent or degree ○ *The hot night had cooled somewhat.*

somewhere /súm wair/ *adv* **1** in, to, or at some unspecified place ○ *He lives somewhere in Scotland.* **2** used in giving approximate amounts, numbers, or times ○ *somewhere around three hundred* ○ *somewhere between three and four o'clock* ◇ **get somewhere** to make progress towards achieving something

somite /sṓ mīt/ *n* **1** one of a series of paired blocks of cells that develop along the back of a vertebrate embryo giving rise to the vertebral column and most of the skeletal muscles **2** a body segment, usually one of several, into which the bodies of certain animals, e.g. earthworms and crayfish, are divided along their length [Mid-19C. < SOMA[1] + -ITE[1].] —**somital** /sṓmit'l/ *adj* —**somitic** /sō míttik/ *adj*

Somme /som/ river in N France, flowing into the English Channel. Length: 241 km/150 mi.

sommelier /sómm'l yay, sə mélli ər/ *n* a wine waiter in a restaurant, hotel, or other licensed establishment, who supervises the ordering, storing, and serving of wine [Early 20C. Via a variant of French *sommerier*, *sommier* 'officer in charge of provisions' < *somme* 'burden' < Greek *ságma* 'covering, packsaddle'.]

sommer /sómmər/ *adv S Africa* just, only, or somewhat (*informal*) [Mid-19C. < Afrikaans *somaar*, *sommer*.]

somn- *prefix* = **somni-** (*before vowels*)

somnambulate /som námbyŏŏ layt/ (**-lates, -lating, -lated**) *vi* to sleepwalk (*technical*) —**somnambulance** /-námbyŏŏlənss/ *n* —**somnambulation** /som námbyŏŏ láysh'n/ *n* —**somnambulator** *n*

somnambulism /som námbyŏŏlizəm/ *n* sleepwalking (*technical*) —**somnambulist** *n* —**somnambulistic** /som námbyŏŏ lístik/ *adj*

somni- *prefix* sleep ○ *somnifacient* [< Latin *somnus*]

somnifacient /sómni fáysh'nt/ *adj* describes a drug designed to induce sleep

somniferous /som níffərəss/ *adj* making somebody, or designed to make somebody, feel sleepy —**somniferously** *adv*

somnolent /sómnələnt/ *adj* **1 SLEEPY** feeling sleepy or tending to fall asleep **2 LACKING ACTIVITY** quiet and with little or no activity **3 SLEEP-INDUCING** making somebody feel sleepy [15C. Via Old French < Latin *somnōlentus* 'sleepy' < *somnus* 'sleep'.] —**somnolence** *n* —**somnolently** *adv*

son /sun/ *n* **1 MALE CHILD** a male child in relation to his parents **2 MALE DESCENDANT** a male descendant **3 MALE CONNECTED WITH SOMETHING** a man or boy referred to in terms of his connection with a place, a time in history, or a sphere of interest ○ *the achievements of the sons of the Industrial Revolution* **4 TERM OF ADDRESS** an affectionate, or sometimes condescending, way of addressing a boy or man (*informal*) [Old English *sunu* < Indo-European, 'give birth'] —**sonless** *adj* —**sonlike** *adj*

LITERARY LINK *Sons and Lovers*, a novel (1913) by D. H. Lawrence. Lawrence's first major novel, it centres on a family living in a Nottinghamshire coalmining community. Gertrude Morel is frustrated by life with her less refined and increasingly drunken husband and devotes herself to her children, focusing on her son Paul. When Paul falls in love, first with a local girl and subsequently with a married woman, he finds it hard to break the bonds of attachment to his mother.

SPELLCHECK Do not confuse ***son*** with ***sun***, which has a similar sound. Beware: your spellchecker will not catch this error.

Son *n* a title that Christians give to Jesus Christ, especially when referred to as the second person in the Holy Trinity

sonant /sṓnənt/ *adj* **1 HAVING SOUND** producing or possessing a sound (*formal*) **2 VOICED** made with vibration of the vocal cords **3 SYLLABIC** describes a consonant that is capable of forming a syllable on its own, without a vowel ■ *n* **1 VOICED SOUND** a sound made with vibration of the vocal cords **2 SYLLABIC CONSONANT** a consonant capable of forming a syllable on its own, without a vowel [Mid-19C. < Latin *sonans*, present participle of *sonare* 'sound'.] —**sonance** *n* —**sonantal** /sō nánt'l/ *adj* —**sonantic** *adj*

sonar /sṓ naar/ *n* **1** a system that determines the position of unseen underwater objects by transmitting sound waves and measuring the time it takes for their echo to return after hitting the object **2** a device that uses sonar [Mid-20C. Acronym < *sound navigation ranging*.]

sonata /sə naátə/ *n* **1** a piece of classical music for a solo instrument or a small ensemble consisting of several movements, at least one of which is in sonata form **2** a piece of baroque keyboard music in a single movement [Late 17C. Via Italian < *sonare* 'sound' < Latin *sonare* (see SONANT).]

sonata form *n* an important musical form developed in the 18th century consisting of three sections, an exposition, development, and recapitulation, and used especially for the first movement of sonatas, concertos, and symphonies

sonatina /sónnə téenə/ *n* a short and usually less technically difficult sonata [Early 18C. Via Italian, 'little sonata' < *sonata* (see SONATA).]

sondage /son daázh/ *n* a deep trench dug in order to study the relative positions of human artefacts in horizontal layers [Mid-20C. French, 'sounding, bore hole' (see SOUND[1]).]

sonde /sónd/ *n* a collection of instruments that can be lowered down a borehole or carried into the upper atmosphere by balloon or rocket to transmit information relating to the conditions encountered [Early 20C. < French, 'plumb line, sound' (see SOUND[1]).]

Sondheim /sónd hīm/, **Stephen** (*b.* 1930) US composer and lyricist

sone /sōn/ *n* a unit measuring the loudness of sound as subjectively perceived, equal to a tone of 1 kilohertz at 40 decibels above the threshold where sounds become audible to the listener [Mid-20C. < Latin *sonus* 'sound'.]

son et lumière /són ay lóomi air/ *n* an outdoor nighttime spectacle that combines dramatic lighting effects with recorded sounds and music, usually staged at the site of a famous and historical building, often telling its history [French, 'sound and light']

song /song/ *n* **1 SET OF WORDS SUNG** a usually relatively short musical composition consisting of words set to music **2 SINGING** the art or practice of singing **3 INSTRUMENTAL WORK IN STYLE OF SONG** an instrumental work written in the style of a vocal song, or, in popular music, any musical work **4 CHARACTERISTIC SOUND OF BIRD OR INSECT** the characteristic sound that a bird or insect makes, usually either to attract a mate or to warn off competing members of its species **5 POETRY** poetry or verse (*literary*) **6 POEM** a poem, especially one that rhymes (*literary*) [Old English *sang* < Indo-European, 'sing'] —**songlike** *adj* ◇ **for a song** very cheaply (*informal*) ◇ **on song** performing well or in good form (*informal*)

Song *n* HIST = **Sung**

song and dance *n* (*informal*) **1** an unnecessary fuss about something **2** *US* a long-winded attempt to explain or justify something

songbird /sóng burd/ *n* a bird with a musical call, especially a perching bird belonging to the suborder that includes larks, finches, and thrushes. Suborder: Oscines.

songbook /sóng bòòk/ *n* a book containing the words and music for a collection of songs

song cycle *n* a set of songs linked by a common subject or underlying musical theme or forming a narrative, often with words by a single poet and music by a classical composer

songfest /sóng fest/ *n US* an informal gathering of people to sing folk or popular songs together

song form *n* the three-part structure of a song consisting of a first section that leads to a contrasting section before the original section returns, either identically or with some variation

songful /sóngfòòl, sóngf'l/ *adj* resembling song, especially in having a pleasing melody —**songfully** *adv* —**songfulness** *n*

Songhai /sóng gī/ (*plural* **-hai** *or* **-hais**), **Songhay** (*plural* **-hay** *or* **-hays**) *n* **1 MEMBER OF W AFRICAN PEOPLE** a member of a people living in West Africa, mainly in Mali and Niger **2 SONGHAI LANGUAGE** the Nilo-Saharan language of the Songhai. Native speakers: 2 million. **3** an ancient empire in W Africa from the 8th to the 16th centuries, in present-day Mali

Song of Songs, Song of Solomon *n* a book of the Bible consisting mainly of love poems. Traditionally attributed to King Solomon, it is now thought to have been written by several later authors.

songsmith /sóng smith/ *n* MUSIC = **songwriter**

song sparrow *n* a brown and white finch with a musical call. Native to: North America. *Melospiza melodia.*

songster /sóngstər/ *n* **1 SINGER** a singer, especially a talented one **2 SONGBIRD** a bird with a musical call **3 POET** a poet (*literary*)

songstress /sóngstrəss/ *n* a woman singer, songwriter, or poet (*dated; offensive in some contexts*)

song thrush *n* a small common songbird with brown upper parts and a white breast speckled with brown. Native to: Europe, Asia. *Turdus philomelos.*

songwriter /sóng rītər/ *n* a writer of songs

sonic /sónnik/ *adj* **1 RELATING TO SOUND OR SOUND WAVES** relating to, using, or producing sound or sound waves **2 AUDIBLE TO HUMAN EAR** able to be heard by the human ear **3 RELATING TO SPEED OF SOUND** relating to or travelling at the speed of sound in air, approximately 1,220 km per hour/760 mi. per hour at sea level [Early 20C. < Latin *sonus* 'sound' + -IC.]

sonic barrier *n* AEROSP = **sound barrier**

sonic boom *n* a noise heard as a loud boom at ground level resulting from the shock waves created by an aircraft flying above the speed of sound

sonics /sónniks/ *n* the study of sound or, more generally, elastic wave motion (+ *singular verb*)

son-in-law (*plural* **sons-in-law**) *n* the husband of somebody's daughter

sonnet /sónnət/ *n* a short poem with fourteen lines, usually ten-syllable rhyming lines, divided into two, three, or four sections ■ *vi* to write sonnets [Mid-16C. Via French and Italian *sonnetto* < Old Provençal *son* 'poem' < Latin *sonus* 'sound'.]

sonneteer /sónnə téer/ *n* **1** a poet who writes sonnets **2** a writer of mediocre poems

sonnet sequence *n* a set of sonnets written by one poet and unified by a single theme or idea

sonny /súnni/ (*plural* **-nies**), **sonny boy** *n* an affectionate, or sometimes condescending, way of addressing a man or boy (*informal*)

sonobuoy /sṓnə boy, sónnə-/ *n* a buoy fitted with equipment for detecting underwater noises and transmitting them by radio [Mid-20C. < Latin *sonus* 'sound' + BUOY[1].]

son of a bitch *n* (*plural* **sons of bitches**) *US, Can* **1 TABOO TERM** a highly offensive term for somebody, usually a man, regarded as hateful, despicable, or intensely annoying (*taboo insult*) **2 ANY PERSON** used as a familiar, humorous, and slightly vulgar term for a person, usually a man, who has the named characteristic (*slang; sometimes considered offensive*) ○ *He's a lucky son of a bitch.* ■ *interj US, Can* **EXCLAMATION OF ANGER** used as a swearword to express anger or defiance (*slang; sometimes considered offensive*)

son of a gun *n* (*plural* **sons of guns**) *US, Can* a person, especially a man, and usually somebody affectionately or kindly regarded (*informal*) ■ *interj US, Can* used to express mild annoyance or surprise (*informal*)

son of God *n* **1** a superhuman, angelic being **2** a believer in the Christian faith

Son of God, Son of Man *n* Jesus Christ, considered as the Messiah

sonogram /sṓnə gram/ *n* a graphical representation of sound, especially in the three dimensions of frequency, time, and intensity

Sonoma /sə nṓmə/ town in W California. Population: 8,121 (1990).

Sonoma Valley region of W California, extending northwards from the town of Sonoma

Sonoran Desert /sə náwrən-/ desert in SW Arizona, S California, and NW Mexico. Area: 310,799 sq. km/120,000 sq. mi.

sonority /sə nórrəti/ (*plural* **-ties**) *n* **1** a sonorous quality **2** a sound, especially a rich deep sound [Early 16C. Via French *sonorité* < medieval Latin *sonoritas* < Latin *sonorus* (see SONOROUS).]

sonorous /sónnərəss/ *adj* **1 PRODUCING SOUND** producing or possessing sound **2 RESONANT** sounding with loud, deep, and clear tones **3 HAVING AN IMPRESSIVE MANNER OF SPEAKING** speaking, spoken, or expressed in a rich, full, and impressive manner [Early 17C. < Latin *sonorus* 'noisy, loud' < *sonor* 'sound' < *sonare* 'make a sound'.] —**sonorously** *adv* —**sonorousness** *n*

Sons of Freedom *npl* a religious group in W Canada involved in antigovernment terrorism during the 1950s and 1960s

sonsy /sónssi/ (**-sier, -siest**), **sonsie** (**-sier, -siest**) *adj Scotland* buxom or chubby [Mid-16C. < *sonse* 'abundance, plentifulness' < Gaelic *sonas* 'good fortune'.]

Sontag /són tag/, **Susan** (*b.* 1933) US writer

sook /sòòk/ *n* **1** *Scotland* **TOADY** an undue or blatant flatterer of somebody (*insult*) **2** *ANZ* **SOMEBODY WEAK OR TIMID** somebody considered to be weak, timid, or cowardly (*insult*) **3** *NZ* **CALF** a calf (*informal*) [Late 19C. Dialect form of SUCK.]

soon /soon/ *adv* **1 AFTER A SHORT TIME** within or after a short time ○ *She soon realized that she had made a mistake.* **2 QUICKLY** quickly or without much delay ○ *How soon will you be ready?* ○ *I'll soon see about that!* **3 EARLY** before a reasonable or the desired length of time has elapsed ○ *Do you really have to go so soon?* ○ *It's a bit soon to be thinking of marriage, isn't it?* **4 WILLINGLY** used when expressing a preference for one alternative over another or an equal willingness to accept either, and often in the comparative form 'sooner' ○ *I'd sooner stay in than go out.* ○ *I'd as soon stay in as go out.* [Old English *sōna*] ◇ **as soon as** immediately after ◇ **no sooner...than** immediately after one thing had happened, another took place ◇ **sooner or later** inevitably or certainly at some as yet unspecifiable time

soot /sòòt/ *n* a black powdery form of carbon produced when coal, wood, or oil is burned, which rises up in fine particles with the flames and smoke ■ *vt* to sprinkle or cover something with soot [Old English *sōt* 'something that sits' < Germanic, 'sit']

sooth /sooth/ *n* truth (*archaic or literary*) [Old English *sōþ* 'true' < Indo-European, 'be'] —**soothly** *adv*

soothe /sooth/ (**soothes, soothing, soothed**) *v* **1** *vt* to make pain or discomfort less severe **2** *vti* to make somebody less angry, anxious, or upset [Old English *sōþian* 'prove to be true, verify' < *sōþ* (see SOOTH). The modern meanings evolved < 'prove true' via 'support' and 'encourage'.] —**soother** *n* —**soothing** *adj* —**soothingly** *adv* —**soothingness** *n*

soothsayer /sòòth sayər/ *n* a predicter of future events —**soothsay** *vi*

sooty /sòòti/ (**-ier, -iest**) *adj* **1** covered in soot, or lined or blocked with soot **2** resembling soot in its blackness, dirtiness, or powdery texture

sooty mould *n* **1** a plant disease characterized by a black velvety fungus **2** a fungus that causes sooty mould. Genus: *Meliola* and *Capnodium.*

sooty tern *n* a medium-sized jet-black tropical seabird with white underparts. *Sterna fuscata.*

sop /sop/ *n* **1 SOMETHING GIVEN TO SATISFY DISCONTENTED PERSON** something offered as a concession or gesture to pacify somebody who is angry or discontented **2 FOOD DIPPED IN LIQUID** a piece of food dipped or soaked in liquid before it is eaten **3 OFFENSIVE TERM** an offensive term that deliberately insults a person's, especially a man's, courage (*dated insult*) ■ *vti* (**sops, sopping, sopped**) **MAKE OR BECOME SOAKING WET** to make something, or become, thoroughly wet [Old English *sopp* 'bread dipped in liquid' < *sūpan* 'swallow, taste'. Ultimately from Germanic 'take liquid'.]

sop up *vt* to soak up a liquid with something absorbent

SOP *abbr* standard operating procedure

sop. *abbr* soprano

sophism /sóffizəm/ *n* an argument or explanation that seems very clever or subtle on the surface but is actually flawed, misleading, or intended to deceive [14C. Via Old French *sophisme* < Greek *sóphisma* 'acquired skill, clever device' < *sophós* (see SOPHIST).]

sophist /sóffist/ *n* **1 sophist, Sophist** a member of a school of ancient Greek professional philosophers who were expert in and taught the skills of rhetoric, argument, and debate, but were criticized for specious reasoning **2** a deceptive person who offers clever-sounding but flawed arguments or explanations [Mid-16C. Via Latin < Greek *sophistḗs* 'master of a craft, man clever in practical affairs', also 'cheat' < *sophós* 'skilled in a craft, clever, wise'.]

sophister /sóffistər/ *n* formerly, a second-year undergraduate student at a British university [14C. Via Old French *sophistre* and Latin *sophista* < Greek *sophós* (see SOPHIST).]

sophistic /sə fístik/, **sophistical** *adj* **1** clever-sounding and plausible but based on shallow or dishonest thinking or flawed logic **2** relating to sophists [Mid-16C. Via Latin < Greek *sophistikós* < *sophós* (see SOPHIST).] —**sophistically** *adv*

sophisticate /sə físti kayt/ *v* (**-cates, -cating, -cated**) **1** *vt* **MAKE SOMEBODY MORE CULTURED OR WORLDLY** to make somebody more cultured or worldly, especially by educating out or destroying his or her naturalness, naivety, or innocence **2** *vt* **MAKE SOMETHING MORE COMPLEX** to make something more advanced or complex than before **3** *vti* **USE SOPHISTRY** to use sophistic arguments, or make reasoning or an argument sophistic **4** *vt* **CORRUPT** to make something impure, false, or adulterated ■ *n* **CULTURED OR WORLDLY PERSON** a person with cultivated tastes and refined manners who knows how the world works [14C. < medieval Latin *sophisticatus*, past participle of *sophisticare* 'deceive with words, disguise' < Greek *sophós* (see SOPHIST).] —**sophisticator** *n*

sophisticated /sə físti kaytid/ *adj* **1 KNOWLEDGEABLE AND CULTURED** knowledgeable about the ways of the world, self-confident, and not easily deceived **2 SUITABLE FOR SOPHISTICATED PEOPLE** appealing to or frequented by sophisticated people **3 ADVANCED** complex, advanced, and very up-to-date —**sophisticatedly** *adv*

sophistication *n* **1 KNOWLEDGEABLENESS AND REFINEMENT** a combination of worldly wisdom, self-confidence, and refinement in a person **2 TECHNICAL ADVANCEDNESS** technical advancedness and complexity **3 SOPHISTICATING** the process of sophisticating something or somebody

sophistry /sóffistri/ (*plural* **-tries**) *n* **1** a method of argumentation that seems clever but is actually flawed or dishonest **2** = **sophism** [14C. Via Old French *sophistrie* < Latin *sophistria* (see SOPHIST).]

Sophocles /sóffə kleez/ (496?–406? BC) Greek dramatist

sophomore /sóffə mawr/ *n US, Can* **1** a second-year student at a high school or university **2** somebody in the second year of a project or activity [Late 17C. Alteration of *sophumer* (probably influenced by Greek *sophos* 'wise' + *mōros* 'dull') < obsolete English *sophum* 'sophism', variant of SOPHISM.]

sophomoric /sóffə máwrik/ *adj* **1** showing the naive lack of judgement that accompanies immaturity **2** relating to sophomores

-sophy *suffix* wisdom, knowledge, science ○ *theosophy* [< Greek *sophia* < *sophos* 'wise']

sopor /sṓpər/ *n* an abnormally deep sleep or state of unconsciousness [Mid-17C. < Latin, 'sleep'.]

soporific /sóppə ríffik/ *adj* **1 MAKING SOMEBODY SLEEPY** causing sleep or drowsiness **2 FEELING SLEEPY** experiencing sleepiness or drowsiness **3 TEDIOUS** dull and boring ■ *n* **SLEEP-INDUCING DRUG** a drug or other substance that induces sleep —**soporifically** *adv*

sopping /sópping/, **sopping wet** *adj* thoroughly wet

soppy /sóppi/ (**-pier, -piest**) *adj* **1** excessively affectionate or sentimental (*informal*) **2** thoroughly wet —**soppily** *adv* —**soppiness** *n*

sopranino /sóppra néenō/ (*plural* **-nos**) *n* a musical instrument, usually a wind instrument, that has a pitch higher than any others in its family [Early 20C. < Italian, 'little soprano' (see SOPRANO).]

soprano /sə praánō/ (*plural* **-os** *or* **-i**) *n* **1 WOMAN OR BOY WITH HIGHEST VOICE** a woman, girl, or boy with the highest register of singing voice **2 HIGHEST SINGING VOICE** the highest register of singing voice a woman, girl, or boy can have **3 SINGING PART FOR SOPRANO VOICE** a singing part written for somebody with the highest register of voice **4 MUSICAL INSTRUMENT WITH HIGH PITCH** a musical instrument, especially a wind instrument, with the highest or second-highest pitch of instruments in its family [Early 18C. < Italian, < *sopra* 'above' < Latin *supra*.]

soprano clef *n* a C clef in which middle C is designated by the first line of the staff, formerly used for the soprano vocal line

Sopwith /sóppwìth/, **Sir Thomas** (1888–1989) British aircraft designer and yachtsman

sora /sáwrə/ *n* a small greyish-brown bird that lives in bogs and swamps, and, though common, is seldom seen. Native to: North America. *Porzana carolina.* [Early 18C. < ?]

sorb /sawrb/ *n* **1** TREES = **service tree 2 sorb, sorb apple** the berry of the service tree [Early 16C. Via French *sorbe* < Latin *sorbum* 'service berry'.] —**sorbic** *adj*

Sorb /sawrb/ *n* a member of a Slavic people living mainly in the upper Spree Valley between E Germany and SW Poland [Mid-19C. Via German *Sorbe* < Wendish *serbje*, related to, or a variant of, SERB.]

sorbet /sáwr bay, sáwrbit/ *n* a frozen dessert, usually made with fruit syrup and sometimes egg whites, whisked until smooth [Late 16C. Via French and Italian *sorbetto* < Turkish *şerbet* 'cool drink' (see SHERBET).]

sorbic acid /sáwrbik-/ *n* $C_6H_8O_2$ a white crystalline solid acid. Source: berries of mountain ash or synthetically manufactured. Use: food preservative, fungicide.

sorbitol /sáwrbi tol/ *n* $C_6H_{14}O_6$ a white crystalline sweet alcohol. Source: berries of mountain ash or synthetically manufactured. Use: sweetener, moisturizer, manufacture of Vitamin C.

Sorbonne /sawr bón/ *n* a part of the University of Paris, founded in 1253, and containing the faculties of science and literature

sorbose /sáwr bóss/ *n* a six-carbon sugar that is an isomer of fructose [Late 19C. < SORBITOL + -OSE[2].]

sorcerer /sáwrssərər/ *n* a person supposed to have magical powers [Early 16C. Via French *sorcier* < Latin *sors* (see SORT).]

sorceress /sáwrsərəs/ *n* a woman who is believed or claims to have magical powers

sorcery /sáwrssəri/ *n* the supposed use of magic —**sorcerous** *adj*

sordid /sáwrdid/ *adj* **1** demonstrating the worst aspects of human nature, e.g. immorality, selfishness, and greed **2** dirty and depressing [Late 16C. Via French *sordide* and Latin *sordidus* < *sordes* 'dirt'.] —**sordidly** *adv* —**sordidness** *n*

sordino /sawr deénō/ (*plural* **-ni** /-ni/) *n* a device used to muffle or soften the tone of a musical instrument, e.g. a mute for a stringed or brass instrument or a damper on a piano [Late 16C. < Italian, < *sordo* 'unable to speak or hear' < Latin *surdus*.]

sore /sawr/ *adj* (**sorer, sorest**) **1 PAINFUL** painful or tender because of an injury, infection, or unaccustomed exercise **2 ANNOYING** causing annoyance or embarrassment ○ *His dismissal has always been a sore point.* **3 DISTRESSING** causing great worry or distress (*literary*) ○ *Her illness was a sore trial to her husband and children.* **4 URGENT** requiring urgent action to provide relief ○ *The survivors of the flood are in sore need of help.* **5 OFFENDED** angry or irritated, especially because of something said or done by another person in the recent past (*informal*) ○ *He was still sore because I kidded him about his tie.* ■ *n* **INFECTED SPOT** a painful open skin infection or wound ■ *adv* **SORELY** sorely (*archaic*) [Old English *sār* < Germanic] —**soreness** *n*

SPELLCHECK See ***saw***

sorehead /sáwr hed/ *n US, Can* an easily offended or angered person (*informal*)

sorely /sáwrli/ *adv* to a great extent or degree ○ *I was sorely tempted to give him the money.*

sorghum /sáwrgəm/ (*plural* **-ghums** *or* **-ghum**) *n* **1** a drought-resistant cereal plant, widely cultivated in tropical and warm areas. Use: grain crop, animal feed. Genus: *Sorghum.* **2** a syrup made from the juice of some varieties of sorghum [Late 16C. Via modern Latin < Italian *sorgo* (see SORGO).]

sorgo /sáwrgō/ (*plural* **-gos**) *n* any sorghum cultivated as a source of syrup [Mid-18C. Via Italian < Vulgar Latin *syricum (granum)* 'Syrian (grain)'.]

sori plural of **sorus**

sorites /so rī́ teez/ (*plural* **-tes**) *n* an argument consisting of a series of premises arranged so that the predicate of each premise forms the subject of the next [Mid-16C. Via Latin < Greek *sōreitēs* < *sōros* 'heap'.]

Soroptimist /sə róptəmist/ *n* a member of an international organization (**Soroptimist International**) of professional women and businesswomen that promotes public service [Early 20C. Blend of Latin *soror* 'sister' and OPTIMIST.]

sororate /sórrə rayt/ *n* a custom in some societies in which a widower marries a younger sister of his deceased wife [Early 20C. < Latin *soror* 'sister'.]

sororicide /sə rórri sīd/ *n* **1** the murder of a sister **2** a killer of his or her sister [Mid-17C. < Latin *soror* 'sister' + -CIDE.] —**sororicidal** /sə rórri sīd'l/ *adj*

sorority /sə rór əti/ (*plural* **-ties**) *n* a social society for women students at an American college or university, with a name made up of Greek letters. ◊ **fraternity** *n.* 4 [Mid-16C. < medieval Latin *sororitas* < Latin *soror* 'sister'.]

sorption /sáwrpsh'n/ *n* the taking in or holding of something, either by absorption or adsorption [Early 20C. Back-formation < ABSORPTION and ADSORPTION.]

sorrel[1] /sórrəl/ (*plural* **-rels** *or* **-rel**) *n* a sharp-tasting plant of the dock family. Use: salad greens, medicines. Genus: *Rumex.* [14C. < Old French *surele* < *sur* 'sour'.]

sorrel[2] /sórrəl/ *adj* **REDDISH-BROWN** of a reddish-brown colour ■ *n* **1 BROWN WITH RED ADDED** a brown colour with a red tone **2 REDDISH-BROWN ANIMAL** a sorrel horse or other animal with a reddish-brown coat [15C. < Old French *sorel* < *sor* 'yellowish'.]

Sorrento /sə réntō/ town in S Italy, on the Bay of Naples. Population: 17,015 (1991).

sorrow /sórrō/ *n* **1 GRIEF** a feeling of deep sadness caused by a loss or misfortune **2 SADDENING BURDEN** an unfortunate event, experience, or other cause of sorrow ■ *vi* **GRIEVE** to feel or express deep sadness over something (*literary*) [Old English *sorg* < Germanic, 'care'] —**sorrower** *n* ◇ **drown your sorrows** to take alcoholic drink in order to try to forget a source of sadness or disappointment

sorrowful /sórrəf'l/ *adj* **1** feeling or expressing sorrow **2** characterized by or causing sorrow —**sorrowfully** *adv* —**sorrowfulness** *n*

sorry /sórri/ *adj* (**-rier, -riest**) **1 APOLOGETIC** feeling or expressing regret for an action that has upset or inconvenienced somebody, or for a similar future action **2 SYMPATHETIC** feeling or expressing sympathy or empathy, especially because of something that has happened ○ *I felt sorry it had to end that way.* ○ *I feel sorry for the disappointed fans who travelled all this way.* ○ *Don't start feeling sorry for yourself.* **3 PITIFUL** pitifully bad or neglected **4 VERY BAD** pathetically or contemptibly unsatisfactory ○ *a sorry excuse for a car* ■ *interj* **1 APOLOGIZING FOR** used as an apology for hurting, interrupting, or inconveniencing somebody ○ *Sorry – I didn't realize that was your foot.* **2 ASKING SOMEBODY TO REPEAT** used with an interrogative inflexion to ask somebody to repeat something (*informal*) **3 CORRECTING A REMARK** used to introduce a correction in speech ○ *The company employs ten thousand – sorry, twelve thousand workers nationwide.* [Old English *sārig* < *sār* (see SORE)] —**sorrily** *adv* —**sorriness** *n* ◇ **say sorry** to apologize to somebody

ϟ **sort** /sawrt/ *n* **1 CATEGORY** a category of persons or things with shared attributes, to which somebody or something can be assigned ○ *What sort of instrument is that?* **2 PARTICULAR TYPE** a particular type of person (*informal*) ○ *She'll help – she's a good sort.* **3 SIMILAR THING** something similar to the thing specified ○ *It's a sort of play with dancing.* **4 SORTING OF DATA** a process of arranging data in a set order **5 LETTER OR SYMBOL** a particular character in a font of type (*often plural*) **6 MANNER** a manner of doing something (*archaic*) ■ *vt* **1 PUT IN CATEGORIES** to place people or things in categories according to shared attributes ○ *clothes sorted into piles* **2 PUT IN SEQUENCE** to arrange things in a set order, especially automatically as some computer programs do with data **3** = **sort out** *v.* 3 [14C. Via French *sorte* < Latin *sors* 'lot, fortune'.] —**sortable** *adj* —**sorter** *n* ◇ **of a sort, of sorts** used to indicate that something is not very good ○ *We had a meal of sorts at the airport.* ◇ **out of sorts 1** slightly unwell **2** not in a very good mood ◇ ⚠ **sort of** rather (*informal*) ○ *This place is sort of strange.*

SYNONYMS See ***type.***

USAGE Overuse of the expression ***sort of*** is not only vague but unduly informal. Avoid usages like this in formal writing: *This character is sort of dishonest, or so the author lets us believe. It was a sort of tragicomedy.* Substitute more formal, more precise expressions, as in: *This character is rather dishonest. It was a tragicomedy of sorts.*

sort out *vt* **1 RESOLVE EFFECTIVELY** to deal effectively with a problem ○ *I think we've sorted out our difficulties with the printer.* **2 REACH CONCLUSION** to think and come to a conclusion about a problem or difficulty **3 PUT IN ORDER** to put something into order, or disentangle something ○ *It took weeks to sort out the library.* **4 SEPARATE** to separate something from the mixture it exists in, or from another group of things **5 PUNISH** to deal with or punish somebody who has behaved badly (*informal*) ○ *Don't worry about him – I'll soon sort him out.*

ϟ **sortation** /sawr táysh'n/ *n* the process of sorting items into categories or into a set order, especially when done by machine or computer

sort code *n* a number that uniquely identifies a financial institution so that banking transactions can be sent to it

sorted /sáwrtid/ *adj* **1 PUT RIGHT** put to rights, repaired, or dealt with satisfactorily (*informal*) **2 WELL-ADJUSTED** socially or emotionally well-adjusted (*slang*) **3 WELL PREPARED** well prepared for something or well provided with something, especially illegal drugs (*slang*)

sortie /sáwrti/ *n* **1 ATTACK ON AN ENEMY** an attack made by a small military force into enemy territory **2 AIRCRAFT MISSION** a mission flown by a combat aircraft **3 SHORT TRIP** a brief trip away from home, especially to an unfamiliar place (*humorous*) **4 PEOPLE ON SORTIE** the personnel engaged in a military sortie ■ *vi* (**-ties, -tieing, -tied**) **MAKE A SORTIE** to make a sortie against an enemy position [Late 17C. < French, past participle of *sortir* 'go out' < ?]

sortilege /sáwrtilij/ *n* **1** the supposed foretelling of the future by drawing lots **2** the supposed practice of magic or sorcery [14C. Via French *sortilège* < Latin *sortilegus* 'prophetic, soothsayer' < *sors* (see SORT) + *legere* 'read'.]

sorting office *n* a place where letters and packages for delivery are sorted according to their destinations

sorus /sáwrəss/ (*plural* **-ri** /-rī/) *n* **1** a cluster of spore cases on the underside of some fern fronds **2** a spore-producing organ in some algae, fungi, and lichens [Mid-19C. Via modern Latin < Greek *sōros* 'heap'.]

SOS *n* **1 DISTRESS SIGNAL** an international radio signal that ships or aircraft in serious distress can use to call for help **2 CALL FOR HELP** a call or signal requesting help **3 BROADCAST TO CONTACT SOMEBODY URGENTLY** a radio broadcast attempting to contact somebody, whose whereabouts are unknown, in an emergency

Sosigenes of Alexandria /so síjjə neez-/ (*fl.* 50 BC) Greek astronomer

so-so *adj* neither very good nor very bad (*informal*) ○ *The food was so-so, but the atmosphere was wonderful.* ■ *adv* neither very well nor very badly (*informal*) ○ *feeling so-so*

sostenuto /sóstə noótō/ *adv* with notes sustained to or beyond the notated value (*musical direction*) ■ *n* (*plural* **sostenutos**) a piece of music, or a section of a piece, played sostenuto [Mid-18C. < Italian, past participle of *sostinere* 'sustain' < Latin *sustinere*.] —**sostenuto** *adj*

sot /sot/ *n* an offensive term for somebody who habitually drinks alcohol to excess (*literary*) [Pre-12C. Via Old French, 'fool' < medieval Latin *sottus*.]

soteriology /sō teéri óllәji/ *n* the Christian doctrine that salvation has been brought about by Jesus Christ [Mid-18C. < Greek *sōtēria* 'salvation' + -LOGY.] —**soteriologic** /sō teéri ə lójjik/ *adj*

Sothic cycle *n* a cycle of 1460 Sothic years in the ancient Egyptian calendar [Early 19C. *Sothic* < Greek *Sōthis*, the star Sirius, used in calendar calculations.]

Sothic year /sṓthik-/ *n* a year of $365\frac{1}{4}$ days in the ancient Egyptian calendar, based on the first appearance of the dog star (**Sirius**) above the horizon [See SOTHIC CYCLE]

Sotho /soó too/ (*plural* **-tho** *or* **-thos**) *n* **1** a member of a large group of peoples who live in southern Africa, mainly in Botswana, Lesotho, and South Africa **2** the

Bantu language of the Sotho people [< stem of BASOTHO and SESOTHO] —**Sotho** *adj*

sotol /sṓtōl/ *n* **1** a prickly-leaved desert plant. Flowers: whitish, in dense clusters. Native to: SW United States, Mexico. Genus: *Dasylirion*. **2** an alcoholic drink made from the sap of the sotol plant [Late 19C. Via American Spanish *sotole* < Nahuatl *tzotolli*.]

sottish /sóttish/ *adj* **1** in the habit of drinking far too much alcohol **2** showing the effects of having drunk too much alcohol

sotto voce /sóttō vṓchi/ *adv* in a soft voice, so as not to be overheard [Mid-18C. < Italian, 'under (the) voice'.] —**sotto voce** *adj*

sou /soo/ *n* **1** a French coin no longer in use, worth only a small amount **2** the least amount of money (*informal; in negatives*) ○ *I haven't a sou.* [15C. < French, back-formation < Old French *sous*, the plural of *sout* 'sou' < Latin *solidus* (see SOLIDUS).]

soubrette /soo brét/ *n* **1** MAIDSERVANT IN COMEDY a pretty, flirtatious woman's role in a comedy, especially one in which she plays a lady's maid involved in romantic intrigues **2** ACTOR PLAYING SOUBRETTE an actor who often plays soubrettes **3** DISMISSIVE TERM a dismissive term for a young woman whose behaviour is interpreted as flirtatious (*dated*) [Mid-18C. Via French, 'maid', and Provençal *soubreto* 'coy' < Latin *superare* 'surpass' < *super* 'above'.]

soubriquet *n* = **sobriquet**

~~**souce**~~ incorrect spelling of **source**

souchong /soo chóng/ *n* black China tea [Mid-18C. < Cantonese *síu-chúng* 'small kind'.]

soucouyant /sóokoo yaan/ *n Carib* a person, usually a woman, who according to legend sucks people's blood and can shed her skin, change into a ball of fire, and fly around by night [Mid-20C. < a West Indian creole < ?]

souffle /sóof'l/ *n* a soft blowing sound inside somebody's chest, heard through a stethoscope and caused by blood flowing through blood vessels [Late 19C. < French, 'breath' < *souffler* (see SOUFFLÉ).]

soufflé /sóof lay/ *n* a sweet or savoury open-textured dish that has been made light by adding whisked egg whites [Early 19C. < French, past participle of *souffler* 'blow, to puff up' < Latin *sufflare*.] —**soufflé** *adj*

Soufriere Hills Volcano /soofri áir-/ volcano on the island of Montserrat, in the Caribbean Sea. Height: 915 m/3,002 ft.

sough /sow/ *vi* to make a soft rustling, sighing, or murmuring sound, like the wind in trees (*archaic or literary*) ■ *n* a sound like that made by a gentle wind through trees (*archaic or literary*) [Old English *swōgan* < Germanic]

sought past tense, past participle of **seek**

sought-after /sáwt aaftər/ *adj* in high demand because scarce ○ *Blue diamonds are among the most sought-after gems.*

souk /sook/, **suq** *n* an open-air market in North Africa or the Middle East [Early 19C. < Arabic *sūq*.]

soukous /sóo kooss/ *n* a style of dance music originally from the Congo, combining guitar, drums, and vocals [Late 20C. Probably via Lingala < French *secouer* 'shake'.]

soul /sōl/ *n* **1** NONPHYSICAL ASPECT OF PERSON the complex of human attributes that manifests as consciousness, thought, feeling, and will, regarded as distinct from the physical body **2** SPIRIT SURVIVING DEATH in some systems of religious belief, the spiritual part of a human being that is believed to continue to exist after the body dies **3** FEELINGS a person's emotional and moral nature, where the most private thoughts and feelings are hidden ○ *Her soul was in turmoil.* **4** SPIRITUAL DEPTH evidence of spiritual or emotional depth and sensitivity, either in a person or in something created by a person ○ *Though technically perfect, the drawing lacked soul.* **5** ESSENCE the deepest and truest nature of people or a nation, or what gives somebody or something a distinctive character ○ *In my travels I hoped to discover the soul of the Russian people.* **6** TYPE OF PERSON somebody of a particular type, especially one regarded sympathetically or with familiarity ○ *Poor soul! What will he do now?* **7** ANYONE anyone at all (*in negatives*) ○ *You have to promise not to tell a soul.* **8** INDIVIDUAL an individual person, especially when thought of as making up the number of a particular group (*usually plural*) ○ *a country of some 10 million souls* **9** PERFECT EXAMPLE a good example, or personification, of a positive quality ○ *The hotel manager was the soul of discretion.* **10** SOMEBODY ESSENTIAL a leader or the most influential person in a group or movement **11** AFRICAN AMERICAN SPIRIT the quality that characterizes African American culture, especially as manifested in a person's natural sympathies and in social customs, speech, and music **12** MUSIC = **soul music** [Old English *sāwol* < Germanic] ◇ **sell your soul** to abandon your principles in order to obtain wealth or success

SPELLCHECK See *sole*.

Soul /sōl/ *n* the name for God in Christian Science

soul-destroying *adj* extremely boring, repetitive, or unfulfilling

soul food *n* the traditional foods of African Americans of the American South

soulful /sṓlf'l/ *adj* deeply or sincerely emotional —**soulfully** *adv* —**soulfulness** *n*

soulless /sṓl ləss/ *adj* **1** lacking warmth, sensitivity, or feeling ○ *soulless bureaucrats* **2** lacking anything that might stimulate or engage the feelings —**soullessly** *adv* —**soullessness** *n*

soul mate *n* somebody with whom somebody else naturally shares deep feelings and attitudes

soul music *n* a style of African American popular music with a strong emotional quality, related to gospel music and rhythm and blues

soul-searching *n* a thorough examination of personal thoughts and feelings, especially when faced with a difficult problem

Soult /soolt/, **Nicolas Jean de Dieu** (1769–1851) French marshal and government official

sound[1] /sownd/ *n* **1** SOMETHING AUDIBLE something that can be heard ○ *not a sound in the whole house* ○ *the sound of gunfire* **2** VIBRATIONS SENSED BY EAR vibrations travelling through air, water, or some other medium, especially those within the range of frequencies that can be perceived by the human ear **3** SENSATION OF VIBRATIONS the sensation produced in the ear by vibrations travelling through air, water, or some other medium **4** REPRODUCED MUSIC OR SPEECH the music, speech, or other sounds heard through an electronic device such as a television, radio, or loudspeaker, especially with regard to volume or quality ○ *Please turn down the sound.* **5** RECORDING MUSIC OR SPEECH the recording, editing, and replaying of music, speech, or sound effects in the broadcast or entertainment industry **6** IMPLICATION an impression of somebody or something formed from limited but significant information, especially information lately received ○ *From the sound of it she's finally found a job she really likes.* **7** NOISE meaningless noise ○ *I didn't care for the poetry – it had more sound than sense.* **8** EARSHOT the distance or area within which something can be heard ○ *Our house was within the sound of the church bells.* **9** ELEMENT OF SPEECH AS HEARD a basic element of speech formed by the vocal tract and interpreted through the ear, or a combination of such sounds **10** TYPE OF MUSIC the distinctive quality that identifies bands or music from a particular place, area, or studio, or belonging to a particular movement or style ■ **sounds** *npl* MUSIC music, especially music that is not classical, such as pop, jazz, or rock (*informal*) ■ *v* **1** *vi* SEEM to give a particular impression when mentioned or described ○ *The meal sounded awful.* **2** *vi* INDICATE CONDITION to give a particular impression about physical or mental condition via speech or writing ○ *He sounded exhausted when I talked to him on the phone.* **3** *vi* HAVE PARTICULAR QUALITY WHEN HEARD to give a particular impression to a hearer about the quality of the noise or the identity of the source of the noise ○ *That sounds like the postman.* **4** *vti* MAKE NOISE to make a particular noise so as to be heard, or make something produce such a noise ○ *Somewhere down the corridor, an alarm sounded.* **5** *vt* ANNOUNCE to spread the news of or signal something by making a noise, or produce a similar effect by saying something ○ *She sounded a note of caution about the likely result of the election.* **6** *vt* ARTICULATE to pronounce a specific letter or sound, especially in a context in which it might be silent ○ *You don't sound the 'p' in 'psychic'.* **7** *vt* TEST BODILY CONDITION BY CAUSING SOUND to make an organ of the body emit a sound for testing or diagnostic purposes [13C. Via Anglo-Norman *soun* and French *son* < Latin *sonus*.]

sound off *vi* **1** to express strong feelings through speech, or complain loudly about something (*informal*) ○ *always sounding off about high property taxes* **2** to chant or count in turn while marching

sound out *vt* to find out somebody's opinions about something before becoming committed to a course of action

sound[2] /sownd/ *adj* **1** NOT DAMAGED without any serious damage or decay **2** HEALTHY free from injury, disease, or illness **3** SENSIBLE based on good sense and valid reasoning ○ *a sound argument* **4** COMPLETELY ACCEPTABLE worthy of approval, especially as agreeing with traditional views or conforming to conventional behaviour **5** DEEP AND PEACEFUL unbroken by waking and untroubled by dreams or discomfort ○ *She had a sound night's sleep.* **6** COMPLETE including all necessary aspects and details ○ *sound knowledge of the subject* **7** THOROUGH painful and thorough **8** WITH LITTLE FINANCIAL RISK financially secure and likely to make money **9** VALID WITH TRUE PREMISES having a true conclusion that follows from true premises **10** LEGALLY VALID legally valid ■ *adv* PEACEFULLY in a deep and peaceful way ○ *sound asleep* [12C. Shortening of Old English *gesund*.] —**soundly** *adv* —**soundness** *n*

SYNONYMS See *valid*.

sound[3] /sownd/ *v* **1** *vti* MEASURE DEPTH to measure the depth of water using a weighted line or sonar **2** *vi* DIVE DOWN to dive suddenly and swiftly downwards **3** *vt* EXAMINE WITH PROBE to use a surgical probe to examine a bodily cavity or passage, e.g. the bladder, or to dilate an abnormal constriction ■ *n* SURGICAL PROBE a surgical probe used to sound bodily cavities [14C. Via French *sonder* < Vulgar Latin *subundare* < Latin *sub* 'under' + *unda* 'wave'.] —**sounder** *n*

sound[4] /sownd/ *n* **1** WIDE CHANNEL a broad channel between two large bodies of water, or between an island and the mainland **2** OCEAN INLET a long wide arm of the sea **3** AIR BLADDER a fish's air bladder [Old English *sund* < Germanic]

sound-alike *n* a performer whose voice or musical style closely resembles that of a particular well-known performer

sound barrier *n* a sudden increase in the force of air opposing an aircraft or other moving body when it approaches the speed of sound, producing a sonic boom

sound bite *n* a very short comment or phrase intended or suitable for broadcasting in a news programme, especially one by a politician ○ *There's no substance to their policy – it's all sound bites.*

soundboard /sównd bawrd/, **sounding board** *n* a thin sheet of wood placed under or above the strings of a musical instrument to increase resonance

sound bow *n* the thick part of a bell, where the clapper strikes

soundbox /sównd boks/ *n* the hollow chamber in a stringed instrument that increases its resonance

ϟ**sound card** *n* a computer circuit board that allows a personal computer to receive sound in digital form and reproduce it through speakers

sound effect *n* a recording or imitation of a particular sound used in a film, radio or television programme, play, or other theatrical performance ■ **sound effects** *npl* all the sounds in a film or broadcast production other than dialogue and music (*hyphenated when used before a noun*)

sound hole *n* an opening near the centre of a hollow stringed instrument that increases resonance

sounding[1] /sównding/ *n* **1** DEPTH MEASUREMENT a measurement of the depth of water, taken using sonar or a weighted line **2** ATMOSPHERIC MEASUREMENT a measurement of the conditions in the atmosphere at a specific altitude ■ **soundings** *npl* **1** PRELIMINARY INQUIRY INTO OPINION a sampling of the views of a group of people taken before somebody becomes committed to a course of action ○ *taking soundings about the popularity of the council's plans* **2** WATER WHERE SOUNDINGS ARE TAKEN a place where the water is shallow enough for a sounding line to be used to determine its depth

sounding[2] /sównding/ *adj* having an impressive or resonant sound (*literary*) —**soundingly** *adv*

sounding board *n* **1** MUSIC = **soundboard** **2** a person or group who gives feedback on preliminary ideas before they are considered for further development **3** a rooflike structure built above a pulpit or platform to direct the speaker's voice to the audience

sounding line *n* a weighted line with measurements marked on it, used for determining the depth of water

soundless /sówndləss/ *adj* not making any noise — **soundlessly** *adv* —**soundlessness** *n*

sound mixer *n* a person or machine that combines or balances sounds for a recording, broadcast, or film soundtrack

soundpost /sównd pōst/ *n* a small piece of wood inside the body of a stringed instrument that supports the bridge and transmits the vibrations to the back

soundproof /sównd proof/ *adj* constructed so that no sound can enter or escape ■ *vt* to line or seal a room so that no sound can enter or escape

sound ranging *n* a method of locating the source of a sound by measuring the travel time of sound waves to a microphone at a fixed position

sound shift *n* a systematic change over time in the pronunciation of a set of sounds in a language

sound spectrograph *n* an electronic instrument that makes a graphic representation of sound qualities

sound stage *n* a large room or studio, usually soundproof, where film scenes are shot

sound system *n* electronic equipment for amplifying sound produced by recording, broadcasting, or live at public gatherings

soundtrack /sównd trak/ *n* 1 **SOUND RECORDING FOR A FILM** the recorded music, dialogue, and sound effects in a film or video production 2 **STRIP CARRYING FILM SOUND** a thin strip at the edge of a film reel or video tape on which sound or the soundtrack is recorded 3 **MUSIC FROM FILM** a commercially released recording of music that has been used in a particular film

sound truck *n US* = **loudspeaker van**

sound wave *n* an audible pressure wave caused by a disturbance in water or air and carried forward in a ripple effect

Souness /sóonəss/, **Graeme** (*b.* 1953) Scottish footballer and team manager

soup /soop/ *n* 1 **LIQUID FOOD** a liquid food made by cooking meat, fish, vegetables, and other ingredients in water, milk, or stock 2 **SOMETHING THICK AND SWIRLING** something with the consistency or appearance of soup, especially a swirling liquid or dense fog ○ *the primordial soup of hydrogen, oxygen, and other gases* 3 **PHOTOGRAPHIC CHEMICALS** chemicals for developing photographs (*slang*) [Mid-17C. Via French *soupe* < late Latin *suppa* < assumed *suppare* 'soak'.] ◇ **in the soup** in difficulties or trouble (*informal*)
soup up *vt* to make changes to a car, motorcycle, engine, or similar machine in order to make it more powerful (*informal*) [< the use of SOUP for 'a drug injected into a horse to increase its speed']

soupçon /sóop son/ *n* a very small amount of something [Mid-18C. Via French, 'suspicion' < Latin *suspicion-* (see SUSPICION).]

soup du jour /sóop dyōō zhóor/ (*plural* **soups du jour** /sóop dyōō zhóor/) *n* a soup featured by a restaurant on a particular day [Mid-20C. < French 'soup of the day'.]

soup kitchen *n* a place that serves free meals to people who have no money

soupspoon /sóop spoon/ *n* a large spoon for eating soup

soupy /sóopi/ (**-ier, -iest**) *adj* 1 **LIKE SOUP** like soup in appearance or consistency 2 **DAMP OR FOGGY** unpleasantly damp or foggy (*informal*) 3 **SENTIMENTAL** highly sentimental (*informal*)

sour /sowr/ *adj* 1 **SHARP-TASTING** having a tart or sharp taste that is acidic though not necessarily unpleasant, like the taste of vinegar, lemons, or unripe apples 2 **BAD THROUGH FERMENTATION** unpleasantly rancid in taste or smell because of fermentation 3 **DISSATISFIED** characterized by ill temper or feelings of bitterness or dissatisfaction ○ *a sour look* 4 **UNFRIENDLY** unpleasant, unfriendly, or ill-disposed, having previously been harmonious, friendly, or approving 5 **UNPLEASANT** causing distaste or discomfort 6 **LACKING LIME** of soil, acidic because of a shortage of lime, and so unfavourable to crops 7 **SULPHUROUS AND ACIDIC** describes crude oil or gas that is foul-smelling, toxic, and acidic because of excessive levels of sulphur compounds ■ *vti* 1 **BECOME OR MAKE SOMETHING SOUR** to become, or make something become, sour in taste, smell, or composition 2 **BECOME OR MAKE SOMEBODY DISSATISFIED** to become, or make somebody become, ill-tempered, embittered, or dissatisfied 3 **BECOME OR MAKE SOMEBODY UNFRIENDLY** to become, or make somebody or something become, unpleasant, unfriendly, or ill-disposed towards somebody or something after having been previously harmonious, friendly, or approving ○ *A breach of diplomacy soured relations between the countries.* ■ *n* 1 *US* **COCKTAIL WITH LEMON OR LIME** a cocktail made with whisky, lemon or lime juice, and often sugar 2 **SOMETHING SOUR OR ACID** something sour or acid, especially an acid solution used in bleaching clothes or in curing skins [Old English *sūr* < Germanic] —**sourly** *adv* —**sourness** *n*

source /sawrss/ *n* 1 **ORIGIN** the place where something begins, the thing from which something is derived, or the person or group that initiated or created something 2 **PROVIDER OF INFORMATION** a person, organization, book, or other text that supplies information or evidence ○ *a reliable source* 3 **WORK ON WHICH ANOTHER IS BASED** a creation such as a story or work of art that forms the basis of or inspiration for a later work 4 **BEGINNING OF RIVER** the spring or fountain from which a river or stream first issues from the ground, or the area around this 5 **ELECTRODE REGION** a region of a transistor from which charge carriers flow ■ *v* (**sources, sourcing, sourced**) 1 *vt* **SPECIFY SOURCES OF SOMETHING WRITTEN** to list the people or materials used in researching a written work 2 *vti* **LOCATE SOMETHING FOR USE** to get or locate parts, materials, or information from elsewhere [14C. Via Old French *sourse* 'spring' < Latin *surgere* 'rise'.]

SYNONYMS See ***origin***.

source book *n* a document or collection of documents that is the main source of information about a subject of study

ϟ **source code** *n* computer code written in a recognized programming language that can be converted into machine code. ◊ **object code**

source language *n* the language from which a translation is made

sour cherry *n* 1 a sharp-tasting red or blackish fruit used mainly in cooking and preserves 2 a shrub or small tree that produces sour cherries. Native to: Europe, Asia. *Prunus cerasus*.

sour cream *n* a smooth thick cream that has been soured artificially, used in cooking and baking and as a topping

sourdine /soor déen/ *n* 1 a reed instrument with a soft tone similar to a bassoon 2 *MUSIC* = **sordino** 3 a stop on an organ that produces a low muted tone [Early 17C. Via French < Italian *sordina*, feminine form of *sordino* (see SORDINO).]

sourdough /sówr dō/ *n* 1 fermenting dough used as a leavening agent in making bread 2 bread made with sourdough

sour grapes *n* the scornful denial that something is attractive or desirable because it is unobtainable [In allusion to Aesop's fable *The Fox and the Grapes* where the fox disparages some grapes as sour when he cannot reach them]

sour mash *n* 1 a grain mash that is a mixture of new and old batches, used in distilling some kinds of whisky 2 whisky distilled using sour mash

sourpuss /sówr pòoss/ *n* a gloomy or bad-tempered person (*informal*)

soursop /sówr sop/ (*plural* **-sops** *or* **-sop**) *n* 1 a spiny fruit with a tart fibrous pulp 2 a tree with spicy fragrant leaves that produces soursops. Native to: tropical America. *Annona muricata*.

sourwood /sówər wòod/ (*plural* **-woods** *or* **-wood**) *n* a tree with thick bark, small white flowers, and sour-tasting leaves. Native to: E United States. *Oxydendrum arboreum*.

Sousa /sóozə/, **John Philip** (1854–1932) US military bandmaster and composer

sousaphone /sóozə fōn/ *n* a large brass instrument with a flaring bell, resembling a tuba [Early 20C. After John Philip SOUSA.] —**sousaphonist** *n*

sous-chef /sóo-/ *n* a head chef's assistant and deputy [Late 17C. *Sous* via French, 'under' < Latin *subtus*.]

souse /sowss/ *v* (**souses, sousing, soused**) 1 *vt* **PICKLE** to steep something in vinegar or brine in order to preserve it (*often passive*) 2 *vti* **PLUNGE INTO LIQUID** to plunge, or plunge something, into a liquid 3 *vti* **SOAK** to make something soaking wet, or become soaking wet 4 *vt* **MAKE SOMEBODY INTOXICATED** to make somebody extremely intoxicated (*slang; usually passive*) ■ *n* 1 **LIQUID USED IN PICKLING** the brine or vinegar used in pickling 2 **PICKLED FOOD** pickled food, especially pork trimmings 3 *Carib* **BROTH MADE WITH PORK** a broth made with a pig's snout, trotters, and sometimes tail, boiled with vegetables and seasonings 4 **HABITUAL ALCOHOL DRINKER** a drunkard (*slang*) 5 **BINGE** a bout of heavy drinking (*dated*) [14C. < Old French *sous*.]

souslik *n ZOOL* = **suslik**

Sousse /sooss/ city and port in east-central Tunisia. Population: 125,000 (1994).

soutache /soo tásh/ *n* a narrow ornamental braid in a herringbone pattern, used for trimming garments [Mid-19C. Via French < Hungarian *sujtás*.]

soutane /soo taán, -tán/ *n* a priest's robe or cassock, especially one with buttons down the front [Mid-19C. Via French < Italian *sottana* < *sotto* 'below' < Latin *subtus*.]

souterrain /sóotə rayn/ *n* an ancient underground room or passage [Mid-18C. < French, 'underground'.]

south /sowth/ *n* 1 **DIRECTION TO RIGHT FACING RISING SUN** the direction that lies directly to the right of somebody facing the rising sun or that is located towards the bottom of a conventional map of the world. See table at **compass** 2 **COMPASS POINT OPPOSITE NORTH** the compass point that lies directly opposite north 3 **south, South AREA IN SOUTH** the part of an area, country, or region that is situated in or towards the south 4 **RIGHT-HAND SIDE OF CHURCH** the right side of a church as you face the altar from the nave 5 **POSITION EQUIVALENT TO SOUTH** the position equivalent to south in any diagram consisting of four points at 90-degree intervals ■ *adj* 1 **IN SOUTH** situated in, facing, or coming from the south of a place, region, or country 2 **BLOWING FROM SOUTH** blowing from the south (*refers to winds*) ■ *adv* **TOWARDS SOUTH** in or towards the south [Old English *sūþ* < Germanic]

South /sowth/ *n* 1 the southern region of England, roughly south of the River Severn and the Wash 2 the nations of the world with less industrialized economies

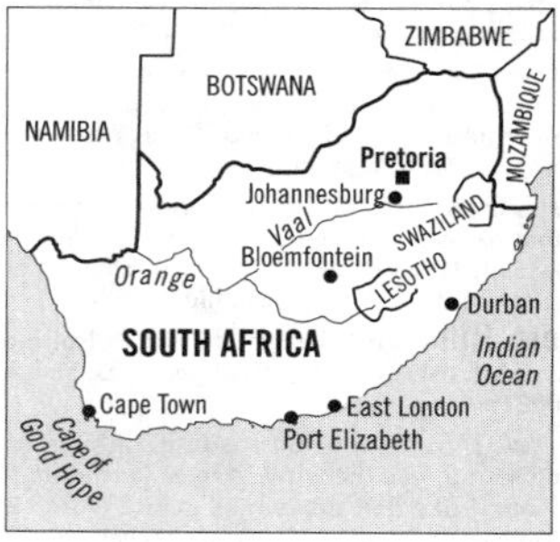

South Africa

South Africa republic in southern Africa. Capital: Pretoria. Population: 42,327,458 (1997). Area: 1,224,691 sq. km/472,731 sq. mi. —**South African** *n, adj*

South African Dutch *n LANG* = **Cape Dutch** *n.* 3 (*not used in South Africa*)

South African English *n* a variety of English spoken in South Africa

South America fourth largest continent in the world, lying between the Atlantic and Pacific oceans southeast of North America and stretching from the isthmus of Panama southwards to Cape Horn. Population: 317,846,000 (1996). Area: 17,819,100 sq. km/6,880,000 sq. mi. —**South American** *adj, n*

South American trypanosomiasis *n MED* = **Chagas' disease**

Southampton /sow thámptən, sowth hámptən/ port in S England. Population: 213,400 (1995).

South Asia region comprising the countries of Bangladesh, Bhutan, India, the Maldives, Nepal, Pakistan, and Sri Lanka

South Asian English *n* a variety of English spoken in South Asia

South Australia state in south-central Australia. Capital: Adelaide. Population: 1,474,000 (1996). Area: 984,377 sq. km/380,070 sq. mi. —**South Australian** *n, adj*

South Ayrshire council area in the former Strathclyde Region of west central Scotland. The administrative centre is Ayr. Population: 14,247 (1997). Area: 1,234 sq. km/766 sq. mi.

South Bend city in N Indiana. Population: 99,417 (1998 estimate).

southbound /sówth bownd/ *adj* leading, going, or travelling towards the south

south by east *n* the direction or compass point midway between south and south-southeast —**south by east** *adj, adv*

south by west *n* the direction or compass point midway between south and south-southwest —**south by west** *adj, adv*

South Carolina state of the SE United States, bordering the Atlantic Ocean. Capital: Columbia. Population: 3,760,181 (1997). Area: 80,779 sq. km/31,189 sq. mi. —**South Carolinian** *n, adj*

South China Sea part of the China Sea, bounded by SE China, Vietnam, Malaysia, and the Philippines. Area: 2,319,086 sq. km/895,400 sq. mi.

South Dakota state of the north-central United States. Capital: Pierre. Population: 737,973 (1997). Area: 199,742 sq. km/77,121 sq. mi. —**South Dakotan** *n, adj*

Southdown /sówth down/ *n* a breed of small-to-medium hornless English sheep with short dense wool, usually kept for mutton [Late 18C. After the SOUTH DOWNS.]

South Downs chalk ridge extending along the south coast of England

southeast /sówth eést/ *n* 1 COMPASS POINT BETWEEN SOUTH AND EAST the direction or compass point midway between south and east. See table at **compass 2 southeast, Southeast AREA IN THE SOUTHEAST** the part of an area, region, or country that is situated in or towards the southeast ■ *adj* 1 **southeast, Southeast IN THE SOUTHEAST** situated in, facing, or lying towards the southeast of a region, place, or country 2 FROM THE SOUTHEAST blowing from the southeast (*refers to winds*) ■ *adv* TOWARDS THE SOUTHEAST in or towards the southeast

Southeast Asia region comprising the countries of Brunei, Cambodia, Indonesia, Laos, Malaysia, Myanmar, the Philippines, Singapore, Thailand, and Vietnam —**Southeast Asian** *n, adj*

Southeast Asia Treaty Organization *n* a former alliance of countries for economic cooperation and defence against communism in Southeast Asia and the South Pacific, formed in 1954 and disbanded in 1977

southeast by east *n* the direction or compass point midway between southeast and east-southeast

southeast by south *n* the direction or compass point midway between southeast and south-southeast

southeaster /sówth eéstər/ *n* a storm or wind that blows from the southeast

southeasterly /sówth eéstərli/ *adj* 1 IN THE SOUTHEAST situated in or towards the southeast 2 BLOWING FROM THE SOUTHEAST blowing from the southeast (*refers to winds*) ■ *n* (*plural* -**lies**) WIND FROM THE SOUTHEAST a wind blowing from the southeast

southeastern /sówth eéstərn/ *adj* 1 IN THE SOUTHEAST situated in the southeast of a region or country 2 FACING SOUTHEAST situated in or facing the southeast 3 **southeastern, Southeastern OF THE SOUTHEAST** native to the southeast of a region or country

southeastward /sówth eéstwərd/ *adj* towards or in the southeast ■ *n* a direction towards or a point in the southeast —**southeastward** *adv* —**southeastwardly** *adv,* **adj** —**southeastwards** *adv*

Southend-on-Sea /sówth end on seé/ town in E England, on the Thames estuary. Population: 172,300 (1996).

souther /sówthər/ *n* a strong wind that blows from the south

southerly /súthərli/ *adj* 1 IN THE SOUTH situated in or towards the south 2 BLOWING FROM THE SOUTH blowing from the south (*refers to winds*) ■ *n* (*plural* -**lies**) WIND FROM THE SOUTH a wind blowing from the south

southern /súthərn/ *adj* 1 IN THE SOUTH situated in the south of a region or country 2 SOUTH OF EQUATOR lying south of the equator or south of the celestial equator 3 FACING SOUTH situated in or facing the south 4 **southern, Southern OF THE SOUTH** native to the south of a region or country 5 FROM THE SOUTH blowing from the south (*refers to winds*)

Southern /súthərn/, **E. M.** (*b.* 1938) British biochemist. Full name **Edwin Mallor Southern**

Southern Alps mountain range on the South Island, New Zealand. Highest peak: Mount Cook 3,754 m/12,316 ft.

Southern blot *n* a technique for transferring DNA restriction fragments onto a membrane filter, enabling them to be identified with a gene probe [Late 20C. After E. M. SOUTHERN.]

Southern Cross *n* a constellation of the southern hemisphere containing four bright stars forming a cross, the smallest of the constellations. See illustration at **constellation**

southerner /súthərnər/ *n* a person who comes from the southern part of a country or region

southern hemisphere *n* 1 the half of the earth that is south of the equator 2 the southern half of an imaginary sphere that contains the universe and is divided horizontally by the celestial equator

Southernism /súthərnizəm/ *n* 1 an expression or pronunciation that is characteristic of the S United States or S England 2 an attitude or custom that is characteristic of the South, especially in the United States

southernmost /súthərnmōst/ *adj* situated farthest south

Southern Paiute, Southern Piute *n* 1 a member of a Native North American people who lived in Utah, Nevada, Arizona, and California, and now live in Utah 2 the Uto-Aztecan language of the Southern Paiute people —**Southern Paiute** *adj*

Southern Rhodesia former name for **Zimbabwe**

southernwood /súthərn wóod/ (*plural* -**woods** or -**wood**) *n* an ornamental shrub with fragrant grey bitter-tasting leaves. Native to: Europe. *Artemisia abrotanum*.

South Georgia uninhabited island in the South Atlantic Ocean, a dependency of the United Kingdom. Area: 3,755 sq. km/1,450 sq. mi.

South Holland province in the west-central Netherlands. Capital: The Hague. Population: 3,313,193 (1994). Area: 3,333 sq. km/1,287 sq. mi.

southing /sówthing/ *n* 1 how far south a point is from a reference latitude 2 the distance covered as a ship sails towards the south

South Island largest island of New Zealand, southwest of the North Island in the SW Pacific Ocean. Population: 931,566 (1996). Area: 151,215 sq. km/58,368 sq. mi.

South Korea country in NE Asia, occupying the S Korean Peninsula. Capital: Seoul. Population: 45,948,811 (1997). Area: 99,268 sq. km/38,328 sq. mi. —**South Korean** *n, adj*

Southland /sówthlənd/ region of the south of the South Island, New Zealand. Capital: Invercargill. Population: 100,758 (1996). Area: 53,132 sq. km/20,514 sq. mi.

southpaw /sówth paw/ *n* a left-handed person, especially a boxer who leads with the left hand (*informal*) [Late 19C. Originally used of left-handed baseball players, from the pitcher's orientation on the mound (since baseball diamonds are traditionally oriented to the same points of the compass).]

South Pole *n* 1 the southern end of the Earth's axis at the latitude of 90° S 2 the point where the southern end of the Earth's axis intersects the celestial sphere

Southport /sówth pawrt/ town in NW England. Population: 88,596 (1991).

Southron /súthrən/ *adj* Scotland relating to England (*dated*) [15C. Variant of SOUTHERN.]

South Saskatchewan river in central Canada, rising in S Alberta and flowing to central Saskatchewan, where it joins the North Saskatchewan. Length: 1,393 km/865 mi.

South Sea Bubble *n* frenzied speculation in the South Sea Company in early 18th-century Britain. In 1720 the company collapsed, ruining many banks and private investors.

South Shields /-sheéldz/ port in NE England. Population: 83,704 (1991).

south-southeast *n* the direction or compass point midway between south and southeast ■ *adj, adv* in, from, facing, or towards the south-southeast —**south-southeasterly** *adv*

south-southwest *n* the direction or compass point midway between south and southwest ■ *adj, adv* in, from, facing, or towards the south-southwest —**south-southwesterly** *adv*

South Taranaki Bight gulf on the southwest coast of the North Island, New Zealand

South Vietnam former country in Southeast Asia, occupying the southern part of modern-day Vietnam —**South Vietnamese** *n, adj*

southward /sówthwərd/ *adj* towards or in the south ■ *n* a direction towards or a point in the south ■ *adv* = **southwards** —**southwardly** *adv, adj*

southwards /sówthwərdz/, **southward** /sówthwərd/ *adv* in a southerly direction

southwest /sówth wést/ *n* 1 COMPASS POINT BETWEEN SOUTH AND WEST the direction or compass point midway between south and west 2 **southwest, Southwest AREA IN THE SOUTHWEST** the part of an area, region, or country that is situated in or towards the southwest ■ *adj* IN THE SOUTHWEST situated in, facing, or lying towards the southwest of a region, place, or country ■ *adv* TOWARDS THE SOUTHWEST in or towards the southwest

southwest by south *n* the direction or compass point midway between southwest and south-southwest

southwest by west *n* the direction or compass point midway between southwest and west-southwest

Southwest Cape southernmost point in New Zealand, at the southern tip of Stewart Island

southwester /sówth wéstər/ *n* a storm or wind that blows from the southwest

southwesterly /sówth wéstərli/ *adj* 1 IN THE SOUTHWEST situated in or towards the southwest 2 FROM THE SOUTHWEST blowing from the southwest (*refers to winds*) ■ *n* (*plural* -**lies**) WIND FROM THE SOUTHWEST a wind blowing from the southwest

southwestern /sówth wéstərn/ *adj* 1 IN THE SOUTHWEST situated in the southwest of a region or country 2 FACING SOUTHWEST situated in or facing the southwest 3 **southwestern, Southwestern OF THE SOUTHWEST** native to the southwest of a region or country

southwestward /sówth wéstwərd/ *adj* towards or in the southwest ■ *n* a direction towards or a point in the southwest —**southwestward** *adv* —**southwestwardly** *adv, adj* —**southwestwards** *adv*

South Yorkshire metropolitan county in N England, including Barnsley, Doncaster, Rotherham, and Sheffield. Area: 1,562 sq. km/603 sq. mi.

souvenir /soóvə neér/ *n* something bought or kept as a reminder of a particular place or occasion [Late 18C. Via French, 'memory' < Latin *subvenire* 'come into mind'.]

souvlakia /soov laáki ə/ *npl* Greek kebabs consisting of pieces of marinated meat, usually lamb, skewered and grilled [Mid-20C. < modern Greek, 'small skewers' < *souvla* 'skewer'.]

sou'wester /sow wéstər/ *n* a waterproof hat with a broad brim covering the back of the neck, originally made of oilskin, now usually of rubber or plastic [Mid-19C. Contraction of *southwester*.]

sovereign /sóvvrin/ *n* 1 MONARCH the ruler or permanent head of a state, especially a king or queen 2 OLD BRITISH GOLD COIN a gold coin worth one pound, used in Britain between the early 17th and the early 20th centuries ■ *adj* 1 INDEPENDENT self-governing and not ruled by any other state 2 WITH COMPLETE POWER having supreme authority or power 3 OUTSTANDING outstanding, e.g. in its excellence or effectiveness [13C. Via Old French *souverein* < Vulgar Latin *superanus* < Latin *super* 'above'.] —**sovereignly** *adv*

sovereignty /sóvvrənti/ (*plural* -**ties**) *n* 1 TOP AUTHORITY supreme authority, especially over a state 2 INDEPENDENCE freedom from outside interference and the right to self-government 3 INDEPENDENT STATE a politically independent state

~~sovereign~~ incorrect spelling of **sovereign**

soviet /sóvi i ət, sóv-/ *n* 1 any of the elected government councils that existed at local, regional, and national levels in the former Soviet Union 2 a council in the early political organization of the Russian Revolution in 1917 [Early 20C. < Russian *sovet* 'council'.] —**sovietism** *n*

Soviet /sóvi ət, sóv-/ *adj* 1 TYPICAL OF USSR relating to the former Soviet Union, or its people, culture, or political system 2 COMMUNIST having Communist views similar to those found in the former Soviet Union ■ *n* SOMEBODY

FROM USSR a person who came from the former Soviet Union

Sovietologist /sóvi ə tólləjist, sóv-/ *n* a scholar who studies the former Soviet Union, especially its government and political history

Soviet Union /sóvi ət yōonyən/ former federation of Communist states in Eastern Europe and northern and Central Asia from 1922 until 1991

sow[1] /sō/ (**sows, sowing, sowed, sown** /sōn/ *or* **sowed**) *v* **1** *vti* **PLANT SEED** to scatter or plant seed on an area of land in order to grow crops **2** *vt* **INTRODUCE IDEA** to cause some feeling or belief to arise or become widespread, especially when negative or divisive ○ *Increased competition will only sow discord among the members of the company.* **3** *vt* **SPREAD THICKLY** to spread something thickly with something (*often passive*) ○ *a sky sown with stars* [Old English *sāwan* < Indo-European] —**sowable** *adj* —**sower** *n*

SPELLCHECK See **sew**

sow[2] /sow/ *n* **1** **FEMALE PIG** an adult female pig **2** **ADULT FEMALE ANIMAL** the adult female of several animals such as the bear, mink, badger, guinea pig, and hedgehog **3** **CHANNEL FOR MOLTEN IRON** a channel through which molten iron runs into a mould in the process of casting pig iron **4** **HARDENED IRON** a mass of iron that has hardened in a channel or mould in the process of casting pig iron [Old English *sugu* < Indo-European]

⚡**SOW** *abbr* speaking of which (*in e-mails*)

Sow. *abbr* S Asia Sowbhagyawati

sowback /sówbak/ *n* a long ridge of earth left by a glacier [Late 19C. < sow[2].]

sowbelly /sów beli/ *n* fatty salt pork

Sowbhagyawati /sə bági ə wótti/ *n* S Asia a title used in India before the name of a married woman whose husband is still alive, roughly equivalent to the English term 'Mrs' [< Sanskrit]

sowbread /sów bred/ (*plural* **-breads** *or* **-bread**) *n* a cyclamen, especially one with a single nodding flower. Native to: S Europe. Genus: *Cyclamen.* [Mid-16C. Because it is supposedly eaten by pigs.]

sow bug /sów-/ *n* US, Can ZOOL = **woodlouse** [< its piglike shape]

Soweto /sə wáytō, sə wéttō/ township in NE South Africa. Population: 596,632 (1991).

sown past participle of **sow**[1]

sow thistle /sów-/ *n* a prickly-leaved plant. Flowers: yellow. Native to: Europe, Asia. Genus: *Sonchus.* [< ?]

soya /sóyə/, **soy** /soy/ *n* **1** the soya bean plant **2** FOOD = **soy sauce** ■ *adj* made or derived from soya beans [Late 17C. Via Dutch, Malay, and Japanese < Chinese *jiàngyóu* 'soyabean oil'.]

soya bean *n* **1** a plant cultivated around the world for its nutritious seeds, for soil improvement, and to provide grazing for animals. Native to: SE Asia. *Glycine max.* **2** the oil- and protein-rich seed of the soya bean plant. Use: soy sauce, soymilk, tofu, textured vegetable protein.

soya milk *n* a milk substitute made from soya beans

soya sauce *n* FOOD = **soy sauce**

soybean /sóy been/ *n* US = **soya bean**

Soyinka /so yíngkə/, **Wole** (*b.* 1934) Nigerian writer and political activist

soy sauce, **soy** *n* a dark, salty liquid made by fermenting soya beans in brine, used to flavour foods

sozzled /sózz'ld/ *adj* extremely intoxicated (*informal*) [Late 19C. < English dialect *sozzle* 'splash'.]

SP *abbr* **1** starting price **2** submarine patrol

spa /spaa/ *n* **1** a resort with mineral springs (*often used in placenames*) **2** a bath with a device for aerating or swirling water [Early 17C. After a resort town in eastern Belgium, famous for its mineral springs.]

KEY DATES IN SPACE TRAVEL

Year	Event	Year	Event
1957	Sputnik 1, first artificial satellite, launched by USSR	1974	US probe Mariner 10 orbits Mercury
1957	Soviet satellite Sputnik 2 carries first animal into orbit, the dog Laika	1974	US/German probe Helios 1 is first to fly close to Sun
1958	Explorer 1, first US satellite, launched	1975	Soviet and US spacecraft Soyuz 19 and Apollo ASTP dock in space for first time
1959	Soviet probe Luna 2 lands on Moon	1976	US Viking probes land on Mars
1961	Soviet cosmonaut Yuri Gagarin is first person in space	1977	US Voyager probes launched to send back data from outer solar system and beyond
1962	First successful interplanetary spacecraft US Mariner 2 probe flies past Venus	1981	US reusable space shuttle Columbia launched
1962	US astronaut John Glenn orbits Earth	1984	13-member European Space Agency begins its own rocket launch programme
1963	Soviet cosmonaut Valentina Tereshkova is first woman in space	1985	European spacecraft Giotto flies close to Halley's comet
1964	US probe Mariner 4 flies past Mars, sending back photographs of Martian craters	1986	Soviet modular space station Mir launched
1965	Soviet cosmonaut Alexei Leonov completes first space walk	1988	Soviet cosmonauts Vladimir Titov and Musa Manarov set new record by spending one year on space station Mir
1966	First Saturn 5 rocket launched by United States	1990	Hubble Space Telescope launched by US space shuttle Discovery, seeing farther into space than any instrument before
1969	USSR achieves first successful docking of two manned spacecraft, Soyuz 4 and Soyuz 5		
1969	US astronauts Neil Armstrong and Buzz Aldrin land on Moon	1992	Russian satellite Progress M-15 tests solar sail to light up night sky from space
1970	Soviet probe Venera 7 transmits information from surface of Venus	1997	US spacecraft Mars Pathfinder lands on Mars and launches robot vehicle Sojourner for exploration
1971	Salyut 1, first space station, launched by USSR		
1973	US Pioneer 10 sends back images of Jupiter	2000	First crew begins extended stay on ISS (International Space Station)

space /spayss/ *n* **1** **REGION BEYOND EARTH'S ATMOSPHERE** the region that lies beyond the Earth's atmosphere, and all that it contains ○ *space travel* **2** **REGION BETWEEN ALL ASTRONOMICAL OBJECTS** the region, usually of negligible density, between all astronomical objects in the universe **3** **THREE-DIMENSIONAL EXPANSE WHERE MATTER EXISTS** the unbounded three-dimensional expanse in which all matter exists **4** **INTERVAL OF TIME** a period or interval of time ○ *In the space of two hours the situation was resolved.* **5** **AREA SET APART** an area set apart or available for use ○ *floor space* **6** **BLANK AREA BETWEEN TYPE** a blank area between characters, words, or lines of type, or an interval the width of a single character **7** **INTERVAL BETWEEN LINES OF MUSICAL STAFF** an interval between the lines of the musical staff **8** **TIME OR AREA AVAILABLE FOR ADVERTISING** broadcast time or an area in a publication available for specific use, e.g. by advertisers **9** **SET OF POINTS GOVERNED BY AXIOMS** in mathematics, a collection of points that have geometric properties in that they obey set rules (**axioms**), e.g. a Euclidian space that is governed by Euclidian geometry **10** **PIECE OF TYPE TO CREATE SPACE** a piece of type used to create a blank interval in printing **11** **FREEDOM TO ASSERT IDENTITY** the freedom or opportunity to assert a personal identity or fulfil personal needs (*informal*) ○ *I need my own personal space.* **12** **INTERVAL IN TELEGRAPHIC TRANSMISSION** an interval during the transmission of a telegraphic message when the key is not in contact ■ *vt* (**spaces, spacing, spaced**) **TO SET THINGS APART** to set things some distance apart or arrange them with gaps between [13C. Via French *espace* < Latin *spatium* 'space, distance'.]

space age *n* the era marked by the exploration of space, often considered as beginning in 1957 when the Soviet Union launched Sputnik —**space-age** *adj*

spaceband /spáyss band/ *n* a device used in printing to provide variable but even spacing between words in a justified line

space-bar *n* a horizontal bar at the bottom of a keyboard or typewriter that is pressed to introduce a space

space biology *n* BIOL = **exobiology**

space blanket *n* a plastic wrapping with aluminium foil coating that is used to restore body heat in people affected by exposure or exhaustion

spacebridge /spáyss brij/ *n* a way of communicating internationally by television, using transmissions from orbiting satellites

space cadet *n* a forgetful or mildly strange person, especially somebody who has taken hallucinogenic drugs (*slang*)

space capsule *n* a vehicle or cabin designed to support life and used for transporting human beings or animals in outer space or at very high altitudes within Earth's atmosphere

space charge *n* the net electric charge distributed in a given volume of space

spacecraft /spáyss kraaft/ *n* a vehicle or device designed for travel or use in space

spaced-out *adj* inattentive, dazed, confused, or light-headed from or as if from drug use (*slang*)

spacefaring /spáyss fairing/ *n* the use of spacecraft for the exploration of outer space —**spacefaring** *adj*

spaceflight *n* flight beyond Earth's atmosphere, or an instance of this

space heater *n* a small portable appliance used to heat a small area

spacelab /spáyss lab/ *n* a laboratory in space used to carry out scientific experiments

space lattice *n* CRYSTALS = **lattice** *n.* 4

spaceless /spáyssləss/ *adj* (*literary*) **1** with no limits **2** not occupying any space

spaceman /spáyss man/ (*plural* **-men** /-mən/) *n* **1** an astronaut or somebody who travels in space **2** a traveller to Earth from outer space, in science fiction

space medicine *n* a branch of medicine dealing with the effects of space flight on the human body

Space Needle *n* a tall tower in central Seattle, Washington State, with a revolving restaurant and observation deck near the top

space opera *n* a science fiction drama involving space travel and, often, extraterrestrial beings

spaceport /spáyss pawrt/ *n* an installation for launching, testing, landing, and maintaining spacecraft

space probe *n* a satellite or other spacecraft that is designed to explore the solar system and transmit data back to earth

spaceship /spáyss ship/ *n* a vehicle designed to transport people or materials through outer space

space shuttle *n* a reusable spacecraft designed to transport people and cargo between Earth and space, with two solid rocket boosters and an external fuel tank that are jettisoned after takeoff

space sickness *n* motion sickness experienced as a result of space flight

space station, space platform *n* a spacecraft or satellite designed to be occupied by a crew for extended periods of time and used as a base for the exploration, observation, and research of space

Spacesuit: Astronaut Buzz
Aldrin on the Moon

spacesuit /spáyss syoot/ *n* a sealed pressurized suit designed to support the wearer's life in space

space-time, space-time continuum *n* a four-dimensional system consisting of three spatial coordinates and one for time, in which it is possible to locate events

spacewalk /spáyss wawk/ *n* an excursion by an astronaut or cosmonaut outside the spacecraft ■ *vi* to go out of a spacecraft in order to perform a task or experiment

spacewoman /spáyss woomɑn/ (*plural* **-en** /-wimin/) *n* 1 a woman astronaut or cosmonaut who travels in space 2 a female who travels to Earth from outer space, in science fiction

space writer *n* a writer paid according to the area of print taken up by what is written

spacey /spáyssi/ *adj* = **spacy** (*informal*)

spacial /spáysh'l/ *adj* = **spatial**

spacing /spáyssing/ *n* 1 the space, or the way this is arranged, between several things, e.g. between words or lines in type 2 the act of arranging things in spaces

spacious /spáyshɑss/ *adj* roomy and containing ample space —**spaciously** *adv* —**spaciousness** *n*

spacy /spáyssi/ (**-ier, -iest**), **spacey** (**-ier, -iest**) *adj* spaced-out (*slang*)

spade[1] /spayd/ *n* a digging tool with a wide shallow blade flattened where it meets the shaft so it can be pushed into the ground with the foot ■ *vti* (**spades, spading, spaded**) to dig or remove something using a spade [Old English *spadu* < Indo-European] —**spader** *n* ◊ **call a spade a spade** to say plainly and bluntly what you mean without being euphemistic

spade[2] /spayd/ *n* 1 SUIT WITH SPEAR-SHAPED SYMBOL one of the four suits used in cards, with a black figure shaped like a stylized spearhead as its symbol 2 CARD OF SPADES SUIT a card of the suit of spades 3 TABOO TERM a highly offensive term for somebody, especially a man, who is of African descent (*taboo*) [Late 16C. Via Italian, the plural of *spada* 'sword' (the sign used on Italian cards), and Latin *spatha* 'broadsword' < Greek *spathē*.] ◊ **in spades** to a very great degree (*informal*)

spadefish /spáyd fish/ (*plural* **-fish** or **-fishes**) *n* a deepbodied bony fish. Native to: Atlantic coastal waters. Family: Ephippidae. [Early 18C. < its shape.]

spade guinea *n* a British gold coin worth 21 shillings issued between 1787 and 1799 [< the spade-shaped shield on its reverse]

spadework /spáyd wurk/ *n* 1 work done using a spade 2 preliminary work that is often hard drudgery

spadille /spa díl/ *n* the highest trump card in some card games, e.g. ombre [Late 17C. Via French and Spanish *espadilla* 'a small sword' < Latin *spatha* (see SPADE[2].)]

spadix /spáydiks/ (*plural* **-dices** /-di seez/) *n* a fleshy or succulent plant spike bearing tiny flowers and usually enclosed in a leafy sheath (**spathe**) [Mid-18C. Via Latin, 'palm branch torn off with its fruit' < Greek, < *span* 'pull']

spaewife /spáy wíf/ (*plural* **-wives** /-wīvz/) *n* Scotland a woman fortune-teller

~~spagetti~~ incorrect spelling of **spaghetti**

spaghetti /spa gétti/ *n* 1 pasta in the shape of long, thin strings 2 a dish of long thin strings of boiled pasta, usually served with a sauce 3 US ELEC = **sleeving** [Mid-19C. < Italian, 'small strings' < *spago* 'string' < ?]

spaghetti junction *n* a motorway interchange with complex systems of intersections, overpasses, and underpasses

spaghettini /spágga teeni/ *n* pasta that is thinner than spaghetti but thicker than vermicelli [Mid-20C. < Italian, 'small spaghetti' (see SPAGHETTI).]

spaghetti western *n* a western made in Europe, usually Spain, by an Italian film company, characterized by extreme and melodramatic violence

spahi /spaà hee, -ee/, **spahee** *n* 1 a cavalryman in the Turkish army in former times 2 a member of a corps of Algerian cavalrymen in French service in former times [Mid-16C. Via French and Turkish < Persian *sipāhī* 'cavalryman' < *sipāh* 'army'.]

Spain

Spain /spayn/ monarchy in SW Europe on the Iberian Peninsula. Capital: Madrid. Population: 39,181,114 (1996). Area: 504,782 sq. km/194,897 sq. mi.

spake past tense of **speak** (*archaic*)

Spalding /spáwl ding/ market town in E England. Population: 20,000 (1993).

spall /spawl/ *n* a small fragment, splinter, or chip of stone or ore ■ *vti* to break up into small chips, flakes, or splinters [15C]

spallation /spaw láysh'n/ *n* 1 a nuclear reaction in which several particles are emitted from the nucleus of an atom after bombardment with high-energy particles or radiation 2 the removal of the surface layers of a rock by meteorite impact

spalpeen /spál peen/ *n* Ireland 1 a mischievous and cunning person 2 an impoverished farm labourer [Late 18C. < Irish *spailpín*.]

⚡ **spam** /spam/ *n* an unsolicited, often commercial, message transmitted through the Internet as a mass mailing to a large number of recipients ■ *vti* (**spams, spamming, spammed**) to post a message many times to a newsgroup, an inappropriate message to several newsgroups, or to send an unsolicited message, often an advertisement, to many people [Late 20C]

Spam *tdmk* a trademark for tinned chopped meat, mainly pork, that is pressed into a loaf

span[1] /span/ *n* 1 DISTANCE BETWEEN LIMITS the distance or expanse between two extremes or limits 2 PERIOD FOR MAINTENANCE OF COGNITIVE FUNCTION the period of time during which a mental function or act can be maintained ○ *a short attention span* 3 DISTANCE BETWEEN BRIDGE

SUPPORTS the extent or space between abutments or supports, e.g. on a bridge or arch, or a portion of the structure that is supported in this way 4 = **wingspan** 5 PERIOD OF TIME a period of time, especially the lifetime of an individual 6 OLD MEASUREMENT an old measurement based on the distance from the end of the thumb to the end of the little finger of a spread hand, approximately 23 cm/9 in ■ *vt* (**spans, spanning, spanned**) 1 EXTEND OVER OR ACROSS to reach or extend over or across something 2 MEASURE SOMETHING WITH HAND to measure something by or as if by the hand with fingers and thumb fully extended 3 ENCIRCLE SOMETHING WITH HANDS to encircle or cover something with the hands, especially in order to estimate its size [Old English *spann* < Germanic]

span[2] /span/ *n* a pair of horses or other animals harnessed and driven together [Mid-18C. < Dutch < *spannen*, 'harness'.]

spanakopita /spánna kóppita, -ka peeta/ *n* a traditional Greek dish of spinach and feta cheese baked in filo pastry [Mid-20C. < modern Greek *spanakopēta* 'spinach pie'.]

Spandau /spán dow/ district of Berlin, Germany, the site of a prison where Nazi war criminals were confined after World War II. Population: 192,895 (1986).

spandex /spán deks/ *n* a synthetic stretch fabric of fibre made from polyurethane [Mid-20C. < EXPAND.]

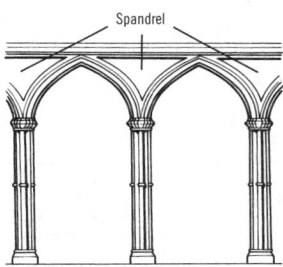

Spandrel

spandrel /spándrɑl/, **spandril** *n* 1 the triangular space between the right or left exterior curve of an arch and the framework of another arch 2 the area between two arches and a horizontal cornice above them [15C. < ?]

spang /spang/ *adv* US completely, squarely, or exactly on target or in the middle of something (*informal*) [Mid-19C. < ?]

spangle /spáng g'l/ *n* 1 SMALL SHINY DECORATION a small shiny piece of metal or plastic used for decoration on clothing 2 SMALL SPARKLING OBJECT a small sparkling spot or object ■ *v* (**-gles, -gling, -gled**) 1 *vt* SPRINKLE SOMETHING WITH SPANGLES to sprinkle or adorn something with spangles 2 *vi* GLITTER WITH SPANGLES to sparkle or glitter as if adorned with spangles [15C. < obsolete *spang* 'glittering ornament' < Dutch *spange* 'clasp'.]

Spanglish /spáng glish/ *n* a variety of Spanish characterized by many borrowings from English [Mid-20C. Blend of SPANISH + ENGLISH.]

Spaniard /spánnyɑrd/ *n* 1 a person who comes from Spain 2 a perennial rock plant with sharp leaves. Native to: New Zealand. [14C. Via Old French *Espaignart* < Latin *Hispania* 'Spain'.]

spaniel /spánnyɑl/ *n* a small or medium-sized dog characterized by a long wavy silky coat, usually short legs, large drooping ears, and feathering on the legs and tail [14C. Via Old French *espaigneul* 'Spanish' < Latin *Hispania* 'Spain'.]

spa night *n* US an evening session at a health and beauty centre booked by a private group

Spanish /spánnish/ *n* ROMANCE LANGUAGE a Romance language spoken in most of Spain and Central and South America ■ *npl* PEOPLE OF SPAIN the people of Spain ■ *adj* 1 RELATING TO SPAIN relating to Spain, or its people or culture 2 RELATING TO SPANISH LANGUAGE relating to the Spanish language [13C. < SPAIN + -ISH.]

Spanish America the part of America that was colonized by the Spanish from the 16th century and where Spanish is still widely spoken, including much of

Central and South America and some Caribbean islands —**Spanish-American** n, adj

Spanish bayonet (plural **Spanish bayonet** or **Spanish bayonets**) n a plant with stiff pointed leaves and a long woody stem. Flowers: white. Native to: America. Genus: Yucca. [< its sword-like leaves]

Spanish customs npl soc sci = **Spanish practices** (dated informal)

Spanish fly (plural **Spanish fly** or **Spanish flies**) n 1 a green European blister beetle, source of the stimulant and irritant cantharides. Lytta vesicatoria and Cantharis vesicatoria. 2 a toxic preparation made from the crushed dried bodies of the Spanish fly. Use: formerly, as an aphrodisiac and to treat skin blisters.

Spanish guitar n the classical six-stringed form of guitar

Spanish Inquisition n an ecclesiastical tribunal of the Roman Catholic Church established in Spain in 1542, and finally suppressed in 1834, under which large numbers of people deemed to be heretics were tortured and executed

Spanish mackerel n 1 a large game fish of the tuna family. Native to: Atlantic coast of North and South America. Scomberomorus maculatus. 2 a mackerel. Native to: Atlantic coastal waters of Europe and North America. Scomberomorus colias.

Spanish Main 1 in the 16th and 17th centuries, region of Spanish America from the isthmus of Panama to the mouth of the Orinoco River, in present-day Venezuela 2 part of the Caribbean Sea crossed by Spanish ships in colonial times

Spanish moss n a plant of the pineapple family that grows on trees in long drooping matted clusters of greyish-green filaments. Native to: SE United States, South America. Tillandsia usneoides.

Spanish needles npl PLANTS = **beggar's lice** n. 1 (+ singular or plural verb) [< its spiny fruit]

Spanish omelette n an omelette filled with a selection of vegetables, usually including tomatoes and cooked potato [Because it contains ingredients typical in Spanish cuisine]

Spanish onion n an onion with yellow skin and a mild flavour. Allium fistulosum.

Spanish practices, **Spanish customs** npl irregular practices that are in the interests of workers and are usually imposed on employers by trade unions, e.g. overstaffing and excessive overtime (dated informal)

Spanish rice n rice cooked with onion, green pepper, tomato, and seasonings

Spanish Sahara former name for **Western Sahara**

Spanish Town second largest city in Jamaica, in the southeast of the island. Population: 110,400 (1995).

spank[1] /spangk/ vt to strike somebody, usually on the buttocks with the open hand in punishment ■ n an open-handed slap on the buttocks [Early 18C. Probably an imitation of the sound.]

spank[2] vi to move briskly, spiritedly, or smartly [Early 19C. Probably a back-formation < SPANKING[2].]

spanker /spángkər/ n the fore-and-aft sail on the sternmost mast of a square-rigged ship [Mid-17C. < ?]

spanking[1] /spángking/ n a beating with the flat of the hand on somebody's buttocks, given as punishment

spanking[2] /spángking/ adj 1 EXCEPTIONAL with an unusual quality that makes something exceptional or remarkable of its kind 2 BRISK lively, or moving briskly, especially a breeze ■ adv VERY extremely and impressively ○ a spanking new car [Mid-17C. < ?]

spanner /spánnər/ n a tool with fixed or movable jaws, used to seize, turn, or twist objects such as nuts and bolts. US term **wrench** n. 3 [Mid-17C. < German, < spannen (see SPAN[1].)] ◇ **put** or **throw a spanner in the works** to ruin or impede a plan or system

spanworm /spán wurm/ n US INSECTS = **measuring worm**

spar[1] /spaar/ n 1 a stout pole used to support rigging on a ship 2 one of the principal lateral members supporting the wing of an aeroplane [14C. Probably < Old French esparre or Old Norse sperra.]

spar[2] /spaar/ vi (**spars**, **sparring**, **sparred**) 1 USE LIGHT BLOWS to engage in a practice or exhibition bout of boxing or martial arts using light blows 2 FIGHT USING FEET AND SPURS to fight using the feet and spurs to strike an opponent (refers to gamecocks) 3 ARGUE to engage in argument ■ n

1 PRACTICE BOUT a practice or exhibition bout of boxing 2 PARTICULAR MOTION IN BOXING a motion in boxing for attack or defence [Late 16C. < ?]

spar[3] /spaar/ n any light-coloured lustrous mineral that cleaves easily —**sparry** adj

sparable /spárrəb'l/ n a small headless nail used to attach the soles of shoes [Early 17C. Alteration of sparrow-bill.]

spare /spair/ v (**spares**, **sparing**, **spared**) 1 vt REFRAIN FROM HARMING to refrain from killing, punishing, or harming somebody 2 vt TREAT SOMEBODY LENIENTLY to treat leniently or refrain from treating somebody harshly 3 vt SAVE SOMEBODY FROM DOING SOMETHING to save or relieve somebody from the effort or trouble of doing something 4 vt WITHHOLD to withhold or avoid something 5 vt USE EFFORT FRUGALLY to use or dispense something frugally 6 vt AFFORD to give up or be able to contribute something from one's resources, especially without inconvenience ○ I can't spare any time to exercise. 7 vt REFRAIN FROM USING to refrain from using something 8 vi BE FRUGAL to be frugal and thrifty (archaic) ■ adj 1 KEPT IN RESERVE kept in reserve for emergency use 2 SUPERFLUOUS more than what is needed 3 LEAN with a muscular physique and no excess fat 4 SCANTY lacking in quantity or extent ■ n 1 SOMETHING EXTRA something extra that is kept in reserve 2 KNOCKING DOWN PINS IN TWO TRIES in tenpin bowling, an instance of knocking down all the pins in two attempts 3 BOWLING SCORE a score made in tenpin bowling by using two rolls to knock down all ten pins 4 UNATTACHED MEMBERS OF OPPOSITE SEX unattached members of the opposite sex who are potential sexual partners (slang) [Old English sparian < Germanic] —**sparely** adv —**spareness** n —**sparer** n ◇ **go spare** become upset, especially to lose your temper (informal) ◇ **to spare** more than what is needed

spare part n a replacement for a defective component in a vehicle or machine (hyphenated when used before a noun)

spare-part surgery n surgery in which defective organs in the body are replaced by transplanted or artificial organs

sparerib /spáir ríb/ n a rib of pork from which most of the meat has been removed, usually cooked in a barbecue or Chinese sauce [Late 16C. By folk etymology < Low German ribbesper 'pickled pork ribs roasted on a spit', by association with SPARE.]

spare time n time not spent working or attending to other day-to-day responsibilities

spare tyre n 1 an extra tyre, mounted somewhere on a motor vehicle and carried in case of a flat tyre 2 a roll of extra flesh around somebody's waist (informal humorous)

sparge /spaarj/ v (**sparges**, **sparging**, **sparged**) vt to scatter, spray, or sprinkle something [Late 16C. Directly or via Old French < Latin spargere (see SPARSE).] —**sparger** n

sparid /spárrid/ (plural **-id** or **-ids**), **sparoid** /spárroyd/ (plural **-oid** or **-oids**) n a warm-water marine fish with a compressed body, large head, and sharp teeth, including porgies and breams. Family: Sparidae. [Late 20C. Via modern Latin Sparidae < Greek sparos 'sea bream'.]

sparing /spáiring/ adj 1 FRUGAL showing careful restraint in the use of resources 2 SCANTY limited or restricted in quantity 3 MERCIFUL inclined to be lenient or merciful

spark[1] /spaark/ n 1 FIERY PARTICLE a small piece of a burning substance thrown off in combustion or produced in friction 2 ELECTRIC DISCHARGE a quick bright discharge of electricity between two conductors 3 SOMETHING THAT ACTIVATES a factor or device that sets off or acts as a stimulant, inspiration, or catalyst 4 SOMETHING CAPABLE OF DEVELOPMENT a latent trace of something capable of development 5 **spark**, **sparks** ELECTRICIAN an electrician (informal) 6 **sparks** RADIO OPERATOR the radio operator on a ship or aircraft (informal; + singular verb) ■ v 1 vi THROW OFF SPARKS to throw off sparks 2 vi PRODUCE SPARKS to have an electric ignition working properly so that it generates sparks 3 vi RESPOND ENTHUSIASTICALLY to respond with lively enthusiasm 4 vt STIMULATE OR INCITE to stimulate or initiate a burst of activity [Old English spærca. < ?]

spark off vt to activate or act as a catalyst for something

spark[2] /spaark/ n 1 DANDY a vain young man, especially one concerned with fashion and appearance (archaic) 2 BOYFRIEND a male who courts a woman (dated informal) ■ vti WOO to try to persuade somebody to become romantically or sexually involved (archaic) [Early 16C. Probably < SPARK[1].]

Spark /spaark/, **Dame Muriel** (b. 1918) British writer

spark chamber n a device for tracking the path of a subatomic particle, consisting of charged plates that cause the particle to ionize the gas present and create sparks

spark coil n the induction coil that produces the spark discharge to start combustion in an internal combustion engine

spark erosion n a process for shaping metal, similar to conventional machining but using an electric arc from a moving electrode to remove metal

spark gap n a space between two electrodes across which a discharge of electricity occurs, e.g. the gap between electrodes of a spark plug in an internal combustion engine

sparking plug n ENG = **spark plug** n.

sparkle /spáark'l/ v (**-kles**, **-kling**, **-kled**) 1 vi THROW OFF SPARKS to throw off sparks 2 vti GLITTER to give off or reflect light in brilliant, glittering sparks, or make something do this 3 vi PERFORM VIVACIOUSLY to perform brilliantly or be vivacious, witty, or enthusiastic 4 vi EFFERVESCE to effervesce, especially a wine or other drink ■ n 1 SHINING PARTICLE a little spark or shining particle 2 ANIMATION lively or brilliant animation and vivacity 3 EFFERVESCENCE effervescence in wine and other drinks [12C. < SPARK[1].] —**sparkly** adj

sparkler /spáarklər/ n 1 a handheld firework that throws off sparks as it burns 2 a diamond or other sparkling gem (informal)

sparkling water n water charged with carbon dioxide to make it effervescent

sparkling wine n wine that is made effervescent naturally through a second fermentation or artificially through the introduction of carbon dioxide

spark plug n a device that ignites the fuel mixture in the cylinder in an internal-combustion engine by emitting a spark

spark transmitter n an obsolete form of radio transmitter that used power generated from the discharge of a condenser across a spark gap

sparky /spáarki/ (**-ier**, **-iest**) adj very lively and enthusiastic

sparling /spáarling/ (plural **-lings** or **-ling**) n 1 a smelt. Native to: Europe. Osmerus eperlanus. 2 an immature herring [14C. < Old French esperlinge < Germanic.]

sparring partner n 1 a person who spars with a boxer to help in training 2 a regular debater or disputer with somebody else

sparrow /spárrō/ n 1 a small dull-coloured songbird with a short stout bill for cracking seeds. Family: Passeridae. 2 US, Can a finch that resembles the true sparrow [Old English spearwa < Germanic]

sparrowgrass /spárrō graass/ n US asparagus (regional) [Mid-17C. By folk etymology < ASPARAGUS.]

sparrowhawk /spárrō hawk/ n 1 a small hawk that preys on smaller birds and has short broad wings, a long tail, and a dark grey to blackish back. Native to: Europe, Asia. Accipiter nisus. 2 a kestrel that hovers over fields and eats mainly insects and mice. Native to: North America. Falco sparverius.

sparse /spaarss/ (**sparser**, **sparsest**) adj thinly spread, or occurring with many spaces in between [Early 18C. < Latin sparsus, past participle of spargere 'scatter'.] —**sparsely** adv —**sparseness** n

Sparta /spáartə/ town in the S Peloponnese, Greece, the site of an ancient city-state that was an important military power between the 6th and 4th centuries BC. Population: 14,390 (1981).

Spartacist /spáartəssist/ n a member of a German revolutionary group organized in 1918 and promoting an extreme socialistic agenda [Early 20C. < German Spartakist < Spartakus 'Spartacus', adopted as pen-name by the German socialist leader Karl Liebknecht.]

Spartacus /spáartəkəss/ (d. 71 BC) Roman enslaved labourer and rebel leader

Spartan /spáart'n/ n 1 NATIVE OF SPARTA somebody who came from ancient Sparta 2 PERSON WITH STRONG CHARACTER a strong and self-disciplined person ■ adj 1 RELATING TO ANCIENT SPARTA relating to the ancient Greek city-state of Sparta, or its people or culture 2 **Spartan**, **spartan** MARKED BY DISCIPLINE AND AUSTERITY marked by stern discipline, frugality, simplicity, or courage —**Spartanism** n —**Spartanly** adv

sparteine /spaárti īn, -in/ *n* a bitter poisonous alkaloid. Source: common broom plant. Use: medicines. [Mid-19C. < modern Latin *Spartium*, broom genus < Greek *sparton* 'esparto'.]

spasm /spázzəm/ *n* **1** an involuntary sudden muscle contraction **2** a sudden brief emotion, sensation, or action ○ *a spasm of pain* [14C. Via French and Latin < Greek *spasmos* < *span* 'pull'.]

spasmodic /spaz móddik/ *adj* **1 AFFECTED BY SPASMS** affected or characterized by spasms **2 RESEMBLING SPASM** resembling a spasm in sudden brief intensity **3 INTERMITTENT** occurring at uneven intervals **4 EXCITABLE** prone to sudden outbursts of emotion [Late 17C. Via modern Latin *spasmodicus* < Greek *spasmōdēs* < *spasmos* (see SPASM).] —**spasmodically** *adv*

spasmolytic /spázmə líttik/ *n, adj* MED, PHARM = **antispasmodic**

spastic /spástik/ *adj* **1 AFFECTED BY SPASMS** relating to or affected by spasms **2 OFFENSIVE TERM** an offensive term meaning lacking physical coordination or the ability to perform competently (*slang*) ■ *n* **1 OFFENSIVE TERM** a former term now considered highly offensive for somebody affected by cerebral palsy (*dated offensive*) **2 OFFENSIVE TERM** an offensive term that deliberately insults somebody's coordination or competence (*slang insult*) [Mid-18C. Via Latin < Greek *spastikos* < *span* (see SPASM).] —**spastically** *adv*

spastic colon *n* MED = **irritable bowel syndrome**

spat[1] /spat/ *n* a brief quarrel usually concerning petty matters ■ *vi* (**spats, spatting, spatted**) *US, Can* to engage in a petty, brief quarrel [Early 19C. < ?]

spat[2] past tense, past participle of **spit**[1]

spat[3] /spat/ *n* a short cloth or leather gaiter, popular in the late 19th and early 20th centuries, worn over a shoe to cover the instep and the ankle [Early 19C. Shortening of SPATTERDASH.]

spat[4] /spat/ *n* an immature bivalve mollusc, e.g. an oyster [Mid-17C. < Anglo-Norman, < ?]

spatchcock /spách kok/ *n* **SPLIT BIRD FOR COOKING** a chicken or other fowl that is split, dressed, and grilled ■ *vt* **1 PREPARE FOWL FOR ROASTING** to prepare a chicken or other fowl for roasting by splitting it open **2 INSERT SOMETHING AWKWARDLY** to introduce or interpose something into a piece of writing, especially in a forced or inappropriate way [Late 18C. < ?]

spate /spayt/ *n* **1 FLOOD** a flood, or a river overflowing its banks ○ *After the heavy rain the river was in spate.* **2 OUTBURST** a sudden strong outburst **3 LARGE QUANTITY** a large quantity of something [15C. < ?]

spathe /spayth/ *n* a leafy sheath (**bract**) that encloses the cluster of flowers (**spadix**) in some plants, e.g. the arum, and sometimes resembles a petal [Late 18C. Via Latin *spatha* < Greek *spathē* (see SPADE[1]).] —**spathaceous** /spə tháyshəss/ *adj* —**spathed** *adj*

spathic /spáthik/, **spathose** /spáthōss/ *adj* resembling spar minerals [Late 18C. < German *Spat(h)* 'spar'.]

spathulate *n* BIOL = **spatulate**

spatial /spáysh'l/, **spacial** *adj* relating to, occupying, or happening in space [Mid-19C. < Latin *spatium* (see SPACE).] —**spatiality** /spáyshi állәti/ *n* —**spatially** *adv*

spatiotemporal /spáyshi ō témpərəl/ *adj* **1** relating to, existing in, or having the qualities of both space and time **2** relating to a four-dimensional space-time system [Early 20C. < Latin *spatium* (see SPACE) + TEMPORAL[1].] —**spatiotemporally** *adv*

spätlese /shpáyt layzə/ (*plural* **-sen** /-layz'n/ *or* **-ses**) *n* a grade of high-quality German table wine made from late-picked grapes, and typically medium sweet [Early 20C. < German, 'late vintage'.]

spatter /spáttər/ *v* **1** *vti* **COME OUT IN DROPS** to expel something or come out in small scattered drops or splashes **2** *vt* **SPLASH WITH LIQUID** to splash something with or as if with a liquid, especially if the liquid leaves a mark or residue **3** *vti* **SCATTER IN DROPLETS** to splash or scatter in droplets **4** *vt* **DEFAME** to defame or sully somebody's character ■ *n* **1 ACT OF SPATTERING** an act of spattering or being spattered **2 SPATTERING SOUND** the sound of spattering **3 DROPLET OF SOMETHING SPATTERED** a droplet or splash of something spattered **4 SMALL AMOUNT** a small amount of something [Mid-16C. < ?]

spatterdash /spáttər dash/ *n* a knee-length cloth or leather legging formerly worn to protect clothing from water or mud spatters

spatula /spáttyōōlə/ *n* **1** a flat flexible metal, plastic, or rubber utensil with a handle, used to scoop, lift, spread, or mix **2** a flat wooden stick used to depress the tongue when the mouth or throat is being examined. US term **tongue depressor** [Early 16C. Via Latin, 'a small broadsword' < Greek *spathē* (see SPADE[1]).] —**spatular** *adj*

spatulate /spáttyōōlət/, **spathulate** /spáth-/ *adj* shaped like a spatula, with a narrow tapering base and a broad rounded tip

spavin /spávvin/ *n* an ailment of horses involving a swelling or enlargement of the hock joint [15C. < Old French *espavin* < ?]

spavined /spávvind/ *adj* **1** having or being lame with a spavin **2** lacking health, vigour, and strength ○ *a spavined horse*

spawn /spawn/ *n* **1 EGG MASS** a mass of eggs of a fish, amphibian, or other aquatic animal **2 OFFSPRING** progeny or offspring, especially if numerous **3 MYCELIUM** a mass of microscopic fungal threads (**mycelium**), especially when prepared on a growth medium for starting a new culture of the fungus **4 SEED** a seed, germ, or the source of something ■ *v* **1** *vi* **DEPOSIT EGGS** to produce and deposit eggs **2** *vi* **PRODUCE YOUNG** to produce offspring in large numbers **3** *vt* **GIVE RISE TO** to generate or give rise to something **4** *vt* **START NEW FUNGUS CULTURE** to start a new culture of a fungus using spawn [15C. Via Anglo-Norman *espaundre* 'shed' and Old French *espandre* < Latin *expandere* 'spread out'.] —**spawner** *n*

spay /spay/ *vt* to surgically remove an animal's ovaries and adjacent parts of the uterus [15C. < Old French *espeer* 'cut with a sword' < *espee* 'sword' < Greek *spathē* (see SPADE[1]).]

spaza /spaázə/ *n S Africa* a small informal shop, often run from a home in a township

SPCK *abbr* Society for Promoting Christian Knowledge

~~**speach**~~ incorrect spelling of **speech**

speak /speek/ (**speaks, speaking, spoke** /spōk/ *or* **spake** *archaic* /spayk/, **spoken** /spókən/) *v* **1** *vti* **TALK** to utter words or articulate sounds with the voice **2** *vi* **EXPRESS THOUGHTS AND OPINIONS** to communicate thoughts, opinions, or feelings by uttering with the voice **3** *vt* **BE ABLE TO USE LANGUAGE** to know and be able to converse in a language **4** *vi* **BE ON GOOD TERMS** to be on good and friendly terms with somebody ○ *It's sad, but they're not speaking anymore.* **5** *vi* **DELIVER SPEECH TO AUDIENCE** to make a speech or deliver an address **6** *vti* **EXPRESS IN WRITING** to express something or make a statement in writing **7** *vti* **COMMUNICATE NONVERBALLY** to communicate by other than verbal means ○ *Actions speak louder than words.* **8** *vi* **MAKE CHARACTERISTIC SOUND** to produce or make a sound typical of its kind **9** *vt* **COMMUNICATE WITH ANOTHER SEA-GOING VESSEL** to communicate with another vessel at sea [Old English *specan, sprecan* < Indo-European] —**speakable** *adj* ◇ **so to speak** used to indicate that you are expressing something in an unusual way, e.g. that you are being euphemistic ◇ **something speaks for itself** something has an obvious meaning and needs no further explanation ◇ **to speak of** significant or worth mentioning

speak for *vt* to act as an advocate for or speak on behalf of

speak out *vi* **1** to express opinions boldly, freely, and frankly **2** to talk loudly or loudly enough to be heard

speak to *vt* to address a particular issue in a speech or discussion ○ *a speech that spoke to the needs of international students*

speak up *vi* **1** to talk loudly enough to be heard **2** to express opinions freely and frankly

speak up for *vt* to speak in support or on behalf of somebody or something

speakeasy /speék eezi/ (*plural* **-ies**) *n US* a place where alcoholic beverages are sold and consumed illegally, especially formerly during Prohibition in the United States [Late 19C. < the custom of speaking softly so as not to attract attention.]

speaker /speékər/ *n* **1** a person who speaks **2** a speechmaker or lecturer **3** BROADCAST = **loudspeaker**

Speaker *n* the presiding officer of a legislative body, e.g. the House of Commons or the US or the Australian House of Representatives

speakerphone /speékər fōn/ *n US* a telephone equipped with a loudspeaker and microphone

speaking /speéking/ *adj* **1 INVOLVING SPEECH** involving speech or speaking **2 ELOQUENT** capable of communicating in an eloquent or impressive way **3 APPARENTLY REAL** resembling a real person or object ○ *the speaking image of her aunt* **4 ABLE TO USE SPECIFIED LANGUAGE** able to speak a particular language (*usually in combination*) ○ *French-speaking students*

speaking clock *n* a telephone service that provides an accurate verbal announcement of the time

speaking in tongues *n* the making of utterances that are not recognizable as any known language and have no formal linguistic content

speaking tube *n* a pipe connecting different parts of something, e.g. a ship or building, through which conversation can be conducted

spear[1] /speer/ *n* **1 LONG-HANDLED WEAPON WITH BLADE** a weapon for throwing or thrusting that has a long handle and a blade or head with a sharpened point **2 WEAPON FOR SPEARING FISH** a weapon with a sharp point and barbs used for catching fish by piercing them ■ *vti* **PIERCE SOMETHING WITH SPEAR** to stab, strike, pierce, or take somebody or something with or as though using a spear [Old English *spere* < Germanic] —**spearer** *n* —**spearman** *n*

spear[2] /speer/ *n* a young blade, shoot, or stalk of a plant such as asparagus or grass [15C. Alteration of SPIRE[1].]

spear carrier *n* **1** a minor member of a cast in a play or opera **2** an unimportant or irrelevant contributor to something (*informal*)

spearfish /speér fish/ (*plural* **-fish** *or* **-fishes**) *n* a large marine swordfish that is related to the marlin and sailfish and has a very long, pointed upper jaw. Genus: *Tetrapturus.*

spear grass *n* PLANTS = **feather grass**

spear gun *n* a gun designed to shoot a barbed spear underwater, used to catch fish

spearhead /speér hed/ *n* **1 POINTED HEAD OF SPEAR** the pointed head of a spear **2 LEADING FORCES IN MILITARY ATTACK** the leading forces in a military attack **3 DRIVING FORCE IN EVENT** the leading or driving element or force in an undertaking ■ *vt* **ACT AS LEADER OF EVENT** to act as the leader or driving force of a military attack, or any event or undertaking

spearmint /speér mint/ (*plural* **-mint** *or* **-mints**) *n* a common mint, the leaves and essential oil of which are used for flavouring. *Mentha spicata.* [Mid-16C. < the stem's resemblance to a spear.]

spear side *n* a husband's or father's side of a family (*literary*) ◊ **distaff side** [*Spear* as a symbol of man's domain]

spearwort /speér wurt/ (*plural* **-wort** *or* **-worts**) *n* a buttercup with spear-shaped leaves. Flowers: small, yellow. Native to: Europe, Asia, E United States. [Old English]

spec /spek/ *n* a detailed description of a particular thing, especially one detailed enough to provide somebody with the information needed to make that thing (*informal*) [Late 18C. Shortening.] ◇ **on spec** with a chance of achieving something but no certainty of it (*informal*)

special /spésh'l/ *adj* **1 UNUSUAL OR BETTER** distinct, different, unusual, or superior in comparison to others of the same kind ○ *a very special occasion* ○ *received special consideration* **2 HELD IN ESTEEM** regarded with particular esteem or affection **3 RESERVED** unique to or reserved for a specific person or thing ○ *It's my special chair.* **4 MADE FOR PARTICULAR PURPOSE** made or used for a particular purpose or occasion ○ *Firefighters used special breathing equipment.* **5 ARRANGED FOR SPECIFIC PURPOSE** planned for a specific occasion or purpose ○ *made a special visit to the factory* **6 ADDITIONAL** in addition to or more than is usual ○ *a special issue of the newspaper* **7 RELATING TO EDUCATING SPECIAL-NEEDS CHILDREN** designed or intended for educating children who have physical disabilities or learning difficulties ■ *n* **1 SOMETHING RESERVED FOR PARTICULAR PURPOSE** something designed or reserved for a particular purpose or occasion **2 TELEVISION PROGRAMME NOT PART OF SCHEDULE** a television programme that is not part of a network's normal schedule **3** *US, Can* **TEMPORARY REDUCTION IN PRICE** a temporary reduction in the price of an item **4 DISH NOT ON USUAL MENU** a dish that a restaurant or other food outlet offers in addition to the standard menu, or one that is available for a low price **5** CRIME = **special constable** [12C. Directly or via Old French *especial* < Latin *specialis* < *species* (see SPECIES).] —**specialness** *n*

Special Air Service *n* full form of **SAS**

Special Boat Service *n* an elite British Royal Marines force that is used to spearhead amphibious operations and to reconnoitre beach landings

Special Branch *n* the branch of the UK police force that is the executive arm of the government intelligence agencies and specializes in matters of political security

special constable *n* in the United Kingdom, somebody who acts as a volunteer to supplement the police force, especially on occasions when a large police force is necessary, e.g. emergencies or demonstrations

special delivery *n* the delivery of mail more quickly than or outside normal delivery times for an extra fee

special drawing rights *n* a method of settling international debts through the International Monetary Fund in order to stabilize exchange rates

special education *n* teaching modified to suit students with special educational needs

special effects *npl* extraordinary visual effects in a film or television programme achieved by technical means, either optically, digitally, or mechanically

special interest group *n* a group seeking to influence government policy in favour of a particular interest or issue

specialise *vi* = **specialize**

specialism /spéshəlizəm/ *n* concentration in a particular field of study ○ *There is a great deal of specialism in their education system.*

specialist /spéshəlist/ *n* **1 SOMEBODY SPECIALIZING IN PARTICULAR INTEREST** a person who specializes in an occupation, interest, or field of study **2** *US* **ENLISTED RANK IN US ARMY** an enlisted person in the US Army with special technical skills, of a rank in a series numbered from 4 to 7 between corporal and sergeant first class **3 TYPE OF PHYSICIAN** a medical doctor who practises in a certain field, e.g. surgery, dermatology, or oncology —**specialistic** /spéshə lístik/ *adj*

speciality /spéshi álləti/ (*plural* **-ties**) *n* **1 SOMETHING SOMEBODY SPECIALIZES IN** a skill, field of study, interest, or activity in which somebody specializes. US term **specialty** *n.* 1 **2 PRODUCT OF SOMEBODY'S SPECIALIZATION** a product or result of somebody's specialization. US term **specialty** *n.* 2 **3 DISTINCTIVE MARK** an unusual, distinctive, or superior mark or quality. US term **specialty** *n.* 4

specialization /spéshə lī záysh'n/ *n* **1 ACT OF BECOMING SPECIALIZED** the act or process of becoming specialized **2** EDUC = **speciality** *n.* 1 **3 ADAPTATION OF ORGANISM** the adaptation of an organism or a part of an organism to a particular function or condition in response to environmental conditions **4 ADAPTED BODY PART** an organism or a part of an organism that has been adapted to a particular function or condition

specialize /spéshə līz/ (**-izes, -izing, -ized**), **specialise** (**-ises, -ising, -ised**) *v* **1** *vi* **DEVOTE TIME TO PARTICULAR ACTIVITY** to devote time exclusively to a particular interest, skill, or field of study **2** *vt* **SPECIFY** to specify or make specific mention of something **3** *vt* **ADAPT TO PARTICULAR PURPOSE** to adapt something to suit a specific purpose **4** *vi* **BECOME ADAPTED** to become adapted to a particular function or condition

~~**speciall**~~ incorrect spelling of **special**

special licence *n* a marriage licence that allows a marriage to take place without the usual legal conditions being enforced

specially /spésh'li/ *adv* for a special or particular purpose, person, or occasion ○ *It was intended specially for preschool children.* ○ *I had it specially made.*

USAGE See ***especially***.

special needs *npl* the particular requirements, especially in education, that some people have because of physical disabilities or learning difficulties

Special Olympics *n* an international athletic competition for athletes who have a physical or mental disability (*+ singular or plural verb*)

special pleading *n* **1** pleading that introduces new or special matter and that avoids allegations of matter pleaded by the opposite side, instead of direct denial of those allegations **2** an argument that presents only one aspect of an issue and avoids any unfavourable aspects

special relativity *n* PHYS = **relativity** *n.* 1

special school *n* a school catering to students who have special educational needs, e.g. because of learning difficulties or physical disabilities

special session *n* a session of a legislature, court, or council held in addition to and outside of regularly scheduled sessions

special sort *n* a character that is not on the usual printing font, e.g. an accented or Greek letter

special theory of relativity *n* PHYS = **relativity** *n.* 1

specialty /spésh'lti/ (*plural* **-ties**) *n* **1** *US* = **speciality** *n.* 1 **2** *US* = **speciality** *n.* 2 **3** an area of medicine in which somebody specializes **4** *US* = **speciality** *n.* 3 **5** a legal agreement made under seal

speciation /speéssi áysh'n/ *n* the evolutionary formation of new biological species, usually by one species that divides into two or more species that are genetically unique [Early 20C. < SPECIES.] —**speciate** /speéssi ayt/ *vi*

specie /speéshi/ *n* money in the form of coins [Mid-16C. Shortening of Latin *in specie* 'in kind' < *species* (see SPECIES).] ◇ **in specie 1** in the form of coins **2** in a similar way or kind **3** in the form specified

~~**speciel**~~ incorrect spelling of **special**

species /speé sheez/ (*plural* **-cies**) *n* **1 TAXONOMIC GROUP** a subdivision of a genus considered as a basic biological classification and containing individuals that resemble one another and that may interbreed **2 ORGANISMS IN SPECIES** the organisms belonging to a particular species **3 KIND OR SORT** a kind, sort, or variety of something **4 ATOM CATEGORY** a category of atomic nucleus, ion, molecule, or atom **5 SUBDIVISION OF GENUS** a collection of objects or individuals that, on the basis of shared features, form a subdivision of a genus **6 BREAD AND WINE IN COMMUNION** the two elements of the Communion, bread and wine, or their outward form after consecration [14C. < Latin, 'appearance, kind', < *specere* 'look'.]

SYNONYMS See ***type***.

speciesism /speé sheezizəm/ *n* the belief that the human race is superior to other species, and that exploitation of animals for the advantage of humans is justified

specif. *abbr* **1** specific **2** specifically

specific /spə síffik/ *adj* **1 PRECISE** particular and detailed, avoiding vagueness ○ *specific instructions* **2 RELATING TO PARTICULAR THING** acting on or relating to a particular thing ○ *The instructions are specific to this task.* **3 DISTINCTIVE** with individual qualities that allow a distinction to be made or make a distinction necessary ○ *discussing these specific problems* **4 OF SPECIES** relating to a biological species **5 EFFECTIVE** specially effective in a particular pathological condition **6 CAUSED BY PARTICULAR INFECTIOUS AGENT** describes a disease caused by a particular infectious agent **7 DENOTING PHYSICAL PROPERTY** used to indicate that a physical property is being expressed with reference to a particular quantity, such as mass, volume, or length **8 LEVIED PER UNIT** describes taxes or duties levied on a per-unit basis using number, weight, or volume ■ *n* **1 DETAIL** a particular item, quality, or detail ○ *didn't go into specifics* **2 EFFECTIVE DRUG** a medicine that is especially effective against a particular disease [Mid-17C. < late Latin *specificus* 'making a kind' < Latin *species* 'kind' (see SPECIES).] —**specifically** *adv* —**specificity** /spéssi físsəti/ *n*

specific absorption rate *n* full form of **SAR**

specification /spéssifi káysh'n/ *n* **1 DETAILED DESCRIPTION** a detailed description of a particular thing, especially one detailed enough to provide somebody with the information needed to make that thing ○ *a look at the engine specification* **2 DETAIL** an item within a specification ○ *The machine's technical specifications are in Appendix A.* **3 SPECIFYING** the specifying of something **4 INTELLECTUAL PROPERTY DESCRIPTION** a detailed description of intellectual property, as required by law **5 TYPOGRAPHICAL INSTRUCTIONS** detailed instructions regarding information such as font, point size, and layout that are sent with material to be typeset and printed

specific charge *n* the ratio of the electric charge of an elementary particle divided by its mass

specific gravity *n* PHYS = **relative density**

specific heat *n* US PHYS = **specific heat capacity**

specific heat capacity *n* (*symbol* c) the amount of heat needed to raise the temperature of one gram of a substance by one degree, usually measured in joules per kelvin per kilogram. US term **specific heat**

specific language impairment *n* an inability to develop normal language skills in a child with normal intelligence and hearing, possibly due to an inability to process sound

~~**specificly**~~ incorrect spelling of **specifically**

specific performance *n* a court order compelling somebody to carry out an obligation, often something stated in a contract

specific resistance *n* ELEC = **resistivity** *n.* 1

specify /spéssi fī/ (**-fies, -fying, -fied**) *vt* **1 STATE EXPLICITLY** to state or identify something in detail or explicitly **2 STIPULATE** to state something or make it a condition ○ *The rules specify that pets cannot be kept here.* **3 INCLUDE IN SPECIFICATION** to include or state something in a specification [13C. Via French *spécifier* or directly < late Latin *specificare* < *specificus* (see SPECIFIC).] —**specifiable** *adj* —**specificative** /spéssifi kaytiv, spə síffi kaytiv/ *adj* —**specifier** *n*

~~**speciman**~~ incorrect spelling of **specimen**

specimen /spéssimin/ *n* **1 REPRESENTATIVE THING** something that is representative because it is typical of its kind or of a whole, especially something that serves as an example ○ *a specimen of the candidate's handwriting* **2 TYPE OF PERSON** a person who displays specific characteristics (*informal*) ○ *'turning away with disgust from the loathsome specimen of humanity before him'* (Baroness Orczy, *The Scarlet Pimpernel*; 1905) **3 SAMPLE OF BODY MATERIAL** a sample, e.g. of urine or blood, used for testing and diagnosis **4 TYPICAL EXAMPLE** an organism or one of its parts preserved as a typical example of its classification [Early 17C. < Latin, < *specere* 'look at'.]

specious /speéshəss/ *adj* **1** appearing to be true but really false **2** superficially attractive but actually of no real interest or value [14C. < Latin *speciosus* 'good-looking' < *species* 'appearance' (see SPECIES).] —**speciously** *adv* —**speciousness** *n*

speck /spek/ *n* **1 SMALL SPOT** a very small mark or stain **2 PARTICLE** a tiny particle of something solid ■ *vt* **MARK WITH SPECKS** to mark something with specks (*usually passive*) [Old English *specca* < ?]

speckle /spék'l/ *n* a small spot or mark, often a small irregular patch of contrasting colour, e.g. on plumage or an egg shell ■ *vt* (**-les, -ling, -led**) to mark something with speckles (*usually passive*) [15C. Probably literally 'little speck'.]

speckled /spék'ld/ *adj* **1** with a pattern of many small spots or small irregular patches, often of a contrasting colour **2** with parts that contrast distinctly with each other ○ *a speckled career* ○ *speckled shadows*

speckle interferometry *n* a technique for reducing distortions in photographic images of celestial objects by combining a number of images of very short exposure

specs /speks/ *npl* (*informal*) **1** spectacles **2** specifications

SPECT *abbr* single photon emission computed tomography

spectacle /spéktək'l/ *n* **1 SOMETHING REMARKABLE THAT CAN BE SEEN** an object, phenomenon, or event that is seen or witnessed, especially one that is impressive, unusual, or disturbing **2 LAVISH DISPLAY** an impressive performance or display, especially something staged as a form of entertainment **3 UNPLEASANT CENTRE OF ATTENTION** somebody or something that attracts attention by being unpleasant or ridiculous ○ *You are making a spectacle of yourself.* [14C. Via French < Latin *spectaculum* < *spectare* 'watch' < *specere* (see SPECIMEN).]

spectacled /spéktək'ld/ *adj* **1** with eyeglasses on **2** with markings on the face that encircle the eyes in a way that resembles spectacles

spectacles /spéktək'lz/ *npl* a pair of glass or plastic lenses worn in a frame in front of the eyes to help correct imperfect vision [15C. Plural of SPECTACLE.]

spectacular /spek tákyoōlər/ *adj* **1 VISUALLY IMPRESSIVE** impressive or dramatic to look at or watch **2 REMARKABLE** remarkably large, great, or speedy ■ *n* **EXTRAVAGANZA** a lavish celebration or artistic production —**spectacularly** *adv*

spectate /spek táyt/ (**-tates, -tating, -tated**) *vi* to watch rather than participate [Early 18C. Back-formation < SPECTATOR.]

spectator /spek táytər/ *n* a watcher or observer, especially somebody who watches an event [Late 16C. Via French *spectateur* or directly < Latin *spectator* < *spectare* 'watch' (see SPECTACLE).] —**spectatorial** /spéktə táwri əl/ *adj* —**spectatorship** *n*

spectator sport *n* a sport that attracts spectators in large numbers

specter *n* US = **spectre**

spectinomycin /spéktinō mísin/ *n* a broad-spectrum antibiotic effective against penicillin-resistant pathogens. Use: treatment of gonorrhoea. [Mid-20C. < modern Latin *spectabilis* < Latin, 'visible' < *spectare* 'watch' (see SPECTACLE), after *actinomycin.*]

spectra plural of **spectrum**

spectral /spéktrəl/ *adj* 1 relating to spectres or in the form of a spectre 2 produced by a spectrum or relating to a spectrum —**spectrality** /spek trálləti/ *n* —**spectrally** *adv* —**spectralness** *n*

spectral class *n* ASTRON = **spectral type**

spectral line *n* any discrete band of light in a spectrum associated with a specific wavelength and used to identify substances

spectral type, spectral class *n* a classification system for stars based on an analysis of the light they emit. This analysis also gives information on a star's temperature and chemical composition.

spectre /spéktər/ *n* 1 a ghostly presence or apparition 2 a threat or prospect of something unpleasant ○ *the spectre of my performance review* [Early 17C. Via French or directly < Latin *spectrum* 'image, apparition' (see SPECTRUM).]

spectrin /spéktrin/ *n* a fibrous protein in the membranes of red blood cells [Mid-20C. < SPECTRE, because the material was first isolated from red blood cells lacking haemoglobin, called 'ghosts'.]

spectro- *prefix* spectrum ○ *spectroscope* [< SPECTRUM]

spectrochemistry /spéktrō kémmistri/ *n* a branch of chemistry dealing with the spectra formed during chemical activity, such as the emission spectra of substances burned in an arc or spark —**spectrochemical** *adj*

spectrogram /spéktrə gram/ *n* a photograph or representation of a spectrum

spectrograph /spéktrə graaf, -graf/ *n* an instrument consisting of a spectrometer and related equipment used to obtain a visual record of a spectrum —**spectrographic** /spéktrə gráffik/ *adj* —**spectrographically** *adv* —**spectrography** /spek tróggrəfi/ *n*

spectroheliogram /spéktrə héeli ə gram/ *n* an image of the sun produced using a narrow wavelength band of the radiation it emits

spectroheliograph /spéktrō héeli ə graaf, -graf/ *n* an instrument used to obtain images of the sun over a narrow band of wavelengths —**spectroheliographic** /spéktrō heeli ə gráffik/ *adj* —**spectroheliography** /spéktrō héeli óggrəfi/ *n*

spectrohelioscope /spéktrō héeli ə skōp/ *n* an instrument that is similar to a spectroheliograph but is used for viewing the sun's spectrum, as distinct from recording it —**spectrohelioscopic** /spéktrō heeli ə skóppik/ *adj*

spectrometer /spek trómmitər/ *n* an instrument used to disperse radiant energy or particles into a spectrum and measure properties such as wavelength, mass, energy, or index of refraction —**spectrometric** /spéktrə méttrik/ *adj* —**spectrometry** *n*

spectrophotometer /spéktrōfə tómmitər/ *n* an instrument used to measure the relative intensities of wavelengths in a spectrum —**spectrophotometric** /spéktrō fōtə méttrik/ *adj* —**spectrophotometrically** *adv* —**spectrophotometry** *n*

spectroscope /spéktrə skōp/ *n* an instrument for dispersing light, usually light in the visible range, into a spectrum in order to measure it —**spectroscopic** /spéktrə skóppik/ *adj* —**spectroscopically** *adv*

spectroscopic analysis *n* the use of spectroscopy to determine the chemical composition, energy levels, and molecular structure of substances

spectroscopy /spek tróskəpi/ *n* the study of spectra, especially to determine the chemical composition of substances and the physical properties of molecules, ions, and atoms —**spectroscopist** *n*

spectrum /spéktrəm/ (*plural* **-tra** /-trə/ *or* **-trums**) *n* 1 **DISTRIBUTION OF COLOURED LIGHT** a continuous distribution of coloured light produced when a beam of white light is dispersed into its components, e.g. by a prism 2 **RADIATION FREQUENCY RANGE WITH SPECIFIED PROPERTY** a range of radiation frequencies that have a specified property 3 **RECORD OF SUBSTANCE'S RADIATION DENSITY** a visual record of the wavelengths of the radiation or particles emitted by a substance, used as a means of analysing its physical properties, e.g. energy and mass 4 **RANGE** any range, especially one with opposite values at its limits ○ *a spectrum of opinions between the two extremes* 5 **RANGE OF DRUG TARGETS** the range of organisms that an antibiotic can kill [Late 19C. < Latin, 'image, apparition' < *specere* 'see' (see SPECIMEN).]

specula plural of **speculum**

specular /spékyŏŏlər/ *adj* 1 relating to mirrors or having the characteristics of a mirror 2 carried out using a speculum [Late 16C. < Latin *specularis* < *speculum* (see SPECULUM).]

speculate /spékyŏŏ layt/ (**-lates, -lating, -lated**) *v* 1 *vti* **CONJECTURE** to conjecture something based on incomplete facts or information 2 *vi* **CONSIDER** to think over possibilities 3 *vi* **MAKE RISKY DEALS FOR PROFIT** to engage in financial transactions such as commodity trading that have an element of risk especially in the short term with the hope of making a profit 4 *vi* **TAKE RISKS** to take risks in an attempt to achieve something or get some benefit [Late 16C. < Latin *speculat-*, past participle of *speculari* 'observe, spy out' < *specere* (see SPECIMEN).]

speculative /spékyŏŏlətiv/ *adj* 1 **USING INCOMPLETE INFORMATION** based on conjecture or incomplete information 2 **FORMING CONCLUSIONS NOT BASED ON FACT** given to forming conclusions or opinions that are not based on fact 3 **RISKY BUT POTENTIALLY PROFITABLE** risky in nature but potentially profitable speculative investments ○ *speculative investments* —**speculatively** *adv* —**speculativeness** *n*

speculator /spékyŏŏ laytər/ *n* a person who speculates, especially financially

speculum /spékyŏŏləm/ (*plural* **-la** /spékyŏŏlə/ *or* **-lums**) *n* 1 **MIRROR** a mirror or other reflective surface in an optical instrument such as a telescope 2 **MEDICAL INSTRUMENT** a medical instrument used to hold open a body passage, e.g. the anus or vagina, so that it can be examined 3 **COLOURED PATCH ON BIRD'S WINGS** a patch of colour on the wings of ducks and some other birds, helpful in identification [Late 16C. < Latin, 'mirror' < *specere* 'see' (see SPECIMEN).]

speculum metal *n* an alloy of copper and tin sometimes with other metals. It is hard, brittle, white, resistant to corrosion and, because it can be highly polished, is used for metal mirrors.

sped past tense, past participle of **speed**

speech /speech/ *n* 1 **SPEAKING ABILITY** the ability to speak (*often before nouns*) 2 **COMMUNICATION BY SPEAKING** the act of communicating by speaking 3 **THINGS SAID** things that are spoken ○ *recordings of human speech* 4 **SPOKEN LANGUAGE** spoken language especially as distinct from writing 5 **ADDRESS** a talk given to an audience 6 **PARTICULAR WAY OF SPEAKING** a particular way of speaking or using language, especially that of an individual or group [Old English *spǣc* < *specan*, an earlier form of SPEAK]

speech community *n* a group that includes all the speakers of a single language or dialect

speech day *n* an annual event in a school during which speeches are given by staff and guests and pupils are presented with prizes for good work and outstanding achievements

speechify /spéechi fī/ (**-fies, -fying, -fied**) *vi* (*informal*) 1 to talk in a tedious and self-important manner, especially in giving an opinion 2 to give a speech or speeches —**speechification** /spéechifi káysh'n/ *n* —**speechifier** *n*

speechless /spéechləss, -liss/ *adj* 1 **TEMPORARILY UNABLE TO SPEAK** temporarily not able to speak or not able to think of something to say, e.g. because of surprise or fear 2 **UNABLE TO SPEAK** lacking the power of speech 3 **REMAINING SILENT** choosing not to say anything 4 **UNSPOKEN** not expressed in words 5 **HARD TO EXPRESS** difficult or impossible to put into words [Old English] —**speechlessly** *adv* —**speechlessness** *n*

speechmaker /spéech maykər/ *n* a maker of a speech or speeches —**speechmaking** *n*

speech pathology *n* the study, diagnosis, and treatment of speech disorders, including failure of normal speech development in children and language disorders resulting from acquired brain dysfunction —**speech pathologist** *n*

speech-reading *n* COMMUNICATION = **lip-reading**

ϟ **speech recognition** *n* a system of computer input and control in which the computer can recognize spoken words and transform them into digitized commands or text

ϟ **speech synthesis** *n* computer-generated audio output that resembles human speech

speech therapy *n* the treatment of speech disorders —**speech therapist** *n*

speechwriter /spéech rītər/ *n* a writer of speeches for other people

speed /speed/ *n* 1 **RATE OF MOVEMENT OR HAPPENING** the rate at which something moves, happens, or functions 2 **RAPIDITY** fast movement, progress, or operation 3 **RATE OF MOVEMENT IRRESPECTIVE OF DIRECTION** rate of movement irrespective of direction. It is equal either to distance travelled divided by travel time, or to rate of change of distance with respect to time. 4 **AMPHETAMINE** an amphetamine drug (*slang*) 5 *US* **SOMETHING SUITABLE** something that matches somebody's tastes, abilities, or inclinations (*informal*) ○ *The intermediate course will be more my speed.* 6 **SUCCESS** success or prosperity (*archaic*) 7 **GEAR RATIO** a gear ratio in a motor, engine, or driving mechanism ○ *a ten-speed bicycle* ○ *operates at three different speeds* 8 **PHOTOGRAPHIC FILM'S SENSITIVITY TO LIGHT** a measure of the sensitivity of photographic film to light, expressed numerically according to any of various rating systems ■ *v* (**speeds, speeding, sped** *or* **speeded**) 1 *vti* **GO OR MOVE QUICKLY** to go or move quickly, or to make something or somebody go or move quickly 2 *vi* **DRIVE FAST** to drive fast, especially exceeding the speed limit 3 *vi* **PASS QUICKLY** to pass or happen quickly or more quickly 4 *vi* **USE AMPHETAMINES** to be under the influence of amphetamines (*slang*) 5 *vti* **MAKE OR BE PROSPEROUS** to prosper or cause somebody or something to prosper (*archaic*) [Old English *spēd* 'success, prosperity' < Indo-European, 'to prosper'] ◇ **be** *or* **get up to speed** 1 to reach the maximum or desirable rate of movement or progress 2 to be or become fully informed about the latest developments

speed up *vti* to increase in rate or speed, or to increase the rate or speed of somebody or something

speedball /spéed bawl/ *n* 1 a team game similar to football, in which the ball can be passed forwards with the hands and caught when in mid-air 2 a combination of illegal drugs such as cocaine and heroin taken by injection (*slang*)

speedboat /spéed bōt/ *n* a motorboat capable of travelling at high speeds

speed brake *n* a flap on an aircraft wing used to decrease speed in flight before landing

speed bump (*plural* **speed bumps** *or* **speed humps**) *n* a raised area or ridge on a road surface designed to limit traffic speed

speed camera *n* a roadside-mounted camera that automatically photographs a vehicle passing by it at excessive speed. It provides traffic police with concrete evidence of speeding offences.

speed demon *n US* a speeder in a motor vehicle (*informal*) ◊ **speed merchant**

speed dial *n* a function on a telephone that enables numbers to be stored in a memory so that they can be dialled by pressing a single button ○ *I have her number on speed dial.*

speeder /spéedər/ *n* a motorist who breaks the speed limit

speedfreak *n* an addict of amphetamines (*slang*)

speed hump *n* TRANSP = **speed bump**

speeding /spéeding/ *n* the offence of driving a vehicle at a speed above the designated speed limit ■ *adj* moving or working quickly

speed limit *n* the maximum permitted speed, usually specified by law, at which a vehicle may travel on a particular stretch of road

speed merchant *n UK, ANZ, Can* a speeder in a motor vehicle (*informal*)

speedo /spéedō/ (*plural* **-os**) *n* a speedometer (*informal*) [Mid-20C. Shortening.]

speedometer /spi dómmitər/ *n* an instrument that continuously measures a vehicle's speed and displays it either numerically or by means of a needle on a dial

speed-read *vti* to read something very fast using a learned technique of skimming the text

speed skate *n* an ice skate designed for racing —**speed skater** *n*

speed skating *n* the sport of racing competitively on speed skates

speed trap *n* a stretch of road kept under hidden surveillance by police officers monitoring vehicle speeds, usually using radar equipment

speedup /spéed up/ *n US* **1** an increase in rate or speed **2** a demand for an increase in productivity from a workforce without a corresponding pay increase

speed walking *n* ATHLETICS = **race walking**

speedway /spéed way/ *n* **1** a motor sport in which lightweight motorcycles race against each other on an oval cinder track (*often before nouns*) **2** a track or stadium used for speedway

speedwell /spéed wel/ *n* a perennial plant of the snapdragon family with opposite leaves. Flowers: blue or pinkish, in clusters. Native to: Europe. Genus: *Veronica*. [Late 16C. < SPEED (verb) + WELL[2].]

speedwriting /spéed rīting/ *n* a system of shorthand writing that uses combinations of standard letters, as distinct from other systems that use symbols

speedy /spéedi/ (**-ier, -iest**) *adj* **1** accomplished or achieved quickly **2** capable of moving very fast —**speedily** *adv* —**speediness** *n*

speiss /spīss/ *n* a compound of arsenic or antimony formed during the smelting of ores such as iron, nickel, and copper [Late 18C. < German *Speise* 'food, speiss'.]

Speke /speek/, **John Hanning** (1827–64) British explorer

spelaean /spi lée ən/, **spelean** *adj* relating to caves, or found in caves [Mid-19C. Via Latin *spelaeum* < Greek *spēlaion* 'cave'.]

speleology /spéeli ólləji/, **spelaeology** *n* **1** the scientific study of caves **2** the sport or pastime of exploring caves. US term **spelunking** —**speleological** /spéeli ə lójjik'l/ *adj* —**speleologist** *n*

spell[1] /spel/ (**spells, spelling, spelt** /spelt/ *or* **spelled**) *v* **1** *vti* **NAME OR WRITE LETTERS OF WORD** to name or write in correct order the constituent letters of a word, part of a word, or group of words **2** *vt* **FORM WORD** to form a word when arranged in the correct order **3** *vt* **SIGNIFY** to be a sign or indication of something ○ *Increased interest rates could spell trouble for some corporate borrowers.* [13C. Via Old French *espeller* < Germanic.]

spell out *vt* **1 MAKE COMPLETELY CLEAR** to state something clearly, allowing no room for misunderstanding **2 READ SLOWLY OR WITH DIFFICULTY** to read something with difficulty or very slowly, especially by reading out words one letter at a time **3 FIGURE OUT** to figure something out by careful study or analysis

spell[2] /spel/ *n* **1 WORDS WITH MAGICAL POWER** a word or series of words believed to have magical power, spoken to invoke the magic **2 SPELL'S INFLUENCE** the influence that a spell has over somebody or something **3 FASCINATION** a compelling fascination or attraction ■ *vt* (**spells, spelling, spelt** /spelt/ *or* **spelled, spelt** *or* **spelled**) **INFLUENCE USING SPELL** to put somebody or something under the influence of a spell [Old English, 'talk, speech' < Germanic]

spell[3] /spel/ *n* **1 SHORT PERIOD** a period of indeterminate but usually short duration (*informal*) ○ *Let's sit a spell.* **2 PERIOD OF PARTICULAR WEATHER** a period of weather of a particular type ○ *a warm spell* **3 BOUT OF ILLNESS** a period of illness ○ *a fainting spell* **4 PERIOD OF WORK** a period of work or purposeful activity **5 TOUR OF DUTY** somebody's turn to work or perform a particular duty **6** *Scotland, ANZ* **REST PERIOD** a period of rest **7** *US* **SHORT DISTANCE** a short but unspecified distance (*informal*) ○ *down the road a spell* ■ *v* (**spells, spelling, spelled, spelt** /spelt/ *or* **spelled**) **1** *vt US, ANZ, Scotland* **RELIEVE** to relieve somebody of a task temporarily, especially in order to allow him or her to rest **2** *vi US* **TAKE TURNS** to take turns working at a job [Late 16C. The noun came from the verb, a variant of obsolete *spele* 'take the place of someone' < Old English *spelian* < ?]

spellbinding /spél bīnding/ *adj* holding attention and interest completely, as if with the influence of a spell —**spellbind** *vt* —**spellbinder** *n* —**spellbindingly** *adv*

spellbound /spél bownd/ *adj* with attention and interest held completely, as if under the influence of a spell [Late 18C. Literally 'bound by a spell' < SPELL[2].]

⚡**spellchecker** /spél chekər/ *n* a computer program that compares words in a text to a file of correctly spelled words to detect misspellings —**spellcheck** *n, vt*

speller /spéllər/ *n* **1** a person who spells words, especially in a specific way **2** a book for teaching or improving spelling

spellican /spéllikən/ *n* HOBBIES = **spillikin** [Mid-18C. Variant.]

spelling /spélling/ *n* **1 ABILITY TO SPELL** the ability to spell words correctly **2 FORMING WORDS BY ORDERING LETTERS** the forming of words with letters in a conventionally accepted order (*often before nouns*) **3 SPECIFIC EXAMPLE OF LETTER ORDER** a specific example of how a word is actually spelt

spelling bee *n* a competition in which the object is to see who can spell the most words correctly

spelling pronunciation *n* a variant pronunciation of a word that differs from the standard pronunciation and is influenced by the way a word is spelt

spelt[1] past tense, past participle of **spell**

spelt[2] /spelt/ *n* a hardy variety of wheat of inferior quality, sometimes grown in mountainous regions. *Triticum spelta*. [Pre-12C. < late Latin *spelta* < ?]

spelter /spéltər/ *n* impure zinc, often used as a cheap alternative for bronze in cast decorative items [Mid-17C. Ultimately related to PEWTER.]

spelunking /spi lúngking/ *n US* = **speleology** *n.* **2** [Mid-20C. < *spelunk* 'cave', via Old French *spelunque* < Latin *spelunca* < Greek *spelunx*.] —**spelunker** *n*

Spemann /shpáy màn/, **Hans** (1869–1941) German embryologist

spencer /spénssər/ *n* **1** a short jacket worn by boys in the late 18th and early 19th centuries **2** a very short jacket worn by women over a high-waisted gown in the late 18th and early 19th centuries [Late 18C. After George John *Spencer*, second Earl Spencer (1758–1834).]

Spencer /spénssər/, **Sir Baldwin** (1860–1929) Australian anthropologist

Spencer, Sir Stanley (1891–1959) British painter

Spencer Gulf large inlet of the Indian Ocean in South Australia. Length: 322 km/200 mi.

Spencerian /spen séeri ən/ *adj* describes a style of handwriting with perfectly formed letters and ornamentation of capitals [Mid-19C. After Platt Rogers *Spencer* (1800–64), US calligrapher.]

spend /spend/ *v* (**spends, spending, spent**) **1** *vti* **PAY MONEY** to pay out money in exchange for goods or services **2** *vt* **DEVOTE TIME OR EFFORT** to devote time, energy, or thought to something ○ *spent a lot of time thinking about it* **3** *vt* **PASS TIME** to pass time in a specified place or way ○ *spend a week in Hawaii* **4** *vt* **USE UP** to deplete something totally **5** *vt* **SACRIFICE** to sacrifice something, especially for a cause ○ *spent her life working for reform* ■ *n* **1 SPREE** a time or trip during which things are bought and money is spent, especially a lot of money **2 AMOUNT OF MONEY SPENT** an amount of money spent or set aside for spending ○ *'...is increasing its advertising spend by 40 per cent...'* (*Marketing Week*; December 1998) [Pre-12C. < Latin *expendere* 'pay' (see EXPEND), but also in part < Old French *despendre* 'expend' < Latin *dispendere* 'distribute by weighing out' (see DISPENSE).] —**spender** *n*

Spender /spéndər/, **Dale** (*b.* 1943) Australian writer and feminist

Spender, Sir Stephen (1909–95) British poet and editor

spending money *n* cash used or available for personal expenses, especially expenditure on nonessential items

spendthrift /spénd thrift/ *n* a reckless or extravagant spender of money ■ *adj* tending to spend money extravagantly and wastefully [Late 16C. < SPEND + THRIFT, in the archaic sense 'savings, earnings'.]

Spenser /spénssər/, **Edmund** (1552?–99) English poet —**Spenserian** /spen séeri ən/ *adj*

Spenserian stanza *n* a stanza devised by Edmund Spenser that contains eight lines of iambic pentameter and a ninth of iambic hexameter, using the rhyme scheme ababbcbcc

spent /spent/ past tense, past participle of **spend** ■ *adj* **1 CONSUMED** used or used up ○ *tossed the spent match into the fire* **2 EXHAUSTED** totally depleted of energy or strength ○ *felt totally spent by the end of the day* **3 FINISHED** at an end **4 EXHAUSTED OF SPAWN OR SPERM** describes a female fish that has deposited all its spawn or a male fish that has used up all its sperm

sperm[1] /spurm/ (*plural* **sperm** *or* **sperms**) *n* **1** used popularly, but technically incorrectly, to refer to semen **2** BIOL = **spermatozoon** [14C. Via late Latin *sperma* < Greek, 'seed, semen'.]

sperm[2] /spurm/ *n* **1** INDUST = **spermaceti** **2** INDUST = **sperm oil** **3** ZOOL = **sperm whale** [Mid-19C. Shortening.]

spermaceti /spúrmə sétti, spúrmə séeti/ *n* a white waxy solid. Source: oil in the head of sperm whales and other cetaceans. Use: formerly in cosmetics, candles, and ointments. [Late 15C. < medieval Latin, < late Latin *sperma* 'semen' (see SPERM[1]) + Latin *ceti* 'of a whale'.]

spermary /spúrməri/ (*plural* **-ries**) *n* an organ in which male reproductive cells are developed. The testes are spermaries.

spermat- *prefix* = **spermato-** (*before vowels*)

spermatheca /spúrmə théekə/ *n* a receptacle for storing sperm in the reproductive tracts of some invertebrates such as insects [Early 19C. < late Latin *sperma* 'seed, semen' (see SPERM[1]) + THECA.] —**spermathecal** *adj*

spermatic /spur máttik/, **spermic** /spúrmik/ *adj* **1** relating to, carrying, or containing semen **2** relating to a sperm-ary or to the spermatic cord —**spermatically** *adv*

spermatic cord *n* a cord by which a testis is suspended in the scrotum. It contains the vas deferens as well as nerves, vessels, and veins.

spermatid /spúrmə tid/ *n* any of the four cells that are formed from a spermatocyte and develop into spermatozoa

spermato- *prefix* **1** sperm, spermatozoon ○ *spermatogenesis* **2** seed ○ *spermatophyte* [< Greek *spermat-*, stem of *sperma* (see SPERM[1])]

spermatocide /spur máttō sīd/ *n* PHARM = **spermicide** —**spermatocidal** /spur máttō sīd'l, spúrmətō-/ *adj*

spermatocyte /spur máttō sīt/ *n* a cell that develops from a spermatogonium

spermatogenesis /spur máttō jénnəsiss, spúrmətō-/ *n* the formation and development of spermatozoa in the testes —**spermatogenetic** /spur máttō jə néttik, spúrmətō-/ *adj*

spermatogonium /spur máttō gṓni əm, spúrmətō-/ (*plural* **-a** /-ni ə/) *n* a cell in the male testes that develops and divides to form spermatocytes. These subsequently divide to form spermatids, from which spermatozoa finally develop. —**spermatogonial** *adj*

spermatophore /spur máttō fawr, spúrmətə fawr/ *n* a capsule or mass that encloses spermatozoa in insects and other lower animals and that is transferred to the female during insemination —**spermatophoral** /spur máttə fáwrəl, spúrmət-/ *adj*

spermatophyte /spur máttō fīt/ *n* any plant that produces seeds, including angiosperms and gymnosperms —**spermatophytic** /spur máttə fíttik, spúrmətō-/ *adj*

spermatorrhoea /spur mátə rée ə/ *n* the involuntary emission of semen without orgasm

spermatozoa plural of **spermatozoon**

spermatozoid /spur máttō zṓ id, spúrmətō-/ *n* a male reproductive cell, resembling a ribbon, produced in algae, ferns, fungi, mosses, and some gymnosperms [Mid-19C. < SPERMATOZOON + -ID.]

spermatozoon /spur máttō zṓ on, spúrmətō-/ (*plural* **-a** /-ə/) *n* a male reproductive cell (**gamete**) that has an oval head with a nucleus, a short neck, and a tail by which it moves to find and fertilize an ovum —**spermatozoan** *adj*

sperm bank *n* a place that stores semen until it is required for use in artificial insemination

sperm count *n* **1** the concentration of sperm in a given volume of seminal fluid, taken as an index of male fertility **2** a test to determine a man's sperm count

spermi- *prefix* = **spermo-**

spermic *adj* BIOL = **spermatic**

spermicide /spúrmi sīd/ *n* a contraceptive cream or gel used in conjunction with a birth-control device. Use: kills spermatozoa. —**spermicidal** /spúrmi sīd'l/ *adj*

spermiogenesis /spúrmi ō jénnəsiss/ *n* the stage of spermatogenesis during which a spermatid is transformed into a spermatozoon —**spermiogenetic** /spúrmi ō jə néttik/ *adj*

spermo- *prefix* seed, sperm ○ *spermophyte* [< Greek *sperma* 'seed']

sperm oil *n* a pale yellow oil obtained from the head of the sperm whale. Use: formerly, industrial lubricant.

spermophile /spúrmə fīl/ *n* a ground squirrel that eats grain and is often regarded as a pest. Native to: North America. Genera: *Citellus* and *Spermophilus*. [Early 19C. < modern Latin *spermophilus* 'seed lover'.]

sperm whale *n* the largest of the toothed whales, whose massive square head has a cavity filled with a mixture of sperm oil and spermaceti [Shortening of *spermaceti whale*]

-spermy *suffix* fertilization ○ *polyspermy* [< Greek *sperma* 'seed' + -Y²]

Sperrin Mountains /spérrin-/ mountain range in Northern Ireland. Highest peak: Sawel Peak 683 m/2,240 ft.

sperrylite /spérri līt/ *n* a silvery white platinum arsenide mineral. Use: source of platinum. [Early 20C. After Francis L. *Sperry* (d. 1906), Canadian chemist.]

spessartine /spéssər teen/, **spessartite** /spéssər tīt/ *n* a yellow or reddish-brown garnet that contains manganese. Use: gems. [Mid-19C. < French, after *Spessart*, S Germany.]

spew /spyoo/ *vti* **1 VOMIT** to vomit something that has been eaten **2 POUR OR FLOW OUT FORCEFULLY** to flow out forcefully, or force something out in a stream ○ *a volcano spewing ash* **3 SAY FORCEFULLY** to utter something in an angry, forceful, or relentless way ■ *n* **VOMIT** something ejected from the mouth, especially vomit [Old English *spīwan* < Indo-European 'to spit', an imitation of the sound] —**spewer** *n*

Spey /spay/ river in N Scotland. Length: 171 km/107 mi.

Speyer /spī ər, shpī ər/ city in SW Germany, scene in 1529 of a protest by supporters of Martin Luther. Population: 45,100 (1989).

SPF *n* the degree to which a sun cream, lotion, screen, or block provides protection for the skin against the sun. Full form **sun protection factor**

Spgs *abbr* Springs (*in place names*)

sphagnum /sfágnəm/ *n* moss growing in wet acid temperate regions that decays and becomes compacted to form peat. Genus: *Sphagnum*. [Mid-18C. Via modern Latin < Greek *sphagnos*, a type of shrub.] —**sphagnous** *adj*

sphalerite /sfállə rīt, sfáylə rīt/ *n* a yellow or brownish zinc sulphide mineral. Use: source of zinc. [Mid-19C. < Greek *sphaleros* 'slippery, uncertain', because the mineral is easily confused with galena.]

sphen- *prefix* = **spheno-** (*before vowels*)

sphene /sfeen/ *n* a brown-black mineral composed of calcium titanium silicate. Source: igneous rocks. [Early 19C. Via French *sphène* < Greek *sphēn* 'wedge'.]

spheno- *prefix* wedge-shaped ○ *sphenogram* [< Greek *sphēn* 'wedge']

sphenodon /sféenə don/ *n* ZOOL = **tuatara** [Late 19C. < modern Latin, 'wedge-toothed' < Greek *sphēn* 'wedge'.]

sphenoid /sfée noyd/ *adj* **1** shaped like a wedge **2** relating to the sphenoid bone

sphenoid bone, sphenoid *n* a bone with prominent wings at the base of the cranium

spher- *prefix* = **sphero-** (*before vowels*)

sphere /sfeer/ *n* **1 GLOBE** any object similar in shape to a ball **2 THREE-DIMENSIONAL SURFACE** a three-dimensional closed surface consisting of all points that are a given distance from a centre **3 ROUND SOLID FIGURE** the solid figure bounded by a sphere, or the volume it encloses **4 FIELD OF KNOWLEDGE OR ACTIVITY** a field of knowledge, interest, or activity **5 AREA OF INFLUENCE** an area of control or influence ○ *took no interest in matters beyond her sphere* **6 GROUP IN SOCIETY** a level or group within a society **7 ASTRONOMICAL OBJECT** an astronomical object, e.g. a planet, moon, or star (*literary*) **8 SKY** the sky or the heavens (*literary*) **9 CELESTIAL LAYER** any revolving concentric transparent shell on which, in early astronomy, the Sun, Moon, planets, and stars were thought to be fixed as they moved around the Earth ■ *vt* (**spheres, sphering, sphered**) **1 ENCIRCLE** to surround, encircle, or enclose something (*literary*) **2 RAISE ALOFT** to place something in the sky or in heaven, among the celestial spheres (*literary*) **3 FORM INTO BALL** to form something into the shape of a ball [13C. Via Old French *espere* < late Latin *sphera* < Latin *sphaera* < Greek *sphaira* 'ball'.] —**spheral** *adj* —**sphericity** /sfe rissəti/ *n*

sphere of influence *n* a geographic region or area of activity in which a particular state, organization, or person is dominant

spherical /sférrik'l/, **spheric** /sférrik/ *adj* **1 ROUND** shaped like a sphere **2 OF SPHERES** relating to a sphere, or to spheres in general **3 OF ASTRONOMICAL OBJECTS** relating to astronomical objects **4 OF ANCIENT ASTRONOMY SPHERES** relating to the spheres of ancient astronomy —**spherically** *adv* —**sphericalness** *n*

spherical aberration *n* a defect in a lens or curved mirror in which light passing through the edge has a different focal point from light passing through the centre, resulting in blurred images

spherical angle *n* an angle formed on a sphere at the point at which any two circles of maximum radius intersect

spherical coordinates *npl* a set of coordinates used for locating a point in space representing its distance from some origin and two angles describing its orientation relative to perpendicular axes extending from that origin

spherical geometry *n* the geometry of figures formed on the surface of a sphere

spherical polygon *n* a geometric figure formed on the surface of a sphere, bounded by three or more arcs of great circles

spherical triangle *n* a spherical polygon that has three sides

spherical trigonometry *n* trigonometry dealing with spherical triangles

spherics /sférriks/ *n* the study of electromagnetic radiation emanating from natural sources in the atmosphere (+ *singular verb*) [Mid-20C. Shortening of ATMOSPHERICS.]

sphero- *prefix* sphere, spherical ○ *spheroid* [Via Latin *sphaero-* < Greek *sphaira* 'sphere']

spheroid /sférroyd, sfeér oyd/ *n* a three-dimensional object that is shaped like a sphere but is not perfectly round, e.g. an ellipsoid —**spheroidal** /sfi róyd'l/ *adj* —**spheroidally** *adv* —**spheroidicity** *n*

spherometer /sfi rómmitər/ *n* an instrument used to measure the curvature of a surface

spheroplast /sférrō plast, -plaast/ *n* a bacterium or yeast cell that has lost part of its cell wall and is as a result spherical in shape and more sensitive to osmosis

spherule /sférrool/ *n* a minute sphere or globule [Mid-17C. < late Latin *spherula* 'small sphere' < Latin *sphaera* (see SPHERE).] —**spherular** *adj*

spherulite /sférrŏŏ līt/ *n* a spherical mass of radiating crystal fibres. Source: volcanic rocks. —**spherulitic** /sférrŏŏ líttik/ *adj*

sphery /sféeri/ *adj* **1** in the shape of a sphere **2** relating to or resembling the planets, the stars, and other astronomical objects (*literary*)

sphincter /sfíngktər/ *n* a circular band of muscle that surrounds an opening or passage in the body and narrows or closes the opening by contracting [Late 16C. Via Latin < Greek *sphigktēr* < *sphiggein* 'bind tight'.] —**sphincteral** *adj*

sphinges plural of **sphinx**

sphingosine /sfíng gə seen, -sin/ *n* a long-chain amino glycol that is part of the lipids found in nerve tissue [Late 19C. < Greek *sphiggos* 'of a sphinx' (see SPHINX) + -INE.]

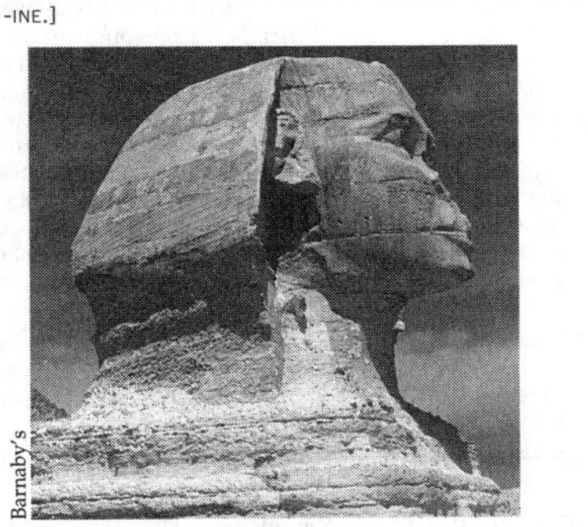

Sphinx, Giza, Egypt

sphinx /sfingks/ (*plural* **sphinxes** *or* **sphinges** /sfín jeez/) *n* **1 GREEK COMPOSITE CREATURE** in Greek mythology, a winged creature with a lion's body and a woman's head. It strangled all who could not answer its riddle, but killed itself when Oedipus answered correctly. **2 EGYPTIAN COMPOSITE CREATURE** in Egyptian mythology, a creature with a lion's body and the head of a man, ram, or bird **3 SPHINX STATUE** a statue of a sphinx **4 MYSTERIOUS PERSON** a mysterious or inscrutable person [Late 16C. Via Latin < Greek *sphigx* < ?]

sphinxlike /sfíngks līk/ *adj* difficult to understand or find out about

sphinx moth *n* = **hawk moth** [*Sphinx* from its appearance, suggestive of a sphinx]

sphragistics /sfrə jístiks/ *n* the study of seals and signet rings (+ *singular verb*) [Mid-19C. Directly or via French *sphragistique* < late Greek *sphragistikos* 'of seals' < *sphragis* 'seal'.] —**sphragistic** *adj*

sphygm- *prefix* = **sphygmo-** (*before vowels*)

sphygmic /sfígmik/ *adj* relating to the pulse [Early 18C. < Greek *sphugmikos* < *sphugmos* (see SPHYGMO-).]

sphygmo- *prefix* pulse ○ *sphygmograph* [< Greek *sphugmos* 'pulsation' < 'sphug-', stem of *spuzein* 'throb']

sphygmograph /sfígmō graaf, -graf/ *n* an apparatus used to make a graphical record (**sphygmogram**) of variations in blood pressure and pulse —**sphygmographic** /sfígmō gráffik/ *adj* —**sphygmography** /sfig móggrəfi/ *n*

sphygmomanometer /sfíg mōmə nómmitər/ *n* an instrument used to measure blood pressure in an artery that consists of a pressure gauge, an inflatable cuff placed around the upper arm, and an inflater bulb or pressure pump

spic /spik/ *n* a highly offensive term for a Spanish or Italian person (*taboo*) [Early 20C. Shortening of *spiggoty* < ?]

spica /spíkə/ (*plural* **-cae** /-see/ *or* **-cas**) *n* a bandage applied to a limb in an overlapping figure-of-eight pattern to immobilize it [14C. < Latin, 'ear of grain'; from its spiralling shape, reminiscent of an ear of grain.]

spic-and-span *adj* = **spick-and-span**

spicate /spí kayt/ *adj* growing in the form of a spike, or with flowers growing in spikes [Mid-17C. < Latin *spicatus*, past participle of *spicare* 'furnish with sharp points' < *spica* 'spike'.]

spiccato /spi kaátō/ *n* (*plural* **-tos**) a technique of playing staccato on stringed instruments, in which the bow is allowed to bounce on the string ■ *adj, adv* played using a technique of allowing the bow to bounce on the string [Early 18C. < Italian, past participle of *spiccare* 'pick off, detach'.]

spice /spīss/ *n* **1 AROMATIC PLANT SUBSTANCE USED AS FLAVOURING** any aromatic plant substance such as nutmeg and ginger used as flavourings **2 FLAVOURINGS FROM PLANTS** food flavourings derived from the nonleafy parts of plants (*often before nouns*) **3 EXCITING OR INTERESTING THING** a source of excitement or interest **4** *US* **STRONG SMELL** a pungent odour or fragrance (*often before nouns*) **5 TRACE OF** the tiniest amount of something ■ *vt* (**spices, spicing, spiced**) **1 SEASON WITH SPICE** to season food or beverages with spice **2 MAKE MORE EXCITING** to introduce excitement or interest into something ○ *spiced the speech with joking asides* [13C. Via Old French *espice* < Latin *species* 'appearance, kind', in late Latin, in plural, 'goods, wares' (see SPECIES).]

spiceberry /spíssbəri/ (*plural* **-ries**) *n* **1** a spicy orange, red, or black berry **2** a tree or shrub that produces spiceberries, e.g. the wintergreen

spicebush /spíssbŏŏsh/ *n* a shrub of the laurel family with aromatic leaves. Flowers: yellow, in dense clusters. Native to: North America. *Lindera benzoin*.

spicey *adj* = **spicy**

spick-and-span /spík-/, **spic-and-span** *adj* **1** very clean and tidy (*not hyphenated after verbs*) **2** showing not the slightest sign of damage or wear and tear [Late 16C. Shortening of *spick-and-span-new* < obsolete *spick*, variant of SPIKE¹ + AND + *span-new* < Old Norse *spánnyr* 'new chip' < *spán* 'chip'.]

spicule /spíkyool/ (*plural* **-ules** *or* **-ulum** /spíkyələm/) *n* **1** a small hard needle-shaped part, especially any of the calcium- or silicon-containing supporting parts of some invertebrates such as sponges and corals **2** a slender column of relatively cool, high-density gas that rapidly erupts from the solar chromosphere and then falls back [Late 18C. < modern Latin *spiculum* 'small spike', Latin *spica* 'spike', ear of grain (see SPIKE²).] —**spicular** *adj* —**spiculate** *adj*

spicy /spíssi/ (**-ier, -iest**) *adj* **1 SEASONED WITH SPICE** smelling or tasting strongly of spices **2 INVOLVING IMPROPRIETY** arousing interest because of its scandalous nature, usually because it deals with sexual impropriety (*informal*) **3 VIVACIOUS** with a very lively personality **4 PRO-**

DUCING SPICES describes plants or plant parts from which spices are obtained —**spicily** *adv* —**spiciness** *n*

ϟ **spider** /spídər/ *n* **1 EIGHT-LEGGED ANIMAL THAT SPINS WEBS** a predatory animal with four pairs of legs and two or more abdominal organs (**spinnerets**) used for spinning webs that serve as nests and traps for prey. Order: Araneae. **2** *US* **TRIVET** a trivet for supporting a pan on a hearth **3 SET OF STRAPS FOR ATTACHING LOADS** a bunch of elastic straps joined at a central point, usually with a hook at each free end, used especially for attaching a load to a rack on a vehicle **4 MECHANICAL DEVICE** a mechanical device that has radiating arms, spokes, or other parts **5 FRAME SECURING REDUNDANT ROPES** a circular frame at the base of a ship's mast, used to secure ropes when sails are not in use **6 PROGRAM SEARCHING INTERNET FOR INFORMATION** a computer program that searches the Internet for newly accessible information to be added to the index examined by a standard search tool (**search engine**) **7 CUE REST** a multi-position cue rest with wide legs designed to lift the cue tip over an intervening ball **8** TRANSP = **spider phaeton** [Old English *spiþra* < *spinnan* 'spin' (see SPIN)]

spider beetle *n* a name given to various wingless beetles, many of which are pests to stored food in households and warehouses. Family: Ptinidae.

spider crab *n* a marine crab with a small triangular body and long slender legs. Family: Majidae.

spider flower *n* **1** PLANTS = **cleome** **2** a name given to various Australian flowering plants whose flowerheads resemble spiders. Genus: *Grevillea.*

spider hole *n* a concealed sniper position (*informal*)

spiderman /spídər man/ (*plural* **-men** /-men/) *n* (*informal*) **1** a construction worker who erects the steel frame of a building **2** a worker who climbs and repairs tall buildings

spider mite *n* any tiny web-spinning mite. Some spider mites are garden and crop pests. Family: Tetranychidae.

spider monkey *n* a tree-dwelling monkey with long slender limbs, a long prehensile tail, and a small head. Native to: Central and South America. Genus: *Ateles.*

spider phaeton *n* a high-bodied lightweight fast horse carriage with large wheels

spider plant *n* a common houseplant grown for its long narrow variegated leaves and clusters of plantlets. Flowers: white. *Chlorophytum variegatum.*

spiderweb /spídər web/ *n* a web that is constructed by a spider to entrap prey, using silk produced from fluid from its abdominal glands

spiderwort /spídər wurt/ *n* a plant widely grown as a houseplant. Flowers: pink, blue, or violet. Genus: *Tradescantia.* ◊ **tradescantia** [*Spider* from the resemblance of the stamens to a spider's legs]

spidery /spídəri/ *adj* **1 THIN AND IRREGULAR** with thin lines or constituent parts that form irregular angles **2 SPIDER-INFESTED** infested with spiders **3 LIKE SPIDER** like a spider in shape or movement

spiegeleisen /speég'l īz'n/, **spiegel** /speég'l/ *n* pig iron containing high concentrations of manganese and carbon [Mid-19C. < German, < *Spiegel* 'mirror' (ultimately < Latin *speculum*; see SPECULUM) + *Eisen* 'iron'.]

spiel /shpeel, speel/ *n* an irritatingly long or predictably glib speech, e.g. a rambling apology or a prepared sales patter (*informal*) ■ *vi* to deliver a spiel (*informal*) [Late 19C. < German, 'play, game'.]

spiel off *vt* to say something very quickly or by rote ○ *spiel off a list of names*

Spielberg /speél burg/, **Steven** (*b.* 1946) US film director and producer

spies **1** plural of **spy** **2** 3rd person singular present of **spy**

spiffing /spíffing/ *adj UK* exceptionally good (*dated informal*) [Late 19C. < ?]

spifflicate *vt* = **spiflicate**

spiff up *vt US* to improve something by adding enhancing features (*informal*) [Late 19C. < ?]

spiffy /spíffi/ (**-ier, -iest**) *adj US* stylish or modern and attractive (*informal*) ○ *'a spiffy collection of supercomputers blinking away in a room of their own'* (Kathleen O'Gorman (*Detroit Free Press; 1997*) [Mid-19C. < ?] —**spiffily** *adv* —**spiffiness** *n*

spiflicate /spíffli kayt/ (**-cates, -cating, -cated**), **spifflicate** (**-cates, -cating, -cated**) *vt* to destroy something, or beat somebody resoundingly (*dated or humorous slang*) [Mid-18C. Nonsense word.] —**spiflication** /spíffli káysh'n/ *n*

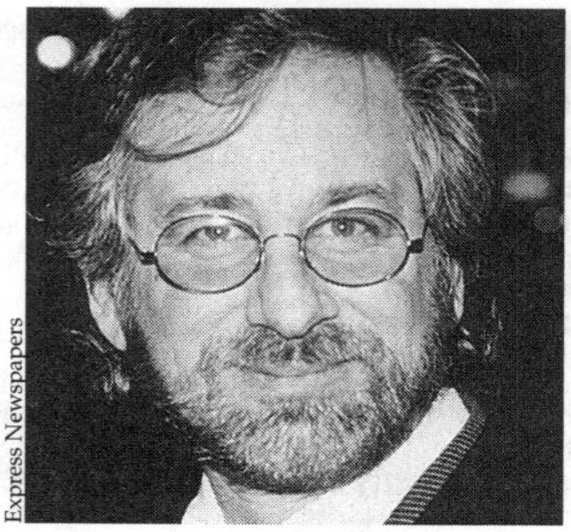

Steven Spielberg

spignel /spígn'l/ *n* a plant with fine aromatic leaves, found mainly in mountain pastures. Flowers: small, white. Native to: Europe. *Meum athamanticum.* [Early 16C. < ?]

spigot /spíggət/ *n* **1** *US* **OUTDOOR TAP** a tap situated outdoors **2 TAP FITTED TO CASK** a tap, usually wooden, that is fitted to a cask **3 PLUG FOR CASK HOLE** a plug for the vent hole of a cask **4 PIPE END JOINING OTHER** the end of a pipe that is joined by insertion into the enlarged end of another pipe [14C. < ?]

spike[1] /spīk/ *n* **1 POINTED METAL OR WOODEN PIECE** a sharply pointed piece of metal or wood, especially one of a number along the top of a railing, fence, or wall **2 LARGE NAIL** a long heavy metal nail **3 METAL POINT ON RUNNING SHOE SOLE** a pointed metal stud, part of a set attached to the sole of an athlete's shoe to give better grip (*often plural*) ◊ **cleat** **4 SHARP POINT** narrow sharp point **5 UNBRANCHED ANTLER OF DEER** the antler of a young deer, straight and without branches **6 VARIATION IN VOLTAGE** an abrupt temporary surge in the voltage or current in an electrical circuit **7 IMAGE OF PEAK AND FALL** a graphic representation of a sharp rise followed by a sharp fall, especially on a graph or as a reading on an instrument **8 DOWNWARD SMASH OF VOLLEYBALL** a hard smash of a volleyball, hit close to the net and straight down into the opponent's court **9 SUDDEN BRIEF INCREASE** a sharp and brief rise in something **10 METAL PART FOR GRIPPING AND CLIMBING** a sharp pointed metal projection strapped to a boot as an aid in gripping and climbing something **11 METAL ROD FOR LOOSE PAPERS** a pointed metal rod mounted on a base onto which loose papers are thrust, especially rejected news stories (*dated*) **12 HYPODERMIC NEEDLE** a hypodermic needle (*slang*) **13 HOSTEL FOR PEOPLE WITHOUT HOMES** a hostel that houses people who have no place to live (*dated slang*) ■ **spikes** *npl* **PAIR OF SHOES WITH METAL STUDS** a pair of athletic shoes whose soles are equipped with pointed metal studs to give better traction ■ *v* (**spikes, spiking, spiked**) **1** *vt* **RENDER USELESS** to make something useless or ineffective (*informal*) **2** *vt* **SNEAKILY ADD SOMETHING TO DRINK** to put alcohol, a drug, or a poison into another person's drink surreptitiously **3** *vt* **DISCARD POTENTIAL NEWS STORY** to reject or decide not to use a news story (*slang*) **4** *vt* **SMASH VOLLEYBALL DOWNWARD** to leap high close to the net and hit a volleyball straight down into an opponent's court **5** *vt* **CAUSE INJURY WITH SPIKES ON SHOE** to injure another player or competitor with the spikes of an athletic shoe **6** *vt* **DISABLE CANNON** to render a cannon useless by driving a spike into its vent **7** *vi* **RISE ABRUPTLY** to rise sharply and briefly [13C. < Indo-European, 'sharp point'.] —**spiked** *adj*

spike[2] /spīk/ *n* **1** a long cluster of flowers attached directly to a stem with the newest flowers at the tip. ◊ **inflorescence, raceme** **2** an ear of corn such as wheat or barley [14C. < Latin *spica* 'ear of grain'.]

spike heel *n* a high pointed heel on a woman's shoe, or a shoe with such a heel

spike lavender *n* a mint related to lavender that yields an oil used in paints. Flowers: light purple. Native to: Europe. *Lavandula latifolia.*

spikelet /spíklət/ *n* a small flower spike, especially any of the basic units of the flower cluster of a grass or sedge

spikenard /spík naard, spíkə naard/ (*plural* **-nards** *or* **-nard**) *n* **1 HIMALAYAN PLANT** a perennial aromatic plant of the valerian family. Flowers: pinkish purple. Native to: Himalayas. *Nardostachys jatamansi.* **2 ANCIENT FRAGRANT OINTMENT** a fragrant ointment derived from spikenard, used in ancient times **3 PLANT WITH AROMATIC ROOT** a plant of the ginseng family with purplish berries and aromatic roots. Flowers: small, whitish. Native to: North America. *Aralia racemosa.* [14C. < medieval Latin *spica nardi* 'spike of nard' (translation of Greek *nardou stakhus*).]

spike-rush *n* a perennial plant with narrow leaves and small flowers that grows in temperate regions. Genus: *Eleocharis.*

spiky /spíki/ (**-ier, -iest**) *adj* **1** with one or more narrow sharp points **2** easily made angry (*informal*) —**spikily** *adv* —**spikiness** *n*

spile /spīl/ *n* **1 HEAVY SUPPORTING POST** a heavy timber post driven into the ground as a foundation or support **2 WOODEN PEG** a wooden peg, especially used as a plug or stopper **3** *US, Can* **TREE-TAPPING SPOUT** a tap for drawing sap from the sugar maple tree ■ *vt* (**spiles, spiling, spiled**) **1 SUPPORT WITH POST** to provide or support something with a heavy post driven into the ground **2** *US, Can* **TAP TREE FOR SAP** to draw sap from a tree with a spout or spigot [Early 16C. Via Dutch *spijl* < Middle Dutch or Middle Low German *spile* 'splinter, wooden pin' (see SPILL[2]).]

spilikin *n* GAMES = **spillikin**

spill[1] /spil/ *v* (**spills, spilling, spilt** /spilt/ *or* **spilled, spilt** *or* **spilled**) **1** *vti* **FLOW FROM CONTAINER** to flow or allow something to flow from a container, especially accidentally and usually resulting in loss or waste **2** *vi* **COME OUT OF CONFINED SPACE** to come out from a building or other confined space in large numbers, often to the wrong place ○ *The fans spilled out onto the pitch* **3** *vt* **DIVULGE** to reveal or divulge something, often unintentionally (*informal*) ○ *spilled the news* **4** *vti* **FALL OFF** to fall off, or make somebody fall off, something onto the ground or floor, especially from a horse, bicycle, or motorbike (*informal*) **5** *vt* **LET WIND OUT OF SAIL** to let the wind escape from a sail ■ *n* **1 ACT OF FALLING** a tumble to the ground or floor, especially from a bicycle, motorbike, or horse (*informal*) **2 SOMETHING THAT RUNS OVER** a quantity of something that flows accidentally or unintentionally from a container or confined area, or an instance of this happening ○ *Workers fought hard to contain the spill.* **3** GEOG = **spillway** [Old English *spillan* 'to kill'] —**spiller** *n*

spill over *vi* **1** to overflow a container or an enclosed area **2** to spread out from a confined space into a nearby area

spill[2] /spil/ *n* **1** a splinter or twist of paper used to light something, e.g. a pipe or candle **2** = **spile** *n.* 2 [14C. < Middle Low German *spile.*]

spillage /spíllij/ *n* **1** the act of spilling something **2** a quantity of something that has been spilled

Spillane /spi láyn/, **Mickey** (*b.* 1918) US writer. Born **Frank Morrison Spillane**

spillikin /spílli kin/, **spilikin, spellican** /spéllikən/ *n* any thin piece used in the game of jackstraws (*dated*) ■ **spillikins, spilikins** *npl* the game of jackstraws (*dated;* + *singular verb*) [Mid-18C. < SPILL[2], literally 'small spill'.]

spillover /spíl ōvər/ *n US, Can* **1** any spread or expansion of something **2** an indirect effect of something

spillway /spíl way/ *n* a channel for carrying away excess water, e.g. at a reservoir or dam

spilt past tense, past participle of **spill**[1]

spin /spin/ *v* (**spins, spinning, spun** /spun/ *or* **span** /span/, **spun**) **1** *vti* **ROTATE QUICKLY** to turn or make something turn round and round rapidly, as if on an axis ○ *He spun a coin.* ○ *dancers spinning round the room* **2** *vi* **FACE ABOUT QUICKLY** to turn round rapidly to face in the opposite direction **3** *vti* **CREATE YARN FROM RAW MATERIALS** to twist raw fibres, e.g. of wool, silk, or cotton, so that they form a continuous yarn or thread **4** *vti* **MAKE WEB OR COCOON** to make a web or cocoon from filaments extruded from the body **5** *vt* **INVENT LONG STORY** to make up an extended story or a series of lies **6** *vti* **ROTATE RAPIDLY IN CHANGED DIRECTION** to strike, throw, or kick something in a way that makes it revolve and change direction when it hits something, or to rotate and change direction in this way **7** *vi* **ROTATE FREELY** to revolve or rotate rapidly around an axis ○ *Our wheels spun on the ice.* **8** *vti* **DIVE STEEPLY** to go into a steep spiral dive, or make an aircraft do this **9** *vi* **BECOME DIZZY** to feel dazed, as if whirling round ○ *My head is spinning.* **10** *vi* **FISH WITH RAPIDLY MOVING BAIT** to fish with a rod, line, and reel, constantly drawing a revolving bait or lure through the water **11** *vi* **DRIVE FAST AND WELL** to drive smoothly and speedily **12** *vt* **PLAY RECORDING** to play a piece of recorded music (*informal*) **13** *vti* **DRY CLOTHES** to remove most of the water from washed clothes in a washing machine by rotating them rapidly ■ *n* **1 ROTATION** a quick rotating movement **2 ROTATION CAUSING CHANGED DIRECTION** rotation given to a ball to make it change direction **3 ROTATION WHILE SKATING** a stationary rotation during figure skating **4 SPIRALLING DIVE** a steep spiral dive in an aircraft **5 DIZZY STATE** a state of mental disorientation or dizziness **6 INTERPRETIVE POINT OF VIEW** a viewpoint, bias, or interpretation, especially one that is presented to influence the public in a desired way (*informal*) ○ *There's no way the government can put a favourable spin on this disaster.* **7 SHORT JOURNEY IN VEHICLE** a brief journey taken for pleasure in a motor vehicle **8 DRYING OPERATION IN WASHING MACHINE** the rapid rotation of washed clothes in a washing machine to remove most of the moisture from them **9 ANGULAR MOMENTUM** the intrinsic angular momentum of an elementary particle or system of such particles independent of its motion **10 QUANTUM PROPERTY OF ANGULAR MOMENTUM** the quantum property or number of an elementary particle that is a measure of its intrinsic angular momentum and magnetic moment [Old English *spinnan* < Indo-European, 'to stretch, spin'] ◇ **in a flat spin** in a state of confusion or panic

spin off *v* **1** *vti* to derive a new product, material, or service from something that already exists, or be derived in this way **2** *vt* to divest a company of a subsidiary by distributing the subsidiary's shares to shareholders in the parent corporation

spin out *v* **1** *vt* **PROLONG** to make an activity last longer than it needs to, usually by adding something unnecessary **2** *vt* **MAKE SUPPLIES LAST** to make something last longer than it ordinarily would, usually by careful management **3** *vi* **LOSE CONTROL OF VEHICLE** to skid out of control

spina bifida /spínə bífidə, spínə bíffidə/ *n* a congenital condition in which part of the spinal cord or meninges protrudes through a cleft in the spinal column, resulting in partial to total loss of voluntary movement in the lower body [< modern Latin, 'spine split in two']

spinach /spínich/ *n* a widely cultivated annual plant that produces spinach. Use: eaten cooked as a vegetable or raw in salads. *Spinacia oleracea.* [14C. Via Old French *espinache* < Persian *aspānāk.*]

spinal /spín'l/ *adj* **1 RELATING TO SPINE** on, in, near, or relating to a spine, especially a backbone **2 LIKE SPINE** resembling a spine ■ *n* **SPINAL ANAESTHETIC** spinal anaesthesia or a spinal anaesthetic (*informal*) —**spinally** *adv*

spinal anaesthesia *n* **1** an anaesthesia of the lower half of the body achieved by injecting an anaesthetic into the fluid surrounding the spinal cord. ◊ **epidural** **2** the loss of sensation in part of the body caused by injury to the spine

spinal canal *n* a passage that runs through the opening in the middle of each vertebra of the spinal column and contains the spinal cord, the meninges, nerve roots, and blood vessels

spinal column *n* the axis of the skeleton of a vertebrate animal, extending from the head and consisting of a series of interconnected vertebrae that enclose and protect the spinal cord

spinal cord *n* a thick whitish cord of nerve tissue extending from the bottom of the brain through the spinal column and giving rise to pairs of spinal nerves that supply the body

spinal meningitis *n* inflammation of the membranes surrounding the spinal cord that particularly affects young children

spin angular momentum *n* PHYS = **spin** *n.* **9**

spin bowler *n* a bowler in cricket who specializes in bowling balls that spin

spindle /spínd'l/ *n* **1 SPECIALLY SHAPED ROD FOR SPINNING THREAD** a handheld stick or rod with a notched end through which strands of natural fibres are drawn, then twisted into thread and wound round the rod **2 THREAD-SPINNING ROD ON SPINNING WHEEL** a device similar to the handheld spindle, attached to a spinning wheel **3 MECHANICAL THREAD-SPINNING DEVICE** a device on a spinning machine for spinning thread and winding it onto bobbins **4 ROTATING ROD FOR DEVICE** a rotating rod on a device such as a lathe, turntable, or door handle **5 SPINDLE-SHAPED PIECE OF WOOD** a long thin piece of wood such as a table leg or baluster that is shaped like a spindle **6 SPINDLE-SHAPED CELL STRUCTURE** a spindle-shaped structure along which chromosomes are distributed and drawn apart during meiosis and mitosis **7 SIGNAL WARNING FOR BOATS** a metal rod surmounted by a ball or lantern and fixed to a rock or shoal. Use: warning for approaching vessels. ■ *v* (**-dles, -dling, -dled**) **1** *vt* **MAKE WITH SPINDLE** to form or equip something with a spindle **2** *vi* **RAPIDLY GROW TALL AND SLENDER** to grow quickly into a high slender stalk or stem [Old English *spinel* < Germanic]

spindle cell *n* a narrow, elongated cell characteristic of some cancers

spindle tree *n* an evergreen or deciduous tree or shrub with small flowers, red fruits, and hard wood. Use: formerly, to make spindles. Genus: *Euonymus.*

spindly /spíndli/ (**-dlier, -dliest**), **spindling** /spíndling/ *adj* long or tall, thin, and weak-looking

spin doctor *n* somebody whose job is to present the actions of a person or organization in the best possible light, especially via the news media (*informal*)

spin-drier *n* UTIL = **spin-dryer**

spindrift /spín drift/ *n* **1** spray that blows from the surface of the sea **2** driving snow or sand in a storm [Early 17C. Alteration (probably influenced by SPIN) of obsolete *spoon* 'run before a sea' + DRIFT.]

spin-dry (**spin-dries, spin-drying, spin-dried**) *vt* to remove most of the water from washed laundry by spinning it in a washing machine or a spin-dryer

spin-dryer, spin-drier *n* a machine that forces most of the water out of wet laundry by spinning it around rapidly in a perforated drum

spine /spīn/ *n* **1** ANAT = **spinal column** **2 VERTICAL BACK OF BOOK COVER** the vertical back of a book's cover or a record's sleeve, usually printed with the title and the name of the author or performer **3 HARD SHARP PROJECTION ON ANIMAL'S BODY** a sharp stiff projection on the body of an animal or a fish, e.g. the quill of a porcupine or the ray of a fish's fin **4 SHARP POINT ON PLANT** a stiff sharp pointed plant part that is a modification of part of a leaf, e.g. in holly, or of an entire leaf, e.g. in cacti **5 RIDGE IN MOUNTAINS** a continuous ridge in a range of mountains or hills **6 FLEXIBLE PAY SCALE** a pay scale used by some professions and large organizations that takes into account individual circumstances such as age and location [14C. Via Old French *espine* < Latin *spina* 'thorn'.]

spine-chiller *n* something, especially a book, film, or story, that is meant to frighten people —**spine-chilling** *adj* —**spine-chillingly** *adv*

spinel /spi nél/ *n* a hard crystalline, usually red, oxide mineral containing magnesium, aluminium, iron, and sometimes manganese. Use: gems. [Early 16C. Via French *spinelle* < Latin *spina* (see SPINE); from its pointed crystals.]

spineless /spínləss/ *adj* **1** lacking willpower, courage, or strength of character **2** lacking a vertebral column —**spinelessly** *adv* —**spinelessness** *n*

SYNONYMS See ***cowardly.***

spinet /spi nét/ *n* a small harpsichord, popular in the 18th century, that has the strings set at a slant to the keyboard [Mid-17C. Via French *espinette* < Italian *spinetta* < ?]

spine-tingling *adj* causing nervous fear or excitement —**spine-tinglingly** *adv*

spinifex /spínni feks/ (*plural* **-fexes** *or* **-fex**) *n* **1** a perennial Australian grass that has sharp pointed leaves and grows in circular mounds in dry inland areas. Genera: *Plectrachne* and *Triodia.* **2** an Australasian plant that has silvery foliage, globular seed heads, and grows on coastal sand dunes. Genus: *Spinifex.* [Early 19C. < modern Latin, 'thorn-maker'.]

spinnaker /spínnəkər/ *n* a large triangular sail set at the front of a racing yacht for running before the wind [Mid-19C. < ?]

spinner /spínnər/ *n* **1 SOMEBODY OR SOMETHING THAT SPINS** a person, object, or device that spins **2 FISHING LURE** an angling lure that spins in the water when the line is reeled in **3** CRICKET = **spin bowler** **4 SPINNING CRICKET BALL** a cricket ball bowled with spin **5 COVER FOR AIRCRAFT PROPELLER** a streamlined dome-shaped cap (**fairing**) that fits over the hub of the propeller of an aircraft

spinneret /spínnə ret/ *n* **1** a tiny tubular structure, usually one of two pairs, that exudes the fluid produced by the abdominal glands of a silk-producing spider **2** a perforated device for extruding filaments of synthetic fibre

spinney /spínni/ (*plural* **-neys**) *n* a small thicket or wood [Late 16C. Via Old French *espinei* 'thorny hedge' < Latin *spinetum* < *spina* (see SPINE).]

spinning frame *n* a machine that draws out fibres, twists them into yarn or thread, and winds them onto spindles

spinning jenny /-jénni/ *n* a spinning machine invented in the 18th century that was the first practical device to wind yarn onto more than one spindle

spinning mule *n* TEXTILES = **mule**[1] *n.* **5**

spinning top *n* HOBBIES = **top**[2] *n.*

spinning wheel *n* a machine used at home for twisting fibres into yarn or thread and winding it onto a spindle by means of a large wheel driven by hand or a treadle

spinode /spínōd/ *n* MATH = **cusp** *n.* **6** [Mid-19C. Blend of SPINE + NODE.]

spin-off *n* **1** a product, material, or service deriving from something that already exists **2** a subsidiary of a company that is divested by means of a distribution of its shares of stock to shareholders of the parent corporation

spin-orbit coupling *n* the interaction between two specific quantum physical properties of a particle

spinous /spínəss/ *adj* **1** with, covered with, or resembling spines **2** sharply pointed, like a spine of a leaf ○ *spinous process of a bone* [Mid-17C. < Latin *spinosus* < *spina* (see SPINE).]

spinous process *n* a long projection at the rear of a vertebra

spinout /spínnowt/, **spin-out** *n* a skid, especially in a motor vehicle that is out of control

Spinoza /spi nṓzə/, **Baruch** (1632–77) Dutch philosopher

Spinozism /spi nṓzizəm/ *n* the philosophical system developed by Baruch Spinoza, defining God as a unique impersonal deity with an infinite number of attributes and modes —**Spinozist** *n*

spinster /spínstər/ *n* **1 OFFENSIVE TERM** an offensive term for a woman, especially one who is no longer young or is of advanced years, who has never married (*dated*) **2 UNMARRIED WOMAN IN LEGAL DOCUMENTS** in some legal documents, a woman who has never married **3 WOMAN SPINNER OF YARN** a woman whose livelihood is spinning yarn (*archaic*) [14C. < SPIN.]

spinthariscope /spin thárri skōp/ *n* an instrument used to detect ionizing radiation such as alpha particles that produces flashes of light on a phosphorescent screen [Early 20C. < Greek *spintharis* 'spark' + -SCOPE.]

spinto /spíntō/ *adj* describes an operatic voice that is both lyric and dramatic [Mid-20C. < Italian, 'pushed'.]

spiny /spíni/ (**-ier, -iest**) *adj* **1 WITH SPINES** with or covered with spines **2 THORNY** with thorns or prickles **3 LIKE A SPINE** shaped like a spine —**spininess** *n*

spiny anteater *n* ZOOL = **echidna**

spiny eel *n* a freshwater fish resembling an eel that has a sensitive elongated snout with tubular nostrils and several sharp spines in front of the dorsal fin. Native to: Africa, Asia. Family: Mastacembelidae.

spiny-headed worm *n* a parasitic unsegmented worm that has a proboscis composed of rows of hooked spines, used for attachment to a vertebrate's intestinal wall. Phylum: Acanthocephala.

spiny lobster *n* a large edible crustacean that is like a lobster but has a spiny shell and lacks enlarged pincers. Family: Palinuridae.

spiracle /spírək'l/ *n* **1 VENT IN LAVA FLOW** a small vent in a lava flow that allows the escape of built-up gases **2 BLOWHOLE** a blowhole (*technical*) **3 SMALL APERTURE IN AN INSECT** a small paired aperture along the side of the thorax or abdomen of an insect or spider through which air enters and leaves **4 SMALL GILL SLIT** a small gill slit or opening behind the eye area of some fishes, such as skates and rays [Early 17C. Via Old French < Latin *spiraculum* < *spirare* 'breathe' (see SPIRIT).] —**spiracular** /spī rákyoōlər/ *adj*

spiraea /spī rée ə/, **spirea** *n* an ornamental flowering shrub. Flowers: small white or pink, in dense clusters. Native to: N hemisphere. Genus: *Spiraea.* [Mid-17C. Via modern Latin < Greek *speiraia* 'privet' < *speira* 'coil, twist'.]

spiral /spírəl/ *n* **1 CONTINUOUS CIRCLING FLAT CURVE** a flat curve or series of curves that constantly increase or decrease in size in circling around a central point **2 HELIX** a helix **3 SOMETHING WITH CURVING CIRCULAR PATTERN** something that has a helical or spiral form **4 FLIGHT MANOEUVRE** a manoeuvre in which an aircraft makes a continuous banking turn as it descends **5 CHANGE IN ECONOMIC CYCLE** a continuous widening increase or decrease of prices, wages, or interest rates ■ *adj* **1 CONTINUOUSLY CIRCLING WITH FLAT CURVES** with a flat curve or series of curves that constantly increase or decrease in size in circling around a central point **2 HELICAL** helical in shape ■ *v* (**-rals, -ralling, -ralled**) **1** *vti* **SHAPE SOMETHING LIKE A SPIRAL** to take on or make something take on a spiral shape **2** *vti* **MOVE IN A SPIRAL** to move or make something move in a spiral **3** *vi* **CHANGE INCREASINGLY** to increase or decrease with ever-increasing speed [Mid-16C. < medieval Latin *spiralis* 'coiled' < Latin *spira* (see SPIRE[2]).] —**spiroid** *adj*

spiral binding *n* a binding, especially for a notebook or booklet, in which pages are fastened together with a spiral of wire or plastic that coils through a series of punched holes —**spiral-bound** *adj*

spiral galaxy *n* a galaxy consisting of an older central nucleus of stars from which extend two spiral arms of gas, dust, and newer stars

spiral of Archimedes *n* a spiral curve formed by a point moving at constant speed to or from a fixed point and along a line rotating, also at a constant speed, about the point [Mid-17C. After ARCHIMEDES.]

spiral staircase *n* a staircase that winds round a central axis, often made of stone or iron

spirant /spīrənt/ *n, adj* PHON = **fricative** [Mid-19C. < Latin *spirant-*, present participle of *spirare* 'breathe' (see SPIRIT).]

spire[1] /spīr/ *n* **1 NARROW TAPERING STRUCTURE** a tall narrow pointed structure on the top of a roof, tower, or steeple **2 POINTED SHOOT OF PLANT** a slender, upward-pointing part of a plant such as a blade of grass or the top of a tree **3 UPWARD-FACING SPIKE** the top part of something narrow and pointed such as a mountain peak ■ *vi* (**spires, spiring, spired**) **RISE TO POINT** to rise to a narrow point [Old English *spīr* < Indo-European, 'sharp point']

spire[2] /spīr/ *n* **1** a spiral or coil **2** a convolution of a spiral or coil [Late 16C. Via Latin *spira* 'coil' < Greek *speira*.]

spirea *n* PLANTS = **spiraea**

spirelet /spīrlət/ *n* ARCHIT = **flèche** *n.* 1 [Mid-19C. < SPIRE[1].]

spirillum /spī ríllәm/ (*plural* **-la** /-lə/) *n* a spiral-shaped or curved bacterium with a rigid body requiring oxygen for respiration. Genus: *Spirillum*. [Late 19C. < modern Latin, 'little spiral' < Latin *spira* (see SPIRE[2]).] —**spirillar** *adj*

spirit /spírrit/ *n* **1 LIFE FORCE OF PERSON** a vital force that characterizes a living being as being alive **2 WILL** a person's will, sense of self, or enthusiasm for living **3 ENTHUSIASM** an enthusiasm and energy for living **4 DISPOSITION** somebody's personality or temperament **5 ATTITUDE** a person's attitude or state of mind **6 GROUP LOYALTY** a sense of enthusiasm and loyalty that somebody feels through belonging to a group **7 IMPORTANT INFLUENCE** somebody or something that is a divine, inspiring, or animating influence **8 REAL MEANING** the intention behind something such as a rule or decree, rather than its literal interpretation **9 SHARED OUTLOOK** a prevailing mood or outlook characteristic of a place or time **10 SUPERNATURAL ENTITY** a supernatural being that does not have a physical body, e.g. a ghost, fairy, angel, or demon **11 PERSON** a person who displays a specific quality **12 SOUL** a person's soul, especially that of a dead person **13 ALCOHOLIC DRINK** a strong alcoholic liquor made by distillation (*often plural*) ○ *We drank a toast with a glass of the local spirit.* **14 DISTILLED LIQUID** any liquid produced by distillation, especially a distilled solution of ethanol and water (*often plural*) **15 ALCOHOLIC SOLUTION** a solution of an essence or volatile substance in alcohol (*often plural*) ■ **spirits** *npl* **MOOD** a particular frame of mind or mood ○ *The group was in high spirits, talking and laughing.* ■ *adj* **BURNING ALCOHOL** using alcohol as fuel ○ *a spirit stove* ■ *vt* **REMOVE SECRETLY** to take somebody or something away quickly in a secret or mysterious way ○ *spirited him out of the room* [13C. Via Anglo-Norman < Latin *spiritus* 'breath' < *spirare* 'breathe' < ?] ◇ **in high spirits** elated and happy ◇ **out of spirits** sad or dejected

Spirit /spírrit/ *n* in Christianity, the Holy Spirit

spirited /spírritid/ *adj* **1 LIVELY** lively and vigorous **2 ANIMATED** with great animation **3 BEHAVING IN SPECIFIED WAY** behaving in a way that has a specified feeling, mood, or character (*usually in combination*) ○ *low-spirited* —**spiritedly** *adv* —**spiritedness** *n*

spirit gum *n* a glue made from a solution of gum in ether, used especially to stick false hair to an actor's skin

spiritism /spírritizəm/ *n* PARANORMAL = **spiritualism** *n.* 1 —**spiritist** *n* —**spiritistic** /spírri tístik/ *adj*

spirit lamp *n* a lamp that uses methylated spirit as fuel

spiritless /spírritləss/ *adj* lacking courage or energy —**spiritlessly** *adv* —**spiritlessness** *n*

spirit level *n* a device laid on something to check whether it is level. US term **level** *n.* 11

spiritoso /spírri tóssō/ *adv* in a lively and vivacious way, or to be played in this way (*musical direction*) [Early 18C. < Italian, 'spirited'.] —**spiritoso** *adj*

spirits of ammonia *n* CHEM = **sal volatile** *n.* 2

spirits of turpentine *n* CHEM = **turpentine** *n.* 3

spiritual /spírrichoo əl/ *adj* **1 OF THE SOUL** relating to the soul or spirit, usually in contrast to material things **2 OF RELIGION** relating to religious or sacred things rather than worldly things **3 TEMPERAMENTALLY OR INTELLECTUALLY AKIN** connected by an affinity of the mind, spirit, or temperament **4 REFINED** showing great refinement and concern with the higher things in life ■ *n* **1 FOLK HYMN** a religious song, especially one arising from African American culture **2 THINGS OF THE SPIRIT** matters concerning the spirit ○ *He was deeply concerned with anything to do with the spiritual.* —**spiritually** *adv* —**spiritualness** *n*

spiritual bouquet *n* in the Roman Catholic Church, a promise of, or performance of, devotional acts, performed on behalf of another, e.g. in memory of somebody who has died

spiritualise *vt* RELIG = **spiritualize**

spiritualism /spírrichoo ə lizəm/ *n* **1 BELIEF IN COMMUNICATION WITH DEAD PEOPLE** the belief that the spirits of dead people can communicate with the living, especially through mediums **2 PRACTICES OF COMMUNICATING WITH DEAD PEOPLE** the practices used among people who believe that communication occurs between the dead and the living **3 BELIEFS EMPHASIZING SPIRITUAL MATTERS** a system of belief that emphasizes the spiritual nature of existence **4 PHILOSOPHY EMPHASIZING SPIRITUAL NATURE OF REALITY** the philosophical doctrine that all reality is spiritual, not material **5 SPIRITUAL STATE** the quality or state of being spiritual

spiritualist /spírrichoo əlist/ *n* **1** a believer in communication between the living and the dead **2** a person who is interested in spiritual matters —**spiritualistic** /spírrichoo ə lístik/ *adj*

spirituality /spírrityoo álləti/ (*plural* **-ties**) *n* **1** the quality or condition of being spiritual **2** the property or revenue belonging to a church or church official (*often plural*)

spiritualize /spírrichoo ə līz/ (**-izes, -izing, -ized**), **spiritualise** (**-ises, -ising, -ised**) *vt* **1** to give something a spiritual content **2** to attribute a spiritual meaning to something —**spiritualization** *n* —**spiritualizer** *n*

spiritualty /spírrichoo əlti/ (*plural* **-ties**) *n* CHR = **spirituality** *n.* 2

spirituel /spírrityoo él/, **spirituelle** *adj* showing a refined and graceful intellect [Late 17C. *Spirituel* < French (see SPIRITUAL), masculine; *spirituelle* < French, feminine.]

spirituous /spírrityoo əss/ *adj* containing alcohol or made by distillation (*formal*) —**spirituousness** *n*

spirit varnish *n* a varnish consisting of a resin dissolved in alcohol

spirketting /spúrkiting/ *n* a thick planking used to line and reinforce the decks and ports of a wooden ship [Mid-18C. < *spurket* 'space between deck and side of a ship' < ?]

spiro- *prefix* breathing, respiration ○ *spirograph* [< Latin *spirare* 'breathe']

spirochaete /spīrō keet/, **spirochete** *n* a coiled rod-shaped bacterium. Order: Spirochaetales. [Late 19C. < modern Latin *Spirochaeta* < Latin *spira* 'coil' + *chaeta* 'hair'.]

spirochaetosis /spīrōki tóssiss/ (*plural* **-ses** /-seez/) *n* a disease caused by a spirochaete

spirochete *n* = **spirochaete**

spirograph /spīrə graaf, -graf/ *n* an instrument that makes a record of the depth and rapidity of somebody's breathing [Late 19C. < Latin *spirare* 'breathe' + -GRAPH.] —**spirographic** *adj* —**spirography** /spī róggrəfi/ *n*

spirogyra /spīrə jīrə/ *n* a multicellular freshwater green alga. Genus: *Spirogyra*. [Late 19C. < modern Latin, < Latin *spira* 'coil' + Greek *guros* 'round'.]

spirometer /spī rómmitər/ *n* an instrument for measuring the capacity of the lungs [Mid-19C. < Latin *spirare* 'breathe' + -METER.] —**spirometric** /spīrə méttrik/ *adj* —**spirometry** *n*

spironolactone /spīrənō láktōn/ *n* $C_{24}H_{32}O_4S$ a steroid that acts as a diuretic. Use: treatment of oedema, hypertension. [Mid-20C. < *spirolactone*, a steroid derivative (< Latin *spira* 'coil' + LACTONE) by inserting -ONE.]

spirt /spurt/ *vti* to spurt (*dated*) ■ *n* a spurt (*dated*) [Mid-16C. Variant of SPURT.]

spirulina /spírroŏ līnə, spī-/ *npl* cyanobacteria valued as a rich source of protein, containing vitamins, minerals, essential fatty acids, and antioxidants. Spirulina are grown in tanks and harvested to make into nutritional supplements. Genus: *Spirulina*. [< modern Latin, < Latin *spirula* 'small spiral shell' < *spira* (see SPIRE[2])]

spiry[1] /spīri/ *adj* shaped like a spiral (*literary*) [Late 17C. < SPIRE[2].]

spiry[2] /spīri/ *adj* shaped like a spire (*literary*) [Early 17C. < SPIRE[1].]

spit[1] /spit/ *v* (**spits, spitting, spat** *or* **spit, spat** /spat/ *or* **spit**) **1** *vi* **EJECT SALIVA** to expel saliva forcefully from the mouth **2** *vi* **EXPEL SALIVA TO SHOW CONTEMPT** to show anger, contempt, or hatred by or as if by expelling saliva **3** *vt* **EXPEL FROM YOUR MOUTH** to eject something harmful or unpleasant such as blood or food forcefully from the mouth **4** *vti* **MAKE SOUND OF SPUTTERING** to make sputtering sounds, such as those made when a fire shoots out sparks **5** *vi* **HISS LIKE CAT** to make a hissing explosive sound like an angry cat **6** *vi* **RAIN OR SNOW LIGHTLY** to rain lightly or in scattered drops or flakes **7** *vt* **UTTER ANGRILY** to utter something sharply and angrily ■ *n* **1 SPITTLE FROM MOUTH** saliva, especially when ejected from the mouth **2 EXPULSION OF SOMETHING FROM THE MOUTH** a forceful ejection of saliva or something else from the mouth **3 LIKENESS** an exact likeness (*informal*) [Old English *spittan*. Ultimately < Indo-European.] —**spitter** *n* ◇ **spit it out** to say something at once, especially something that has been withheld (*informal; usually a command*)

spit up *vt* to regurgitate or cough up something

spit[2] /spit/ *n* **1 THIN ROD FOR ROASTING** a thin rod on which something is impaled for roasting over a fire **2 LAND PROJECTING FROM SHORE** an elongated point of land or shoal projecting into a body of water ■ *vt* (**spits, spitting, spitted**) **IMPALE** to impale somebody or something on a roasting spit or on any long sharp pointed thing [Old English *spitu* < Indo-European, 'sharp point']

spit and polish *n* meticulous care in presenting a neat appearance, especially in the armed forces (*informal*)

spitball /spít bawl/ *n* **1** *US, Can* a tiny wad of paper chewed and moistened with saliva that is thrown as a prank **2** *US* in baseball, an illegal pitch that is made to curve deceptively because it has been moistened with saliva

spitchcock /spích kok/ *n* an eel split and then grilled or fried [Early 17C. < ?]

spit curl *n US* = **kiss curl** [< its being fixed in place with saliva]

spite /spīt/ *n* a malicious, usually small-minded desire to harm or humiliate somebody ■ *vt* (**spites, spiting, spited**) to harm, hinder, or humiliate somebody out of small-minded malice [13C. Shortening of DESPITE.] ◇ **in spite of** notwithstanding, or without taking account of something

spiteful /spítf'l/ *adj* full of or showing petty maliciousness —**spitefully** *adv* —**spitefulness** *n*

spitfire /spít fīr/ *n* a quick-tempered person

Spitfire /spít fīr/ *n* a British fighter plane used by the Royal Air Force during World War II

spitting cobra *n US* ZOOL = **ringhals**

spitting distance *n* a short enough distance to seem within reach (*informal*)

spitting image *n* an exact likeness of somebody (*informal*) [Alteration of *spit and image* < SPIT[1] in the meaning 'an exact likeness']

spitting snake *n* = **ringhals** [< its spitting of venom]

spittle /spítt'l/ *n* **1** saliva, especially that has been or is about to be expelled from the mouth **2** something that looks like frothy saliva, especially the secretions from spittlebugs deposited on plants (**cuckoo spit**) [15C. Alteration (under the influence of SPIT[1]), of *spattle* < Old English *spātl* 'spittle' < Germanic.]

spittlebug /spítt'l bug/ *n* INSECTS = **froghopper**

spittoon /spi tóon/ *n* a container for people to spit into [Mid-19C. < SPIT[1].]

spitz /spits/ *n* dog belonging to a breed that has a pointed muzzle, erect pointed ears, and a tightly curled tail [Mid-19C. Shortening of German *Spitzhund* 'pointed dog'.]

spiv /spiv/ *n UK* an offensive term for a man whose way of dressing is considered ostentatiously smart and whose integrity is doubted (*slang insult*) [Mid-20C. < ?] —**spivvy** *adj*

splanchnic /splángknik/ *adj* relating to the intestines (*technical*) [Late 17C. < modern Latin *splanchnicus* < Greek *splagkhna* 'entrails'.]

splash /splash/ *v* 1 *vti* **SPATTER LIQUID** to make a liquid scatter or fall in drops or larger amounts ○ *The children were splashing in the pool.* ○ *She splashed water over the side of the bath.* 2 *vi* **BE SPATTERED ABOUT** to scatter or fly up in drops or larger amounts ○ *The waves splashed against the rocks.* 3 *vt* **SPATTER DROPS OF LIQUID ON** to wet or dirty something by spattering it with liquid ○ *She splashed her blouse with the hot tea.* 4 *vti* **MOVE WHILE SPLASHING** to make your way through water or another liquid, scattering it about ○ *They splashed through the puddles.* 5 *vt* **ADD CONTRASTS TO** to apply contrasting colour or light to something 6 *vt* **DISPLAY PROMINENTLY** to display something such as a news headline, story, or photograph conspicuously (*usually passive*) ○ *The story was splashed across the front page.* ■ *n* 1 **NOISE OF WATER SCATTERING** an act or sound of splashing 2 **SOMETHING SPLASHED** something that is splashed ○ *The bathroom floor was covered with splashes.* 3 **MARK CAUSED BY SPLASH** a mark or stain made by something splashing or being splashed ○ *The backs of her legs were covered with splashes.* 4 **PATCH OF COLOUR** an area of contrasting colour or light, often irregular ○ *The dark forest was dappled with splashes of moonlight.* 5 **TINY AMOUNT OF LIQUID** a very small quantity of one liquid added to another (*informal*) ○ *She added a splash of milk to her tea.* 6 **PROMINENT DISPLAY** a conspicuous display, e.g. a prominent news headline, story, or photograph [Early 18C. Probably a variant of PLASH[1].] ◇ **make a splash** to attract a great deal of attention or publicity
splash down *vi* to land in the sea after a flight in space

splashback /splásh bak/ *n* a sheet of something such as glass or plastic attached to a wall behind a basin or cooker to protect the wall from splashes

splashboard /splásh bawrd/ *n* 1 a screen for preventing water from splashing into a boat 2 a protective guard that prevents mud or water from splashing the upper part of a motor vehicle and the people travelling in it

splashdown /splásh down/ *n* the landing of a spacecraft or missile in the sea after a flight

splashguard /splásh gaard/ *n US* AUTOMOT = **mud flap**

splashy /spláshi/ (**-ier, -iest**) *adj* 1 **COLOURFUL** with lots of bright colours 2 **ATTRACTING NOTICE** attracting a lot of attention (*informal*) 3 **MAKING SPLASHES** with great splashing of liquid —**splashily** *adv* —**splashiness** *n*

splat /splat/ *n* **WET SMACKING SOUND** a sound made when something soft and wet hits something hard ■ *adv* **WITH SMACK** with a wet smacking sound ■ *interj* **IMITATING IMPACT** used to imitate the sound made when something soft and wet hits something hard [Late 19C. An imitation of the sound.]

splatter /splátter/ *vti* to spatter or splash something, or to be spattered or splashed ■ *n* a spatter or splash [Late 18C. < ?]

splatterpunk /splátter pungk/ *n* a form of narrative such as a story, film, or comic strip that contains a lot of gory violence (*slang*)

splay /splay/ *vti* 1 **SPREAD WIDE AND OUTWARDS** to spread out something such as the fingers or toes 2 **TURN OUT AWKWARDLY** to turn something awkwardly outwards 3 **MAKE SIDES OF SOMETHING SLANT** to give something or have obliquely sloping edges, e.g. an opening in a wall that is bigger on one side than the other ■ *adj* **splay, splayed** 1 **SPREAD FLAT AND OUTWARDS** sloping, turning, or spread flatly and outwards 2 **TURNED AWKWARDLY OUTWARDS** turned awkwardly outwards ■ *n* **SLANT TO SIDES OF OPENING** an oblique slope given to the edges of something such as an opening in a wall, so that the opening is bigger on one side than the other [14C. Shortening of DISPLAY.]

splayed *adj* = **splay** *adj.* 1, **splay** *adj.* 2

splayfoot /spláy fòòt/ (*plural* **-feet** /-feet/) *n* 1 a foot with fallen arches, often with widely spread toes, or the condition that causes this. ◊ **flatfoot** *n.* 1 2 a foot that is excessively turned outwards, or the condition causing it —**splayfooted** /spláy fòòtid/ *adj* —**splayfootedly** /-fòòtidli/ *adv*

spleen /spleen/ *n* 1 a ductless vascular organ in the left upper abdomen of humans and other vertebrates that helps to destroy old red blood cells, form lymphocytes, and store blood 2 anger or bad temper [13C. Via Latin < Greek *splēn*.] —**spleenful** *adj* —**spleenish** *adj* —**spleeny** *adj*

spleenwort /spleén wurt/ *n* an evergreen fern of temperate and tropical regions that has feathery fronds. Genus: *Asplenium*. [Late 16C. < the former belief that it cured illnesses of the spleen.]

splendent /spléndənt/ *adj* (*literary*) 1 reflecting light so that it shines 2 distinguished in a particular field [15C. < Latin *splendere* 'shine'.]

splendid /spléndid/ *adj* 1 **MAGNIFICENT** impressive because of quality or size 2 **RADIANT** reflecting light brilliantly 3 **EXCELLENT** excellent or highly enjoyable 4 **ACCLAIMED** very well known and acclaimed [Early 17C. < Latin *splendidus* < *splendere* 'shine'.] —**splendidness** *n*

splendidly /spléndidli/ *adv* in a fine or admirable way ○ *The restoration work is coming along splendidly.*

splendiferous /splen dífferəss/ *adj* magnificent and wonderful (*humorous*) [Mid-19C. < SPLENDOUR.] —**splendiferously** *adv* —**splendiferousness** *n*

splendor *n US* = **splendour**

splendour /spléndər/ *n* 1 the condition of being magnificent, impressive, or brilliant 2 something that is magnificent, impressive, or brilliant ○ *the splendours of Ancient Greece* [15C. Directly and via Old French < Latin *splendor* < *splendere* 'shine'.] —**splendorous** *adj*

splenectomy /spli néktəmi/ (*plural* **-mies**) *n* surgical removal of the spleen [Mid-19C. < Greek *splēn* 'spleen' + -ECTOMY.]

splenetic /spli néttik/ *adj* 1 **BAD-TEMPERED** extremely bad-tempered or spiteful (*literary*) 2 **RELATING TO SPLEEN** relating to the spleen (*dated*) ■ *n* **SOMEBODY BAD-TEMPERED** a bad-tempered or spiteful person (*literary or dated*) [Mid-16C. < Latin *spleneticus* < *splen* 'spleen'.] —**splenetically** *adv*

splenic /splénnik, spleé-/ *adj* relating to, in, or near the spleen [Early 17C. < Greek *splēn* 'spleen'.]

splenius /spleéni əss/ (*plural* **-i**) *n* either of two muscles on each side of the neck that reach from the base of the skull to the upper back and rotate and extend the head and neck [Mid-18C. Via modern Latin < Greek *splēnion* 'bandage, compress'.] —**splenial** *adj*

splenomegaly /spleénō méggəli/ *n* abnormal enlargement of the spleen [Early 20C. < Greek *splēn* 'spleen' + *megal-* 'great'.]

splice /splīss/ *vt* (**splices, splicing, spliced**) 1 **INTERWEAVE STRANDS OF TWO ROPES** to join two pieces of rope or wire by weaving the strands of each into the other 2 **JOIN ENDS OF FILM OR TAPE** to join the ends of two pieces of film or magnetic tape, e.g. in editing 3 **JOIN PIECES OF WOOD** to join two pieces of wood together by overlapping them and bolting or otherwise attaching them 4 **JOIN GENETIC MATERIAL** to join together or insert pieces of DNA when altering the genetic structure of something 5 **MARRY TWO PEOPLE** to join a couple in marriage (*slang; often passive*) ■ *n* 1 **CONNECTION** a join made by connecting two pieces of something 2 **JUNCTION OF SPLICING** the junction where something has been spliced 3 **END OF BAT HANDLE** the wedge-shaped end of the handle of a cricket bat where it fits into the striking part [Early 16C. < Middle Dutch *splissen*.] —**splicer** *n*

spliff /splif/ *n* a marijuana cigarette (*slang*) [Mid-20C. < ?]

spline /splīn/ *n* 1 a flat, relatively narrow key that is integral to a shaft, produced by milling a longitudinal groove 2 = **slat** *n.* 1 3 a thin narrow piece of wood, metal, or plastic that fits onto or into the edges of tiles or boards and connects them together [Mid-18C. < ?]

splint /splint/ *n* 1 **DEVICE TO IMMOBILIZE BROKEN BONE** a strip of rigid material used to keep a broken bone or other injured body part from moving 2 **STRIP OF WOOD USED IN BASKETRY** a thin strip of wood used to weave something such as a basket or chair seat 3 WOODWORK = **splinter** *n.* 1 4 **WOOD SLIVER FOR LIGHTING FIRES** a sliver of wood used to carry a flame, e.g. to light a fire or a candle 5 **METAL PLATE IN ARMOUR** any overlapping metal plate or strip used in making a suit of armour 6 **ENLARGEMENT OF HORSE'S LEG BONE** a condition that occurs in young horses, consisting of painful bony outgrowths in or near the splint bones on the inner sides of the legs ■ *vt* 1 **IMMOBILIZE INJURED PART** to immobilize a broken bone or injured body part with a rigid support 2 **STRENGTHEN** to give support or added strength to something [13C. < Middle Low German or Middle Dutch *splinte*.]

splint bone *n* either of a pair of thin bones on either side of the cannon bone in the lower legs of horses and other hoofed animals

splinter /splíntər/ *n* 1 **THIN SHARP FRAGMENT** a small thin sharp piece of wood, metal, stone, glass, or other material broken from a larger piece 2 **BOMB FRAGMENT** a metal fragment thrown from an exploding bomb or shell 3 POL = **splinter group** ■ *vti* 1 **BREAK INTO SHARP FRAGMENTS** to break something or be broken into thin sharp fragments 2 **DIVIDE GROUP** to split a larger group into factions or independent groups, or to be split in this way [14C. < Middle Dutch.] —**splintery** *adj*

splinter group *n* a group formed by individuals who have dissociated themselves from a larger organization, usually because of disagreement

split /split/ *v* (**splits, splitting, split**) 1 *vti* **DIVIDE LENGTHWISE** to divide something or be divided lengthwise into two or more parts, usually by force 2 *vti* **BURST** to burst apart or rip something apart 3 *vt* **AFFECT VIOLENTLY** to disturb or disrupt something with a violently jarring presence 4 *vti* **SEPARATE INTO PARTS** to divide a whole into parts, or to be separated from the rest or from a whole 5 *vt* **SEPARATE BY ADDING SOMETHING BETWEEN** to separate a whole into its components by interposing something 6 *vti* **DIVIDE INTO FACTIONS** to separate from a main group, or make a group divide into factions, because of disagreement 7 *vt* **SHARE** to share something among a group 8 *vti* **DEPART** to leave a place (*slang*) ■ *n* 1 **ACT OF BREAKING APART** the action of breaking or splitting something 2 **CRACK** a crack or break in something, especially one that runs lengthways 3 **FRAGMENT** a piece broken off from the whole 4 **DIVISION THROUGH DISAGREEMENT** a breach in a group, caused by a disagreement between members 5 **PORTION** a share, especially a share of money (*informal*) 6 **ICE CREAM DESSERT** a dessert of fruit with ice cream and a topping of flavoured syrup, nuts, and whipped cream 7 **STRIP OF WOOD FOR BASKETRY** a strip of flexible wood, usually willow, used for basketry 8 **LAYER OF ANIMAL HIDE** a single thickness of animal hide other than the outermost layer 9 **LEATHER** leather made from a single inner layer of animal hide 10 **ARRANGEMENT OF STANDING BOWLING PINS** in ten-pin bowling, a batch of remaining pins in which the pins are clustered into two groups with a large gap in between ■ **splits** *npl* **GYMNASTIC ACTION** a gymnastic action in which the legs are fully extended in opposite directions until the body is sitting on or very close to the floor (+ *singular verb*) ○ *do the splits* ■ *adj* 1 **BROKEN** broken, divided, or separated into parts 2 **DISUNITED** divided because of disagreement [Late 16C. < Dutch *splitten*.] —**splitter** *n*
split on *vt* to inform on somebody (*informal*)
split up *v* 1 *vi* **END RELATIONSHIP** to end a relationship or a marriage 2 *vti* **SEND PEOPLE DIFFERENT WAYS** to go off in a different direction or send individuals off in different directions 3 *vt* **DIVIDE INTO PARTS** to divide something into separate parts

Split /split/ port in S Croatia, on the Adriatic Sea. Population: 189,388 (1991).

split brain *n* a brain that has the corpus callosum surgically severed or missing from birth, so that the two hemispheres of the brain are not connected

split decision *n* in boxing, a win awarded by a majority of judges, rather than by a unanimous decision

split end *n* 1 a hair with a damaged end that has separated into strands 2 in American football, a player at the end of an offensive line that lines up some distance outside the rest of the line

split infinitive *n* an infinitive in which the 'to' and the verb are separated by another word, as in the phrase 'to seriously think'

LANGUAGE NOTE What is wrong with a split infinitive? The ***split infinitive*** is a stylistic issue that has been rationalized into a grammatical one. There is no grammatical basis for rejecting split infinitives, since to regard an infinitive with *to* as an inseparable unit has no support in the typical structures of English grammar, which freely separates particles, auxiliary verbs, and other qualifiers from the words to which they belong (e.g., *I have never been to Paris* separates *have* from *been*). The issue is one of style and not of grammar. If splitting an infinitive produces awkwardness, it is better to avoid it, but if the split is natural and supports or clarifies the meaning, there can be no objection to it. The adverb belongs closely with the verb in the infinitive in cases such as *They agreed to flatly forbid such actions.* and *They were plotting to secretly copy the files*, but can be moved to a more comfortable position in other cases such as *We expect to further modernize our services* (revise as: ... *to modernize* *our services further*) and *I would like to briefly mention a few points* (revise as: *I would like briefly to . . .*). It is usually advisable to avoid splitting the infinitive with an adverbial phrase (e.g. *They were trying to in some way improve the situation*). In some cases, however, even an adverbial phrase cannot be separated from its verb: *Prices are likely to more than double* (in which *more than double* is effectively regarded as a set verb phrase). The guiding principle is that the split infinitive has a long history of use; it is acceptable when the rhythm and meaning of the sentence call for it or when its use is that of a set verb phrase. It should be avoided (either by repositioning or by rephrasing) when it seems stilted or awkward, or creates ambiguity, especially in formal writing where its inclusion may draw criticism.

split-level *adj* **1** describes the floor of a room that is on different levels with steps between them **2** having the oven and hob in separate units (*refers to a cooker*) — **split-level** *n*

split-new *adj Scotland* brand-new (*informal*) [Referring to a strip of wood]

split pea *n* a pea that has been shelled, dried, and split in half, used especially in soup

split personality *n* **1** PSYCHIAT = **multiple personality** **2** a tendency towards erratic mood or temperament changes

split pin *n* a two-pronged metal pin that holds things together when its prongs are passed through holes on both parts and then bent back

split ring *n* a small steel ring with two spiral turns, often used as a key ring or as a means of fastening two parts together

split screen *n* a cinema or television screen frame divided into more than one image

split second *n* an extremely brief amount of time

split-second *adj* carried out instantly, or depending on instant skill or judgment

split shift *n* a single work period that is divided into two or more sessions of work, separated by an interval that is longer than a normal rest or meal break

split stitch *n* a back stitch in which each new stitch is made through the centre of the previous one

⚡**splitter** /splíttər/ *n* an electronic or other device that divides something into parts, e.g. a software device that enables a long file to be divided into sections or a device that splits a telephone signal so that it can carry voice and data transmissions simultaneously

split tin *n* a long narrow loaf of bread with a shallow lengthwise split along the top [< its being baked in a tin]

splitting /splítting/ *adj* causing intense pain ○ *a splitting headache* ■ *n* a Freudian defence mechanism in which somebody separates something unpleasant such as an idea into parts that are each less threatening than the whole

split-up *n* an instance or the act of separating, e.g. the ending of a relationship between two people

splodge /sploj/ *n* a large irregular spot, stain, or discoloration. US term **splotch** *n.* ■ *vt* (**splodges, splodging, splodged**) to mark or dirty something with splodges. US term **splotch** *v.* [Early 17C. < ?]

splotch /sploch/ *n* = **splodge** *n.* ■ *vt* = **splodge** *v.* [Early 17C. < ?]

splurge /splurj/ *v* (**splurges, splurging, splurged**) **1** *vi* **INDULGE** to indulge in something extravagant or expensive (*informal*) **2** *vt* **SPEND MONEY EXTRAVAGANTLY** to spend money in an extravagant or wasteful way ■ *n* (*informal*) **1 BOUT OF EXTRAVAGANCE** a period of indulgence or extravagant spending **2 GRAND DISPLAY** a showy display of something such as wealth [Early 19C. < ?]

splutter /splúttər/ *v* **1** *vi* **MAKE SPITTING SOUND** to make a spitting or choking sound **2** *vti* **SAY INCOHERENTLY** to say something in a choking incoherent manner **3** *vti* **SPIT SOMETHING OUT** to scatter saliva, liquid, or particles of food from the mouth ■ *n* **1 INCOHERENT SPEECH** a burst of choking incoherent speech **2 CHOKING NOISE** a spitting choking noise [Late 17C. < ?] —**splutterer** *n* —**spluttering** *n, adj*

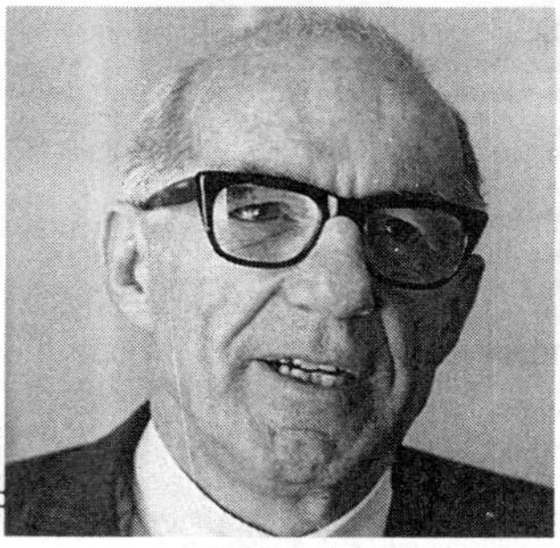

Popperfoto

Dr Spock

Spock /spok/, **Dr** (1903–98) US paediatrician and political activist. Full name **Benjamin McLane Spock**

spodumene /spóddyoo meen/ *n* a crystalline aluminosilicate mineral containing lithium that occurs in grayish white, greenish, or lilac forms. Use: source of lithium, gems. ◊ **hiddenite, kunzite** [Early 19C. Via French < Greek *spodoumenos* 'burnt to ashes' < *spodos* 'ashes'; from its greyish colour.]

spoil /spoyl/ *v* (**spoils, spoiling, spoiled** *or* **spoilt, spoiled** *or* **spoilt** /spoylt/) **1** *vt* **IMPAIR** to damage or ruin something in such a way that a quality such as worth, beauty, or usefulness, is diminished **2** *vt* **HARM BY OVERINDULGENCE** to harm a person's character, especially a child's, by repeated overindulgence **3** *vt* **TREAT INDULGENTLY** to treat somebody with indulgence out of a desire to please ○ *The hotel staff really spoiled us.* **4** *vt* **CAUSE TO SEEM UNSATISFACTORY** to make somebody dissatisfied with what is usually offered by greatly exceeding it in quality ○ *All that sun spoils you for holidays at home.* **5** *vi* **BECOME ROTTEN** to become unfit to eat because of decay **6** *vt* **TAKE PROPERTY FROM** to take somebody's property by force or violence (*archaic*) ■ *n* **1 WASTE FROM EXCAVATION** waste material removed from an excavation **2 STEALING** the act of plundering (*archaic*) ■ **spoils** *npl* **1 PROPERTY SEIZED BY VICTOR** valuables or property seized by the victor in a conflict **2 SOMETHING GAINED THROUGH EFFORT** something valuable or desirable gained through effort, opportunism, or other means [13C. Via Old French *espoillier* 'plunder, despoil' < Latin *spoliare* < *spolium* 'booty'.] ◇ **be spoiling for something** be eager for something, usually a conflict or confrontation

spoilage /spóylij/ *n* **1 DECAYING** the process of decaying or becoming damaged, or such a condition **2 WASTE** waste arising from decay or damage **3 AMOUNT WASTED** the amount of something wasted because of decay or damage

spoiled /spoyld/, **spoilt** /spoylt/ *adj* **1** severely or irrevocably impaired, e.g. by damage or decay **2** wilful or selfish because of having been overindulged

spoiled priest *n Ireland* a student of the priesthood who withdrew or was dismissed

spoiler /spóylər/ *n* **1 AEROFOIL FOR CONTROLLING LIFT AND DRAG** a narrow hinged aerofoil attached lengthwise to the upper surface of an aircraft wing **2 CAR AIR DEFLECTOR** a fixed air deflector on the rear of a car, designed to keep it on the ground during high speeds **3 SOMEBODY WHO CAN RUIN ANOTHER'S WIN** a candidate for office, or a competitor in sport, who cannot win but can or does prevent an opponent from doing so **4 RIVAL PUBLICATION** a newspaper or magazine whose release is calculated to coincide with that of a rival publication in order to divert interest in it and reduce its sales **5 SOMEBODY WHO WRECKS** somebody or something that ruins or wrecks something **6 ROBBER** somebody or something that robs or pillages

spoilsport /spóyl spawrt/ *n* somebody whose conduct spoils the plans or pleasure of others

spoils system *n* the practice of a winning political party giving government jobs and public appointments to its supporters

spoilt *adj* = **spoiled** ■ *v* past tense, past participle of **spoil**

Spokane /spō kán/ **1** river in N Idaho and E Washington State. Length: 195 km/120 mi. **2** city in E Washington State, on the Spokane River. Population: 177,196 (1990).

spoke¹ /spōk/ *n* **1 SUPPORTING ROD FOR WHEEL RIM** any bar or rod that extends from the hub of a wheel to support or brace the rim **2 KNOB ON SHIP'S WHEEL** a knob that sticks out from the rim of a ship's wheel **3 RUNG** a rung of a ladder [Old English *spāca* < Indo-European, 'pointed object'] ◇ **put a spoke in somebody's wheel** to hinder or thwart somebody's plans

spoke² *v* past tense of **speak**

spoken /spōkən/ *v* past participle of **speak** ■ *adj* **1** expressed with the voice ○ *the spoken word* **2** speaking in a stated way, e.g. with a particular voice quality, accent, command of the language, or attitude (*in combination*) ○ *well-spoken* ◇ **be spoken for 1** to be already owned or reserved by somebody **2** to be already married, engaged or romantically committed to somebody (*dated*)

SYNONYMS See ***verbal***.

spokeshave /spōk shayv/ *n* a small carpenter's plane consisting of a blade with a handle at each end, once used to shape spokes, now used to shape and smooth convex and concave wooden surfaces

spokesman /spōksmən/ (*plural* **-men** /-mən/) *n* somebody authorized to speak on behalf of another person or other people [Mid-16C. < SPOKE².]

spokesperson /spōks purss'n/ *n* a spokesman or spokeswoman [Late 20C. After SPOKESMAN.]

spokeswoman /spōks wŏŏmən/ (*plural* **-en** /-wimin/) *n* a woman authorized to speak on behalf of another person or other people [Mid-17C. After SPOKESMAN.]

spoliation /spōli áysh'n/ *n* **1 PLUNDERING** the seizing of things by force **2 SEIZURE OF SHIPS** the seizure or plundering of neutral ships at sea by a belligerent power in time of war **3 ALTERATION OF DOCUMENT** the alteration or destruction of a document so as to make it invalid or unusable as evidence **4 TAKING OF POSITION'S PRIVILEGES** the taking of the income or privileges that go with a religious position by somebody who is not entitled to them [15C. < Latin *spoliation-* < *spoliare* (see SPOIL).] — **spoliatory** /spōli ətəri/ *adj*

spondaic /spon dáy ik/ *adj* relating to spondees or written in spondees [Late 16C. < French *spondaïque* < Greek *spondeios* (see SPONDEE).]

spondee /spón dee/ *n* a unit of rhythm in poetry (**foot**), consisting of two long or stressed syllables [14C. Via French < Greek *spondeios* 'libational' < *spondē* 'libation'; so called because the spondee was often used in songs accompanying libations.]

spondylitis /spóndi lítiss/ *n* inflammation of the vertebrae and the attached discs and ligaments [Mid-19C. < Latin *spondylus* 'vertebra' < Greek *spondulos* < ?]

sponge /spunj/ *n* **1 MARINE ANIMAL** a chiefly marine invertebrate animal with a porous fibrous skeleton composed of calcium carbonate, silica, and spongin. Phylum: Porifera. **2 NATURAL MATERIAL USED FOR WASHING** a lightweight porous absorbent piece of the skeleton of some sponges. Use: washing, cleaning. **3 SYNTHETIC MATERIAL USED FOR WASHING** a piece of cellulose or synthetic material resembling a true sponge. Use: washing, cleaning. **4 GAUZE PAD** a folded gauze pad. Use: in surgery or medicine to absorb discharges, dress wounds, or apply medications. **5 HEAVY DRINKER** a drunkard (*informal*) **6 MASS OF RISING YEAST DOUGH** a small amount of yeast dough that is allowed to rise before being kneaded with the rest of the batch **7** FOOD = **sponge cake** **8** FOOD = **sponge pudding** **9 ACT OF CLEANING** the act of rubbing or bathing somebody or something with a wet sponge or cloth **10 POROUS METAL** a porous metal capable of absorbing large quantities of gas, obtained by reduction without melting of a metal compound, or by electrolysis ■ *v* (**sponges, sponging, sponged**) **1** *vt* **CLEAN** to wipe something or clean somebody with a wet sponge or cloth **2** *vt* **REMOVE** to remove or destroy something by rubbing **3** *vt* **ABSORB** to absorb liquids with a sponge or with the efficiency of a sponge **4** *vt* **GET BY IMPOSING ON GENEROSITY** to get something by imposing on the generosity of others **5** *vi* **LIVE OFF OTHERS** to live at the expense of others, repeatedly imposing on them and making no effort to live independently **6** *vi* **COLLECT SPONGES** to dive for sponges under the sea [Pre-12C. Via Latin *spongia* < Greek *sphoggos*.] —**sponger** *n*

sponge bag *n* a small waterproof bag used to carry toiletries when travelling. US term **ditty bag** *n.* **2**

sponge bath *n US* = **bed bath**

sponge cake *n* a light open-textured cake made of flour, eggs, sugar, flavouring, and traditionally no fat

sponge pudding *n* a light steamed or baked pudding made from a basic cake mixture

spongiform encephalopathy /spúnji fawrm en keffə lóppəthi/ *n* a brain disease in humans and animals in which areas of the brain slowly degenerate and take on a spongy appearance

spongin /spúnjin/ *n* a protein that forms the skeletal framework of sponges [Mid-19C. < SPONGE + -IN.]

spongioblast /spúnji ō blast/ *n* an embryonic cell in the brain and spinal cord that develops into supporting connective tissue (**glia**) [Early 20C. < Latin *spongia* 'sponge' + -BLAST.] —**spongioblastic** /spúnji ō blástik/ *adj*

spongy /spúnji/ (**-ier, -iest**) *adj* **1 OPEN-TEXTURED** with a light open texture full of holes or cavities **2 ABSORBENT** absorbent and elastic **3 SOFT AND WET** soft and full of water —**sponginess** *n*

~~**sponser**~~ incorrect spelling of **sponsor**

sponson /spónss'n/ *n* **1 SHIP'S GUN PLATFORM** a gun platform sticking out from the side of a ship **2 AIR CHAMBER IN CANOE** an air chamber that runs along each side of a canoe to help keep it afloat **3 STABILIZER FOR SEAPLANE** an air-filled structure or small wing projecting from the lower hull of a seaplane to stabilize it in water **4 GUN TURRET** a gun turret mounted on the side of an early tank **5 SUPPORT FOR PADDLE WHEEL** a structural support for a paddle wheel on a ship [Mid-19C. < ?]

sponsor /spónssər/ *n* **1 CONTRIBUTOR TO EVENT'S FUNDING** a person or organization that provides or pledges money to help fund an event, especially an event run by another person or group **2 CONTRIBUTOR TO CHARITY** a person or organization that donates money to a charity on the basis of the performance of a participant in an organized fundraising event **3 LEGISLATOR** a legislator who proposes and supports the passage of a bill **4 SUPPORTER** a country, organization, or group that supports or organizes an activity, or one who vouches for the acceptability of another **5 SOMEBODY ANSWERING AT CHILD'S BAPTISM** a person who answers for a child at baptism and becomes responsible for the child's religious upbringing (*formal*) **6** *US* **SOMEBODY RESPONSIBLE FOR ANOTHER** a person who becomes responsible for somebody else, especially during education, apprenticeship, or probation **7 RADIO OR TELEVISION ADVERTISER** an individual or a business that pays for radio or television programming by buying advertising time ■ *vt* **ACT AS SPONSOR TO** to act as a sponsor to somebody or something [Mid-17C. < late Latin, 'baptismal sponsor' < Latin *spons-*, past participle of *spondere* 'pledge'.] —**sponsorial** /spon sáwri əl/ *adj* —**sponsorship** *n*

SYNONYMS See ***backer***.

spontaneity /spóntə née əti, -náy-/ *n* **1** behaviour that is natural and unconstrained and is the result of impulse, not planning **2** the generating or provoking of activity from within, rather than as a result of external influences

spontaneous /spon táyni əss/ *adj* **1 ARISING FROM INTERNAL CAUSE** resulting from internal or natural processes, with no apparent external influence **2 ARISING FROM IMPULSE** arising from natural impulse or inclination, rather than from planning or in response to suggestions from others **3 UNRESTRAINED** naturally unrestrained or uninhibited **4 GROWING UNCULTIVATED** growing without cultivation [Mid-17C. < late Latin *spontaneus* 'of your own accord' < Latin *sponte*.] —**spontaneously** *adv* —**spontaneousness** *n*

spontaneous abortion *n* MED = **miscarriage** *n.* 1

spontaneous combustion *n* the ignition of a combustible material such as hay as a result of internal heat generation usually caused by rapid oxidation

spontaneous generation *n* BIOL = **abiogenesis**

spontaneous ignition *n* PHYS = **spontaneous combustion**

spontaneous recovery *n* in psychology, the return of an extinguished conditioned response without reinforcement

~~**spontanious**~~ incorrect spelling of **spontaneous**

spontoon /spon to͞on/ *n* a type of halberd used by some infantry officers in the 18th century [Mid-18C. Via obsolete French *sponton* < Italian *spontone* < *punto* 'point' < Latin *punctum* (see POINT).]

spoof /spoof/ *n* **1 HOAX** a good-humoured hoax **2 AMUSING SATIRE** a light amusing satire ■ *vt* **1 DECEIVE** to fool or deceive somebody **2 SATIRIZE** to satirize somebody or something good-naturedly [Late 19C. Invented name for a game involving hoaxing.] —**spoofer** *n*

spook /spook/ *n* (*informal*) **1 GHOST** a ghost or a ghostly figure **2** *US* **SPY** a spy ■ *v* **1** *vt* **HAUNT** to haunt somebody as a ghost **2** *vt US* **STARTLE** to startle or make an animal or person feel uneasy **3** *vi US* **BE FRIGHTENED** to feel frightened or uneasy [Early 19C. < Dutch < ?]

spooky /spo͝oki/ (**-ier, -iest**) *adj* **1 FRIGHTENINGLY SUGGESTIVE OF SUPERNATURAL INVOLVEMENT** frightening or unnerving because suggesting the presence of supernatural forces (*informal*) **2 AMAZING** strange or amazing, often because it seems that supernatural influences may have been at work (*informal*) **3** *US* **EASILY FRIGHTENED** easily frightened or startled —**spookily** *adv* —**spookiness** *n*

spool[1] /spool/ *n* **1 CYLINDER ON WHICH SOMETHING IS WOUND** a cylinder around which thread, tape, or film is wound **2 AMOUNT ON SPOOL** the amount of something wound on a spool ■ *vti* **WIND SOMETHING ON SPOOL** to wind something on a spool or on something similar to a spool such as a reel or bobbin [14C. Directly and via Old French *espole* < Middle Dutch *spoele*.]

ϟ **spool**[2] *vi* to transfer computer data for printing into a computer's memory store so that it can be printed later without slowing down the computer's operations [Late 20C. < SPOOL[1]; sometimes thought to be an acronym < *simultaneous peripheral operation on line*.] —**spooling** *n*

spoon /spoon/ *n* **1 EATING UTENSIL** a utensil used for eating or preparing food, consisting of a shallow oval bowl attached to a handle **2 SHINY FISHING LURE** a bright oval metal fishing lure with a hook attached **3 GOLF CLUB** a number three wood, used for hitting long high drives from the fairway (*dated*) **4 QUANTITY OF DRUG** a quantity of hard drugs, especially a two-gram measure of heroin (*slang*) ■ *v* **1** *vt* **EAT FOOD USING SPOON** to eat, scoop, or carry something with a spoon or with the action of somebody using a spoon **2** *vt* **HOLLOW OUT** to dig or scrape a hollow in something, or dig something out to leave a hollow **3** *vt* **HIT BALL UP** in golf, to hit a ball upwards with a scooping action, often as a result of an imperfect stroke **4** *vi* **USE SPOON FISHING LURE** to fish with a spoon lure **5** *vi* **BE AMOROUS** to indulge in amorous behaviour such as kissing and cuddling (*dated slang*) [Old English *spōn* 'wood chip' < Indo-European, 'flat piece of wood'] —**spoonful** *n*

spoonbill /spo͞on bil/ *n* a tropical wading bird with a long flat bill shaped like a spoon. Family: Threskiornithidae.

spoonerism /spo͞onərizəm/ *n* an accidental transposition of initial consonant sounds or parts of words, especially in an amusing way, e.g. 'half-warmed fish' for 'half-formed wish' [Early 20C. After Reverend William *Spooner* (1844–1930), British educationalist.]

spooney *adj* = **spoony**

spoon-feed (**spoon-feeds, spoon-feeding, spoon-fed**) *vt* **1 FEED WITH SPOON** to feed somebody, especially a child or hospital patient, using a spoon **2 GIVE EVERYTHING NEEDED TO SOMEBODY** to cater to somebody completely, requiring him or her to make no effort at all **3 DEPRIVE OF INDEPENDENT THOUGHT** to provide somebody with ideas, opinions, and judgments to an extent that independent thought becomes unnecessary or impossible for that person

spoonworm /spo͞on wurm/ *n* a marine worm that burrows in mud or rock crevices, with a soft plump body and spoon-shaped mouthpart that it extends to trap food particles. Phylum: Echiura.

spoony /spo͞oni/, **spooney** (**-ier, -iest**) *adj* foolishly sentimental or amorous (*dated*)

spoor /spoor, spawr/ *n* the visible trail of an animal, especially an animal that is being hunted for sport ■ *vti* to track an animal by following its trail [Early 19C. Via Afrikaans < Middle Dutch.] —**spoorer** *n*

spor- = **sporo-**

Sporades /spórrədiz/ group of Greek islands in the Aegean Sea

sporadic /spə ráddik/ *adj* **1** occurring occasionally at intervals that have no apparent pattern **2** describes a disease that appears in scattered or isolated instances or locations [Late 17C. Via medieval Latin < Greek *sporad-*, stem of *sporas* 'scattered'.]

SYNONYMS See ***periodic***.

sporangiophore /spə ránji ə fawr/ *n* a thread (**hypha**) from a fungus or a projection from the cone of a horsetail from which spore-forming sacs develop

sporangium /spə ránji əm/ (*plural* **-a** /-ə/) *n* a hollow spore-producing organ in fungi, ferns, and some other plants [Early 19C. < modern Latin, 'spore-vessel' < Greek *spora* (see SPORE) + *aggeion* 'small vessel' (see ANGIO-).]

spore /spawr/ *n* **1 ASEXUAL REPRODUCTIVE STRUCTURE** a small, usually one-celled reproductive structure produced by seedless plants, algae, fungi, and some protozoans that is capable of developing into a new individual **2 DORMANT BACTERIUM** a dormant resistant form taken by some bacteria in response to adverse conditions ■ *vi* (**spores, sporing, spored**) **PRODUCE SPORES** to produce or release spores [Mid-19C. Via modern Latin < Greek *spora* 'sowing, seed'.]

spore case *n* PLANT SCI = **sporangium**

sporiferous /spə ríffərəss/ *adj* producing or releasing spores

sporo- *prefix* spore ○ *sporoplasm* ○ *sporocyte* [< Greek *spora* 'seed']

sporocarp /spórrō kaarp, spáwrō-/ *n* **1** the spore-producing organ in red algae and some fungi and slime moulds **2** the hard round spore-producing organ of some aquatic ferns

sporocyst /spáwrō sist/ *n* **1 CASE PROTECTING SPOROZOITES** a protective case produced by sporozoans in which sporozoites develop **2 ENCASED SPOROZOITE** an encased sporozoite **3 FIRST STAGE OF A TREMATODE** the first sac-like reproductive stage in many trematode worms that buds off cells that develop into rediae **4 DORMANT SPORE-PRODUCING STRUCTURE** a dormant or resting sac-like structure that produces spores **5 LARVAL STAGE OF PARASITIC FLUKE** an immobile larval stage of a parasitic fluke that develops inside a snail following entry of the free-swimming miracidium larva. It gives rise to the next larval stage (**redia**).

sporocyte /spórrō sīt, spáwrō-/ *n* a cell from which spores are produced

sporogenesis /spórrō jénnəsiss, spáwrō-/ *n* **1** the production or formation of spores **2** reproduction by means of spores —**sporogenous** /spə rójjənəss/ *adj*

sporogony /spo róggəni, spə-/ *n* the process in sporozoans by which sporozoites are formed from multiple fission of an encysted zygote

sporophore /spórrə fawr, spáwrə-/ *n* an organ in fungi that produces spores

sporophyll /spórrə fil, spáwrə-/, **sporophyl** *n* a leaf or modified leaf that bears spore-producing organs, e.g. the fertile leaf of a fern or club moss

sporophyte /spórrə fīt, spáwrə-/ *n* in plants that alternate between sexual and asexual phases, a plant in its asexual spore-producing phase —**sporophytic** /spórrə fíttik, spáwrə-/ *adj*

sporoplasm /spórrə plazəm, spáwrə-/ *n* an infective mass of protoplasm contained inside a spore that is injected into a host cell by various parasitic organisms

sporopollenin /spórrə póllənin, spáwrə-/ *n* a polymer found in the outer layer of pollen and some spores [Mid-20C. < SPORO- + POLLEN + -IN).]

sporotrichosis /spórrə trī kṓssiss, spáwrə-/ *n* a serious infectious disease caused by a fungus *Sporothrix schenckii* that enters the body from soil or wood via a skin wound [Early 20C. < modern Latin *Sporotrichum* < *spora* (see SPORE) + Greek *thrix* 'hair'.]

sporozoan /spórrə zṓ ən, spáwrə-/ *n* a parasitic single-celled organism (**protozoan**) that has alternating sexual and asexual generations and reproduces by means of spores. Class: Sporozoa. [Late 19C. < modern Latin *Sporozoa* < Greek *spora* (see SPORE) + *zōion* 'animal'.]

sporozoite /spáwrə zṓ īt/ *n* any small infectious motile individual produced in sporozoans by sporogony, usually within a host [Late 19C. < modern Latin *Sporozoa*, class name (see SPOROZOAN).]

sporran /spórrən/ *n* a leather pouch, sometimes decorated with fur, worn hanging from a belt in front of the kilt in men's traditional Scottish Highland dress [Mid-18C. Via Scottish Gaelic < Middle Irish *sporán*.]

sport /spawrt/ *n* **1 COMPETITIVE PHYSICAL ACTIVITY** an individual or group competitive activity involving physical exertion or skill, governed by rules, and sometimes engaged in professionally **2 COMPETITIVE PHYSICAL ACTIVITIES AS A GROUP** competitive physical activities considered collectively as a group **3 PASTIME** an active pastime participated in for pleasure or exercise **4 SOMEBODY CHEERFUL** a person who remains cheerful when losing or in an unpleasant situation (*informal*)

5 SOMEBODY WHO PLAYS FAIRLY somebody noted for abiding by the rules in a game or for generally honourable behaviour (*informal*) **6 GOOD COMPANION** a good-natured, easy-going, or sociable person (*informal*) **7 JOKING** good-natured joking (*formal*) ○ *a harmless prank done in sport* **8 DERISION** contemptuous mockery (*formal*) **9 OBJECT OF RIDICULE** an object of ridicule or mockery (*formal*) **10 SOMEBODY OR SOMETHING MANIPULATED BY OTHERS** somebody or something manipulated by external forces (*literary*) **11 GAMBLER** a gambler, especially somebody who gambles on sporting events (*informal*) **12** *ANZ, US* **FORM OF ADDRESS** a casual form of address, especially used between men or boys (*informal*) **13 MUTATED ORGANISM** a plant or animal that deviates markedly from its parent stock or type, usually as a result of mutation, especially mutation of somatic tissue **14 UNUSUAL CHARACTER** the mutant character of a mutated organism **15 AMOROUS BEHAVIOUR** amorous behaviour such as kissing or cuddling (*archaic*) ■ *v* **1** *vt* **WEAR** to wear or display something, usually proudly or with the intention of impressing others (*informal*) **2** *vi* **PLAY HAPPILY** to romp and play happily (*formal*) **3** *vi* **ENJOY YOURSELF** to enjoy yourself, especially by taking part in outdoor physical activity (*formal*) **4** *vi* **MAKE JOKES** to joke or trifle with somebody (*formal*) **5** *vi* **MUTATE** to produce or undergo a mutation [14C. Shortening of *disport* 'diversion, amusement' < Old French *desport* < *desporter* (see DISPORT).] —**sporter** *n* —**sportful** *adj* —**sportfully** *adv* —**sportfulness** *n*

sport climbing *n* a sport in which competitors ascend walls, often artificial ones, on difficult routes that have bolts in place

sporting /spáwrting/ *adj* **1 USED IN SPORTS** relating to or used in sports activities ○ *sporting dogs* **2 FAIR** in keeping with the principles of fair competition, respect for other competitors, and personal integrity **3 OF GAMBLING** relating to gambling, or taking an interest in gambling **4 RISKING** willing to take a risk —**sportingly** *adv*

sporting chance *n* an even or good chance of succeeding

sportive /spáwrtiv/ *adj* **1 PLAYFUL** playful and frolicsome **2 JOKING** done as a joke **3 FOND OF SPORT** regularly taking part in sport **4 SEXUALLY ACTIVE** frequently indulging in sexual activity or tending to enjoy it (*archaic*) —**sportively** *adv* —**sportiveness** *n*

sports /spawrts/ *adj* **1 FOR SPORTING ACTIVITIES** relating to or used in physical or recreational activities ○ *sports equipment* ○ *sports ground* **2 FOR INFORMAL WEAR** designed for informal or outdoor wear ○ *sports shirt* ■ *npl* **SPORTS MEETING** a meeting for athletics or other sports activities, especially for school pupils ○ *It's the school sports next week.*

sports car *n* a small car with a low centre of gravity designed for fast acceleration and for handling at high speeds

sportscast /spáwrts kaast/ *n* a radio or television broadcast of a sports event or of sports news [Mid-20C. Blend of SPORTS + BROADCAST.] —**sportscaster** *n*

sports day *n UK, Can* a day on which a school stages races and other sports competitions for its pupils

sports drink *n* a soft drink that is intended to quench thirst faster than water and replenish the sugar and minerals lost from the body during physical exercise

sports jacket *n* a man's jacket similar in style to a suit jacket but worn on more informal occasions with trousers of a different material or colour

sportsman /spáwrtsmən/ (*plural* **-men** /-mən/) *n* **1** a man who participates in and gets pleasure from sport **2** a person who behaves fairly, observing rules, respecting others, and accepting defeat graciously —**sportsmanlike** *adj*

sportsmanship /spáwrtsmən ship/ *n* **1** conduct considered fitting for a sportsperson, including observance of the rules of fair play, respect for others, and graciousness in losing **2** participation in sports

sports medicine *n* the branch of medicine concerned with preventing and treating injuries resulting from sport

sportsperson /spáwrts purss'n/ *n* a sportsman or sportswoman

sports supplement *n* a dietary supplement used by athletes to enhance bursts of high performance [Late 20C]

sportswear /spáwrts wair/ *n* clothes worn for sport or outdoor leisure activities

sportswoman /spáwrts wòomən/ (*plural* **-en** /-wimin/) *n* **1** a woman who participates in and gets pleasure from sport **2** somebody who behaves according to principles of fairness, and who observes rules, shows respect for others, and accepts defeat graciously

sportswriter /spáwrts rītər/ *n* a writer about sport, especially for a newspaper or magazine

sport ute *n US* a sport-utility vehicle (*informal*)

sport-utility vehicle, sport-utility *n US* a four-wheel-drive vehicle used for everyday driving but suitable for rough terrain

sporty /spáwrti/ (**-ier, -iest**) *adj* **1 FOR SPORT** designed or appropriate for sport or leisure activities **2 ENTHUSIASTIC ABOUT SPORT** enthusiastic about sport or outdoor activities and regularly taking part in them **3 SIMILAR TO SPORTS CAR** with features resembling the style or performance of a sports car

sporulate /spórryòo layt/ (**-lates, -lating, -lated**) *vi* to produce spores [Late 19C. < modern Latin *sporula* 'small spore' < *spora* (see SPORE).] —**sporulation** /spórryòo láysh'n/ *n*

spot /spot/ *n* **1 SMALL ROUND AREA** a small defined area, especially one that is more or less circular, that is different in colour, material, or texture from the surrounding area **2 STAIN** a dirty mark or stain **3 MARK ON SKIN** a mark or blemish on the skin, especially a pimple **4 PARTICULAR PLACE** a particular place or location ○ *Do you remember the exact spot?* **5 GEOGRAPHICAL LOCATION** a geographical location or area ○ *a local beauty spot* **6 ASPECT** a particular aspect or part of something larger ○ *a weak spot in her argument* **7 SMALL AMOUNT** a small amount, e.g. of liquid to drink or of work to do ○ *What about a spot of lunch?* **8 ANNOUNCEMENT OR ADVERTISEMENT** a brief announcement or advertisement inserted between regular radio or television programmes **9 PERFORMER'S TIME SLOT** a performer's appearance in a variety show, or the scheduled or regular time for that appearance **10 AWKWARD SITUATION** an awkward or difficult situation (*informal*) **11 ENTERTAINMENT VENUE** a place of entertainment (*dated slang*) **12** *US* **POSITION** a position in a series or sequence **13** *US* **MONEY** a piece of paper money worth a particular amount (*dated slang; usually in combination*) ○ *She handed me a ten spot.* **14** ARTS = **spotlight** *n.* 1 **15 CHARACTER BLEMISH** a blemish on somebody's character or reputation (*archaic*) **16 MARKED WHITE BILLIARD BALL** in billiards, the white ball that is marked with a black dot **17 BILLIARD PLAYER** the player in billiards who is using the white ball with the black mark **18 DOT ON BILLIARD TABLE** any small black dot on the table in billiards, snooker, and pool that marks where a ball should be placed **19** *US* **SYMBOL ON PLAYING CARD** one of the traditional symbols, heart, diamond, spade, or club, on a playing card **20** *US* **PLAYING CARD** any playing card from two to ten of any of the four suits ○ *a six spot* **21** *US* **DOT ON GAME PIECE** one of the dots on a domino or dice **22 ILLUMINATED POINT ON CATHODE-RAY TUBE** the point on the face of a cathode-ray tube at which the phosphor is illuminated by the impact of an electron beam ■ *adj* **1 AVAILABLE IMMEDIATELY** describes goods or currencies that are paid for and delivered immediately after a sale **2 ORIGINATING LOCALLY** describes a news report that is broadcast from the place where it happens ■ *v* (**spots, spotting, spotted**) **1** *vt* **SEE** to see or detect something suddenly **2** *vt* **IDENTIFY AS PROMISING** to identify somebody, especially a performer, as having a promising talent worthy of being developed to a high, often professional standard **3** *vti* **MAKE OR BECOME STAINED** to mark or dirty something with stains, or to become marked or dirtied with stains **4** *vt* **MARK WITH DOTS** to mark something with dots **5** *vti* **ADJUST FIRE** to adjust gunfire for accuracy by observation **6** *vt* **BLEMISH SOMEBODY'S CHARACTER** to blemish somebody's character or reputation **7** *vi* **FALL LIGHTLY** to fall in light drops (*refers to rain*) **8** *vt US* **LEND TO OR BUY FOR** to give or lend money to somebody, or pay for something for somebody (*slang*) ○ *Will somebody spot me twenty bucks?* [12C. < ?] ◇ **hit the spot** to be absolutely what is required for total satisfaction, especially in terms of food or drink (*informal*) ◇ **in a spot** in a difficult or embarrassing position (*informal*) ◇ **on the spot 1** in the exact place where something is happening **2** immediately **3** in a difficult situation or under pressure ◇ **put somebody on the spot** to put somebody in a difficult or embarrassing position, especially a position of having to make an instant judgment or decision

spot check *n* a quick random inspection usually made without prior notice —**spot-check** *vt*

spotless /spótləss/ *adj* **1** impeccably clean ○ *a spotless kitchen* **2** beyond reproach ○ *a spotless reputation* —**spotlessly** *adv* —**spotlessness** *n*

spotlight /spót līt/ *n* **1 FOCUSED BEAM OF LIGHT** a strong beam of light that can be directed to illuminate a small area, especially one focusing attention on a stage performer **2 LAMP** a lamp that produces a strong narrow beam of light that can be directed at will, e.g. one mounted on a police car **3 FOCUS OF ATTENTION** the focus of public attention ■ *vt* (**-lights, -lighting, -lit** /spót lit/ *or* **-lighted**) **1 ILLUMINATE WITH LIGHT BEAM** to direct a beam of light on somebody or something **2 FOCUS ATTENTION ON** to focus public attention on somebody or something

spot market *n* a market in which commodities, securities, or currencies are traded for immediate payment and delivery

spot-on *adj* (*informal*) **1** absolutely correct or perfectly accurate **2** exactly what is needed

spot price *n* the market price for goods, currencies, or securities at a given time

spotted /spóttid/ *adj* **1** with a pattern of spots **2** stained or soiled with spots of something

spotted crake *n* a wading bird of the rail family with buff speckled plumage and dark brown wings. Native to: marshes of Europe and Asia. *Porzana porzana.*

spotted dick *n* a steamed suet pudding containing dried fruit [< its spotted appearance]

spotted fever *n* any fever accompanied by skin eruptions, e.g. Rocky Mountain spotted fever, typhus, or epidemic cerebrospinal meningitis

spotter /spóttər/ *n* **1 SOMEBODY WATCHING OUT** somebody or something that watches for and locates something (*often before nouns*) **2 LOCATER OF ENEMY POSITIONS** a person or aircraft that locates and reports enemy positions **3 TALENT SCOUT** a locator of new talent or material **4 SOMEBODY WHO MARKS** a person who puts marks or dots on something **5 SOMEBODY WHOSE HOBBY IS WATCHING** somebody whose hobby is watching for and noting down sightings of things, especially trains and aircraft (*usually in combination*)

spotty /spótti/ (**-tier, -tiest**) *adj* **1 PIMPLY** covered in pimples **2 SPOTTED** with a pattern of spots **3** *US* **INCONSISTENT** inconsistent in quality or character —**spottily** *adv* —**spottiness** *n*

spot-weld *vt* to join overlapping pieces of metal by making a series of small welds dotted about, rather than by making a large continuous weld ■ *n* a joint between overlapping metal parts, formed using the technique of spot-welding —**spot-welder** *n*

spouse /spowss, spowz/ *n* somebody's husband or wife [12C. Via Old French *spous* < Latin *sponsus* 'pledged', past participle of *spondere* 'betroth'.] —**spousal** /spówz'l/ *adj* —**spousally** *adv*

spout /spowt/ *vti* **1 DISCHARGE** to discharge a substance forcibly in a jet or stream **2 DISCHARGE AIR FROM BLOWHOLE** to discharge air and water through a blowhole (*refers to whales or dolphins*) **3 TALK AT GREAT LENGTH** to talk about something tediously and at great length, usually with no regard for the listener's interest ■ *n* **1 TUBE FOR POURING LIQUID** a tube or pipe out of which a liquid is poured **2 CHUTE FOR DISCHARGE OF SOLID SUBSTANCE** a chute through which something solid such as grain is discharged **3 STREAM OF LIQUID** a continuous and forceful stream of liquid **4** BUILDING = **waterspout** *n.* 2 **5** METEOROL = **waterspout** *n.* 1 **6 AIR AND WATER FROM BLOWHOLE** a burst of air and water from a whale or other marine animal's blowhole [14C. < Middle Dutch *spouten* 'spout'.] ◇ **up the spout 1** ruined or useless (*informal*) **2** an offensive phrase meaning pregnant (*slang*)

spouting /spówting/ *n NZ, Northeast US* the system of gutters and downpipes that carry rainwater from the roof of a building

spp. *abbr* species (*plural*)

SPQR *abbr* the senate and people of Rome [Latin, *Senatus Populusque Romanus*]

Spr *abbr* Sapper

spraddle /sprádd'l/ (**-dles, -dling, -dled**) *vti US* to sprawl, or cause somebody to sprawl [Mid-17C. < ?]

sprain /sprayn/ *n* a painful injury to the ligaments of a joint caused by wrenching or overstretching ■ *vt* to injure a joint by a sudden wrenching of its ligaments [Early 17C. < ?]

sprang *v* past tense of **spring**

sprat /sprat/ *n* **1** (*plural* **sprats** *or* **sprat**) **SMALL EDIBLE FISH** a small fish of the herring family. Native to: NE Atlantic Ocean, North Sea. *Sprattus sprattus.* **2 SMALL HERRING** a small or young herring or similar fish such as an anchovy **3 SPRAT AS FOOD** the flesh of a sprat as food **4 SOMEBODY YOUNG OR UNIMPORTANT** a young, small, or insignificant person (*dated*) [Old English *sprot*]

sprawl /sprawl/ *vi* **1 LIE AWKWARDLY** to sit or lie with the arms and legs spread awkwardly in different directions **2 EXTEND IN A DISORDERED WAY** to extend over or across something in a disordered, awkward, or ugly way ○ *handwritten notes sprawled across the page* ■ *n* **1 AWKWARD SITTING OR LYING POSITION** a sitting or lying position in which the arms and legs are spread out awkwardly **2 UNCHECKED GROWTH OF URBAN AREA** the scattered, unplanned, and unchecked expansion of a town or city into the surrounding countryside **3 URBANIZED AREAS ON CITY'S EDGE** the urbanized areas on the edge of a town or city that have developed as a result of unplanned and unchecked expansion [Old English *sprēawlian* 'move convulsively' < Indo-European, 'to strew'] —**sprawler** *n* —**sprawling** *adj* —**sprawly** *adj*

spray[1] /spray/ *n* **1 LIQUID PARTICLES** a moving cloud or mist of water or other liquid particles **2 JET OF LIQUID** a jet of fine particles of liquid from an atomizer or pressurized container **3 CONTAINER FOR RELEASING LIQUID** an atomizer or pressurized container that releases fine particles of a liquid (*often before nouns*) **4 SOMETHING IN PRESSURIZED CONTAINER** a liquid product such as a deodorant, paint, or insecticide that is packaged in an atomizer or pressurized container (*often before nouns*) ■ *v* **1** *vt* **DISCHARGE FROM PRESSURIZED CONTAINER** to disperse a liquid in the form of fine particles, or apply a liquid in this form to the surface of something **2** *vt* **PAINT WITH PAINT SPRAY** to paint or mark something using a paint spray ○ *spray the car red* ○ *He sprayed his name on the wall.* **3** *vi* **URINATE** to put out a stream of urine, e.g. as a cat does when marking its territory [Early 17C. < Middle Dutch *sprayen* 'sprinkle'.]

spray[2] /spray/ *n* **1 PLANT SPRIG** a shoot or branch of a plant, with flowers, leaves, or berries on it **2 FLOWER ARRANGEMENT** a decorative arrangement of flowers and foliage **3 DECORATION IMITATING FLOWERS AND FOLIAGE** something decorative such as a brooch, made in imitation of a sprig of flowers and foliage [13C. < assumed Old English *spræg*, probably related to SPRIG and Old English *spræc* 'shoot'.]

spray can *n* a small pressurized container used to disperse liquids in a fine mist

sprayer /spráy ər/ *n* a device that is capable of spraying liquid over an area

spray gun *n* a device that uses pressure to apply atomized paint or other liquids, operated by means of a trigger

spread /spred/ *v* (**spreads, spreading, spread**) **1** *vt* **OPEN FULLY** to open or extend something to its fullest area **2** *vti* **EXTEND WIDELY** to extend, or cause something to extend, over a large area ○ *A vast plain spread out before them.* **3** *vti* **EXTEND IN TIME** to extend something over a period of time **4** *vti* **EXTEND IN RANGE** to extend over a wider range, or cause something to cover a wider range than before **5** *vt* **SEPARATE THINGS BY STRETCHING** to separate things by stretching or pulling, so that they become far apart **6** *vti* **BECOME OR MAKE KNOWN** to become widely known, or make something widely known **7** *vt* **APPLY COATING TO** to coat something with a layer of a substance, especially one smoothly applied **8** *vti* **DISPERSE** to disperse something over a wide area, or to be dispersed in this way **9** *vti* **SEND OUT IN ALL DIRECTIONS** to send out something, or to be sent out, in all directions ○ *The lamp spread its light.* **10** *vt* **DISPLAY** to exhibit or display something in its fullest extent **11** *vt* **DIVIDE UP** to divide, share, or split something up among several people or groups ○ *They decided to spread out the money more evenly among the various departments.* **12** *vt* **GET TABLE READY FOR MEAL** to prepare a table for a meal **13** *vt* **PUT FOOD ON TABLE** to lay out food or a meal on a table ■ *n* **1 EXTENSION OF** the extension, diffusion, or distribution of something over an area, range, or time **2 VARIETY** a wide variety of things **3 LIMIT OF EXTENSION** the limit to which something can be extended **4 DISTANCE BETWEEN THINGS** the distance or range between two points or things **5** *US* **RANCH OR FARM** a piece of land and its buildings used for ranching or farming **6 BED OR TABLE COVER** a covering for a bed or table **7 SPREADABLE FOOD** a food with a soft texture, designed to be spread on bread or crackers **8 PAIR OF FACING PAGES** two facing pages in a newspaper, magazine, or book, often with material printed across the fold **9 EXTENSIVE STORY** an advertisement or story that occupies two or more columns in a newspaper or magazine **10 MEAL** a large meal laid out on a table (*informal*) **11 WIDENING OF BODY** a widening of the hips and waist owing to weight gain (*informal*) **12 PLANE'S WINGSPAN** the wingspan of an aeroplane (*informal*) **13 DIFFERENCE BETWEEN BID AND OFFER** the difference between the asking price and the bid price of a security **14 GEMSTONE SIZE** the size of a gemstone when viewed from above, expressed in carats ■ *adj* **1 EXTENDED** extended or stretched out **2 SHALLOW** describes a gemstone that is shallow and flat **3 SAID WITH LIPS STRAIGHT** describes a speech sound that is pronounced with the lips forming a horizontal line [Old English *sprǣdan* < Indo-European, 'to strew'] —**spreadable** *adj*

spread betting *n* a form of gambling that involves betting on the movement of a stock price in relation to a given range of high and low values. If the stock price moves outside the values on a given day the bettor wins a multiple of the original stake times the number of points above or below the set range.

spread eagle *n* **1 SYMBOLIC IMAGE OF EAGLE** the image of an eagle with its wings and legs outstretched, especially when used as an emblem of the United States **2 SKATING FIGURE** in ice skating, a figure performed with the blades touching heel to heel **3 POSTURE WITH SPREAD LIMBS** a way of standing or lying with arms and legs spread apart

spread-eagle *v* (**spread-eagles, spread-eagling, spread-eagled**) **1** *vt* **FORCE INTO SPREAD-OUT POSITION** to force somebody to stand or lie with arms and legs spread apart, especially when being arrested or searched **2** *vi* **PERFORM SKATING FIGURE** in ice skating, to perform a spread eagle **3** *vt* **STRETCH BODY ACROSS** to stand or lie with limbs spread wide across a gap or an object **4** *vi* **ADOPT POSITION WITH SPREAD LIMBS** to stand or lie with arms and legs spread apart ■ *adj US* = **spread-eagled**

spread-eagled *adj* standing or lying with arms and legs spread apart. US term **spread-eagle** *adj.*

spreader /spréddər/ *n* **1 DEVICE FOR DISTRIBUTING SEED OR FERTILIZER** a machine used by farmers and gardeners to spread manure, fertilizer, seed, or similar material over the ground (*usually in combination*) **2 IMPLEMENT FOR SPREADING** an implement such as a spatula, trowel, or broad-bladed knife, used for spreading soft substances (*usually in combination*) **3 DEVICE FOR SEPARATING THINGS** a device such as a bar, used to hold things such as cables or wires apart

spreading factor *n* BIOL = **hyaluronidase**

⚡**spreadsheet** /spréd sheet/ *n* **1** a computer program that displays numerical data in cells in a simulated accountant's worksheet of rows and columns in which hidden formulas can perform calculations on the visible data **2** the display or printout of a spreadsheet, showing the many lines and columns of a ledger

sprechgesang /shprékgə zang, shprékh-/, **Sprechgesang** *n* a style of singing that blends elements of normal nonmusical speech into the voice [Early 20C. < German, 'speech song'.]

sprechstimme /shprék shtimə, shprékh-/, **Sprechstimme** *n* **1** the voice used to sing sprechgesang **2** MUSIC = **sprechgesang** [Early 20C. < German, 'speech voice'.]

spree /spree/ *n* **1** a session of extravagant self-indulgent activity, especially of spending or drinking, but also of criminal activity **2** a fun-filled sociable outing (*dated*) [Late 18C. < ?]

sprier /sprī́r/ comparative of **spry**

spriest superlative of **spry**

sprig /sprig/ *n* **1 SMALL BRANCH** a shoot, stem, or twig cut or broken from a plant ○ *garnished with a sprig of parsley* **2 DECORATION** an artistic representation of a sprig that is usually repeated in rows on fabric or wallpaper to produce a decorative pattern **3 YOUTH** a young man (*dated*) **4 SMALL NAIL** a small headless tack that tapers to a point **5 STUD** a stud or spike in the sole of a boot used for various sports ■ *vt* (**sprigs, sprigging, sprigged**) **1 PATTERN WITH SPRIGS** to decorate fabric, wallpaper, or pottery with a pattern of sprigs ○ *a dress of sprigged cotton* **2 CUT TWIGS FROM PLANT** to cut small twigs or branches from a plant **3 NAIL WITH TACKS** to nail something using brads or tacks [14C. < ?] —**sprigger** *n* —**spriggy** *adj*

sprightly /sprī́tli/ *adj* (**-lier, -liest**) full of life and vigour, especially with a light and springy step ■ *adv* in a lively and vigorous way [Early 16C. < variant of SPRITE.] —**sprightliness** *n*

spring /spring/ *v* (**springs, springing, sprang** /sprang/, **sprung** /sprung/) **1** *vi* **MOVE SUDDENLY IN SINGLE MOVEMENT** to move rapidly upwards or forwards in a single movement or in a series of rapid movements ○ *He sprang to his feet.* **2** *vt* **LEAP OVER** to leap over a barrier **3** *vi* **RAPIDLY RESUME ORIGINAL POSITION** to move back rapidly to an original position after being forced in another direction ○ *A branch sprang back and hit me in the face.* **4** *vi* **EMERGE RAPIDLY** to appear or come into existence quickly ○ *new houses springing up* **5** *vi* **COME FROM SOMEBODY'S LIPS** to be uttered, especially as a sudden and almost involuntary reaction to something **6** *vi* **ORIGINATE FROM** to originate from a particular source ○ *reform that springs from discontent* **7** *vi* **BE DESCENDED** to be descended from a person or family **8** *vt* **SUDDENLY REVEAL TO** to make something known to somebody unexpectedly or suddenly (*informal*) ○ *You can't just spring a decision like that on me!* **9** *vt* **MAKE SOMETHING OPERATE** to operate a device or trap by releasing a mechanism that was held in check **10** *vi* **JUMP OUT OF PLACE** to move suddenly out of place or come suddenly loose within a mechanism **11** *vt* **GET OUT OF PRISON** to release somebody from prison or help somebody escape from prison (*slang*) **12** *vt* **MOVE ANIMAL FROM COVER** to move an animal or bird out into the open during a hunting expedition, or be moved in this way **13** *vti* **DETONATE MINE** to explode or detonate a mine, or be detonated **14** *vti* **WARP OR SPLIT** to crack, split, or warp, or cause wood to do this **15** *vi* **EXTEND UPWARDS** to extend upwards from the topmost part of a column **16** *vi US* **PAY FOR** to pay for something, usually for another person (*slang*) ○ *I'll spring for lunch.* ■ *n* **1 COIL OF METAL** a resilient metal coil used especially for cushioning and in clockwork **2 ABILITY TO REGAIN SHAPE** the ability of an object to revert rapidly to its original position after being extended, compressed, or under tension ○ *a mattress with a lot of spring left in it* **3 ONWARD OR UPWARD LEAP** a rapid forward or upward movement **4 WATER EMERGING FROM UNDERGROUND** a source of water that flows out of the ground as a small stream or pool **5 SOURCE OF** the source of something such as a particular quality or state (*literary*) **6 FORCE CAUSING ACTION** a strong motivation that causes somebody to act in a particular way (*formal*) ○ *the springs of her ambition* **7 SEASON OF YEAR** the season of the year between winter and summer during which many plants bring forth leaves and flowers **8 TIME OF RENEWAL** a time of new growth and regeneration **9 WARPING OR BENDING** warping, cracking, or bending, especially when caused by great force **10** METEOROL = **spring tide** *n.* 1 ■ *adj* **1 HAPPENING IN SPRINGTIME** relating to, occurring in, or appropriate to the season of spring ○ *spring fashions* **2 GROWN IN SPRINGTIME** normally grown or growing in the season of spring ○ *spring flowers* **3 FULL OF SPRINGS** having or containing springs, especially for cushioning or as part of a clockwork mechanism **4 RECOILING** acting like a spring in being held back then quickly releasing energy [Old English *springan* < Indo-European, 'rapid movement']

spring balance *n* a device to determine the weight of something by measuring the tension it creates on a spring

spring beauty *n* a spring-flowering succulent herbaceous plant of the purslane family. Flowers: white or pinkish. Native to: E North America. Genus: *Claytonia.*

springboard /spríng bawrd/ *n* **1 FLEXIBLE DIVING BOARD** a flexible board secured to a base at one end and projecting over the water at the other, used for diving **2 GYMNASTIC EQUIPMENT** a flexible board on which gymnasts bounce in order to gain height for vaulting **3 EVENT OR FACTOR HELPING ADVANCEMENT** an event, activity, or plan that helps to further somebody's career

springbok /spríng bok/ (*plural* **-bok** *or* **-boks**) *n* a small swift gazelle noted for its ability to leap high in the air repeatedly when startled. Native to: semi-arid regions of southern Africa. *Antidorcas marsupialis.* [Late 18C. < Afrikaans, 'leaping he-goat'.]

Springbok /spríng bok/ *n* **1** a member of the South African national rugby team **2** an athlete who has represented South Africa in any of various international sporting competitions (*dated*)

spring break *n* a holiday, usually lasting a week, during the spring term at school

springbuck /spríng buk/ (*plural* **-buck** *or* **-bucks**) *n* ZOOL = **springbok**

spring chicken *n* a chicken less than ten months old, formerly available for eating only in spring ◇ **no spring chicken** no longer young, inexperienced, or agile

spring-clean *vti* to clean a house or room thoroughly, usually including all the contents and furnishings, at the end of the winter or during spring ■ *n* a thorough cleaning of a house or room at the end of the winter or during spring —**spring-cleaning** *n*

springe /sprinj/ *n* a snare or trap for small animals, consisting of a noose attached to a branch under tension [13C. < assumed Old English *sprencg*.]

springer /spríngər/ *n* **1 WEDGE-SHAPED STONE** the first wedge-shaped stone (**voussoir**) of an arch resting on the top section of the arch's supporting pillar (**impost**) **2 COW READY TO GIVE BIRTH** a cow that is on the point of giving birth to a calf **3** ZOOL = **springer spaniel 4 SOMEBODY OR SOMETHING THAT LEAPS** a person or animal that springs or leaps

springer spaniel *n* a hunting dog with a long wavy coat, short legs, and floppy ears, belonging to either an English or a Welsh breed

spring fever *n* a feeling of restlessness, yearning, lust, or sometimes laziness, believed to be brought on by the coming of spring

Springfield /spríng feeld/ **1** city in central Illinois. Population: 117,098 (1998 estimate). **2** city in south-central Massachusetts. Population: 148,144 (1998 estimate). **3** town in NE Virginia. Population: 23,706 (1990).

Springfield rifle *n* a bolt-action .30-calibre rifle developed at the federal arsenal in Springfield, Massachusetts, used by the US Army in World War I.

springhaas /spríng haass/ (*plural* **-haas**) *n* a jumping mammal with hind legs like a kangaroo's and a long black-tufted tail. Native to: semi-arid regions of southern Africa. *Pedestes capensis*. [Late 18C. < Afrikaans, 'leaping hare'.]

springhead /spríng hed/ *n* **1** the source of a stream **2** the source of a particular way of thinking

springhouse /spríng howss/ (*plural* **-houses** /-howziz/) *n* a storehouse built over a spring, formerly used to keep meat and dairy products fresh and cool

springing /spríngíng/ *n* the point at which an arch, vault, or dome rises from its support

spring line *n* a rope by means of which a sailing vessel is made fast to an anchorage, usually one of two

spring-loaded *adj* fixed in place or controlled by a spring (*refers to a part of a mechanism*)

spring lock *n* a lock that is bolted automatically by means of a spring

spring onion *n* a young onion with a small white bulb and a long green shoot

spring peeper *n* a small brownish tree frog that has an X-shaped marking on its back and makes a shrill peeping call early in the spring. Native to: E North America. *Hyla crucifer*.

spring roll *n* a hot oriental snack or starter of mixed savoury ingredients formed into a slightly flattened cylindrical shape in a wrapping and fried until crisp and golden [Translation of Chinese *chūn juǎn*]

Springs /springz/ town in NE South Africa. Population: 170,000 (1991).

spring scale *n* = **spring balance**

Springsteen /spríng steen/, **Bruce** (*b.* 1949) US singer and songwriter

springtail /spríng tayl/ *n* a primitive wingless insect with a forked abdominal structure that helps it spring through the air. Order: Collembola.

spring tide *n* **1** a tide that occurs near the times of the new moon and full moon and has a greater than average range **2** a great rush of emotion (*literary*)

springtide /spríng tīd/ *n* springtime (*literary*)

springtime /spríng tīm/ *n* **1** the season of spring, between winter and summer **2** the earliest, freshest, and most pleasant stage of somebody's life, a relationship, or a period of time (*literary*)

springwood /spríng wŏŏd/ *n* young relatively soft wood that develops just beneath the bark of trees in spring

springy /spríngi/ (**-ier, -iest**) *adj* **1** springing back strongly to its original shape after being compressed or extended **2** tending to make a lot of springing movements (*informal*) —**springily** *adv* —**springiness** *n*

sprinkle /spríngk'l/ *v* (**-kles, -kling, -kled**) **1** *vt* **DISTRIBUTE SMALL AMOUNTS OF** to scatter small drops of a liquid or particles of a fine or powdery substance such as sugar, ashes, or flour over the surface of something **2** *vt* **SCATTER OR BE SCATTERED THROUGHOUT THINGS** to scatter things in amongst other things, at random or as though at random, or be scattered amongst other things in this way ○ *hedgerows sprinkled with poppies* **3** *vt* **GIVE OUT IN SMALL AMOUNTS** to distribute a substance, emotion, or commodity in small amounts **4** *vi US* **RAIN VERY SLIGHTLY** to rain very gently in fine drops, usually for a short period ■ *n* **1 ACT OF SPRINKLING** the action of scattering small drops of liquid or particles of a fine or powdery substance **2** *US* **FINE RAIN** a light rain falling in fine or sporadic drops [14C. < ?]

sprinkler /spríngklər/ *n* **1** a device that sends out a moving spray of water, used for watering gardens or for suppressing fires ○ *a ban on the use of hosepipes and sprinklers* **2** a plastic or metal nozzle perforated with many small holes that fits onto a watering can or hose

sprinkler system *n* **1** a system for extinguishing fires, designed to release water from overhead nozzles that open automatically when a particular temperature is reached **2** a system of sprinklers for watering a garden or lawn, operated by a single control

sprinkling /spríngkling/ *n* **1** a small quantity of a fine or powdery substance such as sugar, snow, dust, or sand scattered on or throughout something **2** a small, thinly distributed amount of a particular emotion or quality ○ *a sprinkling of wit*

sprint /sprint/ *n* **1 SHORT SWIFT RACE** a short race run or cycled at a very high speed **2 FAST FINISHING RUN** a burst of fast running or cycling during the last part of a longer race **3 BURST OF ACTIVITY** a sudden burst of activity or speed ■ *vi* **GO AT TOP SPEED** to run, swim, or cycle as rapidly as possible [Mid-16C. < Old Norse *spretta* 'jump'.] —**sprinter** *n*

sprit /sprit/ *n* a pole that crosses a fore-and-aft sail diagonally [Old English *sprēot* < Germanic]

ϟ **sprite** /sprīt/ *n* **1 SUPERNATURAL ELFIN CREATURE** in folklore, a small supernatural being like an elf or a fairy, especially one associated with water **2 SOMEBODY LIKE AN ELF** a small or delicately built person who is likened to an elf or a fairy **3 GHOST** in folklore, a ghost or spirit **4 INDEPENDENT GRAPHIC OBJECT** an independent graphic object that moves freely across a computer screen [14C. Via Old French *esp(i)rit* < Latin *spiritus* (see SPIRIT).]

spritsail /sprít sayl/; *nautical* /sprítś'l/ *n* a sail that is extended by being mounted on a sprit

spritz /sprits/ *vt* to spray a fine jet of liquid through a nozzle ■ *n* a fine spray of liquid squirted through a nozzle [Early 20C. < German *spritzen* 'squirt'.]

spritzer /sprítsər/ *n* a drink consisting of wine, generally white, diluted with sparkling water or lemonade [Mid-20C. < German, 'splash'.]

sprocket /sprókit/ *n* **1** a projecting tooth on a wheel or cylinder that engages with the links of a chain or with perforations in film to make the chain or film move forward **2 sprocket, sprocket wheel** a wheel with sprockets [Mid-16C. < ?]

sprog /sprog/ *n* (*slang*) **1** a child or baby **2** in the RAF, a new recruit [Mid-20C. < ?]

sprout /sprowt/ *v* **1** *vti* **DEVELOP SHOOTS** to develop buds or shoots **2** *vi* **GERMINATE** to begin to grow from a seed **3** *vti* **GROW** to grow or cause something or somebody to grow **4** *vti* **EMERGE** to emerge and grow rapidly, or cause something to emerge and grow rapidly ■ *n* **1 NEW GROWTH ON A PLANT** a new growth on a plant, e.g. a bud or shoot **2** PLANTS, FOOD = **Brussels sprout 3 SOMETHING LIKE A SPROUT** a person who or thing that grows rapidly ■ **sprouts** *npl US* **EDIBLE SHOOTS OF PLANTS** newly sprouted seeds or beans, eaten especially in sandwiches, salads, and stir-fries [Old English *-sprūtan* < Germanic]

spruce[1] /sprooss/ (*plural* **spruces** *or* **spruce**) *n* **1** an evergreen tree of the pine family with a pyramid shape, short needles, drooping cones, and soft light wood. Genus: *Picea*. **2** the soft light wood of a spruce tree [Early 17C. Shortening of *Spruce fir* 'Prussian fir'; *Spruce* alteration of *Pruce* < medieval Latin *Prussia*.]

spruce[2] /sprooss/ *adj* having a clean, smart, and well-cared-for appearance ○ *a spruce young man* ■ *vti* (**spruces, sprucing, spruced**) to make a person, usually yourself, or a place cleaner and smarter in appearance ○ *The city was getting spruced up for the celebrations.* [Late 16C. < ?] —**sprucely** *adv* —**spruceness** *n*

spruce beer *n* a fermented drink whose ingredients include spruce leaves and twigs

spruce grouse *n* a common plump game bird with a black throat and breast. Native to: coniferous forests of North America. *Dendragapus canadensis*.

sprue[1] /sproo/ *n* a vertical channel in a mould, used to pour in molten material [Early 19C. < ?]

sprue[2] /sproo/ *n* a tropical disease of unknown origin involving deficient absorption of nutrients from the intestine and marked by persistent diarrhoea, weight loss, and anaemia [Late 19C. < Dutch *spruw* 'the disease thrush'.]

spruik /sprook/ *vi Aus* **1** to promote goods or services by addressing passing members of the public from the door of a shop or similar establishment (*informal*) **2** to promote goods, services, or a cause by addressing people in a public place (*humorous*) [Early 20C. < ?]

spruiker /sprŏŏkər/ *n Aus* **1** a salesperson who addresses passing members of the public from the door of a shop, bar, or other establishment (*informal*) **2** a promoter of goods, services, or a cause who addresses people in a public place (*humorous*)

sprung past participle of **spring**

sprung rhythm *n* a system of prosody that always places the accent on the first syllable of any foot in an effort to evoke the rhythms of ordinary speech

spry /sprī/ (**spryer** /sprīr/ *or* **sprier, spryest** /sprī əst/ *or* **spriest**) *adj* markedly brisk and active, especially at an advanced age [Mid-18C. < ?] —**spryly** *adv* —**spryness** *n*

SPUC *abbr* Society for the Protection of the Unborn Child

spud /spud/ *n* **1 POTATO** a potato (*informal*) **2 GARDEN IMPLEMENT** a spade with a sharp narrow blade, used for cutting through roots and digging up weeds **3 TOOL FOR REMOVING BARK FROM TREES** a tool resembling a chisel that is used to peel bark from trees ■ *v* (**spuds, spudding, spudded**) **1** *vi* **START DRILLING AN OIL WELL** to use a large bit to drill the upper part of the bore of a new oil well **2** *vt* **REMOVE BARK** to remove bark from trees by the use of a tool like a chisel **3** *vt* **DIG WITH A SPUD** to use a spud to dig up weeds or cut through roots [15C. < ?]

spud-bashing *n* in the British armed forces, the task of peeling potatoes as a punishment (*slang*)

spume /spyoom/ *n* a mass of fine bubbles on the surface of a liquid, especially on the sea (*literary*) ■ *vi* (**spumes, spuming, spumed**) to produce or have a mass of fine bubbles on the surface (*literary*) [14C. Directly or via Old French < Latin *spuma* 'foam'.] —**spumous** *adj* —**spumy** *adj*

spumone /spoo mṓni/, **spumoni** *n* **1** an Italian ice cream composed of differently coloured and flavoured layers, often containing nuts and candied fruit **2** an Italian light mousse dessert [Early 20C. < Italian, < *spuma* 'foam'.]

spun past tense, past participle of **spin**

spun glass *n* **1** INDUST = **fibreglass** *n*. 1 **2** glass that is blown in such a way as to incorporate slender threads of glass

spunk /spungk/ *n* **1 PLUCKINESS** spiritedness or eager willingness (*informal*) **2 TABOO TERM** a highly offensive term for semen (*taboo*) **3 TINDER** a combustible material, especially soft wood or twigs, that can be used to kindle fires **4** *Aus* **SEXUALLY DESIRABLE PERSON** a sexually desirable person (*informal*) [Mid-16C. < ?]

spunky /spúngki/ (**-ier, -iest**) *adj* very lively, determined, and courageous (*informal*) —**spunkily** *adv* —**spunkiness** *n*

spun silk *n* inexpensive fabric or yarn made from short-fibred silk combined with silk waste

spun sugar *n US* FOOD = **candyfloss**

spun yarn *n* rope or cord made from several light yarns twisted or spun together

spur /spur/ *n* **1 DEVICE ATTACHED TO A RIDER'S HEEL** a small spike or spiked wheel attached to the heel of a rider's boot that is nudged into the horse's sides to encourage it to go faster **2 INDUCEMENT** something such as the hope of a reward or the fear of punishment that encourages a person or organization to take action or to make a greater effort **3 PROJECTING PLANT PART** a tubular extension from a flower part, e.g. that in larkspur and columbine **4 SHORT BRANCH OR SHOOT** a short branch or lateral shoot from a stem or branch of a plant **5 HORNY PROJECTION** a sharp horny projection on the legs of some male birds, e.g. cocks, above the claws **6 PROJECTING ANIMAL PART** a pointed extension or projecting part (**process**) on some animals, e.g. the stiff outgrowth on the legs of some insects and birds **7 SHORT BONY OUTGROWTH** a bony outgrowth, usually a normal part of the body but sometimes one that develops such as that on the bottom of the heel after an injury **8 SPIKE FASTENED TO THE LEG OF A GAMECOCK** a sharp metal spike attached to the leg of a gamecock **9 PROP** a timber or masonry prop or support **10 MOUNTAIN RIDGE** a ridge that projects outwards from a mountain range and descends towards a valley floor **11 SHORT JETTY** a small jetty extending from a shore to protect a beach against erosion or to trap shifting sands **12 PART OF A RAILWAY** a short section of railway track leading off a main line **13 ROAD OFF A MAJOR ROAD** a short side road leading off a main road **14 CERAMIC SUPPORT IN A KILN** a small ceramic support placed beneath a pot in a kiln ■ *v* (**spurs, spurring, spurred**) **1** *vt* **ENCOURAGE SOMEBODY TO TRY HARDER** to stimulate a person or organization to take action or make greater efforts in the hope of a reward or in the fear of punishment ○ *'Public schools are spurred to perform better thanks to new reforms'.* (*US News & World Report*; December 1998) **2** *vt* **MAKE A HORSE GO FASTER** to encourage a horse to go faster by nudging spurs into its sides **3** *vi* **RIDE FAST** to ride fast, using spurs (*literary*) **4** *vi* **GO QUICKLY** to go or proceed hastily (*literary*) **5** *vt* **CAUSE INJURY TO A HORSE WITH SPURS** to injure a horse by using spurs too strongly and too frequently **6** *vt* **PUT SPURS ON** to equip somebody or something with spurs [Old English *spura* < Indo-European, 'to kick'] —**spurred** *adj* ◇ **win** *or* **gain your spurs 1** to gain recognition and respect for the first time **2** in the past, to be given the rank of knight ◇ **on the spur of the moment** without thinking about what you are going to do or making preparations beforehand

SYNONYMS See *motive*.

spurge /spurj/ *n* a herbaceous plant or shrub that has flowers without petals and a bitter milky juice. Genus: *Euphorbia*. [14C. < Old French *espurge* < *espurgier* 'purge' < Latin *expurgare* 'cleanse'.]

spur gear *n* a gear whose teeth are arranged along the rim parallel to its axis of rotation

spurge laurel *n* a low-growing evergreen shrub with elongated glossy leaves. Flowers: yellow. Native to: Europe, Asia. *Daphne laureola*.

spurious /spyóori əs/ *adj* **1 NOT GENUINE** being different from what it claims to be **2 RESEMBLING ANOTHER PLANT PART** having the outward appearance of another plant part but not its function or origin **3 BORN OUT OF WEDLOCK** born to parents not legally married to each other (*archaic*) [Late 16C. < Latin *spurius* 'illegitimate child'.] —**spuriously** *adv* —**spuriousness** *n*

spurn /spurn/ *v* **1** *vti* **REJECT SOMEBODY OR SOMETHING WITH DISDAIN** to reject a person, offer, gift, or advances with scorn and contempt **2** *vt* **THRUST SOMETHING AWAY WITH THE FOOT** to reject something by pushing it away with the foot (*archaic*) ■ *n* (*archaic*) **1 SCORNFUL REJECTION** a contemptuous or scornful rejection **2 KICK** a kick [Old English *spurnan* < Indo-European] —**spurner** *n*

spur-of-the-moment *adj* happening, made, or done in haste, without reflection or preparation ○ *a spur-of-the-moment purchase*

spurrey /spúrr i/ (*plural* **-reys**), **spurry** (*plural* **-ries**) *n* a low-growing plant with linear whorled leaves. Flowers: small, white. Native to: Europe. Genus: *Spurgula*. [Late 16C. < Dutch *spurrie*.]

spurt /spurt/ *n* **1 JET OF LIQUID OR GAS** a sudden stream of liquid or gas, forced out under pressure **2 SUDDEN INCREASE** a short intense burst of energy, interest, action, or speed ○ *I had a spurt of energy as I was digging.* ■ *vti* **GUSH OUT** to gush out or cause a liquid or gas to gush out in a pressurized stream or jet ○ *Blood spurted from the wound.* [Mid-16C. < ?]

spurtle /spúrt'l/ *n Scotland* a short turned stick, frequently with a decorative end, used for stirring porridge [Early 16C. < ?]

spur wheel *n* MECH ENG = **spur gear**

sputa plural of **sputum**

sputnik /spóotnik, spút-/ *n* one of a series of ten artificial Earth-orbiting satellites launched by the former Soviet Union starting in 1957 [Mid-20C. < Russian, 'fellow traveller'.]

sputter /spúttər/ *v* **1** *vi* **MAKE POPPING SOUND** to make a popping, spitting sound **2** *vi* **SPIT OUT FOOD AND SALIVA** to spray out drops of saliva or food particles, especially when talking or laughing while eating **3** *vi* **SPEAK EXPLOSIVELY** to make sounds or pronounce words in an explosive way, especially when angry or excited **4** *vti* **REMOVE SURFACE ATOMS BY ION BOMBARDMENT** to cause or experience the effect in which the atoms of a surface are removed through bombardment by ions, e.g. in cathode evaporation in a discharge tube **5** *vti* **USE A METAL TO COAT SOMETHING** to use a metal to coat something by the process of sputtering, or be coated in this way ■ *n* **1 NOISE OF SPUTTERING** the noise of a person, fire, candle, or other object sputtering **2 INCOHERENT SPEECH** the confused or incoherent speech of somebody who is angry or excited **3 SOMETHING EMITTED WHILE SPUTTERING** drops of saliva or food particles sprayed out of the mouth while sputtering [Late 16C. < Dutch *sputteren* 'spray', thought to suggest the action.] —**sputterer** *n*

sputum /spyóotəm/ (*plural* **-ta** /-tə/) *n* a substance such as saliva, phlegm, or mucus coughed up from the respiratory tract and usually ejected by mouth [Late 17C. < Latin, 'saliva' < *spuere* 'spit'.]

spy /spī/ *n* (*plural* **spies**) **1 SOMEBODY EMPLOYED TO OBTAIN SECRET INFORMATION** an employee of a government who seeks secret information in or from another country, especially about military matters **2 EMPLOYEE WHO OBTAINS INFORMATION ABOUT RIVALS** an employee of a company who seeks secret information about rival organizations **3 SECRET OBSERVER OF OTHERS** a watcher of other people in secret ■ *v* (**spies, spying, spied**) **1** *vi* **ACT AS A SPY** to work, operate, or function as a spy **2** *vi* **ENGAGE IN ESPIONAGE** to maintain a network of spies and gather intelligence in other clandestine ways **3** *vi* **OBSERVE IN SECRET** to observe somebody or something secretly ○ *Have you been spying on us again?* **4** *vt* **SEE SUDDENLY** to catch sight of somebody or something **5** *vt* **DISCOVER BY OBSERVATION** to discover something by close observation **6** *vi* **INVESTIGATE** to investigate something intensively [13C. < Old French *espie* < *espier* 'to spy' < Germanic.]

spy out *vt* to discover something by close and discreet examination

spyglass /spī glaass/ *n* a telescope that is small enough to be held in the hand

spyhole /spī hōl/ *n* = **peephole** *n*. 2

spy-in-the-cab (*plural* **spies-in-the-cab**) *n* a tachograph (*informal*)

spymaster /spī maastər/ *n* the leader of espionage and intelligence-gathering activities for a country or organization, especially in fictional spy stories

⚡**spyware** /spī wair/ *n* software surreptitiously installed on a hard disk without the user's knowledge that relays encoded information on his or her identity and Internet use via an Internet connection

sq. *abbr* **1** sequence **2** sequens **3** square [Latin, 'the one that follows']

Sq. *abbr* **1** Squadron **2** Square (*in addresses*)

⚡**SQL** *n* a standardized language that approximates the structure of natural English for obtaining information from databases. Full form **structured query language**

squab /skwob/ *n* (*plural* **squabs** *or* **squab**) **1 YOUNG BIRD** a fledgling bird, especially a pigeon, sometimes cooked as a delicacy **2 SOFA** a couch ■ *adj* (**squabber, squabbest**) **1 NEWLY HATCHED** newly hatched and not flying yet **2 SHORT AND STOUT** short and somewhat stout [Late 17C. < ?] —**squabby** *adj*

squabble /skwóbb'l/ *n* a noisy argument over a petty matter ■ *vi* (**-bles, -bling, -bled**) to have a petty argument over a trivial matter [Early 17C. An imitation of the sound.] —**squabbler** *n*

squad /skwod/ *n* **1 GROUP OF PLAYERS** a number of players from which a team is selected ○ *dropped from the England squad* **2 MILITARY FORMATION** a small military formation, especially one that is doing a drill **3 GROUP OF POLICE OFFICERS** a group of police officers, generally assigned to a particular task **4 TEAM OF PEOPLE** a small group of people engaged in the same activity, especially in a sport ○ *a squad of volunteers* [Mid-17C. Via French *escouade* and Italian *squadra* or Spanish *escuadra* < assumed Vulgar Latin *exquadra* (see SQUARE).]

squad car *n* a police car linked by radio with police headquarters

squaddie /skwóddi/ *n* a private soldier (*slang*)

squadron /skwóddrən/ *n* **1 NAVAL UNIT** a naval unit containing two or more divisions of a fleet **2 AIR FORCE UNIT** an element of a tactical air force belonging to a group and containing two or more flights **3 CAVALRY UNIT** an armoured cavalry unit belonging to a regiment and containing two or more troops **4 GROUP** an organized group of people, animals, or objects [Mid-16C. < Italian *squadrone* 'large squad' < *squadra* (see SQUAD).]

squadron leader *n* in the RAF, the commander of a squadron of military aircraft

squalene /skwáy leen/ *n* a hydrocarbon that is an intermediate in the formation of cholesterol. Source: human sebum, shark-liver oil. [Early 20C. < modern Latin *Squalus* < Latin, 'a sea fish'.]

squalid /skwóllid/ *adj* **1** dirty and shabby because of neglect and lack of money **2** lacking in honesty, dignity, and morals ○ *a squalid little scandal* [Late 16C. < Latin *squalidus* 'filthy, rough' < *squalere* 'be filthy' < *squalus* 'filthy'.] —**squalidly** *adv* —**squalidness** *n*

SYNONYMS See *dirty*.

squall[1] /skwawl/ *n* **1 WINDSTORM** a sudden strong wind, often with heavy rain or snow **2 BRIEF DISTURBANCE** a short but noisy disturbance **3 SHOW OF TEMPER** a brief but intense outburst of temper ■ *vi* **BLOW STRONGLY** to blow strongly and suddenly (*refers to the wind*) [Late 17C. < ?]

squall[2] /skwawl/ *vi* to cry or yell hoarsely ■ *n* a noisy cry or yell [Mid-17C. < ?] —**squaller** *n*

squall line *n* a series of small storms that occur along a cold front

squally /skwáwli/ (**-ier, -iest**) *adj* **1** occurring in or characterized by strong gusts, often accompanied by rain or snow **2** marked by sudden short noisy arguments

squalor /skwóllər/ *n* **1** shabbiness and dirtiness resulting from poverty or neglect **2** a state of moral degradation [Early 17C. < Latin, 'dirtiness, roughness' < *squalere* (see SQUALID).]

squama /skwáymə/ (*plural* **-mae** /-mi/) *n* a scale, or a structure resembling a scale, of the type that make up the covering of fish, reptiles, and some mammals [Early 18C. < Latin, 'scale'.]

squamate /skwáy mayt/ *n* a reptile of the order that comprises all lizards and snakes and includes about 6,000 species. Order: Squamata. ■ *adj* having scales or structures resembling scales of the type that make up the covering of fish, reptiles, and some mammals —**squamation** /skway máysh'n/ *n*

squamosal /skwə móss'l/ *n* a thin plate-shaped bone of the vertebrate skull that forms the forward and upper part of the temporal bone in humans [Mid-19C. < Latin *squamosus* 'squamous'.]

squamous /skwáyməss/, **squamose** /-mōss/ *adj* **1 OF SCALES ON THE BODY** covered with, consisting of, or resembling scales or thin plates of the type that make up the covering of fish, reptiles, and some mammals **2 CONSISTING OF SCALE-SHAPED CELLS** describes a layer of skin (**epithelium**) made up of small scale-shaped cells **3 OF THE SKULL BONE** relating to the squamosal in the vertebrate skull —**squamously** *adv* —**squamousness** *n*

squamous cell carcinoma *n* a common type of cancer that usually develops in the epithelial layer of the skin but sometimes in various mucous membranes of the body

squamulose /skwáymyoo lōs, -lōz/ *adj* having or consisting of tiny scales of the type that make up the covering of fish, reptiles, and some mammals [Mid-19C. < *squamule* 'small scale' < Latin *squamula* < *squama* 'scale'.]

squander /skwóndər/ *vt* to spend or use something precious in a wasteful and extravagant way ■ *n* extravagant spending [Late 16C. < ?] —**squanderer** *n*

square /skwair/ *n* **1 EQUILATERAL RECTANGLE** a geometric figure with four right angles and four equal sides **2 RECTANGULAR OBJECT** an object in the shape of a square or a rectangle that is nearly a square **3 DIVISION OF A GAMES BOARD** any one of the squares marked on the board used to play chess, draughts, or other games **4 OPEN SPACE IN A CITY** an open area in a city or town where two or more streets meet, often containing trees, grass, and benches for recreational use **5** *US* **CITY BLOCK** a block of buildings surrounded by four streets **6 MILITARY DRILL AREA** an open space within an army barracks where soldiers practise marching and handling weapons **7 PART OF CRICKET PITCH** an area in the middle of a cricket pitch where the grass is kept shorter, from which the wicket area is chosen **8 RESULT OF MULTIPLICATION** the product resulting from multiplying a number or term by itself ○ *The square of 7 is 49.* **9 DRAWING INSTRUMENT** an L- or T-shaped instrument made of plastic, wood, or metal, used for drawing or measuring right angles **10 BODY OF SOLDIERS** formerly, a tactical formation of soldiers in a solid or hollow rectangle, with the soldiers on the sides facing outwards **11 UNFASHIONABLE PERSON** an unfashionable person who is out of touch with current popular culture (*slang dated*) ■ *adj* **1 SHAPED LIKE A SQUARE** having the shape of a square, with four more or less equal sides and angles **2 FORMING A RIGHT ANGLE** intersecting at, having, or making a right angle **3 CUBIC** in the shape of a cube ○ *a square block of stone* **4 VAGUELY SQUARE IN SHAPE** roughly square or angular in shape, and looking firm and solid **5 OF THE MEASUREMENT OF SURFACE AREA** describes a measurement of area in which the specified unit refers to the length of each side of a square whose surface area constitutes the measurement ○ *One box contains enough tiles to cover 100 square metres.* **6 WITH SIDES OF A SPECIFIED LENGTH** describes a square area with sides of a particular length ○ *a room ten feet square* **7 STRAIGHT OR LEVEL** adjusted or made to be perfectly straight, even, level, or lined up with something else ○ *Make sure the picture is square on the wall.* **8 COMPLETELY FAIR** completely fair, honest, and direct ○ *a square deal* **9 AT RIGHT ANGLES TO WICKET** in cricket, positioned at right angles to the wicket **10 BORING AND OLD-FASHIONED** dressing and behaving in an unfashionable way and out of touch with current popular culture (*slang dated*) **11 NOT OWING MONEY** with all outstanding debts paid up ○ *She paid me back this morning – we're square now.* **12 CLEAN** clean and tidy (*informal*) ○ *The kitchen still needs getting square.* **13 LACKING COMPLEXITY** in jazz and popular music, lacking swing or complexity ■ *v* (**squares, squaring, squared**) **1** *vt* **MAKE SOMETHING SQUARE** to make something into a square or rectangular shape **2** *vt* **MULTIPLY A NUMBER BY ITSELF** to multiply a number or term by itself ○ *Seven squared equals 49.* **3** *vt* **DIVIDE SOMETHING INTO SQUARES** to divide a surface, sheet of paper, or other object into squares **4** *vt* **SET SOMETHING STRAIGHT** to move an object, item of clothing, or part of the body so that it is straight or level **5** *vti* **PUT OR BE AT RIGHT ANGLES** to adjust something or be adjusted so that it is at right angles to something else, or test something for this alignment **6** *vt* **SETTLE THINGS FAIRLY** to arrive at a fair and equal agreement with somebody about something, especially about paying off money owed ○ *He squared all his bills and left town.* **7** *vt* **BRING SCORES LEVEL** to level the scores, especially in a ball game **8** *vti* **CONCUR OR MAKE SOMETHING AGREE** to agree with another person, fact, event, or idea, or make two facts, events, or ideas concur ○ *That does not square with what we know.* **9** *vt* **BRIBE** to bribe another person (*slang*) **10** *vt* **IMPROVE IMPRESSION** to try to improve the impression that somebody has of you ■ *adv* **1 AT RIGHT ANGLES** so as to be even, straight, level, or at right angles to something **2 NOT FORWARDS OR BACKWARDS** in ball games, to or at another point at the same distance up or down the pitch **3 DIRECTLY** in a direct or forceful way (*informal*) ○ *She drove square into the wall.* **4 HONESTLY** in an honest and straightforward way (*informal*) [13C. Via Old French *esquare* and assumed vulgar Latin *exquadra* < Latin *quadrum* < Latin *quat-* 'four'.] —**squarer** *n* —**squareness** *n* —**squarish** *adj* ◇ **all square 1** in a situation in which the scores are even **2** in a situation whereby all debts and obligations to each other have been cleared and nobody owes anybody anything ◇ **on the square 1** at right angles to something, or constructed with right angles **2** in an honest and direct manner, or direct and honest **3** done on equal terms, or being on equal terms with somebody **4** being a member of the order of Freemasons ◇ **out of square 1** not at right angles to something **2** not in agreement with each other

square off *vi* to take the proper stance for beginning to fight

square up *v* **1** *vi* **SETTLE DEBTS** to pay bills, accounts, or other sums of money owed to somebody **2** *vti* **ARRANGE OR BE ARRANGED SATISFACTORILY** to arrange something or be arranged in an acceptable or pleasing way **3** *vi* **FACE SOMETHING UNPLEASANT** to confront something unpleasant or frightening **4** *vi* **ADOPT AN AGGRESSIVE POSTURE** to put up fists or adopt a similar posture that shows a readiness to fight **5** *vt* **ENLARGE SOMETHING USING A GRID OF SQUARES** to enlarge or transfer a drawing using a grid of squares

square-bashing *n* the training of soldiers in marching and handling arms on a barracks square (*slang*)

square bracket *n* either of a pair of symbols, [ ], used in keying, printing, or writing to indicate the insertion of special commentary, e.g. that made by an editor. US term **bracket** *n.* 2

PUNCTUATION ***Square brackets*** are used around text that is added by somebody other than the original writer or speaker, especially to explain or comment on a word or phrase used in a quotation: *He wrote 'As we travelled across Rhodesia [now Zimbabwe] the weather changed for the worse'.* They are also used to provide information needed when a quotation is taken out of its original context: *She said 'I have never seen him [the accused] before'.* The word *sic* (Latin for 'thus'), enclosed in square brackets, indicates that the preceding word, although wrong, is the one actually used: *The notice read 'In case of fire please excite [sic] the building by the nearest door'.*

square dance *n* **1** a country dance featuring dancers in pairs or sets, lively music played on fiddles and other instruments, and a caller who announces the steps **2** a country dance in which four couples form a square —**square dancing** *n*

square knot *n* = **reef knot**

square leg *n* a fielding position in cricket more or less at right angles to the batsman, or somebody who holds this position

squarely /skwáirli/ *adv* **1 DIRECTLY** in a direct or forceful way ○ *She met my gaze squarely.* **2 HONESTLY** in an honest and straightforward way **3 AT RIGHT ANGLES** in or into a position that is at right angles to something else

square matrix *n* a mathematical matrix that has equal numbers of rows and columns

square meal *n* a filling and nourishing meal

square measure *n* a unit or system of units for measuring an area, e.g. a hectare or an acre

square pyramid *n* a solid figure with a base that forms a square and four faces made up of triangles meeting at a common point

square-rigged *adj* having principal sails that are at right angles to the length of the ship

square-rigger *n* a sailing vessel equipped with square-shaped sails

square root *n* a number or quantity that when multiplied by itself gives the stated number or quantity

square sail *n* a sail with four sides that is usually suspended horizontally on the mast

squarrose knapweed /skwárrōss-/ *n* a low-growing shrubby plant of the sunflower family with pink flowers and recurved bract tips, now becoming a pest in some states of the W United States. Native to: E Mediterranean.

squash[1] /skwosh/ *v* **1** *vt* **FLATTEN SOMETHING WITH PRESSURE** to apply pressure to something so that its shape is altered ○ *managed to squash it flat before packing it* **2** *vti* **ENTER OR PUT SOMETHING INTO A SMALL SPACE** to force your way into a confined space, or force something into a confined space ○ *people trying to squash into the lift* **3** *vt* **PUT DOWN A REBELLION** to suppress a revolt or uprising completely by using force **4** *vt* **MAKE SOMEBODY FEEL SMALL** to silence somebody with a crushing answer **5** *vi* **BECOME FLAT** to become flat, often making a squelching sound ■ *n* **1 JUICE-BASED DRINK** a soft drink made from fruit juice or syrup diluted with water **2 MANY PEOPLE IN A SMALL SPACE** a situation in which a lot of people are crushed into a small space ○ *It was a terrible squash in the back seat.* **3 ACTION OR NOISE OF SQUASHING** the action or noise that results when something is being squashed **4 SOMETHING SQUASHED** a squashed object or number of objects **5 BALL GAME IN A WALLED COURT** a game for two or four participants played in an enclosed court with long-handled rackets and a small ball that may be hit off any of the walls **6 GAME LIKE SQUASH WITH TENNIS BALLS** a ball game for two players resembling squash but played with a tennis ball and rackets shaped more like conventional tennis rackets [Mid-16C. Via Old French *esquasser* < assumed Vulgar Latin *exquassare* < Latin *quassare* (see QUASH[1]).] —**squasher** *n*

squash[2] /skwosh/ (*plural* **squash** *or* **squashes**) *n* **1** the fruit of any plant of the gourd family, cooked and eaten as a vegetable **2** any plant yielding or cultivated for its edible gourds. Genus: *Cucurbita*. [Mid-17C. Shortening of Narraganset *asquutasquash* 'green things that may be eaten raw'.]

squash rackets *n* = **squash**[1] *n.* 5 (+ *singular verb*)

squash tennis *n* RACKET GAMES = **squash**[1] *n.* 6

squashy /skwóshi/ (**-ier, -iest**) *adj* **1 EASILY SQUASHED** soft and easily squashed **2 OVERRIPE** overripe and full of juice **3 SOFT AND WET** soft and waterlogged **4 LOOKING SQUASHED** having a squashed appearance

squat /skwot/ *vi* (**squats, squatting, squatted**) **1 CROUCH DOWN** to crouch down with the knees bent and the thighs resting on the calves **2 CROUCH DOWN LOW** to crouch close

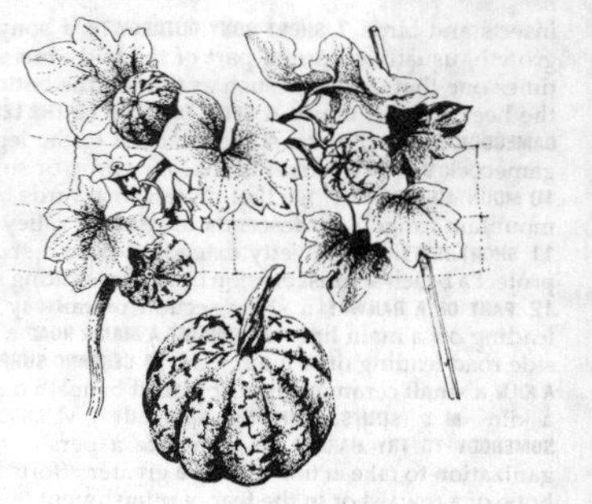

Squash

to the ground like an animal, especially in order to avoid being seen **3 OCCUPY PROPERTY WITHOUT A LEGAL CLAIM** to occupy land or buildings without permission of the owner or other rights holder ■ *adj* (**squatter, squattest**) **1 SHORT AND SOLID** short and solidly built **2 IN A CROUCHED POSTURE** in a crouched position ■ *n* **1 ACTION OF SQUATTING** the action of crouching down with the knees bent and the thighs resting on the calves **2 SQUATTING POSITION** a crouched posture with knees bent and thighs resting on calves **3 WEIGHTLIFTING EXERCISE** an exercise in weightlifting in which the lifter raises a barbell while rising from a crouching position **4 PROPERTY OCCUPIED BY SQUATTERS** a piece of property that is occupied by squatters **5 HARE'S LAIR** the den of a hare [14C. Via Old French *esquatir* 'crush' < Latin *coactus*, past participle of *cogere* 'force together'.] —**squatness** *n*

squatly /skwótli/ *adv* in a solid unyielding manner ○ *The piano stood squatly by the window.*

squatter /skwóttər/ *n* **1 ILLEGAL OCCUPANT OF LAND OR PROPERTY** an illegal occupant of land or property, especially somebody who takes over and lives in somebody else's empty house **2 HOMESTEADER** an early North American homesteader **3** *Aus* **TENANT ON AUSTRALIAN GRAZING LAND** an early Australian settler who farmed supposedly vacant land and subsequently obtained a lease for it from the government **4** *Aus* **LANDOWNER** a wealthy landowner **5** *NZ* **SETTLER IN NEW ZEALAND** an early settler in New Zealand who leased a large area of government-owned land **6 SOMEBODY OR SOMETHING THAT CROUCHES** a person or animal that crouches down

squattocracy /skwo tókrəssi/ *n* *Aus* wealthy landowners regarded as a powerful and influential social class (*disapproving*)

squaw /skwaw/ *n* **1** an offensive term for a Native North American woman or wife (*dated*) **2** an offensive term for a woman or wife (*slang*) [Mid-17C. < Narraganset *squaws* 'woman' or Massachuset *squa*.]

squawk /skwawk/ *v* **1** *vi* **UTTER A HARSH CRY** to utter a loud harsh cry **2** *vti* **COMPLAIN LOUDLY** to complain or protest about something noisily and annoyingly (*informal*) **3** *vi* **CRY LOUDLY** to cry or wail loudly and annoyingly (*informal*) **4** *vti* **SAY SOMETHING LOUDLY AND SHRILLY** to say something in a loud harsh voice (*informal*) ■ *n* **1 RAUCOUS CRY** a loud raucous cry **2 NOISY COMPLAINT** a noisy and annoying complaint or protest (*informal*) [Early 19C. An imitation of the sound.] —**squawker** *n*

squawk box *n* a public-address system or one of its speakers, originally box-shaped (*dated slang*)

squeak /skweek/ *v* **1** *vi* **MAKE A HIGH-PITCHED SOUND** to make a short high-pitched sound or cry **2** *vt* **SAY SOMETHING SHRILLY** to say something in a high-pitched voice **3** *vi* **BE AN INFORMER** to give information or evidence about somebody to the police (*slang disapproving*) **4** *vi* **MANAGE SOMETHING WITH NARROW MARGIN** to only just manage to pass, win, or survive something (*informal*) ○ *squeaked through her final exams* ■ *n* **HIGH-PITCHED CRY** a short high-pitched sound or cry [14C. An imitation of the sound.] ◇ **a narrow squeak** an escape or success achieved by an extremely narrow margin

squeaker /skweekər/ *n* **1 SOMEBODY OR SOMETHING THAT SQUEAKS** a person, animal, or device that makes a short high-pitched sound or cry **2 SNITCH** a person who informs on somebody to the police (*slang disapproving*) **3** *US* **NARROWLY WON VICTORY** a competition, election, race, or other event that is won by a very slight margin (*informal*)

squeaky /skweéki/ (**-ier, -iest**) *adj* **1** having a tendency to squeak **2** designed to make a squeaking noise when pressed —**squeakily** *adv* —**squeakiness** *n*

squeaky-clean *adj* **1** so clean that it squeaks when rubbed ○ *His hair was squeaky-clean.* **2** appearing to be almost unnaturally free from general human shortcomings (*informal*)

squeal /skweel/ *n* **1 SHRILL CRY** a short high cry expressing pain, excitement, delight, or other strong emotion **2 LOUD HIGH SOUND** the screaming sound made by tyres when a vehicle brakes suddenly ■ *v* **1** *vti* **GIVE A SHORT HIGH CRY** to say something, speak, or make a sound in a loud high-pitched tone **2** *vi* **BECOME AN INFORMER** to give information or evidence against somebody to the police (*slang disapproving*) **3** *vi* **PROTEST LOUDLY** to protest or complain loudly and annoyingly (*informal*) [13C. An imitation of the sound.] —**squealer** *n*

squeamish /skweémish/ *adj* **1 EASILY MADE TO FEEL SICK** easily sickened by such sights as blood or physical injuries **2 EASILY OFFENDED** easily shocked by such things as violence, the mention of bodily functions, or strong language **3 FASTIDIOUS** excessively scrupulous about manners or behaviour [14C. < Anglo-Norman *escoymous*.] —**squeamishly** *adv* —**squeamishness** *n*

squeegee /skweé jee/ *n* **1** a T-shaped implement edged with plastic or rubber that is drawn across the surface of windows to remove water after washing **2** an implement, usually a rubber roller, that is used in printing and photography to remove excess water or ink [Mid-19C. < obsolete *squeege* 'press', alteration of SQUEEZE.]

squeegee man *n* a man or youth who enters stopped traffic without invitation, attempting to wash motorists' windscreens for money (*slang*)

squeeze /skweez/ *v* (**squeezes, squeezing, squeezed**) **1** *vt* **PRESS SOMETHING FROM TWO SIDES** to press something hard in the hand or between two other objects, especially in order to reduce its size or alter its shape **2** *vt* **PRESS SOMEBODY ENCOURAGINGLY** to exert slight pressure on part of somebody's body such as the hand, knee, or shoulder, usually as a sign of affection and reassurance **3** *vti* **APPLY PRESSURE** to exert pressure on something ○ *Come on, squeeze harder!* **4** *vt* **HUG** to hold somebody tightly in your arms **5** *vt* **PUSH A PERSON OR OBJECT INTO A GAP** to force a person, object, or part of the body into or through a small or narrow space **6** *vi* **PUSH INTO OR THROUGH SMALL SPACE** to push into or through a small, narrow, or crowded space ○ *I squeezed through a gap in the hedge.* **7** *vt* **PRESS FRUIT TO OBTAIN JUICE** to compress a piece of fruit, especially a citrus fruit, in order to extract its juice **8** *vt* **FIND TIME FOR** to find time or space for somebody or something in a busy schedule ○ *I could squeeze you in at 9.30.* **9** *vt* **OBTAIN USING PHYSICAL PRESSURE** to extract something by exerting physical pressure on somebody or something **10** *vt* **EXTORT MONEY OR FAVOURS** to obtain something such as money or favours from somebody by means of psychological pressure or threats **11** *vt* **DEMAND MONEY FROM** to make excessive financial demands on somebody, especially for rent and taxes **12** *vt* **EXCLUDE** to put an end to somebody's participation in a field of activity ○ *squeezed them out by means of aggressive marketing* **13** *vt* **PRODUCE WITH DIFFICULTY** to make an effort to produce something ○ *He managed to squeeze out a timid 'thank you'.* **14** *vi* **JUST MANAGE** just narrowly to succeed in winning, passing, or surviving something ○ *managed to squeeze through the exam with a D* **15** *vt* **PLAY A CARD** to lead a card in bridge or whist that may force an opponent to discard a valuable card **16** *vi* **COLLAPSE** to condense or collapse under pressure **17** *vi* **MAKE AN IMPRESSION OF** to make an impression or mould of an object using a soft material such as wax or plaster of Paris ■ *n* **1 PHYSICAL PRESSING** a pressing action ○ *gave the sponge a quick squeeze* **2 SOMETHING PRESSED OUT** an amount pressed out of something ○ *Add a squeeze of lemon.* **3 HUG** a hug or close embrace **4 TOUCH THAT SHOWS AFFECTION** the action of briefly clasping somebody's hand, arm, knee, or other part of the body, usually as a sign of affection or reassurance **5 CROWD OF PEOPLE OR THINGS** a group of people or objects crowded together **6 RESTRICTION IN FINANCIAL CRISIS** a government-imposed restriction on credit and investment to counteract inflation or some other financial crisis **7 FINANCIAL PRESSURE TO ACT** an action by business competitors that influences or forces others to make some type of transaction **8 SOMETHING EXTORTED** money or goods obtained from somebody as a result of threats or the use of force **9 SQUEEZE PLAY** a squeeze play (*informal*) **10 IMPRESSION OF AN OBJECT** an impression of an object made by using a soft material such as wax or plaster of Paris [Mid-16C. Alteration of obsolete *quease*.] —**squeezability** /skweéza bílləti/ *n* —**squeezable** *adj* ◇ **put the squeeze on somebody 1** to exert pressure on somebody by means of force and threats in order to extort money or goods or to obtain some other end, e.g. a confession (*informal*) **2** to place somebody in a difficult situation, especially financially, or pressure somebody to do something (*informal*)

squeeze off *vt* to fire a bullet from a gun

squeezebox /skweéz boks/ *n* a concertina or small accordion (*informal*)

squeeze play *n* a play in bridge or whist in which an opponent is forced to discard a valuable and potentially winning card

squelch /skwelch/ *v* **1** *vi* **MAKE A SUCKING SOUND** to move with or make a sucking or gurgling sound like that of somebody treading on muddy ground **2** *vt* **CRUSH BY TRAMPLING** to crush something by trampling, or as if by trampling **3** *vt* **SILENCE** to silence something such as a rumour or an unwanted remark (*slang*) ■ *n* **1 SUCKING SOUND** a sucking or gurgling sound like that of somebody treading on muddy ground **2 CRUSHING RETORT** a clever or cutting answer to something somebody has said (*slang*) **3 ELECTRONIC CIRCUIT** an electronic circuit that automatically reduces the gain of a receiver in response to an input signal that exceeds a predetermined level [Early 17C. An imitation of the sound.] —**squelcher** *n* —**squelchy** *adj*

squeteague /skwi teég/ (*plural* **-teague** *or* **-teagues**) *n* a large fish of the croaker family, especially an Atlantic weakfish. Native to: Atlantic Ocean. Genus: *Cynoscion*. [Early 19C. < Algonquian.]

squib /skwib/ *n* **1 SMALL FIREWORK** a small firework, especially a banger **2 DUD FIREWORK** a faulty firework that burns without exploding **3 PIECE OF SATIRE** a short satirical piece of writing or speech **4 SHORT JOURNALISTIC PIECE** a short humorous piece that acts as a filler in a newspaper **5 DEVICE FOR FIRING A ROCKET ENGINE** a small device for firing a rocket engine ■ *v* (**squibs, squibbing, squibbed**) **1** *vt* **SATIRIZE** to write a satirical piece about somebody **2** *vt* **KICK A BALL LOW** in American football, to kick the ball in such a way that it wobbles as it bounces along the ground **3** *vi* **SET OFF A FIREWORK** to set off a small firework, especially a banger [Early 16C. < ?]

squid /skwid/ (*plural* **squid** *or* **squids**) *n* **1** a marine cephalopod mollusc that has two long tentacles and eight shorter arms, a long tapered body, two triangular fins, and an internal shell. Order: Teuthoidea. **2** a dish of squid that has been prepared and cooked for eating [Late 16C. < ?]

squidgy /skwíjji/ (**-gier, -giest**) *adj* **1** being or feeling soft and damp **2** feeling unpleasantly soft and squashy (*informal*) [Late 19C. < ?]

squiffy /skwíffi/ (**squiffier, squiffiest**) *adj* slightly drunk (*informal*) [Mid-19C. < ?]

squiggle /skwígg'l/ *n* **1 WAVY LINE** a wavy or curly line or movement **2 ILLEGIBLE WORD** an illegible handwritten word or words ■ *vi* (**-gles, -gling, -gled**) (*informal*) **1 SQUIRM** to twist, squirm, or wriggle **2 DRAW SQUIGGLES** to draw wavy or curly lines [Early 19C. < ?] —**squiggler** *n* —**squiggly** *adj*

squill /skwil/ *n* **1** a plant grown from a bulb. Flowers: small, blue, white, pink, or purple, drooping. Native to: Europe, Asia, Africa. Genus: *Scilla* and *Pushkinia*. **2** PLANTS = **sea squill 3** dried slices of a sea squill's bulb. Use: expectorant, diuretic. [14C. Via Latin *squilla* 'shrimp, squill' < Greek *skilla*.]

squilla /skwílla/ *n* a burrowing marine crustacean that has eyes on stalks and large grasping appendages. Genus: *Squilla*. [Early 16C. < modern Latin, < Latin, 'shrimp' (see SQUILL).]

squillion /skwíllyan/ *pron* a number of people or things so huge it cannot be counted or determined (*slang*) [Mid-20C. After *million* and *billion*.] —**squillion** *det*

squinch[1] /skwinch/ *n* an arch, corbelling, or lintel built across the upper inside corner of a square tower to support the weight of a spire or other structure above [Mid-19C. Alteration of *scuncheon* < Old French *escoinson* 'corner out' < *coin* 'corner' (see COIN).]

squinch[2] /skwinch/ *v* *US* **1** *vt* to screw up the eyes or face **2** *vti* to crouch so as to take up less space [Early 19C. Probably blend of SQUINT + PINCH.]

squint /skwint/ *v* **1** *vi* **PARTLY CLOSE THE EYES** to half-close the eyes so as to see better ○ *a photo of them squinting into the camera in bright sunlight* **2** *vti* **HAVE EYES NOT LOOKING IN PARALLEL** to have eyes that are not aligned in parallel **3** *vi* **GLANCE ASIDE** to glance or look at something sideways **4** *vi* *US* **LOOK ASKANCE** to regard something with disapproval (*disapproving*) ○ *Congress clearly is squinting at the prospect of increased funding for the program.* ■ *n* **1 EYE CONDITION** a condition in which the eyes are not aligned in parallel, causing a cross-eyed appearance. Technical name **strabismus 2 QUICK GLIMPSE** a quick look or glance at something, often to the side **3 ACTION OF NARROWING EYES** the act of narrowing the eyes to try to see better **4** ARCHIT = **hagioscope** ■ *adj* **1 CROSS-EYED** with a squint or a cross-eyed appearance **2 ASKEW** not level or properly aligned (*informal*) [Mid-16C. Shortening of *asquint* < ?] —**squinter** *n* —**squinty** *adj* ◇ **have** *or* **take a squint at something** to have a look at something (*informal*)

squint-eyed *adj* **1 WITH SQUINT** with one or both eyes looking slightly inwards or outwards rather than in parallel **2 LOOKING WITH EYES PARTLY CLOSED** looking with the eyes partly closed to see better **3 ASKANCE** looking askance or sidelong

squirarchy *n* HIST = **squirearchy**

squire /skwīr/ *n* **1 RURAL LANDOWNER** a country landowner in England, often the main local landowner **2 ATTENDANT TO A KNIGHT** a young apprentice knight who acted as an attendant to a knight in the Middle Ages **3 MAN WHO ESCORTS A WOMAN** a man who is escorting a woman or going out with her regularly (*dated*) **4 FORM OF ADDRESS** a term used by a man to address another (*informal*) ■ *vt* (**squires, squiring, squired**) **ESCORT** to escort or go out with a man or a woman (*dated; often passive*) [13C. < Old French *esquier* (see ESQUIRE).]

squirearchy /skwīr aarki/ (*plural* **-chies**), **squirarchy** (*plural* **-chies**) *n* the main rural landowners collectively, especially the social, economic, or political class formed by such landed proprietors [Late 18C. < SQUIRE + HIERARCHY.] —**squirearchal** /skwīr aárk'l/ *adj* —**squirearchic** /skwīr aárkik/ *adj*

squireen /skwī reén/ *n* *Ireland* a rural landowner owning a relatively small amount of land (*archaic*) [Early 19C. < SQUIRE + the suffix *-een* 'little' < Irish *-ín*.]

squirm /skwurm/ *vi* **1 WRIGGLE FROM DISCOMFORT** to wriggle the body, especially because of discomfort or in an attempt to break free from being held **2 FEEL EMOTIONAL DISTRESS** to feel very uncomfortable, especially because of shame, embarrassment, or revulsion ○ *a tough question that made the press office squirm* ■ *n* **WRIGGLING MOVEMENT** a wriggling movement, especially from discomfort or as an attempt to break free from being held [Late 17C. < ?] —**squirmer** *n* —**squirmy** *adj*

squirrel /skwírrəl/ *n* **1 SMALL BUSHY-TAILED RODENT** a small rodent that has a long bushy tail, lives in trees, and eats nuts and seeds. Family: Sciuridae. ◊ **grey squirrel, red squirrel 2 RODENT LIKE A SQUIRREL** a rodent related to or resembling the squirrel, e.g. the ground squirrel, flying squirrel, or chipmunk **3 US CRIMINAL SUSPECT** a person who is a criminal or who is suspected of having committed a crime (*slang*) **4 HOARDER** a hoarder of something (*informal*) ■ *vt* (**-rels, -relling, -relled**) **HOARD** to hoard or save things [14C. Via Anglo-Norman *esquirel* 'little squirrel' < Greek *skiouros* 'shady-tail' < *skia* 'shadow' + *oura* 'tail'.]

squirrel cage *n* **1 ROTATING FRAMEWORK FOR AN ANIMAL** a cage containing a cylindrical framework that goes round when a small pet rodent runs inside it **2 DULL TASK** a dull, repetitive, seemingly purposeless task **3 WINDING IN INDUCTION MOTORS** a rotor of an induction motor consisting of copper bars mounted in slots around the periphery

squirrelfish /skwírrəl fish/ (*plural* **-fish** *or* **-fishes**) *n* a brightly coloured nocturnal fish. Native to: tropical reefs. Family: Holocentridae. [< ?]

squirrelly /skwírrəli/ *adj* **1** *US* an offensive term meaning very irrational or odd **2** resembling or characteristic of a squirrel

squirrel monkey *n* a small long-tailed monkey that has soft yellowish-grey, brown, or reddish fur, a white face, and a black muzzle. Native to: Central and South America. Genus: *Saimiri*.

squirt /skwurt/ *v* **1** *vti* **FORCE SOMETHING OUT FROM A NARROW OPENING** to force something or be pushed out of a narrow opening in a strong quick stream ○ *The ketchup squirted all over the table.* ○ *managed to squirt the last of the toothpaste out of the tube* **2** *vt* **SQUIRT LIQUID OVER** to hit or cover somebody or something with liquid that is forced out of a narrow opening in a strong quick stream ○ *She squirted me with her water bottle.* ■ *n* **1 STREAM OF EJECTED LIQUID** a small stream of liquid forced out of a narrow opening ○ *a squirt of body lotion* **2 OFFENSIVE TERM** an offensive term that deliberately insults somebody's young age or small size, especially in response to perceived impudence (*informal insult*) **3 INSTRUMENT FOR SQUIRTING LIQUID** an instrument such as a syringe that is used to dispense liquid in a thin quick stream [15C. An imitation of the sound of something being squirted.]

squirt gun *n US* = water pistol

squirting cucumber *n* a vine of the gourd family with oblong fruits that burst when ripe, ejecting seeds and juice. Native to: Mediterranean. *Ecballium elaterium.*

squish /skwish/ *v* **1** *vt* **SQUEEZE** to squeeze or crush something soft **2** *vi* **MAKE A SOFT SPLASHING NOISE** to make a sucking or soft splashing sound when subjected to pressure, as when being walked on or squeezed ■ *n* **1 SOFT SPLASHING NOISE** a sucking or soft splashing sound **2** *US* **OFFENSIVE TERM** an offensive term for somebody perceived as weak or cowardly (*slang insult*) [Mid-17C. Probably alteration of SQUASH[1].]

squishy /skwishi/ (**-ier, -iest**) *adj* soft and giving under pressure, like mud or a soft fruit

squit /skwit/ *n* **1 OFFENSIVE TERM** an offensive term that deliberately insults somebody's status and importance (*informal insult*) **2 NONSENSE** nonsense (*dated informal*) ■ **squits** *npl* **DIARRHOEA** diarrhoea (*slang*) [Early 19C. < ?]

squiz /skwiz/ (*plural* **squizzes**) *n ANZ* a quick inquisitive look at something (*informal*) ○ *Can I have a squiz at your paper?* [Early 20C. < ?]

sr[1] *symbol* steradian

⚡**sr**[2] *abbr* Suriname (*in Internet addresses*)

Sr[1] *symbol* strontium

Sr[2] *abbr* **1** Senhor **2 Sr, sr** senior **3** Señor **4** Sir **5** sister

Sra *abbr* **1** Senhora **2** Señora

sraddhaa /shrāad aa/, **shraddh** /shraad/ *n S Asia* a ceremonial offering of food and water to the dead [Late 18C. < Sanskrit *śraddha* < *śraddhā* 'faith, trust'.]

⚡**SRAM** *abbr* static random access memory

Sranantongo /sraanan tóngó/, **Sranan** /sraanan/ *n* a creole language based on English that is the lingua franca of Suriname [Mid-20C. < Sranantongo, 'Suriname tongue'.]

S-R connection *n* the relationship between a stimulus and a response

Srebrenica /srébbra neétsa/ town in E Bosnia-Herzegovina. Population: 37,211 (1991).

Sri /sree/ *n* **1** a title of respect for a man in South Asia, equivalent to 'Mr' **2** a title of respect for a Hindu deity or holy man **3** RELIG = Lakshmi [Late 18C. Via Hindi < Sanskrit *śrī* 'lord', literally 'beauty, wealth, majesty'.]

Sri Lanka

Sri Lanka /shri láng ka/ island republic in South Asia, off the tip of SE India in the Indian Ocean. Capital: Colombo. Population: 18,318,000 (1996). Area: 65,610 sq. km/25,326 sq. mi. —**Sri Lankan** *n, adj*

Sriman /sreémən/ *n* = Sri *n*. 1

Srinagar /sri núggər, shrínna gaar/, **Srīnager** capital of the state of Jammu and Kashmir, NW India. Population: 595,000 (1991).

SRN *abbr* State Registered Nurse

sRNA *abbr* soluble RNA

SRO *abbr* **1** single room occupancy **2** standing room only **3** Statutory Rules and Orders **4** self-regulatory organization

Srta *abbr* **1** Senhorita **2** Señorita

SS[1] *abbr* **1** Saints **2** Social Security **3** steamship **4** Sunday school **5** sworn statement

SS[2] *n* a paramilitary organization founded by Hitler in 1925 as a personal bodyguard [Early 20C. < German *Schutzstaffel* 'defence squadron'.]

SS. *abbr* Saints

SSB *abbr* single sideband (transmission)

SSC *abbr* **1** *Scotland* Solicitor to the Supreme Court **2** *S Asia* Secondary School Certificate

SSE *abbr* south-southeast

SSG *abbr US* Staff Sergeant

SSM *abbr* surface-to-surface missile

SSN *abbr US* Social Security Number

SSP *abbr* statutory sick pay

ssp. *abbr* subspecies

SSRI *abbr* selective serotonin reuptake inhibitor

SSS *abbr* selective serotonin reuptake inhibitor

SSSI *abbr* site of special scientific interest

SSW *abbr* south-southwest

st *abbr* short ton

St *abbr* **1** Saint **2** Strait **3** Street (*in addresses*)

Sta *abbr* Santa

stab /stab/ *v* (**stabs, stabbing, stabbed**) **1** *vt* **THRUST A KNIFE INTO** to thrust a knife or other sharp pointed instrument into somebody or something **2** *vti* **JAB FINGER OR OBJECT AT** to thrust a finger or an object sharply at something ○ *He stabbed his potato angrily with his fork.* **3** *vi* **HURT LIKE A KNIFE WOUND** to cause a sudden sharp hurting sensation, like that of a knife wound ○ *Pain stabbed at her temples.* ■ *n* **1 ACT OF STABBING** the action or result of thrusting a knife or other sharp implement into somebody (*often before nouns*) ○ *a stab wound* **2 SEVERE CRITICISM** a severe criticism of somebody **3 SUDDEN PAINFUL FEELING** a sudden brief sensation, especially of pain ○ *felt a sudden stab of loss* **4 ATTEMPT** an attempt at something (*informal*) ○ *Each of us made a stab at solving the problem.* [15C. < ?] —**stabber** *n* ◇ **a stab in the back** a betrayal or act of treachery (*informal*) ◇ **stab somebody in the back** to betray or harm somebody that trusts you

~~**stabalize**~~ incorrect spelling of **stabilize**

Stabat Mater /staa bat maàtər/ *n* **1** a Latin hymn that was composed in the 13th century and concerns the grief of the Virgin Mary at the crucifixion of Jesus Christ **2** a musical setting of the Stabat Mater [Mid-19C. < Latin *stabat mater dolorosa* 'the mother stood, full of grief', the first words of the hymn.]

stabbing /stábbing/ *n* an incident in which somebody is deliberately stabbed with a knife or sharp object ■ *adj* brief, sharp, and sudden, as if from the thrust of a knife ○ *a stabbing pain in the side*

stabile /stáy bīl/ *n* **SCULPTURE ATTACHED TO SOMETHING** an abstract sculpture made of wire, metal, or other materials and attached to fixed supports ■ *adj* **1 STABLE** in a fixed position **2 NOT CHANGING CHEMICALLY** not readily undergoing chemical change [Late 18C. < Latin *stabilis* (see STABLE[1]).]

stabilise *vti* = stabilize

stabiliser *n* = stabilizer

stability /stə bílləti/ *n* **1 STABLE QUALITY** the condition of being stable ○ *policies aimed at creating economic stability* **2 MENTAL FIRMNESS** mental or psychological firmness **3 RESISTANCE TO CHANGE** resistance to sudden change or deterioration **4 ABILITY TO ADJUST TO LOAD CHANGES** a property of a transmission system that allows changes in load to be met without any reduction in performance **5 AIR MASS WITHOUT UPWARD MOVEMENT** a condition of no upward movement in an air mass **6 RESISTANCE TO AIR CURRENTS** a measure of the tendency of an air mass to be influenced by convection currents **7 ABILITY TO MAINTAIN A BALANCE** the ability of an ecological community to resist disturbance caused by changes in, e.g., climate, or the ability to return to its original state after disturbance **8 RESISTANCE TO A CHANGED POSITION** the capability of an aircraft, rocket, or ship to maintain a position and to return to it if displaced **9 RESISTANCE TO A CHEMICAL CHANGE** a resistance to chemical change **10 MEASURE OF MAINTAINING EQUILIBRIUM** a measure of the difficulty of displacing an object or system from equilibrium

stabilization fund *n* a reserve of money that a country

uses to maintain its official exchange rate by buying and selling foreign exchange

stabilize /stáybi līz/ (**-lizes, -lizing, -lized**), **stabilise** (**-lises, -lising, -lised**) *v* **1** *vti* to become stable, or make something stable ○ *The patient's condition has stabilized.* **2** *vt* to maintain something at an unfluctuating level —**stabilization** /stáybilī záysh'n/ *n*

stabilizer /stáybi līzər/, **stabiliser** *n* **1 AEROFOIL THAT STABILIZES AN AIRCRAFT** an aerofoil or combination of aerofoils, e.g. in the tail assembly of an aeroplane, that keeps an aircraft or missile aligned with the direction of flight **2 FINS TO CONTROL A SHIP'S ROLLING** one or more pairs of submerged fins, often gyroscopically controlled, used to minimize the rolling of a ship in rough waters **3 ADDITIVE THAT MAINTAINS CHEMICAL PROPERTIES** a chemical compound added to another substance to make it resistant to change **4 DEVICE TO PRODUCE A CONSTANT VOLTAGE** a device used to maintain a constant voltage from a source of direct current **5 SOMETHING ADDED TO DISPERSE PAINT** a substance added to a fast-drying paint to improve the dispersion of pigment **6 STABILIZING PERSON OR THING** something that or somebody who acts to bring stability ■ **stabilizers, stabilisers** *npl* **EXTRA WHEELS TO BALANCE BICYCLE** a pair of small wheels fitted to the back wheel of a bicycle to help balance it while somebody is learning to ride

stable[1] /stáyb'l/ *adj* **1 NOT CHANGING** steady and not liable to change ○ *Prices have remained stable.* **2 NOT LIKELY TO MOVE** steady or firm and not liable to move **3 NOT EXCITABLE** having a calm and steady temperament rather than being excitable or given to apparently irrational behaviour **4 NOT READILY UNDERGOING CHANGE** not subject to changes in chemical or physical properties **5 NOT NATURALLY RADIOACTIVE** incapable of becoming a different isotope or element by radioactive decay [13C. Via Anglo-Norman and Old French < Latin *stabilis*.] —**stableness** *n* —**stably** *adv*

stable[2] /stáyb'l/ *n* **1 BUILDING FOR HORSES** a building in which horses, and sometimes other large types of livestock, are kept **2 HORSES OWNED BY SOMEBODY** the group of horses, especially racehorses, owned by one person or kept and trained at one establishment **3 PEOPLE WORKING IN A STABLE** the people who work in a stable **4 GROUP UNDER MANAGEMENT** a group of people managed by the same person or organization ○ *a stable of bestselling authors* ■ *vti* (**stables, stabling, stabled**) **PUT OR LIVE IN A STABLE** to keep or put a horse or other large animal in a particular building, or be kept in a particular building ○ *We stabled our horses in the barn.* [13C. Via Old French *estable* < Latin *stabulum*.]

stable boy *n* a youth or man who looks after horses in a racing stable

stable door *n* a door split into upper and lower sections that can be closed separately

stable equilibrium *n* **1** the state of a system that will return to its original condition after experiencing a slight disturbance **2** an economic equilibrium that is restored quickly if it is disrupted by an outside influence, e.g. a change in one of the factors affecting demand or supply

stable fly *n* a biting bloodsucking fly resembling a housefly that attacks humans and domestic animals. *Stomoxys calcitrans.*

stable girl *n* a woman or girl who looks after horses in a racing stable

stablemate /stáyb'l mayt/ *n* **1** a horse that belongs to the same owner or is kept and trained at the same racing stable as another **2** an associate of somebody or something, e.g. an author who shares the same publisher as another

stabling /stáybling/ *n* **1** a stable or stables **2** accommodation for horses, usually but not always in a stable

~~**stablize**~~ incorrect spelling of **stabilize**

stab stitch *n* a very small straight stitch designed to hold pieces of fabric together without showing as more than a dot on the surface

stacc. *abbr* staccato

staccato /stə kaátō/ *adv* **IN QUICK SEPARATE NOTES** to be played, as rapid short detached notes (*musical direction*) ■ *adj* **QUICK AND CLIPPED** rapid, brief, and clipped in sound ■ *n* (*plural* **-tos**) **STACCATO PASSAGE** a staccato passage in music [Early 18C. < Italian, 'detached'.]

stachys /stáykiss/ *n* a plant with spiked whorls of purple, reddish, or white flowers, e.g. lamb's ears or betony. Genus: *Stachys*. [Mid-16C. Via modern Latin < Greek *stakhus* 'ear of corn'.]

stack /stak/ *n* 1 HEAPED PILE OF THINGS a pile of things more or less neatly arranged one on top of another ○ *a stack of chairs* 2 LARGE PILE OF SOMETHING STORED OUTDOORS a large pile of hay, straw, or grain often conical in shape, stored outdoors 3 CHIMNEY OR CHIMNEYS a tall chimney or group of chimneys arranged together 4 LARGE NUMBER a large number or amount (*informal*) ○ *She has stacks of money.* 5 AIRCRAFT WAITING TO LAND a queue of aircraft waiting a turn to land at an airport, circling at different heights 6 ROCKY PILLAR RISING FROM COASTAL WATERS a steep-sided pillar of rock that has been isolated from nearby cliffs at the shoreline by the erosion of the waves 7 LIST IN A COMPUTER MEMORY an area in a computer memory where data can be stored temporarily in a list in which the last item entered is the first one removed 8 ARRANGEMENT OF FIREARMS a group of firearms formed in a pyramid, especially three rifles with their muzzles leaning against each other 9 VERTICAL PIPE a vertical duct or waste pipe 10 MEASURE FOR COAL OR WOOD a nonmetric measure of coal or firewood equal to 108 cubic feet ■ **stacks** *npl* BOOK STORAGE IN A LIBRARY an area of a library, usually not open to the public, where books are stored on shelves ■ *v* 1 *vti* PUT IN AN ORGANIZED PILE to put things one on top of another to form a pile, or to be arranged in this way 2 *vt* PUT THINGS ON A SHELF to arrange objects on a shelf 3 *vi* HEAP WITH PILES OF OBJECTS to load or heap something with large piles of articles or objects ○ *The bins were stacked with bargains.* 4 *vt* MANIPULATE A SITUATION UNETHICALLY to arrange something underhandedly to ensure a desired outcome 5 *vti* KEEP AIRCRAFT WAITING IN A STACK to keep aircraft waiting to land at an airport circling at different heights, or be kept in this position [13C. < Old Norse *stakkr* < Germanic, 'stick, pole'.] —**stackable** *adj* —**stacker** *n* ◇ **be stacked against somebody** to amount to an unfair disadvantage for somebody ◇ **blow your stack** to become suddenly furious (*slang*) ◇ **stack the deck** *or* **cards** 1 to arrange playing cards in a deck for the purposes of cheating (*slang*) 2 to arrange something dishonestly or unethically so as to gain an unfair advantage (*slang*)

stack up *vi* 1 *US* to be measurable against or comparable to something 2 *US, Aus* to add up to a total

stacked /stakt/ *adj* 1 *US* OFFENSIVE TERM an offensive term meaning having large breasts (*slang*) 2 DISHONESTLY ARRANGED unfairly or dishonestly manipulated or arranged 3 DISPOSED AT DIFFERENT HEIGHTS disposed at different heights prior to landing

stacked heel *n* a wide high heel made of different coloured layers of wood or material simulating wood

stacte /stákti/ *n* a sweet spice mentioned in the Bible as being used by the ancient Jews in making incense [14C. Via Latin < Greek *staktē* < *staktos*, past participle of *stazein* 'drip, ooze'.]

staddle /stádd'l/ *n* a supporting base to keep stored hay off the ground (*regional or archaic*) [Old English *staþol* < Indo-European, 'to stand']

stadholder /stád hōldər/, **stadtholder** *n* 1 the chief magistrate of the Dutch republic from the 16th to 18th centuries 2 formerly, a governor or viceroy of a province in the Netherlands [Mid-16C. Partial translation of Dutch *stadhouder* 'place-holder'.] —**stadholderate** *n* —**stadholdership** *n*

stadia[1] plural of **stadium**

stadia[2] /stáydi ə/ *n* a method of measuring distances or differences in elevation using a telescopic instrument calibrated to correspond to distances from the surveyor [Mid-19C. Directly or via Italian < Latin, plural of *stadium* (see STADIUM).]

stadium /stáydi əm/ (*plural* **-ums** *or* **-a** /-ə/) *n* 1 ARENA WITH TIERED SEATS a place where people watch sports or other activities, usually a large enclosed flat area surrounded by tiers of seats for spectators 2 ANCIENT GREEK RACECOURSE a racecourse for foot races in ancient Greece that had tiers of seats at each side and one end 3 ANCIENT GREEK MEASUREMENT UNIT a unit of linear measure in ancient Greece equal to about 185 m/607 ft [14C. Via Latin < Greek *stadion* 'racetrack, unit of measure'.]

stadtholder *n* HIST, LAW = **stadholder**

Staël /staal/, **Madame de** (1766–1817) French writer. Born **Anne Louise Germaine Necker**

staff[1] /staaf/ *n* 1 WORKERS people who are employed by a company or individual 2 SPECIFIC BODY WITHIN A LARGER GROUP a specific group of employees within a company, institution, or organization 3 TEACHERS the teachers in a school or other educational institution, as opposed to the students. US term **faculty** *n.* 5 4 PEOPLE WHO WORK FOR A LEADER a group of people who serve a leader or an executive of a company, organization, or institution 5 GROUP OF AIDES TO A COMMANDER a group of officers in the armed services who assist a commanding officer or work at headquarters as advisers or planners 6 *Malaysia, Singapore* MEMBER OF STAFF a member of staff working for a company, organization, or school 7 (*plural* **staffs** *or* **staves**) LARGE HEAVY STICK a stick, rod, or pole, such as a stick used as a support while walking, or a rod used as a symbol of authority in ceremonies 8 (*plural* **staffs** *or* **staves**) = **flagpole** *n.* 9 SET OF LINES FOR WRITING MUSIC a set of five horizontal lines, together with the four spaces between them, on which the notes of music are written 10 **staff** (*plural* **staffs** *or* **staves**) GRADUATED ROD USED FOR MEASURING a graduated rod used for testing or measuring something, e.g. in surveying ■ *adj* 1 EMPLOYED WITH SALARY employed full-time, not on a freelance basis 2 CONCERNED WITH STAFF for or relating to the staff of a company, institution, or organization ■ *vt* PROVIDE WITH WORKERS to provide a place or organization with employees (*often passive*) [Old English *stæf* 'stick, rod' < Indo-European, 'to support']

staff[2] /staaf/ *n* a building material of plaster and fibrous material used as a temporary, especially decorative, finish on the outside of a structure [Late 19C. < ?]

Staffa /stáffə/ uninhabited island in the Inner Hebrides, W Scotland. Area: 0.5 sq. km/0.2 sq. mi.

staff college *n* a school in which military officers are prepared for higher positions, e.g. as staff officers or commanders

staffer /staáfər/ *n* a member of the staff of an organization (*informal*) ○ *White House staffers*

staffing /staáfing/ *n* the number of people working in a place or organization, or the act of providing workers

staffman /staáf man/ (*plural* **-men** /-men/) *n* somebody who holds a levelling staff during surveying. US term **rodman**

staff nurse *n* a fully qualified hospital nurse of a rank below team leader

staff of Aesculapius /-eéskyoŏ láypi əss/ *n* a symbol for the medical profession consisting of a staff with a single snake entwined round it. ◊ **caduceus**

staff officer *n* a military officer who assists a commanding officer or works as a planner or adviser at a headquarters

staff of life *n* bread, or sometimes another food, considered as an essential part of the human diet (*literary*) [*Staff* < STAFF[1], in the sense 'staple, support']

Stafford /stáffərd/ town in central England. Population: 61,885 (1995).

Stafford, Sir Edward William (1819–1901) Irish-born New Zealand statesman

Staffordshire /stáffərdshər/ county in central England. Area: 2,716 sq. km/1,049 sq. mi.

Staffordshire bull terrier, Staffordshire terrier *n* a bull terrier belonging to a breed with a short broad head and ears that hang down [After the county of STAFFORDSHIRE]

staffroom /staáf room, -rŏom/ *n* a room used only by the teachers in a school, e.g. for relaxation between classes

Staffs. /stafs/ *abbr* Staffordshire

staff sergeant *n* 1 BRITISH ARMY RANK a noncommissioned officer in the British Army, of a rank above sergeant 2 US ARMY RANK a noncommissioned officer in the US Army of a rank above sergeant 3 US AIR FORCE RANK a noncommissioned officer in the US Air Force, of a rank above sergeant 4 US MARINE RANK a noncommissioned officer in the US Marine Corps of a rank above sergeant

stag /stag/ *n* 1 MATURE MALE DEER an adult male deer, especially a male red deer 2 *US* UNACCOMPANIED MAN AT A SOCIAL EVENT a man who goes to a social function without a partner (*informal*) 3 CASTRATED ADULT ANIMAL a male animal, e.g. a pig, castrated after it reaches maturity 4 SPECULATOR IN NEW ISSUES OF SHARES a speculator who applies for a new issue of a security in the hope of making a quick profit when it begins to be traded ■ *adj* RESTRICTED TO MEN for men only, and usually involving activities that would not be appropriate in mixed company (*informal*) ■ *adv US* WITHOUT A WOMAN DATE without a woman companion on a social occasion (*informal*) ■ *v* (**stags, stagging, stagged**) 1 *vt* BUY SHARES FOR QUICK PROFIT to buy a new issue of a security in the hope of making a quick profit when it begins to be traded 2 *vi US* ATTEND AN EVENT WITHOUT A WOMAN DATE to attend a social event without a woman companion (*informal*) [Old English (assumed) *stagga* < Indo-European, 'pointed']

stag beetle *n* a large beetle, the male of which has long extended jaws (**mandibles**) shaped like a stag's antlers. Family: Lucanidae.

stage /stayj/ *n* 1 PERIOD OR STEP DURING A PROCESS a step, level, or period in the development or progress of something ○ *The project is still in its early stages.* 2 AREA IN A THEATRE the area in a theatre where a performance takes place, especially a platform on which actors perform a play 3 PLATFORM a raised platform, e.g. in a hall or auditorium, where speeches are made and ceremonies are carried out 4 DRAMATIC PROFESSION the profession of acting, drama, or the theatre 5 SETTING IN WHICH SOMETHING HAPPENS the scene of an event or series of events ○ *The summit marks her first appearance on the world stage.* 6 PART OF BUS ROUTE any division of a bus route that is used to calculate fares 7 PART OF JOURNEY a distinct section of a journey, especially one after which a stop is made 8 DETACHABLE ROCKET UNIT a separable unit of a rocket or spacecraft that contains fuel and can be jettisoned after the fuel is exhausted 9 *US, Can* PLATFORM FOR WORKERS a raised platform, especially a scaffolding for workers during the construction of a building 10 SUBJECT STUDIED FOR A YEAR a subject studied for one year at a university or college 11 PLATFORM FOR DRYING a platform used to dry fish or meat 12 RECORDING = **sound stage** 13 PERIOD OF DEVELOPMENT OF AN ORGANISM a distinct period of development in the life of an organism when its form is different from earlier or later periods 14 SIGNIFICANT PHASE an important phase of cultural, economic, or social development 15 ELEVATION OF A RIVER SURFACE a measure of how much the surface of a river or stream rises above a given point 16 PLATFORM FOR MOUNTING MICROSCOPIC SPECIMEN the small platform of an optical microscope on which a specimen is placed for examination 17 PERIOD OF ROCK STRATA a relatively short distinct period, a subdivision of a series, during which rock strata are deposited during an age of geological time 18 UNIT OF ELECTRICAL COMPONENTS a group of components that form part of an electronic or electrical system 19 TRANSP = **stagecoach** ■ *vt* (**stages, staging, staged**) 1 ORGANIZE A PERFORMANCE FOR THE PUBLIC to put on a play, concert, exhibition, or similar event for an audience 2 ORGANIZE EVENT to organize or carry out something, e.g. an event that will attract attention or publicity 3 SET PLAY IN PLACE OR TIME to set a play in a particular place or time ○ *staged the drama in the regency period* 4 CLASSIFY PHASES OF DISEASE to classify the progress of a disease [13C. Via Old French *estage* < assumed Vulgar Latin *staticum* 'standing place' < Latin *stat-*, past participle of *stare* 'stand'.] —**stageability** /stáyjə bíllәti/ *n* —**stageable** *adj* —**stageably** *adv* ◇ **by** *or* **in easy stages** in an unhurried, undemanding way ◇ **hold the stage** to continue to be the centre of attention ◇ **on stage** performing in something, especially as an actor ◇ **take centre stage** to draw people's or public attention

stage brace *n* a brace used to support upright pieces of scenery in a play

stage business *n* THEATRE = **business** *n.* 8

stagecoach /stáyj kōch/ *n* a large four-wheeled horse-drawn coach formerly used to carry passengers and mail over a regular route

stagecraft /stáyj kraaft/ *n* the technique or art of writing, adapting, or putting plays on stage

stage direction *n* an instruction for an actor in the script of a play

stage door *n* a door in the back or side of a theatre that leads directly backstage and is usually used by performers

stage effect *n* a special visual or auditory effect created on a theatrical stage by lighting, scenery, or sound

stage fright *n* fear or nervousness that somebody feels before going in front of an audience to speak or perform

stagehand /stáyj hand/ *n* a manual worker in a theatre, e.g. somebody who sets up and removes stage sets

stage left *n* the side of a stage that is to a performer's left when facing the audience. ◊ **stage right**

stage-manage *v* **1** *vt* to control an organized event, especially in a way that is not public, so that it happens exactly as planned **2** *vti* to carry out the work of a stage manager, especially on a particular production —**stage-management** *n*

stage manager *n* an assistant of the director of a play who supervises backstage activities

stager /stáyjər/ *n* an actor (*archaic*) [Late 16C. < ?]

stage right *n* the part of a stage that is to the performer's right when facing the audience. ◊ **stage left**

stage-struck *adj* loving theatre and intensely wanting to be part of it, especially as a performer

stage wait *n* an unintentional pause in the action of a play, especially one caused by an actor's missing a cue

stage whisper *n* **1** something said on stage that for the purposes of the play is supposed to be a whisper but is intended to be heard by the audience **2** a loud whisper intended to be overheard

stagey *adj* = **stagy**

stagflation /stag fláysh'n/ *n* a period of rising prices and unemployment but little growth in consumer demand and business activity [Mid-20C. Blend of STAGNATION + INFLATION.] —**stagflationary** *adj*

stagger /stággər/ *v* **1** *vi* **MOVE UNSTEADILY, NEARLY FALLING** to move or walk unsteadily, almost but not quite falling over **2** *vt* **MAKE PERSON OR ANIMAL STUMBLE** to make a person or animal stumble or nearly fall, especially by a blow **3** *vt* **ASTONISH** to completely astonish or amaze somebody (*often passive*) **4** *vi* **CONTINUE IMPERFECTLY** to keep going or operating in a defective or incompetent way **5** *vt* **ARRANGE ACTIVITIES FOR SEPARATE TIMES** to arrange activities so that they do not overlap **6** *vt* **MAKE INTO ALTERNATING OR ZIGZAG PATTERN** to arrange things so that they do not form a straight line, especially in an alternating or zigzag pattern (*often passive*) **7** *vi* **HESITATE** to hesitate or falter **8** *vt* **ADJUST THE EDGE OF BIPLANE'S WING** to make the leading edge of one wing of a biplane project beyond the leading edge of the other wing ■ *n* **1 STUMBLE NEARLY RESULTING IN A FALL** an unsteady movement in which a person or animal almost falls **2 ARRANGEMENT OF BIPLANE WINGS** a design in which the leading edge of one wing of a biplane is ahead of that of the other wing [Mid-16C. Alteration of obsolete *stacker* < Old Norse *stakkra* < *staka* 'push' < Germanic 'pole' (see STACK).] —**staggerer** *n*

staggerbush /stággər bŏŏsh/ (*plural* **-bushes** *or* **-bush**) *n* a deciduous shrub of the heath family with poisonous leaves. Flowers: white or pink, in clusters. Native to: E United States. *Lyonia mariana.*

staggered /stággərd/ *adj* **1** shocked or astounded at something **2** not arranged in sequence or in a straight line

staggered hours *npl* an arrangement in a business in which employees arrive and leave at different times but work hours that overlap for part of the time

staggering /stággəring/ *adj* with the effect of shocking or astounding people —**staggeringly** *adv*

staggers /stággərz/ *n* a form of vertigo associated with decompression sickness, with symptoms including dizziness, weakness, and confusion (*+ singular or plural verb*)

staghorn /stág hawrn/, **stag's horn** *n* **1** a stag's antler, or a piece of this used as material for carved objects **2** PLANTS = **staghorn fern 3** = **staghorn moss** ■ *adj* made from a piece of a stag's antlers

staghorn coral *n* a form of stony coral branched like a deer's antlers. Genus: *Acropora.*

staghorn fern *n* a fern with broad leaves like antlers and smaller clinging leaves, often cultivated as a houseplant. Genus: *Platycerium.*

staghorn moss *n* a plant with creeping stems like antlers and tiny overlapping leaves. *Lycopodium clavatum.*

staghound /stág hownd/ *n* a hound like a large foxhound, used especially formerly in hunting stags

staging /stáyjing/ *n* **1 TECHNIQUE OF PRESENTING STAGE PLAY** the activity, process, or style of presenting a play on a stage **2 SCAFFOLDING FOR BUILDING** a temporary structure of supports and platforms used in building or working on something **3 TECHNIQUE FOR INCREASING SPACECRAFT'S VELOCITY** a technique to increase the velocity achieved by a spacecraft's launch vehicle by using multiple propulsive stages, each being jettisoned after use

staging area *n* a place where soldiers and military equipment are gathered for final organization, outfitting, and training before deployment on an operation

staging post *n* a place where people on a long journey stop off to take a break from travel, especially on an air route

stagnant /stágnənt/ *adj* **1 STILL AND UNMOVING** not flowing or moving **2 FOUL OR STALE** stale or impure from lack of motion **3 NOT DEVELOPING** not developing or making progress **4 INACTIVE** not active or lively ○ *a stagnant week on the share market* [Mid-17C. < Latin *stagnant-*, present participle of *stagnare* (see STAGNATE).] —**stagnancy** *n* —**stagnantly** *adv*

stagnate /stag náyt/ (**-nates, -nating, -nated**) *vi* **1 STOP FLOWING** to stop flowing or moving **2 BECOME FOUL** to become stale or impure through not flowing or moving **3 NOT DEVELOP OR MAKE PROGRESS** to fail to develop, progress, or make necessary changes **4 BECOME INACTIVE** to become listless and inactive [Mid-17C. < Latin *stagnat-*, past participle of *stagnare* < *stagnum* 'pool, swamp'.] —**stagnation** *n* —**stagnatory** *adj*

stag night *n* a social occasion that only men attend, especially an evening of drinking with male friends spent by a man about to be married (*informal*) US term **stag party**

stag party *n* = **stag night** (*informal*)

stag's horn *n* PLANTS = **staghorn**

stagy /stáyji/ (**-ier, -iest**), **stagey** (**-ier, -iest**) *adj* exaggerated or artificial in manner, as if in a play (*disapproving*) —**stagily** *adv* —**staginess** *n*

staid /stayd/ *adj* sedate and settled in habits or temperament, sometimes to the point of dullness [Mid-16C. An obsolete past participle of STAY[1], literally 'fixed, settled'.] —**staidly** *adv* —**staidness** *n*

stain /stayn/ *n* **1 DISCOLOURED PATCH** a discoloured mark made by something e.g. blood, wine, or ink **2 COLOUR FINISH** a liquid that is applied to something, especially wood, to darken it or change its colour without hiding its texture or grain **3 DYE USED TO COLOUR MICROSCOPIC SPECIMENS** a dye used to colour tissues and cells to make features more visible under a microscope **4 DYE FOR TEXTILES OR LEATHER** a dye that is used in liquid form to colour textiles or leather **5 CHARACTER BLEMISH** something that detracts from a person's good reputation ■ *v* **1** *vti* **LEAVE MARK ON** to make a discoloured mark on something (*often passive*) **2** *vt* **DYE** to dye something a different or deeper colour using liquid or pigment that penetrates the surface **3** *vt* **TARNISH** to disgrace or detract from something ○ *reprehensible acts that stained his reputation* **4** *vt* **COLOUR ORGANIC SPECIMENS** to colour organic materials with dyes to make features more visible under a microscope [15C. Partly < Old Norse *steina* 'paint' (< *steinn* 'stone, paint'), partly < Old French *desteindre* 'discolour' (< Latin *tingere* 'to dye').] —**stainability** /stáynə bílləti/ *n* —**stainable** *adj* —**stainer** *n*

stained glass *n* glass that has been coloured so that it can be used to make a mosaic picture, especially in a window (*hyphenated before nouns*)

Staines /staynz/ town in S England. Population: 51,167 (1991).

stainless /stáynləss/ *adj* **1 ENTIRELY REPUTABLE** without any blemishes, especially of character or reputation **2 WITHOUT STAINS** without a stain or discoloured mark **3 RESISTANT TO RUST** resisting rust or corrosion ■ *n* METALL = **stainless steel** —**stainlessly** *adv*

stainless steel *n* a corrosion-resistant steel containing at least 12 per cent chromium that has many domestic and industrial uses, e.g. cutlery, ball bearings, and turbine blades (*hyphenated before nouns*)

stair /stair/ *n* **1 SINGLE STEP** a step in a series of steps leading from one floor or level to another **2 SERIES OF STEPS** a flight of steps leading from one floor or level to another ■ **stairs** *npl* **SET OF STEPS** a set or several sets of steps leading from one floor or level to another [Old English *stǣger* < Indo-European, 'to step'] ◇ **above stairs** in the upper part of a large house, formerly occupied by the employers but not the servants (*archaic*) ◇ **below stairs** in the lower part of a house, formerly occupied by the servants (*archaic*)

SPELLCHECK Do not confuse ***stair*** with ***stare***, which has a similar sound. Beware: your spellchecker will not catch this error.

---

staircase /stáir kayss/ *n* a set of stairs in a building, usually with banisters or handrails

stairhead /stáir hed/ *n* the landing at the top of a flight of stairs

stair rod *n* a rod laid to hold a carpet in place against the bottom of a riser in a staircase

stairway /stáir way/ *n* a passageway from one floor or level of a building to another, consisting of stairs or a staircase

stairwell /stáir wel/ *n* the vertical space in a building where stairs are located

stake[1] /stayk/ *n* **1 THIN POINTED POST IN THE GROUND** a thin wooden or metal post that is driven into the ground to mark or support something **2 POST TO TIE SOMEBODY** a wooden post used in an old form of execution to which the person was tied and burnt **3 FORM OF EXECUTION** the method of execution in which somebody was tied to a post and burnt **4 POST TO RETAIN A LOAD** an independent upright post inserted into sockets of a flat wagon or lorry to keep long loads such as logs in place **5 MORMON CHURCH DISTRICT** an administrative district in the Church of Jesus Christ of Latter-Day Saints that consists of wards, each governed by a president and two counsellors ■ *v* (**stakes, staking, staked**) **1** *vt* **SUPPORT OR STRENGTHEN WITH STAKE** to support or strengthen something using a stake **2** *vt* **TIE OR TETHER TO STAKE** to tie or tether something to a stake **3** *vi* **MARK OR FENCE AREA WITH STAKES** to mark out, confine, or fence off an area using stakes driven into the ground round the boundary **4** *vt* **ASSERT RIGHTS OVER** to assert something, usually rights, over something such as an area of land [Old English *staca* < Germanic, 'stick, pole'] ◇ **(pull) up stakes** *US* to leave and move to another place

stake out *vt* **1 WATCH CONTINUOUSLY** to watch a place continuously from a hidden vantage point (*informal*) **2 ESTABLISH BOUNDARIES** to establish the boundaries of an area intended to be used or controlled **3 ESTABLISH AND CLARIFY POSITION** to establish and clarify a personal position in a situation

stake[2] /stayk/ *n* **1 MONEY RISKED IN GAMBLING** an amount of money risked in a bet or game **2 SHARE OR INTEREST IN SOMETHING** a share or interest in something, particularly through money risked in it **3 PERSONAL INVOLVEMENT** a personal or emotional interest, concern, or involvement ○ *We had a huge stake in his success.* **4** *US, Can* MIN EXTRACT = **grubstake** *n.* 1 ■ **stakes** *npl* **1 DEGREE OF RISK** the degree of hazard or danger involved in a situation **2 PRIZE AVAILABLE** the prize, reward, or success available in a gamble or competition **3 PRIZE MADE UP OF CONTRIBUTIONS** the total of bets made by players in a gambling game that is taken by the winner **4 AMOUNT OF BETS IN POKER** in poker, the cash values assigned to chips, bets, or raises ■ *vt* (**stakes, staking, staked**) **1 WAGER** to bet something, especially money, on something **2 RISK THE LOSS OF** to risk the loss of something valuable **3 SUPPLY SOMEBODY WITH REQUIREMENTS** to give or lend somebody something needed or wanted **4 INVEST IN** to put money into something, especially initial capital [Mid-16C. < ?] ◇ **at stake** at risk of being lost

stakeholder /stáyk hōldər/ *n* **1** a person or group with a direct interest, involvement, or investment in something, e.g. the employees, shareholders, and customers of a business concern ○ *'...demonstrating how to build powerful stakeholder relationships based on trust...'* (*Marketing Week*; December 1998) **2** a holder and payer of bets in a gambling game —**stakeholding** *n*

stakeholder pension *n* in the United Kingdom, a pension intended to help especially low-paid people to supplement their state pension, administered by the private financial sector but regulated by government

stakeout /stáyk owt/ *n US* (*informal*) **1** hidden surveillance of somebody or something, especially by the police **2** the place from which surveillance is carried out, especially by the police

stakes /stayks/ (*plural* **stakes**) *n* a horse race in which a prize is offered, especially a sum of money made up of contributions from owners of horses that take part (*+ singular verb*)

Stakhanovite /stə kánnə vīt/ *n* a worker in the former Soviet Union who received a reward for increasing production ■ *adj* rewarding people who work very hard, especially in the former Soviet Union [Mid-20C. After Aleksei Grigorevich *Stakhanov* (1906–77), Soviet mine worker.]

stalactite /stállək tīt/ *n* a conical hanging pillar in a limestone cave that has gradually built up as a deposit from ground water seeping through the cave's roof. ◊ **stalagmite** [Late 17C. Via modern Latin *stalactites* < Greek *stalaktos* 'dripping' < *stalak-*, stem of *stalassein* 'drip'.] —**stalactitic** /stálləkˈ títtik/ *adj* —**stalactitically** *adv*

stalag /stálag/ *n* a German prisoner of war camp in World War II for officers or lower ranks [Mid-20C. < German, contraction of *Stammlager* 'main camp'.]

stalagmite /stálləg mīt/ *n* a conical pillar in a limestone cave that is gradually built upwards from the floor as a deposit from ground water seeping through and dripping from the cave's roof. ◊ **stalactite** [Late 17C. Via modern Latin *stalagmites* < Greek *stalagmos* 'something dropped' < *stalak-*, stem of *stalassein* 'drip'.] —**stalagmitic** /stálləg míttik/ *adj* —**stalagmitically** *adv*

stale[1] /stayl/ *adj* (**staler, stalest**) **1 KEPT TOO LONG** no longer fresh **2 LOW IN OXYGEN** stagnant and low in oxygen owing to lack of circulation or ventilation **3 FREQUENTLY HEARD AND BORING** heard too often before and no longer interesting or amusing **4 OUT OF CONDITION** ineffective, enervated, or bored because of doing too much of the same thing **5 LEGALLY EXPIRED** having lost legal force through lack of use or elapse of time **6 NOT NEGOTIABLE BECAUSE OF DELAY** describes financial statements or cheques that are not negotiable by a bank because a time limit has expired ■ *vti* (**stales, staling, staled**) **1 LOSE FRESHNESS** to become, or make something become, stale **2 LOSE EFFECTIVENESS** to lose effectiveness or energy **3 BECOME BORING** to become dull and uninteresting over time [13C. < Old French *estale* 'settled', literally 'standing still' < *estal* 'standing place' < Germanic (see STALL[1]).]

stale[2] /stayl/ *vi* (**stales, staling, staled**) to urinate (*refers to livestock*) ■ *n* the urine of livestock, especially horses and cattle [14C. < ?]

stalemate /stáyl mayt/ *n* **1 SITUATION WITH NO POTENTIAL WINNERS** a situation in a contest in which neither side can take any further worthwhile action **2 CHESS SITUATION WITH NO WINNER** a situation in chess in which no winner is possible because neither player can move a piece without placing the king in check ■ *vt* (**-mates, -mating, -mated**) **PUT INTO STALEMATE** to put somebody or something into a stalemate (*often passive*) [Mid-18C. < Anglo-Norman *estale* 'fixed position' (< Old French *estaler* 'take up a position' < *estal*; see STALE[1]) + MATE[2].]

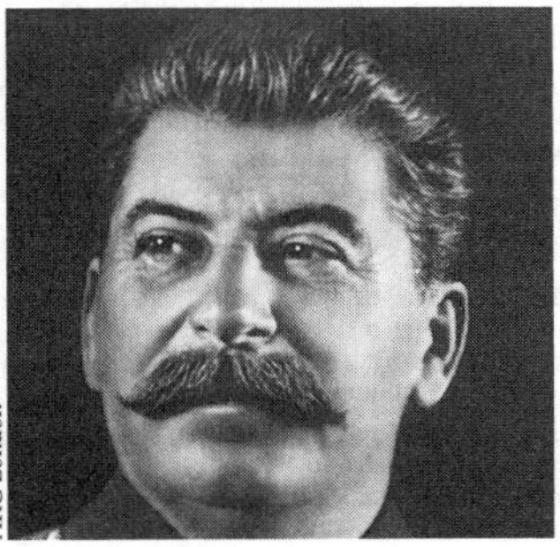

AKG London

Joseph Stalin

Stalin /staálin/, **Joseph** (1879–1953) Georgian-born Soviet statesman. Born **Iosif Vissarionovich Dzhugashvili**

Stalingrad /staálin grad/ former name for **Volgograd**

Stalinism /staálinizəm/ *n* the political principles and economic policies developed by Joseph Stalin from Marxist-Leninist thought, which included centralized autocratic rule and total suppression of dissent —**Stalinist** *n, adj*

Stalin Peak /staálin-/ former name for **Ismail Samani Peak**

stalk[1] /stawk/ *n* **1 STEM OF PLANT** the main stem or axis of a plant that is fleshy rather than woody **2 SUPPORTING PART OF PLANT** a supporting part of a plant, e.g. a leaf stem (**petiole**) or flower stalk (**pedicel**) **3 SLENDER SUPPORTING PART** a thin cylindrical part of something that acts as a support, e.g. of a glass **4 SLENDER STRUCTURAL PART OF ANIMAL** a slender supporting structure for an organ or body of an animal [14C. Probably alteration of obsolete *stale* 'stile of a ladder, handle' < Old English *stalu* 'upright piece'.] —**stalked** *adj* —**stalkless** *adj*

stalk[2] /stawk/ *v* **1** *vt* **FOLLOW STEALTHILY** to follow or try to get close to a person or animal unobtrusively **2** *vi* **WALK STIFFLY AND ANGRILY** to walk in a stiff, angry, or proud way **3** *vt* **PROCEED STEADILY AND MALEVOLENTLY** to proceed in a steady and sinister way **4** *vt* **PERSISTENTLY HARASS** to harass somebody by persistent and inappropriate attention, e.g. by constantly following, telephoning, or writing to him or her ■ *n* **1 STEALTHY PURSUIT** a stealthy pursuit or hunt of something **2 STIFF WALK** a stiff, angry, or proud walk [Old English (assumed) *stealcian* < Germanic, 'to steal'] —**stalkable** *adj* —**stalker** *n*

stalking /stáwking/ *n* **1** the act or process of stealthily following or trying to approach somebody or something **2** the crime of harassing somebody with persistent and inappropriate attention —**stalkingly** *adv*

stalking horse *n* **1 MEANS TO DISGUISE AN OBJECTIVE** something used as a means of disguising a real objective **2 DECEPTIVE CANDIDATE FOR ELECTION** a candidate who is in an election only to conceal the potential candidacy of somebody else, to divide the opposition, or to determine how strong the opposition is **3 FAKE HORSE** a horse or figure of a horse that is used as cover in the hunting of game

stalky /stáwki/ (**-ier, -iest**) *adj* **1** long or tall and thin like a stalk **2** with stalks, especially a lot of stalks —**stalkily** *adv* —**stalkiness** *n*

stall[1] /stawl/ *n* **1 SMALL AREA SELLING OR DISPENSING GOODS** a booth, table, counter, or compartment set up to display goods for sale or information to give out **2 COMPARTMENT FOR A LARGE ANIMAL** a compartment in a building where a single large animal lives or is fed or milked **3 SITUATION IN WHICH ENGINE HALTS** a situation in which an engine stops abruptly because of insufficient fuel, being braked too suddenly, or mechanical failure **4 SMALL ROOM** a very small room, or partitioned area in a room, for a shower or toilet **5 SUDDEN DIVE BY AN AIRCRAFT** a situation in which an aircraft suddenly dives because the airflow is so obstructed that lift is lost **6 SEAT IN A CHURCH** a pew or enclosed seat in a church **7 SHEATH FOR FINGER** a protective covering for a finger or thumb **8 COMPARTMENT OF STARTING GATE** a partitioned compartment at the starting gate of a racecourse that holds a horse before the start of a race ■ **stalls** *npl* **SEATS CLOSEST TO STAGE** the seats in a theatre or cinema on the ground floor nearest the stage or screen ■ *v* **1** *vti* **STOP OR MAKE AN ENGINE STOP** to stop working suddenly, or make an engine do this **2** *vti* **PLUNGE OR CAUSE TO PLUNGE** to go into a sudden dive, or cause a sudden dive in an aircraft **3** *vt* **PUT LARGE ANIMAL INTO STALL** to put a large animal into a compartment where it will live or be fed or milked **4** *vti US* **BECOME STUCK** to cause something to get stuck, or become immovable ○ *stalled the project* ○ *a project that stalled* [Old English *steall* 'standing place' < Germanic]

stall[2] /stawl/ *vti* to delay or obstruct somebody, or to use delaying tactics ■ *n* a pretext or ruse used to delay or deceive somebody [Early 19C. Alteration of obsolete *stale* 'decoy, pickpocket's accomplice' < Anglo-Norman *estale* 'something set up'.]

stall-feed *vt* to keep an animal in a stall while fattening it for slaughter

stallholder /stáwl hōldər/ *n* a person who has a stall at a market or fair

stalling angle *n* the angle relative to the horizontal at which the flow of air around an aerofoil changes abruptly, resulting in significant changes in the lift and drag of an aircraft

stallion /stályən/ *n* **1** an uncastrated adult male horse, especially one kept for breeding. ◊ **gelding 2** a man with supposed great sexual prowess (*informal*) [14C. < Anglo-Norman *estaloun*.]

Stallone /stə lṓn, -lṓni/, **Sylvester** (*b.* 1946) US actor

stalwart /stáwlwərt/ *adj* **1 DEPENDABLE** dependable and loyal **2 STRONG** sturdy and strong ■ *n* **HARD-WORKING LOYAL SUPPORTER** a faithful, dependable, and hard-working supporter of somebody or something ○ *phones manned by party stalwarts* [15C. Variant of *stealwurthe* < Old English *stǣlwierþe* 'good', literally 'having a worthy foundation' < *staþol* 'foundation' (see STADDLE) + *weorþ* (see WORTH).] —**stalwartly** *adv* —**stalwartness** *n*

stamen /stáy men, -mən/ (*plural* **-mens** *or* **-mina** /stámminə/) *n* the male reproductive organ of a flower, typically consisting of a stalk (**filament**) bearing a pollen-producing anther at its tip [Mid-17C. < Latin, 'thread in the warp of a loom'.] —**staminal** /stámmin'l/ *adj* —**staminiferous** /stámmi níffərəss/ *adj*

Stamford /stámfərd/ **1** market town in E England. Population: 17,492 (1991). **2** city in SW Connecticut. Population: 110,689 (1998 estimate).

Stamford Bridge village near York, N England. Nearby King Harold II defeated an invasion by his brother Tostig and King Harald Hardraada of Norway in 1066. Population: 3,099 (1991).

stamina /stámminə/ *n* enduring physical or mental energy and strength that allows somebody to do something for a long time [Early 18C. < Latin, plural of *stamen* 'thread in woven cloth' (see STAMEN).] —**staminal** *adj*

staminate /stámminət/ *adj* describes plants that have stamens, especially flowers with stamens but without female parts (**carpels**)

staminode /stámmi nōd/, **staminodium** /stámmi nṓdi əm/ (*plural* **-a** /-di ə/) *n* a sterile or vestigial stamen. It forms a conspicuous part of some flowers, e.g. in the iris. [Early 19C. < modern Latin *staminodium* < *stamen* 'thread' (see STAMEN).]

stammel /stámm'l/ *n* **1** a coarse woollen cloth, usually red. Use: in medieval times, undergarments. **2** a bright red colour, like that of stammel cloth [Mid-16C. Alteration of earlier *stamin*, via Old French *estamine* < Latin *stamineus* 'consisting of threads' < *stamen* 'thread'.] —**stammel** *adj*

stammer /stámmər/ *vti* to speak, or say something, with many quick hesitations and repeated consonants or syllables because of a speech condition or a strong emotion ■ *n* a speech condition that makes somebody speak with involuntary hesitations and repetition of consonants or syllables [Old English *stamerian* < Germanic, 'halt, stutter'] —**stammerer** *n*

stamp /stamp/ *n* **1 GUMMED PAPER PAYING FOR POSTAGE** a small piece of gummed paper that is stuck on an envelope or parcel to show that postage has been paid **2 CANCELLATION ACROSS A POSTAGE STAMP** a mark put across a postage stamp on an envelope or parcel to show that the stamp has been used **3 SMALL BLOCK FOR PRINTING DESIGN** a small block with a raised design or lettering that can be printed onto paper by inking the block and pressing it to the paper **4 DESIGN PRINTED ONTO PAPER WITH A STAMP** a design printed onto paper using a stamp in order to show that a document has been read, cancelled, or officially approved **5 GUMMED PAPER AS AN OFFICIAL MARK** a piece of printed gummed paper fixed to a document as an official sign of something, e.g. approval or validity **6 CHARACTERISTIC OF** a characteristic or distinguishing sign or impression **7 TYPE OR KIND** a class or type of something **8 WAY OF PAYING FOR** a piece of paper that can be purchased as a way of redeeming part or all of the amount charged for goods or a service. ◊ **trading stamp 9 NATIONAL INSURANCE CONTRIBUTION** a contribution to national insurance, recorded formerly by means of a stamp on an official card (*informal*) **10 ACT OF BANGING DOWN A FOOT** the action of bringing a foot down forcefully on a surface **11 MACHINE FOR CRUSHING ROCKS AND ORES** a machine that crushes rocks and ores by a weight being lifted and dropped ■ *v* **1** *vt* **PUT A STAMP ON A DOCUMENT** to press a stamp onto a document leaving a design or lettering on it in order to show that it has been seen, dated, cancelled, or officially approved **2** *vti* **BANG A FOOT DOWN FORCIBLY** to bring a foot down forcefully on a surface **3** *vt* **STICK A POSTAGE STAMP ON SOMETHING** to stick a stamp on an envelope or parcel **4** *vi* **WALK FORCEFULLY** to walk by taking short forceful steps **5** *vt* **HAVE A LASTING EFFECT ON SOMEBODY** to have a lasting effect or influence on somebody **6** *vt* **SUPPRESS SOMETHING OR SOMEBODY** to suppress or eradicate something or somebody ○ *He stamped on any suggestion he should resign.* **7** *vt* **CRUSH ROCKS** to crush or pound rocks and ores [12C. Probably < assumed Old English *stampian* 'pound' < Germanic.] —**stampable** *adj* —**stamped** *adj*

stamp out *vt* **1 ERADICATE** to put an end to something **2 EXTINGUISH** to extinguish something by stamping on it with the feet **3 CUT SOMETHING OUT USING A SHARP TOOL** to cut out a shape or object by pressing a sharp-edged machine or tool onto a material

Stamp Act *n* a law passed in the British parliament in 1765 introducing a tax on legal documents, commercial contracts, licences, publications, and playing cards in the North American colonies

stamp collecting *n* the collecting of postage stamps as a hobby or investment. ◊ **philately** —**stamp collector** *n*

stamp duty *n* a duty applied to some legal documents

stampede /stam peéd/ *n* **1 HEADLONG RUSH OF ANIMALS** an uncontrolled headlong rush of frightened animals **2 HEADLONG SURGE OF CROWD** an uncontrolled surging rush of a crowd of people **3 SUDDEN RUSH OF PEOPLE** a sudden rush of many people all doing or wanting to do something at the same time ○ *There was a stampede to take advantage of the low prices.* **4** *US, Can* **FESTIVAL INCLUDING A RODEO** a celebration in the W United States and especially in Canada, usually held annually, that includes a rodeo along with contests, exhibitions, dancing, and entertainment ■ *v* (**-pedes, -peding, -peded**) **1** *vti* **RUSH FORWARDS IN FRIGHTENED SURGE** to rush forwards in a frightened headlong surge, or make animals or people surge forward **2** *vt* **FORCE SOMEBODY INTO DOING SOMETHING** to force somebody to do something before he or she is ready or has properly thought about it [Early 19C. < Mexican Spanish *estampida* < Spanish, 'uproar'.] —**stampeder** *n*

stamper /stámpər/ *n* **1 SOMEBODY OR SOMETHING THAT STAMPS** a person or device used for stamping **2 MACHINE FOR STAMPING** a tool or machine that stamps something, especially ore being pulverized **3 MOULD FOR DISC RECORDINGS** a mould from which disc recordings are pressed

stamping ground *n* a place where somebody or a group of people is habitually found (*informal*)

stamp mill *n* a machine in which ores and rocks are finely crushed, usually operated by hydraulic power, or a building housing one or more such machines

stance /stanss, staanss/ *n* **1 ATTITUDE** an attitude or view that somebody takes about something **2 WAY OF STANDING** the way a person or an animal stands **3 POSITION OF WHEELS** the position of a vehicle's wheels in relation to its bodywork ○ *The newer model has a wider stance and a taller cab.* **4 POSITION OF PLAYER** the position in which a player holds the body in attempting to hit a ball, e.g. in cricket or golf **5 PLACE FOR PITCHING AND BELAYING** a place where a mountain climber can pitch and belay **6** *Scotland* **TRANSPORT WAITING PLACE** a place where buses or taxis wait for passengers [Mid-16C. Via French, 'position' < Italian *stanza* (see STANZA).]

stanch *vt* = **staunch**[1]

stanchion /staánchən/ *n* **1 UPRIGHT SUPPORTING POLE** a vertical pole, bar, or beam used to support something **2 FRAME FOR CONFINING A COW** an upright frame in which the neck of a cow is loosely fitted, usually to confine the cow for milking ■ *vt* **SUPPORT SOMETHING WITH A POLE** to support something using a vertical pole, bar, or beam [15C. < Old French *estanchon* < *estance* 'prop, support'.]

stand /stand/ *v* (**stands, standing, stood** /stŏŏd/, **stood**) **1** *vti* **BE OR SET UPRIGHT** to be in an upright position, or put something in an upright position ○ *I was standing behind him.* ○ *Stand the box in the corner.* **2** *vi* **GET UP ON FEET** to get up into an upright position from a sitting or lying position ○ *The newborn foal tried to stand but only collapsed again.* **3** *vi* **BE IN PARTICULAR PLACE** to be situated or positioned in a particular place ○ *The castle stands on a headland.* **4** *vi* **MEASURE IN HEIGHT** to be of a particular height when upright ○ *He stood six feet tall.* **5** *vi* **BE IN PARTICULAR STATE** to be in a particular condition or state ○ *The old place stands in need of a few repairs.* ○ *The document can't be published as it stands.* **6** *vi* **REMAIN MOTIONLESS** to remain in a particular place without moving or being used ○ *The car stood outside the office all morning.* **7** *vi* **REMAIN VALID** to continue to be in effect or existence ○ *Her world record still stands.* **8** *vi* **STOP** to come to a halt ○ *I had to stand and catch my breath.* **9** *vi* **GATHER WITHOUT FLOWING AWAY** to gather somewhere and not flow away ○ *rainwater standing in pools* **10** *vi* **BE AT PARTICULAR POINT** to be at a particular point while subject to change or fluctuation ○ *The balance of the account stands at four hundred pounds.* **11** *vt* **TOLERATE** to accept or put up with something ○ *He can't stand being kept waiting.* **12** *vt* **UNDERGO WITHOUT HARM** to resist or bear something without being harmed or damaged ○ *The mechanism is too delicate to stand rough handling.* **13** *vt* **SUBMIT TO** to submit or be subjected to something ○ *I am prepared to stand trial.* **14** *vi* **SEEK ELECTION** to enter an election as a candidate ○ *She decided not to stand at the next election.* **15** *vi* **FIGHT** to fight resolutely or give battle, often after having been in retreat ○ *The general was convinced the enemy would not stand if attacked.* **16** *vt* **BUY SOMETHING FOR SOMEBODY** to pay for something, e.g. a drink, for somebody else to have ○ *My uncle offered to stand dinner for all of us.* **17** *vt* **BENEFIT FROM** to benefit from something, or be no worse for something ○ *I could stand to lose a few more pounds.* ■ *n* **1 ACT OF STANDING** the act or an example of standing ○ *a long stand in the airport* **2 ATTITUDE** an opinion that somebody has or an attitude that somebody adopts on a particular subject ○ *Management took a tough stand on absenteeism.* **3 SUPPORTING STRUCTURE** a framework or structure on which something is supported ○ *a music stand* **4 PIECE OF FURNITURE** a piece of furniture on which clothes or accessories are hung or supported (*often in combination*) ○ *an umbrella stand* ○ *a hat stand* **5 PLACE FOR SPECTATORS** a large seating area for spectators in a sports stadium ○ *a ticket for the North stand* **6 STATIONARY CONDITION** a state of having stopped or being stationary ○ *The runaway vehicle came to a stand in a field.* **7 PLACE WHERE SOMETHING IS SOLD** a booth or stall where something is sold or given out (*often in combination*) ○ *a refreshment stand* **8 EXHIBITION AREA** one of several places in an exhibition where something is displayed **9 AREA OF GROWING THINGS** a group of several plants, especially trees, growing together in one place ○ *a stand of trees* **10 HALT TO FIGHT** a halt made, especially by a force that has been retreating, to give battle ○ *Custer's last stand* **11** *US* **PLACE FOR WAITING VEHICLES** a place where vehicles, especially taxis, wait to pick up passengers (*usually in combination*) ○ *a taxi stand* **12 STOP FOR PERFORMANCE** a halt made to give a performance during a tour by a performer or theatrical company ○ *a three-week stand out of town* **13 TIME AT WICKET** a period at a wicket involving two batsmen during which both bat and are not out, or the score they make [Old English *standan* < Indo-European] —**standee** /stan deé/ *n* ◇ **stand or fall by something** to succeed or fail depending on particular circumstances

stand by *vi* **1 REMAIN READY** to wait in a state of readiness to act if required ○ *Stand by for further orders.* **2 BE PRESENT WITHOUT ACTION** to be present while something is happening but play no part in it ○ *I'm not prepared to stand by and let this go on.* **3 SUPPORT** to support or remain faithful to somebody ○ *Her friends all stood by her.* **4 ADHERE TO** to continue to assert or believe in something ○ *I stand by what I said yesterday.*

stand down *v* **1** *vi* **RESIGN** to resign from office or withdraw from a contest **2** *vi* **END TESTIMONY** to leave a witness box after having been questioned **3** *vti* **END DUTY** to end somebody's period of duty, or to go off duty, especially military duty **4** *vti* **GO OFF ALERT** to go off alert or be taken off alert or out of a combat zone

stand for *vt* **1 MEAN** to mean or represent something else **2 BELIEVE IN** to believe in something strongly and fight for it ○ *To agree with this would go against everything I stand for.* **3 BECOME A CANDIDATE FOR** to enter an election as a candidate for a particular office **4 PUT UP WITH** to tolerate or put up with something ○ *She won't stand for any nonsense.* **5 HEAD FOR A PLACE** to set a course for a particular destination ○ *The fleet stood for home.*

stand in *vi* to take the place of somebody or something else as a substitute ○ *I'm looking for someone to stand in for me next week.*

stand off *v* **1** *vti* **KEEP AWAY** to keep at a distance from something, or to make somebody or something stay at a distance **2** *vti* **SAIL AWAY** to sail a vessel away from something such as a shore **3** *vt* **SUSPEND FROM WORK** to suspend somebody from work, usually temporarily

stand on *v* **1** *vt* to insist on something or see it as being important ○ *We don't stand on ceremony in this house.* **2** *vi* to continue sailing on a particular course

stand out *vi* **1 BE CONSPICUOUS** to be conspicuous or prominent **2 STICK OUT** to project or protrude from something **3 REFUSE TO ACCEPT** to refuse to accept or comply with something, especially after others have done so

stand to *vti* to take up position in readiness for military action, or to make somebody do this

stand up *v* **1** *vti* to rise to an upright position, or make something do this **2** *vi* to be seen as still valid or right despite being closely examined or criticized ○ *I don't think her testimony will stand up in court.*

stand up for *vi* to defend or act to protect the interests of somebody

stand up to *vi* **1** to resist or refuse to be cowed by somebody ○ *He'll back down if you stand up to him.* **2** to undergo something that is potentially damaging without being badly affected ○ *These cars won't stand up to being driven on rough terrain.*

stand up with *vi US* to act as best man or maid of honour for somebody who is getting married

ϟ **stand-alone** *adj* able to operate as a self-contained unit independently of a computer network or system

standard /stándərd/ *n* **1 LEVEL OF QUALITY OR EXCELLENCE** the level of quality or excellence attained by somebody or something ○ *I hadn't expected work of such a high standard from trainees.* **2 LEVEL OF QUALITY ACCEPTED AS NORM** a level of quality or excellence that is accepted as the norm or by which actual attainments are judged (*often plural*) ○ *By present-day standards the sound quality of this recording is very poor.* **3 FLAG** a flag with a distinctive design that is the emblem of, and often a focus of loyalty to, a particular nation, person, or group **4 DEVICE USED AS BATTLE RALLYING POINT** a flag or other symbolic device attached to a pole and used as a rallying point for troops in battle **5 LONG TAPERING FLAG** a long tapering flag ending in two points and with heraldic devices on it, used in heraldry as an emblem of a person or group **6 AUTHORIZED MODEL OF UNIT OF MEASUREMENT** an authorized model used to define a unit of measurement **7 PROPORTION OF METAL IN COIN** the proportion of gold or silver and of nonprecious metal that a coin is legally required to contain **8 COMMODITY MONEY HAS VALUE BASED ON** the commodity or commodities on which the value of a currency or monetary system is based **9 UPRIGHT POLE OR POST** an upright pole or post, usually serving as a support for something **10 PLANT WITH STRAIGHT BARE STEM** a plant, especially a fruit tree or rose, trained so that its leaves and flowers grow at the top of a straight bare stem **11 ITEM IN USUAL REPERTOIRE** something, especially a song or other piece of music, that is very popular or is performed as part of the usual repertoire of a performer or performers ○ *played all the old standards* **12 LARGE UPPER PETAL OF PEA** the large upper petal in the flowers of plants of the pea family ■ *adj* **NORMAL** constituting or not differing from the norm for a particular thing ○ *This clause is absolutely standard in a contract of this type* ■ **standards** *npl* **PRINCIPLES** principles or values that govern a persons behaviour ■ *adj* **1 WIDELY USED AND RESPECTED** very widely used and generally regarded as authoritative ○ *the standard text in thermodynamics* **2 GRAMMATICALLY CORRECT** regarded as correct or acceptable by the majority of educated speakers of or authorities on a language **3 TRAINED TO GROW WITH STRAIGHT STEM** trained in such a way that the leaves and flowers grow at the top of a straight bare stem [12C. Via Anglo-Norman *estaundart* 'flag to which troops rally' < Old French *estandart.*] —**standardly** *adv*

standard assessment task *n* a test used to assess the progress of children in a core subject of the UK national curriculum

standard atmosphere *n* MEASURE = **atmosphere** *n.* **6**

standard-bearer *n* **1** the bearer of a standard or flag, especially for a military unit **2** a leader or prominent and inspiring representative of a movement, cause, or party

Standardbred /stándərd bred/, **standard-bred** *n* a horse belonging to a North American breed specially bred for speed and stamina in harness races

standard candle *n* MEASURE = **candela**

standard cell *n* an electric cell that produces a constant known voltage and can be used to calibrate voltage-measuring equipment

standard cost *n* the budgeted expenditure of a regular manufacturing process against which the actual cost is measured

standard deviation *n* a statistical measure of the amount by which a set of values differs from the arithmetical mean, equal to the square root of the mean of the differences' squares

standard electrode potential *n* the voltage developed by an electrode of a particular element placed in a solution of the element's ions, measured against that of hydrogen under standardized conditions

Standard English *n* the form of the English language used by educated speakers and regarded as representing correct usage in grammar, spelling, vocabulary, and punctuation

standard error *n* the standard deviation of the sample in a frequency distribution divided by the square root of the number of values in the sample

standard gauge *n* the gauge used for most public railway systems worldwide, the distance between the rails being 143.5 cm/4 ft $8\frac{1}{2}$ in

ϟ **Standard Generalized Markup Language** *n* full form of **SGML**

Standard Grade *n* **1** the lower-level public examination for the Scottish Certificate of Education in Scotland, usually taken by school students at the age of 15 or 16 **2** a subject studied, an examination taken, or a pass achieved at Standard Grade

standardize /stándər dīz/ (**-izes, -izing, -ized**), **standardise** (**-ises, -ising, -ised**) *v* **1** *vti* to remove variations and irregularities and make all types or examples of something the same or bring them into conformity with one another **2** *vt* to assess something or determine its properties by comparing it with a standard —**standardization** /stándər dī záysh'n/ *n* —**standardizer** *n*

standard lamp *n* a tall lamp with a base that stands on the floor. US term **floor lamp**

standard of living *n* the level of material comfort enjoyed by a person, group, or society

standard operating procedure *n* a procedure that is usually followed when carrying out a particular operation or dealing with a particular situation

Standards Australia *n* in Australia, a government-funded independent organization that sets, monitors, and certifies standards in a wide range of fields such as building and manufacturing

standard state *n* the pure form of a chemical substance that is stable at a given pressure and temperature

standard time *n* a system of measuring time in relation to the natural day usually based on the mean solar time at the central meridian of a particular time zone

stand-by *n* **1 PERSON OR THING READILY AVAILABLE** somebody or something that can always be relied on to be available and useful, especially if needed as a substitute or in an emergency **2 UNRESERVED TICKET OR PASSENGER WITHOUT RESERVATION** an unreserved ticket or a passenger having no prior reservation on a mode of public transport such as an airline ■ *adj* **1 RESERVE** able to be used as a replacement **2 UNRESERVED AND SUBJECT TO AVAILABILITY** made available, usually at a lower price, shortly before the departure of a flight when there are seats remaining unsold, or using a ticket made available in this way ■ *adv* **ON STAND-BY BASIS** on the basis of stand-by ○ *flew standby from Washington to Amsterdam* ◇ **on stand-by** available for use or service if necessary

stand-down *n* a return to normal status after being on alert, or the withdrawal of a military presence ○ *After three weeks on alert in the riot-torn city the UN forces were finally put on stand-down.*

stand-in *n* **1** somebody or something that acts as a temporary replacement **2** a replacement for an actor in a film, e.g. during preparatory or dangerous action —**stand-in** *adj*

standing /stánding/ *n* **1 STATUS AND REPUTATION** somebody's reputation or position, e.g., in society or business ○ *a person of some standing in computer electronics* **2 DURATION** the period over which something has been in existence ■ *adj* **1 UPRIGHT** performed while standing rather than sitting or moving **2 PERMANENT** remaining permanently in existence or in force **3 NOT FLOWING** not flowing, or containing water that cannot flow or run away **4 NOT CUT DOWN** growing where planted, having not been cut down

standing army *n* a permanent professional military force maintained by a country in times of peace as well as war

standing committee *n* a committee that remains in existence permanently in order to deal with a particular issue

standing crop *n* the total mass of living things of all kinds or of one particular kind found in a particular area at a particular time

standing order *n* **1** an instruction given by an account holder to a bank to pay a specified sum of money at specified intervals to a specified person or account **2** an order or rule, especially one governing military or parliamentary procedures, that remains in force on all relevant occasions until it is specifically revoked

standing rigging *n* the wires and ropes holding the masts and spars of a sailing ship that are more or less permanently fixed in place

standing room *n* space where people can only stand, not sit

standing stone *n* a large stone set upright in the ground in prehistoric times, singly or as part of a larger structure

standing wave *n* a stationary wave characterized by points of zero vibration and points of maximum vibration, occurring when two waves of equal frequency and intensity travelling in opposite directions combine [Because the points of minimum and maximum vibration remain stationary]

standoff /stánd of/ *n* **1** a situation in which no result or conclusion can be reached because the two sides in a contest or dispute are equally matched or are equally intransigent **2** *US* a draw or tie

stand-off half, stand-off *n* in rugby, a player who plays behind the forwards and the scrum half, provides a link between them and the three-quarter backs, and often has control of the team's tactics

standoff insulator *n* an insulator that supports an electrical conductor and keeps it at a distance from other conducting elements

standoffish /stand óffish/ *adj* reluctant to show friendship or enter into conversation with other people —**standoffishly** *adv* —**standoffishness** *n*

standoff missile *n* a guided missile that can be fired from an aircraft at a sufficient distance from its target to be out of range of enemy defences

stand oil *n* a thick drying oil used in oil enamel paints, made by heating linseed or another oil to a high temperature [Translation of German *Standöl*; it was formerly prepared by allowing linseed oil to stand]

standout /stánd owt/ *n US* somebody or something that is especially prominent or outstanding (*informal*)

standpipe /stánd pīp/ *n* **1** a vertical pipe with a tap on the top, used to enable householders to draw water from a water main in the street when the normal supply is disrupted **2** a vertical, open-ended pipe attached to a pipeline to act as a pressure regulator, ensuring that the pressure head at that point cannot exceed the length of the pipe

standpoint /stánd poynt/ *n* the particular way an individual or a group thinks about or is affected by an event or an issue, usually as opposed to the way others view the same thing ○ *From the ecological standpoint, this is an utter disaster.*

standstill /stánd stil/ *n* a situation in which all movement or activity ceases and further movement or activity is prevented ○ *Traffic is at a standstill.*

standstill agreement *n* an agreement that things should remain as they are, especially one between a creditor country and a debtor country that needs extra time to repay its debt

stand-to *n* the act of taking up positions ready for action

standup /stánd up/, **stand-up** *adj* **1 ERECT** standing erect and not folded down **2 AT WHICH PEOPLE STAND** where or at which people stand, especially to eat or drink ○ *A large stand-up buffet was laid out for the reception.* **3 NOISY AND INTENSE** intense and involving a lot of noise and sometimes violence **4 INVOLVING SOLO PERFORMANCE BY COMEDIAN** involving a performance by a comedian standing alone on stage telling jokes or stories to an audience **5** *US* **TRUSTWORTHY** showing the qualities of honesty, loyalty, and dependability (*informal*) ■ *n* **1 STANDUP COMEDY** comedy in which the performer stands alone on stage telling jokes or stories to an audience **2** an often life-size freestanding cardboard figure of a film or television character, used for promotional purposes

Stanford /stánfərd/, **Sir Charles Villiers** (1852–1924) British composer and teacher

Stanford-Binet test /stánfərd bi náy-/ *n* an intelligence test commonly used with children in the United States [Early 20C. After *Stanford* University, California, + Alfred *Binet*, (1857–1911), French psychologist.]

stanhope /stán hōp/ *n* a light open horse-drawn carriage with a single seat and two or four wheels [Early 19C. After Fitzroy H. R. *Stanhope* (1787–1864), English clergyman for whom one was first made.]

Stanislavsky /stánni slávski/, **Stanislavski, Konstantin Sergeyevich Alexeyev** (1863–1938) Russian actor and theatre director —**Stanislavskian** *adj*

Stanislavsky method *n* THEATRE = **Method**

stank past tense of **stink**

Stanley[1] /stánli/ town in N England. Population: 18,905 (1991).

Stanley[2] capital of the Falkland Islands, on East Falkland Island. Population: 1,232 (1986).

Stanley, Sir H. M. (1841–1904) British journalist and explorer. Full name **Sir Henry Morton Stanley**. Born **John Rowlands**

Stanley knife *tdmk* a trademark for a type of knife that is very sharp and has a retractable blade

Stanley Pool former name for **Malebo Pool**

stann- *prefix* tin ○ *stanniferous*

Stannaries /stánnəriz/ *npl* a former tin-mining district in the English counties of Devon and Cornwall

stannary /stánnəri/ (*plural* **-naries**) *n* a district with tin mines [15C. Via medieval Latin *stannaria* 'stannaries' < late Latin *stannum* 'tin'.]

stannic /stánnik/ *adj* relating to or containing tin, especially with a valency of four [Late 18C. < late Latin *stannum* 'tin'.]

stannic sulphide *n* a yellow or gold-coloured solid compound of sulphur and tin. Use: pigment.

stanniferous /sta níffərəss/ *adj* containing or yielding tin [Early 19C. < obsolete English *stannum* 'tin'.]

stannite /stánnīt/ *n* a grey metallic oxide mineral containing copper, iron and tin. Use: source of tin. [Mid-19C. < late Latin *stannum* 'tin'.]

stannous /stánnəss/ *adj* relating to or containing, especially with a valency of two [Mid-19C. < late Latin *stannum* 'tin'.]

stannous fluoride *n* SnF_2 a white crystalline powder with a bitter salty taste. Use: fluoride toothpaste.

Stansted /stán sted/ village in SE England, home to London's third airport. Population: 4,943 (1991).

Stanton /stántən/, **Elizabeth Cady** (1815–1902) US social reformer

stanza /stánzə/ *n* a number of lines of verse forming a separate unit within a poem [Late 16C. Via Italian < assumed Vulgar Latin *stantia* 'a standing, stopping place' < Latin *stare* 'stand'.] —**stanzaic** /stan záy ik/ *adj*

stapedectomy /stáypi déktəmi/ (*plural* **-mies**) *n* surgical removal of the stapes of the ear [Late 19C. < modern Latin *staped-*, stem of *stapes* (see STAPES).]

stapedes plural of **stapes**

stapelia /stə peéli ə/ (*plural* **-as** *or* **-a**) *n* plant similar to the cactus, with thick fleshy four-angled stems and no leaves. Flowers: large, mottled, foul-smelling. Native to: Africa. Genus: *Stapelia*. [Late 18C. < modern Latin, after Jan Bode van *Stapel*, (died 1636), Dutch botanist.]

stapes /stáy peez/ (*plural* **-pes** *or* **-pedes** /-peédeez/) *n* a small stirrup-shaped bone in the middle ear of mammals, the innermost of the three small bones that transmit vibration to the inner ear. ◊ **incus** *n.*, **malleus** [Mid-17C. Via modern Latin < medieval Latin, 'stirrup'.] —**stapedial** /stə peédi əl/ *adj*

staph /staf/ *n* a staphylococcus (*informal*) [Early 20C. Shortening.]

staphylococcus /stáffilə kókəss/ (*plural* **-ci** /-kók sī/) *n* a bacterium that typically occurs in clusters resembling grapes, normally inhabits the skin and mucous membranes, and may cause disease. Genus: *Staphylococcus*. [Late 19C. Via modern Latin < Greek *staphulē* 'bunch of grapes' + *kokkos* 'berry'.] —**staphylococcal** *adj* —**staphylococcic** /-kóksik/ *adj*

staple[1] /stáyp'l/ *n* **1 BENT WIRE TO FASTEN PAPERS** a small thin piece of metal wire bent into the shape of a flattened U with square corners, used to fasten things together, especially sheets of paper **2 U-SHAPED FASTENER FOR WOOD OR MASONRY** a small U-shaped piece of strong metal wire with two sharp points, usually driven into a surface to hold something such as a bolt or cable in place ■ *vt* (**-ples, -pling, -pled**) **FASTEN WITH STAPLES** to fasten something to something else or in position with staples [Old English *stapol* 'post, pillar' < Germanic]

staple[2] /stáyp'l/ *n* **1 MOST IMPORTANT ARTICLE OF TRADE** the commodity or product that is most important to the trade of a country, region, or organization **2 BASIC INGREDIENT OF DIET** a food that forms the basis of the diet of the people of a particular country or region or of a particular animal **3 PRINCIPAL OR RECURRING INGREDIENT** a principal or continually recurring ingredient or feature of something ○ *I'd hardly describe opera as a staple of the entertainment offered in this theatre.* **4 WOOL, COTTON, OR FLAX FIBRE** the fibre of wool, cotton, or flax graded according to its length and fineness ■ *adj* **BASIC AND MOST IMPORTANT** used or depended on as the basic and most important element of something, especially diet or trade ■ *vt* (**-ples, -pling, -pled**) **GRADE FIBRES** to grade the fibres of wool, cotton, or flax according to their length and fineness [14C. Via Old French *estaple* < Middle Low German, Middle Dutch *stapel* 'shop; pillar' < Germanic.]

staple gun *n* a powerful device used to project heavy metal staples into wood or masonry

stapler /stáyplər/ *n* a device that fastens paper and other materials together using staples, usually consisting of a flat metal base, a spring-loaded magazine of staples, and a top section

star /staar/ *n* **1 POINT OF LIGHT IN NIGHT SKY** an astronomical object usually visible as a small bright point of light in the night sky **2 MASS OF GAS IN SPACE** a gaseous mass in space such as the Sun, ranging in size from that of a planet to larger than the Earth's orbit, which generates energy by thermonuclear reactions **3 STAR SHAPE** a shape representing or based on that of a star as seen in the night sky, usually having four or five triangular points radiating from a centre **4 STAR-SHAPED SYMBOL OF MERIT OR RANK** a star-shaped object or symbol used as a sign of merit, quality, or rank **5** PRINTING, LING = **asterisk** *n.* **1**, **asterisk** *n.* **2** **6 POPULAR PERFORMER** a very famous, successful, and popular performer, especially in a field of entertainment or in sport **7 MOST IMPORTANT OR PROFICIENT PERSON** an especially proficient or important member of a group ○ *the star of the French class* **8 HELPFUL PERSON** a very nice or helpful person (*informal*) ○ *Thanks, Ben. You're a star!* **9 ASTRONOMICAL OBJECT IN RELATION TO FATE** a planet or constellation believed to influence a person's character or fate on Earth ■ **stars** *npl* **DESTINY** somebody's future, especially as supposedly revealed in a horoscope (*informal*) ■ *v* (**stars, starring, starred**) **1** *vt* **HAVE AS LEADING ACTOR** to have somebody as the leading performer or as one of the leading performers **2** *vi* **BE LEADING PERFORMER** to be the leading performer or one of the leading performers in something such as a film or play ○ *starring in his first major film* **3** *vt* PRINTING, LING = **asterisk** *v.* **4** *vt* **COVER OR DECORATE SOMETHING WITH STARS** to cover or decorate something with stars, or with many brilliant or colourful objects so as to give an effect comparable to that of the stars in the night sky ■ *adj* **OUTSTANDING** very or most important, skilful, or successful [Old English *steorra* < Indo-European] ◇ **see stars** see flashes of light, e.g. after receiving a hard blow to the head

star anise *n* **1** a star-shaped fruit, consisting of 6 to 12 woody single-seeded carpels, and with an aniseed-flavour. Use: in Chinese cookery and medicine, source of oil. **2** an evergreen tree that yields star anise. Native to: China. *Illicium verum.*

star-apple *n* **1** an apple-shaped fruit with a smooth greenish-purple skin and star-shaped arrangement of seeds inside **2** an evergreen tree that produces star-apples. Native to: tropical America. *Chrysophyllum cainito.*

Stara Zagora /stárrə zə górrə/ city in central Bulgaria. Population: 151,218 (1995).

star billing *n* the fact of being advertised as the leading performer in something

starboard /staárbərd/ *n* **RIGHT-HAND SIDE** the direction to the right of somebody facing the front of a ship or aircraft ■ *adj* **ON RIGHT-HAND SIDE** on, towards, or from the right-hand side of somebody facing the front of a ship or aircraft ■ *adv* **TOWARDS STARBOARD** towards starboard or the starboard side of a ship or aircraft ■ *vt* **TURN TOWARDS STARBOARD** to turn or move something, especially the helm, towards starboard [Old English *stēorbord* < *stēor* 'paddle' + *bord* 'board']

starburst /staár burst/ *n* a pattern of lines or light rays radiating outwards from a centre

starburst galaxy *n* a galaxy in a stage of intense star production

starch /staarch/ *n* **1 CARBOHYDRATE SUBSTANCE** a natural substance composed of chains of glucose units, made by plants and providing a major energy source for animals **2 STIFFENING SUBSTANCE FOR FABRICS** a white powder extracted from potatoes and grain. Use: fabric stiffener. **3 STARCHY FOODSTUFF** a foodstuff that contains a large amount of starch **4 STIFF AND FORMAL MANNER** behaviour marked by a stiff manner and formality **5** *US* **COURAGE** great courage or energy ■ *vt* **STIFFEN WITH STARCH** to stiffen fabric with starch [Old English (assumed) *stercan* 'stiffen' < Germanic, 'be rigid']

star chamber *n* a court or tribunal noted for being harsh, arbitrary, and unaccountable in its proceedings

Star Chamber *n* a court established by King Henry VII of England to try civil and criminal cases, especially those involving the security of the state, in secret [*Star* because the ceiling of the original courtroom was decorated with stars]

starch syrup *n* a syrup created through the incomplete hydrolysis of glucose that contains dextrose, maltose, and dextrine

starchy /staárchi/ (**-ier, -iest**) *adj* **1** containing a large amount of starch, or like starch, especially in consistency **2** very formal and unbending, and apparently lacking in warmth or a sense of humour —**starchily** *adv* —**starchiness** *n*

star connection *n* an electrical connection in a polyphase system in which the windings have one end connected to a common junction and the other ends connected to separate load points

star-crossed *adj* believed to be destined by fate to be unhappy [< the belief in the influence of the stars over human lives]

stardom /staárdəm/ *n* **1** the status of a star performer in sport or entertainment, and the fame and prestige that go with it **2** star performers considered as a group

stardust /staár dust/ *n* **1** a dreamy romantic sentimental feeling, or an imaginary substance, usually represented as starry and twinkling, that is supposed to induce this feeling **2** far distant stars in a cluster or strewn like a cloud of bright dust in the night sky

stare /stair/ *v* (**stares, staring, stared**) **1** *vti* **LOOK FIXEDLY** to look directly at somebody or something for a long time without moving the eyes away, usually as a result of curiosity or surprise, or to express rudeness or defiance ○ *'What is this life if, full of care,/ We have no time to stand and stare?'* (W. H. Davies *Leisure*; 1911) **2** *vi* **BE WIDE OPEN WITH SHOCK** to look wide open with shock, fear, or amazement (*refers to eyes*) **3** *vi* **BE OBVIOUS** to be obvious or blatant ○ *The answer was staring at you all the time you just couldn't see it.* ■ *n* **1 LONG CONCENTRATED LOOK** a long concentrated look at somebody or something, often full of curiosity or hostility **2 FACIAL EXPRESSION** a facial expression in which the eyes are wide open with shock or amazement and looking fixedly at somebody or something [Old English *starian* < Germanic, 'be rigid'] —**starer** *n*

SPELLCHECK See ***stair.***

SYNONYMS See ***gaze.***

stare down *vt US* = **stare out**

stare out *vt* to look somebody directly in the eyes until he or she is forced to look away. US term **stare down** *v.*

starets /staárits/ (*plural* **startsy** /staártsi/) *n* a religious teacher or spiritual adviser in the Eastern Orthodox Church, especially one who is a monk or holy man [Early 20C. < Russian, 'elderly man, elder'.]

star facet *n* one of the eight small triangular facets that surround the table of a gem cut in the brilliant style

starfish /staár fish/ (*plural* **-fish** *or* **-fishes**) *n* a marine invertebrate animal (**echinoderm**) whose body consists of five or more arms radiating from a central disc. Class: Asteroidea.

starfish flower *n* PLANTS = **stapelia**

star fruit *n* FOOD = **carambola** *n.* **2**

stargaze /staár gayz/ (**-gazes, -gazing, -gazed**) *vi* **1** to observe the stars at night **2** to engage in daydreaming

stargazer /staár gayzər/ *n* **1** a daydreamer **2** a bottom-dwelling tropical marine fish that has eyes and mouth on the top of its head. Families: Uranoscopidae and Dactyloscopidae.

star grass *n* a plant of the daffodil family with long leaves that look like grass. Flowers: star-shaped, white or yellow. Native to: tropical and temperate regions. Genus: *Hypoxis.*

stark /staark/ *adj* **1 FORBIDDINGLY BARE AND PLAIN** forbidding in its bareness and lack of any ornament, relieving feature, or pleasant prospect ○ *the stark interior of a dungeon cell* **2 UNAMBIGUOUS AND HARSH** presented in plain, unambiguous, and usually rather harsh terms ○ *Faced with the stark choice, we had either to change or go under.* **3 COMPLETE** having reached the fullest extent or degree of something **4 WITHOUT CLOTHES** completely unclothed and uncovered **5 RIGID** showing or affected by rigor mortis (*archaic*) ■ *adv* **UTTERLY** to the utmost degree [Old English *stearc* < Germanic, 'be rigid'] —**starkly** *adv* —**starkness** *n*

Stark /staark/, **Dame Freya** (1893–1993) British writer

starkers /staárkərz/ *adj* completely unclothed and uncovered (*informal*) [Early 20C. Shortening and alteration of STARK-NAKED.]

stark-naked *adj* completely unclothed and uncovered

starlet /staárlət/ *n* a young woman actor seen as a possible major film star of the future

starlight /staár līt/ *n* the light that comes from the stars

starling[1] /staárling/ *n* a common bird with glossy greenish-black plumage, a short tail, and pointed wings. Native to: Europe. *Sturnus vulgaris.* [Old English *stærlinc* 'little starling' < *stær* 'starling' < Germanic]

starling[2] /staárling/ *n* a structure made of piles surrounding a pier of a bridge to protect the pier from floating debris [Late 17C. < ?]

starlit /staár lit/ *adj* lit by light from the stars

star-nosed mole *n* a mole that has a ring of small pink fleshy tentacles surrounding its nose. Native to: North America. *Condylura cristata.*

star-of-Bethlehem (*plural* **stars-of-Bethlehem** *or* **star-of-Bethlehem**) *n* a perennial plant of the lily family that has long slender leaves. Flowers: white, star-shaped, in clusters on a central stalk. Native to: Europe. Genus: *Ornithogalum.* [Late 16C. < its abundance in Palestine.]

Star of David *n* a symbol of the Jewish faith and of the state of Israel consisting of two equilateral triangles superimposed on each other to form a six-pointed star

Starr /staar/, **Ringo** (*b.* 1940) British musician, drummer of Beatles. Born **Richard Starkey**

star ruby *n* a ruby that reflects light in a star shape when cut with a convex surface

starry /staári/ (**-rier, -riest**) *adj* **1 WITH MANY STARS SHINING** bright with many shining stars **2 COVERED WITH STARS** covered or decorated with stars **3 SIMILAR TO STAR** relating to or similar in shape or brightness to a star

starry-eyed *adj* having a happy and enthusiastic or romantic attitude that is naïve and unrealistic

Stars and Bars *n* the first flag of the Confederacy during the American Civil War, which had two red stripes and one white, and a circle of white stars representing the seceded states (+ *singular or plural verb*)

Stars and Stripes *n* the national flag of the United States, which has 13 alternating red and white stripes and one star for each state on a blue field (+ *singular or plural verb*)

star sapphire *n* a sapphire that reflects light in a star shape when cut with a convex surface

star shell *n* an artillery shell designed to burst in midair and release a flare or a shower of lights

starship /staár ship/ *n* a spaceship designed to travel between stars or star systems, and as yet existing only in science fiction

star sign *n* a sign of the zodiac, especially the sun sign under which somebody was born

star-spangled *adj* **1** covered or decorated with stars **2** attended by many important people, including politicians, company directors, and film stars

Star-Spangled Banner *n* **1** the national anthem of the United States **2** the national flag of the United States

starstruck /staár struk/, **star-struck** *adj* feeling or showing an awed fascination with stars, especially from the world of entertainment, and stardom

star-studded *adj* containing many well-known actors or performers

star system *n* the system of deliberately exploiting an individual star, both on screen and off, to sell films

start /staart/ *v* **1** *vti* **BEGIN** to begin doing something or begin something ○ *She started to laugh.* ○ *I'd better start getting ready.* **2** *vti* **BEGIN HAPPENING** to begin happening, or to make something begin happening ○ *The film starts at 7 o'clock.* **3** *vt* **CREATE** to bring something into being as an entity or operation **4** *vti* **MAKE ENGINE BEGIN TO WORK** to begin working, or make an engine begin to operate ○ *The car won't start.* ○ *I can't start the car.* **5** *vt* **BEGIN WORKING** to commence work on something **6** *vt* **HELP SOMEBODY BEGIN** to help somebody out in beginning an activity such as a journey or career ○ *It was a university professor who started her on her law career.* **7** *vti* **PLAY FIRST IN A SPORTS MATCH** to be or select somebody to be in a race or to play at the beginning of a sports match **8** *vi* **BEGIN ARGUING** to begin arguing or making a fuss (*informal*) ○ *Please don't start.* **9** *vi* **MAKE SUDDEN MOVEMENT** to make a sudden movement out of surprise, pain, fear, or anger **10** *vti* **MOVE SUDDENLY** to go or cause a person or animal to go very quickly from being still to moving ○ *start to your feet* **11** *vi* **GO FROM A PARTICULAR LEVEL** to begin at a particular level ○ *Prices start at fifteen pounds.* **12** *vt* **RAISE** to raise or care for something in the early stages of its growth ○ *start some plants in early spring* **13** *vi* **FLOW VIOLENTLY OUT** to flow violently or suddenly out of something ○ *water starting from the barrel's seams* **14** *vt* **CAUSE AN ANIMAL TO APPEAR** to cause a hunted animal to appear suddenly from its hiding place or den **15** *vti* **COME LOOSE** to come loose, or cause something to come loose, from its proper place ○ *timbers starting at the joints* ■ *n* **1 BEGINNING** the first part of something that proceeds through time ○ *We missed the start of the play.* **2 PLACE OR TIME OF START** the place or time at which something starts ○ *The start of the race is scheduled for noon.* **3 QUICK SUDDEN MOVEMENT** a quick sudden movement from being still to moving **4 SUDDEN INVOLUNTARY MOVEMENT** a sudden involuntary movement caused by fear, pain, surprise, or anger **5 INSTANCE OF PARTICIPATING** the fact or an instance of participating in a race or game ○ *winning three out of five starts* **6 POSITION AHEAD OF OTHERS** a position of being ahead of other competitors ○ *get a start on the rest* **7 POSITION AT THE BEGINNING** a set of circumstances at the beginning of something ○ *He needed a better start in life.* **8 SIGNAL TO BEGIN** the signal to begin something such as a race **9 SOMETHING SURPRISING** something surprising (*informal*) [12C. Probably < Old English *styrtan* 'jump' < Germanic.] ◇ **for a start** used in an argument to indicate that you are making the first point of many ◇ **to start with** at the beginning

start in *vi US* to begin to scold or criticize somebody ○ *As soon as she'd finished tearing a strip off Doreen, she started in on me.*

start off *v* **1** *vti* **BEGIN** to begin to do something, or cause or help somebody to begin to do something ○ *Let's start off by introducing ourselves.* **2** *vi* **SET OFF** to begin moving in a particular direction, or begin a journey ○ *She turned and started off up the hill.* **3** *vt* **MAKE SOMEBODY START TALKING OR LAUGHING** to do something that causes somebody else to start doing something such as talking, laughing, crying, or misbehaving (*informal*) ○ *Stop it, or you'll start her off again.*

start on *vt* **1** to begin to work on or deal with something or somebody, usually something that will take a long time to finish ○ *As soon as I've finished cleaning the kitchen, I'm going to start on the bathroom.* **2** to begin to scold, criticize, or attack somebody (*informal*) ○ *Look, don't start on me. It's not my fault!*

start out *vi* **1 BEGIN JOURNEY** to set off on a journey ○ *If we start out at about nine, we should be there in time for lunch.* **2 BEGIN** to do something at the beginning of a process ○ *He starts out trying to prove she's guilty and ends up convincing everyone she's innocent.* **3 INTEND** to intend to do something, or have something as an initial intention ○ *I didn't start out to cause a lot of trouble.* **4 BEGIN STAGE OF LIFE** to make a start in something such as adult life or a career ○ *young people who are starting out in journalism*

start up *v* **1** *vti* **BEGIN TO OPERATE** to begin to operate, or make something begin to operate ○ *start the engine up* **2** *vti* **OPEN BUSINESS** to begin something such as a business venture ○ *started up her own accountancy firm* **3** *vi* **BEGIN TO MAKE SOUND** to begin to make a sound, especially a characteristic sound, or begin to speak ○ *First a solitary blackbird started up, and soon the whole wood was alive with birdsong.* **4** *vi* **RISE SUDDENLY** to rise suddenly to a standing or upright position ○ *He started up from his chair at the loud sound and rushed to the window.*

START /staart/ *abbr* Strategic Arms Reduction Talks

starter /stáartər/ *n* **1 STARTING DEVICE FOR AN ENGINE** a device for starting a machine or engine, especially an electrically operated device that causes the internal-combustion engine in a motor vehicle to fire **2 SOMEBODY SIGNALLING START OF RACE** a person who gives the signal for a race to start **3 COMPETITOR WHO STARTS** a horse or competitor who starts in a race **4 PLAYER AT BEGINNING OF A GAME** a player who takes the field for a team at the beginning of a game **5** *US* **FIRST PITCHER** in baseball, the pitcher who pitches first for a team, either regularly or in a particular game **6 FIRST COURSE OF A MEAL** a first course of a meal, or something suitable to be eaten as a first course of a meal ■ *adj* **USED TO START** used to start something or as an introduction to something for people with little experience of it ○ *a starter set of paints* ◇ **for starters** as the first thing to be done, considered, or dealt with (*informal*)

starter home *n* a small property suitable for somebody who is buying a home for the first time

star thistle *n* a plant belonging to the daisy family. Flowers: purple, encircled by radiating spines. Native to: Europe, Asia. Genus: *Centaurea.*

starting block *n* either of a pair of objects used by runners to brace their feet against at the start of a sprint race

starting gate *n* **1 STARTING STALLS** a line of starting stalls **2 TAPES RAISED AT START OF HORSERACE** a set of tapes spanning the width of a racetrack that are raised by the starter to begin a race **3 BARRIER CONNECTED TO TIMER** a physical barrier or electronic beam that automatically starts a timing device when a competitor passes through it, e.g. at the start of a skiing race

starting grid *n* a pattern of lines marked on a motor racing track, with numbered starting positions

starting gun *n* a gun fired as the signal for a race to start

starting line *n* a line marked across a racetrack to show runners where to start

starting pistol *n* SPORTS = **starting gun**

starting price *n* the odds being offered by a bookmaker on a particular horse just before the start of the race

starting stalls *npl* a line of stalls into which racehorses are put at the start of a race that have gates at the front that spring open simultaneously when operated by the starter

startle /stáart'l/ (**-tles, -tling, -tled**) *vt* to disconcert or frighten a person or an animal into making an involuntary movement, or become disconcerted or frightened by a sudden shock ○ *gave a startled cry and dropped the plate on the floor* [Old English *steartlian* < Germanic] —**startler** *n*

startling /stáartling/ *adj* provoking surprise, fright, wonder, or alarm —**startlingly** *adv*

startsy plural of **starets**

startup /stáart up/, **start-up** *n* **1 SOMETHING JUST BEGINNING** something such as a company that is just beginning operations **2 COMMENCEMENT** the beginning of an activity such as the construction of a building ■ *adj* **INVOLVED IN STARTING SOMETHING UP** involved in or used for the establishment of a business venture

star turn *n* the most striking or popular item or performer in a show

starvation /staar váysh'n/ *n* **1** the state of having not enough food, or of losing strength or dying through lack of food **2** *Scotland, N England, Ireland* extreme cold

starve /staarv/ (**starves, starving, starved**) *v* **1** *vti* **WEAKEN OR DIE BECAUSE OF HUNGER** to weaken or die through lack of food, or cause somebody to do this ○ *The besieged city was starved into submission.* **2** *vi* **BE HUNGRY** to be very hungry (*informal*) ○ *I'm starving! What's for dinner?* **3** *vt* **DEPRIVE** to deprive somebody or something of something vitally needed ○ *starved of affection* **4** *vi* **NEED** to feel deprived of something, or feel a great need or desire for something ○ *starving for a kind word* **5** *vi Scotland, N England, Ireland* **BE VERY COLD** to be feeling extremely cold [Old English *steorfan* 'die' < Germanic, 'be stiff'] —**starver** *n*

starve out *vt* to force an enemy to surrender by making necessary food and supplies inaccessible

starveling /stáarvling/ *n* a very thin and hungry-looking person or animal (*archaic*)

stash /stash/ *n* **1 HIDDEN STORE** a secret or hidden store of something such as money or valuables (*informal*) **2 HIDING PLACE** a secret hiding place (*informal*) **3 SECRET STORE OF DRUGS** a store of illegal drugs kept for personal consumption (*slang*) ■ *vt* **1 HIDE** to put something into a secret hidden storage place (*informal*) **2** *US* **PUT SOMETHING AWAY** to put something somewhere, e.g. in a convenient place or where it belongs ○ *We'll eat after we've stashed our gear.* [Late 18C. < ?]

stasis /stáyssiss/ *n* **1 MOTIONLESS STATE** a state in which there is neither motion nor development, often resulting from opposing forces balancing each other **2 STOPPAGE OF FLOW OF BODY FLUIDS** a condition in which body fluids, such as blood or the contents of the bowel, are prevented from flowing normally through their channels **3 STATE OF NO CHANGE** a state in which there is little or no apparent change in a species of organism over a long period of time [Mid-18C. Via modern Latin < Greek, 'standing, stoppage'.]

stat[1] /stat/ *n* a statistic (*informal*) [Mid-20C. Shortening.]

stat[2] /stat/, **stat.** *adv* used in prescriptions to indicate that a drug is to be given immediately ■ *adj* urgent ○ *The doctor received a stat page while on call.* [Late 19C. Shortening of Latin *statim* 'immediately'.]

-stat *suffix* **1** device for stabilizing or regulating ○ *humidistat* ○ *rheostat* **2** a device for focusing something in a single direction ○ *siderostat* **3** a substance or device that inhibits the growth or flow of something ○ *fungistat* ○ *haemostat* [Via modern Latin *-stata* < Greek *statos* 'standing' and *statēs* 'one that causes to stand']

state /stayt/ *n* **1 CONDITION** the condition that something or somebody is in at a particular time ○ *What sort of state was he in after hearing the news?* ○ *in an unhappy emotional state* **2 FORM OR ENERGY LEVEL** any form, such as solid or liquid, or quantifiable condition, such as energy level, that a physical substance can be in depending on its temperature and other circumstances **3 PHYSICAL STAGE** a growth or developmental stage of an animal or plant **4 COUNTRY** a country or nation with its own sovereign independent government **5 MOSTLY AUTONOMOUS REGION OF FEDERAL COUNTRY** an area forming part of a federal country such as the United States or Australia with its own government and legislature and control over most of its own internal affairs **6 GOVERNMENT** a country's government and those government-controlled institutions that are responsible for its internal administration and its relationships with other countries ○ *state-owned companies* **7 CEREMONIOUS STYLE** a very formal, dignified or grand way of doing something in which all the appropriate ceremonies are observed **8 NERVOUS, UPSET, OR EXCITED CONDITION** a very nervous, upset, or excited frame of mind or manner of behaving ○ *He was in a state by the time she finally arrived.* ○ *Don't get into a state worrying about money.* **9 BAD PHYSICAL CONDITION** a very untidy or disreputable condition (*informal*) ○ *The house is in such a state that we'll never get it tidy.* ■ *adj* **1 RELATING TO GOVERNMENT** involving or relating to a nation or an autonomous federal region within a nation its government **2 HELD OR RUN BY A STATE** owned, operated, or financed by a nation or an autonomous region within a federalized nation **3 DONE WITH FULL CEREMONY** involving many grand rituals and ceremonies, especially those appropriate to a head of state ■ *vt* (**states, stating, stated**) **1 EXPRESS IN WORDS** to express something in spoken or written words, especially to announce something publicly in a deliberate, formal way ○ *We have already stated our position on this issue.* **2 DECLARE WITH FORCE OF LAW** to declare something officially so that it has the force of a law or regulation ○ *It is expressly stated in your contract that you must not undertake work for another employer.* **3 PLAY MUSICAL THEME FOR FIRST TIME** to play a particular musical theme or motif for the first time before it is repeated and developed within a piece of music [12C. Directly or via Old French *estat* < Latin *status* 'way of standing, condition' (as in *status rei publicae* 'condition of the republic').] ◇ **the state of play** a stage reached in a situation or activity

state benefit *n* money given by the government to people who do not have enough money to live on

state capitalism *n* an economic system in which the state controls the use of capital and the means of production

statecraft /stáyt kraaft/ *n* the art of governing or managing the affairs of a country well

stated /stáytid/ *adj* **1** laid down by an official agreement or in a legal document **2** announced previously, especially in a public medium

stated case *n* LAW = **case stated**

State Department *n* the department of the United States government that deals with foreign affairs and is headed by a Cabinet secretary and staffed by career foreign service officers

state earnings-related pension scheme *n* full form of **SERPS**

State Enrolled Nurse *n* in the United Kingdom, a nurse certified as competent to carry out many of the functions of a nurse, but who is less qualified than and junior to a State Registered Nurse

statehood /stáyt hood/ *n* the status of a state in a federal union, especially in the United States, as opposed to that of a territory or dependency

statehouse /stáyt howss/ (*plural* **-houses** /-howziz/), **state house, Statehouse** (*plural* **-houses**) *n* a building in which a state legislature convenes in any of the US state capitals

stateless /stáytləss/ *adj* not being a citizen of any country and having no nationality

state line *n* the official boundary between two US states

stately /stáytli/ (**-lier, -liest**) *adj* **1** characterized by an impressively weighty and dignified but graceful manner **2** grand and imposing in appearance

stately home *n* a large and impressive country house, especially one that is owned by a famous or aristocratic family and is open to the public

ϟ**statement** /stáytmənt/ *n* **1 EXPRESSION IN WORDS** the expression in spoken or written words of something such as a fact, intention, or policy, or an instance of this **2 SOMETHING SAID** something that somebody says that is not a question or an exclamation and that expresses an idea or facts in definite terms ○ *We were unable to verify* *the truth of that statement.* **3 SPECIALLY PREPARED PUBLIC ANNOUNCEMENT** a specially prepared announcement or reply that is made public ○ *Has she made a statement to the press?* **4 ACCOUNT OF FACTS** an account of the facts relating to a crime or case given to the police or in a court of law, usually for use as evidence ○ *The police asked me if I wished to make a statement.* **5 WORDLESS EXPRESSION OF IDEA** a bold or conspicuous expression of an idea, opinion, or concept made in a nonverbal way ○ *Her art is a powerful statement of her political beliefs.* **6 PRINTED RECORD OF BANK ACCOUNT** a printed record of all transactions that have taken place over a period of time in a bank account and of the amount of the holder's current credit or debt **7 CUSTOMER'S ACCOUNT** an account issued to a customer showing charges made, payments received, and any balance owing **8 ASSESSMENT OF CHILD'S SPECIAL EDUCATIONAL NEEDS** an official and legally binding assessment made by a local authority of the help required by a child with special educational needs **9 FIRST PRESENTATION OF MUSICAL THEME** the first presentation of a theme or idea that is to be developed later in a piece of music **10 COMPUTER INSTRUCTION** a computer instruction written in a source language ■ *vt* **DRAW UP STATEMENT FOR CHILD** to draw up an official statement of a child's special educational needs, thus ensuring that the local education authority will have to make provision for those needs

statement of attainment *n* a programme of the objectives that school students should be able to attain within their own ability range in a particular subject

statement of case *n* a formal statement of the facts relating to either of the parties involved in a legal case

statement of claim *n* = **declaration** *n.* 5

Staten Island /státt'n-/ one of the five boroughs of New York City. Population: 378,977 (1990).

state of affairs *n* a particular set of circumstances ○ *This regrettable state of affairs cannot be allowed to continue.*

State of Origin *n* in Australia, a policy stating that players must have been born in the state they represent in annual interstate rugby league matches

state of the art *n* the most advanced level of knowledge and technology currently achieved in any field at any given time ■ *adj* **state-of-the-art** representing the most advanced level of knowledge or technology currently achieved in any field at any given time

state of war *n* **1** armed conflict between states or other groups, with or without a formal declaration of war **2** the situation brought about by a declaration of war, with or without the commencement of actual armed conflict, in which special internationally-agreed laws apply

state prayers *npl* the prayers for the sovereign, royal family, clergy, and Parliament, said at services in the Anglican Church

stater /stáytər/, **Stater** *n* a person who comes from a specific state or type of state, especially in the United States (*usually in combination*) ○ *Bay Staters are from Massachusetts.*

State Registered Nurse *n* in the United Kingdom, a nurse who has obtained a higher qualification in nursing than a State Enrolled Nurse and is certified as competent to carry out all the functions of a nurse

stateroom /stáyt room, stáyt rōōm/ *n* **1** a large and luxuriously furnished private cabin on a ship or a private sleeping compartment on a train **2** a large imposing room in a palace or government building, used for large-scale functions and entertaining important guests

state room *n* a large imposing room in a palace or government building, used for large-scale functions and entertaining important guests

States /stayts/ *npl* **1** the United States of America (*informal*) **2** the name of the legislative bodies in Jersey, Guernsey, and Alderney in the Channel Islands

state's attorney, state attorney *n* a US attorney who acts as prosecutor in court cases on behalf of a state

state school *n* a school controlled and financed by a public authority in which education is free

state secret *n* a piece of information, usually considered important to national security, that is supposed to be known only to people authorized by the state

state services *npl* special forms of service for use in Anglican churches on days of national celebration

state's evidence *n* evidence given for the prosecution in a criminal trial in the United States and other nations, sometimes by one of the accused or by an accomplice to the crime

States General *npl* **1** the legislative assembly of the Netherlands **2** the legislative body in France before 1789, consisting of representatives of the three estates of the realm

stateside /stáyt sīd/ *adv US* in or towards the continental United States ■ *adj US* relating to, in, or towards the continental United States

statesman /stáytsmən/ (*plural* **-men** /-mən/) *n* **1** a senior male politician who plays an important role in his country's government or in international affairs **2** a senior male politician who is widely respected for his integrity and impartial concern for the public good —**statesmanlike** *adj* —**statesmanship** *n*

state socialism *n* a political and economic system in which the state controls major industries and banks and plans its economic and social welfare programmes in order to bring about an egalitarian society —**state socialist** *n*

states' rights *npl* **1** the powers and rights not granted by the US Constitution to the federal government and not forbidden to the states by the Constitution **2** a political doctrine that advocates the reduction of federal rights and powers and a maximization of those of the US states —**states' righter** *n*

stateswoman /stáyts wŏŏmmən/ (*plural* **-men** /-wimmin/) *n* **1** a senior politician who plays an important role in her country's government or in international affairs **2** a senior woman politician who is widely respected for her integrity and impartial concern for the public good

state trooper *n* a member of the highway patrol police of a US state

statewide /stáyt wīd/ *adj US* affecting or happening throughout an entire state ○ *a statewide search for the escaped prisoner* ■ *adv US* throughout an entire state

ϟ **static** /státtik/ *adj* **1 MOTIONLESS** not moving or changing, or fixed in position **2 OF FORCES NOT CAUSING MOVEMENT** relating to forces, weight, or pressure that act without causing movement **3 INVOLVING STATICS** relating to, involving, or characteristic of statics **4 INVOLVING STATIONARY ELECTRIC CHARGES** relating to, involving, or characteristic of stationary electric charges **5 CAUSED BY ELECTRICAL INTERFERENCE** relating to or caused by electrical interference in a radio or television broadcast **6 NOT NEEDING TO BE REFRESHED** retaining its contents without having to be refreshed by the central processor (*refers to a random-access-memory computer chip*) ■ *n* **1 ELECTRICAL INTERFERENCE** electrical interference in a radio or television broadcast, causing a random crackling noise or disruption of a picture **2** ELEC = **static electricity** **3** *US* **OPPOSITION OR INTERFERENCE** criticism, opposition, or unwanted interference by somebody else (*informal*) ○ *getting a lot of static from the boss* [Mid-19C. Via modern Latin < Greek *statikos* 'causing to stand' < *statos* 'standing' (see STATO-).] —**statically** *adv*

statice /státtissi/ *n* PLANTS = **sea lavender** [Mid-18C. Via modern Latin < Greek *statikos* 'causing to stand or stop' (see STATIC), because it stops the flow of blood.]

static electricity *n* a stationary electric charge that builds up on an insulated object, e.g. on a capacitor or a thundercloud

static line *n* a rope attached to an aircraft and a parachutist's parachute that automatically opens the parachute

static pressure *n* pressure not caused by motion at a point on the surface of an object moving freely in a flowing fluid

statics /státtiks/ *n* a branch of mechanics that deals with forces and systems in equilibrium (+ *singular verb*)

static tube *n* a tube used to measure the static pressure present in a moving fluid

station /stáysh'n/ *n* **1 STOP ON RAILWAY ROUTE** a place along a train or bus route where passengers are picked up or set down, often with amenities such as ticket offices, waiting rooms, refreshments, toilets, and facilities for goods and parcels **2 LOCAL BRANCH OF AN ORGANIZATION** a local branch or headquarters of an official organization such as the police force, fire brigade, or ambulance service **3 SPECIALLY EQUIPPED BUILDING** a building or group of buildings that provides a particular function or service ○ *a pumping station* **4 BROADCASTING BUILDING** a place equipped to make and broadcast radio or television programmes **5 BROADCASTING CHANNEL** a television or radio channel **6 USUAL PLACE** the place or position where somebody or something is usually to be found or is supposed to be found **7 POSITION FOR PERFORMING TASK** a position where somebody performs a task, e.g. in a factory, or the equipment used in performing a task **8 RANK** the position somebody holds in society or in an organization in terms of rank **9 MILITARY POSTING** a place where military personnel are sent to carry out duties **10 PLACE ON SHIP FOR CREW MEMBER** a place on board a ship where a crew member carries out duties **11 PLACE WHERE SHIP IS SENT** a place where a naval ship or fleet is sent for a period of duty **12** *ANZ* **SHEEP OR CATTLE FARM** a large farm in Australia or New Zealand where sheep or cattle are raised **13 SURVEYOR'S REFERENCE POINT** a fixed point used by surveyors as a reference **14 STATION OF THE CROSS** in Christianity one of the Stations of the Cross **15 MILITARY OR GOVERNMENT SETTLEMENT IN INDIA** a place where military officers or government officials lived in India while it was under British rule ■ *vt* **PUT IN OR SEND TO A PLACE** to assign somebody to a particular place, or put something in a particular place (*often passive*) [Mid-16C. Via Old French < Latin *station-* 'standing still' < *stare* 'stand'.]

stationary /stáysh'nəri/ *adj* **1 NOT MOVING** not moving, especially at a standstill after being in motion **2 IMMOBILE** fixed in position and not able to be moved **3 UNCHANGING** not changing **4 STAYING IN ONE PLACE** showing a tendency to remain in the same place [15C. Directly or via French *stationnaire* 'motionless' < medieval Latin *stationarius* < Latin, 'of a military station', < *station-* (see STATION).]

SPELLCHECK Do not confuse ***stationary*** with ***stationery***, which has a similar sound. The two words are distantly related but have quite different meanings. ***Stationary*** is an adjective meaning 'not moving' (normally used of vehicles), whereas ***stationery*** is a noun meaning 'things used in writing'. Beware: your spellchecker will not catch this error.

stationary bicycle *n* SPORTS = **exercise bike**

stationary front *n* a weather condition in which the boundary between a cold air mass and a warm air mass is stationary

stationary orbit *n* an orbit around a celestial body that has the same period as one revolution of the celestial body

stationary wave *n* PHYS = **standing wave**

stationer /stáysh'nər/ *n* a person or shop that sells stationery

stationery /stáysh'nəri/ *n* paper, envelopes, pens, pencils, and other things used in writing

SPELLCHECK See ***stationary***.

station hand *n Aus* a worker on a large sheep or cattle farm

station house *n US* a building housing a police department or precinct office, or a fire department

stationmaster /stáysh'n maastər/, **station manager** *n* somebody whose job is to oversee the running of a railway station

Stations of the Cross *npl* **1** a series of 14 images around the inside of a Roman Catholic church, each representing a stage in Jesus Christ's road to Calvary **2** a Roman Catholic devotion in which a prayer is said before each of the Stations of the Cross

station-to-station *adj US* charged from the time somebody answers the telephone (*dated*) ■ *adv US* by a station-to-station call

station wagon *n US, Can, ANZ* a car with an extended area behind the rear seats that provides extra seating or carrying capacity, usually with a tailgate [Originally a covered carriage for transporting passengers to and from train stations]

statism /stáytizəm/ *n* the theory, or its practice, that economic and political power should be controlled by a central government leaving regional government and the individual with relatively little say in political matters [Early 17C. < STATE.]

statist /stáytist/ *n* an advocate, believe in, or practitioner of statism ■ *adj* belonging or relating to, or characteristic of, statism

statistic /stə tístik/ *n* **1 ELEMENT OF DATA** a single element of data from a collection **2 NUMERICAL VALUE OR FUNCTION** a numerical value or function, such as a mean or standard deviation, used to describe a sample or population **3 PIECE OF INFORMATION** somebody or something treated as a piece of data or information [Late 18C. Back-formation < STATISTICS.] —**statistical** *adj* —**statistically** *adv*

statistical mechanics *n* the branch of physics that analyses macroscopic systems by applying statistical principles to their microscopic constituents (+ *singular verb*)

statistics /stə tístiks/ *n* a branch of mathematics that deals with the analysis and interpretation of numerical data in terms of samples and populations (+ *singular verb*) ■ *npl* a collection of numerical data ○ *this month's sales statistics* [Late 18C. Via German *Statistik* < Latin *status* (see STATE).] —**statistician** /státti stísh'n/ *n*

stative /stáytiv/ *adj* describes a verb, e.g. 'know' or 'own', that deals with states, as opposed to one, e.g. 'listen', 'talk', or 'go', that deals with actions ■ *n* a verb dealing with states not actions [Mid-17C. < Latin *stativus* < *stat-*, past participle of *stare* (see STATION).]

stato- *prefix* 1 balance, equilibrium ○ *statoscope* 2 resting ○ *statoblast* [< Greek *statos* 'standing' < Indo-European, 'to stand']

statoblast /státtō blast/ *n* a chitin-encased body that serves as a means of asexual reproduction for freshwater bryozoans

statocyst /státtō sist/ *n* a fluid-filled organ of balance in some invertebrates such as the lobster containing suspended bony granules that, along with sensory cells, help it to determine its position

statolith /státtō lith/ *n* 1 any tiny bony granule that is suspended in fluid within a statocyst and whose movement is detected by sensory hairs that determine an invertebrate's position 2 a starch grain or other particle inside plant cells that moves in response to gravity, and is thought to influence the way shoots or other organs grow —**statolithic** /státtō líthik/ *adj*

stator /stáytər/ *n* a stationary part in a machine, such as a motor or generator, about which or in which a rotor rotates [Late 19C. < modern Latin, 'one that stands' < Latin *stat-*, past participle of *stare* (see STATION).]

statoscope /státtō skōp/ *n* a sensitive aneroid barometer used to detect small changes in atmospheric pressure, often used in aircraft to determine changes in altitude

statuary /státtyoo əri/ *n* 1 statues considered collectively 2 the art and techniques of making statues [Mid-16C. < Latin *statuarius* 'of a statue' < *statua* (see STATUE).]

statue /státtyoo/ *n* a three-dimensional image of a human being or animal that is sculpted, modelled, cast, or carved [14C. Via Old French < Latin *statua* < *statuere* 'set up' (see STATUTE).]

Statue of Liberty *n* a huge statue of a woman holding a torch and a book inscribed 'July 4, 1776'. It stands in New York Harbour.

statuesque /státtyoo ésk/ *adj* like a statue, especially in having classical beauty, elegance, or proportions —**statuesquely** *adv*

statuette /státtyoo ét/ *n* a small usually portable statue

stature /stáchər/ *n* 1 the standing height of somebody or something 2 somebody's standing or level of achievement [13C. Via Old French < Latin *statura* < *stat-*, past participle of *stare* (see STATION).]

status /stáytəss/ *n* 1 RANK the relative position or standing of somebody or something in a society or other group 2 PRESTIGE high rank or standing, especially in a community, workforce, or organization 3 CONDITION a condition that is subject to change ○ *What's the current status of the investigation?* 4 LEGAL STANDING somebody's standing in terms of the law [Late 18C. < Latin (see STATE).]

status bar *n* a bar on a computer screen that displays information about an application being used

status quo /-kwṓ/ *n* the condition or state of affairs that currently exists [< Latin, 'the state in which']

status symbol *n* a possession that is a sign of wealth or prestige

statute /státtyoot/ *n* 1 a law established by a legislative body, e.g. an Act of Parliament 2 a permanent established rule or law, especially one involved in the running of a company or other organization [13C. Via Old French < late Latin *statutum* 'something set up' < Latin *statuere* 'set up' < *status* 'position'.] —**statutable** *adj* —**statutably** *adv*

statute book *n* a record of the acts that have been passed by a legislature and remain in force

statute law *n* the body of law that has been enacted by a legislature, or a specific law so enacted

statute mile *n* MEASURE = **mile** *n.* 1 [Because it is fixed by law]

statute of limitations *n* a statute that lays down the time within which legal proceedings must be started

statutory /státtyŏŏtəri/ *adj* 1 OF A STATUTE relating to a statute 2 CONTROLLED BY STATUTE regulated or imposed by statute 3 SUBJECT TO PENALTY covered by a statute, and subject to the penalty laid down by that statute —**statutorily** *adv*

statutory declaration *n* a declaration that somebody makes on oath according to statute

statutory order *n* a statute that augments an existing statute

statutory rape *n US* the offence under US law of having sexual relations with somebody who has not reached the legal age of consent

Stauffenberg /stówfən burg, shtówfən bŏŏrk/, **Claus Schenk, Count** (1907–44) German army officer, leader of a plot to assassinate Adolf Hitler

staunch[1] /stawnch/, **stanch** /staanch/ *v* 1 *vti* STOP LIQUID FLOW to stop the flow of a liquid, particularly blood, or be stopped from flowing 2 *vt* STOP WOUND BLEEDING to stop a wound from bleeding or exuding pus 3 *vt* ASSUAGE to assuage or allay something that is bad (*archaic*) [14C. Via Old French *estanchier* < assumed Vulgar Latin *stanticare* 'cause to stand' < Latin *stant-*, present participle of *stare* (see STATION).] —**staunchable** *adj* —**stauncher** *n*

staunch[2] /stawnch/ *adj* 1 showing loyalty, dependability, and enthusiasm 2 solidly built or substantial [15C. Via Anglo-Norman *estaunche* < Old French *estanchier* 'stop'.] —**staunchly** *adv* —**staunchness** *n*

staurolite /stáwrə līt/ *n* a reddish-brown or black aluminosilicate mineral containing iron and magnesium that often occurs in cross-shaped crystals. Source: metamorphic rocks. Use: gems. [Late 18C. < Greek *stauros* 'cross' (because it often forms twin crystals in the shape of a cross).] —**staurolitic** /stáwrə líttik/ *adj*

Stavanger /stə vángər/ port in SW Norway. Population: 103,590 (1995).

stave /stayv/ *n* 1 BAND OF WOOD a long thin piece of wood, one of several fixed together to make the hull of a boat, or the body of a container such as a barrel 2 RUNG OR BAR OF WOOD a bar or strip of wood or other material, especially one that forms a rung in a ladder or a cross-piece between the legs of a chair 3 = **staff**[1] *n.* 7 4 MUSIC = **staff**[1] *n.* 9 5 POETRY STANZA a stanza of poetry 6 *Scotland* SPRAIN an injury to a part of the body, e.g. a toe, finger, or elbow, caused by spraining or twisting ■ *v* (**staves, staving, staved** *or* **stove** /stōv/, **staved**) 1 *vti* BREAK STAVES to break a barrel, a tub, or a boat's hull by smashing its staves in, or to break by having the staves smashed in 2 *vti* BREAK A HOLE IN AN OBJECT to smash a hole in the side of a boat or a barrel 3 *vt* BREAK INWARDS to strike something such as a door or a rib making it break inwards 4 *vt* FIT A STAVE TO to fit a stave to something such as a chair or a ladder 5 *vt Scotland* SPRAIN PART OF BODY to injure a part of the body, e.g. a toe, finger, or elbow, by spraining it or twisting it [14C. Back-formation < *staves*, the plural of STAFF[1].]

stave off *vt* to avoid or prevent something unpleasant, often only temporarily ○ *stave off hunger*

staves plural of **staff**[1] *n.* 7, **staff**[1] *n.* 8, **staff**[1] *n.* 10, **stave**

stavesacre /stáyvz aykər/ *n* a delphinium with poisonous seeds. Flowers: purple. Use: formerly, cathartic, emetic. Native to: Europe, Asia. *Delphinium staphisagria.* [14C. Alteration of *staphisagre*, via Latin < Greek *staphis agria* 'wild raisin'.]

Stavropol /stávrəpol/ city in SW Russia. Population: 418,112 (1995).

stay[1] /stay/ *v* 1 *vi* REMAIN to continue to be in the same place, condition, or state 2 *vi* RESIDE FOR A SHORT TIME to spend some time or live temporarily in a specified place 3 *vi Scotland* RESIDE to live permanently in a place 4 *vti* PASS SOME TIME to spend a specified length of time at a place or in doing something 5 *vi* REMAIN IN CONTENTION to keep up with somebody or something, especially by going along with the leader or leaders of a race 6 *vt* PERSEVERE to continue to do something, especially to support something, e.g. an idea, plan, or project ○ *stay the course until the task is completed* 7 *vt* UNDERGO to endure, put up with, or survive something, especially something trying, difficult, or unpleasant ○ *The runner had trouble staying the final mile.* 8 *vi* BE AROUND FOR SOMETHING to be present long enough to take part in something, especially a meal 9 *vi* LINGER to linger or wait somewhere ○ *Stay a moment.* 10 *vt* STOP to put a stop to something 11 *vt* POSTPONE OR HINDER to postpone, hinder, or delay something ○ *stay a trip until the weather improves* 12 *vt* ALLEVIATE IN THE SHORT TERM to relieve or ease something temporarily, e.g. hunger, thirst, or other physical need 13 *vt* RESTRAIN to hold something back or in check 14 *vt* SUSPEND LEGAL PROCESS TEMPORARILY to suspend a judgment or proceedings temporarily 15 *vi* STAKE SAME AMOUNT to stake the same amount of money on a poker hand as the person who last raised the stake ■ *n* 1 A VISIT a short spell of being away from home ○ *a weekend stay in the country* 2 CURB OR CHECK something that acts to stop or delay something negative happening 3 TEMPORARY HALT a temporary halt in legal proceedings, or a period during which a judgment may not be carried out [15C. Via Old French *ester* < Latin *stare* 'stand'.] ◇ **stay put** to remain in a place or position

stay on *vi* to remain somewhere after others have left or after the expected time of leaving

stay out *vi* to be away from home, usually for or until a specified time

stay up *vi* to remain awake and not go to bed at the normal time

stay[2] /stay/ *n* 1 A SUPPORT something that gives extra support to something else, e.g. a brace, prop, or buttress 2 CORSET BONE a small bone or piece of metal or plastic used as a stiffener in corsets and girdles ■ **stays** *npl* STIFFENED CORSET a corset that is stiffened with strips of whalebone, metal, or other material ■ *vt* 1 SUPPORT to support something (*archaic*) 2 COMFORT to give somebody comfort or strength (*formal*) [Early 16C. < Old French *estaye* < Germanic.]

stay[3] /stay/ *n* 1 ROPE SUPPORTING MAST a rope or cable used to support a mast 2 STEADYING ROPE a rope used for steadying or guiding something, especially on a chimney or flagpole ■ *vti* TURN ONTO OTHER TACK to turn onto the other tack, or make a vessel turn [Old English *stæg* < Indo-European, 'make stand']

stay-at-home *adj* preferring a quiet domestic routine to travelling or to leading a busy social life —**stay-at-home** *n*

stayer /stáy ər/ *n* 1 SOMEBODY WHO STAYS somebody or something that stays 2 SOMEBODY PERSISTENT a person with much stamina and persistence 3 HORSE OR DOG THAT RACES PERSISTENTLY a racehorse or greyhound that has stamina and competes to the end of a race, even under difficult conditions

staying power *n* the ability to keep doing something or keep trying, especially over long periods of time

staysail /stáy sayl/; *nautical* /stáyss'l/ *n* an extra sail hoisted on one of the stays of a sailing vessel

stay stitching *n* an extra line of stitches reinforcing a seam, used to prevent stretching and fraying

STD *abbr* 1 sexually transmitted disease 2 subscriber trunk dialling

Ste *abbr* Sainte [French, '(female) Saint']

stead /sted/ *n* the position or role of somebody or something else [Old English *stede* 'place' < Indo-European, 'to stand'] ◇ **stand somebody in good stead** to be useful to somebody, especially at a later time

Stead /sted/, **Christina Ellen** (1902–83) Australian writer

Stead, C. K. (*b.* 1932) New Zealand writer. Full name **Christian Karlson Stead**

steadfast /stéd faast/ *adj* 1 firm and unwavering in purpose, loyalty, or resolve 2 firmly fixed or constant [Old English *stedefæst* 'fixed in place'] —**steadfastly** *adv* —**steadfastness** *n*

steading /stédding/ *n* 1 a farm, especially a small one 2 a farm outbuilding or all of the outbuildings of a farm [15C. < STEAD.]

steady /stéddi/ *adj* (**-ier, -iest**) 1 STABLE fixed, stable, or not easily moved 2 STAYING THE SAME showing no tendency to change or fluctuate 3 CONSTANT OR CONTINUOUS coming in a regular nonstop flow 4 REGULAR OR ORDINARY reliable, but often rather dull or routine 5 UNRUFFLED not easily upset or excited 6 STAID OR SERIOUS having a serious and calm attitude or character 7 REGULAR OR INDUSTRIOUS regular, habitual, or industrious ■ *adv* (**-ier, -iest**) CONTINUOUSLY in a constant or continuous way (*informal*) ■ *vti* (**-ies, -ying, -ied**) MAKE OR BECOME STEADY to become steady or make something steady ■ *n* (*plural* **-ies**) SOMEBODY DATED REGULARLY the person with whom somebody regularly goes on dates (*informal*) ■ *interj* 1 BE

CAREFUL used to tell somebody to be careful or be calm **2** KEEP TO PRESENT COURSE used to tell somebody steering a ship or boat to keep to the present course [Mid-13C. < STEAD.] —**steadier** *n* —**steadily** *adv* —**steadiness** *n* ◇ **go steady** to go out together regularly as a couple (*informal*)

steady state *n* a condition of stability or equilibrium in a system, e.g. in the energy levels of an atom, in which there is little or no change over time

steady-state theory *n* a theory in astronomy that the universe has always existed at a uniform density that is maintained because new matter is created continuously as the universe expands

steak /stayk/ *n* **1** CUT OF BEEF a thick slice of beef from a lean part of a cow **2** PIECE OF MEAT OR FISH a piece of meat other than beef, e.g. pork, gammon, venison, or veal, or of a large fish, e.g. cod, salmon, or tuna **3** SERVING OF MINCED MEAT minced meat formed into a solid shape, usually a flat roundish shape, and served grilled, fried, or barbecued [15C. < Old Norse *steik* 'meat roasted on a spit'.]

steakhouse /stáyk howss/ (*plural* **-houses** /-howziz/) *n* a restaurant that specializes in serving beef steaks

steak knife *n* a table knife with a sharp usually serrated blade, suitable for cutting steak

steak tartare /-taar taár/ *n* freshly minced beef that is served uncooked with raw egg and chopped onions [*Tartare* < French, 'Tatar']

steal /steel/ *v* (**steals, stealing, stole** /stōl/, **stolen** /stólən/) **1** *vti* TAKE UNLAWFULLY to take something that belongs to somebody else, illegally or without the owner's permission **2** *vt* TAKE FURTIVELY to take or get something secretly, surreptitiously, or through trickery ○ *steal a glance* **3** *vi* SNEAK to move quietly, especially in the hope of not been seen or caught **4** *vt* TAKE AND USE ANOTHER'S IDEAS to take something that another person has created, especially ideas, theories, or a piece of writing, and present it as your own **5** *vi* PASS UNNOTICED to pass or move without being noticed (*literary*) ○ *Dawn was stealing over the mountaintops.* **6** *vti* GAIN A BASE WITHOUT HIT to gain a base by running without the ball being hit by the batter and in the absence of an error by the fielding team **7** *vt* SUCCEED AT UNEXPECTEDLY to win or succeed at something unexpectedly, luckily, or dishonestly at the expense of another or others (*informal*) ■ *n* **1** ACT OF STEALING an act of stealing **2** BARGAIN something that does not cost very much or that costs a lot less than would be expected (*informal*) [Old English *stelan* < Germanic] —**stealer** *n*

SPELLCHECK Do not confuse ***steal*** with ***steel*** which has a similar sound. Beware: your spellchecker will not catch this error.

SYNONYMS ***steal, pinch, nick, filch, purloin, pilfer, embezzle, misappropriate***

CORE MEANING: the taking of property unlawfully

steal to take something that belongs to somebody else, illegally or without the owner's permission; **pinch** (*informal*) to steal something; **nick** (*slang*) to steal something; **filch** (*informal*) to steal something furtively and opportunistically, usually a small item or something of little value; **purloin** (*formal*) to steal something, sometimes used humorously or euphemistically; **pilfer** to steal small items of little value, especially habitually; **embezzle** to take for personal use money or property that has been given on trust by others, without their knowledge; **misappropriate** to take something, especially money, dishonestly or in order to use it for an improper or illegal purpose.

stealth /stelth/ *n* **1** ACTION TO AVOID DETECTION the action of doing something slowly, quietly, and covertly, in order to avoid detection **2** FURTIVENESS secretive, dishonest, or cunning behaviour or actions ■ *adj* VIRTUALLY UNDETECTABLE BY RADAR designed or constructed in such a way and using requisite technology and materials so as to be invisible to enemy radar ○ *stealth bombers* ■ SECRET done in a highly secret way so as to be unnoticed (*slang*) ○ *conducted a stealth money raising campaign* [13C. < assumed Old English *stǣlþ* < Germanic.] —**stealthful** *adj*

stealth car *n* a car designed to be untraceable by electronic tracking and monitoring devices

stealth tower *n* a wireless telecommunications tower camouflaged so as to be ecologically friendly and aesthetic, e.g. one configured as a pine tree, and intended to soften the environmental and visual impact of proliferating antenna sites (*informal*)

stealthy /stélthi/ (**-ier, -iest**) *adj* **1** done in a deliberately slow, careful, and quiet way **2** secretive, furtive, or cunning —**stealthily** *adv* —**stealthiness** *n*

SYNONYMS See ***secret***.

steam /steem/ *n* **1** VAPORIZED WATER the vapour that is formed when water is boiled **2** MIST OF WATER VAPOUR the visible mist that forms when water vapour condenses in the air **3** VAPOUR any visible form of vapour **4** POWER stamina, strength, or speed (*informal*) ○ *running out of steam* ■ *adj* **1** DRIVEN BY STEAM driven or powered by steam **2** USING STEAM using steam to do something **3** OUTMODED old-fashioned or obsolete, like the steam engine (*humorous*) ■ *v* **1** *vi* PRODUCE STEAM to produce or be produced as steam **2** *vi* MOVE BY STEAM to move or be powered by steam **3** *vti* COOK IN STEAM to cook something or be cooked in the steam of boiling water **4** *vi* MOVE FAST to move very quickly and energetically (*informal*) **5** *vi* GENERATE STEAM to generate steam (*refers especially to boilers*) [Old English *stēam*] ◇ **get up steam** to gather together enough energy and speed to do something (*informal*)

steam up *vti* to become, or make something become, clouded with condensation

steam bath *n* a steam-filled room or compartment that people go into to relax and refresh themselves through sweating

steamboat /steém bōt/ *n* a boat with an engine powered by steam

steam chest *n* a compartment in a steam engine from which steam is supplied to the valve of the engine

steam distillation *n* the process of separating or purifying a liquid by passing steam through it

steam engine *n* an engine powered by steam, typically incorporating a flywheel attached to a reciprocating piston that in turn is driven by the expansive action of steam generated in a boiler

steamer /steémər/ *n* **1** BOAT POWERED BY STEAM a boat or ship that is powered by a steam engine or engines **2** PAN FOR STEAMING FOOD a covered pan with a perforated base that fits on top of a saucepan of boiling water so that the food inside is cooked by steam **3** CONTAINER FOR STEAMING WOOD a container in which wood is treated with steam to make it pliable **4** MUGGER a member of a large group of youths who go to crowded areas and do mass muggings (*slang*) **5** *US* SOFT-SHELL CLAM a soft-shell clam, especially when steamed and eaten **6** WET SUIT FOR COLD CONDITIONS a wet suit with long sleeves and legs, for use in cold conditions (*slang*)

steamer rug *n US* a warm blanket that can be put over the knees and legs for warmth, used especially by passengers sitting on the deck of a ship

steamer trunk *n* a traveller's trunk, especially one that is shallow enough to fit underneath a bunk on a ship

steam-generating heavy-water reactor *n* a nuclear reactor that uses ordinary water as the coolant, which produces steam, and heavy water as the moderator

steaming /steéming/ *adj* **1** VERY ANGRY very angry or upset (*informal*) **2** DRUNK extremely drunk (*slang*) ■ *n* MASS MUGGING mass mugging carried out by a large group of youths, in crowded areas such as busy streets or shopping malls, or on trains, buses, or the underground (*slang*)

steam iron *n* an electric iron with a chamber for water. As the iron heats up steam is produced and channelled through holes in the face of the iron to dampen the laundry.

steam jacket *n* a covering or casing surrounding the cylinders and heads of a steam engine to keep the surfaces hot and dry

steam organ *n* a musical organ with whistles sounded by steam. It is played manually by keyboard or automatically using a punched card and it used to be a popular fairground attraction. US term **calliope**

steamroller /steém rōlər/ *n* **1** VEHICLE FOR FLATTENING ROADS a specialized vehicle, originally steam-powered, with large heavy rollers for wheels, designed to flatten and compress newly-laid road surfaces **2** CRUSHING FORCE somebody or something that is a powerful driving force, often crushing or dismissing anybody or anything that might stand in the way ■ *vt* **steamroller, steamroll 1** FLATTEN ROAD to flatten and compress a newly-laid road surface using a steamroller **2** RUTHLESSLY CRUSH to crush or dismiss anybody or anything that might stand in the way ○ *steamroller everyone else's ideas* **3** COMPEL to force somebody to do something

steam room *n* a room with a steam bath in it, or a room that can be filled with steam and used as a steam bath

steamship /steém ship/ *n* a ship with an engine powered by steam

steam shovel *n* a large steam-powered excavating machine, especially an earth-mover that has a bucket on a boom fixed to a jib that can be rotated

steamtight /steém tīt/ *adj* designed or sealed so that steam cannot escape —**steamtightness** *n*

steam turbine *n* a turbine that uses the heat energy of steam to generate the power for mechanical rotation

steamy /steémi/ (**-ier, -iest**) *adj* **1** covered with, full of, affected by, or like steam **2** with an exaggerated emphasis on sexual relations or sexuality (*informal*) —**steamily** *adv* —**steaminess** *n*

stearate /steér ayt/ *n* a salt or ester of stearic acid [Mid-19C. < Greek *stear* (see STEATO-) + -ATE.]

stearic /sti árrik/ *adj* **1** relating to, containing, or typical of stearin or fat **2** about, derived from, or containing stearic acid [Mid-19C. < Greek *stear* (see STEATO-).]

stearic acid *n* $C_{18}H_{36}O_2$ a colourless odourless waxy crystalline fatty acid. Source: animal tallow, vegetable oils. Use: manufacture of candles, cosmetics, soaps, lubricants, medicines.

stearin /steérin/, **stearine** /steéreen/ *n* **1** a colourless ester of glycerol and stearic acid. Use: manufacture of soap, candles, adhesives. **2** BIOCHEM = **stearic acid 3** the solid form of fat [Early 19C. < Greek *stear* (see STEATO-) + -IN.]

steatite /steé ə tīt/ *n* = **soapstone** [Mid-18C. Via Latin < Greek *steatitis (lithos)* 'tallow-like (stone)' < *stear* (see STEATO-).] —**steatitic** /steé ə títtik/ *adj*

steato- *prefix* fat ○ *steatopygia* [< Greek *steat-*, stem of *stear* 'solid fat, tallow']

steatopygia /steé ətō píjji ə, -píji ə/ *n* an accumulation of fat on the buttocks [Early 19C. < STEATO- + Greek *pugē* 'buttocks' < ?] —**steatopygous** /steé ətō pígəss, steé ə tóppigəss/ *adj*

steatorrhea *n US* = **steatorrhoea**

steatorrhoea /steé ətə reé ə/ *n* an unusual condition in which an excess of fat is present in stools

steed /steed/ *n* a horse, especially a lively spirited one (*literary*) [Old English *stēda* 'stallion' < Germanic]

steel /steel/ *n* **1** STRONG ALLOY OF IRON AND CARBON a strong alloy of iron containing up to 1.5 per cent carbon along with small amounts of other elements such as manganese, chromium, and nickel **2** SOMETHING MADE OF STEEL something made of steel, e.g. a weapon **3** KNIFE SHARPENER a steel rod, often with a handle, that knives are drawn back and forward along in order to sharpen them **4** TOUGHNESS determination, toughness, or great strength of character ■ *adj* STRONG OR HARD like steel, especially in strength or hardness ■ *vt* **1** TREAT WITH STEEL to coat, plate, edge, or point something with steel **2** PREPARE BY HARDENING to make somebody unfeeling, or tough enough to withstand a setback or trial ○ *steeled myself for the news* [Old English *stēli* < Indo-European, 'stand, be solid']

SPELLCHECK See ***steal***.

steel band *n* a group of musicians who play steel drums and often specialize in calypsos

steel-blue *adj* of a cold greyish-blue colour —**steel blue** *n*

steel drum, steel pan *n* a Caribbean percussion instrument made by hammering an oil drum into a concave shape with flattened areas that make musical notes when struck

Steele, Mount /steel/ peak in the Saint Elias Range, in SW Yukon Territory, Canada. Height: 5,073 m/16,644 ft.

steel engraving *n* **1** the art, technique, or process of engraving on a steel plate **2** a print made from an engraved steel plate

steel-grey *adj* of a dark bluish-grey colour —**steel grey** *n*

steel guitar *n* a fretless guitar played on a horizontal stand with a plectrum and a movable metal slide. ◊ **pedal steel**

steelhead /stéel hed/ (*plural* **-heads** *or* **-head**) *n* an anadromous rainbow trout with a silver coloration, popular for sport fishing. Native to: North Pacific Ocean.

steel pan *n* MUSIC = **steel drum**

steel wool *n* thin strands of steel tangled together to form an abrasive mass, used for cleaning and polishing

steelwork /stéel wurk/ *n* something made from steel, especially a structural framework

steelworker /stéel wurkər/ *n* a worker at making steel

steelworks /stéel wurks/ *n* a factory where steel is made (*+ singular or plural verb*)

steely /steeli/ *adj* **1** like steel, especially in colour or in being tough or determined **2** made of steel (*dated or literary*) —**steeliness** *n*

steelyard /stéel yaard/ *n* a portable balance for weighing objects [Mid-17C. < YARD[1] 'rod, spar'.]

Steen /stayn/, **Jan** (1626–79) Dutch painter

steenbok /stéen bok/ (*plural* **-boks** *or* **-bok**), **steinbok** /stín bák/ *n* a small slender antelope with short straight horns, long legs, and a reddish-brown coat. Native to: grasslands of southern Africa. *Raphicerus campestris.* [Late 18C. Via Afrikaans < Middle Dutch *steenboc* 'stone buck'.]

steep[1] /steep/ *adj* **1** SLOPING SHARPLY sloping very sharply, often to the extent of being almost vertical **2** EXCESSIVE unreasonably or excessively high, especially in cost (*informal*) **3** UNREASONABLE unreasonable, unfair, or expecting too much (*informal*) **4** RAPID OR HUGE faster or greater than is usual, or might be expected ○ *There's been a steep decline in the number of people out of work.* **5** TAXING very ambitious or difficult [Old English *stēap* 'high' < Germanic, 'lofty, deep'] —**steeply** *adv* —**steepness** *n*

steep[2] /steep/ *v* **1** *vti* IMMERSE IN LIQUID to soak something, or be soaked, in a liquid, especially for cleaning or softening, or in order to extract something **2** *vt* PERMEATE to permeate somebody or something with a substance or quality, usually over a long period (*usually passive*) ○ *steeped in tradition* ■ *n* **1** A SOAKING an act or the process of steeping something in a liquid **2** LIQUID FOR SOAKING a liquid that something is or can be steeped in [14C. < assumed Old English *stiepan* < Germanic.] —**steeper** *n*

steepen /stéepən/ *vti* to become, or make something become, steep or steeper

steeple /stéep'l/ *n* **1** a tower and spire forming part of a church, or a spire found on the top of a church tower or roof **2** a spire [Old English *stēpel* < Germanic, 'lofty, deep'] —**steepled** *adj*

steeplechase /stéep'l chayss/ *n* **1** HORSERACE WITH JUMPS ON TRACK a horse race, e.g. the Grand National, run over a course that has obstacles, e.g. hedges, ditches, and water jumps, that the horses must jump over. ◊ **flat race** *n.* 1 **2** TRACK EVENT WITH WATER JUMP a track event in which the runners must jump over a water jump as well as hurdles ■ *vi* (**-chases, -chasing, -chased**) RUN A STEEPLECHASE to compete in a steeplechase [Late 18C. Because a church steeple was originally the competitors' goal.] —**steeplechaser** *n*

steeplejack /stéep'l jak/ *n* a builder or repairer of tall structures, especially steeples and chimneys

steer[1] /steer/ *v* **1** *vti* DIRECT to guide something such as a motor vehicle or ship in a direction using a steering wheel, rudder, or other device **2** *vt* INFLUENCE DIRECTION to try to influence people to follow a particular course of action by unobtrusively guiding them towards it **3** *vi* FOLLOW PARTICULAR COURSE to follow a specified course **4** *vi* MANOEUVRE IN A CERTAIN WAY to go or move in a specified way or direction when being driven or propelled ○ *This car steers to the left.* ■ *n US* PIECE OF ADVICE a piece of information or advice (*informal*) [Old English *stīeran* < Germanic, 'steer'] —**steerable** *adj* —**steerer** *n*

steer[2] /steer/ *n* a male of the cattle family that has been castrated before reaching sexual maturity and is kept for beef, especially a young bull [Old English *stēor*]

steerage /stéerij/ *n* **1** the cheapest passenger accommodation on board a ship, usually in the area near the rudder and steering gear **2** the act or process of steering a boat

steerageway /stéerij way/ *n* a rate of forward movement that is fast enough to allow a boat to be steered from the helm

steering column *n* the part in a motor vehicle that connects the steering wheel, or the handlebars on a motorcycle, with the steering gear

steering committee *n* a group of selected people who decide agendas and topics for discussion, and prioritize urgent business, especially one acting for a legislative body or other assembly

steering gear *n* the mechanism in a vehicle or ship that allows it to be steered

steering wheel *n* a wheel in a vehicle or ship that is connected by way of the steering column to the steering gear and is turned to change direction

steersman /stéerzmən/ (*plural* **-men** /-mən/) *n* a steerer of a boat or ship [Old English *stēoresman* 'man for steering' < *stēor* 'steering']

steeve[1] /steev/ *n* a spar with a pulley block at one end that is used for stowing cargo on a boat or ship ■ *vt* (**steeves, steeving, steeved**) to stow cargo in the hold of a boat or ship and make it secure [Mid-19C. < ?]

steeve[2] /steev/ *vti* (**steeves, steeving, steeved**) to incline upwards, or make a bowsprit incline upwards ■ *n* the angle at which a bowsprit inclines upwards from the horizontal [Mid-17C. < ?]

stegosaur /stéggə sawr/, **stegosaurus** /stéggə sáwrəss/ *n* a plant-eating dinosaur that lived in the Jurassic and Early Cretaceous periods and had tough bony dorsal plates and spikes. Genus: *Stegosauria.* [Early 20C. < modern Latin *Stegosaurus* < Greek *stegos* 'plate' + *sauros* 'lizard'.]

stein /stīn/ *n* **1** a large beer mug, especially a German earthenware or pewter one, often with a hinged lid **2** the amount of beer or other liquid that a stein holds [Mid-19C. < German, shortening of *Steinkrug* 'stoneware mug'.]

Stein /stīn/, **Gertrude** (1874–1946) US writer

Stein /steen/, **Jock** (1922–85) Scottish football manager. Born **John Stein**

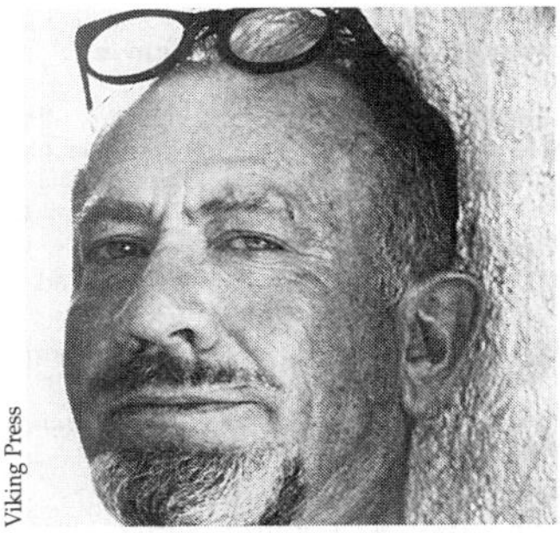

Viking Press

John Steinbeck

Steinbeck /stín bek/, **John Ernst** (1902–68) US writer

steinbok *n* ZOOL = **steenbok**

Steinem /stínəm/, **Gloria** (*b.* 1934) US feminist

Steiner /shtínər, stínər/, **Rudolf** (1861–1925) Austrian philosopher

stela /stéelə/ (*plural* **-lae** /stée lee/) *n* ARCHAEOL = **stele** *n.* 1 [Late 18C. Via Latin < Greek *stēlē* 'standing stone'.]

stele /steel, stéeli/ (*plural* **-lae** /stée lee/ *or* **-les**) *n* **1** an ancient stone slab or pillar, usually engraved, inscribed, or painted, and set upright **2** the cylindrical core of the stem and roots of a plant that contains the sap-conducting vascular tissues and varying amounts of packing tissue (**pith**) [Early 19C. < Greek *stēlē* 'standing stone'.] —**stelar** *adj*

stellar /stéllər/ *adj* **1** INVOLVING STARS relating to, consisting of, or like a star or stars **2** *US* EXCEPTIONAL exceptionally good **3** INVOLVING FAMOUS PEOPLE about, involving, characteristic of, or full of famous people, especially those in the film or entertainment industries [Mid-17C. < late Latin *stellaris* < Latin *stella* 'star'.]

stellar wind *n* a stream of ionized particles ejected from the surface of a star. ◊ **solar wind**

stellate /stéllət, -ayt/, **stellated** /ste láytid/ *adj* **1** shaped like a star **2** having a central part with smaller parts radiating out from it, like a starfish, some flower heads, and some crystal formations [Mid-17C. < Latin *stella* (see STELLAR).] —**stellately** *adv*

stem[1] /stem/ *n* **1** MAIN AXIS OF PLANT the main axis of a plant that bears buds and shoots **2** SECONDARY PLANT BRANCH a slender part of a plant other than its main axis that supports a leaf, flower, or fruit **3** NARROW CONNECTING PART any long slim part of an object, e.g. the part that connects the base of a wine glass to its bowl, or the hollow tube on a smoker's pipe **4** GENEALOGICAL LINE the major line of descent in a family tree **5** CYLINDRICAL WATCH PART a short rod, usually with an expanded crown at the end of it, that is used in winding a watch **6** BASE OF A WORD the base of a word, to which affixes are added **7** VERTICAL LETTER PART an upright stroke, especially the main one, in a letter or character **8** VERTICAL PART OF MUSIC NOTE the vertical part that extends from the head of a written musical note **9** UPRIGHT BOW TIMBER the main upright timber at the bow of a ship ■ *v* (**stems, stemming, stemmed**) **1** *vi* ORIGINATE to derive, originate, or be caused by something ○ *This behaviour stems from some trauma in his childhood.* **2** *vt* REMOVE STEM OF to take off the stem or part of the stem from something, especially a flower, fruit, or vegetable **3** *vt* GIVE STEM TO to give something a stem, e.g. a smoker's pipe or a wineglass **4** *vt* MAKE HEADWAY to make headway in a ship or boat against a tide or wind [Old English *stefn* < Indo-European, 'to stand'] —**stemless** *adj* —**stemmed** *adj* —**stemmer** *n* ◇ **from stem to stern** through the whole of a place, especially a ship

stem[2] /stem/ *v* (**stems, stemming, stemmed**) **1** *vt* PREVENT FROM FLOWING to hinder, obstruct, or stop something from flowing, especially by creating a dam or plug **2** *vt* STOP UP to plug something such as a blast or drill hole by packing it **3** *vti* TURN SKI IN to turn the tip of a ski or skis inwards in order to turn or slow down ■ *n* **stem, stem turn** TURNING IN OF SKI an act or the technique of turning the tip of a ski or skis inwards to turn or slow down [13C. < Old Norse *stemma* < Germanic, 'halt, stammer'.]

stem cell *n* an undifferentiated cell that can give rise to other cells of the same type indefinitely or from which specialized cells, e.g. blood cells, develop

stem christie /-krísti/ *n* a skiing turn performed by stemming one ski and then bringing the other parallel to it during the turn [*Stem* < STEM[2]; *christie* a shortening and alteration of *christiania*]

stem ginger *n* round portions of the underground stem of a ginger plant, cooked until tender and preserved in syrup

stemma /stémmə/ (*plural* **-mata** /-mətə/) *n* **1** FAMILY TREE a family tree **2** DIAGRAM OF TEXTS OF LITERARY WORK a diagram like a family tree, showing the relationships between different texts of a literary work **3** EYE OF ARTHROPOD a simple eye or facet of a compound eye of some arthropods [Mid-17C. Via Latin < Greek *stemma* 'garland'; from the ancient Roman practice of placing garlands on images of their ancestors.]

stemson /stémss'n/ *n* a timber attached to the stem and keelson in the bow of a wooden ship [Mid-18C. < STEM[1], after KEELSON.]

stem turn *n* SKIING = **stem**[2] *n.*

stemware /stém wair/ *n* glasses, goblets, and other glass vessels that have stems

stench /stench/ *n* a really disgusting smell, especially a strong lingering one [Old English *stenc* 'odour' < Germanic]

SYNONYMS See ***smell.***

stench trap *n* a device used in a sewer to prevent foul-smelling gases from rising, especially one that has a water seal

stencil /sténss'l/ *n* **1** PLATE WITH CUT-OUT DESIGN a thin sheet of material with a shape cut out of it that is marked on a surface when paint or ink is applied **2** PATTERN the design, lettering, or other characters marked using a stencil ■ *vt* (**-cils, -cilling, -cilled**) **1** MAKE PATTERN USING STENCIL to apply a design, lettering, or other characters to a surface using a stencil **2** DECORATE USING STENCIL to decorate or mark a surface, e.g. a wall or paper, using a stencil [Early 18C. Via Old French *estenceler* 'decorate with bright colours' < Latin *scintilla* 'spark'.] —**stenciller** *n*

stengah /sténg gə/ *n* BEVERAGES = **stinger**[2] *n.* 2 [Late 19C. < Malay *satĕngah* 'half'.]

Sten gun /stén-/ *n* a light, cheaply manufactured submachine gun formerly used by the British Army, especially in World War II [After R. V. V. *Shepherd* and H. J. *Turpin* + *Enfield* in Greater London (after BREN GUN).]

steno /sténnō/ (*plural* **-os**) *n US* (*informal*) **1** a stenographer **2** stenography [Early 20C. Shortening.]

steno- *prefix* narrow, small ○ *stenothermal* [< Greek *stenos*]

stenobathic /sténnō báthik/ *adj* able to live only within a narrow range of depth of water [Early 20C. < STENO- + Greek *bathos* 'depth'.] —**stenobath** /sténnō bath/ *n*

stenograph /sténnə graaf, -graf/ *n* **1 SHORTHAND TYPEWRITER** a machine like a small typewriter with keys for shorthand characters **2 SHORTHAND CHARACTER** a character in a system of shorthand writing ■ *vt* **WRITE OR TYPE IN SHORTHAND** to record something in shorthand by writing or using a stenograph

stenography /stə nóggrəfi/ (*plural* **-phies**) *n* **1** the act, process, or skill of recording something in shorthand by writing or by using a stenograph **2** something that has been recorded in written shorthand or by using a stenograph —**stenographer** *n* —**stenographic** /sténnə gráffik/ *adj* —**stenographical** *adj* —**stenographically** *adv*

stenohaline /sténnō háy leen, -līn/ *adj* unable to tolerate wide variations in salinity of water [Mid-20C. < STENO- + the Greek stem *hal-* 'salt'.]

stenosis /stə nṓssiss/ *n* an abnormal constriction or narrowing of a duct, passage, or opening in the body [Late 19C. Via modern Latin < Greek *stenos* 'narrow'.] —**stenosed** /stə nṓzd, -nṓst/ *adj* —**stenotic** /stə nóttik/ *adj*

stenothermal /sténnə thúrm'l/ *adj* able to live only within a narrow temperature range

stenotype /sténnə tīp/ *n* a machine whose keyboard is used to record speech by means of phonetic shorthand

stenotypy /sténnə tīpi/ *n* a form of phonetic shorthand that uses combinations of letters to represent sounds and short words —**stenotypic** /sténnə típpik/ *adj* —**stenotypist** /sténnə tīpist/ *n*

stentor /stén tawr/ *n* **1** somebody with a loud powerful voice **2** a trumpet-shaped protozoan with a mouth at the broad end. Genus: *Stentor*. [Early 17C. After *Stentor*, a strong-voiced Greek herald in the Trojan war.]

stentorian /sten táwri ən/ *adj* loud, powerful, or declamatory in tone

step /step/ *n* **1 SHORT MOVEMENT WITH FOOT** a short movement made by raising one foot and lowering it ahead of the other foot **2 DISTANCE OF STEP** the distance travelled in taking a step **3 SOUND OF FOOTFALL** the sound made by moving the foot on a horizontal surface **4 FOOTPRINT** the footprint made by putting down the foot on a surface **5 WAY OF WALKING** a particular manner of walking **6 SHORT WAY** a very short distance **7 RAISED SURFACE** a raised surface for the foot, especially in a series going up or down **8 STAGE IN PROGRESS** a stage in a progression towards some goal or target **9 DEGREE OR GRADE** a degree, rank, or grade, especially on a scale **10 DANCE MOVE** a movement of the feet and body that forms part of a dance **11 DEGREE OR INTERVAL** a degree of a musical staff or scale, or the interval between two degrees **12 STEP AEROBICS** step aerobics (*informal*) ○ *a step class* ■ **steps** *npl* **1 OUTDOOR STAIRS** a flight of stairs, usually outdoors, and made of stone or a similar material **2 PATH MADE BY SOMEBODY ELSE** a route, path, or course set by somebody else ○ *She followed in her mother's steps and became an architect.* ■ *v* (**steps, stepping, stepped**) **1** *vti* **MOVE FOOT** to move a foot on top of something or in a particular direction ○ *Please step aside.* **2** *vi* **WALK A FEW STEPS** to walk a short distance or to a specific place **3** *vi* **TO MOVE FORWARD WITH FOOT** to move forward by raising one foot and setting it down in front of the other **4** *vi* **MOVE IN REGULAR RHYTHM** to move at a measured pace, e.g. in a dance **5** *vi* **TREAT SOMEBODY WITHOUT RESPECT** to show or treat somebody with arrogant disregard and unkindness ○ *She is stepping on other people's feelings constantly.* **6** *vi* **EASILY WALK INTO SITUATION** to come into a new situation with ease or with little preparation **7** *vt* **ARRANGE IN STEPS** to arrange or organize something in steps, or to furnish something with steps **8** *vt* **MEASURE BY STEPS** to measure something by walking or pacing its length [Old English *stæpe* < Germanic, 'to tread'] —**stepped** *adj* —**stepper** *n* ◇ **be in** *or* **out of step 1** to agree or disagree with somebody or something in your attitudes or opinions **2** to move in unison with or at a different pace and rhythm from other people ◇ **step by step** gradually ◇ **step on it** to hurry (*informal*) ◇ **take steps** to take action ◇ **watch your step 1** to be careful and cautious **2** to tread carefully

SPELLCHECK Do not confuse ***step*** with ***steppe***, which has a similar sound. Beware: your spellchecker will not catch this error.

step down *v* **1** *vi* to resign, retire, or withdraw from a position **2** *vti* to lower or decrease in stages

step in *vi* to intervene or become involved in something

step out *vi* **1 LEAVE BRIEFLY** to leave a place for a brief period **2 WALK WITH LONG STRIDES** to walk fast, with longer strides than usual **3 DATE** to go on a date or to a social gathering with somebody (*informal*) **4 TO BE UNFAITHFUL** to be unfaithful to a spouse or partner (*informal*)

step up *v* **1** *vt* **RAISE IN STAGES** to raise or increase something in stages **2** *vt* **RAISE VOLTAGE** to raise voltage using a transformer **3** *vi* **TO COME FORWARD** to come forward, e.g. to stand for something or to take responsibility for something

step- *prefix* related because of remarriage, not by blood ○ *stepson* [Old English *stēop-*]

step aerobics *n* an exercise programme done to music that involves performing different movements with the arms and legs while stepping onto and off a small portable platform (+ *singular or plural verb*)

stepbrother /stép bruth̲ər/ *n* a boy or man who has brothers or sisters through the remarriage of a parent to somebody who has children

stepchild /stép chīld/ (*plural* **-children** /-children/) *n* the son or daughter of a stepparent

step dance *n* a dance in which feet and leg movements are important, often performed with the dancer remaining in one spot

stepdaughter /stép dawtər/ *n* the daughter of somebody's spouse by a previous marriage

step-down *adj* **1** decreasing in quantity, size, or status, especially in stages **2** serving to lower voltage —**step-down** *n*

stepfamily /stép famli/ (*plural* **-lies**) *n* a family in which there is a stepparent

stepfather /stép faath̲ər/ *n* a man who has married somebody's mother after the death of or divorce from the person's father

step function *n* a mathematical function such as a waveform that remains constant in value over a given interval but changes abruptly in value from one interval to the next

stephanotis /stéffə nṓtiss/ (*plural* **-tises** *or* **-tis**) *n* an ornamental vine or shrub with leathery leaves. Flowers: fragrant, white, waxy. Genus: *Stephanotis*. [Mid-19C. < Greek *stephanōtis* 'fit for a crown' < *stephanos* 'crown, wreath' < *stephein* 'to crown'.]

Stephen /stéev'n/ (1090?–1154) king of England (1135–54)

Stephen, Sir Ninian Martin (*b.* 1923) British-born Australian lawyer and statesman

Stephen, St (*d.* AD 36) Christian martyr. Known as **the Protomartyr**

Stephen I, St (975?–1038) king of Hungary

Stephens /stéev'nz/, **Frederick George** (1828–1907) British art critic

Stephenson /stéevənss'n/, **George** (1781–1848) British railway engineer

Stephenson, Robert (1803–59) British civil engineer and politician

step-in *adj* without fastenings and put on by stepping into it ■ **step-ins** *npl* a step-in article of clothing, especially panties with wide legs worn by women in the 1920s and 1930s (*dated*)

stepladder /stép laddər/ *n* a folding ladder that has flat broad steps and a hinged supporting frame

stepmother /stép mut̲hər/ *n* a woman who has married somebody's father after the death of or divorce from the person's mother

stepparent /stép pairənt/ *n* a stepfather or a stepmother —**stepparenting** *n*

steppe /step/ *n* an extensive, usually treeless plain, often semiarid and grass-covered [Late 17C. Via German < Russian *step*.]

SPELLCHECK See ***step***.

Steppes /steps/ *n* the vast grassy plains of Russia and the Ukraine

stepping stone *n* **1** one of a series of stones on which somebody is able to step, e.g. to cross shallow water **2** a stage or step that helps achieve a goal

stepsister /stép sistər/ *n* a girl or woman who has brothers or sisters through the remarriage of a parent to somebody who has children

stepson /stép sun/ *n* the son of somebody's spouse by a previous marriage

step stool *n* a stool with hinged steps that can be folded

step turn *n* a turn in which a skier lifts one ski in a desired direction, brings it down, and then aligns the other ski with it

step-up *adj* **1** increasing in quantity, size, or status, usually in stages **2** serving to raise voltage —**stepped-up** *adj* —**step-up** *n*

stepwise /stép wīz/ *adj* arranged in or resembling steps

-ster *suffix* **1** associated with, doing, or making a specific thing ○ *gangster* ○ *punster* **2** having a specific characteristic ○ *youngster* [Old English *-estre*, originally a feminine suffix]

steradian /stə ráydi ən/ *n* (*symbol* **sr**) the basic SI unit of measurement of solid angle [Late 19C. < STEREO- + RADIAN.]

stercoraceous /stúrkə ráyshəss/ *adj* consisting of or resembling dung or faeces [Mid-18C. < Latin *stercor-* 'dung'.]

stere /steer/ *n* a cubic metre, equal to 35.32 cubic ft [Late 18C. Via French *stère* < Greek *stereos* (see STEREO-).]

stere- *prefix* = **stereo-** (*before vowels*)

stereo /stérri ō, steér-/ (*plural* **-os**) *n* **1 DEVICE PRODUCING STEREOPHONIC SOUND** an audio system or device that reproduces stereophonic sound **2 STEREOPHONIC REPRODUCTION** stereophonic sound reproduction **3 STEREOSCOPIC PHOTOGRAPHY** photography using stereoscopy **4** PRINTING = **stereotype** *n.* 3 [Late 19C. Shortening.]

stereo- *prefix* **1** three-dimensional ○ *stereology* **2** solid ○ *stereotaxis* [< Greek *stereos* 'solid' < Indo-European, 'stiff']

stereobate /stérri ō bayt, steéri-/ *n* **1** a masonry platform that supports a building **2** BUILDING = **stylobate** [Mid-19C. < Latin *stereobates* < Greek *stereos* 'solid' + *-batēs* 'walker'.]

stereochemistry /stérri ō kémmistri, steéri-/ *n* the study of the spatial distribution of atoms in a compound and its effects on the compound's properties

stereochrome /stérri ə krōm, steéri-/ *n* a wall painting that uses water glass as a medium or preservative [Mid-19C. < German *Stereochrom* < Greek *stereos* 'solid' + *khroma* 'colour'.] —**stereochromy** *n*

stereogram /stérri ə gram, steéri-/ *n* **1** PHOTOGRAPHY = **stereograph 2** a diagram or picture that shows objects as though in relief **3** a stereo radiogram (*dated*)

stereograph /stérri ə graaf, steéri ə-, -graf/ *n* a picture with two superimposed images or two almost identical pictures placed side-by-side which when viewed through special glasses or a stereoscope produce a three-dimensional image

stereography /stérri óggrəfi, steéri-/ *n* **1** the technique or art of depicting or drawing a three-dimensional object on a flat surface **2** the study and construction of defined geometric objects —**stereographic** /stérri ə gráffik, steéri-/ *adj* —**stereographically** *adv*

stereoisomer /stérri ō íssəmər, steéri-/ *n* one of a group of molecules having identical atoms connected in the same order but in different spatial arrangements

stereoisomerism /stérri ō ī sómmərizəm, steéri-/ *n* isomerism in which the atoms in molecules are connected in the same order but in different spatial arrangements —**stereoisomeric** /-íssə mérrik/ *adj*

stereology /stérri ólləji, steéri-/ *n* the study of the properties of three-dimensional structures and objects based on two-dimensional views of them —**stereological** *adj*

stereometry /stérri ómmətri, steéri ō-/ *n* the measurement of volume —**stereometric** /stérri ō méttrik, steérri ō méttrik/ *adj*

stereomicroscope /stérri ō míkrəskōp, steéri-/ *n* a microscope with two optically separate eyepieces to make viewed objects look three-dimensional

stereophonic /stérri ə fónnik, steéree-/ *adj* using an audio system based on two or more soundtracks to make recorded sound seem more natural when reproduced —**stereophonically** *adv* —**stereophony** /stérri óffəni, steéri-/ *n*

stereopsis /stérri ópsiss, steéri-/ *n* three-dimensional vision

stereopticon /stérri óptikən, steéri-/ *n* a slide projector able to allow one image to gradually replace another [Mid-19C. < modern Latin, < Greek *stereos* 'solid' + *optikos* 'optic'.]

stereoscope /stérri əskōp, steéri-/ *n* a device resembling a pair of binoculars in which two-dimensional pictures of a scene taken at slightly different angles are viewed concurrently, one with each eye, creating the illusion of three dimensions

stereoscopic /stérri ə skóppik, steéri ə-/ *adj* **1** involving, producing, or resembling the effects of seeing something as three-dimensional **2** produced by or relating to a stereoscope —**stereoscopically** *adv*

stereoscopy /stérri óskəpi, steéri-/ *n* the visual perception of objects as being three-dimensional

stereospecific /stérri ō spə síffik, steéri ō-/ *adj* relating to a process in which atoms are in a fixed spatial position

stereotaxis /stérri ō táksiss, steéri ō-/ *n* **1** BIOL = **thigmotaxis** **2** neurological surgery involving the insertion of delicate instruments that are guided to a specific area by the use of three-dimensional scanning techniques —**stereotactic** /-táktik/ *adj* —**stereotactically** *adv* —**stereotaxic** /-táksik/ *adj* —**stereotaxically** *adv*

stereotype /stérri ə tīp, steéri ə-/ *n* **1 OVERSIMPLIFIED CONCEPTION** an oversimplified standardized image or idea held by one person or group of another **2** PSYCHOL = **stereotypy** *n.* 1 **3 METAL PRINTING PLATE** a metal printing plate cast from a mould in another material such as papier-mâché ■ *vt* (**-types, -typing, -typed**) **1 REDUCE TO OVERSIMPLIFIED CATEGORIES** to categorize individuals or groups according to an oversimplified standardized image or idea **2 USE STEREOTYPE IN PRINTING** to cast or print using a stereotype [Late 18C. < French *stéréotype* 'solid-block printing'.] —**stereotyper** *n* —**stereotypical** /stérri ə típpik'l, steéri ə-/ *adj* —**stereotypically** *adv* —**stereotypist** *n*

stereotypy /stérri ə tīpi, steéri ə-/ *n* **1 stereotypy, stereotype** a pattern of persistent, fixed, and repeated speech or movement that is apparently meaningless and is characteristic of some mental conditions **2** the process of casting or printing stereotypes

steric /stérrik, steér-/ *adj* related to the way atoms are spatially arranged [Late 19C. < STEREO-.] —**sterically** *adv*

sterile /stérrīl/ *adj* **1 BARREN** incapable of supporting vegetation **2 INFERTILE** incapable of becoming pregnant or of inducing pregnancy **3 NOT PRODUCING SEEDS** not producing seeds, fruit, or spores **4 FREE FROM INFECTIVE ORGANISMS** free from living bacteria and other microorganisms **5 DULL AND UNCREATIVE** unstimulating, uncreative, and lacking in ideas that will lead to any useful outcome [15C. Via Old French < Latin *sterilis*.] —**sterilant** /stérrilənt/ *n* —**sterilely** *adv* —**sterility** /stə rílləti, ste r-/ *n*

sterilise *vt* = **sterilize**

sterilize /stérri līz/ (**-izes, -izing, -ized**), **sterilise** (**-ises, -ising, -ised**) *vt* **1** to kill all living microorganisms in order to make something incapable of causing infection **2** to stop a person or animal from reproducing, e.g. by surgical removal or alteration of reproductive organs —**sterilizable** *adj* —**sterilization** /stérri lī záysh'n/ *n* —**sterilizer** *n*

sterlet /stúrlit/ (*plural* **-lets** *or* **-let**) *n* a small caviar-bearing sturgeon. Native to: Black and Caspian Seas. *Acipenser ruthenus*. [Late 16C. < Russian *sterlyad*, ultimately < Germanic.]

sterling /stúrling/ *n* **1 BRITISH CURRENCY** British money **2 BRITISH STANDARD FOR COIN METAL PURITY** the official standard of purity in terms of precious metal content for gold and silver coins in Britain, being 91.666% (22 carat) or 74.999% (18 carat) for gold and 92.5% for silver **3** = **sterling silver** ■ *adj* **1 OF STERLING SILVER** made of sterling silver **2 ADMIRABLE** admirable or valuable ○ *sterling efforts* [13C. Probably literally 'small star' < an earlier form of STAR.]

sterling area *n* the group of countries that use British currency, or that link the value of their own currency to that of sterling

sterling silver, sterling *n* an alloy containing at least 92.5% silver with the remainder usually copper

stern[1] /stern/ *adj* **1 STRICT** rigid, strict, and uncompromising **2 SEVERE** severe and allowing no leeway **3 FORBIDDING** grim, austere, or forbidding in appearance [Old English *styrne* < Indo-European, 'stiff'] —**sternly** *adv*

stern[2] /stern/ *n* **1 REAR OF SHIP** the rear part of a vessel **2 BACK PART** the rear part of something ■ *adj* **IN REAR** located at or resembling the stern [13C. Probably < Old Norse *stjórn* 'rudder' < Germanic.]

Stern /sturn/, **Isaac** (*b.* 1920) Russian-born US violinist

sterna plural of **sternum**

Sterne /sturn/, **Laurence** (1713–58) Irish novelist

sterno- *prefix* the sternum ○ *sternotomy* [< Greek *sternon* (see STERNUM)]

sternoclavicular /stúrnōklə víkyŏŏlər/ *adj* relating to or connecting the sternum and clavicle

sternocostal /stúrnō kóst'l/ *adj* situated between or relating to the sternum and ribs [Late 18C. < STERNO- + Latin *costa* 'rib'.]

sternpost /stúrnpōst/ *n* the main upright timber in the stern of a vessel

sternsheets /stúrn sheets/ *npl* the space at the rear of an open boat that is behind the rowers' bench [Mid-17C. < SHEET[2] 'forward or after section of a boat'.]

sternson /stúrnss'n/ *n* a reinforcing timber at the joint of a sternpost and keelson at the stern of a wooden vessel [Mid-19C. < STERN[2], after KEELSON.]

sternum /stúrnəm/ (*plural* **-na** /-nə/ *or* **-nums**) *n* **1** the breastbone (*technical*) **2** the chitinous ventral plate covering the abdomen of an arthropod [Mid-17C. Via modern Latin < Greek *sternon* 'breastbone'.] —**sternal** *adj*

sternutation /stúrnyŏŏ táysh'n/ *n* the act of sneezing, or a sneeze (*formal*) [Mid-16C. < Latin *sternutation-* < *sternutare* 'keep sneezing' < *sternuere* 'sneeze'.]

sternutatory /stur nyóotətəri/ *adj* causing or resulting in sneezing ■ *n* (*plural* **-ries**) any substance that causes sneezing [Early 17C]

sternwards /stúrnwərdz/, **sternward** /-wərd/ *adv* in the direction of the stern

sternway /stúrn way/ *n* any backward movement of a vessel

stern-wheeler /stúrn weelər/ *n* a boat propelled by a large paddle wheel at the rear, especially a river boat

steroid /steér oyd, stérroyd/ *n* any of a large group of natural or synthetic fatty substances containing four carbon rings, including the sex hormones [Mid-20C. < STEROL + -OID.] —**steroidal** /ste róyd'l/ *adj*

sterol /steér ol, stérrol/ *n* a steroid alcohol, widespread in animal and plant lipids, e.g. cholesterol [Early 20C. Shortening of CHOLESTEROL.]

-sterone *suffix* steroid hormone ○ *androsterone* [< STEROL + -ONE]

stertor /stúrtər, stúr tawr/ *n* noisy or laborious snoring, heard when somebody is deeply unconscious or when there are obstructed air passages [Early 19C. < modern Latin, < Latin *stertere* 'snore'.] —**stertorous** *adj* —**stertorously** *adv* —**stertorousness** *n*

stet /stet/ *vti* (**stets, stetting, stetted**) to restore or direct somebody to restore something that has previously been deleted from a printed or written text ■ *n* a word or mark indicating that previously deleted printed or written matter should be restored [Mid-18C. < Latin, 'let it stand'.]

stethoscope /stéthə skōp/ *n* a medical instrument used for listening to breathing, heartbeats, and other sounds made by the body [Early 19C. < Greek *stēthos* 'chest'.] —**stethoscopic** /stéthə skóppik/ *adj* —**stethoscopy** /ste thóskəpi/ *n*

Stetson /stéts'n/ *tdmk* a trademark for hats with wide brims and high crowns

stevedore /steévə dawr/ *n* somebody whose job is to load and unload ships ■ *vti* (**-dores, -doring, -dored**) to work as a dockworker, loading and unloading ships [Late 18C. Via Spanish *estibador* or Portuguese *estivador* < Latin *stipare* (see STEEVE[1]).]

stevedore's knot *n* a knot that forms a lump to prevent a line from passing through a hole

Stevens /steév'nz/, **Siaka Probin** (1905–88) Sierra Leone statesman

Stevens, Wallace (1879–1955) US poet

Stevens-Johnson syndrome /steév'nz jónss'n-/ *n* a severe inflammation of the skin and mucous membranes, often after a respiratory infection or as an allergic reaction to drugs [Mid-20C. After Albert Mason *Stevens* (1884–1945) and Frank Chambliss *Johnson* (1894–1934), US paediatricians.]

Stevenson /steévənss'n/, **Robert Louis** (1850–94) Scottish writer

stew[1] /styoo/ *n* **1 SIMMERED DISH** a dish of meat, fish, or vegetables, or a combination of them, that is cooked by slow simmering **2 MIXTURE** any widely assorted mixture **3 BROTHEL** a brothel (*archaic*) ■ *v* **1** *vti* **COOK BY SIMMERING** to cook something by long slow simmering **2** *vi* **BE UPSET** to be deeply troubled or agitated **3** *vi* **BE VERY HOT** to swelter or become uncomfortably hot **4** *vti* **MAKE TEA BITTER** to cause tea to become bitter by infusing it for too long [14C. Via Old French *estuve* 'steam bath' < assumed Vulgar Latin *extufa*.] ◇ **in a stew** agitated, anxious, or in a difficult situation (*informal*)

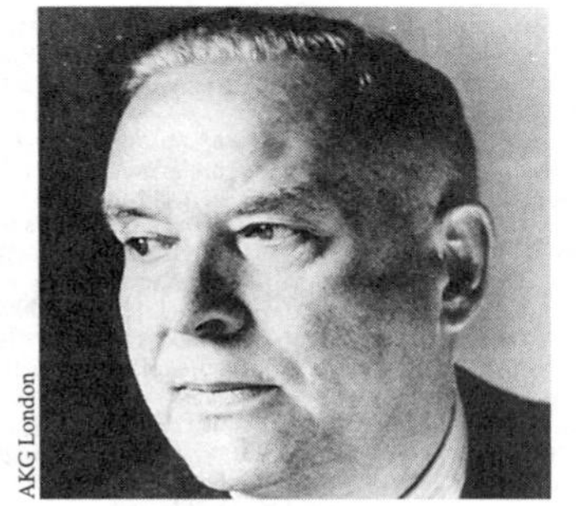

Wallace Stevens

stew[2] /styoo/ *n* **1** a fishpond (*archaic*) **2** an artificial oyster bed [14C. Via Old French *estui* 'confinement' < Latin *studium* (see STUDY).]

steward /styoó ərd/ *n* **1 PLANE OR SHIP ATTENDANT** an attendant of passengers on an aircraft or ship, or a manager of provisions and dining aboard a ship **2 PROPERTY MANAGER** a manager of somebody else's property, finances, or household **3 HOTEL OR CLUB MANAGER** a manager of details concerning meals or lodging at a hotel, club, college, or other establishment **4** POL = **shop steward** **5 OFFICIAL AT PUBLIC EVENT** a marshal or official at a large public event ■ *v* **1** *vti* **ACT AS STEWARD** to act as a steward **2** *vt* **DIRECT OR GUIDE SOMETHING** to guide or direct something such as a project to completion ○ *successfully stewarded the fundraising campaign to completion on time* ○ *stewarded the bill through Congress to the President* [Old English *stigweard* < *stig* 'house, hall' + *weard* 'keeper' (see WARD)] —**stewardship** *n*

stewardess /styoó ərdiss/ *n* a female flight attendant on a large passenger aeroplane (*dated*)

Stewart /styoó ərt/, **Jackie** (*b.* 1939) British racing driver. Born **John Young Stewart**

Stewart, Jimmy (1908–97) US actor and Air Force general. Full name **James Maitland Stewart**

Stewart Island island in New Zealand, south of the South Island. Population: 417 (1996). Area: 1,735 sq. km/670 sq. mi.

stewed /styood/ *adj* **1 SIMMERED** cooked by slow simmering **2 INTOXICATED** very intoxicated (*slang*) **3 MADE BITTER** made bitter by being infused for too long ○ *stewed tea*

stey /stay/ *adj* *Scotland* very steep ○ *a stey brae* [14C. < ?]

Sth *abbr* South

stibine /stíbbeen, -īn/ *n* SbH_3 a highly toxic, foul-smelling gas, or a derivative of one, produced by the action of hydrochloric acid on an antimony and zinc alloy. Use: fumigant. [Mid-19C. < Greek *stibi* 'antimony' + -INE.]

stibnite /stíb nīt/ *n* a soft greyish antimony sulphide mineral. Use: source of antimony. [Mid-19C. < STIBINE + -ITE[1].]

stich /stik/ *n* a line of poetry [Early 18C. < Greek *stikhos* 'row, rank, line of verse'.]

Stich /stik, stikh/, **Michael** (*b.* 1968) German tennis player

stichomythia /stíkō míthi ə/ *n* a form of dramatic dialogue in which characters speak single lines alternately [Mid-19C. < Greek *stikhomuthia* 'speaking in lines'.] —**stichomythic** *adj*

stick[1] /stik/ *n* **1 THIN BRANCH** a thin branch or shoot cut or broken from a tree **2 WOOD USED FOR FUEL OR CONSTRUCTION** wood pieces used as fuel or as construction material **3 SPECIALLY SHAPED WOOD** a shaped piece of wood used for a specified purpose ○ *a hockey stick* **4 ROD** a rod, wand, or baton **5 CANE** a cane, club, or cudgel **6 SHORT THIN THING** a short slender part or piece ○ *a stick of celery* **7 SOMETHING USED TO SECURE COMPLIANCE** something used to intimidate or coerce somebody into compliant behaviour ○ *carrot and stick* **8 PERSON** somebody of a particular kind (*dated* *informal*) ○ *He's a decent old stick.* **9** US **BORING PERSON** a dull, formal, or stuffily conventional person (*informal*) **10 CRITICISM** strong adverse criticism (*informal*) **11 FURNITURE** a piece of furniture (*informal*) ○ *We need a few sticks to furnish the flat* **12 BOMBS FALLING ON TARGET AT INTERVALS** a group of bombs that are arranged to fall on a target at regular intervals **13** US **CAR WITH GEARSTICK** a car with a manual transmission (*informal*) **14 SHIP'S MAST** a mast or spar on a ship **15 PARACHUTISTS JUMPING TOGETHER** a group of parachutists all jumping at the same time **16** *Aus* **SURFBOARD** a surfboard (*slang*) **17** US **CANNABIS CIGARETTE** a marijuana cigarette (*dated slang*) ■ **sticks** *npl* **REMOTE PLACE** a rural or remote place or district, especially one that is unsophisticated or unfashionable (*informal*) ○ *living out in the sticks* ■ *vt* **SUPPORT PLANT WITH STICK** to support a plant with a stake or stick [Old English *sticca* 'peg', < Indo-European, 'to stick, stab'] ◇ **in a cleft stick** in a situation where no possible course of action will bring a good result

stick[2] /stik/ *v* (**sticks, sticking, stuck** /stuk/, **stuck**) **1** *vti* **PENETRATE** to pierce, stab, or puncture something, or be pierced, stabbed, or punctured **2** *vt* **FASTEN WITH POINTED OBJECT** to fasten something in position by thrusting a pointed object such as a pin or nail through something **3** *vti* **FASTEN WITH ADHESIVE** to fasten or fix something, or remain attached, by means of an adhesive **4** *vti* **PROTRUDE** to protrude or cause something to protrude ○ *She stuck out her hand.* **5** *vt* **PUT SOMEWHERE** to place or put something in a location or position (*informal*) ○ *Stick it on the shelf.* **6** *vti* **BE UNABLE TO MOVE** to be at or cause to be at a standstill or unable to move or proceed ○ *be stuck in traffic* **7** *vt* **PUZZLE** to bewilder or perplex (*usually passive*) ○ *stuck for an answer* **8** *vi* **STAY IN THE MIND** to remain in the mind ○ *He told me all the facts but they didn't stick.* **9** *vt* **BE ABLE TO TOLERATE** to be able to tolerate or put up with a particular thing or person (*informal*) ○ *I can't stick him.* **10** *vt* **USE** to impose on or exploit somebody (*usually passive*) ○ *stuck with the boring jobs* **11** *vt* **KILL ANIMAL** to kill an animal by stabbing ○ *stick a pig* ■ *n* **ABILITY TO ADHERE** adhesive quality, e.g. of glue or tape [Old English *stician* < Indo-European] ◇ **stick in your craw** *or* **throat** to go against your sense of what is right, making you feel anger or resentment (*informal*) ◇ **stick it to somebody** US to exploit somebody or treat somebody unfairly (*informal*) ◇ **stick it out** to persist with something to the end, even when doing so is difficult ◇ **stuck on somebody** infatuated with somebody (*informal*)

stick around, stick about *vti* to linger or wait for somebody or something (*informal*)

stick at *vt* to persist at something ○ *stick at a job until it's done*

stick by *vt* to remain loyal to something or somebody ○ *I'll stick by you no matter what.*

stick out *vt* **1** to make something protrude **2** to endure something disagreeable ○ *stick out a long wait*

stick to *v* **1** *vti* **ADHERE TO** to adhere to something, or make something adhere to something **2** *vt* **BE LOYAL TO** to be loyal or close to somebody or something **3** *vt* **PERSIST WITH** to persist with something **4** *vt* **CONTINUE WITH** to keep to without digression

stick together *vi* to stay close physically or to remain unified ○ *stuck together through thick and thin*

stick up *v* **1** *vti* to protrude or point upwards, or to make something protrude or point upwards **2** *vt* US to carry out an armed robbery on somebody (*informal*)

stick up for *vt* to defend a belief or a person

stick with *vt* **1** to continue an enterprise rather than succumb to the temptation to cease **2** to remain loyal or faithful to somebody or something

sticker /stíkər/ *n* **1 SOMETHING WITH ADHESIVE** an adhesive label, poster, or paper **2 SOMETHING THAT STICKS** something that sticks **3 SOMEBODY PERSISTENT** a person who perseveres

stick figure *n* a simple or crude drawing of a person or animal with single lines for the torso, arms, and legs, and a circle for the head

stickhandle /stík hand'l/ (**-dles, -dling, -dled**) *vt* to control and manoeuvre a ball or puck using a lacrosse or ice hockey stick —**stickhandler** *n* —**stickhandling** *n*

sticking plaster *n* a plaster

sticking point *n* an issue, detail, or item likely to cause difficulty or prevent progress from being made, e.g. in a negotiation

stick insect *n* a long brown or green insect that resembles a twig. Family: Phasmidae.

stick-in-the-mud *n* somebody who resists new ideas and practices (*informal*)

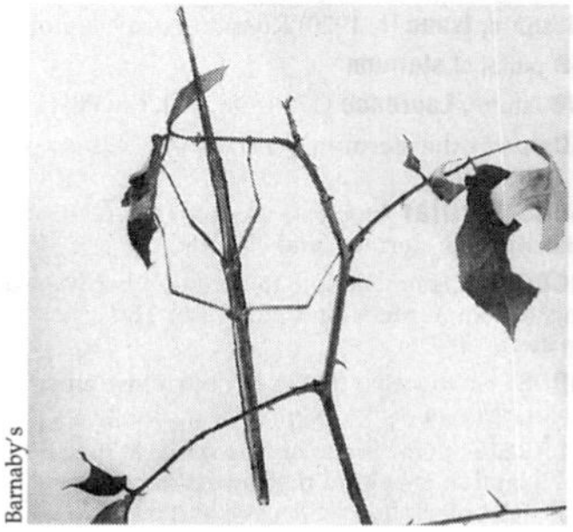

Barnaby's

Stick insect

stickleback /stík'l bak/ (*plural* **-backs** *or* **-back**) *n* **1** a small spiny-backed fish found in both salt and fresh water that has distinctive nest-building and courtship behaviour. Family: Gasterosteidae. **2** a minnow (*informal regional*) [15C. *stickle* < Old English *sticel* 'thorn, sting'.]

stickler /stíklər/ *n* a person who insists that every detail must be correct [Mid-16C. < *Stickle*, alteration of obsolete *stightle* 'keep trying to control things' < Old English *stihtian* 'arrange, settle'.]

stick pin *n* US an ornamental pin with a long shaft and a decoration or design at one end

stickseed /stík seed/ *n* a plant with prickly seeds that can stick to clothing. Native to: Europe, Asia, North America. Genus: *Lappula.*

stick shift *n* US a manually operated transmission in a motor vehicle, the gear stick that operates it, or a motor vehicle with a manual transmission

stick tackle *n* an illegal challenge in hockey when a player hits another player's stick instead of the ball

sticktight /stík tīt/ *n* a plant with barbed fruits that can stick to clothing or fur

stickup /stík up/, **stick-up** *n* US an armed robbery (*informal*)

stickweed /stík weed/ (*plural* **-weeds** *or* **-weed**) *n* a plant with clinging seeds, especially ragweed. Native to: North America.

⚡**sticky** /stíki/ (**-ier, -iest**) *adj* **1 COVERED IN GLUEY STUFF** covered in something gluey or viscous **2 ADHESIVE** having adhesive qualities **3 HUMID AND HOT** uncomfortably warm and humid ○ *sticky weather* **4 DIFFICULT** difficult, unpleasant, or involving problems (*informal*) ○ *a sticky situation* **5** US **SENTIMENTAL** cloying or excessively sentimental (*informal*) **6 ATTRACTING VISITORS** describes an Internet site that attracts and especially retains visitors (*informal*) —**stickily** *adv* —**stickiness** *n*

stickybeak /stíki beek/ *n ANZ* (*informal*) **1 SOMEBODY NOSY** a prier or snooper into somebody else's private business **2 NOSY LOOK** an inquisitive look ■ *vi ANZ* **SNOOP** to pry or snoop into the affairs of others (*informal*)

sticky-fingered *adj* having a tendency to steal things (*informal*)

sticky wicket *n* **1** wetted by rain and then dried by sun, making the ball bounce awkwardly **2** an awkward or difficult situation (*informal*)

Stieglitz /steéglits/, **Alfred** (1864–1946) US photographer

stiff /stif/ *adj* **1 RIGID** rigid, inflexible, or hard to move **2 NOT SUPPLE** painful and not supple ○ *stiff muscles* **3 SEVERE** very harsh or severe ○ *a stiff punishment* **4 TAXING** difficult or demanding ○ *stiff competition* **5 FORCEFUL** having force or power ○ *a stiff breeze* **6 STRONG** strong or potent to the taste or in effect on the body **7 RESOLUTE** showing determination and resolve ○ *stiff resistance* **8 TOO HIGH** higher than is justified or normal ○ *stiff prices* **9 FORMAL** rigidly formal or distant in manner ○ *a stiff manner* **10 NOT LIKELY TO CAPSIZE** relatively stable in the water **11 INTOXICATED** having had too much alcohol to drink (*slang*) ■ *adv* **1 TOTALLY** totally or utterly ○ *bored stiff* ○ *scared stiff* **2 IN A STIFF WAY** in a stiff way or manner ■ *n* **1 CORPSE** a dead body (*slang*) **2** US **PERSON** a person, especially somebody of a particular type (*slang*) ○ *a lucky stiff* **3** US **OFFENSIVE TERM** an offensive term for somebody regarded as unpleasant or excessively formal (*slang insult*) **4** US **OFFENSIVE TERM** an offensive term for somebody who leaves insufficient tips (*slang insult*) **5 FLOP** something that is an utter failure (*slang*) ■ *vt* US **RENEGE** to fail to pay somebody an amount due or expected (*slang*) ○ *He stiffed me on the tip.* [Old English *stīf* < Indo-European, 'to compress, pack'] —**stiffish** *adj* —**stiffly** *adv* —**stiffness** *n*

stiff-arm *adj* US = **straight-arm**

stiffen /stíff'n/ *vti* **1** to become or make something rigid or inflexible **2** to make something stronger or more effective or to become stronger or more effective ○ *Local opposition to the plan had stiffened.* —**stiffener** *n*

stiff-necked *adj* extremely obstinate and arrogant

stiffy[1] /stíffi/ (*plural* **-fies**), **stiffie** *n* an offensive term for an erect penis (*slang*)

stiffy[2] (*plural* **-fies**), **stiffie** *n* a formal invitation card printed on high-quality stiff paper (*slang*) [Late 20C. < the stiff card that they are printed on.]

stifle[1] /stīf'l/ (**-fles, -fling, -fled**) *v* **1** *vti* **SUFFOCATE** to impair somebody's breathing or find it hard to breathe **2** *vt* **CHECK OR REPRESS** to curb, repress, or prevent the development of something ○ *stifled the spreading discontent* **3** *vt* **REPRESS PHYSICAL ACT** to cut off a physical act, e.g. a yawn or laugh, before it develops [14C. Probably alteration of Old French *estouffer* 'smother' (influenced by Old Norse *stífla* 'stop up').] —**stifler** *n*

stifle[2] /stīf'l/ *n* the joint, corresponding to the human knee, in the hind leg of a four-legged animal [14C. < ?]

stifling /stīfling/ *adj* **1** uncomfortably hot and stuffy **2** repressive in not allowing full expression —**stiflingly** *adv*

stigma /stígmə/ *n* **1 SIGN OF SOCIAL UNACCEPTABILITY** the shame or disgrace attached to something regarded as socially unacceptable **2 PLANT PART** the part of a flower's female reproductive organ (**carpel**) that receives the male pollen grains **3 stigma** (*plural* **-mata**) **MARK ON SKIN** a mark on the skin indicating, e.g. a medical condition **4 SPOT ON BUTTERFLIES** a coloured mark or spot, often resembling an eye, found on some protozoans and invertebrates, especially butterflies and other lepidopterans [Late 16C. Via Latin < Greek, 'mark on the skin' < *stig-*, stem of *stizein* 'prick'.]

stigmasterol /stig mástərol/ *n* a sterol found in plants. Use: manufacture of progesterone. [Early 20C. < shortening of *Physostigma* + STEROL.]

stigmata /stígmətə, stig maátə/ *npl* marks on the hands and feet resembling the wounds from Jesus Christ's crucifixion [Mid-17C. < Greek, the plural of stigma (see STIGMA).]

stigmatic /stig máttik/ *adj* **1** socially unacceptable **2** OPTICS = **anastigmatic** ■ *n* a person affected with stigmata [Late 16C. < Greek *stigmat-*, stem of *stigma* (see STIGMA).]

stigmatise *vt* = **stigmatize**

stigmatism /stígmətizəm/ *n* **1 PROPERTIES OF AN ANASTIGMATIC LENS** the properties of an anastigmatic lens **2 BEING ANASTIGMATIC** the condition in which the eye focuses normally **3 HAVING STIGMATA** the condition of having stigmata [Mid-19C. In senses 1 and 2, back-formation < ASTIGMATISM.]

stigmatist /stígmətist/ *n* CHR = **stigmatic** *n.*

stigmatize /stígmə tīz/ (**-tizes, -tizing, -tized**), **stigmatise** (**-tises, -tising, -tised**) *v* **1** *vt* to label somebody or something as socially undesirable **2** *vti* to mark somebody or be marked with a stigma or stigmata —**stigmatization** /stígmə tī záysh'n/ *n* —**stigmatizer** *n*

stilb /stilb/ *n* a unit of luminescence equal to 1 candela per square centimetre [Mid-20C. Via French < Greek *stilbein* 'glitter' < ?]

stilbene /stíl been/ *n* $C_{14}H_{12}$ a crystalline solid. Use: manufacture of dyes. [Mid-19C. < Greek *stilbein* 'glitter' + -ENE.]

stilbestrol *n* CHEM = **stilboestrol**

stilbite /stíl bīt/ *n* a white or yellow zeolite mineral containing calcium and sodium [Early 19C. < Greek *stilbein* 'glitter' + -ITE[1]; from its lustrous crystals.]

stilboestrol /stil beéss trol/, **stilbestrol** *n* CHEM = **diethylstilboestrol** [Mid-20C. < STILBENE + OESTRUS + -OL.]

stile[1] /stīl/ *n* a step or rung that enables people to climb over a fence or wall [Old English *stigel* < Indo-European, 'to step, climb']

SPELLCHECK Do not confuse ***stile*** with ***style***, which has a similar sound. Beware: your spellchecker will not catch this error.

stile² /stīl/ *n* a vertical piece in a door, frame, or panel [Late 17C. Probably via Dutch *stijl* 'prop, doorpost' < Latin *stilus* 'column, post' (see STYLUS).]

stilet /stílət/ *n* **1** a wire inserted in a catheter to give it rigidity **2** a fine wire used as a probe in surgery [Late 17C. Via French < Italian *stiletto* (see STILETTO).]

stiletto /sti léttō/ *n* (*plural* **stilettos** *or* **stilettoes**) **1 SMALL DAGGER** a small dagger with a narrow tapering blade **2 POINTED TOOL** a pointed tool for making holes in fabric or leather **3** CLOTHING = **stiletto heel** ■ *vt* (**stilettos, stilettoing, stilettoed**) **TO STAB WITH A STILETTO** to stab somebody with a stiletto [Early 17C. < Italian, 'small dagger' < *stilo* 'dagger' < Latin *stilus* (see STYLUS).]

stiletto heel *n* a high pointed heel on a woman's shoe, or a shoe with such a heel

Stilicho /stíllikō/, **Flavius** (359?–408) Roman general and politician

still¹ /stil/ *adj* **1 NOT MOVING** motionless and undisturbed **2 NOT CARBONATED** not sparkling or bubbly **3 QUIET** subdued, gentle, or quiet **4 TAKING STATIC PHOTOGRAPHS** designed for, or relating to the process of, taking photographs as opposed to making films ■ *adv* **SILENTLY OR WITHOUT MOTION** without sound or movement ■ *n* **1 PEACE** silence or peace (*literary*) **2 SCENE FROM A FILM** a photographic print, either made from a single frame of a film or shot independently with a still camera during production ■ *v* **1** *vti* **MAKE CALM** to make somebody or cause somebody to become quiet, calm, soundless, or immobile **2** *vt* **RELIEVE** to allay or relieve ○ *stilled our fears* [Old English *stille* < Indo-European, 'stay put'] —**stillness** *n*

SYNONYMS See ***calm***.

still² /stil/ *adv* **1 EXISTING NOW** an adverb used to indicate that a situation that used to exist has continued, and exists now ○ *The original is still my favourite.* ○ *I still believe it's a mistake.* ○ *It was still light.* **2 EVEN AT THIS TIME** used to emphasize that something is the case even up to the point mentioned ○ *Her birthday is still a month away.* ○ *He may still be around.* ○ *Still to come…* **3 EVEN MORE** used to emphasize that there is even more of a quality or quantity (*often used with a comparative*) ○ *Profits next year will be larger still.* ○ *The market for flour is equal to almost any in the West, and it will be still better.* **4 NEVERTHELESS** used to emphasize that something remains the case in spite of the situation mentioned ○ *How am I going to do your work and still have time to do my own?* [13C. < STILL¹.]

still³ /stil/ *n* **1** an apparatus for distilling liquids, especially alcohol **2** BEVERAGES = **distillery** [Mid-16C. Shortening of DISTIL.]

stillage /stíllij/ *n* a frame, stand, or platform for keeping goods off the floor in a warehouse [Late 16C. Probably from obsolete Dutch *stellagie* 'scaffolding' < *stellen* 'set up'.]

still and all *adv* nonetheless or notwithstanding (*informal*)

stillbirth /stíl búrth/ *n* the birth of a dead foetus or baby after the 28th week of pregnancy

stillborn /stíl bawrn/ *adj* **1** dead at birth **2** useless or ineffectual from the start [Mid-16C. < STILL¹ in the obsolete meaning 'dead'.]

~~**stilleto**~~ incorrect spelling of **stiletto**

~~**stilletto**~~ incorrect spelling of **stiletto**

still frame *n* a single frame from a film or television programme displayed as a photograph

still life (*plural* **still lifes**) *n* **1** a representation of inanimate objects, e.g. fruit, flowers, or food, often in a domestic setting, in paintings, pictures, and photographs (*hyphenated before nouns*) ○ *a still-life class* **2** the style or genre of still life used in the various arts such as painting and photography

still room *n* **1** a room in which distilling is done **2** a pantry or storeroom off the kitchen of a large house

Still's disease /stílz-/ *n* chronic arthritis that develops in children under the age of 16 [Early 20C. After Sir George *Still* (1868–1941), British physician.]

stilt /stilt/ *n* **1 POLE FOR WALKING** either of two poles with footrests high off the ground on which somebody balances and walks **2 SUPPORTING POST** a tall post or column that supports a structure above land or water **3 LONG-LEGGED WADING BIRD** a three-toed, straight-billed, black-and-white shore bird that lives near ponds and marshes. Genera: *Himantopus* and *Cladorhynchus.* ■ *vt* **RAISE ON STILTS** to place or raise something up on stilts [14C. Probably < Low German < Indo-European, 'to set up'.]

stilted /stíltid/ *adj* **1 NOT FLUENT** lacking fluency in being halting or unnatural in flow **2 FORMAL** pompous or unduly formal **3 RESTING ON VERTICAL PIECES OF STONE** describes an arch that is joined to its supporting impost by vertical pieces of stone —**stiltedly** *adv* —**stiltedness** *n*

Stilton¹ /stíltən/ *n* either of two strong-flavoured British white cheeses made from whole milk, one veined with blue mould, the other plain [Mid-18C. After STILTON².]

Stilton² /stíltən/ village in E England, after which Stilton cheese is named. Population: 2,219 (1991).

stimulant /stímmyŏŏlənt/ *n* **1 SOURCE OF STIMULUS** something that provides a stimulus, incentive, or quickening **2 AGENT PRODUCING INCREASE IN FUNCTIONAL ACTIVITY** a drug or other agent that produces a temporary increase in functional activity of a body organ or part ■ *adj* **INCREASING ACTIVITY** increasing bodily activity or acting as a stimulus or incentive

stimulate /stímmyŏŏ layt/ (**-lates, -lating, -lated**) *vt* **1 ENCOURAGE** to encourage something, e.g. an activity or a process, so that it will begin, increase, or develop **2 MAKE INTERESTED** to cause somebody to become interested in or excited about something **3 CAUSE TO RESPOND** to cause physical activity in something such as a nerve or an organ [Early 16C. < Latin *stimulat-*, past participle of *stimulare* 'goad' < *stimulus* (see STIMULUS).] —**stimulable** *adj* —**stimulating** *adj* —**stimulatingly** *adv* —**stimulation** /stímmyŏŏ láysh'n/ *n* —**stimulative** *adj* —**stimulator** *n* —**stimulatory** *adj*

stimulus /stímmyŏŏləss/ (*plural* **-li** /stím yŏŏ lī/) *n* **1 INCENTIVE** something that encourages an activity or a process to begin, increase, or develop **2 SOMETHING AROUSING INTEREST** an agent or factor that provokes interest, enthusiasm, or excitement **3 CAUSE OF A RESPONSE** something, e.g. a drug or an electrical impulse, that causes a physical response in an organism [Late 17C. < Latin, 'goad, stake' < ?]

sting /sting/ *v* (**stings, stinging, stung** /stung/) **1** *vti* **INJECT WITH TOXIN** to prick the skin and inject a small quantity of a poisonous or irritant substance, causing a sharp pain often followed by itchiness and swelling **2** *vti* **PRODUCE SHARP PAIN** to feel, or cause somebody to feel, a sharp pain, usually only for a short period of time ○ *His eyes were stinging with the onions.* **3** *vt* **UPSET** to make somebody feel upset, hurt, or annoyed ○ *I was stung by her harsh criticisms.* **4** *vt* **GOAD** to urge somebody on, usually with criticism ○ *words that stung them into action* **5** *vt* **OVERCHARGE** to overcharge somebody (*informal*) ○ *They stung me £800 for repainting the wall.* **6** *vt* **BORROW MONEY FROM** to borrow money from somebody (*informal*) ○ *I might be able to sting my old man for a tenner.* ■ *n* **1 WOUND CAUSED BY STING** a skin wound that may hurt, swell up, and itch, caused by an insect, plant, or animal piercing the skin and injecting a small quantity of poison **2 POISON-INJECTING ORGAN** the sharp organ through which an insect or other animal injects poison to immobilize its prey or for defence. US term **stinger**¹ *n.* 3 **3 SHARP PAIN** a short sharp pain, e.g. that caused by the application of an antiseptic to a fresh wound **4 HURTFULNESS** the hurtful nature of something, e.g. criticism **5 POWER TO UPSET** the power to inflict mental or emotional discomfort ○ *threats that have lost their sting* **6** *US* **TRICK** an underhand scheme, especially a carefully planned and orchestrated swindle (*slang*) [Old English *stingan* < Germanic] —**stinging** *adj* —**stingingly** *adv*

Sting /sting/ (*b.* 1952) British singer, songwriter, and actor. Born **Gordon Sumner**

stinger¹ /stíngər/ *n* **1 SOMETHING STINGING** something that stings, especially a hurtful or critical comment **2** *ANZ* **STINGING ANIMAL OR PLANT** an animal or plant that stings, especially the box jellyfish **3** *US* ZOOL = **sting** *n.* 2 **4 BLOW** a sharp blow or slap that causes a smarting pain (*informal*) **5** *US* **UNDERCOVER OFFICER** a law enforcement officer who is taking part in an undercover operation (*informal*)

stinger² /stíngər/ *n* **1** *US* a cocktail consisting of crème de menthe and brandy **2** a whisky and soda with crushed ice [Early 20C. Alteration of STENGAH.]

stinging nettle *n* PLANTS = **nettle** *n.* 1

stingo /stíng gō/ *n* strong beer, especially an English beer originally made in Yorkshire (*archaic slang*) [Mid-17C. < STING; from the beer's sharp taste.]

stingray /stíng ray/ (*plural* **-rays** *or* **-ray**) *n* a ray with a flexible tail shaped like a whip with poisonous spines. Native to: shallow warm waters. Family: Dasyatidae.

stingy¹ /stínji/ (**-gier, -giest**) *adj* (*informal*) **1** not generous in giving or spending money **2** ungenerously small or inadequate ○ *a stingy tip* [Mid-17C. < ?] —**stingily** *adv* —**stinginess** *n*

stingy² /stíngi/ *adj* (**-ier, -iest**) stinging or capable of stinging (*informal*) ■ *n* (*plural* **-ies**) *Wales* a nettle (*informal*)

stink /stingk/ *vi* (**stinks, stinking, stank** /stangk/ *or* **stunk** /stungk/, **stunk**) **1 SMELL HORRIBLE** to have a very strong and extremely unpleasant smell **2 BE WORTHLESS** to be loathsomely bad or worthless (*informal*) ○ *This poetry stinks.* **3 BE CORRUPT** to be despicably corrupt or dishonest (*informal*) ○ *The whole admissions process stinks.* **4 HAVE TOO MUCH** to have, or be suspected of having, been assisted by improper influence (*informal*) ○ *a career that stinks of nepotism* ■ *n* **1 TERRIBLE SMELL** a very strong and unpleasant smell **2 SCANDAL** a scandalous revelation (*informal*) ○ *'even if there was a stink, he had plenty good friends in San Francisco'* (Robert Louis Stevenson, *The Wrecker*; 1896) [Old English *stincan* 'smell'] ◇ **like stink** very hard or fast (*informal*) ◇ **kick up** *or* **make** *or* **raise a stink** to cause trouble, especially by protesting (*informal*)

SYNONYMS See ***smell***.

stink out *vt* **1** to give something a very strong and unpleasant smell ○ *The smell of rotting cabbage stank the whole place out.* US term **stink up** **2** to drive a person or animal out of a place by introducing a strong and unpleasant smell

stink up *vt US* = **stink out** *v.* 1

stink bomb *n* a practical joker's toy in the form of a small glass or plastic capsule that, when smashed, emits a horrible smell

stinkbug /stíngk bug/ *n* an insect that emits foul-smelling secretions. It typically has a flattish body, and is often camouflaged to blend with its surroundings. Family: Pentatomidae.

stinker /stíngkər/ *n* **1 SOMETHING UNPLEASANT** something that is very difficult or unpleasant (*informal*) ○ *That last exam was a real stinker.* **2 OFFENSIVE TERM** an offensive term for a person considered obnoxious or hateful (*slang insult*) **3 SPITTING SEABIRD** a fulmar or petrel that feeds on offal and carrion and spits a foul-smelling oil at aggressors (*informal*)

stinkhorn /stíngk hawrn/ *n* a fungus with a thick white stalk and a thimble-shaped foul-smelling cap containing spores. The smell attracts flies, which disperse the spores. Order: Phallales.

stinking /stíngking/ *adj* **1 SMELLY** having or giving off a very strong and unpleasant smell **2 EXTREMELY BAD** describes an action or behaviour regarded as unpleasant or contemptible (*informal*) ○ *'This was, of course, a stinking lie'.* (Richard Kadrey, *Metrophage*; 1995) **3 INTOXICATED** very intoxicated (*slang*) ■ *adv* **USED FOR EMPHASIS** used to emphasize the contemptible extent of something (*informal*) —**stinkingly** *adv*

stinking ash *n* a deciduous tree with fragrant greenish-white flowers and fruits that are used in brewing. Native to: E North America. *Ptelea trifoliata.*

stinking badger *n* = **teledu** [< the foul-smelling secretion that the animal ejects]

stinking camomile *n* a weed similar to a daisy, with foul-smelling leaves. Native to: Europe. *Anthemis cotula.*

stinko /stíngkō/ *adj* **1** very intoxicated (*dated slang*) **2** *US* of the poorest quality (*informal*) ○ *a stinko bowl of stew*

stinkpot /stíngk pot/ *n* **1 SOMETHING WITH HORRIBLE SMELL** somebody or something that has a foul smell (*informal humorous*) **2 OFFENSIVE TERM** an offensive term for somebody considered very unpleasant or unpopular (*slang insult*) **3 SMALL N AMERICAN TURTLE** a small species of musk turtle that emits a foul-smelling secretion from its cloacal glands. Native to: ponds and sluggish streams of the United States. *Sternotherus odoratus.* **4 STINKING WEAPON** a military weapon used in former times, consisting of an earthenware pot that released a suffocating vapour when thrown into an enemy position or onto an enemy ship

stinkweed /stíngk weed/ (*plural* **-weeds** *or* **-weed**) *n* **1** PLANTS = **wall rocket** **2** a plant with unpleasant-smelling flowers or foliage, e.g. mayweed or pennycress

stinkwood /stíngk wŏŏd/ (*plural* **-woods** *or* **-wood**) *n* **1** a tree with unpleasant-smelling wood, in particular a South African deciduous tree whose hard wood is used for making furniture **2** the hard durable wood of any of the stinkwood trees [Mid-18C. Translation of Dutch *stinkhout*.]

stinky /stíngki/ *adj* (*informal*) **1** with a strong and unpleasant smell ○ *one of those stinky cheeses* **2** unfair, dishonest, or devious —**stinkily** *adv*

stint[1] /stint/ *v* **1** *vi* **BE MISERLY** to be ungenerous in offering, providing, or giving ○ *For a really good mousse, don't stint on the chocolate.* **2** *vt* **DENY** to deny somebody something out of miserliness, or deny something of the self, usually in an act of sacrifice ○ *'your mother and me economizing and stinting ourselves to give you a University education'* (Thomas Hardy, *Tess of the d'Urbervilles*; 1891) ■ *n* **1 ALLOTTED TIME** a fixed period of time spent on a particular task or job ○ *do a two-year stint as an apprentice* **2 LIMITATION** limitation or restriction, especially one of time or amount ○ *'I gave him time and thought without stint'* (Willa Cather, *The Professor's House*; 1925) [Old English *styntan* 'blunt', later reinforced by Old Norse *stytta* 'shorten'] —**stinter** *n*

stint[2] /stint/ (*plural* **stints** *or* **stint**) *n* any one of various sandpipers [15C. < ?]

stipe /stīp/ *n* **1** the stalk of a mushroom or fern **2** ZOOL = **stipes** *n.* 1 [Late 18C. Via French < Latin *stipes* 'post'.]

stipel /stíp'l/ *n* a structure shaped like a tiny leaf or scale located at the base of a leaflet of a compound leaf [Early 19C. Via French < modern Latin *stipella* 'small stipule' < *stipula* (see STIPULE).] —**stipellate** /sti péllət/ *adj*

stipend /stī pend/ *n* a fixed amount of money paid at regular intervals as a salary or to cover living expenses, especially one paid to a member of the clergy [15C. Directly or via Old French < Latin *stipendium* 'soldier's pay' < *stips* 'payment' + *pendere* 'weigh out' (see PENSIVE).]

SYNONYMS See *wage*.

stipendiary /stī péndi əri/ *adj* **1 PROVIDED WITH ALLOWANCE** receiving a fixed amount of money on a regular basis as a salary or to cover living expenses **2 WITH STIPEND** paying a stipend or paid for by a stipend ■ *n* (*plural* **-ies**) **SOMEBODY RECEIVING STIPEND** a person who regularly receives a fixed amount of money as a salary or to cover living expenses, e.g. a priest or magistrate

stipes /stī peez/ (*plural* **stipites** /stíppi teez/) *n* **1** the second or bottom mouthpart of some insects and crustaceans **2** the eyestalk of a crayfish or crab **3** PLANT SCI = **stipe** *n.* 1 [Mid-18C. Via modern Latin < Latin, 'post'.] —**stipitiform** /stíppiti fawrm/ *adj*

stipites plural of **stipes**

stipple /stípp'l/ *vt* (**-ples, -pling, -pled**) **1 PAINT BY DABBING** to paint, draw, or engrave something using dots or short dabbing strokes **2 APPLY WITH DABBING STROKES** to apply paint or any other substance in dots or short dabbing strokes **3 MAKE SURFACE MATERIAL APPEAR GRAINY** to give something, e.g. wet paint or plaster, a rough grainy texture with dabbing strokes **4 DAPPLE** to mark something with dots or speckles (*literary; usually passive*) ○ *its lime-green weatherboard stippled with sunlight* ■ *n* **1 ARTISTIC TECHNIQUE** the technique of painting, engraving, or drawing using dots or short dabbing strokes **2 DABBED FINISH** an irregular or grainy finish in paint or wet plaster, produced using dabbing strokes [Mid-18C. < Dutch *stippelen* 'keep pricking' < *stip* 'point, dot'.] —**stippler** *n* —**stippling** *n*

stipulate[1] /stíppyoo layt/ (**-lates, -lating, -lated**) *v* **1** *vt* **SPECIFY** to specify something such as a condition when making an agreement or an offer ○ *The contract stipulates which expenses will be covered.* **2** *vti* **DEMAND** to make a specific demand for something, usually as a condition in an agreement ○ *stipulate a price* **3** *vt* **MAKE FORMAL PROMISE** to promise something formally or legally **4** *vi* **AGREE** to agree, in terms of the conduct of a legal proceeding ○ *We will stipulate to our receipt of all pertinent discovery documents, my lord.* **5** *vti* **MAKE ORAL CONTRACT** in Roman Law, to make an oral contract in the form of question and answer [Early 17C. < Latin *stipulat-*, past participle of *stipulari* 'demand, bargain'.] —**stipulable** *adj* —**stipulation** /stíppyoo láysh'n/ *n* —**stipulator** /stíppyoo laytər/ *n* —**stipulatory** *adj*

stipulate[2] /stíppyoo layt/ *adj* describes a stem or stalk that has a pair of growths resembling leaves (**stipules**) at the base [Late 18C. < STIPULE.]

stipule /stíppyool/ *n* either of a pair of small growths at the base of a leaf stalk or stem that resemble leaves [Late 18C. Directly or via French < Latin *stipula* 'straw, stalk' < ?] —**stipular** /stíppyoolər/ *adj*

stir[1] /stur/ *v* (**stirs, stirring, stirred**) **1** *vt* **MIX INGREDIENTS** to move a spoon, stick, or some other implement through a liquid in order to mix or cool the contents ○ *Slowly stir the cream into the soup.* **2** *vi* **BE ABLE TO BE STIRRED** to be of a consistency that allows a spoon or other implement to be moved around **3** *vti* **MOVE** to move gently or cause something to move gently **4** *vi* **LEAVE** to move or leave, especially from a favourite or usual place ○ *The guards were told not to stir from their posts.* **5** *vi* **MOVE AFTER RESTING** to get up and move about, especially after a rest ○ *anyone stirring at this early hour* **6** *vt* **GOAD INTO ACTION** to rouse somebody into action **7** *vt* **AROUSE FEELING** to arouse something, e.g. an emotion or a memory (*formal*) **8** *vi* **BE FELT** to begin to be experienced as an emotion (*formal*) ○ *Deep-seated bitterness began to stir within him.* **9** *vti* **MAKE EMOTIONAL** to arouse strong emotions in somebody ○ *music that never fails to stir me* **10** *vi* **HAPPEN** to happen or be current (*informal*) ○ *What's stirring this week at Westminster?* ■ *n* **1 ACT OF STIRRING** an act or instance of stirring a liquid **2 COMMOTION** a fervent reaction, usually either excitement or controversy **3 SLIGHT MOVEMENT** a gentle movement **4** *Aus* **TROUBLE** trouble (*informal*) **5** *NZ* **NOISY PARTY** a raucous party (*informal*) [Old English *styrian* 'agitate' < Indo-European, 'to whirl'] —**stirrable** *adj* ◇ **for a stir** *Aus* with the aim of making mischief (*informal*)

stir up *vt* **1** to cause trouble or a confrontation deliberately **2** to cause something such as dust to rise and swirl around

stir[2] /stur/ *n* prison (*slang*) [Mid-19C. < ?]

stir-crazy *adj* mentally unsettled as a result of spending a long time in a confined space, e.g. a prison cell (*informal or humorous*) [< STIR[2]]

stir-fry *vt* to fry small tender pieces of food rapidly in a small amount of oil over high heat, stirring continuously ■ *n* a dish of food prepared by stir-frying

stirk /sturk/ *n* a young cow or bullock of varying age (*regional*) [Old English *stīrc* < ?]

Stirling /stúrling/ **1** town in central Scotland, on the River Forth. Population: 30,515 (1991). **2** town in S South Australia. Population: 16,150 (1996).

Stirling, Sir James (1926–92) British architect

Stirling engine *n* an external-combustion engine in which heat generated on the outside of the cylinders causes either air or an inert gas within the cylinders to expand and drive the pistons [Mid-19C. After Revd Robert *Stirling* (1790–1878), Scottish minister and engineer.]

Stirling Ranges mountain range in SW Western Australia. Highest peak: Bluff Knoll 1,073 m/3,520 ft.

Stirling's formula *n* a mathematical formula used to calculate the approximate value of the factorial of a very large number [Mid-20C. After James *Stirling* (1692–1770), Scottish mathematician.]

stirps /sturps/ (*plural* **stirpes** /stúr peez/) *n* **1** a line of descendants from a common ancestor **2** a plant variety in which the characters are fixed through cultivation [Late 17C. < Latin, 'stem, lineage' < ?]

stirrer /stúrər/ *n* a maker of trouble or confrontation, often by spreading rumours or divulging confidences (*informal*)

stirring /stúring/ *adj* **1 CAUSING EMOTIONAL REACTION** causing an emotional or excited reaction **2 LIVELY** full of energy and vitality ○ *a stirring rendition of a Chopin mazurka* ■ *n* **1 MOVEMENT** a slight movement **2 AROUSING OF FEELING** the awakening of something, especially an emotion or memory (*formal*) [Old English *styrend, styring*] —**stirringly** *adv*

stirrup /stírrəp/ *n* **1 HORSERIDER'S FOOT SUPPORT** a flat-bottomed metal ring hanging from a strap on each side of a horse's saddle to provide support for a rider's foot **2 STRAP** a loop or strap that supports a foot or passes under a foot, such as the straps supporting a woman's feet in childbirth **3 SHIP'S ROPE** one of a set of ropes hanging from a sail-supporting spar (**yard**) on a ship [Old English *stīgrāp* 'rope for getting up' < *stīgan* 'go up' + *rāp* 'rope']

stirrup bone *n* the stapes [< its shape]

stirrup cup *n* a farewell drink of alcohol, originally one shared with a departing horserider

stirrup iron *n* the metal ring of a riding stirrup

stirrup leather *n* a leather strap that attaches a stirrup to the saddle

stirrup pants *npl* = **ski pants** *npl.* 1

stirrup pump *n* a portable hand-operated pump, held on the ground with the feet, which draws water from a bucket, and sprays it out [< the shape of the foot-piece used to hold the pump in place]

stishovite /stíshə vīt/ *n* a rare crystalline form of quartz. Source: meteor craters. [Mid-20C. After Sergey Mikhailovich *Stishov* (*b.* 1937), Russian mineralogist.]

stitch /stich/ *n* **1 LENGTH OF THREAD IN MATERIAL** a short length of thread that has been passed through one or more pieces of material, either for decoration or to join pieces together **2 SURGICAL THREAD** a single loop of surgical thread used to close up a wound **3 LOOP OF WOOL** a single loop of wool or similar material, passed around a knitting needle or a crochet hook **4 STYLE OF NEEDLEWORK** a specified style of sewing or knitting ○ *lock stitch* **5 ACHING PAIN** cramp in the side of the abdomen caused e.g. by exercising or laughing **6 ARTICLE OF CLOTHING** a single article of clothing (*informal*) ○ *didn't have a stitch on* **7 RIDGE BETWEEN FURROWS** the ridge between two adjacent furrows in a field ■ *vt* **1 SEW** to join, finish, or decorate something with stitches **2 CLOSE WOUND** to close a wound with one or more stitches **3 BIND PAGES** to bind the pages of a book, pamphlet, or other publication with thread or staples [Old English *stice* 'prick' < Indo-European, 'jab'] —**stitcher** *n* ◇ **in stitches** laughing a great deal

stitch up *vt* **1 SEW** to sew fabric or an article, or repair something by sewing it **2 CLOSE A WOUND** to close a wound with stitches (*informal*) **3 CAUSE TO APPEAR GUILTY** to deliberately make somebody appear guilty when he or she is innocent (*slang*) ○ *He claimed the police had stitched him up.*

stitchery /stíchəri/ *n* needlework, especially when it is functional rather than decorative

stitchwort /stích wurt/ (*plural* **-worts** *or* **-wort**) *n* a low-growing herbaceous plant. Flowers: small, white, star-shaped. Genus: *Stellaria*. [Old English *sticwyrt*; < its former use to cure sharp pains in the side]

STM *abbr* scanning tunnelling microscope

stoa /stṓ ə/ (*plural* **-as** *or* **-ae** /stṓ ee/) *n* in ancient Greece, a covered walkway, usually with a row of columns on one side and a wall on the other [Early 17C. < Greek.]

stoat /stōt/ (*plural* **stoats** *or* **stoat**) *n* a small mammal similar to a weasel, with a sleek brown coat. Native to: Europe, Asia, North America. *Mustela erminea*. ◊ **ermine** *n.* 1 [15C. < ?]

stob /stob/ *n* *UK, Southern US* a stake or stump (*regional*) [14C. Probably a variant of STUB.]

stochastic /stə kástik/ *adj* **1 RANDOM** involving or showing random behaviour **2 INVOLVING PROBABILITY** involving or subject to probabilistic behaviour **3 INVOLVING GUESSWORK** involving guesswork or conjecture (*formal*) [Mid-20C. < Greek *stokhastikos* < *stokhos* 'target, aim', literally 'pointed stake'.] —**stochastically** *adv*

stock /stok/ *n* **1 SUPPLY OF SALEABLE GOODS** a supply of goods for sale, kept on the premises by a shop or business **2 SUPPLY** a supply held in reserve for future use **3 AVAILABLE AMOUNT** the amount of something, e.g. a natural resource or a service, available in a particular area ○ *an alarming fall in North Atlantic fish stocks* **4 INVESTOR'S CAPITAL SHARE** the share of capital held by an individual investor (*often plural*) **5 TOTAL SHARE ISSUE** the total number of shares issued by a company or sector **6 MONEY RAISED** the amount of money raised by a company through the sale of shares, entitling holders to dividends, certain rights of ownership, and other benefits. US term **capital stock** *n.* 1 **7 SOMEBODY'S REPUTATION** a person's standing or reputation ○ *Her stock is high in terms of public opinion because of her aid work.* **8** AGRIC = **livestock** **9 DESCENT** ancestry, usually with reference to race, ethnic group, class, region, or profession **10 ORIGINAL VARIETY** the original variety from which other similar plants, animals, or languages are descended **11 RELATED ORGANISMS** a race, family, breed, or other related group of animals or plants **12 BROTH** a liquid made by simmering meat, fish, bones, or vegetables with herbs in water, used in soups, stews, and sauces **13 TRUNK** the trunk of a tree or the main stem of a plant **14 PLANT RECEIVING GRAFT** a plant or plant stem onto which a shoot or bud is grafted **15 PLANT USED FOR CUTTINGS** a plant or part of a plant from which cuttings are taken **16 ANIMAL PEN** a small pen or frame where a single animal can be confined, e.g. for veterinary examination or treatment (*often plural*) **17 PART OF FIREARM** the part of a firearm to which the barrel and firing mechanism are attached **18 PART OF GUN CARRIAGE** the long beam on a field artillery carriage that extends behind it **19 PART OF PLOUGH** the frame of a horse-drawn plough **20 HANDLE** a handle, e.g. the handle of a fishing rod, whip, or carpentry tool **21 WOODEN BLOCK** a block of wood **22 SUPPORTING PART** any upright supporting part **23 ANCHOR PART** the crosspiece on some types of anchor **24 RAW MATERIAL** the basic material from which anything is manufactured **25 UNEXPOSED FILM** cinema film that has not yet been exposed **26 PIECE OF METAL** a piece of cut metal ready to be processed, especially by forging **27** (*plural* **stocks** *or* **stock**) **FLOWERING PLANT** a widely-grown ornamental plant. Flowers: fragrant, brightly coloured, in clusters. Native to: Europe, Asia. Genus: *Matthiola.* **28** (*plural* **stocks** *or* **stock**) PLANTS = **Virginia stock 29 CLERICAL SHIRT FRONT** a broad piece of cloth worn on the chest below a clerical collar by members of the clergy in some denominations of the Christian Church **30 UNDISTRIBUTED CARDS OR COUNTERS** a pile of cards or counters not dealt out at the start of a game, but picked up during it **31** *US* THEATRE = **repertory** *n.* 1 **32 HUB** the hub of a wheel **33 ROCK MASS** a roughly circular mass of exposed igneous rock **34** RAIL = **rolling stock** *n.* 1 ■ *adj* **UNORIGINAL** typical or familiar and therefore lacking originality ○ *When pushed for an answer, he gave the stock response.* ■ *v* **1** *vt* **HAVE PRODUCT IN STOCK** to have an item available for sale **2** *vt* **FILL WITH SUPPLY** to fill something with goods ○ *stocked the supermarket shelves with their new product* **3** *vt* **FILL UP** to fill with a plentiful supply of something ○ *We've stocked the fridge with cold cuts for the big game.* **4** *vt* **SUPPLY FARM WITH LIVESTOCK** to supply a farm with livestock **5** *vi* **SPROUT** to sprout new shoots [Old English *stocc* 'tree trunk'] —**stocker** *n* ◇ **take stock 1** to think carefully about something so that you can form an opinion about it **2** make an inventory of the stock, especially at the end of a season in a shop or business. ◊ **stocktaking** *n.* 2

stock up *vti* to collect a large supply for future use

stockade /sto káyd/ *n* **1 DEFENSIVE BARRIER** a tall fence or enclosure made of wooden posts driven into the ground side by side, to keep out enemies or intruders **2 AREA INSIDE STOCKADE** an area surrounded by a stockade **3** *US* **MILITARY PRISON** a prison on a military base ■ *vt* (**-ades, -ading, -aded**) **SURROUND AREA WITH STOCKADE** to enclose an area with a stockade [Early 17C. Via obsolete French *estocade* < Spanish *estacada* < *estaca* 'stake' < Germanic.]

stockbreeder /stók breedər/ *n* a breeder and rearer of livestock —**stockbreeding** *n*

stockbroker /stók brōkər/ *n* a dealer in stocks, shares, and other securities for clients —**stockbrokerage** *n* —**stockbrokering** *n*

stockbroker belt *n* an affluent residential area outside a city, typically inhabited by middle-class professional people who commute to the city to work

stock car *n* **1** a standard passenger car that has been modified for professional racing **2** *US* RAIL = **cattle truck**

stock certificate *n US* FIN = **share certificate**

stock company *n US* **1** a company that has its capital divided into shares that are freely tradable **2** THEATRE = **repertory company**

stock cube *n* a small cube of dried and concentrated food extracts that, when added to hot water, makes a stock for use in soups, stews, and sauces

stock dove *n* a greyish dove that nests in holes in trees and cliffs. Native to: Europe. *Columba oenas.* [Probably < STOCK 'tree trunk'; from its nesting in trees]

stock exchange *n* **1** FIN = **stock market** *n.* 1 **2** a building in which a stock exchange is sited

stock farm *n* a farm on which animals, e.g. cattle, sheep, and pigs, are bred and raised

stockfish /stók fish/ (*plural* **-fish** *or* **-fishes**) *n* fish, usually cod or haddock, that has been cured by being split and air-dried without the addition of salt [13C. Translation of Low German and Middle Dutch *stokvisch* < *stok* 'stick, tree trunk' + *visch* 'fish'.]

Stockhausen /shtók howz'n/, **Karlheinz** (*b.* 1928) German composer

stockholder /stók hōldər/ *n* **1** *US* FIN = **shareholder 2** *Aus* a farmer who keeps livestock —**stockholding** *n*

Stockholm /stók hōm/ capital of Sweden, on the east coast of the country. Population: 711,119 (1996).

Stockholm syndrome /stók hōm-/ *n* a condition experienced by people who have been held as hostages for some time in which they begin to identify with and feel sympathetic towards their captors [Late 20C. After STOCKHOLM, Sweden, where a bank employee taken hostage in a robbery became attached to one of her captors.]

stockhorse /stók hawrss/ *n Aus* a horse trained for the herding of livestock

stockinette /stóki nét/, **stockinet** *n* a stretchy knitted fabric. Use: bandages, dishcloths. [Late 18C. Probably alteration of *stocking net.*]

stockinette stitch *n US* HANDICRAFT = **stocking stitch**

stocking /stóking/ *n* **1 COVERING FOR WOMAN'S LEG** either of a pair of tightly fitting leg coverings for women, made of silk, nylon, or wool (*often plural*) **2 SOCK** a sock (*dated or formal*) **3 CHRISTMAS STOCKING** a Christmas stocking (*informal*) **4 DIFFERENTLY COLOURED PART OF ANIMAL'S LEG** a differently coloured part of the lower leg of an animal, especially a horse [Late 16C. < STOCK in the obsolete sense 'stocking' < ?] —**stockinged** *adj*

stocking cap *n* a tightly fitting, cone-shaped knitted cap with a tapering tail that often has a tassel on the end

stocking filler *n* a small and usually inexpensive Christmas gift, especially one put into a child's Christmas stocking. US term **stocking stuffer**

stocking frame *n* an early type of knitting machine

stocking mask *n* a nylon stocking pulled over the head to disguise the features, usually worn by somebody committing a crime

stocking stitch *n* a pattern in knitting that alternates rows of plain and purl stitches. US term **stockinette stitch**

stocking stuffer *n US* = **stocking filler**

stock-in-trade *n* **1** a resource that somebody needs and regularly makes use of, especially at work ○ *Courtesy and composure are the receptionist's stock-in-trade.* **2** the goods and equipment that need to be kept on the premises for a business or shop to run

stockist /stókist/ *n* a seller or shop that stocks a particular product

stockjobber /stók jobbər/ *n* **1** formerly, a dealer on the stock exchange who dealt only with brokers, not with members of the public **2** *US* a stockbroker, especially an unscrupulous dealer trading worthless securities (*dated*) —**stockjobbery** *n* —**stockjobbing** *n*

stockman /stókmən/ (*plural* **-men** /stókmən/) *n* **1** a man who owns or breeds farm animals, especially cattle **2** a man who looks after the livestock on a farm

stock market *n* **1** an organized market where brokers meet to buy and sell stocks and shares **2** the activity of buying and selling stocks and shares, or the global market for stocks and shares (*hyphenated before nouns*)

stockpile /stók pīl/ *vti* (**-piles, -piling, -piled**) to accumulate large quantities of something, e.g. food or weapons ■ *n* a large supply of something, e.g. food or weapons, often accumulated in anticipation of future difficulties —**stockpiler** *n*

SYNONYMS See ***collect.***

Stockport /stók pawrt/ town in NW England. Population: 132,813 (1991).

stockpot /stók pot/ *n* a large pot for cooking stock

stockroom /stók room, -rŏŏm/ *n* a room where goods are stored in a shop, office, or factory

stocks /stoks/ *n* (+ *singular or plural verb*) **1 PUNISHMENT DEVICE** a wooden frame in which, in former times, an offender was secured by the hands and feet or head and hands and left in public to be ridiculed or abused **2 CONSTRUCTION STAND** a frame that supports a boat or ship while it is being built **3 RUDDER SHAFT** the vertical shaft at the forward edge of a rudder, attached to the steering controls [14C. < the plural of STOCK in the meaning 'post'.] ◇ **on the stocks** in the process of being made, prepared, or arranged

stock saddle *n US* RIDING = **western saddle** [< a Scottish phrase meaning 'saddle with a wooden tree']

stock-still *adv* absolutely motionless

stocktaking /stók tayking/ *n* **1** evaluating a personal situation, or that of somebody else **2** making an itemized list of all merchandise in a shop or business. US term **inventory** *n.* 5

Stockton-on-Tees /stóktən on teéz/ port in NE England. Population: 83,576 (1991).

stockwoman /stók wŏŏmən/ (*plural* **-men** /stók wimin/) *n* **1** a woman who owns or breeds farm animals, especially cattle **2** a woman who looks after the livestock on a farm

stocky /stóki/ (**-ier, -iest**) *adj* **1** having a broad strong-looking physique, and usually short in stature **2** *US* somewhat overweight —**stockily** *adv* —**stockiness** *n*

stockyard /stók yaard/ *n* a large enclosed yard with pens or covered stables where livestock are kept before being sold, slaughtered, or shipped on

stodge /stoj/ *n* **1 HEAVY FOOD** food that is heavy, filling, and usually fairly tasteless (*informal*) **2 ANYTHING DULL** dull or unimaginative matter of any kind, especially writing **3 SPONGE PUDDING** baked or steamed sponge pudding [Late 17C. < ?]

stodgy /stójji/ (**-ier, -iest**) *adj* (*informal*) **1 FILLING** heavy, filling, and usually fairly tasteless **2 FORMAL OR POMPOUS** boringly or laughably conventional, formal, or pompous ○ *another of his stodgy dinner parties* **3 UNIMAGINATIVE** lacking originality, flair, or imagination ○ *another sheaf of stodgy poems* —**stodgily** *adv* —**stodginess** *n*

stoep /stoop/ *n S Africa* a porch or veranda [Late 18C. Via Afrikaans < Dutch (see STOOP[2]).]

stogy /stṓgi/ (*plural* **-gies**), **stogie, stogey** (*plural* **-geys**) *n US* **1** a long slim inexpensive cigar **2** a heavy boot or shoe that is crudely made [Mid-19C. Shortening of *Conestoga*, supposedly because drivers of Conestoga wagons used such cigars and shoes.]

stoic /stṓ ik/ *n* an unemotional person, especially somebody who shows patience and endurance during adversity ■ *adj* **stoic, stoical** tending to remain unemotional, especially showing admirable patience and endurance in the face of adversity [Late 16C. < STOIC.] —**stoically** *adv*

SYNONYMS See ***impassive.***

Stoic /stṓ ik/ *n* a member of an ancient Greek school of philosophy that asserted that happiness can only be achieved by accepting life's ups and downs as the products of unalterable destiny [14C. < Latin *Stoicus* < Greek *stoa* 'porch', referring to the Painted Porch in Athens, where Zeno taught.] —**Stoic** *adj*

stoical *adj* = **stoic**

stoichiometry /stóyki ómmətri/ *n* **1** the branch of chemistry concerned with measuring the proportions of elements that combine during chemical reactions **2** a measure of the relative proportions of the elements that take part in a chemical reaction [Mid-19C. < Greek *stoikheion* 'element' after German *Stöchiometrie.*] —**stoichiometric** /stóyki ə méttrik/ *adj* —**stoichiometrically** *adv*

stoicism /stṓ isizəm/ *n* emotional indifference, especially admirable patience and endurance shown in the face of adversity

Stoicism /stṓ issizəm/ *n* an ancient Greek school of philosophy that asserted that happiness can only be achieved by accepting life's ups and downs as the products of unalterable destiny

stoke /stōk/ (**stokes, stoking, stoked**) *vti* **1** to add fuel to a fire and stir it up to make it burn more intensely **2** to be responsible for adding fuel to and tending the boiler of a furnace [Mid-17C. Back-formation < STOKER.]

stoke up *v* **1** *vt* **ADD FUEL TO FIRE** to add fuel to a fire or a furnace and stir it up so that it burns more intensely **2** *vt* **INTENSIFY EMOTION** to cause an emotion, e.g. anger or fear, to be felt more strongly **3** *vi* **EAT IN BULK** to eat food in large quantities, because or as if more food may not be had (*informal*)

stoked /stōkt/ *adj* **1** *Aus* delighted or exhilarated (*informal*) ○ *She said she was stoked about the new job.* **2** *US* in an excited or euphoric state, especially from having taken drugs

stokehold /stṓk hōld/ *n* **1** the boiler room of a steamship **2** a coal bunker for a steamship's boiler

stokehole /stṓk hōl/ *n* **1** the opening through which fuel is added to a boiler or furnace **2** NAUT = **stokehold** [Mid-17C. Translation of Dutch *stookgat.*]

Stoke-on-Trent /stṓk on trént/ city in central England. Population: 244,600 (1997).

stoker /stṓkər/ *n* somebody whose job it is to add fuel to and tend a furnace or boiler, e.g. on a steamship or a steam train [Mid-17C. < Dutch, < Middle Dutch *stoken* 'poke with a stick'.]

Stokes-Adams syndrome /stṓks áddəmz-/ *n* episodes of temporary dizziness or fainting, due to disruption or extreme slowing of the heartbeat and consequent brief stoppage of blood flow [Early 20C. After William

Stokes (1804–75) and Robert *Adams* (1791–1875), Irish physicians.]

Stokowski /stə kófski/, **Leopold** (1882–1977) British-born US conductor

stokvel /stók fel/ *n S Africa* an informal savings society in which members contribute regularly and receive payouts in rotation [< Afrikaans, alteration of English *stock-fair* 'livestock market']

STOL /stol, éss tol/ *n* **1** a flying system that gives an aircraft the ability to take off and land on a very short runway. Full form **short takeoff and landing 2** an aircraft fitted with the STOL system

stole[1] past tense of **steal**

stole[2] /stōl/ *n* **1** a woman's scarf or shawl of fur or worn as part of evening wear **2** a long, narrow, and usually embroidered scarf made of silk or linen, worn by various members of the clergy [Pre-12C. Via Latin < Greek *stolē* 'robe, equipment'.]

stolen past participle of **steal**

stolen children *npl Aus* Aboriginal children who, in line with Australian government policy to integrate Aboriginals, were taken from their families and placed in state homes or with white foster families

stolid /stóllid/ *adj* solemn and showing little or no emotion [Late 16C. Directly or via French < Latin *stolidus* 'dense, stupid'.] —**stolidity** /stə líddəti/ *n* —**stolidly** *adv* —**stolidness** *n*

SYNONYMS See *impassive*.

stollen /stóllən/ (*plural* **-len** *or* **-lens**) *n* a rich sweet German fruit bread made with nuts, raisins, and other dried fruits [Early 20C. Via German < Old High German *stollo* 'post, support'.]

stolon /stō lon/ *n* **1** a long stem or shoot that arises from the central rosette of a plant and droops to the ground **2** a budding of the body wall in simple organisms, especially an extension of some colonial organisms, e.g. hydroids, that anchors the colony to a rock or other substrate [Early 17C. < Latin *stolon-*.] —**stolonate** *adj* —**stoloniferous** /stōlə níffərəss/ *adj*

stoma /stómə/ (*plural* **-mata** /-mətə/) *n* **1 PLANT PORE** a tiny pore in the outer layer (**epidermis**) of a plant leaf or stem that controls the passing of water vapour and other gases into and out of the plant **2 MOUTH OR SIMILAR STRUCTURE** a mouth, or an opening that acts as or is shaped like a mouth **3 SURGICAL OPENING** an artificial opening made in an organ, especially an opening in the colon or ileum made via the abdomen [Late 17C. Via modern Latin < Greek, 'mouth'.] —**stomal** *adj* —**stomatal** *adj* —**stomatous** *adj*

stomach /stúmmək/ *n* (*plural* **-achs**) **1 VERTEBRATES' DIGESTIVE ORGAN** an organ resembling a sac in which food is mixed and partially digested. It forms part of the digestive tract of vertebrates and is situated between the oesophagus and the small intestine. **2 ABDOMEN** the abdomen (*informal*) **3 INVERTEBRATES' DIGESTIVE ORGAN** a digestive organ in some invertebrate animals in which food is mixed, stored, and partially digested **4 COMPARTMENT OF ANIMAL'S STOMACH** any of the four digestive chambers that make up the stomach in ruminant animals (*informal*) **5 SEAT OF UNPLEASANT FEELINGS** the part of the body in which disgust, nausea, and fear are experienced ○ *The very idea makes me sick to my stomach.* **6 RESISTANCE TO UNPLEASANTNESS** the ability to withstand disgust, nausea, or fear ○ *This is not a job for someone with a weak stomach.* ■ *vt* **1 TOLERATE** to put up with something ○ *I find their gloating hard to stomach.* **2 EAT FOOD WITHOUT ILL EFFECTS** to eat a particular food without ill effects ○ *for those of you who don't stomach seafood* [14C. Via Old French *stomaque* < Greek *stomakhos* 'throat, gullet' < *stoma* 'mouth'.]

stomachache /stúmmək ayk/ *n* a pain in the abdominal region, caused, e.g., by indigestion or an infection

stomach-churning *adj* producing feelings of disgust, nausea, or fear

stomach crunch *n* an exercise in which you lie flat on your back with your legs bent and then raise the upper part of your body a few centimetres off the ground without using your hands

stomachic /stə mákik/ *adj* **stomachic, stomachical 1 RELATING TO THE STOMACH** associated with the stomach **2 BENEFICIAL FOR STOMACH** good for the stomach, especially in stimulating digestion (*archaic*) ■ *n* **STOMACH MEDICINE** a tonic that stimulates gastric activity or appetite (*archaic*) —**stomachically** *adv*

stomach pump *n* a popular name for the equipment, consisting of a simple tube, funnel, and bucket, used to flush out the stomach contents of somebody who has, e.g., ingested a poison (*informal*)

stomach tooth *n* either of the first canine teeth in the lower jaw of humans, whose appearance is popularly believed to be hastened by stomach upsets in infants

stomach-turning *adj* producing feelings of disgust or nausea

stomata plural of **stoma**

stomatitis /stómə títiss/ *n* inflammation of the mucous tissue lining the mouth [Mid-19C. < Greek *stomat-*, stem of *stoma* 'mouth'.] —**stomatitic** /-títtik/ *adj*

stomatology /stṓmə tólləji/ *n* the branch of medicine or dentistry that is concerned with the study of the mouth and diseases of the mouth [Late 19C. < Greek *stomat-*, stem of *stoma* 'mouth'.] —**stomatological** /stṓmətə lójjik'l/ *adj* —**stomatologist** *n*

-stome *suffix* mouth, stoma ○ *peristome* [< Greek *stoma* 'mouth'] —**-stomous** *suffix*

stomodaeum /stṓmə dée əm/ (*plural* **-a** /-dée ə/), **stomodeum** (*plural* **-a**) *n* a depression in the surface of an early embryo that develops into the mouth [Late 19C. < modern Latin, < Greek *stoma* 'mouth' + *hodaios* 'on the way, becoming' (< *hodos* 'way, road').] —**stomodaeal** *adj*

stomp /stomp/ *vti* **WALK WITH HEAVY STEPS** to tread heavily and noisily, often in anger ■ *n* **1 JAZZ DANCE** a jazz dance with stamping foot movements **2 JAZZ MUSIC** jazz music accompanying the stomp [Early 19C. Variant of STAMP.] —**stomper** *n* —**stompingly** *adv*

-stomy *suffix* a surgical operation that creates an artificial opening ○ *gastrostomy* [< Greek *stoma* 'mouth, opening' + -Y[2]]

stone /stōn/ *n* **1 HARD NON-METALLIC MATERIAL** the hard solid non-metallic substance that rocks are made of. Use: building material. **2 ROCK FRAGMENT** a small piece of rock of any shape **3 SHAPED ROCK FRAGMENT** a piece of rock that has been shaped for a particular purpose, e.g. a gravestone or a paving stone (*often in combination*) **4 SMALL HARD MASS** a small hard mass, e.g. a hailstone (*usually in combination*) **5 GEMSTONE** a gemstone **6 HARD MASS INSIDE FRUIT** the hard central part of some fruits, such as cherries, plums, olives, and peaches, that contains the seed **7** (*plural* **stone** *or* **stones**) **UNIT OF WEIGHT** in the United Kingdom, a unit of weight equivalent to 6.35 kg/14lb. It is used especially for expressing somebody's weight. ○ *He's trying to get down to 12 stone.* **8 MINERAL MASS INSIDE ORGAN** a small hard mass of mineral material formed in an organ, e.g. the kidney or gall bladder. Technical name **calculus** *n.* 3 **9 LIGHT GREY OR BEIGE** a dull light grey or beige colour **10 PRINTER'S TABLE** a very smooth flat table used for arranging printing type (*dated*) **11 CURLING BLOCK** the shaped and polished mass of granite or iron that is slid along the ice in the game of curling ■ *adj* **1 OF STONEWARE** made of stoneware **2 LIGHT GREY TO BEIGE IN COLOUR** of the colour stone ■ *adv* **1 USED FOR EMPHASIS** used to emphasize the degree of a quality, usually a quality associated with stone, such as coldness, stillness, or lifelessness ○ *stone drunk* **2 USED FOR EMPHASIS** used to emphasize the degree of a quality (*slang*) ○ *stone fine* ○ *stone tired* ■ *vt* (**stones, stoning, stoned**) **1 THROW STONES AT** to throw stones at somebody or something, especially as a form of punishment, execution, or vandalism **2 REMOVE STONE FROM FRUIT** to remove the hard central part from a piece of fruit, e.g. a plum **3** *US* **RUB WITH STONE** to polish or sharpen something on a stone or with a stone [Old English *stān*. < Indo-European.] ◇ **be carved** *or* **set** *or* **cast in (tablets of) stone** to be so firmly established as to make changes impossible or unthinkable ◇ **cast** *or* **throw the first stone** to be the first person to quarrel with, accuse, or criticize somebody else ◇ **leave no stone unturned** to be very thorough in making a search or in carrying out a task

Stone, Oliver (*b.* 1946) US film director

Stone Age *n* the earliest period of human history, in which tools and weapons were made of stone rather than metal. It is divided into the Palaeolithic, Mesolithic, and Neolithic periods.

Stone-Age *adj* **1** dating from the Stone Age, the earliest period of human history **2 Stone-Age, stone-age** hopelessly behind the times

stone bass *n* a large dark-brown and yellow fish of the perch family. Native to: Atlantic and Mediterranean waters. *Polyprion americanus.* [< its inhabiting rocky ledges and wrecks]

stone-blind *adj* an offensive term meaning completely unable to see —**stone-blindness** *n*

stone bramble *n* a prickly herbaceous plant like the wild raspberry that produces deep-red berries. Flowers: white. Native to: Europe, Asia. *Rubus saxatilis.* [< its growing in rocky places]

stone-broke *adj US* = **stony-broke** (*informal*)

stonecast /stṓn kaast/ *n* = **stone's throw**

stonecat /stṓn kat/ (*plural* **-cats** *or* **-cat**) *n* a slender yellowish-brown catfish that inhabits the beds of streams, rivers, and lakes, typically under stones. Native to: North America. *Noturus flavus.*

stonechat /stṓn chat/ (*plural* **-chats** *or* **-chat**) *n* a small songbird, the male of which has a black head, brown back, chestnut breast, and white rump. Native to: grassy regions and dry plains of Europe and N Africa. *Saxicola torquata.* [Late 18C. *Stone* from the resemblance of the bird's call to the sound of colliding stones.]

stone-cold *adj* completely cold, especially too cold to be palatable ■ *adv* completely and utterly (*informal*) ○ *stone-cold sober*

stone crab *n* a large crab that lays several million eggs and can be a serious pest to oyster beds. Native to: coast of S United States. *Menippe mercenaria.*

stonecrop /stṓn krop/ (*plural* **-crops** *or* **-crop**) *n* **1** an annual or perennial flowering plant with fleshy leaves. Native to: N temperate regions. Genus: *Sedum.* **2** a plant related or similar to the stonecrop [Old English *stāncropp* < an earlier form of STONE (because the plant grows on rocks) + CROP in the obsolete sense 'flower cluster, ear of grain']

stone curlew *n* a brownish, mostly nocturnal wading bird with a large head and eyes and thick knee joints. Native to: open dry stony regions of N Europe. *Burhinus oedicnemus.*

stonecutter /stṓn kuttər/ *n* **1** a cutter and carver of stone **2** a machine that is used to cut stone and concrete, especially a hand-held power tool with a circular blade —**stonecutting** *n*

stoned /stōnd/ *adj* **1** relaxed, excited, or euphoric from taking illegal drugs, especially cannabis (*slang*) **2** very intoxicated (*informal*)

stone-dead *adj* definitely or completely lifeless

stone-deaf *adj* an offensive term meaning completely unable to hear

stone-faced *adj* **1** = **stony-faced 2** having a facing of stone

stonefish /stṓn fish/ (*plural* **-fishes** *or* **-fish**) *n* a tropical marine fish whose mottled and knobbly body serves as camouflage in its rocky habitat. Genus: *Synanceja.*

stonefly /stṓn flī/ (*plural* **-flies** *or* **-fly**) *n* an insect that, in its wingless juvenile stage, lives among stones in rivers and streams. The adults have long antennae and usually two pairs of wings. Order: Plecoptera.

stone fruit *n* PLANT SCI = **drupe**

stoneground /stṓn grownd/ *adj* ground in the traditional way with millstones rather than with metal rollers

Stoneham /stṓnəm/ town in NE Massachusetts. Population: 22,203 (1996 estimate).

Stonehenge /stṓn hénj/ prehistoric monument on Salisbury Plain, S England, consisting of two concentric circles of large standing stones

stone lily *n* a fossil of a sea lily

stone marten *n* **1** a marten with dark-brown fur with a lighter throat and undersides. Native to: woods of Europe and Asia. *Martes foina.* **2** the fur of the stone marten [< its inhabiting rocky inlets and crevices]

stonemason /stṓn mayss'n/ *n* a maker and repairer of stone structures or stone used as a building material —**stonemasonry** *n*

stone parsley *n* a roadside plant with leaves that smell like a mixture of petrol and nutmeg when crushed. Flowers: small, white. Native to: W Europe, Mediterranean. [Translation of Greek *petroselinon* (see PARSLEY)]

stone pine *n* a pine tree with an umbrella-shaped crown that is cultivated for its seeds, eaten raw or roasted. Native to: Mediterranean region. *Pinus pinea.*

stoner /stṓn ər/ *n* a regular smoker of marijuana (*slang*)

stone shoot *n* a strip of loose stones that extends up a steep hillside or mountainside

stone's throw *n* not very far away at all

stonewall /stṓn wáwl/ *v* **1** *vti* **REFUSE TO COOPERATE** to refuse to cooperate with somebody else by avoiding answering questions or providing desired information (*informal*) ○ *a press secretary who stonewalled the reporters' questions* **2** *vi* **DELIBERATELY CREATE DELAY** to create obstructions or employ delaying tactics, especially in order to hinder parliamentary business **3** *vi* **PLAY DEFENSIVELY IN CRICKET** to play persistently defensive batting strokes in cricket —**stonewaller** *n*

Stonewall Generation *n* the generation of activists who campaigned in the early 1970s in favour of more liberal treatment of homosexuals [After *Stonewall (Inn)*, scene of a riot in June 1969 in which homosexuals resisted police harassment]

stoneware /stṓn wair/ *n* dense opaque non-porous pottery that is fired at a very high temperature

stonewashed /stṓn wosht/ *adj* washed with small pumice pebbles to give a worn faded look

stonework /stṓn wurk/ *n* **1** the parts of a building or other structure that are made of stone **2** using stone as a building material —**stoneworker** *n*

stonewort /stṓn wurt/ (*plural* **-wort** *or* **-worts**) *n* green algae that grow in fresh or slightly salty water. They have jointed branches, often encrusted with lime. Genus: *Chara*.

stoney *adj* = **stony**

stonk /stongk/ *vt* to subject something, e.g. a building or enemy position, to a heavy artillery bombardment (*dated slang*) ■ *n* a heavy artillery barrage (*dated slang*) [Mid-20C. < ?]

stonker /stóngkər/ *n* an excellent example of something, often something impressively large or powerful (*slang*) ○ *played a stonker of a shot* [Early 20C. < STONK.]

stonkered /stóngkərd/ *adj* (*slang*) **1** exhausted, defeated, or out of action **2** extremely drunk [Early 20C. < Scots and N English dialect *stonk* 'game of marbles, marble' < ?]

stonking /stóngking/ *adv* used to emphasize how good or enjoyable something is (*slang*) ○ *hit a stonking drive straight down the middle* ○ *a stonking good party* [Late 20C. < STONK.]

stony /stṓni/ (**-ier, -iest**), **stoney** (**-ier, -iest**) *adj* **1 OF OR LIKE STONE** made of stone or similar to stone in appearance, texture, or colour **2 COVERED WITH STONES** covered with or having a great many stones **3 EMOTIONLESS** expressing no emotion, especially no friendliness or pity **4** stony-broke (*slang*) —**stonily** *adv* —**stoniness** *n*

stony-broke *adj* having no money at all (*informal*) US term **stone-broke**

stony coral *n* a coral with a robust external calcium-based skeleton that forms reefs and islands. Order: Scleractinia and Madreporaria.

stony-faced, stone-faced *adj* showing not the slightest emotion, especially no sign of friendliness

stony-hearted /-haártid/, **stonehearted** /stṓn haártid/ *adj* having or showing no compassion or kindness

stony-iron meteorite *n* a meteorite consisting of metal and stony material

stony meteorite *n* a meteorite that is composed mainly of rock-forming silicate minerals, especially olivine, plagioclase, and pyroxine

stood past tense, past participle of **stand**

stooge /stooj/ *n* **1 COMIC LOSER** a comic actor, usually part of a double act, who acts as the butt of most of the jokes **2 SOMEBODY EXPLOITED** a person who is exploited by others, especially somebody used by criminals in committing their crimes (*slang insult*) **3** US BIRDS = **stool pigeon** *n*. 1 (*slang*) ■ *vi* (**stooges, stooging, stooged**) **BE TAKEN ADVANTAGE OF** to be taken advantage of by another (*informal*) [Early 20C. < ?]

stook /stook, stŏŏk/ *n* AGRIC = **shock**² *n*. ■ *vt* AGRIC = **shock**² *v*. [14C. < ?] —**stooker** *n*

stookie /stŏŏki/ *n Scotland* **1** a plaster cast on a broken limb **2** a statue ○ *stood there like a stookie* [Late 18C. Variant of STUCCO.]

stool /stool/ *n* **1 SIMPLE SEAT** a simple seat with three or four legs and no back or arm rests **2 EXCREMENT** a piece of excrement **3 PLANT BASE** the base of a plant, from which shoots or suckers sprout **4 CLUMP OF SHOOTS** a clump of shoots or suckers sprouting from the base of a plant **5** US **HUNTER'S DECOY** a real or artificial bird used by hunters as a decoy **6** *W Africa* **CHIEF'S THRONE** a chief's throne **7 TOILET** a toilet or toilet seat (*slang*) ■ *vi* **1 SPROUT SHOOTS** to sprout shoots or suckers from a stool **2** US **EVACUATE BOWELS** to evacuate the bowels **3 BE DECOY OR HUNT WITH DECOY** to be a decoy for a hunter of wildfowl, or to hunt wildfowl using decoys **4** US **BE STOOL PIGEON** to provide information to law enforcement agencies about criminals (*slang*) [Old English *stōl* 'chair' < Indo-European, 'to stand'] ◇ **fall between two stools 1** to fail to achieve either of two objectives by hesitating between them and failing to take action, or by trying for both and ending up with neither **2** to be a possible member of two categories but a true member of neither

stoolie /stŏŏli/ *n* US a stool pigeon (*informal*) [Early 20C. Shortening.]

stool pigeon *n* **1 POLICE INFORMER** a person who informs on criminals or their activities to the police (*slang*) **2 HUNTER'S DECOY PIGEON** a pigeon, or a dummy of a pigeon, used by a hunter as a decoy **3 DECOY CRIMINAL** a criminal working as a decoy for a gang of criminals, with the job of distracting attention or throwing the police off the scent (*slang*) [Because such decoys were originally tied to a wooden platform]

stoop¹ /stoop/ *v* **1** *vti* **BEND BODY** to bend the top half of the body forwards and downwards **2** *vi* **WALK OR STAND BENT OVER** to walk or stand with the head and shoulders bent forwards and downwards **3** *vi* **BEHAVE UNETHICALLY** to act in an unethical or self-degrading way ○ *I never imagined you would stoop so low.* **4** *vi* **CONDESCEND** to do something reluctantly and with the attitude of somebody who does not normally do something that is so unworthy ○ *'He could not stoop to love; No lady in the land had power His frozen heart to move'*; (Sir Walter Scott, *Waverley*; 1814) **5** *vi* **SWOOP DOWN** to swoop down with wings folded, e.g. when attacking prey (*refers to birds*) ■ *n* **1 BENT POSTURE** a posture in which the head and shoulders are bent forwards and downwards **2 BIRD'S DOWNWARDS SWOOP** the downwards swoop of a bird of prey [Old English *stūpian* < Germanic] —**stooper** *n* —**stooping** *adj* —**stoopingly** *adv*

LITERARY LINK ***She Stoops to Conquer***, a play (1773) by Oliver Goldsmith. An enduringly popular comedy of manners, it is the story of a shy young gentleman, Marlow, who reluctantly travels to the country to woo a young woman. Mistaking her home for an inn, he assumes she is the maid, treats her accordingly, and wins her heart with his frankness.

stoop² /stoop/ *n* US, *Can* a small porch or verandah at the entrance to a house [Mid-18C. < Dutch *stoep*.]

stoop³ *n* CHR = **stoup**

stop /stop/ *v* (**stops, stopping, stopped**) **1** *vti* **DISCONTINUE** to cease doing something or make somebody cease doing something ○ *She's trying to stop smoking.* **2** *vti* **CEASE MOVING** to come to a standstill or bring something to a standstill ○ *Stop the car!* **3** *vti* **END** to come to an end or bring something to an end ○ *The snow has stopped.* **4** *vt* **PREVENT FROM HAPPENING** to prevent something from happening or continuing ○ *We couldn't stop the roof from caving in.* **5** *vt* **PREVENT AN ACTION** to prevent somebody or something from doing something ○ *a way of stopping the children from climbing the fence* **6** *vi* **PAUSE** to pause in order to do something before continuing ○ *I urge you to stop and think before deciding.* **7** *vi* **INTERRUPT JOURNEY** to interrupt a journey in order to make a brief visit somewhere ○ *Stop at the post office on the way into town.* **8** *vt* **FILL HOLE** to fill or block a hole ○ *We need to stop the cracks in the wall.* **9** *vt* **BLOCK** to block or plug something, e.g. a pipe or a wound, so that nothing can pass through it ○ *Grease has stopped the drain.* **10** *vt* **INTERDICT CHEQUE** to instruct a bank not to honour a cheque **11** *vt* **DEDUCT** to deduct money or a payment from somebody's salary ○ *have the cost of breakages stopped off your wages* **12** *vt* **PRESS MUSICAL STRING** to press a string on a stringed instrument in order to produce a particular note **13** *vt* **COVER HOLE ON INSTRUMENT** to use a finger to close a hole on a wind instrument in order to produce a particular note **14** *vt* **PUT HAND INSIDE FRENCH HORN** to alter the tone and pitch of a French horn by putting a hand inside the bell **15** *vt* **KNOCK OUT** to defeat an opponent in boxing by a knockout **16** *vti* **BLOCK BRIDGE SUIT** to block the winning of a suit in bridge **17** *vt* **BE HIT BY** to be hit by something, usually a punch or a bullet (*informal*) **18** *vt* **DEFEAT** to defeat an opponent or competitor or overcome an obstacle (*informal*) ○ *Nothing's going to stop us now.* ■ *n* **1 STANDSTILL** a complete end or lack of movement **2 BREAK IN JOURNEY** a short break in a journey, e.g. to rest or to visit somebody **3 PLACE VISITED ON THE WAY** a place visited while on a journey **4 PAUSE MADE ON ROUTE** a place where a bus or a train regularly pauses on its route ○ *Is this your stop?* **5 BLOCKAGE** a blockage or obstruction **6 PLUG THAT BLOCKS** something, e.g. a plug or a stopper, that is used to block the flow or passage of something **7 DEVICE PREVENTING MOVEMENT** a device or control that prevents movement (*often in combination*) **8 FULL STOP** in punctuation, a full stop (*informal*) ○ *Send help. Stop.* **9 ORDER INTERDICTING CHEQUE** an order to a bank not to honour a cheque ○ *had to put a stop on the lost check* **10 STOPPING ON MUSICAL INSTRUMENT** an act of stopping a string or a hole on a musical instrument **11 SUBSET OF ORGAN PIPES** a subset of organ pipes or harpsichord strings with a common tone colour that can be played in isolation **12 ORGAN CONTROL** a knob or lever on an organ or harpsichord that isolates a subset of pipes or strings **13 CAMERA'S APERTURE SETTING** one of the graded settings for the size of the aperture of a camera lens **14 CAMERA'S DIAPHRAGM** the diaphragm of a camera **15 SHORT ROPE** a short length of line used to tie up something, e.g. a sail **16 SPEECH SOUND** a consonant sound made by closing the passage of air through the mouth and then suddenly opening it again. ◊ **continuant 17 PART OF ANIMAL'S FACE** the area between the nose and the forehead of a cat or a dog **18 FENCING COUNTERTHRUST** a swift counterthrust made at the time of a fencing opponent's thrust that seeks to make contact first **19 CARVING** a carving that finishes the end of a moulding [Old English *-stoppian* 'block up', via Germanic < Latin *stuppa* 'plug, stopper' < Greek *stuppē*] —**stoppable** *adj* ◇ **pull out all the stops** to make every possible effort in order to accomplish something ◇ **put a stop to something** to bring something to an end, usually quickly and permanently

stop by *v* to interrupt a journey in order to make a brief visit somewhere ○ *Can you stop by the supermarket on your way home?*

stop down *vti* to make the aperture of a camera lens smaller

stop off *vi* to interrupt a journey briefly in order to do something or see somebody ○ *We stopped off at the supermarket on the way home.*

stop out *vi* to remain out of the house, or stay out late (*informal*)

stop bath *n* an acid solution in which a negative or print is immersed in order to halt the developing process

⚡**stop bit** *n* in serial communications, a bit that signals the end of a transmission unit

stopcock /stóp kok/ *n* a valve or tap used to turn on, turn off, or regulate the flow of a fluid in a pipe

stope /stōp/ *n* an excavation that resembles steps, used especially in the mining of ore ■ *vti* (**stopes, stoping, stoped**) to make stopes in a mine, or to extract ore in this way [Mid-18C. < ?]

~~**stoped**~~ incorrect spelling of **stopped**

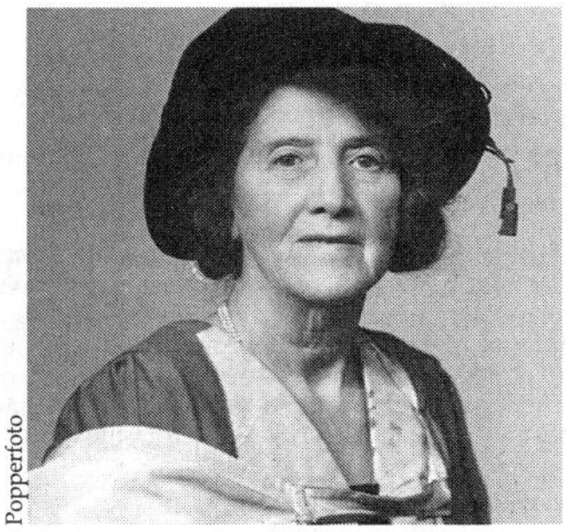

Popperfoto

Marie Stopes

Stopes /stōps/, **Marie** (1880–1958) Scottish pioneer advocate of birth control and writer

stopgap /stóp gap/ *n* something used as a temporary substitute for something that is really needed ■ *adj* used as a temporary substitute for something that is really needed ○ *a stopgap spending bill*

stop-go *adj* alternating deliberately between discouragement and encouragement of economic demand so as to control inflation

stoplight *n* 1 *US* TRANSP = **traffic light** 2 AUTOMOT = **brake light**

stop light *n* 1 a red traffic light 2 AUTOMOT = **brake light**

stop-loss order *n* an order to a stockbroker to stop selling a stock when its price has fallen below a specified level

stop-off *n* = **stopover**

stop order *n* an order to a stockbroker to buy or sell a stock when it has risen or fallen to a specified price

stopover /stópp ővər/ *n* 1 a usually brief halt on a journey 2 a place where somebody makes a brief halt on a journey

stoppage /stóppij/ *n* 1 **STRIKE** a strike, especially a brief one 2 **DEDUCTION FROM PAY** an amount of money deducted from an employee's pay, e.g. for tax, national insurance, or pension contributions 3 **TIME WHEN PLAY IS HALTED** a time during which the play in a game, especially football or rugby, is briefly halted, e.g. because of an injury to a player 4 **ACT OF STOPPING** the act of stopping the movement of something 5 **SITUATION WHERE THINGS ARE STOPPED** a situation in which something has been stopped or blocked ○ *a work stoppage*

stoppage time /stóppij-/ *n* extra time played at the end of a game, especially in football or rugby, to make up for time lost in dealing with injured players or through other interruptions

Stoppard /stóppard/, **Sir Tom** (*b.* 1937) Czech-born British dramatist. Born **Tom Straussler**

stopper /stóppər/ *n* 1 **CORK OR PLUG** something that is put into an opening in order to close it 2 **SOMEBODY OR SOMETHING THAT STOPS** a person or thing that brings something to a stop 3 **CARD THAT PREVENTS TAKING OF SUIT** a card held by somebody that will prevent the opponents from taking all the tricks in that card's suit during a hand of bridge ■ *vt* **CLOSE WITH STOPPER** to close or secure something with a stopper

stopple /stópp'l/ *n* = **stopper** *n.* 1 [15C. < STOP.] —**stopple** *vt*

stop press *n* 1 news that is inserted into an edition of a newspaper after printing has begun (*hyphenated before nouns*) 2 a space in a newspaper kept for the insertion of late news

stopwatch /stópp woch/ (*plural* **-watches**) *n* a special watch that can be started and stopped instantly and is used to measure the amount of time somebody or something takes, e.g. a runner in a race

⚡**storage** /stáwrij/ *n* 1 **STORING OR BEING STORED** the act of storing something, or the condition of being stored 2 **SPACE FOR STORING** space in which to store things, especially the amount of such space 3 **PRICE FOR STORING** the price charged for storing something 4 **MEDIUM FOR STORING DATA** any device or medium used for deposit, retention, and retrieval of data, especially a hard disk or floppy disk

storage battery (*plural* **storage batteries**) *n US* ELEC ENG = **accumulator** *n.* 1

storage cell *n* ELECTRONICS = **secondary cell**

⚡**storage dump** *n* a printout of all the data held in system storage in a computer

storage heater *n* an electrical device that accumulates energy during off-peak times and later releases it as heat

storax /stáwr aks/ *n* 1 **TREE WITH DROOPING WHITE FLOWERS** a tree or shrub, some species of which are grown as ornamentals. Flowers: white, drooping in long clusters. Native to: tropical or subtropical regions. Genus: *Styrax.* 2 **VANILLA-SCENTED BALSAM** a vanilla-scented balsam obtained from a species of storax tree 3 **FRAGRANT BALSAM** a fragrant liquid balsam obtained from the bark of an Asian tree [14C. < Latin, alteration of *styrax.*]

⚡**store** /stawr/ *v* (**stores, storing, stored**) 1 *vt* **PUT AWAY** to put something away for use in the future ○ *stored old clothes in the attic* ○ *squirrels storing up reserves of nuts for the winter* 2 *vt* **PUT SOMETHING INTO SAFEKEEPING** to put or hold something somewhere for safekeeping, e.g. in a warehouse 3 *vi* **SURVIVE STORAGE** to survive or stay fresh while being kept in storage ○ *Apples will store well in a cool, humid building.* 4 *vt* **STOCK ITEMS** to fill or provide something with other things 5 *vt* **HOLD DATA** to enter or save data or programs into a computer memory ■ *n* 1 **PLACE SELLING GOODS** a place where goods are offered for retail sale to customers 2 **QUANTITY SAVED FOR FUTURE USE** a quantity or collection put away for future use ○ *a store of grain in a silo* 3 **PLACE WHERE GOODS ARE KEPT** a place where goods are kept in quantity, e.g. a warehouse 4 **GREAT QUANTITY** a great quantity or large collection ○ *a rich store of memories* ○ *a weapon store* 5 **ANIMAL BEING FATTENED** an animal that is being fattened for sale ■ **stores** *npl* **SUPPLIES** items or materials needed for something, e.g. a business, expedition, or vessel ■ *adj US* **COMMERCIALLY BOUGHT** purchased from a shop [13C. Via Old French *estorer* 'build, supply' < Latin *instaurare.*] —**storable** *adj* ◇ **in store** 1 about to happen in the future ○ *She has a surprise in store for you.* 2 in a large amount ○ *He has come back with money in store.* ◇ **set** *or* **lay** *or* **put great store by something** to consider something to be important, valuable, or worthwhile

store-bought *adj US* = **shop-bought**

⚡**store builder** *n* a computer program used to create a virtual storefront for a retailer (*in e-commerce*)

store card *n* = **charge card**

storefront /stáwr frunt/ *n* 1 *US* COMM = **shopfront** 2 *US* **ROOM OR BUILDING WITH STOREFRONT** a room, suite of rooms, or building that has a storefront 3 **VIRTUAL SHOP ON WEB** a virtual shop on the World Wide Web providing product information, ordering capability, and provision for secure transfer of payment ■ *adj US* 1 **LOCATED ON STOREFRONT** located on or near the side of the store where the main entrance is 2 **BASED IN STOREFRONT** working or based in a storefront rather than in a more professional or expensive location ○ *a storefront clinic*

storehouse /stáwr howss/ (*plural* **-houses** /-howziz/) *n* 1 a place where things are stored 2 an abundant source, collection, or supply ○ *She's a storehouse of information on local history.*

storekeeper /stáwr keepər/ *n* 1 a manager of the supplies or stores of a military unit, ship, or organization 2 *US* = **shopkeeper**

storeroom /stáwr room, -rŏŏm/ *n* a room or enclosed space where things are stored

storey /stáwri/ *n* 1 a floor or level in a building 2 a set of rooms, or space, on a particular floor of a building [14C. Via Anglo-Latin *historia* < Latin (see HISTORY).]

SPELLCHECK Do not confuse ***storey*** with ***story***, which has a similar sound. Beware: your spellchecker will not catch this error.

Storey /stáwri/, **David** (*b.* 1933) British novelist and playwright

storeyed /stáwrid/ *adj* with stories, usually of a given number (*often in combination*) [Early 17C. < STOREY.]

storied[1] /stáwrid/ *adj* 1 interesting, famous, or celebrated in stories and books (*literary*) ○ *the storied outlaw Robin Hood* 2 decorated with images of scenes from history or legend [14C. < STORY[1].]

storied[2] *adj* US = **storeyed**

stork /stawrk/ (*plural* **storks** *or* **stork**) *n* large wading bird related to the heron and ibis having a long neck, a long straight bill, and black-and-white plumage. Family: Ciconiidae. [Old English *storc*, < Indo-European, 'stiff']

storksbill /stáwrks bil/ *n* a plant of the geranium family with lobed leaves and fruits with a beak-shaped tip. Flowers: pink or purple, in clusters. Genus: *Erodium.*

storm /stawrm/ *n* 1 **VIOLENT WEATHER** a disturbance in the air above the Earth, with strong winds and usually also with rain, snow, sleet, or hail and sometimes lightning and thunder 2 **HEAVY RAIN OR SNOW** a heavy fall of rain, snow, or sleet, often occurring with strong winds 3 **RAIN OF OBJECTS** a heavy bombardment of solid objects 4 **OUTBURST OF FEELING** a sudden strong outpouring of feeling in reaction to something ○ *a storm of anger* 5 **SUDDEN STRONG ATTACK** a sudden strong attack on a defended place or position 6 **STRONG WIND** a gale that has a speed of 103 to 106 km/64 to 72 mi. per hour ■ *v* 1 *vti* **ATTACK VIOLENTLY** to attack or capture a place, especially a well defended one, suddenly and with great force ○ *stormed the barricades* 2 *vti* **BE ANGRY** to be violently and noisily angry 3 *vi* **RUSH WITH VIOLENCE OR ANGER** to go somewhere in a rush, violently or angrily ○ *stormed out of the room in a huff* 4 *vi* **BLOW WITH OR WITHOUT PRECIPITATION** to blow strongly, to drop large amounts of rain, snow, or sleet, or to do both together [Old English, < Indo-European, 'to whirl'] ◇ **a storm in a teacup** a fuss or row over something trivial ◇ **take somebody** *or* **something by storm** 1 to capture a place *or* overwhelm a body of enemies suddenly and with great force 2 to make a great and immediate impression on somebody or something

storm beach *n* an accumulation of coarse sand and stones that is built up by storm action on a shore above the high-water mark

storm belt *n* a region on the surface of the Earth where there are frequent storms

stormbound /stáwrm bownd/ *adj* unable to leave, go out, or get in touch with anyone because of a strong storm

storm cellar *n* a shelter underground used as a refuge during a windstorm

storm centre *n* 1 the central region of a cyclonic storm, with a low barometric pressure and relatively calm conditions 2 a focus of trouble, disturbance, or controversy

storm cloud *n* 1 a large dark cloud that is a sign of approaching heavy rain or a storm 2 a sign that violence, especially war, is soon to break out

storm-cock *n* a mistle thrush (*regional*) [So called because it sings even in bad weather]

storm cone *n* a cone-shaped canvas signal hoisted on a mast as a warning of approaching high winds

storm door *n* a door added outside the main door of a house to provide additional protection against extremes of weather

storm drain *n* a large drain built to carry away excess water from a road during heavy rain. US term **storm sewer**

stormer /stáwrmər/ *n* a person or thing that is excellent or impressive (*slang*)

storm glass *n* a glass tube containing a solution that is supposed to indicate weather changes by changes in its appearance. US term **weatherglass** *n.* 2

storming /stáwrming/ *adj* excellent or impressive (*informal*) ■ *n* the act of suddenly and violently attacking or capturing a place

storm petrel *n* a small seabird with black or brown plumage and a white rump. Native to: N Atlantic, Mediterranean. *Hydrobates pelagicus.* [Because the bird's appearance was thought to forebode a storm]

stormproof /stáwrm proof/ *adj* able to withstand the wind, rain, or other elements of a storm, or providing protection from them

storm sewer *n US* = **storm drain**

storm trooper *n* 1 a member of the SA, a private militia of the Nazi party that used tactics of violence and brutality 2 a member of a military shock force specially trained to carry out attacks [< *storm troop*, a translation of German *Sturmabteilung*]

storm window *n* a window added outside an ordinary house window to provide additional protection against extremes of weather

stormy /stáwrmi/ (**-ier, -iest**) *adj* 1 affected by or experiencing a storm or frequent storms 2 dominated by or subject to strong emotions or disturbances —**stormily** *adv* —**storminess** *n*

stormy petrel *n* 1 BIRDS = **storm petrel** 2 a person who causes or brings trouble

Stornoway /stáwrnə way/ port on the island of Lewis-with-Harris, in the Outer Hebrides, Scotland. Population: 5,975 (1991).

Storrier /stórri ər, stáwri ər/, **Tim** (*b.* 1949) Australian painter

story[1] /stáwri/ *n* (*plural* **-ries**) 1 **FACTUAL OR FICTIONAL NARRATIVE** a factual or fictional account of an event or series of events 2 **SHORT FICTIONAL PROSE PIECE** a work of fiction in prose that is shorter than a novel 3 **PLOT OF FICTION OR DRAMA** the plot of a novel, play, film, or other fictional narrative work 4 **ACCOUNT OF FACTS** what somebody says has happened ○ *changed her story several times* 5 **FALSEHOOD** something that one person tells another that is not true (*informal*) ○ *Don't give me any stories.* ○ *You're telling stories again.* 6 **NEWS REPORT** a report in the news of something that has happened 7 **SUBJECT FOR REPORT** a subject or material for a news report 8 **LEGEND OR ROMANCE** traditional tales and legends, or the literature based on such tales ■ *vt* (**-ries, -rying, -ried**) **DECORATE WITH LEGENDARY SCENES** to decorate something with images of scenes from history or legend [13C. Via Anglo-Norman *estorie* < Latin *historia* (see HISTORY).] ◇ **the same old story** what always happens or is said (*informal disapproving*) ◇ **to cut a long story short** to say something in a brief rather than a longer and more detailed way

SPELLCHECK See *storey.*

story[2] *n US* = **storey**

storyboard /stáwri bawrd/ *n* a set of sketches, arranged in sequence on panels, outlining the scenes that will make up something to be filmed, e.g. a film, television show, or advertisement

storybook /stáwri bŏŏk/ *n* a book of stories for children ■ *adj* typical of or like something found in children's stories rather than the real world

story line *n* = **story**[1] *n.* 3

storyteller /stáwri tellər/ *n* 1 a teller or writer of stories 2 a liar (*informal*) —**storytelling** *n*

stoss /stoss/ *adj* describes a mountain, hill, or slope that faces the direction of an oncoming glacier [Late 19C. < German, 'thrust, push'.]

stot[1] /stot, stōt/ (**stots, stotting, stotted**) *v Scotland* 1 *vti* to bounce, or make something bounce 2 *vi* to stagger or walk unsteadily [Early 16C. < ?]

stot[2] /stot/ *n Scotland* a bullock [Old English *stot(t)* 'bull']

stotin /sto teén/ *n* see table at **currency** [< Slovene, 'hundredth']

stotinka /sto tíngkə/ (*plural* **-ki** /-ki/) *n* see table at **currency** [Late 19C. < Bulgarian, 'hundredth' < *sto* 'hundred'.]

stotious /stṓshəss/ *adj Scotland, Ireland* very drunk (*slang*) [< STOT[1]]

stoup /stoop/, **stoop** *n* a basin for holy water in a church [14C. < Old Norse *staup* 'drinking vessel'.]

stour /stowr, stoor/ *n Scotland* dust, in a deposit or as a cloud [15C. < ?] —**stoury** *adj*

Stourbridge /stówrbrij/ town in central England. Population: 55,624 (1991).

stoush /stowsh/ *n ANZ* a fight or dispute (*informal*) ■ *vt ANZ* to fight somebody (*informal*) [Early 20C. < ?]

stout /stowt/ *adj* 1 **THICKSET OR HEAVY** thicker and heavier in body than an average person of the same height 2 **COURAGEOUS AND DETERMINED** possessing or showing courage and determination 3 **STRONG** strong and substantial ■ *n* **DARK STRONG BEER** a strong, very dark, almost black beer made from roasted malted barley [13C. < Anglo-Norman, < Germanic.] —**stoutly** *adv* —**stoutness** *n*

Stout /stowt/, **Sir Robert** (1844–1930) Scottish-born New Zealand statesman

stouten /stówt'n/ *vti* to become, or make somebody or something, stout or stouter

stouthearted /stówt haártid/ *adj* having or showing courage and resolution —**stoutheartedly** *adv* —**stoutheartedness** *n*

stove[1] /stōv/ *n* 1 **APPLIANCE FOR COOKING OR HEATING** an appliance that uses electricity or burns a fuel to produce heat for cooking or for heating 2 **WOOD-BURNING COOKING APPLIANCE** a cooking appliance that runs on solid fuel such as wood 3 **HEAT-PRODUCING CHAMBER OR DEVICE** a device or chamber that is used to heat or dry something, e.g. a kiln ■ *vt* (**stoves, stoving, stoved**) **HEAT IN A STOVE** to treat something by heating it in a stove in order to coat it with a surface such as enamel [15C. Probably < Middle Dutch or Middle Low German, 'heated room'.]

stove[2] past tense, past participle of **stave**

stovepipe /stṓv pīp/ *n* 1 a pipe used as a chimney for a fuel-burning stove, usually made of sheet steel formed into a tube 2 CLOTHING = **stovepipe hat**

stovepipe hat *n* a tall tube-shaped silk hat for a man

stovies /stṓviz/ *npl Scotland* a dish of sliced potatoes and onions stewed together, sometimes with a little meat

stow /stō/ *vt* 1 **PUT SOMETHING AWAY** to pack something or put something away 2 **FILL SOMETHING WITH TIGHTLY PACKED THINGS** to fill something with other things, especially things packed tightly ○ *to stow a boat's hold with cargo* 3 **STORE SOMETHING FOR LATER USE** to store something for use in the future 4 **HOLD** to be capable of containing something 5 **STOP** to stop doing something (*slang*) ○ *Stow this silly chatter.* [14C. < Old English *stōw* 'place'.]

stow away *vi* to hide on a ship or aircraft in the hope of being taken somewhere without having to pay

Stow /stō/, **Randolph** (*b.* 1935) Australian writer

stowage /stṓ ij/ *n* 1 **STOWING OF THINGS** a loading, packing, or storing of something, or a way of doing this 2 **SITUATION OR ARRANGEMENT OF THINGS PACKED** the condition of being stowed, or the way this has been done 3 **THINGS STOWED** something that is stowed somewhere or is to be stowed 4 **PLACE OR SPACE FOR STOWING** a place, container, or space for stowing things 5 **FEE FOR STOWING** a fee or fees for stowing something

stowaway /stṓ ə way/ *n* a person who hides on a ship or aircraft in the hope of being taken somewhere without cost

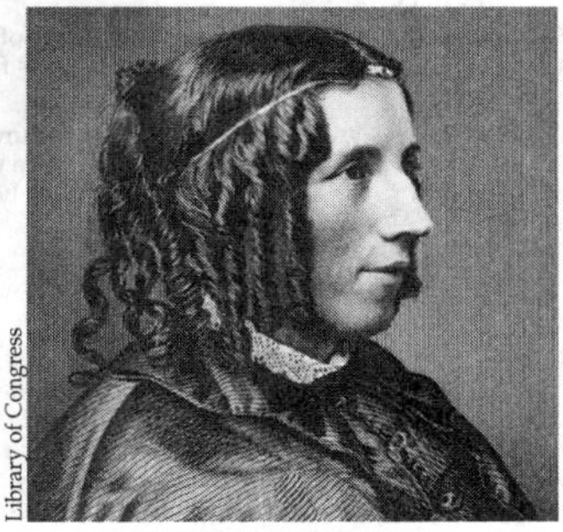

Library of Congress

Harriet Beecher Stowe

Stowe /stō/, **Harriet Beecher** (1811–96) US writer and abolitionist. Born **Harriet Elizabeth Beecher**

STP *abbr* standard temperature and pressure

str. *abbr* 1 **str., Str.** strait 2 stroke

Strabane /strə bán/ town in W Northern Ireland. Population: 11,981 (1991).

strabismus /strə bízməss/ *n* a squint (*technical*) [Late 17C. Via modern Latin < Greek *strabizein* 'squint' < *strabos* 'squinting'.] —**strabismal** *adj* —**strabismic** *adj* —**strabismical** *adj*

Strabo /stráybō/ (63? BC–AD 24) Greek geographer and historian

Strachey /stráychi/, **Lytton** (1880–1932) British writer

Strad /strad/ *n* a Stradivarius violin (*informal*) [Late 19C. Shortening.]

straddle /strádd'l/ *v* (**-dles, -dling, -dled**) 1 *vt* **SIT OR STAND WITH LEGS ASTRIDE** to sit or stand so that one leg is on one side and the other leg is on the other side of something or somebody 2 *vt* **BE OVER OR ACROSS** to be on both sides of something ○ *The city straddles the river.* 3 *vt* **APPLY TO MORE THAN ONE THING** to exist in, belong to, or apply to more than one situation or category ○ *The rule of the dynasty straddled the end of one century and the beginning of the next.* 4 *vt* **STRIKE AND NARROWLY MISS TARGET** to strike a target as well as miss it on either side 5 *vt* **SPREAD LEGS APART** to spread your legs apart, usually so that they are on either side of something 6 *vi* **SIT OR WALK WITH LEGS APART** to sit, stand, or walk with your legs spread apart or on either side of something 7 *vt* **FIRE SHELLS FOR RANGE** to fire artillery shells in front of and behind a target to find the correct range ■ *n* 1 **POSITION ACROSS OR OVER** a position in which something is over or across something else, or somebody's legs are apart or on either side of something 2 **ACT OF STRADDLING** the act of putting one leg on either side of something 3 **STOCK TRANSACTION** the simultaneous holding of options to buy and sell a commodity at a set price during a specific period of time 4 **JUMPING TECHNIQUE** a technique used in the high jump, in which the body is held parallel to the bar and the legs straddle it [Mid-16C. Probably a variant of obsolete *stridlen* 'keep striding' < an earlier form of STRIDE.] —**straddler** *n*

Stradivari /stráddi vaári/, **Antonio** (1644–1737) Italian violin maker

Stradivarius /stráddi váiri əss/ *n* a violin or other stringed instrument that was made by the Italian violin maker Antonio Stradivari or his sons [Mid-19C. Latinized form of STRADIVARI.]

strafe /straaf, strayf/ *vt* (**strafes, strafing, strafed**) 1 **ATTACK SOMETHING WITH GUNFIRE** to attack a position or troops on the ground with machine gun or cannon fire from a low-flying aircraft 2 **PUNISH** to punish somebody, especially severely (*slang*) ■ *n* **AIR ATTACK** a machine gun or cannon attack by low-flying aircraft on a ground target [Early 20C. < German *strafen* 'punish'.] —**strafer** *n*

Strafford /stráffərd/, **Thomas Wentworth, 1st Earl of** (1593–1641) English soldier and courtier

straggle /strágg'l/ *vi* (**-gles, -gling, -gled**) 1 **STRAY FROM PATH** to stray from a path, or wander away from or become separated from a group 2 **MOVE OR BECOME SPREAD OUT** to move or become spread out over a large area 3 **COME OR GO IRREGULARLY** to come or go in an irregular or disorganized way 4 **GROW UNTIDILY** to grow or hang in an untidy or irregular way ■ *n* **STRAGGLED GROUP OR ARRANGEMENT** a group or arrangement that lacks order, is spread out, or is untidy [15C. < ?] —**straggler** *n* —**straggly** *adj*

straggling /strágg'ling/ *adj* 1 **WANDERING** wandering, or having fallen behind or become separated from a group 2 **SPREAD OUT** spread out over a large area 3 **GROWING UNTIDILY** growing or hanging in an untidy or irregular way

straight /strayt/ *adj* 1 **NOT CURVED** without bends, curves, irregularities, or deviations 2 **CANDID** making no attempt to deceive or soften the truth ○ *Give a straight answer.* 3 **LEVEL** level, even, or properly positioned ○ *Your tie isn't straight.* 4 **ACCURATE** accurate or correct ○ *You can rely on her for the straight figures.* 5 **HONESTLY STRAIGHTFORWARD** honest, fair and upright ○ *straight dealings* 6 **CONSECUTIVE** following one after another, without interruption ○ *The team celebrated its tenth straight win.* 7 **NOT DILUTED** not diluted or mixed with any other drink 8 **NEAT AND TIDY** neat and tidy, or in order 9 **NOT FUNNY** not intended to be funny or unconventional ○ *playing both straight and comic roles* 10 **CONSISTENT** not leaving or differing from a principle or political party ○ *the straight party line* 11 **DELIVERED WITH UNBENT ARM** delivered with the arm unbent ○ *a straight left to the body* 12 **HETEROSEXUAL** heterosexual (*slang*) 13 **CONVENTIONAL** unremarkable or conventional in outlook, style, or way of life (*slang*) ○ *gave up being a rock musician and got a straight job* 14 **NOT USING DRUGS** not using or addicted to drugs (*slang*) ■ *adv* 1 **WITHOUT BENDING** without bending, curving, or diverging from a course 2 **IMMEDIATELY** without delay or detour ○ *She went straight home.* 3 **IN A LEVEL POSITION** in a level, even, or proper position ○ *Put your hat on straight.* 4 **CANDIDLY** without any attempt to deceive or soften the truth ○ *Give it to me straight.* 5 **WITH NO INTERRUPTION** one after another, without interruption ○ *three nights straight* 6 **UNDILUTED** without being diluted or mixed with any other drink 7 **INTO NEAT CONDITION** in or into a neat, tidy, or orderly condition ○ *We'll have to put the place straight after the party.* 8 **WITHOUT BEING FUNNY** without trying to be funny or unconventional ■ *n* 1 **SOMETHING STRAIGHT** something that is straight, e.g. a line 2 **FIVE CARDS IN SEQUENCE** a poker hand in which the cards form a continuous sequence but are not all of the same suit 3 **UNBENDING PART OF RACING TRACK** a part of a racing track that does not bend. US term **straightaway** *n.* 4 **HETEROSEXUAL PERSON** a heterosexual person (*slang*) 5 **CONVENTIONAL PERSON** a person of conventional outlook, style, or way of life (*slang*) 6 **CIGARETTE WITHOUT ADDED DRUG** an ordinary tobacco-filled cigarette to which no marijuana or other drug has been added (*dated slang*) [14C. Originally past participle of STRETCH.] —**straightly** *adv* —**straightness** *n*

SPELLCHECK Do not confuse ***straight*** with ***strait***, which has a similar sound. Beware: your spellchecker will not catch this error.

straight-ahead *adj US* showing little variation from what is usual or typical ○ *straight-ahead Italian opera*

straight and narrow *n* the orthodox and law-abiding way to live life (*informal*)

straight angle *n* an angle of 180 degrees

straight-arm *adj* describes a rugby tackle executed with the arm stretched fully out ■ *vt* in rugby football, to push an opponent away with the arm stretched fully out and the hand upturned and stiff

straight arrow *n US* an honest and upright person (*informal*) —**straight-arrow** *adj*

straightaway /stráyt ə wáy/ *adv* **straight away** immediately and without hesitation ■ *n US* SPORTS = **straight** *n.* 3

straight chain *n* an open chain of atoms in a molecule that has no side branches

straightedge /stráyt ej/ *n* a rigid strip of wood, metal, or plastic that is used in drawing a straight line or checking for straightness

straighten /stráyt'n/ *vti* to make something straight, or become straight —**straightener** *n*

straighten out *vti* 1 to make something straight, or become straight 2 to become, or make something, clear, satisfactory, or less complicated

straighten up *vti* to become, or make something, upright or in line

straight face *n* a serious expression on somebody's face that does not betray the fact that he or she really wants to laugh —**straight-faced** *adj*

straight fight *n* a contest, especially in politics, between only two opponents

straight flush *n* a poker hand in which all the cards are of the same suit and form a continuous sequence

straightforward /stráyt fáwrwərd/ *adj* **1 FRANK** truthful and to the point, rather than evasive **2 EASY** not complicated, difficult, or hard to understand **3 STRAIGHT OR DIRECT** following a straight or direct path ■ *adv* **straightforwards IN STRAIGHTFORWARD WAY** in a straightforward way or direction —**straightforwardly** *adv* —**straightforwardness** *n*

straightjacket *n, vt* = **straitjacket**

straight-line *adj* with components that are designed to move or make something move in a straight line, or are arranged in a straight line

straight man *n* a comedian whose role is to say or do things that allow another comedian to deliver a punch line or make witty or humorous comments in response

straight off *adv* right away or at once (*informal*)

straight out *adv* without hesitating or trying to lead up to something gradually

straight-out *adj* (*informal*) **1** showing directness or bluntness rather than restraint ○ *a straight-out refusal* **2** *US* complete and thoroughgoing, without mitigation ○ *a straight-out jerk*

straight razor *n US* = **cutthroat razor**

straight shooter *n US* an honest, frank, and ethical person (*informal*)

straight stitch *n* a simple stitch that forms a straight line on the surface of the fabric

straight ticket *n US* a ballot where all the candidates selected by the voter are from the same political party

straight-to-video *adj* released only in video format rather than shown in cinemas, usually because of perceived low audience appeal

straight up *interj* used to affirm that something is definitely true or, as a question, to ask if something is true (*slang*)

straightway /stráyt way/ *adv* at once and without delay (*archaic*)

strain[1] /strayn/ *v* **1** *vti* **PULL OR STRETCH TIGHT** to pull or stretch something until it is tight, or be pulled or stretched until tight **2** *vi* **WORK VERY HARD** to work extremely hard or exert yourself to the limit of your power **3** *vt* **USE SOMETHING TO THE UTMOST** to make the greatest possible use of or demands on something **4** *vt* **INJURE** to damage a part of the body through using it too hard or too much **5** *vti* **BE OR MAKE SOMETHING TENSE** to put something or somebody under stress, or be put under stress **6** *vti* **PASS SOMETHING THROUGH STRAINER** to pass something through a filter in order to remove some of its contents, or be passed through a filter **7** *vt* **REMOVE SOMETHING USING STRAINER** to remove part of something from the rest of it with a filter **8** *vt* **HUG** to hold somebody closely and tightly **9** *vt* **DEFORM STRUCTURE** to deform a body or material by applying an external force to it ■ *n* **1 STRAINING** an act of straining something ○ *Give the sauce a thorough strain.* **2 BEING STRAINED** the state of being strained **3 FORCE THAT STRAINS** a pulling or stretching force **4 MENTAL OR PHYSICAL STRESS** mental or physical stress caused by an intense or extreme pressure or demand **5 DEMAND THAT CAUSES STRESS** an intense or extreme demand or pressure that causes mental or physical stress **6 GREAT EXERTION** a great, taxing, or extreme exertion or effort **7 PHYSICAL INJURY** an injury to a part of the body caused by excessive use or by a twisting or stretching of muscles or tendons beyond their normal range **8 DEFORMATION OF STRUCTURE** the deformation of a body or material caused by applying an external force to it [14C. Via Old French *estreindre* 'draw tight' < Latin *stringere* (see STRINGENT).]

strain[2] /strayn/ *n* **1 LINE OF ANCESTRY** a line of ancestry or a group of descendants from a common ancestor **2 VARIETY OF ORGANISM** a subgroup of a species of organism that shows particular characteristics, sometimes developed by breeders for those characteristics **3 INHERITED QUALITY OR TRAIT** an inherited tendency, character, or trait **4 TRACE** a trace, or small amount of something mixed in with something else **5 CHARACTER OR MOOD** the style, character, mood, or theme of something **6 MUSICAL THEME** a musical theme or melody [Old English *strēon* 'offspring', originally 'gain' < Indo-European, 'to spread flat']

strained /straynd/ *adj* **1 PASSED THROUGH STRAINER** having been passed through a strainer to remove part of its content **2 NOT NATURAL** not natural or spontaneous but produced by an effort **3 TENSE** full of tension and often on the verge of hostility

strainer /stráynər/ *n* a device for removing part of the content of something, especially lumps or solids from a liquid

strain gauge *n* a device that measures pressure or stress, using the change of electrical resistance in a wire that is subjected to the same stress as the object being measured

straining beam, straining piece *n* a horizontal beam that connects the tops of two vertical posts (**queen posts**) in a roof truss

strait /strayt/ *n* (*often plural*) **1 CHANNEL JOINING TWO SEAS** a narrow body of water that joins two larger bodies of water, usually a body of salt water **2 DIFFICULT SITUATION** a situation that is difficult or involves hardship ■ *adj* (*archaic*) **1 NARROW OR CONFINED** narrow or with very little room **2 STRICT OR RIGID** very strict or severe [14C. Via Old French *estreit* < Latin *strictus* 'narrow', past participle of *stringere* 'draw tight' (see STRINGENT).] —**straitly** *adv* —**straitness** *n*

SPELLCHECK See ***straight***.

straitened /stráyt'nd/ *adj* made very difficult, restricted, or narrow ○ *had lost all their money and were living in straitened circumstances*

straitjacket /stráyt jakit/, **straightjacket** *n* **1 CONFINING JACKET-SHAPED GARMENT** a jacket-shaped garment with long sleeves that can be tied, used to restrict the arm movements of a resisting person, e.g. a prisoner **2 THING THAT RESTRICTS** something that limits somebody's freedom of action or initiative ○ *a bureaucratic straitjacket of regulations* ■ *vt* **1 PUT SOMEBODY INTO STRAITJACKET** to put a resisting person into a straitjacket **2 RESTRICT** to limit somebody's freedom of action or initiative

strait-laced *adj* prudish, or very strict in morals —**strait-lacedly** /stráyt láyssidli, -láystli/ *adv* —**strait-lacedness** /-láyssidnəss/ *n*

strake /strayk/ *n* **1** a continuous band of wooden planks or metal plates along the hull of a boat or ship **2** a curved metal plate that is part of a rubber tyre or metal wheel rim [15C. < assumed Old English *straca*; ultimately related to STRETCH.]

stramash /strə másh/ *n Scotland* an uproar, commotion, or rowdy dispute [Late 18C. < ?]

stramonium /strə mṓni əm/ *n* a preparation of dried leaves and flowers of the thorn apple containing alkaloids. Use: formerly, as a medicine. [Mid-17C. < modern Latin, < ?]

strand[1] /strand/ *n* **LAND AT WATER'S EDGE** a strip of land along the edge of a body of water ■ *v* **1** *vti* **RUN ASHORE OR AGROUND** to leave or run a ship or aquatic animal aground, or be left or driven aground **2** *vt* **LEAVE SOMEBODY IN DIFFICULTY** to leave somebody in a strange place without the capability or resources to get out of it (*often passive*) ○ *stranded without any means of getting home* [Old English < ?] —**stranded** *adj*

strand[2] /strand/ *n* **1 FIBRE, THREAD, WIRE, OR FILAMENT** any of the fibres, threads, wires, or other filaments that are twisted or braided together to form a rope, cable, or yarn **2 LONG THIN PIECE** a single length of something long and thin such as wire, string, rope, or wool **3 HUMAN HAIR OR HAIRS** a human hair, or a tress of hair **4 LENGTH OF TISSUE RESEMBLING THREAD** a length of animal, plant, or mineral fibre or tissue that resembles a thread **5 STRING OF BEADS** a length of strung pearls or beads **6 ELEMENT OF WHOLE** any of the elements that together make up a larger complex whole ■ *vt* **MAKE SOMETHING BY TWISTING** to make something such as a rope or cable by braiding or twisting threads, wires, or other filaments together ○ *to strand a rope* [15C. < ?]

stranded cotton *n* an embroidery cotton made up of six strands of thread loosely twisted together

strandline /stránd līn/, **strand line** *n* a shoreline, usually one that the sea, a lake, or a river had at an earlier point in time and that is higher than the present shoreline

strange /strayṇj/ *adj* (**stranger, strangest**) **1 UNEXPECTED OR EXTRAORDINARY** not expected, normal, or ordinary **2 UNFAMILIAR** not known or experienced previously **3 HARD TO EXPLAIN** difficult to explain or understand **4 EXOTIC** coming from a different place or environment, or belonging to a different kind **5 UNACCUSTOMED** not yet used to or familiar with something ○ *strange to these new surroundings* **6 RESERVED** reserved or shy, often because of being unfamiliar with people **7 ILL AT EASE** uncomfortable, embarrassed, or slightly ill ○ *I've been feeling a little strange since I took the medicine.* **8 SHOWING QUANTUM CHARACTERISTIC OF STRANGENESS** showing or having the quantum characteristic of strangeness ■ *adv* **IN UNUSUAL WAY** in a strange way (*nonstandard*) [13C. Via Old French *estrange* < Latin *extraneus* 'foreign' < *extra*, feminine of *exter* 'outside' (see EXTERIOR).]

strangely /stráynjli/ *adv* **1** in an unusual or puzzling way **2** it is odd or puzzling that ○ *Strangely, they seemed to have no definite plan of action.*

strangeness /stráynjnəss/ *n* **1** the condition or quality of being strange **2** a quantum characteristic of some elementary particles that is conserved in strong and electromagnetic, but not weak, interactions and has a value (**strangeness number**) of zero for most particles

strangeness number *n* the value of the quantum characteristic of strangeness, equal to the hypercharge minus the baryon number

strange particle *n* an elementary particle having a strangeness number other than zero [Because such particles' long lifetimes were hard to explain]

strange quark *n* a quark that has an electric charge equal to $-\frac{1}{3}$ that of the electron and a strangeness number of −1

stranger /stráynjər/ *n* **1 UNFAMILIAR PERSON** a person whom somebody does not know **2 NEWCOMER** a person who is new to a specific place **3 OUTSIDER** a person who does not belong to a specific organization or group **4 VISITOR OR GUEST** a person who does not live in a specific house or community but is a visitor or guest **5 PERSON UNACCUSTOMED TO SOMETHING** a person who is not familiar or acquainted with something specified ○ *Being a stranger to hard physical work, he found the job exhausting.* **6 ALIENATED PERSON** a person who has become distanced or alienated from somebody or something ○ *She is a stranger to her former colleagues.* **7 PERSON NOT PRIVY TO TRANSACTION** a person who is neither privy nor party to a transaction [14C. < Old French *estrangier* < *estrange* 'foreign' (see STRANGE).]

stranger's gallery *n* a gallery from which members of the public may observe the business of a legislature, especially in the British House of Commons

Strangford Lough /strángfərd lókh/ inlet of the Irish Sea in E Northern Ireland. Length: 40 km/25 mi.

strangle /stráng g'l/ (**-gles, -gling, -gled**) *vti* **1 KILL OR DIE BY CHOKING** to kill a person or an animal by squeezing the throat so that air cannot pass through it into the lungs, or die in this way **2 SUPPRESS UTTERANCE** to suppress suddenly a sound that is being uttered, or be suppressed suddenly ○ *I managed to strangle my giggles.* **3 STIFLE OR BE STIFLED IN DEVELOPMENT** to hinder or stop the growth or development of something, or be hindered or stopped [13C. Via Old French *estrangler* < Latin *strangulare* (see STRANGULATE).] —**strangler** *n*

stranglehold /stráng g'l hōld/ *n* **1** an illegal hold in wrestling that chokes an opponent **2** power over something or somebody that is complete and prevents any movement or change

strangles /stráng g'lz/ *n* an infectious disease of horses in which they experience inflammation and abscesses of the mucous membranes of the respiratory tract, causing strangling. It is caused by the bacterium *Streptococcus equi*. (+ *singular verb*)

strangulate /stráng gyōō layt/ (**-lates, -lating, -lated**) *v* **1** *vt* to strangle a person or animal **2** *vti* to constrict a part of the body, or become constricted, until the natural flow of blood or air is prevented [Mid-17C. Via Latin *strangulare* < Greek *straggalan* < *straggalē* 'halter, cord'.] —**strangulation** /stráng gyōō láysh'n/ *n*

strangury /stráng gyōōri/ *n* painful and slow urination caused by spasms that make urine come out drop by drop [14C. Via Latin < Greek *straggouria* < *stragx* 'drop' + *ouron* 'urine'.]

Stranraer /stran raar/ port in SW Scotland. Population: 11,348 (1991).

strap /strap/ *n* **1 FLEXIBLE STRIP USED FOR BINDING** a narrow flexible strip of leather, nylon webbing, plastic, metal, or other material used to bind or secure something **2 LOOP OF MATERIAL USED AS HANDLE** a loop of flexible material attached to something so that it can be grasped or slung over a shoulder and used in lifting or carrying something **3 LOOP TO HANG ON TO** a loop of leather, rubber, or plastic suspended from the roof inside a bus or train for standing passengers to hold for support **4 RAZOR STROP** a strop for a razor **5 LEATHER STRIP FOR FLOGGING** a long narrow strip of leather used for flogging or beating ■ *vt* (**straps, strapping, strapped**) **1 SECURE WITH STRAP** to secure or bind somebody or something with a strap **2 BANDAGE TIGHTLY** to tie a bandage tightly around an injured body part. US term **tape** *v.* 3 **3 FASTEN STRAPS OF** to secure the straps that are used to fasten something ○ *stood up without strapping her shoes* **4 BEAT WITH STRAP** to beat or flog somebody with a strap **5 SHARPEN WITH STROP** to sharpen something, e.g. a razor, with a strop [Early 17C. Originally a Scottish dialect form of STROP.]

strap up *vt* = **strap** *v.* 2

straphanger /stráp hangər/ *n* a passenger who stands in a bus or train and holds onto a strap that is suspended from the roof (*informal*)

strap hinge *n* a hinge with a flap fastened to the exposed surface of a door, lid, or gate

strapless /strápləss/ *adj* without straps, other supports, or covering over the shoulders

strapline /stráp līn/ *n* a subheading in a piece of print, e.g. in a newspaper article

strappado /strə páydō, -paádō/ (*plural* **-does**) *n* **1** a form of torture in which somebody is hoisted by a rope round the wrists, which are bound behind the back, and then dropped, but not to the ground **2** an apparatus or machine that is used to deliver a strappado [Mid-16C. Alteration of French *(e)strapade* < Italian *strappata* < *strappare* < ?]

strapped /strapt/ *adj* very short of or in need of something, especially money (*informal*)

strapper /stráppər/ *n* a big and powerfully built person (*informal*)

strapping /strápping/ *adj* **ROBUST** tall and powerfully built (*informal*) ■ *n* **1 STRAPS** straps in general, or a set of straps **2 MATERIAL FOR STRAPS** material for making straps or for use as straps

strappy /stráppi/ (**-pier, -piest**) *adj* with straps, especially when they are an important part of the look or design of something (*informal*) ○ *strappy sandals*

strap work *n* decorative work in the form of crossing or interlaced bands on the outside of a building, especially in Tudor architecture

Strasberg /stráz burg, stráss-/, **Lee** (1901–82) Austro-Hungarian-born US actor and teacher. Born **Israel Strassberg**

Strasbourg /stráz burg/ city in NE France, the site of the headquarters of the European Parliament and the Council of Europe. Population: 252,338 (1990).

Strassman /stráss màn/, **Fritz** (1902–80) German chemist

strata plural of **stratum**

stratagem /stráttəjəm/ *n* **1 RUSE FOR DECEIVING ENEMY** a military tactic or manoeuvre that is designed to deceive an enemy **2 CLEVER SCHEME** clever ruse or scheme that is designed to deceive others or achieve something **3 USE OF CLEVER SCHEMES** the use of stratagems to deceive an enemy or others, or skill in using stratagems [15C. Via French *stratagème* < Greek *stratēgēma* < *stratēgos* 'general' (see STRATEGY).]

strategic /strə teéjik/, **strategical** /-teéjik'l/ *adj* **1 TYPICAL OF STRATEGY** relating to involving, or typical of strategy or a strategy **2 DONE FOR REASONS OF STRATEGY** necessary to a strategy, or done because a strategy requires it ○ *a strategic retreat* **3 DISPLAYING SOUND STRATEGY** displaying a sound strategy or plan of action ○ *showing strategic timing in selling a stock short* **4 DESTROYING ENEMY'S FIGHTING CAPACITY** done to destroy, or having the capability to destroy, an enemy's ability to fight a war ○ *strategic bombing* **5 NECESSARY FOR FIGHTING WAR** necessary for fighting a war, or essential to the military forces fighting a war ○ *strategic metals* ○ *strategic air bases*

strategically /strə teéjikli/ *adv* **1** as part of, or in a way useful to, a strategy **2** in a clever or useful way

strategics /strə teéjiks/ *n* the science or art of military strategy (+ *singular verb*)

strategist /stráttəjist/ *n* a person who develops and executes strategy, especially to win something

strategize /stráttə jīz/ (**-gizes, -gizing, -gized**) *vi US* to plan or decide on a strategy

strategy /stráttəji/ (*plural* **-gies**) *n* **1 PLANNING OF WAR** the science or art of planning and conducting a war or a military campaign **2 PLANNING IN ANY FIELD** a carefully devised plan of action to achieve a goal, or the art of developing or carrying out such a plan **3 ADAPTATION IMPORTANT TO EVOLUTIONARY SUCCESS** in evolutionary theory, a behaviour, structure, or other adaptation that improves viability [Early 19C. Via French *stratégie* < Greek *stratēgia* 'generalship' < *stratēgos* 'general' < *stratos* 'army' + *agein* 'lead'.]

Stratford /strátfərd/ **1** city in SE Ontario, Canada, on the Avon River. Population: 28,987 (1996). **2** town in SW Connecticut, on Long Island Sound. Population: 49,389 (1990).

Stratford-upon-Avon /strátfərd ə pon áyvən/ town in west-central England, birthplace of William Shakespeare. Population: 22,375 (1991).

strath /strath/ *n Scotland* a river valley that is wide and flat (*often in placenames*) [Mid-16C. Via Scottish Gaelic < Old Irish *srath*.]

Strathclyde /strath klīd/ former administrative region in SW Scotland between 1975 and 1996

Strathern /strath úrn/, **Marilyn** (*b.* 1941) Australian anthropologist

strathspey /strath spáy/ (*plural* **-speys**) *n* **1** a Scottish dance that is similar to a reel but has a slower tempo **2** the music for a strathspey [Mid-18C. After *Strathspey*, the valley of the River Spey in Scotland.]

strati plural of **stratus**

strati- *prefix* stratum, layer ○ *stratigraphy* [< STRATUM]

stratificational grammar *n* a form of grammar in which language is analysed in terms of layers linked to one another by rules

stratified charge engine *n* an internal combustion engine with two layers of fuel density within the cylinder

stratiform /strátti fawrm/ *adj* **1 COMPOSED OF LAYERS** composed of layers, or with a layered appearance or arrangement **2 FORMED AS LAYER** forming or formed as a layer **3 LIKE STRATUS CLOUD** like or having the form of a stratus cloud

stratify /strátti fī/ (**-fies, -fying, -fied**) *v* **1** *vti* **FORM INTO LAYERS** to form something into a layer or layers, or become formed into a layer or layers **2** *vti* **FORM INTO STATUS GROUPS** to form or be formed into castes, classes, or other groups based on status **3** *vt* **STORE SEEDS IN CHILLED MOIST ENVIRONMENT** to store seeds in chilled moist sand, peat moss, or other material to induce germination or preserve the seeds —**stratification** /stráttifi káysh'n/ *n* —**stratificational** *adj*

stratigraphic /strátti gráffik/, **stratigraphical** /-gráffik'l/ *adj* relating to stratigraphy —**stratigraphically** *adv*

stratigraphy /strə tíggrəfi/ (*plural* **-phies**) *n* **1 STUDY OF ROCK STRATA** the study of the origin, composition, and development of rock strata **2 VERTICAL SECTION THROUGH GROUND** a section cut vertically through the earth showing its different layers and allowing artefacts to be dated according to the layers in which they are found **3 DISPOSITION OF ROCK STRATA** the way in which rock strata are arranged, and the chronology of their formation —**stratigrapher** *n* —**stratigraphist** *n*

stratocumulus /stráytō kyoómyooləss, stráttō-/ (*plural* **-li** /-lī/) *n* a cloud formation in a low-lying extensive layer with large dark round or rolling masses

stratopause /stráttō pawz/ *n* the boundary layer between the stratosphere and the mesosphere, at about 50 km/30 mi. above the Earth's surface [Mid-20C. < STRATOSPHERE, after *tropopause*.]

stratosphere /stráttə sfeer/ *n* **1** the region of the Earth's atmosphere between the troposphere and mesosphere, from 10 km/6 mi. to 50 km/30 mi. above the Earth's surface **2** a very high or the highest level or position [Early 20C. < STRATUM + SPHERE.]

stratospheric /stráttə sférrik/, **stratospherical** /-sférrik'l/ *adj* **1** relating or belonging to the stratosphere **2** very or excessively high —**stratospherically** *adv*

stratovolcano /stráytō vol káynō/ (*plural* **-noes** *or* **-nos**) *n* a volcano consisting of layers of lava alternating with ash or cinder

stratum /straáatəm, stráy-/ (*plural* **-ta** /-tə/ *or* **-tums**) *n* **1 LAYER** any parallel layer or level of something (*formal*) ○ *We found several strata of archaeological material on the site.* **2** GEOL = **bed** *n.* 12 **3 LAYER OF ATMOSPHERE OR SEA** a layer of the atmosphere or the sea **4 LAYER OF CELLS** a layer of living cells **5 LAYER OF SOCIETY** a social class or level of society consisting of people of similar cultural, economic, or educational status **6 LEVEL WITHIN SYSTEM** a layer or level within an ordered system ○ *the various strata of meaning within the text* [Late 16C. < modern Latin, < Latin, 'something thrown down' < *sternere* (see STREW).] —**stratal** *adj*

USAGE The plural of ***stratum*** is *strata*, reflecting the word's Latin history. Do not use the false plural *stratas* or the incorrect false Latin plural *stratae*, as in *on all stratas* or *stratae of society*. Use instead *on all strata of society*. A variant plural *stratums* exists but is relatively infrequent.

stratus /stráytəss, straá-/ (*plural* **-ti** /-tī/) *n* a low-lying flat grey cloud formation [Early 19C. < modern Latin, which evolved from Latin, past participle of *sternere* (see STREW).]

Strauss /strowss/, **Johann** (1804–49) Austrian conductor and composer. Known as **Johann Strauss the Elder**

Strauss, Johann (1825–99) Austrian composer. Known as **Johann Strauss the Younger**

Strauss, Richard (1864–1949) German conductor and composer

stravaig /strə váyg/, **stravage** *vi* (**-ages, -aging, -aged**) *Scotland, Ireland, N England* to wander about in an aimless manner ■ *n Scotland, Ireland, N England* an aimless ramble [Late 18C. < ?]

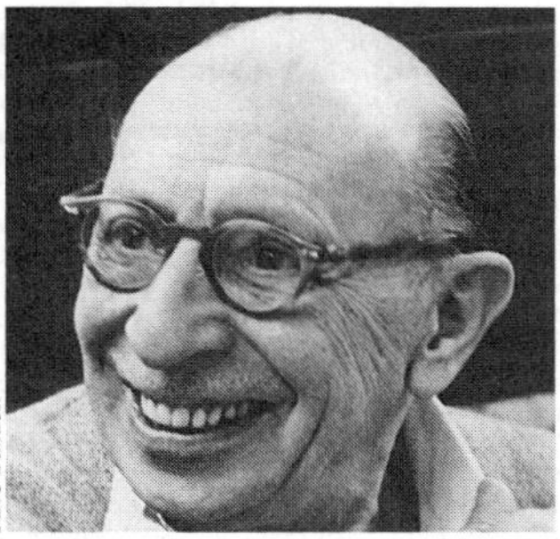

AKG London

Igor Stravinsky

Stravinsky /strə vínski/, **Igor** (1882–1971) Russian-born US composer

straw /straw/ *n* **1 STALKS OF THRESHED CEREAL CROPS** the stalks of threshed cereal crops such as wheat or barley **2 DRIED GRASS STALK** a single dried stalk of a cereal crop or grass **3 ITEM MADE OF STRAW** something made of straw, e.g. a hat or basket **4 THIN TUBE FOR SUCKING UP DRINK** a long thin tube, often made of paper or plastic, used for sucking up a drink **5 SOMETHING WORTHLESS** anything of little or no importance or value **6** COLOURS = **straw colour** ■ *adj* **OF STRAW COLOUR** of the brownish-yellow colour of straw [Old English *strēaw*. Ultimately < Indo-European 'spread'.] —**strawy** *adj* ◇ **a straw in the wind** a relatively minor incident or thing that gives some indication of what is likely to happen ◇ **clutch** *or* **grasp at straws** to be willing to try anything that may help in a situation that is unlikely to succeed ◇ **draw the short straw** to be chosen from a group of people to do a difficult or unpleasant task

strawberry /stráwbəri/ (*plural* **-ries**) *n* **1** a small sweet red fruit covered with tiny seeds **2** a plant that spreads by means of rooting stems and bears strawberries. Genus: *Fragaria*.

strawberry blonde *adj* describes hair that is very pale in colour with a reddish or pinkish tinge ■ *n* a person with strawberry blonde hair

strawberry bush *n* a bush or small tree with tiny flowers and scarlet pods and seeds. Native to: E North America. *Euonymus americanus*.

strawberry mark *n* a raised red birthmark, often found on the scalp or face, containing small blood vessels

strawberry roan *n* a horse that has coat of reddish hairs mixed with white

strawberry tree *n* an evergreen tree of the heath family with berries resembling strawberries. Flowers: white or pink. Native to: S Europe. *Arbutus unedo*.

strawboard /stráw bawrd/ *n* a coarse cardboard made of straw pulp and used in making packaging materials and book covers

straw colour *n* a pale brownish-yellow colour —**straw-coloured** *adj*

strawflower /stráw flowər/ *n* a plant with flower heads that remain colourful when dried. Native to: Australia. *Helichrysum bracteatum.*

straw-hat *adj US* describes a theatre that operates only in the summer [< the relatively rustic beginnings of these theatres]

straw man *n* **1** a straw figure made to resemble a human being **2** = **man of straw** *n.* 1 **3** = **man of straw** *n.* 2

straw mushroom *n* a small brown or pale-coloured edible mushroom used in Chinese cookery

straw poll, straw vote *n* an unofficial poll or vote used to discover the likely result of an election or the trend of opinion regarding a particular issue

straw wine *n* a sweet wine made from grapes that have been partially dried in the sun, especially on a bed of straw

stray /stray/ *vi* **1 WANDER AWAY** to leave the correct course or wander away from the correct place, often unintentionally **2 BECOME SEPARATED FROM GROUP** to move away from or become separated from a flock or group **3 WANDER ABOUT AIMLESSLY** to roam or wander without a particular aim or destination **4 DIGRESS FROM SUBJECT** to digress or become diverted from the main subject **5 DEPART FROM ACCEPTED STANDARDS** to depart from traditional or accepted standards of behaviour **6 MEANDER** to take an indirect course ■ *adj* **1 LOST OR HOMELESS** homeless, lost, or wandering **2 SCATTERED OR SEPARATED** scattered, separated, or happening accidentally or randomly ■ *n* **1 SOMEBODY LOST** somebody, especially a child, who is lost **2 LOST OR HOMELESS DOMESTIC ANIMAL** a domestic animal that is lost, has been turned loose, or has wandered away from the place where it lives ■ **strays** *npl* **ELECTRICAL INTERFERENCE** electrical interference in a radio or television broadcast, causing a random crackling noise or disruption of a picture [13C. Shortening of *astray* < Old French *estraier* < ?] —**strayer** *n*

streak /streek/ *n* **1 THIN STRIPE OF CONTRASTING COLOUR** a long thin stripe or band that is a different colour from its background or surroundings **2 LAYER** a layer or strip of something **3 CONTRASTING CHARACTERISTIC** a characteristic of somebody or something, especially one that is only occasionally evident or that contrasts with other characteristics ○ *a happy-go-lucky streak* **4 SHORT PERIOD OR UNBROKEN RUN** a short period or unbroken run, especially of good or bad luck ○ *The team is finally having a winning streak.* **5 RUN IN PUBLIC BY NAKED PERSON** a quick run through a public place by a person with no clothes on, usually as a joke or publicity stunt (*informal*) **6 LIGHTNING FLASH** a flash of lightning **7 MARK OF MINERAL POWDER** the characteristically coloured mark that a mineral makes when scratched on unglazed porcelain **8 VIRAL PLANT DISEASE** a viral disease of plants such as potatoes or tomatoes that produces discoloured markings on stems and leaves **9 LINEAR GROWTH OF BACTERIA** a linear growth of bacteria on the surface of a culture medium, produced by drawing a contaminated needle across the medium ■ *v* **1** *vt* **MARK WITH STREAKS** to mark or cover something with streaks **2** *vt* **LIGHTEN HAIR** to lighten strands or sections of hair with a bleach or dye **3** *vi* **BECOME STREAKED** to become streaked or form streaks **4** *vi* **DASH OR RUSH** to move at great speed **5** *vi* **RUN NAKED THROUGH PUBLIC PLACE** to run through a public place with no clothes on, usually as a joke or publicity stunt (*informal*) [Old English *strica* < Germanic, 'touch lightly'] —**streaked** *adj*

streaker /streékər/ *n* a person who runs naked through a public place, usually as a joke or publicity stunt (*informal*)

streaky /streéki/ (**-ier, -iest**) *adj* **1 MARKED WITH STREAKS** covered or marked with streaks ○ *I cleaned the windows twice but they still looked streaky.* **2 OCCURRING AS STREAKS** occurring in the form of streaks **3 INCONSISTENT** variable and uneven in quality ○ *Her work's a bit streaky.* —**streakily** *adv* —**streakiness** *n*

streaky bacon *n* bacon that consists of alternate layers of meat and fat

ϟ **stream** /streem/ *n* **1 SMALL RIVER** a narrow and shallow river **2 CONSTANT FLOW** a constant flow of liquid or gas **3 AIR OR WATER CURRENT** a current of air or water **4 CONTINUOUS SERIES** a continuous series or procession of people, things, or events, usually moving in a line or in a certain direction **5 QUICK OR UNBROKEN FLOW** a quick or uninterrupted burst, flow, or succession ○ *a stream of questions* **6 PREVAILING ATTITUDE** a general or prevailing attitude, drift, or trend **7 BEAM OF LIGHT** a steady ray or beam of light **8 GROUP OF PUPILS OF SIMILAR ABILITY** a group or level in which pupils of similar ability are placed and taught together ■ *v* **1** *vi* **FLOW IN LARGE QUANTITIES** to flow continuously or quickly in large quantities **2** *vi* **MOVE IN SAME DIRECTION** to move continuously in large numbers in the same direction **3** *vti* **PRODUCE FLOW OF LIQUID** to emit or produce liquid in a continuous flow ○ *His eyes streamed tears.* **4** *vti* **FLOAT FREELY** to float or trail freely in air, wind, or water, or cause something to do this ○ *an advertising banner streaming behind the plane* **5** *vi* **POUR OUT IN TRAIL OR BEAM** to issue in a beam or move forward leaving a trail **6** *vti* **PUT PUPILS IN ABILITY GROUPS** to place pupils in groups according to their ability **7** *vt* **BROADCAST ON INTERNET** to broadcast something via the Internet [Old English *strēam* < Indo-European, 'to flow']

streambed /streém bed/ *n* a channel through which a stream flows or used to flow

streamer /streémər/ *n* **1 NARROW FLAG** a long narrow flag or banner **2 DECORATIVE PAPER STRIP** a long narrow strip of coloured paper or other material that is used for decoration **3 LUMINOUS STREAK IN SKY** any one of the luminous streaks that make up the aurora borealis and the aurora australis **4 HEADLINE RUNNING ACROSS A FULL PAGE** a large headline that extends the entire width of a newspaper page

ϟ **streaming** /streéming/ *n* **1** the practice of placing pupils in groups according to ability. US term **tracking** *n.* 4 **2** BIOL = **cyclosis 3** the playing of sound or video over the Internet in real time

streamlet /streémlət/ *n* a small stream

streamline /streém līn/ *vt* (**-lines, -lining, -lined**) **1 DESIGN OR BUILD WITH SMOOTH SHAPE** to design or build something with a smooth shape so that it moves with minimum resistance through air or water **2 MAKE SOMETHING MORE EFFICIENT** to make something such as a business, organization, or manufacturing process more efficient, especially by simplifying or modernizing it ■ *n* **1 CONTOUR DESIGNED TO MINIMIZE RESISTANCE** a contour of a body, e.g. of a car, boat, or aeroplane, designed to minimize resistance when moving through air or water **2 LINE IN FLUID** a line in a fluid indicating the direction of the velocity of a particle —**streamlined** *adj* —**streamlining** *n*

streamline flow *n* a flow of fluid in which the particles follow continuous paths and the fluid velocity at a particular point either remains constant or varies regularly with time. ◊ **turbulent flow**

stream of consciousness *n* **1** a literary style that presents a character's continuous random flow of thoughts as they arise (*hyphenated before nouns*) **2** the continuous uninterrupted flow of thoughts and feelings through somebody's mind

~~**strech**~~ incorrect spelling of **stretch**

Streep /streep/, **Meryl** (*b.* 1949) US actor. Born **Mary Louise Streep**

street /street/ *n* **1 PUBLIC ROAD IN TOWN** a public road, especially in a town or city, usually lined with buildings **2 BUILDINGS ON STREET** the buildings on a particular street **3 PART OF ROAD BETWEEN PAVEMENTS** the part of a road that lies between the pavements and is used by vehicles **4 PEOPLE LIVING IN A STREET** the people who live or work in a particular street ■ *adj* **RELATED TO MODERN URBAN SOCIETY** widely found or used in a modern urban environment or fashionable in its culture, especially among young people or the underworld ○ *Street language has worked its way into the mainstream language.* [Old English *strǣt*. Via West Germanic < late Latin *strata* 'paved road' < Latin *sternere* 'pave, throw down'.] ◇ **on the street** having nowhere to live ◇ **on the streets** working as a prostitute ◇ **right up somebody's street** exactly suitable or appropriate for somebody ◇ **streets ahead (of somebody *or* something)** much better in some way than somebody or something ◇ **the man *or* person *or* woman in the street** the average man or person or woman

street Arab, street arab *n* an offensive term for a child who has run way from home and lives on the streets (*archaic*) [< the perception of Arabs as nomadic]

streetcar /streét kaar/ *n US, Can* TRANSP = **tram**[1] *n.* 1

street credibility, street cred *n* popularity and acceptance among fashionable urban people, especially the young —**street-credible** *adj*

street door *n* the door of a house or other building that opens onto the street

street fashion *n* fashion invented and worn by young people rather than by fashion designers, often associated with popular styles of music and dance or with urban subcultures

street fighter *n* **1** somebody whose fighting skills were learnt on the streets rather than through formal training as a boxer **2** a tough, cunning, and aggressive person (*informal*)

street furniture *n* objects that are placed in the street for public use, such as pillar boxes, litter bins, benches, and streetlights

street hockey *n* a variety of hockey played on a paved surface using sticks and a ball

streetlight /streét līt/, **streetlamp** /-lamp/ *n* a light, normally attached to the top of a tall post and one of a series, that illuminates a road or street at night

street luge *n* a sport in which one or two people speed downhill on a dry surface in a small toboggan with runners

street name *n* an informal or colloquial name given to an illegal drug by those who sell or use it ○ *'Smack' has long been used as a street name for heroin.*

Streeton /streét'n/, **Sir Arthur Ernest** (1867–1943) Australian painter

streetscape /streét skayp/ *n* an artistic portrayal of a street and its activities, especially a busy city street

street-smart *adj* = **streetwise**

street theatre *n* dramatic entertainment usually performed outdoors, e.g. in a park or shopping precinct

street value *n* the price that something illegal would fetch if sold to a customer

street virus *n* the natural virulent strain of a virus as distinguished from a less virulent strain of the same organism that has been grown or treated in a laboratory

streetwalker /streét wawkər/ *n* a prostitute who solicits in the streets (*informal*) —**streetwalking** *n*

streetwise /streét wīz/ *adj* shrewd and experienced enough to be able to survive in the often difficult and dangerous environment of a modern city (*informal*)

Strehlow /stráylō/, **T. G. H.** (1908–78) Australian anthropologist and linguist. Full name **Theodor George Henry Strehlow**

Streisand /strī sand/, **Barbra** (*b.* 1942) US singer, actor, and film director. Born **Barbara Joan Streisand**

strelitzia /stre lítsi ə/ (*plural* **-as** *or* **-a**) *n* a widely cultivated perennial plant. Flowers: showy, often unusual or irregular in shape. Native to: southern Africa. Genus: *Strelitzia.* [Late 18C. After Charlotte of Mecklenburg-*Strelitz*, queen of George III of England.]

strength /strength/ *n* **1 PHYSICAL POWER** the physical power to carry out demanding tasks ○ *It took all our strength to lift the heavy table.* **2 EMOTIONAL TOUGHNESS** the necessary qualities required to deal with stressful or painful situations such as loss or failure ○ *she showed great strength of mind during the trial* **3 RESISTANCE** the ability to withstand force, pressure, or stress ○ *tensile strength* **4 DEFENSIVE ABILITY** the ability to resist attack **5 DEGREE OF INTENSITY** degree of intensity, e.g. of colour, light, smell, or sound **6 FORCE OF FEELING** degree of force or effectiveness, e.g. of beliefs or feelings **7 PERSUASIVE POWER** power to convince or persuade, e.g. by argument or suggestion **8 INTENSITY OF EXPRESSION** the intensity of the way somebody expresses ideas or feelings **9 POTENCY** the potency of something such as an alcoholic drink or a drug **10 NUMBER OF PEOPLE NEEDED** the number of people required to make something such as an army, team, or workforce complete, used as a measure of capability **11 ASSET OR QUALITY** an extremely valuable or useful ability, asset, or quality ○ *One of the strengths of this system is its adaptability.* **12 MAINTENANCE OF PRICES** tendency of stock or overall market prices to be stable or rise due to sufficient demand at current prices [Old English *strengþu* < Germanic, 'strong'] ◇ **go from strength to strength** to go on from one success or achievement to another and get progressively better ◇ **in strength** in large numbers ◇ **on the strength of something** on the basis of something

strengthen /stréngth'n/ *vti* to make something stronger or more powerful, or increase in strength or force —**strengthener** *n*

~~**strenth**~~ incorrect spelling of **strength**

strenuous /strénnyoo əss/ *adj* **1** requiring great effort, energy, stamina, or strength **2** active, energetic, or determined [Early 17C. < Latin *strenuus* 'brisk, active' < ?]

—**strenuosity** /strénnyoo óssəti/ *n* —**strenuously** *adv* —**strenuousness** *n*

SYNONYMS See ***hard.***

strep /strep/ *n* a streptococcus (*informal*) ■ *adj* streptococcal (*informal*)

strepsipteran /strep síptərən/ *n* a tiny insect whose larvae and adult females live entirely as parasites within the larvae of other insects. The males have stout antennae and a single pair of large wings. Order: Strepsiptera. [Mid-19C. < modern Latin *Strepsiptera* < Greek *strepsi-* < *strephein* 'twist' + *pteron* 'wing'.]

strep throat *n* an acute sore throat caused by the bacterium *Streptococcus pyogenes* and accompanied by fever and inflammation

strepto- *prefix* **1** streptococcus ○ *streptokinase* **2** twisted chain ○ *streptococcus* **3** streptomyces ○ *streptothricin* [< Greek *streptos* 'twisted' < *strephein* 'turn']

streptobacillus /stréptō bə sílləss/ (*plural* **-li** /-lī/) *n* a rod-shaped bacterium that often causes disease, e.g. rat-bite fever. Genus: *Streptobacillus.*

streptocarpus /stréptə kaárpəss/ (*plural* **-puses**) *n* a plant that often has only one large leaf. Flowers: brightly coloured, tubular. Native to: subtropical regions. Genus: *Streptocarpus.* [Early 19C. Via modern Latin < Greek *streptos* 'twisted' + *karpos* 'fruit', because its fruit is spirally twisted.]

streptococcus /stréptə kókəss/ (*plural* **-ci** /-kók sī/) *n* a spherical bacterium that often causes disease, e.g. scarlet fever or pneumonia. Genus: *Streptococcus.* [Late 19C. Via modern Latin, 'twisted berry' < Greek *streptos* 'twisted' + *coccus* 'berry'.] —**streptococcal** *adj* —**streptococcic** /-kóksik/ *adj*

streptodornase /stréptə dáwr nayz, -nayss/ *n* an enzyme derived from streptococci that can liquefy pus [Mid-20C. < STREPTOCOCCUS + contraction of *deoxyribonuclease.*]

streptokinase /stréptə kī nayz, -nayss/ *n* an enzyme produced by streptococci that dissolves blood clots [Mid-20C. < STREPTOCOCCAL + KINASE.]

streptolysin /stréptə lī́ssin/ *n* a substance that breaks down red blood cells and is produced by streptococci

streptomyces /stréptə mī seez/ (*plural* **-ces**) *n* an aerobic soil bacterium. Some streptomyces produce antibiotics. Genus: *Streptomyces.* [Mid-20C. < modern Latin, < Greek *strepto-* 'twisted' + *mukēs* 'fungus', because it forms twisted chains and resembles mould.]

streptomycin /stréptə mī́ssin/ *n* an antibiotic produced from the soil bacterium *Streptomyces griseus.* Use: treatment of bacterial infections such as tuberculosis.

streptothricin /stréptə thrī́ssin/ *n* any of a group of antibiotics produced by the soil bacterium *Streptomyces lavendulae.* Use: treatment of bacterial and some fungal infections. [Mid-20C. < modern Latin *Streptothric-*, stem of *Streptothrix* < Greek *strepto-* 'twisted' + *thrix* 'hair', because it grows in hair-like filaments.]

Stresemann /stráyzə man, shtráyzə-/, **Gustav** (1878–1929) German statesman

stress /stress/ *n* **1 STRAIN** mental, emotional, or physical strain caused, e.g. by anxiety or overwork **2 CAUSE OF STRAIN** something that causes mental or emotional strain **3 SPECIAL IMPORTANCE** special emphasis, importance, or significance attached to something **4 EMPHASIS ON SYLLABLE** the emphasis placed on a particular sound or syllable by pronouncing it more loudly or forcefully than those surrounding it in the same word or phrase **5 EMPHASIS IN POETRY** the emphasis placed on a particular syllable or word as part of the rhythm of a poem or line **6 ACCENT IN MUSIC** the emphasis placed on a particular note as part of the rhythm of a piece of music, or a mark representing this **7 FORCE DEFORMING BODY** a force or system of forces exerted on a body and resulting in deformation or strain ■ *vt* **1 EMPHASIZE** to place emphasis on or attach importance to something **2 PRONOUNCE FORCEFULLY** to pronounce a word or syllable more loudly or forcefully than those surrounding it **3 SUBJECT TO STRESS** to cause somebody or something to experience mental or physical stress [14C. Partly shortening of DISTRESS, and partly via Old French *estresse* 'narrowness' < Latin *strictus* 'compressed'.] —**stressed** *adj* —**stressor** *n*

SYNONYMS See ***worry.***

stress out *vti* to affect somebody with emotional, mental, or physical stress, or be so affected (*informal*)

stressed out *adj* unable to relax or function properly as the result of experiencing mental or emotional stress (*informal; hyphenated before nouns*)

stress fracture *n* a small fracture of a bone caused by repeated physical strain, sometimes experienced, e.g. by gymnasts, long-distance runners, or marching soldiers

stressful /stréssf'l/ *adj* causing or involving mental or physical stress —**stressfully** *adv* —**stressfulness** *n*

stress management *n* physical and psychological techniques designed to enable people to cope with strain and anxiety

stress mark *n* a mark placed before, on, or after a syllable that is to be stressed when the word containing it is pronounced

stretch /strech/ *v* **1** *vti* **EXTEND** to lengthen, widen, or extend something, or become lengthened, widened, or extended, especially by force **2** *vi* **EXPAND AND REGAIN ORIGINAL SHAPE** to be capable of expanding and returning to its original shape afterwards **3** *vti* **EXTEND EXCESSIVELY** to extend something or be extended excessively so that the shape is permanently altered ○ *The sleeves of this sweater have stretched.* **4** *vti* **EXTEND TO FULL LENGTH** to straighten or extend the body or part of it, especially the limbs, to full length ○ *She woke up, yawned, and stretched.* ○ *The cat lay stretched out by the fire.* **5** *vt* **STRAIN BODY PART** to strain a part of the body such as a muscle **6** *vti* **MAKE TAUT** to make something taut or tight, or become taut or tight **7** *vt* **SUSPEND BETWEEN TWO POINTS** to suspend something, or make something reach, between two points **8** *vi* **EXTEND IN SPACE** to spread out or extend over an area or in a particular direction **9** *vti* **EXTEND OVER TIME** to last or continue over a period of time, or prolong something **10** *vt* **MAKE SMALL AMOUNT GO FURTHER** to make limited supplies or resources go further than usual, planned, or expected **11** *vi* **BE ENOUGH** to be sufficient to allow something ○ *Will the budget stretch to hiring a temporary assistant?* **12** *vt* **EXCEED LIMIT OR BREAK RULE** to exceed a limit or break a rule that would usually prohibit something **13** *vt* **PUSH SOMETHING TO LIMIT** to strain or push something to the limit ○ *You're stretching my patience.* **14** *vt* **PUSH SOMEBODY TO LIMIT OF ABILITY** to cause somebody to make full use of abilities or intellect, e.g. with challenging or demanding work **15** *vt* **EXAGGERATE** to make something sound better or worse than it really is, especially in order to make it seem more impressive (*informal*) ○ *To call his house a mansion is stretching it a bit.* **16** *vt* **KNOCK DOWN** to knock somebody down with a blow (*informal*) ■ *n* **1 STRETCHING EXERCISE** the straightening and extending of a part of the body, e.g. as an exercise **2 EXPANSE** a large expanse of something, especially land or water **3 PERIOD OF TIME** an uninterrupted period of time **4 PRISON TERM** a term of imprisonment (*informal*) **5 ELASTICITY** the ability to expand and return to the original shape afterwards **6 CHALLENGE** something that is difficult to achieve (*informal*) **7 STRAIGHT PART OF RACECOURSE** the straight part of a racecourse, especially the final section approaching the finishing line **8 FINAL STAGE** the final stage of an event, task, process, or period of time, especially one that has been difficult or challenging ■ *adj* **EXTENDED TO PROVIDE EXTRA SPACE** extended or enlarged in order to prove extra space, e.g. for additional seating [Old English *streccan*, probably < Germanic, 'rigid'] —**stretchability** /stréchə bílləti/ *n* —**stretchable** *adj* ◇ **at a stretch 1** continuously ○ *worked five hours at a stretch* **2** with great difficulty or effort ○ *could get there by six at a stretch* ◇ **at full stretch** using all the energy or resources available

stretcher /stréchər/ *n* **1 DEVICE FOR CARRYING SOMEBODY LYING DOWN** a device consisting of a sheet of material such as canvas stretched over a frame, used to carry somebody in a lying position who is sick, injured, or dead **2** *ANZ* **CAMP BED** a camp bed consisting of a folding tubular metal frame and a canvas covering **3 FRAME FOR ARTIST'S CANVAS** a wooden frame over which a canvas for an oil painting is stretched **4 BAR BRACING FURNITURE LEGS** a bar that joins and braces the legs of a chair, table, or other piece of furniture **5 STRONG BEAM USED AS BRACE** a strong, usually horizontal beam or bar that is used as a brace in the framework of a structure **6 STONE WITH LONG EDGE FACING OUT** a brick or stone laid in a wall so that its longer edge forms part of the face of the wall. ◊ **header** *n.* 5 **7 BOARD FOR BRACING ROWER'S FEET** a board fixed across the width of a boat, on which a rower's feet can be braced **8 EXAGGERATED STORY** an exaggerated story or a lie based partly on the truth (*slang*) ■ *vt* **CARRY ON STRETCHER** to carry a sick, injured, or dead person on a stretcher ○ *Their star player was stretchered off in the first half.*

stretcher-bearer *n* a bearer of a stretcher, especially a soldier given the task in wartime

stretch knit *n* knitted fabric that can stretch and return to its original shape afterwards (*hyphenated before nouns*)

stretch mark *n* a mark left on the skin of the abdomen, breasts, buttocks, or thighs after pregnancy or weight loss (*often plural*)

stretchy /stréchi/ (**-ier, -iest**) *adj* capable of being stretched, usually returning to its original shape afterwards, or tending to stretch —**stretchiness** *n*

stretto /stréttō/ (*plural* **-tos** *or* **-ti** /-ti/) *n* **1** in a fugue or similar work, the successive statements of the theme very close together in time **2** the speeding up of a piece of music at a climactic moment [Mid-18C. Via Italian, 'narrow, tight' < Latin *strictus* (see STRICT).]

strew /stroo/ (**strews, strewing, strewed, strewn** /stroon/ *or* **strewed**) *v* **1** *vt* to scatter something, especially carelessly or untidily ○ *Clothes were strewn all over the floor.* **2** *vti* to spread or become spread over a large area ○ *areas strewn with landmines* ○ *a rock-strewn path* [Old English *strewian.* Ultimately < Indo-European.] —**strewer** *n*

strewth /strooth/, **struth** *interj* used to express surprise or irritation (*slang*) [Late 19C. Shortening of *God's truth,* an oath.]

stria /strī ə/ (*plural* **-ae** /-ee/) *n* **1** a thin narrow groove or channel in the surface of something, e.g. a decorative feature on a column **2** a stripe, streak, or narrow band, e.g. a band of nerve fibres or stretch marks seen in pregnancy (**striae gravidarum**) **3** GEOL = **striation** *n.* 3 [Mid-16C. < Latin, 'furrow, channel' (originally 'something grazed').]

striate /strī áyt/ *vt* (**-ates, -ating, -ated**) to mark something with parallel grooves, ridges, stripes, or narrow bands ■ *adj* = **striated** [Late 17C. < Latin *striare* < *stria* (see STRIA).]

striated /strī áytid/ *adj* marked with parallel grooves, ridges, stripes, or narrow bands

striated muscle *n* a muscle or muscle tissue that shows light and dark bands within the muscle fibres

striation /strī áysh'n/ *n* **1 STRIPY PATTERN** patterning or marking with parallel grooves or narrow bands **2 BANDING OR BAND WITHIN MUSCLE FIBRE** the striped pattern of striated muscle, or any of the light and dark bands that make up this effect **3 GROOVE OR SCRATCH** a narrow groove or scratch on an exposed rock face, caused by abrasion by hard rock fragments embedded in a moving glacier

stricken /stríkən/ past participle of **strike** *v.* 21 (*archaic*) ■ *adj* **1 DEEPLY OR BADLY AFFECTED BY** deeply or very badly affected by something such as grief, misfortune, or trouble **2 AFFECTED BY ILLNESS** experiencing severe physical symptoms caused by illness or injury **3 HIT BY MISSILE** injured, struck, or wounded, e.g. by a missile [Originally past participle of STRIKE] —**strickenly** *adv*

strickle /strík'l/ *n* **1 BOARD FOR LEVELLING OFF EXCESS MATERIAL** a board used to level off excess grain or other material in a container or measuring device **2 TOOL FOR SHAPING MOULD SURFACE** a tool used to shape the surface of a mould ■ *vt* (**-les, -ling, -led**) **USE STRICKLE ON** to level or shape something with a strickle [Old English *stricel* < Germanic]

~~**strickly**~~ incorrect spelling of **strictly**

~~**stricly**~~ incorrect spelling of **strictly**

strict /strikt/ *adj* **1 SEVERE IN MAINTAINING DISCIPLINE** severe in maintaining discipline or rigorous in ensuring that rules are obeyed **2 ENFORCED RIGOROUSLY** needing to be closely obeyed **3 PRECISE** exact, precise, or narrowly interpreted **4 FAITHFUL** closely observing rules, principles, or practices **5 ABSOLUTE** complete, utter, or absolute **6 GROWING UPRIGHT** growing upward at or very close to the vertical [15C. < Latin *strictus*, past participle of *stringere* 'draw tight'.] —**strictly** *adv* —**strictness** *n*

stricture /stríkchər/ *n* **1 SEVERE CRITICISM** a severe criticism or strongly critical remark (*formal*) **2 LIMIT OR RESTRICTION** a limit or restriction, especially one that seems unfair or too harsh (*formal*) **3 CONSTRICTION OF BODY PASSAGE** an abnormal constriction or narrowing of a body passage [14C. < Latin *strictura* < *stringere* 'draw tight'.] —**strictured** *adj*

stride /strīd/ *v* (**strides, striding, strode** /strōd/, **stridden** /strídd'n/) **1** *vi* **WALK WITH LONG REGULAR STEPS** to walk with long regular steps, often briskly or energetically **2** *vti* **TAKE LONG STEP OVER** to cross or step over something with a long step ■ *n* **1 LONG STEP** a long step, especially one taken briskly or energetically **2 DISTANCE COVERED BY LONG**

STEP the distance covered when somebody or something takes a long step **3 ADVANCE TOWARDS IMPROVING** an advance or step towards improving or developing something **4 WAY OF WALKING** a way of walking or running in long regular steps, often taken briskly or energetically **5 COORDINATED FORWARD MOVEMENT BY ANIMAL** an act of forward motion by a four-legged animal consisting of a coordinated cycle of movements that brings the legs back to their original positions **6** MUSIC = **stride piano** ■ **strides** *npl Aus* **TROUSERS** a pair of trousers (*informal*) [Old English *strīdan* 'straddle'] —**strider** *n* ◇ **get into your stride** to become familiar and at ease with something so that you can do it easily and well ◇ **take something in your stride** to accept something without being unduly upset or worried about it

strident /strīd'nt/ *adj* **1** harsh, loud, grating, or shrill **2** loudly, strongly, or urgently expressed [Mid-17C. < Latin, present participle of *stridere* 'creak'.] —**stridence** *n* —**stridency** *n* —**stridently** *adv*

stride piano *n* a style of jazz piano-playing in which the right hand plays the melody while the left hand alternates between playing a single note and a related chord [*Stride* in the sense 'straddle'; from the movements of the left hand]

stridor /strī dawr, strīdər/ *n* **1** a harsh, grating, or creaking noise **2** a harsh high-pitched wheezing sound made when breathing in or out, caused by obstruction of the air passages [Mid-17C. < Latin, < *stridere* (see STRIDENT).]

stridulate /stríddyōō layt/ (**-lates, -lating, -lated**) *vi* to make a chirping or grating sound by rubbing parts of the body together, as male crickets and grasshoppers do [Mid-19C. Via French *striduler* < Latin *stridere* (see STRIDENT).] —**stridulance** *n* —**stridulant** *adj* —**stridulantly** *adv* —**stridulation** /stríddyōō láysh'n/ *n* —**stridulator** *n* —**stridulatory** *adj* —**stridulous** *adj* —**stridulously** *adv* —**stridulousness** *n*

strife /strīf/ *n* **1** bitter and sometimes violent conflict, struggle, or rivalry **2** *ANZ* trouble or difficulty (*informal*) [12C. < Old French *estrif* < ?] —**strifeless** *adj*

strigil /stríjjil/ *n* an instrument with a curved blade used in ancient Greece and Rome to scrape dirt and sweat from the skin after bathing or exercising [Late 16C. < Latin *strigilis*.]

strigose /strígōss, -gōz/ *adj* **1** covered with fine scales or short bristles **2** with thin, closely spaced grooves or ridges [Late 18C. < modern Latin *strigosus* < Latin *striga* 'row'.]

strike /strīk/ *v* (**strikes, striking, struck** /struk/, **struck**) **1** *vti* **HIT** to hit somebody or something, e.g. with a hand, tool, or weapon ○ *She was struck on the arm by a piece of falling masonry.* **2** *vti* **DELIVER BLOW** to deliver or inflict something such as a blow or punch **3** *vti* **COLLIDE WITH** to crash into, knock hard against, or collide with somebody or something ○ *The car swerved and struck a tree.* **4** *vti* **PENETRATE** to penetrate or seem to go right through something ○ *The pain struck deep into my shoulder blade.* **5** *vti* **DAMAGE** to hit and damage or injure something or somebody **6** *vt* **KNOCK AWAY** to remove something with a blow ○ *She struck the wasp from the child's head.* **7** *vti* **PRODUCE FIRE** to produce fire by friction, or be produced by friction **8** *vti* **LIGHT MATCH** to cause a match to light or to be lit by friction ○ *The matches won't strike if they get damp.* **9** *vt* **OPERATE BY PRESSING KEY** to operate, produce, or play something by pressing a key or touching a string, e.g. on a a computer keyboard or musical instrument **10** *vti* **INDICATE TIME BY MAKING SOUND** to indicate the time by making a sound such as chiming **11** *vt* **MAKE SOMETHING BY STAMPING** to make or form something such as a coin by stamping or punching **12** *vti* **SHINE ON** to fall or shine on something ○ *Moonbeams struck the placid water on the lake.* **13** *vt* **BE NOTICED** to catch somebody's attention, or be noticed by somebody or something **14** *vt* **BE PERCEIVED** to be perceived by or become audible to somebody **15** *vt* **MAKE PARTICULAR IMPRESSION** to have a particular effect on or make a particular impression on somebody **16** *vt* **ENTER SOMEBODY'S MIND** to enter somebody's mind or occur to somebody, especially suddenly **17** *vt* **AFFECT WITH EMOTION** to affect somebody or cause somebody to be affected with an emotion in a deep, painful, or sudden way **18** *vti* **FIND OR DISCOVER** to come across, find, or discover something, especially suddenly or unexpectedly **19** *vti* **ATTACK** to make an attack on somebody or something ○ *The enemy struck under cover of darkness.* **20** *vi* **BITE OR STING SUDDENLY** to deliver a sudden, fast bite or sting, typically resulting in injury to the one bitten or stung ○ *Suddenly the snake struck.* **21** (*past participle* **stricken** *or* **struck**) *vti* **AFFECT SOMEBODY SUDDENLY** to affect somebody suddenly or unexpectedly ○ *The illness can strike at any age.* **22** *vti* **HAPPEN SUDDENLY** to happen to somebody or something suddenly or unexpectedly **23** *vi* **STOP WORKING AS PROTEST** to stop working as a collective form of protest against an employer **24** *vt US, Can* **STOP WORKING FOR SOMEBODY** to undertake strike action against an employer ○ *They're striking the auto plant.* **25** *vt* **CROSS OUT** to cancel, delete, or cross something out ○ *The judge ordered that the preceding remark be struck from the record.* **26** *vt* **AGREE TO TERMS** to agree on the terms of something ○ *struck a deal* **27** *vt* **REACH AGREEMENT** to achieve something such as a balance or a compromise by careful consideration or calculation **28** *vt* **ADOPT POSE** to adopt or assume something such as a pose or attitude **29** *vti* **TAKE BAIT** to take or attempt to take a bait ○ *The fish are striking today.* **30** *vti* **GROW ROOTS** to send out and establish roots **31** *vt* **DISMANTLE** to dismantle something such as a tent or stage set **32** *vt* **LOWER MAST OR SAIL** to lower a mast or sail **33** *vt* **LOWER IN RESPECT OR SURRENDER** to lower something such as a flag or sail as a sign of respect or surrender **34** *vt* **LOWER INTO SHIP'S HOLD** to lower something into the hold of a ship **35** *vi US* **ATTEMPT TECHNICAL RATING IN US NAVY** to work hard with the aim of achieving a certain technical rating in the US Navy **36** *vt* TECH = **strickle** *v.* ■ *n* **1 HIT OR BLOW** a blow delivered by striking **2 SOUND OF HIT** a sound produced by striking somebody or something **3 WORK STOPPAGE** a work stoppage by employees as a protest against an employer **4 REFUSAL TO DO SOMETHING AS PROTEST** a refusal to carry out a regular action or activity, for such as eating or paying rent, as a form of protest **5 MILITARY ATTACK USING AIRCRAFT** a military attack, especially one using aircraft **6 SUCCESS IN FINDING** a success in finding or discovering something, especially a valuable mineral source such as gold or oil **7 KNOCKING DOWN OF ALL BOWLING PINS** the knocking down of all the pins with the first ball in a session of tenpin bowling **8 COINS STRUCK AT SAME TIME** the number of coins or medals struck at one time **9 DIRECTION OF GEOLOGICAL FORMATION** the compass direction of a horizontal line on a sloping rock surface, used to define geological features such as bedding or faults **10** TECH = **strickle** *n.* 1 **11 ANIMAL DISEASE CAUSED BY FLIES** an animal disease caused by an infestation of flies or fly eggs in open wounds or moist areas of the skin **12 PULL ON FISHING LINE BY FISH** a pull on a fishing line indicating that a fish has taken the bait **13 SENDING OUT OF PLANT ROOTS** the establishment of roots by a plant cutting or seedling [Old English *strīcan* < Germanic, 'touch lightly'] ◇ **strike it rich** to be extremely lucky or successful, particularly in money matters

strike down *vt* **1 CAUSE TO FALL** to cause somebody or something to fall by hitting **2 CAUSE SOMEBODY TO BECOME VERY ILL** to affect somebody or cause somebody to become seriously ill, especially suddenly **3 KILL** to cause somebody to die, especially suddenly

strike off *vt* **1 PREVENT PROFESSIONAL FROM PRACTISING** to prevent somebody, such as a doctor or lawyer, from continuing to practise a particular profession by removing his or her name from the register of authorized practitioners ○ *The surgeon who performed this operation should be struck off.* **2 DELETE** to cancel or remove something from a list, record, or register by crossing it out ○ *A steward struck off the names of the passengers as they boarded the plane.* **3 PRINT** to print something

strike on, strike upon *vt* to think of something, especially suddenly or by chance

strike out *v* **1** *vt* **DRAW LINE THROUGH** to draw a line through something in order to cancel or delete it **2** *vt* **SET OUT ENERGETICALLY** to set out energetically, especially for a particular destination or in a particular direction ○ *We struck out at sunrise, determined to get there by nightfall.* **3** *vi* **BEGIN** to begin doing something, especially independently **4** *vi* **ATTACK** to attack somebody or something, either physically or verbally **5** *vi US, Can* **FAIL** to be unsuccessful (*informal*) ○ *I tried three times to get that job, but struck out completely.*

strike up *v* **1** *vti* to begin playing or singing something ○ *struck up the band and played a waltz* **2** *vt* to begin something, or cause something to begin

strike upon *vt* = **strike on**

strikebound /strīk bownd/ *adj* closed or unable to operate because people have stopped work as a form of protest

strikebreaker /strīk braykər/ *n* **1** a worker who continues on the job while other employees are on strike **2** somebody hired to do the work of somebody who is on strike

strikebreaking /strīk brayking/ *n* **1** the act of working for an employer while other employees are on strike **2** action intended to break up a workers' strike

strike fault *n* a fault with a strike parallel to the rock strata

strike pay *n* money paid by a trade union to members who are on strike

strike price *n* the price at which the holder of stock options or warrants has the right to buy or sell. US term **striking price**

striker /strīkər/ *n* **1 SOMEBODY ON STRIKE** a person who has joined others in ceasing work in protest against working conditions or to compel an employer to accept their demands **2 ATTACKING PLAYER IN FOOTBALL TEAM** an attacking player in a football team whose main role is to score goals **3 DEVICE THAT STRIKES TO TELL TIME** a device that strikes to tell the time, e.g. a hammer in a clock or a clapper in a bell **4 MECHANISM THAT DRIVES FIRING PIN** the mechanical part of a firearm that drives the firing pin forwards

strike-slip fault *n* a geological fault that moves in a direction parallel to its strike

striking /strīking/ *adj* **1 CONSPICUOUS** conspicuous, marked, or noticeable **2 ATTRACTIVE OR IMPRESSIVE** attracting attention, especially in an impressive or unusual way **3 ON STRIKE** not working as a form of protest —**strikingly** *adv* —**strikingness** *n*

striking distance *n* closeness to something or to achieving something

striking price *n US* FIN = **strike price**

Strindberg /strínd burg/, **August** (1849–1912) Swedish dramatist —**Strindbergian** /strind búrgi ən/ *adj*

Strine /strīn/, **strine** *n* Australian English, especially a humorous representation in writing of Australian pronunciation, e.g. 'Emma Chisit' for 'How much is it?' (*humorous*) [Mid-20C. Imitation of the supposed Australian pronunciation of AUSTRALIAN.]

string /string/ *n* **1 STRONG THIN CORD** a strong thin cord or twine, usually made of twisted fibres. Use: binding, fastening, hanging, tying. **2 SOMETHING RESEMBLING STRING** something that resembles string in form or texture **3 SUCCESSION OF ITEMS** a series of similar or connected acts, events, or things **4 LINE OF THINGS** a series of things forming or arranged in a line, usually one behind another **5 GROUP OF ASSOCIATED THINGS** a group of similar things belonging to, managed by, or connected with a single person or a set of people **6 SEQUENCE OF SIMILAR ELEMENTS** a sequence of elements of the same nature, such as letters, numbers, symbols, binary digits, sounds, or words **7 OBJECTS THREADED TOGETHER** a set of objects connected with a single thread **8 CORD STRETCHED ACROSS MUSICAL INSTRUMENT** a cord made of nylon, wire, or gut that is stretched across a musical instrument and plucked, bowed, or otherwise vibrated to produce sound **9 THIN CORD STRETCHED ACROSS SPORTS RACQUET** any of the thin cords that are tightly stretched across the face of a sports racquet and interwoven to form a mesh **10 CORD STRETCHED ACROSS ARCHER'S BOW** the cord stretched between the ends of a bow in archery **11 PLANT FIBRE** a tough chewy fibre in a fruit or vegetable **12** BUILDING = **stringboard 13** BUILDING = **string course 14 PERSON CHOSEN AND RANKED ON ABILITY** a person or group of people chosen, especially for a sports team, and ranked at a specified level on the basis of their ability **15 HIT DETERMINING PLAYING ORDER IN BILLIARDS** an act of hitting the cue ball in billiards towards the head cushion (**lag**) to determine who will play first **16** CUE GAMES = **baulk line** *n.* 1 **17 TEN FRAMES OF BOWLING** a game of tenpin bowling consisting of ten frames **18 HYPOTHETICAL ONE-DIMENSIONAL ENTITY** a hypothetical one-dimensional entity that vibrates as it moves through space and is held to be a fundamental component of matter ■ **strings** *npl* **1 MUSICIANS PLAYING STRINGED INSTRUMENTS** the section of an orchestra consisting of musicians who play stringed instruments **2 STRINGED INSTRUMENTS OF ORCHESTRA** the stringed instruments of an orchestra or other musical ensemble ■ *v* (**strings, stringing, strung** /strung/, **strung**) **1** *vt* **THREAD ONTO STRING** to thread things onto a string **2** *vt* **HANG SOMETHING BETWEEN TWO POINTS** to hang or stretch something between two points **3** *vt* **ARRANGE OR EXTEND SOMETHING IN LINE** to arrange or extend something in a line or series **4** *vt* **PROVIDE SOMETHING WITH STRING OR STRINGS** to provide something, e.g. a sports racquet or musical instrument, with a string or strings **5** *vt* **FASTEN OR TIE SOMETHING WITH STRING** to bind, fasten, hang, or tie something with a string or strings **6** *vt* **REMOVE FIBRES** to remove the stringy fibres from vegetables **7** *vt* **REMOVE CURRANTS** to remove currants from their stalks by sliding them off between the prongs of a fork **8** *vi* **BECOME STRINGY** to form strings or become stringy **9** *vti* **DETERMINE PLAYING**

ORDER IN BILLIARDS to hit the cue ball in billiards towards the head cushion (**lag**) to determine who will play first ■ *adj* **MADE OF STRING** made of a mesh of string or similar material [Old English *streng* < Germanic, 'stiff'] —**stringed** *adj* —**stringless** *adj* ◇ **have somebody on a string** to be able to control somebody easily ◇ **pull strings** to use influence to try to gain an advantage ◇ **pull the strings** to be in control, although not obviously so ◇ **with no strings (attached)** without any conditions or restrictions

string along *v* (*informal*) **1** *vt* **DECEIVE OVER A LONG TIME** to deceive or fool somebody over an extended period of time, especially by keeping him or her in a state of false hope **2** *vi* **ACCOMPANY OR STAY WITH** to accompany or stay with somebody, often in a casual manner ○ *She wanted to string along with us when we went to the shops.* **3** *vi* **AGREE WITH** to agree or go along with another or another person's idea or suggestion

string up *vt* **1** to kill somebody by hanging (*informal*) **2** to suspend somebody or something on a string or strings

string band *n* a group of musicians who play folk or country music on stringed instruments

string bass *n* MUSIC = **double bass**

string bean *n* **1** *US* FOOD = **French bean** *n.* **2 2** *US* PLANTS = **French bean** *n.* **1 3** PLANTS, FOOD = **runner bean 4** a tall thin person (*informal*)

stringboard /stríng bawrd/ *n* a board that covers the ends of the steps on a staircase [Because the board 'strings' the steps together]

string course /stríng kawrss/ *n* a decorative feature on a building in the form of a horizontal band or moulding

stringed instrument, string instrument *n* a musical instrument in which bowing or plucking causes the vibration of a string or strings tightly stretched across a soundboard, e.g. a violin or guitar

stringendo /strin jéndō/ *adv* at an accelerating tempo (*musical direction*) [Mid-19C. Via Italian, present participle of *stringere* 'press, squeeze' < Latin, 'draw tight'.] —**stringendo** *adj*

stringent /strínjənt/ *adj* strictly controlled or enforced [Early 17C. < Latin, present participle of *stringere* 'draw tight, bind'.] —**stringency** *n* —**stringently** *adv*

stringer /stríngər/ *n* **1 FREELANCE OR PART-TIME JOURNALIST** a journalist, often covering a particular geographic area, who works on a freelance or part-time basis for a newspaper or news agency **2 HORIZONTAL TIMBER** a heavy horizontal timber used for structural purposes **3** BUILDING = **stringboard 4 AUXILIARY MEMBER OF WING** a light auxiliary part parallel with the main structural members of a wing or fuselage, used mainly for bracing and stabilizing **5 PLAYER OF SPECIFIED ABILITY** a member of a team who is ranked according to excellence or skill (*usually in combination*) **6 NARROW MINERAL VEIN** a narrow or discontinuous linear vein of ore mineral

stringhalt /stríng hawlt/ *n* a condition of horses marked by sudden lifting of and lameness in the hind legs, caused by muscle spasms [Early 16C. < STRING in the sense 'tendon' + HALT 'limp'.] —**stringhalted** *adj*

string instrument *n* MUSIC = **stringed instrument**

string line *n* CUE GAMES = **baulk line** *n.* **1**

string orchestra *n* a small orchestra of stringed instruments including violins, violas, cellos, and double basses

stringpiece /stríng peess/ *n* a beam of wood placed horizontally to support a framework

string quartet *n* **1** a group of four musicians playing stringed instruments, traditionally two violins, a cello, and a viola **2** a piece of music composed for four stringed instruments, traditionally two violins, a cello, and a viola

string quintet *n* an ensemble of five string instruments, usually two violins, two violas, and a cello, or a piece of music written for this combination

string theory *n* a mathematical theory that provides a unified structure to explain the properties and behaviour of elementary particles and fundamental forces

QUICK FACTS ON... **STRING THEORY**

Key elements: quantum theory that describes gravity as well as the weak, strong, and electromagnetic interactions; each known elementary particle is described mathematically as a different mode of vibration and the interactions between vibrating 'strings' correspond to the observed interactions of particles; mathematical theory of supersymmetry between fermions and bosons results in a theory of superstrings, unifying all forces and particles; prediction of the existence of many more spatial dimensions, up to eleven including time

Key dates: 1919 Kaluza in a letter to Einstein proposes that the universe might have more than three dimensions; 1926 Klein theorizes that the extra dimensions might be extended and/or curled up; 1970 Nambu, Nielsen, and Susskind first propose string theory; 1971 supersymmetry is incorporated into string theory; 1985 supersymmetry is extended to five different string structures; 1996 Strominger and Vafa use string theory to calculate the entropy of certain black holes; 1996 M-theory is suggested to unite competing superstring theories, implying the existence of seven additional dimensions, most of which are tightly curled up and unobservable

string tie *n* **1** a narrow tie made of ribbon, tied in a bow, briefly popular in the 1890s **2** a narrow thong held by a sliding clip, worn as a tie, especially by cowboys

string trio *n* an ensemble of a violin, a viola, and a cello, or a piece of music written for this combination

string vest *n* a vest knitted or woven with an open mesh

stringy /stríngi/ (**-ier, -iest**) *adj* **1 FIBROUS** containing strands of fibre and unpleasant to chew **2 UNATTRACTIVELY THIN** unattractively thin, with bones or muscles showing beneath the skin **3 RESEMBLING PIECES OF STRING** looking like pieces of string or hanging in long thin strands ○ *a stringy beard* **4 FORMING STRANDS** forming long sticky threads —**stringiness** *n*

stringy-bark *n Aus* a eucalyptus tree with thick fibrous grey and brown bark

strip[1] /strip/ *v* (**strips, stripping, stripped**) **1** *vi* **GET UNDRESSED** to remove your clothes, either completely or to a particular extent **2** *vt* **UNDRESS** to remove somebody's clothes, either completely or to a particular extent **3** *vi* **DO STRIPTEASE** to do a striptease, or be a striptease artist **4** *vt* **REMOVE COVERING** to take off a covering, or take the covering off something ○ *strip the wallpaper* **5** *vt* **REMOVE PAINT OR VARNISH FROM SURFACE** to remove old paint or varnish from a surface by scraping or burning it or by using a chemical **6** *vt* **REMOVE CONTENTS** to remove all the contents from a room, building, or similar place **7** *vt* **REMOVE ALL LEAVES OR PLANTS** to remove all the leaves or flowers from a plant, or remove all the plants from an area **8** *vt* **DEPRIVE OF STATUS OR POSSESSIONS** to take status or possessions away from somebody ○ *stripped him of his rank* **9** *vt* **TAKE SOMETHING APART** to take a machine, engine, or weapon to pieces in order to clean or repair it **10** *vti* **DAMAGE SCREW THREAD OR GEAR TEETH** to damage a screw or gearwheel by breaking the thread or teeth, or undergo this damage **11** *vt* **REMOVE VOLATILE CONTENT** to separate one or more components from a solution or mixture, especially by distillation or evaporation **12** *vt* **MAKE INTO PRINTING PLATE** to put pieces of photographic film or paper together to make a plate for printing ■ *n* **ACT OF STRIPPING** the performance of a striptease [Old English *-strȳpan* < Germanic]

strip off *vi* to take off all your clothes

strip out *vt* to take out parts of a machine for cleaning or repair

strip[2] /strip/ *n* **1 LONG FLAT PIECE** a long flat narrow piece of something **2** AIR = **airstrip 3** PUBL = **comic strip 4 SPORTS CLOTHES** the distinctive clothes worn by a particular sports team, e.g. a football team **5** *US* **ROAD LINED WITH BUSINESSES** a road lined with stores, shopping centres, restaurants, and other businesses ■ *vt* (**strips, stripping, stripped**) **DIVIDE INTO STRIPS** to cut, tear, or divide something into strips [15C. Probably < Low German *strippe* 'strap, thong'.] ◇ **tear a strip off somebody** to rebuke somebody angrily

strip[3] /strip/ (**strips, stripping, stripped**) *vt* to remove the last remaining milk from the udder of a cow or goat by hand after machine-milking [Early 17C. < ?]

strip cartoon *n* PUBL = **comic strip**

strip club *n* a club or bar where people can watch striptease acts

strip cropping *n* the growing of different crops in an arrangement of lines or bands to prevent soil erosion

stripe[1] /strīp/ *n* **1 LONG NARROW BAND** a long narrow band of a different colour, composition, or texture from the surrounding surface or background **2 PATTERN** a pattern of stripes **3 FABRIC** a fabric with a pattern of stripes **4 INDICATION OF RANK** a narrow band or V-shaped piece of fabric, sewn on to a uniform as a symbol of rank **5** *US* **TYPE OF PERSON** a recognizable type of person with a particular character or set of opinions **6** *US* **SET OF CHARACTERISTICS** a particular set of characteristics ○ *'...portals of all stripes face a challenging future...'* (*Washington Post*; November 1998) ■ *vt* (**stripes, striping, striped**) **MARK WITH STRIPES** to put stripes on something [15C. Probably < Middle Dutch or Middle Low German *strīpe.*] —**stripy** /strīpi/ *adj*

stripe[2] /strīp/ *n* a blow from a whip, lash, cane, or belt [15C. Probably < Low German or Dutch.]

striped /strīpt/ *adj* patterned or marked with stripes

striped bass /-báss/ *n* a large game fish that travels up rivers to breed, and has black stripes. Native to: US coastal waters. *Morone saxatilus.*

striped muscle *n* ANAT = **striated muscle**

striped skunk *n* a common skunk that has a white cap on its head and white stripes down either side of the spine. Native to: North America. *Mephitis mephitis.*

striper /strīpər/ *n* **1** a member of the armed forces whose stripes on a uniform indicate rank or length of service (*slang*) **2** ZOOL = **striped bass**

strip-grazing *n* a system in which cattle or other livestock are periodically allocated a fresh strip of pasture to graze by moving an electrified fence across the field

strip joint *n US* a strip club (*informal*)

striplight /stríp līt/ *n* **1** a fluorescent lamp in the form of a long tube, especially on a ceiling **2** a row of shaded lamps used to light a theatre stage

stripling /strípling/ *n* a boy in his early teenage years, who has not yet grown to his full size [14C. Probably < STRIP[2].]

strip mall *n US* a long building facing a road, divided into separate stores and businesses with parking spaces at the front of each of them

strip mill *n* an industrial building where steel is rolled into strips

strip mine *n US* a mine where mineral seams near the surface of the ground are exposed by stripping away soil and land —**strip mining** *n*

stripped-down *adj* deprived of all but the most essential or simple features

stripper /stríppər/ *n* **1 STRIPTEASE ARTIST** a performer of striptease acts **2 PAINT OR WALLPAPER REMOVER** a tool or substance used for removing paint, varnish, wallpaper, or other substances from a surface **3 SOMEBODY WHO STRIPS** somebody whose job is to strip something

strip poker *n* a variety of the card game poker in which, at each round, players who lose have to remove an item of their clothing

strippy /stríppi/ *n* patchwork in which broad strips of fabric are pieced together in vertical bands, then quilted ■ *adj* consisting of strips

strip-search (**strip-searches, strip-searching, strip-searched**) *vti* to compel somebody to undress completely while searching for concealed drugs, weapons, or contraband —**strip search** *n*

striptease /stríp teez, stríp téez/ *n* an entertainment in which the performer slowly undresses in an erotic way, usually with music as an accompaniment —**stripteaser** *n*

strive /strīv/ (**strives, striving, strove** /strōv/, **striven** /strívv'n/) *vi* **1 TRY HARD** to try hard to achieve or get something **2 OPPOSE** to fight in opposition to something **3 COMPETE** to compete resolutely against somebody or something [12C. < Old French *estriver* 'contend' < *estrif* (see STRIFE).] —**striver** *n*

strobe /strōb/ *n* **1** ELECTRONICS = **strobe light 2** ELECTRONICS = **stroboscope 3** an electronic pulse of short duration used to examine the characteristics of a periodic waveform **4** the process of viewing vibrations or rotational motion with a stroboscope [Mid-20C. Shortening of STROBOSCOPE.]

strobe light, strobe *n* a high intensity flashing beam of light produced by charging a capacitor to a very high voltage then discharging it as a high-intensity flash of light in a tube

strobe lighting *n* the effect produced by strobe lights or by a perforated disc rotating in front of a high intensity light source, as used in discotheques

strobila /strə bīlə/ (*plural* **-lae** /-lee/) *n* **1** the segmented body of a tapeworm, usually excluding the head (**scolex**) and neck **2** a chain of buds that are attached to the body of certain jellyfish and that later develop into individual offspring [Mid-19C. Via modern Latin < Greek *strobilē* 'twisted plug of lint', feminine of *strobilos* (see STROBILUS).]

strobilus /strṓbələss/ (*plural* **-luses** *or* **-li** /-lī/) *n* **1** the cone of a coniferous plant, or a similar cone-shaped structure in some lower plants that consists of closely packed fertile leaves bearing spore-producing organs (*technical*) **2** a cone-shaped structure in flowering plants, e.g. the fruit of the hop [Mid-18C. Via late Latin < Greek *strobilos* 'twisted object, pine cone' < *strobos* 'whirling'.]

stroboscope /strṓbə skōp/ *n* a flashing lamp of precisely variable periodicity that can be synchronized with the frequency of moving machinery to give the appearance of being stationary [Mid-19C. < Greek *strobos* 'whirling' + -SCOPE.] —**stroboscopic** /strṓbə skóppik, stróbbə-/ *adj*

strobotron /strṓbə tron, -trən/ *n* the triggered gas-discharge tube used as the pulsed light source in a stroboscope [Mid-20C. < STROBOSCOPE + -TRON.]

strode past tense of **stride**

Stroessner /strṓssnər/, **Alfredo** (*b.* 1912) Paraguayan soldier and dictator

stroganoff /stróggə nof/, **Stroganoff** *adj* cooked in a wine sauce with sour cream [Mid-20C. < French, after Count Pavel Aleksandrovich *Stroganov* (1772–1817), Russian diplomat.]

stroke /strōk/ *n* **1 STOPPAGE OF BLOOD FLOW TO BRAIN** a sudden blockage or rupture of a blood vessel in the brain resulting in, e.g. loss of consciousness, partial loss of movement, or loss of speech. Technical name **cerebrovascular accident** **2 SUDDEN OCCURRENCE** a sudden instance or occurrence of something that has a strong or unexpected effect ○ *a stroke of luck* **3 STRIKING OF CLOCK** a single sound made by a clock that is striking ○ *at the stroke of seven* **4 HITTING OF BALL** the hitting of a ball in racket games or golf, or the way in which this is done **5 SWIMMING STYLE** a style of swimming, using the arms and legs in a particular way ○ *a difficult swimming stroke* **6 SINGLE MOVEMENT IN SWIMMING** a single complete movement of the arms and legs when swimming **7 SINGLE PULL** a single movement of the oars through the water in rowing **8 ROWER WHO KEEPS TIME** a rower in a racing boat who sets the pace for the crew **9 ROWING STYLE** a particular rowing style **10 SINGLE MOVEMENT IN SERIES** a single movement forming part of a series of movements such as the beat of a wing or the swing of a pendulum ○ *a wing stroke* **11 MOVEMENT OF PISTON** a single movement, up or down, of a piston in an engine or the distance that it travels in a single movement **12 HIT** a hit or blow made by the hand, a cane, or a tool **13** PRINTING = **slash** *n.* 5 **14 BRUSH OR PEN LINE** a single line or mark made with a pen or brush ○ *a brush stroke* **15 SINGLE MOVEMENT OF PEN OR BRUSH** a single movement of a pen or brush to make a line or mark **16 CARESSING MOVEMENT** a gentle caressing movement of the hand over fur, hair, or skin **17 ADDITIONAL FEATURE** a small additional feature that has an effect on the style or nature of something ○ *a stroke of sarcasm* **18 VERBAL ENCOURAGEMENT** a usually positive comment or statement such as a compliment made by one person to another ○ *I need all the positive strokes I can right now.* **19 ELEMENT OF SOCIAL RECOGNITION** in transactional analysis, a unit of social recognition between two or more people that, in its simplest form, can be a one-word greeting such as 'hello' ■ *v* (**strokes, stroking, stroked**) **1** *vt* **CARESS** to move the hand gently over something as if caressing it ○ *stroked the cat gently* **2** *vt* **HIT BALL SMOOTHLY** to hit or kick a ball smoothly in various sports **3** *vt* **PUSH GENTLY** to push something somewhere gently with a light movement of the hand **4** *vt* **CROSS OUT** to draw a line through something **5** *vt* **SET ROWING PACE** to be the rower who sets the pace for the crew **6** *vi* **MOVE OARS** to row at a particular speed or rate of the oars **7** *vt* **COMPLIMENT** to behave encouragingly or solicitously towards somebody ■ *adj US* **PORNOGRAPHIC** pornographic (*slang*) [Old English *strācian*. Ultimately < Indo-European 'to rub, press'.] ◇ **different strokes for different folks** emphasizes that people are all individuals and that what suits one will not necessarily suit another

stroke play *n* a way of scoring in golf in which the total number of strokes taken for the round is counted rather than the number of holes won. US term **medal play**

stroll /strōl/ *v* **1** *vti* **WALK UNHURRIEDLY** to walk in a slow unhurried way, especially for enjoyment **2** *vi* **DO EFFORTLESSLY** to do, obtain, or achieve something in a casual effortless way ○ *she strolled through the exam* ■ *n* **LEISURELY WALK** a slow leisurely walk for pleasure ○ *went for a stroll in the park* [Early 17C. Probably < German *strollen* 'wander', a variant of *strolchen* < *Strolch* 'vagabond, fortune-teller'.] ◇ **stroll on** used as an expression of disbelief or frustration (*informal*)

stroller /strṓlər/ *n* **1** somebody who is walking in a slow leisurely way for pleasure **2** *US, Can, Aus* a light chair with wheels in which a young child can be pushed around

strolling /strṓling/ *adj* going from place to place to earn a living, especially by entertaining ○ *strolling minstrels*

stroma /strṓmə/ (*plural* **-mata** /-mətə/) *n* **1** the connective tissue that provides the framework of an organ or other anatomical structure rather than carrying out its functions **2** the fluid-filled interior of a chloroplast containing enzymes and other components required for photosynthesis, including the light-trapping components [Mid-19C. Via modern Latin < Greek *strōma* 'bed, cushion'.] —**stromatic** /strō máttik/ *adj*

stromatolite /strō máttə līt/ *n* a very old fossil formed in sedimentary rock by marine blue-green algae and consisting of a rounded or columnar calcium-containing mass of many layers [Mid-20C. < late Latin *stromat-*, stem of *stroma* 'bed-covering' + -LITE.] —**stromatolitic** /strō máttə líttik/ *adj*

Stromboli /strom bṓli/ volcanic island in the Lipari Islands in the Tyrrhenian Sea, north of Sicily. Area: 13 sq. km/5 sq. mi.

Strominger /strómminjər/, **Andrew** (*b.* 1955) US physicist

strong /strong/ *adj* **1 PHYSICALLY POWERFUL** having the physical strength needed to exert considerable force, e.g. in lifting, pulling, or pushing something **2 USING FORCE** using great physical force **3 ROBUST AND STURDY** sturdy, well made, and not easily damaged or broken **4 EMOTIONALLY RESILIENT** having the necessary emotional qualities to deal with stress, grief, loss, risk, and other difficulties **5 HEALTHY AND WELL** in good health, especially after an illness ○ *getting stronger every day* **6 THRIVING** thriving, developing well, and likely to continue so ○ *a strong economy* **7 LIKELY TO SUCCEED** very likely to succeed, win, or come to be something ○ *a strong candidate for the post.* **8 CONVINCING** supported by facts or good evidence and likely to be correct or effective ○ *a strong argument* **9 KNOWLEDGEABLE** very skilful or knowledgeable in a particular subject or area **10 EXERTING INFLUENCE** influential or authoritative by virtue of having or holding power **11 EFFECTIVE** having a powerful effect ○ *strong painkillers* **12 FELT OR EXPRESSED POWERFULLY** felt or expressed with a powerful effect ○ *She has strong views on the subject.* **13 DISTINCTIVE** bold, clearly defined, and prominent ○ *strong features* **14 EXTREME** unusually severe of its kind ○ *Strong measures were taken to prevent a riot.* **15 INTENSE IN IMPRESSION** having an intense, powerful, or vivid effect on the senses ○ *a strong smell of garlic* **16 EASY TO DETECT** easy to detect or receive ○ *The signal gets stronger as you get closer.* **17 CONCENTRATED** containing a lot of the main ingredient and not diluted or watery ○ *strong black coffee* **18 ALCOHOLIC** containing much alcohol **19 FAST MOVING** flowing or blowing at high speed ○ *a strong current* **20 FULLY IONIZED** producing ions freely in solution **21 WELL DEFENDED** well defended and difficult to capture ○ *a strong fortress* **22 WITH SPECIFIED NUMBER** having a particular number of members ○ *a force 50,000 strong* **23 WITH HIGH MAGNIFICATION** having a powerful magnifying or corrective ability ○ *a strong lens* **24 WITH HIGH PRICES** characterized by high or rising prices ○ *a strong currency* **25 WITH CHANGED VOWEL** describes an irregular verb that changes the vowel in the stem in its different forms, e.g. 'ring', 'rang', 'rung' [Old English *strang*. Of Germanic origin.] —**strongly** *adv* ◇ **come on strong** to behave or express something aggressively (*slang*) ◇ **going strong** thriving and doing well

strong-arm *adj* using or prepared to use coercion or physical force (*informal*) ○ *ready to use strong-arm tactics* ■ *vt* (**strong-arms, strong-arming, strong-armed**) to use coercion against somebody to induce cooperation (*informal*)

strongbox /stróng boks/ *n* a secure metal box or safe where money or valuables can be kept

strong breeze *n* a wind with a speed between 40 and 50 km/25 and 31 mi. per hour

strong force *n* PHYS = **strong interaction**

strong gale *n* a wind with a speed between 76 and 87 km/47 and 54 mi. per hour

stronghold /stróng hōld/ *n* **1** a place that is fortified or that can easily be defended **2** a place where a particular group, activity, or set of opinions is concentrated

strong interaction, strong force *n* a fundamental force between elementary particles that is responsible for binding protons and neutrons together in an atomic nucleus and other interactions between elementary particles (**hadrons**)

strong language *n* language that expresses something in a forceful way, especially with abusive words or swearing

strongman /stróng man/ (*plural* **-men** /-men/) *n* **1** a performer of feats of strength, e.g. at a fair or circus **2** a powerful, typically dictatorial, leader who rules by force

strong meat *n* behaviour or attitudes that generally upset or offend people and that are acceptable only to a robust minority

strong-minded *adj* **1** determined and persevering in the face of difficulty **2** confident, intelligent, and independent in thought —**strong-mindedly** *adv* —**strong-mindedness** *n*

strong point, strong suit *n* a particular area for which somebody has a talent ○ *Tact was never his strong point.*

strongroom /stróng room, -rŏŏm/ *n* a reinforced room designed to withstand fire or theft and used for the storage of valuables

strong suit *n* **1** = **strong point** **2** in various card games the suit in which a player or team holds the most cards or the most face cards. ◊ **long suit**

strong-willed *adj* determined to prevail in the face of difficulty or opposition

strongyle /strónjil/, **strongyl** /strónjəl/ *n* a parasitic nematode worm related to the hookworms that infests the intestinal tract of mammals. Superfamily: Strongyloidea. [Mid-19C. Anglicization of modern Latin *Strongylus* < Greek *stroggulos* 'round, compact' < ?]

strongyloidiasis /strónji loy dī́ əssis/ *n* intestinal infection in mammals by strongyles, producing various severe and sometimes fatal intestinal disorders, especially in individuals with weakened immune systems [Mid-20C. < modern Latin *Strongyloidea*, superfamily name < *Strongylus* (see STRONGYLE).]

strongylosis /strónji lṓssiss/ *n* an illness, usually of horses, caused by infection with strongyles

strontia /strónti ə, -shi ə/ *n* CHEM = **strontium monoxide** [Early 19C. Back-formation < STRONTIAN.]

strontian /strónti ən, strónshi-/ *n* **1** MINERALS = **strontianite** **2** CHEM = **strontium monoxide** **3** CHEM = **strontium** [Late 18C. Shortening of *Strontian earth*; after the parish of *Strontian* in Scotland.]

strontianite /strónti ə nīt, strónshi ə nīt/ *n* a variously coloured strontium carbonate mineral. Use: source of strontium.

strontium /strónti əm, -shi-/ *n* (*symbol* **Sr**) a soft yellow or silvery-white metallic element of the alkaline-earth group, found only in combination with other substances. Source: strontianite, celestite. Use: fireworks, flares, alloys. [Early 19C. < STRONTIA.]

strontium 90 *n* a radioactive isotope of strontium with a mass number of 90, present in nuclear fallout and assimilated like calcium in bone formation

strontium monoxide *n* **SrO** a white insoluble solid resembling quicklime. Use: purification of sugar.

strontium unit *n* a unit of measurement of the amount of strontium 90 in an organic substance such as soil or bone, in relation to the concentration of calcium in the same substance

Stroop effect /strŏŏp-/ *n* difficulty identifying the colours in which names of colours are written [Mid-20C. After J. R. *Stroop*, US psychologist.]

strop /strop/ *n* **1 LEATHER STRAP FOR SHARPENING** a leather strap used for sharpening a cutthroat razor **2 STRAP FOR CARGO** a strap of leather or rope used for lifting cargo ■ *vt* (**strops, stropping, stropped**) **SHARPEN RAZOR** to sharpen a straight razor on a strop [Assumed Old English *strop* 'band, cord', via Latin *stroppus* < Greek *strophos* (see STROPHOID).] ◇ **in a strop** in a bad temper or sulk (*informal*)

strophe /strṓfi/ *n* **1** the first type of metrical form in a poem that uses two contrasting metrical forms. ◊ **antistrophe** *n.* 2 **2** the first of two movements made by the chorus in a classical Greek drama, or the part of a ode sung during this. ◊ **antistrophe** *n.* 1 [Early 17C. < Greek *strophē* 'turning'.] —**strophic** /strŏffik, strṓfik/ *adj*

strophoid /strṓ foyd/ *n* a plane curve symmetric to the x-axis, generated by a point whose distance from the y-axis along a straight line is equal to the y-intercept [Late 19C. < Greek *strophos* 'twisted cord'.]

stroppy /stróppi/ (**-pier, -piest**) *adj* bad-tempered and uncooperative (*informal*) [Mid-20C. < ?]

stroud /strowd/ *n* a rough woollen fabric [Late 17C. < ?]

Stroud /strowd/ town in central England. Population: 38,835 (1991).

strove past tense of **strive**

struck /struk/ past tense, past participle of **strike** ■ *adj US* closed temporarily or working at reduced output because of a labour dispute

struck measure *n* a quantity of something such as grain, measured by levelling the substance with the top of a container

structural /strúkchərəl/ *adj* 1 **RELATING TO STRUCTURE** relating to the way that the parts of something are put together or how they work together 2 **RESULTING FROM STRUCTURE** resulting from the interrelationship of constituent parts, e.g. in a political or economic system 3 **BASIC TO A STRUCTURE** constituting an important or essential part of a structure 4 **USED IN CONSTRUCTION** suitable for use in construction ○ *structural fibreglass* 5 **CAUSED BY ATOMIC ARRANGEMENT** relating to or caused by the arrangement of atoms in a molecule 6 **OF ROCK STRUCTURE** relating to or caused by movement of the Earth's surface —**structurally** *adv*

structural formula *n* an expanded chemical formula representing the arrangement of atoms and bonds within a molecule

structural gene *n* a gene that codes for a protein required for the cell's own use

structuralise *vt* = **structuralize**

structuralism /strúkchərəlizəm/ *n* 1 a method of sociological analysis based on the notion of human society as a network of interrelated elements whose patterns and significance can be analysed 2 LING = **structural linguistics** 3 PSYCHOL = **structural psychology** —**structuralist** *n, adj*

structuralize /strúkchərə līz/ (**-izes, -izing, -ized**), **structuralise** (**-ises, -ising, -ised**) *vt* to arrange or organize something so that it has a structure

structural linguistics *n* a branch of linguistics that emphasizes the significance of the interrelations between the elements that constitute a linguistic system (+ *singular verb*) —**structural linguist** *n*

structural psychology *n* a school of psychology of the early part of the 20th century that sought to organize the components of subjective experience in a hierarchy from simplest to most complex —**structural psychologist** *n*

structural steel *n* strong steel shaped and suitable for use in construction

structure /strúkchər/ *n* 1 **SOMETHING BUILT OR ERECTED** a building, bridge, framework, or other object that has been put together from many different parts 2 **ORDERLY SYSTEM OF PARTS** a system or organization made up of interrelated parts functioning as an orderly whole 3 **WAY THAT PARTS LINK OR FUNCTION** the way in which the different parts of something link or work together, or the fact of being linked together ○ *the structure of local government* ○ *The essay is interesting, but it lacks structure.* 4 **ORGANIC FEATURE** a part of a body or organism, e.g. an organ or tissue, identifiable by its shape and other properties 5 **ARRANGEMENT OF ATOMS** the specific arrangement of atoms in a molecule 6 **COMPONENT PARTS OF ROCKS** the physical disposition of a rock mass, e.g. its folding and faulting, or the disposition of its mineral components, e.g. its texture ■ *vt* (**-tures, -turing, -tured**) **GIVE STRUCTURE TO** to organize or arrange something so that it works as a cohesive whole [15C. Directly or via French < Latin *structura* < *struct-*, past participle of *struere* 'build'.]

structured /strúkchərd/ *adj* 1 planned, organized, and controlled 2 with a definite shape, form, or pattern ○ *For business wear, suits need a more structured look.*

⚡**structured programming** *n* a style of computer programming in which a program consists of a hierarchy of simple subroutines

⚡**structured query language** *n* full form of **SQL**

strudel /strooˈd'l/ *n* a pastry made with very thin pastry rolled and baked with a filling, usually of chopped apples, raisins, and sugar [Late 19C. Via German < Middle High German, 'whirlpool'.]

struggle /strúgg'l/ *vi* (**-gles, -gling, -gled**) 1 **TRY TO OVERCOME A PROBLEM** to try very hard to deal with a challenge, problem, or difficulty ○ *He was struggling with his maths homework.* 2 **MAKE A GREAT PHYSICAL EFFORT** to make a great physical effort to achieve or obtain something ○ *A rescue party struggled to reach the stranded climbers.* 3 **FIGHT BY WRESTLING** to fight with somebody by grappling and wrestling 4 **WRITHE TO ESCAPE** to move and wriggle forcefully in an attempt to escape 5 **MOVE WITH DIFFICULTY** to move with great effort ○ *so weak I just managed to struggle out of bed* ■ *n* 1 **GREAT EFFORT TO OVERCOME DIFFICULTIES** a great effort made over a period of time to overcome difficulties or achieve something 2 **HARD TASK** a strenuous physical or mental effort, or something requiring this 3 **FIGHT** a prolonged fight or conflict [14C. < ?] —**struggler** *n*

struggle for existence *n* the ongoing effort to survive and reproduce in an environment of competing organisms

strum /strum/ *v* (**strums, strumming, strummed**) 1 *vti* **PLAY AN INSTRUMENT BY BRUSHING THE STRINGS** to play a guitar or other stringed instrument by brushing the strings with the fingers or a plectrum 2 *vt* **PLAY TUNE** to play a tune by strumming an instrument ■ *n* **SOUND OF STRUMMING** the sound of somebody strumming an instrument [Late 18C. An imitation of the sound.] —**strummer** *n*

struma /stroōmə/ (*plural* **-mae** /-mee/) *n* 1 a swelling at the base of a moss capsule 2 MED = **goitre** [Mid-16C. Via modern Latin < Latin, 'scrofulous tumour'.] —**strumatic** /stroo máttik/ *adj* —**strumose** *adj* —**strumous** *adj*

strumpet /strúmpit/ *n* an offensive term for a prostitute or woman regarded as too sexually active (*archaic*) [14C. < ?]

strung past tense, past participle of **string**

strung out *adj* 1 **OVERWROUGHT** tired, tense, or overwrought (*informal*) 2 **DRUGGED** under the influence of a drug, especially a narcotic drug (*slang*) 3 **WEAKENED** debilitated by long-term drug use (*slang*)

strung up *adj* very tired, tense, and overwrought (*informal*)

strut /strut/ *v* (**struts, strutting, strutted**) 1 *vi* **WALK IN ARROGANT WAY** to walk in a conspicuously stiff or proud way, suggesting arrogance or pomposity 2 *vt* **SUPPORT WITH PLANKS** to prop something up with supporting planks or boards ■ *n* 1 **SUPPORTING MEMBER** a long rigid plank, board, or other structural member used as a support in building 2 **PROUD WALKING** a stiff, proud, pompous way of walking [Old English *strūtian* 'protrude stiffly' < Indo-European, 'stiff']

struth *interj* = **strewth** (*slang*)

struthious /strúthi əss/ *adj* relating to flightless birds, especially the ostrich [Late 18C. < late Latin *struthio* 'ostrich', via late Greek *strouthiōn* < Greek *strouthos*.]

strychnine /strík neen, -nin/ *n* $C_{21}H_{22}N_2O_2$ a bitter white poisonous alkaloid obtained from nux vomica and related plants. Use: rodenticide, nervous system stimulant. [Early 19C. < French, < modern Latin *Strychnos*, via Latin *strychnon* 'nightshade' < Greek *strukhnos* < ?] —**strychnic** *adj*

Strzelecki Range /strez léki-/ range of hills in S Victoria, Australia. Highest peak: 500 m/1,640 ft.

Stuart /styoō ərt/, **Charles Edward** (1720–88) grandson of James II of England, Scotland, and Ireland and claimant to the British throne. Known as **Bonnie Prince Charlie, the Young Pretender**

Stuart, James Francis Edward (1688–1766) son of James II of England, Scotland, and Ireland and claimant to the British throne. Known as **the Old Pretender**

Stuart, John McDouall (1815–66) British-born Australian explorer

stub /stub/ *n* 1 **SHORT REMAINING PART** a short part of something that is left after the main part has been removed or used 2 **SMALL SECTION OF A TICKET OR CHEQUE** a small detachable section of a ticket, cheque, or voucher, retained as a record of a transaction 3 **STUMP OF A TREE OR PLANT** the stump of a tree or plant 4 **SMALL PROJECTION** a small projection from a surface ■ *vt* (**stubs, stubbing, stubbed**) 1 **BANG THE TOE** to bang your toe against something accidentally 2 **DIG UP BY THE ROOTS** to dig up a plant or tree by the roots 3 **CLEAR LAND OF STUMPS** to clear land of tree stumps [Old English *stubb* 'tree stump' < Germanic]

stub out *vt* to put out a cigarette or cigar by pushing the burning end against something

stubble /stúbb'l/ *n* 1 short stalks left in the ground after a grain crop has been harvested 2 the short spiky growth of beard on a man's face when he has not shaved [13C. Via Old French *estuble* < Latin *stupula* 'straw', alteration of *stipula* (see STIPULE).] —**stubbly** *adj*

stubborn /stúbbərn/ *adj* 1 **DOGGED** carried out in a determined, persistent way ○ *met with stubborn resistance* 2 **UNREASONABLY DETERMINED** unreasonably and obstructively determined to persevere or prevail 3 **HARD TO REMOVE** difficult to remove or deal with ○ *a stubborn stain* [14C. < ?] —**stubbornly** *adv* —**stubbornness** *n*

Stubbs /stubz/, **George** (1724–1806) British painter and engraver

stubby /stúbbi/ *adj* 1 **SHORT AND STOUT** short and stout in build 2 **SHORT AND THICK** short and thick, broad, or blunt ○ *stubby fingers* 3 **WITH MANY STUBS** with projecting stubs or short bristles ■ *n Aus* **BEER BOTTLE** a small squat bottle of beer (*informal*)

stub nail *n* a short thick nail

STUC *abbr* Scottish Trades Union Congress

stucco /stúkō/ *n* 1 **WALL PLASTER** plaster used for surfacing interior or exterior walls, often used in association with classical mouldings 2 **DECORATIVE PLASTER WORK** decorative work moulded from stucco ■ *vt* (**-coes** or **-cos, -coing, -coed**) **COVER WITH STUCCO** to apply a coating of stucco to a wall [Late 16C. < Italian, < Germanic.] —**stuccoer** /stúkō ər/ *n*

stuck /stuk/ past tense, past participle of **stick**[2] ■ *adj* 1 **JAMMED OR CAUGHT** jammed, caught, or held in a position from which it is impossible to move ○ *the drawer was stuck fast* 2 **UNABLE TO FIND A SOLUTION** not able to find a solution or way out of a situation 3 **PIERCED** pierced by a sharp object

stuckie /stúki/ *n Scotland* a starling

stuck-up *adj* snobbish and conceited (*informal*)

stud[1] /stud/ *n* 1 **METAL KNOB** a small metal knob or the head of a nail protruding slightly from a surface, especially for decorative effect 2 **EARRING** an earring for pierced ears that has a simple rounded head or is set with a single gemstone 3 **COLLAR FASTENER** a fastener for collars or dress shirts consisting of a small disc attached to a short rod 4 **KNOB ON FOOTBALL BOOT** one of several knobs fitted to the sole of a football boot or other sports shoe to give a firmer grip on slippery ground 5 **VERTICAL SUPPORT** a vertical post that is one of the uprights supporting a timber wall or partition 6 **HEADLESS BOLT** a headless bolt with threads on both ends separated by a threadless section 7 **PROJECTION ON MACHINE** a short rod or other projection on a machine serving as support for something else ■ *vt* (**studs, studding, studded**) 1 **SUPPLY WITH STUDS** to fit or decorate something with studs ○ *a studded leather jacket* 2 **OCCUR THROUGHOUT** to be present or visible in all parts of something [Old English *studu* < Indo-European, 'to stand'] ◇ **studded with** scattered or dotted with something

stud[2] /stud/ *n* 1 **BREEDING STALLION** a male animal, especially a stallion, used for breeding 2 **ESTABLISHMENT WITH STALLIONS** a stable or farm where male animals, especially stallions, are kept for breeding 3 **GROUP OF STALLIONS** a group of male animals, especially stallions, used for breeding 4 **SEXUALLY ACTIVE MAN** a man considered to be sexually active or good at sex (*informal*) 5 CARDS = **stud poker** [Old English *stōd* 'standing place'] ◇ **at stud** available for breeding with female animals, especially mares

studbook /stúd bŏŏk/ *n* a book containing a record of the parentage of purebred animals, especially horses or dogs

studdingsail /stúdding sayl, stúnss'l/ *n* an additional sail on an extra yard and boom at either side of a square sail, for use in light winds [Mid-16C. *Studding* < ?]

student /styoōd'nt/ *n* 1 **PERSON STUDYING** a person who studies at school, college, or university 2 **KNOWLEDGEABLE OR INTERESTED PERSON** a person who has studied or takes much interest in a specific subject ○ *a student of human foibles* ■ *adj* **IN TRAINING FOR JOB** studying as part of the training for a job or profession ○ *student pilots* [15C. Alteration of Old French *estudiant* < Latin *student-*, present participle of *studere* (see STUDY).]

student body *n US* the students of a school collectively

student loan *n* a loan taken by a student to pay for

educational expenses, usually at a favourable rate of interest that is subsidized by the government

studentship /styoōd'nt ship/ *n* EDUC = **scholarship** *n.* 1

Student's t-test *n* STATS = **t-test** [After *Student*, pen name of W. S. Gosset (1876–1937), British statistician.]

students' union *n* **1** an organization of students in a college or university that represents students' interests **2** a building or area at a college or university with a bar and other facilities for the social or recreational activities of students. US term **student union**

student teacher *n* somebody who is studying and training to become a teacher

student union *n* US EDUC = **students' union** *n.* 2

studhorse /stúd hawrss/ *n* a stallion used for breeding [Old English *stod hors*]

studied /stúddid/ *adj* thought about or planned in advance rather than being spontaneous ○ *an air of studied nonchalance*

~~**studing**~~ incorrect spelling of **studying**

studio /styoōdi ō/ *n* **1** ARTIST'S WORKPLACE a place where an artist, photographer, or musician works **2** RECORDING PRODUCTION ROOM a room or building equipped for making films, television or radio productions, or musical recordings **3** US = **studio flat** **4** DANCE SCHOOL a place where dance is taught or can be practised **5** FILM COMPANY a commercial film production company ■ **studios** *npl* FILM PRODUCTION BUILDINGS all the buildings connected with a film production company, used for shooting and producing films [Early 19C. Via Italian < Latin *studium* (see STUDY).]

studio apartment *n* US = **studio flat**

studio couch *n* a usually backless sofa that can be converted into a double bed by sliding out a frame from underneath

studio flat *n* a small one-roomed flat, perhaps with a separate kitchen and bathroom

studio system *n* a process for making a large number of films economically, efficiently, and simultaneously, as used by the major Hollywood studios from the silent era into the 1950s

studious /styoōdi əss/ *adj* **1** having a thoughtful nature and given to studying **2** careful and painstaking, with considerable attention to detail ○ *a studious investigation* [14C. < Latin *studiosus* < *studium* (see STUDY).] —**studiously** *adv* —**studiousness** *n*

studmuffin /stúd mufin/ *n* US a man regarded as being physically attractive (*slang*)

stud poker *n* a variety of poker in which all but the first card are dealt face up, allowing players to see one another's hands [Mid-19C. Probably shortening of earlier *studhorse poker* < ?]

study /stúddi/ *v* (**-ies, -ying, -ied**) **1** *vti* LEARN ABOUT to learn about a particular subject by reading and researching **2** *vti* TAKE EDUCATIONAL COURSE to follow a course at college or university **3** *vt* INVESTIGATE to discover facts about something by doing research or experiments ○ *a team of researchers studying the effects of sleep deprivation* **4** *vt* LOOK AT AND CONSIDER to look at or read something and think about it carefully ○ *He studied the map, frowning.* **5** *vt* LEARN LINES to learn the lines spoken by a character in a play ■ *n* (*plural* **-ies**) **1** PROCESS OF LEARNING the process of learning about a subject by reading, thought, intuition, or research ○ *devoted the afternoons to study* **2** INVESTIGATION an investigation or research project designed to discover facts about something **3** REPORT ON RESEARCH a report or book describing an investigation or piece of research **4** ROOM FOR STUDYING a room used for work that involves reading, thinking, or writing **5** PREPARATORY WORK OF ART a small drawing or sculpture done as preparation for a larger work **6** INSTRUMENTAL WORK an instrumental work intended for teaching or practice **7** ACTOR LEARNING LINES a learner of a role in a play, relative to the amount of time needed to learn it ○ *she's a quick study* ■ **studies** *npl* SUBJECT OF STUDY a particular subject of study, especially as an educational course or academic specialization ○ *social studies* [12C. Via Old French *estudier* (verb) and *estudie* (noun) < Latin *studium* 'zeal, care' < *studere* 'be diligent'.] ◇ **in a brown study** deep in thought (*dated*)

study hall *n* US **1** a period during the school day assigned for study rather than classroom instruction **2** a schoolroom used for independent study rather than instruction

stuff /stuf/ *vt* **1** FILL to fill something by pushing things into it ○ *What are you stuffing the cushions with?* **2** PUSH THINGS INTO CONTAINER to push things into a container, often hurriedly or forcefully **3** PUT HURRIEDLY to put something somewhere in a quick careless way ○ *stuffed it under the pillow, out of sight* **4** EAT TOO MUCH to eat or feed somebody a lot of food **5** FILL FOOD WITH STUFFING to put stuffing or filling into food such as pasta, meat, or vegetables **6** PRESERVE DEAD ANIMAL to fill a dead animal's skin with material to make it look lifelike and suitable for display **7** US, Can SUBMIT INVALID VOTES to put invalid ballots into a ballot box to rig an election **8** BEAT OPPONENT THOROUGHLY to beat an opponent or opposing team easily and thoroughly **9** OFFENSIVE TERM an offensive term meaning to have sex with a woman (*taboo*) **10** TREAT LEATHER to treat leather with chemicals that preserve and soften it ■ *n* **1** THINGS material things generally, especially when unidentified, worthless, or unwanted ○ *What's all this stuff doing in my office?* **2** WORDS OR ACTION action, speech, or writing of a particular kind ○ *all that stuff in the news about changing weather patterns* ○ *I really like her stuff.* **3** POSSESSIONS personal possessions ○ *called by to collect her stuff* **4** PERSONAL QUALITIES personal qualities of a particular kind ○ *She's got the stuff heroes are made of.* **5** SPECIALITY something that somebody does uniquely or very well **6** FOOLISH WORDS OR ACTION foolish or blameworthy action, speech, or writing **7** MONEY money (*slang*) **8** DRUGS a drug, especially heroin (*informal*) **9** WOOLLEN FABRIC woollen fabric, especially as distinguished from fabric made from other natural fibres ■ *interj* USED TO DISMISS used, often with 'it', to dismiss something angrily or carelessly (*slang*) [14C. < Old French *estoffer* 'equip' < Germanic.] —**stuffer** *n* ◇ **get stuffed** an offensive phrase expressing disagreement or impatience (*slang*) ◇ **do your stuff** to do what is required or expected ◇ **strut your stuff** **1** US to do something impressively, suggesting talent for it or thorough preparation (*slang*) **2** to dance, especially in an expressive way (*informal*) ◇ **that's the stuff** used to indicate satisfaction with what has been done or given

stuff up *vti* to make a mess of something (*informal*)

stuffed /stuft/ *adj* **1** filled with stuffing or some other filling **2** completely full, especially after eating too much (*informal*)

stuffed shirt *n* a pompous, formal, or self-important person (*informal*)

stuffing /stúffing/ *n* **1** a mixture of well-flavoured or highly seasoned ingredients used to stuff meat or vegetables **2** feathers, fabric, or artificial fibre used as filling for cushions or pillows ◇ **knock the stuffing out of somebody** **1** to beat or defeat somebody severely (*informal*) **2** to have a sudden or immediate weakening effect on somebody (*informal*)

stuffing box *n* an enclosure containing compressed packing that is used to prevent leakage around a moving part such as a piston rod

stuffy /stúffi/ (**-ier, -iest**) *adj* **1** AIRLESS without any fresh air, and often too warm **2** STRAIT-LACED too old-fashioned, strict, or conventional **3** BLOCKED WITH MUCUS blocked up with mucus, making breathing difficult ○ *a stuffy nose* —**stuffily** *adv* —**stuffiness** *n*

stull /stul/ *n* a supporting timber in a mine or mineshaft [Late 18C. < ?]

stultify /stúlti fī/ (**-fies, -fying, -fied**) *vt* **1** DIMINISH INTEREST to diminish somebody's interest and liveliness of mind by being repetitive, tedious, and boring **2** MAKE SOMEBODY SEEM STUPID to cause somebody or something to seem unintelligent or silly **3** RENDER USELESS to render something useless or ineffectual **4** PROVE SOMEBODY INCAPABLE OF LEGAL RESPONSIBILITY to show or allege somebody to be not legally responsible because of a psychiatric disorder or instability [Mid-18C. < late Latin *stultificare* 'make foolish' < Latin *stultus* 'foolish', literally 'immovable'.] —**stultification** /stúltifi káysh'n/ *n* —**stultifier** *n*

stum /stum/ *n* WINE = **must**[2] ■ *vt* (**stums, stumming, stummed**) to ferment wine by adding stum to it while it is in a cask or vat [Mid-17C. < Dutch *stom* 'dumb', a translation of French *muet*.]

stumble /stúmb'l/ *vi* (**-bles, -bling, -bled**) **1** TRIP OVER to trip when walking or running **2** WALK UNSTEADILY to walk unsteadily, as if intoxicated **3** SPEAK OR ACT HESITATINGLY to speak or act hesitatingly, confusedly, or incompetently ○ *spoke the verse without stumbling* **4** FIND BY CHANCE to find or come across something by chance ○ *I stumbled across the note while I was cleaning the closet.* ■ *n* **1** ACT OF TRIPPING an instance of tripping over something **2** MISTAKE a mistake or hesitation [14C. Probably < assumed Old Norse *stumla*, variant of *stumra* 'walk unsteadily' < Germanic.] —**stumbler** *n* —**stumblingly** *adv*

SYNONYMS See ***hesitate***.

stumblebum /stúmb'l bum/ *n* US an offensive term for somebody who appears to do things in a blundering unskilful way (*slang insult*)

stumbling block *n* something that stands in the way of achieving a goal or of understanding something [Early 16C. Translation of Greek *proskomma* 'something you stumble against'.]

stumer /styoōmər/ *n* a forged or fraudulent item such as a banknote (*slang*) [Late 19C. < ?]

stumm *adj* = **shtoom** (*informal*)

stump /stump/ *n* **1** BASE OF A TREE the base of a tree trunk and its roots after the tree has been felled **2** REMAINING SMALL PART the part of something such as a limb that is left after the main part has been cut off or removed **3** PART OF WICKET in cricket, each of the three upright posts that form part of the wicket **4** CYLINDRICAL IMPLEMENT USED IN DRAWING a short cylindrical piece of rolled paper, cork, rubber, or leather with ends formed into a point, used in drawing especially to soften lines and in representing shade and shadow ■ **stumps** *npl* LEGS somebody's legs (*slang*) ■ *v* **1** *vt* BAFFLE to baffle somebody by presenting a problem that seems impossible to solve **2** *vt* DISMISS BATSMAN BY TOUCHING THE STUMPS to get a batsman out by knocking a bail off the wicket with the ball while the batsman is out of the crease **3** *vi* US CAMPAIGN to campaign for elective office (*informal*) **4** *vi* WALK HEAVILY to walk heavily and often angrily **5** *vt* LOP to lop the top off a tree, leaving a stump **6** *vt* REMOVE STUMPS to clear an area of land of tree stumps [13C. < Middle Low German, < Germanic.] —**stumper** *n* ◇ **on the stump** US, Can engaged in making political speeches to win office (*informal*)

stump up *vt* to pay the amount of money that is asked (*informal*) [Originally, 'dig up by the roots']

stumpage /stúmpij/ *n* US standing timber, or the amount of money it would bring if felled

stumpwork /stúmp wurk/ *n* raised embroidery, with small decorative stitches made over pieces of padding [Early 20C. Because the designs are raised upon stumps of wood.]

stumpy /stúmpi/ (**-ier, -iest**) *adj* short, thick, and unattractive —**stumpiness** *n*

stun /stun/ (**stuns, stunning, stunned**) *vt* **1** MAKE UNCONSCIOUS to make a person or animal unconscious for a short time with a blow or by using a drug **2** SHOCK to shock, upset, or amaze somebody ○ *a tragedy that left the nation stunned and bewildered* **3** OVERWHELM to overwhelm one of the senses, e.g. with loud noise or very bright light [14C. Via Anglo-Norman *estuner* < assumed Vulgar Latin *extonare* < Latin *tonare* 'thunder'.]

stung past tense, past participle of **sting**

stun gun *n* a gun used for stunning animals or people for a short while without causing injury

stunk past tense, past participle of **stink**

stunner /stúnnər/ *n* **1** an impressive or beautiful person or thing (*informal*) **2** ARMS = **stun gun**

stunning /stúnning/ *adj* strikingly impressive or attractive in appearance ○ *They looked stunning at the reception.* —**stunningly** *adv*

stunsail /stúnss'l/ *n* NAUT = **studdingsail** [Mid-18C. Contraction of STUDDINGSAIL.]

stunt[1] /stunt/ *vt* RESTRICT GROWTH to restrict the growth of something so that it does not develop to its normal size ■ *n* **1** SOMETHING NOT FULLY DEVELOPED something that has not grown to its normal size because its growth has been restricted **2** PLANT DISEASE a plant disease resulting in retarded growth [Old English, 'unintelligent, dull' < Germanic]

stunt[2] /stunt/ *n* **1** DANGEROUS FEAT something dangerous that is done as a challenge or to entertain people **2** SOMETHING UNUSUAL DONE FOR ATTENTION something silly or unusual that is done to attract attention ○ *a publicity stunt* ■ *vi* PERFORM STUNTS to perform dangerous feats as a challenge or to entertain people [Late 19C. < ?]

stuntman /stúnt man/ (*plural* **-men** /-men/) *n* a man whose job is to take the place of an actor in a scene involving danger or requiring acrobatic skill

stuntwoman /stúnt wŏŏmən/ (*plural* **-en** /-wimin/) *n* a woman whose job is to take the place of an actor in a scene involving danger or requiring acrobatic skill

stupa /stóopə/ *n* a Buddhist shrine, temple, or pagoda that houses a relic or marks the location of an auspicious event [Late 19C. < Sanskrit *stūpah*.]

stupe /styoop/ *n* a hot, damp, sometimes medicated, cloth or sponge applied in former times to the skin as a compress or a counterirritant to relieve pain [14C. Via Latin *stuppa* 'tow' < Greek *stuppē*; from the use of tow in making compresses.]

stupefacient /styòopi fáysh'nt/ *adj* causing stupor ■ *n* a drug or other agent that causes stupor [Mid-17C. < Latin *stupefacient-*, present participle of *stupefacere* (see STUPEFY).]

stupefaction /styòopi fáksh'n/ *n* **1** great amazement or astonishment (*literary*) **2** the inability to think clearly because of boredom, tiredness, or amazement [15C. Via French < Latin *stupefacere* (see STUPEFY).]

stupefy /styóopi fī/ (**-fies, -fying, -fied**) *vt* **1** to amaze or astonish somebody **2** to make somebody unable to think clearly because of boredom, tiredness, or amazement [15C. Via French *stupéfier* < Latin *stupefacere* < *stupere* 'be stunned' (see STUPID) + *facere* 'make'.] —**stupefier** *n* —**stupefyingly** *adv*

stupendous /styoo péndəss/ *adj* impressively large, excellent, or great in extent or degree ○ *a stupendous achievement* [Mid-17C. < Latin *stupendus*, the gerundive of *stupere* 'be stunned'.] —**stupendously** *adv* —**stupendousness** *n*

stupid /styóopid/ *adj* **1 UNINTELLIGENT** thought to show a lack of intelligence, perception, or common sense ○ *a stupid mistake* **2 SILLY** irritatingly silly or time-wasting ○ *had us playing stupid games* **3 EXPRESSING IRRITATION** used to express anger, annoyance, or frustration (*informal*) ○ *I can't get the stupid thing to work!* **4 DAZED** in a dazed state, e.g. from shock, fatigue, or from the effects of drugs or alcohol ○ *almost stupid with tiredness* [Mid-16C. < Latin *stupidus* < *stupere* 'be stunned'.]

stupidity /styoo píddəti/ (*plural* **-ties**) *n* **1** lack of intelligence, perception, or common sense **2** extremely rash or thoughtless behaviour

stupidly /styóopidli/ *adv* **1** in a way that demonstrates lack of intelligence, perception, or common sense ○ *I had stupidly forgotten to note down the date I mailed it.* **2** in a way that suggests diminished ability to perceive or reason ○ *He gazed stupidly after her.*

~~**stupify**~~ incorrect spelling of **stupefy**

stupor /styóopər/ *n* **1** an acute lack of mental alertness brought on e.g. by shock or lack of sleep **2** a state of near-unconsciousness induced by e.g. drugs or alcohol [14C. < Latin, < *stupere* 'be stunned'.] —**stuporous** *adj*

sturdy /stúrdi/ (**-dier, -diest**) *adj* **1 WELL MADE** solidly made and likely to withstand prolonged use **2 WITH A STRONG BUILD** having a well-developed strong-looking body and limbs **3 RESOLUTE** having or displaying decisiveness, resoluteness, or firmness of purpose ○ *sturdy defenders of the right to free speech* [13C. Via Old French *estourdir* 'dazed' < Latin *turdus* 'thrush', formerly associated with drunkenness. The earliest sense was 'recklessly violent'.] —**sturdily** *adv* —**sturdiness** *n*

sturgeon /stúrjən/ (*plural* **-geons** *or* **-geon**) *n* **1** a large bottom-feeding fish with a long snout and tough bony-plated skin. Native to: northern rivers, coastal waters. Family: Acipenseridae. **2** the flesh of a sturgeon as food [13C. < Old French *esturgeon* < Germanic.]

Sturluson /stúrlòoss'n/, **Snorri** (1179–1241) Icelandic poet and historian

Sturmer /stúrmər/ *n* a pale green English variety of eating apple [Mid-19C. After a village on the border of Essex and Suffolk.]

Sturm und Drang /shtóorm òont dráng/ *n* **1** a movement in late 18th-century German literature whose works typically portray the tortured emotions of a central character who violently rejects society **2** a state of extreme emotional upheaval (*literary*) ○ *films that explore his own personal Sturm und Drang* [Late 18C. < German, 'storm and stress'.]

Sturt /sturt/, **Charles** (1795–1869) British explorer and administrator

Sturt's desert pea *n* an Australian plant of the bean family whose bright red flower is the emblem of South Australia. *Clianthus formosus.* [Mid-19C. After Charles STURT.]

Sturt's desert rose *n* an Australian shrub whose pink flower is the emblem of the Northern Territory. *Gossypium sturtianum.* [Mid-20C. After Charles STURT.]

stushie /stóoshi/, **stishie** /stíshi/ *n Scotland* (*informal*) **1** a bout or scene of heated discussion or argument **2** a nervous, anxious, or upset state ○ *She was in a right stushie about the exam.* [Early 19C. < Scots dialect < ?]

stutter /stúttər/ *v* **1** *vti* **SAY OR SPEAK WITH STAMMER** to say something haltingly, repeating sounds frequently when attempting to pronounce them, either from nervousness or as the result of a speech disorder ○ *managed to stutter an apology* **2** *vi* **MAKE SHORT NOISES** to make repeated short noises that suggest mechanical inefficiency or failure ○ *The motor stuttered briefly and then died again.* ■ *n* **1 STAMMERING AS A SPEECH DISORDER** a speech disorder that makes the speaker repeat certain speech sounds that are found difficult to pronounce ○ *has a slight stutter* **2 BURST OF REPEATED SOUNDS** a burst of repeated short sounds [Early 16C. Alteration of obsolete *stut* < Germanic.] —**stutterer** *n* —**stuttering** *adj* —**stutteringly** *adv*

Stuttgart /stóot gaart/ capital of Baden-Württemberg State, SW Germany. Population: 592,000 (1994).

STV *abbr* **1** Scottish Television **2** single transferable vote

sty[1] /stī/ *n* (*plural* **sties**) an enclosure in which pigs are kept ■ *vt* (**sties, stying, stied**) to put or keep a pig in a sty [Old English *stī* 'pen'. Variant of *stig* (see STEWARD).]

sty[2] /stī/ (*plural* **sties**), **stye** *n* a temporary swelling on an eyelid at the base of an eyelash [Early 17C. By folk etymology from obsolete *styanye*, as if 'sty-on-eye'.]

Stygian /stíjji ən/ *adj* **1 PITCH-BLACK** unremittingly dark and frightening, as hell is imagined to be (*literary*) **2 OF THE STYX** relating to the Styx, the river in Greek mythology that the souls of the dead were ferried across into Hades **3 BINDING** eternally binding, as were promises sworn on the banks of the river Styx in Greek mythology (*literary*) [Mid-16C. Via Latin *Stygius* < Greek *Stugios* < *Stux* (see STYX).]

styl- *prefix* = **stylo-** (*before vowels*)

stylar /stílər/ *adj* relating to or using a stylus

style /stīl/ *n* **1 DISTINCTIVE FORM** a distinctive and identifiable form in an artistic medium such as music, architecture, or literature ○ *a facade in the neoclassical style* ○ *a different style of jazz* **2 WAY OF DOING** a way of doing something, especially a way regarded as expressing a particular attitude or typifying a particular period (*often in combination*) ○ *a hands-on management style* ○ *old-style politics* ○ *Confrontation just isn't his style.* ○ *Self-catering holidays were not really her style.* **3 WAY OF WRITING OR PERFORMING** the way in which something is written or performed as distinct from the content of the writing or performance **4 FLAIR** impressive flair in the way something is done, especially a quality that suggests a self-confident willingness to exhibit skill or good taste ○ *furnished with impeccable style* **5 FASHIONABLE STATUS** fashionable status or quality ○ *a look that has gone out of style* **6 FASHION** an example of cut or shape of garment or way of wearing the hair ○ *dressed in all the latest styles* **7 LUXURIOUSNESS** extravagance or lavishness ○ *dining in style* **8 PUBLISHING CONVENTIONS** the ways in which written material is presented, usually in a particular publication or by a particular publisher ○ *editing text into the publisher's house style* **9 FLOWER PART** an extension of a flower's ovary, shaped like a stalk, that supports the stigma **10** ZOOL = **stylet** *n.* 2 **11** ARTS = **stylus** *n.* 3 **12 TITLE** a name or title, especially one that is official or legally correct (*formal*) ■ *vt* (**styles, styling, styled**) **1 SHAPE** to give something a particular shape or design **2 CAUSE TO CONFORM** to bring something into conformity with a particular style **3 NAME** to give somebody or something a name or title (*formal*) [13C. Via Old French < Latin *stilus* 'writing instrument, style'.] —**styler** *n* ◇ **cramp somebody's style** to restrict what somebody is able to do, often by limiting the person's capacity to impress others (*informal*)

SPELLCHECK See ***stile***.

stylebook /stíl bòok/ *n* a publishing company's gathered conventions in presenting printed material, used as a guide by writers and editors

stylet /stílət/ *n* **1 WIRE PREVENTING BLOCKAGE IN A NEEDLE** a fine wire inserted into a catheter or hollow needle to prevent it from becoming blocked when not in use **2 PART SHAPED LIKE A BRISTLE** a thin long organ or appendage shaped like a bristle, e.g. any of the mouthparts of some insects **3 LONG POINTED INSTRUMENT** any long thin pointed instrument (*formal*) [Late 17C. Via French < Italian *stiletto* (see STILETTO).]

styli plural of **stylus**

styli- *prefix* = **stylo-**

styling *n* **1** the act or an instance of giving a particular shape or design to somebody's hair (*often before nouns*) ○ *styling mousse* **2** an instance of creating something, especially something artistic, in a particular or idiosyncratic way (*informal*) ○ *the zany comedy stylings of the country's favourite stand-up*

stylise *vt* = **stylize**

stylish /stílish/ *adj* **1** having confident good taste and appreciation of what is fashionable **2** having or showing impressive skill or accomplishment ○ *the most stylish player in the team* —**stylishly** *adv* —**stylishness** *n*

stylist /stílist/ *n* **1 HAIRDRESSER** a hairdresser, especially a more senior hairdresser in a salon **2 ACCOMPLISHED ARTIST** somebody whose creative work shows a distinctive and accomplished style **3 DESIGNER** a designer who is consulted on matters of style, especially somebody responsible for creating a distinctive visual image for a product or company **4 SOMEBODY WHO PREPARES A SCENE TO BE PHOTOGRAPHED** somebody employed to set up scenes to be photographed in a magazine, including supplying any accessories or decorative objects required

stylistic /stī lístik/ *adj* relating to matters of style, especially in literature and the arts ○ *stylistic brilliance compromised by a certain thinness of content* —**stylistically** *adv*

stylistics /stī lístiks/ *n* the branch of linguistics that deals with determining which features of written or spoken language characterize particular groups or contexts, especially particular literary genres or works (+ *singular verb*)

stylite /stí līt/ *n* a Christian ascetic in ancient times who lived alone on top of a tall pillar [Mid-17C. < late Greek *stulitēs* < Greek *stulos* 'pillar'.] —**stylitic** /stī líttik/ *adj*

stylize /stí līz/ (**-izes, -izing, -ized**), **stylise** (**-ises, -ising, -ised**) *vt* to give something a distinctive, often artificial artistic style —**stylization** /stí lī záysh'n/ *n* —**stylized** *adj* —**stylizer** *n*

stylo- *prefix* style, column ○ *stylograph* ○ *styloid* [< Latin *stylus* (see STYLUS)]

stylobate /stílə bayt/ *n* a continuous raised platform of masonry supporting a row of columns [Mid-16C. Via Latin *stylobata* < Greek *stulobatēs* 'column step'.]

stylograph /stílō graaf, -graf/ *n* a fountain pen that has a thin hollow tube as its writing point instead of the traditional nib

stylography /stī lóggrəfi/ *n* the art of drawing or engraving using a stylus —**stylographic** /stílō gráffik/ *adj* —**stylographically** *adv*

styloid /stí loyd/ *adj* describes a bony protuberance (**process**) that is long and thin

stylophone /stílə fōn/ *n* a small battery-operated musical instrument with a surface like a keyboard, played using an electronic pen

stylus /stíləss/ (*plural* **-li** /-lī/) *n* **1 RECORD PLAYER NEEDLE** the jewel-tipped needle of a record player that rests in the grooves of a record as it revolves and transmits vibrations to the cartridge **2 MACHINE'S TRACING PEN** the tracing pen on an electronic device such as a seismograph or polygraph that converts an electrical signal into a written record **3 ENGRAVING TOOL** a pointed instrument used for engraving, especially one used in ancient times for writing on clay or wax tablets [Early 18C. < Latin, a spelling variant of *stilus* 'stake, pointed writing instrument' < Greek *stulos* 'pillar'.]

stymie /stími/, **stymy** *vt* (**-mies, -mieing, -mied**; **-mies, -mying, -mied**) **1 HINDER THE PROGRESS OF** to prevent somebody or something from making further progress **2 BLOCK AN OPPONENT'S LINE** to obstruct the line between a golf opponent's ball and the hole (*dated*) ■ *n* (*plural* **-mies**) **1 PROBLEM SITUATION** a situation in which obstacles hinder progress **2 OBSTRUCTION OF AN OPPONENT'S BALL** a situation in which one golf player's ball blocks another's. In the modern game, the obstructing ball is lifted and replaced by a marker. (*dated*) [Mid-19C. < ?]

stypsis /stípsiss/ *n* the use of a styptic substance, or its antibleeding effect [Late 19C. Via late Latin < Greek *stupsis* < *stuphein* 'contract'.]

styptic /stíptik/ *adj* slowing down the rate of bleeding or stopping bleeding altogether, whether by causing the blood vessels to contract or by accelerating clotting ■

n a styptic drug, cream, or lotion [14C. Via late Latin *stypticus* < Greek *stuptikos* < *stuphein* 'contract'.]

styptic pencil *n* an astringent substance in solid form in a small cylindrical container that is applied to stop bleeding in small cuts, e.g. after shaving

styrax *n* TREES = **storax** *n.* 3

styrene /stī reen/ *n* C_8H_8 a colourless flammable liquid hydrocarbon. Use: manufacture of synthetic rubber, plastic. [Late 19C. < Latin *styrax* (see STORAX) + -ENE.]

Styrofoam /stīrə fōm/ *tdmk* a trademark for a light plastic material used to make disposable items, insulation, and packing materials

Styron /stīrən/, **William** (*b.* 1925) US writer

STYS *abbr* speak to you soon (*in e-mails*)

Styx /stiks/ *n* in Greek mythology, the river across which the souls of the dead were ferried into the underworld [14C. Via Latin < Greek *Stux*.]

SU *abbr* strontium unit

Suárez González /swaar ez gon zaal ez/, **Adolfo** (*b.* 1932) Spanish statesman

suave /swaav/ (**suaver, suavest**) *adj* **1** polite and charming, especially in a way that seems affected or insincere **2** well groomed and smartly dressed (*informal*) [Early 16C. Via French or directly < Latin *suavis* 'sweet, agreeable' < Indo-European.] —**suavely** *adv* —**suaveness** *n* —**suavity** /swaavəti/ *n*

sub[1] /sub/ *n* (*informal*) **1 A SUBSTITUTE** a substitute, especially a substitute player in a game **2 SUBEDITOR** a subeditor **3 SUBALTERN** a subaltern **4 SMALL LOAN** a small sum of money borrowed, especially a small advance on wages due ○ *You could ask her for a sub.* **5 SUBSCRIPTION FEE** a subscription fee ○ *Have you paid your subs for this season?* **6 SUBTITLE** a subtitle to a document or printed matter ■ *v* (**subs, subbing, subbed**) (*informal*) **1** *vi* **REPLACE** to take the place of somebody temporarily, usually in a work situation **2** *vti* **SUBCONTRACT** to subcontract work, or work as a subcontractor **3** *vt* **SUBTITLE** to add subtitles to something **4** *vti* **SUBEDIT** to subedit something, or work as a subeditor **5** *vt* **LEND MONEY** to lend somebody a small amount of money, especially as an advance on wages due ○ *He could have subbed me a few quid until payday.* [Late 17C. Shortening.]

sub[2] /sub/ *n* (*informal*) **1** a submarine **2** *US* a sandwich made with a long roll cut horizontally

sub- *prefix* **1** under, below, beneath ○ *subcutaneous* ○ *subfloor* **2** subordinate, secondary ○ *subparagraph* **3** less than completely ○ *subliterate* **4** subdivision ○ *subkingdom* ○ *subcontinent* **5** bordering on ○ *subequatorial* **6** smaller or younger than ○ *subcompact* ○ *subteen* **7** nearly, partly, somewhat ○ *subfossil* **8** containing less than the normal amount of an element ○ *suboxide* [< Latin *sub* 'under']

subacid /súb ássid/ *adj* mildly unkind or critical in tone (*literary*) —**subacidity** /súbbə síddəti/ *n* —**subacidly** *adv*

subacute /súbə kyoōt/ *adj* describes a medical condition that develops less rapidly and with less severity than an acute condition —**subacutely** *adv*

subacute sclerosing panencephalitis /-pán en seffə lītiss/ *n* a severe, usually fatal, inflammatory disease of the brain, chiefly affecting children and linked to infection from measles

subaerial /súb airi əl/ *adj* formed or situated on or just below the surface of the soil ○ *a plant with subaerial roots*

subalpine /súb ál pīn/ *adj* relating to or growing naturally on the lower slopes of mountains, especially the areas below the tree line

subaltern /súbb'ltərn/ *n* **1 JUNIOR OFFICER** an officer in the British Army of a rank below captain, especially a second lieutenant **2 SUBORDINATE PERSON** a person holding a subordinate or inferior position **3 IMPLIED PROPOSITION** a particular proposition that is implied by a universal proposition ■ *adj* **1 SUBORDINATE** in a subordinate or inferior position **2 IMPLIED** in logic, implied as a particular proposition by a universal proposition [Late 16C. < late Latin *subalternus* < Latin *alternus* 'alternate' (see ALTERNATE).]

subalternate /sub áwltərnət, -ól-/ *adj* **1** describes a leaf whose leaflets are arranged in semistaggered rows, neither fully alternate nor fully opposite **2** in a subordinate or inferior position —**subalternation** /sub áwltər náysh'n, sub ól-/ *n*

subantarctic /súb ant áarktik/ *adj* relating to the area between the Antarctic Circle and the South Pole

subapostolic /súb apə stóllik/ *adj* belonging to the period in the history of the Christian Church that immediately followed the time of the Apostles

subaqua /súb ákwə/ *adj* relating to or providing facilities for underwater sports such as scuba diving [Mid-20C. < SUB- + Latin *aqua* 'water'.]

subaquatic /súbə kwáttik/ *adj* **1** existing or able to exist partly in water and partly on land **2** relating or belonging to underwater regions

subaqueous /súb áykwi əss/ *adj* living, found, or formed under water

subarachnoid /súbə ráknoyd/ *adj* situated beneath the middle of the three membranes (**arachnoids**) that cover the brain and spinal cord

subarctic /súb áarktik/ *adj* **1** relating to the area bordering the Arctic Circle to the south **2** similar to the regions that border the Arctic Circle, e.g. in landscape or weather conditions

subassembly /súbə sémbli/ (*plural* **-blies**) *n* a group of pieces assembled separately and incorporated into a larger assembled structure

subatomic /súbə tómmik/ *adj* **1** occurring as part of an atom, or smaller than an atom ○ *a subatomic particle* **2** on a scale smaller than the atom, or involving phenomena at this level

subaudition /súb awdísh'n/ *n* **1** the act of understanding a word or thought that is implied but not actually expressed in speech or writing **2** a word, idea, or thought understood by a hearer or reader that is implied but not expressed [Mid-17C. < late Latin *subaudition-*, stem of *subauditio* < Latin *audire* 'hear'.]

subaxillary /súb ak sílləri/ *adj* **1** located beneath the armpit **2** growing beneath the axil in plants

subbase /súb bayss/ *n* **1** a deep layer of large stones that forms the lowest level of a roadbed or of the foundation of a building **2** the lowest section of any base or foundation, e.g. the bottom part of a pedestal

subbasement /súb bayssmənt/ *n* a storey below the basement in a building

sub-bituminous /súb bi tyoōminəss/ *adj* describes a type of soft coal that has an intermediate carbon content

subcalibre /sub kállibər/ *adj* describes ammunition whose calibre is smaller than that of the gun from which it is fired

subcartilaginous /súb kaarti lájjinəss/ *adj* **1** lying beneath cartilage or a body part composed of cartilage **2** made up partly of cartilage

subcategory /súb katəgəri/ (*plural* **-ries**) *n* any one of the smaller sections into which a main category is divided

subcellular /súb séllyoōlər/ *adj* **1** existing inside a cell, or relating to the component parts of cells **2** on a scale smaller than a cell, or involving phenomena at this level

subcentre /súb sentər/ *n* US a centre that is subsidiary to a main one, particularly an out-of-town shopping centre —**subcentral** *adj* —**subcentrally** *adv*

subclass /súb klaass/ *n* **1** any of the smaller groups into which a main class is divided **2** a subdivision of a class in the classification of plants and animals **3** MATH = **subset**

subclavian /sub kláyvi ən/ *adj* located under the collarbone (**clavicle**) [Mid-17C. < modern Latin *subclavius* < Latin *clavis* 'key'.]

subclinical /sub klínnik'l/ *adj* describes an early stage or mild form of a medical condition, no symptoms of which are detectable —**subclinically** *adv*

subcommittee /súbkəmiti/ *n* a committee set up by and consisting of members of an existing committee to deal with a particular issue

subcompact *n* US a small car, usually the smallest and lightest model in a manufacturer's range

subconscious /sub kónshəss/ *adj* present in your mind without you being aware of it ■ *n* mental activity not directly perceived by your consciousness, from which memories, feelings, or thoughts can influence your behaviour without you realizing it —**subconsciously** *adv* —**subconsciousness** *n*

subcontinent /sub kóntinənt/, **Subcontinent** *n* a large area that is an identifiably separate part of a continent, especially the area encompassing the countries of India, Pakistan, and Bangladesh regarded as a distinct part of Asia —**subcontinental** /súb konti nént'l/ *adj, n*

subcontract /súb kon trakt/ *n* **SECONDARY CONTRACT** a secondary contract in which the person or company originally hired in turn hires somebody else to do all or part of the work ■ /súbkən trákt/ *v* **1** *vt* **GIVE WORK UNDER A SUBCONTRACT** to pass on work to a second person or company under the terms of a subcontract **2** *vi* **TAKE ON WORK FROM A CONTRACTOR** to work on contract with a person or company who is a contractor to somebody else —**subcontractor** *n*

subcontrary /sub kóntrəri/ *adj* describes logical propositions that are related to each other in such a way that both cannot be false at the same time, although both may be true ■ *n* (*plural* **-ies**) a subcontrary logical proposition [Early 17C. < late Latin *subcontrarius*, a translation of Greek *hupenantios* 'contrary'.]

subcortex /sub káwrteks/ (*plural* **-tices** /-seez/) *n* the parts of the brain that lie immediately beneath the cerebral cortex —**subcortical** *adj*

subcranial /sub kráyni əl/ *adj* located beneath the dome of the skull

subculture /súb kulchər/ *n* **1** an identifiably separate social group within a larger culture, especially one regarded as existing outside mainstream society **2** a bacterial culture that is grown from another culture —**subcultural** *adj*

subcutaneous /súbkyoō táyni əss/ *adj* located, living, or made beneath the skin —**subcutaneously** *adv*

subdeacon /sub deēkən/ *n* **1** a member of the Roman Catholic clergy who acts as a deacon's assistant, e.g. by preparing the vessels that are to be used in celebrating Mass **2** a clergyman ranking just above a lector in an Eastern Church

subdiaconate /súb dī ákənət, -nayt/ *n* the position or term of office of a subdeacon —**subdiaconal** *adj*

subdirectory /súbdi rektəri, -dī-/ (*plural* **-ries**) *n* a directory created within another directory on a magnetic storage device such as a hard disk

subdivide /súbdi vīd/ (**-vides, -viding, -vided**) *v* **1** *vt* to divide a section, or all the sections of something into sections that are smaller still **2** *vi* to be divided, or be able to be divided, into sections that are smaller still —**subdivider** *n*

subdivision /súb divizh'n/ *n* **1** the dividing of a divided part into units that are smaller still **2** a section of something that is itself a division of a larger thing —**subdivisional** *adj*

subdomain /sub də máyn, sub dō-/ *n* ONLINE = **subdomain name**

subdomain name *n* **1** a second level of Internet domain names created by the administrator of the domain **2** a subdivision of the two-letter country domain names into two- or three-letter organizational subdomains, e.g. *ac.uk* for United Kingdom academic sites and *com.au* for Australian commercial sites.

subdominant /sub dómminənt/ *n* **1** the fourth note in a major or minor scale **2** a key, chord, or harmony based on a subdominant

subduct /səb dúkt/ *vi* to be carried under the edge of an adjoining continental or oceanic plate, causing tensions in the Earth's crust that can produce earthquakes or volcanic eruptions [Late 16C. < Latin *subduct-*, past participle of *subducere* 'draw up' < *ducere* 'lead'.] —**subduction** *n*

subdue /səb dyoō/ (**-dues, -duing, -dued**) *vt* **1 BRING UNDER FORCIBLE CONTROL** to bring a person or group of people under control using force **2 SOFTEN** to soften something or make it less intense ○ *idealism subdued by experience* **3 REPRESS** to repress or control feelings or emotions ○ *worked hard to subdue her irritation* [14C. Via Old French *souduire* 'seduce' < Latin *subducere* 'draw up' (see SUBDUCT).] —**subduable** *adj* —**subduer** *n*

subdued /səb dyoōd/ *adj* **1 NOT HARSH** not bright, loud, or intense, or made less bright, loud, or intense ○ *subdued lighting* **2 LOW-SPIRITED** sad or in low spirits **3 QUIET** quiet and restrained ○ *speaking in subdued tones*

subdural /sub dyoórəl/ *adj* beneath the dura mater that covers the brain and spinal cord

subedit /súb éddit/ *vt* to read and correct written material before it is published, particularly for newspapers and magazines, under the general supervision of an editor [Mid-19C. Back-formation < SUBEDITOR.]

subeditor /súb édditər/ *n* **1** an assistant editor helping to prepare material for publication **2** somebody whose job is to read and correct written material before it is published, particularly for newspapers and magazines, under the general supervision of an editor. US term **copyreader**

subequatorial /súbekwə táwri əl/ *adj* relating to or situated in the regions that lie just north and south of the equator

suberin /syoóbərin/ *n* a waxy waterproof substance found in the cell walls of many plants, especially cork [Early 19C. < French *subérine* < Latin *suber* 'cork'.]

subfamily /súb famli/ (*plural* **-lies**) *n* **1** a subdivision of a family in the classification of plants and animals **2** a smaller group of related languages within a language family

subfield /súb feeld/ *n* a mathematical field that is a subset of another field

subfloor /súb flawr/ *n* an underlying layer of rough or unfinished material supporting a finished floor —**subflooring** *n*

subfossil /súb foss'l/ *adj* partially fossilized ■ *n* a partially fossilized organism

subframe /súb fraym/ *n* the underlying metal frame on which a vehicle's bodywork is built

subfreezing /sub freézing/ *adj* lower than 0° Celsius or 32° Fahrenheit

subfusc /súb fusk, sub fúsk/ *adj* dark or drab in colour (*literary*) [Mid-18C. < Latin *subfuscus* 'darkish' < *fuscus* 'dark'.]

subgenus /súb jeenəss, -jenəss/ (*plural* **-genera** /-jénnərə/) *n* a category in the classification of plants and animals that is larger than a species but smaller than a genus

subglacial /sub gláysh'l/ *adj* formed below or at the bottom of a glacier —**subglacially** *adv*

subgrade /súb grayd/ *n* the bed of ground on which the foundations of a road, railway, or building are laid

subgroup /súb groop/ *n* **1** a smaller group distinguished in some way from the larger group of which it is a part **2** a mathematical group whose members are also members of a larger group

subhead /súb hed/, **subheading** /-heding/ *n* a heading or title subordinate to the main one

subhuman /sub hyoómən/ *adj* **1** relating to or displaying behaviour that is distastefully inferior in sophistication, moral standards, or intelligence to what is regarded as normal for human beings ○ *a subhuman thug* **2** at the level of development that is considered just below humans

subindex /sub índeks/ (*plural* **-dexes** *or* **-dices** /-índi seez/) *n* an index to a section of a main classification

subirrigate /sub írri gayt/ (**-gates, -gating, -gated**) *vt* to irrigate land from below the surface of the ground, e.g. with porous pipes laid underground —**subirrigation** /súb iri gáysh'n/ *n*

subito /soóbitō/ *adv* suddenly or abruptly (*musical direction*) [Early 18C. Via Italian < Latin *subire* 'come over'.]

subjacent /sub jáyss'nt/ *adj* (*formal*) **1** lying under or just below something **2** next to something and at a lower level than it ○ *'in the damper tracts of subjacent country and along the river-courses'* (Thomas Hardy, *Jude the Obscure*; 1895) [Late 16C. < Latin *subjacent-*, present participle of *subjacere* 'lie under'.] —**subjacency** *n* —**subjacently** *adv*

subject /súb jékt/ *n* **1 TOPIC** a matter that is being discussed, examined, studied, or otherwise dealt with ○ *the subject of our conversation* **2 COURSE OF STUDY** a branch of learning that forms a course of study (*often plural*) **3 PERSON RULED BY ANOTHER** a person who is ruled by a king, queen, or other authority ○ *British subjects* **4 SOMEBODY TREATED OR ACTED UPON** a person who receives treatment or is the focus of an activity ○ *not an appropriate subject for hypnosis* **5 THING REPRESENTED BY ARTIST** a person who or thing that an artist or photographer represents in a piece of work **6 SOMEBODY FEATURED IN A BIOGRAPHY** the main person written about in a biography **7 GRAMMATICAL PERFORMER OF VERB'S ACTION** the part of a sentence or utterance, a noun, noun phrase, or equivalent, that the rest of the sentence asserts something about and that agrees with the verb. The subject typically performs the action expressed by the verb. 'She' and 'The dog' are the subjects of 'She gave me the book' and 'The dog was found asleep' respectively. **8 MUSICAL THEME** the principal theme or melodic phrase that is developed in a musical composition ■ *adj* **1 PRONE TO** likely to be affected by or with a tendency to be affected by a particular thing ○ *areas subject to flooding* ○ *a child subject to mood swings* **2 RULED** under the control of somebody or something such as a ruler or a law, and obliged to obey ○ *a subject nation* ○ *not subject to the laws that apply in this country* ■ *adv* **DEPENDING** depending on or conditional on somebody or something ○ *The plans have been drawn up, subject to your final approval.* ■ *vt* **1 CAUSE TO HAVE UNPLEASANT EXPERIENCE** to cause somebody to undergo something unpleasant ○ *recruits subjected to rigorous physical training* **2 SUBMIT TO TREATMENT** to make something undergo treatment of a particular kind ○ *proposals subjected to detailed scrutiny* **3 OVERPOWER** to bring a person or group under the power or influence of another person or group ○ *a nation subjected to rule from overseas* [14C. Via Old French < Latin *subjectus* < *subicere* 'place under' < *jacere* 'throw'.]

SYNONYMS ***subject, topic, subject matter, matter, theme, burden***

CORE MEANING: what is under discussion

subject a matter that is under discussion or investigation; **topic** a matter dealt with in a text or discussion; **subject matter** the material dealt with in a film, discussion, or other medium; **matter** the material that is dealt with in speech or writing, as opposed to its presentation; **theme** a distinct, recurring, and unifying idea in music, literature, art, or film; **burden** (*literary*) the main argument or recurrent theme in music or literature.

subjection /səb jéksh'n/ *n* **1** the bringing of a person or people under the control of another, usually by force **2** the subjecting of somebody to something

subjective /səb jéktiv/ *adj* **1 NOT IMPARTIAL** based on somebody's opinions or feelings rather than on facts or evidence ○ *Of course, that's only my subjective impression.* **2 EXISTING BY PERCEPTION** existing only in the mind and not independently of it **3 OBSERVED ONLY BY THE PATIENT** describes a medical condition that is perceived to exist only by the patient and is not recognizable to anyone else **4 RELATING TO THE SUBJECT OF VERB** relating to or forming the subject of a verb —**subjectively** *adv* —**subjectiveness** *n*

subjective idealism *n* a philosophical theory arguing that the external world only exists because it is perceived to exist, and does not have existence of its own

subjectivism /səb jéktivizəm/ *n* **1 THEORY OF VALIDITY OF KNOWLEDGE** a theory stating that people can only have knowledge of what they experience directly **2 THEORY OF VALIDITY OF MORAL STANDARDS** a theory stating that the only valid moral standard is the one imposed by somebody's own conscience, and therefore that society's moral codes are invalid **3 EMPHASIS ON PERSONAL INTERPRETATION** emphasis on personal feelings or responses as opposed to external facts or evidence —**subjectivist** *adj* —**subjectivistic** /səb jékti vístik/ *adj* —**subjectivistically** *adv*

subjectivity /súb jek tívvəti/ *n* **1** interpretation based on personal opinions or feelings rather than on external facts or evidence **2** concentration on personal, individual responses in artistic expression

⚡**subject line** *n* a line in an e-mail that indicates the subject of the message

subject matter *n* the matter dealt with in a book, film, discussion, or other pursuit ○ *contains subject matter unsuitable for children*

SYNONYMS See ***subject***.

subjoin /sub jóyn/ *vt* to add something at the end of what has already been written or said (*formal*)

sub judice /súb joódəssi/ *adj* currently under consideration by a judge or a court of law and therefore not to be commented upon publicly [Early 17C. < Latin, 'under a judge'.]

subjugate /súbjoō gayt/ (**-gates, -gating, -gated**) *vt* to bring somebody, especially a people or nation, under the control of another, e.g. by military conquest [15C. < Latin *subjugat-*, past participle of *subjugare* < *jugum* 'yoke'.] —**subjugable** /súbjəgəb'l/ *adj* —**subjugator** *n*

subjugation /súbjoō gáysh'n/ *n* the act or process of bringing somebody, especially a people or nation, under the control of another, e.g. by military conquest

subjunctive /səb júngktiv/ *n* **1 GRAMMATICAL MOOD** a grammatical mood that expresses doubts, wishes, and possibilities. The verb 'were' is in the subjunctive in the phrase 'if I were you'. **2 SUBJUNCTIVE VERB** a verb or form in the subjunctive ■ *adj* **RELATING TO SUBJUNCTIVE** in or relating to the subjunctive [Mid-16C. Via late Latin *subjunctivus* < Latin *subjungere* 'subordinate' < *jungere* 'join'.] —**subjunctively** *adv*

LANGUAGE NOTE Use of the ***subjunctive*** in English: Most people associate the subjunctive with Latin and Greek, and are sometimes surprised to realize that they are using it themselves as a regular (if now limited) feature of English grammar. The subjunctive is distinguishable from the regular form of verbs (called the *indicative*) only in the third person singular present tense, which omits the final *-s* (as in *make* rather than *makes*), and in the forms *be* and *were* of the verb *to be*. A typical use of the subjunctive is in clauses introduced by *that* expressing a wish or suggestion, of the type *I suggested to her that she drop by for a drink before the concert. They demanded that he answer their questions.* The form *were* is used in clauses introduced by *if*, *as if*, *as though*, or *supposing*, as in: *If you were to go, you might regret it. It's not as though he were an expert. Supposing I were to meet you outside the theatre.* The subjunctive also occurs in fixed expressions such as *as it were*, *be that as it may*, *come what may*, and *far be it from me*.

subkingdom /sub kíngdəm/ *n* a category in the classification of plants and animals that is smaller than a kingdom and larger than a phylum

sublease /sub leéss/ *n* an arrangement to rent a property from somebody who is already renting it from somebody else ■ *vt* (**-leases, -leasing, -leased**) = **sublet** *v.* —**sublessee** /súb le seé/ *n* —**sublessor** /súb le sáwr/ *n*

sublet /sub lét/ *vti* (**-lets, -letting, -let**) to rent a property to or as a subsidiary tenant ■ *n* a property that is rented from somebody who is renting it from somebody else

sublimate *v* /súbbli mayt/ (**-mates, -mating, -mated**) **1** *vt* to channel impulses or energies regarded as unacceptable, especially sexual desires, towards an activity that is more socially acceptable, often a creative activity **2** *vti* CHEM = **sublime** *v.* 1 ■ *n* /súbbli mayt, -mət/ a chemical substance formed as a result of sublimation [15C. < Latin *sublimat-*, past participle of *sublimare* 'elevate' < *sublimis* 'elevated'.]

sublimation /súbbli máysh'n/ *n* **1** a process in which a substance is converted directly from a solid to a gas or from a gas to a solid without an intermediate liquid phase **2** the channelling of impulses or energies regarded as unacceptable, especially sexual desires, towards activities regarded as more socially acceptable, often creative activities

sublime /sə blím/ *adj* (**-limer, -limest**) **1 BEAUTIFUL** so awe-inspiringly beautiful as to seem almost heavenly ○ *Monteverdi at his most sublime* **2 MORALLY WORTHY** of the highest moral or spiritual value **3 EXCELLENT** excellent or particularly impressive (*informal*) ○ *a sublime pasta creation* **4 COMPLETE** complete or utter ○ *in sublime ignorance* ■ *n* **SOMETHING SUBLIME** something that is sublime ○ *going from the sublime to the ridiculous* ■ *v* (**-limes, -liming, -limed**) **1** *vti* **CONVERT SOLID SUBSTANCE TO GAS** to convert a substance directly from a solid to a gas or from a gas to a solid without an intermediate liquid phase, or to undergo this process **2** *vti* **CONVERT THEN RECONVERT** to convert a solid directly into a gas and then back to a solid again without an intermediate liquid phase, or to undergo this process **3** *vt* **MAKE PURE** to make something such as an emotion finer or purer [14C. < Latin *sublimis* 'elevated'.] —**sublimely** *adv* —**sublimeness** *n* —**sublimity** /sə blímməti/ *n*

Sublime Porte *n* HIST = **Porte** [Early 17C. < French, 'High Gate', a translation of Turkish *Babiâli*, referring to the palace gate where justice was administered.]

subliminal /sub límmin'l/ *adj* entering, existing in, or affecting the mind without conscious awareness ○ *subliminal messages* [Late 19C. < SUB- + Latin *limin-*, stem of *limen* 'threshhold'.] —**subliminally** *adv*

subliminal advertising *n* advertising in the form of images flashed onto the screen during a film or television programme that are too brief to be noticed but long enough to be registered subconsciously

sublingual /sub líng gwəl/ *adj* **1** situated under the tongue **2** describes medicines that are administered by being placed under the tongue to dissolve —**sublingually** *adv*

subliterate /sub líttərət/ *adj* having or demonstrating a level of language competence that is below the level regarded as literate

sublittoral /sub líttərəl/ *adj* relating to, living near, or located in the shallow water near a shoreline ■ *n* the area of a sea that lies between the shore and the continental shelf

sublunary /sub loónəri/ *adj* **1** relating to or found in the area of space that lies between the Moon and the Earth

2 belonging to the material world rather than to the spiritual or intellectual world (*archaic or literary*)

subluxation /súb luk sáysh'n/ *n* a partial dislocation of bones that leaves them misaligned but still in some contact with each other

submachine gun /súbmə sheén-/ *n* a lightweight portable machine gun fired from the hip or the shoulder

submandibular /súb man díbbyŏŏlər/ *adj* relating to or located under the lower jaw

submarginal /sub maárjinəl/ *adj* falling below a necessary minimum, especially the minimum conditions necessary for profitability —**submarginally** *adv*

submarine /súbmə reen, súbmə reén/ *n* **1 UNDERWATER BOAT** a boat built to operate and travel for long periods underwater **2** *US* **LONG SANDWICH** a sandwich made with a long roll cut horizontally ■ *adj* **UNDERWATER** taking place or growing underwater, especially in the sea ○ *submarine research* —**submariner** /sub márrinər/ *n*

submaxillary /súb mak sílləri/ *adj* ANAT = **submandibular**

submediant /sub meédi ənt/ *n* **1** the sixth note in a major or minor scale **2** a key, chord, or harmony based on a submediant

submerge /səb múrj/ (**-merges, -merging, -merged**) *v* **1** *vt* **PLUNGE IN LIQUID** to put something into water or some other liquid so that all of it is under the surface **2** *vi* **GO UNDER WATER** to go under the surface of water or another liquid **3** *vt* **SUPPRESS** to keep something such as feelings or a secret hidden from others [Early 17C. < Latin *submergere* < *mergere* 'dip'.] —**submerged** *adj* —**submergence** /səb múrjənss/ *n*

submerged tenth *n* the ten per cent of any population that, according to some economic theories, will always remain in poverty

submerse /səb múrss/ (**-merses, -mersing, -mersed**) *vt* = **submerge** *v.* 1 [Early 18C. < Latin *submers-*, past participle of *submergere* (see SUBMERGE).] —**submersion** /sub múrsh'n/ *n*

submersible /səb múrssəb'l/ *adj* **1 FOR UNDERWATER USE** designed for use underwater **2 NOT DAMAGED UNDERWATER** capable of being put underwater without being damaged ■ *n* **UNDERWATER BOAT** an underwater vessel, especially a small craft designed for use at deep levels

submicroscopic /súb míkrə skóppik/ *adj* too small to be seen with an optical microscope —**submicroscopically** *adv*

subminiature /sub mínnichər/ *adj* smaller in size than miniature ■ *n* **subminiature, subminiature camera** a camera substantially smaller than a compact camera, using film smaller than the 35mm miniature format

subminiaturize /sub mínnichə rīz/ (**-izes, -izing, -ized**), **subminiaturise** (**-ises, -ising, -ised**) *vt* to manufacture something that is very small in scale —**subminiaturization** /sub mínnichə rī záysh'n/ *n*

submission /səb mísh'n/ *n* **1 YIELDING, OR READINESS TO YIELD** a willingness to yield or surrender to somebody, or the act of doing so ○ *demanded nothing less than total submission to his authority* **2 IDEA SUBMITTED** something put forward for consideration or approval, e.g. a suggestion, proposal, or plan **3 ACT OF SUBMITTING** the act of submitting or handing in something, e.g. a proposal to be considered or written work to be judged **4 AGREEMENT TO ARBITRATE** an agreement between parties in a dispute to have a contested matter arbitrated **5 WITHDRAWAL FROM WRESTLING BOUT** an acknowledgment by a wrestler that he or she cannot continue a bout because of pain

submissive /səb míssiv/ *adj* giving in or tending to give in to the demands or the authority of others —**submissively** *adv* —**submissiveness** *n*

submit /səb mít/ (**-mits, -mitting, -mitted**) *v* **1** *vt* **PROPOSE OR HAND IN** to hand something in or put something forward for consideration, approval, or judgment ○ *Applications must be submitted in triplicate.* **2** *vi* **YIELD** to give in to somebody's authority, control, or demands **3** *vi* **AGREE** to agree to undergo something ○ *had to submit to intensive questioning* **4** *vi* **DEFER** to defer to another's knowledge, judgment, or experience **5** *vt* **ARGUE POINT** to state or argue that something is the case (*formal*) [14C. < Latin *submittere* 'send under' < *mittere* 'send'.] —**submittable** *adj* —**submittal** *n* —**submitter** *n*

SYNONYMS See *yield*.

submolecular /súb mə lékyŏŏlər/ *adj* relating to, consisting of, or involving a particle smaller than a molecule

submontane /sub món tayn/ *adj* **1** relating to or found in the foothills or on the lower slopes of a mountain **2** passing under or through a mountain —**submontanely** *adv*

submucosa /súb myoo kóssə/ *n* a layer of loosely meshed microscopic fibres and associated cells occurring beneath a mucous membrane, e.g. in the small intestine [Late 19C. < modern Latin, < Latin *mucosa* 'mucous', the feminine of *mucosus* < *mucus*.]

submultiple /sub múltip'l/ *n* a number that can be divided into another an exact number of times and leave no remainder ■ *adj* able to be divided into another number an exact number of times without leaving a remainder [Late 17C. < late Latin *submultiplus* < *multiplus* (see MULTIPLE).]

subnormal /sub náwrm'l/ *adj* **1** with a level of intelligence that is lower than the level regarded as normal **2** lower or less than normal or average —**subnormality** /súb nawr mállәti/ *n* —**subnormally** *adv*

⚡**subnotebook** /sub nṓtbŏŏk/ *n* a portable personal computer that is smaller and lighter than a notebook

suboceanic /súb ōshi ánnik/ *adj* found, formed, or occurring beneath the sea or the sea bed

suborbital /sub áwrbit'l/ *adj* **1** relating to the region below the eye socket (**orbit**) **2** not designed to make a complete orbit of the Earth or another celestial body

suborder /súb awrdər/ *n* a taxonomic category that is a subdivision of an order and usually contains several similar families

subordinary /sub áwrd'nəri/ (*plural* **-ies**) *n* in heraldry, a small shape or design such as a lozenge that can appear on a coat of arms and is smaller than the most prominent shape (**ordinary**)

subordinate *adj* /sə báwrdinət/ **1 LOWER IN RANK** lower than somebody in rank or status **2 OF SECONDARY IMPORTANCE** secondary in importance **3 MODIFYING** acting as a modifying noun, adjective, or adverb within a sentence ■ *n* **SOMEBODY IN JUNIOR POSITION** a person who is lesser in rank or status ■ *vt* /sə báwrdi nayt/ (**-ates, -ating, -ated**) **1 MAKE SOMETHING SECONDARY** to treat something as less important and allow something else to dominate or take priority ○ *had increasingly subordinated her research to the demands of her busy work schedule* **2 PLACE IN LOWER RANK** to give or regard somebody as having a more junior rank or status [15C. < medieval Latin *subordinare* 'place below' < Latin *ordinare* 'place' < *ordo* (see ORDER).] —**subordinately** *adv* —**subordinateness** *n* —**subordination** /sə báwrdi náysh'n/ *n*

subordinate clause *n* a clause that cannot stand alone as a separate sentence since its meaning depends on the meaning of the main clause and simply gives additional information. In the sentence 'We had to run because we were late', the clause 'because we were late' is the subordinate clause and 'We had to run' is the main clause.

subordinate conjunction, subordinating conjunction *n* a conjunction that introduces a subordinate clause, either one word such as 'although', 'because', or 'since', or a group of words such as 'in order that' or 'as long as'

subordinator /sə báwrdi naytər/ *n* GRAM = **subordinate conjunction**

suborn /sə báwrn/ *vt* to persuade somebody to commit a crime or other wrongdoing, e.g. to bribe another party to tell lies in court [Early 16C. < Latin *subornare* 'equip secretly' < *ornare* (see ORNATE).] —**subornation** /súbbawr náysh'n/ *n* —**subornative** *adj* —**suborner** *n*

suboxide /sub ók sīd/ *n* an oxide containing less oxygen than the normal oxide formed by a particular element

subparagraph /súb parə graaf, -graf/ *n* a section of a paragraph, especially a numbered section of a paragraph in a legal document

subphylum /sub fíləm/ (*plural* **-la** /-lə/) *n* a subcategory of a phylum, used in the classification of animals and containing one or more similar classes [Mid-20C. < modern Latin, < *phylum* 'phylum'.] —**subphylar** *adj*

subplot /súb plot/ *n* **1** a second and less prominent story within a book, play, or film **2** a division of a plot of land, used especially for crop husbandry experiments

subpoena /sə peénə, səb-/ *n* a written legal order summoning a witness or requiring evidence to be submitted to a court ■ *vt* (**-nas, -naing, -naed**) to issue a written legal order summoning a witness or requiring something to be submitted in evidence to a court [15C. < Latin *sub poena* 'under penalty' (the first words of the writ) < *sub* 'under' + *poena* 'penalty'.] —**subpoenaed** *adj*

subpolar /sub pṓlər/ *adj* **1** being near the Arctic or the Antarctic polar region **2** relating to, belonging to, or found in the areas that border the Arctic and Antarctic

subpopulation /súb popyŏŏ láysh'n/ *n* a section of a statistical population that is identifiably separate or distinctive

sub-post office *n* a small post office offering limited postal services, located inside a larger shop and managed by somebody who is an agent but not an employee

subprincipal /sub prínssəp'l/ *n* an assistant principal or a vice-principal in a school, college, or other place of education

subregion /súb reej'n/ *n* a part of a region, especially an ecological or zoogeographical division —**subregional** /sub reéj'nəl/ *adj*

subring /súbring/ *n* in mathematics, a ring that is a subset of a larger ring

subrogate /súbbrə gayt/ (**-gates, -gating, -gated**) *vt* to substitute one person for another, especially in transferring a right or claim [15C. < Latin *subrogare* (see SURROGATE).]

subrogation /súbbrə gáysh'n/ *n* the substitution of one claim for another, especially the transfer of the right to receive payment of a debt to somebody other than the original creditor

sub rosa /-rṓzə/ *adv* in a secret or private way [Mid-17C. < Latin, 'under the rose', because the rose was an emblem of confidentiality hung above council tables.]

⚡**subroutine** /súb roo teen/ *n* a sequence of programming statements that performs a single task and can be used repeatedly

sub-Saharan *adj* relating to the area of Africa south of the Sahara desert

subscribe /səb skrī́b/ (**-scribes, -scribing, -scribed**) *v* **1** *vi* **MAKE ADVANCE PAYMENT FOR SOMETHING** to agree to pay for and receive something over a particular period of time, e.g. a periodical, series of books, or set of tickets to musical or dramatic performances **2** *vti* **PROMISE TO GIVE MONEY REGULARLY** to pledge to make regular donations to something, especially a charity **3** *vti* **GUARANTEE TO INVEST IN SOMETHING** to promise to pay for something when it will occur, e.g. the financing of a new business or a new issue of shares **4** *vi* **SUPPORT VIEW** to support or believe in a theory or view **5** *vt* **SIGN NAME ON LEGAL DOCUMENT** to sign a legal document to indicate agreement or approval of its terms (*formal*) [15C. < Latin *subscribere* 'write underneath' < *scribere* (see SCRIBE).] —**subscriber** *n*

subscriber trunk dialling *n* the facility to make long-distance telephone calls directly, without the help of an operator (*dated*)

subscript /súb skript/ *n* a character that is printed on a level lower than the rest of the characters on the line, e.g. the '2' in the chemical formula 'H_2O' ■ *adj* printed below a character in a line of type [Early 18C. < Latin *subscript*, past participle of *subscribere* (see SUBSCRIBE).]

subscription /səb skrípsh'n/ *n* **1 ADVANCE PAYMENT** an agreement to pay for and receive something over a particular period of time, e.g. a periodical, series of books, or set of tickets to musical or dramatic performances ○ *a subscription film channel* **2 MEMBERSHIP FEE** a fee paid for membership in a club or society **3 PLEDGE TO PAY FOR** a promise to pay for something when it will occur, e.g. the financing of a new business or a new issue of shares **4 SIGNING OF DOCUMENT OR SIGNATURE** the process of signing, or a signature on, a legal document as an indication of approval of its terms (*formal*) **5 TOTAL AGREEMENT OR APPROVAL** a full agreement with or approval of something (*literary*) [15C. Originally in the sense 'writing at the end of a document'.]

subscription library *n* a library that lends books in return for a regular fee

subsection /súb seksh'n/ *n* one of the smaller parts into which a section may be divided, e.g. in a legal or official document

subsellium /sub sélli əm/ (*plural* **-lia** /-li ə/) *n* = **misericord** [Early 18C. < Latin, 'low seat' < *sella* 'seat'.]

subsequence[1] /súbsikwənss/ *n* something that happens after something else, or the occurrence of something after something else

subsequence[2] /súb seekwənss/ *n* a sequence within another mathematical sequence

subsequent /súb ssikwənt/ *adj* happening or existing after something [15C. Directly or via French *subséquent* < Latin *subsequent-*, present participle of *subsequi* 'follow closely' < *sequi* (see SEQUENCE).]

subsequently /súbs sikwəntli/ *adv* occurring or happening after something else

subsere /súb seer/ *n* a secondary development of natural plant and animal communities after these have been destroyed by fire, flood, or human action [Early 20C. < SUB- + SERE[2].]

subserve /səb súrv/ (**-serves, -serving, -served**) *vt* to help to further, promote, or bring something about [Early 17C. < Latin *subservire* 'serve under' < *servire* (see SERVE).]

subservient /səb súrvi ənt/ *adj* **1 TOO EAGER TO OBEY** too eager to follow the wishes or orders of others **2 SECONDARY IN IMPORTANCE** in a position of secondary importance **3 INSTRUMENTAL** helping to achieve or bring something about [Mid-17C. < Latin *subservire* 'serve under' < *servire* (see SERVE).] —**subservience** *n* —**subserviently** *adv*

subset /súb set/ *n* a mathematical set whose elements are contained in another set

subshell /súb shel/ *n* an orbital within an electron energy level (**shell**)

subshrub /súb shrub/ *n* a low-growing plant with woody stems and main branches and nonwoody tips that die back each year [Mid-19C. Translation of modern Latin *suffrutex* < Latin *frutex* 'shrub'.] —**subshrubby** *adj*

subside /səb sīd/ (**-sides, -siding, -sided**) *vi* **1 DIMINISH IN INTENSITY** to become less active or intense **2 DROP TO LOWER LEVEL** to sink to a low or lower level **3 SINK TO BOTTOM OF LIQUID** to sink to the bottom of a liquid **4 GRADUALLY SIT OR LIE DOWN** to sink into a sitting or lying position, e.g. out of exhaustion (*formal*) [Mid-17C. < Latin *subsidere* 'settle down' < *sidere* 'settle'.] —**subsider** *n*

subsidence /səb sīd'nss, súbz sidənss/ *n* **1** the sinking down of land resulting from natural shifts or human activity, frequently causing structural damage to buildings **2** the waning or lessening of something

subsidiarity /səb síddi árrəti/ *n* **1** the principle that political power should be exercised by the smallest possible unit of government **2** the fact or quality of being subsidiary [Mid-20C. Translation of German *Subsidiarität*.]

subsidiary /səb síddi əri/ *adj* **1 SECONDARY IN IMPORTANCE** having secondary importance or occupying a subordinate position **2 HELPING OR SUPPORTING** serving to aid, supplement, or support ■ *n* (*plural* **-aries**) **1 SOMEBODY OR SOMETHING AUXILIARY** somebody or something that occupies a secondary or subordinate position **2 COMPANY CONTROLLED BY LARGER ONE** a company controlled or owned by a larger one —**subsidiarily** *adv* —**subsidiariness** *n*

subsidiary coin *n* a coin that has a lower denomination than that of a standard unit of currency

subsidize /súb si dīz/ (**-dizes, -dizing, -dized**), **subsidise** (**-dises, -dising, -dised**) *vt* to contribute money to somebody or something, especially in the form of a government grant to a private company, organization, or charity to help it to continue to function —**subsidizable** *adj* —**subsidization** /súbssi dī záysh'n/ *n* —**subsidizer** *n*

subsidy /súbssidi/ (*plural* **-dies**) *n* **1 MONEY GIVEN BY GOVERNMENT** a grant or gift of money from a government to a private company, organization, or charity to help it to function **2 HELP WITH EXPENSES** a monetary gift or contribution to somebody or something, especially to pay expenses **3 FORMER PARLIAMENTARY GRANT TO CROWN** a grant of money formerly given by the English Parliament to the Crown [14C. Via Anglo-Norman < Latin *subsidium* 'reserve troops' < *sedere* (see SEDENTARY).]

subsist /səb síst/ *v* **1** *vi* **MANAGE TO LIVE** to remain alive or viable, especially with the help of something **2** *vt* **MAINTAIN** to support or maintain somebody by providing something that is needed, e.g. by supplying troops with food or businesses with capital (*formal*) **3** *vi* **BE ATTRIBUTABLE TO** to have something as its reason or origin (*formal*) **4** *vi* **INHERE IN** to reside in or consist of something (*formal*) **5** *vi* **HAVE ABSTRACT EXISTENCE** to have a timeless conceptual existence (*refers to numbers or mathematical sets*) [Mid-16C. Directly or via French *subsister* < Latin *subsistere* 'stand up to' < *sistere* (see ASSIST).] —**subsistent** *adj* —**subsister** *n*

subsistence /səb sístənss/ *n* **1 CONDITION OF MANAGING TO STAY ALIVE** the condition of being or managing to stay alive, especially when there is only just enough food or money for survival **2 CONTINUING TO EXIST** the condition of continuing to exist **3 QUALITY OF ABSTRACT EXISTENCE** the quality that something possesses of existing independently, timelessly, or by virtue of its essence

subsistence allowance *n* **1** a sum of money given to an employee to cover special expenses incurred in the performance of his or her work **2** an advance paid to a new employee or soldier to help to meet living costs until wages begin to be paid

subsistence crop *n* a crop grown by a farmer principally to feed his or her family, with little or nothing left over to sell

subsistence farming *n* farming that generates only enough produce to feed the farmer's family, with little or nothing left over to sell —**subsistence farmer** *n*

subsistence level *n* a standard of living that provides barely enough food and money on which to survive

subsistence wage *n* a wage so low that it is barely enough to live on

subsocial /sub sṓsh'l/ *adj* describes insects that associate with others but without any fixed or organized social structure —**subsocially** *adv*

subsoil /súb soyl/ *n* the compacted soil beneath the topsoil ■ *vt* to turn, break, or stir the compacted soil beneath the topsoil

subsoiler /súb soylər/ *n* **1** a farm implement consisting of a frame with long stout vertical tines **2** an operator of a subsoiler

subsolar /sub sṓlər/ *adj* **1** located directly below the Sun on the Earth's surface when the Sun is at its highest point **2** located in the equatorial region that lies between the Tropics of Cancer and Capricorn

subsonic /sub sónnik/ *adj* **1** slower than 1,220 kmph/760 mph, the speed at which sound travels in air **2** flying at speeds slower than the speed of sound, especially not designed to fly above the speed of sound —**subsonically** *adv*

subspecialise *vi* = **subspecialize**

subspeciality /súb speshi álləti/ (*plural* **-ties**) *n* a very narrow or specialized field of study, within an existing speciality

subspecialize /sub spéshə līz/ (**-izes, -izing, -ized**), **subspecialise** (**-ises, -ising, -ised**) *vi* to work in a very narrow field or area of study within an existing speciality

subspecies /súb spee sheez/ (*plural* **-cies**) *n* a category used to classify plants and animals whose populations are distinct, e.g. in distribution, appearance, or feeding habits, but can still interbreed —**subspecific** /súb spə síffik/ *adj* —**subspecifically** *adv*

substage /súb stayj/ *n* a component assembly in a microscope that contains the condenser, mirror, or other accessories and is located below the stage

substance /súbstənss/ *n* **1 MATERIAL** a particular kind of matter or material **2 TANGIBLE PHYSICAL MATTER** physical reality that can be touched and felt **3 PRACTICAL VALUE** real or practical value or importance ○ *There was nothing of substance in the document.* **4 MATERIAL WEALTH** wealth in the form of money and possessions **5 GIST OF MEANING** the actual meaning of something said or written ○ *the substance of their argument* **6 UNCHANGING ESSENCE** the unchanging essence of something **7 SOMETHING INDIVIDUAL AND CAUSED** something that is individual and caused [13C. Via French < Latin *substantia* 'essence' (a translation of Greek *hupostasis*) < Latin *substare*, literally 'stand under' < *stare* (see STAND).]

substance abuse *n* the excessive consumption or misuse of any substance for the sake of its non-therapeutic effects on the mind or body, especially drugs or alcohol

substance P *n* a peptide found in body tissues, especially nervous tissue, that is involved in the transmission of pain and in inflammation

~~**substancial**~~ incorrect spelling of **substantial**

substandard /sub stándərd/ *adj* below the expected or required standard of quality

substantial /səb stánsh'l/ *adj* **1 CONSIDERABLE** considerable in amount, extent, value, or importance **2 SOLID OR STURDY** solidly built **3 FILLING** providing a lot of nourishment **4 RICH** wealthy and prosperous **5 REAL AND TANGIBLE** actual and real in a palpable way **6 CONSISTING OF SUBSTANCE** consisting of or involving substance ■ *n* **IMPORTANT PART** an important or essential part [14C. Directly or via French *substantiel* < ecclesiastical Latin *substantialis* 'having substance' (a translation of Greek *hupostatikos*) < *substare* 'stand under' < *stare* (see STAND).] —**substantiality** /səb stánshi álləti/ *n* —**substantialness** *n*

substantialise *vt* = **substantialize**

substantialism /səb stánshlizəm/ *n* the philosophical doctrine that beings or entities of substantial reality underlie all phenomena —**substantialist** *n*

substantialize /səb stánsh'l īz/ (**-izes, -izing, -ized**), **substantialise** (**-ises, -ising, -ised**) *vti* to make something that is imaginary, theoretical, or spiritual become palpable, or to become palpable

substantially /səb stánsh'li/ *adv* **1** in an extensive, substantial, or ample way **2** generally or in essence

substantiate /səb stánshi ayt/ (**-ates, -ating, -ated**) *vt* **1** to confirm that something is true or valid **2** to give something an actual physical existence [Mid-17C. < medieval Latin *substantiare* 'give substance to' < Latin *substantia* 'substance' < *stare* (see STAND).] —**substantiable** *adj* —**substantiation** /səb stánshi áysh'n/ *n* —**substantiative** *adj* —**substantiator** /səb stánshi aytər/ *n*

substantive *n* /súbstəntiv/ **NOUN** a noun, or a word or group of words used like a noun ■ *adj* /səb stántiv, súbstəntiv/ **1 WITH PRACTICAL IMPORTANCE** with practical importance, value, or effect ○ *a substantive agreement* **2 ESSENTIAL** relating to the substance of something **3 USED LIKE NOUN** relating to or used like a noun **4 EXPRESSING EXISTENCE** expressing existence, as, e.g., the verb 'to be' **5 INDEPENDENT** continuing independently **6 SUBSTANTIAL** substantial in amount or quantity ○ *a substantive meal* **7 RELATING TO LEGAL PRINCIPLES** relating to the essential principles that a court applies in its work, not to the rules of procedure and practice. ◊ **adjective 8 DIRECTLY ATTACHING AS DYE COLOUR** attaching as a colour directly to a material being dyed without the use of a fixing substance **9 PERMANENT** describes a rank or appointment that is permanent —**substantival** /súbstən tīv'l/ *adj* —**substantivally** *adv* —**substantively** *adv*

substantive right *n* a basic human right such as the right to life or liberty that is regarded as existing naturally and indispensably

substantivize /súbstənti vīz/ (**-vizes, -vizing, -vized**), **substantivise** (**-vises, -vising, -vised**) *vt* to make a word or words function like a noun —**substantivization** /súbstənti vī záysh'n/ *n*

substation /súb staysh'n/ *n* **1** a branch of a main electrical power station where electrical current is converted, redistributed, or modified in strength **2** any office, building, or installation that is a branch of something larger, especially one attached to a larger station

substituent /səb stíttyoo ənt/ *n* an atom or group of atoms that replaces another atom or group in a molecule [Late 19C. < Latin *substituere* 'set up under' < *statuere* (see STATUE).]

substitute /súbsti tyoot/ *v* (**-tutes, -tuting, -tuted**) **1** *vti* **REPLACE OR TAKE PLACE OF** to put somebody or something in place of another, or to take the place of another (*often passive*) **2** *vt* **REPLACE ATOM OR ATOMS IN MOLECULE** to replace an atom or group of atoms in a molecule with another atom or group **3** *vt* **REPLACE MATHEMATICAL ELEMENT WITH EQUIVALENT** to replace one mathematical element with another of equal value ■ *n* **1 REPLACEMENT** somebody or something that takes the place of another ○ *Herb teas can be a pleasant substitute for coffee or tea.* **2 REPLACEMENT PLAYER** a team member in a game who is ready to replace another on the field **3** GRAM = **pro-form** [15C. < Latin *substitutus*, past participle of *substituere* 'set up under' < *statuere* (see STATUE).] —**substitutability** *n* —**substitutable** *adj* —**substituter** *n*

USAGE See ***replace***.

substitute teacher *n US* EDUC = **supply teacher**

substitution /súbsti tyóo sh'n/ *n* **1 ACT OF REPLACING** the replacement of somebody or something with another, especially one team member with another **2 SOMEBODY OR SOMETHING THAT REPLACES** somebody or something that replaces another, especially one team member who replaces another **3 MATHEMATICAL ELEMENT REPLACING EQUIVALENT** the replacement of one mathematical element with another of equal value **4 REPLACEMENT OF LOGICAL EXPRESSION** the replacement of one logical expression with another, or the expression so replaced —**substitutional** *adj* —**substitutionally** *adv*

substitutive /súbsti tyootiv/ *adj* acting or usable as a substitute [Early 17C. Partly < SUBSTITUTE, partly < Latin *substitutivus* < past participle of *substituere* (see SUBSTITUTE).] —**substitutively** *adv* —**substitutivity** /súbsti tyoo tívvəti/ *n*

substrate /súb strayt/ *n* **1** a substance that is acted upon in a biochemical reaction **2** a single crystal of a semiconductor used as the basis for an integrated circuit or transistor **3** BIOL = **substratum** *n.* 6 **4** BIOL = **medium** *n.* 9 [Early 19C. Anglicization of SUBSTRATUM.]

substratosphere /sub stráttə sfeer/ *n* the lowest layer of the Earth's atmosphere, at a height of about 20 km/12 mi. above the Earth

substratum /-straátəm, -stráytəm/ (*plural* **-ta** /-tə, -stráytə/) *n* **1** UNDERLYING BASE an underlying base, layer, or element **2** AGRIC = **subsoil** *n.* **3** GEOL = **bedrock** *n.* 1 **4** BASE FOR EMULSION a layer of a substance placed on a film or plate as a foundation for an emulsion **5** SET OF RETAINED INDIGENOUS LINGUISTIC FEATURES a set of linguistic features retained from the speech of an indigenous culture, especially one that influences the language of a colonizer. ◊ **superstratum** *n.* 2 **6** NON-LIVING FOUNDATION FOR GROWING ORGANISM the non-living material or base on which an organism lives or grows **7** ESSENTIAL SUBSTANCE the essential substance of something [Mid-17C. < modern Latin, a noun use of neuter past participle of Latin *substernere* 'spread underneath' < *sternere* (see STRATUM).] —**substratal** *adj* —**substrative** *adj*

substructure /súb strukchər/ *n* **1** the foundation of an erected structure **2** any underlying structure that supports or gives strength to something —**substructural** /sub strúkchərəl/ *adj*

subsume /səb syoóm/ (**-sumes, -suming, -sumed**) *vt* **1** to include or incorporate something into a larger order, category, or classification **2** to show that a rule applies to something [Mid-16C. < medieval Latin *subsumere* 'take up so as to include' < Latin *sumere* (see SUMPTUOUS).] —**subsumable** *adj*

subsumption /səb súmpsh'n/ *n* **1** the act of subsuming or the fact of being subsumed **2** something that is subsumed [Mid-17C. < medieval Latin *subsumption-* < *subsumere* (see SUBSUME).] —**subsumptive** *adj*

subsurface /súb surfiss/ *adj* relating to or located in an area that lies just below the surface of something, especially of the Earth or a body of water ■ *n* material that is located just below the surface of something, especially of the Earth or a body of water

subsystem /súb sistəm/ *n* a system that forms part of a larger system

subtangent /súb tanjənt/ *n* the part of the x-axis included by the ordinate of a given point on a curve and the tangent at that point

subteen /súb teén/ *n US, Can* = **preteen** [Mid-20C]

subtemperate /sub témpərət/ *adj* relating to or occurring in the colder areas of the Temperate Zone

subtenant /súb tenənt/ *n* a renter of a property from a tenant who in turn rents it from the owner —**subtenancy** *n*

subtend /səb ténd/ *vt* **1** to extend from one side to the other, opposite an angle or side of a geometric figure **2** to lie underneath something so as to surround or enclose it [Late 16C. < Latin *subtendere* 'stretch underneath' < *tendere* (see TEND[1]).]

subterfuge /súbtər fyooj/ *n* a plan, action, or device designed to hide a real objective, or the process of hiding a real objective [Late 16C. Directly or via French < late Latin *subterfugium* < Latin *subterfugere* 'flee secretly' < *fugere* (see FUGITIVE).]

subterminal /sub túrmin'l/ *adj* positioned very near the end of something

subterranean /súbtə ráyni ən/, **subterraneous** /-ráyni əss/ *adj* **1** existing or situated below ground level **2** existing or carried on in secret [Early 17C. < Latin *subterraneus* 'underground' < *terra* (see TERRACE).] —**subterraneanly** *adv*

subtext /súb tekst/ *n* an underlying meaning or message —**subtextual** /sub tékschoo əl/ *adj*

subthreshold /súb thresh hōld, -thresh ōld/ *adj* describes a stimulus that is not strong or large enough to have an effect

subtilise *vt* = **subtilize**

subtilisin /súbti líssin/ *n* a protein-digesting enzyme produced by bacteria. Use: detergents. [Mid-20C. < modern Latin *subtilis* 'subtle' < Latin (see SUBTLE).]

subtilize /sútt'l īz/ (**-izes, -izing, -ized**), **subtilise** /sútt'līz/ (**-ises, -ising, -ised**) *v* **1** *vti* to make or use subtle distinctions in discussing something **2** *vt* to make something increasingly refined —**subtilization** *n* —**subtilizer** *n*

subtitle /súb tīt'l/ *n* **1** CAPTION FOR FOREIGN-LANGUAGE FILM a printed translation of the dialogue in a foreign-language film, usually appearing at the bottom of the screen **2** PRINTED WORDS FOR HEARING-IMPAIRED the printed text of what is being said in a television programme, provided for the hearing-impaired and usually at the bottom of the screen **3** CAPTION IN SILENT FILM a caption for the action or dialogue of a silent film, appearing at intervals as a full-screen panel **4** LESSER TITLE a second and subsidiary title for something such as a book ■ *vt* (**-tles, -tling, -tled**) **1** PROVIDE SUBTITLES FOR to provide subtitles for a film or television programme **2** to give a subtitle to something such as a book —**subtitular** /sub tíchoolər/ *adj*

subtle /sútt'l/ *adj* **1** SLIGHT slight and not obvious **2** PLEASANTLY UNDERSTATED pleasantly delicate and understated **3** ABLE TO MAKE REFINED JUDGMENTS intelligent, experienced, or sensitive enough to make refined judgments and distinctions **4** INGENIOUS cleverly indirect and ingenious [14C. Via Old French *sutil* < Latin *subtilis* 'fine, thin' < *sub tela* 'beneath the weaving' < *sub* 'beneath' + *tela* 'weaving'.] —**subtly** *adv* —**subtleness** *n*

subtlety /sútt'lti/ (*plural* **-ties**) *n* **1** the quality or state of being subtle **2** a distinction that is difficult to make but is important (*often plural*)

subtopia /sub tōpi ə/ *n* suburban development, especially when viewed as falling short of the ideals of city planners [Mid-20C. Blend of SUBURB + UTOPIA.] —**subtopian** *adj*

subtotal /súb tōt'l/ *n* a sum or total of part of a set of figures ■ *vt* (**-tals, -talling, -talled**) to calculate the total of part of a set of figures

subtract /səb trákt/ *v* **1** *vti* to perform the arithmetical calculation of deducting one number or quantity from another **2** *vt* to withdraw or take away something from a larger unit [Mid-16C. < Latin *subtract-*, past participle of *subtrahere* 'pull away' < *trahere* (see TRACTOR).] —**subtracter** *n*

subtraction /səb tráksh'n/ *n* **1** DEDUCTION OF NUMBER (*symbol* –) the act or process of deducting one number or quantity from another **2** REMOVAL FROM SOMETHING LARGER a withdrawal or deduction of something from a larger whole **3** WITHDRAWAL OF BENEFIT the withdrawal or withholding of a benefit

subtractive /səb tráktiv/ *adj* **1** ABLE TO SUBTRACT with the power to subtract something **2** INDICATING SUBTRACTION indicating or needing subtraction **3** REMAINING AFTER ABSORPTION BY TINTED FILTERS describes the colour that remains after all other components of the visible spectrum have been absorbed by tinted filters

subtrahend /súbtrə hend/ *n* a number that is to be deducted from another number. ◊ **minuend** [Late 17C. < Latin *subtrahendus* , literally 'be subtracted', a form of *subtrahere* 'pull away' < *trahere* (see TRACTOR).]

subtropical /sub tróppik'l/ *adj* relating to or found in areas between tropical and temperate regions, and experiencing tropical conditions at some times of the year or near-tropical conditions all year round

subtropics /sub tróppiks/ *npl* the regions of the Earth adjacent to the tropics

subtype /súb tīp/ *n* a type that is a subdivision of a larger type —**subtypical** /sub típpik'l/ *adj*

subulate /súbbyoolət/ *adj* describes a plant part that is long and thin and tapers to a point [Mid-18C. < modern Latin *subulatus* < Latin *subula* 'awl'.]

subunit /súb yoonit/ *n* **1** a unit that forms part of a larger unit **2** a part of a large molecule or complex that can be dissociated from the whole without rupture of covalent chemical bonds

subunit vaccine *n* a vaccine that creates a bodily immunity to a virus or bacterium from whose DNA the vaccine is made

suburb /súbburb/ *n* a district, especially a residential one, on the edge of a city or large town [14C. Directly or via French *suburbe* < Latin *suburbium* 'near a city' < *urbs* (see URBAN).]

suburban /sə búrbən/ *adj* **1** RELATING TO SUBURB relating to, belonging to, or located in a suburb **2** RESEMBLING SUBURB resembling a suburb or its residents **3** UNEXCITING AND CONVENTIONAL typical of the undesirable aspects of a suburb or its residents, especially in being dull, conventional, and materialistic (*disapproving*)

suburbanise *vt* = **suburbanize**

suburbanite /sə búrbə nīt/ *n* a dweller in the suburbs

suburbanize /sə búrbə nīz/ (**-izes, -izing, -ized**), **suburbanise** (**-banises, -banising, -banised**) *vt* to give something the appearance or character of a suburb —**suburbanization** /sə búrbə nī záysh'n/ *n*

suburbia /sə búrbi ə/ *n* suburbs collectively, or the people who live in them

subvention /səb vénsh'n/ *n* (*formal*) **1** a sum of money given by an official body such as a government, especially to an institution of learning, study, or research **2** the giving of help or support, especially financial —**subventionary** *adj*

subversion /səb vúrsh'n/ *n* **1** an action, plan, or activity intended to undermine or overthrow a government or other institution **2** the destruction or ruining of something [14C. Directly or via French < late Latin *subversion-* < *subvertere* (see SUBVERT).]

subversive /səb vúrssiv/ *adj* intended or likely to undermine or overthrow a government or other institution ■ *n* somebody involved in activities intended to undermine or overthrow a government or other institution —**subversively** *adv* —**subversiveness** *n*

subvert /səb vúrt/ *vt* to undermine or overthrow a government or other institution [14C. Directly or via Old French *subvertir* < Latin *subvertere* 'turn from below' < *vertere* (see VERSE).] —**subverter** *n*

subvirus /súb vīrəss/ *n* an infective agent such as a prion that is structurally more primitive than a virus —**subviral** /súb vīrəl/ *adj*

subvocal /sub vōk'l/ *adj* mouthed or mentally pictured but not sounded out loud —**subvocally** *adv*

subvocalize /sub vōkə līz/ (**-izes, -izing, -ized**), **subvocalise** (**-calises, -calising, -calised**) *vti* to mouth words or other speech sounds without saying them out loud —**subvocalization** /sub vōkə lī záysh'n/ *n*

subway /súb way/ *n* **1** a passage under a road or railway for pedestrians to get to the other side **2** *US, Can, Scotland* TRANSP = **underground** *n.* 1

subzero /sub zeérō/ *adj* being below zero degrees in temperature

succah *n* JUDAISM = **sukkah**

~~**succede**~~ incorrect spelling of **succeed**

succeed /sək seéd/ *v* **1** *vi* ACHIEVE INTENTION to manage to do what is planned or attempted ○ *We succeeded in persuading them to change their decision.* **2** *vi* GAIN FAME, WEALTH, OR POWER to realize a goal, especially to gain fame, wealth, or power **3** *vi* MAKE SIGNIFICANT PROGRESS to do well in an activity, making admirable progress or recording impressive achievements ○ *She was one of the first women to succeed in the sciences.* **4** *vi* PROSPER to thrive or prosper **5** *vti* BE NEXT AFTER to be the next person to occupy a post or position after somebody ○ *Mary succeeded him as president over a year ago.* **6** *vt* FOLLOW IN TIME to come after something in time (*often passive*) **7** *vi* BE INHERITED BY to pass to somebody as an inheritance (*formal*) [14C. Directly or via French *succéder* < Latin *succedere* 'go after' < *cedere* (see CEDE).] —**succeedable** *adj* —**succeeder** *n*

succentor /sək séntər/ *n* a deputy to a precentor [Mid-17C. < late Latin, < Latin *succinere* 'sing to' < *canere* (see CANT[2]).] —**succentorship** *n*

succès de scandale /syoók sáy də skaan daál/ (*plural* **succès de scandale**) *n* something such as a book, film, or play that is successful because it is controversial, or the success that is gained as a result of controversy [< French, 'success of scandal']

succès d'estime /syoók sáy des teém/ (*plural* **succès d'estime**) *n* something such as a book, film, or play that is successful with the critics but not with the public, or the success that is gained through critical acclaim [< French, 'success of esteem']

succès fou /syoók sáy foó/ (*plural* **succès fous** /syoók say foó/) *n* an overwhelming success [< French, 'mad success']

~~**succesful**~~ incorrect spelling of **successful**

~~**succesive**~~ incorrect spelling of **successive**

success /sək séss/ *n* **1** ACHIEVEMENT OF DESIRED AIM the achievement of something planned or attempted **2** ATTAINMENT OF FAME, WEALTH, OR POWER impressive achievement, especially the attainment of fame, wealth, or power **3 SOMETHING THAT TURNS OUT WELL** something that turns out as planned or intended **4 SOMEBODY OF SIGNIFICANT ACHIEVEMENT** a person who is wealthy, famous, or powerful because of a record of achievement [Mid-16C. < Latin *successus* < *success-*, past participle of *succedere* (see SUCCEED).]

successful /sək séssf'l/ *adj* **1 TURNING OUT WELL** having the intended result **2 POPULAR** popular and making a lot of money **3 WITH RECORD OF SIGNIFICANT ACHIEVEMENTS** having achieved or gained much, especially wealth, fame, or power —**successfully** *adv* —**successfulness** *n*

succession /sək sésh'n/ *n* **1 SERIES IN TIME** a sequence of people or things coming one after the other in time ○ *rented a succession of dingy flats around town* **2 FOLLOWING ON** the following on of one thing after another ○ *three wins in succession.* **3 TAKING UP OF TITLE OR POSITION** the assumption of a position or title, the right to take it up, or the order in which it is taken up **4 DEVELOPMENT OF PLANT AND ANIMAL COMMUNITY** the series of changes that create a full-fledged plant and animal community, e.g. from the colonization of bare rock to the establishment of a forest —**successional** *adj* —**successionally** *adv*

succession crop *n* a crop that follows another crop as a successive planting, or a crop of a variety with a different rate of growth

succession state *n* a nation created from territory once ruled by another, larger nation

successive /sək séssiv/ *adj* following in an uninterrupted sequence —**successively** *adv* —**successiveness** *n*

successor /sək séssər/ *n* somebody or something that follows another and takes up the same position —**successoral** *adj*

success story *n* somebody or something that is very successful

succinate /súksi nayt/ *n* an ester of succinic acid [Late 18C. < *succinic* < Latin *succinum* 'amber'.]

succinct /sək síngkt/ *adj* showing or expressed with brevity and clarity, with no wasted words [15C. Directly or via French < Latin *succinctus*, past participle of *succingere* 'encompass from below' < *cingere* (see PRECINCT).] —**succinctly** *adv* —**succinctness** *n*

succinic acid /sək sínnik-/ *n* $C_4H_6O_4$ a colourless odourless acid. Source: amber, plant and animal tissues, artificially synthesized. Use: manufacture of lacquers, perfumes, pharmaceuticals.

succinylcholine /súksi nīl kṓ leen/ *n US* PHARM = **suxamethonium** [Mid-20C. < SUCCINIC (ACID) + -YL + CHOLINE.]

succor /súkə/ *n, vt* US = **succour**

succory /súkəri/ *n* PLANTS = **chicory** *n.* 1 [Mid-16C. Alteration of obsolete French *cicorée* (see CHICORY) after Middle Low German *suckerie* and Middle Dutch *sūkerie*.]

succotash /súkə tash/ *n* in the United States, sweetcorn and butter beans cooked together, often with tomatoes [Mid-18C. < Narragansett *msiquatash* 'boiled corn or maize and beans'.]

Succoth *n* JUDAISM = **Sukkoth**

succour /súkər/ *n* (*literary*) **1 HELP** help or relief for somebody or something **2 SOMEBODY OR SOMETHING GIVING HELP** somebody or something that provides help or relief ■ *vt* **GIVE HELP** to provide help or relief to somebody or something (*literary*) [13C. Via Old French *socorre* < Latin *succurrere* 'run under' < *currere* 'run'.] —**succourable** *adj* —**succourer** *n*

succubus /súkyoobəss/ (*plural* **-bi** /-bī/ *or* **-buses**) *n* a woman demon that was believed in medieval times to have sexual intercourse with men while they were asleep [14C. < medieval Latin, an alteration (after English *incubus*) of late Latin *succuba* 'one who lies under another' < *cubare* 'lie'.]

succulent /súkyoolənt/ *adj* **1 JUICY AND TASTY** juicy and pleasant to the taste **2 WITH FLESHY WATER-STORING PARTS** with thick fleshy leaves and stems that can store water **3 INTERESTING** exciting and interesting (*informal*) ■ *n* **SUCCULENT PLANT** a plant with thick fleshy leaves and stems that can store water, e.g. cacti and aloes [Early 17C. Directly or via French < Latin *succulentus* < *succus* (see SUCCUS).] —**succulence** *n* —**succulently** *adv*

succumb /sə kúm/ *vi* **1** to yield to somebody or something powerful **2** to die from an illness or injury [15C. Directly or via French *succomber* < Latin *succumbere* 'lie under' < *cumbere* 'lie'.] —**succumber** *n*

SYNONYMS See ***yield***.

succus /súkəss/ (*plural* **-ci** /súk sī, -see/) *n* a fluid, especially a secretion, of plant or animal origin [Late 18C. < Latin, 'juice, moisture, sap'.]

succuss /sə kúss/ (**-cusses, -cussing, -cussed**) *vt* to shake a patient in order to detect the abnormal presence of air or fluid in a body cavity, especially the space between the lungs and the chest wall [Mid-19C. < Latin *succuss-* 'shaken', past participle of the verb *succutere* < *sub* 'away' + *quatere*, 'shake'.] —**succussion** *n* —**succussive** *adj*

~~**suceed**~~ incorrect spelling of **succeed**

~~**sucessful**~~ incorrect spelling of **successful**

~~**sucessive**~~ incorrect spelling of **successive**

such /such/ *adj* **1 OF PARTICULAR KIND** of a particular kind ○ *I've never heard such nonsense.* **2 SO MUCH** to so great an extent or degree ○ *Don't be such a fool.* ■ *adv* **VERY** extremely or to a great degree ○ *I had never seen such lovely flowers.* ■ *n* **THIS** this, or something of this kind ○ *Such was his fate.* [Old English *swilc* < Germanic, 'so formed'] ◇ **such as 1** for example **2** resembling something ◇ **such as it is** being what it is and no more

USAGE such as or **such that**? *We are such stuff as dreams are made on* (Shakespeare, *The Tempest*, Act 4, scene 1, modernized spelling). In sentences of this type ***such*** is followed by *as* and not by a relative pronoun *that, who*, etc.: *The new law affects only such people as* [not *that*] *are eligible for supplementary benefit.* However, the construction *such ... that ...* is used to indicate the consequence of a stated circumstance: *The country faces such hardship that it will need a great deal of foreign aid.*

such and such *adj* not specified or named ■ *pron* something that is not specified or named

suchlike /súch līk/ *pron* others of the same kind as those just mentioned (*informal*) ■ *det* similar to the kind just mentioned

suchness /súchnəss/ *n* an essential quality or condition [Old English *swilcnes*]

suck /suk/ *v* **1** *vti* **DRAW LIQUID OUT WITH MOUTH** to draw the liquid out of something with the mouth ○ *The baby sucked on her bottle.* **2** *vti* **MAKE PULLING MOUTH MOVEMENTS** to hold something in the mouth and make movements with the tongue and lips as if drawing liquid out of it ○ *sucked his thumb* **3** *vti* **DISSOLVE IN MOUTH** to consume something by making it slowly dissolve in the mouth, rolling the tongue around it and making pulling movements with the cheeks and lips ○ *sucking lozenges for a sore throat* **4** *vt* **EXTRACT** to draw something out of a container (*often passive*) ○ *Fuel is sucked into the cylinder.* **5** *vt* **PULL IRRESISTIBLY** to pull or draw something somewhere with a powerful or irresistible force ○ *The swirling currents suck swimmers under.* **6** *vi US, Can* **BE VERY BAD** to be very bad or inferior (*slang*) ○ *The movie really sucked, so we walked out.* ■ *n* **ACT OF SUCKING** an act of sucking something [Old English *sūcan* < Indo-European, 'to take liquid']

suck in *v* **1** *vt* **INVOLVE SOMEBODY** to make somebody become more and more involved in something in a way that he or she is unable to prevent **2** *vti* **BREATHE IN** to breathe in sharply **3** *vt* **DECEIVE** to trick or deceive somebody (*slang*)

suck off *vt* an offensive term meaning to perform fellatio on a man (*slang*)

suck up to *vt* to try to please or win the favour of somebody important by being extremely flattering or helpful (*informal*)

sucker /súkər/ *n* **1 SOMEBODY EASILY FOOLED** an easily fooled or tricked person (*informal*) **2 SOMEBODY WHO GIVES IN EASILY** a person who has little resistance to and is easily influenced by something (*informal*) ○ *a sucker for a pair of big blue eyes* **3** *US* **ANY PERSON OR THING** used to refer, usually with emphasis or some degree of irritation, to any person or thing somebody happens to be dealing with (*slang*) ○ *Let's see if we can get this sucker to work.* **4 ORGAN THAT CLINGS BY SUCTION** a muscular organ, found on the tentacles of octopuses and similar sea animals, used to cling to or hold things such as prey **5 ORGAN FOR SUCKING IN FOOD** the mouth of an animal such as the leech or lamprey that is adapted for sucking in food **6 SHOOT GROWING FROM ROOT** a shoot that grows from the underground root or stem of a plant, and that is often able to produce its own roots and grow into a new plant **7 SOMETHING THAT ADHERES BY SUCTION** a round, slightly cupped piece of plastic or rubber that when pressed onto a flat surface sticks to it by suction. US term **suction cup 8 ANIMAL LIVING ON MOTHER'S MILK** a young animal such as a young pig or whale that is still taking milk from its mother **9 SUCTION PUMP PISTON** the piston of a suction pump, or the valve of the piston in a suction pump **10 SUCTION PIPE** a pipe that a liquid is drawn through by means of suction **11 FRESHWATER FISH** a bony bottom-feeding freshwater fish with a downward-facing sucking mouth without teeth that resembles the carp. Native to: North America. Family: Catostomidae. ■ *v* **1** *vt US* **TRICK** to take advantage of somebody's ignorance, innocence, or foolishness to trick him or her (*informal*) ○ *got suckered into the scheme* **2** *vi* **PRODUCE SUCKERS** to produce or form suckers **3** *vt* **REMOVE SUCKERS** to remove the suckers from a plant

suckerfish /súkər fish/ (*plural* **-fish** *or* **-fishes**) *n* ZOOL = **remora**

sucker punch *n US* a blow delivered when somebody is not expecting it

sucker-punch *vt US* to hit somebody with a sucker punch

sucking /súking/ *adj* still feeding on its mother's milk and not yet weaned ○ *sucking pig* [Old English *sūcende*]

sucking louse *n* a wingless primitive parasitic insect with mouth parts specially adapted for sucking body fluids, e.g. the head louse and pubic louse that infest human beings. Suborder: Siphunculata.

suckle /súk'l/ (**-les, -ling, -led**) *v* **1** *vti* to take milk from a mother's breast, teat, or udder, or to allow a young child or animal to feed on milk from the breast, teat, or udder **2** *vt* to nourish somebody or something (*literary*) [14C. Probably a back-formation < SUCKLING.] —**suckler** *n*

suckling /súkling/ *n* a human baby or young animal such as a calf or pig that is still feeding on its mother's milk [13C. < SUCK.]

sucks /suks/ *interj* used to express disappointment, contempt, or derision (*informal*) ○ *Sucks to her! Who cares what she thinks?*

sucrase /sóo krayz, syóo-/ *n* BIOCHEM = **invertase** [Early 20C. < SUCROSE + -ASE.]

Sucre /sóok ray/, **Antonio José de** (1795–1830) Venezuelan-born South American soldier and statesman

sucrose /sóo krōss, syóo-/ *n* a disaccharide found naturally in many plants. Use: production of sugar. [Mid-19C. < French *sucre* 'sugar' < Old French *sukere* (see SUGAR).]

suction /súksh'n/ *n* **1** physical force created by a difference in pressure such as that caused by sucking a liquid through a straw **2** the act or process of sucking [Early 17C. < late Latin *suction-* < Latin *suct-*, past participle of *sugere* 'suck'.] —**suctional** *adj*

suction cup *n US* = **sucker** *n.* 7

suction pump *n* a pump that works by means of the suction created when a piston is moved up and down inside a cylinder

suction stop *n* PHON = **click**[1] *n.* 3

suctorial /suk táwri əl/ *adj* **1** specially adapted for sucking or for clinging on by suction **2** having one or more suckers for feeding or for clinging on to something [Mid-19C. < modern Latin *suctorius* < Latin *suct-*, past participle of *sugere* (see SUCTION).]

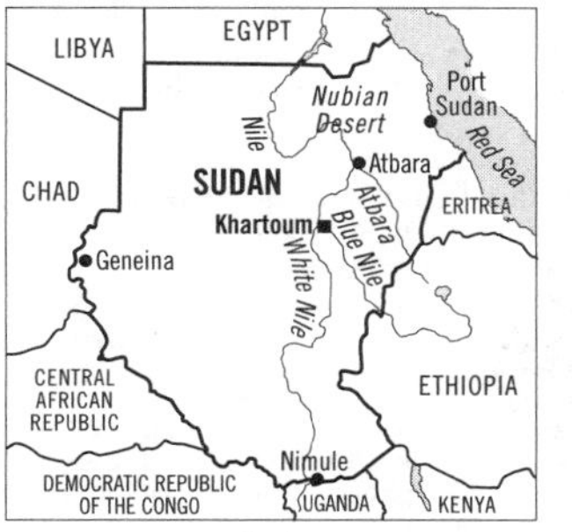

Sudan

Sudan /soo dán/ **1** republic in NE Africa. Capital: Khartoum. Population: 31,065,000 (1996). Area: 2,505,813 sq.

km/967,500 sq. mi. 2 region of savanna and dry grassland in north-central Africa, south of the Sahara —**Sudanese** *n, adj*

Sudanic /soo dánnik/ *n* **GROUP OF LANGUAGES SPOKEN IN SUDAN** a group of Chari-Nile languages spoken in Sudan ■ *adj* 1 **RELATING TO SUDANIC LANGUAGES** relating to the Sudanic group of languages 2 **RELATING TO SUDAN** relating to Sudan, or its people or culture

sudatorium /soódə táwri əm, syoódə táwri əm/ (*plural* **-a** /-ə/) *n* a room, especially in an ancient Roman bathhouse, in which people are made to sweat by hot air or steam [Mid-18C. < Latin, a noun use of the neuter singular of *sudatorius* (see SUDATORY).]

sudatory /soódətəri, syoó-/ *n* (*plural* **-ries**) PHARM = **sudorific** *n.* ■ *adj* PHARM = **sudorific** *adj.* [Early 17C. < Latin *sudatorius* 'for sweating' < *sudare* 'sweat'.]

Sudbury /súdbəri, súdbri/ city in east-central Ontario, Canada. Population: 92,059 (1996).

sudd /sud/ *n* a floating mass of reeds and weeds that obstructs some tropical rivers, especially the White Nile [Late 19C. < Arabic, 'obstruction' < *sadda* 'obstruct'.]

sudden /súdd'n/ *adj* done or happening quickly, unexpectedly, and often without warning [13C. Via Anglo-Norman *sudein* < Latin *subitaneus* < *subire* 'go secretly' < *ire* 'go'.] —**suddenly** *adv* —**suddenness** *n* ◇ **all of a sudden** in a sudden and unexpected way

sudden death *n* the continuation of play in a tied sports contest until one team or player scores, that team or player being declared the winner

sudden infant death syndrome *n* cot death (*technical*)

sudoriferous /soódə ríffərəss, syoódə-/ *adj* producing sweat [Late 16C. < late Latin *sudorifer* 'sudorific' < Latin *sudor* 'sweat'.] —**sudoriferousness** *n*

sudorific /soódə ríffik, syoódə-/ *adj* causing the production of sweat ■ *n* a drug or other agent that causes sweating [Early 17C. < modern Latin *sudorificus* < late Latin *sudorifer* (see SUDORIFEROUS).]

Sudra /soódrə/ *n* 1 the lowest of the four main Hindu castes, traditionally comprising artisans and labourers and their families 2 a member of the Sudra caste [Mid-17C. < Sanskrit *śūdra*.]

suds /sudz/ *npl* a froth of bubbles on the surface of soapy water ■ *n US, Can* beer (*slang*) [Mid-16C. Probably < Middle Dutch *sudse* 'marsh, bog'.] —**sudsy** *adj*

sue /syoo, soo/ (**sues, suing, sued**) *v* 1 *vti* to take legal action against somebody to obtain something, usually compensation for a wrong 2 *vi* to make a humble, earnest, or begging request for something (*formal*) [12C. Via Anglo-Norman *suer* 'follow' < Latin *sequi*.] —**suability** *n* —**suable** *adj* —**suer** *n*

suede /swayd/ *n* 1 **LEATHER WITH VELVETY SURFACE** leather with the flesh side outward and rubbed up to make a velvety nap 2 **FABRIC LIKE SUEDE** a woven fabric that looks like suede ■ *vti* (**suedes, sueding, sueded**) **GIVE LEATHER A VELVETY NAP** to give leather a velvety nap [Mid-17C. < French *gants de Suède* 'gloves of Sweden' < *Suède* 'Sweden', where it originated.]

suet /soó it/ *n* a hard white fat found on the kidneys and loins of sheep and cattle. Use: cooking, tallow. [14C. Probably < Anglo-Norman, 'small suet' < *sue, seu* 'tallow, suet' < Latin *sebum*.] —**suety** *adj*

Suetonius /swee tṓni əss/, **Gaius Tranquillus** (69?–140) Roman biographer and historian

suet pudding *n* a sweet or savoury pudding made with suet, usually cooked by boiling or steaming

Suez /soó əz/ port in NE Egypt, at the head of the Gulf of Suez. Population: 388,000 (1992).

Suez Canal canal in NE Egypt, connecting the Mediterranean and the Red Sea. Length: 195 km/121 mi.

Suff. *abbr* 1 Suffolk 2 Suffragan

suffer /súffər/ *v* 1 *vti* **FEEL PAIN** to feel pain or great discomfort in body or mind 2 *vti* **UNDERGO SOMETHING UNPLEASANT** to experience or undergo something unpleasant or undesirable 3 *vti* **ENDURE** to endure or put up with something painful or unpleasant ○ *I do not suffer fools gladly.* 4 *vi* **HAVE ILLNESS** to have a disease or a physical or psychological condition 5 *vi* **HAVE AS WEAKNESS** to have as a bad quality, weakness, or flaw ○ *Their whole manifesto suffers from a lack of vision.* 6 *vi* **APPEAR TO BE LESS GOOD** to become or appear to be less good 7 *vi* **BE ADVERSELY AFFECTED** to be adversely affected by something ○ *The business suffered when the partnership was dissolved.* 8 *vt* **ALLOW** to allow somebody to do something (*archaic or literary*) [12C. Via Anglo-Norman *suffrir* < Latin *sufferre* 'carry up from underneath', hence 'sustain' < *ferre* 'carry'.] —**sufferer** *n* —**sufferable** *adj*

~~**sufferage**~~ incorrect spelling of **suffrage**

sufferance /súffərənss/ *n* 1 **TOLERANCE OF SOMETHING PROHIBITED** tacit permission for or tolerance of something, because no action is taken to prevent it 2 **ENDURANCE OF DIFFICULTY OR PAIN** the capacity to withstand difficulty or pain 3 **PATIENT ENDURANCE** the fact of enduring hardship patiently (*archaic*) ◇ **on sufferance** as a result of permission or consent given reluctantly and liable to be withdrawn

suffering /súffəring/ *n* physical or psychological pain and distress, or an experience of it

suffice /sə físs/ (**-fices, -ficing, -ficed**) *vti* to be enough for somebody or something [14C. < Old French *suffic-* < Latin *sufficere* 'make up to' < *facere* 'make'.] ◇ **suffice it to say that** used to indicate that what you are saying is all that needs to be said on a subject

~~**sufficiant**~~ incorrect spelling of **sufficient**

sufficient /sə físh'nt/ *adj* as much as is needed [14C. Directly or via Old French < Latin *sufficient-*, present participle of *sufficere* (see SUFFICE).] —**sufficiently** *adv* —**sufficiency** *n*

sufficient reason *n* the philosophical principle that nothing happens by chance and that an explanation must be available for everything

suffix *n* /súffiks/ a letter or group of letters added at the end of a word or word part to form another word, e.g. '-ly' in 'quickly' or '-ing' in 'talking' ■ *vt* /súffiks, sə fíks/ to add something as a suffix [Early 17C. Via modern Latin *suffixum* < Latin *suffigere* 'fasten underneath' < *figere* (see FIX).] —**suffixal** *adj* —**suffixation** /súffik sáysh'n/ *n*

suffocate /súffə kayt/ (**-cates, -cating, -cated**) *vti* 1 **STOP BREATHING** to deprive somebody of air or prevent somebody from breathing, or to be unable to breathe 2 **DIE FROM LACK OF AIR** to die from lack of air or kill somebody by stopping him or her from breathing 3 **MAKE OR FEEL TOO WARM** to feel uncomfortable or make somebody feel uncomfortable through excessive heat and lack of fresh air 4 **NOT ALLOW TO DEVELOP** to confine and restrict somebody or something with adverse effects, or be or feel confined and restricted in development or self-expression [15C. < Latin *suffocat-*, past participle of *suffocare* 'narrow up' < *fauc-* 'throat, narrow entrance'.] —**suffocating** *adj* —**suffocatingly** *adv* —**suffocation** /súffə káysh'n/ *n* —**suffocative** *adj*

Suffolk[1] /súffək/ county in E England. Area: 3,800 sq. km/1,467 sq. mi.

Suffolk[2] /súffək/ *n* a large black-faced hornless sheep belonging to a breed originating in England and kept for meat [Mid-19C. After SUFFOLK[1].]

Suffolk punch *n* a powerful horse with short legs and a chestnut-brown coat, belonging to a breed originating in England, used for pulling loads such as ploughs or carts [*Punch* < English dialect, 'stocky draught horse', shortening of PUNCHINELLO]

suffragan /súffrəgən/ *n* 1 a bishop appointed to assist the main bishop in a diocese 2 the bishop of a diocese who is an assistant to the archbishop of the province to which the diocese belongs [14C. Via Anglo-Norman and Old French < medieval Latin *suffraganeus* 'assisting' < Latin *suffragium* (see SUFFRAGE).] —**suffragan** *adj* —**suffraganship** *n*

suffrage /súffrij/ *n* 1 **RIGHT TO VOTE** the right to vote in public elections 2 **ACT OF VOTING** a vote or the act of voting (*literary*) 3 **SHORT PRAYER** a short prayer on behalf of somebody, especially a prayer said as part of a litany [14C. Directly and partly via French < Latin *suffragium* 'support, vote'.]

suffragette /súffrə jét/ *n* a woman campaigning for the right of women to vote in elections, especially one who took part in militant protests in the United Kingdom in the early 20th century —**suffragettism** *n*

suffragist /súffrəjist/ *n* a supporter of the extension of the right to vote to a particular group, especially to women, or to all people above a particular age —**suffragism** *n*

suffuse /sə fyoóz/ (**-fuses, -fusing, -fused**) *vt* to spread over or through something (*usually passive*) ○ *A blush suffused his face with colour.* [Late 16C. < Latin *suffus-*, past participle of *suffundere* 'pour from below' < *fundere* 'pour'.] —**suffusion** /sə fyoózh'n/ *n* —**suffusive** /sə fyoóssiv/ *adj*

Sufi /soófi/ (*plural* **-fis**) *n* a Muslim mystic [Mid-17C. < Arabic *ṣūfī* 'woollen' (because of their woollen garments).] —**Sufi** *adj* —**Sufic** *adj* —**Sufism** *n* —**Sufistic** *adj*

~~**suficient**~~ incorrect spelling of **sufficient**

sugar /shóoggər/ *n* 1 **SWEET-TASTING SUBSTANCE** a sweet-tasting substance, usually in the form of tiny hard white or brown grains. Source: sugar cane, sugar beet. Use: sweetener for food and drinks. 2 **PORTION OF SUGAR** a spoonful, lump, cube, or other portion of sugar ○ *likes his coffee black with two sugars* 3 **SWEET CARBOHYDRATE** any simple carbohydrate that is sweet-tasting, crystalline, and soluble in water 4 **TERM OF ENDEARMENT** used as a term of endearment (*informal*) 5 **WAY OF MAKING SOMETHING MORE AGREEABLE** something used as a means of persuasion or to make a difficult or unpleasant thing seem less so 6 **STRONG DRUG** a strong drug such as heroin or LSD (*dated slang*) ■ *v* 1 *vt* **ADD SUGAR TO** to add sugar to food or a drink 2 *vi* **MAKE SUGAR** to make sugar or form sugar crystals 3 *vt* **TRY TO MAKE SOMETHING MORE AGREEABLE** to try to make something more appealing or flattering or to make something unpleasant seem less so ■ *interj* **EXPRESSION OF ANNOYANCE** used to express annoyance [13C. Via Old French *çukre, sukere* < medieval Latin *succarum*, via Arabic *sukkar* < Sanskrit *śarkarā* 'grit, ground sugar'.] —**sugared** *adj*

sugar apple *n* = **sweetsop**

sugar beet *n* a variety of beet with a large whitish conical root that is an important commercial source of sugar. *Beta vulgaris.*

sugar candy *n* sugar in the form of large crystals made by suspending a string or stick in a strong sugar solution and allowing crystals to form and grow

sugar cane *n* a tall tough-stemmed species of grass grown in warm regions throughout the world as a source of sugar, which is obtained from its sweet sap. *Saccharum officinarum.* (*hyphenated before nouns*)

sugarcoat /shóoggər kṓt/ *vt* 1 to enclose something in a hard sugar shell or coat something with sugar 2 to make something unpleasant seem less so

sugar daddy *n* a rich man who gives money and gifts to a younger partner in a relationship (*informal*)

sugar diabetes *n* diabetes mellitus (*not in technical use*)

sugar glider *n* a possum that feeds on flowers, sap, and insects and has flaps of skin attached to its limbs enabling it to glide from tree to tree. Native to: E Australia. *Petaurus norfolcensis.*

sugar gum *n* a small eucalyptus tree with smooth bark, barrel-shaped fruit, and sweet-tasting leaves. *Eucalyptus cladocalyx.*

sugar loaf *n* 1 a solid cone-shaped mass of refined sugar 2 something that has a conical shape like a cone of sugar, e.g. a hill

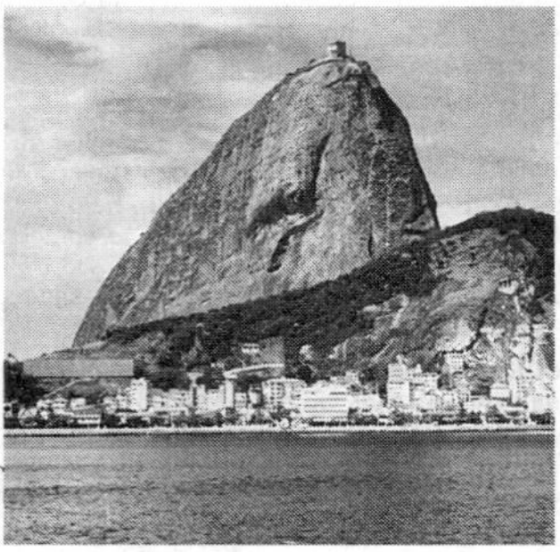

Barnaby's

Sugarloaf Mountain

Sugarloaf Mountain /shóoggər lṓf-/ peak on the edge of Rio de Janeiro, Brazil, that provides a panoramic view of the city. Height: 395 m./1,296 ft.

sugar maple *n* a maple from whose sweet sap maple sugar and maple syrup are made. Native to: North America. *Acer saccharum.*

sugar of lead *n* INDUST = **lead acetate**

sugar pea *n* a variety of garden pea with an edible thin flat pod. *Pisum sativum.*

sugarplum /shóoggər plum/ *n* a small round sweet made of boiled and flavoured sugar

sugar soap *n* a strong alkaline mixture of soap and washing soda used, e.g. for stripping paint or for cleaning surfaces before they are painted

sugary /shóoggəri/ *adj* **1 CONTAINING SUGAR** containing a great deal of sugar **2 LIKE SUGAR** looking or tasting like sugar **3 EXAGGERATEDLY PLEASANT** exaggeratedly and often insincerely pleasant or amiable **4 SENTIMENTAL** excessively sentimental —**sugariness** *n*

suggest /sə jést/ *vt* **1 PROPOSE FOR CONSIDERATION** to state or refer to somebody or something as a possible choice, plan, or course of action for somebody else to consider **2 REMIND SOMEBODY OF SOMETHING** to remind somebody of something or make somebody think of something **3 IMPLY** to imply or hint at something **4 INDICATE AS LIKELY** to indicate that something is likely [Early 16C. Back-formation < SUGGESTION.] —**suggester** *n*

SYNONYMS See ***recommend***.

suggestible /sə jéstəb'l/ *adj* **1** easily influenced by other people **2** capable of being suggested —**suggestibility** /sə jéstə bílləti/ *n* —**suggestibleness** *n* —**suggestibly** *adv*

suggestion /sə jéschən/ *n* **1 IDEA OR PROPOSAL** an idea or proposal put forward for consideration ○ *If I might make a suggestion, why don't we ask Ed to help us?* **2 SLIGHT TRACE** a slight trace, indication, or hint of something **3 ACT OF SUGGESTING** the act or process of suggesting something ○ *He was roused to fury by the mere suggestion of their innocence.* **4 ABILITY TO CONJURE UP ASSOCIATIONS** the ability of words or images to conjure up ideas or feelings, the process by which they do this, or a particular idea or image conjured up by something **5 PUTTING IDEAS INTO SOMEBODY'S MIND** the deliberate introduction into somebody's mind of an opinion, belief, or instruction, e.g. through hypnosis or advertising, so that it is accepted or acted on as that person's own idea ○ *The power of suggestion is used in TV commercials to make us want a product.* [14C. Directly or via French < Latin *suggestion-* < *suggerere* 'bring up' < *gerere* 'bring'.]

suggestive /sə jéstiv/ *adj* **1** able to conjure up ideas or images in the mind or start a train of thought **2** implying or hinting at something rude or improper —**suggestively** *adv* —**suggestiveness** *n*

Suharto /sóo haártō/ (*b.* 1921) Indonesian statesman

Sui /sway/ *n* a Chinese dynasty lasting from AD 581 to AD 618 that succeeded the Han dynasty, united all of N China, and reconquered S China

suicidal /sóo i sīd'l/ *adj* **1 WANTING TO COMMIT SUICIDE** intending or wishing to commit suicide **2 RELATING TO SUICIDE** produced by or involving a wish to commit suicide **3 EXTREMELY DANGEROUS** likely to lead to death, destruction, or ruin, or very much against somebody's own best interests **4 VERY UNHAPPY** deeply unhappy or frustrated (*informal*) —**suicidally** *adv*

suicide /sóo i sīd/ *n* **1 KILLING YOURSELF** the act of deliberately killing yourself **2 SOMEBODY WHO COMMITS SUICIDE** a person who intentionally kills himself or herself **3 DOING SOMETHING AGAINST OWN BEST INTERESTS** the act of doing something that seems contrary to your own best interests and likely to lead to a disaster such as financial ruin or loss of position or reputation [Mid-17C. < modern Latin *suicidium* 'killing of yourself' and *suicida* 'somebody who kills himself or herself', both < Latin *sui* 'of yourself'.]

suicide bombing *n* a bomb attack in which the person carrying out the attack deliberately allows himself or herself to be killed in the process of attempting to destroy something or kill somebody —**suicide bomber** *n*

suicide pact *n* an agreement between two or more people that they will kill themselves at the same time

suicide watch *n* the regular checking by prison warders of the cells of prisoners who are thought likely to commit suicide

sui generis /sóo ī jénnəriss/ *adj* unique, or in a class of its own [< Latin, 'of its own kind']

sui juris /sóo ī jóoriss/ *adj* competent to assume legal responsibility for his or her own affairs [< Latin, 'of its own right']

suint /swint/ *n* the grease found in sheep's wool, formed from dried perspiration [Late 18C. < French < *suer* 'sweat' < Latin *sudare* (see SUDATORY).]

suit /soot, syoot/ *n* **1 CLOTHES MADE OF SAME MATERIAL** a set of clothes made from the same material, consisting of a jacket and trousers or a skirt, sometimes together with a waistcoat **2 CLOTHES FOR PARTICULAR PURPOSE** a piece of clothing or set of clothes worn for a particular purpose (*often in combination*) ○ *a diving suit* **3 SET OF PLAYING CARDS** one of the four different sets of playing cards in a pack **4 LEGAL PROCEEDINGS** a case brought to a law court **5 PETITION** a petition, especially to somebody in authority (*formal*) **6 BUSINESS EXECUTIVE** a business executive, especially when seen as an anonymous bureaucrat (*slang*) **7 SET OF SAILS OR TOOLS** a set of sails or tools **8 WOOING OF WOMAN** a man's wooing of a woman and attempts to persuade her to marry him (*archaic*) ■ *v* **1** *vti* **BE RIGHT** to be appropriate to or the right thing for somebody or something **2** *vti* **BE CONVENIENT** to be convenient or acceptable to somebody **3** *vt* **LOOK GOOD ON** to look good on somebody or go well with something ○ *The colour suits you.* **4** *vt Scotland* **LOOK GOOD IN** to look good in a particular colour or garment ○ *Emma really suits purple.* **5** *vt* **BE SATISFYING** to be something that a person likes or enjoys **6** *vt* **MAKE SUITABLE** to adapt something in order to meet requirements or circumstances **7** *vr* **PLEASE YOURSELF** to do what you prefer [13C. Via Anglo-Norman *siute* < assumed Vulgar Latin *sequere* 'follow', alteration of Latin *sequi*.] ◇ **be somebody's strong suit** to be something at which somebody is particularly good ◇ **follow suit 1** to do the same as somebody else has done **2** to play a card of the same suit as the previous player

suitable /sóotəb'l, syóo-/ *adj* of the right type or quality for a particular purpose or occasion —**suitability** /sóotə bílləti, syóot-/ *n* —**suitableness** *n*

suitably /sóotəbli, syóot-/ *adv* **1** in a way that is right for a particular purpose or occasion **2** to an appropriate or the expected extent

suitcase /sóot kayss, syóot-/ *n* a rectangular case used for carrying clothes and other belongings during travel

ϟ **suite** /sweet/ *n* **1 SET OF MATCHING FURNITURE** a set of matching furniture for a room, e.g. a sofa and two armchairs (**a three-piece suite**) for a lounge **2 SET OF ROOMS** a set of rooms, e.g. in a hotel **3 SET OF INSTRUMENTAL WORKS PERFORMED TOGETHER** a set of instrumental pieces, especially dances, intended to be performed together **4 PEOPLE WITH VIP** a group of followers, servants, or advisers accompanying somebody important **5 INTEGRATED SOFTWARE PACKAGE** a collection of integrated application programs functioning as a single program, each of which can incorporate data from the others, eliminating the need for re-entry or transfer of data [Late 17C. Via French < assumed Vulgar Latin *sequere* (see SUIT).]

SPELLCHECK Do not confuse ***suite*** with ***sweet***, which has a similar sound. Beware: your spellchecker will not catch this error.

suiting /sóoting, syóot-/ *n* material for making suits

suitor /sóotər, syóotər/ *n* **1 MAN WOOING WOMAN** a man who is trying to persuade a woman to marry him (*formal*) **2 SOMEBODY WHO BRINGS LAWSUIT** somebody on whose behalf a case is brought to a law court **3 SOMEBODY SEEKING TO TAKE OVER BUSINESS** a person who seeks to buy or take over a business [13C. Via Anglo-Norman *seutor, suitour* < Latin *secutor* 'follower' < *sequi* (see SUIT).]

Sukarno /soo kaárnō/ (1901–70) Indonesian statesman and president of Indonesia (1945–68)

sukiyaki /sóoki yaáki/ *n* a Japanese dish consisting of thin slices of meat, vegetables, and noodles, cooked quickly in a sweet soy sauce [Early 20C. < Japanese, 'slice-grill'.]

sukkah /sóokə/, **succah** *n* a temporary light shelter with a roof of branches built in Jewish homes, gardens, or temples for the festival of Sukkoth [Late 19C. < Hebrew *sukkāh* 'hut'.]

Sukkoth /sóokəss, sóo kōt, sóo kōth, sóo kōss/, **Succoth, Sukkot** *n* an eight-day Jewish autumn harvest festival. Date: from the eve of the 15th of Tishri. [Late 19C. < Hebrew *sukkōṯ*, the plural of *sukkāh* (see SUKKAH).]

Sukkur /súkər/ city and district in SE Pakistan, on the banks of the Indus. Population: 190,551 (1981).

Sulawesi /soolə wáysi/ island in Indonesia, in the Malay Archipelago east of Borneo. Population: 13,732,500 (1995). Area: 189,040 sq. km/72,989 sq. mi.

Sulayman I /sóolli maán, sóoli maán, sóol ay maán/ = **Suleiman I**

sulcate /súl kayt/ *adj* marked with lengthwise parallel grooves ○ *a sulcate shell/stem* [Mid-18C. < Latin *sulcatus*, past participle of *sulcare* 'furrow' < *sulcus* (see SULCUS).] —**sulcation** /sul káysh'n/ *n*

sulcus /súl kəss/ (*plural* **-ci** /-sī/) *n* a shallow groove or depression, especially any of those separating the convolutions of the surface of the brain [Mid-17C. < Latin, 'furrow, trench'.]

Suleiman I (the Magnificent) /sóolli maán, sóoli maán, sóol ay maán/, **Sulayman I** (1494–1566) Ottoman sultan

sulfamethazine /súlfə méthə zeen/ *n US* PHARM = **sulphadimidine** [Mid-20C. < *sulfa-* (see SULPHA DRUG) + METH- + AZINE.]

sulfonyl /súlfənil/ *n* US = **sulphonyl**

sulfur *n* **1** US = **sulphur 2** sulphur (*technical*)

sulk /sulk/ *vi* **BE ANGRILY SILENT** to refuse to talk to or associate with others as a show of resentment for a real or imagined grievance ■ *n* **1 BAD-TEMPERED SILENCE** a period, state, or show of resentfulness and refusal to communicate **2 SOMEBODY WHO SULKS** a person who sulks [Late 18C. Back-formation < SULKY.] —**sulker** *n*

sulky /súlki/ *adj* (**-ier, -iest**) in a bad mood and refusing to communicate because of resentment for a real or imagined grievance ■ *n* (*plural* **-ies**) a light open two-wheeled vehicle for one person, pulled by one horse [Mid-18C. < ?] —**sulkily** *adv* —**sulkiness** *n*

Sulla /súllə, sóollə/, **Lucius Cornelius** (138–78 BC) Roman general

sullage /súllij/ *n* **1** sewage or any other form of waste or refuse **2** solid material deposited by flowing water, e.g. by a river [Mid-16C. < ?]

sullen /súllən/ *adj* **1 HOSTILELY SILENT** showing bad temper or hostility by a refusal to talk, behave sociably, or cooperate cheerfully **2 CLOUDY AND DULL** dull and grey because of clouds, fog, or haze (*literary*) **3 SLOW-MOVING** moving slowly (*literary*) ○ *a sullen stream* [14C. < Anglo-Norman *sulein* 'alone' < *sol* 'sole, single' < Latin *solus* (see SOLE[2]).] —**sullenly** *adv* —**sullenness** *n*

Sullivan /súllivən/, **Sir Arthur** (1842–1900) British composer

Sullivan, Louis (1856–1924) US architect

Sullom Voe /súlləm vṓ/ inlet on Mainland island, Shetland Islands, NE Scotland. Length: 13 km/8 mi.

sully /súlli/ (**-lies, -lying, -lied**) *v* **1** *vti* to spoil or detract from something, especially somebody's reputation, that has previously been pure and honourable, or to become spoiled or tarnished **2** *vt* to make something dirty (*literary*) [Late 16C. < ?] —**sullied** *adj*

sulph- *prefix* sulphur ○ *sulphite* [< SULPHUR]

sulphadiazine /súlfə dī ə zeen/ *n* $C_{10}H_{10}N_4O_2S$ a sulpha drug. Use: treatment of bacterial infections, especially in weakened patients. [Mid-20C. < *sulpha-* (see SULPHA DRUG) + DIAZINE.]

sulphadimidine /súlfə dímmi deen/ *n* $C_{12}H_{14}N_4O_2S$ a sulphonamide. Use: treatment of bacterial infections. US term **sulfamethazine** [Mid-20C. < SULPH- + DI-[1] + *pyrimidine*.]

sulpha drug /súlfə-/ *n* any bacteriostatic drug synthesized from sulphonamide. Use: treatment of bacterial infections, but now rarely used because of their toxicity and the resistance of bacteria to them. [*Sulpha* shortening of SULPHANILAMIDE]

sulphamic acid /sul fámmik-/ *n* H_3NSO_3 a colourless crystalline solid. Use: manufacture of weedkillers, flame-proofing agents, and artificial sweeteners. [*Sulphamic* contraction of SULPH- + AMIDIC]

sulphanilamide /súlfə níllə mīd/ *n* $C_6H_8N_2O_2S$ the first sulpha drug. Use: formerly, treatment of bacterial infections. [Mid-20C. < SULPH- + ANILINE + AMIDE.]

sulphatase /súlfə tayz/ *n* an enzyme that accelerates the decomposition of sulphuric esters

sulphate /súl fayt/ *n* **SULPHURIC ACID SALT OR ESTER** a salt or ester of sulphuric acid ■ *v* (**-phates, -phating, -phated**) **1** *vti* **MAKE LAYER OF LEAD SULPHATE** to make a layer of lead sulphate form on the plates of an accumulator, or become covered with lead sulphate **2** *vt* **TREAT SOMETHING WITH SULPHUR** to treat something with sulphur, sulphuric acid, or a sulphate **3** *vt* **CONVERT TO SULPHATE** to convert something to a sulphate —**sulphation** /sul fáysh'n/ *n*

sulphide /súl fīd/ *n* a compound in which sulphur is typically combined with one or more electropositive elements or groups

sulphite /súl fīt/ *n* a salt or ester of sulphurous acid —**sulphitic** /sul fíttik/ *adj*

sulphon- *prefix* sulphonic ○ *sulphonyl* [< SULPHONE]

sulphonamide /sul fónnə mīd/ *n* any of a group of compounds responsible for the antibacterial action of sulpha drugs, which work by depriving bacteria of the ability to synthesize folic acid [Late 19C. < SULPHONE + AMIDE.]

sulphonate /súlfə nayt/ *n* a salt or ester of sulphonic acid ■ *vt* to treat an organic substance with sulphuric acid [Late 19C. < SULPHONIC.] —**sulphonation** /súlfə náysh'n/ *n*

sulphone /súlfōn/ *n* any compound containing the sulphonyl group in which sulphur is attached to two carbon atoms [Late 19C. < German *Sulfon* < *Sulfur* 'sulphur'.]

sulphonic /sulfónnik/ *adj* relating to, containing, or derived from the acid group SO_2OH [Late 19C. < German *Sulfon* (see SULPHONE).]

sulphonic acid *n* a strong organic acid. Use: manufacture of dyes, drugs.

sulphonium /sul fṓni əm/ *n* an ion or radical containing sulphur with a valency of three [Late 19C. < SULPHUR.]

sulphonmethane /súl fon mée thayn/ *n* $C_7H_{16}O_4S_2$ a colourless, crystalline, potentially addictive drug. Use: hypnotic.

sulphonyl /súlfənil/ *n* the bivalent chemical group SO_2 [Early 20C. < SULPHONIC.]

sulphonylurea /súlfə nīl yŏŏ rée ə/ *n* an oral drug. Use: lowers blood sugar in diabetics.

sulphoxide /sul fóksīd/ *n* an organic chemical compound in which a group consisting of a sulphur and an oxygen atom is bonded to two carbon atoms

sulphur /súlfər/ *n* **1** (*symbol* **S**) a non-metallic yellow element that occurs alone in nature or combined in sulphide and sulphate minerals. Use: manufacture of sulphuric acid, matches, fungicides, and gunpowder. **2** a yellowish-green colour [14C. Via Anglo-Norman *sulf(e)re* < Latin *sulfur, sulphur*.] —**sulphur** *adj* —**sulphury** *adj*

USAGE In chemistry, the spelling with **-f-** is now the agreed international standard for **sulfur** and all related words.

sulphurate /súlfyŏŏ rayt/ (**-rates, -rating, -rated**) *vt* to treat or combine something with sulphur —**sulphuration** /súlfyŏŏ ráysh'n/ *n*

sulphur bacterium *n* a bacterium that is capable of metabolizing sulphur or inorganic sulphur compounds. Genus: *Thiobacillus*.

sulphur butterfly *n* a butterfly that has yellow or orange wings with black markings. Genus: *Colias*.

sulphur-crested cockatoo *n* a large white cockatoo that lives in large noisy flocks and has a distinctive yellow crest. Native to: N and E Australia, Tasmania. *Cacatua galerita*.

sulphur dioxide *n* a colourless pungent toxic gas and air pollutant formed by burning sulphur or fuels containing sulphur. Use: food preservative, fumigant, bleaching agent, manufacture of sulphuric acid.

sulphureous *adj* = **sulphurous** —**sulphureously** *adv* —**sulphureousness** *n*

sulphuric /sul fyŏŏrik/ *adj* relating to or containing sulphur, especially with a valency of six

sulphuric acid *n* H_2SO_4 a strong colourless oily corrosive acid. Use: batteries, manufacture of fertilizers, explosives, detergents, dyes, chemicals.

sulphurize /súlfyŏŏ rīz/ (**-izes, -izing, -ized**), **sulphurise** (**-ises, -ising, -ised**) *vt* to treat or combine something with sulphur or a sulphur compound —**sulphurization** /súlfyŏŏ rī záysh'n/ *n*

sulphurous /súlfərəss/, **sulphureous** /sul fyŏŏri əss/ *adj* **1 CONTAINING SULPHUR** relating to or containing sulphur, especially with a valency of four **2 SIMILAR TO BURNING SULPHUR** with the colour or acrid smell of burning sulphur **3 RELATING TO HELL** relating to hell or hellfire (*literary*) **4 FIERY** fiery, especially in having or showing a violent temper or in being emotionally charged and containing many swearwords or blasphemies (*literary*) [15C. < Latin *sulphurosus*, or < SULPHUR.] —**sulphurously** *adv* —**sulphurousness** *n*

sulphurous acid *n* H_2SO_3 a weak colourless acid made by dissolving sulphur dioxide in water. Use: disinfectant, food preservative, bleaching agent.

sulphur pearl *n* a very large bacterium, typically between 0.1 and 0.3 mm in size but sometimes larger, found in sediments off the coast of W Namibia. It uses nitrates as its source of oxygen in oxidizing and breaking down sulphur compounds. *Thiomargarita namibiensis*.

sulphur spring *n* a spring with significant amounts of sulphur compounds in the water

sulphur trioxide *n* a toxic, irritating liquid occurring in three forms with different melting points. Use: chemical synthesis.

sulphuryl /súllfyooril/ *n* CHEM = **sulfonyl** [Mid-19C. < SULPHUR + -YL.]

sultan /súltən/ *n* **1** formerly, the sovereign ruler of a Muslim country, especially the head of the Ottoman Empire **2** a man who is powerful in some sphere of activity, especially one who behaves in a domineering or tyrannical fashion (*literary*) [Mid-16C. Directly or via French < medieval Latin *sultanus* < Arabic *sulṭān* 'ruler, power' < Aramaic *saliṭa* 'rule'.] —**sultanic** /sul tánnik/ *adj* —**sultanship** *n*

sultana /sul taánə/ *n* **1** a small dried seedless white grape **2** a wife, mother, sister, daughter, or mistress of a sultan [Late 16C. < Italian, the feminine of *sultano* 'sultan' < Arabic *sulṭān* (see SULTAN).]

sultanate /súltənət/ *n* **1 COUNTRY RULED BY SULTAN** a country ruled by a sultan **2 RANK OF SULTAN** the rank or position of sultan **3 SULTAN'S REIGN** the period of a particular sultan's reign

sultry /súltri/ *adj* **1** oppressively hot and damp **2** giving a suggestion of underlying passion and sensuality [Late 16C. < Earlier *sulter* 'swelter' < ?] —**sultrily** *adv* —**sultriness** *n*

sum /sum/ *n* **1 AMOUNT OF MONEY** an amount of money **2 ARITHMETICAL CALCULATION** a mathematical problem involving adding, subtracting, multiplying, or dividing numbers, especially one given to students to solve **3 TOTAL** the total amount resulting when two or more numbers or quantities are added together **4 COMBINED TOTAL** the combined total amount of anything **5 GIST** the essential point of something that somebody has said or written (*literary*) **6 LIMIT OF SUM OF SERIES** the limit, as n increases indefinitely, of the sum of the first n terms of an infinite series ■ **sums** *npl* **ARITHMETIC** simple arithmetical work, especially for schoolchildren, involving addition, subtraction, multiplication, and division (*informal*) ■ *vt* (**sums, summing, summed**) **ADD UP** to add together two or more amounts to find their total (*formal*) [13C. Via Old French *summe* < Latin *summa* 'sum, substance' (literally 'highest (thing)'), a noun use of the feminine of *summus* 'highest' < *super* 'above' < Latin *summa* 'sum'.] ◇ **in sum** in short or as a summary

sum up *vti* **1** to present the main points or substance of something concisely **2** to summarize the main points of a court case for a jury (*refers to a judge*)

sumach /shŏŏ mak, sŏŏ/, **sumac** *n* **1** a tree or bush of the cashew family with red hairy fruit, and feathery leaves. Flowers: green, in clusters. Genus: *Rhus*. **2** the ground dried leaves of one species of sumach. Use: tanning, dyeing. [14C. Directly or via French *sumac* < medieval Latin *sumac(h)* < Arabic *summāḳ*.]

~~**sumary**~~ incorrect spelling of **summary**

Sumatra /soo maátrə/ island in W Indonesia, separated from the Malay Peninsula by the Strait of Malacca. Population: 36,881 (1990). Area: 473,605 sq. km/182,860 sq. mi. —**Sumatran** *n, adj*

Sumer /sŏŏmər/ ancient country of S Mesopotamia, in present-day Iraq

Sumerian /soo méeri ən/ *n* **1** a member of an ancient people that built the civilization of Sumer **2** the language of ancient Sumer, unrelated to any other known language —**Sumerian** *adj*

summa /súmmə, sŏŏmə/ (*plural* **-mae** /-mee, -mee/) *n* a summary of what is known of a subject, especially a medieval treatise on theology, philosophy, canon law, or alchemy [15C. < Latin, 'main thing, substance, gist', a noun use of the feminine of *summus* (see SUM).]

summa cum laude /súmmə kum láwdi, sŏŏmə kŏŏm lów day/ *adv US* achieving the highest academic honours at graduation, usually awarded on the basis of the average of the candidates' marks. ◊ **cum laude, magna cum laude** [< Latin, 'with highest praise'] —**summa cum laude** *adj*

summae plural of **summa**

summand /súmmand, su mánd/ *n* any number or quantity in a sum [Mid-19C. < medieval Latin *summandus* 'for adding', a form of *summare* 'add' < *summa* (see SUM).]

summarily /súmmərəli/ *adv* immediately and without discussion or attention to formalities

summarize /súmmə rīz/ (**-rizes, -rizing, -rized**), **summarise** (**-rises, -rising, -rised**) *vti* to make or give a shortened version of something that has been said or written, stating its main points —**summarist** *n* —**summarizable** *adj* —**summarization** /súmmə rī záysh'n/ *n* —**summarizer** *n*

summary /súmməri/ *n* (*plural* **-ries**) **SHORT VERSION CONTAINING GIST OF SOMETHING** a shortened version of something that has been said or written, containing only the main points ■ *adj* **1 IMMEDIATE** done immediately and with little discussion or attention to formalities **2 GIVING ONLY MAIN POINTS** shortened and giving only the main points of something **3 RELATING TO MAGISTRATES' COURTS** relating to, dealt with, or given by magistrates' courts operating without the formality of full proceedings [15C. < Latin *summarium* < *summa* (see SUM).] —**summariness** *n*

summation /su máysh'n/ *n* **1 ADDITION** the process of adding something up to find a total **2 TOTAL** a total amount or aggregate **3 SUMMARY OF SOMETHING SAID** a summary of something that has been said or written **4** *US* **FINAL ARGUMENT IN COURT** the final summing-up of an argument in a court of law [Mid-18C. < the modern Latin stem *summation-* < medieval Latin *summare* (see SUMMAND).] —**summational** *adj* —**summative** /súmmətiv/ *adj*

summer[1] /súmmər/ *n* **1 WARMEST SEASON** the warmest season of the year, falling between spring and autumn, and reckoned astronomically from the summer solstice to the autumn equinox **2 WARM WEATHER** the warm weather associated with the summer season **3 PERIOD OF GREAT HAPPINESS** a period of greatest happiness, success, or fulfilment in the life of somebody or something **4 YEAR** a year, especially of somebody's age (*literary*) ■ *v* **1** *vi* **SPEND SUMMER** to spend the summer ○ *They summer at the lake.* **2** *vt* **PASTURE FOR SUMMER** to keep cattle or other animals on a particular pasture during the summer [Old English *sumor, sumer* < Germanic] —**summery** *adj*

summer[2] /súmmər/ *n* **1** a principal horizontal beam in a building used to support floor joists **2** a stone that lies on top of a pier, column, or wall and supports one or more arches **3** BUILDING = **lintel** [13C. Via Anglo-Norman *sumer*, Old French *som(i)er* 'main beam' (originally 'pack horse') < late Latin *sagmarius* 'pack horse' < *sagma* 'pack-saddle' < Greek. The semantic development resulted from analogy between a burdened pack horse and a main supporting beam in a structure.]

summer camp *n* a place, usually residential, offering outdoor recreational activities and skill development for children during the summer

summerhouse /súmmər howss/ (*plural* **-houses** /súmmər howziz/) *n* a small building or structure in a garden or park to give seating and shade during the summer [Old English *sumerhūs*]

summer pudding *n* a cold pudding consisting of soft fruits such as blackberries, raspberries, and strawberries, cooked together and placed inside a casing of white bread that absorbs their juice

summersault *n, vi* = **somersault**

summer school *n* a course of study held during the summer vacation or holiday, in Britain usually a course of university lectures

summer squash *n* a squash eaten as a vegetable shortly after picking in the summer. *Cucurbita pepo melopepo*.

summer time *n* time that is one hour ahead of standard time, used in order to extend the hours of daylight in the evening

summertime /súmmər tīm/ *n* the season of summer

summer tree *n* BUILDING = **summer**[2] *n.* 1

summit /súmmit/ *n* **1 HIGHEST POINT OF MOUNTAIN** the highest point or top of something, especially a mountain **2 HIGHEST POINT OF SOMETHING** the highest point, level, or degree of something such as a career **3 TOP-LEVEL DIPLOMATIC CONFERENCE** a meeting between heads of government or other high-ranking officials to discuss a matter of great importance [14C. < Old French *som(m)ete*, *sumet* 'small top' < *som, sum* 'top' < Latin *summum*, the neuter of *summus* (see SUM).] —**summital** *adj*

summit conference *n* a meeting between heads of government to discuss some important matter such as disarmament

summiteer /súmmi tèer/ *n* a participant in a summit conference

summitry /súmmitri/ *n US* the practice of holding, or deciding matters of international importance through, summit conferences

summon /súmmən/ *v* **1** *vt* **CALL INTO COURT** to order somebody to attend court by serving a summons **2** *vt* **SEND FOR** to send or be a signal for somebody to come ○ *We were summoned to his presence.* **3** *vt* **CONVENE GROUP** to call together a formal or official body ○ *They summoned a meeting to debate the issue.* **4** *vt* **CALL UPON** to request or require somebody to do something ○ *She summoned him to help her.* **5** *vi* **MANAGE TO GET** to gather the resources, especially courage or strength, to cope with or do something ○ *trying to summon up the courage to tell him the news* [13C. Via Old French *sumondre* < Latin *summonere* 'remind secretly' < *sub-* 'under' + *monere* 'warn'.]

summons /súmmənz/ *n* **1** **COURT ORDER TO DEFENDANT** a written order to somebody to attend court to answer a complaint **2** **COURT ORDER TO WITNESS** a written order to a witness to attend court **3** **ORDER BY AUTHORITY TO APPEAR** an authoritative demand to appear at a particular place for a particular purpose ■ *vt* **SERVE SOMEBODY WITH SUMMONS** to serve somebody with a summons to attend court [13C. < Old French *somonse*, feminine past participle of *somondre* (see SUMMON).]

sumo /sóomō/ *n* traditional Japanese wrestling in which each contestant tries to force the other outside a circle or to touch the ground other than with the soles of his feet [Late 19C. < Japanese *sumō*.]

sump /sump/ *n* **1** **RESERVOIR FOR LIQUID** a low area such as a pit or reservoir into which a liquid drains **2** **LOWEST PART OF CRANKCASE** a part located at the bottom of the crankcase of an internal-combustion engine that serves as a lubricating oil reservoir. US term **oil pan** **3** = **cesspool** *n.* 1 **4** **DRAINAGE RESERVOIR IN MINE** an area at the bottom of a mineshaft into which water drains and is then pumped away **5** **ADVANCE EXCAVATION** an excavation ahead of the main excavation of a mineshaft or tunnel [15C. < Middle Dutch *somp* or Middle Low German *sump*.]

sumpter /súmptər/ *n* a packhorse, mule, or other pack animal (*archaic*) [Late 16C. Via Old French *sommetier* 'packhorse driver' < assumed Vulgar Latin *saumatarius* < Latin *sagma* 'packsaddle' < Greek, < *sattein* 'pack' < ?]

~~sumptious~~ incorrect spelling of **sumptuous**

sumptuary /súmptyoo əri/ *adj* **1** relating to or controlling personal spending **2** intended to regulate personal behaviour on moral or religious grounds [Early 17C. < Latin *sumptuarius* < *sumptus* 'expense', past participle of *sumere* 'spend', literally 'take up' < *emere* (see EXAMPLE).]

sumptuous /súmptyoo əss/ *adj* **1** magnificent or grand in appearance **2** entailing great expense [15C. Via Old French *somptueux* < Latin *sumptuosus* < *sumptus* 'expense' (see SUMPTUARY).] —**sumptuously** *adv* —**sumptuousness** *n*

sum total *n* **1** a combined total of separate elements ○ *The sum total of his belongings is the clothes on his back.* **2** a numerical amount obtained by adding sums

sun /sun/ *n* **1** **Sun, sun STAR AROUND WHICH EARTH REVOLVES** the star at the centre of our solar system around which the Earth and the eight other planets orbit **2** **STAR** any star or bright astronomical object, especially one around which planets orbit **3** **SUN'S RADIATION** the light or heat emitted by the Sun **4** **SOMEBODY LIKE SUN** somebody or something thought to resemble the Sun in radiance, glory, or warmth, or in being the centre of a society (*literary*) **5** **DAY OR YEAR** a day or year (*literary*) ■ *v* (**suns, sunning, sunned**) **1** *vr* **BASK IN SUN** to expose the body to the sun's rays for warmth or for a suntan ○ *The cat lay sunning herself on the lawn.* **2** *vt* **WARM OR DRY IN SUN** to expose something to the sun's rays for warmth or drying [Old English *sunne*. Ultimately < Indo-European.] ◇ **catch the sun** to become a little tanned or sunburnt through exposure to the sun ◇ **take the sun** to go out in the sunshine, especially with the aim of gaining some benefit to your health or wellbeing ◇ **under the sun** in the whole world

SPELLCHECK See ***son***.

Sun. *abbr* Sunday

sunbaked /súnn baykt/ *adj* **1** hard and dry from prolonged exposure to the sun **2** baked by a process of exposure to the sun

sunbath /sún baath/ *n* an act or period of exposing the body to the sun or a sun lamp, especially in order to get a tan

sunbathe /súnn bayth/ *vi* to expose the body to sun or a sun lamp, especially in order to get a tan —**sunbather** *n*

sunbeam /sún beem/ *n* a ray of light emitted by the Sun —**sunbeamy** *adj*

sun bear *n* a small bear with sleek black fur, a light-coloured muzzle, and a yellowish breast marking. Native to: forests of SE Asia. *Helarctos malayanus*.

sunbed /sún bed/ *n* **1** an apparatus resembling a bed with a special canopy that emits rays of ultraviolet light so that the person lying on it develops a suntan. US term **tanning bed** **2** FURNITURE = **sunlounger**

sunbird /sún burd/ *n* a small brightly coloured songbird with a long thin curved bill. Native to: S and SE Asia, Africa, Australia. Family: Nectariniidae.

sun bittern *n* a semiarboreal solitary tropical wading bird with mottled brownish plumage featuring a chestnut marking like a sunburst when its wings are spread. Native to: Central and South America. *Eurypyga helius*.

sun blind *n* a blind or awning that shades a room from bright sunlight

sunblock /sún blok/ *n* a substance applied to the skin as a cream or lotion to protect it from the sun's ultraviolet rays

sunbonnet /sún bonit/ *n* a bonnet with a wide brim and a flap at the back, worn by babies and, formerly, by women to protect the face and neck from the sun

sunbow /sún bō/ *n* a spectrum of colours similar to a rainbow produced by sunlight refracting through spray, mist, or water vapour, e.g. above a waterfall [After 'rainbow']

sunburn /sún burn/ *n* an inflammation and sometimes blistering of the skin caused by overexposure to ultraviolet radiation from the sun ■ *vi* (**-burns, -burning, -burned** *or* **-burnt**) to cause the skin to become inflamed and sometimes blistered as a result of overexposure to ultraviolet radiation from the sun

sunburnt /sún burnt/, **sunburned** /-burnd/ *adj* **1** affected by sunburn **2** with a suntan

sunburst /sún burst/ *n* **1** **SUDDEN BURST OF SUNSHINE** a sudden appearance of the sun from behind clouds **2** **SUN-SHAPED DESIGN** a design meant to resemble the sun, consisting of a series of rays extending outwards from a central circle **3** **SUN-SHAPED BROOCH** a brooch or other ornament designed as a sunburst

Sunbury /súnbri/ town in S Victoria, Australia. Population: 18,533 (1991).

Sunbury-on-Thames /súnbəri on témz/ town in S England. Population: 27,392 (1991).

sundae /sún day, -di/ *n* an ice-cream dessert served with toppings [Late 19C. Alteration of SUNDAY.]

Sunda Islands /súndə-/ island group of the Malay Archipelago comprising the Greater Sunda Islands, which include Sumatra, Java and Borneo, and the Lesser Sunda Islands, which include Bali and Timor

sun dance *n* an important ceremonial dance of Native North American peoples living on prairies, held annually in honour of the sun

Sundanese /súndə néez/ (*plural* **-nese**) *n* **1** a member of a people living in the western part of Java, most of whom are Muslims **2** the Austronesian language of the Sundanese people. Native speakers: 27,000,000. [Late 19C. < Sundanese *Sunda*, W part of Java.] —**Sundanese** *adj*

Sunday /sún day, -di/ *n* **1** **7TH DAY OF WEEK** the day of the week after Saturday and before Monday **2** **CHRISTIAN SABBATH DAY** in Christian tradition, the day set aside for the Sabbath ■ *adj* **1** **OF SUNDAY** relating to or occupying a Sunday **2** **FOR SPECIAL OCCASIONS** worn or used for special occasions **3** **ONLY AT WEEKENDS OR AS HOBBY** lacking experience, efficiency, or professional skill ○ *These Sunday drivers are a menace on the roads.* [Old English *sunnandæg* 'day of the sun', a translation of Latin *dies solis*] ◇ **nine ways from Sunday** *US* in every possible way and to the greatest extent (*informal*) ○ *The potential cross-examination questions were covered nine ways from Sunday during pretrial preps.*

Sunday best *n* somebody's best clothes, traditionally worn on a Sunday to go to church

Sunday punch *n US* **1** a boxer's most powerful punch, especially a knockout blow **2** a means of delivering a devastating blow to an opponent

Sundays /sún dayz, -diz/ *adv* every Sunday ■ *npl* special format newspapers published on Sundays ○ *It's in all the Sundays.*

Sunday school *n* a school or class offering children religious education or activities on Sundays

sun deck *n* **1** an open upper deck on a passenger ship **2** *US, ANZ* a balcony, terrace, or platform attached to a building, used for sunbathing

sunder /súndər/ *vti* to separate or make something separate into parts, especially with force (*literary*) [Old English *sundrian* < *sundor* 'apart'. Ultimately < Indo-European.] —**sunderer** *n*

Sunderland /súndərlənd/ port in NE England. Population: 295,800 (1995).

sundew /sún dyoo/ *n* a plant that produces a rosette of hairy sticky leaves that are used to trap and digest insects. Native to: Australia, New Zealand. Family: Droseraceae. [Translation of Latin *ros solis*; so called because the drops of juice the plant secretes resemble dew]

sundial /sún dī əl/ *n* an instrument that shows the time of day by the position of a sun-generated shadow cast by a fixed arm (**gnomon**) onto a graduated plate or surface

sun disc *n* an ancient Egyptian sun-god symbol, consisting of a disc with wings and two serpents

sundog /sún dog/ *n* **1** ASTRON = **parhelion** **2** a small spectrum of light occasionally visible in the sky at the same altitude as the sun, either to the left or right of the sun and sometimes on both sides simultaneously

sundown /sún down/ *n* the time when the sun sets

sundowner /sún downər/ *n UK, S Africa* an alcoholic drink taken early in the evening, around sunset (*informal*)

sundrenched /sún drencht/ *adj* enjoying much hot sunshine

sundress /sún dress/ *n* a light sleeveless summer dress with a low bodice that exposes the shoulders, back, and arms to the sun

sun-dried *adj* dried out naturally by the sun, not by applying artificial heat

sundries /súndriz/ *npl* **1** small miscellaneous items, often of too little value to be enumerated **2** items of food, especially breads or other small extras, that can be ordered in a restaurant as an accompaniment to a meal

sundry /súndri/ *adj* assorted but, perhaps for convenience, being considered as a single category or group ○ *and other sundry items.* ◊ **sundries** ■ *n Aus* an extra [Old English *syndrig* 'separate'] ◇ **all and sundry** everyone without exception (+ *plural verb*)

Sundsvall /sóondz val/ town in east-central Sweden, on the Gulf of Bothnia. Population: 94,531 (1995).

sunfish /sún fish/ *n* **1** a large brownish-blue marine fish that is nearly oval and has high dorsal and anal fins that it uses like oars for locomotion. Family: Molidae. **2** a small to medium sized spiny-finned freshwater fish, often with iridescent colours. Native to: North America. Family: Centrarchidae.

sunflower /sún flowər/ *n* **1** a tall annual plant with edible seeds, grown commercially for oil. Flowers: large heads of yellow petals with dark centre. *Helianthus annuus*. **2** any plant related to the sunflower. Genus: *Helianthus*. [Mid-16C. Translation of modern Latin *flos solis* and Greek *helianthos*.]

sung past participle of **sing**

Sung /sóong/, **Song** /song/ *n* a Chinese imperial dynasty lasting from AD 960–1279, under which science, philosophy, and the arts thrived [Late 17C. < Chinese *Song*.]

sungazer /sún gayzər/ *n* a lizard that grows to about 355 cm/14 in and is known for its habit of basking in the sun. Native to: southern Africa. *Cordylus giganteus*.

sunglass /sún glaass/ *n* a convex lens used to focus the sun's rays to produce heat, especially in order to start a fire ■ **sunglasses** *npl* glasses with tinted or darkened lenses to protect the eyes from sunlight or its glare

sunglow /sún glō/ *n* a pale pink or yellow glow seen in the sky just before sunrise or just after sunset

sun-god *n* **1** the sun worshipped as a god **2** a god that personifies or is seen as controlling the sun

sunhat /sún hat/ *n* a hat with a broad brim that is designed to keep the sun off the face and neck

suni /sóni/ (*plural* **-nis** *or* **-ni**) *n* a small antelope, growing to only about 355 cm/14 in long, that has small straight horns and a strong musky odour from facial glands. Native to: Southern Africa. *Neotragus moschatus.* [Late 19C. Of Bantu origin.]

sunk /sungk/ past participle, past tense of **sink** ■ *adj* without hope of success (*informal*)

USAGE See ***sink***.

sunken /súngkən/ *adj* **1 SUBMERGED** having sunk beneath the surface of something **2 HOLLOW-LOOKING** appearing hollow or concave ○ *sunken cheeks* **3 SUNK LOWER** having settled to a lower level **4 AT LOWER ELEVATION** at a lower level than something adjoining

USAGE See ***sink***.

sunk fence *n* a ditch containing a fence or wall that separates lands without marring the appearance of the landscape

sunlamp /sún lamp/ *n* **1** a lamp that emits ultraviolet light, used to get a suntan or for therapeutic purposes **2** a lamp with parabolic mirrors that are directed to focus light, used in cinema photography

sunless /súnləss/ *adj* **1** deprived of or lacking sunlight **2** without joy or happiness

sunlight /sún līt/ *n* light emitted by the sun —**sunlit** /súnlit/ *adj*

sun lounge *n* a room with large windows designed to receive the maximum sunlight. ◊ **sunroom**

sunlounger /sún lownjər/ *n* a light folding chair with an extended section for the legs, used for sunbathing

sunn /sun/ *n* **1** a strong light plant fibre. Use: rope, sacks. **2** a thin-branched tropical plant whose inner bark yields sunn. Native to: Asia, Australia. *Crotalaria juncea*. [Late 18C. Via Hindustani *san* < Sanskrit *śāṇa-* 'hempen'.]

Sunna /sóonə, súnnə/ *n* one of the basic sources of Islamic law, based on Muhammad's words and deeds as recorded in the Hadith [Early 18C. < Arabic, 'rule, custom'.]

Sunni /sóoni, súnni/ (*plural* **-ni** *or* **-nis**) *n* **1** the largest branch of Islam, which believes in the traditions of the Sunna and accepts the first four caliphs as rightful successors to Muhammad. ◊ **Shia 2** a member of the Sunni branch of Islam [Late 16C. < Arabic, 'lawful' < *sunna* 'rule, custom'.]

Sunnite /sóonīt, súnn-/ *n* ISLAM = **Sunni** *n.* **2**

sunny /súnni/ (**-nier, -niest**) *adj* **1 FULL OF SUNSHINE** with a lot of sunshine **2 FULL OF SUNLIGHT** bright with or exposed to sunlight **3 CHEERFUL** characterized by or showing happiness or cheerfulness —**sunnily** *adv* —**sunniness** *n*

sunny-side up *adj* describes fried eggs that are not turned over in cooking and so have a visible yellow yolk uppermost

sun protection factor *n* full form of **SPF**

sunrise /sún rīz/ *n* **1 COMING UP OF SUN** the rising of the sun above the eastern horizon each morning **2 GLOW FROM RISING SUN** an atmospheric glow and colouring near the horizon as the sun rises **3 TIME SUN RISES** the time at which the sun rises above the horizon in the morning

sunroof /sún roof/ *n* a small panel in the roof of a car that can be raised or slid back to let in air and light

sunroom /sún room, -ròom/ *n US, ANZ* a room with large windows designed to receive the maximum sunlight. ◊ **sun lounge**

sunscreen /sún skreen/ *n* a substance applied to the skin as a cream, lotion, or oil to protect it from burning without preventing tanning

sunset /sún set/ *n* **1 GOING DOWN OF SUN** the setting of the sun below the western horizon in the evening **2 GLOW FROM SETTING SUN** an atmospheric glow and colouring near the horizon as the sun sets **3 TIME SUN SETS** the time at which the sun sets below the horizon in the evening **4 LAST PART** the period during which something is declining or coming to an end

sunshade /sún shayd/ *n* something, e.g. an awning or parasol, under which somebody is protected from the sun

sunshine /sún shīn/ *n* **1 DIRECT SUNLIGHT** direct rays of the sun, producing heat and light ○ *a ray of sunshine* **2 SUNNY PLACE** a place where the sun's rays are falling ○ *Let's sit in the sunshine.* **3 SOURCE OF GOOD FEELINGS** somebody or something producing joy, happiness, or warmth ○ *bringing a little bit of sunshine into people's lives* **4 FAMILIAR TERM OF ADDRESS** used to address somebody in a cheerful or familiar way (*informal; often used ironically*) ○ *Listen, sunshine, you just watch what you're saying, okay?* —**sunshiny** *adj*

Sunshine Coast /sún shīn-/ region in SE Queensland, Australia

sunspecs /sún speks/ *npl* sunglasses (*informal*)

sunspot /sún spot/ *n* **1** one of the relatively cool dark patches that appear in cycles on the Sun's surface and possess a powerful magnetic field **2** a place that has a warm and sunny climate and is usually popular as a holiday destination (*informal*)

sunstone /súnstōn/ *n* MINERALS = **aventurine** *n.* **2** [Translation of Latin *gemma solis*]

sunstroke /súnstrōk/ *n* a condition caused by prolonged and excessive exposure to the sun and characterized by feverishness, faintness, convulsions, and coma. Technical name **insolation**

sunsuit /sún soot, -syoot/ *n* a child's one-piece garment usually consisting of shorts and a bib top with shoulder straps, worn in hot weather

suntan /sún tan/ *n* = **tan**[1] *n.* **2** —**suntanned** *adj*

suntrap /sún trap/ *n* a sheltered area with bright sunlight and little or no wind

sunup /súnnup/ *n US* = **sunrise** *n.* **3**

sunward /súnwərd/ *adj* turned towards or in the direction of the sun ■ *adv* **sunward, sunwards** in the direction of the sun

Sun Yat-sen /sòon yát sén/ (1866–1925) Chinese statesman

Suomi /sòo omi/ *n* Finnish name for **Finland**

sup[1] /sup/ *vti* (**sups, supping, supped**) **1 SIP LIQUID** to drink small amounts of liquid at one time **2 EAT BY SPOONFUL** to eat something that is swallowed directly, e.g. soup or porridge, with a spoon ■ *n* **SIP OF LIQUID** a small amount or mouthful of liquid [Old English *sūpan* < Germanic]

sup[2] /sup/ (**sups, supping, supped**) *vi* to eat the evening meal (*archaic*) [14C. < Old French *souper* < *soupe* (see SOUP).]

supari /sòopaari/ *n S Asia* areca palm nuts chewed with betel leaves, especially after meals as a digestive [Mid-17C. < Hindi *supārī*.]

super /sóopər/ *adj* **1 EXCELLENT** with outstanding or excellent qualities (*informal*) ○ *a super idea* **2 VERY GREAT** exceptionally large or powerful (*informal*) **3 EXCESSIVE** greater than what is normal ■ *adv* **ESPECIALLY** to or in a high or extreme degree (*informal*) ○ *Everyone has been super helpful.* ■ *n* **1 SUPERINTENDENT** a superintendent (*informal*) **2 SUPERVISOR** a supervisor (*informal*) **3** *US* **SOMETHING BIGGER OR BETTER** something superior in grade or quality or large in size **4** *ANZ* **SUPERANNUATION** superannuation (*informal*) **5 ACTOR EMPLOYED AS WALK-ON** a supernumerary, especially an actor with a walk-on part (*informal*) **6 HIGH-OCTANE PETROL** high-octane petrol ■ *interj* **GREAT!** used to express enthusiasm, approval, or agreement (*informal*) [Mid-19C. < SUPER-, or shortening of various words beginning with SUPER-.]

super. *abbr* **1** superfine **2** superior

super- *prefix* **1** something larger, stronger, or faster than others of its kind ○ *superstore* **2** over, above, on ○ *supernatant* ○ *superstructure* **3** exceeding the usual or normal limits ○ *superheat* **4** a more inclusive group or category ○ *superclass* **5** in addition to, over and above ○ *superfetation* **6** greater in size, quality, number, or degree, superior ○ *superhuman* [< Latin *super* 'over, above'. Ultimately < Indo-European.]

superable /sóopərəb'l/ *adj* capable of being overcome [Early 17C. < Latin *superabilis* < *superare* 'overcome' < *super* (see SUPER-).] —**superability** /sòopərə bíllәti/ *n* —**superableness** *n* —**superably** *adv*

superabound /sòopərə bównd/ *vi* to be too numerous or abundant [14C. < late Latin *superabundare* < *abundare* (see ABOUND).]

superabundant /sòopərə búndənt/ *adj* present in excess of what is sufficient [15C. < late Latin *superabundant-*, present participle of *superabundare* (see SUPERABOUND).] —**superabundance** *n* —**superabundantly** *adv*

superacid /sóopər ássid/ *n* an acid that has a proton-donating ability greater than or equal to sulphuric acid

superadd /sòopər ád/ *vt* to add something onto what has already been added [15C. < Latin *superaddere* < *addere* (see ADD).] —**superaddition** /sòopərə dísh'n/ *n* —**superadditional** *adj*

superalloy /sóopər álloy/ *n* a heat-resistant alloy with superior mechanical properties, often having aerospace applications

superannuate /sòopər ánnyoo ayt/ (**-ates, -ating, -ated**) *v* **1** *vti* to become retired or retire somebody with a pension **2** *vt* to reject something or cause something to be rejected because of obsolescence [Mid-17C. Back-formation < SUPERANNUATED.]

superannuated /sòopər ánnyoo aytid/ *adj* **1 RETIRED** having been retired with a pension **2 TOO WORN** too much used for more useful service **3 OUT-OF-DATE** no longer in fashion [Mid-17C. < medieval Latin *superannuatus* 'more than a year old' < *annus* 'year'.]

superannuation /sòopər anyoo áysh'n/ *n* **1 DEDUCTION FOR PENSION SCHEME** the amount contributed regularly from an employee's pay towards a pension **2 RETIREMENT PENSION** the pension paid on retirement to a contributing employee **3 RETIREMENT** the process of retiring or the state of being retired with a pension

superb /soo púrb, syoo/ *adj* **1 EXCELLENT** of the highest quality **2 GRAND** impressive in size or appearance **3 SUMPTUOUS** rich and sumptuous in appearance or detail [Mid-16C. Via French < Latin *superbus* 'proud, superior' < *super* (see SUPER-).] —**superbly** *adv* —**superbness** *n*

Super Bowl a proprietary name for the championship game of the US National Football League, played each year between the champions of the National Football Conference and the American Football Conference

superbug /sóopər bug/, **supergerm** /sóopər jurm/ *n* a bacterium that has become resistant to the antibiotics normally used to treat it

supercalender /sóopər kálləndər/ *n* a machine with an extra large number of rollers to give a glossy finish to paper ■ *vt* to produce a glossy finish on paper using a supercalender

supercargo /sóopər kaargō/ (*plural* **-gos**) *n* an officer who is in charge of the cargo and commercial matters aboard a merchant ship [Late 17C. Alteration (influenced by SUPER-) of earlier *supracargo*, an alteration (influenced by SUPRA-) of Spanish *sobrecargo* < *sobre-* 'over' (from Latin *super-*) + Spanish *cargo* (see CARGO).]

~~**supercede**~~ incorrect spelling of **supersede**

supercharge /sóopər chaarj/ (**-charges, -charging, -charged**) *vt* **1** to increase the power of an internal-combustion engine by means of a supercharger **2** to charge something, e.g. the atmosphere or a remark, with excessive emotion or energy

supercharger /sóopər chaarjər/ *n* a device that supplies air to an internal-combustion engine at a pressure greater than the ambient atmospheric pressure in order to increase its power

superciliary /sòopər sílli əri/ *adj* **1** relating to or in the region of the eyebrow **2** describes markings above an animal's eye [Mid-18C. < Latin *supercilium* 'eyebrow' (see SUPERCILIOUS).]

supercilious /sòopər sílli əss/ *adj* full of contempt and arrogance [Early 16C. < Latin *superciliosus* < *supercilium* 'eyebrow' < *super* 'above' + *cilium* 'eyelid', referring to raised eyebrows as a sign of haughty disdain.]

superclass /sóopər klaass/ *n* a taxonomic category of related organisms of a rank above class

supercluster /sóopər klustər/ *n* an association of clusters of galaxies

supercollider /sòopər kə līdər/ *n* a very large high-energy particle accelerator

supercolumnar /sòopərkə lúmnər/ *adj* with one order of columns above another —**supercolumniation** /sòopər kə lùmni áysh'n/ *n*

ϟ **supercomputer** /sóopər kəm pyootər/ *n* a computer with the very highest processing speeds, used for solving complex problems and creating simulations

superconductivity /sòopər kon duk tívvəti/ *n* the ability of some metals, alloys, and ceramics to conduct electric current with negligible internal resistance at temperatures near absolute zero and, in some cases, at higher temperatures —**superconducting** /sòopər kən dúkting/ *adj* —**superconduction** *n* —**superconductive** *adj* —**superconductor** *n*

supercontinent /sóopər kontinənt/ *n* one of the large continental masses believed to have broken into several parts that drifted apart to form the present continents

supercool /sóopər kóol/ *vti* to cool a liquid below its freezing point without change to a solid, or to cause a liquid to become so cooled ■ *adj* extremely fashionable in attitude or image (*informal*)

supercrip /sóopər krip/ *n US* a disabled person who is very fit and takes part in strenuous sports (*informal*) [< shortening of CRIPPLE]

supercritical /sóopər krítik'l/ *adj* **1 HIGHLY CRITICAL** highly critical of something, e.g. a person's work **2 SELF-SUSTAINING AS NUCLEAR REACTION** describes a nuclear chain reaction that sustains itself explosively because a single transformation produces more than one other transformation **3 ABOVE A CRITICAL TEMPERATURE AND PRESSURE** describes a fluid at temperatures and pressures higher than those at which the liquid and gaseous states of the given substance would have the same density

super-duper /sóopər dóopər/ *adj* of the greatest excellence, size, or efficiency (*informal; often used ironically*) [Doubling of SUPER]

superego /sóopər éegō/ (*plural* **-gos**) *n* according to Freudian theory, the part of the mind that acts as a conscience to the ego, developing moral standards and rules through contact with parents and society [Early 20C. Translation of German *Über-Ich*.]

superelevation /sóopər eli váysh'n/ *n* the distance in height between the inside and outside edges of the bed of a banked road or track

supererogation /sóopər erə gáysh'n/ *n* the performance of work beyond what is required or expected [Early 16C. < Late Latin *supererogation-* < *supererogare* 'pay over and above' < *erogare* 'spend' < Latin *rogare* 'ask, beg'.]

supererogatory /sóopər i róggətəri/ *adj* **1** performed to an extent beyond what is required or expected **2** beyond what is sufficient or necessary, and not wanted —**supererogatorily** *adv*

superfamily /sóopər famli/ (*plural* **-lies**) *n* a taxonomic category of related organisms of a rank above family

superfecundation /sóopər fekən dáysh'n/ *n* **1** the fertilization of two or more ova at different times during one menstrual cycle by sperm from the same or different males **2** the fertilization of an unusually large number of ova at the same time

superfetation /sóopər fee táysh'n/ *n* the fertilization of a second ovum after the start of pregnancy, resulting in the presence of two foetuses at different stages of development in the same uterus [Early 17C. Via French < modern Latin *superfetare* 'conceive a second time' < Latin *foetus* (see FOETUS).]

superficial /sóopər físh'l/ *adj* **1 NOT PROFOUND** concerned with or understanding only the obvious ○ *a superficial knowledge of the text* **2 RELATING TO THE SURFACE** on, near, relating to, or affecting the surface of something ○ *a superficial wound* **3 WITHOUT DEPTH OF CHARACTER** shallow in character or attitude ○ *I find her quite superficial.* **4 CURSORY** swift and not thorough ○ *after a superficial examination of the injury* **5 ONLY APPARENTLY SO** only seeming to be real or the case ○ *The picture bears a superficial resemblance, nothing more.* **6 INSIGNIFICANT** with little significance or substance ○ *superficial changes to the policy* [14C. < Latin *superficies* (see SUPERFICIES).] —**superficiality** /-fishi álləti/ *n* —**superficially** *adv*

superficies /sóopər físhi eez/ (*plural* **-cies**) *n* **1** an outer surface or area of something **2** the outward appearance or form of something [Mid-16C. < Latin, < *super* 'above' + *facies* (see FACE).]

superfine /sóopər fīn/ *adj* **1 FINEST IN TEXTURE** of extremely fine grain or texture **2 FINEST IN QUALITY** of the highest quality or grade **3 AFFECTEDLY REFINED** excessively refined in manner —**superfineness** *n*

superfluid /sóopər floo id/ *n* a fluid characterized by the absence of viscosity at temperatures near absolute zero ■ *adj* relating to or exhibiting the properties of a superfluid —**superfluidity** /sóopər floo íddəti/ *n*

superfluity /sóopər flóo əti/ (*plural* **-ties**) *n* **1** an excessive or overabundant supply of something **2** something beyond what is necessary

superfluous /soo púr floo əss/ *adj* **1** that is in excess of what is needed ○ *a lot of superfluous detail* **2** not essential ○ *superfluous to the discussion* [14C. Directly or via Old French *superflueux* < Latin *superfluus* < *superfluere* 'overflow' < *fluere* (see FLUENT).] —**superfluously** *adv* —**superfluousness** *n*

supergene /sóopər jeen/ *n* a group of genes that lie close together on a chromosome, function as a unit, and are rarely separated

supergerm *n* MICROBIOL = **superbug**

supergiant /sóopər jī ənt/ *n* an extremely large brilliant star with a luminosity thousands of times greater than that of the Sun

superglue /sóopər gloo/ *n* a fast-acting glue that forms a strong bond by polymerization

supergrass /sóopər graass/ *n* an informer who gives information to the police implicating a large number of criminals (*informal*)

supergravity /sóopər grávvəti/ *n* a theory in physics that encompasses all known fundamental interactions, using hypothetical particles (**gravitons**) to carry the gravitational force

supergroup /sóopər groop/ *n* a rock music group whose performers are already famous from having performed individually or in other groups

superheat /sóopər héet/ *vt* **1 HEAT LIQUID WITHOUT VAPORIZATION** to heat a liquid above its pressure-related boiling point without causing it to vaporize **2 HEAT VAPOUR TO SATURATION** to heat a vapour not in contact with its liquid to the point at which a lowering of temperature or increase in pressure will not change it to a liquid **3 GET SOMETHING VERY HOT** to heat something to an extremely high temperature ■ *n* **HEAT FOR SUPERHEATING** the heat used to superheat a vapour —**superheater** *n*

superheavy /sóopər hévvi/ *adj* describes a chemical element having more than 110 protons in the nucleus, and, according to theoretical studies, likely to have special stability

superheavyweight /sóopər hévvi wayt/ *n* an athlete, especially a boxer, wrestler, or weightlifter, who competes in the heaviest weight division —**superheavyweight** *adj*

superhelix /sóopər heeliks/ (*plural* **-helices** /-heeli seez/) *n* a form of DNA in which the helical molecule is coiled in on itself

superhero /sóopər heerō/ (*plural* **-roes**) *n* a fictional character, e.g. from a cartoon, who has superhuman powers and uses them to fight crime or evil

superheterodyne /sóopər héttərō dīn/ *adj* relating to a method of receiving radio signals in which the incoming signal is mixed with a frequency generated by the receiver ■ *n* a radio receiver that operates using the superheterodyne method of receiving signals [Early 20C. < SUPERSONIC + HETERODYNE.]

superhigh frequency /sóopərhī-/ *n* a radio frequency between 3,000 and 30,000 megahertz

⚡**superhighway** /sóopər hī way/ *n* **1** ONLINE = **information superhighway** **2** *US* a motorway in the United States designed for high-speed traffic, with several lanes in each direction

superhuman /sóopər hyóomən/ *adj* **1** beyond ordinary human capability **2** with higher or greater powers than those within human experience ○ *a superhuman being* [Early 17C. < late Latin *superhumanus* < *humanus* (see HUMAN).] —**superhumanity** /-hyoo mánnəti/ *n* —**superhumanly** *adv* —**superhumanness** *n*

superimpose /sóopərim pṓz/ (**-poses, -posing, -posed**) *vt* **1** to place something, e.g. a transparent image, on or over something else, often with the result that both things appear simultaneously, although one may partially obscure the other **2** to add a feature or element without incorporating it ○ *superimpose one culture on another* —**superimposition** /sóopər impə zísh'n/ *n*

superincumbent /sóopərin kúmbənt/ *adj* lying or resting on or above something [Mid-17C. < Latin *superincumbere* 'lie on top of' < *incumbere* (see INCUMBENT).] —**superincumbence** *n* —**superincumbency** *n* —**superincumbently** *adv*

superinduce /sóopərin dyóoss/ (**-duces, -ducing, -duced**) *vt* to introduce somebody or something additional [Mid-16C. < Latin *superinducere* 'bring in upon' < *inducere* (see INDUCE).] —**superinduction** /-dúksh'n/ *n*

superinfection /sóopərin féksh'n/ *n* an infection that develops during drug treatment for another infection, caused by a different microorganism that is resistant to the treatment used for the first infection —**superinfect** *vt*

superintend /sóopərin ténd/ *vt* to be responsible for and supervise something, e.g. a project or job [Early 17C. Back-formation < SUPERINTENDENT.]

~~**superintendant**~~ incorrect spelling of **superintendent**

superintendent /sóopərin téndənt/ *n* **1 SOMEBODY IN CHARGE** an administrator or manager of something, such as an office or organization **2 HIGH-RANKING POLICE OFFICER** in the United Kingdom and Canada, a police officer of a rank above inspector, and in the United States a police officer of high rank, especially the head of a police department **3** *US* = **porter**[2] *n.* 3 ■ *adj* **IN CHARGE** acting in an administrative or supervisory capacity [Mid-16C. < ecclesiastical Latin *superintendere* 'oversee' < *intendere* (see INTEND), as a translation of Greek *episkopos* 'overseer'.]

superior /soo péeri ər/ *adj* **1 HIGHER IN QUALITY** above average or better than another in quality or grade **2 BETTER THAN OTHERS** surpassing others in something, e.g. intellect, achievement, or ability **3 HIGHER IN RANK** higher in rank, position, or authority than another **4 CONDESCENDING** adopting or showing an attitude of condescension towards others ○ *He gave a superior smile.* **5 UNCONCERNED** above being affected or influenced by something ○ *A player has to be superior to such taunts.* **6 LARGER** greater in number or amount ○ *a quantity superior to our needs* **7 HIGHER** upper, or situated higher up **8** PRINTING = **superscript** *adj.* **9 ABOVE OTHER FLOWER PARTS** describes an ovary of a flower whose stamens, petals, and sepals arise either beside or below it **10 NEARER THE HEAD** nearer the head than another body part ■ *n* **1 SOMEBODY OR SOMETHING HIGHER OR BETTER** somebody or something higher in rank, position, authority, or quality than another ○ *Don't argue with your superiors.* **2** PRINTING = **superscript** *n.* **3 SOMEBODY IN CHARGE OF RELIGIOUS ORDER** a head of a religious order or institution [14C. Via Old French < Latin, 'higher' < *superus* 'above' < *super* (see SUPER-).] —**superiority** /soo péeri órrəti/ *n* —**superiorly** *adv*

Superior, Lake /soo péeri ər/ westernmost of the Great Lakes, between the north-central United States and S Ontario, Canada. Area: 82,100 sq. km/31,700 sq. mi. Depth: 406 m/1,333 ft. Length: 563 km/350 mi.

superior conjunction *n* a position of a celestial body in which it is opposite the Earth on the far side of the Sun

superior court *n* a court in some states of the United States that is higher than an inferior court but lower than an appellate court

superiority complex *n* an exaggerated sense of being better than other people

superior planet *n* a planet whose distance from the Sun is greater than that of the Earth

superjacent /sóopər jáyss'nt/ *adj* lying on or above something [Late 16C. < Latin *superjacere* 'lie above' < *jacere* 'lie, throw' (see JET[2]).]

superjet /sóopər jet/ *n* a large supersonic jet plane

superlative /soo púrlətiv/ *adj* **1 EXCELLENT** of the highest quality or degree **2 HIGHEST IN DEGREE OF COMPARISON** expressing the highest degree of grammatical comparison of an adjective or adverb ○ *The superlative form of an adjective or adverb typically has the ending '-est'.* ■ *n* **1 GRAMMATICAL FORM** the grammatical form expressing the highest degree of comparison ○ *Put 'tiny' into the superlative and you get 'tiniest'.* **2 SUPERLATIVE ADJECTIVE OR ADVERB** a superlative form of an adjective or adverb ○ *the difference between a comparative and a superlative* **3 SOMEBODY OR SOMETHING SUPERLATIVE** somebody or something of the highest quality **4 EXAGGERATED PRAISE** an exaggerated description or way of referring to somebody or something, usually expressing admiration ○ *heaping superlatives on their performance* [14C. Via Old French < Latin *superlativus* < *superlat-*, past participle of *superferre* 'carry above'.] —**superlatively** *adv* —**superlativeness** *n*

Super League *n* an international rugby league competition that was introduced alongside or superseded various national rugby league competitions

superliner /sóopər līnər/ *n* a large luxurious ocean-going passenger ship

superload /sóopər lōd/ *n US* a vehicle load that exceeds the permitted weight or dimensions and requires a special permit to be transported over streets and public roads

superlunary /sóopər lóonəri/, **superlunar** /-lóonər/ *adj* **1** located beyond the Moon **2** belonging to a higher world or celestial plane [Early 17C. After SUBLUNARY.]

superman /so͝opər man/ (*plural* **-men** /-men/) *n* **1** a man possessing exceptional or superhuman strength, abilities, or powers **2** according to the philosophy of Nietzsche, an ideal man who through creativity and integrity is able to transcend good and evil and is the goal of human evolution [Early 20C. Translation of German *Übermensch*.]

supermarket /so͝opər maarkit/ *n* a large self-service retail store selling food and household goods

supermassive black hole /so͝opər mássiv-/ *n* an extremely large black hole having a mass between a few million to more than several billion solar masses, and held to be at the centre of many large galaxies driving quasar formation

supermax /so͝opər maks/ *n US* protected or made secure by the most extensive and elaborate security arrangements that are available or in current use ○ *a supermax penitentiary*

supermodel /so͝opər mod'l/ *n* one of an elite group of fashion models who are very well paid and in high demand by fashion designers and photographers

supernal /soo púrn'l/ *adj* (*literary*) **1** coming from or located in the heavens **2** suited to or characteristic of the heavens [15C. Via Old French < Latin *supernus* 'heavenly' < *super* (see SUPER-).] —**supernally** *adv*

supernatant /so͝opər náyt'nt/ *n* the usually clear liquid left above a precipitate or sediment ■ *adj* describes the liquid left above a precipitate or sediment [Mid-17C. < Latin *supernatant-*, present participle of *supernatare* 'float above' < *natare* (see NATANT).]

supernatural /so͝opər náchərəl/ *adj* **1 NOT OF NATURAL WORLD** relating or attributed to phenomena that cannot be explained by natural laws **2 RELATING TO A DEITY** relating or attributed to a deity **3 MAGICAL** relating or attributed to magic or the occult ■ *n* **1 SUPERNATURAL THINGS** supernatural beings or phenomena **2 WORLD OF SUPERNATURAL THINGS** the realm of supernatural beings or phenomena —**supernaturally** *adv* —**supernaturalness** *n*

supernaturalism /so͝opər náchərəlizəm/ *n* **1** the quality or condition of being supernatural **2** the belief that supernatural or divine beings and phenomena intervene in human events —**supernaturalist** *n, adj* —**supernaturalistic** *adj*

supernormal /so͝opər náwrm'l/ *adj* **1** exceeding what is normal or usual **2** = **paranormal** *adj.* —**supernormality** /-nawr mállәti/ *n* —**supernormally** *adv*

supernova /so͝opər nōvə/ (*plural* **-vae** /-vee/ *or* **-vas**) *n* a catastrophic explosion of a large star in the latter stages of stellar evolution, with a resulting short-lived luminosity from 10 to 100 million times that of the Sun

supernumerary /so͝opər nyo͝omərəri/ *adj* **1 EXTRA** exceeding the usual number **2 SUBSTITUTING** employed as a substitute or extra worker ■ *n* (*plural* **-ies**) **1 SOMEBODY OR SOMETHING EXTRA** somebody or something in addition to the usual number **2 WALK-ON ACTOR** an actor who appears on stage but has no lines to speak **3 SUBSTITUTE EMPLOYEE** somebody employed as a substitute or extra worker [Early 17C. < late Latin *supernumerarius* < Latin *super* 'above' + *numerus* 'number'.]

superorder /so͝opər awrdər/ *n* a taxonomic category of related organisms of a rank above order

superordinate /so͝opər áwrdinət/ *n* **1** a word whose meaning encompasses the meaning of another more specific word. 'Animal' is a superordinate of 'cat'. ◊ **hyponym 2** somebody or something of superior rank, status, or class [Early 17C. < SUPER- + SUBORDINATE.] —**superordinate** *adj*

superorganism /so͝opər áwrgənizəm/ *n* a group of organisms functioning as a social unit, e.g. an insect colony

superovulation /so͝opər ovjo͝o láysh'n/ *n* increased frequency of ovulation or production of a large number of ova at one time —**superovulate** /so͝opər óvvjo͝o layt/ *vi*

superoxide /so͝opər ók sīd/ *n* an inorganic chemical compound containing the O_2^- ion, an oxygen molecule with an extra electron

superphosphate /so͝opər fóssfayt/ *n* a commercially produced fertilizer that is a mixture of phosphates, prepared by reacting phosphate mineral deposits with sulphuric acid

superplastic /so͝opər plástik/ *adj* describes alloys that are capable of being easily deformed and moulded at high temperatures without fracturing —**superplasticity** /-pla stíssəti/ *n*

superpose /so͝opər póz/ (**-poses, -posing, -posed**) *vt* **1** to place or lay one object on top of or above another **2** to move one geometric figure so that it coincides exactly with another [Early 19C. Probably < French *superposer*, a back-formation < *superposition* 'superposition' < Latin *superponere* 'place over' < *super-* (see SUPER-) + *ponere* 'place'.] —**superposable** *adj* —**superposed** *adj* —**superposition** /so͝opər pə zísh'n/ *n*

superpower /so͝opər powər/ *n* **1** an extremely powerful nation with greater political, economic, or military power than most other nations, or with all three **2** extremely high electrical or mechanical power —**superpowered** *adj*

supersaturated /so͝opər sáchə raytid/ *adj* **1** describes a chemical solution containing a greater amount of solute than normally possible at a given temperature and pressure **2** describes a vapour containing more gaseous material than normally possible at a given temperature and pressure —**supersaturation** /-sachə ráysh'n/ *n*

supersaver /so͝opər sáyvər/ *n* an airline, coach, or train ticket that is cheaper than the normal price and must usually be bought a given amount of time before the date of travel [Late 20C]

superscribe /so͝opər skrī́b/ (**-scribes, -scribing, -scribed**) *vt* to write or print something such as a name or address above, outside, or on the surface of something else

superscript /so͝opərskript/ *n* a letter, character, or symbol that is written above, or above and to the right or left of, another character ■ *adj* written or printed as a superscript

superscription /so͝opər skrípsh'n/ *n* **1** something that is written, printed, or engraved above, outside, or on the surface of something else **2** the act of writing or printing something above, outside, or on the surface of something else

supersede /so͝opər seéd/ (**-sedes, -seding, -seded**) *vt* **1** to take the place or position of something that is less efficient, less modern, or less appropriate, or cause something to do this **2** to succeed somebody or something in a particular role, office, or function (*formal*) [15C. Via Old French *superceder* 'refrain from' < Latin *supersedere* 'be superior to' < *super-* (see SUPER-) + *sedere* 'sit'.] —**supersedable** *adj* —**supersedence** *n* —**superseder** *n*

supersensible /so͝opər sénssəb'l/, **supersensory** /-sénssəri/ *adj* above or beyond the perception of the senses —**supersensibly** *adv*

supersensitive /so͝opər sénssətiv/ *adj* = **hypersensitive** —**supersensitively** *adv* —**supersensitivity** /-sénssə tívvəti/ *n*

supersensory *adj* = **supersensible**

ϟ **superserver** /so͝opər survər/ *n* an extremely powerful computer that controls a network or networks of other computers

superset /so͝opər set/ *n* in mathematics, a set that contains one or more other sets

supersonic /so͝opər sónnik/ *adj* produced by, capable of reaching, or relating to a speed that is faster than the speed at which sound travels through the air [Early 20C. < SUPER- + Latin *sonus* 'sound'.] —**supersonically** *adv*

supersonics /so͝opər sónniks/ *n* the science or study of supersonic motion or phenomena (+ *singular verb*)

supersonic transport *n* a transport aircraft that travels at supersonic speed

superstar /so͝opər staar/ *n* an extremely famous or successful person, especially in sports or entertainment —**superstardom** *n*

superstition /so͝opər stísh'n/ *n* **1** an irrational but usually deep-seated belief in the magical effects of a particular action or ritual, especially in the likelihood that good or bad luck will result from performing it **2** irrational and often quasi-religious belief in and reverence for the magical effects of particular actions and rituals or the magical powers of particular objects [15C. Via Old French < Latin *superstition-* < *superstes* 'standing over' (in awe) < *stare* 'stand' (see STATION).]

superstitious /so͝opər stíshəss/ *adj* **1** convinced that performing or not performing certain actions brings good or bad luck, that certain events or phenomena are omens, and, generally, fearfully believing in a supernatural dimension to events **2** based on a false or irrational belief in, or fear of, the supernatural

superstore /so͝opər stawr/ *n* **1** a very large supermarket or store offering a wider and more varied range of consumer goods than other stores of the same type **2** a retail chain or single store that specializes in a range of related products offered at discount prices ○ *a computer superstore*

superstratum /so͝opər straatəm, -straytəm/ (*plural* **-ta** /-tə/) *n* **1** a layer, especially of rock or sedimentation, on top of another one **2** the language of an invading or colonizing population in relation to the language of an indigenous population that it changes or influences. ◊ **substratum** *n.* **5**

superstring /so͝opər string/ *n* a hypothetical one-dimensional entity (**string**) of extremely short length held to be a fundamental component of matter in some theories of elementary particles involving supersymmetry

superstructure /so͝opər strukchər/ *n* **1 UPPER PART OF SHIP** the part of a ship above the main deck **2 VISIBLE PART OF BUILDING** the part of a building above its foundations **3 PART DEVELOPED ON BASE** any physical or intellectual structure built on or developed from a fundamental form, base, or concept **4 INSTITUTIONS ASSOCIATED WITH TYPE OF ECONOMY** in Marxist theory, the complex of social, legal, and political institutions that are an extension and reflection of the type of economy operating in a given society —**superstructural** *adj*

supersymmetry /so͝opər símmətri/ *n* a theory in physics proposing a type of symmetry that would apply to all elementary particles, both bosons and fermions

supertanker /so͝opər tangkər/ *n* a very large tanker ship, usually with a capacity of 275,000 tonnes/300,000 tons or more

supertax /so͝opər taks/ *n* ECON = **surtax** *n.* **2**

supertitle /so͝opər tīt'l/ *n* THEATRE = **surtitle** [Late 20C. After *subtitle*.]

supertonic /so͝opər tonik/ *n* the note one step above the tonic in a major or minor scale, or the harmony built upon this note

superunleaded /so͝opər un léddid/ *n* unleaded petrol to which aromatic hydrocarbons have been added in order to give it a higher octane rating, and thus better performance, than standard unleaded petrol —**superunleaded** *adj*

supervene /so͝opər veén/ (**-venes, -vening, -vened**) *vi* (*formal*) **1** to follow or come about unexpectedly, usually interrupting or changing what is going on **2** to follow immediately after something [Mid-17C. < Latin *supervenire* 'come above' < *venire* 'come' (see VENUE).] —**supervenience** *n* —**supervenient** *adj* —**supervention** /-vénsh'n/ *n*

supervise /so͝opər vīz/ (**-vises, -vising, -vised**) *vti* **1** to watch over a particular activity or task being carried out by other people and ensure that it is carried out correctly **2** to be in charge of a group of people engaged in some activity and to keep order or ensure that they carry out a task adequately [Late 16C. < medieval Latin *supervis-*, past participle of *supervidere* 'look over, oversee' < Latin *videre* 'see' (see VISION).] —**supervision** /so͝opər vízh'n/ *n*

~~**superviser**~~ incorrect spelling of **supervisor**

supervision order *n* an order mandating the personal supervision by a named social worker or probation officer of a child involved in care proceedings

supervisor /so͝opər vīzər/ *n* **1 BOSS** somebody whose job is to oversee and guide the work or activities of a group of other people **2** *US* **MAIN TEACHER OF SUBJECT** a teacher or other school official who oversees the teaching and teachers of a single subject area **3 TUTOR FOR A GRADUATE** in some British universities, a teacher assigned to supervise the work of an individual student, especially research done by a postgraduate student —**supervisorship** *n* —**supervisory** /-vīzəri, -vízəri/ *adj*

superweed /so͝opər weed/ *n* an indestructible or ineradicable weed that could hypothetically evolve as a hybrid of ordinary weeds and genetically modified plants

superwoman /so͝opər wo͝omən/ (*plural* **-en** /-wimin/) *n* **1** a woman who succeeds triumphantly in combining several roles, such as worker, wife, mother, and homemaker, and does it all with apparent ease (*informal*) **2** an imaginary or fictional woman with superhuman powers

supinate /sóopi nayt, syóo-/ (**-nates, -nating, -nated**) *v* **1** *vti* **TURN PALM UPWARDS** to turn the hand so that the palm faces upwards, or be turned in this way **2** *vti* **TURN SOLE UPWARDS** to turn the foot so that the sole is facing upwards, or be turned in this way **3** *vi* **LIE FACING UPWARDS** to turn the face upwards, or lie in a supine position with the face upwards [Mid-19C. < Latin *supinat-*, past participle of *supinare* 'turn backwards' < *supinus* 'backwards' (see SUPINE).] —**supination** /sóopi náysh'n, syóo-/ *n*

supinator /sóopi naytər, syóo-/ *n* a muscle, especially of the forearm, that brings about supination

supine /sóo pīn, syóo-/ *adj* **1 LYING ON THE BACK** lying on the back and with the face upwards **2 PALM UPWARDS** with the palm of the hand facing upwards or away from the body **3 LETHARGIC** utterly passive or inactive, especially in a situation where a vigorous reaction is called for ■ *n* **TYPE OF LATIN NOUN** a Latin noun formed from a past participle stem and having only accusative and ablative inflections [15C. < Latin *supinus* 'lying on the back'.]

~~**supose**~~ incorrect spelling of **suppose**

supper /súppər/ *n* **1 EVENING MEAL** a light meal eaten in the evening **2 MAIN EVENING MEAL** the main meal of the day when taken in the evening **3 SOCIAL EVENT** an evening social event that includes a meal [13C. < Old French *soper* 'eat supper' < *soupe* 'sop, broth' (see SOUP).] ◇ **sing for your supper** to work or do something in exchange for your food and board, or for something that you want

supper club *n* **1** *US* a restaurant serving evening meals and sometimes featuring entertainment **2** a group of people who get together periodically to dine in restaurants

suppertime /súppər tīm/ *n* the time at which supper is served or eaten

supplant /sə pláant/ *vt* **1** to take somebody's place or position by force or intrigue **2** to take the place of something, especially something much used, inferior, outmoded, or irrelevant [13C. Directly or via French < Latin *supplantare* 'trip up, overthrow' < *sub-* 'up from beneath' + *planta* 'sole of the foot' (see PLANT).] —**supplantation** /súpplaan táysh'n/ *n* —**supplanter** *n*

supple /súpp'l/ (**-pler, -plest**) *adj* **1 FLEXIBLE** flexible and elastic **2 MOVING EASILY** capable of bending, stretching, and moving with ease, fluidity, and grace **3 ADAPTABLE** adaptable and responsive in grappling with problems or dealing with new challenges **4 COMPLIANT** excessively compliant and agreeable (*literary*) [13C. Via French < Latin *supplex* 'submissive', literally 'bending under' < *-plex* 'fold'.] —**supplely** *adv* —**suppleness** *n*

supplejack /súpp'l jak/ (*plural* **-jacks** *or* **-jack**) *n* **1** a woody vine with bluish fruits. Flowers: tiny, white. Native to: SE United States. *Berchemia scandens.* **2** a tropical vine whose wood is used for walking sticks. Native to: Central and South America. *Paullinia curvassica.* [*Supple* from its pliant stem]

supplement *n* /súpplimənt/ **1 ADDITION** an addition to something to increase its size or make up for a deficiency ○ *a useful supplement to the family income* **2 PUBLICATION** a publication that amplifies or corrects one already published **3 PERIODICAL PART** an additional section included in or sold with a magazine or newspaper, especially an additional section that appears regularly **4 FOOD** a substance with a particular nutritional value taken to make up for a real or supposed deficiency in diet **5 EXTRA CHARGE** a charge payable in addition to the basic charge for a special service or under certain conditions **6 ANGLE OR ARC** an angle or arc that, when added to another, makes 180° or a semicircle ■ *vt* /súppli ment/ **1 MAKE ADDITION TO** to increase, extend, or improve something by adding something to it ○ *supplemented their meagre diet with vitamins* **2 BE ADDITIONAL PART** to be a supplement to something ○ *Her remarks supplemented the report.* [14C. < Latin *supplementum* < *supplere* 'fill out, complete' (see SUPPLY).] —**supplemental** /súppli mént'l/ *adj* —**supplementally** *adv* —**supplementation** /súppli men táysh'n/ *n* —**supplementer** *n*

supplementary /súppli méntəri/ *adj* **1 ADDITIONAL** additional to an existing one, or to the normal number or amount **2 COMPLETING** making up for something that is lacking ■ *n* (*plural* **-ries**) **SOMETHING ADDITIONAL** an additional thing, person, or question —**supplementarily** *adv*

supplementary angle *n* an angle that when added to another angle makes up 180°

supplementary benefit *n* an allowance formerly paid weekly by the state to bring a person's or family's income up to what was considered to be a minimum acceptable level

suppletion /sə pleésh'n/ *n* the use of an unrelated word to fill the gap when some inflected or derived forms of a word are missing, as 'was' forms the past tense of 'to be' —**suppletive** /sə pleétiv/ *adj*

suppliant /súppli ənt/ *adj* expressing a humble heartfelt appeal to somebody who has the power to grant a request (*formal*) ■ *n* = **supplicant** *n.* [15C. < French, present participle of *supplier* 'supplicate' < Latin *supplicare* 'bend under' < *supplex* (see SUPPLE).] —**suppliance** *n* —**suppliantly** *adv*

supplicant /súpplikənt/ *n* a person who makes a humble and sincere appeal to somebody who has the power to grant the request (*formal*) ■ *adj* = **suppliant** *adj.* [Late 16C. < Latin *supplicant-*, present participle of *supplicare* (see SUPPLIANT).] —**supplicatory** /súpplikətəri, -kaytəri/ *adj*

supplication /súppli káysh'n/ *n* (*formal*) **1** a humble appeal to somebody who has the power to grant a request **2** the addressing of humble requests and prayers to somebody with the power to grant them —**supplicate** /-kayt/ *vti*

~~**suppliment**~~ incorrect spelling of **supplement**

supply /sə plī/ *vt* (**-plies, -plying, -plied**) **1 PROVIDE** to give, sell, or make available something that is wanted or needed by somebody or something ○ *supplied equipment for the expedition* **2 SATISFY A NEED** to satisfy a need or requirement (*formal*) **3 MAKE UP FOR A LACK** to make up for a deficiency, loss, or lack **4 SERVE AS A SUBSTITUTE** to act as a substitute for somebody, especially in a church or a school (*formal*) ■ *n* (*plural* **-plies**) **1 AVAILABLE AMOUNT** an amount or quantity of something available for use ○ *a plentiful supply of food and drink* **2 PROVISION** the act or business of bringing something needed to the people or things that need it, or the system that brings something needed ○ *the supply of electric power to villages in the mountains* **3 QUANTITY AVAILABLE IN A MARKET** the quantity of a type of goods or services available in a market at a given time **4 SUBSTITUTE** a replacement for somebody, especially for a preacher (*formal*) **5 SUPPLY TEACHER** a supply teacher (*informal*) ■ **supplies** *npl* **NEEDED THINGS** the things, especially food and equipment, that a group of people need to survive and operate, or that are needed to carry out a particular task or activity ○ *Our supplies were running very low.* [14C. Via Old French *supplier* 'meet a deficiency' < Latin *supplere* 'fill up' < *plere* 'fill'.] —**suppliable** *adj* —**supplier** *n* ◇ **in short supply** present or available only in small or insufficient quantities

supply and demand *n* the relationship between the availability of a good or service and the need or desire for it among consumers

supply-side economics *n* economic policies that promote conditions favouring the producers of goods and services (+ *singular or plural verb*)

supply teacher *n* a teacher who takes the place of another temporarily. US term **substitute teacher**

⚡**support** /sə páwrt/ *vt* **1 KEEP FROM FALLING** to keep something or somebody upright or in place, or prevent something or somebody from falling ○ *Those pillars support the roof.* **2 BEAR WEIGHT** to be strong enough to hold a particular object or weight in place without breaking or giving way ○ *Are you sure the ice is thick enough to support the weight?* **3 SUSTAIN FINANCIALLY** to provide somebody with money and the other necessities of life over a period of time ○ *She succeeds in supporting her family on what she earns* **4 GIVE ACTIVE HELP AND ENCOURAGEMENT** to give active help, encouragement, or money to somebody or something ○ *We support the charity through voluntary work.* **5 BE IN FAVOUR OF** to be in favour of something such as a cause, policy, organization, or sports team and wish to see it succeed **6 BE PRESENT AND GIVE ENCOURAGEMENT** to give encouragement to somebody or something by being present at an event **7 GIVE ASSISTANCE OR COMFORT** to give assistance or comfort to somebody in difficulty or distress ○ *He supported me throughout my crisis.* **8 PROVIDE TECHNICAL SUPPORT** to provide technical support for a computing system or package **9 CORROBORATE** to give something greater credibility by being consistent with it or providing further evidence for it ○ *There is further evidence that supports the defendant's claim.* **10 PLAY SMALL ROLE ALONGSIDE** to play a subsidiary role in a play or film alongside another actor with a leading part **11 TOLERATE** to put up with something unpleasant (*literary*) ■ *n* **1 SOMETHING THAT SUPPORTS** a means of holding something upright or in place, or of preventing it from falling ○ *If you remove those supports the plank will fall down.* **2 REINFORCEMENT TO HOLD THINGS IN PLACE** physical force or reinforcement used to hold things steady or in place ○ *Stakes give the plant extra support.* **3 ACTIVE ASSISTANCE OR ENCOURAGEMENT** active assistance and encouragement to, or an approving and encouraging attitude towards, somebody or something ○ *Support for the cause continues to rise.* **4 HELP IN CRISIS** the encouragement and help somebody gets from others, e.g. friends, family, and charitable organizations, especially during times of crisis and change **5 SUPPORTIVE PERSON** a provider of help, money, encouragement, or comfort **6 SUPPORTERS** the supporters of an organization such as a political party, or of an individual, considered as a group ○ *His support is drawn mainly from the rural areas.* **7 SUPPORTING BANDS OR ENTERTAINERS** the other band or bands, or the other entertainers, appearing in a programme along with the main attraction **8 SUPPORTING GARMENT** a garment that supports or protects a part of the body, especially one used by male athletes to protect the genitals [14C. Via French < Latin *supportare* 'bear up' < *portare* 'carry' (see PORT[1]).] —**supportability** /sə páwrtə bílləti/ *n* —**supportable** *adj* —**supportably** *adv* ◇ **in support of** in order to support somebody or something

support area *n* an area with a supply of military material and personnel standing ready for use

supporter /sə páwrtər/ *n* **1** a person who supports somebody or something, such as a cause, idea, course of action, or sports team ○ *greeted by a crowd of supporters* **2** either of a pair of standing figures on either side of a shield in a coat of arms

support group *n* a group of people with a problem or concern in common who meet regularly to discuss it and support one another

support hose *npl US* MED = **support stockings**

supporting /sə páwrting/ *adj* **1** accompanying and assisting, but secondary to, the main action or the main participants in something ○ *a supporting role* **2** appearing in the same film, play, or programme as the main star or attraction

supportive /sə páwrtiv/ *adj* giving support, especially moral or emotional support —**supportiveness** *n*

support level *n* the price at which a security whose price has been falling begins to attract investors again because of its intrinsic worth

support stockings *npl* elasticized stockings that support the veins in the lower legs, used by people with varicose veins or bad circulation. US term **support hose**

support system *n* the group of friends, colleagues, or professionals available to help a person or organization when required

suppose /sə pōz/ (**-poses, -posing, -posed**) *v* **1** *vti* **BELIEVE TO BE TRUE** to believe or imagine something to be the case ○ *I suppose you haven't heard the news.* **2** *vi* **IMAGINE AS POSSIBLE** to consider or imagine something to be a possibility ○ *Suppose that he doesn't know about your plan.* **3** *vt* **TAKE AS PRECONDITION** to require something as a precondition ○ *Your plan supposes that there are enough presents to go around.* **4** *vt* **BE REQUIRED TO DO SOMETHING** to be expected to do something as the result of a previous agreement or arrangement or an obligation (*usually passive*) ○ *You're supposed to leave tomorrow.* **5** *vti* **AGREE TO SOMETHING RELUCTANTLY** used when agreeing to do something or that something is the case, reluctantly, uncertainly, or noncommittally ○ *I suppose we'd better get going.* [14C. Via French < Latin *supponere* 'place under' < *ponere* 'place' (see POSITION).] —**supposable** *adj* —**supposably** *adv* —**supposer** *n*

supposed to *v* to be expected to do something or to happen as a consequence of a particular action or set of conditions ○ *The light's supposed to come on when the tank is almost empty.* ○ *I'm not supposed to know that.*

supposed /sə pōzd, -pōzid/ *adj* accepted, at least by some, as correct, real, or having a particular quality, but on slender or uncertain evidence ○ *Frankly, I'm very dubious about this supposed brilliant idea of his.*

supposedly /sə pōzidli/ *adv* as some people believe, or as people were led to believe ○ *He was supposedly going to pick us up after work.* ○ *a supposedly instant remedy*

~~**suppose to**~~ incorrect spelling of **supposed to**

supposing /sə pōzing/ *conj* imagining or assuming something to be the case ○ *Supposing she comes, will you let her in?*

supposition /súppə zísh'n/ *n* **1** something that it is suggested might be true, or that is accepted as true, on the basis of some evidence but without proof **2** the mental act of supposing something to be the case, or ideas that result from supposing, especially as opposed to ideas based on firm evidence ○ *All this is mere supposition.* [Late 16C. Directly and via French < Latin *supposition-* < *supposit-*, past participle of *supponere* (see SUPPOSE).] —**suppositional** *adj* —**suppositionally** *adv*

suppositious /súppə zíshəss/ *adj* based on some evidence but without proof (*formal*)

supposititious /sə pózzi tíshəss/ *adj* substituted for something else in order to deceive (*formal*) [Early 17C. < Latin *supposititius* < *suppositus*, past participle of *supponere* (see SUPPOSE).] —**supposititiously** *adv*

suppositive /sə pózzitiv/ *adj* expressing or relating to supposition, or introducing a clause expressing a supposition ■ *n* a conjunction such as 'if', 'provided that', or 'supposing' that introduces a clause expressing a supposition

suppository /sə pózzitəri/ (*plural* **-ries**) *n* a medicated mass that melts at body temperature, designed to be inserted into the rectum, vagina, or urethra [14C. < medieval Latin *suppositorium* < Latin *supposit-*, past participle of *supponere* 'place under' (see SUPPOSE).]

suppress /sə préss/ *vt* **1 PUT AN END TO** to put an end to something, especially something perceived as a threat, by the use of force or a prohibition ○ *suppressed all complaints with a gagging order* **2 PREVENT** to prevent something from happening, operating, or becoming apparent, or restrain something and limit its effects **3 STOP SPREAD OR PUBLICATION OF** to prevent information or evidence from becoming known, or written material from being published ○ *The report was suppressed for political reasons.* **4 RESIST SOMETHING CONSCIOUSLY** to resist particular thoughts or feelings consciously as they arise, and try to banish them from the mind ○ *Try to suppress your anger.* **5 DIMINISH OSCILLATION** to reduce unwanted noise or oscillation in a circuit or unwanted frequencies in a signal **6 REDUCE BODILY FUNCTION** to cause or undergo the reduction or cessation of a normal bodily function, e.g. menstruation or growth **7 INHIBIT GENE EFFECT** to cancel or reverse the effects of a gene [14C. < Latin *suppress-*, past participle of *supprimere* 'push down' < *premere* 'press' (see PRESS[1]).] —**suppresser** *n* —**suppressibility** /sə préssə bílləti/ *n* —**suppressible** *adj*

suppressant /sə préssənt/ *n* a substance, medication, or activity that restrains or limits the effects of something (*often in combination*) ○ *an appetite suppressant*

suppression /sə présh'n/ *n* **1 FORCEFUL PREVENTION** conscious and forceful action to put an end to something, destroy it, or prevent it from becoming known **2 STATE OF CONSTRAINT** the state of being forcefully restrained or held back **3 AVOIDANCE OF THOUGHTS AND FEELINGS** conscious avoidance or inhibition of particular memories, desires, or thoughts **4 DIMINISHING OF OSCILLATION** reduction of unwanted noise or oscillation in a circuit or of unwanted frequencies in a signal **5 DEVELOPMENTAL FAILURE** the failure of an organ, tissue, or part to develop **6 CESSATION OF BODILY FUNCTION** the reduction or stoppage of a normal bodily function, e.g. secretion or excretion. ◊ **immunosuppression 7 REMOVAL OF SYMPTOMS** the lessening or abolition of a symptom or the outward signs of a disease **8 REVERSAL OF MUTATION** the cancellation or reversal of the effect of a gene, especially of one genetic mutation by another

suppressive /sə préssiv/ *adj* having the effect of suppressing something —**suppressively** *adv*

suppressor /sə préssər/ *n* **1** a gene that prevents the expression of another gene **2** a device that reduces unwanted interference or current in a circuit

suppressor T cell, suppressor cell *n* a T cell that diminishes or suppresses the immune response to an antigen of B cells and other T cells

suppurate /súppyōō rayt/ (**-rates, -rating, -rated**) *vi* to produce or discharge pus as a result of an injury or infection [Mid-16C. < Latin *suppurat-*, past participle of *suppurare* < *pus* (see PUS).] —**suppuration** *n* —**suppurative** *adj*

supra /sóōprə/ *adv* used in formal writing to refer the reader back to something at an earlier point in the same text [Early 16C. < Latin, 'above'.]

supra- *prefix* **1** over, on top of ○ *suprarenal* **2** transcending ○ *supranational* [< Latin *supra* 'above, beyond']

supralapsarian /sóōprə lap sáiri ən/ *n* a believer that prior to the general fall of humanity God preordained the salvation of some souls [Mid-17C. < SUPRA- + Latin *lapsus* 'sin, fall' (see LAPSE).] —**supralapsarianism** *n*

supraliminal /sóōprə límmin'l/ *adj* at or above the threshold of consciousness —**supraliminally** *adv*

supramolecular /sóōprə mə lékyōōlər/ *adj* **1** more complex in form than a molecule **2** composed of more than one molecule

supranational /sóōprə násh'nəl/ *adj* not limited by the concerns or boundaries of a single nation —**supranationalism** *n* —**supranationally** *adv*

supraorbital /sóōprə áwrbit'l/ *adj* located above the bony socket (**orbit**) of the eye

suprarenal /sóōprə réen'l/ *adj* located above the kidneys

suprasegmental /sóōprə seg mént'l/ *adj* connected with features of speech such as pitch and stress that accompany rather than constitute phonemes —**suprasegmentally** *adv*

supremacist /sōō prémməssist, syōō-/ *n* a believer that a group is innately superior to others and therefore is entitled to dominate them (*usually in combination*)

supremacy /sōō prémməssi, syōō-/ *n* a position of superiority or authority over all others [Mid-16C. < SUPREME, after *primacy*.]

suprematism /sōō prémmətizəm, syōō-/ *n* a school of cubist painting from early 20th-century Russia [Mid-20C. < Russian *suprematizm* < French *suprématie* 'supremacy'.] —**suprematist** *n*

supreme /sōō préem, syōō-/ *adj* **1 ABOVE ALL OTHERS** above all others in power, authority, rank, status, or skill ○ *holding supreme authority* **2 HIGHEST IN DEGREE** of the greatest or most admirable kind ○ *a supreme example of the architect's skill* **3 ULTIMATE** greater than any that have gone before, or the greatest possible ○ *the supreme sacrifice* **4 IN THE HIGHEST DEGREE** in the highest degree or of the most unmitigated kind ○ *viewed them with supreme contempt* [15C. < Latin *supremus* 'uppermost' < *superus* 'upper' < *super* 'above' (see SUPER-).] —**supremely** *adv*

suprême /sōō préem, syōō-, -prém/ *n* the finest cut from any piece of meat, especially boneless breast of chicken ■ *adj* served with a suprême sauce ○ *chicken suprême* [Early 19C. < French, 'supreme'.]

Supreme Being *n* God

supreme commander *n* a military commander in charge of all allied forces in a theatre of war

Supreme Court *n* **1** LAW = **Supreme Court of Judicature 2 HIGHEST COURT** in the United States, the highest federal court, consisting of nine justices appointed by the president and making decisions solely on constitutional matters **3 HIGHEST STATE COURT** the highest appellate court in many states of the United States **4 HIGHEST COURT IN COUNTRY** the highest court in a country, or in a state or territory of a federation

Supreme Court of Judicature, Supreme Court *n* the highest national court in England and Wales consisting of two divisions, the High Court of Justice and the Court of Appeal

suprême sauce *n* a rich sauce made of chicken or veal stock with added cream and egg yolks

Supreme Soviet *n* the two-chamber national legislature of the former Soviet Union, or a similar legislature in any of the former Soviet republics

supremo /sōō préemō, syōō-/ (*plural* **-mos**) *n* somebody with overriding authority in a particular sphere (*informal*) [Mid-20C. < Spanish (*generalísimo*) *supremo* 'supreme commander'.]

~~**supress**~~ incorrect spelling of **suppress**

~~**suprise**~~ incorrect spelling of **surprise**

suq *n* COMM = **souk**

Suquamish /sə kwáamish, skwáamish/ (*plural* **-mishes** *or* **-mish**) *n* **1** a member of a Native North American people who live along the Puget Sound in Washington State **2** the Salish language of the Suquamish people [Mid-19C. < a Salish language.]

sur- *prefix* **1** over, above, on top of ○ *surprint* **2** additional, extra ○ *surcharge* [Via French < Latin *super* (see SUPER-)]

sura /sóōrə/ *n* a chapter of the Koran [Early 17C. < Arabic *sūra* < ?]

Surabaya /sóōrə bī́ ə/ city on NE Java Island, Indonesia. Population: 2,473,272 (1990).

surah /sóōrə/ *n* a twilled silk or rayon fabric. Use: women's clothing. [Late 19C. Anglicization of French *surat* 'Surat', town in India.]

sural /sóōrəl, syōō-/ *adj* relating to the calf of the leg (*technical*) [Early 17C. < Latin *sura* 'calf of the leg' < ?]

Surat /sōō rát, sóōrət/ port in W India. Population: 1,496,943 (1991).

surbase /súr bayss/ *n* an architectural moulding at the top of a base such as a pedestal or baseboard —**surbasement** /sur báyssmənt/ *n* —**surbased** *adj*

surbased /sur báyst/ *adj* describes an arch with a rise of less than half its span [Mid-18C. < French *surbaissé*, past participle of *surbaisser* 'flatten' < *baisser* 'lower' < medieval Latin *bassus* 'low'.]

surcease /sur séess/ *vti* (**-ceases, -ceasing, -ceased**) to cease, or bring something to an end or stop doing it (*formal*) ■ *n* a cessation, especially a temporary one (*literary*) [15C. Via Anglo-Norman *surseser* (influenced by CEASE) < Latin *supersedere* 'refrain' (see SUPERSEDE).]

surcharge /súr chaarj/ *v* (**-charges, -charging, -charged**) **1** *vti* **CHARGE EXTRA** to add an additional charge to the amount somebody has to pay **2** *vti* **OVERCHARGE** to charge somebody too much for something **3** *vt* **RAISE STAMP VALUE BY OVERPRINTING** to overprint an existing postage stamp so as to increase its face value **4** *vt* **OVERBURDEN** to overburden somebody or something, or overload something such as a ship (*literary*) ■ *n* **1 EXTRA CHARGE** an excess or extra charge **2 MARK ON STAMP** a mark on a postage stamp increasing its face value [15C. < Old French *surcharger* < *chargier* 'charge' (see CHARGE).] —**surcharger** *n*

surcingle /súr sing g'l/ *n* a broad band fastened around the body of a horse to hold a rug or pack in place [14C. < Old French *surcengle* 'belt over' < *cengle* 'belt, girdle' < Latin *cingulum* (see CINGULUM).]

surcoat /súr kōt/ *n* **1** a short tunic worn over armour in medieval times **2** a short sleeveless garment worn as part of the ceremonial costume of an order of knighthood [14C. < Old French *surcote* 'overcoat' < *cote* 'coat' (see COAT).]

surd /surd/ *n* **1** in mathematics, an irrational root or irrational number, or an expression containing one or the other **2** a consonant pronounced without vibration of the vocal cords [Mid-16C. < Latin *surdus* 'unable to hear or speak'.]

sure /shoor, shawr/ *adj* (**surer, surest**) **1 DEFINITELY TRUE** unquestionably true or real and not in doubt ○ *One thing is sure, we'll never make the same mistake again!* **2 FIRMLY BELIEVING** believing strongly and for a good reason, or knowing for a fact that something is true or the case ○ *Are you sure that she understood you?* **3 BOUND TO** inevitably going to do something or to happen, or confidently expected to be going to do something or to happen ○ *He's sure to notice something's missing.* **4 CERTAIN TO OBTAIN** definitely able to or definitely going to obtain or achieve something ○ *Many people book early in order to be sure of the best seats.* **5 VERY CONFIDENT** very confident about something, especially personal beliefs or abilities ○ *It was her self-confidence that made her so sure of her answer.* **6 ALWAYS EFFECTIVE** effective, accurate, and reliable at all times ○ *His aggressive manner is a sure sign that he is frightened.* **7 FIRM AND SECURE** firm, secure, and steady ○ *The fashion had gained a sure hold on every boy.* **8 UNERRING** showing both confidence and competence ○ *a sure grasp of the complexities of the situation* **9 DEPENDABLE** able to be safely relied on ○ *a sure friend in times of trouble* ■ *adv US* (*informal*) **1 UNDOUBTEDLY** used to give emphasis to something that somebody is saying and to indicate that somebody does not expect anyone to disagree with it ○ *This sure tastes good.* **2 YES** used to indicate emphatic or enthusiastic assent ○ *I asked him if he'd like to come and he said, 'Sure!'* [14C. Via Old French < Latin *securus* (see SECURE).] —**sureness** *n* ◇ **be sure and do** *or* **to do something** used to tell somebody to remember to do something ○ *Be sure and introduce us.* ◇ **for sure 1** without a doubt, or inevitably (*informal*) **2** definitely and precisely ◇ **make sure (that) 1** to take the necessary action to have something done or make something happen **2** to check that something is the case, or that something has been done as instructed or requested ◇ **sure enough** as was expected ◇ **sure of yourself** extremely confident ◇ **to be sure** used when admitting or agreeing that something is true, even though it may not agree with most of what you are saying

USAGE The use of ***sure*** as an intensifying adverb, as in the sentence *We sure are glad to see you!* is characteristic of informal US usage and has not fully entered British use except as a conscious Americanism. Note that it does not mean the same as *surely*, which is more judgmental in tone: *They surely don't want us to pay for this?*

sure-fire *adj* always successful or effective (*informal*)

sure-footed *adj* **1** skilled and confident in moving or climbing, and so unlikely to stumble or fall **2** confident and competent, and so unlikely to err —**surefootedly** *adv* —**surefootedness** *n*

surely /shoórli, sháwr-/ *adv* **1 USED TO INVITE A RESPONSE** used as a means of getting somebody to confirm, deny, agree, or disagree with something being said, by adding in an element of challenging self-assurance or considerable hesitancy ○ *Surely you've met before.* **2 WITHOUT FAIL** definitely or unavoidably ○ *slowly but surely* **3** *US* **WITHOUT DOUBT** without a doubt or without fail ○ *Did he get his message across? He surely did.* **4** *Southern US* **YES** used to show ready agreement

sure thing *n* something that can be relied on to happen or to be successful (*informal*) ■ *adv US* used to express assent, agreement, or willingness to do something (*informal*)

surety /shoórəti, sháwr-/ (*plural* **-ties**) *n* **1 LEGAL INSTRUMENT** a pledge, bond, or guarantee against loss or damage **2 GUARANTOR** a person who pledges that another's obligations will be met in case of default **3 CERTAINTY** the condition or quality of being sure (*formal*) [14C. Via Old French *surete* < Latin *securitas* < *securus* 'secure' (see SECURE).] —**suretyship** *n*

⚡**surf** /surf/ *n* **FOAMY WAVES** the lines of foamy waves that break on a seashore or reef ○ *play in the surf* ■ *v* **1** *vi* **USE A SURFBOARD** to ride waves on a surfboard **2** *vt* **RIDE WAVES IN A PARTICULAR AREA** to go surfing in a particular place ○ *Have you surfed Waikiki?* **3** *vti* **SEARCH MEDIUM FOR ENTERTAINMENT** to go on the Internet for recreation, education, or entertainment, frequently changing the site [Late 17C. < ?] —**surfable** *adj* —**surfer** *n* —**surfing** *n* —**surfy** *adj* ◇ **surf's up** *US* used to indicate that it is time to start doing something (*slang*)

surface /súrfiss/ *n* (*plural* **-faces**) **1 OUTER PART** the outermost or uppermost part of a thing, the one that is usually presented to the outside world, and can be seen and touched **2 UPPER PART OF EARTH, SEA, WATER** the part of the Earth, the sea, or any water that meets the atmosphere **3 SOLID FLAT AREA** a solid flat area, e.g. on top of a fitment or piece of furniture, especially an area on which it is suitable to work **4 THIN APPLIED OUTER LAYER** a relatively thin outer layer or coating applied to something, usually to give it a smooth finish ○ *a nonstick surface* **5 SUPERFICIAL PART** the superficial parts or aspects of something, especially when contrasted with the essence of the thing **6 TWO-DIMENSIONAL EXTENT** a flat or curved continuous area definable in two dimensions ○ *the surface of a sphere* ■ *adj* **1 USED ON SURFACE** occurring or used on, or relating to, the surface of something ○ *surface lubricants* **2 SUPERFICIAL** applying only to the outermost or uppermost part **3 APPARENT** put on for effect and not natural, deep-seated, or deeply felt **4 ON LAND OR SEA** operating or transported over land or sea but not in the air ■ *v* (**-faces, -facing, -faced**) **1** *vi* **COME TO THE TOP** to come to or appear at the surface, especially of water ○ *She surfaced after a dive of 20 minutes.* **2** *vi* **APPEAR** to reappear after being hidden or out of reach for a time ○ *She surfaced in Berlin after the war.* **3** *vi* **BECOME KNOWN** to become apparent or known ○ *The information surfaced during a routine investigation.* **4** *vi* **WAKE UP OR GET UP** to wake up, or get out of bed (*informal*) ○ *She didn't surface till three o'clock the next afternoon.* **5** *vt* **GIVE A SURFACE TO** to provide something with a surface, especially with a smooth outer layer ○ *surfacing the road* **6** *vt* **TREAT A SURFACE** to treat a surface, especially in order to smooth or perfect it **7** *vi* **WORK NEAR THE TOP** to mine at or near the Earth's surface [Early 17C. < French, < *sur-* 'upon' and *face* (see FACE), after Latin *superficies* 'surface' (see SUPERFICIES).] —**surfaceless** *adj* —**surfacer** *n* ◇ **on the surface** to outward appearances or when examined superficially ○ *appears cool and collected on the surface* ◇ **scratch the surface** to deal with only a very small or relatively unimportant part of something

surface-active *adj* having the property of reducing the surface tension of a liquid so that the liquid spreads out

surface lift *n* a ski lift that carries skiers uphill while they are standing on their skis

surface mail *n* mail that is transported by sea or land, as opposed to by air

surface noise *n* noise produced as a record player stylus travels over a revolving record, caused by friction, dust, scratches, or static electricity on the record

surface runoff *n* the flow of water over the surface of the ground occurring when rainfall is not absorbed into the soil or evaporated

surface structure *n* in certain types of grammar, a representation of the sequence of syntactic elements that constitute an actual phrase or sentence. ◊ **deep structure**

surface tension *n* (*symbol* γ *or* σ) the property of liquids that gives their surfaces a slightly elastic quality and enables them to form into separate drops

surface-to-air *adj* launched from a ship or from the ground against a target in the air ○ *surface-to-air missiles*

surface-to-surface *adj* launched from a ship or from the ground against another ship or a target on the ground ○ *a surface-to-surface missile*

surfactant /sur fáktənt/ *n* **1** an agent such as a detergent or a drug that reduces the surface tension of liquids so that the liquid spreads out, rather than collecting in droplets **2** a surface-active lipoprotein substance secreted naturally in the lungs, lack of which causes respiratory problems especially in premature babies [Mid-20C. < SURFACE + ACTIVE + -ANT.]

surf and turf *n US, Aus* a meal, menu, or dish including both seafood and meat, especially steak and lobster [*Surf* in reference to the seafood; *turf* in reference to the beef]

surfboard /súrf bawrd/ *n* a long narrow board, with a rounded or pointed front end, on which a surfer stands while riding waves —**surfboarder** *n* —**surfboarding** *n*

surfboat /súrf bōt/ *n* a light sturdy boat, often with a raised prow and stern and buoyancy chambers, suitable for use in high surf

surf carnival *n* an Australian sports festival held at a beach and involving surfing, swimming, canoeing, and running events

surfcasting /súrf kaasting/ *n* a method of fishing in which a baited line is tossed into the surf from the shore or a boat —**surfcaster** *n*

surfeit /súrfit/ *n* **1 EXCESSIVE NUMBER** an excessive number or quantity of something, especially so much of it that people become sickened, repelled, or bored by it **2 OVERINDULGENCE** overindulgence, or a bout of overindulgence, in something, especially food or drink **3 DISGUST OR REVULSION** disgust or revulsion resulting from overindulgence (*literary*) ■ *vt* **GIVE SOMEBODY SURFEIT** to give somebody a surfeit of something [13C. < Old French, past participle of *surfaire* 'overdo' < *faire* 'do' (see AFFAIR).] —**surfeiter** *n*

Surfers Paradise /súrferz párrə dīss/ coastal town in SE Queensland, Australia. Population: 24,086 (1996).

surfie /súrfi/ *n ANZ* somebody whose main interest is surfing (*informal*)

surf-lifesaver *n Aus* somebody, usually a volunteer, who patrols a beach and assists swimmers or surfers who get into difficulties in the water

surf scoter *n* a large marine duck, the male of which is mostly black with white patches on its head. Native to: North America. *Melanitta perspicillata.*

surge /surj/ *vi* **1 MOVE LIKE WAVES** to move in or like a wave, rising up and subsiding and sweeping forwards or back ○ *The boat surged in the rising swell.* **2 MAKE CONCERTED RUSH** to move in a body with a sudden rush in a particular direction **3 INCREASE SUDDENLY** to increase strongly and suddenly **4 SLIP** to slip while being turned on a capstan or windlass (*refers to ropes and cables*) ■ *n* **1 LARGE MOTION** a powerful rising and falling, or forward rushing movement, like that of the sea **2 SUDDEN INCREASE** a sudden increase in something, especially one that seems to rush through somebody or something like a wave **3 POWER INCREASE** a sudden and temporary increase in electrical current or voltage **4 ENERGETIC SOLAR PROMINENCE** an energetic solar prominence lasting for several minutes, which accompanies a solar flare **5 SLIP OF ROPE** a sudden slipping or slackening of a rope or cable on a boat or ship [Early 16C. < French *surgir* 'rise up' and *sourge-*, stem of *sourdre* 'spring up', both ultimately < Latin *surgere* 'rise up from below'.] —**surger** *n*

surgeon /súrjən/ *n* **1** a doctor specializing in operations that involve gaining access to the patient's body, e.g. by making incisions into it, in order to correct defects, repair injuries, or treat diseases **2** a medical officer in the armed services or on board a ship [14C. Via Anglo-Norman < Old French *cirurgien* < *cirurgie* (see SURGERY).]

surgeonfish /súrjən fish/ (*plural* **-fish** *or* **-fishes**) *n* a tropical fish that is often brightly coloured and has spines at the base of its tail that it uses to inflict wounds. Family: Acanthuridae. [*Surgeon* from an imagined resemblance of its spines to a surgeon's needle]

surgeon general (*plural* **surgeons general**) *n* **1** the chief medical officer in many branches of the military service **2** the cabinet-level chief public health officer of the United States, or the chief public health officer of some individual states. The Surgeon General is roughly the equivalent of the UK Chief Medical Officer.

surgeon's knot *n* a surgical knot of a type that can be relied on to remain tight

⚡**surge protector** *n* an electrical device designed to protect a computer against the harmful effects of power surges and spikes

surgery /súrjəri/ (*plural* **-ies**) *n* **1 MEDICAL PROCEDURES INVOLVING OPERATIONS** medical treatment that involves operations or manipulations on the patient's body and, usually, cutting the body open to perform these **2 BRANCH OF MEDICINE** the branch of medicine that deals with diseases and conditions treated by operation or manipulation, or the range of diseases treated in this way **3 SURGEON'S ART OR ACTIVITY** the art or activity of performing surgery **4 DOCTOR'S OFFICE** a doctor's, dentist's, or veterinary surgeon's office **5 DOCTOR'S CONSULTATION TIME** a time when a doctor, dentist, or veterinary surgeon is available for consultation by patients at a surgery **6 POLITICIAN'S OR LAWYER'S CONSULTATION TIME** a time when a Member of Parliament, a councillor, or a professional such as a lawyer is available for consultation by members of the general public **7** *US, Can* **OPERATING ROOM** a hospital or clinic room where surgery is performed [14C. Via Old French *cirurgerie* < Greek *kheirourgia* 'working with the hands' < *kheir* 'hand' + *ergon* 'work'.]

surgical /súrjik'l/ *adj* **1 OF SURGERY** relating to or accomplished by surgery **2 RESULTING FROM SURGERY** due to or as a consequence of surgery **3 PRECISE** like surgery in requiring or being characterized by great skill or great precision [Late 18C. Alteration (under the influence of SURGEON) of French *cirurgical* < *cirurgien* 'surgeon' (see SURGERY).] —**surgically** *adv*

surgical boot *n* a specially fitted shoe that compensates for physical deformity. US term **corrective shoe**

surgical spirit *n* methylated spirits mixed with castor oil and oil of wintergreen. Use: to prevent bed sores, harden the skin of the feet, and formerly to sterilize the skin before injections and operations.

suricate /syoóri kayt/ *n* ZOOL = **meerkat** [Late 18C. Via French < obsolete Dutch *surikat* < ?]

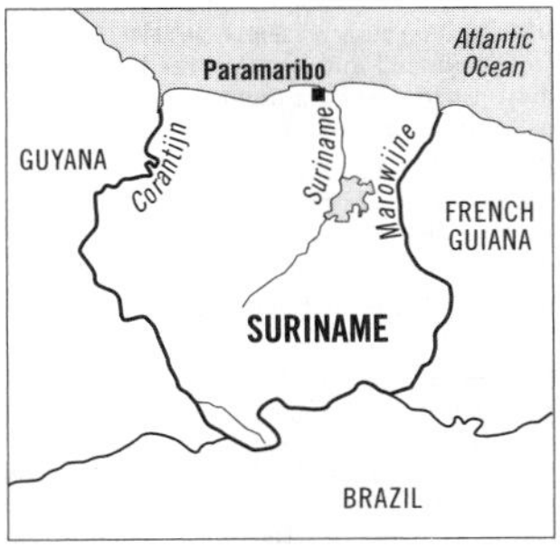

Suriname

Suriname /soóri nám, -náamə/ republic in NE South America, on the Atlantic Ocean. Capital: Paramaribo. Population: 436,418 (1996). Area: 163,265 sq. km/63,037 sq. mi. —**Surinamese** /soóri na meéz/ *n, adj*

Suriname toad *n* AMPHIB = **pipa**[1] *n.*

surjection /sur jéksh'n/ *n* a mathematical function for which each element of a set is the image of at least one element of another set [Mid-20C. < SUR-, after INJECTION.] —**surjective** *adj*

surly /súrli/ (**-lier, -liest**) *adj* bad-tempered, unfriendly, rude, and somewhat threatening ○ *a person with a surly manner* [Late 16C. Alteration of obsolete *sirly* 'lordly, imperious' < SIR.] —**surliness** *n*

surmise /sur míz/ *vti* to conclude that something is the case on the basis of only limited evidence or intuitive feeling ■ *n* a conclusion drawn on only limited evidence or intuitive feeling [Early 16C. < Anglo-Norman *surmis*, past participle of *surmettre* 'accuse', literally 'put over' < Latin *mittere* 'send'.] —**surmisable** *adj* —**surmiser** *n*

surmount /sur mównt/ *vt* **1 OVERCOME DIFFICULTY** to deal with a difficulty successfully **2 GET TO TOP OF** to get over the top of a physical obstacle (*formal*) **3 BE PLACED ON TOP OF** to be positioned on top of something or rise above it (*formal*) ○ *the statues surmounting the parapet* **4 PUT SOMETHING ON TOP OF** to place something on top of or above something (*formal*) ○ *surmount the parapet with a row of statues* [14C. < French *surmonter* 'climb over' < *monter* 'mount' (see MOUNT[1]).] —**surmountability** /sur mówntə bíllәti/ *n* —**surmountable** *adj* —**surmounter** *n*

surname /súr naym/ *n* **1 SOMEBODY'S FAMILY NAME** the name that identifies somebody as belonging to a particular family and that he or she has in common with other members of the family **2 DESCRIPTIVE ADDITION TO NAME** a descriptive addition to somebody's name e.g. 'the Great' in 'Catherine the Great' (*archaic*) ■ *vt* (**-names, -naming, -named**) **GIVE SOMEBODY A SURNAME** to give or transmit a surname to somebody (*usually passive*) [14C. Translation of Old French *surnom* 'name above' < *nom* 'name'.] —**surnamer** *n*

surpass /sur paáss/ *vt* **1 EXCEED EXPECTATIONS** to go beyond what was expected or hoped for, usually by being bigger, better, or greater **2 DO BETTER THAN** to be bigger, greater, better, or worse than somebody or something else **3 BE BEYOND SOMEBODY'S ABILITY** to be beyond somebody's ability to deal with or understand (*formal*) [Mid-16C. < French *surpasser* 'transgress', literally 'pass beyond' < *passer* 'pass' (see PASS).] —**surpassable** *adj*

surpassing /sur paássing/ *adj* of a quality far superior to others (*literary*) ○ *a view of surpassing beauty* —**surpassingly** *adv*

surplice /súrpliss/ *n* a white ecclesiastical outer garment like a smock, with wide, often flared sleeves, and varying in length [13C. Via Anglo-Norman *surpliz* < medieval Latin *superpellicium* '(vestment worn) over a fur garment' < *pellicium* 'fur coat'.]

surplus /súrpləss/ *n* **1 EXCESS AMOUNT** an amount remaining after the original purpose has been served or the original requirement met **2 EXCESS MONEY** an amount of money remaining after all liabilities have been met ○ *The government is predicting a trade surplus this year.* **3 EXTRA WORTH** the amount by which the net worth of a company's assets exceed the value of its owned stock ■ *adj* **ADDITIONAL TO REQUIREMENTS** not required to meet existing needs, or left over after these have been met ○ *be surplus to requirements* [14C. Via Anglo-Norman < medieval Latin *superplus* 'more beyond' < Latin *plus* 'more'.]

surplusage /súrpləssij/ *n* **1 IRRELEVANT MATTER** an irrelevant matter introduced into legal proceedings **2 VERBIAGE** redundant words or arguments (*formal*) **3 SURPLUS** an excess of something (*formal*)

surplus value *n* in Marxist economic theory, the difference between the price of a product produced by labour and the value of labour itself in terms of the wages paid to workers

surprint /sur prínt/ *vt* PRINTING = **overprint** *v.* ■ *n* PRINTING = **overprint** *n.* 1

surprise /sər príz/ *vt* (**-prises, -prising, -prised**) **1 MAKE SOMEBODY AMAZED** to cause somebody to feel sudden wonder or amazement, especially because of something unexpected **2 TAKE SOMEBODY OR SOMETHING UNAWARES** to attack, come upon, or catch somebody or something unexpectedly **3 GIVE SOMEBODY SOMETHING UNEXPECTEDLY** to make an unexpected gift to somebody ○ *surprised me with flowers* **4 TRICK** to cause somebody to do something unexpected by trickery or deceit **5 ELICIT SOMETHING FROM SOMEBODY** to cause somebody to admit something unexpectedly by trickery or deceit ■ *n* **1 AMAZING EVENT** the act or an instance of causing somebody to feel unexpected wonder or delight **2 SOMETHING UNEXPECTED** an unexpected gift or event **3 AMAZEMENT** a feeling of unexpected amazement or delight [15C. < French, feminine past participle of *surprendre* 'overtake' < *sur-* 'over' + Latin *prehendere* (see PREHENSION).] —**surpriser** *n* —**surprising** *adj* —**surprisingly** *adv* ◇ **take somebody by surprise** to happen unexpectedly to somebody ○ *Their arrival took everybody by surprise.*

surra /sóorə/ *n* a tropical disease similar to sleeping sickness that affects camels and horses, and occasionally cattle and dogs [Late 19C. < Marathi *sūra* 'air breathed through the nostrils'.]

surreal /sə reé el/ *adj* suggesting or having qualities associated with surrealism, such as bizarre landscapes and distorted objects ■ *n* the bizarre or unreal qualities associated with surrealism [Mid-20C. Back-formation < SURREALISM.] —**surreally** *adv*

surrealism /sə reé əlizəm/ *n* **1** an early 20th-century movement in art and literature that tried to represent the subconscious mind by creating fantastic imagery and juxtaposing elements that seem to contradict each other **2** surreal art or literature [Early 20C. < French *surréalisme* 'beyond realism'.] —**surrealist** *n, adj* —**surrealistic** /sə reé ə lístik/ *adj* —**surrealistically** *adv*

QUICK FACTS ON... **SURREALISM**

Key dates: early–mid-20th century
Key locations: France, Italy
Key elements: artistic access to the unconscious using dreams, fantasies, myths, and metaphors; unusual techniques and media like automatic writing and collages
Key figures: André Breton, Jean Cocteau, Paul Éluard, Federico García Lorca (literature); Salvador Dali, René Magritte, Max Ernst, Man Ray, Roberto Matta Echaurren, Joan Miró (art); Luis Buñuel (film)
Key works: *Celebes* (Ernst) 1921, *Pleasure* (Magritte) 1927, *Nadja* (Breton) 1928, *Gypsy Ballads* (Lorca) 1928, *Un chien Andalou* (Buñuel and Dali) 1929, *The Persistence of Memory* (Dali) 1931, *Orpheus* (Cocteau) 1933
Key developments: Dada, Theatre of the Absurd, existentialism

surrebuttal /súrri bútt'l/ *n* in a civil court action, an act of giving evidence to support the third reply (**surrebutter**) of the person bringing the action (**plaintiff**) (*archaic*)

surrebutter /súrri búttər/ *n* in a civil court action, the third reply of the person bringing the action (**plaintiff**), in response to the defendant's third statement (**rebutter**) (*archaic*) [Late 16C. < REBUTTER, after SURREJOINDER.]

surrejoinder /súrri jóyndər/ *n* in a civil court action, the second reply of the person bringing the action (**plaintiff**), in response to the defendant's second statement (**rejoinder**)

surrender /sə réndər/ *v* **1** *vi* **STOP FIGHTING BECAUSE UNABLE TO WIN** to declare to an opponent that he or she has won and that fighting can cease **2** *vt* **GIVE UP POSSESSION OF** to relinquish possession or control of something because of coercion or force **3** *vt* **GIVE SOMETHING OUT OF COURTESY** to give somebody a seat, position, or office as a courtesy or as a gesture of goodwill **4** *vt* **GIVE SOMETHING UP** to give up or abandon something such as an idea or intention **5** *vi* **GIVE SELF UP TO SOMETHING** to yield to a strong emotion, influence, or temptation **6** *vt* **ABANDON RIGHTS TO** to give up or abandon rights to something, especially to give up a lease before it has expired ■ *n* **1 GIVING UP A FIGHT** an act of declaring defeat at the hands of an opponent ○ *The French demanded an unconditional surrender.* **2 GIVING UP CONTROL** a relinquishment of control to somebody or something **3 DELIVERY INTO LEGAL CUSTODY** the delivery of a prisoner or fugitive into legal custody **4 ABANDONMENT OF LEGAL RIGHTS** the abandonment of legal rights, especially the giving up of a lease or an insurance policy before it has expired **5 GIVING SELF UP TO AUTHORITIES** an act of willing submission to authorities [15C. < Anglo-Norman, 'give over' < *render* 'give (back)', a variant of Old French *rendre* (see RENDER).] —**surrenderer** *n*

SYNONYMS See ***yield***.

surreptitious /súrrəp tíshəss/ *adj* **1** done, made, or acquired by secret or sneaky methods **2** operating with or characterized by stealth [15C. Via Latin *surreptitius* < *surripere* 'seize secretly', literally 'seize from beneath' < *rapere* (see RAPE[1]).] —**surreptitiously** *adv* —**surreptitiousness** *n*

SYNONYMS See ***secret***.

surrey /súrri/ (*plural* **-reys**) *n* a late 19th-century horse-drawn four-wheeled carriage with two or four seats, used for short pleasure trips [Late 19C. After SURREY.]

Surrey /súrri/ county in SE England. Area: 1,677 sq. km/648 sq. mi.

surrogate *adj* /súrrəgət, -gayt/ **TAKING PLACE OF SOMEBODY OR SOMETHING** taking the place of somebody or something else ■ *n* **1 SUBSTITUTE** a person who acts as a replacement for somebody else **2 WOMAN WHO GIVES BIRTH FOR ANOTHER** a woman who bears a child for a couple, with the intention of handing it over at birth **3 SUBSTITUTE AUTHORITY FIGURE** a respected person, e.g. a teacher or older sibling, who replaces a lost or nonexistent parent in somebody's unconscious ■ *vt* /súrrə gayt/ (**-gates, -gating, -gated**) **APPOINT AS A STAND-IN** to put somebody in somebody else's place [Mid-16C. < Latin *surrogatus*, past participle of *surrogare* 'ask for in place of' < *rogare* (see ROGATION).] —**surrogacy** /súrrəgəssi/ *n* —**surrogateship** *n* —**surrogation** /súrrə gáysh'n/ *n*

surround /sə równd/ *vt* **1 ENCLOSE** to occupy the space all around something **2 CLOSE OFF MEANS OF ESCAPE** to encircle something completely, especially an enemy's military position **3 BE AROUND** to associate closely with somebody ■ *n* **1 OUTSIDE BORDER** an area around the edge of something, especially the space between the edge of a carpet and the walls of the room **2 AREA AROUND** an area or border around a particular thing or place **3 SURROUNDINGS** the immediate environment of something or somebody (*often plural*) [Early 17C. Via Old French *suronder* 'overflow' < late Latin *superundare* < Latin *unda* 'wave' (see UNDULATE).]

surroundings /sə równdingz/ *npl* the immediate environment of somebody or something, including events, circumstances, scenery, conditions, people, and objects

surround sound *n* a system of recording and reproducing sound that uses three or more channels and speakers in order to create the effect of the listener being surrounded by sound sources

sursum corda /súr ssəm káwrdə, -sóom-/ *n* **1** in the Roman Catholic Church, a short sentence (**versicle**) spoken by a priest during Mass, just before the preface **2** a cry or exhortation, especially of hope (*literary*) [< late Latin, '(lift) up (your) hearts', the versicle's opening words]

surtax /súr taks/ *n* **1 ANOTHER TAX** a tax that is charged in addition to other taxes **2 HIGHER TAX** a higher level or levels of tax imposed on individuals and corporations when income or profits exceed a certain amount ■ *vt* **CHARGE SOMEBODY SURTAX** to charge somebody with an additional or higher tax [Late 19C. < French *surtaxe* 'over tax' < *taxe* 'tax' < *taxer* (see TAX).]

Surtees /súrt eez/, **John** (*b.* 1934) British motorcyclist and motor racing driver

surtitle /súr tīt'l/ *n* a translation of words being spoken in a foreign language during the performance of a play or opera, projected on a screen above the stage (*often used in the plural*) US term **supertitle** —**surtitled** *adj*

~~**surveilance**~~ incorrect spelling of **surveillance**

surveillance /sur váylənss/ *n* continual observation of a person or group, especially one suspected of doing something illegal [Early 19C. < French, < *surveiller* 'watch over' < *veiller* 'keep watch' < Latin *vigilare* (see VIGILANT).] —**surveillant** *adj, n*

survey *vt* /sur váy, súr vay/ (**-veys, -veying, -veyed**) **1 CONSIDER SOMETHING GENERALLY** to look at or consider something in a general or very broad way **2 LOOK AT SOMETHING CAREFULLY** to look at or consider somebody or something closely, especially in order to form an opinion **3 PLOT A MAP OF SOMEWHERE** to make a detailed map of an area of land, including its boundaries, area, and elevation, using geometry and trigonometry to measure angles and distances **4 INSPECT A BUILDING** to inspect a building in order to determine its structural soundness or assess its value **5 QUESTION PEOPLE IN A POLL** to do a statistical study of a sample population by asking questions about age, income, opinions, buying preferences, and other aspects of people's lives **6 GAZE AT** to look at or over something in a casual or leisurely way ■ *n* /súr vay/ (*plural* **-veys**) **1 ANALYSIS OF POLL SAMPLE** a statistical analysis of answers to a poll of a sample of a population, e.g. to determine opinions, preferences, or knowledge **2 INSPECTION OF A BUILDING** an inspection of a building to determine its condition and assess its value **3 REPORT FROM INSPECTING BUILDING** a report that results from inspecting the condition and assessing the value of a building **4 GENERAL VIEW** a very broad or general view of a subject or situation **5 CRITICAL INSPECTION** a very detailed, critical examination of something such as a situation or event **6 ACT OF MEASURING LAND** an act of taking detailed measurements of an area of land **7 REPORT ON**

LAND MEASUREMENT a report that shows the results of a survey undertaken to measure an area of land **8** GROUP DOING A SURVEY a team of surveyors working together **9** AREA SURVEYED an area of land that is being or has been surveyed [15C. Via Anglo-Norman *surveier* < medieval Latin *supervidere* 'oversee' < Latin *videre* (see VISION).] —**surveyable** *adj*

~~**surveyer**~~ incorrect spelling of **surveyor**

surveyor /sur váyər/ *n* **1** somebody whose occupation is taking accurate measurements of land areas in order to determine boundaries, elevations, and dimensions **2** somebody whose occupation is inspecting buildings to determine the soundness of their construction or to assess their value **3** CONSTR = **quantity surveyor**

surveyor's chain *n* MEASURE = **chain** *n.* **7**

surveyor's level *n* an instrument with a telescope and a spirit level attached, mounted on a tripod and rotating around the vertical axis, used for measuring elevations of land

surveyor's measure *n* a system of measurement based on the unit the surveyor's chain, 22 yd (about 20 m)

survival /sur vív'l/ *n* **1** STAYING ALIVE continuation in life or existence **2** FACT OF LIVING THROUGH the fact of having managed to live through something **3** SOMETHING FROM THE PAST a custom, idea, or belief that remains when other similar things have been lost or forgotten

survival bag *n* a protective bag that climbers or hikers get into to protect themselves from exposure

survivalist /sə vívəlist/ *n* a person who seeks to survive an impending disaster by hoarding weapons and food, often going off to live alone or with a like-minded group —**survivalism** *n*

survive /sər vív/ (**-vives, -viving, -vived**) *v* **1** *vi* REMAIN ALIVE OR IN EXISTENCE to manage to stay alive or continue to exist, especially in difficult situations **2** *vt* STAY ALIVE LONGER THAN to remain alive after the death of somebody else **3** *vt* LIVE THROUGH to remain alive or in existence after something such as an accident or war that threatens life [15C. Via Anglo-Norman *survivre* < Latin *supervivere* 'live beyond' < *vivere* (see VIVID).] —**survivability** /sər vívə bílləti/ *n* —**survivable** *adj*

survivor /sə vívər/ *n* **1** SOMEBODY WHO SURVIVES a person who lives through an accident, illness, war, or bad experience **2** INHERITOR the one of two or more people having joint interests in property who lives longer than the other or others and is, therefore, entitled to the entire property **3** SOMEBODY OVERCOMING TRAUMATIC EXPERIENCE a person who has been psychologically damaged by a trauma, e.g. rape or an addiction, and seeks to overcome its effects ○ *an incest survivor*

sus[1] /suss/ *n* a state of doubt or misgiving about somebody or something (*slang*) ■ *adj* acting like somebody who has done something wrong or illegal (*slang*) [Mid-20C. Shortening of SUSPICION and SUSPICIOUS.]

sus[2] /suss/ *n* a person who is suspected of a wrongdoing (*slang*) [Mid-20C. Shortening of SUSPECT.]

Susann /soo zán/, **Jacqueline** (1926–74) US writer

Susanna /soo zánnə/ *n* in the Apocrypha, a woman of Babylon who was saved by the prophet Daniel after being falsely accused of adultery

~~**susceptable**~~ incorrect spelling of **susceptible**

susceptibility /sə séptə bílləti/ (*plural* **-ties**) *n* **1** LIKELIHOOD OF BEING AFFECTED the likelihood of being affected by something **2** SENSITIVITY the ability to be affected by strong feelings and emotions **3** FEELINGS somebody's feelings, especially those of somebody who easily becomes upset **4** PHYS = **magnetic susceptibility**

susceptible /sə séptəb'l/ *adj* **1** EASILY AFFECTED easily influenced or affected by something **2** LIKELY TO BE AFFECTED liable to being affected by something ○ *susceptible to hay fever and other allergies* **3** EMOTIONAL easily affected emotionally **4** CAPABLE OF SOMETHING capable or permitting of something [Early 17C. Directly or via French < Latin *suscipere* 'take up' < *capere* (see CAPTURE).] —**susceptibleness** *n* —**susceptibly** *adv*

susceptive /sə séptiv/ *adj* **1** easily affected by something **2** open to new ideas and suggestions [Mid-15C. < Latin *suscept-*, past participle of *suscipere* (see SUSCEPTIBLE).] —**susceptiveness** *n* —**susceptivity** /sússep tívvəti/ *n*

~~**suseptible**~~ incorrect spelling of **susceptible**

sushi /sóo shee/ *n* small cakes of cold boiled rice, shaped by hand or wrapped in seaweed and topped with pieces of raw or cooked fish, vegetables, or egg [Late 19C. < Japanese.]

sus laws *npl* laws that permit the arrest and prosecution of people suspected of frequenting or loitering in public places for the purpose of committing a crime (*dated informal*)

suslik /sóoss lik/ (*plural* **-liks** *or* **-lik**), **souslik** (*plural* **-liks** *or* **-lik**) *n* a ground squirrel with large eyes and small ears that lives in dry open areas. Native to: Europe, Asia. *Citellus citellus.* [Late 18C. < Russian.]

suspect *v* /sə spékt/ **1** *vt* BELIEVE SOMEBODY IS GUILTY to believe that somebody may have committed a crime or wrongdoing without having any proof **2** *vt* DOUBT to doubt the truth or validity of something **3** *vt* BELIEVE SOMETHING TO BE SO to think that something is probable or likely **4** *vti* HAVE SUSPICIONS to be suspicious about something ■ *n* /súss pekt/ SOMEBODY WHO MIGHT BE GUILTY a person who is suspected of a wrongdoing ■ *adj* /súss pekt/ **1** SUSPICIOUS thought or likely to be false or untrustworthy ○ *All his claims about the wealth of his family are rather suspect.* **2** LIKELY TO CONTAIN SOMETHING ILLEGAL looking likely to contain something dangerous or illegal [14C. < Latin *suspect-*, past participle of *suspicere* 'look up at' < *specere* (see SPECTACLE).] ◇ **the usual suspects** people, businesses, or organizations frequently mentioned in the context of a particular activity

USAGE ***Suspect*** denotes somebody who is suspected of wrongdoing, and who is entitled to seek to prove his or her innocence, as opposed to somebody who has been found guilty. But unless the word is referring to a specific individual, its refusal to affirm guilt may be beside the point, as it is in *The day after the burglary the police began searching for suspects.* When guilt is evident, even though the use of ***suspect*** acknowledges that a legal defence may yet be possible, it may seem foolish: *After the jewels were found in his house and he confessed to the burglary, the suspect was remanded for trial.*

~~**suspence**~~ incorrect spelling of **suspense**

suspend /sə spénd/ *v* **1** *vt* HANG SOMETHING FROM ABOVE to hang something from above, especially so that it can swing freely **2** *vt* STOP SOMETHING FOR A PERIOD to stop something or make something ineffective, usually for a short time **3** *vt* BAR SOMEBODY FOR A PERIOD to bar somebody from a privilege, a position, or an organization, usually when under suspicion of wrongdoing **4** *vt* POSTPONE to delay or defer action on a decision or a judgment until more of the facts are known **5** *vt* HANG ABOVE to hang over or above something **6** *vt* DISPERSE SOMETHING IN LIQUID to cause particles to be dispersed in a liquid or gas **7** *vt* SUSTAIN A NOTE to hold a note until the next note or chord is sounded, so that they are heard together **8** *vi* STOP MAKING PAYMENTS to cease payment on something, especially because of an inability to meet financial obligations [13C. Directly or via French *suspendre* < Latin *suspendere* 'hang up' < *pendere* (see PENDANT).] —**suspendibility** *n* —**suspendible** *adj*

suspended animation *n* **1** the stopping or slowing of the vital functions of an organism for some period of time, especially by freezing **2** a state, often caused by asphyxia, in which an organism loses consciousness and stops breathing so that it appears to be dead

suspended sentence *n* a sentence imposed on somebody found guilty of a crime that need not be served as long as the individual commits no other crime during the term of the sentence

suspender /sə spéndər/ *n* **1** STRAP FOR WOMAN'S STOCKINGS an elastic strap, usually attached to a girdle or belt, with a clamp at one end to hold up a woman's stockings. US term **garter** *n.* **2** **2** STRAP FOR MAN'S SOCK an elastic strap with a clamp on one end that attaches to and holds up a man's sock **3** *US* STRAP FOR HOLDING UP TROUSERS a strap, usually made of elastic, worn over the shoulders and with a clip at either end to attach to trousers so that they do not fall down (*usually plural*) **4** SOMETHING THAT LETS SOMETHING HANG something that allows something else to hang, e.g. one of the cables on a suspension bridge

suspender belt *n* a belt with four elastic straps hanging from it, one down the back and front of each leg, with clamps on the ends to hold up a woman's stockings. US term **garter belt**

suspense /sə spénss/ *n* **1** UNCERTAINTY the state or condition of being unsure or in doubt about something **2** ENJOYABLE TENSION a feeling of tense excitement about how something such as a mystery novel or film will end **3** ANXIETY a state of anxiety or intense worry about something [15C. Via Anglo-Norman < Latin *suspensus*, past participle of *suspendere* (see SUSPEND).] —**suspenseful** *adj*

suspense account *n* an account in which entries are made temporarily, until it is determined where they belong

suspension /sə spén sh'n/ *n* **1** TEMPORARY STOP an interruption of something for a period of time **2** POSTPONEMENT OF A SENTENCE a delay in the carrying out of a sentence or the making of a decision or judgment **3** TEMPORARY REMOVAL the temporary removal of somebody from a team, position, school, or organization, especially as punishment **4** END TO REPAYING DEBTS an end to the repayment of financial obligations because of a lack of money **5** SYSTEM REDUCING VEHICLE'S VIBRATION a system of springs and shock absorbers on a wheeled vehicle that reduces the impact of bumps and uneven running surfaces on the occupants and gives the wheels better contact **6** DISPERSION OF PARTICLES a dispersion of fine solid particles in a liquid or gas, removable by filtration **7** TECHNIQUE FOR CREATING DISSONANCE a technique in which a note of the first chord is held into the second chord, the dissonance created being resolved by moving a step lower in the third chord

suspension bridge *n* a bridge that has the roadway suspended from cables that are anchored by towers at either end and, sometimes, with supporting structures for the cables placed at regular intervals

suspension point *n US* one of a series of dots, usually three, used in printed and written material to indicate an omission from text being reproduced or an incomplete phrase (*often plural*)

suspensive /sə spénsiv/ *adj* **1** STOPPING causing or tending to cause something to stop or be deferred **2** CAUSING TENSION causing, arousing, or relating to a feeling of doubt or anxious excitement **3** UNDECIDED inclined to delay making a decision or judgment —**suspensively** *adv* —**suspensiveness** *n*

suspensoid /sə spén soyd/ *n* a solution of very fine solid particles dispersed throughout a liquid [Early 20C. < SUSPENSION.]

suspensory /sə spénsəri/ *n* (*plural* **-ries**) **1** LIGAMENT OR MUSCLE a ligament or muscle from which a structure or part is suspended **2** BANDAGE OR SLING something such as a bandage or a sling that holds part of the body in position while it heals ■ *adj* TEMPORARILY STOPPING temporarily interrupting or delaying the completion of something

suspensory ligament *n* a ligament that provides support for an organ or another body part, especially a fibrous membrane that holds the lens of the eye in place

suspicion /sə spísh'n/ *n* **1** FEELING OF SOMETHING WRONG an unsubstantiated belief that something is the case, especially a belief that something wrong has happened or that somebody may have committed a crime ○ *a sneaking suspicion that she was the one who ate the last biscuit* **2** MISTRUST a feeling of mistrust or doubt, especially because something wrong has happened and has not been explained ○ *an atmosphere of suspicion* **3** CONDITION OF BEING SUSPECTED the condition of being suspected of something, especially wrongdoing ○ *under suspicion* **4** SMALL AMOUNT OF a tiny amount of something, e.g. a colour or flavour [13C. Via Anglo-Norman *suspeciun* < Latin *suspicere* (see SUSPECT).] —**suspicional** *adj*

suspicious /sə spíshəss/ *adj* **1** AROUSING SUSPICION creating or liable to create suspicion **2** TENDING TO SUSPECT inclined or tending to believe that something is wrong ○ *a suspicious nature* **3** SUGGESTING DOUBT showing or indicating suspicion —**suspiciously** *adv* —**suspiciousness** *n*

suspire /sə spír/ (**-pires, -piring, -pired**) *vi* (*dated literary*) **1** to draw in breath **2** to give a sigh [15C. < Latin *suspirare* 'breathe up' < *spirare* (see SPIRIT).] —**suspiration** /súspi ráysh'n/ *n*

Susquehanna /súskwə hánnə/ river in New York State and Pennsylvania, emptying into the Chesapeake Bay in Maryland. Length: 715 km/444 mi.

suss /sus/, **sus** *vt* to discover or understand something, e.g. somebody's motives, a situation, or how to use something (*informal*) ○ *I think I've finally got this camera sussed.* [Mid-20C. Shortening of SUSPECT.]
suss out *vt* to get to the bottom of something, or discover what somebody is up to (*informal*)

Sussex /sússiks/ former county of SE England, now divided into the counties of East Sussex and West Sussex

Sussex Downs hilly region in SE England that has been designated an Area of Outstanding Natural Beauty. Area: 983 sq. km/379 sq. mi.

Sussex Drive, 24 Sussex Drive *n* the address of the official residence of the Prime Minister of Canada

Susskind /súss kind/, **Leonard** (*b.* 1940) US physicist

sustain /sə stáyn/ *vt* **1 WITHSTAND SOMETHING** to manage to withstand something and continue doing something in spite of it **2 BE AFFECTED BY** to experience a setback, injury, damage, loss, or defeat ○ *The child who fell sustained no more than several broken bones.* **3 MAINTAIN** to make something continue to exist **4 NOURISH** to provide somebody with nourishment or the necessities of life **5 SUPPORT FROM BELOW** to keep something in position by holding it from below ○ *The floor will not sustain the weight of a grand piano.* **6 PROVIDE WITH MORAL SUPPORT** to keep somebody going with emotional or moral support **7 VALIDATE** to decide that a statement or objection is valid or justified **8 CONFIRM** to confirm that something is true or valid **9 KEEP A PRETENCE GOING** to maintain a pretence successfully ■ *n* **PROLONGED NOTE** a note that is prolonged [13C. Via Anglo-Norman *sustein-*, stem of *sustenir* < Latin *sustinere* 'hold up' < *tenere* (see TENANT).] —**sustainment** *n*

sustainable /sə stáynəb'l/ *adj* **1** able to be maintained **2** exploiting natural resources without destroying the ecological balance of a particular area —**sustainability** *n* —**sustainably** *adv*

sustainable development *n* economic development maintained within acceptable levels of global resource depletion and environmental pollution ○ *'Sustainable development is the principle which should guide politicians in planning the future...'* (*BBC website*; April 1999)

sustained yield *n* **1** the ongoing supply of a natural resource, e.g. timber, by scheduled harvesting **2** the amount of a natural resource obtained by scheduled harvesting

sustainer /sə stáynər/ *n* a person who sustains another, or a person or thing that supports and upholds something

sustaining pedal *n* the right pedal of a piano, which is used to keep the dampers off the strings so that they can vibrate freely

sustenance /sússtənənss/ *n* **1 NOURISHMENT** something, especially food, that supports life ○ *There isn't much sustenance in a small chocolate bar.* **2 CONDITION OF BEING SUSTAINED** the condition of being supported ○ *'I have hardly a penny in the world – I am staying with my aunt for my bare sustenance'.* (Thomas Hardy, *Far from the Madding Crowd*; 1874) **3 LIVELIHOOD** a means of supporting somebody financially [13C. < Anglo-Norman *sustenaunce* < *sustenir* (see SUSTAIN).]

sustentacular /súss ten tákyoolər/ *adj* describes cells or fibres that serve as a support and have no other function [Late 19C. < modern Latin *sustentaculum* 'support' < Latin *sustentare* (see SUSTENTATION).]

sustentation /súss ten táysh'n/ *n* (*formal*) **1** something that supports or sustains something **2** a means of support [14C. Via French < Latin *sustentare* 'keep holding up' < *sustinere* (see SUSTAIN).] —**sustentative** /sústən taytiv, sə sténtativ/ *adj*

Susu /sóo soo/ (*plural* **-su** *or* **-sus**) *n* **1** a member of a people who live in West Africa, mainly in Guinea and Sierra Leone **2** the Mande language of the Susu people. Native speakers: 700,000. [Late 18C. < Susu.] —**Susu** *adj*

susurrate /sússə rayt/ (**-rates, -rating, -rated**) *vi* to whisper or rustle softly [Early 17C. Back-formation < *susurration* < Latin *susurrare* < *susurrus* 'whisper', ultimately an imitation of the sound.] —**susurrant** *adj* —**susurration** /sússə ráysh'n/ *n*

susurrus /sússərəss/ *n* a whispering or murmuring sound (*literary*) [15C. < Latin (see SUSURRATE).]

Sutcliffe /sútklif/, **Herbert** (1894–1978) British cricketer

Sutherland /súthərlənd/ former county of N Scotland, part of Highland council area

Sutherland, Graham (1903–80) British painter

Sutherland, Dame Joan (*b.* 1926) Australian singer

Sutherland Falls waterfall on South Island, New Zealand. Height: 580 m/1,904 ft.

Sutlej /sút lij/ river in S Asia, flowing through SW Tibet, N India, and E Pakistan. Length: 933 km/850 mi.

sutler /sútt lər/ *n* a person who follows an army and sells goods to the soldiers (*archaic*) [Late 16C. < obsolete Dutch *soeteler* < *soetelen* 'befoul, do menial work'.] —**sutlership** *n*

sutra /sóotrə/ *n* **1** a short aphoristic summary of the teachings of Hinduism, created to be memorized and later incorporated into Hindu literature **2 sutra, sutta** a classic religious text of Buddhism, especially one regarded as a discourse of the Buddha [Early 19C. < Sanskrit *sūtram* 'aphorism', literally 'thread'.]

suttee /súttee, su teé/, **sati** *n* **1** in the Indian subcontinent, the practice, now illegal, of a widow throwing herself on her husband's funeral pyre **2** a Hindu widow who throws herself on her husband's funeral pyre [Late 18C. < Sanskrit *satī* 'good woman', feminine present participle of *as-* 'be'.] —**sutteeism** *n*

Sutton /sútt'n/, **Henry** (1856–1912) Australian inventor

Sutton Coldfield /sútt'n kṓld feeld/ town in central England. Population: 90,325 (1991).

suture /sóo chər/ *n* **1 MATERIAL FOR SURGICAL STITCHING** a piece of material, e.g. catgut, thread, or wire, used to close a wound or connect tissues **2 SURGICAL SEAM** the line formed where a wound has been closed or tissues have been joined **3 SEAM** any seam or line at which two edges have been joined **4 IMMOVABLE JOINT** a joint, found especially in the skull, in which the bones are tightly bound together by fibrous connective tissue, permitting no movement between them **5 LINE AT POINT OF JUNCTURE** a distinguishable line at the junction of adjacent structures, e.g. between the chambers of a mollusc shell or between the exoskeletal plates of an insect **6 LINE ON SEED POD OR FRUIT** a line along which a seed pod or fruit will split to release its seeds ■ *vt* (**-tures, -turing, -tured**) **CLOSE A WOUND** to close a wound by joining the edges [15C. < Latin *sutura* < *sut-*, past participle of *suere* 'sew'.] —**sutural** *adj* —**suturally** *adv*

SUV *abbr US* sport-utility vehicle

Suva /sóovə/ capital of Fiji, on the SE coast of Viti Levu island. Population: 69,665 (1986).

Suwannee /sə wónni/ river in the SE United States, flowing from SE Georgia through N Florida to the Gulf of Mexico. Length: 306 km/190 mi.

suxamethonium *n* an intravenous drug. Use: muscle relaxant during surgery. US term **succinylcholine**

suzerain /sóo zə rayn/ *n* a nation that controls a dependent nation's international affairs but otherwise allows it to control its internal affairs [Early 19C. < Old French *suserain* < ?] —**suzerainty** /-rənti/ *n*

Suzhou /sóo jṓ/ city in E China, west of Shanghai. Population: 706,459 (1990).

Suzman /sóozmən, sóozmən/, **Helen** (*b.* 1917) South African politician

sv *abbr* El Salvador (*in Internet addresses*)

Sv *symbol* sievert

SV *abbr* **1** Holy Virgin **2** Your Holiness

s.v., sv *abbr* **1** sailing vessel **2** side valve **3** under the word or term

SV40 /éss veé fáwrti/ *n* a virus that causes cancer in monkeys and is widely used in genetic and medical research [*SV* < *simian virus*]

Svalbard /svál baard/ Norwegian archipelago north of the mainland, in the Arctic Ocean. Population: 2,864 (1996). Area: 62,050 sq. km/23,958 sq. mi.

svelte /svelt/ *adj* graceful and slender in figure or contour [Early 19C. Via French < Italian *svelto* 'stretched', past participle of *svellere* 'pluck out' < assumed Vulgar Latin *exvellere* < Latin *vellere* 'pull'.]

Svengali /sven gaáli/ *n* somebody who controls and manipulates somebody else, usually for evil purposes [Early 20C. After a villainous hypnotist in the novel *Trilby* (1894), by George du Maurier.]

Sverdrup Islands /sfáirdrəp-/ island group in N Nunavut, Canada, comprising Axel Heiberg, Ellef Ringnes, and Amund Ringnes

SVGA a modified specification for video display controllers used in personal computers. Full form **super video graphics array**

SW *abbr* **1** short wave **2** southwest **3** southwestern

Sw. *abbr* Sweden

swab /swob/ *n* **1 SOFT MATERIAL FOR MOPPING UP BLOOD** a small piece of gauze, cotton, or other soft material, used to mop up blood during surgery **2 SMALL STICK WITH COTTON WOOL** a small stick, wire, or plastic wand with cotton wool attached to one or both ends, often used to clean wounds, apply medicine, or obtain a specimen of something **3 SPECIMEN** a specimen of mucus or another secretion obtained by using a swab **4 PIECE OF MATERIAL FOR CLEANING GUN** a small piece of absorbent material that is used to clean the bore of a firearm **5 MOP** a mop used to clean decks or floors **6 SOMEBODY WHO MOPS** a user of a mop to clean, especially on a ship **7 WORTHLESS PERSON** an uncouth or worthless person (*archaic slang*) ■ *vt* (**swabs, swabbing, swabbed**) **1 CLEAN WITH A SWAB** to clean out or apply medicine to a wound with a soft piece of material **2 MOP** to clean something such as a floor or a deck with a mop **3 CLEAN SOMETHING UP** to clean up something such as a spill [Mid-17C. Back-formation from obsolete *swabber* 'deck mop' < assumed Dutch *zwabber* < obsolete Dutch *zwabben* 'mop'.]

swaddle /swódd'l/ (**-dles, -dling, -dled**) *vt* **1 WRAP SOMEBODY IN SOMETHING** to wrap or bandage somebody or something with something **2 WRAP BABY UP TIGHTLY** to wrap a baby tightly in soft material **3 SMOTHER** to restrain somebody or something with a complete wrapping [15C. Probably a back-formation < Middle English *swadling band* < an earlier form of SWATHE[1].]

swaddling clothes, swaddling bands *archaic npl* long strips of linen or some other soft material, used in some cultures to wrap babies in order to keep them still and calm

Swadeshi /swə dáyshi/ *adj S Asia* used in India to describe goods produced within the country of India ■ *n S Asia* the practice of favouring domestic products and refusing to buy imported goods as part of the struggle for independence in India [Early 20C. Via Hindi *svadeśī* < Sanskrit *svadeśaḥ* 'your own country'.]

swag /swag/ *n* **1 CURTAIN** an ornamental drapery or curtain that hangs in a curve between two points **2 FESTOON** an ornamental draping of fruit or flowers **3 LOOT** stolen property (*slang*) **4 PROPERTY** somebody's goods or valuables (*slang*) **5** *Aus* **PACK** a pack or rolled-up blanket containing the personal belongings of a wanderer **6 LURCHING MOVEMENT** a lurching or swaying movement ■ *vi* (**swags, swagging, swagged**) **MOVE WITH LURCH** to move with a lurching or swaying movement [Early 16C. Probably < N Germanic.]

swagbelly /swág beli/ *n* a large overhanging stomach (*informal*) —**swagbellied** *adj*

swage /swayj/ *n* **1** a tool or die used to shape cold metal by hammering or applying pressure **2** ENG = **swage block** ■ *vt* (**swages, swaging, swaged**) to bend or shape metal with a swage [14C. < Old French *souage* 'decorative moulding' < ?] —**swager** *n*

swage block *n* a metal block with holes or grooves used to work cold metal

swagger /swággər/ *vi* **1 STRUT AROUND** to walk in an arrogant or proud way **2 BRAG** to talk boastfully about personal accomplishments ■ *n* **ARROGANT WALK** an arrogant way of walking or behaving [Early 16C. Probably < SWAG.] —**swaggerer** *n* —**swaggeringly** *adv*

swagger stick *n* a short stick often carried by army officers

swagman /swág man/ (*plural* **-men** /-men/) *n Aus* a tramp or itinerant worker who carries his belongings in a pack or rolled-up blanket (*informal*)

Swahili /swə heéli, swaa-/ (*plural* **-li** *or* **-lis**) *n* **1** a member of a people who live mainly along the eastern coasts and islands of eastern and southern Africa **2** LANG = **Kiswahili** [Early 19C. Via Kiswahili < Arabic *sawāḥilīy* 'of the coasts' < *sāḥil* 'coast'.] —**Swahili** *adj*

swain /swayn/ *n* **1** a young man who lives in the country (*archaic or literary*) **2** a woman's male admirer or lover (*literary*) [Late 16C. < Old Norse *sveinn* 'boy, servant' < Germanic, 'your own'.]

swale /swayl/ *n* a depression between slopes that provides for drainage [Early 16C. < ?]

Swaledale /swáyl dayl/ (*plural* **-dales** *or* **-dale**) *n* a hardy sheep of a breed originating in N England and noted for its long fleece. It has long curled horns, a black face, and mottled or grey legs. [Early 20C. After *Swaledale*, an area in North Yorkshire.]

SWALK /swawlk, swolk/ *abbr* sealed with a loving kiss (*sometimes written on the back of an envelope containing a letter to a beloved person*)

swallow[1] /swóllō/ *v* **1** *vti* **TAKE IN FOOD** to take in food or liquid through the mouth and pass it down the throat into the stomach **2** *vi* **GULP** to perform the act of swallowing, usually as an emotional response to something ○ *swallowing hard to hold back the tears* **3** *vt* **DESTROY** to engulf or destroy something **4** *vt* **SUPPRESS FEELINGS** to refrain from expressing thoughts or feelings ○ *Swallow your pride and apologize.* **5** *vt* **BELIEVE** to accept something as true without questioning it (*informal*) ○ *They'll never swallow anything so far-fetched.* **6** *vt* **ENDURE** to put up with something unpleasant without saying or doing anything to stop it **7** *vt* **RETRACT A REMARK** to withdraw a statement or remark as false or unjustified **8** *vt* **SPEAK UNCLEARLY** to say words in such a way that you cannot be understood ■ *n* **1 ACT OF TAKING SOMETHING DOWN THROAT** the act of taking something in through the mouth and down the throat **2 AMOUNT PASSED DOWN THROAT** an amount taken into the mouth and passed down the throat [Old English *swelgan*. Ultimately < Indo-European.]

swallow[2] /swóllō/ *n* a small graceful swift-flying migratory bird with long pointed wings and a notched or forked tail. Family: Hirundinidae. [Old English *swealwe* < Germanic]

swallow dive *n* a dive performed with the back arched, the legs held together straight, and the arms outstretched. US term **swan dive**

swallow hole *n* GEOG = **sinkhole** *n.* 1 [Old English *geswelg* 'deep hole']

swallowtail /swóllō tayl/ (*plural* **-tails** *or* **-tail**) *n* **1** a colourful butterfly distinguished by the small tails that extend from the ends of its hind wings. Family: Papilionidae. **2** the tail of a swallow or similar bird —**swallow-tailed** *adj*

swallow-tailed coat *n* a man's evening tail coat with a split rounded tail

swam past tense of **swim**

swami /swáami/ *n* a title of respect for a Hindu saint or religious teacher [Late 18C. Via Hindi < Sanskrit *svāmin-* 'being your own master'.]

swamp /swomp/ *n* **WETLAND** an area of land, usually fairly large that is always wet and is overgrown with various shrubs and trees ■ *v* **1** *vt* **INUNDATE AN AREA** to submerge an area in water **2** *vti* **SINK A BOAT** to cause a boat to fill with water and sink, or become full of water and sink **3** *vt* **OVERBURDEN** to overwhelm somebody by being too much or too many to cope with (*usually passive*) [Early 17C. < ?] —**swampy** *adj*

swamp boat *n* a flat-bottomed boat used to travel in swamps and shallow water. It is powered by an aeroplane propeller.

swamp cypress *n* TREES = **bald cypress**

swamper /swómpər/ *n* *US* **1 SWAMP DWELLER OR WORKER** a dweller or worker in a swamp, especially in the S United States **2 SOMEBODY WHO CLEARS SWAMP** a worker who clears a swamp of trees and undergrowth or who clears a path through a forest so that logs can be moved **3 LORRY DRIVER'S ASSISTANT** an assistant to a lorry driver **4 HELPER IN RESTAURANT** a helper in a restaurant

swamp fever *n* **1** *US* any disease such as malaria or leptospirosis that is liable to be contracted by people in swampy areas **2** equine infectious anaemia (*dated*)

swampland /swómp land/ *n* an area of land that is always moist or that has many swamps in it

swamp pink *n* an orchid found in the NE United States. Flowers: rose-coloured, marked with purple. Genus: *Arethusa*.

swan /swon/ *n* a large graceful water bird with webbed feet and a long slender neck and usually with white plumage. Family: Anatidae. ■ *vi* (**swans, swanning, swanned**) to wander around in a relaxed way, especially one regarded as irresponsible or selfish (*informal*) [Old English, 'singer' < Indo-European, 'to make a sound']

Swan /swon/ river in SW Western Australia. Length: 386 km/240 mi.

swan dive *n* *US* SWIMMING = **swallow dive**

swank /swangk/ *n* an arrogant or conceited person (*informal*) ■ *vi* to behave or swagger in a pretentious way (*informal*) [Early 19C. Originally dialect.]

swanky /swángki/ *adj* (*informal*) **1** very stylish and expensive **2** conceited and boastful —**swankily** *adv* —**swankiness** *n*

swannery /swónnəri/ (*plural* **-ies**) *n* a place where swans are bred and reared

swansdown /swónz down/, **swan's-down** *n* **1** the soft down feathers of a swan **2** a soft woollen fabric. Use: baby clothes. **3** TEXTILES = **flannelette**

Swansea /swónzi/ port in S Wales. Population: 230,000 (1996 estimate).

swanskin /swón skin/ *n* any cotton or woollen fabric that is very soft to the touch

swansong /swón song/ *n* **1** a final appearance, performance, or work, as a farewell to a career or profession **2** a song of legendary beauty said to be sung only once by a swan during its lifetime, when it is dying

swap /swop/, **swop** *vti* (**swaps, swapping, swapped; swops, swopping, swopped**) **EXCHANGE** to trade or exchange one thing or person for another (*informal*) ○ *Let's swap over and you can have my seat.* ■ *n* **1 AN EXCHANGE** the exchanging of one thing or person for another (*informal*) **2 SOMETHING EXCHANGED** somebody or something that is traded or exchanged (*informal*) **3 CONTRACT** a contract in which the parties exchange liabilities on outstanding debts, either as a means of managing debt or in the business of trading [14C. Probably from an earlier meaning 'strike' (ultimately an imitation of the sound), from the practice of striking hands together to seal an agreement.] —**swappable** *adj*

swap contract *n* a contract that involves a reciprocal exchange of some kind, e.g. one in which the contracting parties agree to exchange cash flows

swap meet *n* **1** a flea market where new, used, and sometimes rare or speciality items are sold **2** *US* a gathering that people, especially hobbyists, attend for the purpose of exchanging things

swaption /swópsh'n/ *n* an option giving the holder the right to enter into a swap [Late 20C. Contraction of *swap option*.]

swaraj /swə ráaj/ *n* *S Asia* self-government as a political objective in the former British India [Early 20C. Via Hindi *svarāj* < Sanskrit *svarājyam* 'own rule'.] —**swarajism** *n* —**swarajist** *n*

sward /swawrd/ *n* an area of turf or grass ■ *vti* to cover or become covered with turf or grass [Old English *sweard* 'hairy skin, rind' < Germanic]

swarf /swawrf/ *n* **1** debris, especially from disintegrating satellites, orbiting the Earth (*informal*) **2** the fine metallic shavings removed by grinding or cutting tools [Mid-16C. < ?]

swarm[1] /swawrm/ *n* **1 GROUP OF INSECTS** a large group of insects, especially bees or gnats, in flight **2 LARGE MASS** a large crowd or group of people or animals moving in a confused or disorderly way ■ *v* **1** *vi* **FORM A FLYING GROUP** to form a flying group, especially to found a new colony ○ *Do bees swarm often?* **2** *vi* **MOVE IN A MASS** to move or gather in a large crowd ○ *people swarmed all over the road* **3** *vi* **BE OVERRUN** to be overrun with a large mass or group ○ *swarming with people* **4** *vt* **CAUSE SOMETHING TO SWARM** to cause something to swarm, or produce a swarm [Old English *swearm*. Ultimately from Germanic that was an imitation of the sound of buzzing.]

swarm[2] /swawrm/ *vi* to climb up somewhere using the arms and legs [Mid-16C. < ?]

swarm cell, swarm spore *n* BIOL = **zoospore**

swart /swawrt/ *adj* swarthy (*archaic or literary*) [Old English *sweart* < Indo-European, 'dirty, black']

swarthy /swáwrthi/ (**-ier, -iest**) *adj* with a dark and often weather-beaten complexion [Late 16C. Alteration of obsolete *swarty* < SWART.] —**swarthily** *adv* —**swarthiness** *n*

swash /swosh/ *n* **1 CHANNEL** a narrow channel through which tides flow **2 SANDBAR** a sandbar that is washed over by waves **3 SPLASH** the motion or sound of the motion of water splashing or washing over something **4** = **swashbuckler** *n.* 1 ■ *v* **1** *vi* **WASH OVER** to strike or move with a splashing sound **2** *vt* **SPLASH** to throw a liquid at or on something, especially with a splashing sound **3** *vi* **STRUT** to move in a swaggering, pretentious way (*dated*) [Early 16C. Probably an imitation of the sound of splashing liquid or of a blow.]

swashbuckler /swósh buklər/ *n* **1** a bold and swaggering swordsman or adventurer **2** a play, novel, or film about an adventurer [Mid-16C. < SWASH + BUCKLER, from the sound of swords striking shields.] —**swashbuckling** *adj*

swash letter /swósh-/ *n* an ornate italic letter with elaborate flourishes and tails [< ?]

swastika /swósstikə/ *n* **1** a Nazi and fascist symbol formed by a Greek cross with the four ends of the arms bent in a clockwise direction **2** an ancient religious symbol formed by a Greek cross, usually with the four ends of the arms bent at right angles in a clockwise or anticlockwise direction [Late 19C. < Sanskrit *svastikaḥ* 'good-luck sign' < *svasti* 'good luck', literally 'well-being'.]

swat /swot/, **swot** *vti* (**swats, swatting, swatted; swots, swotting, swotted**) to strike or slap somebody or something sharply ■ *n* **1** a sharp blow or slap **2** = **swatter** [Early 17C. Alteration of SQUAT, in the obsolete meaning 'crush, flatten'.]

SWAT /swot/ *n* *US* a police unit that is trained in the use of military weapons and tactics. Full form **Special Weapons and Tactics**

swatch /swoch/ *n* a piece cut from a material, e.g. fabric or carpeting, used as a sample [Early 16C. Originally a northern English dialect word meaning 'counterfoil', later 'tally attached to cloth sent for dyeing' < ?]

swath /swoth/, **swathe** /swayth/ *n* **1 WIDTH CUT** the width cut by a single passage of a scythe or mowing machine **2 PATH CUT** the path through a crop made during a single passage of a scythe or mowing machine **3 AMOUNT CUT** the amount of grass or corn left in the path made by a single passage of a scythe or mowing machine [Old English *swæþ* 'track' < Germanic] ◇ **cut a swath through something** to destroy or use up a large part of something

swathe[1] /swayth/ *vt* **1 WRAP COMPLETELY** to wrap or cover somebody or something completely with bandages or as if with bandages **2 ENFOLD** to envelop somebody or something ■ *n* **WRAPPING** a bandage, wrapping, or other binding [Old English *swaþian* 'wrap up': < ?]

swathe[2] *n* = **swath**

Swati /swáati/ *n* LANG = **Swazi** *n.* 2

swatter /swóttər/, **swotter** *n* a flat meshed flexible piece of metal or plastic attached to a long handle, used to kill insects, especially flies

sway /sway/ *v* **1** *vti* **SWING** to swing or cause something to swing back and forth **2** *vi* **LEAN OVER** to lean or bend to one side or in different directions in turn **3** *vti* **WAVER BETWEEN OPINIONS** to go back and forth or cause somebody to go back and forth between two or more opinions **4** *vt* **INFLUENCE** to persuade or influence somebody to believe or do something (*usually passive*) ○ *Don't let yourself be swayed.* **5** *vi* **MOVE GRACEFULLY** to move back and forth in a graceful way **6** *vi* **STAGGER** to move from side to side in a clumsy and unsteady way **7** *vt* **HOIST** to hoist a yard, mast, or other spar (*technical*) ■ *n* **1 SWINGING MOTION** the act of swinging back and forth **2 CONTROL OVER** rule or control over a person, group, or area [13C. Probably < N Germanic.] —**swayable** *adj* —**swayer** *n* ◇ **hold sway** to have control or influence over a person or place

sway-back *n* an extreme inward or downward curving of the spine in horses and human beings

sway bar *n* *US* AUTOMOT = **anti-roll bar**

Swazi /swáazi/ (*plural* **-zi** *or* **-zis**) *n* **1** a member of an African people who live in Swaziland and parts of Transvaal in South Africa **2** an official language of Swaziland, belonging to the Benue-Congo family of languages. Native speakers: 2 million. [Late 19C. Alteration of Nguni *Mswati*, former Swazi king.] —**Swazi** *adj*

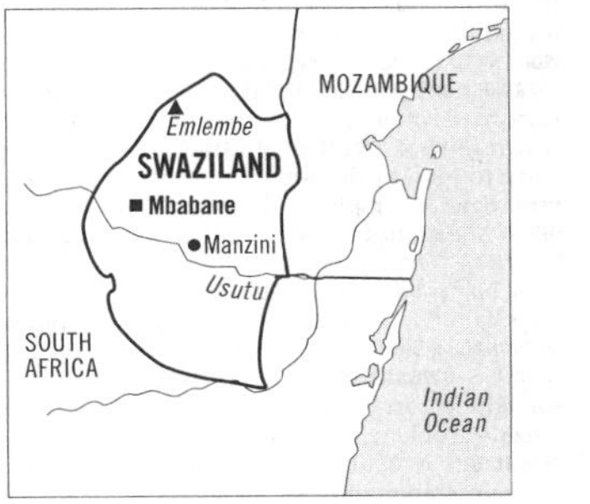

Swaziland

Swaziland /swázi land/ landlocked monarchy in southern Africa. Capital: Mbabane. Population: 934,000 (1996). Area: 17,363 sq. km/6704 sq. mi.

swear /swair/ *v* (**swears, swearing, swore** /swawr/, **sworn** /swawrn/) **1** *vti* **AFFIRM TRUTH OF SOMETHING** to declare solemnly or forcefully that what is said is true, sometimes calling somebody or something thought to be sacred as a witness ○ *She swore on her mother's grave that she had done as she had been asked.* **2** *vti* **SOLEMNLY PROMISE** to promise something very solemnly ○ *He swore that he would serve humanity.* **3** *vi* **SAY SOMETHING OFFENSIVE** to use blasphemous or obscene language, usually as an expression of strong feelings or with the intention of giving offence **4** *vti* **TAKE AN OATH** to make a formal promise in a court of law or when taking up an official position **5** *vti* **DECLARE SOMETHING ON OATH** to make a solemn statement under oath, especially in a court of law, or cause somebody to make such a statement **6** *vt* **MAKE SOMEBODY PROMISE SOLEMNLY** to cause somebody to take an oath or make a promise ■ *n* **BURST OF OFFENSIVE LANGUAGE** a short spell of using blasphemous or obscene language [Old English *swerian.* Ultimately < Indo-European.] —**swearer** *n* ◇ **swear blind** to assert something vehemently ○ *He swore blind he knew nothing about it.*

swear by *vt* **1** to have great faith or complete confidence in the effectiveness of something or the ability of somebody for a particular purpose or task **2** to use the name of a person or thing thought to be sacred to reinforce a solemn declaration or promise

swear in *vt* to cause somebody to make a formal promise in a court of law or when taking up an official position

swear off *vt* to make a solemn promise to give something up, especially a bad habit

swearword /swáir wurd/ *n* a word or phrase that is considered unacceptable in polite language, especially one that is blasphemous or obscene, used to express strong feelings or give offence

sweat /swet/ *n* **1** **MOISTURE ON SKIN** the clear salty liquid that passes to the surface of the skin when somebody is hot or as a result of strenuous activity, fear, anxiety, or illness **2** **STATE OF HAVING SWEAT ON SKIN** the production or secretion of sweat, e.g. during strenuous activity or illness, or a state of fear or anxiety that causes this **3** **MOISTURE CONDENSED ON SURFACE** drops of liquid that appear on the surface of something, usually by condensation of water vapour from the surrounding warmer air **4** **LIQUID EXUDED TO THE SURFACE** drops of liquid that ooze through and collect on the surface of something, e.g. sap on a tree **5** **HARD OR BORING WORK** hard, unpleasant, or tedious work **6** **RUN BEFORE RACE** a run that a horse has before a race, as exercise **7** **EXPERIENCED PERSON** an experienced person, especially a soldier (*dated informal*) ■ **sweats** *npl US* **TWO-PIECE SPORTS OUTFIT** a sweatshirt and sweatpants made of matching fabric and worn together for sport or casual activities ■ *v* **1** *vt* **MAKE SOMEBODY SWEAT** to make somebody sweat, e.g. as a medical treatment, **2** *vt* **WET OR MARK WITH SWEAT** to make something damp or stained with sweat **3** *vti* **FORM OR APPEAR AS MOISTURE** to produce or form as moisture on the surface of something, usually by condensation of water vapour from the surrounding warmer air **4** *vti* **EXUDE LIQUID AT THE SURFACE** to produce or form as liquid beads by oozing through the surface of something and collecting there **5** *vti* **REMOVE MOISTURE** to remove moisture, e.g. when fermenting fruits or tobacco or when curing animal hides **6** *vti* **COOK SOMETHING IN OWN JUICES** to cook something in a covered pan in its own juices until tender **7** *vt* **HEAT SOLDER UNTIL IT MELTS** to heat solder until it melts and runs between surfaces to bond them **8** *vi* **WORK HARD** to work very hard or overwork (*informal*) **9** *vt* **OVERWORK OR UNDERPAY EMPLOYEES** to make somebody work very hard, often in poor conditions or for low wages (*informal*) **10** *vt US* **EXTORT INFORMATION FROM** to force somebody to give up information, especially by relentless interrogation or physical violence (*informal*) **11** *vi* **BE UNDER STRESS** to be very anxious, impatient, or afraid (*informal*) ○ *He left them sweating in the corridor while he made up his mind.* **12** *vi* **SUFFER FOR WRONGDOING** to suffer physically or mentally, especially as a punishment (*informal*) [Old English *swāt.* Ultimately < Indo-European.] —**sweatless** *adj* ◇ **no sweat** used to say that something can be done with ease and without foreseeable problems (*informal*)

sweat out *vt* **1** to relieve the symptoms of an illness by maintaining a raised body temperature, and hence cause profuse sweating **2** to carry on doing something difficult or put up with something unpleasant until it is over (*informal*)

sweatband /swét band/ *n* **1** a strip of terry cotton worn around the head or wrists to stop sweat running into the eyes or onto the hands while playing sport **2** a strip of fabric or leather sewn inside a hat to protect it from damage by sweat

sweatbox /swét boks/ *n* **1** **DEVICE FOR REMOVING WATER FROM HIDES** a device in which hides or some fruits are placed to remove water **2** **CONFINED PLACE** a very small room, especially a narrow cell where a prisoner is confined for punishment (*informal*) **3** **PLACE WHERE SOMEBODY SWEATS** a place where somebody is made to sweat through heat or fear (*informal*)

sweated /swéttid/ *adj* **1** made to work very hard in poor conditions for low wages **2** performed or produced by employees who are made to work very hard in poor conditions for low wages

sweater /swéttər/ *n* **1** CLOTHING = **jumper**[2] *n.* 1 **2** a person who visibly sweats, or who sweats in a specific way **3** an employer who makes people work very hard in poor conditions for low wages

sweat gland *n* any small tube-shaped gland in the skin of most parts of the body from which sweat is released

sweat lodge *n* a hut, cavern, or building heated by steam from water poured over hot rocks and used, especially by Native Americans, for therapeutic or ritual sweating

sweatpants /swét pants/ *npl US* long trousers made of a soft knitted fabric, often with elastic at the waist and ankles, worn casually or for exercising

sweatshirt /swét shurt/ *n* a long-sleeved pullover or zipped jacket made of soft knitted fabric, worn casually or for sport

sweatshop /swét shop/ *n* a small factory or other establishment where employees are made to work very hard in poor conditions for low wages

sweaty /swétti/ (**-ier, -iest**) *adj* **1** **DAMP WITH SWEAT** damp with or smelling of sweat **2** **CAUSING SWEAT** making somebody sweat **3** **WITH MOISTURE ON SURFACE** with drops of exuded or condensed liquid on the surface —**sweatily** *adv* —**sweatiness** *n*

swede /sweed/ *n* **1** a large round root with yellowish flesh that is cooked and eaten as a vegetable. US term **rutabaga** *n.* 2 **2** a plant that produces swedes. *Brassica napus napobrassica.* US term **rutabaga** *n.* 1 [Early 19C. < SWEDE, from its introduction (into Scotland) from Sweden.]

Swede /sweed/ *n* a person who comes from Sweden [Early 17C. < Middle Low German or Middle Dutch *Swēde*, probably < Old Norse *Svíar* (plural) 'Swedes' + *þjóð* 'people'.]

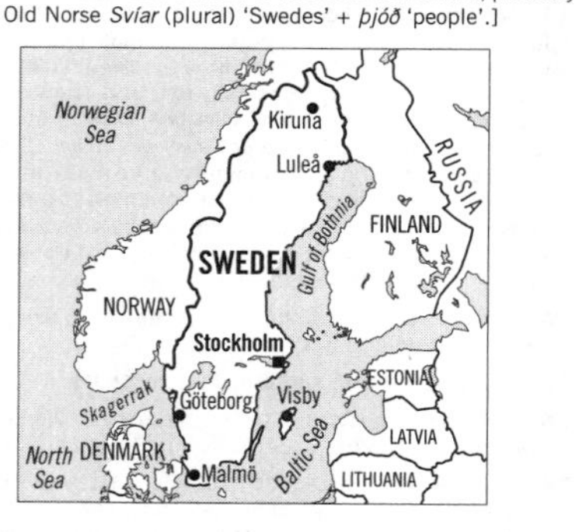

Sweden

Sweden /swéed'n/ monarchy in NW Europe. Capital: Stockholm. Population: 8,858,000 (1996). Area: 449,964 sq. km/173,732 sq. mi.

Swedenborg /swéed'n bawrg/, **Emanuel** (1688–1772) Swedish scientist and theologian. Born **Emanuel Swedberg** —**Swedenborgian** /swéed'n báwrji ən, -gi ən/ *n, adj*

Swedish /swéedish/ *n* **OFFICIAL LANGUAGE OF SWEDEN** the official language of Sweden and an official language of Finland, belonging to the North Germanic branch of the Indo-European family of languages. Native speakers: 8.5 million. ■ *adj* **1** **OF SWEDEN** relating to Sweden, or its people or culture **2** **OF SWEDISH** relating to the Swedish language [Early 17C. < either SWEDEN or SWEDE.]

Swedish massage *n* a system of massage employing both active and passive exercising of the muscles and joints [*Swedish* from the system of massage having originated in Sweden]

Swedish mile *n* a unit of measure used in Sweden equal to 10 km/6.2 mi

sweeny /swéeni/, **sweeney** *n* atrophy of the shoulder muscles of horses due to harness pressure on nerves going to these muscles [Early 19C. < ?]

sweep /sweep/ *v* (**sweeps, sweeping, swept** /swept/, **swept**) **1** *vti* **CLEAN A PLACE WITH A BROOM** to remove something such as dust, dirt, debris, or snow from the floor or ground with a broom, brush, or similar implement **2** *vt* **CLEAR A CHIMNEY** to remove soot from the inside of a chimney with a long-handled brush **3** *vt* **MOVE SOMETHING WITH A HORIZONTAL STROKE** to move something with a long smooth stroke or a quick brushing stroke ○ *I swept the papers off the desk.* **4** *vti* **BRUSH AGAINST THE GROUND** to brush against a horizontal surface such as the floor or the ground **5** *vi* **MOVE WITH SPEED AND FORCE** to move quickly, smoothly, and forcefully, often in a large body or group ○ *the crowd swept across the bridge* **6** *vi* **MOVE WITH DIGNITY** to move quickly and smoothly with a proud, majestic, or self-important air ○ *swept angrily out of the room* **7** *vti* **MOVE ACROSS A PLACE** to move quickly and forcefully across an area ○ *the gales that are sweeping the country* **8** *vti* **SPREAD THROUGH A PLACE** to pass or spread quickly through a place ○ *the news swept through the city* **9** *vt* **CARRY SOMEBODY OR SOMETHING ALONG** to carry somebody or something quickly and forcefully in the same direction ○ *swept along by the current* **10** *vt* **STRONGLY INFLUENCE** to strongly influence or overwhelm somebody (*often passive*) ○ *We were swept along by their enthusiasm.* **11** *vti* **WIN SOMETHING OVERWHELMINGLY** to win something easily and overwhelmingly, or win all the games in a series or set of games for a championship ○ *watched them sweep to victory* **12** *vi* **STRETCH OUT IN AN ARC** to extend in a long smooth graceful curve or a wide circle ○ *plains sweeping down to the coast* **13** *vti* **EXTEND OVER A WIDE AREA** to be directed over a wide range or the entire area of something ○ *Her eyes swept around the room.* **14** *vti* **SEARCH A PLACE FOR** to search a place for something, e.g. an area of water for mines or a room for hidden recording devices **15** *vti* **HIT BALL WITH HORIZONTAL BAT** in cricket, to hit a ball from a half-kneeling position by bringing the bat, held almost horizontally, across the body with a long smooth stroke ■ *n* **1** **BOUT OF CLEANING WITH A BRUSH** a cleaning of something with a brush, broom, or similar implement **2** **BRUSHING STROKE** a quick brushing stroke **3** **LONG SMOOTH MOVEMENT** a long smooth curved movement ○ *with a sweep of her arm* **4** **LONG SMOOTH CURVE** a long smooth graceful curve ○ *the sweep of the coastline* **5** **WIDE EXPANSE** a wide expanse or extent ○ *the sweep of the horizon* **6** **CURVED RANGE** the range over which something is directed, usually a wide arc or circle ○ *stay out of the sweep of the searchlights* **7** **BROAD RANGE** the broad range or comprehensive nature of something ○ *the sweep of history* **8** **SEARCH** a thorough search ○ *a sweep of the neighbourhood* **9** **OVERWHELMING VICTORY** an overwhelming or absolute victory ○ *their sweep to power* **10** **SWEEPSTAKE** a sweepstake (*informal*) **11** OCCUPATIONS = **chimney sweep** **12** **SHOT WITH BAT HORIZONTAL** in cricket, a shot in which the ball is hit from a half-kneeling position, bringing the bat, held almost horizontal, across the body with a long smooth stroke **13** **OAR FOR PROPELLING A BOAT** a long oar that is used to propel small boats or sometimes act as a rudder **14** **ELECTRON BEAM MOTION IN CATHODE-RAY TUBE** the steady movement of the electron beam across the fluorescent surface of a cathode-ray tube **15** **WINDMILL SAIL** a sail of a windmill **16** **POLE FOR LIFTING A BUCKET IN A WELL** a long pole used as a lever to raise or lower a bucket in a well ■ **sweeps** *npl US* **TELEVISION RATINGS IN A PARTICULAR PERIOD** a periodic survey of television ratings that is used to determine advertising rates, or the period when these ratings are done [13C. Probably < the past tense of Old English *swāpan* 'sweep' < Germanic, 'to swing'.] —**sweepy** *adj* ◇ **make a clean sweep (of something)** **1** to have a complete change by getting rid of everything or everyone unwanted or unnecessary **2** to win everything

sweep away, sweep aside *vt* to remove, dismiss, or destroy something quickly, forcefully, and completely

sweep up *vti* to remove dust, dirt, or debris from the floor or ground with a brush or similar implement

sweepback /swéep bak/ *n* an aircraft wing that slants backwards towards the tail assembly, forming an acute angle with the fuselage

sweeper /swéepər/ *n* **1** **SOMEBODY WHO SWEEPS** somebody whose job involves sweeping something, usually floors or roads **2** **SOMETHING THAT SWEEPS** a device or machine, usually fitted with brushes, that sweeps something such as a floor or a road **3** **ROVING DEFENSIVE PLAYER** in soccer, a defensive player who is not assigned to cover an attacking player but plays across the pitch in the space between other defenders and the goalkeeper

sweep hand *n* a long hand, mounted concentrically with the minute hand of an analogue watch or clock, that indicates seconds as it sweeps around the same dial as the minute hand

sweeping /swēeping/ *adj* **1 ON A LARGE SCALE** wide-ranging and comprehensive, usually affecting a large number of things or people ○ *sweeping reforms* **2 TOO GENERAL** failing to take specific exceptions or details into consideration ○ *a sweeping condemnation of modern youth* **3 OVERWHELMING** complete, overwhelming, or decisive ○ *a sweeping victory* **4 WITH BROAD EXTENT** covering a large area, usually a wide arc or circle ○ *included in her sweeping glance* ■ *n* **ACT OF USING A BROOM** the action of somebody who sweeps with a broom or brush —**sweepingly** *adv* —**sweepingness** *n*

sweepings /swēepingz/ *npl* dirt and refuse swept up

sweep-saw *n* a thin-bladed saw that is held taut in a frame and used for cutting curves

sweep-second hand *n* TIME = **sweep hand**

sweepstake *n* a lottery in which the payout is determined by the amount paid in and the winner determined by the outcome of a horserace, or the prize itself [< the obsolete meaning 'person who takes (sweeps) all the stakes in a game']

sweet /sweet/ *adj* **1 TASTING OR SMELLING OF SUGAR** tasting or smelling of sugar or a similar substance **2 CONTAINING OR RETAINING SUGAR** containing a relatively large amount of sugar, or retaining some natural sugars ○ *sweet cider* **3 NOT SALT, BITTER, OR SOUR** associated with the basic taste sensation that is not bitter, salt, or sour **4 FRESH** not stale, rancid, or soured ○ *sweet water* **5 NOT SALTY** not salty or saline ○ *sweet butter* **6 PLEASING TO THE SENSES** pleasing to any of the senses ○ *the sweet strains of the violin* **7 SATISFYING** desirable, gratifying, or satisfying ○ *Revenge turned out not to be sweet after all.* **8 KIND** kind, thoughtful, or generous ○ *He's so sweet, he never forgets my birthday.* **9 VERY PLEASING TO LOOK AT** having an appearance that is charming or endearing ○ *a sweet little cottage by the lake* **10 NOT ACIDIC** describes land that contains no acid or corrosive substances **11 CONTAINING LITTLE OR NO SULPHUR** describes petrol or oil that contains little or no sulphur **12** *Aus* **OK** satisfactory (*informal*) **13 RESPECTED** dear, respected, or beloved (*archaic*) ○ *Indeed, my sweet lord.* ■ *adv* **PLEASANTLY** in a pleasant manner ○ *sing sweet* ■ *n* **1 SHAPED ITEM OF CONFECTIONERY** a small hard, chewy, or soft piece of food made from sugar and other ingredients or flavourings such as chocolate, nuts, fruit, or peppermint. US term **candy** *n.* 2 **2 DESSERT** a course or dish of sweet food served at or near the end of a meal ○ *Would you like a sweet?* **3 SWEET FOOD** any item of sweet food **4** *US* **SWEET POTATO** a sweet potato (*informal*) **5 SENSATION OF SWEETNESS** a sweet taste or smell **6 SOMETHING PLEASANT** a pleasant thing or experience (*literary*) ○ *squander the sweets of life* **7 DEAR** used as a term of endearment ○ *Come to me, my sweet.* **8 SULPHUR-FREE NATURAL GAS OR OIL** a natural gas or crude oil that is essentially free from acidic or odorous sulphur compounds [Old English *swēte*. Ultimately < Indo-European.] —**sweetly** *adv* —**sweetness** *n* ◇ **be sweet on somebody** to be in love with somebody (*dated*) ◇ **keep somebody sweet** to treat somebody with particular kindness or indulgence as a tactic to win favour or secure help or support (*informal*)

SPELLCHECK See ***suite***.

---

sweet alyssum *n* a widely-cultivated perennial plant. Native to: Europe. Flowers: low-growing, fragrant white, pink, or purple, in clusters. *Lobularia maritima.*

sweet-and-sour *adj* cooked in or served with a sauce that has sugar and vinegar among the ingredients

sweet basil *n* a herb with aromatic leaves used for seasoning. *Ocimum basilicum.*

sweet bay *n* **1** TREES = **bay**³ *n.* 1 **2** a magnolia bush or tree with yellow-green leaves and red fruit. Flowers: fragrant, white. Native to: E United States. *Magnolia virginia.*

sweet birch *n* **1** the hard dark wood from the sweet birch tree **2** a birch with smooth blackish-brown bark and aromatic stems that yield methyl salicylate. Native to: E United States. *Betula lenta.*

sweetbread /swēet bred/ *n* the pancreas or thymus of a calf, lamb, or other young animal soaked, fried, and eaten as food [The element *-bread* probably < Old English *brǣd* 'flesh']

sweetbriar /swēet brīr/ (*plural* **-ars** *or* **-ar**), **sweetbrier** (*plural* **-ers** *or* **-er**) *n* a rose that has a long stem with stout prickles and fragrant leaves. Flowers: rosy pink or white, single. Native to: Europe, Asia. *Rosa rubiginosa.*

sweet cherry *n* **1** the sweet firm-fleshed fruit of a sweet cherry tree **2** a cultivated variety of cherry tree, e.g. a bigarreau

sweet chestnut *n* TREES = **chestnut** *n.* 1, **chestnut** *n.* 2

sweet cicely /-síssəli/ (*plural* **sweet cicely**) *n* **1** a plant with aromatic fleshy roots. Flowers: small, white, in clusters. Native to: America, Asia. Genus: *Osmorhiza.* **2** a perennial plant with aromatic compound leaves. Flowers: small, white, in umbels. Native to: Europe. *Myrrhis odorata.*

sweet clover *n* PLANTS = **melilot**

sweetcorn /swēet kawrn/ *n* **1** a variety of maize with kernels that contain a high concentration of sugar and are yellowish in colour. *Zea mays rugosa.* **2** the sweet yellowish kernels of some varieties of maize plant, cooked and eaten as a vegetable

sweeten /swēet'n/ *v* **1** *vti* **INCREASE IN SWEETNESS** to make something taste sweet or sweeter by adding sugar or some other natural or artificial substance, or to become sweet or sweeter in flavour **2** *vt* **IMPROVE THE TASTE OR SMELL OF** to make something taste or smell more pleasant **3** *vt* **MAKE SOMETHING MORE DESIRABLE** to make something more attractive, agreeable, or acceptable ○ *sweeten the offer* **4** *vt* **SOFTEN OR PERSUADE** to make somebody kinder, gentler, friendlier, or calmer, or persuade somebody by flattery, cajolery, or bribery to accept or agree to something ○ *might sweeten his temper* **5** *vti* **IMPROVE THE PROPERTIES OF** to improve a product such as petroleum by making it less corrosive and foul-smelling, or by making its colour more acceptable **6** *vt US* **INCREASE THE VALUE OF COLLATERAL** to add securities to collateral so that its value is increased **7** *vt* **INCREASE VALUE OF A POT** in poker, to add stakes to a pot remaining from a previous deal (*informal*)

sweetener /swēet'nər/ *n* **1** a natural or artificial substance that is added to food or drink to make it sweet or sweeter, especially a synthetic substance used in place of sugar **2** something given as a bribe, incentive, or means of persuading somebody to accept or agree to something (*informal*)

sweetening /swēet'ning/ *n* **1** a substance that makes food or drink sweet or sweeter, especially an artificial additive **2** the act of making something sweet or sweeter

sweet FA /-ef áy/, **sweet Fanny Adams** /-fanni áddəmz/ *n* nothing at all (*slang*)

sweet fern *n* a bush with aromatic leaves similar to those of a fern. Flowers: small, brownish, in heads. Native to: E North America. *Comptonia peregrina.*

sweet flag *n* a perennial marsh plant with narrow sword-shaped leaves and an aromatic rootstock. Flowers: tiny, greenish. *Acorus calamus.*

sweet gale *n* a bush of the bayberry family that grows in marshy regions and has aromatic lance-shaped leaves. Native to: Europe, Asia, North America. *Myrica gale.*

sweet gum *n* **1** the amber aromatic resin of the sweet gum tree **2** a tree of the witch hazel family with lobed leaves, hard wood, and round prickly fruit clusters. Native to: North America. *Liquidambar styraciflua.*

sweetheart /swēet haart/ *n* **1 BOYFRIEND OR GIRLFRIEND** a boyfriend, girlfriend, or lover (*dated*) **2 AFFECTIONATE TERM OF ADDRESS** used as a term of endearment, usually addressed to a lover or child **3 KIND PERSON** a kind or obliging person ○ *Be a sweetheart and make me a cup of coffee, will you?* **4 SOMETHING CHERISHED** something cherished for its fine qualities and often considered one of a kind

sweetheart agreement *n* **1** an arrangement arrived at secretly to benefit some at the expense of the rest, especially an industrial agreement between union and management representatives that is not in the workers' best interest **2** *Aus* in industrial relations, an agreement reached through direct discussions between workers and their employer without recourse to arbitration [*Sweetheart* from the privileged treatment of one party]

sweetheart neckline *n* on women's clothing, a low-cut neckline with two curves over the bust, making the bodice look heart-shaped

sweetie /swēeti/ *n* **1 PIECE OF CONFECTIONERY** a boiled sweet, toffee, or other piece of confectionery (*informal; except in Scotland, usually used by or to children*) **2 TERM OF ENDEARMENT** used as a term of endearment (*informal*) **3 ENDEARING PERSON OR ANIMAL** a likeable or lovable person or animal (*informal*) **4 SWEET GRAPEFRUIT** a seedless variety of grapefruit with a greenish rind and sweet juicy flesh

sweetie pie *n* a lovable or likeable person (*informal*)

sweeting /swēeting/ *n* loved or cherished person (*archaic*)

sweet marjoram *n* a herb with aromatic leaves used as a seasoning in cookery and salads. Flowers: small, purple. Native to: Mediterranean. *Origanum majorana.*

sweetmeal /swēet meel/ *adj* made with wholemeal flour that has been sweetened, usually by adding sugar

sweetmeat /swēet meet/ *n* a superior type of sweet or confectionery served at the end of a meal or with tea (*archaic*)

sweetness and light *n* pleasantness and friendliness or peace and harmony, especially in contrast to normal behaviour or circumstances ○ *He has a vile temper, but when he gets his way, he's all sweetness and light.*

sweet nothings *npl* romantic words and phrases

sweet oil *n* any mild-flavoured oil, e.g. sweet almond oil or grapeseed oil

sweet pea *n* a widely cultivated climbing plant of the legume family. Flowers: sweet-scented, butterfly-shaped. Native to: Italy. *Lathyrus odoratus.*

sweet pepper *n* **1** a bell-shaped red, green, or orange fruit eaten raw or cooked as a vegetable **2** a plant that produces sweet peppers. *Capsicum frutescens grossum.*

sweet potato *n* **1** the fleshy orange root of the sweet potato plant cooked and eaten as a vegetable **2** a vine that produces sweet potatoes. Flowers: funnel-shaped, purplish. Native to: tropical America. *Ipomoea batatas.*

sweetshop /swēet shop/ *n* a shop that sells sweets and sometimes other items, e.g. cigarettes or newspapers. US term **candy store**

sweet-smelling *adj* having a pleasant smell

sweetsop /swēet sop/ (*plural* **-sops** *or* **-sop**) *n* **1** the fruit of the sweetsop plant with a hard green rind and a sweet edible pulp **2** an evergreen shrub that produces sweetsops. Native to: tropical America. *Annona squamosa.* [< the sweet pulp of its fruit]

sweet sorghum *n* PLANTS = **sorgo**

sweet spot *n* the most effective place to hit the ball on a racket, bat, club, or other piece of sports equipment [*Sweet* in the sense of 'desirable']

sweet sultan (*plural* **sweet sultans** *or* **sweet sultan**) *n* a shrub with large variously coloured flowers. Native to: E Mediterranean region. *Centaurea moschata.* [Ultimately < *sultan's flower*]

sweet talk *n* flattering or pleasing words used to persuade somebody (*informal*)

sweet-talk *vti* to use flattering or pleasing words to persuade somebody to do something (*informal*)

sweet tooth *n* a particular fondness for sweet food

sweet william /-wíllyəm/ (*plural* **sweet williams** *or* **sweet william**) *n* a plant widely grown for its flat clusters of white, pink, red, or purple flowers with banded or mottled patterns. Native to: Europe, Asia. *Dianthus barbatus.*

swell /swel/ *v* (**swells, swelling, swelled, swollen** /swṓlən/ *or* **swelled**) **1** *vti* **INCREASE IN SIZE** to make something larger, fuller, or rounder, or to expand in size or shape, usually as a result of pressure from within ○ *the wind swelled the sails* **2** *vi* **BECOME LARGER THAN NORMAL** to increase in size temporarily, typically as a result of injury, infection, or other medical condition ○ *my ankles had swelled in the heat* **3** *vti* **INCREASE IN QUANTITY** to increase something in number or amount, usually by adding to it, or to increase in this way ○ *new members to swell the ranks of the Party* **4** *vti* **INCREASE IN DEGREE** to make something stronger or more intense, or become stronger or more intense ○ *could feel indignation swelling inside her* **5** *vti* **INCREASE AND DECREASE IN LOUDNESS** in music, to alternate in growing gradually louder and softer, or alternately increase and decrease in volume **6** *vti* **FILL WITH EMOTION** to be filled, or cause somebody's heart or soul to be filled, with a strong feeling or emotion ○ *His heart swelled with pride.* **7** *vi* **UNDULATE ON A SURFACE** to rise and fall in long large waves ■ *n* **1 UNDULATION OF THE SEA SURFACE** the rising and falling movement of a large area of the sea as a long wave travels through it without breaking ○ *There's quite a swell out there today.* **2 ROUND SHAPE** the full, round shape of something **3 BULGE** a bulge or protuberance **4 INCREASING OF SIZE** an increase in size, fullness, or roundness **5 INCREASING OF NUMBER** an increase in number, amount, or degree **6 CRESCENDO THEN DIMINUENDO** a gradual increase in the loudness of music followed by a gradual decrease, or the sign indicating this **7** MUSIC = **swell box** **8 GENTLE SLOPE** a low hill or gentle slope **9 FASHIONABLE PERSON** a fashionably and expensively dressed person (*dated informal*) **10 SOMEBODY OF HIGH STATUS** a very important person, especially in society or politics (*dated informal*) ■ *adj US* **GOOD** very good (*dated informal*) [Old English *swellan* < Germanic]

swell box *n* a device on an organ, usually an enclosed box with pipes, that permits crescendo and diminuendo, a characteristic otherwise lacking on this instrument

swelled head *n US* = **swollen head**

swellhead /swél hed/ *n US* a conceited and arrogant person (*informal*) —**swellheaded** /-héddid/ *adj* —**swellheadedness** *n*

swelling /swélling/ *n* **1** an increase in size of part of the body, typically as a result of injury, infection, or other medical condition ○ *The swelling should go down in a couple of days.* **2** a bulge or protuberance caused by swelling

swelter /swéltər/ *vi* to feel uncomfortably hot ○ *We had been sweltering in a hot car all afternoon.* ■ *n* excessive or oppressive heat, or the uncomfortable feeling it produces [15C. 'Faint repeatedly' < *swelten* 'faint' < Old English *sweltan* 'die' < Germanic, 'to burn'.]

sweltering /swéltəring/ *adj* **1** oppressively hot **2** feeling uncomfortably hot —**swelteringly** *adv*

swept past tense, past participle of **sweep**

sweptback /swépt bák/ *adj* describes a wing that is angled backwards towards the aircraft's tail

sweptwing /swépt wing/ *adj* describes an aircraft or missile that has sweptback wings

swerve /swurv/ *vti* to make a sudden change in direction, often to avoid a collision, or make something change direction suddenly ○ *had to swerve to avoid a pedestrian* ■ *n* a sudden change in direction [Old English *sweorfan* 'file, scour, turn aside' < Indo-European, 'to turn'] —**swerver** *n*

Sweyn I /swayn/ (960?–1014) king of Denmark (1016–35). Known as **Sweyn Forkbeard**

SWG *abbr* standard wire gauge

swidden /swídd'n/ *n* a place temporarily cleared for agriculture by cutting back and burning off previous growth [Late 18C. Variant of *swithen* 'burn' < Old Norse *sviðna* 'be singed'.]

swift /swift/ *adj* **1 HAPPENING FAST** happening or done very quickly or suddenly ○ *issued a swift denial* **2 ACTING FAST** acting very quickly or promptly ○ *they were swift to respond* **3 MOVING FAST** moving or able to move very quickly ■ *adv* **QUICKLY** very quickly ○ *a swift-flowing river* ■ *n* **1** (*plural* **swift** *or* **swifts**) **SMALL BIRD RESEMBLING SWALLOW** a small dark bird with long narrow wings, related to the hummingbirds and resembling a swallow. Family: Apodidae. **2 SMALL FAST LIZARD** a small fast-running lizard. Native to: North America. Genera: *Sceloporus* and *Uta*. **3 REEL OR CYLINDER ON A MACHINE** the reel on which yarn is placed while it is wound off, or the cylinder on a machine that cards flax [Old English, 'quick, moving along a course' < a Germanic base meaning 'swing, bend'] —**swiftly** *adv* —**swiftness** *n*

Swift /swift/, **Jonathan, Dean** (1667–1745) Irish author and clergyman —**Swiftian** *adj*

Swift Current /swíft kúrrənt/ town in SW Saskatchewan, Canada. Population: 14,890 (1996).

swift fox *n* a small fox with large ears. Native to: W North America. *Vulpes velox*.

swiftie /swífti/ *n ANZ* a trick or deception (*informal*)

swiftlet /swíftlət/ *n* a small cave-dwelling swift whose nest is used in making birds' nest soup. Native to: Asia. Genus: *Collocalia*.

swig /swig/ *vti* (**swigs, swigging, swigged**) to drink something in large gulps (*informal*) ■ *n* a large gulp of drink (*informal*) [Mid-16C. < ?] —**swigger** *n*

swill /swil/ *v* **1** *vt* **WASH SOMETHING WITH WATER** to wash or rinse something by flooding or filling it with water **2** *vti* **MOVE LIQUID AROUND IN** to make liquid move around or over something, or move in this way ○ *He swilled the water around in the bucket.* **3** *vti* **DRINK A LOT OF SOMETHING** to drink large amounts of something (*disapproving*) **4** *vt* **FEED PIGS WITH WATERY FEED** to feed animals, especially pigs, with a watery feed typically containing kitchen waste or food by-products ■ *n* **1 PIG FEED** a watery feed for livestock, especially pigs, typically containing kitchen waste or food by-products **2 KITCHEN WASTE** kitchen waste or general refuse **3 WASHING OF SOMETHING WITH WATER** a wash or rinse using a large amount of water **4 LARGE DRINK** a large drink or mouthful of drink **5 INFERIOR FOOD OR DRINK** inferior or unpleasant food or drink **6 SLOPPY LIQUID MIXTURE** a sloppy liquid mixture or mess **7 NONSENSE** talk or writing that is utter nonsense (*informal*) [Old English *swillan*. Ultimately < Indo-European.] —**swiller** *n*

swim /swim/ *v* (**swims, swimming, swam** /swam/, **swum** /swum/) **1** *vi* **MOVE THROUGH WATER** to move or propel yourself unsupported through water using natural means of propulsion such as legs, tails, or fins **2** *vt* **TRAVEL A DISTANCE BY SWIMMING** to cross a particular stretch of water or travel a particular distance by swimming **3** *vt* **COMPETE IN A SWIMMING RACE** to take part as a competitor in a swimming race **4** *vt* **SWIM WITH A PARTICULAR STROKE** to swim using a particular stroke **5** *vi* **BE DIZZY** to be dizzy or confused ○ *The noise made my head swim.* **6** *vi* **SEEM TO MOVE OR SPIN** to appear to move, whirl, or sway ○ *words swimming on the page* **7** *vi* **FLOAT ON THE SURFACE** to float on the surface of a liquid ○ *oil swimming on the water* **8** *vi* **BE COVERED IN LIQUID** to be surrounded or covered with a large quantity of liquid ○ *mushrooms swimming with garlic butter* **9** *vi* **HAVE PLENTY** to have a large amount of something ○ *not exactly swimming in offers* ■ *n* **1 SPELL OF SWIMMING** a period of time spent swimming, usually for pleasure or exercise ○ *went for her morning swim* **2 SMOOTH MOVEMENT** a smooth gliding movement **3 DIZZINESS** dizziness or confusion ○ *with my head in a swim* **4 PLACE WITH MANY FISH** a place where fish are found in abundance [Old English *swimman* < Germanic] —**swimmable** *adj* —**swimmer** *n* ◇ **be in the swim** to be involved with the latest fashions or trends (*informal*)

⚡**SWIM** *abbr* see what I mean? (*in e-mails*)

swim bladder *n* ZOOL = **air bladder** *n*. 1

swimmeret /swímmə rét, swímmə ret/ *n* an abdominal appendage of shrimp, lobsters, and some other crustaceans that is adapted for swimming and, in females, for carrying eggs

swimmers /swímmərz/ *npl Aus* a swimming costume (*informal*)

swimmer's itch *n* an inflammation of the skin caused by the larvae of some schistosomes that penetrate the skin and cause itching

swimming /swímming/ *n* the action or activity of making progress unsupported through water using the arms and legs, usually for pleasure, exercise, or sport

swimming baths, swimming bath *n* a building containing a swimming pool for public use (+ *singular or plural verb*)

swimming costume *n* a piece of clothing worn for swimming, especially by women

swimmingly /swímmingli/ *adv* very smoothly, easily, and successfully ○ *The whole evening went swimmingly.*

swimming pool *n* a water-filled structure in which people can swim, usually set into the ground outdoors or the floor indoors, or a building that houses such a structure

swimming trunks *npl* a piece of clothing worn by men and boys for swimming. Swimming trunks may be brief, like close-fitting underpants, or larger and looser, like shorts.

swimsuit /swím soot, -syoot/ *n* a piece of clothing worn for swimming, especially a one-piece garment worn by women

swimwear /swím wair/ *n* any type of clothing worn for swimming

Swinburne /swín burn/, **Algernon Charles** (1837–1909) British poet

swindle /swínd'l/ *vt* to obtain something from somebody, especially money, by deception or fraud ○ *I've been swindled!* ■ *n* a transaction in which one person or organization obtains something from another by deception or fraud [Late 18C. Back-formation < *swindler* < German *Schwindler* 'cheat' < *schwindeln* 'be dizzy', literally 'vanish repeatedly' < Old High German *swintan* 'vanish'.] —**swindler** *n*

swine /swīn/ (*plural* **swine**) *n* **1** (*plural* **swine** *or* **swines**) an offensive term that deliberately insults somebody's manners or behaviour (*insult*) **2** a pig, boar, or similar animal [Old English *swīn*. Ultimately < Indo-European.] —**swinish** *adj* —**swinishly** *adv*

swine fever *n* a very infectious and often fatal viral disease of pigs marked by fever, weakness, lesions, loss of appetite, and diarrhoea. US term **hog cholera**

swineherd /swīn hurd/ *n* a person who tends pigs (*archaic or literary*)

swinepox /swīn poks/ *n* an infectious viral disease of pigs marked by lesions of the skin

swine vesicular disease *n* a mild viral disease in pigs that causes lesions on the feet and in the mouth

swing /swing/ *v* (**swings, swinging, swung** /swung/) **1** *vti* **MOVE TO AND FRO** to move freely from side to side or backwards and forwards, usually hanging from a fixed point, or make something move in this way **2** *vti* **PIVOT OR ROTATE** to move or turn in a circle or an arc, usually pivoting around a fixed point, or make something move or turn in this way ○ *The door swung open.* **3** *vti* **SUSPEND OR HANG** to fix something so that it can swing, or be fixed in this way **4** *vti* **MOVE IN A CURVE** to move in a smooth curve, or make something move in this way ○ *The limousine swung into the drive.* **5** *vi* **WALK WITH A SWAYING MOTION** to walk with a swaying motion in a relaxed or easy manner **6** *vti* **STRIKE WITH A SWEEPING BLOW** to hit or attempt to hit somebody or something with a sweeping blow or stroke ○ *swung at the ball wildly* **7** *vti* **RIDE ON A SWINGING SEAT** to move backwards and forwards on a swinging seat, or make somebody move in such a way by pushing the person or the seat **8** *vti* **FLUCTUATE OR VACILLATE** to change from one feeling or condition to another, sometimes quickly or suddenly, or make something or somebody change in this way ○ *Their mood swung between elation and gloom.* **9** *vt* **ARRANGE OR MANIPULATE** to achieve a desired change or result by using influence, persuasion, or other means (*informal*) ○ *You want the job? I can swing it for you.* **10** *vi* **BE HANGED FOR** to be hanged as punishment for something (*informal*) **11** *vi* **SWAP SEXUAL PARTNERS** to have a number of sexual partners, especially by exchanging them within a group (*slang*) **12** *vi* **BE LIVELY** to be lively or animated (*informal*) ○ *The party was really swinging by the time we arrived.* **13** *vi* **BE MODERN AND FASHIONABLE** to be interested in and involved in modern or fashionable trends (*informal*) **14** *vti* **PLAY JAZZ** to play a passage or musical work in big-band jazz music **15** *vti* **BOWL BALL WITH SIDEWAYS CURVE** to bowl a ball in such a way that it moves sideways in the air, or move in this way **16** *vi* **DANCE SWING** to dance the swing ■ *n* **1 HANGING SEAT** a seat hung from a frame or branch for somebody to sit on and move backwards and forwards, especially one on which children play **2 SWINGING MOVEMENT** the process of swinging, or a swinging movement **3 RANGE OF MOVEMENT** the curve or distance covered by something as it swings **4 SWEEPING STROKE OR BLOW** a sweeping stroke, blow, or punch ○ *took a swing at the ball* **5 RELAXED SWINGING MOTION** a relaxed or graceful swaying motion **6 WAY OF SWINGING** the manner of movement used to swing a bat or club or bowl a ball ○ *practising her golf swing* **7 SIDEWAYS MOVEMENT OF BOWLED BALL** the sideways movement through the air of a bowled ball **8 PUNCH FROM SIDE** a wide punch from the side **9 SHIFT OR FLUCTUATION** a sudden or significant change, especially in the way people think or act ○ *frequent mood swings* ○ *a massive swing in popularity towards the younger candidate* **10 UP-AND-DOWN CYCLICAL CHANGES** the up-and-down cycles of something such as business profits, economic growth, or share prices **11 STEADY PROGRESSION** a steady progression or advance across territory, or through a process, activity, or phase **12 swing, swing music STYLE OF JAZZ MUSIC** jazz music of the 1930s and 1940s, suitable for dancing and generally played by big bands **13 swing, swing dance LIVELY DANCE STYLE** lively dancing for couples involving syncopated steps, spins, and jumps, with one partner often swinging and lifting the other off the ground [Old English *swingan* 'flog, rush' < Germanic, 'violent circulatory movement'] —**swingy** *adj* ◇ **in full swing** in vigorous progress ◇ **get into the swing of things** to get into rhythm or routine ◇ **go with a swing** to be lively and animated ○ *The evening really went with a swing.* ◇ **swings and roundabouts** used to indicate that a situation has both advantages and disadvantages, or is sometimes good and sometimes bad

swing around, swing round *vi* **1** to turn around quickly or suddenly **2** to change direction quickly or suddenly

swingboat /swíng bōt/ *n* a boat-shaped carriage with seats in which people swing backwards and forwards for fun, usually at a fairground or amusement park

swing bridge *n* a low movable bridge that pivots horizontally on a pier in midstream and is swung parallel to the stream to allow a ship to pass

swing-by *n* a deliberate change in the course of an interplanetary vehicle caused by moving through the gravitational field of an astronomical object, especially that of a planet

swing door *n* a door that can be opened by pushing from either side, especially one that swings shut automatically. US term **swinging door**

swinge /swinj/ (**swinges, swingeing** *or* **swinging, swinged**) *vt* to punish somebody severely, especially by beating or flogging (*literary*) [Mid-16C. < Germanic.]

swingeing /swínjing/ *adj* causing great harm or hardship ○ *swingeing cuts in spending*

swinger /swíngər/ *n* a person who lives an unconventional and hedonistic life, especially somebody who exchanges sexual partners with others (*slang*)

swinging /swínging/ *adj* 1 FASHIONABLE lively and fashionable (*dated*) 2 LIVELY lively and animated 3 OFTEN CHANGING SEXUAL PARTNERS frequently changing or exchanging sexual partners (*slang*)

swinging chad /swínging-/ *n* a rectangular chad still attached to a ballot paper but with the perforations broken through on two sides

swinging door *n US* = **swing door**

swingle /swíng g'l/ *n* a wooden instrument like a knife or paddle used to beat hemp or flax and scrape woody portions out of the material ■ *vt* to beat and scrape hemp or flax with a swingle [15C. < Middle Dutch *swinghel*.]

swingletree /swíng g'l tree/ *n* a horizontal crossbar by means of which the harness traces of a draught animal are attached to a vehicle or device. US term **whiffletree**

swingometer /swing ómmitər/ *n* a device used on television during an election to show the swing of votes from one political party to another [Mid-20C. Coined after BAROMETER.]

swing shift *n US* 1 = **back shift** *n.* 1 2 = **back shift** *n.* 2

swing voter *n US* POL = **floating voter**

swing-wing *adj* describes an aircraft whose wings are constructed to allow them to move backwards and forwards relative to the fuselage during flight ■ *n* an aeroplane with variable-sweep wings

swipe /swīp/ *v* 1 *vti* HIT SOMEBODY OR SOMETHING HARD to strike or attempt to strike somebody or something with a forceful swinging or sweeping blow 2 *vt* STEAL to steal something, often with a snatching movement (*informal*) 3 *vt* PUT A CARD THROUGH MACHINE to pass a card on which data has been stored magnetically through an electronic reading device, e.g. to gain access to a building or to initiate a banking transaction, or to be read successfully by such a device ○ *the card won't swipe through the machine* ■ *n* 1 SWINGING BLOW a forceful swinging or sweeping blow ○ *took a swipe at me but missed* 2 CRITICAL ATTACK a critical remark or attack (*informal*) 3 PIVOTED POLE a long pole used as a lever to raise or lower a bucket in a well [Early 19C. Partly from a Scottish variant of SWEEP and partly from obsolete English *swip* 'stroke, blow' < SWEEP.] —**swiper** *n*

swipe card *n* a plastic card such as a credit card on which data has been stored magnetically and that can be passed through and read by an electronic reading device and decoded

swirl /swurl/ *v* 1 *vti* TURN WITH A CIRCULAR MOTION to turn around and around with a twisting or spiralling movement, or to make something move in this way ○ *caught up in a swirling throng of dancers and musicians* 2 *vi* BE DIZZY to be dizzy or confused ■ *n* 1 CIRCULAR MOTION a turning, twisting, spiralling movement, or something that moves in this way 2 SPIRAL a curl, twist, or spiral ○ *a carpet with black swirls on a red background* 3 CONFUSION dizziness or confusion [15C. Originally 'whirlpool' < ?] —**swirly** *adj*

swish /swish/ *v* 1 *vi* MAKE OR MOVE WITH A WHISTLING SOUND to make the soft smooth whistling or rustling sound of something moving quickly through the air, or to move with such a sound 2 *vt* MOVE SOMETHING WITH A WHISTLING SOUND to cause something to make or move with a swishing sound ○ *swishing a sword* 3 *vt* CUT WITH A SWIFT SHARP BLOW to cut or strike something or somebody with a swift sharp swishing blow ■ *n* 1 SWISHING SOUND OR MOVEMENT a soft smooth whistling or rustling sound, or a movement that makes such a sound ○ *the angry swish of its tail* 2 STICK OR STROKE a rod used to beat or flog a person or animal, or a blow from such a rod 3 US OFFENSIVE TERM an offensive term for a homosexual man that deliberately insults his manner or behaviour as being more characteristic of a woman (*slang insult*) ■ *adj* 1 ELEGANT elegant and fashionable (*informal*) 2 US OFFENSIVE TERM an offensive term that deliberately insults a homosexual man whose manner or behaviour is regarded as more characteristic of a woman (*insult*) [Mid-18C. Probably an imitation of the sound made when moving through or brushing against something.] —**swishy** *adj*

Swiss /swiss/ *n* (*plural* **Swiss**) 1 SOMEBODY FROM SWITZERLAND a person who comes from Switzerland 2 DIALECT SPOKEN IN SWITZERLAND any dialect of German, French, or Italian spoken in Switzerland ■ *adj* OF SWITZERLAND relating to Switzerland, or its people or culture [Early 16C. < French *Suisse* < Middle High German *Swīz* 'Switzerland'.]

Swiss army knife *n* a pocketknife with a number of additional items that fold into the handle, e.g. a corkscrew, nail file, bottle opener, and scissors

Swiss chard, chard *n* a variety of beet with large edible leaves and stems that are similar to spinach, cooked and eaten as a vegetable. *Beta vulgaris cicla.*

Swiss cheese plant *n* a houseplant with large perforated leaves. *Monstera deliciosa.*

Swiss Guard *n* a group of Swiss-born soldiers employed to protect the pope at the Vatican, or a member of this group

swiss muslin *n* a fine cotton fabric, often with a raised pattern. Use: clothes, curtains.

swiss roll, Swiss roll *n* a thin light sponge spread with jam or cream and rolled up into a cylinder before it cools

switch /swich/ *n* 1 BUTTON OR LEVER CONTROLLING AN ELECTRICAL CIRCUIT a mechanical or electronic device that opens, closes, or changes the connections in an electrical circuit, e.g. one used to turn a light or machine on or off 2 SUDDEN CHANGE a quick or sudden change 3 SUBSTITUTION an exchange or substitution 4 THIN ROD OR CANE a thin flexible stick, especially one used for punishment, or a blow or beating with such a stick 5 PONYTAIL HAIRPIECE a hairpiece in the form of a false ponytail 6 TIP OF AN ANIMAL'S TAIL a tuft of hair at the end of the tail of a cow or other animal 7 CARD GAME any card game in which the suit can be changed during play 8 ROUTING DEVICE USED WITHIN TELEPHONE EXCHANGES a device used within a telephone exchange to route transmissions between network nodes 9 TECHNIQUE FOR CONTROLLING A PROGRAM'S LOGIC in computing, a programmed technique for indicating which alternative path to take at a decision point in a program's logic ■ *v* 1 *vti* CHANGE, SHIFT, OR TRANSFER to change from one time, activity, or situation to another, often quickly or suddenly, or to cause somebody or something to make such a change ○ *The dancing class has been switched from Friday afternoon to Saturday morning.* 2 *vti* MAKE AN EXCHANGE OR SUBSTITUTION to exchange two similar or related things, or put one in the place of the other, sometimes secretly or surreptitiously 3 *vti* CHANGE AN ELECTRICAL FUNCTION to make an electrical device do something different by operating a switch to cause current to stop or start flowing or change its path ○ *He switched the radio to a different station.* 4 *vti* FLICK OR SWING TO AND FRO to move quickly from side to side or backwards and forwards, or make something move in this way 5 *vt* BEAT SOMEBODY WITH SWITCH to beat somebody with a switch, especially as a punishment [Late 16C. Probably < Middle Dutch *swijch* 'twig'.] —**switchable** *adj* —**switcher** *n*

switch off *vti* to stop paying attention, lose interest, or stop thinking about something, or make somebody do this (*informal*)

switch on *v* 1 *vti* to start the flow of electricity to something by operating a switch or other device 2 *vt* to suddenly and automatically produce something, e.g. a smile, charm, or tears, for effect and without sincerity

Switch /swich/ *tdmk* a trademark for a type of debit card

switchback /swích bak/ *n* 1 a road or track with many steep uphill and downhill slopes and sharp bends 2 a sharp bend on a road or track going steeply uphill or downhill 3 LEISURE = **roller coaster** *n.* 1 [Mid-19C. Originally a zigzag railway track used on steep slopes, where the individual tracks were connected by switches (points) at each of which the train was reversed in direction.]

switchblade /swích blayd/, **switchblade knife** *n US* = **flick knife**

switchboard /swích bawrd/ *n* 1 a manually operated device for interconnecting telephone lines and routing telephone calls, usually within a telephone exchange or in a workplace, hotel, or other large building 2 one or more insulating panels containing the electrical devices and instruments, e.g. switches, circuit breakers, fuses, and meters, required to operate electrical equipment

switched-on *adj* 1 AWARE alert or aware (*informal*) 2 MODERN modern in outlook or appearance (*dated informal*) 3 DRUGGED intoxicated by drugs (*dated informal*)

switchgear /swích geer/ *n* a device used solely to open and close electric circuits, especially one used to control a high-current application, e.g. a power and transforming station or electric motor

swither /swíthər/ *vi Scotland* to hesitate or be indecisive ■ *n Scotland* a state of hesitation or indecision [Early 16C. < ?]

Swithun /swíth'n, swíth'n/, **St** (*d.* 862) English bishop

Switzer /swítsər/ *n* a member of the Swiss Guard [Mid-16C. < Middle High German *Swītzer* < *Swīz* 'Switzerland'.]

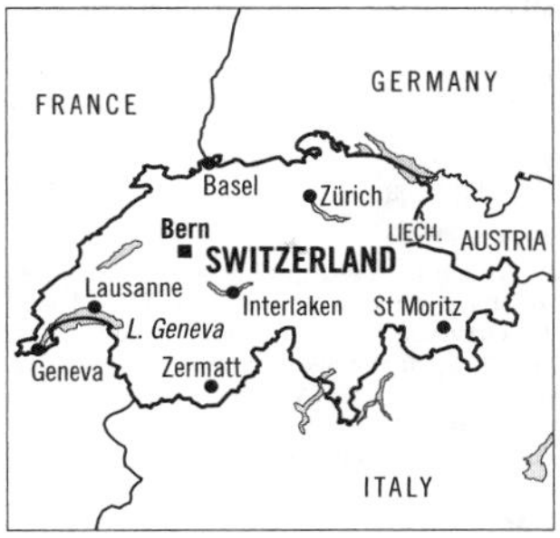

Switzerland

Switzerland /swítsər lənd/ federal republic in west-central Europe. Capital: Bern. Population: 7,207,060 (1996). Area: 41,284 sq. km/15,940 sq. mi.

swive /swīv/ *vti* to have sexual intercourse with somebody (*archaic*) [14C. Via Old English *swīfan* 'to sweep' < Germanic.]

swivel /swívv'l/ *v* (**-els, -elling, -elled**) 1 *vti* PIVOT OR ROTATE to turn freely or horizontally in a circle, or make something turn in this way 2 *vt* PROVIDE SOMETHING WITH A PIVOTING JOINT to fit, attach, or support something with a joint that allows complete freedom of movement ■ *n* 1 DEVICE ALLOWING PARTS TO TURN a joint or fastening that allows something attached to it to turn freely 2 SUPPORT ALLOWING SOMETHING TO PIVOT a pivoting support that allows something such as a gun, chair, or camera to turn from side to side or up and down, sometimes in a full circle 3 PIVOTING GUN a gun that can be turned from side to side horizontally because of the pivoting mount supporting it [14C. < Old English *swīfan* 'sweep'.]

swivel chair *n* a chair, generally an office chair, mounted on a central support with a device that enables it to turn horizontally in a circle

swivel-hipped *adj* moving with loosely swinging hips, usually in an exaggerated manner

swivel pin *n* AUTOMOT = **kingpin** *n.* 2

swiz /swiz/, **swizz** *n* (*plural* **swizzes**) (*informal*) 1 DISAPPOINTMENT a great disappointment, especially something that makes somebody feel cheated 2 SWINDLE a swindle ■ *vt* (**swizzes, swizzing, swizzed**) CHEAT to swindle or cheat somebody (*informal*) [Early 20C. Shortening of SWIZZLE.]

swizzle /swízz'l/ *n* 1 US an iced cocktail, usually containing rum, that is stirred to make it frothy or to frost the glass 2 = **swiz** *n.* 1, **swiz** *n.* 2 (*informal*) ■ *v* 1 *vt* to stir a drink with a swizzle stick to mix the ingredients, make it frothy, or reduce its effervescence 2 *vti* = **swiz** *v.* (*informal*) [Early 19C. < ?]

swizzle stick *n* a small thin plastic rod used for stirring a drink to mix the ingredients, make it frothy, or reduce its effervescence

swollen past participle of **swell**

swollen head *n* a feeling of conceited self-importance, usually stimulated by personal success or by praise received from others. US term **swelled head** —**swollen-headed** *adj* —**swollen-headedness** *n*

swoon /swoon/ *vi* **1 FEEL FAINT WITH JOY** to be overwhelmed by happiness, excitement, adoration, or infatuation **2 FALL IN A FAINT** to experience a sudden and usually brief loss of consciousness ■ *n* **LOSS OF CONSCIOUSNESS** a sudden and usually brief loss of consciousness [13C. Probably < Old English *iswowen* 'in a swoon' < *geswōgen*, past participle of assumed *swōgan* 'suffocate' < ?]

swoony /swoōni/ (**-ier, -iest**) *adj* (*informal*) **1** romantically or sentimentally affectionate or in love **2** very attractive —**swooniness** *n*

swoop /swoop/ *v* **1** *vi* **MAKE SWEEPING DESCENT** to descend quickly and suddenly with a sweeping movement, usually from the air **2** *vi* **POUNCE** to make a sudden swift attack or raid on something or somebody ○ *The police swooped in on the terrorists.* **3** *vt* **SEIZE QUICKLY OR SUDDENLY** to seize or snatch something in a sudden swift attack ■ *n* **1 SUDDEN DESCENT** a quick sudden sweeping descent **2 SUDDEN ATTACK** a sudden swift attack or raid [Mid-16C. Probably from a variant of Old English *swāpan*, an earlier form of SWEEP.] ◇ **at** *or* **in one fell swoop** in a single action

swoosh /swoosh, swoōsh/ *v* **1** *vi* **MAKE OR MOVE WITH RUSHING SOUND** to make the rushing or swirling sound of fast-moving water or air, or move with such a sound **2** *vt* **MOVE SOMETHING WITH RUSHING SOUND** to cause something to make or move with a swooshing sound ■ *n* **SWOOSHING SOUND** a swooshing sound or movement [Mid-19C. An imitation of the sound.]

swop *vti, n* = **swap**

sword /sawrd/ *n* **1** a hand-held weapon with a long blade that is sharp on one or both edges and sometimes slightly curved **2** the use of force, violence, or military power ○ *The pen is mightier than the sword.* [Old English *sweord* < Germanic] —**swordless** *adj* ◇ **cross swords (with somebody)** to argue or come into conflict with somebody ◇ **put somebody to the sword** to kill somebody violently, especially in war (*literary*)

sword and sorcery *adj* set in a fantasy place or time with a technology that has not advanced beyond bladed weapons and in which magic is important (*informal*)

sword bayonet *n* a bayonet with a very long blade

swordbearer /sáwrd bairər/ *n* an official who carries a sword that is a symbol of somebody's authority, e.g. a sovereign's sword

sword cane *n* ARMS = **swordstick**

sword dance *n* a dance in which swords are used, especially a Highland dance in which somebody dances over swords crossed on the floor

sword fern *n* a fern with long fronds shaped like swords

swordfish /sáwrd fish/ (*plural* **-fish** *or* **-fishes**) *n* **1** a large ocean fish with an upper jaw that extends into a long point. *Xiphias gladius.* **2** the flesh of a swordfish as food

sword grass *n* a grass with leaves that have very sharp edges

sword knot *n* a decorative ribbon or tassel on the hilt of a sword

sword lily *n* PLANTS = **gladiolus** *n.* 1 [< its sword-shaped leaves]

Sword of Damocles *n* something that threatens to bring imminent disaster [(See DAMOCLES)]

swordplay /sáwrd play/ *n* fighting with a sword, especially when done with skill

swordsman /sáwrdzmən/ (*plural* **-men** /-mən/) *n* a fighter who uses a sword —**swordsmanship** *n*

swordstick /sáwrd stik/ *n* a hollow walking stick or cane whose handle is also the handle of a narrow sword hidden inside the stick. US term **sword cane**

sword-swallower /sáwrd swolōwər/ *n* a performer who passes or creates an illusion of passing a sword down his or her throat to its hilt

swordswoman /sáwrdz woōmən/ (*plural* **-en** /-wimin/) *n* a woman who fights with a sword with a particular degree of skill

swordtail /sáwrd tayl/ *n* a small brightly coloured freshwater fish with a long sword-shaped tail, popular as an aquarium fish. Native to: Central America. *Xiphophorus helleri.*

swore past tense of **swear**

sworn[1] past participle of **swear**

sworn[2] /swawrn/ *adj* **1** made under oath ○ *a sworn statement* **2** determined to maintain a particular situation ○ *sworn enemies*

swot[1] /swot/, **swat** *vi* (**swots, swotting, swotted; swats, swatting, swatted**) **STUDY VERY HARD** to study very hard and intensively, especially for an examination (*informal*) ■ *n* **1 HARD-WORKING STUDENT** an unduly industrious student (*disapproving informal*) **2 PERIOD OF HARD STUDY** a period of time spent studying hard, especially for an examination (*informal*) [Mid-19C. Originally a Scottish variant of SWEAT.]

swot[2] *vti, n* = **swat**

swotter *n* = **swatter**

swotty /swótti/ *adj* given to studying very hard or excessively (*informal disapproving*)

swum past participle of **swim**

swung past participle, past tense of **swing**

swung dash *n* a character (~) used in printing to represent all or part of a word previously spelt out

swy /swī/ *n* ANZ the gambling game two-up (*informal*) [Early 20C. < German *zwei* 'two'.]

ϟ **sy** *abbr* Syria (*in Internet addresses*)

sybarite /síbbə rīt/ *n* somebody devoted to luxury and the gratification of sensual desires [Mid-16C. Via Latin *Sybarita* < Greek *Subaris* 'Sybaris', an ancient Greek city in S Italy known as a place of luxury and indulgence.] —**sybaritic** /síbbə ríttik/ *adj* —**sybaritical** *adj* —**sybaritically** *adv* —**sybaritism** /síbbə rītizəm/ *n*

syboe /sī bō/ *n* Scotland a spring onion [Late 16C. Via French *ciboule* < Latin *caepa* 'onion'.]

sycamore /síkə mawr/ (*plural* **-mores** *or* **-more**) *n* **1 TYPE OF MAPLE TREE** a tree of the maple family, naturalized in N Europe and North America, with five-lobed leaves and two-winged fruits. Native to: central and S Europe, Asia. *Acer pseudoplatanus.* **2** *US* **LARGE SPREADING PLANE TREE** a large spreading plane tree with lobed leaves, round spiked fruit clusters, and flaking bark. Native to: central and E North America. *Platanus occidentalis.* **3 FIG TREE** a fig tree with edible fruit. Native to: Africa, SW Asia. *Ficus sycomorus.* [14C. Via Old French *sicamor* < Greek *sukomoros* 'fig-mulberry'.]

syce /sīss/, **saice, sice** *n* formerly in India, a groom, stable hand, or other attendant [Mid-17C. Via Persian and Urdu *sā'is* < Arabic, < *sūs* 'tend a horse'.]

syconium /sī kōni əm/ (*plural* **-a** /-ni ə/) *n* a fleshy fruit, e.g. a fig, in which numerous seeds are borne inside the enlarged hollow tip of the flower stalk [Mid-19C. Via modern Latin < Greek *sukon* 'fig'.]

sycophant /síkəfənt, -fant/ *n* a servile or obsequious flatterer of a powerful person for personal gain [Mid-16C. Via Latin *sycophanta* < Greek *sukophantēs* 'informer' < *sukon* 'fig, obscene gesture' + *-phantes* 'shower' (< *phanein* 'show').] —**sycophancy** *n* —**sycophantic** /síkə fántik/ *adj* —**sycophantically** *adv*

sycosis /sī kóssiss/ *n* inflammation of hair follicles, especially of the beard, caused by bacterial infection and marked by pustules and encrustations [Late 16C. Via modern Latin < Greek *sukōsis* < *sukon* 'fig'.]

Sydenham's chorea /sídd'nəmz-/ *n* a neurological disease of children and pregnant women, sometimes following rheumatic fever, in which those affected experience involuntary jerking movements of the body [Late 19C. After Thomas *Sydenham* (1624–89), English physician.]

Sydney /sídni/ capital of New South Wales, SE Australia. Population: 3,276,207 (1996).

Sydney Opera House *n* an arts centre in Sydney Harbour, Australia, that was designed by Jörn Utzon and completed in 1973

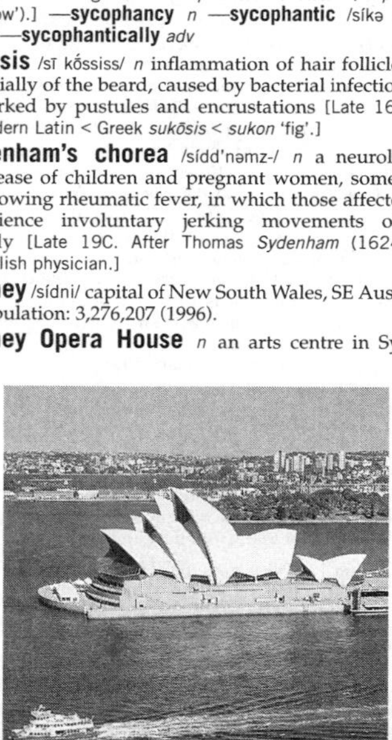
AKG London
Sydney Opera House

syenite /sī ə nīt/ *n* a light-coloured coarse-grained igneous rock consisting mainly of feldspar [Late 18C. < Latin *syenites (lapis)* '(stone of) Syene'.]

~~**sylabus**~~ incorrect spelling of **syllabus**

Sylhet /sil hét/ city in NE Bangladesh. Population: 114,284 (1991).

syllabary /sílləbəri/ (*plural* **-ies**) *n* a list or set of written characters in which each character represents a single syllable e.g. the Japanese kana

syllabi plural of **syllabus**

syllabic /si lábbik/ *adj* **1 INVOLVING SYLLABLES** relating to, involving, or typical of a syllable or syllables **2 BEING A SYLLABLE WITHOUT A VOWEL** describes a consonant that acts as a syllable without a vowel, as does the 'l' in 'bottle' **3 MARKED BY CLEAR ENUNCIATION** clearly enunciated with every syllable distinct **4 BASED ON THE NUMBER OF SYLLABLES** describes verse in which the rhythm is set by the number of syllables rather than accents, stresses, or vowel strengths. ◊ **accentual** *adj.* 2 ■ *n* **SYLLABIC CONSONANT OR SOUND** a syllabic consonant, character, or sound

syllabify /si lábbi fī/ (**-fies, -fying, -fied**), **syllabicate** /si lábbi kayt/ (**-cates, -cating, -cated**) *vt* to break a word down into syllables in speech or writing [Early 20C. Back-formation < *syllabification* < Latin *syllaba* 'syllable'.] —**syllabication** /si lábbi káysh'n/ *n* —**syllabification** /si lábbifi káysh'n/ *n*

syllabism /síllәbizәm/ *n* **1** the use of characters that stand for individual syllables in writing **2** the breaking down of words into syllables, in speech or writing

syllable /sílləb'l/ *n* **1 UNIT OF SPOKEN LANGUAGE** a unit of spoken language that consists of one or more vowel sounds alone, a syllabic consonant alone, or any of these with one or more consonant sounds **2 LETTERS CORRESPONDING TO SPOKEN SYLLABLE** one or more letters in a word that roughly correspond to a syllable of spoken language **3 MENTION** the slightest mention of something (*usually in negative statements*) ■ *vt* (**-bles, -bling, -bled**) **PRONOUNCE SOMETHING CLEARLY** to pronounce something in distinct or separate syllables [14C. Via Anglo-Norman *sillable* and Old French *sillabe* < Greek *sullabē* < *sullambanein* 'bring together' < *lambanein* 'take'.]

syllabogram /si lábbō gram/ *n* a written or printed symbol that stands for a single syllable

syllabub /síllə bub/ *n* **1** a light soft cold dessert made from cream whipped with brandy, wine or sherry, lemon juice, and a little sugar **2** a drink made of sweetened milk or cream curdled with wine or cider (*dated*) [Mid-16C. < ?]

syllabus /sílləbəss/ (*plural* **-bi** /-bī/ *or* **-buses**) *n* **1** a summary or list of the main topics of a course of study, text, or lecture **2** the subjects offered for study by a school, college, or university, or a list of these [Mid-17C. < modern Latin, originally a misprint of Latin *sittybas* 'indexes' < Greek *sittuba* 'index, label'.]

Syllabus, Syllabus of Errors *n* a list of religious doctrines condemned by the Roman Catholic Church as erroneous

syllepsis /si lépsiss/ (*plural* **-ses** /-seez/) *n* **1** the use of a word that relates to, qualifies, or governs two or more other words but agrees in number, gender, or case with only one of them **2** the use of a word that relates to, qualifies, or governs two or more other words but has a different meaning in relation to each, as in the example 'He picked up his hat and a taxi' [Late 16C. Via late Latin and Greek *sullēpsis* 'a taking together' < *lambanein* (see SYLLABLE).]

syllogise *vti* = **syllogize**

syllogism /síllə jizəm/ *n* **1 ARGUMENT INVOLVING THREE PROPOSITIONS** a formal deductive argument made up of a major premise, a minor premise, and a conclusion. An example is 'all birds have feathers, penguins are birds, therefore penguins have feathers'. **2 DEDUCTIVE REASONING** reasoning from the general to the specific, or an example of this **3 SPECIOUS ARGUMENT** a subtle piece of reasoning, or one that seems true but is actually false or deceptive [14C. Via Latin < Greek *sullogismos* < *sullogizesthai* 'infer' < *logos* 'reason'.]

syllogistic /síllə jístik/ *adj* relating to, using, or typical of syllogisms [Mid-17C. Via Latin < Greek *sullogistikos* < *sullogizesthai* (see SYLLOGISM).] —**syllogistically** *adv*

syllogize /síllə jīz/ (**-gizes, -gizing, -gized**), **syllogise** (**-gises, -gising, -gised**) *vti* to reason or infer something by means of syllogisms [15C. Via late Latin *syllogizare* < Greek *sullogizesthai* (see SYLLOGISM).] —**syllogization** /sílla jī záysh'n/ *n* —**syllogizer** *n*

sylph /silf/ *n* **1** a woman or girl who is slight and graceful **2** an elemental soulless female being imagined to inhabit the air [Mid-17C. < modern Latin *sylpha* < ?] —**sylphic** *adj* —**sylphish** *adj* —**sylphy** *adj*

sylphlike /sílf līk/ *adj* slight and graceful figure

sylvan /sílvən/, **silvan** *adj* **1 OF A FOREST** relating to, typical of, or found in a forest (*literary*) **2 WOODED** covered in or full of trees (*literary*) **3 RURAL** typical of the countryside, especially in an idyllic way ■ *n* **INHABITANT OF A FOREST** a person, animal, or spirit that lives in a forest

sylvanite /sílvə nīt/ *n* a mixed telluride mineral containing gold and silver [Late 18C. After TRANSYLVANIA.]

Sylvanus *n* = **Silvanus**

sylvatic /sil váttik/ *adj* **1** affecting wild animals ○ *sylvatic plague* **2** = **sylvan** *adj.* 1, **sylvan** *adj.* 2

sylviculture *n* AGRIC = **silviculture**

sylvite /síl vīt/, **sylvine** /-vīn/ *n* a colourless transparent potassium chloride mineral. Use: source of potassium. [Mid-19C. < modern Latin *(sal digestivus) Silvii* '(digestive salt) of Silvius'.]

sym- *prefix* = **syn-** (*before b, m, and p*)

symbion /símbi on, -bī on/ *n* a tiny marine organism that lives in the mouth hairs of the Norwegian lobster. *Symbion pandora*. [Late 20C. < SYM- + Greek *bioun* 'live', because it lives in symbiosis with the lobster.]

symbiont /símbi ont, -bī-/ *n* an animal or plant living in close and often mutually beneficial association with another of a different species [Late 19C. < Greek *bioun* 'live' < *bios* (see SYMBIOSIS).] —**symbiontic** /símbi óntik, -bī-/ *adj* —**symbiontically** *adv*

symbiosis /sím bī óssiss, -bi-/ (*plural* **-ses** /-ó seez, -/) *n* **1** a close association of animals or plants of different species that is often, but not always, of mutual benefit **2** a cooperative, mutually beneficial relationship between two people or groups [Early 17C. Via modern Latin and Greek *sumbiōsis* 'a living together' < *bios* 'life'.] —**symbiotic** /sím bī óttik, -bi-/ *adj* —**symbiotical** *adj* —**symbiotically** *adv*

symbiote /símbī ōt/ *n* an organism, person, or thing that exists in or depends on a symbiotic relationship with something or someone else [Late 19C. Back-formation < SYMBIOTIC.]

symbol /símb'l/ *n* **1 SOMETHING THAT REPRESENTS SOMETHING ELSE** something that stands for or represents something else, especially an object representing an abstraction **2 SIGN WITH SPECIFIC MEANING** a written or printed sign or character that represents something in a particular context, e.g. an operation or quantity in mathematics or music **3 OBJECT REPRESENTING SOMETHING REPRESSED IN UNCONSCIOUS** an object or act that represents an impulse or wish in the unconscious mind that has been repressed [15C. Via Latin < Greek *sumbolon* 'mark' < *sumballein* 'compare' < *ballein* 'throw'.]

SPELLCHECK See ***cymbal***.

symbolic /sim bóllik/, **symbolical** /-bóllik'l/ *adj* **1 OF SYMBOLS** relating to or typical of symbols **2 USING SYMBOLS** using a symbol or symbols to represent something else **3 REPRESENTING SOMETHING ELSE** acting as a symbol ○ *a gesture symbolic of repentance* **4 INVOLVING USE OF SYMBOLS** characterized by or involving the use of symbols or symbolism ○ *symbolic art* —**symbolically** *adv*

⚡**symbolic language** *n* **1** an artificially constructed language with many symbols, used for precise formulations, e.g. in symbolic logic or mathematics **2** a computer programming language that expresses memory addresses and operation codes in symbols recognizable to the programmer rather than in machine language

symbolic logic *n* the branch of formal logic that studies the meaning and relationships of statements through precise mathematical methods and a standardized system of symbols and rules of inference

symbolise *vt* = **symbolize**

symbolism /símbəlizəm/ *n* **1 USE OF SYMBOLS** the use of symbols to invest things with a representative meaning or to represent something abstract by something concrete **2 SYSTEM OF SYMBOLS** a set or system of symbols **3 SYMBOLIC MEANING** symbolic meaning or quality **4 ARTISTIC USE OF SYMBOLS** the artistic method of revealing ideas or truths through the use of symbols **5 symbolism, Symbolism 19C LITERARY AND ARTISTIC MOVEMENT** a 19th-century literary and artistic movement that sought to evoke, rather than describe, ideas or feelings through the use of symbolic images **6 BELIEF IN SYMBOLIC NATURE OF COMMUNION** the belief that the bread and wine used in the Communion are symbols and not literally the flesh and blood of Jesus Christ

QUICK FACTS ON... **SYMBOLISM**

Key dates: 1870–1900
Key locations: France
Key elements: rejection of artistic conventions, rationalism, and naturalism; primacy of imagination; subjectivity, formalism, interest in different cultures, interest in mythology and the supernatural; synaethesia, interlinking of art, literature, and music
Key figures: Paul Verlaine, Arthur Rimbaud, Stéphane Mallarmé, Jules Laforgue, Joris Karl Huysmans, Maurice Maeterlinck (literature); Gustave Moreau, Odilon Redon, Pierre Puvis de Chavannes, Paul Gauguin, Vincent van Gogh, Edvard Munch (art)
Key works: *A Season in Hell* (Rimbaud) 1873, *Songs Without Words* (Verlaine) 1874, *Against Nature* (Huysmans) 1884, *Ramblings* (Mallarmé) 1897; *Salomé* (Moreau) 1876, *Vision after the Sermon, or Jacob Wrestling with the Angel* (Gauguin) 1888, *The Scream* (Munch) 1893
Key developments: Nabis, aestheticism, art nouveau, fauvism, expressionism, surrealism, the Beat poets

symbolist /símbəlist/ *n* **1 SOMEBODY USING SYMBOLS** a user of symbols or symbolism **2 SOMEBODY SKILLED AT INTERPRETING SYMBOLS** somebody skilled in the study or interpretation of symbols **3 symbolist, Symbolist SOMEBODY INVOLVED IN 19C ARTISTIC SYMBOLISM** a writer or artist involved in or associated with the 19th-century movement of symbolism **4 SOMEBODY BELIEVING COMMUNION USES SYMBOLS** a believer that the bread and wine used in the Communion are symbols and not literally the flesh and blood of Jesus Christ ■ *adj* **1 OF OR USING SYMBOLS** relating to, involving, or using symbols **2 symbolist, Symbolist ASSOCIATED WITH 19C ARTISTIC SYMBOLISM** involved in, associated with, or typical of the 19th-century movement of symbolism —**symbolistic** /símbə lístik/ *adj* —**symbolistically** *adv*

symbolize /símbə līz/ (**-izes, -izing, -ized**), **symbolise** (**-ises, -ising, -ised**) *v* **1** *vt* **BE SYMBOL OF** to serve as a symbol of something **2** *vt* **REPRESENT** to represent something by means of a symbol **3** *vi* **USE SYMBOLS** to use symbols or symbolism —**symbolization** /símbə lī záysh'n/ *n*

symbology /sim bólləji/ *n* **1** the study or interpretation of symbols **2** the use of symbols to represent things —**symbological** /símbə lójjik'l/ *adj* —**symbologist** *n*

~~**symetrical**~~ incorrect spelling of **symmetrical**

symmetallism /si métt'lizəm/ *n* a system of coinage in which the unit of currency consists of a combination of two or more metals in fixed relative proportions

symmetrical /si méttrik'l/, **symmetric** /si méttrik/ *adj* **1 EXHIBITING SYMMETRY** having both sides of a central dividing line correspond or be identical to each other **2 BALANCED** relating to or having balanced proportions, especially in two halves of a whole **3 WITH PARTICULAR PAIRS OF POINTS** describes two points that can be joined by a line bisected by a given point or perpendicular, or a shape that has such pairs of points **4 WITH INTERCHANGEABLE TERMS** describes an equation or function in which terms or variables may be interchanged without altering its value or form **5 WITH SYMMETRICAL MOLECULAR STRUCTURE** with atoms or groups that display symmetry about a plane in a chemical structure **6 ON OPPOSITE SIDES** describes body parts that have the same function but are situated on opposite sides, either of the same organ or the same body —**symmetrically** *adv*

symmetric matrix *n* a square matrix that is identical to the matrix formed by transposing its rows and columns

symmetrize /símmə trīz/ (**-trizes, -trizing, -trized**), **symmetrise** (**-trises, -trising, -trised**) *vt* to give symmetry to something —**symmetrization** /símmə trī záysh'n/ *n*

symmetry /símmə tri/ (*plural* **-tries**) *n* **1 PROPERTY OF SAMENESS** the property of being the same or corresponding on both sides of a central dividing line **2 BALANCED PROPORTIONS** harmony or beauty of form that results from balanced proportions **3 EXACT CORRESPONDENCE IN POSITION** a correspondence in the position of pairs of points of a geometric object that are equally positioned about a point, line, or plane that bisects the object **4 STATE OF INVARIANCE** a state of invariance shown by some phenomena when changes of orientation, charge, or parity are made [Mid-16C. Via Latin and Greek *summetria* 'similar measure' < *metron* 'measure'.]

sympathectomy /símpə théktəmi/ (*plural* **-mies**) *n* formerly, the surgical interruption of a pathway in the sympathetic nervous system, e.g. by cutting out a nerve segment [Early 20C. < SYMPATHETIC + -ECTOMY.]

sympathetic /símpə théttik/ *adj* **1 FEELING OR SHOWING SYMPATHY** showing, having, or resulting from shared feelings, pity, or compassion **2 APPROVING** showing favour, agreement, or approval **3 PROVOKING SYMPATHY** provoking sympathy, interest, or compassion **4 SUITED** agreeably suited to somebody's tastes or mood **5 PRODUCED BY OTHER SOUNDS** describes vibrations such as musical tones that are produced in something as a result of similar vibrations at the same frequency from something else **6 OF SYMPATHETIC NERVOUS SYSTEM** relating or belonging to the sympathetic nervous system or one of its components [Mid-17C. < SYMPATHY after PATHETIC.] —**sympathetically** *adv*

sympathetic magic *n* magic based on the belief that somebody or something can be supernaturally affected by something done to an object representing the person or thing

sympathetic nervous system *n* the part of the autonomic nervous system that is active during stress or danger and is involved in regulating pulse and blood pressure, dilating pupils, and changing muscle tone

sympathetic string *n* a string on a musical instrument that other strings cause to vibrate when bowed or plucked

sympathize /símpə thīz/ (**-thizes, -thizing, -thized**), **sympathise** (**-thises, -thising, -thised**) *vi* **1** to share the feelings of somebody else or show pity or compassion for another ○ *I can sympathize; the same thing happened to me.* **2** to share the ideas or ideals of another person or group —**sympathizer** *n*

sympatholytic /símpə thō líttik/ *adj* describes a drug that opposes or blocks the effects of the sympathetic nervous system ■ *n* a drug or agent that acts against the sympathetic nervous system [Mid-20C. < SYMPATHETIC + -LYTE.]

sympathomimetic /símpə thō mi méttik/ *adj* describes a drug that stimulates the sympathetic nervous system or produces physiological effects similar to it ■ *n* a drug or agent that stimulates the sympathetic nervous system [Early 20C. < SYMPATHETIC + MIMETIC.]

sympathy /símpəthi/ (*plural* **-thies**) *n* **1 CAPACITY TO SHARE FEELINGS** the ability to enter into, understand, or share somebody else's feelings **2 FEELINGS CAUSED BY SYMPATHY** the feelings of somebody who enters into or shares another's feelings **3 SORROW FOR ANOTHER'S PAIN** the feeling or expression of pity or sorrow for the pain or distress of somebody else ○ *We extended our sympathies to the widow.* **4 INCLINATION TO FEEL ALIKE** the inclination to think or feel the same as somebody else ○ *A sympathy exists between them.* **5 AGREEMENT** agreement or harmony with something or somebody else **6 ALLEGIANCE OR LOYALTY** allegiance or loyalty to a group or cause (*often plural*) ○ *nationalist sympathies* [Late 16C. Via Latin < Greek *sumpatheia* < *sumpathēs* 'feeling with' < *pathos* 'feeling'.] ◇ **come out in sympathy** to go on strike in support of other strikers (*informal*)

sympathy strike *n* a strike by workers demonstrating their support for another group of strikers rather than against their own employer

sympathy vote *n* a vote that people give to somebody for whom they feel pity or affection

sympatric /sim páttrik/ *adj* describes species that occupy roughly the same area of land but do not interbreed [Early 20C. < Greek *patra* 'fatherland' < *patēr* 'father'.] —**sympatrically** *adv*

symphonic /sim fónnik/ *adj* **1** relating to, involving, or typical of a musical symphony, or resembling one in form or content **2** harmonious in sound, colour, or composition —**symphonically** *adv*

symphonic poem *n* an extended piece of music for a symphony orchestra that is based on a literary, artistic, or ideological theme, e.g. a folktale or landscape

symphonist /símfənist/ *n* a composer of symphonies or symphonic works

symphony /símfəni/ (*plural* **-nies**) *n* **1 COMPLEX MUSICAL COMPOSITION** a major work for an orchestra, including wind, string, and percussion instruments, usually composed in four movements, at least one of which is in sonata form **2** MUSIC = **symphony orchestra 3 CONCERT BY SYMPHONY ORCHESTRA** a concert performed by a symphony orchestra **4 HARMONIOUS COMPOSITION OR ARRANGEMENT** something that is harmoniously composed of various elements ○ *The colour scheme was a symphony of blues, greens, and yellows.* [13C. Via Latin and Greek *sumphōnia* 'harmony', literally 'sounding together' < *phōnē* 'sound'.]

symphony orchestra *n* a large orchestra that includes wind, string, and percussion instruments and plays symphonies and other works scored for these instruments

symphysis /símfəssiss/ (*plural* **-ses** /-seez/) *n* **1 GROWING TOGETHER OF BONES OR PARTS** the natural merging of two or more separate bones or parts of the body, or a point where this occurs **2 ABNORMAL CONDITION** an abnormal condition in which two or more separate bones or parts of the body have merged **3 JOINT WITH LITTLE MOVEMENT** a joint in which the bones are connected by tough cartilage (**fibrocartilage**) and there is very little movement between them, e.g. between adjacent vertebrae in the spinal column **4 FUSION OF PLANT PARTS** a fusion of two similar organs or parts of a plant, or a line marking such a fusion [Late 16C. Via modern Latin < Greek *sumphusis* 'growing together' < *phusis* 'growth'.] —**symphyseal** /sim fízzi əl/ *adj* —**symphystic** /sim fístik/ *adj* —**symphytic** /sim fíttik/ *adj*

sympodium /sim pṓdi əm/ (*plural* **-a** /-di ə/) *n* a main plant stem, e.g. the stem of a grapevine, that develops from a series of lateral branches, often in a zigzag pattern [Mid-19C. < modern Latin < the Greek stem *pod-* 'foot'.] —**sympodial** *adj* —**sympodially** *adv*

symposia plural of **symposium**

symposiarch /sim pṓzi aark/ *n* a supervisor of a symposium [Early 17C. < Greek *sumposiarkhos* < *sumposion* (see SYMPOSIUM).]

symposiast /sim pṓzi ast/ *n* a participant in a symposium [Mid-17C. < Greek *sumposiazein* 'drink together' < *sumposion* (see SYMPOSIUM).]

symposium /sim pṓzi əm/ (*plural* **-ums** *or* **-a** /-ə/) *n* **1 FORMAL MEETING FOR DISCUSSION OF SUBJECT** a formal meeting held for the discussion of a particular subject and during which individuals may make presentations **2 PUBLISHED COLLECTION OF OPINIONS** a published collection of opinions or writings on a subject, often in a periodical **3 DRINKING PARTY IN ANCIENT GREECE** a drinking party in ancient Greece, usually with music and philosophical conversation [Late 16C. Via Latin < Greek *sumposion* 'drinking party' < *sumpotēs* 'fellow drinker' < *potēs* 'drinker'.] —**symposiac** *adj*

symptom /símptəm/ *n* **1** an indication of some disease or other disorder, especially one experienced by the patient, e.g. pain, dizziness, or itching, as opposed to one observed by the doctor (**sign**) **2** a sign or indication of the existence of something, especially something undesirable [Mid-16C. Via late Latin < Greek *sumptōma* 'occurrence' < *sumpiptein* 'fall together' < *piptein* 'fall'.] —**symptomless** *adj*

symptomatic /símptə máttik/ *adj* **1 INDICATING ILLNESS** indicating or typical of a specific illness **2 CHARACTERISTIC** typical or indicative of something, especially something undesirable ○ *symptomatic of the breakdown in communication between children and parents* **3 OF SYMPTOMS** relating to, affecting, or based on a symptom or symptoms of bodily disorder ○ *Only symptomatic relief is available for the common cold.* [Late 17C. < late Latin *symptomaticus* < Greek *sumptoma* (see SYMPTOM).] —**symptomatically** *adv*

symptomatology /símptəmə tólləji/ (*plural* **-gies**) *n* **1** the study of the relationships between symptoms and diseases **2** the set of symptoms that are associated with a particular disease or that affect a patient [Late 18C. < Greek *sumptōmat-* stem of *sumptōma* (see SYMPTOM) + -LOGY.]

symptomize /símptəmīz/ (**-izes, -izing, -ized**), **symptomise** (**-ises, -ising, -ised**) *vt* to be an indication of the existence of something

syn- *prefix* together, together with, united ○ *syncarpous* [< Greek *sun* 'together']

synaeresis *n* CHEM = **syneresis**

synaesthesia /sínnəss theézhə/ *n* **1 SENSATION FELT ELSEWHERE IN BODY** the feeling of sensation in one part of the body when another part is stimulated **2 STIMULATION OF ONE SENSE ALONGSIDE ANOTHER** the evocation of one kind of sense impression when another sense is stimulated, e.g. the sensation of colour when a sound is heard **3 RHETORICAL DEVICE** in literature, the description of one kind of sense perception using words that describe another kind of sense perception, as in the phrase 'shining metallic words' (*literary*) [Late 19C. < modern Latin, < *syn-* (see SYN-) + stem of Greek *aisthēsis* 'sensation', after ANAESTHESIA.] —**synaesthetic** /-théttik/ *adj*

synagogue /sínnə gog/ *n* **1** the place of worship and communal centre of a Jewish congregation **2** a body of followers of Judaism who worship together [12C. Via French and late Latin *synagoga* < Greek *sunagōgē* 'assembly' < *sunagein* 'bring together' < *agein* 'lead'.] —**synagogal** /sínnə gógg'l/ *adj* —**synagogical** /-gójjik'l/ *adj*

synalepha /sínnə leéfə/, **synaloepha** *n* the blending of two adjacent vowels into one, e.g. when a word ending in a vowel is immediately followed by a word beginning with a vowel [Mid-16C. Via late Latin < Greek *sunaloiphē* < *sunaleiphein* 'smear together' < *aleiphein* 'smear'.]

synapse /sī naps, sínnaps/ *n* a junction between two nerve cells, where the club-shaped tip of a nerve fibre almost touches another cell in order to transmit signals ■ *vi* (**-apses, -apsing, -apsed**) to form a synapse between nerve cells [Late 19C. Anglicization of SYNAPSIS.]

synapsis /si nápsiss/ (*plural* **-ses** /-seez/) *n* the pairing of homologous chromosomes from each parent during the initial phase (**prophase**) of cell division [Mid-17C. Via modern Latin and Greek *sunapsis* 'connection' < *haptein* 'join'.]

synaptic /si náptik/ *adj* **1** relating to or involving a junction between nerve cells **2** relating to, involving, or typical of synapsis [Late 19C. < SYNAPSIS or SYNAPSE after Greek *sunaptikos* 'connective'.]

synarthrosis /sín aar thrṓssiss/ (*plural* **-ses** /-seez/) *n* a rigid joint formed by the union of two bones and connected by fibrous tissue —**synarthrodial** /-thrṓ di əl/ *adj* —**synarthrodially** *adv*

sync /singk/, **synch** *n* (*informal*) **1 SYNCHRONIZATION** the relationship between things that are happening or working at the same time, especially the correspondence of sound and image in a film **2 HARMONY** harmony or agreement ■ *vti* **SYNCHRONIZE** to synchronize something, or be synchronized (*informal*) [Early 20C. Shortening.]

SPELLCHECK See ***sink***.

syncarpous /sin kaárpəss/ *adj* describes the female reproductive parts (**gynoecium**) of a flower in which the carpels are fused —**syncarpy** /sín kaarpi/ *n*

syncategorematic /sín kátəgərə máttik/ *adj* describes an expression that has meaning only in conjunction with another expression [Early 19C. Via medieval Latin *syncategorematicus* and Greek *sugkatēgorēmatikos* 'predicating jointly' < *katēgorein* 'predicate'.]

synch *n*, *vti* = **sync**

synchondrosis /síng kon drṓssiss/ (*plural* **-ses** /-seez/) *n* **1** a joint in which there is slight movement between bones that are held together by cartilage, e.g. between the ribs and the breastbone **2** a joint in which the cartilage linking two bones in childhood is replaced by bone as development progresses [Late 16C. Via modern Latin < late Greek *sugkhondrōsis* < *khondros* 'cartilage'.]

synchro /síngkrō/ (*plural* **-chros**) *n* ELEC ENG = **selsyn** [Mid-20C. Shortening of *synchronizing* (see SELSYN).]

synchro- *prefix* synchronous, synchronized ○ *synchroscope* [< SYNCHRONOUS]

synchrocyclotron /síngkrō sīklə tron/ *n* a particle accelerator that compensates for increases in the relativistic mass of accelerated particles, and so achieves greater energies, by using the synchronizing effects of a frequency-modulated electric field

synchroflash /síngkrō flash/ *n* a mechanism in a camera that opens the shutter at the moment when the light from the flashbulb or electronic flash is brightest

synchromesh /síngkrō mesh/ *n* a gear system in which the speeds of the driving and driven parts are synchronized before they engage, making gear changes smoother —**synchromesh** *adj*

synchronal /síngkrən'l/ *adj* happening at the same time [Mid-17C. < late Latin *synchronus* (see SYNCHRONOUS).]

synchronic /sin krónnik/ *adj* relating to something, especially a language, as it exists at a certain point in time and not historically. ◊ **diachronic** [Mid-19C. < late Latin *synchronus* (see SYNCHRONOUS).] —**synchronically** *adv*

synchronicity /síngkrə níssəti/ *n* **1** the coincidence of events that seem related but are not obviously caused one by the other **2** = **synchronism** *n*. **1**

synchronise *vti* = **synchronize**

synchronism /síngkrənizəm/ *n* **1** the simultaneous occurrence of two or more things **2** an arrangement in chronological order showing historical events that happened or people who were alive around the same time [Late 16C. < Greek *sugkhronismos* < *sugkhronos* (see SYNCHRONOUS).] —**synchronistic** /síngkrə nístik/ *adj* —**synchronistically** *adv*

synchronize /síngkrə nīz/ (**-nizes, -nizing, -nized**), **synchronise** (**-nises, -nising, -nised**) *v* **1** *vi* **HAPPEN TOGETHER** to happen at the same time **2** *vi* **GO TOGETHER** to go or work together or in unison **3** *vt* **MAKE THINGS WORK AT SAME TIME** to make something work at the same time or the same rate as something else **4** *vt* **ALIGN SOUND AND IMAGE OF FILM** to make the soundtrack of a film match up with the action **5** *vt* **REPRESENT CONTEMPORARY HISTORICAL EVENTS AND PEOPLE** to represent historical events or people in an arrangement that shows which of them happened or lived around the same time [Early 17C. < SYNCHRONISM.] —**synchronization** /síngkrə nī záysh'n/ *n*

synchronized swimming *n* a sport in which swimmers perform coordinated movements in time to music in the manner of a dance

synchronous /síngkrənəss/ *adj* **1 OCCURRING SIMULTANEOUSLY** happening at the same time **2 WORKING AT SAME RATE** working or moving at the same rate **3 WITH SAME PERIOD AND PHASE** with the same period and phase of oscillation or cyclical movement [Mid-17C. < late Latin *synchronus* < Greek *sugkhronos* < *khronos* 'time'.] —**synchronously** *adv* —**synchronousness** *n*

synchronous motor *n* an electric motor that operates at a speed directly proportional to the frequency of the applied voltage source

synchronous orbit *n* an orbit that keeps time with the rotation of the orbited object, so that the orbiting body is always directly over the same point on the surface of the orbiting body

synchrony /síngkrəni/ (*plural* **-nies**) *n* occurrence at the same time or movement at the same rate, or an example of this phenomenon

synchroscope /síngkrə skōp/, **synchronoscope** /síng krónnə skōp/ *n* **1** an instrument used to find whether or not two things such as moving machine parts are synchronous **2** an instrument used to indicate the difference in frequency between two alternating current supplies

synchrotron /síngkrə tron/ *n* a very high-energy circular particle accelerator that operates by using a high-frequency electric field and a magnetic field in synchrony with the movement of the particles

synchrotron radiation *n* the electromagnetic radiation emitted by charged particles, usually electrons, moving in curved paths in a magnetic field at speeds approaching that of light

syncline /síng klīn/ *n* a fold in a rock formation that is shaped like a basin or trough and contains younger rocks in its core —**synclinal** /sing klīn'l/ *adj*

syncopate /síngkə payt/ (**-pates, -pating, -pated**) *vt* **1** to modify a musical rhythm by shifting the accent to a weak beat of the bar **2** to shorten a word by the loss of one or more sounds or letters from the middle —**syncopator** *n*

syncopation /síngkə páysh'n/ *n* **1** a rhythmic technique in music in which the accent is shifted to a weak beat of the bar **2** PHON = **syncope** *n*. **2**

syncope /síngkəpi/ *n* **1** a loss of consciousness due to lack of oxygen to the brain (*technical*) **2** the shortening of a word by the loss of sounds or letters from its middle [Mid-16C. Via late Latin < Greek *sugkopē* < *sugkoptein* 'cut short' < *koptein* 'cut'.] —**syncopal** *adj* —**syncopic** /sing kóppik/ *adj*

syncretise *vti* = **syncretize**

syncretism /síngkrətizəm/ *n* **1** the attempted combination of different systems of philosophical or religious belief or practice **2** the use of a single inflectional form of a word to cover functions previously covered by two separate forms, e.g. 'spun' in English, now used for both the past tense and the past participle although the past tense used to be 'span' [Early 17C. Via modern Latin *syncretismus* < Greek *sugkrētismos* 'union' < *sugkrētizein* (see SYNCRETIZE).] —**syncretic** /sing kréttik/ *adj*—**syncretist** *n* —**syncretistic** /singkrə tístik/ *adj*

syncretize /síngkrə tīz/ (**-tizes, -tizing, -tized**), **syncretise** (**-cretises, -cretising, -cretised**) *vti* to combine, or try to combine, elements from different systems of philosophical or religious belief or practice [Late 17C. < Greek *sugkrētizein* 'unite (against a common enemy)' < ?] —**syncretization** /síngkrə tī záysh'n/ *n*

~~**syncronous**~~ incorrect spelling of **synchronous**

syncytium /sin sítti əm/ (*plural* **-a** /-tti ə/) *n* a mass of cytoplasm within a cell membrane that contains multiple nuclei and is often the result of cellular fusion, e.g. in some slime moulds [Late 19C. < Greek *kutos* (see -CYTE).] —**syncytial** /-sítti əl/ *adj*

synd /sīnd/, **syne** /sīn/ *vt* (**synes, syning, syned**) *Scotland* to rinse something, usually with water ■ *n Scotland* an act of rinsing something [14C. < ?]

syndactyl /sin dáktil/ *adj* having two or more fingers or toes joined together. This may be a natural condition, as in some animals, or a congenital abnormality, as in people with webbed toes. —**syndactyl** *n* —**syndactylism** *n* —**syndactyly** *n*

syndesis /sin deéssiss/ *n* the use in grammar of constructions in which clauses are joined by conjunctions [Early 20C. < German, < Greek *desis* 'binding' < *dein* (see SYNDETIC).]

syndesmosis /sín dess mṓssiss/ (*plural* **-ses** /-seez/) *n* an immovable joint in which the bones are held firmly by fibrous tissue but are not very close together, e.g. at the lower ends of the tibia and fibula [Late 16C. < Greek *sundesmos* 'ligament' < *sundein* (see SYNDETIC).] —**syndesmotic** /-móttik/ *adj*

syndetic /sin déttik/ *adj* describes a construction in grammar in which two clauses are joined by a conjunction [Early 17C. < Greek *sundetikos* < *sundein* 'bind together' < *dein* 'bind'.] —**syndetically** *adv*

syndeton /sində toón, síndətən/ *n* a grammatical construction in which two clauses are joined by a conjunction [Mid-20C. Back-formation < ASYNDETON and POLYSYNDETON.]

syndic /síndik/ *n* **1** somebody appointed to represent an organization, e.g. a corporation or a university, in business transactions **2** a government official, especially a civil magistrate, in some European countries [Early 17C. Via French, 'delegate' < Greek *sundikos* 'defendant's advocate' < *dikē* 'judgment'.] —**syndical** *adj* —**syndicship** *n*

syndicalism /síndikəlizəm/ *n* **1** a revolutionary political doctrine that advocates the seizure of the means of production by workers organized in trade unions **2** a system of government in which workers organized in unions control the means of production [Early 20C. Via French *syndicalisme* < *syndic* (see SYNDIC).] —**syndical** *adj*—**syndicalist** *adj, n* —**syndicalistic** /síndikə lístik/ *adj*

syndicate *n* /síndi kət/ **1 GROUP OF BUSINESSES** an association of businesses jointly contributing capital to a major project **2 BUSINESS THAT SELLS NEWS MATERIALS** a business or agency that sells news stories or photographs to the media **3 GROUP OF NEWSPAPERS UNDER SAME OWNER** a group of newspapers that have the same owner **4 GROUP OF PEOPLE** a group of people who combine to carry out a business, enterprise, or some other common purpose **5 ASSOCIATION OF GANGSTERS** an association of gangsters that controls a particular area of organized crime **6 COUNCIL OR JURISDICTION OF CIVIL MAGISTRATE** a council or body of syndics, or the office or jurisdiction of a government official, especially a civil magistrate, in some European countries ■ *v* /síndi kayt/ (**-cates, -cating, -cated**) **1** *vt* **SELL SOMETHING FOR MULTIPLE PUBLICATION** to sell something, e.g. an article or a cartoon strip, for publication in a number of newspapers or magazines simultaneously **2** *vt US* **SELL TV PROGRAMMES TO INDEPENDENT STATIONS** to sell television or radio programmes directly to independent stations **3** *vt* **CONTROL SOMETHING AS SYNDICATE** to control or manage something as a syndicate **4** *vi* **COME TOGETHER AS SYNDICATE** to come together to form a syndicate

syndrome /síndrōm/ *n* **1** a group of signs and symptoms that together are characteristic or indicative of a specific disease or other disorder **2** a group of things or events that form a recognizable pattern, especially of something undesirable [Mid-16C. Via modern Latin and Greek *sundromē* 'running together' < *dramein* 'run'.]

syne[1] /sīn/ *adv Scotland* **AGO** since then ■ *prep Scotland* **SINCE** from a particular time onward ■ *conj Scotland* **FROM WHEN** from the time that [14C. Contraction of *sithen* (see SINCE).]

syne[2] *vt, n* = **synd**

synecdoche /si nékdəki/ *n* a figure of speech in which the word for part of something is used to mean the whole, e.g. 'sail' for 'boat', or vice versa [14C. Via Latin < Greek *sunekdokhē* < *sunekdekhesthai* 'take on a share of' < *ekdekhesthai* 'take'.] —**synecdochic** /sínnek dókik/ *adj*—**synecdochical** *adj*

synecology /sínni kólləji/ *n* a branch of ecology dealing with the structure and development of entire ecological communities and the interrelationships of the plants and animals within them —**synecologic** /sínnikə lójjik/ *adj* —**synecological** *adj* —**synecologically** *adv*

synectics /si néktiks/ *n* an approach to solving problems based on the creative thinking of a group of people from different areas of experience and knowledge (+ *singular verb*) [Mid-20C. < late Latin *synecticus* 'producing an effect immediately', via Greek *sunektikos* < *ekhein* 'hold'.]

syneresis /si neérəssiss/, **synaeresis** *n* **1 LIQUID SEPARATION IN GEL** the process by which a liquid is separated from a gel **2 MERGING OF VOWELS INTO DIPHTHONG** the merging of two vowels into a diphthong **3 MERGING OF VOWELS INTO ONE SYLLABLE** the merging of two vowels into one syllable without making it into a diphthong [Late 16C. Via late Latin and Greek *sunairesis* 'contraction' < *hairein* 'take'.]

synergism /sínnərjizəm/ *n* **1** = **synergy 2** the doctrine in Christian theology that the human will and the Holy Spirit work together to bring about spiritual regeneration or salvation [Mid-18C. See SYNERGY.] —**synergistic** /sínnər jístik/ *adj* —**synergistically** *adv*

synergist /sínnərjist/ *n* something that works in combination with something else to increase its effect, e.g. a drug that increases the effect of another drug

synergy /sínnərji/ (*plural* **-gies**) *n* **1** the working together of two or more things, people, or organizations, especially when the result is greater than the sum of their individual effects or capabilities **2** the phenomenon in which the combined action of two things, e.g. drugs or muscles, is greater than the sum of their effects individually [Mid-17C. Via Latin < Greek *sunergia* < *sunergein* 'work together' < *ergos* 'work'.] —**synergetic** /sínnər jéttik/ *adj* —**synergetically** *adv* —**synergic** /si núrjik/ *adj*

synesis /sínnəssiss/ *n* grammatical agreement according to meaning rather than strict syntax, e.g. the use of a plural form of a verb or a plural pronoun with a collective noun [Late 19C. Via modern Latin < Greek *sunesis* 'union' < *sunienai* 'bring together' < *hienai* 'send'.]

synesthesia *n* = **synaesthesia**

synfuel /sín fyoo əl/ *n* a liquid fuel synthesized from a nonpetroleum source such as coal, oil shale, or waste plastics, and used as a substitute for a petroleum product [Late 20C. Blend of SYNTHETIC + FUEL.]

syngamy /síng gəmi/ *n* sexual reproduction through the fusion of gametes [Early 20C. < SYN- + Greek *gamos* 'marriage'.] —**syngamic** /sing gámmik/ *adj* —**syngamous** /síng gəməss/ *adj*

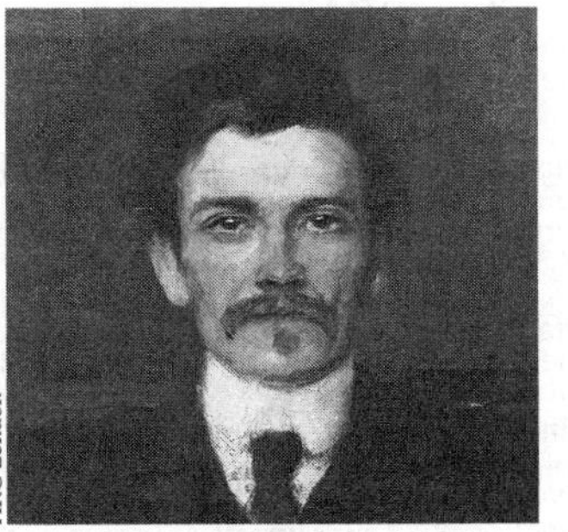

AKG London

J. M. Synge: Portrait by John B. Yeats

Synge /sing/, **J. M.** (1871–1909) Irish dramatist. Full name **John Millington Synge**

syngeneic /sínji neé ik, -náyik/ *adj* having an identical or closely similar genetic make-up, especially one that will allow the transplantation of tissue without provoking an immune response [Mid-20C. < Greek *sungeneia* 'kinship' < *genos* 'kind'.] —**syngeneically** *adv*

syngenesis /sin jénnəssiss/ *n* reproduction involving fusion of male and female genetic material —**syngenetic** /sínjə néttik/ *adj*

synkaryon /sin kárri on/ *n* a cell nucleus formed through the fusion of male and female nuclei [Early 20C. < Greek *karuon* 'seed'.] —**synkaryonic** /sín kari ónnik/ *adj*

synkinesis /sínki neéssiss, -kī-/, **synkinesia** /sínki neézi ə, -kī-/ *n* the performing of an unintended movement when making a voluntary one —**synkinetic** /-néttik/ *adj*

synod /sínnəd/ *n* **1 CHURCH COUNCIL** a special council of church members that holds regular meetings to discuss religious issues **2 PRESBYTERIAN CHURCH COURT** a Presbyterian church court between the Presbytery and the General Assembly **3 ASSEMBLY OR COUNCIL** an assembly or council held for the discussion of issues (*formal*) [14C. Via late Latin < Greek *sunodos* 'meeting' < *hodos* 'way'.] —**synodal** *adj*

synodic /si nóddik/, **synodical** /-ik'l/ *adj* **1** relating to the alignment of astronomical objects, or the interval between occasions when the same astronomical objects are aligned **2** relating to or having the character of a church synod —**synodically** *adv*

synodic month *n* ASTRON = **lunar month**

synoecious /si neéshəss/ *adj* with male and female organs on the same flower or other structure [Mid-19C. < Greek *oikos* 'house'.]

~~**synonim**~~ incorrect spelling of **synonym**

synonym /sínnənim/ *n* **1 WORD MEANING SAME AS ANOTHER** a word that means the same, or almost the same, as another word in the same language, either in all of its uses or in a particular context **2 ALTERNATIVE NAME** a word or expression that is used as another name for something in certain styles of speaking or writing or to emphasize a particular aspect or association **3 REJECTED DUPLICATE TAXONOMIC NAME** a duplicate taxonomic name that has been rejected or replaced [15C. Via Latin *synonymum* < Greek *sunōnumos* 'synonymous' < *onuma* 'name'.] —**synonymic** /sínnə nímmik/ *adj* —**synonymity** /-nímməti/ *n*

synonymize /si nónni mīz/ (**-mizes, -mizing, -mized**), **synonymise** (**-mises, -mising, -mised**) *vt* to provide an analysis or listing of the synonyms of a word or expression

synonymous /si nónniməss/ *adj* **1** meaning the same, or almost the same, as another word in the same language, or being an alternative name for somebody or something **2** having an implication similar to the idea expressed by another word ○ *Andy Warhol is synonymous with pop art.* —**synonymously** *adv* —**synonymousness** *n*

synonymy /si nónnimi/ (*plural* **-mies**) *n* **1 EQUIVALENCE OF MEANING** the state or quality of being synonymous **2 STUDY OF SYNONYMS** the study, classification, and distinguishing of synonyms **3 ANNOTATED LIST OF SYNONYMS** a list or book of synonyms, with emphasis on the discrimination of meanings

synopsis /si nópsiss/ (*plural* **-ses** /-seez/) *n* **1** a condensed version of a text, e.g. a summary of the plot of a book, film, or television programme **2** a concise outline or survey of a subject [Early 17C. Via late Latin < Greek *sunopsis* 'general view' < *opsis* 'view'.]

synopsize /si nóp sīz/ (**-sizes, -sizing, -sized**), **synopsise** (**-sises, -sising, -sised**) *vt* to summarize or make a synopsis of something

synoptic /si nóptik/ *adj* **1 PERTAINING TO SYNOPSIS** constituting a general view of the whole of a subject **2 DISPLAYING WIDESPREAD WEATHER** pertaining to or showing simultaneous weather conditions over a large area **3 Synoptic, synoptic SHARING VIEWS OF JESUS CHRIST'S LIFE** describes the gospels of Matthew, Mark, and Luke that tell the story of Jesus Christ's life and ministry from a similar point of view and are similar in structure ■ *n* **1 Synoptic, synoptic SYNOPTIC GOSPEL** any one of the Synoptic gospels of Matthew, Mark, or Luke **2 Synoptic** = **synoptist** [Early 17C. Via modern Latin < Greek *sunoptikos* < *sunopsis* (see SYNOPSIS).] —**synoptical** *adj* —**synoptically** *adv*

synoptist /si nóptist/, **synoptic** *n* an author of one of the Synoptic gospels

synostosis /sín o stṓssiss/ (*plural* **-ses** /-seez/) *n* the formation of a single bone from the fusion of two adjacent bones —**synostotic** /-stóttik/ *adj*

synovia /sī nṓvi ə/ *n* a clear viscous fluid that lubricates the linings of joints and the sheaths of tendons [Mid-17C. < modern Latin *sinovia* < ?]

synovial fluid *n* ANAT = **synovia**

synovitis /sīnō vītiss/ *n* inflammation of the sinovial membrane of a joint —**synovitic** /-vittik/ *adj*

syntactic /sin táktik/, **syntactical** /-ik'l/ *adj* **1** relating to the rules or patterns of syntax **2** correctly formed according to the rules or accepted structures of syntax [Early 19C. Via Latin < Greek *suntaktikos* < *suntassein* (see SYNTAX).] —**syntactically** *adv*

syntagma /sin tágmə/ (*plural* **-mata** /-tágmətə/ *or* **-mas**), **syntagm** /sín tam/ *n* a linguistic unit made up of sets of phonemes, words, or phrases that are arranged sequentially [Mid-17C. Via late Latin < Greek *suntagma* < *suntassein* (see SYNTAX).]

syntagmatic /sín tag máttik/, **syntagmic** /sin tágmik/ *adj* relating to syntactic units, or the function and behaviour of a word or phrase within a syntactic unit

ϟ **syntax** /sín taks/ *n* **1 ORGANIZATION OF WORDS IN SENTENCES** the ordering of and relationship between the words and other structural elements in phrases and sentences **2 BRANCH OF GRAMMAR** the branch of grammar that studies syntax **3 RULES OF SYNTAX** an exposition of or set of rules for producing grammatical structures according to the syntax of a language **4 RULES FOR DERIVING LOGICAL FORMULAS** the part of logic that gives the rules that define which combinations of expressions in the logical system yield well-formed formulas **5 RULES GOVERNING PROGRAM STRUCTURE** the rules governing which statements and combinations of statements in a programming language will be acceptable to a compiler for that language **6 RULE-BASED ARRANGEMENT** the arrangement of any group of elements in a systematic or rule-based manner [Late 16C. Via French or late Latin < Greek *suntaxis* < *suntassein* 'put in order' < *tassein* 'arrange'.]

synth /sinth/ *n* a synthesizer (*informal*)

synthesis /sínthəssiss/ (*plural* **-ses** /-seez/) *n* **1 RESULT OF COMBINING DIFFERENT ELEMENTS** a new unified whole resulting from the combination of different ideas, influences, or objects **2 COMBINING OF DIFFERENT ELEMENTS INTO WHOLE** the process of combining different ideas, influences, or objects into a new whole (*formal*) **3 FORMATION OF CHEMICAL COMPOUNDS** the formation of compounds through one or more chemical reactions involving simpler substances **4 PRODUCING OF SOUND WITH SYNTHESIZER** the production of music or speech using an electronic synthesizer **5 USE OF INFLECTIONS** the expression of syntactic relationships by means of inflections rather than word order or prepositions and other function words **6 IDEA RESOLVING CONTRADICTIONS** in Hegelian philosophy, the new idea that resolves the conflict between the initial proposition (**thesis**) and its negation (**antithesis**) **7 DEDUCTIVE REASONING** the process of deductive reasoning from first principles to a conclusion [15C. Via Latin, 'collection' < Greek *sunthesis* < *suntithenai* 'put together' < *tithenai* 'put'.] —**synthesist** *n*

synthesise *vti* = **synthesize**

synthesiser *n* = **synthesizer**

synthesis gas *n* a mixture of carbon monoxide and hydrogen derived from the breakdown of carbon- and hydrogen-containing materials. Use: manufacture of ammonia, other chemicals.

synthesize /sínthə sīz/ (**-sizes, -sizing, -sized**), **synthesise** (**-sises, -sising, -sised**), **synthetize** /sínthə tīz/ (**-tizes, -tizing, -tized**), **synthetise** (**-tises, -tising, -tised**) *v* **1** *vti* to combine different ideas, influences, or objects into a new whole, or be combined in this way **2** *vt* to produce a substance or material by chemical or biological synthesis —**synthesization** /sínthə sī záysh'n/ *n*

synthesizer /sínthə sīzər/, **synthesiser** *n* **1 ELECTRONIC MUSICAL INSTRUMENT** a device that generates and modifies sounds electronically, often a musical instrument **2 MANUFACTURER OF SYNTHETIC SUBSTANCES** somebody or something involved in the synthesis of substances or materials **3 SOMEBODY WHO COMBINES DIFFERENT ELEMENTS** a combiner of ideas, influences, or objects into a new whole

synthetic /sin théttik/ *adj* **1 MADE BY A CHEMICAL PROCESS** made artificially by chemical synthesis, especially so as to resemble a natural product **2 INSINCERE** not genuine, especially expressed but not genuinely felt ○ *synthetic expressions of sympathy* **3 WITH TRUTH DEPENDING ON FACTS** describes a proposition whose truth or falsity is a matter of facts and not merely a matter of the meaning of the words in the sentence **4 USING INFLECTIONS TO EXPRESS SYNTAX** describes a language that expresses syntactic relationships by means of inflections rather than word order or prepositions and other function words ■ *n* **CHEMICALLY PRODUCED SUBSTANCE OR MATERIAL** a substance or material produced by chemical processes rather than occurring naturally [Late 17C. Via French or modern Latin < Greek *sunthetikos* 'component' < *sunthetos* 'combined' < *suntithenai* (see SYNTHESIS).] —**synthetical** *adj* —**synthetically** *adv*

synthetic resin *n* a resin produced by polymerization of simple molecules rather than obtained directly from plant substances

synthetic rubber *n* a compound synthesized from unsaturated hydrocarbons that resembles rubber

synthetize /sínthə tīz/, **synthetise** *vti* = **synthesize** —**synthetization** /sínthə tī záysh'n/ *n*

syntonic /sin tónnik/ *adj* **1** describes somebody who is normally attuned to the environment **2** in ego psychology, used to describe behaviour that does not conflict with somebody's basic attitudes and beliefs and, therefore, is not anxiety-provoking (*in combination*) ○ *ego-syntonic* [Late 19C. < Greek *suntonos* 'attuned' < *suntenein* 'draw tight'.] —**syntonically** *adv*

syphilis /síffəliss/ *n* a serious sexually transmitted disease caused by the spirally twisted bacterium *Treponema pallidum* that affects many body organs and parts, including the genitals, brain, skin, and nervous tissue [Early 18C. < modern Latin, after the person allegedly first affected (according to Girolamo Fracastoro (1483–1553), Veronese physician).] —**syphiloid** *adj*

syphilitic /síffə líttik/ *adj* relating to, caused by, or affected by syphilis ■ *n* an offensive term for somebody who has been infected with the spirochaete that causes syphilis [Late 18C. < modern Latin *syphiliticus* < SYPHILIS.] —**syphilitically** *adv*

syphiloma /síffə lṓmə/ (*plural* **-mata** /-mətə/ *or* **-mas**) *n* MED = **gumma**

syphon *n*, *vt* = **siphon**

Syracuse /sírrə kyooz/ capital of Syracuse Province, SE Sicily, Italy. Population: 126,800 (1992).

syrah /sírrə/ *n* **1** a black grape grown mainly in the Rhône valley of France but also in California and Australia, and used to make wine **2** a typically strong full-bodied wine made from the syrah grape variety [Early 19C. Alteration of SHIRAZ.]

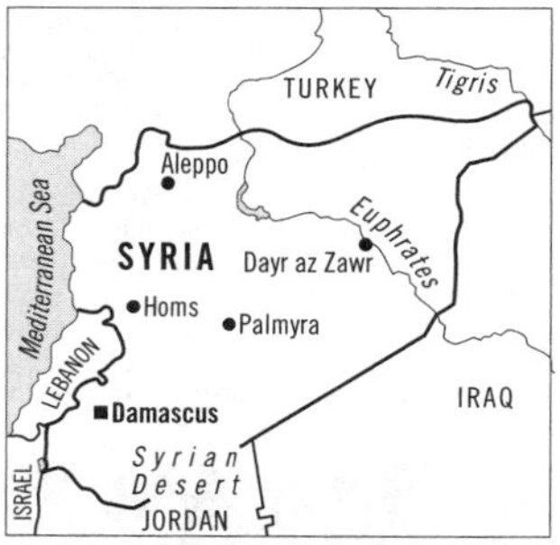

Syria

Syria /sírri ə/ republic in the Middle East, bordered by Turkey, Iraq, Jordan, Israel, Lebanon, and the Mediterranean Sea. Capital: Damascus. Population: 14,798,000 (1996). Area: 185,050 sq. km/71,498 sq. mi. —**Syrian** *n*, *adj*

Syriac /sírri ak/ *n* a form of Aramaic used in the 3rd to 13th centuries that survives in some Eastern Orthodox churches —**Syriac** *adj*

syringa /si ríng gə/ *n* **1** TREES = **mock orange** *n*. 1 **2** a lilac flower or shrub. Genus: *Syringa*. [Mid-17C. Modern Latin, < Greek *surigx* 'panpipe'.]

syringe /si rínj/ *n* **1 INSTRUMENT FOR WITHDRAWING AND EJECTING FLUIDS** an instrument consisting of a piston in a small tube, used in conjunction with a hollow needle or tube for the withdrawal and ejection of fluids and for cleaning wounds. ◊ **hypodermic syringe 2 DEVICE FOR PUMPING AND SPRAYING LIQUIDS** a device similar to a medical syringe that is used for spraying or extracting fluids by means of pressure or suction ■ *vt* (**-ringes, -ringing, -ringed**) **USE SYRINGE ON** to clean, spray, or inject something using a syringe [15C. Via medieval Latin *syringa* < Greek *surigx* 'panpipe'.]

syringes plural of **syrinx**

syringomyelia /si ríng gō mī éeli ə/ *n* a chronic progressive disease of the spinal cord in which tubular fluid-filled cavities form in the nerve tissue, causing sensory disturbances and, eventually, loss of voluntary movement [Late 19C. < SYRINGE + MYEL- + -IA.]—**syringomyelic** *adj*

syrinx /sírringks/ (*plural* **syrinxes** *or* **syringes** /si rín jeez/) *n* **1 PANPIPES** a set of panpipes **2 VOCAL ORGAN OF BIRDS** the vocal organ of a bird, usually situated near the junction between the trachea and bronchi **3 CORRIDOR IN EGYPTIAN TOMB** a narrow corridor or gallery in an ancient Egyptian tomb **4 CAVITY IN SPINAL CORD** one of the tubular fluid-filled cavities formed in the nerve tissue of the spinal cord in cases of syringomyelia [Early 17C. Via Latin < Greek *surigx* (see SYRINGE).] —**syringeal** /si rínji əl/ *adj*

syrphid /súrfid/ *n* a dipteran fly that hovers and darts, feeds on nectar and pollen, and has coloration mimicking that of a bee or wasp. Family: Syrphidae. [Late 19C. < modern Latin *Syrphidae* < *Syrphus*, via modern Latin < Greek *surphos* 'gnat'.] —**syrphid** *adj*

Syrtis Major /súrtiss-/ wedge-shaped dark area on the surface of Mars in the equatorial region

syrup /sírrəp/ *n* **1 SWEET LIQUID** a liquid made of sugar dissolved in water by heating, widely used in sweet cookery **2 FLAVOURED SWEET LIQUID** a flavoured thick sweet liquid **3 PHARMACEUTICAL LIQUID** a thick sweet liquid used to convey oral medicines **4 GOLDEN SYRUP** golden syrup **5 SENTIMENTALITY** excessive sentimentality (*informal*) [14C. Via French *sirop* or medieval Latin *siropus* < Arabic *šarāb* 'drink'.]

syrupy /sírrəpi/ (**-ier, -iest**) *adj* **1** resembling syrup in taste, quality, or consistency **2** excessively sentimental in a cloying saccharine fashion

ϟ **SYS** *abbr* see you soon (*in e-mails*)

ϟ **sysop** /sís sop/ *n* a system operator, usually one who runs a bulletin board (*informal*) [Late 20C. Contraction.]

systaltic /si stáltik/ *adj* describes an organ such as the heart that undergoes alternating rhythmic contraction and dilation [Late 17C. Via late Latin < Greek *sustaltikos* < *sustellein* (see SYSTOLE).]

ϟ **system** /sístəm/ *n* **1 COMPLEX BODY** a combination of related elements organized into a complex whole ○ *a social system* **2 SET OF PRINCIPLES** a scheme of ideas or principles, e.g. for classification or for forms of government or religion **3 WAY OF PROCEEDING** a method or set of procedures for achieving something **4 TRANSPORT NETWORK** a physical network of roads, railways, and other routes for travel, transport, or communication **5 GROUP OF RELATED BODY PARTS** a set of organs or structures in the body that have a common function ○ *the nervous system* **6 WHOLE BODY** the human or animal body as a unit ○ *My grandmother used to insist that liquorice was good for the system.* **7 ASSEMBLY OF COMPONENTS** an assembly of mechanical or electronic components that function together as a unit **8 SET OF COMPUTER COMPONENTS** an assembly of computer hardware, software, and peripherals functioning together ○ *A turnkey system has all the hardware and software installed and is ready to run.* **9 ORDERLINESS** the use or result of careful planning and organization of elements **10 GROUP OF ASTRONOMICAL OBJECTS** a group of astronomical objects or other gravitationally linked objects **11 MINERAL CLASSIFICATION** any of various divisions used to classify minerals according to their crystal structures **12 STRATIGRAPHIC UNIT OF ROCK** a stratigraphic division of rocks larger than a series but smaller than a stage, used to distinguish formations of a specific era or period **13 ASSEMBLY OF SUBSTANCES IN EQUILIBRIUM** an assembly of substances in chemical or physical equilibrium **14 GROUP OF MUSICAL STAVES** a number of musical staves that are grouped together by a line or brace in a score and are played simultaneously **15 system, System THE WAY THINGS ARE** the established order, especially regarded as thwarting the individual [Early 17C. Via French or late Latin < Greek *sustēma* < *sunistanai* 'combine' < *histanai* 'set up'.] —**systemless** *adj* ◇ **all systems go** used to indicate that everything is functioning and an operation or activity can start

systematic /sístə máttik/, **systematical** /-k'l/ *adj* **1 DONE METHODICALLY** carried out in a methodical and organized manner **2 WELL ORGANIZED** habitually using a method or system for organization **3 METHODICAL** deliberate and regular in a methodical manner **4 BASED ON SYSTEM** constituting, based on, or resembling a system **5 PERTAINING TO TAXONOMIC CLASSIFICATION** in accordance with a system of taxonomic classification (**systematics**) [Mid-17C. Via late Latin < Greek *sustēmatikos* < *sustēma* (see SYSTEM).] —**systematically** *adv*

systematic desensitization *n* a therapy for phobias and other anxiety disorders in which patients are gradually given longer and longer exposures to the object of their fears

systematics /sístə máttiks/ *n* the study of systems and classification, especially the science of classifying organisms (*takes a singular verb*)

systematise *vt* = **systematize**

systematism /sístəmətizəm/ *n* **1** the practice of classifying information in a systematic manner **2** adherence to a system

systematist /sístəmətist/ *n* **1** SOMEBODY WHO CONSTRUCTS SYSTEMS somebody engaged in constructing a system or systems **2** SOMEBODY WHO CLASSIFIES ORGANISMS somebody engaged in classifying organisms according to a taxonomic system **3** SOMEBODY ADHERING TO SYSTEM a conformer to a method or system

systematize /sístəmə tīz/ (**-tizes, -tizing, -tized**), **systematise** (**-tises, -tising, -tised**), **systemize** (**-izes, -izing, -ized**) *vti* to arrange something, or be arranged, according to a system [Mid-18C. < the Greek stem *sustēmat-* (see SYSTEM).] —**systematization** /sístəmə tī záysh'n/ *n* —**systematizer** *n*

system building *n* building with prefabricated components —**system-built** *adj*

systemic /si stémmik, si steémmik/ *adj* **1** OF A SYSTEM affecting or relating to a system as a whole **2** AFFECTING WHOLE BODY affecting the whole body as distinct from having a local effect ○ *a systemic infection* **3** AFFECTING WHOLE PLANT describes an herbicide or other chemical that works by spreading through all the tissues of a plant rather than just staying on the surface ■ *n* SYSTEMIC CHEMICAL a systemic herbicide, pesticide, or other chemical —**systemically** *adv*

systemic circulation *n* the main part of the blood circulation as distinct from the pulmonary circulation

systemize /sísta mīz/ *vt* = **systematize** —**systemization** /sísta mī záysh'n/ *n* —**systemizer** *n*

⚡**system operator** *n* a manager or maintainer of an online bulletin board or a computer network

⚡**systems analysis** *n* the determination of the data-processing requirements of a company, project, procedure, or task, and the designing of computer systems to fulfil them —**systems analyst** *n*

systems engineering *n* the design and implementation of production systems that require the integration of diverse and complex tasks, e.g. motor car assembly lines —**systems engineer** *n*

⚡**system software** *n* the operating system and utility programs used to operate and maintain a computer system and provide resources for application programs such as word processors and spreadsheets

systole /sístəli/ *n* the contraction of the heart, during which blood is pumped into the arteries [Mid-16C. Via late Latin < Greek *sustolē* < *sustellein* 'contract' < *stellein* 'put'.] —**systolic** /si stóllik/ *adj*

syzygy /sízzəji/ (*plural* **-gies**) *n* **1** CONJUNCTION OF THREE ASTRONOMICAL OBJECTS the straight-line conjunction or opposition of three astronomical objects, e.g. the Sun, Earth, and Moon **2** TWO CONNECTED THINGS a pair of related things that are either similar or opposite (*formal*) **3** TWO METRICAL FEET a metrical unit of two feet in classical Greek and Latin verse [Early 17C. Via late Latin < Greek *suzugia* < *suzugos* 'paired' < *zugon* 'yoke'.] —**syzygetic** /sízzə jéttik/ *adj* —**syzygetically** *adv* —**syzygial** /si zíjji əl/ *adj*

⚡**SZ** *abbr* Swaziland (*in Internet addresses*)

Szczecin /shtét shin/ capital of Szczecin Province, NW Poland. Population: 419,300 (1995).

Szechuan pepper /séch waan-/, **Szechwan pepper** *n* a pepper with a hot aniseed flavour, one of the spices used in Chinese five spice powder [Mid-20C. After Szechuan (now Sichuan).]

Szechwan /séch waan/ = **Sichuan**

Szeged /ségged/ port in SE Hungary, on the River Tisza. Population: 178,878 (1994).

Szell /sel/, **George** (1897–1970) Hungarian-born US conductor

t¹ /tee/ (plural **t's**), **T** (plural **T's** or **Ts**) n the 20th letter of the English alphabet, representing a consonant sound

t² symbol **1** Student's t distribution **2** time **3** troy

t³ abbr **1** tare **2** teaspoon **3** teaspoonful **4** tempo **5** tenor **6** tense **7** ton **8** tons **9** transitive

T¹ /tee/ (plural **T's** or **Ts**) n something shaped like a letter 'T' ◇ **to a T** exactly

T² symbol **1** absolute temperature **2** kinetic energy **3** period **4** surface tension **5** temperature **6** tesla **7** tritium

T³ abbr **1** tablespoon **2** tablespoonful **3** tera- **4** Tuesday

⚡T1 line, T-1 line n a dedicated telephone line for high-speed digital access to the Internet, handling 24 voice or data channels simultaneously

ta /taa/ interj thank you (informal) [Late 18C. Baby-talk alteration of thank you.]

Ta symbol tantalum

⚡TA abbr **1** Territorial Army **2** thanks again (in e-mails) **3** transactional analysis **4** Transit Authority

tab¹ /tab/ n **1 FLAP FOR HOLDING** a small strip, loop, or other attachment to something, used for lifting, moving, hanging, opening, or closing **2 FLAP ON GARMENT** a small strip or square of fabric attached to a garment for decoration **3 TAG OR LABEL** a small piece of paper, cloth, or plastic attached to something and containing information about the object **4 AUXILIARY AEROFOIL** a small auxiliary aerofoil on a control surface such as an aileron or rudder, used as a stabilizer **5 STAFF OFFICER'S INSIGNIA** the insignia on a staff officer's collar **6** BEVERAGES = **ring-pull 7 RESTAURANT BILL** the bill for a meal or drinks in a restaurant or bar (informal) ■ vt (**tabs, tabbing, tabbed**) **ATTACH TAB TO** to attach a tab to something [Early 17C. < ?] ◇ **keep tabs on somebody** or **something** to watch somebody or something closely (informal) ◇ **pick up the tab** to pay the bill (informal)

tab² /tab/ n a key on a computer keyboard, or a device or key on a typewriter, that advances the next character to a predetermined position, used to align lines or columns [Early 20C. Shortening of TABULATOR.]

tab³ /tab/ n a tablet or piece of paper containing a drug, especially one that is illegal [Mid-20C. Shortening of TABLET.]

tab⁴ /tab/ n THEATRE = **tableau curtain** [Early 20C. Shortening.]

TAB abbr typhoid-paratyphoid A-paratyphoid B (vaccine) ■ n ANZ in New Zealand, the state-run agency that runs legal betting on horseracing, greyhound-racing, and other sporting events, or a branch of this. Full form **Totalizator Agency Board**

tabanid /tábbənid/ n a stout-bodied bloodsucking fly such as a horsefly. Family: Tabanidae. [Late 19C. < Latin tabanus 'horsefly'.]

tabard /tábbaard/ n **1 SLEEVELESS OVERGARMENT** a sleeveless tunic with slits at the sides, worn by women and girls **2 HERALD'S COAT** an official coat worn by a herald, bearing the sovereign's coat of arms **3 KNIGHT'S JACKET** a sleeveless or short-sleeved garment worn by a knight over his armour [13C. < Old French tabart.]

tabaret /tábbərit/ n a hard-wearing fabric with alternate satin and watered-silk stripes. Use: upholstery. [Late 18C. Probably < TABBY.]

Tabasco /tə báskō/ tdmk a trademark for a hot-tasting sauce made from peppers, vinegar, and spices

tabbouleh /tə boò lay/ n a Middle Eastern salad made with bulgur wheat and finely chopped tomatoes, mint, and parsley [Mid-20C. < Arabic tabbūla.]

tabby /tábbi/ n (plural **-bies**) **1 STRIPED CAT** a brown or grey cat with a striped or mottled coat **2 PET FEMALE CAT** a domestic cat, especially a female one **3 GOSSIP** a woman who is thought to be gossipy, spiteful, and interfering (literary insult) **4 SILK WITH STRIPED PATTERN** watered silk or taffeta with a striped or wavy pattern **5 PLAIN WEAVE FABRIC** a plain-woven fabric ■ adj **1 HAVING STRIPED COAT** describes a cat having a brown or grey coat with a striped or mottled pattern **2 STRIPED OR BRINDLED** having a striped or wavy pattern **3 RESEMBLING TABBY** resembling or made of tabby [Late 16C. Via French tabis < Arabic 'attābī.]

tabernacle /tábbər nak'l/ n **1 tabernacle, Tabernacle TENT FOR CARRYING ARK OF COVENANT** a portable tent used as a sanctuary for the Ark of the Covenant by the Israelites during the Exodus **2 tabernacle, Tabernacle JEWISH TEMPLE** the Jewish Temple, regarded as representing the presence of God **3** JUDAISM = **sukkah 4 NONCONFORMIST PLACE OF WORSHIP** a place of worship, especially in some nonconformist Christian denominations **5 CONTAINER FOR HOLY BREAD AND WINE** a box or case in which the consecrated elements of Communion are kept **6 NICHE FOR ICON** a canopied recess or niche for an icon **7 HUMAN BODY** the human body considered as a place temporarily housing the soul or principle of life (literary) **8 SOCKET FOR MAST** a support for the foot of a ship's mast [13C. Directly or via French < Latin tabernaculum 'tent' < taberna 'hut'.] — **tabernacular** /tábbər nákyoolər/ adj

Tabernacles /tábbər nak'lz/ n CALENDAR = **Sukkoth**

tabes /táy beez/ n (plural **-bes**) **1** progressive wasting of the body, usually as a result of a chronic disease **2** MED = **tabes dorsalis** [Late 16C. < Latin, 'wasting away'.] — **tabetic** /tə béttik/ adj

tabes dorsalis /-dawr sáyliss/ n a disorder of the nervous system characteristic of late-stage syphilis and marked by degeneration of nerve fibres, wasting, pain, and inability to move the leg muscles [< late Latin, 'dorsal tabes']

tabi /táabi/ n (plural **-bis** or **-bi**) n a Japanese sock with a thick sole and a separate section for the big toe [Early 17C. < Japanese.]

tabla /táblə/ n an Indian musical instrument consisting of a pair of hand-played small drums [Mid-19C. Via Persian and Hindi < Arabic ṭabl 'drum'.]

tablature /táblachər/ n **1** a special kind of musical notation in which the notes themselves are not represented but rather the hand positions required to play them **2** a tablet or other flat surface that has been engraved or painted [Late 16C. Via French < Italian tavolatura < tavolare 'set to music' < tavola 'table'.]

table /táyb'l/ n **1 ITEM OF FURNITURE WITH FLAT TOP** a piece of furniture with a flat top and one or more legs, used for placing things on or doing things at **2 TABLE FOR FOOD** a table at which people sit to eat meals, or a similar structure provided outdoors at which birds may feed **3 FLAT SURFACE FOR PARTICULAR PURPOSE** a raised flat surface with a nondomestic or office use, e.g. one at which a surgeon operates or one on which a piece of machinery rests **4 FOOD SERVED** the food provided in a household or restaurant in terms of its quality or quantity **5 PEOPLE SITTING AT TABLE** a group of people sitting at a table, especially for a meal ○ The whole table erupted in laughter. **6 ARRANGEMENT OF INFORMATION IN COLUMNS** an arrangement of information or data into columns and rows or a condensed list **7 MULTIPLICATION TABLE** a multiplication table (informal) **8** GEOG = **tableland 9 BAND OR PANEL ON WALL** a band of masonry or a rectangular panel on a wall either raised or depressed and with ornamentation or inscriptions **10 FLAT SURFACE OF GEM** the upper horizontal surface of a cut gem **11 SLAB FOR INSCRIPTION** a slab of wood, stone, or metal for inscription **12 PART OF BACK-GAMMON BOARD** either of the two hinged halves of a backgammon board **13 FRONT PART OF STRINGED INSTRUMENT** the part of the body of a stringed instrument that acts as a sounding board **14 PLATE OF BONE** a flat layer of bone, especially either of the inner or outer surfaces of the skull that are separated by a more spongy bone (**diploë**) **15 AREA ON PALM** an area on the palm defined by four lines, regarded as significant in palmistry ■ **tables** npl ANCIENT TABLETS WITH LAWS INSCRIBED tablets on which certain ancient Greek, Roman, and Hebrew laws were inscribed, or the laws themselves ■ vt (**-bles, -bling, -bled**) **1** PROPOSE to put forward a bill or proposal for discussion at a meeting **2** US POSTPONE DISCUSSION OF to postpone discussion of a bill or motion for a later time **3 ENTER INFORMATION INTO TABLE** to enter information in a tabular form **4 PUT SOMETHING ON TABLE** to place or lay something on a table [Pre-12C. Directly or via French < Latin tabula 'board, slab'.] — **tableful** n ◇ **on the table** put forward for discussion at a meeting ◇ **turn the tables (on somebody)** to reverse a situation and gain the advantage from somebody who had previously held it

tableau /tábblō/ (plural **-leaux** /-lōz/ or **-leaus**) n **1** a vivid and wide-ranging description or display **2** THEATRE = **tableau vivant 3** a visually dramatic scene or situation that suddenly arises [Late 17C. Via French < Old French tablel 'small table' (see TABLE).]

tableau curtain n either of a pair of stage curtains that are drawn to each side and upwards by a cord

tableau vivant /-vee vaàN/ (plural **tableaux vivants**) n a representation of a scene by a group in appropriate costume posing silent and motionless [< French, 'living picture']

Table Bay /táyb'l-/ inlet of the Atlantic Ocean in SW South Africa, forming the harbour of Cape Town. Length: 19 km/12 mi.

tablecloth /táyb'l kloth/ n a cloth for covering a table, especially before it is set for a meal

table d'hôte /taàb'l dōt/ n a restaurant meal or menu offering a series of courses at a fixed price [Early 17C. < French, 'host's table'.]

table football n a game based on football that is played on a table with rows of small model players. US term **foosball**

table knife n a knife used at table with a fork for cutting food, especially the food of a main course

tableland /táyb'l land/ n an extensive elevated region of flat land

table licence n a licence authorizing a restaurant to serve alcoholic drinks only with meals

table mat n a mat placed under hot dishes to protect the table

Table Mountain flat-topped mountain overlooking Cape Town, SW South Africa. Height: 1,086 m/3,563 ft.

table salt n fine salt suitable for use at table

tablespoon /táyb'l spoon/ n **1 SERVING SPOON** a large serving spoon a size larger than a dessertspoon **2 tablespoon,**

tablespoonful MEASURE BASED ON CAPACITY OF TABLESPOON a unit of capacity used in recipes, equal to 15 ml/half a fluid ounce or three teaspoons **3 tablespoon, tablespoonful** AMOUNT HELD BY TABLESPOON the amount of food or liquid that a tablespoon can hold

tablet /tábləṭ/ *n* **1** COMPRESSED POWDERED DRUG FOR SWALLOWING a small solid pill containing a measured medicinal dose, usually intended to be taken orally **2** SMALL FLAT CAKE a small compressed cake of a substance such as soap **3** INSCRIBED STONE OR WOODEN SLAB a slab of stone, wood, or metal used for inscription or engraving **4** SHEETS OF PAPER FASTENED TOGETHER a number of sheets of paper for writing or drawing, fastened together along one edge **5** SHEET OF MATERIAL TO WRITE ON a thin stiff sheet of wood, slate, or ivory on which somebody writes **6** ARCHIT = **table** *n.* 9 **7** *Scotland* SWEET CONFECTIONERY a confectionery similar to fudge made from sugar, butter, and condensed milk **8** *NZ* TOKEN USED BY TRAIN DRIVER a token held by train drivers on single lines, giving them the right of way [14C. < Old French, 'little table' < *table* (see TABLE).]

table talk *n* **1** informal conversation on subjects considered suitable during a meal **2** in bridge, the discussion of bidding and strategy across the table with a partner, which is not permitted

table tennis *n* a game that resembles tennis and is played with small bats and a light hollow ball on a table divided by a net

tabletop /táyb'l top/ *n* the flat upper surface of a table

tableware /táyb'l wair/ *n* dishes, plates, glasses, cutlery, and other articles used at meals

table wine *n* an unfortified wine for drinking with meals

tabloid /tábbloyd/ *n* **1 tabloid, tabloid newspaper** SMALL NEWSPAPER WITH SHORT ARTICLES a small-format popular newspaper with a simple style, many photographs, and sometimes an emphasis on sensational stories **2** CONDENSED PIECE OF WRITING a piece of writing, especially a news story, in a condensed form ■ *adj* SENSATIONALIST relating to or characteristic of tabloid newspapers, especially in having a popular sensationalist style [Late 19C. < proprietary name for tablets of condensed medicine.]

taboo /tə bóó/, **tabu** *adj* **1** SOCIALLY OR CULTURALLY PROSCRIBED forbidden to be used, mentioned, or approached because of social or cultural rather than legal prohibitions **2** SACRED AND PROHIBITED set apart as sacred and at the same time forbidden to be used ■ *n* (*plural* **-boos**) **1** PROHIBITION a prohibition or rejection of particular types of behaviour or language because they are considered socially unacceptable **2** FORBIDDEN BEHAVIOUR a subject or behaviour that is forbidden or disapproved of because it is considered socially unacceptable **3** PROHIBITION ON GROUNDS OF BEING SACRED the practice, especially in some Polynesian societies, of regarding particular things, people, or types of behaviour as sacred and therefore forbidden to be used, made contact with, or engaged in ■ *vt* (**-boos, -booing, -booed**) **1** FORBID OR DISCOURAGE to prohibit or disapprove of particular types of behaviour or language because they are considered socially unacceptable **2** PROHIBIT BECAUSE SACRED to regard particular things, people, or types of behaviour as sacred and therefore forbidden to be used, made contact with, or engaged in [Late 18C. < Polynesian *tabu*.]

tabor /táybər/, **tabour** *n* a small drum played with one hand while the other hand plays a pipe [13C. < Old French *tabour*.] —**taborer** *n*

Tabor, Mount /táyb awr/ peak in N Israel, site of the transfiguration of Jesus Christ in the Bible. Height: 588 m/1,929 ft.

Tabora /ta báwrə/ capital of Tabora Region, west-central Tanzania. Population: 214,000 (1986 estimate).

taboret /tábbə rét/, **tabouret** *n* **1** a low solid seat without arms or a back **2** HANDICRAFT = **tambour** *n.* 1 **3** a small tabor or tambourine [Mid-17C. < French, 'small tabor'.]

tabour *n* MUSIC = **tabor**

tabu *adj, n, vt* ANTHROP = **taboo**

tabular /tábbyóólər/ *adj* **1** ARRANGED IN TABLE arranged in a table or in columns and rows **2** HAVING FLAT SURFACE having a flat surface that resembles a table **3** BROAD AND FLAT describes crystals that are broad and flat **4** SPLITTING INTO THIN PLATES made up of and splitting into thin horizontal plates **5** COMPUTED USING TABLE calculated with or making use of a table, e.g. of logarithms [Mid-17C. < Latin *tabularis* < *tabula* 'board, slab'.] —**tabularly** *adv*

tabula rasa /tábbyóólə raázə/ (*plural* **tabulae rasae** /-lee raá zee/) *n* **1** the mind at birth, regarded as having no innate conceptions **2** an opportunity to make a clean break or a fresh start [Mid-16C. < Latin, 'scraped table'.]

tabularize /tábbyóólə rīz/ (**-izes, -izing, -ized**), **tabularise** (**-ises, -ising, -ised**) *vt* = **tabulate** *v.* 1 —**tabularization** /-rī záysh'n/ *n*

tabulate /tábbyoo layt/ *vt* (**-lates, -lating, -lated**) **1** ARRANGE INFORMATION IN TABLE to arrange information systematically in a table or in columns and rows **2** MAKE SOMETHING FLAT to give a flat top or upper surface to something (*usually passive*) ■ *adj* FLAT with a flat surface that resembles a table [Late 16C. < late Latin *tabulatus* < Latin *tabula* 'board, slab'.] —**tabulable** *adj* —**tabulation** /tábbyoo láysh'n/ *n*

tabulator /tábbyoo laytər/ *n* **1** a person or device that tabulates information **2** OFFICE = **tab**[2] *n.*

tabun /taa bóón/ *n* $C_5H_{11}N_2O_2P$ an organic phosphorus compound. Use: lethal chemical weapon. [Mid-20C. < German.]

tacamahac /tákəmə hak/, **tacmahack** /tákmə-/ *n* **1** a resinous tree gum. Use: ointments, incense. **2** a tree that yields tacamahac resin, especially the balsam poplar [Late 16C. Via obsolete Spanish *tacamahaca* < Nahuatl *tecomahiyac*.]

Tacan /ták an/ *n* an aircraft navigation system using UHF signals emitted from a transmitting station to determine distance and bearing [Mid-20C. Acronym < TACTICAL + AIR + NAVIGATION.]

tacet /táy set/ *n* a musical direction instructing a musician not to play or sing a certain passage [Early 18C. < Latin, '(it) is silent' < *tacere* 'be silent'.]

tach[1] /tak/ *n US* a tachometer (*informal*) [Mid-20C. Shortening.]

tach[2] /tash/ *n US* = **tache** (*informal*)

tache /tash/, **tash** *n* a moustache (*informal*) [Late 19C. Shortening.]

tacheometry /táki ómmətri/ *n* BUILDING = **tachymetry** —**tacheometer** *n* —**tacheometric** /táki ə méttrik/ *adj* —**tacheometrical** *adj* —**tacheometrically** *adv*

tachina fly /tákinə-/ *n* a bristly fly whose larvae live as parasites on other insects. Family: Tachinidae. [< modern Latin *Tachina* < Greek *takhinos* 'swift']

tachinid /tákənid/ *n* INSECTS = **tachina fly** ■ *adj* relating to the family of insects that the tachina fly belongs to [Late 19C. < modern Latin *Tachinidae* < *Tachina* (see TACHINA FLY).]

tachism /táshizəm/, **tachisme** *n* action painting in which random blotches of colour are used as a method of instinctive expression [Mid-20C. < French *tachisme* < *tache* 'spot'.] —**tachist** *n, adj*

tachistoscope /tə kístə skōp/ *n* an instrument for displaying visual images very briefly, used to test perception and memory [Late 19C. < Greek *takhistos* 'swiftest' < *takhus* 'swift'.] —**tachistoscopic** /tə kístə skóppik/ *adj* —**tachistoscopically** *adv*

tachogram /tákə gram/ *n* a record in graph form produced by a tachograph

tachograph /tákə graaf, -graf/ *n* an instrument that produces a record of the use and readings of a tachometer, especially one in a commercial vehicle or coach recording speeds and distances travelled [Early 20C. < Greek *takhos* 'speed'.]

tachometer /ta kómmitər/ *n* a device used to determine speed of rotation, typically of a vehicle's crankshaft and usually in revolutions per minute [Early 19C. < Greek *takhos* 'speed'.] —**tachometric** /tákə méttrik/ *adj* —**tachometrically** *adv* —**tachometry** *n*

tachy- *prefix* accelerated, rapid ○ *tachygraphy* [< Greek *takhus* 'swift']

tachyarrhythmia /táki ə ríthmi ə/ *n* a medical condition in which the heartbeat is fast and irregular

tachycardia /táki kaárdi ə/ *n* an excessively rapid heartbeat, typically regarded as a heart rate exceeding 100 beats per minute in a resting adult [Late 19C. < TACHY- + Greek *kardia* 'heart'.] —**tachycardiac** *adj*

tachygraphy /ta kíggrəfi/ *n* **1** the shorthand system used by the ancient Greeks and Romans **2** the abbreviated cursive writing used in medieval times for Latin and Greek —**tachygrapher** *n* —**tachygraphic** /táki gráffik/ *adj* —**tachygraphically** *adv* —**tachygraphist** *n*

tachymetry /ta kímmətri/ *n* the measurement of distances, elevations, and directions using a type of theodolite (**tachymeter**) —**tachymeter** *n* —**tachymetric** /táki méttrik/ *adj* —**tachymetrically** *adv*

tachyon /táki on/ *n* a hypothetical elementary particle that always travels faster than the speed of light

tachypnea *n* US = **tachypnoea**

tachypnoea /tákip neé ə/ *n* abnormally fast breathing, usually considered to be over 20 breaths per minute in a resting adult [Late 19C. < TACHY- + Greek *pnoiē* 'breathing' < *pnein* 'breathe'.]

tacit /tássit/ *adj* understood or implied without being stated openly [Early 17C. < Latin *tacitus*, past participle of *tacere* 'be silent'.] —**tacitly** *adv* —**tacitness** *n*

taciturn /tássi turn/ *adj* habitually uncommunicative or reserved in speech and manner [Late 18C. Via French *taciturne* < Latin *taciturnus* < *tacitus* (see TACIT).] —**taciturnity** /tássi túrnəti/ *n* —**taciturnly** *adv*

SYNONYMS See ***silent***.

Tacitus /tássitəss/ (55?–117?) Roman historian

tack[1] /tak/ *n* **1** SMALL NAIL a small sharp nail with a broad head **2** TEMPORARY STITCH a long loose temporary stitch, often used to align seams in preparation for final sewing **3** CHANGE IN DIRECTION OF SAILING a change in the direction of movement of a sailing ship or sailing boat made in order to maximize the benefit from the wind **4** PART OF ZIGZAG SAILING COURSE a stage or series of stages in the zigzag movement of a sailing ship or sailing boat that is changing direction in order to maximize the benefit from the wind **5** COURSE OF ACTION a course of action or method of approach intended to achieve something, especially one adopted after another has failed **6** DIRECTION OF SAILING the direction of movement of a sailing ship or sailing boat in relation to the side from which the wind is blowing, effected by the position of its sails **7** ROPE HOLDING DOWN SAIL a rope holding down the corner of some sails, or the corner that is held down **8** SLIGHT STICKINESS slight stickiness, e.g. of glue or paint that has not yet dried ■ *v* **1** *vt* FASTEN WITH TACKS to attach something with small sharp broad-headed nails **2** *vt* ATTACH WITH DRAWING PIN to attach something light to a board or wall with a drawing pin **3** *vt* SEW TEMPORARILY to sew something with long loose temporary stitches **4** *vt* PUT TOGETHER ARBITRARILY to bring different things together to form an arbitrary or illusory whole **5** *vti* CHANGE DIRECTION OF SAILING SHIP to change the direction or course of a sailing ship or sailing boat, or to steer it on alternate tacks **6** *vi* CHANGE APPROACH to take a different course of action or use a different method [14C. < Old N French *taque* 'fastening' < Germanic.]
tack on *vt* to add something to something else either as a supplement or an afterthought

tack[2] /tak/ *n* saddles, bridles, and other parts of a horse's harness [Late 18C. Shortening of TACKLE.]

tack[3] /tak/ *n* goods that are tasteless and vulgar or cheap and shoddy (*informal*) [Late 20C. Back-formation < TACKY[2].]

tack[4] /tak/ *n* foodstuff, especially of the poor quality fed to a ship's crew in the days of sailing ships (*slang*) ◊ **hardtack** [Late 16C. < ?]

tackboard /ták bawrd/ *n US* a bulletin board (*informal*)

tacket /tákit/ *n Scotland, N England* a nail or hobnail

tackety boots /tákəti-/ *npl Scotland* hobnail boots (*informal*)

tackle /ták'l/ *n* **1** ATTEMPT TO STOP OPPONENT'S PROGRESS a physical challenge against an opposing player who has the ball in football, hockey, and some other games **2** SPORTS EQUIPMENT the equipment used for a particular activity such as angling, or rock climbing **3** ROPES AND PULLEYS equipment consisting of ropes and pulleys used for lifting heavy weights through increased mechanical advantage **4** SHIP'S RIGGING the gear and rigging of a ship **5** MAN'S GENITALS a man's genitals (*slang; sometimes offensive*) **6** LINEMAN NEXT TO END in American football, a lineman positioned between a guard and an end, or the position of such a player ■ *vt* (**-les, -ling, -led**) **1** EMBARK ON DOING to undertake or deal with something that requires effort **2** CONFRONT to open a conversation or discussion on a difficult issue with somebody who would prefer to avoid it **3** MAKE TACKLE ON to challenge an opposing player **4** HARNESS AN ANIMAL to put a harness on an animal, especially a horse [13C. Probably < Low German *takel* 'ship's rigging' < *taken* 'seize'.] —**tackler** *n*

tack welding *n* the welding of two metals by individual welds at isolated points

tacky[1] /táki/ (**-ier, -iest**) *adj* slightly sticky to the touch [Late 18C. < TACK[1].] —**tackily** *adv* —**tackiness** *n*

tacky[2] /táki/ (**-ier, -iest**) *adj* (*informal*) **1** perceived of as vulgar, lacking in taste, or no longer fashionable **2** appearing to be cheaply made or in need of repair [Early 19C. < ?] —**tackily** *adv* —**tackiness** *n*

taco /tákō/ (*plural* **-cos**) *n* a crisp fried maize tortilla usually filled with meat, lettuce, tomatoes, cheese, and hot sauce [Mid-20C. Via American Spanish < Spanish, 'wad'.]

Tacoma /tə kṓmə/ city in W Washington State. Population: 179,814 (1998 estimate).

taconite /tákə nīt/ *n* a banded iron formation consisting of layers of the iron oxides magnetite and haematite that may be extracted from pulverized rock using a magnet [Early 20C. After *Taconic*, mountain range in New York State.]

tact /takt/ *n* **1** skill in situations in which other people's feelings have to be considered **2** an intuitive sense of what is right or appropriate [Early 17C. Via French < Latin *tactus* '(sense of) touch' < *tangere* 'to touch'.]

tactful /táktf'l/ *adj* having or showing concern about upsetting or offending people —**tactfully** *adv* —**tactfulness** *n*

tactic /táktik/ *n* a method used or a course of action followed in order to achieve an immediate or short-term aim [Mid-17C. Via modern Latin < Greek *taktikos* 'of arrangement' < *taktos* 'arranged' < *tassein* 'arrange'.]

tactical /táktik'l/ *adj* **1 OF TACTICS** relating to or involving tactics **2 AS MEANS TO END** done or made for the purpose of trying to achieve an immediate or short-term aim **3 SHOWING SKILFUL PLANNING** showing skilful planning in order to accomplish something **4 WITH LIMITED MILITARY OBJECTIVE** used or made to support limited military operations **5 SUPPORTING OTHER MILITARY OBJECTIVE** undertaken or for use in support of other military and naval operations —**tactically** *adv*

tactical voting *n* the act of voting for the second strongest candidate in an election with a view to preventing the strongest candidate from winning

tactics /táktiks/ *n* (+ *singular verb*) **1** the science of organizing and manoeuvring forces in battle to achieve a limited or immediate aim **2** the art of finding and implementing means to achieve particular immediate or short-term aims —**tactician** /tak tísh'n/ *n*

tactile /ták tīl/ *adj* **1 OF TOUCH** relating to or used for the sense of touch **2 TANGIBLE** capable of perception by the sense of touch **3 APPARENTLY THREE-DIMENSIONAL** giving an illusion of physical solidity and tangibility **4 PLEASANT TO TOUCH** pleasing or interesting to the sense of touch **5 HABITUALLY TOUCHING PEOPLE** inclined to touch people a lot, e.g. while talking to them [Early 17C. Directly or via French < Latin *tactilis* < *tactus* (see TACT).] —**tactilely** *adv* —**tactility** /tak tílləti/ *n*

tactile corpuscle, tactile bud *n* a tiny egg-shaped touch receptor that responds to light pressure and is found in the skin of the palms, lips, soles, and other hairless sensitive areas

tactless /táktləss/ *adj* lacking or showing a lack of concern about upsetting or offending people —**tactlessly** *adv* —**tactlessness** *n*

tactual /tákchoo əl/ *adj* relating to the sense of touch, or imparting the sensation of contact [Mid-17C. < Latin *tactus* (see TACT).] —**tactually** *adv*

tad /tad/ *n* a very slight amount or degree of something (*informal*) [Late 19C. < ?] ◇ **a tad** somewhat (*informal*)

tadpole /tád pōl/ *n* the aquatic larva of a frog, toad, or salamander that has a limbless round body, gills, and a tail [15C. < earlier forms of TOAD + POLL.]

Tadzhik *n, adj* PEOPLES, LANG = **Tajik**

Tadzhiki *n, adj* LANG, PEOPLES = **Tajiki**

Tadzhikistan = **Tajikistan**

Tae Bo /tī bṓ/ *n* a fitness regime based on exercising to music and performing movements that derive from martial arts such as karate [Late 20C. < TAE KWON DO + BOXING.]

taedium vitae /tēedi əm vēe tī/ *n* the feeling of being weary of or disgusted with life [Mid-18C. < Latin.]

tae kwon do /tī kwon dṓ/ *n* a Korean martial art resembling karate but also employing a wide range of kicking moves [Mid-20C. < Korean, 'art of hand and foot fighting'.]

tael /tayl/ *n* **1** a varying unit of weight used in East Asia, usually around 38 g/1.75 oz **2** a silver coin that was a unit of currency in China between 1889 and 1912, equivalent to a tael of silver [Late 16C. Via Portuguese < Malay *tahil*, unit of weight.]

ta'en /tayn/ *v* taken (*archaic or literary*)

taenia /tēeni ə/ (*plural* **-ae** /-ee/) *n* **1 PART SHAPED LIKE RIBBON** a body part that resembles a ribbon, especially muscle or nervous tissue **2 HORIZONTAL BAND IN DORIC ARCHITECTURE** in the Doric order of ancient Greek architecture, a narrow band (**fillet**) between the main beam (**architrave**) across the top of the columns and the frieze above **3 PARASITIC TAPEWORM** a large parasitic tapeworm. Genus: *Taenia*. **4 NARROW HEADBAND** a fillet or headband worn in ancient Greece [Mid-16C. Via Latin < Greek *tainia* 'band'.]

taeniacide /tēeni ə sīd/ *n* a substance for killing tapeworms

taeniafuge /tēeni ə fyooj/ *n* a drug or other agent that expels tapeworms from the body

taeniasis /tee nī əssiss/ *n* infestation with adult tapeworms, usually following the eating of raw or undercooked meat containing tapeworm larvae

TAFE /tayf/ *n* in Australia, a system of higher education providing instruction in technical subjects. Full form **Technical and Further Education**

taffeta /táffitə/ *n* a stiff lustrous silk or a silky fabric with a slight rib. Use: women's clothes. [14C. Via medieval Latin or Old French *taffetas* < Persian *tāftah* < *tāftan* 'to shine'.]

taffrail /táf rayl/ *n* **1** the rail round the stern of a ship **2** the upper flat and often carved part of a ship's stern [Early 19C. < Dutch *taffereel* 'a small table' < *tafel* 'table'.]

taffy /táffi/ (*plural* **-fies**) *n* **1** *US, Can* a chewy confectionery made of sugar or molasses boiled down and pulled until glossy and light in colour **2** flattery of an insincere kind (*informal dated*) [Early 19C. Probably dialect form of TOFFEE.]

Taffy /táffi/ (*plural* **-fies**) *n* an offensive term for a Welsh person (*slang*) [Mid-17C. < the alleged Welsh pronunciation of the forename *David*.]

Taft /taft/, **William Howard** (1857–1930) US statesman and 27th president of the United States (1909–13)

⚡**tag**[1] /tag/ *n* **1 LABEL** a small piece or strip of cloth, paper, plastic, or other material attached to something, especially by one end, or hung on it as a label or means of identification **2 ELECTRONIC DEVICE WORN BY OFFENDER** an electronic device worn, usually on the ankle or wrist, by a convicted offender serving a sentence in the community to allow his or her movements to be monitored **3 CLASSIFYING LABEL FOR DATA** a label that classifies a piece of data, e.g. by its type, to facilitate later retrieval **4 TIP AT END OF SHOELACE** a plastic or metal tip attached to the end of a shoelace or cord to prevent it from fraying **5 TIP OF ANIMAL'S TAIL** the tip of an animal's tail, especially if in a contrasting colour with the rest of the tail **6 SMALL LOOSE OR RAGGED PIECE** a small piece of a material hanging loosely or raggedly from the main piece **7 MATTED LOCK OF WOOL** a dirty matted lock of wool or hair in an animal's fleece or coat **8 ATTACHMENT TO ARTIFICIAL FLY** a piece of usually brightly coloured material tied around the shank of the hook in the body of an artificial fly **9 WELL-KNOWN QUOTATION** a well-known or hackneyed quotation, often in Latin, usually intended to add dignity or weight to a speech or piece of writing **10 EPITHET** a descriptive word or phrase used, especially frequently, about somebody or something **11 ENDING FOR PIECE OF WRITING** something ending or added to a piece of writing, e.g. a refrain, the cue line ending an actor's speech, or a final speech addressed to the audience **12** LING = **tag question 13 GRAFFITI ARTIST'S SIGNATURE** a signature or identifying symbol used by a graffiti artist ■ *v* (**tags, tagging, tagged**) **1** *vt* **LABEL WITH TAG** to attach a tag to something or label something with a tag **2** *vt* **ADD AT END** to add an additional piece or section to the end of something, especially a piece of writing ○ *tagged on a couple of extra lines at the end* **3** *vt* **ATTACH EPITHET TO** to give somebody a nickname, or assign a verbal label to somebody **4** *vt* **ATTACH ELECTRONIC TAG TO OFFENDER** to make an offender wear an electronic tag **5** *vt US* **TICKET CAR** to attach a ticket to a vehicle to notify the driver that a traffic or parking offence has been committed **6** *vt US* **CHARGE SOMEBODY WITH CRIME** to charge somebody with a crime (*often passive*) ○ *He was tagged for theft.* **7** *vt* **ATTACH RHYMES TO** to put unrhymed verse or prose into rhyme **8** *vt* **REMOVE TAGS FROM WOOL** to remove tags from an animal's fleece or coat **9** *vti* **FOLLOW CLOSELY** to follow along close behind somebody [15C. < ?]

tag along *vi* to accompany or follow somebody, often when your presence is unwanted

tag[2] /tag/ *n* **1 CHILDREN'S CHASING AND TOUCHING GAME** a children's game in which one player is chosen to chase the others and try to touch one of them. Anyone touched becomes 'it' and is then the player who does the chasing. **2 INSTANCE OF TAGGING RUNNER OUT** an instance of tagging a runner out in baseball **3** WRESTLING = **tag wrestling 4 INSTANCE OF TAGGING IN WRESTLING** an instance of tagging a partner in wrestling ■ *vt* (**tags, tagging, tagged**) **1 CATCH PLAYER IN GAME OF TAG** to touch a player in the children's game of tag, making that player 'it' **2 TOUCH RUNNER WITH BALL** to get a runner out in baseball by touching him or her with the ball before he or she reaches the base **3 TOUCH PARTNER'S HAND IN WRESTLING** to touch the hand of a partner in tag wrestling in order to switch places **4** *Aus* **MARK OPPONENT** in Australian Rules football, to mark an opponent [Mid-18C. < ?]

tag up *vi* in baseball, to touch a base before running to the next one after a fly ball is caught

Tagalog /tə gáalog, -gáaləg, -gálog/ (*plural* **-logs** *or* **-log**) *n* **1** a member of a Malayan people who originally lived in the Manila area of the Philippines **2** the Austronesian language of the Tagalog people, the basis of Filipino. Native speakers: 17 million. [Early 19C. < Tagalog *tagá* 'native' + *ilog* 'river'.] —**Tagalog** *adj*

tag day *n US* = **flag day**

tag end *n* **1** a loose or detached piece of something **2** *US* the very last or last remaining part of something

tagetes /ta jēe teez/ *n* a marigold, especially an African or French marigold. Genus: *Tagetes*. [Late 18C. < modern Latin *Tagetes* < Latin *Tages*, an Etruscan god.]

tagger /tággər/ *n* a graffiti artist who spray-paints his or her name or symbol on a public structure (*slang*)

taggers /tággərz/ *npl* iron or steel in thin sheets coated with tin [Mid-19C. Perhaps because used to make shoelace tags.]

tagine /tə zhēen/ *n* **1** a cooking pot with a high cone-shaped earthenware lid and a cast-iron or earthenware base, used especially for stews in Moroccan cookery **2** a Moroccan stew cooked very slowly in a tagine and consisting usually of meat or poultry combined with fruit [< Arabic *tajin*]

tagliatelle /tállyə télli/ *n* pasta in the form of long narrow ribbons [Late 19C. < Italian, < *tagliare* 'cut into strips'.]

tag line *n US* **1** the final line of a joke, story, or drama, delivering a humorous or dramatic point **2** a phrase repeatedly used in connection with a person, organization, or product, especially in publicity

tagma /tágmə/ (*plural* **-mata** /-mətə/) *n* a distinct functional region of the body of an arthropod, e.g. a thorax [Early 20C. < Greek, 'something arranged' < *tag-*, stem of *tassein* 'arrange'.]

tagmeme /tág meem/ *n* any of the various positions in the structure of a sentence into which a word or phrase of a particular grammatical type can fit [Mid-20C. < Greek *tagma* (see TAGMA).] —**tagmemic** /tag mēemik/ *adj*

tagmemics /tag mēemiks/ *n* a grammatical analysis of language based on the way in which the different elements that make up a sentence are arranged within it (+ *singular verb*)

Tagore /tə gáwr/, **Rabindranath** (1861–1941) Indian writer

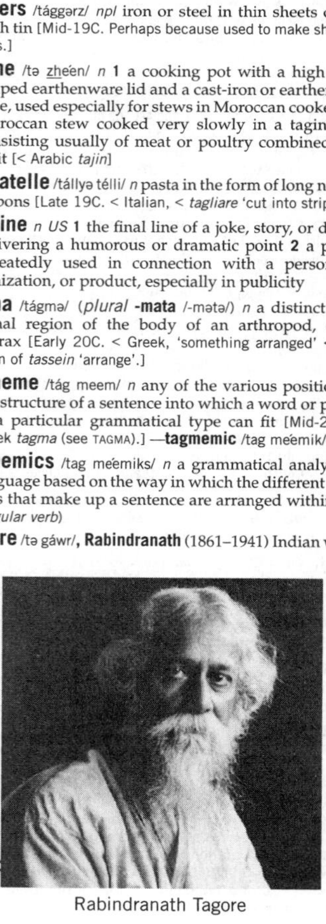

Popperfoto

Rabindranath Tagore

tag question *n* a short clause added on to a statement to turn it into a question, e.g. 'don't you?' or 'isn't it?', or a statement with a question clause attached

tag team *n* a team of two or more wrestlers, only one of whom may wrestle at a time

taguan /tág wan/ *n* a large nocturnal flying squirrel that leaps from tree to tree with the help of skin flaps that stretch between its limbs. Native to: Southeast Asia. *Petaurista petaurista*. [Early 19C. Probably < local name in the Philippines.]

tague *n Ireland* = **taig** (*slang offensive*)

Tagus /táygəss/ river flowing through central Spain and central Portugal to the Atlantic Ocean. Length: 1,007 km/626 mi. Portuguese **Tejo**. Spanish **Tajo**

tag wrestling *n* a form of wrestling in which wrestlers compete in teams of two or more, taking it in turns to enter the ring, a touch of hands being required for a changeover

tahini /tə héeni, -nə/, **tahina** /-nə/ *n* an oily paste made from crushed sesame seeds. Use: seasoning. [Mid-20C. < Arabic *ṭaḥīnā* < *ṭaḥana* 'grind'.]

Tahiti /tə héeti/ island of French Polynesia, in the S Pacific Ocean. Population: 115,820 (1998). Area: 1,000 sq. km/400 sq. mi. —**Tahitian** *n, adj*

Tahoe, Lake /taʹahō/ lake in the W United States, on the border of Nevada and California. Area: 500 sq. km/193 sq. mi.

tahr /taar/ *n* a cud-chewing mammal similar to a goat, with a shaggy coat and curved horns. Native to: mountains in South Asia. Genus: *Hemitragus*. [Mid-19C. < Nepalese *thār*.]

tahsil /taa séel/ *n* an administrative district in some states of India [Mid-19C. Via Urdu and Persian < *taḥṣīl* 'revenue' < Arabic *ḥaṣala* 'collect'.]

tahsildar /taa séel daar/ *n* in India, a government official in charge of collecting taxes and other revenues in a tahsil [Late 18C. Via Urdu *taḥṣīldār* < Persian, 'revenue-holder' < *taḥṣīl* (see TAHSIL).]

Tai /tī/ (*plural* **Tai** *or* **Tais**) *n* a group of tonal languages spoken in Southeast Asia, including Thai and Lao [Late 17C. Variant of THAI.] —**Tai** *adj*

T'ai Chi /tī chee/, **t'ai chi ch'uan** /-chwaán/, **T'ai Chi Ch'uan, Tai Chi Chuan** *n* a Chinese form of physical exercise characterized by a series of very slow and deliberate balletic body movements [Mid-18C. < Chinese, literally 'extreme limit'.]

taig /tayg/, **tague, teigue** *n N Ireland* an offensive term for a Roman Catholic (*slang*) [Late 20C. < the Irish name *Tadhg*.]

taiga /tīgə/ *n* the subarctic coniferous forests of North America, N Europe, and Asia located south of the tundra [Late 19C. < Russian.]

tail /tayl/ *n* **1 REAR PART OF ANIMAL'S BODY** the flexible rear part, or a movable extension to the rear part, of a vertebrate animal's body, that begins above the anus and often contains the terminal vertebrae **2 LAST PART** the rear, last, or lowest part of something ○ *the tail of the procession* **3 REAR OF AIRCRAFT** the rear part of an aircraft together with the fin and the tailplane **4 REAR OF MISSILE** the rear part of a missile or bomb, including structures for controlling the angle of the trajectory **5 STREAM OF GAS FROM COMET** the luminous stream of gas and dust particles driven by the solar wind from a comet as it approaches and then recedes from the Sun **6 PEOPLE IN A QUEUE** a queue of people or things **7 LONG LOCK OR BRAID OF HAIR** a long lock or braid of hair **8 BOTTOM OF PAGE** the bottom of a printed page, or the margin between the bottom of the page and the lowest line of type **9 SOMEBODY FOLLOWING ANOTHER** a secret follower or observer of somebody (*informal*) ○ *The police put a round-the-clock tail on the suspect.* **10 TRAIL** somebody's trail, especially when being followed or pursued (*informal*) **11** HIST = **horsetail** *n.* 2 **12 BUTTOCKS** the buttocks (*informal*) **13 TABOO TERM** a highly offensive term for a woman's genitals (*taboo*) **14** *US* **TABOO TERM** a highly offensive term used by some men for sexual intercourse with a woman (*taboo*) **15 TABOO TERM** a highly offensive term used by some men for a woman perceived only as a potential partner for sexual intercourse (*taboo*) ■ **tails** *npl* **1 MAN'S FORMAL COAT WITH TAILS** a formal, usually black coat for a man, cut short at the front and with two long tails at the back **2 MAN'S EVENING CLOTHES** full evening clothes for a man **3 REVERSE OF COIN** the reverse side of a coin ■ *v* **1** *vt* **FOLLOW SECRETLY** to follow somebody secretly in order to keep watch on him or her (*informal*) ○ *Someone must have tailed you back to the house.* **2** *vi* **FOLLOW** to follow behind somebody or something ○ *She strode out purposefully, leaving the rest of the party to tail along behind.* **3** *vi* **FORM LINE** to form a long line when moving, especially a long spread-out line **4** *vt* **REMOVE TAIL OF ANIMAL** to remove or cut short the tail of an animal **5** *vt* **REMOVE STALK FROM FRUIT** to remove the stalk from something such as a piece of fruit **6** *vt* **JOIN THINGS END TO END** to join two or more things end to end **7** *vti* **BUILD INTO WALL** to build one end of something such as a joist, beam, or brick, into a wall, or be fixed into a wall at one end **8** *vi* **LIE WITH STERN IN PARTICULAR DIRECTION** to lie with the stern pointing in a particular direction when moored (*refers to a boat or ship*) [Old English *tægel* < Germanic] —**tailless** *adj* ◇ **turn tail** to turn and walk or run away ◇ **with your tail between your legs** in an abject ashamed manner

SPELLCHECK Do not confuse ***tail*** with ***tale***, which has a similar sound. Beware: your spellchecker will not catch this error.

tail off, tail away *vi* to grow less, smaller, or fainter, usually gradually

tailback /táyl bak/ *n* a queue of stationary or slow-moving traffic caused by an obstruction ahead

tail beam *n* BUILDING = **tailpiece** *n.* 4

tailboard /táyl bawrd/ *n* TRANSP = **tailgate** *n.* 1

tailbone /táyl bōn/ *n* ANAT = **coccyx**

tail coat *n* a formal, usually black coat for a man, cut short at the front and with two long tails at the back

tail covert *n* any one of the small feathers on a bird's tail that cover the bases of the tail feathers

tail end *n* **1** the last or hindmost part of something **2** the buttocks (*informal*)

tailender /tayl éndər/ *n* somebody or something that comes at or towards the end of something or in last place (*informal*)

tail fan *n* a fan-shaped structure at the rear end of some crustaceans such as the lobster

tailgate /táyl gayt/ *n* **1 GATE AT BACK OF VEHICLE** a gate at the back of a lorry that can be laid flat or dropped down during loading or unloading **2 tailgate, tail gate GATE IN WATERWAY** a gate controlling the flow of water at the lower end of a lock in a waterway ■ *vti* (**-gates, -gating, -gated**) **DRIVE CLOSE BEHIND** to drive very close behind another vehicle —**tailgater** *n*

tailgate party *n US* a social gathering before a sports event held in a car park outside the stadium

tail grab *n* in snowboarding, a move in which the back of the board is manoeuvred upwards and grabbed with the hand

tailing /táyling/ *n* the end of something such as a beam that is built into a wall during construction ■ **tailings** *npl* the waste left after something has been processed from rock

tail lamp *n US* CARS = **rear light**

taille /tīl, tayl/ *n* a tax levied by the French monarch on his subjects before the French Revolution [Mid-16C. < French, 'tax', literally 'a cut'.]

tailor /táylər/ *n* **1 CLOTHES MAKER** a maker or repairer of clothes, especially men's clothes **2** *Aus* **FISH WITH SHARP TEETH** a fast-moving, aggressive fish with a large, strong mouth containing sharp teeth that resemble scissors. Native to: Australia. *Pomatomus saltatrix*. ■ *v* **1** *vti* **MAKE CLOTHES TO MEET PARTICULAR NEED** to make clothes to meet a particular need or for a particular person **2** *vt* **ADAPT** to adapt something to make it suitable for a particular purpose **3** *vi* **WORK AS TAILOR** to work as a tailor [13C. Via Anglo-Norman *taillour*, Old French *tailleur* 'cutter' < *taillier* 'to cut' < late Latin *taliare* < Latin *talea* 'twig, cutting'.]

tailorbird /táylər burd/ *n* a warbler that makes a nest by sewing leaves together with plant fibres. Native to: tropical Asia. Genus: *Orthotomus*.

tailored /táylərd/ *adj* **1 MADE BY TAILOR** made by a tailor **2 MADE TO FIT NEATLY** describes clothes marked by a neat fit with trim lines and a clean and formal or severe look **3 MADE FOR PARTICULAR PURPOSE** made or adapted for a particular purpose

tailor-made *adj* **1 IDEAL** perfectly suited to somebody or for a particular purpose **2 MADE BY TAILOR** made by a tailor rather than in a factory ■ *n* **1 SOMETHING MADE BY TAILOR** a garment made by a tailor **2 MANUFACTURED CIGARETTE** a cigarette bought ready-made rather than rolled by hand (*informal*)

tailpiece /táyl peess/ *n* **1 END** something that forms an end or is added at the end of something **2 DECORATION AT BOTTOM OF PAGE** a decoration at the bottom of a page, e.g. at the end of a chapter **3 PART OF STRINGED INSTRUMENT** a piece of wood or metal at the lower end of a stringed instrument such as a violin, to which the strings are attached **4 BEAM EMBEDDED IN WALL** a beam that has one end embedded in a wall

tailpipe /táyl pīp/ *n US* ENG = **exhaust pipe**

tailplane /táyl playn/ *n* the horizontal part of the tail of an aircraft, designed to give stability

tailrace /táyl rayss/ *n* **1** a channel that carries away water that has passed through a mill wheel or turbine **2** a channel that carries away mine tailings in water

tail rotor *n* a small propeller on the tail of a helicopter that counteracts the main rotor, preventing the body of the helicopter from rotating in the opposite direction to it

tailskid /táyl skid/ *n* **1** a support or runner on the underside of the tail of an aircraft **2** a skidding of the rear wheels of a motor vehicle

tailspin /táyl spin/ *n* **1** a rapid spiral descent of an aircraft **2** a state of great confusion or distress (*informal*)

tailstock /táyl stok/ *n* a movable part of a lathe, used to support the free end of the workpiece and permitting it to rotate freely

tailwind /táyl wind/ *n* a wind that is blowing in the same direction as a ship or aircraft is travelling

Taino /tī nō/ (*plural* **-nos** *or* **-no**) *n* **1** a member of an extinct Native Central American people who lived on the Caribbean islands of the Greater Antilles and the Bahamas **2** the Arawak language of the Taino people [Mid-19C. < Taino.] —**Taino** *adj*

taint /taynt/ *v* **1** *vt* **POLLUTE** to pollute or contaminate something with something undesirable or dangerous **2** *vt* **CORRUPT MORALLY** to corrupt somebody morally, or detract from somebody's reputation by associating him or her with something reprehensible **3** *vt* **FLAVOUR** to give a scent or flavour of one thing to another **4** *vi* **SPOIL** to spoil or become rotten ■ *n* **1 IMPERFECTION DETRACTING FROM QUALITY** an imperfection that detracts from the quality of somebody or something ○ *a taint on her reputation* **2 SOMETHING THAT POLLUTES** something that detracts from the purity or cleanliness of something [Late 16C. Partly < Anglo-Norman *teint* 'coloured, dyed' < Latin *tingere* 'moisten, dye', partly < Old French *ataint* 'convicted', past participle of *ateindre* (see ATTAIN).] —**taintless** *adj*

taipan[1] /tī pan/ *n* a foreigner in charge of a business or trading operation in China, especially a powerful business tycoon [Mid-19C. < Chinese (Cantonese) *daaih-bāan*.]

taipan[2] /tī pan/ *n* a large, rare, highly venomous snake, brown in colour with a lighter brown belly, that can grow to 3.3 m/11 ft in length. Native to: N Australia. *Oxyuranus scutellatus*. [Mid-20C. < Aboriginal.]

Taipei /tī páy/, **T'aipei** capital and largest city of Taiwan, on the northern part of the island. Population: 2,605,374 (1997 estimate).

Taiping /tī píng/ *n* a supporter or participant in a rebellion against the Manchu dynasty in China between 1850 and 1864 [Mid-19C. < Chinese *tài píng* 'great peace'.]

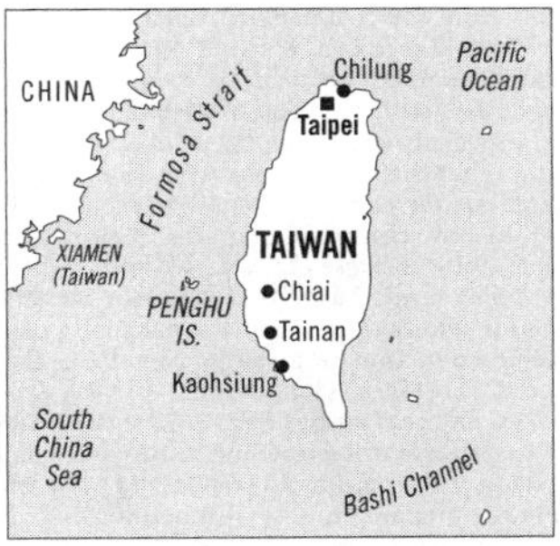

Taiwan

Taiwan /tī waán/ island country of Southeast Asia, administered independently since 1949 by the Chinese Nationalist government. It is claimed as a province by the People's Republic of China. Capital: Taipei.

Population: 21,703,304 (1997). Area: 36,000 sq. km/13,900 sq. mi. —**Taiwanese** /tī waa neez/ *n, adj*

Taiyuan /tī ywán, tī yoo án/ capital of Shanxi Province, east-central China. Population: 1,711,709 (1991).

taj /taaj/ *n* a tall brimless conical cap, often richly decorated, worn by Muslims as a mark of distinction [Late 19C. Via Arabic < Persian *tāj* 'crown'.]

Tajik /taa jeek/ (*plural* **-jiks** *or* **-jik**), **Tadzhik** (*plural* **-dzhiks** *or* **-dzhik**) *n* **1** a person who comes from Tajikistan **2** the official Iranian language of Tajikistan. Native speakers: 4.5 million. [Early 19C. < Persian.] —**Tajik** *adj*

Tajiki /taa jeeki/, **Tadzhiki** *n* LANG = **Tajik** *n.* 2 ■ *adj* relating to the Tajik people, or their language or culture

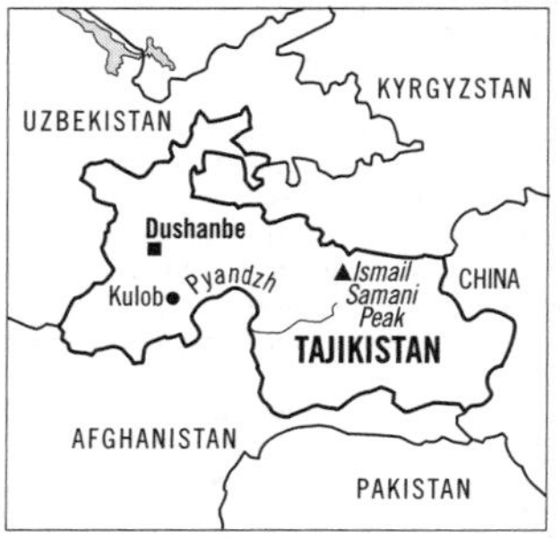

Tajikistan

Tajikistan /tə jeeki staan/, **Tadzhikistan** republic in SE Central Asia. Capital: Dushanbe. Population: 5,945,903 (1997). Area: 143,100 sq. km/55,250 sq. mi.

Taj Mahal /taaj mə haal, taazh-/ *n* a white marble mausoleum in Agra, N India, completed in 1643 in memory of Mumtaz Mahal, the wife of Mughal emperor Shah Jahan

taka /taakə/ *n* see table at **currency** [Late 20C. Via Bengali *ṭākā* < Sanskrit *ṭaṅkah* 'stamped coin'.]

takahe /taakə hee/ *n* a rare and endangered flightless bird of the rail family with a large stout bill and sturdy legs, thought to be extinct until rediscovered in 1948. Native to: New Zealand. *Notornis mantelli* and *Porphyrio mantelli*. [Mid-19C. < Maori.]

Takakkaw Falls /tá kək aw-/ Canada's highest waterfall, in SE British Columbia. Height: 503 m/1,650 ft.

take /tayk/ *v* (**takes, taking, took** /to͝ok/, **taken** /táykən/) **1** *vt* REMOVE to remove or steal something belonging to somebody else ○ *Did you take my gardening gloves?* ○ *I wish you wouldn't take things without asking.* **2** *vt* CARRY to carry or transport something or somebody from one place to another ○ *I took a notebook with me.* ○ *We decided to take him to the doctor.* **3** *vt* WIN to capture or gain possession of a place, area, or object, or win something in a contest or competition ○ *took the town after a long siege* ○ *took first prize in the competition.* **4** *vt* GET HOLD OF to get hold of something or somebody using a hand, or receive something into your hand ○ *She took him by the arm and steered him out of the room.* **5** *vt* SELECT to choose an individual object or person from a number available ○ *Here, take a chocolate.* **6** *vt* GET INTO OR ONTO to place yourself in something, or start to occupy something ○ *Please take a seat.* **7** *vt* CLAIM OR ASSUME to obtain something, especially credit, glory, or blame, or accept or maintain that this is deserved ○ *He doesn't mind taking the credit for the party's recent successes.* **8** *vt* REGULARLY RECEIVE to buy, consume, or perform something as a regular habit ○ *We take the Sunday papers.* ○ *I've stopped taking lunch breaks.* **9** *vt* LEAD SOMEBODY SOMEWHERE to enable somebody to go towards a particular place or in a specified direction, or go along something that leads to a particular place ○ *Will this road take us to the beach?* ○ *Take the first road on the left.* **10** *vt* AGREE TO PERFORM to agree to perform or assume the duties associated with something ○ *I decided to take the job.* **11** *vt* BE WILLING TO ACCEPT to be prepared to accept something as valid, true, or satisfactory ○ *The machine refused to take my card.* **12** *vt* BE ABLE TO BEAR to endure, deal with, accept, or put up with something, especially when it is unpleasant or unavoidable ○ *She cannot take criticism.* **13** *vt* REACT TO to behave, feel, or act in response to being told or finding out about something ○ *I don't know how they will take the news.* **14** *vt* HAVE STRENGTH TO HOLD UP to be capable of supporting something physically, without collapsing or breaking ○ *Will the shelf take the weight of all those books?* **15** *vt* TRAVEL BY MEANS OF to use a particular means of transport to make a journey ○ *Let's take a taxi.* **16** *vt* HAVE ROOM FOR to be capable of containing a specified amount or quantity of something ○ *The tank takes 20 gallons.* **17** *vt* WRITE to record something in a written form ○ *Do you mind if I take notes?* **18** *vt* CAPTURE ON CAMERA to use a camera to make a photograph ○ *Let's take a few photos to record the event.* **19** *vt* STUDY to study something, or teach somebody or something, on a formal basis ○ *We both took French in the sixth form.* ○ *Do you remember that teacher who took the French class?* **20** *vt* START TO DO to start to perform or occupy something ○ *The new treasurer takes office next month.* **21** *vt* CARRY OUT to perform or carry out something ○ *I'll take action on this immediately.* **22** *vt* TRAVEL OVER OR ROUND to travel over or round something, especially in a vehicle or on a motorcycle or horse and in a particular way ○ *He took the bend too fast.* **23** *vt* DERIVE FROM to copy or derive something from a particular text or author (*often passive*) ○ *That quote is taken from Shakespeare.* **24** *vt* CONSIDER to use somebody or something as an example or as a subject for consideration or discussion ○ *Let's take your last point first.* **25** *vt* REQUIRE PARTICULAR LENGTH OF TIME to need a particular amount of time to be completed or performed ○ *The journey usually takes about three hours.* **26** *vt* NEED IN ORDER TO FUNCTION to need a particular thing in order to operate ○ *This cassette recorder takes four batteries.* **27** *vt* REQUIRE to require something, especially a particular quality or characteristic, for something to be achieved ○ *It took a lot of courage to admit that you were wrong.* **28** *vt* EXPERIENCE EMOTION OR HAVE VIEW to experience a particular emotion, have a particular reaction, or adopt a particular opinion with regard to something ○ *They looked so pathetic that I took pity on them.* **29** *vt* INTERPRET IN PARTICULAR WAY to interpret, recognize, or understand something, especially somebody's words or actions, in a particular way ○ *I took you to mean that the loan would be approved.* **30** *vt* ASSUME to make an assumption, usually a mistaken one, about somebody's identity or about the nature of a thing or a situation ○ *I took you for his daughter.* **31** *vt* CONSUME to swallow or receive something into the body or system ○ *He refuses to take his medicine.* **32** *vt* EXPOSE BODY TO ELEMENTS to go or sit out in the sun, or expose the body to other elements ○ *She was lying on the beach, taking the sun.* **33** *vi* WORK OR BE SUCCESSFUL to work or have an effect in the intended way ○ *The perm didn't take because you rinsed out the solution too soon.* **34** *vi* START TO GROW to start to grow by producing roots ○ *The plant has taken nicely.* **35** *vt* MEASURE to measure something in an accurate way using a special instrument or procedure ○ *His temperature was normal when I took it this morning.* **36** *vi* BECOME ILL to become noticeably or suddenly unwell or more unwell ○ *The whole family took sick and it turned out to be food poisoning.* **37** *vt* SUBTRACT NUMBER to subtract a number or quantity from something ○ *Take 19 from 36 and you get 17.* **38** *vt* ASSUME CHARGE OF to assume control of something as a person who holds authority or has the attention of others ○ *She took the chair at the meeting.* **39** *vt* HAVE SEX WITH to penetrate somebody in an act of sexual intercourse, especially perfunctorily or without the person's consent (*literary or dated*) **40** *vti* BITE to bite the hook or fly at the end of an angler's line or the bait containing the hook ○ *The fish just weren't taking that morning.* **41** *vt US* CHEAT SOMEBODY to cheat or swindle somebody, especially out of a particular amount of money ■ *n* **1** MONEY OBTAINED IN BUSINESS TRANSACTIONS the amount of money received from customers or clients during a specified period of time ○ *What was the take last week?* **2** CAMERA SHOT a single uninterrupted recording of a piece of the action in a film by a camera ○ *This is the 15th take of this scene.* **3** SINGLE UNINTERRUPTED SOUND RECORDING a single uninterrupted session in which a work or section of a work is recorded by audio recording equipment **4** GRABBING OF BAIT the action of a fish in picking up or grabbing a bait or lure **5** IMPRESSION a personal impression or opinion of something (*informal*) ○ *What's your take on his presentation?* [Pre-12C. < Old Norse *taka*.] —**takable** *adj* —**taker** *n* ◇ **be taken with somebody** *or* **something** to find somebody or something pleasing or attractive ◇ **on the take** taking or willing to take bribes (*informal*) ◇ **take it** **1** to be able to tolerate a situation, usually one involving hardship, punishment, or criticism **2** to assume that something is true ○ *I take it that you want some breakfast.* ◇ **take it or leave it** **1** used to indicate that somebody can either accept or refuse something, but cannot alter the conditions **2** to be able either to accept or do something, or decline or not do something

USAGE See *bring*.

take after *vt* **1** to look or behave like somebody else, especially within the same family **2** to begin to pursue somebody

take apart *vt* **1** DISMANTLE to reduce something whole to its individual parts or pieces **2** CRITICIZE to criticize somebody or something in a severe and detailed way (*informal*) **3** BEAT SEVERELY to give somebody a severe beating or inflict a heavy defeat on somebody (*informal*)

take away *vt* **1** to remove or take something or somebody elsewhere **2** to subtract a number or quantity

take back *v* **1** *vt* WITHDRAW to withdraw something said or written **2** *vt* REGAIN POSSESSION OF to gain possession of something previously held but lost or given up **3** *vt* RETURN SOMETHING BOUGHT AS UNACCEPTABLE to return an unwanted or unsatisfactory article to the place where it was bought for a refund or exchange **4** *vt* ACCEPT GOODS BACK to accept an article returned as unwanted or unsatisfactory and offer a refund or exchange **5** *vt* REACCEPT to reaccept somebody into a relationship or home **6** *vt* REMIND OF THE PAST to remind somebody of an earlier time **7** *vti* MOVE COPY to move a portion of text back to the previous line

take down *vt* **1** WRITE DOWN to make a note of something in writing ○ *take down the names and addresses of the witnesses* **2** DISMANTLE to dismantle or demolish something **3** HUMILIATE to make somebody less arrogant or powerful **4** FORCE OPPONENT TO FALL to force an opponent to the mat during a wrestling match **5** REMOVE ACCUSED FROM DOCK to remove the accused from the dock to the cells at the end of or during a trial

take for *vt* to think of somebody or something as being of a particular description, often mistakenly ○ *Do you take me for a fool?*

take in *vt* **1** UNDERSTAND to understand and remember something ○ *Children can't be expected to take in so much new information in one lesson.* **2** ACCEPT AS REAL to accept something as real or true ○ *The news was such a shock that we still haven't taken it in.* **3** INCLUDE to include something within its scope ○ *The study takes in the whole postwar period.* **4** DECEIVE to deceive or cheat somebody by presenting a false appearance ○ *We were all taken in by her plausible manner.* **5** ACCEPT AS PAYING GUESTS to accept people as paying guests into a home **6** GIVE SHELTER to give somebody shelter in your home **7** WORK ON AT HOME to do paid work on something at home ○ *takes in ironing twice a week* **8** MAKE GARMENT NARROWER to alter a garment to make it narrower **9** *US* GO AND SEE to go and see some kind of entertainment or sport ○ *take in a movie*

take off *v* **1** *vt* REMOVE A GARMENT to remove something you are wearing **2** *vt* HAVE AS A BREAK FROM WORK to spend a particular amount of time not working ○ *I took a day off for the wedding.* **3** *vt* DEDUCT AN AMOUNT to deduct an amount from a price or sum **4** *vt* IMITATE to imitate somebody or something, especially for comic effect (*informal*) **5** *vt* STOP SOMETHING OPERATING to end the operation of something ○ *took off regular flights to the island* **6** *vi* BEGIN FLYING to leave the ground and begin flying **7** *vi* JUMP to leave the ground at the beginning of a jump **8** *vi* DEPART to leave, especially in a hurry or at short notice (*informal*) **9** *vi* SUCCEED to begin suddenly to be very successful or popular (*informal*)

SYNONYMS See *imitate*.

take on *v* **1** *vt* UNDERTAKE to begin doing something, or accept responsibility for something ○ *I can't take on any more projects at the moment.* **2** *vt* HIRE to hire additional people to do work **3** *vt* ADOPT to acquire or display a different character ○ *Her voice took on a kindlier tone.* **4** *vt* OPPOSE to oppose somebody or something in a competition or fight ○ *took on the city council* **5** *vt* TAKE ON BOARD to have people or things loaded on board a vessel or vehicle **6** *vi* BE UPSET to show extreme feelings, especially grief (*dated informal*) **7** *vti Carib* WORRY ABOUT to pay attention to or worry about somebody or something (*slang*)

take out *v* **1** *vt* BRING INTO THE OPEN to bring something into the open from a place where it was contained or concealed **2** *vt* REMOVE to remove or extract something from another substance **3** *vt* OBTAIN to obtain something such as a permit, mortgage, or insurance by applying for it **4** *vt* HAVE AS COMPANION to take somebody as a companion or guest to a social event or function **5** *vt* DIRECT ANGER AT SUBSTITUTE to express or relieve a strong feeling such as anger or frustration by directing it against somebody or something that is not the actual cause of it ○ *Don't take it out on me because you didn't get the job.* **6** *vt* DESTROY to destroy, kill, or neutralize somebody or something (*slang*) ○ *took out enemy artillery* **7** *vt Aus* **WIN** to win something, especially a sporting event (*informal*) ○ *They took out this year's premiership.* **8** *vi US* **BEGIN JOURNEY** to start out on a journey ○ *took out for the frontier*

take over *vti* **1 TAKE CONTROL** to obtain or assume control of something, or gain control of something from somebody else ○ *taken over by a larger company* **2 TAKE SOMEBODY'S PLACE** to begin to do something or operate something in place of somebody else ○ *She takes over when I finish my shift.* **3 MOVE COPY FORWARD** to move a portion of text forward to the next line

take to *vt* **1 FORM LIKING FOR** to develop a liking for somebody or something, especially quickly **2 START DOING OR USING** to start doing or using something as a habit, especially for help or consolation ○ *I've taken to checking that all the windows are locked before I leave the house.* **3 ADAPT YOURSELF** to adapt yourself to something, or become comfortable with something new ○ *quickly took to the new procedure* **4 GO TO A PLACE** to go to a place, especially for safety ○ *The slightest cough or sneeze would make him take to his bed.* ○ *took to their cars and fled*

take up *vt* **1 BEGIN DOING REGULARLY** to begin doing something regularly either as an occupation or a hobby **2 BEGIN DOING AGAIN** to begin doing something again after a break ○ *take up where you left off* **3 ACCEPT** to accept something offered **4 LIFT** to lift or raise something or somebody **5 SHORTEN GARMENT** to raise the hem of a garment such as a skirt to make the garment shorter **6 USE WASTEFULLY** to make use of or occupy something, especially in a wasteful or unwelcome way **7 ABSORB** to absorb a liquid **8** *US* **PAY OFF** to pay off a debt, e.g. a mortgage

take up on *vt* **1** to accept somebody's offer or wager **2** to argue with somebody on a point

take up with *vt* **1** to raise a matter for discussion with somebody **2** to begin associating with a particular person or people

takeaway /táykə way/ *adj* **1 FOR EATING ELSEWHERE** bought ready-cooked and taken away to be eaten elsewhere. US term **takeout** *adj.* 1 **2 SELLING TAKEAWAY FOOD** selling ready-cooked food to be eaten elsewhere. US term **takeout** *adj.* 2 ■ *n* **1 RESTAURANT SELLING TAKEAWAY FOOD** a restaurant or shop that sells ready-cooked food for eating elsewhere. US term **takeout** *n.* 1 **2 TAKEAWAY MEAL** a meal or food bought ready-cooked for eating elsewhere. US term **takeout** *n.* 2

take-down *adj* capable of being disassembled quickly

take-home pay *n* the amount of pay left to an employee after all deductions, e.g. for tax, have been made

taken past participle of **take**

take-no-prisoners *adj* persistent in an assertive way

takeoff /táyk of/ *n* **1 BEGINNING OF FLIGHT** the process of leaving the ground and beginning to fly **2 BEGINNING OF JUMP** the act or point of leaving the ground at the beginning of a jump **3 POINT OF RAPID GROWTH** a point at which substantial success or economic expansion is achieved and the prospect of further success or growth seems assured **4 IMITATION** an imitation of somebody or something, especially for comic effect (*informal*)

takeout /táyk owt/ *adj US* **1** FOOD = **takeaway** *adj.* 1 **2** = **takeaway** *adj.* 2 ■ *n US* **1** = **takeaway** *n.* 1 **2** FOOD = **takeaway** *n.* 2

takeover /táyk ōvər/ *n* an assumption or seizure of control of something, especially of a company, political entity, or organization

take-up *n* **1** the degree to which something offered or made available is accepted or made use of by people **2** a part of a mechanism onto which something passing through it, e.g. tape, is wound

takin /taá keen/ *n* a large ruminant mammal with a heavy build, shaggy coat, and heavy horns that curve back. Native to: mountainous regions of South Asia. *Budorcas taxicolor.* [Mid-19C. Probably < Tibeto-Burman.]

taking /táyking/ *adj* **1** displaying a charming or fascinating appeal **2** infectious (*informal*)

takings /táykingz/ *npl* money received through sales by a business

taki-taki /taáki taaki/ *n* LANG = **Sranantongo** [Alteration of TALK]

tala /taálə/ (*plural* **-la** *or* **-las**) *n* see table at **currency** [Mid-20C. < Polynesian.]

talapoin /tállə poyn/ *n* **1** a small olive-green guenon monkey. Native to: swampy forests in western equatorial Africa. *Cercopithecus talapoin* and *Miopithecus talapoin.* **2** in Myanmar and Thailand, a Buddhist monk [Late 16C. Via French and Portuguese < Mon *tala pói* 'lord of merit'.]

talaria /tə láiri ə/ *npl* winged sandals worn by characters in Greek myth, especially by Hermes [Late 16C. < Latin, plural of *talaris* 'of the ankles' < *talus* 'ankle'.]

Talbot /táwlbət, tól-/, **William Henry Fox** (1800–77) British photographic pioneer

talc /talk/ *n* **1 SOFT HYDRATED MINERAL** a soft mineral consisting of hydrated magnesium silicate. Source: igneous and metamorphic rocks. Use: talcum powder. **2 COSMETIC POWDER** talcum powder (*informal*) ■ *vt* (**talcs, talcking** *or* **talcing, talcked** *or* **talced**) **APPLY TALC** to put talc onto something [Late 16C. Via French *talc* and medieval Latin *talcum* < Persian *ṭalḳ*.] —**talcose** /tál kōss/ *adj* —**talcous** *adj*

talcum powder /tálkəm-/ *n* a powder made from purified talc, often scented, that is put onto the skin to perfume it and absorb moisture [< medieval Latin (see TALC)]

tale /tayl/ *n* **1 NARRATIVE** a narrative or account of events **2 SHORT PIECE OF FICTION** a short piece of fiction, often one of a connected series **3 PIECE OF GOSSIP** an item of gossip, or a malicious rumour **4 FALSEHOOD** a story or report that is untrue [Old English *talu* < Germanic] ◇ **tell tales (out of school)** to report acts of wrongdoing to somebody in authority

LITERARY LINK ***The Canterbury Tales***, a collection of stories (1387–1400) by Geoffrey Chaucer. The tales, mainly in verse, are told by a group of pilgrims travelling to the shrine of St Thomas à Becket in Canterbury. They range from the bawdy 'Miller's Tale' to reworkings of traditional stories, for example the 'Nun's Priest's Tale' about Chanticleer the cock.

SPELLCHECK See ***tail.***

Taleban *npl* ISLAM = **Taliban**

talebearer /táyl bairər/ *n* a person who informs against other people or spreads malicious rumours —**talebearing** *n*

talent /tállənt/ *n* **1 ABILITY** a natural ability to do something well **2 SOMEBODY WITH AN EXCEPTIONAL ABILITY** a person or people with an exceptional ability **3 POSSIBLE ROMANTIC PARTNERS** people considered collectively as possible romantic or sexual partners (*slang*) **4 ANCIENT UNIT** an ancient unit of weight and money [14C. Via Old French, 'mental inclination' < Latin *talentum* 'balance, sum of money' < Greek *talanton.*] —**talentless** *adj*

SYNONYMS ***talent, gift, aptitude, flair, bent, knack, genius***

CORE MEANING: the natural ability to do something well

talent a natural ability to do something well that can be developed by training; **gift** a natural ability, especially an artistic ability, or a social skill; **aptitude** a natural ability to do or learn something, especially one that is not yet fully developed; **flair** a natural ability to do something well, especially creative or artistic ability; **bent** a natural ability, inclination, or liking for something; **knack** an intuitive ability to do something well, especially one that might not be developed by training; **genius** exceptional intellectual or creative ability.

talent contest *n* ARTS = **talent show**

talent scout *n* somebody whose job is to search for people who have exceptional abilities in some field, e.g. entertainment or sport, and recruit them for professional work

talent show *n* a public performance made up of acts by amateur entertainers who compete for a prize and are sometimes given professional opportunities

taler *n* COINS = **thaler**

tales /táy leez/ *n* (*plural* **-les**) a writ used to summon people to court to fill vacancies on a jury (+ *singular verb*) ■ *npl* a group of people summoned to court to fill vacancies on a jury [15C. < Latin *tales de circumstantibus* 'such of the bystanders', phrase in the writ.]

talesman /táy leezmən/ (*plural* **-men** /-mən/) *n* somebody selected from a group to fill a vacant seat in a jury

taleteller /táyl tellər/ *n* **1** a teller of stories **2** a person who informs against other people or spreads malicious rumours —**taletelling** *n*

tali plural of **talus**[2]

Taliban /tálli ban/, **Taleban** *npl* a strict Islamic group that took over the government of Afghanistan in 1996 after its militia had gained control of most of the country [Late 20C. Via Pashto < Persian, 'students'.]

Taliesin /tal yéssin/ (*fl.* AD 6th century) Welsh poet

talion /tálli ən/ *n* a punishment that has the same nature as the crime, e.g. the death penalty for murder [15C. Via Anglo-Norman < Latin *talion-*.]

talipes /tállə peez/ *n* club foot (*technical*) [Mid-19C. < modern Latin, < Latin *talus* 'ankle' + *pes* 'foot'.]

talipot /tálli pot/ *n* a palm tree with large fan-shaped leaves. Native to: Southeast Asia. *Corypha umbraculifera.* [Late 17C. Via Malayalam < Sanskrit *tālīpatra* < *tālī* 'fan palm' + *patra* 'leaf'.]

talisman /tállizmən/ *n* **1** an object, e.g. a stone or jewel, believed to give magical powers to somebody who carries or wears it **2** anything believed to have magical properties [Mid-17C. Via French or Spanish < Greek *telesma* 'something consecrated' < *telein* 'complete, consecrate' < *telos* 'result'.] —**talismanic** /tálliz mánnik/ *adj*

⚡**TALISMAN** /tállizmən/ *n* a computer system used for buying and selling securities on the London Stock Exchange. Full form **Transfer Accounting Lodgement for Investors and Stock Management**

talk /tawk/ *v* **1** *vti* **EXPRESS SOMETHING BY SPEAKING** to speak, or express something using speech **2** *vi* **HAVE CONVERSATION ABOUT** to address spoken words to somebody, or have a conversation with somebody **3** *vt* **DISCUSS SUBJECT** to discuss a particular subject ○ *talk business* **4** *vi* **COMMUNICATE** to communicate in a way other than by speaking ○ *talk in sign language* **5** *vti* **SPEAK IN SPECIFIED LANGUAGE** to use, or be able to use, a particular language to communicate with people ○ *talks Italian with his grandmother* **6** *vi* **REVEAL INFORMATION** to reveal information, especially when being pressured to do so ○ *They interrogated her for hours but she wouldn't talk.* **7** *vi* **GOSSIP** to discuss the affairs of others, or spread rumours ○ *People are starting to talk.* **8** *vi* **MAKE SOUNDS LIKE SPEECH** to imitate the sounds of speech ○ *The baby is beginning to talk.* **9** *vi* **BE PERSUASIVE** to have the power to influence or persuade people (*informal*) ○ *Money talks!* **10** *vi* **LECTURE** to give a speech or lecture on a subject **11** *vt* **SPEAK IN TERMS OF SOMETHING PARTICULAR** to have to do or deal with something when discussing a particular topic (*informal*) ○ *You're talking big money for a job like that.* **12** *vi* **BE FRIENDLY** to be on sufficiently friendly terms with somebody to be able to have a conversation (*informal*) ○ *Don't bother asking me how she is, because we're not talking.* ■ *n* **1 CONVERSATION** a conversation or exchange of ideas or information between two or more people **2 THINGS SAID** the things said by somebody or by a group of people in conversation ○ *The talk after dinner was mostly about politics.* **3 SPEECH ON PARTICULAR SUBJECT** a speech or lecture on a particular subject, given before an audience **4 GOSSIP ABOUT AFFAIRS OF OTHERS** idle or malicious conversation about the affairs of others **5 EMPTY SPEECH** speech about something without any intention of taking action ○ *He's all talk; he won't do anything!* **6 THING TALKED ABOUT** a subject of discussion or gossip among a group of people ○ *the talk of the town* **7 WAY OF SPEAKING** a particular way of speaking ■ **talks** *npl* **NEGOTIATIONS** formal discussions among parties to bring about a resolution to a problem ■ *adj* **USING INFORMAL INTERVIEWS** made up mainly of informal interviews with guests or telephone calls from viewers or listeners ○ *talk radio* [13C. Ultimately < Germanic.] —**talker** *n*

talk at *vt* to speak to somebody without showing any interest in listening to the person's reply

talk back *vi* to make an impudent reply

talk down *vt* **1 PREVENT FROM SPEAKING** to prevent somebody from speaking by speaking loudly and ignoring attempts to interrupt **2 TELL HOW TO LAND AIRCRAFT** to give radio guidance to somebody on how to land an aircraft **3 MAKE SEEM LESS IMPRESSIVE** to discuss something in a way that makes it seem less important or successful than it is

talk down to *vt* to speak to somebody in a superior or condescending way

talk into *vt* to persuade somebody to do something by talking to him or her ○ *We talked her into staying for dinner.*

talk out *vt* **1** to settle a difference of opinion through discussion **2** to prevent the passage of a piece of legislation, especially a bill in Parliament, by prolonging the discussion of it until it is too late to vote on it

talk out of *vt* to dissuade somebody from doing some-

thing by talking to him or her ○ *talked him out of buying a car*
talk over *vt* **1** to discuss something at length or thoroughly **2** to persuade somebody to agree with an opinion or point of view ○ *talked them over to our side*
talk round *vt* **1** to persuade somebody to agree with an opinion ○ *She didn't like the idea but we talked her round in the end.* **2** to talk about matters relating to a topic without discussing the topic itself or the really central issue and without coming to any conclusions
talk up *vt* to praise something in the hope of making it popular or successful

talkathon /táwkə thon/ *n* US a long period of discussion [Mid-20C. < TALK + MARATHON.]

talkative /táwkətiv/ *adj* tending to talk readily and at length —**talkatively** *adv* —**talkativeness** *n*

SYNONYMS ***talkative, chatty, gossipy, garrulous, loquacious***
CORE MEANING: talking a lot
talkative willing to talk readily and at length; **chatty** talking freely about unimportant things in a friendly way; **gossipy** talking with relish about other people and their lives, often unkindly or maliciously; **garrulous** excessively or pointlessly talkative; **loquacious** (*formal*) tending to talk a great deal.

talkback /táwk bak/ *n* a system of communication in a broadcasting studio that enables the staff to speak to each other without the speech being broadcast

talkie /táwki/ *n* an early film with a soundtrack (*dated*) [Early 20C. Shortening of *talking picture*, after MOVIE.]

talking book *n* a book that has been recorded onto an audio cassette, originally designed for people who cannot see

talking head *n* somebody such as a newsreader who talks at length into a camera in a television broadcast, usually shown only from the shoulders up

talking point *n* **1 INTERESTING ITEM FOR DISCUSSION** a topic, or aspect of something, that provokes a lot of discussion **2** US **SOMETHING SUPPORTING AN ARGUMENT** something that supports an argument, e.g. a particularly convincing point **3 PUBLICITY POINT** a claim made about a product in publicity material that is considered particularly interesting or persuasive to potential customers

talking-to *n* a scolding given to somebody, especially by somebody in authority (*informal*)

talk show *n* US BROADCAST = **chat show**

talky /táwki/ (**-ier, -iest**) *adj* containing too much dialogue and not enough action ○ *a talky and dull film*

tall /tawl/ *adj* **1 VERY HIGH** reaching or having grown to a considerable or above-average height ○ *tall trees* **2 OF CERTAIN HEIGHT** having reached a particular height ○ *five foot tall* **3 LARGE** substantial, demanding, or difficult to deal with ○ *a tall order* **4 INCREDIBLE** exaggerating the events of something beyond the bounds of probability ○ *a tall story* **5 POMPOUS** having an excessively grand or boastful style ■ *adv* **PROUDLY** in a proud or courageous way ○ *There are times when you must stand tall and defend your beliefs.* ■ *n* **SIZE FOR TALL PEOPLE** a clothing size for tall people, or a garment in this size [Old English *getæl* 'quick, ready' < Germanic, 'to count'.] —**tallish** *adj* —**tallness** *n*

tallage /tállij/ *n* **1 ROYAL TAX** a tax levied by the Norman and Angevin kings of England on royal lands and towns **2 TAX LEVIED BY LORD** in feudal times, a tax levied by a lord on his vassals or tenants ■ *vt* (**-lages, -laging, -laged**) **LEVY TAX ON** to levy a tax, especially a tallage, on somebody or something [13C. < Old French *taillage* < *taillier* 'to cut'.]

Tallahassee /tállə hássi/ capital of Florida, in the northern part of the state. Population: 136,628 (1998 estimate).

tallboy /táwl boy/ *n* **1** a high set of drawers, made up of two chests of drawers set one on top of the other. US term **highboy 2** a narrow fitting at the top of a chimney to prevent smoke being carried back down

Talleyrand /tálli ránd/, **Charles Maurice de** (1754–1838) French statesman

Tallinn /tállin, ta lín, -leén/ capital of Estonia, on the Bay of Tallinn, an inlet of the Gulf of Finland. Population: 490,000 (1994).

tallis *n* JUDAISM = **tallith**

Tallis /tálliss/, **Thomas** (1510?–85) English composer

tallith /tállith/ (*plural* **-lithim** /tali theém/ *or* **-liths**), **tallis** /tálliss/ (*plural* **-lisim** /-seém/) *n* a Jewish four-cornered fringed prayer shawl of white material with a black, blue, or purple stripe, worn at morning prayers [Early 17C. < Rabbinic Hebrew *ṭallīt* < biblical Hebrew *ṭillel* 'to cover'.]

tall oil *n* an oily liquid produced as a by-product of a chemical process in the manufacture of wood pulp. Use: making soaps and emulsions. [Early 20C. Partial translation of German *Tallöl* < Swedish *tallolja* < *tall* 'pine' + *olja* 'oil'.]

tallow /tá lō/ *n* **1 FATTY SUBSTANCE** a hard fatty substance extracted from the fat of sheep and cattle. Use: candles, soap. **2 SUBSTANCE MADE FROM VEGETABLE MATTER** a substance similar to tallow, made from vegetable matter ■ *vt* **COVER WITH TALLOW** to cover or grease something with tallow [13C. < Low German.] —**tallowy** *adj*

tall poppy syndrome *n* Aus a tendency among the media and the public to denigrate the achievements of prominent members of society

tall ship *n* a square-rigged sailing ship

tally /tálli/ *v* (**-lies, -lying, -lied**) **1** *vti* **AGREE** to agree, correspond, or come to the same amount, or cause two or more things to agree **2** *vi* **KEEP SCORE** to keep a record of a score or account **3** *vt* **COUNT** to count or reckon items **4** *vt* **REGISTER IN AN ACCOUNT** to register something in an account of items **5** *vt* **PUT LABEL OR TAG ON** to put an identifying label or tag on something ■ *n* (*plural* **-lies**) **1 RECORD OF ITEMS** a record or account of items, e.g. things bought or points scored ○ *keep a tally* **2 SCORE ACHIEVED** the total or current number of things achieved by somebody, especially somebody's score in a game or competition ○ *added to his personal tally of nine goals for the season* **3** US **SINGLE SCORE** a single score, e.g. a run or a touchdown, in a contest **4 IDENTIFYING LABEL OR MARK** something, e.g. a label or mark, that identifies something **5 COUNTERPART** something that corresponds to or is the counterpart of something else **6 NOTCH CUT TO RECORD NUMBER** a notch cut into a stick as a record of a number **7 MARK REPRESENTING NUMBER** a mark or marks representing a number, especially a set of four short vertical lines crossed by a diagonal fifth line used for numbering things in fives [15C. Via Anglo-Norman < Latin *talea* 'twig, cutting'.] —**tallier** *n*

tally-ho /tálli hō/ *interj* **EXCLAMATION THAT FOX HAS BEEN SIGHTED** used by a participant in a fox hunt to let others know that a fox has been sighted ■ *n* (*plural* **tally-hos**) **1 FOX HUNTER'S CRY** a cry by a participant in a fox hunt to let others know that a fox has been sighted **2** TRANSP = **four-in-hand** *n.* 1 ■ *vi* (**tally-hos, tally-hoing, tally-hoed**) **SHOUT 'TALLY-HO'** to give a shout of 'tally-ho' [Probably alteration of French *taïaut*]

tallyman /tállimən/ (*plural* **-men** /-mən/) *n* **1** a person who records or accounts for something, e.g. items bought on credit or points scored **2** a travelling sales representative who sells goods to be paid for in instalments

Talmud /tálmòod, -məd/ *n* the collection of ancient Jewish writings that forms the basis of Jewish religious law, consisting of the early scriptural interpretations (**Mishnah**) and the later commentaries on them (**Gemara**) [Mid-16C. < post-biblical Hebrew *talmūḏ* 'instruction' < Hebrew *lāmaḏ* 'learn'.] —**Talmudic** /tal mòodik, -myòodik/ *adj* —**Talmudical** *adj* —**Talmudism** *n* —**Talmudist** *n*

talon /tállən/ *n* **1 HOOKED CLAW** a hooked claw, especially of a bird of prey **2 SOMETHING LIKE A CLAW** something that looks like a claw, e.g. a curled human finger **3 PART OF A LOCK** the part of a lock that the key is pressed against when turned and that causes the bolt to slide out **4** ARCHIT = **ogee** *n.* 2 **5 UNDEALT CARDS** the remainder of the deck of cards after a deal in particular games, e.g. in piquet or solitaire [14C. Via French < assumed Vulgar Latin *talon-* 'heel, spur' < Latin *talus* 'ankle'.] —**taloned** *adj*

taluk /taa lòok/ (*plural* **-luka** /-lòokə/) *n* S Asia **1** a subdivision of a district in South Asia **2** a piece of hereditary land in South Asia [Late 18C. < Urdu, Persian *ta'alluḳ* 'estate' < Arabic *ta'allaḳa* 'be attached'.]

talus[1] /táyləss/ *n* **1 AREA OF RUBBLE** a sloping area of rock rubble **2 ROCK RUBBLE** rock rubble, e.g. at the base of a cliff **3 BASE OF FORTIFICATION** the sloping base of a fortification [Mid-17C. < ?]

talus[2] /táyləss/ (*plural* **-li** /-lī/) *n* the bone in the ankle that connects with the lower leg bones to form the ankle joint [Late 16C. < Latin, 'ankle'.]

talweg /taál veg/ *n* GEOG = **thalweg**

tam /tam/ *n* a tam-o'-shanter (*informal*) [Shortening]

TAM /tam/ *abbr* Television Audience Measurement

tamale /tə maáli/ *n* a Mexican dish made by mixing fried chopped meat with peppers and seasonings, rolling the mixture in cornmeal dough, wrapping it in maize husks, and then steaming it [Late 17C. Back-formation < American Spanish *tamales*, plural of *tamal* < Nahuatl *tamalli*.]

tamandua /támmən dòo ə/, **tamandu** /-dòo/ *n* a small tree-living toothless anteater with a long prehensile tail. Native to: Central and South America. *Tamandua tetradactyla* and *Tamandua mexicana*. [Early 17C. Via Portuguese < Tupi *tamanduá* 'ant hunter'.]

Tamar /táym aar/ **1** river in SW England, emptying into the English Channel. The Tamar valley is an Area of Outstanding Natural Beauty. Length: 97 km/60 mi. **2** river in N Tasmania, Australia. Length: 65 km/40 mi.

tamarack /támmə rak/ *n* **1** a deciduous larch with bluish-green needles and oval cones. Native to: North America. *Larix laricina*. **2** the wood of the tamarack tree [Early 19C. < Canadian French *tamarac*.]

tamari /tə maári/ *n* a rich Japanese soy sauce [Late 20C. < Japanese.]

tamarillo /támmə ríll ō/ (*plural* **-los**) *n* US FOOD, TREES = **tree tomato** [Mid-20C. Alteration of TOMATILLO.]

tamarin /támmərin/ *n* a small monkey that has a long tail and is highly vocal. Native to: South America. Genus: *Saguinus*. [Late 18C. Via French < Galibi.]

tamarind /támmərind/ *n* **1 FRUIT** a pod containing many seeds within an acid-tasting pulp. Use: preserves, drinks, medicines. **2 TROPICAL TREE** a tropical evergreen tree that produces tamarinds. Flowers: yellow with red streaks. *Tamarindus indica*. **3 WOOD FROM TAMARIND** the wood of the tamarind tree [Mid-16C. Via Old French < Arabic *tamr hindī* 'Indian date'.]

tamarisk /támmərisk/ *n* a tree or shrub with leaves resembling scales. Flowers: white to pink, in terminal spikes. Native to: Europe, Asia, Africa. Genus: *Tamarix*. [14C. < late Latin *tamariscus*, variant of Latin *tamarix*.]

Tamatave /tamataáv/ former name for **Toamasina**

tambac *n* METALL = **tombac**

tambala /taam baálə/ (*plural* **-la** *or* **-las**) *n* see table at **currency** [Late 20C. < Chewa, 'cockerel'.]

Tambo /támbō/, **Oliver** (1917–93) South African political leader

tambour /tám boor, -bawr/ *n* **1 EMBROIDERY FRAME** a round frame on which material is stretched while it is being embroidered **2 EMBROIDERY** embroidery done on a tambour **3 FLEXIBLE ROLLING TOP OF DESK** a flexible rolling top of a desk or sliding front of a cabinet, made of thin strips of wood attached to canvas **4 DRUM** a drum, especially a side drum **5 CIRCULAR WALL** a circular wall, especially one supporting a dome ■ *vti* **EMBROIDER DESIGN USING FRAME** to embroider using a round frame [15C. Via Old French < Persian *tabīra* 'drum'.]

tamboura /tam bòorə, -báwrə/ *n* an Asian stringed instrument resembling a lute without frets, played to produce a harmonic drone [Late 16C. Via Arabic and Persian < Persian *dunbara* 'lamb's tail'.]

tambourin /támbòorin/ *n* **1 DANCE** an 18th-century Provençal dance in a two-beat rhythm, usually accompanied by a drum **2 MUSIC FOR TAMBOURIN** the music for a tambourin **3 DRUM** a small Provençal drum [Late 18C. < French, 'small drum' < *tambour* (see TAMBOUR).]

tambourine /támbə reén/ *n* a shallow single-headed drum with jingling metallic discs in its frame, held in one hand and played by shaking it or striking it with the free hand [Late 16C. < French, 'small drum' < *tambour* (see TAMBOUR).] —**tambourinist** *n*

Tamburlaine = **Tamerlane**

tame /taym/ *adj* (**tamer, tamest**) **1 NO LONGER WILD** changed from a wild or uncultivated state to one suitable for domestic use or life **2 FRIENDLY TOWARDS PEOPLE** describes an animal or bird unafraid of human contact **3 WITHOUT SPIRIT** lacking in spirit or vigour **4 BLAND** showing little of the qualities that make something interesting, e.g. imagination, adventurousness, or inspiration ○ *Considering the controversial nature of his other films, this latest one is very tame.* **5 SLOW-MOVING** describes a river with very little current ○ *a tame stretch of river* ■ *vt* (**tames, taming, tamed**) **1 DOMESTICATE** to make a wild animal or uncultivated land suitable for domestic life or use **2 SUBDUE** to remove the wildness, spirit, or energy from somebody or something **3 MODERATE** to make something much less harsh or extreme **4 BRING UNDER HUMAN CONTROL** to bring a natural force under human control ○ *a series of dams to tame the raging river* [Old English *tam* < Indo-European, 'constrain'] —**tamable** *adj* —**tamableness** *n* —**tamely** *adv* —**tameness** *n* —**tamer** *n*

Tamerlane /támmər layn/, **Tamburlaine** /támbər layn/ (1336–1405) Turkic ruler and conqueror. Born **Timur**

Tamil /támmil/ (*plural* **-ils** *or* **-il**) *n* **1** a member of a Dravidian people who live in S India and N Sri Lanka **2** the Dravidian language of the Tamil people. Native speakers: 50 million. [Mid-18C. < Tamil *Tamil*.] —**Tamil** *adj*

Tamil Nadu /támmil naa dóo/ state in S India. Capital: Chennai. Population: 58,840,000 (1994). Area: 130,058 sq. km/50,215 sq. mi.

Tamil Tiger *n* a member of a movement that seeks to found a separate state for the Tamil people in NE Sri Lanka and uses armed resistance and terror tactics against the Sri Lankan authorities

Tammany Hall /támməni-/ *n* a political organization formed as a fraternal society in New York in 1789 but mainly known for political corruption in the early 20th century [Mid-19C. After a Native North American leader said to have welcomed William Penn.] —**Tammanyism** *n* —**Tammanyite** *n*

tammar /támmər/ *n* a rabbit-sized wallaby that has a reddish-brown coat with whitish underparts. Native to: dry scrub of southern Australia. *Wallabia eugenii.* [Mid-19C. < Aboriginal.]

Tammuz /taá mooz/ *n* in the Jewish calendar, the tenth month of the civil year and the fourth month of the religious year [Mid-16C. Via Hebrew *Tammūz* < Babylonian *Du'uzu*, a deity.]

tammy[1] /támmi/ (*plural* **-mies**) *n* a tam-o'-shanter (*informal*) [Late 19C. < TAM.]

tammy[2] /támmi/ *n* **tammy** (*plural* **-mies**), **tammy cloth** a fine strainer made of woollen cloth ■ *vt* (**-mies, -mying, -mied**) to strain something such as a sauce using a tammy [Mid-18C. Probably < French *tamis*.]

tam-o'-shanter /támmə shántər/ *n* a brimless Scottish woollen hat, usually with a bobble at the centre of the crown [Mid-19C. < *Tam O' Shanter*, eponymous hero of a poem by Robert BURNS.]

tamoxifen /tə móksi fen/ *n* $C_{26}H_{29}NO$ a drug that inhibits the actions of oestrogen. Use: treatment of breast cancer, some types of infertility. [Late 20C. < TRANS- + AMINE + OXY- + PHENOL.]

tamp /tamp/ *vt* **1** to pack or push something down, especially by tapping it repeatedly **2** to pack a substance such as sand or earth into a drill hole above an explosive ■ *n* = **tamper**[2] *n.* 2 [Early 19C. < ?]

Tampa /támpə/ seaport in west-central Florida, on Tampa Bay, an arm of the Gulf of Mexico. Population: 289,156 (1998 estimate).

tamper[1] /támpər/ *vi* **1** to interfere with something in a way that damages it or has harmful results **2** to try to corrupt or influence somebody or affect the outcome of something [Mid-16C. Probably variant of TEMPER.] —**tamperer** *n*

tamper[2] /támpər/ *n* **1 SOMEBODY OR SOMETHING THAT TAMPS** somebody or something that packs something down with repeated blows **2 TAMPING DEVICE** a device for pushing tobacco down into the bowl of a pipe. US term **tamp** *n.* **3 CASING ON NUCLEAR WEAPON** the casing around the core of a nuclear weapon that reflects neutrons back into the core, slowing the expansion of the nuclear reaction and increasing the weapon's power

Tampere /támpərə, támp e re/ city in SW Finland. Population: 191,254 (1999).

tamper-proof *adj* designed to be difficult to tamper with

Tampico /tam peékō/ seaport in E Mexico. Population: 262,690 (1990).

tampion /támpi ən/, **tompion** /tómpi-/ *n* a plug or cover for the muzzle of a gun to keep out moisture and dust when it is not in use [15C. < French *tampon* (see TAMPON).]

tampon /tám pon/ *n* **1 PLUG OF MATERIAL USED DURING MENSTRUATION** a cylindrical plug of soft material inserted in the vagina during menstruation to absorb blood **2 PAD TO CHECK BLEEDING** a pad of cotton or other absorbent fabric that is used for plugging wounds or for controlling blood flow in body cavities, especially during surgery ■ *vt* **CONTROL BLOOD FLOW** to use a tampon to plug a wound or to control blood flow in a body cavity, especially during surgery [Mid-19C. < French, 'plug, bung', variant of *tapon* 'piece of cloth to stop a hole' < assumed Frankish *tappo* 'stopper'.]

tamponade /támpə náyd/ *n* the insertion of a tampon during surgery to check bleeding

tam-tam /tám tam/ *n* a large gong [Mid-19C. < ?]

Tamworth[1] /tám wurth/ *n* a reddish-gold pig with a long snout belonging to a hardy breed developed in the Midlands. Kept for: meat. [Mid-19C. After TAMWORTH[2] 1.]

Tamworth[2] /tám wurth, támmwərth/ **1** market town in central England. Population: 68,440 (1991). **2** city in NE New South Wales, Australia. Population: 31,865 (1996).

tan[1] /tan/ *n* **1 LIGHT BROWN COLOUR** a light brown orange-tinged colour **2 SUNTAN** the brownish colour that the skin takes on after being exposed to ultraviolet light, especially from the Sun or a sunlamp **3** MANUF = **tanbark** *n.* **4** CHEM = **tannin** ■ *v* (**tans, tanning, tanned**) **1** *vti* **GET OR GIVE SOMEBODY A SUNTAN** to give somebody's skin a brownish colour, or take on such a colour **2** *vt* **CONVERT HIDE TO LEATHER** to convert an animal skin or hide into leather by treating it with something such as tannin **3** *vt* **BEAT** to give a beating to somebody (*informal*) ■ *adj* (**tanner, tannest**) **1 OF LIGHT BROWN COLOUR** of a light brown orange-tinged colour **2** *US* = **tanned 3 OF PROCESS OF TANNING HIDES** relating to or used in the process of tanning animal skins and hides [Pre-12C. < medieval Latin *tannare* 'tan, dye a tawny colour' < *tannum* 'tanbark'.] —**tannable** *adj* —**tannish** *adj*

tan[2] /tan/ *abbr* tangent

tana /taánə/ *n* **1** a small lemur with a grey-brown back, whitish underparts, and a dark stripe that runs along the back and encircles each eye. Native to: Madagascar. *Phaner furcifer.* **2** a mainly ground-dwelling tree shrew with a brownish coat that has a black stripe along the back. Native to: Borneo, Sumatra. Genus: *Lyongale.* [Early 19C. Via modern Latin < Malay *tūpai tāna* 'ground-squirrel'.]

Tana, Lake /taánə/ largest lake in Ethiopia, in the north-central Ethiopian highlands. Area: 2,156 sq. km/1,219 sq. mi.

Tanabata /taánə baátə/ *n* in Japan, an annual festival during which people write down their wishes and hang them with other decorations on branches of bamboo. Date: 7 July. [Early 20C. < Japanese.]

Tanach /taa naákh/, **Tanakh** *n* the sacred book of Judaism consisting of the Torah, Prophets, and Hagiographa [Mid-20C. < Hebrew *tĕnak*, acronym < *tōrāh* 'law' + *nĕbī'īm* 'prophets' + *kĕtūbīm* 'hagiographa'.]

tanager /tánnəjər/ *n* a songbird that is usually fairly small and brightly coloured in bold patterns and has a conical bill. Native to: forests of North and South America. Family: Thraupidae. [Early 17C. < modern Latin *Tanagra* < Tupi *tangará*.]

Tanakh *n* JUDAISM = **Tanach**

Tananarive /tə nánnə reév/ former name for **Antananarivo**

tanbark /tán baark/ *n* the bark of some trees, especially oak and hemlock, used as a source of tannin

T & E *abbr* tired and emotional (*informal*)

tandem /tándəm/ *n* **1 BICYCLE FOR TWO RIDERS** a bicycle with two saddles and two sets of handlebars and pedals, one behind the other, so that it can be ridden by two people at the same time. US term **tandem bicycle 2 HORSE-DRAWN CARRIAGE** a two-wheeled carriage drawn by two horses harnessed one behind the other **3 HORSE TEAM HARNESSED IN SINGLE FILE** a team of two horses harnessed one behind the other **4 ARRANGEMENT IN SINGLE FILE** a setup in which two things are arranged one behind the other ■ *adv* **ONE BEHIND ANOTHER** with one behind the other ○ *We'll ride tandem.* [Late 18C. < Latin, 'at length' (< *tam* 'so' + demonstrative suffix *-dem*), humorously interpreted as 'in a straight line'.] ◇ **in tandem 1** in partnership or co-operation **2** with one behind the other

tandem bicycle *n US* CYCLING = **tandem** *n.* 1

tandoor /tan dóor/ *n* a clay oven used especially in the cuisine of the N Indian subcontinent for cooking food quickly at high temperature [Mid-19C. Via Urdu *tandūr*, Persian *tanūr* < Arabic *tannūr* 'oven, furnace'.]

tandoori /tan dóori/ *adj* **COOKED IN CLAY OVEN** baked or cooked in a tandoor after being marinated in a mixture of yoghurt and spices ■ *n* **TANDOORI MEAL** a dish or meal of tandoori food (*informal*) ■ *vt* **COOK IN TANDOORI STYLE** to cook something in a tandoor, or after marinating the food in the mixture of yoghurt and spices traditionally used for such dishes [Mid-20C. < Persian and Urdu, < Urdu *tandūr*, Persian *tanūr* (see TANDOOR).]

tang[1] /tang/ *n* **1 STRONG TASTE** a distinctively sharp strong taste **2 PUNGENT SMELL** a smell that has a sharp biting quality **3 SUGGESTION** a slight hint or flavour of a particular thing ○ *a cake with a tang of lemon* **4 SHARP END GOING INTO HANDLE** the sharp part at one end of a chisel, knife blade, or other similar tool that secures it to the handle or shaft [14C. < N Germanic.] —**tangy** *adj*

tang[2] /tang/ *n* a loud, often harsh, ringing noise [Early 17C. An imitation of the sound.] —**tang** *vti*

Tang /tang/, **T'ang** *n* a wealthy Chinese dynasty that lasted from AD 618–907 and was renowned for its encouragement and patronage of the arts, especially poetry and ceramics, and the development of printing [Mid-17C. < Chinese *táng*.] —**Tang** *adj*

tanga /táng gə/ *n* an undergarment or the lower part of a bikini made of two small triangles of fabric fastened with ties [Early 20C. Via Portuguese, 'triangular loincloth' < Bantu.]

Tanga /táng gə/ town in NE Tanzania, on the Indian Ocean. Population: 188,000 (1994).

Tanganyika /táng gən yeékə/ former country in East Africa, constituting the mainland part of what is now Tanzania —**Tanganyikan** *n, adj*

Tanganyika, Lake lake in east-central Africa, with shorelines in Burundi, Tanzania, Zambia, and the Democratic Republic of the Congo. Area: 32,900 sq. km/12,700 sq. mi. Length: 680 km/420 mi.

Tange Kenzo /táng gay kénnzō/ (*b.* 1913) Japanese architect

tangelo /tánjəlō/ (*plural* **-los**) *n* **1** a citrus fruit with smooth easily peeled skin and sharp-tasting orange flesh **2** a hybrid between a tangerine tree and a grapefruit tree that produces tangelos [Early 20C. Blend of TANGERINE + POMELO.]

tangent /tánjənt/ *n* **1 LINE OR SURFACE THAT TOUCHES ANOTHER** a line, curve, or surface that touches another curve or surface but does not cross or intersect it **2 TRIGONOMETRIC FUNCTION** for a given angle in a right-angled triangle, a trigonometric function equal to the length of the side opposite the angle divided by the length of the adjacent side **3 PART OF SURVEY LINE** the part of a survey line that is straight **4 PART OF CLAVICHORD** a part of the clavichord that resembles a small hammer and strikes the strings ■ *adj* **1** MATH = **tangential** *adj.* 1 **2 TOUCHING AT A SINGLE POINT** touching only at a single point **3 TOUCHING BUT NOT CROSSING** in contact, but not crossing or intersecting **4 AWAY FROM THE POINT** not relevant to the subject currently under consideration [Late 16C. < Latin *tangent-*, present participle of *tangere* 'touch'.] —**tangency** *n* ◇ **go off at** *or* **on a tangent** to change quickly and suddenly to a different subject or line of thought

tangent galvanometer *n* a device with a compass needle suspended horizontally in a vertical coil through which a direct current is passed, causing deflection of the needle proportional to the current size

tangential /tan jénsh'l/ *adj* **1** relating to or involving a tangent **2** with only slight relevance to the current subject —**tangentiality** /tan jénshi álləti/ *n* —**tangentially** *adv*

tangerine /tánjə reén/ *n* **1 CITRUS FRUIT** a citrus fruit with easily peeled orange skin and sweet flesh **2 CITRUS TREE** a citrus tree, widely cultivated in tropical and warm regions, that produces tangerines. Native to: Southeast Asia. *Citrus reticulata.* **3 BRIGHT ORANGE COLOUR** a bright orange colour like that of a tangerine [Early 17C. Probably after Spanish *Tangerino* 'of or from Tangier'.] —**tangerine** *adj*

tangi /túng ee/ (*plural* **-gis**) *n NZ* a Maori funeral ceremony and the feast that accompanies it [Mid-19C. < Maori, 'lament, action of crying'.]

tangible /tánjəb'l/ *adj* **1 ABLE TO BE TOUCHED** able to be touched or perceived through the sense of touch ○ *a tangible coldness* **2 ACTUAL** capable of being understood and evaluated, and therefore regarded as real ○ *There is no tangible evidence to support this claim.* **3 ABLE TO BE REALIZED** capable of being given a physical existence ○ *some very tangible financial benefits* ■ *n* **SOMETHING TANGIBLE** something that has a physical form, especially a financial asset (*often plural*) [Late 16C. Directly or via French < late Latin *tangibilis* 'that may be touched' < Latin tangere 'to touch'.] —**tangibility** /tánjə bílləti/ *n* —**tangibleness** *n* —**tangibly** *adv*

Tangier /tán jéer/ city in N Morocco. Population: 526,215 (1994).

tangle[1] /tángg'l/ *v* (**-gles, -gling, -gled**) **1** *vti* **BECOME TWISTED** to become or make something become twisted together into a jumbled mass **2** *vt* **CATCH AND HOLD** to catch and entwine somebody or something in something that is difficult to get out of, e.g. a net or trap ○ *I got my jacket tangled in the branches.* **3** *vt* **TRAP SOMEBODY IN DIFFICULT SITUATION** to trap somebody in a complicated, awkward, or dangerous situation ○ *tangled in a web of controversy* **4** *vi* **COME INTO CONFLICT** to become involved in a confrontation or disagreement with somebody, especially somebody powerful or important ○ *You'll regret it if you tangle with them.* ■ *n* **1 JUMBLED MASS** a mass of fibres, lines, or other things twisted together **2 DIFFICULTY** a complicated situation or problem **3 STATE OF MENTAL UPSET** a state of mental or emotional confusion or upset [14C. < ?] —**tanglement** *n* —**tangler** *n* —**tangly** *adj*

tangle[2] /tángg'l/, **tangle weed** *n* any large brown seaweed that grows on shores at or below the level of low tide [Mid-16C. Probably via Norwegian *tångel* < Old Norse *þongull* < *þang* 'bladder wrack'.]

tango /táng gō/ *n* (*plural* **tangos**) **1 DANCE OF LATIN AMERICAN ORIGIN** a stylized Latin American ballroom dance in 2/4 time in which the steps are marked by glides and sudden pauses **2 MUSIC FOR TANGO** the music for a tango ■ *vi* (**tangos, tangoing, tangoed**) **DANCE TANGO** to dance a tango [Late 19C. < Argentine Spanish.] —**tangoist** *n*

Tango *n* a word used to represent the letter 'T' in international radio communications

tangram /tán gram/ *n* a puzzle of Chinese origin that involves putting together seven pieces, usually a square, a parallelogram, and five triangles, to form different shapes [Mid-19C. < ?]

Tangshan /táng shán/ city in NE China. Population: 1,500,000 (1991).

Tanguy /taang gée/, **Yves** (1900–55) French-born US artist

Tang Yin /táng yín/ (1470–1523) Chinese painter and poet

Tani /taáni/, **Buncho** (1763–1840) Japanese artist

tanist /tánnist/ *n* the heir apparent to a Celtic chieftain, usually a member of the chieftain's own clan and elected by the tribe during the chieftain's lifetime [Mid-16C. < Irish Gaelic *tánaiste* 'second in excellence or rank'.]

tanistry /tánnistri/ *n* the process of selecting an heir apparent to a Celtic chieftain while the current chieftain is still alive

Tanizaki Junichiro /taán ee zaák ee jóon ee chéer aw/ (1886–1965) Japanese writer

tank /tangk/ *n* **1 LARGE CONTAINER** a large container for storing liquids or gases **2 AMOUNT HELD BY TANK** the amount of liquid or gas that a particular tank holds ○ *We should get there and back on a couple of tanks of petrol.* **3 ARMOURED VEHICLE** a large armoured combat vehicle with tracks, a rotating turret, and a heavy gun **4** *US* **JAIL** prison, or a prison cell (*informal*) **5 CONTAINER FOR DEVELOPING FILM** a lightproof container for developing film, designed so that processing chemicals can be poured in and out without light entering **6 TRAY FOR PROCESSING SHEETS OF FILM** a large tray or container for processing a number of sheets of film together **7 POND OR RESERVOIR** a fairly small body of water, especially one used for water storage ■ *v* **1** *vt* **PUT IN A TANK** to put or keep something in a tank **2** *vi* **GO FAST** to move quickly or heavily, often with great purpose or determination ○ *He tanked up the road to the bus stop.* **3** *vt* **BEAT IN COMPETITION** to defeat a person or team heavily in a sport, competition, or election (*informal*) **4** *vi US* **DROP SHARPLY IN PRICE** to drop sharply in price to the point of bottoming out ○ *Tech stocks tanked.* [Early 17C. < Gujarati *tākū*, Marathi *ṭākē* 'pond, cistern'.] —**tankful** *n*

tank up *v* **1** *vti* to fill the fuel tank of a motor vehicle (*informal*) **2** *vi* to drink enough alcohol to become drunk (*slang*)

tanka /tángkə/ (*plural* **-kas** *or* **-ka**) *n* **1** a five-line Japanese verse form in which the first and third lines have five syllables each and the other lines have seven syllables each. ◊ **haiku 2** a poem with a tanka verse structure [Late 19C. < Japanese, < *tan* 'short' + *ka* 'song'.]

tankage /tángkij/ *n* **1 TANK CAPACITY** the amount that can be held by a tank or tanks **2 STORAGE IN TANK** the storage of something in a tank, or the cost of this **3 FERTILIZER** a byproduct of the slaughter of livestock consisting of carcass trimmings cooked to reduce moisture and drained of surplus fat. Use: feed supplement, fertilizer.

tankard /tángkərd/ *n* **1** a large mug with a handle and sometimes a hinged lid, made of glass, pewter, or silver plate, typically used for drinking beer **2** the amount of liquid that a tankard holds [14C. < ?]

tank car *n US* RAIL = **tank wagon**

tanked /tangkt/, **tanked-up** *adj* extremely drunk (*slang*)

tank engine, tank locomotive *n* a steam engine that carries its water supply in tanks at the sides of the boiler instead of carrying it in a tender

tanker /tángkər/ *n* a ship, lorry, or aeroplane designed to carry large quantities of liquid or gas

tank farm *n* a site with several large storage tanks, especially ones containing oil

tank farming *n* AGRIC = **hydroponics**

tank locomotive *n* RAIL = **tank engine**

tank session *n US* an intense brainstorming policymaking meeting, especially one held between senior members of the armed forces [After a room in the Pentagon nicknamed 'the Tank']

tank top *n* a close-fitting, sleeveless, usually knitted garment with a low U-shaped or V-shaped neck [Probably because it resembles a garment worn by the crews of armoured tanks]

tank trap *n* something such as a concrete block designed to stop or slow the movement of military tanks

tank wagon *n* a railway wagon that has a large tank for transporting liquids or gases in bulk. US term **tank car**

tannage /tánnij/ *n* **1** the tanning of animal hides or skins **2** an animal skin or hide that has been tanned

tannate /tánnayt/ *n* a salt or ester of tannic acid [Early 19C. < TANNIC.]

tanned /tand/ *adj* with a tan from the Sun or an artificial source of ultraviolet light. US term **tan**[1] *adj.* **2**

tanner[1] /tánnər/ *n* a person who tans animal skins [Pre-12C. Both < TAN[1] and via Old French *tanere* < medieval Latin *tannator.*]

tanner[2] /tánnər/ *n* a sixpence, or the sum of sixpence (*dated informal*) [Early 19C. < ?]

tannery /tánnəri/ (*plural* **-ies**) *n* a building or factory where animal skins and hides are tanned

tannic /tánnik/ *adj* relating to, containing, or derived from tannin [Mid-19C. < French *tannique* < *tanin* (see TANNIN).]

tannic acid *n* CHEM = **tannin**

tannin /tánnin/ *n* a brownish or yellowish compound found in plants. Use: tanning, dyes, astringents. [Early 19C. < French *tanin* < *tan* 'tanbark' < medieval Latin *tannum.*]

tanning /tánning/ *n* **1 CONVERSION OF ANIMAL SKIN INTO LEATHER** the conversion of animal skins and hides into leather **2 BROWNING OF SKIN** the browning of skin when it is exposed to the Sun or some other ultraviolet light source **3 SOUND BEATING** a sound beating or whipping

tanning bed *n US* LEISURE = **sunbed** *n.* **1**

Tannoy /tánnoy/ *tdmk UK* a trademark for a public-address system

Tanoan /tə nō ən/ *n* a group of languages spoken mainly in New Mexico and Arizona. Native speakers: 3,000. [Late 19C < Spanish *Tano* 'Tewa'] —**Tanoan** *adj*

tanrec *n* ZOOL = **tenrec**

tansy /tánzi/ (*plural* **-sies**) *n* **1** an aromatic perennial plant of the daisy family with leaves divided into toothed leaflets. Flowers: yellow, in flat-topped clusters. Use: formerly, in cooking and medicine. Native to: Europe, Asia. *Tanacetum vulgare.* **2** any plant similar to the tansy, e.g. ragwort [13C. < ?]

Tanta /tántə/ city in NE Egypt, in the Nile delta. Population: 380,000 (1992).

tantalic /tan tállik/ *adj* relating to or containing tantalum, especially with a valency of five

tantalise *vt* = **tantalize**

tantalite /tántə līt/ *n* a reddish-black mixed oxide mineral containing tantalum, iron, and manganese. Source: granites, pegmatites. Use: source of tantalum.

tantalize /tántə līz/ (**-lizes, -lizing, -lized**), **tantalise** (**-lises, -lising, -lised**) *vt* to tease or torment people by letting them see, but not have, something they desire [Late 16C. < Latin *Tantalus* 'Tantalus'.] —**tantalization** /tántə lī záysh'n/ *n* —**tantalizer** *n*

tantalizing /tántə līzing/ *adj* tempting but unavailable or unattainable ○ *a really tantalizing offer* —**tantalizingly** *adv*

tantalum /tántələm/ *n* (*symbol* **Ta**) a dense blue-grey metallic element. Use: electronic components, alloys, in plates and pins for orthopaedic surgery. [Early 19C. Via modern Latin < Latin *Tantalus* 'Tantalus', because of its inability to absorb acid even when it is immersed in it.]

tantalus /tántələss/ *n* a lockable stand or case for decanters of alcoholic drinks, especially spirits [Late 19C. < Latin *Tantalus* 'Tantalus'.]

Tantalus *n* in Greek mythology, a king who was condemned to stand in water under a fruit tree. Whenever he tried to drink or eat, the water or fruit receded beyond his reach. [Mid-18C. Via Latin < Greek.]

tantamount /tántə mownt/ *adj* equivalent to a particular thing in effect, outcome, or value, especially something unpleasant ○ *an answer that was tantamount to a refusal* [Mid-17C. < Anglo-French *tant amunter* 'amount to as much' < Old French *tant* 'as much' + *amonter* 'to amount'.]

tantara /tántə raá/ *n* a fanfare or blast on a horn, or a sound that resembles this, especially when used to announce something important [Mid-16C. An imitation of the sound.]

tantie /tánti/, **Tantie** *n Carib* an older aunt, or any older woman [Late 19C. < French Creole, blend of French *tante* + AUNTIE.]

tantivy /tan tívvi/ *n* (*plural* **-ies**), *interj* **HUNTER'S SHOUT** a hunting cry, especially one given by a hunter riding a horse at full gallop ■ *n* (*plural* **-ies**) **FAST MOVEMENT** a fast ride, especially on a horse going at full gallop ■ *adj* **SPEEDY** moving very fast, especially when on a horse going at full gallop [Mid-17C. Probably an imitation of the sound of galloping horses, influenced by TANTARA.] —**tantivy** *adv*

tant mieux /taáN myő/ *interj* so much the better [Mid-18C. < French.]

tant pis /taáN pée/ *interj* so much the worse [Late 18C. < French.]

Tantra /tántrə, tún-/ *n* the sacred books of Tantrism [Late 18C. < Sanskrit, 'loom, warp, groundwork, system, doctrine'.]

Tantrism /tántrizəm, tún-/ *n* a movement in Hinduism and Buddhism, especially a variety based on yoga and intended to release energy through sexual intercourse in which the orgasm is withheld or delayed —**Tantric** *adj* —**Tantrist** *n*

tantrum /tántrəm/ *n* an outburst of anger, especially a childish display of rage or bad temper [Early 18C. < ?]

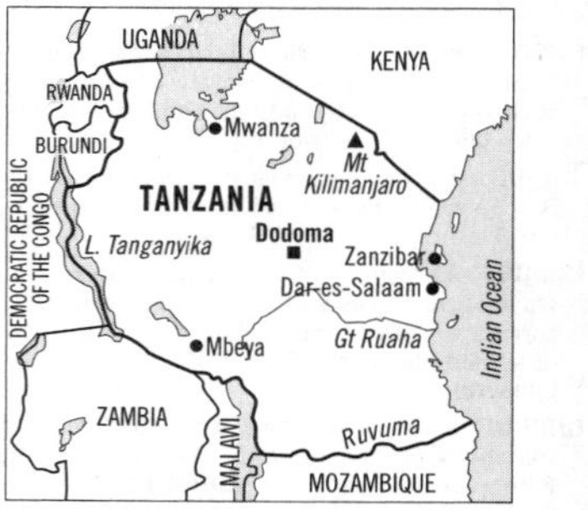

Tanzania

Tanzania /tánzə née ə/ republic in SE Africa. Capital: Dodoma. Population: 29,898,774 (1997). Area: 945,100 sq. km/364,900 sq. mi. —**Tanzanian** *n, adj*

Tao /tow, dow/ *n* **1 ULTIMATE REALITY** in Taoist philosophy, the ultimate reality in which all things are located or happen **2 Tao, tao UNIVERSAL ENERGY** in Taoist philosophy, the universal energy that makes and maintains everything that exists **3 RELATIONSHIP BETWEEN INDIVIDUAL AND UNIVERSE** in Taoist philosophy, the order and wisdom of individual life, and the way that this harmonizes with the universe as a whole [Mid-18C. < Chinese *dào* 'way, path, right way (of life), reason'.]

Taoiseach /téeshək/ *n* the prime minister of the Republic of Ireland [Mid-20C. < Irish, 'chief, leader'.]

Taoism /tówizəm, dów-/ *n* **1** a Chinese philosophy that advocates a simple life and a policy of noninterference with the natural course of things **2** a popular Chinese religion that seeks harmony and long life through the philosophy of Taoism combined with pantheism and magical practices —**Taoist** *n, adj* —**Taoistic** /tow ístik, dow-/ *adj*

taonga /ta óngə/ *n NZ* something that should be cherished and is considered very valuable [< Maori]

Taormina /towr meénə/ town in E Sicily, Italy. Population: 9,979 (1991).

Tao Te Ching /tów tə chíng, dów də jíng/ *n* the most important Taoist text, a collection of 81 poems by the mystic and philosopher Lao-tzu, the founder of Taoism [< Chinese, 'the Book of the Way']

tap[1] /tap/ *v* (**taps, tapping, tapped**) **1** *vti* **HIT SOMETHING LIGHTLY** to hit something or somebody lightly, especially more than once **2** *vt* **HIT OBJECT AGAINST SOMETHING ELSE** to hit an object lightly against something else **3** *vt* **MAKE SOUND** to produce something such as a noise or rhythm by tapping **4** *vi* **MOVE MAKING LIGHT SOUNDS** to move making a series of light noises **5** *vt* **REINFORCE SHOE** to attach a small piece of leather or metal to the toe or heel of a shoe to cover worn parts or to protect against wear **6** *vi* **DO A TAP DANCE** to perform a tap dance **7** *vt US* **GIVE POST TO** to select and appoint somebody for a particular role or office (*usually passive*) ○ *'The coal industry was tapped to lead the way for reform'* (*US News & World Report*; December 1998) ■ *n* **1 LIGHT BLOW** a light blow, especially one that produces a noise **2 SOUND OF BLOW** the sound made by a light blow **3 REINFORCEMENT FOR SHOE** a small piece of leather or metal attached to the toe or heel of a shoe to cover a worn part or to protect against wear **4 METAL PART ON TAP-DANCING SHOE** a metal tip attached to the toe or heel of a tap-dancing shoe so that it can produce sounds **5 TAP-DANCING** tap-dancing (*informal*) **6 TOUCH OF TONGUE TO MOUTH TOP** the production of a speech sound made when any flexible speech organ hits any hard part of the mouth, e.g. when the tongue is brought into contact with the hard palate [12C. < ?] —**tappable** *adj* —**tapper** *n*

tap[2] /tap/ *n* **1 VALVE ON PIPE** a valve on a pipe that is operated by a handle and used to draw off or control the flow of liquid, especially from a water supply. US term **faucet** **2 BARREL PLUG** a stopper in a cask or barrel, used to seal in the contents and also to allow liquid to be drawn off at a controlled rate **3 BEER FROM CASK** liquid, especially beer, that has been drawn from a tap in a cask or barrel and is regarded as having particular qualities because of this **4** = **taproom** **5 LISTENING DEVICE** a device put into a telephone or other telecommunication equipment in order to secretly listen to or record other people's conversations **6 SURGICAL FLUID EXTRACTION** a surgical procedure that involves drawing off a body fluid using a hollow needle or tube **7 TOOL FOR MAKING INTERNAL SCREW THREADS** a tool used to make an internal screw thread **8** *US* ELEC = **tapping** **9 SECURITY ON MARKET AT PREDETERMINED PRICE** a government security made available gradually on the stock market when its price reaches a predetermined level ■ *v* (**taps, tapping, tapped**) **1** *vt* **ATTACH TAP** to attach a tap to something in order to draw off or control the flow of liquid **2** *vt* **DRAW LIQUID FROM BARREL** to draw off liquid, e.g. wine or beer, from a barrel by means of a tap **3** *vt* **DRAW FLUID FROM BODY** to surgically draw off fluid from a part of the body **4** *vt* **OBTAIN SAP** to cut into a tree in order to draw off sap or resin **5** *vt* **GET INTO POWER SUPPLY** to connect to a power supply and divert energy from it, usually illegally **6** *vt* **PLACE LISTENING DEVICE ON PHONE LINE** to fit a device into a telephone or other telecommunication equipment in order to secretly listen to or record other people's conversations **7** *vt* **SECRETLY LISTEN TO PHONE CONVERSATIONS** to secretly listen to or record other people's conversations using a device fitted into a telephone or other telecommunication equipment **8** *vti* **PUT RESOURCE TO USE** to make use of a resource or supply of something (*informal*) ○ *tapping into the reserves of goodwill that exist in the community* **9** *vt* **BORROW MONEY** to borrow a sum of money from somebody (*informal*) ○ *She tapped me for 20 quid.* **10** *vt* **MAKE INTERNAL SCREW THREAD** to cut an internal screw thread into something [Old English *tæppa* (noun), *tæppian* (verb) < Germanic.] —**tappable** *adj* —**tapper** *n* ◇ **on tap** **1** available for immediate use (*informal*) **2** on draught (*informal*)

tapa /taapə/ *n* **1** the inner bark of the paper mulberry tree **2** a strong fabric made from the inner bark of the paper mulberry tree [Early 19C. < Polynesian.]

tapas /táppəss/ *npl* small savoury snacks that are often served as an appetizer along with alcoholic drinks, originally in Spain [Mid-20C. Plural of Spanish *tapa* 'cover, lid'.]

tap dance *n* a step dance performed by a person wearing shoes with metal tips to make a rhythmic sound —**tap-dance** *vi* —**tap-dancer** *n* —**tap-dancing** *n*

tape /tayp/ *n* **1 LONG NARROW STRIP OF MATERIAL** a long narrow strip of material such as paper, fabric, or plastic used to secure or tie something **2 STRIP OF STICKY MATERIAL** a long strip of plastic or cloth with adhesive on one or both sides, usually on a roll **3 MAGNETIC TAPE** magnetic tape used in cassettes and some computers **4** RECORDING = **tape recording** **5 VIDEO OR AUDIO CASSETTE** a cassette used for audio or video recording or playback ○ *Put the tape in the player.* **6 FINISHING LINE MARKER** a long strip of material that marks the finishing line in a race **7 TAPE MEASURE** a tape measure **8 STRIPE** a stripe (*informal*) ■ *v* (**tapes, taping, taped**) **1** *vti* **RECORD SOMETHING** to record something, especially music or a television programme on magnetic tape **2** *vt* **FIX USING TAPE** to secure, fasten, or strengthen something using tape **3** *vt* MED = **strap** *v.* 2 **4** *vt* **MEASURE USING TAPE MEASURE** to measure something using a tape measure [Old English *tæppe* 'narrow strip of cloth' < ?] ◇ **have somebody** *or* **something taped** to have a clear understanding of somebody or something (*informal*)

tape up *vt* MED = **strap** *v.* 2

tape deck *n* an electrical device that plays and records tapes, especially audio cassettes

tape grass *n* a perennial grass that grows largely submerged in fresh water, forming tufts of long narrow leaves and bearing inconspicuous pinkish-white flowers. *Vallisneria spiralis.*

tapeline /táyp līn/ *n* MEASURE = **tape measure**

tape machine *n* an electronic machine that receives and displays or prints current stock quotations. US term **ticker** *n.* 3

tape measure *n* a long roll or strip of fabric, plastic, paper, or thin metal that is marked off in inches or centimetres for measuring

tapenade /táppə naad/ *n* a paste made from puréed black olives, capers, and anchovies [< French, < Provençal *tapeno* 'caper']

taper /táypər/ *vti* **1 GET OR MAKE NARROWER** to become or make something narrower at one end, especially gradually **2 REDUCE GRADUALLY** to become or make something smaller in size or amount, or less important, especially gradually ○ *Sales of the first album are beginning to taper off.* ■ *n* **1 SLIM CANDLE** a slim candle that is narrower at the top than at the bottom **2 STRIP FOR TRANSFERRING FLAME** a strip of wood or waxed paper used for taking a flame to light something else **3 NARROWING OF SHAPE** a gradual narrowing in the shape of something ○ *a spire with a pronounced taper* **4 DIM LIGHT** a faint source of light, e.g. from a small candle [Pre-12C. Alteration of Latin *papyrus* 'papyrus', whose pith was used for candle wicks.] —**tapering** *adj* —**taperingly** *adv*

tape recorder *n* a machine that can record and play audio tapes, especially one with its own speaker

tape recording *n* a recording made on magnetic tape, especially an audio recording —**tape-record** *vt*

tapestry /táppistri/ (*plural* **-tries**) *n* **1** a heavy fabric with a woven pattern or picture. Use: wall hanging, upholstery. **2** HANDICRAFT = **needlepoint** *n.* 1 **3** something that is considered to be rich, varied, or intricately interwoven ○ *the rich tapestry of life* [14C. < French *tapisserie* < *tapis* 'carpet' < Greek *tapēt-*.] —**tapestried** *adj*

tapestry moth *n* a moth whose caterpillars eat fabrics made from wool and other natural fibres. *Trichophaga tapetzella.*

tapetum /tə peétəm/ (*plural* **-ta** /-tə/) *n* **1** a specialized membrane or layer of cells **2** a layer of cells in the wall of the eye of nocturnal and deep-sea animals that reflects light back onto the retina, enhancing visual sensitivity in dim light [Early 18C. < late Latin, < Latin *tapete*, < Greek *tapēt-*.] —**tapetal** *adj*

tapeworm /táyp wurm/ *n* a flatworm with a long ribbon-shaped segmented body that exists in many varieties and lives mainly as a parasite in the gut of vertebrate animals. Class: Cestoda. Technical name **cestode**

taphole /táp hōl/ *n* a hole at the bottom of a furnace for drawing off molten metal or slag

taphonomy /tə fónnəmi/ *n* the scientific study of fossilization [Mid-20C. < Greek *taphos* 'grave'.] —**taphonomic** /táffə nómmik/ *adj* —**taphonomist** *n*

taphouse /táp howss/ (*plural* **-houses** /-howziz/) *n* an inn, bar, public house, or other place where alcohol is served (*archaic*)

tap-in *n* **1** BASKETBALL = **tip-in** *n.* 1 **2** in soccer, a goal scored with minimum effort by a player who is very close to the opposition's goal **3** in golf, a short putt to put the ball in the hole

tapioca /táppi ṓkə/ *n* **1** a starch obtained from the roots of a cassava plant. Use: puddings, thickener for sauces. **2** a milk pudding made from tapioca [Mid-17C. Via Portuguese or Spanish < Tupi *tipioca* < *tipi* 'residue, dregs' + *ok* 'squeeze out'.]

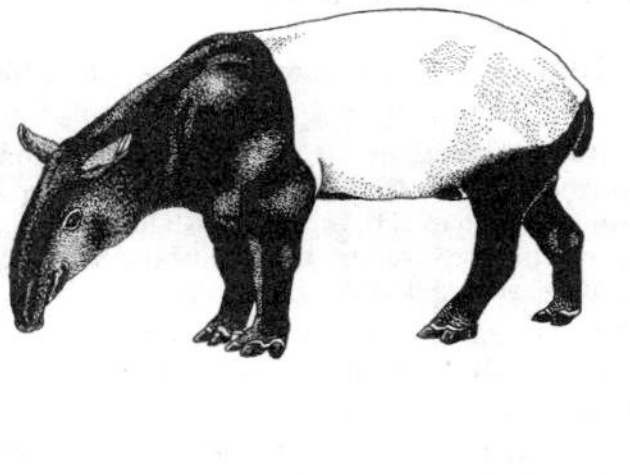

Tapir

tapir /táypər/ (*plural* **-pirs** *or* **-pir**) *n* a nocturnal hoofed forest-dwelling mammal that has short limbs and a fleshy snout and feeds on fruit and vegetation. Native to: Central and South America, Southeast Asia. Family: Tapiridae. [Late 18C. Via Portuguese or Spanish < Tupi *tapira*.]

tap-off *n* BASKETBALL = **tip-off**[2] *n.*

tappet /táppit/ *n* a lever, arm, or other machine part that transfers motion from a cam to a part such as a valve or push rod [Mid-18C. < TAP[1].]

tapping /tápping/ *n* a point in an electrical circuit where a temporary connection may be made. US term **tap**[2] *n.* 8

taproom /táp room, -rŏom/ *n UK* a bar in a place such as a hotel or pub

taproot /táp root/ *n* a long tapering root that extends downwards below the stem of some plants and has fine lateral roots [Early 17C. < TAP[2].]

taps /taps/ *n* (+ *singular verb*) **1 SIGNAL FOR LIGHTS OUT** a bugle call or other signal given at the end of the day, especially in a military camp, as an order that lights should be put out **2 SIGNAL AT FUNERAL** a bugle call or other signal given at a funeral or memorial service, especially a military one **3 GUIDE SONG** a song sung by members of the Guide movement at the close of a meeting or around a campfire at the end of the day [Early 19C. < TAP[1], or alteration of *taptoo*, variant of TATTOO[1].]

tapster /tápstər/ *n* a person who serves drinks in a bar or pub (*archaic*) [Old English *tæpestre*, originally feminine of *tapper* < TAP[2]]

tapu /taá poo/ *adj NZ* taboo [Mid-19C. < Maori.]

tap water *n* water that comes out of the tap, from a domestic or commercial water supply, as opposed to water from some other source, e.g. mineral water or rainwater

tar[1] /taar/ *n* **1 THICK BLACK LIQUID** a thick black liquid obtained through the destructive distillation of an organic substance such as wood or coal **2 RESIDUE FROM TOBACCO SMOKE** the residue from tobacco smoke ■ *vt* (**tars, tarring, tarred**) **COVER WITH TAR** to coat or cover something, especially a road surface, with tar [Old English *teoru* < Indo-European] —**tarriness** *n* —**tarry** *adj*

tar[2] /taar/ *n* a sailor (*archaic informal*) [Late 17C. < ?]

Tara, Hill of /taárə/ hill in E Republic of Ireland. It was the seat of the Irish kings until about AD 560. Height: 155 m/507 ft.

taradiddle *n* = **tarradiddle**

tarakihi /tárrə kee/, **terakihi** /térrə-/ *n* an edible fish with a silvery body and a black saddle behind the head. Native to: New Zealand. *Nemadactylus macropterus.* [< Maori]

taramasalata /tàrrəməssə làatə/ *n* a creamy pink or beige paste made from smoked fish roe [Early 20C. < modern Greek, < *taramas* 'preserved roe' (< Turkish *tarama* 'preparation of soft roe or red caviar') + *salata* 'salad'.]

Taranaki /tàrrə náki/ region in the southwest of the North Island, New Zealand. Population: 106,570 (1996). Area: 12,640 sq. km/4,880 sq. mi.

Taranaki, Mount dormant volcano near the coast of the west of the North Island, New Zealand. Height: 2,518 m/8,260 ft.

tarantass /tàarən táss/ *n* a large Russian horse-drawn carriage with four wheels and no springs [Mid-19C. < Russian *tarantas.*]

tarantella /tàrrən téllə/ *n* **1** a whirling dance from S Italy in 6/8 time **2** the music for a tarantella [Late 18C. < Italian, < TARANTO.]

Tarantino /tàrrən teénō/, **Quentin** (*b.* 1963) US film director and screenwriter

tarantism /tárrəntìzəm/ *n* a nervous condition characterized by uncontrollable body movements, common during the 15th to 17th centuries in S Italy and formerly believed to be caused by the bite of the tarantula [Mid-17C. < Italian *tarantismo* < TARANTO.]

Taranto /ta rántō/ port in Taranto Province, Apulia Region, S Italy. Population: 230,207 (1992).

tarantula /tə rántyŏolə/ (*plural* **-las** *or* **-lae** /-lee/) *n* **1** a large spider that has a hairy body and legs and feeds on invertebrates, toads, small reptiles, and young birds. Native to: tropical and subtropical America. Family: Theraphosidae. **2** a wolf spider formerly believed to cause tarantism with its bite. Native to: Europe. *Lycosa tarentula.* [Mid-16C. Via medieval Latin < Italian *tarantola* < TARANTO.]

Tararua Range /tárrə rŏo ə-/ mountain range in the south of the North Island, New Zealand. Highest peak: Mitre Peak 1,571 m/5,154 ft.

taraxacum /tə ráksəkəm/ *n* **1** a herbal remedy extracted from dandelion roots or leaves. Use: mild laxative, liver tonic, diuretic. **2** a plant such as the dandelion that produces flower heads made up of numerous florets and with seeds attached to whitish hairs. Genus: *Taraxacum.* [Early 18C. Via medieval Latin *altaraxacon* < Arabic. Persian *ṭaraḵšaḵūn* 'dandelion, wild endive' < Persian *talḵ* 'bitter' + *čaḵūk* 'purslane'.]

tarboosh /taar bŏosh/, **tarbush, tarbouche** *n* a brimless usually red felt hat, similar to a fez, that has a silk tassel and is worn by Muslim men by itself or with a turban [Early 18C. Via Egyptian Arabic *ṭarbūš* < Ottoman Turkish *terpōş*, Turkish *tarbuş* < Persian *sarpūš* < *sar* 'head' + *pūš* 'cover'.]

tardigrade /tàardi grayd/ *n* **TINY WATER CREATURE** a tiny aquatic invertebrate animal with a short body and four pairs of stubby legs. Phylum: Tardigrada. ■ *adj* **1 RELATING TO TARDIGRADES** relating or belonging to the tardigrades **2 SLUGGISH** sluggish or slow-moving [Early 17C. Directly or via French < Latin *tardigradus* 'walking slowly' < *tardus* 'slow'.]

tardis /tàar diss/, **Tardis** *n* a room or building that seems to be much larger than it actually is or appears to be from the outside [Late 20C. < *Tardis*, time machine used in the British television series *Dr Who.*]

tardive dyskinesia /-díski neé zi ə/ *n* a condition marked by involuntary movements of the tongue and facial muscles, especially after prolonged treatment with phenothiazine tranquillizers and similar drugs [< French *tardif* (see TARDY)]

tardy /tàardi/ (**-dier, -diest**) *adj* **1** later than the expected or usual time **2** slow to move or react (*archaic or literary*) [Mid-16C. < French *tardif* < Latin *tardus* 'slow, sluggish'.] —**tardily** *adv* —**tardiness** *n*

tare[1] /tair/ *n* **1 VETCH PLANT** a trailing or scrambling vetch plant that has compound leaves with paired leaflets and tendrils. Flowers: bluish or purplish, in spikes. Native to: Europe, North Africa. Genus: *Vicia.* **2 VETCH SEED** the seed of a vetch or tare **3 PROBLEMATIC WEED** in the Bible, a weed found growing among crops, usually considered to be darnel [13C. < ?]

tare[2] /tair/ *n* **1 WEIGHT OF PACKAGING** the weight of a container or packaging used to wrap goods **2 ALLOWANCE FOR WEIGHT OF PACKAGING** an allowance for the packaging around goods, deducted from the total weight and not included in transportation costs **3 VEHICLE'S UNLADEN WEIGHT** the weight of a motor vehicle without fuel, cargo, passengers, or equipment **4 CONTAINER OF KNOWN WEIGHT** a container of known weight that is used as a counterbalance when calculating the net weight of a cargo ■ *vt* (**tares, taring, tared**) **WEIGH PACKAGING** to weigh packaging in order to calculate the amount of tare to be deducted from a particular cargo [15C. Via French, 'waste in goods, deficiency' < Arabic *ṭarḥ* 'that which is deducted' < *ṭaraḥa* 'reject, subtract'.]

Taree /taa reé/ town in E New South Wales, Australia. Population: 16,297 (1991).

targe /taarj/ *n* a round shield, especially used by Scottish Highlanders (*archaic*) [Pre-12C. Probably < Old Norse *targa* 'shield'; reinforced by Old French *targe* 'light shield'.]

target /tàargit/ *n* **1 OBJECT AIMED AT IN SHOOTING** a round object or surface marked with concentric circles that is aimed at in archery, rifle shooting, and similar sports **2 SOMETHING AIMED AT** an area, surface, object, or person aimed at ○ *The bird's bright plumage makes it an easy target.* **3 GOAL** a goal or objective towards which effort is directed ○ *Our target is to raise £20,000 for cancer research.* **4 SOMEBODY OR SOMETHING ON RECEIVING END** somebody or something that is the focus or object of the behaviour or actions of others ○ *the target of her anger* **5 MARKER FOR TAKING LEVELS** a sliding weight on a surveyor's levelling rod that is used to help determine proper levels **6 SOMETHING HIT BY PARTICLE ACCELERATOR BEAM** a substance that is hit by a beam of electrons or other elementary particles or ions from a particle accelerator in order to start a nuclear reaction **7 SURFACE HIT BY ELECTRONS** a surface or electrode, often luminescent, that is hit by an electron beam to produce an output signal, e.g. in an X-ray tube or a television camera tube **8 SMALL SHIELD** a small round shield (*archaic*) ■ *vt* **1 MAKE TARGET** to make a particular person or thing the focus or object of something ○ *a campaign that targets under-35s* **2 AIM** to aim something at or direct something towards a particular person, group, or thing ○ *The missiles were targeted on the enemy capital.* [13C. < TARGE.]

⚡**targetcast** /tàargit kaast/ (**-casts, -casting, -cast** *or* **-casted**) *vi* to broadcast a website to a particular group of people who are known to be potentially interested, rather than to everyone on the Internet [Late 20C. Blend of TARGET + BROADCAST.]

target date *n* a date by which it is expected that something such as a project or piece of work will be completed

⚡**target language** *n* **1 TRANSLATION LANGUAGE** the language into which a particular text is to be translated **2 LANGUAGE BEING LEARNED** a foreign language that is being learned **3 SOURCE CODE COMPILATION LANGUAGE** the machine-readable instructions into which a computer program written in a high-level language is to be compiled

target man *n* a football forward whose role is to receive high passes and crosses, especially in front of the goal

Targum /tàargəm/ *n* a translation of part of the Bible in Aramaic [Late 16C. Via Hebrew < Aramaic *targūm* 'interpretation' < *targēm* 'interpret'.] —**Targumic** /taar gŏomik/ *adj* —**Targumist** *n*

tariff /tárrif/ *n* **1 DUTY LEVIED ON GOODS** a duty or duties levied by a government on imported or sometimes exported goods **2 LIST OF TARIFFS** a list or system of tariffs **3 LIST OF COSTS** a list of fees, fares, or other prices charged by a business **4 PRICED MENU** a list of the available dishes at a restaurant together with their prices **5 SYSTEM OF CHARGING FOR UTILITIES** a system of charging for utility services such as gas and electricity, or a list of such charges ■ *vt* **SET COST** to fix a specified tariff or price on something [Late 16C. Via Italian *tariffa* < Arabic *ta'rif* 'notification, inventory of fees to be paid' < *'arrafa* 'notify'.]

tariff office *n* an insurance company that charges premiums according to a schedule established by a group of companies

Tarkington /tàarkingtən/, **Booth** (1869–1946) US writer

Tarkovsky /taar kófski/, **Andrey** (1932–86) Russian film director

tarlatan /tàarlətən/ *n* an open-weave transparent highly starched cotton muslin. Use: stiffener for collars and other parts of clothes. [Early 18C. < French *tarlatane.*]

Tarmac /tàar mak/ *tdmk* a trademark for a material used for surfacing roads

tarmacadam /tàar mə káddəm/ *n* a mixture of broken stone and tar used for surfacing roads

tarn /taarn/ *n* a small mountain lake, especially one formed by the action of glaciers [14C. < N Germanic.]

tarnish /tàarnish/ *vti* **1 BECOME DULL AND DISCOLOURED** to lose or make something lose its shine and become dull because of oxidation or rust **2 DAMAGE SOMEBODY'S REPUTATION** to damage somebody's reputation or good name, or become damaged ■ *n* **1 DISCOLORATION** the dullness or discoloration of metal affected by oxidation or rust **2 FILM OF DISCOLORATION ON METAL** the film of discoloration that forms on metal **3 SULLIED CONDITION** the damaged condition of somebody's reputation or good name [15C. < French *terniss-*, stem of *ternir* 'make dull'.] —**tarnishable** *adj*

taro /tàarō/ (*plural* **-ros**) *n* a perennial plant cultivated in tropical regions for its edible starchy tubers and also widely grown as an ornamental plant. Native to: Southeast Asia. *Colocasia esculenta.* [Mid-18C. < Polynesian.]

tarot /tárrō/ *n* **1** a system of fortune-telling using a special pack of 78 cards that consists of 4 suits of 14 cards together with 22 picture cards **2 tarot, tarot card** a card used in tarot [Late 19C. < French, < Italian *tarocchi*, plural of *tarocco.*]

tarp /taarp/ *n* a tarpaulin (*informal*) [Early 20C. Shortening.]

tarpan /tàar pan/ *n* a small grey-brown horse with a short thick neck, erect mane, and a stripe along the back, now extinct. Native to: S Russia, Poland. [Mid-19C. < Turkic.]

tarpaper /tàar paypər/ *n* a heavy paper coated with tar. Use: waterproofing in building.

tarpaulin /taar páwlin/ *n* **1** a heavy waterproof material, especially treated canvas, used as a covering and to protect things from moisture **2** a sheet of tarpaulin [Early 17C. Probably < TAR[1] + PALL[2] + -ING[2].]

Tarpeian Rock /taar peé ən-/ *n* a rock on the Capitoline Hill in ancient Rome, from which traitors were hurled to their deaths [Early 17C. After *Tarpeia*, legendary betrayer of the Roman citadel to the Sabines, reputedly buried at the foot of the rock.]

tar pit *n* an area where tar or asphalt naturally accumulates, trapping animals and preserving their bones

tarpon /tàarpən/ (*plural* **-pon** *or* **-pons**) *n* a sea fish with a streamlined body and thick silvery scales. Native to: tropical and subtropical waters. Genus: *Megalops.* [Late 17C. Probably < Dutch *tarpoen.*]

Tarquinius Superbus /taar kwínni əss soo púrbəss/, **Lucius** (*fl.* 6th century BC) king of Rome (534–510 BC)

tarradiddle /tárrədid'l/, **taradiddle** *n* (*informal*) **1** nonsense or idle talk **2** a small lie [Late 18C. Probably suggesting unintelligible speech.]

tarragon /tárrəgən/ *n* a perennial herb with aromatic leaves. Use: flavouring food. Native to: temperate Asia. *Artemisia dracunculus.* [Mid-16C. < medieval Latin *tragonia, tarchon.*]

Tarragona /tàrrə gṓnə/ port in Tarragona Province, NE Spain. Population: 114,931 (1995).

~~**tarrif**~~ incorrect spelling of **tariff**

~~**tarriff**~~ incorrect spelling of **tariff**

tarry /tárri/ (**-ries, -rying, -ried**) *vi* **1 REMAIN** to stay temporarily at a place **2 LINGER** to delay a departure or arrival, especially in an idle way **3 WAIT** to wait [13C. < ?] —**tarrier** *n*

tarsal /tàarss'l/ *adj* relating to the tarsus of the ankle or eyelid [Early 19C. < TARSUS.]

tarsier /tàarsi ər/ *n* a small nocturnal animal with large eyes and delicate grasping fingers and toes ending in pads, that lives in trees. Native to: Philippines, Indonesia, and neighbouring islands. Genus: *Tarsius.* [Late 18C. < French, < *tarse* 'tarsus'; from its long tarsal bones.]

tarsometatarsus /tàar sō méttə tàarsəss/ (*plural* **-si** /-sī/) *n* the bone in the lower leg of birds that connects to the toes [Mid-19C. < TARSUS.]

tarsus /tàarssəss/ (*plural* **-si** /-sī/) *n* **1 ANKLE BONES** the group of bones that forms the ankle joint in vertebrates, located between the inner bone of the lower leg (**tibia**) and the main skeleton of the foot (**metatarsus**) **2 PART OF EYELID** the small section of connective tissue along the edge of the eyelid **3** ZOOL = **tarsometatarsus** **4 PART OF ARTHROPOD LEG** the part of the leg of an arthropod that is furthest from the tibia [Late 17C. Via modern Latin < Greek *tarsos* 'eyelid, flat part of the foot'.]

Tarsus /tàarsəss/ city in S Turkey, near the Mediterranean Sea. Population: 146,502 (1985).

tart[1] /taart/ *adj* **1** with a sharp and sour but usually pleasant flavour **2** sharp, cutting, or critical [14C. < Old English *teart* 'painful, severe' < ?] —**tartness** *n*

tart up *vt* (*informal*) **1 TRY TO IMPROVE PLACE'S APPEARANCE** to change the decor of a place in an attempt to improve its appearance **2 TRY TO IMPROVE PERSONAL APPEARANCE** to use makeup, accessories, or different clothing in order to try to improve your appearance **3 DECORATE** to try to improve the appearance of something by decorating it, especially in an excessively ornate way

tart[2] /taart/ *n* a pie that has no top crust and is usually filled with something sweet such as fruit or custard [14C. < Old French *tarte*.]

tart[3] /taart/ *n* an offensive term for a woman thought to be a prostitute or to behave like one (*slang*) [Mid-19C. Probably shortening of SWEETHEART.]

tartan[1] /taárt'n/ *n* **1 WOOL FABRIC** a Scottish wool or worsted fabric woven in a wide range of checked or plaid patterns, many of which are associated with particular Scottish clans **2 PATTERN OF TARTAN** a particular pattern of tartan, officially registered and associated with a particular clan, regiment, or other organization **3 TARTAN GARMENT** a piece of clothing made of tartan **4 TRADITIONAL HIGHLAND DRESS** the traditional dress of the Scottish Highlands ○ *wearing the tartan with pride* ■ *adj* **SCOTTISH** relating to Scotland (*informal*) [15C. < ?]

tartan[2] /taárt'n/ *n* a Mediterranean sailing ship with a single mast and a lateen sail [Early 17C. Via French *tartane* < Old Provençal *tartana* 'buzzard'.]

tartar /taártər/ *n* **1** a hard deposit of mostly organic material that forms on teeth at the gum line and contributes to dental decay if not regularly removed **2** a substance consisting mostly of potassium bitartrate deposited in wine casks during fermentation [14C. Via medieval Latin *tartarum* < medieval Greek *tartaron*.] —**tartarous** *adj*

Tartar /taártər/ *n* **1** PEOPLES, LANG = **Tatar 2 tartar, Tartar** a fearsome or ferocious person (*offensive in some contexts*) [14C. Directly or via French *Tartare* < medieval Latin *Tartarus* < Turkish.] —**Tartar** *adj* —**Tartarian** /taar táiri ən/ *adj* —**Tartaric** /taar tárrik/ *adj*

tartare sauce, tartar sauce *n* mayonnaise mixed with capers and chopped pickles that is served as an accompaniment to fish [< French (see TARTAR)]

tartaric acid /taar tárrik-/ *n* $(CHOH)_2(COOH)_2$ a white crystalline organic acid. Source: wine vat tartar. Use: foods, beverages, photographic processes.

tartar sauce *n* FOOD = **tartare sauce**

tartar steak *n* FOOD = **steak tartare**

Tartarus /taártərəss/ *n* **1** in Greek mythology, the lowest part of the underworld where the worst evildoers were imprisoned **2** in Greek mythology, Hades or the underworld in general [Mid-16C. Via Latin < Greek *Tartaros*.]

tartlet /taártlət/ *n* a miniature tart, usually for one person [15C. < French *tartelette*, diminutive of *tarte* 'tart'.]

tartly /taártli/ *adv* in a tone of voice or with words conveying strong but tight-lipped disapproval or annoyance

tartrate /taár trayt/ *n* a salt or ester of tartaric acid [Late 18C. < French, < *tartre* 'tartar'.]

tartrated /taár traytid/ *adj* in the form of a tartrate

tartrazine /taártrə zeen/ *n* a dye widely used in processed foods to give a yellow colour [Late 19C. < French *tartrate* 'tartrate' + AZO-.]

Tartu /taártoo/ city in E Estonia. Population: 101,901 (1997).

Tartuffe /taar toóf, -tyoóf/, **Tartufe** *n* a religious hypocrite [After the main character in Molière's play *Tartuffe* (1664)] —**Tartuffian** *adj*

tarty /taárti/ (**-ier, -iest**) *adj* an offensive term that deliberately insults a woman's appearance as vulgar or gaudy (*slang*)

tarweed /taár weed/ *n* a strong-smelling resinous plant. Flowers: yellow, like daisies. Native to: W North America, Chile. Genus: *Madia*.

Tarzan /taárz'n/ *n* a man who is very strong and looks rugged and muscular (*informal*) [Early 20C. < *Tarzan*, character raised in the jungle by apes in the stories of Edgar Rice BURROUGHS.]

TAS *abbr* true air speed

Tas. *abbr* Tasmania

tash /tash/ *n* HAIR = **tache** (*informal*)

Tashkent /tásh ként/ capital of Uzbekistan, in the east of the country. Population: 2,100,000 (1994).

task /taask/ *n* **1 JOB ASSIGNED** a piece of work that is assigned to somebody **2 ANY JOB TO BE DONE** a piece of work or an assignment, especially one that is important or difficult ■ *vt* **1 ASSIGN WORK** to assign a task to somebody **2 BURDEN** to burden somebody excessively with work or duties [13C. Via Old N French *tasque* 'duty, tax' < medieval Latin *tasca* < Latin *taxare* (see TAX).] ◇ **take somebody to task** to scold or criticize somebody

task force *n* **1** a group of people and resources temporarily brought together for a particular purpose **2** a formation of military units put together on a temporary basis to accomplish a particular mission

taskmaster /taásk maastər/ *n* **1** a person who assigns and supervises work, especially in a demanding way **2** a responsibility or discipline that is very demanding or requires a lot of hard work

taskwork /taásk wurk/ *n* unpleasant, hard, or difficult work

Tasman /tázmən/ region in the northwest of the South Island, New Zealand. Population: 40,036 (1996). Area: 14,538 sq. km/5,613 sq. mi.

Tasman, Mount /tázmən, taáss maan/ peak in the S Alps, in the west-central part of the South Island, New Zealand. Height: 3,498 m/11,476 ft.

Tasman, Abel Janszoon (1603?–59) Dutch navigator

Tasman Bay inlet of the Tasman Sea on the northern coast of the South Island, New Zealand

Tasman Glacier largest glacier in New Zealand, in the S Alps of the South Island. Length: 29 km/18 mi.

Tasmania /taz máyni ə/ Australian state, occupying the island of Tasmania off SE Australia. Capital: Hobart. Population: 475,000 (1996). Area: 68,331 sq. km/26,383 sq. mi. —**Tasmanian** *n, adj*

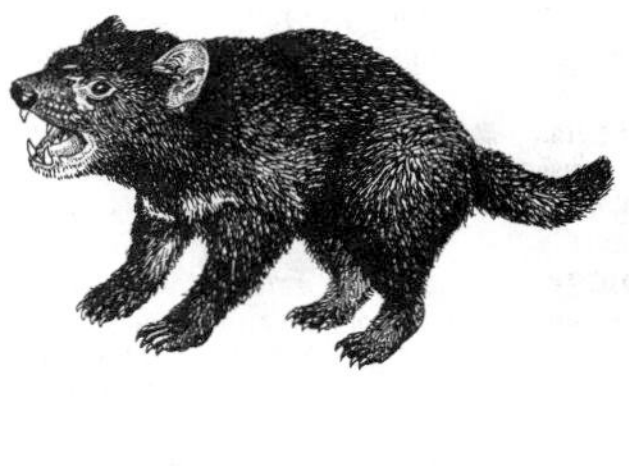

Tasmanian devil

Tasmanian devil *n* a burrowing carnivorous marsupial characterized by a black coat with white markings and large powerful jaws. Native to: formerly, all Australia, but now confined to remote regions of Tasmania. *Sarcophilus harrisii*.

Tasmanian tiger, Tasmanian wolf *n* ZOOL = **thylacine**

Tasman Peninsula peninsula in SE Tasmania, Australia. Area: 520 sq. km/200 sq. mi.

Tasman Sea region of the South Pacific Ocean lying between Australia and New Zealand

tasse /tass/ *n* = **tasset** [Mid-16C. < ?]

tassel /táss'l/ *n* **1 DECORATION MADE OF BUNCHED LOOSE THREADS** a bunch of loose parallel threads that are tied together at one end and used as a decoration, e.g. on curtains, cushions, or clothes **2 TUFT AT END OF MAIZE** something resembling a tassel, especially the tuft of male flowers at the top of the main stem of a maize plant ■ *v* (**-sels, -selling, -selled**) **1** *vt* **DECORATE SOMETHING WITH TASSELS** to decorate something with tassels **2** *vi* **PRODUCE A TUFT ON MAIZE** to produce a tuft of stamens at the end of a flower cluster, especially as seen on an ear of maize **3** *vt* **REMOVE TASSEL FROM MAIZE** to remove the tassel from an ear of maize [14C. < Old French, 'clasp'.] —**tasselly** *adj*

tassie /tássi/ *n Scotland, N England* a small cup, glass, or goblet (*archaic*) [Early 18C. < *tass*, via French *tasse* < Arabic *ṭasa* 'cup' < Persian *tašt* 'bowl'.]

taste /tayst/ *n* **1 SENSE THAT IDENTIFIES FLAVOURS** the sense that perceives the particular qualities of something such as a food by means of the sensory organs in the tongue (**taste buds**) **2 SENSATION STIMULATED IN TASTE BUDS** the sensation stimulated in the taste buds when food, drink, or other substances are in contact with them ○ *has a salty taste* **3 ACT OF TASTING** an act of tasting something **4 SMALL QUANTITY TASTED** a very small quantity of something eaten, drunk, or tasted ○ *Can I have a taste of that?* **5 FIRST EXPERIENCE** a brief sample, preview, or first experience of something ○ *a taste of freedom* **6 LIKING** a tendency to like or enjoy a particular thing or type of thing ○ *She has developed a taste for modern art.* **7 ABILITY TO JUDGE AESTHETICALLY** the faculty of making discerning judgments in aesthetic matters ○ *He has good taste.* **8 SENSE OF THE SOCIALLY ACCEPTABLE** a sense of what is proper or acceptable socially ○ *The remark was in poor taste.* ■ *v* (**tastes, tasting, tasted**) **1** *vt* **DISCERN FLAVOUR** to discern the flavour of a substance by means of the taste buds **2** *vt* **HAVE PARTICULAR FLAVOUR** to have a particular flavour ○ *This tastes horrible.* **3** *vt* **TEST FOR FLAVOUR** to put a small amount of food or drink into the mouth in order to try it or to test its flavour ○ *Taste this for salt.* **4** *vti* **EXPERIENCE** to experience something, especially for the first time or only briefly ○ *He had tasted success.* [13C. < Old French *taster* 'to touch'.] —**tastable** *adj*

taste bud *n* a sensory receptor on the surface of the tongue or in the mouth that sends signals to the brain when stimulated by certain chemicals, producing the sense of taste

tasteful /táystf'l/ *adj* **1** having or exhibiting good aesthetic taste **2** having a pleasant flavour —**tastefully** *adv* —**tastefulness** *n*

tasteless /táystləss/ *adj* **1** having little or no flavour **2** showing a lack of taste or judgment in aesthetic or social matters —**tastelessly** *adv* —**tastelessness** *n*

tastemaker /táyst maykər/ *n US* a person who influences decisions in what is tasteful or stylish, e.g. in fashion or the arts

taster /táystər/ *n* **1 JUDGE OF FOOD OR DRINK QUALITY** a specialist who tastes food or drink to judge its quality **2 SHORT PREVIEW** a sample or short preview of something **3 FREE SAMPLE OF FOOD** a small quantity of food or drink given free as a sample **4 DEVICE USED FOR TASTING** a device or container used for tasting, e.g. a small cup for tasting wine **5 PERSON TESTING FOR POISON** somebody engaged to test an important person's food or drink by sampling it first in case it contains poison

tasty /táysti/ (**-ier, -iest**) *adj* **1** having a pleasant flavour **2** attractive or interesting (*informal*) —**tastily** *adv* —**tastiness** *n*

tat[1] /tat/ *n* **1 THINGS IN POOR CONDITION** articles in very poor condition (*informal*) **2 TASTELESS THINGS** tasteless or very low quality articles (*informal*) **3 KNOTTED MASS** a knotted mass of something, especially hair [Mid-19C. < ?]

tat[2] /tat/ (**tats, tatting, tatted**) *vti* to work at or produce tatting [Late 19C. Back-formation < TATTING.]

ϟ**TAT** *abbr* **1** thematic apperception test **2** *US* turnaround time (*in e-mails*)

ta-ta /tə taá/ *interj* used as a childish or familiar way of saying goodbye (*informal*) [Early 19C. < ?]

tatami /tə taámi, taa-/ (*plural* **-mi** *or* **-mis**) *n* a straw mat, used especially in Japanese homes as a floor covering [Early 17C. < Japanese.]

Tatar /taátər/ *n* **1** a member of a people who came from E Central Asia, founded an empire stretching into Serbia, Russia, and Ukraine, and now live mainly between the Volga River and the Ural Mountains, and in Crimea and Siberia **2** the Turkic language of the Tatars. Native speakers: 6 million. [Early 17C. < Turkish.] —**Tatar** *adj* —**Tatarian** /taa táiri ən/ *adj* —**Tataric** /taa tárrik/ *adj*

Tatarstan /taátər staán/ autonomous republic in central Russia. Capital: Kazan. Population: 3,743,600 (1994). Area: 68,000 sq. km/26,255 sq. mi.

Tate Britain /táyt-/ *n* a museum in London that houses a collection of British art from 1500 to the present day

Tate Modern /táyt-/ *n* a museum in London that houses a collection of international modern art from 1900 to the present day

tater /táytər/ *n* a potato (*regional*) [Mid-18C. Alteration.]

Tati /ta teé/, **Jacques** (1908–82) French actor and film director. Born **Jacques Tatischeff**

Tatlin /tátlin/, **Vladimir** (1885–1953) Russian sculptor and painter

~~**tatoo**~~ incorrect spelling of **tattoo**

Tatra Mountains /taátrə-, táttrə-/ range of the Carpathian Mountains in central Europe, extending along the border between Poland and Slovakia. Highest peak: Gerlachovka 2,655 m/8,711 ft.

tatter /táttər/ *n* **1 RAGGED PIECE OF CLOTH** a torn or ragged piece of cloth **2 RUINED STATE** a ruined or damaged state (*usually plural*) ○ *The policy was in tatters.* ■ *vti* **BECOME OR MAKE RAGGED** to become ragged, or make something ragged or torn to shreds [15C. < Old Norse *totrar* (plural) 'rags'.]

tatterdemalion /táttərdə máyli ən, -málli-/ *adj* raggedly dressed and unkempt ■ *n* somebody wearing ragged clothes [Early 17C. < TATTERED + ?]

tattered /táttərd/ *adj* **1 RAGGED** ragged or torn to shreds **2 DRESSED IN RAGS** dressed in ragged clothes **3 SHABBY** shabby and run-down

tattersall /táttər sawl/ *n* **1** a pattern of squares or checks formed by dark lines on a light or brightly coloured background **2** cloth with a tattersall pattern [Late 19C. After *Tattersall's* horse market, London, from the traditional design of horse blankets.]

tattie-bogle /tátti bóg'l/ *n Scotland* a scarecrow (*informal*)

tatting /tátting/ *n* **1** a form of lace made with a shuttle **2** the process or craft of making tatting [Mid-19C. < ?] —**tatter** *n*

tattle /tátt'l/ *v* (**-tles, -tling, -tled**) **1** *vi* **GOSSIP** to gossip about the personal secrets or plans of others **2** *vti* **DISCLOSE SECRET** to disclose somebody's personal or private information **3** *vi* **TALK IDLY** to talk or chatter idly ■ *n* **1 SOMEBODY WHO GOSSIPS** a gossip or informer **2 IDLE GOSSIP** idle talk, chatter, or gossip [15C. Probably < Middle Flemish *tatelen*, an imitation of the sound.]

tattler /táttlər/ *n* **1 tattler, tattle-tongue** a gossip, revealer of secrets, or idle talker **2** a long-legged shore bird related to the sandpipers and noted for its loud cries. Genus: *Heteroscelus*.

tattletale /tátt'l tayl/ *n US* = **telltale** *n.* 1 (*often by or to children*) ■ *adj US* = **telltale** *adj.*

tattoo[1] /ta tóo, tə-/ *n* (*plural* **-toos**) a permanent picture, design, or other marking made on the skin by pricking it and staining it with an indelible dye ■ *vt* to mark the skin with a tattoo, or form a tattoo on the skin [Mid-18C. < Polynesian.] —**tattooer** *n* —**tattooist** *n*

tattoo[2] /ta tóo, tə-/ *n* (*plural* **-toos**) **1 CALL TO RETURN TO QUARTERS** a bugle or drum call that tells soldiers to return to their quarters in the evening **2 EVENING MILITARY DISPLAY FOR ENTERTAINMENT** a military display, often with a variety of items, performed as an entertainment, usually in the evening ■ *vti* **BEAT ON WITH STEADY RHYTHM** to beat a steady rhythm, or beat rhythmically on something such as a drum [Mid-17C. < Dutch *taptoe* 'shut the tap (of the beer barrel)', a signal at closing time in taverns.]

tatty /tátti/ (**-tier, -tiest**) *adj* shabby, run-down, or in poor condition [Mid-20C. < TAT[1].] —**tattily** *adv* —**tattiness** *n*

Tatum /táytəm/, **Edward Lawrie** (1909–75) US geneticist

tau /taw, tow/ *n* the 19th letter of the Greek alphabet [14C. < Greek.]

tau cross *n* a cross shaped like a T

taught past tense, past participle of **teach**

tau neutrino *n* a subatomic particle of the lepton family with no electric charge and a mass less than 69 times that of an electron, created during the decay of a tauon

taunt[1] /tawnt/ *vt* **1 PROVOKE OR RIDICULE** to provoke, ridicule, or tease somebody in a hurtful or mocking way **2 TANTALIZE** to tantalize somebody, e.g. by refusing to disclose a secret ■ *n* **HURTFUL REMARK** a hurtfully mocking or provocative remark [Early 16C. < French *tant (pour tant)* 'so much (for so much)' < Latin *tantus* 'so great'.] —**taunter** *n* —**taunting** *adj* —**tauntingly** *adv*

taunt[2] /tawnt/ *adj* describes a ship's mast that is taller than normal [Early 17C. < ?]

Taunton /táwntən/ town in SW England. Population: 60,300 (1993 estimate).

Taunus /táwnəss, tównəss/ mountain range in west-central Germany. Highest peak: 880 m/2,887 ft.

tauon /tów on/ *n* an unusually massive subatomic particle of the lepton family with the same charge as an electron but nearly 3,500 times its mass [Late 20C. < TAU.]

taupe /tōp/ *n* a dark brownish-grey colour [Early 20C. Via French < Latin *talpa* 'mole'.] —**taupe** *adj*

Taupo /tówpō/ city in the centre of the North Island, New Zealand, on Lake Taupo. Population: 21,044 (1996).

Taupo, Lake largest lake in New Zealand, in the centre of the North Island. Area: 606 sq. km/234 sq. mi.

Tauranga /tów rungə/ port in the northern part of the North Island, New Zealand, on the Bay of Plenty. Population: 89,800 (1998 estimate).

taurine[1] /táw rīn/ *adj* relating to or resembling a bull [Early 17C. < Latin *taurinus* < *taurus* 'bull'.]

taurine[2] /táw reen, -rin/ *n* a crystalline derivative of cysteine found in bile and nervous tissue [Mid-19C. < TAUROCHOLIC ACID.]

taurocholic acid /táw rō kolik-/ *n* a bile acid present as a sodium salt in humans that breaks down to produce taurine [Mid-19C. < Greek *tauros* 'bull' + *kholē* 'bile'.]

tauromachy /taw rómməki/ *n* the activity or skill of bullfighting —**tauromachian** /táwrə máyki ən/ *adj*

Taurus /táwrəss/ (*plural* **-ruses** *or* **-ri** /-rī/) *n* **1 CONSTELLATION IN N HEMISPHERE** a constellation of the northern hemisphere containing the bright star Aldebaran, the Pleiades and Hyades, and the Crab Nebula. See illustration at **constellation 2 SIGN OF THE ZODIAC** the second sign of the zodiac, represented by a bull and lasting from approximately 20 April to 20 May **3 SOMEBODY BORN UNDER TAURUS** somebody whose birthday falls between 20 April and 20 May [14C. < Latin *taurus* 'bull'.] —**Taurean** /táwri ən, taw rée ən/ *n* —**Taurus** *adj*

ϟ **TAURUS** /táwrəss/ *n* a computerized system used for buying and selling securities on the International Stock Exchange. Full form **Transfer of Automated Registration of Uncertified Stock**

Taurus Mountains /táwrəss-/ mountain range in S Turkey. Highest peak: Aladag 3,734 m/12,251 ft.

taut /tawt/ *adj* **1 STRETCHED TIGHTLY** pulled or stretched tightly **2 FIRM AND FLEXED** flexed and working, as opposed to being in a relaxed state ○ *taut muscles* **3 STRESSED** stressed, tense, or anxious **4 CONCISE** concise and efficient in its use of language or reasoning **5 KEPT IN GOOD ORDER** trim, tidy, and well-run ○ *runs a taut ship* [13C. < ?] —**tautly** *adv* —**tautness** *n*

taut- *prefix* = **tauto-** (*before vowels*)

tauten /táwt'n/ *vti* to become tightly stretched, or pull something such as a rope tight

tauto- *prefix* the same, identical ○ *tautomer* [< Greek *t' auto* 'the same thing' < *to* 'the' + *autos* 'same']

tautog /taw tóg/ *n* a large dark-coloured edible fish of the wrasse family. Native to: Atlantic coast of North America. *Tautoga onitis*. [Mid-17C. < Narraganset *tautauog*.]

tautology /taw tólləji/ (*plural* **-gies**) *n* **1 REDUNDANCY** a redundant repetition of a meaning in a sentence, using different words **2 INSTANCE OF TAUTOLOGY** an instance of redundant repetition **3 LOGICAL TRUE PROPOSITION** a proposition or statement that, in itself, is logically true —**tautological** /táwtə lójjik'l/ *adj* —**tautologically** *adv* —**tautologist** *n* —**tautologize** *vi*

tautomer /táwtəmər/ *n* a compound exhibiting tautomerism [Early 20C. < TAUTO- + ISOMER.]

tautomerism /taw tómmərizəm/ *n* the property permitting some compounds to exist as a mixture of two isomers that are interconvertible and thus in equilibrium —**tautomeric** /táwtə mérrik/ *adj*

tautonym /táwtənim/ *n* a species name in which the epithet for the species is the same as that of the genus, e.g. the name of the filarial worm *Loa loa* —**tautonymic** /táwtə nímmik/ *adj* —**tautonymy** /taw tónnəmi/ *n*

tav /taav, taaf/ *n* the 23rd and final letter of the Hebrew alphabet [Mid-17C. < Hebrew *tāw*.]

Tavel /taa vél/ *n* a dry rosé wine produced in the Rhône region of France [Late 19C. After *Tavel*, France.]

Tavener /távvənər/, **John** (*b.* 1944) British composer

tavern /távvərn/ *n* a pub or inn (*archaic*) [13C. Via French *taverne* < Latin *taberna* 'hut, inn'.]

taverna /tə vúrnə/ *n* **1** a small restaurant or café in Greece **2** a guesthouse in Greece that has a bar [Early 20C. Via modern Greek < Latin *taberna* 'hut, inn'.]

taverner /távvərnər/ *n* a person who runs a tavern (*archaic*)

Taverner /távvərnər/, **John** (1490?–1545) English composer

taw[1] /taw/ *vt* to whiten animal skins by applying alum or other mineral salts [Old English *tawian* < Germanic, 'make'] —**tawer** *n*

taw[2] /taw/ *n* **1 MARBLE USED TO HIT OTHERS** a fancy marble that is shot at others **2 LINE FROM WHICH PLAYER SHOOTS MARBLES** in a game of marbles, the line from which a player must shoot **3 GAME PLAYED WITH MARBLES** a game of marbles in which the object is to shoot as many marbles as possible out of a circular area where they have been placed [Early 18C. < ?]

tawa /taáwə/ *n* a tree of the laurel family with purple fruit. Native to: New Zealand. *Beilschmiedia tawa*. [Mid-19C. < Maori.]

tawdry /táwdri/ *adj* (**-drier, -driest**) **1 GAUDY AND POOR QUALITY** gaudy, cheap in appearance, and of inferior quality **2 SHABBY BUT WITH PRETENSIONS** shabby and worthless, though possibly with a superficial air of grandeur **3 MEAN-SPIRITED** mean-spirited and lacking in human decency ■ *n* **CHEAP GAUDY FINERY** gaudy finery of inferior quality [Early 17C. Shortening of *tawdry lace*, alteration of *St Audrey's lace*.] —**tawdrily** *adv* —**tawdriness** *n*

tawny /táwni/, **tawney** (**-nier, -niest**) *adj* **1** of an orange-brown colour tinged with gold **2** describes port wine that has matured for at least ten years in the barrel before bottling, and is therefore paler than ruby port [14C. Via Anglo-Norman *tauné* < Old French *tané* < *tan* 'tanbark'.] —**tawniness** *n*

tawny owl *n* a common round-headed owl with brown or grey plumage, black eyes, and tawny markings. Native to: forests from Europe to China. *Strix aluco*.

Tawny Owl *n* formerly, the official name for an assistant to the woman in charge of a group of Brownies

tawse /tawz/, **taws** *n Scotland* a leather strap split at the end, formerly used to punish school pupils with a blow to the palm of the hand ■ *vti Scotland* to hit a pupil on the hand with a tawse [Early 16C. Plural of *taw* 'lash, whip' < TAW[1].]

tax /taks/ *n* **1 MONEY PAID TO A GOVERNMENT** an amount of money levied by a government on its citizens and used to run the government, the country, a state, a county, or a municipality **2 CHARGE PAID BY MEMBERS** an amount charged to members of a club or organization to be used for expenses **3 STRAIN** a strain or heavy demand ■ *v* **1** *vt* **CHARGE TAX** to charge a tax on something such as a company's or person's income **2** *vt* **PAY TAX FOR CAR** to pay the annual tax required in order to drive a motor vehicle **3** *vt* **STRAIN OR MAKE HEAVY DEMANDS ON** to strain or make heavy demands on something or somebody ○ *You're starting to tax my patience.* **4** *vt* **ACCUSE OR CHARGE** to accuse or charge somebody **5** *vt* **DETERMINE COSTS OF LITIGATION** to determine the costs of litigation and the total amount of costs payable at the end of a trial (*dated or literary*) **6 ENTER ONTO LIST** to enter a name or names onto a list, e.g. for census-taking (*archaic*) [13C. Via French *taxer* < Latin *taxare* 'censure, assess' < *tangere* 'touch'.] —**taxability** *n* —**taxable** *adj, n* —**taxableness** *n* —**taxably** *adv* —**taxer** *n* —**taxless** *adj*

tax- *prefix* = **taxo-** (*before vowels*)

taxa plural of **taxon**

taxation /tak sáysh'n/ *n* **1 SYSTEM OF LEVYING TAXES** the system whereby taxes are levied upon certain types of income, earnings, or purchases **2 MONEY COLLECTED IN TAXES** the amount of money raised by collecting taxes **3 TAX** an amount levied as a tax on something —**taxational** *adj*

tax avoidance *n* the practice of paying as little tax as possible by claiming all allowable deductions from income. ◊ **tax evasion**

tax-deductible *adj* describes an expenditure that can be deducted from taxable income to lower the amount of tax owed by an individual or business

tax-deferred *adj* not taxable until a later time, often after retirement

tax disc *n* a small circular official document displayed on a motor vehicle, typically on the inside of the windscreen, showing that the annual road tax has been paid

taxeme /ták seem/ *n* a small linguistic feature such as selection, order, or phonetic modification [Mid-20C. < TAXIS.] —**taxemic** /tak séemik/ *adj*

tax evasion *n* an illegal activity in which a taxpayer seeks to hide taxable income or claim unauthorized tax deductions. ◊ **tax avoidance**

tax-exempt *adj* legally exempt from taxation

tax exile *n* a person who leaves a country in order to avoid paying taxes there

tax file number *n* in Australia, a numeric code required by all employers, and obtained when an individual registers with the Tax Office

tax-free *adj* not subject to taxation

tax haven *n* a country with favourable tax rates

tax holiday *n* a period during which a company is exempt from taxation, e.g. when just starting out in business

taxi /táksi/ *n* (*plural* **-is** *or* **-ies**) CAR TAKING PAYING PASSENGERS a car, usually with a taximeter, whose driver is paid to transport passengers, typically for short distances ■ *vti* (**-ies, -iing** *or* **-ying, -ied**) **1** MOVE AIRCRAFT ON GROUND to make an aircraft move under its own power on the ground, typically before take-off or after landing, or move on the ground in this way **2** TRAVEL IN TAXI to transport somebody or something in a taxi, or travel in a taxi **3** TRANSPORT SOMEBODY OR BE TRANSPORTED to transport somebody or something or be transported, especially in a car (*informal*) ○ *taxi the children to school* [Early 20C. Shortening of *taximeter cab*.]

taxi- *prefix* = taxo-

taxicab /táksi kab/ *n* CARS = **taxi** *n*. [Early 20C. Contraction of *taximeter cab*.]

taxidermy /táksi durmi/ *n* the art or skill of preparing, stuffing, and presenting dead animal skins so that they appear lifelike [Early 19C. < Greek *taxis* 'arrangement' (see TAXIS).] —**taxidermal** /táksi dúrm'l/ *adj* —**taxidermist** *n*

taximeter /táksi meetər/ *n* a device installed in a taxi that automatically computes the fare, which is usually based on time, distance travelled, or a combination of both [Late 19C. < French *taximètre* < *taxe* 'charge, tariff'.]

taximetrics /táksi metriks/ *n* BIOL = **numerical taxonomy**

taxing /táksing/ *adj* placing numerous or severe demands on somebody —**taxingly** *adv*

taxiplane /táksi playn/ *n* US an aircraft that is available for hire

taxi rank *n* an area reserved for parked taxis awaiting customers. US term **taxi stand**

taxis /táksiss/ *n* **1** movement of a cell or microorganism towards or away from the source of a stimulus **2** the manipulating of a displaced body part to return it to its normal position, e.g. in a case of hernia [Late 16C. < Greek, 'order, arrangement' < *tassein* 'arrange'.]

-taxis *suffix* **1** movement in response to a stimulus ○ *hydrotaxis* **2** arrangement, order of parts ○ *phyllotaxis* [< Greek *taxis* (see TAXIS)]

taxi stand *n* US TRANSP = **taxi rank**

taxiway /táksi way/ *n* a path used by aircraft when taxiing to and from a runway or other ground facility

tax loss *n* a transaction that results in a reduced tax liability, even though it may not be associated with an actual cash loss, e.g. the loss associated with depreciation expenses

taxman /táks man/ (*plural* **-men** /-men/) *n* **1** the taxing authority of a region or nation (*informal*) **2** a person who collects taxes

taxo- *prefix* order, arrangement ○ *taxonomy* [< Greek *taxis* (see TAXIS)]

taxon /ták son/ (*plural* **taxa** /-sə/) *n* any group to which organisms are assigned according to the principles of taxonomy, including species, genus, family, order, class, and phylum [Early 20C. Back-formation < TAXONOMY.]

taxonomy /tak sónnami/ *n* (*plural* **-mies**) **1** GROUPING OF ORGANISMS the science of classifying plants, animals, and microorganisms into increasingly broader categories based on shared features **2** PRINCIPLES OF CLASSIFICATION the practice or principles of classification **3** STUDY OF CLASSIFICATION the study of the rules and practice of classifying living organisms [Early 19C. < French *taxonomie* < Greek *taxis* 'arrangement' (see TAXIS).] —**taxonomic** /táksə nómmik/ *adj* —**taxonomically** *adv* —**taxonomist** *n*

taxpayer /táks pay ər/ *n* a payer of taxes, especially income taxes —**taxpaying** *adj*

tax rate *n* the percentage of income paid in income tax

tax relief *n* a reduction in the amount of tax that a person or company is legally required to pay

tax return *n* the collection of government forms on which earnings and expenses are recorded in order to calculate the tax liability of an individual or business

tax shelter *n* an investment activity that tends to reduce income tax liability —**tax-sheltered** *adj*

-taxy *suffix* order, arrangement ○ *epitaxy* [< Greek *-taxia* < *tag-*, stem of *tassein* 'arrange']

tay /tay/ *n* Ireland tea [Mid-17C. Variant.]

Tay /tay/ longest river in Scotland, flowing through Loch Tay and the Firth of Tay into the North Sea. Length: 190 km/120 mi.

Tay, Firth of estuary of the River Tay on the coast of E Scotland

tayberry /táybəri, -berri/ (*plural* **-ries**) *n* **1** a sweet dark red berry **2** a shrub that bears tayberries, produced by crossing a blackberry with a raspberry [Late 20C. After the River Tay.]

Taylor /táylər/, **Dennis James** (*b.* 1949) UK snooker player

Taylor, **Elizabeth** (*b.* 1932) British-born US film actor

Taylor, **Sir Gordon** (1896–1966) Australian aviator

Taylor, **Zachary** (1785–1850) US military leader and 12th president of the United States (1849–50). Known as **Old Rough and Ready**

Taylor's series /táylərz-/ *n* a basic theorem of calculus relating an approximation of the value of a continuous function at a point to the successive derivatives of the function evaluated at the point [Early 19C. After Brook *Taylor* (1685–1731), English mathematician.]

Taymyria /tay míri ə/ autonomous region in north-central Siberia, Russia. Capital: Dudinka. Population: 47,300. Area: 862,100 sq. km/332,850 sq. mi.

Tay-Sachs disease /tay sáks-/ *n* a genetic disease that principally affects Jewish people of E European ancestry, marked by accumulation of lipids in the brain and nerves and resulting in loss of sight and brain functions [Early 20C. After Warren *Tay* (1843–1927), English ophthalmologist, and Bernard *Sachs* (1858–1944), US neurologist.]

tazza /tátsə/ *n* an ornamental vessel that has a shallow bowl, usually mounted on a pedestal [Early 19C. Via Italian < Arabic *ṭasa* (see TASSIE).]

Tb *symbol* terbium

TB *abbr* **1** torpedo boat **2** TB, t.b. trial balance **3** tuberculosis

t.b.a. *abbr* **1** to be agreed **2** to be announced

T-bar *n* **1** T-SHAPED METAL BAR a metal bar that is T-shaped in cross section **2** SKI TOW FOR TWO PEOPLE a ski tow for two people, shaped like an inverted T, in which skiers rest against a horizontal bar on either side of a central shaft **3** T-SHAPED STRAP ON SHOE a T-shaped strap cut from the upper part of a shoe

⚡**TBC** *abbr* to be continued (*in e-mails*)

TBD *abbr* to be discussed

Tbilisi /tibi leéssi/ capital of the Republic of Georgia, in the east-central part of the country. Population: 1,268,000 (1990 estimate).

T-bone steak *n* a large thick sirloin steak containing a T-shaped bone

tbs., **tbsp.** *abbr* tablespoon

⚡**tc** *abbr* Turks and Caicos Islands (*in Internet addresses*)

Tc *symbol* technetium

TCCB *abbr* Test and County Cricket Board

TCDD *n* an extremely toxic byproduct of herbicide manufacture. Full form **tetrachlorodibenzodioxin**

T-cell *n* a white blood cell (**lymphocyte**) that matures in the thymus and is essential for various aspects of immunity, especially in combating viral infections and cancers [Abbreviation of *thymus-derived*]

AKG London

Peter Ilich Tchaikovsky

Tchaikovsky /chī kófski/, **Peter Ilich** (1840–93) Russian composer

⚡**TCOB** *abbr* taking care of business (*in e-mails*)

⚡**TCP/IP** *abbr* transmission control protocol/Internet protocol

TD *abbr* **1** Member of the Dáil **2** tank destroyer **3** technical drawing **4** Territorial Decoration **5** touchdown

t.d.c. *abbr* top dead-centre

TDD *abbr* telecommunications device for the deaf

TDM *abbr* time-division multiplexing

te /tee/ *n* a syllable that represents the seventh note in a scale, used for singing solfeggio. US term **ti**[1]

Te *symbol* tellurium

Tea

tea /tee/ *n* **1** PLANT'S DRIED LEAVES FOR MAKING DRINK the dried leaves of an Asian plant, often shredded, used to make a drink by adding boiling water **2** TEA DRINK a tea drink, usually served hot but sometimes with ice **3** DRINK MADE BY INFUSION any drink made by infusion of particular plant leaves, or the dried leaves used as the basis of a drink ○ *a herbal tea* **4** ASIAN EVERGREEN SHRUB an evergreen shrub with toothed leathery leaves that are dried to make tea. Flowers: fragrant, cup-shaped. Native to: Asia. *Camellia sinensis.* **5** EVENING MEAL a meal eaten early in the evening **6** AFTERNOON MEAL OF CAKES AND TEA a light meal taken in the afternoon, usually consisting of cakes, sandwiches, and tea or other nonalcoholic drinks; or an afternoon social event at which this meal is eaten **7** BREAKFAST IN GUYANA in Guyana, the first meal of the day **8** US, Can MARIJUANA marijuana (*dated slang*) [Mid-17C. Probably via Dutch *tee* < Chinese (Amoy dialect) *te*.]

SPELLCHECK Do not confuse *tea* with *tee*, which has a similar sound. Beware: your spellchecker will not catch this error.

tea bag *n* a small bag made of permeable paper or cloth containing tea leaves that is placed in boiling water to make one serving of tea

tea ball *n* a small perforated metal ball for holding tea leaves that is placed in boiling water to make tea

tea bread *n* a lightly sweetened bread, usually containing dried fruit, that is served sliced and buttered

tea break *n* a break from work in order to have a drink, usually of tea or coffee

tea caddy *n* a small container, usually with a tight-fitting lid, for holding tea leaves

teacake /teé kayk/ *n* a large round flattened yeast bun made with currants and chopped mixed peel or other fruit, sometimes spiced

tea ceremony *n* a Japanese ritual in which tea is prepared, served, and drunk in a prescribed manner

teach /teech/ (**teaches, teaching, taught** /tawt/, **taught**) *v* **1** *vt* IMPART KNOWLEDGE OR SKILL to impart knowledge or skill to somebody by instruction or example **2** *vti* GIVE LESSONS to give lessons in a subject, or give lessons to a person or animal **3** *vt* MAKE UNDERSTAND BY EXPERIENCE to bring understanding to somebody, especially through an experience ○ *The episode taught me a lesson I'll never forget.* **4** *vt* TEACH REGULARLY to engage in imparting knowledge or instruction for a period of time in a particular place ○ *teaches college* **5** *vt* ADVOCATE OR PREACH to advocate or preach something [Old English *tæcan*, < Indo-European 'to show'] —**teachable** *adj*

SYNONYMS *teach, educate, train, instruct, coach, tutor, school, drill*
CORE MEANING: to impart knowledge or skill in something
teach to impart knowledge or skill to somebody by instruction or example; **educate** to increase the knowledge or develop

the abilities of somebody by formal teaching or training, especially in a school or college context; **train** to teach the skills necessary for a particular task or job by means of instruction, observation, and practice; **instruct** to teach somebody a subject, methodology, or skill, not necessarily in a school or college context; **coach** to give special tuition to one person or a small group of people, especially in preparation for an exam, or to teach sports, artistic, or life skills; **tutor** to give somebody individual tuition in a particular subject or skill; **school** to train somebody in a particular skill or area of expertise in a thorough and detailed way; **drill** to teach something by means of repeated exercises and practice.

teacher /teéchər/ *n* **1** a person who teaches, especially as a profession **2** anything from which something may be learnt ○ *Experience is a great teacher.* —**teacherless** *adj* —**teacherly** *adj*

teacher bird *n* BIRDS = **ovenbird** *n.* 1 [An imitation of its call]

teachers' centre *n* a resource centre where all the teachers in a particular area can go for materials and assistance

teacher's pet *n* **1** a student who is specially favoured by a teacher and consequently resented by other students (*insult*) **2** a special favourite of somebody in authority

tea chest *n* a large box made of thin wood lined with metal in which tea is packed for transport after drying

teach-in *n* an extended period of speeches, lectures, and discussions, usually held at a college or university as part of a political or social protest

teaching /teéching/ *n* **1 PRACTICE OR PROFESSION OF A TEACHER** the profession or practice of being a teacher **2 SOMETHING TAUGHT** something that is taught, e.g. a point of doctrine (*often plural*) ■ *adj* **1 USED FOR TEACHING** used for or in teaching **2 THAT TEACHES** being a person or establishment that teaches

teaching fellow *n* a postgraduate student in a university who teaches, especially undergraduates, in return for tuition and usually a small stipend —**teaching fellowship** *n*

teaching hospital *n* a hospital that provides supervised practical training for medical students, student nurses, or other health-care professionals, often in conjunction with a medical school

teaching practice *n* the part of a student teacher's training that consists of a placement at a school where classroom teaching is undertaken by the student. US term **practice teaching**

tea cloth *n* HOUSEHOLD = **tea towel**

tea cosy *n* a soft padded cover for keeping a teapot warm, usually with slits to fit over the handle and spout

teacup /teé kup/ *n* **1** a small to medium-sized cup, usually used with a saucer, especially for serving tea **2 teacup, teacupful** the amount a teacup holds

tea dance *n* an afternoon social event at which people dance with partners and tea may be served

tea egg *n* HOUSEHOLD = **tea ball**

tea garden *n* **1** a garden or outdoor restaurant where tea and light refreshments are served to the public **2** a plantation where tea is grown

teahouse /teé howss/ (*plural* **-houses** /-howziz/) *n* a restaurant, especially in China or Japan, that serves tea and light refreshments

teak /teek/ *n* **1 teak, teakwood DURABLE WOOD** the durable red-brown wood of an Asian tree. Use: furniture, shipbuilding. **2 TALL ASIAN TREE** a tall tree valued for its timber. Native to: South Asia, Myanmar, Malay Archipelago. *Tectona grandis.* **3 WOOD OR TREE SIMILAR TO TEAK** a wood or tree similar to teak **4 YELLOWISH-BROWN COLOUR** a yellowish-brown colour [Late 17C. Via Portuguese *teca* < Tamil or Malayalam *tēkku.*] —**teak** *adj*

teakettle /teé kett'l/ *n* a kettle used for boiling water for making tea

teal /teel/ (*plural* **teals** *or* **teal**) *n* **1** a small freshwater surface-feeding duck with bright iridescent blue or green patches on the wings. Genus: *Anas.* **2** a greenish-blue colour [13C. < ?] —**teal** *adj*

tea lady *n* a woman employed to make tea during tea breaks, e.g. in a factory or office

tea leaf *n* **1 DRIED LEAF OF TEA PLANT** a dried leaf or shredded part of the dried leaf of the tea plant, used to make tea **2 TEA LEAF AFTER INFUSION** a tea leaf, or part of a leaf, after it has been infused (*often plural*) **3 THIEF** a thief (*slang*)

team /teem/ *n* **1 SIDE IN SPORTS COMPETITION** a group of people forming one side in a sports competition **2 COOPERATIVELY FUNCTIONING GROUP** a number of people organized to function cooperatively as a group **3 ANIMALS WORKED TOGETHER** two or more animals worked together, especially to pull a vehicle or agricultural equipment **4 TEAM OF ANIMALS WITH VEHICLE** a team of animals and the vehicle harnessed to them **5 GROUPING OF ANIMALS** a grouping of animals such as a flock, brood, or herd ■ *v* **1** *vti* **FORM INTO A TEAM** to form a team, or form people or animals into a team ○ *Tiffany, why don't you team up with Michael for the next game?* **2** *vt US, Can* **TRANSPORT BY A TEAM** to transport something using a team of animals **3** *vi US, Can* **DRIVE A TEAM** to drive a team of farm animals or a truck [Old English *tēam* < Indo-European, 'to lead']

SPELLCHECK Do not confuse ***team*** with ***teem***, which has a similar sound. Beware: your spellchecker will not catch this error.

tea-maker *n* **1** a machine that is designed to make tea automatically, usually with a timer so that it turns itself on at the required time **2** = **tea ball**

team leader *n* a senior nurse in charge of a ward and of the junior nurses working on the ward

team-mate *n* a player on the same team

tea money *n Hong Kong* money offered to another person as a bribe or in return for services provided (*informal*)

team player *n* a member of a group who cooperates with other people and who subordinates personal interests in order to achieve a common goal

team spirit *n* an enthusiastic attitude towards working productively with a team or work group

teamster /teémstər/ *n* **1** a driver of a team of animals used for hauling **2** *US, Can* a driver of a lorry that is used commercially for hauling loads

Teamster *n US* a member of the Teamsters Union

Teamsters Union /teémstərz-/ *n* trade union whose members are mainly lorry drivers. Full form **International Brotherhood of Teamsters, Chauffeurs, Warehousemen, and Helpers of America**

team teaching *n* an instructional programme involving two or more subjects that are taught in a coordinated way by specialist teachers

teamwork /teém wurk/ *n* **1** a cooperative effort by a group or team **2** work produced by a group or team

Te Anau /te únnow/ town in the southwest of the South Island, New Zealand, on Lake Te Anau. Population: 2,209 (1991).

Te Anau, Lake lake in the southwest of the South Island, New Zealand. Area: 344 sq. km/133 sq. mi.

tea party *n* an afternoon social event at which tea is served

teapot /teé pot/ *n* a covered container with a spout and handle, used for making and serving tea

teapoy /teé poy/ *n* **1** a small three-legged ornamental table or stand **2** a small table used to hold a tea caddy and tea service [Early 19C. By folk etymology (after TEA) < Hindi *tipāī*, alteration of Persian *si-pāya* 'three-footed'.]

tear[1] /tair/ *v* (**tears, tearing, tore** /tawr/, **torn** /tawrn/) **1** *vti* **PULL OR COME APART** to pull something such as paper or cloth into pieces, or come apart or rip ○ *She tore open the parcel.* **2** *vt* **MAKE A HOLE IN** to make a hole or opening in something such as a garment ○ *tore her skirt on a nail* **3** *vt* **CUT LEAVING JAGGED EDGES** to cut something, especially flesh, leaving jagged edges **4** *vt* **SPRAIN BODY PART** to injure a muscle or ligament so that some of the tissue is pulled apart and separated **5** *vt* **SEPARATE USING FORCE** to remove or separate something using force **6** *vti* **UPSET OR DISTRESS** to upset or distress somebody ○ *the memory tore at his heart* **7** *vt* **DIVIDE** to divide or fragment something ○ *an organization that was torn by internal conflict* **8** *vi* **MOVE OR ACT QUICKLY OR CARELESSLY** to move or act with great or careless speed (*informal*) ○ *He went tearing off down the road.* ■ *n* **1 SPLIT CAUSED BY TEARING** a hole or split caused by tearing **2 ACT OF TEARING** an act of tearing **3 HURRY** a hurry or rush [Old English *teran* < Indo-European, 'to split'] —**tearable** *adj* —**tearer** *n* ◇ **that's torn it!** used to indicate that something unfortunate has happened, often something that will lead to trouble (*dated informal*)

SYNONYMS ***tear, rend, rip, slit***

CORE MEANING: to pull apart forcibly

tear to pull something apart, either by accident or on purpose, leaving jagged edges; **rend** to pull something apart violently; **rip** to tear something with a sudden rough splitting action, accompanied by a distinctive noise, especially accidentally; **split** to divide something into two parts with a single movement, usually by force.

tear apart *vt* **1 FRAGMENT** to cause division, separation, or conflict in a group or organization ○ *a family torn apart by war* **2 DISTRESS** to cause somebody distress or emotional conflict ○ *the strain of separation was tearing us apart* **3 SEARCH** to search a place thoroughly, often causing disruptions and mess ○ *The police tore apart the house looking for the weapon.*

tear away *vt* to force or persuade yourself or somebody else to leave a place or object

tear down *vt* to demolish, destroy, or dismantle something such as a building

tear into *vt* to attack somebody or something vigorously, either physically or verbally

tear off *vt* **1** to remove a covering quickly and carelessly ○ *He tore off his shirt.* **2** to produce something quickly and carelessly

tear up *vt* to tear something into small pieces, e.g. in order to destroy it

tear[2] /teer/ *n* **1 SINGLE DROP OF FLUID FROM THE EYE** a single drop of salty fluid secreted by the lacrimal gland of the eye **2 DROP OF LIQUID** a drop of liquid or hardened fluid, especially one with a round base and narrower top ■ **tears** *npl* **1 CRYING** weeping accompanied by intense emotion **2 LIQUID BATHING THE EYE** the salty liquid secreted by the lacrimal gland that moistens and protects the surface of the eye and its surrounding tissue **3 EXCESS OF LIQUID IN THE EYES** a greater than usual amount of liquid produced by the eye or eyes, often accompanying intense emotions, or caused by irritation of the eye ■ *vi* **PRODUCE TEARS** to produce tears, especially in excessive amounts ○ *My eyes tear a lot during the hay fever season.* [Old English *tēar* < Indo-European] —**tearless** *adj*

SPELLCHECK Do not confuse ***tear*** with ***tier***, which has a similar sound. Beware: your spellchecker will not catch this error.

tearaway /táirə way/ *n* a reckless, impulsive, and undisciplined person, often a child

teardrop /teér drop/ *n* **1** = **tear**[2] *n.* 1 **2** a shape that resembles a tear, or something having this shape

tear duct /teér-/ *n* a passage that conveys tears, especially the duct that drains tears from the inner corner of the eye into the nasal cavity

tearful /teérf'l/ *adj* **1** crying, about to cry, or feeling like crying, usually because of an emotion such as great sadness **2** sad enough to cause weeping ○ *a tearful occasion* —**tearfully** *adv* —**tearfulness** *n*

tear gas /teér-/ *n* a chemical agent, delivered by a grenade or other means, that incapacitates a person by irritating the eyes —**tear-gas** *vt*

tearing /táiring/ *adj* violent or frenzied ○ *in a tearing hurry*

tear-jerker /teér-/ *n* a story or artistic work that is excessively sentimental (*informal*) —**tear-jerking** *adj*

tear-off /táir-/ *adj* produced in a block of paper in sheet form, or perforated, so that individual pieces can be removed easily

tearoom /teé room, -ro͝om/ *n* **1** a restaurant or café serving tea and other beverages, and usually cakes and other light refreshments (*often plural*) **2** *S Africa* a small shop in which some staple groceries, newspapers, and small consumer goods are sold

tea rose *n* a cultivated bushy or climbing rose. Flowers: large, tea-scented, pale pink or yellow. Native to: China. *Rosa odorata.*

tear sheet /táir-/ *n* a single page taken from a magazine or other periodical, often used to prove to an advertiser that an advertisement has been published

tearstain /teér stayn/ *n* a mark or track left by tears —**tear-stained** *adj*

teary /teéri/ (**-ier, -iest**) *adj* **1 WET WITH TEARS** wet with or full of tears **2 ABOUT TO CRY** seeming to be about to cry **3 CAUSING WEEPING** causing or sad enough to cause weeping **4 LIKE TEARS** resembling tears —**tearily** *adv* —**teariness** *n*

teary-eyed *adj* **1** with tears in the eyes, especially caused by emotion **2** characterized by weeping, especially when caused by sadness

tease /teez/ *v* (**teases, teasing, teased**) **1** *vti* **MAKE FUN OF** to make fun of somebody, either playfully or maliciously **2** *vti* **DELIBERATELY ANNOY OR IRRITATE** to deliberately annoy or irritate a person or an animal **3** *vt* **PERSUADE BY COAXING** to urge somebody, especially to do something, by continual coaxing **4** *vt* **AROUSE PHYSICAL DESIRE WITHOUT GIVING SATISFACTION** to arouse hope, curiosity, or especially physical desire in somebody with no intention of giving satisfaction **5** *vt* **PULL FIBRES APART** to pull fibres apart by combing or carding **6** *vt* **RAISE A NAP BY COMBING** to raise the nap on cloth by combing it with a wire brush **7** *vt* **SEPARATE TISSUE** to separate the parts of a tissue specimen gently with a needle in preparation for examination under a microscope **8** *vt US* HAIR = **backcomb** ■ *n* **1 PERSON WHO TEASES** a person who has a tendency to tease others **2 PERSON WHO TEASES SEXUALLY** a person who teases somebody else sexually **3 PROVOCATIVE OPENING REMARK** an opening remark or action intended to stimulate curiosity or interest **4 ACT OF TEASING** an act of teasing [Old English *tǣsan* < W Germanic] —**teasing** *adj* —**teasingly** *adv*

tease out *vt* **1 tease out, tease apart** to gradually separate things that are tangled up, or gradually separate something from an object with which it is entangled **2** to extract something gradually, e.g. the truth or information

teasel /teéz'l/, **teazel, teazle** *n* **1 PRICKLY PLANT OF EUROPE AND ASIA** a prickly plant with flowers covered with hooked leaves (**bracts**). Native to: Europe, Asia. Genus: *Dipsacus.* **2 TEASEL FLOWER HEADS** the flower heads of the teasel. Use: formerly, to raise fabric nap in the textile industry. **3 IMPLEMENT USED TO RAISE NAP** an industrial implement or device used to raise the nap on fabric [Old English *tǣsel* < W Germanic] —**teaseller** *n*

teaser /teézər/ *n* **1 TRICKY PROBLEM** a tricky or difficult problem or question **2** = **tease** *n.* 1 **3 ADVERTISEMENT OFFERING A GIFT** an advertisement offering something free such as a bonus or gift **4 IMPLEMENT FOR TEASING WOOL** an implement for teasing fibres, especially wool

tea service, tea set *n* a set of matching articles such as cups, saucers, and a teapot, used for serving tea

teashop /teé shop/ *n* = **tearoom** *n.* 1

teaspoon /teé spoon/ *n* **1 SMALL SPOON** a small spoon, used especially for stirring tea and other beverages and for eating desserts **2 teaspoon, teaspoonful AMOUNT HELD BY A TEASPOON** the amount held by a teaspoon **3 teaspoon, teaspoonful ONE THIRD OF A TABLESPOON** a standard household measure equal to one-third of a tablespoon or 5 ml

tea strainer *n* a small utensil consisting of a usually round head surrounding a mesh, through which tea is poured to separate the leaves from the liquid

teat /teet/ *n* **1** a protuberance on the breast or udder of a female mammal through which milk is excreted for the nourishment of young **2** a part designed to resemble a nipple or teat on a baby's or baby animal's feeding bottle. US term **nipple** *n.* 2 [12C. < Old French *tete* < Germanic.] —**teated** *adj*

tea table *n* a small table at which tea is served

tea-time *n* the usual time at which tea is served, typically mid- or late afternoon

tea towel, tea cloth *n* a cloth for drying dishes and other kitchen items. US term **dishtowel**

tea tray *n* a tray intended for carrying a tea service

tea tree *n* a tree or shrub from whose leaves an antiseptic oil (**tea tree oil**) is obtained, used in cosmetics and lotions. Native to: Australia, New Zealand. Genus: *Leptospermum.*

tea trolley *n* a small household trolley from which tea can be served. US term **tea wagon**

tea wagon *n US* HOUSEHOLD = **tea trolley**

teazel, teazle *n* PLANTS, TEXTILES, TECH = **teasel**

Tebet *n* JUDAISM, CALENDAR = **Tevet**

TEC /tek/ *abbr* Training and Enterprise Council

tech /tek/ *n* (*informal*) **1** a technical college or institute **2** a technical rehearsal [Early 20C. Shortening.]

tech. *abbr* **1** technical **2** technician **3** technology

tech city *n* a town or city where a large number of people are employed in advanced technology industries, especially those connected with computing and electronic engineering

⚡**techie** /téki/, **tekkie** *n* a person who is interested in, adept at, or a student of a technology, especially one based on computing or electronics (*informal*) [Mid-20C. < TECHNICAL.]

technetium /tek neéshi əm/ *n* (*symbol* **Tc**) a silvery-grey radioactive metallic element. Source: fission products of uranium, made artificially by particle bombardment of molybdenum. Use: tracer, corrosion-resistant materials. [Mid-20C. < modern Latin, < Greek *tekhnētos* 'artificial' < *tekhnē* 'art, skill'.]

technetronic /tékni trónnik/ *adj* associated with or marked by the changes brought about by modern technology and electronics [Mid-20C. Blend of Greek *tekhnē* 'art, skill' + ELECTRONIC.]

technic /téknik/ *n* **1** INDUST = **technics 2** the way in which the basics of something are treated, or skill in handling a technique (*dated*) [Early 17C. < Greek *tekhnikos* (see TECHNICAL).]

technical /téknik'l/ *adj* **1 RELATING TO INDUSTRY OR APPLIED SCIENCE** relating to or specializing in industrial techniques or subjects or applied science **2 SKILLED IN PRACTICAL SUBJECTS** skilled in practical or scientific subjects **3 BELONGING TO PARTICULAR SUBJECT OR PROFESSION** belonging to or involving a particular subject, field, or profession ○ *technical glossaries* **4 STRICTLY INTERPRETED** according to a strict interpretation of rules or words **5 EXHIBITING TECHNIQUE** exhibiting or deriving from technique or the use of technique ○ *a high level of technical expertise* **6 ANALYSING PRICES AND MARKET INDICATORS** describes a type of security analysis based on past prices and volume levels as well as other market indicators **7 HIGH-TECH** describes outdoor clothing that has been made using state-of-the-art materials and techniques ○ *Our technical fleece jacket has advanced dual construction.* ■ *n* BASKETBALL = **technical foul** [Early 17C. < Greek *tekhnikos* 'of art' < *tekhnē* 'art, skill'.] —**technicalness** *n*

technical drawing *n* **1** the technique or practice of drawing objects and plans in a precise and detailed way, especially as taught in school **2** a precise scale drawing of something, usually prepared by a draughtsperson for architectural, engineering, or industrial purposes, showing dimensions or quantities

technical foul *n* in basketball, a foul against a player or coach for unsporting behaviour or language rather than for physical contact with an opponent

technicality /tékni kálləti/ (*plural* **-ties**) *n* **1 INFORMATION UNDERSTOOD ONLY BY SPECIALISTS** information such as a detail or a term that is understood by or relevant only to a specialist **2 TRIVIAL POINT FROM STRICTLY APPLYING RULES** a minor point arising from a rigorous interpretation of laws or rules ○ *the case was dismissed on a legal technicality* **3 QUALITY OF BEING TECHNICAL** the quality or condition of being technical

technical knockout *n* a decision in boxing that ends a match because one of the participants is too badly injured to continue fighting

technically /téknikli/ *adv* **1 STRICTLY INTERPRETED** according to a very strict, even unnecessarily strict, interpretation of rules or regulations ○ *Technically, you shouldn't be here at all.* **2 IN TECHNIQUE** as regards a particular skill or ability in technique **3 SCIENTIFICALLY OR TECHNOLOGICALLY** as regards the use of technology ○ *technically advanced*

technical rehearsal *n* a rehearsal of a play or other theatrical presentation for the purpose of making sure that lights, sound, and any other technical effects are cued correctly and in working order

technical sergeant *n* a noncommissioned officer in the US Air Force of a rank above staff sergeant

⚡**technical support** *n* a repair or advice service offered to customers by some computer hardware and software manufacturers, usually by telephone, fax, or e-mail

technician /tek nísh'n/ *n* **1 SPECIALIST IN INDUSTRIAL TECHNIQUES** a person who is skilled in specific industrial techniques **2 LABORATORY EMPLOYEE** somebody employed to do practical work in a laboratory **3 PERSON SKILLED RATHER THAN EXPERT** a person who has skills but lacks originality or flair

Technicolor /tékni kulər/ *tdmk* a trademark for an early colour process for making films that used three-colour separation negatives and a dye transfer process with three matrices made from the negatives

technics /tékniks/ *n* the science or rules of a particular field of knowledge, especially a technical one (+ *singular or plural verb*)

technique /tek neék/ *n* **1 PROCEDURE OR SKILL REQUIRED** the procedure, skill, or art used in a particular task **2 TREATMENT OF BASICS** the way in which the basics of something, e.g. an artistic work or a sport, are treated **3 SKILL POSSESSED** skill or expertise in doing something particular ○ *a pianist with superb technique* **4 SPECIAL ABILITY** a special ability or knack [Early 19C. Via French < Greek *tekhnikos* (see TECHNICAL).]

techno /ték nō/ *n* electronic dance music characterized by its quick tempo and use of digitally synthesized instruments [Shortening of TECHNOLOGY]

techno- *prefix* technology, technological ○ *technophobia* [Shortening]

technobabble /téknō bab'l/ *n* language in which technical terms are overused

technocracy /tek nókrəssi/ (*plural* **-cies**) *n* **1** a social system in which scientists, engineers, and technicians have high social standing and political power **2** a philosophy that advocates the enlistment of a bureaucracy of highly trained engineers, scientists, or technicians to run the government and society

technocrat /téknə krat/ *n* **1** a bureaucrat who is intensively trained in engineering, economics, or some form of technology **2** a proponent of government by technicians —**technocratic** /téknə kráttik/ *adj*

⚡**technofreak** /téknō freek/ *n* a technical expert in, or obsessive enthusiast of, information systems (*informal*)

technol. *abbr* technology

technologize /tek nóllə jīz/ (**-gizes, -gizing, -gized**), **technologise** (**-gises, -gising, -gised**) *vti* to modify or modernize something by introducing technology —**technologization** /tek nóllə jī záysh'n/ *n*

technology /tek nólləji/ (*plural* **-gies**) *n* **1 APPLICATION OF TOOLS AND METHODS** the study, development, and application of devices, machines, and techniques for manufacturing and productive processes ○ *recent developments in seismographic technology* **2 METHOD OF APPLYING TECHNICAL KNOWLEDGE** a method or methodology that applies technical knowledge or tools ○ *a new technology for accelerating incubation* ○ '...*Maryland-based firm uses database and Internet technology to track a company's consumption of printed goods...*' (*Forbes Global Business and Finance*; November 1998) **3 SUM OF PRACTICAL KNOWLEDGE** the sum of a society's or culture's practical knowledge, especially with reference to its material culture [Early 17C. < Greek *tekhnologia* 'systematic treatment' < *tekhnē* 'art, craft'.] —**technologic** /téknə lójjik/ *adj* —**technological** *adj* —**technologically** *adv* —**technologist** *n*

⚡**technophile** /téknō fīl/ *n* a lover of new technology or computerization

⚡**technophobe** /téknə fōb/ *n* somebody who dislikes new technology or computerization —**technophobia** /téknō fṓbi ə/ *n*

technostructure /téknō strukchər/ *n* a network of controlling technocrats in an organization or society

technothriller /téknō thrilər/ *n* a suspenseful book or film in which the plot turns on seemingly plausible technological wonders

techy *adj* = **tetchy**

~~**tecnical**~~ incorrect spelling of **technical**

tecta plural of **tectum**

tectonic /tek tónnik/ *adj* **1** relating to the forces that produce movement and deformation of the Earth's crust **2** relating to construction and architecture [Mid-17C. Via late Latin < Greek *tektonikos* < *tekton* 'builder, carpenter'.] —**tectonically** *adv*

tectonic plate *n* a segment of the Earth's crust that moves relative to other segments and is characterized by volcanic and seismic activity around its margins

tectonics /tek tónniks/ *n* **1** the study of the mechanisms and results of large-scale movement of the Earth's crust, e.g., that producing mountain ranges and extensive fault systems (+ *singular verb*) ◊ **plate tectonics 2** the science or practice of building construction

tectrix /téktriks/ (*plural* **-trices** /-tri seez/) *n* ZOOL = **covert** *n.* 3 [Late 19C. < modern Latin, < Latin *tect-*, past participle of *tegere* 'to cover'.] —**tectricial** /tek trísh'l/ *adj*

tectum /téktəm/ (*plural* **-ta** /-tə/) *n* a part in the body that forms a covering or is arranged like a roof, especially the back upper section of the midbrain [Early 20C. < Latin, 'roof' < *tegere* 'to cover'.] —**tectal** *adj*

Tecumseh /tə kúmssə/ (1768?–1813) Native North American leader

ted[1] /ted/ *n* a teddy boy (*informal*) [Mid-20C. Shortening.]

ted[2] /ted/ (**teds, tedding, tedded**) *vt* to spread or shake up mown grass in order to dry it when making hay [15C. < Old Norse *teðja* 'spread (manure)'.]

tedder /téddər/ *n* a machine or person that spreads or shakes mown grass so that it can dry during hay making

Tedder /téddər/, **Arthur William, 1st Baron** (1890–1967) British air force commander

teddy[1] /téddi/ (*plural* **-dies**) *n* = **teddy bear**

teddy[2] /téddi/ (*plural* **-dies**) *n* a woman's one-piece undergarment serving as both bra and panties [Early 20C. < ?]

teddy[3] /téddi/ (*plural* **-dies**) *n W Country* a potato [Early 20C. Alteration of *tattie* 'potato'.]

teddy bear *n* a furry stuffed toy in the shape of a stylized bear cub [Early 20C. After Theodore ('Teddy') ROOSEVELT, who was fond of bear-hunting.]

teddy boy *n* **1** a young man in Britain in the 1950s and early 1960s who followed the fashion of dressing in Edwardian style with tight narrow trousers, pointed shoes, and long sideboards **2** any rebellious and tough young man (*dated*) [Mid-20C. Pet form of *Edward*, alluding to EDWARD VII.]

teddy girl *n* a teddy boy's woman companion

Te Deum /tay dáy əm, tee dée əm/ *n* **1** an ancient Christian hymn praising God that is sung or recited at matins in the Roman Catholic Church or at morning prayers in the Church of England **2** a Christian service of thanksgiving that uses the Te Deum [Pre-12C. < Latin *Te Deum laudamus* 'Thee God, we praise', the first words of the hymn.]

tedious /téedi əss/ *adj* boring because of being long, monotonous, or repetitive [15C. Directly or via Old French < late Latin *taediosus* < Latin *taedium* (see TEDIOUS).] —**tediously** *adv* —**tediousness** *n*

tedium /téedi əm/ *n* the quality of being boring, monotonous, too long, or repetitive [Mid-17C. < Latin *taedium* 'weariness, disgust' < *taedere* 'be wearisome'.]

tee[1] /tee/ *n* **1 LETTER T** the letter T **2 T-SHAPED THING** something with the shape or form of a capital T, e.g. two pipes joined to form this shape **3** *US* **T-SHIRT** a T-shirt (*informal*) **4 TARGET** the mark aimed at in curling, quoits, and some other games

SPELLCHECK See ***tea***.

tee[2] /tee/ *n* **1 PEG** a small wooden or plastic peg with one pointed and one cupped end, inserted in the ground to hold a golf ball **2 STARTING AREA** an area on a golf course where play for a new hole begins **3 BALL STAND** a plastic device that supports a football or rugby ball on the ground in kicking position ■ *vti* (**tees, teeing, teed**) **POSITION THE BALL** to place a ball on a tee ready for striking [Late 17C. < ?]

tee off *vi* **1** to hit the ball from a tee at the start of a hole of golf **2** to start a new activity (*informal*)

TEE *abbr* Trans-Europe Express (train)

teed off /téed-/ *adj US* angry, especially because of something that somebody has done (*informal*) [Probably alteration of *peed (pissed) off*]

tee-hee /tée hée/, **te-hee** *interj* used to indicate brief, especially mocking or gloating laughter [14C. An imitation of the sound.] —**tee-hee** *vi*

tee-joint *n* CONSTR = **T-joint**

teem[1] /teem/ *vi* to have an extremely large number of people or animals in a place ○ *streets teeming with people* [Old English *tēman* < Germanic]

SPELLCHECK See ***team***.

teem[2] /teem/ *v* **1** *vi* to rain very hard **2** *vt* to pour out or empty something [14C. < Old Norse *tœma* 'to empty' < *tómr* 'empty'.]

teen /teen/ *adj* teenage (*informal*) ■ *n* a teenager (*informal*) [Early 19C. Shortening.]

teenage /téen ayj/, **teenaged** /-ayjd/ *adj* **1** aged between 13 and 19 ○ *teenage girls* **2** relating to teenagers ○ *teenage styles*

teenager /téen ayjər/ *n* a young person between the ages of 13 and 19

SYNONYMS See ***youth***.

teens /teenz/ *npl* **1** the years in somebody's life between the ages of 13 and 19 **2** the numbers ending in '-teen' [Late 16C. < TEEN.]

teensy /téenzi/ (**-sier, -siest**) *adj* very small (*informal*) [Late 19C. Probably < TEENY.]

teensy-weensy /téenzi wéenzi/ *adj* very small (*informal*) [After TEENY-WEENY]

teeny /téeni/ (**-nier, -niest**) *adj* very small (*informal*) [Early 19C. Variant of TINY, after WEENY.]

teenybopper /téeni bopər/ *n* a young teenager, usually a young girl, who follows the latest fads in fashion and music

teeny-weeny *adj* very small (*informal*)

teepee *n* ANTHROP = **tepee**

tee-plate *n* CONSTR = **T-plate**

Tees /teez/ river of NE England, flowing into the North Sea. Length: 128 km/80 mi.

tee shirt *n* CLOTHING = **T-shirt**

tee-square *n* ART = **T-square**

Teesside /téez sīd/ industrial region in NE England, around the mouth of the River Tees

teeter /téetər/ *vi* **1** to walk or move unsteadily and as if about to fall ○ *teetering along in her high heels* **2** to be in a precarious position in which things could imminently go badly wrong ○ *For 24 hours the country teetered on the brink of war.* [Mid-19C. Variant of TITTER.]

teeth plural of **tooth**

teethe /teeth/ (**teethes, teething, teethed**) *vi* to grow milk teeth [15C. < TEETH.]

teething ring /téething-/ *n* a ring of hard rubber or plastic on which a baby can bite when teething

teething troubles *npl* temporary difficulties that arise at the outset of a new activity

teethridge /téeth rij/ *n US* = **alveolar ridge**

teetotal /tee tṓt'l/ *adj* **1** completely abstaining from alcoholic beverages **2** complete and absolute [Mid-19C. < initial letter of TOTAL + TOTAL.] —**teetotalism** *n* —**teetotaller** *n* —**teetotally** *adv*

teetotum /tee tṓtəm/ *n* a top spun with the fingers, once used in a game of chance [Early 18C. < Latin *totum* 'all' + its initial letter 'T', inscribed on one side of the toy.]

teff /tef/, **tef** *n* an annual North African grass cultivated for its seed, which is used as a grain. *Eragrostis tef*. [Late 18C. < Amharic *ṭēf*.]

tefillin /tə fíllin/ *npl* the small leather boxes containing Hebrew texts ritually worn by orthodox Jewish men. ◊ **phylactery** *n.* 1 [Early 17C. < Aramaic *tēpillīn* 'prayers'.]

TEFL /téff'l/ *abbr* Teaching (of) English as a Foreign Language

Teflon /téf lon/ *tdmk* a trademark for polytetrafluoroethylene, a plastic with nonstick properties that is used as a coating, e.g. for cookware

teg /teg/ *n* **1** a sheep of either sex between weaning and first shearing **2** *US* a doe that is in the second year of life [Early 16C. < ?]

tegmen /tégmən/ (*plural* **-mina** /-mənə/), **tegmentum** /tegméntəm/ *n* **1 INNER LAYER IN A SEED** the inner layer of a seed's coat **2 INSECT FOREWING** the forewing of a primitive insect such as the cockroach **3 COVERING PART** a covering part in a plant or animal [Early 19C. < Latin, < *tegere* 'to cover'.] —**tegminal** *adj*

tegu /ti góo/ (*plural* **-gus** *or* **-gu**) *n* a fast-running lizard that grows up to 120 cm/4 ft long. Native to: Central and South America. Genus: *Tupinambis*. [Mid-20C. Shortening of *teguexin* < Nahuatl *tecoixin* 'lizard'.]

Tegucigalpa /te góossi gálpə/ capital of Honduras, in the south-central part of the country. Population: 738,500 (1993).

tegular /téggyoolər/, **tegulated** /téggyoo làytid/ *adj* relating to or resembling tiles [Early 19C. < Latin *tegula* 'tile' < *tegere* 'to cover'.] —**tegularly** *adv*

tegument /téggyoomənt/ *n* the protective outer covering of an organism [15C. < Latin *tegumentum* 'covering' < *tegere* 'to cover'.] —**tegumental** /téggyoo mént'l/ *adj* —**tegumentary** /-méntəri/ *adj*

te-hee *interj, vi* = **tee-hee**

Tehran /te raán/, **Tehrān** capital of Iran, in the north of the country. Population: 6,475,527 (1991).

Teide, Pico de /peékō day táythə/ highest mountain in Spain, on the island of Tenerife. Height: 3,715 m/12,188 ft.

te igitur /táy íggitoor/ *n* the first prayer of the Roman Catholic Mass, beginning 'te igitur clementissime Pater' [Early 19C. < Latin, 'thee, therefore'.]

teiglach /táyg laakh, tī́g-/ (*plural* **teiglachs** *or* **teiglach**) *n* a Jewish or German biscuit made from spiced dough shaped into small balls and simmered in honey, nuts, and spices [Early 20C. < Yiddish *teyglekh* < *teyg* 'dough' < Old High German *teic*.]

teigue *n Ireland* = **taig** (*slang offensive*)

teiid /tée id, tī́ id/ *adj* describes a member of a reptile family of large carnivorous lizards with forked tongues. Native to: Central and South America. Family: Teiidae. [Mid-20C. < modern Latin *Teiidae* < Portuguese *teiu* 'lizard' < Tupi *tejú*.]

Teilhard de Chardin /táy jaa də shaárdan/, **Pierre** (1881–1955) French priest, palaeontologist, and theologian

teind /teend/ *n Scotland* a tithe ■ *vti Scotland* to tithe income or produce [13C. Alteration of TENTH.]

Te Kanawa /tə kaánəwə, tay-/, **Dame Kiri** (*b.* 1944) New Zealand opera singer

Tekapo, Lake /tékəpō/ lake in the centre of the South Island, New Zealand. Area: 83 sq. km/32 sq. mi.

tekkie *n* = **techie** (*informal*)

Te Kooti /te kóoti/, **Arikirangi Te Turuki** (1830?–93) New Zealand Maori leader

tektite /ték tīt/ *n* a small dark-coloured glassy object, possibly resulting from meteoric impact, found in groups at various locations throughout the world [Early 20C. < Greek *tēktos* 'molten' < *tēkein* 'melt'.]

tel. *abbr* **1** telegram **2** telegraph **3** telegraphic **4** telephone

tela /téelə/ (*plural* **-ae** /-lee/) *n* a delicate part or tissue in the body with a fine or intricate pattern like a web [Early 20C. < Latin, 'web'.]

telaesthesia /télliss theézhə, -theézi ə/ *n* the supposed perception of phenomena or events considered beyond the range of normal senses [Late 19C. < TELE- + Greek *aisthēsis* 'perception'.] —**telaesthetic** /télliss théttik/ *adj*

telamon /téllə mon, -mən/ (*plural* **telamones** /téllə mṓneez/ *or* **telamons**) *n* ARCHIT = **atlas** *n.* 3 [Early 17C. < Greek, after *Telamon*, Greek mythical hero.]

telangiectasia /te lánji ek táyzi ə/, **telangiectasis** /-ek táyssiss/ *n* permanent dilation of the capillaries and small blood vessels, especially in the face and thighs, producing dark red blotches [Mid-19C. < Greek *telos* 'end' + *aggeion* 'vessel' + *ektasis* 'extension'.] —**telangiectatic** /-táttik/ *adj*

Tel Aviv /tél ə veév/, **Tel Aviv-Jaffa** /-jáffə/ city in west-central Israel, on the Mediterranean Sea. Population: 353,100 (1997).

⚡**telco hotel** /tél kō-/ *n* ONLINE = **Internet hotel**

tele- *prefix* **1** distant, operating at a distance ○ *telepathy* **2** television ○ *telecourse* **3** telegraph, telephone ○ *teleprinter* [< Greek *tēle* 'far away']

telebanking /télli bangking/ *n* a system of transacting business with a bank by telephone

telebridge /télli brij/ *n* a telephone system that enables three or more people to be connected simultaneously ○ *'Group classes are limited to 15 participants and are held on a telebridge.'* (*The Washington Post*; July 1998)

telecast /télli kaast/ *n* a television broadcast ■ *vti* (**-casts, -casting, -cast** *or* **-casted**) to broadcast a programme on television —**telecaster** *n*

telecom /télli kom/ *n* telecommunication (*informal*) [Mid-20C. Shortening.]

telecommunication /télli kə myóoni káysh'n/ *n* the transmission of encoded sound, pictures, or data over significant distances, using radio signals or electrical or optical lines

telecommunications /télli kə myóoni káysh'nz/ *n* the science and technology of transmitting information electronically by wires or radio signals with integrated encoding and decoding equipment (+ *singular or plural verb*)

⚡**telecommute** /télli kə myóot/ (**-commutes, -commuting, -commuted, -commuted**) *vi* to work from home on a computer linked to the workplace via modem —**telecommuter** *n* —**telecommuting** *n*

telecoms /télli komz/ *n* telecommunications (*informal; + singular or plural verb*) [Contraction]

teleconferencing /télli konfərənssing/ *n* a system of video-conferencing that uses a restricted band of frequencies and allows participants to be connected by telephone lines —**teleconference** *n, vi*

telecottage /télli kotij/ *n* a place, often in a rural area, where people can use computers and other electronic equipment to telecommute —**telecottaging** *n*

teledensity /télli dénssəti/ *n* a measure of telephone availability, expressed as the number of main lines per 100 inhabitants in a country

teledu /télli doo/ (*plural* **-dus** *or* **-du**) *n* a carnivorous mammal of the weasel family with a dark coat and a white stripe down its back. Native to: Southeast Asia. *Mydaus javanensis.* [Early 19C. < Javanese.]

téléférique *n* TRANSP = **téléphérique**

telefilm /télli film/ *n* a film made for television

teleg. *abbr* **1** telegram **2** telegraph **3** telegraphic **4** telegraphy

telega /te láygə/ *n* a simple four-wheeled Russian cart [Mid-16C. < Russian.]

telegenic /télli jénnik/ *adj* pleasant and attractive when viewed on television —**telegenically** *adv*

telegnosis /téllə nṓssiss, télləg-/ *n* knowledge of phenomena beyond the range of normal sense perception —**telegnostic** /-nóstik/ *adj*

telegony /ti léggəni/ *n* the now discredited idea that characteristics from the sire of a female's earlier pregnancy can be inherited by offspring from a subsequent sire —**telegonic** /télli gónnik/ *adj* —**telegonous** *adj*

telegram /télli gram/ *n* a message sent by telegraph [Mid-19C. After TELEGRAPH.] —**telegrammatic** /télli grə máttik/ *adj* —**telegrammic** /télli grámmik/ *adj*

telegraph /télli graaf, -graf/ *n* **1** LONG-DISTANCE COMMUNICATION METHOD THROUGH WIRES a method of long-distance communicating by coded electric impulses transmitted through wires **2** TELECOM = **telegram** ■ *v* **1** *vti* SEND BY WIRE to send a message to somebody by telegraph **2** *vt* INDICATE to communicate a thought or feeling indirectly or without words **3** *vt* SHOW INTENTION to give advance notice of intentions, especially unwittingly, to an audience or opponent [Early 18C. < French *télégraphe* 'something that writes far' < *-graphe* (see -GRAPH).] —**telegrapher** /ti léggrəfər/ *n* —**telegraphist** /ti léggrəfist/ *n*

telegraphese /télli gra féez/ *n* language reduced to its essential elements without regard to elegance or grammar, as typically found in telegrams

telegraphic /télli gráffik/ *adj* **1** relating to telegraphy or telegrams **2** concise or elliptical in spoken or written expression —**telegraphically** *adv*

telegraph plant *n* a leguminous shrub, with small leaflets that jerk spasmodically under solar radiation. Native to: tropical Asia. *Desmodium gyrans.*

telegraph pole, telegraph post *n* a high wooden pole for supporting telephone wires. US term **telephone pole**

telegraphy /ti léggrəfi/ *n* the system, study, or operation of telegraph communications

Telegu *n, adj* LANG, PEOPLES = **Telugu**

telekinesis /télli ki néessiss, -kī-/ *n* the supposed psychic power to move or deform inanimate objects without the use of physical force —**telekinetic** /télli ki néttik, -kī-/ *adj* —**telekinetically** *adv*

Telemachus /tə lémmәkəss/ *n* in Greek mythology, the son of Odysseus, who waited with his mother, Penelope, for his father's return after the Trojan War

Telemann /táylə man, téllə-/, **Georg Philipp** (1681–1767) German composer

telemark /télli maark/ *n* a turn in cross-country skiing accomplished by putting the outside ski forwards and turning it slowly inwards [Early 20C. After *Telemark*, region in Norway.]

telemarketing /télli maarkiting/ *n* selling or promoting goods and services by telephone —**telemarketer** *n*

telematics /telli máttiks/ *n* the study of the processes involved in the long-distance transmission of computer data (*+ singular verb*) [Late 20C. Blend of TELECOMMUNICATION + INFORMATICS.] —**telematic** *adj*

telemedicine /télli medəss'n/ *n* the use of video links, e-mail, telephone, or another telecommunications system to transmit medical information, e.g. in consultations between a doctor and patient or supervision of medical staff

telemeter *n* /ti lémmitər, télli meetər/ **1** REMOTE MEASURING DEVICE a device used to record information about a remote object or event and transmit it to an observer **2** DEVICE FOR MEASURING DISTANCES DIRECTLY a device used for measuring distances directly that does not use rods or chains across the distance to be measured ■ *vt* /télli meetər/ TRANSMIT DATA to collect and transmit data about a remote object, especially using a satellite —**telemetric** /télli méttrik/ *adj* —**telemetrical** *adj* —**telemetrically** *adv* —**telemetry** /ti lémmətri/ *n*

telencephalon /téll en séffə lon/ *n* the frontmost part of the brain, consisting of the cerebral hemispheres —**telencephalic** /téll enssə fállik/ *adj*

teleological /télli ə lójjik'l, teeli ə lójjik'l/, **teleologic** *adj* relating to the study of ultimate causes in nature or of actions in relation to their ends or utility —**teleologically** *adv*

teleological argument *n* an argument for God's existence from the existence of order and design in the universe

teleology /teeli óllәji/ *n* **1** STUDY OF CAUSES the study of ultimate causes in nature **2** APPROACH TO ETHICS an approach to ethics that studies actions in relation to their ends or utility **3** GOAL-DIRECTED ACTIVITY any activity that tends towards the achievement of a goal [Mid-18C. < modern Latin *teleologia* 'science of ends' < Greek *telos* 'end'.] —**teleologism** *n* —**teleologist** *n*

teleost /télli ost/, **teleostean** /télli ósti ən/ *n* any bony fish with rayed fins in a suborder that includes most living species, numbering around 20,000, but excluding sturgeons, gars, sharks, rays, and related fish. Subclass: Teleostei. [Mid-19C. < Greek *telos* 'end' + *osteon* 'bone'.]

telepath /télli path/ *n* somebody who claims to communicate by telepathy

telepathize /tə léppə thīz/ (**-thizes, -thizing, -thized**), **telepathise** (**-thises, -thising, -thised**) *vi* to claim or be believed to communicate by telepathy

telepathy /tə léppəthi/ *n* supposed communication directly from one person's mind to another's without speech, writing, or other signs or symbols —**telepathic** /télli páthik/ *adj* —**telepathically** *adv*

téléphérique /téllifə reek/, **téléférique** *n* **1** a cable car **2** a cableway [Early 20C. < French, 'carrying far' < Greek *pherein* 'carry'.]

telephone /télli fōn/ *n* **1** ELECTRONIC COMMUNICATIONS DEVICE an electronic apparatus containing a receiver and transmitter that is connected to a telecommunications system, enabling the user to speak to and hear others with similar equipment **2** COMMUNICATION USING TELEPHONES a system of communications using telephones ○ *a telephone company* ■ *vti* (**-phones, -phoning, -phoned**) **1** USE TELEPHONE to contact and speak to somebody using the telephone **2** CONVEY SOMETHING BY TELEPHONE to send a message by telephone ○ *Bob couldn't come to the party and telephoned his regrets.* —**telephoner** *n* —**telephonic** /télli fónnik/ *adj* —**telephonically** *adv*

telephone answering machine *n* TELECOM = **answering machine**

telephone book *n* TELECOM = **telephone directory**

telephone booth *n US* TELECOM = **telephone box**

telephone box *n* an enclosed or partly enclosed space with a pay telephone in it. US term **telephone booth**

telephone directory *n* an alphabetical listing of individuals or groups who have telephones, along with their addresses and telephone numbers. US term **telephone book**

telephone exchange *n* a centre that houses equipment used for interconnecting telephone lines

telephone pole *n US* TELECOM = **telegraph pole**

telephone tag *n* a situation in which two people repeatedly return each other's telephone calls and leave recorded messages without succeeding in speaking directly to each other (*informal*)

telephonist /tə léffənist/ *n* a telephone switchboard operator

telephony /tə léffəni/ *n* the science, technology, or system of communication by telephone

telephoto /télli fōtō/ *adj* producing a large image of a distant object ■ *n* (*plural* **-tos**) **1** PHOTOGRAPHY = **telephoto lens** **2** a photograph taken using a telephoto lens

telephotography /télli fə tóggrəfi/ *n* the photographing of distant objects with the use of special lenses or electronic equipment —**telephotographic** /télli fōtə gráffik/ *adj*

telephoto lens *n* a camera lens that integrates a telescope

teleplay /télli play/ *n* a treatment or script for a play written for presentation on television

teleport /télli pawrt/ *v* **1** *vt* MOVE SOMETHING USING MENTAL POWER to move an object supposedly using telekinesis **2** *vi* MOVE SOMEWHERE WITHOUT TRAVELLING in science fiction and fantasy, to move instantly from one place to another by some paranormal or magical means **3** *vt* DUPLICATE OBJECT USING LIGHT BEAMS to duplicate the properties of a physical object using light beams [Mid-20C. < TELE- + Latin *portare* 'carry'.] —**teleportation** /télli pawr táysh'n/ *n*

teleprinter /télli printər/ *n* a piece of equipment for telegraphic communication that uses a device like a typewriter for data input and output. US term **teletypewriter**

teleprocessing /télli prṓ sessing/ *n* the use of computer terminals in different locations, connected to a main computer, to process data

TelePrompTer /télli promptər/ *tdmk US* a trademark for a device showing text for somebody speaking on television to read

telerecording /télli ri káwrding/ *n* the recording of a television programme on tape or film as it is being broadcast

telesales /télli saylz/ *n* MARKETING = **telemarketing**

telescience /télli sī ənss/ *n* the technology of making observations and performing experiments from a great distance

telescope /télli skōp/ *n* **1** DEVICE FOR LOOKING AT DISTANT OBJECTS a device for making distant objects appear nearer and larger by means of compound lenses or concave mirrors **2** ASTRON = **radio telescope** ■ *v* (**-scopes, -scoping, -scoped**) **1** *vi* COLLAPSE NEATLY to slide neatly one inside another like the sections of a telescope **2** *vt* CONDENSE to make something shorter in time or length ○ *telescoped his adventure into a one-hour talk* [Mid-17C. < Italian *telescopio* or modern Latin *telescopium*, both literally 'looking far' < Greek *skopein* 'look'.]

telescopic /télli skóppik/ *adj* **1** OF TELESCOPES relating to or visible only by using a telescope **2** ENLARGING with the ability to make something distant seem nearer or larger ○ *a telescopic lens* **3** ABLE TO SEE FAR able to see great distances ○ *telescopic vision* **4** COLLAPSIBLE consisting of parts that slide one inside another ○ *a tripod with telescopic legs* —**telescopically** *adv*

telescopic sight *n* a telescope mounted on a rifle and used for sighting, especially on distant targets

Telescopium /téllə skṓpi əm/ *n* a constellation of the southern hemisphere

telescopy /tə léskəpi/ *n* the science and technology of making and using telescopes

teleshopping /télli shoping/ *n* the practice or activity of ordering goods advertised on television by phone or computer

telestereoscope /télli stérri ə skōp, -steeri-/ *n* a binocular telescope or telescopic stereoscope adapted to provide a three-dimensional view of distant objects or landscapes

telesthesia *n* US = **telaesthesia**

telestich /ti léstik, télli stik/ *n* an acrostic or poem in which the last letters in each line spell a word [Mid-17C. < Greek *telos* 'end' + *stikhos* 'row, line of verse'.]

Telesto /ti léstō/ *n* a very small natural satellite of Saturn

teletext /télli tekst/ *n* a system of broadcasting news and other information in written form that can be viewed on specially equipped television sets, superimposed on, or in place of, the picture

telethon /téllə thon/ *n* a lengthy television broadcast that combines entertainment with appeals to donate to a particular charity [Mid-20C. Blend of TELE- + MARATHON.]

teletypewriter /télli tīp rītər, télli tīp-/ *n US* TELECOM = **teleprinter**

teleutospore /ti lootə spawr/ *n* BIOL = **teliospore** [Late 19C. < Greek *teleutē* 'completion' < *telos* 'end'.] —**teleutosporic** /ti lootə spáwrik, -spórrik/ *adj*

televangelist /télli vánjəlist/ *n* a Christian evangelist whose services and revivals are broadcast on television [Late 20C. Blend of TELEVISION + EVANGELIST.] —**televangelism** *n*

televise /télli vīz/ (**-vises, -vising, -vised**) *vt* to broadcast something on television [Early 20C. Back-formation < TELEVISION.]

television /télli vizh'n, -vízh'n/ *n* **1 VIDEO BROADCASTING SYSTEM** a system of capturing images and sounds, broadcasting them via a combined electronic audio and video signal, and reproducing them to be viewed and listened to **2 TV SET** an electronic device for receiving and reproducing the images and sounds of a television signal **3 TV INDUSTRY** the television industry ○ *works in television* **4 BROADCAST CONTENT** the image, sound, or content of a television broadcast ○ *appearing on television for the first time* —**televisual** /télli vízhyoo əl, téllə-, -víz-/ *adj* —**televisually** *adv*

television set *n* = **television** *n.* 2

television tube *n* = **tube** *n.* 7

⚡**teleworking** /télli wurking/ *n* HR = **telecommuting**

telex /télleks/ *n* **1 COMMUNICATIONS SYSTEM** a communications system using teleprinters that communicate via telephone lines **2 MESSAGE** a message sent or received by telex ■ *vti* **SEND BY TELEX** to send a message to somebody by telex [Mid-20C. Blend of TELEPRINTER + EXCHANGE.]

telfer *n* TRANSP = **telpher**

telferage *n* TRANSP = **telpherage**

Telford /télfərd/ town in west-central England. Population: 115,000 (1991).

Telford, Thomas (1757–1834) British civil engineer

telia plural of **telium**

telic /téllik/ *adj* directed towards a definite end or purpose [Mid-19C. < Greek *telikos* 'final' < *telos* 'end'.]

teliospore /teéli ə spawr/ *n* a resting spore that develops in rust and smut fungi in the autumn and germinates in the spring [Early 20C. < TELIUM.] —**teleosporic** /teéli ə spáwrik, -spórrik/ *adj*

telium /teéli əm, télli-/ (*plural* **-a** /-ə/) *n* the spore case of a rust or smut fungus that bears teliospores [Early 20C. < Greek *telos* 'end'.] —**telial** *adj*

tell /tel/ (**tells, telling, told** /tōld/) *v* **1** *vt* **INFORM** to inform somebody, or inform somebody of something ○ *Who told you?* ○ *Jim told us the news.* **2** *vt* **RELATE EVENTS OR FACTS** to give an account in speech or writing of events or facts ○ *tell a story* **3** *vti* **EXPRESS IN WORDS** to express thoughts or feelings to somebody in words **4** *vt* **EXPRESS** to speak, expressing a particular thing ○ *tell a lie* **5** *vt* **ORDER** to command or order somebody to do something **6 DISTINGUISH** to be able to distinguish two or more things ○ *couldn't tell one from the other* **7** *vt* **REVEAL THE FUTURE** to purport to reveal future events ○ *tell your fortune* **8** *vt* **COUNT THINGS** to count things, e.g. votes cast or beads as part of a prayer ○ *tell a rosary* **9** *vi* **REVEAL A SECRET** to reveal secret or damaging information, especially to an authority [Old English *tellan* < Germanic, 'put in order'] —**tellable** *adj* ◇ **all told** altogether, or when everything else is taken into consideration ◇ **tell it like it is** to give a frank and accurate account of something (*informal*) ◇ **tell me about it! 1** used to indicate heartfelt agreement (*informal*) **2** used wryly to indicate to a speaker that you too have had a similar, usually negative, experience to the one being described (*informal*) ◇ **you're telling me!** used to indicate agreement with an observation (*informal*)

tell against *vt* to play a part in determining a negative outcome for somebody ○ *His extreme nervousness told against him in the interview.*

tell apart *vt* to distinguish two or more similar things or people

tell off *vt* to scold or rebuke somebody, especially in anger (*informal*)

tell on *vt* **1** to have an adverse effect on somebody or something **2** to report damaging or incriminating information to an authority

Tell, William /tel/ *n* in Swiss legend, a patriot who liberated Switzerland from Austrian rule in the 14th century

tell-all *adj* not withholding any information, even what may be considered secret, private, or unsuitable

teller /téllər/ *n* **1 BANK EMPLOYEE** an employee in a bank or savings institution who receives and pays out money **2 COUNTER OF VOTES** a counter of votes in an election or legislature **3 SOMEBODY WHO TELLS** a person who tells something ○ *a teller of tales*

Teller /téllər/, **Edward** (*b.* 1908) Hungarian-born US physicist

tellin /téllin/ (*plural* **-lins** *or* **-lin**) *n* a marine bivalve mollusc that lives in intertidal sand. Genus: *Tellina.* [Early 18C. Via Latin < Greek *tellinē* 'type of shellfish'.]

telling /télling/ *adj* **1** revealing information inadvertently or indirectly ○ *a telling glance* **2** very effective or expressive ○ *a telling indictment* —**tellingly** *adv*

telling-off (*plural* **tellings-off**) *n* a scolding or reprimand (*informal*)

telltale /tél tayl/ *adj* **CLEARLY SHOWING** clearly showing or indicating something that is secret or hidden ○ *telltale signs* ■ *n* **1 SOMEBODY WHO TELLS SECRETS** a person, especially a child, who tells people about another person's secrets or bad behaviour **2 DEVICE** a device or signal intended to monitor a machine or system **3 WIND STRIPS** strips of ribbon hung aloft on a sailing boat to show apparent wind direction **4 METAL STRIP** a horizontal metal strip across the front wall of a squash or racquetball court, above which the ball must be bounced

tellurate /téllyoo rayt/ *n* a salt or ester of telluric acid [Early 19C. < TELLURIUM.]

tellurian /te loori ən/ *adj* relating to the Earth or life on Earth ■ *n* an inhabitant of the Earth, as described in science fiction [Mid-19C. < Latin *tellus* 'earth'.]

telluric[1] /te loorik/ *adj* **1** originating or proceeding from the Earth or its atmosphere **2** GEOG = **tellurian** *adj.* [Mid-19C. < Latin *tellus* 'earth'.]

telluric[2] /te loorik/ *adj* relating to or containing tellurium, especially in a high valency [Early 19C. < TELLURIUM.]

telluric acid *n* H_6TeO_6 a white crystalline inorganic acid. Use: chemical reagent. [< TELLURIC[2]]

telluride /téllyoo rīd/ *n* a binary compound of tellurium with an electropositive element or group [Mid-19C. < TELLURIUM.]

tellurion /te loori on, -lyoori ən, -lyoori on/ *n* a model that shows how day and night and the seasons result from the Earth's orbit and its tilted axis in relation to the Sun [Mid-19C. < Latin *tellus* 'earth'.]

tellurise *vt* CHEM = **tellurize**

tellurium /te loori əm/ *n* (*symbol* **Te**) a semimetallic element that occurs naturally, both in a native state and in mineral ores. Source: refining of copper and lead. Use: alloys, various manufacturing processes. [Early 19C. < Latin *tellus* 'earth', after URANIUM.]

tellurize /téllyoo rīz/ (**-izes, -izing, -ized**), **tellurise** (**-ises, -ising, -ised**) *vt* to cause something to combine with tellurium

tellurometer /téllyoo rómmitər/ *n* a device that measures distances from the travel time of microwaves or radio waves transmitted across the distance to be measured [Mid-20C. < Latin *tellus* 'earth'.]

tellurous /téllyoorəss, te loorəss/ *adj* relating to or containing tellurium, especially in a low valency [Mid-19C. < TELLURIUM, after FERROUS.]

Tellus /téllәss/ *n* in Roman mythology, the goddess of the earth and of fertility [< Latin, 'earth']

telly /télli/ (*plural* **-lies**) *n* television, or a television set (*informal*) [Mid-20C. Shortening.]

⚡**TELNET** /tél net/, **Telnet** *n* a terminal emulation program that allows computer users to connect interactively to a server and access remote sites, e.g. on the Internet ■ *vti* to access a remote computer [Late 20C. < TELETYPE + NETWORK.]

telo- *prefix* end, terminal ○ *telophase* [< Greek *telos* 'end']

telocentric /téllə séntrik/ *adj* describes a chromosome whose centromere is located at or near one end

telomere /téllə meer/ *n* a region of DNA at the end of a chromosome that protects the start of the genetic coding sequence against shortening during successive replications

telophase /téllə fayz/ *n* the final stage of cell division, in which daughter cell nuclei form around chromosomes at opposite ends of the dividing mother cell —**telophasic** /téllə fáyzik/ *adj*

telpher /télfər/, **telfer** *n* a car or other carrying unit suspended from a cable in a telpherage ■ *vt* to transport something in a container suspended from cables [Late 19C. Contraction of *telephore.*] —**telpheric** *adj*

telpherage /télfərij/, **telferage** *n* a transport system in which cargoes or passengers are carried in containers suspended from cables

telson /télss'n/ *n* the terminal segment of an arthropod or arachnid body, e.g. the stinger of a scorpion [Mid-19C. < Greek, 'limit'.] —**telsonic** /tel sónnik/ *adj*

Telstar /tél staar/ *n* a communications satellite used for transmitting television programmes and telephone messages [Mid-20C. Blend of TELE- + STAR.]

Telugu /téllə goo/ (*plural* **-gu** *or* **-gus**), **Telegu** (*plural* **-gu** *or* **-gus**) *n* **1** a Dravidian language of central and SE India. Native speakers: over 10 million. **2** a member of a Telugu-speaking people [Late 18C. < Kannada and Tamil.] —**Telugu** *adj*

Tema /teémə/ city in SE Ghana, on the Gulf of Guinea. Population: 180,600 (1990 estimate).

temazepam /tə mázzə pam/ *n* a benzodiazepine drug used for the short-term treatment of insomnia [Late 20C. < *tem-* < ? + OXAZEPAM.]

temblor /témblər, -blawr/ *n* US an earthquake or tremor [Late 19C. < American Spanish, 'trembling' < Vulgar Latin *tremulare* 'tremble'.]

temerity /tə mérrəti/ *n* reckless confidence that might be offensive [15C. < Latin *temeritas* 'rashness' < assumed *temus* 'darkness'.] —**temerarious** /témmə ráiri əss/ *adj*

temmoku /témmō koo/ *n* a Japanese iron glaze that is black in colour but breaks into rust where the glaze coat is thin [Late 19C. Via Japanese < Chinese *tiān mù* 'eye of heaven'.]

Temne /témni/ (*plural* **-nes** *or* **-ne**) *n* **1** a member of an African people living in Sierra Leone **2** the Niger-Congo language of the Temne people. Native speakers: 1 million. [Late 18C. < Temne.] —**Temne** *adj*

temp /temp/ *n* a temporary worker, especially one hired from an agency [Early 20C. Shortening.] —**temp** *vi*

temp. *abbr* **1** temperance **2** temperate **3** temperature **4** template **5** temporal **6** temporary

tempeh /tém pay/, **tempe** *n* fermented soya beans, popular as a health food and in some Asian cuisines [Mid-20C. < Indonesian *tempe.*]

temper /témpər/ *n* **1** (*plural* **-pers** *or* **-per**) **TENDENCY TO ANGER** a tendency to get angry easily and suddenly ○ *has quite a temper* **2 ANGRY STATE** a state of anger or ill temper ○ *got himself into a terrible temper* **3 EMOTIONAL CONDITION** an emotional condition or predisposition of a particular kind ○ *an even temper* **4 CALM STATE** a state of calm and balance ○ *lost your temper* **5 HARDNESS OF METAL** the degree of hardness of a metal **6 ADDITIVE** something added to improve the consistency or strength of something ■ *vt* **1 SOFTEN** to make something less harsh or unacceptable, especially by adding something to it ○ *temper criticism with kindness* **2 HARDEN METAL** to harden metal by heating it to very high temperatures and then cooling it ○ *temper steel* **3 MAKE SOMEBODY STRONGER** to make somebody stronger through exposure to hardship ○ *tempered by combat duty* **4 TUNE EARLY KEYBOARD INSTRUMENT** to tune a baroque keyboard instrument so that consistent harmonic intervals are achieved throughout its range [Pre-12C. < Latin *temperare* 'mix, restrain yourself' < *tempus* 'time'.] —**temperability** /témpərə bílləti/ *n* —**temperable** *adj* —**temperer** *n*

tempera /témpərə/ *n* **1** a technique of painting with colours made from powdered pigments mixed with water and egg yolk, size, or casein **2** a painting done in tempera [Mid-19C. < Italian, < Latin *temperare* (see TEMPER).]

temperament /témprəmənt/ *n* **1 QUALITY OF MIND** a prevailing or dominant quality of mind that characterizes a person **2 MOODINESS** excessive moodiness, irritability, or sensitivity **3 MEDIEVAL PHYSIOLOGICAL CLASSIFICATION** in medieval physiology, the quality of mind resulting from various proportions of the four cardinal humours in an individual **4 NOTE INTERVAL SETTING** the subtle relationship of the pitches of notes of keyboard instruments, and the consequences this has on harmony

temperamental /témprə mént'l/ *adj* **1 EASILY UPSET** easily upset or irritated **2 UNPREDICTABLE** unpredictable and erratic in behaviour **3 OF TEMPERAMENT** relating to temperament —**temperamentally** *adv*

temperance /témpərənss/ *n* **1** total abstinence from alcoholic drink **2** self-restraint in the face of temptation or desire

~~**temperary**~~ incorrect spelling of **temporary**

temperate /témpərət/ *adj* **1 MILD** mild or restrained in behaviour or attitude **2 WITHOUT EXTREMES** describes a climate that has a range of temperatures within moderate limits **3 NOT SPREADING** describes viruses that exist in host cells but do not cause lysis —**temperately** *adv* —**temperateness** *n*

Temperate Zone *n* the parts of the Earth that lie between the tropics and the polar circles and have generally hot summers, cold winters, and intermediate autumns and springs

temperature /témprichər/ *n* **1 DEGREE OF HEAT** the degree of heat as an inherent quality of objects expressed as hotness or coldness relative to something else **2 RELATIVE DEGREE OF HEAT** (*symbol* T *or* t) the heat of something measured on a particular scale such as the Fahrenheit or Celsius scale **3 BODY HEAT** the degree of heat in a living organism **4 FEVER** human body heat in excess of 37.0° C/98.6° F or somebody's normal body heat ○ *running a temperature* [15C. Directly or via French < Latin *temperatura* < *temperare* (see TEMPER).]

temperature gradient *n* the rate of change in air temperature over distance, especially elevation

temperature-humidity index *n* a measure of ambient humidity relative to heat as it affects human comfort

temperature inversion *n* METEOROL = **inversion** *n.* 4

tempered /témpərd/ *adj* **1 WITH A PARTICULAR TEMPER** with a temper or temperament of a particular quality (*usually in combination*) ○ *even-tempered* **2 HARDENED** hardened through a tempering process ○ *tempered steel* **3 WELL PROPORTIONED** with elements combined in balanced and suitable proportion **4 TUNED TO A TEMPERAMENT** describes a keyboard instrument tuned to a particular temperament, especially equal temperament

~~**temperment**~~ incorrect spelling of **temperament**

~~**temperture**~~ incorrect spelling of **temperature**

tempest /témpist/ *n* **1** a severe storm with very high winds and often rain, hail, or snow (*literary*) **2** a severe commotion or disturbance, especially an emotional upheaval [13C. Via Old French < Latin *tempestas* < *tempus* 'time'.] ◇ **a tempest in a teapot** *US* a commotion raised about an unimportant matter

LITERARY LINK ***The Tempest***, a play (1611) by William Shakespeare. An elaborate blend of comedy, drama, and fantasy, it is set on an enchanted island where Prospero, rightful duke of Milan, has lived since being usurped by his brother Antonio. Using his magical powers, Prospero conjures up a storm that forces Antonio and his companions onto the island, paving the way for an ingenious reconciliation.

tempestuous /tem péstyoo əss/ *adj* **1** having or affected by frequent or violent storms ○ *tempestuous seas* **2** frequently turbulent and giving rise to many emotions ○ *a tempestuous relationship* —**tempestuously** *adv* —**tempestuousness** *n*

tempi plural of **tempo**

Templar /témplər/ *n* **1** HIST = **Knight Templar 2** a barrister or law student with offices in the Temple, London [13C. < the place in Jerusalem (*Temple of Solomon*) where the medieval order had its headquarters.]

template /tém playt, -plət/ *n* **1 MASTER** something that serves as a master or pattern from which other similar things can be made **2 PATTERN** a mechanical pattern or mould with one or more shapes used to guide the manufacture or drawing of objects with a similar shape **3 SHORT BEAM** a short beam of metal, wood, or stone, used to distribute weight or pressure in a structure **4 MASTER MOLECULE** a molecule that provides a pattern for the synthesis of other molecules **5 MASTER FILE** a computer file that is used as a master for creating others similar to it [Late 17C. Alteration of TEMPLET, after PLATE.]

temple[1] /témp'l/ *n* **1 BUILDING FOR WORSHIP** a building used as a place of worship **2 SPECIAL PLACE** an institution or building considered as a guardian of, or reservation for, a particular activity ○ *a temple of learning* **3 MEETING PLACE** a building where a fraternal order holds meetings and rites **4 HOLY DWELLING** a place where something holy or divine is thought to dwell, e.g. the body of a holy person **5** *US* **SYNAGOGUE** a synagogue **6 MORMON CHURCH** a place of worship for the Church of Jesus Christ of Latter-Day Saints where sacred ordinances such as marriage are executed [Pre-12C. < Latin *templum* 'sacred place, place for worship'.]

temple[2] /témp'l/ *n* the part of either side of the head between the eye and the ear [14C. Via Old French < Latin *tempora*, plural of *tempus* 'temple, time'.]

temple[3] /témp'l/ *n* the part of a loom that keeps the cloth being woven stretched to the proper width [15C. < French.]

Temple[1] *n* either of two groups of buildings in Paris and London built on sites that once belonged to the Knights Templar

Temple[2] *n* either of two successive temples in Jerusalem. The First Temple, built by Solomon in 957 BC, was destroyed by Nebuchadnezzar II in 586 BC. The Second Temple was destroyed by the Romans in AD 70.

Temple /témp'l/, **Shirley** ♦ **Black, Shirley Temple**

templet /témplət/ *n* a template (*archaic*) [< TEMPLE[3]]

tempo /témpō/ (*plural* **-pos** *or* **-pi** /-pee/) *n* **1** the speed at which a musical composition or passage is performed **2** the pace or rate of something ○ *the tempo of urban life* [Mid-17C. Via Italian < Latin *tempus* 'time'.]

tempolabile /témpō láy bīl/ *adj* changing at an uneven rate [Mid-20C. < Latin *tempus* 'time' + *labilis* < *labi* 'to slip'.]

temporal[1] /témpərəl/ *adj* **1 RELATING TO TIME** relating to measured time **2 RELATING TO LAITY** relating to the laity rather than the clergy in the Christian Church **3 OF THIS WORLD** relating to life in the world, rather than spiritual life **4 BRIEF** lasting only a short time **5 RELATING TO TENSES** relating to grammatical tenses or the expression of time in a language [14C. Directly or via French < Latin *temporalis* < *tempus* 'time'.] —**temporally** *adv*

temporal[2] /témpərəl/ *adj* relating to or located in the region of the temples on the head [Late 16C. < late Latin *temporalis* < Latin *tempus* 'temple, time'.]

temporal bone *n* either of a pair of bones that form part of the sides and base of the skull and contain the middle and inner ears

temporality /témpə rálləti/ *n* the quality or state of being connected with time or the world ■ **temporalities** *npl* the secular property and assets of a church

temporal lobe *n* either of two lobes of the brain, located on the side of each cerebral hemisphere, that contain the auditory centres responsible for hearing

temporary /témpərəri/ *adj* lasting for or involving a limited period of time ■ *n* (*plural* **-ies**) a paid worker in an office or other workplace hired for a limited time only [Mid-16C. < Latin *temporarius* < *tempus* 'time'.] —**temporarily** *adv* —**temporariness** *n*

SYNONYMS ***temporary, fleeting, passing, transitory, ephemeral, evanescent, short-lived***

CORE MEANING: lasting only a short time

temporary lasting or designed to last for a short time; **fleeting** very brief or rapid; **passing** superficial and not long-lasting; **transitory** existing only for a short time; **ephemeral** lasting for a short time and leaving no permanent trace; **evanescent** (*literary*) disappearing after a short time and soon forgotten; **short-lived** lasting only for a short time.

temporize /témpə rīz/ (**-rizes, -rizing, -rized**), **temporise** (**-rises, -rising, -rised**) *vi* to use delaying tactics to gain time, especially in order to avoid coming to a decision or committing yourself —**temporization** /témpə rīzáysh'n/ *n* —**temporizer** *n*

temporomandibular joint /témpərō man díbbyōōlər-/ *n* either of the joints connecting the lower part of the jaw (**mandible**) with the temporal bone on each side of the head [< TEMPORAL[2]]

temporomandibular syndrome *n* a painful condition involving the temporomandibular joint and the muscles used for chewing, sometimes causing clicking sounds and restricted jaw movement

~~**tempory**~~ incorrect spelling of **temporary**

~~**temprature**~~ incorrect spelling of **temperature**

tempt /tempt/ *vt* **1 INCITE DESIRE** to cause desire or craving to arise in somebody ○ *I was tempted by that chocolate cake!* **2 INCITE TO TRANSGRESSION** to persuade or attempt to persuade somebody to do something considered wrong **3 INVITE** to invite or attract somebody ○ *The sightseeing tour tempted us.* **4 RISK** to risk the possible destructive powers of something ○ *tempt fate* [13C. Via Old French *tempter* < Latin *temptare* 'feel, try, test'.] —**temptable** *adj* —**tempter** *n*

temptation /temp táysh'n/ *n* **1 FEELING** a craving or desire for something, especially something thought wrong ○ *yield to temptation* **2 ENTICING ACT** the enticing of desire or craving in somebody **3 ENTICING THING** something that or somebody who tempts somebody ○ *too many temptations for me here*

Tempter /témp tər/ *n* Satan

tempting /témp ting/ *adj* causing craving or desire to arise ○ *a tempting offer* —**temptingly** *adv* —**temptingness** *n*

temptress /témp triss/ *n* an offensive term for a woman that deliberately insults her sexuality and public behaviour

tempura /tém pōōrə/ *n* a Japanese dish of vegetables or seafood coated in light batter and deep-fried [Mid-20C. < Japanese.]

tempus fugit /témpōōs fyōōjit/ time flies [Latin]

ten /ten/ *n* see table at **number** [Old English *tēn(e)*, *tīen(e)* < Indo-European] —**ten** *adj*

tenable /ténnəb'l/ *adj* **1 WITH REASONABLE ARGUMENTS TO SUPPORT IT** justified in a fair or rational way and able to be defended because there is sufficient evidence or reason behind it **2 ABLE TO BE OCCUPIED** capable of being occupied or held, usually by a particular person or for a particular period of time (*formal*) **3 CAPABLE OF BEING DEFENDED IN BATTLE** able to be held successfully against an enemy attack [Late 16C. < French *tenir* 'to hold'.] —**tenability** /ténnə bílləti/ *n* —**tenableness** *n* —**tenably** *adv*

tenace /ténn ayss/ *n* a combination of two high cards in the same suit that do not form a sequence, e.g. a jack and a king [Mid-17C. Via French < Spanish *tenaza* 'pincers, tongs'.]

tenacious /tə náyshəss/ *adj* **1 VERY DETERMINED OR STUBBORN** tending to stick firmly to any decision, plan, or opinion without changing or doubting it **2 TIGHTLY HELD** difficult to loosen, shake off, or pull away from **3 ABLE TO REMEMBER MANY THINGS** capable of absorbing and retaining a large store of information and of recalling details accurately **4 STICKY OR CLINGING** sticking or clinging to something else, especially a surface **5 NOT EASILY DISCONNECTED** holding together tightly or fused solidly [Early 17C. < Latin *tenax* 'holding fast' < *tenere* 'to hold'.] —**tenaciously** *adv* —**tenaciousness** *n* —**tenacity** /tə nássəti/ *n*

tenaculum /tə nákyōōləm/ (*plural* **-la** /-lə/ *or* **-lums**) *n* a long-handled instrument with a slender sharp hook, used especially in surgery to grasp and hold arteries or other bodily parts [Late 17C. < Latin, 'holder' < *tenere* 'to hold'.]

tenancy /ténnənssi/ (*plural* **-cies**) *n* **1 OCCUPATION OF PROPERTY FOR RENT** exclusive possession of property or land owned by somebody else for a fixed period, in return for an agreed rent **2 TIME OF SOMEBODY'S TENANCY** a period of time when a piece of property, e.g. a house or farm, is legally occupied and used by somebody paying an agreed rent **3 PLACE LIVED IN BY A TENANT** a piece of property that somebody is entitled to use or occupy on condition that an agreed rent is paid to the owner [15C. < TENANT.]

tenant /ténnənt/ *n* **1 RENTER OF PROPERTY** a renter of a building, house, set of rooms, plot of land, or piece of property for a fixed period of time **2 OCCUPIER OF A PLACE** somebody living in or on a particular piece of property (*dated literary*) ■ *vti* **PAY RENT TO OCCUPY PROPERTY** to live in or on another person's property as a tenant [14C. < Anglo-Norman *tenaunt*, Old French *tenant* < *tenir* 'to hold' < Latin *tenere* 'hold, keep'.] —**tenantable** *adj* —**tenanted** *adj* —**tenantless** *adj*

tenant farmer *n* a farmer who rents a farm, smallholding, or agricultural land, and pays the owner in cash or with produce

tenantry /ténnəntri/ *n* **1** all tenants or tenant farmers, especially all those renting property from a particular landowner (*formal*) **2** tenancy (*dated*)

tenants' association *n* an official representative body formed by tenants to negotiate with their landlord, e.g. to ensure that tenants' rights are protected, and to represent the tenants in disputes or when they want improvements made or changes introduced

tenants' charter *n* in the United Kingdom, the legal rights of tenants in new towns, local authorities, and housing associations

tench /tench/ (*plural* **tench** *or* **tenches**) *n* a freshwater game fish related to the carp, with a heavy greenish body, small scales, and a barbel on each side of its mouth. Native to: Europe, W Asia. *Tinca tinca.* [14C. Via Old French *tenche* < late Latin *tinca.*]

Ten Commandments *npl* the ten laws given by God to Moses, according to the Bible

tend[1] /tend/ *vi* **1** to be generally inclined or likely to react or behave in a particular way, or be in the habit of doing something **2** to make a gentle steady movement in a particular direction [14C. Via Old French *tendre* 'move towards' < Latin *tendere* 'stretch, extend'.]

tend[2] /tend/ *vt* **1** to do or provide the things that a person, animal, or plant needs for health, comfort, and welfare **2** to manage something, especially something that needs constant supervision [12C. Shortening of ATTEND.] —**tendance** *n*

~~**tendancy**~~ incorrect spelling of **tendency**

tendencious *adj* = **tendentious**

tendency /téndənssi/ (*plural* **-cies**) *n* **1 GENERAL INCLINATION** a way that somebody or something typically behaves or is likely to react or behave **2 PREDISPOSITION** a character or quality that makes it likely that something will happen ○ *My ankle has a tendency to twist.* **3 MOVEMENT** a gradual but steady progress, development, or shift of opinion in a particular direction (*dated or formal*) [Early 17C. < medieval Latin *tendentia* < Latin *tendere* 'tend, be inclined to'.]

tendentious /ten dénsshəs/, **tendencious** *adj* written or spoken by somebody who obviously wants to promote a particular cause or who supports a particular viewpoint [Early 20C. < TENDENCY.] —**tendentiously** *adv* —**tendentiousness** *n*

tender[1] /téndər/ *adj* **1 PHYSICALLY PAINFUL** hurting or unusually sensitive when touched or pressed **2 WITH GENTLE FEELING** showing care, gentleness, and feeling **3 KIND AND SYMPATHETIC** sensitive and caring towards others and often feeling emotions intensely **4 EMOTIONALLY PAINFUL** particularly uncomfortable, hurtful, or upsetting to discuss or think about, and so best avoided **5 PLEASANTLY SOFT FOR EATING** soft enough for the teeth to go through easily without much chewing ○ *a tender juicy steak* **6 NEEDING PROTECTION FROM HARSH WEATHER** easily damaged or killed by unsuitable weather or conditions, especially frost and cold ○ *a tender plant* **7 YOUNG AND DEFENCELESS** vulnerably young, weak, and inexperienced ○ *at a tender age* **8 FRAGILE** so delicate, soft, or weak as to be hurt, crushed, or broken easily (*literary*) [13C. Via French *tendre* < Latin *tener* 'delicate, tender'.] —**tenderly** *adv* —**tenderness** *n*

LITERARY LINK ***Tender is the Night***, a novel (1934) by US writer F. Scott Fitzgerald. Set on the French Riviera in the 1930s, it focuses on a group of glamorous US expatriates. Psychologist Richard Diver's attempts to nurse his wife and former patient, Nicole, and his involvement with a visiting woman actor, lead to his mental collapse. A powerful depiction of human frailty, it is also admired for the elegance of its prose.

tender[2] /téndər/ *v* **1** *vt* **OFFER SOMETHING FORMALLY IN WRITING** to present something formal or official, in the form of a document ○ *tender a resignation* **2** *vi* **OFFER TO SUPPLY** to offer to undertake a job or supply particular goods ○ *tender for a contract* **3** *vt* **OFFER A SUM IN SETTLEMENT** to offer to pay money or goods as a way of settling a debt or claim ■ *n* **1 FORMAL OFFER TO UNDERTAKE A JOB** a formal offer to undertake a job or supply particular goods ○ *Their tender was accepted because it was the lowest.* **2 ACT OF TENDERING** the act of tendering for a contract **3 OFFER MADE TO SETTLE** a formal offer to settle legal proceedings on payment of an amount of damages [Mid-16C. Via Old French *tendre* < Latin *tendere* 'hold out, stretch'.] —**tenderable** *adj* —**tenderer** *n*

tender[3] /téndər/ *n* **1 SMALL BOAT FERRYING TO LARGE BOAT** a small boat used to go to and from a larger one such as a yacht **2 VEHICLE CARRYING STEAM ENGINE'S SUPPLIES** the permanently coupled rear part of a large steam locomotive, which carries its coal and water **3 EMERGENCY VEHICLE** a road vehicle that carries tools and specialized equipment and personnel to assist in an emergency (*usually in combination*) [15C. Shortening of *attender* (< ATTEND), or < TEND[2].]

tenderfoot /téndər fòòt/ (*plural* **-foots** *or* **-feet** /-feet/) *n* **1** somebody just starting to do or try something, with little or no previous experience of it (*informal*) **2** a new member of a Scout troop or Guide company (*dated*)

tenderhearted /téndər haártid/ *adj* quick to show compassion and sympathy to other people —**tenderheartedly** *adv* —**tenderheartedness** *n*

tenderize /téndə rīz/ (**-izes, -izing, -ized**), **tenderise** (**-ises, -ising, -ised**) *vt* to make meat tender by beating it, soaking it in a marinade, or sprinkling it with a special substance (**tenderizer**) that breaks down its fibres —**tenderization** /téndə rī záysh'n/ *n*

tenderizer /téndə rīzər/, **tenderiser** *n* **1** a commercial preparation containing enzymes that break down fibrous tissue in meat **2** a wooden or metal mallet used to tenderize meat

tenderloin /téndər loyn/ *n* a prime cut of lean tender pork or lamb taken from the curve of the ribs at the backbone

tendinitis /téndə nítiss/, **tendonitis** *n* inflammation of a tendon usually occurring after excessive use, as in a sports injury [Early 20C. < modern Latin *tendin-*, stem of *tendo* 'tendon'.]

tendon /téndən/ *n* an inelastic cord or band of tough white fibrous connective tissue that attaches a muscle to a bone or other part [Mid-16C. Directly and via French < medieval Latin *tendon-*, stem of *tendo*, translation of Greek *tenōn* 'sinew' < *teinein* 'stretch'.] —**tendinous** /téndinəss/ *adj*

tendon hammer *n* MED = **plexor**

tendonitis *n* MED = **tendinitis**

tendril /téndrəl/ *n* **1** a modified stem, leaf, or other part of a climbing plant, usually in the form of a thread, that coils around and attaches the plant to supporting objects **2** a slim, wispy, curling, or winding piece of something, especially hair (*literary*) [Mid-16C. < Middle French *tendrillon* 'little shoot, little cartilage' < *tendron* 'shoot, cartilage' < Old French *tendre* (see TENDER[1]).]

Tenebrae /ténnə bray/ *n* in the Roman Catholic Church, the office of matins and lauds for the last three days of Holy Week (+ *singular or plural verb*) [Mid-17C. < Latin, 'darkness', because candles are extinguished during the service in memory of the darkness at the crucifixion.]

tenebrionid /tə nébbri ənid/ (*plural* **-nids** *or* **-nid**) *n* INSECTS = **darkling beetle** [Early 20C. < modern Latin.]

tenebrious *adj* = **tenebrous**

tenebrism /ténnəbrizəm/, **Tenebrism** *n* a style of painting, popular in 17th-century Naples and Spain and largely associated with Caravaggio, that uses large areas of shadow and dark colours, sometimes with a shaft of light [Mid-20C. < Italian *tenebroso* 'dark'.] —**tenebrist** *n*

tenebrous /ténnəbrəss/, **tenebrious** /tə nébbri əss/ *adj* dark, murky, or obscured by shadows (*literary*) [15C. < Old French *tenebrus* < Latin *tenebrae* 'darkness'.] —**tenebrosity** /ténnə bróssəti/ *n* —**tenebrousness** *n*

tenement /ténnəmənt/ *n* **1 LARGE MULTIPLE-OCCUPANCY RESIDENTIAL BUILDING** a large residential building in a town, usually of three or more storeys, divided into flats for separate householders, or the section of such a building served by one stair **2 RENTED ACCOMMODATION IN MULTISTOREY BUILDING** in England and Wales, a room or flat in a multistorey residential building, especially one used by a tenant (*dated regional*) **3 ITEM OF PROPERTY** a piece of property such as land or houses held by somebody [14C. Via Old French, 'tenure' < medieval Latin *tenementum* < Latin *tenere* 'to hold'.]

~~**tenent**~~ incorrect spelling of **tenant**

Tenerife /ténnə reéf, ténnə reéfay/, **Teneriffe** largest of the Canary Islands, Spain, off the coast of NW Africa. Population: 759,388 (1986). Area: 2,034 sq. km/785 sq. mi.

tenesmus /tə nézməss/ *n* an urgent, painful, and unsuccessful attempt to defecate or urinate [Early 16C. Via medieval Latin < Greek *tēnesmos* < *teinein* 'stretch, strain'.]

~~**Tenessee**~~ incorrect spelling of **Tennessee**

tenet /ténnit/ *n* any established and fundamental belief, especially one relating to religion or politics ○ *a basic tenet of Christianity* [Late 16C. < Latin, 'he or she holds', form of *tenere* 'to hold'.]

tenfold /tén fōld/ *adj* **1 WITH TEN PARTS** made up of ten parts **2 TIMES TEN** multiplied by ten ■ *adv* **TEN TIMES OVER** to ten times the amount or number, or multiplied by or up to that amount or number

ten-four, 10-4 *interj US* used to express affirmation or confirmation [< US police code 'message received']

ten-gallon hat *n* a cowboy hat with a high round uncreased crown and a wide brim

tenge /téngay/ (*plural* **-ge**) *n* see table at **currency** [Late 20C. < Kazakh.]

Tenn. *abbr* Tennessee

Tennant /ténnənt/, **Kylie** (1912–88) Australian writer

Tennant Creek /ténnənt-/ town in central Northern Territory, Australia. Population: 3,114 (1991).

tenner /ténnər/ *n* (*informal*) **1** ten pounds sterling, either as cash or as a sum **2** *US, ANZ, Can* ten dollars, either as cash or as a sum

~~**Tennesee**~~ incorrect spelling of **Tennessee**

Tennessee /ténnə seé/ **1** state in the east-central United States. Capital: Nashville. Population: 5,368,198 (1997). Area: 109,158 sq. km/42,146 sq. mi. **2** river of the SE United States, rising in E Tennessee and flowing through N Alabama, W Tennessee, and W Kentucky to the Ohio River. Length: 1,050 km/652 mi. —**Tennessean** *n, adj*

Tennessee Walking Horse, Tennessee Walker *n* a saddle horse of a breed developed in Tennessee from Standardbred and Morgan stock, with a characteristic fast, easy gait

Tenniel /ténni əl/, **Sir John** (1820–1914) British illustrator

tennis /ténniss/ *n* a game played on a rectangular court by two, or two pairs of, players who use rackets to hit a ball back and forth over a net stretched across a marked-out court [14C. Probably < Old French *tenez* 'hold!', form of *tenir* 'to hold, receive'.]

tennis ball *n* a white or yellow fuzzy cloth-surfaced hollow rubber ball about 7.5 cm/3 in in diameter, used in tennis

tennis elbow *n* painful inflammation of the tendon in the outer elbow region caused by excessive and repetitive strain from overuse, e.g. as a result of playing tennis and similar sports

tennis shoe *n* a rubber-soled white canvas shoe with long laces, worn for playing tennis

Tennyson /ténniss'n/, **Alfred, 1st Baron Tennyson of Freshwater and Aldworth** (1809–92) British poet. Known as **Alfred, Lord Tennyson** —**Tennysonian** /ténni sṓni ən/ *n, adj*

tenon /ténnən/ *n* **PROJECTION ON WOOD FOR MAKING JOINT** a projection made on the end of one piece of wood that fits into a mortise on another piece, making a joint ■ *vt* **1 MAKE A TENON** to make a tenon on a piece of wood **2 JOIN PIECES OF WOOD USING TENON** to join two pieces of wood using a tenon [Early 17C. < Old French, < *tenir* 'to hold'.] —**tenoner** *n*

tenon saw *n* a small thin saw with a strong back, used especially for cutting tenons

tenor /ténnər/ *n* **1 HIGH MALE VOICE** the highest natural male singing voice, or an adult whose voice is in this register **2 HIGH OR FAIRLY HIGH INSTRUMENT** an instrument with a range similar to a tenor voice (*often before nouns*) **3 WAY SOMETHING IS PROGRESSING** the direction in which something is steadily moving (*formal*) **4 WHAT SOMETHING IS MAINLY ABOUT** the overall nature, pattern, or meaning of something, especially a written or spoken statement (*formal*) ○ *The general tenor of the reply was positive.* **5 EXACT WORDS OF DEED** the exact wording of a document, rather than its effect **6 EXACT COPY** an exact copy or transcript of a document **7 TIME FOR BILL TO BE PAID** the period of time over which cash flows are exchanged with a swap contract [13C. Via Anglo-Norman, Old French < Latin, 'continuous course' < *tenere* 'to hold'.]

tenor clef *n* one of the C clefs in which middle C is represented by the second highest line on the staff, formerly used to notate the tenor voice

tenorite /ténnə rīt/ *n* a black copper oxide mineral [Mid-19C. After Michelo *Tenore* (1781–1861), president of the Naples Academy of Sciences.]

tenosynovitis /ténnō sīnə vítiss/ *n* inflammation of a tendon sheath, usually in the wrist, with swelling and audible creaking on movement. ◊ **RSI** [Late 19C. < modern Latin, < Greek *tenōn* 'tendon'.]

tenotomy /tə nóttəmi/ (*plural* **-mies**) *n* the surgical cutting of a tendon

tenpin /tén pin/ *n* one of the ten skittles used in tenpin bowling

tenpin bowling *n* an indoor game in which players try to knock down ten skittles at the far end of a special bowling alley by rolling a heavy ball at them

tenpounder /ténn pówndər/ *n US* ZOOL = **ladyfish** *n.* 1

tenrec /tén rek/ (*plural* **-recs** *or* **-rec**), **tanrec** /tán-/ (*plural* **-recs** *or* **-rec**) *n* a small to medium-sized insect-eating mammal with a long, pointed snout. Native to: Madagascar, the Comoro Islands. Family: Tenrecidae. [Late 18C. Via French *tanrec* < Malagasy *tàndraka, tràndraka.*]

TENS /tens/ *n* a method of treating chronic pain by applying electrodes to the skin and passing small electric currents through sensory nerves and the spinal cord, thus suppressing the transmission of pain signals. Full form **transcutaneous electrical nerve stimulation**

tense[1] /tenss/ *adj* (**tenser, tensest**) **1 WORRIED AND NERVOUS** affected by anxious feelings or mental strain, so that it is impossible to behave in a natural relaxed way **2 RESTRAINED AND UNNATURAL** making people feel unusually anxious, nervous, and uncertain, so that they do not talk or behave in a natural relaxed way **3 TIGHT AND STIFF** stretched or held tight and stiff **4 PRONOUNCED WITH TAUT MUSCLES** describes a speech sound that is pronounced with muscular effort, is relatively long in duration, and is accurate in articulation ■ *vti* (**tenses, tensing, tensed**) **BECOME OR MAKE TENSE** to become tense, or make something tense [Late 17C. < Latin *tensus* 'stretched', past participle of *tendere* 'stretch'.] —**tensely** *adv* —**tenseness** *n*

tense up *vti* = **tense**[1] *v.*

tense[2] /tenss/ *n* the facet of a verb that expresses the different times at which action takes place relative to the speaker or writer, e.g. the present, past, or future [14C. Via Old French *tens* 'time' < Latin *tempus*.] —**tenseless** *adj*

tensile /tén sīl/ *adj* **1** relating to or involving tension **2** capable of being stretched or pulled out of shape [Early 17C. < medieval Latin *tensilis* < Latin *tendere* 'stretch'.] —**tensilely** *adv* —**tensileness** *n* —**tensility** /ten síllәti/ *n*

tensile strength *n* the maximum stretching force that a material, e.g. wire, can withstand before breaking

tensimeter /ten símmitәr/ *n* an instrument used to measure differences in vapour pressure [Early 20C. < TENSION.]

tensiometer /ténssi ómmitәr/ *n* **1** an instrument used to measure tensile stress **2** an instrument used to measure the surface tension of liquids [Early 20C. < TENSION.]

tension /ténsh'n/ *n* **1 ANXIOUS FEELINGS** mental worry or emotional strain that makes natural relaxed behaviour impossible **2 UNEASY FEELING IN RELATIONSHIP** a state of wariness, mistrust, controlled hostility, or fear of hostility felt by countries, groups, or individuals in their dealings with one another (*often plural*) **3 SENSE OF DIFFERENT ELEMENTS CONFLICTING** the way that opposing elements or characters clash or interact in an interesting way with each other in a literary work **4 BUILDUP OF SUSPENSE** the buildup of suspense in a fictional work, leading to the denouement **5 TAUTNESS** how tightly something such as wire, string, thread, or a muscle is stretched **6 DEVICE CONTROLLING TIGHTNESS OF THREAD** a device on a sewing machine or a loom that regulates how tight the thread is **7 PULLING FORCE** a force that pulls or stretches something **8 STRESS FROM TENSION** the stress resulting from a force of tension, or a measure of it **9 VOLTAGE** voltage or electromotive force (*often in combination*) [Mid-16C. Directly or via French < Latin *tension-* 'stretching' < *tendere* 'stretch'.] —**tensional** *adj*

tensity /ténssәti/ *n* the state or quality of being tense

tensive /ténssiv/ *adj* causing or relating to tension [Early 18C. < French *tensif* < Latin *tendere* 'stretch'.]

tensometer /ten sómmitәr/ *n* **1** = **tensiometer** *n.* 1 **2** = **tensiometer** *n.* 2

tensor /ténssәr, -sawr/ *n* **1** a muscle that tenses or stretches a part of the body **2** the generalization of a vector, a mathematical entity specified with respect to a given coordinate system and able to undergo transformation to other coordinate systems [Early 18C. < modern Latin, < Latin *tendere* 'stretch'.] —**tensorial** /ten sáwri әl/ *adj*

ten-strike *n* BOWLING = **strike** *n.* 7

tent[1] /tent/ *n* **1 COLLAPSIBLE SHELTER** a collapsible movable shelter consisting of a tough fabric or plastic cover held up by poles and kept in place by ropes and pegs **2 TENT-SHAPED OBJECT** something that looks like a tent, is constructed in a similar way, or serves a similar purpose ○ *an oxygen tent* ■ *v* **1** *vt* **COVER AS A TENT DOES** to form a raised nonrigid cover over something ○ *Tent the roast with aluminium foil.* **2** *vi* **CAMP** to live or camp in a tent **3** *vt* **SUPPLY A TENT FOR** to accommodate a person or group of people in tents, or provide somebody or something with tents [13C. Via Old French *tente* < Latin *tenta* 'tent' < *tendere* 'stretch'.]

tent[2] /tent/ *n* a cone-shaped expandable plug of soft material, e.g. gauze, used to keep a wound or orifice open ■ *vt* to open or expand a wound or orifice with a tent [14C. < French *tente* < *tenter* < Latin *temptare* 'feel, try'.]

tentacle /téntәk'l/ *n* **1 LONG FLEXIBLE ORGAN** a long flexible organ around the mouth or on the head of some animals, especially invertebrates such as squid, used in holding, grasping, feeling, or moving **2 HAIR ON A PLANT LEAF** a sticky glandular hairy projection from the leaf of an insect-eating plant such as the sundew, whose secretions trap and digest prey **3 SOMETHING FAR-REACHING** something that gradually or unnoticeably insinuates its way into and around things and has a definite presence or effect (*literary*) [Mid-18C. < modern Latin *tentaculum* < Latin *temptare* 'feel, try'.] —**tentacled** *adj* —**tentacular** /ten tákyŏŏlәr/ *adj*

tentage /tént ij/ *n* tents in general or as a group

tentative /téntәtiv/ *adj* **1** said or done in a slow, hesitant, and careful way, revealing a lack of confidence **2** likely to have many later changes before becoming final and complete ○ *a tentative draft of the document* [Late 16C. < medieval Latin *tentativus* < Latin *tentare*, variant of *temptare* 'feel, try'.] —**tentatively** *adv* —**tentativeness** *n*

tent caterpillar *n* a destructive caterpillar that builds large tent-shaped communal webs in the branches of trees. Genus: *Malacosoma.*

tent dress *n* a wide full dress that hangs loose from the shoulders

tented /téntid/ *adj* **1 WITH TENT SHAPE** constructed or shaped like a tent **2 CAMPED IN TENTS** staying in tents, or supplied with tents as shelter **3 WITH TENTS** covered in tents (*literary*)

tenter /téntәr/ *n* a frame on which cloth is held taut during various phases of its manufacture, especially while it dries ■ *vt* to stretch cloth on a tenter [13C. < medieval Latin *tentorium* < Latin *tendere* 'stretch'.]

tenterhook /téntәr hŏŏk/ *n* any one of the hooks used to hold cloth taut on a frame during manufacture, especially while it dries ◇ **be on tenterhooks** to be anxious or in great suspense

tenth /tenth/ *n* **1** see table at **number 2** a musical interval equal to an octave plus a third [Old English *teogoþa, tēoþa* < Germanic; later < TEN] —**tenth** *adj, adv*

tent stitch *n* a short parallel diagonal stitch used to fill in an area in needlepoint or embroidery

tenuis /ténnyoo iss/ (*plural* **-es** /-eez/) *n* a voiceless stop consonant in classical Greek grammar [Mid-17C. < Latin, 'thin, fine', translation of Greek *psilon* 'bare, smooth'.]

tenuous /ténnyoo әss/ *adj* **1 WEAK AND UNCONVINCING** not based on anything significant or substantial, and so unlikely to withstand a challenge ○ *That's an extremely tenuous argument.* **2 EXTREMELY DELICATE AND FINE** thin and fine and so easily broken (*literary*) **3 DILUTED** thin or diluted in consistency [Late 16C. < Latin *tenuis* 'thin, fine'.] —**tenuity** /te nyóo әti/ *n* —**tenuously** *adv* —**tenuousness** *n*

tenure /ténnyәr, ténnyoor/ *n* **1 APPOINTMENT OR PERIOD OF APPOINTMENT** the occupation of an official position, or the length of time a position is occupied (*formal*) ○ *during her tenure of the presidency* **2 PROPERTY RIGHTS** the rights of a tenant to hold property, or the holding of property as a tenant **3** *US, Can* **PERMANENT STATUS** the position of having a formal secure appointment until retirement, especially at an institution of higher learning after working there on a temporary or provisional basis [15C. < Old French, 'tenure, estate' < Latin *tenere* 'to hold'.] —**tenured** *adj*

tenure-track *adj US* guaranteed consideration for tenure in the US and Canadian system of academic employment ○ *offered a tenure-track position at the university*

tenuto /te nyóotō/ *adv, adj* indicating that a musical note should be held for its full value (*musical direction*) [Mid-18C. < Italian, past participle of *tenere* 'to hold' < Latin.]

Tenzing Norkay /ténssing náwrk ay/ (1914?–86) Nepalese mountaineer

teocalli /tee ō kálli/ *n* a temple in ancient Mexico or Central America, or the pyramidal mound on which one was built [Early 17C. Via American Spanish < Nahuatl *teokalli* 'deity's house'.]

teosinte /táy ō sínti/ *n* a tall annual grass grown for forage, related to, and perhaps the ancestor of, maize. Native to: Mexico, Central America. *Zea mexicana*. [Late 19C. Via French *téosinté* < Nahuatl *teocintli*.]

tepa /téepә/ *n* $C_6H_{12}N_3OP$ a soluble crystalline compound. Use: insect sterilization, cancer treatment, textile fireproofing. [Mid-20C. Acronym < TRI- + ETHYLENE + PHOSPH- + AMIDE.]

tepal /téep'l/ *n* any part that forms the outer whorl (**perianth**) of flowers such as the tulip, in which there is no differentiation into petals and sepals [Mid-19C. < French, blend of *sépale* 'sepal' + *pétale* 'petal'.]

Te Papa Tongarewa /te púppә tóngә ray wә/ *n* a museum in Wellington that contains the New Zealand national collections [Late 20C. < Maori.]

tepary bean /téppәri-/ *n* an annual twining bean grown for its round edible seeds. Native to: SW United States, Mexico. *Phaseolus acutifolius latifolius.*

tepee /tée pee/, **teepee, tipi** *n* a conical tent built around several long branches or wooden poles that meet and cross at the top [Mid-18C. < Dakota *tīpi* 'dwelling'.]

tephra /téffrә/ *n* solid material ejected explosively from a volcano, e.g. ash, dust, and boulders [Mid-20C. < Greek, 'ashes'.]

tepid /téppid/ *adj* **1** slightly warm **2** showing little enthusiasm or warmth ○ *tepid applause* [14C. < Latin *tepidus* < *tepere* 'be warm'.] —**tepidity** /te píddәti/ *n* —**tepidly** *adv* —**tepidness** *n*

TEPP /tep/ *n* $C_8H_{20}O_7P_2$ a crystalline compound (**organophosphate**). Use: insecticide, stimulant for nervous system. Full form **tetraethyl pyrophosphate**

Te Puea Herangi /te póo i ә hérrungi/ (1884–1952) New Zealand Maori leader

tequila /ti kéelә, te-/ *n* a strong Mexican spirit made by redistilling the fermented juice of the agave plant (**mescal**) [Mid-19C. < Mexican Spanish, after *Tequila*, town in central Mexico.]

tequila sunrise *n* a cocktail based on tequila that also contains orange juice and grenadine

ter. *abbr* **1** territorial **2** territory

Ter. *abbr* Terrace (*in addresses*)

ter- *prefix* three, threefold ○ *terpolymer* [< Latin *ter* 'three times' < Indo-European, 'three']

tera- *prefix* **1** (*symbol* **T**) one million million (10^{12}) **2** a binary trillion ○ *terabyte* [< Greek *teras* 'monster']

⚡**terabyte** /térrә bīt/ *n* an information unit of one million million bytes in computing

⚡**teraflop** /térrә flop/ *n* one million million floating-point operations per second, a measure of computer speed [Late 20C. < TERA- + acronym < *floating-point operations per second.*]

terahertz /térrә hurts/ (*plural* **-hertz**) *n* a unit of frequency equal to one million million hertz

Terai /tә rí/ an area of marshy land in the foothills of the Himalayas in N India and S Nepal [Late 19C. < Hindi *tarāī* 'marshy lowlands'.]

terakihi *n* ZOOL = **tarakihi**

teraph /térrәf/ (*plural* **-aphim** /térrәfim/) *n* an image or idol worshipped by ancient Semitic peoples [Early 19C. Back-formation < *teraphim*, via late Latin *theraphim*, Greek *theraphin* < Hebrew *tĕrāpīm*.]

terato- *prefix* **1** malformed, grotesque ○ *teratogen* **2** tumour ○ *teratoma* [< Greek *terat-*, stem of *teras* 'monster']

teratocarcinoma /térrәtō kaárssi nṓmә/ (*plural* **-mas** *or* **-mata** /-mәtә/) *n* a malignant teratoma, most often occurring in the testes

teratogen /tә ráttәjәn/ *n* an agent, e.g. a chemical, virus, or ionizing radiation, that interrupts or alters the normal development of a foetus, with results that are evident at birth —**teratogenesis** /tәrrәtә jénnәsiss/ *n* —**teratogenic** /térrәtō jénnik/ *adj*

teratoid /térrә toyd/ *adj* affected by a visible condition caused by the interruption or alteration of normal development

teratology /térrә tólləji/ *n* the scientific study of visible conditions caused by the interruption or alteration of normal development —**teratologic** /térrәtә lójjik/ *adj* —**teratologist** *n*

teratoma /térrә tṓmә/ (*plural* **-mata** /-mәtә/ *or* **-mas**) *n* a tumour composed of various tissues, e.g. bone, hair, and teeth, not normally found together at the site of origin and probably derived from embryonic remnants —**teratomatous** *adj*

Te Rauparaha /te rówprә haa/ (1768?–1849) New Zealand Maori leader

terbium /túrbi әm/ *n* (*symbol* **Tb**) a silvery-grey metallic element of the rare-earth group. Source: monazite, bastnaesite. Use: lasers, X-rays, television tubes. [Mid-19C. After *Ytterby*, village in Sweden.] —**terbic** *adj*

terce /turss/ *n* in the Roman Catholic Church, the third of the seven prayer times (**canonical hours**) when specific prayers are said [14C. < Old French, variant of *tierce* (see TIERCE).]

Terceira /tər sáyrə, -sīrə/ second largest island in the Azores archipelago, in the North Atlantic Ocean. Population: 55,800 (1987). Area: 397 sq. km/153 sq. mi.

tercel /túrss'l/ (*plural* **-cels** *or* **-cel**), **tiercel** /téerss'l/ (*plural* **-cels** *or* **-cel**) *n* a male falcon or hawk used in falconry [14C. < Old French *terçuel* < Latin *tertius* 'third'.]

tercentenary /túr sen teénəri, -ténnəri/ *n* (*plural* **-ries**) a year, or an exact day, 300 years after a specific thing happened, usually something of special historic significance ■ *adj* coinciding with the 300th anniversary of a particular event, and often celebrating or commemorating this [Mid-19C. < Latin *ter* 'three times'.]

tercet /túrssit, tur sét/ *n* a group of three lines of verse that rhyme with each other or with another group of three [Late 16C. Via French < Italian *terzetto* < Latin *tertius* 'third'.]

terebinth /térr əbinth/ (*plural* **-binths** *or* **-binth**) *n* a tree of the cashew family that yields turpentine. Native to: Mediterranean. *Pistacia terebinthus*. [14C. Directly and via Old French < Latin *terebinthus* < Greek *terebinthos*.]

terebinthine /térrə bín thīn/ *adj* **1** relating to the terebinth tree **2** like or consisting of turpentine [Early 16C. < Latin *terebinthinus* < *terebinthus* (see TEREBINTH).]

teredo /te reédō/ (*plural* **-dos** *or* **-do**) *n* MARINE BIOL = **shipworm** [14C. Via Latin < Greek *terēdōn* < *teirein* 'rub hard, wear away, bore'.]

Terence /térrənss/ (185–159 BC) Roman playwright

Teresa (of Ávila) /tə reézə əv áwvilə/, **St** (1515–82) Spanish nun. Born **Teresa de Cepeda y Ahumada**

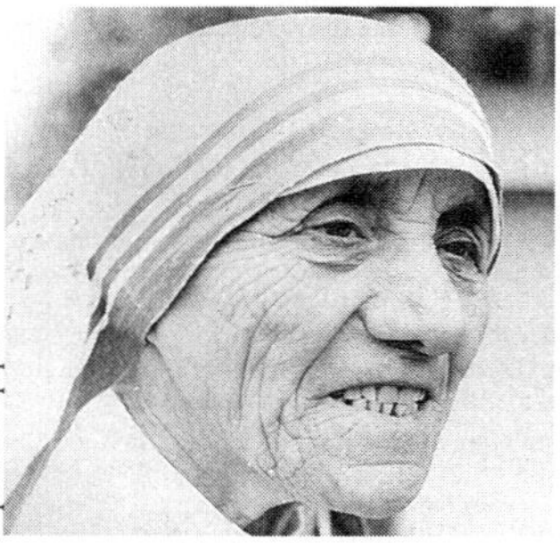

Express Newspapers

Mother Teresa

Teresa (of Calcutta) /tə reéssə-, -ráyzə-/, **Mother** (1910–97) Albanian-born nun. Born **Agnes Gonxha Bojaxhiu**

Tereshkova /térrish kṓvə/, **Valentina** (*b.* 1937) Soviet cosmonaut

~~**terestrial**~~ incorrect spelling of **terrestrial**

terete /té reet/ *adj* describes a plant part that is smooth, cylindrical, and tapering, e.g. a grass stem [Early 17C. < Latin *teret-* 'rounded'.]

terga plural of **tergum**

tergiversate /túrjivər sayt/ (**-sates, -sating, -sated**) *vi* (*formal*) **1** to make deliberately unclear, ambiguous, or contradictory statements **2** to change sides or loyalties [Mid-17C. < Latin *tergiversare* 'turn your back' < *tergum* 'back' + *vertere* 'turn'.] —**tergiversant** /-vurs'nt/ *n* —**tergiversator** *n* —**tergiversatory** /túrji vúrssətəri/ *adj*

tergum /túrgəm/ (*plural* **-ga** /-gə/) *n* a thick plate covering the dorsal surface of a body segment of an arthropod, or the movable segments of a barnacle's shell [Early 19C. < Latin, 'back'.] —**tergal** *adj*

teriyaki /térri yáki/ *n* a Japanese dish consisting of grilled shellfish or meat brushed with a marinade of soy sauce, sugar, and rice wine [Mid-20C. < Japanese, 'glaze grill'.]

term /turm/ *n* **1 NAME OR WORD FOR SOMETHING** a particular word or combination of words, especially one used to mean something very specific or one used in a specialized area of knowledge or work ○ *The correct legal term is 'easement'.* **2 PERIOD OF TIME SOMETHING LASTS** the length of time that something lasts, with a fixed or specified beginning and end, often a period during which a person holds a specific appointment or office or spends time in prison (*formal*) ○ *during her term of office* **3 PERIOD OF TIME BODY CONTINUES MEETING** a length of time over which a political or legal body, e.g. a parliament or court of law, regularly assembles and carries out its formal duties **4 DIVISION OF ACADEMIC YEAR** one of the sections of the academic year during which students attend a school, college, or university and receive regular tuition **5 EXPECTED TIME FOR BIRTH OF CHILD** the time at the end of a woman's pregnancy when the baby is expected to be born ○ *A post-term pregnancy lasts two weeks longer than term.* **6 SUBJECT OR PREDICATE OF PROPOSITION** in traditional Aristotelian logic, the subject or the predicate of a categorical proposition **7 NAME OR INDIVIDUAL VARIABLE** in modern logic, a name or individual variable **8 MATHEMATICAL EXPRESSION** a mathematical expression that forms part of a fraction or proportion, is part of a series, or is associated with another by a plus or minus sign **9 SCULPTURED PILLAR** a sculptured pillar, especially one with a bust without arms or an animal portrait on top of a square post **10 ESTATE RUNNING FOR LIMITED PERIOD** an estate limited to a prescribed period ■ **terms** *npl* **1 WAY PEOPLE GET ON TOGETHER** the treatment given by one person, nation, or power to another, or the opinions or attitudes they have or express towards each other ○ *on good terms with the neighbours* **2 PARTS THAT MAKE UP AN AGREEMENT** the particular requirements laid down formally in an agreement or contract, or proposed by one side when negotiating an agreement **3 LANGUAGE** the words that somebody uses, or specifically chooses to use, when speaking or writing ○ *defended his position in robust terms* ■ *vt* **USE A PARTICULAR WORD FOR** to describe or refer to something using a particular name or expression ○ *His followers were termed 'Roundheads'.* [13C. Via French *terme* 'limit of time or space' < Latin *terminus* 'end, boundary, limit'.] ◇ **come to terms (with something)** to reach a state of acceptance or agreement about something ◇ **in terms of (something)** in relation to something ◇ **not be on speaking terms (with somebody)** to have had a quarrel or disagreement with somebody, so that neither one will speak to the other

LITERARY LINK ***For the Term of His Natural Life***, a novel (1874) by Australian writer Marcus Clark. An epic work set in early 19th-century England and Australia, it tells the story of a young man transported to Australia. He endures the horrors of various penal settlements before drowning during an escape attempt.

term. *abbr* terminal

termagant /túrməgənt/ *n* an offensive term that deliberately insults a woman's temperament suggesting a propensity for arguing, criticizing, and quarrelling [13C. Via Old French *Tervagant*, an overbearing non-Christian deity in medieval mystery plays < Italian *Trivigante*.] —**termagancy** *n*

term assurance *n* life assurance that pays a sum of money only if the person who is covered dies within a particular period of time

-termer *suffix* a person who serves a term as a political appointee or in prison ○ *a second-termer*

terminable /túrminəb'l/ *adj* **1** able to be terminated (*formal*) ○ *The contract is terminable at any time.* **2** ending or capable of being ended after a given period or on a given date ○ *a terminable annuity* [15C. < obsolete *termine* 'terminate', via French *terminer* < Latin *terminare*.] —**terminability** /túrminə bílləti/ *n* —**terminably** *adv*

ϟ**terminal** /túrminəl/ *adj* **1 CAUSING DEATH** inevitably, but often gradually, leading to the death of the patient affected ○ *a terminal illness* **2 DYING** affected by a fatal illness or condition that is approaching its final stages ○ *a terminal cancer patient* **3 RELATING TO DYING PATIENTS** for or concerned with patients with terminal conditions ○ *terminal care* **4 EXTREME** extremely intense or overwhelming (*informal humorous*) ○ *terminal boredom* **5 AT THE VERY END** forming or found at the extreme point or limit of something, or relating to the very end of something **6 AT END OF STEM** at the end of a stem, stalk, or branch **7 RELATING TO AN ACADEMIC TERM** taking place during or after an academic term, or every term (*formal*) ■ *n* **1 STATION AT END OF TRANSPORT ROUTE** a building or complex containing facilities needed by transport operators and passengers at either end of a travel or shipping route by air, rail, road, or sea **2** TRANSP = **terminus** *n.* 1 **3 ONSHORE INDUSTRIAL SITE FOR OFFSHORE PRODUCTS** an industrial installation where raw material is brought onshore and often also processed, e.g. for the offshore gas or oil industry **4 ELECTRICAL CONDUCTOR** a conductor attached at the point where electricity enters or leaves a circuit, e.g. on a battery **5 DEVICE LINKED TO COMPUTER** a remote input or output device linked to a computer, or a combination of such devices, e.g. a keyboard and video display **6 ORNAMENTAL CARVING** an ornamental carving or figure at the end of a larger structure [15C. < Latin *terminalis* < *terminus* 'end, boundary, limit'.]

SYNONYMS See ***deadly***.

terminal moraine *n* a ridge of rock, gravel, and soil across a valley at the end of a glacier or ice field

terminal platform *n* an offshore platform from which gas or petroleum is piped ashore

terminal velocity *n* the constant speed that a falling object reaches when the downward gravitational force equals the frictional resistance of the medium through which it is falling, usually air

terminate /túrmi nayt/ (**-nates, -nating, -nated**) *vti* to come to an end, or bring something to an end [Late 16C. < Latin *terminare* < *terminus* 'end, boundary, limit'.] —**terminative** /-nətiv/ *adj* —**terminatory** *adj*

terminating decimal *n* a decimal fraction with a finite number of digits

termination /túrmi náysh'n/ *n* **1 ENDING** the process of bringing something to an end or of being brought to an end, or an individual example of this (*formal*) **2 ABORTION** an induced abortion **3 WORD ENDING** a word ending such as a suffix or an inflection **4 TIP OR EDGE** something that forms the end or final limit of something (*formal*) **5 FINAL OUTCOME** something that happens or is produced as a result of something else (*formal*) [14C. Directly or via French < Latin *termination-* < *terminare* (see TERMINATE).] —**terminational** *adj*

terminator /túrmi naytər/ *n* **1** a person who or thing that puts an end to something (*formal*) **2** the boundary between the part of a moon or planet that is illuminated and the part that is dark

terminator gene *n* a gene inserted into genetically modified plants that makes them unable to produce seed after one season

terminology /túrmi nólləji/ (*plural* **-gies**) *n* **1** the expressions and words, or a set of expressions and words, used by people involved in a specialized activity or field of work **2** the systematic study of names and terms [Early 19C. < German *Terminologie* < medieval Latin *terminus* 'term'.] —**terminological** /túrminə lójjik'l/ *adj* —**terminologically** *adv* —**terminologist** *n*

terminus /túrminəss/ (*plural* **-ni** /-nī/ *or* **-nuses**) *n* **1** a town, city, or location at the end or beginning of a fixed transport route such as a railway line or bus route **2** a point where something stops or reaches its end (*literary or formal*) **3** SCULPTURE = **term** *n.* 9 [Mid-16C. < Latin, 'end, boundary, limit'.]

terminus ad quem /túrminəss ad kwém/ *n* the aim or finishing point of something [< Latin, 'end to which']

terminus a quo /túrmənəss aa kwṓ/ *n* the starting point of something [< Latin, 'end from which']

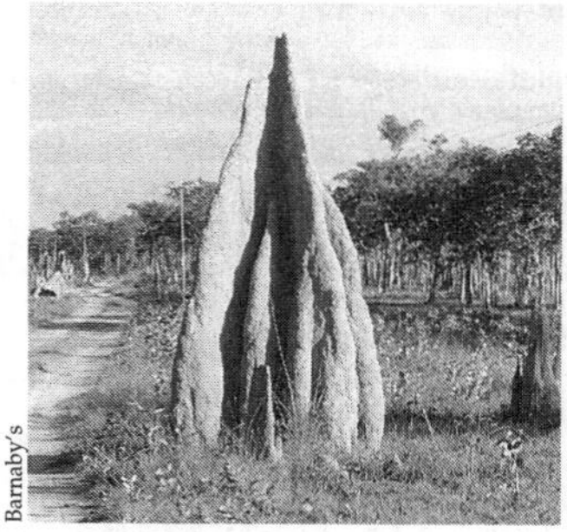

Barnaby's

Termitarium: Queensland, Australia

termitarium /túrmi táiri əm/ (*plural* **-a** /-ri ə/) *n* a nest, sometimes extremely large, made by a group of termites

termite /túr mīt/ *n* a light-coloured social insect that forms large colonies. Many species live in warm or tropical regions, feed on wood, and are highly destructive to trees and wooden structures. Order: Isoptera. [Late 18C. < Latin *termit-*, stem of *termes* 'woodworm'.] —**termitic** /tur míttik/ *adj*

termless /túrmləss/ *adj* **1** having no end or limit (*literary*) **2** not depending on any particular terms and conditions (*formal*)

termly /túrmli/ *adj* **1** taking place once every academic term **2** for each fixed or agreed time period (*formal*)

term paper *n US* a long essay required of a student during an academic term

terms of trade *npl* the ratio of a nation's export prices to its import prices, used to measure the country's trading position

tern[1] /turn/ (*plural* **terns** *or* **tern**) *n* a seabird, typically black and white, related to the gulls but with a more slender body and wings, a pointed bill, and a forked tail. Subfamily: Sterninae. [Late 17C. < N Germanic.]

tern[2] /turn/ *n* **1** a set of three things, especially three numbers that together form a winning combination in a lottery or other gambling game **2** a schooner with three masts [14C. < French *terne* < Latin *terni* 'three each'.]

ternary /túrnəri/ *adj* **1 THREEFOLD** consisting of three things or parts, or arranged in groups of three (*formal*) ○ *ternary form* **2 WITH A BASE OF THREE** describes a number system, or a number belonging to it, that has three as its base ○ *a ternary logarithm* **3 WITH THREE VARIABLES** involving or having three variables **4 WITH THREE COMPONENTS** describes an alloy that consists of three components **5 WITH THREE ATOMS OR MOLECULES** describes compounds consisting of three active elements, e.g. three atoms, molecules, or radicals [15C. < Latin *ternarius* < *terni* 'three at a time' < *ter* 'three times'.]

ternary form *n* in musical composition, a three-part form in which the first section is repeated or slightly varied in the last section, following a second, contrasting section

ternary system, ternary number system *n* the number system that uses 3 as a basis for counting or ordering

ternate /túr nayt/ *adj* describes a compound leaf that is divided into three more or less equal parts [Mid-18C. < modern Latin *ternatus* < medieval Latin, past participle of *ternare* 'make threefold'.] —**ternately** *adv*

terne /turn/ *n* **1** an alloy of lead and tin with antimony. Use: coating. **2** METALL = **terneplate** [Mid-19C. Probably < French, 'dull, tarnished'.]

terneplate /túrn playt/ *n* a steel or iron plate coated with terne

Terni /túrni/ capital of Terni Province, Umbria Region, central Italy. Population: 108,150 (1992).

ternion /túrni ən/ *n* three sheets of paper folded once to make 12 pages [Late 16C. < Latin *ternion-* < *ter* 'three times'.]

terotechnology /teérō tek nólləji/ *n* a branch of technology that uses managerial and financial expertise as well as engineering skills when installing and running machinery [Late 20C. < Greek *tērein* 'watch over, take care of'.]

terpene /túr peen/ *n* an aromatic hydrocarbon obtained from plant oils [Late 19C. < German *Terpentin* 'turpentine'.] —**terpenic** /tur peénik/ *adj*

terpineol /tur pínni ol/ *n* a derivative of pine oil that has a distinctive lilac smell. Use: perfumery. [Late 19C. < *terpin*, an organic compound < TERPENE.]

terpolymer /tur póllimər/ *n* a polymer consisting of three monomers [Mid-20C. < Latin *ter* 'three times'.]

Terpsichore /turp síkəri/ *n* the Muse of choral songs and dance in Greek mythology

terpsichorean /túrpsikə reé ən/ *adj* relating to or like dance (*formal* or *humorous*) ■ *n* a dancer (*formal* or *humorous*) [Early 19C. < Greek *Terpsikhorē* 'delighting in dance' < *terpein* 'to delight' + *khoros* 'dance'.] —**terpsichoreal** *adj*

terr. *abbr* **1** territorial **2** territory

Terr. *abbr* Terrace (*in addresses*)

terra /térrə/ (*plural* **terrae** /-ree/) *n* a light-coloured highland or mountainous area of the Moon or of a planet [Early 17C. Directly or via Italian < Latin, 'earth, land'.]

terra alba /térrə álbə/ *n* a white substance such as kaolin or gypsum, used in the making of paints and paper [< Latin, 'white earth']

terrace /térrəss/ *n* **1 PORCH OR WALKWAY WITH PILLARS** a promenade or portico, usually with columns or a balustrade along the side or sides **2 STRIP OF AGRICULTURAL LAND ON HILLSIDE** a flat, fairly narrow, level strip of ground, bounded by a vertical or steep slope and constructed on a hillside so that the land can be cultivated **3 AREA OF NATURAL GROUND ALONG COAST** a flat raised strip of beach or ground that has been formed naturally along the coast, beside a river or lake, or along the side of a valley by erosion or the changing sea level **4 ROW OF IDENTICAL HOUSES JOINED TOGETHER** a long row of houses built together in the same style, separated only by shared dividing side-walls (**party walls**) **5 CONSTRUCTED BANK OF GROUND** a raised bank of ground, artificially constructed **6** *US* **ROOFTOP PATIO** a flat roof used as living space **7 FLAT AREA BESIDE A BUILDING** a paved or grassy area immediately outside and on a level with a building, used for sitting or eating outdoors **8 BUILDINGS SET ON RAISED GROUND** a row of houses facing down from a raised position on or along the top of a piece of sloping ground, or built on a raised bank of ground ■ **terraces** *npl* **1 STANDING AREAS AROUND FOOTBALL PITCHES** the broad shallow open-air steps built around football pitches to provide cheap standing areas for spectators, outlawed at larger football grounds in the United Kingdom in the early 1990s **2 FOOTBALL SPECTATORS ON THE TERRACES** the football spectators standing on the terraces (*informal*) ■ *vt* (**-races, -racing, -raced**) **FORM TERRACE ON LAND** to convert land into a terrace or terraces [Early 16C. < Old French, 'rubble, platform' < Latin *terra* 'earth, land'.]

terraced house, terrace house *n* any house in a row of similar houses joined side by side and facing the street. US term **row house** —**terraced housing** *n*

terracing /térrəss ing/ *n* **1 STRIPS OF AGRICULTURAL LAND IN STEPS** a series of level, fairly narrow strips of ground constructed on a hillside that would otherwise be too steep for cultivation **2 TERRACED AREA OR STRUCTURE** something built in shallow, gradually rising steps or tiers such as the open-air terraces in a football ground or an area of landscaped garden **3 TERRACED HOUSES** a group of buildings designed or built as a terrace or terraces **4 MAKING OF TERRACES** the act or process of creating a terrace or terraces

terracotta /térrə kóttə/ *n* **1 REDDISH-BROWN POTTERY CLAY** unglazed reddish-brown hard-baked clay, often used to make pottery objects **2 SOMETHING MADE OF TERRACOTTA** a work of art or craft modelled in terracotta, or terracotta items generally **3 BROWNISH-RED COLOUR** a reddish-brown colour, like that of terracotta [Early 18C. < Italian, 'baked earth'.] —**terracotta** *adj*

terrae plural of **terra**

terra firma /-fúrmə/ *n* solid ground, in contrast to water or air (*literary or humorous*) [< Latin, 'firm land']

terraform /térrə fawrm/ *vt* to create an environment similar to that of Earth on another planet, or make it habitable for beings from Earth [Mid-20C. < Latin *terra* 'earth, land'.]

terrain /tə ráyn/ (*plural* **-rains** *or* **-rain**) *n* ground or a piece of land seen in terms of its surface features or general physical character, especially when crossing it or using it for military purposes [Early 18C. Via French < Latin *terrenum* 'land, ground' < *terrenus* 'of the earth' < *terra* 'earth, land'.]

terra incognita /-in kógnitə/ (*plural* **terrae incognitae** /térree in kógni tee/) *n* **1** a country or region that is unknown or has not been explored **2** a subject or area of knowledge that has not been explored and about which nothing is known [< Latin, 'unknown land']

terra nullius /térrə noólli əss/ *n* in Australia, the idea and legal concept that when the first Europeans arrived in Australia the land was owned by no one and therefore open to settlement [< Latin, 'land belonging to no one']

terrapin /térrəpin/ (*plural* **-pins** *or* **-pin**) *n* **1** a moderate-sized turtle. Native to: brackish water in E North America. *Malaclemys terrapin.* **2** a freshwater turtle with four webbed feet, a shell like that of a tortoise, and a retractable head. Family: Emydidae. [Early 17C. < Algonquian.]

terraqueous /te ráykwi əss/ *adj* consisting of areas of water and areas of dry land (*archaic or literary*) [Mid-17C. < Latin *terra* 'earth, land' + AQUEOUS.]

terrarium /tə ráiri əm/ (*plural* **-ums** *or* **-a** /-ə/) *n* **1** an enclosure that is used for keeping or observing small land animals or reptiles such as lizards in a simulated natural environment **2** a sealed glass container used for growing ornamental plants that require a high level of humidity [Late 19C. < medieval Latin, < Latin *terra* 'earth, land' (after AQUARIUM).]

terrazzo /te rátsō/ *n* mosaic that is made by laying marble or stone chips in mortar and grinding them to a polished level surface. Use: floor or wall coverings. [Early 20C. < Italian, 'terrace'.]

terreplein /táir playn/ *n* a raised embankment or platform behind a parapet where heavy guns are positioned [Late 16C. Via French < Italian *terrapienare* 'fill with earth' < *terra* 'earth' + *pieno* 'full'.]

~~**terrestial**~~ incorrect spelling of **terrestrial**

terrestrial /tə réstri əl/ *adj* **1 RELATING TO EARTH** relating to Earth rather than other planets **2 BELONGING TO THE LAND** belonging to the land rather than the sea or air **3 LIVING OR GROWING ON LAND** living or growing on land rather than in the sea or the air **4 BROADCAST BY A LAND-BASED TRANSMITTER** broadcast by a land-based transmitter rather than by satellite ○ *a terrestrial TV channel* **5 WORLDLY OR MUNDANE** worldly or mundane as opposed to heavenly ■ *n* **DWELLER ON PLANET EARTH** a person or creature who lives on the Earth, especially in science fiction [14C. < Latin *terrestris* < *terra* 'earth, land'.] —**terrestrially** *adv* —**terrestrialness** *n*

terrestrial guidance *n* a missile or rocket guidance system in which the missile is given precise details of its flight path, enabling it to follow a predetermined route. ◊ **inertial guidance**

terrestrial link *n* a telecommunications connection that runs on or below the ground

terrestrial planet *n* any of the four planets, Mars, Venus, Mercury, and Earth, that are nearest the Sun and are similar in density and composition

terret /térrit/ *n* **1** either of two metal rings attached to the driving harness of a horse, through which the reins are passed to prevent them from slipping round the horse's flanks **2** a metal ring on a dog's collar to which a leash can be attached [Late 15C. < Old French *toret* 'little ring' < *tour* (see TOUR).]

terre verte /táir vúrt/ *n* a greyish-green pigment of powdered glauconite. Use: in paints. [< French, 'green earth']

terrible /térrəb'l/ *adj* **1 EXTREME** very serious or severe ○ *a terrible cold* **2 VERY UNPLEASANT** very unpleasant or harrowing ○ *The past few days have been a terrible time.* **3 EXTREMELY LOW IN QUALITY** of a very low standard or quality ○ *My cooking isn't that great, but it's not terrible.* **4 ILL OR UNHAPPY** unwell, or extremely unhappy ○ *You look terrible. Are you ill?* **5 TROUBLING** causing considerable fear or anxiety ○ *a terrible sight* **6 FORMIDABLE** causing awe or dread ○ *a terrible responsibility* [14C. Via Old French < Latin *terribilis* < *terrere* 'frighten'.] —**terribleness** *n*

terribly /térrəbli/ *adv* **1** to an extreme degree ○ *I'm terribly pleased that you can come.* **2** in a way that is extremely difficult or painful ○ *affected terribly by the news*

terricolous /te ríkələss/ *adj* living in or on the soil [Mid-19C. < Latin *terricola* 'earth-dweller' < *terra* 'earth, land'.]

terrier[1] /térri ər/ *n* any small lively dog of a type initially bred to hunt animals living in underground burrows, but now common as a pet [15C. < Old French *(chien) terrier* 'terrier (dog)' < Latin *terra* 'earth'.]

terrier[2] /térri ər/ *n* in English legal history, a land register or survey [15C. Via Old French < Latin *terra* 'earth, land'.]

Terrier /térri ər/ *n* a member of the British Army's Territorial and Volunteer Reserve (*informal*) [Early 20C. < TERRITORIAL.]

terrific /tə ríffik/ *adj* **1 VERY GOOD** exceptionally good in a way that inspires enthusiasm (*informal*) **2 VERY GREAT** very great in size, force, or degree ○ *terrific speed* **3 VERY FRIGHTENING** inspiring a sense of terror (*archaic*) [Mid-17C. < Latin *terrificus* 'frightening' < *terrere* 'frighten'.]

terrifically /tə ríffikli/ *adv* to a very high degree or very great extent

terrify /térri fī/ (**-fies, -fying, -fied**) *vt* **1** to make somebody feel very frightened or alarmed **2** to coerce somebody to do something by using threats ○ *terrified into naming the members* [Late 16C. < Latin *terrificare* < *terrificus* (see TERRIFIC).] —**terrifier** *n* —**terrifying** *adj* —**terrifyingly** *adv*

terrine /te reén/ *n* **1** a small dish with a tight-fitting lid that is used for cooking and serving food, especially cooked pâtés **2** the food that is cooked and served in a terrine dish, often a coarse pâté **3** HOUSEHOLD = **tureen** [Early 18C. < French, form of Old French *terrin* 'earthen' < Latin *terra* 'earth'.]

territorial /térrə táwri əl/ *adj* **1 RELATING TO OWNED LAND** relating to land or water owned or claimed by an entity, especially a government **2 ASSERTING OWNERSHIP OF AN AREA** having a tendency to appropriate an area or territory and to protect that area or territory against intruders of the same species, particularly other males **3 RELATING TO RESERVE ARMY** relating to a reserve army that has been trained for use in emergencies —**territorially** *adv*

Territorial *n* a member of a reserve army that has been trained for use in emergencies, especially the British Army's Territorial and Volunteer Reserve. ◆ **Territorial Army**

Territorial Army *n* the British Army's Territorial and Volunteer Reserve, a reserve army established in 1907 to 1908 to assist with national defence in emergencies

territorialise *vt* = **territorialize**

territorialism /térrə táwri əlizəm/ *n* **1** a social system in which the landowners hold or control most of the positions of power and authority **2** a system of civil government in which the citizens of a territory are penalized unless they adopt the same religion as their civil ruler —**territorialist** *n*

territoriality /térrə táwri álləti/ *n* **1** the ranking of a region as a territory **2** a pattern of animal behaviour marked by the establishment, demarcation, and defence of an area that can support the growth and activity of an animal or group of animals

territorialize /térrə táwri ə līz/ (**-izes, -izing, -ized**), **territorialise** (**-ises, -ising, -ised**) *vt* **1** to organize something on a territorial basis **2** to enlarge a country by adding more territory or territories to it —**territorialization** /térrə táwri ə lī záysh'n/ *n*

territorial waters *npl* the area of sea around a country's coast recognized as being under that country's jurisdiction

territory /térrətəri/ (*plural* **-ries**) *n* **1 LAND** land, or an area of land **2 GOVERNED GEOGRAPHICAL AREA** a geographical area that is owned and controlled by a particular government or country **3 territory, Territory AREA OF COUNTRY WITH SEPARATE GOVERNMENT** an area of a country or empire such as the United States, Canada, or Australia that is not a state or province but has a separate organized government **4 FIELD OF INQUIRY** a field of knowledge, investigation, or experience **5 AREA THAT ANIMAL CONSIDERS ITS OWN** an area that an animal considers as its own and that it defends against intruders of the same species **6 DISTRICT THAT AGENT COVERS** the district that an agent, especially a sales representative, is responsible for **7 AREA DEFENDED BY TEAM** the area of a playing field defended by a team [14C. < Latin *territorium* < *terra* 'earth, land'.] ◇ **come** *or* **go with the territory** to be an inseparable part of or accompaniment to something else

terror /térrər/ *n* **1 INTENSE FEAR** intense or overwhelming fear **2 TERRORISM** violence or the threat of violence carried out for political purposes **3 SOMETHING CAUSING FEAR** something such as an event or situation that causes intense fear ○ *a rabid dog that became the terror of the neighbourhood* **4 ANNOYING PERSON** an annoying, difficult, or unpleasant person, particularly a naughty child (*informal*) [14C. Via Old French < Latin, < *terrere* 'frighten'.] —**terrorful** *adj*

Terror *n* HIST = **Reign of Terror**

terrorise *vt* = **terrorize**

terrorism /térrərizəm/ *n* violence or the threat of violence, especially bombing, kidnapping, and assassination, carried out for political purposes

terrorist /térrərist/ *n* a person who uses violence, especially bombing, kidnapping, and assassination, to intimidate others, often for political purposes —**terroristic** /térrə rístik/ *adj*

terrorize /térrə rīz/ (**-izes, -izing, -ized**), **terrorise** (**-ises, -ising, -ised**) *vt* **1** to intimidate or coerce somebody with violence or the threat of violence **2** to fill somebody with feelings of intense fear over a period of time —**terrorization** /térrə rī záysh'n/ *n* —**terrorizer** *n*

terror-stricken, terror-struck *adj* filled with a feeling of intense fear

terry /térri/ (*plural* **-ries**) *n* **1** TEXTILES = **terry towelling 2** an uncut loop of thread in the pile of a fabric that consists of such loops **3** a square of terry towelling. Use: nondisposable nappy. [Late 18C. < ?]

Terry /térri/, **Dame Ellen** (1847–1928) British actor

terry towelling *n* a fabric with uncut loops of thread on both sides. Use: towels, bath mats, nappies. US term **terry** *n.* 1

terse /turss/ (**terser, tersest**) *adj* **1** brief and unfriendly, often conveying annoyance **2** concise and economically phrased [Early 17C. < Latin *tersus* 'wiped off, clean', past participle of *tergere* 'wipe'.] —**tersely** *adv* —**terseness** *n*

tertial /túrsh'l/ *adj, n* BIRDS = **tertiary** *adj.* **3** [Mid-19C. < Latin *tertius* 'third'.]

tertian /túrsh'n/ *adj* describes a fever, especially a malarial fever, with symptoms that appear every other day ■ *n* a tertian fever or set of symptoms [14C. < Latin *(febris) tertiana* '(fever) of the third (day)' < *tertius* 'third'.]

tertiary /túrshəri/ *adj* **1 THIRD** third in degree, order, place, or importance (*formal*) **2 RELATING TO BIRD'S SHORT FLIGHT FEATHERS** relating to the short flight feathers nearest the body on the rear edge of a bird's wing, making up the third row of feathers **3 FROM EARLY CENOZOIC ERA** formed in, occurring in, or relating to the first period of the Cenozoic era, during which mammals became dominant and modern plants evolved **4 CHARACTERIZED BY REPLACEMENT IN THIRD DEGREE** characterized by replacement in the third degree, particularly the replacement of the three hydrogens in either a methyl group or in ammonia with three other groups ■ *n* (*plural* **-ies**) **1 BIRD'S SHORT FLIGHT FEATHER** a bird's tertiary feather, on the rear edge of its wing **2 FIRST PERIOD OF CENOZOIC ERA** the first period of the Cenozoic era during which mammals became dominant and modern plants evolved, 65 million to 1.6 million years ago **3 tertiary, Tertiary MEMBER OF LAY GROUP** in the Roman Catholic Church, a member of a group of the laity associated with a religious order [Mid-16C. < Latin *tertiarius* 'of the third part or rank' < *tertius* 'third'.]

tertiary colour *n* a colour made by mixing two secondary colours together or by mixing a primary colour with the secondary colour closest to it

tertiary education *n* education at college or university level

tertiary industry *n* the field of industry that provides services, e.g. transport or finance, rather than manufacturing or extracting raw materials

tertiary syphilis *n* the final stage of syphilis in which the disease spreads throughout the body, affecting the brain, spinal cord, heart, skin, bones, and joints

tertium quid /túrshi əm kwíd/ *n* an unknown or indefinite thing or factor that is related to but cannot be classified as belonging to either of two other areas or categories [< late Latin, 'some third thing']

Tertullian /tər túlli ən/ (160?–225?) Roman theologian

tervalent /tur váylənt/ *adj* CHEM = **trivalent** —**tervalency** *n*

terza rima /táirtsə réemə/ (*plural* **terze rime** /táirt say rée may/) *n* a rhyming verse form of Italian origin, consisting of three-line, 11-syllable verses (**tercets**), with the middle line of one verse rhyming with the first and third lines of the next [< Italian, 'third rhyme']

terzetto /tur tséttō/ (*plural* **-tos** *or* **-ti** /-tsétti/) *n* a musical trio for instruments or voices [Early 18C. < Italian (see TERCET).]

TES *n* a weekly magazine published in the United Kingdom that covers all aspects of education. Full form **Times Educational Supplement**

TE score *n* in Australia, a score awarded on the basis of final secondary school examinations that determines whether or not a student is accepted into some tertiary education institutions. Full form **Tertiary Entrance Score**

TESL /téss'l/ *abbr* Teaching (of) English as a Second Language

tesla /tésslə/ *n* (*symbol* **T**) the derived unit of magnetic flux density in the SI system, equal to a flux of one weber in an area of one square metre [Late 19C. After Nikola TESLA.]

Tesla /tésslə/, **Nikola** (1856–1943) Croatian-born US electrical engineer

tesla coil *n* an air-core transformer that is used to produce high voltages at high frequencies, e.g. in X-ray tubes [After Nikola TESLA]

TESOL /tée sol/ *abbr* **1** Teaching (of) English to Speakers of Other Languages **2** Teachers of English to Speakers of Other Languages

TESSA /téssə/, **Tessa** *abbr* Tax-Exempt Special Savings Account

tessellate /téssə layt/ (**-lates, -lating, -lated**) *v* **1** *vt* to construct, pave, or decorate something with small pieces of stone or glass to give a mosaic effect **2** *vi* to fit together without leaving any spaces (*refers to geometric shapes*) [Late 18C. < Latin *tessellatus* 'made of small square stones' < *tessera* (see TESSERA).] —**tessellation** /téssə láysh'n/ *n*

tessera /téssərə/ (*plural* **-ae** /-ree/) *n* **1** a small square of stone, tile, or glass used to make a mosaic **2** a piece of bone or wood that was used in ancient Greece and Rome as a dice, tally, or ticket [Mid-17C. Via Latin < Greek *tesseres*, a variant of *tessares* 'four'; from the sides of the square.] —**tesseral** *adj*

tesseract /téssə rakt/ *n* the four-dimensional extension of a cube [Late 19C. < Greek *tesseres* (see TESSERA) + *aktis* 'ray'.]

tessitura /téssi tóórə/ (*plural* **-turas** *or* **-ture** /-ray/) *n* the pitch range that predominates in a particular piece of music [Late 19C. Via Italian < Latin *textura* 'web, structure'.]

test[1] /test/ *n* **1 EXAMINATION** a series of questions, problems, or practical tasks to gauge somebody's knowledge, ability, or experience **2 TRIAL RUN-THROUGH OF A PROCESS** a trial run-through of a process or on equipment to find out if it works **3 BASIS FOR EVALUATION** a basis for evaluating or judging something or somebody **4 DIFFICULT SITUATION** an often difficult situation or event that will provide information about somebody or something **5 EXAMINATION OF PART OF THE BODY** an examination of part of the body or of a body fluid or specimen in order to find something out, e.g. whether it is functioning properly or is infected ○ *an eye test* **6 PROCEDURE TO DETECT PRESENCE** a procedure to ascertain the presence of or the properties of a substance ○ *a test for nitrates in drinking water* **7 REACTIVE SUBSTANCE** a substance or a reagent that reacts in a particular way to show the presence of a substance **8 RESULT OF A PROCEDURE** a result of a procedure to ascertain the presence of a substance ○ *Your test hasn't come back yet.* **9** SPORTS = **test match** ■ *v* **1** *vt* **TRY SOMETHING OUT** to try something out, e.g. by touching, operating, or experiencing it, in order to find out what it is like, how well it works, or what it feels like **2** *vt* **EVALUATE** to use something on a trial basis in order to evaluate it **3** *vt* **ASK SOMEBODY QUESTIONS** to ask somebody questions or make somebody do a practical activity in order to gauge knowledge, skill, or experience **4** *vt* **CARRY OUT A MEDICAL TEST** to carry out a test on part of the body or on a bodily specimen **5** *vti* **EXAMINE SOMETHING TO DETECT A PRESENCE** to examine something in order to ascertain the presence of or the properties of a particular substance ○ *tested the water for bacteria* **6** *vi* **ACHIEVE PARTICULAR TEST RESULT** to achieve a particular result on a test ○ *She tested positive for rubella immunity.* **7** *vt* **MAKE DEMANDS ON** to make considerable demands on somebody, particularly somebody's skills or abilities [14C. Via Old French, 'pot' < Latin *testum* 'earthenware pot'.] —**testability** /téstə bílləti/ *n* —**testable** *adj*

test[2] /test/ *n* the hard outer covering or shell of some invertebrates such as molluscs and crustaceans [Mid-16C. < Latin *testa* 'tile, shell'.]

testa /téstə/ (*plural* **-tae** /-tee/) *n* the protective covering of a seed from a flowering plant [Late 18C. < Latin 'tile, shell'.]

testaceous /te stáyshəss/ *adj* **1** made of shell, or having a shell or other hard covering **2** of a brownish-red colour like a brick (*technical*)

Test Act *n* an act passed by the English Parliament in 1673 that barred from public office anyone who would not take Anglican Communion or renounce transubstantiation [< TEST[1] in the archaic sense of 'oath']

testae plural of **testa**

testament /téstəmənt/ *n* **1** something that shows that something else exists or is true ○ *His remarkable recovery is a testament to the doctor's skill.* **2** a formal statement or speech outlining beliefs (*formal*) [13C. < Latin *testamentum* 'will' < *testis* 'witness'.] —**testamental** /téstə mént'l/ *adj*

Testament *n* **1** either of the two major divisions of the Bible, known as the Old Testament and the New Testament **2** a printed copy of the New Testament [13C. Mistranslation of Greek *diathēkē* 'covenant', as well as 'will, testament'.]

testamentary /téstə méntəri/ *adj* **1** relating to a will (*formal*) **2** bequeathed or set out in a will

testate /tés tayt/ *adj* having made a legally valid will ■ *n* a person who has made a legally valid will [15C. < Latin *testatus*, past participle of *testari* 'bear witness, make your will' < *testis* 'witness'.] —**testacy** /téstəssi/ *n*

testator /tes táytər/ *n* somebody, especially a man, who has made a legally valid will [14C. Via Anglo-Norman < Latin, < *testari* (see TESTATE).]

testatrix /tes táytriks/ (*plural* **-trices** /-trə seez/) *n* a woman who has made a legally valid will [Late 16C. < late Latin, feminine of Latin *testator* (see TESTATOR).]

test ban *n* an agreement between nations to suspend testing of some or all nuclear weapons

test bed *n* a facility designed and equipped to test engines and machinery under circumstances as close to actual operating conditions as possible

test card *n* a geometric pattern usually incorporating areas of different colours, transmitted by a television broadcasting organization to help viewers to tune in their television sets and obtain optimum reception. US term **test pattern**

test case *n* **1** an important legal case that establishes a precedent referred to in future cases **2** an event that provides an opportunity to prove or disprove a hypothesis

testcross /tést kross/ *n* **1 GENETIC CROSS TECHNIQUE** a procedure used especially in plant breeding whereby a plant's genetic constitution is inferred by examining the progeny resulting from crossing it with another individual of known genetic makeup **2 RESULT OF TESTCROSS** an organism produced by a testcross ■ *vt* **SUBJECT ORGANISM TO TESTCROSS** to subject an organism to a testcross

test drive *n* a short drive in a car or other motor vehicle in order to see what it is like, usually with a view to buying it

test-drive *vt* to drive a car or other motor vehicle for a short period in order to see what it is like, usually with a view to buying it

tester[1] /téstər/ *n* **1 SOMEBODY WHO TESTS NEW PRODUCTS** somebody whose job it is to try out new products **2 SAMPLE OF PRODUCT** a sample of a product, especially a cosmetic **3 EQUIPMENT TO CHECK PROPER FUNCTIONING** a piece of equipment that tests if a machine or device is working properly **4 SMALL FOOD THERMOMETER** a small thermometer inserted into something that is cooking to determine if it is done **5 SOMEBODY WHO TESTS** a person who administers or carries out tests ○ *a water tester*

tester[2] /téstər/ *n* a canopy, especially one over a four-poster bed or a pulpit [14C. Via medieval Latin *testerium* < late Latin *testa* 'head' < Latin, 'tile, shell'.]

testes plural of **testis**

testicle /téstik'l/ *n* the male gonad or sperm-producing gland (**testis**) usually with its surrounding membranes, particularly in humans or other higher vertebrates [15C. < Latin *testiculus* 'small testis' < *testis* (see TESTIS).] —**testicular** /te stíkyŏŏlər/ *adj*

testify /tésti fī/ (**-fies, -fying, -fied**) *vi* **1 MAKE FACTUAL STATEMENT BASED ON EXPERIENCE** to make a factual statement based on personal experience or to declare something to be true from personal experience **2 DECLARE SOMETHING UNDER OATH IN COURT** to declare something that can be taken as evidence under oath in a court of law **3 PROVE OR DEMONSTRATE** to be clear evidence of something (*formal*) **4 TALK ABOUT EXPERIENCE AS A CHRISTIAN** to talk to an audience or group of listeners about personal experience as a Christian [14C. < Latin *testificari* 'make yourself a witness' < *testis* 'witness'.] —**testification** /téstifi káysh'n/ *n* —**testifier** *n*

testimonial /tésti mṓni əl/ *n* **1 RECOMMENDATION** a favourable report on the qualities and virtues of somebody or something **2 STATEMENT BACKING UP CLAIM** a statement backing up a claim or supporting a fact **3 TRIBUTE** something given, held, or done in order to honour or thank somebody ■ *adj* **RELATING TO TESTIMONY OR TESTIMONIAL** relating to or consisting of testimony or a testimonial

testimony /téstiməni/ (*plural* **-nies**) *n* **1 EVIDENCE GIVEN BY WITNESS IN COURT** evidence that a witness gives to a court of law **2 PROOF** something that supports a fact or a claim ○ *This win is testimony to the tactical skill of the coach.* **3 TEN COMMANDMENTS** the Ten Commandments inscribed on two stone tablets, or the Ark of the Covenant in which the tablets were stored **4 PUBLIC AVOWAL** a public profession of Christian faith or religious experience [14C. < Latin *testimonium* < *testis* 'witness'.]

testing /désting/ *adj* subjecting somebody or something to challenging difficulties ○ *A testing time lies ahead for the new administration.*

testis /téstiss/ (*plural* **-tes** /-steez/) *n* either of the paired male reproductive glands, roundish in shape, that produce sperm and male sex hormones, and hang in a small sac (**scrotum**) [Early 18C. < Latin, 'witness', because it 'bears witness' to a man's virility.]

test marketing *n* the use of a sample of a larger market to try out a particular marketing strategy or product

test match, test *n* one of a series of cricket or rugby matches between two international teams

testosterone /te stóstərōn/ *n* $C_{19}H_{28}O_2$ a male steroid hormone produced in the testicles and responsible for the development of secondary sex characteristics [Mid-20C. < TESTIS + -*sterone* (blend of STEROL + KETONE).]

test paper *n* **1** a sheet of paper with examination questions or the student's answers on it **2** a small piece of paper soaked in reagent, e.g. litmus, that is used to show the presence of or properties of a substance

test pattern *n* US MEDIA = **test card**

test pilot *n* a pilot who flies new aircraft in order to assess their performance

test-screening *n* a screening of a provisional version of a film to test audience reaction

test tube *n* a small glass tube-shaped container that is closed and rounded at one end and open at the other, used to mix, heat, and store chemicals in laboratories ■ *adj* **test-tube** made in a test tube or by other artificial means, rather than occurring or arising naturally

test-tube baby *n* a baby that has been conceived by fertilizing a woman's egg in a laboratory (**in vitro fertilization**) and then inserting it in her womb to develop normally for the remainder of the pregnancy (*informal*)

testudinal /te styŏŏdinəl/, **testudinary** /-əri/ *adj* resembling a tortoise or the shell of a tortoise

testudo /te styŏŏdō/ (*plural* **-dines** /-dineez/) *n* a shelter against missiles from above, used by the ancient Roman army in siege warfare [14C. < Latin, 'tortoise-shell, shelter' < *testa* 'pot, shell'.]

testy /tésti/ (**-tier, -tiest**) *adj* impatient and easily upset or annoyed (*informal*) [14C. < Anglo-Norman *testif* < Latin *testa* 'tile, pot', later 'head'.] —**testily** *adv* —**testiness** *n*

Tet /tet/ *n* in Vietnam, and in Vietnamese communities, a festival held over three days to mark the lunar New Year [Late 19C. < Vietnamese.]

tetanic /te tánnik/ *adj* **1** relating to tetanus or to the sustained contraction of the muscles that is characteristic of tetanus **2** capable of producing muscle spasms such as are seen in tetanus [Early 18C. Via Latin < Greek *tetanikos* < *tetanos* (see TETANUS).] —**tetanically** *adv*

tetanize /téttə nīz/ (**-nizes, -nizing, -nized**), **tetanise** (**-nises, -nising, -nised**) *vt* to cause tetanic spasms in a muscle —**tetanization** /téttə nī záysh'n/ *n*

tetanus /téttənəss/ *n* **1** an acute infectious disease, usually contracted through a penetrating wound, that causes severe muscular spasms and contractions, especially around the neck and jaw **2** sustained muscle contraction, e.g. induced by electrical stimulation [14C. Via Latin < Greek *tetanos* 'muscular spasm' < *teinein* 'stretch'.] —**tetanal** *adj* —**tetanoid** *adj*

tetany /téttəni/ *n* repeated prolonged contraction of muscles, especially of the face and limbs, caused by low blood calcium arising from, e.g. an underactive parathyroid gland or vitamin D deficiency [Late 19C. Via French, 'intermittent tetanus' < Latin *tetanus* (see TETANUS).]

tetchy /téchi/ (**-ier, -iest**), **techy** (**-ier, -iest**) *adj* oversensitive and easily upset or annoyed (*informal*) [Late 16C. Probably < *tache* 'blemish, defect' < French.] —**tetchily** *adv* —**tetchiness** *n*

tête-à-tête /tét ə tét/ *n* **1 INTIMATE CONVERSATION FOR TWO** a private conversation between two people **2 TYPE OF SOFA** a two-seater sofa shaped like an S, allowing those seated to face each other ■ *adv* **INTIMATELY** in private with only two people present [< French, 'head-to-head']

tête-bêche /tét bésh/ *adj* describes a pair of stamps, one of which is printed the right way up and the other upside-down [< French, '(sleeping) head to foot']

teth /teth, tess, tet/ *n* the ninth letter of the Hebrew alphabet [Early 19C. < Hebrew.]

tether /té*th*ər/ *n* a rope or chain attached to an animal and attached to something at the other end, thus restricting the animal's movement ■ *vt* to tie something, especially an animal, with a rope or chain in order to restrict its movement [14C. < Old Norse *tjóðr* < Germanic, 'fasten'.] ◇ **at the end of your tether** having reached the limit of your patience, strength, or endurance

tetherball /té*th*ər bawl/ *n* US GAMES = **bumble-puppy** *n.* 1

Tethys /teéthiss, téth-/ *n* **1 TITAN** a Titan in Greek mythology who was the wife of Oceanus and the mother of thousands of sea and river gods and nymphs **2 SATELLITE OF SATURN** a moon of the planet Saturn **3 ANCIENT SEA** an ancient sea that is thought to have separated Laurasia and Gondwanaland, surviving vestigially today as the Mediterranean [Late 19C. Via Latin < Greek *Tēthus*.]

Tetley /téttli/, **Glen** (*b.* 1926) US-born Canadian dancer and choreographer

Teton[1] /teét'n, teé ton/ (*plural* **-ton** *or* **-tons**), **Teton Dakota** *n* **1** a member of a group of Native North American peoples who lived in western parts of the Great Plains, and now live mainly in North and South Dakota **2** the Siouan language of the Teton people. Native speakers: 6,000. [Early 19C. < Dakota *thíthuwa* 'dwellers on the prairie'.] —**Teton** *adj*

Teton[2] /teéton, teét'n/ range of the Rocky Mountains in NW Wyoming and SW Idaho. Highest peak: Grand Teton 4,197 m/13,770 ft.

Teton Dakota *n* PEOPLES, LANG = **Teton**[1]

Tétouan /te twaán/, **Tetuán** city in N Morocco on the Mediterranean Sea. Population: 272,000 (1992).

tetr- *prefix* = **tetra-** (*before vowels*)

tetra /téttrə/ (*plural* **-ras** *or* **-ra**) *n* a brightly-coloured freshwater fish that lives in tropical regions and is kept as an aquarium fish. Family: Characidae. [Mid-20C. Shortening of modern Latin *Tetragonopterus* < late Latin *tetragonum* (see TETRAGON) + Greek *pteron* 'wing'.]

tetra- *prefix* four ○ *tetrastich* [< Greek *tetra-* < Indo-European]

tetrabasic /téttrə báyssik/ *adj* containing four atoms of replaceable hydrogen in a molecule (*refers to acids*) —**tetrabasicity** /téttrə bay síssəti/ *n*

tetrabrach /téttrə brak/ *n* a word consisting of four short syllables in Latin or classical Greek literature [< Greek *tetrabrakhus* 'four short' < *brakhus* 'short']

tetracaine /téttrə kayn/ *n* $C_{15}H_{24}N_2O_2$ a crystalline compound chemically related to procaine. Use: local anaesthetic.

tetrachloride /téttrə kláwr īd/ *n* a compound that has four chlorine atoms in each molecule

tetrachloromethane /téttrə kláwrō meé thayn/ *n* CHEM = **carbon tetrachloride**

tetrachord /téttrə kawrd/ *n* a group of four notes, the first and last of which form a perfect fourth, used principally in ancient Greek music —**tetrachordal** *adj*

tetracid /te trássid/ *n* **1** a base that can react with four molecules of a monobasic acid to form a salt **2** an alcohol with four OH groups per molecule

tetracyclic /téttrə sīklik/ *adj* describes a compound whose molecular structure contains four rings

tetracycline /téttrə sī kleen/ *n* $C_{22}H_{24}N_2O_8$ a broad-spectrum antibiotic. Source: bacteria of the genus *Streptomyces*, synthesized from chlortetracycline. Use: treatment of acne, general infections. [Mid-20C. < TETRA- + CYCLIC.]

tetrad /té trad/ *n* **1 SERIES OF FOUR** a group or series of four things or people **2 GROUP OF FOUR CHROMOSOMES** a group of four chromosomes in a diploid cell that is about to undergo the cell division (**meiosis**) that produces sex cells **3 GROUP OF FOUR CELLS** a group of four cells produced by the division (**meiosis**) of a single parent cell, e.g. as it occurs in the formation of pollen and spores **4 ATOM WITH VALENCY OF FOUR** an atom or chemical group with a valency of four [Mid-17C. < Greek *tetrad-*, stem of *tetras* 'four'.]

tetradactyl /téttrə dáktil/ *adj* with four toes or fingers

tetradymite /te tráddi mīt/ *n* a grey metallic sulphide mineral containing tellurium and bismuth. Use: source of tellurium. [Mid-19C. Via German < Greek *tetradumos* 'fourfold'; from the double twin crystals in which it is usually found.]

tetraethyl lead /téttrə eé thīl-/ *n* $Pb(C_2H_5)_4$ a colourless, extremely poisonous, oily liquid. Use: petrol antiknock agent now often restricted or banned because it produces air pollution and poisons catalytic converters.

tetragon /téttrə gon/ *n* a geometric figure with four sides and four angles [Early 17C. < late Latin *tetragonum* < Greek *tetragōnos* 'four-angled' < *gōnos* 'angled'.] —**tetragonal** *adj* —**tetragonally** *adv*

tetragram /téttrə gram/ *n* a word that has four letters

Tetragrammaton /téttrə grámmətən/ *n* a four-letter Hebrew name for God revealed to Moses, usually written YHVH or YHWH (Exodus 3:13–14) [14C. < Greek, neuter of *tetragrammatos* 'having four letters' < *gramma* 'letter'.]

tetrahedrite /téttrə heé drīt/ *n* a grey to black metallic sulphide mineral containing copper, iron, and antimony. Use: source of copper and other metals. [Mid-19C. Directly < TETRAHEDRON or < Greek *tetraedron*.]

tetrahedron /téttrə heédrən/ (*plural* **-drons** *or* **-dra** /-drə/) *n* a solid figure that has four faces [Late 16C. < Greek *tetraedron*, neuter of *tetraedros* 'four-sided' < *hedra* 'face'.] —**tetrahedral** /téttrə heédrəl/ *adj* —**tetrahedrally** *adv*

tetrahydrocannabinol /téttrə hīdrō kə nábbi nol/ *n* full form of **THC**

tetrahydroxy /téttrə hī dróksi/ *adj* describes a molecule having four hydroxyl groups

tetralogy /te trálləji/ (*plural* **-gies**) *n* a series of four related literary, dramatic, artistic, or musical works [Mid-17C. < Greek *tetralogia* 'four dramas' < *-logia* 'discourse'.]

tetramer /téttrəmər/ *n* a polymer that is formed from four identical monomers —**tetrameric** /téttrə mérrik/ *adj*

tetramerous /te trámmərəss/ *adj* with four parts, or with parts arranged in multiples of four —**tetramerism** *n*

tetrameter /te trámmitər/ *n* **1** VERSE LINE WITH FOUR FEET a line of verse that has four metrical feet **2** LINE WITH FOUR PAIRS OF FEET in classical poetry, a line of verse made up of four pairs of feet **3** VERSE IN TETRAMETER verse written in tetrameters [Early 17C. Via late Latin < Greek *tetrametron*, form of *tetrametros* 'having four measures' < *metron* 'measure'.]

tetraploid /téttrə ployd/ *adj* possessing four matched sets of chromosomes in the cell nucleus ■ *n* a tetraploid cell, nucleus, or organism —**tetraploidy** *n*

tetrapod /téttrə pod/ *n* **1** a vertebrate animal that has four limbs or legs **2** a device comprising four arms projecting from a central point at 120° to each other, making a tripod with the fourth arm projecting vertically upwards [Early 19C. Via modern Latin *tetrapodus* < Greek *tetrapod-* 'four-footed' < *pous* 'foot'.]

tetrapody /te tráppədi/ (*plural* **-dies**) *n* a poetic measure of four feet —**tetrapodic** /téttrə póddik/ *adj*

tetrapterous /te tráptərəss/ *adj* describes insects that have four wings

tetrarch /té traark/ *n* **1** the ruler of a quarter of a country or province **2** one of four joint rulers [Pre-12C. Via late Latin *tetrarcha* < Greek *tetrarkhēs* 'four ruling' < *arkhēs* 'ruler'.] —**tetrarchic** /te traárkik/ *adj*

tetrarchy /té traarki/ (*plural* **-chies**), **tetrarchate** /te traá kayt/ *n* **1** government by four rulers **2** the rule or domain of one of four joint rulers

tetraspore /téttrə spawr/ *n* an asexual spore that occurs after cell division (**meiosis**), usually in groups of four, in red algae —**tetrasporic** /téttrə spórrik/ *adj*

tetrastich /téttrə stik/ *n* a poem, verse, or strophe that has four lines [Late 16C. Via Latin *tetrastichon* < Greek *tetrastikhos* 'containing four rows' < *stikhos* 'row, line of verse'.] —**tetrastichic** /téttrə stíkik/ *adj*

tetrasyllable /téttrə sílləb'l/ *n* a word with four syllables —**tetrasyllabic** /téttrə si lábbik/ *adj*

tetratomic /téttrə tómmik/ *adj* **1** with four atoms per molecule **2** with four replaceable atoms or radicals

tetravalent /téttrə váylənt/ *adj* with a valency of four —**tetravalency** /téttrə váylənssi/ *n*

tetri /téttri/ (*plural* **-ri**) *n* see table at **currency** [Late 20C. < Georgian.]

tetrode /téttrōd/ *n* a four-element electron tube containing an anode, a cathode, a control grid, and an additional electrode or screen grid

tetrodotoxin /te trṓdə tóksin/ *n* a potent neurotoxin found in puffers

tetrose /téttrōss/ *n* a natural sugar that contains four carbon atoms [Early 20C. < TETRA- + -OSE[2].]

tetroxide /te tróksīd/, **tetroxid** /-tróksid/ *n* a compound having four oxygen atoms per molecule [Mid-19C. < TETRA-.]

tetryl /téttrīl, -tril/ *n* $C_7H_5N_5O_8$ a yellow crystalline compound. Use: explosives detonator.

teuchter /tyoókhtər, tyoóktər/ *n Scotland* used by Lowlanders in Scotland to refer to a Highlander in a disrespectful or teasing way (*informal*) [Mid-20C. < ?]

Teucrian /tyoókri ən/ *n* a Trojan (*literary*) [< Greek *Teukros* 'Teucer', first king of Troy] —**Teucrian** *adj*

Teutoburg Forest /tóytō burg-/, **Teutoburger Wald** /tóytō burgər vált/ ridge of wooded hills in NW Germany, scene of a major Roman defeat in AD 9

Teuton /tyoót'n/ *n* **1** a member of an ancient Germanic people that originally came from Jutland and invaded Gaul in the 2nd century BC, where they were wiped out **2** somebody from a German-speaking culture, especially from Germany, Switzerland, or Austria (*informal or humorous*) [Early 18C. < Latin *Teutoni* or *Teutones* (plural) 'the Teutons'.]

Teutonic /tyoo tónnik/ *adj* **1** relating to German-speaking cultures or people (*informal or humorous*) **2** relating to the ancient Teuton people, or their culture —**Teutonically** *adv*

Teutonic Knights, **Teutonic Order** *n* a German religious and military order that was founded as a charitable order in Palestine in 1190 during the Third Crusade, but became a military organization operating in Eastern Europe

Teutonise *vti* = **Teutonize**

Teutonism /tyoótənizəm/ *n* **1** a German characteristic, custom, or idiom **2** German society or civilization —**Teutonist** *n*

Teutonize /tyoótə nīz/ (**-izes, -izing, -ized**), **Teutonise** (**-ises, -ising, -ised**) *vti* to become German or to make something German —**Teutonization** /tyoótə nī záysh'n/ *n*

Tevet /te vét/, **Tebet** *n* in the Jewish calendar, the fourth month of the civil year and the tenth month of the religious year

Tewa /táywə/ (*plural* **-was** *or* **-wa**) *n* **1** a member of a group of Pueblo peoples who live in N New Mexico **2** the Tanoan language of the Tewa people. Native speakers: under 3,000. [Mid-19C. < Tewa *téwa* 'moccasins'.] —**Tewa** *adj*

Te Whiti /te fítti/ (1830–1907) New Zealand Maori leader and prophet

Tewkesbury /tyoóksbəri/ market town in west-central England. Population: 9,600 (1994 estimate).

Tex. *abbr* **1** Texan **2** Texas

Texas /téks əss/ state of the SW United States, bordering the Gulf of Mexico. Capital: Austin. Population: 19,439,337 (1997). Area: 691,201 sq. km/266,873 sq. mi. —**Texan** *n, adj*

Texas fever *n* an infectious disease of cattle characterized by high fever, anaemia, and severe weight loss, that is transmitted by tick bites and caused by a protozoan

Texel /téks'l/ *n* a sheep of a breed originally from the Netherlands that has a heavy white fleece and a short neck and is raised for meat and milk production [Mid-20C. After an island off the north coast of the Netherlands.]

Tex-Mex /téks méks/ *adj* showing a blend of Texan and Mexican cultures or cuisines [Shortening]

⚡**text** /tekst/ *n* **1** MAIN BODY OF BOOK the main body of a book or other printed material as distinct from the introduction, index, illustrations, and headings **2** WRITTEN MATERIAL words that have been written down, typed, or printed **3** WRITTEN VERSION OF a complete written, typed, or printed version of something such as a speech or a statement ○ *the full text of the President's speech* **4** EDITION one among the extant forms or versions of a written work ○ *compared various texts to arrive at this reading* **5** BOOK FOR STUDY a book or piece of writing that is used for academic study or discussion **6** EDUC = **textbook** *n.* **7** BIBLE PASSAGE a short passage from the Bible that is read aloud and on which a sermon is based **8** ORIGINAL WORDING the original wording of a piece of writing, especially the Bible, as opposed to a translation, summary, or revision **9** TYPEFACE FOR TEXT a style of type that is suitable for printing running text **10** WORDS APPEARING ON COMPUTER SCREEN computer data that represents words, numbers, and other typographic characters, typically stored in ASCII format ■ *adj* USING WORDS associated with or designed for use with words in written form ■ *vt* to send a text message to a recipient's mobile phone [14C. Via Old French < Latin *textus* 'woven material, literary composition' < past participle of *texere* 'weave'.]

textbook /tékst book/ *n* a book that treats a subject comprehensively and is used by students as a basis for study ■ *adj* typical overall and in detail, and thus a suitable example for study ○ *a textbook case of superpower aggression*

⚡**text box** *n* a box within a dialog box in which characters, e.g. text, dates, or numbers, can be typed and edited

⚡**text chat** *n* a real-time communication between users in which messages are typed via a keyboard

⚡**text editor** *n* a computer program that permits the creation and editing of stored text

⚡**text file** *n* a computer file consisting of alphanumeric characters exclusive of transmission characters

textile /téks tīl/ *n* **1** cloth or fabric that is woven, knitted, or otherwise manufactured **2** raw material such as fibre or yarn that is used for making fabrics [Early 17C. < Latin *textilis* < past participle of *texere* 'weave'.]

⚡**text index** *n* an index of some or all of the words in, e.g. a computer file or database field, used to aid searching and retrieval

⚡**text message** *n* a message sent in textual form, especially one designed to appear on the viewing screen of a mobile phone or pager —**text-messaging** *n*

⚡**text processing** *n* the use of a computer to create, store, edit, and print or display text

textual criticism *n* **1** the study of a group of manuscripts, especially of the Bible or works of literature, in order to determine which is the original or most authentic one **2** the critical study of a work of literature involving a detailed analysis of the way in which it was written, e.g. its context, use of language, and principal themes —**textual critic** *n*

textualism /tékschoo əlizəm/ *n* **1** unswerving adherence to a text, especially a text from the Bible **2** detailed and critical analysis of a text —**textualist** *n*

textuary /tékschoo əri/ *adj* textual (*formal*) [Early 17C. < medieval Latin *textuarius* < Latin *textus* (see TEXT).]

texture /tékschər/ *n* **1** FEEL OF A SURFACE the feel and appearance of a surface, especially how rough or smooth it is **2** STRUCTURE OF the structure of a substance or material such as soil or food, especially how it feels when touched or chewed **3** ROUGH QUALITY the rough quality of a surface or fabric ○ *a fabric that has plenty of texture* **4** DISTINCTIVE CHARACTER the typical and distinctive character of something complex ○ *The book captures the texture of 1950s provincial England.* **5** WAY AN ARTIST DEPICTS A SURFACE the way in which an artist depicts the quality or appearance of a surface **6** EFFECT OF DIFFERENT COMPONENTS OF MUSIC the effect of the different components of a piece of music, e.g. melody, harmony, rhythm, or the use of different instruments ■ *vt* (**-tures, -turing, -tured**) GIVE A SURFACE A PARTICULAR FEEL to give a surface a particular feel, usually one that is rough and grainy [15C. Via Old French < Latin *textura* 'a weaving' < past participle of *texere* 'weave'.] —**textural** *adj* —**texturally** *adv* —**textured** *adj*

textured vegetable protein *n* full form of **TVP**

⚡**tg** *abbr* Togo (*in Internet addresses*)

TG *abbr* transformational grammar

⚡**TGAL** *abbr* think globally, act locally (*in e-mails*)

TGIF, **T.G.I.F.** *abbr* Thank God It's Friday *or* Thank Goodness It's Friday (*informal*)

TGV *n* in France and some other countries, a very high-speed train [< French, abbreviation of *train (à) grande vitesse* 'high-speed train']

TGWU *abbr* Transport and General Workers' Union

⚡**th** *abbr* Thailand (*in Internet addresses*)

Th *symbol* thorium

Th. *abbr* **1** Thessalonians **2** Thursday

Thackeray /thákə ray/, **William Makepeace** (1811–63) British novelist

Thaddaeus /tháddi əss/ *n* in the Bible, one of the 12 apostles. He is traditionally identified with St Jude (Mark 3:16–19) (Matthew 10:2–4).

Thai /tī/ (*plural* **Thais** *or* **Thai**) *n* **1** a person who comes from Thailand **2** the Tai official language of Thailand. Native speakers: 25 million. [Early 19C. < Thai, 'free'.] —**Thai** *adj*

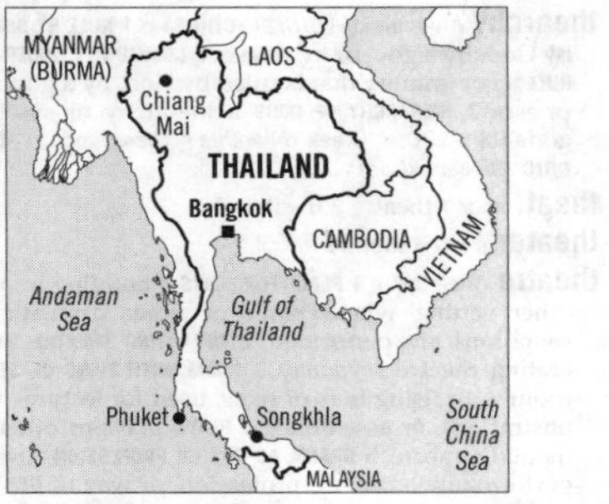

Thailand

Thailand /tī land, tīlənd/ kingdom in Southeast Asia, on the Gulf of Thailand. Capital: Bangkok. Population: 59,450,818 (1997). Area: 513,115 sq. km/198,115 sq. mi.

Thailand, Gulf of wide inlet of the South China Sea in S Thailand. Length: 800 km/500 mi.

Thaïs /tháy iss/ (*fl.* 4th-century BC) Greek courtesan

thalamus /thálləməss/ (*plural* **-mi** /-mī/) *n* **1** either of a pair of egg-shaped masses of grey matter lying beneath each cerebral hemisphere in the brain that relay sensory information to the cerebral cortex **2** PLANT SCI = **receptacle** *n*. 2 [Late 17C. Via Latin, 'inner chamber' < Greek *thalamos*.] —**thalamic** /thə lámmik/ *adj* —**thalamically** *adv*

Thalassa /thə lássə/ *n* a small inner natural satellite of Neptune, discovered in 1989 by the space probe Voyager 2. It is approximately 80 km/50 mi. in diameter.

thalassaemia /thállə seémi ə/ *n* a hereditary form of anaemia, particularly prevalent around the Mediterranean, that is caused by a dysfunction in the synthesis of the red blood pigment haemoglobin [Mid-20C. < Greek *thalassa* 'sea' (from its discovery in Mediterannean countries) + *haima* 'blood'.] —**thalassaemic** *adj*

thalassic /thə lássik/ *adj* **1** living in or growing in the sea **2** relating to a sea or ocean, especially a smaller inland sea [Mid-19C. < French *thalassique* < Greek *thalassa* 'sea'.]

thalassocracy /thállə sókrəssi/ (*plural* **-cies**), **thalattocracy** /-tókrəssi/ (*plural* **-cies**) *n* naval or commercial supremacy over a large area of sea or ocean [Mid-19C. < Greek *thalassokratia* 'authority over the sea' < *thalassa* 'sea'.] —**thalassocrat** /thə lássə krat/ *n*

thalassotherapy /thállәssō thérrəpi/ *n* a therapeutic treatment that involves bathing in sea water [Late 19C. < Greek *thalassa* 'sea'.]

thalattocracy *n* POL = **thalassocracy**

thaler /taálər/ (*plural* **-ler** *or* **-lers**), **taler** (*plural* **-ler** *or* **-lers**) *n* a former silver coin used in Austria, Germany, and Switzerland [Late 18C. < archaic German (now *Taler*).]

Thales (of Miletus) /tháy leez əv mī leétəss/ (625?–546? BC) Greek philosopher

Thalia /thə lī ə/ *n* **1** the muse of comedy in Greek mythology. ◊ **Muse 2** one of the three Graces in Greek mythology who lived on Mount Olympus and tended the goddess Aphrodite. ◊ **Grace**

thalidomide /thə líddə mīd/ *n* a synthetic drug found to cause physical deformities in foetuses when taken by pregnant women. Use: formerly, sedative and hypnotic. [Mid-20C. < alteration of PHTHALIC ACID + (IM)ID(E) + (IM)IDE, elements of its chemical name.]

thallic /thállik/ *adj* relating to or containing thallium, especially with a valency of three

thallium /thálli əm/ *n* (*symbol* **Tl**) a soft highly toxic white metallic element. Source: lead and zinc smelting. Use: manufacture of low-melting glass, photocells, infrared detectors. [Mid-19C. < Greek *thallos* 'green shoot' (because its spectrum is marked by a green band).]

thallophyte /thállə fīt/ *n* a plant that has no stem, roots, or leaves, e.g. algae, lichens, and fungi [Mid-19C. < modern Latin *Thallophyta* < Greek *thallos* 'green shoot' + *phuton* 'plant'.] —**thallophytic** /thállə fíttik/ *adj*

thallous /thálləss/ *adj* relating to or containing thallium, especially with a valency of one

thallus /thálləss/ (*plural* **-li** /-lī/ *or* **-luses**) *n* the body of an organism such as an alga or liverwort that is not differentiated into leaves, stems, and roots [Early 19C. < Greek *thallos* 'green shoot' < *thallein* 'to bloom'.] —**thalloid** /thálloyd/ *adj*

thalweg /taal veg/, **talweg** *n* a line connecting the lowest points of successive cross sections through a river channel or valley [Mid-19C. < German, < obsolete *Thal* 'valley' (now *Tal*) + *Weg* 'path'.]

Thames /temz/ major river of S England, flowing through London and emptying into the North Sea. Length: 338 km/210 mi.

than *stressed* /t͟han/; *unstressed* /t͟hən/ CORE MEANING: used after a comparative adjective or adverb in order to introduce the second element of a comparison ○ (prep) *paying more than £490 a year in fees* ○ (prep) *The hole was no deeper than 12 ft.* ○ (conj) *The risk may be higher than the figures indicate.*
conj used to introduce a rejected alternative in a contrast between two alternatives, in order to state a preference ○ *more a state of mind than a physical condition* [Old English *þanne, þonne, þænne, þan* < Germanic]

USAGE than he or **than him**? Because ***than*** is a preposition as well as a conjunction, either construction is possible, as is the fuller form *than he is*. The form *than him* is common in conversation and other spoken contexts (*We're older than him*) but is still frowned upon in formal writing where *We're older than he is* is preferred.

thanatology /thánnə tólləji/ *n* the study of the medical, psychological, and sociological aspects of death and the ways in which people deal with it [Mid-19C. < Greek *thanatos* 'death'.] —**thanatological** /thánnətə lójjik'l/ *adj* —**thanatologist** *n*

Thanatos /thánnə toss/ *n* **1** in Greek mythology, the personification of death and the son of Nyx, goddess of the night. Roman equivalent **Mors 2** the universal death instinct theorized by Sigmund Freud [Mid-20C. < Greek, 'death'.]

thane /thayn/ *n* **1** an Anglo-Saxon nobleman of low rank who held lands in return for military service to a lord **2** a baron in feudal Scotland, or a hereditary tenant of the Scottish crown [Old English *þegn* < Germanic, 'boy, man'] —**thanage** *n* —**thaneship** *n*

Thanet, Isle of /thánnit/ coastal region in SE England. It was formerly an island.

thank /thangk/ *vt* **1 EXPRESS GRATITUDE** express feelings of gratitude to somebody **2 BLAME SOMEBODY FOR** to blame somebody or hold somebody responsible for something ○ *You have only yourself to thank for this situation.* **3 BE GRATEFUL** to be grateful to somebody or something because of something that has happened ○ *Thank goodness you got here in time.* [Old English *þancian* < Indo-European] ◇ **I'll thank you (not) to** used in an ironic or angry way to ask somebody to do or not do something ○ *I'll thank you not to bring any more of your friends round.* ◇ **thank you** used to express gratitude to somebody

thankful /thángkf'l/ *adj* **1** feeling or expressing gratitude ○ *We must be thankful for small mercies.* **2** glad or relieved about something —**thankfulness** *n*

thankfully /thángkf'li/ *adv* **1** used to express approval or relief about a situation (*informal*) ○ *Thankfully, he didn't fall.* **2** with feelings or expressions of gratitude ○ *They thankfully accepted her offer of a room for the night.*

LANGUAGE NOTE See sentence adverb.

USAGE *Thankfully* is used in two ways: as a conventional adverb of manner (*They received the good news thankfully*), and as a sentence adverb (*Thankfully, the news was good*). Some people dislike the second use, although the objection is not as strong as that to *hopefully* used in a corresponding way.

USAGE see hopefully.

thankless /thángkləss/ *adj* **1** not likely to be appreciated or rewarded ○ *a thankless task* **2** not showing or feeling gratitude —**thanklessly** *adv* —**thanklessness** *n*

thank-offering *n* something offered or given to somebody as a sign of gratitude

thanks /thangks/ *interj* **USED TO EXPRESS GRATITUDE** used to express gratitude to somebody (*informal*) ○ *Goodbye, and thanks!* ■ *npl* **1 EXPRESSION OF GRATITUDE** an expression of gratitude for something ○ *Many thanks for your help yesterday.* **2 GRATITUDE FOR** gratitude or appreciation for something ◇ **no thanks to somebody** *or* **something** despite somebody *or* something or without somebody's assistance ◇ **thanks a lot** used to express great gratitude (*informal; sometimes used ironically*) ○ *Thanks a lot for coming over.* ○ *You took my glass? Thanks a lot!* ◇ **thanks to somebody** *or* **something** because of somebody *or* something

thanksgiving /thángks giving/ *n* **1 PRAYER OF THANKS** a prayer that offers thanks to God **2 GIVING OF THANKS** an expression or an act of giving thanks **3 PUBLIC ACKNOWLEDGMENT OF DIVINE GOODNESS** a public acknowledgment or celebration of divine goodness

Thanksgiving Day, Thanksgiving *n* **1** *US* in the United States, a public holiday marking the feast given in thanks for the harvest by the Pilgrim colonists in 1621. Date: fourth Thursday in November. **2** *Can* in Canada, a public holiday observed as a day of giving thanks for the harvest and other good things received. Date: second Monday in October.

thank-you *n* an expression of gratitude to somebody ○ *a big thank-you to all our readers* ■ *adj* expressing gratitude to somebody for something ○ *Send a thank-you note promptly.*

Thant /thant/, **U** (1909–74) Burmese statesman

Thar Desert /taar-/ desert in NW India, extending across the border into Pakistan. Area: 199,429 sq. km/77,000 sq. mi.

Tharp /thaarp/, **Twyla** (*b.* 1941) US dancer and choreographer

Tharsis /thaársiss/ *n* an extensive shallow bulge on the surface of Mars in the northern hemisphere about 2000 km/1200 mi. across and 8 km/5 mi. high, supporting several volcanoes

Thásos /táss oss/, **Thassos** /thάss oss/ island in NE Greece, in the Aegean Sea. Population: 13,111 (1981). Area: 378 sq. km/146 sq. mi.

that *stressed* /t͟hat/; *unstressed* /t͟hət/ CORE MEANING: a grammatical word used to indicate somebody or something that has already been mentioned or identified, or something that is understood by both the speaker and hearer ○ (det) *Do you remember that discussion we had?* ○ (det) *Later that week I saw her again.* ○ (pron) *Is that why you're here?* ○ (pron) *Don't touch that!*
1 *det, pron* **INDICATING DISTANCE FROM THE SPEAKER** indicating somebody or something a distance away from you, or farther away from another, referred to as 'this' ○ (det) *You see that girl over there?* ○ (det) *That bag looks more spacious than this one.* ○ (pron) *What's that you're doing?* ○ (pron) *That looks much nicer than this.* **2** *det, pron* **INDICATING A FAMILIAR PERSON OR THING** used to refer to somebody or something not described, but familiar to the speaker and hearer and not requiring identification ○ (det) *Did you read that e-mail I sent?* ○ (det) *that woman we met yesterday* ○ (pron) *That was a great year.* **3** *det* **INDICATING A TYPE** used to characterize a particular type, person, or thing ○ *I really want a sleep that goes on forever.* **4** *pron* **IDENTIFYING** used to introduce a clause giving more information to identify the person or thing mentioned ○ *the committee that deals with such matters* ○ *Take the road that forks to the left.* ○ *on the day that he left.* **5** *conj* **EXPRESSING A COMMENT OR FACT** used to introduce a noun clause expressing a comment on a situation or a supposed or real fact ○ *It was clear that she wanted to see the concert.* ○ *The report stated that sales were improving.* **6** *conj* **EXPRESSING A RESULT** used to introduce a clause expressing result or effect ○ *It made such a noise that we had to cover our ears.* **7** *conj* **EXPRESSING A CAUSE** used to introduce a clause expressing the cause of a feeling ○ *I feel hurt that you should think such a thing.* ○ *He's sorry that he told her now.* **8** *conj* **EXPRESSING PURPOSE** used to introduce a clause expressing purpose ○ *We continue to give, that others will receive and live.* **9** *conj* **EXPRESSING DESIRE OR AMAZEMENT** used after an understood but unspoken statement such as 'I wish' or 'If only' to introduce a clause expressing desire, amazement, or indignation ○ *Oh that I had never set eyes on her!* ○ *That you could think such a thing!* **10** *adv* **TO THE STATED DEGREE** used to specify the extent of something ○ *I came that close to hitting the car in front.* **11** *adv* **SO VERY** used before adjectives to emphasize the quality they are describing (*informal*) ○ *I didn't think she'd be that upset.* **12** *adv Scotland* **SO** so ○ *I was that angry!* [Old English *þæt* < Indo-European] ◇ **that is** in other words, or to be specific ○ *You need a further qualification, that is, a PhD.* ◇ **that's that 1** used to say that something is finished or dealt with **2** used to say that something has been settled and there will be no more discussion on it

USAGE That in reference to people: For centuries ***that*** has been used to refer to people as well as things. Sometimes this usage can be clumsy: *He's the one that did it.* But it is not incorrect, and occasionally ***that*** is the most appropriate choice of relative pronoun: *Anything or anyone that helps me is my friend.*

USAGE that or **which**? As relative pronouns the two words are often interchangeable: *The house that/which stands on the corner is up for sale. The school that/which they go to is several miles away.* When ***that*** or ***which*** is the object of a following verb, it can be omitted altogether, as in *The school they go to ....* When the relative clause adds information that is additional rather than necessary for identifying the noun it follows, ***which*** is used and is preceded by a comma: *The largest house, which stands on the corner, is up for sale.* Some usage guides, especially American ones, advocate the use of ***that*** in defining relative clauses (where the information added is essential to identify the noun it follows) and ***which*** in nondefining clauses (where the information added is incidental), and this is the practice followed in this dictionary.

USAGE that not **that there**: Avoid using ***there*** in formal writing as an adjectival intensifier of a noun preceded by ***that***: That [not That there] house is for sale.

thataway /thátta way/ *adv US* in that direction, or over there (*humorous* or *regional*) ○ *The masked man went thataway, Sheriff.* [Mid-19C. Alteration of *that way*.]

thatch /thach/ *n* **1 PLANT MATERIAL USED FOR A ROOF** a plant material such as straw or rushes used as roofing on a house **2 ROOF OF THATCH** a roof made of thatch **3 HAIR ON SOMEBODY'S HEAD** the hair on somebody's head, especially when it is thick ○ *The child had an unmistakable thatch of red hair.* **4 LAYER OF DEAD MATERIAL IN GRASS** a matted layer of dead plant material that builds up next to the soil at the base of lawn grasses ■ *vti* **ROOF BUILDING WITH THATCH** to put a roof of thatch on a building, or to work at doing this [Old English *þeccan*. < Indo-European 'to cover'.] —**thatched** *adj* —**thatcher** *n*

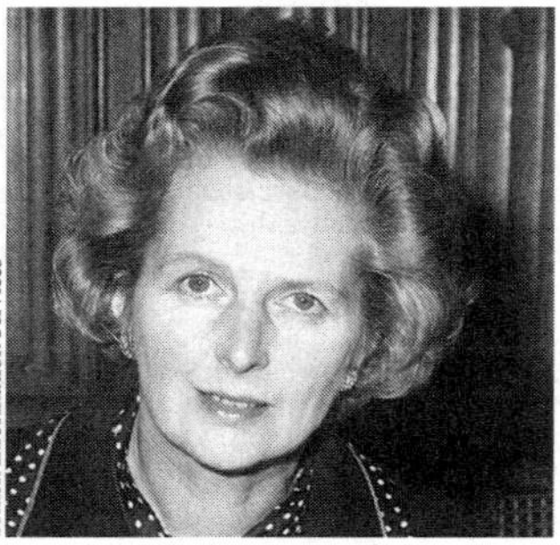

British Information Services

Margaret Thatcher

Thatcher /tháchər/**, Margaret, Baroness Thatcher of Kesteven** (*b.* 1925) British stateswoman and first woman prime minister of Great Britain (1979–90). Born **Margaret Hilda Roberts**

Thatcherism /tháchərizəm/ *n* the political policies and style of government of Margaret Thatcher, typified by privatization, monetarism, and hostility to trade unions —**Thatcherite** *n, adj*

thatching /tháching/ *n* **1** the craft or process of constructing or repairing thatched roofs **2** BUILDING = **thatch** *n.* 1

thaumato- *prefix* miracle ○ *thaumatology* [< Greek *thaumat-*, stem of *thauma* 'marvel, wonder']

thaumatology /tháwmə tólləji/ *n* the study or description of miracles

thaumatrope /tháwmə trōp/ *n* a card with different pictures on either side so that when the card is rapidly twirled, the images appear to combine [Early 19C. < Greek *thauma* 'wonder' + *tropos* 'turning'.] —**thaumatropical** /tháwmə tróppik'l/ *adj*

thaumaturge /tháwmə turj/, **thaumaturgist** /tháwmə turjist/ *n* a performer of magic or supposed miracles [Early 18C. Via medieval Latin < Greek *thaumatourgos* < *thauma* 'wonder' + *-ergos* 'working'.]

thaumaturgy /tháwmə turji/ *n* the performance of miracles or magic —**thaumaturgic** *adj*

thaw /thaw/ *v* **1** *vti* **MELT** to melt or make something melt **2** *vti* **DEFROST** to defrost frozen food or become defrosted ○ *Leave the gateau out to thaw.* **3** *vi* **BECOME LESS COLD** to become less cold or numb through exposure to heat ○ *Come and thaw out by the fire.* **4** *vi* **BE WARM ENOUGH TO MELT ICE** to be warm enough that snow and ice will melt **5** *vi* **BECOME LESS HOSTILE** to become less hostile, tense, or aloof ○ *The atmosphere thawed.* ■ *n* **1 PROCESS OF THAWING** the action or process of thawing **2 WARMER WEATHER** a period of weather warm enough to melt snow and ice **3 LESSENING OF HOSTILITY** a lessening of hostility, tension, or aloofness [Old English *þawian* < Germanic]

Thayer /tháy ər, thair/**, Sylvanus** (1785–1872) US soldier and educator. Known as **Father of West Point**

THC *n* the main active chemical in cannabis. Full form **tetrahydrocannabinol**

ThD *abbr* Doctor of Theology [Latin *Theologiae Doctor*]

the (*stressed/emphatic*) /thee/; (*unstressed*)(*before a vowel*) /thi/; (*unstressed*)(*before a consonant*) /thə/ CORE MEANING: a determiner, the definite article, used before somebody or something that has already been mentioned or identified, or something that is understood by both the speaker and hearer, as distinct from 'a' or 'an' ○ *The film ended with the hero riding off into the desert.* ○ *The food was excellent but the service was poor.*

1 *det* **INDICATING ONE AS DISTINCT FROM ANOTHER** used to refer to a particular one of a number of things or people, identified as distinct from all others by the use of some kind of modifier ○ *Put them in the small bag.* ○ *the door on the left* ○ *the girl who answered the phone* ○ *the right to vote* ○ *the points made earlier* **2** *det* **INDICATING GENERIC CLASS** used to refer to a person or thing considered generically or universally ○ *Exercise is good for the heart.* ○ *she played the violin* ○ *The dog is a loyal pet.* **3** *det* **INDICATING SHARED EXPERIENCE** used to refer to objects and concepts associated with the shared experience of a culture, society, or community ○ *go to the hospital* ○ *thinking about the future* ○ *lying in the sun* **4** *det* **ALL PEOPLE OF A PARTICULAR TYPE** used before adjectives to refer generically to people of a particular type or class ○ *new measures to help the unemployed* ○ *They say the good always die young.* **5** *det* **TITLES AND NAMES** used before titles and some names, e.g. placenames ○ *the King of Spain* ○ *the Times newspaper* ○ *the President of the United States* **6** *det* **QUALIFYING NAMES AND TITLES** used in names and titles before adjectives and nouns that distinguish somebody from others of the same name or title ○ *Ivan the Terrible* ○ *Henry the Fifth* **7** *det* **INDICATING PARTS OF THE BODY** used instead of 'my', 'your', etc., to refer to a part of somebody's body ○ *patted him on the head* ○ *took her by the hand* **8** *det* **INDICATING MOST FAMOUS OR IMPORTANT** the best, only, or most outstanding ○ *It's the place to be.* **9** *det* **EXPRESSING RATES AND RATIOS** used to indicate how many units apply to the particular items being measured ○ *ordered in at £60 the ton* **10** *det* **INDICATING A FAMILY RELATIONSHIP** used instead of 'your', 'my', etc (*informal*) ○ *Give my regards to the family.* ○ *How's the wife?* **11** *det* **PERIOD OF TIME** used to refer to a specified period of time, especially a decade or an era ○ *living in the sixties* **12** *adv* **TO THAT EXTENT** used adverbially to emphasize that somebody or something is true to a particular extent (*before comparatives*) ○ *She looks the better for her holiday.* ○ *the worse for wear* **13** *adv* **BY HOW MUCH OR BY THAT MUCH** used adverbially to indicate how one amount or quality changes in relation to another (*before each of two comparative adjectives or adverbs*) ○ *the cheaper the better* ○ *The more you exercise, the fitter you'll feel.* **14** *det Scotland* used in various constructions where standard English requires no article, particularly before public institutions like 'the school' and 'the church', and names of diseases, e.g. 'the mumps' (*informal*) **15** *det Scotland* used before a surname to indicate the chief of a clan, e.g. 'the MacGregor'; also historical, e.g. 'Hughie the Graham', with surnames other than Highland ones **16** *det Scotland* used in various constructions, notably 'the baith' (also, in informal Scottish English, 'the both'), 'the maist' (also, 'the most'); 'the day', 'the morn', 'the nicht', that is today, tomorrow, tonight [Old English *þe*, earlier *se* < Indo-European]

the- *prefix* = **theo-** (*before vowels*)

theanthropism /thi ánthrəpizəm/ *n* **1** the assigning of human characteristics to a god or gods **2** the Christian doctrine that the human and the divine are united in Jesus Christ [Early 19C. < Greek *theanthrōpos* 'god-man' < *theos* 'god' + *anthrōpos* 'man'.] —**theanthropic** /thee ən thróppik/ *adj* —**theanthropist** *n*

thearchy /thee aarki/ (*plural* **-chies**) *n* **1 RULE BY GOD** rule by God, by a god, or by priests **2 COMMUNITY UNDER DIVINE RULE** a community that is ruled by God, by a god, or by priests **3 HIERARCHY OF GODS** a hierarchy or system of gods [Mid-17C. < Greek *thearkhia* < *theos* 'god'.] —**thearchic** /thi aarkik/ *adj*

theat. *abbr* **1** theatre **2** theatrical

theater *n* US = **theatre**

theatre /theertər/ *n* **1 PLACE FOR PLAYS** a building, room, or other setting where plays or other dramatic presentations are performed **2 OPERATING THEATRE** an operating theatre (*informal*) **3 ROOM WITH TIERS OF SEATS** a room with rising tiers of seats, used for lectures, demonstrations, or assemblies **4 PLAYS** plays or other dramatic literature **5 DRAMA AS ART OR PROFESSION** dramatic performance as an art, profession, or way of life ○ *She decided to make the theatre her life.* **6 DRAMATIC QUALITY** dramatic or theatrical quality or effectiveness ○ *As a public speaker he has a great sense of theatre.* **7 PLACE OF SIGNIFICANT EVENTS** the place or realm where significant actions or events take place ○ *the political theatre* ■ *adj* **FOR USE IN THEATRE OF OPERATIONS** relating to or for use in a military theatre of operations [14C. Via Old French and Latin < Greek *theatron* < *theasthai* 'to watch'.]

theatregoer /theertər gō ər/ *n* a person who goes to the theatre —**theatregoing** *n, adj*

theatregoing /theé ətər gō ing/ *n* the practice of going to the theatre, especially regularly ■ *adj* attending the theatre, especially regularly ○ *The theatregoing public is being shortchanged by plays of this standard.* —**theatregoer** *n*

theatre-in-the-round (*plural* **theatres-in-the-round**) *n* **1** a theatre in which the stage is in the centre with the seats around it on all sides **2** drama or the style of drama written for performance in a theatre-in-the-round

theatre of cruelty *n* a form of surrealist drama emphasizing that human beings live in a threatening world with precarious moral values

theatre of operations *n* an area where fighting takes place during a war

Theatre of the Absurd *n* a form of drama that represents the absurdity of human life in a meaningless universe by deliberately unrealistic means and by ignoring or distorting conventions of plot and characterization

QUICK FACTS ON... **THEATRE OF THE ABSURD**

Key dates: mid-1940s–early 1960s
Key locations: Paris
Key elements: existentialism, pessimism, scepticism; rejection of naturalistic theatrical conventions; minimal plot, illogical situations, unconventional or absurd dialogue
Key figures: Samuel Beckett, Eugène Ionesco, Arthur Adamov, Jean Genet, Fernando Arrabal, Harold Pinter
Key works: *The Bald Soprano* (Ionesco) 1950; *Waiting for Godot* (Beckett) 1953; *The Balcony* (Genet) 1956; *The Caretaker* (Pinter) 1960
Key developments: experimental theatre, performance art

theatre of war *n* a large area of land, sea, and air in which warfare may take place. ◊ **theatre of operations**

theatrical /thi áttrik'l/ *adj* **1 RELATING TO THEATRE** relating to or typical of the theatre or dramatic performance **2 MARKED BY ARTIFICIAL EMOTION** full of exaggerated or false emotion ■ *n* **ACTOR** a professional actor —**theatricalism** *n* —**theatricality** /thi áttri kálləti/ *n* —**theatrically** *adv* —**theatricalness** *n*

theatricals /thee áttrik'lz/, **theatrics** /thi áttriks/ *npl* **1** the performance of plays, often by amateurs **2** showy dramatic gestures and actions

thebaine /theebə een, thi báy-/ *n* $C_{19}H_{21}NO_3$ a poisonous alkaloid that causes convulsions similar to those caused by strychnine. Source: opium. Use: formerly, as medicine. [Mid-19C. < Greek *Thēbai* 'Thebes'; because Upper Egypt was an important source of opium.]

thebe /tébbe/ (*plural* **-be**) *n* see table at **currency** [Late 20C. < Setswana, 'shield'.]

Thebe /theebee/ *n* a moon of the planet Jupiter [Mid-18C. Via Latin, a nymph < Greek.]

Thebes /theebz/ **1** city of ancient Greece, northwest of present-day Athens **2** capital of ancient Egypt, on both sides of the River Nile, south of present-day Cairo —**Theban** *n, adj*

theca /theéka/ (*plural* -**cae** /-see, -keef/) *n* an enclosing organ, capsule, or sheath, e.g. the spore case of a moss or the horny covering of the pupa of an insect [Early 17C. Via Latin < Greek *thēkē* 'case'.] —**thecal** *adj* —**thecate** /theé kayt/ *adj*

thecodont /theéka dont/ *adj* **WITH TEETH IN SOCKETS** describes animals whose teeth are set in sockets ■ *n* **1 EXTINCT PREHISTORIC REPTILE** an extinct reptile that lived in the Triassic period, had teeth set in sockets, and was the ancestor of the dinosaur. Order: Thecodontia. **2 THECODONT REPTILE** a thecodont reptile [Mid-19C. < Latin *theca* (see THECA).]

thé dansant /táy daaN saáN/ (*plural* **thés dansants**) *n* a tea dance [< French, 'dancing tea']

thee /theé/ *pron* **1** the objective form of 'thou' used as the object of a verb or preposition to mean 'you' (*archaic*) **2** a subjective form of 'thou' as used by members of the Christian denomination, the Society of Friends ○ *See that they thee keepest silence.* [Old English *þē*, objective form of *þū* (see THOU²)]

theft /theft/ *n* the stealing of somebody else's property [Old English *þēoft* < Germanic]

~~theif~~ incorrect spelling of **thief**

theine /theé een, -in/ *n* caffeine, particularly as found in tea [Mid-19C. < modern Latin *Thea*, former genus name of the tea plant < Dutch *t(h)ee* (see TEA).]

their /thair/ *det* **1** belonging to or relating to a particular group of people or things ○ *They have sold their house and moved to London.* **2** ⚠ belonging to an individual person ○ *Everyone should make their own way home.* [12C. < Old Norse *þeirra* 'theirs'.]

USAGE their/there/they're Do not confuse these three words, as they have different meanings and spellings, and they function differently. **Their** is a possessive determiner: *Their* [not *They're* or *There*] *decisions have been made.* **There** can be an adverb or a pronoun, e.g. *Look over there* [not *their* or *they're*] *quickly. There* [not *They're* or *Their*] *are several unanswered questions.* **They're** is a contraction of 'they are', as in *They're* [not *There* or *Their*] *sitting in the front row.*

USAGE See **they**.

theirs /thairz/ *pron* **1** belonging to a particular group of people or things ○ *Theirs was the biggest house in the town.* **2** belonging to an individual person ○ *I have spare copies of the agenda if anyone has forgotten theirs.*

theism /theé izam/ *n* **1** belief that one God created and rules humans and the world, not necessarily accompanied by belief in divine revelation such as through the Bible **2** belief in the existence of a god or gods [Late 17C. < Greek *theos* 'god'.] —**theist** *n* —**theistic** /thee ístik/ *adj* —**theistical** *adj* —**theistically** /-ístikli/ *adv*

them *stressed* /them/; *unstressed* /thəm/ *pron* **1 OBJECTIVE FORM OF 'THEY'** used to refer to a group of people or things other than the speaker or people addressed ○ *I'll put them in a box for you.* **2 HIM OR HER** used instead of 'him' or 'her' to refer to a person without specifying gender ○ *If anyone is looking for me, tell them I'll be back soon.* **3 THOSE** a dialect form of 'those' (*nonstandard*) ○ *Give me one of them oranges.* [12C. < Old Norse *þeim*.]

thematic /thi máttik/ *adj* **1 RELATING TO THEME** relating to or being a theme **2 RELATING TO WORD STEM** relating to the stem of a word **3 LAST BEFORE INFLECTION** being the last part of a word stem before the inflectional ending [Late 17C. < Greek *thematikos* < *thema* 'proposition'.] —**thematically** *adv*

thematic apperception test *n* a test for exploring aspects of personality in which somebody is shown pictures of people in various situations and asked to describe what is happening

theme /theem/ *n* **1 SUBJECT OF DISCUSSION OR COMPOSITION** a subject of a discourse, discussion, piece of writing, or artistic composition **2 DISTINCT AND UNIFYING IDEA** a distinct, recurring, and unifying quality or idea ○ *Efficiency will be the theme of this organization.* **3 REPEATED MELODY** a melody that is repeated, often with variations, throughout a piece of music ○ *one of the themes of the concerto* **4 MUSIC IN FILM** a song or tune that is played at the beginning or end of, or during, a film or television programme, and is identified with it ○ *the theme from 'The Magnificent Seven'* **5 ESSAY OR WRITTEN EXERCISE** a short essay or written exercise for a student ■ **stem**¹ *n.* **6** GRAM ■ *adj* **WITH DISTINCT SUBJECT** with one distinct and recurring subject, organizational principle, or idea ○ *We ate at a Wild West theme restaurant.* ■ *vt* (**themes, theming,**

themed) **GIVE SOMETHING DISTINCT CHARACTER** to give something a single distinct character or subject ○ *The local bar has been themed as an Irish pub.* [13C. Via Old French and Latin < Greek *thema* 'proposition'.] —**themed** *adj*

SYNONYMS See **subject**.

USAGE Do not use the noun **theme** as a verb in formal contexts. Like some other nouns that have undergone *functional shift* to become verbs, **theme** has not gained wide acceptance (it is associated with the lingo of commerce and popular culture). Therefore, avoid sentences like these: *She worked hard to theme her keynote speech. The party was themed as a Renaissance ball.* Use instead: *She worked hard to develop the theme of her keynote speech. The party theme was a Renaissance ball.* Similarly, avoid using the adjective *themed* alone or in combination with other words, as in *a baroque-themed concert*, where *a concert with a baroque theme* is the safer choice.

theme park *n* an amusement park in which all of the entertainments and facilities are designed around a particular subject or idea

theme song *n US* MUSIC = **signature tune**

Themistocles /thə místa kleez/ (527?–460? BC) Greek general and statesman

themselves /them sélvz/ *pron* **1 REFLEXIVE OF 'THEY' OR 'THEM'** used to refer to a group of people or things when the object of a verb is the same as the subject ○ *They all made themselves at home.* **2 THEIR NORMAL SELVES** their real or normal selves (*usually in negative statements*) ○ *They haven't been themselves since the accident.* **3 EMPHASIZING** used to emphasize the people or things being referred to ○ *They themselves would rather have gone to a movie.* **4 HIMSELF OR HERSELF** used to refer to an individual person without using 'himself' or 'herself' (*informal*) ○ *Everyone needs to take care of themselves.*

USAGE Themselves is the correct form; do not add the singular -*self* to *them*, a plural reflexive pronoun. If you need a singular, choose from the following: *himself, herself, oneself, yourself,* or *itself*.

then /then/ *adv* CORE MEANING: an adverb used to indicate a particular time in the past or future ○ *We were much happier then.* ○ *Until then, he'll be staying with me.* **1** *adv* **AFTER THAT** after that or subsequently in time, order, or position ○ *Fry the onions and garlic, then the vegetables.* ○ *We went for a walk, then came home.* **2** *adv* **THEREFORE** that being the case, or in that case ○ *Then why don't you go back?* **3** *adv* **ON THE OTHER HAND** on the other hand, or at the same time ○ *It was a brave thing to do, but then I would have expected no less of her.* **4** *adv* **IN ADDITION** in addition to something else, or besides what has been mentioned ○ *I have to pay the money, then a penalty on top of that!* **5** *adj* **BEING AT THAT TIME** being at that time, or existing or belonging to the time mentioned ○ *the then governor* [Old English *þænne* < Indo-European] ◇ **(but) then again** used to introduce a contrasting and additional fact that has to be taken into account ○ *It was a brave thing to do, but then again I would have expected no less of her.* ◇ **then and there** immediately and in that very place (*informal*) ○ *Did you expect me to hand over the money then and there?*

thenar /theé naar/ *n* **1 PALM OF HAND** the palm of the hand (*technical*) ■ *adj* **BASE OF THUMB** the fleshy area at the base of the thumb ■ *adj* **IN PALM OR BALL OF THUMB** relating to or in the palm of the hand or the fleshy area at the base of the thumb [Mid-17C. < Greek, 'palm of the hand'.]

thence /thenss/ *adv* (*formal or literary*) **1 FROM THERE** from that place ○ *We went by boat to Rotterdam and thence to Amsterdam.* **2 THEREFORE** from that fact, or therefore **3 THEREAFTER** from that time, or thereafter [13C. < obsolete *thenne* < W Germanic.]

thenceforth /thénss fáwrth/ *adv* from that time on

thenceforward /thénss fáwrwərd/ *adv* from that place or time on or forwards

theo- *prefix* god ○ *theocentric* [< Greek *theos* < Indo-European, 'to shine, sky, heaven']

theobromine /theé ō brố meen, -brố min/ *n* C₇H₈N₄O₂ a white alkaloid powder that has effects similar to caffeine. Source: cocoa beans. Use: diuretic, vasodilator, treatment of cardiovascular disorders. [Mid-19C. < modern Latin *Theobroma*, genus name of the cacao tree, literally 'food of the gods' < Greek *brōma* 'food'.]

theocentric /theé ō séntrik/ *adj* with God, a god, or gods as the focal point —**theocentricism** /-séntrissizəm/ *n* —**theocentricity** /-sen tríssəti/ *n*

theocracy /thi ókrəssi/ (*plural* -**cies**) *n* **1** government by a god or by priests **2** a community governed by a god or priests [Early 17C. < Greek *theokratia* 'rule of the gods'.] —**theocrat** /theé ə krat/ *n* —**theocratic** /-kráttik/ *adj* —**theocratical** *adj* —**theocratically** *adv*

Theocritus /thi ókrətəs/ (310?–250? BC) Greek poet

theodicy /thee óddisi/ (*plural* -**cies**) *n* argument in defence of God's goodness despite the existence of evil [Late 18C. Anglicization of French *Théodicée*, title of a book by Gottfried LEIBNIZ, literally 'justice of the gods' < Greek *dikē* 'justice'.] —**theodicean** /thee óddi seè ən/ *adj*

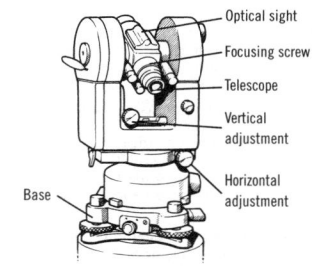

Optical sight
Focusing screw
Telescope
Vertical adjustment
Horizontal adjustment
Base

Theodolite

theodolite /thi óddə līt/ *n* an optical instrument consisting of a rotating telescopic sight, used by a surveyor to measure horizontal and vertical angles [Late 16C. < modern Latin *theodelitus*.] —**theodolitic** /thi óddə líttik/ *adj*

Theodora /theé ə dáwrə/ (508?–548) Byzantium empress

Theodorakis /theé ə daw raákiss/, **Mikis** (b. 1925) Greek composer

Theodore I Lascaris /theé ə dawr láskərəss/ (1174?–1221) Byzantine emperor

Theodoric /thi óddərik/ (AD 454?–526) king of the Ostrogoths (AD 474–526). Known as **Theodoric the Great**

Theodosius I /theé ə dốssi əss/ (AD 346?–395) Roman emperor (AD 379–95). Known as **Theodosius the Great**

Theodosius II /theé ə dốssi əss/ (AD 401–450) Roman emperor (AD 408–450)

theogony /thi óggəni/ (*plural* -**nies**) *n* the origin and descent of the gods, or an account of this [Early 17C. < Greek *theogonia* 'birth of the gods'.] —**theogonic** /theé ə gónnik/ *adj* —**theogonist** *n*

theol. *abbr* **1** theologian **2** theological **3** theology

theologian /theé ə lốjən/ *n* an expert in, or student of, theology

theological /theé ə lójjik'l/, **theologic** /-lójjik/ *adj* about, using, engaged in, or typical of theology —**theologically** *adv*

theological virtues *npl* faith, hope, and charity, the three spiritual graces that, according to Christian theology, are given directly by God

theologize /thi ólla jīz/ (-**gizes, -gizing, -gized**), **theologise** (-**gises, -gising, -gised**) *v* **1** *vt* to give a theological or religious significance to something **2** *vi* to theorize, speculate, or discourse on religious topics —**theologizer** *n*

theology /thi ólləji/ (*plural* -**gies**) *n* **1 STUDY OF RELIGION** the study of religion, especially the Christian faith and God's relation to the world **2 RELIGIOUS THEORY** a religious theory, school of thought, or system of belief **3 COURSE OF RELIGIOUS TRAINING** a course of specialized religious training, especially one intended to lead students to a vocation in the Christian Church [14C. Via French and Latin < Greek *theologia* 'study of divine things'.] —**theologist** *n*

theomachy /thi ómməki/ (*plural* -**chies**) *n* a battle among gods or against gods [Late 16C. < Greek *theomakhia* 'fighting of the gods'.]

theomorphic /theé ə máwrfik/ *adj* in the form or likeness of a deity [Late 19C. < Greek *theomorphos* 'of divine form'.] —**theomorphism** *n*

theonomy /thi ónnəmi/ *n* the state of being governed by God, a god, or priests —**theonomous** *adj*

theophany /thi óffəni/ (*plural* -**nies**) *n* the appearance of a god in a visible form to a human being [Mid-17C.

Via medieval Latin < Greek *theophaneia* 'appearance of the gods'.] —**theophanic** /theē ə fánnik/ *adj*

Theophilus /thee óffiləs/ *n* a crater on the Moon northwest of Mare Nectaris. It is approximately 100 km/60 mi. in diameter and has a central mountain 2200 m/7200 ft in height.

Theophrastus /theē ə frástəs/ (372?–287 BC) Greek philosopher

theophylline /theē ə filleen, -fillin, -leen, -lin/ *n* C$_7$H$_8$N$_7$O$_2$.H$_2$O a white crystalline alkaloid. Source: tea leaves or synthetically made. Use: vasodilator, diuretic, treatment of bronchial asthma. [Late 19C. < modern Latin *Thea* (see THEINE) + PHYLLO-.]

theorbo /thi áwr bō/ *n* a stringed instrument from the 17th century similar to the lute except larger and with an extra set of bass strings longer than the main set [Early 17C. Via Italian *tiorba* < Turkish *torba* 'bag'.] —**theorbist** *n*

theorem /theērəm/ *n* 1 a proposition or formula in mathematics or logic that is provable from a set of axioms and basic assumptions 2 an idea accepted or proposed as true [Mid-16C. Via late Latin *theōrēma* 'speculation' < Greek *theōrein* 'look at' < *theōros* 'spectator'.] —**theorematic** /theērə máttik/ *adj* —**theorematically** *adv* —**theoremic** /theer reèmik/ *adj*

theoretical /theēr réttik'l/, **theoretic** /-réttik/ *adj* 1 BASED ON THEORY about, involving, or based on theory 2 DEALING WITH THEORY dealing with theory or speculation rather than practical applications 3 SPECULATIVE inclined to or skilled in speculative contemplation or theorizing 4 HYPOTHETICAL existing only in theory [Early 17C. < late Latin *theoreticus* < Greek *theoretikos* < *theōrētos* 'observable' < *theorein* 'look at'.]

theoretically /theēr réttiklí/ *adv* 1 IN THEORY NOT REALITY in theory only, not in reality ○ *Time travel is theoretically possible.* 2 IN TERMS OF WHAT IS POSSIBLE in terms of what is possible in theory ○ *Theoretically speaking, it could be done.* 3 SUPPOSEDLY supposedly or ideally, but probably not in reality ○ *Can we still win the election? Yes, theoretically.*

theoretician /theēra tísh'n/ *n* a person who is skilled in considering theories, or is learned in the theoretical aspect of a subject

theoretics /theēr réttiks/ *n* the theoretical or speculative aspect of a subject (*takes a singular or plural verb*)

theorise *vi* = theorize

theorist /theē e rīst, theèrist/ *n* a holder or expounder of a theory

theorize /theē ə rīz, theèr īz/ (**-rizes, -rizing, -rized**), **theorise** (**-rises, -rising, -rised**) *v* 1 *vi* to speculate or form a theory about something 2 *vt* to conceive of something in a theoretical way ○ *Research scientists were able to theorize the existence of the particle before it was actually discovered.* —**theorization** /theē ə rī záysh'n, theèr ī-/ *n* —**theorizer** /theē ə rīzər, theèr īzər/ *n*

theory /theēri/ (*plural* **-ries**) *n* 1 RULES AND TECHNIQUES the body of rules, ideas, principles, and techniques that applies to a particular subject, especially when seen as distinct from actual practice ○ *economic theories* 2 SPECULATION abstract thought or contemplation 3 IDEA FORMED BY SPECULATION an idea of or belief about something arrived at through speculation or conjecture ○ *She believed in the theory that you catch more flies with honey than with vinegar.* 4 HYPOTHETICAL CIRCUMSTANCES a set of circumstances or principles that is hypothetical ○ *That's the theory, but it may not work out in practice.* 5 SCIENTIFIC PRINCIPLE TO EXPLAIN PHENOMENA a set of facts, propositions, or principles analysed in their relation to one another and used, especially in science, to explain phenomena [Late 16C. Via late Latin < Greek *theōria* 'contemplation, theory' < *theōros* 'spectator'.] ◇ **in theory** under hypothetical or ideal circumstances but perhaps not in reality

theory of games *n* MATH = game theory

theos. *abbr* 1 theosophical 2 theosophy

theosophy /thi óssəfi/ (*plural* **-phies**) *n* any religious philosophy based on intuitive insight into the nature of God [Mid-17C. Via medieval Latin < late Greek *theosophia* 'knowledge of the gods'.] —**theosophic** /theē ə sóffik/ *adj*—**theosophical** *adj* —**theosophically** *adv* —**theosophism** *n* —**theosophist** *n*

Theosophy *n* the teachings of the Theosophical Society, a religious movement founded in New York in 1875, incorporating chiefly Buddhist and Brahmanic theories

such as reincarnation and karma —**Theosophical** *adj*—**Theosophist** *n*

Thera /theerə/ island in the Greek Cyclades group, north of Crete. Population: 10,000 (1994). Area: 76 sq. km/29 sq. mi.

therap., **therapeut.** *abbr* 1 therapeutic 2 therapeutics

therapeutic /thérrə pyóotik/ *adj* 1 relating to, involving, or used in the treatment of disease or disorders 2 working or done to restore or maintain somebody's health [Mid-16C. < French *therapeutique* or late Latin *therapeutica* < Greek *therapeutēs* 'somebody who treats' < *therapeuein* (see THERAPY).] —**therapeutically** *adv*

therapeutic index *n* the ratio of the dose of a drug that causes cell damage to the dose typically needed to effect a cure. Use: indicates relative drug safety.

therapeutics /thérrə pyóotiks/ *n* the branch of medicine that deals with methods of treatment and healing, especially the use of drugs to treat diseases (+ *singular verb*)

therapist /thérrəpist/ *n* 1 somebody trained to treat disease, disorders, or injuries, especially somebody who uses methods other than drugs and surgery 2 a psychoanalyst or a professional from another school of psychotherapy who is trained to treat mental and emotional problems with psychological methods

therapsid /thə rápsid/ *n* any extinct reptile of an order that lived during the Permian and Triassic periods. Many of them are thought to be ancestors of the mammals. Order: Therapsida. [Early 20C. < modern Latin *Therapsida* < Greek *thēr* 'wild animal' + *hapsis* 'vault'.]

therapy /thérrəpi/ (*plural* **-pies**) *n* 1 treatment of physical, mental, or behavioural disorders that is meant to cure or rehabilitate somebody (*often in combination*) ○ *radiation therapy* 2 US psychoanalysis or techniques from another school of psychotherapy, intended to treat mental and emotional problems with psychological methods [Mid-19C. Via modern Latin < Greek *therapeia* < *therapeuein* 'treat medically' < *theraps* 'attendant'.]

therapy dog *n* US a dog that is taken to visit patients in, e.g. hospitals or nursing homes to provide a source of comfort and distraction

Theravada /thérrə vaàdə/ *n* the doctrines of the Hinayana Buddhists [Late 19C. < Pali, 'doctrine of the elders'.]

there stressed /thair/; unstressed /thər/ CORE MEANING: an adverb used to indicate a place, either one that has already been mentioned or is understood, or one indicated by pointing or looking ○ *I don't know how to get there by car.* ○ *May I sit there?*

1 *adv* AT THAT POINT used to refer to a point reached in an activity or process ○ *I suggest we pause there and have coffee.* ○ *And there we end our news bulletin.* 2 *adv* ON THAT MATTER on that matter, or with respect to that ○ *I can't agree with you there.* 3 *adv* AT A SUCCESSFUL POINT used to indicate that something has reached a final or successful point or stage ○ *We're not the best yet, but we're getting there.* 4 USED TO IDENTIFY used to identify somebody or something emphatically ○ *They ran into that house there.* 5 *pron* INTRODUCING A SENTENCE used to introduce a sentence stating that something exists, develops, or can be seen ○ *There's a stain on this sweater.* ○ *There remain several important issues to be discussed.* 6 *interj* USED TO EXPRESS FEELINGS used to express strong feelings such as anger, satisfaction, relief, finality, or reassurance ○ *There! I told you she would make it.* [Old English *þær* < Indo-European] ◇ **be there for somebody** to be ready to give your support, sympathy, or friendship to somebody ◇ **not all there** not fully conscious, rational, or aware of something ◇ **there and then** immediately and in that very place ◇ **there or thereabouts** there or somewhere nearby (*informal*) ◇ **there, there** used to console, soothe, or comfort somebody ○ *There, there. Don't cry.* ◇ **there you are** 1 used when giving somebody something 2 used to express triumph at having been seen to be right 3 used to express resignation or sorrow at something that has happened

children in the hall. An easy way to ensure the correct agreement between the verb and the subject is to reorder the words in your sentences mentally: *Three cars are in the garage. A lot of children are in the hall.* By contrast, you would never say *Three cars is in the garage. A lot of children is in the hall.* With compound grammatical subjects *there* used with a singular linking verb is acceptable only when the compound subject is regarded not as two separate entities but as a single compound noun, or when two indefinite noun phrases are linked together. Thus it is acceptable to say: *There is/There's food and drink for everybody. There is a pen and a book on the table.* Stylistically, *There is/are* sentences tend to be flat and lacking in emphasis, so it is wise to avoid overusing them.

USAGE See *their*.

thereabouts /tháirə bowts, -bówts/, **thereabout** US/-bowt/ *adv* near that place, amount, number, or time ○ *We're expecting twenty guests or thereabouts.*

thereafter /tháir aàftər/ *adv* after that time or from that time on ○ *She graduated from college, and shortly thereafter found a good job.*

thereat /tháir át/ *adv* (*archaic*) 1 at that time or place 2 because of that

thereby /tháir bī, -bī/ *adv* 1 by means of or because of that ○ *Interest rates may fall, thereby discouraging investment.* 2 in connection with or with reference to that ○ *Thereby hangs a tale.*

~~**therefor**~~ incorrect spelling of **therefore**

therefore /tháir fawr/ *adv* 1 and so, or because of that ○ *This statement is true; therefore that statement must be false.* 2 accordingly, or to that purpose ○ *We were forbidden to attend and therefore stayed at home.*

USAGE *Therefore* and *thus* are both fairly formal words that introduce a statement that is a consequence of the previous statement. Avoid using these words as empty connectors when what follows them does not derive from what precedes them: *Your mark in the test was 20%; therefore, you have failed.* Do not use *so therefore,* but just *therefore.* Be careful about punctuation around *therefore.* Do not put a comma between clauses where *therefore* is in the second clause, but instead use a semicolon or begin a new sentence: *She left the library at 4 o'clock. She was therefore not there when the murder took place.*

therefrom /tháir fróm/ *adv* from that place or thing (*archaic or formal*)

therein /tháir ín/ *adv* 1 in or into that place (*formal*) 2 in that matter, respect, or detail ○ *Therein lies the problem.*

thereinafter /tháirin aàftər/ *adv* from then on in something, especially a legal document (*formal*)

theremin /thérrə min/ *n* an early electronic musical instrument producing a tremulous sound [Early 20C. After Leo *Theremin* (1896–1993), Russian engineer.]

thereof /tháir óv/ *adv* (*formal*) 1 of or about that ○ *a levy of £50 per annum or part thereof* 2 from that as a reason or cause

thereon /tháir ón/ *adv* 1 on the place or surface just mentioned (*formal*) ○ *a metal plate with an inscription thereon* 2 regarding the point just mentioned (*archaic*) ○ *income and capital expense, including tax thereon*

Theresa of Lisieux /tə reèzə əv lee zyő/ (1873–97) French nun

thereto /tháir toò/ *adv* to that thing just mentioned (*formal*)

theretofore /tháirtoò fáwr/ *adv* before or up to that time (*formal*)

thereunder /tháir úndər/ *adv* below that, or after that, especially in a legal document (*formal*)

thereupon /tháirə pón/ *adv* 1 at that point in time (*archaic*) ○ *She was found to have leaked information to a rival firm, and he thereupon insisted on her dismissal.* 2 upon or concerning that point (*formal*)

therewith /tháir with, -with/, **therewithal** /tháir with áwl/ *adv* 1 with that, or as well as that (*formal*) 2 at that point, or immediately

~~**therfore**~~ incorrect spelling of **therefore**

therianthropic /theēri ən thróppik/ *adj* describes a mythological creature such as a centaur that is partly human and partly animal [Late 19C. < Greek *thērion* 'small wild animal' + *anthrōpos* 'human being'.] —**therianthropism** /theèri ánthrəpizəm/ *n*

heriomorphic /theéri ō máwrfik/ *adj* in the form of an animal, or thought of as being in animal form [Late 19C. < Greek *thērion* 'small wild animal'.]

herm /thurm/ *n* a unit of heat equal to 100,000 British thermal units or 1.055 x 10^8 joules [Early 20C. < Greek *thermē* 'heat'.]

herm- *prefix* = **thermo-** (*before vowels*)

hermae /thúr mee/ *npl* hot springs or baths, especially the public baths of ancient Rome [Mid-16C. Via Latin < Greek *thermai* < *thermē* 'heat'.]

hermaesthesia /thúrməss theézi ə/ *n* sensitivity to heat and cold, or to changes in temperature [Late 19C. < modern Latin, < Greek *thermē* 'heat' + *aisthēsis* 'perception'.]

hermal /thúrm'l/ *adj* **1 INVOLVING HEAT** about, involving, affected by, or producing heat ○ *thermal energy* **2 HOT OR WARM** hot or warm, especially because of the presence of hot springs ○ *thermal baths* **3 USING HEAT FOR PRODUCTION** using heat to produce something **4 FOR RETENTION OF BODY HEAT** designed to retain body heat ○ *thermal underwear* ■ *n* **AIR COLUMN** a current of warm air rising through cooler surrounding air ○ *watching hawks ride thermals* ■ **thermals** *npl* **THERMAL CLOTHING** thermal clothing, especially underwear (*informal*) [Mid-18C. < French < Greek *thermē* 'heat'.] —**thermally** *adv*

hermal barrier *n* the problematic heating effect caused by air friction on an aircraft flying at high speed

hermal conductivity *n* (*symbol* **λ** *or* **k**) the rate at which heat flows through a material between points at different temperatures, measured in watts per metre per degree

hermal cracking *n* the breaking down of a hydrocarbon (**cracking**) using heat

hermal efficiency *n* the work done by a heat engine divided by the thermal energy required to operate it

hermal imaging *n* the use of a device that detects the different levels of infrared energy given off by areas of different temperatures and displays these as a pattern on a screen

hermalize /thúrmə līz/ (**-izes, -izing, -ized**), **thermalise** (**-ises, -ising, -ised**) *vt* to slow neutrons in a nuclear reactor to give them thermal energy and thus produce fission —**thermalization** /thúrmə lī záysh'n/ *n*

hermal neutron *n* PHYS = **slow neutron**

hermal noise *n* noise in an electronic circuit, e.g. an amplifier, caused by electrons in conducting elements that are agitated by the absorption of heat

hermal pollution *n* the discharge into a natural body of water of heated water or other liquid that is hot enough to harm aquatic life

hermal printer *n* an output device that produces visible characters by moving heated wires over specially treated heat-sensitive paper

hermal reactor *n* a nuclear reactor in which the chain reaction, and thus fission, is brought about mainly by thermal neutrons

hermal shock *n* stress in a material caused by rapid changes in temperature, often resulting in fractures

hermesthesia *n* US = **thermaesthesia**

hermic /thúrmik/ *adj* PHYS = **thermal** *adj*. 1 —**thermically** *adv*

thermic *suffix* having to do with heat ○ *exothermic* [< Greek *thermē* 'heat']

hermic lance *n* a cutting tool that works by heating steel wool held inside a steel tube

hermion /thúrmi ən, -on/ *n* a positive ion or electron given off by a very hot material such as a hot cathode —**thermionic** /thúrmi ónnik/ *adj*

hermionic current *n* an electric current generated by the flow of electrons leaving a heated cathode and flowing to other electrodes

hermionic emission *n* the emission of electrons or ions from a solid or liquid as a result of its thermal energy

hermionics /thúrmi ónniks/ *n* a branch of electronics that deals with the emission of electrons from hot bodies (+ *singular verb*)

hermionic tube *n US* ELECTRONICS = **thermionic valve**

hermionic valve *n* an electronic component that consists of an evacuated glass tube containing a heated cathode that emits electrons, an anode that collects the electrons, and other electrodes. US term **thermionic tube**

thermistor /thur místər/ *n* a semiconductor device with a resistance that is very sensitive to temperature, resistance decreasing as the temperature increases [Mid-20C. Contraction of *thermal resistor*.]

thermite process *n* INDUST = **aluminothermy**

thermo- *prefix* **1** heat ○ *thermochemistry* **2** thermoelectricity ○ *thermocouple* [< Greek *thermē* 'heat']

thermobarometer /thúrmō bə rómmitər/ *n* an instrument that measures both air temperature and pressure

thermocautery /thúrmō káwtəri/ *n* the use of a heated instrument, e.g. a hot wire, to destroy tissue, especially in cauterizing wounds

thermochemistry /thúrmō kémmistri/ *n* a branch of chemistry concerned with the relationship between chemical action and heat —**thermochemical** /thúrmō kémmik'l/ *adj* —**thermochemically** *adv* —**thermochemist** *n*

thermocline /thúrmō klīn/ *n* a layer of water, e.g. in a lake, where there is an abrupt change in temperature that separates the warmer surface water from the colder deep water

thermocouple /thúrmō kup'l/ *n* a device for measuring temperature in which two wires of different metals are joined

thermoduric /thúrmō dyoórik/ *adj* describes a microorganism that is capable of surviving high temperatures or pasteurization [Early 20C. < THERMO- + Latin *durare* 'endure'.]

thermodynamic /thúrmō dī námmik/, **thermodynamical** /-námmik'l/ *adj* **1** about or involving thermodynamics **2** obeying or affected by the laws of thermodynamics —**thermodynamically** *adv*

thermodynamics /thúrmō dī námmiks/ *n* the branch of physics that deals with the conversions from one to another of various forms of energy and how these affect temperature, pressure, volume, mechanical action, and work (+ *singular verb*) ■ *npl* thermodynamic processes or phenomena —**thermodynamicist** *n*

thermodynamic temperature *n* PHYS = **absolute temperature**

thermoelectric /thúrmō i léktrik/, **thermoelectrical** /-léktrik'l/ *adj* involving a direct relationship between temperature of materials and electricity —**thermoelectrically** *adv*

thermoelectricity /thúrmō ilek tríssəti, -éllek-/ *n* electricity produced by maintaining a temperature difference at the point where two different materials come into contact, e.g. in a thermocouple

thermoelectron /thérmō i lék tron/ *n* an electron emitted by a material that is at high temperature

thermoform /thúrmō fawrm/ *vt* to shape plastic using heat and pressure —**thermoformable** *adj*

thermogenesis /thúrmō jénnəssiss/ *n* the production of heat in a person's or animal's body by physiological processes, especially metabolic processes —**thermogenetic** /thúrmō jə néttik/ *adj*

thermogram /thúrmə gram/ *n* **1** an image or record of the heat radiating from the body, made by thermography **2** a record of temperatures made by a thermograph

thermograph /thúrmə graaf, -graf/ *n* **1** an instrument that continuously records temperature readings **2** a device that shows patterns of heat radiated from a person's or an animal's body, used in diagnostic thermography

thermography /thər móggrəfi/ (*plural* **-phies**) *n* **1** the recording of a visual image of the heat that bodies emit as infrared radiation. The technique is used to diagnose disease and tumours, especially breast tumours. **2** the process of producing a raised image on a printed surface by using heat to fuse a resinous powder and wet ink to the surface —**thermographer** *n* —**thermographic** /thúrmə gráffik/ *adj* —**thermographically** *adv*

thermojunction /thúrmō júngksh'n/ *n* a point at which two dissimilar metals of differing temperatures come into contact, producing a thermoelectric current

thermolabile /thúrmō láy bīl/ *adj* describes substances such as some enzymes that are easily destroyed or altered by heat

thermoluminescence /thúrmō loómi néss'nss/ *n* phosphorescence released by certain previously irradiated substances when they are heated —**thermoluminescent** *adj*

thermolysis /thər móllәssiss/ *n* **1** loss of body heat, e.g. by sweating **2** the breaking down of a substance by heat —**thermolytic** /thúrmə líttik/ *adj*

thermomagnetic /thúrmō mag néttik/ *adj* relating to the relationship between heat and magnetism, and especially the effects of heat upon the magnetic properties of a substance

thermometer /thər mómmitər/ *n* an instrument for measuring temperature, e.g. an instrument with a graduated glass tube and a bulb containing mercury or alcohol that rises in the tube when the temperature increases [Mid-17C. < French *thermomètre* < Greek *thermos* 'warm' < *thermē* 'heat' + *-mètre* (see -METER).]

thermometry /thər mómmətri/ *n* temperature measurement and the branch of physics concerned with measuring temperature —**thermometric** /thúrmō méttrik/ *adj* —**thermometrical** *adj* —**thermometrically** *adv*

thermonuclear /thúrmō nyoókli ər/ *adj* relating to nuclear fusion or making use of nuclear fusion ○ *thermonuclear energy* ○ *thermonuclear war*

thermophile /thúrmə fīl/, **thermophil** /-fil/ *n* an organism that thrives in a warm environment, e.g. a bacterium —**thermophile** *adj* —**thermophilic** /thúrmə fíllik/ *adj* —**thermophilous** /thər móffələss/ *adj*

thermopile /thúrmə pīl/ *n* a set of thermocouples, either joined in series for increased voltage or in parallel for increased current, used to measure radiant energy or to convert radiant energy into electric current

thermoplastic /thúrmo plástik/ *n* a substance that becomes soft and pliable when heated, without a change in its intrinsic properties. Polystyrene and polythene are thermoplastics. —**thermoplastic** *adj* —**thermoplasticity** /thúrmō pla stíssəti/ *n*

Thermopylae /thə móppəli/ pass in ancient Greece, northwest of Athens, that was the site of a major battle between the Greeks and Persians in 480 BC

thermoreceptor /thúrmō ri séptər/ *n* a sensory receptor, usually a nerve ending in the skin, that is stimulated by heat or cold

thermoregulation /thúrmo réggyoo láysh'n/ *n* the maintenance of a particular body temperature regardless of changes in the environment —**thermoregulate** /thúrmo réggyoo layt/ *vi* —**thermoregulator** *n*

thermoremanent /thúrmō rémmənənt/ *adj* describes the permanent magnetism molten rock acquires from the Earth's magnetic field as it cools and hardens

Thermos /thúrməss/ *tdmk* a trademark for an insulated or vacuum container used to hold a liquid and maintain it at a constant temperature

thermoscope /thúrməskōp/ *n* an instrument that measures changes in temperature by their effects on a substance, e.g. the change in volume of a gas —**thermoscopic** /thúrmə skóppik/ *adj* —**thermoscopical** *adj* —**thermoscopically** *adv*

thermosetting /thúrmō seting/ *adj* describes a plastic that sets permanently when heated

thermosphere /thúrmə sfeer/ *n* the region of the atmosphere above the mesosphere in which temperature steadily increases with height, beginning at about 85 km/53 mi. above the earth's surface

thermostable /thúrmō stáyb'l/ *adj* describes substances such as some toxins that are able to withstand heat without being destroyed or altered —**thermostability** /thúrmō stə bílləti/ *n*

thermostat /thúrmə stat/ *n* **1** a device that regulates temperature by means of a temperature sensor, e.g. a bimetallic strip. Thermostats are used in vehicle engines and domestic heating systems. **2** a device that activates a mechanism or system, e.g. a fire alarm or a sprinkler system, in response to a change in temperature —**thermostatic** /thúrmə státtik/ *adj* —**thermostatically** *adv*

thermotaxis /thúrmə táksiss/ *n* movement of a living organism towards or away from a heat source —**thermotactic** *adj* —**thermotaxic** *adj*

thermotherapy /thúrmō thérrəpi/ (*plural* **-pies**) *n* the use of heat to alleviate pain and stiffness, especially in joints and muscles, and to increase circulation

thermotropism /thúrmō trṓpizəm/ *n* the movement of a plant part towards or away from a source of heat —**thermotropic** /-trṓpik, -tróppik/ *adj*

-thermy *suffix* heat ○ *diathermy* [Via modern Latin *-thermia* < Greek *thermē* 'heat']

theropod /thééra pod/ *n* any carnivorous dinosaur with strong hind legs and short front limbs. Tyrannosaurs and megalosaurs are theropods. Suborder: Theropoda. [Early 20C. < modern Latin *Theropoda* < Greek *thēr* 'wild animal' + *pod-* 'foot'.] —**theropodan** /thi róppədən/ *adj*

Theroux /thə roó/, **Paul** (*b.* 1941) US writer

~~**thesarus**~~ incorrect spelling of **thesaurus**

thesaurus /thə sáwrəss/ (*plural* **-ri** /-rī/ *or* **-ruses**) *n* **1 BOOK OF WORD GROUPS** a book that lists words related to each other in meaning, usually giving synonyms and antonyms **2 BOOK OF SPECIALIST VOCABULARY** a dictionary of words relating to a particular subject **3 TREASURY** a place in which valuable things are stored [Early 19C. Via Latin, 'treasury' < Greek *thēsauros* 'storehouse'.]

these /theez/ *pron, det* the form of 'this' used before a plural noun or with a multiple referent ○ (pron) *These are the people I was telling you about.* ○ (det) *These delays, along with the paperwork demanded by government, can be costly for banks.* [Old English *þæs, þās*, plural of *þes* (see THIS)]

Theseus /théessi əss, théesyooss/ *n* in Greek mythology, a hero who performed many brave deeds, including slaying the Minotaur, defeating the Amazons, and descending into Hades to rescue Persephone

thesis /théesiss/ (*plural* **-ses** /-seez/) *n* **1 LENGTHY ACADEMIC PAPER** a dissertation based on original research, especially as work towards an academic degree **2 PROPOSITION** a proposition advanced as an argument **3 STATEMENT** an unproved statement, especially one serving as a premise in an argument **4 ESSAY SUBJECT** a subject for an essay **5 DOWNBEAT** the downbeat of a bar of music **6 STRESSED SYLLABLE** a long syllable, on which the stress naturally falls, in classical Greek and Latin poetry. ◊ **arsis** *n.* 1 **7 UNSTRESSED SYLLABLE** a short unstressed syllable in modern accentual poetry. ◊ **arsis** *n.* 2 **8 FIRST STAGE OF DIALECTIC** the first of three stages in Hegelian dialectic [14C. Via Latin < Greek, 'proposition, stressed beat'.]

thespian /théspi ən/ *n* an actor or actress ■ *adj* relating to the ancient Greek poet Thespis [Early 19C. < *Thespis*, Greek poet (6C BC), regarded as the father of Greek tragedy.]

Thess. *abbr* Thessalonians

Thessalonian /théssa lṓni ən/ *n* a person who came from the ancient Greek city of Thessaloníki —**Thessalonian** *adj*

Thessalonians *n* either of two letters written to the Christians of Thessaloníki by the Apostle Paul, included as books of the Christian Bible (+ *singular verb*)

Thessaloníki /théssələ neéki/ city in NE Greece. Population: 377,951 (1991).

Thessaly /théssəli/ region in north-central Greece. Area: 13,940 sq. km/5,382 sq. mi. —**Thessalian** *n, adj*

theta /théetə/ *n* the eighth letter of the Greek alphabet [Early 17C. < Greek, < Phoenician.]

theta rhythm, theta wave *n* a pattern of brain waves with a frequency between 4 and 7 Hz seen on an electroencephalogram

Thetford /thétfərd/ town in E England. Population: 20,058 (1991).

thetic /théttik/, **thetical** /théttik'l/ *adj* **1** relating to or having stress in classical poetry **2** imposed arbitrarily [Late 17C. < Greek *thetikos* < *thetos* 'placed, stressed' < *tithenai* 'to place'.] —**thetically** *adv*

theurgy /theé urji/ *n* **1 SUPERNATURAL OR DIVINE INTERVENTION** intervention of supernatural or divine powers in human affairs **2 PERSUADING THE SUPERNATURAL TO INTERVENE** the art of securing the intervention of supernatural or divine powers in human affairs **3 MAGIC PERFORMED FOR GOOD** magic with the help of benevolent spirits, as practised by neo-Platonists [Mid-16C. Via late Latin *theurgia* < Greek *theourgia* 'ritual, mystery' < *theos* 'god' + *ergon* 'work'.] —**theurgic** /thi úrjik/ *adj* —**theurgically** *adv* —**theurgist** /theé urjist/ *n*

thew /thyoo/ *n* muscle or muscular strength (*archaic; often plural*) [Old English *þēaw* 'custom, habit' < Indo-European, 'to watch'] —**thewy** *adj*

they /thay/ *pron* **1** used to refer to people in general when making statements about the things people do, think, or say ○ *As people and businesses move out of inner cities, bank branches follow, they say.* **2** ⚠ used instead of 'he' or 'she' to refer to a person without specifying gender (*informal*) ○ *A friend phoned the other day and they told me what you had said.* [12C. Old Norse *þeir*.]

USAGE Because English does not have a gender-neutral third person singular pronoun that can be used to refer to people, ***they***, together with associated words such as *their*, is often used in this role and is a revival of an older use that was once well established in English. In more formal contexts, and when the individuality of the subject is significant, it is necessary to use *he or she*, but this phrase is too cumbersome to provide a solution in informal conversational usage, e.g. *Everyone taking the test should do the best they can.* A way of avoiding the need to use ***he*** or ***she*** in writing can be to use a plural: *Students taking the test should do the best they can.*

they'd /thayd/ *contr* **1** a short form of 'they had' **2** a short form of 'they would'

they'll /thayl/ *contr* **1** a short form of 'they will' **2** a short form of 'they shall'

they're /thair/ *contr* they are

USAGE See ***their***.

they've /thayv/ *contr* a short form of 'they have'

THI *abbr* temperature-humidity index

thi- *prefix* = **thio-** (*before vowels*)

thiabendazole /thī ə béndəzōl/ *n* $C_{10}H_7N_3S$ a white compound. Use: treatment of parasitic worm infestations, fungal infections. [Mid-20C. Contraction of THIAZOLE + BENZENE + IMIDAZOLE.]

thiamine /thī əmeen, -əmin/, **thiamin** /thī əmin/ *n* a B vitamin that plays a role in carbohydrate metabolism. Source: grains, meat, yeasts. [Mid-20C. < THIO- + AMINE.]

thiazide /thī ə zīd/ *n* one of a group of compounds that inhibit the reabsorption of sodium and increase the release of calcium by the kidneys, promoting greater water excretion. Use: diuretic, treatment of high blood pressure. [Mid-20C. < THIO- + AZINE + OXIDE.]

thiazine /thī ə zeen/ *n* any organic compound containing a ring composed of four carbon atoms, a sulphur atom, and a nitrogen atom. Use: dyes, tranquillizers. [Early 20C. < THIO- + AZINE.]

thiazole /thī ə zōl/, **thiazol** /thīəzol/ *n* **1** C_3H_3NS a volatile colourless liquid with a sharp odour. Use: dyes, fungicides. **2** any compound derived from thiazole. Use: dyes, fungicides, chemical-reaction accelerators. [Late 19C. < THIO- + AZOLE.]

thick /thik/ *adj* **1 DEEP OR BROAD** of relatively large extent from surface to surface or side to side ○ *a thick carpet* ○ *The child wrote her name in thick capital letters.* **2 LARGE IN DIAMETER** having a large diameter ○ *a thick cable* **3 OF STATED DEPTH OR BREADTH** having a specified depth or breadth ○ *a wall two feet thick* **4 VISCOUS** having a liquid consistency that is not free-flowing ○ *thick paint* **5 DENSE** composed of many densely packed objects ○ *a thick forest* ○ *thick hair* **6 OF HEAVY FABRIC** made of thick material ○ *thick socks* **7 FILLED** densely covered or filled ○ *The air was thick with mosquitoes.* **8 HARD TO SEE THROUGH** permitting little or no light to enter ○ *a thick mist* **9 PRONOUNCED** readily noticeable or distinct ○ *a thick country accent* **10 SLOW TO LEARN OR UNDERSTAND** lacking the ability to learn and understand quickly (*informal insult*) **11 NOT CLEAR** not articulating words clearly ○ *a voice thick with emotion* **12 FRIENDLY** allied in a close relationship (*informal*) ○ *They seem very thick with each other.* **13 PREVENTING CLEAR THOUGHT** feeling numb and not conducive to clear thought or perception, e.g. because of a cold or a hangover (*informal*) ○ *woke up with a thick head* ■ *adv* **MAKING DEEP LAYER** in a way that produces something deep, broad, or dense ■ *n* **1 MOST ACTIVE PART** the most intense, crowded, or busiest part of something ○ *in the thick of the battle* **2 DENSEST PART** the part of something with the greatest depth, density, or breadth ○ *in the thick of the jungle* [Old English *þicce* < Germanic] —**thickly** *adv* ◇ **be a bit thick** to go beyond what is fair or reasonable (*informal*) ○ *It's a bit thick, expecting me to look after the baby for nothing.* ◇ **thick and fast** in large numbers and with great frequency ◇ **through thick and thin** no matter what might happen

thicken /thíkən/ *v* **1** *vti* to become thick or thicker or to make something thick or thicker **2** *vi* to become more complicated or puzzling —**thickener** *n* —**thickening** *n*

thicket /thíkit/ *n* a dense or tangled growth of small trees or bushes

thickfilm technology /thík film-/ *n* a method of fabricating electronic circuitry in which a glaze is printed onto a glass or ceramic support, then wiring and components such as microchips are added. ◊ **thinfilm technology**

thickhead /thík hed/ *n* an offensive term that deliberately insults somebody's intelligence (*slang insult*) —**thickheaded** /thík héddid/ *adj* —**thickheadedness** *n*

thickie /thíki/, **thicky** (*plural* **-ies**) *n* an offensive term that deliberately insults somebody's intelligence (*slang insult*)

thick-knee *n* a large long-legged shore bird with distinctive enlarged knee joints. Native to: mainly semidesert regions. Family: Burhinidae. ◊ **stone curlew**

thickness /thíknəss/ *n* **1 THICK QUALITY** the quality or state of being thick **2 DIMENSION** the dimension between two surfaces of an object, especially the shortest dimension as opposed to the width or the length **3 LAYER** an individual layer **4 THICK PART** a part of something that is thick

thicko /thíkō/ (*plural* **-os**) *n* an offensive term that deliberately insults somebody's intelligence (*slang insult*)

thickset /thík sét/ *adj* **1** with a stocky physique **2** growing closely together

thick-skinned *adj* **1** insensitive to other people's feelings or circumstances **2** not easily offended by criticism or insults

thick-witted *adj* regarded as lacking intelligence (*insult*) —**thick-wittedly** *adv* —**thick-wittedness** *n*

thicky *n* = **thickie**

thief /theef/ (*plural* **thieves** /theevz/) *n* a person who steals something, especially one who intends to escape notice [Old English *þēof* < Germanic] —**thievish** *adj* —**thievishly** *adv* —**thievishness** *n*

thief ant *n* any small ant that pillages the colonies of other ants, taking food stores and even the young of the colony

Thiele /teéli/, **Colin Milton** (*b.* 1920) Australian writer

~~**thier**~~ incorrect spelling of **their**

thieve /theev/ (**thieves, thieving, thieved**) *vti* to steal things [Old English *þēofian* < *þēof* 'thief'] —**thievery** (*plural* **-ries**) *n*

thigh /thī/ *n* **1** the top of the leg between the knee and the hip **2** the part of an animal's leg that corresponds to the human thigh [Old English *þēoh* < Indo-European, 'to swell']

thighbone /thíbōn/ *n* ANAT = **femur** *n.* 1

thigmotaxis /thígmo táksiss/ *n* movement of a cell or organism in response to a touch stimulus from a specific direction, e.g. contact with a surface. US term **stereotaxis** [Early 20C. < Greek *thigma* 'touch'.] —**thigmotactic** *adj* —**thigmotactically** *adv*

thigmotropism /thig móttrəpizəm/ *n* a directional growth movement (**tropism**) of a plant part, especially a tendril, in response to physical contact with a surface [Early 20C. < Greek *thigma* 'touch'.] —**thigmotropic** /-trṓpik, -tróppik/ *adj*

thill /thil/ *n* one of the two shafts of a carriage or cart [15C. < ?]

thimble /thímb'l/ *n* **1 COVER FOR FINGER WHEN SEWING** a small protective cap for a finger, used to push a needle through fabric **2 RING PROTECTING LOOP FROM WEAR** a metal ring, concave on the outside, that fits into a loop in a rope or an eye in a sail **3 METAL SLEEVE** any small metal tube or sleeve used in machinery [Old English *þȳmel* 'leather thumb protector' < *þūma* (see THUMB)]

thimbleberry /thímb'l beri/ (*plural* **-ries**) *n* **1** a red or dark-purple thimble-shaped raspberry **2** a bush that bears thimbleberries. Native to: North America. *Rubus parviflorus, Rubus occidentalis*, and *Rubus odoratus*.

thimbleful /thímb'lfŏŏl/ *n* a very small amount of liquid

thimblerig /thímb'lrig/ *n* **1 GUESSING GAME USING TRICKERY** a trick in which a participant guesses which of three cups covers an object after somebody has moved them about using sleight of hand to change the object's location **2** *US* **SOMEBODY MOVING CUP** somebody moving the cup in thimblerig ■ *vt* (**-rigs, -rigging, -rigged**) **SWINDLE** to cheat or swindle somebody —**thimblerigger** *n*

Thimbu = **Thimphu**

thimerosal /thī mérrə sal/ *n* $C_9H_9HgNaO_2S$ a cream-coloured mercury compound. Use: local antiseptic. [Mid-20C. Probably contraction of THIO- + MERCURY SALICYLATE.]

Thimphu /thímfoo/, **Thimbu** /thímboo/ capital of Bhutan, in the western part of the country. Population: 30,340 (1993).

thin /thin/ *adj* (**thinner, thinnest**) **1 SHALLOW OR NARROW** of relatively small extent from surface to surface or side to side ○ *A thin layer of snow covered the path.* ○ *Draw a thin line.* **2 OF SMALL DIAMETER** having a small diameter ○ *thin wire* **3 SLIM** with little body fat **4 SPARSE** composed of few things widely spaced ○ *thin hair* ○ *a thin forest* **5 WATERY** with a free-flowing consistency similar to that of water ○ *a thin soup* ○ *thin paint* **6 LIGHTWEIGHT** made of light or flimsy material ○ *a thin summer dress* ○ *thin cotton socks* **7 EASY TO SEE THROUGH** permitting light to enter or pass through ○ *thin mist* **8 QUIET** lacking volume or resonance ○ *a thin sound* **9** *US* **WEAK** lacking intensity or colour **10 UNCONVINCING** lacking credibility or adequacy ○ *a thin excuse* **11 LACKING CONTRAST** of a photographic negative, lacking density or contrast ■ *adv* **MAKING THIN LAYER** in a way that produces something shallow, narrow, or sparse ○ *Spread the paint thin.* ■ *vti* (**thins, thinning, thinned**) **MAKE OR BECOME THINNER** to reduce something in thickness or number or to become reduced in thickness or number ○ *You can thin down the paint before you use it.* ○ *The crowd started to thin out in the evening.* [Old English *þynne* < Indo-European, 'stretch'] —**thinly** *adv* —**thinness** *n*

SYNONYMS ***thin, lean, slim, slender, emaciated, scraggy, scrawny, skinny***
CORE MEANING: without much flesh, the opposite of fat
thin having little body fat; **lean** muscular and fit-looking, without excess fat; **slim** pleasingly thin and well-proportioned; **slender** gracefully and attractively thin; **emaciated** unhealthily thin, usually because of illness or starvation; **scraggy** or **scrawny** unpleasantly or unhealthily thin and bony; **skinny** extremely thin.

thine /thīn/ *pron, det* belonging to or associated with you, when 'you' is singular (*archaic; before vowels*) ○ (pron) *Thine is the womb where our riches have birth.* ○ (det) *Know thine enemy.* [Old English *þīn*, possessive form of *þū* (see THOU[2])]

thinfilm technology /thín film-/ *n* a method of fabricating electronic circuitry in which a thin layer of semiconductor is applied to a glass or ceramic support, then wiring and passive components, e.g. resistors, are added. ◊ **thickfilm technology**

thing /thing/ *n* **1 OBJECT** an inanimate object ○ *What's that thing over there?* **2 UNSPECIFIED ITEM** an unnamed or unspecified object ○ *I need a few things in town.* **3 OCCURRENCE** something that occurs or something that is done ○ *The fire was a terrible thing.* **4 WORD OR THOUGHT** a thought or an utterance ○ *Don't say another thing!* **5 DETAIL** a piece of information ○ *You forgot one important thing.* **6 AIM** the objective of an action ○ *The thing is to win.* **7 CONCERN** a matter of responsibility or concern ○ *I have several things to do.* **8 DEED** an act or deed ○ *She promises to do great things.* **9 LIVING CREATURE** a person or animal, often spoken of affectionately ○ *The poor thing was soaked to the bone.* **10 GARMENT** an article of clothing ○ *This old thing?* **11 PREFERRED ACTIVITY** a favourite activity or special interest (*informal*) ○ *Golf's not really my thing.* **12 SOMETHING THAT CAN BE POSSESSED** an object or right that can be possessed or owned **13 FASHION** the fashion (*informal*) ○ *When we were young, we considered it the latest thing.* **14 STRONG LIKE OR DISLIKE** a particularly strong feeling of attraction or repulsion (*informal*) ○ *He's got a thing about spiders.* **15 IDEAL** something that is needed or desirable (*informal*) ○ *Iced tea would be just the thing.* ■ **things** *npl* **1 BELONGINGS** personal items owned or carried ○ *You can leave your things in my room.* **2 APPARATUS** equipment for a particular activity ○ *a drawer for all my writing things* **3 AFFAIRS** general matters or circumstances ○ *How are things today?* [Old English *þing* 'assembly' < Germanic, 'time'] ◇ **all** *or* **other things being equal** in a situation in which there is little difference between two or more people or things ○ *Other things being equal, I would choose the cheaper holiday.* ◇ **be on to a good thing** to be in an advantageous or desirable situation ◇ **it comes to the same thing** it has the same result ◇ **make a (big) thing of something** to exaggerate the importance of something and make a fuss about it

thingamabob /thíngəmə bob/, **thingumabob** *n* a word used when the proper word for something is not known or does not come to mind [Mid-18C. Alteration of *thingumbob* < obsolete *thingum* (see THINGUMMY).]

thingamajig /thíngəməjig/, **thingumajig, thingummy** /thíngəmi/ (*plural* **-mies**), **thingy** /thíngi/ (*plural* **-ies**) *n* a word used when the proper word for something is not known or does not come to mind (*informal*) [Early 19C. < obsolete *thingum* (see THINGUMMY).]

thing-in-itself (*plural* **things-in-themselves**) *n* an object that exists even though we have no experience or perception of it [Translation of German *Ding an sich*]

thingness /thíngnəss/ *n* status as a material thing, as distinct from something that is abstract

thingumabob *n* = **thingamajig**

thingumajig *n* = **thingamajig**

thingummy *n* = **thingamajig** [Late 18C. Alteration of obsolete *thingum* < THING.]

thingy *n* = **thingamajig**

think /thingk/ *v* (**thinks, thinking, thought, thought** /thawt/) **1** *vti* **FORM THOUGHTS** to use the mind to consider ideas and make judgments ○ *Think carefully before you start writing.* **2** *vt* **HAVE AS AN OPINION** to believe something or have something as an opinion ○ *I don't think it will rain today.* ○ *She seems to think she's a good dancer.* **3** *vti* **HAVE IN MIND** to bring something to mind ○ *I can't think what the date is today.* ○ *I hadn't thought about him for months.* **4** *vti* **COMPREHEND** to imagine or understand something or the possibility of something ○ *I can't think of letting you leave so soon.* **5** *vt* **CONCENTRATE ON** to focus the attention on something ○ *He thinks golf day and night.* **6** *vi* **HAVE REGARD** to regard somebody with care or concern ○ *You need to think of your family.* **7** *vt* **VIEW IN CERTAIN WAY** to regard somebody or something in a specified way ○ *Don't think me unkind.* **8** *vti* **INTEND** to have something as a plan ○ *She thought she'd go out after dinner.* **9** *vt* **FORESEE** to anticipate something happening ○ *I didn't think he'd actually do it.* **10** *vt* **BE HEEDFUL OF** to be attentive or considerate enough to do something ○ *Didn't you think to ask about her mother?* **11** *vi* **CHOOSE** to make a mental choice ○ *Think of a card and I'll try to guess what it is.* **12** *vt* **INFLUENCE WITH THE MIND** to bring something to a particular condition using the mind ○ *Try to think the pain away.* ■ *n* **SPELL OF THINKING** an act of thinking or a period of time spent thinking (*informal*) ○ *She sat down to have a think.* [Old English *þencan* < Indo-European] —**thinkable** *adj* —**thinkably** *adv* —**thinker** *n* ◇ **have got another think coming** used to say that somebody is mistaken (*informal*) ○ *If he thinks I'm going to help him he's got another think coming.* ◇ **I don't think** used to indicate that the opposite is true (*informal*) ○ *You can rely on him to be generous – I don't think!* ◇ **not think much of somebody** *or* **something** to regard somebody or something as not being very good ◇ **think better of something** to change your mind and decide not to do something ○ *She was about to speak her mind, but then thought better of it.* ◇ **think nothing of something** to regard something as not being unusual ○ *She thinks nothing of working all night to finish a project.* ◇ **think twice** to consider something very carefully ○ *You should think twice about lending them so much money.*

think out *vt* to consider something carefully, taking account of possible problems or consequences ○ *He hadn't really thought the policy out properly.*

think over *vt* to reflect on something ○ *Maybe you'd like to think it over before you sign.*

think through *vt* to consider or reflect on something carefully, especially in order to reach a decision ○ *I needed some time to think it through.*

think up *vt* to invent or devise something ○ *I've thought up an easy way to do it.*

thinking /thíngking/ *adj* **RATIONAL** capable of using the mind to reason or reflect ○ *the thinking person's choice* ■ *n* **1 FORMING OF THOUGHTS** use of the mind to form thoughts ○ *There's a lot of thinking to do before we make that decision.* **2 JUDGMENT** opinions or conclusions arrived at ○ *What's your thinking on the political situation?*

thinking cap ◇ **put your thinking cap on** to think carefully about something, especially to find a solution to a problem

think piece *n* an article giving somebody's analysis or opinion of a situation or event, written to provoke thought

think-tank *n* a committee of experts that undertakes research or gives advice, especially to a government

thinner /thínnər/ *n* a liquid used to dilute paint or varnish. Turpentine is a thinner.

thin-skinned *adj* **1** easily offended by criticism or insults **2** covered in a thin peel or rind

thio- *prefix* containing sulphur ○ *thiophene* [< Greek *theion* 'sulphur']

thiocarbamide /thí ō kaárbə mīd/ *n* CHEM = **thiourea**

thiocyanate /thí ō sí ə nayt/ *n* a salt or ester of thiocyanic acid

thiocyanic acid /thí ō sī ánnik-/ *n* **HSCN** an unstable colourless liquid. Use: as salts or esters in insecticides.

thiol /thí ol/ *n* an organic compound similar to an alcohol but in which the oxygen atom has been replaced by a sulphur atom

thionic /thī ónnik/ *adj* relating to or containing sulphur [Late 19C. < Greek *theion* 'sulphur'.]

thionyl /thí ənil/ *n* containing the chemical group SO [Mid-19C. < Greek *theion* 'sulphur'.]

thiopentone sodium /thí ə pén tōn-/, **thiopental sodium** /-t'l-/ *n* $C_{11}H_{17}N_2O_2SNa$ a fast-acting barbiturate. Use: general anaesthetic, hypnotic.

thiophen /thí ə fen/, **thiophene** /-feen/ *n* C_4H_4S a colourless liquid with a faint odour of benzene. Use: solvent, manufacture of dyes, resins, pharmaceuticals. [Late 19C. < THIO- + PHENO-.]

thiophene *n* CHEM = **thiophen**

thiosulphate /thí ō súl fayt/ *n* a salt or ester of thiosulphuric acid

thiosulphuric acid /thí ō sul fyóórik-/ *n* $H_2S_2O_3$ an unstable acid known only in the form of salts or esters or in solution

thiotepa /thí ō téépə/ *n* $C_6H_{12}N_3PS$ a compound used in the treatment of malignant tumours

thiouracil /thí ō yóórəssil/ *n* $C_4H_4N_2OS$ a bitter-tasting white crystalline compound. Use: treatment of hyperthyroidism.

thiourea /thí ō yoo rée ə, -yóóri ə/ *n* $CS(NH_2)_2$ a soluble crystalline substance. Use: manufacture of resins, photographic processes.

third /thurd/ *n* **1** see table at **number 2 ONE AFTER SECOND IN IMPORTANCE** somebody or something ranking next after second in authority or precedence **3 VEHICLE GEAR** in a motor vehicle, the forward gear between second and fourth **4 MUSICAL INTERVAL** in a standard musical scale, the interval between one note and another that lies two notes above or below it **5 MUSICAL NOTE A THIRD AWAY** in a standard musical scale, a note that is a third away from another **6 HARMONIC** a harmonic of a combination of two tones a third apart **7 UNIVERSITY DEGREE** the lowest class of honours degree awarded by a British university **8** BALLET = **third position** [Old English *þirdda, þridda* < Indo-European, 'three'] —**third** *adj, adv*

third class *n* **1 THIRD IN A CLASSIFICATION SYSTEM** the next below second in grade or category **2 CHEAPEST ACCOMMODATION** formerly, the least expensive and least luxurious accommodation on a ship or train **3 EXAMINATION DIVISION** the third highest division in an examination. For British honours degrees, third class is the lowest class. **4 MAIL CLASS** a class of mail in the United States and Canada for unsealed printed matter —**third-class** *adj, adv*

third degree *n* intensive interrogation, often also implying rough treatment (*informal*) ○ *The interrogators gave the suspects the third degree.* [< the interrogation required to reach the 'third degree', the highest rank in Freemasonry]

third-degree burn *n* a burn of the most serious kind, in which the skin and the tissues beneath it are severely damaged

third dimension *n* **1** the added dimension of depth that distinguishes a solid object from one that is two-dimensional or planar **2** a quality that makes something more vivid —**third-dimensional** *adj*

third estate *n* the third social class, traditionally the commons, in a society divided into estates

third eyelid *n* ZOOL = **nictitating membrane**

third force *n* a group that mediates between two opposing political groups or parties

thirdhand /thúrd hánd/ *adj, adv* **1** used by, or after having been used by, two previous owners **2** from or through two intermediate sources

thirdly /thúrdli/ *adv* used to introduce the third point in an argument or discussion

third man *n* **1** in cricket, a deep fielder on the off side behind the slips **2** the position played by a third man

third market *n* a market on the London Stock Exchange trading in the shares of companies not on the main market or the Unlisted Securities Market, e.g. new or small companies

third party *n* a person who is involved in a legal matter but not as a principal party ○ *The signatures need to be witnessed by a third party.* ○ *third-party motor-vehicle insurance*

third person *n* **1 VERB OR PRONOUN FORM** the form of a verb or a pronoun indicating somebody or something being spoken about. In English, the third-person singular subject pronouns are 'he', 'she', 'it', and 'one', and the third-person plural subject pronoun is 'they'. **2 SET OF GRAMMATICAL FORMS** the grammatical set containing the forms indicating the third person **3 WRITING IN THIRD PERSON** a style of writing using third-person forms ○ *Write your account in the third person.*

third position *n* a position in ballet in which the feet are turned outwards with the heel of the front foot touching the instep of the back foot

third rail *n* a rail from which some electrically powered trains pick up current

third-rate *adj* of a low or the lowest quality

third reading *n* the third presentation of a bill to a legislative assembly

Third Reich *n* the Nazi regime in Germany between 1933 and 1945

Third Republic *n* the French system of government set up after Napoleon III's reign

thirdstream /thúrd streem/ *n* music that draws from both classical music and jazz [Mid-20C. After MAINSTREAM.] —**third-stream** *adj*

Third World, third world *n* the nations outside the capitalist industrial nations of the First World and the industrialized Communist nations of the Second World, generally less economically advanced but with varied economies (*hyphenated before nouns*) [Translation of French *tiers monde*] —**Third Worlder** *n*

thirl /thurl/ *vt Scotland* to bind or subject somebody, e.g. to a lease [Mid-16C. Alteration of *thrill*, alteration of THRALL.]

Thirlmere, Lake /thúrl meer/ lake in NW England. Length: 5 km/3.25 mi.

thirst /thurst/ *n* **1 NEED FOR LIQUID** a desire or need to drink a liquid, or the feeling of dryness in the mouth and throat caused by a need for a liquid **2 CRAVING** a strong desire for something ○ *a thirst for knowledge* ■ *vi* **1 EXPERIENCE THIRST** to feel a thirst for a liquid **2 TO DESIRE** to desire something strongly ○ *thirsted for news of home* [Old English *þurst* < Indo-European, 'be dry'] —**thirster** *n*

thirst snake *n* a small non-poisonous snake with long needle-shaped teeth for preying on slugs and snails. Native to: Southeast Asia, tropical America. Genus: *Dipsas*.

thirsty /thúrsti/ (**-ier, -iest**) *adj* **1 NEEDING LIQUID** feeling the need to drink a liquid ○ *Gardening always makes me thirsty.* **2 LACKING WATER** having insufficient water, especially in the form of irrigation ○ *The land was thirsty for rain.* **3 DESIRING** having a strong desire or craving ○ *thirsty for companionship* **4 CAUSING THIRST** causing the need to drink a liquid (*informal*) ○ *thirsty work* —**thirstily** *adv* —**thirstiness** *n*

thirteen /thúr téen/ *n* see table at **number** [Old English *þrēotīne* < *þrēo* 'three' + *-tīne* 'ten']

thirteenth /thúr téenth/ *n* **1** see table at **number 2** the note an octave and a sixth above the principal note in a musical scale —**thirteenth** *adj, adv*

thirteenth chord *n* a complex musical chord that, in addition to a seventh, also contains the interval of a thirteenth

thirtieth /thúrti əth/ *n* see table at **number** —**thirtieth** *adj, adv*

thirty /thúrti/ *n* (*plural* **-ties**) **1** see table at **number 2 SCORE IN TENNIS** in a game of tennis, the score awarded to a player with a score of 15 on winning a further point ■ **thirties** *npl* **1 NUMBERS 30 TO 39** the numbers 30 to 39, particularly as a range of Fahrenheit temperatures ○ *in the low thirties* **2 YEARS FROM 30 TO 39** the years from 30 to 39 in a century or in somebody's life [Old English *þrītig* < Indo-European, 'three']

thirty-eight *n US* a handgun with a .38 calibre.

Thirty-nine Articles *npl* the basic teachings and beliefs of the Church of England, written in the 16th century and still the basis of its doctrines

thirty-second note *n US, Can* MUSIC = **demisemiquaver**

thirty-twomo /-tóomō/ (*plural* **thirty-twomos**) *n* **1** a size of page that is formed when a standard printing sheet is cut or folded into 32 leaves or 64 pages **2** a book made with thirty-twomo pages [Late 18C. Pronunciation of the printers' abbreviation *32mo.*]

this /thiss/ CORE MEANING: a grammatical word used to indicate somebody or something that has already been mentioned or identified or something that is understood by both the speaker and hearer ○ (det) *This book is brilliant.* ○ (det) *This holiday – how much is it going to cost?* ○ (pron) *Is this why you've been so happy lately?* ○ (pron) *I first encountered this while travelling abroad.*

1 *det, pron* **CLOSE BY** indicating somebody or something present or close by, especially as distinct from somebody or something further away, referred to as 'that' ○ (det) *I much prefer this painting to that one.* ○ (pron) *What's this?* **2** *det, pron* **INDICATING WORDS TO FOLLOW** used to indicate a phrase or statement about to be said ○ (det) *All I can say is this – he hadn't called by the time I left.* ○ (pron) *Hey, listen to this!* **3** *pron, det* **A STATED TIME** used to refer to a particular time in the past or present ○ (pron) *I expected him back before this.* ○ (det) *At this particular moment she felt she'd never experience such happiness again.* **4** *det* **NOT PREVIOUSLY MENTIONED** used to indicate somebody or something not previously mentioned, especially when telling a story to give a sense of immediacy (*informal*) ○ (det) *Then this woman came running up to me, shouting at the top of her voice.* **5** *adv* **TO THIS DEGREE** used to emphasize the degree of a feeling or quality ○ *I was this close to walking out.* [Old English *þis, þes* < Indo-European] ◇ **this and that** miscellaneous unimportant things

USAGE In formal writing, avoid using ***this*** as an intensifier modifying a noun, where the definite article *the* or the indefinite articles *a/an* are the appropriate choices. Avoid usages like these: *After the exam I had this terrifying thought that I had not answered the third essay question. You've just got to call this person in the main office to straighten out your scheduling problem. Suddenly this woman selling cosmetics appeared at my door.* Use instead *the terrifying thought; a person I know in the main office; a woman selling cosmetics.*

Thisbe /thízbi/ *n* ♦ **Pyramus and Thisbe**

thistle /thíss'l/ *n* **1** a plant with prickly stems and leaves. Flowers: dense, rounded, usually purple, flower heads surrounded by thorny bracts. Genera: *Carduus, Cirsium*, and *Onopordum*. **2** the representation of a thistle that is the national emblem of Scotland [Old English *þistel* < Germanic]

thistledown /thíss'l down/ *n* **1** the fluffy mass of hairs attached to the seeds of the mature flower head of a thistle **2** anything fine and silky that resembles thistledown, e.g. a baby's hair or a delicate fabric

thistly /thíss'li/ (**-lier, -liest**) *adj* **1** full or consisting of thistles **2** difficult to deal with

thither /thíthər/ *adv* to or in the direction of that place (*archaic formal*) ○ *'I will set thee on thy way to Benares, if thou goest thither, and tell thee what must be known by us'.* (Rudyard Kipling, *Kim*; 1901) [Old English *þider*, alteration (after *hider* 'hither') of *þæder* 'that place' < Germanic]

thitherward /thíthərwərd/ *adv* = **thither** *adv.*

thixotropic /thíksə tróppik/ *adj* becoming fluid when shaken or stirred and returning to a gel state when allowed to stand [Early 20C. < Greek *thixis* 'touch'.] —**thixotropy** /thik sóttrəpi/ *n*

tho' /thō/ *adv, conj* though (*informal or literary*)

~~**thoght**~~ incorrect spelling of **thought**

thole[1] /thōl/ *n* ROWING = **tholepin** [Old English *þol* < Indo-European, 'stick out']

thole[2] /thōl/ *vt Scotland, N England* to experience or bear something such as pain or grief patiently or uncomplainingly [Old English *þolian* < Indo-European, 'support, lift up']

tholepin /thōl pin/ *n* a small upright wooden peg in the side of a rowing boat, usually provided in pairs to support an oar and act as a pivot when the oar is used

tholos /thō loss/ (*plural* **-loi** /thō loy/) *n* an ancient Greek circular domed building, especially a Mycenaean dry-stone tomb [Mid-17C. < Greek.]

Thomas /tómməss/ *n* in the New Testament, one of the 12 apostles of Jesus Christ. His reluctance to recognize Jesus Christ's resurrection until he had seen and touched his wounds gave rise to the phrase 'doubting Thomas' (John 14:1–7, John 20:19–29).

Thomas (of Erceldoune) /tómməss/ (1220?–97?) Scottish poet and seer. Known as **Thomas the Rhymer**

Thomas, Dylan (1914–53) Welsh poet

Thomas à Kempis /-ə kémpiss/ (1379?–1471) German monk and writer. Born **Thomas Hemerken**

Thomism /tómizəm/ *n* the philosophical and theological doctrines of Thomas Aquinas, which formed the basis of medieval scholasticism [Early 18C. After St *Thomas* AQUINAS.] —**Thomist** *n, adj* —**Thomistic** /tō místik/ *adj* —**Thomistical** *adj*

Thompson /tómps'n/ main tributary of the Fraser River in S British Columbia, Canada. Length: 489 km/304 mi.

Thompson, Daley (*b.* 1958) British athlete. Born **Francis Morgan Thompson**

Thompson, Hunter S. (*b.* 1939) US journalist and writer

Thompson, Jack (*b.* 1940) Australian actor. Full name **John Payne Thompson**

Thompson submachine gun *n* a relatively lightweight submachine gun introduced in 1915. It was intended as an infantry weapon. [Early 20C. After the US manufacturing company.]

Thomson /tómssən/ river in SW Queensland, Australia. Length: 380 km/236 mi.

Thomson /tómss'n/, **Sir Joseph John** (1856–1940) British physicist

Thomson, Peter (*b.* 1929) Australian golfer

Thomson effect *n* the phenomenon of temperature differences within a conductor or semiconductor causing an electric potential gradient [Late 19C. After William *Thomson* (1st Baron KELVIN).]

Thomson's gazelle *n* a small gazelle that has a broad black stripe on its side. Native to: grasslands and dry woodlands of Africa. *Gazella thomsoni*. [Late 19C. After the Scottish explorer Joseph *Thomson* (1858–94).]

-thon *suffix* a long session devoted to a single activity ○ *talkathon* [< MARATHON]

thong /thong/ *n* **1 LONG THIN PIECE OF LEATHER** a thin strip of something, especially leather, used for fastening or supporting things **2 WHIP** a whip made of plaited leather, cord, or some other material **3 LIGHT SANDAL** a light sandal held on by strips of material that join the sole of the sandal at either side of the foot and between the first and second toes **4 BIKINI OR UNDERWEAR BOTTOM** a narrow piece of cloth or leather that goes between the legs and is attached to a band around the hips, worn as a bikini bottom or as underwear [Old English *þwong* < Germanic]

Thor /thawr/ *n* in Norse mythology, the god of thunder and eldest son of Odin

thoracentesis /tháwrə sen téesiss/ (*plural* **-ses** /-téeseez/) *n* a surgical procedure in which a needle is inserted through the chest wall in order to withdraw fluid, blood, or air [Mid-19C. < THORACO- + Greek *kentēsis* 'pricking' (< *kentein* 'to prick').]

thoraces plural of **thorax**

thoracic /thaw rássik/ *adj* involving or located in the chest —**thoracically** *adv*

thoracic duct *n* the main duct of the lymphatic system that drains lymph from smaller lymph vessels in the trunk and returns it to the bloodstream by emptying into a major vein

thoraco- *prefix* chest, thorax ○ *thoracolumbar* [< Greek *thōrak-*, stem of *thōrax*]

thoracolumbar /tháwrəkō lúmbər/ *adj* **1** describes the thoracic and lumbar areas of the body **2** including parts of and behind the vertebral column in the chest and lower back but excluding the pelvis

thoracotomy /tháwrə kóttəmi/ (*plural* **-mies**) *n* a surgical incision made in the chest wall

thorax /tháw raks/ (*plural* **-raxes** *or* **-races** /tháw rə seez/) *n* **1 UPPER PART OF TORSO** the part of the human body between the neck and abdomen, enclosed by the ribs and containing the heart and lungs **2 UPPER PART OF ANIMAL'S BODY** the area corresponding to the human thorax in other vertebrates **3 PART BETWEEN HEAD AND ABDOMEN** the middle division of the body of an insect, crustacean, or arachnid [14C. Via Latin < Greek *thōrax* 'chest, breastplate'.]

Thorburn /tháwr burn/, **Archibald** (1860–1935) British artist

Library of Congress

Henry David Thoreau

Thoreau /thawr ṓ, tháwr ō/, **Henry David** (1817–62) US essayist and philosopher

thoria /tháwri ə/ *n* CHEM = **thorium dioxide** [Mid-19C. < THORIUM, after MAGNESIA.]

thorianite /tháwri ə nīt/ *n* a rare black radioactive mineral that is an oxide of thorium mixed with rare-earth metals. Use: source of thorium and uranium. [Early 20C. < THORIA + -ITE[1].]

thorite /tháw rīt/ *n* a rare brown, black, or yellow radioactive thorium silicate mineral. Use: source of thorium. [Mid-19C. < THOR.]

thorium /tháwri əm/ *n* (*symbol* **Th**) a soft silvery-white radioactive metallic element. Source: thorite, thorianite. Use: alloys, source of nuclear energy. [Mid-19C. < THOR.] —**thoric** *adj*

thorium dioxide *n* ThO_2 an insoluble white powder. Use: catalyst, manufacture of gas mantles, refractories, ceramics, optical glass.

thorium series *n* one of the natural radioactive decay series that shows how the unstable isotope thorium-232 changes by stages into the stable isotope lead-208

thorn /thawrn/ *n* **1 SHARP POINT ON A PLANT STEM** a sharply pointed woody growth projecting from the stem of some trees, shrubs, and woody plants **2 PLANT WITH THORNS** a tree, shrub, or woody plant that has thorns **3 WOOD OF TREE WITH THORNS** the wood of a tree or shrub with thorns **4 RUNIC LETTER** a runic letter used to represent both of the 'th' sounds, as in 'this' and 'thick', in Old English and Middle English [Old English *þorn* < Germanic] —**thornless** *adj* ◇ **be a thorn in (somebody's) flesh** *or* **side** to be a source of constant irritation to somebody

thorn apple *n* a tall poisonous weed with foul-smelling foliage and spiny capsule fruits. Flowers: large, trumpet-shaped, white or purple. *Datura stramonium*. US term **jimsonweed**

thornback /tháwrn bak/ (*plural* **-backs** *or* **-back**) *n* a ray with one to three rows of large hooked spines on its back. *Raja clavata* and *Platyrhinoidis triseriatis*.

thornbill /tháwrn bil/ (*plural* **-bills** *or* **-bill**) *n* **1** a small bird of the warbler family with a short sharp bill. Native to: Australia. Genus: *Acanthiza*. **2** a hummingbird with a bill that resembles a thorn. Native to: South America. *Ramphomicron microrhynchum*.

Thorndike /tháwrn dīk/, **Dame Sybil** (1882–1976) British actor

Thornhill /tháwrn hil/, **Sir James** (1675–1734) British painter

thorny /tháwrni/ (**-ier, -iest**) *adj* **1** complicated and difficult to resolve **2** covered in or full of thorns —**thornily** *adv* —**thorniness** *n*

thorny devil *n Aus* ZOOL = **moloch**

thoron /tháw ron/ *n* a radioactive isotope of radon with a half-life of 55 seconds, formed by the radioactive decay of thorium [Early 20C. < THORIUM, after RADON.]

thorough /thúrrə/ *adj* **1 EXTREMELY CAREFUL** extremely careful and accurate in doing something ○ *She's very thorough in her research methods.* **2 DONE FULLY** complete in every detail and carried out with care ○ *The doctor gave me a thorough examination.* **3 ABSOLUTE** that is so to the fullest extent or in the truest sense of the word ○ *a thorough bore* [Old English *þuruh* 'from end to end', variant of *þurh* (see THROUGH)] —**thoroughly** *adv* —**thoroughness** *n*

SYNONYMS See ***careful***.

thoroughbass /thúrrə bayss/ *n* MUSIC = **continuo** [Mid-17C. < THOROUGH 'all the way through'.]

thorough brace *n US* a strong leather strap running underneath a carriage from front to back, forming, with several other such straps, the carriage's support and springs [< THOROUGH 'from end to end'] —**thorough-braced** *adj*

thoroughbred /thúrrə bred/ *n* **1 PUREBRED ANIMAL** a purebred animal, especially a horse **2 ARISTOCRAT** somebody descended from ancestors of high social status ■ *adj* **1 PUREBRED** bred from pure stock **2 OF AN ARISTOCRATIC FAMILY** descended from ancestors of high social status [Early 18C. < THOROUGH 'all the way through'.]

Thoroughbred *n* a pure breed of horse descended from English mares and Arab stallions, originally bred in Britain and most often used for racing —**Thoroughbred** *adj*

thoroughfare /thúrrə fair/ *n* **1 PUBLIC ROAD** a public highway that passes through a place ○ *a lorry blocking a busy thoroughfare* **2 MEANS OF ACCESS** a way or passage from one place to another **3 RIGHT OF PASSAGE** the right to go from one place to another along a certain route **4 HEAVILY USED ROUTE** a stretch of road or water, or a pathway between two places, that is used by many people [14C. < THOROUGH 'from end to end' + obsolete *fare*, 'way, journey'.]

thoroughgoing /thúrrə gṓ ing/ *adj* **1** carried out in an extremely careful and thorough way ○ *not very thoroughgoing when it comes to housework* **2** that is so to the fullest extent or in the truest sense of the word ○ *a thoroughgoing pragmatist* [Early 19C. < THOROUGH 'all the way through'.]

thoroughpaced /thúrrə páysst/ *adj* describes a horse that is thoroughly trained so as to be able to perform all paces well

thoroughpin /thúrrə pin/ *n* inflammation and swelling above the hock joint on both sides of a horse's leg, affecting the flexor tendon and causing lameness [Late 18C. < THOROUGH 'all the way through'; from the appearance of the swelling, like a pin passing through the tendon.]

thorp /thawrp/, **thorpe** *n* a small village (*archaic; often in placenames*) [Old English *þorp* < Germanic]

those /thōz/ *pron, det* the form of 'that' used before a plural noun or with a multiple referent ○ *Those are the ones I prefer.* ○ *Do you remember those outings to the seaside?* [Old English *þās* (see THESE)]

Thoth /thoth/, **Thot** *n* in ancient Egyptian mythology, the god of the moon, associated with writing and wisdom. He is usually depicted as a man with the head of an ibis, or as a baboon. ➧ **Hermes Trismegistus**

thou[1] /thow/ (*plural* **thous** *or* **thou**) *n* **1** one thousandth of an inch **2** a thousand, especially when referring to money (*informal*) [Mid-19C. Shortening of THOUSAND.]

thou[2] /thow/ *pron* **1** you (*archaic or regional; in familiar address*) **2 thou, Thou** used to address God, e.g. in prayers and hymns [Old English *þū* < Indo-European]

though /thō/ *conj* **ALTHOUGH** in spite of the fact that ○ *He didn't receive any special treatment, even though he is close friends with the chairman.* ○ *Though she served as president of the student union, she was attracted to journalism rather than politics.* ■ *adv* **1 AND YET** indicating a statement that modifies a statement just made ○ *The weather has improved a lot, though it still doesn't feel like spring.* **2 NEVERTHELESS** follows a statement modifying the statement that preceded it ○ *It rained all the time. We still enjoyed ourselves, though.* [Old English *þeah* < Indo-European; partly < Old Norse *þó*]

USAGE See ***although***.

thought[1] /thawt/ *n* **1 THINKING** the activity or process of thinking ○ *deep in thought* **2 IDEA PRODUCED BY MENTAL ACTIVITY** an idea, plan, conception, or opinion produced by mental activity ○ *The thought had crossed my mind.* **3 SET OF IDEAS** the intellectual, scientific, and philosophical ideas associated with a particular place, time, or group ○ *medieval religious thought* **4 REASONING POWER** the ability to think and reason ○ *felt incapable of rational thought* **5 PROCESS OF CONSIDERING** the process of applying the mind to thinking about a particular person or subject ○ *I didn't give it another thought.* **6 INTENTION** an intention or desire to do something ○ *I had no thought of offending anybody.* **7 EXPECTATION** an expectation or hope that something will happen ○ *entertained no thoughts of failure* **8 COMPASSIONATE CONSIDERATION** a feeling of respect, affection, or consideration for somebody or something ○ *no thought for other people* **9 SMALL AMOUNT** a small amount on a comparative scale ○ *Could you be a thought quieter, please?* [Old English *þōht* < Germanic]

thought[2] past participle, past tense of **think**

thought disorder *n* disorder affecting the thought processes or the way they are composed or connected, e.g. delusions or an inability to concentrate or think clearly

thoughtful /tháwtf'l/ *adj* **1 CONSIDERATE** treating people in a kind and considerate way, especially by anticipating their wants or needs **2 PENSIVE** appearing to be deep in thought **3 CAREFULLY THOUGHT OUT** showing the application of careful thought —**thoughtfully** *adv* —**thoughtfulness** *n*

thoughtless /tháwtləss/ *adj* **1 INCONSIDERATE** showing a lack of consideration for other people or for consequences **2 DONE WITHOUT THOUGHT** showing a lack of planning or forethought **3 UNABLE TO THINK** not having or using the faculty of thought —**thoughtlessly** *adv* —**thoughtlessness** *n*

thought police *n* an oppressive and intrusive police force or similar group that tries to monitor and regulate people's thoughts in order to stamp out any original or potentially subversive ideas

thought-provoking *adj* interesting and causing somebody to engage in careful thought

thousand /thówz'nd/ (*plural* **-sand** *or* **-sands**) *n* **1** see table at **number** **2** the fourth digit to the left of the decimal point in the decimal number system **3** a very large number or amount (*informal*) ○ *must have told him a thousand times* [Old English *þūsend* < Germanic, 'swollen hundred'< Indo-European, 'to swell']

Thousand Guineas, 1,000 Guineas *n* a flat horse race for fillies run annually since 1814 at Newmarket, England (+ *singular verb*)

Thousand Island dressing *n* a salmon-pink salad dressing containing mayonnaise, tomato sauce, chopped gherkins, onions, and spices [Early 20C. < ?]

Thousand Islands /thówz'nd-/ group of more than 1,000 small islands in the St Lawrence River, between SE Ontario, Canada, and N New York State

thousandth /thówz'nth/ *n* see table at **number** —**thousandth** *adj*

~~**thousend**~~ incorrect spelling of **thousand**

Thrace /thrayss/ region in SE Europe, including parts of present-day Greece, Bulgaria, and Turkey. Area: 8578 sq. km/3,312 sq. mi. —**Thracian** *adj, n*

thrall /thrawl/ *n* **1 DOMINATION** a condition of being controlled by a more powerful person or force (*literary*) ○ *caught in the thrall of greed* **2 SOMEBODY WHOSE LIFE IS CONTROLLED** somebody whose life is completely controlled by a more powerful person or a moral or intellectual force **3 SOMEBODY CONTROLLED BY** a person who is controlled by a specific physical or mental need ○ *a thrall to alcohol* **4 ANCIENT SLAVE** a person of the lowest, and enslaved, class of ancient N Europe, particularly one held in bondage [Old English *þræl* < Old Norse *þræll* < Germanic, 'run'] —**thraldom** *n*

thrapple /thrápp'l/ *n Scotland* the human throat or windpipe ■ *vt* (**-ples, -pling, -pled**) *Scotland* to throttle somebody [14C]

thrash /thrash/ *v* **1** *vt* **BEAT PERSON OR ANIMAL** to beat a person or animal with a whip or stick **2** *vt* **DEFEAT PERSON OR TEAM DECISIVELY** to defeat a person or team decisively, especially in a sporting competition ○ *The home team got thrashed in the final.* **3** *vti* **TOSS ABOUT** to toss or move the body and limbs about in an uncontrolled or restless way ○ *thrashed around unable to sleep* **4** *vi* **PADDLE WITH LEGS** to move the legs up and down in the water while performing a swimming stroke **5** *vti* AGRIC = **thresh** *v.* 1 **6** *vti* **SAIL BOAT AGAINST TIDE OR WIND** to sail a boat so that it is forcing its way against the direction of the tide or wind ■ *n* **1 BEATING** a blow or beating with a whip or stick **2 SOCIAL PARTY** a party or celebration (*dated informal*) **3** MUSIC = **thrash metal** [Late 16C. Variant of THRESH.]

thrash out *vt* to discuss and develop all the possibilities of a situation in order to reach a decision about it. US term **hash out**

thrasher /thráshər/ *n* **1** a long-tailed brownish bird with a downward-curved bill and a speckled breast. Native to: North America. Genus: *Toxostoma*. **2** ZOOL = **thresher** *n*. **3 3** a person or machine that threshes crops

thrashing /thrάshing/ *n* **1** a physical beating, e.g. with a whip or stick **2** a decisive defeat in a sporting competition

thrash metal *n* a very fast, often discordant, type of heavy metal music, strongly influenced by punk

thrawn /thrawn/ *adj Scotland, N England* **1** stubborn and uncooperative or ill-tempered **2** twisted or crooked (*archaic*) [15C. < an archaic past participle of THROW.]

ϟ**thread** /thred/ *n* **1 FINE TWISTED CORD** fine cord made of two or more twisted fibres. Use: sewing, weaving. **2 PIECE OF THREAD** a length of thread **3 VERY THIN STRIP** a fine strand of solid material, trickle of liquid, or wisp of gas **4 RIDGE ON SCREW** the continuous helical ridge on a screw or pipe **5 FILAMENT OF SPIDER'S WEB** one of the filaments of a spider's web **6 SOMETHING CONNECTING ELEMENTS** a continuous unifying element running through a story, argument, discussion, or series of events **7 DISCUSSION ON INTERNET** a series of messages in an Internet discussion group (**forum**), commenting on or replying to a previous message **8 HUMAN LIFE** the course of human life, believed by the ancient Greeks to be spun, measured out, and cut by the Fates **9 VEIN OF ORE** a thin seam of ore or coal ■ **threads** *npl US* **CLOTHING** clothes (*slang*) ■ *v* **1** *vt* **PASS THROUGH** to pass something, e.g. thread, photographic film, magnetic tape, or ribbon through a hole or gap in something else **2** *vt* **STRING ON THREAD** to string beads or pearls on a thread **3** *vt* **INTERSPERSE** to distribute something at intervals in something else ○ *hair threaded with grey* **4** *vti* **GO CAREFULLY** to move along carefully, following a winding route ○ *We threaded our way through the crowded streets.* **5** *vt* **PRODUCE SCREW THREAD** to produce a thread on a screw or bolt, or within a material into which a bolt or screw may be inserted **6** *vi* **FORM THREAD** to form a fine thread when dropped from a spoon (*refers to sugar syrup*) [Old English *þrǣd* 'twisted cord' < Indo-European, 'to turn, twist'] —**thread-like** *adj* ◇ **lose the thread (of something)** to cease to follow or understand the connection between the parts of a story or argument

threadbare /thréd bair/ *adj* **1 WORN AWAY TO REVEAL THREADS** so heavily used that the soft part of the fabric has been worn away to reveal the threads beneath **2 OVERUSED SO NO LONGER CONVINCING** having been used so often as to be no longer convincing ○ *the same old threadbare excuses* **3 MEAGRE** not large, varied, or substantial enough to be satisfactory ○ *eked out a threadbare existence* **4 SHABBILY DRESSED** wearing worn-out shabby clothes —**threadbareness** *n*

threader /thréddər/ *n* a device for threading a needle, consisting of a loop of extremely fine wire attached to a flat metal disc that is held between the thumb and forefinger

threadfin /thréd fin/ (*plural* **-fins** *or* **-fin**) *n* a tropical marine fish with long rays resembling threads on the lower part of its pectoral fin. Family: Polynemidae.

thread mark *n* a strand of silk fibres put inside a paper banknote during manufacture to make it more difficult to counterfeit

thread snake *n* a small nonvenomous snake resembling a worm. Native to: Africa, Asia, Central and South America. Genus: *Leptotyphlops*.

threadworm /thréd wurm/ *n* a long nematode worm, such as a pinworm

thready /thréddi/ (**-ier, -iest**) *adj* **1 THREADLIKE** resembling thread **2 HAVING MANY THREADS** consisting of or containing many threads, especially loose or visible ones **3 FORMING THREADS** thick and sticky enough to form threads when dropped from a spoon or other utensil **4 SOUNDING WEAK** sounding thin and lacking in power and tone **5 ONLY JUST PERCEPTIBLE** describes a weak and barely perceptible pulse —**threadiness** *n*

threap /threep/, **threep** *vt Scotland, N England* **1** to scold or criticize somebody harshly **2** to state something vehemently or persistently, especially something that somebody else has contradicted [Old English *þrēapian* < ?] —**threaper** *n*

threat /thret/ *n* **1 DECLARATION OF INTENT TO CAUSE HARM** the expression of a deliberate intention to cause harm or pain **2 INDICATION OF SOMETHING BAD** a sign or danger that something undesirable is going to happen ○ *a threat of severe thunderstorms* **3 SOMEBODY OR SOMETHING LIKELY TO CAUSE HARM** a person, animal, or thing likely to cause harm or pain ○ *The dog is no threat.* [Old English *þrēat* 'crowd, menace' < Indo-European, 'press in']

threaten /thrétt'n/ *v* **1** *vti* **EXPRESS A THREAT TO** to express a deliberate intention to harm or hurt somebody unless the person does what is demanded **2** *vti* **ENDANGER WELLBEING** to be a threat to the wellbeing, safety, or happiness of somebody or something **3** *vti* **SIGNIFY SOMETHING BAD HAPPENING** to signify that something bad is going to happen, especially that bad weather is going to arrive **4** *vt* **SUGGEST IN A THREAT** to suggest or announce something by means of a threat [Old English *þrēatnian* 'press in on' < *þrēat* (see THREAT)] —**threatener** *n*

threatened /thrétt'nd/ *adj* describes an organism or species that is in danger of becoming extinct

threatening /thrétt'ning/ *adj* **1 EXPRESSING A THREAT** expressing an intention to cause somebody deliberate harm or pain **2** likely to bring rain or severe weather ○ *a threatening sky* **3 MAKING SOMEBODY FEEL ANXIOUS OR FEARFUL** causing somebody to feel anxious, fearful, and unconfident —**threateningly** *adv*

Thredbo /thrédbō/ ski resort in the Australian Alps, New South Wales, Australia. Population: 2,100 (1996).

three /three/ *n* see table at **number** [Old English *þrī*, *þrēotīne* < Indo-European] —**three** *adj*

three-card monte *n* a game in which three cards are dealt face up and then turned face down and moved round

three-card trick *n* a game in which three cards are dealt face up, and then turned face down and moved round

three-colour *adj* using, produced by, or relating to a colour printing process in which the print is produced by superimposing separate plates for the colours yellow, magenta, and cyan

three-D, 3-D *n* a three-dimensional effect ■ *adj* = **three-dimensional** *adj*. 1, **three-dimensional** *adj*. 2 (*informal*)

three-day event *n* a competition for horses and riders consisting of dressage, cross-country, and show-jumping events, held over a three-day period

three-day measles *n* rubella (*not in technical use*)

three-decker *n* **1 SOMETHING WITH THREE LEVELS** a vehicle, building, or other construction with three levels or floors **2 SHIP WITH THREE DECKS** a warship with three decks set with guns, or any ship with three decks **3 SANDWICH WITH THREE SLICES OF BREAD** a sandwich consisting of two layers of filling between three slices of bread

three-dimensional *adj* **1 WITH THREE DIMENSIONS** possessing or appearing to possess the dimensions of height, width, and depth **2 APPEARING TO HAVE DEPTH** creating the illusion of depth behind a flat surface **3 BELIEVABLE** represented with sufficient complexity to be convincing

three-field system *n* a system of crop rotation that was in operation in W Europe by the 9th century. One-third of land was left fallow, one-third planted in spring grains, and one-third in the season's crops such as barley and vegetables.

threefold /thrée fōld/ *adj* **1 CONSISTING OF THREE** made up of three parts or elements **2 THREE TIMES AS MANY OR MUCH** being or having three times as many or as much ■ *adv* **BY THREE TIMES** by three times as many or as much

Three Kings Islands group of uninhabited islands 50 km/31 mi. northwest of the North Island, New Zealand. The islands are a wildlife refuge. Area: 8 sq. km/3 sq. mi.

three-legged race *n* a race in which pairs of runners compete with their adjacent legs bound together

three-line whip *n* a notice, underlined three times for emphasis, issued to members of a political party requiring them to attend and vote in a specified way in a specified vote in the British Parliament

Three Mile Island /thrée mīl-/ island in the Susquehanna River in SE Pennsylvania, site of a major nuclear reactor accident in 1979

three-mile limit *n* the outer limit of a country's territorial waters, three nautical miles from shore

threep *vt N England, Scotland* = **threap**

threepence /thréppənss, thrúp-/, **thruppence** /thrúppənss, thrŏŏp-/ *n* a former British coin worth three old pennies

threepenny /thrépni, thrúp-/, **thruppenny** /thrúpni, thrŏŏp-/ *adj* (*dated*) **1** worth or costing three pennies, especially old pence **2** worth or costing very little

threepenny bit, thruppenny bit *n* a 12-sided former British coin worth three old pennies

three-phase *adj* **1** consisting of three separate phases **2** describes an electrical system or circuit of three alternating voltages that have the same frequency but are separated by one third of a cycle

three-piece *adj* consisting of three matching or coordinated pieces ■ *n* a suit consisting of matching trousers or skirt, waistcoat or blouse, and jacket

three-piece suite *n* a set of living-room furniture consisting of a sofa with two matching armchairs

three-ply *adj* **1 WITH THREE LAYERS** consisting of three layers or laminations **2 WITH THREE STRANDS** made up of three twisted strands ■ *n* **THREE-PLY KNITTING YARN** knitting yarn made up of three twisted strands

three-point landing *n* an aircraft landing in which the two main wheels of the landing gear and the nose or tail wheel touch the ground at the same time

three-point turn *n* a turn to reverse the direction of travel of a motor vehicle that involves two forward movements and one reverse movement

three-quarter *adj* **1 BEING THREE QUARTERS OF** being three quarters of something measurable or countable, e.g. length, an area, or a time interval **2 BEING THREE QUARTERS OF FULL LENGTH** being three quarters of the full or usual length **3 WITH FACE SLIGHTLY TURNED** showing the subject's face turned slightly to one side (*refers to a portrait*) ■ *n* **RUGBY PLAYER** a rugby player in one of the four positions between the forwards and the full back, or this position

three-quarter binding *n* bookbinding in which the spine and most of the sides of a book are covered in the same material

three-ring circus *n US* **1** a circus in which performances take place simultaneously in three separate rings **2** a situation full of activity and confusion (*informal*)

three Rs /-άarz/, **3 Rs** *npl* the skills of reading, writing, and arithmetic, considered as the basis of primary education [Presumed to have originated with a toast proposed by Sir William Curtis (1752–1829), illiterate Lord Mayor of London]

threescore /thrée skáwr/ *adj*, *n* sixty (*archaic*) ○ *threescore years and ten*

threesome /threéssəm/ *n* **1 GROUP OF THREE** a group of three people **2 ACTIVITY FOR THREE** a game or activity for three people **3 SEXUAL EXPERIENCE** a sexual experience involving three people **4 TYPE OF GOLF GAME** a golf game involving three players, one playing one ball and the other two taking alternate shots to play another ball

three-spine stickleback, three-spined stickleback *n* a small stickleback of temperate fresh and salt water that has three dorsal spines. *Gasterosteus aculeatus*.

three-square *adj* shaped like an equilateral triangle when viewed in cross section

three strikes and you're out *n* a law that requires mandatory life sentences for criminals convicted three times for major capital offences

three-way *adj* **1** involving three participating people or things **2** providing routes to three different places from one point ○ *a three-way junction*

three-wheeler *n* a vehicle with three wheels such as a small car or a tricycle

Three Wise Men *n* BIBLE = **Magi**

thremmatology /thrémmə tólləji/ *n* the science of breeding domesticated plants and animals [Late 19C. < Greek *thremmat-* 'nursling'.]

threnody /thrénnədi/ (*plural* **-dies**), **threnode** /thrénnōd/ *n* a song, poem, or speech of lament for the dead [Mid-17C. < Greek *thrēnōidia* < *thrēnos* 'lament' + *ōidē* 'song'.] —**threnodial** /thri nṓdi əl/ *adj* —**threnodic** /-nóddik/ *adj* —**threnodist** *n*

threonine /thrée ə nīn/ *n* an essential amino acid [Mid-20C. < *threose*, kind of sugar + -INE.]

thresh /thresh/ *v* **1** *vti* **SEPARATE SEEDS FROM PLANT** to use a machine, flail, or other implement to separate the seeds of a harvested plant from the straw and chaff, husks, or other residue **2** *vt* **BEAT** to beat a person, animal, or object **3** *vi* **FLAIL ABOUT** to move the body and limbs about in an uncontrolled or restless way **4** *vt* **EXAMINE EXHAUSTIVELY** to examine something such as an issue or a proposal, exhaustively ■ *n* **THRESHING** an act of threshing a harvested crop [Old English *þerscan* < Indo-European, 'to rub']

thresher /thréshər/ *n* **1** a harvester of a crop with a machine, flail, or other implement **2** AGRIC = **threshing machine 3 thresher, thresher shark** a large, widely distributed shark that has a curved elongated upper lobe on the tail with which it agitates or threshes the water. Family: Alopiidae.

~~**threshhold**~~ incorrect spelling of **threshold**

threshing machine *n* a static power-driven agricultural machine formerly used to beat or rub harvested plants in order to separate the seeds from the rest of the plant

threshold /thrésh hōld, -ōld/ *n* **1 WOOD OR STONE BELOW DOOR** a piece of stone or hardwood that forms the bottom of a doorway **2 DOORWAY** a doorway or entrance **3 STARTING POINT** the point where a new era or experience begins ○ *on the threshold of maturity* **4 LEVEL AT WHICH AN EFFECT STARTS** the level at which a psychological or physiological effect or state starts ○ *the threshold of consciousness* [Old English *þerscold*. Ultimately from Germanic whose first element meant 'tread'.]

threshold agreement *n* an agreement that raises wages in order to compensate for increases in the cost of living that reach a specified level

threw past tense of **throw**

thrice /thrīss/ *adv* **1 THREE TIMES** three times over (*archaic or literary*) **2 THREEFOLD** by three times as many or as much (*archaic or literary*) **3 GREATLY** to a high degree (*archaic*) [12C. Alteration of *thries* < Old English *þriga* 'three times' < *þrī* (see THREE).]

thrift /thrift/ *n* **1 PRUDENT USE OF MONEY AND GOODS** the sensible and cautious management of money and goods in order to waste as little as possible and obtain maximum value **2 PLANT WITH PINK OR WHITE FLOWERS** a perennial evergreen plant of the plumbago family. Flowers: dense, round, pink or white. Genus: *Armeria*. **3 STRONG GROWTH** vigorous and healthy growth of living things such as plants (*formal*) [13C. < Old Norse *þrift* 'prosperity' < *þrífask* (see THRIVE).]

thriftless /thríftləss/ *adj* showing carelessness and wastefulness in the handling of money and other resources —**thriftlessly** *adv* —**thriftlessness** *n*

thrift shop *n US* a shop that sells used goods, particularly clothing, usually for charity

thrifty /thrífti/ (**-ier, -iest**) *adj* **1** managing money and resources in a cautious and sensible way so as to waste as little as possible **2** prosperous and thriving (*archaic*) —**thriftily** *adv* —**thriftiness** *n*

thrill /thril/ *vti* **1 BE OR MAKE SOMEBODY VERY EXCITED** to feel or make somebody experience intense excitement ○ *The children were thrilled by the amusement park.* **2 BE PLEASURABLE** to feel or make somebody feel great pleasure ○ *It thrilled me to see my old friends.* **3 VIBRATE OR CAUSE TO VIBRATE** to vibrate or make something or somebody quiver or vibrate ■ *n* **1 CAUSE OF GREAT EXCITEMENT** a source or cause of great excitement, and often pleasure **2 FEELING OF EXCITEMENT** a feeling of great excitement, which may be experienced as a quivering or trembling sensation **3 TREMOR ASSOCIATED WITH HEART-VALVE DEFECTS** a slight vibration of the chest wall often associated with some types of heart-valve defect [Old English *þyrlian* 'go through' < *þyrel* 'hole' < *þruh* 'through']

thriller /thríllər/ *n* **1** a book, play, or film that has an exciting plot involving crime, mystery, or espionage **2** somebody or something that thrills people

thrilling /thrílling/ *adj* **1** causing intense excitement **2** characterized by trembling or vibrating —**thrillingly** *adv*

thrips /thrips/ (*plural* **thrips**) *n* a tiny sucking insect with four long thin wings fringed with hairs. It feeds on the sap of plants. Order: Thysanoptera. [Late 18C. Via Latin < Greek, 'woodworm'.]

thrive /thrīv/ (**thrives, thriving, thrived** *or* **throve** /thrōv/, **thrived** *or* **thriven** /thrívv'n/) *vi* **1** to grow vigorously and healthily **2** to be successful and often profitable [13C. < Old Norse *þrífask* 'grasp for yourself' < *þrífa* 'seize'.] —**thriver** *n*

thrive on *vt* to enjoy and be stimulated by something generally considered difficult or undesirable

thro' /throo/, **thro** *prep, adv* through (*informal or literary*) [15C. Variant.]

throat /thrōt/ *n* **1 DIGESTIVE AND BREATHING PASSAGE** the part of the airway and digestive tract between the mouth and both the oesophagus and the windpipe **2 FRONT OF NECK** the front part of the neck of an animal or human being **3 NARROW PART** a narrow part or passage that resembles a human's or animal's throat in shape or function **4 OPENING OF TUBULAR ORGAN OF FLOWER** the opening of a tubular organ of a flower, e.g. of a corolla **5 SORE THROAT** a throat infection (*informal*) [Old English *þrote* < Germanic] ◇ **jump down somebody's throat** to speak angrily and impatiently to somebody ◇ **ram** *or* **force something down somebody's throat** to make repeated and emphatic attempts to get somebody to listen to or accept a view or belief

throatlash /thrōt lash/, **throatlatch** /-lach/ *n* the strap that passes under a horse's jaw to hold its bridle in place

throat microphone, throat mike *informal n* a microphone that is placed in contact with the throat to pick up the vibrations produced by speech

throaty /thrṓti/ (**-ier, -iest**) *adj* **1** sounding deep and husky **2** deep or rough in tone, as though having been produced in the throat —**throatily** *adv* —**throatiness** *n*

throb /throb/ *vi* (**throbs, throbbing, throbbed**) **1 BEAT RAPIDLY AND FORCEFULLY** to beat or pulsate in a rapid forceful way ○ *My head is throbbing.* **2 BEAT REGULARLY** to have a regular rhythmic beat ■ *n* **1 SINGLE BEAT** a single beat or pulsation **2 REGULAR BEAT** a regular beat or pulsation ○ *a heart throb* [14C. Probably an imitation of pulsating.] —**throbbingly** *adv*

throe /thrō/ *n* **PANG** a spasm of pain ■ **throes** *npl* **1 EFFECTS OF PANGS** the effects of severe physical pain **2 EFFECTS OF UPHEAVAL** the effects of an upheaval or struggle [12C. < ?] ◇ **in the throes of something** in the process of doing something, usually something difficult or unpleasant

thromb- *prefix* = **thrombo-** (*before vowels*)

thrombi plural of **thrombus**

thrombin /thrómbin/ *n* an enzyme in blood that causes clotting by catalysing the conversion of fibrinogen to fibrin [Late 19C. < THROMBO-.]

thrombo- *prefix* blood clot ○ *thromboplastic* [< Greek *thrombos* 'clot']

thrombocyte /thrómbō sīt/ *n* BIOL = **platelet** —**thrombocytic** /thrómbō síttik/ *adj*

thrombocytopenia /thrómbō sītō peéni ə/ *n* the state of having fewer than the normal number of blood platelets per unit volume of blood, often associated with haemorrhaging [Early 20C. < THROMBOCYTE + Greek *penia* 'poverty'.] —**thrombocytopenic** *adj*

thromboembolism /thrómbō émbəlizəm/ *n* the blockage of a blood vessel by a blood clot (**thrombus**) that has broken away from its site of origin —**thromboembolic** /-em bóllik/ *adj* —**thromboembolitic** /-émbə líttik/ *adj*

thrombokinase /-kī nay, thrómbokīnayss/ *n* BIOCHEM = **thromboplastin**

thrombolysis /throm bólləssiss/ *n* the breaking down of a blood clot by infusion of a specific enzyme into the blood —**thrombolytic** /thrómbō líttik/ *adj*

thrombophlebitis /thrómbō fli bítiss/ *n* inflammation of a vein with the formation of a blood clot

thromboplastic /thrómbō plástik/ *adj* causing or increasing blood-clot formation —**thromboplastically** *adv*

thromboplastin /thrómbō plástin/ *n* a blood-clotting factor in blood platelets that converts prothrombin to thrombin

thrombose /throm bṓz, thrombṓss/ (**-boses, -bosing, -bosed**) *vti* to affect something such as a coronary artery with thrombosis, or to be affected by thrombosis

thrombosis /throm bṓssiss/ (*plural* **-ses**) *n* the formation or presence of one or more blood clots that may partially or completely block an artery, e.g. flowing to the heart or brain, or a vein [Early 18C. < modern Latin, < Greek *thrombos* 'clot'.] —**thrombotic** /throm bóttik/ *adj*

thromboxane /throm bók sayn/ *n* a substance in platelets that causes blood clotting and constriction of blood vessels

thrombus /thrómbəss/ (*plural* **-bi** /thróm bī/) *n* a blood clot that forms in a blood vessel and remains at the site of formation [Late 17C. Via modern Latin < Greek *thrombos* 'clot'.]

throne /thrōn/ *n* **1 CHAIR OF MONARCH OR BISHOP** an ornate chair, often raised on a platform and covered by a canopy, occupied by a monarch or bishop on ceremonial occasions **2 POWER OF ROYAL PERSON** the power, rank, and privileges of a monarch **3 TOILET** the part of a lavatory on which people sit (*informal humorous*) ■ **Thrones, thrones** *npl* **ORDER OF ANGELS** the third group of angels, ranking after the Seraphim and Cherubim, in the first circle of the traditional Christian hierarchy (*literary*) ■ *vti* (**thrones, throning, throned**) **PUT SOMEBODY ON THRONE** to place somebody or be placed on a throne [12C. Via Old French *trone* < Greek *thronos*.]

throng /throng/ *n* **CROWD** a large crowd of people or objects (*literary*) ■ *v* **1** *vt* **CROWD INTO PLACE** to crowd into or fill a place **2** *vi* **MOVE IN CROWD** to move or gather in a throng **3** *vt* **CROWD AROUND** to surround and push against somebody [Old English *geþrang* < Germanic, 'to press, crowd']

throstle /thróss'l/ *n* a thrush, especially a song thrush (*literary*) [Old English *þrostle* < Indo-European]

throttle /thrótt'l/ *n* **1 VALVE CONTROLLING FLUID FLOW** a valve used to control the flow of a fluid, especially the amount of fuel and air entering the cylinders of an internal-combustion engine **2 CONTROL FOR THROTTLE** a pedal or lever for controlling a throttle valve ■ *vt* (**-tles, -tling, -tled**) **1 REGULATE FUEL FLOW USING THROTTLE** to regulate the amount of fuel entering an engine using a throttle **2 REGULATE ENGINE SPEED** to regulate the speed of an engine by using a throttle **3 KILL PERSON OR ANIMAL BY CHOKING** to kill or injure a person or animal by squeezing the throat **4 SILENCE OR SUPPRESS** to prevent somebody or something from expressing an opinion freely or from engaging in an activity [14C. < THROAT.] —**throttler** *n*

through /throo/ CORE MEANING: a grammatical word used to indicate movement from one side or end of something to or past the other side or end

1 *prep, adv* **TRAVELLING ACROSS** travelling across or to various places in a town, country, or area ○ *He spent the summer travelling through Europe.* ○ *We're not stopping long; we're just passing through.* **2** *prep, adv* **AMONG** in the midst of, or having things or people all around or on either side of ○ *She wandered through the crowds milling around outside the cathedral.* ○ *Massage the conditioner through to the ends of the hair.* **3** *prep, adv* **PAST A BARRIER** past the limitations or difficulties of something such as a barrier or a problem ○ *the problems involved in wading through acres of bureaucracy* ○ *The road has been narrowed to prevent larger vehicles getting through.* **4** *prep, adv* **FROM BEGINNING TO END** from the beginning until the end or conclusion of ○ *Martin and Johanson's works will be on view through June.* ○ *I can't come I'm afraid; I'm working through.* **5** *adv, prep* **TO CONCLUSION** to a successful conclusion ○ *We've been trying to get through all morning but the lines are busy.* ○ *The bill will never get through the House of Lords.* **6** *prep* **VIA** by way or means of ○ *How the marketing is done, through a branch or telemarketing or a future service, is up to each bank.* **7** *prep* **OVER THE EXTENT OF** happening or existing over the entire extent of or affecting all of ○ *A flu of epidemic proportions swept through the town.* **8** *prep* **BECAUSE OF** as a result of ○ *Through his mishandling of our affairs, we'll be lucky to be in credit at all this year.* **9** *adv* **THOROUGHLY** completely and in every part **10** *prep US* **UP TO** up to and including that time ○ *Museum hours are 2–4:30 p.m. Tuesdays through Fridays.* **11** *adj* **GOING DIRECTLY** going directly without stopping or requiring a change ○ *The through train leaves on the hour.* [Old English *þurh* < Indo-European, 'pass through'] ◇ **be through with somebody** to want to have nothing else to do with somebody (*informal*) ◇ **be through with something** to have finished with something (*informal*) ◇ **through and through** completely

through-composed *adj* describes a song with different music for each verse, especially without pauses between the verses, or an opera that is not clearly divided into arias and recitatives

through-other *adj Scotland, Ireland* (*informal*) **1** in a state of confusion or disorder **2** in a dishevelled, disorderly, or agitated state —**through other** *adv*

throughout /throo ówt/ *prep, adv* **1** through or during the whole of ○ *Societies throughout history believed they had reached the frontiers of human accomplishment.* ○ *Throughout, they maintained their dignity.* **2** happening or existing in all parts of ○ *The group is seeking experts of any age throughout the area.* ○ *The house is carpeted throughout.*

⚡**throughput** /throo poot/ *n* the amount of something such as data or raw material that is processed over a given period [After INPUT and OUTPUT]

throughway /throo way/, **thruway** *n US* TRANSP = **expressway**

throve past tense of **thrive**

throw /thrō/ *vt* (**throws, throwing, threw** /throo/, **thrown** /thrōn/) **1 PROPEL SOMETHING FROM THE HAND** to make something move relatively quickly from the hand and through the air **2 DROP SOMETHING CARELESSLY** to put or drop something somewhere without paying proper attention to where it is left ○ *throws magazines all over the place* 3 **FORCE SOMEBODY OR SOMETHING SOMEWHERE** to move somebody or something forcefully or suddenly into a particular position or in a particular direction 4 **PUT SOMEBODY OR SOMETHING IN DIFFERENT CIRCUMSTANCES** to bring somebody or something suddenly or unexpectedly into a particular state, especially an undesirable one ○ *thrown out of a job* 5 **HURL SOMEBODY TO THE GROUND** to make a movement that causes somebody, e.g. an opponent in wrestling or judo or a horserider, to fall to the ground 6 **PROJECT LIGHT** to send out light to illuminate a particular place, or create a shadow by blocking light 7 **CAST DOUBT OR SUSPICION** to cause doubt or suspicion in people's minds by saying or doing something 8 **DIRECT THE EYES** to direct a look or glance quickly or suddenly in a particular direction ○ *She threw me a warning look.* 9 **DISCONCERT** to take somebody by surprise to the extent that he or she does not know how to react (*informal*) ○ *His unexpected arrival threw me.* 10 **MOVE AN OPERATING SWITCH OR LEVER** to move something, usually a switch or lever, to make a machine or system operate or to connect up a system 11 **HAVE AN EXTREME REACTION** to be affected by a sudden outburst of strong emotion such as anger or ill-temper ○ *throw a tantrum* 12 **SEND SOMETHING ACROSS** to make something that extends from one point to another, especially hastily ○ *The enemy threw a bridge across the moat.* 13 **DELIVER A PUNCH** to deliver a punch or blow with a movement of the arm 14 **MAKE AN OBJECT ON POTTER'S WHEEL** to produce a ceramic object by turning clay on a potter's wheel 15 **TURN MATERIAL ON LATHE** to turn wood or metal on a lathe 16 **HOST A PARTY** to organize and be the host at a party 17 **LOSE SOMETHING INTENTIONALLY** to lose a fight, race, or contest deliberately, e.g. by not trying or by committing a foul 18 **MAKE MATERIAL INTO YARN** to make silk or filaments into thread by twisting or spinning 19 **PROJECT VOICE** project a vocal sound so that it seems to be coming from elsewhere 20 **ROLL DICE** to tip or roll dice onto a flat surface to obtain a score, or score a particular number in this way 21 **GIVE BIRTH TO YOUNG** to give birth to young (*refers especially to cows*) 22 *Malaysia, Singapore* **THROW AWAY** to throw something away ○ *Once you get your new card you can throw the old one.* ■ *n* 1 **ACT OF THROWING** an act of throwing something, e.g. a ball or missile, or dice in a game 2 **DISTANCE THROWN** the distance that something is thrown or can be thrown 3 **WAY OF THROWING** an act of being thrown, or a way of throwing an opponent, in wrestling or judo 4 **SCORE THROWN** the score obtained by throwing something, e.g. dice or darts, in a game 5 **EACH** each item or attempt (*informal*) ○ *I didn't buy any – they were ten pounds a throw.* 6 **COVER FOR FURNITURE** a light cover or rug that covers and protects furniture 7 **MOVEMENT OF MACHINE PART** the maximum movement in a single direction of a machine part driven by a crank, cam, or eccentric 8 **DEFLECTION OF MEASURING INSTRUMENT** the distance moved by the tip of the needle of a measuring instrument 9 **VERTICAL DISPLACEMENT ALONG GEOLOGICAL FAULT** the vertical displacement up or down produced by movement along a geological fault [Old English *þrāwan* 'twist, hurl' < Indo-European, 'to twist'] — **thrower** *n* ◇ **throw yourself into something** to start doing something with great energy and commitment

SYNONYMS ***throw, chuck, fling, heave, hurl, toss, cast***
CORE MEANING: to send something through the air
throw to cause something to go through the air using a physical movement; **chuck** (*informal*) to throw something in a reckless or aimless way; **fling** to throw something fast using a lot of force; **heave** (*informal*) to throw something large or heavy with effort in a particular direction; **hurl** to throw something with great force; **toss** to throw something small or light in a casual or careless way; **cast** to throw something to a particular place or into a particular thing, or to throw a fishing line or net.

throw about *vt* to spend money in an extravagant, ostentatious way

throw away *vt* 1 **DISCARD** to get rid of something no longer wanted 2 **WASTE** to fail to take advantage of an opportunity to do something 3 **SAY SOMETHING IN OFFHAND MANNER** to say a line in a play in a way that makes it seem unimportant, even though it may be crucial to the plot

throw in *vt* 1 **ADD SOMETHING TO DISCUSSION** to contribute a comment to a conversation or discussion 2 **ADD SOMETHING AS EXTRA** to add something as an extra, especially another item at no extra cost when selling something 3 **RETURN BALL INTO PLAY BY HAND** to return a football to the pitch by means of an overhead throw after it has gone out of play ◇ **throw in the towel** *or* **sponge** to admit or accept defeat when something is proving difficult (*informal*)

throw off *vt* 1 **FREE YOURSELF FROM** to get rid of something troublesome or oppressive 2 **TAKE CLOTHES OFF HASTILY** to remove an item of clothing in a hurried or careless way 3 **GIVE OFF** to emit a substance into the air 4 **ESCAPE FROM SOMEBODY** to elude a pursuer 5 **SAY SOMETHING IN OFFHAND WAY** to say or write something in a casual manner 6 **MAKE SOMEBODY FLUSTERED** to confuse or unsettle somebody by doing something unexpected

throw on *vt* to put an item of clothing on in a hurried or careless way

throw out *vt* 1 **DISCARD** to get rid of something no longer wanted, especially something that has been kept for a while 2 **EJECT** to eject somebody forcibly from a place 3 **DISMISS** to expel somebody from membership of an organization 4 **SUGGEST** to make a suggestion, proposal, or hint, especially in an informal way 5 **REJECT BILL** to reject a bill in Parliament 6 **REJECT LAWSUIT** to reject a lawsuit so that the defendant does not have to stand trial 7 **DISCONCERT** to confuse or unsettle somebody by doing something unexpected 8 **BUILD A PROJECTING CONSTRUCTION** to build something in such a way that it sticks out 9 **GIVE OFF** to emit a substance into the air 10 **PUT CRICKET PLAYER OUT** in cricket, to cause a batsman to be run out by throwing the ball and hitting the wicket 11 **PUT BASEBALL PLAYER OUT** in baseball, to throw the ball to a team-mate who puts the runner out

throw over *vt* to end a romantic or sexual relationship with somebody (*informal*)

throw together *vt* (*informal*) 1 to make something in a hurry or carelessly 2 to cause people to meet and become acquainted with each other in a casual or unplanned way

throw up *v* 1 *vt* **ABANDON** to give something up, especially something important or valuable (*informal*) 2 *vt* **BUILD SOMETHING HASTILY** to erect a building or structure quickly 3 *vt* **BRING SOMETHING TO NOTICE** to produce or reveal somebody or something, especially unexpectedly or indirectly 4 *vti* **VOMIT** to vomit the contents of the stomach (*informal*)

throwaway /thrṓ ə way/ *adj* 1 **DISPOSABLE** designed to be thrown away after use 2 **WASTEFUL** tending to discard things too readily ○ *a throwaway society* 3 **OFFHAND** said or written in an apparently offhand manner ■ *n* **SOMETHING TO BE DISCARDED** an object designed to be thrown away after use

throwback /thrṓ bak/ *n* 1 **ORGANISM REPRESENTING REVERSION TO EARLIER TYPE** an organism with the characteristics of an earlier type 2 **REVERSION TO EARLIER TYPE** reversion to an earlier ancestral type 3 **ANIMAL OR PERSON RESEMBLING ANCESTOR** an animal or person bearing a striking resemblance to an ancestor 4 **SOMETHING BELONGING TO THE PAST** something contemporary that seems to belong to the past

throw-in *n* 1 **RETURN OF FOOTBALL TO PLAY** an act of returning a football to play from the sideline by propelling it from behind the head with both hands 2 **RETURN OF BALL FROM OUTFIELD** an act of returning a baseball or cricket ball after it has been hit to the outfield 3 **RETURN OF BASKETBALL TO PLAY** an act of returning a basketball to play by passing it onto the court

throwing stick *n* a stick, often with a handgrip, used as a weapon to hurl at birds or small game

thrown past participle of **throw**

throw pillow *n US, Can* DIY = **scatter cushion**

throw rug *n US, Can* DIY = **scatter rug**

throwster /thrṓstər/ *n* somebody who twists filaments into thread

throw weight *n* the total weight of a missile's payload, including the warhead and guidance system but not the rocket

thru /throo/ *prep, adv, adj US* through (*informal*)

thrum[1] /thrum/ *v* (**thrums, thrumming, thrummed**) 1 *vti* **STRUM** to strum on a stringed instrument 2 *vi* **TAP STEADILY** to drum on something, especially with the fingers 3 *vti* **SAY OR SPEAK MONOTONOUSLY** to say something or talk monotonously ■ *n* **MONOTONOUS BEAT** a low monotonous beating sound [Late 16C. An imitation of the sound.] — **thrummer** *n*

thrum[2] /thrum/ *n* 1 **THREAD END LEFT ON LOOM** an unwoven end or row of ends from warp threads that are left on a loom after the web has been cut off 2 **FRINGE** a short fringe or thread end ■ **thrums** *npl* **YARN PIECES ADDED TO CANVAS** short pieces of yarn inserted in canvas in order to create a rough surface and prevent chafing or leaks ■ *vt* (**thrums, thrumming, thrummed**) 1 **ADD FRINGES TO** to put fringes on something 2 **INSERT YARN PIECES IN CANVAS** to insert pieces of yarn in canvas in order to create a rough surface and prevent chafing or leaks [Old English *þrum* < Indo-European]

~~**thruogh**~~ incorrect spelling of **through**

thruppence *npl* = **threepence**

thruppenny *adj* = **threepenny**

thruppenny bit *n* MONEY = **threepenny bit**

thrush[1] /thrush/ (*plural* **thrushes** *or* **thrush**) *n* 1 a small to medium-sized songbird with a slender bill, including the song thrush, mistle thrush, or blackbird. Family: Turdidae. 2 a bird that resembles a thrush, e.g. the North American water thrush [Old English *þrysce*]

thrush[2] /thrush/ *n* 1 **FUNGAL DISEASE OF MOUTH** a fungal infection of the mouth characterized by white patches 2 **FUNGAL INFECTION OF VAGINA** a fungal infection of the vagina characterized by a white discharge and itching 3 **DISEASE OF HORSE'S HOOF** infection of the fleshy part of a horse's foot (**frog**), causing softening of the horn and a foul-smelling discharge [Mid-17C. < ?]

thrust /thrust/ *v* (**thrusts, thrusting, thrust**) 1 *vt* **PUSH SOMEBODY OR SOMETHING FORCEFULLY** to push somebody or something with great force 2 *vti* **FORCE WAY** to force a way 3 *vt* **STRETCH OR EXTEND** to stretch or extend something, or be stretched or extended ○ *towers thrusting skywards* 4 *vt* **FORCE SOMEBODY INTO** to force somebody to accept or deal with something ○ *He was thrust into the limelight.* 5 *vt* **ATTACK BY STABBING** to attack somebody with a piercing or stabbing movement with a weapon 6 *vt* **INSERT** to add or insert material, usually inappropriately, into a context ■ *n* 1 **FORCEFUL PUSH** a forceful push or shove 2 **FORWARD MOVEMENT** a forward movement or impetus 3 **STABBING ACTION** a piercing or stabbing action 4 **MILITARY ATTACK** a military assault or offensive 5 **GIST OR AIM** the chief meaning, direction, or purpose of something 6 **FORCE OF PROPELLER** a propulsive force produced by a rotating propeller, e.g. on a ship or aircraft 7 **REACTIVE FORCE OF EXPELLED GASES** the reactive force of expelled gases, e.g. those generated by a rocket or jet engine 8 **FORCE EXERTED BY STRUCTURE** the continuous force exerted sideways or downwards by one structure on another, e.g. by an arch on an abutment or a rafter against a wall 9 **FORCE IN EARTH'S CRUST** a force in the earth's crust that results in recumbent folding of rock strata 10 GEOL = **thrust fault** [12C. < Old Norse *þrýsta*.] —**thrustful** *adj*

thrust bearing *n* a bearing designed to withstand axial loading and to prevent movement along the axis of a loaded shaft

thruster /thrústər/ *n* 1 **ROCKET THAT CONTROLS ALTITUDE** a rocket on a spacecraft or high-altitude aircraft that controls an altitude or flight path 2 **MANOEUVRING DEVICE ON OIL-DRILLING VESSEL** a jet or propeller on an oil-drilling ship or offshore rig, used to manoeuvre it into position 3 **SOMEBODY AGGRESSIVELY AMBITIOUS** an aggressive pursuer of personal ambitions 4 **SURFBOARD OR SAILBOARD WITH EXTRA FIN** a surfboard or sailboard equipped with one or more extra fins designed to give it greater speed or manoeuvrability 5 **FOX HUNTER GETTING TOO FAR FORWARDS** a fox hunter who gets too close to the pack during a hunt (*slang*)

thrust fault *n* an inclined fault in which rocks on the lower side of the slope are displaced downwards

thrusting /thrústing/ *adj* tending to pursue ambitions aggressively

thrust stage *n* a stage surrounded on three sides by the audience

thruway *n US* TRANSP = **throughway**

Thucydides /thyoo síddi deez/ (460?–400? BC) Athenian historian

thud /thud/ *n* 1 **DULL HEAVY SOUND** a loud dull sound made by a heavy object impacting with a surface 2 **DULL HEAVY BLOW** a blow that makes a dull heavy sound ■ *vi* (**thuds, thudding, thudded**) **MAKE A THUD** to make a dull heavy sound [Early 16C. Probably < Old English *þyddan* 'thrust'.]

thug /thug/ *n* 1 somebody, especially a criminal, who is brutal and violent 2 **thug, Thug** a member of a former secret organization of robbers in India, worshippers of the goddess Kali, who strangled their victims [Early 19C. < Hindi *ṭhag* 'swindler, cheat, robber' < Sanskrit *sthagayati* 'covers, conceals'.] —**thuggery** *n* —**thuggish** *adj*

thuggee /thu gée/ *n* the method of robbery and murder by strangulation, characteristic of the former thugs of India [Mid-19C. < Hindi *ṭhagī* < *ṭhag* (see THUG).]

huja /thyoòya/ (*plural* **-jas** *or* **-ja**), **thuya** (*plural* **-yas** *or* **-ya**) *n* TREES = **arbor vitae** [Mid-18C. Via modern Latin *Thuja* < medieval Latin *thuia* 'cedar' < Greek.]

hulium /thyoòli əm/ *n* (*symbol* **Tm**) a very rare soft bright silvery-grey metallic element of the lanthanide series. Source: monazite, bastnaesite. Use: X-ray source. [Late 19C. After *Thule*, most northerly region to the ancients; because first found in Norway.]

humb /thum/ *n* **1** THICKEST DIGIT ON HUMAN HAND the shortest thickest digit of the human hand, located next to the forefinger **2** ANIMAL'S DIGIT RESEMBLING HUMAN THUMB a short thick digit in some animals, e.g. many primates, that is adapted for grasping and corresponds to the human thumb **3** SECTION OF GLOVE FOR THUMB the part of a glove or mitten that covers the thumb **4** ARCHIT = **ovolo** ■ *v* **1** *vti* HITCH LIFT to obtain or try to obtain a lift by signalling with the thumb to passing drivers **2** *vt* MAKE SOMETHING DIRTY BY USE to soil or cause wear on something, especially a book, by repeated handling (*often passive*) ○ *a well-thumbed book* **3** *vti* FLIP THROUGH PRINTED MATTER to glance through pages of a book or magazine [Old English *þúma* < Indo-European] —**thumbless** *adj* ◇ **all thumbs** extremely awkward or clumsy ◇ **stick out like a sore thumb** to be completely obvious, or conspicuously out of place ◇ **twiddle your thumbs** to be idle or unoccupied, especially involuntarily ◇ **under somebody's thumb** under the influence and control of somebody

humbhole /thúm hōl/ *n* **1** a hole in something such as a bowling ball into which a thumb can be inserted in order to provide a grip **2** a hole in a wind instrument that is covered and uncovered by the thumb to produce notes

humb index *n* a series of labelled indentations cut into the pages of a book down the edge opposite the binding to facilitate quick location of divisions or sections — **thumb-index** *vt*

humb knot *n* = **overhand knot**

humbnail /thúm nayl/ *n* **1** NAIL OF THUMB the hard growing plate of keratin on the surface of the tip of the thumb **2** MINIATURE GRAPHIC IMAGE a small version of a larger graphic image displayed on a computer monitor so as to save space ■ *adj* CONCISE covering the salient points concisely ○ *a thumbnail sketch*

humbnut /thúm nut/ *n* DIY, CONSTR = **wing nut**

humb piano *n* a box-shaped African musical instrument with a row of tuned metal or wooden strips that vibrate when plucked by the thumb

humbprint /thúm print/ *n* an impression of the fleshy pad near the tip of the thumb, often used to identify people

humbscrew /thúm skroo/ *n* **1** an instrument of torture used to crush the thumbs **2** a screw with a flat head to be turned with the thumb and forefinger

humbs-down /ˌ/ *n* an indication of disapproval or rejection (*informal*)

humbstall /thúm stawl/ *n* a sheath of rubber, leather, or fabric used to protect the thumb, e.g. by covering a dressing

humbs-up /ˌ/ *n* an indication of approval or acceptance (*informal*)

humbtack /thúm tak/ *n* US, Can COMM = **drawing pin**

Thummim *n* ↓ **Urim and Thummim** [Mid-16C. < Hebrew *tummīm*, plural of *tōm* 'completeness'.]

hump /thump/ *v* **1** *vti* STRIKE HEAVILY to strike somebody or something heavily with the fist or an object **2** *vi* PALPITATE OR POUND to beat very fast or loudly because of fear or excitement (*refers to the heart*) **3** *vi* MAKE DULL HEAVY SOUND to make the loud dull sound that a heavy object makes when it impacts with a surface **4** *vti* DEFEAT CONVINCINGLY to inflict a humiliating defeat upon somebody (*informal; often passive*) ○ *Our team was thumped 9–0.* ■ *n* **1** HEAVY BLOW a heavy blow struck with the fist or an object **2** DULL HEAVY SOUND the loud dull sound made by a heavy object impacting with a surface ○ *I heard a loud thump from next door.* [Mid-16C. An imitation of the sound.] —**thumper** *n*

humping /thúmping/ *adj* **1** LARGE huge, resounding, or impressive (*informal*) ○ *won by a thumping majority* **2** PAINFUL very painful and throbbing ■ *adv* VERY extremely or exceptionally (*informal*) ○ *a thumping good read* —**thumpingly** *adv*

Thun /toon/ *n* town in central Switzerland. Population: 39,854 (1998).

thunbergia /thun búrji ə/ *n* a widely cultivated ornamental plant of the acanthus family with opposite pairs of simple leaves. Flowers: five-lobed, tubular. Native to: Africa, South Asia. Genus: *Thunbergia*. [Late 18C. < modern Latin *Thunbergia*, after C. P. *Thunberg* (1743–1822), Swedish botanist.]

thunder /thúndər/ *n* **1** LOUD NOISE FOLLOWING LIGHTNING a loud rumbling noise caused by the rapid expansion of air suddenly heated by lightning **2** NOISE RESEMBLING THUNDER a loud deep rumbling noise resembling thunder **3** THREATENING OR VEHEMENT UTTERANCE a manifestation of somebody's anger in an explosion of strong words ■ *v* **1** *vi* MAKE LOUD NOISE FOLLOWING LIGHTNING to make a loud rumbling noise caused by the rapid expansion of air suddenly heated by lightning **2** *vi* RUMBLE LOUDLY LIKE THUNDER to make a loud deep rumbling noise resembling thunder **3** *vti* SHOUT VEHEMENTLY to shout something loudly and angrily [Old English *þunor* (noun), *þunrian* (verb) < Indo-European] ◇ **steal somebody's thunder** to prevent somebody from receiving acclaim for doing something by doing it or something similar first

Thunder Bay /thúndər-/ city in SW Ontario, Canada, on Thunder Bay, an arm of Lake Superior. Population: 113,662 (1996).

Thunderbird: Totem pole, Stanley Park, Vancouver, Canada

The Purcell Team/Corbis

thunderbird /thúndər burd/ *n* in Native North American mythology, a bird that produces thunder

thunderbolt /thúndər bōlt/ *n* **1** FLASH OF LIGHTNING WITH THUNDER a flash of lightning accompanied by a crash of thunder **2** STARTLING OCCURRENCE a sudden shocking action, occurrence, pronouncement, or piece of news **3** MYTHOLOGICAL WEAPON WIELDED BY GODS in mythology, a destructive missile hurled to earth by a god in a flash of lightning **4** FORMIDABLE PERSON OR THING a person who or thing that resembles a thunderbolt, especially in energy and destructive power

thunderbox /thúndər boks/ *n* a toilet, especially a primitive or portable one (*dated informal humorous*)

thunderclap /thúndər klap/ *n* **1** CRASH OF THUNDER a loud crashing noise produced by thunder **2** STARTLING OCCURRENCE a sudden shocking occurrence or piece of news **3** NOISE RESEMBLING THUNDER a sudden loud sound resembling thunder

thundercloud /thúndər klowd/ *n* a large dark cumulonimbus cloud that produces thunder and lightning

thunderhead /thúndər hed/ *n* US, Can the upper rounded mass of a cumulonimbus cloud associated with the development of a thunderstorm

thundering /thúndəring/ *adj* very great (*dated informal*) ■ *adv* extremely or exceptionally (*dated informal*) —**thunderingly** *adv*

thunderous /thúndərəss/ *adj* **1** resembling thunder in its loudness ○ *thunderous applause* **2** angry and threatening —**thunderously** *adv*

thunder sheet *n* a large sheet of metal shaken to simulate thunder as a theatrical sound effect

thundershower /thúndər showər/ *n* a shower of rain during a thunderstorm

thunderstone /thúndər stōn/ *n* a naturally occurring long tapering piece of rock, formerly believed to be a thunderbolt

thunderstorm /thúndər stawrm/ *n* a storm with thunder, lightning, heavy rain, and sometimes hail

thunderstruck /thúndər struk/ *adj* so surprised, incredulous, or startled as to be in a state of shock

thundery /thúndəri/ *adj* **1** causing or indicating the onset of thunder or a thunderstorm **2** resembling thunder in sound

thunk /thungk/ *n* a thud (*informal*) ■ *vi* to make a thud (*informal*) [Mid-20C. An imitation of the sound.]

Thur. *abbr* Thursday

Thurber /thúrbər/, **James** (1894–1961) US writer and cartoonist

thurible /thyoóríb'l/ *n* RELIG = **censer** [15C. Directly or via French < Latin *t(h)uribulum* < Greek *thuos* 'sacrifice, incense'.]

thurifer /thyoóríifər/ *n* a bearer of the censer in religious ceremonies [Mid-19C. < late Latin < Greek *thuos* 'sacrifice, incense'.]

Thurs. *abbr* Thursday

Thursday /thúrz day, -di/ *n* the fourth day of the week, coming after Wednesday and before Friday [Old English *þu(n)resdæg* 'day of thunder', translation of late Latin *Jovis dies* 'day of Jupiter (the god of thunder)']

Thursday Island island off the coast of NE Australia. Area: 3.6 sq. km/1.4 sq. mi.

Thursdays /thúrz dayz, -diz/ *adv* every Thursday

Thurso /thúrssō/ *n* seaport on the coast of N Scotland. Population: 8,488 (1991).

thus /thuss/ *adv* **1** CONSEQUENTLY as a result (*formal*) **2** LIKE THIS in this way (*formal*) **3** TO THIS DEGREE to this degree or extent [Old English *þus* < ?] ◇ **thus far** up to this point ○ *The evidence thus far suggested that he was innocent.*

thusly /thússli/ *adv* US thus (*humorous*)

Thutmose III /thoot mōsə/ (*d.* 1450 BC) Egyptian pharaoh

thuya *n* TREES = **thuja**

thwack /thwak/ *vt* to strike somebody or something with a flat object such as the flat of the hand ■ *n* a sharp smacking blow with a flat object [Early 16C. An imitation of the sound.] —**thwacker** *n*

thwaite /thwayt/ *n* a piece of reclaimed wasteland (*archaic or regional; often in placenames*) [Early 17C. < Old Norse *þveit(i).*]

thwart /thwawrt/ *vt* FRUSTRATE to prevent somebody or somebody's plan from being successful ■ *adj* EXTENDING ACROSS situated or extending across something ■ *n* CROSSWISE SEAT IN BOAT a crosswise seat or transverse member on a rowing boat, canoe, or similar small boat ■ *prep* ATHWART athwart (*archaic*) [13C. < Old Norse *þvert.*] —**thwartedly** *adv* —**thwarter** *n*

⚡ **THX, TX** *abbr* thanks (*in e-mails*)

thy /thī/ *det* belonging or relating to you, the second person singular possessive corresponding to 'thou' (*archaic*) [12C. Shortening of THINE.]

Thyestes /thī ést eez/ *n* in Greek mythology, the brother of Atreus and king of Mycenae. After usurping the throne from his brother, he was tricked into eating the flesh of his own sons. —**Thyestean** *adj*

thylacine /thíla seen/ *n* a large carnivorous marsupial that resembles a dog and has brownish fur and black stripes across the back. Native to: Tasmania. *Thylacinus cynocephalus.* [Mid-19C. < modern Latin *Thylacinus* < Greek *thulakos* 'pouch'.]

thylakoid /thíla koyd/ *n* any of a group of chlorophyll-containing membranous structures resembling sacs in which photosynthesis takes place. Thylakoids are stacked one on top of the other in the chloroplast layers (**grana**) of most plants. [Mid-20C. < Greek *thulakos* 'sac'.]

thyme /tīm/ *n* a small low-growing shrub with narrow aromatic leaves. Use: cooking, thymol extraction. Genus: *Thymus*. [15C. Via Old French *thym* < Greek *thumon* < *thuein* 'burn, sacrifice'; from its use as incense.] —**thymy** *adj*

SPELLCHECK See *time*.

thymectomy /thī méktəmi/ (*plural* **-mies**) *n* surgical removal of the thymus gland [Early 20C. < THYMUS.]

thymi *plural of* **thymus**

-thymia *suffix* condition or state of mind ○ *dysthymia* [Via modern Latin < Greek *thumos* 'mind']

thymic /thí mik/ *adj* relating to the thymus

thymidine /thími deen/ *n* a nucleoside in DNA, consisting of thymine linked to deoxyribose [Early 20C. < THYMINE + -IDINE.]

thymine /thī meen/ n (*symbol* **T**) one of the four nitrogenous bases in DNA in which it pairs with adenine [Late 19C. < THYMIC.]

thymocyte /thīma sīt/ n a small white blood cell (**lymphocyte**) occurring in the thymus that is a precursor of a T-cell

thymol /thī mol/ n $C_{10}H_{14}O$ a colourless crystalline phenol with an aromatic odour. Source: thyme oil, synthetically made. Use: fungicide, preservative, vermifuge, perfumes. [Mid-19C. < Greek *thumon* (see THYME).]

thymoma /thī mōma/ (*plural* **-mas** *or* **-mata** /-mata/) n a tumour of the thymus [Early 20C. < Greek *thumos* (see THYMUS).]

thymosin /thīmassin/ n a hormone that influences the development and differentiation of T-cells in the thymus [Mid-20C. < Greek *thumos* (see THYMUS).]

thymus /thīmass/ (*plural* **-muses** *or* **-mi** /-mī/), **thymus gland** n an organ, located at the base of the neck, that is involved in development of cells of the immune system, particularly T-cells [Late 16C. Via modern Latin < Greek *thumos* 'warty growth resembling a bunch of thyme' < *thumon* (see THYME).]

thyratron /thīra tron/ n a gas-filled hot-cathode tube that acts as an electronic switch or relay in which a signal applied to the control grid initiates anode current but does not limit it [Early 20C. < Greek *thura* 'door'.]

thyristor /thī rīstar/ n a semiconductor device that has two stable switches used for conductive and non-conductive modes [Mid-20C. Blend of THYRATRON + TRANSISTOR.]

thyro- *prefix* thyroid ○ *thyrotropin* [< THYROID]

thyrocalcitonin /thīrō kálssi tōnin/ n BIOCHEM = **calcitonin**

thyroid /thī royd/ n 1 ANAT = **thyroid gland** 2 = **thyroid cartilage** 3 MEDICINE OBTAINED FROM ANIMAL THYROID GLAND a preparation obtained from the thyroid gland of certain animals. Use: treating conditions of the thyroid gland. ■ adj 1 thyroid, thyroidal OF THYROID GLAND relating to, situated in, supplying, or secreted by the thyroid gland 2 thyroid, thyroidal OF THYROID CARTILAGE relating to the thyroid cartilage [Early 18C. < obsolete French *thyroide* < Greek *thura* 'door'; from the oblong shape of the cartilage in front of the throat.]

thyroid cartilage n the largest cartilage of the larynx, forming the projection called the Adam's apple

thyroidectomy /thī roy déktami, thīra-/ (*plural* **-mies**) n surgical removal of the thyroid gland or part of it

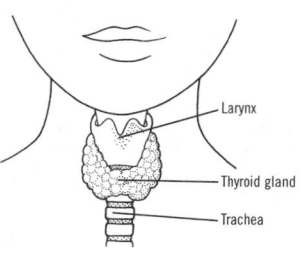

Thyroid gland

thyroid gland n an endocrine gland located in the neck of human beings and other vertebrate animals that secretes the hormones responsible for controlling metabolism and growth

thyroid hormone n either of the two hormones, thyroxine and triiodothyronine, that are secreted by the thyroid gland and regulate body metabolism and growth

thyroiditis /thī roy dītiss/ n inflammation of the thyroid gland

thyroid-stimulating hormone n BIOCHEM = **thyrotropin**

thyrotoxicosis /thīrō tókssi kṓssiss/ n MED = **hyperthyroidism** n. 1

thyrotropin /thīrō trṓpin/, **thyrotrophin** /-fin/ n a hormone that is secreted by the anterior lobe of the pituitary

gland and stimulates release of hormones by the thyroid gland [Mid-20C. < THYRO- + -TROPIC + -IN.]

thyrotropin-releasing hormone n a peptide hormone that is produced by the hypothalamus and controls the release of thyrotropin by the pituitary gland

thyroxine /thī rók seen/, **thyroxin** /-sin/ n the principal hormone secreted by the thyroid gland, which stimulates metabolism and is essential for normal growth and development [Early 20C. < THYRO- + OXY- + INDOLE (from a misunderstanding of its chemical structure), altered after -INE.]

thyrse /thurss/ n a flower head, e.g. in lilacs, that consists of numerous branching clusters of individual flowers arising from a single main stem [Early 17C. Via French < Latin *thyrsus* 'stalk of plant'.] —**thyrsoid** adj

thyrsus /thúrssass/ (*plural* **-si** /-sī/) n 1 in Greek mythology and art, a staff tipped with a pine cone, carried by the Greek god Dionysus and his followers 2 PLANT SCI = **thyrse** [Late 16C. Via Latin < Greek *thursos* 'stalk of a plant, staff carried by Dionysus'.]

thysanuran /thíssa nyōōran/ n INSECTS = **bristletail** [Mid-19C. < modern Latin *Thysanura* < Greek *thusanos* 'tassel, fringe' + *oura* 'tail'.] —**thysanurous** adj

thyself /thī sélf/ pron the form of 'thy' used to refer to the same individual who is being addressed and is the subject of the verb (*archaic*) [Old English. Originally < THEE + SELF (adjective), but interpreted as being < THY + SELF (noun).]

THz abbr terahertz

ti[1] /tee, te/ n US MUSIC = **te** [Mid-19C. Alteration of SI.]

ti[2] /tee/ (*plural* **tis**) n a woody plant with leaves that yield a useful fibre, and roots that are used as food or in beverages. Native to: Polynesia, Australia. Genus: *Cordyline*. [Mid-19C. < Tahitian and Maori.]

Ti *symbol* titanium

⚡**TIA** abbr thanks in advance (*in e-mails*)

Tiananmen Square /tyén a mən-/ n a large square in central Beijing, China, that is a traditional site for festivals, rallies, and demonstrations

Tian Shan /tyén shán/ = **Tien Shan**

tiara /ti áara/ n 1 WOMAN'S JEWELLED CORONET a small jewelled semicircular headdress worn by a woman on formal occasions 2 POPE'S CROWN a headdress consisting of three coronets with an orb and a cross on top, worn by the pope or carried before him on ceremonial occasions 3 PERSIAN KING'S CROWN a high headdress worn by an ancient Persian king [Mid-16C. Directly and via Italian < Latin, < Greek *tiara(s)*.] —**tiaraed** adj

Tiber /tībar/ n river of central Italy, emptying into the Tyrrhenian Sea. Length: 405 km/252 mi.

Tiberius /tī beéri ass-/ (42 BC–AD 37) Roman emperor (AD 14–37)

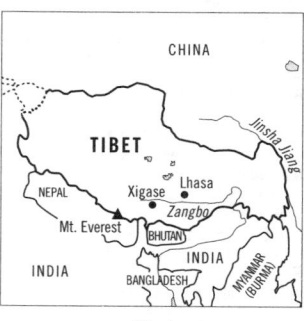

Tibet

Tibet /ti bét/ n former independent state and provincial-level administrative area of SW China. With an average elevation of more than 4,000 m/12,000 ft, it is the highest region in the world. Capital: Lhasa. Population: 2,220,000 (1990). Area: 1,200,000 sq. km/463,320 sq. mi.

Tibetan /ti bétt'n/ n 1 a person who comes from Tibet 2 the Tibeto-Burman language of Tibet, spoken also in neighbouring parts of China, Nepal, and India. Native speakers: 6 million. —**Tibetan** adj

Tibetan Buddhism n RELIG = **Lamaism**

Tibeto-Burman /ti béttō-/ n a branch of the Sino-Tibetan family of languages that includes Tibetan, Burmese, and many other languages of south and Southeast Asia —**Tibeto-Burman** adj

tibia /tíbbi a/ (*plural* **-ae** /-ee/ *or* **-as**) n 1 INNER BONE IN LOWER LEG the inner and larger of the two bones in the lower leg, extending from the knee to the ankle bone alongside the fibula 2 BONE IN ANIMAL'S LEG a bone in the lower leg of vertebrates corresponding to the human tibia 3 PART OF INSECT'S LEG the fourth segment of an insect's leg, between the femur and the tarsus 4 PART OF BIRD'S LEG the lower feathered segment or drumstick of a bird's leg 5 ANCIENT WIND INSTRUMENT an ancient flute originally made from an animal's tibia [Late 17C. < Latin, 'shinbone, pipe'.] —**tibial** adj

tibiofibular /tíbbi ō fíbbyōōlar/ adj relating to the tibia and fibula, the bones of the lower leg

tic /tik/ n 1 a sudden involuntary spasmodic muscular contraction, especially of facial, neck, or shoulder muscles, which may become more pronounced when somebody is stressed 2 a distinctive behavioural trait or quirk [Early 19C. Via French < Italian *ticchio*.]

⚡**TIC** abbr tongue in cheek (*in e-mails*)

tic douloureux /-doola rṓ/ n MED = **trigeminal neuralgia** [< French, 'painful tic']

tich n = **titch**

tichy adj = **titchy**

Ticino /ti cheénō/ river in south-central Switzerland and NW Italy, a tributary of the River Po. Length: 248 km/154 mi.

tick[1] /tik/ n 1 RECURRING CLICK a slight quiet recurring clicking sound, especially one made by a clock or watch 2 VERY SHORT TIME a very short time (*informal*) ○ *I'll be back in a tick.* 3 MARK NOTING ITEM'S STATUS a mark (✓) or electronic signal put beside an item as a record or reminder, or as an indication that something is correct. US term **check** n. 4 DEGREE ON SCALE an increment on a scale, especially the smallest amount by which a security may rise or fall in a stock or bond market ■ v 1 vi MAKE RECURRING CLICKING SOUND to make a slight quiet recurring clicking sound 2 vi REGISTER TAXI FARE BY CLICKING to make a clicking sound while registering the progressive increase of a taxi fare 3 vt MARK SOMETHING WITH TICK to put a tick beside an item as a record or reminder, or as an indication that something is correct. US term **check** v. 4 vi FUNCTION PROPERLY to function well or in the specified way [13C. < ?] ○ **what makes somebody tick** what causes somebody to behave and think in a particular way (*informal*)

tick away, tick by vi to pass or elapse at a steady pace (*refers to time*)

tick off vt 1 MARK WITH TICK to mark something with a tick, especially an item in a list. US term **check off** 2 SCOLD to tell somebody off for doing something wrong (*informal*) 3 US ANNOY to make somebody angry (*informal*)

tick over vi 1 to function slowly without causing a vehicle to move (*refers to a motor-vehicle engine*) 2 to keep going or continue to function without any significant progress or achievement

tick[2] /tik/ n 1 a small wingless bloodsucking insect that lives on the skin of humans and warm-blooded animals and may transmit diseases. Families: Argasidae and Ioxidae. 2 a parasitic fly that lives on the skin of sheep, cattle, horses, and other animals [Old English *ticia* < Germanic]

tick[3] /tik/ n the system of owing somebody money for goods that are acquired (*dated informal*) ○ *bought it on tick* [Mid-17C. Shortening of TICKET 'note of goods received on credit'.]

tick[4] /tik/ n the cloth case or covering that is filled with cotton, feathers, or other materials to form a pillow or mattress [15C. Via Middle Dutch *tēke* < Greek *thēkē* 'cover, case'.]

tick-bird n a bird that feeds on ticks, e.g. the oxpecker

tick-borne adj describes a disease in which the causative microorganism is transmitted by the bite of a tick, e.g. Lyme disease or many forms of encephalitis

ticker /tíkar/ n 1 somebody's heart (*informal*) 2 a wristwatch or pocket watch (*dated informal*) 3 US fin = **tape machine**

ticker tape n formerly, a continuous paper ribbon on which a tape machine automatically printed stock quotations

ticker-tape parade *n* in the United States, a parade honouring a visiting celebrity who is showered with shredded paper, formerly ticker tape, from buildings while being driven through the streets

ticket /tíkit/ *n* **1 TRAVEL PASS** a printed piece of cardboard or paper showing that the holder is entitled to be travelling on a means of transport **2 PASS FOR ENTERTAINMENT** a printed piece of cardboard or paper showing that the holder is entitled to admission to a place of public entertainment or a sports ground **3 NOTIFICATION OF TRAFFIC OFFENCE** a printed notice that a traffic or parking offence has been committed and a fine must be paid ○ *a parking ticket* **4 LABEL OR TAG** a small piece of card attached to an article, showing the price or other details **5 QUALIFICATION OF PILOT OR SHIP'S OFFICER** a certificate of qualification as a ship's captain or an aircraft pilot **6 ARMY DISCHARGE** a certificate of discharge from the army (*informal*) **7** *US* **GROUP OF CANDIDATES RUNNING TOGETHER** a list of candidates put forward by one party or group in an election **8 LIST OF STOCK PURCHASERS** a list of investors who have purchased securities during a specified period for the purpose of settling accounts **9 PRECISELY WHAT IS NEEDED** the right, just, desired, or appropriate thing (*informal*) ○ *A week in France would be just the ticket.* ■ *vt* **1 ATTACH A TICKET TO** to attach a ticket to an article, showing the price or other details **2 ISSUE A PASS TO** to issue a ticket for admission to something **3 GIVE A PARKING TICKET TO** to issue a motor vehicle or its driver with a ticket for a traffic or parking violation **4 CATEGORIZE** to assign somebody to a particular category, or designate something for a particular purpose [Early 16C. < obsolete French *étiquet* 'ticket, label' < Old French *estiquier* 'to stick'; from the idea of sticking on a label.]

ticket day *n* a day on which purchasers of securities during a preceding specified period are listed so that accounts may be settled

ticket of leave *n* formerly, a permit allowing a convict to leave prison before completion of a sentence, under certain restrictions (*hyphenated before nouns*) ○ *a ticket-of-leave man*

ticket scalper *n US* BUSINESS = **ticket tout**

ticket tout *n* somebody who buys tickets for a theatrical or sporting event and sells them on at a profit. US term **ticket scalper**

tickety-boo /tíkəti bo͞o/ *adj UK, Can* perfectly fine (*dated informal*)

tickey /tíki/ (*plural* **-eys**) *n* a small silver threepenny coin in use in South Africa between 1806 and 1961 [Late 19C. < ?]

tick fever *n* an acute infectious disease transmitted by the bite of a tick, e.g. Rocky Mountain spotted fever or Texas fever

ticking /tíking/ *n* a strong cotton fabric, often twilled. Use: mattress and pillow covers. [Mid-17C. < TICK[4].]

ticking-off (*plural* **tickings-off**) *n* an act of telling somebody off for doing something wrong (*informal*)

tickle /tík'l/ *v* (**-les, -ling, -led**) **1** *vt* **MAKE SOMEBODY LAUGH AND TWITCH** to touch, prod, stroke, or caress lightly a sensitive part of somebody's body, usually so as to produce involuntary laughter and wriggling **2** *vti* **CAUSE ITCHINESS** to cause an itchy or scratchy feeling by lightly touching a sensitive part of the body ○ *This feather boa tickles.* **3** *vt* **PLEASE OR AMUSE** to make somebody pleased, or appeal to somebody's sense of humour (*often passive*) **4** *vt* **CATCH TROUT WITH HANDS** to catch a trout by stroking it gently so that it moves backwards into the hands ■ *n* **1 TOUCH THAT MAKES SOMEBODY LAUGH** a light touch, prod, stroke, or caress applied to a sensitive part of somebody's body, usually so as to produce involuntary laughter and wriggling **2 ITCHY FEELING** an itchy or scratchy feeling caused when a sensitive part of the body is touched lightly by something, especially material [14C. Probably < TICK[1] 'touch lightly'.] ◇ **tickled pink** *or* **silly** *or* **to death** extremely pleased (*informal*)

tickler /tík'lər/ *n* **1** ELEC ENG = **tickler coil 2** a difficult, delicate, or puzzling problem or situation (*informal*)

tickler coil *n* a small coil connected in series with a radio vacuum tube's plate circuit and inductively coupled to a coil located in a grid circuit to provide regenerative feedback

tickler file *n US* a file consisting of reminders of matters that must be dealt with

ticklish /tík'lish/ *adj* **1 SENSITIVE TO TICKLING** sensitive to being tickled **2 PROBLEMATIC** requiring careful or delicate handling because of its risk or difficulty **3 TOUCHY** easily irritated, angered, or upset —**ticklishly** *adv* —**ticklishness** *n*

tickly /tík'li/ (**-lier, -liest**) *adj* **1** producing a tickling or itching sensation on the surface of the skin **2** *Scotland* ticklish

tickseed /tík seed/ *n* an annual or perennial plant with opposite-lobed leaves, sometimes grown as an ornamental. Flowers: resembling daisies. Native to: North America. Genus: *Coreopsis*. [Because their seeds resemble the insects]

ticktack /tík tak/, **tictac** *n* **1** a system of sign language used by bookmakers to convey information at racecourses **2** a clicking or tapping sound [Mid-16C. An imitation of the sound.]

tick-tack-toe, tic-tac-toe *n US* HOBBIES = **noughts and crosses** [Probably an imitation of the sound of an earlier game in which players brought pencils down on slates with their eyes closed]

ticktock /tík tok/ *n* the clicking sound made by a clock or watch ■ *vi* to make a quiet recurring clicking sound (*refers to a timepiece*) [Mid-19C. An imitation of the sound.]

ticky-tacky /tíki táki/, **ticky-tack** *adj US* dull, unimaginative, and often of uniform quality or design (*informal*) ■ *n US* dull, unimaginative, or inferior materials, or something made from them (*informal*) [Reduplication of TACKY[2] 'shoddy']

Ticonderoga /tíkondə rṓgə/ village in NE New York State, site of Fort Ticonderoga, an important strategic fortification in the French and Indian War (1754–63) and the American War of Independence (1775–83). Population: 2,770 (1990).

tictac *n* GAMBLING = **ticktack**

tic-tac-toe *n US* HOBBIES = **tick-tack-toe**

tidal /tíd'l/ *adj* **1 OF TIDES** relating to or affected by tides **2 DEPENDENT ON TIDE** having a time of departure dependent on the phase of a tide ○ *a tidal ferry* **3 DEFINED BY TIDE LEVEL** changing in character or accessibility according to the level of the tide **4 FLUCTUATING** not constant but fluctuating between periods of intense activity and periods of little activity —**tidally** *adv*

tidal air *n* the volume of air that passes in and out of the body during normal breathing

tidal basin *n* an artificial basin cut in rock that fills up at high tide

tidal power, tidal energy *n* the generation of electricity using the force created by the rise and fall of ocean tides

tidal volume *n* PHYSIOL = **tidal air**

tidal wave *n* **1** an enormous and destructive ocean wave caused by extremely strong winds or seaquakes. ◊ **tsunami 2** a powerful widespread expression or surge of something ○ *a tidal wave of public emotion*

tidbit /tídbit/ *n* US = **titbit**

tiddle /tídd'l/ *vi* (**-dles, -dling, -dled**) to urinate (*babytalk*) ■ *n* an act of urination (*babytalk*) [Mid-19C. Alteration of PIDDLE.]

tiddler /tídd'lər/ *n* (*informal*) **1** a very small fish, especially a minnow or a stickleback **2** somebody or something that is small compared to most others [Late 19C. Probably related to TIDDLY[2].]

tiddly[1] /tídd'li/ (**-dlier, -dliest**) *adj* slightly intoxicated from having drunk a small amount of alcohol (*informal*) [Mid-19C. < ?]

tiddly[2] /tídd'li/ (**-dlier, -dliest**) *adj* very small (*informal*) [Mid-19C. Variant of obsolete *tiddy* < ?]

tiddlywink /tídd'li wingk/ *n* a plastic counter used in the game of tiddlywinks [Mid-19C. < ?]

tiddlywinks /tídd'li wingks/ *n* a game in which players try to flip plastic counters into a cup by pressing them on the side with a larger counter (+ *singular verb*)

tide /tīd/ *n* **1 RISE AND FALL OF SEA** the cyclical rise and fall of the sea or another body of water produced by the attraction of the Moon and Sun, occurring about every twelve hours **2 INFLOW OR OUTFLOW OF WATER** the ebb or flow of water at a particular place resulting from the cyclical rise and fall of the sea **3** GEOG = **flood tide** *n.* 1 **4 GRAVITATIONAL STRESS** a stress on something caused by a gravitational attraction, e.g. in the atmosphere or on an astronomical object **5 GENERAL TREND** something that rises and falls, especially a tendency or trend **6 CRUCIAL POINT** an extreme or critical point or position **7 PERIOD OF TIME** a period of time or a season (*archaic; usually in combination*) ○ *Yuletide* ■ *v* **1** *vti* **CARRY ALONG ON TIDE** to carry somebody or something along on the tide, or be carried along in this way **2** *vi* **EBB AND FLOW** to ebb and flow like the tide [Old English *tīd* 'time' < Indo-European, 'to divide'] —**tideless** *adj* ◇ **swim against the tide** to have an opinion or take a stance that is different from or opposite to that taken by others ◇ **swim with the tide** to follow the opinions and attitudes of other people ◇ **turn the tide** to reverse the way things happen

SPELLCHECK Do not confuse ***tide*** with ***tied***, which has a similar sound. Beware: your spellchecker will not catch this error.

tide over *vt* to help somebody through a difficult time, especially with a loan or gift of money

tide gauge *n* a gauge used to measure the level of tidal movement

tideland /tíd land/ *n US* land that is covered by water at high tide

tideline /tíd līn/ *n* a line made on a shore by the highest point of a tide

tidemark /tíd maark/ *n* **1 MARK LEFT BY TIDE** a mark made by the highest or lowest point of a tide **2 MARKER INDICATING LEVELS OF TIDES** a marker indicating the highest or lowest point of a tide **3 POINT MARKING RISE OR FALL** a point that somebody or something has reached, risen above, or fallen below **4 RING ROUND BATH** a usually grimy mark left in a bath showing the level of water it contained (*informal*) **5 DIRTY MARK ON BODY** a dirty mark on the skin showing where somebody has stopped washing (*informal*)

tide race *n* a fast tidal current

tide-rip *n* GEOG = **riptide**

tide table *n* a table showing the expected times and levels of tides

tidewaiter /tíd waytər/ *n* formerly, an officer who boarded incoming ships to enforce customs regulations

tidewater /tíd wawtər/ *n* **1 WATER AFFECTED BY TIDES** water whose movement or level is affected by tides **2 WATER COVERING LAND AT HIGH TIDE** water at high tide covering land that is dry at low tide **3** *US* **SEACOAST** a coastal region, especially that of E Virginia

tideway /tíd way/ *n* **1** a channel in which a tide runs **2** a current in a tidal channel

tidings /tídingz/ *npl* news or information (*literary*) ○ *I bring you glad tidings.* [Old English *tīdung*, alteration of Old Norse *tíðendi* 'events']

tidy /tídi/ *adj* (**-dier, -diest**) **1 NEAT IN APPEARANCE** having a neat orderly appearance **2 METHODICAL** tending to perform tasks in a systematic way **3 CONSIDERABLE** considerable and significant (*informal*) ○ *cost a tidy sum* **4** *NZ, US* **SATISFACTORY** adequate or satisfactory, especially when circumstances are taken into account (*informal*) ○ *negotiated a tidy redundancy package* ■ *vti* (**-dies, -dying, -died**) **MAKE TIDY** to make somebody or something neat and orderly ○ *We need to tidy the place up before they arrive.* ■ *n* (*plural* **-dies**) **1 ACT OF MAKING SOMETHING TIDY** an act of making something neat and orderly (*informal*) **2 BOX FOR HOLDING SMALL OBJECTS** a box for holding small objects that would otherwise lie around and look untidy ○ *a desk tidy* **3 SMALL RECEPTACLE FOR WASTE SCRAPS** a small receptacle kept beside or in a kitchen sink for the collection of waste scraps ○ *a sink tidy* **4** *US* **COVERING FOR BACK OF CHAIR** an ornamental protective covering for the back of a chair or sofa [13C. < TIDE 'time'.] —**tidily** *adv* —**tidiness** *n*

tidy-up *n* = **tidy** *n.* 1 (*informal*)

tie /tī/ *v* (**ties, tying, tied**) **1** *vt* **FASTEN WITH ROPE** to fasten things together with a rope, string, or cord ○ *They tied his hands together.* **2** *vt* **FASTEN BY KNOTTING** to fasten something with a knot or bow ○ *Tie your shoelaces.* **3** *vt* **MAKE A KNOT** to make a knot or bow with rope, string, or cord ○ *All Scouts learn how to tie knots.* **4** *vt* **CONNECT** to make a connection or link between people or things **5** *vt* **RESTRICT** to restrict somebody to certain conditions **6** *vi* **HAVE AN EQUAL SCORE** to achieve the same score or place as somebody else in a game, race, or competition **7** *vt* **SUSTAIN A MUSICAL NOTE** to hold a musical note from one bar to the next, thereby extending its value **8** *vt* **CONNECT NOTES WITH A CURVED LINE** in musical notation, to connect two notes with a curved line ■ *n* (*plural* **ties**) **1 STRIP OF FABRIC WORN ROUND NECK** a long thin piece of fabric worn round the neck, under a shirt collar, and tied at the front so that the ends hang down. ◊ **bow tie, bolo tie 2 SOMETHING FOR ATTACHING** a long thin piece of material such as rope or wire used to fasten or close something else ○ *ties for bin bags* ○ *Where are the ties for the garbage* *bags?* **3 CONNECTION** something that links or unites people or things **4 RESTRICTION** something that restricts or confines somebody or something **5 EQUAL OUTCOME** an equal score or result in a game, race, or competition **6 MATCH IN KNOCKOUT COMPETITION** a match in a knockout competition, especially in football ○ *a cup tie* **7 STRENGTHENING BEAM** a connecting, strengthening, or supporting beam or rod **8 CURVED LINE INDICATING EXTENSION OF NOTES** a curved line shown above or below two musical notes of the same pitch, indicating that they are to be sounded without a break for their combined duration **9** *US, Can* RAIL = **sleeper** *n.* 4 **10 SURVEYING MEASUREMENT** either of two measurements on a survey line used to fix the position of a reference point [Old English *tīgan* < Germanic, 'pull']

tie down *vt* prevent somebody from acting freely

tie up *v* **1** *vt* **BIND** to fasten or bind something using rope or string **2** *vti* **DOCK A BOAT** to moor a boat or ship by securing lines, or be moored in this way **3** *vt* **OCCUPY** to keep somebody or something busy ○ *I'm going to be tied up all afternoon in meetings.* **4** *vt* **COMPLETE** to complete the work needed for something **5** *vti* **STOP** to bring something to a halt, or come to a halt **6** *vt* **INVEST MONEY WITH RESTRICTIONS** to invest money in such a way that it cannot be used for other purposes **7** *vt* **PLACE RESTRICTIONS ON PROPERTY** to place legal restrictions on the selling or alienation of property

tieback /tī bak/ *n* a length of cord or fabric used to hold a curtain to one side

tie beam *n* a beam such as the bottom horizontal member of a roof truss that pulls together a structure and stops it spreading outwards

tiebreaker /tī braykər/, **tie-break** /-brayk/ *n* a means of deciding the winner of a game or competition when there is a tie —**tiebreaking** *adj*

tie clip, tie clasp *n* an ornamental clasp that holds a tie in place against a shirt

tied /tīd/ *adj* **1 SELLING ONLY OWNER'S PRODUCTS** owned by a producer, especially a brewery, and obliged to sell only its products **2 OWNED BY OCCUPANT'S EMPLOYER** owned by the occupant's employer and lived in only for the duration of the employment **3 LOANED TO BUY LENDER'S GOODS** loaned on condition of being spent only on goods or services supplied by the lender

SPELLCHECK See *tide.*

tie-dye *vt* **DYE DESIGNS USING BUNCHED CLOTH** to dye designs on cloth by tightly tying portions of it with waxed thread so that the dye only affects the exposed areas ■ *n* **1 FABRIC WITH TIE-DYED DESIGNS** a piece of fabric whose designs are made by tie-dyeing (*informal*) **2** the process of tie-dyeing cloth —**tie-dyeing** *n*

tie-dyeing *n* a method of dyeing textiles to produce patterns by tightly tying waxed thread round sections of the fabric so that they will not become impregnated with the dye

tie-in *n* **1 LINK** a link or relationship with something **2 JOINT PROMOTION OF PRODUCTS** an arrangement by which related products are sold, promoted, or marketed together, e.g. a book or toy along with a film **3 RELATED PRODUCT** a product that is sold, promoted, or marketed in close connection with another **4** *US* **SALE REQUIRING DUAL PURCHASES** a sale in which items are advertised or sold with the stipulation that they must be purchased together, or a product sold in this way

~~**tieing**~~ incorrect spelling of **tying**

tie line *n* a telephone line that connects two private exchanges

tiemannite /téemə nīt/ *n* a dark grey mineral form of mercury selenide [Mid-19C. < German *Tiemannit*, after J. C. W. F. *Tiemann* (1848–99), German scientist.]

Tien Shan /tyén shaán/ mountain range in Central Asia, stretching from Kyrgyzstan through NW China to Mongolia. Highest peak: Victory Peak 7,439 m/24,406 ft. Length: 2,400 km/1,500 mi.

tiepin /tī pin/ *n* an ornamental pin that holds a tie in place against a shirt. US term **tie tack**

tier /teer/ *n* **1 ROW OF SEATS IN RISING SERIES** any of a series of rows placed one above and behind another, e.g. seats in a theatre **2 LAYER** any of a series of layers or levels placed one above the other (*often in combination*) ○ *a three-tier cake* **3 LEVEL IN HIERARCHY** a hierarchical level in an organization (*often in combination*) ■ *vt* **ARRANGE IN RISING ROWS** to arrange something in rows rising one above the other [15C. < French *tire* 'rank, sequence, order' < *tirer* 'draw out, elongate'.] —**tiered** *adj*

SPELLCHECK See *tear.*

tierce /teerss, turss/ *n* **1** CHR = **terce 2 THREE CARDS OF THE SAME SUIT** a sequence of three cards of the same suit **3 PARRYING POSITION** the third of eight positions from which a fencing parry can be made **4 FORMER MEASURE OF CAPACITY** a former measure of capacity equal to 42 wine gallons [15C. Via Old French < Latin *tertia*, form of *tertius* 'third'.]

tiercel *n* BIRDS = **tercel**

tie rod *n* a metal rod that joins or supports two parts such as one used as a linkage in the steering mechanism of a motor vehicle

Tierra del Fuego /ti érrə del fwáygō/ archipelago off the southern tip of South America, belonging partly to Argentina and partly to Chile. Area: 71,500 sq. km/27,600 sq. mi. —**Fuegian** /fyoo éeji ən, fwáyji-/ *adj, n*

tie tack, tie tac *n US* CLOTHING = **tiepin**

tie-up *n* **1** something that connects one thing with another **2** *US* a temporary delay or obstruction, e.g. in the flow of traffic

tiff /tif/ *n* **1 QUARREL** a minor quarrel **2 ILL HUMOUR** a brief period of bad temper ■ *vi* **1 ARGUE** to have a minor quarrel with somebody **2 BE ILL-HUMOURED** to be in a bad temper [Early 18C. Probably suggesting the sound of escaping gas.]

ϟ**TIFF** *abbr* tagged image file format

tiffany /tíffəni/ (*plural* **-nies**) *n* a fine gauzy fabric [Early 17C. Via Old French *tifanie* < Greek *theophaneia* 'vision of God'.]

ϟ**TIFF file, TIF file** *n* a graphic file in a format often used for storing bit-mapped images

tiffin /tíffin/ *n S Asia* **1** a light midday meal or snack of savouries and sweets **2** = **tiffin-carrier** [Early 19C. Variant of *tiffing* < obsolete *tiff* 'to drink' < ?]

tiffin-carrier *n S Asia* a carrier consisting of several metal containers stacked one on top of another, used to carry prepared food

tig /tig/ *n* GAMES = **tag**² *n.* 1 ■ *vt* (**tigs, tigging, tigged**) GAMES = **tag**² *v.* 1 [15C. Variant of TICK¹ 'touch lightly'.]

tiger /tígər/ (*plural* **-gers** *or* **-ger**) *n* **1** a carnivorous cat, the largest member of the cat family, that has a tawny coat and black stripes. Native to: Asia. *Panthera tigris.* **2** a fierce, brave, or forceful person [13C. Via Old French *tigre* < Greek *tigris.*] —**tigerish** *adj* —**tigerishly** *adv* —**tigerishness** *n* ◇ **ride a tiger** be in a very difficult, precarious, or dangerous position

Tiger *n* FIN = **TIGR**

tiger beetle *n* a fast-running predatory beetle with strong sharp jaws for digging and brightly coloured patterned wing covers. Native to: warm regions. Family: Cicindelidae. [< its predatory habits]

tiger cat *n* **1** a small striped or spotted cat such as the margay, serval, or ocelot **2** a domestic cat with blotched or striped markings resembling those of a tiger

tigereye /tígər ī/ *n* MINERALS = **tiger's-eye**

tigerfish /tígər fish/ (*plural* **-fish** *or* **-fishes**) *n* **1** a small to medium-sized food fish characterized by bold dark curved stripes that extend to the tail. Native to: Indian and Pacific oceans. *Therapon jarbua.* **2** a freshwater fish of the piranha family that has sharp teeth and grows to about 1.4 m/4.5 ft in length. Native to: Africa. *Hydrocynus goliath.*

tiger lily *n* **1** an Asian lily. Flowers: red or orange, with dark purple or brown spots. *Lilium lancifolium* and *Lilium tigrinium.* **2** any lily that resembles the Asian tiger lily [< its colouring]

tiger moth *n* a moth that has bold black and yellow or orange markings, especially on its wings. Family: Arctiidae.

tiger salamander *n* a large black salamander with yellow or green stripes. Native to: North America. *Ambystoma tigrinum.* [< its stripes]

tiger's-eye *n* a striped yellow-brown rock composed of bands of quartz and crocidolite. Use: gems.

tiger shark *n* a large striped or spotted shark with a voracious and indiscriminate appetite. Native to: tropics. *Galeocerdo cuvieri.*

tiger snake *n* a highly venomous brown and yellow snake. Native to: SE Australia, Tasmania. Genus: *Notechis.*

tiger swallowtail *n* a large butterfly with a deeply forked tail and yellow wings with black stripes. Native to: North America. *Palilio glaucus* and *Palilio rutilus.*

tight /tīt/ *adj* **1 SNUG** fitting the body very closely ○ *a tight sweater* **2 TAUT** stretched so that there is no slack ○ *pulled the rope tight* **3 FIXED** firmly secured or held ○ *a tight knot* **4 SEALED** sealed against gas or liquid leaks ○ *An airlock must have a tight seal.* **5 STRICT** strictly controlled or administered ○ *security was tight for the conference* **6 CRAMPED** lacking sufficient space to move freely ○ *It's going to be tight in the back seat.* **7 HAVING NO EXTRA TIME** allowing no time beyond what is needed to do something ○ *a tight schedule* **8 HAVING NO EXTRA MONEY** allowing no money beyond what is required ○ *working to a tight budget* **9 MISERLY** excessively frugal with money **10 HARD TO GET OUT OF** difficult or dangerous to handle ○ *We're in a tight fix now.* **11 WITH CLOSE RIVALS** characterized by well-matched competitors or teams ○ *a tight race* **12 DRUNK** intoxicated with alcohol (*slang*) **13 WELL DONE** arranged or performed with style and precision ○ *a tight performance by the whole team* **14 SUCCINCT** characterized by clear concise expression ○ *tight prose* **15** *US* **INTIMATE** having a very close relationship with somebody (*informal*) ○ *He's tight with his boss.* **16 HARD TO GET** characterized by conditions in which demand exceeds supply, often with concomitant rising prices ○ *a tight economy* ■ *adv* **FIRMLY** in a firm, close, snug, or secure way ○ *hold on tight* [14C. Alteration of obsolete *thight* 'dense, thick' < Old Norse *þéttr* 'watertight, dense'.] —**tightly** *adv* —**tightness** *n* ◇ **in a tight spot** *or* **corner** in a difficult or dangerous situation

tighten /tīt'n/ *vti* to become or cause something to become tight or tighter —**tightener** *n*

tight end *n* in American football, a player who lines up near to the tackle

tightfisted /tīt fístid/ *adj* disinclined to spend money —**tightfistedly** *adv* —**tightfistedness** *n*

tight-fitting *adj* **1** fitting closely to the body ○ *tight-fitting jeans* **2** fitting closely on to a container so that its contents are not exposed to the air ○ *a tight-fitting lid*

tight head *n* in rugby, the prop forward positioned to the right of the hooker in the front row of the scrum

tightknit /tīt nít/ *adj* **1** closely united by love, friendship, or common interests ○ *a tightknit community* **2** arranged or functioning as a well-structured whole

tight-lipped /-lípt/ *adj* **1** unwilling to communicate ○ *He is remaining tight-lipped in the face of intense press speculation.* **2** having the lips firmly closed, e.g. in anger or pain

tightrope /tīt rōp/ *n* a rope or wire stretched taut and suspended above the ground, on which somebody walks or performs a balancing act ◇ **walk a tightrope** to have to deal cautiously with a precarious situation, often one involving a choice or compromise

tights /tīts/ *npl* **1 SHEER ONE-PIECE GARMENT** a light tight-fitting sheer covering for a woman's legs that stretches from the toes up to an elastic waistband. US term **pantyhose 2 THICK ONE-PIECE GARMENT** a one-piece close-fitting garment made of opaque coloured material, covering the body from the waist to the feet and worn by women and girls for warmth and casual wear **3 DANCER'S ONE-PIECE GARMENT** a one-piece close-fitting garment covering the body from the neck or waist to the feet, worn by men and women dancers and acrobats

tightwad /tīt wod/ *n US, Can* a miser (*insult*)

Tiglath-pileser I /tíg lath pī léezər/ (*b.* 1115?-1077? BC) Assyrian king

tiglic acid /tígglik-/ *n* $C_5H_8O_2$ a viscous poisonous colourless liquid. Source: croton oil. Use: pharmaceutical preparations, manufacture of perfumes. [< modern Latin *(Croton) tiglium*, scientific name of the tree from whose seeds croton oil is obtained]

tigon /tígən/, **tiglon** /tíglən/ *n* the offspring of a male tiger and a female lion. ◊ **liger** [Mid-20C. Blend of TIGER + LION.]

TIGR /tígər/, **Tiger** *n* a bond linked to US treasury bonds, profits from which are subject to UK tax when the bond is cashed or redeemed. Full form **Treasury Investment Growth Receipts**

Tigray /tée gray/, **Tigre** region in NE Ethiopia. Capital: Mekele. Population: 3,136,267 (1994). Area: 65,786 sq. km/25,400 sq. mi.

tigress /tígrəss/ *n* **1** a female tiger **2** a fierce, brave, or passionate woman [Late 16C. < TIGER after French *tigresse* 'tigress'.]

Tigrinya /ti greénya/ *n* a Semitic language of N Ethiopia. Native speakers: 4 million. [Mid-19C. < Tigrinya.] — **Tigrinya** *adj*

Tigris /tígriss/ river in SW Asia, rising in SE Turkey and flowing through Iraq to the River Euphrates. Length: 1,900 km/1,180 mi.

Tijuana /ti waána/ city in NW Mexico, near the United States border. Population: 747,381 (1990).

tike *n* = **tyke**

tiki /teéki/ *n* **1** a small carved human foetal figure, especially in greenstone, representing an ancestor and worn as an amulet by some Maori and Polynesian peoples **2** a stone or wooden representation of a Polynesian god [Late 18C. < Maori, 'image'.]

tikka /teéka/ *adj* a South Asian dish of skewered meat that is marinated and then dry-roasted in an oven [Mid-20C. < Punjabi *ṭikkā*.]

til /til/ *n* FOOD = **sesame** *n.* 2 [Mid-19C. < Sanskrit *tila*.]

'til *conj, prep* = **till**[1] [Mid-20C. Shortening.]

Tilak /tíllak/, **B. G.** (1856–1920) Indian journalist and political activist. Full name **Balwantrao Gangadhar Tilak**

tilapia /ti láppi a, -láy-/ (*plural* **-as** *or* **-a**) *n* a freshwater fish of the cichlid family, introduced and cultivated worldwide. Native to: tropical Africa. Genus: *Tilapia*. [Mid-19C. < modern Latin.]

Tilburg /tíl burg/ city in S Netherlands. Population: 163,383 (1994).

tilde /tílda/ *n* a mark (~) placed over a letter to show that the pronunciation is nasalized, e.g. 'ã' or 'õ' in Portuguese, or palatalized, e.g. over 'n' in Spanish [Mid-19C. Via Spanish < Latin *titulus* 'heading'.]

tile /tīl/ *n* **1 COVERING FOR FLOORS, ROOFS, OR WALLS** a thin flat or curved piece of baked, sometimes glazed, clay or synthetic material used to cover roofs, floors, and walls, or for decoration **2 SHORT PIPE IN A DRAIN** a short pipe of baked clay, concrete, or plastic used in making a drain **3** *US* **HOLLOW BLOCK** a hollow block of baked clay, concrete, or gypsum used as a building material for walls or floors **4 TILES COLLECTIVELY** tiles considered collectively **5 PLAYING PIECE** a rectangular playing piece in various games such as mahjongg **6 HAT** a hat (*dated informal*) ■ *v* (**tiles, tiling, tiled**) **1** *vt* **LAY TILES ON** to cover a surface with tiles **2** *vt* **FIT WITH DRAINAGE TILES** to put drainage tiles in something **3** *vti* **ARRANGE WINDOWS ON COMPUTER SCREEN** to arrange the windows on a computer screen side by side so that all are visible [Pre-12C. < Latin *tegula*.] — **tiler** *n* ◇ **on the tiles** in pursuit of drinking and pleasure (*informal*)

tilefish /tīl fish/ (*plural* **-fish** *or* **-fishes**) *n* a long blue deep-water fish with yellow spots on its upper body. Native to: Atlantic coast of North America. *Lopholatilus chamaeleonticeps*.

tiling /tīling/ *n* **1 LAID TILES** tiles that have been laid **2 LAYING OF TILES** the laying of tiles on a wall or floor **3 TILES** tiles collectively

till[1] /til/, **'till, 'til** *conj, prep* until [Old English *til* 'up to a particular point' < Germanic, 'aim, goal']

USAGE till or **until**? Both words have the same meaning and function (conjunction and preposition), and are largely interchangeable. ***Till*** is more likely to be heard in speech: *Just wait till we get home!* ***Until*** is more usual at the beginning of a sentence: *Until last week there was no one here that we knew.* The spellings *'til* and *'till* reflect the commonly held belief that ***till*** is a shortened form of ***until***, but ***till*** is in fact the older form.

till[2] /til/ *n* **1** a box, drawer, or tray, e.g. in a cash register, in which money is kept **2** COMM = **checkout** *n.* 1 [15C. < ?]

till[3] /til/ *vt* to prepare land for the growing of crops by ploughing or harrowing [Old English *tilian* 'cultivate, strive to obtain something' < Germanic, 'aim, purpose'] — **tillable** *adj*

till[4] /til/ *n* sediment of various particle sizes deposited by the direct action of ice [Late 17C. < ?]

tillage /tíllij/ *n* **1** the ploughing or harrowing of land in preparation for growing crops **2** land that has been tilled

tillandsia /ti lándzi a/ *n* an epiphytic plant of the pineapple family such as Spanish moss. Native to: tropical or subtropical America. Genus: *Tillandsia*. [Mid-18C. < modern Latin, after Elias *Tillands* (1640–93), Swedish botanist.]

tiller[1] /tíllar/ *n* the means by which a small boat is steered, consisting of a handle attached to the rudder [14C. < Anglo-Norman *telier* 'weaver's beam' < Latin *tela* 'web'.]

tiller[2] /tíllar/ *n* a person or machine that ploughs or cultivates the soil

tiller[3] /tíllar/ *n* a shoot growing from the base of a stem, especially the stem of a grass [Mid-17C. Probably < Old English *telgor* 'extended' < *telga* 'branch'.]

tillerman /-man/ (*plural* **-men** /-man/) *n* a handler of a tiller who steers a boat

Tillich /tíllik/, **Paul** (1886–1965) German-born US philosopher and theologian

Tilly /tílli/, **Johann Tserclaes, Count** (1559–1632) Flemish soldier

tilt[1] /tilt/ *v* **1** *vti* **SLOPE** to slant, or cause something to slant ○ *She tilted her head as she listened.* **2** *vi US* **HAVE AS A PREFERENCE** to tend towards favouring a particular opinion, course of action, or side in a dispute **3** *vi* **CRITICIZE** to make a spoken or written attack on somebody or something **4** *vi* **COMBAT** to combat or struggle against somebody or something **5** *vti* **CHARGE WITH A LANCE** to attack an opponent using a lance **6** *vi* **JOUST WITH SOMEBODY** to take part in a joust against somebody **7** *vi* **POINT A LANCE** to hold a lance ready for combat in a joust **8** *vt* **USE A TILT HAMMER ON** to work on something using a tilt hammer ■ *n* **1 ACT OF TILTING** an act of tilting or of causing something to tilt **2 INCLINE** a slanted surface or position ○ *His hat was at a rakish tilt.* **3 CRITICISM** a spoken or written attack on somebody or something **4** *US* **PREFERENCE** a tendency to favour a particular opinion, course of action, or side in a dispute **5 JOUST** a jousting contest **6 LANCE THRUST** a thrust made with a lance in a jousting contest **7** ENG = **tilt hammer** [14C. Probably < assumed Old English *tyltan* 'fall over' < Germanic, 'unsteady'.] —**tilter** *n* ◇ **(at) full tilt** at full speed

tilt[2] /tilt/ *n* a canvas cover or canopy used to cover an otherwise open boat, booth, or trailer of a lorry [15C. < Old English *teld*.]

tilth /tilth/ *n* **1 TILLING OF LAND** the ploughing of land in preparation for growing crops **2 TILLED LAND** land under cultivation **3 CONDITION OF LAND** the condition of a piece of tilled land, in terms of its cultivation history and suitability for crops **4 DEGREE OF FINENESS OF SOIL** the degree of fineness of soil particles in the topmost soil layer [Old English *tilþ(e)* < *tilian* (see TILL[3])]

tilt hammer *n* a heavy drop hammer used to forge metal, pivoted by a lever

tiltyard /tílt yaard/ *n* a place, usually enclosed, where a jousting contest was held

Tim. *abbr* Timothy

Timaru /tímmaroo/ city on the east-central coast of the South Island, New Zealand. Population: 27,100 (1998 estimate).

timbal /tímb'l/, **tymbal** *n* a kettledrum (*archaic*) [Late 17C. < French *timbale*, alteration (after *cymbale* 'cymbal') of obsolete *tamballe* < (influenced by *tambour* 'drum') Spanish *atabal* < Arabic *aṭ-ṭabl* 'the drum'.]

timbale /tam baál/ *n* **1 DISH MADE IN A MOULD** a dish consisting of a mixture of ingredients, often set with eggs, made in a mould **2 COOKING MOULD** a small deep or tall mould in which a timbale is cooked ■ **timbales** *npl* **LATIN AMERICAN DRUMS** a pair of cylindrical drums, commonly played in Latin American dance music [Early 19C. < French (see TIMBAL).]

timber /tímbar/ *n* **1 WOOD CONSTRUCTION MATERIAL** wood that has been sawn into boards, planks, or other materials for use in building, woodworking, or cabinetmaking **2 GROWING TREES** standing trees or their wood **3 WOODED LAND** land covered with trees **4 LARGE WOODEN BUILDING SUPPORT** a large piece of wood, usually squared, used in a building, e.g. as a beam **5 PART OF SHIP'S FRAMEWORK** a large piece of wood used in the framework of a wooden ship ■ *adj* **WOODEN** constructed of wood ■ *interj* **WARNING OF A FALLING TREE** used by a lumberjack to warn others that a tree has been cut and is about to fall ■ *vt* **PROVIDE WITH TIMBERS** to build, cover, or support something with timbers [Old English, 'a building' < Indo-European, 'build']

timbered /tímbard/ *adj* **1** made of timber, or having timbers (*often in combination*) ○ *a half-timbered house* **2** covered with growing trees

timberhead /tímbar hed/ *n* the top of a timber of a ship that projects above the deck and is used as a tall post (**bollard**) for securing the ship to a wharf or dock

timber hitch *n* a knot used to tie a rope around a spar or log that is to be hoisted or hauled

timbering /tímbaring/ *n* timber, or objects made of timber

timberland /tímbar land/ *n US* an area of wooded land, especially one with trees that have commercial value as timber

timberline /tímbar līn/ *n US* ECOL = **tree line** *n.* 1

timber rattlesnake *n* a poisonous rattlesnake that is yellow-brown with wide dark bands and feeds on small mammals. Native to: E United States. *Crotalus horridus*.

timber wolf *n* ZOOL = **grey wolf**

timberwork /tímbar wurk/ *n* something constructed of timber, or the timber parts of something

timberyard /tímbar yaard/ *n* a place where timber and other building materials are stored and sold. US term **lumberyard**

timbre /támbar, tímbar, táNbra/ *n* **1** the quality of a speech sound that comes from its tone rather than its pitch or volume **2** the quality or colour of tone of an instrument or voice [Mid-19C. Via French, originally 'drum, bell hit with a hammer' < Greek *tumpanon* 'drum'.]

timbrel /tímbral/ *n* in the Bible, a tambourine or small hand drum [Early 16C. < ?]

Timbuktu[1] /tìmb uk toó/, **Timbuctoo** *n* anywhere that is far away or extremely remote (*informal*) [After TIMBUKTU[1]]

Timbuktu[2] /tìmb uk toó/ ♦ **Tombouctou**

time /tīm/ *n* **1 SYSTEM OF DISTINGUISHING EVENTS** (*symbol t*) a dimension that enables two identical events occurring at the same point in space to be distinguished, measured by the interval between the events **2 PERIOD WITH LIMITS** a limited period during which an action, process, or condition exists or takes place ○ *elapsed time* **3 METHOD OF MEASURING INTERVALS** a system for measuring intervals of time ○ *sidereal time* ○ *British Summer Time* **4 MINUTE OR HOUR** the minute or hour as indicated by a clock ○ *What time is it?* **5 TIME AS A CAUSATIVE FORCE** time conceived as a force capable of acting on people and objects ○ *time's ravages* **6 MOMENT SOMETHING OCCURS** a moment or period at which something takes place ○ *at the time of her 90th birthday* **7 SUITABLE MOMENT** a moment or period chosen as appropriate for something to be done or to take place ○ *The times for the games will be announced.* **8 UNALLOCATED PERIOD** a period that is not allocated for a particular purpose ○ *I had time on my hands.* **9 PERIOD NEEDED** a period required, allocated, or taken to complete an activity ○ *How much time?* **10 PERIOD WITH A PARTICULAR QUALITY** a period, activity, or occasion that has a particular quality or characteristic (*often plural*) ○ *They've been through some rough times.* ○ *We had an interesting time there.* **11 APPOINTED MOMENT** a designated or customary moment or period at which something is done or takes place ○ *It's time to get up.* **12 CLOSING TIME** the time at which a pub or bar is legally required to close **13 CERTAIN INTERVAL** a limited but unspecified period ○ *We stayed for a time.* **14 HISTORICAL PERIOD** a period in history, often characterized by a particular event or person (*often plural*) ○ *in Shakespeare's time* ○ *ancient times* **15 NOW** the present as distinguished from the past or future (*often plural*) ○ *technology that is ahead of the times* **16 GEOLOGICAL DIVISION** a chronological division of geological history **17 ANTICIPATED MOMENT** a moment in which some important event such as a birth or death is expected to happen ○ *He knew his time had come.* **18 SOMEBODY'S LIFETIME** a period during which somebody is alive, especially the most active or productive period in somebody's life ○ *She'd been a well-known athlete in her time.* ○ *We didn't worry about such trifles in my time.* **19 APPRENTICESHIP PERIOD** a period during which somebody is an apprentice ○ *had served his time* **20 PRISON TERM** a term in prison (*informal*) ○ *serve time for robbery* **21 MILITARY SERVICE** a term of military service **22 SEASON** a period during which particular climatic conditions prevail ○ *the rainy times of the year* **23 INSTANCE** a separate occasion of a recurring event ○ *I told you three times.* **24 TEMPO OF MUSIC** the relative speed at which a musical composition is played **25 MUSICAL BEAT** the number of beats per bar of a musical composition **26 PERIOD WORKED** the period during a day or week that somebody works ○ *working half time* **27 PAY** a rate of pay ○ *paid double time* **28 PLAYING PERIOD** a period of play in a game **29** *US* SPORTS = **timeout** *n.* 1 ■ *v* (**times, timing, timed**) **1** *vt* **MEASURE HOW LONG SOMETHING TAKES** to measure or record the duration, speed, or rate of something **2** *vt* **SCHEDULE** to plan the moment or occasion for something, especially in order to achieve the best result or effect ○ *time an entrance* **3** *vt* **SET THE TIME OF** to regulate or set the time of something such as a clock or a train's schedule **4** *vi* **STAY IN RHYTHM** to keep time to a rhythmic or musical beat [Old English *tīma* 'period of time' < Germanic, 'extend'] ◇ **all in good time** no sooner than is appropriate ◇ **all the time** continuously ◇ **at one time 1** at a time in the past **2** simultaneously ◇ **at the same time 1** simultaneously **2** nevertheless ◇ **at times** sometimes ◇ **behind the times** out of touch with modern fashions, methods, or attitudes ◇ **bide your time** to wait patiently for the right opportunity ◇ **for the time being** for a short period of time starting from now ◇ **from time to time** occasionally ◇ **have no time for somebody** *or* **something** to regard somebody or something with dislike or contempt ◇ **have the time of your life** to have a very enjoyable experience ◇ **in good time 1** early enough ○ *got there in good time so we could find a parking space* **2** quickly ◇ **in (less than) no time** in a very short period of time ◇ **in time 1** early enough ○ *We were in time for the concert.* **2** after some time has passed ○ *He'll understand in time that you were trying to help him.* **3** in the correct rhythm ○ *clapping in time to the music* ◇ **in your own time 1** not during working hours **2** at a speed or pace that feels natural and comfortable ◇ **keep time 1** to show the time accurately **2** to do something in the correct rhythm, or in the same rhythm as somebody or something else ◇ **live on borrowed time** to enjoy an unexpected extension of life ◇ **make time with somebody** *US* to pursue somebody as a sexual partner (*informal*) ◇ **mark time 1** to continue marching in rhythm without moving forwards **2** to do something that makes no contribution towards achieving a goal or ambition while awaiting an opportunity to make progress ◇ **on time** at the scheduled time ◇ **once upon a time** used at the beginning of fairy tales and children's stories to indicate that something happened a long time ago or in an imaginary world ◇ **pass the time of day (with somebody)** to engage in casual conversation with somebody ◇ **play for time** to delay action or a decision in the hope that conditions will be more favourable later on ◇ **take your time 1** to take whatever time is necessary **2** to do something unacceptably slowly ◇ **time after time, time and (time) again** repeatedly ◇ **time out of mind** for an extremely long time ◇ **time was** there was a time in the past

---

LITERARY LINK ***A Brief History of Time***, (1988) by Stephen Hawking. This best-selling text aims to describe fundamental concepts in physics in terms that the general reader can understand. It covers a wide range of subjects, from the origin of the universe to the nature of time itself, and explains the theories put forward by other scientists such as Galileo, Newton, and Einstein.

SPELLCHECK Do not confuse ***time*** with ***thyme***, which has a similar sound. Beware: your spellchecker will not catch this error.

---

time and a half *n* a rate of pay equal to one and a half times the normal rate, usually paid for overtime work

time and motion study *n* an analysis of the working practices of, e.g. a person, department, or factory, done with the aim of finding ways to increase efficiency

⚡**time bomb** *n* **1 BOMB EXPLODING AT A FIXED TIME** a bomb with a timing mechanism that allows it to explode at a specified time **2 FUTURE DANGER** something that is not dangerous or harmful at the moment but is likely to become so **3 TIME-TRIGGERED COMPUTER VIRUS** a computer virus either existing independently or included in a larger program that is triggered by date or by the length of time a computer application is used

time capsule *n* a container of articles representative of the present, placed in a building's foundations or buried for a future generation to find and learn about the period it represents

timecard /tīm kaard/ *n* a card that an employee has stamped by a time clock when starting and finishing work

time clock *n* a clock with a mechanism for stamping employees' timecards when they start and finish work

time-consuming *adj* taking up or wasting a great deal of time

time deposit *n* a bank deposit from which a withdrawal can be made only after a specified period of time or after giving notice. ◊ **demand deposit**

time dilation, time dilatation *n* the principle that time elapsed is relative to motion, so that time passes more slowly for a system in motion than for one at rest relative to an outside observer

timed-release, time-release *adj* formulated to release an active ingredient gradually to prolong its effect

time exposure *n* **1** the exposure of photographic film for an unusually long time to achieve a desired effect **2** a photograph taken by time exposure

time frame *n* a period of time during which something takes place or is planned to take place ○ *What's the time frame for the project?*

time-honoured *adj* respected or continued because of having been the custom for a long time

time immemorial *n* **1** time so distant in the past as to be beyond memory or record **2** the time prior to the keeping of official legal records in England, fixed at 1189, the beginning of Richard I's reign

timekeeper /tīm keepər/ *n* **1 SOMEBODY RECORDING THE TIME ELAPSED** a recorder of the time elapsed during a sporting event **2 SOMEBODY RECORDING THE TIME WORKED** a recorder of time worked by employees **3 SOMEBODY CONSIDERED IN TERMS OF PUNCTUALITY** an employee considered in terms of his or her punctuality ○ *She's a hard worker and a good timekeeper.* **4 WATCH OR CLOCK** an instrument for recording or showing the time such as a watch or clock **5 WATCH CONSIDERED IN TERMS OF ACCURACY** a watch or clock considered in terms of its accuracy —**timekeeping** *n*

time lag *n* an amount of time that passes between two connected events

time-lapse photography *n* a method of filming a slow process such as the opening of a flower by taking a series of single exposures, then showing them at higher speed to simulate continuous action

timeless /tīmləss/ *adj* **1** remaining invariable throughout time ○ *fiction that has a timeless appeal* **2** having no beginning or end —**timelessly** *adv* —**timelessness** *n*

time limit *n* a period of time within which something must be done or is effective

time line *n* a linear representation of significant events in a subject area, e.g. the history of art, shown in chronological order

time loan *n* a loan that has to be repaid by or on a given date. ◊ **call loan**

time lock *n* a lock on a device such as a safe or bank vault with a timing mechanism that allows it to open only at set times

timely /tīmli/ (**-lier, -liest**) *adj* happening or done at the right time or an appropriate time ○ *a timely invention* —**timeliness** *n* —**timely** *adv*

time machine *n* a fictional or hypothetical machine that can be used to travel backwards or forwards in time

time note *n US* a legal document such as a promissory note that specifies a date for repayment

time-off *n* time that somebody spends away from work, study, or other usual duties

time-on *n Aus* in Australian Rules football, a period of time added on at the end of each quarter to make up for time lost through stoppages

timeous /tīməss/ *adj Scotland* happening or done in good time —**timeously** *adv*

⚡**timeout** /tīm owt/ *n* **1 TIME DURING WHICH GAME STOPS** in some games, a break taken to allow players to rest, receive medical treatment, confer, or be substituted **2 LACK OF COMPUTER RESPONSE** an interruption in the operation of a computer when a device such as a printer or disk drive does not respond to a command in a predetermined amount of time ■ *interj* **REQUEST FOR A BREAK** used to ask for or suggest a break in a game or an activity

time out *n US* a short break or rest from work or other activities ○ *took time out from her studies to travel for a year*

timepiece /tīm peess/ *n* an instrument such as a watch or clock for recording or showing the time, especially one that does not strike or chime

timer /tīmər/ *n* **1 TIME-SETTING DEVICE** a device that can be preset to start or stop something at a given time or that sounds after a set period of time **2 TIME-RECORDING DEVICE** a device such as a stopwatch for recording, showing, or measuring time **3 SOMEBODY TRACKING TIME** a measurer or recorder of elapsed time **4 DEVICE CONTROLLING IGNITION** a device in an internal-combustion engine that controls the timing of the spark in the cylinders

time-release *adj* PHARM = **timed-release**

times /tīmz/ *prep* used to indicate that a number is to be multiplied by another ○ *Three times two is six.*

timesaving /tīm sayving/ *adj* designed to reduce the length of time taken to do something —**timesaver** *n*

timescale /tīm skayl/ *n* **1** a period of time scheduled for something to be completed **2** a measurement of time relative to the time in which a typical event occurs, e.g. in geological or cosmic time

time series *n* a sequence of data gathered at uniformly spaced intervals of time

time-served *adj* having completed an apprenticeship and therefore fully competent to work as a tradesperson

timeserver /tīm survər/ *n* somebody whose opinions and behaviour change to suit the times and circumstances without regard for principle —**timeserving** *n, adj*

timeshare /tīm shair/ *n* **1** = **time sharing** *n.* 1 **2** a property, usually an apartment in a resort area, that is jointly owned by people who use it at different times

⚡**time sharing** *n* **1** the joint ownership of a property such as an apartment in a resort area, in which each owner may occupy the property for a specific time during the year **2** a technique for the concurrent use of a computer by many people working at remote terminals, each apparently operating as the only user of the computer's resources —**time-share** *vti* —**time-sharer** *n*

time sheet *n* a sheet or card on which the hours worked by an employee are recorded

time signature *n* a sign used in music to show metre, represented by a fraction in which the upper figure shows beats to the bar and the lower figure shows each beat's time value

times sign *n* a multiplication sign (*informal*)

times table *n* a multiplication table (*informal; often in combination*)

time-stamp *n* a part of the financial order-routing process in which the time of day is stamped on an order when it is received on the trading floor and when it is completed

time study *n* INDUST = **time and motion study**

time switch *n* an electrical switch that can be set to turn an appliance on or off at a particular time

timetable /tīm tayb'l/ *n* a list of the times at which events are to occur, e.g. the arrival and departure times of trains or the times of school classes. US term **schedule** *n.* 3 ■ *vti* (**-bles, -bling, -bled**) to put something in its chronological place in a list of events

time-tested *adj US* proved to be effective over a long period

time trial *n* a race in which competitors compete individually for the fastest time

time warp *n* a hypothetical distortion in the continuum of space-time, popular in science fiction, allowing time to stand still or people to travel from one time to another

time-wasting *n* **1** the wasting or frittering away of time **2** the employment of negative tactics to prevent an opponent from scoring towards the end of a sports event —**time-waster** *n*

timework /tīm wurk/ *n* work paid according to the time it takes, especially by the hour or the day —**timeworker** *n*

timeworn /tīm wawrn/ *adj* **1** showing the effects of having been used for a long period of time **2** having lost effectiveness through overuse ○ *a timeworn phrase*

time zone *n* any of the 24 longitudinal areas into which the world is divided and within which the same standard time is used

timid /timmid/ *adj* demonstrating a lack of courage or self-assurance [Mid-16C. Directly or via French < Latin *timidus* 'fearful' < *timere* 'to fear'.] —**timidity** /ti míddəti/ *n* —**timidly** *adv*

timing /tīming/ *n* **1 JUDGMENT OF WHEN TO ACT** the ability to choose or the choice of the best moment to do or say something, e.g. in performing music or comedy or in sport ○ *a comedian with an immaculate sense of timing* ○ *split-second timing* **2 RECORDING OF TIME** the measurement and recording of the time taken to do something **3 ADJUSTMENT OF VALVES OF ENGINE** the adjustment of the sequence and relative position of the valves and crankshaft of an automobile engine so that maximum output power is achieved

Timişoara /timmi swaarə/ city in W Romania. Population: 327,830 (1994).

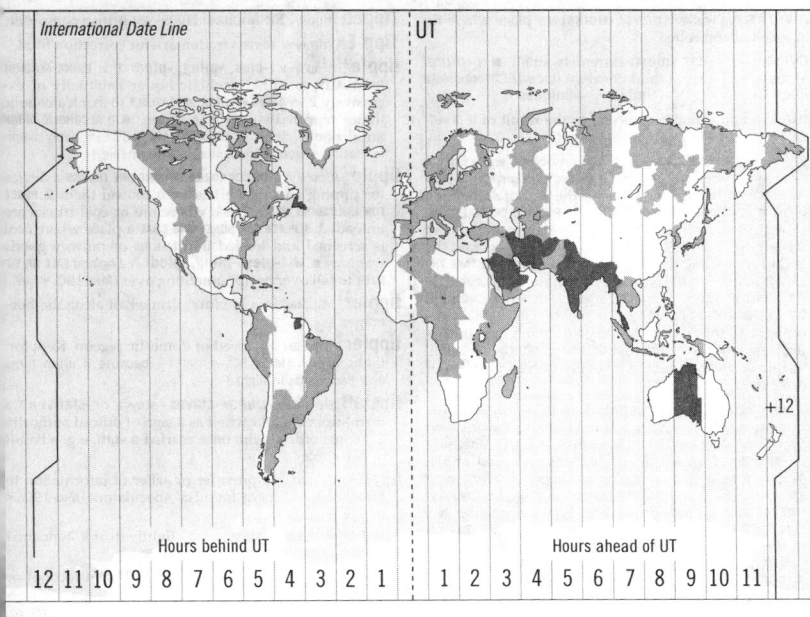

International Date Line UT

Hours behind UT | Hours ahead of UT

+12

12 11 10 9 8 7 6 5 4 3 2 1 | 1 2 3 4 5 6 7 8 9 10 11

Even numbered hours from Universal Time (UT)

Odd numbered hours from Universal Time

Varies from relevant time zone by half hour

Time zone

timocracy /ti mókrəssi/ (*plural* **-cies**) *n* **1** government in which the possession of property is a qualification for holding office **2** a form of government in which honour is the guiding principle [15C. Via French *timocratie* < Greek *timokratia* < *timē* 'honour, value'.] —**timocratic** /tímmə kráttik/ *adj*

Timor /tèe mawr/ largest and easternmost of the Lesser Sunda Islands, in the Malay Archipelago. Population: 1,382,207 (1980). Area: 30,820 sq. km/11,900 sq. mi.

timorous /tímmərəss/ *adj* showing fear or hesitancy [15C. Via Old French < medieval Latin *timorosus* < Latin *timere* 'to fear'.] —**timorously** *adv* —**timorousness** *n*

Timor Sea arm of the Indian Ocean separating the island of Timor from N Australia. Area: 450,000 sq. km/174,000 sq. mi.

timothy /tímməthi/, **timothy grass** *n* a perennial grass with a cylindrical flower spike, widely cultivated for hay and pasture. Native to: temperate regions. *Phleum pratense*. [Mid-18C. After *Timothy* Hanson, American farmer who introduced the grass to the Carolinas around 1720.]

Timothy /tímməthi/ *n* two books in the Bible, in the form of epistles addressed to Timothy, traditionally believed to be from St Paul. They are concerned with the organization of Christian doctrine and codes of Christian behaviour.

Timothy, St *n* in the Bible, an early Christian missionary, and friend and disciple of St Paul

timpani /tímpəni/, **tympani** *n* a set of two or more kettledrums, usually played as part of an orchestra (+ *singular or plural verb*) [Late 19C. < Italian, plural of *timpano* 'kettledrum' < Greek *tumpanon* 'drum'.] —**timpanist** *n*

timps /timps/ *npl* timpani (*informal*) [Mid-20C. Shortening.]

tin /tin/ *n* **1** METALLIC ELEMENT (*symbol* **Sn**) a silvery, easily shaped metallic element. Source: oxide ore. Use: alloys, e.g. solder, bronze, and pewter, protective coating for steel. **2** CONTAINER a sealed container for food or drink, made of thin sheet metal coated with tin or of other thin metal, e.g. aluminium. US term **can**[1] *n*. **1** **3** SHEET-

METAL CONTAINER a container with a lid, made of thin sheet metal and often decorated **4** AMOUNT IN TIN the amount that a tin holds **5** CORRUGATED IRON corrugated or galvanized iron **6** MONEY money (*dated informal*) ■ *adj* **1** MADE OF TIN made from thin sheet metal coated with tin **2** MADE OF CORRUGATED IRON made of corrugated or galvanized iron ■ *vt* (**tins, tinning, tinned**) **1** PUT FOOD IN TINS to preserve or seal food in tins. US term **can**[1] **2** COAT WITH TIN to coat or plate something with tin [Old English, < Germanic]

tinamou /tínni moo/ (*plural* **-mous** *or* **-mou**) *n* a short round-bodied ground-dwelling bird. Native to: grassy and jungle areas of Central and South America. Family: Tinamidae. [Late 18C. Via French < Carib *tinamu*.]

Tinbergen /tín burgən/, **Jan** (1903–94) Dutch economist

tincal /tíngk'l/ *n* a sodium borate mineral formed by the weathering of borax [Mid-17C. Probably via Portuguese < Persian, Urdu *tinkār* < Sanskrit *ṭaṅkaṇa*.]

tin can *n* **1** a container made of tin or aluminium, especially one used for food **2** US a naval destroyer (*informal*)

tinct /tingkt/ *n* TINT a tint (*archaic*) ■ *vti* TINT to tint (*archaic*) ■ *adj* TINTED tinted or coloured (*literary*) [15C. < Latin *tinctus* 'a dyeing' (see TINT).]

tincture /tíngkchər/ *n* **1** ALCOHOL SOLUTION a solution of a plant extract or chemical in alcohol ○ *tincture of iodine* **2** TINGE OR COLOUR a tint or slight coloration **3** TINY AMOUNT a hint or small amount of something **4** HERALDIC COLOUR a colour, metal, or fur used in heraldry ■ *vt* (**-tures, -turing, -tured**) **1** ADD A TINT TO to give something a hint of colour **2** IMBUE to suffuse something with a quality or property ○ *praise tinctured with criticism* [14C. < Latin *tinctura* 'dyeing' < past participle of *tingere* 'dye'.]

Tindal /tínd'l/ ♦ **William Tyndale**

tinder /tíndər/ *n* material such as dry sticks that is easily combustible and can be used for lighting a fire [Old English *tynder* < Germanic, 'ignite, kindle']

tinderbox /tíndər boks/ *n* **1** a metal box containing tinder, often fitted with a flint and steel, formerly used for lighting fires **2** a person, place, or situation that is likely to become violent

tine /tín/ *n* **1** a thin pointed projection of a utensil or implement such as a fork or pitchfork **2** a pointed branch of a deer's antler [Old English *tind*] —**tined** *adj*

tinea /tínni ə/ *n* an infection of the skin caused by any of several species of fungi that live as parasites on the outer layer of the skin, nails, or hair [14C. < Latin, 'gnawing worm, moth'.] —**tineal** *adj*

tinea barbae /-baarbi/ *n* barber's itch (*technical*) [< Latin, 'tinea of the beard']

tinea cruris /-króoriss/ *n* dhobi itch (*technical*) [< Latin, 'tinea of the leg']

tinea pedis /-péddiss/ *n* athlete's foot (*technical*) [< Latin, 'tinea of the foot']

tin ear *n* an inability to perceive differences in musical sounds or subtleties in speech (*informal*)

tineid /tínni id/ *n* a very small moth found worldwide whose larvae either eat fabrics of animal origin or are scavengers. Family: Tineidae. [Mid-19C. < modern Latin *Tineidae* (plural), < Latin *tinea* 'moth'.]

tinfoil /tín foyl/ *n* **1** aluminium in a very thin sheet, used to wrap food **2** tin, or an alloy of tin and lead, in a very thin sheet

ting /ting/ *n* a light high-pitched ringing sound, like that of a small bell ■ *vti* to produce or cause something to produce a light high-pitched ringing sound [Early 17C. An imitation of the sound.]

ting-a-ling /tíngə ling/ *n* a tinkling sound resembling that made by a small bell [An imitation of the sound]

tinge /tinj/ *n* **1** SLIGHT ADDED COLOUR a slight amount of a colour added to something **2** SLIGHT ADDED ELEMENT a slight amount of something, e.g. an emotion or a flavour ○ *with a tinge of regret in her voice* ■ *vt* (**tinges, tingeing** *or* **tinging, tinged**) **1** ADD COLOUR TO to add a slight amount of colour to something **2** MIX IN AN ELEMENT OF SOMETHING to mix a slight amount of something with something else (*often passive*) ○ *celebrations tinged with sadness* [15C. < Latin *tingere* 'moisten, dye'.]

tingle /tíng g'l/ *vti* (**-gles, -gling, -gled**) to feel or to cause somebody to feel a sensation of stinging, pricking, or vibration, e.g. from cold or a slight electric shock ○ *The frost made our faces tingle* ■ *n* a sensation of stinging, pricking, or vibration [14C. Variant of TINKLE.] —**tingler** *n* —**tinglingly** *adv* —**tingly** *adj*

tin god *n* **1** somebody, often in a position of minor authority, who behaves in a self-important, overbearing way **2** somebody or something mistakenly or unjustifiably considered to be worthy of admiration

tin hat *n* a steel helmet (*informal*)

tinhorn /tín hawrn/ *n* US somebody relatively insignificant who pretends to be wealthy, influential, or important, especially a gambler (*informal*) [Late 19C. < the horn-shaped metal can used to shake the dice in chuck-a-luck, a gambling game.]

tinker /tíngkər/ *n* **1** TRAVELLING POT MENDER formerly, somebody who travelled from place to place mending metal household items such as pots and pans **2** UNSKILFUL WORKER a clumsy or unskilful worker, especially at repair work **3** ACT OF FIDDLING WITH SOMETHING an act of fiddling with something in an attempt to repair it **4** SOMEBODY GOOD AT MANY TASKS somebody able to do many different kinds of work successfully **5** Ireland, Scotland ITINERANT a person who travels from place to place as a way of life **6** NAUGHTY CHILD a mischievous or badly-behaved child (*informal*) **7** YOUNG MACKEREL a mackerel that is not fully grown ■ *vi* **1** FIDDLE WITH SOMETHING to fiddle with something in an attempt to repair it ○ *had been tinkering with the car all morning* **2** HANDLE SOMETHING UNSKILFULLY to handle something clumsily or unskilfully **3** BE TRAVELLING POT MENDER to work as a travelling pot mender [13C. < ?] —**tinkerer** *n*

tinker's damn, **tinker's cuss** *n* the slightest possible amount of care, heed, or value (*informal; in negatives*) ○ *This car isn't worth a tinker's damn.* [Probably < the reputation of tinkers for swearing]

tinkle /tíngk'l/ *v* (**-kles, -kling, -kled**) **1** *vti* JINGLE to make or cause something to make light metallic ringing sounds **2** *vi* URINATE to urinate (*informal*) ■ *n* **1** JINGLING SOUND a series of light metallic ringing sounds **2** ACT OF URINATING an act of urinating (*informal*) **3** TELEPHONE CALL a call on the telephone (*informal*) [14C. < obsolete *tink* 'make a faint metallic sound' < ?] —**tinkly** *adj*

tin lizzie /-lízzi/ *n* a cheap, old, or dilapidated motor car (*informal*) [< *Tin Lizzie*, nickname for the Model T Ford car]

tinned /tind/ *adj* packed in a tin for storage or sale. US term **canned** *adj*. 1

tinner /tínnər/ *n* **1** a worker in a tin mine **2** INDUST = **tinsmith** **3** a person or company that packs food into tins

tinnie /tínni/, **tinny** (*plural* **-nies**) *n Aus* a can of beer (*informal*)

tinnitus /tínnitəss/ *n* a continual noise in the ear such as a ringing or roaring, usually caused by damage to the hair cells of the inner ear [Mid-19C. < Latin, < *tinnire* 'to ring, tinkle', an imitation of the sound.]

tinny[1] /tínni/ (**-nier, -niest**) *adj* **1** HAVING A THIN METALLIC SOUND lacking a full resonant sound ○ *banging out tunes on a tinny old piano* **2** CONSISTING OF TIN yielding, containing, or having the characteristics of tin **3** TASTING OF METAL having a metallic taste **4** INFERIOR IN QUALITY cheaply or shoddily made **5** *ANZ* LUCKY lucky (*informal*) —**tinnily** *adv* —**tinniness** *n*

tinny[2] *n Aus* = **tinnie** (*informal*)

tin-opener *n* a device for opening tins, especially tins of food. US term **can opener**

Tin Pan Alley *n* (*dated*) **1** a city district in which the business of composing and publishing popular music is carried on **2** popular music composers and publishers considered collectively [*Tin pan* 'tinny piano', from the cheap pianos associated with music publishers' offices]

tin plate *n* steel or iron in thin sheets coated with tin —**tin-plate** *vt* —**tin-plater** *n*

tinpot /tín pot/ *adj* inferior in quality or importance (*informal insult*)

tinsel /tínss'l/ *n* **1** GLITTERING MATERIAL a thin strip of glittering metal foil, paper, or plastic, used for decoration **2** SOMETHING SHOWY something worthless that appears glamorous ■ *vt* (**-sels, -selling, -selled**) **1** DECORATE WITH TINSEL to decorate something with tinsel or other glittering material **2** MAKE SHOWY to give something a gaudy, flashy quality ■ *adj* **1** MADE OF TINSEL made of or decorated with tinsel **2** GAUDY appearing glamorous but in fact worthless [15C. < French *étincelé* 'sparkling' (especially with metallic thread) < Old French *estincele* 'spark' < Latin *scintilla*.] —**tinselly** *adj*

Tinseltown /tínsəl town/ *n* Hollywood and the US film industry regarded as a place of substantial glamour (*informal disapproving*)

tinsmith /tín smith/ *n* a maker or repairer of objects made of tin or other easily worked metals

tin snips *npl* shears used for cutting sheet metal

tinstone /tín stōn/ *n* MINERALS = **cassiterite**

tint /tint/ *n* **1** PALE SHADE a shade of a colour, especially a pale one **2** COLOUR WITH WHITE ADDED a colour mixed with white to give low saturation and high lightness **3** TRACE OF COLOUR a slight amount of a colour **4** HAIR DYE a dye for the hair **5** SMALL ADDITION a barely noticeable addition of something **6** BACKGROUND COLOUR a pale colour printed as a background onto which another colour is printed **7** SHADING IN ENGRAVING a shading effect in engraving, produced by a series of parallel lines ■ *vti* GIVE A TINT TO to colour or shade something with a tint, or acquire a tint [Early 18C. Variant of TINCT, < Latin *tinctus*, past participle of *tingere* 'soak, dye'.] —**tinter** *n*

Tintagel /tin tájjəl/ coastal village in SW England, said to be the birthplace of the legendary King Arthur. Population: 1,800 (1998 est.).

tintinnabulation /tínti nábbyoo láysh'n/ *n* the ringing of bells [Mid-19C. < Latin *tintinnabulum* (see TINTINNABULUM).] —**tintinnabular** /tínti nábbyoolər/ *adj*

tintinnabulum /tínti nábbyooləm/ (*plural* **-la** /-lə/) *n* a small bell with a high clear ring [Late 16C. < Latin, 'bell' < *tintinnare* 'ring repeatedly' < *tinnire* 'to ring', an imitation of the sound.]

Tintoretto /tíntə réttō/ (1518?–94) Italian painter. Born **Jacopo Robusti**

tintype /tín tīp/ *n* PHOTOGRAPHY = **ferrotype**

tinware /tín wair/ *n* objects made of tin plate, especially utensils

tin whistle *n* MUSIC = **penny whistle**

tinwork /tín wurk/ *n* things made of tin

tinworks /tín wurks/ (*plural* **-works**) *n* a place where tin is smelted and rolled

tiny /tīni/ *adj* (**-nier, -niest**) extremely small ■ *n* (*plural* **-nies**) a very young child (*informal*) [Late 16C. < obsolete *tine* 'very small' < ?] —**tinily** *adv* —**tininess** *n*

-tion *suffix* an action or process, or the result of it ○ *pollution* [Directly or via French < Latin *-tion-*]

tip[1] /tip/ *n* **1** POINTED END the end of an object, especially a narrow or pointed end ○ *a pencil with a sharp tip* **2** PART FITTED ON AN END a piece fitted to the end of something else ■ *vt* (**tips, tipping, tipped**) **1** PROVIDE OR BE END to provide something with an end, or form the end of something **2** COVER THE END OF to cover or decorate the end of something ○ *shoes with steel-tipped toes* **3** TAKE THE END OFF to remove the end from something [15C. Probably < Old Norse *typpi* < Germanic, 'upper extremity'.] ◇ **on the tip of somebody's tongue** **1** nearly, but not quite, brought to mind **2** on the verge of being said but remaining unsaid ◇ **the tip of the iceberg** the small visible or obvious part of a largely unseen problem or difficulty

tip[2] /tip/ *v* (**tips, tipping, tipped**) **1** *vti* TILT to cause something to slant, or become slanted ○ *sitting with his chair tipped back* **2** *vti* KNOCK SOMETHING OVER to turn something on its side or upside down, or become turned on the side or upside down ○ *High winds caused the truck to tip over on its side.* **3** *vti* DUMP RUBBISH to dispose of refuse **4** *vt* TAKE OFF YOUR HAT to touch or lift a hat as a greeting ■ *n* **1** ACT OF TIPPING an act of tipping something **2** TILT an incline from vertical or horizontal **3** RUBBISH DUMP a place to dump refuse **4** UNTIDY PLACE an extremely untidy or dirty place (*informal*) [14C. < ?] —**tippable** *adj*

tip[3] /tip/ *n* **1** GRATUITY a gift of money for a service, especially as an amount above what is owed **2** WARNING OR INFORMATION an item of advance, inside, or confidential information given, e.g., to warn of something about to occur or to help in solving a crime **3** HELPFUL HINT a useful suggestion or idea for doing something ○ *cooking tips* ■ *vti* (**tips, tipping, tipped**) **1** GIVE A GRATUITY to give somebody a gift of money in return for a service, especially in addition to what is owed **2** INFORM to give somebody advance, inside, or confidential information [Early 17C. < ?] —**tipper** *n*

tip off *vt* to give somebody a warning or some useful advance information ○ *The police had been tipped off about the girl's whereabouts.*

tip[4] /tip/ *n* **1** LIGHT HIT a light glancing blow **2** DEFLECTED BALL IN CRICKET a stroke in cricket in which the ball glances off the bat ■ *vt* (**tips, tipping, tipped**) **1** HIT LIGHTLY to strike somebody or something with a light glancing blow **2** DEFLECT CRICKET BALL WITH BAT to hit a ball in cricket so that it glances off the bat [15C. < ?]

tip and run *n* a variety of cricket in which the batter must run if his or her bat strikes the ball [< TIP[4]]

tip-and-run *adj* striking quickly then withdrawing immediately

tipcart /típ kaart/ *n* a cart whose load is emptied by tilting its body

tipi *n* ANTHROP = **tepee**

~~tipical~~ incorrect spelling of **typical**

tip-in *n* **1** in basketball, a goal scored by lightly pushing a rebound into the basket with the fingertips **2** in hockey, a goal scored at very close range by giving a short stroke with the stick

tip-off[1] *n* advance information or a warning given in an effort to help (*informal*)

tip-off[2] *n* in basketball, the start of a period of play in which two players try to tap a jump ball to one of their team-mates

Tipperary /típpə ráiri/ former county in Munster Province, S Republic of Ireland

tipper truck, tipper lorry *n* a lorry built so that the front of the platform carrying the load can be raised to allow the load to slide off

tippet /típpit/ *n* **1** STOLE WITH HANGING ENDS a stole or cape, often made of fur, with long ends that hang down the front **2** STOLE OF ANGLICAN CLERGY the long stole worn around the shoulders and over the robes of Anglican clergy during services **3** HANGING END OF A GARMENT a long hanging end worn attached to a sleeve, hood, or cape up to the 16th century **4** BIRD'S RUFF the ruff of a bird **5** PART TO WHICH A FLY IS TIED in angling, the thin end section of a leader to which a fly is tied [14C. Probably < TIP[1].]

Tippett /típpit/, **Sir Michael** (1905–98) British composer

Tipp-Ex /típ eks/ *tdmk* a trademark for correction fluid

tipple[1] /típp'l/ *v* (**-ples, -pling, -pled**) **1** *vi* DRINK ALCOHOL HABITUALLY to drink alcoholic liquor habitually or excessively **2** *vti* DRINK ALCOHOL REPEATEDLY to drink alcoholic liquor repeatedly a little at a time ■ *n* ALCOHOLIC DRINK an alcoholic drink (*informal*) [Mid-16C. Probably back-formation < *tippler* 'ale seller' < N Germanic.]

tipple[2] /típp'l/ *n* **1** DEVICE FOR UNLOADING ORE TRUCKS a device for tipping coal or ore trucks to unload them **2** PLACE FOR UNLOADING ORE a place where ore or coal trucks are unloaded **3** PLACE FOR SCREENING COAL a place where coal is screened and loaded into trucks or railway goods wagons ■ *vti* (**-ples, -pling, -pled**) *N England* FALL OR TIP OVER to fall over or tip something over [Mid-19C. < TIP[2].]

tippler[1] /típplər/ *n* a habitual drinker of alcoholic beverages

tippler[2] /típplər/ *n* a breed of domestic pigeon. Kept for: flight, show. [Mid-19C. < TIPPLE[2], because it often turns over backwards in flight.]

tipstaff /típ staaf/ (*plural* **-staves** /-stayvz/ *or* **-staffs**) *n* **1** a metal-tipped staff carried as a sign of official authority **2** a court official who once carried a staff, e.g. a bailiff or constable

tipster /típstər/ *n* a provider or seller of information to horse-race betters or financial speculators [Mid-19C. < TIP[3].]

tipsy /típsi/ (**-sier, -siest**) *adj* **1** slightly drunk **2** inclined to tilt or tip —**tipsily** *adv* —**tipsiness** *n*

tipsy cake *n* a sponge cake soaked with alcohol or alcohol-laced syrup

tip-tilted *adj* describes a person's nose that is slightly turned up

tiptoe /típ tō/ *vi* (**-toes, -toeing, -toed**) **1** WALK WITH HEELS RAISED to walk on the toes and the balls of the feet with the heels off the ground **2** MOVE CAUTIOUSLY to move or proceed quietly or cautiously ■ *n* POSITION WITH HEELS RAISED a standing position in which the heels are raised off the ground and the weight is on the front part of the feet, with the body often also stretched up to gain extra height ○ *walking on tiptoe* ■ *adj* **1** WALKING ON THE TOES walking or standing on the toes or balls of the feet **2** CAUTIOUS proceeding with caution or stealth ■ *adv* ON THE TIPS OF TOES on the toes or the balls of the feet [14C. < TIP[1].]

tiptop /típ tóp/ *adj* OF TOP QUALITY of the highest quality or rank (*informal*) ■ *adv* WELL exceptionally well (*informal*) ■ *n* (*informal*) **1** HIGHEST POINT the highest point **2** HIGHEST IN QUALITY the highest degree of quality or excellence [Early 18C. Doubling of TOP[1], after TIP[1].]

tip-up *adj* designed to tilt upward or fold up

TIR *abbr* Transports Internationaux Routiers [French, 'international road transport']

tirade /tī ráyd, ti-/ *n* a long angry speech, usually of criticism or denunciation [Early 19C. < French, 'volley' < *tirer* 'to draw' < assumed Vulgar Latin *tirare*.]

tiramisu /tírrə mee sóo, -mée soo/ *n* an Italian dessert made with layers of sponge cake soaked in espresso coffee, Marsala, mascarpone cheese, and chocolate [Late 20C. < Italian *tira mi sù* 'pick me up'.]

Tirana /ti raánə/ capital of Albania, in the central part of the country. Population: 251,000 (1991).

tire[1] /tīr/ (**tires, tiring, tired**) *vti* **1** to make somebody feel in need of rest or sleep, or grow weaker and less energetic and feel a need for rest or sleep **2** to lose interest in and become bored and impatient with somebody or something, or cause somebody to do this [Old English *tyrian* < ?]

tire[2] /tīr/ *n* US = **tyre**

tire[3] /tīr/ *n* a woman's head covering or ornament (*archaic*) [14C. Shortening of ATTIRE.]

tired /tīrd/ *adj* **1** NEEDING REST in need of rest or sleep, or weakened and made less active by exertion **2** NO LONGER INTERESTED having lost patience or interest ○ *grew tired of hearing the same complaints* **3** OVERUSED no longer new or fresh because of overuse ○ *a tired old slogan* —**tiredly** *adv* —**tiredness** *n* ◇ **tired and emotional** drunk (*humorous*)

tired out *adj* thoroughly tired

Tiree /tī rée/ island of the Inner Hebrides, W Scotland. Population: 950 (1991). Area: 76 sq. km/29 sq. mi.

tireless /tīrləss/ *adj* never slackening or stopping, and apparently immune to tiredness or fatigue —**tirelessly** *adv* —**tirelessness** *n*

Tiresias /tī reési əss/ *n* in Greek mythology, a blind seer from Thebes who often delivered prophecies to Oedipus

tiresome /tīrsəm/ *adj* causing weariness, annoyance, or boredom —**tiresomely** *adv* —**tiresomeness** *n*

Tirgu Mures /túrgoo moor esh/ city in central Romania. Population: 165,534 (1997 estimate).

tiring /tīring/ *adj* causing somebody to feel tired, usually because requiring great physical or mental exertion

Tír na n-Óg /teér na nog/ *n* in Irish legend, a land of eternal youth [Late 19C. < Irish *tír na n-óg* 'land of the young'.]

Tirol /tirṓl/, **Tyrol** province in W Austria. Capital: Innsbruck. Population: 660,000 (1996). Area: 12,648 sq. km/4,883 sq. mi. —**Tirolean** /tirrə leé ən/ *n, adj* —**Tirolese** /tirrə leéz/ *n, adj*

Tiros /tī rōss/ (*plural* **-ros**) *n* a satellite with infrared and television equipment for transmitting weather data to Earth [Late 20C. Acronym < *television infrared observational satellite*.]

Tirso de Molina /teérss ō day mə leénə/ (1571?–1648) Spanish playwright and theologian. Pseudonym of **Gabriel Téllez**

Tirthankara /teer tàngkərə/ *n* a traditional holy man of Jainism, belonging to a group who have attained personal immortality through enlightenment, and by their teaching have made a path for others to follow [Mid-19C. < Sanskrit *tīrthaṁkaraḥ* 'ford maker' < *tīrtham* 'ford, passage' + *kṛ-* 'make'.]

Tiruchchirappalli /tirrə chirə púlli, ti roóchi raápəli/ city in S India. Population: 387,223 (1991).

Tirunelveli /tirroō nélvəli/ town in S India. Population: 135,825 (1991).

Tiryns /tírrinz/ ancient city in the E Peloponnese, S Greece

'tis /tiz/ *contr* it is (*archaic or literary*)

Tisha b'Av /ti shaá bə áv/ *n* in Judaism, a fast on the ninth day of the month of Av to commemorate the destruction of the First and Second Temples [< Hebrew *tišāh bĕāḇ* 'ninth of Av']

Tishri /tíshri/ (*plural* **-ris**) *n* in the Jewish calendar, the first month of the civil year and the seventh month of the religious year [Mid-17C. < Hebrew *tišrī*.]

Tisiphone /tī síffəni/ *n* in Greek mythology, one of the three Furies

Tissot /teéssō/, **Jacques-Joseph** (1836–1902) French painter

tissue /tíshoo, tíssyoo/ *n* **1** PIECE OF ABSORBENT PAPER a piece of soft absorbent paper that can be used as a handkerchief, toilet paper, or a towel **2** INDUST = **tissue paper** **3** GROUP OF CELLS IN AN ORGANISM organic body material in animals and plants made up of large numbers of cells that are similar in form and function and their related intercellular substances **4** INTRICATE SERIES an intricate interrelated series of things ○ *a tissue of lies* **5** GAUZY FABRIC a thin, finely woven fabric with a gauzy texture [14C. < Old French *tissu* < past participle of *tistre* 'weave' < Latin *texere*.]

tissue culture *n* **1** the growth of tissue outside an organism in a nutrient medium, or the techniques involved in this process **2** the tissue grown in a culture medium

tissue paper *n* a thin soft paper. Use: wrapping and protecting delicate items.

tissue plasminogen activator *n* an anticlotting enzyme that is produced naturally in blood vessel linings and is genetically engineered for use in treating heart attacks, to dissolve blood clots, and to prevent heart muscle damage

tissue type *n* the chemical characteristics of the body tissue of an individual that determine whether or not the tissue is immunologically compatible with the tissue of another individual

Tisza /tíss aw/ river in E Europe, rising in W Ukraine and flowing through E Hungary and N Yugoslavia to the River Danube. Length: 970 km/600 mi.

tit[1] /tit/ *n* **1** OFFENSIVE TERM an offensive term for a woman's breast (*slang*) **2** TEAT a teat **3** OFFENSIVE TERM a highly offensive term for somebody who is regarded as unintelligent or obnoxious (*slang*) [Old English *titt* < Germanic]

tit[2] /tit/ *n* a small active songbird with a short bill and strong feet, e.g. the bluetit or great tit. Native to: N hemisphere. [Early 18C. Shortening of TITMOUSE.]

Tit. *abbr* Titus

titan /tít'n/ *n* somebody whose power, achievement, intellect, or physical size is extraordinarily impressive [Early 19C. < TITAN.]

Titan /tít'n/ *n* **1** in Greek mythology, one of the twelve children of Uranus and Gaea, supreme rulers of the universe until they were overthrown by Zeus **2** the largest natural satellite of Saturn, discovered in 1655. It is 5,150 km/3,198 mi. in diameter and has a significant atmosphere that is composed mainly of nitrogen. [15C. Via Latin < Greek.]

titanate /títə nayt/ *n* a compound that is a salt or an ester of titanic acid

Titania /ti taáni ə/ *n* **1** in medieval folklore, the wife of Oberon and queen of the fairies **2** the largest moon of the planet Uranus, the fourth most distant satellite observable from the Earth

titanic[1] /tī tánnik/ *adj* **1** having extraordinary physical strength or size **2** of extraordinary power, scope, or impressiveness —**titanically** *adv*

titanic[2] /tī tánnik/ *adj* relating to or containing titanium, especially with a valency of four [Early 19C. < TITANIUM.]

Titanic *adj* relating to or like the Titans of mythology

titanic oxide *n* CHEM = **titanium dioxide**

titaniferous /títəníffərəss/ *adj* yielding or containing titanium [Early 19C. < TITANIUM.]

Titanism /títənizəm/ *n* a spirit of defiance of authority, conventional society, and the established order

titanite /títənīt/ *n* MINERALS = **sphene** [Mid-19C. < TITANIUM.]

titanium /tī táyni əm, ti-/ *n* (*symbol* **Ti**) a strong, lightweight, corrosion-resistant silvery metallic element. Source: rutile, ilmenite. Use: manufacture of alloys for aerospace industry. [Late 18C. < TITAN *n.* 2, after URANIUM.]

titanium dioxide *n* TiO_2 a white crystalline compound. Source: rutile, ilmenite, other minerals. Use: pigment for durable paints and plastics.

titanium white *n* **1** CHEM = **titanium dioxide** **2** a brilliant white paint pigment consisting primarily of titanium dioxide

titanosaur /tī tánnə sawr/ *n* a huge herbivorous sauropod dinosaur of the Cretaceous and Jurassic periods, found especially in South America. Genus: *Titanosaurus*. [Late 19C. < modern Latin *Titanosaurus* < Greek *Titan* 'Titan' + *sauros* 'lizard'.]

titanothere /tī tánnə theer/ *n* a large mammal similar to a rhinoceros that lived in North America during the Tertiary Period [Mid-20C. < modern Latin *Titanotherium* < Greek *Titan* 'Titan' + *therion* 'wild beast'.]

titanous /títənəss/ *adj* relating to or containing titanium with a valency of three [Mid-19C. < TITANIUM.]

titbit /tít bit/ *n* **1** a small, usually bite-sized, piece of delicious food **2** a small piece of interesting information or gossip [Mid-17C. < ?]

titch /tich/, **tich** *n* a very small person (*informal*) [Mid-20C. < Little *Tich*, stage name of the English comedian Harry Relph (1868–1928), who was very small.]

titchy /tíchi/ (**-ier, -iest**), **tichy** (**-ier, -iest**) *adj* very small (*informal*)

titer *n* US = **titre**

titfer /títfər/ *n* a hat (*slang*) [Early 20C. Shortening of rhyming slang *tit for tat*.]

tit for tat *n* the process or act of repaying a wrong or injury suffered by inflicting equivalent harm on the doer (*hyphenated before nouns*) ○ *tit-for-tat strikes* [Mid-16C. < ?]

tithe /tīth/ *n* **1** INDIVIDUAL'S FINANCIAL SUPPORT FOR A CHURCH one tenth of somebody's income or produce paid voluntarily or as a tax for the support of a church or its clergy **2** OBLIGATION OF SUPPORTING A CHURCH FINANCIALLY the obligation to pay a tithe to a church or its clergy **3** ASSESSMENT OR CONTRIBUTION any voluntary contribution or tax payment, especially when it constitutes one tenth of somebody's income **4** SMALL PART one tenth or a small part of anything ■ *v* (**tithes, tithing, tithed**) **1** *vti* PAY ONE TENTH OF INCOME to contribute or pay one tenth of your income or produce, especially to support a church **2** *vt* COLLECT ONE TENTH OF SOMEBODY'S INCOME to assess or collect the payment of one tenth of somebody's income [Old English *tēopa* 'tenth, tithe'] —**tithable** *adj* —**tither** *n*

tithe barn *n* formerly, a barn that served as a store for the produce contributed by the parish to the church as a tithe

tithing /tīthing/ *n* **1** PAYING OF TITHES the assessing or paying of tithes **2** TEN HOUSEHOLDERS a small district in medieval England composed of ten householders and their households, each bearing responsibility for the conduct of the others **3** RURAL DIVISION a rural administrative region in medieval England equal to one tenth of the county division known as a hundred **4** ONE TENTH one tenth part of anything [Old English *tēoþung* < TITHE]

titi[1] /teé tee/ (*plural* **-tis**) *n* an arboreal monkey with a round face, thick soft fur, and a long tail. Native to: tropical South America. Genus: *Callicebus*. [Mid-18C. Via Spanish *tití* < Aymara.]

titi[2] /teé tee/ *n* **1** an evergreen shrub or small tree with glossy leathery leaves. Flowers: fragrant, white or pinkish. Native to: SE United States. *Cliftonia monophylla*. **2** a small evergreen tree or shrub with leathery leaves and yellow fruit. Native to: SE United States, Central and South America. *Cyrilla racemiflora*. [Early 19C. < ?]

titian /tísh'n/, **Titian** *adj* of a gold-tinged auburn colour ○ *titian hair* [Late 19C. After TITIAN, who used the colour frequently.]

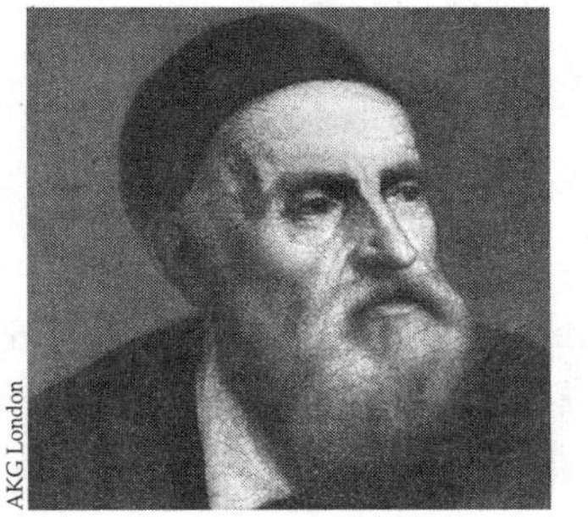

Titian: Self-portrait (1555)

Titian /tísh'n/ (1477?–1576) Italian painter. Born **Tiziano Vecellio**

Titicaca, Lake /títti kaá kaa/ largest lake in South America, extending from SE Peru to W Bolivia. Area: 8,288 sq. km/3,200 sq. mi.

titillate /títti layt/ (**-lates, -lating, -lated**) *v* **1** *vti* to excite or stimulate somebody pleasurably, usually in a mildly sexual way **2** *vt* to cause a tingling sensation in somebody by touching him or her lightly [Early 17C. < Latin *titillare* 'tickle'.] —**titillating** *adj* —**titillatingly** *adv* —**titillation** /títti láysh'n/ *n* —**titillative** *adj*

titivate /títti vayt/ (**-vates, -vating, -vated**), **tittivate** (**-vates, -vating, -vated**) *vti* to improve the appearance of somebody or something by neatening or adding decoration [Early 19C. Alteration of earlier *tidivate* < ?] —**titivation** /títti váysh'n/ *n* —**titivator** *n*

titlark /tít laark/ *n* BIRDS = **pipit** [Mid-17C. < TIT² + LARK¹.]

title /tít'l/ *n* **1** NAME a name that identifies a book, film, play, painting, musical composition, or other literary or artistic work **2** DESCRIPTIVE HEADING a descriptive heading for something such as a book chapter, a magazine article, or a speech **3** PUBL = **title page** **4** PUBLISHED WORK a work published or recorded by a company ○ *this spring's new titles* **5** DESIGNATION ADDED TO A NAME a word such as 'Mr', 'Ms', 'Dr', or 'Lord' added to and usually preceding a person's name to indicate his or her rank, social status, or profession, or as a courtesy **6** NAME DESCRIBING A POSITION a name that describes somebody's job or position in a company or organization ○ *a job title* **7** CHAMPIONSHIP the status of champion in a sport or competition ○ *a title fight* **8** RIGHT OR PROOF OF RIGHT any legitimate right or anything providing proof or justification for that claim **9** REQUIREMENT OF ORDINATION a source of income or office in the church required of a candidate by the Church of England before ordination **10** CLAIM BASED ON A RIGHT a claim based on a legitimate right **11** ROMAN CATHOLIC CHURCH IN ROME a Roman Catholic church in or near Rome that has a bishop or cardinal as its nominal head **12** RIGHT TO POSSESS PROPERTY a legal right to possess and dispose of property **13 EVIDENCE OF PROPERTY RIGHTS** the evidence of legal right to property **14 DOCUMENT** a document giving the legal right to property **15 DIVISION** a division of a law, statute, or law book **16 LAW HEADING** a heading for a lawsuit or legal action, or one that names a document or statute ■ **titles** *npl* **CREDITS OR SUBTITLES ON SCREEN** the written presentation on the screen of credits, narration, or subtitles in a film or television programme ■ *vt* (**-tles, -tling, -tled**) **1 NAME SOMETHING** to give a name or title to a person or thing **2 CALL BY A TITLE** to call a person by a title [Pre-12C. Via Old French < Latin *titulus* 'inscription'.] —**titled** *adj*

title deed *n* a deed or document that is evidence of somebody's legal right to property

titleholder /tī́t'l hōldər/ *n* **1** a holder of a sports championship title **2** a holder of legal title to property —**titleholding** *n*

title page *n* a page at the beginning of a book that gives its title and the name of the author and publisher

title role *n* the role in a play or film that gives the work its name

titmouse /tít mowss/ (*plural* **-mice** /-mīss/) *n* a small bird widespread in Europe, Asia, Africa, and North America. Genus: *Parus*. [14C. Alteration (influenced by *mouse*) of *titmose* < obsolete *tit* 'something small, runt' + *mose* 'titmouse' (< Old English *māse*).]

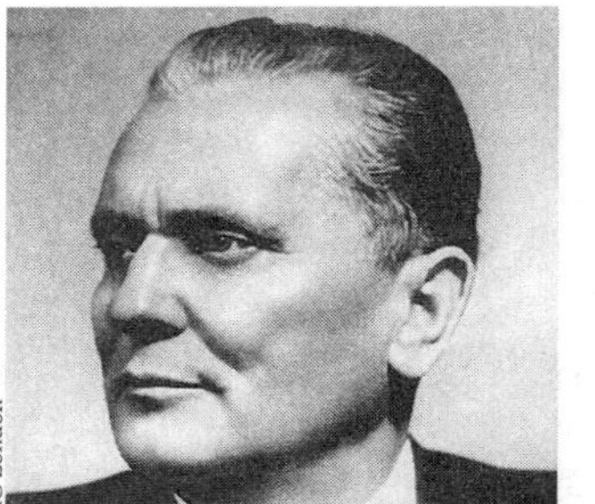

Tito

Tito /teétō/ (1892–1980) Yugoslav patriot and statesman. Known as **Marshal Tito**. Born **Josip Broz**

Titoism /teétō izəm/ *n* the form of Communism associated with Tito and practised by him in Yugoslavia, especially involving the pursuit of national interests independent of the then Soviet Union and its satellites —**Titoist** *n, adj*

titrant /tī́trənt/ *n* a reagent, e.g. a solution of known concentration, that is added in titration [Mid-20C. < TITRATE.]

titrate /tī tráyt/ (**-trates, -trating, -trated**) *vt* to measure the concentration of a solution by titration [Late 19C. < French *titrer* < *titre* (see TITRE).] —**titratable** *adj*

titration /tī tráysh'n/ *n* a method of calculating the concentration of a dissolved substance in a known volume of test solution by adding measured quantities of a reagent of known concentration until a specific reaction occurs

titre /tī́tər, teétər/ *n* **1** the concentration of a substance in solution as determined by titration **2** the concentration of an antibody in serum [Mid-19C. < French *titre* 'qualification, quality (of gold or silver alloy)', variant of *title* (see TITLE).]

titrimetric /tī́tri méttrik/ *adj* using or calculated by titration [Late 19C. < TITRATION.] —**titrimetrically** *adv*

titter /títtər/ *vi* to laugh in a nervous self-conscious way ■ *n* a short high-pitched nervous laugh or giggle [Early 17C. An imitation of the sound.] —**titterer** *n* —**tittering** *n* —**titteringly** *adv*

tittivate *vti* = **tivitate**

tittle /títt'l/ *n* **1** a small mark used in printing and writing such as an accent, punctuation, or diacritical mark **2** the tiniest bit [14C. < medieval Latin *titulus* 'small superscript mark' < Latin, 'title'.]

tittle-tattle *n* idle gossip ■ *vi* (**tittle-tattles, tittle-tattling, tittle-tattled**) to gossip or chatter idly [Early 16C. Doubling of TATTLE.] —**tittle-tattler** *n*

tittup /títtəp/ *vi* (**-tups, -tupping, -tupped**) to move in a lively prancing way ■ *n* a sometimes exaggerated lively prancing movement [Late 17C. < ?]

titubation /títtyōō báysh'n/ *n* an unsteady or stumbling gait or a head tremor, often caused by a disorder of the cerebellum [Mid-17C. < Latin *titubare* 'stagger'.]

titular /títtyōōlər/ *adj* **1 IN NAME ONLY** having a particular title, rank, or position but not possessing the power or exercising the functions usually associated with it **2 WITH A TITLE OF RANK** holding a title of rank **3 FROM A TITLE** derived from or figuring in the title of a work such as a book or film **4 FROM AN INACTIVE SEE** bearing the title of a see or monastery that is no longer active ■ *n* **1 SOMEBODY WITH A TITLE OF RANK** a holder of a title of rank **2 HOLDER OF A NOMINAL TITLE** a holder of a title in name only [Late 16C. < Latin *titulus* 'title'.] —**titularly** *adv* —**titulary** *n*

Titus[1] /tī́təss/ *n* in the Bible, an early Christian leader, and a disciple of St Paul

Titus[2] *n* in the Bible, a letter addressed to Titus, traditionally believed to be from St Paul

Titus /tī́təss/ (39–81) Roman general and emperor (79–81). Full name **Titus Flavius Sabinus Vespasianus**

Tiv /tiv/ (*plural* **Tivs** *or* **Tiv**) *n* **1** a member of a people living in West Africa, mainly in S Nigeria and neighbouring Cameroon **2** the Benue-Congo language of the Tiv people. Native speakers: 1.5 million. [Mid-20C. < Bantu.] —**Tiv** *adj*

TiVo box /teé vō-/ *tdmk* a trademark for a box attached to a television and a phone line that permits interactive TV viewing, e.g. by allowing the viewer to freeze a programme while it is in progress or to record all the programmes in a series without specifically setting the machine to record each one separately

Tivoli /tívvəli/ town in central Italy. Population: 54,352 (1990).

Tizard /tíz aard/, **Dame Cath** (*b.* 1931) New Zealand stateswoman and governor general (1990–96). Full name **Dame Catherine Anne Tizard**

tizzy /tízzi/, **tizz** /tíz/, **tiz-woz** /tíz woz/ *n* a nervous agitated state (*informal*) [Mid-20C. < ?]

⚡**tj** *abbr* Tajikistan (*in Internet addresses*)

T-joint, **tee-joint** *n* a joint in wood or other material forming the letter T

T-junction *n* a junction where a road joins another road, especially at a right angle, but does not cross it

TKO *abbr* technical knockout

Tl *symbol* thallium

Tlaxcala /tlass kaálə, -kállə/ capital of Tlaxcala State in east-central Mexico. Population: 911,696 (1997 estimate).

TLC *abbr* tender loving care (*informal*)

Tlemcen /tlem sén/ town in NW Algeria. Population: 126,882 (1987).

Tlingit /tlíng git/ (*plural* **-gits** *or* **-git**) *n* **1** a member of a group of Native North American peoples who lived on coastal SE Alaska, and who now live mainly there and in British Columbia **2** the Na-Dene language of the Tlingit people. Native speakers: 2,000. [Mid-19C. < Tlingit, 'person'.] —**Tlingit** *adj*

TLS *n* a weekly literary magazine published in the United Kingdom. Full form **Times Literary Supplement**

T-lymphocyte *n* BIOL = **T-cell**

⚡**tm** *abbr* Turkmenistan (*in Internet addresses*)

Tm *symbol* thulium

TM *abbr* **1** trademark **2** transcendental meditation

T-man *n* a special investigator of the US Department of the Treasury (*informal*)

tmesis /tmeé siss, meé-, tə meé-/ *n* the separation of the parts of a word by inserting a word or words between them, as in 'pretty un-bloody-likely' [Mid-16C. < Greek *tmēsis* 'cutting' < *temnein* 'cut'.]

TMJ syndrome *n, abbr* temporomandibular joint syndrome

TMT *abbr* tech, media, and telecom

⚡**tn** *abbr* Tunisia (*in Internet addresses*)

TN *abbr* Tennessee

TNT *n* $C_7H_5N_3O_6$ a yellow flammable crystalline compound. Use: explosive. Full form **trinitrotoluene**

⚡**TNX** *abbr* thanks (*in e-mails*)

to[1] *stressed* /too/; *unstressed* /tōō, tə/ CORE MEANING: a preposition or adverb indicating the direction, destination or position of somebody or something ○ *I met him on his way to school.* ○ *She climbed all the way to the top.* ○ *You'll see a supermarket to your left.*

1 INDICATES DIRECTION indicates the direction or destination of somebody or something ○ *He was on his way to the party.* ○ *You hit the space bar and go to the next screen* **2 INDICATES POSITION** indicates the position of somebody or something ○ *To the right of the door you will see a noticeboard.* **3 FORMS INFINITIVE** used before the base form of a verb to make the infinitive of that verb ○ *I want to leave now.* **4 INDICATES PURPOSE** used with the base form of a verb to indicate the intention or purpose of an action ○ *The news system is used to distribute information to large groups of people.* **5 INDICATES RECIPIENT** indicates the recipient of something (*with a noun phrase to form the indirect object*) ○ *Give it to me.* ○ *mail sent to another user on the same computer* **6 INDICATES DIRECTION OF FEELING OR ACTION** indicates who or what a particular feeling or action is directed towards ○ *I was very grateful to her for everything she did for me.* **7 INDICATES ATTACHMENT** indicates that two things are joined together ○ *Each triangle consists of three square faces joined to one another along two edges.* **8 UNTIL** indicates that something goes on until a certain time or until it reaches a certain amount ○ *He shuts the shop on Mondays and opens from Tuesday to Saturday.* **9 INDICATES RANGE** indicates a range of things or topics ○ *Studies have explored everything from pollution to pesticides to genetics to parental occupations to electromagnetic fields and proven nothing.* **10 INDICATES RESULT OF CHANGE** indicates what somebody or something is changing into or becoming ○ *Their excitement soon turned to gloom when they saw what the climb entailed.* **11 INDICATES SIMULTANEITY** indicates that two things are happening at the same time, especially that a particular sound or music accompanies another action ○ *I woke up to the sound of the telephone ringing.* **12 INDICATES EQUALITY** indicates equality, e.g. of two weights, amounts, or measurements ○ *There are 12 inches to the foot.* **13 AS COMPARED WITH** indicates comparison between two things, e.g. scores in a game ○ *The score was 5 to 3 in favour of our team.* **14 BEFORE HOUR** indicates the number of minutes before the hour ○ *It was five to seven before they arrived home.* **15 AT** at (*regional*) ○ *Where's he to?* ○ *He's over to the doctor's.* ■ *adv* **1 SHUT OR ALMOST SHUT** indicates that a door is shut or across the opening but not completely or firmly shut ○ *He pulled the door to after him.* **2 CONSCIOUS AGAIN** into a state of lucidity and consciousness ○ *came to in the recovery room* ○ *brought the patient to* **3 INTO WIND** into the direction from which the wind is blowing ○ *turned the yacht to* [Old English *tō*. < Germanic.]

SPELLCHECK Do not confuse ***to*** with ***too*** or ***two***, which may sound similar. Beware: your spellchecker will not catch this error.

⚡**to**[2] *abbr* Tonga (*in Internet addresses*)

toad /tōd/ *n* **1 TERRESTRIAL AMPHIBIAN SIMILAR TO FROG** a small squat tailless amphibian distributed nearly worldwide. It is similar to a frog but has dry warty skin and, except for breeding in water, lives mostly on land. Family: Bufonidae. **2 SIMILAR AMPHIBIAN** an amphibian similar to a toad such as the midwife toad but belonging to a different taxonomic family **3 OFFENSIVE TERM** an offensive term for somebody considered loathsome or disgusting [Old English *tādige* < ?] —**toadish** *adj*

toadfish /tṓd fish/ (*plural* **-fish** *or* **-fishes**) *n* a scaleless spiny bottom-feeding fish with a broad flattened head and wide mouth. Native to: tropical and temperate seas. Family: Batrachoididae.

toadflax /tṓd flaks/ (*plural* **-flaxes** *or* **-flax**) *n* **1** a common narrow-leaved plant. Flowers: spurred, two-lipped, orange-and-yellow, similar to snapdragon's. Native to: Europe. *Linaria vulgaris*. **2** a plant related to the common toadflax and similar to it. Flowers: lilac-coloured. Genus: *Linaria*.

toad-in-the-hole *n* a dish consisting of sausages or sausage meat baked in a batter similar to Yorkshire pudding

toadstone /tṓd stōn/ *n* **1** a dark brownish-grey type of basalt found in the limestone regions of Derbyshire **2** a stone or similar object believed to have formed in the head or body of a toad, formerly worn around the neck as a charm against evil and disease

toadstool /tṓd stool/ *n* a poisonous umbrella-shaped fungus with a spore-producing round flat cap on a stalk [14C. Because it resembles a small stool and grows where toads are found.]

toady /tṓdi/ *n* (*plural* **-ies**) a self-serving person who behaves in a servile sycophantic manner, fawning on and flattering people with power or influence ■ *vi* (**-ies, -ying, -ied**) to behave in an obsequious and ingratiating manner [Early 19C. Shortening of *toadeater* 'toady'.] —**toadyish** *adj* —**toadyism** *n*

Toamasina /twàamə seénə/ major port in E Madagascar, on the Indian Ocean. Population: 127,441 (1993).

to and fro *adv* **1** moving backwards and forwards **2** moving about here and there —**to-and-fro** *adj, n* —**toing and froing** *n*

toast /tōst/ *n* **1 BREAD BROWNED WITH HEAT** sliced bread that has been browned on both sides with heat, in a toaster, under a grill, or in front of an open fire **2 CALL TO HONOUR** a call to a gathering to honour somebody or something by raising glasses and drinking **3 RAISING OF GLASSES TO HONOUR** an act of raising a glass and drinking in honour of somebody or something **4 SOMEBODY OR SOMETHING HONOURED** somebody or something honoured by a toast **5 ADMIRED PERSON** a person who is the object of much attention or admiration ○ *the toast of Hollywood* ■ *v* **1** *vti* **HEAT AND BROWN FOOD** to heat and brown bread or other food, or to become browned, on a grill, over an open fire, or in a toaster **2** *vt* **WARM BODY** to warm the body or a part of the body near a source of heat **3** *vti* **DRINK IN SOMEBODY'S HONOUR** to drink or propose a drink in honour of somebody or something [14C. Via Old French *toster* 'roast' < Latin *tost-*, past participle of *torrere* 'scorch'.] ◇ **be toast** *US* to be in serious trouble (*slang*) ○ *Do that again and you're toast!*

toaster /tṓstər/ *n* a small electrical appliance for making toast that works by exposing the bread to heated electrical coils

toastie *n* FOOD = **toasty** *n.*

toastmaster /tṓst maastər/ *n* a proposer of toasts who introduces speakers at a banquet or reception

toastmistress /tṓst mistrəss/ *n* a woman who proposes toasts and introduces speakers at a banquet or reception

toast rack *n* a stand that holds slices of toast on end and separate from each other

toasty /tṓsti/ *adj* (**-ier, -iest**) pleasantly warm ■ *n* (*plural* **-ies**) **toasty, toastie** a sandwich that has been toasted (*informal*)

Tob. *abbr* Tobit

tobacco /tə bákō/ (*plural* **-cos** *or* **-coes** *or* **-co**) *n* **1** a plant cultivated for its large leaves that are dried and processed primarily for smoking. Native to: tropical America. Genus: *Nicotiana*. **2** the dried processed leaves of the tobacco plant [Late 16C. < Spanish *tabaco*.]

tobacco mosaic virus *n* a retrovirus that causes mosaic disease in tobacco and other plants belonging to the nightshade family

tobacconist /tə bákənist/ *n* a person or shop that specializes in selling tobacco products and supplies such as cigarettes, tobacco, and pipes [Mid-17C. < TOBACCO + -IST.]

tobacco road *n US* a shabby poverty-stricken rural community [Mid-20C. < the title of a novel by Erskine CALDWELL.]

~~**tobaco**~~ incorrect spelling of **tobacco**

Tobago /tə báygō/ island in the Caribbean, part of Trinidad and Tobago. Population: 50,282 (1990). Area: 300 sq. km/120 sq. mi.

Toba Sojo /tṓbə sṓjō/ (1053–1140) Japanese artist and Buddhist high priest

Tobit /tṓbit/ *n* **1** in the Bible, a pious Israelite living in Nineveh at the end of the 8th century BC **2** a book in the Roman Catholic Bible and the Protestant Apocrypha

toboggan /tə bóggən/ *n* a long narrow sledge without runners, made of strips of wood running lengthwise and curled up at the front, used for coasting downhill on snow ■ *vi* to ride on a toboggan [Early 19C. Via Canadian French *tabagane* < Mi'kmaq *topağan* 'sled'.] —**tobogganer** *n* —**tobogganist** *n*

Tobruk /tə bròok/ city in NE Libya, on the Mediterranean Sea. Population: 94,006 (1984).

toby jug, toby /tṓbi/ (*plural* **-bies**), **Toby** (*plural* **-bies**) *n* a beer mug or jug in the shape of a stout man wearing a three-cornered hat [Mid-19C. < *Toby* (nickname for *Tobias*), common 19C name for a man or boy.]

TOC /tok/ *n* in the United Kingdom, a train company that has been franchised to provide passenger services over particular routes as part of the arrangements by which the national railway system was privatized. Full form **train operating company**

toccata /tə kaátə/ (*plural* **-tas**) *n* a composition for a keyboard instrument written in a free style that includes full chords and elaborate runs and is intended to show off the player's technique [Early 18C. < Italian, < feminine past participle of *toccare* 'touch' < assumed Vulgar Latin.]

Toc H /tók áych/ *n* an interdenominational association formed in England after World War I to encourage Christian fellowship [Early 20C. < telegraphic code for *TH* 'Talbot House', Belgian recreation centre on which it was modelled.]

Tocharian /to kaári ən, tə-/, **Tokharian** *n* **1** a member of a Central Asian people who lived in the Tarim Basin in W China before being defeated by the Uigurs during the 9th century AD **2** the extinct language of the Tocharian people that forms a separate branch of the Indo-European family [Early 20C. < Latin *Tochari* < Greek *Tokharoi* 'the Tocharians'.] —**Tocharian** *adj*

tocher /tókhər, tókər/ *n Scotland* a bride's dowry (*literary*) ■ *vt Scotland* to give something as a dowry (*literary*) [15C. < Scottish Gaelic *tochradh*.]

tocopherol /to kóffə rol/ *n* one of a group of fat-soluble compounds that make up vitamin E, present in vegetable oils and leafy greens [Mid-20C. < Greek *tokos* 'childbirth' + *pherein* 'to bear'.]

tocsin /tóksin/ *n* **1 ALARM** an alarm sounded by means of a bell **2 BELL** a bell that sounds an alarm **3 WARNING** any warning signal [Late 16C. Via French < Old Provençal *tocasenh* < *tocar* 'to strike' (< assumed Vulgar Latin *toccare*) + *senh* 'bell' (< Latin *signum* 'signal').]

tod[1] /tod/ *n* **1 UNIT OF WEIGHT FOR WOOL** a unit of weight for wool, usually equal to 12.7 kg/28 lb **2 MASS OF FOLIAGE** a mass of foliage, especially ivy **3** *Scotland, N England* **FOX** a fox [15C. < ?]

tod[2] /tod/ [Shortening of *Tod Sloan*, US jockey (1874–1933), rhyming slang for *alone*] ◇ **on your tod** alone (*informal*)

today /tə dáy/ *n* **1 THIS DAY** this day, as distinct from yesterday or tomorrow **2 PRESENT AGE** the present time or age ○ *the fashions of today* ■ *adj* **MODERN** modern or of the present day ○ *a today look* ■ *adv* **1 ON THIS DAY** on or during this day ○ *She is working today.* **2 IN PRESENT TIME** during the present time or age ○ *Children today have far more sophisticated toys than we ever had.* [Old English *tō dæge* '(this) day']

Todd /tod/, **Alexander R., Baron Todd of Trumpington** (1907–97) British chemist

toddle /tódd'l/ *vi* (**-dles, -dling, -dled**) **1 TAKE SHORT UNSTEADY STEPS** to walk with short unsteady steps, as a child does when learning to walk **2 WALK UNHURRIEDLY** to walk at a leisurely pace (*informal*) ■ *n* **1 UNHURRIED WALK** a leisurely walk (*informal*) **2 UNSTEADY STEPS** an unsteady, tottering gait [Late 16C. < ?]

toddler /tódd'lər/ *n* a young child who is learning to walk

toddy /tóddi/ (*plural* **-dies**) *n* **1** a drink made with alcoholic liquor, hot water, sugar, and sometimes spices **2** the sweet sap of a variety of Asian palm tree used as a beverage, either fresh or fermented [Late 18C. Via Hindi *tāṛī* 'palm sap' < Sanskrit *tālaḥ* 'palm', probably < Dravidian.]

to-do /tə dóo/ *n* a fuss, especially an angry complaint or protest (*informal*)

tody /tṓdi/ (*plural* **-dies**) *n* a small bird with a short tail and round wings, a bright green back, red throat, and a long straight beak. Native to: Caribbean. Family: Todidae. [Late 18C. Probably via French *todier* < Latin *todus*, a small bird.]

toe /tō/ *n* **1 FOOT PART** any one of the digits of the foot, equivalent to the fingers and thumb of the hand **2 VERTEBRATE'S FOOT PART** a part corresponding to the human toe in other vertebrates **3 PART OF HOOF** the forepart of an animal's hoof **4 PART OF SHOE OR SOCK** the part of a shoe, boot, sock, or stocking that covers the toes and the front part of the foot **5 PART OF GOLF CLUB** the end of the head of a golf club **6 PART RESEMBLING TOE** a part that resembles the front part of a foot in form or position ○ *the toe of Italy* **7 LOWER END OF SHAFT** the lower end of a vertical shaft that turns in a bearing **8 BASE OF EMBANKMENT** the base of an embankment, cliff, wall, or dam ■ *v* (**toes, toeing, toed**) **1** *vt* **TOUCH SOMETHING WITH TOES** to touch, kick, reach, or mark something with the toes or the front part of the foot **2** *vt* **STRIKE GOLF BALL** to strike a golf ball with the front part of the head of the club **3** *vt* **DRIVE NAIL AT ANGLE** to drive in a nail or spike at an angle **4** *vt* **FASTEN SOMETHING WITH ANGLED NAIL** to fasten something with a nail or spike driven in at an angle **5** *vi* **STAND WITH TOES POINTED** to stand or move with the toes pointed in a particular direction [Old English *tā*. < Indo-European, 'to point'.] —**toed** *adj* ◇ **on your toes** alert and ready for action ◇ **tread on somebody's toes** to offend or upset somebody by interfering with something considered to be that person's own responsibility ◇ **turn up your toes** to die (*informal*)

toea /tṓ i ə, tṓ aa/ (*plural* **-a** *or* **-as**) *n* see table at **currency** [Late 20C. < Motu, 'conical shell', used as currency.]

toe and heel *n* a technique used by racing drivers for operating the brake and accelerator simultaneously with the right foot, using the heel for one pedal and the toe for the other

toecap /tṓ kap/ *n* a metal or leather covering reinforcing the toe of a shoe or boot

toe dance *n* a dance performed on tiptoe ■ *vi* to perform a toe dance —**toe dancer** *n*

TOEFL /tṓf'l/ *tdmk* a trademark for a standardized English language test taken by speakers of other languages who are applying to universities in the United States. Full form **Test of English as a Foreign Language**

toehold /tṓ hōld/ *n* **1 SMALL RECESS IN ROCK** a small recess or ledge in a rock giving support for the toes **2 SMALL ADVANTAGE** a small advantage or gain in an endeavour **3 HOLD ON FOOT** a wrestling hold in which one competitor holds the foot and twists the leg of the other

toe-in *n* the alignment of a motor vehicle's front wheels so that the front edges are slightly closer together than the rear edges to improve its steering capabilities and reduce tyre wear

toe loop *n* a jump in which an ice skater, skating backwards, takes off from one skate, makes one rotation in the air, and lands on the outer edge of the same skate

toenail /tṓ nayl/ *n* **1 NAIL ON TOE** the nail of a toe **2 NAIL DRIVEN IN AT ANGLE** a nail driven in at an angle, e.g. to join intersecting structural parts **3 PARENTHESIS** a parenthesis (*slang*) ■ *vt* **JOIN WITH ANGLED NAILS** to join parts of a structure with nails driven in at an angle

toerag /tṓ rag/ *n* an offensive term for a person regarded as worthless, despicable, or generally no good (*insult*)

toe ring *n* a ring worn on the toe, particularly a silver ring worn by married Hindu women

toe-to-toe *adj US* being in direct opposition ■ *adv US* in direct opposition as if in close combat

toey /tṓ i/ *adj Aus* easily annoyed or irritated (*informal*)

toff /tof/ *n* a rich or upper-class person, especially somebody who is elegantly dressed (*informal*) [Mid-19C. Probably variant of *tuft*, golden plume worn by titled students at Oxford and Cambridge.]

toffee /tóffi/ *n* a sweet that can be soft and chewy or hard and brittle, made by boiling brown sugar or treacle with butter [Early 19C. Variant of TAFFY.] ◇ **somebody cannot do something for toffee** used to emphasize somebody's lack of ability or competence (*informal*)

toffee apple *n* a caramel-coated apple mounted on a stick. US term **candy apple**

toffee-nosed *adj* behaving in an aloof condescending way (*informal*) [Alteration of TOFF]

toft /toft/ *n* a house with its adjoining buildings and land (*archaic*) [Old English, < Old Norse *topt*]

tofu /tṓ foo/ *n* a soft food with no particular flavour made from soya milk curd pressed into a cake [Late 18C. Via Japanese < Chinese *dòufǔ* 'fermented beans'.]

tog /tog/ *vti* (**togs, togging, togged**) **DRESS UP** to dress up, or dress somebody up, usually in smart clothing (*informal*) ■ *n* **MEASURE OF THERMAL INSULATION** a measure of the thermal insulation properties of fabrics, quilts, and clothes ■ **togs** *npl* (*informal*) **1 CLOTHES** clothes of any kind **2** *ANZ, Ireland* **SWIMMING COSTUME** swimming clothes [Late 18C. Shortening of obsolete slang *togeman* < obsolete French *togue* 'cloak' < Latin *toga* (see 'toga').]

toga /tṓgə/ *n* **1** an outer garment worn by the citizens of ancient Rome, consisting of a semicircular piece of cloth draped around the body **2** a robe of office [Early 17C. < Latin.] —**togaed** *adj*

together /tə gé*th*ər/ CORE MEANING: an adverb indicating that people are with one another, or that something is done with another person or other people, or by joint effort ○ *My brother and I always walked to school together.* **1 WITH OTHERS** in company with others in a group or in a place ○ *We only come together on family occasions.* **2 INTERACTING WITH ONE ANOTHER** interacting, communicating, or in a relationship with one another ○ *They get on well together.* **3 BY JOINT EFFORT** cooperating with one another or by joint or combined effort ○ *Let's work together on this one.* **4 INTO CONTACT** indicates that two or more things are put into contact with one another, or unite to form a single whole ○ *The moccasins were sewn together roughly.* **5 COLLECTIVELY** considered collectively or as a whole ○ *Taken together, these developments add up to a significant change in policy.* **6 UNINTERRUPTEDLY** without interruption ○ *It has been raining for all of four days together.* **7 IN AGREEMENT** in or into agreement or harmony ○ *They can't seem to get together on anything.* **8 IN INTEGRATED COHERENT STRUCTURE** in or into a unified structure or a coherent integrated whole ○ *If you understand how something is put together, you will use it better.* **9 INTO ORDERLY CONDITION OR STATE** into an orderly condition or a stable and effective emotional state (*informal*) ○ *"I'm just trying to get my life together," he said quietly.* **10 IN A COUPLE** indicates that two people are married, having a sexual relationship, or form an established and recognized couple (*informal*) ○ *got back together again after a trial separation* ■ *adj* **STABLE AND SELF-CONFIDENT** emotionally stable, self-confident, and well-organized (*informal*) ○ *She's a very together person.* [Old English *tōgædere* < to 'to' + Germanic, 'joined together'] ◇ **together with** as well as or in addition to

USAGE When *together with* forms an addition to the grammatical subject of a verb, the verb agrees with the grammatical subject. In the following sentence the grammatical subject is *remark*: *This remark, together with earlier comments of the same kind, was not well received.*

togetherness /tə gé*th*ərnəss/ *n* a feeling of closeness in being with others

toggery /tóggəri/ *n* (*informal*) **1** clothes **2** *US* a clothes shop [Early 19C. < TOG.]

toggle /tógg'l/ *n* **1 PEG INSERTED IN LOOP** a peg or rod that is inserted crosswise into a loop at the end of a rope, chain, or strap to hold or fasten something **2 FASTENER ON CLOTHES** a small peg sewn on clothes or on a bag, inserted crosswise into a loop or buttonhole and used as a fastener **3 KEY FOR SWITCHING BETWEEN OPERATIONS** a key or command that switches back and forth between computer operations each time it is used **4 PIN INSERTED INTO KNOT** a pin inserted into a nautical knot to keep it from coming undone **5 SOMETHING WITH TOGGLE JOINT** a toggle joint or a device with a toggle joint ■ *v* (**-gles, -gling, -gled**) **1** *vti* **SWITCH BETWEEN OPERATIONS WITH ONE KEY** to switch back and forth between two computer operations using the same key or command **2** *vt* **SUPPLY OR FASTEN SOMETHING WITH TOGGLES** to supply or fasten something with a toggle or toggles [Late 18C. < ?] —**toggler** *n*

toggle bolt *n* a threaded bolt that has a nut with spring-loaded hinged wings attached and is used especially for securing things to hollow walls

toggle iron, toggle harpoon *n* a whaling harpoon with a pivoting barb that keeps the whale from freeing itself

toggle joint *n* a device with two arms hinged together so that pressure applied at the pivot point to straighten the device exerts force along the two arms

toggle switch *n* **1** a small spring-loaded mechanical switch that opens and closes an electric circuit by manual operation **2** COMPUT = **toggle** *n.* **3**

Togliatti /to lyátti/ city in S European Russia, on the Volga River. Population: 642,000 (1990).

Togo /tṓgō/ republic in West Africa, on the Gulf of Guinea. Capital: Lomé. Population: 4,735,610 (1997). Area: 56,785 sq. km/21,925 sq. mi. —**Togolese** /tṓgə leéz/ *n, adj*

Togrul Beg /tógril bég/ (993?–1063) Turkish Seljuk leader

toheroa /tṓ ə rṓ ə/ (*plural* **-a** *or* **-as**) *n* **1** a large edible mollusc with a hinged shell. Native to: New Zealand coasts. *Amphidesma ventricosum.* **2** a greenish soup made from the toheroa [Late 19C. < Maori.]

toil[1] /toyl/ *n* **HARD WORK** hard exhausting work or effort ■ *vi* **1 WORK HARD** to work long and hard **2 PROGRESS SLOWLY** to progress slowly and with difficulty [13C. < Anglo-Norman *toiler* 'drag around' < Latin *tudicula* 'machine for bruising olives' < *tudes* 'hammer'.] —**toiler** *n*

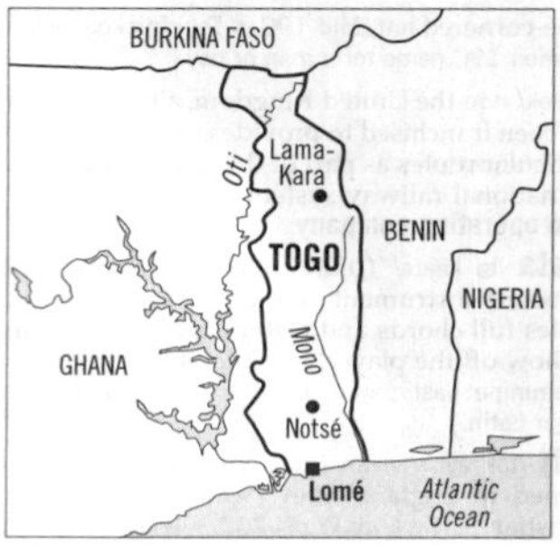

Togo

toil[2] /toyl/ *n* a net, snare, or other thing that entraps or entangles (*archaic or literary; often plural*) [Early 16C. Via Old French *toile* 'cloth, web' < Latin *tela*.]

toile /twaal/ *n* **1** a sheer cotton or linen fabric **2** a prototype of a designer garment made up in a cheap fabric so that alterations can be made [Late 18C. Via French < Latin *tela* 'web'.]

toile de Jouy /-də jweé/ *n* a fabric with a white or light-coloured background and a floral or pastoral print usually in one colour only. Use: curtains, upholstery. [Mid-18C. < French, after *Jouy*-en-Josas, town near Paris, France.]

toilet /tóylət/ *n* **1 FIXTURE FOR DISPOSING OF BODILY WASTE** a bowl-shaped fixture with a waste drain and a flushing device connected to a water supply, used for defecating and urinating **2 ROOM WITH TOILET** a room with a toilet and usually a washbasin **3 WASHING AND DRESSING** the process of attending to your personal appearance and making it presentable, e.g. by washing, dressing, shaving, and tidying your hair (*formal*) **4 CLEANSING ASSOCIATED WITH A SURGICAL PROCEDURE** a cleansing of part of the body after a medical or surgical procedure, often in preparation for applying dressings or bandages [Late 17C. < French *toilette* 'bag for clothing' < Old French *teile* 'cloth' < Latin *tela* 'web'.]

toilet paper *n* a usually soft absorbent paper, especially in a roll, used for cleaning the body after defecating or urinating

toilet roll *n* a length of toilet paper wound around a cardboard cylinder, or the cardboard cylinder on which the paper is wound

toiletry /tóylətri/ (*plural* **-ries**) *n* an article such as shampoo, deodorant, or soap, used in washing or caring for the appearance (*usually plural*)

toilette /twaa lét/ *n* the process of attending to your personal appearance and making it presentable [Mid-16C. < French (see TOILET).]

toilet tissue *n* INDUST = **toilet paper**

toilet training *n* the process of teaching a young child to control bladder and bowel movements and to use the toilet

toilet water *n* a lightly perfumed liquid used to freshen or scent the skin

toilsome /tóylssəm/ *adj* requiring long hard work (*literary*) —**toilsomely** *adv* —**toilsomeness** *n*

toilworn /tóyl wawrn/ *adj* worn, damaged, or exhausted from hard work

toitoi /tóy toy/ (*plural* **-tois**), **toetoe** *n* a tall grass with feathery fronds. Native to: New Zealand. Genus: *Cortederia.* [Mid-19C. < Maori.]

Tojo Hideki /tṓjō hee déki/ (1884–1948) Japanese general and prime minister (1941–44)

Tokaj /tō káy, to-, -kī/ town in NE Hungary. Population: 5,000 (1989 estimate).

tokamak /tókə mak/ *n* an experimental doughnut-shaped nuclear reactor for producing fusion using an electric current and a magnetic field to heat and contain a gaseous plasma [Mid-20C. < Russian, contraction of *toroidal'naya kamera s aksial'nym magnitnym polem* 'toroidal chamber with axial magnetic field'.]

tokay /tṓ kay/ *n* a small lizard that has a retractile claw a the tip of each digit. Native to: southern and Southeas Asia. *Gekko gecko.* [Mid-18C. Via Malay dialect *toke'* < Javanese *tekèk*.]

Tokay /tō káy, to-, tō kī/ *n* **1** a large sweet variety of grap originally grown near Tokaj, Hungary **2** a sweet win made near Tokaj, Hungary, from the Tokay grape, or a similar sweet wine produced elsewhere [Early 18C. Afte TOKAJ (Tokay).]

toke /tōk/ *n* a puff on a cigarette or pipe containin marijuana (*slang*) ■ *vti* (**tokes, toking, toked**) to puff or a cigarette or pipe containing marijuana (*slang*) [Mid-20C. < ?]

token /tṓkən/ *n* **1 SOMETHING REPRESENTING SOMETHING ELSE** something that represents, expresses, or is a symbol o something else ○ *Please accept this gift as a token of ou appreciation.* **2 DISC USED LIKE MONEY** a disc of metal o plastic used instead of money, e.g. in slot machine **3 KEEPSAKE** an object kept in memory of somethin **4 PAPER EXCHANGED FOR GOODS** a paper or card certificat that can be exchanged for goods up to the stated valu ○ *a book token for £10* **5 INSTANCE OF EXPRESSION** a particula instance of a word or expression **6 CONCRETE EXAMPLE** a written or spoken expression considered as a concret example ■ *adj* **EXISTING AS GESTURE ONLY** made, given, or existing merely because expected or required, not because sincere or serving a real purpose ○ *the toke student on the committee* [Old English *tācen* < Indo-Europear 'to point, show']

tokenism /tṓkənizəm/ *n* the practice of making only a symbolic effort at something, especially in order to meet the minimum requirements of the law —**tokenistic** /tṓkə nístik/ *adj*

Tokharian *n, adj* PEOPLES, LANG = **Tocharian**

tokoloshe /tóko lósh, -lóshi/ *n* a small mischievous evi spirit or water sprite in African folklore that takes o human or animal appearance [Mid-19C. < Nguni.]

tokonoma /tṓkə nṓmə/ *n* an alcove in the living room of a Japanese house where a decoration such as flowers or an ornament is displayed [Early 18C. < Japanese.]

Tokoroa /tṓkō rṓ ə/ town in the northwest of the North Island, New Zealand. Population: 15,528 (1996).

Tok Pisin /tók píssin/ *n* a creole, originating as a pidgin based on English, that is widely spoken in Papua New Guinea. Native speakers: 2 million. [Mid-20C. < Pidgin English, 'talk pidgin'.] —**Tok Pisin** *adj*

Tokyo /tṓki ō/ capital of Japan, on Tokyo Bay, on the coast of E Honshu Island. Population: 8,019,938 (1995).

tola /tṓlə/ *n* an Indian unit of weight equal to 180 grains troy weight or 11.7 grams [Early 17C. Via Hindi *tolā* < Sanskrit *tulā* 'weight'.]

tolar /tólaar/ *n* see table at **currency** [Via Slovene < German *Taler* 'thaler']

tolbooth /tṓl booth, -boo*th*/ *n* **1** *Scotland* a town hall or a prison, or a building that performed both functions (*archaic*) **2** = **tollbooth**

tolbutamide /tol byoótə mīd/ *n* $C_{12}H_{18}N_2O_3S$ a drug that lowers blood-glucose levels by stimulating the islets in the pancreas to produce more insulin. Use: treatment of adult-onset diabetes. [Mid-20C. Contraction of TOLUENE + BUTYL + AMIDE.]

told past tense, past participle of **tell**

tole /tōl/ *n* lacquered or enamelled metal used to make decorative objects, usually brightly painted or gilded or both, or objects made of this kind of decorated metal [Mid-20C. Via French *tôle* 'sheet iron' < Latin *tabula* 'board'.]

Toledo[1] /to láydō/ (*plural* **-dos**) *n* a sword or sword blade of highly tempered steel, made in Toledo, Spain

Toledo[2] /to láydō/ historic city and administrative centre of Toledo Province, central Spain. Population: 63,561 (1991).

tolerable /tóllərəb'l/ *adj* **1** not too unpleasant or severe to put up with **2** moderately good, but not outstanding —**tolerability** /tóllərə bílləti/ *n* —**tolerableness** *n* —**tolerably** *adv*

tolerance /tóllərənss/ *n* **1 ACCEPTANCE OF DIFFERENT VIEWS** the acceptance of the differing views of other people, e.g. in religious or political matters, and fairness towards the people who hold these different views **2 TOLERATING OF** the act of putting up with something or somebody irritating or otherwise unpleasant **3 ABILITY TO ENDURE HARDSHIP** the ability to put up with harsh or difficult conditions **4 ALLOWANCE MADE FOR DEVIATION** allowance made for something to deviate in size from a standard, or the limit within which it is allowed to deviate **5 ABILITY TO REMAIN UNAFFECTED** the loss of or reduction in the normal response to a drug or other agent, following use or exposure over a prolonged period **6 ABILITY TO WITHSTAND EXTREMES** the ability of an organism to survive in extreme conditions

tolerant /tóllərənt/ *adj* **1 ACCEPTING DIFFERENT VIEWS** accepting the differing views of others, e.g. different religious or political beliefs **2 WITHSTANDING HARSH TREATMENT** able to put up with harsh conditions or treatment **3 NOT AFFECTED BY A DRUG** no longer responding to a drug that has been taken over a prolonged period, or suffering no ill effects from exposure to a harmful substance —**tolerantly** *adv*

tolerate /tóllə rayt/ (**-ates, -ating, -ated**) *vt* **1 PERMIT** to be willing to allow something to happen or exist **2 ENDURE** to withstand the unpleasant effects of something **3 ACCEPT EXISTENCE OF** to recognize other people's right to have different beliefs or practices without attempting to suppress them **4 BE UNAFFECTED BY** to fail to respond to a drug because the body has built up a resistance to it, or to suffer no ill effects from being exposed to a harmful substance [Early 16C. < Latin *tolerat-*, past participle of *tolerare* 'bear, endure'.] —**tolerative** *adj* —**tolerator** *n*

toleration /tóllə ráysh'n/ *n* **1** official acceptance by a government of religious beliefs and practices that are different from those it upholds **2** the act of tolerating something —**tolerationism** *n* —**tolerationist** *n, adj*

tolidine /tóllə deen/ *n* $C_{14}H_{16}N_2$ an isomeric derivative of toluene. Use: manufacture of dyes. [Late 19C. < TOLYL + *benzidine*.]

Tolkien /tól keen/, **J. R. R.** (1892–1973) South African-born British scholar and writer. Full name **John Ronald Reuel Tolkien**

toll[1] /tōl/ *n* **1 FEE FOR USING A ROAD** a fee charged for a privilege, usually crossing a bridge or using a road **2 BOOTH** a tollbooth, where tolls are paid (*often plural*) **3 DAMAGE SUSTAINED** the damage done by an accident or disaster in terms of, e.g. people killed, property destroyed, or financial loss ○ *The toll on the environment was significant.* **4 CHARGE FOR A TELEPHONE CALL** in the United States a charge for a long-distance telephone call, or, in New Zealand, for a call made to a place outside a free-dialling area **5 FEE FOR SERVICES** a fee charged for services, e.g. transport ■ *vti* **CHARGE A TOLL ON A ROAD** to charge a toll for the use of a road or bridge [Pre-12C. Via medieval Latin *toloneum* < Greek *telōnion* 'toll house' < *telos* 'tax'.]

toll[2] /tōl/ *v* **1** *vti* **RING SLOWLY AND REPEATEDLY** to ring a bell, repeatedly and with long pauses between each ring, especially to announce a death, or be rung in this way ○ *'never send to know for whom the bell tolls; it tolls for thee'* (John Donne, *Devotions*; 1624) **2** *vt* **ANNOUNCE SOMETHING WITH A BELL** to announce something or call somebody with the repeated slow ringing of a bell ○ *bells tolling the death of the king* ■ *n* **ACT OR SOUND OF BELL TOLLING** the act of ringing a bell slowly and repeatedly, or the sound so made [15C. Probably < Old English *-tyllan* 'pull'.] —**toller** *n*

tollbooth /tōl booth, -booth/, **tolbooth** *n* a booth on a road or bridge where tolls for use of the road or bridge are collected

toll bridge *n* a bridge where a toll is charged for crossing

toll call *n* **1** *US, NZ* a long-distance telephone call charged at a higher rate than a local call **2** *NZ* a telephone call made to a place outside a free-dialling area, and therefore charged for

Tollens reagent /tóllənz-/ *n* a solution of silver nitrate, ammonia, and sodium bicarbonate. Use: testing for aldehydes. [After Bernhard *Tollens* (1841–1918), German chemist]

Toller /tóllər/, **Ernst** (1893–1939) German playwright

toll-free *adj US* describes a telephone call that is charged to the person called, not to the caller —**toll-free** *adv*

tollgate /tōl gayt/ *n* a gate barring the way on a road or bridge where a toll must be paid to proceed

tollhouse /tōl howss/ (*plural* **-houses** /-howziz/) *n* a shelter or kiosk for a toll collector at a tollgate

tollhouse cookie *n US* a biscuit made with flour, brown sugar, chocolate chips, and often chopped nuts

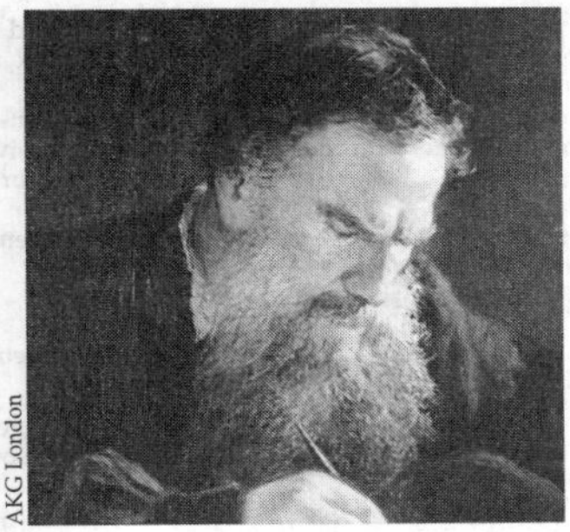

Count Leo Nikolayevich Tolstoy

Tolstoy /tólstoy/, **Count Leo Nikolayevich** (1828–1910) Russian writer

Toltec /tól tek/ (*plural* **Toltecs** *or* **Toltec**) *n* a member of a Native Central American people who formerly lived in central Mexico and were succeeded by the Aztecs [Late 18C. Via Spanish *tolteca* < Nahuatl *toltecatl* 'somebody from Tula', ancient Toltec city.] —**Toltec** *adj*

tolu /tə lóo, tō-, to-/ *n* an aromatic resin. Source: South American tree. Use: perfumes, cough medicines. [Late 17C. < Spanish *tolú*, after the town of Santiago de *Tolú* in Colombia, from which it was exported.]

toluene /tóllyoo een/ *n* C_7H_8 a colourless liquid aromatic hydrocarbon resembling benzene but less flammable. Use: solvent, high-octane fuel, organic synthesis. [Late 19C. < TOLU.]

toluidine /tol yóo i deen/ *n* C_7H_9N any of three isomeric derivatives of toluene. Use: manufacture of dyes.

toluol /tóllyoo ol/ *n* CHEM = **toluene**

tolyl /tóllil/ *n* C_7H_7 any of three chemical groups derived from toluene

tom /tom/ *n* the male of various animals, especially the domestic cat [14C. < the name *Tom* (short for *Thomas*).]

Tom, Dick, and Harry /tóm dík ənd hárri/, **Tom, Dick, or Harry** *n* anyone at all

tomahawk /tómmə hawk/ *n* **1 NATIVE N AMERICAN WEAPON** a small axe, formerly used as a weapon by some Native North American peoples **2** *ANZ* **SMALL AXE** a small short-handled axe ■ *vt* **ATTACK SOMEBODY WITH TOMAHAWK** to attack or kill somebody with a tomahawk [Early 17C. < Virginia Algonquian *tamahaac*.]

tomalley /tóm alli, tə málli/ *n* a soft green part of the insides of a cooked lobster, often called the liver but technically an organ called the hepatopancreas, eaten as a delicacy [Mid-17C. Via French *taumalin* < Carib *taumali*.]

toman /tə maán/ *n* **1** an Iranian coin worth ten rials **2** a gold coin and former unit of Persian currency [Mid-16C. Via Persian *tūmān* < W Tocharian *tmān*.]

tomatillo /tṓmə tée yō/ (*plural* **-los**) *n* **1** a purplish sticky edible fruit that grows on a Mexican ground cherry **2** the ground cherry plant that bears tomatillos. *Physalis ixocarpa*. [Early 20C. < Spanish, 'small tomato' < *tomate* (see TOMATO).]

tomato /tə maátō/ (*plural* **-toes**) *n* **1** a round fruit with bright-red skin and pulpy seedy flesh, eaten cooked or raw as a vegetable **2** a climbing plant that produces tomatoes and is grown throughout the world, in northern regions usually in greenhouses. Native to: South America. Genus: *Lycopersicon*. [Early 17C. Alteration of Spanish *tomate* < Nahuatl *tomatl*.]

tomb /toom/ *n* **1 GRAVE** a grave or other place for burying a dead person **2 BURIAL CHAMBER** a cave or chamber used for burial of a dead person **3 MONUMENT** a monument to a dead person, often built over the place where he or she is buried **4 DEATH** death (*literary*) ○ *go to the tomb unrepentant* **5 HARDENED ENCLOSURE** a hardened enclosure for a closed nuclear reactor, designed to contain radioactive emissions [12C. Via French *tombe* < Greek *tumbos* 'mound, tomb'.] —**tombless** *adj*

Tomba /tómba/, **Alberto** (*b.* 1966) Italian skier

tombac /tóm bak/, **tambac** /tám-/ *n* an alloy of copper and zinc, often with tin and arsenic, originally used in eastern countries to make gongs and bells and now used worldwide to make inexpensive jewellery [Early 17C. Via French < Malay *tembaga* 'copper, brass'.]

tombola /tom bṓlə/ *n* a small-scale lottery, often held at a community event, with tickets drawn from a revolving drum turned by hand [Late 19C. Directly or via French < Italian, *tombolare* 'to tumble'.]

tombolo /tómbəlō/ (*plural* **-los**) *n* a narrow strip of sand or shingle that links one island to another or to the mainland [Late 19C. Via Italian, 'sand dune' < Latin *tumulus* (see TUMULUS.)]

Tombouctou /tóN book tóo/, **Timbuktu** /tím buk-/ city in central Mali, on the southern edge of the Sahara Desert. Population: 19,165 (1976).

tomboy /tóm boy/ *n* a girl who dresses or behaves in a way regarded as boyish, especially a girl who enjoys rough boisterous play [Mid-16C. < the name *Tom* (short for *Thomas*).] —**tomboyish** *adj* —**tomboyishly** *adv* —**tomboyishness** *n*

tombstone /tóom stōn/ *n* an ornamental stone on or at the site of a grave, often with the dead person's name and dates of birth and death engraved on it

Tombstone /tóomstōn/ city in SE Arizona, famous as a lawless mining town of the American West. Population: 1,460 (1998 estimate).

tomcat /tóm kat/ *n* **1 MALE CAT** a male domestic cat **2** *US* **OFFENSIVE TERM** an offensive term for a man who seeks many sexual partners, or who has casual sex with many partners (*slang*) ■ *vi* (**-cats, -catting, -catted**) *US* **OFFENSIVE TERM** an offensive term meaning to seek many sexual partners, or have casual sex with many partners (*slang; refers to a man*)

tomcod /tóm kod/ *n* each of two small sea fishes of the cod family. Native to: North American Atlantic and N Pacific waters. *Microgradus tomcod* and *Microgradus proximus*.

Tom Collins *n* an alcoholic cocktail consisting of gin, lemon or lime juice, soda water, and sugar [Late 19C. < ?]

tome /tōm/ *n* **1** a book, especially a large heavy book on a serious subject (*formal or humorous*) **2** a single volume of a book made up of several volumes [Early 16C. Via French < Greek *tomos* 'section, volume'.]

-tome *suffix* **1** segment, part ○ *myotome* **2** cutting instrument ○ *microtome* [Via modern Latin *-tomus* < Greek *tomos* 'cutting, section']

tomentum /tə méntəm/ (*plural* **-ta** /-tə/) *n* a downy covering of tiny hairs on leaves and other plant parts [Late 17C. < Latin, 'stuffing for a cushion'.] —**tomentose** /tə méntōss, tṓ men-/ *adj*

tomfool /tóm fóol/ *n* a very foolish person (*dated informal*) [14C. < the name *Tom* (short for *Thomas*).] —**tomfool** *adj* —**tomfoolish** *adj* —**tomfoolishness** *n*

tomfoolery /tom fóoləri/ (*plural* **-ies**) *n* **1** silly behaviour (*informal*) **2** a foolish action or statement (*dated informal*)

Tomlinson /tómlinsən/, **Ray** US computer programmer

Tommy /tómmi/ (*plural* **-mies**), **Tommy Atkins** /-átkinz/ *n* a private in the British army (*dated slang*) [Late 19C. < *Thomas Atkins*, name used on specimen forms in the British army.]

tommy bar *n* a rod used to provide leverage in turning a box spanner [< the name *Tommy* (short for *Thomas*)]

Tommy gun *n* a hand-held machine gun, especially a Thompson submachine gun (*informal*)

tommyrot /tómmi rot/ *n* complete nonsense (*dated informal*) [Late 19C. < the name *Tommy* (short for *Thomas*), used for somebody considered foolish.]

tommy rough, **tommy ruff** *n* a fish that is green on the top and silver on its undersides and is related to the Australian salmon. Native to: S Australia. *Arripis georgianus*. [Early 20C. the name *Tommy* (short for *Thomas*) meaning 'little'; *rough* because it is considered inadequate for sport and food.]

tomogram /tṓmə gram/ *n* an image, especially one of the body, made using tomography

tomography /tō móggrəfi/ *n* the technique of using ultrasound, gamma rays, or X-rays to produce a focused image of the structures across a certain depth within the body, while blurring details at other depths [Mid-20C. < Greek *tomos* 'section'.]

tomorrow /tə mórrō/ *n* **1 THE NEXT DAY** the day after today **2 THE FUTURE** a future time, or the future in general ○ *the leaders of tomorrow* ■ *adv* **1 ON THE NEXT DAY** on the day after today **2 IN FUTURE** in the future, or at some time in the future [Old English *tō morgenne* 'in the morning'] ◇ **like** *or* **as if there was** *or* **were no tomorrow** used to emphasize the degree of speed, intensity, or carelessness with which somebody is doing something (*informal*) ○ *ran from the fire like there was no tomorrow*

tompion *n* MIL = **tampion**

toms /toms/ *npl* MUSIC = **tom-tom** *n.* 2 [Early 20C. Shortening.]

Tomsk /tomsk/ city in S Siberian Russia, on the River Tom. Population: 502,000 (1990).

Tom Thumb *n* a character in English folklore who was no taller than his father's thumb

tomtit /tómtit/ *n* a bird of the tit family, especially the blue tit (*informal*) [Early 18C. < name *Tom* (short for *Thomas*).]

tom-tom *n* **1 DRUM HIT WITH THE HANDS** a drum hit with the hands, especially a drum with a long narrow shell and a small head, first used as a signalling instrument **2 DEEP-SIDED DRUM IN MODERN DRUM KIT** a deep-sided drum that forms part of a modern drum kit, deeper in tone than a snare drum but not as deep as a bass drum **3 SOUND OF BEATING DRUM** the sound of a drum being repeatedly beaten, especially slowly and monotonously [Late 17C. < Telugu *ṭamaṭama* or Hindi *ṭam ṭam*, an imitation of the drum's sound.]

-tomy *suffix* cutting, incision ○ *lobotomy* [Via modern Latin *-tomia* < Greek *tomos* 'cutting']

ton[1] /tun/ *n* **1 US UNIT OF WEIGHT** an imperial unit of weight, equal to 907 kilograms in the United States **2 UK UNIT OF WEIGHT** an imperial unit of weight, equal to 1016 kg/2,240 lb in the United Kingdom **3** MEASURE = **metric ton 4** MEASURE = **displacement ton 5 UNIT MEASURING SHIP'S INTERNAL CAPACITY** a unit used to measure the capacity of the inside of a ship, equal to 28.3 cu. m/100 cu. ft **6** MEASURE = **freight ton 7 LARGE AMOUNT** a very great number of things or of something (*informal; often plural*) ○ *tons of things to do* **8 FIGURE OF HUNDRED** a figure of a hundred, especially a hundred miles per hour or a score of a hundred in cricket (*slang*) ■ *adv* **tons A GREAT DEAL** to a great degree or extent [13C. Variant of TUN.] ◇ **come down on somebody like a ton of bricks** to scold or punish somebody severely (*informal*)

USAGE See Usage at ***tonne***.

ton[2] /toN/ *n* the current trend in fashion, or the group of people who like to stay at the cutting edge of fashion [Mid-18C. < French, 'tone'.]

tonal /tṓn'l/ *adj* **1** relating to tone or tonality **2** relating to music written in a harmonic system in which there is a key. ◊ **atonal** —**tonally** *adv*

tonality /tō nálləti/ *n* **1 QUALITY OF TONE** the quality of tone, especially that of an instrument or voice **2 SYSTEM OF MUSICAL TONES** the relationship between the notes and chords of a passage or work that tends to establish a central note or harmony as its focal point. ◊ **atonality 3 ARRANGEMENT OF COLOURS** the scheme connecting the colour tones in a work of art such as a painting

Tonbridge /túnbrij/ town in SE England. Population: 34,260 (1991).

tondo /tóndō/ (*plural* **-dos**) *n* a circular painting or relief carving [Late 19C. < Italian, shortening of *rotondo* 'round' < Latin *rotundus* (see ROTUND).]

tone /tōn/ *n* **1 PARTICULAR KIND OF SOUND** a sound with a particular quality ○ *The first bell has a clearer tone.* **2 WAY OF SPEAKING** the way somebody says something as an indicator of what that person is feeling or thinking ○ *a defiant tone in her voice* **3 GENERAL QUALITY** the general quality or character of something as an indicator of the attitude or view of the person who produced it ○ *the optimistic tone of the report* **4 MACHINE SOUND** a sound, especially one produced by a machine **5 PREVAILING CHARACTER** the characteristic style that something has, particularly in relation to elegance or standing ○ *neon signs that lower the tone of the place* **6 SHADE OF COLOUR** any shade of a particular colour ○ *a green with a more vibrant tone* **7 COMBINATION OF COLOUR AND SHADING** the overall blend of colour and light and shade in a painting or photograph **8 FIRMNESS OF MUSCLES** the natural firmness of muscles when they are not being flexed, or of the body generally **9 INTONATION** the way a syllable of a word is spoken in terms of pitch ○ *the rising tone signifying a question* **10 TIMBRE** the quality of a sound that makes it distinctive, e.g. in a voice or musical instrument **11** MUSIC = **whole tone 12 PLAINSONG** a melody used in singing plainsong, e.g. in psalms **13** *Can, US* MUSIC = **note** *n.* 9 ■ *v* (**tones, toning, toned**) **1** *vi* **BLEND IN** to be similar to something else, especially in colour or brightness, and fit well with it **2** *vti* **CHANGE COLOUR OF PHOTOGRAPH** to develop the colour image of a silver negative in making a photograph **3** *vt* **SAY WITH PARTICULAR PITCH** to say a syllable or word with a particular pitch [13C. Via French *ton* < Greek *tonos* 'tension, tone'.]

tone down *vt* **1** to make something less intense or extreme, usually in order to make it less offensive or controversial **2** to make something less intense, bright, or loud

tone up *vt* to make muscles, or the body in general, firmer and stronger

Tone /tōn/, **Wolfe** (1763–98) Irish revolutionary

tone arm *n* a record player's pivoting, or sometimes sliding, arm with a stylus on its end

tone cluster *n* a group of adjacent notes played together and forming a chord, usually resulting in a dissonant sound

tone colour *n* MUSIC = **timbre** *n.* 2

tone control *n* a control on a radio, record player, or other piece of audio equipment that adjusts the tone it produces, accentuating the higher or lower sound frequencies

tone-deaf *adj* unable to hear the differences between musical notes —**tone-deafness** *n*

tone language *n* a language in which the meaning of a fixed sequence of sounds depends on the pitch in which it is pronounced, different tones identifying different words

toneless /tṓnləss/ *adj* **1** lacking expression in speech **2** lacking brightness or vitality —**tonelessly** *adv* —**tonelessness** *n*

toneme /tṓ neem/ *n* a phoneme in a tone language in which the distinctive feature is a tone [Early 20C. After PHONEME.] —**tonemic** /tō neémik/ *adj*

tone poem *n* MUSIC = **symphonic poem**

toner /tṓnər/ *n* **1 SKIN COSMETIC** a lotion or light astringent used to improve the look or feel of the skin, especially of the face **2 INK** ink in powder or liquid form for a photocopier or computer printer **3 PHOTOGRAPHIC CHEMICAL** a chemical solution used in photograph development

tone row, tone series *n* a sequence of notes that is the basis of a piece of serial music, especially a series of 12 notes

tonetic /tō néttik/ *adj* relating to a language in which changes in pitch distinguish meaning [Early 20C. After PHONETIC.] —**tonetically** *adv*

tong[1] /tong/ *vt* to lift or move something with tongs

tong[2] /tong/ *n* a Chinese secret society thought to be involved in criminal activity [Late 19C. < Chinese (Cantonese) *t'ōng* 'hall, meeting place'.]

tonga /tóng gə/ *n* a light horse-drawn carriage in southern and central India [Late 19C. < Hindi *tāgā*.]

Tonga[1] /tóng gə/ (*plural* **-gas** *or* **-ga**) *n* **1** a member of a people living in south central Africa, mainly in SW Zambia and NW Zimbabwe **2** the Bantu language of the Tonga people [Mid-19C. < Tonga.] —**Tonga** *adj*

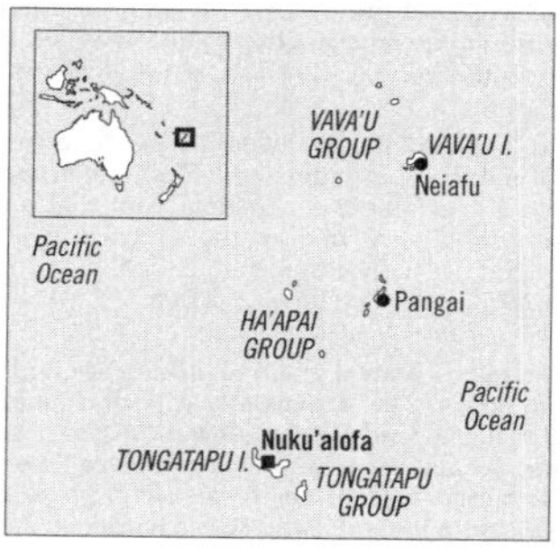

Tonga

Tonga[2] /tóngə, tóng gə/ independent island nation consisting of more than 150 islands in the S Pacific Ocean. Capital: Nukualofa. Population: 107,335 (1997). Area: 750 sq. km/290 sq. mi. —**Tongan** *n, adj*

Tongariro, Mount /tóngə reérō/ active volcano in the central part of the North Island, New Zealand. Height: 1,967 m/6,453 ft.

tongs /tongz/ *npl* **1** a utensil for handling things that consists of two hinged or sprung arms that press together in a pinching movement around the object to be lifted **2** curling tongs [Old English *tang* < Indo-European 'to bite']

tongue /tung/ *n* **1 FLESHY ORGAN INSIDE MOUTH** the movable fleshy organ attached to the bottom of the inside of the mouth of humans and most animals, used for tasting, licking, swallowing, and, in humans, speech. Technical name **glossa** *n.* 1 **2 ANIMAL'S TONGUE AS FOOD** the tongue of an animal, especially a cow, used as food **3 LANGUAGE** a language or dialect **4 WAY OF SPEAKING** somebody's manner of speaking (*formal*) **5 ABILITY TO SPEAK** the power of speech ○ *She found that her tongue had deserted her.* **6 FLAP IN SHOE** the middle flap in the opening of a shoe or boot **7 PIN IN BUCKLE** the pivoting pin in a buckle **8 CLAPPER IN BELL** the small swinging hammer inside a bell that hits against the inside of the bell to make the sound **9 STRIP OF LAND** a narrow strip of land sticking out into a sea, lake, or river **10 VIBRATING END OF MUSICAL REED** the vibrating end of a reed in a wind instrument **11 POLE ON CARRIAGE** the pole at the front of a coach or carriage to which the horses' harnesses are fastened **12 PROJECTING STRIP FITTING INTO GROOVE** a strip that sticks out along the edge of a wooden board and is designed to fit into a corresponding groove along the edge of another board **13 SOMETHING LIKE TONGUE** something shaped or moving like a tongue ■ **tongues** *npl* **SPEECH RESULTING FROM RELIGIOUS ECSTASY** speech in no known language that results from religious ecstasy ■ *v* **1** *vt* **TOUCH WITH TONGUE** to touch or lick something with the tongue **2** *vt* **KISS USING TONGUE** to kiss somebody with the lips open and the tongue touching the inside of the other person's mouth (*informal*) **3** *vti* **USE TONGUE TO ARTICULATE INSTRUMENT'S NOTES** to use the tongue to block the flow of air on a wind or brass instrument, thereby separating one note from another **4** *vt* **CUT TONGUE ALONG BOARD'S EDGE** to cut a tongue along the edge of a wooden board, to make one half of a tongue-and-groove joint [Old English *tunge* < Indo-European] —**tongued** *adj* —**tongueless** *adj* ◇ **hold your tongue** to keep silent ◇ **trip off the tongue** to be easy or pleasant to say

SYNONYMS See ***language***.

tongue-and-groove joint *n* a joint made between two wooden boards consisting of a projecting strip or tongue along the edge of one board and a groove along the edge of the other

tongue depressor *n* *US* MED = **spatula** *n.* 2

tongue-in-cheek *adj* spoken with gentle irony and meant as a joke

tongue-lashing *n* a severe scolding

tongue-tie *vt* to make somebody unable to speak, especially because of awe, shyness, or embarrassment ■ *n* the inability to move the tongue with the normal amount of freedom, because the small membrane (**frenulum**) that attaches the tongue to the floor of the mouth is unusually short

tongue-tied *adj* **1** unable to speak because of awe, shyness, or embarrassment **2** unable to move the tongue freely because of tongue-tie

tongue twister *n* a word, phrase, or sentence that is difficult to say because of its unusual sequence of sounds, especially an invented sentence such as 'She sells seashells on the seashore'

tongue worm *n* a tongue-shaped parasite with a hooked mouth that infests the lungs or nostrils of mammals, reptiles, and birds. Phylum: Arthropoda.

tonic /tónnik/ *n* **1 SOMETHING THAT LIFTS THE SPIRITS** something that lifts the spirits or makes somebody feel better generally **2 MEDICINE PRODUCING SENSE OF WELL-BEING** a medicine that purports to make patients feel stronger, more energetic, and generally healthier **3** BEVERAGES = **tonic water 4 FIRST NOTE OF SCALE** the first note in a scale and the harmony built on this note **5 STRESSED SYLLABLE** the syllable that has the main stress in a word ■ *adj* **1 LIFTING THE SPIRITS** lifting the spirits and generally creating a feeling of well-being **2 BOOSTING ENERGY** designed or serving to boost energy and generally create a feeling of strength and health **3 RELATING TO MUSCLE TONE** relating to or affecting muscular tone or contraction **4 RELATING TO FIRST NOTE** based on the first note of a scale **5 OF A STRESSED SYLLABLE** constituting or relating to the main stressed syllable in a word **6** LING = **tonetic** [Mid-17C. Via French *tonique* < Greek *tonikos* 'of stretching' < *tonos* 'tension, tone'.] —**tonically** *adv*

tonic accent *n* **1** a musical accent produced by higher pitch rather than by stress **2** stress on a syllable created through a change in pitch

tonicity /tō nìssəti/ *n* **1** the state or quality of being tonic **2** the state or quality of muscles being slightly contracted or ready to contract

tonic sol-fa *n* a system of using syllables to denote degrees of a musical scale, and in which the syllables are movable depending on the key of the piece

tonic water *n* a carbonated drink with a bitter taste, originally and still sometimes containing quinine, drunk on its own as a soft drink or used as an ingredient in cocktails. US term **quinine water** [So called because it was originally drunk to stimulate the appetite or digestion]

tonight /tə nít/ *n* the night or evening of the present day ■ *adv* on or during the night or evening of the present day [Old English *tō niht* 'at night']

tonka bean /tóngkə-/ *n* **1** a fragrant black almond-shaped seed. Use: perfume, scenting tobacco and snuff. **2** a leguminous tree that produces tonka beans. Native to: tropical America. *Dipteryx odorata.*

Tonkin, Gulf of /tón kin, tóng-/ arm of the South China Sea, on the coast of NE Vietnam and SE China

Tonle Sap /tón lay sáp/ largest lake in Southeast Asia, in W Cambodia. It swells from 2,600 sq. km/1,000 sq. mi. in the dry season to 10,400 sq. km/4,020 sq. mi. in the monsoon season.

tonnage /túnnij/, **tunnage** *n* **1** WEIGHT IN TONS weight measured in imperial or metric tons **2** SHIP'S SIZE OR CAPACITY the size of a ship measured in tons or cubic feet or metres of seawater displaced, or the capacity of a ship measured in cubic feet or metres **3** WEIGHT OF SHIP'S CARGO the weight of a ship's cargo, measured in tons **4** DUTY CHARGED ON SHIP'S CARGO the duty charged at a rate per ton on a ship's cargo **5** SIZE OF FLEET OF SHIPS the size of a fleet of ships, e.g. a merchant company's fleet or a nation's warships, calculated as the combined weights or carrying capacities of all ships [15C. < TON¹.]

tonne /tun/ *n* MEASURE = **metric ton** [Late 19C. Via French < medieval Latin *tunna.*]

USAGE tonne, ton, or **tun**? All three words are pronounced the same way (tun). A ***tonne*** is a metric unit equal to 1000 kilograms. A ***ton*** is an imperial unit, and differs in value in British and American usage (see ***ton***). A ***tun*** is a large beer or wine cask or a unit of liquid capacity equal to 955 litres/210 gallons.

tonneau /tónnō/ (*plural* **-neaus** *or* **-neaux** /tónnō, -nōz/) *n* the back-seat compartment of an open-top vintage car, or a flexible cloth cover protecting it when it is not being used [Late 18C. < French, 'barrel' (because of its shape) < *tonne* (see TONNE).]

tonometer /tō nómmitər/ *n* **1** an instrument, often one fitted with a range of tuning forks, that measures the exact pitch of a sound **2** an instrument that measures pressure in a part of the body such as the blood vessels, or the eyeball as a test for glaucoma [Early 18C. < Greek *tonos* 'tension, tone'.] —**tonometric** /tónnə méttrik, tōnə-/ *adj* —**tonometry** *n*

tonsil /tónss'l, -sil/ *n* **1** each of two small oval masses of tissue, one on each side of the back of the mouth, that are important for the body's immune system **2** any lump of tissue shaped like the tonsils of the mouth, e.g. either of two small lumps in the brain (**tonsils of the cerebellum**) [Late 16C. < Latin *tonsillae* 'tonsils'.] —**tonsillar** *adj*

~~**tonsilitis**~~ incorrect spelling of **tonsillitis**

tonsillectomy /tónssi léktəmi/ (*plural* **-mies**) *n* a surgical procedure to remove the tonsils of the mouth

tonsillitis /tónssi lítiss/ *n* inflammation of the tonsils of the mouth, caused either by bacteria or a virus, which makes the throat very sore and can lead to fever and earache —**tonsillitic** /-líttik/ *adj*

tonsorial /ton sáwri əl/ *adj* relating to barbers or their work (*formal or humorous*) [Early 19C. < Latin *tonsorius* < *tonsor* 'barber' < *tondere* 'to clip'.]

tonsure /tónshər, -syər/ *n* a shaved patch on the crown of the heads of priests and monks in some religious orders, or the shaving of the head in this way ■ *vt* (**-sures, -suring, -sured**) to shave the crown of the head [14C. Directly or via French < Latin *tonsura* < *tondere* 'to clip'.]

tontine /tón tīn, -teen, -teén/ *n* an investment or insurance scheme in which contributors pay equal amounts into a common fund and receive equal dividends and benefits from it, with the final surviving contributor receiving everything [Mid-18C. < French, after Lorenzo *Tonti* (1630–95), Neapolitan banker.]

tonto /tón tō/ *adj* an offensive term that deliberately insults somebody who is thought to be mentally ill (*insult*) [Late 20C. < Spanish.]

ton-up *adj* (*dated informal*) **1** CAPABLE OF OVER 100 MPH describes a motorcycle travelling at or capable of travelling at over 100 miles per hour **2** FOND OF RIDING MOTORCYCLES FAST fond of riding motorcycles at high speeds, especially recklessly ■ *n* SPEED OVER 100 MPH a speed in excess of 100 miles per hour, or a motorcyclist who frequently rides at these speeds (*dated informal*)

tonus /tōnəss/ *n* the normal state of a healthy muscle when resting in a state of slight contraction [Late 19C. Via Latin < Greek *tonos* 'tension, tone'.]

tony /tōni/ *adj Can, US* having an aristocratic, expensive, or stylish presentation (*informal*)

Tony /tōni/ (*plural* **-nys** *or* **-nies**) *n* an award made annually in the United States for achievement in the theatre [Mid-20C. < *Tony*, nickname of Antoinette Perry (1888–1946) US actor and producer.]

too /too/ *adv* **1** AS WELL used to indicate that a person, thing, or aspect of a situation applies in addition to the one just mentioned ○ *Can cats be affected by it too?* ○ *You ought to see a doctor, and quickly too!* **2** MORE THAN IS DESIRABLE more of an amount or degree of something than is desirable, necessary, or fitting ○ *He's a little too conservative for me.* **3** EXTREMELY used to emphasize a quality ○ *She's only too aware of how this will affect her career.* **4** VERY used to modify the force of a negative statement in order to sound polite or cautious ○ *It didn't look too good.* **5** *Can, US* INDEED used to emphasize the force of a statement or command ○ *'I didn't touch it'. – 'You did too!'* [Old English *tō* (see TO), in the sense 'in addition, furthermore'] ◇ **too right** used to express emphatic agreement with a statement that has just been made ○ *'So you're leaving?' – 'Too right I am!'*

SPELLCHECK See ***to***.

toodle-oo /toòd'l oò/, **toodle-pip** *interj* farewell (*dated informal or humorous*) [Early 20C. < ?]

took past tense of **take**

tool /tool/ *n* **1** DEVICE FOR DOING WORK an object designed to do a particular kind of work, e.g. cutting or chopping, by directing manually applied force or by means of a motor **2** CUTTING PART OF MACHINE the cutting or shaping part of a power-driven device, e.g. the blade on a lathe **3** BOOKBINDER'S IMPLEMENT an implement that a bookbinder uses to make a design on leather, or the design made by such an implement **4** MEANS TO AN END something used as a means of achieving something **5** SOMETHING USED FOR A JOB an item people use in the course of their everyday work ○ *Words are the poet's tool.* **6** SOMEBODY MANIPULATED an easily manipulated person, especially in carrying out unsavoury or dishonest tasks somebody else is unwilling to do **7** GUN a criminal's gun (*slang*) **8** OFFENSIVE TERM an offensive term for a man's penis (*slang*) ■ *v* **1** *vt* WORK USING HAND TOOLS to cut, shape, or form something, especially to press a design into the leather cover of a book, using hand tools **2** *vt* GIVE TOOLS TO to equip somebody or something with tools **3** *vti* DRIVE A CAR to drive a car in a particular way, especially at high speeds (*slang*) ○ *tooling along at a cool 65* [Old English *tōl* < Germanic, 'manufacture'] —**tooler** *n*

tool up *vti* on a large scale, to provide a factory or an industry with the equipment needed to manufacture many things ○ *tooled up the automotive industry for the war effort*

ϟ**toolbar** /toòl baa/ *n* a row of icons on a computer screen that are clicked on to perform certain frequently used functions

tooled up *adj* (*slang*) **1** equipped, especially well enough equipped to do a particular job **2** carrying a gun

tooling /toòling/ *n* any kind of decorative work done with hand tools, especially the carving of stone or the pressing or stamping of designs onto leather

toolkit /toòl kit/ *n* a set of tools, especially for a particular type of work, kept in a special box or bag

toolmaker /toòl maykər/ *n* a maker or repairer of precision tools, especially the cutting or shaping parts of industrial machines —**toolmaking** *n*

tool pusher *n* a supervisor of drilling operations on an oil rig (*informal*)

toolroom /toòl room, -ròom/ *n* a room in a machine shop where tools are stored, maintained, or made

tool shed *n* a small outbuilding where tools are kept, especially one in a garden used for storing gardening tools

tool steel *n* hard steel used to make the cutting or shaping parts of hand tools and power tools

toon[1] /toon/ *n* **1** a fragrant hard reddish mahogany. Use: furniture, joinery. **2** a tree of the mahogany family and bears red flowers that yields toon. Native to: Australia, tropical Asia. *Cedrela toona.* [Early 19C. Via Hindi *tūn* < Sanskrit *tunnaḥ*.]

toon[2] /toon/ *n* any kind of cartoon or cartoon character, or the whole of the cartoon-making industry

toon[3] *n* = **toun** *n.* 1

toot[1] /toot/ *n* SOUND OF VEHICLE HORN the high-pitched hooting sound that a vehicle's horn makes, or a similar sound ■ *v* **1** *vti* MAKE SHORT HOOTING SOUND to make, or cause the horn of a vehicle to make, a short high-pitched hooting sound **2** *vi* PASS GAS to pass gas noisily (*slang*) [Early 16C. An imitation of the sound.] —**tooter** *n*

toot[2] /toot/ *n* a quantity of an illegal drug, especially cocaine, taken by inhaling through the nose (*slang*) ■ *vti US* to inhale an illegal drug, especially cocaine (*slang*) [Late 17C. < ?]

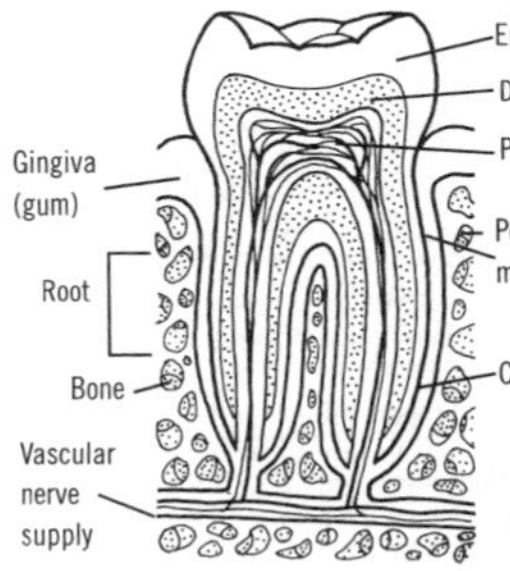
Enamel
Dentine
Pulp
Gingiva (gum)
Pendental membrane
Root
Cementum
Bone
Vascular nerve supply

Tooth: Cross-section of a human tooth

tooth /tooth/ *n* (*plural* **teeth** /teeth/) **1** WHITISH BONY OBJECT IN THE MOUTH a hard whitish bony object inside a human or vertebrate animal's mouth, used for biting and chewing food **2** INVERTEBRATE PART RESEMBLING A TOOTH a sharp part on an invertebrate made of horny, calcareous, or chitinous material and functioning like or resembling a vertebrate tooth **3** INDENTATION an object resembling the shape of or performing the function of a tooth, e.g. one of the jagged indentations along the edge of a saw or leaf **4** PART STICKING OUT ON GEAR WHEEL any of the parts that stick out from the edge of a gear wheel or sprocket, designed to interlock with another set **5** SURFACE ROUGHNESS the roughness of a surface, especially the surface of paper, which allows paints, glues, and other substances to stick to it **6** SOMETHING DESTRUCTIVE something that has the power to destroy (*usually plural*) ○ *the teeth of the gale* **7** TASTE a liking for the taste of something ○ *a sweet tooth* ■ **teeth** *npl* EFFECTIVE POWER the power or ability to accomplish something ○ *Sanctions without teeth won't do any good.* ■ *v* **1** *vt* PUT TEETH ON to give something teeth, especially to cut teeth into a saw blade or around the edge of a gear wheel or sprocket **2** *vti* FIT TOGETHER WITH INTERLOCKING TEETH to interlock by means of teeth that fit one set inside the other [Old English *tōþ* < Indo-European] —**toothed** *adj* ◇ **armed to the teeth (with something)** extremely well armed or equipped with something (*informal*) ◇ **cut your teeth (on something)** to learn how to do something and gain experience from it ◇ **get your teeth into something** to start doing something that will be challenging and satisfying ◇ **in the teeth of** against opposition or contradiction from ◇ **set your teeth on edge** to irritate ◇ **show your teeth** to indicate that you have power and intend to use it

toothache /tòoth ayk/ *n* pain in or around a tooth, especially because the tooth is decaying

tooth and nail *adv* very aggressively, or with every available means

toothbrush /tóoth brush/ *n* a small brush for cleaning the teeth, with a long handle and a comparatively small head —**toothbrushing** *n*

toothed whale /toótht-/ *n* a smallish whale that has teeth and feeds on fish and molluscs. Suborder: Odontoceti.

tooth fairy *n* in children's folklore, a fairy who takes away the milk tooth that a child leaves under the pillow and replaces it with a coin or small gift

toothless /tóothləss/ *adj* **1** lacking teeth, especially because the teeth have decayed and fallen out **2** lacking power, authority, or a forceful manner

toothless whale *n* a whale without teeth but with thin horny plates hanging from the upper jaw through which it filters plankton. Toothless whales are larger than toothed ones. ◊ **toothed whale**

toothpaste /tóoth payst/ *n* paste brushed onto the teeth to clean them and protect them from decay

toothpick /tóoth pik/ *n* a thin pointed stick of wood or plastic used to remove pieces of food from between the teeth

tooth powder *n* powder that is mixed to a lather with a damp toothbrush and used to clean the teeth and protect them from decay

tooth shell *n* MARINE BIOL = **tusk shell**

toothsome /tóothsəm/ *adj* **1** having a pleasing smell, taste, and appearance **2** attractive, especially sexually (*dated informal; offensive in some contexts*) —**toothsomely** *adv* —**toothsomeness** *n*

toothwort /tóoth wurt/ (*plural* **-worts** *or* **-wort**) *n* **1** a leafless plant that grows on tree roots and has horizontal underground stems (**rhizomes**) covered with scales resembling teeth. Flowers: pinkish. Native to: Europe. *Lathraea squamaria.* **2** a flowering plant with scaly rhizomes. Flowers: showy, pink or purple. Native to: North America. *Cardamine bulbifera.*

toothy /tóothi/ (**-ier, -iest**) *adj* having or showing a lot of teeth, large teeth, or protruding teeth —**toothily** *adv* —**toothiness** *n*

tootle /tóot'l/ *v* (**-tles, -tling, -tled**) (*informal*) **1** *vi* **DRIVE SLOWLY** to proceed slowly or aimlessly, especially in a car **2** *vti* **MAKE HOOTING SOUND** to make or cause something to make repeated high-pitched tooting sounds ■ *n* (*informal*) **1 LEISURELY DRIVE** a drive at a leisurely pace **2 REPEATED SOUND** a gentle repeated tooting sound [Early 19C. < TOOT[1].] —**tootler** *n*

toots /tóots/, **tootsie** /tóotsi/ *n US* an affectionate or patronizing way of addressing somebody, especially a woman (*dated informal; offensive in some contexts*) [Mid-20C. < ?]

tootsy (*plural* **-sies**) *n* **1** a child's word for foot or toe (*babytalk or humorous*) **2** *US* = **toots** [Mid-19C. Alteration of FOOTSIE.]

Toowoomba /tə wóombə/ city in SE Queensland, Australia. Population: 83,350 (1996).

top[1] /top/ *n* **1 HIGHEST PART** the highest part or point (*often in combination*) ○ *snow on the mountain tops* **2 UPPER SURFACE** the upper side or surface ○ *dust on the top of the cupboard* **3 LID OR COVER** the part covering and sealing the open upper side of an object or an opening on the upper side (*often in combination*) ○ *bottle tops* **4 GARMENT COVERING UPPER BODY** a piece of clothing, especially women's clothing, covering the upper body **5 MOST IMPORTANT POSITION OR PERSON** the most important position or most senior rank, or the person occupying it ○ *at the top of her profession* ○ *He's top of the class.* **6 BEST PART** the best part or section ○ *They only take the top of the group.* **7 MOST EXCELLENT LEVEL** the level of highest excellence ○ *not at the top of his game* **8 MOST INTENSE LEVEL** the level of greatest intensity, power, or force ○ *at the top of her voice* **9 FARTHEST END** the farthest end of something, e.g. a road or street **10 BEGINNING** the beginning or the first or earliest section ○ *Take it from the top.* **11 CROWN OF HEAD** the crown of the head ○ *from top to toe* **12 CAR ROOF** the roof of a car, especially a convertible **13 TOP GEAR** top gear in a motor vehicle (*informal*) US term **high** *n.* 7 **14** SPORTS = **topspin** **15 STROKE HITTING BALL ABOVE CENTRE** a stroke that puts topspin on a ball by hitting the ball above its centre **16 PLAYER'S BEST CARD** the best card or group of cards in a player's hand **17 HIGH-FREQUENCY PART OF SOUND** the high-frequency element of any sound **18 VOLATILE PART OF A SOLUTION** that fraction of a volatile solution that is collected first during distillation **19 PLATFORM ON A MAST** a platform around the head of a lower mast on a sailing ship, used to stand on or to support rigging ■ **tops** *npl* **ROOT VEGETABLE'S VISIBLE PARTS** the parts of a root vegetable that are visible above the ground when it is growing (*often in combination*) ■ *adj* **1 HIGHEST** situated at the top, or higher than all others ○ *the top shirt on the pile* **2 MOST SUCCESSFUL** most important, senior, successful, or respected ○ *a convention of top academics* **3 OF BEST QUALITY** of the finest quality available ○ *one of the city's top hotels* **4 MAXIMUM** being at the highest level or degree ○ *at top speed* ■ *vt* (**tops, topping, topped**) **1 ADD TOPPING TO** to put a topping on something (*often passive*) ○ *topped with a layer of melted cheese* **2 CUT TOP OFF** to cut the top off something, especially a vegetable prior to cooking ○ *First top and tail the carrots.* **3 OUTRANK ALL OTHERS IN** to be at the head of something such as a list or hierarchy ○ *They've topped the music charts for the fifth week in a row.* **4 EXCEED** to do better than something, or be greater than something ○ *profits topping $500 million* **5 REACH APEX OF** to reach or go over the top of something, e.g. a mountain **6 KILL** to kill somebody or kill yourself (*slang*) **7 PUT TOPSPIN ON** to hit a ball above its centre, putting topspin on it **8 HIT ABOVE CENTRE** to hit a golf ball too far above its centre, so that it runs along the ground instead of rising into the air **9 DISTIL VOLATILE PART OF** to distil the most volatile part of a solution [Old English *topp* < Germanic, 'tuft, crest'] ◇ **blow your top** to lose your temper and fly into a rage (*informal*) ◇ **off the top of your head** without thinking deeply, checking, or planning something

top out *vi* to add the final storey or other structural feature to a building under construction, usually as part of an official ceremony

top up *vt* **1 FILL CONTAINER** to fill or refill a container that is partly empty **2 INCREASE SUM BY ADDING MONEY** to give extra money to augment a sum or fund of money, especially in order to bring it up to a required or desirable level **3 GIVE SOMEBODY MORE TO DRINK** to refill somebody's drink, especially when it is not yet finished (*informal*)

top[2] /top/ *n* a toy that spins round on a rounded or pointed base, traditionally a conical wooden toy that is set spinning by pulling a string wrapped round it [Pre-12C. < ?]

top- *prefix* = **topo-** (*before vowels*)

topaz /tố paz/ *n* **1 TRANSPARENT BROWN GEMSTONE** a usually brown, transparent precious stone. Source: pegmatite. Use: gems. **2 YELLOWISH GEMSTONE** a yellowish gemstone, especially yellow sapphire or a yellow variety of quartz **3 HUMMINGBIRD WITH YELLOWISH THROAT** each of two vividly coloured yellowish-throated hummingbirds of the South American rainforest. *Topaza pyra* and *Topaza pella.* **4 YELLOWISH-BROWN COLOUR** a light yellowish-brown colour [13C. Via Old French *topace* < Greek *topazos.*] —**topaz** *adj*

topazolite /tō pázzə līt/ *n* a yellowish-green variety of garnet. Use: gems.

top banana *n US* the main person in a group (*slang*)

top billing *n* **1** a performer's status as the star attraction in a show with his or her name appearing first in any list of performers or promotional material **2** the position of greatest prominence in something

top boot *n* a knee-length boot with a band of differently coloured leather around the top

top brass *n* the highest-ranking officers or officials (*informal*)

top-class *adj* belonging to or characteristic of the highest category of something ○ *a top-class tennis player*

topcoat /tópkōt/ *n* **1** a finishing coat of paint, applied over an undercoat **2** a coat for outdoor wear (*dated*)

top dead-centre *n* the position of a piston in an engine or pump when it is at the top of its stroke

top dog *n* the most important or powerful person, often somebody who has beaten all other competitors (*informal*)

top dollar *n* a high price, or the highest price (*informal*)

top-down *adj* **1** having all control in the hands of the people at the most senior levels **2** starting at the most general level and working towards details or specifics ○ *a top-down approach*

top drawer *n* **1** the highest level of excellence, or the people at this level **2** the upper class or highest class in society —**top-drawer** *adj*

top-dress *vt* to spread a thin layer of something on the ground, especially fertilizer on the surface of soil, a growing crop, or a lawn

top dressing *n* **1 SURFACE FERTILIZER** fertilizer spread thinly on the surface of soil, a growing crop, or a lawn **2 LOOSE GRAVEL AS A ROAD SURFACE** loose gravel spread thinly on the surface of a road or path **3 SUPERFICIAL COVERING** a thin or superficial covering, especially a deceptively pleasant façade hiding an unpleasant reality

tope[1] /tōp/ (**topes, toping, toped**) *vti* to drink alcohol heavily and habitually (*archaic or literary*) [Mid-17C. < ?]

tope[2] /tōp/ (*plural* **topes** *or* **tope**) *n* a small grey widely distributed shark with a long snout. *Galeorhinus galeus.* [Late 17C. < ?]

tope[3] /tōp/ *n* RELIG = **stupa** [Early 19C. < Hindi *top.*]

topee /tố pee/ *n* ACCESSORIES = **pith helmet** [Mid-19C. < Hindi *topī* 'hat'.]

Topeka /tō peékə/ capital of Kansas, in the northeastern part of the state. Population: 118,977 (1998 estimate).

top end *n* MECH ENG = **little end**

toper /tốpər/ *n* a heavy and habitual drinker of alcoholic beverages (*literary or informal*)

top-flight *adj* of the highest quality or status

topgallant /top gállənt/ *n* **1 topgallant mast, topgallant** a ship's mast that is taller than a topmast or is an extension of a topmast **2 topgallant sail, topgallant** a sail set on a topgallant mast

top gear *n* **1** the highest of a motor vehicle's gears, selected for the fastest speed of travel. US term **high gear** **2** the state of greatest intensity, e.g. the fastest working rate or the highest level of enthusiasm (*informal*)

top gun *n US* a person who is the best in his or her field (*informal*)

top-hamper *n* the uppermost sails, spars, and other equipment on a sailing ship, especially when regarded as weight to be minimized or monitored because of the destabilizing effect it can have

top hat *n* a man's tall cylindrical hat with a flat top and a narrow brim. It is usually black, is often made of silk, and is worn as part of formal dress.

top-heavy *adj* **1** unbalanced or unstable owing to excessive weight at the top **2** with too many executives or managers in proportion to the numbers of staff at junior levels —**top-heavily** *adv* —**top-heaviness** *n*

Tophet /tốfət/, **Topheth** *n* according to the Bible, a place of torment and punishment where the wicked are sent after death [14C. < Hebrew *Tōpet*, area near Jerusalem.]

top-hole *adj UK* first-rate or excellent (*dated informal*) [Late 19C. Probably after TOPNOTCH.]

tophus /tốfəss/ (*plural* **-phi** /-fī/) *n* a hard deposit of crystalline uric acid and its salts in cartilage, joints, or skin [Mid-16C. < Latin, 'tufa'.] —**tophaceous** /tō fáyshəss/ *adj*

topi[1] /tố pee/ (*plural* **-pis** *or* **-pi**) *n* an African antelope that has curved horns, a long muzzle, and bluish-black and yellow markings. It is said to be the fastest of all the antelopes. *Damaliscus lunatus.* [Late 19C. < ?]

topi[2] /tốpi/ *n* ACCESSORIES = **pith helmet** [Mid-19C. Variant of TOPEE.]

topiary /tốpi əri/ (*plural* **-ies**) *n* **1 ART OF SHAPING BUSHES** the art of trimming bushes, hedges, and trees into decorative shapes **2 SHAPED BUSH** a bush, hedge, or tree trimmed into a decorative shape **3 TOPIARY GARDEN** a garden in which topiaries feature prominently [Late 16C. Via French < Latin *topiarius* < Greek *topos* 'place'.] —**topiarist** *n*

topic /tóppik/ *n* **1** a subject written or spoken about **2** a class of arguments used as a source of proofs in formal reasoning [15C. < *Topics*, title of Aristotle's treatise on rhetorical commonplaces < Latin *Topica* < Greek *topos* 'place'.]

SYNONYMS See ***subject***.

TOPIC /tóppik/ *abbr* Teletext Output of Price Information by Computer

topical /tóppik'l/ *adj* **1 OF CURRENT INTEREST** relating to something that is of particular interest at the moment **2 OF TOPICS** relating to topics or in the form of topics **3 LOCAL** relating to, or situated in, a particular place or part **4 APPLIED EXTERNALLY** describes drugs or medications that are applied directly to the surface of the part of the body being treated —**topically** *adv*

topicality /tóppi kálləti/ *n* relevance to matters that are of interest at the moment

topic sentence *n* a sentence that states the main idea of a paragraph or larger section of writing, usually placed at or near the beginning

topknot /tóp not/ *n* **1 HAIR DECORATION** a decorative arrangement of hair, or of hairbands or bows, worn on top of the head **2 FLATFISH** a flatfish, especially a species that has an oval, dark-brown body with darker patches. Native to: Europe. *Zeugopterus*. **3 BIRD'S CREST** a small tuft of feathers on the head of some birds, e.g. the quail

topless /tópləss/ *adj* **1 WITH NOTHING COVERING BREASTS** wearing no covering over the breasts or upper torso **2 WHERE WOMEN SHOW BREASTS** where women can or do expose their breasts in public ○ *a topless beach* **3 WITH NO TOP PART** with no covering for the upper torso **4 MISSING A TOP** without or missing a top —**toplessness** *n*

top-level *adj* **1** involving the most senior or influential people **2** at the highest level of influence or authority

top-level domain *n* the part of an Internet address that identifies an Internet domain, such as .edu (education), .com (commercial), or a two-letter country code.

toplofty /tóp lofti/ **(-ier, -iest)** *adj US* haughty, pretentious, or condescending (*informal*) —**toploftily** *adv* —**toploftiness** *n*

topmast /tóp maast/ *n* a mast that is taller than the lowest mast and is usually the tallest mast on a ship whose sails run fore-and-aft

topminnow /tópminō/ (*plural* **-nows** *or* **-now**) *n* a small freshwater fish that swims near the surface in warmer waters and has an upturned mouth for catching prey. Families: Cyprinodontidae, Poeciliidae, and Goodeidae.

topmost /tópmōst/ *adj* highest or uppermost

topnotch /tòp nóch/ *adj* meeting the highest standards of excellence and quality (*informal*) —**topnotcher** *n*

topo /tóppō/ (*plural* **-pos**) *n* a photograph of a mountain that has possible routes for climbing marked on it [Late 20C. Shortening of *topographic*.]

topo- *prefix* place, region ○ *topotype* [< Greek *topos* 'place']

top of mind *adj US* first among the things a person thinks about (*informal*) ○ *how to keep food safety top of mind among your employees*

top-of-the-range *adj* the most expensive and sophisticated available and considered to be the best of its kind (*not hyphenated after verbs*) ○ *bought the top-of-the-range model*

topography /tə póggrəfi/ (*plural* **-phies**) *n* **1 MAPPING OF SURFACE FEATURES** the study and mapping of the features on the surface of land, including natural features such as mountains and rivers and constructed features such as roads and railways **2 AREA'S FEATURES** the features on the surface of a particular area of land **3 DESCRIPTION OF STRUCTURE** a study or detailed description of the various features of any object or entity and the relationships between them **4 MAP** a map or chart of an area's topography —**topographer** *n* —**topographic** /tóppə gráffik/ *adj* —**topographical** *adj* —**topographically** *adv*

topoi plural of **topos**

topoisomerase /tóppō ī sómmə rayss, -rayz/ *n* an enzyme that controls the manipulation of the structure of DNA necessary for replication

topology /tə pólləji/ *n* **1 STUDY OF GEOMETRICAL PROPERTIES** the study of the properties of figures that are independent of size or shape and are not changed by stretching, bending, knotting, or twisting **2 FAMILY OF SUBSETS** the family of all open subsets of a mathematical set, including the set itself and the empty set, which is closed under set union and finite intersection **3 ANATOMY OF BODY PART** the anatomy of a specific part of the body **4 STUDY LINKING TOPOGRAPHY AND TIME** the study of changes in topography that occur over time and, in particular, of how such changes taking place in a particular area affect the history of that area **5 RELATIONSHIPS BETWEEN LINKED ELEMENTS** the relationships between elements linked together in a system, e.g. a computer network (*formal*) —**topologic** /tóppə lójjik/ *adj* —**topological** *adj* —**topologically** *adv* —**topologist** /tə pólləjist/ *n*

Topolski /tə pólski/, **Feliks** (1907–89) Polish-born British artist

toponym /tóppənim/ *n* **1** a name given to a place (*formal*) **2** a name, e.g. a personal name, that is derived from the name of a place [Late 19C. < TOPO- after SYNONYM.]

toponymy /tə pónnəmi/ *n* the study of the place names of a specific region or language —**toponymic** /tóppə nímmik/ *adj*

topos /tópposs/ (*plural* **-poi** /tóppoy/) *n* a traditional theme, especially one developed in literature or rhetoric [Mid-20C. < Greek, 'place, rhetorical commonplace'.]

topotype /tóppə tīp/ *n* a biological specimen taken from its typical habitat

topper /tóppər/ *n* **1 TOP HAT** a top hat (*informal*) **2 SOMEBODY OR SOMETHING DEALING WITH TOPS** a person or machine that removes or adds tops **3 CROWNING COMMENT** a remark or joke that improves on or triumphs over a preceding one (*informal*) **4 PLEASANT PERSON** an outstandingly kind or popular person (*dated informal*) **5 BEST OF ITS KIND** something that surpasses all others of its kind (*dated informal*)

topping /tópping/ *n* **1 GARNISH FOR FOOD** something put on top of food, especially a sauce or garnish **2 FEATHER FOR A FISHING FLY** a feather from the crest of a golden pheasant put at the top of a fishing fly ■ *adj UK* **FIRST-RATE** excellent (*dated informal*)

topple /tópp'l/ **(-ples, -pling, -pled)** *v* **1** *vti* **FALL OR MAKE SOMETHING FALL OVER** to fall forward or tip over, or make something fall forward or tip over **2** *vi* **TOTTER** to lean or sway precariously, as if about to fall over **3** *vt* **OVERTHROW** to overthrow somebody or something from a position of authority [Mid-16C. < TOP[1].]

top quark *n* a quark with an electric charge of +2/3 and zero strangeness and charm

top-ranking *adj* of a senior rank or the highest rank

top-rated *adj* considered highest in quality or rank ○ *the city's ten top-rated restaurants*

top round *n US* FOOD = **topside** *n.* **2**

tops /tops/ *n* **BEST PERSON OR THING** somebody or something ranking highest in quality, importance, or popularity (*dated informal*) ■ *adv* **AT MOST** at the most (*informal*) ■ *n* (*plural* **tops**) **BEST PERSON OR THING** the very best person or thing (*informal*) ○ *Thanks, mum, you're the tops.*

topsail /tóp sayl, tópss'l/ *n* a sail set above the lowermost sail on a mast on a square-rigged sailing vessel, or above the gaff on a fore-and-aft-rigged vessel

top-secret *adj* requiring complete secrecy or containing information that must be kept completely secret, especially because its disclosure would endanger national security

top-shelf *adj* **1** relating to pornographic magazines that are very sexually explicit and are therefore displayed on the top shelf in a shop, out of direct view **2** *Aus* of the finest quality

topside /tóp sīd/ *n* **1 UPPER SIDE** the uppermost side of something **2 CUT OF BEEF** a lean boneless cut of beef from the outer thigh. US term **top round** **3 UPPER HULL** the part of a ship's hull that lies above the water ■ *adj* **ON THE TOPSIDE OF A SHIP** relating to or situated on the topside of a ship ■ *adv* **topside, topsides** /-sīdz/ *US* **TO A SHIP'S DECK** up on or to the deck of a ship

topsoil /tóp soyl/ *n* **SOIL'S TOP LAYER** the upper fertile layer of soil, from which plant roots take nutrients ■ *vt* **1 SPREAD LAND WITH TOPSOIL** to spread topsoil onto farming or gardening land **2 REMOVE TOPSOIL FROM LAND** to remove the top layer of soil from farming or gardening land

topspin /tópspin/ *n* forward spin given to a ball by hitting it on its upper half, making it arc more sharply in the air or bounce higher on impact

topstitch /tópstich/ *n* a row of stitching on the outer or upper side of a garment, near the seam ■ *vt* to sew a topstitch on a garment —**topstitching** *n*

topsy-turvy /tópsi túrvi/ *adj, adv* **1 UPSIDE DOWN** with the bottom at the top and the top at the bottom **2 IN OR INTO CONFUSION** in or into a confused or chaotic state, especially one in which the natural order or arrangement of things is inverted ■ *n* **DISORDER OR CONFUSION** a state of complete disorder or confusion [Early 16C. < ?] —**topsy-turvily** *adv* —**topsy-turviness** *n*

top-up *n* **1** a refilling of a glass or cup out of which somebody has drunk all or part of the contents **2** an additional sum of money, especially one that brings a fund up to a required or desirable level (*often before nouns*) ○ *a top-up loan*

toque /tōk/ *n* **1 BRIMLESS HAT** a close-fitting brimless hat worn by women **2 CHEF'S HAT** a tall white hat worn by chefs **3 HAT WORN IN THE PAST** a velvet hat with a narrow brim and pouched crown, popular in the 16th century with men and women [Early 16C. < French.]

tor /tawr/ *n* a rocky peak of a hill or mountain, specifically one exposed by the weathering of surrounding rock (*often in placenames*) [Old English *torr* < ?]

Torah /táwrə/ *n* **1** the Jewish Pentateuch, or a parchment scroll on which the Pentateuch is written for use in services in synagogues **2** the collective body of Jewish teaching embodied in the Hebrew Bible and the Talmud [Late 16C. < Hebrew *tôrāh* 'law'.]

torbernite /táwrbə nīt/ *n* a green mineral containing uranium and copper. Use: source of uranium. [Mid-19C. After *Torbern* Olof Bergman (1735–84), Swedish chemist.]

torc *n* MEASURE = **torque**[2]

torch /tawrch/ *n* **1 PORTABLE LIGHT SOURCE** a small hand-held lamp usually powered by batteries. US term **flashlight** *n.* 1 **2 BURNING STICK** a stick of wood dipped in wax or with one end wrapped in combustible material, set on fire and carried, especially formerly, as a source of light **3 DEVICE EMITTING FLAME** a portable device that emits an extremely hot flame, e.g. one used in welding or for stripping paint **4 SOURCE OF ENLIGHTENMENT** a source of guidance or enlightenment (*literary*) ■ *vt* **SET ON FIRE** to set fire to something, especially as an act of arson or terrorism (*informal*) [13C. Via French *torche* < Latin *torques* 'torque' < *torquere* 'to twist'.] —**torcher** *n* ◇ **carry a torch for somebody** to be in love with somebody, especially when this feeling is secret or unrequited (*informal*)

torchbearer /táwrch bairər/ *n* **1** a bearer of a torch, usually in a procession or ceremony **2** a provider of leadership or inspiration

torchère /tawr sháir/ *n* a tall decorated stand for holding a candle or candelabrum [Early 20C. < French, < *torche* (see TORCH).]

torchier /táwrchi ər/, **torchiere** *n* a tall floor lamp that gives indirect upward lighting [Early 20C. Variant of TORCHÈRE.]

torchlight /táwrch līt/ *n* **1** the light from a torch or torches **2** = **torch** *n.* **2**

torchon lace /táwrsh'n-/ *n* lace made from coarse linen or cotton, with a simple open pattern

torch song *n* a popular sentimental song about unrequited love [< the torch as a symbol of unrequited love] —**torch singer** *n*

torchwood /táwrch wŏŏd/ *n* **1** a resinous wood once used to make torches **2** a tree yielding torchwood. Native to: Florida, Caribbean. Genus: *Amyris*.

tore[1] past tense of **tear**[1]

tore[2] /tawr/ *n* ARCHIT = **torus** *n.* **2** [Mid-17C. Via French < Latin *torus* 'bulge'.]

toreador /tórri ə dawr/ *n* a bullfighter, especially one on horseback [Early 17C. < Spanish, < *torear* 'fight bulls' < *toro* 'bull' (see TORERO).]

torero /to ráirō/ (*plural* **-ros**) *n* a bullfighter, especially one on foot [Early 18C. < Spanish, < *toro* 'bull' < Latin *taurus*.]

toreutics /tə rŏŏtiks/ *n* the art of making detailed reliefs in metal using the techniques of embossing and engraving (+ *singular verb*) [Mid-19C. < Greek *toreutikos* < *toreus* 'boring tool'.] —**toreutic** *adj*

tori plural of **torus**

toric /tórrik/ *adj* ring- or doughnut-shaped like a torus, or relating to tori

toric lens *n* a spectacles lens used to correct the vision of somebody with astigmatism

torii /táwri ee/ (*plural* **-i**) *n* a form of gateway to a Japanese Shinto temple that has two posts and two cross-pieces [Early 18C. < Japanese, 'bird's perch'.]

torment *vt* /tawr mént/ **1 INFLICT PAIN ON** to inflict torture, pain, or anguish on somebody or something **2 TEASE** to tease a person or an animal persistently ■ *n* /táwr ment/ **1 TORTURE** severe mental anguish or physical pain **2 CAUSE OF ANGUISH** a source of severe mental anguish or physical pain **3 CAUSE OF ANNOYANCE** a source of annoyance or anxiety [13C. Via Old French < Latin *tormentum* 'catapult, torment' < *torquere* 'to twist'.] —**tormented** *adj* —**tormentedly** *adv* —**tormentingly** *adv*

tormenter *n* = **tormentor**

tormentil /táwrməntil/ (*plural* **-tils** *or* **-til**) *n* a downy plant with an astringent root. Flowers: yellow. Use: medicine, tanning, dyeing. *Potentilla erecta*. [14C. < French *tormentille* < Latin *tormentum* (see TORMENT).]

tormentor /tawr méntər/, **tormenter** *n* **1 CAUSE OF TORMENT** a causer or cause of mental anguish, physical pain, annoyance, or anxiety **2 CURTAIN MASKING STAGE WINGS** a curtain or screen at each side of a theatre stage that hides the wings from the audience **3 ECHO-REDUCING DEVICE** a panel of sound-absorbent material used to eliminate echo on a film set [13C. < Anglo-Norman *tormentour*, Old French *tormenteor* < Latin *tormentum* (see TORMENT).]

torn past participle of **tear**[1] ■ *adj* favouring or tending towards both options and therefore unable to choose between them ◇ **that's torn it** an expression of annoyance at, or fear of the consequences of, a sudden and unexpected problem (*dated informal*)

tornado /tawr náydō/ (*plural* **-dos** *or* **-does**) *n* **1 COLUMN OF SWIRLING WIND** an extremely destructive funnel-shaped rotating column of air that passes in a narrow path over land **2 AFRICAN WIND** a short-lived but severe windstorm, especially one that occurs on the West African coast **3 FRANTIC PERSON OR STATE** a state of frenzied activity or intense emotion, or somebody in such a state (*informal*) [Mid-16C. Probably alteration of Spanish *tronada* 'thunderstorm' < Latin *tonare* 'to thunder'.] —**tornadic** /tawr náddik/ *adj*

~~**tornament**~~ incorrect spelling of **tournament**

toroid /táw royd/ *n* MATH = **torus** *n.* 1

Toronto /tə róntō/ capital of Ontario Province, Canada, on the shore of NW Lake Ontario. Population: 653,734 (1996). —**Torontonian** /tə ron tṓnee ən/ *n, adj*

torose /táwrōz/, **torous** /táwrəss/ *adj* cylindrical and knotted or bulging [Mid-18C. < Latin *torosus* 'brawny' < *torus* 'bulge'.] —**torosity** /taw róssəti/ *n*

torpedo /tawr péedō/ *n* (*plural* **-does**) **1 SELF-PROPELLED UNDERWATER WEAPON** a cylindrical self-propelled missile that is launched from an aircraft, ship, or submarine and travels underwater to hit its target **2 UNDERWATER MINE** an underwater explosive mine (*dated*) **3** *US* **FIREWORK** a gravel-filled firework that explodes when thrown against a hard surface **4** *US* **RAILWAY DANGER SIGNAL** a detonating device placed on a railway track that acts as a danger signal to the crew of a train that runs over it **5** *US* **EXPLOSIVE FOR OIL WELLS** an explosive device used to release the oil from an oil well **6** ZOOL = **electric ray** ■ *vt* (**-does, -doing, -doed**) **1 HIT WITH TORPEDO** to hit or destroy a ship with a torpedo **2 DESTROY** to spoil, thwart, or destroy something completely (*informal*) [Early 16C. < Latin, 'numbness' < *torpere* 'be stiff'.]

torpedo boat *n* a small light fast boat used to launch torpedoes

torpedo bomber *n* an aircraft that carries and launches torpedoes

torpedo tube *n* a tube from which torpedoes are fired from submarines or ships

torpid /táwrpid/ *adj* **1 SLUGGISH** lacking physical or mental energy **2 DORMANT** in a dormant state, especially when hibernating **3 NUMB** describes a part of the body that has lost the ability to move or feel [Early 17C. < Latin *torpidus* < *torpere* 'be stiff'.] —**torpidity** /tawr píddəti/ *n* —**torpidly** *adv*

torpor /táwrpər/ *n* **1 LACK OF ENERGY** lack of mental or physical energy **2 DORMANCY** dormancy, especially in hibernation **3 NUMBNESS** absence of the ability to move or feel [13C. < Latin, < *torpere* 'be stiff'.] —**torporific** /táwrpə ríffik/ *adj*

Torquay /táwr kée/ town in SW England. Population: 59,587 (1991).

torque[1] /tawrk/ *n* **1** force that causes rotation, twisting, or turning, e.g. the force generated by an internal-combustion engine to turn a vehicle's drive shaft **2** the measurement of the ability of a rotating gear or shaft to overcome turning resistance [Late 19C. < Latin *torquere* 'to twist'.]

torque[2] /tawrk/, **torc** *n* a metal collar or armband worn by the ancient Gauls and Britons [Mid-19C. Via French < Latin *torques* (see TORCH).]

torque converter *n* a hydraulic coupling designed to change the mechanical advantage or torque speed between an input and an output shaft

Torquemada /táwrkwi maádə/, **Tomás de** (1420–98) Spanish monk and grand inquisitor

torques /tawrks/ (*plural* **torques**) *n* a ring of colour, hair, or feathers around the neck of an animal [Mid-16C. < Latin (see TORCH).]

torque spanner *n* a spanner with a gauge attached for regulating the amount of torque applied to a bolt. US term **torque wrench**

torr /tawr/ (*plural* **torr**) *n* a unit of pressure equal to about 133.3 pascals or one millimetre of mercury supported in a column [Mid-20C. After Evangelista TORRICELLI.]

Torre del Greco /tór ay del grékō/ coastal city near Naples, S Italy. Population: 100,688 (1992).

torrefy /tórri fī/ (**-fies, -fying, -fied**) *vt* to subject something to intense heat, especially an ore or a chemical, for the purpose of removing excess water [Early 17C. < French *torréfier* < Latin *torrere* 'scorch'.] —**torrefaction** /tórri fáksh'n/ *n*

Torremolinos /tórrimə léen oss/ major resort in S Spain, on the Mediterranean Sea. Population: 37,235 (1998).

Torrens, Lake /tórrənz/ salt lake in South Australia. Area: 5,780 sq. km/2,230 sq. mi.

Torrens title /tórrənz-/ *n* in Australia, a system of registering land ownership in which ownership occurs when the document that transfers the property is lodged at the local land office [Mid-19C. After the British administrator Sir Robert *Torrens* (1814–84).]

torrent /tórrənt/ *n* **1** a fast and powerful rush of liquid, especially water **2** a violent or tumultuous flow [Late 16C. < Latin *torrent-* 'hot, rushing' < *torrere* 'scorch'.]

torrential /tə rénsh'l/ *adj* **1** flowing or falling fast and in great quantities ○ *torrential rain* **2** intense or abundant —**torrentially** *adv*

Torres Strait /tórriss-/ body of water between Cape York, Australia, and Papua New Guinea

Torres Strait Islands group of about 60 Australian islands located in the Torres Strait. Population: 8,905 (1996).

Torricelli /tórri chélli/, **Evangelista** (1608–47) Italian mathematician and physicist

Torricellian vacuum /torri chélli ən-/ *n* the partially evacuated space above a column of mercury in a tube that is closed at one end and has been placed open end down onto a mercury reservoir [After Evangelista TORRICELLI]

torrid /tórrid/ *adj* **1 FULL OF PASSION** full of passion, especially sexual passion **2 SCORCHING HOT** describes weather that is hot and dry enough to scorch land **3 SCORCHED** describes land that has been scorched by extremely hot and dry weather [Late 16C. Directly or via French < Latin *torridus* < *torrere* 'scorch'.] —**torridity** /to ríddəti/ *n* —**torridly** *adv* —**torridness** *n*

Torrid Zone *n* the region of the Earth that lies between the Tropics of Cancer and Capricorn

torsade /tawr saád, -sáyd/ *n* a decorative twist of beads, cord, or fabric [Late 19C. < French, < Latin *tors-* (see TORSION).]

Tórshavn /tawrs hówn/ administrative headquarters of the Faroe Islands, on the island of Streymoy. Population: 15,272 (1995).

torsi plural of **torso**

torsibility /táwrsə bílləti/ *n* the ability to undergo or resist twisting [Mid-19C. < TORSION.]

torsion /táwrsh'n/ *n* **1 TWISTING OF AN OBJECT** the twisting of an object by applying equal and opposite torques to its ends **2 MECHANICAL STRESS** the stress placed on an object that has been twisted **3 TWISTING** the twisting of something, or a twisted state (*technical*) [15C. Directly or via French < late Latin *torsion-* < Latin *tors-*, past participle of *torquere* 'twist'.] —**torsional** *adj* —**torsionally** *adv*

torsion balance *n* an instrument that measures small electrical or magnetic forces by the degree of twist they produce in a filament

torsion bar *n* a metal bar that acts as a spring when subjected to torsion, e.g. in a motor vehicle's suspension system

torsk /tawrsk/ (*plural* **torsks** *or* **torsk**) *n* a soft-finned marine fish of the cod family. Native to: northern coastal waters. *Brosmius brosme.* US term **cusk** *n.* 1 [Early 18C. Via Norwegian < Old Norse *þorskr.*]

torso /táwrssō/ (*plural* **-sos** *or* **-si** /táwr see/) *n* **1 UPPER BODY** the upper part of the human body, not including the head and arms **2 SCULPTURE** a sculpture of a torso, or a broken statue of a human figure, with the head, arms, and legs missing **3 SOMETHING WITH PARTS MISSING** something that has parts missing, either because it has been mutilated or because it has not been completed (*literary*) [Late 18C. Via Italian, 'trunk of a statue' < Latin *thyrsus* (see THYRSUS).]

tort /tawrt/ *n* in civil law, a wrongful act for which damages can be sought by the injured party [14C. Via Old French < medieval Latin *tortum* < Latin *torquere* 'to twist'.]

torte /táwrtə, tawrt/ *n* a very rich cake consisting of layers sandwiched together with a cream filling [Mid-18C. Via German < Italian *torta* 'cake' < late Latin, type of bread.]

Tortelier /tawr télli ay/, **Paul** (1914–90) French cellist

tortellini /táwrtə léeni/ *npl* small filled pasta that is shaped into rings, boiled, and served in a soup or sauce [Mid-20C. < Italian, plural of *tortellino* 'little cake' < *torta* (see TORTE).]

tort-feasor /táwrt feezər/ *n* a committer of a tort [Mid-17C. < Old French *tort-fesor* 'wrong-doer'.]

torticollis /táwrti kólliss/ *n* a twisting of the neck to one side, resulting in the head being tilted [Early 19C. < modern Latin, < Latin *tortus* 'twisted' + *collum* 'neck'.] —**torticollar** *adj*

tortilla /tawr tée ə/ (*plural* **-las**) *n* **1** a thin flat Mexican bread made with either corn meal or wheat flour, cooked on a hot griddle and eaten folded, with a filling of beans, cheese, or shredded meat **2** a thick omelette made with eggs, potatoes, and fried onion [Late 17C. < Spanish, < *torta* 'cake' < late Latin, type of bread.]

tortilla chip *n* a thin crunchy crisp made of maize meal, often served with dips, e.g. salsa or guacamole

tortillon /tawr tíllyən/ *n* ART = **stump** *n.* 4 [Late 19C. < French, < *tortiller* 'to twist' < Latin *torquere.*]

tortious /táwrshəss/ *adj* involving or constituting a tort in civil law —**tortiously** *adv*

tortoise /táwrtəss/ *n* **1** a slow-moving land-dwelling reptile with a large dome-shaped shell into which it can retract its head and limbs. Family: Testudinidae. **2** MIL, HIST = **testudo 3** a person who moves very slowly [15C. Alteration of obsolete *tortuce* < medieval Latin *tortuca.*]

tortoise beetle *n* a brightly-coloured beetle that has a flat rounded body and whose larvae eat leaves. Subfamily: Cassidinae.

tortoiseshell /táwrtəss shel/ *n* **1 OUTER PART OF TURTLE SHELL** the hard mottled outer layer of the shell of a hawksbill turtle. Use: combs, ornaments, jewellery. **2 SYNTHETIC TORTOISESHELL** a synthetic substance made to resemble tortoiseshell **3 TYPE OF CAT** a domestic cat with black, cream, and brownish markings **4 ORANGE-BROWN BUTTERFLY** a butterfly that has jagged orange-brown wings with black markings. Family: Nymphalidae. **5** ZOOL = **hawksbill** ■ *adj* **MOTTLED YELLOW AND BROWN** with mottled yellow and brown markings

tortoni /tawr tṓni/ *n* rich Italian ice cream often flavoured with sherry or rum and chopped cherries or almonds [Early 20C. Probably after an Italian café-owner of 18C Paris.]

tortricid /táwrtrissid/ *n* a small moth whose larvae live in coiled leaves and are often destructive to plants. Family: Tortricidae. [Late 19C. < modern Latin *Tortrix*, genus name < Latin *tortus* 'twisted'.]

Tortuga Island /tawr tóogə-/ island off N Haiti, in the Caribbean. Population: 22,880 (1982). Area: 180 sq. km/70 sq. mi.

tortuosity /táwrtyoo óssəti/ (*plural* **-ties**) *n* **1** the state of being twisted or crooked **2** a twist or turn

tortuous /táwrtyoo əss/ *adj* **1 TWISTING AND WINDING** with many turns or bends **2 INTRICATE** extremely complex or intricate **3 DEVIOUS** devious or deceitful [14C. Via Anglo-Norman < Latin *tortuosus* < *torquere* 'to twist'.] —**tortuously** *adv* —**tortuousness** *n*

USAGE tortuous or **torturous**? Even though both words come ultimately from a Latin word meaning 'twist', their meanings diverge in English. A mountain pass is ***tortuous*** ('with many turns or bends'), and by figurative extension, a legal argument can be ***tortuous*** ('complex or intricate') as well. A severe illness, and by figurative extension a decision, may be ***torturous*** ('causing anguish').

torture /táwrchər/ *vt* (**-tures, -turing, -tured**) **1 INFLICT PAIN ON** to inflict extreme pain or physical punishment on people **2 CAUSE SOMEBODY ANGUISH** to cause somebody mental or physical anguish ○ *This headache is torturing me.* **3 DISTORT** to twist or distort something into an unnatural form ■ *n* **1 INFLICTING OF PAIN** the inflicting of severe physical pain on somebody, e.g. as punishment or to persuade somebody to confess or recant something **2 METHODS OF INFLICTING PAIN** the methods used to inflict physical pain on people **3 ANGUISH** mental or physical anguish [Mid-16C. Directly or via French < late Latin *tortura* < Latin *tortus* 'twisted' < *torquere* 'to twist'.] —**torturer** *n* —**torturingly** *adv*

torturous[1] /táwrchərəss/ *adj* **1** inflicting, or designed to inflict, severe physical pain, e.g. as punishment **2** causing great physical or mental anguish [15C. < Anglo-Norman, < Old French *torture* (see TORTURE).] —**torturously** *adv*

USAGE See **tortuous**.

torturous[2] incorrect spelling of **tortuous**

torula /tórryələ/ (*plural* **-lae** /-lee/ *or* **-las**) *n* **1 torula, torula yeast** an edible yeast that is cultivated for use as a medicine and food additive. *Candida utilis.* **2** a yeast fungus that does not have sexual spores. Many of them grow on dead vegetation and fermented sugars. Genus: *Torula.* [Mid-19C. < modern Latin, < Latin *torus* 'bulge'.]

torus /táwrəss/ (*plural* **-ri** /-rī/) *n* **1 RING-SHAPED SURFACE** a doughnut-shaped geometric surface generated by rotating a circle about a line in the same plane as the circle but not intersecting it **2 MOULDING** a large convex moulding, especially at the base of a classical column **3 RIDGED BODY PART** a body part in the shape of a rounded ridge or bulge, e.g. the bony ridge below an eyebrow **4 FLOWER PART** the receptacle of a flower [Mid-16C. < Latin, 'bulge'.]

Torvill /táwrvil/, **Jayne** (*b.* 1957) British ice-skater

Tory /táwri/ *n* (*plural* **-ries**) **1 UK CONSERVATIVE** in the UK, a member of the Conservative and Unionist Party **2 CANADIAN CONSERVATIVE** in Canada, a member of the Progressive Conservative Party **3 ENGLISH ROYALIST** a member of an English political party, active from the late 17th century until the 1830s, that supported the social order represented by the monarchy and the Church of England **4 Tory, tory SUPPORTER OF CONSERVATIVE PRINCIPLES** a holder of politically conservative views **5 AMERICAN SUPPORTER OF BRITAIN** a resident of the American colonies of Great Britain who supported the British Crown during the War of Independence in the 18th century **6 17C IRISH OUTLAW** in 17th-century Ireland, any of the Irish people who became outlaws harrying the English settlers who had displaced and dispossessed them ■ *adj* **1 CONSERVATIVE** relating to, belonging to, or supporting any Conservative Party **2 Tory, tory VERY CONSERVATIVE** politically conservative or reactionary [Mid-17C. Via Irish *tóraidhe* 'highwayman' < Old Irish *tóir* 'chase'.] —**Toryism** *n*

Tosa Mitsunobu /tṓssə mítsoo nṓ boo/ (1434–1525) Japanese artist

Toscanini /tóskə neéni/, **Arturo** (1867–1957) Italian-born US conductor

tosh /tosh/ *n* nonsense or foolishness (*informal*) [Mid-19C. < ?]

toss /toss/ *v* **1** *vt* **LIGHTLY THROW** to throw something lightly, especially with the palm of the hand upwards ○ *tossed the letter on the table* **2** *vti* **THROW OR BE THROWN UP AND DOWN** to be thrown, or throw something, repeatedly up and down or to and fro ○ *tossed by the waves* **3** *vti* **THROW COIN** to throw a coin upwards, usually spinning it with the thumb on the way, the side it falls on being a way of deciding between two options **4** *vt* **MIX** to mix something, especially a salad with its dressing, by lifting and turning its parts rather than by stirring **5** *vt* **THROW RIDER** to throw the rider of a horse or other animal off its back **6** *vt* **THROW SOMEBODY OR SOMETHING UPWARDS** to hurl somebody or something upwards with apparent ease **7** *vt* **JERK HEAD UPWARDS** to jerk the head upwards, e.g. in a gesture of anger or impatience **8** *vi* **MOVE RESTLESSLY** to move about restlessly, especially in sleep **9** *vi* **MOVE QUICKLY** to move abruptly, e.g. in anger ■ *n* **1 THROWING** an act of throwing somebody or something **2 HEAD JERK** an abrupt jerk of the head **3 DECIDING THROW OF COIN** a spinning of a coin in the air as a method of deciding between two options [Early 16C. < ?] ◇ **argue the toss** to take part in a prolonged argument, especially in disputing a decision ◇ **not give a toss** not to care in the least (*informal*)

SYNONYMS See *throw*.

toss off *v* **1** *vti* **TABOO TERM** a highly offensive term meaning to masturbate (*taboo*) **2** *vt* **DO SOMETHING QUICKLY** to do something quickly and easily **3** *vt* **DRINK SOMETHING QUICKLY** to drink something quickly, often in one gulp

tosser /tóssər/ *n* an offensive term for a person, especially a man, regarded as unintelligent or contemptible (*slang*) [Mid-20C. < TOSS OFF.]

tosspot /tósspot/ *n* **1** a drunken person (*archaic or literary*) **2** an offensive term for somebody regarded as inferior or unintelligent (*slang insult*)

toss-up *n* **1** a throw of a coin into the air that decides, by which side it falls on, between two options **2** an even risk or chance

tostada /to staádə/, **tostado** /to staádō/ *n* a crisply fried Mexican-style tortilla, usually served with several meat and vegetable toppings [Mid-20C. < Spanish, < past participle of *tostar* 'toast'.]

tot /tot/ *n* **1** a small child (*informal*) **2** a small amount of something, especially alcoholic spirit [Early 18C. < ?]

total /tṓt'l/ *n* **SUM** the sum of several amounts added or considered together ■ *adj* **1 USED FOR EMPHASIS** used to emphasize how good, bad, or complete something is ○ *a total success* **2 OVERALL** with all elements added or considered together ○ *the total price* ■ *vt* (**-tals, -talling, -talled**) **1 ADD THINGS TOGETHER** to add several amounts together to arrive at a total **2 AMOUNT TO TOTAL** to amount to a total when added or considered together ○ *The numbers totalled in the hundreds.* **3** *US* **KILL SOMEBODY OR DESTROY** to kill, destroy, wreck, or demolish somebody or something (*slang*) [14C. Via Old French < medieval Latin *totalis* < Latin *totus* 'entire'.]

total eclipse *n* an eclipse in which the entire surface of an astronomical object, e.g. the Sun or the Moon, is obscured

total football *n* a style of football in which players' positions are interchangeable as part of a general method of attack

total heat *n* PHYS = **enthalpy**

total internal reflection *n* the complete reflection of a light ray at the boundary of the medium in which it is travelling, when the angle of incidence exceeds the critical angle

totalisator *n* BETTING = **totalizator**

totalise *vt* = **totalize**

totaliser /tṓtə līzər/ *n* BETTING = **totalizator** *n.* 2

totalitarian /tō tálli táiri ən/ *adj* relating to or operating a centralized government system in which a single party without opposition rules over political, economic, social, and cultural life [Early 20C. < TOTALITY after AUTHORITARIAN.] —**totalitarian** *n* —**totalitarianism** *n*

totality /tō tálləti/ (*plural* **-ties**) *n* **1 COMPLETENESS** the state of being complete or total **2 TOTAL AMOUNT** the sum or total amount of something **3 FULLNESS OF ECLIPSE** the stage of an eclipse at which light is completely obscured

totalizator /tṓtə lī zaytər/, **totalisator** *n* **1** a system of betting on horse races using an electronic machine that totals all bets, deducts management charges and taxes, and determines the final odds and payouts **2** a machine that records bets, odds, and totals, and calculates winnings in the tote betting system [Late 19C. After French *totalisateur.*]

totalize /tṓtə līz/ (**-izes, -izing, -ized**), **totalise** (**-ises, -ising, -ised**) *vt* to add several amounts to make a total —**totalization** /tṓtə lī záysh'n/ *n*

totalizer /tṓtə līzər/ *n* GAMBLING = **totalizator** *n.* 2

totally /tṓt'li/ *adv* **1** in a complete or utter way **2** used to emphasize how good, bad, or complete something is (*informal*) ○ *I totally hate this!*

total recall *n* the ability to remember accurately in every detail

total reflection *n* PHYS = **total internal reflection**

totaquine /tṓtə kween/ *n* a mixture of quinine and other alkaloids from cinchona bark. Use: treatment of malaria. [Mid-20C. < modern Latin *totaquina* < Latin *totus* 'whole' + Spanish *quina* 'cinchona bark'.]

totara /tṓtərə/ *n* a tall coniferous tree that produces dark-red, durable but light wood. Native to: New Zealand. *Podocarpus totara.* [Mid-19C. < Maori *tōtara.*]

tote[1] /tōt/ *vt* (**totes, toting, toted**) (*informal*) **1 CARRY** to carry or haul something, especially something heavy **2 HAVE SOMETHING ON YOUR PERSON** to carry something, especially a gun, on your person ■ *n* **HEAVY LOAD** a heavy load that is hauled or carried [Late 17C. < ?] —**toter** *n*

tote[2] /tōt/ *n* a system of betting on horse races using an electronic machine that totals all bets, deducts management charges and taxes, and determines the final odds and payouts (*informal*) [Late 19C. Shortening of TOTALIZATOR.]

tote bag *n* a soft open bag with handles, often made of canvas, leather, plastic, or straw

totem /tṓtəm/ *n* **1 IMPORTANT TRIBAL OBJECT** an object, animal, plant, or other natural phenomenon revered as a symbol of a tribe and often used in rituals among some tribal or other traditional groups of people **2 CARVING** a carving or other representation of a totem **3 SYMBOLIC THING** something regarded as a symbol, especially something treated with the kind of respect normally reserved for religious icons [Mid-18C. < Ojibwa *nindoodem* 'my totem'.] —**totemic** /tō témmik/ *adj*

totemism /tṓtəmizəm/ *n* **1** the use of totems as symbols of kinship **2** the organizing of societies into groups whose members share a common totem —**totemist** *n* —**totemistic** /tṓtə místik/ *adj*

totem pole *n* **1** among some Native North American peoples, a tall wooden pole carved with totems that symbolize family and historical relationships **2** *US* a hierarchy, e.g. in a company or organization (*informal*)

tother /tú*th*ər/, **t'other** *adj, pron* the or that other (*informal*) [14C. Contraction of *the other.*]

totipalmate /tṓti pál mayt/ *adj* describes birds that have all four toes webbed, e.g. pelicans and gannets [Late 19C. < Latin *totus* 'whole'.] —**totipalmation** /tṓti pal máysh'n/ *n*

totipotent /tō típpətənt/ *adj* describes a cell, e.g. a fertilized ovum, that is capable of generating new tissue, organs, or individuals [Early 20C. < Latin *totus* 'whole'.] —**totipotency** *n*

Totonac /tṓtə nák/ (*plural* **-nac** *or* **-nacs**) *n* **1** a member of a Native Central American people inhabiting east-central Mexico **2** one of two languages spoken by the Totonac people [Late 18C. < Spanish *Totonaca* < Nahuatl, plural of *Totonacatl.*] —**Totonac** *adj* —**Totonacan** *adj*

totter /tóttər/ *vi* **1 WALK UNSTEADILY** to move or walk unsteadily **2 WOBBLE** to sway or wobble as if about to fall **3 BE UNSTABLE** to be unstable or on the point of collapse ○ *an economic system tottering on the brink of collapse* ■ *n* **WOBBLING GAIT** a wavering or wobbling gait [13C. < ?] —**totterer** *n* —**tottering** *adj* —**totteringly** *adv* —**tottery** *adj*

tottie /tótti/, **totty** (*plural* **-ties**) *n* an offensive term that deliberately insults a woman or women collectively regarded only as objects for sexual pleasure (*slang*) [Early 19C. < TOT.]

totting /tótting/ *n* the salvaging of items from rubbish for re-use or sale [Late 19C. < obsolete *tot* 'bone, rubbish' < ?]

totty *adj, n* = **tottie**

tot up (**tots up, totting up, totted up**) *v* **1** *vi* to grow larger in amount or amount to a large total **2** *vt* to add several amounts together to arrive at a total [Mid-18C. < *tot*, shortening of TOTAL, or < Latin *tot* 'this number, so many'.]

toucan /tóokən/ (*plural* **-cans** *or* **-can**) *n* a fruit-eating bird with bright plumage and a very large curved beak. Native to: tropical Central and South America. Family: Ramphastidae. [Mid-16C. Via French < Portuguese *tucano* < Tupi *tucan.*]

touch /tuch/ *n* **1 FEELING SENSE** the sense by which the texture, shape, and other qualities of objects are felt through contact with parts of the body, especially the fingertips ○ *the sense of touch* **2 FELT QUALITIES** the quality or combination of qualities experienced through the sensation of touch **3 CONTACT MADE** a coming into contact with a part of the body ○ *felt the touch of her hand on my face* **4 LIGHT STROKE** a light pushing or pressing stroke **5 SMALL AMOUNT** a small but noticeable amount ○ *a touch of malice in her voice* **6 DISTINCTIVE STYLE** a distinctive style or general facility in doing something ○ *a sure touch* **7 DETAIL** a detail that adds to or completes something **8 ATTACK OF ILLNESS** a mild attack of an illness or disease ○ *a touch of bronchitis* **9 COMMUNICATION** the fact of getting into communication, or the state of being in communication ○ *I completely lost touch with my brother.* ○ *Keep in touch.* ○ *I'll get in touch with them if I find anything out.* **10 LENDER OF MONEY** somebody considered in terms of his or her willingness to lend money (*informal*) ○ *He's always been a soft touch.* **11 REQUEST FOR MONEY** an act of asking for money or a sum of money given (*informal*) **12 AREA OUT OF PLAY** in some team sports, the area beyond the touchlines in which the ball is out of play **13 FENCING SCORE** in competitive fencing, a scoring hit delivered to a specified part of an opponent's body ■ *v* **1** *vti* **PUT BODY IN CONTACT WITH** to put a part of the body, especially the fingertips, in contact with something so as to feel it **2** *vti* **BE OR PUT IN CONTACT** to be in, or bring something into, physical contact with an object ○ *so that the ends are just touching* **3** *vt* **PRESS SOMETHING LIGHTLY** to apply the slightest pressure to something ○ *You only have to touch the brake.* **4** *vt* **INTERFERE WITH** to interfere with or disturb something by handling it ○ *told the kids not to touch anything on my desk* **5** *vt* **HAVE AN EFFECT ON** to have an effect or influence on somebody or something ○ *events that touched all our lives* **6** *vt* **AFFECT SOMEBODY EMOTIONALLY** to affect somebody emotionally, usually arousing gratitude, affection, pity, or compassion ○ *Your concern for my welfare touches me greatly.* **7** *vt* **CONSUME** to consume something, especially food or drink, or otherwise make use of something ○ *You've hardly touched your meal.* **8** *vt* **HAVE DEALINGS WITH** to have dealings or become involved with something ○ *Don't touch that issue; it's very controversial.* **9** *vt* **MATCH** to come close to somebody or something in level of excellence ○ *Others may have more technique, but nobody can touch her style.* **10** *vt* **APPROACH A LEVEL** to approach or reach a level ○ *profits touching 2 billion* **11** *vt* **APPROACH SOMEBODY FOR MONEY** to ask somebody for a loan or gift of money (*informal*) [13C. Via Old French *to(u)chier* < assumed Vulgar Latin *toccare* 'to strike'.] —**touchability** /túchə bíllәti/ *n* —**touchable** *adj* —**touchableness** *n* —**toucher** *n* ◇ **a touch** somewhat

touch down *v* **1** *vi* to land in an aircraft or spacecraft **2** *vt* to touch the ball to the ground, either in scoring a try or when behind your own goal line as a way of forcing a restarting of play

touch off *vt* **1** to make something explode, especially by touching it with a flame or smouldering match **2** to make something begin, especially something that is difficult to control ○ *touched off a bitter disagreement between them*

touch on, touch upon *vt* **1** to write or talk about something briefly during the course of a discussion ○ *The report only touches on the financial implications.* **2** to come close to a particular quality, state, or condition ○ *a sympathetic attitude touching on pity*

touch up *vt* **1** **IMPROVE** to make slight improvements to something, e.g. with paint **2** **FALSIFY** to make changes to something, especially a photograph, so that it is no longer an accurate representation (*disapproving*) **3** **CARESS** to fondle somebody sexually (*slang*)

touch-and-go *adj* highly uncertain or unpredictable (*not hyphenated after verbs*) ○ *a touch-and-go situation*

touchback /túchbak/ *n* a play in American football in which the defence recovers and downs a ball that has been kicked or passed into its end zone

touchdown /túch down/ *n* **1** **LANDING** a landing made by an aircraft or spacecraft, or the precise moment when it lands **2** **TOUCHING THE BALL ON THE GROUND** in rugby, a touching of the ball on the ground that scores a try **3** **SCORING PLAY** in American football, a scoring of six points achieved by being in possession of the ball behind an opponent's goal line

touché /tōo shay/ *interj* **1** in fencing, a word used to acknowledge that somebody has made an especially witty, penetrating, or cogent remark, usually in retaliation **2** a word used to acknowledge that an opponent has made a scoring hit [Early 20C. < French, past participle of *toucher* 'touch' < Old French *touchier* (see TOUCH).]

touched /tucht/ *adj* **1** **AFFECTED EMOTIONALLY** affected emotionally, usually with gratitude, affection, pity, or compassion **2** **MODIFIED BY** slightly marked or modified by something (*literary*) ○ *blonde hair touched with grey* **3** **OFFENSIVE TERM** an offensive term meaning unable to behave in a reasonable or conventional way

touch football *n* an informal noncompetitive version of American football in which touching replaces tackling

touchhole /túch hōl/ *n* the opening in the breech of an early cannon or gun where a flame or smouldering material was applied to set off the gunpowder

touching /túching/ *adj* giving rise to feelings of sympathy, tenderness, or tearfulness ■ *prep* concerning or relating to something (*archaic or literary*) —**touchingly** *adv* —**touchingness** *n*

touch-in-goal *n* the area at each end of a rugby pitch, behind the goal line and bounded by the dead-ball line, where the ball may be touched down to score a try

touch judge *n* either of the two assistant referees in rugby, whose main task is to decide when and where the ball has gone into touch

touchline /túch līn/ *n* either of the lines that mark the side boundaries of a playing area, especially in rugby or football

touchmark /túch maark/ *n* a mark stamped on something made of pewter that identifies the maker

touch-me-not *n* **1** a flowering plant with seed pods that burst open if touched when they are ripe. Genus: *Impatiens.* **2** *US* PLANTS = **sensitive plant** *n.* **1**

ϟ**touch pad** *n* **1** an electronic device, e.g. an input device in a computer system or a control panel on a microwave oven, on which somebody can choose options by touching the display **2** a small flat stationary surface on a laptop computer which a user touches to move the cursor

touchpaper /túch paypər/ *n* paper soaked in saltpetre that is lit to set off gunpowder, especially used for the part of a firework that is lit

ϟ**touch screen** *n* an input device that allows a user to choose options and commands on a computer by touching the screen

touchstone /túch stōn/ *n* **1** a standard by which something is judged **2** a hard black stone formerly used to test the purity of gold and silver according to the colour of the streak left when the metal was rubbed against it

touch-tone *adj* describes a type of telephone with keys that produce tones when pressed, each of which is decoded as a number at the telephone exchange

touch-type *vi* to type without having to look at the keyboard —**touch-typist** *n*

touch-up *n* **1** an improvement to something such as makeup or paintwork **2** an alteration, especially one made to cover up or repair a flaw

touchwood /túch wŏŏd/ *n* dry decayed wood that can be used as tinder

touchy /túchi/ (**-ier, -iest**) *adj* **1** **EASILY UPSET** liable to become, or make somebody, angry or upset ○ *a touchy subject* **2** **TRICKY** needing care or tact to prevent an undesirable outcome **3** **FLAMMABLE** easily catching fire —**touchily** *adv* —**touchiness** *n*

touchy-feely /-feeli/ *adj* (*informal*) **1** physically and emotionally demonstrative, e.g. in hugging other people or crying openly, often in a way that is considered excessive **2** encouraging demonstrativeness, especially in losing inhibitions about touching other people and the free expression of emotions

tough /tuf/ *adj* **1** **DURABLE** able to withstand much use, strain, or wear without breaking, tearing, or other damage ○ *boots made of tough leather* **2** **HARD TO CHEW OR CUT** not easily chewed or cut ○ *This steak is pretty tough.* **3** **VERY STRONG** physically or mentally strong and possessing great endurance ○ *Is he tough enough to make the climb?* **4** **THREATENING** characterized by antisocial behaviour, crime, and social deprivation ○ *a tough neighbourhood* **5** **RESOLUTE** having or showing firm resolve ○ *She's a tough person to negotiate with.* **6** **DIFFICULT** difficult to do or deal with, or needing great effort to do ○ *That's a tough question.* **7** **SEVERE** involving or inflicting severe punishment or strict rules ○ *the police policy of being tough on drink-driving* **8** **HARD TO ENDURE** unfortunate or hard to bear (*informal*) ○ *a tough break* ■ *n* **THUG** an aggressive or antisocial person ■ *adv* **AGGRESSIVELY** in an aggressive way that makes the person appear to be strong, forceful, and unafraid (*informal*) ○ *act tough* ■ *interj* **BAD LUCK!** used to comment that something is unfortunate but cannot be helped, and often that the speaker does not really care that this is so [Old English *tōh* < Germanic] —**toughly** *adv* ◇ **tough it out** to be strong and hold out during a time of difficulty (*informal*)

SYNONYMS See ***hard***.

toughen /túff'n/ *vti* **1** **MAKE OR BECOME TOUGHER** to become, or make something, less easy to cut or chew or less liable to wear or damage **2** **MAKE OR BECOME STRONGER** to become, or make somebody, more resolute, hardier, or physically or emotionally stronger **3** **MAKE OR BECOME MORE SEVERE** to become, or make somebody or something, stricter or more severe —**toughener** *n*

toughie /túffi/ *n* (*informal*) **1** something that is difficult to deal with **2** a tough person, especially a child, regarded with some affection or amusement because he or she is rather self-assertive and resilient

tough love *n* a caring but strict attitude adopted towards a friend or loved one with a problem, as distinct from an attitude of indulgence

tough-minded *adj* able to face hardship and misfortunes in a realistic, determined, and unsentimental way —**tough-mindedly** *adv* —**tough-mindedness** *n*

toughness /túffnəss/ *n* **1** the fact or quality of being tough **2** the resistance of a metal to breaking under repeated twisting and bending forces, measured in kilojoules

Toulon /too lóN/ city in SE France, on the Mediterranean Sea. Population: 160,639 (1999).

Toulouse /too lōoz/ city in SW France. Population 390,350 (1999).

Toulouse-Lautrec /too lōoz lō trék/, **Henri de** (1864–1901) French artist

toun /toon/ *n* **1** **toun, toon** a town (*regional*) **2** *Scotland* a farm, including all of its buildings and land [Old English *tūn* (see TOWN)]

toupee /tōo pay/ *n* a wig or partial wig worn to cover a bald area [Early 18C. Alteration of French *toupet* 'tuft of hair' < Germanic, 'topknot'.]

tour /toor, tawr/ *n* **1** **PLEASURE TRIP** a journey visiting several places, usually taken for pleasure, e.g. on holiday **2** **PERFORMING TRIP** a long series of performances in different places, e.g. by a rock band or a theatre company ○ *The band are on tour at the moment.* **3** **PLAYING TRIP** a series of games or tournaments played by the same team in different places, often overseas **4** **BRIEF TRIP TO SEE** a short trip, especially for the purpose of viewing or inspecting different items **5** **PERIOD OF DUTY** a period of duty, especially in a particular place or for a specific length of time ■ *vti* **TAKE PART IN A TOUR** to take part in a tour, for some purpose or of a specified place [14C. Via Old French < Latin *tornus* 'lathe'.]

touraco /tōorə kō/ (*plural* **-cos**), **turaco** (*plural* **-cos**) *n* a bird with brightly coloured feathers and a long tail that is a weak flyer. Native to: Africa. Family: Musophagidae. [Mid-18C. Via French < a W African language.]

tour de force /tōor də fáwrss, táwr-/ (*plural* **tours de force** /tōor də fáwrss, táwr-/) *n* something done with supreme skill or brilliance [Early 19C. < French, 'feat of strength'.]

Touré /tōor ay/, **Sékou** (1922–84) Guinean statesman and president (1958–84)

tourer /tōorər, táw-/ *n* a convertible car designed for long-distance leisure driving

Tourette syndrome /toor rét-/, **Tourette's syndrome** /toor réts-/ *n* a condition in which somebody experiences multiple tics and twitches, and utters involuntary vocal grunts and obscene speech [Late 19C. After Gilles de la *Tourette* (1857–1904), French neurologist.]

touring car /tōoring-/ *n* a convertible car, popular in the 1920s, designed for long-distance leisure driving

touring company *n* a theatre company that takes part in performing tours rather than performing solely in one venue

tourism /tōorizəm, táw-/ *n* **1** the visiting of places away from home for pleasure **2** the business of organizing travel and services for people travelling for pleasure

tourist /tōorist, táw-/ *n* **1** **SOMEBODY WHO TRAVELS FOR PLEASURE** a traveller who visits places away from home for pleasure **2** **MEMBER OF A TOURING TEAM** a member of a team that is making a playing tour **3** TRANSP = **tourist class** ■ *adj* **FOR OR OF TOURISTS** typical of or involving tourists, or suitable or intended for tourists, e.g. in terms of cheapness or exploitative prices —**touristic** /toor rístik, taw-/ *adj*

tourist class, tourist *n* the cheapest class of accommodation on an aircraft or ship

tourist trap *n* a place that is popular with tourists but where, as a result, the prices of goods and services are higher than average

touristy /tōoristi, táw-/ *adj* relating to, appealing to, or full of tourists, especially when this is looked down on (*informal*)

tourmaline /tōormə leen, túr-/ *n* a hard, variously coloured crystalline borosilicate mineral. Use: electronics, optics, gems. [Mid-18C. < Sinhalese *tōramalli* 'cornelian'.] —**tourmalinic** /tōormə línnik, túr-/ *adj*

Tournai /toor náy/ city in SW Belgium. Population: 67,939 (1996).

tournament /tōornəmənt, táwr-/ *n* **1** **SERIES OF GAMES** a sports event made up of a series of games, rounds, or contests **2** **MOCK FIGHTING** a sporting contest popular in the Middle Ages in which knights took part in jousting or combat, generally with blunted weapons **3** **MILITARY SHOW** a military show with competitions [12C. < Old French *torneiement* 'act of jousting' < *torneier* (see TOURNEY).]

tournedos /tōornə dō/ (*plural* **-dos**) *n* a small round cut of fillet steak [Late 19C. < French, < *tourner* 'to turn' + *dos* 'back'.]

tournement incorrect spelling of **tournament**

tourney /tŏorni, túr-, táwr-/ *n* (*plural* **-neys**) HIST = **tournament** *n.* 2 ■ *vi* (**-neys, -neying, -neyed**) to take part in a tournament [13C. Via Old French *torneier* 'joust, tilt' < Latin *tornare* 'to turn'.] —**tourneyer** *n*

tourniquet /tŏorni kay, táwr-/ *n* a tight encircling band applied around an arm or leg in an emergency to stop severe arterial bleeding that cannot be controlled in any other way [Late 17C. < French.]

tour of duty *n* MIL = **tour** *n.* 5

tour operator *n* a person or company that organizes package holidays

Tours /toor, toorz/ city in west-central France. Population: 132,820 (1999).

tousle /tówz'l/ *vt* (**-sles, -sling, -sled**) to make hair or fur tangled or ruffled ■ *n* a tangled mass of something, especially hair or fur [15C. < obsolete and dialect *touse* 'pull, handle roughly' < Germanic.] —**tousled** *adj*

Toussaint L'Ouverture /tŏo saN loov air chŏor, -tür/, **François Dominique** (1743?–1803) Haitian soldier and statesman. Born **François Dominique Toussaint**

tout /towt/ *v* 1 *vi* **ATTRACT CUSTOMERS** to try to attract customers or support, especially in an aggressive or persistent way ○ *street traders touting for business* 2 *vt* **OFFER OR ADVERTISE** to claim to have something available or to hand, or offer something for sale 3 *vt* **PRAISE** to praise or recommend somebody or something enthusiastically (*usually passive*) ○ *was touted as the next champion* 4 *vi* **SPY ON RACEHORSES** to spy on racehorses in training to gain information useful to people who bet on horse races 5 *vti* **SELL INFORMATION ABOUT RACEHORSES** to sell information about racehorses to potential gamblers ■ *n* 1 **SOMEBODY WHO SELLS INFORMATION ABOUT RACEHORSES** a spy on racehorses in training who obtains information and sells it to people who bet on horse races 2 **AGGRESSIVE SELLER** an aggressive person who tries to attract customers or sell things 3 BUSINESS = **ticket tout** [14C. Ultimately < Germanic, 'poke out, project'.] —**touter** *n*

tout à fait /tŏot aa fáy/ *adv* in a complete or thorough manner [< French]

tout court /tŏo kŏor/ *adv* without qualification or additional information [< French, 'very short']

tout de suite /tŏot swéet/ *adv* as quickly as possible [< French, 'completely in succession']

tout ensemble /tŏot on sómb'l/ *adv* all together at the same time or all in all ■ *n* the total appearance or effect of something [Early 18C. < French, 'all together'.]

tout le monde /tŏo lə móNd/ *n* everyone [< French, 'all the world']

tovarish /tə vaárish/ (*plural* **-rishes**), **tovarich** /tə vaárich/ (*plural* **-riches**), **tovarisch** /tə vaárish/ (*plural* **-risches**) *n* a friend or comrade, often used as a term of address, especially in the former Soviet Union [Early 20C. < Russian *tovarishch*.]

tow[1] /tō/ *vt* **PULL** to pull something such as a barge or a broken-down car along by a rope or chain attached to it ■ *n* 1 **ACT OF PULLING SOMETHING ALONG** the act of pulling something along by a rope or chain attached to it 2 **STATE OF BEING PULLED ALONG** the state of being towed by a rope or chain 3 **ROPE** a rope or chain used for towing something 4 **SOMETHING THAT PULLS** something that tows something else 5 **SOMETHING TOWED** something that is towed [Old English *togian* < Indo-European, 'to lead'] —**towable** *adj* — **tower** *n* ◇ **have** *or* **take somebody in tow** 1 to follow or accompany somebody 2 *US* to act as a protector or guide for somebody

SYNONYMS See *pull*.

tow[2] /tō/ *n* fibres of flax, hemp, or jute, or of a synthetic material such as rayon [Old English *tow-* < Germanic] — **towy** *adj*

towage /tō ij/ *n* 1 the act or process of towing somebody or something, or the state of being towed 2 a charge made for towing something

towards /tə wáwrdz/, **toward** /tə wáwrd/ *prep* 1 **IN A PARTICULAR DIRECTION** used to indicate that some person or thing is moving or facing in the direction of another person or thing ○ *They headed off towards town.* 2 **SHORTLY BEFORE** shortly before a particular time ○ *towards midnight* 3 **WITH SPECIFIC AUDIENCE INTENDED** with a particular target group in mind ○ *remarks slanted towards those sitting in the front row* 4 **REGARDING** concerning or with regard to ○ *his attitude towards her* 5 **CONTRIBUTING TO** as a contribution to or means of achieving something ○ *a grant towards the cost of refurbishment* [Old English *tōweardes*]

towbar /tō baar/ *n* a rigid metal bar or frame attached to the back of a vehicle and used for towing other vehicles

towboat /tō bōt/ *n* 1 SHIPPING = **tug** *n.* 3 2 *US* a powerful boat with a broad bow, designed for pushing barges on rivers or canals

tow-coloured *adj* having a pale yellow colour like hemp or flax

towel /tówəl/ *n* 1 **ABSORBENT CLOTH** a usually rectangular piece of absorbent cloth or paper, used to dry the body 2 **DISHTOWEL** a towel used in the kitchen to dry dishes ■ *vti* **DRY SOMEBODY WITH TOWEL** to use a towel to dry somebody or something [13C. < Old French *toaille* < Germanic, 'wash'.]

towelette /tówə lét/ *n* *US* a small moistened piece of paper or cloth used for cleaning the hands and face

towelling /tówəling/ *n* a soft absorbent usually looped cotton fabric. Use: towels, bathrobes.

tower[1] /tówər/ *n* 1 **TALL BUILDING** a tall structure, sometimes the upper part or a tall part of a building or structure and sometimes a separate building 2 **FORTRESS** a building designed to withstand attack 3 **CD STAND** a tall wooden, plastic, or metal case in which to store CDs or videos ■ *vi* 1 **BE TALL** to be very high or tall, or much higher or taller than somebody or something else 2 **BE SUPERIOR** to be considerably superior to somebody or something [12C. Via Latin *turris* < Greek.] ◇ **a tower of strength** somebody who is reliable and supportive (*informal*)

tower[2] /tō ər/ *n* somebody or something such as a vehicle that tows something by a rope or chain

tower block *n* a tall modern building, especially a residential one

tower crane *n* a crane mounted on top of a very high steel frame, used on building sites

towering /tówəring/ *adj* 1 **HIGH OR TALL** rising very high or standing very tall 2 **OUTSTANDING** being of the highest quality or importance 3 **INTENSE** characterized by extreme or intense emotion or pain ○ *a towering rage* — **toweringly** *adv*

Tower of Babel /-báyb'l/ *n* according to the Book of Genesis, an overambitious tower that people on earth started to build, causing God to show his anger by making them speak different languages, which led to the collapse of the project and ultimately to the scattering of people across the world

tower of silence *n* in Zoroastrianism, an open tower in which the dead are exposed to be eaten by vultures, the bones then being deposited in the centre of the tower

tow-haired /tō-/ *adj* having blond or tousled hair [< TOW[2]]

towhead /tō hed/ *n* 1 somebody with fair or tousled hair 2 a head that is covered with light blond hair [< TOW[2]] — **towheaded** *adj*

towhee /tów hi, tō-/ *n* a large long-tailed sparrow, typically a ground feeder. Native to: North America. Genera: *Pipilo* and *Chlorura*. [Mid-18C. An imitation of the bird's call.]

towline /tō līn/ *n* TRANSP = **towrope**

town /town/ *n* 1 **LARGE AREA OF BUILDINGS** a densely populated area with many buildings, larger than a village and smaller than a city 2 **URBAN AREA** a large urban area, either a town, a city, or a borough 3 *US, Can* **UNIT OF LOCAL GOVERNMENT** in certain parts of the United States and Canada, a unit of local government that is smaller than a county or city 4 **LOCAL TOWN** the nearest large town or city, or the town or city in which somebody lives ○ *moving into town* 5 **CENTRE OF SETTLED AREA** the centre of a town or city 6 **POPULATION OF SETTLED AREA** the people who live in a town ○ *The whole town's talking about it.* 7 **NONACADEMIC POPULATION** the permanent residents of a town that has a university, as opposed to the staff and students of the university ○ *town and gown* 8 **PRAIRIE DOG BURROWS** a group of prairie dog burrows [Old English *tūn* 'yard, buildings within an enclosure' < Germanic] —**townish** *adj* ◇ **go to town (on somebody or something)** to do something with great enthusiasm or thoroughness (*informal*) ◇ **on the town** spending time enjoying the entertainment available in a town or city, especially if a lot of money is spent (*informal*) ◇ **paint the town red** to go out and celebrate, especially by spending a lot of money for entertainment (*informal*)

SYNONYMS See *city*.

town-and-gown *adj* relating to a town that has a large population of students in higher education, especially Oxford or Cambridge

town clerk *n* 1 the secretary and chief administrative officer of a town in the United Kingdom before the reorganization of local government in 1974 2 *US* a public official responsible for such things as keeping the records of a town and issuing licences

town council *n* the people elected or appointed to govern a town

town crier *n* somebody employed by a town, especially formerly, to make public announcements in the streets

townee *n* = **townie**

town gas *n* gas manufactured from coal, for domestic and industrial use

town hall *n* a building that houses the offices of the local administration and often has a public hall that can be used for meetings

town house *n* 1 **HOUSE IN TOWN** a house in a town or city, especially one that belongs to somebody who also has a house in the country 2 **TERRACED HOUSE** a terraced house in a town or city, especially one in a fashionable area 3 *US* ARCHIT = **row house** 4 *ANZ* **MODERN TOWN DWELLING** in New Zealand, a modern, usually two-storey town dwelling of superior quality, semidetached or in a block of three or four and with limited garden space

townie /tówni/, **towny** (*plural* **-ies**), **townee** /tow neé/ *n* 1 a permanent resident of a town (*informal*) 2 a non-academic town resident as opposed to a student or member of staff at a university in the town

townland /tównlənd/ *n* *Ireland* 1 an area of land that is a subdivision of a parish, or an area of land consisting of a town and the region around it 2 a land division, used in postal addresses, averaging about 865 hectares/350 acres

town manager *n* *US* an official in charge of the administrative activities of a town

town meeting *n* 1 **MEETING OF INHABITANTS** a public meeting involving all of the inhabitants of a town 2 *US* **MEETING OF VOTERS** a public meeting involving all of the voters of a town, with the authority to make legislative decisions 3 *US* **TELEVISED GATHERING** a television programme centring on an issue of national interest, in which people from a particular area ask questions of debaters or speakers ○ *a televised national town meeting on the role of the military in global peacekeeping*

town planning *n* the organized planning and control of the construction or extension of a town. US term **urban planning** —**town planner** *n*

townscape /tówn skayp/ *n* 1 the part of a town within the sight of somebody looking at it 2 a painting or photograph of an urban scene

townsfolk /tównz fōk/ *npl* = **townspeople**

township /tówn ship/ *n* 1 **SMALL TOWN** a small town 2 *US, Can* **SUBDIVISION OF A COUNTY** a subdivision of a county, often serving as a unit of local government 3 *US* **AREA GOVERNED BY TOWN MEETING** in some parts of the United States, an area governed by a town meeting 4 *US* **36 SQUARE MILES** an area of surveyed public land equal to 36 sections or 36 square miles 5 *Scotland* **CROFTING COMMUNITY** a small community of crofts in the Highlands and Islands 6 *S Africa* **URBAN SETTLEMENT FOR BLACK PEOPLE** an urban settlement planned for people classed as Black or of mixed ethnic origin by the apartheid system, usually implying inferior facilities and services 7 **PARISH** a former term for an English parish or subdivision of a parish 8 *ANZ* **VILLAGE** a small town or village

townsman /tównzmən/ (*plural* **-men** /-mən/) *n* 1 a man who lives in a town 2 a man who lives in the same town as somebody else

townspeople /tównz peep'l/ *npl* the people who live in a town or who have lived in a town and are used to the ways of town life

Townsville /tównzvil/ city on the eastern coast of Queensland, Australia. Population: 101,398 (1996).

townswoman /tównz wŏomən/ (*plural* **-en** /-wimin/) *n* 1 a woman who lives in a town 2 a woman who lives in the same town as somebody else

towny *n* = **townie**

towpath /tṓ paath/ (*plural* **-paths** /-paath̲z/) *n* a path beside a canal or river for people or animals to walk along, originally as they pulled a barge or boat

towrope /tṓ rōp/, **towline** /tṓ līn/ *n* a rope used to tow something, e.g. a boat or a broken-down car

tox- *prefix* = **toxi-** (*before vowels*)

toxaemia /tok seémi ə/ *n* a condition produced by the presence of bacterial toxins in the blood, usually with tissue or organ damage, fever, and severe intestinal upset [Mid-19C. < TOX- + Greek *haima* 'blood'.] —**toxaemic** *adj*

toxalbumin /toks álbyoŏmin, -al byoŏmin/ *n* a toxic albumin found in some plants and snake venom

toxaphene /tóksə feen/ *n* $C_{10}H_{10}Cl_8$ a waxy amber-coloured poisonous compound that smells of pine and is used as an insecticide [Mid-20C. < TOXI- + shortening of *chlorinated camphene*.]

toxemia *n* US = **toxaemia**

toxi- *prefix* poison, poisonous ○ *toxigenic* [< TOXIC]

toxic /tóksik/ *adj* **1 INVOLVING SOMETHING POISONOUS** relating to or containing a poison or toxin **2 DEADLY** causing serious harm or death ■ *n* **POISONOUS SUBSTANCE** a toxic substance [Mid-17C. Via medieval Latin *toxicus* 'poisoned' < Greek *toxikos* 'of the bow' (Greek *toxikon pharmakon* meant 'poison for smearing arrows').] —**toxically** *adv*

toxicant /tóksikənt/ *n* a toxic substance, especially one used as a pesticide

toxic boy *n* the sort of boy a girl's parents are bound to disapprove of (*slang*)

toxicity /tok síssəti/ (*plural* **-ties**) *n* **1** the degree to which something is poisonous **2** the state of being poisonous to somebody or something

toxico- *prefix* poison ○ *toxicogenic* [< Greek *toxicon* (see TOXIC)]

toxicogenic /tóksi kō jénnik/ *adj* BIOCHEM = **toxigenic**

toxicology /tóksi kólləji/ *n* the scientific study of poisons, their effects, and their antidotes —**toxicologic** /tóksikə lójjik/ *adj* —**toxicologically** *adv* —**toxicologist** *n*

toxicosis /tóksi kóssiss/ (*plural* **-ses** /-seez/) *n* the harmful effects of a poison, including any disease caused by toxins

toxic shock syndrome *n* acute, potentially fatal circulatory failure, commonly associated with the use of vaginal tampons, which can create conditions promoting the growth of a toxin-producing staphylococcal bacterium

toxigenic /tóksi jénnik/ *adj* **1** producing poisonous substances **2** caused or produced by a toxin —**toxigenicity** /tóksijə níssəti/ *n*

toxin /tóksin/ *n* **1** a poison produced by a living organism, causing disease **2** any substance that accumulates in the body and causes it harm ○ *drinking plenty of water to eliminate toxins* [Late 19C. < TOXIC.]

toxin-antitoxin *n* a mixture containing a toxin and slightly less of its antitoxin. Use: formerly, vaccine.

toxocariasis /tóksōkə rī́ əssiss/ *n* an infestation of the larvae of a kind of roundworm in human beings, from worm eggs picked up from contaminated soil or domestic pets [Mid-20C. < alteration of TOXI- + Greek *kara* 'head'.]

toxoid /tók soyd/ *n* a preparation of an inactive toxin that can still stimulate antibody production to the toxin. Use: vaccine. [Early 20C. < shortening of TOXIN.]

toxophilite /tok sóffi līt/ *n* an archer or archery enthusiast (*humorous*) [Late 18C. < *Toxophilus*, 'lover of the bow'.] —**toxophily** *n*

toxoplasma /tóksō plázmə/ *n* a microscopic protozoan organism that lives as a parasite in the organs of vertebrates, especially birds and mammals, and can cause disease. Genus: *Toxoplasma*. [Early 20C. < alteration of TOXI-.] —**toxoplasmic** *adj*

toxoplasmosis /tóksō plaz mṓssiss/ (*plural* **-ses** /-seez/) *n* a disease of mammals caused by a toxoplasma transmitted to humans via undercooked meat or through contact with infectious animals, especially cats

toy /toy/ *n* **1 THING TO PLAY WITH** something meant to be played with, especially by children **2 REPLICA** a replica of a real object, meant to be played with or used as an ornament **3 MINIATURE BREED** an animal, especially a dog, that is a miniature version of another animal (*before nouns*) ○ *a toy poodle* **4 SOMETHING UNIMPORTANT** something of little value or importance ■ *adj* **EASILY DISMISSED** regarded as irrelevant or of inferior quality (*informal*) [14C. < ?] —**toyer** *n*

toy with *vt* **1 PLAY WITH** to play or fiddle with something, especially because of a lack of real interest in it or preoccupation with something else **2 THINK ABOUT** to consider doing something **3 TREAT SOMEBODY OR SOMETHING CRUELLY** to behave in a cruelly insincere or offhand way towards somebody or something **4 TREAT SOMEBODY INSINCERELY** to treat somebody in an insincere or flirtatious way, merely for amusement

⚡**TOY** *abbr* thinking of you (*in e-mails*)

toy boy *n* an offensive term for a young man who is the lover of an older person

toyi-toyi /tóy toy/ *n* S Africa a dance with high steps performed by a circle of protesters, accompanied by singing and chanting of slogans [Late 20C. < an African language.]

Toynbee /tóyn bee/, **Arnold** (1889–1975) British historian

toyon /tóy on/ *n* an evergreen shrub with red berries. Flowers: white. Native to: California. *Heteromeles arbutifolia*. [Mid-19C. < Mexican Spanish *tollón*.]

Toyotomi Hideyoshi /tṓyō tōmi híddə yóshi/ (1537–98) Japanese general

⚡**tp** *abbr* East Timor (*in Internet addresses*)

TP *abbr* triple play

TPI *abbr* tax and price index

Tpke *abbr* US turnpike (*in place names*)

T-plate, **tee-plate** *n* a metal plate, shaped like a letter T, used to strengthen a right-angled joint, e.g. between two beams

Tpr *abbr* Trooper

TQM *abbr* total quality management

⚡**tr** *abbr* Turkey (*in Internet addresses*)

TR *abbr* transmit-receive

tr. *abbr* **1** transitive **2** translator **3** transpose **4** transposition **5** treasurer **6** trill **7** troop **8** trust **9** trustee

trabeated /tráybi aytid/, **trabeate** /tráybi ət, -ayt/ *adj* built using horizontal beams rather than arches [Mid-16C. < Latin *trab-* 'beam'.] —**trabeation** /tráybi áysh'n/ *n*

trabecula /trə békyoŏlə/ (*plural* **-lae** /-lee/) *n* **1 ROD-SHAPED SUPPORT IN AN ORGAN** a rod-shaped body part that forms an internal support of an organ and divides it into separate chambers **2 BAR OF BONY TISSUE** any of the thin bars of bony tissue in spongy bone that form a meshwork with interconnecting spaces that contain bone marrow **3 ROD-SHAPED CELL** a rod-shaped cell or structure that bridges a cavity, e.g. between cells [Mid-19C. < Latin, 'small beam' < *trab-* 'beam'.] —**trabecular** *adj* —**trabeculate** *adj*

trace[1] /trayss/ *n* **1 REMAINING SIGN** a sign that remains to show the former presence of a person or thing no longer there **2 TINY QUANTITY** a tiny amount or the slightest amount **3 JUST DETECTABLE AMOUNT** an amount of something that is detectable but too small to be quantified **4 FOOTPRINT** a footprint or physical sign of the passage of a person or animal **5** *US* **PATH** a path or track left by people or animals regularly passing **6 LINE MARKING SOMETHING** a line made by a recording instrument, e.g. one drawn by a seismograph or one formed on the screen of a cathode ray tube, or the record made in this way **7 DRAWING** a drawing, especially one made using tracing paper **8 ATTEMPT TO FIND ANOTHER** an attempt to find or follow somebody or something **9** PSYCHOL = **engram** **10 INTERSECTION** the point of intersection of a line or plane with the surface of a coordinate plane **11 SUM OF DIAGONAL ENTRIES** the sum of the diagonal entries of a square matrix **12 AMOUNT OF PRECIPITATION** an amount of precipitation that is too small to be recorded by instruments, or the record of such an amount ■ *v* (**traces, tracing, traced**) **1** *vt* **FIND** to find out where somebody or something is or who or what somebody or something was **2** *vti* **FOLLOW OR BE FOLLOWED** to follow or show a course or series of developments, or be able to be followed back in time or to a source **3** *vti* **COPY** to copy writing, a design, or drawing by putting translucent paper on top of it and drawing the visible outlines on this paper **4** *vt* **DRAW SOMETHING CAREFULLY** to draw or write something with great care **5** *vt* **OUTLINE** to give an outline or brief description of something **6** *vt* **DECORATE** to decorate something with tracery **7** *vi* **SEARCH** to search through something [13C. Via Old French *tracier* 'make your way' < Latin *trahere* 'pull'.] —**traceability** *n* —**traceable** *adj* —**traceableness** *n* —**traceably** *adv* —**traceless** *adj* —**tracelessly** *adv*

trace[2] /trayss/ *n* **1 HORSE'S PULLING STRAPS** either of the two straps or chains connected to a horse's harness by means of which it pulls something such as a cart (*often plural*) **2 BAR TRANSFERRING MOTION** a hinged bar that enables motion to be transferred from one part of a machine to another **3 FLY-TYING THREAD** in angling, thread or wire for attaching a fly to a line [14C. < Old French *trais*, plural of *trait* 'strap for harnessing' < Latin *tractus* 'drawing' < *trahere* 'pull'.] ◇ **kick over the traces** to reject restrictions and controls and do something unconventional (*informal*)

trace element *n* **1 ELEMENT PRESENT IN TINY AMOUNT** a chemical element present in minute but detectable amounts in something such as a metal or ore **2 ELEMENT ESSENTIAL FOR HEALTH** an element such as zinc, iodine, or manganese that is required in minute amounts for normal growth and development and the functioning of vital enzyme systems **3 MINUSCULE AMOUNT** a very tiny amount ○ *only a trace element of truth to that statement*

trace fossil *n* a feature in sedimentary rocks that resulted from the activity of an animal, e.g. a worm cast or footprint

tracer /tráyssər/ *n* **1** ARMS = **tracer bullet** **2 AMMUNITION ACTING AS TRACERS** ammunition that has been treated to act as tracers ○ *a gun loaded with tracer* **3** MED = **tracer element** **4 INVESTIGATION OR INVESTIGATOR** an investigation into the whereabouts of something missing, e.g. an item of mail or a cargo shipment, or somebody who carries out such an investigation **5 SOMEBODY OR SOMETHING THAT MAKES TRACINGS** somebody or something that makes tracings **6 TRACKING DEVICE** a device that gives out a signal that can be tracked and followed when attached to a vehicle or person

tracer bullet, **tracer** *n* a bullet that has been treated with chemicals to make it leave a glowing or smoky trail as it flies

tracer element, **tracer** *n* a radioactive element used in experiments so that its movements can be monitored

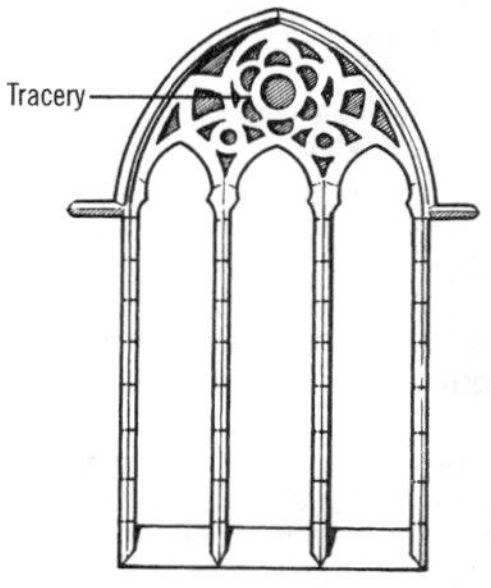

Tracery

tracery /tráyssəri/ (*plural* **-ies**) *n* **1** decorative ribs in windows, especially medieval church windows, and screens **2** a decorative pattern of interlaced lines, especially one that resembles the form or patterns found in church windows —**traceried** *adj*

trachea /trə keé ə/ (*plural* **-ae** /-keé ee/ *or* **-as**) *n* **1 WINDPIPE** a windpipe (*technical*) **2 BREATHING TUBE** a tube in insects and related air-breathing animals through which air is drawn into the body by the pumping action of the abdominal muscles **3 TUBE OF PLANT CELLS** a tubular part of water-conducting plant tissue that provides mechanical support and transport of water and nutrients [14C. < medieval Latin, < Greek (*artēria*) *trakheia* 'rough (artery)'.] —**tracheal** *adj* —**tracheate** /trə keé ət/ *adj*

tracheid /tráyki id/, **tracheide** *n* a cell in the trachea of conifers and other gymnosperm plants, with bands of lignin thickening the cell walls and adding structural support [Late 19C. < German *Tracheïde* 'something belonging to the trachea'.] —**tracheidal** /trə keé id'l, tráyki íd'l/ *adj*

tracheitis /tráyki ī́tiss/ *n* inflammation of the trachea

tracheo- *prefix* trachea ○ *tracheostomy*

tracheobronchial /tráyki ō bróngki əl/ *adj* relating to or in both the trachea and the bronchi

tracheole /tráyki ōl/ *n* a fine channel that branches off from an insect's trachea and carries oxygen to its tissues [Early 20C. < TRACHEA.]

tracheo-oesophogeal *adj* relating to or in both the trachea and the oesophagus

tracheophyte /tráyki ō fīt/ *n* a plant that has a system of vascular tissues for conducting water and nutrients through it [Mid-20C. < TRACHEA + Greek *phuton* 'plant'.]

tracheoscopy /tráki óskəpi/ (*plural* **-pies**) *n* the examination of the inside of the trachea, e.g. using a laryngoscope —**tracheoscopic** /tráki ə skóppik/ *adj*

tracheostomy /tráki óstəmi/ (*plural* **-mies**) *n* **1** a hole cut in the trachea, e.g. to ensure the airway is unblocked and to suck out secretions **2** an operation to cut a hole in the trachea

tracheotomy /tráki óttəmi/ (*plural* **-mies**) *n* the making of an incision through the neck into the trachea to assist breathing when the upper airways are blocked

trachoma /trə kṓmə/ *n* a contagious bacterial eye disease in which scar tissue forms inside the eyelid, eventually causing it to curve inwards and the eyelashes to scrape the eye, often leading to infection [Late 17C. < Greek *trakhōma* 'roughness'.] —**trachomatous** *adj*

trachyte /tráy kīt, trák-/ *n* fine-grained volcanic rock, characterized by the presence of alkaline feldspar minerals [Early 19C. < Greek *trakhus* 'rough' + -ITE[1].] —**trachytoid** /tráki toyd, tráyki-/ *adj*

trachytic /trə kíttik/ *adj* describes igneous rocks in which the crystals are arranged in parallel and show the flow of the molten lava from which they were formed

tracing /tráyssing/ *n* **1** a copy of something made by tracing it onto a sheet of translucent paper laid on top of it **2** a graphic record made by an instrument such as a seismograph

tracing paper *n* paper through which it is possible to see what is underneath, and on which it is possible to draw a copy of something underneath

track /trak/ *n* **1 MARK LEFT** a mark left by a moving person, animal, or thing, e.g. a footprint, an animal's paw print, or the mark of a wheel **2 PATH** a path or road, especially one made by the continual passing of people or animals or one specially created for some purpose **3 RAIL STRUCTURE** a rail or pair of parallel rails on which a vehicle, especially a train, runs, along with supporting structures **4 COURSE OF TRAVEL** the path taken by somebody or something while travelling **5 LINE OF ACTION OR THOUGHT** a line of thought or investigation, or a course of action ○ *realized our research was on the wrong track* **6 RACE COURSE** a course laid out for racing **7** *US, Can* **SPORTS TAKING PLACE ON SPORTS TRACK** a collective term for all sports that take place on a sports track **8 SEPARATE RECORDING OF MUSIC** a separate piece of music or song on a disc, tape, or record **9 PATH FOR RECORDING** a separate section of a magnetic tape where the input of a single channel is recorded **10 RECORDED INPUT** a recording on separate tracks of a magnetic tape that are combined to give a final version, e.g. of a piece of recorded music or a film **11** RECORDING = **soundtrack** *n.* 1 **12 SECTION OF COMPUTER DISK** a path on the surface of a storage medium such as a diskette or CD-ROM on which information is recorded and from which recorded information is read **13** CINEMA = **tracking shot** **14 TREADS OF A TANK OR BULLDOZER** a continuous loop of rubber or metal plates driven by wheels, giving great traction over soft or rough ground, used especially on bulldozers and heavy military vehicles such as tanks **15** *US* **COURSE OF STUDY** a course of study tailored to the relative abilities or needs of students **16 CAREER PATH** the course or projected course of a career **17 MOVING ASSEMBLY LINE** a moving belt carrying things along a factory assembly line **18 SUPPORTING RAIL** a usually grooved rail along which something moves, e.g. a lighting fitment or the supporting hooks of a curtain **19 PATH OF A PARTICLE** the path taken by a particle of ionizing radiation in a cloud chamber, bubble chamber, or photographic emulsion **20 DISTANCE BETWEEN WHEELS** the distance between a pair of wheels, e.g. the front wheels of a motor vehicle ■ **tracks** *npl* **NEEDLE MARKS** marks or scars on the body of a drug user caused by frequent injections (*slang*) ■ *v* **1** *vti* **FOLLOW A TRAIL** to follow a trail made by somebody or something, or try to find somebody or something by following a trail left behind **2** *vt* **FOLLOW THE FLIGHT PATH OF** to follow the flight path of a vehicle such as a spacecraft using electronic equipment or radar **3** *vt* **FOLLOW PROGRESS OF** to follow the progress or development of something **4** *vti* **FOLLOW A PATH** to follow a path through a place **5** *vti* **FOLLOW A MOVING OBJECT** to film a moving person or object with a mobile camera **6** *vi* **ALIGN** to be in alignment or the correct distance apart, especially as wheels on a motor vehicle **7** *vi* **FOLLOW THE GROOVE ON A RECORD** to follow the groove on a gramophone record **8** *vi US* **TRAVEL** to travel, especially on a long or laborious journey (*informal*) **9** *vt US* **BRING AND LEAVE DIRT** to carry something, especially mud, on the shoes or feet and leave some of it on a floor **10** *vt US* **ASSIGN TO A COURSE** to assign a student to a course of study tailored to his or her abilities or needs [15C. < French *trac* 'footprint, mark'.] —**trackable** *adj* ◇ **cover your tracks** to remove all signs of having been somewhere or done something (*informal*) ◇ **in your tracks** suddenly and immediately, just where somebody or something is or in the middle of what somebody or something is doing (*informal*) ◇ **keep track (of)** to follow, pay attention to, or keep a check on the position or progress of somebody or something ◇ **lose track (of)** to fail to follow or pay attention, or fail to keep an adequate check on the position or progress of somebody or something ◇ **make tracks** to leave (*informal*) ◇ **off the beaten track** away from main roads and busy populated areas, and perhaps difficult to find or gain access to as a result (*informal*) ○ *The cottage is lovely but it's a bit off the beaten track.* ◇ **on track** on the correct or desired path or schedule

track down *vt* to find a person, animal, or object by searching or following a trail

trackage /trákij/ *n US* railway tracks collectively

track and field *n US, Can* SPORTS = **athletics** *n.* 1

⚡**trackball** /trák bawl/ *n* a computer pointing device consisting of a freely rotating ball in a socket with sensors that translate its rotation into movements of an on-screen cursor

tracked /trakt/ *adj* moving on tracks, as a military tank or bulldozer does, or along a fixed track, as a dockside crane does

tracked vehicle *n* a vehicle such as a military tank or a bulldozer that is propelled by tracks instead of wheels

tracker /trákər/ *n* a follower of a trail made by somebody else or an animal, especially in order to guide police, soldiers, or hunters

tracker dog *n* a dog trained to find people, e.g. fugitives or people who are lost, by following the trail of their scent

tracker fund *n* an investment fund made up of quantities of all shares listed in a stock market index, whose value automatically follows the market's performance

track event *n* a sports competition that takes place on a running track

tracking /tráking/ *n* **1 FOLLOWING OF A TRAIL** the act or process of following the trail of a person or animal **2 FINDING BEST PICTURE** the finding by a video player of the best quality picture **3 LEAKING OF CURRENT** the leaking of current between two insulated points, e.g. caused by damp or dirt **4** *US* EDUC = **streaming** *n.* 1

tracking radar *n* a radar system that emits a beam that oscillates about an object being tracked, allowing the system to detect sudden changes of direction

tracking shot *n* a camera shot filmed from a moving dolly, following the movement of somebody or something

tracking station *n* a place from which the movement of something such as a launched missile or a space vehicle can be followed using radar or radio signals

trackless /trákləss/ *adj* **1 LACKING PATHS** so isolated that there are no trails or paths **2 LEAVING NO TRAIL** leaving no track or trail **3 RUNNING WITHOUT RAILS** not needing rails on which to run —**tracklessly** *adv* —**tracklessness** *n*

track light *n* an electric light that can be moved and repositioned anywhere along the length of an electrified track mounted on a wall or ceiling —**track lighting** *n*

trackman /trákmən/ (*plural* **-men** /-mən/) *n US* RAIL = **platelayer**

track meet *n US* an athletic competition in which teams from several places participate in track events

track record *n* **1** a record of the past performance of a person, organization, or thing (*informal*) **2** a record for a particular sports arena, as opposed to a national or international record

track rod *n* the rod that connects the two front wheels of a motor vehicle

track shoe *n* either of a pair of lightweight spiked running shoes

trackside /trák sīd/ *n* the area immediately beside a running track or racetrack

tracksuit /trák soot, -syoot/ *n* a loose-fitting long-sleeved top and matching trousers in knitted nylon or cotton, worn by athletes over their sports clothes and by other people as casual wear

trackwalker /trák wawkər/ *n* somebody employed to inspect railway track

tract[1] /trakt/ *n* **1 AREA OF LAND OR WATER** an unmeasured expanse of land or water, or a measured area, especially of land **2 GROUP OF ORGANS** a system of organs or body parts that work together to provide for the passage of something such as food or bodily waste products **3 BUNDLE OF NERVES** a group of nerve fibres that forms a pathway from one part of the brain or spinal cord to another [15C. < Latin *tractus* 'a drawing out, duration' < *trahere* 'pull'.]

tract[2] /trakt/ *n* an anthem sung in some Roman Catholic masses [14C. Via medieval Latin *tractus* < Latin (see TRACT[1]).]

tract[3] /trakt/ *n* a pamphlet that sets out a position or an analysis, especially one dealing with a political or religious issue [Pre-12C. < Latin *tractatus* < *tractare* 'handle' < *trahere* 'pull'.]

tractable /tráktəb'l/ *adj* **1** being very easy to control or persuade **2** being very easy to bend or work with [15C. < Latin *tractabilis* < *tractare* (see TRACT[3]).] —**tractability** /tráktə bílləti/ *n* —**tractably** *adv*

Tractarianism /trak táiri ənizəm/ *n* CHR = **Oxford Movement** [Mid-19C. < the tracts distributed.] —**Tractarian** *n, adj*

tractate /trák tayt/ *n* a short essay on a particular subject (*formal*) [15C. < Latin *tractatus* (see TRACT[3]).]

tract house *n US* one of many similar houses built on a tract of land —**tract housing** *n*

tractile /trák tīl/ *adj* able to be stretched into another shape without breaking [Mid-19C. < Latin *tract-*, past participle of *trahere* 'pull'.] —**tractility** /trak tílləti/ *n*

traction /tráksh'n/ *n* **1 APPLICATION OF WEIGHTS** application of a pulling force for surgical purposes, e.g. to reduce a fracture, maintain bone alignment, relieve pain, or prevent spinal injury **2 FRICTION ALLOWING MOVEMENT** the adhesive friction between a moving object and the surface on which it is moving, e.g. between a tyre and the ground, without which the object cannot move **3 PULLING** the act or process of pulling something, especially by means of a motor, or the fact or state of being pulled along **4 WAY TO MOVE VEHICLES** a means of moving vehicles **5 WAY TO ACHIEVE PROGRESS** a means by which, or the degree to which, progress can be made ○ *could not get any traction in trying to push through the legislation* [Early 17C. Directly or via French < medieval Latin *traction-* < Latin *tract-*, past participle of *trahere* 'pull'.] —**tractional** *adj*

traction engine *n* a steam-powered road locomotive used for hauling heavy loads by road, as a source of power in fairgrounds, and for ploughing

traction load *n* the coarse-grained fraction of a river's sedimentary load, carried along the riverbed by sliding and rolling

tractive force /tráktiv-/ *n* the force exerted by a tractor or locomotive through a drawbar as it pulls a load

⚡**tractor** /tráktər/ *n* **1 FARM VEHICLE** a motor vehicle used for pulling heavy loads, especially on farms, where its typically large deep-treaded rear wheels enable it to move in fields **2 FRONT PART OF ARTICULATED LORRY** the powered, self-contained front section of an articulated lorry, with driving cab, engine, and coupling for trailers **3 AIRCRAFT WITH THE PROPELLER IN FRONT** an aircraft that has its propeller in front of the engine, exerting a pull through the air rather than a pushing force **4 PROPELLER** a propeller at the front of an aircraft engine **5** COMPUT = **tractor feed** [Late 18C. < Latin *tract-* (see TRACTION).]

⚡**tractor feed** *n* a mechanism for feeding paper into a printer, using toothed wheels to mesh with the perforations in continuous stationery

tractor-trailer *n US* a truck for pulling heavy loads, consisting of a tractor attached to a trailer or semitrailer

Tracy /tráyssi/, **Spencer** (1900–67) US actor

trad[1] /trad/ *n* traditional jazz (*informal*) [Mid-20C. Shortening.]

trad[2] *abbr* traditional

trade /trayd/ *n* **1 AREA OF BUSINESS OR INDUSTRY** a particular area of business or industry ○ *the book trade* **2 OCCUPATION** somebody's particular occupation, especially one that involves a skill ○ *learn a trade* **3 PEOPLE IN BUSINESS** the people who work in a particular area of business or industry ○ *You'll never convince the trade that this tax is fair.* **4 BUYING AND SELLING** the activity of buying and selling, or sometimes bartering, goods ○ *a suspension of trade between the two countries* **5 WORK IN COMMERCE** work in commerce as opposed to a profession ○ *graduates going into trade* **6 CUSTOMERS** customers or business generated by customers ○ *losing trade to their competitors* **7 COMMERCIAL CUSTOMERS** customers in business and industry, as opposed to the general public, who purchase products related to their business or industry ○ *This counter is for trade only.* **8** *US, Can* **EXCHANGE** an exchange of somebody or something for another ○ *If neither of you likes your room, why don't you do a trade?* **9 TRADE WIND** a trade wind ○ *the southern trades* **10 BUSINESS PUBLICATION** a publication meant for people in a particular line of business ○ *advertising in all the trades* ■ *v* (**trades, trading, traded**) **1** *vi* **BUY AND SELL GOODS** to take part in buying and selling goods for trade **2** *vt* **EXCHANGE** to give and receive something alternately with somebody else ○ *trading punches* **3** *vt* **DEAL IN** to buy and sell a particular commodity **4** *vti* **MAKE AN EXCHANGE** to make an exchange, or exchange somebody or something for another ○ *Each had something the other wanted and they were happy to trade.* **5** *vi US* **SHOP OR BUY REGULARLY FROM BUSINESS** to shop or buy something regularly at a particular place of business [14C. < Middle Low German, 'track'.] —**tradable** *adj* —**tradeless** *adj*

trade down *vi* to sell something large or expensive and buy something smaller or less expensive in its place

trade in *vt* to give an old or used item, especially a car, in part payment for a new one

trade on *vt* to take advantage of a personal quality or situation, often unfairly or excessively

trade up *vi* to sell something small or inexpensive and buy something larger and more expensive in its place

trade acceptance *n* a bill of exchange for the amount of a purchase drawn by the seller on the buyer, signed by the buyer and often specifying the place and date of payment

trade agreement *n* a treaty between two or more countries to regulate trade between them

trade association *n* an organization formed to represent the collective interests of a number of businesses in the same trade

trade book, trade edition *n* a standard edition of a book, meant for sale to the general public, as opposed to a deluxe or book-club edition

trade cycle *n* the recurrent fluctuation between depression and prosperity in a capitalist economy. US term **business cycle**

trade discount *n* a reduction in the standard price of something, offered by one business to another, e.g. by a manufacturer to a retailer, especially within the same trade

traded option *n* a stock option that is marketable

trade edition *n* PUBL = **trade book**

trade gap *n* the difference, measured in monetary value, between a nation's imports and its exports when the imports exceed the exports. US term **trade deficit**

trade-in *n* **1** a used item such as a car that is used as partial payment for something new **2** a transaction in which an old or used item serves as partial payment for something new

trade journal *n* a periodical devoted to news and features relating to a particular trade or profession

trade language *n* a language used between native speakers of different languages to allow them to communicate so that they can trade with each other

trade-last *n US* an exchange in which somebody repeats an overheard compliment to the complimented person if that person will first offer an overheard compliment about the other (*informal*)

trademark /tráyd maark/ *n* **1 COMPANY SYMBOL** a name or symbol used to show that a product is made by a particular company and legally registered so that no other manufacturer can use it **2 DISTINCTIVE CHARACTERISTIC** a distinctive characteristic associated with a particular person ○ *Quick exits are her trademark.* ■ *vt* **1 REGISTER SOMETHING AS A TRADEMARK** to register a name or symbol as a trademark **2 LABEL PRODUCT WITH A TRADEMARK** to place a trademark on a product

trade name *n* **1 PRODUCT NAME** a name given by a manufacturer to a product or service **2 NAME USED IN A TRADE** a name for something that is usually known or used only by people working in a particular trade **3 COMPANY NAME** a name under which a company or business operates

trade-off, tradeoff *n* a situation in which somebody is prepared to compromise by giving up all or part of one thing in exchange for another ○ *a trade-off between quality and price*

trade paperback *n* a paperback edition of a book that is superior in production quality to a mass-market paperback edition and is similar to a hardback in size

trade plates *npl* temporary number plates given to a vehicle before it is registered. US term **dealer plates**

trader /tráydər/ *n* **1 SOMEBODY TRADING IN GOODS** a buyer and seller of retail goods **2 SOMEBODY TRADING IN STOCKS** a dealer in stocks and securities, especially somebody who tries to profit by making frequent deals, each netting a small profit **3 SHIP** a merchant ship

trade reference *n* a person or company that furnishes a report concerning somebody's credit standing in response to an inquiry by somebody else in the same trade, especially a supplier

trade route *n* a route used by merchant ships or trading vehicles

Tradescant /trə déskənt, tráddə skant/, **John** (1570–1638?) English naturalist

tradescantia /tráddi skánti ə/ (*plural* **-tias** *or* **-tia**) *n* a plant grown for its striped leaves and blue, white, or pink flowers. Genus: *Tradescantia.* ◊ **spiderwort** [Early 18C. < modern Latin, after John Tradescant (1570–1634), English naturalist, or his son.]

trade school *n* a school that gives instruction in a particular trade or that offers vocational courses in general

trade secret *n* **1** a secret formula or technique that is used to make a product, known only to the company that manufactures it **2** any secret (*informal*) ○ *Which shampoo do you use – or is it a trade secret?*

trades holiday *n Scotland* an annual two-week summer holiday taken by industries in a particular town

tradesman /tráydzmən/ (*plural* **-men** /-mən/) *n* **1** a man who works in a skilled trade, especially one related to the building trade such as plumbing or carpentry **2** a man involved in retail trade, especially a shopkeeper (*dated*)

tradespeople /tráydz peep'l/ *npl* **1** people who work in retail trade, especially shopkeepers (*dated*) **2** people who work in a skilled trade, especially one related to the building trade such as plumbing or carpentry

tradesperson /tráydz purss'n/ *n* **1** a retail dealer, especially a shopkeeper (*dated*) **2** a skilled worker, especially in a trade related to the building trade such as plumbing or carpentry

trades union *n* POL = **trade union**

Trades Union Congress *n* an association of trade unions in Britain, to which most of the largest unions belong

tradeswoman /tráydz wòommən/ (*plural* **-en** /-wimmin/) *n* a woman who works in a skilled trade, especially one related to the building trade such as plumbing or carpentry

trade union, trades union *n* an organized association of people who work in a particular trade or profession, formed to represent their interests and help them improve their working conditions. US term **labor union** —**trade unionism** *n* —**trade unionist** *n*

trade wind *n* a prevailing tropical wind blowing towards the equator from the northeast in the northern hemisphere or from the southeast in the southern hemisphere [< *blow trade* 'blow in a constant direction']

~~tradgedy~~ incorrect spelling of **tragedy**

trading card *n* a card with a picture or information on it that is one of a set designed to be collected

trading estate *n* COMM = **industrial estate**

trading post *n* **1** especially formerly, a shop in a remote area, where local products can be bartered for supplies **2** a location where a particular security is traded on the floor of a stock exchange

trading stamp *n* a stamp that can be exchanged for goods, given by a shop to customers each time they spend a certain amount of money

tradition /trə dísh'n/ *n* **1 CUSTOM OR BELIEF** a long-established custom or belief, often one that has been handed down from generation to generation **2 BODY OF CUSTOMS** a body of long-established customs and beliefs viewed as a set of precedents **3 HANDING DOWN OF CUSTOMS** the handing down of customs, practices, and beliefs that are valued by a particular culture **4 tradition, Tradition ACCEPTED UNWRITTEN CHRISTIAN DOCTRINES** the body of Christian doctrines that are accepted as the teachings of Jesus Christ and the apostles without written evidence **5 tradition, Tradition TEACHINGS SUPPLEMENTING KORAN** the body of Islamic beliefs and customs that are not written in the Koran, e.g. the words of Muhammad **6 TRANSFER OF OWNERSHIP** especially in Roman and Scots law, the formal transfer of ownership of movable property [14C. Via Old French < Latin *tradition-* < *tradere* 'hand over, betray' < *trans-* 'across, over' + *dare* 'give'.] —**traditionless** *adj*

SYNONYMS See ***habit***.

traditional /trə dísh'nəl/ *adj* **1** based on or relating to tradition **2** describes older styles of jazz, usually played by small ensembles featuring clarinet, trumpet, trombone, and rhythm sections —**traditionality** /trə dísh'n állәti/ *n* —**traditionalize** *vt* —**traditionally** *adv*

traditionalism /trə dísh'nəlizəm/ *n* **1** deep respect for tradition, especially cultural or religious practices **2** the idea that all knowledge comes from divine revelation and is passed on by tradition —**traditionalist** *n* —**traditionalistic** /trə dísh'nə lístik/ *adj*

traditional option *n* on the Stock Exchange, an option that cannot be resold after it has been bought

traditional policy *n* a life assurance policy in which premiums are paid into a general fund and benefits are based on actuarial statistics

traditor /trádditər/ (*plural* **-tores** /-táw reez/) *n* an early Christian who betrayed other Christians during the Roman persecutions [14C. < Latin (see TRAITOR).]

traduce /trə dyóoss/ (**-duces, -ducing, -duced**) *vt* to say very critical or disparaging things about somebody [Late 16C. < Latin *traducere* 'convert, transfer, scorn, disgrace' < *trans-* 'across, over' + *ducere* 'to lead'.] —**traducement** *n* —**traducer** *n* —**traducible** *adj*

traducianism /trə dyóosh'nizəm/ *n* the belief that a child inherits a soul as well as its bodily characteristics from its parents [Mid-18C. < late Latin *traducianus* 'believer in traducianism' < Latin *tradux* 'inheritance, transmission' < *traducere* (see TRADUCE).] —**traducian** *n, adj* —**traducianist** *n, adj* —**traducianistic** /trə dyóosh'n ístik/ *adj*

Trafalgar, Cape /trə fálgər/ cape in SW Spain between Cádiz and the Strait of Gibraltar

traffic /tráffik/ *n* **1 MOVEMENT OF VEHICLES** the movement of vehicles along the roads in a particular area **2 SEA OR AIR TRANSPORT** the movement of ships, trains, or aircraft between two places, or the volume of passengers or goods transported by sea, rail, or air **3 BUSINESS OF TRANSPORTATION** the business of transporting goods or people **4 TRADE** illegal trade in goods such as drugs or weapons **5 FLOW OF COMMUNICATIONS** the volume or flow of messages carried by a communications system in a particular period **6 NEGOTIATIONS** dealings or negotiations between people (*formal*) ■ *v* (**-fics, -ficking, -ficked**) **1** *vi* **TRADE ILLEGALLY** to engage in illegal trading **2** *vi* **HAVE DEALINGS** to have dealings with somebody or something **3** *vt* **TRADE** to trade or exchange anything ○ *We spent the afternoon trafficking gossip.* [Early 16C. Via obsolete French *trafique* < Old Italian *traffico* < *trafficare* 'carry on trade'.]

trafficator /tráffi kaytər/ *n* an illuminated signal on either side of an old motor vehicle, raised by the driver to signal a turn [Mid-20C. Blend of TRAFFIC + INDICATOR.]

traffic calming *n* the use of obstructions such as speed bumps to force drivers to slow down, especially in residential areas (*hyphenated before nouns*)

traffic circle *n US, Can* TRANSP = **roundabout** *n.* **2**

traffic cone *n* a marker in the shape of a cone, usually made of orange plastic, used to separate lines of traffic during road repairs or to prevent vehicles from entering an area

traffic cop *n* (*informal*) **1** a police officer who supervises traffic **2** *NZ* a traffic officer

traffic court *n* a court that deals with people who have committed traffic offences

traffic engineering *n* the design and planning of roads and walkways, considering such factors as pedestrian and vehicular capacity and means for controlling traffic

traffic island *n* a raised area in the centre of a road to separate lanes of traffic and allow pedestrians to wait safely until they can cross

traffic jam *n* a line of traffic that cannot move or moves very slowly or spasmodically because of overcrowding or an obstruction —**traffic-jammed** *adj*

traffic light *n* a signal that uses red, green, and amber lights to control traffic, especially at a junction

traffic officer *n NZ* a member of an official force responsible for enforcing traffic regulations and controlling the flow of traffic

traffic pattern *n* the pattern of routes to which an aircraft is restricted when approaching or circling an airport

traffic signal *n* TRANSP = **traffic light**

traffic warden *n UK* a uniformed public official who enforces parking restrictions on the highway and may also direct traffic

tragacanth /trággə kanth/ *n* **1** a reddish or white gum extracted from a plant grown in Asia. Use: pills, adhesives, textile printing, stabilizer, thickener for sauces. **2** a plant from which tragacanth is obtained, especially a spiny Asian plant with white, yellow, or purple flowers. Genus: *Astragalus.* [Late 16C. Via French < Greek *tragakantha* 'goat's thorn' < *tragos* 'goat' + *akantha* 'thorn'.]

tragedian /trə jéedi ən/ *n* **1** a playwright who specializes in tragedies **2** an actor who plays tragic roles

tragedienne /trə jéedi én/ *n* a woman actor who plays tragic roles (*dated*) [Mid-19C. < French, < *tragédie* (see TRAGEDY).]

tragedy /trájjədi/ (*plural* **-dies**) *n* **1 VERY SAD EVENT** an event in life that evokes feelings of sorrow or grief **2 DISASTROUS EVENT** a disastrous circumstance or event such as serious illness, financial ruin, or fatality **3 TRAGIC PLAY** a serious play with a tragic theme, often involving a heroic struggle and the downfall of the main character **4 TRAGIC PIECE OF LITERATURE** a literary work that deals with a tragic theme **5 TRAGEDIES AS A GENRE** the genre of plays or other literary works that deal with tragic themes [14C. Via French *tragédie* < Greek *tragōidia* 'goat's song' < *tragos* 'goat' + *aeidein* 'sing'.]

tragi plural of **tragus**

tragic /trájjik/, **tragical** /-ik'l/ *adj* **1** provoking deep sadness, distress, or grief **2** relating to tragedies as a dramatic genre [Mid-16C. Via Latin < Greek *tragikos* 'of tragedy' < *tragos* 'goat'.] —**tragically** *adv*

tragic flaw *n* a character flaw that causes the downfall of the protagonist in a tragedy

tragic irony *n* the revealing to an audience of a tragic event or consequence that remains unknown to the character concerned

tragicomedy /trájji kómmədi/ (*plural* **-dies**) *n* **1 WORK COMBINING TRAGEDY AND COMEDY** a play or other literary work that combines elements of tragedy and comedy **2 TRAGICOMIC PLAYS AS A GENRE** tragicomic plays or literary works considered as a genre **3 EVENT MIXING TRAGEDY AND COMEDY** an event or situation that has both tragic and comical aspects [Late 16C. Via French *tragicomédie* < late Latin *tragicomoedia* < *tragicus* (see TRAGIC) + *comoedia* (see COMEDY).] —**tragicomic** *adj* —**tragicomical** *adj* —**tragicomically** *adv*

tragopan /trággə pan/ *n* a brightly coloured pheasant, the male of which has a bright blue bare throat and fleshy appendages on its head that look like horns. Native to: Asia. *Tragopan temminckii.* [Early 17C. Via Latin < Greek, type of hornbill < *tragos* 'goat' + *pan* 'Pan'.]

tragus /tráygəss/ (*plural* **-gi** /-jī, -gī/) *n* the pointed flap of cartilage that lies above the earlobe and partly covers the entrance to the ear passage [Late 17C. Via modern Latin < Greek *tragos* 'goat, hairy part of the ear'.] —**tragal** *adj*

trail /trayl/ *v* **1** *vti* **DRAG SOMETHING OR BE DRAGGED** to be pulled or dragged along, or pull or drag something along **2** *vi* **DRAPE** to hang, grow, or float loosely ○ *Her curly hair trailed along her shoulders and down her back.* **3** *vi* **LAG** to walk slowly, usually from tiredness or boredom **4** *vt* **FOLLOW SOMEBODY SECRETLY** to follow a person or animal either by staying close but out of sight or by looking for signs of movement left behind, e.g. footprints or scent **5** *vti* **FALL BEHIND IN ATHLETIC COMPETITION** to be losing in a race, match, or competition **6** *vt* **SHOW EXCERPT OF IN ADVANCE** to advertise an upcoming film or programme by showing a clip from it **7** *vt* **DECORATE SOMETHING BY DRIZZLING LIQUID CLAY** to decorate ceramics with liquid clay (**slip**) that is drizzled or sprayed on **8** *vt* **TOW** to tow something such as a caravan behind a vehicle **9** *vt* **CARRY WEAPON IN LOW POSITION** to carry a weapon horizontally or with the butt near to the ground **10** *vti* **MAKE TRACK** to make a track through a place ■ *n* **1 ROUTE THROUGH COUNTRYSIDE** a route through the countryside that links paths and points of interest ○ *a nature trail* **2 MARKS WHERE SOMEBODY OR SOMETHING MOVED** a sequence of marks left by somebody or something moving along a surface **3 SCENT FOLLOWED** a scent or track that is followed in a hunt **4 PATH** a path or track, especially one that has been beaten through a wild area **5 BOTTOM OF GUN CARRIAGE** the part of a gun carriage that rests on the ground **6 DISTANCE FROM STEERING WHEEL** the distance between the centre of a steering wheel and a line intersecting the steering axis and the ground [14C. Via Old French *trailler* 'tow' < Latin *tragula* 'dragnet, sledge', probably < *trahere* 'pull'.]

trail away, trail off *vi* to become quieter or fainter in sound and gradually fade away

trail bike *n* a lightweight motorcycle for use on rough terrain

trailblazer /tráyl blayzər/ *n* **1** a pioneer or innovator in a particular field **2** a person who makes a new path through a wilderness —**trailblazing** *adj, n*

trailer /tráylər/ *n* **1 TOWED VEHICLE** a vehicle that is towed by another vehicle, e.g. a small open cart or a platform used for transporting a boat **2 PART OF LORRY** the rear part of an articulated lorry **3** *Can, US* TRANSP = **caravan** *n.* 1 **4 ADVERTISEMENT FOR FILM** an advertisement for a film consisting of extracts from it, shown on television or in a cinema **5 END OF REEL OF FILM** a blank piece of film at the end of a reel **6 SOMEBODY OR SOMETHING THAT TRAILS** a person who or thing that trails, especially somebody who lags behind others **7 PLANT** a trailing plant ■ *vt* **1 MOVE BY TRAILER** to transport something using a trailer **2 ADVERTISE WITH TRAILER** to advertise a film with extracts from it

trailer park *n US* a caravan site

trailer tent *n* a large tent that packs into a trailer. When erected, the trailer's base becomes a raised sleeping or living area.

trailing arbutus *n* a trailing evergreen shrub with leathery leaves. Flowers: fragrant, pink-and-white, in clusters. Native to: E North America. *Epigaea repens.*

trailing edge *n* **1** the rear edge of a wing, aerofoil, or propeller blade **2** the part of a pulsed signal during which its amplitude decreases

trail mix *n* a snack containing nuts, dried fruit, and seeds [< its use by walkers]

trail rope *n* **1** a rope that hangs from a balloon or airship and is used for mooring or as a brake **2** a long rope attached to the trail of a gun carriage

train /trayn/ *n* **1 LINKED RAILWAY CARRIAGES** a number of railway carriages or trucks pulled by a locomotive (*often before nouns*) **2 TRAILING PART OF GOWN** a long part at the back of a gown or robe that trails on the ground **3 LONG MOVING LINE** a long moving line of people or animals **4 ARMY FOLLOWERS** the people and military vehicles supporting or supplying an army unit **5 SEQUENCE OF EVENTS** a series or sequence of events, actions, or things **6 MECHANICAL SERIES** a series of connected wheels or other mechanical parts **7 LINE OF GUNPOWDER** a line of gunpowder or other combustible material **8 ENTOURAGE** a retinue or group of followers **9 SOMETHING DRAGGED BEHIND** something that is pulled or dragged along or that follows something else ■ *v* **1** *vti* **LEARN OR TEACH SKILLS** to learn or teach somebody the skills necessary to do a particular job, especially through practical experience **2** *vt* **DOMESTICATE ANIMAL** to teach an animal to behave in ways acceptable to people, especially by repetition or practice **3** *vti* **PREPARE FOR SPORTING COMPETITION** to prepare or prepare somebody for a sporting competition, usually with a planned programme of appropriate physical exercises **4** *vt* **MAKE PLANT GROW AS WANTED** to make a plant, bush, or tree grow in a particular way, e.g. by pruning or tying it **5** *vt* **SHAPE HAIR TO ENCOURAGE PARTICULAR GROWTH** to comb or otherwise arrange hair to encourage it to grow in a particular direction **6** *vt* **AIM** to aim something such as a weapon or a camera at somebody or something **7** *vt* **PRODUCE IMPROVEMENT** to improve something, especially the mind, with discipline **8** *vi* **TRAVEL BY TRAIN** to make a journey by train (*informal*) [Mid-15C. < Old French *traïn* 'something that drags or trails behind' < *traïner* 'draw, pull'.]

SYNONYMS See ***teach***.

trainband /tráyn band/ *n* a company of trained civilian militia operating in England and North America from the 16th to the 18th centuries [Mid-17C. Contraction of *trained band*.]

trainbearer /tráyn bairər/ *n* an attendant who holds up the train of somebody walking in a procession or other ceremony

trainee /tray née/ *n* a person who is being trained to do a job (*often before a noun*) ○ *a trainee hairdresser* —**traineeship** *n*

trainer /tráynər/ *n* **1 SOMEBODY WHO TRAINS ANIMALS OR PEOPLE** a person who trains animals or people, especially racehorses or athletes **2 TRAINING APPARATUS** an apparatus or device used in training, especially a simulation cockpit in which pilots train **3 SPORTS SHOE** a sports shoe with a thick cushioned sole, often worn as leisurewear

training /tráyning/ *n* **1** the process of teaching or learning a skill or job (*often before nouns*) ○ *a training programme* **2** the process of improving physical fitness by exercise and diet

Training Agency *n* an organization that provides training and retraining for adults

training college *n* a college that trains people for a particular profession, especially the teaching profession

training shoe *n* CLOTHING = **trainer** *n.* 3

training wheels *npl* a pair of small wheels fitted to the back wheel of a bicycle to help balance it while somebody is learning to ride. US term **stabilizer** *npl.*

trainload /tráyn lōd/ *n* the number of people or the amount of cargo that a train can carry ○ *a trainload of tourists*

trainman /tráynmən/ (*plural* **-men** /-mən/) *n* a man who is a member of a train crew, especially a brakeman, who works to assist the conductor

train oil *n* oil from the blubber of a whale or other marine animal [< Low German *trān* or Middle Dutch *traen* 'train oil']

train operating company *n* full form of **TOC**

trainspotter /tráyn spotər/ *n* **1** somebody whose hobby is collecting the numbers of railway locomotives **2** somebody who is considered boring because of his or her staid outlook, narrow interests, or unfashionable appearance (*slang insult*)

trainspotting /tráyn spoting/ *n* **1** a hobby that consists of collecting the numbers of railway locomotives **2** the search for a vein that is prominent enough to inject drugs into (*slang*)

traipse /trayps/ *vi* (**traipses, traipsing, traipsed**) to trudge in a weary way (*informal*) ■ *n* a tiring or wearisome walk [Late 16C. < ?]

trait /trayt, tray/ *n* **1 INDIVIDUAL CHARACTERISTIC** a particular characteristic or quality that distinguishes somebody **2 INHERITED CHARACTERISTIC** a quality or characteristic that is genetically determined **3 INDICATION** a hint or trace of something (*literary*) [Late 16C. Via French, 'act of pulling or drawing, line drawn, feature' < Latin *tractus* < *trahere* 'pull'.]

traitor /tráytər/ *n* a disloyal or treacherous person [13C. Via Old French < Latin *traditor* 'betrayer' < *tradere* (see TRADITION).] —**traitorous** *adj* —**traitorously** *adv* —**traitorousness** *n*

Trajan /tráyjən/ (53?–117) Roman emperor (98–117). Full name **Marcus Ulpius Trajanus**

trajectory /trə jéktəri/ (*plural* **-ries**) *n* **1** the path a projectile makes through space under the action of given forces such as thrust, wind, and gravity **2** a curve or surface that intersects all of a family of curves or surfaces at a constant angle [Late 17C. < medieval Latin *trajectorius* 'relating to throwing across' < Latin *traject-* (see TRAJECT).]

Tralee /trə lée/ town in the SW Republic of Ireland. Population: 20,000 (1996).

Tralee Bay /trə lée-/ inlet of the Atlantic Ocean on the southwestern coast of the Republic of Ireland

tram[1] /tram/ *n* **1** a passenger vehicle that runs along rails on a road. It has an overhead wire from which it draws electricity. US term **streetcar** **2** a small vehicle on rails used to carry coal and other materials in a coal mine [Early 16C. < ?]

tram[2] /tram/ *n* a fine adjustment that keeps a machine functioning correctly ■ *vt* (**trams, tramming, trammed**) to adjust or align mechanical parts accurately [Late 19C. < *tram-staff* 'straight edge used to adjust a millstone spindle' < *tram* 'instrument for drawing ellipses', shortening of TRAMMEL.]

tram[3] /tram/ *n* heavy silk thread. Use: horizontal weave in velvet or silk. [Late 17C. Via French *trame* < Latin *trama* 'woof of a web'.]

tramcar /trám kaar/ *n* TRANSP = **tram**[1] *n.* 1

tramline /trám līn/ *n* 1 **TRAM TRACK** a track for a tram 2 **TRAM ROUTE** the route driven by a tram ■ *npl* 1 **tramlines MARKINGS ON TENNIS COURT** a pair of parallel lines at either side of a tennis court delimiting the singles and doubles courts (*informal*) 2 **tramlines MARKINGS ON BADMINTON COURT** a pair of parallel lines at either side and either end of a badminton court delimiting the singles and doubles courts

trammel /trámm'l/ *n* 1 **LIMITATION TO FREEDOM** something that limits a person's freedom 2 **FISHING NET** a fishing net consisting of a fine net between two layers of coarse mesh 3 **DRAWING INSTRUMENT** an instrument used to draw ellipses 4 MECH ENG = **tram**[2] *n.* 5 **FIREPLACE HOOK** a hook in a fireplace on which a kettle or pot can be hung and raised or lowered ■ *vt* (**-mels, -melling, -melled**) 1 **CONFINE** to restrain somebody or something 2 **ENSNARE** to catch or entangle somebody or something 3 MECH ENG = **tram**[2] *v.* [14C. Via Old French *tramail* < late Latin *tremaculum* < Latin *tres* 'three' + *macula* 'mesh'.]

tramontana /trámmon taána/ *n* a cold dry wind that blows down from mountains, especially a north wind that blows into Italy from the Alps [Late 18C. Via Italian, 'north wind' < Latin *transmontanus* 'beyond the mountains' < *trans-* 'across, over' + *mont-* 'mountain'.]

tramontane /trə món tayn/ *adj* 1 **BEYOND MOUNTAINS** living or situated on the far side of the mountains, especially the Alps as seen from Italy 2 **FOREIGN** foreign and uncivilized, originally from an Italian point of view ■ *n* 1 METEOROL = **tramontana** 2 **FOREIGNER** a person from beyond mountains, especially from beyond the Alps as seen from Italy [Late 16C. Via Italian *tramontano* < Latin *transmontanus* (see TRANSMONTANE).]

tramp /tramp/ *n* 1 **VAGRANT** a homeless person who travels on foot, often begging for a living 2 *UK* **LONG JOURNEY ON FOOT** a long journey on foot, e.g. as part of a walking tour 3 **SOUND OF FEET** the sound of heavy footsteps or horses' hooves 4 **HEAVY STEP** a heavy step or tread 5 **OFFENSIVE TERM** an offensive term that deliberately insults a woman who is considered sexually promiscuous or who works as a prostitute 6 **METAL PLATE ON BOOT** a metal plate that protects the sole of a boot when the wearer is digging 7 **PART OF SPADE** the part of a spade on which the digger's foot presses ■ *v* 1 *vi* **TREAD HEAVILY** to tread heavily or noisily 2 *vi* **WALK** to walk, especially a long way 3 *vi* **LIVE AS VAGRANT** to live or wander about as a vagrant 4 *vt* **COVER DISTANCE ON FOOT** to traverse an area, especially wearily, or cover a distance in a steady weary way 5 *vt* **CRUSH UNDERFOOT** to crush something by treading on it 6 *vi NZ* **HIKE IN BUSH** to go hiking in the countryside for recreation [14C. < Middle Low German *trampen* 'to stamp'.] —**tramper** *n* —**tramping** *n* —**trampish** *adj*

trample /trámp'l/ (**-ples, -pling, -pled**) *vti* 1 to tread heavily, or to tread heavily on something or somebody so as to cause damage or injury 2 to behave in an insulting contemptuous way or to treat somebody in a hurtful insulting way [14C. < TRAMP.] —**trampler** *n*

trampoline /trámpə leen/ *n* a strong sheet, usually of canvas, that is stretched tightly on a horizontal frame to which it is connected by springs and on which gymnasts and acrobats jump [Late 18C. < Italian *trampolino* 'springboard' < *trampoli* 'stilts'.] —**trampoline** *vi* —**trampoliner** *n* —**trampolinist** *n*

tramp steamer *n* a merchant ship that carries cargo but does not follow a fixed route

tramway /trám way/ *n* 1 TRANSP = **tramline** *n.* 1 2 a light-rail system that uses trams, or a company that operates such a system

trance /traanss/ *n* 1 **DAZED STATE** a state in which somebody is dazed or stunned or in some other way unaware of the environment and unable to respond to stimuli 2 **HYPNOTIC STATE** a hypnotic or cataleptic state 3 **RAPTUROUS STATE** a state of rapture or exaltation in which somebody loses consciousness 4 **SPIRITUAL MEDIUM'S STATE** the state of apparent semi-unconsciousness that a spiritual medium enters into in an attempt to communicate with the dead 5 **HYPNOTIC ELECTRONIC DANCE MUSIC** electronic dance music with a repetitive hypnotic beat ■ *vt* (**trances, trancing, tranced**) **ENTRANCE** to put somebody in a trance (*literary*) [14C. < Old French *transe* < *transir* 'be numb with fear' < Latin *transire* (see TRANSIENT).]

tranche /traansh/ *n* a portion or section, often a division of something in financial terms, e.g. a single repayment of a loan or an individual class of securities [Mid-20C. < French, 'slice' < Old French *trenchier* 'to cut'.]

trannie /tránni/, **tranny** (*plural* **-nies**) *n* 1 **RADIO** a transistor radio (*informal*) 2 **TRANSSEXUAL** a transsexual (*slang*) 3 **TRANSVESTITE** a transvestite (*slang*) [Mid-20C. Shortening.]

tranquil /trángkwil/ *adj* 1 free of any disturbance or commotion ○ *a tranquil morning* 2 free from or showing no signs of anxiety or agitation [Mid-15C. Via French < Latin *tranquillus.*] —**tranquilly** *adv* —**tranquilness** *n*

SYNONYMS See ***calm.***

tranquilize *vti* US = **tranquillize**

tranquillise *vti* = **tranquillize**

tranquilliser *n* = **tranquillizer**

tranquillity /trang kwílləti/ *n* a state of peace and calm [14C. Via Old French < Latin *tranquillitas* 'quietness' < *tranquillus* 'tranquil'.]

tranquillize /trángkwi līz/ (**-quillizes, -quillizing, -quillized, -quillized**), **tranquillise** (**-lises, -lising, -lised**) *v* 1 *vt* **MAKE SOMEBODY CALM** to induce calmness in a person or an animal, usually with medication 2 *vi* **BECOME CALM** to become calm or calmer 3 *vi* **HAVE CALMING EFFECT** to have a calming effect —**tranquilization** /trángkwi lī záysh'n/ *n*

tranquillizer /trángkwi līzər/, **tranquilliser** *n* 1 a medication that reduces anxiety and tension without affecting mental clarity. Use: treatment of anxiety, neuroses, psychoses. 2 anything that renders a person or animal calm

trans. *abbr* 1 transaction 2 transferred 3 transitive 4 translated 5 translation 6 transport 7 transpose 8 transverse

trans- *prefix* 1 across, on the other side of, beyond ○ *transcontinental* ○ *transfinite* 2 through ○ *transdermal* 3 indicating change, transfer, or conversion ○ *transliterate* [< Latin *trans* 'across, over, through']

transact /tran zákt, -sákt/ *vti* to conduct or carry out something such as business [Late 16C. Back-formation < TRANSACTION.] —**transactor** *n*

transactinide /transs ákti nīd/ *n* an element with an atomic number greater than 103 (*often before nouns*)

ϟ**transaction** /tran záksh'n, -sák-/ *n* 1 **BUSINESS** a business deal that is being negotiated or has been settled 2 **ACT OF NEGOTIATING** the act of negotiating something or carrying out a business deal 3 **INTERACTION** a communication or activity between two or more people that influences and affects all of them (*formal*) 4 **ADDITION TO DATABASE** an action that adds, removes, or changes data in a database or other computer program ■ **transactions** *npl* **PROCEEDINGS** the published records of a learned society [Mid-15C. Via French < late Latin *transactiion-* < Latin *transigere* 'drive through, accomplish' < *agere* 'drive, do'.] —**transactional** *adj* —**transactionally** *adv*

transactional analysis *n* a form of psychotherapy that emphasizes the interactions within and between individuals and classifies these interactions as 'adult', 'parent', or 'child'

transactivation /tránss akti váysh'n, tránz-/ *n* the process whereby an infecting virus activates another virus's genes that are already integrated into the chromosome of the host bacterium, inducing the host cell to replicate the initial virus

transalpine /tranz ál pīn/ *adj* 1 **BEYOND THE ALPS** relating to or found in the area beyond the Alps, especially as seen from Italy 2 **CROSSING ALPS** relating to or engaged in crossing the Alps ■ *n* **SOMEBODY FROM BEYOND THE ALPS** a person who comes from beyond the Alps, especially as seen from Italy [Late 16C. < Latin *transalpinus* < *alpes* 'the Alps'.]

transaminase /tranz ámmi nayz, -nayss/ *n* an enzyme that catalyses the transfer of an amino group in the process of transamination

transamination /tranz ámmi náysh'n/ *n* the formation of one amino acid from another

transatlantic /tránzət lántik/ *adj* 1 situated on or coming from the other side of the Atlantic 2 relating to or engaged in crossing the Atlantic

transaxle /tránz aks'l/ *n* a combined front axle and transmission in a motor vehicle with front-wheel drive [Mid-20C. < TRANSMISSION + AXLE.]

transboundary /tránz bówndəri/ *adj* crossing or existing across national boundaries

trans-butanedoic acid /tránz byootanə dōik-/ *n* CHEM = **fumaric acid**

Transcaucasia /tránz kaw káyzhə, -káyzi ə/ region in SE Europe, between the Black and Caspian seas. It consists of the republics of Georgia, Armenia, and Azerbaijan. Area: 186,100 sq. km/71,853 sq. mi. —**Transcaucasian** *adj*

ϟ**transceiver** /tran séevər/ *n* 1 a radio transmitter and receiver combined in a single, often portable unit 2 a device that can receive and transmit data, e.g. a modem [Mid-20C. Blend of TRANSMITTER + RECEIVER.]

transcend /tran sénd/ *vt* 1 **GO BEYOND LIMIT** to go beyond a limit or range, e.g. of thought or belief 2 **SURPASS** to go beyond something in quality or achievement 3 **BE INDEPENDENT OF WORLD** to exist above and apart from the material world [14C. Via Old French < Latin *transcendere* 'climb over or beyond' < *scandere* 'climb, mount'.]

transcendent /tran séndənt/ *adj* 1 **BETTER** superior in quality or achievement 2 **BEYOND LIMITS OF EXPERIENCE** in Kant's philosophical system, exceeding the limits of experience and therefore unknowable except hypothetically 3 **BEYOND CATEGORIES** above or outside all known categories 4 **INDEPENDENT OF THE WORLD** existing outside the material universe and so not limited by it —**transcendence** *n* —**transcendency** *n* —**transcendent** *n* —**transcendently** *adv* —**transcendentness** *n*

transcendental /trán sen dént'l/ *adj* 1 = **transcendent** *adj.* 1 2 **NOT EXPERIENCED BUT KNOWABLE** independent of human experience of phenomena but within the range of knowledge 3 **MYSTICAL** relating to mystical or supernatural experience and therefore beyond the material world 4 **NOT ALGEBRAIC** describes a number or function that is not algebraic and is not the root of an algebraic equation ■ *n* **NUMBER IMPOSSIBLE TO EXPRESS AS INTEGER** a number that cannot be expressed as an integer, e.g. a nonrepeating decimal such as pi [Early 17C. < late Latin *transcendentalis* 'transcending the bounds of all categories' < *transcendere* (see TRANSCEND).] —**transcendentality** /trán sen den tálləti/ *n* —**transcendentally** *adv*

transcendentalism /trán sen dént'lizəm/ *n* 1 **PHILOSOPHY EMPHASIZING REASONING** a system of philosophy, especially that of Kant, that regards the processes of reasoning as the key to knowledge of reality 2 **PHILOSOPHY EMPHASIZING DIVINE** a system of philosophy, especially that associated with Ralph Waldo Emerson and other New England writers, that emphasizes intuition or the divine 3 **TRANSCENDENTAL THOUGHT** transcendental thought or language 4 **TRANSCENDENTAL NATURE** the state or quality of being transcendental —**transcendentalist** *n, adj*

QUICK FACTS ON... **TRANSCENDENTALISM**

Key dates: 1836–60
Key locations: United States, especially Massachusetts
Key elements: rejection of religious dogmatism and 18th-century rationalism; individualism, Romanticism; celebration of nature, beauty, and human goodness; intuition as means of experiencing the divine; Platonism, neo-Platonism, deism
Key figures: Ralph Waldo Emerson, Henry David Thoreau, Margaret Fuller, William Ellery Channing, Bronson Alcott, Theodore Parker
Key events: formation of the Transcendental Club in Boston, 1836; establishment of cooperative Brook Farm 1841; Thoreau withdraws to Walden pond 1845–47; Thoreau jailed for not paying taxes to protest about war 1846
Key works: *Nature* (Emerson) 1836, 'Self-Reliance' (Emerson) 1841, *The Dial [journal]* 1840–44, *Walden, or Life in the Woods* (Thoreau) 1854
Key developments: American Renaissance, environmentalism, feminism, civil disobedience and passive resistance, hippie movement

transcendental meditation *n* a form of meditation in which a mantra is repeated silently

transcontinental /tránz konti nént'l/ *adj* 1 **ACROSS CONTINENT** extending across a continent 2 **BEYOND CONTINENT** situated on or coming from the other side of a continent ■ *n* **TRAIN CROSSING CONTINENT** a train or railway that crosses a continent —**transcontinentally** *adv*

ϟ**transcribe** /tran skrīb/ (**-scribes, -scribing, -scribed**) *vt* 1 **COPY OUT** to write out an exact copy of something 2 **EXPAND SOMETHING IN WRITING** to write something out in full from notes or shorthand 3 **WRITE SOUNDS PHONETICALLY** to write speech sounds phonetically 4 **TRANSLATE** to translate or transliterate something 5 **REARRANGE MUSIC** to arrange a piece of music for a different instrument, voice, or combination **6 RECORD SOMETHING FOR LATER BROADCASTING** to record something so that it can be broadcast at a later time **7 BROADCAST SOMETHING TRANSCRIBED** to broadcast something that has been transcribed earlier **8 TRANSFER SOMETHING TO OTHER STORAGE FORMAT** to transfer information from one way of storing it on computer to another, or from a computer to an external storage device **9 CONVERT CODE FOR TRANSMISSION TO RNA** to convert the genetic code carried by DNA into an equivalent form carried by a molecule of messenger RNA **10 CONVERT GENETIC CODE INTO DNA MOLECULE** to convert the genetic code carried by the RNA of a retrovirus into a molecule of DNA [Mid-16C. < Latin *transcribere* 'copy, convey' < *scribere* 'write'.] —**transcribable** *adj* —**transcriber** *n*

transcript /trán skript/ *n* **1 WRITTEN RECORD** a written record of something, e.g. a copy of the script of a broadcast programme or a record of court proceedings **2** *US* **STUDENT'S ACADEMIC HISTORY** an official document showing the educational work of a student in a North American school or college **3 COPY** any copy or record **4 RNA WITH TRANSCRIBED CODE** a molecule of messenger RNA that carries coded genetic information converted from the genetic code held by the DNA during the process of transcription in living cells **5 DNA CARRYING CODED RETROVIRUS** the DNA that carries the coded information of a retrovirus, converted from the genetic code held by the virus's RNA during transcription following the infection of a living cell [Mid-15C. < Latin *transcriptum* < past participle of *transcribere* (see TRANSCRIBE).]

transcriptase /tran skríp tayz, -tayss/ *n* an enzyme that catalyses the synthesis of messenger RNA from a DNA template during transcription

transcription /tran skrípsh'n/ *n* **1 TRANSCRIBING** the act or process of transcribing something **2 TRANSCRIPT** something that has been transcribed **3 PHONETIC REPRESENTATION** a phonetic representation of speech using special symbols **4 TRANSFER OF GENETIC CODE** the first step in carrying out genetic instructions in living cells, in which the genetic code is transferred from DNA to molecules of messenger RNA, which subsequently direct protein manufacture **5 TRANSFER OF GENETIC INFORMATION** the first step in the replication of a retrovirus following its infection of a living cell, in which its genetic code is transferred from RNA to a molecule of DNA —**transcriptional** *adj* —**transcriptionally** *adv*

transcriptive /tran skríptiv/ *adj* used for transcribing or in the form of a transcript —**transcriptively** *adv*

transcultural /tranz kúlchərəl/ *adj* extending across cultures or involving more than one culture

transculturation /tránz kulchə ráysh'n/ *n* the change in a culture brought about by the diffusion within it of elements from other cultures

transcurrent /tranz kúrrənt/ *adj* running across something, especially perpendicular to an expected direction or flow [Early 17C. < Latin *transcurrent-*, present participle of *transcurrere* 'run across, traverse' < *currere* 'run'.]

transcutaneous /tránz kyoō táyni əss/ *adj* MED = **transdermal**

transcutaneous electrical nerve stimulation *n* full form of **TENS**

transdermal /tranz dúrm'l/ *adj* describes something, especially a drug, that is introduced into the body through the skin

transdermal patch *n* a medicated patch applied to the skin. Use: controlled release of medicine into the body.

transduce /tranz dyoōss/ (**-duces, -ducing, -duced**) *vt* **1** to change one type of energy into another type **2** to effect the transfer of genetic material from one bacterium to another using a bacteriophage [Mid-20C. Back-formation < TRANSDUCER.]

transducer /tranz dyoōssər/ *n* **1** a device that transforms one type of energy into another, e.g. a microphone, a photoelectric cell, or a car horn **2** a biological entity that converts energy in one form to another, e.g. the rods and cones of the eye or the hair cells of the ear [Early 20C. < Latin *transducere* 'lead across, transfer' (see TRADUCE).]

transduction /tranz dúksh'n/ *n* **1** the transfer of genetic material from one bacterium to another using a bacteriophage **2** the conversion of stimuli detected in receptor cells to electrical impulses that are then transported by the nervous system, as occurs when the ear converts sound waves into nerve impulses —**transductional** *adj*

transect /tran sékt/ *vt* to divide something by running or cutting across it ■ *n* a strip of ground along which ecological measurements, e.g. of the number of organisms, are made at regular intervals [Mid-17C. < TRANS- + INTERSECT.] —**transection** *n*

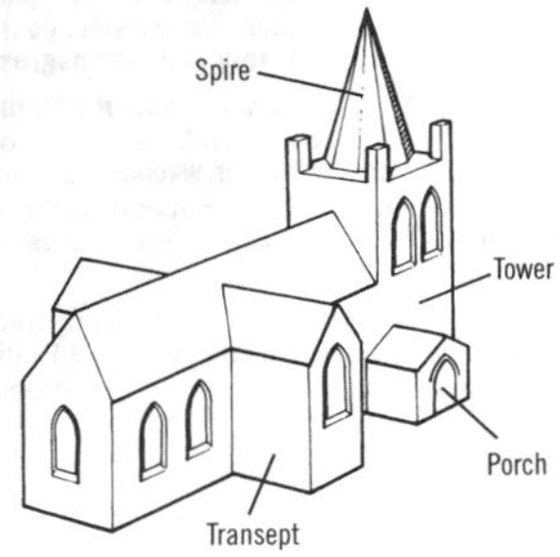
Spire
Tower
Porch
Transept

Transept

transept /trán sept/ *n* **1** the part of a cross-shaped church that runs at right angles to the long central part (**nave**) **2** either of the two arms of a transept [Mid-16C. < modern Latin *transeptum* < Latin *trans-* 'across' + *saeptum* 'enclosure, wall, fence'.] —**transeptal** /tran sépt'l/ *adj*

transeunt /tránzi ənt/, **transient** *adj* that produces effects outside the mind

trans-fatty acid /tránss fátti-/, **trans-fat** /tránss fat/ *n* an unsaturated fat formed during the hydrogenation of vegetable oils to produce margarine

transfection /transs féksh'n/ *n* the infection of a cell with viral DNA leading to production of the virus in the cell [Mid-20C. < TRANS- + INFECTION.] —**transfection** *v*

transfer *v* /transs fúr/ (**-fers, -ferring, -ferred**) **1** *vti* **MOVE FROM ONE PLACE TO ANOTHER** to move from one place to another, or cause somebody or something to do so **2** *vti* **PASS FROM ONE PERSON TO ANOTHER** to pass from one person, group, or organization to another, or cause something to be passed from one person, group, or organization to another ○ *not clear when power will transfer to the new government* **3** *vti* **START WORKING ELSEWHERE** to employ somebody, or begin employment, at a different job or in a different place while working for the same company ○ *transfer to the Chicago branch* **4** *vti* **START PLAYING FOR DIFFERENT CLUB** to sign, or sign somebody, for a different sports club, especially in professional football **5** *vti* **CHANGE VEHICLES** to change from one vehicle or method of transport to another, or cause somebody to do this **6** *vt* **GIVE OWNERSHIP OF** to pass ownership rights in something to somebody else ○ *transfer a deed* **7** *vt* **PUT IMAGE ON ANOTHER SURFACE** to copy a design or image from a piece of paper onto a different material **8** *vti* **CHANGE SCHOOLS OR SUBJECTS** to move from one school or university to another, or change from one course to another ■ *n* /tránss fur/ **1 CHANGE OF PLACE** the conveying of somebody or something from one place, e.g. one department of an organization, to another **2 DESIGN APPLIED TO SURFACE** an image on a piece of film or paper that is specially designed to be lifted off by heat or pressure and applied permanently to the surface of a material **3 SOMEBODY TRANSFERRED** a person who is transferred, e.g. a football player moving from one team to another **4 CONVEYANCE** the passing of rights or property from one person to another, or a document that conveys rights or property between persons **5 RECORDING OF SALE** the recording of a change of ownership of shares or bonds in the books of the issuer **6** *US* **TICKET ALLOWING PASSENGER TO TRANSFER** a ticket that allows a passenger to change from one vehicle to another on a journey, or the place where this is done [14C. < Latin *transferre* 'carry across' < *ferre* 'carry'.] —**transferral** *n* —**transferee** /tránss fur reé/ *n*

transferable /transs fúrəb'l/, **transferrable** *adj* able to be transferred, especially to somebody else's ownership —**transferability** /transs fúrə bílləti/ *n*

transferable vote *n* a vote that will be given to a voter's second choice if his or her first choice candidate is eliminated from the ballot

transferase /tránssfə rayz, -rayss/ *n* any enzyme that catalyses the transfer of a chemical group from one molecule to another

transfer characteristic *n* a graphic illustration of the relationship between the input and output of an electronic system

~~transfered~~ incorrect spelling of **transferred**

transference /tránssfərənss/ *n* **1 ACT OF TRANSFERRING** the transferring of something from one place or person to another **2 PROCESS OF BEING TRANSFERRED** the change from one person or place to another that happens when something is transferred **3 REDIRECTION OF FEELING** the process in psychoanalysis or other psychotherapy whereby somebody unconsciously redirects feelings, fears, or emotions onto a new object, often the analyst or therapist —**transferential** /tránssfə rénsh'l/ *adj*

transfer factor *n* a polypeptide that is produced by white blood cells and can transfer immunity from one cell to another or from one person to another

transfer fee *n* a fee that is paid for a professional footballer or rugby player who is transferred from one club to another before his or her contract has expired

transfer list *n* a list of footballers who are available to be transferred

transferor /transs fúrər/, **transferrer** *n* a person who transfers a title, right, or property to somebody else

transfer payment *n* an item of personal income that comes from the state or a financial institution and is not included in calculating the national income

transferrable *adj* = **transferable**

transferrer *n* = **transferor**

transferrin /transs férrin/ *n* a serum protein that transports iron to bone marrow for the production of red blood cells [Mid-20C. < TRANS- + Latin *ferrum* 'iron'.]

transfer RNA *n* RNA that attaches amino acids to protein chains being made at ribosomes

transfiguration /transs figgə ráysh'n/ *n* **1** a dramatic change in appearance, especially one that glorifies or exalts somebody **2** the transfiguring of somebody or something, or the changed state that results

Transfiguration *n* **1** the radiant appearance of Jesus Christ on a mountaintop before three of his disciples, as recorded in the Bible **2** a Christian festival marking the Transfiguration of Jesus Christ. Date: 6 August or, in the Eastern Orthodox Church, 19 August.

transfigure /transs fíggər/ (**-ures, -uring, -ured**) *vt* to transform the appearance of somebody or something, revealing great beauty, spirituality, or magnificence [14C. < Latin *transfigurare* 'change the shape of' < *figura* 'shape' (see FIGURE).] —**transfigurement** *n*

transfinite /transs fí nīt/ *adj* describes a mathematical entity such as a number, group, or quantity that extends beyond infinity [Early 20C. < German *transfinit* < Latin *trans-* 'across, over' + *finitus* 'finite, limited'.]

transfinite number *n* a system of cardinal and ordinal numbers, used in the comparison of infinite sets, to which several types of infinity can be assigned concurrently

transfix /transs fíks/ *vt* **1 PIERCE THROUGH** to pierce somebody or something through with a weapon or other sharp object **2 MAKE SOMEBODY IMMOBILE WITH SHOCK** to shock or terrify somebody so much as to induce a momentary inability to move **3 CUT COMPLETELY THROUGH LIMB** to cut through a part of the body completely, e.g. when amputating a limb [Late 16C. Directly or via Old French *transfixer* < Latin *transfix-*, past participle of *transfigere* 'pierce, run through' < *figere* 'to fix'.] —**transfixion** *n*

transform[1] /transs fáwrm/ *v* **1** *vt* **CHANGE SOMETHING DRAMATICALLY** to change people or things completely, especially improving their appearance or usefulness **2** *vi* **UNDERGO TOTAL CHANGE** to change completely for the better **3** *vt* **CONVERT SOMETHING TO DIFFERENT ENERGY** to convert one form of energy to another **4** *vt* **CHANGE ELECTRICAL CURRENT BY TRANSFORMER** to increase or decrease current or voltage by means of a transformer **5** *vt* **CHANGE MATHEMATICAL EXPRESSION BY OPERATOR** to change the form of a mathematical expression in keeping with a mathematical rule, especially by the substitution of variables or the change of coordinates **6** *vt* **CHANGE CONSTRUCTION BY LINGUISTIC TRANSFORMATION** to apply transformational rules to a linguistic construction [14C. Directly or via French *transformer* < Latin *transformare* 'form across' < *formare* < *forma* 'mould, shape'.] —**transformable** *adj* —**transformative** *adj*

SYNONYMS See ***change***.

transform[2] /tránss fawrm/ *n* **1** LING = **transformation** *n.* 8 **2** a process or rule by which one mathematical entity such as a line or expression can be derived from another

transformation /tránsfər máysh'n/ *n* **1 COMPLETE CHANGE** a complete change, usually into something with an improved appearance or usefulness **2 TRANSFORMING** the act or process of transforming somebody or something **3 SUBSTITUTION OF VARIABLES** the mathematical conversion of an expression, equation, or function into another equivalent entity, e.g. by the substitution of one set of variables with another **4 CELL MODIFICATION** the conversion of a normal cell into a malignant cell brought about by the action of a carcinogen or virus **5 CHANGE IN POSITION OF AXIS** a change in the position or direction of the axes of a mathematical coordinate system without changing their relative angles **6 CHANGE IN ATOMIC NUCLEUS** the change of one type of atom to another, resulting from a nuclear reaction **7 STAGE IN GRAMMATICAL CONVERSION** in transformational grammar, the process of converting one linguistic construction or structure to another, following the rules that convert deep structure to surface structure **8 STAGE IN TRANSFORMATIONAL PROCESS** in transformational grammar, a construction or structure generated by using the rules that convert deep structure into surface structure **9 SUDDEN SET CHANGE** a sudden changing of a stage set that takes place in sight of the audience **10 GENETIC CHANGE** a permanent change in the genetic make-up of a cell when it acquires foreign DNA —**transformational** *adj* —**transformationally** *adv*

USAGE transformation, transmigration, or **transmutation?** ***Transformation*** means 'a complete change from one thing or state to another, often for the better' (*a complete transformation of the dingy attic into a sunny loft*). ***Transmutation*** is 'a change, or the process of changing, from one form, substance, nature, or state into another' (*the transmutation of society from industrial to postindustrial; the transmutation of base metals into gold by alchemy*). It is rather close in meaning to ***transformation***. ***Transmigration*** has two senses not shared by ***transformation*** and ***transmutation***: 'movement from one place to another' (*a huge transmigration of geese from Canada to Florida*), and 'in some religions, the supposed passage of a decedent's soul into another body at or after death' (*transmigration of the soul*). Problems occur when people use ***transmigration*** when either ***transformation*** or ***transmutation*** is the correct choice: *an obvious transformation/transmutation* [not *transmigration*] *in attitude from liberal to conservative.*

---

transformational grammar *n* grammar that is based on the theory that language has a deep structure and that there are rules that transform the deep structure into the surface structure

transformational rule /tránsfər máysh'nəl-/ *n* **1** in transformational grammar, a rule that generates one stage from another in the conversion of deep structure into surface structure **2** in logic, a rule for deriving theorems from axioms

transformer /tránss fáwrmər/ *n* **1** a device that transfers electrical energy from one alternating circuit to another with a change in voltage, current, phase, or impedance **2** a person who or thing that effects a transformation

transfuse /tránss fyo͞oz/ (**-fuses, -fusing, -fused**) *vt* **1 SPREAD THROUGHOUT** to spread throughout something and affect every part of it **2 TRANSFER SOMETHING BY POURING** to pour something from one container into another (*formal or technical*) **3 GIVE BLOOD TO** to administer blood obtained from one person into the bloodstream of another person **4 PUT FLUID INTO SOMEBODY'S BLOODSTREAM** to administer a fluid such as saline or plasma into somebody's bloodstream [Early 15C. < Latin *transfus-*, past participle of *transfundere* 'decant, transfer' < *fundere* 'pour'.] —**transfusable** *adj* —**transfuser** *n* —**transfusive** *adj*

transfusion /tránss fyo͞ozh'n/ *n* **1** the act or process of transfusing something **2** the transfer of whole blood, blood components, or bone marrow from a healthy donor into the bloodstream of somebody who has lost blood or who has a blood disorder

transgene /tránss jeen/ *n* a gene transferred from one organism to another

transgenic /tranz jénnik/ *adj* **1** describes an animal or plant that contains genes from a different species, transferred using genetic engineering techniques **2** describes the technique of transferring genetic material from one organism into the DNA of another —**transgenically** *adv*

transgress /tranz gréss/ *v* **1** *vi* **DO WRONG** to commit a crime or do wrong by disobeying a law, command, or moral code ○ *He transgressed against the organization's code of conduct.* **2** *vt* **BREAK LAW** to break a law, rule, or moral code ○ *transgress the law* **3** *vt* **OVERSTEP PROPER LIMIT** to go beyond a limit, usually in a blameworthy way ○ *She'd transgressed the bounds of civil behaviour.* [15C. Directly or via French *transgresser* < Latin *transgress-*, past participle of *transgredi* 'step across, go over' < *gradi* 'step, go'.] —**transgressive** *adj* —**transgressively** *adv* —**transgressor** *n*

transgression /tranz grésh'n/ *n* **1 ACTION VIOLATING LAW OR CODE** a crime or any act that violates a law, command, or moral code **2 COMMISSION OF WRONGS** the committing of acts that violate a law, command, or moral code **3 OVERSTEPPING A LIMIT** an act or the process of overstepping a limit

transgressive fiction *n* a literary genre traceable to such writers as the Marquis de Sade and William Burroughs, characterized by graphic exploration of taboo topics

tranship *vti* TRANSP = **transship**

transhumance /tránss hyo͞omənss/ *n* the practice of moving livestock between different grazing lands according to season, especially up to mountain pastures in summer and back down into the valleys in winter [Early 20C. < French, < *transhumer* 'go across ground' < Latin *humus* 'ground'.] —**transhumant** *adj*

transient /tránzi ənt/ *adj* **1 SHORT IN DURATION** lasting for only a short time and quickly coming to an end, disappearing, or changing ○ *a transient emotion* ○ *transient sunlight on an otherwise cloudy day* **2 NOT PERMANENTLY SETTLED** staying in a place for only a short period of time ○ *transient workers* **3** PHILOS = **transeunt** ■ *n* **1 SOMEBODY STAYING BRIEFLY** a person who stays in a place only briefly, e.g. a migrant labourer or hotel guest **2 BRIEF DISTURBANCE IN ELECTRICAL CIRCUIT** an oscillation or brief disturbance in a system, e.g. a sudden pulse of current or voltage in an electrical circuit [Late 16C. Alteration of Latin *transiens* (stem *transeunt-*), present participle of *transire* 'pass away, go across' < *ire* 'go'.] —**transience** *n* —**transiency** *n* —**transiently** *adv*

transilluminate /tránzi lo͞omi nayt/ (**-nates, -nating, -nated**) *vt* to shine a bright light through a body organ or cavity to detect disease or other abnormality —**transillumination** /tránzi loomi náysh'n/ *n* —**transilluminator** *n*

transistor /tran zístər/ *n* **1** a small low-powered solid-state electronic device consisting of a semiconductor and at least three electrodes, used as an amplifier and rectifier and frequently incorporated into integrated circuit chips **2** a transistor radio [Mid-20C. Blend of TRANSFER + RESISTOR.]

transistorize /tran zístə rīz/ (**-izes, -izing, -ized**), **transistorise** (**-ises, -ising, -ised**) *vt* to equip a device or circuit with transistors

transistor radio *n* a small portable radio using transistors in its circuits

transit /tránzit/ *n* **1 TRAVELLING** the act of travelling or being transported through or across an area, over a distance, or from one place to another ○ *a transit permit* **2 ROUTE** a particular route or method used in travelling through or across an area ○ *overland transit* **3** *US* **PUBLIC TRANSPORT** the transportation of passengers by means of a local public transport system ○ *travelled by rapid transit* **4 PLANET'S CROSSING OF SUN** the movement of Venus or Mercury across the face of the Sun, or of a moon or its shadow across the face of a planet, as seen from Earth **5 PASSAGE OF STAR ACROSS MERIDIAN** the apparent movement of a star or planet across the meridian from which it is being observed, caused by the Earth's rotation **6 PLANET'S CROSSING OF ZODIAC** the passing of a planet across a particular point on the zodiac **7 TRANSITION** a transition or passing, e.g. from life to a supposed spiritual existence after death **8** *US* CIV ENG = **transit theodolite** ■ *v* **1** *vti* **PASS THROUGH** to pass through or over something ○ *They transited the area on foot.* **2** *vti* **MAKE A TRANSIT** to make a transit across the face of the Sun or a planet, or across a meridian **3** *vt* **REVERSE DIRECTION OF SURVEYING TELESCOPE** to rotate the telescope of a surveying instrument horizontally through 180°, thus reversing its direction [15C. < Latin *transitus* 'passage' < *transire* 'go across' < *ire* 'go'.] —**transitable** *adj* ◇ **in transit** in the process of travelling or being transported from one place to another

transit camp *n* a camp set up to accommodate people such as refugees, soldiers, or prisoners of war temporarily, until they can be sent on to a final destination

transit circle *n* an astronomical telescope that moves in a north-south plane enabling it to be used to determine the exact time a star, planet, or other astronomical object passes most nearly overhead

transit instrument *n* a telescopic instrument that can move only in the plane of a meridian, used to determine the exact time a star, planet, or other astronomical object crosses that meridian

transition /tran zísh'n/ *n* **1 PROCESS OF CHANGE** a process or period in which something undergoes a change and passes from one state, stage, form, or activity to another **2 MUSICAL PASSAGE** a passage connecting two sections of a musical composition **3 CHANGE OF KEY** a progression from one key to another in a piece of music **4 LINKING WORD OR PHRASE** a word, phrase, or passage that links one subject or idea to another in speech or writing **5 CHANGE BETWEEN PHASES** a change between phases such as solid to liquid or liquid to gas **6 ARCHITECTURAL STYLE BETWEEN ROMANESQUE AND GOTHIC** a style of architecture in many buildings dating from the 12th century in W Europe, in which elements of the Romanesque and Gothic styles are combined **7 CHANGE IN AN ATOMIC NUCLEUS** a change in the energy level or state of an atomic nucleus in which a single quantum of electromagnetic radiation is either lost or gained [15C. < Latin *transition-* < *transire* (see TRANSIT).] —**transitional** *adj* —**transitionally** *adv*

transition element, transition metal *n* any of the metallic elements such as copper and gold that have an incomplete penultimate electron shell, variable valencies, and typically form coloured compounds

transition point *n* **1** the point at which laminar flow in a moving fluid changes to turbulent flow **2** PHYS = **transition temperature**

transition temperature *n* the temperature at which a substance loses or gains a particular property, especially superconductivity

transitive /tránssətiv/ *adj* **1** needing or usually taking a direct object ○ *a transitive verb* **2** in logic or maths, describes a given relation between terms such that if it exists between 'a' and 'b' and between 'b' and 'c' then it also exists between 'a' and 'c' —**transitively** *adv* —**transitiveness** *n* —**transitivity** /tránssə tívvəti/ *n*

LANGUAGE NOTE ***transitivity*** A common way of classifying verbs is by what, if anything, follows them. Some verbs can have no object (a noun or noun phrase) after them and they cannot form passives. They are ***intransitive*** verbs: *You'd better go. He snores.* In this dictionary, such verbs are indicated by the letters *vi*. Some verbs are followed by an object, which is the one acted upon by the verb. They are ***transitive*** verbs: *Do you love me? Put your books away.* In this dictionary, such verbs are indicated by the letters *vt*. A few transitive verbs can have two objects: a direct object, which is the one acted directly upon by the verb; and an indirect object, which is the one affected by the action of the verb: *I gave him $100* (the direct object is $100, the indirect object is him).

Many verbs are both transitive and intransitive, depending on how they are used and what they mean. In *The dealer sells used cars*, the verb *sell* is ***transitive***, but in *This used car won't sell*, the same verb is intransitive. In this dictionary, such verbs are indicated by the letters *vti*. A small number of intransitive verbs are followed by a complement, which relates back to the subject. The verb describes the relationship between the subject and the complement (which can be a noun or an adjective). Such verbs are known as *linking verbs* or *copulas*: *I* **am** *Fred. I* **feel** *sick.* Others are *grow, act, look, smell, taste* and *sound*. A few transitive and intransitive verbs can be followed by complements, which are added words that complete the predicates. There are two kinds of complement – objective and subjective. An objective complement, used with transitive verbs, is a noun, adjective, or pronoun that qualifies the direct object of the verb: *I find her books fascinating* (the object is *her books*, the complement is *fascinating*). *The team elected Sarah captain* (the object is *Sarah*, the complement is *captain*). A subjective complement, used with intransitive verbs, relates to and further describes the subject of the verb, as in *She has fallen ill*, where *she* is the subject, *has fallen* is the intransitive verb, and *ill* is the subjective complement. A few verbs are placed in front of other verbs to indicate their tense, or to convey concepts such as possibility or conditionality. They are called *auxiliary* verbs: *You* **have** *won. She* **may** *relent.*

LANGUAGE NOTE See ***auxiliary verb***.

---

transit lounge *n* a waiting room at an international airport used mainly by passengers transferring from one flight to another without presenting themselves to customs or immigration officials

transitory /tránssətəri/ *adj* not permanent or lasting, but existing only for a short time ○ *a transitory infatuation* —**transitorily** *adv* —**transitoriness** *n*

transit passenger *n* a passenger who is only at an airport to change flights

transit theodolite *n* a surveying instrument surmounted by a telescope that can be rotated completely around its horizontal axis, used for measuring vertical and horizontal angles. US term **transit** *n.* 8

Transkei /tránss kī/ former autonomous Black African homeland in E South Africa

transl. *abbr* 1 translated 2 translation 3 translator

translate /transs láyt/ (**-lates, -lating, -lated**) *v* 1 *vti* TURN WORDS INTO DIFFERENT LANGUAGE to give an equivalent in another language for a particular word or phrase, or reproduce a written or spoken text in a different language while retaining the original meaning ○ *Can you translate that phrase?* 2 *vi* BE CAPABLE OF BEING TRANSLATED to be capable of being translated, or have an equivalent in another language ○ *The idiom doesn't translate well.* 3 *vt* CONVERT CODE to convert data to a different form following an algorithm ○ *translate the program into machine code* 4 *vt* SAY SOMETHING IN UNDERSTANDABLE TERMS to say or explain something in terms that are easier to understand ○ *Which means translated 'We don't know what happened to your car'.* 5 *vt* INTERPRET MEANING to explain the meaning of something not expressed in words, e.g. an action, gesture, or look ○ *I translated his silence as approval.* 6 *vti* CHANGE FORM OF to change something, or be changed, from one form or effect into another ○ *'Microchips controlled by software now translate the flick of a pilot's wrist into the movement of a wing flap'* (Evan I. Schwartz, *Trust Me, I'm Your Software,* (*Discover Magazine; May 1996*) 7 *vt* MOVE to move or carry somebody or something from one place to another, usually involving a complete change of condition or scene ○ *She was translated from her small country home to a high-rise city apartment.* 8 *vt* TRANSFER CLERGY to transfer a member of the clergy to another office, especially to transfer a bishop to another see 9 *vt* MOVE SAINT'S REMAINS to move the remains or relics of a saint from one place to another 10 *vt* CONVEY SOMEBODY TO HEAVEN to convey somebody to heaven, especially in a way that is believed not to involve death 11 *vt* DECIPHER GENETIC INSTRUCTIONS FOR MAKING PROTEIN to decipher the genetic message carried by a molecule of messenger RNA and assemble the amino acids of a protein chain according to the instructions 12 *vt* MOVE BODY SIDEWAYS IN STRAIGHT LINE to move a body sideways through space in a direct straight line without rotation [14C. < Latin *translatus,* used as past participle of *transferre* 'carry across' < *ferre* 'carry'.] —**translatability** /transs láytə bílləti/ *n* —**translatable** *adj*

translation /transs láysh'n/ *n* 1 VERSION IN ANOTHER LANGUAGE a word, phrase, or text in another language that has a meaning equivalent to that of the original 2 EXPRESSING OF SOMETHING IN A DIFFERENT LANGUAGE the rendering of something written or spoken in one language in words of a different language ○ *She read the novel in translation.* 3 CHANGE OR TRANSFERENCE a change in form or state, or transference to a different place, office, or sphere 4 PROCESS DETERMINING AMINO ACID SEQUENCE the process by which information in messenger RNA directs the sequence of amino acids assembled by a ribosome during protein synthesis 5 MOTION IN STRAIGHT LINE the movement of a body in a straight line so that every point on the body follows a parallel path and no rotation takes place —**translational** *adj*

⚡**translator** /transs láytər/ *n* 1 SOMEBODY WHO TRANSLATES somebody or something that translates, in writing or speech, from one language into another 2 TRANSMITTER THAT ALTERS SIGNAL FREQUENCY a radio transmitter that receives a signal on one frequency and retransmits it on another 3 CONVERTING COMPUTER PROGRAM a computer program that converts other programs from one computer language into another —**translatorial** /tránslə táwri əl/ *adj*

transliterate /transs líttə rayt, tranz-/ (**-ates, -ating, -ated**) *vt* to represent letters or words written in one alphabet using the corresponding letters of another [Mid-19C. < TRANS- + Latin *littera* 'letter of the alphabet'.] —**transliteration** /transs líttə ráysh'n, tranz-/ *n* —**transliterator** *n*

translocate /tráns lō káyt/ (**-cates, -cating, -cated**) *vt* to move somebody or something from one place or position to another

translocation /tráns lō káysh'n/ *n* 1 MOVEMENT FROM ONE PLACE TO ANOTHER movement, or the act of moving something or somebody, from one place or position to another 2 MOVEMENT OF FOOD IN PLANTS the movement of soluble materials within a plant 3 TRANSFER OF PART OF CHROMOSOME the transfer of part of a chromosome to a new position on the same or on a different chromosome with resultant rearrangement of the genes

translucent /transs lóoss'nt/ *adj* 1 allowing light to pass through, but only diffusely, so that objects on the other side cannot be clearly distinguished ○ *a translucent membrane* 2 having a glowing appearance, as if light were coming through ○ *translucent skin* [15C. < Latin *translucent-,* present participle of *translucere* 'shine through' < *lucere* 'shine' (see LUCID).] —**translucence** *n* —**translucency** *n* —**translucently** *adv*

translunar /transs lóonər/, **translunary** /-lóonəri/ *adj* situated or coming from beyond the Moon or its orbit around the Earth

transmarine /tránzmə réen/ *adj* 1 involving crossing a sea or ocean 2 situated or coming from across a sea or ocean [Late 16C. < Latin *transmarinus* < *marinus* (see MARINE).]

transmigrate /tránz mī gráyt/ (**-grates, -grating, -grated**) *vi* 1 to move from one place or country to another 2 in some religions, to pass into another body at or after death (*refers to the soul*) [15C. < Latin *transmigrat-,* past participle of *transmigrare* < *migrare* 'migrate'.] —**transmigrant** *adj, n* —**transmigrative** /-mígrətiv/ *adj* —**transmigrator** *n* —**transmigratory** /tranz mígrətəri/ *adj*

transmigration /tránz mī gráysh'n/ *n* 1 movement by a person or group from one place or country to another 2 in some religions, the supposed passage of the dead person's soul into another body at or after death [Directly or via French < late Latin *transmigration-* < Latin *transmigrare* (see TRANSMIGRATE)] —**transmigrational** *adj*

USAGE See ***transformation.***

transmissible spongiform encephalopathy *n* full form of **TSE**

transmission /tranz mísh'n/ *n* 1 ACT OF TRANSMITTING the act or process of transmitting something, especially radio signals, radio or television broadcasts, data, or a disease 2 SOMETHING TRANSMITTED something transmitted, e.g. a radio or signal 3 RADIO OR TV BROADCAST a radio or television broadcast 4 MECHANISM TRANSFERRING POWER TO WHEELS the mechanical system, including gears and shafts, by which power is transmitted from the engine of a motor vehicle to the drive wheels 5 *US* AUTOMOT = **gearbox** *n.* 2 6 ABILITY TO LET RADIATION THROUGH the ability of a material to let incoming radiation pass completely through it [Early 17C. Directly or via French < Latin *transmission-* < *mission-* 'a letting go, release' (see MISSION).] —**transmissibility** /tranz míssə bílləti/ *n* —**transmissible** *adj* —**transmissive** *adj* —**transmissively** *adv* —**transmissiveness** *n*

transmission line *n* a conductor such as a coaxial cable that carries electricity or other electromagnetic waves, usually over long distances

transmissometer /tránzmi sómmitər/ *n* an instrument used to measure the ability of a substance or body to transmit light [Mid-20C. < TRANSMISSION.]

transmit /tranz mít/ (**-mits, -mitting, -mitted**) *v* 1 *vt* SEND to send something, pass something on, or cause something to spread, from one person, thing, or place to another ○ *The disease is transmitted by droplet infection.* 2 *vt* COMMUNICATE INFORMATION to communicate a message, information, or news ○ *Data was quickly transmitted.* 3 *vti* SEND A SIGNAL to send a signal by radio waves, satellite, or wire 4 *vti* BROADCAST A PROGRAMME to broadcast a radio or television programme 5 *vt* MAKE RADIATION PASS THROUGH to make heat, sound, light, or other radiation pass or spread through space or a medium 6 *vt* ALLOW RADIATION THROUGH to allow heat, sound, or light or other radiation to pass through 7 *vt* TRANSFER POWER to transfer power, force, or movement from one part of a mechanism to another [14C. < Latin *transmittere* 'send across' < *mittere* 'send'.] —**transmittable** *adj* —**transmittal** *n* —**transmittible** *adj*

transmittance /tranz mítt'nss/ *n* 1 the act or process of transmitting something 2 the ability of a material to let incoming radiation pass completely through it, measured as the ratio of incident radiation to transmitted radiation

transmitter /tranz míttər/ *n* 1 AGENT OR MEANS OF TRANSMISSION somebody or something that transmits something 2 PART OF BROADCASTING EQUIPMENT a piece of broadcasting equipment that generates a radio-frequency wave, modulates it so that it carries a meaningful signal, and sends it out from an antenna 3 TELEPHONE PART the part of a telephone that converts sound waves to electrical impulses

transmogrify /tranz móggri fī/ (**-fies, -fying, -fied**) *vt* to change the appearance or form of something, especially in a grotesque or bizarre way [Mid-17C. < ?] —**transmogrification** /tranz móggrifi káysh'n/ *n*

transmontane *adj, n* GEOG = **tramontane** *adj.* 1, **tramontane** *adj.* 2, **tramontane** *n.* 2

transmundane /tranz mún dayn/ *adj* not belonging to this material world and its concerns, or extending beyond them (*literary*)

transmute /tranz myóot/ (**-mutes, -muting, -muted**) *vti* 1 CHANGE to change something, or be changed, from one form, nature, substance, or state to another 2 CHANGE FROM ONE ELEMENT TO ANOTHER to change one chemical element into another through disintegration or nuclear bombardment, or undergo a change of this kind 3 CONVERT BASE METAL TO GOLD in alchemy, to convert a base metal into gold or silver, or be converted in this way [14C. < Latin *transmutare* 'change thoroughly' < *mutare* 'to change'.] —**transmutability** /tranz myóotə bílləti/ *n* —**transmutable** *adj* —**transmutably** *adv* —**transmutation** /tránzmyoo táysh'n/ *n* —**transmutational** *adj* —**transmutative** *adj* —**transmuter** *n*

SYNONYMS See ***change.***

transnational /tranz násh'nəl/ *adj* not confined to a single nation or state, but including, extending over, or operating within several of them —**transnationally** *adv*

transoceanic /tránz ōshi ánnik/ *adj* 1 involving crossing an ocean 2 situated or coming from across an ocean

transom /tránssəm/ *n* 1 STRUCTURAL BEAM ABOVE A WINDOW a horizontal beam or stone above a window that supports the structure above 2 CROSSPIECE ABOVE DOOR a crosspiece over a door or between the top of a door and a window above 3 CROSSBAR THAT DIVIDES WINDOW a crossbar of wood or stone that divides a window horizontally 4 *US* ARCHIT = **fanlight** *n.* 2 5 BEAM FOR STRENGTHENING STERN a transverse beam for strengthening the stern of a ship 6 PLANKING AT SHIP'S STERN the planking forming a flat surface across the stern of a ship 7 HORIZONTAL BEAM OF CROSS OR GALLOWS the horizontal beam of a cross or gallows [14C. Probably alteration of Latin *transtrum* 'crossbeam'.] —**transomed** *adj*

transonic /tran sónnik/ *adj* relating to speeds close to the speed of sound or conditions encountered when travelling at those speeds [Mid-20C. < TRANS- + SONIC after SUPERSONIC and ULTRASONIC.]

transonic barrier *n* the sound barrier (*technical*)

transp. *abbr* 1 transport 2 transportation

transpacific /tránzpə síffik/ *adj* 1 involving crossing the Pacific Ocean 2 situated or coming from across the Pacific Ocean

transpadane /tránzpə dayn/ *adj* from or on the northern side of the River Po in N Italy [Early 17C. < Latin *transpadanus* < *padanus* 'of the Padus (River Po)'.]

transparency /transs párrənsi/ (*plural* **-cies**) *n* 1 the quality or state of being transparent 2 a positive photographic image on a transparent material, especially film or a slide, that can be viewed when light is shone through it [Late 16C. < medieval Latin *transparentia* < *transparent-* (see TRANSPARENT).]

transparent /transs párrənt/ *adj* 1 EASILY SEEN THROUGH allowing light to pass through with little or no interruption or distortion so that objects on the other side can be clearly seen ○ *transparent plastic* 2 FINE ENOUGH TO SEE THROUGH thin or fine enough in texture to see through ○ *transparent fabric* 3 OBVIOUS AND EASY TO RECOGNIZE clearly recognizable as what it, he, or she really is ○ *a transparent motive* 4 FRANK completely open and frank about things ○ *was grateful for the transparent honesty of the reply* 5 LETTING RADIATION THROUGH allowing electromagnetic radiation of specified wavelengths to pass through [15C. Directly or via French < medieval Latin *transparent-,* present participle of *transparere* 'shine through' < Latin *parere* 'appear'.] —**transparently** *adv* —**transparentness** *n*

transparent context *n* in logic, an expression in which the truth-value is not changed when any term is replaced by another with the same reference

transpierce /transs péerss/ (**-pierces, -piercing, -pierced**) *vt* to pierce through something (*archaic*)

transpire /tran spír/ (**-spires, -spiring, -spired**) *v* **1** *vt* **COME TO LIGHT** to become known or be disclosed ○ *It later transpired that they had been furious at what had happened.* **2** ⚠ *vi* **HAPPEN** to take place ○ *What transpired after they left remains a secret.* **3** *vti* **GIVE OFF VAPOUR THROUGH SKIN** to give off water vapour through the pores of the skin **4** *vti* **LOSE WATER VAPOUR** to lose water vapour from a plant's surface, especially through minute surface pores (**stomata**) [15C. Directly or via French *transpirer* < medieval Latin *transpirare* 'breathe through' < Latin *spirare* 'breathe'.] —**transpirable** *adj* —**transpiration** /tránsspi ráysh'n/ *n* —**transpiratory** *adj*

USAGE The use of ***transpire*** to mean 'happen', as in the sentence *Tell me what transpired at the meeting*, is sometimes criticized, although it has been in common use for several centuries and conveys something of the sense inherent in its uncontroversial meaning 'become known or be disclosed': *It transpired that the police had known about the plan all along.*

transplant *v* /transs pla̋ant/ **1** *vt* **RELOCATE PLANT** to remove a plant from the place where it is growing and replant it somewhere else **2** *vt* **MOVE TO ANOTHER PLACE** to move somebody or something to another place or position **3** *vt* **TRANSFER BODY ORGAN** to transfer an organ or tissue from one body to another, or from one place in somebody's body to another **4** *vi* **BE CAPABLE OF BEING MOVED** to be capable of being transplanted ○ *Poppies do not transplant well.* ■ *n* /tránss plaant/ **1 SURGICAL PROCEDURE** a surgical operation or procedure to transplant an organ or tissue **2 TRANSPLANTED ORGAN OR TISSUE** an organ or tissue that has been transplanted **3 TRANSPLANTED PLANT** a plant that has been transplanted [15C. Directly or via French *transplanter* < late Latin *transplantare* 'plant across' < *plantare* 'to plant'.] —**transplantable** *adj* —**transplantation** /tránss plaan táysh'n/ *n* —**transplanter** *n*

transpolar /tranz pólər/ *adj* crossing or extending across either of the polar regions

transponder /tran spóndər/, **transpondor** *n* **1** a radio or radar transceiver that automatically transmits a signal of its own when it receives a predetermined signal from elsewhere, used especially for locating and identifying objects **2** a receiving and transmitting device in a communication or broadcast satellite that relays the signals it receives back to Earth [Mid-20C. < TRANSMIT + RESPOND.]

transpontine /tranz pón tīn/ *adj* on or from the other side of a bridge (*dated*) [Mid-19C. < TRANS- + Latin *pont-*, stem of *pons* 'bridge'.]

transport *vt* /transs páwrt/ **1 CARRY** to carry people or goods from one place to another, usually in a vehicle **2 MAKE SOMEBODY IMAGINE BEING ELSEWHERE** to take somebody on a mental or imaginative journey to another place or time ○ *The sounds of the game transported him back to his youth.* **3 AFFECT SOMEBODY WITH STRONG EMOTION** to put somebody in a state of intense or uncontrollable emotion, especially joy ○ *She was transported with joy.* **4 SEND SOMEBODY TO PENAL COLONY** to exile somebody to a penal colony ■ *n* /tráns pawrt/ **1 CONVEYANCE OF SOMEBODY OR SOMETHING** the act or business of carrying people or goods from one place to another, especially in vehicles. US term **transportation** *n.* 1 **2 MEANS OF TRAVELLING** a means of travelling, or of carrying people or goods, from one place to another ○ *It'll be quicker by public transport.* US term **transportation** *n.* 2 **3 A CRAFT CARRYING PEOPLE OR FREIGHT** a ship or aircraft for carrying passengers, especially military personnel, or freight **4 EXPERIENCE OR DISPLAY OF INTENSE EMOTION** an experience or display of intense and uncontrollable emotion, especially joy (*often plural*) ○ *in transports of delight* **5 SOMEBODY SENT TO PENAL COLONY** somebody exiled to a penal colony [14C. Directly or via French *transporter* < Latin *transportare* 'carry across' < *portare* 'carry'.] —**transportability** /tránss pawrtə bílləti/ *n* —**transportable** *adj* —**transportive** *adj*

transportation /tránsspawr táysh'n/ *n* **1** *US* TRANSP = **transport** *n.* 1 **2** *US* TRANSP = **transport** *n.* 2 **3** *US* the fare paid or charge made for travelling in a bus, train, or other public vehicle **4** exile to a penal colony

transport café *n* a roadside café that offers plain and inexpensive meals, used mainly by long-distance lorry drivers. US term **truck stop**

transporter /transs páwrtər/ *n* **1** somebody or something that transports something **2** a large vehicle used to carry heavy loads, often other vehicles

transporter bridge *n* a bridge consisting of a high overarching framework from which a moving platform is suspended on cables

transpose /trans pōz/ *v* (**-poses, -posing, -posed**) **1** *vt* **REVERSE ORDER** to make two things change places or reverse their normal order, e.g. to reverse the order of two letters in a word **2** *vt* **MOVE SOMETHING TO DIFFERENT POSITION** to move something to a different position, especially in a sequence ○ *transposed that section to the end of the essay* **3** *vt* **CHANGE SETTING OF** to take something such as a story, incident, or play out of its usual setting or time and relocate it in another ○ *transposing the action from Shakespeare's time to the present* **4** *vti* **CHANGE MUSIC TO A DIFFERENT KEY** to rewrite or play a musical composition in a key or at a pitch other than the one in which it was originally written or in which it is usually performed **5** *vt* **MOVE TERM IN EQUATION** to transfer a term from one side of an equation to the other, reversing its sign ■ *n* **TYPE OF MATRIX** a matrix created by interchanging the rows and columns of a previously given matrix [14C. < French *transposer*, alteration (by association with *poser* 'to place') of Latin *transponere* < *ponere* 'to place'.] —**transposability** /transs pōzə bílləti/ *n* —**transposable** *adj* —**transposal** *n* —**transposer** *n* —**transpositive** /-pózzətiv/ *adj*

transposing instrument *n* a musical instrument such as a horn or clarinet whose part is written in a different key of the sounds it produces when it plays

transposition /tránsspə zísh'n/ *n* **1 REVERSAL OF ORDER** a reversal or alteration of the positions or order in which things stand **2 RECASTING** a placing of something in a different setting, or its recasting in a different language, style, or medium **3 PUTTING IN DIFFERENT KEY** a rewriting or playing of a piece of music in a key or at a pitch other than the original or usual one **4 TRANSFER OF TERM IN EQUATION** a transfer of a term from one side of an equation to another, reversing the sign —**transpositional** *adj*

transposon /transs pō zon/ *n* a segment of DNA that can move to a new position on the same or another chromosome, often modifying the action of neighbouring genes [Late 20C. < TRANSPOSITION.]

⚡**transputer** /tranz pyóotər/ *n* a powerful microchip with the functions of a microprocessor, having its own memory and the capability of parallel processing

transsexual /tranz sékshoo əl/ *n* **1** a person who has undergone treatment to change his or her anatomical sex **2** a person who identifies himself or herself as a member of the opposite sex —**transsexual** *adj* —**transsexualism** *n*

transship /transs shíp/ (**-ships, -shipping, -shipped**), **tranship** (**-ships, -shipping, -shipped**) *vti* to transfer goods, or be transferred, from one means of transportation to another —**transshipment** *n*

transubstantiate /tránssəb stánshi ayt/ (**-ates, -ating, -ated**) *v* **1** *vi* in Roman Catholic and Eastern Orthodox doctrine, to undergo a change in substance, from bread and wine to the body and blood of Jesus Christ during Communion **2** *vti* to change, or change something, from one substance into another (*formal*) [15C. < medieval Latin *transubstantiat-*, past participle of *transubstantiare* 'change the substance of thoroughly' < Latin *substantia* (see SUBSTANCE).] —**transubstantial** *adj* —**transubstantially** *adv*

transubstantiation /tránssəb stanshi áysh'n/ *n* **1** the Roman Catholic and Eastern Orthodox doctrine that the bread and wine of Communion become, in substance but not appearance, the body and blood of Jesus Christ at consecration. ◊ **consubstantiation** *n.* 1 **2** a process whereby one substance changes into another (*formal*) —**transubstantiationalist** *n*

transudate /tránss yoo dayt/ *n* a fluid that passes through the pores or interstices of a membrane

transude /tran syóod/ (**-sudes, -suding, -suded**) *vi* to pass through pores, interstices, or a membrane, as a fluid such as sweat does [Early 17C. Via French *transsuder* 'sweat through' < Latin *sudare* 'to sweat'.] —**transudation** /trán syoo dáysh'n/ *n* —**transudatory** *adj*

transuranic /tránzyoo ránnik/, **transuranian** /-ráyni ən/, **transuranium** /-ráyni əm/ *adj* having a higher atomic number than uranium

Transvaal /tránz vaal/ former province of South Africa, in the northeastern part of the country

transvalue /tranz vállyoo/ (**-ues, -uing, -ued**) *vt* to re-evaluate something using a different standard, especially one that differs from conventional or accepted standards and results in a very different assessment of the worth of something —**transvaluation** /tránz valyoo áysh'n/ *n* —**transvaluer** *n*

transversal /tranz vúrss'l/ *n* a line that intersects two or more other lines ■ *adj* = **transverse** *adj.* 1, **transverse** *adj.* 2 —**transversally** *adv*

transverse /tranz vúrss/ *adj* **1 CROSSWISE** lying or going crosswise or at right angles to something **2 PASSING THROUGH THE FOCI OF A HYPERBOLA** passing through a hyperbola's foci ■ *n* **CROSSWISE THING** something lying or extending crosswise [14C. < Latin *transversus*, past participle of *transvertere* 'turn across' < *vertere* 'to turn'.] —**transversely** *adv* —**transverseness** *n*

transverse colon *n* the part of the colon that passes from right to left across the upper abdominal cavity just beneath the liver and stomach

transverse flute *n* a flute with the mouth hole on top of the barrel near one end, so that the player blows across the hole while holding the flute in a sideways-on position

transverse process *n* either of the two bony projections on the sides of a vertebra

transverse wave *n* a wave that makes the medium through which it travels vibrate in a direction at right angles to the direction of its travel

transvestite /tranz vés tīt/ *n* a person who adopts the dress and often the behaviour of the opposite sex [Early 20C. < German *Transvestit* 'cross-dresser' < Latin *vestire* 'clothe, dress' (see VEST).] —**transvestism** *n* —**transvestitism** *n*

Transylvania /tránssil váyni ə/ historic region in E Europe that now forms the central and northwestern parts of Romania. Area: 62,000 sq. km/24,000 sq. mi. —**Transylvanian** *adj*

Transylvanian Alps /tránssil váyni ən-/ mountain range in the Carpathian Mountains, extending through south-central Romania. Highest peak: Mount Moldoveanu 2,544 m/8,395 ft.

trap[1] /trap/ *n* **1 SOMETHING DESIGNED TO CATCH ANIMALS** a device designed to catch an animal and kill it or prevent it escaping, e.g. a concealed pit or a mechanical device that springs shut **2 SCHEME TO CATCH SOMEBODY OUT** an ambush, scheme, or trick intended to catch somebody unawares and put the person at a disadvantage or in somebody else's power **3 CONFINING SITUATION** a situation from which it is difficult to escape and in which somebody feels confined, restricted, or in another person's power ○ *wanted to avoid the trap of being typecast in the same roles* **4 SECTION OF DRAINPIPE BLOCKING GAS** a curved section of a drainpipe that holds a quantity of water to act as a barrier to prevent sewer gas from rising up the pipe **5 DEVICE PREVENTING THE PASSAGE OF GAS** any device designed to prevent gas, vapour, or other substances passing through or escaping from something **6** = **trapdoor** **7 MOUTH** the mouth (*informal*) ○ *If the cops ask questions, keep your trap shut.* **8 DEVICE USED IN TRAPSHOOTING** a device that throws clay pigeons into the air for trapshooting **9 GOLF BUNKER** a hazard, especially a bunker, on a golf course **10 STARTING STALL FOR A GREYHOUND** one of the set of stalls from which greyhounds are released at the start of a race **11 CARRIAGE** a light horse-drawn carriage with two wheels ■ **traps** *npl* **PERCUSSION INSTRUMENT** a set of percussion instruments, especially the drum set used in a dance orchestra or jazz band (*informal*) ■ *v* (**traps, trapping, trapped**) **1** *vt* **CATCH SOMETHING IN TRAP** to catch an animal in a trap so that it is killed or unable to escape **2** *vi* **SET TRAPS FOR ANIMALS** to set traps for animals or make a living by catching animals in traps **3** *vt* **HOLD SOMETHING IN A TIGHT GRIP** to catch or hold something in a tight grip or narrow space so that it cannot be moved or is painfully squeezed ○ *I trapped my finger in the door.* **4** *vt* **PLACE SOMEBODY IN A CONFINING SITUATION** to put somebody in a situation from which it is difficult or impossible to escape ○ *They were trapped inside the burning building.* ○ *felt trapped in a dead-end job* **5** *vt* **TAKE SOMEBODY BY SURPRISE** to put somebody at a disadvantage by means of an ambush, surprise, clever plan, or trick ○ *She was trapped into admitting the truth.* **6** *vt* **CONTROL A BALL** to bring a moving ball quickly under control using a part of the body **7** *vt* **CATCH AN OFFENDER** to identify or catch an offender by means of a speed trap or a security device **8** *vt* **PREVENT AIR FROM ESCAPING** to prevent air, gas, heat, or a fluid from escaping **9** *vt* **EQUIP SOMETHING WITH A TRAP** to put a trap into a drainpipe [Old English *træppe* (in *coltetræppe*, plant name), *treppe* 'trap, snare' < Germanic]

trap[2] /trap/ *n* any of various types of dark fine-grained igneous rock, e.g. basalt. US term **traprock** [Late 18C. < Swedish *trapp* < *trappa* 'stair' (from the rock's appearance).]

trap[3] /trap/ *npl* **traps** somebody's personal belongings (*informal*) ■ *vt* (**traps, trapping, trapped**) to provide somebody or something with trappings or adornments ○ *They were all trapped out in the gaudiest of clothes.* [14C. Alteration of French *drap* 'cloth' < late Latin *drappus*.]

Trapani /tra paàni/ seaport in Trapani Province, NW Sicily, Italy. Population: 69,497 (1996).

trapdoor /tráp dawr/ *n* a hatch covering a horizontal or sloping opening in a floor, ceiling, or roof

trapdoor spider *n* a spider that constructs a tubular silk-lined burrow with a hinged lid like a trapdoor. Native to: warm regions. Family: Ctenizidae.

trapeze /trə peéz/ *n* a horizontal bar attached to the ends of two ropes hanging parallel to each other, used for gymnastics or for acrobatics, especially in a circus [Mid-19C. Via French *trapèze* < late Latin *trapezium* (see TRAPEZIUM).]

trapeze artist *n* an acrobat who performs on a trapeze, especially in a circus

trapezia plural of **trapezium**

trapeziform /trə peézi fawrm/ *adj* shaped like a trapezium

trapezii plural of **trapezius**

trapezium /trə peézi əm/ (*plural* **-ums** *or* **-a** /-zi ə/) *n* **1** a quadrilateral that has two parallel sides. US term **trapezoid** *n*. 2 **2** *US* MATH = **trapezoid** *n*. 1 **3** a small bone in the wrist at the base of the thumb [Late 16C. Via late Latin < Greek *trapezion* 'small table' < *trapeza* 'table' < *peza* 'foot'.] —**trapezial** *adj*

trapezius /trə peézi əss/ (*plural* **-uses** *or* **-i**) *n* either of the two large flat triangular muscles that run from the back of the neck and cover each shoulder [Early 18C. < modern Latin, < late Latin *trapezium* (see TRAPEZIUM).]

trapezohedron /trə peézō heédrən/ (*plural* **-drons** *or* **-dra** /-drə/) *n* a form of crystal with faces that are all trapeziums in shape [Early 19C. < TRAPEZIUM.] —**trapezohedral** *adj*

trapezoid /tráppi zoyd/ *n* **1** a quadrilateral that has no parallel sides. US term **trapezium** *n*. 2 **2** *US* MATH = **trapezium** *n*. 1 **3** a small bone in the wrist near the metatarsal bone that connects with the index finger —**trapezoidal** *adj*

trapper /tráppər/ *n* a person who professionally traps animals for their fur or hides

trappings /tráppingz/ *npl* **1** the dress, accessories, insignia, and other outward signs associated with an office, position, or status ○ *the trappings of power* **2** an ornamental or ceremonial rig for a horse, including a decorated harness, saddle, and cloth covering

Trappist /tráppist/ *n* a member of the main reformed branch of the Cistercian order of Christian monks, established in 1664 at La Trappe monastery in Normandy and noted for its vow of silence [Early 19C. < French *trappiste* < *La Trappe*.]

traprock /tráp rok/ *n* MINERALS = **trap**[2]

trapshooting /tráp shooting/ *n* the sport of shooting at clay pigeons thrown by a trap —**trapshooter** *n*

trapunto /trə poóntō/ *n* quilting in which only the design, which is outlined with parallel lines of stitches, is padded to give it a raised look [Early 20C. < Italian, past participle of *trapungere* 'embroider' < Latin *pungere* 'to prick'.]

Traralgon /trə rálgən/ town in SE Victoria, Australia. Population: 19,699 (1991).

trash /trash/ *n* **1 NONSENSE** something spoken or written that is viewed as meaningless, absurd, or very inaccurate ○ *You're talking trash!* **2 POOR QUALITY LITERATURE OR ART** literature or art considered worthless or offensive ○ *How can you read such trash?* **3** *US* **DISCARDED MATERIAL** discarded, unwanted, or worthless material or objects **4** *US* **OFFENSIVE TERM** an offensive term that deliberately insults somebody's social position or morals **5 TRIMMINGS FROM PLANTS** twigs, branches, or leaves that have fallen or been trimmed from trees and plants **6 SUGAR CANE REFUSE** the dry refuse of sugar cane after it has been crushed for the juice, often used as fuel ■ *vt* **1 DESTROY** to destroy, severely damage, or vandalize something deliberately (*informal*) ○ *wondered whether rock stars still trashed their hotel rooms* ○ *'The storm trashed bridges in Honduras and Central America'.* (*US News & World Report*; December 1998) **2** *US* **DISCARD** to throw away or discard something (*informal*) **3** *US* **CRITICIZE SOMEBODY SAVAGELY** to criticize something or somebody savagely, or condemn something or somebody as worthless (*informal*) **4 REMOVE TWIGS AND BRANCHES** to remove twigs, branches, or leaves from plants **5 STRIP LEAVES FROM SUGAR CANE** to strip the outer leaves from sugar cane [14C. Probably < N Germanic.] ◇ **talk trash** *US* to try to intimidate somebody, especially a rival or an opponent in a sporting contest, by being boastful or insulting (*slang*)

trash can *n US* a dustbin (*informal*)

trashy /tráshi/ (**-ier, -iest**) *adj* of very little worth or merit ○ *a trashy novel* —**trashily** *adv* —**trashiness** *n*

Trasimeno, Lake /trázzi meénō/ lake in central Italy. Area: 128 sq. km/49 sq. mi.

trass /trass/ *n* a light-coloured volcanic rock (**tuff**) used in making cement and mortar [Late 18C. Via Dutch *tras* or German *Trass* < Latin *terra* 'earth'.]

trattoria /tráttə reé ə/ (*plural* **-as** *or* **-e** /-reé ay/) *n* an Italian restaurant, especially one that is simple in style [Early 19C. < Italian, < *trattore* 'restaurateur' < Latin *tractare* 'drag, manage' < *trahere* 'pull'.]

trauchled /traákh'ld, traák'ld/ *adj Scotland* exhausted or overburdened with physical or mental work or with responsibilities and cares [Early 20C. Past participle of *trauchle* 'tire out, trudge' < ?]

trauma /tráwmə/ (*plural* **-mas** *or* **-mata** /-mətə/) *n* **1** an extremely distressing experience that causes severe emotional shock and may have long-lasting psychological effects **2** a physical injury or wound to the body [Late 17C. < Greek, 'wound'.]

traumatic /traw máttik/ *adj* **1 EXTREMELY DISTRESSING** extremely distressing, frightening, or shocking, and sometimes having long-term psychological effects **2 RELATING TO TRAUMA** relating to or caused by psychological trauma **3 RELATING TO INJURIES** relating to wounds or injuries [Mid-17C. Via late Latin *traumaticus* < Greek *traumatikos* < *traumat-*, stem of *trauma* 'wound'.] —**traumatically** *adv*

traumatise *vt* = **traumatize**

traumatism /tráwmətizəm/ *n* the condition resulting from a physical injury or wound or from an emotional shock [Mid-19C. < Greek *traumat-* (see TRAUMATIC).]

traumatize /tráwmə tīz/ (**-tizes, -tizing, -tized**), **traumatise** (**-tises, -tising, -tised**) *vt* **1** to cause somebody to experience severe emotional shock or distress, often resulting in long-lasting psychological damage **2** to cause physical injury to somebody or something [Early 20C. < Greek *traumat-* (see TRAUMATIC).] —**traumatization** *n*

traumatology /tráwmə tólləji/ *n* the branch of medicine that deals with serious injuries and wounds and their long-term consequences [Late 19C. < Greek *traumat-* (see TRAUMATIC).] —**traumatologist** *n*

travail /trávvayl/ *n* **1 HARD WORK** work, especially work that involves hard physical effort over a long period **2 CHILDBIRTH** labour pains (*archaic*) ■ *vi* **1 WORK LONG AND HARD** to work long and hard (*literary*) **2 BE IN LABOUR** to be in labour (*archaic*) [13C. < French, 'pain', *travailler* 'to toil' < assumed Vulgar Latin *tripalium* 'instrument of torture' < Latin *tripalis* 'having three stakes' < *palus* 'stake'.]

trave /trayv/ *n* **1** BUILDING = **crossbeam** **2** a section of a building, e.g. in a ceiling, formed by crossbeams **3** a frame to restrain a difficult horse while it is being shod [14C. Via Old French, 'beam' < Latin *trab-*.]

travel /trávv'l/ *v* (**travels, travelling, travelled**) **1** *vi* **GO ON A JOURNEY** to go on a journey to a particular place, usually using some form of transport **2** *vi* **GO FROM PLACE TO PLACE** to go from place to place or visit various places and countries for business or pleasure ○ *We hope to travel more when we retire.* **3** *vt* **JOURNEY THROUGH** to go on journeys through, around, or within a particular area ○ *They travelled the world.* **4** *vt* **COVER A PARTICULAR DISTANCE** to go or cover a particular distance ○ *travel 10 miles* **5** *vi* **GO AT A PARTICULAR SPEED** to move at a particular speed or in a particular way ○ *The train was travelling at 90 mph when it had to stop.* **6** *vi* **MOVE FAST** to move swiftly (*informal*) **7** *vi* **GO TO DIFFERENT PLACES TO DO BUSINESS** to go from place to place as a salesperson or as part of a business ○ *After five years travelling, she wanted an office job.* **8** *vi* **TOLERATE BEING TRANSPORTED** to retain its quality or freshness while being transported ○ *Some products do not travel well.* **9** *vi* **BE TRANSMITTED** to be transmitted or communicated ○ *News travelled fast.* **10** *vi* **SCAN** to scan an object or scene in the process of observing or filming it **11** *vi* **MOVE IN A FIXED PATH** to move in a fixed path while operating (*refers to a machine part*) **12** *vi US* **ASSOCIATE WITH A SPECIFIC GROUP** to associate with a particular person or group ○ *They've been travelling with a new crowd.* **13** *vi* **TAKE AN ILLEGAL NUMBER OF STEPS** in basketball or netball, to take more steps while holding the ball than the rules allow ■ *n* **1 ACTIVITY OF TRAVELLING** the activity of going on journeys, often using a particular form of transport, or visiting different places ○ *air travel* **2 TOTAL DISTANCE A MECHANICAL PART MOVES** the total distance that a mechanical part such as a piston inside a cylinder moves **3** *US* **TRAFFIC** the amount of traffic at a given place along a route ■ **travels** *npl* **1 SERIES OF JOURNEYS** a series of journeys undertaken by a particular person or group ○ *She's off on her travels again.* **2 ACCOUNT OF SOMEBODY'S JOURNEYS** an account of the journeys undertaken by a particular person or group ■ *adj* **FOR TRAVELLERS** designed for use by travellers, especially by being lightweight and smaller than usual ○ *a travel kettle* [14C. Variant of TRAVAIL.] —**travellable** *adj*

LITERARY LINK ***Gulliver's Travels***, a satire (1726) by Jonathan Swift. It is a four-part account of the adventures of a castaway, ship's surgeon Lemuel Gulliver. First washed ashore in Lilliput, peopled by tiny inhabitants, he subsequently finds himself in Brobdingnag, the kingdom of giants. The third part of the novel deals with his time on the flying island of Laputa and the neighbouring continent, occupied by scientists and philosophers, while the final part takes him to the land of the Houyhnhms, where horses rule with benevolent reason over the brutish human Yahoos.

travel agency *n* a business that arranges transport, accommodation, and tours for travellers —**travel agent** *n*

travelator *n* = **travolator**

travel bureau *n* COMM = **travel agency**

travelcard /trávv'l kaard/ *n* a ticket entitling the user to an unlimited number of journeys on a public transport system within a specified area and over a specified period of time

traveled *adj* US = **travelled**

traveler *n* US = **traveller**

travelled /trávv'ld/ *adj* **1** having been on many journeys, or being experienced as a traveller **2** used by many travellers ○ *Keep to the travelled roads.*

traveller /trávv'lər/ *n* **1 SOMEBODY ON A JOURNEY** a person who journeys to a specific place or who uses a specific form of transport **2 SOMEBODY WHO HAS TRAVELLED** a person who has travelled or travels extensively ○ *an experienced traveller* **3** OCCUPATIONS = **travelling salesman** **4 MEMBER OF TRAVELLING FOLK** a Rom or other person living an itinerant lifestyle **5 MOVING PART** a part of a mechanism that is designed to move in a fixed path **6 RING ON A ROPE** a metal ring that moves freely on a rope, spar, or rod **7 ROPE** a rope, spar, or rod on which a metal ring moves

traveller's cheque *n* an internationally accepted cheque for a sum in a particular currency that can be exchanged elsewhere for local currency or for goods and is usually guaranteed against loss or theft

traveller's joy *n* a climbing plant of the buttercup family that has feathery fruits. Flowers: white. Native to: Europe. *Clematis vitalba.*

traveller's tale *n* a fantastic, unlikely, or obviously untrue account of something, as given by a traveller to people who do not travel

travelling folk, travelling people *npl* a term for Romany and other itinerant people, most often used by themselves

travelling salesman *n* a salesperson whose work consists of travelling around calling on potential customers within a territory

travelling saleswoman *n* a woman salesperson whose work consists of travelling around calling on potential customers within a territory

travelling wave *n* a wave that continuously carries energy away from its source

travelogue /trávvə log/ *n* a film, video tape, or piece of writing, or a lecture accompanied by pictures, video or film, about travel, especially to interesting or remote places, or about one particular person's travels

travel sickness *n* a feeling of nausea caused by movement, especially by the movement of the vehicle, train, ship, or aircraft in which somebody is travelling. US term **motion sickness** —**travel-sick** *adj*

Travers, Mount /trávvərz/ mountain in the north of the South Island, New Zealand. Height: 2,338 m/7,671 ft.

Travers, Ben (1886–1980) British playwright

traverse /trávvurss, trə vúrss/ *v* (**-verses, -versing, -versed**) **1** *vt* **MOVE ACROSS AN AREA** to travel or move across, over, or through an area or a place ○ *traverse the countryside* **2** *vti* **MOVE BACK AND FORTH** to move backwards and forwards across something ○ *Volunteers traversed the field looking for clues.* **3** *vt* **REACH ACROSS** to extend or reach across something ○ *traverse the river* **4** *vti* **MOVE AT AN ANGLE** to move at an angle across a rock face while ascending or descending it **5** *vti* **FOLLOW A ZIGZAG COURSE** to ski in diagonal runs following a zigzag course down a slope **6** *vti* **SWIVEL A GUN** to swivel something, especially a gun, from side to side on a pivot **7** *vi* **SLIDE A BLADE TOWARDS AN OPPONENT'S HILT** in fencing, to slide the blade of a sword towards an opponent's hilt while at the same time applying pressure to his or her blade **8** *vt* **THWART** to thwart somebody or something (*literary*) **9** *vt* **DENY ALLEGATIONS** to deny the opposing party's allegations as set out in the pleading in a lawsuit, formally and, usually, in their entirety ■ *n* **1 JOURNEY** a movement or journey across, over, or through something **2 ROUTE** a route or way across or over something **3 MOVEMENT ACROSS A ROCK FACE** a horizontal or oblique movement across a rock face in climbing **4 DIAGONAL RUN** a diagonal zigzag skiing run down a ski slope **5 CROSSBEAM** something that is fixed across a gap or lies crosswise such as a structural member of a building **6 GALLERY** a gallery or loft that crosses from side to side inside a building **7 BARRIER WITHIN A BUILDING** a railing, curtain, screen, or partition forming a barrier **8 BARRIER ACROSS A TRENCH** a defensive barrier of earth across a trench **9 OBSTRUCTION** something that thwarts or obstructs (*literary*) **10** MATH = **transversal** *n.* **11 ZIGZAG COURSE** the zigzag course of a sailing vessel in contrary winds **12 LATERAL MOVEMENT** the horizontal movement of a machine part such as a lathe or grinding tool as it moves across the work piece **13 DENIAL OF ALLEGATIONS** a formal denial of the opposing party's allegations as set out in their pleading in a lawsuit **14 TYPE OF SURVEY** a survey made using a series of intersecting straight lines of known length whose angles of intersection are measured for recording on a map or in a table of data ■ *adj* **CROSSWISE** lying across something [14C. Via French *traverser* < late Latin *tra(ns)versare* < Latin *transversus*, past participle of *transvertere* 'turn across' < *vertere* 'to turn'.] —**traversable** *adj* —**traversal** *n* —**traverser** *n*

travertine /trávvərtin/, **travertin** *n* a hard white or light-coloured limestone precipitated in hot springs and caves and used as a facing material in building [Late 18C. Via Italian *travertino* < Latin *(lapis) tiburtinus* '(stone) of Tibur (Tivoli)'.]

travesty /trávvəsti/ *n* (*plural* **-ties**) **1 FALSE REPRESENTATION** a distorted or debased version of something ○ *It was a kangaroo court, a travesty of justice.* **2 GROTESQUE IMITATION** a literary or artistic work, usually meant as a parody, that ridicules something serious by imitating it in a grotesque or distorted manner ■ *vt* (**-ties, -tying, -tied**) **MAKE A TRAVESTY OF** to imitate or mock something in a grotesque or distorted manner [Mid-17C. < French *travesti* 'dressed in disguise' < *travestir* 'disguise, ridicule' < Italian *travestire* < Latin *trans-* 'across', + *vestire* 'clothe, dress' (see VEST).]

travois /trə vóy, trávvoy/ (*plural* **-vois**) *n* a sledge made of two poles connected by a frame and pulled by an animal, formerly used by Native North Americans of the Great Plains [Mid-19C. < Canadian French variant of French *travail* < Latin *trabs* 'beam'.]

travolator /trávvə laytər/, **travelator** *n* a moving walkway for pedestrians, e.g. in an airport or shopping precinct [Mid-20C. < TRAVEL, after ESCALATOR.]

trawl /trawl/ *n* **1 FISHING NET** a large net that is dragged along the sea bottom behind a commercial fishing boat **2 SUSPENDED FISHING LINE** a long fishing line suspended between buoys that has several shorter lines with baited hooks attached **3 SEARCH** a search for something, especially information ■ *vti* **1 FISH WITH A TRAWL** to use or put out a trawl to catch fish **2 SEARCH THROUGH LARGE AMOUNT OF INFORMATION** to search for something through a large amount of information or many possibilities [Mid-16C. < Middle Dutch *traghelen* 'drag' < *traghel* 'trawl net' < Latin *tragula* < *trahere* 'pull'.]

trawler /tráwlər/ *n* **1** a boat that is used in trawling for fish **2** a person who fishes by trawling —**trawlerman** *n*

tray /tray/ *n* **1 FLAT CARRIER FOR SMALL OBJECTS** a flat piece of plastic, wood, or metal with a raised edge, used for carrying or displaying light objects **2 TRAY AND THINGS IT CARRIES** a tray and the objects on it ○ *brought in the tea tray* **3 CONTAINER IN WHICH TO ORGANIZE THINGS** a shallow container, sometimes part of a desk drawer or cabinet, in which to keep items such as stationery or jewellery [Old English *trīg* < Indo-European]

tray table *n* a small table that folds down from the back of the seat in front of you in a plane or train

treacherous /tréchərəss/ *adj* **1** betraying or ready to betray somebody's trust, confidence, or faith **2** involving hidden dangers or hazards ○ *treacherous seas* [14C. < Old French *trecheros* 'deceitfulness' < *trechier* 'cheat, trick'.] —**treacherously** *adv* —**treacherousness** *n*

treachery /tréchəri/ (*plural* **-ies**) *n* **1** betrayal or deceit **2** an act or instance of betrayal or deceit [12C. < Old French *trecherie* < *trechier* 'cheat, trick'.]

treacle /treek'l/ *n* **1 SYRUP FROM SUGAR REFINING** a thick brown sticky sweet liquid, produced during the process of refining raw sugar. Use: to make cakes, sweets, and puddings. (*often before a noun*) ○ *treacle toffee.* US term **molasses** *n.* **2 2 SOMETHING CLOYING** something cloying or excessively sentimental **3 FORMER ANTIDOTE TO POISON** a preparation used in the past as an antidote to poison [14C. Via Old French *triacle*, Latin *theriaca* < Greek *thēriakē (antidotos)* '(antidote to) poisonous animals' < *thērion* 'wild or poisonous animal' < *thēr* 'wild'.]

treacly /treek'li/ *adj* **1** sticky and sweet like treacle **2** cloying or excessively sentimental —**treacliness** *n*

tread /tred/ *v* (**treads, treading, trod** /trod/, **trodden** /trόdd'n/ *or* **trod**) **1** *vi* **TRAMPLE** to step or put a foot on something, especially so as to crush or damage it ○ *She trod on his toe.* **2** *vti* **WALK OR STEP ON** to take a step or steps, or walk or step on, across, or along something ○ *Don't tread on the wet concrete.* **3** *vt* **SPREAD SOMETHING DIRTY BY WALKING** to spread something unwanted from the feet or footwear by walking, often grinding it in ○ *food trodden into the carpet* **4** *vt* **FORM A PATH** to form something such as a path by trampling or walking **5** *vt* **DANCE STEPS** to perform the steps of a dance (*dated*) **6** *vi* **ACT IN STATED WAY** to proceed or behave in a particular way ○ *You'll have to tread carefully at the next meeting.* **7** *vi* **CRUSH** to repress or treat somebody or something harshly ■ *n* **1 WAY OF TREADING** a way or sound of walking or stepping ○ *heard the heavy tread of marching feet* **2 ACT OF TREADING** an act of walking or of trampling something **3 HORIZONTAL PART OF A STEP** the horizontal part of a step in a staircase **4 WIDTH OF A STEP** the width of the horizontal part of a step, measured from front to back **5 OUTER SURFACE OF A TYRE** the part of the surface of a tyre or wheel that comes in contact with a road or rail **6 DEPTH OF GROOVES ON A TYRE SURFACE** the depth of grooves on the surface of a tyre **7 PART OF SHOE THAT TOUCHES THE GROUND** the part of the sole of a shoe that touches the ground [Old English *tredan* < Germanic] —**treader** *n* —**treadless** *adj*

treadle /trédd'l/ *n* a lever pushed repeatedly by the foot to provide drive for a machine such as a sewing machine or potter's wheel ■ *vti* (**-les, -ling, -led**) to operate a treadle, or operate a machine by using a treadle [Old English *tredel* 'step, stair' < *tredan* (see TREAD)] —**treadler** *n*

treadmill /trédmil/ *n* **1 CYLINDER PROVIDING POWER** a continuous belt or series of steps kept moving by people or animals walking on it that is used to provide power to a machine, e.g. to grind grain or raise water from a well **2 EXERCISE MACHINE** a machine with an endless belt on which somebody can walk, jog, or run, used for exercise and stress testing **3 NEVER-ENDING ROUTINE** a monotonous and seemingly endless task, job, or routine

treas. *abbr* **1** treasurer **2** treasury

treason /treez'n/ *n* **1 BETRAYAL OF COUNTRY** violation of the allegiance owed by a person to his or her own country, e.g. by aiding an enemy. ◊ **high treason 2 TREACHERY** betrayal or disloyalty **3 ACT OF BETRAYAL** an act of betrayal or disloyalty [12C. Via Anglo-Norman *treisoun* 'treacherous handing over, betrayal' < Latin *tradition-* (see TRADITION).]

treasonable /treez'nəb'l/, **treasonous** /treez'nəss/ *adj* involving, being, or punishable as treason —**treasonableness** *n* —**treasonably** *adv*

treasure /trézhər/ *n* **1 JEWELS AND PRECIOUS OBJECTS** wealth, especially in the form of jewels and precious objects, often accumulated or hoarded **2 SOMETHING VALUABLE** something of great value or worth **3 SOMEBODY HIGHLY VALUED** a highly valued or much loved person ○ *an actor considered as one of our national treasures* ■ *vt* (**-ures, -uring, -ured**) **1 REGARD AS VALUABLE** to prize somebody or something as being of great value or worth ○ *treasured the memory of that day* **2 ACCUMULATE AND STORE** to accumulate and store something regarded as valuable [12C. Via French *trésor* < Latin *thesaurus* < Greek *thēsauros* 'treasure'.] —**treasurable** *adj*

LITERARY LINK ***Treasure Island***, a novel (1883) by Scottish writer Robert Louis Stevenson. This classic romance recounts young Jim Hawkins' adventures with a treacherous band of pirates searching for lost treasure on a distant island. The book's most memorable character is one-legged pirate Long John Silver.

treasure house *n* **1** a place or collection in which many valuable things are located **2** a building in which treasure is kept

treasure hunt *n* a game in which competitors attempt to solve a series of clues, sometimes leading to a hidden prize

treasurer /trézhərər/ *n* a manager of the finances of an organization, e.g. a club, society, government, or corporation —**treasurership** *n*

Treasurer *n Aus* the finance minister in the federal government and in each of the state governments

treasure-trove /-trōv/ *n* **1** silver or gold coins or bullion found buried in the earth and for which there is no known owner. In the United Kingdom such finds become Crown property. **2** something discovered that is valuable or the source of something valuable ○ *The new shop is a treasure-trove of antiques.* [Mid-16C. < Anglo-Norman *tresor trove* < Old French *tresor* 'treasure' + *trove*, past participle of *trover* 'find'.]

treasury /trézhəri/ (*plural* **-ies**) *n* **1 PLACE FOR THINGS OF VALUE** a place in which treasure or other valuable items are stored and preserved **2 STORE OF MONEY** the funds or revenues of a government, organization, or corporation, or the place in which they are deposited and disbursed **3 COLLECTION OF VALUABLE THINGS** a source or collection of valuable things, e.g. literary or artistic works [13C. < Old French *tresorie* < *trésor* (see TREASURE).]

Treasury (*plural* **-ies**) *n* in many countries, the government department in charge of collecting and managing public revenue

Treasury Bench *n* the front bench of the row to the Speaker's right in the British House of Commons, where members of the government sit

Treasury bill *n* a financial security issued by the Treasury payable to the bearer after a fixed period, usually three months

Treasury bond *n* an interest-bearing debt security issued by the US government, with an initial life of between ten and thirty years

Treasury note *n* **1** an intermediate-term, interest-paying debt instrument issued by the US government, with an initial life of between one and ten years **2** a currency note issued by the British Treasury in 1914 and valid until 1928

treasury tag *n* a short length of cord with metal ends that is passed through punched holes in sheets of paper to hold them together

treat /treet/ *v* **1** *vt* **REGARD SOMEBODY IN A PARTICULAR WAY** to behave towards or think of somebody or something in a particular way ○ *They treated us practically like family.* **2** *vt* **UNDERTAKE TO CURE** to give medical aid to somebody or apply medical techniques to a disease or symptom in order to provide a cure **3** *vt* **SUBJECT SOMETHING TO PROCESS OR AGENT** to subject something to a physical, chemical, or biological process or agent such as a chemical reaction or the application of a coating **4** *vt* **PAY FOR SOMEBODY ELSE** to pay for somebody else's food, drink, entertainment, or gifts ○ *I'll treat you to lunch at the hotel.* **5** *vt* **PROVIDE SOMEBODY WITH SOMETHING PLEASURABLE** to give somebody or yourself something enjoyable ○ *They treated their mother to breakfast in bed.* **6** *vt* **DEAL WITH SOMETHING IN A PARTICULAR WAY** to present or handle a subject, especially in art or literature, in a particular way ○ *treat a delicate subject with great sensitivity* **7** *vi* **DISCUSS A TOPIC** to discuss or deal with a topic in writing or speech ○ *a play that treats of greed and revenge* **8** *vi* **NEGOTIATE TERMS** to negotiate, especially in order to reach a settlement (*formal*) ○ *refusing to treat with the enemy* ■ *n* **1 ENTERTAINMENT PAID FOR BY SOMEBODY ELSE** something such as food, entertainment, or a gift that is given to somebody and paid for by somebody else **2 ACT OF PAYING**

FOR SOMEBODY ELSE an act of paying for something such as food, entertainment, or a gift, for somebody else **3** SOMETHING ENJOYABLE something enjoyable, especially when a surprise ○ *It's a treat to see a smile on his face again.* [13C. Via Old French *traitier* 'bargain with, negotiate' < Latin *tractare* 'handle' < *trahere* 'pull'.] —**treatable** *adj* —**treater** *n* ◇ **a treat** in a pleasing or successful way (*informal*) ○ *The woodwork's come up a treat.*

treatise /treétiss, -iz/ *n* a formal written work that deals with a subject systematically and usually extensively [14C. < Anglo-Norman *tretiz* < Old French *traitier* (see TREAT).]

treatment /treétmənt/ *n* **1** PROVISION OF MEDICAL CARE the application of medical care to cure disease, heal injuries, or ease symptoms **2** MEDICAL CARE a particular remedy, procedure, or technique for curing or alleviating a disease, injury, or condition ○ *a new treatment for asthma* **3** WAY OF HANDLING the particular way in which somebody or something is dealt with or handled ○ *had pretty rough treatment* **4** PRESENTATION OF A SUBJECT the way of presenting or handling a subject, especially in art or literature **5** SCHEMATIC VERSION OF A FILM a schematic version of a film script, generally without dialogue and individual shots, indicating how the story is to be dealt with in a screenplay **6** TREATING SOMETHING WITH AGENT an act of subjecting something to a physical, chemical, or biological process or agent **7** USUAL ACTIONS TAKEN the usual way of dealing with somebody or something in a particular situation (*informal*) ○ *As guests of the government we got the full VIP treatment.*

treaty /treéti/ (*plural* **-ties**) *n* **1** a formal contract or agreement negotiated between countries or other political entities **2** an agreement or contract between two or more parties [14C. Via Old French *traité* 'assembly, agreement, treaty' < Latin *tractatus* < *tractare* (see TREAT).]

treaty port *n* formerly, a port where foreign trade was allowed by a treaty, especially in China, Japan, and Korea

treble /trébb'l/ *adj* **1** TRIPLE three times as many or much **2** OF THE HIGHEST MUSICAL RANGE relating to or intended for a soprano voice or a high-pitched instrument **3** HIGH-PITCHED high-pitched or shrill ■ *n* **1** HIGH-PITCHED INSTRUMENT OR VOICE a treble voice, singer, instrument, or part **2** HIGH-PITCHED SOUND a high-pitched or shrill sound **3** AUDIO FREQUENCY RANGE the higher audio frequencies electronically reproduced by a radio, recording, or sound system **4** CONTROL FOR HIGH-FREQUENCY AUDIO RESPONSE a control for increasing or decreasing the high-frequency response on a radio or audio amplifier **5** SOMETHING TRIPLED something three times as many or as much **6** RING ON DARTBOARD the narrow inner ring on a dartboard, or a hit landing within this ring, which scores three times the stated value **7** SET OF THREE WINS the winning of three major competitions in one season, especially in football **8** BET ON THREE RACES a bet on three races in which the winnings and stake from each race are placed on the next ■ *vti* (**-les, -ling, -led**) TRIPLE to become or make something become three times as many or as much ○ *output has trebled over the past year* [13C. Via Old French < Latin *triplus* 'triple'.] —**trebleness** *n* —**trebly** *adv*

treble chance *n* a way of betting on football pools

treble clef *n* a clef that puts G above middle C on the second line of the staff, used for soprano and alto voices, high-pitched instruments, and the right hand of keyboard instruments

Treblinka /tre blíngkə/ site of two Nazi concentration camps in E Poland

trebuchet /trébbyoo shet/, **trebucket** /treé bukit/ *n* a medieval siege engine with a sling attached to a wooden arm for hurling large stones [14C. < French *trébuchet* < *trébucher* 'overturn'.]

trecento /tray chéntō/ *n* the 14th century, used especially in referring to Italian art and literature [Mid-19C. < Italian, shortening of *mil trecento* 'one thousand three hundred'.] —**trecentist** *n*

~~**trecherous**~~ incorrect spelling of **treacherous**

⚡**tree** /tree/ *n* **1** LARGE PERENNIAL WOODY PLANT a woody perennial plant that grows to a height of several metres and typically has a single erect main stem with side branches **2** PLANT RESEMBLING A TREE a large shrub or nonwoody plant that resembles a tree, e.g. a palm tree or tree fern **3** SOMETHING BRANCHED LIKE A TREE something that has branches or pegs on which to hang things ○ *a mug tree* **4** WOODEN SUPPORT a wooden beam, bar, or post that supports or is part of a structure **5** DIAGRAM OF A HIERARCHICAL STRUCTURE a diagram of a hierarchical structure that shows the relationships between components as branches **6** HIERARCHICAL DATA STRUCTURE a hierarchical data structure in which each element contains data and may be linked by branches to two or more other elements **7** CRYSTALLINE GROWTH a branching growth of crystals, particularly of a metal **8** GALLOWS a gallows (*archaic*) **9** CROSS JESUS CHRIST DIED ON in Christianity, the cross on which Jesus Christ was crucified (*archaic*) ■ *vt* (**trees, treeing, treed**) **1** FORCE UP A TREE to chase or force an animal or person to climb a tree **2** *US, Can* PUT IN A DIFFICULT SITUATION to force somebody into a position of difficulty or disadvantage (*informal*) **3** STRETCH ON A SHOE-TREE to stretch or shape a shoe or a boot on a shoe-tree [Old English *trēo(w)* < Indo-European, 'oak tree'] —**treeless** *adj* —**treelessness** *n* ◇ **be barking up the wrong tree** to be mistaken, especially as regards the best way to achieve something ◇ **out of your tree** behaving irrationally (*slang*) ◇ **up a tree** *US* in a position of difficulty or disadvantage (*informal*)

LITERARY LINK ***The Tree of Man***, a novel (1955) by Australian writer Patrick White. The story of a pioneer couple who settle in New South Wales, Australia, it charts the establishment of their farm, the birth of their children, and their gradual estrangement as they search for greater fulfilment in their respective lives.

tree creeper *n* a small forest bird with large claws for climbing tree trunks in search of insects. Family: Certhidae.

tree diagram *n* = **tree** *n.* 5

tree farm *n* an area where trees are grown commercially for their wood products

tree fern *n* a tropical fern that grows to the height of a tree and has a crown of fronds. Family: Cyatheaceae and Marattiaceae.

tree frog *n* a small frog that has long digits with adhesive discs that allow it to climb trees. Native to: America, Asia, Australia. Family: Hylidae.

tree heath *n* TREES = **briar**[1] *n.* 1

treehopper /treé hopər/ *n* a small tree-dwelling insect that feeds on the sap of trees. Many species have grotesque projections on their backs. Family: Membracidae.

tree house *n* a platform, often with a roof and walls, built among the branches of a tree, especially for children to play in

tree kangaroo *n* a kangaroo that has sharp claws and grasping forepaws that allow it to climb trees. Native to: New Guinea, N Australia. Genus: *Dendrolagus*.

tree line *n* **1** the limit of altitude, or northern or southern latitude, beyond which no trees can grow. US term **timberline 2** the edge of a wood or forest

treen /treen/ *n* tableware and other household utensils made of wood ■ *adj* made of wood (*archaic*) [Old English *trēowen* 'made of wood' < TREE]

treenail /treé nayl, trénn'l/, **trenail, trunnel** /trúnn'l/ *n* a large cylindrical peg made of dry wood that expands to give a tight fit when it is wet and is used to fasten timbers together, e.g. in ships

treenware /treén wair/ *n* HOUSEHOLD = **treen** *n.*

tree of heaven *n* a quick-growing deciduous tree, tolerant of pollution and often planted in urban areas. Native to: China. *Ailanthus altissima* and *Ailanthus glandulosa*.

tree of knowledge *n* in the Bible, the tree that grew in the Garden of Eden and produced the fruit that was forbidden to Adam and Eve (Genesis 2:9, 3)

tree of life *n* in the Bible, the tree that grew in the Garden of Eden and produced a fruit that gave eternal life to somebody who ate it (Genesis 3:22–24)

tree ring *n* PLANT SCI = **growth ring**

tree shrew *n* a small insect-eating mammal resembling a squirrel with a long snout. Native to: forests of Southeast Asia. Family: Tupaiidae.

tree snake *n* a slender tree-living snake. Native to: East Indies. Family: Colubridae

tree sparrow *n* **1** a small sparrow that differs from the house sparrow in having a black spot near its ear and a chestnut crown. Native to: Europe, Asia. *Passer montanus*. **2** a large sparrow with a chestnut cap and a grey breast with a single dark chest spot. Native to: North America. *Spizella arborea*.

tree spiking *n US* the act of hammering long nails into trees as a form of environmental protest, making it dangerous to cut down the trees using a chain saw

tree surgeon *n* somebody trained in pruning trees or treating diseased or damaged trees, e.g. by cutting off branches or filling cavities —**tree surgery** *n*

tree toad *n* ZOOL = **tree frog**

tree tomato *n* US term **tamarillo** *n.* **1** the edible red fruit of a plant of the nightshade family **2** a cultivated bush that bears tree tomatoes. Native to: South America. *Cyphomandra betacea* and *Cyphomandra crassifolia*.

treetop /treé top/ *n* the highest branches of a tree

treeware /teé wair/ *n* books and other material printed on paper made from wood pulp

trefoil /tréffoyl/ *n* **1** PLANT WITH THREE-LOBED LEAVES a plant of the pea family that has three-lobed leaves, especially clover **2** THREE-LOBED LEAF OR PART a leaf or other plant part with three lobes **3** THREE-LOBED SHAPE OR OBJECT an object or design with three lobes or connected parts, such as an emblem used in heraldry **4** ORNAMENT IN THE SHAPE OF A CLOVER LEAF an architectural ornament or form resembling a clover leaf [14C. Via Anglo-Norman *trifoil* < Latin *trifolium* 'with three leaves' < *folium* 'leaf'.]

trehala /tri haálə/ *n* an edible sugary substance that comes from the pupal case of an Asian beetle [Mid-19C. Via Turkish *tigale* < Persian *tīğāl*.]

trehalase /tri haá layss, -layz/ *n* an enzyme that catalyses the breakdown of trehalose

trehalose /tri haá lōss, -lōz/ *n* a disaccharide found in yeast, lichen, bacteria, and insects

treillage /tráylij/ *n* a trellis or latticework [Late 17C. < French, < *treille* < Latin *trichila* 'bower, arbour'.]

trek /trek/ *vi* (**treks, trekking, trekked**) **1** MAKE A LONG DIFFICULT JOURNEY to make a long difficult journey, especially on foot and often over rough or mountainous terrain **2** GO SLOWLY OR LABORIOUSLY to go somewhere slowly or with difficulty ○ *I had to trek across town to the other bookshop.* **3** *S Africa* GO BY OX WAGON to travel in a wagon pulled by an ox ■ *n* **1** LONG DIFFICULT JOURNEY a long difficult journey, especially on foot and often over rough or mountainous terrain **2** *S Africa* OX WAGON JOURNEY a journey or migration by ox wagon [Mid-19C. Via Afrikaans < Dutch *trekken* 'draw, pull, travel'.] —**trekker** *n*

Trekkie /tréki/ *n* a fan of the science-fiction television series 'Star Trek' (*informal*)

trellis /trélliss/ *n* **1** LATTICE FOR SUPPORTING A PLANT a lattice of wood, metal, or plastic used to support plants, usually fixed to a wall **2** LATTICEWORK STRUCTURE a structure made of latticework, especially an arch ■ *vt* **1** TRAIN A PLANT ON A LATTICE to support or train a plant such as a vine on a trellis **2** MAKE SOMETHING INTO A TRELLIS to interweave pieces of wood, metal, or plastic to make a trellis [14C. Via Old French *trelis* < Latin *trilix* 'three threads' < *licium* 'thread of a warp'.]

trelliswork /trélliss wurk/ *n* latticework, usually for supporting plants

trematode /trémmətōd, treé-/ *n* a flatworm that lives as a parasite in the liver, gut, lungs, or blood vessels of vertebrates, attaching itself by suckers or hooks and sometimes causing serious disease. Class: Trematoda. [Mid-19C. Via modern Latin *Trematoda* < Greek *trēmatōdēs* 'perforated' (because many have perforated skins) < *trēma* 'hole, orifice'.]

tremble /trémb'l/ *vi* (**-bles, -bling, -bled**) **1** SHAKE SLIGHTLY BUT UNCONTROLLABLY to shake with slight movements, continuously and uncontrollably, e.g. from fear, cold or anger **2** VIBRATE to shake or vibrate as a result of an external force ○ *We felt the house tremble as the train passed.* **3** BE AFRAID to be afraid or anxious about something ■ *n* QUIVERING a shaking, vibration, or quivering [14C. Via Old French *trembler* < medieval Latin *tremulare* 'shake' < Latin *tremulus* 'shaking' < *tremere* 'shake'.] —**tremblingly** *adv* —**trembly** *adj*

trembles /trémb'lz/ *n* poisoning in sheep and cattle that have fed on white snakeroot. Affected animals tremble and become weak. (+ *singular verb*)

trembling poplar *n* TREES = **aspen**

tremendous /trə méndəss/ *adj* **1** extremely large, powerful, or great ○ *There was a tremendous clap of thunder.* **2** extremely good, successful, or impressive ○ *a tremendous improvement* [Mid-17C. < Latin *tremendus* 'fearful' < *tremere* (see TREMBLE).] —**tremendously** *adv* —**tremendousness** *n*

tremie /trémmi/ *n* a device consisting of a funnel-shaped hopper at the top connected to a large metal pipe with a valve at the bottom, used to spread concrete underwater [Early 20C. Via French, '(mill-)hopper' < Latin *trimodia* 'three-peck measure' < *modius* 'peck'.]

tremolite /trémmə līt/ *n* a white, grey, or pale green hydrated silicate mineral containing calcium, magnesium, and some iron. Source: metamorphic rocks. Use: substitute for asbestos. [Late 18C. After *Tremola*, valley in Switzerland.]

tremolo /trémmələ̄/ (*plural* **-los**) *n* **1** the rapid repetition of a tone or the rapid alternation between two tones in singing or playing a musical instrument, which produces a quavering effect **2** a device in an organ for producing tremolo [Mid-18C. Via Italian < Latin *tremulus* (see TREMBLE).]

tremolo arm *n* a lever attached to the bridge of an electric guitar and used to move the bridge slightly, so as to stretch the strings to alter the pitch of a note

tremor /trémmər/ *n* **1 MINOR EARTHQUAKE** a quivering or vibration caused by slippage of the Earth's crust at a fault, especially before or after a major earthquake **2 TREMBLING** a slight shaking or trembling movement **3 SHUDDER** a quiver or shudder, e.g. from fear, illness, or nervousness **4 SUDDEN SENSATION** a sudden and usually brief feeling of excitement, nervousness, or anticipation **5 WAVERING SOUND OR LIGHT** a fluctuation in a sound or light [14C. Directly or via Old French < Latin, 'trembling, terror' < *tremere* 'shake'.] —**tremorous** *adj*

tremulant /trémmyoolənt/ *adj* shaking or trembling ■ *n* MUSIC = **tremolo** *n.* 2 [15C. < TREMULOUS.]

tremulous /trémmyooləss/ *adj* **1** shaking, trembling, or quavering, e.g. from fear or nervousness ○ *in a tremulous voice* **2** showing fear or nervousness about something [Early 17C. < Latin *tremulus* (see TREMBLE).] —**tremulously** *adv* —**tremulousness** *n*

trenail *n* CONSTR = **treenail**

trench /trench/ *n* **1 DITCH WITH STEEP SIDES** a long deep hole dug in the ground, usually with steep or vertical sides **2 PROTECTION AGAINST ENEMY FIRE** a long excavation, often with the excavated earth banked up in front, used as a defence against enemy fire ○ *warfare conducted in the trenches* **3 VALLEY ON THE OCEAN FLOOR** a long narrow valley on an ocean or sea floor ■ *v* **1** *vti* **DIG A TRENCH IN** to dig a long deep hole in or through something **2** *vt* **FORTIFY SOMETHING WITH TRENCHES** to fortify a position with trenches as a defence against enemy fire **3** *vt* **PUT SOMETHING IN A TRENCH** to place something such as a pipe in a trench [14C. < Old French *trenche* 'ditch, cutting, slice' < *trenchier* 'to cut' < Latin *truncare* 'cut (off)' < *truncus* 'tree trunk'.]

trenchant /trénchənt/ *adj* **1** direct, incisive, and deliberately hurtful ○ *trenchant criticism* **2** effective and relevant in the pursuit or achievement of a goal ○ *trenchant opinions* [14C. < Old French, 'cutting' < *trenchier* (see TRENCH).] —**trenchancy** *n* —**trenchantly** *adv*

Trenchard /trénch aard, trénchərd/, **Hugh Montague, 1st Viscount** (1873–1956) British air force commander

trench coat *n* a belted double-breasted raincoat, originally modelled on a military coat of World War I

trencher[1] /trénchər/ *n* formerly, a wooden platter used to serve or cut food (*archaic*) [14C. < Anglo-Norman *trenchour*, Old French *trenchoir* < *trenchier* (see TRENCH).]

trencher[2] /trénchər/ *n* somebody or something that digs trenches, especially a machine that cuts a furrow or ditch in which to lay cables or pipes

trencherman /trénchərmən/ (*plural* **-men** /-mən/) *n* a hearty eater

trench fever *n* a contagious illness whose symptoms include fever, headaches, and muscle aches, common among soldiers fighting in trenches in World War I and caused by the bacterium *Rochalimaea quintana*

trench foot *n* a painful condition of the feet caused by prolonged exposure of the feet to cold and wet. It results in loss of sensation, tissue damage, and sometimes gangrene.

trench mortar *n* a small cannon capable of firing shells at high trajectories over short distances, often used in trench warfare

trench mouth *n* MED = **Vincent's angina**

trench warfare *n* **1** a form of warfare in which armies conduct attacks on each other from opposing positions in fortified trenches **2** long-standing and bitter conflict in which opposing parties continually attack each other

trend /trend/ *n* **1 TENDENCY** a general tendency, movement, or direction ○ *a report documenting recent such trends* **2 PREVAILING STYLE** a current fashion or mode ○ *the latest trends in designer kitchens* ■ *vi* **TEND OR MOVE** to show a tendency or movement towards something or in a particular direction ○ *public opinion trending towards reunification* [Late 16C. < Old English *trendan* 'revolve, turn, turn in a particular direction' < Germanic, 'roundness'.]

trendoid /trénd oyd/ *n* a slavish follower of the latest trends or fashions (*informal*) —**trendoid** *adj*

trendsetter /trénd setər/ *n* somebody or something that starts or popularizes a new trend or fashion —**trendsetting** *adj*

trendy /tréndi/ *adj* (**-ier, -iest**) (*informal*) **1 CURRENTLY FASHIONABLE** relating to or exemplifying the latest fashion ○ *a trendy restaurant* **2 REFLECTING THE LATEST FAD** deliberately reflecting or adopting fashionable, often faddish, ideas or tastes ■ *n* (*plural* **-ies**) **SOMEBODY FOLLOWING CURRENT FASHION** a follower of the latest trends or fashions, often slavishly (*informal*) —**trendily** *adv* —**trendiness** *n*

Trent /trent/ river in central England, flowing into the North Sea via the Humber Estuary. Length: 270 km / 170 mi.

trente et quarante /tróNt ay ka róNt/ *n* GAMBLING = **rouge et noir** [Late 17C. < French, 'thirty and forty' (winning and losing numbers).]

Trenton /tréntən/ capital of New Jersey, in the west-central part of the state. Population: 88,675 (1990).

trepan /tri pán/ *n* **1 EARLY TYPE OF TREPHINE** an early cylindrical surgical instrument (**trephine**) used especially to cut a hole in the skull **2 TOOL FOR CUTTING DISC OR CYLINDER** a machine tool used to remove a circular disc from a metal sheet or a shallow cylindrical core from a metal ingot or block **3 ROCK-BORING TOOL** a tool for boring holes in rock ■ *vt* (**-pans, -panning, -panned**) **1 REMOVE A CIRCLE OF BONE** to remove a circular section from a bone, especially the skull, with a trepan **2 CUT SOMETHING OUT USING A TREPAN** to cut a disc or cylindrical core from something using a trepan **3 BORE HOLE IN ROCK WITH TREPAN** to bore a hole in rock using a trepan [14C. Via medieval Latin *trepanum* 'rotary saw' < Greek *trupanon* 'borer' < *trupan* 'pierce' < *trupē* 'hole'.] —**trepanation** /tréppə náysh'n/ *n* —**trepanner** *n*

trepang /tri páng/ *n* a large sea cucumber that is eaten in soups, especially in China and Indonesia. Native to: South Pacific, Indian Ocean. Genera: *Holothuria* and *Actinopyga*. [Late 18C. < Malay *teripang*.]

trephine /tri feén, -fīn/ *n* a cylindrical sharp or sawtooth-edged surgical instrument used especially to cut a hole in the skull ■ *vt* (**-phines, -phining, -phined**) to remove a circular section from a bone, especially the skull, or from corneal tissue with a trephine [Early 17C. < Latin *tres fines* 'three ends', partly after TREPAN.] —**trephination** /tréffi náysh'n/ *n*

trepidation /tréppi dáysh'n/ *n* **1** fear or uneasiness about the future or a future event **2** an involuntary trembling (*archaic*) [15C. < Latin *trepidation-* < *trepidare* 'startle, be agitated'.]

treponema /tréppə neémə/ (*plural* **-mas** /-mətə/ or **-mata**), **treponeme** /tréppə neem/ *n* a spirochaete bacterium that lives as a parasite in warm-blooded animals. One species causes syphilis in humans. Genus: *Treponema*. [Early 20C. < modern Latin, < Greek *trepein* 'turn', + *nēma* 'thread'.] —**treponemal** *adj*

trespass /tréspəss/ *vi* **1 ENTER SOMEBODY ELSE'S LAND UNLAWFULLY** to go onto somebody else's land or enter somebody else's property without permission **2 CAUSE INJURY** to cause injury to the person, property, or rights of another **3 ENCROACH ON** to intrude on somebody's privacy or time **4 BREAK A MORAL OR SOCIAL LAW** to commit a sin or break a social law (*archaic*) ■ *n* **1 UNLAWFUL ENTRY ONTO SOMEBODY ELSE'S LAND** the act or an instance of going onto somebody else's land or entering somebody else's property without permission **2 ENCROACHMENT** an intrusion into somebody's privacy or time **3 SIN** a sin or act of wrongdoing (*archaic*) [14C. < Old French *trespas* 'transgression' < *trespasser* 'pass beyond or across' < medieval Latin *transpassare*.] —**trespasser** *n*

tress /tress/ *n* **LOCK OF HAIR** a lock of long hair, especially a woman's hair ■ **tresses** *npl* **HAIR** somebody's hair, especially a woman's long hair ■ *vt* **STYLE HAIR IN TRESSES** to arrange or style hair in tresses [13C. < Old French *tresse*.]

tressure /tréshər, tréss yoor/ *n* an inner border with ornamental fleur-de-lis on a heraldic shield [14C. < Old French *tressour* < *tresse* 'tress'.] —**tressured** *adj*

trestle /tréss'l/ *n* **1 SUPPORTING FRAMEWORK** a supporting framework consisting of a horizontal beam held up by a pair of splayed legs at each end **2 TOWER FOR SUPPORTING A BRIDGE** timber, steel, or reinforced concrete tower that supports a bridge **3 BRIDGE SUPPORTED BY TOWERS** a bridge consisting of multiple short spans supported by braced towers [14C. < Old French *trestel* 'small beam' < Latin *transtrum* 'beam, crossbar'.]

trestle table *n* a table whose top is supported on trestles

trestletree /tréss'l tree/ *n* either of two horizontal timbers fixed to the masthead to support the crosstrees

trestlework /tréss'l wurk/ *n* a system of supporting trestles, e.g. one that supports a bridge

tretinoin /trə tínnō in, trétti noyn/ *n* a drug related chemically to vitamin A. Use: topical treatment of acne and other skin disorders. [Late 20C. < TRANS- + *retinoic (acid)* (< RETINO-) + -IN.]

trevally /tri válli/ (*plural* **-lies**) *n* a marine fish with a slender body and sharply forked tail. Native to: Australia. Family: Carangidae. [Late 19C. Alteration of *cavalla*.]

Trevino /trə veénō/, **Lee** (*b.* 1939) US golfer

Treviso /tre veéssō/ capital of Treviso Province, NE Italy. Population: 84,100 (1990).

Trevithick /trə víthik/, **Richard** (1771–1833) British engineer and inventor

trews /trooz/ *npl* close-fitting trousers, usually made of tartan cloth, worn by some Scottish army regiments [Mid-16C. < Irish *triús* or Gaelic *triubhas* 'close-fitting shorts'.]

trey /tray/ (*plural* **treys**) *n* a card, or the face of a dice or domino, with three spots [14C. Via Old French *trei(s)* < Latin *tres* 'three'.]

TRH *abbr* **1** Their Royal Highnesses **2** thyrotropin-releasing hormone

tri- *prefix* three, third ○ *trilateral* [< Latin and Greek < Indo-European]

triable /trí əb'l/ *adj* **1** subject to or fit for trial in a court of law **2** able to be tested or tried [15C. < Anglo-Norman, < Old French *trier* (see TRY).] —**triableness** *n*

triacid /trī ássid/ *adj* **1** describes a base capable of reacting with three hydrogen atoms or three molecules of a monobasic acid **2** describes an acid or a salt containing three replaceable hydrogen atoms

triad /trí ad, -əd/ *n* **1 SET OF 3** a group of three people or things **2 MUSICAL CHORD** a musical chord consisting of three notes, especially a chord made up of a tonic, a third, and a fifth **3 ATOM WITH VALENCY OF 3** an atom or chemical group with a valency of three **4 US STRATEGIC MISSILE FORCE** a US strategic missile force made up of bombers, land-based ballistic missiles, and submarine-launched ballistic missiles **5 WELSH LITERARY FORM** a form of composition in ancient Welsh literature in which subjects or statements are arranged in groups of three [Mid-16C. Via French *triade* or late Latin *triad-* < Greek *triados* 'of three'.] —**triadic** /trī áddik/ *adj*

Triad /trí ad/ *n* a Chinese secret society, especially one involved in organized crime [Mid-20C. Said to be from the early rituals of such societies, using a triangle as a symbol, where the *Triad* refers to a trinity of heaven, earth, and humankind.]

triage /treé aazh, trí ij/ *n* the process of prioritizing sick or injured people for treatment according to the seriousness of the condition or injury [Early 18C. < French, < *trier* (see TRY).]

trial /trí əl/ *n* **1 FORMAL LEGAL PROCESS** a formal examination of the facts and law in a civil or criminal action before a court of law in order to determine an issue **2 USE OF A COURT TRIAL** the use of a court trial to determine an issue or somebody's guilt or innocence ○ *standing trial for fraud* **3 TEST** a test or experiment to determine the quality, safety, performance, usefulness, or public acceptance of something **4 PAINFUL EXPERIENCE** an instance of trouble or hardship, especially one that tests somebody's ability to endure **5 SOMEBODY OR SOMETHING TROUBLESOME** somebody or something that causes trouble or annoyance to somebody ○ *He's such a trial!* **6 EFFORT** an earnest attempt to do something (*formal*) ○ *a trial to circle the globe in a hot-air balloon* **7 PRELIMINARY COMPETITION** a sports competition or preliminary test to select candidates for a later competition ■ **trials** *npl* **COMPETITION FOR ANIMALS** a competition to test the skills of a working animal or one used in sport ○ *sheepdog trials* ■ *adj* **1 EXPERIMENTAL** done as a test or experiment ○ *a trial separation* **2 OF A COURT TRIAL** relating to or used in a court trial ○ *a trial judge* ■ *vt* (**-als, -alling, -alled**) **TEST** to test something, especially under the conditions in which it is intended to be used [Mid-15C. < Anglo-Norman *triallum* < Old French *trier* (see TRY), or < medieval Latin.]

LITERARY LINK ***The Trial***, a novel (1925) by Czech writer Franz Kafka. It is the story of Josef K, a young bank clerk who is abruptly arrested for an unspecified misdemeanour. After a long, unsuccessful attempt to discover the nature of his crime, Josef is executed. This enigmatic work is seen as a disturbing allegory of the human condition.

trial and error *n* a method of finding a satisfactory solution or means of doing something by experimenting with alternatives and eliminating failures

trial balance *n* a statement used to check that the debits and credits in a double-entry book-keeping ledger are equal

trial balloon *n* a tentative suggestion, proposal, or plan put forward to test opinion or reaction

trial by fire *n* a thorough test of somebody's abilities or character under pressure

trial court *n* a court in which a case is first decided, as opposed to a court of appeal

trial lawyer *n US* a lawyer who practises in a trial court as opposed to an appeal court

triallist /trī́ əlist/ *n* a sports player or competitor who is given a chance to prove worthy of being included in a team for a major competition

trial of strength *n* a contest between two individuals or sides to decide which is the stronger

trialogue /trī́ ə log/, **trialog** *n* discussion involving three people or groups [Mid-16C. Blend of TRI- + DIALOGUE.]

trial run *n* a test of something new or untried, especially to assess its performance

triamcinolone /trī am sínnəlōn/ *n* $C_{21}H_{27}FO_6$ a synthetic drug (**corticosteroid**). Use: treatment of skin, oral, and joint inflammations. [Mid-20C. < TRI- + *amyl* + *cinene* + *prednisolone*.]

triangle /trī́ ang g'l/ *n* **1 3-SIDED PLANE POLYGON** a plane figure that has three sides and three angles **2 OBJECT WITH 3 SIDES** something shaped like a triangle **3** *US* MATH = **set square** **4 PERCUSSION INSTRUMENT** a metal bar bent into the shape of a triangle with one angle open, used as a percussion instrument **5 3-PERSON RELATIONSHIP** an emotional relationship involving three people. ◊ **eternal triangle** [14C. Directly or via Old French < Latin *triangulum* < *triangulus* 'three-cornered'.]

triangular /trī áng gyoõlər/ *adj* **1 OF A TRIANGLE** relating to or in the shape of a triangle **2 WITH A TRIANGULAR BASE** having a base in the shape of a triangle **3 HAVING 3 ELEMENTS** consisting of or involving three parts or people [14C. < late Latin *triangularis* < Latin *triangulum* (see TRIANGLE).] —**triangularity** /trī áng gyoõ lárrəti/ *n* —**triangularly** *adv*

triangulate *vt* /trī áng gyoõ layt/ (**-lates, -lating, -lated**) **1 MEASURE SOMETHING USING TRIGONOMETRIC RELATIONSHIPS** to measure something using the trigonometric relationships between pairs of the sides and angles of triangles **2 SURVEY OR MAP SOMETHING BY TRIANGULATION** to survey or map an area by the process of triangulation **3 SPLIT SOMETHING INTO TRIANGLES** to divide a surface into triangles **4 MAKE SOMETHING TRIANGULAR** to make something into the shape of a triangle ■ *adj* /trī áng gyoõlit, -layt/ **MADE UP OF TRIANGLES** shaped like a triangle or made up of triangles [15C. < Latin *triangulum* (see TRIANGLE).] —**triangulately** *adv*

triangulation /trī áng gyoõ láysh'n/ *n* **1 METHOD FOR DETERMINING LOCATION TRIGONOMETRICALLY** a navigation technique that uses the trigonometric properties of triangles to determine a location or course by means of compass bearings from two points a known distance apart **2 DIVIDING OF AN AREA INTO TRIANGLES FOR SURVEYING** the division of a large area into adjacent triangles for survey purposes using trigonometric relationships to calculate the dimensions of an area bounded by each triangle **3 SYSTEM OF TRIANGLES USED IN TRIANGULATION** the system of triangles laid out in triangulation

Triangulum /trī áng gyoõləm/ *n* a small constellation of the northern hemisphere. See illustration at **constellation**

Triangulum Australe /-o stráayli/ *n* a small constellation of the southern hemisphere. See illustration at **constellation**

triarchy /trī́ aarki/ (*plural* **-chies**) *n* **1** a system in which a country is ruled by three leaders **2** a country ruled by three leaders [Early 17C. < Greek *triarkhia* 'triumvirate', or < TRI- + -ARCH.]

Triassic /trī ássik/ *n* the period of geological time when reptiles flourished and dinosaurs, modern corals, and coniferous forests first appeared, 245 to 208 million years ago [Mid-19C. < German *Trias* < Latin, 'three, triad' < Greek.] —**Triassic** *adj*

triathlon /trī áthlən, -lon/ *n* an athletic contest in which the contestants take part in three events, usually swimming, cycling, and running. ◊ **pentathlon** *n.* **2, heptathlon, decathlon** [Late 20C. < TRI- + Greek *athlon* 'contest'.] —**triathlete** *n*

triatomic /trī́ ə tómmik/ *adj* **1** containing three atoms in each molecule **2** having three replaceable atoms or chemical groups —**triatomically** *adv*

triaxial /trī áksi əl/ *adj* having or involving three axes —**triaxiality** /trī áksi álləti/ *n*

triazine /trī́ ə zeen, trī áy-/ *n* **1** $C_3H_3N_3$ an organic compound with a six-membered ring containing three carbon and three nitrogen atoms **2** a derivative of a triazine isomer. Use: herbicides, pesticides, dyes.

triazole /trī́ ə zol, -zōl, trī ázzol, -zōl/ *n* **1** $C_2H_3N_3$ an organic compound with a five-membered ring containing two carbon and three nitrogen atoms **2** a derivative of triazole. Use: photocopying.

tribade /tríbbəd/ *n* a lesbian, especially one who takes part in tribadism [Early 17C. Via French or Latin < Greek *tribas* < *tribein* 'rub'.]

tribadism /tríbbədizəm/ *n* a lesbian practice in which one partner rubs her genitals against the other's

tribalism /trī́bəlizəm/ *n* **1** the customs, beliefs, and social organization of a tribe **2** loyalty to a tribe or social group —**tribalist** *n, adj* —**tribalistic** /trī́bə lístik/ *adj*

tribasic /trī báyssik/ *adj* **1** describes an acid containing three replaceable hydrogen atoms and capable of reacting with three hydroxyl ions per molecule **2** describes a compound that contains three univalent metal atoms or groups in each molecule

tribe /trīb/ *n* **1 SOCIAL DIVISION OF PEOPLE** a society or division of a society whose members have ancestry, customs, beliefs, and leadership in common **2 FAMILY** a large family (*informal humorous*) **3 GROUP WITH SOMETHING IN COMMON** a group of people who have something in common such as an occupation, social background, or political viewpoint (*disapproving*) ○ *rebelled against the whole tribe of earnest policy makers* **4 TAXONOMIC DIVISION** a division in the scientific classification of animals and plants, between a subfamily and a genus **5 ANCIENT ROMAN SOCIAL GROUP** any of the three groups, Latins, Sabines, and Etruscans, into which ancient Roman society was divided [13C. Via Old French *tribu* < Latin *tribus* 'one of three ethnic divisions of the Roman people' < *tri-* 'three'.] —**tribal** *adj* —**tribally** *adv*

Tribeca /trī béekə/, **TriBeCa** area of lower Manhattan, New York

tribesman /trī́bzmən/ (*plural* **-men** /-mən/) *n* a man who is a member of a tribe

tribespeople /trī́bz peep'l/ *npl* people who belong to a tribe

tribeswoman /trī́bz wŏomən/ (*plural* **-en** /-wimin/) *n* a woman who is a member of a tribe

triblet /tríbblət/ *n* a cylindrical or tapered rod used for making annular and cylindrical items such as rings or nuts or in drawing tubes [Early 17C. < French *triboulet*.]

tribo- *prefix* friction ○ *triboelectricity* [< Greek *tribos* 'rubbing' < *tribein* 'rub']

triboelectricity /trībō i lek tríssəti, -éllek-/ *n* an electric charge generated by friction, e.g. by rubbing materials together —**triboelectric** /-léktrik/ *adj*

tribology /trī bólləji/ *n* the science and technology of interacting surfaces in relative motion, including the study of friction, lubrication, and wear —**tribological** /trībə lójjik'l/ *adj* —**tribologist** *n*

triboluminescence /trībō loomi néss'nss/ *n* luminescence caused by friction —**triboluminescent** *adj*

tribrach /trī́ brak, trí-/ (*plural* **-brachs**) *n* a metrical foot made up of three short syllables [Late 16C. Via Latin *tribrachys* < Greek *tribrakhus* < *tri-* 'three' + *brakhus* 'short'.] —**tribrachic** *adj*

tribromoethanol /trī brōmō éthə nol/ *n* CBr_3CH_2OH a white crystalline organic compound. Use: general anaesthetic.

tribulation /tríbbyoõ láysh'n/ *n* **1** great difficulty, affliction, or distress **2** something such as an ordeal that causes difficulty, affliction, or distress ○ *the trials and tribulations of the struggling author* [13C. Via Old French < ecclesiastical Latin *tribulation-* < Latin *tribulare* 'afflict, press' < *tribulum* 'threshing tool' < *terere* 'rub'.]

tribunal /trī byóon'l, tri-/ *n* **1 LAW COURT** a court of justice **2 JUDGING BODY** a body that is appointed to make a judgment or inquiry ○ *an industrial tribunal* **3 COURT CONVENED BY GOVERNMENT** a court convened, under English law, by the British government to judge or investigate a particular matter **4 RAISED SEAT** a bench or seat on a platform where a judge or magistrate sits [15C. Directly and via Old French < Latin *tribunal* 'platform for magistrates' < *tribunus* (see TRIBUNE[1]).]

tribunate /tríbbyoõnət/ *n* the office, rank, or authority of a tribune in ancient Rome [Mid-16C. < Latin *tribunatus* < *tribunus* (see TRIBUNE[1]).]

tribune[1] /tríbyoon/ *n* **1** a representative of the common people in the ancient Roman republic, elected annually **2** a person or institution that defends the rights of the people [14C. Via Old French < Latin *tribunus* 'magistrate' < *tribus* (see TRIBE).] —**tribunary** *adj* —**tribuneship** *n*

tribune[2] /tríbyoon/ *n* **1 BISHOP'S THRONE OR SITE OF IT** a bishop's throne, or an apse of a Christian basilica containing the throne **2 CHURCH GALLERY** a gallery in a Christian church **3 PLATFORM** a raised platform for a speaker [Mid-18C. Via French < Italian *tribuna* 'raised platform', alteration of Latin *tribunal* < *tribunus* (see TRIBUNE[1]).]

Tribune Group *n* a left-wing group of British Labour Members of Parliament, founded in 1966 (+ *singular or plural verb*) —**Tribunite** /tríbbyoõ nīt/ *n, adj*

tributary /tríbbyoõtəri/ *n* (*plural* **-ies**) **1 STREAM FEEDING A LARGER BODY OF WATER** a stream, river, or glacier that joins a larger stream, river, or glacier, or a lake **2 PAYER OF TRIBUTE** a person or nation that pays a monetary tribute to another ■ *adj* **1 FLOWING INTO A LARGER BODY OF WATER** joining a larger stream, river, or glacier, or a lake **2 PAID AS TRIBUTE** paid or owed as a tribute **3 PAYING TRIBUTE** paying tribute in praise, money, or goods [14C. < Latin *tributarius* 'liable to tax or tribute' < *tributum* (see TRIBUTE).] —**tributarily** *adv*

tribute /tríbyoot/ *n* **1 EXPRESSION OF GRATITUDE OR PRAISE** something said or given to show gratitude, praise, or admiration **2 EVIDENCE OF GOOD** something that is indicative of a value, benefit, or good quality in somebody or something ○ *The result is a tribute to her powers of persuasion.* **3 PAYMENT BY ONE RULER TO ANOTHER** a payment made by one ruler or state to another as a sign of submission **4 PAYMENT TO A FEUDAL LORD** in medieval society, a payment made by a vassal to a lord, or an obligation for such payment [14C. Directly or via Old French < Latin *tributum* < *tribuere* 'give out among the tribes' < *tribus* (see TRIBE).]

tricarboxylic acid cycle /trī kaár bok síllik-/ *n* BIOCHEM = **Krebs cycle**

trice[1] /trīss/ *n* a very short period of time [15C. < TRICE[2].]

trice[2] /trīss/ *vt* to haul up or fasten something, especially with a rope [14C. < Middle Dutch *trīsen* 'pull' < *trīse* 'pulley'.]

tricentenary /trī sen téenəri, -tén-/ *adj, n* TIME = **tercentenary**

tricentennial *adj, n* TIME = **tercentenary**

triceps /trī́ seps/ (*plural* **-cepses** *or* **-ceps**) *n* a muscle that has three points of anchorage, especially the large muscle running along the back of the upper arm that straightens the elbow [Late 16C. < Latin, 'three-headed' < *caput* 'head'.]

triceratops /trī sérrə tops/ *n* a plant-eating dinosaur of the Cretaceous Period, somewhat similar in appearance to a rhinoceros, with a bony crest on the back of its neck and three horns. Genus: *Triceratops*. [Late 19C. < modern Latin, < Greek *trikeratos* 'three-horned' + *ōps* 'face'.]

trich- *prefix* = **tricho-** (*before vowels*)

tri-chad /trī chad/ *n US* a rectangular chad still attached to a ballot paper and with the perforations unbroken on three sides

trichiasis /tri kī́ ə siss/ *n* the inward growth of hair around a body opening, especially inward growth of the eyelashes, causing irritation of the eyeball [Mid-17C. Via late Latin < Greek *trikhiasis* < *trikhian* 'be hairy'.]

trichina /tri kī́nə/ (*plural* **-nae** /-nee/) *n* a small slender nematode worm that infests the intestines of meat-eating mammals, and whose larvae form cysts in skeletal muscle. *Trichinella spiralis.* [Mid-19C. < modern Latin, < Greek *trikhinos* 'hairy' < *thrix* 'hair'.] —**trichinal** *adj* —**trichinous** *adj*

trichinize /tríki nīz/, **trichinise** *vt* to infest a person, an animal, or meat with trichinae (*often passive*) [Mid-19C. < TRICHINA.] —**trichinized** *adj* —**trichinization** *n*

Trichinopoly /trínchin óppəli/ former name for **Tiruchchirappalli**

trichinosis /tríki nṓssiss/ *n* a disease caused by infestation with trichinae and marked by fever, muscle pain, and diarrhoea, often resulting from eating undercooked pork infected with the larvae

trichlorethylene *n* CHEM = **trichloroethylene**

trichlorfon, trichlorphon *n* $C_4H_8Cl_3O_4P$ a crystalline organic compound. Use: insecticide. [Mid-20C. < TRI- + CHLORO- + -*fon*, shortening of *phosphonate*.]

trichloride /trī kláw rīd/, **trichlorid** /-rid/ *n* any compound with three chloride atoms per molecule

trichloroacetic acid /trī́ klawrō a ssée̍tik-/ *n* $C_2Cl_3HO_2$ a corrosive toxic acid. Use: astringent, antiseptic, herbicide.

trichloroethane /trī́ klawrō ée thayn/ *n* $C_2H_3Cl_3$ a volatile colourless nonflammable liquid. Use: industrial solvent.

trichloroethylene /trī́ klawrō éthə leen/, **trichlorethylene** /-klawr éthə-/ *n* C_2HCl_3 a volatile colourless nonflammable liquid. Use: solvent, degreaser, anaesthetic.

trichlorphon *n* CHEM = **trichlorfon**

tricho- *prefix* hair, filament, thread ○ *trichoid* [< Greek *trikh-*, stem of *thrix* 'hair']

trichocyst /tríkə sist/ *n* a stinging or grasping organ resembling a thread that protrudes from minute cavities on the surface of some protozoans, especially ciliates —**trichocystic** /tríkə sístik/ *adj*

trichology /tri kóllə ji/ *n* the study and treatment of hair and its diseases —**trichological** /tríkə lójjik'l/ *adj* —**trichologist** *n*

trichome /trī́kōm, tríkōm/ *n* **1** an outgrowth of a plant's outer cell layer (**epidermis**). Trichomes have various shapes and functions, and include root hairs. **2** a filamentous chain of cells of bacteria or cyanobacteria [Late 19C. < Greek *trikhōma* 'growth of hair' < *thrix* 'hair'.] —**trichomic** /tri kómmik/ *adj*

trichomonad /tríkō mónnad/ *n* a flagellated protozoan that lives as a parasite in the digestive and reproductive tracts of humans and animals. Genus: *Trichomonas.* —**trichomonadal** *adj* —**trichomonal** *adj*

trichomoniasis /tríkō mō nī́ əssiss/ *n* **1** a sexually transmitted infection, especially of the vagina, marked by persistent discharge and intense itching. It is caused by a protozoan parasite *Trichomonas vaginalis.* **2** an infection of animals caused by parasitic protozoans (**trichomonads**) [Early 20C. < TRICHOMONAD.]

trichopteran /trī kóptərən/ *n* INSECTS = **caddis fly** [Mid-19C. < modern Latin *Trichoptera* < Greek *trikho-* (see TRICHO-) + *ptera*, plural of *pteron* 'wing'.]

trichotomy /trī́ kóttə mi/ (*plural* **-mies**) *n* **1** the division of something into three categories, classes, elements, or parts (*formal*) **2** the division of human nature into body, soul, and spirit [Early 17C. < modern Latin *trichotomia* < Greek *trikha* 'in three parts'.] —**trichotomic** /tríkə tómmik/ *adj* —**trichotomous** *adj* —**trichotomously** *adv*

trichroism /trī́ krō izəm/ *n* the property possessed by some crystals of showing three different colours when viewed along each of their three axes [Mid-19C. < Greek *trikhroos* 'three-coloured'.] —**trichroic** /trī krṓ ik/ *adj*

trichromat /trī́krō mat, trī́krə-/ *n* a person who has normal colour vision and is able to perceive red, green, and blue [Early 20C. Back-formation < TRICHROMATIC.]

trichromatic /trī́ krō máttik/, **trichrome** /trī́ krōm/, **trichromic** /trī-/ *adj* **1** 3-COLOUR relating to, involving, or using three colours **2** COMBINING PRIMARY COLOURS involving the combination of the three primary colours to produce the other colours **3** RELATING TO NORMAL COLOUR VISION relating to normal colour vision, which is able to perceive red, green, and blue —**trichromatism** /trī krṓmətizəm/ *n*

trichuriasis /tríkyoo rī́ ə siss/ *n* intestinal infection with nematodes of the genus *Trichuris.* It usually produces no symptoms, but may cause diarrhoea and bleeding in severely infected children. [Early 20C. < modern Latin *Trichuris* < Greek *trikh* 'hair' + *oura* 'tail'.]

trick /trik/ *n* **1** CUNNING DECEPTION a cunning action or plan that is intended to cheat or deceive **2** PRANK a prank, joke, or mischievous action or plan ○ *played a trick on his sister* **3** SPECIAL SKILL a special, effective, or ingenious knack, skill, or technique ○ *taught me the tricks of the trade* **4** SKILFUL ACT DESIGNED TO AMUSE a skilful act or feat, designed to amuse or entertain ○ *taught the dog to do tricks* **5** ACT OF MAGIC an act of magic or illusion, especially one involving sleight of hand, designed to puzzle or entertain ○ *a conjuring trick* **6** DECEPTIVE EFFECT OF LIGHT an illusion, especially one caused by the light **7** PECULIAR HABIT a peculiar characteristic, habit, mannerism, or way of behaving ○ *He has this trick of scratching his ear when he's being evasive.* **8** UNFORESEEN EVENT a strange event or development that was not anticipated or that seems unfair or sad ○ *a cruel trick of fate* **9** CARDS FROM EACH PLAYER IN A ROUND the cards played by all the players participating in one round of a card game and won by an individual player **10** GOOD CARD a card likely to win a trick, especially in bridge **11** PERIOD OF DUTY a period of duty, e.g. at the helm of a ship **12** *US* PROSTITUTE'S CUSTOMER a customer of a prostitute (*slang*) **13** *US* SEX WITH SOMEBODY FOR MONEY an individual engagement between a prostitute and a client (*slang*) ■ *vti* CHEAT to cheat or deceive somebody ○ *Hundreds of readers were tricked into sending them money.* ■ *adj* **1** OF TRICKS involving or intended to be used for tricks or trickery ○ *trick photography* **2** MADE AS AN IMITATION FOR A JOKE made as an imitation of something so that it can be used to play a joke on somebody **3** *US, Can* OCCASIONALLY SYMPTOMATIC displaying symptoms of injury from time to time (*informal*) ○ *a trick ankle* [15C. < Old N French *trique.*] —**tricker** *n* —**trickless** *adj* ◇ **be unable to take a trick** *Aus* to have a run of back luck (*informal*) ◇ **do the trick** to be effective and do what is needed (*informal*) ◇ **how's tricks?** used as a greeting (*informal*) ◇ **never** *or* **not miss a trick** to notice everything that is happening, or any opportunity that is advantageous (*informal*) ◇ **show somebody a trick or two** to demonstrate more skill than somebody else ◇ **up to one's (old) tricks** acting in a characteristically idiosyncratic manner in a way that is disapproved of (*informal*)

trick out, trick up *vt* **1** to decorate or dress somebody or something up, especially in a fancy or garish way **2** to modify something such as a vehicle or piece of electronic equipment, and add a large number of additional features to it

trick cyclist *n* **1** a performer of stunts on a bicycle or monocycle, especially in a circus **2** a psychiatrist (*dated humorous informal*)

trickery /tríkəri/ (*plural* **-ies**) *n* a trick, or the use of tricks, especially in order to cheat or deceive

trickle /trík'l/ *v* (**-les, -ling, -led**) **1** *vti* FLOW SLOWLY IN A THIN STREAM to flow or cause something to flow in a thin stream or in drops ○ *sweat trickled down his face* **2** *vi* MOVE SLOWLY OR GRADUALLY to move, come, or go slowly or gradually ○ *The crowd trickled slowly away and the park emptied.* ■ *n* **1** THIN SLOW FLOW a thin slow flow, movement, or stream ○ *a trickle of blood* **2** ACT OF FLOWING IN THIN STREAM an act of flowing or of causing a liquid to flow in a thin stream [14C. < ?] —**trickling** *adj* —**tricklingly** *adv* —**trickly** *adj*

trickle charger *n* a small low-current device used to recharge batteries slowly and maintain them in a fully charged state —**trickle charge** *n*

trickle-down theory *n* the economic theory that financial and other benefits received by big businesses gradually spread to benefit the rest of society

trick or treat *n* a Halloween custom in which children call at neighbours' houses and threaten to play a trick on the householder unless they are given a treat such as sweets ■ *interj* used as a greeting by children when they call on a house in order to ask for sweets at Halloween

trick-or-treat *vi* to go to neighbours' houses and ask for sweets at Halloween

trickster /tríks tər/ *n* a deceiver, swindler, or player of tricks

tricksy /tríksi/ *adj* **1** MISCHIEVOUS mischievous, playful, or inclined to play tricks **2** NOT STRAIGHTFORWARD intricate, complicated, or overelaborate **3** GIMMICKY new and ingenious —**tricksiness** *n*

tricky /tríki/ (**-ier, -iest**) *adj* **1** difficult to do or deal with and requiring skill, caution, or tact ○ *a tricky manoeuvre* ○ *a tricky situation* **2** likely to cheat or outwit somebody —**trickily** *adv* —**trickiness** *n*

triclad /trī́ klad/ *n* a flatworm with an intestine that is divided into three sections. Order: Tricladida. [Late 19C. Shortening of modern Latin *Tricladida* < Greek *tri-* 'three' + *klados* 'branch'.]

triclinic /trī klínnik/ *adj* describes a crystal that has three unequal axes, none of which is perpendicular to another

triclinium /tri klínni əm, trī-, tri klī́n-/ (*plural* **-a** /-ni ə/) *n* **1** a couch arranged around three sides of a table and used by ancient Romans to recline on at meals **2** an ancient Roman dining room, especially one containing a triclinium [Mid-17C. Via Latin < Greek *triklinion* < *triklinos* 'room with three couches' < *klinē* 'couch'.]

tricolour /tríkələr, trī́ kulər/ *n* **1** 3-COLOURED FLAG a flag with three colours **2** **tricolour, Tricolour** FRENCH NATIONAL FLAG the French national flag, consisting of three equal vertical bands of blue, white, and red **3** 3-COLOURED DOG a black, tan, and white dog ■ *adj* **tricolour, tricoloured** **1** 3-COLOURED with, involving, or using three colours **2** PIEBALD having a coat of black, tan, and white

tricorn /trī́ kawrn/, **tricorne** *n* **1** COCKED HAT a hat with its brim turned up on three sides that was worn by men in the 18th century **2** MYTHICAL ANIMAL an imaginary animal with three horns ■ *adj* 3-HORNED having three horns or corners [Mid-18C. Directly or via French *tricorne* < Latin *tricornis* 'three-horned' < *cornu* 'horn'.]

tricornered /trī́ kawrnərd/ *adj* having three corners

tricot /tríkō, tréekō/ *n* **1** a plain close-knit fabric of natural or artificial fibre. Use: underwear. **2** a soft ribbed wool or wool and cotton mix fabric. Use: dresses. [Late 18C. < French *tricoter* 'to knit' < Germanic.]

tricotine /tríkə téen, trée-/ *n* a strong woollen fabric woven with a double twill

tricuspid /trī kúss pid/ *adj* **tricuspid, tricuspidal, tricuspidate** having three cusps or points ■ *n* something such as a tooth, valve, or leaf that has three cusps

tricuspid valve *n* a heart valve consisting of three flaps that prevents blood from flowing back into the right atrium when the right ventricle contracts

tricycle /trī́ssik'l/ *n* **1** PEDAL-DRIVEN 3-WHEELED VEHICLE a pedal-driven vehicle with two wheels at the back and one at the front, ridden now especially by young children **2** MOTOR-DRIVEN THREE-WHEELED VEHICLE a motor-driven vehicle with three wheels ■ *vi* (**-cles, -cling, -cled**) RIDE A TRICYCLE to ride a tricycle —**tricyclist** *n*

tricyclic /trī sī́klik/ *adj* having a molecular structure containing three rings ■ *n* PHARM = **tricyclic antidepressant drug**

tricyclic antidepressant drug *n* any of a group of drugs having chemical structures based on linked six-carbon rings. Use: treatment of depression.

tridactyl /trī dáktil/, **tridactylous** /trī dáktiləss/ *adj* having three claws, fingers, or toes on each limb

trident /trī́d'nt/ *n* **1** 3-PRONGED SPEAR an instrument, spear, or weapon with three prongs **2** 3-PRONGED SPEAR OF POSEIDON OR NEPTUNE in classical mythology, the three-pronged spear carried by the Greek sea god, Poseidon, or his Roman equivalent, Neptune ■ *adj* **trident, tridental, tridentate** 3-PRONGED having three prongs, points, or teeth [15C. < Latin *trident-*, stem of *tridens* < *dens* 'tooth'.]

Trident /trī́d'nt/ *n* a US-manufactured ballistic missile system fired from nuclear submarines and in service with the US Navy and the British Royal Navy

Tridentine /trī dén tīn, tri-/ *adj* relating to the Council of Trent or its decrees, in which the traditional doctrines of Roman Catholicism were reasserted and the Counter Reformation was begun ■ *n* a Roman Catholic who adheres to doctrines laid down by the Council of Trent, especially in opposition to the reforms of the Second Vatican Council [Mid-16C. < medieval Latin *Tridentinus* < Latin *Tridentum* 'Trent'.]

tridimensional /trī́ dī ménsh'nəl, -di-/ *adj* having three dimensions —**tridimensionality** /trī́ dī ménsh'n álleti, -di-/ *n* —**tridimensionally** *adv*

triduum /tríddyoo əm, trī́-/ *n* a period of three days of prayer before a Roman Catholic feast [Early 18C. < Latin, < *dies* 'day'.]

tried /trīd/ past tense, past participle of **try** ■ *adj* (*often in combination*) **1** proved through experience or testing to be good, effective, or reliable ○ *using this tried and tested method* ○ *a tried and tested formula for successful game shows* **2** subjected to considerable strain, stress, or worry ○ *the sorely tried teacher of a class of noisy pupils*

triene /trī́ een/ *n* a chemical compound having three double bonds

triennial /trī énni əl/ *adj* **1 HAPPENING EVERY 3 YEARS** taking place once every three years **2 LASTING 3 YEARS** lasting for a period of three years ■ *n* **1 THIRD ANNIVERSARY** a third anniversary of an event **2 THREE-YEARLY EVENT** an event that takes place every three years **3 3-YEAR PERIOD** a period of three years [Mid-16C. < Latin *triennis* < *triennium* (see TRIENNIUM).] —**triennially** *adv*

triennium /trī énni əm/ (*plural* **-ums** *or* **-a** /trī énni ə/) *n* a period of three years [Mid-19C. < Latin, < *annus* 'year'.]

trier /trī́ ər/ *n* **1 SOMEBODY WHO TRIES** somebody who or something that tries, e.g. a tester of new things **2 SOMEBODY WHO PERSEVERES** a person who perseveres in doing something despite limited ability or lack of success **3 TOOL FOR TESTING MATERIALS** a tool or implement designed and used for testing materials, particularly food products, during manufacture

Trier /treer/ city in SW Germany. Population: 98,900 (1992).

Trieste /tri ést/ seaport of Friuli-Venezia Region, NE Italy. Population: 228,398 (1992).

Trieste, Gulf of inlet of the N Adriatic Sea, bordered by Italy, Slovenia, and Croatia

trifecta /trī féktə/ *n Aus, US* a bet, especially on a horse race, that involves selecting the competitors that will come in the first three places in the correct order [Late 20C. Blend of TRI- + PERFECTA.]

triffid /tríffid/ *n* a very large fictional plant capable of moving about and killing people, or any large plant thought to resemble a triffid [Mid-20C. Invention.]

trifid /trífid/ *adj* describes a tail or organ that is deeply divided into three parts [Mid-18C. < Latin *trifidus* 'having three clefts' < *findere* 'to split'.]

trifle /trī́f'l/ *n* **1 SOMETHING TRIVIAL** something that has little or no importance, significance, or value ○ *dismissed the complaint as a mere trifle* **2 SMALL QUANTITY** a small amount of something ○ *What he'd earned seemed a trifle beside his mountain of debts.* **3 COLD DESSERT** a cold dessert typically consisting of sponge cake soaked in sherry or fruit juice, spread with jam, jelly, or fruit, and topped with custard, whipped cream, or both **4 MEDIUM-HARD PEWTER** pewter of medium hardness ■ **trifles** *npl* **PEWTER UTENSILS** objects or utensils made of trifle [13C. < Old French *trufle*, variant of *truffe* 'deception'.] —**trifler** *n* ◇ **a trifle** slightly or somewhat (*formal or humorous*)

trifle with *vt* to treat or take advantage of somebody or something thoughtlessly or without due respect or consideration ○ *had trifled with her affections*

trifling /trī́fling/ *adj* **1** insignificant, trivial, or of little value **2** concerned with matters of little importance ○ *'He is not a trifling, silly young man'* (Jane Austen, *Emma*; 1816) —**triflingly** *adv*

trifocal /trī fṓk'l/ *adj* describes a lens that has three different sections, each with a different focal point ■ **trifocals** *npl* spectacles with trifocal lenses whose three sections correct separately for near, medium, and distant vision

trifold /trī́ fōld/ *adj* consisting of three parts

trifoliate /trī fṓli ət, -ayt/, **trifoliated** /trī fṓli aytid/ *adj* **1 trifoliate, trifoliated, trifolioate** /-ə layt/ describes a compound leaf consisting of three leaflets that arise from the same point, e.g. a clover leaf **2** with leaves composed of three leaflets or shaped like such a leaf

triforium /trī fáwri əm/ (*plural* **-a** /-ri ə/) *n* an arcaded storey in a church between the nave arches and the clerestory [13C. < Anglo-Latin.] —**triforial** *adj*

triform /trī́ fawrm/, **triformed** /trī́ fawrmd/ *adj* having or consisting of three different forms or parts

trifurcate *adj* **trifurcate, trifurcated** divided into three branches or forks ■ *vi* to divide into three branches or forks [Early 18C. < Latin *trifurcus* < *furca* 'fork'.] —**trifurcation** /trī fur káysh'n/ *n*

trig /trig/ *n* trigonometry, especially as a school subject (*informal*) [Mid-19C. Shortening.]

trig. *abbr* **1** trigonometrical **2** trigonometry

trigeminal /trī jémmin'l/ *adj* relating to or involving the trigeminal nerve [Mid-19C. < modern Latin *trigeminus* 'three twins' < Latin *geminus* 'twin'.]

trigeminal nerve, trigeminal *n* either of the fifth pair of cranial nerves that provide the jaw, face, and nasal cavity with motor and sensory functions

trigeminal neuralgia *n* a condition involving recurring sudden sharp pain in the face along the branches of the trigeminal nerve

trigger /tríggər/ *n* **1 SMALL LEVER THAT FIRES A GUN** a small lever that is pressed with a finger to fire a gun **2 LEVER THAT OPERATES A MECHANISM** a small lever or device that is pressed or squeezed to operate a mechanism, e.g. by releasing a spring **3 STIMULUS FOR** a stimulus that sets off an action, process, or series of events **4 SIGNAL FOR STARTING AN OPERATION** an automatic or manual pulse or signal for an operation to start ■ *vt* **1 MAKE SOMETHING HAPPEN** to set something off, bring something about, or make something happen ○ *memories triggered by the sight of old photos* **2 FIRE A WEAPON BY PULLING A TRIGGER** to fire a weapon or initiate an explosion by operating a trigger **3 SET SOMETHING IN MOTION** to initiate electrical or mechanical activity that will then allow a device to function for a time under its own control [Early 17C. < Dutch *trekker* < *trekken* 'pull'.]

trigger finger *n* **1** the finger used to pull the trigger on a gun, usually the right-hand forefinger **2** a disorder, caused by inflammation of the fibrous sheath around a tendon, in which one or more fingers are locked in a bent position and click if forcibly straightened

triggerfish /tríggər fish/ (*plural* **-fish** *or* **-fishes**) *n* a tropical marine fish found on coral reefs with a thin body and a dorsal fin spine that locks in an erect position as a protection against predators. Family: Balistidae.

trigger-happy *adj* (*informal*) **1** likely or overeager to shoot a firearm without considering the consequences **2** liable to act in a rash or violent way without considering the consequences

triggerman /tríggər man/ (*plural* **-men** /-men/) *n US* (*informal*) **1** a person who shoots somebody else, usually as part of a gang committing a crime **2** a bodyguard, especially one working for a gangster

triglyceride /trī glíssə rīd/ *n* an ester formed from a molecule of glycerol and three molecules of fatty acids, considered to have adverse effects on human health when consumed in excessive amounts. Source: animal and plant fats and oils.

triglyph /trī́ glif/ *n* in classical architecture, a block carved with three vertical grooves that separates the square panels (**metopes**) in a Doric frieze [Mid-16C. Via Latin < Greek *trigluphos* < *gluphē* 'carving'.] —**triglyphic** /trī glíffik/ *adj*

trigon /trī́ gon/ *n* **1** a triangular harp or lyre of ancient Greece and Rome **2** ZODIAC = **triplicity** *n.* **3** [Mid-16C. Via Latin *trigonum* < Greek *trigōnon* 'triangle' < *gōnia* 'angle'.]

trigonal /tríggən'l/ *adj* **1** in the shape of a triangle **2** describes a crystal that has threefold symmetry —**trigonally** *adv*

trigonometric function /tríggənə méttrik-/ *n* a function of an angle or arc expressed as a ratio of the two sides of a right triangle containing the angle

trigonometry /tríggə nómmətri/ *n* a branch of mathematics dealing with properties of trigonometric functions and their applications, e.g. in surveying —**trigonometric** /tríggənə méttrik/ *adj* —**trigonometrical** *adj* —**trigonometrically** *adv*

trig point *n* a land surveyor's reference point on high ground, usually marked by a stone pillar set into the ground [Mid-19C. Shortening of *trigonometrical point*.]

trigram /trī́ gram/ *n* **1** a group of three alphabetical letters **2** one of eight combinations of three solid or broken lines that are joined in pairs to form hexagrams of the I Ching —**trigrammatic** /trīgrə máttik/ *adj* —**trigrammatically** *adv*

trigraph /trī́ graaf, -graf/ *n* a group of three successive letters, especially one representing a single sound such as 'igh' in 'might' —**trigraphic** /trī gráffik/ *adj* —**trigraphically** *adv*

trihalomethane /trī háylō mée thayn/ *n* a methane-derived compound such as chloroform that contains three halogen atoms, formed especially during the chlorination of drinking water

trihedron /trī héedrən/ (*plural* **-drons** *or* **-dra** /-drə/), **trihedral** /-héedrəl/ *n* a figure formed by the intersection of three planes —**trihedral** *adj*

triiodothyronine /trī ī ṓdō thī́rə neen/ *n* an iodine-containing hormone produced by the thyroid gland

trijet /trī́ jet/ *n* an aeroplane propelled by three jet engines

trike /trīk/ *n* a tricycle (*informal*) [Late 19C. Shortening and alteration of TRICYCLE.]

trilateral /trī láttərəl/ *adj* **1 3-SIDED** describes a geometric figure that has three sides **2 TRIPARTITE** involving three countries or parties ■ *n* **3-SIDED FIGURE** a geometric figure with three sides —**trilaterally** *adv*

trilateralism /trī láttərəlizəm/ *n* three-sided relations or discussions between nations, areas, or groups —**trilateralist** *n*

trilby /trílbi/ (*plural* **-bies**) *n* a soft felt hat with a deep crease in the crown and a narrow brim [Late 19C. After *Trilby*, novel by George Du Maurier with such a hat in his original illustrations.]

trilinear /trī línni ər/ *adj* consisting of, contained by, or involving three lines

trilingual /trī líng gwəl/ *adj* **1** able to speak or use three languages, especially fluently **2** relating to three languages —**trilingual** *n* —**trilingualism** *n* —**trilingually** *adv*

triliteral /trī líttərəl/ *adj* **1** having three alphabetical letters **2** having three consonants —**triliteral** *n*

trilithon /trī lí thon, trī́li-/, **trilith** /trī́ lith/ *n* a prehistoric structure consisting of two large vertical stones supporting a horizontal stone laid on top of them [Mid-18C. < Greek, < *lithos* 'stone'.] —**trilithic** /trī líthik/ *adj*

trill[1] /tril/ *n* **1 WARBLING SOUND** a high-pitched warbling sound, especially one made by a bird **2 MELODIC ORNAMENT** a musical ornament consisting of rapid alternation between two adjacent notes **3 SOUND MADE BY VIBRATING VOCAL ORGANS** a sound or consonant made by two vocal organs vibrating rapidly against each other, e.g. the tip of the tongue vibrating against the ridge behind the front teeth ■ *vti* **UTTER SOMETHING WITH A TRILL** to play, sing, pronounce, or utter something with a trill or sound resembling a trill [Mid-17C. < Italian *trillare*.]

trill[2] /tril/ *vi* to spin or twirl around [14C. < ?]

trillion /tríllyən/ (*plural* **-lion** *or* **-lions**) *n* **1 1 FOLLOWED BY 12 ZEROS** the number equal to 10^{12}, written as 1 followed by 12 zeros. See table at **number 2 1 FOLLOWED BY 18 ZEROS** the number equal to 10^{18}, written as 1 followed by 18 zeros (*dated*) See table at **number 3 LARGE NUMBER** an exceptionally large but unspecified number or amount of something (*informal; often plural*) ○ *had trillions of fans wanting to meet her* [Late 17C. < French, after *million*.] —**trillion** *det*

USAGE See ***billion***.

trillionth /tríllyənth/ *n* see table at **number** —**trillionth** *adj, adv*

trillium /trílli əm/ *n* a plant with a cluster of three leaves at the top of the stem. Flowers: single, large, white, pink, or purple, three-petalled. Native to: North America, Asia. [Mid-19C. < modern Latin.]

trilobate /trī lṓ bayt/, **trilobated** /trī́lə baytid/, **trilobed** /trī́ lōbd/ *adj* describes a leaf that has three lobes

trilobite /trī́lə bīt/ *n* an extinct Palaeozoic marine arthropod with a flat oval body and a dorsal exoskeleton divided into three vertical sections. Class: Trilobita. [Mid-19C. < modern Latin *Trilobites* < Greek *lobos* 'lobe'.] —**trilobitic** /-bíttik/ *adj*

trilocular /trī lókyŏŏlər/ *adj* having or consisting of three cavities, cells, or chambers [Mid-19C. < TRI- + Latin *loculus* 'little place' < *locus* 'place'.]

trilogy /tríllə ji/ (*plural* **-gies**) *n* **1** a group or series of three related works, especially of literature or music **2** a set of three related things [Mid-17C. < Greek *trilogia* < *logos* 'word'.]

trim /trim/ *v* (**trims, trimming, trimmed**) **1** *vt* **MAKE SOMETHING TIDY BY CUTTING** to make something neat and tidy by clipping, cutting, or pruning **2** *vt* **CUT SOMETHING TO THE REQUIRED SIZE** to reduce something by cutting it to the required shape or size ○ *The editor said I needed to trim the manuscript down to 40,000 words.* **3** *vt* **REMOVE EXCESS BY CUTTING** to reduce or remove something, especially something excess, by cutting ○ *We had to trim the budget.*

4 *vt* **DECORATE** to decorate or embellish something ○ *He trimmed the hat with fur.* 5 *vt* **SHAPE TIMBER** to shape and finish the edges of wood or timber 6 *vt* **EDIT A FILM** to cut pieces from a film during editing 7 *vti* **CHANGE THE ARRANGEMENT OF SAILS** to change the position or arrangement of the sails so that a ship is ready to set sail 8 *vti* **CHANGE THE DISTRIBUTION OF CARGO** to improve, alter, or maintain a vessel's balance by changing the way the ballast or cargo is distributed 9 *vi* **BE BALANCED IN THE WATER** to be or become well-balanced in the water (*refers to a vessel*) 10 *vt* **MAKE ADJUSTMENTS TO IMPROVE AIRCRAFT STABILITY** to improve the stability of an aircraft, e.g. by redistributing the load before takeoff or by transferring fuel during flight 11 *vti* **ALTER AN OPINION TO SUIT CIRCUMSTANCES** to alter opinions or behaviour to suit the circumstances of a particular time as an expedient means of gaining an advantage 12 *vi* **ADOPT A NEUTRAL POSITION** to adopt a neutral position between two parties that are in dispute 13 *vt* **BEAT SOMEBODY THOROUGHLY** to beat or overwhelm somebody completely (*informal*) ○ *got trimmed regularly at tennis by her partner* 14 *vt* **SCOLD** to reprimand or scold somebody (*informal*) 15 *vt* **DEFEAT** to inflict a heavy defeat on somebody or something (*informal*) 16 *vt* **CHEAT** to cheat or deceive somebody (*informal*) ■ *adj* (**trimmer, trimmest**) 1 **FIT** fit, healthy, slim, or in good physical condition ○ *had a trim figure* 2 **NEAT AND TIDY** neat and tidy, compact, or in good order ■ *n* 1 **ACT OF CUTTING** the cutting of something in order to make it neater or tidier ○ *gave the hedge a trim* 2 **HAIRCUT** a haircut that tidies rather than changes a hairstyle 3 **SOMETHING USED AS DECORATION** something used for decoration such as contrasting material attached to a piece of clothing 4 **DECORATIVE PARTS OF A VEHICLE** the accessories and decorative parts added to the interior or exterior of a vehicle 5 **DECORATIVE ADDITIONS TO A BUILDING** the nonstructural decorative additions to a building, especially mouldings around doorways, windows, and walls 6 *US* **WINDOW DRESSING** the goods, props, and other items placed in a shop window 7 **SOMETHING TRIMMED OFF** a piece of something removed by trimming 8 **FILM CUT DURING EDITING** a piece of film eliminated from a shot during editing 9 **ADJUSTMENT OF AN AIRCRAFT FOR STABILITY** adjustment of the controls of an aircraft to give stability 10 **FLIGHT POSITION** the position of an aircraft in flight relative to the horizon 11 **APPEARANCE OF A VESSEL** the way a vessel appears when it is fitted out and prepared for sailing 12 **RELATION BETWEEN A SAIL AND A DIRECTION** the relation between the plane of a sail and the direction in which the vessel is pointing 13 **POSITION OF A VESSEL** the position of a ship or boat, especially with reference to the horizontal and to the difference between the depth in water at the front and back of the vessel 14 **BUOYANCY** the relative buoyancy of a submarine [Old English *trymman* 'strengthen'. < Indo-European, 'be solid'.] —**trim** *adv* —**trimly** *adv* —**trimness** *n*

trimaran /trī́mə ran, trī́mə rán/ *n* a sailing boat with three hulls arranged side by side [Mid-20C. Blend of TRI- + CATAMARAN.]

Trimble /trímb'l/, **David** (*b.* 1944) British politician

trimer /trī́mər/ *n* a polymer formed by combining three identical molecules —**trimeric** /trī mérrik/ *adj*

trimerous /trímmərəss/ *adj* 1 having or consisting of three similar parts or segments 2 describes a flower with parts arranged in groups of three [Early 19C. < Greek *trimerēs* < *meros* 'part'.]

trimester /trī méstər/ *n* 1 a period of three months, especially one of the three three-month periods into which human pregnancy is divided for medical purposes 2 *US* one of the three terms into which the academic year is divided by some US colleges, schools, and universities [Early 19C. Via French *trimestre* < Latin *trimestris* 'of three months' < *mensis* 'month'.] —**trimestral** *adj* —**trimestrial** *adj*

trimeter /trímmitər/ *n* a line of verse made up of three metrical feet

trimethadione /trī́ methə dī́ ōn/ *n* $C_6H_9NO_3$ a white, crystalline, bitter-tasting compound with an odour similar to camphor. Use: epileptic anticonvulsant. [Contraction of TRI- + METHYL + DI-[1] + -ONE]

trimethoprim /trī méthə prim/ *n* $C_{14}H_{18}N_4O_3$ a synthetic drug. Use: bactericide, treatment of malaria. [Mid-20C. Contraction of TRI- + METHYL + OXY- + PYRIMIDINE.]

trimetric /trī méttrik/, **trimetrical** /trī méttrik'l/ *adj* 1 consisting of one or more trimeters 2 CRYSTALS = **orthorhombic**

trimetric projection *n* a geometric projection in which the three axes are measured on different scales and are at arbitrary angles

trimetrogon /trī méttrə gon/ *n* a technique in which three aerial photographs are taken at the same time, one vertical and two at oblique angles, in order to obtain more topographical detail [Mid-20C. < TRI- + *Metrogon*, commercial lens.]

trimmer /trímmər/ *n* 1 **SOMEBODY OR SOMETHING THAT TRIMS** somebody or something that trims, e.g. a machine for trimming hedges, lawns, or timber 2 **SOMEBODY ALTERING AN OPINION ACCORDING TO CIRCUMSTANCES** somebody whose opinions or behaviour change to suit the circumstances of a particular time in order to gain an advantage (*disapproving*) 3 **VARIABLE CAPACITOR** a small variable capacitor used, usually in parallel with a larger capacitor, to adjust the overall capacitance of the combination 4 **CROSSWISE JOIST** a joist or beam that is set crosswise and has the ends of the joists running lengthwise fitted into it 5 **SOMEBODY WHO STOWS CARGO** a person who stows cargo on a ship to ensure good stability 6 AEROSP = **trim tab**

trimming /trímming/ *n* 1 **SOMETHING ATTACHED AS DECORATION** a piece of material used as a decoration on clothing or furnishings, e.g. a strip of lace, fur, or braid along the edge of a piece of clothing 2 **ACT OF SOMETHING THAT TRIMS** the act of somebody or something that trims 3 **BEATING** a vigorous beating or thrashing (*dated informal*) ■ **trimmings** *npl* 1 **FOOD ACCOMPANYING A MAIN DISH** the items of food traditionally served as accompaniments to a main dish 2 **EXTRAS** things added to something as accessories or extras 3 **PIECES CUT OFF DURING TRIMMING** the parts or pieces cut off when something is trimmed 4 *NZ* **CHRISTMAS DECORATIONS** Christmas decorations

trimming capacitor *n* ELECTRONICS = **trimmer** *n.* 3

trimming tab *n* AEROSP = **trim tab**

trimolecular /trī́mə lékyŏŏlər/ *adj* relating to or consisting of three molecules

trimonthly /trī múnthli/ *adj* occurring or done every three months —**trimonthly** *adv*

trimorph /trī́ mawrf/ *n* 1 a substance, especially a mineral, that occurs in three distinct crystalline forms 2 one of the crystalline forms in which a trimorph exists

trimorphism /trī máwrfizəm/ *n* 1 the property of existing in three different crystalline forms 2 the adoption of three successive forms during a life cycle, e.g. the forms of larva, pupa, and adult in some insects [Mid-19C. < Greek *trimorphos* < *morphē* 'form'.] —**trimorphic** *adj* —**trimorphically** *adv* —**trimorphous** *adj*

trimotor /trī́ mōtər/ *n* a vehicle, typically an aeroplane, with three engines

trim tab *n* a flight control surface that can be adjusted in flight by the pilot, for trimming out control forces

Trimurti /tri mŏŏrti/ *n* the Hindu gods Brahma, Vishnu, and Shiva, the creator, preserver, and destroyer respectively, who represent the three forms of the supreme being [Mid-19C. < Sanskrit, < *mūrti* 'form'.]

trinary /trī́nəri/ *adj* 1 consisting of three parts 2 progressing in threes

Trincomalee /tríngkōmə lée/ port in NE Sri Lanka. Population: 44,313 (1981).

trine /trīn/ *adj* 1 **TRIPLE** consisting of three parts 2 **120° APART** in astrology, describes two planets or astronomical objects separated by an angle of 120° as seen from the Earth ■ *n* 1 **GROUP OF 3** a group of three, or something consisting of three parts 2 **ASPECT OF 120°** in astrology, an aspect of 120° between two planets or astronomical objects as seen from the Earth [14C. Via Old French < Latin *trinus*, singular of *trini* 'in threes'.] —**trinal** *adj*

Trinidad /trínni dad/ island in the Caribbean, part of Trinidad and Tobago. Population: 1,065,245 (1998). Area: 4,828 sq. km/1,864 sq. mi. —**Trinidadian** /trínni dáddi ən/ *n, adj*

Trinidad and Tobago /trínni dad ənd tə báy gō/ republic in the Caribbean, comprising two islands off the NE coast of Venezuela. Capital: Port-of-Spain. Population: 1,116,595 (1998). Area: 5,128 sq. km/1,980 sq. mi.

Trinil man /tréenil man/ *n* ANTHROP = **Java man** [Early 20C. After *Trinil*, village in Java.]

Trinitarian /trínni táiri ən/ *n* a believer in the Christian doctrine of the Trinity —**Trinitarian** *adj* —**Trinitarianism** *n*

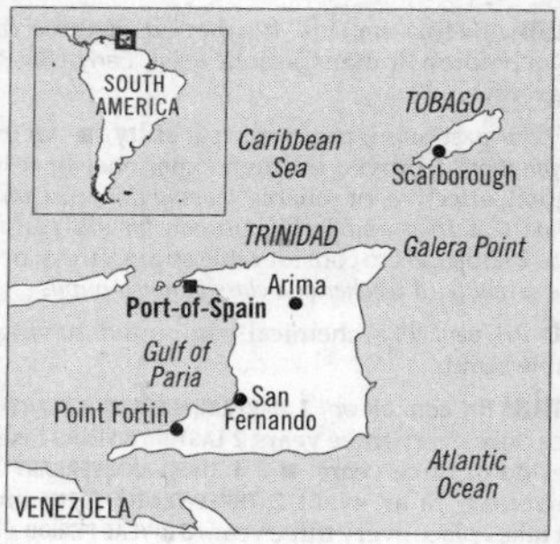

Trinidad and Tobago

trinitrobenzene /trī́ nītrō bén zeen/ *n* $C_6H_3(N_3O_2)_3$ a yellow crystalline compound. Use: explosives.

trinitroglycerin /trī́ nītrō glíssərin/ *n* CHEM = **nitroglycerine**

trinitrotoluene /trī́ nītrō tóllyoo een/, **trinitrotoluol** /-tóllyoo ol/ *n* full form of **TNT**

trinity /trínnə ti/ (*plural* **-ties**) *n* 1 a group of three 2 the condition of existing as three persons or things [13C. Via Old French *trinité* < Latin *trinitas* < *trinus* 'threefold' (see TRINE).]

Trinity *n* 1 the union of the three persons of the Christian God, the Father, Jesus Christ, the Son, and the Holy Spirit, in a single Godhead 2 CHR = **Trinity Sunday** 3 EDUC = **Trinity term**

Trinity Brethren *npl* the members of Trinity House

Trinity House *n* an association that licenses maritime pilots and maintains lighthouses and buoys around the coasts of England, Wales, the Channel Islands, and Gibraltar

Trinity Sunday, Trinity *n* the Sunday eight weeks after Easter when Christians celebrate the doctrine of the Trinity

Trinity term, Trinity *n* 1 the term at some universities that begins after Easter 2 one of the English court terms, beginning in the early summer after Trinity Sunday

Trinitytide /trínnə ti tīd/ *n* the season from Trinity Sunday to Advent

trinket /tríngkit/ *n* 1 a small article of little value such as an ornament or piece of jewellery 2 something trivial or unimportant [Mid-16C. < ?] —**trinketry** *n*

trinomial /trī nṓmi əl/ *adj* 1 **HAVING 3 MATHEMATICAL EXPRESSIONS** consisting of three mathematical terms or expressions 2 **HAVING 3 NAMES** relating to or consisting of three taxonomic names, denoting the genus, species, and subspecies or variety of an organism ■ *n* **POLYNOMIAL WITH 3 TERMS** a polynomial made up of three terms linked by plus or minus signs [Late 17C. Blend of TRI- + BINOMIAL.] —**trinomially** *adv*

trinucleotide /trī nyŏŏkli ə tīd/ *n* a chemical compound consisting of three linked mononucleotides

trio /trée ō/ (*plural* **-os**) *n* 1 **GROUP OF 3** a group or set of three 2 **GROUP OF 3 MUSICIANS** a group of three musicians who perform together 3 **MUSIC FOR 3 MUSICIANS** a piece of music composed for a group of three musicians 4 **MIDDLE SECTION OF A MUSICAL PIECE** the middle section of a minuet, march, or other piece of music, composed in a contrasting style and originally written for three instruments 5 **SET OF 3 PIQUET CARDS** a set of three equal-ranking cards in piquet [Early 18C. < Italian, < *tri-* after *duo* 'duet'.]

triode /trī́ ōd/ *n* an electron valve that has an anode, a cathode, and a grid that controls electron flow between the two

triol /trī́ ol/ *n* a chemical compound that has three hydroxyl groups

triolet /trée ə let, trī́-, -ōlet, -əlit/ *n* a poem consisting of eight lines with a rhyme scheme of abaaabab in which the first, fourth, and seventh lines are the same, as are the second and eighth lines [Mid-17C. < French, 'small trio'.]

triose /trī́ ōz/ *n* a simple sugar containing three carbon atoms

trio sonata *n* a baroque sonata composed for three instruments, usually two violins and one cello or bass viol, with keyboard continuo accompaniment

trioxide /trī ók sīd/ *n* an oxide containing three oxygen atoms per molecule

trip /trip/ *n* 1 **JOURNEY** a journey of relatively short duration, especially to a place and back again, usually for a specific purpose such as a holiday or business meeting 2 **FALL CAUSED BY CATCHING THE FOOT** a fall or stumble caused by catching the foot on something 3 **ACTION THAT CAUSES A FALL** an action that causes somebody to fall or stumble 4 **LIGHT STEP** a light or nimble skip, step, or tread 5 **ERROR** a blunder, error, or mistake 6 **SOMETHING ACTING AS A SWITCH** a catch or switch that activates a mechanism 7 **DRUG-INDUCED HALLUCINATION** the experience produced by taking a hallucinogenic drug (*informal*) 8 **STIMULATING EXPERIENCE** an intense, emotional, or stimulating experience (*informal*) ○ *a nostalgia trip* 9 **INTENSE INTEREST** an obsessive and often shortlived interest in something (*informal*) 10 *US* **UNUSUAL OR AMUSING THING** something such as an experience, event, or person that somebody enjoys or takes pleasure in (*slang*) ○ *living abroad may not be your trip* ■ *v* (**trips, tripping, tripped**) 1 *vti* **STUMBLE OR CAUSE SOMEBODY TO STUMBLE** to stumble or fall as a result of catching the foot on something, or to cause somebody to stumble or fall by making the person's foot catch on something ○ *The player tripped up his opponent deliberately.* ○ *I tripped and fell.* 2 *vt* **CATCH SOMEBODY IN A MISTAKE** to detect or catch somebody out through a mistake ○ *He's trying to trip them up with his questions.* 3 *vti* **MAKE A MISTAKE** to make or cause somebody to make a mistake 4 *vi* **MOVE WITH RAPID LIGHT STEPS** to move, run, walk, or dance with rapid light steps ○ *went tripping off down the road* 5 *vt* **CAUSE A DEVICE TO OPERATE** to operate or to cause a device or system to operate 6 *vi* **EXPERIENCE DRUG EFFECTS** to experience the effects of a hallucinogenic drug (*informal*) 7 *vi* **GO ON A JOURNEY** to go on a journey, tour, or excursion 8 *vt* **FREE AN ANCHOR** to free an anchor from the sea bed so that it hangs loose on the end of its rope or chain 9 *vt* **TIP UP A YARD** to tilt or tip up a yard or mast so that it can be lowered 10 *vt* **RAISE AN UPPER MAST** to raise one of the upper masts of a sailing ship to remove the bar (**fid**) that supports it so that it can be lowered [14C. < Old French *tripper* < Germanic.]

tripalmitin /trī pálmitin/ *n* CHEM = **palmitin**

tripartite /trī paár tīt/ *adj* 1 **INVOLVING 3 PARTIES** involving, made between, or ratified by three parties, groups, or nations ○ *a tripartite agreement* 2 **IN 3 PARTS** divided into or made up of three parts 3 **WITH 3 LOBES** describes a leaf that has three deeply divided lobes —**tripartitely** *adv*

tripartition /trī paar tísh'n/ *n* a division of something into three parts or among three parties

tripe /trīp/ *n* 1 the stomach lining of a ruminant such as a cow or sheep, used as food 2 something absurd, untrue, or worthless (*informal*) [14C. < Old French.]

trip hammer, triphammer /tríp hamər/ *n* a power hammer with a massive head raised by a cam

triphenylmethane /trī feé nīl meé thayn, trī fénnīl-/ *n* $CH(C_6H_5)_3$ a colourless crystalline hydrocarbon. Use: manufacture of dyes.

triphibian /trī fíbbi ən/ *n* 1 a craft that can operate on water, on land, and in the air 2 a competitor in a triathlon ■ *adj* = **triphibious** [Mid-20C. Blend of TRI- + AMPHIBIAN.]

triphibious /trī fíbbi əss/, **triphibian** *adj* operating or occurring in the water, on the land, and in the air [Mid-20C. Blend of TRI- + AMPHIBIOUS.]

trip hop *n* a rhythmic dance music developed from hip-hop in the 1990s and using electronic sampling to create a psychedelic effect

triphosphate /trī fóss fayt/ *n* a salt or ester with three phosphate groups

triphosphopyridine nucleotide /trī fosfō pírri deen-/ *n* BIOCHEM = **NADP**

triphthong /tríf thong, tríp thong/ *n* 1 a vowel sound that combines three elements in one syllable 2 LING = **trigraph** [Mid-16C. Via French *triphtongue* < medieval Greek *triphthongos* < Greek *phthongos* 'sound'.] —**triphthongal** /trif thóng g'l, trip-/ *adj*

tripinnate /trī pínnət, -pínnayt/ *adj* describes a leaf in which the main stalk bears opposite pairs of leaflets that themselves have a similar arrangement of secondary leaflets that are also similarly subdivided —**tripinnately** *adv*

Tripitaka /tríppi taákə/ *n* the three long canonical texts of Buddhism, the *Vinayapitaka*, the *Suttapitaka*, and the *Abhidhammapitaka* [Late 19C. < Sanskrit < *piṭaka* 'basket'.]

triplane /trī playn/ *n* an aeroplane with three main wings positioned one above the other

triple /trípp'l/ *adj* 1 **HAVING 3 PARTS** consisting of three parts, members, or units 2 **3 TIMES AS MUCH** three times as great, as much, or as many 3 **DONE 3 TIMES** done or occurring three times 4 **WITH 3 SIMILAR SYLLABLES** having three similar or corresponding syllables in a verse 5 **WITH 3 BEATS** having three musical beats in a bar ■ *vti* (**-ples, -pling, -pled**) **MAKE 3 TIMES AS MUCH** to become or cause something to become three times as great, as much, or as many ■ *n* 1 **SOMETHING 3 TIMES GREATER** a number or amount that is three times greater than another or than usual 2 **TREBLE MEASURE** a measure, usually of spirits, containing three times the amount of a single measure 3 **SET OF 3** a group, series, or set of three things 4 *US* HORSERACING = **trifecta** [14C. Via French or directly < Latin *triplus* < Greek *triplous*.]

triple bond *n* a chemical bond composed of three covalent bonds between two atoms

triple crown, Triple Crown *n* 1 **VICTORY IN SPORTS EVENTS** victory in all three of a set of major events in certain sports 2 **HORSERACING VICTORY** in horseracing, victory in the Derby, St Leger, and 2000 Guineas in the same season 3 **VICTORY OVER THREE TEAMS** in rugby, victory in the home championships contested between England, Ireland, Scotland, and Wales by one team over the other three in the same season 4 **POPE'S TIARA** the tiara that the Pope wears as a symbol of the papacy

triple-decker /-dékər/ *n* something such as a structure or sandwich with three levels or layers

Triple Entente *n* an understanding that developed between Britain, France, and Tsarist Russia for dealing with their various colonial differences, formalized as a military pact in 1914

triple jump *n* an event requiring an athlete to perform a short run and three consecutive jumps, landing first on one foot, then the opposite foot, and finally both feet, in continuous motion

triple measure *n* US = **triple time**

triple point *n* the temperature and pressure at which the solid, liquid, and gaseous phases of a substance exist in equilibrium

triple rhyme *n* a rhyme in which three syllables rhyme with another three, e.g. 'snobbery' and 'robbery'

triple sec *n* a sweet colourless liqueur that is orange-flavoured

triplet /trípplət/ *n* 1 **GROUP OF 3** three things that are connected or related to each other in some way 2 **ONE OF 3 OFFSPRING** one of three children or animals that are delivered by the same mother during one birth 3 **GROUP OF 3 NOTES** a group of three notes played in the time usually taken by two notes of the same value 4 **VERSE OF 3 LINES** a poetic stanza of three lines, usually with a single rhyme and sometimes sharing the same metrical pattern 5 **CHEMICAL UNIT WITH 2 UNPAIRED ELECTRONS** an atom, molecule, or radical with two unpaired electrons 6 **GROUP OF 3 ELEMENTARY PARTICLES** a group of three elementary particles with similar characteristics that differ only in their charge 7 GENETICS = **codon** [Mid-17C. < TRIPLE, after *doublet*.]

triple-team *vti US* to use three members of a sports team to guard only one opponent, e.g. in basketball or American football —**triple team** *n*

triple time *n* a musical metre or time signature with three beats to the bar ○ *a waltz in triple time*

triple-tonguing *n* production of a rapid series of notes on a wind or brass instrument by alternating tongue movements to repeat a pattern of three articulated sounds —**triple-tongue** *vi*

triple witching hour *n* a time when stock options, stock index futures, and options on such futures all mature at once

triplex /trípplekś/ *n US, Can* a building divided into three flats on three separate floors, or a single flat that occupies three floors [Early 17C. < Latin, 'threefold'.]

triplicate *n* /trípplikət/ **WITH 3 IDENTICAL PARTS** something that has three identical parts to it or that exists in three identical copies ■ *adj* /trípplikət/ **THREEFOLD** triple or tripled ■ *v* /trípli kayt/ (**-cates, -cating, -cated**) 1 *vt* **MAKE 3 COPIES OF** to make three identical copies of something 2 *vti* **MULTIPLY SOMETHING BY 3** to multiply, or cause something to be multiplied, by three [15C. < Latin *triplicat-*, past participle of *triplicare* 'triple' < *triplex* 'threefold'.] —**triplication** /tríppli káysh'n/ *n*

triplicity /tri plíssəti, trī-/ (*plural* **-ties**) *n* 1 **EXISTENCE OF 3 IDENTICAL COPIES** the condition of existing in three identical copies 2 **GROUP OF 3** a group or combination of three 3 **ZODIACAL DIVISION** one of the four groups that the zodiac is traditionally divided into, each separated from the other by 120° and consisting of three astrological signs [14C. < late Latin *triplicitas* < Latin *triplex* 'threefold'.]

triploid /trí ployd/ *adj* possessing three representatives of each chromosome ■ *n* a triploid cell, nucleus, or organism —**triploidy** *n*

triply /tríppli/ *adv* threefold or in a triple number, measure, or degree

tripod /trī pod/ *n* 1 a frame or stand with three legs that are usually collapsible, used for supporting something such as a camera, compass, theodolite, or other piece of equipment 2 a piece of furniture such as a pot, cauldron, stool, or table with three legs [Early 17C. < Latin *tripod-*, stem of *tripus* < Greek *tripous* 'three-footed' < *pous* 'foot'.] —**tripodal** /tríppəd'l/ *adj*

tripoli /tríppəli/ *n* a light porous siliceous sedimentary rock containing schist or shells of diatoms and used in powdered form for polishing [Early 17C. < French after TRIPOLI.]

Tripoli /tríppəli/ 1 capital of Libya, on the Mediterranean Sea. Population: 1,500,000 (1994). 2 city in NW Lebanon, on the Mediterranean Sea. Population: 160,000 (1998 estimate).

Tripolitania /tríppəli táyni ə/ ancient region surrounding Tripoli in NW Libya —**Triplotanian** *n, adj*

tripos /trī poss/ (*plural* **-poses**) *n* a final honours examination for the BA degree at Cambridge University [Late 16C. Alteration of Latin *tripus* (see TRIPOD).]

tripper /tríppər/ *n* 1 a person who takes a journey or outing, especially one for pleasure (*informal*) 2 *US* a person who takes a hallucinogenic drug such as LSD (*slang*) 3 ELEC ENG = **trip** *n*. 6

trippet /tríppit/ *n* a mechanism that strikes another part at regular intervals or is struck by it [15C. < TRIP.]

trippingly /tríppingli/ *adv* in a manner that is nimble, lively, or fluent

trippy /tríppi/ (**-pier, -piest**) *adj* accompanied by or producing distorted visual or sound effects similar to those associated with psychedelic drugs, especially LSD (*slang*)

trip switch *n* an electric switch designed to interrupt a circuit, or the power to a machine, quickly

triptane /tríp tayn/ *n* C_7H_{17} a colourless flammable liquid alkane. Use: antiknock compound in aviation fuel. [Mid-20C. Contraction of *trimethylbutane*.]

triptych /tríptik/ *n* 1 a painting or carving consisting of three panels, often made as an altarpiece hinged together so that when the smaller outer panels are folded the middle part is entirely covered 2 in ancient times, a set of three writing tablets hinged or tied together [Mid-18C. < Greek *triptukhos* 'threefold' < *ptux* 'fold'.]

tripwire /tríp wīr/ *n* 1 a wire that is attached to a trap, mine, weapon, alarm, camera, or other device in such a way that it will set the device off if disturbed 2 a concealed length of wire or rope stretched across a piece of land at ground level for an enemy or intruder to trip over

triquetral bone /trī kweétrəl-, -kwéttrəl-/, **triquetral** *n* a pyramid-shaped bone in the wrist that connects with the inner bone of the forearm (**ulna**) on the side of the little finger [Mid-17C. < Latin *triquetrus* 'three-cornered'.]

triquetrous /trī kweétrəss, -kwét-/ *adj* triangular, especially in a cross section of something [Mid-17C. < Latin *triquetrus* 'three-cornered'.]

triradiate /trī ráydi ət, -ayt/ *adj* having three rays or radiating branches —**triradiately** *adv*

Triratna /tree rátnə/ *n* the three principal components of Buddhism, namely the Buddha or teacher, the teaching, and the priesthood [< Sanskrit, 'three jewels' < *ratna* 'jewel']

trireme /trī reem/ *n* a galley, originally used by the ancient Greeks as a warship and later adopted by the Romans, that had three rows of oars on each side, arranged one above the other [Early 17C. Directly or via French *trirème* < Latin *triremis* 'having three banks of oars' < *remus* 'oar'.]

trisaccharide /trī sákə rīd/ *n* a sugar that has three linked monosaccharide units

trisect /trī sékt/ *vt* to divide something into three parts, especially equal parts —**trisection** /-séksh'n/ *n* —**trisector** *n*

trishaw /trī shaw/ *n* TRANSP = **rickshaw** *n.* 2

triskaidekaphobia /tríss kī dékə fōbi ə/ *n* an irrational or obsessive fear of the number 13 [Early 20C. < Greek *triskaideka* 'thirteen'.] —**triskaidekaphobe** /-fōb/ *n* —**triskaidekaphobic** /-fōbik/ *adj*

triskelion /tri skélli on, trī-/ (*plural* **-a** /-li ə/), **triskele** /trī skeel, tríss-/ *n* a symbol in the form of three bent or curved lines or limbs radiating from a common centre [Mid-19C. < modern Latin, < Greek *triskelēs* 'three-legged' < *skelos* 'leg'.]

trismus /trízməss/ *n* a sustained spasm of the jaw muscles, characteristic of the early stages of tetanus [Late 17C. Via modern Latin < Greek *trismos* 'grinding'.] —**trismic** *adj*

trisoctahedron /triss óktə heédrən/ (*plural* **-drons** *or* **-dra** /-drə/) *n* a solid with 24 identical triangular faces, each triplet of which rests on a face of an underlying octahedron [Mid-19C. < Greek *tris* 'thrice'.] —**trisoctahedral** *adj*

trisodium /trī sōdi əm/ *adj* containing three sodium atoms in a molecule

trisomy /trī sōmi/ *n* the genetic condition of having one or more sets of three chromosomes instead of the usual two chromosomes —**trisomic** /trī sōmik/ *adj*

Tristan and Iseult /trístən ənd i soólt, trí stan-/, **Tristram and Isolde** /trístrəm ənd i sóldə, -zóldə/ *n* a pair of lovers in medieval legend. Tristan was a knight who fell in love with Iseult, his uncle's bride, after drinking a love potion.

Tristan da Cunha /trístən də koónə/ group of volcanic islands in the South Atlantic Ocean, part of the British dependency of St Helena. Population: 313 (1988). Area: 202 sq. km/78 sq. mi.

tristate /trī stayt/ *adj US* relating to three adjacent states of the United States or the adjoining parts of them

tristearin /trī steérin/ *n* CHEM = **stearin** *n.* 1

tristich /trístik/ *n* a poem, stanza, refrain, or other division of poetry that consists of three lines [Early 19C. After DISTICH.] —**tristichic** /tri stíkik/ *adj*

tristimulus values /trī stímyooləss-/ *npl* the three values representing the amounts of red, green, and blue light that in combination match a particular colour

Tristram *n* ◊ **Tristan and Iseult**

trisulphide /trī súl fīd/ *n* a sulphide that has three sulphur molecules per atom

trisyllable /trī sílləb'l/ *n* a word of three syllables, e.g. 'enormous' —**trisyllabic** /trī si lábbik/ *adj* —**trisyllabically** *adv*

tritanopia /trītə nōpi ə, trít-/ *n* a rare condition in which perception of blue and green becomes confused [Early 20C. < Greek *tritos* 'third' + *anōpia* 'blindness'.] —**tritanopic** *adj*

trite /trīt/ (**triter, tritest**) *adj* overused and consequently lacking in interest or originality [Mid-16C. < Latin *tritus*, past participle of *terere* 'wear out'.] —**tritely** *adv* —**triteness** *n*

tritheism /trī thi izəm/ *n* belief in three gods, especially the belief or doctrine that the Christian Trinity of Father, Son, and Holy Spirit consists of three distinct divinities —**tritheist** *n* —**tritheistic** /-ístik/ *adj*

tritiate /trítti ayt/ (**-ates, -ating, -ated**) *vt* to replace normal hydrogen atoms, or chemically combine something, with tritium —**tritiation** /-áysh'n/ *n*

triticale /trítti kaáli, -káyli/ *n* a high-protein high-yielding cereal plant that is a hybrid of wheat and rye [Mid-20C. Blend of modern Latin *Triticum* 'wheat' + *Secale* 'rye'.]

tritium /trítti əm/ *n* (*symbol* **T**) a radioactive isotope of hydrogen occurring naturally in trace amounts and having atomic mass 3 and a half-life of 12.3 years [Mid-20C. < modern Latin, < Greek *tritos* 'third'.]

triton[1] /trīt'n/ *n* a large tropical marine gastropod mollusc with a heavy multicoloured spiral shell. Family: Cymatiidae. [Late 18C. Via modern Latin < Latin *Triton* 'the god Triton'.]

triton[2] /trī ton/ *n* the nucleus of a tritium atom, consisting of one proton and two neutrons [Mid-20C. < TRITIUM.]

Triton[1] /trīt'n/ *n* a god of the sea in Greek mythology, the son of Poseidon and Amphitrite, represented as having the tail of a fish and the upper body of a man [Late 16C. Via Latin < Greek *Tritōn*.]

Triton[2] *n* the largest moon of the planet Neptune, about 2,700 km/1,680 mi. in diameter, and revolving in a direction counter to that of the planet [< its dependence on the planet Neptune, like the god Triton's dependence on the sea god Neptune]

tritone *n* a dissonant musical interval composed of three whole tones

triturate *vt* /tríttyoo rayt/ (**-rates, -rating, -rated**) to grind or rub a substance into a fine powder ■ *n* /tríttyoorət/ a finely ground powder, especially a drug [Mid-18C. < late Latin *triturat-*, past participle of *triturare* 'thresh' < Latin *terere* 'rub'.] —**triturable** *adj* —**triturator** *n*

trituration /tríttyoo ráysh'n/ *n* **1** GRINDING OF SOMETHING INTO POWDER the process of grinding or rubbing a substance into a fine powder **2** BEING A FINE POWDER the condition of having been ground or rubbed into a fine powder **3** POWDERED DRUG MIXTURE a mixture of powdered drugs prepared pharmaceutically **4** MIXING OF AMALGAM the mixing of an amalgam, usually of silver and mercury, for use in filling cavities in teeth

triumph /trī umf/ *n* **1** SUCCESS an act or occasion of winning, being victorious, or overcoming something **2** JOY ABOUT SUCCESS the happiness, pride, or feeling of elation that comes from winning, being victorious, or overcoming something **3** OUTSTANDING SUCCESS something that is notable for its exceptional quality or for being a great achievement ○ *The reviews hailed the company's new production of Hamlet as a triumph.* **4** ROMAN VICTORY PARADE in ancient Rome, a procession through the streets of Rome to the Capitoline Hill to mark a general's victory over a foreign army ■ *vi* **1** ACHIEVE SUCCESS to be successful, especially against an adversary or in combating the odds against success ○ *triumphed over life's setbacks* **2** BECOME EXULTANT to experience the happiness, pride, or feeling of elation that comes from winning, being victorious, or overcoming something [14C. Via Old French *triumphe* < Latin *triumphus*.] —**triumphal** /trī úmf'l/ *adj*

triumphal arch *n* a monument, usually in the form of an ornamental free-standing arch spanning a street, built to commemorate something, especially an outstanding military victory

triumphalism /trī úmf'lizəm/ *n* **1** a display or feeling of often excessive pride in having achieved a victory or been proved right **2** the conviction that one belief or set of beliefs, especially religious or political ones, is victorious and far superior to any others —**triumphalist** *n, adj*

triumphant /trī úmfənt/ *adj* **1** FULL OF PRIDE AT VICTORY displaying or feeling great pride in having achieved a victory **2** VICTORIOUS successful or victorious **3** VERY IMPRESSIVE outstandingly successful ○ *made a triumphant reappearance in the role he made famous* —**triumphantly** *adv*

triumvir /trī úmvər/ (*plural* **-virs** *or* **-viri** /-vi reel/) *n* **1** each of the three people who made up a triumvirate, especially in ancient Rome **2** a person who shares power with two other people (*formal*) [Late 16C. < Latin, back-formation < *triumviri* 'board of three men' < *trium virum* 'of three men'.] —**triumviral** *adj*

triumvirate /trī úmvərət/ *n* **1** ROMAN COMMITTEE OF 3 RULERS a group of three men who together were responsible for public administration or civil authority in the government system of ancient Rome **2** 3 SHARING AUTHORITY a group of three people who jointly share some responsibility, authority, or power **3** POSITION OF SHARING POWER the position of being one of three who exercise power or authority **4** TERM OF OFFICE OF SHARED POWER the duration of the term of office for somebody who shares power or authority with two others **5** RULE BY A GROUP OF 3 government or rule by a group of three [Late 16C. < Latin *triumviratus* < *triumviri* (see TRIUMVIR).]

triune /trī yoon/, **Triune** *adj* consisting of or being three in one, e.g. in the Christian Trinity ■ *n* a group consisting of three members, especially the Christian Trinity [Early 17C. < TRI- + Latin *unus* 'one'.]

triunity /trī yoónəti/ (*plural* **-ties**) *n* = **trinity** *n.* 1

trivalent /trī váylənt/, **tervalent** /tur-/ *adj* **1** having a chemical valency of three **2** with three chemical valencies —**trivalency** *n*

Trivandrum /tri vándrəm/ capital of Kerala State, S India. Population: 483,086 (1991).

trivet /trívvit/ *n* **1** a stand or support, usually metal with three legs, for hot pans and dishes **2** a device, usually metal with three legs, that fits over the grate of a fire to support a pan or kettle [15C. Probably alteration of Latin *triped-*, stem of *tripes* 'three-footed' < *pes* 'foot'.]

trivia[1] /trívvi ə/ *npl* a collection of insignificant or obscure items, details, or information (+ *singular or plural verb*) [Early 20C. Latinized back-formation < TRIVIAL.]

trivia[2] plural of **trivium**

trivial /trívvi əl/ *adj* **1** HAVING LITTLE VALUE lacking in seriousness, significance, or value **2** COMMONPLACE lacking any qualities that are unique or interesting **3** CONCERNED WITH TRIVIA relating to or concerned with trivia **4** WITH ZERO VALUES describes the simplest possible case mathematically, especially with all mathematical variables equal to zero **5** CONCERNING TRIVIUM belonging or relating to the trivium [15C. < Latin *trivialis* 'relating to the trivium division of subjects', hence 'commonplace' (because the trivium was considered to incorporate the less important subjects) < *trivium* (see TRIVIUM).] —**trivially** *adv* —**trivialness** *n*

trivialise *vt* = **trivialize**

triviality /trívvi álləti/ (*plural* **-ties**), **trivialism** /-əlizəm/ *n* **1** the condition or quality of having little importance or seriousness **2** something that is considered to lack importance or seriousness

trivialize /trívvi ə līz/ (**-izes, -izing, -ized**), **trivialise** (**-ises, -ising, -ised**) *vt* to treat something as, or make it appear, less important, significant, or valuable than it really is —**trivialization** *n*

trivial name *n* **1** a common or popular name for a substance that does not describe its exact chemical composition **2** the noun or adjective that follows the genus name in a taxonomic binomial

trivium /trívvi əm/ (*plural* **-a** /-vi ə/) *n* grammar, rhetoric, and logic, three of the seven liberal arts that formed the basis of medieval university study, traditionally considered to be less important than the other four. ◊ **quadrivium** [Early 19C. Via medieval Latin < Latin, 'place where three roads cross'.]

triweekly /trī weékli/ *adj* **1** APPEARING OR DONE EVERY 3 WEEKS occurring, published, or performed once every three weeks **2** APPEARING OR DONE 3 TIMES WEEKLY occurring, published, or performed three times each week ■ *adv* **1** EVERY 3 WEEKS once every three weeks **2** 3 TIMES A WEEK three times each week ■ *n* (*plural* **-lies**) **1** 3-WEEKLY PUBLICATION a publication that comes out every three weeks **2** PUBLICATION 3 TIMES A WEEK a publication that comes out three times each week

-trix *suffix* **1** a woman who performs a particular function ○ *administratrix* **2** a geometric element that performs a particular function ○ *directrix* [< Latin, feminine form of *-tor*]

tRNA *abbr* transfer RNA

Trobriand Islands /tró bri ənd-/ island group of Papua New Guinea, in the Solomon Sea. Area: 440 sq. km/170 sq. mi.

trocar /trō kaar/ *n* a sharply pointed steel rod sheathed with a tight-fitting cylindrical tube (**cannula**), used together to drain or extract fluid from a body cavity [Early 18C. < French *trocart* < *carre*, 'side of an instrument' < Latin *quadrum* 'square'.]

trochaic /trō káy ik/ *adj* relating to, belonging to, or consisting of trochees ■ *n* **1** LITERAT = **trochee** **2** a poem, or part of a poem, written in trochees —**trochaically** *adv*

trochal /trók'l/ *adj* shaped like a wheel [Mid-19C. < Greek *trokhos* 'wheel' (see TROCHOID).]

trochanter /trō kántər/ *n* **1** one of two rough knobs on the upper thigh bone (**femur**), where the muscles between the thigh and pelvis are attached in humans and other vertebrates **2** the second segment from the base of an insect's leg [Early 17C. Via French < Greek *trokhantēr* 'ball on which the hip bone turns in its socket' < *trekhein* 'run'.]

troche /trōsh/ *n* a medicinal lozenge [Late 16C. Alteration of obsolete *trochisk* < Greek *trokhiskos* 'small wheel' < *trokhos* 'wheel' (see TROCHOID).]

trochee /tróki/ *n* a metrical foot that consists of one stressed syllable followed by an unstressed syllable, e.g. the word 'human' [Late 16C. Via Latin *trochaeus* < Greek *trokhaios* 'running' < *trekhein* 'run'.]

trochlea /trókli ə/ n an anatomical part or structure with a grooved surface that resembles a pulley, especially that of a bone over which a tendon passes [Late 17C. Via Latin < Greek *trokhileia* 'pulley'.]

trochlear /trókli ər/ adj relating to, situated near, or resembling a trochlea or trochlear nerve

trochlear nerve n either of the fourth pair of cranial nerves serving the muscle that is used to rotate the eyeball outward and downward

trochoid /tró koyd/ n CURVE FORMED BY POINT ON RADIUS a curve formed by a point on the radius of a circle, or on the extended radius, as the circle rolls along a straight line ■ adj trochoid, trochoidal 1 ROTATING ABOUT CENTRAL AXIS rotating, showing rotation, or able to rotate about a central axis 2 RESEMBLING PIVOT resembling or functioning in the body like a pivot or pulley [Early 18C. < Greek *trokhoeidēs* 'wheel-like' < *trokhos* 'wheel' < *trekhein* 'run'.] —**trochoidally** /tró kóyd'li/ adv

trochophore /tróka fawr/, **trochosphere** /tróka sfeer/ n a free-swimming ciliated larval form of certain invertebrates such as molluscs and rotifers [Late 19C. < Greek *trokhos* 'wheel'.]

trockenbeerenauslese /trókən bairən owss layzə/ n the highest grade of German table wine, made from individually selected shrivelled grapes and typically very sweet [Mid-20C. < German *Trockenbeerenauslese* 'picking out dry grapes'.]

trod past tense, past participle of **tread**

trodden past participle of **tread**

trog /trog/ (**trogs, trogging, trogged**) vi to walk slowly and heavily (*informal*) [Late 20C. < ?]

troglodyte /trógglə dīt/ n 1 somebody living in a cave, especially somebody who belonged to a prehistoric cave-dwelling community 2 a solitary person who lives alone, especially somebody who is antisocial or unconventional [Late 15C. Via Latin *Troglodyta* < Greek *Troglodutai* 'ones who enter a hole', alteration of *Trōgodutai*, an Ethiopian people.] —**troglodytic** /-dittik/ adj

trogon /tró gon/ n a tropical or subtropical tree-dwelling bird with a short hooked bill, long tail, and brightly coloured plumage. Family: Trogonidae. [Late 18C. < modern Latin, < Greek *trōgein* 'gnaw'.]

troika /tróykə/ n 1 a carriage of Russian origin drawn by three horses harnessed abreast of each other 2 a team of three horses harnessed abreast of each other 3 = **triumvirate** n. 2 [Mid-19C. < Russian, < *troe* 'group of three'.]

troilism /tróylizəm/ n sexual activity involving three people [Mid-20C. < ?] —**troilist** n

troilite /tróy līt/ n a variety of iron sulphide found in some meteorites [Mid-19C. After Domenico *Troili*, 18C Italian who described meteorite containing it.]

Troilus /tróylass/ n in Greek mythology, the son of the Trojan king Priam

Trois-Rivières /twaà rívvi áir/ city in S Quebec Province, Canada, on the St Lawrence River. Population: 48,419 (1996).

Trojan /trójan/ n 1 a person who came from ancient Troy 2 a determined, strong, or courageous person —**Trojan** adj

Trojan asteroid n a member of either of the two groups of asteroids that share the same orbit as Jupiter but precede or follow it by about 60 degrees [Early 20C. Because the asteroids take their names from characters in Homer's *Iliad*.]

⚡**Trojan Horse** n 1 HOLLOW HORSE CONCEALING GREEKS in Greek legends, a hollow wooden horse that hid Greek soldiers, left at the gates of Troy 2 CONCEALED STRATAGEM somebody or something that is meant to disrupt, undermine, subvert, or destroy an enemy or rival, especially somebody or something that operates while concealed within an organization 3 DESTRUCTIVE COMPUTER PROGRAM a computer program containing a hidden function that causes damage to other programs while appearing to perform a valid function. ◊ **virus** n. 3, **worm** n. 8

troll[1] /trōl/ v 1 vti DRAG BAITED LINE THROUGH WATER to drag a baited line through water, often from the back of a boat moving slowly 2 vti TROLL IN ONE AREA to troll a particular area 3 vti TROLL FOR PARTICULAR FISH to try to catch a particular kind of fish by trolling 4 vi AMBLE ABOUT to walk casually about 5 vti WANDER AROUND SEARCHING FOR to wander round a particular area or place, especially in search of a sexual partner (*slang*) 6 vti ROLL OR CAUSE SOMETHING TO ROLL to roll or rotate, or cause something to

roll or rotate ■ n ACTIVITY OF DRAGGING BAITED FISHING LINE the act or process of fishing by trolling [14C. < ?] —**troller** n

troll[2] /trōl, trol/ n a supernatural being in Scandinavian legends depicted as either a dwarf or giant and living in caves or under bridges [Early 17C. Via Swedish or Norwegian < Old Norse, 'demon'.]

trolley /trólli/ n (*plural* -**leys**) 1 UK, Can WHEELED CART PUSHED BY HAND a wheeled cart that is pushed by hand and used for transporting things, especially luggage at an airport or railway station or goods in a supermarket 2 WHEELED HOSPITAL BED a wheeled bed used for taking patients from one part of a hospital to another, e.g. from the ward to the operating theatre. US term **gurney** 3 UK, Can WHEELED TABLE a small wheeled table used for serving or moving food and drinks 4 TRANSP= **trolleybus** 5 DEVICE COLLECTING POWER FROM AN OVERHEAD WIRE a device such as a wheel or pulley carried at the end of a pole that collects current from an overhead electric wire in order to power a vehicle 6 WAGON ON RAILS a small open cart that runs on rails and carries materials, especially goods in a factory or coal or other minerals in a mine or quarry 7 SUSPENDED TRUCK a small cart or basket suspended from an overhead rail and used, especially in factories and mines, for transporting loads ■ vti (-**leys, -leying, -leyed**) MOVE BY TROLLEY to travel by or transport something using a wheeled cart on a track or a vehicle powered by electrical current from overhead wires [Early 19C. Probably < TROLL[1] 'roll'.] ◊ **be off your trolley** to be mentally ill or intoxicated (*slang*)

trolleybus /trólli buss/ n (*plural* -**buses**) an electric bus that takes its power from overhead wires by means of a trolley on a pole

trolley car n US, Can a tram

trollop /tróllap/ n 1 an offensive term that deliberately insults a woman who is a prostitute or who is reputed to be sexually immoral 2 an offensive term that deliberately insults a girl's or a woman's appearance or her indifference to household chores [Early 17C. < ?] —**trollopy** adj

Trollope /tróllap/, **Anthony** (1815–82) British novelist —**Trollopian** /trólla pée ən/ adj

trombiculiasis /trom bíkyoo lī əssiss/, **trombidiasis** /trómbi dī əssiss/ n infestation with mite larvae (**chiggers**) that often causes severe rickettsial disease or viral disease [Early 20C. < modern Latin *Trombicula*, genus of mites.]

trombone /trom bṓn/ n 1 a brass wind instrument of varying size with a U-shaped slide that is moved to produce different pitches 2 a player of a trombone [Early 18C. Directly or via French < Italian, 'big trumpet' < *tromba* 'trumpet' < Germanic.]

trombonist /trom bṓnist/ n a person who plays the trombone

trommel /trómm'l/ n a rotating sieve for sizing or screening crushed rock or ore [Late 19C. < German *Trommel* 'drum'.]

trompe /tromp/ n a device formerly used for supplying air in a forge by means of a thin column of falling water [< French, 'trumpet']

Trompe l'oeil: Fresco (1561?) by Paolo Veronese at the Villa Barbaro, Maser, Italy

AKG London

trompe l'oeil /trómp lóya/ (*plural* **trompe l'oeils** /trómp lóya/) n 1 a technique used in realistic paintings to trick the eye, especially through the use of perspective to

create an illusion of three-dimensionality 2 a painting or other artistic object that uses trompe l'oeil [Late 19C. < French, 'deceives the eye'.]

Tromsø /trómssö/ fishing port in N Norway, on the island of Tromsø. Population: 57,485 (1998).

tron /tron/ n Scotland formerly, a public weighing machine set up in the marketplace of a burgh for weighing merchandise, now the place or building where the tron stood, particularly in Edinburgh and Glasgow [13C. Via Old French *trone* < Latin *trutina* < Greek *trutanē* 'balance'.]

-tron suffix 1 a device for manipulating atoms or subatomic particles, accelerator ○ *cyclotron* 2 a vacuum tube ○ *klystron*

trona /trṓnə/ n a greyish-white or yellowish hydrated sodium carbonate mineral. Source: salt deposits. [Late 18C. < Swedish.]

Trondheim /trónd hīm/ city in central Norway, on Trondheim Fjord. Population: 140,718 (1993).

Troon /troon/ coastal resort in SW Scotland, on the Firth of Clyde. Population: 15,231 (1991).

troop /troop/ n 1 BIG GROUP a large group of similar people, animals, or things 2 MILITARY UNIT a unit of soldiers that forms a subdivision of a cavalry or armoured cavalry squadron or artillery battery and is about the size of a platoon (*often before nouns*) ○ *troop movements in the area* 3 SCOUTING UNIT a unit of Boy Scouts or Guides under an adult leader and usually subdivided into several patrols 4 COLLECTIVE NAME FOR SOME ANIMALS a collective name for some animals, especially monkeys and kangaroos ■ **troops** npl 1 MILITARY GROUP a body of soldiers ○ *Order was restored by flooding the area with troops.* 2 LARGE NUMBER OF PEOPLE OR THINGS a large number of people or things ■ vi 1 GO AS A LARGE ORDERLY GROUP to move or gather together as a large orderly group 2 GO AS IF MARCHING to walk somewhere in a deliberate or heavy-footed way, as if marching ○ *After breakfast the family trooped off to church.* [Mid-16C. < French *troupe*.] ◊ **troop the colour** to parade a military flag ceremonially along ranks of soldiers

SPELLCHECK Do not confuse **troop** with **troupe**, which has a similar sound. Beware: your spellchecker will not catch this error.

trooper /troopar/ n 1 MEMBER OF A CAVALRY UNIT a member of a cavalry unit 2 CAVALRY HORSE a cavalry horse 3 TROOPSHIP a troopship (*informal*) 4 US MOUNTED POLICE OFFICER a member of a mounted police unit 5 US STATE TROOPER a state trooper

troopship /troop ship/ n a ship, sometimes one originally in the merchant navy, used for transporting military personnel

troostite /troost īt/ n a greyish or reddish manganese-containing form of the mineral willemite [Mid-19C. After Gerard *Troost* (1776–1850), US geologist.]

trop. abbr 1 tropic 2 tropical

trop- prefix = **tropo-** (*before vowels*)

troparion /trō párri on, -páiri-/ n a short hymn or stanza sung in Eastern Orthodox services [Mid-19C. < Greek, 'little trope' < *tropos* 'turn'.]

trope /trōp/ n 1 a word, phrase, expression, or image that is used in a figurative way, usually for rhetorical effect 2 in the medieval Christian church, a phrase or text interpolated into the service of the Mass [Mid-16C. Via Latin *tropus* < Greek *tropos* 'turn'.]

troph- prefix = **tropho-** (*before vowels*)

trophic /tróffik/ adj relating to the nutritive value of food —**trophically** adv

-trophic suffix 1 needing or pertaining to a particular kind of food or nutrition ○ *autotrophic* 2 = **-tropic** [< Greek *trophē* (see TROPHO-)]

trophic level n a stage in a food chain that reflects the number of times energy has been transferred through feeding, e.g. when plants are eaten by animals that are in turn eaten by predators

tropho- prefix nutrition, feeding ○ *trophoblast* [< Greek *trophē* 'food, nutrition' < *trephein* 'nourish']

trophoblast /tróffa blast/ n a thin outer layer (**ectoderm**) that encloses the embryo of mammals, attaches the fertilized ovum to the wall of the womb, and absorbs nutrients —**trophoblastic** /tróffa blástik/ adj

trophoderm /tróffa durm/ n a trophoblast and its underlying layer (**mesoderm**)

trophozoite /trṓffə zṓ īt/ *n* the active or feeding form of a protozoan, especially a parasite, as opposed to the resting or reproductive form

trophy /trṓfi/ *n* (*plural* **-phies**) **1 TOKEN OF VICTORY** a cup, shield, plaque, medal, or other award given in acknowledgment of a victory, success, or some other achievement, especially in a sporting contest **2 HUNTING OR WAR SOUVENIR** a memento that symbolizes victory or success, e.g. the head of an animal killed during a hunting expedition or something taken from an enemy killed in battle **3 MEMENTO OF SUCCESS** something that symbolizes a personal victory or achievement **4 GREEK OR ROMAN VICTORY MEMORIAL** in ancient Greece or Rome, a victory memorial in a public place or near a battlefield, originally a display of enemy weapons **5 GREEK OR ROMAN BATTLE COMMEMORATION** a representation of a Greek or Roman battle trophy, e.g. on a commemorative medal, plaque, or monument **6 DECORATIVE CARVING OF WEAPONS** a decorative casting or carving showing weapons or armour on a square or circular base ■ *adj* **ENHANCING SOMEBODY'S STATUS** describes a romantic or sexual partner apparently chosen by somebody to impress others and enhance his or her status (*disapproving*) ○ *a trophy wife* [Early 16C. Via French *trophée* < Latin *tropaeum* 'monument to victory' < Greek *tropaion* < *tropē* 'a turning'.]

-trophy *suffix* **1** nutrition, food ○ *dystrophy* **2** growth ○ *hypertrophy* [< Greek *-trophia* < *trophē* (see TROPHO-)]

tropic[1] /tróppik/ *n* **1 LINE OF LATITUDE** a line of latitude on the Earth's globe either 23° 26′ north of the equator (**tropic of Cancer**) or 23° 26′ south (**tropic of Capricorn**) **2 CIRCLE ON THE CELESTIAL SPHERE** either of two circles on the celestial sphere that have the same latitudes and mark the limits of the apparent north-and-south movement of the Sun ■ **tropics, Tropics** *npl* **AREA BETWEEN THE TROPICS** the area between or near the tropic of Cancer and the tropic of Capricorn [Early 16C. Via Old French *tropique* < Latin *tropicus* < Greek *tropē* 'turn'; from the ancient belief that the sun 'turned back' at the tropics of Cancer and Capricorn.] —**tropic** *adj*

LITERARY LINK ***Tropic of Cancer***, a novel (1934) by US writer Henry Miller. It is an autobiographical account of a struggling US writer's sojourn in 1930s Paris. Its focus on the protagonist's erotic encounters gained it notoriety and led to it being banned in both the United States and Britain until the 1960s, but its openness was an inspiration for many contemporary writers.

tropic[2] /trṓ pik/ *adj* relating to or showing tropism

-tropic *suffix* **1** turning, changing, or reacting in a particular way ○ *dexiotropic* **2** attracted to, having an affinity for, or moving towards a particular thing ○ *neurotropic* **3** acting on something in a particular way ○ *vagotropic* [< Greek *tropē* 'turn' (see TROPIC[1])]

tropical /tróppik'l/ *adj* **1** relating to or characteristic of the tropics **2** very hot and often combined with a high degree of humidity —**tropicality** /tróppi kálləti/ *n* —**tropically** *adv*

tropical cyclone *n* a cyclone that develops over tropical oceans and has winds up to hurricane force

tropical fish *n* a fish, usually small and brightly coloured, that occurs naturally in tropical waters but is often kept in aquariums because of its attractive appearance

tropicalize /tróppikə līz/ (**-izes, -izing, -ized**), **tropicalise** (**-ises, -ising, -ised**) *vt* to make or adapt something so that it becomes tropical in character or appearance or can be used under tropical conditions —**tropicalization** *n*

tropical storm *n* a severe storm that develops offshore over tropical seas with less than hurricane force winds but with the ability to develop into a hurricane

tropical year *n* TIME = **solar year**

tropicbird /tróppik burd/ *n* a tropical web-footed water bird, related to the pelicans, with long slender tail feathers, small legs, and white plumage with black markings. Family: Phaethontidae.

tropic of Cancer *n* a line of latitude that is about 23.5° north of the equator [< the constellation that its celestial projection intersects]

tropic of Capricorn *n* a line of latitude that is about 23.5° south of the equator [< the constellation that its celestial projection intersects]

tropine /trṓ peen, -pin/ *n* $C_8H_{15}NO$ a colourless crystalline alkaloid formed by heating atropine with barium hydroxide [Mid-19C. Shortening of ATROPINE.]

tropism /trṓpizəm/ *n* the involuntary response of an organism or one of its parts towards or away from a stimulus such as heat or light [Late 19C. < Greek *tropos* 'turning' < *trepein* 'turn'.] —**tropismatic** /trṓpiz máttik/ *adj* —**tropistic** /trō pístik/ *adj* —**tropistically** *adv*

tropo- *prefix* **1** turning, change ○ *tropopause* **2** tropism ○ *tropotactic* [< Greek *tropē*]

tropology /tro póllәji/ (*plural* **-gies**) *n* **1 USE OF FIGURATIVE LANGUAGE** the use of figurative language in speaking or writing **2 TREATISE ON FIGURATIVE LANGUAGE** a piece of discursive writing on the use of figurative language **3 METHOD OF INTERPRETING THE BIBLE** a method of interpreting the moral teaching of the Bible through its use of figurative language [Early 16C. < TROPE.] —**tropologic** /tróppə lójjik/ *adj* —**tropologically** *adv*

tropomyosin /tróppə mī́ əssin/ *n* a protein in muscle that interacts with other proteins to regulate contraction

troponin /tróppənin/ *n* a protein complex that plays a role in muscle contraction [Mid-20C. Contraction < TROPOMYOSIN + -IN.]

tropopause /tróppə pawz/ *n* the transitional region of the atmosphere between the troposphere and stratosphere, 16 km/10 mi. above the equator and 9 km/6 mi. above polar regions [Early 20C. Blend of TROPOSPHERE + PAUSE.]

troposphere /tróppə sfeer/ *n* the lowest and most dense layer of the atmosphere, extending 10 to 20 km/6 to 12 mi., in which temperature decreases with rising altitude and most weather occurs —**tropospheric** /-sférrik/ *adj*

tropotaxis /tróppə táksiss/ *n* the movement of an organism towards or away from a stimulus as a result of comparing sensory input received from paired receptors on both sides of the body —**tropotactic** /-táktik/ *adj* —**tropotactically** *adv*

-tropous *suffix* turning or growing in a particular way ○ *anatropous* ○ *orthotropous* [< Greek *tropos* 'turning, changing' < *trepein* 'turn']

troppo[1] /tróppō/ *adv* excessively or too much (*in musical directions*) ◊ **non troppo** [< Italian, 'too much']

troppo[2] /tróppō/ *adj Aus* mentally disturbed or ill (*slang*) ○ *He's been acting very strange – gone a bit troppo, I think.* [Mid-20C. < TROPIC[1].]

-tropy *suffix* the condition of taking a particular molecular form ○ *allotropy* [< Greek *-tropia* < *tropos* (see -TROPOUS)]

trot /trot/ *v* (**trots, trotting, trotted**) **1** *vti* **MOVE AT PACE SLOWER THAN CANTERING** to move or cause a four-legged animal such as a horse to move at a rate that is faster than walking but slower than cantering, and in which diagonal pairs of feet are off the ground alternately **2** *vi* **MOVE AT A JOGGING PACE** to move at a jogging pace that is faster than walking but not as fast as running ○ *The team trotted onto the field.* ■ *n* **1 PACE FASTER THAN A WALK** the forward movement of a four-legged animal, especially a horse, in which it trots **2 TROTTING PACE** a ride on a horse in which it trots **3 JOGGING PACE** a jogging pace that is faster than a walk but slower than a run **4 TROTTERS' RACE** a race for horses who run in harness **5** FISHING = **trotline** ■ **trots** *npl* (*informal*) **1 DIARRHOEA** a prolonged bout of diarrhoea **2** *ANZ* **TROTTER RACES** races for trotters in harness [13C. < Old French *troter* < Germanic.] ◇ **on the trot 1** one after the other in succession **2** *UK, Can* busy, especially doing something that involves walking about a lot

trot out *vt* to bring something out or display something repeatedly, especially in the expectation of gaining admiration or approval (*informal*) ○ *He trots out the same old excuses every time he's late.*

Trot /trot/ *n* a follower of Leon Trotsky (*slang disapproving*) [Mid-20C. Shortening of TROTSKYIST or TROTSKYITE.]

troth /trōth/ *n* a solemn pledge, especially the promise to remain faithful exchanged by a bride and groom or an engaged couple (*formal*) [13C. Variant of TRUTH.]

trotline /trót līn/ *n* a long fishing line with shorter baited lines attached, used in streams or near the shore [Mid-19C. < ?]

Trotsky /trótski/, **Leon** (1879–1940) Russian revolutionary leader. Born **Lev Davidovich Bronstein**

Trotskyism /trótski izəm/ *n* an interpretation of socialism advanced by Leon Trotsky, asserting that fully developed Marxist principles and practices would culminate in a world revolution by the proletariat —**Trotskyist** *n, adj* —**Trotskyite** *n, adj*

trotter /tróttər/ *n* **1** the foot of an animal, especially that of a pig or sheep, when used as food **2** a person who or thing that trots, especially a horse that has been specially trained to trot in harness

trotting race *n ANZ* a harness race for trotters

trotyl /trṓtil, -tīl/ *n* the explosive TNT [Early 20C. < TRINITROTOLUENE + -YL.]

troubadour /tróobə dawr, -door/ *n* **1 MEDIEVAL POET OR SINGER** a writer or singer of lyric verses about courtly love, especially in parts of Europe in the 11th to 13th centuries **2 LOVE POET OR SINGER** a writer or singer of love poems or songs **3** *US* **SINGER** a singer who performs while strolling, especially in a restaurant [Early 18C. Via French < Old Provençal *trobador* < *trobar* 'compose'.]

trouble /trúbb'l/ *n* **1 CONDITION OF DISTRESS** a condition of distress, anxiety, or danger ○ *When the bills started to come in they realized they were in serious trouble.* **2 SOMEBODY OR SOMETHING UPSETTING** a source or cause of worry, distress, or concern ○ *This car has been nothing but trouble.* **3 SOURCE OF DIFFICULTY** something that is extremely difficult or presents a problem ○ *Sorry I'm late – I had trouble getting the car to start.* **4 REAL OR APPARENT WEAKNESS** an actual or perceived failing or drawback ○ *Your trouble is that you give up too easily.* **5 MEDICAL PROBLEMS** an illness or physical condition involving a particular body part that is not functioning as it should ○ *off work with back trouble* **6 EFFORT** the effort or exertion involved in doing something ○ *I hope you like your CD – I went to a lot of trouble to find it.* **7 DISORDER OR UNREST** disorder or unruly behaviour in a public place **8 MALFUNCTIONING** a condition in which something mechanical or electronic is not functioning or operating as it should ○ *My car has engine trouble.* ■ *v* (**-bles, -bling, -bled**) **1** *vt* **WORRY OR UPSET** to cause worry, distress, or concern to somebody or something ○ *I'm troubled by the fact that she hasn't been in touch.* **2** *vt* **PHYSICALLY AFFECT** to cause pain or discomfort to somebody or something ○ *My arthritis troubles me from time to time.* **3** *vt* **IMPOSE ON** to put somebody to the inconvenience of doing something ○ *Could I trouble you to open the window?* **4** *vti* **TO MAKE AN EFFORT** to make an effort to do something or take pains in doing it ○ *He hadn't troubled to check the figures.* **5** *vt* **MAKE WATER ROUGH** to agitate or disturb something, especially the surface of water (*often passive*) [13C. Via Old French *troubler* < late Latin *turbidare* < Latin *turbidus* 'confused, muddy'.] —**troubler** *n* —**troubling** *adj* —**troublingly** *adv* ◇ **in trouble 1** discovered in wrongdoing and liable to be punished **2** pregnant and unmarried (*dated informal; used euphemistically*)

SYNONYMS See ***bother***.

troubled /trúbb'ld/ *adj* **1 ANXIOUS OR UPSET** experiencing worry or distress **2 MARKED BY PROBLEMS** characterized by difficulties or adversity ○ *The bill has had a troubled passage through Parliament.* **3 LACKING INNER CALM** experiencing or prone to emotional conflict or psychological difficulties

troublemaker /trúbb'l maykər/ *n* a person who constantly causes problems —**troublemaking** *n, adj*

Troubles /trúbb'lz/ *npl* the political and civil unrest in Northern Ireland during the period from 1919 to 1923 and after 1969

troubleshoot /trúbb'l shoot/ (**-shoots, -shooting, -shot** /-shot/, **-shot**) *vti* to act or operate as somebody who finds and eliminates problems [Mid-20C. Back-formation < TROUBLESHOOTER.]

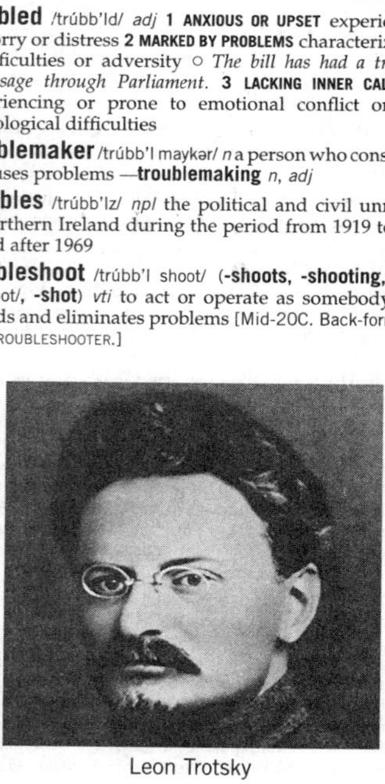

AKG London

Leon Trotsky

troubleshooter /trúbb'l shootər/ *n* **1** a person who is hired to find and eliminate problems, difficulties, or flaws **2** a person who is asked to settle political, industrial, or diplomatic disagreements

troubleshooting /trúbb'l shooting/ *n* **1 FINDING AND ELIMINATING OF PROBLEMS** the act or process of identifying and eliminating problems, difficulties, or faults, especially in electronic or computer equipment **2 MEDIATION** the act or process of mediating in political, industrial, or diplomatic disagreements **3 OCCUPATION OF FINDING AND SOLVING PROBLEMS** the occupation of finding and eliminating problems, e.g. in an organization

troublesome /trúbb'lssəm/ *adj* **1** causing difficulties or taking a great deal of time ○ *Fixing the bug in the program proved more troublesome than I thought.* **2** producing annoyance, discomfort, or anxiety, especially in a recurrent way ○ *a troublesome knee injury* —**troublesomely** *adv* —**troublesomeness** *n*

trouble spot *n* a place where trouble occurs, especially a place that is notorious for disruption to civil order or a lack of political control

troublous /trúbbləss/ *adj* (*archaic or literary*) **1** fraught with difficulty or many problems **2** full of uneasiness or anxiety —**troublously** *adv* —**troublousness** *n*

trough /trof/ *n* **1 CONTAINER FOR ANIMAL FOOD OR WATER** a long low narrow open container that holds feed or water for animals **2 INDUSTRIAL CONTAINER** a long, low, narrow, open container used in industry, e.g. in washing, kneading, or mixing substances **3 CHANNEL FOR LIQUID** a narrow channel, gully, or gutter in which liquid passes, especially one under the eaves of a roof for catching rainwater **4 AREA OF LOW PRESSURE** an elongated area of low atmospheric pressure that may be associated with a front. ◊ **ridge** *n.* 4 **5 SUNKEN AREA** a long hollow area in the surface of the ground or the sea bed, or between waves **6 LOW POINT** any low or negative point, especially a temporary one **7 LOWEST POINT OF AN ECONOMIC CYCLE** the lowest point or period of an economic cycle **8 LOW PART OF A WAVE OR SIGNAL** the low or negative half of the amplitude in the cycle of a periodic wave or alternating signal [Old English *trog.* < Indo-European, 'wood, tree'.]

trounce /trownss/ (**trounces, trouncing, trounced**) *vt* **1** to defeat an opponent or team convincingly **2** to beat somebody or something severely (*dated*) [Mid-16C. < ?]

troupe /troop/ *n* a group of actors, circus people, or other entertainers, especially one that travels around ■ *vi* (**troupes, trouping, trouped**) to travel as or perform in a troupe of actors or entertainers [Early 19C. < French.]

SPELLCHECK See ***troop***.

trouper /tróopər/ *n* **1 MEMBER OF A TROUPE** somebody who is a member of a group of travelling entertainers **2 SOMEBODY RELIABLE AND DEDICATED** somebody who is conscientious, dependable, and selfless **3 VETERAN THEATRICAL PERFORMER** somebody who has been involved in the theatre for many years, especially an actor or entertainer

troupial /tróopi əl/ *n* **1** a large oriole with bright black-and-orange plumage. Native to: South America. *Icterus icterus.* **2** a member of a family of gregarious birds that includes the bobolinks, blackbirds, and orioles. Native to: North and South America. Family: Icteridae. [Early 19C. < French *troupiale*, alteration (influenced by *troupe* 'flock') of American Spanish *turpial.*]

trouser /trówzər/ *adj* belonging to, concerning, suitable for, or part of trousers ○ *a trouser pocket* ■ *n* a pair of trousers, especially one suitable for a smart or formal occasion [Mid-19C. Back-formation < TROUSERS.] —**trousered** *adj*

trousers /trówzərz/ *npl* a garment for the lower body that covers the area from the waist to the ankles and has separate tube-shaped sections for each leg [Early 17C. < Gaelic *triubhas.*] ◇ **be caught with your trousers down** *UK* to be caught in an unprepared or embarrassing position ◇ **wear the trousers** *UK* be the member of a household who makes the important decisions (*informal*)

trouser suit *n* a woman's suit of matching or co-ordinating trousers and jacket or top

trousseau /tróossō/ (*plural* **-seaus** *or* **-seaux** /tróossōz/) *n* a bride's clothes and linen, especially items such as nightdresses, underwear, and bedclothes, that she has collected during the period of her engagement [Early 19C. < French, 'little bundle' < *trousser* 'truss'.]

trout /trowt/ (*plural* **trouts** *or* **trout**) *n* **1 FRESHWATER FISH SIMILAR TO A SALMON** a freshwater fish that is typically smaller than the related salmon and has a speckled body, small scales, and soft fins. Genus: *Salmo.* **2 GAME FISH OF THE SALMON FAMILY** a game fish of the salmon family such as the sea trout. Genus: *Salvelinus.* **3 FISH UNRELATED TO THE TROUT** a fish similar to but unrelated to, the trout such as the troutperch **4 OFFENSIVE TERM** an offensive term that deliberately insults a woman's age, appearance, or behaviour (*informal insult*) [Pre-12C. < late Latin *tructa.*]

troutperch /trówt purch/ (*plural* **-perch**) *n* a small freshwater fish with a spotted body, an adipose fin, and rough scales. Native to: North America. Family: Percopsidae.

trouvaille /troo vī/ *n* something interesting, amusing, or beneficial discovered by chance ○ *The anecdote was one of her many literary trouvailles.* [< French, 'a find']

trouvère /troo váir/ *n* a poet-musician of N France during the 12th and 13th centuries who wrote poems and songs of courtly love, as well as narrative and satirical works [Late 18C. Via French < Old French *trovere* < *trover* 'compose' (see TROVER).]

trove /trōv/ *n* **1** a collection of discovered valuable items **2** a discovery of great importance or monetary value [Late 19C. Shortening.]

trover /trṓvər/ *n* a common law action to recover goods that have been wrongly appropriated by somebody else (*archaic*) [Late 16C. < Anglo-Norman, < Old French, 'to find'.]

trow /trō/ *vti* to think, believe, or suppose that something is the case (*archaic*) [Old English *trēowian.* < Germanic.]

Trowbridge /trṓbrij/ town in SW England. Population: 29,334 (1991).

trowel /trówəl/ *n* **1 FLAT-BLADED HAND TOOL** a small hand tool with a short handle and a flat, usually pointed blade used for spreading, shaping, and smoothing plaster, cement, or mortar **2 GARDENER'S SHORT-HANDLED TOOL** a hand tool with a short handle and a curved tapering blade, used for making holes to put plants and seedlings in and for other light digging work ■ *vt* (**trowels, trowelling, trowelled**) **WORK MATERIAL WITH A TROWEL** to dig, spread, or level something such as earth or mortar using a trowel [14C. Via Old French *troele* < late Latin *truella* 'dipper' < Latin *trua* 'ladle'.] —**troweller** *n* ◇ **lay it on with a trowel** to exaggerate, especially in order to flatter somebody (*informal*)

troy /troy/ *adj* measured in or using the troy weight system [14C. Probably < TROYES, which had a fair at which this weight was used.]

Troy /troy/ city of ancient Greece in present-day NW Turkey, on the Aegean Sea

Troyes /trwa/ city in NE France, on the River Seine. Population: 60,958 (1999).

troy weight *n* a system of weights used for precious metals and gemstones, based on a 12-ounce pound, a 20-pennyweight ounce, and a 24-grain pennyweight

trs *abbr* transpose

truant /tróo ənt/ *n* **1 SOMEBODY ABSENT FROM SCHOOL** somebody who is absent without permission or good reason, especially from school **2 SHIRKER** somebody who avoids work or shirks responsibilities (*dated*) ■ *adj* **ABSENT** absent without permission ■ *vi* **BE ABSENT** to be absent without permission, especially from school [14C. < Old French, 'beggar, vagabond', of Celtic origin.] —**truancy** *n*

truce /trooss/ *n* **1 AGREED BREAK IN FIGHTING** a cessation of military hostilities that both sides agree to hold to, usually for a fixed period ○ *Both sides called a truce.* **2 AGREEMENT TO STOP FIGHTING** an agreement to suspend military hostilities **3 AGREED BREAK IN ARGUING** an agreed break in any kind of dispute or feud, or the agreement to stop arguing [14C. Variant of earlier *trewes*, the plural of *trewe* 'treaty, pledge' < Old English *trēow* (see TRUE).]

Trucial States /tróosh'l-/ former name for **United Arab Emirates**

truck[1] /truk/ *n* **1 LARGE GOODS VEHICLE** a large vehicle for transporting goods by road **2 CART PUSHED BY HAND** any kind of cart or barrow with two or more wheels that is pushed by hand and is used for moving heavy objects **3 RAILWAY GOODS WAGON** an open railway wagon that carries freight **4 TRAIN'S WHEEL UNIT** a swivelling frame that the wheels and springs are mounted on at either end of a railway vehicle **5 ROPE GUIDE ON A SHIP'S MAST** a guide for a ship's ropes, in the form of a disc with holes, fitted horizontally to the top of the mast **6 SKATEBOARD WHEEL UNIT** either of a pair of swivelling wheel units on a skateboard ■ *v* **1** *vti* **TAKE BY TRUCK** to transport, or transport something, by truck **2** *vi US, Can* **DRIVE A TRUCK** to drive a truck, especially as a job (*informal*) [Early 17C. < ?] ◇ **keep on trucking** to carry on with work or life in a cheerful and relaxed way, in spite of problems (*informal*)

truck[2] /truk/ *n* **1 DEALINGS** dealings or involvement (*informal*) ○ *We'll have no truck with that kind of behaviour.* **2** *US, Can* **MARKET PRODUCE** vegetables and fruit grown for market **3 GOODS** traded goods of any kind **4 TRADE** the buying, selling, or bartering of goods **5 STUFF** miscellaneous items (*informal*) ○ *'Now I wanted thirty dollars' worth of artist truck, for I was always sketching in the woods'.* (Robert Louis Stevenson, *The Wrecker*; 1896) **6 PAYMENT IN KIND** payment in goods rather than with money (*archaic*) ■ *vti* (*dated*) **1 EXCHANGE** to exchange or barter something, or take part in the business of bartering **2 BE INVOLVED WITH** to have dealings with somebody, especially secret or dishonest dealings [12C. < Old French dialect *troquer* 'to barter'.]

trucker /trúkər/ *n* somebody who drives a truck, especially somebody whose job is transporting goods by truck over long distances

trucking /trúking/ *n* the carrying of freight on roads in trucks

truckle[1] /trúk'l/ (**-les, -ling, -led**) *vi* to behave in a weak or servile way [Early 17C. Shortening of TRUCKLE BED, from the use of such beds by servants.] —**truckler** *n*

truckle[2] /trúk'l/ *n* **1** a small wheel on which something runs **2** a small cylindrical cheese [14C. Via Anglo-Norman *trocle* < Greek *trokhileia* 'system of pulleys' < *trokhos* 'wheel'.]

truckle bed *n* a low bed on casters that can be stowed away under another bed. US term **trundle bed**

truckload /trúk lōd/ *n* the quantity carried by a truck, or a quantity large enough to fill a truck

truck stop *n US* TRANSP = **transport café**

truculent /trúkyoolənt/ *adj* aggressively or sullenly refusing to accept something or do what is asked [Mid-16C. < Latin *truculentus* < *trux* 'fierce'.] —**truculence** *n* —**truculently** *adv*

Trudeau /tróodō/, **Pierre** (1919–2000) Canadian statesman

trudge /truj/ *vti* (**trudges, trudging, trudged**) to walk, or walk a particular path or distance, with slow heavy weary steps ■ *n* a long and exhausting walk [Mid-16C. < ?] —**trudger** *n*

true /troo/ *adj* (**truer, truest**) **1 REAL OR CORRECT** conforming with reality or fact **2 GENUINE** genuine, not pretended, insincere, or artificial **3 PERSONALLY FAITHFUL** showing loyalty to another person ○ *a true friend* **4 COMMITTED** faithful to a cause, purpose, or religious belief ○ *a true believer* **5 CONFORMING TO A STANDARD OR MEASURE** conforming to a standard, measure, or pattern ○ *a true fit* **6 RIGHTFUL** conforming to the way things should be by right ○ *returned to the true owners* **7 IN RELATION TO EARTH'S POLES** measured in relation to geographical points on the earth's surface, rather than to points of magnetic attraction ○ *true north* **8 CONFORMING TO INCLUSION CRITERIA** meeting the criteria for inclusion in a particular category, in contrast to being given the same name because of superficial resemblance to members of that category ○ *A shooting star is not a true star.* **9 NOT RELATIVE** not relative as a value and corrected for all error factors, e.g. the difference between true time and mean time **10 IN TUNE** perfectly in tune ○ *The orchestra maintained true pitch throughout.* ■ *adv* **1 SO AS TO CORRESPOND WITH REALITY** in a way that corresponds with reality or fact ○ *His explanations just didn't ring true.* **2 ACCURATELY** so as to arrive at the precise position aimed for ○ *The arrow flew straight and true.* **3 HONESTLY** in a frank and open way that seeks to hide nothing ○ *Tell me true.* **4 CERTAINLY** used to admit the validity or accuracy of a statement, often in a discussion or when considering the advantages and disadvantages of something ○ *True, it does rain a lot here.* **5 WITHOUT LOSS OF ANCESTRAL FEATURES** without variation from the ancestral form, or producing offspring with the same hereditary characteristics ○ *breed true* ■ *vt* (**trues, truing, trued**) **ADJUST POSITION OF** to adjust something to make it straight or level or put it in any other required position ■ *n* **1 ALIGNMENT** a correct position, especially a position in relation to the horizontal or vertical **2 REALITY** the absolute truth [Old English *trēowe* 'trustworthy'. < Indo-European, 'be solid'.] —**trueness** *n* ◇ **come true** to happen as hoped or expected ◇ **not true**

impossible to believe or accept (*informal*) ◇ **true to life** conforming accurately with reality

true bill *n US* a legal document requesting a criminal trial (**bill of indictment**), formally endorsed by a grand jury and certifying that somebody can be brought to trial

true blue *n* somebody with staunchly loyalist, royalist, or conservative views (*informal*)

true-blue *adj* completely loyal or faithful ○ *a true-blue pal*

true-born *adj* having one's true social position or nationality beyond doubt, because it was established at birth ○ *a true-born Londoner*

true bug *n* ZOOL = **bug** *n.* 1

true-life *adj* presenting matters, especially human relationships, as they are or have been in reality ○ *a true-life adventure story*

truelove /tro͞o luv/ *n* a person who is deeply loved by another

truelove knot, true lovers' knot *n* a complicated bowknot that is difficult to untie, symbolizing lovers' faithfulness

~~truely~~ incorrect spelling of **truly**

Trueman /tro͞omən/, **Fred** (*b.* 1931) British cricketer

true rib *n* a rib that is attached to the breastbone (**sternum**) by cartilage

Truffaut /tro͞ofō/, **François** (1932–84) French film director and critic

truffle /trúff'l/ *n* **1** an underground fungus whose fleshy edible fruiting body is highly valued as a delicacy. Genus: *Tuber.* **2** a rich ball-shaped chocolate with a centre of soft chocolate [Late 16C. Alteration of French *trufe*, via Provençal *trufa* < Latin *tuber* 'swelling'.]

trug /trug/ *n* a shallow rectangular basket made from curved strips of wood, used especially for carrying garden produce [14C. < ?]

Truganini /tro͞ogə neéni/ (1812?–76) Australian Aboriginal associated with resettlement of Tasmanian Aboriginal communities

truism /tro͞o izəm/ *n* a statement that is so obviously true and so often repeated that people find it trite or meaningless —**truistic** /troo ístik/ *adj*

~~truley~~ incorrect spelling of **truly**

trull /trul/ *n* a prostitute (*archaic*) [Early 16C. < Middle High German *trulle*.]

truly /tro͞oli/ *adv* **1 SINCERELY** honestly, without affectation or pretence ○ *feel truly sorry* **2 USED FOR EMPHASIS** used to emphasize the extent or degree of something ○ *a truly remarkable achievement* **3 COMPLETELY** to the fullest extent or in the fullest degree ○ *Only she can truly appreciate how happy I feel.* ◇ **yours truly 1** used as a rather formal way of signing off in a letter **2** used to refer to yourself (*humorous*) ○ *Doubtless they're expecting yours truly to pick them up from the airport.*

Truman /tro͞omən/, **Bess** (1885–1982) US first lady. Born **Elizabeth Virginia Wallace**

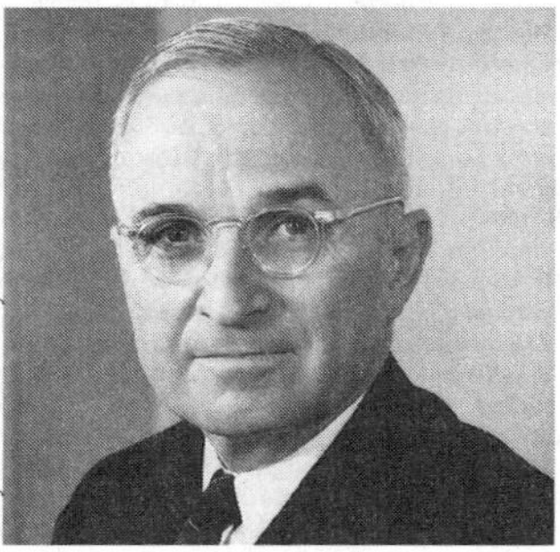

Harry S. Truman Library

Harry S. Truman

Truman, Harry S. (1884–1972) US statesman and 33rd president of the United States (1945–53)

Trumbull /trúmbəl/, **John** (1750–1831) US lawyer and poet

trumeau /tro͞o mṓ/ (*plural* **-meaux** /tro͞o mṓz/) *n* a pillar or a section of wall that separates two doors or two sections of a door [Late 19C. < French, 'calf of the leg'.]

trump[1] /trump/ *n* **1 CARD FROM HIGHEST SUIT** in card games, a card from a suit declared to be higher in value than any other suit, or the suit itself **2 KEY RESOURCE** a highly valuable resource or advantage, especially one held in reserve for future use **3 FINE PERSON** an admirable or reliable person (*informal*) ■ *vt* **1 DEFEAT SOMEBODY BY PLAYING A TRUMP** in card games, to beat an opponent or an opponent's card by playing a trump **2 OUTDO** to defeat or outdo a competitor by bringing a valuable resource or advantage into play [Early 16C. Alteration of TRIUMPH.] ◇ **turn up trumps** to prove unexpectedly to be a valuable asset, especially one that plays a decisive role in the success of something

trump up *vt* to invent false accusations or false evidence in order to incriminate somebody wrongly

trump[2] /trump/ *n* a trumpet, or the sound of a trumpet (*archaic*) [13C. < Old French *trompe* (see TRUMPET).]

trump card *n* CARDS = **trump**[1] *n.* 1, **trump**[1] *n.* 2 ◇ **play your trump card** to make use of a highly valuable resource or advantage that has been held in reserve

trumped-up *adj* false and deliberately invented, usually in order to incriminate somebody wrongly ○ *trumped-up charges* [< TRUMP[1] in the obsolete sense 'fabricate, invent']

trumpery /trúmpəri/ (*plural* **-ies**) *n* (*archaic or literary*) **1** something worthless or useless, often something showy that seems appealing at first glance **2** empty or ridiculous talk [15C. < French *tromperie* 'trickery' < *tromper* 'deceive'.]

trumpet /trúmpit/ *n* **1 BRASS INSTRUMENT** a brass musical instrument, either straight or coiled, with three valves and a flared bell **2 SOMETHING SHAPED LIKE A TRUMPET** something shaped like the flared bell of a trumpet **3 SOUND LIKE TRUMPET'S** a loud high sound made by a trumpet, or a sound such as the call of an elephant **4 PLAYER OF TRUMPET** a player of a trumpet **5** MED = **ear trumpet 6 ORGAN STOP** a solo organ stop that imitates the sound of a trumpet ■ *v* **1** *vti* **ANNOUNCE** to announce something loudly, proudly, or with great ceremony **2** *vt* **SPEAK IN PRAISE OF SOMETHING** to speak of somebody or something with ostentatious admiration or pride **3** *vi* **MAKE ELEPHANT'S CALL** to make an elephant's characteristically high-pitched, penetrating call **4** *vt* **EXPRESS BY TRUMPETING** to convey something with a trumpeting call ○ *The elephant trumpeted a warning.* [14C. < Old French *trompette* 'small horn' < *trompe* 'horn' < Germanic, probably an imitation of the sound of a horn.] ◇ **blow your own trumpet** to speak confidently, proudly, or boastfully about your own achievements, qualities, or possessions (*informal*)

trumpet creeper, trumpet vine *n* a woody deciduous vine with compound leaves. Flowers: large, red, trumpet-shaped. Native to: North America. *Campsis radicans.*

trumpeter /trúmpitər/ *n* **1 TRUMPET PLAYER** a musician who plays the trumpet **2 TROPICAL BIRD** a medium-sized bird that rarely flies and has long legs, a short stout bill, dark glossy plumage, and a loud call. Native to: South America. Family: Psophidae. **3 PIGEON** a domestic pigeon with a long ruff, heavily feathered feet, and a loud call

trumpeter swan *n* a large white swan with a black bill and a loud call. Native to: W Canada, Alaska. *Cygnus buccinator.*

trumpet flower *n* a plant with trumpet-shaped flowers, e.g. the trumpet creeper

trumpet vine *n* PLANTS = **trumpet creeper**

trumps /trumps/ *npl* in card games, the suit that is chosen at the outset to be the highest in value (+ *singular or plural verb*) ○ *Diamonds are trumps.*

truncate /trung káyt/ *vt* (**-cates, -cating, -cated**) **1 SHORTEN SOMETHING BY REMOVING PART** to shorten something by cutting off or removing a part **2 SHORTEN DECIMAL NUMBER** to restrict the precision of a decimal number by limiting the digits to the right of the decimal point without rounding ■ *adj* **1** = **truncated** *adj.* 1 **2 NOT POINTED** describes a leaf that has a blunt end, giving the impression that a part has been cut off [15C. < Latin *truncare* 'cut short, mutilate' < *truncus* 'something cut off'.] —**truncately** *adv* —**truncation** /-káysh'n/ *n*

truncated /trung káytid/ *adj* **1 WITH END REMOVED** shortened by having a part cut off or removed **2 WITH END REPLACED BY PLANE** describes a geometric figure that has the apex or an end removed and replaced with a plane section, often parallel to the base **3 HAVING INCOMPLETE CORNERS** describes a crystal lacking the fully formed corners or faces that would be present in a simple form of the crystal **4 WITH ONE SYLLABLE FEWER** describes a line of poetry that has one syllable fewer in one of its feet than in others in the line

truncheon /trúnchən/ *n* **1 POLICE OFFICER'S CLUB** a short heavy stick carried by a police officer **2 SYMBOLIC STICK** a baton carried as a symbol of rank or authority **3 SPEAR'S SHAFT** the shaft of a spear ■ *vt* **HIT SOMEBODY WITH A TRUNCHEON** to hit somebody or something with a truncheon [13C. Via Old Northern French *tronchon* < Latin *truncus* 'something cut off'.]

trundle /trúnd'l/ *vti* (**-dles, -dling, -dled**) **MOVE HEAVILY ON WHEELS** to move, or move something, slowly and heavily, especially on wheels or rollers ■ *n* **1 WHEEL** a small wheel or roller by which something is moved along **2 ROLLING MOVEMENT** a slow heavy movement, especially a rolling movement **3 CART WITH WHEELS** a trolley or cart with small wheels [Mid-16C. Variant of *trendle* 'wheel' < Old English *trendel* 'circle' < Germanic.]

trundle bed, trundle *n* FURNITURE = **truckle bed**

trunk /trungk/ *n* **1 TREE'S MAIN STEM** the main stem of a tree, excluding branches and roots **2 LARGE TRAVELLING CASE** a large strong travelling case or box with a hinged lid that is bigger, more rigid, and less portable than a suitcase **3 UPPER BODY** the main part of the body of a human being or an animal, excluding the head, neck, and limbs **4 ELEPHANT'S PROBOSCIS** the long muscular proboscis of an elephant, used for grasping, feeding, and drinking **5 MAIN PART** the main part of something that has branches or subsidiary parts leading off it, e.g. a transport network or an electrical or communications network **6** *US* CARS = **boot**[1] *n.* 2 **7 STEM OF BLOOD VESSEL** the main stem of a blood vessel or nerve, with branches leading off it **8 PART OF CABIN ABOVE DECK** the part of a boat's cabin that sits above the deck **9 DUCT** any kind of duct in a building, e.g. a ventilation duct or a duct carrying electrical wires **10 PART OF COLUMN** the shaft of an architectural column, excluding the base and the capital ■ **trunks** *npl* **MEN'S SWIMWEAR** men's shorts worn for sports, especially swimming [15C. Via French *tronc* 'tree trunk, alms box' < Latin *truncus* 'something cut off'.]

trunk call *n* formerly, a long-distance telephone call (*dated*)

trunkfish /trúngk fish/ (*plural* **-fishes** *or* **-fish**) *n* a brightly coloured tropical fish that has a body covered in bony plates. Family: Ostraciidae.

trunking /trúngking/ *n* **1** casing used to anchor, conceal, and protect cables and small pipes **2** a freight transport system in which bulk deliveries are made to local distribution centres. Individual stores or customers order or collect items from these centres as required.

trunk road *n* a designated major long-distance A road used by high volumes of traffic

trunnel *n* CONSTR = **treenail**

trunnion /trúnni ən/ *n* either of a pair of pivots, especially the cylindrical knobs on the side of a cannon's barrel that allow it to pivot on the gun carriage [Early 17C. < French *trognon* 'fruit core, tree stump'.] —**trunnioned** *adj*

Truro /tro͞orō/ **1** city in SW England. Population: 17,200 (1994 estimate). **2** town in central Nova Scotia, Canada. Population: 11,938 (1996).

truss /truss/ *vt* **1 BIND** to tie something or somebody tightly **2 TIE SOMETHING FOR COOKING** to prepare meat for roasting by tying it into a neat shape **3 SUPPORT SOMETHING WITH LOAD-BEARING MEMBERS** to support or strengthen a roof, bridge, or other elevated structure with a network of beams and bars **4 SUPPORT A HERNIA** to support a hernia with a specially designed device ■ *n* **1 CORBEL** a corbel **2 SUPPORT FOR A HERNIA** a device designed to apply pressure to a hernia to stop it enlarging or protruding **3 FRUIT CLUSTER** a cluster of flowers or fruit on a single branching stem, e.g. on a tomato plant **4 MAST FITTING** a metal fitting used to attach a ship's beam (**yard**) to a mast **5 BUNDLE** a bundle, especially a bundle of hay of varying weight [12C. < Old French *trousse* < *trousser* 'to truss'.] —**trusser** *n*

truss bridge *n* a bridge whose supporting structure consists of a network of beams in a series of triangular sections

trussing /trússing/ *n* a framework of beams arranged in triangular sections and supporting a roof, bridge, or other structure, or the beams themselves

trust /trust/ *n* **1 RELIANCE** confidence in and reliance on good qualities, especially fairness, truth, honour, or ability **2 CARE** responsibility for taking good care of somebody or something ○ *We put our children in the trust of a good child-minder.* **3 POSITION OF OBLIGATION** the position of somebody who is expected by others to behave responsibly or honourably ○ *breached the public trust* **4 HOPE FOR THE FUTURE** hopeful reliance on what will happen in the future **5 HOLDING OF ANOTHER'S PROPERTY** the legal holding and managing of money or property belonging to somebody else, e.g. that of a minor **6 ARRANGEMENT TO MANAGE ANOTHER'S PROPERTY** a legal arrangement by which one person (**trustee**) holds and manages money or property belonging to somebody else **7 CREDIT** credit given to somebody on purchases made ○ *Let me have it on trust.* ■ *v* **1** *vti* **RELY ON** to place confidence in somebody's good qualities, especially fairness, truth, honour, or ability **2** *vt* **CONFIDENTLY ALLOW SOMEBODY TO HAVE** to allow somebody to do or use something in confidence that the person will behave responsibly or properly ○ *I trust you to do the right thing.* **3** *vt* **PLACE IN SOMEBODY'S CARE** to place somebody or something in the care of another person ○ *You could certainly trust him with such an important job.* **4** *vt* **SUPPOSE** to hope or suppose something ○ *I trust you had a good holiday.* **5** *vt Carib* **GIVE CREDIT TO** to give somebody credit on a purchase ○ *wouldn't even trust me a carton of milk* [12C. < Old Norse *traust* 'confidence', *treysta* 'to trust'.] —**trustability** /trústə bílləti/ *n* —**trustable** *adj* —**truster** *n* ◇ **take something on trust** to accept something as true or honest without checking that this is the case

trustafarian /trústə fáiri ən/ *n* a young person from an affluent background who is temporarily living in circumstances less comfortable than he or she can expect to enjoy in the future, typically in a bohemian or socially disadvantaged area (*humorous informal*) [Late 20C. Blend of TRUST + RASTAFARIAN.]

trust company *n* a bank or other commercial organization that sets up and operates trusts for private individuals and businesses

trustee /tru stée/ *n* **1 MANAGER OF ANOTHER'S PROPERTY** a person who is given the legal authority to manage money or property on behalf of somebody else **2 FINANCE MANAGER** a member of a group of people responsible for managing the financial affairs of an institution or organization **3 COUNTRY SUPERVISING TRUST TERRITORY** a country responsible for administering a trust territory

trusteeship /tru stée ship/ *n* **1** the status or responsibilities of a trustee, or the period of time for which a trustee holds office **2** the administration of a country that is not self-governing by a foreign country under terms laid down by the United Nations

trustful /trústf'l/ *adj* = **trusting** —**trustfully** *adv* —**trustfulness** *n*

trust fund *n* an investment fund managed on behalf of somebody, particularly a minor, by one or more people given legal authority to do so

trusting /trústing/, **trustful** /trústf'l/ *adj* willing or tending to trust people —**trustingly** *adv* —**trustingness** *n*

trust territory *n* a country that does not have its own government but is run by a foreign country under terms laid down by the United Nations

trustworthy /trúst wurthi/ *adj* deserving trust, or able to be trusted —**trustworthily** *adv* —**trustworthiness** *n*

trusty /trústi/ *adj* (**-ier, -iest**) **RELIABLE** able to be relied on (*dated or humorous*) ■ *n* (*plural* **-ies**) **1 TRUSTED PERSON** a trusted person **2 TRUSTED PRISONER** a prisoner regarded by the prison authorities as trustworthy and given special privileges —**trustily** *adv* —**trustiness** *n*

truth /trooth/ *n* **1 TRUE QUALITY** correspondence to fact or reality **2 SOMETHING FACTUAL** something that corresponds to fact or reality ○ *If you tell the truth, you have nothing to fear.* ○ *spoke the truth* **3 TRUE STATEMENT** a statement that corresponds to fact or reality **4 OBVIOUS FACT** something that is so clearly true that it hardly needs to be stated **5 SOMETHING GENERALLY BELIEVED** a statement that is generally believed to be true ○ *a religious truth* **6 HONESTY** honesty, sincerity, or integrity **7 DESCRIPTIVE ACCURACY** accuracy in description or portrayal ○ *a criticism that had an element of truth in it* **8 CONFORMITY** adherence to a standard or law **9 LOYALTY** faithfulness to a person or a cause (*dated*) **10 ACCURACY** accuracy of alignment, setting, position, or shape (*dated*) [Old English *trēowth* 'faithfulness' < *trēow*(see TRUE)] ◇ **be economical with the truth** to tell lies (*used euphemistically*)

Truth /trooth/ *n* in Christian Science, the word used to refer to God

truth-condition *n* the condition that must apply if a given philosophical proposition is to be true

truth drug *n* a sedative such as thiopentone sodium that is supposed to make the person taking it tell the truth, either by reducing inhibitions or causing hypnosis. US term **truth serum**

truthful /troóthf'l/ *adj* **1** telling the truth, or tending to tell the truth **2** corresponding to fact or reality —**truthfulness** *n*

truthfully /troóthf'li/ *adv* **1** in a way that corresponds to fact or reality or that expresses the truth **2** used to reinforce the truth of what has just been said or is about to be said ○ *Truthfully, I did not know she was there.*

truth serum *n US* PHARM = **truth drug**

truth set *n* a set of all the values that make a given mathematical or logic statement true when substituted in the statement

truth table *n* **1** a table used to work out the truth or falsity of a compound statement in logic **2** in electronics and computing, a table used to indicate the value of the output signal from a logic circuit or device for every possible input

truth-value *n* in logic, the truth or falsity of a proposition or of a compound statement consisting of two or more propositions

try /trī/ *v* (**tries, trying, tried**) **1** ⚠ *vti* **MAKE AN EFFORT** to make an effort or an attempt to do or achieve something. **2** *vt* **TEST SOMETHING FOR PURPOSE OF ASSESSMENT** to test, sample, or experiment with something in order to assess its usefulness, worth, or quality ○ *You get to try the software out at home.* **3** *vt* **STRAIN OR VEX** to subject somebody or something to great strain ○ *The long wait tried her patience.* **4** *vt* **SUBJECT SOMEBODY TO LEGAL TRIAL** to carry out the trial in court of somebody accused of a crime or offence **5** *vt* **CONDUCT A CASE IN COURT** to conduct a legal case in court ○ *asked when the case would be tried* **6** *vt* FOOD = **render** *v.* **8** ■ *n* (*plural* **tries**) **1 EFFORT** an attempt made to do or achieve something **2 SCORE IN RUGBY** a score achieved by touching the ball on the ground behind the line of the opponent's posts (**goal line**) [13C. Via Old French *trier* 'sift out' < assumed Vulgar Latin *triare*.]

SYNONYMS ***try, attempt, endeavour, strive***

CORE MEANING: to make an effort to do something

try to make an effort or an attempt to do or achieve something; **attempt** to make an effort to do something, especially without much expectation of success; **endeavour** to make a serious and sincere effort to do or achieve something; **strive** to make persistent efforts to achieve something.

USAGE try and or **try to**? The two expressions are often interchangeable (*We'll try and come* or *We'll try to come*), although ***try and*** is rather more informal. In the past tense and in negative and progressive constructions, however, ***try to*** is needed: *They tried to deliver the package on Friday. Are you trying to tell me something?*

try on *vt* to put on an item of clothing to test its fit or suitability ◇ **try it on** to behave in an unacceptable way, or make an unjustified claim or request, in order to find out whether this will be allowed or accepted (*informal*)

try out *vi US, Can* to undergo a competitive test of suitability, especially for a place on a sports team or for a part as an actor ○ *plans to try out for the play*

trying /trī ing/ *adj* placing great strain on somebody's patience, composure, or good nature, and often physically exhausting as a result —**tryingly** *adv*

trying plane *n* a woodworking plane with a long body, used for planing long surfaces [< *try up* 'to smooth rough-planed wood']

try-on *n* a test of a person's gullibility or patience (*informal*)

try-out *n* a trial to test somebody's suitability, especially to play on a sports team or play a specific role as an actor

trypan blue /tríppən-/ *n* a blue dye used to distinguish live cells from dead cells [Shortening of TRYPANOSOME]

trypanosome /tríppənə sōm/ *n* a simple microscopic organism (**protozoan**) that lives as a parasite in the blood of certain vertebrates, including human beings. It is transmitted by insect bites and causes serious diseases. Genus: *Trypanosoma*. [Early 20C. < modern Latin, < Greek *trupanon* 'borer' + *sōma* 'body'.] —**trypanosomal** /-sōm'l/ *adj*

trypanosomiasis /tríppənō sō mī əssiss/ *n* a disorder caused by infestation with a microscopic organism that lives as a parasite in the blood, especially sleeping sickness

trypsin /trípsin/ *n* a pancreatic enzyme that digests proteins [Late 19C. Probably < Greek *tripsis* 'rubbing', because first obtained by rubbing a pancreas with glycerine.] —**tryptic** *adj*

trypsinogen /trip sínnəjən/ *n* an inactive substance secreted in the juices of the pancreas and converted into trypsin in the duodenum

tryptamine /tríptə meen/ *n* an amine formed by the decomposition of tryptophan [Early 20C. < TRYPTOPHAN + -AMINE.]

tryptophan /tríptō fan/ *n* an essential amino acid found in proteins [Late 19C. < *tryptic* 'of trypsin' + -PHANE.]

trysail /trī sayl/ *n* a strong sail used in stormy weather that is either square or triangular and is set to run parallel to the length of the ship (**fore-and-aft**) [Mid-18C. < *a-try* 'hove to'.]

try square *n* a woodworking tool used to test and mark out right angles, consisting of a rectangular handle with a thin flat rectangular metal blade fitted perpendicular to it

tryst /trist/ *n* (*archaic or literary*) **1 ARRANGEMENT TO MEET** an arrangement to meet, especially one made privately or secretly by lovers **2 SECRET MEETING** a secret meeting, or place of meeting, especially between lovers ■ *vi* **MEET OR ARRANGE TO MEET** to arrange a meeting with somebody or keep an arrangement to meet, especially secretly with a lover (*archaic or literary*) [14C. < Old French *triste* 'place to lie in wait' < Germanic.] —**tryster** *n*

TS, ts *abbr* transsexual

tsaddik *n* JUDAISM = **tzaddik**

tsade *n* ALPH = **sadhe**

tsar /zaar/, **czar, tzar** *n* **1 RUSSIAN EMPEROR** an emperor of Russia, before 1917 **2 TYRANT** an autocrat **3 PERSON IN AUTHORITY** an official or a person in a position of authority, especially in a particular area (*informal*) ○ *a drugs tsar* [Mid-16C. Via Russian *tsar'*, Old Slavic *tsěsarĭ*, and Gothic *kaisar* < Latin *Caesar* (see CAESAR).] —**tsardom** *n*

tsarevitch /zaárə vich/, **czarevitch** *n* a son of a Russian emperor, especially the eldest son [Early 18C. < Russian *tsarevich* < *tsar'* (see TSAR).]

tsarevna /zaa révnə/, **czarevna** *n* **1** the wife of a tsarevitch **2** the daughter of a tsar [Late 19C. < Russian, < *tsar'* (see TSAR).]

tsarina /zaa réenə/, **tsaritsa** /zaa réetsə/, **czarina** /zaa réenə/, **czaritza** *n* **1** an empress of Russia, before 1917 **2** the wife or widow of a tsar [Early 18C. < Italian or Spanish *zarina*, feminine of *zar* < Russian *tsar'* (see TSAR).]

tsarism /zaár izəm/, **czarism, tzarism** *n* **1** government by an emperor who has absolute power **2** absolute rule of any kind, especially the cruel abuse of absolute power by a despot —**tsarist** *adj, n*

tsaritsa *n* HIST = **tsarina**

Tsavo National Park /tsaávō-/ national park and game reserve in S Kenya. Area: 20,700 sq. km/8,000 sq. mi.

Tselinograd /tsə línnə grad/ former name for **Astana** (1960–91)

tsetse fly /tétsi-, tsétsi-/, **tzetze fly** *n* a two-winged biting fly that feeds on the blood of humans and animals and is responsible for transmitting several diseases, including sleeping sickness. Native to: central Africa. Genus: *Glossina*. [Mid-19C. Via Afrikaans < Setswana.]

TSH *abbr* thyroid-stimulating hormone

T-shirt, tee shirt *n* **1** a collarless usually short-sleeved top without fastenings usually made of cotton and worn for leisure and sports **2** *US* a man's short-sleeved vest [Early 20C. < its T-shape when spread out.]

Tshombe /chómbi/, **Moise** (1919–69) Congolese statesman

tsimmes *n* FOOD = **tzimmes**

tsitses *n* JUDAISM = **tzitzith**

tsk tsk /tisk tísk/ *interj* used in writing to represent a sucking or clicking sound made to express disappointment, disgust, or sympathy [Mid-20C. An imitation of the sound.] —**tsk-tsk** *vti*

Tsonga /tsóng gə/ (*plural* **-ga** *or* **-gas**) *n* **1** a member of a people who live in southern Africa, mainly in Mozambique, Swaziland, and South Africa **2** the Bantu language of the Tsonga people. Native speakers: 4 million. [Early 20C. < Bantu.] —**Tsonga** *adj*

tsp. *abbr* teaspoon

T-square, tee-square *n* a drawing-board ruler consisting of a rectangular handle with a straight-sided wooden or plastic blade attached perpendicular to it, to form a T shape

TSS *abbr* toxic shock syndrome

T-strap *n* a style of shoe, usually worn by women or children, with a T-shaped strap cut from the upper part of the shoe

tsunami /tsoo náami/ (*plural* **-mis**) *n* a large destructive ocean wave caused by an underwater earthquake or some other movement of the earth's surface [Late 19C. < Japanese, 'harbour wave'.] —**tsunamic** *adj*

tsuris /tsóorriss/, **tzuris** *n* problems or difficulties (*informal*) [Early 20C. Via Yiddish *tsores* 'troubles' < Hebrew *ṣārāh* 'trouble'.]

Tsushima /tsoo shéema/ island group of SW Japan, in the Korea Strait. Population: 48,875 (1985). Area: 700 sq. km/270 sq. mi.

tsutsugamushi disease /tsóotsəgə móoshi-/ *n* MED = **scrub typhus** [Early 20C. < Japanese, 'disease tick'.]

Tswana /tswáanə/ (*plural* **-na** *or* **-nas**) *n* **1** a member of a people living in southern Africa, mainly in Botswana **2** the Sotho language of the Tswana people [Mid-20C. < Bantu.] —**Tswana** *adj*

ϟ**tt** *abbr* Trinidad and Tobago (*in Internet addresses*)

TT *abbr* **1** teetotal **2** tuberculin-tested **3** telegraphic transfer ■ *n* **MOTORCYCLE RACES IN ISLE OF MAN** a series of motorcycle races held every year in the Isle of Man. Full form **Tourist Trophy**

t-test *n* a test of whether a sample of observations comes from a larger sample with a normal distribution of statistical properties

TTL[1] *n* a method of constructing electronic logic circuits. Full form **transistor transistor logic**

TTL[2] *abbr* through-the-lens

ϟ**TTL4N** *abbr* that's the lot for now (*in e-mails*)

TU *abbr* trade union

Tu. *abbr* Tuesday

tuan /tóo aan/ *n* in Malay-speaking countries, a respectful form of address for a man [Early 18C. < Malay.]

Tuareg /twáa reg/ (*plural* **-reg** *or* **-regs**) *n* **1** a member of a nomadic people who live in NW Africa, mainly in the Sahara and Sahel regions **2** the Berber language of the Tuareg people [Early 19C. < Berber.] —**Tuareg** *adj*

tuart /tóo ərt/ *n* a variety of eucalyptus grown for its very pale durable wood [Mid-19C. < Aboriginal.]

tuatara /tóo ə táarə/ *n* a large spiny greenish-grey reptile resembling an iguana. Native to: islands off New Zealand. *Sphenodon punctatum*. [Late 19C. < Maori, 'with spines on its back'.]

tub /tub/ *n* **1 LOW OPEN CONTAINER** a low open, often round, container of any size that is used for purposes such as storage and washing **2 ROUND CONTAINER FOR LIQUIDS** a small, often round, plastic or cardboard container for liquid, semi-liquid, or soft substances such as ice cream or margarine **3 AMOUNT HELD BY TUB** the contents of a tub **4 BATH** a bath for washing in (*informal*) **5 POOR QUALITY BOAT** a slow unreliable boat (*informal*) **6 MINE VEHICLE** an open-top vehicle on rails used to transport coal and other excavated minerals in a mine ■ *v* (**tubs, tubbing, tubbed**) **1** *vt* **STORE IN TUB** to store or package something in a tub **2** *vti* **BATHE** to wash, or wash something or yourself, in a bath (*informal*) [14C. < Middle Low German or Middle Dutch.]

tuba /tyóobə/ *n* a low-pitched brass musical instrument held vertically with the bell pointing upwards and the mouthpiece set horizontally [Mid-19C. Via French or Italian < Latin, 'large war trumpet'.]

tubal /tyóob'l/ *adj* **1** relating to or in the form of a tube or tubes **2** relating to or developing in a fallopian tube

tubal ligation *n* a sterilization technique in which a woman's fallopian tubes are tied to prevent ova entering the uterus

tubate /tyóo bayt/ *adj* tubular in shape

tubby /túbbi/ (**-bier, -biest**) *adj* **1 OVERWEIGHT** carrying more bodyweight than is desirable or advisable (*informal; sometimes offensive*) **2 TUB-SHAPED** like a tub in shape **3 LACKING RESONANCE** describes a violin or other string instrument that lacks resonance —**tubbiness** *n*

tube /tyoob/ *n* **1 CYLINDER FOR TRANSPORTING OR STORING LIQUIDS** any long hollow cylinder used to transport or store liquids **2 CYLINDRICAL BODY ORGAN** any hollow cylindrical organ that transports liquids or gases around the body **3 COLLAPSIBLE CONTAINER WITH CAP** a collapsible, generally cylindrical container sealed at one end and closed with a cap at the other. It is used for packaging semi-liquid substances such as toothpaste. **4 UNDERGROUND RAILWAY** the underground railway system in London (*informal*) **5** *UK* **UNDERGROUND TRAIN** a train on an underground railway system **6 INNER TUBE** an inner tube of a pneumatic tyre **7 CATHODE RAY TUBE IN TV** a cathode ray tube used to reproduce television images **8** *US, Can* MEDIA = **boob tube**[2] *n.* **9** *Aus* **CAN OF BEER** a can of beer (*informal*) **10** *Scotland* **OFFENSIVE TERM** an offensive term for a foolish or unintelligent person **11 CHANNEL IN PLANT** any narrow enclosed channel in a plant, e.g. the organ in a germinating pollen grain that conveys the male gametes to the ovule **12 FLOWER PART** a roughly cylindrical fusion of the petals of a flower such as a daffodil **13 VALVE** a valve (*informal*) **14 BODY OF WIND INSTRUMENT** the hollow cylinder that forms the main body of a wind instrument, through which the player's breath passes **15 PART OF A WAVE** the tunnel formed when a large rolling wave prepares to break ■ *vt* (**tubes, tubing, tubed**) **1 FIT SOMETHING WITH TUBE** to supply or fit something with a tube **2 ENCLOSE SOMETHING IN TUBE** to put something in a tube [Early 17C. Via French < Latin *tubus*.]

tubectomy /tyoo béktəmi/ (*plural* **-mies**) *n* the surgical removal of a fallopian tube (*informal*)

tube foot *n* an outgrowth of the body wall of marine invertebrates of the sea urchin family (**echinoderms**), used for feeding, moving around, or performing other functions depending on the species

tubeless tyre /tyóobləss-/ *n* a pneumatic tyre that does not require an inner tube because the casing and wheel rim form an airtight seal

tubenose /tyóob nōz/ *n* **1** a seabird with large tubular nostrils on the upper bill, e.g. the albatross or petrel. Family: Procellariiform. **2** a small marine fish related to the stickleback that has its ribs fused to lateral bony plates. Native to: E Pacific. *Aulorhynchus flavidum*. —**tubenose** *adj*

tube pan *n US* a round cooking pan with a hollow cylinder or cone in the middle, used for baking or moulding foods in a ring shape

tuber /tyóobər/ *n* **1** a fleshy swollen part of a root, e.g. a dahlia root, or of an underground stem, e.g. a potato, that stores food over winter and produces new growth in spring **2** a small raised area or swelling on the body [Mid-17C. < Latin, 'swelling'.]

tubercle /tyóobərk'l/ *n* **1** a small raised area on a plant or animal part **2** a small rounded swelling on the skin or on a mucous membrane, caused by a disease, especially a nodule in the lungs that is the characteristic symptom of tuberculosis [Late 16C. < Latin *tuberculum* 'small swelling' < *tuber* 'swelling'.]

tubercle bacillus *n* a rod-shaped bacterium that causes tuberculosis. *Mycobacterium tuberculosis*.

tubercular /tyoo búrkyoolər/, **tuberculous** /tyoo búrkyooləs/ *adj* **1 OF TUBERCULOSIS** relating to, characteristic of, or affected by tuberculosis **2 CAUSED BY TUBERCLE BACILLUS** caused by the tubercle bacillus ○ *tubercular meningitis* **3 NODULE-SHAPED** taking the form of a small rounded swelling or nodule [Late 18C. < Latin *tuberculum* (see TUBERCLE).]

tuberculate /tyoo búrkyoolət/ *adj* covered with small rounded swellings or nodules (**tubercles**) [Late 18C. < Latin *tuberculum* (see TUBERCLE).] —**tuberculately** *adv* —**tuberculation** /tyoo búrkyoo láysh'n/ *n*

tuberculin /tyoo búrkyoolin/ *n* a sterile liquid obtained from cultures of the tubercle bacillus and used in a scratch test to establish whether somebody has or has had tuberculosis [Late 19C. < Latin *tuberculum* (see TUBERCLE).]

tuberculin-tested *adj* describes a dairy herd that has been certified as not having tuberculosis, or to describe milk from such a herd

tuberculosis /tyoo búrkyoo lóssiss/ *n* an infectious disease that causes small rounded swellings (**tubercles**) to form on mucous membranes, especially a disease (**pulmonary tuberculosis**) that affects the lungs [Mid-19C. < Latin *tuberculum* (see TUBERCLE).] —**tuberculoid** /tyoo búrkyoo loyd/ *adj*

tuberculous *adj* MED = **tubercular**

tuberose[1] /tyóob rōz, tyóobə rōz/ *n* a perennial agave with blade-shaped leaves. Flowers: fragrant, white, in spikes. Native to: Mexico. *Polianthes tuberosa*. [Mid-17C. < modern Latin *tuberosa* < Latin *tuberosus* < *tuber* 'swelling'.]

tuberose[2] /tyóobə róss/ *adj* PLANT SCI, MED = **tuberous**

tuberosity /tyóobə róssəti/ (*plural* **-ties**) *n* a rounded protuberance, especially at a point on a bone where muscles or ligaments are attached

tuberous /tyóobərəss/, **tuberose** /tyóobərōss/ *adj* **1** relating to tubers or in the form of tubers **2** producing or covered with knobbly growths [Mid-17C. < Latin *tuberosus* (see TUBEROSE[1]).]

tube sock *n* a straight sock made without a shaped heel for greater comfort

tube top *n US* a short strapless stretchy top for women

tube worm *n* a worm that builds itself a tube-shaped shelter that sticks out of the soil

tubifex /tyóobi feks/ *n* a thin reddish freshwater worm that builds a tube-shaped shelter in the sand of riverbeds and is used as food for aquarium fish. Genus: *Tubifex*. [Mid-20C. < modern Latin, < Latin *tubus* 'tube' + *-fex* 'maker'.]

tubing /tyóobing/ *n* **1** a system or series of tubes **2** the hollow, cylindrical material that tubes are made of **3** HANDICRAFT = **piping** *n.* **2**

Tübingen /tóobingən/ city in SW Germany. Population: 82,900 (1992).

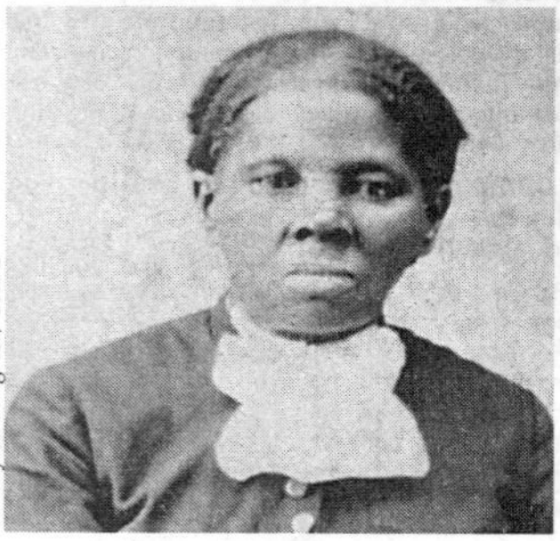

Library of Congress/Corbis

Harriet Tubman

Tubman /túbmən/, **Harriet** (1830–1913) US abolitionist

Tubman, William (1895–1971) Liberian statesman

tubocurarine /tyóobō kyoo ráarin/ *n* **1** a toxic alkaloid that is the active constituent of curare. Use: muscle relaxant. **2** the hydrochloride salt of tubocurarine [Late 19C. < TUBE (because shipped in bamboo tubes) + CURARE.]

tuboplasty /tyóobō plasti/ (*plural* **-ties**) *n* the surgical repair of one or both fallopian tubes, especially when these have been cut and tied for contraceptive reasons

tub-thump *vi* to speak out in favour of somebody or something in a passionate or aggressive way (*informal*) —**tub-thumper** *n* —**tub-thumping** *adj*

tub-thumper *n* a passionate or aggressive public speaker (*informal*) —**tub-thumping** *adj, n*

tubular /tyóobyoolər/, **tubulate, tubulous** *adj* **1** shaped like a tube **2** having a tube or tubes [Late 17C. < Latin *tubulus* (see TUBULE).]

tubular bells *npl* a set of tuned metal tubes, usually arranged in a scale and hung from a frame, that are struck with a mallet

tubulate *adj* /tyóobyoolət/ = **tubular** [Mid-18C. < Latin *tubulatus* < *tubulus* (see TUBULE).]

tubule /tyóob yool/ *n* a very small tubular part in a plant or animal organism [Late 17C. < Latin *tubulus* 'small tube' < *tubus* 'tube'.]

tubulin /tyóobyoolin/ *n* a globular protein found in microscopic filamentous tubes (**microtubules**) in cells

tubulous /tyóobyooləss/ *adj* = **tubular**

TUC *abbr* Trades Union Congress

Tucana /too káanə/ *n* a small faint constellation of the southern hemisphere containing much of the smaller Magellanic Cloud. See illustration at **constellation**

Tucanoan /tóokə nō ən/ *n* a family of languages spoken by Native South Americans in Peru, Colombia, Brazil, and Ecuador [Late 20C. < Tucanoan.] —**Tucanoan** *adj*

tuck[1] /tuk/ *v* **1** *vt* **FOLD INTO POSITION** to push, fold, or bend something such as a flap of material into a particular place or position **2** *vti* **DRAW TOGETHER** to pull or draw something together, or be pulled or drawn together **3** *vt* **SEW FOLD** to sew a fold into fabric, e.g. to reduce its length or for decoration **4** *vt* **TIGHTEN WITH SURGERY** to perform a surgical operation to remove loose or wrinkled skin, usually for cosmetic reasons ■ *n* **1 TUCKED PART** a part that is tucked safely or neatly into position **2 PLEAT** a fold sewn into a piece of fabric, e.g. to reduce its length or for decoration **3 FOOD** food, especially sweets and cakes (*often before nouns*) **4 SURGICAL REMOVAL OF LOOSE SKIN** a surgical operation to remove loose or wrinkled skin, especially for cosmetic reasons **5 BODY POSITION** a compact body position, adopted in sports such as diving and gymnastics, with the knees drawn up to the chest, the hands round the shins, and the chin held on the chest **6 PART OF SHIP'S STERN** the part of a ship's hull where the side planks or plates join the spar or spars forming the stern [15C. Probably < Middle Dutch *tucken* 'draw up'.]

tuck away *vt* **1** to put something in a safe or secluded place **2** to eat large quantities of food heartily or hungrily (*informal*)

tuck in *v* **1** *vt* to make somebody, especially a child, comfortable in bed by tucking the bedclothes snugly around the body **2 tuck in, tuck into** *vti* to eat, or eat something, hungrily (*informal*)

tuck up *vt* = **tuck in** *v.* **1**

tuck^{2} /tuk/ *n* a beating of a drum or a blast on a trumpet as a flourish [15C. Via Old N French *toquer* 'to strike' < assumed Vulgar Latin *toccare*.]

tuckahoe /túkəhō/ *n* **1** any plant of the arum family with arrow-shaped leaves and edible roots. Use: formerly, as food by Native North Americans. **2** a large edible fungus that grows underground on the roots of trees. Native to: S United States. *Poria cocos*. [Early 17C. < Virginia Algonquian *tockawhoughe*.]

tucker^{1} /túkər/ *n* **1** *ANZ* **FOOD** food (*informal; often before nouns*) **2 SEWING-MACHINE ATTACHMENT** an attachment for a sewing machine, used to sew tucks **3 DETACHABLE PART OF DRESS** a detachable lace or linen cover for the neck and chest, formerly worn by women under a low-cut dress [13C. < TUCK¹.]

tucker^{2} /túkər/ *vt US, Can* to tire a person or animal out completely (*informal*) [Mid-19C. < ?]

Tucker /túkər/, **Albert** (*b.* 1914) Australian painter

tucket /túkit/ *n* a fanfare played on a trumpet (*archaic*) [Late 16C. < TUCK².]

tuck-in *n* a large and delicious meal (*dated*)

tuck-point *vt US* to finish a wall by sealing the facing joints between the bricks or stones with a thin line of putty or very fine lime-based mortar

tuck shop *n* a small shop, especially one in or near a school, selling sweets, drinks, and snacks

tucotuco /tōokō tōokō/ (*plural* **-cos**) *n* a South American rodent that closely resembles the North American gopher. It uses its sharp claws to dig complex systems of burrows in sandy soils. *Ctenomys talarum*. [Mid-19C. An imitation of its call.]

Tucson /tōo son/ city in S Arizona. Population: 460,466 (1998 estimate).

Tucuman /tōokoo man, tōokoo mán/ province in N Argentina. Capital: San Miguel de Tucuman. Population: 1,142,105 (1991). Area: 22,524 sq. km/8,694 sq. mi.

'tude /tood/ *n* an arrogant or assertive manner or stance assumed as a challenge or for effect (*slang*) [Late 20C. Shortening of ATTITUDE.]

-tude *suffix* state, condition, or quality ○ *decrepitude* [Via French < Latin *-tudo*]

Tudor /tyōodər/ *adj* **1 OF ENGLISH ROYAL FAMILY** belonging or relating to the English royal family that ruled between 1485 and 1603, from Henry VII to Elizabeth I, or to this period of English history **2 RELATING TO TUDOR ARCHITECTURAL STYLE** relating to or being a style of architecture popular throughout the Tudor period characterized by timber frameworks, visible from the outside, filled in with plaster or brick ■ *n* **MEMBER OF TUDOR FAMILY** a member of the Tudor royal family [Mid-18C. Named after the Welsh squire Owen *Tudor* (d.1461), father of Henry VII.]

Tue., Tues. *abbr* Tuesday

Tuesday /tyōoz day, -di/ *n* the second day of the week, coming after Monday and before Wednesday [Old English *Tīwesdæg* 'Tiu's day' < *Tīw*, Germanic god of war (translation of Latin *Martis dies* 'Mars' day')]

Tuesdays /tyōoz dayz, -diz/ *adv* every Tuesday

tufa /tyōofə/ *n* porous rock formed from deposited calcium carbonate and found near mineral springs. Use: as a basis on which to grow alpine plants. [Late 18C. Via obsolete Italian < late Latin *tofus* 'porous rock'.] —**tufaceous** /tyoo fáyshəss/ *adj*

tuff /tuf/ *n* rock made up of very small volcanic fragments compacted together [Mid-16C. Via French < Latin *tofus*.] —**tuffaceous** /tu fáyshəss/ *adj*

tuffet /túffit/ *n* **1** a small mound or clump of grass **2** a low seat or stool [Mid-16C. Alteration of TUFT.]

tuft /tuft/ *n* **1 BUNCH OF FIBRES OR GRASS** a small bunch of hair, grass, feathers, or fibres held or growing together at the base **2 CLUMP OF PLANTS** a small clump of plants or trees **3 BUNCH OF THREADS DRAWN THROUGH UPHOLSTERY** a group of threads drawn through fabric and tied to secure it to material beneath ■ *v* **1** *vti* **FORM INTO TUFTS** to grow in tufts, or form something into tufts **2** *vt* **SEW TUFTS IN** to sew tufts in fabric, either for decoration or to secure one surface to another [14C. Alteration of Old French *toffe*.] —**tufted** *adj* —**tufty** *adj*

tufted duck *n* a common diving duck, the male of which is black with white flanks and belly and has feathery crests dangling over the back of the neck. Native to: Europe, Asia. *Aythya fuligula*.

Tu Fu /dōo fōo/ (710?–770) Chinese poet

tug /tug/ *v* (**tugs, tugging, tugged**) **1** *vti* **PULL AT OR MOVE** to pull at or haul something with a sharp forceful movement **2** *vt* **TOW SHIP** to tow a ship with a tugboat **3** *vi* **MAKE LABORIOUS EFFORT** to work hard or struggle to do something ■ *n* **1 STRONG PULL** a quick sharp or forceful pull ○ *gave it a tug* **2 STRUGGLE OR CONTEST** a struggle or strenuous contest between opposing forces or individuals **3 BOAT USED FOR TOWING SHIPS** a small powerful boat used to tow ships and barges. US term **tugboat** **4 VEHICLE THAT PULLS ANOTHER** any type of vehicle, whether land, sea, air, or space, that is used to pull another **5 CHAIN OR STRAP FOR HAULING** a chain, rope, or strap that is used for hauling or pulling something [13C. Ultimately < Indo-European, 'pull'.] —**tugger** *n*

SYNONYMS See ***pull***.

tugboat /túg bōt/ *n* SHIPPING = **tug** *n.* **3**

Tugela /too gáylə/ river in E South Africa, flowing into the Indian Ocean. Length: 502 km/312 mi.

Tugela Falls series of waterfalls on the River Tugela, E South Africa. Height: 948 m/3,110 ft.

tughrik /tōog reek/ (*plural* **-ghrik** *or* **-ghriks**), **tugrik** (*plural* **-grik** *or* **-griks**) *n* see table at **currency** [Mid-20C. < Mongolian *dughurik* 'round thing'.]

tug of love *n* a struggle between divorced parents or between natural and foster or adoptive parents over custody of a child (*informal*)

tug of war *n* **1** an athletic contest in which two teams pull at opposite ends of a rope, the winner being the one who drags the other across a specified line **2** any struggle between two evenly-matched people, parties, or influences

tugrik *n* MONEY = **tughrik**

tui /tōo i/ *n* a bird with iridescent dark blue-green plumage, white tufts at the throat, and white spots on the wings. Native to: New Zealand. *Prosthemadera novaeseelandiae*. [Mid-19C. < Maori.]

Tuileries Gardens /twéeləri-/ formal gardens in central Paris, beside the River Seine. Area: 25 hectares/63 acres.

tuition /tyoo ísh'n/ *n* **1** instruction or teaching, especially instruction given individually or in a small group **2** a sum charged for instruction at a school or university [15C. Via Old French < Latin *tuition-* 'support' < *tueri* 'protect'.] —**tuitional** *adj*

tularaemia /tōolə réemi ə/ *n* an acute infectious disease of rabbits and rodents caused by the bacterium *Francisella tularensis* that can be spread to other animals and humans by insect bites, animal contact, or water [Early 20C. < *Francisella tularensis*, the causative bacterium (after *Tulare* County, California).] —**tularaemic** *adj*

tularemia *n* US = **tularaemia**

tule /tōoli/ (*plural* **-les** *or* **-le**) *n* each of two bulrushes found in marshes and flooded land. Native to: SW North America. *Scirpus californicus* and *Scirpus acutus*. [Mid-19C. Via American Spanish < Nahuatl *tullin*.]

tulip /tyōolip/ *n* a spring-flowering plant that grows from a bulb and has lance-shaped leaves. Flowers: large, usually single, cup-shaped, variously coloured. Native to: W Asia. Genus: *Tulipa*. [Late 16C. Via French *tulipe* < Turkish *tülbend* (see TURBAN); from the shape of the expanded flower.]

tulip tree *n* a deciduous tree of the magnolia family with large greenish-yellow tulip-shaped flowers and soft light wood. Native to: North America, China. *Liriodendron tulipifera* and *Liriodendron chinense*.

tulipwood /tyōolip wōod/ *n* the light soft wood of the tulip tree, or the striped wood of similar trees, used in making wooden objects or in cabinetmaking

tulle /tyool/ *n* a thin netted, often stiffened, silk, nylon, or rayon fabric. Use: ballet costumes, evening dresses, veils. [Early 19C. After the French city *Tulle*.]

Tulsa /túlssə/ city in NE Oklahoma. Population: 367,302 (1990).

tulu /tōo loo/ *n* a camel that is a hybrid between a dromedary and a Bactrian camel. Native to: W Asia.

tum^{1} /tum/ *n* somebody's stomach (*informal*) [Mid-19C. Shortening of TUMMY.]

tum^{2} /toom/ *adj Scotland, N England* empty of all contents [Old English *tōm* &lt Germanic]

tumble /túmb'l/ *v* (**-bles, -bling, -bled**) **1** *vti* **FALL OR MAKE FALL OVER** to fall suddenly and awkwardly, especially rolling over and over, or cause something to fall in this way **2** *vi* **MOVE HASTILY** to move heedlessly or hastily ○ *The puppies tumbled from the room.* **3** *vi* **ROLL ABOUT** to roll about, especially in play **4** *vi* **DROP STEEPLY** to fall quickly and by a significant amount ○ *Prices have tumbled on the stock market.* **5** *vi* **CASCADE OVER** to flow, fall, or spill out over something **6** *vi* **REALIZE** to realize the full significance of something, or see through a deceit (*informal*) ○ *She finally tumbled to it.* **7** *vi* **LEAP OR ROLL** to perform athletic or gymnastic leaps, rolls, or somersaults **8** *vt* **ROTATE IN TUMBLER** to roll or spin something in a drum or tumbler ■ *n* **1 BAD FALL** an awkward or sudden fall ○ *He had a nasty tumble.* **2 DISORDERLY HEAP** a disorderly or disorganized heap or arrangement **3 ATHLETIC MOVEMENT** an athletic or gymnastic leap, roll, or somersault [13C. < obsolete Low German *tummelen*.]

tumblebug /túmb'l bug/ *n* a dung beetle of the scarab family that forms animal dung into balls, in which the female lays her eggs. The dung provides food for the larvae. Family: Scarabaeidae.

tumbledown /túmbl down/ *adj* ruined or dilapidated and falling down

tumble-dry (**tumble-dries, tumble-drying, tumble-dried**) *vt* to dry washing in a tumble dryer —**tumble-dryer** *n*

tumble dryer, tumble drier *n* a machine that dries wet laundry by revolving it through heated air in the rotating metal drum of a dryer

tumblehome /túmb'l hōm/ *n* **1** the inward upward slope of a ship's topsides **2** the inward slope of the hull of a canoe from the water line up to the gunwales

tumbler /túmblər/ *n* **1 DRINKING GLASS** a drinking glass with a thick flat bottom and no stem or handle **2 ROUND-BOTTOMED GLASS** a drinking glass, used in the past, that had a rounded or pointed bottom and so could not be put down until it was empty **3 AMOUNT IN TUMBLER** the amount of liquid that a tumbler holds **4 ACROBAT** a performer of athletic or gymnastic leaps, rolls, and somersaults **5 PART OF LOCK** the part of a lock that must be engaged by a key in order to move the bolt **6** HOUSEHOLD = **tumble dryer** **7 ROTATING CONTAINER** a box, drum, or barrel that pivots or rotates, e.g. one used to polish gemstones. US term **tumbling barrel** **8 MACHINE PART** a part of a machine that moves or engages a gear **9 PART OF GUNLOCK** a lever in a gunlock that forces the hammer forward when a trigger is pressed **10 PIGEON THAT DOES SOMERSAULTS IN FLIGHT** a domestic pigeon that can perform backward somersaults in flight

tumbler dryer *n* HOUSEHOLD = **tumble dryer**

tumbleweed /túmb'l weed/ (*plural* **-weeds** *or* **-weed**) *n* any densely branched plant such as the Russian thistle that grows in arid regions and in late summer withers and breaks from its roots to be blown about by the wind

tumbling /túmbling/ *n* the art, practice, or act of performing leaps, rolls, and somersaults

tumbling barrel, tumbling box *n US* TECH = **tumbler** *n.* **7**

tumbrel /túmbrəl/, **tumbril** /-bril/ *n* **1** a tiltable farm cart used to carry manure **2** a covered cart formerly used to carry ammunition and equipment for the artillery [14C. < Old French *tumberel* < *tomber* 'fall'.]

tume /tyoom/ (**tumes, tuming, tumed**) *vti Scotland* to empty or empty something [Early 16C. < variant of TOOM.]

tumefaction /tyo͝omi fáksh'n/ *n* **1** the swelling of tissue as a result of a build-up of fluid within it **2** a swollen part or area [15C. < French *tuméfaction* < Latin *tumefacere* (see TUMEFY).]

tumefy /tyo͝omi fī/ (**-fies, -fying, -fied**) *vti* to swell, or cause tissue to swell [Late 16C. Via French *tuméfier* < Latin *tumefacere* 'make swollen' < *tumere* 'swell' + *facere* 'make'.] —**tumefacient** /tyo͝omi fáyshi ənt/ *adj*

tumescent /tyoo méss'nt/ *adj* swollen or showing signs of swelling, usually as a result of a build-up of blood or water within body tissues [Mid-19C. < Latin *tumescent-*, present participle of *tumescere* 'become swollen' < *tumere* 'swell'.] —**tumescence** *n*

tumid /tyo͝omid/ *adj* **1** SWOLLEN describes a body part or organ that is swollen **2** BULGING bulging or sticking out **3** POMPOUS IN STYLE having language or a style that is bombastic or inflated [Mid-16C. < Latin *tumidus* < *tumere* 'swell'.] —**tumidity** /tyoo míddəti/ *n* —**tumidness** *n*

tummler /túmmlər/ *n US* a man employed as a comedian and host to encourage audience participation, especially one hired to amuse guests at resorts in the Catskill Mountains, north of New York City [Mid-20C. < American Yiddish, < Yiddish *tumlen* 'to bustle'.]

tummy /túmmi/ (*plural* **-mies**) *n* somebody's stomach (*informal*) [Mid-19C. Baby talk alteration of STOMACH.]

tummy button *n* the human navel (*informal*)

tummy tuck *n* a cosmetic surgical operation to remove excess fat, skin, and tissue from the abdomen (*informal*)

tumor *n* US = **tumour**

tumorigenic /tyo͝oməri jénnik/ *adj* describes a drug or other agent that may initiate or promote the growth of tumours —**tumorigenesis** *n* —**tumorigenicity** /tyo͝omərijə níssəti/ *n*

tumour /tyo͝omər/ *n* **1** an uncontrolled growth or mass of body cells, which may be malignant or benign and has no physiological function **2** any unusual swelling in or on the body [15C. < Latin *tumor* < *tumere* 'swell'.] —**tumorous** *adj*

tumour necrosis factor *n* a protein that can cause the destruction of tumours

tumpline /túmp līn/ *n US, Can* a band or strap strung across the forehead or chest to support a backpack [Late 18C. < Algonquian *mattump*.]

tumular /tyo͝omyo͝olər/ *adj* resembling or in the form of a mound or tumulus

tumuli plural of **tumulus**

tumulose /tyo͝omyo͝olōss/, **tumulous** /-ləss/ *adj* **1** having many mounds or small hills **2** forming or resembling a mound —**tumulosity** /tyo͝omyo͝o lóssəti/ *n*

tumult /tyo͝omult/ *n* **1** a violent or noisy commotion **2** a psychological or emotional upheaval or agitation [14C. Directly or via French *tumulte* < Latin *tumultus* 'commotion' < *tumere* 'swell'.]

tumultuous /tyoo múlchoo əss/ *adj* **1** noisy and unrestrained in a way that shows excitement or great happiness **2** involving great excitement, confusion, and emotional agitation —**tumultuously** *adv* —**tumultuousness** *n*

tumulus /tyo͝omyo͝oləss/ (*plural* **-li** /-lī/) *n* ARCHAEOL = **barrow**² *n.* [15C. < Latin, 'mound' < *tumere* 'swell'.]

tun /tun/ *n* **1** a large cask for beer or wine **2** a measure of liquid volume, especially one for wine equal to 955 litres/210 gallons [Pre-12C. < medieval Latin *tunna* 'cask'.]

Tun. *abbr* Tunisia

tuna¹ /tyo͝onə/ (*plural* **-na** *or* **-nas**) *n* **1** a large fast-swimming, widely distributed marine fish with a tapering body, large forked tail, and pointed head. Native to: warm and temperate waters. Genus: *Thunnus.* **2** the firm meaty flesh of the tuna, used as food [Late 19C. < American Spanish.]

tuna² /tyo͝onə/ *n* **1** a tropical prickly pear cactus that has coloured flowers and sweet edible fruit. *Opuntia tuna.* **2** the edible fruit of the tuna cactus [Mid-16C. Via Spanish < Taino.]

tuna fish *n* FOOD = **tuna**¹ *n.* **2**

Tunbridge Wells /túnbrij wélz/ spa town in SE England. Population: 60,272 (1991).

tundish /túndish/ *n* **1** a trough at the top of a mould into which molten metal is poured **2** *N Ireland* a funnel

tundra /túndrə/ *n* the level or nearly level treeless plain between the ice cap and the timber line of North America and Eurasia that has permanently frozen subsoil [Late 16C. Via Russian < Sami *tundar*.]

tune /tyoon/ *n* **1** SIMPLE MELODY a series of musical notes that make a simple melody **2** SONG a melodious song or short piece of music ■ *vt* (**tunes, tuning, tuned**) **1** ADJUST INSTRUMENT FOR PITCH to adjust an instrument so that a note is at the required pitch **2** ADJUST ENGINE to adjust an engine or machine to make it run better **3** ADJUST STATION OR CHANNEL to adjust a radio or television set to a particular station or channel (*usually passive*) **4** ADAPT TO to bring yourself into harmony or accord with something **5** ADJUST ELECTRONIC INSTRUMENT to adjust an electronic device or instrument to the required frequency [14C. Alteration of TONE.] —**tunable** *adj* —**tuneable** *adj* ◇ **call the tune** to be in charge ◇ **change your tune** to change your attitude or opinion ◇ **in tune 1** played or sung at the appropriate pitch **2** in accord or agreement with somebody or something **3** adjusted to the correct frequency ◇ **out of tune 1** played or sung at the wrong pitch **2** out of harmony or in disagreement with somebody or something **3** not adjusted to the correct frequency ◇ **to the tune of something** to the stated exact or approximate amount

tune in *v* **1** *vti* to adjust a radio or television to receive a signal, programme, or channel **2** *vi* to be attentive or receptive to somebody or something (*informal*)

tune out *v* **1** *vt* to adjust a radio or television set to eliminate the reception of something undesired such as interference **2** *vi* to ignore or be unreceptive to somebody or something (*informal*) ○ *'The country was tuning out all things when suddenly there was focus on scandal'.* (*US News & World Report*; December 1998)

tune up *vti* **1** to adjust one or more musical instruments to an accurate or common pitch **2** to test and improve something as a preparation, e.g. for a competition or meeting

tuneful /tyo͝onf'l/ *adj* having a pleasant melody —**tunefully** *adv* —**tunefulness** *n*

tuneless /tyo͝onləss/ *adj* unmusical, lacking a tune, or not producing a tune —**tunelessly** *adv* —**tunelessness** *n*

tuner /tyo͝onər/ *n* **1** a person who tunes musical instruments, especially pianos **2** a device, e.g. in a radio or television set containing one or more resonant circuits, used for accepting a desired signal from a mixture of signals

tunesmith /tyo͝on smith/ *n US* a composer of popular songs or music (*informal*)

tune-up *n* a set of adjustments to an engine to make it run better

tung oil /túng-/ *n* a quick-drying yellow oil extracted from the seeds of the tung tree, used in paints and varnishes to speed up drying, and also as a waterproofing agent [< Chinese *tóng* 'tung tree']

tung-oil tree *n* TREES = **tung tree**

tungstate /túng stayt/ *n* a salt or ester of tungstic acid. Source: tungsten ore.

tungsten /túngstən/ *n* (*symbol* **W**) a hard lustrous grey metallic element with a very high melting point. Source: wolframite, scheelite. Use: high-temperature alloys, lamp filaments, high-speed cutting tools. [Late 18C. < Swedish, 'heavy stone'.]

tungsten carbide *n* a fine, very hard, grey crystalline powder made by heating tungsten and carbon together. Use: manufacture of dies, cutting and abrasion tools, durable machine parts.

tungsten lamp *n* an incandescent electric lamp with a filament made of tungsten

tungsten steel *n* a hard heat-resistant steel containing between 1% and 20% tungsten, used in tools and high-temperature engineering equipment

tungstic /túngstik/ *adj* relating to or containing tungsten, especially with a valency of six. ◊ **tungstous**

tungstic acid *n* H_2WO_4 a yellow powder that forms a weak acid. Use: manufacture of textiles, plastics.

tungstite /túng stīt/ *n* a rare yellow-green tungsten oxide mineral. Source: tungsten ores.

tungstous /túngstəss/ *adj* relating to or containing tungsten, especially with a valency of two. ◊ **tungstic**

tung tree /túng-/ *n* a tree whose large round fruit contain hard seeds that yield tung oil. Native to: E Asia. Genus: *Aleurites*. [See TUNG OIL]

Tungus /to͝ong go͝oss, to͝ongəss/ (*plural* **-gus** *or* **-guses**) *n* PEOPLES, LANG = **Evenki** [Early 17C. < Yakut.]

Tungusic /to͝ong go͝ossik/ *n* a group of languages spoken in northern parts of the People's Republic of China and E Asiatic Russia. Native speakers: 50,000. —**Tungusic** *adj*

tunic /tyo͝onik/ *n* **1** LOOSE GARMENT a loose wide-necked garment that extends to the hip or knee and is usually worn with a belt or gathered at the waist **2** GARMENT WORN IN PAST a knee-length garment with sleeves, a round neck, and a loose body worn by men in ancient Rome, or a similar garment worn during the Middle Ages **3** POLICE OR MILITARY JACKET a close-fitting high-collared jacket worn as part of a police or military uniform **4** SPORTS DRESS a short belted dress worn when playing sports **5** ENVELOPING MEMBRANE a covering or membrane that envelops an organ or part **6** ANAT = **tunica** **7** PAPERY COVERING ON BULB a dry, often brown and papery covering around a bulb or corm such as of an onion **8** RELIG = **tunicle** [Pre-12C. Directly or via French *tunique* < Latin *tunica*.]

tunica /tyo͝onikə/ (*plural* **-cae** /-see/) *n* a layer of tissue that covers or lines a body part or organ, especially tubular parts such as the blood vessels. US term **tunic** *n.* **6** [Late 17C. < Latin, 'tunic'.]

tunicate /tyo͝onikət/ *n* MARINE ANIMAL a sac-shaped marine chordate animal such as a sea squirt or ascidian that has a tough leathery or rubbery outer coat. Subphylum: Urochordata. ■ *adj* **1** RELATING TO TUNICATES relating to or classified as a tunicate **2 tunicate, tunicated** WITH DRY PAPERY COVERING describes a bulb or corm that has a dry, often brown and papery covering **3 tunicate, tunicated** WITH COVERING OF TISSUE describes an organ or body part that is covered or lined with a layer of tissue [Mid-18C. < Latin *tunicatus* 'covered with a tunic' < *tunica* 'tunic'.]

tunicle /tyo͝onik'l/ *n* in Christian worship, a short vestment worn over the alb by a subdeacon at a Mass, or under the dalmatic by a bishop or cardinal at other ceremonies [14C. Directly or via Old French < Latin *tunicula* 'small tunic' < *tunica* 'tunic'.]

tuning /tyo͝oning/ *n* **1** the standard range of pitches to which a musical instrument is tuned **2** the degree to which musical instruments or the voices of a choir are adjusted to a norm

tuning fork *n* an instrument with a stem and two prongs that produces a constant pitch when struck, used to tune musical instruments and in acoustics

Tunis /tyo͝oniss/ capital of Tunisia, on a shallow lake near the Gulf of Tunis. Population: 674,100 (1994).

Tunis, Gulf of arm of the Mediterranean Sea in NE Tunisia

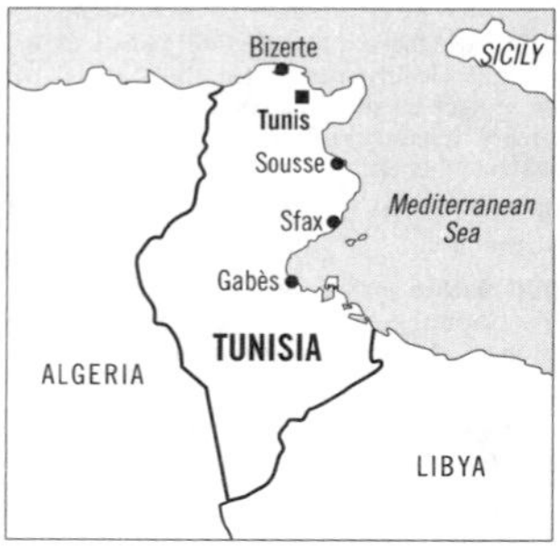

Tunisia

Tunisia /tyoo nízzi ə/ republic in North Africa, on the Mediterranean Sea. Capital: Tunis. Population: 9,245,284 (1997). Area: 164,418 sq. km/63,482 sq. mi. —**Tunisian** *n, adj*

tunnage *n* MEASURE, SHIPPING = **tonnage**

tunnel /túnn'l/ *n* **1** PASSAGEWAY UNDER OBSTRUCTION a long passage that allows pedestrians or vehicles to proceed under or through an obstruction such as a river, mountain, or congested area **2** ANIMAL'S UNDERGROUND PASSAGE an underground passage or system of passages dug by a burrowing animal **3** PART OF MINE a corridor or working area in a mine **4** PASSAGE any passage, channel, or route through or under something ■ *v* (**-nels, -nelling, -nelled**) **1** *vti* MAKE TUNNEL to make, burrow, or excavate a tunnel under or through something **2** *vt* MAKE SOMETHING

LIKE TUNNEL to produce or dig something that resembles or is shaped like a tunnel [15C. < Old French *tonel* 'small barrel' < medieval Latin *tunna* 'cask'.] —**tunneller** *n*

unnel disease *n* MED = **ancylostomiasis** [Because caused by tunnel worms]

unnel effect *n* a quantum mechanical effect in which elementary particles can pass through an energy barrier such as a thin layer even if they do not have enough energy to do so

unnelling /túnn'ling/ *n* PHYS = **tunnel effect**

unnel vault *n* ARCHIT = **barrel vault**

unnel vision *n* **1** a condition in which peripheral vision is lost or severely limited, so that only objects directly in line with the eyes can be seen **2** a very limited viewpoint or conception of things

unny /túnni/ (*plural* **-ny** *or* **-nies**) *n* ZOOL = **tuna**[1] *n.* 1 [Mid-16C. Via French *thon* and Latin *thunnus* < Greek *thunnos*.]

up /tup/ *vt* (**tups, tupping, tupped**) **MATE WITH A EWE** to copulate with a ewe ■ *n* **1** *Scotland, N England* **RAM** a male sheep used for breeding **2 HEAD OF HAMMER** the head of a power hammer or a mechanism resembling a hammer [14C. < ?]

upek /tóopək/, **tupik** /-pik/ *n* a tent made of animal skins, used in the summer by the Inuit in the Arctic [Mid-19C. < Inuit *tupiq*.]

upelo /tyóopəlō/ (*plural* **-los**) *n* **1** the soft pale wood of a deciduous tree **2** a deciduous tree that grows in swamps and on river banks and yields tupelo. Native to: North America, Asia. Genus: *Nyssa*. [Mid-18C. < Creek *ito opilwa* 'swamp tree'.]

'upi /tóo pee/ (*plural* **-pi** *or* **-pis**) *n* **1** a member of a group of Native South American peoples who live in the Amazon valley **2** the Tupi-Guarani language of the Tupi people. Native speakers: 3,000. [Mid-19C. < Tupi, 'comrade'.] —**Tupi** *adj*

'upian /tóopi ən/ *n* **1** LANG = **Tupi** *n.* 2 **2** a family of Native South American languages that includes Tupi-Guarani —**Tupian** *adj*

'upi-Guarani *n* a Native South American language family whose principal members are Tupi and Guarani —**Tupi-Guarani** *adj*

upik *n* ANTHROP = **tupek**

uppence *n* MONEY = **twopence**

uppenny *adj* MONEY = **twopenny**

u quoque /tóo kwṓ k way/ *interj* used when accused of a crime to accuse the accuser of the same crime [Late 17C. < Latin, 'you too'.]

'ur. *abbr* **1** Turkey **2** Turkish

uraco *n* BIRDS = **touraco**

'uranian /tyoo ráyni ən/ *n* a member of any of the peoples who speak a Ural-Altaic language ■ *adj* relating to ancient Turkestan, or its people or culture [Late 18C. < Persian *Tūrān* 'Turkestan'.]

urban /túrbən/ *n* **1** a man's headdress that consists of a long piece of fabric wrapped around the head or around a small cap, completely covering the hair, worn especially by Sikhs and Muslims **2** a woman's hat that is similar in shape to a man's turban [Mid-16C. Via obsolete French *turbant*, Italian *turbante* < Turkish *tülbend* < Persian *dulband*.] —**turbaned** *adj*

urbary /túrbəri/ *n* an area of land where turf or peat may be cut or dug [14C. < Anglo-Norman *turberie* < French *tourbe* 'turf' < Germanic.]

urbellarian /túrbi láiri ən/ *n* a free-living flatworm such as a planarian that inhabits wet soil, freshwater, and marine environments. Class: Turbellaria. [Late 19C. < modern Latin *Turbellaria* < Latin *turbella* 'small commotion'.] —**turbellarian** *adj*

urbid /túrbid/ *adj* **1 MUDDY** opaque and muddy as when particles and sediment are stirred up **2 FOGGY** dense and cloudy or dark **3 CONFUSED** confused and muddled ○ *turbid thought processes* [Early 17C. < Latin *turbidus* 'troubled' < *turba* 'disorder'.] —**turbidity** /tur bíddəti/ *n* —**turbidly** *adv* —**turbidness** *n*

USAGE turbid or **turgid**? The two words are unrelated in form but can both describe water in their literal meanings (either 'opaque and muddy' in the case of ***turbid*** or 'swollen and overflowing' in the case of ***turgid***), and can both describe literary styles in their figurative meanings. ***Turgid*** is the more common and means 'pompous and overcomplicated' (as in *turgid prose*), whereas ***turbid*** means 'confused and muddled'.

turbidimeter /túrbi dímmitər/ *n* an instrument that determines the amount of material in suspension in a liquid or gas by measuring the decrease in light transmittance through the fluid —**turbidimetric** /túrbidi méttrik/ *adj* —**turbidimetrically** *adv* —**turbidimetry** /túrbi dímmətri/ *n*

turbidite /túrbi dīt/ *n* a sedimentary deposit laid down by a turbidity current, e.g. on the ocean floor at the bottom of the continental shelf

turbidity current *n* a rapidly moving current containing dispersed sediments, sometimes started off by seismic shocks or slumping

turbinate /túrbinət, -nayt/, **turbinal** /-n'l/ *adj* **1 OF BONE IN NASAL PASSAGE** describes any of the three scroll-shaped bones found on the walls of the nasal passages of mammals **2 SPIRAL IN SHAPE** having a shape like a spiral or scroll **3 SHAPED LIKE INVERTED CONE** describes a shell that spirals and is shaped like an inverted cone ■ *n* **1 TURBINATE BONE** a turbinate bone in the nasal passage of mammals **2 MOLLUSC SHELL** a turbinate mollusc shell [Mid-17C. < Latin *turbinatus* < Latin *turbin-* 'spiral, spinning top'.] —**turbination** /túrbi náysh'n/ *n*

turbine /túrb īn, -bin/ *n* a machine in which a moving fluid such as steam acts upon the blades of a rotor to produce rotational motion that can be transformed to electrical or mechanical power [Mid-19C. Via French < Latin *turbin-* 'spiral, spinning top'.]

turbit /túrbit/ *n* a domestic pigeon of a breed with a ruffed neck and breast [Late 17C. < ?]

turbo[1] /túrbō/ (*plural* **-bos**) *n* **1** = **turbine** **2** = **turbocharger**

turbo[2] /túrbō/ (*plural* **-bos**) *n* a gastropod mollusc that has a whorled spiral shell. Genus: *Turbo*. [Mid-17C. < Latin, 'spiral, spinning top'.]

turbo- *prefix* **1** using the principle of a turbine, or driven by a turbine ○ *turbocharger* **2** turbojet ○ *turboprop* [< TURBINE]

turbocharger /túrbō chaarjər/ *n* a specialized turbine driven by the exhaust gases of an engine that supplies air under pressure to the engine for combustion [Mid-20C. Contraction of TURBOSUPERCHARGER.] —**turbocharged** *adj*

turbo-electric *adj* using or relating to an electric generator driven by a turbine

turbofan /túrbō fan/ *n* US term **fanjet** **1** a jet engine in which fans driven by a turbine force air into the exhaust gases, thereby increasing the propelling thrust of the engine **2** a jet aircraft that has turbofan engines

turbogenerator /túrbō jénnə raytər/ *n* a machine used to generate electricity in which steam from coal, oil, or gas, is used to drive the turbine

turbojet /túrbō jet/ *n* **1** an aircraft powered by jet engine with a gas turbine that uses exhaust gases to provide the propulsive thrust **2** a jet engine with a gas turbine that uses exhaust gases to provide the propulsive thrust for an aircraft

turboprop /túrbō prop/ *n* **1** an aircraft whose propellers are driven by a gas turbine **2** a turbojet engine that powers a propeller

turboramjet /túrbō rám jet/ *n* **1** a turbojet engine in which forward motion is achieved by compression of the fuel, used, e.g., in guided missiles **2** an aircraft powered by a turboramjet

turbosupercharger /túrbō sóopər chaarjər/ *n* ENG = **turbocharger**

turbot /túrbət/ (*plural* **-bot** *or* **-bots**) *n* **1 EUROPEAN FLATFISH** a flatfish that is almost circular with bony tubercles on its body and both eyes on the left side. Native to: Europe. *Scophthalmus maximus*. **2 TURBOT AS FOOD** the flesh of a turbot as food **3 FLATFISH** a flatfish in the same family as the European turbot, e.g. the spotted turbot of the Pacific. Family: Pleuronectidae. [13C. Via Old French < Old Swedish *törnbut* 'thorn-flatfish'; from the bony tubercles on its back.]

turbulence /túrbyŏŏlənss/, **turbulency** /-lənssi/ *n* **1 UNREST** a state of confusion characterized by unpredictability and uncontrolled change **2 INSTABILITY IN ATMOSPHERE** an instability in the atmosphere that disrupts the flow of the wind, causing gusty, unpredictable air currents **3 EDDIES** eddies or secondary motion within a moving fluid

turbulent /túrbyŏŏlənt/ *adj* **1 MOVING VIOLENTLY** full of violent motion and agitation ○ *turbulent rapids* **2 CHAOTIC AND RESTLESS** marked by disturbances, changes, and unrest ○ *a turbulent year in politics* **3 ATMOSPHERICALLY UNSTABLE** atmospherically unstable, with variations in wind speed and direction [15C. < Latin *turbulentus* < *turba* 'disorder'.] —**turbulently** *adv*

turbulent flow *n* a form of fluid flow in which particles of the fluid move with irregular local velocities and pressures

Turcoman *n, adj* PEOPLES, LANG = **Turkmen**

turd /turd/ *n* **1** a highly offensive term for a piece of excrement or dung (*taboo*) **2** a highly offensive term for somebody who is seen as contemptible (*taboo insult*) [Old English *tord* < Indo-European]

tureen /tyoo réen/ *n* a wide deep bowl with a lid that is used especially to serve soups, stews, and casseroles [Mid-18C. Alteration of TERRINE.]

turf /turf/ *n* (*plural* **turfs** *or* **turves** /turvz/) **1 DENSE LAYER OF GRASS** a dense thick even cover of grass and roots in the top layer of soil **2 ARTIFICIAL GRASS** artificial grass, used, e.g., on a playing field **3 PIECE OF SOIL WITH GRASS** a piece of soil with grass growing in it put down to form lawns and new grassed surfaces **4 PEAT FOR FUEL** peat, especially when sold for fuel **5 HORSERACING** horseracing as a sport or industry **6 HORSERACING TRACK** a track where horses are raced **7 AREA OF EXPERTISE** an area in which somebody feels confident or has authority or expertise (*informal*) **8 TERRITORY** a territory or geographical area (*informal*) **9 GANG TERRITORY** an area or territory that a gang claims to be its own (*informal*) ■ *vt* **COVER WITH TURF** to cover an area with pieces of turf (*informal*) [Old English, < Indo-European] —**turfy** *adj*

turf out *vt* to eject somebody from a place or organization (*informal*)

turf accountant *n* a bookmaker

Turgenev /tur gáy nyef/, **Ivan** (1818–83) Russian writer. Full name **Ivan Sergeyevich Turgenev**

turgescent /tur jéss'nt/ *adj* swollen or becoming swollen, usually as a result of an accumulation of blood or other fluids [Early 18C. < Latin *turgescent*, present participle of *turgescere* 'begin to swell' < *turgere* 'swell'.] —**turgescence** *n* —**turgescency** *n*

turgid /túrjid/ *adj* **1 POMPOUS AND OVERCOMPLICATED** pompous, boring, and overcomplicated ○ *a turgid speech* **2 DISTENDED** swollen or distended by a build-up of fluid **3 OVERFLOWING** swollen and overflowing [Early 17C. < Latin *turgidus* < *turgere* 'swell'.] —**turgidity** /tur jíddəti/ *n* —**turgidly** *adv* —**turgidness** *n*

USAGE See ***turbid***.

turgor /túrgər/ *n* the normal rigid state of plant cells, caused by outward pressure of the water content of each cell on its membrane [Late 19C. < late Latin, < Latin *turgere* 'swell'.]

Turin /tyoor rín/ capital of Turin Province, Piedmont Region, NW Italy. Population: 952,736 (1992).

Turing /tyóoring/, **Alan** (1912–54) British mathematician

⚡**Turing machine** /tyóoring-/ *n* a mathematical model of a hypothetical computer that can modify its instructions and read from, write on, or erase a potentially infinite tape [After Alan TURING]

turion /tyóori ən/ *n* **1** a bud that breaks off from an aquatic plant and lies submerged and dormant until the following spring, when it produces a new plantlet that floats to the surface **2** a shoot from an underground root or stem, e.g. in asparagus [Early 18C. Via French < Latin *turion-* 'young sprig'.]

Turk /turk/ *n* **1 SOMEBODY FROM TURKEY** a person who comes from Turkey **2 MEMBER OF TURKISH ETHNIC GROUP** a member of the Turkish-speaking ethnic group in Turkey, or, formerly, in the Ottoman Empire **3 TURKIC SPEAKER** a member of a people speaking a Turkic language [14C. Via French *Turc*, medieval Latin *Turcus* < Turkish *Türk*.]

Turk. *abbr* **1** Turkey **2** Turkish

Turkana, Lake /tur kaánə/ lake in NW Kenya, bordering Ethiopia at its N end. Area: 7,100 sq. km/2,700 sq. mi.

Turkestan /túrki stán, -staán/, **Turkistan** mountainous region of Central Asia that stretches from the Caspian Sea to the Gobi Desert

turkey /túrki/ (*plural* **-keys**) *n* **1 LARGE N AMERICAN BIRD** a large bird with a bare wattled head and neck and brownish feathers. Kept for: meat. Native to: North

America. *Meleagris gallopavo*. **2 TURKEY MEAT** the meat of the turkey used for food **3 LARGE CENTRAL AMERICAN BIRD** a large bird similar to the North American turkey. Native to: Central and N South America. *Agriocharis ocellata*. **4** *US* **FAILURE** something that fails or flops, especially a bad play or film (*slang*) **5** *US* **OFFENSIVE TERM** an offensive term that deliberately insults somebody regarded as unintelligent, incompetent, or socially inept (*slang*) **6 THREE CONSECUTIVE BOWLING STRIKES** three strikes in a row in the sport of bowling (*informal*) [Mid-16C. < its resemblance to the guinea fowl, imported through Turkish territory.] ◇ **talk turkey** *US* to talk honestly and bluntly (*informal*)

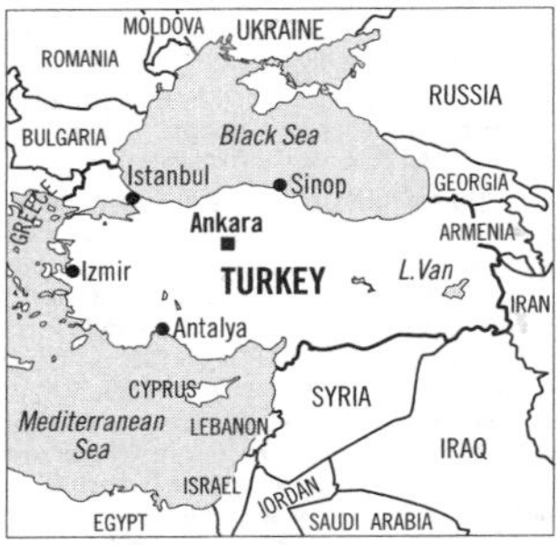

Turkey

Turkey /túrki/ republic in SE Europe and SW Asia. Capital: Ankara. Population: 63,528,225 (1997). Area: 779,452 sq. km/300,948 sq. mi.

turkey buzzard *n* BIRDS = **turkey vulture**

Turkey carpet *n* a handwoven woollen carpet with rich colours and a deep pile

turkey cock *n* **1** a male turkey, especially when fully grown **2** a person regarded as arrogant or conceited (*insult*)

Turkey red *adj* of the vibrant red colour produced using alizarin as a dye [Late 18C. < fabrics made in the Ottoman Empire.] —**Turkey red** *n*

turkey shoot *n* *US* **1** a marksmanship contest in which rifles are fired at moving targets **2** something easily accomplished (*slang*)

turkey trot *n* a round dance to ragtime music in which dancers walk springily and make birdlike movements with their upper body

turkey vulture *n* a blackish-brown vulture with a bare wrinkled red head and neck. Native to: Americas. *Cathartes aura*.

Turkic /túrkik/ *n* a subgroup of the Altaic family of languages spoken in western and central Asia, including Turkish and Azeri —**Turkic** *adj*

Turkish /túrkish/ *adj* **1 OF TURKEY** relating to Turkey, or to its people or culture **2 OF LANGUAGE OF TURKEY** relating to the Turkish language ■ *n* **OFFICIAL LANGUAGE OF TURKEY** the Turkic language that is the official language of Turkey, also spoken in Cyprus and several European countries. Native speakers: 50 million. —**Turkishness** *n*

Turkish bath *n* **1** a bath in which the bather sweats freely in hot air or steam, followed by a shower and often a massage **2** a commercial establishment where somebody can have a Turkish bath

Turkish coffee *n* a strong coffee, usually sweetened, made by simmering finely ground coffee and serving the liquid with the grounds

Turkish delight *n* a sweet made with flavoured gelatin, cut into cubes and dusted with icing sugar

Turkish tobacco *n* an aromatic dark tobacco grown in SE Europe and Turkey

Turkish towel *n* a large coarse-fibred cotton towel

Turkmen /túrk men/ (*plural* **-men** *or* **-mens**), **Turkoman** (*plural* **-mans**), **Turcoman** /túrkəmən/ (*plural* **-mans**) *n* **1** a member of an originally nomadic Turkic-speaking people who now live mainly in Turkmenistan and Afghanistan **2** the Turkic official language of Turkmenistan. Native speakers: 4 million. [Early 20C. Via Persian *turkmān* < Turkish *türkmen*.] —**Turkmen** *adj*

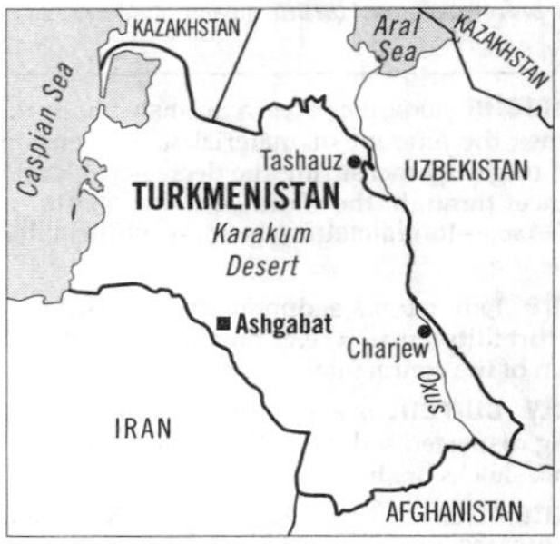

Turkmenistan

Turkmenistan /turk ménni staan/ republic in SW Central Asia, on the Caspian Sea. Capital: Ashgabat. Population: 4,229,249 (1997). Area: 488,100 sq. km/188,500 sq. mi.

Turkoman *n, adj* PEOPLES, LANG = **Turkmen**

Turks and Caicos Islands /túrks ənd káykoss īləndz/ British dependency consisting of two island groups in the West Indies. Capital: Cockburn Town. Population: 14,302 (1996). Area: 430 sq. km/166 sq. mi.

Turk's-cap lily /túrks kap-/ *n* either of two lilies that have bright nodding flowers with petals that bend sharply backwards. *Lilium martagon* and *Lilium superbum*.

Turk's-head *n* a knot shaped like a turban, made by weaving a smaller rope around a larger rope or spar

turmeric /túrmərik/ *n* **1** a yellow spice made from the dried rhizomes of an Asian plant. Use: cooking, yellow dye. **2** a tropical Asian plant of the ginger family with yellow flowers and rhizomes that are dried to produce turmeric. *Curcuma longa*. [Mid-16C. < French *terre-mérite* 'worthy earth'.]

turmeric paper *n* a strip of test paper impregnated with turmeric. Use: turns brown in the presence of alkalis and red-brown in the presence of boric acid.

turmoil /túr moyl/ *n* **1** a state of great confusion, commotion, or disturbance **2** a disruptive event that causes confusion, commotion, or disturbance ○ *a leader untroubled by the nation's turmoils* [Early 16C. < ?]

turn /turn/ *v* **1** *vti* **MOVE TO FACE DIFFERENT DIRECTION** to move to face in a particular direction or towards a particular location, or move something so that it does this ○ *She turned to see what was happening.* ○ *turning his eyes skywards* **2** *vti* **MOVE ROUND AN AXIS** to move around an axis or point in a particular direction, or move something in this way ○ *Turn the handle to the left.* **3** *vt* **USE CONTROL TO OPERATE** to control something such as a machine or an appliance or some aspect of its performance by moving a knob, switch, or slider to a particular setting ○ *Turn the heat to high.* **4** *vti* **TRAVEL IN NEW DIRECTION** to go in a different direction when moving or travelling, or make a vehicle change direction ○ *Turn left at the crossroads.* **5** *vt* **GO AROUND** to change direction and go round something ○ *to turn a corner* **6** *vi* **FOLLOW DIFFERENT COURSE** to change direction and follow a different course ○ *The path turns uphill.* **7** *vti* **MOVE PAGE OVER** to move a page so that the other side, or another page, can be read or looked at ○ *He turned the pages slowly.* **8** *vti* **CHANGE** to change or be transformed, or change or transform somebody or something, into somebody or something different **9** *vti* **CHANGE COLOUR** to change colour, or cause something to change colour **10** *vti* **ALTER FOCUS** to direct the focus of something towards something else, or be focused on something ○ *Her thoughts turned to the past.* **11** *vi* **START DOING SOMETHING DIFFERENT** to start doing something new or different, especially as a way of solving a problem or improving a situation **12** *vi* **APPEAL** to seek or appeal for help from somebody ○ *He turned to his mother for advice.* **13** *vi* **CHANGE IN WEATHER** to change to become a different temperature or type of weather ○ *It's turned cold again.* **14** *vti* **MAKE SOMEBODY FEEL SLIGHTLY SICK** to be sufficiently unpleasant or upsetting to make somebody feel nauseated, or respond with feelings of nausea ○ *The scenes of carnage turned his stomach.* **15** *vt* **PERFORM CARTWHEEL** to rotate the body to perform a physical action such as a cartwheel or somersault **16** *vt* **TWIST ANKLE** to injure the ankle or wrist by twisting or spraining it ○ *She turned her ankle getting off the bus.* **17** *vt* **SEARCH EXTENSIVELY** to search a place extremely thoroughly ○ *They turned the house upside down looking for the ticket.* **18** *vt* **PASS TIME OR AGE** to pass a particular age, time, or speed ○ *She's just turned sixty.* **19** *vi* **BECOME SOUR** to become sour (*refers to milk*) **20** *vi* **START TO EBB OR FLOW** to reach high tide and start to ebb, or reach low tide and start to rise ○ *The tide has turned.* **21** *vt* **SHAPE ON LATHE** to shape or cut something on a lathe **22** *vt* **FORM INTO ROUND SHAPE** to shape clay or a pot into a rounded form with the hands or with tools **23** *vt* **EARN MONEY** to earn or achieve a monetary gain ○ *The business should turn a profit in this financial year.* **24** *vti* **CHANGE SOMEBODY'S ALLEGIANCE** to cause a change in somebody's allegiance or undergo a change of allegiance ○ *a diplomat who turned spy* **25** *vt* **SAY OR WRITE SOMETHING WELL** to give a distinctive or pleasing form to something said or written **26** *vt* **DIG UP LOWER LEVELS OF SOIL** to dig soil so as to bring lower layers up to the surface **27** *vt* **PASS ROUND ENEMY** to pass round an enemy in order to attack from the flank or rear **28** *vt* **SPIN A BALL** to make a cricket ball spin **29** *vt* **BLUNT A WEAPON** to blunt the edge of a weapon (*archaic*) ■ *n* **1 OPPORTUNITY** a time when somebody gets an opportunity to do something or somebody is asked to do something, especially when this is rotated among other people ○ *It's your turn to do the washing up.* **2 CHANGE OF DIRECTION** a change of direction in something such as a road or the plot of a book ○ *Slow down for the turn in the road ahead.* **3** TRANSP = **turning** *n.* 1 **4 MOVEMENT OF ROTATION** a full or partial rotation ○ *Give the screw a few more turns.* **5 PARTICULAR INCLINATION** a particular inclination or tendency ○ *She has an academic turn of mind.* **6 SUDDEN SCARE** a sudden shock or scare ○ *It gave me quite a turn.* **7 SPELL OF ILLNESS** a short period of feeling unwell or faint ○ *She had a nasty turn but she's OK now.* **8 SHORT OUTING** a short walk, excursion, or dance (*dated*) ○ *They took a turn around the park.* **9 END OF TIME PERIOD** the point at which one period of time ends and another begins **10 GOOD OR BAD DEED** a deed that helps or harms another person ○ *a good turn* **11 MELODIC EMBELLISHMENT** a melodic embellishment that is played around a given note using one note above and one note below the principal note **12 INDIVIDUAL THEATRICAL PERFORMANCE** a short theatrical solo performance, e.g. in a cabaret or variety show **13 STOCK MARKET TRANSACTION** a stock market transaction that includes both a sale and a purchase **14 ADVANCE PASSING ROUND ENEMY** a military advance that passes around an enemy in order to attack from the flank or rear [Pre-12C. < Latin *tornare* 'turn on a lathe' < *tornus* 'lathe' < Greek *tornos*.] —**turnable** *adj* ◇ **at every turn** everywhere, or at every significant moment ◇ **a turn of phrase** a particular way of expressing yourself ◇ **be on the turn 1** to be on the point of going sour **2** to be on the point of changing **3** to be at high or low tide and just about to ebb or return ◇ **by turns** one after the other, alternately ◇ **in turn** in a regular order, one after the other ◇ **out of turn 1** not in a regular or correct order **2** in an inappropriate way, or at an inappropriate time ◇ **to a turn** perfectly ○ *meat done to a turn* ◇ **turn and burn** *US* to change direction and increase speed rapidly, as in an aircraft, or make a major change in policy or approach

turn against *vt* to stop approving of something or being friendly towards somebody and show definite disapproval or unfriendliness instead, or make somebody change attitude in this way

turn away *v* **1** *vti* **TURN TO FACE SOMEWHERE ELSE** to change position so as to face away from somebody or something, or move somebody or something so as to face in another direction **2** *vt* **REFUSE ADMISSION TO** to send somebody away, refusing to see, entertain, or accommodate him or her **3** *vt* **REFUSE TO ACCEPT** to refuse to listen to somebody or to what somebody wants to say or offer **4** *vi* **REJECT** to reject something as unworthy or undesirable ○ *to turn away from a life of sin*

turn back *v* **1** *vti* to stop and return in the direction you have come from, or stop people or vehicles and make them return in the direction they have come from **2** *vt* to fold something over and down ○ *turned back the top sheet on the bed*

turn down *vt* **1 REJECT** to reject or refuse something such as an offer or application **2 REDUCE VOLUME OR INTENSITY** to make something less powerful, bright, loud, or hot, especially by moving a knob, switch, or slider **3 FOLD SOMETHING DOWNWARDS** to fold something or the top part of something towards the bottom, so that a double layer is formed

turn in *v* **1** *vt* **RETURN SOMETHING AFTER USE** to hand something over or give something back to its owner or to whoever is responsible for it ○ *turn in your key at reception before leaving* **2** *vt* **SUBMIT** to hand in or send in something such as work assigned in school **3** *vt* **TAKE**

SOMEBODY TO THE POLICE to hand over somebody or something to the police or other authorities 4 *vi* GO TO BED to go to bed at the end of the day (*informal*) 5 *vt* PRODUCE RESULT to achieve a particular outcome ○ *turned in a creditable performance* 6 *vti* FOLD INWARDS to arrange something so that it bends or points inwards, or be arranged in this way

turn off *v* 1 *vt* OPERATE SWITCH TO STOP to make a machine or appliance stop working, or something stop flowing, by operating a control 2 *vt* SET TO OFF POSITION to move a device such as a button, knob, or lever so that a machine stops working or something stops flowing 3 *vti* DIMINISH ENTHUSIASM to diminish or destroy somebody's interest, enthusiasm, or sexual arousal, or lose interest or become unresponsive (*informal*) 4 *vti* GO IN A NEW DIRECTION to split off from a road or path and head a different way, or take a road or path that goes in a new direction

turn on *v* 1 *vt* OPERATE SWITCH TO START to make a machine or appliance operate, or make something start flowing, by operating a control 2 *vt* SET SOMETHING TO ON POSITION to move a device such as a button, knob, or lever so that a machine starts working or something starts flowing 3 *vt* BEHAVE IN CALCULATED WAY to display a particular behaviour or emotion in a way that people find calculated, irritating, or insincere ○ *He'll really turn on the charm if he thinks he's losing the sale.* 4 *vt* REACT AGGRESSIVELY TO to react aggressively or violently to somebody 5 *vt* MAKE SOMEBODY EXCITED to interest somebody greatly or fill somebody with pleasure, energy, or excitement (*informal*) 6 *vt* AROUSE to make somebody feel sexually excited (*informal*) 7 *vti* TAKE ILLEGAL DRUGS to take drugs, especially a hallucinogenic drug, or cause somebody to take a hallucinogen or similar drug (*informal*)

turn out *v* 1 *vt* SWITCH LIGHT OFF to make an electric light go out by operating its power switch 2 *vi* COME TO EVENT to assemble in a particular place, especially for a special event or public occasion ○ *Hardly anybody turned out for the reunion.* 3 *vt* MAKE SOMEBODY LEAVE to force somebody to leave a room, building, or residence 4 *vi* HAPPEN IN PARTICULAR WAY to happen in a particular way, often in a way that was not expected 5 *vi* END UP to have a particular result ○ *The birthday party turned out OK, despite our fears.* 6 *vt* MAKE to create or produce something, especially in a consistent way or by mass production ○ *a factory that turns out tennis rackets* 7 *vt* DRESS SOMEBODY UP to clothe yourself or somebody else in a particular way (*often passive*) ○ *a well-turned-out young man* 8 *vti* SIGNAL GROUP TO ASSEMBLE to call an organized group of people, usually soldiers, to assemble for duty or for a military parade 9 *vt* EMPTY CONTENTS to take out the contents of a pocket or bag, usually to check or reorganize what is there 10 *vti* FOLD OUTWARDS to be arranged so as to bend or point outwards, or arrange something in this way 11 *vi* GET UP to get out of bed (*informal*)

turn over *v* 1 *vt* TURN SOMETHING THE OTHER WAY UP to alter the position of the body or of an object, bringing the underside uppermost, or move so that the underside is uppermost 2 *vt* THINK ABOUT to give something slow and careful thought, considering different aspects or possibilities 3 *vt* GIVE SOMETHING TO SOMEBODY ELSE to hand something over to the police or other authorities, especially when required to do so 4 *vt* DELEGATE to give the responsibility for something to somebody else ○ *turned over some duties to her assistant* 5 *vt* PUT SOMEBODY UNDER SOMEBODY'S RESPONSIBILITY to transfer the responsibility for somebody to another person or authority ○ *The principal turned him over to his parents.* 6 *vt* ROB A PLACE to break into a building or premises and steal anything thought to be valuable (*slang; often passive*) 7 *vti* START to start an engine or motor, or be started ○ *couldn't get it to turn over* 8 *vt* HAVE SALES OF to have sales or other business transactions totalling a specified amount ○ *The firm turns over several million a month.* 9 *vti* SELL AND RESTOCK GOODS to sell and restock all items for sale ○ *The produce usually turns over in 10 days.*

turn round, turn around *vt* 1 COMPLETE ALL NECESSARY PROCEDURES to carry out all the necessary procedures between receiving an order or task and shipping the order or completing the task ○ *How long will it take you to turn this work round?* 2 PREPARE VEHICLE BETWEEN JOURNEYS to prepare an aircraft for its next flight or a ship for its next sailing 3 IMPROVE SOMETHING SIGNIFICANTLY to cause a significant improvement in something, especially in the profits made by a company or organization ○ *moves to turn the debt round*

turn to *vi* to set to work, especially vigorously (*dated*)

turn up *v* 1 *vt* INCREASE to make something louder, brighter, hotter, or more powerful, especially by operating its control 2 *vti* UNFOLD UPWARDS to unfold something so that it stands up instead of lying in a flat double layer, or be capable of unfolding in this way 3 *vt* SHORTEN GARMENT to fold and sew the bottom edge of a garment or piece of fabric, so as to shorten it 4 *vi* BE FOUND to reappear or be rediscovered after being lost or in an unknown place, often in a surprising or unexpected way ○ *It'll turn up sooner or later.* 5 *vt* FIND SOMETHING BY SEARCHING to uncover something that was hidden or previously unknown by investigating, hunting, or digging ○ *He didn't expect to turn up such an interesting story.* 6 *vi* ARRIVE to come or appear somewhere, especially in a casual or unplanned way ○ *She just turned up yesterday morning.* 7 *vi* HAPPEN to take place luckily or unexpectedly to settle matters or put things right ○ *They manage to get along somehow ... something always seems to turn up.*

turnabout /túrn ə bowt/ *n* 1 a shift from one situation, opinion, policy, or attitude to another that is the complete opposite 2 the act of turning to face in the opposite direction

turnaround *n* = **turnround**

turnbuckle /túrn buk'l/ *n* a device to tighten or loosen rope or wire, consisting of a sleeve through which the rope or wire is threaded and held so that the tension can be adjusted

turncoat /túrnkōt/ *n* a person who abandons or betrays a group or cause and joins its opponents

turndown /túrn down/ *adj* folded down or over from the top ■ *n* 1 ECON = **downturn** 2 *US* a rejection of something such as an offer or application

turned-on *adj* 1 SEXUALLY EXCITED sexually aroused or excited (*informal*) 2 UP-TO-DATE aware of or involved in the most modern trends in culture and fashion (*dated informal*) 3 HIGH ON DRUGS under the influence of a drug such as cannabis or LSD, or familiar with its effects as a result of having taken it (*dated informal*)

turner /túrnər/ *n* 1 somebody or something that turns or that is used for turning something else, e.g. a device for turning food while it is cooking ○ *a pancake turner* 2 somebody whose job involves operating a lathe

Turner /túrnər/, **J.M.W.** (1775–1851) British painter and watercolourist. Full name **Joseph Mallord William Turner**

Turner, John Napier (*b.* 1929) Canadian statesman

Turner, Lana (1920–95) US actor. Born **Julia Jean Mildred Frances Turner**

Turner, Ted (*b.* 1938) US business executive and philanthropist. Full name **Robert Edward Turner III**

Turner's syndrome *n* a genetic disorder affecting women in which only one X chromosome per cell is present instead of the usual two, resulting in underdeveloped ovaries and underdevelopment of the womb, vagina, and breasts [Mid-20C. After Henry Hubert Turner (1892–1970), US physician.]

turnery /túrnəri/ (*plural* **-ies**) *n* 1 WORK ON LATHE the technique, art, or skill of forming and contouring using a lathe 2 ARTICLES TURNED ON LATHE articles that have been made or turned on a lathe 3 WORKSHOP a room or building where lathes are used

turning /túrning/ *n* 1 JUNCTION a road or path that joins the main road or the road that is being travelled. US term **turn** *n.* 3 2 DEVIATION a deviation from a straight or planned course 3 TECH = **turnery** *n.* 1 4 FABRIC THAT FORMS HEM the amount of fabric that will be turned back to form a hem at the edge of a piece of sewing ■ **turnings** *npl* WASTE MATERIAL FROM LATHE the waste material produced when something is turned on a lathe

turning circle *n* the smallest circle in which a vehicle can complete a 360-degree turn. US term **turning radius**

turning point *n* 1 a particular time or incident that marks the beginning of a completely new, and usually better, stage in somebody's life or in the development of something 2 a minimum or maximum point on a plane curve

turning radius *n US* AUTOMOT = **turning circle**

turnip /túrnip/ *n* 1 a white rounded fleshy root that is cooked and eaten as a vegetable 2 a plant that produces turnips. *Brassica rapa.* [Mid-16C. < *tur-* (< ?) + NEEP.]

turnkey /túrn kee/ *adj* complete and ready to use upon delivery or installation ○ *a turnkey operation* ■ *n* (*plural* **-keys**) a keeper of keys, especially in a jail (*archaic*)

turn-off /túrn óf/ *n* 1 ROAD BRANCHING OFF MAIN ROAD a road that branches off a main road 2 ROAD JUNCTION a junction formed by two roads, especially a larger and a smaller one 3 SOMETHING DISGUSTING OR OFF-PUTTING somebody or something that causes a complete loss of interest, enthusiasm, or sexual arousal (*informal*)

turn-on *n* somebody or something that causes sexual arousal (*informal*)

turnout /túrn owt/ *n* 1 ATTENDANCE the number of people who attend or take part in a particular event ○ *expecting a huge turnout for the carnival this weekend* 2 NUMBER OF VOTERS the number or proportion of voters who register their vote in an election 3 AMOUNT OF WORK PRODUCED the total quantity or amount produced, e.g. by a particular company or manufacturing process 4 OUTFIT the clothes or equipment somebody is wearing ○ *a smart turnout* 5 *US* WIDENED PART OF STREET a section where a narrow roadway is broader, allowing vehicles to pass each other, pull over, or park 6 OUTWARD ROTATION OF DANCER'S LEGS the outward rotating movement from the hip sockets of a classical ballet dancer's legs

turnover /túrnōvər/ *n* 1 AMOUNT OF BUSINESS the amount of business transacted over a given period of time, especially when expressed as gross revenue 2 THROUGHPUT OF STOCK the rate at which business stock is sold and replaced 3 CHANGE IN EMPLOYEES the number of employees in an organization who leave and are replaced over a given period ○ *job dissatisfaction that results in high turnover* 4 *US* LOSS OF POSSESSION in basketball and football, a loss of possession of the ball resulting from error or violation of rules 5 FILLED PASTRY a filled pastry, made by folding a square or circle of pastry in half over a filling to form a semicircle or triangle ■ *adj* ABLE TO BE FOLDED OVER designed to be turned or folded over

turnpike /túrn pīk/ *n* 1 TOLL ROAD in the United States, a motorway on which a toll is charged 2 ROAD BARRIER a gate formerly used to bar the way onto a section of road or a bridge until a toll had been paid 3 ROAD WITH TURNPIKE in former times, a road that travellers were allowed to use only after paying a toll at the turnpike [14C. < TURN + PIKE[5].]

turnround /túrn rownd/, **turnaround** /túrn ə rownd/ *n* 1 TIME TAKEN TO DO ENTIRE JOB the time it takes to carry out all the necessary procedures between receiving an order or task and the shipment of the order or completion of the task 2 PREPARATION OF VEHICLE BETWEEN JOURNEYS the process of unloading and reloading, refuelling, and checking an aircraft, ship, or vehicle between journeys 3 BIG IMPROVEMENT a dramatic improvement in a bad or unsatisfactory situation 4 *US* PLACE FOR TURNING CAR ROUND a circular or curved driveway or section of road where vehicles can turn round

turnsole /túrnsōl/ *n* 1 a purple dye obtained from a Mediterranean plant 2 an annual plant that yields turnsole. Native to: Mediterranean. *Chrozophora tinctoria.* [14C. Via Old French *tournesole* < Old Italian *tornasole* < *tornare* 'turn' + *sol* 'sun'.]

turnstile /túrn stīl/ *n* a mechanical barrier designed to let people pass through a narrow opening one at a time between bars that revolve around a central post

turnstone /túrn stōn/ *n* a wading bird with mottled black or tortoiseshell markings. Native to: Arctic coast, migrating south. Genus: *Arenaria.* [Late 17C. Because it turns over stones to find food.]

turntable /túrn tayb'l/ *n* 1 REVOLVING PLATFORM ON RECORD PLAYER the flat round revolving plate on which the record rests on a record player 2 RECORD PLAYER DECK a record player deck, especially without the amplifier and speakers, and as distinct from a separate tape player, CD player, or tuner 3 ROTATING PLATFORM a rotating platform for turning round a vehicle such as a railway locomotive, so that it is facing the opposite way

turntable ladder *n* an extending ladder mounted on a rotating platform on the back of a fire engine. US term **aerial ladder**

turn-up *n* 1 *UK* FOLD AT BOTTOM OF TROUSER LEG a fold of material that is turned up at the bottom of a trouser leg 2 SOMETHING SURPRISING an unexpected, unlikely, or unusual event (*informal*) ○ *That's a turn-up for the books!* ■ *adj* FOR TURNING UP designed to be folded or turned up

turpentine /túrpən tīn/ *n* 1 SUBSTANCE FROM PINE TREES a viscous substance obtained from coniferous trees. Use: manufacture of paint solvent. 2 STICKY SUBSTANCE FROM TEREBINTH TREE a brownish yellow sticky mixture of essential oil and resin that comes from the terebinth tree 3 LIQUID FROM TURPENTINE a colourless, flammable, strong-smelling essential oil distilled from turpentine. Use: paint solvent, in medicine. 4 PAINT THINNER a colourless petroleum-based liquid used as a thinner for paint and varnish ■ *vt* (**-tines, -tining, -tined**) **1 TREAT WITH TURPENTINE** to treat or thin something with turpentine **2 EXTRACT TURPENTINE FROM** to extract turpentine from trees [14C. Via Old French *terbentine* 'terebinth resin' < Greek *terebinthos* 'terebinth tree'.]

turpentine tree *n* **1** a tree such as the terebinth that yields turpentine **2** a tree of the eucalyptus family that yields a viscous resin and is often planted as a shade tree. Native to: Australia. Genus: *Syncarpia.*

turpeth /túrpith/ (*plural* **-peths** *or* **-peth**) *n* **1** a plant belonging to the bindweed family whose roots are turpeths. Native to: Asia. *Operculina turpethum.* **2** root of an Asian plant. Use: formerly, as a laxative. [14C. Via medieval Latin *turbithum* < Persian *turbid* < Sanskrit *triputin* 'castor-oil plant'.]

Turpin /túrpin/, **Dick** (1706–39) British highwayman. Full name **Richard Turpin**. Known as **the King of the Road**

turpitude /túrpi tyood/ *n* extreme immorality or wickedness (*formal*) [15C. Directly or via French < Latin *turpitudo* < *turpis* 'repulsive'.]

turps /turps/ *n* (*informal*) **1** turpentine **2** *Aus* beer or other alcoholic drink [Early 19C. Shortening.]

turquoise /túrkwoyz, -kaaz/ *n* **1** a semiprecious stone that is a greenish-blue form of aluminium copper phosphate. Source: igneous rocks. Use: gems. **2** a bright greenish-blue colour [15C. < Old French *(pierre) turqueise* 'Turkish (stone)'; because first found in Turkestan.] —**turquoise** *adj*

turret /túrrit/ *n* **1 SMALL TOWER** a small rounded tower that projects from a wall or corner of a large building such as a castle **2 DOME CONTAINING GUN** a rotating armoured structure on a ship or tank, or a dome projecting from the fuselage of an aircraft, containing one or more guns and a gun crew **3 PART OF LATHE** a device on a lathe, used for holding a range of tools [14C. < Old French *tourete* 'small tower' < *tour* 'tower' < Latin *turris*.]

turreted /túritid/ *adj* **1** constructed or designed to include turrets **2** shaped like a long pointed spiral

turret lathe *n* MECH ENG = **capstan lathe**

turtle[1] /túrt'l/ *n* **1 WARM-WATER MARINE TURTLE** a large turtle with limbs shaped like paddles that is usually found in tropical and subtropical seas. Family: Cheloniidae and Dermochelyidae. US term **sea turtle 2** *US* **REPTILE WITH SHELL** a water- or land-dwelling reptile such as a tortoise or terrapin with a body protected by a bony shell **3 TURTLE MEAT** the flesh of any edible type of turtle, tortoise, or terrapin [Mid-16C. < ?] ◊ **turn turtle** to turn upside down

turtle[2] /túrt'l/ *n* a turtledove (*archaic*) [Pre-12C. < Latin *turtur*, an imitation of its call.]

turtleback /túrt'l bak/ *n* an arched cover for protecting the deck of a ship in heavy seas

turtledove /túrt'l duv/ *n* a slender dove with black-and-chestnut upper parts, a pink breast, and a black-and-white neck, noted for its purring call. Native to: N Europe, migrating to Africa. *Streptopelia turtur.* [13C. < TURTLE[2].]

turtlehead /túrt'l hed/ (*plural* **-heads** *or* **-head**) *n* a perennial plant found near running water. Flowers: white, purplish, greenish, or yellowish. Native to: E North America. Genus: *Chelone.* [Mid-19C. < the shape of its flowers.]

turtleneck /túrt'l nek/ *n* **1** *US* = **polo neck** *n.* **1 2** *US* = **polo neck** *n.* **2 3** a high tight-fitting round collar on a garment such as a sweater. US term **mock turtle** *n.* **1 4** a sweater with a turtleneck. US term **mock turtle** *n.* **2**

turves plural of **turf**

Tuscan /túskən/ *adj* **1 OF TUSCANY** relating to the Italian region of Tuscany, or its people or culture **2 OF STYLE OF ARCHITECTURE** relating to a classical order of architecture characterized by plain bases and capitals and unfluted columns ■ *n* **1 SOMEBODY FROM TUSCANY** a person who comes from Tuscany **2 STANDARD ITALIAN** the standard and literary form of Italian, principally based on the dialect of Florence [14C. Via Old French *tuscan*, Italian *toscano* < Latin *Tuscanus* < *Tuscus* 'Etruscan'.]

Tuscany /túskəni/ region in N Italy. Capital: Florence. Population: 3,526,031 (1995). Area: 22,993 sq. km/8,878 sq. mi.

Tuscarora /túska ráwrə/ (*plural* **-ras** *or* **-ra**) *n* a member of an Iroquois people who lived in North Carolina, and who now live mainly in New York State and Ontario [Mid-17C. < Iroquois, 'hemp gatherer'.]

tusche /toosh/ *n* a thick black liquid that is used as a drawing medium in lithography and as a resist in silk-screen printing and etching [Late 19C. < German, a back-formation < *tuschen* 'draw in ink', via French *toucher* < Old French *touchier* (see TOUCH).]

tush[1] /toosh/ *n* *US* somebody's buttocks or bottom (*slang*) [Mid-20C. Alteration of Yiddish *tokhes*.]

tush[2] /tush/ *interj* an expression of mild disapproval or disdain (*archaic*) [Mid-16C. Natural exclamation.]

tusk /tusk/ *n* **1 ENLARGED TOOTH** an enlarged pointed front tooth that projects from the mouth in animals such as the elephant, walrus, and wild boar and is often used for fighting **2 TENON JOINT** in joinery, a form of tenon that has a short projecting part to make it stronger ■ *vti* **JAB TUSK INTO** to use a tusk or tusks to attack, dig at, or stab somebody or something [Old English *tūsc, tux* < Indo-European, 'tooth'.] —**tusked** *adj*

tusker /túskər/ *n* a wild boar, elephant, or other animal with large tusks (*informal*)

tusk shell *n* a marine mollusc with a slender, tapering, and often curved shell that is open at both ends. Order: Scaphopoda. US term **tooth shell**

tussah /tússə/ (*plural* **-sahs** *or* **-sah**) *n* **1** INSECTS = **tussore** *n.* **1 2** TEXTILES = **tussore** *n.* **2 3** TEXTILES = **tussore** *n.* **3**

Tussaud /tooss ó/, **Madame** (1760–1850) Swiss wax-modeller. Born **Marie Grosholtz**

tussis /tússiss/ *n* a cough or coughing (*technical*) [< Latin] —**tussal** *adj* —**tussive** *adj*

tussle /túss'l/ *vi* (**-sles, -sling, -sled**) to have a vigorous physical or verbal struggle with somebody ■ *n* a vigorous physical or verbal struggle [15C. Probably < N English dialect *touse* 'pull about'.]

tussock /tússək/ *n* a small thick clump of growing vegetation, usually coarse grass [Mid-16C. < ?] —**tussocky** *adj*

tussock grass *n* a grass that grows in clumps. Native to: New Zealand, Australia.

tussock moth *n* a moth whose caterpillars are covered in tufts of brightly coloured hairs. Family: Lymantriidae.

tussore /tússər/ (*plural* **-sores** *or* **-sore**) *n* **1 SILKWORM** the silkworm of an Asian moth, from which a coarse silk is obtained. *Antheraea paphia.* US term **tussah** *n.* **1 2 SILK THREAD** the silk thread produced by the tussore silkworm. US term **tussah** *n.* **2 3 SILK FABRIC** the silk fabric woven from tussore. US term **tussah** *n.* **3** [Early 17C. < Hindi *tasar* (see TUSSAH).]

tut /tut/, **tut-tut** *interj* a clicking sound made with the tongue, or a spoken imitation of this sound, used as an expression of annoyance or disapproval, sometimes ironically ■ *vi* (**tuts, tutting, tutted; tut-tuts, tut-tutting, tut-tutted**) to make a clicking sound with the tongue to express annoyance or dissatisfaction, or to express these feelings in some other way [Early 16C. Natural exclamation.]

Tutankhamen /tootən ka'amən/, **Tutankhamun** /tootən kaa moon/ (1346?–1328 BC) Egyptian pharaoh

tutee /tyoo teé/ *n* the student of a particular tutor, or somebody being tutored [Early 20C. < TUTOR + -EE.]

tutelage /tyootalij/ *n* **1 TEACHING** instruction and guidance provided by somebody such as a tutor ◊ *Under her tutelage, he became a first-rate marksman.* **2 BEING A TUTOR** the condition of being a tutor or guardian **3 SUPERVISION BY A TUTOR** the condition of being supervised or protected by a tutor or guardian ◊ *continued my studies under private tutelage* [Early 17C. < Latin *tutela* 'guardianship' < *tut-*, past participle of *tueri* 'watch over'.]

tutelary /tyootələri/, **tutelar** /tyootələr/ *adj* (*formal or literary*) **1 ACTING AS PROTECTOR** acting in the role of a protector or guardian ◊ *tutelary saints* **2 OF GUARDIAN** relating to or belonging to a guardian ■ *n* (*plural* **-ies**) **GUARDING PRESENCE** a tutelary being or person, especially a saint or deity (*literary*) [Early 17C. < Latin *tutelarius* < *tutela* (see TUTELAGE).]

tutor /tyootər/ *n* **1 TEACHER** a teacher who instructs an individual pupil or a small group of pupils **2 BRITISH UNIVERSITY TEACHER** an academic who is responsible for teaching and advising an allocated group of students **3** *US* **LOW-RANKING US UNIVERSITY TEACHER** in some US universities, a teacher of a rank below instructor **4 GUARDIAN OF PUPIL** in Scottish law, somebody who is the guardian of a pupil (*formal*) ■ *v* **1** *vti* **ACT AS TUTOR** to act as a tutor to somebody or in a particular discipline **2** *vi* *US* **RECEIVE PRIVATE TUITION** to study under a tutor [14C. Via Anglo-

Norman < Latin, 'guardian' < *tut-* (see TUTELAGE).] —**tutorage** *n* —**tutorship** *n*

tutorial /tyoo táwri əl/ *n* **1 LESSON WITH TUTOR** a teaching session spent individually or in a small group under the direction of a tutor **2 LESSON FROM BOOK** a chapter of a book or manual, or a section of a computer program, designed to provide instruction or training using exercises and assignments ■ *adj* **RELATING TO TUTOR** relating to or belonging to a tutor, or to the role and responsibilities of a tutor

tutsan /túts'n/ (*plural* **-sans** *or* **-san**) *n* a woodland plant with large stalkless leaves, yellow flowers, and small rounded red fruits that turn black when ripe. Native to: Europe, Asia. *Hypericum androsaemum.* [14C. < French *toute-saine* < *toute* 'all' + *saine* 'healthy'.]

Tutsi /tootsi/ (*plural* **-si** *or* **-sis**) *n* a member of an African people living in Rwanda and Burundi. ♦ **Hutu** *n.* **1** [Mid-20C. < Bantu.] —**Tutsi** *adj*

tutti /tootti/ *n* the part of a concerto or other orchestral composition in which all the musicians play, as opposed to a solo section [Early 18C. Via Italian < Latin *totus* 'entire'.]

tutti-frutti /tooti footi/ (*plural* **tutti-fruttis**) *n* an ice cream, dessert, or type of confectionery containing a variety of chopped, usually dried or candied, fruit [Mid-19C. < Italian, 'all fruits'.]

tut-tut *interj, vi* = **tut**

tutu[1] /too too/ *n* a ballet dancer's skirt that is very short and made of layers of stiffened net so that it stands out from the body [Early 20C. < French, baby-talk alteration of *cucu* < *cul* 'buttocks' < Latin *culus.*]

tutu[2] /too too/ (*plural* **-tus** *or* **-tu**) *n* a tree with poisonous sap and seeds. Native to: New Zealand. *Coriaria arborea.* [Mid-19C. < Maori.]

Desmond Tutu

Tutu /tootoo/, **Desmond** (*b.* 1931) South African archbishop and political activist

tutulbay *adj* Carib utterly confused or bewildered, especially by love (*slang*)

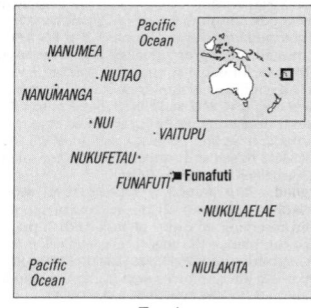

Tuvalu

Tuvalu /too va'aloo/ country consisting of coral islands in the W Pacific Ocean. Capital: Funafuti. Population: 10,297 (1997). Area: 26 sq. km/10 sq. mi. —**Tuvaluan** *n, adj*

uwhare /too fúrray/, **Honi** (b. 1922) New Zealand poet

u-whit tu-whoo /ə wit tə woō/ *interj* used to represent the sound of an owl hooting (*informal*) [Late 16C. An imitation of the sound.]

UX /tuks/ *n US* a tuxedo (*informal*) [Early 20C. Shortening.]

uxedo /tuk seédō/ (*plural* **-dos**) *n US* 1 = **dinner jacket** 2 a formal set of clothing for a man including a tuxedo jacket and matching trousers, usually with a band of silk down each leg, dress shirt, bow tie, and cummerbund [Late 19C. After the town of *Tuxedo Park*, New York.]

uyère /twee air/, **twyer** /twí ə/ *n* an opening in the refractory lining and shell of a furnace through which air is forced to promote combustion [Late 18C. < French, < *tuyau* 'pipe'.]

v *abbr* Tuvalu (*in Internet addresses*)

'V[1] *n* television or a television set (*informal*)

'V[2] *abbr* transvestite (*informal*)

'V dinner *n* a precooked frozen or chilled meal that can be reheated in the oven or microwave and eaten straight from the tray or dish

'VEI *abbr* technical and vocational initiative

'ver /vair/ *city in W Russia*, at the confluence of the Volga and Tvertsa rivers. Population: 454,000 (1990).

'VP *n* a high-protein product made from processed soya beans that are formed into chunks or minced and flavoured to taste like meat. Full form **textured vegetable protein**

'VRO *n* an antenna used for receiving television signals from a broadcasting satellite. Full form **television receive only**

w *abbr* Taiwan (*in Internet addresses*)

wa /twaw/ *n Scotland* two [Variant of TWO]

waddle /twódd'l/ *n* nonsensical or pretentious speech or writing (*informal*) ■ *vi* (**-dles, -dling, -dled**) to speak or write twaddle (*dated informal*) [Late 18C. < ?] —**twaddler** *n*

wain /twayn/ *npl* two (*archaic or literary*) ○ 'Oh, East is East, and West is West, and never the twain shall meet'. (Rudyard Kipling, *The Ballad of East and West*) [Old English *twēgen* < Germanic, 'two']

Library of Congress

Mark Twain

wain /twayn/, **Mark** (1835–1910) US writer. Pseudonym of **Samuel Langhorne Clemens**

wang /twang/ *n* 1 **SOUND OF TIGHT STRING VIBRATING** the sharp resonating noise made when something such as a tight string on an instrument is plucked or released 2 **SOUND IN CERTAIN ACCENTS** a nasal quality of voice associated with various accents ○ *a Texas twang* ■ *vti* 1 **VIBRATE WITH A TWANG** to make a twang or cause something to make a twang 2 **STRUM SOMETHING CARELESSLY** to play a stringed instrument, or a tune on a stringed instrument, in a rough amateur style 3 **MOVE WITH A TWANG** to move, spring, or be released suddenly with a twang ○ *The lid of the box twanged shut.* 4 **SPEAK WITH A TWANG** to speak or say something with a twang [Mid-16C. An imitation of the sound.] —**twangy** *adj*

twas /twoz/ *contr* it was (*archaic or literary*)

wat /twot/ *n* 1 a highly offensive term for a woman's vagina or genital area (*taboo*) 2 a highly offensive term for somebody regarded as unintelligent, worthless, or detestable (*taboo insult*) [Mid-17C. < ?]

wayblade /twáy blayd/ *n* an orchid that has only two leaves, arranged opposite each other, at the base.

Genera: *Listera* and *Liparis* and *Ophrys*. [Late 16C. < obsolete variant of TWAIN.]

tweak /tweek/ *vt* 1 **TWIST SOMETHING QUICKLY** to take hold of something between the finger and thumb and twist it sharply 2 **ADJUST SOMETHING SLIGHTLY** to make a slight adjustment or change in something, especially in order to improve it or fix it (*informal*) ○ *tweaked the engine to refine its performance* ■ *n* 1 **SHARP PINCH** a sharp pinch or twist 2 **SLIGHT ADJUSTMENT** a slight adjustment or change in something, especially in order to improve it or fix it (*informal*) [Early 17C. Probably variant of obsolete *twick* < Old English *twiccian* < Germanic.] —**tweaky** *adj*

twee /twee/ *adj* dainty or pretty in an overdone and affected way ○ *Those frilly curtains are a bit twee for my taste.* [Early 20C. Baby-talk alteration of SWEET.] —**tweely** *adv* —**tweeness** *n*

tweed /tweed/ *n* a fairly rough, thick woollen fabric often made with several different shades of wool to give it a distinctive flecked appearance. Use: warm clothing. ■ **tweeds** *npl* a tweed suit or outfit [Mid-19C. Alteration of *tweel*, Scottish variant of TWILL, after the river TWEED.]

Tweed /tweed/ *river of S Scotland and NE England*, flowing into the North Sea at Berwick-upon-Tweed. Length: 160 km/97 mi.

tweedy /tweédi/ (**-ier, -iest**) *adj* 1 made of tweed, or looking or feeling like tweed 2 showing a liking for the attitudes and outdoor lifestyle traditionally associated with the upper classes, especially activities such as hunting and shooting (*informal*) —**tweediness** *n*

'tween /tween/ *contr* between (*archaic or literary*) [13C. Shortening.]

tweenager /tweén ayjər/ *n* somebody aged roughly between 8 and 12, no longer a small child and not yet a teenager (*informal*) [Late 20C. Alteration of TEENAGER, after BETWEEN.]

tweet /tweet/ *n* a light high-pitched note, especially one sung by a small bird ■ *vi* to make the light high-pitched sound of a small bird [Mid-19C. An imitation of the sound.]

tweeter /tweétər/ *n* a loudspeaker used to reproduce high-frequency sounds, e.g. in a hi-fi system. ◊ **woofer**

tweeze /tweez/ *vt US* to pull out or manipulate something using tweezers [Mid-20C. Back-formation < TWEEZERS.]

tweezers /tweézərz/ *npl* a metal tool consisting of two narrow slightly curved arms joined at one end, typically used for extracting or holding small objects [Mid-17C. Alteration of obsolete *tweeze* 'tweezer case' < French *étuis*, plural of *étui* (see ÉTUI).]

twelfth /twelfth/ *n* see table at **number** [Old English *twelfta*. < Germanic, 'twelve'.] —**twelfth** *adj, adv*

Twelfth Day *n CHR* = **Epiphany**

twelfth man *n* a reserve player in a cricket team

Twelfth Night *n* the Christian feast of the Epiphany. Date: 6 January.

LITERARY LINK *Twelfth Night* a play (1600?) by William Shakespeare. A comedy set in Illyria, it tells of shipwrecked Viola, who disguises herself as a young man called Cesario and enters the service of Orsino. Orsino loves Olivia, who falls in love with Cesario, while Viola herself is attracted to Orsino. The reappearance of Viola's twin brother Sebastian ultimately brings a happy conclusion to the complicated plot.

twelth incorrect spelling of **twelfth**

twelve /twelv/ *n* see table at **number** [Old English *twelf* < Germanic, 'two left', that is 'two left beyond ten''] —**twelve** *adj, pron*

Twelve Apostles, **the Twelve** *n* eleven of the twelve followers originally chosen by Jesus Christ, according to the Bible, together with Matthias who was chosen to replace Judas

twelve-inch *n* a record that is 30.5 cm/12 in diameter and played at 45 rpm, usually containing a single, often extended, track (*informal*)

twelve-mile limit *n* an offshore boundary 12 miles from a country's coast, claimed by some countries as marking the territorial limit of their jurisdiction in order to safeguard fishing rights and limit the approach of foreign vessels. ◊ **three-mile limit**

twelvemo /twélvmō/ (*plural* **-mos**) *n PRINTING* = **duodecimo** [Early 18C. Pronunciation of the printers' abbreviation *12mo*.]

twelvemonth /twélvmunth/ *n* a year (*archaic*)

twelve-step programme *n* a programme for recovery from addiction, based on the methods of Alcoholics Anonymous and involving gradual self-improvement techniques

Twelve Tables *n* the earliest code of Roman law on civil, criminal, and religious matters, dating back to 451–450 BC

twelveth incorrect spelling of **twelfth**

twelve-tone *adj* relating to or using compositional techniques based on strict sequences of notes selected from the 12 notes of the chromatic scale

twelve-tone row *n MUSIC* = **tone row**

twentieth /twénti əth/ *n* see table at **number** [Old English *twentigoþa* < Germanic, 'twenty'] —**twentieth** *adj, adv*

twentieth man *n Aus* in Australian Rules football, the second of two substitutes that can be used during a regular match

twenty /twénti/ *n* (*plural* **-ties**) 1 see table at **number** 2 £20 **NOTE** a banknote worth twenty pounds (*informal*) ■ **twenties** *npl* 1 **NUMBERS 20 TO 29** the numbers 20 to 29, particularly as a range of Fahrenheit temperatures ○ *in the low twenties* 2 **YEARS FROM 20 TO 29** the years from 20 to 29 in a century or somebody's life [Old English *twēntig* < Germanic, 'twice ten'] —**twenty** *adj, pron*

twenty-first *n* somebody's 21st birthday, formerly marking the person's legal coming of age

24/7 /twénti fawr sévv'n/ *adj* occurring, happening, or appearing 24 hours a day, 7 days a week (*slang*) —**24/7** *adv*

twenty-one *n CARDS* = **pontoon**[2]

twenty questions *n* a game in which one player thinks of an object and others try to work out what it is by asking questions that can be answered only with 'yes' or 'no'

twenty-six counties *npl* the counties of the Republic of Ireland

twenty-twenty, **20/20** *adj* describes normal vision or eyesight [< the figures denoting normal eyesight at a distance of 20 feet]

'twere /twur/ *contr* it were (*archaic or literary*) [Early 17C. Contraction.]

twerp /twurp/, **twirp** *n* an offensive term for somebody who is seen as silly or insignificant (*informal insult*) [Late 19C. < ?]

Twi /twee/ (*plural* **Twi** or **Twis**) *n* 1 a member of an African people who live in S Ghana 2 the Kwa language of the Twi people, a dialect of Akan [Late 19C. < Kwa.] —**Twi** *adj*

twibill /twíbil/ *n* 1 a large pick (**mattock**) with one blade shaped like an axe and one blade like an adze 2 a double-edged battleaxe, formerly used as a weapon [Old English *twibil* < *twi-* 'two' + *bill* 'bladed weapon']

twice /twīss/ *adv* 1 on two occasions, or in two instances 2 double in amount or degree [Old English *twige* < Indo-European]

twice-laid *adj* describes ropes or cables that are made from previously used rope

Twickenham /twíkənəm/ *residential district in W London*,

twiddle /twídd'l/ *vti* (**-dles, -dling, -dled**) 1 **TURN SOMETHING BACK AND FORTH** to turn something round or back and forth repeatedly ○ *twiddling the dial on the radio to get a better reception* 2 **TWIST OR TURN SOMETHING ABSENT-MINDEDLY** to keep twisting something or turning it round in a bored or absent-minded way ○ *sitting at a desk twiddling his pencil and staring out of the window* ■ *n* 1 **TWISTING ACTION** a to-and-fro turning or twisting action 2 **LITTLE PIECE OF EXTRA DECORATION** a small extra twist or curve added to something for ornamentation, e.g. a small flourish on a letter of script, or a musical ornament such as a mordent or trill [Mid-16C. < ?] —**twiddler** *n* — **twiddly** *adj*

twig[1] /twig/ *n* 1 a small branch or shoot, especially one from a tree or shrub 2 a structure that resembles a branch, e.g. a minute offshoot of a nerve or blood vessel [Old English *twigge* 'forked branch' < Germanic] — **twiglet** *n*

twig[2] /twig/ (**twigs, twigging, twigged**) *vti* to understand or realize something (*informal*) ○ *finally twigged what was going on* [Mid-18C. < ?]

twiggy /twíggi/ (**-gier, -giest**) *adj* **1** covered in twigs rather than branches or leaves ○ *a twiggy shrub* **2** very thin or fragile ○ *twiggy legs*

twilight /twí lìt/ *n* **1** TIME AFTER SUNSET the time of day just after sunset or before dawn, when the Sun is below the horizon **2** HALF-LIGHT the faint diffuse light that occurs at twilight **3** PERIOD OF OFFICIAL TWILIGHT the period during which the sun is at a specified angle below the horizon **4** FINAL PERIOD the time when something is declining or approaching its end, especially in a gentle or peaceful way ○ *the twilight of the empire* ■ *adj* OUTSIDE NORMAL SOCIETY existing or operating beyond the laws and morals of normal society ○ *the twilight world of prostitution* [15C. < archaic *twi-* 'two, half' < Germanic.]

Twilight of the Gods *n* **1** = **götterdämmerung** *n.* 1 **2** = **Ragnarök** [Translation of German *Götterdämmerung*]

twilight sleep *n* a state of partial consciousness in which awareness of pain is diminished or abolished, formerly induced during childbirth by injecting morphine and scopolamine

twilight zone *n* **1** UNCERTAIN STATE an ambiguous or unsettled state or condition, especially between two opposing conditions **2** RUN-DOWN AREA a neglected or run-down area, especially one on the edge of a city or town between the business centre and residential areas **3** LOWEST PART OF THE SEA WITH LIGHT the lowest layer of the sea that natural light can reach

twilit /twílit/ *adj* lit by twilight or a similar kind of half-light, especially when this creates a feeling of mystery [Mid-19C. Past participle of earlier *twilight*, verb.]

twill /twil/ *n* **1** STRONG FABRIC a strong woven material with diagonal ridges or ribs across its surface **2** TEXTILE WEAVE the weave used to produce twill ■ *vt* WEAVE TWILL to weave fabric with diagonal ridges or ribs across its surface [14C. < N English dialect variant of Old English *twilic* 'having two threads'.]

'twill /twil/ *contr* it will (*archaic or literary*)

twin /twin/ *n* **1** EITHER OF TWO OFFSPRING BORN TOGETHER either of two people or animals born to the same mother at the same time (*often before nouns*) ○ *twin boys* **2** ONE OF TWO SIMILAR THINGS somebody or something similar or identical to another, or unusually closely associated with another **3** TOWN LINKED WITH ANOTHER either of a pair of towns in two different countries with cultural and administrative links (*often before nouns*) ○ *twin towns* **4** COMPOUND CRYSTAL a compound crystal consisting of two mirror-image crystals that share a common plane ■ *adj* DOUBLE describes two identical things that operate together ○ *the streamlined twin hulls of a racing catamaran* ■ *v* (**twins, twinning, twinned**) **1** *vti* PAIR PEOPLE OR THINGS to group people or things in pairs, or to link them very closely **2** *vt* LINK UP TOWN WITH ANOTHER to create a cultural and administrative link in one town or city with another town or city in a different country **3** *vi* HAVE TWINS to give birth to twins [Old English *twinn* < Indo-European, 'two by two']

twin bed *n* either of a pair of matching single beds

twinberry /twínbəri/ (*plural* **-ries**) *n* **1** PLANTS = **partridgeberry** *n.* 1 **2** a shrub of the honeysuckle family. Flowers: purple. Native to: North America. *Lonicera involucrata.*

twin bill *n* US SPORTS = **double-header**

twine /twīn/ *n* **1** STRING string or cord made from threads or strands that have been twisted together **2** SOMETHING MADE BY TWISTING something that is formed by twisting or coiling separate strands together **3** TWISTING ACTION a twisting or weaving action ■ *v* (**twines, twining, twined**) **1** *vti* TWIST AROUND to grow, wind, or twist around or together, or make something grow, wind, or twist around something else ○ *the ivy twining around the old oak tree* **2** *vi* HAVE WINDING COURSE to take or follow a winding route (*literary*) **3** *vt* WEAVE to make something by weaving or twisting separate strands together [Old English *twīn* 'double thread'. < Germanic.] —**twiner** *n*

twinflower /twín flow ər/ *n* a creeping plant of the honeysuckle family with opposite oval leaves. Flowers: pinkish-white, bell-shaped, in pairs. Native to: North America. *Linnaea borealis.*

twinge /twinj/ *n* **1** BRIEF PAIN a sudden brief stab of pain **2** BRIEF UNCOMFORTABLE EMOTION a brief uncomfortable pang of an emotion such as guilt or fear ■ *vti* (**twinges, twingeing, twinged**) FEEL A TWINGE to feel a twinge, or make somebody feel a twinge, either physical or emotional [Old English *twengan* 'pinch' < Germanic]

twinkle /twíngk'l/ *vi* (**-kles, -kling, -kled**) **1** SHINE WITH FLICKER to give out or reflect a bright but unsteady light, especially from a small or distant source **2** SHINE WITH AMUSEMENT to be bright because of a feeling such as amusement, delight, or mischief (*refers to people's eyes*) ■ *n* **1** FLICKERING SHINE a bright unsteady light, especially one that is small or seen from a distance **2** BRIGHTNESS IN SOMEBODY'S EYES a brightness in somebody's eyes, caused by a feeling such as amusement, delight, or mischief **3** = **twinkling** *n.* [Old English *twinclian* 'keep blinking' < *twincan* 'blink' < Germanic] —**twinkler** *n* —**twinkly** *adj*

twinkling /twíngkling/ *n* an instant of time ■ *adj* giving out or reflecting light brightly but unsteadily, especially from a small or distant source ◇ **in the twinkling of an eye** very quickly or very soon

twin-lens reflex *n* a camera that has two forward-facing lenses, one for focusing through and one for taking pictures

twinned /twind/ *adj* **1** EXISTING AS MATCHING PAIR linked together as or like a couple **2** SHARING CULTURAL LINK describes towns or cities in different countries that share cultural and administrative links **3** SYMMETRICAL describes a compound crystal consisting of two mirror-image crystals that share a common plane

Twins /twinz/ *n* the constellation or zodiac sign Gemini

twin-screw *adj* describes a ship that has two propellers

twinset /twín set/ *n* a woman's matching short-sleeved jumper and cardigan designed to be worn together

twin town *n* a town or city that has special cultural and administrative links with another town or city in a different country

twin-tub *n* a washing machine with two separate compartments, one for washing and the other for spin-drying

twirl /twurl/ *v* **1** *vti* SPIN ROUND QUICKLY to turn lightly and rapidly round in a circle, or spin something so that it turns rapidly round and round ○ *twirled his partner around the dance floor* **2** *vt* TURN SOMETHING ROUND to fiddle with something by turning or spinning it between the fingers **3** *vi* TURN AND FACE OTHER WAY to turn round suddenly to face somebody or face the other way ○ *She twirled round, her eyes blazing.* ■ *n* **1** QUICK SPINNING MOVEMENT a quick turning or spinning movement, e.g. when somebody is dancing or modelling clothes **2** SPIRAL a twisting or spiral shape, pattern, or line, especially something used for decoration [Late 16C. Probably alteration of *tirl*, variant of TRILL, after WHIRL.] —**twirler** *n* —**twirly** *adj*

twirp *n* = **twerp**

twist /twist/ *v* **1** *vti* MAKE ENDS TURN IN OPPOSITE DIRECTIONS to make one part or end of something turn in the opposite direction to the other, or turn in this way ○ *I twisted my handkerchief into a knot.* **2** *vti* DISTORT to distort the shape or position of something, or become distorted ○ *His face was twisted in a grimace of disgust.* **3** *vti* WIND to wind something, make something wind, or wind things together ○ *constantly twisting her hair round her fingers* **4** *vt* INJURE PART OF BODY to injure part of the body by turning or moving it out of position ○ *I've twisted my ankle.* **5** *vti* ROTATE to rotate, or turn something so that it rotates ○ *The lid just twists and comes off.* **6** *vt* DISTORT MEANING to distort the meaning of something ○ *keeps twisting what I'm saying to make it sound as if I agree* **7** *vt* AFFECT SOMETHING ADVERSELY to distort somebody's mind or outlook **8** *vi* CONSTANTLY CHANGE DIRECTION to change direction constantly instead of continuing in a direct or straight line **9** *vi* SQUIRM to squirm or wriggle ○ *a child twisting restlessly in her chair* **10** *vi* DANCE to dance the twist **11** *vt* CHEAT to cheat somebody (*informal*) ■ *n* **1** TWISTING MOVEMENT the action or movement performed when somebody twists something ○ *a twist of the screw* **2** SOMETHING SHAPED BY BEING TWISTED something that has been shaped, split, or gathered together by being twisted ○ *a twist of paper* **3** UNEXPECTED DEVELOPMENT an unexpected development in a narrative or a sequence of events ○ *The story had a strange twist.* **4** BEND a bend in something such as a road or river ○ *a road full of twists and turns* **5** 1960S DANCE a 1960s dance that involved rotating the hips **6** SLICE OF LEMON a thin slice of lemon, lime, or some other peel that is cut and twisted and added to a drink **7** BREAD OR ROLL a roll or loaf of bread made by twisting pieces of dough **8** PAINFUL WRENCH a painful wrench or pull in a wrist, ankle, or some other body part **9** LENGTH OF YARN a length of yarn or thread whose strands have been twisted together **10** FORCE a force that causes stress or strain by twisting **11** SPIN GIVEN TO BALL spin imparted to a hit or thrown ball **12** ROTATION OF THE BODY a complete turn of the body around a vertical axis, e.g. in gymnastics or diving **13** DISTORTION a contortion or distortion in the shape of something **14** QUIRK OF CHARACTER an eccentricity or strange personal characteristic **15** CIGAR OR TOBACCO a cigar made from three cigars twisted together, or chewing tobacco twisted into a roll [Mid 16C. < Old English, 'something split in two, twisted yarn' < Germanic.] —**twistability** /twìstə bíllәti/ *n* —**twistable** *adj* —**twisting** *adj* —**twistingly** *adv* —**twisty** *adj* ◇ **be or go round the twist** to be or become mentally ill (*slang*)

LITERARY LINK ***Oliver Twist***, a novel (1837–39) by Charles Dickens. It tells the tale of an abandoned child who runs away from his workhouse home to London, where he falls in with a band of criminals led by Fagin and his young assistant a streetwise pickpocket called the Artful Dodger.

twist drill *n* a drill bit with one or more helical grooves along its axis to expel cuttings or swarf

twisted /twístid/ *adj* **1** AFTER TWISTING having undergone twisting ○ *twisted strands of fibre* **2** DISTORTED IN SHAPE severely distorted in shape or form ○ *The force of the blast reduced the car to a twisted heap of metal.* **3** BADLY AFFECTED BY EXPERIENCES badly affected by unpleasant experiences or constant disappointment (*informal*) ○ *The experience left her bitter and twisted.* **4** CORRUPT morally unacceptable ○ *What kind of twisted mind could think up a thing like that?*

twister /twístər/ *n* **1** US TORNADO a tornado, cyclone, or whirlwind (*informal*) **2** SOMEBODY OR SOMETHING THAT TWISTS a person or device that twists **3** CHEAT a cheater or misleader of others (*dated informal insult*) **4** BALL WITH TWIST a ball that has been thrown or hit with a twist

twist grip *n* a control mounted in one of the handlebar grips of a motorcycle or bicycle, allowing the rider to change gear or accelerate by twisting the grip

twist-tie *n* a piece of wire sealed in a paper or plastic strip, used as a fastener, especially for a plastic bag

twit /twit/ *n* an offensive term for somebody who is regarded as unthinking or silly (*informal insult*) ■ *vt* (**twits, twitting, twitted**) to make fun of or criticize somebody in a playful friendly way (*dated*) [Mid-16C. Shortening of Old English *ætwītan* 'find fault' < *æt-* 'at' + *wītan* 'reproach' < Germanic.] —**twitter** *n*

twitch /twich/ *v* **1** *vi* JERK SLIGHTLY to move with a slight jerk, either once or repeatedly ○ *His eyebrow twitches when he's nervous.* **2** *vt* PULL SOMETHING LIGHTLY AND QUICKLY to give something a sudden light tug or jerk **3** *vi* HURT SHARPLY to hurt with a sharp or sudden pain ■ *n* **1** JERKY MOVEMENT a very quick jerky movement **2** MUSCLE CONTRACTION a brief, rapid contraction of a muscle **3** HORSE RESTRAINT a restraint used on a horse during a veterinary procedure, consisting of a cord loop that can be pulled tight around the animal's upper lip [12C. < ?]

twitcher /twíchər/ *n* **1** a person, animal, or thing that twitches **2** a birdwatcher who will go to excessive lengths to spot rare birds (*informal*)

twitch grass *n* PLANTS = **couch grass** [Alteration of QUITCH GRASS]

twitchy /twíchi/ (**-ier, -iest**) *adj* **1** nervous and jittery (*informal*) **2** twitching frequently

twite /twīt/ *n* a finch with streaked brown plumage, the male of which has a pink rump. Native to: N Europe. *Acanthis flavirostris.* [Mid-16C. An imitation of the bird's call.]

twitter /twíttər/ *v* **1** *vi* CHIRP to sing in a succession of light high-pitched chirping sounds (*refers to birds*) **2** *vi* CHATTER to chatter or giggle in an overexcited or nervous way **3** *vti* USE SMALL HIGH VOICE to sing or say something in a light shaky high-pitched voice **4** *vi* TREMBLE to quiver or move about nervously and quickly ■ *n* **1** REPETITIVE HIGH-PITCHED SONG a continuous light string of high sounds made by a small bird or other small animal **2** EXCITEMENT a state of great agitation or excitement ○ *all of a twitter* [14C. An imitation of birds chirping.] —**twitterer** *n* —**twittery** *adj*

'twixt /twikst/ *prep* between (*archaic*) [14C. Shortening of BETWIXT.]

twizzle /twízz'l/ *vt* (**-zles, -zling, -zled**) to twirl or twist something vigorously (*informal*) ■ *n* a vigorous twirl or twist (*informal*) [Late 18C. Probably alteration of TWIST or TWIRL.]

two /too/ (*plural* **twos**) *n* see table at **number** [Old English *twā* < Indo-European] —**two** *adj, pron* ◇ **it takes two to tango** used to indicate that both of the people involved in an awkward or unpleasant situation are responsible or to blame, not just one ◇ **put two and two together** to work something out from the available evidence ◇ **that makes two of us** used to indicate agreement with something expressed, or acknowledged of something shared

SPELLCHECK See *to*.

wo-bit *adj US* of very low quality or importance (*informal*)

wo-by-four, 2 x 4 *n* BUILDING = **four-by-two**

woc /twok/, **twock** *vt* (**twocs, twoccing, twocced**) to steal a car, often only temporarily for the purpose of joyriding (*slang*) ■ *n* a theft of a car (*slang*) [Late 20C. Acronym < *taken without owner's consent.*] —**twoccer** *n*

wo cents worth *n US* an opinion, when expressed assertively as one of many ○ *just had to add her two cents worth*

wock *vt, n* = **twoc**

wo-cycle *adj US* ENG = **two-stroke**

wo-dimensional *adj* **1 HAVING TWO DIMENSIONS** describes a figure that has length and width but no depth, e.g. a geometric figure on a single plane **2 DONE ON A FLAT SURFACE** describes works of art such as paintings and drawings that exist on a flat surface, as opposed to art forms such as sculpture that also have depth **3 HAVING NO DEPTH OF CHARACTER** lacking the emotional or psychological depth that creates the impression of realism ○ *a two-dimensional character* —**two-dimensionality** *n* —**two-dimensionally** *adv*

wo-edged *adj* **1** having two sharp edges for cutting in opposite directions **2** having two effects, one positive and one negative, especially two possible and opposite interpretations or meanings

wo-faced *adj* **1** insincere in dealings with people, especially by being outwardly friendly but secretly disloyal **2** having two faces or surfaces —**two-facedly** *adv* —**two-facedness** *n*

wofer /to͞ofər/ *n US* a set of two items sold together, often for the price of one, or a coupon giving entitlement to such a discount (*informal*) [Late 19C. Alteration of *two for (one).*]

wo-fisted /-fístid/ *adj US* characterized by energy, enthusiasm, assertiveness, or aggression

wofold /to͞ofōld/ *adj* **1 HAVING TWO ELEMENTS** consisting of two parts or elements **2 DOUBLE** twice as much or as many ■ *adv* **DOUBLY** by the same amount over again

2,4,5-T /too fawr fīv tee/ *n* $C_8H_5Cl_3O_3$ an insoluble crystalline compound. Use: chemical weedkiller, plant hormone. [Mid-20C. *T* < TRI-.]

2,4-D /to͞o fawr dee/ *n* $C_8H_6Cl_2O_3$ a white crystalline compound. Use: weedkiller. [Mid-20C. *D* < DI-¹.]

wo-four time *n* a rhythm with two crotchet beats to the bar

wo-handed *adj* **1 USING TWO HANDS** using, or requiring the use of, two hands **2 DESIGNED FOR TWO** designed for two people, especially for two players or operators **3 AMBIDEXTROUS** able to use either the left or right hand with equal skill —**two-handedly** *adv* —**two-handedness** *n*

wo-hander *n* a play written for and performed by two actors

wo-master *n* a sailing ship with two masts

wo-pack *n* a set of two identical products packaged together and sold as one

wopence /túppənss/, **tuppence** *n* **1** the value of two pence, especially two pennies in the predecimal British monetary system **2** the least amount (*in negatives*) ○ *I don't care twopence what they think.*

wopenny /túppəni/, **tuppenny** *adj* **1** costing or worth twopence **2** cheap and of the poorest quality

two-phase *adj* describes an electrical system in which there are two alternating voltages of the same frequency, with a phase difference of 90° between them

two-piece *adj* consisting of two parts or pieces, especially pieces of clothing ■ *n* a suit consisting of two garments such as a bikini

two-ply *adj* consisting of two layers or strands

two-seater *n* **1** a vehicle with seats for two people, especially a sports car **2** a seat for two people, especially a sofa

two-shot *n* a film or television shot in which two people more or less fill the screen

two-sided *adj* **1 HAVING TWO SURFACES** having two sides or surfaces **2 USING TWO SIDES** using both sides of a page **3 HAVING TWO CONTESTING SIDES** consisting of two contesting sides, e.g. two groups opposing each other, or two equally valid opinions

twosome /to͞ossəm/ *n* **1** a pair of people, especially two golfers paired to play together, a couple on a date together, or a team consisting of two players **2** GOLF = **single** *n.* **6**

two-spot *n* **1** a game piece such as a playing card or a domino with two marks on it **2** *US* a two-dollar bill (*informal*)

two-step *n* **1 BALLROOM DANCE** a ballroom dance in 2/4 time with sliding steps **2 DANCE MUSIC** the music for a two-step ■ *vi* (**two-steps, two-stepping, two-stepped**) **DANCE TWO-STEP** to dance the two-step

two-stroke *adj* used to describe an internal-combustion engine in which the piston makes two movements, usually one upwards and one downwards, in each power cycle. US term **two-cycle**

two-tier *adj* having two levels, especially two levels of administration or two standards of treatment or privilege

two-time (**two-times, two-timing, two-timed**) *vt* (*informal*) **1** to be unfaithful to a romantic or sexual partner **2** to deceive or betray a partner in an undertaking —**two-timer** *n*

two-tone *adj* **1** consisting of two colours or two shades ○ *toe-tone shoes* **2** consisting of two sounds with different frequencies ○ *a two-tone siren*

.22 *n* a gun or rifle that uses a bullet with a diameter of .22 in., typically used for killing small game.

'twould /two͝od/ *contr* it would (*archaic or literary*)

two-up *n Aus* an Australian gambling game in which bets are placed on how two tossed coins will land

two-way *adj* **1 MOVING IN BOTH DIRECTIONS** moving in opposite directions or allowing for movement in opposite directions **2 INVOLVING TWO CONTESTANTS** involving two people or teams ○ *a two-way race* **3 ABLE TO TRANSMIT AND RECEIVE** able both to transmit and receive radio signals ○ *two-way radio* **4 RECIPROCAL** requiring cooperation between two people or groups

two-way mirror *n* a sheet of glass that is a mirror on one side and can be seen through from the other. US term **one-way mirror**

two-wheeler *n* a vehicle with two wheels, especially a bicycle

twyer *n* ENG = **tuyère**

TX *abbr* Texas

ϟ**TY** *abbr* thank you (*in e-mails*)

Tycho /tíkō/ *n* a crater on the south of the Moon that is the centre of the Moon's most extensive ray system. It is 84 km/52 mi. in diameter, 4500 m/14,750 ft high, and is surrounded by terraced walls.

tycoon /tī ko͞on/ *n* **1** an amasser of great wealth and power, especially in business **2** a shogun (*archaic*) [Mid-19C. < Japanese *taikun* 'great lord, shogun' < Chinese *dà* 'great' + *jūn* 'prince'.]

tyiyn /ti yeén/ (*plural* **-iyn** *or* **-iyns**) *n* see table at **currency** [Late 20C. < Kyrgyz.]

tyke /tike/, **tike** *n* **1 NAUGHTY CHILD** a little child, especially one who is naughty or mischievous (*informal*) **2 MONGREL** a dog of mixed breed **3 BOOR** a man regarded as having coarse manners (*dated insult*) **4 YORKSHIREMAN** a Yorkshireman (*regional*) [14C. < Old Norse *tík* 'bitch'.]

tylectomy /tī léktəmi/ (*plural* **-mies**) *n* MED = **lumpectomy** [Late 20C. < Greek *tulos* 'lump'.]

Tyler /tílər/, **Anne** (*b.* 1941) US writer

Tyler, John (1790–1862) US statesman and 10th president of the United States (1841–45)

Tyler, Wat (*d.* 1381) English revolutionary leader

tylosis /tī lóssiss/, **tylose** /tílōss/ (*plural* **tyloses** /-seez/) *n* **1** a callus or thickening, especially of the eyelids **2** a sac that forms in the water-conducting vessels of the older wood of a tree, often in response to drought or disease [Late 19C. Via modern Latin < Greek *tulōsis* 'formation of a callus or lump' < *tulē* 'callus, swelling'.]

tymbal *n* MUSIC = **timbal**

tympan /tímpən/ *n* **1** a padding device that fits between the impression cylinder of a printing press and the paper to be printed so as to ensure a uniform image **2** ARCHIT = **tympanum** *n.* **1** **3** a membrane or diaphragm that vibrates to produce or transmit sound, e.g. as the skin on a drum or the diaphragm in a telephone receiver [Pre-12C. < Latin *tympanum* 'drum' (see TYMPANUM).]

tympani MUSIC = **timpani**

tympanic /tim pánnik/ *adj* relating to a tympanum

tympanic bone *n* the part of the temporal bone that supports and partly surrounds the auditory canal

tympanic membrane *n* the eardrum (*technical*)

tympanites /tímpə nī teez/ *n* swelling of the abdominal wall caused by gas trapped in the intestines or peritoneal cavity [14C. Via late Latin < Greek *tumpanitēs* < *tumpanon* 'drum'.] —**tympanitic** /-níttik/ *adj*

tympanitis /tímpə nítis/ *n* inflammation of the eardrum [Mid-19C. < TYMPANUM.]

tympanoplasty /tímpə nō plasti/ (*plural* **-ties**) *n* the surgical repair or reconstruction of the eardrum, usually in order to close a perforation [Mid-20C. < TYMPANUM.]

tympanum /tímpənəm/ (*plural* **-nums** *or* **-na** /-nə/) *n* **1 RECESSED SPACE** a recess, especially the recessed space between the top of a door or window and the arch above it, or between the cornices forming a classical triangular gable (**pediment**) **2 EAR PART** the eardrum or the cavity of the middle ear (*technical*) **3 INSECT ORGAN** a vibrating membrane in some insects that serves as a hearing organ **4** ACOUSTICS = **tympan** *n.* **3** [Early 16C. Via Latin < Greek *tumpanon* 'drum'.]

tympany /tímpəni/ *n* MED = **tympanites** [Early 16C. < Greek *tumpanias* < *tumpanon* 'drum'.]

Tyndale /tínd'l/, **Tindal, William** (1492?–1536) English religious reformer

Tyndall effect /tínd'l-/ *n* the scattering of light by minute particles in its path, such as dust in the air [Early 20C. After John *Tyndall* (1820–93), British physicist.]

tyndallimetry /tínd'l ímmətri/ *n* the measurement of the concentration of suspended particles in a liquid by gauging the amount of light they scatter [See TYNDALL EFFECT]

Tyne /tīn/ river in NE England, flowing through Newcastle upon Tyne to the North Sea. Length: 48 km/30 mi.

Tynemouth /tīn mowth, tínməth/ town in NE England, at the mouth of the River Tyne. Population: 17,422 (1991).

Tyneside /tīn sīd/ industrial and shipbuilding region in NE England, along the lower River Tyne

typ. *abbr* **1** typographer **2** typographical **3** typography

type /tīp/ *n* **1 KIND OR SORT** a category of things or people whose members share some qualities **2 PERSON OR THING** somebody or something regarded as belonging to a group or category by virtue of having the main qualities associated with it ○ *the paraffin type of burner* **3 KIND OF PERSON** a person regarded as having the stated characteristics or temperament (*informal*) ○ *a gathering of sporty types* **4 SOMEBODY WHO APPEALS** somebody with the qualities that appeal to somebody else (*informal*) ○ *He's really not my type.* **5 TEMPLATE** something used as a pattern or template for making other things of the same kind **6 PRINTING BLOCK** a small metal block with, on one of its sides, a raised figure that is the mirror image of a number or letter, used with others for printing **7 SET OF PRINTING BLOCKS** printing blocks collectively **8 PRINTED LETTERS** printed words, letters, or symbols on a page **9 REPRESENTATIVE GENUS OR SPECIES** a genus or species of plant or animal whose characteristics best represent the next higher category of taxonomic classification **10 REPRESENTATIVE ORGANISM** a plant or animal that represents its genus by having the main qualities that define it **11 LINGUISTIC UNIT** a letter, word, or other linguistic unit regarded as representing all units that are forms of it, as distinct from an individual form (**token**) **12 GENERAL EXPRESSION** an expression regarded not as a physical object but as an abstract pattern that individual expressions can conform to **13 SIGN OF SOMETHING TO COME** an event, figure, or sign taken as foreshadowing something in the future ■ *v* (**types, typing, typed**) **1** *vti* **KEY WORDS ON KEYBOARD** to key words using a computer keyboard, word processor, or typewriter **2** *vt* **CLASSIFY** to classify something, especially blood, according to its type **3** *vt* **TYPECAST** to characterize somebody as being a person who plays a particular kind of role **4** *vt* **FORE-**

SHADOW to foreshadow a future event or fact [15C. Via Latin *typus* < Greek *tupos* 'blow, impression'.] —**typal** *adj*

SYNONYMS ***type, kind, sort, category, class, species, genre***

CORE MEANING: a group having a common quality or qualities

type a group of individuals or items with strongly marked and readily defined similarities; **kind** a group of individuals or items connected by shared characteristics; **sort** a general word used in the same way as *kind*; **category** a set of things that are classified together because of common characteristics; **class** used in the same way as *category*; **species** a specific group of animals, plants, insects, or other organisms, used in formal taxonomic classification; **genre** a particular style of painting, writing, dance, or other art form.

USAGE See ***kind***[2].

type A *n* an anxious, hard-working person who has a strong drive to succeed and finds it hard to delegate or share tasks with colleagues

type B *n* a patient and friendly person

typebar /tīp baar/ *n* a lever operated by a typewriter key

typecase /tīp kayss/ *n* a tray or box for storing printer's type

typecast /tīp kaast/ (**-casts, -casting, -cast**) *vt* **1** to give an actor a series of parts of the same type, to the extent that the performer becomes associated with that kind of role and is overlooked for others **2** to give an actor a part that suits his or her physical or emotional type —**typecaster** *n*

typeface /tīp fayss/ *n* **1** a particular style of printed character such as Helvetica or bold **2** the side of a printing block that has the shape of the printed character on it

type founder *n* a manufacturer of metal printing type —**type foundry** *n*

type genus *n* the genus of a family or other higher taxonomic category that is most typical of it and usually bears the same name

type-high *adj* as high as the standard height of a block of printer's type, 23.3 mm/0.9186 in

type I error *n* in statistics, the error of rejection of a null hypothesis when it is true

type II error *n* in statistics, the failure to reject a false null hypothesis

type locality *n* a place where a rock formation or other geological feature was first found and described, and after which it is named

type metal *n* the alloy from which printing type is made, consisting mostly of lead, antimony, and tin

typescript /tīp skript/ *n* a typewritten document or other text [Late 19C. < TYPE + MANUSCRIPT.]

typeset /tīp set/ (**-sets, -setting, -set**) *vt* to prepare text for printing, either by the use of computers or by arranging blocks of type manually

typesetter /tīp setər/ *n* **1** a person who sets type for printing **2** a mechanical or electronic device that prepares text for printing

type-site *n* an archaeological site that is thought to typify a culture and that gives the culture its name

type species *n* a species of plant or animal that is most typical of its genus and bears the same name or a related name

type specimen *n* an individual plant or animal that serves as the basis for the description of its species

type style *n* PRINTING = **typeface** *n.* 1

typewrite /tīp rīt/ (**-writes, -writing, -wrote** /-rōt/, **-written** /-rit'n/) *vti* to type [Late 19C. Back-formation < TYPEWRITER.]

typewriter /tīp rītər/ *n* **1** an electrical or mechanical device for printing words on individual sheets of paper **2** a printing typeface that looks like characters produced by a typewriter

typewriting /tīp rīting/ *n* **1** the process or skill of writing on a typewriter **2** the output of text produced on a typewriter

typhlitis /ti flītiss/ *n* inflammation of the entrance to the large intestine (**caecum**) [Mid-19C. < Greek *tuphlon* 'caecum' < *tuphlos* 'sightless'.] —**typhlitic** /ti flíttik/ *adj*

typhlology /ti flólləji/ *n* the scientific study of sightlessness [Late 19C. < Greek *tuphlos* 'blind'.]

Typhoeus /tī feé əss/ *n* in Greek mythology, a monster with a hundred dragon heads who fought with Zeus and was thrown down into the ground under Mount Etna —**Typhoean** *adj*

typhoid /tī foyd/ *n* a serious and sometimes fatal bacterial infection of the digestive system, caused by ingesting food or water contaminated with the bacillus *Salmonella typhi* ■ *adj* relating to typhoid or typhus —**typhoidal** /tī fóyd'l/ *adj*

typhoid fever *n* MED = **typhoid** *n.*

Typhoid Mary *n* **1** an offensive term for somebody who spreads a disease or is held to be responsible for spreading it **2** an offensive term for somebody who spreads something undesirable such as pessimism or bad news, and is generally avoided (*insult*) [Early 20C. Nickname of *Mary* Mallon (d. 1938), Irish-born cook in the United States who was found to be a typhoid carrier.]

typhoon /tī foón/ *n* a violent tropical storm in the W Pacific and Indian oceans [Late 16C. Partly < Chinese (Cantonese) *toi fung* 'big wind', and partly via Portuguese *tufão*, Urdu *ṭūfān*, Arabic < Greek *tuphōn*.] —**typhonic** /tī fónnik/ *adj*

typhus /tīfəss/, **typhus fever** *n* an infectious disease that causes fever, severe headaches, a rash, and often delirium [Late 18C. < Greek *tuphos* 'smoke, stupor' < *tuphein* 'to smoke'.] —**typhous** *adj*

typical /típpik'l/ *adj* **1** REPRESENTATIVE having all or most of the characteristics shared by others of a type and therefore suitable as an example of the type **2** CONFORMING TO EXPECTATION conforming to what is expected **3** RESEMBLING OTHERS IN TAXONOMIC GROUP describes an organism, species, or genus that has most of the characteristics that identify the larger taxonomic group to which it belongs [Early 17C. < medieval Latin *typicalis* < late Latin *typicus* < Greek *tupikos* < *tupos* 'blow, impression'.] —**typicality** /típpi kálləti/ *n* —**typicalness** *n*

typically /típpikli/ *adv* **1** IN THE USUAL WAY with all or many of the usual or expected characteristics **2** IN MOST CASES in most cases or on most occasions **3** PREDICTABLY as is to be expected ○ *not her typically cheerful self today*

typify /típpi fī/ (**-fies, -fying, -fied**) *vt* **1** to have all or most of the characteristics of others of a type and therefore be a suitable example of the type **2** to be a typical representation of something [Mid-17C. < Latin *typus* (see TYPE).] —**typification** /típpifi káysh'n/ *n* —**typifier** *n*

typist /tīpist/ *n* a user of a typewriter, especially somebody who produces documents using a typewriter or computer keyboard

typo /tīpō/ (*plural* **-pos**) *n* a typographical error (*informal*) [Early 19C. Shortening.]

typo., typog. *abbr* **1** typographer **2** typographical **3** typography

typographical /tīpə gráffik'l/, **typographic** /tīpə gráffik/ *adj* **1** relating to the activity of preparing texts for printing **2** relating to the appearance of printed characters on the page

typographical error *n* a printing error such as a misspelled word, that results from striking the wrong key or keys on a keyboard

typography /tī póggrəfi/ *n* **1** the activity or business of preparing texts for printing **2** the appearance of printed characters on the page [Early 17C. Via French < modern Latin *typographia* < Greek *tupos* 'blow, impression'.] —**typographer** *n*

typology /tī pólləji/ *n* **1** CLASSIFICATION OF TYPES the study or systematic classification of types **2** LANGUAGE STUDY the study of syntactic and morphological similarities in languages without regard to their history **3** STUDY OF RELIGIOUS TEXTS the study of religious texts for the purpose of identifying episodes in them that appear to prophesy later events [Mid-19C. < Greek *typos* 'blow, impression'.] —**typologic** /tīpə lójjik/ *adj* —**typological** *adj* —**typologically** *adv* —**typologist** /tī pólləjist/ *n*

typw. *abbr* **1** typewriter **2** typewritten

tyramine /tīrəmin/ *n* $C_8H_{11}NO$ an amine, found in some foods and formed from the breakdown of the amino acid tyrosine, that has the effect of simulating sympathetic nervous system action [Early 20C. Blend of TYROSINE + AMINE.]

tyrannical /ti ránnik'l/, **tyrannic** /ti ránnik/ *adj* **1** ruling with absolute power over a population cruelly kept submissive and fearful **2** cruelly or irrationally insisting on complete obedience and giving harsh punishment to those who disobey [Mid-16C. < French *tyrannique* < Greek *turannikos* < *turannos* 'tyrant'.] —**tyrannically** *adv* —**tyrannicalness** *n*

tyrannicide /ti ránni sīd/ *n* **1** the killing of a tyrant **2** the killer of a tyrant [Mid-17C. < Latin *tyrannicidium* 'tyrant killing', *tyrannicida* 'tyrant-killer' < *tyrannus* (see TYRANT) + *caedere* 'kill' (see -CIDE).] —**tyrannicidal** *adj*

tyrannize /tírrə nīz/ (**-nizes, -nizing, -nized**), **tyrannise** (**-nises, -nising, -nised**) *vti* **1** to govern with extreme cruelty and harshness **2** to treat somebody in a cruelly unfair way [15C. < French *tyranniser* < Old French *tyran* (see TYRANT).] —**tyrannizer** *n*

tyrannosaur /ti ránnə sawr/, **tyrannosaurus** /-əss/, **tyrannosaurus rex** /-réks/ *n* a large fierce flesh-eating dinosaur that walked on powerful hind legs and had small front legs [Early 20C. < modern Latin *Tyrannosaurus* < Greek *turannos* 'tyrant' + *sauros* 'lizard'.]

tyranny /tírrəni/ (*plural* **-nies**) *n* **1** CRUEL USE OF POWER cruelty and injustice in the exercising of power or authority over others **2** OPPRESSIVE GOVERNMENT oppressive government by one or more people who exercise absolute power cruelly and unjustly **3** STATE RULED BY TYRANT a country or state under the power of an oppressive ruler **4** CRUEL ACT an act of cruelty committed by somebody with great power **5** OPPRESSIVE FORCE a harsh or oppressive force [14C. Via French < late Latin *tyrannia* < Latin *tyrannus* 'tyrant'.] —**tyrannous** *adj*

tyrant /tīrənt/ *n* **1** ABSOLUTE RULER an absolute ruler who exercises power cruelly and unjustly **2** AUTHORITARIAN PERSON an unjust and oppressive exerciser of authority **3** SOMETHING THAT OPPRESSES something that oppresses harshly or cruelly **4** ANCIENT GREEK RULER in ancient Greece, a ruler who took control of a state without legal sanction and governed with absolute power [13C. Via Old French < Latin *tyrannus* < Greek *turannos*.]

tyrant flycatcher *n* BIRDS = **flycatcher** *n.* 2 [Translation of modern Latin *Tyrannidae*, family name]

~~**tyrany**~~ incorrect spelling of **tyranny**

tyre /tīr/ *n* **1** HOLLOW RUBBER EDGING a circular hollow band of rubber fitted around the edge of a vehicle's wheel to ease movement and help absorb bumps in road surfaces **2** SOLID RUBBER EDGING a circular solid band of rubber fitted to a wheel's edge, e.g. on prams and children's bicycles **3** METAL EDGING a band of metal fitted for reinforcement to the rims of wheels on various vehicles, e.g. handcarts and railway carriages

Tyre /tīr/ town in S Lebanon, on the Mediterranean Sea. It was the most important city of ancient Phoenicia. Population: 14,000 (1988). —**Tyrian** /tírri ən/ *adj*

Tyree, Mount /tī reé/ peak in the Ellsworth Mountains, Antarctica. Height: 4,965 m/16,290 ft.

Tyrian purple *n* **1** a deep purple dye extracted from molluscs **2** a rich crimson-purple colour —**Tyrian purple** *adj*

tyro /tīrō, tiro/ (*plural* **-ros**) *n* a person who is beginning to learn something [Early 17C. Via medieval Latin, 'squire' < Latin *tiro* 'young soldier, recruit'.] —**tyronic** /tī rónnik/ *adj*

SYNONYMS See ***beginner***.

tyrocidine /tīrō sīdeen/, **tyrocidin** /-sīdin/ *n* an antibiotic polypeptide that is the main constituent of the antibiotic tyrothricin. Source: the soil bacillus *Bacillus brevis*. [Mid-20C. Contraction of TYROTHRICIN + GRAMICIDIN + -INE.]

Tyrol /tiról/ = **Tirol**

Tyrolienne /ti rōli én/ *n* **1** a lively folk dance of Tirolese origin **2** the music for a Tyrolienne [Late 19C. < French *tyrolienne*, feminine of *tyrolien* 'Tirolean'.]

tyropitta /tírrə pittə/ *n* a Greek cheese pie usually made with filo pastry [Late 20C. < modern Greek *turopēta* 'cheese pie'.]

tyrosinase /tī róssə nayz/ *n* a copper-containing enzyme involved in the production of dopa from tyrosine [Late 19C. < TYROSINE.]

tyrosine /tīrō seen/ *n* an amino acid that is the precursor of adrenalin, thyroxine, and melanin [Mid-19C. < Greek *turos* 'cheese'.]

tyrothricin /tīrō thríssin/ *n* an antibiotic drug made from tyrocidine and gramicidin. Use: against gram-positive bacteria in local infections. [Mid-20C. < modern Latin *Tyrothric-* < Greek *turos* 'cheese' + *thrix* 'hair'.]

~~**tyrrany**~~ incorrect spelling of **tyranny**

yrrhenian Sea /ti reeni ən-/ arm of the Mediterranean Sea between the coast of W Italy and the islands of Corsica, Sardinia, and Sicily. Area: 155,000 sq. km/60,000 sq. mi.

yson /tiss'n/, **Mike** (*b.* 1966) US boxer. Born **Michael Gerald Tyson**

z *abbr* Tanzania (*in Internet addresses*)

zaddik /tsaadik/ (*plural* **-dikim** /tsaadi keem/), **tsaddik** (*plural* **-dikim**), **zaddik** (*plural* **-dikim**) *n* **1** in Judaism, a righteous man **2** JUDAISM = **rebbe** [Late 19C. < Hebrew *şaddîq* 'righteous'.]

tzar *n* = tsar

Tzara /tsaarə/, **Tristan** (1896–1963) French essayist and poet

tzarism *n* = tsarism

tzatziki /sat seeki, tsat-/ *n* a dip of Greek origin made from yogurt, chopped cucumber, mint, and garlic [Mid-20C. Via modern Greek *tsatsiki* < Turkish *cacik*.]

tzetze fly *n* INSECTS = **tsetse fly**

tzigane /tsi gaan, si/ *n* a member of a Romany people, especially one from Hungary [Mid-18C. Via French < Hungarian *czigany*.] —**tzigane** *adj*

tzimmes /tsimməss/ (*plural* **-mes**), **tsimmes** (*plural* **-mes**) *n* **1** a stew of meat, vegetables, and dried fruits, baked in a casserole **2** *US* a confused, muddled, or agitated state (*slang*) [Late 19C. < Yiddish *tsimes*.]

tzitzith /tsitsiss/, **tzitzit, tzitzes, tsitses** *n* the fringes on the corners of a Jewish prayer shawl (**tallis**) to remind Jews of God's commandments (Numbers 15:38) [Late 17C. < Hebrew *şîştt*.]

tzuris *n* = tsuris

Uu

u /yoo/ (*plural* **u's**), **U** (*plural* **U's** *or* **Us**) *n* the 21st letter of the English alphabet, representing a vowel sound

U[1] /yoo/, **u** *pron* a written form of 'you' (*informal*) [Because the letter *U* and *you* are pronounced the same]

U[2] /yoo/ (*plural* **U's** *or* **Us**) *n* **1** something shaped like a letter 'U' **2** a British film classification for films that can be seen by everybody, regardless of age. Full form **universal**

U[3] /oo/ *n* a title of respect for a man used in Myanmar, equivalent to 'Mr' [Mid-20C. < Burmese.]

U[4] *symbol* **1** internal energy **2** **U**, Ⓤ kosher certification **3** potential difference **4** uranium

U[5] *abbr* **1** united **2** university **3** unsatisfactory

u., **U.** *abbr* **1** uncle **2** unit **3** upper

⚡**ua** *abbr* Ukraine (*in Internet addresses*)

UAE *abbr* United Arab Emirates

uakari /wə kaäri/ (*plural* **-ri**) *n* a South American short-tailed monkey that lives high in the forest canopy, seldom coming down onto the ground. Genus: *Cacajao*. [Mid-19C. < Tupi.]

UAM *abbr* underwater-to-air missile

⚡**UART** /yoo aart/ *abbr* universal asynchronous receiver/transmitter

Ubangi /yoo báng gi/ river in central Africa. The chief tributary of the River Congo, it is formed by the confluence of the Bomu and Uele rivers. Length: 1,130 km/700 mi.

Ubangi-Shari /yoo báng gi shaäri/ former name for **Central African Republic**

U-bend *n* a U-shaped section of water pipe inserted in a waste system, e.g. beneath a basin, to trap water and so prevent the backflow of noxious vapours

Übermensch /oöbar mensh, yoöbar-/ (*plural* **-menschen** /-mensh'n/) *n* a superior kind of human being, especially in Nietzschean philosophy or Nazi ideology [Late 19C. < German, back-formation < *übermenschlich* 'superhuman'.]

ubiety /yoo bí əti/ *n* the condition of existing in a particular place (*literary*) [Late 17C. < medieval Latin *ubietas* < Latin *ubi* 'where'.]

ubiquinone /yoo bíkwinón/ *n* an electron transporter in energy-producing reactions that take place in mitochondria [Mid-20C. Blend of UBIQUITOUS + QUINONE.]

ubiquitarianism /yoo bíkwi táiri ənizəm/ *n* the Christian belief, held particularly by the Lutheran Church, that Jesus Christ is present in all places and at all times, not just in Communion —**ubiquitarian** *n*, *adj*

ubiquitous /yoo bíkwitəss/ *adj* present everywhere at once, or seeming to be [Mid-19C. < modern Latin *ubiquitas* 'presence everywhere' < Latin *ubique* 'everywhere' < *ubi* 'where'.] —**ubiquitously** *adv* —**ubiquitousness** *n* —**ubiquity** *n*

U-boat *n* a German submarine, especially one used during World Wars I and II [Early 20C. Partial translation of German *U-Boot*, shortening of *Unterseeboot* 'undersea boat'.]

U-bolt *n* a U-shaped bolt, threaded at the two ends

ubuntu /oö boön too/ *n* S Africa humanity, compassion, and goodness, regarded as fundamental to the way Africans approach life [Late 20C. < Xhosa.]

u.c. *abbr* uppercase

UCAS /yoo kass/ *abbr* Universities and Colleges Admissions Service

UCATT /yoo kat/ *abbr* Union of Construction, Allied Trades, and Technicians

Ucayali /oö kaa yaäli/ river in E Peru. Length: 1,900 km/1,200 mi.

UCCA /úka/ *abbr* Universities Central Council on Admissions. Now called **UCAS**

UCLA *abbr* University of California at Los Angeles

UCW *abbr* Union of Communication Workers

UDA *abbr* Ulster Defence Association

Udaipur /yoo dípoor, yoö dΐpoor/ city in NW India. Population: 308,571 (1991).

udder /úddər/ *n* a bag-shaped structure containing two or more milk-secreting glands, each with its own teat, found in mammals such as cows, sheep, and goats [Old English *üder* < Indo-European]

UDI *abbr* unilateral declaration of independence

Udjung Pandang /oo joöng pan dáng/, **Ujungpandang** capital of Sulawesi Selantan Province, on S Sulawesi, Indonesia. Population: 944,372 (1990).

UDM *abbr* Union of Democratic Mineworkers

Udmurt /oöd moort/ (*plural* **-murt** *or* **-murts**) *n* **1** a member of a people who live mainly in Udmurtia in central Russia **2** the Finno-Ugric language of the Udmurt people. Native speakers: 500,000.

Udmurtia /oöd moörti ə/ republic in E European Russia. Capital: Izhevsk. Population: 1,640,700 (1994). Area: 42,100 sq. km/16,300 sq. mi.

udo /oödō/ (*plural* **udos**) *n* a perennial plant of the ginseng family whose tender shoots are cooked and eaten as a vegetable. Native to: Asia. *Aralia cordata*. [Late 20C. < Japanese.]

udometer /yoo dómmitər/ *n* a gauge that measures rainfall (*technical*) [Early 19C. < French *udomètre* < Latin *udus* 'wet' + *mètre* 'meter'.]

UDR *abbr* Ulster Defence Regiment

UEFA /yoo áyfə/ *abbr* Union of European Football Associations

Ufa /oo faä/ city in SE European Russia. Population: 1,097,200 (1992).

Uffington /úffingtən/ village in south-central England. A large figure of a white horse cut in the chalk hill nearby is believed to date from the Iron Age. Population: 748 (1991).

Uffizi /yoo fítsi/ *n* a museum in Florence that contains one of the world's finest collections of Italian paintings [Mid-19C. < Italian, 'offices', because built to house the administrative centre of the Florentine state.]

UFO /yoö ef ō, yoöfō/ (*plural* **UFOs**) *n* a flying object that cannot be identified and is thought by some to be an alien spacecraft [Mid-20C. Acronym < *unidentified flying object*.]

ufology /yoö fólləji/ *n* the study of UFOs, especially the investigation of recorded sightings of them

⚡**ug** *abbr* Uganda (*in Internet addresses*)

Uganda

Uganda /yoo gándə/ republic in E Africa. Capital: Kampala. Population: 19,136,000 (1996). Area: 236,034 sq. km/91,134 sq. mi. —**Ugandan** *n*, *adj*

Ugaritic /oögə ríttik/ *n* an extinct Semitic language of the region that is now N Syria, closely related to Hebrew and Phoenician [Mid-20C. < *Ugarit*, ancient city in N Syria.] —**Ugaritic** *adj*

ugh /ug, oökh, u/ *interj* used as the written form of a grunting exclamation of disgust, strain, or horror [Mid-19C. Representing an involuntary utterance.]

uglify /úggli fī/ (**-fies**, **-fying**, **-fied**) *vt* to make somebody or something physically unappealing —**uglification** /úgglifi káysh'n/ *n* —**uglifier** /úggli fī ər/ *n*

ugly /úggli/ (**-lier**, **-liest**) *adj* **1** UNATTRACTIVE lacking appealing physical features, especially facial ones **2** ANGRY characterized by anger or hostility ○ *an ugly mood* **3** POTENTIALLY VIOLENT threatening or involving violence ○ *Things were turning ugly.* **4** UNPLEASANT generally unpleasant ○ *a dull ugly afternoon* [13C. < Old Norse *ugglig* 'frightful' < *uggr* 'fear'.] —**uglily** *adv* —**ugliness** *n*

ugly American *n* a loud, boorish, nationalistic American, especially one travelling abroad, who is regarded as conforming to a stereotype that gives Americans a bad reputation

ugly duckling *n* **1** somebody or something regarded as physically unappealing in comparison to others **2** somebody or something whose true beauty or value is yet to be revealed or appreciated [< *The Ugly Duckling*, children's story by Hans Christian Andersen in which a cygne raised by a duck is considered ugly until it grows into a beautiful swan]

Ugrian /yoögri ən/ *n* a member of a group of peoples including the Magyars and Voguls, who live in Hungary and parts of Siberia [Mid-19C. < Russian *Ugry* 'Hungarians' < Turkic.] —**Ugrian** *adj*

Ugric /yoögrik/ *n* a branch of the Finno-Ugric family of languages that includes Hungarian [Mid-19C. < Russian *Ugry* 'Hungarians' (see UGRIAN).] —**Ugric** *adj*

uh /u/ *interj* used as the written form of a grunting exclamation made to express surprise or request something to be said again [Early 17C. Representing an inarticulate sound.]

UHF *n* any or all radio frequencies between 300 and 3000 megahertz, typically used for television transmission. Full form **ultrahigh frequency**

h-huh /u húl *interj* used as the written form of a grunting exclamation made to express agreement or to answer affirmatively [Representing an inarticulate sound]

h-oh /ú ō/ *interj* used as the written form of a grunting exclamation made to express apprehension [Representing an articulate sound]

HT *adj* sterilized and having a long shelf-life as a result of being heated to a very high temperature. Full form **ultra heat treated**

h-uh /u ú, ú, ù/ *interj* used as the written form of a grunting exclamation made to express disagreement or to answer in the negative [An imitation of an inarticulate sound]

huru /oo hoōroo/ *n* freedom or national independence, especially for the people of E Africa [Mid-20C. < Ki-swahili.]

I *abbr* user interface

-ie /yoō i/ (*plural* **U-ies**) *n* a U-turn (*informal*) [Late 20C. Shortening and alteration of U-TURN.]

Jigur /weegar, -goorl/ (*plural* **Uigur** *or* **Uigurs**), **Uighur** *n* **1** a member of a people who live in W China, mainly in NW Xinjiang Uygur Autonomous Region **2** the Turkic language of the Uigur people. Native speakers: 7 million. [Mid-18C. < E Turkic.] —**Uigurian** /wee gooʻri ən/ *adj* —**Uiguric** /wee gooʻrik/ *adj*

iilleann pipes /oōli ən-/ *npl* Irish bagpipes played by squeezing the bellows under the arm [Early 20C. < Irish *píob uilleann* 'elbow pipe' < *uille* 'elbow' < Old Irish *uilind*.]

intaite /yoō ínta ʔt/ *n* a bitumen mined in the Uinta mountains in Utah in the United States. Use: manufacturing industries.

k *abbr* United Kingdom (*in Internet addresses*)

K *abbr* United Kingdom

JKAEA *abbr* United Kingdom Atomic Energy Authority

kase /yoo káyz/ *n* **1** in pre-Revolutionary Russia, an order from the tsar that had the force of law **2** any order or ruling, especially one handed down by a self-styled expert or guru [Early 18C. < Russian *ukaz* 'edict' < *ukazat* 'show'.]

ke /yook/ *n* a ukulele (*informal*) [Early 20C. Shortening.]

kelele *n* MUSIC = **ukulele**

kiyo-e /oóo kee yō yáyl/, **ukiyo-ye** *n* a movement in Japanese painting dating from the 17th to 19th centuries in which scenes and objects from ordinary life were depicted [Late 19C. < Japanese, 'transitory-world picture'.]

Ukraine

Ukraine /yoo kráyn/ republic in E Europe, with a coastline on the Black Sea. Capital: Kiev. Population: 51,639,000 (1995). Area: 603,700 sq. km/233,090 sq. mi.

Ukrainian /yoo kráyni ən/ *n* **1** a person who comes from Ukraine **2** a Balto-Slavic language, the official language of the Ukraine, also spoken in Poland and the Czech Republic. Native speakers: 45 million. —**Ukrainian** *adj*

ukulele /yoōka láyli/, **ukelele** *n* an instrument like a small guitar with four strings [Late 19C. < Hawaiian *'ukulele* 'jumping flea'.]

Ulaanbaatar /oō laan baátar/, **Ulan Bator** capital of the Republic of Mongolia, in the north-central part of the country. Population: 600,900 (1992).

ulama /oōlima/, **ulema** *npl* a body of Islamic scholars who have jurisdiction over legal and social matters for the people of Islam [Late 17C. Via Turkish *'ulemā* < Arabic *'ulamā* 'learned men'.]

Ulan Bator = **Ulaanbaatar**

Ulan-Ude /oo laán oo də/ port city in S Siberian Russia. Population: 366,000 (1992).

Ulbricht /oōl brikht/, **Walter** (1893–1973) German statesman

ulcer /úlssar/ *n* **1** INTERNAL SORE a slow-healing sore on the surface of a mucous membrane, especially the membrane lining the stomach or other part of the digestive tract **2** EXTERNAL SORE a suppurating sore on the skin that does not heal and results in the destruction of tissue **3** BAD INFLUENCE a corrupting or debilitating influence [14C. < Latin *ulcer-*, stem of *ulcus* 'a sore'.] —**ulcerous** *adj*

ulcerate /úlssa rayt/ (*-ates, -ating, -ated*) *vti* to cause or undergo the formation of an ulcer or ulcers —**ulceration** /úlssa ráysh'n/ *n* —**ulcerative** *adj*

ulcerative colitis *n* inflammation of the walls of the bowel accompanied by the formation of ulcers

ulcerative gingivitis *n* painful inflammation of the gums accompanied by the formation of ulcers

-ule *suffix* small one, miniature ○ *lobule* [Via French < Latin *-ulus*]

ulema *npl* ISLAM = **ulama**

-ulent *suffix* having a great deal of something ○ *flocculent* [< Latin *-ulentus*]

ullage /úllij/ *n* (*formal*) **1** the amount or volume by which a container, especially one for liquids, is short of being full **2** the amount of liquid lost from a container through evaporation or leakage [15C. < Anglo-Norman *ulliage* < Old French *ouillier* 'fill a barrel to the bunghole' < *oeil* 'eye, bunghole' < Latin *oculus* 'eye'.]

Ullswater /úlz wawtar/ lake in the Lake District, NW England. Area: 8 sq. km/3 sq. mi.

Ulm /oólm/, **Charles** (1898–1934) Australian aviator

ulmaceous /ul máysh əss/ *adj* belonging or relating to the family of temperate and tropical deciduous trees that includes the elms [Mid-19C. < modern Latin *Ulmaceae* < Latin *ulmus* 'elm'.]

ulna /úlna/ (*plural* **-nae** /úlnee/ *or* **-nas**) *n* **1** the longer of the two bones in the human forearm, situated on the inner side **2** a bone in the lower forelimb of vertebrate animals, roughly corresponding to the human ulna [Mid-16C. < Latin, 'elbow, forearm'.] —**ulnar** *adj*

ulnar nerve *n* a major nerve of the arm that runs down the inner side of the upper arm and is situated just under the skin at the elbow

-ulose *suffix* ketose ○ *ribulose*

ulotrichous /yoo lóttrikəss/ *adj* with hair that is naturally tightly curled, especially belonging to a group of people with this kind of hair [Mid-19C. < Greek *oulos* 'crisp, curly' + *trikh-*, stem of *thrix* 'hair'.]

ulster /úlstər/ *n* a man's long heavy double-breasted overcoat [Mid-19C. After ULSTER.]

Ulster /úlstər/ **1** historic province in the north of Ireland, comprising nine counties, including the six that make up Northern Ireland **2** informal name for Northern Ireland —**Ulsterman** *n* —**Ulsterwoman** *n*

ult. *abbr* **1** ultimate **2** ultimo

ulterior /ul teéri ər/ *adj* **1** UNDERLYING existing in addition to or being other than what is apparent or assumed **2** LYING OUTSIDE lying beyond or outside a point or area **3** HAPPENING IN THE FUTURE happening or expected in the future [Mid-17C. < Latin, 'further' < assumed *ulter* 'beyond'.] —**ulteriorly** *adv*

ulterior motive *n* a second and underlying motive, usually a selfish or dishonourable one

ultima /última/ *n* the final syllable of a word [Early 20C. < Latin, form of *ultimus* (see ULTIMATE).]

ultimata *plural of* **ultimatum**

ultimate /últimat/ *adj* **1** FINAL coming or expected as the very last ○ *our ultimate destination* **2** FUNDAMENTAL existing as an underlying reality, when all other things are disregarded ○ *the ultimate truth* **3** GREATEST greatest, most nearly perfect, or highest in quality (*informal*) ○ *the ultimate home entertainment system* **4** FARTHEST AWAY outermost or most remote ■ *n* GREATEST THING the greatest or most nearly perfect thing (*informal*) ○ *seats that were the ultimate in passenger comfort* [Mid-17C. < late Latin *ultimatus*, past participle of *ultimare* 'be at an end' < Latin *ultimus* 'last, final' < assumed *ulter* 'beyond'.] —**ultimacy** *n* —**ultimateness** *n*

ultimately /últimatli/ *adv* **1** most importantly, when all things are considered **2** in the end, as the culmination of a process or event

ultima Thule /-thyoōli/ *n* (*literary*) **1** a distant or very remote place **2** an ultimate or distant goal [Late 18C. < Latin, 'farthest Thule', the northernmost part of the inhabited world.]

ultimatum /últi máytəm/ (*plural* **-tums** *or* **-ta** /-tə/) *n* a demand accompanied by a threat to inflict some penalty if the demand is not met [Mid-18C. < modern Latin, < *ultimatus* (see ULTIMATE).]

ultimo /últimō/ *adj* used in formal correspondence to refer to the previous month (*dated*) ○ *your letter of the 20th ultimo* [Late 16C. < Latin *ultimo (mense)* 'in the last (month)' < *ultimus* (see ULTIMATE).]

ultimogeniture /últimō jénnichər/ *n* the principle of inheritance or succession by the youngest son [Late 19C. < Latin *ultimus* 'last', after *primogeniture*.]

ultra /últra/ *adj* **1** EXTREME going beyond all else **2** HOLDING EXTREMIST VIEWS holding extremist views, especially in religious or political matters **3** EXCELLENT excellent or superior (*slang*) ■ *n* EXTREMIST somebody with extremist views, especially in religious or political matters [Late 19C. Via French < Latin, 'beyond'.]

ultra- *prefix* **1** more than normal, excessively, completely ○ *ultrasophisticated* **2** outside the range of ○ *ultrasound* [< Latin *ultra* 'beyond' < Indo-European]

ultrabasic /últra báyssik/ *adj* describes igneous rock that is high in iron and magnesium and contains no free quartz. ◊ **ultramafic** ■ *n* a rock of ultrabasic composition. ◊ **ultramafic**

ultracentrifuge /últra séntri fyooj/ *n* a centrifuge for separating microscopic or submicroscopic particles by using a force many times greater than gravity ■ *vt* (*-fuges, -fuging, -fuged*) to subject something to the action of an ultracentrifuge —**ultracentrifugal** /últra séntri fyoogˈl/ *adj* —**ultracentrifugally** *adv* —**ultracentrifugation** /últra séntrifyoo gáyshˈn/ *n*

ultraconservative /últrakən súrvətiv/ *adj* extremely conservative in religious or political views —**ultraconservative** *n*

ultrafiche /últra feesh/ *n* **1** a sheet of microfilm of similar size to a microfiche but with a much greater number of documents on it **2** a device for viewing ultrafiches that has much greater magnification than a microfiche

ultrafilter /últra fíltər/ *n* a filter for separating extremely small particles from a solution or colloid

ultrafiltrate /últra fíl trayt/ *n* the material that is not filtered out and remains in the liquid phase after ultrafiltration

ultrafiltration /últra fil tráyshˈn/ *n* a filtration process that uses a porous membrane to isolate and remove particles such as bacteria and viruses

ultra-heat-treated *adj* full form of UHT

ultrahigh frequency /últra hī-/ *n* full form of UHF

ultraism /últra izəm/ *n* religious or political extremism —**ultraist** *n* —**ultraistic** /-ístik/ *adj*

ultralarge crude carrier *n* a very large oil tanker, larger than a supertanker, that has a capacity greater than 400,000 tons

ultramafic /últra máffik/ *adj* describes a dark igneous rock, over 90% of whose content consists of ferromagnesian minerals, including olivine and pyroxenes. ◊ **ultrabasic** ■ *n* a rock of ultramafic composition. ◊ **ultrabasic**

ultramarine /últrama reén/ *n* **1** BLUE PIGMENT a deep blue pigment or dye, especially one made from lapis lazuli **2** DEEP BLUE COLOUR a brilliant deep blue colour ■ *adj* **1** OF A DEEP BLUE of the colour ultramarine **2** BEYOND THE SEA coming from or lying beyond or beyond the sea (*literary*) [Late 16C. < medieval Latin *ultramarinus* 'beyond the sea'.]

ultramicrometer /últra mī krómmitər/ *n* a measuring device designed to measure spaces and thicknesses more minute than those measurable using a standard micrometer

ultramicroscope /últra míkrəskōp/ *n* a microscope that uses scattered light to make submicroscopic objects visible

ultramicroscopic /últra míkrə skóppik/ *adj* **1** = submicroscopic **2** involving the use of an ultramicroscope

ultramodern /últra móddərn/ *adj* more modern than anything comparable, especially in using the very latest designs or making use of the most advanced technology —**ultramodernism** *n* —**ultramodernist** *n*

ultramontane /últrə món tayn/ *adj* **1 BEYOND MOUNTAINS** coming from or lying beyond mountains, especially beyond the Alps as viewed from ancient Rome **2 SUPPORTING THE POPE** supporting the power and authority of the pope within the Roman Catholic Church ■ *n* **1 DWELLER BEYOND MOUNTAINS** a person who lives beyond mountains, especially beyond the Alps as viewed from ancient Rome **2 PAPAL SUPPORTER** a supporter of the power and authority of the pope in the Roman Catholic Church [Late 16C. < medieval Latin *ultramontanus* 'beyond the mountains'.]

ultramontanism /últrə móntənizəm/ *n* in the Roman Catholic Church, the policy of investing all power and authority in the pope

ultramundane /últrə mun dáyn/ *adj* (*literary*) **1** coming from or lying beyond the Earth or its solar system **2** belonging or relating to heaven or to the realm of the spirit, and not to the physical world [Mid-16C. < Latin *ultramundanus* 'beyond the world' < *ultra* 'beyond' + *mundus* 'world'.]

ultranationalism /últrə násh'nəlizəm/ *n* nationalism that is so extreme as to be detrimental to international interests or cooperation —**ultranationalist** /últrə násh'nəlist/ *n* —**ultranationalistic** /-násh'nə lístik/ *adj*

ultraprecise /últrə pri síss/ *adj* showing, capable of, or characterized by extreme or excessive precision

ultrarealistic /últrə ree ə lístik/ *adj* characterized by extreme or excessive realism

ultrareligious /últrə ri líjjəss/ *adj* showing great devotion to religious rites and rituals

ultraroyalist /últrə róy əlist/ *n* an extreme or overzealous supporter of royalism, especially a member of the extreme right wing of the royalist movement in France from 1815 to 1830

ultrashort /últrə sháwrt/ *adj* **1** describes wavelengths that are shorter than 10 m **2** extremely short in length or duration

ultrasonic /últrə sónnik/ *adj* describes sound waves that have frequencies above the upper limit of the normal range of human hearing, which is about 20 kilohertz —**ultrasonically** *adv*

ultrasonics /últrə sónniks/ *n* the study of sound waves that have frequencies above the upper limit of the normal range of human hearing, which is about 20 kilohertz (+ *singular verb*)

ultrasonic testing *n* the scanning of surfaces with high-frequency sound waves in order to gauge their integrity and check for defects or to measure the thickness of materials

ultrasonic welding *n* the bonding of two components by bombarding them with ultrasonic waves to cause vibrations between them

ultrasonogram /últrə sṓnə gram/ *n* a picture made with ultrasound for the purpose of medical examination or diagnosis

ultrasonography /últrə sə nóggrəfi/ *n* the use of ultrasound to make pictures for the purpose of medical examination or diagnosis —**ultrasonigraphic** /últrə sṓnə gráffik/ *adj*

ultrasound /últrə sownd/ *n* **1** sound of a frequency above the upper limit of the normal range of human hearing, which is about 20 kilohertz **2** an imaging technique that uses high-frequency sound waves reflecting off internal body parts to create images, especially of the foetus in the womb, for medical examination **3** MED = **ultrasound scan**

ultrasound scan *n* a medical examination of an internal body part, especially a foetus in the womb, using ultrasound technology

ultrastructure /últrə strúkchər/ *n* the minute structure of an organic substance or object that becomes evident only under electron microscopy —**ultrastructural** *adj*

ultraviolet /últrə ví ələt/ *adj* relating to or producing electromagnetic radiation of wavelengths from about 5 to about 400 nanometers, beyond the violet end of the visible light spectrum ■ *n* radiation with ultraviolet wavelengths

ultra vires /últrə ví reez/ *adj, adv* beyond the legal capacity of a person, company, or other legal entity [< Latin, 'beyond the powers']

ultravirus /últrə vírəss/ *n* a virus small enough to pass through an ultrafilter —**ultraviral** *adj*

ulu /oo lóo/ *adj Malaysia, Singapore* rural and not economically or technologically advanced (*informal*)

ululate /yóolyoo layt/ (**-lates, -lating, -lated**) *vi* to howl or wail, in grief or in jubilation [Early 17C. < Latin *ululare*, an imitation of the sound.] —**ululation** /yóolyoo láysh'n/ *n*

Uluru /óolə róo/ largest rock mass in the world, in S Northern Territory, Australia. Height: 868 m/2,848 ft.

Ulverstone /úlvərstən/ coastal town in N Tasmania, Australia. Population: 9,935 (1991).

Ulysses /yoo lísseez, yóoli seez/ *n* the name used by the Romans for the Greek hero Odysseus [Early 17C. < Latin.] —**Ulyssean** /yoo líssi ən/ *adj*

um /um/ *interj* a word used in writing to represent the kind of grunting sound that people make when they hesitate in speaking [Early 17C. Representing an inarticulate sound.]

Umayyad /oo mí yad/, **Omayyad** *n* the family that dominated the politics and commercial economy of Mecca and later established a dynasty as rulers (**caliphs**) of Islam [Mid-18C. < *Umayya*, cousin of Muhammad's grandfather.] —**Umayyad** *adj*

umbel /úmb'l/ *n* an umbrella-shaped flower head in which the individual flowers are borne on short stems arising from the top of a main stem [Late 16C. Directly or via Old French *umbelle* < Latin *umbella* 'parasol' < *umbra* 'shade'.] —**umbellar** /um béllər/ *adj* —**umbellate** /úmbələt, -layt/ *adj* —**umbellated** *adj*

umbelliferous /úmbə líffərəss/ *adj* with flower heads shaped like an opened umbrella [Mid-17C. < Latin *umbella* 'parasol' (see UMBEL).]

umber /úmbər/ *n* **1 PIGMENT** pigment or dye made from soil that contains oxides of iron and manganese **2 SOIL USED FOR PIGMENTS AND DYES** a soil that yields umber ■ *adj* **OF BROWN PRODUCED BY UMBER PIGMENT** of any shade of brown produced by umber pigment ■ *vt* **PAINT WITH UMBER** to paint or dye something with umber, or colour something dark brown [Mid-16C. Via French *terre d'ombre* or Italian *terra di ombre* < Latin *umbra* 'shadow'.]

Umberto I /óom búrtō/ (1844–1900) king of Italy (1878–1900)

Umberto II (1904–83) king of Italy (1946)

umbilical /um bíllik'l/ *adj* **1 OF THE UMBILICAL CORD** relating to or situated in the umbilical cord, the navel, or the area of the abdomen that surrounds the navel **2 RESEMBLING A NAVEL** resembling a navel (**umbilicus**) in appearance **3 PROVIDING A LIFELINE** providing a link to something essential, e.g. supplies or services in wartime, or connecting an astronaut to a spacecraft while outside of it ■ *n* ANAT = **umbilical cord** *n.* 1 [Mid-16C. < obsolete French, 'navel' < Latin *umbilicus* (see UMBILICUS).]

umbilical cord *n* **1** the flexible, often spirally twisted tube that connects the abdomen of a foetus to the mother's placenta in the womb, and through which nutrients are delivered and waste expelled **2** a cable, tube, or pipe attaching somebody or something to an essential supply, e.g. the tube that connects a deep-sea diver to an oxygen supply on a ship

umbilicate /um bíllikət/, **umbilicated** /um bílli kaytid/ *adj* **1** with a mark, depression, or perforation that resembles a navel **2** shaped like a navel [Late 17C. < UMBILICUS.] —**umbilication** /um bílli káysh'n/ *n*

umbilicus /um bíllikəss/ (*plural* **-ci** /-li sī/) *n* **1** a navel (*technical*) **2** a dip or hollow, e.g. the hollow at each end of the shaft of a feather, that resembles a navel [Late 17C. < Latin, < Indo-European.]

umbo /úmbō/ (*plural* **-bones** /um bṓ neez/ *or* **-bos**) *n* **1 BUMP ON PLANT OR ANIMAL PART** a small protuberance on a plant or animal part, e.g. the hump on the caps of some mushrooms, or the bump just above the hinge of a bivalve shell **2 SMALL HOLLOW IN THE EARDRUM** a small hollow in the centre of the outer surface of the eardrum, at the point where the malleus joins it on the inside **3 KNOB ON SHIELD** a knob at the centre of a round shield, especially a Saxon shield [Early 18C. < Latin, 'shield boss'.] —**umbonal** /um bṓn'l/ *adj* —**umbonate** /úmbənət/ *adj*

umbra /úmbrə/ (*plural* **-brae** /úm bree/ *or* **-bras**) *n* **1 COMPLETE SHADOW** an area of complete shadow caused by light from all points of a source being prevented from reaching the area, usually by an opaque object **2 DARKEST PART OF MOON'S SHADOW** the darkest portion of the shadow cast by an astronomical object during an eclipse, especially that cast on the Earth during a sola eclipse **3 DARK PART OF SUNSPOT** the inner, darker area of sunspot [Late 16C. < Latin, 'shadow'.] —**umbral** *adj*

umbrage /úmbrij/ *n* **1 OFFENCE** resentment or annoyanc arising from some offence ○ *took umbrage* **2 GIVER OF SHA** something that gives shade, e.g. a tree (*literary*) **3 VAGU SHAPE** a vague or shadowy shape, or simply an outlir (*archaic*) [15C. < Old French, < Latin *umbra* 'shadow'.]

umbrageous /um bráyjəss/ *adj* **1** providing shade an coolness (*literary*) **2** easily offended or likely to becom irritated —**umbrageously** *adv* —**umbrageousness** *n*

umbrella /um brélə/ *n* **1 COLLAPSIBLE CANOPY THAT PROTECT FROM RAIN** a round collapsible canopy of plastic or wate proof material on a frame at the top of a handle, hel in the hand to protect somebody from rain or su **2 OBJECT LIKE AN UMBRELLA** an object that looks like an ope umbrella, or that collapses like an umbrella, e.g. th folding paper decoration sometimes served in cocktai **3 JELLYFISH'S BODY** the rounded body of a jellyfis **4 AIRCRAFT FLYING OVERHEAD FOR PROTECTION** a group of ai craft patrolling the sky above a place where troops ar carrying out operations, to give them protection **5 SHIE OF GUNFIRE** gunfire used to suppress enemy fire and th shield friendly forces making a movement or attac **6** *US* **PARACHUTE** a parachute (*slang*) **7 SUPPORT OR AUTHORI** something that gives support, protection, or authorit ○ *under the umbrella of the United Nations* ■ *adj* **1 UNIFYI MEMBER ORGANIZATIONS** acting to coordinate or protect number of member organizations or bodies **2 INCLUDI SEVERAL THINGS** including or containing a number c things ○ *an umbrella term for a variety of plants* [Early 17C Via Italian *ombrella* < late Latin *umbrella*, alteration of Lati *umbella* 'parasol' (see UMBEL) after *umbra* 'shadow'.]

umbrella bird *n* a bird with a large feathered cres Native to: Central and South America. Genus: *C phalopterus.*

umbrella pine *n* TREES = **stone pine**

umbrella plant *n* a plant of the sedge family that ha thin leaves radiating from the top of long stems. Nativ to: Africa. *Cyperus alternifolius.*

umbrella stand *n* an upright stand or rack for holdin walking sticks and folded umbrellas

umbrella tree *n* **1** a magnolia tree with large leave clustered around the ends of the branches. Native tc SE United States. *Magnolia fraseri* and *Magnolia tripetala* **2** a bush or tree with umbrella-shaped clusters of leave Flowers: red, clustered on long spikes. Native to: Aus tralia. *Schefflera actinophylla.*

umbrette /um brét/ *n* BIRDS = **hammerhead** *n.* 1

Umbria /úmbri ə/ region in central Italy. Populatior 822,972 (1991). Area: 8,456 sq. km/3,265 sq. mi.

Umbrian /úmbri ən/ *n* **1** a person who comes from Umbri **2** an extinct Italic language of ancient S Italy —**Umbria** *adj*

Umbriel /úmbri əl/ *n* one of the five major moons circlin the planet Uranus [Named after a sprite in the poem 'Th Rape of the Lock' by Alexander POPE]

umiak /óomi ak/ *n* a large Inuit boat made of animal skin stretched across a wooden frame, larger and more ope than a kayak and traditionally paddled by women [Mid 18C. < Inuit *umiaq*.]

UMIST /yóomist/ *abbr* University of Manchester Institut of Science and Technology

umlaut /óom lowt/ *n* **1 CHANGE IN A VOWEL SOUND** in German languages, a change in the way a vowel is pronounce caused by the influence of another vowel in a syllabl immediately after it **2 TWO DOTS ABOVE A VOWEL** the mar (¨) that is placed above a vowel in Germanic language to show that it is pronounced differently ■ *v* **1** *vti* **CHANG A VOWEL SOUND** to change a sound, or make a vowe change its sound, because of other vowel sounds ne to it **2** *vt* **MARK A VOWEL WITH TWO DOTS** to write or print vowel with an umlaut above it [Mid-19C. < German, < *um-* 'about, change' + *Laut* 'sound'.]

umma /óomə/, **ummah** *n* within Islam, the community o the faithful that transcended long established triba boundaries to create a degree of political unity [Lat 19C. < Arabic, 'people, community'.]

umpire /úm pīr/ *n* **1 OFFICIAL ENFORCING A SPORT'S RULES** ar official who supervises play and enforces the rules o the game in some sports such as cricket and basebal **2 SOMEBODY SETTLING A DISPUTE** somebody called in to settl a dispute ■ *vti* (**-pires, -piring, -pired**) **1 ACT AS AN UMPIR IN SPORT** to supervise play in a game or sport and enforc the rules **2** SETTLE A DISPUTE to give a ruling on a dispute as an impartial arbitrator [Late 16C. By false division < *noumper* < Old French *nonper* < *non* 'not' + *per* 'pair'.]

umpteen /ùmp teén/ *det* a large but unspecified number of (*informal*) [Early 20C. Humorous formation after *thirteen, fourteen*, etc.] —**umpteenth** *det*

Umtata /um taáta/ town in SE South Africa. Population: 67,000 (1995 estimate).

un /ən, 'n/, **'un** *pron* a spelling of the pronoun 'one' designed to reflect the way it is sometimes pronounced in informal speech (*informal*) [Early 19C. Alteration of ONE.]

UN *abbr* United Nations

un-[1] *prefix* **1** not ○ *unavoidable* **2** opposite of, lack of ○ *unrest* [Old English, < Indo-European]

USAGE un- or **non-**? Many adjectives formed with ***un-*** have special (usually unfavourable) meanings, for example, *uncooperative* and *unprofessional*. In these cases neutral equivalents that mean simply 'not ...' are formed by means of ***non-***, for example, *noncooperative, nonprofessional*.

un-[2] *prefix* **1** to do the opposite of, reverse ○ *unclose* **2** to deprive of, remove something from ○ *unfrock* **3** to release from ○ *unchain* **4** completely ○ *unloose* [Old English *on-*, alteration of *ond-*, *and-* 'against' < Germanic after UN-[1]]

unabashed /ùnnə básht/ *adj* not ashamed or embarrassed by something

unabated /ùnnə báytid/ *adj* still as forceful or intense as before —**unabatedly** *adv*

unable /un áyb'l/ *adj* not able to do something

unabridged /ùn ə bríjd/ *adj* complete and not shortened or summarized

unabsorbed /ùn əb sáwrbd, -záwrbd/ *adj* not taken up, soaked up, or incorporated into something else

unaccented /ùn ək séntid/ *adj* **1** HAVING NO DIACRITICAL MARK describes a letter that has no accent or diacritical mark **2** HAVING NO ACCENTUAL STRESS describes a syllable that has no stress **3** HAVING NO SPEECH ACCENT describes speech that is without any foreign or regional accent

unacceptable /ùn ək séptəb'l/ *adj* **1** not good enough to win approval or meet a required standard ○ *Such conduct is completely unacceptable in a police officer.* **2** not of a kind that can be accepted or agreed to ○ *The terms were unacceptable to us.* —**unacceptability** /ùn ək séptə bílləti/ *n* —**unacceptably** /-séptəbli/ *adv*

unaccommodated /ùnnə kómmə daytid/ *adj* (*formal*) **1** not adapted to or for something ○ *unaccommodated to the dryness of the desert* **2** lacking accommodation, equipment, or supplies

unaccommodating /ùn ə kómmə dayting/ *adj* unwilling to adjust actions in response to the needs of others —**unaccommodatingly** *adv*

unaccompanied /ùnnə kúmpənid/ *adj, adv* **1** alone, especially when a companion would be expected **2** playing or singing alone, without any other instruments or voices

unaccomplished /ùnnə kúmplisht/ *adj* **1** not carried out or completed **2** lacking talents or abilities, especially those abilities educated people may be expected to have

unaccountable /ùnnə kówntəb'l/ *adj* **1** impossible to explain or give a reason for **2** not answerable or responsible to anyone —**unaccountability** /ùnnə kówntə bílləti/ *n*

unaccountably /ùnnə kówntəbli/ *adv* for some unknown and usually puzzling reason

unaccounted-for *adj* **1** missing or absent, for unknown reasons **2** not explained or understood

unaccredited /ùnnə kréddìtid/ *adj* **1** with the source or origin not given **2** not officially declared to be of the required standard, or with no official status

unaccustomed /ùnnə kústəmd/ *adj* **1** not used or accustomed to something **2** not usual or known before —**unaccustomedness** *n*

unachievable /ùn ə chéevəb'l/ *adj* unable to be done or gained successfully

unacknowledged /ùnnək nóllijd/ *adj* **1** not recognized as existing or having a particular function ○ *the unacknowledged leader of the movement* **2** receiving no answer, response, or reaction ○ *The letter went unacknowledged.*

una corda /òonə káwrdə/ *adj, adv* in piano music, using only one string per pitch, achieved by depressing the soft pedal [< Italian, 'one string']

unacquainted /ùn ə kwáyntid/ *adj* **1** having no knowledge of something **2** unknown to somebody or to each other from a previous introduction

unaddicted /ùn ə díktid/ *adj* not physiologically or mentally dependent on something, especially a drug

unadmitted /ùn əd míttid/ *adj* not confessed, or not acknowledged to exist or be true

unadopted /ùnnə dóptid/ *adj* **1** not adopted by new parents **2** describes a road that is not maintained or repaired by a local authority

unadorned /ùn ə dáwrnd/ *adj* plain and simple, without any decoration or embellishment

unadulterated /ùnnə dúltə raytid/ *adj* **1** not mixed or diluted with something else **2** free from any element that would spoil or detract from it —**unadulteratedly** *adv*

unadventurous /ùn əd vénchərəss/ *adj* **1** cautiously unwilling to take risks or try new things **2** not involving or offering anything new, unusual, or exciting ○ *an unadventurous repertoire* —**unadventurously** *adv* —**unadventurousness** *n*

unadvised /ùnnəd vízd/ *adj* **1** done without being carefully considered **2** without asking the advice of others —**unadvisedly** *adv* —**unadvisedness** *n*

unaffected /ùnnə féktid/ *adj* **1** sincere and genuine, with no intention to mislead or deceive **2** not influenced or affected by something —**unaffectedly** *adv* —**unaffectedness** *n*

unaffecting /ùn ə fékting/ *adj* failing to stir people's emotions

unaffiliated /ùn ə fílli aytid/ *adj* not attached to or connected with any organization or with another particular organization

unaffordable /ùn ə fáwrdəb'l/ *adj* **1** not within somebody's financial means ○ *housing that remains unaffordable to most people* **2** involving unacceptable consequences ○ *an unaffordable risk*

unafraid /ùn ə fráyd/ *adj* feeling or showing no fear

unaggressive /ùn ə gréssiv/ *adj* **1** unlikely to attack or do harm **2** showing little energy, drive, or determination —**unaggressively** *adv* —**unaggressiveness** *n*

unaided /un áydid/ *adj* acting or done entirely without help

Unaipon /oo nī pon/, **David** (1873–1967) Australian writer and inventor

Unalaska /ùnnə láskə/ island in SW Alaska, second largest of the Aleutian Islands. Population: 4,285. Area: 1,287 sq. km/800 sq. mi.

unalienable /un áyli ənəb'l/ *adj* not alienable

unaligned /ùn ə línd/ *adj* not allied with any major world power or any political party

unalleviated /ùn ə léevi aytid/ *adj* not lessened or made more bearable

unallocated /un állə kaytid/ *adj* set aside for no particular person, group, or purpose

unalloyed /ùnnə lóyd/ *adj* **1** containing no impurities, and not mixed or alloyed with other metals **2** not mixed with anything else, especially anything that would dilute it or any other feeling that would diminish it ○ *unalloyed pleasure*

unalterable /un áwltərəb'l/ *adj* unable to be changed in any way —**unalterability** /un àwltərə bílləti/ *n* —**unalterableness** *n* —**unalterably** *adv*

unaltered /un áwltərd/ *adj* still the same, without having changed or having been changed

unambiguous /ùn am bíggyoo əss/ *adj* completely clear in meaning or intention and unable to be misunderstood —**unambiguously** *adv*

unambitious /ùn am bíshəss/ *adj* **1** having no strong desire to be highly successful in life **2** not requiring great effort or risk in order to succeed ○ *an unambitious project* —**unambitiously** *adv* —**unambitiousness** *n*

un-American *adj* **1** at odds with the customs, traditions, or ways of the people of the United States ○ *It's practically un-American not to like apple pie.* **2** unpatriotic or disloyal to the United States

unamplified /un ámpli fīd/ *adj* not made louder by electronic amplification

unanalysable /un ánnə līzəb'l/ *adj* impossible or very difficult to analyse

unaneled /ùnnə neéld/ *adj* in the Roman Catholic Church, not having received the last rites given to people who are dying or very ill (*archaic*) [Early 17C. < UN-[1] + *aneled*, past participle of obsolete *anele* 'anoint' < Old English *ele* 'oil' < Latin *oleum*.]

unanimous /yoo nánniməss/ *adj* **1** shared or taken as a view by all of the people concerned, with nobody disagreeing **2** with all members in agreement with each other ○ *Board members were unanimous in their rejection of the proposed merger.* [Early 17C. < Latin *unanimus* < *unus* 'one' + *animus* 'mind'.] —**unanimity** /yòonə nímməti/ *n* —**unanimously** *adv*

unannounced /ùn ə nównsst/ *adj* **1** without giving or being the subject of previous notification of arrival or intentions **2** not publicly reported

unanswerable /un áanssərəb'l/ *adj* **1** impossible to answer or solve **2** so clearly true that nobody could contradict or deny it —**unanswerableness** *n* —**unanswerably** *adv*

unanswered /un áanssərd/ *adj* not having received an answer or response ○ *The letter went unanswered.*

unanticipated /ùn an tíssi paytid/ *adj* **1** not foreseen or prepared for in advance **2** ⚠ not expected or scheduled in advance.

USAGE See ***anticipate***.

unapologetic /ùn ə pollə jéttik/ *adj* showing no regret for a previous action, or offering no apology for it —**unapologetically** *adv*

unappealable /ùnnə peéləb'l/ *adj* describes a case or judgment that is not open to appeal —**unappealably** *adv*

unappealing /ùnnə peéling/ *adj* not attractive or likely to be enjoyable —**unappealingly** *adv*

unappeased /ùn ə peézd/ *adj* not pacified or satisfied

unappetizing /un áppi tīzing/, **unappetising** *adj* **1** not looking good to eat, or not stimulating the appetite **2** not appealing, good-looking, or wholesome in form, function, or use —**unappetizingly** *adv*

unappreciated /ùn ə preéshi aytid/ *adj* not fully and properly valued, recognized, or understood

unappreciative /ùn ə preéshətiv/ *adj* failing to express or feel gratitude, approval, or full understanding

unapproachable /ùnnə próchəb'l/ *adj* **1** TOO UNFRIENDLY TO APPROACH OR CONTACT characterized by a formal, unfriendly, or hostile manner that discourages communication **2** INACCESSIBLE difficult to get to **3** UNRIVALLED so excellent that nothing or nobody else is nearly as good —**unapproachability** /ùnnə prócha bílləti/ *n* —**unapproachableness** *n* —**unapproachably** /ùnnə próchəbli/ *adv*

unappropriated /ùnnə própri aytid/ *adj* **1** not yet set aside for a specific purpose and therefore still available or free **2** not yet brought under the ownership or control of a particular person or organization

unapt /un ápt/ *adj* **1** lacking the qualities suitable or appropriate to a particular context **2** not likely or liable to do something (*formal*) ○ *unapt to cause any problems* —**unaptly** *adv* —**unaptness** *n*

unarable /un árrəb'l/ *adj* unsuitable for the cultivation of crops

ϟ**unarchive** /un áar kīv/ *vt* to retrieve a computer file from archive storage

unarguable /un áargyoo əb'l/ *adj* **1** so clearly true or correct that nobody can argue with it or deny it **2** not sound or convincing enough to be put forward as an argument —**unarguably** *adv*

unarm /un áarm/ *vt* to take arms away from a country, armed force, or person

unarmed /un áarmd/ *adj* **1** WITHOUT WEAPONS not carrying or using weapons **2** WITH NO OBVIOUS MEANS OF SELF-DEFENCE with no horns, claws, shells, thorns, prickles, or other means of self-protection **3** UNABLE TO FIRE describes a missile or projectile whose fuse or firing mechanism has been disabled

unarmoured /un áarmərd/ *adj* not protected by armour, especially not covered in armour plate

unaroused /ùn ə rówzd/ *adj* not having been stimulated or excited

unary /yoͻ́nəri/ *adj* describes a mathematical operation that is applied to only one member of a set at a time, e.g. squaring a number [Early 20C. < Latin *unus* 'one'.]

unashamed /únnə sháymd/ *adj* 1 not ashamed or embarrassed, and not feeling the need to apologize to others 2 not limited, restrained, or avoided out of a feeling of shame or embarrassment —**unashamedly** /-sháymidli/ *adv* —**unashamedness** /-sháymidnəss/ *n*

unasked /un áaskt/ *adj* 1 NOT ASKED not having been asked 2 NOT INVITED coming to a gathering without an invitation 3 NOT ASKED FOR providing something, e.g. assistance, that has not been asked for

unaspirated /un áspi raytid/ *adj* describes a letter 'h' at the beginning of a word that is not pronounced when the word is spoken, as in 'hour' or 'honour'

unassailable /únnə sáyləb'l/ *adj* 1 so sound or well established that it cannot be challenged or overtaken ○ *an unassailable lead* 2 so strong or impregnable that it cannot be successfully attacked —**unassailability** /únnə sáylə bílləti/ *n* —**unassailably** *adv*

unassertive /ún ə súrtiv/ *adj* not tending to act self-confidently or insist on a share of attention —**unassertively** *adv* —**unassertiveness** *n*

unassigned /ún ə sínd/ *adj* not having been designated for a particular task or purpose or for a particular person or group

unassisted /ún ə sístid/ *adj* 1 not given any help, or performed without help ○ *his own unassisted efforts* 2 *US* scored by a player without any help from a team mate

unassuming /únnə syoͻ́oming/ *adj* acting in a way that does not assume superiority —**unassumingly** *adv* —**unassumingness** *n*

unattached /únnə tácht/ *adj* 1 WITHOUT A SPOUSE OR PARTNER not married and not in a long-term romantic or sexual relationship 2 NOT JOINED not joined or attached, especially to other or larger organizations or bodies 3 NOT SEIZED FOR SECURITY describes property that is not taken away from its owner for security under the orders of a court of law

unattainable /ún ə táynəb'l/ *adj* impossible to reach or achieve —**unattainability** /-tayná bílləti/ *n* —**unattainableness** /-táynəb'lnəss/ *n* —**unattainably** *adv*

unattended /únnə téndid/ *adj* 1 WITH NO ONE THERE with no one present to listen, watch, or participate 2 NOT CARED FOR not looked after or seen to 3 NOT ESCORTED not accompanied or escorted (*formal*) 4 NOT HEEDED not listened to or heeded (*formal*) 5 NOT HAVING SOMETHING AS CONSEQUENCE not accompanied by something, or not having something as a result or consequence (*formal*)

unattractive /ún ə tráktiv/ *adj* 1 not having a beautiful, pleasing, or desirable appearance 2 not having any obvious advantages or interesting aspects —**unattractively** *adv* —**unattractiveness** *n*

~~unatural~~ incorrect spelling of **unnatural**

unau /yoͻ́ now/ (*plural* **unaus** *or* **unau**) *n* ZOOL = **two-toed sloth** [Late 18C. Via French < Tupi *unáu*.]

unauthorized /un áwthə rīzd/, **unauthorised** *adj* not having permission to do or say something, or for which permission has not been granted ○ *'No unauthorized entry'*

unavailable /ún ə váyləb'l/ *adj* 1 not obtainable or able to be used 2 unable to undertake something, or to be consulted —**unavailability** /ún ə vaylə bílləti/ *n*

unavailing /únnə váyling/ *adj* done but failing to achieve the desired result —**unavailingly** *adv*

unavenged /ún ə vénjd/ *adj* for which no one has been punished or no retaliatory action has been taken ○ *resolved his murder would not go unavenged*

unavoidable /únnə vóydəb'l/ *adj* that cannot be avoided —**unavoidability** /únnə vóydə bílləti/ *n* —**unavoidably** *adv*

unaware /únnə wáir/ *adj* 1 not conscious or aware of something 2 lacking important information or analysis ○ *a politically unaware generation* ■ *adv* = **unawares** —**unawarely** *adv* —**unawareness** *n*

USAGE unaware or **unawares**? ***Unaware*** is normally used as an adjective (*They were unaware of the danger*) whereas ***unawares*** is an adverb, used especially in the idiom *to catch* (or *take*) *somebody unawares*, but also in other ways: *They crept up on us unawares.*

unawares /únnə wáirz/ *adv* 1 without any warning or anticipation ○ *His question caught me unawares.* ○ *You took me completely unawares.* 2 without planning or intending to do something ○ *He took the wrong coat, unawares.* [Mid-16C. < UNAWARE + *-s*, adverbial suffix.]

USAGE See ***unaware***.

unb. *abbr* unbound

unbacked /un bákt/ *adj* 1 NOT SUPPORTED OR BACKED with no support or backing, especially financial backing 2 WITHOUT A BACK describes a chair that has been made without a back 3 NEVER RIDDEN describes a horse that has never been ridden ○ *an unbacked mare* 4 NOT BET ON describes a horse that has had no bets placed on its performance

unbaited /un báytid/ *adj* relating to a fishing hook or trap that does not have any bait

unbalance /un bállənss/ *vt* (**-ances, -ancing, -anced**) 1 KNOCK SOMETHING OFF BALANCE to make something lose its balance or equilibrium 2 MAKE SOMEBODY PSYCHOLOGICALLY UNSTABLE to make somebody psychologically or emotionally unstable ■ *n* STATE OF INSTABILITY the state of being unstable and out of balance —**unbalanceable** *adj*

unbalanced /un bállənst/ *adj* 1 WITHOUT EQUILIBRIUM lacking the proper distribution of weight or forces that would provide balance 2 PSYCHOLOGICALLY UNSTABLE unable to make sound judgments 3 ONE-SIDED done or provided from only one perspective ○ *unbalanced reporting* 4 WITH UNEQUAL DEBITS AND CREDITS in which the totalled debits and credits are not equal

unbaptized /un bap tízd/, **unbaptised** *adj* not having been accepted into the Christian religion through the sacrament of baptism

unbar /un báar/ (**-bars, -barring, -barred**) *vt* 1 to unlock or open a door or gate 2 to remove the bars or obstructions from something

unbd *abbr* unbound

unbearable /un báirəb'l/ *adj* difficult, unpleasant, or impossible to bear or tolerate —**unbearableness** *n* —**unbearably** *adv*

unbeatable /un beétəb'l/ *adj* too good or favourable to be beaten or surpassed —**unbeatably** *adv*

unbeaten /un beét'n/ *adj* 1 UNDEFEATED never having been defeated or outdone 2 NOT WHIPPED OR POUNDED not subjected to pounding, whipping, or beating as part of the preparation for cooking or eating 3 NOT TRAVELLED not made smooth from pedestrian or vehicular traffic 4 NOT OUT without being got out

unbecoming /ún bi kúmming/ *adj* 1 unsuitable or unattractive on the wearer 2 not suitable, especially as not conforming with accepted attitudes or behaviour —**unbecomingly** *adv* —**unbecomingness** *n*

unbeknown /únbi nṓn/, **unbeknownst** /únbi nṓnst/ *adj* 1 WITHOUT SOMEBODY KNOWING happening without a particular person knowing about it 2 NOT KNOWN TO not known or familiar to somebody ■ *adv* **unbeknownst** WITHOUT BEING SEEN without being noticed or seen by anybody ○ *slipped away unbeknownst* [Mid-17C. < UN-[1] + *beknown*, past participle of obsolete *beknow* 'know thoroughly' < KNOW.]

unbelief /únbi leéf/ *n* lack of religious or political belief

unbelievable /únbi leévəb'l/ *adj* 1 too unrealistic or improbable to be believed 2 used to emphasize that something is very great, or very good, bad, or impressive ○ *reacted with unbelievable agility* —**unbelievably** *adv*

unbeliever /únbi leévər/ *n* a person who does not believe in a specific religious faith or in conventional beliefs

unbelieving /únbi leéving/ *adj* 1 lacking belief or expressing disbelief about something 2 with no religious faith or doctrinal beliefs —**unbelievingly** *adv*

unbelt /un bélt/ *vt* 1 to unfasten the belt on a garment 2 to remove somebody or something from a supporting or restraining belt

unbenched /un bénch t/ *adj* describes a dog show where the entered dogs need to be present only for the judging of their breed or obedience class and are not assigned benches

unbend /un bénd/ (**-bends, -bending, -bent** /-bént/) *v* 1 *vti* MAKE OR BECOME RELAXED to become, or make somebody become, more informal, relaxed, or friendly 2 *vti* MAKE OR BECOME STRAIGHT to become, or make something become, straight after being bent, twisted, or flexed 3 *vt* UNFASTEN SAIL OR ROPE to free a sail, rope, or mooring line that was fastened —**unbendable** *adj*

unbending /un bénding/ *adj* 1 RESOLUTE not willing to change opinions, beliefs, or attitudes 2 STRICTLY OBSERVED strictly applied or observed 3 ALOOF formal or unfriendly in manner or behaviour —**unbendingly** *adv*

unbent[1] /un bént/ *adj* 1 not forced into submitting or giving in 2 not bent or twisted

unbent[2] past tense, past participle of **unbend**

unbiased /un bí əst/, **unbiassed** *adj* 1 fair and impartial rather than biased or prejudiced 2 in statistics, with an expected value that is equal to the parameter being estimated —**unbiasedly** *adv* —**unbiasedness** *n*

unbiblical /un bíbblik'l/ *adj* opposed or in contrast to the teachings of the Bible, or not present or approved in biblical teaching

unbidden /un bídd'n/ *adj, adv* (*literary*) 1 not wished for or willed 2 not asked for or invited

unbind /un bínd/ (**-binds, -binding, -bound, -bound** /-bównd/) *vt* (*literary*) 1 to free somebody from something restraining or restricting, e.g. a duty or obligation 2 to untie a person or animal

unbleached /un bleécht/ *adj* not treated with a bleach or whitener

unblemished /un blémmisht/ *adj* 1 not marked by any damage or imperfection such as a stain, scar, or scratch 2 not spoiled by wrongdoing or error ○ *an unblemished record*

unblessed /un blést/ *adj* 1 WITHOUT A BLESSING not given a blessing 2 UNFORTUNATE unfortunate or wretched (*literary*) 3 REGARDED AS EVIL in particular religions, regarded as behaving in unrighteous ways (*literary*) —**unblessedness** /un bléssidnəss/ *n*

unblinking /un blíngking/ *adj* 1 showing no emotion, reluctance, or hesitation 2 failing or unable to close and open the eyes in quick succession —**unblinkingly** *adv*

unblock /un blók/ *vt* to remove an obstruction from something in order to allow free access to it or a passage through it

unblushing /un blúshing/ *adj* feeling or showing no shame or embarrassment —**unblushingly** *adv* —**unblushingness** *n*

unbolt /un bṓlt/ *vt* to pull back the bolt or bolts on a door or gate, so that it can be opened

unbolted /un bṓltid/ *adj* 1 not fitted with bolts, or with bolts not fastened 2 describes flour or grain that has not had the coarse particles sifted from the fine ones

unbordered /un báwdərd/ *adj* 1 not having a border, especially one that is decorative ○ *unbordered photos* 2 not limited or otherwise restricted in any way ○ *unbordered access to government files*

unborn /ún báwrn/ *adj* 1 not yet born, but usually already conceived and gestating ○ *behaviour that could benefit the unborn child* 2 not thought of or begun yet (*literary*)

unbosom /un boͻ́ozzəm/ *v* (*literary*) 1 *vti* to express something previously suppressed or hidden 2 *vr* to reveal the thoughts, feelings, or secrets you have been keeping inside yourself

unbound[1] /ún bównd/ *adj* 1 WITHOUT A COVER not fastened inside a permanent cover 2 UNRESTRICTED having had restraints or fetters removed 3 NOT IN CHEMICAL COMBINATION free from chemical or physical combination 4 CONSTITUTING A WORD describes a morpheme that can form a word on its own without any added elements

unbound[2] past tense, past participle of **unbind**

unbounded /un bówndid/ *adj* 1 not controlled or restrained in any way 2 not subject to limits, boundaries, or restrictions —**unboundedly** *adv* —**unboundedness** *n*

unbowed /un bṓwd/ *adj* 1 having refused to submit or admit defeat 2 remaining in an erect position, not bent or bowed

unbrace /un bráyss/ (**-braces, -bracing, -braced**) *vt* to make something less tense or strained (*literary*)

unbranched /un bráancht/, **unbranching** /un bráanching/ *adj* not dividing into or producing branches

unbranded /un brándid/ *adj* 1 relating to goods that do not carry a maker's brand name 2 relating to a calf, cow, steer, horse, or similar animal that does not have an owner's brand marked on its hide ○ *unbranded cattle*

unbreakable /un bráykəb'l/ *adj* 1 impossible to break or smash 2 not able to be disobeyed, escaped from, or reneged on

nbred /un bréd/ *adj* **1 NOT TRAINED** not given training or instruction (*literary*) **2 NOT WELL BRED** lacking refinement or breeding (*literary*) **3 NOT YET MATED** not yet mated with another animal

nbridgeable /un bríjjəb'l/ *adj* **1** impossible to span by building a bridge across **2** impossible to reduce in distance or significance ○ *a seemingly unbridgeable gulf between the two delegations*

nbridle /un brīd'l/ (**-dles, -dling, -dled**) *vt* **1** to take the bridle from a horse **2** to take away the limits, controls, or restraints that apply to something

nbridled /un brīd'ld/ *adj* **1** freely and openly expressed **2** not fitted with a bridle —**unbridledly** *adv* —**unbridledness** *n*

nbroken /un brṓkən/ *adj* **1 WITHOUT GAPS OR PAUSES** with no gaps or pauses **2 ONGOING** continued without interruption **3 UNDEFEATED** not beaten or subdued **4 UNTAMED** not yet having submitted to human control ○ *an unbroken horse* **5 NOT FRAGMENTED** remaining intact or in one piece **6 NOT VIOLATED** having remained viable or in force —**unbrokenly** *adv* —**unbrokenness** *n*

nbundle /un búnd'l/ *vt* to sell or charge for related products and services separately, rather than as a unit

nburden /ún búrd'n/ *v* **1** *vr* to relieve yourself of something that has been worrying you by telling somebody about it (*formal*) **2** *vt* to take off a load that a person or animal has been carrying (*literary*)

nburnable /un búrnəb'l/ *adj* not able to be destroyed by burning ○ *Do not deposit unburnable material in the stoves or fireplaces.*

nburnt /un búrnt/, **unburned** /un búrnd/ *adj* not consumed, destroyed, or damaged by fire

nbutton /un bútt'n/ *v* **1** *vt* to undo a garment by unfastening the buttons **2** *vi* to relax and become more talkative (*informal*)

ncaged /un káyjd/ *adj* **1** no longer restrained in a cage **2** allowed to fly or roam freely

ncalled-for /un káwld-/ *adj* beyond what is necessary or expected, especially in being unjustifiably unkind or impolite

ncanny /un kánni/ (**-nier, -niest**) *adj* **1** too strange or unlikely to seem merely natural or human **2** unexpectedly accurate or precise ○ *an uncanny resemblance to the president* —**uncannily** *adv* —**uncanniness** *n*

ncap /un káp/ (**-caps, -capping, -capped**) *vt* to remove an upper limit or restriction from something

ncared-for /ùn káird-/ *adj* neglected and allowed to deteriorate

ncaring /un káiring/ *adj* **1** showing or feeling no compassion or sympathy for others **2** uninterested in or unworried about something ○ *totally uncaring of what the others might think of her* —**uncaringly** *adv* —**uncaringness** *n*

ncarpeted /un kaárpitid/ *adj* not covered with a carpet

ncastrated /un ka stráytid/ *adj* not having had the testicles removed

nceasing /un seéssing/ *adj* continuing without stopping, pausing, or diminishing —**unceasingly** *adv* —**unceasingness** *n*

ncensored /un sénssərd/ *adj* published, reported, or broadcast without being subject to censorship

nceremonious /ún serri mṓni əss/ *adj* **1** sudden and rather rude, with no concern for politeness or good manners **2** done without formality or ceremony —**unceremoniously** *adv* —**unceremoniousness** *n*

ncertain /un súrt'n/ *adj* **1 WITHOUT KNOWLEDGE** lacking clear knowledge or a definite opinion **2 NOT KNOWN OR SETTLED** not yet known, or remaining undecided **3 CHANGEABLE** likely to change, and therefore not reliable or stable **4 LACKING SELF-ASSURANCE** lacking self-assurance or confidence —**uncertainly** *adv* —**uncertainness** *n*

SYNONYMS See ***doubtful***.

ncertainty /un súrt'nti/ (*plural* **-ties**) *n* **1** the quality or state of being uncertain **2** something that nobody can predict or guarantee (*often plural*)

ncertainty principle *n* a principle in quantum mechanics holding that it is impossible to determine both the position and momentum of a particle at the same time

unchain /un cháyn/ *vt* **1** to take off the chain or chains holding a person or animal **2** to take away the limits, controls, or restraints that apply to something or somebody

unchallenged /un chállənjd/ *adj* **1 NOT CALLED INTO QUESTION** not subjected to opposition or demands for explanation and justification **2 PREDOMINANT** without opposition or competition **3 NOT HALTED** not stopped and asked to produce identification or account for your presence or actions ○ *The journalist gained unchallenged access to the cargo-handling area.*

unchangeable /un cháynjəb'l/ *adj* unable to be changed —**unchangeability** /un cháynjə bíllәti/ *n* —**unchangeably** /un cháynjəbli/ *adv*

unchanged /un cháynjd/ *adj* not having changed or having been changed

unchanging /un cháynjing/ *adj* not varying or showing signs of alteration but always remaining the same —**unchangingly** *adv*

uncharacteristic /ún karrəktə rístik/ *adj* not typical of the nature or behaviour of a person or thing —**uncharacteristically** *adv*

uncharged /un chaárjd/ *adj* with no electric charge

uncharitable /un chárritəb'l/ *adj* lacking in kindness or mercy —**uncharitably** *adv*

uncharted /un chaártid/ *adj* **1** not surveyed or recorded on a map **2** not previously encountered, experienced, or investigated

unchartered /un chaártərd/ *adj* not officially authorized or permitted

unchaste /un cháyst/ *adj* **1** freely indulging in sexual activity, especially in a way that is considered immoral **2** having extramarital sexual relations

unchecked /ún chékt/ *adj* **1** not limited or controlled, especially when restraint or control is required **2** remaining unverified or untested, especially for problems or imperfections

unchristian /ún krístyən/ *adj* **1** unkind or selfish, and therefore against Christian principles and teachings **2** not belonging to the Christian church

unchurch /ún chúrch/ *vt* **1** to expel somebody from a church **2** to remove the status of being a church from a building

uncial /únssi əl/ *n* **1 STYLE OF LETTER USED IN MANUSCRIPTS** a letter of the kind used in Greek and Latin manuscripts written between the third and ninth centuries that resembles a modern capital letter but is more rounded **2 MANUSCRIPT IN UNCIALS** a manuscript written in uncials ■ *adj* **WRITTEN IN UNCIALS** relating to or written in uncials [Mid-17C. < late Latin *unciales (litterae)* 'inch-high (letters)' < Latin *uncia* 'twelfth part, inch'.] —**uncially** *adv*

unciform /únssi fawrm/ *adj* shaped like a hook ■ *n* ANAT = **hamate** [Mid-18C. < Latin *uncus* 'hook'.]

uncinariasis /únssinə rī́ əssiss/ *n* infestation of the intestines with hookworms [Early 20C. < modern Latin *Uncinaria*, genus of hookworms < Latin *uncus* 'hook'.]

uncinate /únssinət/ *adj* shaped like a hook at the end [Mid-18C. < Latin *uncinatus* < *uncus* 'hook'.]

uncinus /un sīnəss/ (*plural* **-ni** /-sīnī/) *n* **1** a small hooked body part, e.g. the hook-shaped tooth of a gastropod or a chitinous hook on the body of an annelid **2** a cirrus cloud that is curled in a hook shape at one of its elongated ends [Mid-19C. < Latin, < *uncus* 'hook'.]

uncirculated /un súrkyōō laytid/ *adj* not distributed or passed from person to person or from place to place

uncircumcised /ún súrkəm sīzd/ *adj* not having had the prepuce of the penis or clitoris removed —**uncircumcision** /ún surkəm sízh'n/ *n*

uncivil /un sívv'l/ *adj* **1** behaving in a way that is seen as hostile or indifferent **2** lacking features thought to reflect a civilized society or individual (*archaic*) —**incivility** /únssi víllәti/ *n* —**uncivilly** *adv* —**uncivilness** *n*

uncivilized /un sívvə līzd/, **uncivilised** *adj* **1 NOT CULTURALLY ADVANCED** existing in a condition or behaving in ways that are thought to be socially or culturally primitive **2 REMOTE** far from civilized or settled areas **3 NOT POLITE, REFINED, OR COMFORTABLE** unacceptable or unbecoming to educated, cultured people used to refinement and comfort (*humorous*) —**uncivilizedly** /un sívvə līzidli/ *adv* —**uncivilizedness** *n*

unclad /un klád/ *adj* not wearing any clothes

unclaimed /un kláymd/ *adj* not demanded, requested, or collected by the owner or winner ○ *an unclaimed prize*

unclasp /un klaásp/ *vt* **1** to separate hands previously held together **2** to unfasten the clasp holding something closed

unclassified /un klássi fīd/ *adj* **1 NOT ARRANGED SYSTEMATICALLY** not arranged or grouped systematically **2 NOT SECRET** remaining open for examination by anyone who wishes access **3 NOT FOR MAIN TRAFFIC** not classed as a motorway, an A-road, or a B-road

uncle /úngk'l/ *n* **1** the brother of somebody's mother or father, or the husband of somebody's aunt (*capitalized before a name*) **2** a pawnbroker (*dated slang*) [13C. Via Old French *oncle* < Latin *avunculus* 'maternal uncle'.]

Uncle *n* a name some children are encouraged to call a man friend of one or both of their parents

unclean /ún kleén/ *adj* **1 DIRTY** dirty or insanitary **2 UNCHASTE** sinful, especially involving or guilty of committing a sexual sin **3 RELIGIOUSLY OR RITUALLY IMPURE** not pure according to religious rules or rituals —**uncleanness** *n*

SYNONYMS See ***dirty***.

uncleanly /un klénnli/ *adj* unclean (*formal or literary*) ■ *adv* in a way that is not clean —**uncleanliness** /un klénlinəss/ *n*

unclear /ún kleér/ *adj* **1** not obvious or easy to understand **2** not sure or not free from doubt

uncleared /un kleérd/ *adj* **1 NOT CLEARED OF OBSTRUCTIONS** not made free from obstacles, obstructions, or other unwanted items ○ *uncleared land* **2 NOT YET REMOVED** not yet removed from an area and still impeding access to it ○ *uncleared vegetation* **3 NOT PAID** not yet settled or paid off ○ *an uncleared debt* **4 NOT AUTHORIZED FOR PAYMENT** not yet passed through a clearing house or credited to the account of a payee ○ *an uncleared cheque* **5 WITH NO SECURITY CLEARANCE** not having been given a security clearance ○ *uncleared military personnel*

unclench /ún klénch/ *vti* to release the muscles in a part of your body that were being held tightly, or to relax from a tightened state

Uncle Sam *n* **1** a personification of the government of the United States, shown as a tall thin man with a white beard, wearing red and white striped trousers, a blue tail coat, and a stovepipe hat with a band of stars **2** the United States or the American people [19C. Invented < *US*, abbreviation of *United States*.]

Uncle Tom /-tóm/ *n* a highly offensive term for a Black man who is thought to be too solicitous of or subservient to white people (*taboo*) [Mid-19C. After a character in Harriet Beecher Stowe's novel *Uncle Tom's Cabin*.] —**Uncle Tomism** *n*

unclog /un klóg/ (**-clogs, -clogging, -clogged**) *vt* to remove a blockage from something such as a pipe

unclose /un klṓz/ (**-closes, -closing, -closed**) *vti* **1** to make or become open rather than closed **2** to reveal something, or to be revealed

unclosed /un klṓzd/ *adj* not in a closed condition

unclothe /un klṓth/ (**-clothes, -clothing, -clothed**) *vt* to remove the clothes or covering from somebody or something —**unclothed** *adj*

uncluttered /un klúttərd/ *adj* not having an excessive amount of objects or details and therefore not appearing untidy, obstructed, or cramped

unco /úngkō/ *adv Scotland* very or extremely ■ *adj Scotland* unusual or unfamiliar [15C. Variant of UNCOUTH.]

uncoagulated /únkō ággyōō laytid/ *adj* **1** not having thickened to form a semisolid mass ○ *uncoagulated blood* **2** not grouped together as a larger mass ○ *uncoagulated particles*

uncoil /ún kóyl/ *vti* to release something, or be released, from a coiled or wound position

uncollected /únkə léktid/ *adj* not yet having been collected

uncolonized /un kóllə nīzd/, **uncolonised** *adj* **1** describes a country or region in which people have not settled **2** describes an area in which a particular organism does not occur ○ *reduce the spread of nonindigenous aquatic organisms into uncolonized waters*

uncoloured /un kúllərd/ *adj* **1** showing or made with no particular colour or colours **2** not influenced or skewed by somebody else's attitude, character, or experiences

uncombined /ún kəm bīnd/ *adj* not joined or mixed together with anything else

uncomfortable /un kúmftəb'l/ *adj* **1** feeling a lack of or not providing physical comfort **2** feeling or making others feel awkward and ill-at-ease —**uncomfortableness** *n* —**uncomfortably** *adv*

uncommercial /únkə múrsh'l/ *adj* **1** NOT CONCERNED WITH COMMERCE OR BUSINESS not involved in commerce, especially not operated or organized for profit **2** AGAINST BUSINESS PRINCIPLES OR PRACTICES contrary to the way things are usually done in commerce or business **3** UNPROFITABLE unappealing to consumers and so not likely to turn a profit

uncommitted /únkə míttid/ *adj* **1** not dedicated to a particular principle, cause, or organization **2** not pledged to a particular cause, purpose, or course of action ○ *uncommitted funds*

uncommon /un kómmən/ *adj* **1** appearing or happening infrequently **2** used to emphasize the great extent of something —**uncommonness** *n*

uncommonly /un kómmənli/ *adv* **1** not frequently **2** to a degree or extent that is unusual or rare

uncommunicative /únkə myóonikətiv/ *adj* not willing to say much or tending not to say much —**uncommunicatively** *adv* —**uncommunicativeness** *n*

SYNONYMS See ***silent***.

uncomplaining /ún kəm pláyning/ *adj* expressing no dissatisfaction or unhappiness, especially in the midst of difficulties or hardship —**uncomplainingly** *adv*

uncompleted /ún kəm pleétid/ *adj* not finished or accomplished

uncomplicated /un kómpli kaytid/ *adj* simple, comprehensible, or easy to deal with

uncomplimentary /un kómpli méntəri/ *adj* expressing or intending to express an unflattering, disapproving, or contemptuous opinion

uncomprehending /ún kompri hénding/ *adj* having or showing an inability to understand something or somebody —**uncomprehendingly** *adv*

uncompromising /un kómprə mīzing/ *adj* feeling or showing no willingness to compromise or back down —**uncompromisingly** *adv* —**uncompromisingness** *n*

unconcealed /ún kən seéld/ *adj* expressed or displayed openly ○ *Members greeted the news with unconcealed delight.*

unconcern /únkən súrn/ *n* lack of concern or interest, especially where concern would be expected or thought appropriate

unconcerned /únkən súrnd/ *adj* **1** not worried or anxious, especially when this seems unexpected or unnatural **2** lacking concern or interest or unwilling to become involved in something —**unconcernedly** /-súrnidli/ *adv* —**unconcernedness** /-súrnidnəss/ *n*

uncondescending /ún kondi sénding/ *adj* implying or conveying no patronizing superiority

unconditional /únkən dísh'nəl/ *adj* complete or guaranteed, with no conditions, limitations, or provisos attached ○ *unconditional love* —**unconditionality** /únkən díshə nálləti/ *n* —**unconditionally** *adv*

unconditioned /únkən dísh'nd/ *adj* **1** without any conditions or limits restricting or affecting it **2** arising spontaneously and not as a result of learning or conditioning ○ *an unconditioned reflex* —**unconditionedness** *n*

unconditioned stimulus *n* a stimulus that evokes a reflexive response without prior conditioning or learning

unconfident /un kónfidənt/ *adj* showing or feeling nervousness or lack of self-assurance —**unconfidently** *adv*

unconfined /ún kən fínd/ *adj* **1** not enclosed or kept within limits or boundaries ○ *in an unconfined space* **2** expressed naturally and uninhibitedly ○ *Let joy be unconfined!*

unconfirmed /ún kən fúrmd/ *adj* not having been proved or officially stated to be true ○ *an unconfirmed sighting*

unconformable /únkən fáwrməb'l/ *adj* unwilling or unable to follow conventional social customs —**unconformability** /únkən fáwrmə bílləti/ *n* —**unconformably** *adv*

unconformity /únkən fáwrməti/ (*plural* **-formities**) *n* **1** LACK OF CONFORMITY behaviour or thinking that refuses to follow conventional social prescriptions **2** BREAK IN CONTINUITY IN SEDIMENTARY ROCKS a break in the continuity of sedimentary rocks resulting from erosion or cessation of deposition **3** SURFACE BETWEEN MISMATCHED STRATA the contact surface between two unconformable strata, often marked by angular discordance

unconfused /ún kən fyóozd/ *adj* able to think about or understand something clearly

uncongenial /ún kən jeényəl/ *adj* **1** not friendly or welcoming **2** not suitable or agreeable and therefore unlikely to find acceptance ○ *found the lifestyle decidedly uncongenial to him* —**uncongenially** *adv* —**uncongenialness** *n*

unconnected /únkə néktid/ *adj* not related or connected to something else or each other ○ *The two incidents are entirely unconnected.* —**unconnectedly** *adv* —**unconnectedness** *n*

unconquerable /un kóngkərəb'l/ *adj* unable to be conquered

unconquered /un kóngkərd/ *adj* not conquered, defeated, or mastered

unconscionable /un kónsh'nəb'l/ *adj* **1** shocking and morally unacceptable **2** far beyond what is considered reasonable —**unconscionableness** *n* —**unconscionably** *adv*

unconscious /un kónshəss/ *adj* **1** EXPERIENCING LOSS OF SENSES unable to see, hear, or otherwise sense what is going on, usually temporarily and often as a result of an accident or injury **2** UNAWARE not aware of something **3** UNINTENTIONAL not intended, or not realized or recognized ○ *unconscious irony* ■ *n* MIND'S HIDDEN PART the part of the mind containing memories, thoughts, feelings, and ideas that the person is not generally aware of but that manifest themselves in dreams and dissociated acts —**unconsciously** *adv* —**unconsciousness** *n*

unconsidered /únkən síddərd/ *adj* done without being properly thought about beforehand

~~**unconsious**~~ incorrect spelling of **unconscious**

unconsolidated /ún kən sólli daytid/ *adj* **1** not combined into a single or solid mass ○ *unconsolidated deposits* **2** not united as a single unit ○ *unconsolidated accounts*

unconstitutional /ún konsti tyóosh'nəl/ *adj* not allowed by or against the principles set down in a constitution, especially a nation's written constitution —**unconstitutionality** /ún konsti tyóosh'n álləti/ *n* —**unconstitutionally** *adv*

unconstrained /ún kən stráynd/ *adj* not restricted or inhibited by circumstances, self-consciousness, or reserve —**unconstrainedly** /ún kən stráynidli/ *adv*

unconstructive /ún kən strúktiv/ *adj* not carefully considered or helpful ○ *unconstructive criticism* —**unconstructively** *adv* —**unconstructiveness** *n*

uncontaminated /ún kən támmi naytid/ *adj* having had no harmful or polluting substances added ○ *uncontaminated waste products*

uncontrollable /únkən trṓləb'l/ *adj* **1** too strongly felt to be suppressed **2** too unruly or wild to discipline or control —**uncontrollability** /únkən trōlə bílləti/ *n* —**uncontrollably** *adv*

uncontrolled /ún kən trṓld/ *adj* **1** allowed free expression and kept under no restraint **2** done in a wild or haphazard way without proper care, skill, or discipline

uncontroversial /ún kontrə vúrsh'l/ *adj* unlikely to provoke argument or disapproval

unconventional /únkən vénsh'nəl/ *adj* different from what is regarded as normal or standard —**unconventionality** /únkən vénshə nálləti/ *n* —**unconventionally** *adv*

unconverted /ún kən vúrtid/ *adj* **1** NOT CONVERTED TO NEW BELIEF not persuaded to adopt a particular religion, belief, or point of view or to exchange a current religion, belief, or opinion for another **2** NOT ALTERED FOR NEW USE not altered so as to be suitable for a different use **3** NOT FOLLOWED BY SUCCESSFUL KICK describes a rugby try that is not followed by a successful kick over the crossbar to gain extra points

unconvinced /ún kən vínst/ *adj* not entirely persuaded that something is true or that somebody is telling the truth

unconvincing /ún kən vínssing/ *adj* **1** unable to persuade people to believe something or to accept something as actual or lifelike **2** not good enough to succeed or impress people —**unconvincingly** *adv*

uncooked /un kóokt/ *adj* not having been cooked

uncool /ún kóol/ *adj* **1** unfashionable, undesirable, or unacceptable, especially in the opinion of young peop[le] (*slang*) **2** not suitably relaxed, casual, or self-assure[d], especially in the opinion of young people (*informal*)

uncooperative /ún kō óppərətiv/ *adj* not willing to hel[p] by doing what is asked or required —**uncooperative[ly]** *adv* —**uncooperativeness** *n*

uncoordinated /ún kō áwrdi naytid/ *adj* **1** awkward wh[en] moving or doing something, as if different parts of th[e] body were not acting in harmony **2** with no o[r]ganization or proper cooperation between individua[ls] or groups

uncork /un káwrk/ *vt* **1** to open a bottle of somethin[g], especially wine, by taking out its cork **2** to release som[e]thing that has been restrained or repressed such as strong emotion

uncorrected /ún kə réktid/ *adj* left unchanged witho[ut] the things that are wrong being rectified or improve[d]

uncorroborated /ún kə róbbə raytid/ *adj* not backed u[p] by supporting facts, evidence, or testimony

uncorrupted /ún kə rúptid/ *adj* **1** not morally tainted [or] compromised by contact with wrongdoing or co[r]ruption **2** describes a computer file or database that [is] free of errors or viruses

uncountable /un kówntəb'l/ *adj* **1** too various or great [a] number to be counted **2** describes a noun that does n[ot] refer to a single object

uncounted /un kówntid/ *adj* **1** too numerous to be count[ed] **2** not, or not yet, subjected to a count

uncouple /un kúpp'l/ (**-ples, -pling, -pled**) *v* **1** *vti* to se[p]arate two things or one thing from another by undoi[ng] a fastening that connects them **2** *vt* to let loose som[e]thing that has been restrained

uncouth /un kóoth/ *adj* **1** behaving in an ill-mannered [or] unrefined way **2** clumsy and ungraceful [Old Engli[sh] *uncūþ* 'unknown' < *cūþ* 'known', past participle of *cunn[an]* 'know' (see CAN²)] —**uncouthly** *adv* —**uncouthness** *n*

uncovenanted /un kúvvənəntid/ *adj* not bound, san[c]tioned, or guaranteed by a covenant

uncover /un kúvvər/ *v* **1** *vti* TAKE THE COVER OFF to remove [a] covering from something **2** *vt* EXPOSE to find, find o[ut] about, or reveal something secret or previously hidd[en] ○ *uncover the truth about somebody* **3** *vti* TAKE OFF YOUR H[AT] to take off a hat or other head covering (*dated*)

uncovered /un kúvvərd/ *adj* **1** WITH NO COVERING witho[ut] any covering or protection **2** NOT INSURED not protect[ed] by insurance or guaranteed by some security **3** WITH T[HE] HEAD BARE with a hat or other head covering remove[d], usually as a sign of respect (*dated*)

uncreased /un kreést/ *adj* having a smooth surfa[ce] without any creases

uncreated /ún kri áytid/ *adj* not yet created, or existi[ng] without having been created ○ *an uncreated and etern[al] force*

uncreative /ún kri áytiv/ *adj* **1** unable to create things, [to] be imaginative, or to generate new ideas **2** offering litt[le] scope for imagination and originality

uncrewed /un króod/ *adj* not having any personnel, e[s]pecially not having a pilot or crew

uncritical /un kríttik'l/ *adj* accepting or approving som[e]thing without analysing or questioning it or di[s]criminating between good and bad —**uncritically** *adv*

uncross /un króss/ *vt* to straighten out from a cross[ed] position ○ *She sat crossing and uncrossing her arms i[m]patiently.*

uncrowned /ún krównd/ *adj* **1** possessing power, status, [or] wide respect but without an official title or recogniti[on] **2** with royal rank but not yet crowned

uncrystallized /un krístə līzd/, **uncrystallised** *adj* n[ot] having been formed into crystals

unction /úngksh'n/ *n* **1** ANOINTING WITH OIL the rubbing [or] sprinkling of oil on somebody as part of a religio[us] ceremony **2** SUBSTANCE USED IN A RITE an oil, ointment, [or] salve used in religious rites **3** REAL OR PRETENDED EAR[NESTNESS] real or pretended earnestness or fervour, e[s]pecially with regard to spiritual matters and especial[ly] when expressed in suitably solemn language **4** FLA[T]TERING EFFORTS TO CHARM excessively ingratiating effor[ts] to charm or convince somebody **5** SOMETHING SOOTHI[NG] something that soothes or comforts somebody [14C. < Latin *unction-* < *unguere* 'smear, anoint'.]

unctuous /úngkchoo əss/ *adj* **1** attempting to charm or convince somebody in an unpleasantly suave, smug, or smooth way **2** resembling or containing oil, fat, or grease [14C. < medieval Latin *unctuosus* < Latin *unctus* 'anointing' < *unguere* 'smear, anoint'.] —**unctuosity** /úngkchoo óssəti/ *n* —**unctuously** *adv* —**unctuousness** *n*

uncultivated /un kúlti vaytid/ *adj* **1** not prepared or used for the growing of crops **2** not having the knowledge, sophistication, or manners of somebody who has received a good academic and social education

uncultured /un kúlchərd/ *adj* not having or showing discriminating taste and cultural sophistication

uncured /un kyóord/ *adj* **1** not successfully treated or restored to health **2** not preserved by smoking, salting, pickling, or drying

uncurl /un kúrl/ *vti* to straighten something that was previously wound in a curl, coil, or spiral, or to become unwound or straight

uncus /úngkəss/ (*plural* **-ci** /ún sī/) *n* a body part shaped like a hook [Early 19C. Via modern Latin < Latin, 'hook'.]

uncut /ún kút/ *adj* **1 NOT CUT** with no part removed or divided by cutting **2 COMPLETE** not abridged, shortened, or censored **3 NOT FACETED** describes a gemstone in its original shape, before facets have been cut **4 WITH UNSEPARATED PAGES** with the edges of the pages not yet trimmed to separate them **5 NOT ADULTERATED** in a pure and unadulterated form (*informal*)

undamaged /un dámmijd/ *adj* not having been harmed physically or psychologically

undamped /un dámpt/ *adj* **1** not subdued or discouraged **2** describes a scientific instrument or system that is allowed to oscillate unchecked

undated /un dáytid/ *adj* **1** not having a date marked **2** not assigned to a particular year or period

undaunted /un dáwntid/ *adj* not afraid or deterred by the prospect of defeat, loss, or failure —**undauntedly** *adv* —**undauntedness** *n*

undead *npl* in fiction, especially vampire stories, people or other beings who are technically dead but still exist, move, and interact with the living in a physical form —**undead** *adj*

undealt /un délt/ *adj* relating to a card or pack of cards that has not been dealt

undecagon /un dékəgən/ *n* a plane figure with eleven sides and eleven angles [Early 18C. < Latin *undecim* 'eleven' + -GON, after DECAGON.]

undecayed /ún di káyd/ *adj* not rotten, deteriorated, decomposed, or disintegrated

undeceive /úndi seév/ (**-ceives, -ceiving, -ceived**) *vt* to tell the truth to somebody who has been misled (*often passive*) —**undeceiver** *n*

undecided /úndi sídid/ *adj* **1 NOT HAVING DECIDED** not yet having made a choice or decision **2 NOT FINALIZED** not yet settled or resolved ■ *n* **SOMEBODY WITHOUT MIND MADE UP** a person who has not yet made a decision or choice about something ○ *She was counted among the undecideds.* —**undecidedly** *adv* —**undecidedness** *n*

undecipherable /ún di sífərəb'l/ *adj* impossible or very difficult to read or understand, usually because of being badly written or in code

undecorated /un dékə raytid/ *adj* **1** not having any ornamentation, or not having been painted or wallpapered **2** not having received any military medals

undefeated /ún di feétid/ *adj* not yet having been beaten by an opponent, especially in a battle or contest

undefended /ún di féndid/ *adj* **1** unprotected against attack or harm ○ *an undefended border* **2** with no legal defence being pleaded, e.g. when a defendant fails to appear in court even though he or she has been legally required to do so ○ *an undefended divorce*

undefiled /ún di fíld/ *adj* pure and free from physical or moral pollution

undefined /úndi fínd/ *adj* **1** for which no definite limits have been decided **2** not given a definition, meaning, or value

undelete /úndi leét/ (**-letes, -leting, -leted**) *vt* to reinstate text or a file that has been deleted on a computer

undelivered /ún di lívvərd/ *adj* not delivered, especially not having reached the addressee

undemanding /ún di maánding/ *adj* **1** not requiring much physical or mental effort **2** not difficult to please or satisfy

undemarcated /un deé maar kaytid/ *adj* lacking fixed or official boundaries or divisions

undemocratic /ún demmə kráttik/ *adj* not in accordance with or not practising democracy —**undemocratically** *adv*

undemonstrative /úndi mónstrətiv/ *adj* tending not to show emotions openly —**undemonstratively** *adv* —**undemonstrativeness** *n*

undeniable /úndi ní əb'l/ *adj* **1 BEYOND QUESTION** unquestionably true or real and beyond dispute **2 UNABLE TO BE REFUSED** not able to be refused because of its importance or impact **3 INDISPUTABLY WORTHY** with worth, merit, or quality that cannot be doubted ○ *a person of undeniable character* —**undeniableness** *n* —**undeniably** *adv*

undependable /ún di péndəb'l/ *adj* not able to be depended upon

under /úndər/ CORE MEANING: a grammatical word used to express the concept of being beneath or below something, e.g. in location, size, age, or price ○ (prep) *Johnny had the book hidden under his tunic.* ○ (prep) *The machine is under a foot high and will fit on to any work surface.* ○ (prep) *The toy should not be given to children under three years old.* ○ (prep) *It's the best meal you can get for under £5.* ○ (adv) *For one week only, kids five and under eat free.*

1 *prep* **BELOW** directly below or underneath the base of something ○ *They were sheltering under a huge umbrella.* **2** *prep* **BENEATH** beneath a layer of something ○ *He had two sweaters on under his jacket.* **3** *prep* **LESS THAN** fewer in number than or less than something, e.g. in age, quantity, size, or price ○ *By the age of sixteen she was still under five feet tall.* **4** *prep* **SUBORDINATE TO** lower in rank or status than somebody ○ *I was under him in the company hierarchy.* **5** *prep* **SUBJECT TO** subject to the control or authority of somebody or something ○ *under existing legislation* ○ *working under a new boss* **6** *prep* **DURING THE RULE OF** during the rule of a person or government ○ *The crime rate had in fact gone down under the new mayor.* **7** *prep* **IN VIEW OF** in view of something or while something, especially conditions or circumstances, prevails ○ *Serious work is impossible under these conditions.* **8** *prep* **UNDERGOING A PROCESS** used to indicate that somebody or something is going through a particular process or experience ○ *the proposals currently under scrutiny by the committee* **9** *prep* **USING THE NAME OF** using a particular name, especially an assumed name ○ *travelling under a false name* **10** *prep* **CLASSIFIED WITHIN** classified as or in something ○ *You should find it in the filing cabinet under 'Miscellaneous'.* **11** *prep* **PLANTED WITH** planted with a particular crop ○ *That field will be under rye next year.* **12** *prep* **POWERED BY** powered or driven by something ○ *under sail* **13** *prep* **IN A SIGN OF THE ZODIAC** during a period in which the sun is in a particular position in the zodiac ○ *I was born under Sagittarius.* **14** *adv* **BELOW A SURFACE OR POINT** at or to a point or place at a lower level, especially one below a surface ○ *lifted the wire and crawled under* **15** *adv* **FEWER OR LESS** fewer or less than a previously given figure ○ *Employers with 50 employees or under are exempt.* **16** *adv, adj* **SUBSERVIENT** in or into a position of submissiveness or subservience (*informal*) ○ *policies designed to keep the masses under* **17** *adv, adj* **UNCONSCIOUS** in or into a state of unconsciousness or hypnosis (*informal*) ○ *could feel myself going under* ○ *waiting for the anaesthetist to put him under* [Old English, < Indo-European]

underachiever /úndər ə cheévər/ *n* **1** a student who does less well than might be expected, given the person's intelligence and aptitude **2** somebody or something that performs below expectations —**underachieve** *vi* —**underachievement** *n*

underact /úndər ákt/ *v* **1** *vti* to fail to play a role with enough power or conviction **2** *vt* to play a role in an understated way deliberately, for dramatic effect

underactive /úndər áktiv/ *adj* less active than is usual or desirable ○ *an underactive thyroid* —**underactivity** /úndər ak tívvəti/ *n*

underage /úndər áyj/ *adj* **1** below the legal or required age for something **2** carried on by people who are below the age at which something is legally permitted

underarm /úndər aarm/ *adj* **1 DONE WITH ARM BELOW SHOULDER** with the arm kept below shoulder height and usually close to the body when performing the action, e.g. throwing, serving, or bowling a ball. US term **underhand** *adj.* 2 **2 BELOW THE ARM** below the arm or for use under the arm, especially the armpit **3 FROM WRIST TO ARMPIT** relating to the area along the underside of the arm from armpit to wrist ■ *adv* **WITH ARM LOW** with the arm kept below shoulder height. US term **underhand** *adv.* 2 ■ *n* **AREA JUST BELOW THE ARM** the area below the arm on the body or on a garment, especially the armpit

underate past tense of **undereat**

underbelly /úndər belli/ (*plural* **-lies**) *n* **1 LOWEST PART OF AN ANIMAL'S BELLY** the underside of an animal, normally the part of the belly that is closest to the ground **2 WEAK POINT** a weak or vulnerable part of something ○ *the soft underbelly of the regime* **3 LOWER SURFACE** the underside of an object, especially an aircraft

underbid /úndər bíd/ *v* (**-bids, -bidding, -bid**) **1** *vti* **OFFER LESS** to offer a lower price than somebody else in competitive bidding **2** *vi* **MAKE TOO LOW A BID** to make a very low bid or too low a bid to obtain something **3** *vti* **BID LESS THAN THE VALUE OF YOUR CARDS** to bid less than the full value of a hand in cards ■ *n* **VERY LOW BID** a bid that is lower than somebody else's, or too low to obtain something —**underbidder** *n*

underbite /úndər bīt/ *n* a dental condition in which the lower incisor teeth overlap the upper. ◊ **overbite**

underbody /úndər boddi/ (*plural* **-ies**) *n* the underside of the body of a motor vehicle or of an animal

underbooked /úndər bóokt/ *adj* **1** not having attracted enough interest as a possible new securities issue in the period before offering **2** not having attracted enough bookings to cover costs, make a profit, or achieve some other desired effect

underbred /úndər bréd/ *adj* **1** not bred from pure stock **2** not brought up well or well-mannered —**underbreeding** /-breéding/ *n*

underbridge /úndər brij/ *n* a bridge built to allow people or vehicles to pass beneath a road, railway line, or canal

underbrush /úndər brush/ *n US, Can* = **undergrowth** *n.* 1

undercapitalize /úndər káppit'l īz/ (**-izes, -izing, -ized**), **undercapitalise** (**-ises, -ising, -ised**) *vti* to fail to supply an organization, especially a business, with enough capital to operate efficiently (*often passive*) —**undercapitalization** /úndər káppit'l ī záysh'n/ *n*

undercarriage /úndər karrij/ *n* **1** the framework of struts and wheels on which an aircraft runs when it moves on the ground **2** the supporting framework underneath a vehicle, to which wheels, tracks, or other means of locomotion are attached

undercharge *v* /úndər chaárj/ (**-charges, -charging, -charged**) **1** *vti* **NOT CHARGE SOMEBODY ENOUGH** to charge somebody too low a price for something **2** *vt* **INSERT TOO WEAK A CHARGE IN** to put an inadequate charge in a firearm ■ *n* /úndər chaarj/ **EXCESSIVELY LOW PRICE** a price charged that is too low

underclass /úndər klaass/ *n* a social class consisting of people so underprivileged that they are seen as being excluded from mainstream society

underclay /úndər klay/ *n* a layer of fine-grained sedimentary clay found beneath a coal seam, containing the fossilized roots of the plants that became the coal

underclothes /úndər klō*thz*/ *npl* = **underwear**

underclothing /úndər klō*thing*/ *n* = **underwear**

undercoat /úndər kōt/ *n* **1 COAT BENEATH THE FINAL PAINT COAT** a coat of paint or emulsion applied to a surface before a top coat is applied **2 PAINT TO BE COVERED** paint or emulsion designed to be used as an undercoat **3 SHORT HAIRS UNDER AN ANIMAL'S COAT** a dense layer of short hairs, fur, or wool beneath the longer growth of an animal's outer coat ■ *vt* **1 PAINT WITH UNDERCOAT** to apply an undercoat to a surface **2** *US* AUTOMOT = **underseal** *v.*

undercoating /úndər kōting/ *n US* AUTOMOT = **underseal** *n.*

underconsumption /úndər kən súmpsh'n/ *n* the use of a smaller amount of something than is expected or appropriate

undercook /úndər kóok/ *vt* to cook something for too short a time or at too low a heat, so that it is less well done that it should be

undercool /úndər kóol/ *vti* CHEM, PHYS = **supercool** *v.*

undercover /úndər kúvvər/ *adj* engaged in or involving the secret gathering of information, especially by somebody who disguises himself or herself as a member of the group whose activities are being investigated ○ *an undercover police officer* —**undercover** *adv*

undercroft /úndər kroft/ *n* an underground room, especially the crypt of a church

undercurrent /úndər kurrənt/ *n* **1** a current in a body of water or air that flows beneath another current or the surface **2** a feeling, opinion, force, or tendency that is felt to be present in somebody, but that is not openly shown or expressed and often differs markedly from the person's outward reaction ○ *an undercurrent of resentment*

undercut *v* /úndər kút/ (**-cuts, -cutting, -cut**) **1** *vt* **CHARGE A LOWER AMOUNT THAN** to charge less for something than somebody else **2** *vt* **REDUCE SOMETHING'S FORCE** to undermine something or detract from its force (*often passive*) **3** *vt* **CUT THE LOWER PART OF** to cut away or cut into the lower part of something, especially so as to leave a portion overhanging **4** *vti* **HIT A BALL WITH BACKSPIN** to hit a ball with a downward oblique stroke, e.g. in golf or tennis, so that it has backspin ■ *n* /úndər kut/ **1 CUT MADE IN A LOWER PART** a cut made below another or into the lower part of something **2 SOMETHING CUT AWAY** a piece of material that has been cut away from the lower part of something **3** *US* **NOTCH IN A TREE TRUNK** a notch cut in a tree that is being felled that helps it make a clean break and directs its fall **4 STROKE WITH BACKSPIN** a stroke that gives backspin to a ball

underdeveloped /úndər di vélləpt/ *adj* **1 NOT FULLY GROWN** not grown to a full or normal extent **2 WITHOUT MEANS FOR ECONOMIC GROWTH** lacking the technology and capital to make efficient use of available resources **3 NOT DEVELOPED ENOUGH** describes a photograph, negative, or film that was inadequately developed during processing, usually through being taken out of the developer too soon, and that lacks contrast as a result —**underdevelopment** *n*

underdog /úndər dog/ *n* **1** a person who is expected to lose a fight or contest **2** an unsuccessful person

underdone /úndər dún/ *adj* **1** not cooked as thoroughly as intended or required **2** cooked only lightly or partially to achieve a desired flavour or texture

underdrain *vt* /úndər dráyn/ to equip an area, especially cultivated land, with a system of underground drains ■ *n* /úndər drayn/ an underground drain or system of drains on agricultural land —**underdrainage** /úndər draynij/ *n*

underdress (*vi*) /úndər dréss/ *vi* to dress less fully or formally than an occasion or circumstance demands, e.g. in cold weather or for a social event (*often passive*) ■ *n* /únder dréss/ a garment or set of garments worn beneath others, especially if designed to be seen when worn

undereat /úndər éet/ (**-eats, -eating, -ate** /-ét, -áyt/, **-eaten** /-éet'n/) *vi* to eat an insufficient amount of food

underemphasize /úndər émfə sīz/ (**-sizes, -sizing, -sized**), **underemphasise** (**-sises, -sising, -sised**) *vt* to fail to give something the emphasis or importance it deserves —**underemphasis** *n*

underemployed /úndər im plóyd/ *adj* **1** not being used to full capacity in a job **2** working part-time but preferring full-time employment —**underemployment** *n*

underestimate *v* /úndər ésti mayt/ (**-mates, -mating, -mated**) **1** *vti* **MAKE TOO LOW AN ESTIMATE** to make an estimate of something that is too low ○ *We underestimated the time it would take.* **2** *vt* **MISJUDGE THE WORTH OF** to judge people or things as being inferior to their real value or ability ○ *Don't underestimate her – she's tougher than she looks.* ■ *n* /úndər éstimət/ **TOO LOW AN ESTIMATE** an estimate that is too low, or a judgment that is too unfavourable to somebody or something —**underestimation** /úndər ésti máysh'n/ *n*

underexploited /úndər ik splóytid/ *adj* not used sufficiently to gain the maximum possible benefit ○ *huge tracts of underexploited land that could be used to grow food*

underexpose /úndər ik spṓz/ (**-poses, -posing, -posed**) *vt* **1** to expose film to light for too short a time or to inadequate light **2** to fail to give somebody or something enough publicity —**underexposure** *n*

underfeed (**-feeds, -feeding, -fed** /-féd/) *vt* **1** to fail to give a person or animal enough to eat **2** to fuel something, e.g. an engine or a furnace, from underneath

underfelt /úndər felt/ *n* a layer of felt or other material put down on a floor before a carpet is laid to give better insulation and wear

underfinanced /úndər fi nánst, úndər fī́ nanst/ *adj* not provided with sufficient capital or funds to be able to run efficiently

underfloor /úndər fláwr/ *adj* locating beneath the flooring of a room or building ○ *underfloor heating*

⚡ **underflow** /úndərflō/ *n* the inability of a location in computer memory to handle data of an excessively small magnitude, or an instance of this. ◊ **overflow** *n.* 5

underfoot /úndər fŏŏt/ *adv* **1 BENEATH THE FEET** under the feet of a person or animal, on the ground, or between the feet and the ground ○ *It was muddy underfoot.* **2 IN THE WAY** creating an obstacle or obstruction **3 WITH ARROGANT DISREGARD OR DESTRUCTIVE INTENT** in a way that shows an arrogant or callous disregard or an intention to destroy ○ *trampled underfoot the feelings of everyone who worked for them*

underframe /úndər fraym/ *n* the supporting frame or chassis on which the body of a railway carriage or motor vehicle is built

underfund /úndər fúnd/ *vt* to fail to provide adequate funding for something such as a project or scheme (*often passive*) ○ *It was an ambitious plan, hopelessly underfunded from the start.*

underfunding /úndər fúnding/ *n* failure to make enough funds available for something ○ *The programme eventually foundered after years of underfunding.*

underfur /úndər fur/ *n* ZOOL = **undercoat** *n.* 3

undergarment /úndər gaarmənt/ *n* a piece of clothing worn beneath outer clothes, especially next to the skin, and not normally seen in public

undergird /úndər gúrd/ (**-girds, -girding, -girded** *or* **-girt** /-gúrt/, **-girded** *or* **-girt**) *vt* **1** to support or secure something from below, e.g. with ropes passed underneath **2** to provide something with support or reinforcement of any kind

underglaze /úndər glayz/ *adj* describes decoration or pigment applied to a piece of pottery before the glaze is put on ○ *an underglaze pigment* ■ *n* something, especially a decoration or pigment, that is applied to a piece of pottery before the glaze is put on

undergo /úndər gṓ/ (**-goes, -going, -went** /-wént/, **-gone** /-gón/) *vt* to experience or endure something, or have something happen to you ○ *You'll be obliged to undergo a thorough medical examination.* ○ *The city underwent a period of great change.*

undergrad /úndər grad/ *n* an undergraduate (*informal; often used before a noun*) ○ *undergrad humour* [Early 19C. Shortening.]

undergraduate /úndər grájjoo ət/ *n* a student at university or college who is studying for a first degree (*often before nouns*) ○ *undergraduate courses*

underground *adj* /úndər grownd/ **1 BENEATH THE EARTH'S SURFACE** located, happening, or operating beneath the surface of the Earth **2 COVERT** concealed and done in secret **3 CONTRARY TO THE PREVAILING CULTURE** separate from a prevailing social or artistic environment, and often exercising a subversive influence ○ *The story had been circulating in the underground press for years.* ■ *n* /úndər grownd/ **1 RAILWAY RUNNING BELOW GROUND** a railway system that runs below ground (*often used before a noun*) US term **subway** *n.* 2 **2 RESISTANCE MOVEMENT** a secret movement that aims to overthrow a government or fight against an occupying enemy **3 MOVEMENT CONTRARY TO THE PREVAILING CULTURE** a movement or group that is separate from the prevailing social or artistic environment and often exerts a subversive influence ■ *adv* /úndər grównd/ **1 BELOW GROUND** below the surface of the ground **2 SECRETLY** in secret or in hiding

Underground Railroad *n* a secret organization that helped enslaved labourers flee from the S United States to Canada or other places of safety prior to the abolition of slavery

undergrown /úndər grōn, úndər grṓn/ *adj* **1** not grown to the expected size **2** having or covered with undergrowth

undergrowth /úndər grōth/ *n* **1** shrubs, small trees, or other vegetation growing beneath the trees in a forest **2** growth that is less than expected **3** ZOOL = **undercoat** *n.* 3

underhand /úndər hánd, úndər hand/ *adj* **1** done secretively and dishonestly or with the intention to deceive or cheat somebody **2** *US* SPORTS = **underarm** *adj.* 1 ■ *adv* **1** in a secretive and dishonest way **2** *US* SPORTS = **underarm** *adv.*

underhanded /úndər hándid/ *adj, adv* = **underhand** *adj.* 1, **underhand** *adv.* 1 —**underhandedly** *adv* —**underhandedness** *n*

underhung /úndər húng/ *adj* **1** describes a lower jaw tha projects beyond the upper jaw **2** running on a rail o track situated underneath ○ *underhung sliding doors*

underinsure /úndərin shóor/ (**-sures, -suring, -sured**) *v* to take out insufficient insurance to cover the value o the article that is being insured

underlain past participle of **underlie**

underlay[1] *vt* /úndər láy/ (**-lays, -laying, -laid** /-láyd/ **PROVIDE WITH SOMETHING UNDERNEATH** to lay somethin underneath something else (*often passive*) ■ *n* /únde lay/ **1 LAYER BENEATH CARPET** a layer of cushioning an insulating material put down on a floor before a carpe is laid **2 SUPPORT FOR** something laid beneath somethin else as a base, support, or foundation —**underlaid** *adj*

USAGE underlay or **underlie**? Unlike the root words *lay* and *lie*, both verbs are transitive (i.e. take an object). The mor common word is ***underlie***, and this has a wider range o meanings including the figurative meaning 'be the basis o cause of something': *This trend underlies all the socia changes of recent times.* The primary meaning of ***underla*** is 'to lay something underneath something else' (*We under laid the carpet with felt*), and in this meaning it also acts as a noun (with the stress on the first syllable).

underlay[2] past tense of **underlie**

underlayer /úndər layər/ *n* a layer that exists or is applied before one or more top layers

underlet /úndər lét/ (**-lets, -letting, -let**) *v* **1** *vt* to let a property for less than its full value **2** *vti* = **sublet** *v.*

underlie /úndər lī́/ (**-lies, -lying, -lay** /-láy/, **-lain** /-láyn/) *v* **1 LIE BENEATH** to lie or be put under something else **2 BE THE FOUNDATION OF** to be the basis or cause of somethin ○ *the assumptions that underlie this argument* **3 HAVE FI NANCIAL PRIORITY OVER** to take priority over other financia rights or securities ○ *This claim underlies yours.*

USAGE See ***underlay***[1].

underline *vt* /úndər lī́n/ (**-lines, -lining, -lined**) **1 PUT LINE BELOW** to draw or type a line under something **2 EMPHASIZE** to give emphasis or extra force to something ■ *n* /úndər līn/ **1 LINE BENEATH** a line drawn or typed unde something **2 CAPTION UNDER AN ILLUSTRATION** a captio placed below an illustration —**underliner** *n*

underling /úndərling/ *n* a servant or subordinate of somebody else, especially one regarded as of little worth o importance

underlip /úndər lip/ *n* the lower lip of a person or anima

underlying /úndər lī́ ing/ *adj* **1 LYING UNDERNEATH** positioned beneath something else ○ *the underlying rock strata* **2 HIDDEN AND SIGNIFICANT** present and important but no immediately obvious ○ *the underlying reasons for his odd behaviour* **3 ESSENTIAL** basic or fundamental to something ○ *at odds with the underlying ideology of the party* **4 FINANCIALLY MOST IMPORTANT** describes financial obligations or assets that take priority over others

undermentioned /úndər mensh'nd/ *adj* named or listed below, or later in a document (*formal*)

undermine /úndər mī́n/ (**-mines, -mining, -mined**) *vt* **1 ERODE** to weaken something by removing or wearing away material from its base or from beneath it ○ *The chalk cliffs are being gradually undermined by the waves.* **2 WEAKEN GRADUALLY** to diminish or weaken something gradually ○ *Successive failures at job interviews began to undermine my confidence.* **3 WEAKEN INSIDIOUSLY** to demoralize somebody or something by covert and malicious action

undermost /úndər mōst/ *adj* lowest or last in position, status, or level ■ *adv* in the lowest or last place

underneath /úndər néeth/ CORE MEANING: a grammatical word indicating that something is below or beneath another thing, and may be covered by it ○ (adv) *Underneath, on the floor, was what appeared to be a heap of black clothes.* ○ (prep) *I left the key underneath the doormat.*

1 *prep, adv* **UNDERLYING** underlying something that is shown on the surface or openly expressed ○ (prep) *Underneath her confident exterior she was a very shy person.* ○ (adv) *There must be deeper problems underneath.* **2** *adv, adj* **ON THE LOWER PART OF** on the bottom of something or the part that faces towards the ground ○ (adv) *brown with white feathers underneath* ○ (adj) *The underneath part is hard to reach.* **3** *n* **LOWER PART** the bottom part of something or the part that faces towards the ground [Old English *underneoþan* < UNDER + *neoþan* 'beneath']

undernourish /úndər núrrish/ *vt* to fail to supply somebody with enough food or other resources to provide for proper development (*often passive*) —**undernourishment** *n*

undernourished /úndər núrrishd/ *adj* without having had enough food or nutrients for good health

underpainting /úndər paynting/ *n* painting on a canvas or frame that is later entirely or partly covered by another layer of paint

underpants /úndər pants/ *npl* briefs or shorts worn as underclothes (+ *plural verb*)

underparts /úndər paarts/ *npl* the belly and sides of an animal, especially a bird

underpass /úndər paass/ *n* **1** a part of a road that crosses under another road or a railway line **2** a tunnel for pedestrians beneath a road or railway

underpay /úndər páy/ (**-pays, -paying, -paid**) *vt* to pay somebody less than he or she deserves or than is usual, or to fail to pay the full amount of something —**underpayment** *n*

underperform /úndər pər fáwrm/ *vi* to do less well than expected or than something or somebody else ○ *underperforming investments* —**underperformance** *n* —**underperformer** *n*

underpin /úndər pín/ (**-pins, -pinning, -pinned**) *vt* **1** to support a weakened wall or structure by propping it up from below **2** to act as a support or foundation for something (*often passive*) ○ *the hard facts that underpin these assumptions*

underpinning /úndər pinning/ *n* **1** a structure built to support a weakened wall or building **2** something that supports or acts as a foundation for something (*usually plural*)

underplay /úndər pláy/ *v* **1** *vti* **ACT A ROLE SUBTLY** to act a role in a deliberately restrained or subtle way **2** *vt* **DO SUBTLY** to present or deal with something in a deliberately restrained or subtle way **3** *vi* **PLAY A LOWER CARD** to play a lower card while holding a higher one

underplot /úndər plot/ *n* a secondary plot in a play, novel, or other work of fiction

underpopulated /úndər póppyoō laytid/ *adj* having a smaller population than is desirable or expected ○ *underpopulated rural areas* —**underpopulation** /úndər poppyoō láysh'n/ *n*

underprice /úndər príss/ (**-prices, -pricing, -priced**) *vt* to put a price on something for sale that is less than its actual value

underprivileged /úndər prívəlijd/ *adj* deprived of many of the rights and privileges enjoyed by most people in society, usually as a result of poverty (*used euphemistically*) ■ *n* underprivileged people considered as a social group (*used euphemistically*)

underproduction /úndər prə dúksh'n/ *n* the production of something in smaller quantities than is desirable or forecast

underproof /úndər proōf/ *adj* describes an alcoholic drink that contains less alcohol than is standard or than is legally required

underprop /úndər próp/ (**-props, -propping, -propped**) *vt* to prop something up from underneath —**underpropper** *n*

underquote /úndər kwṓt/ (**-quotes, -quoting, -quoted**) *v* **1** *vti* to offer something for sale at a lower price than the market value **2** *vt* to quote a price for something that is lower than that quoted by somebody else

underrate /úndər ráyt/ (**-rates, -rating, -rated**) *vt* to judge the value, degree, or worth of somebody or something to be less than it really is ○ *a greatly underrated writer*

underreport /úndər ri páwrt/ *vt* to declare or report a number or amount to be smaller than is actually the case

underrepresent /úndər réppri zént/ *vt* **1** to contain a disproportionately small number of representatives of a particular population group or a particular type of thing (*often passive*) ○ *addressing the problem of women being underrepresented in government* **2** to present something as smaller, less widespread, or less important than it actually is —**underrepresentation** /úndər réppri zen táysh'n/ *n*

underrun *v* /úndər rún/ (**-runs, -running, -ran** /-rán/, **-run**) **1** *vt* **MOVE UNDER** to run, pass, or go under something **2** *vti* **PASS SOMETHING OVER A BOAT FOR INSPECTION** to pass something such as a net or cable over the deck of a boat, hauling it in on one side and putting it back into the water on the other, so that it can be inspected or repaired ■ *n* /úndər run/ **1 LOWER-THAN-ESTIMATED COST** a cost or expense that is less than anticipated **2 LOWER-THAN-REQUIRED PRODUCTION RUN** a production run of a manufactured or printed item that is less than the quantity ordered

undersaturated /úndər sáchə raytid/ *adj* describes igneous rock that contains low levels of combined silica and no free silica

underscore *vt* /úndər skáwr/ (**-scores, -scoring, -scored**) **1 DRAW A LINE UNDER** to draw a line underneath something **2 EMPHASIZE** to give emphasis or extra force to something ■ *n* /úndər skawr/ **1 LINE UNDER** a line drawn underneath something **2 BACKGROUND MUSIC** a piece of background music accompanying action or dialogue in a film

undersea /úndər see/ *adj* existing, carried out, or designed for use below the surface of the sea ■ *adv* **undersea, underseas** in or into the area below the surface of the sea

underseal *n* /úndər seel/ a coating applied to the underside of a motor vehicle to retard rust and corrosion. US term **undercoating** ■ *vt* /úndər seél/ to apply an underseal to the underside of a motor vehicle. US term **undercoat** *v.* 2

undersecretary /úndər sékritəri/ (*plural* **-ies**) *n* **1** a secretary who ranks just below a chief secretary in a government or bureaucratic organization **2** a government minister who is subordinate to the secretary of state for a government department —**undersecretariat** /úndər sékri táiri ət/ *n* —**undersecretaryship** *n*

undersell /úndər sél/ (**-sells, -selling, -sold**) *vt* **1 SELL BELOW ITS PROPER VALUE** to sell something at a price below its full or usual value **2 SELL MORE CHEAPLY THAN** to sell something more cheaply than a competitor **3 ADVERTISE WITH TOO LITTLE ENTHUSIASM** to present the merits of something or somebody with too little enthusiasm or conviction or in too restrained or understated a way —**underseller** *n*

underset *n* /úndər set/ **1 OCEAN UNDERCURRENT** an ocean undercurrent that runs in a direction contrary to the direction of the surface waves **2 UNDERLYING ORE** a vein of ore lying beneath another layer ■ *vt* /úndər sét/ (**-sets, -setting, -set**) **PROVIDE A PROP FOR** to support something from below

undersexed /úndər sékst/ *adj* having less sex drive or less interest in sex than some other people

undershirt /úndər shurt/ *n US* CLOTHING = **vest** *n.* 2

undershoot /úndər shoōt/ (**-shoots, -shooting, -shot, -shot** /-shót/) *vti* **1** to land an aircraft short of a landing area ○ *The pilot undershot the runway.* **2** to shoot something, e.g. an arrow, so that it lands short of the target

undershorts /úndər shawrts/ *npl US* shorts or briefs worn as underclothes by men and boys (*informal; + plural verb*)

undershot /úndər shot/ *adj* **1** = **underhung** *adj.* 1 **2** describes a device, especially a waterwheel, that is driven by water flowing beneath it

undershrub /úndər shrub/ *n* PLANT SCI = **subshrub**

underside /úndər sīd/ *n* **1** the lower side or bottom of something **2** an aspect of something that is undesirable or unpleasant and usually hidden

undersigned /úndər sīnd/ *n* (*plural* **-signed**) a person whose signature appears on the document being read (*formal*) ■ *adj* with their signatures appearing below

undersized /úndər sīzd/ *adj* smaller than the prevailing or preferred size

underskirt /úndər skurt/ *n* a skirt worn under another skirt

underslung /úndər slúng/ *adj* suspended or supported from above, like a motor vehicle chassis that is suspended from the axles

undersoil /úndər soyl/ *n* = **subsoil** *n.*

undersold past tense, past participle of **undersell**

underspend /úndər spénd/ (**-spends, -spending, -spent** /-spént/) *vi* to spend less money than is required or expected —**underspend** *n*

understaff /úndər staáf/ *vt* to provide a workplace or an organization with inadequate or insufficient staff

understand /úndər stánd/ (**-stands, -standing, -stood** /-stoōd/) *v* **1** *vti* **GRASP THE MEANING OF SOMETHING** to know or be able to explain to yourself the nature of somebody or something, or the meaning or cause of something ○ *I can't understand what all the fuss is about.* **2** *vti* **COME TO KNOW** to realize or become aware of something ○ *Only then did she understand the urgency of the situation.* **3** *vt* **BE ABLE TO HANDLE** to know and be able to use something such as a foreign language ○ *She thoroughly understood the workings of the system.* **4** *vti* **KNOW AND SYMPATHIZE** to recognize somebody's character or somebody's situation, especially in a sympathetic, tolerant, or empathetic way ○ *It's such a relief to find someone who understands.* **5** *vt* **TAKE AS MEANT** to interpret something in a particular way, or to infer or deduce a particular meaning from something ○ *I understood it as a peacemaking gesture.* ○ *Am I to understand from this that you are refusing our offer?* **6** *vt* **TAKE AS SETTLED** to believe something to be agreed, settled, or firmly communicated ○ *The bank was given to understand that you would repay the loan in six months.* **7** *vt* **KNOW BY LEARNING OR HEARING** to gather or assume something on the basis of having heard or been told it ○ *They're not due back, so I understand, until next Tuesday.* [Old English *understandan* < UNDER + *standan* (see STAND)]

understandable /úndər stándəb'l/ *adj* **1** having a meaning or nature that can be understood ○ *Try to make it understandable to a nonspecialist.* **2** able to be accepted as normal, reasonable, or forgivable ○ *Under the circumstances it was a perfectly understandable reaction.* —**understandability** /úndər stándə bílləti/ *n* —**understandably** *adv*

understanding /úndər stánding/ *n* **1 ABILITY TO GRASP A MEANING** the ability to perceive and explain the meaning or the nature of somebody or something ○ *Surely even someone with a very limited understanding could see the logic in that.* **2 INTERPRETATION OF SOMETHING** somebody's interpretation of something, or a belief or opinion based on an interpretation of or inference from something ○ *It was my understanding that the costs would be shared equally.* **3 MUTUAL COMPREHENSION** an agreement, often an unofficial or unspoken one ○ *I'm sure we can come to an understanding about this.* **4 KNOWLEDGE OF ANOTHER'S NATURE** a sympathetic, empathetic, or tolerant recognition of somebody else's nature or situation ○ *I thought you of all people would show a little understanding.* ■ *adj* **1 SYMPATHETICALLY AWARE** sympathetic, empathetic, or tolerant in recognizing somebody's or something's character and situation ○ *fortunate in having understanding parents* **2 ABLE TO KNOW** able to comprehend the sense or meaning of something (*archaic*) —**understandingly** *adv*

understate /úndər stáyt/ (**-states, -stating, -stated**) *vt* **1** to express something in a deliberately less dramatic, emphatic, or emotional way than it seems to warrant, often in order to increase its actual effect or for the sake of irony **2** to describe something as being smaller in quantity or number than it really is ○ *The official account understates the true costs of the delay.*

understated /úndər stáytid/ *adj* achieving its effect through restraint, subtlety, and good taste ○ *understated elegance* —**understatedness** *n*

understatement /úndər staytmənt, úndər stáytmənt/ *n* **1** a statement, or a way of expressing yourself, that is deliberately less forceful or dramatic than the subject would seem to justify or require **2** a statement that underrepresents or underreports something

understeer *vi* /úndər steér/ to turn less sharply than the turning of a steering wheel would lead the driver to expect ■ *n* /úndər steer/ a motor vehicle's tendency to turn less sharply than expected

understood /úndər stoōd/ past tense, past participle of **understand** ■ *adj* agreed, assumed, or implied, especially without being openly or officially expressed

understorey /úndər stawri/ (*plural* **-reys**) *n* a layer of small trees and shrubs below the level of the taller trees in a forest

understrapper /úndər strapər/ *n* a subordinate (*dated formal*) [Early 18C. < *strapper* 'person who straps or harnesses horses'.]

understrength /úndər stréngth/ *adj* having inadequate strength, especially less than the usual or desirable number of personnel

understudy /úndər studi/ *n* (*plural* **-ies**) **1 SUBSTITUTE ACTOR** an actor who learns the role of another actor so as to be able to act as a replacement if necessary **2 TRAINED SUBSTITUTE** a trained replacement or substitute for somebody ■ *vti* (**-ies, -ying, -ied**) **BE A SUBSTITUTE ACTOR** to learn the role of another actor so as to be able to replace him or her if necessary

undersubscribed /úndər səb skríbd/ adj with fewer than the expected number of people subscribing or showing an interest, often not enough people to make something viable ○ We couldn't offer the course as it was undersubscribed.

undersurface /úndər surfiss/ n the lower or downward-facing surface of something

undertake /úndər táyk/ (-takes, -taking, -took /-tŏok/, -taken /-táykən/) v 1 vti to make a commitment to do something ○ Jo undertook to find out the cost of flights. 2 vt to begin to do something or to set out on something ○ They were prepared to undertake the work at the formerly agreed price.

undertaker n 1 somebody whose profession is to prepare the dead for burial or cremation and to arrange funerals. US term **funeral director** 2 a person who sets about doing a task

undertaking n 1 TASK a task or project ○ It was a colossal undertaking. 2 PLEDGE TO DO SOMETHING a promise or agreement to do something ○ She gave an undertaking to keep it for a year. 3 FUNERAL BUSINESS the business of preparing the dead for burial or cremation and arranging funerals

under-the-counter adj sold or obtained clandestinely or illegally (not hyphenated after verbs)

under-the-table adj done or organized clandestinely and often illegally (not hyphenated after verbs)

underthings /úndər thingz/ npl underwear, especially women's underwear

underthrust /úndər thrust/ n a reverse fault in which a lower layer of rock is driven underneath a higher, relatively passive layer

undertint /úndər tint/ n a slight or subtle tint

undertone /úndər tōn/ n 1 LOW TONE a quiet, subdued, or background tone, especially of the voice ○ He spoke in an undertone. 2 UNDERLYING QUALITY OR ELEMENT something that is suggested or implied rather than stated openly ○ undertones of menace 3 MUTED COLOUR a subdued colour

undertow /úndər tō/ n 1 the seaward pull of water away from a shore after a wave has broken 2 an underlying tendency or force that runs in the opposite direction to the apparent one ○ An undertow of dissatisfaction made it difficult to carry everyone with us.

undertrick /úndər trik/ n in bridge, a trick short of the number declared by a player

undertrump /úndər trúmp/ vi in cards, to play a trump that is lower than a trump that has already been played in a hand

underused /úndər yŏozd/ adj not used as much as is expected, appropriate, or desirable —**underuse** /úndər yŏoss/ n

underutilized /úndər yŏoti ītzd/, **underutilised** adj not used as much as expected, appropriate, or desirable —**underutilization** /úndər yŏoti īt záysh'n/ n

undervalue /úndər vállyoo/ (-ues, -uing, -ued) vt 1 to judge the value of something or somebody as being lower than it really is ○ buy up stock that is undervalued 2 to hold too low an opinion of something or somebody —**undervaluation** /úndər vállyoo áysh'n/ n

underwater adj /úndər wawtər/ 1 BELOW THE WATER SURFACE existing, carried out, or designed for use below the surface of water 2 UNDER A SHIP'S WATERLINE below the waterline in a ship ■ adv /úndər wáwtər/ BELOW THE WATER SURFACE on or to a place below the surface of a body of water ■ n /úndər wawtər/ WATER UNDERNEATH THE SURFACE the water beneath the surface of a river, lake, or sea

under way, **underway** /úndər wáy/ adj in motion or progress ○ not long before the project was under way

USAGE **under way** or **underway**? Although the form **underway** is often seen, and has long been in use, **under way** is still widely preferred. The only exception to this is the adjectival use that precedes the noun: The submarine received underway servicing.

underwear /úndər wair/ n clothes worn beneath outer clothes, usually next to the skin and not normally seen in public

underweight /úndər wáyt/ adj weighing less than is normal or required

underwent past tense of **undergo**

underwhelm /úndər wélm/ vt to fail notably to impress or excite somebody (humorous) [Mid-20C. After OVER-WHELM.] —**underwhelming** adj

underwing /úndər wing/ n 1 HIND WING OF AN INSECT a hind wing of an insect such as a beetle, especially when covered by a forewing while the insect is not in flight 2 MOTH WITH BRIGHT WINGS a moth that has brightly coloured hind wings that become visible only in flight. Genus: Catocala. 3 LOWER SIDE OF A BIRD'S WING the underside of a bird's wing

underwire /úndər wīr/ n a wire sewn into the lining under each cup of a brassiere to provide support — **underwired** adj

underwood /úndər wŏod/ n ECOL = **undergrowth** n. 1

underworld /úndər wurld/ n 1 the part of society that lives by crime (often before nouns) ○ an underworld shooting 2 in classical mythology, the place beneath the earth where the souls of the dead go

underwrite /úndər rīt, úndər rīt/ (-writes, -writing, -wrote /úndər rōt, úndər rōt/, -written /úndər ritt'n, úndər ritt'n/) v 1 vti ISSUE INSURANCE to insure somebody or something by accepting liability for specified losses, or to be in the business of doing this 2 vti AGREE TO BUY UNSOLD SECURITIES to guarantee the sale of an issue of securities at a fixed price 3 vti SUBSIDIZE to agree to provide funds for something and to cover any losses ○ The tour was underwritten by an electronics company. 4 vt LEND SUPPORT TO to give support to somebody or something, especially by signing a document 5 vt WRITE BENEATH OTHER WRITING to write something, or add a signature, underneath other written matter [15C. After Latin subscribere 'write underneath, sign'.]

underwriter /úndər rītər/ n 1 INSURER COVERING LIABILITIES a person, firm, or organization that issues insurance and accepts liability for specified risks 2 SOMEBODY ASSESSING RISKS ON INSURANCE somebody employed by an insurance company to assess risks and fix premiums 3 GUARANTOR OF A SECURITIES ISSUE a person or organization that agrees to buy at a fixed price any unsold part of an issue of securities

undescended /úndi séndid/ adj describes a testicle that has remained in the inguinal canal and has not descended into the scrotum

undeserved /úndi zúrvd/ adj unfairly awarded or endured, or not merited on the basis of the facts — **undeservedly** /úndi zúrvidli/ adv

undeserving /úndi zúrving/ adj unworthy of receiving benefits or rewards

undesigning /úndi zíning/ adj not trying to deceive or manipulate

undesirable /úndi zírəb'l/ adj not wanted, liked, or approved of ■ n somebody or something regarded as undesirable —**undesirability** /úndi zírə bílləti/ n —**undesirably** adv

undesired /úndi zírd/ adj not wanted, especially because of being troublesome, superfluous, or interfering

undetailed /un dée tayld/ adj containing or characterized by little or no detail

undetectable /úndi téktəb'l/ adj impossible to detect, or so small or slight as to be unnoticed —**undetectability** /úndi tektə bílləti/ n —**undetectably** adv

undetected /úndi téktid/ adj not discovered or noticed

undetermined /úndi túrmind/ adj 1 not resolved, decided, or fixed 2 unknown or undiscovered

undeterred /úndi túrd/ adj not discouraged by obstacles or difficulties

undeveloped /úndi vélləpt/ adj 1 UNEXPLOITED not exploited or made ready for use in a productive way 2 WITHOUT MEANS FOR ECONOMIC GROWTH lacking the technology and capital to make efficient use of available resources (offensive in some contexts) 3 NOT PROCESSED not yet chemically treated to produce a negative or print 4 NOT MATURE not having undergone a process of growth and change

undeviating /un dée vi ayting/ adj remaining loyal or constant —**undeviatingly** adv

undiagnosed /un dī´ əgnōzd/ adj not identified as a specific illness, disorder, or problem

undid past tense of **undo**

undies /úndi diz/ npl underclothes, especially women's underclothes (informal) [Late 19C. Shortening.]

undifferentiated /úndi diffə rénshi aytid/ adj not having distinguishing characteristics, or not made up of distinguishable components

undigested /úndi jéstid, -dī-/ adj 1 not having undergone the process of digestion 2 not fully analyzed, considered, or understood

undignified /un dígni fīd/ adj lacking dignity and appearing foolish or making the person involved appear foolish ○ made an undignified exit

undiluted /úndi lŏotid, -lyŏotid/ adj 1 not thinned or weakened by the addition of water or another substance 2 in a pure and simple form, without the presence of any moderating or weakening factor ○ There was undiluted panic in his voice.

undiminished /úndi mínnisht/ adj not lessened or weaker or smaller ○ Despite the years of attending plays his appetite for the theatre was undiminished.

undiminishing /úndi mínnishing/ adj not becoming smaller or less

undine /úndeen/ n a female spirit that lives in water, especially one that could become human by bearing the child of a human male [Early 19C. < modern Latin undina < Latin unda 'wave'.]

undiplomatic /úndi diplə máttik/ adj lacking in tact and diplomacy —**undiplomatically** adv

undirected /úndi réktid, úndī-/ adj 1 without a purpose or object 2 not marked with an address in the proper way

undiscerning /úndi súrning, -zúrn-/ adj not showing insight, good judgment, or good taste

undischarged /úndi diss chaárjd/ adj 1 NOT FIRED not having discharged a bullet or ammunition ○ an undischarged firearm 2 NOT BROUGHT TO COMPLETION not carried out, paid in full, or relieved from an obligation or liability ○ an undischarged bankrupt ○ undischarged debts 3 NOT GIVEN VENT TO not freely expressed or relieved by free expression ○ undischarged emotion 4 NOT EMITTED not given off or emitted as a discharge ○ undischarged gas

undisciplined /un díssəplind/ adj showing a lack of proper control and orderliness

undisclosed /úndiss klōzd/ adj not revealed or made generally known

undiscovered /úndis kúvərd/ adj not found or widely known about ○ undiscovered inland Spain

undiscriminating /úndi skrímmi nayting/ adj unable or unwilling to identify differences between things and to exercise good judgment and taste

undisguised /úndiss gīzd/ adj expressed fully and openly —**undisguisedly** /úndiss gízidli/ adv

undisposed /úndi spózd/ adj 1 not resolved or dealt with 2 not prepared or inclined to do something

undisputable /úndi di spyóotab'l/ adj impossible to doubt, question, or deny —**undisputably** adv

undisputed /úndi di spyóotid/ adj accepted as true, valid, or rightfully deserving the description by everyone concerned ○ the undisputed champion of the world

undissociated /úndi sōshi aytid, -sōssi-/ adj describes a molecule not broken down into simpler molecules, atoms, or ions

undissolved /úndi di zólvd/ adj remaining in solid form, not absorbed into a liquid

undistinguished /úndi sting gwisht/ adj 1 MEDIOCRE not very good or ever rising above the ordinary ○ an undistinguished career 2 COMMONPLACE not at all striking or likely to stand out from others ○ undistinguished appearance 3 NOT MADE SEPARATE not differentiated from others 4 NOT ATTRACTING NOTICE not noticeable or noticed

undistorted /úndi stáwrtid/ adj clearly seen or accurately presented

undistributed /úndi stríbbyŏotid/ adj 1 not paid out as a dividend to shareholders, but invested back into the business ○ undistributed profits 2 describes a term that does not refer to all members of the class it designates. The term 'dogs' is undistributed in the statement 'Some dogs are unfriendly'.

undisturbed /úndi stúrbd/ adj 1 not interrupted or disrupted by anybody or anything 2 not touched or moved ○ The plate of food had been left undisturbed.

undivided /úndi ví dídid/ adj 1 not separated or split into several parts or sections 2 concentrated solely on one person or thing ○ I gave her my undivided attention.

⚡ **undo** /un dŏo/ (-does /-dúz/, -doing, -did /-díd/, -done /-dún/) v 1 vti UNFASTEN to open, unfasten, untie, or unwrap something ○ I can't undo this button. 2 vt NULLIFY to cancel or reverse the effect of an action ○ What's done can't be *undone.* **3** *vt* REVERSE AN ACTION to cancel the effect of the last command or action done on a computer, restoring the material being worked on to its previous condition **4** *vt* RUIN to bring somebody or something to ruin or disaster (*formal*)

undock /un dók/ *vti* to detach, or become detached, from a space station, or another spacecraft, in space

undocumented /un dókyoō mentid/ *adj* **1** not recorded in a document or supported by written evidence ○ *undocumented accusations* **2** *US* not having the necessary identification papers, permits, or other legally required documents ○ *undocumented refugees*

undoing *n* the ruin, downfall, or destruction of somebody or something, or something that causes this ○ *Pride was our undoing.*

undomesticated /ún də mésti kaytid/ *adj* **1** wild and not tamed or accustomed to living with or near people **2** unaccustomed or unsuited to carrying out ordinary domestic tasks (*humorous*)

undone *adj* **1** UNCOMPLETED not yet done or completed **2** UNFASTENED not tied or fastened **3** BROUGHT TO RUIN ruined, destroyed, or brought to the brink of collapse (*formal or humorous*)

undoubted /un dówtid/ *adj* not subject to doubt or dispute

undoubtedly /un dówtidli/ *adv* without any doubt or question

~~undoubtly~~ incorrect spelling of **undoubtedly**

undrained /ún dráynd/ *adj* not emptied of liquid or dried out

undramatic /ún drə máttik/ *adj* **1** unlikely to or not seeking to excite people or generate strong feelings ○ *He went about things in his usual undramatic way.* **2** lacking in excitement, tension, or any of the other qualities associated with drama

undraw /un dráw/ (**-draws, -drawing, -drew** /un droō/, **-drawn** /un dráwn/) *vt* to draw something such as a curtain back or open

undreamed-of /un dreémd ov/, **undreamt-of** /un drémt ov/ *adj* impossible to imagine in advance, usually through being so wonderful and so unlikely

undress *v* /un dréss/ **1** *vti* TAKE CLOTHES OFF to remove the clothes from somebody's body **2** *vt* TAKE DRESSING OFF to remove a dressing from a wound **3** *vt* REMOVE ORNAMENTATION to strip something of its decoration ■ *n* **1** CONDITION OF HAVING NO CLOTHES ON a condition of nakedness or of being scantily clothed **2** INFORMAL CLOTHING informal attire or an everyday uniform ■ *adj* /ún dress/ INFORMAL not full or formal in dress, or for which informal clothing can be worn ○ *an undress uniform*

undressed /un drést/ *adj* **1** WITHOUT CLOTHES naked or scantily clothed **2** UNTREATED not processed or treated in some way ○ *undressed leather* **3** NOT READY FOR TABLE not fully prepared for cooking or eating **4** WITHOUT DRESSING not covered with a dressing or sauce **5** INFORMALLY DRESSED appropriately but not formally dressed for an event or occasion **6** WITHOUT A BANDAGE without a dressing or bandage ○ *an undressed wound*

undrinkable /un dríngkəb'l/ *adj* unsuitable for drinking, or too unpleasant to drink

undue /ún dyoō/ *adj* **1** going beyond the limits of what is proper, normal, justified, or permitted ○ *using undue force to disperse the crowd* **2** not owed or payable at present

undulant /úndyoōlənt/ *adj* resembling waves in motion or form (*formal*) [Early 19C. < UNDULATE.]

undulant fever *n* MED = **brucellosis** (*in humans*)

undulate *v* /úndyoō layt/ (**-lates, -lating, -lated**) **1** *vti* MOVE SINUOUSLY LIKE WAVES to move, or cause something to move, in waves or in a movement resembling waves **2** *vi* GO UP AND DOWN GRACEFULLY to rise and fall gracefully in volume or pitch ■ *adj* /úndyoōlət, -layt/ **undulate, undulated** WAVY IN APPEARANCE with a wavy appearance, edge, or markings [Mid-17C. < Latin *undulatus* 'wavy' < *unda* 'wave'.] —**undulation** /úndyoō láysh'n/ *n* —**undulatory** *adj*

unduly /un dyoōli/ *adv* to a very great extent, or to an excessive, improper, or unjustifiable degree ○ *We were not unduly concerned.*

undutiful /un dyoōtif'l/ *adj* **1** lacking a sense of moral or legal obligation **2** unwilling to fulfil moral or legal obligations —**undutifully** *adv* —**undutifulness** *n*

undyed /un díd/ *adj* not coloured with a dye

undying /un dí ing/ *adj* describes an emotion that does not diminish but continues forever

unearned /un úrnd/ *adj* **1** not acquired by labour or service ○ *unearned income* **2** not deserved ○ *unearned criticism*

unearned increment *n* an increase in property value resulting from factors other than labour or improvements made by the owner

unearth /un úrth/ *vt* **1** DIG SOMETHING UP to bring something up out of the ground **2** DISCLOSE to discover or disclose something, especially after an investigation **3** FIND SOMETHING LOST to find something that has been lost or hidden

unearthly /un úrthli/ *adj* **1** NOT FROM THIS WORLD not being or seeming to be from this world **2** EERIE looking or sounding so strange as to be frightening **3** UNREASONABLE completely inappropriate or unreasonable (*formal*) ○ *at this unearthly hour* —**unearthliness** *n*

uneasy /un eézi/ (**-ier, -iest**) *adj* **1** ANXIOUS anxious or afraid **2** UNCERTAIN not certain enough to let people relax completely ○ *an uneasy truce* **3** ILL AT EASE awkward or lacking confidence **4** RESTLESS not allowing somebody to rest properly —**unease** *n* —**uneasily** *adv* —**uneasiness** *n*

uneaten /un eét'n/ *adj* not having been consumed as food

~~unecessary~~ incorrect spelling of **unnecessary**

uneconomic /ún eekə nómmik, -ekə-/ *adj* **1** not making or not likely to make a profit **2** **uneconomic, uneconomical** not efficient or worth the expense

unedited /un édditid/ *adj* **1** not corrected or revised **2** not adapted to a particular audience, purpose, or medium

uneducated /un éddyoō kaytid/ *adj* lacking the learning that is usually acquired in schools

unelectable /únni léktəb'l/ *adj* certain to be defeated as a candidate for public office, e.g. because of extreme positions on controversial issues

unelected /ún i léktid/ *adj* having been chosen by some other means than an election, especially having been appointed to an office by a higher authority ○ *unelected officials*

unembarrassed /ún im bárrəst/ *adj* not experiencing self-consciousness or shame

unembellished /ún im béllisht/ *adj* **1** without ornamentation **2** without enhancing or exaggerated details ○ *gave a sober unembellished account of the event*

unembroidered /ún em bróydərd/ *adj* **1** not decorated with embroidery ○ *unembroidered bed linen* **2** having no exaggerated or fictitious details added ○ *just the plain unembroidered facts*

unemotional /únni mósh'nəl/ *adj* **1** showing little or no feeling **2** involving reason or intellect rather than feelings —**unemotionally** *adv*

unemployable /únnim plóy əb'l/ *adj* lacking the skills, education, or ability to get a job

unemployed /únnim plóyd/ *adj* **1** JOBLESS not in paid employment **2** NOT IN USE not being used ■ *npl* JOBLESS PEOPLE people who are out of work

unemployment /únnim plóymənt/ *n* **1** the condition of having no job **2** the number of people who are unemployed in an area, often given as a percentage of the total labour force

unemployment benefit *n* a regular payment made by the government to somebody who is out of work

unenclosed /ún in klózd/ *adj* not enclosed by fences, walls, or other boundaries

unencumbered /ún in kúmbərd/ *adj* not impeded by obstructions or a heavy or awkward load

unending /un énding/ *adj* continuing or seeming to continue forever, especially when an end would be welcome

unendurable /ún in dyoōrəb'l/ *adj* too painful, disturbing, or injurious to be tolerated —**unendurably** *adv*

unenforceable /ún in fáwrssəb'l/ *adj* unable to be enforced as a law, regulation, or command

unenforced /ún in fáwrst/ *adj* **1** not imposed on somebody by force or by circumstances **2** not put into effect and backed up by legal or other sanctions

un-English /un íng glish/ *adj* **1** not characteristic of the English **2** not considered standard English usage

unenjoyable /ún in jóyəb'l/ *adj* not providing or capable of providing pleasure

unenlightened /ún in lít'nd/ *adj* **1** NOT ENLIGHTENED having or showing ignorance, prejudice, and a narrow outlook **2** NOT AWARE not having been informed about something in particular ○ *remained unenlightened as to how the policy was to be implemented* **3** NOT GRANTED UNDERSTANDING not having been granted insight or understanding, especially in religious matters

unenlightening /ún in lít'ning/ *adj* providing no useful information or insight ○ *The press handout was singularly unenlightening.*

unentangle /ún in táng g'l/ (**-gles, -gling, -gled**) *vt* **1** FREE SOMETHING FROM TANGLES to free things that are knotted or tied **2** STRAIGHTEN OUT SOMETHING COMPLEX to clarify or resolve something that is intricate or puzzling **3** FREE SOMEBODY FROM BAD SITUATION to release another person, or yourself from a confused, complicated, or undesired situation

unenthusiastic /ún in thyoozi ástik/ *adj* showing no eagerness, interest, or excitement about something —**unenthusiastically** *adv*

unenviable /un énvee əb'l/ *adj* not pleasant, easy, or likely to be wished for ○ *had the unenviable task of breaking the bad news*

unequal /un eékwəl/ *adj* **1** NOT MEASURABLY THE SAME not measurably the same, e.g. in size or number **2** NOT OF SAME SOCIAL POSITION not of the same status, rank, or position in society **3** NOT EVENLY MATCHED not evenly matched in competition **4** VARIABLE uneven or variable in quality or character **5** ASYMMETRICAL not evenly balanced **6** UNABLE TO DO having less than the required ability to do something ○ *unequal to the task* ■ *n* SOMEBODY NOT EQUAL TO ANOTHER somebody or something not equal to another —**unequally** *adv*

unequalled /un eékwəld/ *adj* without equal or parallel among things of its kind

unequivocal /únni kwívvək'l/ *adj* allowing for no doubt or misinterpretation —**unequivocally** *adv*

uneroded /ún i ródid/ *adj* not eaten away or reduced by erosion

unerring /un úr ing/ *adj* accurate or correct —**unerringly** *adv*

UNESCO /yoo néskō/, **Unesco** a trademark for a UN agency that promotes international collaboration on culture, education, and science

unessential /únni sénsh'l/ *adj* not absolutely needed ■ *n* something that is not necessary or important

unethical /un éthik'l/ *adj* not conforming to agreed standards of moral conduct, especially within a particular profession —**unethically** *adv*

uneven /un eév'n/ *adj* **1** NOT LEVEL without a level or smooth surface **2** VARYING varying and inconsistent, e.g. in quality, thoroughness, or duration **3** NOT PARALLEL not straight or parallel **4** NOT FAIRLY MATCHED not fairly matched in competition **5** ODD not divisible by two **6** NOT THE SAME SIZE unequal in number or measurement to another —**unevenly** *adv* —**unevenness** *n*

uneventful /únni véntf'l/ *adj* not marked by any unusual or momentous occurrence —**uneventfully** *adv* —**uneventfulness** *n*

unexamined /ún ig zámmind/ *adj* not having been subjected to close investigation, study, or analysis ○ *a mass of hitherto unexamined evidence*

unexampled /únnig zaámp'ld/ *adj* without a similar case or occurrence

unexcelled /únnik séld/ *adj* never having been excelled, and often conspicuously better than somebody or something comparable ○ *Her record remained unexcelled.*

unexceptionable /únnik sépsh'nəb'l/ *adj* good enough to provide no reason for criticism or objection —**unexceptionability** /únnik sépsh'nə bílləti/ *n* —**unexceptionableness** *n* —**unexceptionably** *adv*

USAGE See ***unexceptional***.

unexceptional /únnik sépsh'nəl/ *adj* not special or unusual —**unexceptionally** *adv*

USAGE **unexceptional** or **unexceptionable**? The distinction in meaning corresponds to that between the positive forms *exceptional* and *exceptionable.* Something is described as ***unexceptional*** when it is not special or unusual, even perhaps a little dull: *Her performance got a good review, but*

I thought it was unexceptional. ***Unexceptionable*** comes close to this in meaning, but its strict meaning is 'good enough to provide no reason for criticism or objection': *Their behaviour has been unexceptionable so far.*

unexcited /únnik sítid/ *adj* **1** not emotionally aroused **2** describes particles that remain at the lowest energy level

unexciting /ún ik síting/ *adj* failing to cause feelings of eagerness, tense anticipation, or pleasurable arousal —**unexcitingly** *adv*

unexpected /únnik spéktid/ *adj* coming as a surprise —**unexpectedly** *adv* —**unexpectedness** *n*

unexperienced /únnik speéri ənst/ *adj* **1** not having been known or undergone before **2** lacking experience

unexpired /ún ik spírd/ *adj* not yet having reached the date of expiry and therefore still valid or in operation

unexplainable /ún ik spláynəb'l/ *adj* not able to be explained

unexplained /ún ik spláynd/ *adj* not known, not made clear, or not able to be explained ○ *the unexplained disappearance of the aircraft*

unexploded /ún ik splṓdid/ *adj* having failed to explode but still capable of exploding ○ *an unexploded bomb*

unexploited /ún ik splóytid/ *adj* **1** not used as raw material, either for profit or to gain an advantage **2** not taken advantage of in a selfish or unfair way

unexplored /ún ik splawrd/ *adj* **1** not visited or not mapped **2** not yet investigated, studied, or discussed

unexposed /ún ik spṓzd/ *adj* **1 COVERED** under a covering and thereby not open to view or to the air **2 SHELTERED** protected or sheltered, e.g. from the weather or the possibility of danger or attack **3 NOT EXPOSED TO LIGHT** describes a film that has not been exposed to light

unexpressed /únnik sprést/ *adj* **1** not spoken or made known **2** describes a gene that does not have an observable effect on the organism that carries it

unexpressive /ún ik spréssiv/ *adj* communicating no feeling or meaning ○ *an unexpressive face*

unfaceted /un fássitid/ *adj* having a surface that has not been cut into facets

unfading /un fáyding/ *adj* retaining the original brightness, colour, or impressiveness ○ *unfading glory*

unfailing /un fáyling/ *adj* **1** able to be relied on at all times ○ *unfailing good humour* **2** totally accurate and without fault ○ *an unfailing eye for symmetry and beauty* —**unfailingly** *adv* —**unfailingness** *n*

unfair /un fáir/ *adj* **1** not equal or just **2** not ethical in business dealings —**unfairly** *adv* —**unfairness** *n*

unfaithful /un fáythf'l/ *adj* **1 UNTRUE TO COMMITMENTS** untrue to commitments, duties, beliefs, or ideals **2 ADULTEROUS** engaging in sexual relations with somebody other than one to whom monogamy has been pledged **3 NOT LIKE ORIGINAL** not true to the original **4 WITH NO RELIGIOUS FAITH** not having religious faith (*archaic*) —**unfaithfully** *adv* —**unfaithfulness** *n*

unfaltering /un fáwltering, -fólte-/ *adj* strong, steady, and not becoming weaker —**unfalteringly** *adv*

unfamiliar /únfə mílli ər/ *adj* **1** not previously known or recognized **2** with no previous knowledge or experience ○ *unfamiliar with the software* —**unfamiliarity** /únfə mílli árrəti/ *n* —**unfamiliarly** *adv*

unfarmed /un faármd/ *adj* not used to grow crops or raise livestock

unfashionable /un fásh'nəb'l/ *adj* **1** not in the current style **2** not socially approved of ○ *an unfashionable suburb* —**unfashionably** *adv*

unfasten /un faáss'n/ *vt* undo something that holds things together, e.g. the buttons of a garment

unfathomable /un fáthəməb'l/ *adj* **1** too deep to be measured **2** so mysterious or complicated that understanding is impossible —**unfathomableness** *n* —**unfathomably** *adv*

unfavourable /un fáyvərəb'l/ *adj* **1** expressing disapproval or opposition **2** unlikely to be beneficial —**unfavourableness** *n* —**unfavourably** *adv*

unfavoured /un fáyvərd/ *adj* not preferred or enjoying advantages

unfeasible /un feézəb'l/ *adj* impractical as a goal, or not easily carried out

unfeathered /un féthərd/ *adj* having no feathers

unfed /un féd/ *adj* given no food to eat

unfederated /un féddə raytid/ *adj* not being or belonging to a federation

unfeeling /un feéling/ *adj* **1** without sympathy for somebody else's feelings **2** unable to experience physical sensation —**unfeelingly** *adv* —**unfeelingness** *n*

unfeminine /un fémmənin/ *adj* conventionally believed to be uncharacteristic of or inappropriate for a woman or girl

unfertilized /un fúrti līzd/, **unfertilised** *adj* **1** not united with a male gamete during a reproductive process and thus unable to develop ○ *an unfertilized egg* **2** not treated with fertilizer

unfetter /un féttər/ *vt* **1** to release somebody or something from fetters **2** to allow somebody to act without restraint

unfettered /un féttərd/ *adj* not subject to limits or restrictions

unfilled /un fíld/ *adj* not having been occupied or filled ○ *All the applicants were unsuitable, so the post remained unfilled.*

SYNONYMS See ***vacant***.

unfinished /un fínnisht/ *adj* **1 NOT COMPLETED** not completed satisfactorily **2 NOT FINALLY TREATED** not finally processed or treated with dye, varnish, paint, or bleach **3 WITH SLIGHT NAP** woven with a slight nap

unfired /un fírd/ *adj* **1** not baked hard in a kiln **2** not discharged from a gun or other weapon, or not used to discharge ammunition ○ *an unfired cartridge* ○ *an unfired rifle*

unfit /un fít/ *adj* **1 UNSUITABLE** unsuitable for a specific purpose **2 UNQUALIFIED** lacking the necessary skills or qualifications to perform a specific task adequately **3 NOT HEALTHY** not physically or mentally healthy —**unfitly** *adv* —**unfitness** *n*

unfitted /un fíttid/ *adj* **1** not suited or adapted for a specific purpose **2** describes furniture that is not fitted

unfitting /un fítting/ *adj* not suitable or appropriate for somebody or something —**unfittingly** *adv*

unfix /un fíks/ *vt* **1** to loosen or detach something **2** to upset the certainty or stability of something

unflagging /un flágging/ *adj* remaining strong and unchanging —**unflaggingly** *adv*

unflappable /un fláppəb'l/ *adj* able to maintain composure under all circumstances —**unflappability** /un fláppə bílləti/ *n* —**unflappably** *adv*

unflattering /un fláttəring/ *adj* showing or depicting a person or thing in an uncomplimentary or unfavourable way —**unflatteringly** *adv*

unflawed /un fláwd/ *adj* not spoiled by any imperfection or defect

unfledged /un fléjd/ *adj* **1** not having developed the feathers required for flight **2** young and inexperienced

unflinching /un flínching/ *adj* strong and unhesitating —**unflinchingly** *adv*

unfluctuating /un flúkchoo ayting/ *adj* not subject to unpredictable changes in level, movement, or intensity

unflustered /un flústərd/ *adj* showing no signs of nervousness or agitation

unfluted /un flootid/ *adj* not decorated with parallel grooves

unfocused /un fṓkəst/, **unfocussed** *adj* **1** not adjusted for a clear image **2** lacking a clear purpose or objective

unfold /un fṓld/ *v* **1** *vti* **OPEN OUT** to open something and spread it out, or to open and spread out **2** *vti* **MAKE SOMETHING UNDERSTOOD** to make something clear and understood by gradual exposure, or to become clear in this way **3** *vi* **DEVELOP** to develop or expand over time ○ *His talent unfolded as he grew older.*

unforced /un fáwrst/ *adj* **1** spontaneous and natural rather than willed ○ *unforced laughter* **2** not resulting from compulsion, irresistible pressure, or an opponent's superior skill ○ *made an unforced error and lost the point*

unforceful /un fáwrssf'l/ *adj* lacking strength and power and making a generally weak impression

unforeseeable /ún fawr seé əb'l/ *adj* not able to be predicted or planned for in advance ○ *a bizarre and unforeseeable chain of events*

unforeseen /ún fawr seén/ *adj* not expected beforehand

unforgettable /únfər géttəb'l/ *adj* remarkable in a way that cannot be forgotten —**unforgettably** *adv*

unforgivable /únfər gívvəb'l/ *adj* so bad that it can never be forgiven —**unforgivably** *adv*

unforgiven /ún fər gívv'n/ *adj* not forgiven, pardoned, or excused

unforgiving /únfər gívving/ *adj* **1** unwilling or unable to forgive **2** providing little or no margin for mistakes or weakness —**unforgivingly** *adv*

unformed /un fáwrmd/ *adj* **1 WITH NO REAL SHAPE** without coherent shape or structure ○ *the unformed restless desire in her mind* **2 UNDEVELOPED** not yet fully developed **3 NOT CREATED** not yet created

unformulated /un fáwrmyoo laytid/ *adj* not given a clear or concise form of expression ○ *creative but as yet unformulated ideas*

unforthcoming /ún fawrth kúmming/ *adj* **1 UNINFORMATIVE** reluctant to talk or reveal information ○ *He was cool, distant, unforthcoming.* **2 UNAVAILABLE** not ready when required or requested ○ *Help was unforthcoming.* **3 FAILING TO HAPPEN** not happening despite being expected ○ *The hoped-for success was unforthcoming.*

unfortified /un fáwrti fīd/ *adj* **1** defended by no walls, earthworks, or other fortifications **2** describes wine that has had no extra alcohol added

unfortunate /un fáwrchənət/ *adj* **1 UNLUCKY** never experiencing good luck **2 WITH BAD LUCK** accompanied by or bringing bad luck **3 INAPPROPRIATE** not appropriate to a given situation ○ *The unfortunate comment was an example of his lack of social polish.* ■ *n* **POOR PERSON** a person who has bad luck or inadequate resources —**unfortunateness** *n*

unfortunately /un fáwrchənətli/ *adv* **1** used when somebody wishes something were not true ○ *I didn't get there before he left, unfortunately.* **2** in a way that is inappropriate to a given situation ○ *an unfortunately worded critique*

unfounded /un fówndid/ *adj* **1** not supported by evidence or facts **2** not yet established

unframed /un fráymd/ *adj* not mounted in a frame

unfree /un freé/ *adj* having no freedom or liberty

unfreeze /un freéz/ (**-freezes, -freezing, -froze** /-frṓz/, **-frozen** /-frṓz'n/) *vt* to remove controls or restrictions fixing wages, hiring, prices, or rents

unfrequented /únfri kwéntid/ *adj* not often visited, especially by tourists or travellers

unfretted /un fréttid/ *adj* relating to a stringed instrument that has no frets on its fingerboard

unfriendly /un fréndli/ *adj* **1** behaving in an obviously cold or hostile way **2** not beneficial or advantageous —**unfriendliness** *n*

unfrock /un frók/ *vt* **1 REMOVE ORDAINED PERSON FROM OFFICE** to remove an ordained person from office and duties as a punishment for doing something considered immoral or heretical **2 TAKE AWAY SOMEBODY'S RIGHT** to take away somebody's right to practise a profession **3 REMOVE SOMEBODY FROM POSITION** to remove somebody from an honorary or privileged position

unfruitful /un fróotf'l/ *adj* **1** not bearing fruit or offspring (*literary*) **2** not having a successful outcome —**unfruitfully** *adv* —**unfruitfulness** *n*

unfulfilled /ún fool fíld/ *adj* **1 NOT REALIZED** not developed or made use of adequately or to the fullest possible extent **2 NOT FULLY CARRIED OUT** not carried out fully or in accordance with the original requirements or stipulations **3 NOT SATISFIED** not satisfied, especially by not having fully realized ambitions or potential

unfulfilling /ún fool fílling/ *adj* unsatisfying and failing to provide scope for the full range of somebody's abilities

unfurl /un fúrl/ *vti* to unroll or spread out something, or to become extended in this way

unfurnished /un fúrnishd/ *adj* not furnished, or available to be rented without furniture ○ *an unfurnished flat*

unfurrowed /un fúrrōd/ *adj* having a smooth flat surface not marked with furrows or wrinkles

unfused /un fyoózd/ *adj* **1** not joined to or combined with something **2** describes electrical devices not fitted with fuses

unfussy /un fússi/ *adj* free from excessively elaborate detail or complication ○ *a refreshingly unfussy guide to American cuisine* ○ *elegant and unfussy decor*

ungainly /un gáynli/ *adj* **1** LACKING GRACE lacking grace while moving **2** AWKWARD awkward to handle **3** GANGLING having an awkward long-limbed appearance ■ *adv* CLUMSILY in a clumsy or graceless way (*archaic*) [Early 17C. < obsolete *gain* 'straight, convenient' < Old Norse *gegn*.]

Ungava /ŏong gaávə/ region in NE Canada, east of Hudson Bay. Area: 912,000 sq. km/352,100 sq. mi.

Ungava Bay inlet of Hudson Strait in NE Quebec, Canada

ungelded /un géldid/ *adj* not gelded or castrated

ungenerous /un jénnərəss/ *adj* **1** slow to give, forgive, or share things **2** mean-spirited and ignoble —**ungenerously** *adv*

unglamorous /un glámmərəss/ *adj* unexciting and lacking style, fashion, and allure

unglazed /un gláyzd/ *adj* **1** not fitted with glass **2** not covered with a glaze

unglued /ún glo͞od/ *adj* **1** having become separated or detached **2** *US* having lost your composure or temper (*informal*)

ungodly /un góddli/ *adj* **1** NOT REVERING GOD not devoted to or obeying God **2** WICKED behaving in a way thought to violate moral strictures **3** UNREASONABLE not meeting standards for reasonableness (*informal*) ○ *at this ungodly hour* —**ungodliness** *n*

ungovernable /un gúvvərnəb'l/ *adj* incapable of being governed or restrained —**ungovernableness** *n* —**ungovernably** *adv*

ungraceful /un gráyssf'l/ *adj* clumsy and inelegant in appearance, manner, or movement —**ungracefully** *adv*

ungracious /un gráyshəss/ *adj* **1** inconsistent with good manners **2** extremely unpleasant or difficult —**ungraciously** *adv* —**ungraciousness** *n*

ungrammatical /ún grə máttik'l/ *adj* not conforming to the accepted rules of grammar —**ungrammatically** *adv*

ungrateful /un gráytf'l/ *adj* **1** not thankful or appreciative **2** unpleasant or unrewarding —**ungratefully** *adv* —**ungratefulness** *n*

ungratified /un grátti fīd/ *adj* having desires or wishes that have not been satisfied

ungrudging /un grújjing/ *adj* without reluctance or reservation —**ungrudgingly** *adv*

ungual /úng gwəl/ *adj* **1** relating to or affecting the fingernails or toenails **2** relating to, occurring in, or supporting a nail, claw, or hoof [Mid-19C. < Latin *unguis* 'nail, claw'.]

unguarded /un gaárdid/ *adj* **1** WITH NO PROTECTION lacking a guard or protection **2** NATURAL free from pretence or guile **3** NOT WARY showing a lack of thought or care —**unguardedly** *adv* —**unguardedness** *n*

unguent /úng gwənt/ *n* a healing or soothing ointment [15C. < Latin *unguentum* < *unguere* 'smear, anoint'.]

unguided /un gīdid/ *adj* **1** NOT LED not led or steered in a particular direction **2** NOT DIRECTED EXTERNALLY OR INTERNALLY not directed by remote control or internal regulatory devices ○ *unguided missiles* **3** LACKING ADVICE OR DIRECTION given no advice or instructions on how to behave or how to carry something out

unguis /úng gwiss/ (*plural* **-gues** /-gweez/) *n* **1** a nail, claw, hook, or hoof on a digit or foot of an animal **2** the claw-shaped base of some petals [Early 18C. < Latin, 'nail, claw'.]

ungulate /úng gyo͝o layt, -lət/ *adj* **1** WITH HOOFS having hoofs **2** SHAPED LIKE HOOF resembling a hoof in shape or function ■ *n* HOOFED MAMMAL a mammal with hoofs, e.g. the horse, rhinoceros, pig, giraffe, deer, or camel [Early 19C. < late Latin *ungulatus* < Latin *ungula* 'hoof, claw' < *unguis* 'nail, claw'.]

unguligrade /úng gyo͝oli grayd/ *adj* describes a mammal that walks on hoofs [Mid-19C. < Latin *ungula* 'hoof' (see UNGULATE).]

unhallowed /un hállōd/ *adj* **1** NOT CONSECRATED not consecrated or blessed **2** IRREVERENT lacking religious reverence **3** IMMORAL not conforming to the standards of a religion

unhampered /un hámpərd/ *adj* able to move or act freely and without obstruction

unhand /un hánd/ *vt* to let somebody go by releasing a grasp (*archaic or humorous*)

unhandy /un hándi/ (**-ier, -iest**) *adj* **1** NOT SKILLED WITH HANDS not skilled at working with the hands or with tools **2** INCONVENIENTLY LOCATED in an inconvenient location **3** DIFFICULT TO USE not easy to use or handle

unhappily /un háppili/ *adv* **1** in a way that expresses or is characterized by unhappiness **2** used to express a wish that something were not true ○ *Unhappily, she was never able to go there.*

unhappy /un háppi/ (**-pier, -piest**) *adj* **1** SAD not cheerful or joyful **2** UNFORTUNATE not bringing good luck **3** INAPPROPRIATE done without proper thought or inappropriate in a specific context **4** DISPLEASED not pleased or satisfied with somebody or something —**unhappiness** *n*

unhardened /un haárd'nd/ *adj* not made hard, tough, or callous

unharmed /un haármd/ *adj* not hurt or damaged in any way

unharness /un haárnəss/ *vt* **1** REMOVE HARNESS FROM HORSE to remove the harness from a horse **2** RELEASE ENERGY OR PASSIONS to release energy or passions from restraints **3** REMOVE ARMOUR to remove the armour from somebody (*archaic*)

UNHCR *abbr* United Nations High Commission for Refugees

unhealthful /un hélthf'l/ *adj US* having a bad effect on somebody's health

unhealthy /un hélthi/ (**-ier, -iest**) *adj* **1** SICK affected by ill health **2** BAD FOR HEALTH not good for the health **3** SYMPTOMATIC OF ILL HEALTH showing the symptoms of or resulting from ill health **4** HARMING CHARACTER harmful to the character **5** CORRUPT morally corrupt or unwholesome **6** RISKY taking unnecessary risks (*informal*) —**unhealthily** *adv* —**unhealthiness** *n*

unheard /un húrd/ *adj* **1** not perceived by the ear **2** not listened to or given a hearing

unheard-of *adj* **1** UNKNOWN not previously known **2** UNPRECEDENTED never having happened before **3** OFFENSIVE extremely offensive or rude

unheated /un heétid/ *adj* not supplied or fitted with any form of heating

unheeded /un heédid/ *adj* not listened to or given serious attention ○ *My warnings went unheeded.*

unhelpful /un hélpf'l/ *adj* not providing or willing to provide help —**unhelpfully** *adv* —**unhelpfulness** *n*

unheroic /ún hi rṓ ik/ *adj* not characteristic of or acting like a hero

unhesitating /un hézzi tayting/ *adj* without pause, indecision or change —**unhesitatingly** *adv*

unhewn /un hyo͞on/ *adj* not cut down, shaped with a cutting implement, or carved

unhindered /un híndərd/ *adj* obstructed by no obstacles or difficulties ○ *allowed them to carry on with the work unhindered*

unhinge /un hínj/ (**-hinges, -hinging, -hinged**) *vt* **1** REMOVE SOMETHING FROM HINGES to remove something from its hinges **2** REMOVE HINGES to remove the hinges of something **3** DISLOCATE to dislodge or detach something **4** DISRUPT to throw something into confusion **5** MAKE PSYCHOLOGICALLY UNSTABLE to cause somebody to become emotionally or mentally unstable

unhitch /un hích/ *vt* to unfasten something that is tied up

unholy /un hṓli/ (**-lier, -liest**) *adj* **1** NOT BLESSED not blessed or consecrated by a church ritual **2** DEFYING RELIGIOUS PRECEPTS deliberately defiant of specific religious precepts **3** EXTREME extremely bad or awful (*used for emphasis*) ○ *This place is an unholy mess!* —**unholiness** *n*

unhook /un ho͝ok/ *vt* **1** to remove something from a hook **2** to unfasten the hooks of something

unhoped-for /un hṓpt-/ *adj* not expected or anticipated ○ *an unhoped-for victory*

unhopeful /ún hṓpf'l/ *adj* lacking confidence that something desired or positive will happen ○ *The situation is bleak, but I am not entirely unhopeful.* —**unhopefully** *adv*

unhorse /un háwrss/ (**-horses, -horsing, -horsed**) *vt* **1** to knock or throw somebody from a horse **2** to bring somebody down from a high office or position

unhurried /un húrrid/ *adj* done in a relaxed and deliberate way —**unhurriedly** *adv*

unhurt /un húrt/ *adj* having received no injury or harm ○ *The driver escaped unhurt from the accident.*

unhygienic /ún hī jeénik/ *adj* not clean, sanitary, or healthy —**unhygienically** *adv*

uni /yo͞oni/ *n* a university (*informal*) [Late 19C. Shortening.]

uni- *prefix* one, single ○ *unicellular* [< Latin, < *unus* 'one'. < Indo-European.]

Uniat /yo͞oni ət, -ayt, yo͞oni at/, **Uniate** *n* a member of any of the Eastern Christian Churches that recognize papal supremacy but keep their own liturgy, language, and canon law ■ *adj* relating to the Uniat Churches [Mid-19C. < Russian *uniyat*, Polish *uniat* < *unia* 'union' (of the Roman Catholic and Greek Churches) < Latin *unio* (stem *union-*: see UNION).]

uniaxial /yo͞oni áksi əl/ *adj* **1** describes a crystal or mineral that has one direction, parallel to the principal axis, along which single refraction occurs **2** describes a plant with an unbranched main stem —**uniaxially** *adv*

unicameral /yo͞oni kámmərəl/ *adj* having only one legislative chamber [Mid-19C. < UNI- + Latin *camera* 'chamber' (see CAMERA).] —**unicameralism** *n* —**unicameralist** *n* —**unicamerally** *adv*

ϟ **unicast** /yo͞oni kast/ *n* a transmission from a single computing terminal to one other terminal

UNICEF /yo͞oni sef/, **Unicef** a trademark for a UN agency that works for the protection and survival of children around the world

unicellular /yo͞oni séllyo͞olər/ *adj* consisting of a single cell —**unicellularity** /yo͞oni séllyo͞o lárrəti/ *n*

unicolour /yo͞oni kúllər/ *adj* composed of or containing only one colour

unicorn /yo͞oni kawrn/ *n* **1** a mythical animal usually depicted as a white horse with a single straight spiralled horn growing from its forehead **2** a horned animal mentioned in the Bible, now believed to be a rhinoceros or aurochs [13C. Via Old French < Latin *unicornis* 'one-horned' < *cornu* 'horn'.]

unicycle /yo͞oni sīk'l/ *n* a pedal-powered vehicle having a single wheel with a seat mounted on a frame above it [Mid-19C. After BICYCLE.] —**unicyclist** *n*

unidealized /únī deé ə līzd/, **unidealised** *adj* realistic and not ignoring imperfections or inconsistencies

unidentified /ún ī dénti fīd/ *adj* **1** unable to be recognized or given a name **2** wishing not to be associated with or held responsible for something

unidirectional /yo͞oni di réksh'nəl, -dī-/ *adj* thinking, moving, or operating in only one direction

UNIDO /yoo neédō/, **Unido** *abbr* United Nations Industrial Development Organization

unifactorial /yo͞oni fak táwri əl/ *adj* describes an inherited characteristic dependent on a single gene

unification /yo͞onifi káysh'n/ *n* **1** the act or process of uniting or joining together **2** a result of uniting or joining

Unification Church *n* a religious denomination founded in 1954 by the South Korean industrialist Sun Myung Moon

unified field theory *n* a single theory capable of defining the nature of the interrelationships among nuclear, electromagnetic, and gravitational forces

uniform /yo͞oni fawrm/ *n* **1** DISTINCTIVE CLOTHES a distinctive set of clothes worn to identify somebody's occupation, affiliation, or status **2** COMPLETE OUTFIT a single outfit of identifying clothes **3** PARTICULAR IDENTIFYING LOOK a particular style or other feature that identifies somebody as a member of a certain group ■ *adj* **1** UNCHANGING always the same in quality, degree, character, or manner **2** CONSISTENT conforming to one standard or rule **3** LIKE ANOTHER being the same as another or others **4** UNVARYING IN DESIGN unvarying in colour, texture, or design ■ *vt* **1** PROVIDE WITH UNIFORMS to provide people or a group with uniforms **2** MAKE THE SAME to make something homogeneous, unvarying, or consistent [Mid-16C. Directly or via French < Latin *uniformis* 'having one form' < *forma* 'shape'.] —**uniformed** *adj* —**uniformity** /yo͞oni fáwrməti/ *n* —**uniformly** *adv*

Uniform /yo͞oni fawrm/ *n* a code word for the letter 'U', used in international radio communications

uniformitarianism /yo͞oni fáwrmi táiri ənizəm/ *n* the theory that the same geological processes occurred in the past as occur today, and that geological formations and structures can be interpreted by observing present-day actions —**uniformitarian** *adj, n*

ϟ **Uniform Resource Locator** *n* full form of **URL**

unify /yo͞oni fī/ (**-fies, -fying, -fied**) *vt* to bring people or things together to form a single unit or entity [Early

16C. Via French *unifier* < Latin *unificare* 'make one'.] —**unifiable** *adj* —**unified** *adj* —**unifier** *n* —**unifying** *adj*

unignorable /ún ig náwrəb'l/ *adj* demanding notice, attention, or comment

unilateral /yóoni láttərəl/ *adj* **1 DECIDED BY ONE PARTY** decided or acted on by only one involved party or nation irrespective of what the others do **2 ACCOUNTING FOR ONE SIDE ONLY** taking into account only one side of a subject **3 BINDING ONLY ONE PARTY** binding or at the insistence of only one party to a contract, obligation, or agreement **4 AFFECTING ONLY ONE SIDE** affecting or involving only one side of the body, only one of a pair of organs, or only one side of an organ **5 WITH PARTS ON ONLY ONE SIDE** having parts that are arranged on only one side of a stem or other axis **6 WITH ONE SIDE** having only one side **7 THROUGH ONE PARENT ONLY** tracing lineage through one parent only —**unilaterally** *adv*

unilateralism /yóoni láttərəlizəm/ *n* the implementation of a foreign policy with little or no regard for the views of allies —**unilateralist** *n*

unilineal /yóoni línni əl/ *adj* = **unilateral** *adj.* 7

unilinear /yóoni línni ər/ *adj* developing or evolving progressively through defined stages from primitive to advanced and excluding any variation on this course

unilingual /yóoni líng gwəl/ *adj* using or knowing only one language

uniliteral /yóoni líttərəl/ *adj* having only a single letter

unillustrated /un íllə straytid/ *adj* having no illustrations

unilocular /yóoni lókyóolər/ *adj* with a single loculus, cell, or cavity

unimaginable /únni májjinəb'l/ *adj* beyond anything that could be imagined or described —**unimaginably** *adv*

unimaginative /únni májjinətiv/ *adj* **1** unable to think of new or interesting ideas, plans, or situations **2** boring and ordinary, without any new ideas

unimpaired /únnim páird/ *adj* not adversely affected by anything unpleasant, dangerous, or different that happens

unimpassioned /únnim pásh'nd/ *adj* unlikely to appeal to the emotions

unimpeachable /únnim péechəb'l/ *adj* **1** impossible to discredit or challenge **2** so good that it is beyond reproach —**unimpeachably** *adv*

unimpeded /ún im péedid/ *adj* providing or affording free unobstructed movement, progress, development, or communication

unimportant /únnim páwrt'nt/ *adj* of little or no significance —**unimportance** *n*

unimposing /ún im pózing/ *adj* unimpressive because of a lack of size or grandeur

unimpressed /ún im prést/ *adj* not having a lasting or favourable impression of somebody or something

unimpressive /ún im préssiv/ *adj* not producing a lasting or favourable impression —**unimpressively** *adv* —**unimpressiveness** *n*

unimproved /únnim próovd/ *adj* **1 NOT MADE BETTER** not made better or not developed ○ *hours of driving on unimproved roads* **2 NOT GETTING HEALTHIER** not showing improvement in health ○ *her condition remains unimproved* **3 WITHOUT IMPROVEMENTS** describes land that is not modified in a way that would increase value, e.g. by cultivation or the addition of buildings, landscaping, or services ○ *an unimproved plot*

unincorporated /únnin káwrpə raytid/ *adj* **1** not organized into a corporation or municipality **2** not included as a part of something

unindented /ún in déntid/ *adj* printed without a space set in from the margin

unindicted /ún in dítid/ *adj* not formally charged with the commission of a crime ○ *a second, unindicted conspirator*

unindustrialized /ún in dústri ə lízd/, **unindustrialised** *adj* having little or no industrial development

uninfected /ún in féktid/ *adj* not affected by a disease or virus, or contaminated with a toxin

uninfluenced /un ín floo ənst/ *adj* not influenced by somebody or something

uninformative /únnin fáwrmətiv/ *adj* not providing adequate information —**uninformatively** *adv*

uninformed /únnin fáwrmd/ *adj* lacking facts or knowledge of a particular situation or subject

uninhabitable /únnin hábbitəb'l/ *adj* unfit as a habitation, especially for human beings —**uninhabitability** /únnin hábbitə bílləti/ *n*

uninhabited /únnin hábbitid/ *adj* without human habitation

uninhibited /únnin híbbitid/ *adj* **1** expressing feelings or views without restraint **2** not subject to social or other constraints —**uninhibitedly** *adv* —**uninhibitedness** *n*

uninitiate /únni níshi ət/ *adj* without experience

uninitiated /únni níshi aytid/ *adj* having no knowledge or experience of a particular subject ■ *npl* people who have no knowledge or experience of a particular subject (+ *plural verb*)

uninjured /un ínjərd/ *adj* having sustained no injuries

uninspired /únnin spírd/ *adj* lacking originality or distinction

uninspiring /únnin spíring/ *adj* not arousing interest or excitement

⚡**uninstall** /únnin stáwl/ *vt* to remove software from a computer

uninstructed /únnin strúktid/ *adj* **1 NOT EDUCATED** not educated or informed **2 NOT TOLD WHAT TO DO** natural or instinctive and not acquired by teaching or instruction **3** not told how to cast a vote

uninsurable /únnin shóorəb'l, -sháwr-/ *adj* considered too great a risk to cover by insurance —**uninsurability** /únnin shóorə bílləti, -sháwrə-/ *n*

uninsured /únnin shóord, -sháwrd/ *adj* not covered against some hazard by insurance ■ *npl* a person or group not covered by insurance (+ *plural verb*)

unintellectual /ún intə lékchoo əl/ *adj* not having, or intended for those who do not have, the power of thinking intelligently on an abstract level

unintelligent /únnin téllijənt/ *adj* **1** lacking or showing a lack of intelligence **2** not having a mind or the ability to think and reason —**unintelligently** *adv*

unintelligible /únnin téllijəb'l/ *adj* difficult or impossible to understand —**unintelligibility** /únnin téllijə bílləti/ *n* —**unintelligibly** *adv*

unintended /únnin téndid/ *adj* neither planned nor wanted

unintentional /únnin ténsh'nəl/ *adj* not on purpose or by plan —**unintentionally** *adv*

uninterest /un íntrəst/ *n* a lack of interest or concern

uninterested /un íntrəstid/ *adj* lacking interest or concern [Mid-17C. The earliest meaning was 'impartial, disinterested'.] —**uninterestedly** *adv* —**uninterestedness** *n*

USAGE See ***disinterested***.

uninteresting /un íntrəsting/ *adj* without interesting qualities —**uninterestingly** *adv*

uninterpreted /ún in túrpritid/ *adj* not having had the meaning or significance explained

uninterrupted /únnintə rúptid/ *adj* **1** without interruption or break **2** free from obstructions ○ *an uninterrupted view* —**uninterruptedly** *adv*

uninucleate /yóoni nyóokli ət/ *adj* describes a cell that has a single nucleus

uninvestigated /ún in vésti gaytid/ *adj* not having undergone a detailed inquiry or examination

uninvited /únnin vítid/ *adj* not invited or welcome

uninviting /únnin víting/ *adj* not appealing or pleasant —**uninvitingly** *adv*

uninvolved /únnin vólvd/ *adj* not participating in something

union /yóonyən/ *n* **1 ACT OF JOINING TOGETHER** the act of joining together people or things to form a whole **2 RESULT OF BRINGING PEOPLE TOGETHER** a result of bringing or joining together people or things **3 AGREEMENT** agreement or unity of interests or opinions **4 MARRIAGE** the state of being married **5 SEX** sexual intercourse **6 POLITICAL ALLIANCE** an alliance formed by the joining of people or organizations for a common political purpose **7 COMM** = **trade union 8 PARISHES UNITED TO AID THE POOR** a number of parishes in 19th-century Britain united to administer relief to the poor **9 WORKHOUSE** a workhouse in 19th-century Britain supported by parishes united to aid the poor **10 SMALL SET OF ELEMENTS** the smallest set that consists of all the elements of any or all of two or more given sets and no other elements **11 union, Union ORGANIZATION PROVIDING RECREATIONAL FACILITIES** an organization that provides recreational facilities for students at a college or university **12 union, Union BUILDIN FOR RECREATION** a building that houses recreational facilities for students at a college or university **13 COUPLIN** a coupling for parts such as pipes and pipe fitting **14 FABRIC OF DIFFERENT YARNS** a fabric made of two or mor different yarns, e.g. cotton and linen **15 union, Unio** *Aus* **RUGBY UNION** Rugby Union, as distinct from Rugb League (*informal*) [15C. Directly or via French < Latin *unio* 'oneness' < *unus* 'one'.]

Union *n* **1 NORTHERN SIDE IN US CIVIL WAR** the side of th northern states in the US Civil War, or its armed force The northern states favoured preservation of the natio as a union of states whereas the southern states de clared their secession from that union. **2 UNION OF BRITA AND NORTHERN IRELAND** the union of Great Britain an Northern Ireland since 1920 **3 UNITED STATES OF AMERIC** the United States of America

union card *n* a card signifying membership in a trad union

union catalogue *n* a library catalogue combining th materials in more than one library or in branches of th same library

Union City /yóonyən-/ **1** city in W California, near Sa Francisco Bay. Population: 64,085 (1998 estimate). **2** cit in NE New Jersey, on the Hudson River. Populatio 57,621 (1998 estimate).

Union flag *n* = **Union Jack**

unionise *vti* = **unionize**

unionism /yóonyə nizəm/ *n* **1** the principles or policies c trade unions **2** the advocacy of forming and joinin trade unions —**unionist** *n, adj*

Unionism /yóonyə nizəm/ *n* **1 SUPPORT FOR UNION WITH NORTH ERN IRELAND** support or advocacy since 1920 for the unio between Northern Ireland and Britain **2 SUPPORT FO IRELAND'S UNION WITH BRITAIN** support or advocacy befor 1920 for the union of all Ireland and Great Britai **3 LOYALTY TO FEDERAL UNION** loyalty to the federal unio during the Civil War in the United States —**Unionist** *n adj*

unionize /yóonyə nīz/ (**-izes, -izing, -ized**), **unionis (-ises, -ising, -ised**) *vti* to organize workers into a trad union, or to join a trade union —**unionization** /yóony nī záysh'n/ *n* —**unionizer** *n*

Union Jack, Union flag *n* the flag of the Unite Kingdom, which united by superposition the flags c England, Scotland, and Ireland

union shop *n* a place of employment where a contrac between the employer and a trade union requires em ployees to be or become members of the union withi a specified time. ◊ **closed shop, open shop**

union territory, Union Territory *n* a territory in Indi ruled directly by the central government

uniparous /yoo níppərəss/ *adj* **1** having given birth t only one child **2** producing a single offspring at eac birth

unipersonal /yóoni púrss'nəl/ *adj* **1** existing or manifeste in the form of only one person **2** existing as an inflecte form in only one person, especially the third perso singular

uniplanar /yóoni pláynər/ *adj* occurring or located in a single plane

unipod /yóoni pod/ *n* a one-legged stand, e.g. for a camera [Mid-20C. After TRIPOD.]

unipolar /yóoni pólər/ *adj* **1 HAVING SINGLE POLE** operatin by means of, having, or produced by a single electri or magnetic pole **2 BRANCHING OUT AT ONLY ONE END** describe a neurone that branches out at only one end **3 WITH ON POLARITY** describes a transistor that has carriers wit only one polarity —**unipolarity** /yóonipō lárrəti/ *n*

unipotent /yóoni pót'nt/ *adj* describes an embryonic ce that is capable of developing into only one type of ce or tissue

~~**uniqe**~~ incorrect spelling of **unique**

unique /yoo néek/ *adj* **1 ONLY ONE** being the only one of it kind **2** ⚠ **UNUSUAL** different from others in a way tha makes something special and worthy of note ○ *a uniqu marketing opportunity.* **3 LIMITED** limited to a specifi place, situation, group, person, or thing ○ *concerns tha are unique to resettled refugees* [Early 17C. Via French < Latin *unicus* < *unus* 'one'.] —**uniquely** *adv* —**uniquenes** *n*

USAGE The use of *unique* in its sense 'worthy of note' is common in marketing and advertising (*Don't miss this unique offer*), as well as in conversation. Many dictionaries and usage guides argue that *unique* is an absolute concept, thereby rejecting the use of qualifying words such as *very* and *rather*, but in many cases this stricture seems a pedantic objection to what is a linguistic rather than a philosophical convention. It is, however, best avoided in formal writing.

unique selling point, **unique selling proposition** *n* full form of **USP**

unirrigated /un írri gaytid/ *adj* not artificially supplied with water in order to help crops to grow

specific function who are part of a larger organization ○ *the cancer research unit* **4 GROUP OF MILITARY PERSONNEL** a group of military personnel with a particular function organized as a subdivision of a larger body **5 COMPONENT OR ASSEMBLY OF COMPONENTS** a component or assembly of components that performs a specific function ○ *a kitchen unit* **6** *US, Can, Aus, NZ* **RESIDENCE** one of a number of similar residences within a building or development **7 PART OF ACADEMIC COURSE** a part of an academic course that focuses on a particular theme **8 MEASUREMENT** a standard measurement, e.g. an inch, degree, calorie, volt, or hour, whose multiples are used in determining quantity **9 DRUG AMOUNT** an amount of an enzyme, hormone, drug, or other agent that produces a given

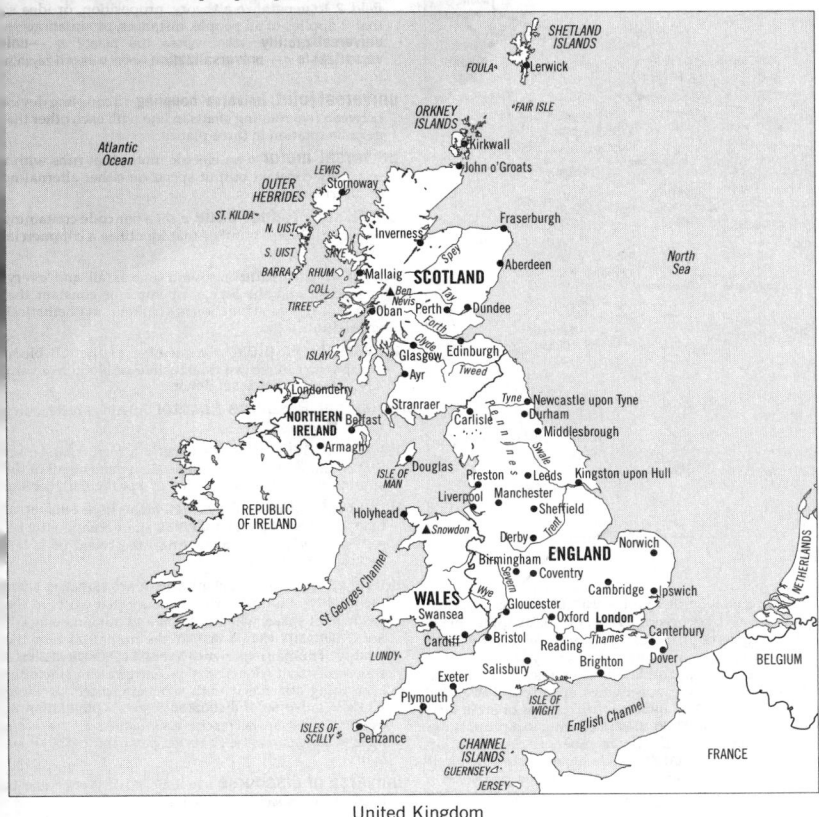

United Kingdom

uniseptate /yoóni sép tayt/ *adj* with a single separating wall or membrane [Mid-19C. < UNI- + SEPTUM.]

uniserial /yoóni seéri əl/, **uniseriate** /-ayt/ *adj* arranged in or consisting of a single row or series

unisex /yoóni seks/ *adj* **1** designed or suitable for people of either sex ○ *unisex fashions* **2** not distinctly of either the male or the female sex

unisexual /yoóni sékshoo əl/ *adj* **1** related to or limited to one sex **2** having either only male or only female reproductive organs —**unisexuality** /yoóni sékshoo állati/ *n* —**unisexually** *adv*

unison /yoóniss'n/ *n* **1** two or more notes sharing the same pitch **2** the performance of two or more parts at the same pitch or an octave apart [Late 16C. Via Old French < late Latin *unisonus* 'having the same sound' < *sonus* 'sound'.] ◇ **in unison 1** in perfect agreement or harmony **2** at the same time as somebody or something else

UNISON /yoóniss'n/ *n* the largest trade union in the United Kingdom, for public service employees

unit /yoónit/ *n* **1 ONE PERSON, THING, OR GROUP** a single person, thing, or group, usually regarded as a whole part of something larger ○ *the family unit* **2 DISCRETE PART** any of the individuals or discrete parts or elements into which something can be divided, especially for analysis **3 GROUP WITH SPECIFIC FUNCTION** a group of people with a

effect, often as specified by an internationally agreed standard **10 MEASURE OF ALCOHOL INTAKE** a measure of alcohol intake used in monitoring the effects of alcohol on the body **11 NATURAL NUMBER** the lowest positive natural number **12 NUMBER LESS THAN TEN** the first digit to the left of the decimal point in decimal notation, representing a whole number less than ten **13 SET WITH SINGLE NUMBER** a set having a single number [Late 16C. < Latin *unus* 'one', after *digit*.]

unitard /yoóni taard/ *n* a one-piece stretchable garment with or without sleeves that covers the body from the neck to the feet [Mid-20C. < UNI- + LEOTARD.]

unitarian /yoóni táiri ən/ *n* a supporter of unity or a unitary system —**unitarianism** *n*

Unitarian /yoóni táiri ən/ *n* **1** a member of the Christian Church that upholds the doctrine of Unitarianism **2 Unitarian, unitarian** a Christian who does not believe in the Trinity —**Unitarian** *adj*

Unitarianism /yoóni táiri ə nizəm/ *n* a religious doctrine that rejects the Christian doctrine of the Trinity, the divinity of Jesus Christ, and formal dogma but stresses reason and individual conscience in belief and practice

unitary /yoónitəri/ *adj* **1 RELATING TO UNIT** relating to or consisting of a unit **2 CHARACTERIZED BY UNITY** based on or characterized by unity **3 EXISTING AS UNIT** undivided and

existing as a unit **4 OF CENTRALIZED GOVERNMENT** of or based on a system of government in which authority is centralized —**unitarily** *adv*

Unitary Authority, **Unitary Council** *n* an administrative body responsible for the provision of all local government services in its area

unit cell *n* the smallest structural unit of a crystal that has all its symmetry and by repetition in three dimensions makes up its full lattice

unit cost *n* the cost of producing a single item

unite /yoo nít/ (**unites, uniting, united**) *v* **1** *vti* **BRING THINGS TOGETHER** to bring things together or to come together to form or act as a unit **2** *vti* **UNIFY PEOPLE** to unify people or to become unified by a common interest or concern **3** *vti* **MARRY** to join a couple in marriage or be married **4** *vti* **ADHERE** to adhere or cause things to adhere **5** *vt* **COMBINE QUALITIES** to combine qualities or traits [15C. < Latin *unit-*, past participle of *unire* 'make one' < *unus* 'one'.] —**uniter** *n*

united /yoo nítid/ *adj* **1 COMBINED INTO ONE** combined into or made one **2 BY OR FROM UNION** formed by or resulting from the union of two or more persons or things **3 IN HARMONY** in agreement or harmony —**unitedness** *n*

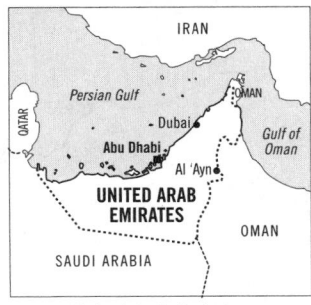

United Arab Emirates

United Arab Emirates /yoo nítid árrəb émmərəts/ federation of seven independent states on the E Arabian Peninsula, including Abu Dhabi, Ajmān, Dubai, Al Fujayrah, Ra's al Khaymah, Ash Sharigah, and Umm Al Qaywayn. Capital: Abu Dhabi. Population: 2,500,000 (1996). Area: 77,700 sq. km/30,000 sq. mi.

United Arab Republic former independent union between Egypt and Syria

United Kingdom /-kíngdəm/ constitutional monarchy in NW Europe, comprising the historic kingdoms of England and Scotland, the principality of Wales, and the province of Northern Ireland. Capital: London. Population: 58,784,000 (1996). Area: 241,752 sq. km/93,341 sq. mi.

United Nations *n* an organization of nations that was formed in 1945 to promote peace, security, and international cooperation (+ *singular or plural verb*)

United States federal republic in central North America, consisting of 50 states. Capital: Washington, D.C. Population: 270,311,758 (1998). Area: 9,629,047 sq. km/3,717,796 sq. mi. See map overleaf.

unitise *vt* = unitize

unitive /yoónitiv/ *adj* **1** having the ability to unite or promoting unity **2** characterized by union or unity [Early 16C. < late Latin *unitivus* < Latin *unit-* (see UNITE).]

unitize /yoóni tíz/ (**-izes, -izing, -ized**), **unitise** (**-ises, -ising, -ised**) *v* **1** *vti* **MAKE ONE** to form or to make something into a single unit **2** *vt* **DIVIDE INTO UNITS** to separate something into units **3** *vt* **CONVERT TRUST** to convert an investment trust into a unit trust —**unitization** /yoóni tī záysh'n/ *n*

unit of account *n* **1** the way money is used to keep financial accounts **2** FIN = **money of account 3** the official currency of a nation

unit operation *n* an operation, e.g. mixing, filtration, chemical reaction, or distillation, that is common in the chemical process industries

unit price *n* the price of goods per item or measure, e.g. per pound or dozen

United States

unit trust *n* a trust company that manages investments for investors with holdings in the form of units representing a fraction of the value of the investments that are issued by and bought back by the managers. US term **mutual fund**

unity /yoónati/ (*plural* **-ties**) *n* 1 BEING ONE the state of being one 2 COMBINING INTO ONE the combining or joining of separate things or entities to form one 3 SOMETHING WHOLE something whole or complete formed by combining or joining separate things or entities 4 HARMONY harmony of opinion, interest, or feeling 5 SINGLENESS AMONG INDIVIDUALS singleness or constancy among individuals or groups 6 ARRANGING OF ARTISTIC ELEMENTS AESTHETICALLY the arranging of separate elements in a literary or artistic work to create an overall aesthetic impression 7 AESTHETIC IMPRESSION the overall aesthetic impression produced by the arrangement of elements in an artistic or literary work 8 PRINCIPLE OF DRAMATIC STRUCTURE any one of the three principles of dramatic structure derived from Aristotle's *Poetics* 9 NUMBER ONE a number by which a given element of a mathematical system can be multiplied with the result being equal to the value of the given element 10 MATH = **identity element** [13C. Via Old French *unite* < Latin *unitas* < unus 'one'.]

univ. *abbr* university

univalent /yoóni váylant, yoo nívvalant/ *adj* 1 CHEM = **monovalent** *adj*. 1 2 describes a chromosome that remains unpaired during the cell division (**meiosis**) that precedes sex cell formation —**univalency** *n*

univalve /yoóni valv/ *adj* 1 WITH SINGLE-PIECE SHELL having a shell that is a single piece or valve ○ *an univalve gastropod* 2 MADE OF SINGLE PIECE describes a shell that is made of a single piece ■ *n* MOLLUSC a mollusc or shell that is univalve

universal /yoóni vúrss'l/ *adj* 1 AFFECTING THE WORLD affecting, relating to, or including the whole world or everyone in the world 2 RELATING TO UNIVERSE relating to the universe or everything 3 AFFECTING THOSE IN PARTICULAR GROUP affecting, relating to, or including everyone in a particular group or situation 4 USED BY EVERYONE used or understood by everyone 5 APPLICABLE TO ALL applicable to all situations or purposes ○ *a universal solution* 6 PRESENT EVERYWHERE present or prevalent everywhere 7 KNOWLEDGEABLE knowledgeable about or encompassing extensive skills, interests, activities, or subjects 8 ADAPTABLE TO DIFFERENT SIZES adaptable to many uses or sizes 9 AFFIRMING OR DENYING EVERY MEMBER relating to a proposition that is true or false of every member of a class or group ■ *n* 1 COMMON CHARACTERISTIC a characteristic or behaviour pattern common to everyone or all the people in a particular group or situation 2 TRUE OR FALSE PROPOSITION FOR ALL a proposition that is true or false for all members of a class or group 3 GENERAL TERM OR CONCEPT a general term or concept or that which it denotes 4 UNCHANGING METAPHYSICAL ENTITY a metaphysical entity that remains unchanged in character through a series of changing relations 5 PLATONIC IDEA OR ARISTOTELIAN FORM a Platonic idea or Aristotelian form 6 GRAMMATICAL CHARACTERISTIC COMMON TO ALL LANGUAGES an actual or possible characteristic common to the grammatical description of all human languages —**universality** /yoóni vur sállati/ *n* —**universally** *adv*

SYNONYMS See **widespread**.

universal beam *n* a strong steel beam suitable as a support, used either vertically or horizontally

universal class *n* MATH = **universal set**

universal coupling *n* ENG = **universal joint**

universal donor *n* somebody with group O blood who can potentially donate blood to anyone, regardless of the recipient's blood group. ◊ **universal recipient**

universal grammar *n* the set of actual or possible rules that form the grammatical description of all human languages

universal indicator *n* a solution that undergoes several colour changes over a wide range of pH values

universalise *vt* = **universalize**

universalism /yoóni vúrss'lizam/ *n* 1 COMPREHENSIVE RANGE a comprehensive range of knowledge, interests, or activities 2 UNIVERSAL FEATURE a universal characteristic or feature 3 PRINCIPLE OF WELFARE SERVICES the principle that welfare services should be publicly funded and available to all strictly on the basis of need —**universalist** *n* —**universalistic** /yoóni vurssa lístik/ *adj*

Universalism /yoóni vúrss'lizam/ *n* the doctrine of salvation for all people —**Universalist** *n*

universalize /yoóni vúrssa líz/ (**-izes, -izing, -ized**), **universalise** (**-ises, -ising, -ised**) *vt* 1 to make something universal in use or distribution, often within a certain field 2 to generalize a theory, proposition, or idea so that it applies to all people, instances, or situations —**universalizability** /yoóni vúrssa líza bíllati/ *n* —**universalizable** *n* —**universalization** /yoóni vurssa lí záysh'n/ *n*

universal joint, universal coupling *n* a coupling device between two rotating shafts in line with each other that permits rotation in three planes

universal motor *n* an electric motor that runs with a relatively constant output speed on either alternating or direct current

Universal Product Code *n* US a bar code containing a unique 12-digit number that identifies a commercial product

universal quantifier *n* a word such as 'all' and 'every' in English and the logical operator or constant that performs the same function in symbolic, mathematical, or predicate logic

universal recipient *n* a member of the AB blood group who can receive transfusions of blood from any ABO group. ◊ **universal donor**

⚡ **Universal Resource Locator** *n* Uniform Resource Locator (*dated*)

universal set, universal class *n* a mathematical set that contains all of the possible elements and all of the subsets relevant to the solution of a particular problem

universal time *n* 1 = Greenwich Mean Time 2 universal time, universal time coordinated an internationally accepted standard for calculating time based on International Atomic Time

universe /yoónivurss/ *n* 1 ALL MATTER AND ENERGY IN SPACE the totality of all matter and energy that exists in the vastness of space, whether known to human beings or not 2 HUMANITY AND ITS HISTORY the human race or the totality of human experience 3 SPHERE OF PERSON OR THING a sphere of activity or field that is centred on and includes everything associated with a person, place, or thing 4 LOGIC = **universe of discourse** 5 STATS = **population** *n*. 5 [14C. Directly or via French < Latin *universum* 'the whole world' < *universus* 'whole', < *versus*, past participle of *vertere* 'turn'.]

universe of discourse *n* in logic, all of a set of objects implied by a specific discussion

university /yoóni vúrssati/ (*plural* **-ties**) *n* 1 UNDERGRADUATE AND POSTGRADUATE EDUCATIONAL INSTITUTION faculties comprising departments offering courses of undergraduate and postgraduate study in many subjects 2 BUILDINGS HOUSING A UNIVERSITY the buildings, other facilities, and grounds of a university 3 STUDENTS AND STAFF the students, teachers, and administrative and other staff of a university [14C. Via French *université* < Latin *universitas* 'the whole, society, guild' < *universus* (see UNIVERSE).]

univocal /yoóni vók'l/ *adj* having only one meaning ■ *n* a word or term with only one meaning [Mid-16C. < late Latin *univocus* 'having one voice' < *vox* 'voice'.] —**univocally** *adv*

⚡ **UNIX** /yoóniks/, **Unix** *tdmk* a trademark for a widely used computer operating system, developed in 1969 at AT&T Bell Laboratories, that can support multitasking in a multiuser environment

unjam /un jám/ (**-jams, -jamming, -jammed**) *vti* to remove a blockage or stoppage from something, or become free from a blockage or stoppage

unjust /un júst/ *adj* contrary to what is right, just, or fair, or lacking fairness or justice —**unjustly** *adv* —**unjustness** *n*

unjustifiable /un jústi fī ab'l/ *adj* incapable of being shown to be, or defended as being, fair, reasonable, or correct —**unjustifiably** *adv*

unjustified /un jústi fīd/ *adj* **1 HAVING NO ACCEPTABLE JUSTIFICATION** shown to have no good or just reason or explanation **2 NOT HAVING A STRAIGHT VERTICAL MARGIN** not arranged evenly in such a way that the ends of the lines on a page form a straight vertical line parallel to the margin **3 NOT PRONOUNCED TO BE RIGHTEOUS** not having been made or declared righteous

unkempt /un kémpt/ *adj* **1 NEEDING GROOMING** tangled, matted, or messy, and needing combing or grooming **2 UNTIDY AND NEGLECTED** untidy or disorderly as a result of neglect or a lack of care **3 UNPOLISHED** lacking in polish or elegance [14C. < UN-¹ + *kempt*, past participle of *kemb* 'comb' < Old English *cemban* < Germanic.]

unkennel /un kénn'l/ (**-nels, -nelling, -nelled**) *vt* **1 LET DOG OUT OF KENNEL** to let a dog out of a kennel **2 FORCE ANIMAL OUT OF LAIR** to make an animal leave its den or lair **3 MAKE SOMETHING KNOWN** to reveal or uncover something secret or hidden

unkind /un kínd/ *adj* **1** lacking or resulting from a lack of kindness, sympathy, or consideration **2** severe, harsh, or inclement —**unkindness** *n*

unkindly /un kíndli/ *adv* in an unkind manner or without showing kindness ■ *adj* lacking in kindliness —**unkindliness** *n*

unkink /un kíngk/ *v* **1** *vti* to remove a kink or kinks from something, or to have a kink or kinks removed **2** *vi US* to become loose or relaxed

unknit /un nít/ (**-knits, -knitting, -knitted** *or* **-knit**) *vti* **1** to unravel something or become unravelled **2** to allow the eyebrows to move back to a natural position after being drawn together, or to be moved apart in this way

unknot /un nót/ (**-knots, -knotting, -knotted**) *vti* to remove the knots or tangles from something

unknowable /un nṓ əb'l/ *adj* impossible to know, often because of lying outside human experience or being inaccessible to human understanding ■ *n* something that cannot be known —**unknowability** /un nṓ ə bíllәti/ *n* —**unknowableness** *n* —**unknowably** *adv*

unknowing /un nṓ ing/ *adj* **1** unwitting or lacking awareness **2** not intended —**unknowingly** *adv*

unknowledgeable /un nóllijəb'l/, **unknowledgable** *adj* not possessing or showing a great deal of knowledge or intelligence

unknown /ún nṓn/ *adj* **1 NOT KNOWN** not forming part of somebody's knowledge or of knowledge in general **2 NOT IDENTIFIED** undetermined or undiscovered **3 NOT WIDELY KNOWN** not known to, or recognized by, many people ■ *n* **1 SOMEBODY OR SOMETHING NOT KNOWN** somebody or something that is not part of somebody's knowledge or of knowledge in general **2 SOMEBODY OR SOMETHING NOT WIDELY KNOWN** somebody or something that is not known or recognized by many people **3 VARIABLE TO BE DETERMINED** a variable in an equation whose values are solutions of the equation

Unknown Soldier *n* an unidentified soldier killed in battle and selected for burial with national honours to represent all those who died fighting for their country but could not be identified

unlabelled /un láyb'ld/ *adj* not provided with a label or identifying term

unlabored *adj* US = **unlaboured**

unlaboured /un láybərd/ *adj* exhibiting a naturalness and ease of accomplishment

unlace /un láyss/ (**-laces, -lacing, -laced**) *vt* **1** to loosen or untie the laces of a shoe, piece of clothing, or other item **2** to loosen or untie laced shoes or clothing on somebody

unlade /un láyd/ (**-lades, -lading, -laded, -laded** *or* **-laden** /-láyd'n/) *vt* **1** to empty a ship or vehicle by removing its cargo or load **2** to remove a cargo or load from a ship or vehicle

unlash /un lásh/ *vt* to loosen or untie the ropes or other lashing holding or restraining something

unlatch /un lách/ *vti* to unfasten or open by lifting or releasing a latch, or become unfastened or open in this way

unlawful /un láwf'l/ *adj* **1** not permitted by the law **2** contrary to religious precepts, ethical standards, or the conventions of society —**unlawfully** *adv* —**unlawfulness** *n*

SYNONYMS ***unlawful, illegal, illicit, wrongful, nonlegal***

CORE MEANING: not in accordance with laws or rules

unlawful the most general and neutral term, meaning not permitted by the law or by the rules of an organization or religion, or not recognized as valid by those laws or rules; **illegal** a stronger term, meaning in contravention of a specific written statute, rule, or law, especially a criminal law; **illicit** not permitted by the law, suggesting especially that something is considered morally wrong or unacceptable; **wrongful** a term often used in civil lawsuits, meaning unjust, unfair, or against conscience, but not punishable by criminal law; **nonlegal** not established or affected under common law or legislation.

unlawful assembly *n* an assembly of people that is not sanctioned by law and is therefore illegal, e.g. a march or picket that is not in compliance with the Public Order Acts

unlay /un láy/ (**-lays, -laying, -laid**) *vti* to separate the strands of a rope by untwisting them, or become separated in this way

unlead /un léd/ *vt* to take out the leading or leads separating lines of type

unleaded /un léddid/ *adj* **1 FREE OF TETRAETHYL LEAD** not containing tetraethyl lead as an antiknock additive and consequently less harmful to the environment ○ *unleaded gas* **2 NOT SEPARATED BY LEADS** not separated by spaces created by inserting leads between the lines of type ■ *n* **UNLEADED PETROL** petrol that does not contain tetraethyl lead as an antiknock additive

unlearn /un lúrn/ (**-learns, -learning, -learnt** *or* **-learned** /-lúrnt/, **-learnt** *or* **-learned**) *vt* **1** to rid the mind of the knowledge or memory of something **2** to break the habit of something or end the practice of something

unlearned /un lúrnid/ *adj* **1 LACKING EDUCATION** not having received an education or schooling **2 DISPLAYING LACK OF EDUCATION** showing or resulting from a lack of education **3 UNSKILLED OR UNFAMILIAR** lacking a knowledge of, skills in, or familiarity with, a specified field **4 unlearned, unlearnt NATURAL OR UNSTUDIED** possessed or known without having been practised, studied, or taught —**unlearnedly** *adv*

unleash /un léesh/ *vt* **1** to set a person or animal free from a leash or other form of restraint or confinement **2** to allow something, especially something previously held in check, to have its full effect

unleavened /un lévv'nd/ *adj* made without yeast or other raising agent

unless /un léss/ *conj* except under the circumstances that ○ *I won't go unless the weather improves.* [15C. < obsolete *on less than* 'on a lower condition, except'.]

unlettered /un léttərd/ *adj* **1 NOT WELL-EDUCATED** lacking a good education or the knowledge and understanding that such an education can provide **2 ILLITERATE** unable to read and write **3 NOT HAVING ANY LETTERING** not containing or inscribed with any lettering

unlicensed /un líss'nst/ *adj* **1 HAVING NO LICENCE** lacking a required official licence, especially an official licence to sell alcohol **2 UNSANCTIONED** done without authorization or permission **3 WITHOUT ETHICAL INHIBITIONS** lacking ethical or religious constraints

unlighted /un lítid/, **unlit** /-lít/ *adj* **1** not lit by electric or natural light **2** not having been set alight

unlike /un lík/ *prep* **1 DISSIMILAR** having qualities and characteristics dissimilar to or different from somebody or something ○ *They were completely unlike each other in appearance.* **2 INDICATES CONTRAST** used to indicate a contrast between two things, people, or situations ○ *Unlike the previous government, we intend to fulfil our manifesto promises.* **3 NOT TYPICAL OF** used to indicate that somebody's words or actions are not typical or characteristic of him or her ○ *It was so unlike her to speak like that.* —**unlikeness** *n*

unlikely /un líkli/ (**-lier, -liest**) *adj* **1 IMPROBABLE** not likely to occur **2 NOT BELIEVABLE** not likely to be true or be believed **3 INCONGRUOUS** not suitable or appropriate **4 PROBABLY NOT SUCCESSFUL** not likely to meet with success —**unlikelihood** *n* —**unlikeliness** *n*

unlimber /un límbər/ (**-bers, -bering, -bered**) *vti* **1** to prepare something for action or use **2** to remove a piece of field artillery from its gun carriage and prepare it for use

unlimited /un límmitid/ *adj* **1 NOT RESTRICTED** without limits, restrictions, or controls **2 INFINITE** lacking or appearing to lack a boundary or end **3 COMPLETE OR TOTAL** not subject to qualification or exception **4 NOT LIMITED IN MONEY PAYABLE** describes a financial liability that is not limited in the amount of money that the members of a company are required to pay out if the company ceases to trade **5 NOT HAVING MEMBERS WITH LIMITED LIABILITY** describes a company in which each of the members is financially liable for his or her full share of the company's debts if the company ceases to trade —**unlimitedly** *adv* —**unlimitedness** *n*

unlined¹ /un línd/ *adj* having no lines or wrinkles

unlined² /un línd/ *adj* not covered or reinforced with a lining

unlink /un língk/ *vti* **1** to undo one or more links of something, or to become undone at one or more links **2** to separate or disconnect, or to become separated or disconnected

unlisted /un lístid/ *adj* **1 NOT ON LIST** not included on a list **2 NOT LISTED ON STOCK EXCHANGE** not registered on a physical stock exchange and consequently not available for trading on that exchange **3** *US, Can, ANZ* **NOT PUBLICLY AVAILABLE** not included in a telephone directory available to the public

unlisted securities market *n* the London market trading in shares that are not included on the official Stock Exchange list

unlit *adj* = **unlighted**

unlive /un lív/ (**-lives, -living, -lived**) *vt* to reverse or undo the effects of an experience, action, or period of life

unload /un lṓd/ *vti* **1 REMOVE CARGO OR LOAD FROM CARRIER** to take off or remove a cargo or load from a ship, lorry, or pack animal **2 DISCHARGE** to discharge passengers or cargo **3 REMOVE CHARGE FROM GUN** to remove a charge or cartridge from a gun **4 TAKE FILM OUT OF CAMERA** to remove a roll of film from a camera **5 SELL ON SOMETHING UNWANTED** to get rid of something, especially by selling a large quantity of it **6 TRANSFER SOMETHING UNWANTED** to pass work, responsibility, or a problem on to somebody else **7 SHARE TROUBLES** to find an outlet for worries or negative feelings by sharing them with somebody else

unlock /un lók/ *v* **1** *vti* **OPEN OR BECOME OPEN AFTER LOCKING** to open a lock or something locked, or to become open after being locked **2** *vt* **GIVE ACCESS TO** to provide access to something previously unavailable **3** *vti* **RELEASE EMOTION** to release or unleash a pent-up feeling or emotion, or to be released or unleashed **4** *vti* **REVEAL OR BE REVEALED** to expose or explain something, or to be exposed or explained **5** *vti* **LOOSEN** to unclench something, or to be unclenched

unlooked-for /un lóokt-/ *adj* not hoped for or expected

unloose /un lóoss/ (**-looses, -loosing, -loosed**), **unloosen** /-lóoss'n/ *vt* **1 UNFASTEN** to untie or undo something, especially a knot **2 SET FREE BY UNTYING** to set a person or animal free by untying restraints **3 RELEASE FROM RESTRAINT OR CONFINEMENT** to restore freedom to somebody held under restraint or in confinement **4 MAKE LOOSER** to relax the tightness of something **5 MAKE SOMETHING LESS INTENSE** to reduce the intensity of something

unloved /un lúvd/ *adj* receiving no love from others

unlovely /un lúvvli/ (**-lier, -liest**) *adj* **1** not beautiful or pleasing to look at **2** not producing pleasure or delight —**unloveliness** *n*

unlucky /un lúki/ (**-ier, -iest**) *adj* **1 HAVING BAD LUCK** not experiencing good luck or good fortune **2 FULL OF MISFORTUNE OR FAILURE** full of bad luck, misfortune, or failure **3 BRINGING MISFORTUNE** causing or heralding misfortune **4 DISAPPOINTING** producing disappointment or regret —**unluckily** *adv* —**unluckiness** *n*

unmade past tense, past participle of **unmake** ■ *adj* **1** not restored to a neat and tidy state after being slept in ○ *an unmade bed* **2** = **unmetalled**

unmailed /un máyld/ *adj US* not having been sent through the post

unmake /un máyk/ (**-makes, -making, -made** /-máyd/, **-made**) *vt* **1 UNDO** to undo the effects of something **2 CHANGE COMPLETELY** to make a fundamental change or changes in something **3 REMOVE FROM POWER** to remove somebody from office or a position of authority

unman /un mán/ (**-mans, -manning, -manned**) *vt* to cause somebody to lose a quality or qualities traditionally attributed to men, especially courage (*literary*)

unmanageable /un mánnijəb'l/ *adj* impossible or difficult to deal with —**unmanageability** /un mánnijə bíllәti/ *n* —**unmanageably** *adv*

unmanly /un mánnli/ (**-lier, -liest**) *adj* not typical or appropriate for of a man, according to traditional perceptions of masculinity —**unmanliness** *n*

unmanned /ún mánd/ adj AEROSP = **uncrewed** (often considered offensive)

unmannered /un mánnərd/ adj 1 lacking or displaying a lack of good manners 2 having an easy unaffected manner —**unmanneredly** adv

unmannerly /un mánnərli/ adj lacking or displaying a lack of good manners ■ adv in a rude or discourteous manner (archaic) —**unmannerliness** n

unmapped /un mápt/ adj 1 NOT ON A MAP not recorded on a map of a geographical area 2 UNEXPLORED not travelled to for exploration 3 NOT MAPPED not mapped as a gene sequence

unmarked /un maárkt/ adj 1 WITHOUT MARK not bearing any mark 2 LACKING IDENTIFYING MARKINGS lacking identifying letters, numbers, or symbols ○ an unmarked police car 3 UNSEEN not seen or spotted 4 LACKING DISTINGUISHING QUALITY having no particular distinguishing quality or character

unmarried /un márrid/ adj not joined to another person by marriage

unmask /un maásk/ v 1 vti TAKE MASK OFF to remove a mask from somebody or somebody's face 2 vt EXPOSE TRUE NATURE OF to expose the true nature or identity of somebody or something 3 vi LET TRUE NATURE BECOME KNOWN to allow somebody's or something's true nature or identity to become known

unmatched /un mácht/ adj 1 not matching, especially not belonging to a matching pair 2 having no equal or rival

unmated /un máytid/ adj not having a mate for breeding purposes

unmaterialistic /ún mə teeri ə lístik/ adj not concerned with or desiring material wealth and possessions

unmatured /ún mə tyoórd, -choórd/ adj describes food or drink that has not yet matured to acquire the maximum flavour

unmeaning /un meéning/ adj 1 MEANINGLESS lacking meaning or significance 2 UNINTENTIONAL not intended or deliberate 3 UNINTELLIGENT devoid of intelligence —**unmeaningly** adv

unmeant /un mént/ adj not intended

unmeasured /un mézhərd/ adj 1 NOT DETERMINED BY MEASURING not found out by measurement 2 NOT RESTRAINED unrestrained, incautious, or ill-considered 3 NOT DIVIDED INTO BARS not marked with bar lines and therefore with no set rhythm

unmechanical /únmi kánnik'l/ adj lacking the ability or skill to work with tools and machinery —**unmechanically** adv

unmechanized /un méka nīzd/, **unmechanised** adj using human or animal labour instead of machines to carry out a task

unmelodic /ún mə lóddik/ adj not pleasantly tuneful, or having no discernible melody

unmentionable /un ménsh'nəb'l/ adj NOT TO BE MENTIONED not to be mentioned or discussed, especially in polite conversation ■ n THING NOT TO BE MENTIONED something that should not be mentioned or discussed, especially in polite conversation ■ **unmentionables** npl UNDERWEAR undergarments (dated or humorous) —**unmentionableness** n —**unmentionably** adv

unmerciful /un múrssif'l/ adj 1 displaying no mercy or characterized by a lack of mercy 2 going beyond what is reasonable —**unmercifully** adv —**unmercifulness** n

unmerited /un mérritid/ adj not earned or deserved ○ unmerited good fortune

unmet /ún mét/ adj not satisfactorily fulfilled

unmetalled /ún métt'ld/ adj not covered with durable road surfacing material

unmethodical /ún mə thóddik'l/ adj unsystematic and badly organized

unmindful /un míndf'l/ adj not aware, attentive, careful, or heedful of somebody or something —**unmindfully** adv —**unmindfulness** n

unmistakable /únmi stáykəb'l/, **unmistakeable** adj easily recognized or understood —**unmistakably** adv

~~unmistakeable~~ incorrect spelling of **unmistakable**

unmitigated /un mítti gaytid/ adj 1 not lessened or eased in any way 2 absolute and unqualified —**unmitigatedly** adv —**unmitigatedness** n

unmixed /ún míkst/ adj not mixed, especially not diminished by the presence or occurrence of something else

unmodifiable /un móddi fī əb'l/ adj not able to be changed or altered

unmodified /un móddi fīd/ adj not having undergone any changes or alterations

unmolested /únmə léstid/ adj not bothered, interfered with, or stopped ■ adv without being bothered, interfered with, or stopped

unmoor /un moór, un máwr/ v 1 vti to free a ship or boat from its moorings, or to be freed from moorings 2 vt to leave a ship or boat moored by only one of its anchors

unmoral /un mórrəl/ adj 1 lacking or displaying a lack of a moral sense 2 not subject to morality or ethics —**unmorality** /únmə rálləti/ n —**unmorally** adv

unmotivated /un móti vaytid/ adj 1 not stimulated by interest or desire to do something 2 not resulting from an understandable reason or motive

unmould /un mōld/ vt to remove something from a mould

unmovable /un moóvəb'l/, **unmoveable** adj 1 not able to be moved to another place or position 2 not able to be swayed or persuaded of another viewpoint

unmoved /un moóvd/ adj having or showing no emotional reaction to something

SYNONYMS See *impassive*.

unmoving /un moóving/ adj 1 STATIONARY not in motion 2 EMOTIONALLY UNAFFECTING not causing an emotional reaction 3 STILL not in motion ○ unmoving vehicles 4 NOT AROUSING EMOTIONS failing to arouse deep emotions ○ an unmoving story

unmown /un mṓn/ adj not mown with a scythe or machine

unmuffle /un múff'l/ (-fles, -fling, -fled) vt to remove a muffle or something that muffles from something

unmusical /un myoózik'l/ adj 1 lacking melodic qualities and consequently unpleasant to hear 2 having no ability for, or no interest in, music —**unmusically** adv —**unmusicalness** n —**unmusicality** /un myoŏzi kálləti/ n

unmuzzle /un múzz'l/ (-zles, -zling, -zled) vt 1 to remove a muzzle from an animal, especially a dog 2 to restore to a person or organization the right to say, publish, or broadcast something

unmyelinated /un mī əli naytid/ adj describes a nerve fibre that lacks a myelin sheath, such as in worms, insects, and other invertebrate animals

unnameable /un náyməb'l/, **unnamable** adj incapable of being named, especially too terrible to name

unnamed /ún náymd/ adj 1 having a name but not specified by it 2 not yet assigned a name

unnatural /un nácherəl/ adj 1 CONTRARY TO LAWS OF NATURE contrary to the physical laws of nature 2 NOT CONFORMING TO THE AVERAGE behaving in ways that contradict conventional assumptions about what constitutes normal or acceptable human behaviour 3 CONTRARY TO EXPECTED BEHAVIOUR contrary to a particular habit, custom, or practice 4 ARTIFICIAL affected, artificial, contrived, or strained —**unnaturally** adv —**unnaturalness** n

unnavigable /un návvigəb'l/ adj 1 NOT PASSABLE BY A VESSEL not wide or deep enough to allow a ship or boat to pass through 2 DIFFICULT TO DRIVE THROUGH so complex as to be very hard to drive through in a motor vehicle ○ the unnavigable narrow streets of an old seaport 3 DIFFICULT TO UNDERSTAND so complex as to be difficult or impossible to read through or understand ○ unnavigable tax laws

unnecessary /un néssəssəri/ adj 1 not essential, needed, or required 2 gratuitous, unjustified, and hurtful —**unnecessarily** adv

unneeded /un neédid/ adj not needed or necessary

unnerve /un núrv/ (-nerves, -nerving, -nerved) vt 1 to deprive somebody of courage, resolve, or self-confidence 2 to cause somebody to feel nervous —**unnerving** adj —**unnervingly** adv

unnoticeable /un nótissəb'l/ adj not easily noticed or observed —**unnoticeably** adv

unnoticed /un nótist/ adv without being seen or spotted by anybody —**unnoticed** adj

unnumbered /un númbərd/ adj 1 too many to be counted 2 not assigned or having an identifying number

UNO abbr United Nations Organization

unobjectionable /ún əb jéksh'nəb'l/ adj unlikely to bring objections or cause offence

unobscured /ún əb skyoórd/ adj not concealed, covered, or darkened

unobservable /ún əb zúrvəb'l/ adj not able to be seen or detected

unobservant /ún əb zúrvənt/ adj 1 not paying close attention or noticing details 2 not strictly adhering to the rules and rituals of a religion

unobserved /ún əb zúrvd/ adj not seen or noticed

unobstructed /ún əb strúktid/ adj having no blockages or obstructions

unobtainable /ún əb táynəb'l/ adj not able to be obtained or acquired

unobtrusive /únnəb troóssiv/ adj not conspicuous, blatant, or assertive —**unobtrusively** adv —**unobtrusiveness** n

unoccupied /un ókyoo pīd/ adj 1 NOT IN USE not being used by anybody 2 NOT DOING ANYTHING not doing anything or anything important 3 NOT INHABITED not lived in by anybody 4 NOT UNDER FOREIGN MILITARY RULE not under the control or military rule of a foreign country

SYNONYMS See *vacant*.

unofficial /únnə físh'l/ adj 1 UNAUTHORIZED not authorized or sanctioned by the proper official or other authority 2 NOT ACTING OFFICIALLY not acting or employed in an official capacity or position 3 NOT DONE OR MADE OFFICIALLY not done or made by somebody acting in an official capacity 4 LACKING UNION APPROVAL not ratified by the trade union to which the strikers belong ○ an unofficial strike 5 NOT ON LIST OF APPROVED DRUGS not included on an official list of medicinal drugs —**unofficially** adv

unopened /un ōpənd/ adj not opened

unopposed /únnə pōzd/ adj, adv 1 MEETING WITH NO OPPOSITION not fought, objected to, or resisted 2 HAVING NO OPPONENT unchallenged by an official opponent in an election or competition ■ adv 1 WITH NO OPPOSITION without being fought, objected to, or resisted 2 WITH NO OPPONENT without being challenged by an official opponent in an election or competition

unorganized /un áwrgə nīzd/, **unorganised** adj 1 NOT DONE IN ORGANIZED WAY not arranged or done in an orderly or systematic way 2 NOT ACTING IN ORGANIZED WAY not acting, thinking, or working in an orderly or systematic manner 3 NOT UNIONIZED not organized in a trade union or unions 4 NOT LIVING lacking the characteristics of a living organism

unoriginal /únnə ríjjin'l/ adj lacking in originality or creativity —**unoriginality** /únnə ríjji nálləti/ n

unornamented /un áwrnə mentid/ adj plain and lacking any decoration or embellishment

unorthodox /un áwrthə doks/ adj 1 not following, or resulting from a failure to follow, conventional or traditional beliefs or practices 2 not practising or conforming to the accepted traditional form of a particular religion —**unorthodoxly** adv —**unorthodoxy** n

unowned /un ōnd/ adj 1 not belonging to anyone ○ unowned dogs roaming the streets 2 not acknowledged or admitted to (literary) ○ unowned fears and anxieties

unp. abbr unpaged

unpack /un pák/ v 1 vt TAKE CONTENTS FROM to take the contents out of something 2 vti TAKE OUT PACKED THINGS to remove something that has been packed from its container or packaging 3 vt TAKE PACK OFF to take a pack or other burden from a person or animal that has been carrying it 4 vt REVEAL WHAT IS HIDDEN IN to reveal what is hidden, buried, or encoded within something

unpackaged /un pákijd/ adj not presented in a wrapper or container

unpaged /un páyjd/, **unpaginated** /un pájji naytid/ adj not marked with page numbers

unpaid /ún páyd/ adj 1 NOT YET SETTLED awaiting payment or settlement 2 HAVING NOT YET RECEIVED PAYMENT not yet in receipt of payment for work done 3 WORKING FOR NO PAY working without wages or a salary 4 NOT PAYING MONEY not paying wages or a salary

unpainted /un páyntid/ adj not having been painted

unpaired /ún páird/ adj 1 not being one of a pair 2 characterized by a lack of pairs

npalatable /un pálletəb'l/ adj 1 having an unpleasant taste 2 not pleasant, agreeable, or acceptable —**unpalatability** /un pálleti billəti/ n —**unpalatably** adv

nparalleled /un párrə leld/ adj not equalled, matched, or paralleled in kind or quality

npardonable /un paárd'nəb'l/ adj so bad as to merit no forgiveness —**unpardonably** adv

nparliamentary /ún paarlə méntəri/ adj not acceptable according to the practice of a parliament

npasteurized /un paáschə rīzd, -páschə-/, **unpasteurised** adj not treated with heat so as to remove harmful bacteria

npatriotic /ún pattri óttik, -paytri/ adj feeling or showing no pride in or devotion to your country —**unpatriotically** adv

npatterned /un pátternd/ adj plain and having no pattern

npaved /un páyvd/ adj not covered with brick, concrete, or other hard materials to provide a suitable surface on which to walk or travel

npeeled /un peéld/ adj not having had the peel removed

npeg /un pég/ (-pegs, -pegging, -pegged) vt 1 TAKE PEG FROM to take a peg or pegs from something 2 RELEASE BY REMOVING PEG to release something by removing a peg or pegs 3 STOP FIXING PRICES OR WAGES to allow something, especially prices or wages, to fluctuate freely by removing the restrictions holding them at a fixed level

npenalized /un peénə līzd/, **unpenalised** adj not having had an official penalty or punishment imposed

npeople /un peép'l/ (-ples, -pling, -pled) vt = depopulate —**unpeopled** adj

nperceptive /ún pər séptiv/ = imperceptive —**unperceptively** adv —**unperceptiveness** n

nperformed /ún pər fáwrmd/ adj not previously performed or played

nperfumed /un púr fyoomd, ún pər fyoómd/ adj having no natural or artificial perfume

nperson /ún purss'n/ n somebody whose existence is not acknowledged officially, especially a public figure whose existence is, for political or ideological reasons, unrecognized by a totalitarian government and the news media it controls

nperturbed /únpər túrbd/ adj not worried, concerned, or upset

nphonetic /ún fə néttik/ adj using a system of writing that does not represent or correspond to the sounds of human speech

npick /un pík/ vt to undo something by pulling out a thread or threads

npigmented /ún pig méntid/ adj having no natural or added colour

npile /un píl/ (-piles, -piling, -piled) vt to take or separate something from a pile

npin /un pín/ (-pins, -pinning, -pinned) vt 1 to take a pin or pins from something 2 to release or unfasten something by removing a pin or pins

npitched /un pícht/ adj describes a musical instrument such as a drum, tambourine, or gong that is not set to a particular pitch or key

nplaced /un pláyst/ adj 1 failing to finish first, second, or third in a race 2 not assigned a particular place or position

nplanned /un plánd/ adj 1 NOT INTENDED not happening according to a plan 2 LACKING AN OVERALL PLAN not following or structured according to an overall plan or programme 3 DONE SPONTANEOUSLY accomplished without advance planning

npleasant /un plézz'nt/ adj 1 not pleasing, enjoyable, or agreeable 2 unfriendly and nasty to somebody —**unpleasantly** adv

npleasantness /un plézz'ntnəss/ n 1 UNPLEASANT CONDITION OR QUALITY the condition or quality of being unpleasant 2 UNPLEASANT EXPERIENCES OR EVENTS experiences or events that are not pleasing or enjoyable 3 UNFRIENDLINESS an unfriendly and nasty attitude or behaviour 4 UNPLEASANT SITUATION a situation that is not pleasing or enjoyable 5 DISAGREEMENT an argument or disagreement

npleasantry /un plézz'ntri/ n (plural -ries) n 1 UNFRIENDLINESS hostility towards somebody 2 UNPLEASANT REMARK OR ACTION a nasty remark or action (often plural)

3 UNPLEASANT ACTION an unfriendly and nasty action (often plural) 4 NASTY SITUATION a situation that is disconcerting or unpleasant (often plural)

unpledged /un pléjd/ adj US not having given a pledge, e.g. not having promised support or a vote to a particular candidate in an election

unploughed /un plówd/ adj relating to land or soil that has not been broken up and turned over into furrows

unplug /un plúg/ (-plugs, -plugging, -plugged) vt 1 TAKE STOPPER FROM to remove a stopper, cork, or other plug from something 2 REMOVE BLOCKAGE FROM to remove a blockage, clog, or other obstruction from something 3 PULL OUT OF ELECTRIC SOCKET to pull an electric plug out of a socket 4 DISCONNECT ELECTRICAL APPLIANCE to disconnect an electrical appliance by pulling its plug out of a socket

unplugged /ún plúgd/ adj performed without the use of amplified musical instruments, especially guitars

unplumbed /un plúmd/ adj 1 NOT FULLY EXAMINED not thoroughly understood or investigated 2 NOT CHECKED FOR VERTICALITY not checked for verticality with a plumb line 3 NOT MEASURED FOR DEPTH not measured with a plumb line to determine depth 4 LACKING PLUMBING having no plumbing or sanitation installed

unplundered /un plúndərd/ adj not having had things of value plundered from it ○ The royal graves remained undisturbed and unplundered for hundreds of years.

unpolarized /un pólə rīzd/, **unpolarised** adj showing no sharp differences, e.g. between groups of people or ideas

unpolished /un póllisht/ adj 1 lacking a shiny surface produced by polishing 2 not brought to a high level of refinement or sophistication

unpolled /un póld/ adj 1 NOT INVITED TO PARTICIPATE IN POLL not invited to participate in a survey of public opinion 2 NOT VOTING not having cast a vote at an election 3 US NOT ON ELECTORAL ROLL not included in a list of electors

unpollinated /un póllə naytid/ adj describes a plant or flower that has not been pollinated

unpolluted /ún pə loótid/ adj free of contamination, especially by any harmful substances

unpopular /un póppyŏŏlər/ adj not liked by, approved of, or acceptable to a person, a group of people, or the general public —**unpopularity** /ún poppyŏŏ lárrəti/ n —**unpopularly** adv

unpopulated /un póppyŏŏ laytid/ adj 1 having no inhabitants 2 describes a printed circuit board that has no fitted components

unposed /un pózd/ adj having subjects who have not been arranged in a special position or who are not adopting a special pose or facial expression ○ The photograph was unposed.

unpowered /un pówərd/ adj not powered or operated by electricity or fuel such as petrol

unpractical /un práktik'l/ adj 1 not effective or problem-free when put into practice ○ an unpractical plan 2 incapable of performing practical tasks or of dealing easily with practical matters ○ an unpractical person

unpractised /un práktist/ adj 1 UNTRAINED OR INEXPERIENCED lacking in training or experience 2 NOT DONE FREQUENTLY not done or not commonly done 3 NOT REHEARSED not prepared and tried out beforehand

unprecedented /un préssi dentid/ adj having no earlier parallel or equivalent

unpredictable /únpri díktəb'l/ adj not easily foreseen or predicted —**unpredictability** /únpri díktə bílləti/ n —**unpredictably** adv

unpredicted /ún prə díktid/ adj not foreseen or anticipated ○ Their success was unpredicted.

unprejudiced /un préjjŏŏdist/ adj having or reflecting opinions that are not based on insufficient knowledge, irrational feelings, or stereotypes

unpremeditated /ún pree méddi taytid/ adj done without advance planning or thought —**unpremeditatedly** adv

unprepared /únpri páird/ adj 1 UNREADY not ready for something or not expecting something to happen 2 NOT MADE READY not having been prepared as required or expected 3 IMPROVISED done without any preparation —**unpreparedly** /únpri páiridli/ adv —**unpreparedness** /-páiridnəss/ n

unprepossessing /ún preepə zéssing/ adj not producing a favourable impression —**unprepossessingly** adv

unpretending /únpri ténding/ adj not pretentious or affected

unpretentious /únpri ténshəss/ adj not putting on a false or showy display of importance, wealth, or knowledge —**unpretentiously** adv —**unpretentiousness** n

unprime /un prím/ adj describes furs or hides that are not of prime quality

unprimed /un prímd/ adj 1 NOT READY not made ready for use 2 NOT PREPARED FOR PAINTING not prepared for painting by the application of an undercoat or sealant 3 WITH NO INDUCED SUSCEPTIBILITY not made susceptible to something by artificial means

unprincipled /un prínssip'ld/ adj lacking, or resulting from a lack of, moral or ethical principles —**unprincipledness** n

unprintable /un príntəb'l/ adj not fit for publication, usually because obscene, libellous, or otherwise illegal or offensive

unprinted /un príntid/ adj not printed or published

unproblematic /ún problə máttik/ adj presenting no difficulties or problems

unprocessed /un prŏ sest/ adj not having undergone processing

unproductive /únprə dúktiv/ adj 1 not producing useful results, decisions, or achievements 2 not producing very much in terms of work or output —**unproductively** adv —**unproductiveness** n

unprofessed /únprə fést/ adj not freely or openly declared

unprofessional /únprə fésh'nəl/ adj 1 CONTRARY TO PROFESSIONAL STANDARDS being or behaving contrary to the expected standards of a profession 2 AMATEURISH unworthy of a professional 3 NOT BELONGING TO PROFESSION not having membership of a profession —**unprofessionalism** n —**unprofessionally** adv

unprofitable /un próffitəb'l/ adj 1 not producing a profit 2 not producing a desirable result or having a useful purpose —**unprofitability** /un próffitə bílləti/ n —**unprofitableness** n —**unprofitably** adv

UNPROFOR /ún prŏ fawr/ abbr United Nations Protection Force

unpromising /un prómmissing/ adj 1 not likely to prove successful 2 not favourable —**unpromisingly** adv

unprompted /un prómptid/ adj said or done without any encouragement or help

unpronounceable /únprə nównssəb'l/ adj very difficult or impossible to pronounce

unpronounced /únprə nównst/ adj 1 not clear or easy to notice 2 not sounded or pronounced

unpropitious /únprə píshəss/ adj not seeming to promise success —**unpropitiously** adv

unprosperous /un próspərəss/ adj not rich or successful at earning or producing wealth

/ **unprotected** /ún prə téktid/ adj 1 HAVING NO PROTECTION FROM HARM having no protection against harm or damage ○ With that insurance policy you're still unprotected against accidental damage. 2 LACKING SAFETY PRECAUTIONS not provided with something to prevent accident or injury ○ an unprotected fire 3 PERFORMED WITHOUT A CONDOM performed without the use of a condom ○ unprotected sex 4 NOT LOCKED AGAINST UNAUTHORIZED CHANGES not locked against changes by unauthorized users ○ an unprotected computer network

unprotesting /ún prə tésting/ adj making no objection or complaint

unprovable /un proóvəb'l/ adj not capable of being proved by evidence or argument ○ unprovable allegations

unproved /un proóvd/ adj not established as true or factual

unproven /un próv'n, un proóv'n/ adj 1 not used or done before and found satisfactory 2 not demonstrated beyond a doubt to be true

unprovided /únprə vídid/ adj 1 not supplied or furnished with something 2 not ready for something —**unprovidedly** adv ◇ **unprovided for** not provided with money or the means to live adequately

unprovoked /ún prə vŏkt/ adj not caused by any particular event or piece of behaviour on the part of another person ○ given to outbursts of unprovoked laughter

unpublishable /un púbblishəb'l/ adj not fit or feasible to publish, usually because of poor quality or expected poor sales

unpublished /un púbblisht/ *adj* 1 not produced in print for distribution to the public ○ *unpublished poems* 2 having had no written works produced in printed form ○ *an unpublished poet*

unpunished /un púnnisht/ *adj* receiving no penalty or punishment

unputdownable /ún pŏŏt dównəb'l/ *adj* so interesting, entertaining, or exciting that the reader cannot stop reading (*informal*)

unqualified /un kwólli fīd/ *adj* 1 LACKING REQUIRED QUALIFICATIONS having no academic, professional, or vocational qualifications 2 GIVEN WITHOUT RESERVATION not limited or modified by any condition or reservation 3 TOTAL complete and absolute —**unqualifiedly** *adv* —**unqualifiedness** *n*

unquantifiable /un kwónti fī əb'l/ *adj* impossible to quantify in respect of amount, extent, or number

unquenchable /un kwénchəb'l/ *adj* 1 INSATIABLE impossible to satisfy 2 INEXTINGUISHABLE impossible to extinguish 3 UNDIMINISHING OR UNDYING impossible to suppress, stifle, or destroy —**unquenchably** *adv*

unquestionable /un kwéschənəb'l/ *adj* 1 impossible to doubt, question, or dispute 2 acknowledged as not subject to doubt or open to question —**unquestionability** /un kwéschənə bílləti/ *n* —**unquestionableness** *n* —**unquestionably** *adv*

unquestioned /un kwéschənd/ *adj* 1 not open to questioning, doubt, or dispute 2 not asked a question or questions

unquestioning /un kwéschəning/ *adj* not asking questions, expressing doubt, or hesitating because of questions or doubts —**unquestioningly** *adv*

unquiet /un kwī ət/ *adj* 1 NOISY OR TURBULENT full of noise or unrest 2 ANXIOUS unsettled or restless, especially in thought or feeling ■ *n* 1 NOISE OR UNREST a state of noisiness or unrest 2 ANXIETY restlessness or uneasiness —**unquietly** *adv* —**unquietness** *n*

unquote /un kwṓt/ *adv* used when speaking to indicate where the end of a quotation falls ○ *He said, quote, You're fired, unquote.*

unquoted /un kwṓtid/ *adj* not listed or quoted on a stock exchange

unraised /ún ráyzd/ *adj* 1 made without yeast and therefore fairly flat and firm in consistency 2 not moved, lifted, or increased to a raised position or level

unravel /un rávv'l/ (**-els, -elling, -elled**) *v* 1 *vti* UNDO STRANDS OF SOMETHING to undo the knitted or woven yarn, thread, or other strands of something, or to become undone by having the strands come apart 2 *vti* DISENTANGLE OR BECOME DISENTANGLED to separate something out from a tangle or other mass, or to become disentangled or separated out 3 *vti* MAKE OR BECOME UNDERSTANDABLE to make clear or understandable all the complex, baffling, or intricate elements or aspects of something, or to become clear or understandable 4 *vi* START TO FAIL to begin to fail or come to an end

unreachable /un réechəb'l/ *adj* 1 impossible to travel to 2 impossible to contact, especially by telephone —**unreachability** /un reechə bílləti/ *n* —**unreachably** *adv*

unreacted /ún ri áktid/ *adj* describes the portion of starting materials in a chemical reaction that do not combine

unreactive /ún ri áktiv/ *adj* 1 failing to react to events, situations, or stimuli 2 not taking part in chemical reactions

unread /un réd/ *adj* 1 NOT READ not read, especially by a usual or intended reader 2 NOT WELL READ having read very little and consequently lacking knowledge acquired from reading 3 LACKING KNOWLEDGE OF SUBJECT not acquainted with a specific subject through reading

unreadable /un réedəb'l/ *adj* 1 ILLEGIBLE consisting of letters, words, or symbols that are difficult to identify 2 NOT ENJOYABLE TO READ impossible to read through being boring, badly written, or intellectually difficult 3 IMPOSSIBLE TO INTERPRET impossible to interpret or make sense of ○ *his unreadable face* —**unreadability** /ún reedə bílləti/ *n* —**unreadableness** *n* —**unreadably** *adv*

unready /un réddi/ *adj* 1 UNAVAILABLE not available or prepared for use 2 NOT PREPARED TO DO SOMETHING not prepared or available to do something or to act 3 LACKING MENTAL ALERTNESS OR QUICKNESS lacking or displaying a lack of mental alertness or quickness —**unreadily** *adv* —**unreadiness** *n*

unreal /un réel, un rée əl/ *adj* 1 NOT EXISTING having no substance, reality, or existence 2 FALSE not true or genuine 3 IMAGINARY imaginary or dream-like 4 EXCELLENT excellent or extremely good (*informal*) 5 INCREDIBLE difficult to believe (*informal*) —**unreally** *adv*

unrealistic /un rée ə lístik/ *adj* not taking into account or based on the way the world actually is and how things are likely to happen —**unrealistically** *adv*

unreality /únri álləti/ (*plural* **-ties**) *n* 1 UNREAL QUALITY an unreal or seemingly unreal state or quality 2 UNREAL THING something that is not real, genuine, or true, or lacks substance 3 INABILITY TO FACE REALITY an inability to accept reality

unrealizable /un rée ə līzəb'l/, **unrealisable** *adj* not able to be achieved ○ *an unrealizable goal*

unrealized /un rée ə līzd/, **unrealised** *adj* not achieved, brought to fruition, or made real

unreason /un réez'n/ *n* lack of reason or rationality

unreasonable /un réez'nəb'l/ *adj* 1 not acting with or subject to reason 2 being or going beyond accepted or reasonable limits —**unreasonableness** *n* —**unreasonably** *adv*

unreasonable behaviour *n* behaviour that is considered unacceptable in a marital relationship and constitutes grounds for divorce

unreasoned /un réez'nd/ *adj* not resulting from sound reasoning

unreasoning /un réez'ning/ *adj* lacking, or resulting from a lack of, sound judgment or reasoning —**unreasoningly** *adv*

unreceptive /ún ri séptiv/ *adj* 1 not willing or able to accept something, especially new ideas or information 2 not reacting favourably to something ○ *an unreceptive audience*

unreciprocated /ún ri sípprə kaytid/ *adj* not given or felt in return ○ *unreciprocated love*

unreckonable /un rékənəb'l/ *adj* impossible to calculate

unrecognizable /un rékəg nīzəb'l/, **unrecognisable** *adj* not identifiable as having been seen or experienced before —**unrecognizably** *adv*

unrecognized /un rékəg nīzd/, **unrecognised** *adj* 1 not identified as having been seen or experienced before ○ *In her headscarf and dark glasses, she could pass through the crowds unrecognized.* 2 receiving no acknowledgment or appreciation ○ *There is plenty of unrecognized talent out there.*

unreconciled /un rékən sīld/ *adj* 1 STILL HOSTILE still feeling hostility towards each other and not having settled a dispute 2 NOT SETTLED not settled or brought to an end by an agreement 3 UNABLE TO ACCEPT SOMETHING UNDESIRABLE not able to accept or come to terms with something undesirable

unreconstructed /ún reekən strúktid/ *adj* 1 retaining beliefs, views, or practices that are outdated or associated with a particular place or group 2 not rebuilt, restored, or recreated

unrecorded /ún ri káwrdid/ *adj* not having been recorded

unredeemed /ún ri déemd/ *adj* 1 not made acceptable or forgivable by the offsetting presence of a good quality 2 not paid off, or not exchanged for cash or goods

unreel /un réel/ *vti* to unwind something from a reel, or to become unwound from it

unreeve /un réev/ (**-reeves, -reeving, -reeved** *or* **-rove, -reeved** *or* **-rove** /-rṓv/) *vti* to pull out a rope or cable from a block or thimble on a ship, or be pulled out from a block or thimble

unrefined /únri fīnd/ *adj* 1 not processed to remove impurities 2 not in accord with socially approved tastes

unreflecting /únri flékting/ *adj* not engaging in or resulting from deep or serious thinking —**unreflectingly** *adv*

unreflective /únri fléktiv/ *adj* not tending to think or reflect, or not resulting from thinking or reflection —**unreflectively** *adv*

unreformed /ún ri fáwrmd/ *adj* 1 not improved by political or social reform 2 persisting in socially unacceptable behaviour ○ *an unreformed criminal*

unregenerate /únri jénnərət/ *adj* 1 NOT REFORMED not reborn spiritually and not repentant 2 VIOLATING SOCIAL OR MORAL STRUCTURES behaving in a way regarded as violating particular social or moral structures 3 CLINGING TO OUTDATED BELIEFS retaining beliefs, views, or practices that are outdated or associated with a particular place or group 4 STUBBORN unyielding or stubborn —**unregenerable** *adj* —**unregeneracy** *n* —**unregeneratel**[y] *adv*

unregistered /un réjjistərd/ *adj* not registered or recorded

unregulated /un réggyŏŏ laytid/ *adj* not controlled by rules, regulations, or laws ○ *Since the profession is completely unregulated, anyone can set up as a practitioner.*

unrehearsed /ún ri húrst/ *adj* not practised beforehand

unrelated /ún ri láytid/ *adj* not connected by similarities, source, or family ○ *The incidents were totally unrelated.*

unrelaxed /ún ri lákst/ *adj* tense, uneasy, and anxious, or producing feelings of tension and unease

unrelenting /únri lénting/ *adj* 1 unyielding or unswerving in determination or resolve 2 not weakening, easing up, or otherwise diminishing in strength, speed, or effort —**unrelentingly** *adv*

unreliable /únri lī əb'l/ *adj* not able to be relied on or trusted —**unreliability** /únri lī ə bílləti/ *n* —**unreliableness** *n* —**unreliably** *adv*

unrelieved /ún ri léevd/ *adj* without any variation or diverting contrast to provide relief ○ *It was a day of unrelieved tedium.* —**unrelievedly** /únri léevidli/ *adv*

unremarkable /ún ri máarkəb'l/ *adj* not unusual, exceptional, or worthy of note —**unremarkably** *adv*

unremarked /únri máarkt/ *adj* not noticed or observed

unremittable gain /ún ri míttəb'l-/ *n* a gain made from an investment abroad that cannot be sent to the investor's own country, e.g. because of currency exchange controls

unremitting /únri mítting/ *adj* continuing, persisting, or recurring without diminishing or ceasing —**unremittingly** *adv* —**unremittingness** *n*

unremorseful /ún ri máwrssfəl/ *adj* showing or feeling no sense of regret or shame —**unremorsefully** *adv* —**unremorsefulness** *n*

unrepeatable /ún ri péetəb'l/ *adj* 1 not able to be done or made again ○ *an unrepeatable performance* 2 too rude and shocking for the hearer to wish to repeat ○ *His answer was unrepeatable!*

unrepeated /ún ri péetid/ *adj* done, made, or said once only

unrepentant /ún ri péntənt/, **unrepenting** /-ing/ *adj* feeling or showing no regret for having done something wrong ○ *an unrepentant sinner* —**unrepentantly** *adv*

unrepresentative /ún reppri zéntətiv/ *adj* not typical of a particular kind or class

unrepresented /ún reppri zéntid/ *adj* not having another individual or organization to speak or act on your behalf ○ *thousands of unrepresented workers*

unrequited /únri kwítid/ *adj* 1 not felt in response, or not returned in the same way or to the same degree 2 not avenged —**unrequitedly** *adv*

unresearched /ún ri súrcht/ *adj* not investigated by methodical study

unresentful /ún ri zéntf'l/ *adj* feeling or showing no sense of being aggrieved

unreserve /únri zúrv/ *n* a lack of reserve in showing and expressing feelings or opinions

unreserved /únri zúrvd/ *adj* 1 NOT RESERVED FOR PARTICULAR USE not set aside or retained for a particular person or group of people to use 2 GIVEN WITHOUT QUALIFICATION not limited or modified by any condition or reservation 3 FRANK OR OPEN not cautious, restrained, or reticent —**unreservedly** *adv* —**unreservedness** /-zúrvidnəss/ *n*

unresolvable /ún ri zólvəb'l/ *adj* not capable of being resolved

unresolved /ún ri zólvd/ *adj* not resolved or decided ○ *a list of unresolved queries*

unresonant /un rézz'nənt/ *adj* not producing or increasing amplification of sound or echoes

unresponsive /ún ri spónssiv/ *adj* not reacting strongly or quickly or showing no reaction at all —**unresponsively** *adv* —**unresponsiveness** *n*

unrest /un rést/ *n* 1 strong social or political discontent or protest that disrupts the established order and is often violent but falls short of true rebellion 2 a disturbed, unsettled, or uneasy mental or emotional state

unrestrained /únri stráynd/ *adj* 1 not subject to control, restriction, or restraint 2 natural and uninhibited —**unrestrainedly** *adv* —**unrestrainedness** /-stráynidnəss/ *n*

unrestraint /únri stráynt/ *n* lack of restraint in actions or behaviour

unrestricted /ún ri stríktid/ *adj* subject to no restrictions or limits ○ *unrestricted access to all areas*

unreturnable /ún ri túrnəb'l/ *adj* not able to be returned

unrevealed /ún ri veéld/ *adj* 1 **NOT VISIBLE** not able to be seen 2 **UNDISCLOSED** not made public ○ *from an unrevealed source* 3 **NOT REVEALED BY DEITY** not based on the supposed word of a supreme deity ○ *unrevealed religion*

unrewarded /ún ri wáwrdid/ *adj* not given any desirable benefit in return for something done ○ *Such dedication should not go unrewarded.*

unrewarding /ún ri wáwrding/ *adj* providing no satisfaction or pleasure ○ *a tedious and unrewarding task*

unrhymed /un rímd/, **unrhyming** /-ing/ *adj* having lines of verse that do not end in similar sounds

unriddle /un ridd'l/ (**-dles, -dling, -dled**) *vt* to find a solution or explanation for something

unrifled /un ríf'ld/ *adj* having no spiral grooves (**rifling**) cut on the inside of the barrel

unrig /un ríg/ (**-rigs, -rigging, -rigged**) *vt* to remove the rigging from a ship

unrighteous /un ríchəss/ *adj* 1 sinful, wicked, or evil 2 not just, fair, or right —**unrighteously** *adv* —**unrighteousness** *n*

unrip /un ríp/ (**-rips, -ripping, -ripped**) *vt* 1 to open something by ripping 2 to reveal or divulge something (*archaic*)

unripe /un ríp/ (**-riper, -ripest**) *adj* 1 **NOT RIPE** not yet ripe or mature 2 **NOT FULLY READY** not yet complete or fully developed 3 **PREMATURE** occurring too soon or too early (*archaic*) —**unripeness** *n*

unrivalled /un rív'ld/ *adj* having no rival or equal

unroll /un ról/ *vti* 1 to unwind, uncoil, or open up something that is rolled up, or become unwound, uncoiled, or opened up 2 to disclose something gradually and smoothly, or to become disclosed in this way

unroofed /un roóft/ *adj* having no roof

unround /un równd/ *vt* to pronounce a sound with the lips kept flat —**unround** *adj*

unrove past tense, past participle of **unreeve**

UNRRA, Unrra *abbr* United Nations Relief and Rehabilitation Administration

unruffled /un rúff'ld/ *adj* 1 calm and poised, especially in a crisis 2 having a smooth surface, especially in having no ripples

SYNONYMS See *calm*.

unruly /un roóli/ (**-lier, -liest**) *adj* difficult to control, manage, discipline, or govern [15C. < archaic *ruly* 'disciplined, observing rules' < RULE.] —**unruliness** *n*

SYNONYMS *unruly, intractable, recalcitrant, obstreperous, wilful, wild, wayward*
CORE MEANING: not submitting to control
unruly boisterous, disruptive, and difficult to control or discipline; **intractable** (*formal*) strong-willed and rebellious, refusing to be controlled or to submit to discipline; **recalcitrant** obstinate and defiant in refusing to submit to discipline or control; **obstreperous** noisy, difficult to control, and uncooperative; **wilful** stubbornly disregarding the opinions or advice of others; **wild** showing a general lack of control or restraint; **wayward** disobedient and uncontrollable.

unruptured /un rúpchərd/ *adj* not having suffered damage, such as a break or tear

unrushed /un rúshd/ *adj* experiencing or showing no sense of haste

UNRWA, Unrwa *abbr* United Nations Relief and Works Agency

unsaddle /un sádd'l/ (**-dles, -dling, -dled**) *v* 1 *vti* to take a saddle from a horse 2 *vt* to throw a rider from a saddle (*refers to a horse*)

unsaddling enclosure *n* an enclosure at a racecourse where the horses are brought after a race to have their saddles removed

unsafe /un sáyf/ (**-safer, -safest**) *adj* 1 causing or exposing somebody to danger 2 in a position of danger or risk

unsaid /un séd/ past tense, past participle of **unsay** ■ *adj* not spoken of or discussed, although thought about

unsalted /un sáwltid, -sólt-/ *adj* containing no salt

unsanctioned /un sángksh'nd/ *adj* not sanctioned, approved, or authorized

unsanitary /un sánnitəri/ *adj* not clean or free from agents that can cause disease or infection

unsatisfactory /un satiss fáktəri/ *adj* not adequate, acceptable, or satisfying —**unsatisfactorily** *adv* —**unsatisfactoriness** *n*

unsatisfied /un sátiss fīd/ *adj* not satisfied, pleased, or contented

unsatisfying /un sátiss fī ing/ *adj* providing little or no satisfaction

unsaturate /un sáchərət/ *n* an unsaturated chemical compound

unsaturated /un sáchə raytid/ *adj* 1 able to dissolve more of a substance 2 having or able to form double and triple carbon bonds

unsaturation /un sáchə ráysh'n/ *n* the presence of one or more double or triple bonds in an organic molecule

unsavoury /un sáyvəri/ *adj* 1 **DISTASTEFUL** not pleasant or agreeable 2 **IMMORAL** morally unacceptable 3 **UNAPPETIZING** tasting or smelling unappetizing —**unsavourily** *adv* —**unsavouriness** *n*

unsay /un sáy/ (**-says, -séz/, -saying, -said** /-séd/) *vt* to take back something said so that it is as if it has never been said

unsayable /un sáy əb'l/ *adj* difficult or impossible to say or speak about

unscathed /un skáythd/ *adj* not hurt, damaged, or harmed in any way

unscheduled /un shéddyoold/ *adj* not forming part of a plan or schedule

unschooled /un skoóld/ *adj* 1 not educated or trained 2 innate and not acquired by education or training

unschooling /ún skooling/ *n US* a form of homeschooling that involves teaching children at home without a preset curriculum, structuring learning around a child's interests and inclinations —**unschool** *vt*

unscientific /únsī ən tíffik/ *adj* 1 not following, or compatible with, the methods and principles of science 2 not possessing knowledge about science and its methods and principles —**unscientifically** *adv*

unscramble /un skrámb'l/ (**-bles, -bling, -bled**) *vt* 1 to restore order to something jumbled or confused 2 to make a message understandable by undoing the effects of scrambling, especially electronic scrambling —**unscrambler** *n*

unscrew /un skroó/ *vti* 1 **REMOVE OR LOOSEN SCREWS OF SOMETHING** to remove or loosen a screw or screws holding something in place, or to have a screw or screws removed or loosened 2 **TURN TO REMOVE OR ADJUST** to remove or adjust something by rotating, or to be removed or adjusted by rotating 3 **OPEN BY REMOVING THREADED LID** to open something by turning and removing a threaded lid or cap, or to be opened in this way

unscripted /un skríptid/ *adj* 1 without a script that was written or agreed on in advance 2 not planned or expected

unscriptural /un skrípchərəl/ *adj* not recorded in, in accordance with, or sanctioned by biblical texts

unscrupulous /un skroópyoóləss/ *adj* not restrained by moral or ethical principles —**unscrupulously** *adv* —**unscrupulousness** *n*

unseal /un seél/ *vt* 1 to break or remove the seal of something, or to open something by breaking a seal or closure 2 to free something from constraint or restriction —**unsealable** *adj*

unseam /un seém/ *vt* to unpick a seam or seams of something

unsearchable /un súrchəb'l/ *adj* not capable of being searched or investigated —**unsearchableness** *n* —**unsearchably** *adv*

unseasonable /un seéz'nəb'l/ *adj* 1 not usual or appropriate for the time of year 2 not occurring at the right time or at a good time —**unseasonableness** *n* —**unseasonably** *adv*

unseasoned /un seéz'nd/ *adj* 1 **NOT DRIED OUT** not dried, aged, or matured 2 **NOT EXPERIENCED** lacking the skills or knowledge that experience provides 3 **PREPARED WITHOUT SALT AND PEPPER** lacking salt and pepper, or other herbs or spices

unseat /un seét/ *vt* 1 to eject somebody from a seat, especially a saddle 2 to remove somebody from office or a position, especially by means of an election

unseaworthy /un seé wurthi/ *adj* not in a fit condition to be able to sail safely on the sea

unsecured /únssi kyoórd, -kyáwrd/ *adj* 1 **NOT MADE SECURE** not fastened, held in place, or otherwise made secure 2 **MADE WITHOUT SECURITY** not protected against financial loss 3 **UNPROTECTED FROM BUGGING** not protected against electronic eavesdropping

unseeded /un seédid/ *adj* not assigned a position in a draw so that the best players or teams can, in theory, avoid meeting until the later rounds

unseemly /un seémli/ *adj* 1 **NOT IN GOOD TASTE** contrary to accepted standards of good taste or appropriate behaviour 2 **INCONVENIENT** occurring at an inconvenient time or place ■ *adv* **IN AN UNSEEMLY MANNER** in an improper or inappropriate manner —**unseemliness** *n*

unseen /un seén/ *adj* 1 **NOT SEEN** not observed, noticed, watched, or seen 2 **DONE WITHOUT PRACTICE** done or comprehended without previous study or practice 3 **TRANSLATED AT SIGHT** translated without preparation, especially in a test or examination ■ *n* **UNSEEN TRANSLATION** a text for translation without preparation, especially in a test or examination

unsegmented /ún seg méntid/ *adj* not divided into parts or sections

unselective /únssi léktiv/ *adj* choosing or chosen without regard for quality or value

unselfconscious /ún self kónshəss/ *adj* not affected, pretentious, or self-conscious —**unselfconsciously** *adv* —**unselfconsciousness** *n*

unselfish /un sélfish/ *adj* putting the general good or the needs or interests of others first —**unselfishly** *adv* —**unselfishness** *n*

unsell /un sél/ (**-sells, -selling, -sold** /un sóld/) *vt US* to convince somebody that something is false or worthless

unsentimental /ún senti mént'l/ *adj* not mawkish or appealing to tender feelings

unseparated /un séppə raytid/ *adj* not separated into distinct parts or elements

unserious /un seéri əss/ *adj* light, trivial, or unworthy of being regarded as serious

unserviceable /un súrvissəb'l/ *adj* not efficient, functional, or suitable for everyday use ○ *The furniture was beautiful but unserviceable.*

unset /un sét/ *adj* 1 **NOT HARDENED** not hardened or firm 2 **NOT READY** not prepared or made ready 3 **NOT MOUNTED** not mounted in a jewellery setting

unsettle /un sétt'l/ (**-tles, -tling, -tled**) *vt* 1 to disrupt the orderly, fixed, or established state of something 2 to make somebody ill at ease or insecure —**unsettlement** *n*

unsettled /un sétt'ld/ *adj* 1 **LACKING ORDER OR STABILITY** characterized by a lack of order or stability ○ *an unsettled political climate* 2 **CHANGEABLE** changing frequently within a given period of time ○ *unsettled weather* 3 **BEING IN MOTION** not being in a condition or position of rest ○ *unsettled sediment in the water* 4 **NOT DECIDED** not resolved, determined, or decided ○ *an unsettled issue* 5 **UNCERTAIN** not sure, or full of doubt ○ *He was unsettled about his future at the firm.* 6 **UNINHABITED** not inhabited or colonized ○ *unsettled territory* 7 **UNPAID** not paid or fulfilled ○ *an unsettled debt* 8 **MOVING ABOUT** not regular or fixed ○ *an unsettled lifestyle* 9 **NOT LEGALLY RESOLVED** not resolved as required by law ○ *an unsettled lawsuit*

unsettling /un séttling/ *adj* producing a feeling of unease or insecurity

unsewn /un són/ *adj* not sewn or stitched

unsex /un séks/ *vt* 1 to strip away from somebody the qualities stereotypically associated with his or her sex ○ *'Come, you spirits /That tend on mortal thoughts, unsex me here'* (William Shakespeare, *Macbeth*; c. 1605) 2 to deprive somebody of the ability to have sex

UNSF *abbr* United Nations Special Fund for Economic Development

unshackle /un shák'l/ (**-les, -ling, -led**) *vt* **1** to release somebody from shackles **2** to release somebody from restrictions or constraints

unshakable /un sháykəb'l/, **unshakeable** *adj* not subject to doubt or uncertainty —**unshakably** *adv*

unshaken /un sháykən/ *adj* firm and unwavering in purpose, loyalty, or resolve ○ *Consumer confidence remains unshaken.*

unshaking /un sháyking/ *adj* not subject to doubt or uncertainty ○ *an unshaking faith*

unshaped /un sháypt/, **unshapen** /-sháp'n/ *adj* **1** not yet shaped, formed, or finished **2** imperfect in its final or finished form or state

unshared /un sháird/ *adj* not shared with anyone else ○ *an unshared belief*

unsheathe /un sheeth/ (**-sheathes, -sheathing, -sheathed**) *vt* to remove a sword from a sheath

unshell /un shél/ *vt* to remove something from a shell

⚡ **unshift** /un shíft/ *vi* to release the depressed shift key on the keyboard of a computer or typewriter

unship /un shíp/ (**-ships, -shipping, -shipped**) *vti* **1** to unload something from a ship, or to be unloaded **2** to move something, or to be moved, out of its normal position on a ship

unshod /un shód/ *adj* not wearing shoes or horseshoes

unshriven /un shrívv'n/ *adj* not having confessed sins to a priest and been given absolution

unsifted /un síftid/ *adj* not sifted or sorted

unsighted /un sītid/ *adj* **1** not fitted with a sight or sights to help with aiming **2** unable to see somebody or something because the view is obstructed

unsightly /un sītli/ *adj* not pleasant to look at —**unsightliness** *n*

⚡ **unsigned** /un sīnd/ *adj* **1** LACKING A SIGNATURE having no signature **2** NOT SIGNED TO PLAY FOR TEAM not having signed a contract to join a sports team as a player **3** LACKING A PLUS OR MINUS SIGN having no plus or minus sign, or having no digit in binary notation representing a positive or negative value

unsinkable /un síngkəb'l/ *adj* capable of surviving any hazard at sea without sinking

unskilful /un skílf'l/ *adj* lacking or done without skill or expertise —**unskilfully** *adv* —**unskilfulness** *n*

unskilled /ún skíld/ *adj* **1** LACKING SKILL lacking skill or the basic or proper skills **2** LACKING TRAINING lacking the skills acquired through technical training or higher education **3** NOT REQUIRING SPECIAL SKILLS not requiring special training, education, or skill **4** DONE WITHOUT SKILL done without skill, or displaying a lack of the basic or proper skills

unslakable /un sláykəb'l/, **unslakeable** *adj* impossible to satisfy or quench

unslaked lime *n* CHEM = **calcium hydroxide**

unsling /un slíng/ (**-slings, -slinging, -slung** /-slúng/, **-slung**) *vt* **1** REMOVE SOMETHING SLUNG to remove something that has been slung, especially over the shoulder or shoulders **2** TAKE OUT OF SLING to take something out of a sling **3** REMOVE SUPPORTING ROPES FROM to remove the supporting ropes or chains (**slings**) from something

unsmiling /un smīling/ *adj* looking serious and showing no signs of pleasure, amusement, or approval ○ *his grim unsmiling manner* —**unsmilingly** *adv*

unsmoked /un smṓkt/ *adj* **1** not cured by or treated with smoking ○ *unsmoked bacon* **2** not lit and smoked ○ *an unsmoked cigar*

unsnag /un snág/ (**-snags, -snagging, -snagged**) *vt* **1** to free something caught on an obstruction **2** to remove a difficulty or difficulties impeding the progress or development of something

unsnap /un snáp/ (**-snaps, -snapping, -snapped**) *vt* to release or open something by unfastening a press stud or press studs

unsnarl /un snaarl/ *vt* to free something from a snarl or snarls

unsociable /un sṓshəb'l/ *adj* **1** not liking or seeking the company of other people **2** not favouring or encouraging social interaction —**unsociability** /ún sōshə bíllәti/ *n* —**unsociableness** *n* —**unsociably** *adv*

unsocial /un sṓsh'l/ *adj* **1** PREFERRING OWN COMPANY not liking or seeking the company of other people **2** OF UNSOCIAL PERSON characterized or caused by a dislike of the company of other people **3** ANTISOCIAL annoying, inconsiderate, or indifferent to the needs of others **4** OUTSIDE NORMAL WORKING HOURS relating to or done at a time outside normal working hours —**unsocially** *adv*

unsold /ún sṓld/ *adj* not bought by anybody ■ past tense, past participle of **unsell**

unsolicited /únssə líssitid/ *adj* given, sent, or received without being requested

unsolvable /un sólvəb'l/ *adj* not capable of being solved ○ *The puzzle was unsolvable.*

unsolved /un sólvd/ *adj* having had no solution or explanation worked out or found ○ *an unsolved mystery*

unsophisticated /únssə físti kaytid/ *adj* **1** naive, inexperienced, and not wise in the ways of the world **2** simple and lacking in refinements, especially those required to solve a particular problem —**unsophisticatedly** *adv* —**unsophisticatedness** *n* —**unsophistication** /únssə fisti káysh'n/ *n*

unsorted /un sáwrtid/ *adj* not systematically arranged in categories or in a particular order ○ *a pile of unsorted clothes*

unsought /un sáwt/ *adj* not looked for or asked for

unsound /un sównd/ *adj* **1** UNHEALTHY not in a healthy physical or psychological state **2** NOT SOLID OR FIRM in a structurally poor or dangerous state ○ *unsound foundations* **3** NOT RELIABLE not based on reliable facts, information, or reasoning ○ *an unsound conclusion* **4** FINANCIALLY INSECURE not safe or secure financially ○ *an unsound investment* **5** DISTURBED AND NOT RESTFUL characterized by periods of restlessness ○ *unsound sleep* —**unsoundly** *adv* —**unsoundness** *n*

unsparing /un spáiring/ *adj* **1** harsh or without mercy **2** not frugal or stingy with something —**unsparingness** *n* —**unsparingly** *adv*

unspeakable /un speékəb'l/ *adj* **1** NOT DESCRIBABLE IN WORDS incapable of being described in words **2** EXTREMELY BAD OR AWFUL so bad or awful as to be impossible to describe in words **3** NOT TO BE SPOKEN OF not allowed to be spoken of, mentioned, or talked about —**unspeakableness** *n* —**unspeakably** *adv*

unspecialized /un spéshə līzd/, **unspecialised** *adj* **1** not having a special use or purpose **2** not concerned or involved with just one specialized area of knowledge or skill

unspecifiable /un spéssi fī əb'l/ *adj* unable to be explicitly stated or identified ○ *unspecifiable causes*

unspecific /ún spə síffik/ *adj* vague and imprecise —**unspecifically** *adv*

unspecified /un spéssi fīd/ *adj* not stated explicitly or in any detail ○ *unspecified amounts*

unsphere /un sfeér/ (**-spheres, -sphering, -sphered**) *vt* **1** to remove a planet or other astronomical object from its sphere in the sky **2** to release somebody or something from a state of confinement (*literary*)

unspiritual /un spírrityoo əl/ *adj* concerned with material or worldly matters as opposed to religion or the soul

unspoiled /ún spóyld/, **unspoilt** /-spóylt/ *adj* **1** UNCHANGED BY DEVELOPMENT not changed for the worse by modern civilization, industry, or tourism **2** NOT DAMAGED not damaged or physically harmed **3** UNFLAWED not lessened or diminished by flaws or imperfections **4** NOT RUINED IN CHARACTER not ruined in character as a result of success, wealth, or being overindulged

unspoilt *adj* = **unspoiled**

unspoken /un spṓkən/ *adj* not uttered or talked about, although thought about

unspontaneous /ún spon táyni əss/ *adj* showing constraint, prior planning, and a rigidness not associated with the expression of natural impulses or candidness

unsporting /un spáwrting/ *adj* being or acting contrary to fair play or the rules and spirit of a sport or of sport in general —**unsportingly** *adv* —**unsportingness** *n*

unsportsmanlike /un spáwrtsmən līk/ *adj* being or acting contrary to fair play or the rules and spirit of a sport or of sport in general

unspotted /un spóttid/ *adj* **1** NOT SPOTTED OR STAINED not soiled with spots or stains **2** MORALLY UNBLEMISHED not marred by moral or ethical lapses or failures **3** UNOBSERVED not seen or observed —**unspottedness** *n*

unsprung /un sprúng/ *adj* having no springs or having the springs removed

unspun /un spún/ *adj* not spun into yarn or thread

unstable /un stáyb'l/ *adj* **1** NOT FIXED not firm, solid, or fixed ○ *unstable ground* **2** LIKELY TO FALL OR COLLAPSE likely to fall, collapse, or sway ○ *unstable scaffolding* **3** CHANGEABLE apt to change ○ *unstable weather* **4** IRREGULAR IN MOVEMENT OR RHYTHM having a movement or rhythm that changes irregularly ○ *an unstable heartbeat* **5** UNSTEADY IN PURPOSE OR INTENT unsteady or unsure in purpose or intent ○ *political support that is unstable* **6** LACKING EMOTIONAL OR PSYCHOLOGICAL STABILITY lacking, or resulting from a lack of, emotional control or psychological stability ○ *unstable behaviour* **7** APT TO DECOMPOSE able or likely to change chemical or biological composition readily **8** HAVING SHORT HALF-LIFE having a brief existence or half-life **9** SUBJECT TO SPONTANEOUS CHANGE describes a particle that is subject to spontaneous change, such as radioactive decay —**unstableness** *n* —**unstably** *adv*

unstable equilibrium *n* **1** the state of a system that will move further from its original condition after experiencing a slight disturbance **2** economic equilibrium that is not restored if it is disrupted by an outside influence, e.g. a change in one of the demand or supply determinants

unstained /un stáynd/ *adj* **1** not having been discoloured or blemished, or having no dye applied ○ *I prefer this wood unstained.* **2** not spoiled by wrongdoing or error ○ *She emerged with her reputation unstained.*

unstated /un stáytid/ *adj* not announced or declared

unsteady /un stéddi/ *adj* **1** NOT FIXED not firm, solid, or fixed **2** TOTTERING staggering or tottering in walking **3** LIKELY TO MOVE likely to move or shift position ○ *an unsteady ladder* **4** CHANGEABLE subject to large and frequent changes ○ *unsteady financial markets* **5** IRREGULAR IN RHYTHM irregular in movement, rhythm, or pitch ○ *a voice that is unsteady* **6** NOT CONSTANT OR RELIABLE not constant in purpose or actions ■ *vt* (**-ies, -ying, -ied**) MAKE UNSTEADY to cause something to become unsteady —**unsteadily** *adv* —**unsteadiness** *n*

unsteel /un steél/ *vt* to soften or weaken a harsh attitude or a firm resolve

unstep /un stép/ (**-steps, -stepping, -stepped**) *vt* to take a mast out of its step or socket

unstick /un stík/ *v* (**-sticks, -sticking, -stuck, -stuck** /-stúk/) **1** *vt* MAKE SOMETHING STOP STICKING to cause something to stop sticking **2** *vti* to cause an aircraft to take off, or to take off in an aircraft (*informal*) ■ *n* TAKEOFF a takeoff in an aircraft (*informal*)

unstiffened /un stíff'nd/ *adj* not made rigid or inflexible ○ *unstiffened collars*

unstimulating /un stímmyoo layting/ *adj* arousing no interest or excitement ○ *an unstimulating conversation*

unstinting /un stínting/ *adj* given or giving generously —**unstintingly** *adv*

unstipulated /un stíppyoo laytid/ *adj* **1** not specified or required ○ *at some unstipulated future date* **2** having no condition attached ○ *an unstipulated surrender*

unstop /un stóp/ (**-stops, -stopping, -stopped**) *vt* **1** REMOVE STOPPER FROM to remove a stopper from something **2** UNBLOCK to remove a blockage from something **3** PULL OUT STOPS to pull out the stops of an organ

unstoppable /un stóppəb'l/ *adj* not capable of being halted, or not easily halted —**unstoppably** *adv*

unstopped /un stópt/ *adj* **1** NOT HALTED able to continue without being halted **2** NOT BLOCKED OR STOPPERED not blocked, closed, or stoppered **3** ARTICULATED WITH VOCAL ORGANS PARTLY OPEN articulated without a complete closure of the vocal organs

unstrained /un stráynd/ *adj* **1** not put through a strainer to remove lumps **2** not subjected to strain

unstrap /un stráp/ (**-straps, -strapping, -strapped**) *vt* to remove something by undoing a strap or straps

unstratified /un strátti fīd/ *adj* **1** not arranged in or forming layers or strata **2** not arranged in or forming social classes, grades, or ranks

unstreamed /ún streémd/ *adj* not split into groups on the basis of ability or educational achievement

unstressed /un strést/ *adj* **1** not subjected to physical, psychological, or emotional pressure **2** not accented or emphasized in pronunciation

unstriated /un strī aytid/ *adj* lacking transverse striations

unstring /un stríng/ (**-strings, -stringing, -strung, -strung** /-strúng/) *vt* **1** REMOVE OR LOOSEN STRINGS OF to remove or loosen a string or strings of something **2** REMOVE FROM

STRING to remove something from a string or wire **3 UPSET** to make somebody upset or nervous

unstructured /un strúkchərd/ *adj* **1 NOT ORGANIZED INTO HIERARCHY** not organized into a hierarchy or similar system **2 NOT ORDERED OR CONVENTIONALLY ARRANGED** not forced to conform to a particular order or arrangement, especially a conventional one **3 LOOSE AND FLOWING** not tailored to fit tightly, but flowing freely

unstrung past tense, past participle of **unstring** ■ *adj* **1 UPSET** emotionally upset or nervous **2 LACKING STRINGS** with a string or strings missing, removed, or loosened **3 NOT ON STRING** not threaded on a string or wire

unstuck past tense, past participle of **unstick** ■ *adj* freed from being stuck or adhering to something ◇ **come unstuck** to fail (*informal*)

unstudied /un stúddid/ *adj* **1 NATURAL** natural or casual in manner **2 NOT LEARNED THROUGH STUDYING** not acquired through studying or training **3 NOT KNOWLEDGEABLE** lacking the knowledge and understanding of a particular field that is acquired through studying or training

unstylish /un stílish/ *adj* having or showing no sense of style or fashion —**unstylishly** *adv*

unsubstantial /únssəb stánsh'l/ *adj* **1 IMMATERIAL** not having physical substance **2 FLIMSY** not strong or firm **3 NOT TRUE OR BASED ON FACT** having no basis in truth or fact —**unsubstantiality** /únssəb stánshi álləti/ *n* —**unsubstantially** *adv*

unsubstantiated /únssəb stánshi aytid/ *adj* not proven factually

unsubtle /un sútt'l/ *adj* obvious, overstated, or lacking in delicacy or refinement ○ *an unsubtle hint* —**unsubtly** *adv*

unsuccess /únsək séss/ *n* a lack of success in achieving something

unsuccessful /únssək sésf'l/ *adj* **1** not resulting in success or turning out favourably **2** not achieving an intended aim or goal —**unsuccessfully** *adv* —**unsuccessfulness** *n*

unsuitable /un sóotəb'l/ *adj* not appropriate or becoming —**unsuitability** /un sóotə bílləti/ *n* —**unsuitableness** *n* —**unsuitably** *adv*

unsuited /un sóotid, -syóot-/ *adj* **1** not having the necessary or appropriate qualities for a particular purpose or situation ○ *unsuited to life in the city* **2** not sharing interests or not having compatible personalities ○ *They were completely unsuited as a couple.*

unsullied /un súllid/ *adj* not spoiled or tarnished ○ *The minister's reputation remained unsullied.*

unsung /un súng/ *adj* **1** not sung or not to be sung **2** not given the praise or honour that is due

unsupervised /un sóopər vīzd/ *adj* subject to no supervision

unsupportable /únssə páwrtəb'l/ *adj* **1 INDEFENSIBLE** impossible to defend or excuse **2 INTOLERABLE** impossible to tolerate or endure **3 IMPOSSIBLE TO SUPPORT PHYSICALLY** impossible to support physically in order to prevent collapse

unsupported /ún sə páwrtid/ *adj* **1 LACKING PHYSICAL SUPPORT** having no physical support to maintain an upright position or prevent a fall or collapse ○ *The patient is too weak to walk unsupported.* **2 LACKING FINANCIAL SUPPORT** given no financial backing or help ○ *They struggled on, unsupported by government grants or private sponsorship.* **3 NOT CORROBORATED** not corroborated or borne out ○ *unsupported evidence* **4 LACKING TECHNICAL SUPPORT** provided with no technical support system ○ *unsupported software*

unsure /un shóor, -sháwr/ *adj* **1 UNCERTAIN** doubtful or uncertain about somebody or something **2 NOT CONFIDENT** lacking in confidence **3 NOT FIXED OR SECURE** not firm or secure **4 UNRELIABLE** not trustworthy or reliable

SYNONYMS See ***doubtful***.

unsurfaced /un súrfist/ *adj* not given a smooth and finished top or outer layer ○ *an unsurfaced road*

unsurpassed /ún sur paast/ *adj* better or greater than anybody or anything else

unsurprising /únssər prízing/ *adj* not causing surprise, usually because not unexpected —**unsurprisingly** *adv*

unsuspected /únssə spéktid/ *adj* **1** not under suspicion of doing something **2** not known or believed to exist —**unsuspectedly** *adv*

unsuspecting /únssə spékting/ *adj* not suspicious of somebody or something —**unsuspectingly** *adv*

unsuspicious /ún sə spíshəss/ *adj* arousing, feeling, or showing no suspicion

unsustainable /ún sə stáynəb'l/ *adj* **1** unable to be maintained at a particular level ○ *unsustainable levels of production* **2** failing to maintain the ecological balance of an area ○ *unsustainable forestry practices*

unswathe /un swáyth/ (**-swathes, -swathing, -swathed**) *vt* to remove bindings or wrappings from somebody or something

unsweetened /un swéet'nd/ *adj* served, cooked, or manufactured with no added sugar or other natural or artificial sweetening agent

unswerving /un swúrving/ *adj* **1** firm and unchanging in intent or purpose **2** not turning to the side or otherwise altering the direction of movement —**unswervingly** *adv*

unsworn /un swáwrn/ *adj* **1** not stated under an oath to tell the truth **2** not having taken an oath to tell the truth

unsymmetrical /únssi méttrik'l/ *adj* lacking symmetry —**unsymmetrically** *adv*

unsympathetic /ún simpə théttik/ *adj* showing no sympathy or approval —**unsympathetically** *adv*

unsystematic /ún sistə máttik/ *adj* **1** following no system, and thus not methodical or well organized **2** not attributable to, based on, constituting, or resembling a system —**unsystematically** *adv*

untainted /un táyntid/ *adj* not spoiled, corrupted, or polluted

untaken /un táykən/ *adj* **1** not captured or seized by force ○ *After a week's fighting the capital was still untaken.* **2** not yet implemented, claimed, or dealt with ○ *untaken annual leave*

untamed /un táymd/ *adj* not domesticated, cultivated, or otherwise controlled by an external influence

untangle /un táng g'l/ (**-gles, -gling, -gled**) *vt* **1 FREE SOMETHING FROM TANGLES** to undo the tangles in something such as yarn or hair **2 STRAIGHTEN OUT SOMETHING COMPLEX** to clarify or resolve something that is intricate or puzzling **3 FREE SOMEBODY FROM BAD SITUATION** to remove somebody from a difficult or complicated situation

untanned /un tánd/ *adj* **1** relating to or having skin that does not have a brownish colour from exposure to the sun **2** not converted into leather by treatment with tannin or a similar substance ○ *untanned cattle hides*

untapped /ún tápt/ *adj* **1** not yet in use, but available ○ *untapped talents* **2** not yet opened or tapped

untarnished /un taarnishd/ *adj* **1** not discoloured by the effects of oxidation ○ *The metal was still bright and untarnished after all these years.* **2** having suffered no taint or loss of status ○ *She emerged from the inquiry with her reputation untarnished.*

untaught *adj* **1** ignorant or not having had a formal education **2** arising from innate or natural talent or ability rather than from instruction

unteach /un téech/ (**-teaches, -teaching, -taught** /un táwt/) *vt US* **1** to cause somebody to forget something previously learned **2** to reverse somebody's opinion or belief about something previously learned

untenable /un ténnəb'l/ *adj* **1** lacking the qualities, e.g. sound reasoning or high ground, that make defence possible ○ *an untenable position* **2** so shabby, filthy, or poorly built as to be unfit for human occupation (*archaic*) —**untenability** /un ténnə bílləti/ *n* —**untenableness** *n* —**untenably** /un ténnəbli/ *adv*

untested /un téstid/ *adj* not subjected to experiments or tests ○ *an untested theory*

untether /un té*th*ər/ *vt* **1** to free something from a restraining rope or other tie **2** to something such as an emotion after suppressing it

unthanked /un thángkt/ *adj* receiving no expression of gratitude

unthankful /un thángkf'l/ *adj US* without feelings of gratitude —**unthankfully** *adv* —**unthankfulness** *n*

unthemed /un théemd/ *adj* given no distinct theme or subject

unthink /un thíngk/ (**-thinks, -thinking, -thought** /un tháwt/) *vt* **1** to stop thinking about something **2** to change a view or opinion about something

unthinkable /un thíngkəb'l/ *adj* **1 OUT OF THE QUESTION** too strange or extreme even to be considered **2 INCONCEIVABLE** impossible even to conceive of **3 UNLIKELY TO HAPPEN** highly unlikely to happen or succeed —**unthinkability** /un thíngkə bílləti/ *n* —**unthinkableness** *n* —**unthinkably** *adv*

unthinking /un thíngking/ *adj* **1 INCONSIDERATE** not thoughtful or considerate of other people **2 HEEDLESS** without proper attention to the effects of what is said or done **3 UNAWARE** unable or unwilling to think deeply about things —**unthinkingly** *adv* —**unthinkingness** *n*

unthought past tense, past participle of **unthink**

unthread /un thréd/ *vt* to remove the thread or threads from something

unthreatened /un thrétt'nd/ *adj* free from any imminent danger or harm, especially the risk of extinction ○ *50% of the stocks of this species are unthreatened.*

untidy /un tídi/ *adj* (**-dier, -diest**) **1 NOT NEAT** not neat or tidy **2 DISORDERED** not properly organized or ordered ■ *vt* (**-dies, -dying, -died**) **MESS SOMETHING UP** to mess up something that was tidy —**untidily** *adv* —**untidiness** *n*

untie /un tí/ (**-ties, -tying, -tied**) *v* **1** *vti* to loosen or unfasten a knot or similar fastening in something such as a string, ribbon, or rope, or to be loosened or unfastened **2** *vt* to release or free somebody or something that is tied up

until /ən tíl, un tíl/ *conj, prep* **1** up to a time or event but not afterwards ○ (conj) *I lived with my grandparents until I was ten.* ○ (prep) *from the late 1980s until 1994* **2** before a time or event (*in negatives*) ○ (conj) *She agreed not to write about the case until a verdict was reached.* ○ (prep) *He did not open his mail until Monday.* [12C. < assumed Old Norse *und* 'till' + TILL[1].]

USAGE See ***till***.

~~**untill**~~ incorrect spelling of **until**

untimely /un tímli/ *adj* **1 OCCURRING AT A BAD TIME** happening or done at a bad or inconvenient time ○ *an untimely decision* **2 PREMATURE TIME** happening before the expected time ○ *his untimely death* ■ *adv* (*formal*) **1 AT AN INAPPROPRIATE TIME** at a bad or inappropriate time **2 PREMATURELY** earlier than wanted or expected —**untimeliness** *n*

untiring /un tíring/ *adj* **1** not becoming weary or exhausted **2** continuing in spite of difficulty or frustration ○ *her untiring efforts* —**untiringly** *adv*

untitled /un tít'ld/ *adj* **1 UNNAMED** not having a name or title **2 NOT BELONGING TO NOBILITY** possessing no aristocratic title **3 WITHOUT PROPER CLAIM** having no legitimate right or claim

unto (*stressed*) /ún too/; (*unstressed*) /úntōō/ *prep* (*archaic*) **1** used to indicate that something is said, given, or done to somebody ○ *the elders of Gilead said unto Jephthah* **2** used to indicate that something continues until a particular time ○ *faithful unto death* [13C. < UNTIL, with TO replacing TILL[1].]

untold /ún tṓld/ *adj* **1** not having been revealed or related **2** too great or numerous to be properly described or counted

untouchable /un túchəb'l/ *adj* **1 NOT TO BE TOUCHED** not able or allowed to be touched **2 OUT OF REACH** completely out of reach **3 ABOVE CRITICISM** too well known or important to be investigated or criticized **4 DISAGREEABLE TO TOUCH** unpleasant or disagreeable to touch ■ *n* **untouchable, Untouchable OFFENSIVE TERM** an offensive term for a member of the hereditary Hindu class that was formerly segregated and regarded as ritually unclean by the four castes, and who performed tasks that were considered polluting —**untouchability** /un túchə bílləti/ *n* —**untouchably** *adv*

untouched /un túcht/ *adj* **1 NOT TOUCHED** not touched or handled **2 UNEATEN** not eaten or consumed **3 UNINJURED** not injured, damaged, or harmed **4 UNALTERED** not changed or altered **5 EMOTIONALLY UNAFFECTED** emotionally unaffected by something **6 NOT MENTIONED** omitted from mention or discussion

untoward /úntə wáwrd/ *adj* **1 INAPPROPRIATE** not appropriate or fitting ○ *untoward rudeness* **2 UNEXPECTED** beyond the ordinary or the expected ○ *an untoward piece of luck* **3 CAUSING MISFORTUNE** causing misfortune or disadvantage ○ *several untoward events* —**untowardly** *adv* —**untowardness** *n*

untraceable /un tráyssəb'l/ *adj* unable to be found or discovered

untraditional /ún trə dísh'nəl/ *adj* not relating to or based on tradition

untrained /un tráynd/ *adj* having received no training, especially in a particular skill

untrammelled /ún trámm'ld/ *adj* not restricted or restrained

untranslatable /ún transs láytəb'l/ *adj* incapable of being translated adequately into another language

untranslated /ún transs láytid/ *adj* not translated into a different language or form

untravelled /un tráv'ld/ *adj* **1** not having wide knowledge or experience of the world **2** never or rarely travelled along

untreatable /un tréetəb'l/ *adj* not treatable, especially medically

untreated /un tréetid/ *adj* **1** subjected to no physical, biological, or chemical process ○ *untreated wood* **2** having received no medical aid

untried /ún tríd/ *adj* **1** not tried, tested, or proved **2** not tried in a court of law

untrimmed /un trímd/ *adj* not having been trimmed or otherwise cut

untroubled /un trúbb'ld/ *adj* **1** not bothered, uneasy, or distracted by something **2** tranquil and without disturbances ○ *untroubled sleep* —**untroubledness** *n*

untrue /un tróo/ *adj* **1 WRONG OR FALSE** not in accordance with the facts or what is known **2 NOT PRECISE** not precise or accurate according to some standard or measure **3 UNFAITHFUL** not faithful or loyal to somebody —**untruly** *adv*

untrusting /un trústing/ *adj* unwilling or disinclined to trust other people

untrustworthy /un trúst wurthi/ *adj* not deserving trust or able to be trusted —**untrustworthiness** *n*

untruth /un tróoth/ *n* **1** something that is presented as being true but is actually false ○ *accused of telling untruths* **2** a lack of truth, especially as a result of lying

SYNONYMS See *lie*.

untruthful /un tróothf'l/ *adj* **1** not in accordance with the facts or what is known **2** lying or failing to tell the truth —**untruthfully** *adv* —**untruthfulness** *n*

untutored /un tyóotərd/ *adj* **1** not formally educated or trained **2** without any awareness of or interest in what is socially acceptable behaviour

untwist /un twíst/ *vti* to straighten out something that was twisted, or become straightened out

untypical /un típpik'l/ *adj* lacking the characteristic qualities shared by others of a particular type —**untypically** *adv*

ununquadium /ún un kwáydi əm/ *n* (*symbol* **Uuq**) the heaviest chemical element currently thought to exist, first discovered in 1998. Source: bombarding plutonium atoms with calcium ions in a cyclotron.

unusable /un yóozəb'l/ *adj* not in a fit state to be used

unused /un yóozd/ *adj* **1 NOT USED** never having been used ○ *unused matches* **2 NOT IN USE** not being put to use ○ *unused land* **3 UNFAMILIAR** not familiar with or accustomed to something ○ *Our dog is unused to city traffic.*

unusual /un yóozhoo əl/ *adj* **1** not common or familiar **2** remarkable or out of the ordinary —**unusualness** *n*

unutterable /un úttərəb'l/ *adj* impossible to express or describe because of emotional intensity —**unutterableness** *n* —**unutterably** *adv*

unvalued /un vállyood/ *adj* **1 NOT VALUED** not regarded as valuable, especially when true value is being overlooked **2 NOT APPRAISED** not having had a value attached **3 PRICELESS** so valuable as to have no price in monetary terms (*archaic*)

unvalved /un válvd/ *adj* describes a brass musical instrument that has no valves to extend the range of notes it can play

unvanquished /un vángkwisht/ *adj* not having been subjugated or conquered

unvaried /un váirid/ *adj* showing no changes, alteration, or diversity

unvarnished /un vaárnisht/ *adj* **1** having no protective or decorative coat of varnish **2** said or presented without any attempt to disguise the truth ○ *the unvarnished facts*

unvarying /un váiri ing/ *adj* constant and unchanging

unveil /un váyl/ *v* **1** *vti* to take off a veil or other covering, especially from somebody's face or from a plaque, monument, or work of art during a formal ceremony of inauguration **2** *vt* to reveal something that has been hidden or kept secret

unveiling /un váyling/ *n* **1** the formal removal of a covering that has hidden a plaque, monument, or work of art in an inauguration ceremony **2** the revelation of something for the first time, especially something kept secret

unventilated /un vénti laytid/ *adj* having inadequate fresh air in circulation ○ *a crowded unventilated room*

unverifiable /un vérri fī əb'l/ *adj* incapable of being proved to be true

unverified /un vérri fīd/ *adj* not checked and found to be true

unvoice /un vóyss/ (**-voices, -voicing, -voiced**) *vt* PHON = **devoice**

unvoiced /un vóyst/ *adj* **1** not spoken or explicitly stated **2** pronounced without vibration of the vocal chords

unwaged /ún wáyjd/ *adj* not in formal paid employment

unwanted /un wóntid/ *adj* not desired or wanted ○ *unwanted advice*

unwarrantable /un wórrəntəb'l/ *adj* unable to be justified or condoned —**unwarrantably** *adv*

unwarranted /un wórrəntid/ *adj* **1** not authorized **2** not justified or deserved

unwary /un wáiri/ *adj* failing to be alert and cautious —**unwarily** *adv* —**unwariness** *n*

unwashed /ún wósht/ *adj* not having been washed ◇ **the great unwashed** an offensive term for the mass of ordinary people

unwatchable /un wóchəb'l/ *adj* too bad to be worth watching, or too unpleasant and distressing to watch

unwatering /un wáwtəring/ *n* the removal of water from a site or an area, e.g. during the construction of the foundations of a dam

unwavering /un wáyvəring/ *adj* firm in your view or purpose and unable to be swayed or diverted from it —**unwaveringly** *adv*

unweaned /un weénd/ *adj* still being fed solely on a mother's milk

unwearied /un weérid/ *adj* **1** performing a task or promoting a cause without ceasing **2** not tired, e.g. from working or playing —**unweariedly** *adv*

unweathered /un wéthərd/ *adj* not worn or eroded by exposure to the weather

unweighted /un wáytid/ *adj* not adjusted by the addition of a statistical value ○ *an unweighted sample*

unwelcome /un wélkəm/ *adj* **1** not wanted in a particular place or at a particular event **2** causing hurt or unpleasantness —**unwelcomely** *adv* —**unwelcomeness** *n*

unwelcoming /un wélkəming/ *adj* unfriendly and inhospitable, or having an appearance or atmosphere that is uninviting

unwell /un wél/ *adj* not in good health

unwept /un wépt/ *adj* **1** not cried over as a loss (*literary*) **2** held back and not allowed to flow from the eyes ○ *unwept tears*

unwholesome /un hṓlssəm/ *adj* **1 UNHEALTHY** harmful to health ○ *unwholesome eating habits* **2 REGARDED AS HARMFUL TO MORALS** regarded as being harmful to character or morals **3 LOOKING UNHEALTHY** unhealthy in appearance ○ *an unwholesome pallor* —**unwholesomely** *adv* —**unwholesomeness** *n*

~~**unwieldly**~~ incorrect spelling of **unwieldy**

unwieldy /un weéldi/ *adj* **1** hard to handle because of being large, heavy, or awkward **2** too complex or extensive to be manageable —**unwieldily** *adv* —**unwieldiness** *n*

unwilled /un wíld/ *adj* involuntary rather than chosen or planned

unwilling /un wílling/ *adj* **1** not willing to do something ○ *unwilling to participate* **2** given reluctantly or grudgingly ○ *unwilling assistance* —**unwillingly** *adv* —**unwillingness** *n*

SYNONYMS ***unwilling, reluctant, disinclined, averse, hesitant, loath***

CORE MEANING: lacking the desire to do something

unwilling not prepared to do something; **reluctant** showing no enthusiasm for doing something and only doing it if forced; **disinclined** showing a lack of enthusiasm for something rather than a strong objection to it; **averse** (*formal*) strongly opposed to or disliking something; **hesitant** not keen to do something because of uncertainty or lack of confidence; **loath** having reservations about doing something.

unwind /un wínd/ (**-winds, -winding, -wound** /un wównd/ **-wound**) *v* **1** *vti* **UNCOIL** to undo something such as tape or cable by winding, or to come undone in this way **2** *vt* **UNTANGLE** to remove or undo the tangles in something **3** *vti* **RELAX** to relieve somebody of, or obtain relief from, tension or worry ○ *It's sometimes hard to unwind at the end of a busy day.*

unwinking /un wíngking/ *adj* never closing the eyes or becoming distracted

unwinnable /un wínnəb'l/ *adj* not able to be won

unwisdom /un wízdəm/ *n* lack of wisdom or thought

unwise /un wíz/ (**-wiser, -wisest**) *adj* lacking wisdom, judgment, or good sense —**unwisely** *adv*

unwish /un wísh/ *vt* **1** to undo or take back a wish **2** to want something not to be or not to happen

unwitting /un wítting/ *adj* **1** unaware of what is happening in a particular situation **2** said or done unintentionally [Old English *unwitende* < present participle of *witan* 'become aware of, learn' < Germanic] —**unwittingly** *adv*

unwonted /un wṓntid/ *adj* **1** not what is expected or usual **2** not used to or in the habit of doing something (*archaic*) —**unwontedly** *adv* —**unwontedness** *n*

unworkable /un wúrkəb'l/ *adj* **1 NOT PRACTICAL** too complicated or ambitious to be accomplished or established **2 NOT ABLE TO BE WORKED** unable to be cut, shaped, or otherwise fashioned **3 IMPOSSIBLE TO FARM** so hard or rocky that it is impossible to farm —**unworkability** /un wúrkə bílləti/ *n* —**unworkableness** *n* —**unworkably** *adv*

unworked /un wúrkt/ *adj* not being exploited or used as the site of an operation or activity ○ *an unworked mine*

unworldly /un wúrldli/ *adj* **1 NOT MATERIALISTIC** not interested in money or material goods **2 INEXPERIENCED** lacking experience of the world **3 NOT OF THIS WORLD** not concerned with or part of the material world —**unworldliness** *n*

unworn /un wáwrn/ *adj* **1** not previously or recently worn ○ *an unworn shirt* **2** in good condition, rather than worn out or ruined ○ *unworn tyres*

unworried /un wúrrid/ *adj* feeling or showing no anxiety or fear

unworthy /un wúrthi/ *adj* **1 UNDESERVING** not deserving a particular benefit, privilege, or compliment ○ *They proved themselves unworthy of our trust.* **2 BENEATH** not typical of somebody's usual standards of behaviour ○ *Such conduct is unworthy of you.* **3 WITHOUT VALUE** lacking value or merit **4 VILE** bad or unpleasant and wholly undeserved —**unworthily** *adv* —**unworthiness** *n*

unwound past tense, past participle of **unwind**

unwoven /un wṓv'n/ *adj* made by a process other than weaving

unwrap /un ráp/ (**-wraps, -wrapping, -wrapped**) *vti* to take off the wrapping from something, or to have the wrapping removed

unwritten /un rítt'n/ *adj* **1** remaining unprinted or not written down **2** generally accepted and understood even though not formally recorded in writing ○ *unwritten law*

unyeasted /un yéestid/ *adj* having undergone no yeast fermentation ○ *unyeasted bread*

unyielding /un yeélding/ *adj* **1** not giving in to persuasion, pressure, or force **2** hard or rigid rather than flexible —**unyieldingly** *adv* —**unyieldingness** *n*

unyoke /un yṓk/ (**-yokes, -yoking, -yoked**) *vt* **1 UNTIE** to release an animal such as a horse from a yoke **2 DISCONNECT** to separate two or more connected things **3 FREE** to set somebody free (*archaic or literary*)

ϟ **unzip** /un zíp/ (**-zips, -zipping, -zipped**) *v* **1** *vti* to open or unfasten something such as clothing or luggage by means of a zip, or to become open or unfastened by this means **2** *vt* to decompress a computer file that has been compressed

up /up/ *adv, prep* **AT A HIGHER LEVEL** in, at, or to a higher level or position ○ (adv) *Put your hand up if you know the answer.* ○ (prep) *We climbed up the hill.* ○ (adv) *Prices are going up all the time.* ○ (prep) *I went up the ladder as far as the first-floor window.* ■ *prep, adv* **ALONG** along ○ (prep) *Go up the road until you come to a school.* ○ (adv) *You'll find her house up at the top of the road* ■ *adv* **1 INDICATING**

COMPLETION used to indicate thoroughness or the completion of an action ○ *I tore up all the photographs.* **2 UPRIGHT** in or to an upright position from a lower or prone position ○ *sitting up in bed* **3 COMING OUT** coming through or out of some medium ○ *The whales came up for air.* **4 OUT** in a way that detaches or removes ○ *Pulling up weeds isn't easy.* ○ *We drew up water from the well.* **5 RISING ABOVE** rising, or seeming to rise, above or over something ○ *When does the moon come up?* **6 INTO CONSIDERATION** so as to be discussed or mentioned ○ *The subject just didn't come up.* **7 IN NORTHERLY POSITION** towards or in a northerly position relative to the speaker ○ *Our cousins live up in Scotland.* **8 TO A HIGHER VALUE** to or at a higher amount or price ○ *The interest rate is going up again.* **9 TO A GREATER INTENSITY** with or to more intensity or higher pitch or volume ○ *His voice goes up when he's nervous.* ○ *Let's turn up the volume.* **10 NEAR** so as to move towards or closer to the speaker ○ *She ran up to me and gave me a big hug.* ○ *They came up to the door and knocked.* ■ *adv, n* **AHEAD** to the better or ahead ○ (adv) *Our team is up by two.* ○ (n) *Sales are on the up this month.* ■ *adj* **1 INCREASED** more than before ○ *Your grades are up this term.* **2 OUT OF BED** awake and out of bed ○ *She was already up when I called.* **3 FACING UPWARDS** having the face or top side upward **4 RAISED UPWARDS** in a raised or lifted position ○ *The switch is in the up position.* **5 GOING HIGHER OR NORTH** located in or moving towards a higher or northern direction ○ *The train is waiting at the up platform.* ○ *Take the up escalator.* **6 CHEERFUL** happy and feeling good ○ *We've been so up since hearing the news.* **7 HAPPENING** going on at a particular time (*informal*) ○ *What's up with you these days?* **8 BEING CONSIDERED** approaching a deadline for an action ○ *The contract is up for renewal.* **9 NOMINATED FOR** in the running for an office or professional achievement ○ *I hear she's up for a promotion.* **10 ON TRIAL** charged with an offence or called into a court of law ○ *The accused is up for first-degree murder.* **11 OVER** over or finished ○ *Your time is up.* **12 HAVING KNOWLEDGE** possessing up-to-date or accurate information ○ *I'm not up on the latest gossip.* ○ *He's well up with recent developments in the field.* **13 FUNCTIONING** able to operate or function ○ *Is the computer up?* **14 BATTING** taking a turn at bat in baseball ○ *Who's up first in this inning?* ■ *n* **1 UPWARD SLOPE** something that gradually rises from a base point ○ *Let's try to avoid the ups on our hike today.* **2 SOURCE OF GOOD FEELING** something that causes excitement or a feeling of euphoria (*informal*) ○ *The news was a real up for her.* ■ *v* (**ups, upping, upped**) **1** *vt* **RAISE** to raise or increase something ○ *The insurance company has upped our premiums again.* **2** *vt* **PROMOTE** to promote or raise somebody or something to a higher level or position (*usually passive*) ○ *He was upped to manager last week.* **3** *vi* **ACT SUDDENLY** to act suddenly or impulsively ○ *She just upped and left.* ○ *He upped and bought a new car without shopping around.* [Old English *up* 'upward', *uppe* 'on high' < Indo-European] ◇ **be up to somebody** to be the duty, responsibility, or job of somebody ◇ **it is all up with somebody *or* something** used to indicate that somebody *or* something is bound to fail, be destroyed, or get into trouble or danger (*informal*) ◇ **on the up and up 1 on the up and up, on the up** making very good progress **2** honest or legitimate (*dated*) ◇ **up against it** facing difficulty or danger ◇ **up and about** active and on your feet again after an illness ◇ **ups and downs** changes of fortune or alternating spells of good and bad experiences ◇ **up to 1** occupied with or involved in something, often in a way that arouses suspicion ○ *I knew what he was up to, but I couldn't do anything about it.* **2** able to undertake or endure ○ *I don't think I'm up to the journey.* **3** as many as, or as long as ○ *anything up to 25 miles a day* **4** until ○ *up to now* ◇ **up yours** an offensive phrase indicating anger, contempt, or strong disagreement ◇ **what's up? 1** what's the matter? **2** what's happening?

USAGE See ***back***.

UP *abbr* Uttar Pradesh

up. *abbr* upper

up-and-coming *adj* successful or improving, and showing signs of continuing to do so

up-and-down *adj* (*not hyphenated after verbs*) **1 GOING UP AND DOWN** moving alternately upwards and downwards **2 VARIABLE** uneven or readily changing **3 VERTICAL** in a vertical position or direction ○ *up-and-down stripes*

up-and-under *n* a rugby kick that sends the ball high into the air for the kicker and team-mates to rush forward and gather as it lands

Upanishad /oo púnnishəd, oo pánnə shad/ *n* any of the sacred texts written in Sanskrit that form the basis for Hindu philosophy and doctrine [Early 19C. < Sanskrit *upaniṣad* 'a sitting down near (something)' < *upa* 'near' + *ni-ṣad* 'sit down'.] —**Upanishadic** /oo púnni sháddik, -pánnə-/ *adj*

upas /yóopəss/ (*plural* **upases** *or* **upas**) *n* **1** a tree with white bark and poisonous sap. Native to: Southeast Asia. *Antiaria toxicaria*. **2** a poison made from the sap of the upas. Use: tipping arrows. [Late 18C. < Malay *(pohun) upas* 'poison (tree)'.]

upbeat /up beet/ *n* **1 UNACCENTED BEAT** an unaccented beat in music, especially one that ends a bar **2 GESTURE OF BATON** the upward movement of a conductor's baton that indicates an upbeat **3 IMPROVEMENT** an increase in happiness, prosperity, or favourable activity ■ *adj* **OPTIMISTIC** full of optimism or cheerfulness (*informal*)

upbow /úp bō/ *n* the movement of the bow across the strings of an instrument in which the tip of the bow moves away from the instrument

upbraid /up bráyd/ *vt* to correct or criticize somebody in a harsh manner [Old English *upbrēdan* < ?] —**upbraider** *n* —**upbraidingly** *adv*

upbringing /úp bringing/ *n* the way somebody has been brought up, or trained and educated early in life

upbuild /up bíld/ (**-builds, -building, -built** /-bílt/, **-built**) *vt* to build up, develop, or enlarge something —**upbuilder** *n*

upcast /up kaást/ *adj* **CAST UPWARDS** thrown, propelled, or looking upwards ■ *n* **1 SOMETHING THROWN UP** material that has been thrown up **2 VENTILATION SHAFT** a ventilation shaft in a mine that brings air up

upchuck /úp chuk/ *vti US* to vomit (*slang*)

upcoming /úp kumming/ *adj US* about to happen or coming soon

upcountry *adj* /úp kuntri/ **COMING FROM THE INTERIOR** coming from, associated with, or located in an inland region of a country ■ *n* /úp kuntri/ **INLAND REGION** an inland area of a country ■ *adv* /up kúntri/ **TOWARDS THE INTERIOR** in, to, or towards the inland region of a country

update *vt* /up dáyt/ (**-dates, -dating, -dated**) to provide somebody or something with the most recent information, or with more recent information than was previously available ○ *The website is updated once a month.* ■ *n* /úp dayt/ the latest available information or more recent information [Mid-20C] —**updatable** *adj* —**updater** *n*

Updike /úp dīk/, **John** (*b.* 1932) US writer

updraught /úp draaft/ *n* a current of air that is moving upwards

upend /up énd/ *vti* to place, stand, or turn something up so that it is standing or resting on one end, or be turned over onto one end

upfield /up feéld/ *adv* towards the opposing goal

up-front /up frúnt/, **upfront, up front** *adj* (*informal*) **1** honest, frank, or straightforward **2** paid in advance —**up front** *adv* —**up-frontness** *n*

upgradation /úp grə dáysh'n/ *n S Asia* the process of upgrading something

ϟ**upgrade** *v* /up gráyd/ (**-grades, -grading, -graded**) **1** *vt* **PROMOTE** to promote somebody or increase the status of somebody's job or position **2** *vti* **IMPROVE QUALITY** to improve the quality, standard, or performance of something, especially by incorporating new advances ○ *upgrade a computer* **3** *vti* **TRADE UP** to exchange something for another of better quality ○ *upgrade a seat on a flight* **4** *vt* **IMPROVE LIVESTOCK** to improve the quality of livestock by breeding with superior animals to introduce desirable traits into the offspring ■ *n* /úp grayd/ **1 IMPROVEMENT OF** an improvement in the quality or performance of something, e.g. computer hardware or software **2 SOMETHING THAT IMPROVES** something that improves the performance or quality of something else, or something that has better performance or qualities **3** *US, Can* **UPWARD SLOPE** an upward slope or incline ■ *vti* /up gráyd/ (**-grades, -grading, -graded**) **INSTALL NEWER VERSION** to install a newer version of hardware or software on a computer —**upgradable** *adj*

upgrowth /úp grōth/ *n* the process of growing upwards, or the result of such a process

Upham /úppəm/, **Charles Hazlitt** (1908–94) New Zealand soldier

upheaval /up heév'l/ *n* **1** a strong or sudden change in political, social, or living conditions **2** a sudden raising of part of the earth's crust

upheave /up heév/ (**-heaves, -heaving, -heaved** *or* **-hove** /-hṓv/, **-heaved**) *vti* to lift something forcefully from underneath, or rise or be thrust upward

uphill *adv* /up híl/ **1 UP A SLOPE** up a slope or towards the top of a hill **2 WITH DIFFICULTY** against great resistance or in spite of difficulty ■ *adj* /úp hil/ **1 SLOPING UP** going up a slope or a hill **2 ON HIGHER GROUND** located farther up a slope or hill **3 DIFFICULT** requiring a lot of effort ○ *an uphill struggle*

uphold /up hṓld/ (**-holds, -holding, -held** /up héld/, **-held**) *vt* **1** to maintain or defend something, especially laws or principles, in the face of hostility **2** to provide somebody with moral support, or inspire somebody with confidence —**upholder** *n*

upholster /up hṓlstər/ *vt* to fit chairs, couches, and similar items of furniture with stuffing, springs, and covering [Mid-19C. Back-formation < UPHOLSTERY.] —**upholsterer** *n*

upholstery /up hṓlstəri/ *n* **1** the stuffing, cushions, fabric, and other materials used to upholster chairs and couches ○ *upholstery fabric* **2** the craft, trade, or business of upholstering furniture [Mid-17C. < obsolete *upholster* 'upholsterer' < UPHOLD.]

~~**upholstry**~~ incorrect spelling of **upholstery**

UPI *abbr* United Press International

upkeep /úp keep/ *n* **1** the maintenance of somebody or something in proper condition or operation **2** the financial cost of providing maintenance for somebody or something

upland /úpplənd, úp land/ *n* **1 HIGH LAND** land that has a high elevation, or a region of such land **2 INLAND REGION** a region that lies in the interior of a country ■ *adj* **HIGH OR INLAND** relating to, located in, or native to a region that is at a high elevation or lies in the interior of a country

upland cotton *n* a low, multibranched cotton plant commercially grown as an annual. Native to: Central America. *Gossypium hirsutum*.

uplift *vt* /up líft/ **1 PHYSICALLY LIFT** to raise or lift somebody or something **2 SPIRITUALLY LIFT** to help somebody attain a higher intellectual or spiritual level, or improve somebody's living conditions **3** *NZ, S Africa, Scotland* **COLLECT** to pick up passengers or baggage ■ *n* /úp lift/ **1 SOMETHING IMPROVING** something that elevates somebody morally or spiritually, or improves somebody's living conditions **2 LIFTING UP** the lifting up of something, or the result of doing so **3 UPWARD MOVEMENT OF EARTH'S CRUST** the slow upward movement of large parts of stable areas of the earth's crust —**uplifter** *n*

uplifting /up lífting/ *adj* raising people's moral or spiritual level or emotions

uplighter /úp lītər/ *n* a lamp or lampshade that directs the light upwards

uplink /úp lingk/ *n* a transmitter on the ground that sends radio or other signals to an aircraft or communications satellite ■ *vti* to transmit something from a ground transmitter to an aircraft or communications satellite

ϟ**upload** /úp lōd/ *vti* to transfer data or programs, usually from a peripheral computer to a central, often remote computer

upmarket /up maárkit/ *adj* intended or designed for wealthy discriminating consumers ■ *adv* towards a higher and more expensive standard that appeals to wealthy, discriminating consumers ○ *The hotel seems to have gone upmarket.*

upmost /úp mōst/ *adj* = **uppermost** *adj.*

upon /ə pón/ CORE MEANING: means the same as 'on' but is more formal ○ *He stretched out his legs upon the sofa.* ○ *She climbed upon her father's knee.*
prep **1 ON SURFACE** on or onto the surface of something (*formal*) ○ *The great beast bounced to a halt upon the parapet.* **2 ONE AFTER ANOTHER** used to indicate two occurrences of the same noun, referring to a large number ○ *They claimed that the report contained 'innuendo upon innuendo'.* **3 FOLLOWED BY** used to indicate that one event is followed immediately by another event ○ *Upon finding the relevant text, they store it in their own electronic files.* **4 ABOUT TO HAPPEN** used to indicate that an event is imminent ○ *The holidays are upon us again.* [12C. < UP + ON; after Old Norse *upp á*.]

upper /úppər/ *adj* **1 HIGHER** located above another part of something ○ *the upper deck* ○ *a muscle in the upper arm* **2 MORE IMPORTANT** higher in social position or importance ○ *upper management* **3 MORE DISTANT** lying farther inland, upstream, or to the north ○ *the upper reaches of the river* **4 LATER** later in a named geological formation, period, or system **5 INDICATING A MATHEMATICAL LIMIT** indicating a limit or bound of a set of numbers equal to or greater than every member of the set ■ *n* **1 THE ONE ABOVE** the higher of two people or objects **2 PART OF SHOE** the part of a boot or shoe that covers the upper surface of the foot **3 STIMULANT** a drug such as an amphetamine that has a stimulating effect (*slang*) ■ **uppers** *npl* **UPPER TEETH** the teeth of the upper jaw or of a top set of dentures (*informal*) ◇ **be on your uppers** to be very short of money (*informal*)

upper atmosphere *n* the part of the Earth's atmosphere above the troposphere, especially at heights unreachable by balloon

upper bound *n* in mathematics, a number that is greater than or equal to all the members of a set

Upper Canada /úppər-/ former British province in Canada, corresponding to present-day S Ontario

uppercase /úppər kayss, úppər káyss/ *n* **CAPITAL LETTERS** capital letters used in writing, typing, typesetting, or printing ○ *printed in uppercase* ■ *adj* **IN CAPITAL LETTERS** belonging to, written, or printed in capital letters ■ *vt* (**-cases, -casing, -cased**) **CAPITALIZE** to write, type, typeset, or print something in capital letters [Mid-18C. Because types for capital letters were kept in the upper of two type cases.]

upper chamber *n* POL = **upper house**

upper circle *n* the gallery of seats at the top of a theatre, above the dress circle

upper class *n* the highest social class, or the people in it, e.g. the aristocracy and the very wealthy (*often plural*) —**upper-class** *adj*

upperclassman /úppər klaássmən/ (*plural* **-men** /úppər klaássmən/) *n* a student who belongs to the junior or senior class of an American high school, college, or university

upper crust *n* the upper class (*informal*)

uppercut /úppər kut/ *n* a swinging upward blow in which the fist is aimed at an opponent's chin ■ *vt* (**-cuts, -cutting, -cut**) to hit or attempt to hit an opponent with an uppercut

upper hand *n* the controlling position in a situation

upper house *n* the house in a two-house legislature that is smaller and less representative of the general population, e.g. the House of Lords

Upper Hutt /úppər hút/ city in the southern part of the North Island, New Zealand. Population: 35,700 (1998 estimate).

uppermost /úppər mōst/ *adj* highest in position, rank, or level ■ *adv* in, at, or towards the highest point, position, or rank

Upper Palaeolithic *n* the latest of the three periods of the Palaeolithic era, about 40,000 to 14,000 years ago, when modern human beings first appeared —**Upper Palaeolithic** *adj*

upper respiratory *adj* relating to or affecting any of the air passages or associated structures that connect the lungs with the exterior, including the nasal passages, trachea, and bronchi

upper school *n* the senior students in a secondary school, particularly those in Year 10 and above

Upper Volta former name for **Burkina Faso**

upper works *npl* the parts of a boat or ship above the water line when it is fully loaded

uppity /úppəti/ *adj* **1** behaving in a way that other people consider presumptuous and more suited to somebody belonging a higher social class or position (*informal*) **2** having a stubborn inflexible personality (*dated informal*) [Late 19C. Fancifully < UP.] —**uppityness** *n*

Uppsala /úp saalə/ city in east-central Sweden. Population: 184,507 (1996).

up quark *n* a quark with an electric charge of +2/3 and zero strangeness and charm

upraise /up ráyz/ (**-raises, -raising, -raised**) *vt* to raise something or cause something to rise, e.g. hands, prayers, or voices (*literary*)

uprate /up ráyt/ (**-rates, -rating, -rated**) *vt* to increase the value, price, rank, or size of something

upright /úp rīt/ *adj* **1 ERECT** standing vertically or straight upwards **2 RIGHTEOUS** behaving in a moral or honourable manner ■ *adv* **VERTICALLY** straight upwards rather than at an angle ■ *n* **1 VERTICAL SUPPORT** something that stands upright, e.g. a stake or post **2** MUSIC = **upright piano** —**uprightly** *adv* —**uprightness** *n*

upright piano, upright *n* a piano with a rectangular upright case in which the strings are mounted vertically, and a keyboard at right angles to the case

uprise *vi* /up rīz/ (**-rises, -rising, -rose** /-rōz/, **-risen** /-rízz'n/) (*literary or archaic*) **1 RISE UP** to stand or get up **2 MOVE UPWARDS** to stand, go, or move in an upward direction ■ *n* /úp rīz/ **UPWARD SLOPE** an upward slope or incline

uprising /úp rīzing/ *n* an act of rebellion or revolt against an authority

upriver /up rívvər/ *adv, adj* towards or closer to the source of a river

uproar /úp rawr/ *n* a loud or noisy disturbance [Early 16C. By folk etymology < Middle Low German *uprōr* or Dutch *oproer* 'stirring up'.]

uproarious /up ráwri əss/ *adj* **1 TUMULTUOUS** characterized by noisy confusion **2 HILARIOUS** extremely funny and causing people to laugh loudly **3 VERY LOUD** loud and boisterous —**uproariously** *adv* —**uproariousness** *n*

uproot /up ro͞ot/ *vt* **1 PULL PLANT FROM SOIL** to pull a plant and its roots from the soil **2 REMOVE OR DESTROY** to remove or destroy something completely **3 DISPLACE** to displace somebody or something from a home or habitual environment ○ *I don't want to uproot the children and move to the other end of the country.* —**uprootedness** *n* —**uprooter** *n*

uprose past tense of **uprise**

uprush /úp rush/ *n* a sudden upwards rush of something

upsadaisy /úpsə dáyzi/ *interj* = **upsy-daisy**

upscale /úp skáyl/ *adj, adv US* = **upmarket**

upset *adj* /up sét/ **1 DISTURBED OR SAD** unhappy, disappointed, or emotionally distressed because of something that has happened **2 OVERTURNED** overturned or spilled ○ *an upset dinghy* **3 DIGESTING POORLY** affected by indigestion or nausea ○ *an upset stomach* ■ *v* /up sét/ (**-sets, -setting, -set**) **1** *vt* **MAKE SOMEBODY UNHAPPY** to cause somebody emotional or mental distress **2** *vt* **MAKE SOMEBODY FEEL SICK** to make somebody feel sick, or cause a disorder of the digestive system ○ *Spicy foods upset my stomach.* **3** *vti* **TURN SOMETHING OVER** to turn or tip over, or knock or tip something over accidentally, usually scattering its contents **4** *vt* **DISTURB ORDER** to disrupt the usual order or course of something **5** *vt* **DEFEAT UNEXPECTEDLY** to defeat a competitor or a team unexpectedly in a sports contest **6** *vt* **THICKEN RIVET END** to make a heated bolt, rivet, or bar shorter and thicker by hammering one end ■ *n* /úp set/ **1 DRAMATIC CHANGE** an unexpected problem that disturbs people or causes them to change their plans **2 UNEXPECTED RESULT** an unexpected result, e.g. in a sporting contest or an election **3 EMOTIONAL OR PHYSICAL DISTURBANCE** a mild illness of the stomach, or an unhappy experience **4 TOOL** a tool used to make a rivet, bar, or other piece of heated metal shorter and thicker at one end **5 RIVET** a rivet, bar, or other piece of metal that has been hammered and made shorter and thicker at one end —**upsetter** *n*

upset price *n US, Can, Scotland* the lowest sale price at which something can be sold or auctioned. ◊ **reserve price**

upsetting /up sétting/ *adj* emotionally distressing or disturbing —**upsettingly** *adv*

upshift /úp shift/ *vi US* to move a vehicle into a higher gear

upshot /úp shot/ *n* the end result or outcome of something [Mid-16C. Originally 'final shot (in archery)'.]

upside /úp sīd/ *n* **1 UPPER SIDE** the upper side or part of something **2 POSITIVE SIDE** the most favourable or positive aspect of a particular situation or event **3** *US* **INCREASE IN VALUE** an increase in business profits or stock prices

upside down *adv* **1** turned so that the part that should be higher is lower or the side that should be underneath is on top **2** in total confusion or great disorder ○ *We turned the house upside down looking for the keys.* —**upside-down** *adj*

upside-down cake *n* a sponge cake baked with a layer of fruit at the bottom, then inverted before it is served so that the caramelized fruit is on top

upsilon /up sīlən, úpsi lon/ *n* the 20th letter of the Greek alphabet [Mid-17C. < Greek *u psilon* 'simple u' (to distinguish it from the diphthong *oi*) < *psilon*, form of *psilos* 'simple'.]

upslope /úp slōp/ *n* **1 ASCENDING SLOPE** a slope considered as being angled upwards **2 COOLING OF RISING AIR** the even cooling of air as it rises and expands ■ *adj* **1 SITUATED ON AN ASCENDING SLOPE** situated on, happening on, or caused by an ascending slope **2 FORMED BY UPSLOPE** describes fog formed by the even cooling of air as it rises and expands ■ *adv* **TOWARDS HIGHER POINT ON SLOPE** at or towards a higher point on a slope

upstage /up stáyj/ *vt* (**-stages, -staging, -staged**) **1 OUTDO SOMEBODY ELSE** to divert, or attempt to divert, attention away from somebody else **2 TURN ACTOR AWAY FROM AUDIENCE** to move towards the back of the stage in order to force another actor to turn his or her back to the audience ■ *adv* **TOWARDS REAR** in, at, or towards the rear part of a stage ■ *adj* **LOCATED AT REAR** located in or relating to the rear part of a stage ■ *n* **BACK OF STAGE** the rear part of the stage —**upstager** *n*

upstairs /úp stáirz/ *adv* **1 UP THE STAIRS** to, towards, or on an upper level or floor **2 MENTALLY** in the mind or brain (*humorous*) ○ *not a lot happening upstairs* **3 TO A HIGHER JOB** to a higher level or job in an organization or hierarchy (*informal*) ■ *n* **1 UPPER FLOOR** an upper floor or the part of a building above the ground floor (*often before nouns*) ○ *an upstairs bathroom* **2 OWNERS OF WEALTHY HOUSEHOLD** used to refer collectively to wealthy householders, as opposed to the servants who lived downstairs (*archaic informal*) ◊ **downstairs** *n.* 2 ◇ **kick somebody upstairs** to promote somebody to a rank or position that is officially superior but in fact carries less power and opportunity for influence (*informal*)

upstanding /up stánding/ *adj* **1** honest and socially responsible **2** in an erect position (*archaic*) —**upstandingness** *n* ◇ **be upstanding** to stand in response to a formal request, particularly for a toast or prayer or in a court of law (*formal*)

upstart *n* /úp staart/ a newly wealthy, powerful, or famous person who does not deserve to be so ■ *vi* /up staárt/ to rise or jump up suddenly or unexpectedly (*archaic*)

upstate /úp stayt/ *adj US* relating to or living in the northern part of a state

upstream /up streém, úp streem/ *adv* **1 AGAINST THE CURRENT** in or towards the source of a river or stream **2 IN OPPOSITE DIRECTION TO TRANSCRIPTION** in a direction along a strand of a DNA molecule counter to that in which transcription takes place ■ *adj* **NEARER THE SOURCE** located farther towards the source of a stream or river

upstretched /úp strécht/ *adj* stretched or raised upwards

upstroke /úp strōk/ *n* **1** an upward or rising movement of a pen or brush, or the mark it makes **2** the upward movement of a piston in a reciprocating engine

upsurge *n* /úp surj/ a rapid increase in something ■ *vi* /up súrj/ (**-surges, -surging, -surged**) to rise or increase rapidly (*archaic or literary*)

upsweep *n* /úp sweep/ **1 UPWARD SWEEP** an upward or curving line or motion **2** *US* **HAIRSTYLE** a hairstyle in which the hair is swept upward from the neck ■ *vti* /up swéep/ (**-sweeps, -sweeping, -swept, -swept** /up swépt/) **MOVE UPWARD** to sweep, curve, or brush something upwards, or move upwards with a sweeping or curving motion

upswept /úp swépt/ *adj* curved or brushed upwards

upswing /úp swing/ *n* an increase or improvement, e.g. in business profits

upsy-daisy /úpsi-/, **upsadaisy** *interj* a reassuring expression usually addressed to a child being lifted or who has fallen or stumbled (*babytalk*) [Mid-19C. Alteration of *up-a-daisy* < UP + *a-day*, expressing surprise.]

uptake /úp tayk/ *n* **1** a passage such as a pipe or chimney, that draws up smoke or air **2** MIN EXTRACT = **upcast** *n.* 2 **3** the process of physically absorbing something into a living organism ◇ **be quick** *or* **slow on the uptake** to be quick or slow to understand things or realize what is happening (*informal*)

uptempo *n* /úp tempō/ a fast or lively musical tempo ■ *adj* /up témpō/ fast-paced and exciting

upthrow /úp thrō/ *n* the upward movement of one block of rock over another in a low-angle fault

upthrust /úp thrust/ *n* an upward push or thrust ■ *adj* raised or lifted up

ptick /úp tik/ *n US* a small increase in something, especially in stock or bond prices

ptight /úp tīt/ *adj (informal)* **1** tense as a result of anger, fear, or annoyance in a way that is difficult to control **2** unable or unwilling to show emotion —**uptightness** *n*

ptime /úp tīm/ *n* the time during which a computer or other machine is operating or ready for use

p-to-date *adj (not hyphenated after verbs)* **1 WITH LATEST KNOWLEDGE** including or possessing knowledge of the latest information **2 CURRENT** extending up to or reflecting the current time **3 FASHIONABLE** familiar with or knowledgeable about current fashions, styles, or ideas

p-to-the-minute *adj* including or relating to the most recent events or things

ptown *adv* /up tówn/ *US* to, towards, or in the upper part of a city

ptrend /úp trend/ *n* an upward improving trend, especially in business or an economy

pturn *v* /up túrn/ **1** *vti* **TURN OVER** to turn over or cause something to turn over, up, or upside down **2** *vt* **TURN UPWARDS** to turn something upwards, e.g. a face or gaze *(usually passive)* ■ *n* /úp turn/ **IMPROVEMENT** an improvement in the economy or in business conditions

pward /úpwərd/ *adv* US = **upwards** ■ *adj* **1** going or directed towards a higher level or position ○ *a steep upward climb* **2** used to indicate that something is rising or becoming better ○ *an upward trend* —**upwardly** *adv*

pwardly mobile *adj* desiring and attempting to move to a higher social class or to obtain greater social or financial status ■ *npl* those who are becoming richer or more powerful and moving up from a lower class

pward mobility *n* the ability or opportunity to move to a higher social class and acquire greater wealth, power, or status

pwards /úppwərdz/, **upward** /-wərd/ *adv* **1 TOWARDS A HIGHER LEVEL** in, to, or towards a higher place, level, or position ○ *She's working her way upwards through the company hierarchy.* ○ *Keep going upwards and you'll soon see the house.* **2 TOWARDS INTERIOR OR SOURCE** towards the interior of a place, or towards an origin or source ○ *The hikers left the path and headed upwards along the river.* **3 TOWARDS A GREATER AMOUNT** towards a larger amount, degree, or position ○ *Sales have gone steadily upwards during the last quarter.* ◇ **upwards of** more than

pwelling /up wélling/ *n* **1** a rising up from or as if from lower depths **2** a process in which cold nutrient-rich water rises to the surface from the ocean depths

pwind /úp wínd/ *adv, adj* **1** against or into the wind **2** on the side towards which the wind is blowing

Ur /ur/ ancient city of Mesopotamia, in present-day SE Iraq

ur-[1] *prefix* = **uro-**[1] *(before vowels)*

ur-[2] *prefix* = **uro-**[2] *(before vowels)*

uracil /yŏŏrə sil/ *n (symbol* **U***)* a pyrimidine base, one of the four bases in RNA in which it pairs with thymine [Late 19C. < ?]

uraemia /yŏŏ reémi ə/ *n* a form of blood poisoning caused by the accumulation in the blood of products that are normally eliminated in the urine [Mid-19C. < modern Latin, < Greek *ouron* 'urine' + *aima* 'blood'.]

uraeus /yŏŏ reé əss/ *n* the sacred serpent found on the headdresses of Egyptian rulers and divinities, representing sovereignty [Mid-19C. Via modern Latin < Greek *ouraios* 'cobra'.]

Ural /yŏŏrəl/ river of S Russia and NW Kazakhstan, flowing southwards into the Caspian Sea. Length: 2,428 km/1,509 mi.

Ural-Altaic *n* a hypothetical language group formerly proposed by scholars as containing the Uralic and Altaic language families —**Ural-Altaic** *adj*

Uralic /yŏŏ rállik/ *n* a family of languages spoken in northern and central Europe and W Siberia, including the branches Finno-Ugric and Samoyed —**Uralic** *adj*

uralite /yŏŏrə līt/ *n* a fibrous blue-green mixture of amphibole minerals. Source: metamorphosed pyroxenes. [Mid-19C. < German *Uralit* < *Ural* 'Ural Mountains'.]

Ural Mountains /yŏŏrəl mówntinz/ mountain system in W Russia, the traditional dividing line between Asia and Europe. Highest peak: Mount Narodnaya 1,894 m/6,214 ft. Length: 2,400 km/1,500 mi.

uran- *prefix* uranium ○ *uranous* [< URANIUM]

uranalysis /yŏŏrə nálləssiss/ *(plural* **-ses** /-seez/*) n* MED = **urinalysis** [Late 19C. Blend of URINE + ANALYSIS.]

Urania /yŏŏ ráyni ə/ *n* in Greek mythology, the Muse of astronomy. ◊ **Muse**

uranic /yŏŏ ránnik/ *adj* relating to or containing uranium, especially with a high valency [Mid-19C. < Latin *uranus* < Greek *ouranos* 'the heavens'.]

uraninite /yŏŏ ránni nīt/ *n* a black uranium oxide mineral containing thorium, radium and lead. Use: source of uranium. [Late 19C. < German *Uranin* < modern Latin *uranium* (see URANIUM).]

uranite /yŏŏrə nīt/ *n* any mineral that contains uranium [Late 19C. < URANIUM.] —**uranitic** /yŏŏrə níttik/ *adj*

uranium /yŏŏ ráyni əm/ *n (symbol* **U***)* a heavy silvery-white radioactive metallic element occurring in three isotopes. Source: uraninite, pitchblende. Use: in one isotope, as fuel in nuclear reactors and weapons. [Late 18C. < modern Latin, < *Uranus*, the planet (discovered eight years before the element was identified).]

uranium 235 /-toŏ thurti fīv/ *n* a uranium isotope having a mass number of 235 that readily undergoes fission when bombarded with neutrons. Use: nuclear energy source.

uranium 238 /-toŏ thurti áyt/ *n* the most abundant, stable isotope of uranium, having a mass number of 238

uranium-lead dating *n* the determination of the age of a uranium-containing mineral by measuring the level of lead isotope produced by the radioactive decay of uranium, which occurs at a known rate

uranography /yŏŏrə nóggrəfi/ *n* the branch of astronomy that deals with making maps of the constellations [Mid-17C. < Greek *ouranographia* 'science of the skies'.] —**uranographer** *n* —**uranographic** /yŏŏrənə gráffik/ *adj* —**uranographist** *n*

uranous /yŏŏrənəss/ *adj* relating to or containing uranium, especially with a low valency

Uranus /yŏŏrənəss, yŏŏ ráynəss/ *n* **1** in Greek mythology, the ruler of the heavens, husband of Gaia, and father of the Titans **2** the seventh smallest planet in the solar system and the seventh planet from the Sun. See table at **planet** [Via Latin < Greek *Ouranos*]

uranyl /yŏŏrənil/ *n* a compound containing the group UO_2

urase /yŏŏ rayss/ *n* BIOCHEM = **urease**

urate /yŏŏr ayt, yáwr-/ *n* a salt of uric acid —**uratic** /yoo ráttik, yaw-/ *adj*

urban /úrbən/ *adj* relating or belonging to a city [Early 17C. < Latin *urbanus* < *urbs* 'city'.]

Urban VIII /úrbən/ (1568–1644) pope (1623–44)

urban blues *n* blues music that has a stronger beat than country blues, often played with electric instruments and featuring songs about life in the city *(+ singular verb)*

urbane /ur báyn/ (**-baner, -banest**) *adj* showing sophistication, refinement, or courtesy [Mid-16C. Directly or via Old French *urbaine* 'urban' < Latin *urbanus* (see URBAN).] —**urbanely** *adv* —**urbaneness** *n*

urban guerrilla *n* a city dweller who carries out violent acts to further a political cause

urbanise *vt* = **urbanize**

urbanism /úrbənizəm/ *n* **1** the typical way of life of people who live in a city or town **2** the study of life in cities and towns

urbanist /úrbənist/ *n* a specialist in city planning and the study of cities —**urbanistic** /úrbə nístik/ *adj* —**urbanistically** /-nístikli/ *adv*

urbanite /úrbə nīt/ *n* a resident of a city or town

urbanity /ur bánnəti/ *n* the quality of being sophisticated, refined, or courteous ■ **urbanities** *npl* polite or courteous actions [Mid-16C. Directly or via French *urbanité* < Latin *urbanitas* < *urbanus* (see URBAN).]

urbanize /úrbə nīz/ (**-izes, -izing, -ized**), **urbanise** (**-ises, -ising, -ised**) *vt* **1 MAKE AREA INTO TOWN** to make an area of countryside or villages into a town or part of one **2 CAUSE COUNTRY PEOPLE TO BECOME URBAN** to cause people who live in the countryside to migrate to a town or city **3 MAKE SOMEBODY URBAN** to accustom somebody to living in a town or city rather than in the country —**urbanization** /úrbə nī záysh'n/ *n*

urban myth *n* a bizarre and untrue story that circulates in a society through being presented to people as something that actually happened, usually to a friend or relative of somebody the speaker knows

urban planning *n US* = **town planning** —**urban planner** *n*

urban renewal *n* the redevelopment of urban areas that have become run down or impoverished, by demolishing or renovating old buildings or building new ones

urban sprawl *n* the expansion of an urban area into areas of countryside that surround it

urbi et orbi /úrbi et áwrbi/ *adv* a phrase used in a papal blessing, meaning 'to the city of Rome and to the world' [< Latin]

URC *abbr* United Reformed Church

urceolate /úrssi ələt, -layt/ *adj* shaped like an urn or pitcher, with a swollen middle and narrowing top [Mid-18C. < Latin *urceolus* 'little pitcher' < *urceus* 'pitcher'.]

urchin /úrchin/ *n* **1 MISCHIEVOUS CHILD** a mischievous child, especially a young one who is unkempt in appearance **2 SEA URCHIN** a sea urchin **3 HEDGEHOG** a hedgehog *(archaic or regional)* [13C. Via Old N French *herichon* < Latin *(h)ericius* 'hedgehog'.]

Urdu /oŏr doo, úr doo/ *n* the Indic official language of Pakistan, spoken also in Bangladesh and India, closely related to Hindi. Native speakers: 40 million. [Late 18C. Via Persian and Urdu *(zabān i) urdū* '(language of the) camp' < Turkish *ordū* 'camp'.] —**Urdu** *adj*

-ure *suffix* **1** process or condition, or something resulting from an action ○ *licensure* ○ *erasure* **2** office or function, or a body performing a particular function ○ *prefecture* ○ *legislature* [Via Old French < Latin *-ura*]

urea /yoo reé ə, yŏŏri ə/ *n* $CO(NH_2)_2$ a nitrogenous compound found in the urine of mammals, produced through protein decomposition. Source: manufactured synthetically. Use: fertilizers, feeds, manufacture of resins. [Early 19C. < modern Latin, alteration of French *urée* < Old French *urine* (see URINE).] —**ureal** *adj*

urea-formaldehyde resin *n* a resin made from urea and formaldehyde, used in making electrical fittings and in cavity insulation

urease /yŏŏri ayss, -ayz/ *n* an enzyme in some bacteria and seeds that breaks down urea to produce carbon dioxide and ammonia [Late 19C. < UREA + -ASE.]

urediniospore /yŏŏri dínni ə spawr/ *n* FUNGI = **uredospore** [Early 20C. < Latin *uredin-*, stem of *uredo* (see UREDO).]

uredinium /yŏŏri dínni əm/ *(plural* **-a** /-ni ə/*)*, **uredium** /yŏŏrí di əm/ *(plural* **-a***)*, **uredosorus** /yŏŏ reédō sáwrəss/ *(plural* **-i** /-rī/*)* *n* a reddish or black mass of spores produced on a plant by a rust fungus [Early 20C. < Latin *uredin-*, stem of *uredo* (see UREDO).]

uredo /yŏŏ reédō/ *(plural* **-dines** /-di neez/*)* *n* MED = **urticaria** [Early 18C. < Latin, < *urere* 'to burn'.]

uredospore /yŏŏ reédō spawr/ *n* a reddish unicellular spore that develops in the uredinia of rust fungi

ureide /yŏŏri īd/ *n* an acyl derivative of urea

uremia *n* US = **uraemia**

ureotelic /yŏŏri ə téllik/ *adj* producing nitrogen-containing waste in the form of urea [Early 20C. < UREA.] —**ureotelism** *n*

ureter /yŏŏ reétər, yŏŏritər/ *n* either of a pair of ducts that carry urine from the kidneys to the bladder in mammals or to the common cavity for wastes (**cloaca**) in lower vertebrate animals [Late 16C. Via modern Latin < Greek *ourētēr* < *ourein* 'urinate' < *ouron* 'urine'.] —**ureteral** /yŏŏ reétərəl/ *adj* —**ureteric** /yŏŏri térrik/ *adj*

urethane /yŏŏri thayn/, **urethan** /yŏŏri thán/ *n* **1** $C_3H_7NO_3$ a colourless odourless crystalline compound, the ethyl ester of carbamic acid. Use: solvents, pesticides, pharmaceuticals. **2** any ester of carbamic acid other than the ethyl ester **3** CHEM = **polyurethane** [Mid-19C. < modern Latin *urea* (see UREA) + ETHANE.]

urethra /yŏŏ reéthrə/ *(plural* **-thras** *or* **-thrae** /-ree/*)* *n* the tube in mammals that carries urine from the bladder out of the body and in the male also carries semen during ejaculation [Mid-17C. Via late Latin < Greek *ourēthra* < Greek *ourein* 'urinate' (see URETER).] —**urethral** *adj*

urethritis /yŏŏri thrítiss/ *n* inflammation of the urethra, usually caused by infection [Early 19C. < URETHRA.] —**urethritic** /-thríttik/ *adj*

urethroscope /yŏŏ reéthrə skōp/ *n* a medical instrument for examining the inside of the urethra, consisting of a fine flexible tube fitted with lenses and a light [Mid-19C. < URETHRA.] **—urethroscopic** /-skóppik/ *adj* **—urethroscopy** /yo͞ori thróskəpi/ *n*

uretic /yo͞o réttik/ *adj* relating to, involving, or in urine [Mid-19C. Via late Latin < Greek *ourētikos* < *ourein* 'urinate' (see URETER).]

Urey /yo͞ori/, **Harold C.** (1893–1981) US chemist

urge /urj/ *vt* (**urges, urging, urged**) **1 ADVISE SOMEBODY STRONGLY** to advise somebody strongly to do something ○ *urged his firm to reconsider* **2 ADVOCATE SOMETHING EARNESTLY** to recommend or advise something earnestly and with persistence ○ *urging restraint* **3 ENCOURAGE** to encourage, drive, or force somebody or something to do something ○ *could hear the crowd urging her on* **4 EXCITE** to excite or stimulate somebody (*archaic literary*) ■ *n* **STRONG NEED** a strong need, wish, or impulse to do something ○ *the urge to travel* [Mid-16C. < Latin *urgere* 'push, press, compel'.] **—urger** *n*

urgent /úrjənt/ *adj* **1** calling for immediate action or attention **2** showing earnestness or the desire for something to be done quickly [15C. Via French < Latin *urgent-*, present participle of *urgere* 'push, press, compel'.] **—urgency** *n* **—urgently** *adv*

-urgy *suffix* technique or art of working with something ○ *metallurgy* [Via modern Latin *-urgia* < Greek *-ourgos* 'working' < *ergon* 'work']

-uria *suffix* **1** the condition of having a particular substance in the urine ○ *aciduria* **2** the condition of having a particular kind of urine ○ *polyuria* [< modern Latin, < Greek *ouron* 'urine']

Uriah /yo͞o rˊi ə/ *n* in the Bible, a Hittite officer purposely killed in battle to allow King David to marry his wife, Bathsheba (2 Samuel 11:2–16)

uric /yo͞orik/ *adj* relating to, involving, or found in urine [Late 18C. < French *urine* (see URINE).]

uric acid *n* a slightly soluble compound in urine and blood, made in the breakdown of nitrogenous waste

uridine /yo͞ori deen/ *n* a nucleoside, consisting of uracil and ribose, that plays a role in the metabolism of carbohydrates [Early 20C. < URACIL + -IDINE.]

Urim and Thummim /yo͞orim and thúmmim/ *npl* oracles on the breastplate of the high priest of ancient Israel [Hebrew 'ūrīm and tummīm']

urin- *prefix* = urino- (*before vowels*)

urinal /yo͞ori rˊin'l, yo͞orin'l/ *n* **1 RECEPTACLE FOR MEN TO URINATE INTO** a receptacle that is fixed to a wall and plumbed in, used for men to urinate into **2 PLACE WITH URINALS** a room or building in which there are urinals **3 PORTABLE CONTAINER FOR URINE** a container used to transport urine [13C. Via French < late Latin *urinalis* 'urinary' < Latin *urina* 'urine'.]

urinalysis /yo͞ori nállessiss/ (*plural* **-ses** /-seez/), **uranalysis** /yo͞ora nállessiss/ *n* analysis of the physical, chemical, and microbiological properties of urine, carried out to help diagnose disease, monitor treatment, or detect the presence of a specific substance [Late 19C. Blend of URINE + ANALYSIS.]

urinary /yo͞orinəri/ *adj* relating to, involving, or affecting urine or the organs that form and discharge urine [Late 16C. < Latin *urina* 'urine'.]

urinary bladder *n* an expanding muscular sac in mammals and some other vertebrates in which urine collects before it is discharged from the body through the urethra

urinate /yo͞ori nayt/ (**-nates, -nating, -nated**) *vi* to discharge urine from the body [Late 16C. < past participle of *urinat-urinare* < Latin *urina* 'urine'.] **—urination** /yo͞ori náysh'n/ *n* **—urinative** *adj* **—urinator** *n*

urine /yo͞orin/ *n* the yellowish liquid containing waste products that is excreted by the kidneys and discharged through the urethra [14C. Directly and via Old French < Latin *urina*.] **—urinous** *adj*

uriniferous /yo͞ori nífferəss/ *adj* describes a tube that carries urine, especially the tubules of the kidneys [Mid-18thC. < URINE.]

urino- *prefix* urine, urinary ○ *urinometer* [< Latin *urina* 'urine']

urinogenital *adj* ANAT = urogenital

urinometer /yo͞ori nómmitər/ *n* a hydrometer for measuring the specific gravity of urine

⚡ **URL** *n* an address identifying the location of a file on the Internet, consisting of the protocol, the computer on

which the file is located, and the file's location on that computer. Full form **Uniform Resource Locator**

Urmia, Lake /úrmi ə/ salt lake in NW Iran. Area: 4,700 sq. km/1,815 sq. mi.

urn /urn/ *n* **1 ORNAMENTAL VASE WITH PEDESTAL** an ornamental vase that usually has a foot or a pedestal **2 VASE FOR SOMEBODY'S ASHES** a sealed vase in which the ashes of somebody who has died and been cremated are kept **3 VESSEL FOR HOT DRINKS** a closed vessel in which a hot drink, especially tea or coffee, is made in a large quantity and poured out through a tap **4 SPORE-PRODUCING PART OF MOSS CAPSULE** the part of a moss capsule where spores are produced [14C. < Latin *urna*.]

LITERARY LINK *Ode on a Grecian Urn*, a poem (1819) by John Keats. It describes the poet's reaction to a Greek vase decorated with reliefs of joyful rural scenes. The urn becomes a symbol of the contrast between the permanence of art and the transience of human life, and inspires the poem's famous proclamation 'Beauty is truth, truth beauty'.

uro-[1] *prefix* **1** urine, urinary tract ○ *uroscopy* ○ *urolithiasis* **2** urea ○ *urease* [< Greek *ouron* 'urine']

uro-[2] *prefix* tail ○ *uropod* [< Greek *oura*]

urochord /yo͞orō kawrd/ *n* **1** a flexible skeletal rod (**notochord**) that supports the posterior part of the body in some marine animals, e.g. sea squirts **2 urochord, urochordate** MARINE BIOL = **tunicate** *n*. [Late 19C. < URO-[2] + CHORD[2].] **—urochordal** /yo͞orō káwrd'l/ *adj* **—urochordate** *adj*

urochrome /yo͞orō krōm/ *n* a yellow pigment that gives urine its normal colour

urodele /yo͞orō deel/ *n* an amphibian that has a tail throughout its adult life, a long body, and short limbs, e.g. the salamander or newt. Order: Caudata and Urodela. [Mid-19C. Directly or via French *urodèle* < modern Latin *Urodela*, < Greek *oura* 'tail' + *dēlos* 'visible'.] **—urodele** *adj*

urogenital /yo͞orō jénnit'l/, **urinogenital** /yo͞orinō jénnit'l/ *adj* relating to or involving the organs of the urinary tract and the reproductive organs when considered together [Mid-19C. < URINO-[1] + GENITAL.]

urogenous /yo͞orō rójjənəss/ *adj* producing, obtained from, or formed in urine

urogram /yo͞orō gram/ *n* an X-ray picture of the urinary tract or some part of it

urography /yo͞orō róggrəfi/ *n* X-ray photography of all or part of the urinary tract **—urographic** /yo͞orō gráffik/ *adj*

urokinase /yo͞orō kˊi nays, -nayss/ *n* an enzyme, produced by the kidneys, that catalyses the conversion of plasminogen to plasmin. Use: medicinally, to dissolve blood clots.

urol. *abbr* urology

urolith /yo͞orōlith/ *n* a stony mass (**calculus**) in the urinary tract **—urolithic** /yo͞orō líthik/ *adj*

urolithiasis /yo͞orōli thˊi əssiss/ *n* the formation or presence of stony masses in the urinary tract, or the medical condition resulting from this

urology /yo͞o róllǝji/ *n* a branch of medicine that deals with the study and treatment of disorders of the urinary tract in women and the urogenital system in men **—urologic** /yo͞orō lójjik/ *adj* **—urologist** *n*

uropod /yo͞orō pod/ *n* either of a pair of flat appendages on the last abdominal segment of a crustacean, e.g. a lobster or shrimp [Late 19C. < URO-[2].] **—uropodal** /yo͞o róppəd'l/ *adj*

uropygial gland /yo͞orō píjji əl-/ *n* a gland in the skin at the base of the tail of most birds that secretes an oil used while preening to condition and waterproof their feathers

uropygium /yo͞orō píjji əm/ *n* the fleshy hindmost part of a bird's body from which the tail feathers grow [Late 18C. Via medieval Latin < Greek *ouropugion* < *oura* 'tail' + *pūgē* 'buttocks'.] **—uropygial** *adj*

uroscopy /yo͞o róskəpi/ (*plural* **-pies**) *n* the medical examination of urine in order to make a diagnosis **—uroscopic** /yo͞orō skóppik/ *adj* **—uroscopist** *n*

-urous *suffix* having a particular kind of tail ○ *anurous* [< Greek *oura* 'tail']

Urquhart /úrkət/, **Sir Thomas** (1611?–60) Scottish writer and soldier

Ursa Major /úrssə-/ *n* a prominent constellation of the

northern hemisphere containing the Plough. See illustration at **constellation**

Ursa Minor *n* a small constellation of the northern hemisphere containing the star Polaris. See illustration at **constellation**

ursine /úr sˊin/ *adj* **1** relating to or typical of bears, or belonging to the bear family **2** having the characteristics usually associated with bears [Mid-16C. < Latin *ursinus* < *ursus* 'a bear'.]

Ursuline /úrssyo͞o lˊin/ *n* a member of a Roman Catholic order of nuns founded by St Angela Merici in Brescia, Italy, in the 16th century and dedicated to teaching [Late 17C. < *Ursula*, patron saint of the order's founder.] **—Ursuline** *adj*

urticaceous /úrti káyshəss/ *adj* describes a plant that belongs to the nettle family [Mid-19C. < Latin *urtica* 'nettle' < *urere* 'to burn']

urticaria /úrti káiri ə/ *n* a skin rash, usually occurring as an allergic reaction, that is marked by itching and small pale or red swellings and often lasts for a few days (*technical*) [Late 18C. < modern Latin, < Latin *urtica* 'nettle'.] **—urticarial** *adj* **—urticarious** *adj*

urticate /úrti kayt/ *vi* (**-cates, -cating, -cated**) to be affected by or cause urticaria ■ *adj* producing weals and itching [Mid-19C. < medieval Latin *urticant-* past participle of *urticare* 'sting' < Latin *urtica* 'nettle'.] **—urticant** *adj, n*

urtication /úrti káysh'n/ *n* **1** the process by which somebody develops the condition urticaria **2** an intensely itchy or burning sensation

Uru. *abbr* Uruguay

Uruguay

Uruguay[1] /yo͞orə gwˊi/ republic in SE South America, bordering the Atlantic Ocean. Capital: Montevideo. Population: 3,238,952 (1996). Area: 176,215 sq. km/68,037 sq. mi. **—Uruguayan** *n, adj*

Uruguay[2] river in SE South America, rising in S Brazil and entering the Atlantic Ocean through the Río de la Plata. Length: 1,600 km/990 mi.

Urumqi /o͞o ro͞omchi/ capital of Xinjiang Uygur Autonomous Region, NW China. Population: 1,046,898 (1991).

urus /yo͞orəss/ *n* ZOOL = **aurochs** [Early 17C. Via Latin < Greek *ouros*.]

urushiol /o͞o ro͞oshi ol, o͞o ro͞oshi ol/ *n* an oily poisonous irritant found in the resin and on the leaves and stems of poison ivy, the lacquer tree, and some related plants [Early 20C. < Japanese *urushi* 'lacquer' + -OL.]

us[1] /uss, əss/ *pron* **1 SELF AND OTHER OR OTHERS** a pronoun used to refer to both yourself and another person or other people (*after a verb or preposition*) ○ *He told us to go away.* ○ *This problem affects all of us.* **2 ROYAL US** used by a king or queen, or the editor of a newspaper, to mean 'me' (*formal*) ○ *It gives us great pleasure to declare this building open.* **3 ME** used by a person to refer to himself or herself (*informal*) ○ *Give us a look, then!* ■ *det* **OUR** our (*nonstandard or regional* [Old English *ūs* = Germanic]

⚡ **us**[2] *abbr* United States (*in Internet addresses*)

US, U.S. *abbr* United States

u.s. *Latin* **1** where mentioned above. Full form **ubi supra 2** as above. Full form **ut supra**

U/S *abbr* unserviceable

USA, U.S.A. *abbr* United States of America

⚡ **usability engineer** *n* somebody employed by, e.g. the design team of a software company to observe users learning to use new products prior to their release in the marketplace, in order to ensure that the products are suitable for the intended market —**usability engineering** *n*

usable /yóozəb'l/, **useable** *adj* capable of being used —**usability** /yóozə bílləti/ *n* —**usableness** *n* —**usably** *adv*

USAF, U.S.A.F. *abbr* United States Air Force

usage /yóossij, yóoz-/ *n* **1 ACT OR WAY OF USING** the act of using something, the way something is used, or how much something is used **2 ACCEPTED PRACTICE** a customary and generally accepted practice or procedure **3 WAY LANGUAGE IS ACTUALLY USED** the way in which words and phrases are actually used in speech or writing **4 EXAMPLE OF LANGUAGE USE** an example of a specific use of language **5 TREATMENT** the handling or treatment of something [13C. < Old French, < Latin *usus* (see USE[1]).]

USAID *tdmk* a trademark for a US government agency that provides humanitarian aid and assistance for development to other countries

~~usally~~ incorrect spelling of **usually**

usance /yóoz'nss/ *n* the customary length of time allowed for payment of a bill of exchange in foreign commerce [14C. < Old French, < assumed Vulgar Latin *usare* 'keep on using' < Latin *uti* 'to use'.]

USDAW /úz daw/ *abbr* Union of Shop, Distributive, and Allied Workers

use[1] *v* /yooz/ (**uses, using, used**) **1** *vt* **EMPLOY SOMETHING FOR SOME PURPOSE** to employ something for some purpose or to put something into action or service ○ *use a hammer* **2** *vt* **DO SOMETHING HABITUALLY** to do something habitually ○ *use common sense* **3** *vt* **CONSUME** to expend or consume something, often until none is left ○ *All of the space on the disk has been used.* **4** *vt* **MANIPULATE OR EXPLOIT** to exploit or manipulate somebody as a means to an end ○ *the type of person who uses others* **5** *vti* **CONSUME DRUGS OR ALCOHOL REGULARLY** to consume something regularly, especially drugs or alcohol **6** *vt* **BEHAVE TOWARDS** to behave towards somebody or something in a particular way ○ *used his employees poorly* **7** *vt* **BENEFIT FROM** to benefit or get satisfaction from something ○ *I could use a good night's sleep.* ■ *n* /yooss/ **1 ACT OF USING** the act of using something for a particular purpose ○ *skilled in the use of computers* **2 STATE OF BEING EMPLOYED** the state or fact of being employed for a particular purpose ○ *no longer in use* **3 WAY OF EMPLOYING** a way of employing something ○ *We admired the artist's use of colour.* **4 RIGHT TO USE** the right to use something or the benefit of using something **5 ABILITY TO USE** the power or ability to use something **6 PURPOSE** the purpose of something ○ *Put your education to good use.* **7 USEFULNESS** the quality of being useful **8 THE NEED TO USE** the occasion or need to use something **9 BENEFIT OF PROPERTY** the benefit or profit of property held by one person for another **10 LEGAL ENJOYMENT OF PROPERTY** the legal enjoyment of property in its employment, occupation, or practice **11 MODIFIED LOCAL LITURGY** a modified liturgical form or observance practised in a particular church or religious order [13C. Via Old French *user* 'to use' < Latin *usus*, past participle of *uti*.] ◇ **have no use for somebody** *or* **something 1** to have no need or purpose for somebody or something **2** to have no liking or respect for somebody or something (*informal*) ◇ **make use of** to exploit or manipulate somebody as a means to an end ◇ **what's the use?** used to suggest that doing something is pointless (*informal*)

SYNONYMS ***use, employ, make use of, utilize***

CORE MEANING: to put something to use

use to put something into action or service; **employ** to make use of something such as a tool or a resource in a particular way; **make use of** to use what is readily available, especially in a sensible or economical way; **utilize** to find a practical or unintended use for something.

USAGE See ***utilize***.

use up *vt* to expend or consume something, often until none is left

use[2] /yooss/ *vi* used to say that somebody or something habitually or usually did something ○ *We used to eat out more often.* ○ *He used not to be so grumpy.* ○ *Did you use to make your own bread?*

useable *adj* = **usable**

~~useage~~ incorrect spelling of **usage**

used /yoozd/ *adj* **1** having been owned by somebody else **2** having been put to a purpose or expended

used to *adj* accustomed to or familiar with something ○ *We're not used to this weather.*

useful /yóosf'l/ *adj* **1** capable of being put to use or serving some purpose **2** having value or benefit, or bringing some advantage —**usefully** *adv* —**usefulness** *n*

~~usefull~~ incorrect spelling of **useful**

~~useing~~ incorrect spelling of **using**

useless /yóossləss/ *adj* **1 UNUSABLE** not able to be used **2 UNSUCCESSFUL** unsuccessful, or unlikely to be worthwhile **3 INEPT** not able to do something properly (*informal*) —**uselessly** *adv* —**uselessness** *n*

⚡**Usenet** /yóoz net/ *n* a worldwide system that uses the Internet and other networks to distribute articles of news or information

user /yóozər/ *n* **1 PERSON OR THING THAT USES** a person or thing that uses something ○ *computer users* **2 DRUG TAKER** a user of illegal drugs (*informal*) **3 EXERCISE OF RIGHT** the exercise of a right to do or use something

user-friendly (**user-friendlier, user-friendliest**) *adj* easy to operate, understand, or deal with —**user-friendliness** *n*

⚡**user group** *n* a group of people with common interests in some aspect of computer hardware or software who share information among themselves and with the hardware manufacturer or software developer

⚡**user interface** *n* the part of the design of a computer or other device or program that accepts commands from and returns information to the user

~~use to~~ incorrect spelling of **used to**

~~usful~~ incorrect spelling of **useful**

usher /úshər/ *n* **1 SOMEBODY WHO SEATS PEOPLE** a person who escorts people to their seats in a place such as a theatre or church **2 DOORKEEPER** a person who is in charge of the door of a court, hall, or chamber **3 COURT OFFICIAL** an official in an English law court who keeps order **4 OFFICER WALKING BEFORE SOMEBODY OF RANK** an officer who walks in front of people of rank in a procession or who introduces strangers at formal events ■ *v* **1** *vt* **ESCORT OR SEAT** to escort or conduct somebody to a place or from a place **2** *vi* **ACT AS USHER** to act as an usher [14C. Via Anglo-Norman *usser* < Latin *ostarius* 'door-keeper' < *ostium* 'door'.]

usher in *vt* to introduce or lead up to something

usherette /úshə rét/ *n* a woman or girl who escorts people to their seats in a theatre, cinema, or church (*dated*)

Usk /usk/ river in SE Wales. Length: 97 km/60 mi.

USM *abbr* **1** unlisted securities market **2** underwater-to-surface missile

USN *abbr* United States Navy

usnea /ússni ə, úzni ə/ (*plural* **-ae** /-ni ee/ *or* **-as**) *n* a common lichen with a hanging body in which the root, stem, and leaf are not distinguished. Genus: *Usnea*. [Late 16C. Via modern and medieval Latin < Arabic, Persian *ušna* 'moss, lichen'.]

USO *abbr* United Service Organizations

USP *n* a characteristic of a product that makes it different from all similar products (*in advertising and marketing*) Full form **unique selling proposition, unique selling point**

usquebaugh /úskwi baw/ *n Scotland, Ireland* Scotch or Irish whisky (*archaic or literary*) [Late 16C. < Gaelic *uisge beatha* 'water of life'.]

USS *abbr* **1** United States Senate **2** United States Ship

USSR *abbr* Union of Soviet Socialist Republics

Ustinov /yóosti nof/, **Sir Peter** (*b.* 1921) British writer, director and actor

usu. *abbr* usually

usual /yóozhoo əl/ *adj* **NORMAL OR TYPICAL** normal, customary, or typical of somebody or something ■ *n* **1 ORDINARY WAY** the ordinary, normal, or customary way of things **2 WHAT SOMEBODY CUSTOMARILY HAS** what somebody customarily has, especially a drink in a bar (*informal*) [14C. Directly or via Old French *usuel* < late Latin *usualis* < Latin *usus* (see USE[1]).] —**usually** *adv* —**usualness** *n* ◇ **as usual** in a normal or customary way

SYNONYMS ***usual, customary, habitual, routine, wonted***

CORE MEANING: often done, used, bought, or consumed

usual normal, common, or typical; **customary** conforming to regular or typical practice; **habitual** done so often or repeatedly that the behaviour or practice has become ingrained; **routine** normal, regular, and usual in every way, even predictable, repetitive, and monotonous; **wonted** (*formal*) usual or typical.

~~usualy~~ incorrect spelling of **usually**

usufruct /yóozyoo frukt, yóoss-/ *n* the legal right to use and enjoy the advantages or profits of another's property [Early 17C. < Latin *usufructus*, variant of *ususfructus* 'use (and) enjoyment' < *usus* (see USE[1]) + *fructus* 'enjoyment'.]

usufructuary /yóozyoo frúktyoo əri, yóoss-/ (*plural* **-ies**) *n* a person who is entitled by usufruct to the use of another's property —**usufructuary** *adj*

usurp /yoo zúrp/ *vti* use something without the right to do so [14C. Via Old French *usurper* < Latin *usurpare* 'seize for use' <, perhaps, *usus* 'use' (see USE) + *rapere* 'seize'.] —**usurpation** /yóo zur páysh'n/ *n* —**usurpative** *adj* —**usurper** *n* —**usurpingly** *adv*

usury /yóozhəri/ (*plural* **-ries**) *n* **1** the lending of money at an exorbitant rate of interest **2** an exorbitant rate of interest [14C. Via assumed Anglo-Norman *usurie* < Latin *usura* 'use of money lent, interest' < *usus* 'use'.] —**usurious** /yoo zhóori əss/ *adj* —**usuriously** *adv* —**usuriousness** *n* —**usurer** *n*

USW *abbr* ultrashort wave

ut /ut, oot/ *n* the note C, equivalent to 'doh' in the solmization system [14C. < Latin, syllable sung to this note in a hymn.]

UT, Ut. *abbr* **1** universal time **2** Utah

Utah /yóot aa, -aw/ state in the W United States. Capital: Salt Lake City. Population: 2,059,148 (1997). Area: 219,902 sq. km/84,904 sq. mi. —**Utahan** *n, adj*

Utamaro /óotə maáró/ (1753–1806) Japanese artist

UTC *abbr* coordinated universal time

ut dict. /út díkt/ *abbr* as directed (*in prescriptions*) [Latin *ut dictum*]

ute /yoot/ *n ANZ* a pick-up truck (*informal*) [Mid-20C. Shortening of UTILITY.]

Ute /yóot, yóoti/ (*plural* **Ute** *or* **Utes**) *n* **1** a member of a Native North American people who mainly live in Colorado, Utah, and New Mexico **2** the Uto-Aztecan language of the Ute people. Native speakers: 2,500. [Early 19C. < Spanish *Yuta*, Native American language.]

utensil /yoo ténss'l/ *n* a tool or container, especially one used in a kitchen [14C. Via Old French *utensile* < Latin *utensilis* 'usable' < *uti* 'to use'.]

uteri plural of **uterus**

uterine /yóotə rīn/ *adj* **1** relating to, in, or affecting the womb **2** related by having the same mother but a different father ○ *a uterine brother* [15C. < late Latin *uterinus* 'from the same womb' < Latin *uterus* 'womb'.]

uterus /yóotərəss/ (*plural* **-uses** *or* **-i** /-rī/) *n* **1** a hollow muscular organ in the pelvic cavity of female mammals, in which the embryo is nourished and develops before birth (*technical*) **2** a structure in some animals that is similar to the mammalian womb, in which eggs or young develop [17C. < Latin, 'belly, womb'.]

UTI *abbr* urinary tract infection

Utica /yóotikə/ city in E New York State. Population: 59,334 (1998 estimate).

util. *abbr* utility

utilise *vt* = **utilize**

utilitarian /yoo tílli táiri ən/ *adj* **1 BELIEVING VALUE LIES IN USEFULNESS** relating to, typical of, or advocating the doctrine that value is measured in terms of usefulness **2 PRACTICAL** designed primarily for practical use rather than beauty ■ *n* **BELIEVER IN UTILITARIANISM** a believer in the doctrine of utilitarianism

utilitarianism /yoo tílli táiri ənizəm/ *n* **1** the ethical doctrine that the greatest happiness of the greatest number should be the criterion of the virtue of action **2** the quality of being designed primarily for practical use rather than beauty

⚡**utility** /yoo tílləti/ *n* (*plural* **-ties**) **1 USEFULNESS** the quality or state of being useful for something **2 SOMETHING USEFUL** something that serves a useful purpose **3** = **public utility** **4 SERVICE PROVIDED BY PUBLIC UTILITY** a service such as electricity, gas, or water that is provided by a public utility **5 SATISFACTION DERIVED FROM CONSUMPTION** the amount of satisfaction or pleasure that somebody gains from consuming a commodity, product, or service **6 utility, utility truck** *Aus* **PICK-UP TRUCK** a pick-up truck ■ *adj* **1 INTENDED**

FOR PRACTICAL USE designed or intended for practical use rather than for show or appearance **2 ABLE TO PERFORM ANY SMALL ROLE** able to perform any small role in a theatre production **3 ABLE TO PLAY SEVERAL POSITIONS** able to substitute for other players in several different positions **4** *US, ANZ* **DESIGNED FOR STRENGTH** built or designed for performing tasks that require strength and versatility ○ *a utility truck* **5** *US* **RAISED FOR FARM USE** grown or raised to be used on a farm ○ *utility livestock* **6** *US* **OF LOWEST GRADE** classified as the lowest grade of beef by the US Government ■ *n* (*plural* **-ties**) COMPUT = **utility program** [14C. Via French < Latin *utilitas* < *utilis* 'usable' < *uti* 'to use'.]

⚡**utility program** *n* a computer program that carries out routine tasks and supports the operation of the computer or another device, as compared to an application program

utility room *n* a room in a house where there are large domestic appliances, e.g. a washing machine or boiler, and where many household tasks are done

utility truck *n Aus* TRANSP = **utility** *n*. **6**

utility vehicle *n* **1** *US* a sport-utility vehicle **2** *NZ* a pick-up truck

utilize /yoÒti līz/ (**-izes, -izing, -ized**), **utilise** (**-ises, -ising, -ised**) *vt* to make use of or find a practical or effective use for something [Early 19C. < French *utiliser* < Latin *utilis* (see UTILITY).] —**utilizable** *adj* —**utilization** /yoÒti līzáysh'n/ *n* —**utilizer** *n*

SYNONYMS See *use.*

USAGE utilize or use? *Utilize* means 'to make use of or find a practical use for something' and so means something more specific than *use*. *Utilize* is more common in technical contexts: *The device utilizes a special plug-in connection.* It can also refer to using things in unusual or unintended ways, as a more formal equivalent of 'make use of' : *When the fan belt broke they had to utilize a leather belt.* In business jargon and in other contexts *utilize* is often found when the meaning intended is simply 'use', and this should be avoided: *Successful applicants will be able to utilize their skills and experience in this field.*

uti possidetis /yoò tī póssi deètiss/ *n* the principle in international law that land and property captured by belligerent parties in war remain their property unless a treaty rules otherwise (*formal*) [< late Latin, 'as you possess']

utmost /útmōst/, **uttermost** /úttərmōst/ *adj* **1 AT THE EXTREMITY** at the most distant point or extremity **2 OF THE GREATEST DEGREE** of the greatest degree, number, or amount ■ *n* **GREATEST DEGREE OR AMOUNT** the greatest degree, number, or amount of something, especially the greatest effort that somebody is capable of ○ *I did my utmost to persuade her.* [Old English *ūt(e)mest* < OUT + -MOST]

Uto-Aztecan /yoòtō áz tekən/ *n* **1** a family of languages, including Ute and Nahuatl, spoken in the W United States and in Mexico **2** a member of a people who speak a Uto-Aztecan language [< UTE] —**Uto-Aztecan** *adj*

utopia /yoo tōpi ə/, **Utopia** *n* an ideal and perfect place or state, where everyone lives in harmony and everything is for the best [Mid-16C. < modern Latin, literally 'noplace', first used in Sir Thomas More's *Utopia* (1516) < Greek *ou* 'not' + *topos* 'place'.]

utopian, Utopian *adj* **1 IDEAL** belonging to or typical of an ideal perfect state or place **2 ADMIRABLE BUT IMPRACTICABLE** admirable but impracticable in real life **3 IMPRACTICALLY IDEALISTIC** tending to deal in admirable but impracticable ideas ■ *n* **PROPOSER OF UTOPIAN REFORMS** a proposer or advocate of visionary but impractical social or political reforms

utopianism /yoo tōpi ənizəm/, **Utopianism** *n* **1** the principles, views, or aims of a utopian **2** the belief that an ideal society can be achieved —**utopianist** *n*

utopian socialism *n* a form of socialism based on the belief that a socialist society can be brought about by peacefully persuading those in power to accept it

Utrecht /yoòt rekt, -rekht, yoo trékt, -trékht/ city in the central Netherlands. Population: 234,254 (1996).

utricle /yoòtrik'l/, **utriculus** /yoo trí kyoòlass/ (*plural* **-li** /-lī/) *n* **1** the larger of two fluid-filled sacs in the labyrinth of the inner ear and into which the semicircular canals open **2** the bladder-shaped fruit of some plants [Mid-18C. Directly or via French *utricule* < Latin *utriculus* 'little leather bottle' < *uter* 'leather bottle'.] —**utricular** /yoo trí kyoòlər/ *adj* —**utriculate** /-layt/ *adj*

Uttar Pradesh /oòttar prə désh/ state in N India. Capital: Lucknow. Population: 139,112,287 (1991). Area: 294,413 sq. km/113,673 sq. mi.

utter[1] /úttər/ *vt* **1 SAY** to say or pronounce something **2 EMIT SOMETHING AS VOCAL SOUND** to emit something as a sound made by the voice **3 PUBLISH** to publish something, e.g. in a book or newspaper ○ *You would not dare to utter this nonsense in print.* **4 TO PUT SOMETHING INTO CIRCULATION** to put something into circulation, especially counterfeit money or a forgery, in the pretence that it is genuine (*formal*) [14C. < Middle Dutch *ūteren* 'drive out, announce, speak' < Old Low German *ūt* 'out'.] —**utterable** *adj* —**utterer** *n*

utter[2] /úttər/ *adj* at the most extreme point or of the highest degree [Old English *ūtera* 'farther out' < OUT]

utterance /úttəranss/ *n* **1 SOMETHING SAID** something said or emitted as a vocal sound **2 EXPRESSION** the expression of something, especially in speech or vocal sound **3 WAY OF SPEAKING** a style, power, or way of speaking **4 ACT OF SAYING** the act of saying something ◇ **give utterance to** express something, especially in speech

utterly /úttərli/ *adv* in an extreme or complete way

uttermost /úttərmōst/ *adj, n* = utmost

U-turn *n* **1** a turn in the shape of a U made by a vehicle to reverse direction **2** a complete reversal in opinion, actions, or policy

Utzon /oòt zon/, **Jørn** (*b.* 1918) Danish architect

UU *abbr* **1** Ulster Unionist **2** Unitarian Universalist

UV *abbr* ultraviolet

UVA *n* ultraviolet radiation, especially from the sun, with a relatively long wavelength

uvarovite /oo vaàrə vīt/ *n* a bright emerald-green garnet containing calcium and chromium. Use: gems. [Mid-19C. < Count Sergei Semenovich *Uvarov* (1785–1855), Russian statesman.]

UVB *n* ultraviolet radiation, especially from the sun, with a relatively short wavelength

uvea /yoòvi ə/ *n* the middle of the three layers of the eyeball, made up of the choroid, ciliary body, and iris surrounding the lens [Early 16C. Via medieval Latin < Latin *uva* 'grape'.] —**uveal** *adj* —**uveous** *adj*

uveitis /yoòvi ītiss/ *n* inflammation of the uvea of the eye

UVF *abbr* Ulster Volunteer Force

UV Index *n* a scale used to indicate the intensity of the sun's ultraviolet rays

uvula /yoòvyoòlə/ (*plural* **-las** or **-lae**) *n* a small fleshy V-shaped extension of the soft palate that hangs above the tongue at the entrance to the throat [14C. < late Latin, 'little grape' < Latin *uva* 'grape'; from its shape.]

uvular /yoòvyoòlər/ *adj* **1 INVOLVING UVULA** relating to or involving the uvula **2 PRONOUNCED VIBRATING THE UVULA** pronounced with vibration of the uvula ■ *n* **UVULAR SOUND** a uvular consonant —**uvularly** *adv*

uvulitis /yoòvyoò lītiss/ *n* inflammation of the uvula

UW *abbr* **1** underwriter **2** underwritten

UWIST /yoòvi wist/ *abbr* University of Wales Institute of Science and Technology

UX. *abbr* wife [Latin *uxor*]

UXB *abbr* unexploded bomb

uxorial /uk sáwri əl/ *adj* relating to, involving, or typical of a wife [Early 19C. < Latin *uxor* 'wife'.] —**uxorially** *adv*

uxoricide /uk sáwri sīd/ *n* **1** murder of a wife by her husband **2** a man who murders his wife [Mid-19C. < Latin *uxor* 'wife'.] —**uxoricidal** /uk sáwri sīd'l/ *adj*

uxorious /uk sáwri əss/ *adj* excessively devoted or submissive to his wife (*describes a man*) [Late 16C. < Latin *uxoriosus* < *uxor* 'wife'.] —**uxoriously** *adv* —**uxoriousness** *n*

⚡**uy** *abbr* Uruguay (*in Internet addresses*)

⚡**uz** *abbr* Uzbekistan (*in Internet addresses*)

Uzbek /oòz bek, úz-/ (*plural* **-bek** or **-beks**) *n* **1** a member of a people who live mainly in Uzbekistan and in neighbouring regions **2** a Turkic language spoken in Uzbekistan and central Asia. Native speakers: 16 million. [Early 17C. Directly or via Persian or Russian *uzbek* < Turkish, Uzbek *özbek.*]

Uzbekistan

Uzbekistan /oòz béki staàn, uz-/ republic in Central Asia. Capital: Tashkent. Population: 23,467,724 (1997). Area: 447,400 sq. km/172,700 sq. mi.

V¹ /vee/ (*plural* **v's**), **V** (*plural* **V's** *or* **Vs**) *n* **1** the 22nd letter of the English alphabet, representing a consonant sound **2** the Roman numeral for 5

V², **V** *symbol* **1** image distance **2** instantaneous potential difference **3** instantaneous voltage **4** specific volume

V³, **V** *abbr* **1** vacuum **2** vagrant **3** vale **4** vector **5** vein **6** velocity component **7** velocity speed **8** ventilator **9** ventral **10** verb **11** verbal **12** verse **13** versed **14** verso **15** versus **16** vertical **17** via **18** vibrational quantum number **19** vicarage **20** victory **21** vide **22** violin **23** virus **24** (abnormally good) visibility **25** vision **26** vocative **27** voice **28** volcano **29** voltage **30** vowel

V¹ /vee/ (*plural* **V's** *or* **Vs**) *n* something shaped like a letter 'V'

V² *symbol* **1** electric potential **2** electromotive force **3** luminous efficiency **4** potential **5** potential efficiency **6** potential energy **7** vanadium

V³ *abbr* **1** valine **2** variable region **3** vatu **4** Venerable **5** version **6** Very (*in titles*) **7** vespers **8** vicar **9** vice **10** victory **11** village **12** Viscount **13** Viscountess **14** volt **15** voltmeter **16** Volunteer **17** Volunteers

v. *abbr* volume

V-1 /vee wún/ (*plural* **V-1's**) *n* a German robot bomb used in World War II, mainly against England [Abbreviation of German *Vergeltungswaffe eins* 'reprisal weapon one']

V-2 /vee toô/ (*plural* **V-2's**) *n* a German liquid-fuelled ballistic missile used in the latter part of World War II, chiefly against London [Abbreviation of German *Vergeltungswaffe zwei* 'reprisal weapon two']

V6 /vee síks/ (*plural* **V6's**) *n* an internal-combustion engine with six cylinders arranged in a V shape

V8 /vee áyt/ (*plural* **V8's**) *n* an internal-combustion engine with eight cylinders arranged in a V shape

Va *abbr* **1** Vatican City (*in Internet addresses*) **2** verb active **3** verbal adjective **4** viola

VA *abbr* **1** value-added **2** value analysis **3** ventricular arrhythmia **4** vicar apostolic **5** Vice-Admiral **6** (Royal Order of) Victoria and Albert **7** visual acuity **8** visual aid **9** volt-ampere **10** Volunteer Artillery

Va. *abbr* Virginia

V/A *abbr* voucher attached

Vaal /vaal/ river in NE South Africa. Length: 1,160 km/720 mi.

Vaasa /vaáss aa/ capital of Vaasa Province, W Finland. Population: 55,502 (1995).

vac /vak/ *abbr* **1** vacancy **2** vacant **3** vacation **4** vacuum **5** vacuum cleaner

vacancy /váykənsi/ (*plural* **-cies**) *n* **1** VACANT OFFICE OR POSITION an office, position, or tenancy that is unfilled or unoccupied **2** MENTAL INACTIVITY mental inactivity or lack of thought or intelligence **3** VACANT STATE the state of being vacant **4** LEISURE a period of leisure (*archaic*) **5** EMPTY SITE IN A CRYSTAL an empty site, normally containing an atom or ion, in a crystal [Late 16C. < VACANT or < late Latin *vacantia* < Latin *vacant-* (see VACANT).]

vacant /váykənt/ *adj* **1** WITHOUT AN OCCUPANT having no occupant or contents ○ *There were several vacant seats on the bus.* **2** UNOCCUPIED BY AN INCUMBENT OR OFFICIAL not occupied by an incumbent, official, or possessor **3** LACKING EXPRESSION showing no signs of thought, intelligence, or expression ○ *a vacant stare* **4** FREE FROM ACTIVITY free from activity, business, or work ○ *a vacant afternoon* [13C. Via Old French < Latin *vacant-*, present

participle of *vacare* 'be empty'.] —**vacantly** *adv* —**vacantness** *n*

SYNONYMS *vacant, unoccupied, empty, void*
CORE MEANING: lacking contents or occupants
vacant without occupants or contents, often temporarily; **unoccupied** not lived in by anybody, or currently without occupants; **empty** not containing or holding anything, or without occupants; **void** having no contents, or having no incumbent, occupant, or holder.

vacant possession *n* ownership of a house whose previous occupants have already moved out

vacate /və káyt, vay-/ (**-cates, -cating, -cated**) *vt* **1** EMPTY OF OCCUPANTS to empty something of incumbents or occupants **2** GIVE UP OCCUPANCY OF to relinquish the possession or occupancy of something ○ *vacate the premises* **3** RESIGN FROM to withdraw from or surrender possession of an office or post ○ *vacate a legislative seat* **4** MAKE INVALID to make something legally void [Mid-17C. < Latin *vacat-*, past participle of *vacare* 'be empty'.] —**vacatable** *adj*

vacation /və káysh'n/ *n* **1** a scheduled period during which the activities of law courts, universities, or other regular businesses are suspended **2** US = holiday *n*. **2 3** an act or an instance or vacating something ○ *vt US* = holiday *v.* [14C. Directly or via Old French < Latin *vacation-* < vacat- (see VACATE).]

vacationer /və káysh'nər/, **vacationist** /və káysh'nist/ *n US, Can* = holidaymaker

vaccinate /váksi nayt/ (**-nates, -nating, -nated**) *vt* to inoculate a person or animal with a vaccine to produce immunity —**vaccination** /váksi náysh'n/ *n* —**vaccinator** *n* —**vaccinatory** /váksinətəri/ *adj*

⚡ vaccine /vák seen/ *n* **1** a preparation containing weakened or dead microbes of the kind that cause a particular disease, administered to stimulate the immune system to produce antibodies against that disease **2** a program that protects a system against a computer virus [Late 18C. < Latin *vaccinus* 'of a cow' < *vacca* 'cow', because originally the cowpox virus used to prevent smallpox.] —**vaccinal** *adj*

vaccinee /váksi neé/ *n* a person who is vaccinated [Late 19C. < VACCINATE.]

vaccinia /vak sínni ə/ *n* a skin eruption in reaction to inoculation with the weakened cowpox virus that was once used to vaccinate people against smallpox [Early 19C. < modern Latin, < Latin *vaccinus* (see VACCINE).] —**vaccinial** *adj*

vaccuum incorrect spelling of **vacuum**
vaccuum incorrect spelling of **vacuum**

vacherin /vásh raN, vash ráN/ *n* a soft cheese from France or Switzerland [Mid-20C. < French.]

vacillate /vássi layt/ (**-lates, -lating, -lated**) *vi* **1** to be indecisive or irresolute **2** to sway from side to side [Late 16C. < Latin *vacillat-*, past participle of *vaccillare* 'sway, totter'.] —**vacillant** *adj* —**vacillation** /vássi láysh'n/ *n* —**vacillator** *n*

SYNONYMS See *hesitate*.

vacua plural of **vacuum**

vacuity /va kyoó əti/ (*plural* **-ties**) *n* (*formal*) **1** EMPTINESS the condition, state, or quality of being empty of all contents **2** EMPTY SPACE an empty area or space **3** MEANINGLESS STATE OR THING a thing or condition that is inane

or devoid of any meaningful content ○ *legislative vacuity* [Mid-16C. Directly or via French *vacuité* < Latin *vacuitas* < *vacuus* 'empty'.]

vacum incorrect spelling of **vacuum**

vacuolar membrane /vákyoo ốlər-/ *n* a membrane containing fluid in the cytoplasm of a cell

vacuolate /vákyoo ələt, -layt/, **vacuolated** /-laytid/ *adj* having small holes —**vacuolation** /vákyoo ə láysh'n/ *n* —**vacuolization** /-īt záysh'n/ *n*

vacuole /vákyoo ōl/ *n* **1** a small cavity in tissue **2** a membrane-bound compartment containing fluid that is found in the cytoplasm of a cell [Mid-19C. < French, 'little empty (space)' < Latin *vacuus* 'empty'.] —**vacuolar** /vákyoo ốlar/ *adj*

vacuous /vákyoo əss/ *adj* **1** LACKING CONTENT having no content **2** EMPTY OF MEANING lacking ideas or intelligence **3** IDLE lacking serious occupation **4** NULL null [Mid-17C. < Latin *vacuus* 'empty'.] —**vacuously** *adv* —**vacuousness** *n*

vacuum /vákyoo əm, vákyoóm/ (*plural* **-ums** *or* **-a** /-á/) *n* **1** SPACE EMPTY OF MATTER a space completely empty of matter but not achievable in practice on the Earth **2** SPACE WITH ALL THE GAS REMOVED a space from which all air or gas has been extracted **3** EMPTINESS CAUSED BY ABSENCE an emptiness caused by somebody or something's absence or removal ○ *Her death left a vacuum in his life.* **4** ISOLATION FROM THE OUTSIDE WORLD isolation from external influences ○ *You can't live in a vacuum.* **5** HOUSEHOLD = vacuum cleaner ▪ *vti* CLEAN SOMETHING USING A VACUUM CLEANER to clean an area or object using a vacuum cleaner [Mid-16C. < modern Latin, < neuter of Latin *vacuus* 'empty'.]

vacuum activity *n* innate behaviour manifested in the absence of the usual stimulus

vacuum bottle *n US* = vacuum flask

vacuum cleaner *n* an electrical appliance that cleans surfaces such as floors, upholstery, and window coverings by sucking dirt and other material into a bag

vacuum distillation *n* a process of distilling liquid at low pressure so that it boils at a lower boiling point

vacuum drying *n* the removal of liquid from a solution or mixture at reduced air pressure so that it dries at a lower temperature than it would at full pressure

vacuum flask *n* a flask with double walls, usually of silvered glass, separated by an airless space, used to hold liquids and maintain them at constant high or low temperatures. US term **vacuum bottle**

vacuum forming *n* **1** the process of shaping sheets of heated thermoplastic by placing them in a mould and removing air by suction **2** a method of shaping plastic by applying suction to heated sheets held above a mould

vacuum gauge *n* an instrument that measures pressures below atmospheric pressure

vacuum-packed *adj* packed in an airtight container or package under low pressure in order to prevent the contents from spoiling or corroding

vacuum pan *n* a device with a vacuum pump that removes moisture quickly by boiling a substance at a low temperature under reduced pressure

vacuum pump *n* **1** a device that creates a partial vacuum **2** ENG = pulsometer

vacuum tube *n US* ELECTRONICS = **valve** *n.* 3

vada *n S Asia* FOOD = **wada**

vade mecum /vaádi máykəm/ *n* 1 a guidebook, handbook, or manual, especially one carried around or designed to be carried around constantly and referred to often 2 an object that a person carries constantly because it is useful [Early 17C. < Latin, 'go with me'.]

Vadodara /wə dṓdərə/ city in W India. Population: 1,115,265 (1991).

vadose /váy dōss/ *adj* describes or relating to water in the unsaturated zone of the Earth's crust that is above the level of ground water [Late 19C. < Latin *vadosus* < *vadum* 'shallow piece of water'.]

vadose zone *n* the unsaturated zone between the ground surface and the water table through which ground water can percolate

Vaduz /fa dóots/ capital of Liechtenstein, on the River Rhine. Population: 4,887 (1991).

Vafa /vaáfə/, **Cumrun** (*b.* 1960) Iranian physicist

vag- *prefix* = **vago-** (*before vowels*)

vagabond /vággə bond/ *n* 1 **HOMELESS WANDERER** a wanderer who has no permanent place to live 2 **BEGGAR** a beggar for food or money ■ *adj* **OF VAGABONDS** relating to or characteristic of a vagabond ■ *vi* **BE A VAGABOND** to wander from place to place [15C. Via French < Latin *vagabundus* < *vagari* 'wander'.] —**vagabondage** *n* —**vagabondism** *n*

vagal /váyg'l/ *adj* relating to the tenth pair of cranial nerves (**vagus nerves**) —**vagally** *adv*

vagary /váygəri/ (*plural* **-ries**) *n* an unpredictable or eccentric change, action, or idea ○ *the vagaries of the weather* [Late 16C. < Latin *vagari* 'wander'.] —**vagarious** /və gáiri əss/ *adj*

vagi plural of **vagus**

vagile /vájjīl/ *adj* able to move around within a specific environment [Early 20C. < VAGUS.] —**vagility** /və jíllәti/ *n*

vagina /və jínə/ (*plural* **-nas** *or* **-nae** /-nee/) *n* 1 in female mammals, a lubricated muscular tube connecting the cervix of the womb to the vulva 2 a plant or animal part that forms a sheath, e.g. that formed by a leaf around a stem [Late 17C. < Latin, 'sheath, scabbard'.] —**vaginal** *adj* —**vaginally** /və jínəli/ *adv*

vaginate /vájji nət, -nayt/, **vaginated** /-naytid/ *adj* having, forming, or resembling a sheath

vaginectomy /vájji néktəmi/ (*plural* **-mies**) *n* 1 the removal of all or part of the vagina by surgery 2 the removal by surgery of all or part of the smooth moist membrane that encloses the testis and epididymis

vaginismus /vájji nízməss/ *n* a painful and often prolonged contraction of the vagina in response to the vulva or vagina being touched

vaginitis /vájji nítiss/ *n* inflammation of the vagina

vago- *prefix* vagus ○ *vagotomy* [< VAGUS]

vagotomy /və góttəmi/ (*plural* **-mies**) *n* the surgical cutting of the tenth pair of cranial nerves (**vagus nerves**) or any of their branches, performed to control duodenal ulcers by decreasing acid secretion of the stomach

vagotonia /váygə tṓni ə/ *n* a pathological condition in which overactivity of the tenth pair of cranial nerves (**vagus nerves**) affects bodily functions controlled by these nerves, such as those in blood vessels and the gut [Early 20C. < VAGO- + Greek *tonos* 'stretching, tension'.] —**vagotonic** /-tónnik/ *adj*

vagotropic /váygə tróppik, -trṓpik/ *adj* describes a drug that has an effect on the tenth pair of cranial nerves (**vagus nerves**)

vagrant /váygrənt/ *n* 1 **HOMELESS WANDERER** a wanderer who has no permanent place to live 2 **WANDERER** a person who never stays in one place for long 3 **SOMEBODY ILLEGALLY LIVING ON THE STREETS** somebody guilty of the legal offence of living on the streets and, in some jurisdictions, begging 4 **BIRD OFF THE NORMAL MIGRATION ROUTE** a migratory bird or insect that deviates from its normal migration route ■ *adj* 1 **HOMELESS** wandering from one place to another and having no permanent place to live 2 **WANDERING** never staying in one place for long 3 **WAYWARD** wayward or capricious in nature 4 **RANDOM** acting or done in a random way 5 **GROWING IN AN UNCONTROLLED WAY** describes plants that grow in a lush uncontrolled way [15C. < Anglo-Norman *varagarant*.] —**vagrancy** *n* —**vagrantly** *adv* —**vagrantness** *n*

vague /vayg/ (**vaguer, vaguest**) *adj* 1 **NOT EXPLICIT** not clear in meaning or intention ○ *a vague proposal* 2 **NOT DISTINCTLY SEEN** not having a clear or perceptible form ○ *a vague form in the shadows* 3 **UNVERIFIED** not properly validated or having no clear or identifiable source 4 **UNCLEAR IN THINKING** unclear or incoherent in thinking or expression 5 **NOT CLEARLY PERCEIVED IN THE MIND** not clearly felt, understood, or recalled ○ *I have a vague recollection of it.* [Mid-16C. Directly or via French < Latin *vagus* 'wandering, inconstant'.] —**vaguely** *adv* —**vagueness** *n*

vagus /váygəss/ (*plural* **-gi** /váy jī, váy gī/), **vagus nerve** *n* either of the tenth pair of cranial nerves that carry sensory and motor neurons serving the heart, lungs, stomach, intestines, and various other organs [Mid-19C. < Latin *vagus* 'wandering, inconstant'.]

vaidya /vídi ə/ *n S Asia* an Ayurvedic Hindu physician [Mid-20C. < Hindi, < *vaidy* 'expert on Ayurvedic medicine'.]

vain /vayn/ *adj* 1 **EXCESSIVELY PROUD** excessively proud, especially of your appearance 2 **UNSUCCESSFUL** failing to have or unlikely to have the intended or desired result ○ *a vain attempt at persuading them* 3 **EMPTY OF SUBSTANCE** devoid of substance or meaning [14C. Via Old French < Latin *vanus* 'empty, without substance'.] —**vainly** *adv* —**vainness** *n* ◇ **in vain** fruitlessly, pointlessly, or unsuccessfully ○ *We searched in vain for a solution.*

SPELLCHECK Do not confuse ***vain*** with ***vane*** or ***vein***, which sound similar. Beware: your spellchecker will not catch this error.

SYNONYMS ***vain, empty, hollow, idle***

CORE MEANING: without substance or unlikely to be carried though

vain failing to have or unlikely to have the intended or desired result; **empty** lacking substance, sincerity, or truthfulness; **hollow** not sincere or genuine; **idle** unlikely to be carried out or impossible to put into effect.

vainglorious /vayn gláwri əss/ *adj* excessively proud or boastful (*literary*) —**vaingloriously** *adv* —**vaingloriousness** *n*

vainglory /vayn gláwri/ (*plural* **-ries**) *n* (*literary*) 1 excessive pride in or boastfulness about yourself, your achievements, or your abilities 2 an excessive display of something in order to draw attention to it [12C. Via Old French < Latin *vana gloria* 'empty glory'.]

vair /vair/ *n* 1 fur used as a trimming on medieval robes 2 a blue-and-white fur used on heraldic shields [14C. Via Old French < Latin *varius* 'speckled, changeable'.]

vairy /váiri/ *n S W England* a weasel (*regional*)

Vaisakha /víss aakə/ *n* in the Hindu calendar, the second month of the year, made up of 29 or 30 days and falling in approximately April to May

Vaishnava /víshnəvə/ *n* a member of a group devoted to the worship of the Hindu god Vishnu or one of his incarnations [Late 18C. < Sanskrit *vaiṣṇava* 'relating to Vishnu'.] —**Vaishnavism** *n*

Vaisya /víssyə, vísh-/ *n* 1 the third of the four Hindu castes, the members of which were merchants and farmers 2 a member of the Vaisya caste [Mid-17C. < Sanskrit *vaiśya* 'farm labourer, tradesman'.]

Vajpayee /vaj páyee/, **Atal Bihari** (*b.* 1924) Indian politician and prime minister (1996 and 1998-)

vakil /vaa kéel/, **vakeel, wakil** *n S Asia* a lawyer or legal representative in a court of law in the Indian subcontinent [Early 17C. Via Persian and Urdu *wakīl*, Turkish *vakīl* < Arabic *wakīl*.]

val. *abbr* 1 valley 2 valuation 3 value

valance /vállənss/, **valence** *n* 1 a plain, pleated, or gathered fabric cover that hangs from a shelf or from the base of a bed to the floor 2 a short decorative piece of drapery or wood hung across a window to cover the rod from which curtains hang [15C. < ?] —**valanced** *adj*

Valdez /val déez/ city in SE Alaska. Population: 4,309 (1996).

vale[1] /vayl/ *n* a valley or dale, often one that has a stream running through it (*often in placenames*) [14C. Via French < Latin *valles* 'valley'.]

SPELLCHECK Do not confuse ***vale*** with ***veil***, which has a similar sound. Beware: your spellchecker will not catch this error.

vale[2] /vaá lay/ *interj* a Latin expression of farewell ■ *n* an act of saying farewell or adieu [Mid-16C. < Latin, 'be well!', form of *valere* 'be strong or well'.]

valediction /válli díksh'n/ *n* (*formal*) 1 the act of saying goodbye or an instance of leave-taking 2 a statement, speech, or letter of farewell [Mid-17C. < Latin *valedicer* 'say goodbye', after BENEDICTION.]

valedictorian /válli dik táwri ən/ *n US* the student who delivers the valedictory address at graduation

valedictory /válli díktəri/ (*plural* **-ries**) *n* 1 a statement or speech of farewell (*formal*) 2 *US* = **valedictory address** ■ *adj* performing the function of saying farewell (*formal*)

valedictory address *n US* a speech delivered at graduation by the student with the best academic record

valence[1] *n* CHEM, IMMUNOL = **valency**

valence[2] *n* DOMESTIC = **valance**

Valencia /və lénshi ə, və lénssi ə, ba lénthyə/ 1 capital of the autonomous region of Valencia in E Spain. Population 739,412 (1998 estimate). 2 city in N Venezuela. Population: 1,034,033 (1992 estimate).

Valenciennes[1] /vállənssi én/ *n* a fine cotton lace made with bobbins in a floral design, originally made of linen [Early 18C. After VALENCIENNES[2].]

Valenciennes[2] /vállənssi én, va laaNss yen/ city in N France. Population: 39,276 (1990).

valency /váylənssi/ (*plural* **-cies**), **valence** /váylənss/ *n* 1 **COMBINING POWER OF ATOMS** the combining power of atoms or groups measured by the number of electrons the atom or group will receive, give up, or share in forming a compound 2 **COMBINING ANTIGENIC DETERMINANTS** the number of different antigenic determinants with which a single antibody molecule can combine 3 **COMBINING POWER OF A VERB** the ability of a verb to combine grammatically with noun phrases in a given clause [Mid-19C. < Latin *valentia* 'power, competence' < *valere* 'be powerful'.]

valency electron *n* an electron in an outer shell of an atom that can be lost to or shared with another atom to form a molecule

valency shell *n* the outer electron shell of an atom, containing one or more electrons (**valency electrons**) that are available to form bonds with other atoms to create molecules

Valens /váyl enz/ (328?–378) ruler of the eastern Roman empire

-valent *suffix* having a particular valency or valencies ○ *divalent* [< VALENCY]

valentine /vállən tīn/ *n* 1 a greeting card or gift sent, traditionally anonymously, to somebody on Valentine's Day as a token of love 2 the person to whom somebody sends a card or gift on Valentine's Day as a token of love [15C. After St VALENTINE.]

Valentine's Day *n* the Christian feast day of St Valentine and the traditional day for sending a romantic card or gift, especially anonymously, to somebody you love. Date: 14 February.

Valentinian I /vállən tínni ən/ (321–375) ruler of the western Roman empire (364–375)

Valentinian II (371?–392) Roman emperor (375–92)

Valentinian III (419–455) Roman emperor (425–455)

Valentino /vállən téenō/, **Rudolph** (1895–1926) Italian-born US actor. Born **Rodolpho Guglielmi di Valentina d'Antonguolla**

valerian /və léeri ən/ (*plural* **-ans** *or* **-an**) *n* 1 an herbaceous perennial plant. Flowers: small, sweet-smelling, white or pinkish. Native to: Europe, Asia. Genus: *Valeriana*. 2 a herbal medicine made from the dried roots of valerian. Use: mild sedative, tranquillizer. [15C. Via Old French < medieval Latin *valeriana*, after *Valeria*, Roman province.]

Valerian /və léeri ən/ (*d.* 260?) Roman emperor (253–260?)

valeric acid /və léerik-/ *n* $C_5H_{10}O_2$ a pungent colourless liquid. Use: flavourings, perfumes, pharmaceuticals. [< VALERIAN]

Valéry /válle ree/, **Paul** (1871–1945) French poet and critic

valet /vállit, vállay/ *n* 1 **MAN SERVANT** a male personal servant of a man, whose duties include looking after his employer's clothes and providing his meals 2 **MALE HOTEL OR PASSENGER SHIP EMPLOYEE** a man employee whose duties include cleaning the clothes of hotel guests or passengers on ships 3 **SOMEBODY PERFORMING CAR PARKING SERVICE** somebody employed to park the cars of people arriving at a hotel, restaurant, or airport and bring the cars back for them on departure ■ *v* 1 *vti* **WORK AS A VALET** to work as a valet or provide valet services to somebody

2 *vt* **CLEAN A CAR** to clean somebody's car in return for payment [15C. < French, < assumed medieval Latin *vassus* 'servant to a knight'.]

valeta *n* DANCE = **veleta**

valet de chambre /vállay də shaaNbrə/ (*plural* **valets de chambre**) *n* OCCUPATIONS = **valet** *n.* 1 [French, 'valet of the room']

valet parking *n* a service provided by some hotels, restaurants, and airports whereby an employee parks people's cars for them on arrival and brings the cars back for them on departure

valetudinarian /válli tyoōdi náiri ən/, **valetudinary** /válli tyoōdinəri/ (*plural* **-ies**) *n* 1 **SOMEBODY WITH POOR HEALTH** somebody who has persistent ill health 2 **SOMEBODY OBSESSED WITH HEALTH** somebody who is excessively concerned with his or her own health ■ *adj* 1 **OF A VALETUDINARIAN** relating to or being a valetudinarian 2 **OF POOR HEALTH** relating to, characterized by, or arising from poor health 3 **TRYING TO BE HEALTHIER** trying to recover or improve health [Late 16C. < Latin *valetudinarius* 'in ill health' < *valetudo* 'state of health' < *valere* 'be well'.] —**valetudinarianism** *n*

valgus /válgəss/ *adj* describes a deformity in which a body part such as the knee or foot is bent or twisted outwards away from the midline of the body. ◊ **varus** ■ *n* the position or state in which a bone or body part is bent or twisted outwards away from the midline of the body. ◊ **varus** [Early 19C. < Latin, 'knock-kneed'.] —**valgoid** *adj*

Valhalla /val hállə/, **Walhalla, Walhall** *n* in Norse mythology, the great hall where the souls of heroes killed in battle spend eternity [Late 17C. Via modern Latin < Old Norse *valhall* 'hall of the slain' < *valr* 'those slain in battle'.]

valiant /válli ənt/ *adj* 1 **COURAGEOUS** brave and steadfast 2 **DONE COURAGEOUSLY** characterized by or performed with bravery but often ending in failure ○ *despite a valiant attempt at rescue* ■ *n* **SOMEBODY COURAGEOUS** a brave and steadfast person [14C. Via Old French < Latin *valent-*, present participle of *valere* 'be strong'.] —**valiance** *n* —**valiancy** /válli ənssi/ *n* —**valiantly** *adv* —**valiantness** *n*

valid /vállid/ *adj* 1 **JUSTIFIABLE** having a solid foundation or justification ○ *It's a perfectly valid argument.* 2 **EFFECTIVE** bringing about the results or ends intended 3 **LEGALLY BINDING** having binding force in law 4 **LEGALLY ACCEPTABLE** acceptable under law 5 **UNEXPIRED** usable or acceptable until a specified expiry date or under specified conditions of use ○ *a valid passport* 6 **LOGICAL** having premises from which the conclusion follows logically 7 **HEALTHY** having good health (*archaic*) [Late 16C. Directly or via French < Latin *validus* 'strong' < *valere* 'be strong'.] —**validity** /və líddəti/ *n* —**validly** *adv* —**validness** *n*

SYNONYMS *valid, cogent, convincing, reasonable, sound*

CORE MEANING: worthy of acceptance or credence

valid having a solid foundation or justification; **cogent** forceful and convincing to the intellect and reason; **convincing** likely to overcome doubts and win the support of those who hear it; **reasonable** acceptable and according to common sense; **sound** based on good sense and acceptable reasoning and worthy of approval.

---

validate /válli dayt/ (**-dates, -dating, -dated**) *vt* 1 **CONFIRM THE TRUTHFULNESS OF** to confirm or establish the truthfulness or soundness of something 2 **MAKE LEGAL** to declare or render something legal or binding ○ *validate a passport* 3 **REGISTER SOMETHING FORMALLY** to register something formally and have its use officially sanctioned [Mid-17C. < Latin *validare* 'render legally valid' < *validus* (see VALID).] —**validation** /válli dáysh'n/ *n* —**validatory** *adj*

valine /váy leen, vál-/ *n* an essential amino acid, required for normal growth [Early 20C. < VALERIC ACID.]

valise /və leéz/ *n* a small piece of luggage (*dated*) [Early 20C. Via French < Italian *valigia*.]

Valkyrie /válkəri, val keéri/, **Walkyrie, Valkyr** /vál keer/ *n* in Norse mythology, one of the 12 handmaids of Odin who ride their horses over the field of battle and escort the souls of slain heroes to Valhalla [Mid-18C. < Old Norse *Valkyrja* 'chooser of the slain' < *valr* 'those slain in battle'.] —**Valkyrian** /val keéri ən/ *adj*

valla plural of **vallum**

Valladolid /vállə do líd, bál a tho líth/ capital of Valladolid Province, N Spain. Population: 334,820 (1995).

vallate /vállayt/ (**-lates, -lating, -lated**) *vt* to plan or build earthworks for defence [Late 19C. Back-formation < VALLATION.]

vallation /va láysh'n/ *n* 1 a defensive fortification or embankment made of earth 2 the planning or building of defensive fortifications or embankments made of earth [Mid-17C. < Latin *vallation-* < *vallare* 'protect' < *vallum* SEE VALLUM.]

vallecula /və lékyoōlə/ (*plural* **-lae** /-lee/) *n* a shallow groove, depression, or furrow in an animal or plant body such as that between the hemispheres of the cerebellum in the brain [Mid-19C. < Latin *vallicula* < *valles* 'valley'.] —**vallecular** *adj* —**valleculate** /və lékyoō layt/ *adj*

Valle d'Aosta /vállay daa óstə/ region in N Italy, on the border with France and Switzerland. Population: 117,208 (1991). Area: 3,262 sq. km/1,260 sq. mi.

Valles Marineris /válless márri náiriss/ system of valleys and canyons in the equatorial region of Mars, 4,000 km/2,500 mi. long, up to 240 km/150 mi. wide, and 6.5 km/4 mi. deep

Valletta /və léttə/ capital and chief port of Malta. Population: 7,172 (1997 estimate).

valley /válli/ (*plural* **-leys**) *n* 1 **LOW-LYING AREA** a long low area of land, often with a river or stream running through it, that is surrounded by higher ground 2 **LOW-LYING LAND AROUND A RIVER** a large area of low-lying land around a river and its tributaries 3 **VALLEY-SHAPED HOLLOW** a long sunken area or groove shaped like a valley 4 **ANGLE BETWEEN ROOF SLOPES** the angle formed where two slopes of a roof intersect [13C. Via Old French *valee* < Latin *valles* 'valley'.] —**valleyed** *adj*

valley fever *n* MED = **coccidioidomycosis** [After the San Joaquin *Valley*, California]

Valley Forge /válli fawrj/ site in SE Pennsylvania that served as the winter headquarters in 1777–78 for George Washington and the Continental Army during the US War of Independence

Valley of the Kings /-əv thə kíngz/ gorge on the western bank of the River Nile, S Egypt. It was the burial site of pharaohs of the New Kingdom (1570–1070 BC).

Vallis Alpes /válliss ál pez/ valley on the Moon, cutting across Montes Alpes

vallum /vállәm/ (*plural* **-lums** *or* **-la** /-ə/) *n* an ancient Roman fortification or embankment, built for military defence [Early 17C. < Latin, < *vallus* 'palisade, stake'.]

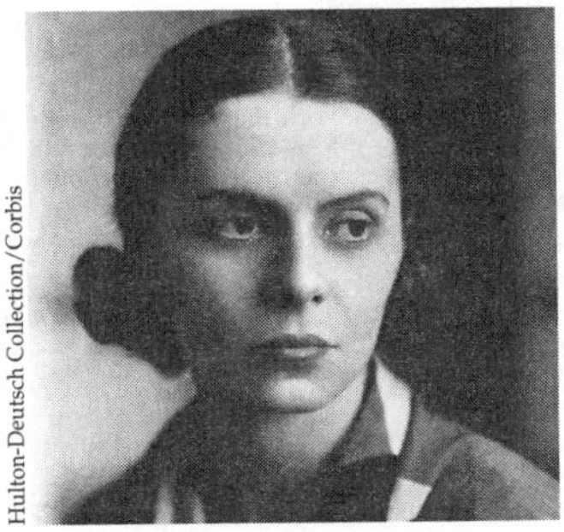

Hulton-Deutsch Collection/Corbis

Dame Ninette de Valois

Valois /vállwaa/, **Dame Ninette de** (1898-2001) Irish-born British dancer and choreographer. Born **Edris Stannus**

valonia /və lṓni ə/ *n* the dried acorn cups and unripe acorns of an oak. Use: tanning, inks, dyes. [Early 18C. Via Italian < Greek *balanos* 'acorn'.]

valor *n* US = **valour**

valorize /vállə rīz/ (**-izes, -izing, -ized**), **valorise** (**-ises, -ising, -ised**) *vt* to set and maintain the price of a commodity at an artificially high level through government action [Early 20C. Via Portuguese *valorizar* < *valor* 'value' < late Latin (see VALOUR).] —**valorization** *n*

valorous /vállərəss/ *adj* having or showing courage, especially in war or battle —**valorously** *adv* —**valorousness** *n*

valour /vállər/ *n* courage, especially that shown in battle [Late 16C. Via Italian *valore* < Latin *valor* < *valere* 'be strong'.]

Valparaiso /válpə ráyzō, -rízō/ capital of Valparaiso Region in central Chile. Population: 293,800 (1998).

Valpolicella /vál polli chéllə/ *n* a light red Italian wine from the northern province of Verona [Early 20C. After the district of *Valpolicella*.]

valproate /válprō ayt/, **valproic acid** /val prṓ ik-/ *n* a synthetic crystalline compound with anticonvulsant properties. Use: treatment of epilepsy. [Late 20C. < *valproic acid* (< VALERIC ACID + PROPYL).]

Valsalva manoeuvre /val sálvə-/ *n* 1 the action of attempting to breathe out when the mouth is closed and the nostrils are held shut, thereby forcing air into the middle ear via the Eustachian tubes 2 the action of attempting to breathe out against a closed glottis, which increases pressure in the thoracic cavity and hinders the return of venous blood to the heart [After Antonio Maria *Valsalva* (1666–1723), Italian anatomist]

valse /valss/ *n* a waltz, especially one of French origin [Late 18C. Via French < German *Walzer* (see WALTZ).]

valuable /vállyoōb'l, -yoo əb'l/ *adj* 1 **WORTH A GREAT DEAL OF MONEY** having significant monetary value 2 **USEFUL** having great importance or usefulness ○ *a valuable insight* 3 **HELD DEAR** cherished or esteemed because of personal qualities 4 **RARE** highly prized because of being in short or limited supply 5 **ABLE TO BE VALUED** capable of being assigned a value ■ *n* **VALUABLE ITEM** a possession, especially a piece of jewellery, that has significant monetary value —**valuableness** *n* —**valuably** *adv*

valuable consideration *n* in English contract law, something given or undertaken as part of an agreement between two parties that has some objective value and so makes the agreement a valid contract

valuate /vállyoo ayt/ (**-ates, -ating, -ated**) *vt* to value something

valuation /vállyoo áysh'n/ *n* 1 **APPRAISAL OF COST** the act of determining the value or price of something, especially property 2 **PRICE** the price of something established by appraisal of its quality, condition, and desirability, or of the cost of replacement 3 **ESTIMATE OF IMPORTANCE** an estimate of the importance or usefulness of something —**valuational** *adj* —**valuationally** *adv*

valuator /vállyoo aytər/ *n* somebody who assesses the value of objects such as jewellery or works of art

~~**valuble**~~ incorrect spelling of **valuable**

value /váll yoo/ *n* 1 **MONETARY WORTH** an amount expressed in money or another medium of exchange that is thought to be a fair exchange for something 2 **FULL RECOVERED WORTH** the adequate or satisfactory return on or recompense for something ○ *it's value for money* 3 **WORTH OR IMPORTANCE** the worth, importance, or usefulness of something to somebody ○ *a ring with great sentimental value* 4 **MEANING** the exact meaning or significance of a word 5 **NUMERICAL QUANTITY** a numerical quantity assigned to a mathematical symbol 6 **LENGTH OF A NOTE** the length of time that a note or pause is held 7 **SHADE OF A COLOUR** in painting and drawing, the lightness or darkness of a colour 8 **SOUND REPRESENTED** the quality or tone of a speech sound that a letter or written character represents, especially in a particular context when in isolation it can represent more than one sound ■ **values** *npl* **PRINCIPLES OR STANDARDS** the accepted principles or standards of an individual or a group ■ *vt* (**-ues, -uing, -ued**) 1 **ESTIMATE THE VALUE OF** to estimate or determine the value of something 2 **RATE** to rate something according to its perceived worth, importance, or usefulness 3 **REGARD HIGHLY** to regard somebody or something as important or useful ○ *I value her as a friend.* [14C. < Old French, < *valoir* 'be worth' < Latin *valere* 'be powerful'.] —**valuer** *n*

value added *n* 1 the difference between the gross profit of a commercial enterprise, such as a firm or industry, and its costs paid to other businesses 2 the amount by which the value of a product increases as it proceeds through the various stages of its manufacture and distribution —**value-added** *adj*

⚡**value-added network** *n* full form of **VAN**

value-added tax *n* full form of **VAT**

value date *n* in the calculation of exchange rates, the date on which a transaction is judged to have occurred

valued policy *n* an insurance policy in which the amount payable for a valid claim is established when the policy is issued and is independent of the value of a loss subsequently incurred

value-free *adj* not affected by or based on value judgments

value judgment *n* a judgment of the worth, appropriateness, or importance of somebody or something made on the basis of personal beliefs, opinions, or prejudices rather than facts

valueless /vállyooləss/ *adj* having no value —**valuelessness** *n*

value system *n* a set of personal principles and standards

valuta /və lóotə/ *n* the value of one nation's currency in terms of its exchange rate with another currency [Late 19C. < Italian, 'value'.]

valval /válvəl/, **valvar** /válvər/ *adj* ANAT = **valvular**

valvate /vál vayt/ *adj* **1 WITH VALVES** having valves or parts similar to valves **2 NOT OVERLAPPING IN BUD** describes sepals or petals that touch but do not overlap in the bud **3 TAKING PLACE BY MEANS OF VALVES** describes the splitting open of the seed capsules of the iris or lily that takes place by means of valves [Early 19C. < Latin *valvatus* 'having folding doors' < *valva* 'leaf of a folding door'.]

valve /valv/ *n* **1 DEVICE THAT CONTROLS LIQUID FLOW** a device that controls the movement of liquids or gases through piping or other passages by opening or closing ports and channels **2 PART ON A BRASS INSTRUMENT** a device in some brass instruments that diverts air down tubes of varying length, thereby altering the pitch **3 ELECTRON TUBE PRODUCING AMPLIFICATION** an electron tube that is either evacuated or filled with low pressure gas and in which electrons are pulled from the cathode by an applied anode voltage. US term **vacuum tube** **4 CLOSABLE FLAP IN AN ORGAN** a membranous structure in a hollow organ or vessel such as the heart or a vein that prevents the return flow of fluid passing through it by folding or closing **5 PART OF A SEED POD** any segment of the wall of a seed pod or other fruit that splits apart to reveal the contents **6 ANTHER FLAP** a flap that acts like a lid in some types of anther **7 PART OF THE CELL WALL** either of the two parts of the silica-impregnated cell wall of a type of alga (**diatom**) that fit together like the lid and base of a box **8 SEPARABLE PART OF A SHELL** a hinged part of the shell of a brachiopod or some molluscs **9 SINGLE-UNIT SHELL** the single-unit shell of a snail and some other molluscs **10 DOOR LEAF** a leaf of a double or folding door (*archaic*) [15C. < Latin *valva* 'leaf of a folding door'.] —**valveless** *adj*

valve gear *n* a mechanical device that controls the valves of a reciprocating engine

valve-in-head engine *n* US MECH ENG = **overhead-valve engine**

valvelet /válvlət/ *n* ANAT = **valvule** *n.*

valve spring *n* **1** a spiral spring that holds a valve closed in the cylinder head of an internal-combustion engine **2** a spring that closes an opened valve

valvula /válvyoolə/ (*plural* **-lae** /-lee/) *n* ANAT = **valvule** [Early 17C. < modern Latin, < Latin *valva* 'leaf of a folding door'.]

valvular /válvyoolər/ *adj* **1** relating to, having, or acting like a valve or set of valves **2** involving or affecting a valve or set of valves

valvule /vál vyool/ *n* a small valve or a part that functions or looks like one [Mid-18C. Variant of VALVULA.]

valvulitis /válvyoo lítiss/ *n* inflammation of a valve in the body, especially one in the heart, often caused by rheumatic fever

valvuloplasty /válvyooló plasti/ (*plural* **-ties**) *n* plastic surgery performed to repair a valve in the body, especially one in the heart [Mid-20C. < VALVULE.]

vambrace /vám brayss/ *n* a piece of armour worn over the forearm as protection [14C. Via Anglo-Norman *vauntbras* < Old French *avantbras* < *avant* 'before' + *bras* 'arm'.]

vamoose /va mooss, və mooss/ (**-mooses, -moosing, -moosed**) *vi* to leave in a hurried way (*slang*) [Mid-19C. < Spanish *vamos* 'let us go'.]

vamp[1] /vamp/ *n* **SEDUCTIVE WOMAN** a woman who is believed to use her sexual attractiveness for the seduction and manipulation of others (*sometimes offensive*) ■ *v* (*sometimes offensive*) **1** *vti* **SEDUCE** to seduce and manipulate somebody by appearing to offer sexual intercourse **2** *vi* **ACT LIKE VAMP** to act like or play the role of a vamp [Early 20C. Shortening of VAMPIRE.] —**vampish** *adj* —**vampishly** *adv* —**vampy** *adj*

vamp[2] /vamp/ *n* **1 UPPER PART OF A SHOE** the upper part of a shoe that covers the front part of the foot **2 SOMETHING PATCHED UP** something repaired so as to appear new **3 REHASHING OF** a reworking of something already used or available, especially a book or article **4 IMPROVISED MUSICAL INTRODUCTION** an improvised musical introduction or accompaniment that is repeated as necessary until the entry of the solo line ■ *v* **1** *vt* **PUT A VAMP ON A SHOE** to put a vamp on a shoe **2** *vti* **IMPROVISE A MUSICAL INTRODUCTION OR ACCOMPANIMENT** to improvise a musical introduction or accompaniment for a solo line [14C. Shortening of Old French *avantpié* < *avant* 'before' + *pié* 'foot'.] —**vamper** *n*

vamp up *vt* **1** to rework or renovate something **2** to make something up or improvise something

vampire /vám pīr/ *n* **1 BLOODSUCKING EVIL SPIRIT** in European folklore, a dead person believed to rise each night from the grave and suck blood from the living for sustenance **2 PREDATORY PERSON** a person who preys on other people for financial or emotional gain **3** ZOOL = **vampire bat** **4 TRAP DOOR** a trap door on the floor of a stage (*technical*) [Mid-18C. Via French or German < Serbo-Croat *vampir*.] —**vampiric** /vam pírrik/ *adj* —**vampirical** *adj* —**vampirish** *adj*

vampire bat *n* a bat that bites the skin of birds or other mammals and laps the blood. Native to: tropical and subtropical Central and South America. Family: Desmodontidae.

vampirism /vám pīrizəm/ *n* **1 BELIEF IN VAMPIRES** the belief that corpses can leave their graves at night and suck the blood of living people **2 STATE OF BEING A VAMPIRE** the supposed state or practices of a vampire **3 FINANCIAL OR EMOTIONAL EXPLOITATION** the act of preying on other people for financial or emotional gain

van[1] /van/ *n* **1 ENCLOSED MOTOR VEHICLE** a motor vehicle that has rear or side doors or sliding side panels and is used for transporting goods or people **2 RAILWAY WAGON** a closed railway wagon for goods, or the section of the carriage for the guard, luggage, parcels, or mail **3 CARAVAN** a caravan [Early 19C. Shortening of CARAVAN.]

van[2] /van/ *n* **1** the leading position **2** MIL = **vanguard** *n.* 1 [Early 17C. Shortening of VANGUARD.]

van[3] /van/ *n* in tennis, a score of advantage (*informal*) [Early 20C. Shortening of ADVANTAGE.] ◇ **van in** *or* **out** in tennis, the score of advantage in favour of *or* against the server (*informal*)

van[4] /van/ *n* **1** a device used for winnowing grain (*archaic*) **2** a bird's wing (*archaic or literary*) [15C. Variant of FAN[1].]

van[5] *abbr* vanilla

Van /van/ capital of Van Province in E Turkey. Population: 153,111 (1990).

Van, Lake saltwater lake in E Turkey. Area: 3,763 sq. km/1,453 sq. mi.

VAN *n* a computer network that enables private companies to exchange information with other registered subscribers (*in e-commerce*) Full form **value-added network**

vanadate /vánnə dayt/ *n* a salt or ester of vanadium [Mid-19C. < VANADIUM.]

vanadic /və náddik, -náyd-/ *adj* relating to or containing vanadium, especially with a high valency. ◊ **vanadous** [Mid-19C. < VANADIUM.]

vanadinite /və náddi nīt/ *n* a rare brown, red, or yellow mineral. Source: lead minerals. Use: source of vanadium. [Mid-19C. < VANADIUM.]

vanadium /və náydi əm/ *n* (*symbol* **V**) a poisonous silvery white metallic element. Source: carnotite, vanadinite. Use: manufacture of tough steel alloys, catalyst. [Mid-19C. < modern Latin, < Old Norse *Vanadis*, Scandinavian goddess.]

vanadium pentoxide *n* V_2O_5 a yellow or red crystalline compound. Use: catalyst, manufacture of glass.

vanadium steel *n* a low-alloy steel containing the element vanadium for added strength

vanadous /vánnədəss/ *adj* relating to or containing vanadium, especially with a low valency. ◊ **vanadic** [Mid-19C. < VANADIUM.]

Van Allen /van állən/, **James** (*b.* 1914) US physicist

Van Allen belt /van állən-/, **Van Allen radiation belt** *n* either of two belts surrounding the Earth and containing charged particles held there by the Earth's magnetic field [Mid-20C. After James VAN ALLEN.]

vanaspati /və náspəti/ *n* a hydrogenated vegetable oil commonly used in Indian cooking instead of butter [Mid-20C. < Sanskrit *vanas-pati* 'lord of the plants'.]

Vanbrugh /vánbrə/, **Sir John** (1664–1726) English playwright and architect

Van Buren /van byóorən/, **Martin** (1782–1862) US statesman and 8th president of the United States (1837–41). Known as **Little Magician, Red Fox of Kinderhook**

Vancouver /van koóvər/ city in SW British Columbia, Canada, opposite Vancouver Island. Population: 514,008 (1996).

Vancouver, Mount peak of the St Elias Range in SW Yukon Territory, Canada. Height: 4,828 m/15,840 ft.

Vancouver, George (1757–98) British naval officer and explorer

Vancouver Island island off SW British Columbia, Canada. Population: 702,000. Area: 31,284 sq. km/12,079 sq. mi.

vanda /vándə/ (*plural* **-das** *or* **-da**) *n* an orchid with strap-shaped leaves. Flowers: flattened with a spur on the lip. Native to: East Asia, Australia. Genus: *Vanda*. [Early 19C. Via modern Latin < Sanskrit *vandā*.]

V and A, V & A *abbr* Victoria and Albert Museum

vandal /vánd'l/ *n* an intentional defacer or destroyer of somebody else's property [Mid-16C. < Latin *Vandalus* 'Vandal' < Germanic.] —**vandalish** *adj*

Vandal *n* a member of an ancient Germanic people who came from Jutland, conquering Gaul, Spain, Rome, and parts of North Africa during the 3rd and 4th centuries AD, before being defeated at Carthage in 533 [Old English *Wendlas* (plural) 'Vandals' < Germanic] —**Vandalic** /van dállik/ *adj*

vandalise *vt* = **vandalize**

vandalism /vánd'lizəm/ *n* the malicious and deliberate defacement or destruction of somebody else's property —**vandalistic** /vándə lístik/ *adj*

vandalize /vándəlīz/ (**-izes, -izing, -ized**), **vandalise** (**-ises, -ising, -ised**) *vt* to deface, destroy, or otherwise damage private or public property maliciously and deliberately —**vandalization** *n*

vanda orchid *n* PLANTS = **vanda**

van de Graaff generator /van də graáf-/ *n* an electrostatic machine that produces electrical discharges at extremely high voltages, used in particle accelerators and for testing electrical insulators [After R. J *van de Graaff* (1901–67), US physicist.]

van der Waals' equation /van dər waálz-/ *n* a modified equation of state describing the physical behaviour of gases that takes into account the volumes of molecules and the interactions between them [After Johannes *van der Waals* (1837–1923), Dutch physicist]

van der Waals' force *n* a weak attractive force between atoms or molecules resulting from the positioning of the electrons within the interacting particles [See VAN DER WAALS' EQUATION]

Van Diemen's Land /van deémənz-/ former name for **Tasmania** (1642–1856)

Van Dongen /van dóngən/, **Kees** (1877–1968) Dutch painter

Vandyke /van dík/ *n* **1** HAIR = **Vandyke beard** **2** CLOTHING = **Vandyke collar** **3** a V-shape forming part of a decorative border on material or clothing **4** a decorative border on material or clothing made up of V-shaped points [Mid-18C. After Sir Anthony van DYCK from various features of his paintings.] —**vandyked** *adj*

Vandyke beard *n* a short, neatly trimmed, pointed beard

Vandyke brown *n* a deep rich brown colour or pigment —**Vandyke brown** *adj*

Vandyke collar *n* a large white collar of linen or lace that has a deeply indented edge

Vandyke stitch *n* a V-shaped variation of cross stitch, used as a filling stitch to form a solid decoration

vane /vayn/ *n* **1 ROTATING BLADE** a flat blade mounted as part of a set in a circle so as to rotate under the action of wind or liquid **2 WEATHER VANE** a weather vane **3 STABILIZER ON A MISSILE** a stabilizing or guiding blade on a missile **4 BLADE OF A FEATHER** the flat part of a feather, consisting of interlocking rows of barbs **5 PART OF A LEVELLING ROD** the moving part on a levelling rod **6 COMPASS OR QUADRANT SIGHT** a sight on a compass or quadrant [15C. Variant of *fane* 'temple'.] —**vaned** *adj*

SPELLCHECK See *vain.*

änern, Lake /vénnərn, váynərn/ largest lake in Sweden, in the southwest of the country. Area: 5,584 sq. km/2,156 sq. mi.

ang /vang/ n a guy rope forming part of a pair that extend from a gaff to the deck [Mid-18C. Variant of FANG.]

an Gogh /van gókh, -góf/, **Vincent** (1853–90) Dutch painter

anguard /ván gaard/ n 1 the military divisions of an army or navy that lead the advance into battle 2 the leading position of a movement, field, or cultural trend, or the people who are foremost in a movement, field, or cultural trend [15C. Shortening of French *avant-garde* < *avant* 'before' + *garde* 'guard'.] —**vanguardism** n — **vanguardist** n

anilla /və nílla/ n 1 **vanilla, vanilla bean** VANILLA POD the long, narrow, fleshy seed pod of a tropical climbing orchid 2 VANILLA FLAVOURING a substance extracted from vanilla seed pods or produced artificially. Use: food flavouring, perfumes. 3 CLIMBING PLANT a climbing plant of the orchid family that produces seed pods from which vanilla is extracted. Native to: tropical America. Genus: *Vanilla*. ■ adj 1 FLAVOURED WITH VANILLA flavoured with vanilla, or having a flavour of vanilla 2 PLAIN OR DULL lacking outstanding or interesting characteristics (*slang*) ○ *vanilla software* [Mid-17C. < Spanish *vainilla* 'small sheath' < *vaina* 'sheath' < Latin *vagina*.]

anillic /və níllik/ adj resembling, containing, or derived from vanilla or vanillin

anillin /və níllin/ n $C_8H_8O_3$ a white aldehyde obtained from vanilla or prepared synthetically. Use: food flavourings, perfumes.

anir /váan eer/ npl in Norse mythology, a race of peace-loving gods [< Old Norse]

anish /vánnish/ vi 1 DISAPPEAR SUDDENLY to disappear suddenly or inexplicably ○ *It can't just have vanished!* 2 STOP EXISTING to cease to exist 3 BECOME ZERO to assume or be given the value of zero (*refers to a function or variable*) [14C. < Old French *esvaniss-* < *esvanir* < Latin *evanescere* 'die out, pass away' < *vanus* 'empty'.] —**vanisher** n —**vanishingly** adv —**vanishment** n

anishing point n 1 a point in a drawing or painting at which parallel lines seem to meet as represented in perspective 2 a point at which something disappears or ceases being

anity /vánnəti/ (*plural* -**ties**) n 1 EXCESSIVE PRIDE excessive pride, especially in your appearance ○ *She is entirely free of personal vanity.* 2 SOMETHING SOMEBODY IS VAIN ABOUT an instance or source of excessive pride 3 FUTILITY the state or fact of being futile, worthless, or empty of significance 4 SOMETHING FUTILE something that is considered futile, worthless, or empty of significance 5 *US* ACCESSORIES = **vanity case** 6 *US* FURNITURE = **dressing table** 7 *US, NZ* CABINET HOLDING A SINK a cabinet that holds a sink and its plumbing, usually with drawers or shelves under the sink for storage [13C. Via Old French < Latin *vanitas* < *vanus* 'empty'.]

LITERARY LINK *Vanity Fair*, a novel (1847–48) by William Makepeace Thackeray. Set in England in the early 19th century, its central characters are the penniless orphan Becky Sharp and Amelia Sedley, the daughter of a rich merchant. The fortunes in life and love of the two young women remain in sharp contrast throughout the complex plot, as Amelia descends into poverty and widowhood while the sharp-witted and unscrupulous Becky enjoys an extravagant lifestyle with a series of lovers.

vanity bag n a vanity case

vanity case n a small case or bag in which somebody carries cosmetics

Vanity Fair, vanity fair n a place, especially a very large city or the world in general, considered to be frivolous and full of idle worthless amusements (*literary*) [Coined by John BUNYAN in his *Pilgrim's Progress* (1678)]

vanity plate n *US* a number plate for a motor vehicle for which the owner has paid extra to be able to choose its numbers and letters

vanity publisher, vanity press n a publishing house that publishes an author's work in return for payment from the author. Vanity publishers do not typically market or distribute their publications. —**vanity publishing** n

vanity table n *US* FURNITURE = **dressing table**

vanity unit n a cabinet that holds a hand basin and its plumbing, usually with drawers or shelves under the sink for storage

vanload /ván lōd/ n the amount of goods or passengers that a van can transport at one time

vanpool /ván pool/ n *US* an arrangement by which a number of people travel together to and from work in a shared van ■ vi to commute in a shared van

vanquish /vángkwish/ vt 1 DEFEAT IN BATTLE to defeat an opponent or opposing army in a battle or fight 2 DEFEAT IN COMPETITION to prove convincingly superior to somebody in a contest, competition, or argument 3 OVERCOME EMOTION to overcome, suppress, or subdue an emotion, feeling, or idea [14C. < Latin *venquis*, form of *veintre* < Latin *vincere* 'conquer'.] —**vanquishable** adj —**vanquisher** n —**vanquishment** n

vantage /váantij/ n 1 a position that provides an advantage 2 superiority in a contest or competition 3 = **vantage point** n. 1 [14C. < Old French *avantage* (see ADVANTAGE).] —**vantageless** adj

vantage ground n a position of superiority over somebody

vantage point n 1 vantage point, vantage a position or location that provides a broad view or perspective of something 2 a personal point of view

Vanuatu

Vanuatu /vánnoo aà too/ republic in the SW Pacific Ocean, comprising approximately 80 islands. Capital: Port-Vila. Population: 172,000. Area: 12,190 sq. km/4,707 sq. mi.

vanward /vánnwərd/ adj in or at the front or edge of something ■ adv moving towards the front or edge of something

vapid /váppid/ adj 1 lacking interest or liveliness 2 lacking strength, taste, or flavour [Mid-17C. < Latin *vapidus* 'insipid'.] —**vapidity** /və píddəti/ n —**vapidly** adv —**vapidness** n

vapor n, vti *US* = **vapour**

vaporescence /váypə réss'nss/ n the formation or creation of vapour —**vaporescent** adj

vaporetto /váppə réttō/ (*plural* -**ti** /váppə rétti/ *or* -**tos**) n a motorboat for transporting passengers along the canals in Venice [Early 20C. < Italian, 'small steamboat' < *vapore* 'steam' < Latin *vapor* (see VAPOUR).]

vaporific /váypə ríffik/ adj 1 PRODUCING VAPOUR producing, causing, or becoming vapour 2 BEING VAPOUR being, containing, or resembling vapour 3 VOLATILE capable of changing easily from a liquid or solid state into vapour

vaporise vti = **vaporize**

vaporiser n = **vaporizer**

vaporize /váypə rīz/ (-**izes**, -**izing**, -**ized**), **vaporise** (-**ises**, -**ising**, -**ised**) vti 1 CHANGE INTO VAPOUR to change into or cause something to change into vapour 2 VANISH OR MAKE VANISH to vanish or cause somebody or something to vanish 3 ANNIHILATE OR BE ANNIHILATED to destroy somebody or something so completely that the person or object is turned into a gas or vapour, or to be destroyed in this way —**vaporizable** adj —**vaporization** /váypə rī záysh'n/ n

vaporizer /váypə rīzər/, **vaporiser** n something used to produce a vapour, especially a device used to vaporize a medication so that it can be inhaled

vaporous /váypərəss/ adj 1 BEING VAPOUR being, containing, or resembling vapour 2 PRODUCING VAPOUR producing, causing, or becoming vapour 3 VOLATILE capable of chan-

ging easily from a liquid or solid state into vapour 4 UNSUBSTANTIAL lacking material existence or permanence 5 FANCIFUL of a fanciful, ridiculous, or implausible nature 6 OBSCURED BY VAPOUR made hard to see because of being obscured by mist or vapour — **vaporosity** /váypə róssəti/ n —**vaporously** adv —**vaporousness** n

vapour /váypər/ n 1 GASEOUS SUBSTANCE a gaseous substance at a temperature lower than that at which it can be liquefied or solidified by an appropriate increase in pressure alone 2 MOISTURE PARTICLES moisture or some other matter visible in the air as mist, clouds, fumes, or smoke 3 GASEOUS STATE OF A SUBSTANCE the gaseous state of a liquid or solid at a temperature below its boiling point 4 VAPORIZED SUBSTANCE a substance prepared for military, industrial, or medical use in vaporized form 5 GAS AND AIR MIXTURE a combination of air with a gaseous substance such as that of air and petrol in an internal-combustion engine 6 SOMETHING UNSUBSTANTIAL something without material existence or permanence (*archaic*) 7 FANCIFUL IDEA a fanciful idea (*archaic*) ■ **vapours** npl LOW SPIRITS a bout of low spirits or sadness (*archaic*) ■ v 1 vti EVAPORATE to change or cause something to change into a vapour 2 vi EMIT VAPOUR to give off or send up vapour 3 vi BRAG to talk boastfully [14C. Directly or via Old French < Latin *vapor* 'steam, heat'.] —**vapourability** /váypərə billəti/ n —**vapourable** /vápərəb'l/ adj —**vapourer** n —**vapoury** n

vapour barrier n a protective layer of material used in building to keep out moisture

vapour density n the density of a gas or vapour in relation to that of hydrogen

vapourer moth /váypərər-/ n a tussock moth that lives in hedges and trees. *Orgyia antiqua*.

vapour lock n a bubble of vaporized petrol that blocks the normal flow of fuel in the line that supplies the carburettor of an internal-combustion engine

vapour pressure, vapour tension n the pressure exerted by a vapour, particularly a vapour in contact with its liquid form

vapour trail n a visible trail of condensed vapour left by an aircraft flying at high altitude

⚡**vapourware** /váypər wair/ n new software that has been announced or advertised but has not yet been, and may never be, produced [Late 20C. After SOFTWARE.]

vaquero /va káirō/ (*plural* -**ros**) n *Southwest US* a cowboy [Early 19C. < Spanish, < *vaca* 'cow'.]

var abbr volt-ampere reactive

⚡**VAR**[1] /vaar/ n a retail seller of computers who adds products to computers produced by manufacturers or performs services such as product integration or customization before selling the computers to customers. Full form **value-added reseller**

VAR[2] abbr 1 visual aural range 2 volt-ampere reactive

var. abbr 1 variable 2 variant 3 variation

vara /váarə/ n a unit of length used in Spain, Portugal, and Latin America that can be from 80 cm/32 in to 108 cm/43 in in length [Late 17C. Via Spanish, 'rod, yardstick' < Latin, 'forked pole, trestle' < *varus* 'bent'.]

varactor /váir aktər/ n a semiconductor diode with a capacitance that varies according to the voltage applied to it, used to regulate the frequency of electronic circuits in amplifiers [Mid-20C. Blend of VARIABLE + REACTOR.]

Varanasi /və ráanəssi/, **Vārānasi** city in N India, on the River Ganges. Population: 929,270 (1991).

Varangian Guard n 1 the body of Scandinavian soldiers who were the Byzantine emperor's bodyguard in the 10th and 11th centuries 2 a Scandinavian soldier in the Varangian Guard

Vardon /váard'n/, **Harry** (1870–1937) British golfer

varec /várrek/ n kelp [Late 17C. < French.]

~~vareity~~ incorrect spelling of **variety**

Vargas Llosa /vaárgass lóssa/, **Mario** (b. 1936) Peruvian writer and critic

vari- prefix = **vario-** (before vowels)

variable /váiri əb'l/ adj 1 ABLE TO CHANGE able or liable to change, especially suddenly and unpredictably 2 INCONSISTENT inconsistent or uneven in quality or performance ○ *a variable performance* 3 FICKLE inconstant and capricious in nature or character 4 LIKELY TO BLOW DIFFERENTLY describes a wind that is likely to change direction or intensity 5 WITH RESISTANCE THAT VARIES describes an electrical device that has a resistance that

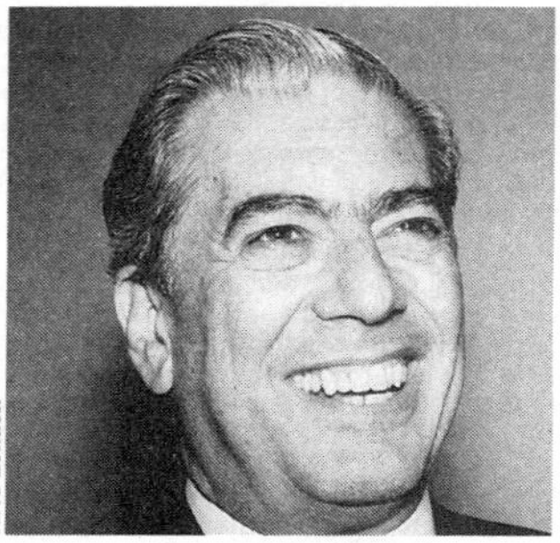

Mario Vargas Llosa

varies **6 DIFFERING FROM THE SPECIES NORM** describes a species that tends to differ in some characteristic from a recognized or known type **7 WITH NO FIXED NUMERICAL VALUE** not having a fixed numerical value ■ *n* **1 SOMETHING THAT CAN VARY** something capable of changing or varying **2 SYMBOL FOR AN UNSPECIFIED QUANTITY** a symbol that represents an unspecified or unknown quantity, such as 'a', 'b', or 'x' **3 RANGE OF VALUES** a range of values, any one of which is a solution to an algebraic expression **4 LOGIC SYMBOL** a symbol, especially 'x', 'y', or 'z', that is used usually in connection with quantifiers to represent individuals in a universe of discourse **5** ASTRON = **variable star 6 VARIABLE WIND** a wind that is likely to change in direction or intensity ■ **variables** *npl* **REGION OF VARIABLE WINDS** a region where variable winds are likely to be encountered [14C. Via Old French < Latin *variabilis* < *variare* (see VARY).] —**variability** /váiri ə bílləti/ *n* —**variableness** *n* —**variably** *adv*

variable cost *n* a cost that varies directly in relation to output

variable-geometry *adj* describes an aircraft with wings that are hinged so that in flight they can move backwards or forwards

variable-rate mortgage *n* a mortgage on which interest is payable at a rate that changes, usually in accordance with market interest rates. US term **adjustable-rate mortgage**

variable star *n* a star whose brightness changes at regular or irregular intervals

variable-sweep *adj* AEROSP = **variable-geometry**

variance /váiri ənss/ *n* **1 CHANGE IN** a change that occurs in something **2 DIFFERENCE BETWEEN THINGS** a difference between two or more things **3 DISAGREEMENT** a difference of opinion or attitude ○ *The project failed because of variances of opinion about the next step.* **4 DISCREPANCY IN** a discrepancy between two statements, documents, or steps in a legal proceeding **5 DIFFERENCE IN COST** a difference between actual costs and the usual costs of production **6 SQUARE OF STANDARD DEVIATION** a statistical measure of the spread or variation of a group of numbers in a sample, equal to the square of the standard deviation **7** *US* **LEGAL DISPENSATION** a dispensation to ignore a rule or law [14C. Via Old French < Latin *variantia* < *variare* (see VARY).]

variant /váiri ənt/ *adj* **1 DIFFERING SLIGHTLY** having or showing a difference from the norm ○ *variant pronunciations of common words* **2 CHANGEABLE** tending or likely to change ■ *n* **1 SLIGHTLY DIFFERENT FORM** something that differs slightly from the norm **2 DIFFERENT FORM OR SPELLING OF WORD** a different form or spelling of a word or phrase from the standard one **3** STATS = **random variable** [14C. French, < *varier* 'vary' < Latin *variare* (see VARY).]

variate /váiri ət, -ayt/ *n* STATS = **random variable** [Late 19C. < Latin *variatus*, past participle of *variare* (see VARY).]

variation /váiri áysh'n/ *n* **1 ACT OF VARYING** the act or a result of varying **2 STATE OF DIFFERING** the state or fact of differing, e.g. from a former state or value, from others of the same type, or from a standard **3 DEGREE OF DIFFERENCE** the degree to which something differs, e.g. from a former state or value, from others of the same type, or from a standard ○ *There is a variation of several marks in the exam results.* **4 SOMETHING DIFFERING SLIGHTLY** something that differs slightly from the norm **5 BIOLOGICAL DEVIATION** a significant deviation from the normal biological form, function, or structure **6 LIVING ORGANISM THAT DIFFERS** a living organism that differs from the normal form for its kind **7 MATHEMATICAL FUNCTION** a mathematical function that relates the values of one variable to those of other variables **8 REPETITION OF A MUSICAL THEME** the repetition of a musical theme with modifications of melody, rhythm, or harmony **9 ALTERED VERSION OF A MUSICAL THEME** an altered version of an original musical theme or melody, such that the rhythm or harmony is varied or melodic embellishment is added **10 SOLO DANCE** a dance performed by a single dancer **11 CHANGE IN ORBIT** a change in or deviation from the average motion or orbit of an astronomical object **12 TERM IN EQUATION DESCRIBING THE MOON'S MOTION** a term representing the gravitational attraction of the Sun on the Earth-Moon system in the mathematical equation for the Moon's motion **13** PHYS = **magnetic declination** [14C. Directly or via French < Latin *variation-* < *variare* (see VARY).] —**variational** *adj* —**variationally** *adv*

~~**variaty**~~ incorrect spelling of **variety**

varic- *prefix* = **varico-** (*before vowels*)

varicella /várri séllə/ *n* chickenpox (*technical*) [Late 18C. < modern Latin, 'lesser smallpox' < late Latin *variola* (see VARIOLA).] —**varicellar** *adj* —**varicellous** *adj*

varicella-zoster virus /várri sellə zóstər-/ *n* a herpes virus that is responsible for chickenpox and shingles

varices plural of **varix**

varico- *prefix* varix, varicose vein ○ *varicotomy* [< Latin *varic-*, stem of *varix*]

varicocele /várrikō seel/ *n* a swelling of the veins in the spermatic cord of the scrotum

varicolored *adj* US = **varicoloured**

varicoloured /váiri kúllərd/ *adj* consisting of or having many colours

varicose /várrikōss/, **varicosed** /várrikōst/ *adj* **1 SWOLLEN** swollen, knotted, or distended to a greater extent than normal **2 WITH VARICOSE VEINS** affected with or having varicose veins **3 PRODUCING SWELLING** relating to or producing swelling **4 RIDGED LIKE A GASTROPOD SHELL** resembling a small longitudinal ridge on the shell of some gastropods [15C. < Latin *varicosus* < *varix* 'dilated vein, varicose vein'.]

varicoses plural of **varicosis**

varicose vein *n* a vein that has become abnormally swollen and knotted as a result of defective valves ■ **varicose veins** *npl* a condition in which the surface veins, especially of the legs, become knotted and swollen, as a result of defects in the valves of the affected veins

varicosis /várri kṓssiss/ (*plural* **-ses** /-seez/) *n* **1** a condition in which a vein or veins become swollen or knotted **2** the formation of small longitudinal ridges on the surface of a gastropod shell

varicosity /várri kóssəti/ (*plural* **-ties**) *n* **1 SWOLLEN STATE** the state of being abnormally swollen or knotted (**varicose**) **2 VARICOSE VEIN** a varicose vein (*technical*) **3 HAVING SWOLLEN VEINS** the condition of suffering from or having abnormally swollen or enlarged veins

varicotomy /várri kóttəmi/ (*plural* **-mies**) *n* a surgical incision into a swollen vein, usually performed to treat varicose veins

varied /váirid/ *adj* **1 DIVERSE** showing or characterized by many different forms or kinds **2 CHANGED** having undergone change or alteration **3 WITH MANY COLOURS** consisting of or having many colours —**variedly** *adv* —**variedness** *n*

variegate /váiri gayt/ (**-gates, -gating, -gated**) *vt* **1** to change the way something looks, especially by adding different colours **2** to add variety to something [Mid-17C. < Latin *variegare* 'make varied' < *varius* 'diverse'.] —**variegation** /váiri gáysh'n/ *n* —**variegator** *n*

variegated /váiri gaytid/ *adj* **1 WITH PATCHES OF DIFFERENT COLOURS** marked with or containing patches of different colours **2 WITH PATCHES OF LIGHTER COLOUR** marked with or containing patches of lighter colour **3 DIVERSE** showing or characterized by many different forms or types

varietal /və rī́ ət'l/ *adj* **1 TYPICAL OF BIOLOGICAL VARIETY** relating to, typical of, or being a variety of something, especially a biological variety **2 MADE FROM SINGLE GRAPE VARIETY** made entirely or principally from a single variety of grape ■ *n* **WINE MADE FROM SINGLE GRAPE VARIETY** a wine that is made entirely or principally from a single variety of grape, and is usually known by the name of the grape variety —**varietally** *adv*

variety /və rī́ əti/ (*plural* **-ties**) *n* **1 QUALITY OF BEING VARIE[D]** the quality of being varied or diversified ○ *It's easy [to] get bored if there's no variety in your work.* **2 PARTICULA[R] TYPE** a particular type or kind within a general grou[p] ○ *a new variety* **3 COLLECTION OF VARIED THINGS** a collectio[n] of varied things, often belonging to the same genera[l] group **4 ENTERTAINMENT MADE UP OF DIFFERENT ACTS** er[n]tertainment made up of a number of different types o[f] act **5 SUBDIVISION OF SPECIES** a taxonomic category o[f] related organisms, especially plants, of a rank above form [Mid-16C. Via Old French < Latin *varietas* < *variu[s]* 'variegated, diverse'.]

variety meat *n US* **1** any meat taken from a slaughtere[d] animal other than flesh removed from the skeleto[n] especially organ meat **2** any meat that is processed, e.g. sausage

variety show *n* a theatrical show made up of a numbe[r] of short performances of different kinds, such a[s] singing, comic sketches, dancing, and magic acts

varifocal /váiri fṓk'l/ *adj* describes composite spectacl[e] lenses with varying focal length that allow differen[t] focusing distances for near, far, and intermediate visio[n] ■ **varifocals** *npl* spectacles with composite lenses fo[r] distant, intermediate, and near vision

variform /váiri fawrm/ *adj* existing in different shapes o[r] forms [Mid-17C. < VARIOUS.] —**variformly** *adv*

~~**varigated**~~ incorrect spelling of **variegated**

vario- *prefix* variation, variance, difference ○ *variolite* [< Latin *varius* 'variegated, diverse']

variola /və rī́ ələ/ *n* smallpox (*technical*) [Early 19C. < late Latin, 'pustule' < Latin *varius* 'variegated, diverse'.] —**varioloid** /váiri ə loyd/ *adj, n*

variolate *vt* /váiri ə layt/ (**-lates, -lating, -lated**) to in[n]oculate somebody with the smallpox virus (*dated*) ■ *adj* /váiri ələt/ with a pitted or scarred appearance, lik[e] the skin of somebody who has had smallpox —**variolation** /váiri ə láysh'n/ *n*

variolous /və rī́ ələss/ *adj* relating to, like, or affected by smallpox

variometer /váiri ómmitər/ *n* **1** an instrument used to measure magnetic fields, especially variations in the Earth's magnetic field **2** an instrument used to measure the rate of climb of an aircraft such as a glider

variorum /váiri áwrəm/ *adj* **1 WITH VARIOUS ANNOTATIONS** with commentary or notes written by various editors or scholars **2 WITH DIFFERENT VERSIONS OF TEXT** containing different versions or readings of a text ■ *n* **VARIORUM EDITION** an edition of a text with commentary or notes written by various editors or scholars, or with various different versions or readings [Early 18C. < Latin genitive plural of *varius* 'variegated, diverse', in *editio cum notis variorum* 'edition with notes of various (commentators)'.]

various /váiri əss/ *det* **ASSORTED** many different ■ *pron* **DIFFERENT EXAMPLES** many different examples of something (*nonstandard*) ■ *adj* **1 OF DIFFERENT KINDS** of different kinds or categories **2 INDIVIDUAL** individual or separate **3 BEING AN ASSORTMENT** being an assortment or variety **4 CHANGING** changing rather than constant (*archaic*) [Mid-16C. < Latin *varius* 'variegated, diverse'.] —**variously** *adv* —**variousness** *n*

varisized /váiri sīzd/ *adj US* being or consisting of different sizes

varistor /və rístər/ *n* a two-element semiconductor with nonlinear resistance in which the resistance drops as the applied voltage increases. Varistors are often used as a safety device to short circuit transient high voltages in electronic circuits. [Mid-20C. < VARIABLE + RESISTOR.]

varix /váiriks/ (*plural* **-ices** /váiri seez/) *n* **1** an abnormally swollen or knotted vessel, especially a vein **2** a ridge along the length of the shell of a gastropod mollusc [14C. < Latin, 'dilated vein, varicose vein'.] —**variceal** /várri seé əl/ *adj*

varlet /vaárlət/ *n* (*archaic*) **1 RASCAL** a rogue or rascal **2 SERVANT** a servant or attendant **3 PAGE** a knight's page [15C. < Old French, variant of VALET (see VALET).]

varmint /vaármint/ *n* a troublesome, unpleasant, or despicable person or animal (*regional*) [Mid-16C. Variant of VERMIN.]

varna /vaárnə/ *n* a caste group in Hindu society. The four Aryan social castes, or varnas, are the priests (**Brahmans**), warriors (**Kshatriyas**), merchants (**Vaisyas**), and workers (**Sudras**), with, beneath these, the untouchables (**Dalits**). [Mid-19C. < Sanskrit, 'colour, cover, class, sort'.]

Varna /vaárnə/ city in E Bulgaria, on the Black Sea. Population: 301,421 (1996).

varnish /vaárnish/ *n* **1 TRANSPARENT RESIN SOLUTION** a solution of a resin in oil or spirits, applied to a surface to give it a protective gloss **2 SMOOTH COATING OF VARNISH** a coating of varnish, applied to something to give it a protective gloss **3 SUPERFICIALLY ATTRACTIVE MANNER OR APPEARANCE** a superficially or deceptively attractive manner or appearance ■ *vt* **1 APPLY VARNISH** to coat something with varnish **2 GIVE SOMETHING SMOOTH SURFACE** to give something a smooth and usually glossy surface **3 MAKE SOMETHING SUPERFICIALLY ATTRACTIVE** to make something superficially or deceptively attractive [14C. Via Old French *vernis* < medieval Latin *vernicium* 'sandarac' < Greek *Bereníkē* 'Berenice', city in Cyrenaica.] —**varnisher** *n*

varnish tree *n* a tree such as the lacquer tree whose sap yields varnish or lacquer

Varro /várrō/, **Marcus Terentius** (116–27BC) Roman scholar

varsity /vaárssəti/ (*plural* **-ties**) *n* a university (*dated*) [Mid-19C. Dialectal variant of *versity*, shortening of UNIVERSITY.]

Varuna /várrōōnə/ *n* the all-seeing creator god of Hindu tradition, who uses the sun as his eye and acts as a life-sustaining force, ever-present in all he has created [< Sanskrit, 'wise one, seer']

varus /váirəss/ *adj* describes an abnormality in which a body part such as the foot is turned or displaced inwards towards the midline of the body or limb [Late 18C. < Latin, 'bent, crooked'.]

varve /vaarv/ *n* a layer or series of layers of sediment deposited annually in a still body of water, e.g. by a glacier [Early 20C. < Swedish *varv* 'layer, turn'.]

vary /váiri/ (**-ies, -ying, -ied**) *v* **1** *vti* **UNDERGO OR MAKE SOMETHING UNDERGO CHANGE** to undergo or make something undergo a change in appearance or characteristics **2** *vi* **BE DIFFERENT** to be different **3** *vt* **GIVE VARIETY TO** to give variety or diversity to something [14C. Via Old French *varier* < Latin *variare* < *varius* 'variegated, diverse'.] —**varying** *adj* —**varyingly** *adv*

SYNONYMS See ***change***.

vas /vass, vaass/ (*plural* **vasa** /váyzə, vaázə/) *n* a vessel or duct in the body of a human or animal [Mid-17C. < Latin, 'vessel'.] —**vasal** /váyss'l, váyz'l/ *adj*

vas- *prefix* = **vaso-** (*before vowels*)

vasa plural of **vas**

Vasarély /vazə ráyli/, **Victor** (1908–97) Hungarian-born French painter, sculptor, and graphic artist

vascular /váskyōōlər/ *adj* relating to fluid-carrying vessels, e.g. blood vessels in animals or the sap-carrying vessels in plants [Mid-17C. < modern Latin *vascularis* < Latin *vasculum* (see VASCULUM).] —**vascularity** /váskyōō lárrəti/ *n* —**vascularly** *adv*

vascular bundle *n* a strand of plant tissue containing the xylem and phloem vessels, responsible for conducting sap through the stems and branches of a plant

vascularization /váskyōōlə rī záysh'n/, **vascularisation** *n* the development of vessels, especially blood vessels, in an organism or tissue

vascular plant *n* any plant that possesses specialized sap-conducting tissues, particularly phloem and xylem, e.g. all flowering plants, conifers, and ferns

vascular tissue *n* plant tissue that is specialized for conducting sap. It comprises phloem, which conveys chiefly dissolved sugars, and xylem, which conveys water and dissolved minerals.

vasculature /váskyōōləchər/ *n* the arrangement of blood vessels in the body or in a particular organ or tissue

vasculitis /váskyōō lítiss/ *n* inflammation of a blood vessel or lymph vessel

vasculum /váskyōōləm/ (*plural* **-la** /-lə/ *or* **-lums**) *n* a small box or case used by botanists in the field for storing collected plants or other specimens [Mid-19C. < Latin, 'little vessel' < vas 'vessel'.]

vas deferens /váss déffə renz, vaáss-/ (*plural* **vasa deferentia** /váyzə deffə rénshə, vaázə-/) *n* either of a pair of ducts that carry sperm from the testes to the urethra during ejaculation [Late 19C. < Latin, 'carrying-away vessel'.]

vase /vaaz/ *n* an open container, usually tall and rounded, used for displaying cut flowers or as an ornament [Mid-16C. Via French < Latin *vas* 'vessel'.]

vasectomize /və séktə mīz/ (**-mizes, -mizing, -mized**), **vasectomise** (**-mises, -mising, -mised**) *vt* to perform a vasectomy on somebody

vasectomy /və séktəmi/ (*plural* **-mies**) *n* a surgical operation in which the vas deferens from each testis is cut and tied to prevent transfer of sperm during ejaculation [Late 19C. < VAS DEFERENS.]

Vaseline /vássə leen/ *tdmk* a trademark for medical petroleum jelly and various skin care products

vaso- *prefix* **1** blood vessels, vascular ○ *vasodilation* **2** vas deferens ○ *vasectomy* [< Latin *vas* 'vessel']

vasoactive /váyzō áktiv/ *adj* making blood vessels contract or dilate —**vasoactivity** /váyzō aktívvəti/ *n*

vasoconstriction /váyzō kən stríksh'n/ *n* narrowing of the blood vessels with consequent reduction in blood flow or increased blood pressure

vasoconstrictor /váyzō kən stríktər/ *n* any agent such as a nerve or hormone that narrows the blood vessels, which in turn increases resistance to blood flow and raises blood pressure —**vasoconstrictive** *adj* —**vasoconstrictor** *adj*

vasodilation /váyzō dī láysh'n/, **vasodilatation** /váyzō dīla táysh'n/ *n* widening of the blood vessels, especially the arteries, leading to increased blood flow or reduced blood pressure

vasodilator /váyzō dī láytər/ *n* an agent, such as a nerve or hormone that widens the blood vessels, which in turn decreases resistance to blood flow and lowers blood pressure —**vasodilator** *adj* —**vasodilatory** *adj*

vasoinhibitor /váyzō in híbbitər/ *n* something that depresses or stops the activity of the nerves that control widening or narrowing of the blood vessels —**vasoinhibitory** *adj*

vasomotor /váyzō mṓtər/ *adj* causing or influencing changes in the diameter of blood vessels

vasopressin /váyzō préssin/ *n* a hormone produced by the pituitary gland that causes narrowing of the arteries and raises blood pressure

vasopressor /váyzō préssər/ *adj* causing or promoting the narrowing of blood vessels, which in turn raises blood pressure ■ *n* something that has the effect of raising blood pressure

vasospasm /váyzō spázzəm/ *n* sustained contraction of the muscular walls of the blood vessels with a resultant reduction in blood flow —**vasospastic** /-spástik/ *adj*

vasovagal /váyzō váyg'l/ *adj* relating to, or involving the influence of the vagus nerve on circulation. Stimulation of the vagus reduces heart rate and, consequently, the amount of blood being pumped by the heart.

vassal /váss'l/ *n* **1** a person who gave loyalty and homage to a feudal lord and received the right to occupy the lord's land and be protected by him **2** a person, nation, or group that is dependent on or subordinate to another [14C. Via Old French < medieval Latin *vassallus* < *vassus* 'servant' < Celtic, 'young man, squire'.] —**vassal** *adj*

vassalage /váss'lij/ *n* **1** the dependent condition of being somebody's vassal **2** any condition of being dependent on or subordinate to somebody or something else (*literary*)

vast /vaast/ *adj* very great in number, size, amount, extent, or degree ■ *n* the immense expanse of space (*literary*) [Late 16C. < Latin *vastus* 'immense, empty'.] —**vastidity** /va stíddəti/ *n* —**vastitude** *n* —**vastity** *n*

vastly /vaástli/ *adv* to a very great extent or degree

vastness /vaástnəss/ *n* **1** the state or quality of being vast **2** an immense expanse or area of space (*literary*)

vat /vat/ *n* **1 LARGE CONTAINER FOR LIQUID** a large container used to hold or store liquid **2 PREPARATION OF DYE** a preparation of weakly coloured soluble dye (**vat dye**) ■ *vt* (**vats, vatting, vatted**) **TREAT OR PUT IN A VAT** to treat, store, or put something in a vat [12C. Alteration of *fat* < Old English *fæt* 'vessel' < Germanic.]

VAT *n* a tax added to the estimated value of a product or material at each stage of its manufacture or distribution, in the end paid by the consumer. Full form **value-added tax**

Vat. *abbr* Vatican

vat dye *n* a dye that is made insoluble and fixed by oxidation after being taken up by fibres —**vat-dyed** *adj*

vatic /váttik/ *adj* relating to, involving, or typical of a prophet [Early 17C. < Latin *vates* 'prophet, seer'.]

Vatican /váttikən/ *n* **1** the palace in the Vatican City that is used as the official residence of the pope and the administrative centre of the papacy **2** the authority and jurisdiction of the pope [Mid-16C. < Latin *(mons) Vaticanus* 'Vatican (hill)'.]

Vatican City /váttikən-/ world's smallest independent nation and headquarters of the Roman Catholic Church. Population: 850 (1996). Area: 44 hectares/110 acres.

Vaticanism /váttikənizəm/ *n* the policies and authority of the pope, especially the idea of absolute papal authority

vaticinate /və tíssi nayt/ (**-nates, -nating, -nated**) *vti* to prophesy something [Early 17C. < Latin *vaticinari* < *vates* 'prophet, seer' + *canere* 'sing'.] —**vaticinal** *adj* —**vaticination** /váttissi náysh'n/ *n* —**vaticinator** *n*

vatu /vaá too/ (*plural* **-tu**) *n* see table at **currency**

Vauban /vō baáN/, **Sebastien le Prestre de** (1633–1707) French marshal of France

vaudeville /váwdəvil/ *n* **1** *US* THEATRE, MUSIC = **music hall** *n*. 1 **2** *US* **VAUDEVILLE SHOW** a vaudeville show **3 COMIC PLAY WITH SONGS** a comic play with songs and dances **4 SATIRICAL POPULAR SONG** a satirical popular song of the type performed in cabarets in the 19th and 20th centuries **5 OPERATIC SONG** a song used as a finale in an opera, with each verse sung by a different character, all joining in a refrain [Mid-18C. < Old French *vaudevire*, shortening of *chanson du Vau de Vire* 'song of the Valley of Vire', region of Normandy noted for satirical folksongs.] —**vaudevillian** /váwdə vílli ən/ *adj*, *n*

Vaudreuil /vō dröi/, **Philippe de Rigaud de Vaudreuil de Cavagnal, marquis de** (1698–1778) French soldier and colonial administrator

Vaughan /vawn/, **Sarah** (1924–90) US jazz singer

Vaughan Williams /vawn wíllyəmz/, **Ralph** (1872–1958) British composer

vault[1] /vawlt, volt/ *n* **1 ARCHED CEILING** an arched structure of stone, brick, wood, or plaster that forms a ceiling or roof **2 ROOM WITH ARCHED CEILING** a room, especially an underground room, with an arched ceiling **3 BURIAL CHAMBER** a burial chamber, usually underground **4 SOMETHING ARCHING OVERHEAD** something that arches overhead, especially the sky (*literary*) **5 ARCHED PART OF BODY** a part of the body with an arched shape ■ *v* **1** *vt* **PUT ARCHED STRUCTURE OVER** to cover a building with an arched ceiling or roof **2** *vt* **BUILD SOMETHING AS VAULT** to build something in the shape of a vault **3** *vi* **FORM VAULT** to arch or curve like a vault [14C. < Old French *vaute* < assumed Vulgar Latin *volvita* 'turn, vault' < Latin *voluta*, feminine past participle of *volvere* 'turn, roll'.] —**vaulted** *adj*

vault[2] /vawlt, volt/ *v* **1** *vti* **SPRING OVER OBJECT** to leap or spring over something, especially by pushing on it with the hands or using a pole **2** *vi* **MOVE WITH A BOUND** to move with a leap or bound **3** *vi* **RISE SUDDENLY TO PROMINENCE** to arrive somewhere or achieve something suddenly ○ *She vaulted to fame with the publication of her first novel.* **4** *vti* RIDING = **curvet** *v.* ■ *n* **1 ACT OF VAULTING** an act of vaulting **2** RIDING = **curvet** *n.* [Mid-16C. Via Old French *volter* < assumed Vulgar Latin *volvitare* 'roll repeatedly' < Latin *volvere* 'turn, roll'.] —**vaulter** *n*

vaulting[1] /váwlting, vólt-/ *n* the structural use of brick, stone, or reinforced concrete to form a ceiling or roof over a space

vaulting[2] /váwlting, vólt-/ *adj* aspiring or confident, especially in an excessive way (*literary*) ○ *vaulting ambition*

vaulting horse *n* a piece of gymnastic equipment with four legs and a solid leather-covered oblong body, used for exercises and especially for vaulting over

vaunt /vawnt/ *v* **1** *vt* **BE BOASTFUL ABOUT** to boast or act boastfully about something such as achievements or possessions **2** *vi* **BOAST** to boast or brag (*literary*) ■ *n* **A BOAST** a boast, or display of boasting [14C. Via Old French *vanter* < late Latin *vanitare* 'be vain' < *vanus* 'empty'.] —**vaunter** *n* —**vauntingly** *adv*

vaunted /váwntid/ *adj* boasted about or praised in an ostentatious way

vav /vawv/, **waw** /waw/ *n* the sixth letter in the Hebrew alphabet [Early 19C. < Hebrew *wāw* 'hook'.]

vavasor /vávvə sawr/, **vavasour** *n* a feudal lord or knight who has power over vassals but is himself a vassal of a more powerful lord [14C. Via Old French < medieval Latin *vavassor*.]

vb *abbr* **1** verb **2** verbal

ϟ**VC** *abbr* St. Vincent and the Grenadines. (*in Internet addresses*)

VC *abbr* 1 vice-chairman 2 vice chancellor 3 vice consul 4 Victoria Cross

VCR *abbr* 1 *US* video cassette recorder 2 visual control room (*on an airfield*)

vd *abbr* 1 vapour density 2 various dates 3 void

VD *abbr* 1 venereal disease 2 Volunteer Decoration

VDR *abbr* 1 video disc recorder 2 video disc recording

VDRL *abbr* venereal disease research laboratory

ϟ**VDT** *abbr* video display terminal

ϟ**VDU** *abbr* visual display unit

ϟ**ve** *abbr* Venezuela (*in Internet addresses*)

've *contr* have

veal /veeʼl/ *n* meat from a young calf, light in colour and texture with a delicate flavour [14C. Via Anglo Norman, Old French *veel* < Latin *vitellus*, diminutive of *vitulus* 'calf'.]

veal calf *n* a calf reared for veal

vealer /véelər/ *n ANZ, Can, US* a veal calf

ϟ**vector** /véktər/ *n* 1 **QUANTITY WITH DIRECTION AND MAGNITUDE** a quantity, e.g. force or velocity, made up of components of both direction and magnitude 2 **ELEMENT OF VECTOR SPACE** an element of a vector space 3 **COURSE OF AIRCRAFT** the course taken by an aircraft or a missile 4 **DISEASE-TRANSMITTING ORGANISM** an organism such as a mosquito or tick that transmits disease-causing microorganisms from infected individuals to other persons, or from infected animals to human beings 5 **GENE TRANSFER AGENT** an agent such as a plasmid or bacteriophage that is used in genetic modification to transfer a segment of foreign DNA into a bacterium or other cell 6 **COMPUTER ARRAY** in computing, an array of any length but only one dimension ■ *vt* 1 **DIRECT AIRCRAFT BY RADIO** to direct an aircraft in flight, or its pilot, by radio, often from the ground 2 **CHANGE THRUST DIRECTION OF AIRCRAFT ENGINE** to change the direction of the thrust of an aircraft engine as a means of steering the aircraft [Early 18C. < Latin, 'carrier' < *vectus*, past participle of *vehere* 'carry'.] —**vectorial** /vek táwri əl/ *adj* —**vectorially** *adv*

ϟ**vector graphics** *npl* COMPUT = **object-oriented graphics**

vector product *n* the result of multiplying two vectors

vector space *n* a mathematical set of vectors associated with a field of scalars comprising a commutative group under addition and in which multiplication of a vector and a scalar is a vector

vector sum *n* the result of adding two vectors, obtained graphically as the directed diagonal of the parallelogram whose sides are the given vectors

Veda /váydə, véedə/ *n* any or all of the collections of Aryan hymns, originally transmitted orally but written down in sacred books from the 6th century BC [Mid-18C. < Sanskrit, 'knowledge, sacred book' Indo-European, *know*.] —**Vedaic** /vi dáy ik/ *adj*

Vedaism /váydə izəm/ *n* RELIG = **Vedism**

Vedanta /vi daántə/ *n* one of the six philosophical schools of Hinduism [Late 18C. < Sanskrit *vedānta* < *veda* (see VEDA) + *anta* 'end'.] —**Vedantic** *adj* —**Vedantism** *n* —**Vedantist** *n*

V-E Day *n* May 8, 1945, designated by the Allies to mark their victory in Europe in World War II after the German surrender of the day before

Vedda /véddə/ (*plural* **-da** *or* **-das**), **Veddah** (*plural* **-dah** *or* **-dahs**) *n* a member of an indigenous forest people of Sri Lanka [Late 17C. < Sinhalese *vaddā* 'hunter'.] —**Veddoid** *adj*

vedette /vi dét/ *n* 1 **vedette, vidette** a mounted soldier posted forwards of a larger force to serve as a scout 2 **vedette, vedette boat** a small fast boat posted forwards of a larger seaborne force to serve as a scout [Late 17C. Via French < Italian *vedetta*, alteration (after *vedere* 'see') of *veletta* < Spanish *vela* 'watch' < Latin *vigilare* (see VIGILANT).]

Vedic /váydik, véedik/ *adj* 1 **IN THE VEDAS** relating to the Vedas 2 **BELONGING TO CULTURE THAT PRODUCED VEDAS** relating to the Hindu culture that produced the Vedas 3 **IN ANCIENT SANSKRIT** relating to the ancient form of Sanskrit in which the Vedas are written ■ *n* **ANCIENT SANSKRIT** the ancient form of Sanskrit in which the Vedas are written

Vedism /váydizəm, véedizəm/ *n* the Hindu religious theory and practice contained in, or based on, the Vedas

vee /vee/ *n* the letter 'V', or something with a similar shape [Late 19C. < the pronunciation of the letter's name.]

vee-jay /vee jáy/ *n* a video jockey (*informal*) ■ *vi* to work or act as a video jockey

veep /veep/ *n US* a vice president (*slang*) [Mid-20C. < VP.]

veer[1] /veer/ *v* 1 *vti* **CHANGE DIRECTION SUDDENLY** to change direction, especially suddenly, or to make something do this 2 *vi* **CHANGE FROM ONE OPINION TO ANOTHER** to change from one opinion or state of mind to another, especially when this is sudden or extreme 3 *vi* **SHIFT IN CLOCKWISE DIRECTION** to shift in a clockwise direction (*refers to a wind*) 4 *vti* **SAIL AWAY FROM WIND** to change course in a sailing vessel away from the wind, or to make a vessel do this ■ *n* **CHANGE IN DIRECTION** a change in direction or course [Late 16C. < French *virer* 'turn'.]

veer[2] /veer/ *vt* to let out a cable or chain or to make it go slack [15C. < Middle Dutch *vieren* 'let out'.]

veery /véeri/ (*plural* **-ries**) *n* a woodland thrush with tawny upper parts and a spotted breast. Native to: E United States. *Catharus fuscescens*. [Mid-19C. < ?]

veg[1] /vej/ (*plural* **veg**) *n* vegetables or a vegetable (*informal*) [Mid-20C. Shortening.]

veg[2] /vej/ *vi* = **veg out**

Vega /véegə/ *n* the brightest star in the constellation Lyra, one of the brightest in the northern hemisphere

Vega /váygə/, **Lope de** (1562–1635) Spanish playwright and poet

vegan /véegən/ *n* a person who does not eat animal products. ◊ **ovolactovegetarian** [Mid-20C. Contraction of VEGETARIAN.] —**vegan** *adj* —**veganism** *n*

vegetable /véjtəbʼl/ *n* 1 **EDIBLE PLANT** any plant with edible parts, especially leafy or fleshy parts that are used mainly for soups and salads and to accompany main courses 2 **FRUIT EATEN AS VEGETABLE** any plant product that is strictly a fruit, e.g. the tomato, but is eaten as, and popularly thought of as, a vegetable 3 **ANY PLANT** any member of the plant kingdom, as opposed to the animal or mineral kingdoms 4 **OFFENSIVE TERM** an offensive term for somebody in whom normal functions are severely reduced or absent, often as a result of injury to the brain 5 **INACTIVE PERSON** somebody regarded as lacking in vitality, alertness, or drive (*insult*) ■ *adj* **CONSISTING OF VEGETABLES** consisting of, made from, using, or like vegetables [14C. Via Old French < medieval Latin *vegetabilis* 'animating, able to grow' < Latin *vegetare* (see VEGETATE).]

vegetable ivory (*plural* **vegetable ivories**) *n* 1 a hard pale material like ivory, used to make decorative items and accessories. It comes from the endosperm of a South American palm nut (**ivory nut**). 2 TREES = **ivory nut**

vegetable marrow *n* 1 FOOD = **marrow** *n.* 1 2 PLANTS = **marrow** *n.* 2

vegetable oil *n* oil that has been extracted from a plant or the seeds of a plant, e.g. olive oil, sunflower oil, sesame oil, and rapeseed oil

vegetable oyster *n* FOOD = **salsify**

vegetable sheep *n* a plant of the daisy family that has dense foliage and white flowers that make it resemble sheep from a distance. Native to: New Zealand uplands. Genus: *Raoulia*.

vegetable wax *n* a waxy material that forms part of the thin film covering the surfaces of most plants and helps reduce their loss of water through evaporation

vegetal /véjjitʼl/ *adj* 1 relating to plants 2 describes processes concerned with the maintenance or growth and development of an organism, rather than sexual reproduction [14C. < medieval Latin *vegetalis*Latin *vegetare* (see VEGETATE).]

vegetal pole *n* the end of an animal egg that contains the greatest concentration of yolk, lying opposite to the animal pole

vegetarian /véjjə táiri ən/ *n* a person who eats vegetables, fruits, grains, seeds, and sometimes eggs and dairy products but not meat or fish [Mid-19C. < VEGETABLE.] —**vegetarian** *adj* —**vegetarianism** *n*

vegetate /véjjə tayt/ (**-tates, -tating, -tated**) *vi* 1 **BEHAVE IN DULL OR INACTIVE WAY** to live or behave in a dull, inactive, or undemanding way 2 **GROW OR SPROUT LIKE PLANT** to grow or sprout like a plant 3 **PRODUCE FLESHY OUTGROWTHS** to grow or spread, especially by producing fleshy outgrowths [Early 17C. < Latin *vegetat-*, past participle of *vegetare* 'grow' < *vegere* 'quicken'.]

vegetation /véjjə táysh'n/ *n* 1 **PLANTS IN GENERAL** plants in general or the mass of plants growing in a particular place 2 **PROCESS OF VEGETATING** the process of vegetating 3 **ABNORMAL OUTGROWTH** an abnormal outgrowth from a body part such as on the membranes surrounding the heart —**vegetational** *adj*

vegetative /véjjətətiv/ *adj* 1 **CONCERNED WITH PLANTS** relating to, involving, typical of, or like vegetation, plants, or plant growth 2 **INVOLVING GROWTH, NOT SEXUAL REPRODUCTION** relating to, involving, or typical of processes in the maintenance or growth and development of an organism, rather than sexual reproduction 3 **REPRODUCING FROM BODY CELLS OF PARENT** describes a method of reproduction, especially in plants, in which new individuals originate from the body cells of the parent rather than from specialized sex cells 4 **DULL OR INACTIVE** dull, inactive, and undemanding in lifestyle 5 **OFFENSIVE TERM** an offensive term meaning that normal functions are reduced or absent because of injury to the brain —**vegetatively** *adv* —**vegetativeness** *n*

vegetative nervous system *n* the part of the body's nervous system that controls involuntary functions, such as the beating of the heart

veggie /véjji/, **vegie** *n* a vegetarian (*informal*) [Mid-20C. Shortening.] —**veggie** *adj*

veggieburger /véjji burgər/ *n* a flat cake made from vegetables and legumes, fried or grilled, and often served in the same way as a hamburger

vegie *n* = **veggie** (*informal*)

veg out, **veg** *vi* to relax, be idle, or loaf, e.g. while watching television (*informal*) [Late 20C. < VEGETATE.]

~~vegtable~~ incorrect spelling of **vegetable**

vehement /vée əmənt/ *adj* 1 expressed with, or showing conviction or intense feeling 2 done with vigour or force [15C. Via Old French < Latin *vehement-* 'forceful, violent'.] —**vehemence** *n* —**vehemently** *adv*

~~vehical~~ incorrect spelling of **vehicle**

vehicle /vée ikʼl/ *n* 1 **MEANS OF LAND TRANSPORT** a usually wheeled conveyance used on land for carrying people or goods, most often by road or rail 2 **STRUCTURE FOR TRANSPORT IN SPACE** a powered structure, device, or rocket used to transport a payload or another craft through space 3 **COMMUNICATION MEDIUM** a medium for communicating, expressing, or accomplishing something 4 **PERFORMANCE FOR PARTICULAR PERFORMER** a film, play, show, or other performance designed or used to show off the talents of a particular performer 5 **MIXTURE FOR PAINT PIGMENT** a substance or mixture such as linseed oil or an acrylic vinyl polymer in which a pigment is mixed for painting 6 **SUBSTANCE BLENDED WITH DRUG** an inactive substance with which a drug is blended to make it easier to apply, administer, or take [Early 17C. Via French *véhicule* < Latin *vehiculum* < *vehere* 'carry'.]

vehicle registration document *n* TRANSP = **registration document**

vehicular /vi hík yŏŏlər/ *adj* relating to, involving, or for use by vehicles, especially motor vehicles [Early 17C. < late Latin *vehicularis* < Latin *vehiculum* (see VEHICLE).]

veil /vayl/ *n* 1 **FACE COVERING WORN BY WOMEN** a length of fabric, usually sheer, worn by women over the head and face as a concealment or for protection 2 **NETTING ATTACHED TO WOMAN'S HAT** a piece of netting or other sheer fabric attached to a woman's hat and covering the eyes 3 **NUN'S HEADDRESS** a part of a nun's headdress covering the sides and back of the head 4 **NUN'S VOWS OR LIFE** the vows that a nun takes or the life that she leads 5 **SOMETHING LIKE CURTAIN** something that acts like a curtain in hiding, disguising, or obscuring something else, or separating one thing from another 6 **COVERING MEMBRANE OF YOUNG MUSHROOM** a thin membrane that covers the stalk and cap of an immature mushroom 7 ANAT = **caul** *n.* 1 8 CHR = **humeral veil** ■ *v* 1 *vt* **COVER WITH A VEIL** to cover something such as a person's face with a veil 2 *vt* **HIDE OR DISGUISE** to hide or disguise something, or separate something from something else 3 *vi* **WEAR A VEIL** to put on or wear a veil [12C. Via Old French *veile* < Latin *vela* 'covering', plural of *velum* 'sail'.] —**veiler** *n* ◇ **draw a veil over something** to ignore something deliberately or refrain from mentioning it, in order to be discreet ◇ **take the veil** to become a nun

SPELLCHECK See ***vale***.

Veil /vīl/, **Simone** (*b.* 1927) French government official and politician

veiled /vayld/ *adj* **1** not open or direct but disguised or suggested **2** covered with or wearing a veil —**veiledly** /váylidli/ *adv*

veiling /váyling/ *n* **1** fabric used for veils **2** a veil

vein /vayn/ *n* **1 VESSEL CARRYING BLOOD TO HEART** any blood vessel that carries blood to the heart **2 ANY BLOOD VESSEL** any vessel that carries blood around the body (*not technical*) **3 SAP-CONDUCTING LEAF STRAND** a distinct strand of tissue in a leaf that contains the sap-conducting vessels **4 LAYER OF MINERAL** a layer of a mineral in rock, especially an ore or a metal **5 PARTICULAR QUALITY** a particular recurrent quality or characteristic **6 STREAK OF DIFFERENT COLOUR** a streak of different colour or material within a substance such as marble, wood, or cheese **7 SUPPORTING STRUCTURE IN INSECT WING** any of the hollow supporting structures in the wing of an insect that carry inside them blood vessels, nerves, and air tubes supplying the wing **8 FISSURE FILLED WITH MATERIAL** a fissure, crack, or channel in rock or ice that has been filled with a crystallized mixture of minerals **9 DISPOSITION** a disposition, tone, or mood ■ *vt* **1 STREAK** to streak or suffuse something of one colour or material with another **2 FORM VEINS IN** to form veins or things like veins in something [13C. Via Old French *veine* < Latin *vena* 'blood vessel, vein of metal, mine'.] —**veinal** *adj* —**veined** *adj* —**veiny** *adj*

SPELLCHECK See *vain*.

veining /váyning/ *n* a distribution or pattern of veins or streaks

veinlet /váynlət/ *n* a small vein

vel. *abbr* **1** vellum **2** velocity

vela plural of **velum**

Vela /veélə/ *n* a constellation of the southern hemisphere. See illustration at **constellation** [Mid-19C. Latin, literally 'sails', from the shape of the constellation.]

velamen /və láy men/ (*plural* **-mina** /və lámminə/) *n* the spongy layer that covers the aerial roots of some plants such as tree-dwelling orchids [Late 19C. < Latin, 'covering' < *velare* 'to cover' < *velum* 'sail'.]

velar /veélər/ *adj* **1 WITH TONGUE NEAR SOFT PALATE** spoken with the back of the tongue close to, or in contact with, the soft palate (**velum**) **2 OF A VELUM** relating to, involving, or typical of a velum ■ *n* **VELAR CONSONANT** a velar consonant [Early 18C. < modern Latin *velaris* < Latin *velum* 'sail'.]

velarise *vt* = **velarize**

velarium /vi láiri əm/ (*plural* **-a** /-ə/) *n* a large awning used in amphitheatres in ancient Rome to shade the audience [Mid-19C. < Latin, 'awning', 'curtain' < *velum* 'sail'.]

velarize /veélə rīz/ (**-izes, -izing, -ized**), **velarise** (**-ises, -ising, -ised**) *vt* to pronounce a speech sound by bringing the back of the tongue close to or against the soft palate (**velum**) —**velarization** *n*

velate /veélət, -layt/ *adj* with or covered by a velum [Mid-19C. < VELUM.]

Velázquez /vi láskwez, ve láthketh/, **Diego** (1599–1660) Spanish painter

Velcro /vélkrō/ *tdmk* a trademark for a fastener consisting of two strips, one with a dense layer of hooks and the other of loops that interlock with them. Use: outerwear, athletic shoes, luggage.

veld /velt/, **veldt** *n* a broad high grassland, especially in southern Africa [Early 19C. Via Afrikaans < Dutch, 'field'.]

Velde /véldə/, **Henry van de** (1863–1957) Belgian architect

veldskoen /vélt skoōn/ *n S Africa* a shoe or boot made of rough hide [Early 19C. < Afrikaans, by folk etymology (after *veld* 'veld') < *velskoen* 'skin shoe' < *vel* 'skin'.]

veldt *n* GEOG = **veld**

veleta /və leétə/, **valeta** *n* a ballroom dance in triple time in which partners sometimes dance side by side and sometimes do a quick waltz

veliger /véllijər/ *n* a larva of some molluscs, e.g. limpets and mussels, that has a protective shell and a ciliated flap-shaped foot used for swimming and feeding [Late 19C. < VELUM + Latin *gerere* 'carry, bear'.]

velleity /ve leé əti/ (*plural* **-ties**) *n* **1** volition or desire at its weakest level (*literary*) **2** a vague wish or desire [Early 17C. < medieval Latin *velleitas-* < Latin *velle* 'to wish'.]

vellum /vélləm/ *n* **1 HIGH QUALITY PARCHMENT OF ANIMAL SKIN** high quality parchment made from calfskin, kidskin, or lambskin **2 MANUSCRIPT ON VELLUM** a manuscript written or printed on vellum **3 PAPER RESEMBLING VELLUM** an off-white heavy paper resembling vellum [15C. < French *vélin* 'of a calf' < Old French *veel* 'calf' (see VEAL).] —**vellum** *adj*

veloce /ve lóchi/ *adv* to be played or performed rapidly (*musical direction*) [Early 19C. Via Italian < Latin *veloc-* 'quick, swift'.]

velocimeter /véllə símmitər, veélō-/ *n* an instrument used to measure the speed of a fluid or sound

velocipede /və lóssi peed/ *n* any early form of bicycle or tricycle, including those that had pedals attached to the front wheel or were propelled by pushing the feet along the ground [Early 19C. < French *vélocipède* 'bicycle' < Latin *veloc-* 'quick, swift', + *ped-* 'foot'.] —**velocipedist** *n*

velocity /və lóssəti/ (*plural* **-ties**) *n* **1** the speed at which something moves, happens, or is done **2** a measure of the rate of change in position of something with respect to time, involving speed and direction [Mid-16C. < Latin *velocitas-* < *veloc-* 'quick, swift'.]

velocity of circulation *n* the rate at which money circulates throughout an economy during a particular period, usually a year

velodrome /vélladrōm/ *n* a stadium that has a banked track for bicycle races [Late 19C. < French *vélodrome* < *vélocipède* (see VELOCIPEDE) + -DROME < Greek *dromos* (see -DROME).]

velours /və loŏr/ (*plural* **-lours** /və loŏr/), **velour** *n* a fabric with a thick pile, similar to velvet. Use: upholstery, clothing. [Early 18C. Via Old French *velous* < Latin *villosus* 'shaggy' < *villus* 'shaggy hair, wool'.]

velouté /və loō tay/ *n* a creamy white sauce based on chicken, veal, or fish stock [Mid-19C. < French, 'velvety' < Old French *vellute* < *velous* (see VELOURS).]

velum /veéləm/ *n* (*plural* **-la** /-lə/) a layer of tissue or other part that covers something like a veil, such as the muscular soft palate in the roof of the mouth ■ PLANT SCI = **veil** *n*. **6** [Late 18C. < Latin, 'sail, covering'.]

velutinous /və loŏtinəss/ *adj* densely covered with short soft hairs [Early 19C. < modern Latin *velutinus* 'velvety' < medieval Latin *velutum* 'velvet' < *villutus* (see VELVET).]

velvet /vélvit/ *n* **1 FABRIC WITH SOFT LUSTROUS PILE** a cotton, silk, or nylon fabric with a dense soft usually lustrous pile and a plain underside **2 SOMETHING LIKE VELVET** something that is smooth and soft like velvet **3 FURRY COVERING ON DEER ANTLERS** the furry layer that covers the growing antlers of deer and is sloughed off when the antlers stop growing and harden ■ *adj* **1 MADE OF VELVET** made of or covered with velvet **2 LIKE VELVET** like velvet, especially in being or looking soft, smooth, or lustrous [14C. < Old French *veluotte* < *velu* 'shaggy (cloth)' < medieval Latin *villutus* < Latin *villus* 'shaggy hair, wool'.] ◇ **on velvet** *US* in an advantageous or enviable position, or prosperous and successful

velvet ant *n* any one of various wasps with bodies covered in soft hair. The females are generally wingless and have a potent sting. Family: Mutillidae.

velveteen /vélvə teén/ *n* a brushed fabric with a soft pile like velvet [Late 18C. < VELVET + variant of -INE.]

velvet glove *n* kind, careful, or gentle treatment, especially when this disguises strength or determination

velvet scoter *n* a large duck, the male of which is black with white patches, and the female dark brown. Native to: Arctic, migrating to Europe and Asia. *Melanitta fusca*.

velvet shank *n* an edible mushroom that grows in clusters on hardwood trees, has a yellow cap, and a velvety dark brown stalk. Native to: Europe, North Africa. *Flammulina velutipes*.

velvety /vélvəti/ *adj* **1** soft and smooth in a way that suggests the feel of velvet **2** smooth and mellow —**velvetiness** *n*

Ven. *abbr* **1** Venerable **2** Venezuela

ven- *prefix* = **veno-** (*before vowels*)

vena /veénə/ (*plural* **-nae** /veén ee/) *n* a vein (*technical*) [14C. < Latin.]

vena cava /-káyvə/ (*plural* **venae cavae** /veé nee káy vee/) *n* either of two major veins that carry circulating blood into the right atrium of the heart [Late 16C. < Latin, 'hollow vein'.] —**vena-caval** *adj*

venal /veén'l/ *adj* **1 OPEN TO BRIBERY** open to persuasion by corrupt means, especially bribery. **2 CORRUPT** characterized by corruption **3 ABLE TO BE BOUGHT** able to be bought, especially in an illegal or unfair way [Mid-17C. < Latin *venalis* < *venum* 'something for sale'.] —**venality** /vee nálləti/ *n* —**venally** *adv*

USAGE venal or **venial**? The two words are derived from entirely different Latin roots: ***venal*** comes from *venum* meaning 'something for sale' and ***venial*** from *venia* meaning 'forgiveness'. ***Venal***, meaning 'open to or characterized by corruption', describes people as well as processes and organizations: *The political system is so venal that bribery is commonplace.* ***Venial***, meaning 'easily forgiven', is used in connection with minor faults or transgressions: *He was inclined to be thoughtless, but that was a venial fault in one so young.* In Roman Catholic theology, a *venial sin* is one that does not deprive the soul of divine grace, as opposed to a *mortal sin*, which does.

venation /vee náysh'n/ *n* **1** the pattern formed by the network of veins in an insect's wing or in a leaf **2** all the veins making up a network —**venational** *adj*

vend /vend/ *v* **1** *vt* to sell something from a vending machine **2** *vti* to sell something, especially in the street, or make a living doing this [Early 17C. Directly or via French *vendre* < Latin *vendere* 'sell'.]

Venda[1] /véndə/ (*plural* **-da** *or* **-das**) *n* **1** a member of a people who live in southern Africa, mainly in N Transvaal **2** a Bantu language spoken mainly in Transvaal in South Africa. Native speakers: 750,000. [Early 20C. < Bantu.] —**Venda** *adj*

Venda[2] /véndə/ former Black African homeland in NE South Africa

vendace /vén dayss/ (*plural* **-daces** *or* **-dace**) *n* a whitefish with a streamlined body and leading lower jaw. Native to: freshwater lakes of NW Europe, Russia. Genus: *Coregonus*. [Late 17C. Probably < Old French *vendoise* < Celtic.]

vendee /vén deé/ *n* a buyer of something

vender *n* COMM = **vendor**

vendetta /ven déttə/ *n* **1** a feud between families started by the killing of a member of one family that is then avenged by a killing of a member of the other family **2** a prolonged bitter feud or quarrel [Mid-19C. Via Italian < Latin *vindicta* 'vengeance'.]

vendible /véndəb'l/ *adj* suitable or fit to be sold ■ *n* something that can be sold or is available for sale —**vendibility** /véndə bílləti/ *n* —**vendibleness** *n*

vending machine *n* a machine from which people can buy such items as packaged food or drinks by inserting money

Vendôme /vaN dṓm/, **Louis Joseph, duc de** (1654–1712) French soldier

vendor /véndər/, **vender** *n* **1** a seller of something **2** a vending machine

vendue /vén dyoo/ *n US* a public sale or auction [Late 17C. Via Dutch *vendu* < French *vendue*, form of *vendre* 'sell' (see VEND).]

veneer /və neér/ *n* **1 THIN LAYER AS SURFACE** a thin layer of a material fixed to the surface of another material that is of inferior quality or less attractive **2 DECEPTIVE APPEARANCE** an outward appearance that is meant to please or impress others but that is false or only superficial **3 OUTER LAYER** an outer layer fixed to something for decoration or protection, e.g. a facing of stone on a brick building **4 LAYER OF PLYWOOD** any of the layers of wood that are glued together to make plywood ■ *vt* **1 FIX VENEER TO** to fix a veneer to a surface **2 HIDE SOMETHING BEHIND DECEPTIVELY PLEASANT APPEARANCE** to hide or disguise something behind a deceptively pleasant or impressive appearance **3 GLUE LAYERS TO MAKE PLYWOOD** to glue layers of wood together to make plywood [Early 18C. < German *Fournier* 'inlay, veneer' < French *fournir* 'furnish, provide'.] —**veneerer** *n*

venepuncture *n* MED = **venipuncture**

venerable /vénnərəb'l/ *adj* **1 WORTHY OF RESPECT** worthy of respect as a result of great age, wisdom, remarkable achievements, or similar qualities **2 REVERED** revered for qualities such as great age or holiness **3 ANCIENT** extremely old **4 USED AS TITLE BEFORE CANONIZATION** used by the Roman Catholic Church to describe somebody who has died and attained the first of the three degrees of canonization **5 USED AS ARCHDEACON'S TITLE** used as a title to describe an archdeacon in the Church of England [15C. Directly or via French < Latin *venerabilis* < *venerari* (see VENERATE).] —**venerability** /vénnərə bílləti/ *n* —**venerably** *adv*

venerate /vénnə rayt/ (**-ates, -ating, -ated**) *vt* **1** to regard somebody with profound respect **2** to honour something or somebody as sacred or special [Early 17C. < Latin *venerat-*, past participle of *venerari* < *vener-*, stem of *venus* 'love, desire'.] —**venerator** *n*

veneration /vénnə ráysh'n/ *n* **1** FEELING OF RESPECT a feeling of great respect or reverence for somebody or something **2** EXPRESSING OF RESPECT the expression of respect or reverence for somebody or something in words or actions **3** BEING RESPECTED the condition of being respected or revered —**venerational** *adj*

SYNONYMS See *regard*.

venereal /və neéri əl/ *adj* **1** PASSED ON THROUGH SEX describes an infection or disease that is caught or transmitted through sexual intercourse **2** ASSOCIATED WITH SEXUALLY TRANSMITTED DISEASE associated with, symptomatic of, or infected with a sexually transmitted disease **3** GENITAL affecting or originating in the genitals **4** ABOUT SEX relating to sex acts or sexual desire (*archaic or literary*) [15C. < Latin *venereus* < *vener-*, stem of *venus* 'love, desire'.]

venereal disease *n* a sexually transmitted disease (*dated*)

venereology /və neéri óllәji/ *n* the branch of medicine involving the study and treatment of sexually transmitted diseases [Late 19C. < VENEREAL.] —**venereological** /və neéri ə lójjik'l/ *adj* —**venereologist** *n*

venery[1] /vénnəri, veén-/ *n* the pursuit of or indulgence in sexual pleasure (*archaic*) [15C. < medieval Latin *veneria* < Latin *vener-*, stem of *venus* 'love, desire'.]

venery[2] /vénnəri, veén-/ *n* the sport or practice of hunting, or the animals hunted (*archaic*) [14C. Via French *vénerie* < Latin *venari* 'to hunt'.]

venesection /vénni seksh'n/ *n* SURG = **phlebotomy** [Mid-17C. < medieval Latin *venae sectio* 'cutting of a vein'.]

Venetian /və neésh'n/ *adj* relating to the Italian city of Venice, or its people or culture ■ *n* a person who comes from Venice [15C. < Old French *Venicien* < Latin *Venetia* 'Venice'.]

Venetian blind, venetian blind *n* a window blind consisting of narrow horizontal slats whose angle can be adjusted to let in more or less light

Venetian glass *n* delicate glassware, often with colourful ornamentation, made in or around Venice, especially at Murano

Venetian red *n* **1** a dark red pigment. Source: hematite, synthetic iron oxide. **2** a strong reddish-brown colour —**Venetian red** *adj*

Venez. *abbr* Venezuela

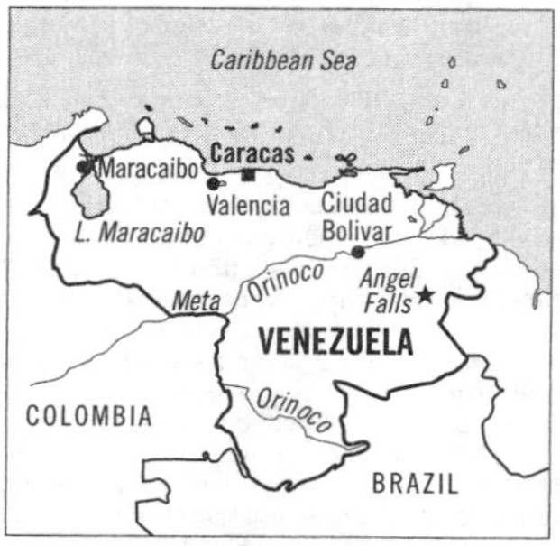

Venezuela

Venezuela /vénnə zwáylə/ republic in NE South America, on the Caribbean Sea and the Atlantic Ocean. Capital: Caracas. Population: 22,311,000 (1996). Area: 912,050 sq. km/352,144 sq. mi. —**Venezuelan** *n, adj*

Venezuela, Gulf of inlet of the Caribbean Sea in NW Venezuela

~~**vengance**~~ incorrect spelling of **vengeance**

vengeance /vénjənss/ *n* punishment that is inflicted in return for a wrong [13C. Via Old French < Latin *vindicare* 'avenge' (see VINDICATE).] ◇ **with a vengeance** in an extreme or intense manner

vengeful /vénjf'l/ *adj* **1** having or showing a strong desire for revenge **2** serving the purpose of revenge or resulting from somebody's desire for revenge —**vengefully** *adv* —**vengefulness** *n*

~~**vengence**~~ incorrect spelling of **vengeance**

V-engine *n* an internal-combustion engine with cylinders arranged in two rows to form a V-shaped angle

veni- *prefix* = **veno-**

venial /veéni əl/ *adj* easily forgiven or excused [13C. Via Old French < late Latin *venialis* < Latin *venia* 'forgiveness'.] —**veniality** /veéni álləti/ *n* —**venially** *adv*

USAGE See *venal*.

venial sin *n* in the Roman Catholic Church, a sin that does not deprive the soul of divine grace, either because it was not serious or because it was committed without intent or without understanding its seriousness. ◊ **mortal sin**

Venice /vénniss/ historic seaport in NE Italy, built on islands in a lagoon in the Gulf of Venice, an arm of the N Adriatic Sea. Population: 294,547 (1997 estimate).

venipuncture /vénni pungkchər, veéni-/, **venepuncture** *n* the puncturing of a vein for any medical purpose, e.g. to take blood, to feed somebody intravenously, or to administer a drug

venire /vi nīri/, **venire facias** /-fáyshi ass/ *n* in the United States, and formerly in the United Kingdom, a judicial writ ordering the summoning of jurors [Mid-17C. < medieval Latin *venire facias* 'you should cause to come'.]

venireman /vi nīrimən/ (*plural* **-men** /-mən/) *n* a citizen summoned for jury duty under a venire

venison /vénniss'n, -z'n/ *n* **1** the meat of a deer used as food **2** the meat of any animal hunted as game (*archaic*) [13C. Via Old French < Latin *venation-* 'hunting' < *venari* 'to hunt'.]

Venite /vi nīti/ *n* **1** the 95th Psalm from the Bible sung as an invitation to morning prayer **2** a musical setting of the 95th Psalm [13C. < Latin, 'come ye', the first word of the psalm.]

Venlo /vénnlō/ city in the SE Netherlands. Population: 64,775 (2000).

Venn diagram /vén-/ *n* a mathematical diagram representing sets as circles, with their relationships to each other expressed through their overlapping positions, so that all possible relationships between the sets are shown [Early 20C. After John *Venn* (1834–1923), British logician.]

vennel /vénn'l/ *n Scotland* an alley or narrow lane between buildings [15C. Via Old French < medieval Latin *venella* 'little vein' < Latin *vena* 'vein'.]

veno- *prefix* vein, venous ○ *venogram* [< Latin *vena* 'vein']

venogram /veénə gram/ *n* an X-ray photograph of a vein or network of veins, taken after injecting a substance that absorbs X-rays and so makes the veins visible

venography /vi nóggrəfi/ *n* the examination of somebody's veins by taking an X-ray photograph (**venogram**) after injecting a substance that absorbs X-rays

venom /vénnəm/ *n* **1** POISONOUS FLUID INJECTED BY ANIMAL a poisonous fluid produced by an animal and injected into prey or attackers by a bite or sting **2** MALICE something that is full of malice, spite, or vicious hostility **3** POISON any kind of poison (*archaic*) [13C. Via Old French *venim* < Latin *venenum* 'poison'.] —**venomous** *adj* —**venomously** *adv* —**venomousness** *n*

venose /veénōss/ *adj* with veins, especially many branched veins e.g. an insect's wing or the leaf of a plant [Mid-17C. < Latin *venosus* < *vena* 'vein'.]

venosity /vi nóssəti/ *n* **1** EXCESSIVE AMOUNT OF BLOOD an excessive amount of blood in the veins, or in an organ or other body part **2** HIGH NUMBER OF VEINS an unusually large number of veins in an organ or other body part **3** QUALITY OF VENOUS BLOOD the deoxygenated state of venous blood **4** VEINED CONDITION the presence or possession of veins, especially many branched veins

venous /veénəss/ *adj* **1** OF VEINS relating to or involving the veins **2** RELATING TO BLOOD IN VEINS describes blood in the veins, which is returning to the heart, as opposed to blood in the arteries, which is leaving the heart **3** WITH VEINS containing or full of veins [Early 17C. < Latin *vena* 'vein'.] —**venously** *adv* —**venousness** *n*

vent[1] /vent/ *n* **1** OPENING FOR AIR a small opening that allows fresh air to enter or stale air, gas, smoke, or steam to escape **2** OPENING IN ANIMAL'S BODY the external opening through which all waste material and eggs pass in fish, amphibians, reptiles, birds, and primitive mammals **3** OPENING IN EARTH'S CRUST an opening in the Earth's crust from which gases or volcanic material escape **4** OPENING IN GUN BREECH a small opening in the breech of an old muzzle-loading gun through which the charge is ignited **5** WAY OF RELEASING STRONG FEELINGS a way of releasing or expressing strong feelings, or a chance to do so ○ *a vent for his anger* ■ *vt* **1** RELEASE EMOTIONS to release or forcefully express strong feelings or emotions **2** LET OUT AIR to let out smoke, gases, steam, or stale air through a vent **3** MAKE VENT to provide a vent for something [14C. Via Old French *esventer* 'let out air' < assumed Vulgar Latin *exventare* < Latin *ventus* 'wind'.] —**ventless** *adj* ◇ **give vent to something** to express a strong feeling or emotion freely

vent[2] /vent/ *n* a vertical slit at the bottom of a seam in a jacket or other garment, that provides room for movement ■ *vt* to put a vent in a jacket or other garment [15C. Old French *fente* 'slit' < Latin *findere* 'to split'.] —**vented** *adj* —**ventless** *adj*

ventage /véntij/ *n* **1** a finger hole in a recorder or other wind instrument **2** a small opening or vent [Early 17C. < VENT[1].]

venter /véntər/ *n* **1** BELLY OF ANIMAL WITH BACKBONE the abdomen of a vertebrate **2** BODY PART RESEMBLING ABDOMEN the part of the body in invertebrates that corresponds to the abdomen in vertebrates **3** SOFT PART OF MUSCLE the soft fleshy area that forms the main part of a muscle **4** HOLLOW OR CAVITY a hollow or cavity, e.g. on a bone **5** FEMALE PLANT PART in plants such as mosses and ferns, the swollen lower part of the female sex organ (**archegonium**) where the ovum develops **6** WOMB in law, a woman's womb. The term is used, e.g., with reference to an unborn child. (*technical*) [Mid-16C. Directly or via French *ventre* < Latin *venter* 'stomach, abdomen'.]

ventifact /vénti fakt/ *n* a rock, stone, or pebble that has been shaped, cut, or polished by wind-blown sand [Early 20C. < Latin *ventus* 'wind', after artifact.]

ventilate /vénti layt/ (**-lates, -lating, -lated**) *vt* **1** PROVIDE FRESH AIR to provide a room or other enclosed space with fresh air or a current of air **2** PROVIDE VENT to provide an enclosed space with a vent or other means of letting fresh air in and stale air out **3** EXPOSE SOMETHING TO MOVING AIR to expose something to moving fresh air, e.g. in order to dry, cool, or preserve it **4** PUBLICLY EXAMINE QUESTIONS to examine freely and publicly or discuss grievances, opinions, or questions **5** SUPPLY OXYGEN TO BLOOD to oxygenate or aerate the blood through the blood vessels of the lungs [15C. < Latin *ventilat-*, past participle of *ventilare* 'fan' < *ventilus* 'to fan' < *ventus* 'wind'.]

ventilation /vénti láysh'n/ *n* **1** CIRCULATION OF AIR the movement or circulation of fresh air **2** MEANS OF SUPPLYING FRESH AIR the means of supplying fresh air to an enclosed space, e.g. an opening or equipment installed in a building **3** PUBLIC DISCUSSION the public discussion or examination of a particular issue

ventilator /vénti laytər/ *n* **1** a device that circulates fresh air in an enclosed space **2** a machine that keeps air moving in and out of the lungs of a patient who cannot breathe normally

ventilatory /véntilətəri, -laytəri/ *adj* relating to or used for breathing or for oxygenating the blood

ventr- *prefix* = **ventro-** (*before vowels*)

ventrad /vén trad/ *adv* towards the ventral surface or side

ventral /véntrəl/ *adj* **1** OF LOWER BODY AT FRONT located on or affecting the lower surface of an animal's body, or the front of the human body **2** OF OR CLOSE TO ABDOMEN relating to or situated in, on, or near the abdomen **3** FACING AXIS describes the upper side of a leaf or other surface that faces towards the stem ■ *n* ZOOL = **ventral fin** [Mid-18C. < Latin *ventr-* 'stomach, abdomen'.] —**ventrally** *adv*

ventral fin, ventral *n* a fin on the underside of a fish, especially a pelvic fin or anal fin. ◊ **dorsal fin**

ventral root *n* the spinal nerve root emerging from the lower surface of the spinal cord in animals and the front surface in humans and in mammals, consisting of motor nerve fibres

ventricle /véntrik'l/ *n* **1** HEART CHAMBER either of the two lower chambers of the heart that receive blood from the upper chambers (**atria**) and pump it into the arteries by contraction of their thick muscular walls **2** BRAIN CAVITY any cavity in the brain that is an enlargement of the central canal of the spinal cord and contains cerebrospinal fluid **3** HOLLOW IN BODY PART a small cavity or chamber in the body or in an organ [14C. < Latin *ventriculus* (see VENTRICULUS).]

ventricose /véntrikōss/ *adj* **1** describes a body part or plant part that is swollen, distended, or protruding on one side **2** corpulent and fleshy, especially around the middle of the body (*formal*) [Mid-18C. < modern Latin *ventricosus* < Latin *venter* 'belly, abdomen'.] —**ventricosity** /véntri kóssəti/ *n*

ventricular /ven tríkyŏŏlər/ *adj* involving, affecting, or relating to a ventricle or a ventriculus

ventricular fibrillation *n* an often fatal heartbeat irregularity in which the muscle fibres of the ventricles work without coordination, resulting in loss of effective pumping action of the heart

ventriculus /ven tríkyŏŏləss/ (*plural* **-li** /-lī/) *n* **1** the part of an insect's gut where digestion takes place **2** the part of a bird's stomach where digestion takes place [Early 18C. < Latin, 'little stomach' < *venter* 'stomach, abdomen'.]

ventriloquise *vi* = **ventriloquize**

ventriloquism /ven trílləkwizəm/, **ventriloquy** /-trílləkwi/ *n* the art or skill of producing vocal sounds that seem to come from somewhere other than the speaker [Late 18C. < modern Latin *ventriloquium* 'speaking from the stomach' < Latin *venter* 'stomach, abdomen' + *loqui* 'speak'.] —**ventriloquial** /véntri lṓkwi əl/ *adj* —**ventriloquially** *adv*

ventriloquist /ven trílləkwist/ *n* a person who performs ventriloquism, especially a performer who makes a puppet or doll appear to speak —**ventriloquistic** /ven trillə kwístik/ *adj* —**ventriloquistically** *adv*

ventriloquize /ven trillə kwīz/ (**-quizes, -quizing, -quized**), **ventriloquise** (**-quises, -quising, -quised**) *vi* to produce vocal sounds that seem to come from something other than the speaker

ventriloquy *n* = **ventriloquism**

Ventris /véntriss/, **Michael** (1922–56) British linguist

ventro- *prefix* ventral, having to do with the stomach or abdomen ○ *ventromedial* [< Latin *venter* 'stomach, abdomen']

ventrodorsal /véntrō dáwrss'l/ *adj* ANAT = **dorsoventral** *adj.* 2 —**ventrodorsally** *adv*

ventrolateral /véntrō láttərəl/ *adj* relating to or extending between the ventral and lateral surfaces of something such as an animal or organ —**ventrolaterally** *adv*

ventromedial /véntrō meédi əl/ *adj* located near or facing the middle of a ventral surface on something such as an animal or organ —**ventromedially** *adv*

venture /vénchər/ *n* **1 RISKY PROJECT** a risky or daring undertaking that has no guarantee of success **2 NEW BUSINESS ENTERPRISE** a business enterprise that involves risk but could lead to profit **3 MONEY RISKED** the money or property risked in a business venture ■ *v* (**-tures, -turing, -tured**) **1** *vi* **MAKE DANGEROUS TRIP** to make a trip that is unpleasant or dangerous ○ *I ventured out into the storm to close the barn doors.* **2** *vt* **RISK DANGERS** to undertake the risks or dangers of a particular task or project **3** *vt* **MAKE SUGGESTION** to offer or express something tentatively at the risk of being contradicted, embarrassed, or ignored **4** *vi* **DARE TO DO** to presume or dare to do something **5** *vt* **PUT MONEY AT RISK** to expose money or property to risk by committing it to a particular project [15C. Shortening of ADVENTURE.] —**venturer** *n*

venture capital *n* money used for investment in projects that involve a high risk but offer the possibility of large profits —**venture capitalist** *n*

Venture Scout /vénchər skowt/, **Venturer** /vénchərər/ *n* a young person aged between 16 and 20 who is a member of the senior branch of the Scouts

venturesome /vénchərssəm/ *adj* (*formal*) **1** willing to take risks or have new experiences **2** involving risk or danger —**venturesomely** *adv* —**venturesomeness** *n*

venturi /ven tyŏŏri/ *n* a constriction in a tube designed to cause a pressure drop when a liquid or gas flows through it [Late 19C. After Giovanni Battista *Venturi* (1746–1822), Italian physicist.]

Venturi /ven tyŏŏri/, **Robert** (*b.* 1925) US architect

venturi tube, **Venturi tube** *n* a tube containing a venturi, that is placed in a fluid to measure its rate of flow

venturous /vénchərəss/ *adj* = **venturesome** *adj.* 1 —**venturously** *adv* —**venturousness** *n*

venue /vénnyoo/ *n* **1 SCENE** a scene or setting in which something takes place **2 PLACE WHERE EVENT IS HELD** a place where an event such as a sports competition or a concert is held, especially one where events are often held **3 SCENE OF CRIME** the place in which a crime takes place or a cause of action arises **4 PLACE OF TRIAL** a county or other area from which a jury is selected and in which a trial is held **5 STATEMENT** a statement that a case is being brought to the proper court or authority [Mid-16C. < Old French, past participle of *venir* 'come' < Latin *venire*.]

venule /vénnyool/ *n* **1** a small blood vessel, especially one that transfers blood from the capillaries to the veins **2** a small branching vein in a leaf or an insect's wing [Mid-19C. < Latin *venula* 'small vein' < *vena* 'vein'.] —**venular** *adj*

Venus /veénəss/ *n* **1** in Roman mythology, the goddess of love and beauty. Greek equivalent **Aphrodite** **2** the fourth smallest planet in the solar system and the second planet from the Sun. See table at **planet** [Pre-12C. < Latin, < *venus* 'love, desire'.] —**Venusian** /və nyóozi ən/ *adj, n*

Venus flytrap *n* PLANTS = **Venus's flytrap**

Venushair *n* MARINE BIOL = **Venus's-hair**

Venus's flower basket *n* a deep-sea sponge with a skeleton of glassy slender pointed structures (**spicules**) that intersect to form a geometrically patterned surface. Native to: W Pacific and Indian oceans. Genus: *Euplectella*.

Venus's flytrap, **Venus flytrap** *n* an insect-eating plant that has leaves ending in hinged lobes that spring shut, entrapping the insect. Native to: North and South Carolina. *Dionaea muscipula*.

Venus's girdle *n* a marine animal (**ctenophore**) that lives in warm seas and has a long virtually transparent belt-shaped body with rows of cilia along the top and bottom edges. *Cestum veneris*.

Venus's-hair /veénəss hair/, **Venushair** *n* a delicate fan-shaped fern, a type of maidenhair fern, that is widely grown as an ornamental plant. Native to: S United States and tropical America. *Adiantium capillus-veneris*.

Venus shell *n* a common marine mollusc that has a hinged shell with rounded ribbed patterning on it. Family: Veneridae.

Venus's-looking-glass *n* an annual plant with hairy oval leaves that grows on cultivated and bare land. Flowers: purple. Native to: Europe, Asia, North Africa. *Legousia hybrida*.

Veps /veps/ (*plural* **Veps**) *n* **1** a Uralic language of the Finno-Ugric group spoken in NW Russia **2** a member of a Finnic people of NW Russia [Mid-19C. Via Russian < Veps *Vepsa* 'the Veps people'.] —**Veps** *adj*

ver. *abbr* **1** verse **2** version

veracity /və rássəti/ (*plural* **-ties**) *n* **1 TRUTH** the truth, accuracy, or precision of something ○ *They questioned the veracity of our claims.* **2 TRUTHFULNESS** the truthfulness or honesty of a person **3 TRUE STATEMENT** a truth or true statement [Early 17C. Directly or via French < medieval Latin *veracitas* < Latin *verax* 'truthful' < *verus* 'true'.] —**veracious** /və ráyshəss/ *adj* —**veraciously** *adv* —**veraciousness** *n*

Veracruz /veérə krooz, vérrə-/ city in E Mexico, on the Gulf of Mexico. Population: 6,856,415 (1997 estimate).

veranda /və rándə/, **verandah** *n* **1** a porch, usually roofed and sometimes partly enclosed, that extends along an outside wall of a building **2** *ANZ* a canopy sheltering a walkway along a shopping street [Early 18C. Via Hindi *varaṇḍā* < Portuguese *varanda* 'railing, balcony'.] —**verandaed** *adj*

verapamil /vi ráppəmil/ *n* a synthetic compound that inhibits the movement of calcium ions across membranes. Use: treatment of angina pectoris, hypertension, irregular heartbeat. [Mid-20C. < *v(al)er(ic)* + *am(ino-)* + *(nitr)il(e)* (with inserted 'p'), its chemical name.]

veratridine /vi ráttri deen/ *n* $C_{36}H_{51}NO_{11}$ a poisonous yellowish-white substance obtained from sabadilla seeds. Use: insecticides. [Early 20C. < Latin *veratrum* 'hellebore'.]

veratrine /vérrə treen, -trin/, **veratrin** *n* a poisonous mixture of alkaloids including veratridine. Use: formerly, to relieve inflammation. [Early 19C. < Latin *veratrum* 'hellebore'.]

verb /vurb/ *n* **1** a word used to show that an action is taking place, or to indicate the existence of a state or condition, or the part of speech to which such a word belongs **2** the part of a clause or sentence that includes the verb but excludes the subject of the verb [14C. Via Old French < Latin *verbum* 'word'.]

verbal /vúrb'l/ *adj* **1 USING WORDS RATHER THAN PICTURES** expressed in or using words or language, especially as opposed to pictorial representation ○ *a verbal picture of the scene outside* **2 USING WORDS RATHER THAN ACTION** relating to or consisting of words rather than physical action or confrontation ○ *verbal protest* **3 ORAL RATHER THAN WRITTEN** relating to or consisting of spoken rather than written words ○ *They made a verbal agreement.* **4 USING WORDS WITHOUT MEANING** using words without conveying meaning or making any meaningful distinctions **5 INVOLVING SKILL WITH WORDS** involving skill in the use and understanding of words and language ○ *verbal dexterity* **6 RELATING TO VERBS** derived from or relating to a verb, or to verbs in general **7 FORMING VERBS** used to form verbs **8 VERBATIM** corresponding word for word (*archaic*) ■ *n* **1 WORD FORMED FROM VERB** a word formed from a verb, especially one used as a noun or an adjective, such as a gerund or participle **2 ADMISSION OF GUILT** an admission of guilt upon being arrested for a crime (*slang*) ■ *vt* (**-bals, -balling, -balled**) **MAKE SOMEBODY SOUND GUILTY** to make somebody sound guilty during police testimony in court by referring to an admission of guilt allegedly given earlier (*slang*) [15C. Via Old French < late Latin *verbalis* < Latin *verbum* 'word'.] —**verbally** *adv*

SYNONYMS ***verbal, spoken, oral***
CORE MEANING: expressed in words
verbal using words, especially spoken words, rather than pictures or physical action; **spoken** expressed with the voice; **oral** expressed in spoken form rather than in writing.

verbal adjective *n* a verb participle ending in -ing or -ed that is used as an adjective

verbalise *vti* = **verbalize**

verbalism /vúrbəlizəm/ *n* **1 VERBAL EXPRESSION** something expressed in words **2 LONG-WINDED EXPRESSION** a wordy expression that has little meaning or relevance **3 USE OF TOO MANY WORDS** the uncritical or undisciplined use of words, especially without any attempt to analyse their meaning or value **4** *US* **WAY SOMETHING IS EXPRESSED** the manner in which something is expressed or communicated

verbalist /vúrbəlist/ *n* **1** a skilled user of words and language **2** a person who emphasizes words or language rather than, e.g. facts, feelings, or ideas —**verbalistic** /vúrbə lístik/ *adj*

verbalize /vúrbə līz/ (**-izes, -izing, -ized**), **verbalise** (**-balises, -balising, -balised**) *v* **1** *vt* **EXPRESS SOMETHING IN WORDS** to express feelings, thoughts, or ideas in words **2** *vt* **MAKE WORD INTO VERB** to make a word that is another part of speech, e.g. a noun or adjective, into a verb **3** *vi* **BE VERBOSE** to speak or write in a way that uses too many words —**verbalization** *n* —**verbalizer** *n*

verbal noun *n* a form of a verb ending in '-ing' used as a noun, e.g. 'dancing' in 'he teaches dancing'

verbatim /vur báytim/ *adj* corresponding word for word with something else ■ *adv* repeated, written down, or copied word for word [15C. < medieval Latin, < Latin *verbum* 'word'.]

verbena /vur beénə/ *n* a common ornamental herbaceous plant. Flowers: colourful, in clusters. Native to: North and South America. Genus: *Verbena*. [Mid-16C. < Latin.]

verbiage /vúrbi ij/ *n* **1** an excess of words, especially in writing or speech with little or no meaning **2** the style of language in which something is expressed ○ *bureaucratic verbiage explaining the regulations* [Early 18C. < French, < Latin *verbum* 'word'.]

verbid /vúrbid/ *n* LING = **verbal** *n.* 1

verbigerate /vur bíjji rayt/ (**-ates, -ating, -ated**) *vi* to repeat the same words or phrases obsessively as a symptom of a psychiatric disorder [Late 19C. < Latin *verbigerat-*, past participle of *verbigerare* 'chat' < *verbum* 'word' + *gerare* 'keep carrying on'.] —**verbigeration** /vur bíjjə ráysh'n/ *n*

verbose /vur bṓss/ *adj* expressed in or using language that is too long-winded or complicated [Late 17C. < Latin *verbosus* < *verbum* 'word'.] —**verbosely** *adv* —**verboseness** *n*

SYNONYMS See ***wordy***.

verboten /fər bṓt'n, vər-/ *adj* forbidden or prohibited [Early 20C. < German.]

verb phrase *n* a grammatical construction consisting of a verb and any direct and indirect objects and modifiers linked to it, but not including the subject of the verb

Vercingetorix /vúrssin jéttəriks/ (*d.* 46 BC) Gaulish leader

verdant /vúrd'nt/ *adj* **1 WITH LUSH GREEN GROWTH** green with vegetation or foliage **2 GREEN** green in colour **3 NAIVE** lacking experience or sophistication (*literary*) [Late 16C.

< Old French *verdeant* 'becoming green' < Latin *viridis* 'green'.] —**verdancy** *n* —**verdantly** *adv*

verd antique /vúrd an teék/, **verde antique** *n* **1** a dark-green mottled or veined variety of serpentine marble that is used in decoration **2** a green marble or stone that resembles verd antique **3** CHEM = **verdigris** *n*. 1 [< obsolete French, 'antique green']

Verde, Cape /vurd/ **1** ◆ **Cape Vert 2** ◆ **Cape Verde**

verderer /vúrdərər/ *n* a judicial official in charge of maintaining the royal forests in medieval England [Mid-16C. < Anglo-Norman, < Latin *viridis* 'green'.]

Verdi /váirdi/, **Giuseppe** (1813–1901) Italian composer

verdict /vúrdikt/ *n* **1** the finding of a jury on the matter that has been submitted to it in a trial **2** a judgment, opinion, or conclusion that is expressed about something [13C. < Anglo-Norman *verdit* 'true speech' < *ver* 'true' + *dit* 'speech, saying'.]

verdigris /vúrdi gree, -greess/ *n* **1** a green or greenish-blue deposit (**patina**) of copper carbonates on copper, brass, and bronze that is caused by atmospheric corrosion **2** a green or greenish-blue poisonous powder formed by the action of acetic acid on copper and consisting of one or more basic copper acetates. Use: paint pigment, fungicide. [14C. < Old French *vert de Grece* 'green of Greece'.]

verditer /vúrditər/ *n* either of two basic copper carbonates, of which one is blue and the other green. Use: pigments. [Early 16C. < Old French *verd de terre* 'green of the earth'.]

Verdun /vur dún/ town in NE France, site of one of the longest and bloodiest battles of World War I. Population: 19,624 (1999).

verdure /vúrjər/ *n* **1** VIVID GREEN OF PLANTS the green colour associated with lush vegetation **2** VEGETATION extremely lush vegetation **3** FRESHNESS a fresh, healthy, or flourishing condition (*literary*) [14C. < French, < Latin *viridis* 'green'.] —**verdured** *adj* —**verdureless** *adj* —**verdurous** *adj* —**verdurousness** *n*

Vereeniging /fə reéniking/ city in NE South Africa. Population: 71,255 (1991).

verge[1] /vurj/ *n* **1** POINT BEYOND WHICH SOMETHING HAPPENS the point beyond which something happens or begins ○ *He was on the verge of tears.* **2** BOUNDARY a line, belt, or strip that acts as a boundary or edge **3** EDGE the edge, rim, or margin of something **4** ROADSIDE BORDER a narrow border that runs alongside a road **5** ROOF EDGE the edge of a sloping roof where it extends beyond the gable **6** CLOCK SPINDLE the spindle of a balance wheel in early clock and watch mechanisms **7** AREA AROUND ROYAL COURT an area around the English royal court that was under the jurisdiction of the Lord High Steward **8** ROD HELD BY TENANT a rod held by a feudal tenant when swearing an oath of loyalty to his or her lord **9** ROD AS SYMBOL OF OFFICE a rod or staff carried as a symbol of authority or an emblem of office [14C. Via French, 'rod' (symbolizing office) < Latin *virga*.]

verge on, verge upon *vt* **1** to border on or be on the edge of a particular place or area ○ *Their property verged on ours.* **2** to approach or come close to a particular quality or condition ○ *The whole performance verged on the ridiculous.*

verge[2] /vurj/ (**verges, verging, verged**) *vi* **1** MOVE IN PARTICULAR DIRECTION to move or lean in a particular direction or towards a certain condition **2** CHANGE GRADUALLY to change gradually from one thing to another (*literary*) **3** SINK FROM VIEW to descend towards the horizon (*literary*) [Early 17C. < Latin *vergere* 'to bend, incline'.]

vergence /vúrjənss/ *n* the inward or outward turning of both eyes when focusing on a near or distant object [Early 20C. Back-formation < CONVERGENCE and DIVERGENCE.]

verger /vúrjər/ *n* **1** a church official who acts as a caretaker and attendant and looks after the inside of a church **2** a church official in the Church of England who carries the staff of office (**verge**) in front of somebody such as a bishop or dean during ceremonies and processions [15C. < Anglo-Norman, < Old French *verge* 'rod of office' (see VERGE[1]).]

Vergil = **Virgil**

verglas /váir glaa/ *n* a thin coating of ice found on rock or exposed ground [Early 19C. < French, < *verre* 'glass' + *glas* 'ice'.]

veridical /və ríddik'l/ *adj* (*formal*) **1** telling the truth **2** corresponding to facts or to reality, and therefore genuine or real [Mid-17C. < Latin *veridicus* 'truth-speaking' < *verus* 'true' + *dicere* 'say'.] —**veridicality** /və ríddi kálləti/ *n* —**veridically** *adv*

verification /vérrifi káysh'n/ *n* **1** ESTABLISHMENT OF TRUTH the establishment of the truth or correctness of something by investigation or evidence **2** EVIDENCE the evidence that proves something true or correct **3** CONFIRMATION OF PROCEDURES in international law, the process of confirming that procedures laid down in an agreement such as a weapons limitation treaty are being followed **4** AFFIDAVIT in law, an affidavit swearing to the accuracy of a pleading **5** CONFIRMATORY EVIDENCE evidence or testimony that confirms something —**verificative** /vérrifi kaytiv/ *adj*

verificationism /vérrifi káysh'nizəm/ *n* the view that every meaningful proposition is capable of being shown to be true or false

verification principle *n* the principle that a proposition or sentence is meaningful only if it is possible to establish whether it is true or false by experience or observation

verify /vérri fī/ (**-fies, -fying, -fied**) *vt* **1** PROVE to prove that something is true **2** CHECK WHETHER SOMETHING IS TRUE to check whether or not something is true by examination, investigation, or comparison **3** SWEAR SOMETHING UNDER OATH in law, to swear or affirm under oath that something is true **4** ATTEST TO TRUTH BY AFFIDAVIT in law, to support the truth of a pleading by affidavit [14C. Via French *verifier* < medieval Latin *verificare* 'make true' < Latin *verus* 'true' + *facere* 'make'.] —**verifiability** /vérri fī ə bíllәti/ *n* —**verifiable** *adj* —**verifiably** *adv* —**verifier** /vérri fī ər/ *n*

verily /vérrili/ *adv* in truth (*archaic*) ○ *Verily, he has admitted it.* [13C. < VERY 'true'.]

verisimilar /vérri símmilər/ *adj* appearing to be true or real (*archaic*) [Late 17C. < Latin *verisimilis* 'like the truth' < *verus* 'true' + *similis* 'like'.] —**verisimilarly** *adv*

verisimilitude /vérrissi mílli tyood/ *n* (*formal*) **1** the appearance of being true or real **2** something that only appears to be true or real, e.g. a statement that is not supported by evidence [Early 17C. < Latin *verisimilitudo* < *verisimilis* (see VERISIMILAR).] —**verisimilitudinous** /vérrissi mílli tyoódinəss/ *adj*

verism /veérizəm/ *n* strict realism or naturalism in art and literature [Late 19C. < Latin *verus* or Italian *vero* 'true'.] —**verist** *n* —**veristic** /veer rístik/ *adj*

verismo /ve rízmō/ *n* a late 19th-century movement in Italian opera that advocated the use of themes drawn from real life and naturalistic portrayal of characters and events [Early 20C. < Italian, 'verism'.]

veritable /vérritəb'l/ *adj* **1** used to emphasize a figurative concept ○ *the business is a veritable gold mine* **2** true as a declaration or statement (*archaic*) [15C. < French, < Latin *veritas* 'truth' (see VERITY).] —**veritableness** *n* —**veritably** *adv*

verity /vérrəti/ (*plural* **-ties**) *n* (*formal*) **1** the quality of being true or real **2** something that is true, especially a statement or principle that is accepted as a fact [14C. Via French < Latin *veritas* < *verus* 'true'.]

verjuice /vúr jooss/ *n* **1** an acid liquid made from crab apples or other sour or unripe fruit. Use: formerly, instead of vinegar. **2** sourness of temper, attitude, or expression [14C. < Old French *vertjus* < *verd* 'green' + *jus* 'juice'.]

Verlaine /vair lén/, **Paul** (1844–96) French poet

Vermeer /vər meér, -máir/, **Jan** (1632–75) Dutch artist

vermeil /vúr mayl/ *n* **1** gilded silver, bronze, or copper **2** the colour vermilion (*literary*) [14C. Via Old French < late Latin *vermiculus*, kermes insect from which red dye was made (see VERMICULAR).]

vermi- *prefix* worm ○ *vermivorous* [< Latin *vermis* 'worm' < Indo-European]

vermicelli /vúrmi chélli/ *n* **1** pasta in long fine threads **2** short thin strands of chocolate that are used to decorate cakes [Mid-17C. < Italian, 'little worms' < Latin *vermis* 'worm'.]

vermicide /vúrmi sīd/ *n* **1** a substance used to kill worms **2** a chemical substance that expels parasitic worms from the small intestines —**vermicidal** /vúrmi sīd'l/ *adj*

vermicomposter /vúrmi kompostər/ *n* a container in which specially bred worms are used to convert organic matter into compost

vermicomposting *n* GARDENING = **vermiculture**

vermicular /vur míkyoolər/ *adj* **1** in wavy lines like the movements, shape, or tracks of worms **2** relating to worms [Late 17C. < medieval Latin *vermicularis* < Latin *vermiculis* 'little worm' < *vermis* 'worm'.] —**vermicularly** *adv*

vermiculate /vur míkyoo layt/ *vt* (**-lates, -lating, -lated**) DECORATE SOMETHING WITH WAVY LINES to decorate something with wavy lines or patterns (*formal*) ■ *adj* **1** WITH WAVY LINES with wavy lines like the movements, shape, or tracks of a worm **2** SINUOUS with many twists and turns (*formal*) **3** LOOKING WORM-EATEN with a worm-eaten appearance (*literary*) [Early 17C. < Latin *vermiculat-*, past participle of *vermiculari* 'be full of worms' < *vermiculus* (see VERMICULAR).]

vermiculation /vur míkyoo láysh'n/ *n* **1** MOVEMENT IN WAVES movement in waves, e.g. the muscular contractions of the intestines (**peristalsis**) **2** WAVY DECORATION decorative wavy lines, patterns, or carvings **3** WORM INFESTATION infestation by worms, or the resulting worm-eaten condition

vermiculite /vur míkyoo līt/ *n* a hydrous silicate of aluminium, magnesium, or iron. Source: altered basic rocks. Use: insulation, lubricant, horticulture. [Early 19C. < Latin *vermiculus* 'little worm' (see VERMICULAR), because of the way flakes of it expand and writhe in long shapes when heated.]

vermiculture /vúrmi kulchər/ *n* the use of specially bred worms to convert organic matter into compost

vermiform /vúrmi fawrm/ *adj* resembling a worm in shape

vermiform appendix, vermiform process *n* ANAT = **appendix** *n*. 1

vermifuge /vúrmi fyooj/ *n* a drug or other substance that causes worms or other parasites to be expelled from the intestines —**vermifugal** /vúrmi fyoóg'l/ *adj*

vermilion /vər mílli ən/, **vermillion** *n* **1** a bright red pigment made from mercuric sulphide or synthetically **2** a bright red colour [13C. < Old French *vermeillon* < *vermeil* (see VERMEIL).] —**vermilion** *adj*

vermin /vúrmin/ (*plural* **-min**) *n* **1** small animals or insects that harm people, livestock, property, or crops and are difficult to control, e.g. rats, weasels, fleas, or cockroaches **2** an offensive term for a person or group considered to be extremely unpleasant or undesirable [13C. Via Old French < assumed Vulgar Latin *verminum* 'noxious life forms' < Latin *vermis* 'worm'.]

vermination /vúrmi náysh'n/ *n* the spreading of or infestation with vermin, especially parasites

verminous /vúrminəss/ *adj* **1** OF OR WITH VERMIN relating to or infested with vermin **2** CAUSED BY VERMIN OR WORMS caused by vermin or parasitic worms **3** DISGUSTING extremely unpleasant or offensive —**verminously** *adv* —**verminousness** *n*

vermis /vúrmiss/ *n* the middle lobe of the brain that connects the two hemispheres of the cerebellum [Late 19C. < Latin, 'worm'.]

Vermont /və mónt/ state in the NE United States. Capital: Montpelier. Population: 588,978 (1997). Area: 24,903 sq. km/9,615 sq. mi. —**Vermonter** *n*

vermouth /vúrməth, vər moóth/ *n* a wine flavoured with aromatic herbs [Early 19C. Via French < German *Wermut* 'wormwood', with which it was originally flavoured.]

vernacular /vər nákyoolər/ *n* **1** ORDINARY LANGUAGE the everyday language of the people in a specific country or region, as opposed to official or formal language **2** SPOKEN LANGUAGE the common spoken language of a people as opposed to formal written or literary language **3** LANGUAGE OF PARTICULAR GROUP the distinctive vocabulary or language of a specific profession, group, or class **4** COMMON NAME a common name of a plant, animal, or other organism as opposed to its scientific name **5** ORDINARY BUILDING STYLE the architecture of a particular place or people, especially the architectural style that is used for ordinary houses as opposed to large official or commercial buildings [Early 17C. < Latin *vernaculus* 'native' < *verna* 'native-born slave'.] —**vernacular** *adj* —**vernacularly** *adv*

vernacularise *vt* = **vernacularize**

vernacularism /vər nákyoolərizəm/ *n* **1** a word or phrase from the everyday language of the people in a particular country or region, as opposed to official or formal language **2** the use of everyday language, as opposed to official or formal language

vernacularize /vər nákyŏŏlə rīz/ (**-izes, -izing, -ized**), **vernacularise** (**-ises, -ising, -ised**) *vt* to make a word or phrase part of ordinary everyday language

vernal /vúrn'l/ *adj* **1** appearing or happening in the season of spring **2** having the freshness or energy associated with being young (*literary*) [Mid-16C. < Latin *vernalis* < *vernus* 'of the spring' < *ver* 'spring'.]

vernal equinox *n* **1** the time when the sun crosses the celestial equator and day and night are of equal length, marking the beginning of spring **2** the point on the celestial sphere where the path of the sun (**ecliptic**) crosses the celestial equator, in the constellation Pisces

vernal grass *n* an early-blooming grass native to Europe and Asia that smells like new-mown hay when crushed. Genus: *Anthoxanthum*.

vernalize /vúrnə līz/ (**-izes, -izing, -ized**), **vernalise** (**-ises, -ising, -ised**) *vt* to expose plant seeds or seedlings to artificially cold temperatures in order to promote development and flowering —**vernalization** *n*

vernation /vur náysh'n/ *n* the way that young leaves are arranged in a bud [Late 18C. < modern Latin *vernation-* < Latin *vernare* 'grow in the spring' < *vernus* (see VERNAL).]

Verne /vurn/, **Jules** (1828–1905) French writer

vernicle /vúrnik'l/ *n* CHR = **veronica**² [14C. < Old French *veronicle*, variant of *veronique* < medieval Latin *veronica* (see VERONICA²).]

vernier /vúrni ər/ *n* **1 SMALL SCALE FOR PRECISE READINGS** a small movable graduated scale parallel to a larger graduated scale, used to obtain smaller or more precise readings from the main scale **2 DEVICE FOR MAKING FINE ADJUSTMENTS** an auxiliary device used to make fine adjustments to a precision instrument ■ *adj* **WITH A VERNIER** relating to or fitted with a vernier [Mid-18C. After Pierre *Vernier* (1580–1637), French mathematician.]

vernier rocket *n* AEROSP = **thruster** *n*. 1 [Mid-20C. See VERNIER.]

vernissage /vúrni saázh/ *n* a private showing or preview before the public opening of an art exhibition [Early 20C. < French, 'varnishing', because originally the day before a public exhibition, when exhibitors varnished paintings after they were in place.]

Vernon /vúrnən/ city in S British Columbia, Canada. Population: 31,817 (1996).

Verny /vúrni/ former name for **Almaty** (1855–1921)

Verona /və rṓnə/ capital of Verona Province, Veneto Region, N Italy. Population: 810,686 (1997 estimate). —**Veronese** /vérrō neéz, vérrō náyzi/ *n, adj*

Veronese /vérrō náyzi/, **Paolo** (1528–88) Italian artist. Born **Paolo Caliari**

veronica¹ /və rónnikə/ *n* a perennial or annual plant or shrub of the figwort family, e.g. the speedwell. Flowers: small, typically blue, in clusters. Genus: *Veronica*. [Early 16C. < modern Latin.]

veronica² /və rónnikə/ *n* **1 IMPRESSION OF JESUS CHRIST'S FACE** the impression of Jesus Christ's face believed by some to have been miraculously left on the cloth with which Saint Veronica wiped it on his way to his crucifixion **2 CLOTH THAT WIPED JESUS CHRIST'S FACE** the cloth with which Saint Veronica is said to have wiped Jesus Christ's face on his way to his crucifixion **3 CLOTH WITH JESUS CHRIST'S FACE** a cloth bearing a representation of Jesus Christ's face, sometimes worn by pilgrims [Late 17C. < medieval Latin, perhaps alteration (after the saint Veronica) of *vera iconica* 'true image'.]

veronica³ /və rónnikə/ *n* a move in bullfighting in which the bullfighter stands in place and slowly swings the cape away from the bull as it charges [Mid-19C. < Spanish *verónica*, after Saint *Veronica*; from the gesture involved in wiping Jesus Christ's face.]

verruca /və rόόkə/ (*plural* **-cas** *or* **-cae** /və rόόsee, -rόόkee/) *n* **1** a wart that grows on the foot, usually on the sole **2** a wart-shaped growth or projection on a plant or the skin of an animal [Mid-16C. < Latin, 'wart'.]

verrucose /vérrookōss/, **verrucous** /vérrookəss, ve rόόkəss/ *adj* covered with warts or similar growths or projections [Late 17C. < Latin *verrucosus* < *verruca* 'wart'.] —**verrucosity** /vérroo kóssəti/ *n*

vers *abbr* versed sine

Versailles /vair sī/ *n* a large and elaborately decorated palace near Paris, built for Louis XIV in the mid-17th century. It is now a museum.

versant /vúrss'nt/ *n* **1** the slope of a mountain or mountain range **2** the slope of a particular region [Mid-19C. < French, present participle of *verser* 'turn over' < Latin *versare* (see VERSATILE).]

versatile /vúrssə tīl/ *adj* **1 WITH MANY USES** able or meant to be used in many different ways **2 MOVING EASILY BETWEEN TASKS** able to move easily from one subject, task, or skill to another **3 CHANGEABLE** subject to rapid or unpredictable change **4 FREE-MOVING** describes a body part or joint that can turn or move freely in more than one direction, e.g. an insect's antenna **5 ATTACHED LOOSELY** describes an anther that is attached to the filament by a small area, allowing it to move more freely [Early 17C. < Latin *versatilis* < *versat-*, past participle of *versare* 'keep turning or changing' < *vertere* 'to turn'.] —**versatilely** *adv* —**versatility** /vúrssə tílləti/ *n*

vers de société /váir də sóssyə táy/ *n* verse or poetry written in a light witty sophisticated style [< French, 'society verse']

verse /vurss/ *n* **1 GROUP OF SONG OR POEM LINES** a section of a poem or song consisting of a number of lines arranged together to form a single unit **2 NUMBERED DIVISION OF BIBLE CHAPTER** a numbered subdivision into which each chapter of the Bible is divided **3 POETRY** poetry as opposed to prose **4 BODY OF POETRY** a body of poetry, e.g. by a single author or from a particular country or period ○ *an anthology of 19th-century verse* **5 KIND OF POETRY** a particular form of poetry **6 BAD POETRY** poetry that is trivial in content or inferior in quality ○ *It's not poetry at all, it's just verse.* **7 SHORT POEM** a poem, especially a short one **8 LINE OF A POEM** a single line of a poem, arranged rhythmically in metrical feet ■ *vt* (**verses, versing, versed**) **VERSIFY PROSE CONTENT** to turn something from prose into poetry (*archaic*) [Pre-12C. Directly and via Old French *vers* < Latin *versus* 'turning (of a plough), furrow, line' < *vertere* 'to turn'.]

versed /vurst/ *n* very knowledgeable about or skilled in something ○ *well versed in the art of flattery* [Early 17C. Directly or via French *versé* < Latin *versatus*, past participle of *versari* 'occupy yourself with' < *versare* (see VERSATILE).]

versed cosine *n* a trigonometric function equal to one minus the sine of the specified angle [After VERSED SINE]

versed sine *n* a trigonometric function equal to one minus the cosine of the specified angle [Translation of modern Latin *sinus versus* 'turned sine']

verset /vúrssit/ *n* a short verse, especially one from a sacred book [Early 17C. < French, 'short verse' < *vers* 'line' (see VERSE).]

versicle /vúrssik'l/ *n* **1** a short sentence spoken or chanted by the minister during a liturgical service and responded to by the congregation or choir **2** a short verse (*literary or archaic*) [14C. < Latin *versiculus* 'short verse' < *versus* 'line' (see VERSE).] —**versicular** /vur síkyŏŏlər/ *adj*

versicolor *adj* US = **versicolour**

versicolour /vúrssi kullər/, **versicoloured** /vúrssi kullərd/ *adj* **1** having various colours **2** varying or changing in colour [Early 17C. < Latin *versicolor* < *versus*, past participle of *vertere* 'turn, change', + *color* 'colour'.]

versification /vúrssifi káysh'n/ *n* **1 ART OF VERSE-WRITING** the art or practice of writing verse **2 METRICAL FORM** the metrical form or structure of a poem **3 TURNING PROSE INTO VERSE** the conversion of prose into verse, or the recounting of something in verse **4 VERSION IN POETRY** a poetic or metrical version of a prose work

versify /vúrssi fī/ (**-fies, -fying, -fied**) *v* **1** *vt* **CHANGE PROSE INTO POETRY** to turn prose into verse **2** *vt* **TELL STORY IN POETRY** to recount something in verse **3** *vi* **WRITE POETRY** to compose verse [14C. Via French < Latin *versificare* 'make verses' < *versus* 'line' (see VERSE).] —**versifier** *n*

versine /vúrsīn/ *n* MATH = **versed sine**

version /vúrsh'n, vúrzh'n/ *n* **1 ACCOUNT** an account of something, given from a particular point of view **2 PARTICULAR VARIETY** a particular form or variety of something that is different from others or from the original **3 ADAPTATION** an adaptation of something for another medium, e.g. a book made into a play or film **4 TRANSLATION** a translation of something into another language **5 version, Version BIBLE TRANSLATION** a particular translation of the Bible **6 MANIPULATION OF FOETUS** the manipulation of a foetus to change its position in the womb, e.g. so it can be delivered safely **7 TILTED CONDITION OF ORGAN** a condition in which an internal organ, especially the womb, is abnormally tilted or turned [Late 16C. Via French < Latin *version-* < *vers-*, past participle of *vertere* 'turn'.] —**versional** *adj*

vers libre /váir leébrə/ *n* LITERAT = **free verse** [< French]

verso /vúrssō/ (*plural* **-sos**) *n* **1** the back of a page or other printed sheet. ◊ **recto** *n*. 1 **2** any left-hand page of a book, usually printed with an even page number. ◊ **recto** *n*. 2 **3** COINS = **reverse** *n*. 3 [Mid-19C. < Latin *verso (folio)* '(with the page) turned' < *versus*, past participle of *vertere* 'turn'.]

verst /vurst/ *n* a Russian measure of length equal to 1.07 km/0.66 mi [Mid-16C. Via French *verste* or German *Werst* < Russian *versta* 'line'.]

versus /vúrssəss/ *prep* **1** against, especially in a competition or court case ○ *The United States versus Canada* **2** as opposed to or contrasted with ○ *such considerations as money versus job satisfaction* [15C. < medieval Latin, 'against' < past participle of Latin *vertere* 'turn'.]

vert /vurt/ *n* **1 GREEN COLOUR** in heraldry, the colour green **2 RIGHT TO CUT WOOD OR VEGETATION** formerly, the right to cut living wood or green vegetation in a forest **3 WOOD OR VEGETATION** formerly, living wood or green vegetation in a forest [15C. Via Old French, 'green' < Latin *viridis*.] —**vert** *adj*

Vert, Cape ♦ **Cape Vert**

vert. *abbr* vertical

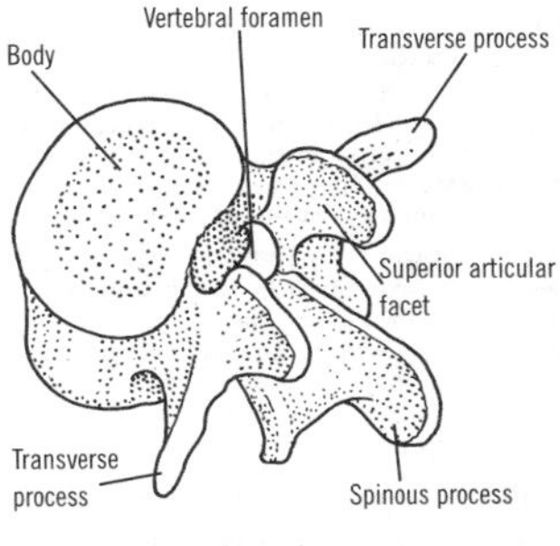

Vertebra

vertebra /vúrtibrə/ (*plural* **-brae** /-bray, -bree/ *or* **-bras**) *n* a bone of the spinal column, typically consisting of a stout body, a bony arch enclosing a hole for the spinal cord, and stubby projections that connect with adjacent bones [Early 17C. < Latin, < *vertere* 'to turn'.] —**vertebral** *adj* —**vertebrally** *adv*

vertebral canal *n* ANAT = **spinal canal**

vertebral column *n* ANAT = **spinal column**

vertebrate /vúrtibrət/ *n* an animal with a segmented spinal column and a well-developed brain such as a mammal, bird, reptile, amphibian, or fish [Early 19C. < Latin *vertebratus* 'having joints' < *vertebra* (see VERTEBRA).] —**vertebrate** *adj*

vertebration /vúrti bráysh'n/ *n* the formation of or division into vertebral segments, or segments resembling vertebrae, during the development of an embryo

vertex /vúrt eks/ (*plural* **-texes** *or* **-tices** /-ti seez/) *n* **1 APEX** the highest point of something **2 TOP OF THE HEAD** the highest point of a body part, especially the top or crown of the head **3 POINT OPPOSITE THE BASE** the point opposite the base of a figure **4 POINT WHERE SIDES OF ANGLE MEET** the point where two sides of a plane figure or an angle intersect **5 POINT WHERE PLANES OF SOLID MEET** the point where three or more planes of a solid figure intersect **6 POINT TOWARDS WHICH STARS MOVE** a point on the celestial sphere towards which or from which a group of stars appears to move [Late 16C. < Latin, 'whirl, spiral of hair at the top of the head' < *vertere* 'to turn'.]

vertical /vúrtik'l/ *adj* **1 AT RIGHT ANGLE TO HORIZON** at a right angle to the horizon **2 UPRIGHT** extending or standing in an upright position, or running straight up or down something such as a piece of paper **3 OVERHEAD** at the vertex or directly overhead **4 INVOLVING ALL STAGES OF PRODUCTION** relating to or involving all the consecutive stages in the production of goods, from design to sale **5 AT THE TOP OF THE HEAD** at or relating to the highest point of a body part, especially the top or crown of the head **6 MADE UP OF MANY LEVELS** involving or made up of successive or many levels ○ *a vertical management structure* ■ *n* **1 SOMETHING VERTICAL** a vertical structure, line, surface, or part **2 VERTICAL POSITION** a position that is upright or at a right angle to the horizon [Mid-16C. Directly or via

French < late Latin *verticalis* 'overhead' < Latin *vertex* (see VERTEX).] —**verticality** /vúrti kállǝti/ *n* —**vertically** *adv*

vertical angle *n* either of the pair of equal angles formed on opposite sides of the point at which two lines intersect

vertical circle *n* a great circle on the celestial sphere whose plane is perpendicular to the horizon and passes through the zenith and the nadir

verticalization /vúrtikǝ lī záysh'n/ *n* the process of making one organization responsible for various stages in a process that were previously overseen by a number of separate organizations

vertical mobility *n* the movement of people or groups in society either upwards or downwards in terms of class or status

vertical stabilizer *n* AEROSP = **fin** *n.* 4

vertices plural of **vertex**

verticil /vúrtissil/ *n* a circular arrangement of similar parts around a central point [Early 18C. < Latin *verticillus* 'whorl of a spindle'.]

verticillate /vur tíssilǝt/ *adj* arranged in whorls, or forming a whorl —**verticillately** *adv*—**verticillation** /vur tíssi láysh'n/ *n*

vertiginous /vur tíjjinǝss/ *adj* **1 DIZZYING** causing dizziness, especially because of being very high or exposed ○ *the mountain's vertiginous summit* **2 SUFFERING FROM VERTIGO** relating to or suffering from the whirling or tilting sensation of vertigo **3 ROTARY** whirling or spinning on an axis **4 FICKLE** tending to change frequently or suddenly —**vertiginously** *adv* —**vertiginousness** *n*

vertigo /vúrtigō/ (*plural* **-tigoes** *or* **-tigos** *or* **-tigines** /vur tíjji neez/) *n* **1** a condition in which somebody feels a sensation of whirling or tilting that causes a loss of balance **2** an instance or episode of vertigo [15C. < Latin (stem *vertigin-*), 'whirling about, giddiness' < *vertere* 'to turn'.]

vertu *n* ARTS = **virtu**

Vertumnus /vur túmnǝss/ *n* the Roman god of gardens

vervain /vúr vayn/ *n* a herbaceous plant that grows wild in temperate regions. Flowers: small, blue, white, or purple. Genus: *Verbena.* [14C. Via French *verveine* < Latin *verbena* 'verbena'.]

verve /vurv/ *n* **1** enthusiasm, energy, or spirit, especially in the expression of artistic ideas **2** lively vigorous spirit [Late 17C. Via French, 'vigour, fanciful expression' < Latin *verba* 'whimsical words', plural of *verbum* 'word'.]

vervet /vúrvit/, **vervet monkey** *n* an African monkey that lives in large groups in savannah woodlands and has a long tail and black face, hands, and feet. *Cercopithecus aethiops.* [Late 19C. < French.]

Verwoerd /fǝr vōōrt/, **Hendrik** (1901–66) Dutch-born South African statesman

very /vérri/ CORE MEANING: an adverb that is used in front of adjectives and adverbs to emphasize their meaning ○ *That is a very, very strong argument.* ○ *Let me very briefly give you some examples.*

1 *adv* **GIVES EMPHASIS** used to give emphasis to adjectives or adverbs that can be graded ○ *I think buying a dog is something we want to be very careful about.* ○ *Someone had copied her style very accurately.* **2** *adj* **EXTREME** indicates an extreme position or extreme point in time ○ *They moved to the very back of the set, smiling at the technicians.* **3** *adj* **RIGHT** exactly the right or appropriate person or thing, or exactly the same person or thing ○ *Hello! The very person I wanted to see!* ○ *He died this very day in 1986.* **4** *adj* **EMPHASIZES IMPORTANCE** used before nouns to emphasize seriousness or importance ○ *An event like this can't help but shake the boxing world to its very foundation.* [13C. Via Old French *verrai* < Latin *verax* 'truthful' < *verus* 'true'.] ◇ **very much so** an emphatic way of saying yes to something or indicating that it is true or correct ○ *'He was a good man, brave and honest'.'Yes, very much so'.* ◇ **very well** indicates that somebody agrees to do something or accepts what somebody has said

very high frequency *n* the radio frequency band between 30 and 300 megahertz, reserved for the transmission of television and FM radio signals

Very light /veéri-/ *n* a coloured flare fired from a pistol, used as a signal [Early 20C. After Edward W. *Very* (1847–1910), US naval officer.]

very low frequency *n* the radio frequency band between 3 and 30 kilohertz

Very pistol /veéri-/ *n* a pistol used for firing coloured flares [Early 20C. See VERY LIGHT.]

Very Reverend *n* the title of a dean and some other religious officials

vesica /véssikǝ/ (*plural* **-cae** /véssi see/) *n* **1** a bladder, especially the urinary bladder (*technical*) **2** a pointed oval shape used in medieval art and sculpture, especially to enclose a figure of Jesus Christ or the Virgin Mary [Mid-17C. < Latin, 'bladder, blister'.]

vesical /véssik'l/ *adj* occurring in or relating to a bladder, especially the urinary bladder ○ *vesical veins*

vesicant /véssikǝnt/, **vesicatory** /véssi kaytǝri/ *n* (*plural* **-ries**) a substance that causes blisters, especially a substance such as mustard gas used in chemical warfare ■ *adj* causing blisters to form

vesicate /véssi kayt/ (**-cates, -cating, -cated**) *vti* to cause or be affected by blisters —**vesication** /véssi káysh'n/ *n*

vesicatory *n* CHEM = **vesicant**

vesicle /véssik'l/ *n* **1 FLUID-FILLED CYST** a small sac or hollow organ in the body, especially one containing fluid **2 FLUID-FILLED BLISTER** a very small blister filled with clear fluid (**serum**) **3 SPHERICAL CAVITY WITHIN A ROCK** a bubble-shaped cavity in an igneous rock, formed by the expansion of gases trapped in lava and often later filled with minerals deposited from percolating solutions **4 CAVITY IN AN AQUATIC PLANT** a cavity filled with air in a seaweed or aquatic plant [Late 16C. Directly or via French *vésicule* < Latin *vesicula* 'small vesica' < *vesica* 'bladder, blister'.]

vesicular /vǝ síkyŏŏlǝr/ *adj* resembling, having, or made up of vesicles —**vesicularly** *adv*

vesiculate *vti* /vǝ síkyŏŏ layt/ (**-lates, -lating, -lated**) to form blisters or vesicles in something, or to become like a vesicle ■ *adj* /vǝ síkyŏŏlǝt/ having or resembling blisters or vesicles —**vesiculation** /vǝ síkyŏŏ láysh'n/ *n*

Vespasian /ve spáyzh'n/ (AD 9–79) Roman emperor (69–79). Born **Titus Flavius Sabinus Vespasianus**

vesper /véspǝr/ *n* **1 vesper, vesper bell BELL RUNG IN THE EVENING** a bell rung in the evening, e.g. to summon worshippers to vespers **2 EVENING** evening (*archaic or literary*) ■ *adj* **RELATING TO VESPERS** relating to the evening or vespers [14C. < Latin, 'evening, evening star'.]

Vesper *n* Venus when seen as a bright star in the evening sky

vesperal /véspǝrǝl/ *n* **1** a book that contains the prayers and hymns used at vespers **2** a covering for an altar cloth

vespers /véspǝrz/, **Vespers** *n* an evening church service, particularly evensong (+ *singular or plural verb*) ■ *npl* the sixth of the seven canonical hours or a service held on Sundays and holy days at this time, especially in the Roman Catholic Church (+ *singular or plural verb*) [14C. Via Old French *vespres* (plural) < Latin *vespera* (singular) 'evening' < *vesper* 'evening star'.]

vesper sparrow *n* a sparrow with white outer feathers on a notched tail, known for its evening song. Native to: grasslands of North America. *Pooecetes gramineus.*

vespertilionid /véspǝr tílli ǝnid/ *n* a common, insect-eating, long-tailed bat. Family: Vespertilionidae. [Late 19C. < modern Latin *Vespertillionidae* < Latin *vespertilio* 'bat' < *vesper* 'evening'.]

vespertine /véspǝr tīn/ *adj* **1 OPENING IN THE EVENING** describes a flower that opens in the evening **2 ACTIVE IN THE EVENING** tending to be most active in the evening **3 APPEARING IN THE EVENING** appearing or setting in the evening

vespiary /véspi ǝri/ (*plural* **-ies**) *n* a nest or colony of social wasps or hornets [Early 19C. < Latin *vespa* 'wasp', after APIARY.]

vespid /véspid/ *n* an insect of the family that includes wasps and hornets. Family: Vespidae. ■ *adj* belonging or related to the family of insects that includes wasps and hornets [Early 20C. < Latin *vespa* 'wasp'.]

Vespucci /ve spŏŏchi/, **Amerigo** (1454–1512) Italian explorer

vessel /véss'l/ *n* **1 RECEPTACLE** a hollow receptacle, especially one that is used as a container for liquids **2 LARGE WATERCRAFT** a ship or large boat **3 AIRSHIP** a flying craft, especially an airship **4 TUBULAR STRUCTURE CONDUCTING BODY FLUID** a duct that carries fluid, especially blood or lymph, around the body **5 TUBE CONDUCTING WATER IN A PLANT** a tube that carries water and dissolved minerals through a plant, forming part of the sap-conducting tissue (**xylem**) **6 SOMEBODY WHO EMBODIES A QUALITY** somebod[y] seen as the recipient or embodiment of a quality [14C. Via Anglo-Norman < Latin *vascellum* 'small dish or vas[e,] ship' < *vas* 'dish, vase'.]

vest /vest/ *n* **1** *US, Can, Aus* **SLEEVELESS GARMENT** a man's o[r] woman's sleeveless and collarless waist-lengt[h] garment, usually with buttons down the front, wor[n] over a shirt and traditionally worn by men under a su[it] jacket **2** *UK, NZ* **SLEEVELESS UNDERGARMENT** a sleeveles[s] garment worn on the upper part of the body, under th[e] clothes. US term **undershirt** ■ *v* **1** *vt* **CONFER POWER ON** t[o] bestow a power on somebody or something (*usual[ly] passive*) ○ *The governor was vested with certain powers.* **2** *v[i]* **CONFER RIGHTS ON** to settle or confer property, power, o[r] rights on somebody, or to be a part of somebody' property, power, or rights ○ *Sovereignty vests in the stat[e]* ○ *by the authority vested in me* **3** *vti* **CLOTHE OR PUT ON CLOTHE[S]** to clothe somebody or to put on clothes, especiall[y] vestments [15C. < Old French *vestu*, past participle of *vest[ir]* 'clothe' < Latin *vestire* < *vestis* 'clothing, garment'.]

Vesta /véstǝ/ *n* **1** the Roman goddess of the hearth. Gree[k] equivalent **Hestia** **2** the brightest and third largest of th[e] asteroids that orbit the Sun [< Latin]

vestal /vést'l/ *adj* **1 CHASTE** chaste, or not having ex[-]perienced sexual intercourse **2 OF VESTA** relating to th[e] Roman goddess Vesta ■ *n* **1 VIRGIN** a woman who is a virgin (*literary*) **2 NUN** a nun (*literary*) **3** = **vestal virgin**

vestal virgin *n* a celibate woman who tended the sacre[d] fire in the temple of Vesta in ancient Rome

vested /véstid/ *adj* **1** having an unquestionable right t[o] the possession of property or a privilege **2** wearin[g] clothes, especially religious vestments

vested interest *n* **1 RIGHT TO POSSESS** a right to the presen[t] or future possession of property **2 SPECIAL INTEREST** a person's particular concern in maintaining or promoting an issue or situation for reasons of private gai[n] **3 INDIVIDUAL OR GROUP HAVING A VESTED INTEREST** an individua[l] or group with a vested interest in maintaining or promoting something (*often plural*)

vestiary /vésti ǝri/ *n* (*plural* **-ies**) a dressing room o[r] storeroom for clothes ■ *adj* relating to clothe[s] (*formal*) [13C. Via Old French *vestiarie* < Latin *vestiarium* 'clothes chest, wardrobe', later 'vestry' < *vestis* 'clothing, garment'.]

vestibular /ve stíbbyoolǝr/ *adj* relating to a vestibule

vestibular nerve *n* a branch of the acoustic nerve that carries nerve impulses from the semicircular canals and other organs in the inner ear, conveying information about posture and balance

vestibule /vésti byool/ *n* **1 ENTRANCE HALL** a small room or hall between an outer door and the main part of a building **2 BODY CAVITY** a cavity or space in the body that serves as the entrance to another cavity or canal, e.g. the part of the mouth between the teeth and lips **3 MIDDLE CAVITY OF THE INNER EAR** the middle cavity of the inner ear between the cochlea and the semicircular canals [Early 17C. Directly or via French < Latin *vestibulum.*]

vestibulocochlear nerve /ve stíbbyŏŏ lō kókli ǝr-/ *n* either of the eighth pair of cranial nerves, critical to the sense of hearing [< Latin *vestibulum* 'entrance']

vestige /véstij/ *n* **1 TRACE OF SOMETHING GONE** a trace or sign of something that is no longer present **2 SLIGHTEST AMOUNT** the slightest amount ○ *There wasn't a vestige of truth in what she wrote.* **3 RUDIMENTARY BODY PART** an organ or part of the body that is now rudimentary and no longer functions, but was formerly fully developed [Early 17C. Via French < Latin *vestigium* 'sole of the foot, footprint, trace'.]

vestigial /ve stíjji ǝl/ *adj* **1** remaining after nearly all the rest has disappeared or dwindled ○ *a vestigial stirring of passion* **2** having become degenerate or functionless in the course of time ○ *the vestigial muscles of the ear* —**vestigially** *adv*

vestment /véstmǝnt/ *n* **1** a garment, especially a robe worn to show rank or office **2** a ceremonial robe worn by members of the clergy during a religious ceremony [13C. Via Old French *vestiment* < Latin *vestimentum* < *vestire* (see VEST).] —**vestmental** /vest mént'l/ *adj* —**vestmented** *adj*

vest-pocket *adj US* small enough to fit into the pocket of a waistcoat ○ *a vest-pocket edition*

vestry /véstri/ (*plural* **-tries**) *n* **1 ROOM FOR VESTMENTS** a room attached to a church, where vestments or sacred objects are kept **2 MEETING ROOM** a room in a church where meetings or classes are held **3 MEETING OF CHURCH MEMBERS** in the Anglican church, a meeting of church members or their representatives [14C. < Anglo-Norman variant of Old French *vestiarie* (see VESTIARY).] —**vestral** *adj*

vestryman /véstrimən/ (*plural* **-men** /-mən/) *n* a member of a church vestry

vesture /véschər/ *n* clothing, or something that covers like clothing (*archaic*) ■ *vt* (**-tures, -turing, -tured**) to clothe or cover somebody or something (*archaic*) [14C. < Old French, < Latin *vestire* (see VEST).] —**vestural** *adj*

vesuvian /və sóovi ən/ *n* MINERALS = **vesuvianite** [Late 17C. After Mount VESUVIUS in Sicily.]

vesuvianite /və sóovi ə nīt/ *n* a semiprecious stone that is a green, brown, or yellow aluminosilicate containing calcium, magnesium and iron. Source: marble. Use: gems. [Late 19C. After Mount VESUVIUS.]

Vesuvius, Mount /və sóovi əss/ active volcano overlooking the Bay of Naples, S Italy. An eruption in AD 79 destroyed the Roman cities of Pompeii and Herculaneum. Height: 1,277 m/4,190 ft.

vet[1] /vet/ *n* VETERINARY SURGEON a veterinary surgeon ■ *vt* (**vets, vetting, vetted**) **1** CHECK UP ON to subject somebody or something to a careful examination or scrutiny, especially when this involves determining suitability for something **2** EXAMINE AN ANIMAL to examine or treat an animal **3** STERILIZE ANIMAL to sterilize an animal by castrating or spaying (*informal*) [Mid-19C. Shortening of VETERINARY or VETERINARIAN.]

vet[2] /vet/ *n* in *US, Can* a former member of the armed forces, especially in a specific conflict (*informal*) ○ *Vietnam vets* [Mid-19C. Shortening of VETERAN.]

vet. *abbr* **1** veteran **2** veterinarian **3** veterinary

vetch /vech/ *n* **1** a leguminous plant with small flowers. Use: silage, fodder. Genus: *Vicia.* **2** a plant related to or similar to vetch, e.g. the kidney vetch [14C. Via Old N French *veche* < Latin *vicia.*]

vetchling /véchling/ *n* a plant with yellow flowers that is related to vetch. *Lathyrus pratensis.*

veteran /véttərən/ *n* **1** SOMEBODY WITH EXPERIENCE a person who is considerably experienced in something **2** EXPERIENCED SOLDIER a long-serving member of the military who has had much active service ○ *a veteran of three foreign wars* **3** *US, Can* SOMEBODY FORMERLY IN THE ARMED FORCES a former member of the armed forces [Early 16C. Directly or via French *vétéran* < Latin *veteranus* < *vetus* 'old'.] —**veteran** *adj*

veteran car *n* a car made before 1919 or, strictly, one made before 1905. ◊ **vintage car**

Veterans Day *n* in the United States, a public holiday honouring former members of the armed forces. Date: 11 November.

veterinarian /véttəri náiri ən/ *n* *US, Can* OCCUPATIONS = **veterinary surgeon** [Mid-17C. < Latin *veterinarius* (see VETERINARY).]

veterinary /véttərinəri/ *adj* relating to diseases of animals and their treatment [Late 18C. < Latin *veterinarius* < *veterinus* 'relating to (mature) cattle' < *veter-*, stem of *vetus* 'old'.]

veterinary medicine, veterinary science *n* the branch of medicine dealing with the health of animals and the diagnosis and treatment of their diseases and injuries

veterinary surgeon *n* *UK, Aus* somebody who is trained and qualified in the medical treatment of animals. US term **veterinarian**

~~**vetinary**~~ incorrect spelling of **veterinary**

vetiver /véttivər/ *n* **1** a tall grass that grows in India, the leaves of which are used to make screens and fans. *Vetiveria zizanioides.* **2** the roots of the vetiver, which produce an oil that is used to make perfume [Mid-19C. Via French *vétiver* < Tamil *vettivēr* < *vēr* 'root'.]

veto /véetō/ *n* (*plural* **-toes**) **1** RIGHT TO REJECT the power to reject something, e.g. a piece of legislation proposed by somebody else **2** EXERCISE OF THE RIGHT TO REJECT MEASURES the exercise of the power or right to reject something, especially a political measure **3** PROHIBITION an order prohibiting something ○ *put her veto on it* ■ *vt* (**-toes, -toing, -toed**) **1** REJECT A MEASURE to reject something such as a measure or government bill by veto **2** PROHIBIT to refuse to consent to or approve something ○ *My teacher vetoed the idea.* [Early 17C. < Latin, 'I forbid'.] —**vetoer** *n*

vex /veks/ *vt* **1** ANNOY to make somebody annoyed or upset **2** AGITATE to cause somebody anxiety or distress **3** CONFOUND to confuse or puzzle somebody [15C. Via French *vexer* < Latin *vexare* 'shake, disturb'.] —**vexingly** *adv*

vexation /vek sáysh'n/ *n* **1** STATE OF BEING VEXED the state of being provoked to irritability or anxiety **2** ACT OF VEXING the act of provoking somebody to irritability or anxiety **3** SOMETHING THAT VEXES something that provokes irritability or anxiety

vexatious /vek sáyshəss/ *adj* **1** provoking irritation or anxiety by causing trouble **2** put forward on insufficient grounds and with the intention of causing annoyance to the defendant —**vexatiously** *adv* —**vexatiousness** *n*

vexed /vekst/ *adj* **1** provoked to irritability or anxiety **2** being the subject of much debate —**vexedly** /véksidli/ *adv* —**vexedness** *n*

vexillology /véksi lólləji/ *n* the study of flags —**vexillologic** /véksilə lójjik/ *adj* —**vexillological** *adj* —**vexillologist** *n*

vexillum /vek síllәm/ (*plural* **-la** /vek síllə/) *n* in ancient Rome, a military standard or the troops serving under a separate standard [Early 18C. < Latin, 'flag, banner' < *vex-*, a stem of *vehere* 'carry'.]

VF *abbr* **1** voice frequency **2** Vicar Forane **3** video frequency

VFR *abbr* visual flight rules

VFT *abbr* very fast train

vg *abbr* **1** very good **2** Virgin Islands, British (*in Internet addresses*)

VG *abbr* Vicar General

VGA *n* a specification for video display controllers used in personal computers. Full form **video graphics array**

VHF, vhf *abbr* very high frequency

VHS *n* a system for recording television programmes in the home

vi[1] *abbr* vide infra

vi[2] *abbr* Virgin Islands of the United States (*in Internet addresses*)

VI, V.I. *abbr* Vancouver Island

via /vī ə, véé ə/ *prep* **1** by way of or through ○ *Can you come home via the post office?* **2** using the means or agency of ○ *removed the obstruction via surgery* [Early 17C. < Latin, 'by way of', form of *via* 'way, road'.]

viable /vī əb'l/ *adj* **1** PRACTICABLE OR WORTHWHILE able to be done or worth doing ○ *a viable proposition* **2** ABLE TO GROW able to germinate or develop normally **3** ABLE TO SURVIVE OUTSIDE THE WOMB describes a foetus that can survive outside the womb [Early 19C. < French *vie*, < Latin *vita* 'life'.] —**viability** /vī ə bílləti/ *n* —**viably** *adv*

Via Dolorosa /véé ə dóllə róssə/ *n* **1** the route taken by Jesus Christ to Calvary to be crucified **2 Via Dolorosa, via dolorosa** a difficult or distressing course or experience [< Latin, 'sorrowful way']

viaduct /vī ə dukt/ *n* a bridge that consists of a series of short masonry or concrete arched spans supported on towers [Early 19C. < Latin *via* 'way, road', after AQUEDUCT.]

Viagra /vī ággrə/ *tdmk* a trademark for sildenafil citrate, an enzyme-inhibiting drug. Use: treatment of male impotence.

vial /vī əl/ *n* a small glass bottle, especially one for medicines [14C. Alteration of PHIAL.]

via media /vī ə méédi ə/ *n* a middle course or choice between extreme possibilities [< Latin]

viand /vī ənd, véé-/ *n* (*formal*) **1** an article of food **2** a store or collection of food, especially the food that makes up a meal or a feast (*often plural*) [14C. Via French *viande* 'food' (now 'meat') < Latin *vivenda* 'things for living' < *vivere* 'to live'.]

viaticum /vī áttikəm, vi-/ (*plural* **-ca** /-kə, -/ *or* **-cums**) *n* **1** Holy Communion given to somebody who is dying or in danger of dying **2** provisions or money for a journey (*literary*) [Mid-16C. < Latin, 'provision for a journey' < *via* 'way, road'.]

vibe /vīb/ *n* a particular kind of atmosphere, feeling, or ambience (*slang; often plural*) ○ *The new decor has a kind of 50s vibe to it.* [Mid-20C. Shortening of VIBRATION.]

vibes /vībz/ (*plural* **vibes**) *n* a vibraphone (*slang*) [Shortening]

vibist /vībist/ *n* a player of the vibraphone (*slang*)

Viborg /véé bawrg/ city in north-central Jutland, Denmark. Population: 39,395 (1990).

vibrant /vībrənt/ *adj* **1** PULSATING WITH ENERGY seeming to quiver or pulsate with energy or activity **2** RESONANT having a full rich sound that tends to continue for some time **3** BRIGHT dazzling or radiantly bright **4** VIBRATING vibrating very rapidly [Mid-16C. < Latin *vibrant-*, past participle of *vibrare* 'shake'.] —**vibrancy** *n* —**vibrantly** *adv*

vibraphone /vībrə fōn/ *n* a percussion instrument with electrically driven resonators beneath a set of metal bars that are struck with small mallets or sometimes played with a bow, causing vibration [Early 20C. < VIBRATE.] —**vibraphonist** *n*

vibrate /vī bráyt/ (**-brates, -brating, -brated**) *v* **1** *vti* MAKE SMALL MOVEMENTS RAPIDLY to shake or move to and fro rapidly, or make something move in this way ○ *The traffic made the whole room vibrate.* **2** *vti* OSCILLATE to oscillate or to make something oscillate with a continuing periodic change relative to a fixed reference point **3** *vi* RESONATE to make a full rich tone that tends to continue for some time **4** *vi* THRILL to experience a rush of emotion in response to something [Early 17C. < Latin *vibrat-*, past participle of *vibrare* 'shake'.] —**vibrative** /vībrətiv/ *adj* —**vibratory** /vī bráytəri, vībrətəri/ *adj*

vibratile /vībrə tīl/ *adj* **1** showing rapid shaking back and forth movements **2** capable of vibrating, or operating by means of vibration [Early 19C. Alteration of *vibratory* after PULSATILE.] —**vibratility** /vībrə tílləti/ *n*

vibration /vī bráysh'n/ *n* **1** INSTANCE OF VIBRATING an instance of shaking or moving to and fro very rapidly **2** PROCESS OF VIBRATING the process of moving or being moved to and fro very rapidly **3** REPETITIVE PERIODIC OSCILLATION a continuing periodic oscillation relative to a fixed reference point, or a single complete oscillation **4** ATMOSPHERE OF A PLACE the atmosphere or aura given off by a place or situation (*informal; often plural*) **5** FEELINGS COMMUNICATED SUBCONSCIOUSLY feelings communicated from one person to another (*informal; often plural*) —**vibrational** *adj*

vibrato /vi braátō/ (*plural* **-tos**) *n* **1** a throbbing effect in the playing of a stringed or wind instrument made by rapidly varying the pitch **2** a throbbing effect in singing produced by rapidly varying the breath pressure or the pitch [Mid-19C. < Italian, 'vibrated'.]

vibrator /vī bráytər/ *n* **1** SOMETHING THAT VIBRATES something that vibrates or makes something vibrate **2** VIBRATING DEVICE an electric device that vibrates, e.g. one used to give a massage or as a sexual aid **3** DEVICE CONVERTING DIRECT TO ALTERNATING CURRENT an electromechanical device, often used in bells and buzzers, that interrupts a direct current to convert it into an alternating current

vibrio /víbbri ō/ (*plural* **-os** *or* **-ones**) *n* a bacterium shaped like a comma or like the letter S. Genus: *Vibrio.* [Mid-19C. < modern Latin, < Latin *vibrare* 'shake'.] —**vibrioid** /víbbri oyd/ *adj*

vibrissa /vī bríssə/ (*plural* **-sae** /-see/) *n* **1** a mammal's hair or whisker, usually on the face or limbs, that vibrates when touched, stimulating nervous tissue in the animal's skin **2** a feather that is like a bristle, near the beak of an insect-eating bird [Late 17C. < Latin, < *vibrare* 'shake'.] —**vibrissal** *adj*

vibronic /vī brónnik/ *adj* relating to the electronic and vibrational energy states of elementary particles and atoms [Mid-20C. < *vibrational* + ELECTRONIC.]

vibrotron /vībrə tron/ *n* a triode valve in which the anode can be vibrated by an external force

viburnum /vī búrnəm/ *n* a shrub or small tree, such as the guelder rose, with flat or rounded flower clusters. Flowers: white, sometimes tinged with pink. Genus: *Viburnum.* [Mid-18C. Via modern Latin < Latin, 'wayfaring tree'.]

vic. *abbr* vicar

Vic. *abbr* Victoria

vicar /víkər/ *n* **1** ANGLICAN PRIEST a priest in the Anglican Church who is in charge of a parish and receives a salary but not the tithes **2** MEMBER OF THE ANGLICAN CLERGY a member of the Anglican clergy who acts in place of a rector or bishop at Communion **3** ROMAN CATHOLIC PRIEST a Roman Catholic priest who represents or deputizes for a bishop **4** *US* EPISCOPAL CHURCH CLERIC a cleric in the Episcopal Church who is in charge of a chapel **5** CHOIR MEMBER a cleric or member of a choir who sings certain parts of a cathedral service in the Church of England **6** SUBSTITUTE a substitute for somebody else (*archaic*) [14C. Via Anglo-Norman *vicare* < Latin *vicarius* 'substitute' < *vic-* 'change, place'; because the vicar acted as a substitute for the rector.] —**vicarly** *adj* —**vicarship** *n*

vicarage /víkərij/ *n* **1** the residence of a vicar **2** the office or duties of a vicar

vicar apostolic (*plural* **vicars apostolic**) *n* a titular bishop or missionary in the Roman Catholic Church

vicarate *n* CHR = **vicariate**

vicar general (*plural* **vicars general**) *n* **1** a priest acting as an assistant to a Roman Catholic bishop **2** a lay official assisting an Anglican bishop with administrative or judicial duties

vicarial /vi káiri əl, vī-/ *adj* **1** being or acting as a vicar **2** relating to a vicar **3** = **vicarious** *adj.* **3**

vicariate /vi káiri ət, vī-/, **vicarate** /víkərət/ *n* **1** the office or authority of a vicar **2** the district that falls under the care of a vicar

vicarious /vi káiri əss, vī-/ *adj* **1 EXPERIENCED THROUGH ANOTHER BY IMAGINING** experienced through another person rather than at first hand, by using sympathy or the power of the imagination **2 ENDURED FOR SOMEBODY ELSE** done or endured by somebody as a substitute for somebody else **3 DELEGATED** delegated to somebody else or performing a function that has been delegated **4 OCCURRING IN AN UNEXPECTED PART OF BODY** occurring in or performed by an unexpected part of the body, e.g. menstrual bleeding in the breasts, nose, or sweat glands [Mid-17C. < Latin *vicarius* (see VICAR).] —**vicariously** *adv* —**vicariousness** *n*

Vicar of Christ *n* the Roman Catholic pope

vice[1] /vīss/ *n* a tool with two jaws that close by a lever or screw that is used to hold an object immobile so that it can be worked on ■ *vt* (**vices, vicing, viced**) to hold something tightly in a vice [13C. Via Old French *vis* 'screw' < Latin *vitis* 'vine'.] —**vice-like** *adj*

vice[2] /vīss/ *n* **1 IMMORAL HABIT** an immoral or wicked habit or characteristic **2 DEPRAVITY** immoral conduct **3 PROSTITUTION** a form of immoral conduct, especially prostitution **4 MILD DEFECT IN CHARACTER** a mild failing or defect in somebody's behaviour or character **5 FAULT IN AN ANIMAL** a fault or undesirable habit in a horse or other domestic animal [13C. Via French < Latin *vitium*.]

vice[3] /vīssi/ *prep* in place of or instead of somebody or something [Late 18C. < Latin *vice* 'in place of' < *vic-* 'change, place'.]

vice admiral *n* a naval officer of a rank above rear admiral —**vice-admiralty** *n*

vice chairperson *n* a person who takes the place of a chairperson in his or her absence

vice chancellor *n* **1 ASSISTANT CHANCELLOR OF A UNIVERSITY** a deputy or assistant chancellor in a university, often the person in charge of administration **2 DEPUTY CHANCELLOR** a deputy for the chancellor of a state **3 JUDGE** a US judge ranking below a chancellor, or an English judge who runs the Chancery Division of the High Court —**vice-chancellorship** *n*

vice consul *n* an officer who acts as the deputy for the official representing a country's commercial interest in an overseas country —**vice-consular** *adj*

vicegerent /vīss jérrənt, -jéer-/ *n* a deputy appointed to act on the authority of a ruler or magistrate, especially in administrative duties [Mid-16C. < medieval Latin, 'deputy' < Latin *gerent-*, present participle of *gerere* 'carry on'.] —**vicegeral** *adj* —**vicegerency** *n*

vicenary /víssinəri/ *adj* **1** being or relating to the number 20 **2** using 20 as a basis for counting or ordering [Early 17C. < Latin *vicenarius* < *viginti* 'twenty'.]

vicennial /vi sénni əl/ *adj* lasting for or occurring every 20 years [Mid-18C. < Latin *vicennium* 'period of twenty years' < *vic-*, stem of *vicies* 'twenty times'.]

Vicenza /vi chéntsə/ capital of Vicenza Province, Veneto Region, N Italy. Population: 107,786 (1995).

vice president *n* an official of a rank below a president, who can take the president's place if necessary —**vice-presidency** *n* —**vice-presidential** *adj*

viceregal /vīss réeg'l/ *adj* **1** relating to a viceroy **2** *Aus, NZ* relating to a governor or a governor general —**viceregally** *adv*

viceregent /vīss réejənt/ *n* a deputy for the regent of a country —**viceregency** *n*

vicereine /vīss rάyn/ *n* a viceroy who is a woman, or the wife of a viceroy [Early 19C. < French, 'vice-queen'.]

viceroy /vīss roy/ *n* **1** a governor who represents a sovereign in a province, colony, or country **2** *US* a brightly coloured orange-and-black butterfly of North America that resembles the monarch butterfly. *Limenitis archippus.* [Early 16C. < French, 'vice-king'.] —**viceroyship** *n*

viceroyalty /vīss róy əlti/ (*plural* **-ties**) *n* **1** the office, term of office, or authority of a viceroy **2** a district that is governed by a viceroy

vice squad *n* a police division in charge of enforcing laws relating to prostitution, gambling, and drug abuse

vice versa /vīss vúrssə, vīssi-/ *adv* the other way round [< Latin, 'the position being reversed']

Vichy /véeshi/ city in central France. It was the seat of a French government that collaborated with the Germans during World War II. Population: 26,528 (1999).

vichyssoise /véeshi swaáz, víshi-/ *n* a creamy soup made from leeks, potatoes, and onions, often served chilled [Mid-20C. Shortening of French *crème vichyssoise glacée* 'iced cream soup from Vichy'.]

Vichy water, Vichy *n* a natural sparkling mineral water from Vichy, France, or a similar sparkling water

vicinage /víssinij/ *n* **1** a neighbourhood, or the people living in it (*archaic*) **2** *US* the area immediately surrounding a place [14C. < Old French *vis(e)nage*, < Latin *vicinus* (see VICINITY).]

vicinal /víssin'l/ *adj* **1 NEIGHBOURING** adjacent or neighbouring **2 LOCAL** relating to or restricted to a local area **3 BEING CONSECUTIVE POSITIONS ON A CARBON CHAIN** relating to two or more adjacent positions on a carbon ring or chain [Early 17C. Directly or via French < Latin *vicinalis* < *vicinus* (see VICINITY).]

vicinity /vi sínnəti/ (*plural* **-ties**) *n* **1 SURROUNDING REGION** a neighbourhood, or the surrounding region of a place ○ *Homes in the vicinity of the fire were evacuated.* **2 PROXIMITY** an area near something else **3 APPROXIMATION** an approximate amount ○ *something in the vicinity of 1,000 jobs* [Mid-16C. < Latin *vicinitas* < *vicinus* 'neighbour' < *vicus* 'village, homestead'.]

vicious /víshəss/ *adj* **1 FEROCIOUS** showing fierce violence **2 DANGEROUS AND AGGRESSIVE** dangerous because of being aggressive ○ *a vicious dog* **3 MALICIOUS** intended to do harm **4 WICKED AND IMMORAL** displaying or tending to immoral behaviour **5 UNSOUND** incorrect or showing faulty logic [14C. < VICE[2].] —**viciously** *adv* —**viciousness** *n*

vicious circle, vicious cycle *n* **1 SITUATION WORSENED BY ATTEMPTS TO SOLVE IT** a situation in which attempts to solve one problem lead to further problems that only make the original position worse **2 REASONING BASED ON AN UNPROVEN ASSUMPTION** a form of reasoning that bases a conclusion on a statement assumed to be true but not proven independently **3 LINKING OF TWO DISEASES** a situation in which two diseases or conditions are linked so that each leads to or aggravates the other

USAGE vicious circle or **vicious cycle**? Until quite recently the invariable choice was ***vicious circle***. Perhaps influenced by such phrases as *the cycle of welfare dependency*, the use of variant ***vicious cycle*** has been gaining ground and is seen in virtually indistinguishable contexts.

vicissitude /vī síssə tyood, vi-/ *n* the fact of being variable (*literary*) ■ **vicissitudes** *npl* unexpected changes, especially in a person's fortunes [Mid-16C. Directly or via French < Latin *vicissitudo* < *vicissim* 'by turns' < *vic-* (see VICAR).] —**vicissitudinary** /vī síssə tyóodinəri, vi-/ *adj* —**vicissitudinous** /-tyóodinəss, -/ *adj*

vicomte /vée koNt/ *n* a French nobleman who is equal in rank to a British viscount [Mid-19C. Via French < Old French *vi(s)conte* (see VISCOUNT).]

vicomtesse /vée koN téss/ *n* a French noblewoman who is equal in rank to a British viscountess [Late 18C. < French, < *vicomte* (see VICOMTE).]

victim /víktim/ *n* **1 SOMEBODY HURT OR KILLED** a person who is hurt or killed by somebody or something **2 SOMEBODY OR SOMETHING HARMED** somebody or something harmed by an act or circumstance ○ *a victim of her own success* **3 SOMEBODY DUPED** a person who is tricked or exploited **4 CREATURE USED FOR SACRIFICE** a living creature used as a sacrifice or in a religious rite **5 HELPLESS PERSON** a person who experiences misfortune and feels helpless to remedy it [15C. < Latin *victima* 'animal offered as a sacrifice'.] ◇ **fall victim to somebody** *or* **something** to be affected, harmed, or deceived by somebody *or* something

victimize /víkti mīz/ (**-izes, -izing, -ized**), **victimise** (**-timises, -timising, -timised, -timised**) *vt* **1** to single somebody out unfairly for punishment or ill treatment **2** to cause somebody to become a victim —**victimization** /víkti mī záysh'n/ *n* —**victimizer** *n*

victimless crime *n* an illegal act such as loitering in which there is no obvious injured party

victor /víktər/ *n* **1** a winner in a contest or battle **2** a code word for the letter 'V', used in international radio communications [14C. Directly or via Anglo-Norman < Latin, < *vic-*, past participle of *vincere* 'conquer'.]

Victor Emmanuel III /víktər i mánnyoo əl/ (1869–1947) king of Italy (1900–46)

victoria /vik táwri ə/ *n* **1 RED-AND-YELLOW PLUM** a large red-and-yellow variety of plum **2 HORSE-DRAWN CARRIAGE WITH A FOLDING HOOD** a horse-drawn carriage with four wheels and a folding hood, accommodating two passengers **3 GIANT WATER LILY** a giant water lily. Flowers: fragrant, red or white. Native to: South America. Genus: *Victoria.* [Mid-19C. After Queen VICTORIA.]

Victoria /vik táwri ə/ **1** river in NW Northern Territory, Australia. Length: 640 km/398 mi. **2** state in SE Australia. Capital: Melbourne. Population: 4,561,000 (1996). Area: 227,620 sq. km/87,884 sq. mi. **3** capital of British Columbia, Canada, on the southern tip of Vancouver Island. Population: 73,504 (1996). **4** capital of the Republic of Seychelles, on the coast of NE Mahé Island. Population: 60,000 (1994 estimate).

Victoria (1819–1901) queen of the United Kingdom (1837–1901)

Victoria, Lake largest lake in Africa, with shorelines in Tanzania, Uganda, and Kenya. Area: 69,490 sq. km/26,830 sq. mi.

Victoria Cross *n* a decoration in the form of a bronze cross, given to members of British and Commonwealth armed forces for conspicuous bravery

Victoria Day *n* in Canada, a statutory holiday marking the birthday of Queen Victoria. Date: 24 May or preceding Monday.

Victoria Falls waterfall in south-central Africa in the River Zambezi, on the border between Zambia and Zimbabwe. Height: 108 m/355 ft.

Victoria Land region of Antarctica, west of Ross Sea

Victorian /vik táwri ən/ *adj* **1 CHARACTERISTIC OF THE TIME OF QUEEN VICTORIA** relating to, belonging to, or typical of the reign of Queen Victoria **2 CONVENTIONAL, HYPOCRITICAL, OR PRUDISH** showing or typical of attitudes commonly associated with the Victorian era, especially prudery or conventionalism **3 ARCHITECTURALLY ELABORATE** in or typical of the elaborate style of architecture popular in Victorian Britain **4 FROM VICTORIA** relating to or from the state of Victoria in Australia, or the cities of Victoria in Canada or the Seychelles ■ *n* **1 SOMEBODY LIVING IN VICTORIA'S REIGN** a person who lived in the reign of Queen Victoria **2 SOMEBODY FROM VICTORIA** a person who comes from the state of Victoria in Australia, or the cities of Victoria in Canada or the Seychelles —**Victorianism** *n*

Victoriana /vik táwri aánə/ *npl* collectible objects dating from the time of Queen Victoria

Victoria Nile section of the upper River Nile in Uganda, between lakes Victoria and Albert

Victoria Peak mountain on Hong Kong Island, overlooking Hong Kong Harbour. Height: 554 m/1,818 ft.

victoria plum *n* TREES = **victoria** *n.* **1**

victorious /vik táwri əss/ *adj* **1** having won something such as a contest or a battle **2** typical of or showing a sense of victory —**victoriously** *adv* —**victoriousness** *n*

victory /víktəri/ (*plural* **-ries**) *n* **1** defeat of an enemy or opponent **2** success attained over a difficult situation or opponent [14C. Via Anglo-Norman *victorie* < Latin *victoria* < *victor* (see VICTOR).]

victory roll *n* an airborne rolling manoeuvre of an aircraft carried out by a pilot as a sign of victory or celebration

victual /vítt'l/ *n* **PROVISIONS** provisions of food (*archaic or formal*) ■ **victuals** *npl* **FOOD** food or other provisions (*often used humorously*) ■ *v* (**-uals, -ualling, -ualled**) (*archaic or formal*) **1** *vt* **FEED** to give food to people or animals **2** *vi* **ASSEMBLE PROVISIONS** to collect a store of food [14C. Via Old French *vitaille* < Latin *victualia* (which later influenced the English spelling) < *victus* 'livelihood, food' < *vivere* 'to live'.]

victualler *n* **1 SUPPLIER OF PROVISIONS** somebody who supplies food or other provisions (*archaic or formal*) **2 INNKEEPER** an innkeeper, especially one licensed to sell spirits (*archaic or formal*) **3 SHIP CARRYING STORES** a ship carrying food or other provisions

icuña /vi kyoóna, -koónya/, **vicuna** n 1 a tawny-coloured mammal related to the llama, with a silky fleece. Native to: Andes. *Vicugna vicugna*. **2** cloth made from the wool of the vicuña, or an imitation of it [Early 17C. Via Spanish < Quechua *wikúña*.]

id n a video cassette (*informal*)

idal /vi daál/, **Gore** (b. 1925) US writer

ide /vídi, vee day/ vt a word used to refer a reader to another place in a text, or tell a musician to skip to a place further ahead in the score [Mid-16C. < Latin, 'see!', form of *videre* 'see'.]

ide infra vt a term used to refer a reader to a place further on in a text [< Latin, 'see below']

idelicet /vi deéli set/ adv full form of **viz** [15C. < Latin, *vide*, stem of *videre* 'see' + *licet* 'it is permissible'.]

ideo /víddi ō/ n (*plural* **-os**) **1 VISUAL PART OF TELEVISION** the visual part of a television broadcast **2 VIDEO RECORDER** a video recorder (*informal*) **3 VIDEO CASSETTE** video tape, or a video cassette (*informal*) ○ *now available to rent or buy on video* **4 SOMETHING RECORDED ONTO VIDEOTAPE** something, especially a film, that has been recorded onto video tape ■ adj **1 RELATING TO TELEVISION** relating to television, especially the reproduction or broadcasting of televised images **2 RELATING TO VIDEO FREQUENCIES** relating to or using video frequencies ■ vt (**-os, -oing, -oed**) **RECORD SOMETHING ON VIDEO** to record something on video tape [Mid-20C. < Latin *videre* 'see', after AUDIO.]

video adapter n COMPUT = **graphics card**

video arcade n a place where people pay to play video games

video camera n a camera that records onto video tape

video card n a circuit board that enables a computer to display screen information

video cassette n a flat rectangular plastic cassette containing two tape reels and a magnetic video tape

video cassette recorder n = **video recorder**

video conferencing n the holding of a meeting in which participants are in different places, connected by audio and video links —**video conference** n

videodisk /víddi ō disk/, **videodisc** n an optical disk that can store full-motion video and audio

video display terminal n US, ANZ a device used to display data from and enter data into a computer, consisting of a visual display such as a cathode-ray tube and a keyboard, mouse, or touch-screen

video frequency n a frequency in the range of signals used to carry the image and synchronizing pulses in a television broadcasting system

video game n an electronic or computerized game, usually controlled by a microprocessor, played by making images move on a computer or television screen or, for hand-held games, on a liquid-crystal display

videography /víddi ógrəfi/ n US the art or practice of using a video camera to make films or programmes —**videographer** n

video jockey n somebody who plays videos, especially music videos, especially on television

video nasty n a film on videotape that contains explicitly violent or pornographic scenes (*informal*)

videophile /víddi ō fīl/ n somebody who enjoys watching or making video recordings

videophone /víddi ō fōn/ n a communications device that can transmit and receive both video and audio signals using a camera, receiver, and screen

video recorder n a tape recorder that can record and play video cassettes through a standard television receiver

videotape /víddi ō tayp/ n magnetic tape on which pictures and sound can be recorded ■ vt (**-tapes, -taping, -taped**) to make a recording of something on videotape

video tape recorder n a tape recorder that can record and play back visual images and sound using magnetic tape

videotext /víddi ō tekst/ n a communications service linked to an adapted television receiver or video display terminal by telephone or cable television lines to allow access to pages of information

video vérité /víddi ō vérri tay/ n the use in video documentaries of the realistic, unrehearsed portrayal of people and situations [After CINÉMA VÉRITÉ]

vide supra vt a term used to refer a reader to an earlier place in a text [< Latin, 'see above']

vidette n ARMY = **vedette** n. 1

vidicon /víddi kon/ n a light-sensitive television camera tube in which an image is stored on a photoconductive plate as an electric charge pattern that is scanned by an electron beam and transmitted [Mid-20C. < VIDEO + ICONOSCOPE.]

Vidor /veéd awr/, **King** (1894–1982) US film director

vie /vī/ (**vies, vying, vied**) vi to strive for superiority or compete with somebody or something for something [Mid-16C. Shortening of obsolete *envie* < Old French *envier* 'raise the bid (at cards), challenge' < Latin *invitare* 'entertain, feast'.] —**vier** n

viel incorrect spelling of **veil**

Vienna /vi énnə/ capital of Austria, in the east of the country. Population: 1,539,848 (1991). —**Viennese** /vee ə neéz/ n, adj

Vienna circle n the leading school of logical positivists of the 1920s and 1930s [Because based at Vienna University]

Vienna sausage n a small, spicy sausage like a frankfurter, often served as a snack or hors d'oeuvre

Vientiane /vyén tyaàn/ capital of Laos, in the central part of the country. Population: 528,109 (1995).

Viet. abbr Vietnam

Vietcong /vyét kóng/ (*plural* **-cong**), **Viet Cong** (*plural* **Viet Cong**) n a member or supporter of the Communist-led armed forces of the National Liberation Front of South Vietnam that fought to unite the country with North Vietnam between 1954 and 1976 [Mid-20C. < Vietnamese *Viêt-công*, shortening of *Viêt-Nam Công Sam* 'Vietnamese Communist'.]

Vietminh /vyét mín/ (*plural* **-minh**), **Viet Minh** (*plural* **Viet Minh**) n a member or supporter of the Vietnamese armed forces led by Ho Chi Minh that resisted and defeated first the Japanese and then the French between 1941 and 1954 [Mid-20C. < Vietnamese *Viêt Minh*, shortening of *Viêt-Nam Dôc-Lâp Dông-Minh* 'Vietnam Independence Federation'.]

Vietnam

Vietnam /vyet nám/ country in Southeast Asia, on the South China Sea. Capital: Hanoi. Population: 75,123,880 (1997). Area: 331,690 sq. km/128,066 sq. mi.

Vietnamese /vyétnə meéz/ adj **OF VIETNAM** relating to Vietnam, or its people or culture ■ n (*plural* **-ese**) **1 SOMEBODY FROM VIETNAM** a person who comes from Vietnam **2 OFFICIAL LANGUAGE OF VIETNAM** the Austro-Asiatic official language of Vietnam. Native speakers: 60 million.

Vietnamese potbellied pig n a small domesticated pig with a rounded shape and a dark skin with a lighter band running around its middle

Vietnam War n a conflict in which the Communist forces of North Vietnam and guerrillas in South Vietnam fought against the non-Communist forces of South Vietnam and the United States

vieux jeu /vyúr zhúr, vyố zhố/ adj no longer fashionable [< French, 'old game']

view /vyoo/ n **1 ACT OF LOOKING AT** an act of looking at or inspecting something **2 RANGE OF VISION** the range or extent of somebody's ability to see something ○ *As we*

rounded the bend the mountains came into view. **3 SCENE** a scene or an area that can be seen from a particular place, especially one that is pleasing or impressive **4 PICTORIAL REPRESENTATION** a painting, drawing, or photograph of a particular scene or building **5 PERSPECTIVE** a particular position or angle from which somebody can look at something **6 OPINION** somebody's opinion on or interpretation of something such as politics or religion **7 SURVEY** a general survey of a particular subject ■ v **1** vt **OBSERVE** to see or look at something, especially with interest **2** vt **INSPECT** to make an inspection or examination of something **3** vt **CONSIDER** to think over or consider something, especially a range of things **4** vt **THINK OF** to regard or assess somebody or something, especially in a particular way **5** vti **WATCH TELEVISION** to watch television, or watch something on television [15C. < Old French *vêue*, past participle of *vêoir* 'see' < Latin *videre*.] —**viewless** adj ◇ **in view of something** because of something, or bearing something in mind ◇ **on view** put somewhere so as to be seen ◇ **take a dim view of somebody** or **something** to consider somebody or something with disapproval ◇ **with a view to something** with the aim, intention, or hope of doing or achieving something

LITERARY LINK *A Room with a View*, a novel (1908) by E.M. Forster. It describes how a young Englishwoman's visit to Italy and her encounter there with a young, unconventional expatriate encourages her to rebel against the emotionally stifling conventions of her upper-class background.

viewable /vyoó əb'l/ adj **1** able to be seen or inspected **2** of a good enough standard, or in a good enough condition, to be watched

viewdata /vyoó daytə/ n an interactive information system in which text and graphic data stored in a central computer are transmitted over telephone lines to be displayed on a modified home television receiver

viewer /vyoó ər/ n **1 SOMEBODY WHO WATCHES** a watcher of something such as television, a film, or an event **2 OPTICAL DEVICE** an optical device for illuminating and magnifying a photographic transparency, video tape, or motion picture film **3 SOMEBODY WHO MAKES A FORMAL INSPECTION** somebody appointed, especially by a court, to inspect something such as property —**viewership** n

viewfinder /vyoó fīndər/ n a device on a camera that lets the user see what is being photographed

view halloo interj used during a fox hunt as a shout to signal that the fox has been seen breaking cover ■ n a shout of 'view halloo!'

viewing /vyoó ing/ n **1** an act or the practice of watching, seeing, or inspecting something **2** television programmes as a body or type

viewpoint /vyoó poynt/ n **1** a personal perspective from which somebody considers something **2** a place or position from which people can look at something

VIF abbr variable import fee

vigesimal /vī jéssim'l/ adj based on or reckoned in units of the number twenty [Mid-17C. < Latin *vigesimus*, variant of *vicesimus* 'twentieth' < *viginti* 'twenty'.]

vigia /vi jeé ə/ n something marked on a chart as a hazard to navigation, although its existence, position, and nature are unconfirmed [Mid-19C. < Portuguese, 'lookout' < Latin *vigilia* (see VIGIL).]

vigil /víjjil/ n **1 NIGHT WATCH** a period spent in doing something through the night, e.g. watching, guarding, or praying **2 FESTIVAL EVE** the eve of some festivals and holy days, spent in prayer ■ **vigils** npl **RELIGIOUS SERVICES AT NIGHT** religious services or prayers at night, especially on the eve of a festival or holy day [13C. Via Old French *vigile* < medieval Latin *vigilia* 'eve of a holy day' < Latin, 'watchfulness' < *vigil* 'awake, alert'.]

vigilance /víjjilənss/ n the condition of being watchful and alert, especially to danger

vigilance committee n US a group of people who pursue and punish suspected or alleged criminals without having the legal authority to do so

vigilant /víjjilənt/ adj watchful and alert, especially to danger or to something that is wrong [15C. < Latin *vigilant-*, present participle of *vigilare* 'keep awake' < *vigil* 'awake, alert'.] —**vigilantly** adv

SYNONYMS See *cautious*.

vigilante /víjji lánti/ n **1** somebody who punishes lawbreakers personally rather than relying on the legal authorities 2 *US* a member of a vigilance committee [Mid-19C. < Spanish, 'watchman' < Latin *vigilant-* (see VIGILANT).]

vign *abbr* vignette

vigneron /véenyə ron, -roN/ *n* a grower of grapes for use in making wine [15C. < French, < *vigne* (see VINE).]

vignette /vin yét/ *n* 1 **DESIGN ON A BOOK PAGE** a small decorative design printed at the beginning or end of a book or chapter of a book, or in the margin of a page 2 **SHORT ESSAY** a short descriptive piece of literary writing 3 **UNBORDERED PICTURE** a painting, drawing, or photograph that has no border but is gradually faded into its background at the edges 4 **BRIEF SCENE** a brief scene from a film or play 5 **ARCHITECTURAL ORNAMENTATION** a carved architectural decoration in the form of tendrils and leaves ■ *vt* (**-gnettes, -gnetting, -gnetted**) 1 **FINISH PICTURE OFF BY SOFTENING EDGES** to finish a painting, drawing, or photograph by gradually fading it into its background at the edges rather than giving it a border 2 **DESCRIBE SOMETHING BRIEFLY** to describe something in a brief but elegant way [Mid-18C. < French, 'small vine' (from such decorations on margins in early books) < *vigne* (see VINE).] —**vignetter** *n* —**vignettist** *n*

Vignola /vin yṓlə/, **Giacomo da** (1507–73) Italian architect. Born **Giacomo Barozzi**

Vigo /veégō/ city in NW Spain, on the Atlantic Ocean. Population: 290,582 (1995).

vigor *n* US = **vigour**

vigorish /víggərish/ *n* *US* (*slang*) 1 a sum of money that a bookmaker or gambling establishment charges a customer for accepting a bet 2 any additional payment that somebody is forced to make, e.g. a bribe or interest paid to a usurer [Early 20C. < ?]

vigoroso /víggə rṓssō/ *adv* to be played with intensity and liveliness (*musical direction*) [Early 18C. < Italian, 'vigorous' < medieval Latin *vigorosus* < Latin *vigor* (see VIGOUR).] —**vigoroso** *adj*

vigorous /víggərəss/ *adj* 1 extremely strong and active, physically and mentally 2 displaying or using great energy —**vigorously** *adv* —**vigorousness** *n*

vigour /víggər/ *n* 1 **VITALITY** great physical or mental strength and energy 2 **INTENSITY** intensity or forcefulness in the way something is done 3 **ABILITY TO GROW** the ability of plants or animals to survive, grow, and thrive 4 *US* **LEGAL VALIDITY** legal validity or force [14C. Via Old French < Latin *vigor* 'liveliness, energy' < *vigere* 'be lively'.]

Vijayawada /veéj ī ə waádə/ town in S India. Population: 701,827 (1991).

Viking /víking/ *n* 1 a member of a Scandinavian people who carried out seaborne raids of NW Europe from the 8th to 11th centuries AD, often settling in the areas they invaded, as in Britain 2 either of two identical, highly instrumented, uncrewed US space probes to Mars, launched in 1975 [Early 19C. < Old Norse *víkingr*, either < *vík* 'creek, inlet' or < Old English *wīc* 'camp'.]

vil. *abbr* village

~~**vilage**~~ incorrect spelling of **village**

vile /vīl/ (**viler, vilest**) *adj* 1 **DISGUSTING** causing disgust or abhorrence 2 **WICKED** very evil or shameful 3 **VERY UNPLEASANT** extremely unpleasant to experience 4 **DEGRADING** so despicable or undesirable as to be degrading 5 **WORTHLESS** of little or no worth (*archaic*) [13C. Via Old French < Latin *vilis* 'of little value, cheap, base'.] —**vilely** *adv* —**vileness** *n*

vilify /vílli fī/ (**-fies, -fying, -fied**) *vt* to make malicious and abusive statements about somebody [15C. < late Latin *vilificare* 'hold cheap' < Latin *vilis* 'worthless'.] —**vilification** /víllifi káysh'n/ *n* —**vilifier** *n*

SYNONYMS See *malign*.

---

vilipend /víllə pend/ *vt* (*literary*) 1 to treat or view somebody with contempt 2 to make malicious or contemptuous statements about somebody [15C. Via Old French *vilipender* < Latin *vilipendere* 'consider base' < *vilis* 'base, cheap'.]

vill *abbr* village

villa /víllə/ *n* 1 **EXPENSIVE HOUSE** a large, luxurious house in the country 2 **HOUSE IN RESIDENTIAL AREA** a detached or semi-detached house in a residential area 3 **HOLIDAY HOME** a house rented for a holiday 4 *NZ* **SUBURBAN HOME** a suburban house with its own land 5 *Aus* = **villa home** 6 **ROMAN HOUSE** a country house in ancient Rome or one of its colonies, with living quarters, farm buildings, and a courtyard [Early 17C. Via Italian < Latin, 'country home, farm'.]

village /víllij/ *n* 1 **RURAL COMMUNITY** a group of houses and other buildings in a rural area, smaller than a town but larger than a hamlet 2 **INHABITANTS OF VILLAGE** all of the people who live in a village 3 **TEMPORARY COMMUNITY** a place where people live temporarily as a community, e.g. an apartment complex for the use of athletes taking part in Olympic games 4 **ANIMAL DWELLINGS** a group of bird or animal dwellings [14C. Via Old French < Latin *villaticum* 'farmstead' < *villa* 'country home, farm'.] —**villager** *n*

village college *n* an educational and recreational centre for a group of villages

Villahermosa /veé ə hair mṓssə/ capital of Tabasco State, NE Mexico. Population: 261,231 (1990).

villa home *n* *Aus* a modern suburban home built on a small allotment and usually separated from a neighbouring home by its garage

villain /víllən/ *n* 1 **EVIL CHARACTER** an evil character in a novel, film, play, or other story, especially one who is the main enemy of the hero 2 **CONTEMPTIBLE PERSON** any person regarded as evil or otherwise contemptible 3 **CAUSE OF PROBLEM** a person who or thing that causes a specific evil or problem 4 **MISCHIEVOUS PERSON** a mischievous or troublesome person (*humorous*) 5 **CRIMINAL** a criminal (*slang*) 6 HIST = **villein** [14C. Via Old French *vilein* 'feudal serf' < medieval Latin *villanus* 'farmhand' < Latin *villa* 'country home, farm'.]

villainage *n* HIST = **villeinage**

villainess /víllə ness/ *n* 1 an evil woman character in a novel, film, play, or other story, especially one who is the main enemy of the hero 2 any woman regarded as evil or otherwise contemptible

villainous /víllənəss/ *adj* 1 typical of an evil or contemptible person 2 obnoxious or unpleasant —**villainously** *adv* —**villainousness** *n*

villainy /vílləni/ *n* 1 **EVIL CONDUCT** behaviour typical of an evil or contemptible person 2 **STATE OF BEING EVIL** the state of being evil or contemptible 3 (*plural* **-ies**) **EVIL ACT** an evil, immoral, or criminal act

Villa-Lobos /víllə lṓb oss/, **Heitor** (1897–1959) Brazilian composer

~~**villan**~~ incorrect spelling of **villain**

villanelle /víllə nél/ *n* a 19-line poem, originally French, that uses only two rhymes and consists of five three-line stanzas and a final quatrain [Late 16C. Via French < Italian *villanella* 'old rustic (Italian) song' < *villano* 'peasant' < medieval Latin *villanus* (see VILLAIN).]

Villanovan /víllə nṓv'n/ *adj* belonging to or typical of an early Iron Age culture that existed near Bologna, Italy, in which bronze was used and also, in a primitive way, iron ■ *n* a member of the Villanovan culture [Early 20C. After *Villanova*, town in NE Italy.]

villein /víllən, víllayn/, **villain** *n* a feudal serf who had the status of a freeman except in relation to his lord, to whom he owed dues and services in exchange for land [14C. Variant of VILLAIN.]

villeinage /víllənij/, **villainage** *n* 1 the status of being a villein in feudal society 2 the form of feudal tenure by which a villein held land

villi plural of **villus**

villiform /vílli fawrm/ *adj* in the form of or resembling a minute projection (**villus**) [Mid-19C. < VILLUS.]

Villon /vee yóN/, **François** (1431?–63?) French poet. Born **François de Montcorbier, François des Loges**

villosity /vi lóssəti/ (*plural* **-ties**) *n* 1 **HAIRINESS** the condition of being covered in long shaggy hairs 2 **BEING COVERED WITH MINUTE PROJECTIONS** the condition of being covered with minute projections 3 **COATING OF FINE PROJECTIONS** a surface or coating of very fine projections resembling hairs 4 **PART RESEMBLING HAIR** a fine projection that resembles a hair [Late 18C. < Latin *villosus* (see VILLOUS).]

villous /vílləss/, **villose** /víllōss/ *adj* 1 covered with long shaggy hairs 2 relating to, resembling, or covered with minute protuberances [14C. < Latin *villosus* 'shaggy' < *villus* 'shaggy hair'.] —**villously** *adv*

villus /vílləss/ (*plural* **-li** /-lī/) *n* 1 any vascular protuberance growing out from some mucous membranes, e.g. from that of the small intestine of some vertebrates or from the chorion that surrounds an embryo 2 a fine part resembling a hair, growing from the surface of plant [Early 18C. < Latin, 'shaggy hair'.]

Vilnius /vílni əss/ capital of Lithuania, in the southeast o the country. Population: 580,100 (1997).

vim /vim/ *n* exuberant vitality and energy (*informal*) [Mid 19C. Probably < Latin, form of *vis* 'power, strength'.]

vin *abbr* vinegar

vin- *prefix* = **vini-**

vina /veénə/, **veena** *n* a S Asian stringed instrumen similar to the sitar, with a long fretted fingerboard and often with a resonating gourd at each end [Late 18C. < Sanskrit *vīṇā*.]

vinaceous /vī náyshəss/ *adj* 1 of the nature of or con taining wine 2 of the colour of red wine [Late 17C. < Latin *vinaceus* < *vinum* 'wine'.]

~~**vinagrette**~~ incorrect spelling of **vinaigrette**

vinaigrette /vínay grét, vínni-/ *n* 1 a salad dressing made with vinegar, oil, salt, pepper, and sometimes other seasonings 2 a small bottle or box with a perforated cap, used to hold aromatic substances such as smelling salts or vinegar [Late 17C. < French, 'little vinegar' < *vinaigre* < Old French *vyn egre* (see VINEGAR).]

vinasse /vi náss/ *n* the residue left in a still after the distillation of an alcoholic beverage, especially brandy [Via French < Provençal *vinassa* < Latin *vinaceus* (see VINACEOUS)]

vinblastine /vin blás teen/ *n* an alkaloid drug from the Madagascar periwinkle. Use: cancer treatment. [Mid-20C. < modern Latin *Vinca* (see VINCA), + LEUKOBLAST.]

vinca /víngkə/ *n* PLANTS = **periwinkle**[2] *n.* [Mid-19C. < modern Latin *Vinca* < late Latin *pervinca* (see PERIWINKLE[2]).]

Vincennes /vin sénz/ town in north-central France. Population: 42,651 (1990).

Vincent de Paul /vínssənt də páwl, vaN saN də páwl/, **St** (1581–1660) French priest

Vincent's angina, Vincent's infection *n* a painful mouth inflammation with ulcers and gum damage [Early 20C. After Jean Hyacinthe *Vincent* (1862–1950), French physician.]

vincible /vínssəb'l/ *adj* able to be defeated or conquered (*literary*) [Mid-16C. < Latin *vincibilis* < *vincere* 'conquer'.] —**vincibility** /vínssə bílləti/ *n* —**vincibleness** *n*

vincristine /vin krís teen/ *n* an alkaloid drug similar to vinblastine [Mid-20C. < modern Latin *Vinca* (see VINCA), + Latin *crista* 'crest'.]

vinculum /víngkyōōləm/ (*plural* **-la** /-lə/) *n* 1 a horizontal line above two or more members of a compound mathematical expression, used like parentheses to show that the expression is to be treated as a single term 2 a band of tissue, especially a ligament [Mid-17C. < Latin, 'fetter, bond' < *vincire* 'tie, fasten'.]

vindaloo /víndə lōō/ (*plural* **-loos**) *n* a very hot curry sauce made with coriander, red chilli, ginger, and other spices, or a dish cooked in this [Late 19C. Via Konkani *vindalu* < Portuguese *vinho de alho*, a wine and garlic sauce, literally 'wine of garlic'.]

vin de pays /ván də páy ee/ (*plural* **vins de pays** /ván də páy ee/) *n* a French wine with the third highest grade of classification, which guarantees that the wine comes from a specified area [< French, 'wine of (the) region']

vindicate /víndi kayt/ (**-cates, -cating, -cated**) *vt* 1 **SHOW TO BE BLAMELESS** to clear somebody or something of blame, guilt, suspicion, or doubt 2 **JUSTIFY** to show that somebody or something is justified or correct 3 **UPHOLD** to defend or maintain something such as a cause or rights [Mid-16C. < Latin *vindicat*, past participle of *vindicare* 'claim, set free, avenge' < *vindic-* 'avenger'.] —**vindicability** *n* —**vindicable** *adj* —**vindication** /víndi káysh'n/ *n* —**vindicator** *n* —**vindicatory** *adj*

vindictive /vin díktiv/ *adj* 1 **VENGEFUL** looking for revenge or done through a desire for revenge 2 **SPITEFUL** feeling, showing, or done through a desire to hurt somebody 3 **MEANT TO PUNISH** describes damages awarded by a court that are set higher than the amount necessary to compensate the victim, in order to punish the defendant [Early 17C. < Latin *vindicta* 'revenge'.]

vin du pays /ván dyoo páy ee/ (*plural* **vins du pays** /ván dyoo páy ee/) *n* a locally produced French wine [< French, 'wine of the region']

vine /vīn/ *n* 1 **CLIMBING PLANT** a plant that supports itself by climbing, twining, or creeping along a surface 2 **STEM** the weak flexible stem of a vine 3 PLANTS = **grapevine** *n.* 1 4 **GRAPEVINES COLLECTIVELY** grapevines considered collectively [13C. Via Old French *vigne* < Latin *vinea* 'vine, vineyard' < *vinum* 'wine'.] —**viny** *adj*

vinedresser /vín dressər/ *n* a tender and pruner of grapevines

vinegar /vínnigər/ *n* **1 SOUR-TASTING LIQUID** a sour-tasting liquid that is a dilute acetic acid made by fermenting beer, wine, or cider, and is used to flavour and preserve foods **2 ILL TEMPER** sourness or ill-tempered behaviour or speech **3** *US* **VITALITY** exuberant energy and enthusiasm [13C. < Old French *vyn egre* 'sour wine' < Latin *vinum acre*.] —**vinegarish** *adj*

vinegar eel, vinegar worm *n* a very small nematode worm that feeds on bacteria that cause fermentation, especially in vinegar. *Anguillula aceti*.

vinegary /vínnigəri/ *adj* **1** with a sour taste or smell like vinegar **2** showing an unpleasant, irritable disposition —**vinegariness** *n*

vinery /vínəri/ (*plural* **-ies**) *n* an area or building, especially a greenhouse, in which grapevines are grown

vineyard /vínnyərd, -yaard/ *n* a piece of land where grapevines are grown

vingt-et-un /vánt ay úN/ *n* the game of pontoon [Late 18C. < French, 'twenty-one'.]

vinho verde /vínnyō vúrdi/ *n* a light, dry, acidic, white or red wine from N Portugal [Mid-20C. < Portuguese, 'green wine' (referring to its youthfulness).]

vini- *prefix* wine, grapes ○ *viniculture* [< Latin *vinum*]

viniculture /vínni kulchər/ *n* AGRIC = **viticulture** —**vinicultural** /vínni kúlchərəl/ *adj* —**viniculturist** /-kúlchrist/ *n*

vinify /vínni fī/ (**-fies, -fying, -fied**) *vt* to ferment grape juice, or another liquid, into wine —**vinification** /vínnəfi káysh'n/ *n*

Vinland /vínlənd/ coastal area of NE North America, now N Newfoundland, visited by Norse voyagers in about AD 986

vino /veénō/ *n* wine, especially cheap wine (*informal*) [Late 19C. < Italian, 'wine'.]

vin ordinaire /ván awrdi náir/ (*plural* **vins ordinaires** /vánz awrdi náir/) *n* cheap table wine, especially from France [Early 19C. < French, 'ordinary wine'.]

vinosity /vī nóssəti/ *n* the distinctive and essential character of wine, including qualities such as body, colour, and taste

vinous /vínəss/ *adj* **1** relating to, typical of, or containing wine **2** tending to drink a lot of wine, or caused by wine-drinking [Mid-17C. < Latin *vinum* 'wine'.] —**vinously** *adv* —**vinousness** *n*

Vinson Massif /vínssən máss eef/ highest mountain in Antarctica, in the central Ellsworth Mountains. Height: 4,897 m/16,066 ft.

vintage /víntij/ *n* **1 WINE PRODUCTION YEAR** the year in which the grapes used in making a particular wine were harvested **2 WINE FROM A PARTICULAR YEAR** wine made from a particular harvest of grapes **3 GRAPE HARVESTING** the harvesting of grapes for wine **4 PERIOD** the period of time when something appeared or began, or when somebody was born or flourished **5 GROUP SHARING CHARACTERISTICS** a group of people or things that are similar or belong to the same period of time (*informal*) ■ *adj* **1 GOOD FOR WINE** produced from or characterized by a good harvest of grapes for wine-making, so that the wine does not have to be improved by blending with wine from another harvest **2 OF THE BEST** representing what is best or most typical of somebody or something **3 CLASSIC** recognized as being of high quality and lasting appeal **4 OUT OF DATE** no longer fashionable or modern ■ *vt* (**-tages, -taging, -taged**) **1 GATHER GRAPES** to harvest grapes to make wine **2 MAKE WINE** to make wine from harvested grapes [14C. Alteration (influenced by VINTNER) of *vendage* < Old French *vendange* < Latin *vindemia* 'grape-gathering' < *vinum* 'wine' + *demere* 'take away'.] —**vintager** *n*

vintage car *n* an old car, especially one built between 1919 and 1930. ◊ **veteran car**

vintage year *n* **1** a year in which the wine that is made is of excellent quality **2** a year of extraordinary accomplishment or success

vintner /víntnər/ *n* a dealer in wines [15C. Via Old French *vinetier* < medieval Latin *vinetarius* < Latin *vinetum* 'vineyard' < *vinum* 'wine'.]

vinyl /vín'l/ *n* **1 CHEMICAL GROUP** CH_2CH a univalent unsaturated chemical group or radical that is formed when one hydrogen atom is removed from ethylene **2 COMPOUND USED IN PLASTICS** a reactive compound that contains the vinyl radical, usually in polymerized form. Use: plastics. **3 PLASTIC MATERIAL** a plastic material, made from a vinyl polymer **4 PLASTIC RECORDS** gramophone records made of a vinyl polymer, as opposed to compact discs [Mid-19C. < VINI- + -YL.] —**vinyl** *adj* —**vinylic** /vī níllik/ *adj*

vinyl chloride *n* CH_2:CHCl a colourless, carcinogenic, explosive, flammable gas. Use: manufacture of polyvinyl chloride, adhesives, organic chemicals.

vinylidene /vī nílli deen/ *n* CH_2:C a bivalent chemical group or radical, made when two hydrogen atoms are removed from one carbon atom of ethylene

vinyl polymer, vinyl resin *n* any odourless, tasteless, thermoplastic material such as PVC made by polymerizing compounds containing vinyl groups

viol /vī əl/ *n* **1** a stringed instrument popular during the 16th and 17th centuries with a fretted fingerboard, a flat-backed body, and six strings, played with a curved bow **2** MUSIC = **viola da gamba** [15C. Via Old French *viole* < Old Provençal *viola*.]

viola[1] /vi ólə/ *n* **1** a stringed instrument slightly larger than a violin held under the chin and played with a long slender bow **2** MUSIC = **viola da gamba** [Late 18C. Via Italian < Old Provençal.]

viola[2] /vī ələ/ *n* a plant related to violets and pansies, especially one with small white, yellow, or purple flowers. Genus: *Viola*. [15C. < Latin, 'violet'.]

violaceous /vī ə láyshəss/ *adj* relating to, belonging to, or typical of the family of plants that includes violets and pansies [Mid-17C. < Latin *violaceus* 'violet-coloured' < *viola* 'violet'.]

viola da braccio /-də bráchō/ (*plural* **violas da braccio**) *n* an old stringed instrument of the viol family, held against the shoulder when played [Mid-19C. < Italian, 'viol for (the) arm'.]

viola da gamba /-də gámbə/ (*plural* **violas da gamba**) *n* an old stringed bass instrument of the viol family, with a range similar to a cello [Late 16C. < Italian, 'viol for (the) leg'.]

viola d'amore /-da máwri/ (*plural* **violas d'amore**) *n* a fretless stringed instrument of the viol family with six or seven strings and a second set of strings that are not played but are made to vibrate by the first set (**sympathetic strings**) [Late 17C. < Italian, 'viol of love'.]

violate /vī ə layt/ (**-lates, -lating, -lated**) *vt* **1 DISREGARD** to act contrary to something such as a law, contract, or agreement, especially in a way that produces significant effects **2 RAPE** to rape or sexually assault somebody **3 DISTURB** to disturb or interrupt something in a rude or violent way **4 DEFILE** to treat something sacred with a lack of respect [15C. < Latin *violatus*, past participle of *violare* 'treat with violence, injure'.] —**violability** *n* —**violable** *adj* —**violableness** *n* —**violably** *adv* —**violation** /vī ə láysh'n/ *n* —**violative** *adj* —**violator** *n*

violence /vī ələnss/ *n* **1 PHYSICAL FORCE** the use of physical force to injure somebody or damage something ○ *threats of violence* **2 ILLEGAL FORCE** the illegal use of unjustified force, or the effect created by the threat of this ○ *robbery with violence* **3 DESTRUCTIVE FORCE** extreme, destructive, or uncontrollable force, especially of natural events ○ *the violence of the storm* **4 FERVOUR** intensity of feeling or expression ○ *the violence of her response to our suggestion* ◇ **do violence to something** to violate, harm, or damage something

violent /vī ələnt/ *adj* **1 USING PHYSICAL FORCE** using physical force to hurt somebody or damage something ○ *violent crime* **2 EMOTIONALLY INTENSE** showing emotional intensity or strong feeling ○ *his violent objections to the plan* **3 SHOWING DESTRUCTIVE FORCE** showing extreme, destructive, or uncontrollable force ○ *a violent thunderstorm* **4 INTENSE** very intense or strong ○ *a violent headache* **5 CAUSED BY FORCE** caused by force rather than natural causes ○ *met a violent death* **6 DISTORTING** distorting or misinterpreting the meaning of something ○ *a violent interpretation of the poem* [14C. < Latin *violentus* 'forcible, vehement'.] —**violently** *adv*

violent storm *n* a storm that causes widespread damage with winds of force 11 on the Beaufort scale, reaching speeds of 103–117 kph/64–72 mph

violet /vī ələt/ *n* **1 FLOWERING PLANT** a low-growing perennial plant. Flowers: irregular, usually purplish-blue. Genus: *Viola*. **2 PLANT RESEMBLING A VIOLET** any of several plants such as the African violet that are like the violet but are not necessarily related to it **3 PURPLISH-BLUE COLOUR** a deep purplish-blue colour [14C. < Old French *violete*, diminutive of *viole* < Latin *viola* 'violet'.] —**violet** *adj*

violin /vī ə lín/ *n* a wooden musical instrument with four strings and an unfretted fingerboard, held under the player's chin and played with a bow [Late 16C. < Italian *violino*, diminutive of *viola* (see VIOLA[1]).] —**violinist** *n*

~~**violincello**~~ incorrect spelling of **violoncello**

violin sonata *n* a sonata for solo violin, usually with piano accompaniment

violist[1] /vi ólist/ *n US* a player of the viola

violist[2] /vī əlist/ *n* a player of the viol

violoncello /vī ələn chéllō/ (*plural* **-los**) *n* a cello (*formal*) [Early 18C. < Italian, diminutive of *violone* (see VIOLONE).]

violone /vī əlōn/ *n* the double-bass viol, larger and with a deeper range than the viola da gamba [Early 18C. < Italian, 'large viola' < *viola* (see VIOLA[1]).]

VIP *abbr* **1** very important person **2** vasoactive intestinal peptide

vipassana /vi pássənə/, **Vipassana** *n* Theravada Buddhist meditation that aims at concentrating the mind on the body

viper /vípər/ *n* **1 POISONOUS SNAKE** a snake with hollow fangs that it uses to inject venom into its victim when it bites. Native to: Europe, Asia, Africa. Family: Viperidae. **2** ZOOL = **adder**[2] *n*. **3 POISONOUS SNAKE NOT OF VIPER FAMILY** a poisonous snake such as the horned viper belonging to a family other than the vipers proper **4** ZOOL = **pit viper** **5 OFFENSIVE TERM** an offensive term for somebody who is considered to be malicious, treacherous, or ungrateful [Early 16C. Via Old French *vipere* < Latin *vipera* 'snake', contraction of assumed *vivipera* 'live-bearing' (from the ancient belief that snakes bore live young) < *vivus* 'alive'.] —**viperine** *adj* —**viperous** *adj* —**viperously** *adv*

viperish /vípərish/ *adj* **1** malicious or spiteful **2** characteristic of or resembling a viper —**viperishly** *adv*

viper's bugloss *n* a widely naturalized weed with rough foliage. Flowers: blue, tubular, in spikes. Native to: Europe, Asia. *Echium vulgare*.

Vir *abbr* **1** Virgil **2** Virgo

VIR *abbr* Victoria Imperatrix Regina

vir- *prefix* = **viro-** (*before vowels*)

viraemia /vī reémi ə/ *n* the presence of viruses in the bloodstream [Mid-20C. < modern Latin, < VIRUS.] —**viraemic** *adj*

virago /vi raágō/ (*plural* **-goes** *or* **-gos**) *n* **1** an offensive term that deliberately insults a woman's temperament or behaviour **2** a woman who is strong and brave (*archaic*) [Pre-12C. < Latin, < *vir* 'man, husband'.] —**viraginous** /vi rájjənəss/ *adj*

viral /vírəl/ *adj* relating to, typical of, or caused by a virus —**virally** *adv*

⚡**viral marketing** *n* a form of marketing in which an organization's customers, wittingly or unwittingly, act as advertisers for its products by spreading knowledge of them by word of mouth e.g. over the Internet (*in e-commerce*) [< the idea of a virus spreading rapidly]

viral pneumonia *n* an infection of the lungs caused by a virus

Virchow /vúrkō/, **Rudolf** (1821–1902) German pathologist and anthropologist

virelay /vírrə lay/ *n* an old French verse form consisting of short lines arranged in stanzas with two rhymes, with the end rhyme repeated as the first line of the next stanza [14C. < French *virelai*.]

virement /veér moN/ *n* an authorized transfer of funds from one use to another [Early 20C. < French, 'turning, transfer' < *virer* 'turn, veer'.]

viremia *n* US = **viraemia**

Viren /veérən/, **Lasse** (*b.* 1949) Finnish athlete

vireo /vírri ō/ (*plural* **-os**) *n* a small insect-eating songbird with greyish or greenish plumage. Native to: Americas. Genus: *Vireo*. [Mid-19C. Via modern Latin < Latin, a bird (probably the greenfinch) < *virere* 'be green'.]

virescent /vī réss'nt/ *adj* **1** being or becoming green **2** describes plant parts that are not normally green but are turned green by disease [Early 19C. < Latin *virescent-*, present participle of *virescere* 'become green'.] —**virescence** *n*

virga /vúrgə/ (*plural* **-ga**) *n* vertical trails of rain, snow, or ice from the underside of a cloud that evaporate before reaching the ground [Mid-20C. < Latin, 'rod, staff, twig'.]

virgate[1] /vúrgət/ *adj* long and thin like a rod [Early 19C. < Latin *virgatus* < *virga* 'rod, staff'.]

virgate[2] /vúrgət/ *n* an old English land measure thought to be the equivalent of about 12 hectares/30 acres [Mid-17C. < medieval Latin *virgata* < Latin *virga* 'rod'.]

Virgil /vúrjil/, **Vergil** (70–19 BC) Roman poet —**Virgilian** /vur jílli ən/ *adj*

virgin /vúrjin/ *n* **1 SOMEBODY WHO HAS NOT HAD SEX** somebody, especially a woman, who has never had sexual intercourse **2 RELIGIOUS WOMAN COMMITTED TO CHASTITY** a woman who has taken a vow of chastity for religious reasons **3 FEMALE ANIMAL** a female animal that has never copulated **4 FEMALE INSECT** a female insect that produces fertile eggs without the help of a male ■ *adj* **1 OF A VIRGIN** relating to, typical of, or being a virgin **2 PURE** in a pure, natural, or clean state **3 NOT TOUCHED BY HUMANS** never having been explored or exploited by humans **4 FIRST** first or happening for the first time **5 FROM FIRST PRESSING** describes vegetable oils that come from the first pressing of fruit, leaves, or seeds without the use of heat **6 PRODUCED DIRECTLY FROM ORE** describes metals produced directly from an ore, not from scrap metal **7 UNALLOYED** found in a pure, unmixed state **8 NEVER HAVING COLLIDED** describes a neutron that has never been in a collision and therefore retains the energy with which it started [12C. Via Old French *virgine* < Latin *virgin-*, stem of *virgo* 'maiden'.]

Virgin *n* **1** CHR = **Virgin Mary 2** ASTRON, ZODIAC = **Virgo** *n*. **1**, **Virgo** *n*. **2**

virginal[1] /vúrjin'l/ *adj* **1 CHASTE** relating to, typical of, or appropriate for somebody, especially a woman, who has never had sexual intercourse **2 LIVING CHASTELY** living in a state of virginity **3 PURE** not corrupted or spoiled in any way —**virginally** *adv*

virginal[2] /vúrjin'l/ *n* a smaller, often legless, oblong version of the harpsichord, popular in the 16th and 17th centuries [Early 16C. Directly or via French < Latin *virginalis* < *virgin* (see VIRGIN).] —**virginalist** *n*

Virgin Birth *n* the Christian doctrine that Jesus Christ was born as the son of God rather than of a human father and that his mother was a virgin

Virginia[1] /vər jínni ə/, **virginia** *n* tobacco of a type originally grown in the state of Virginia

Virginia[2] /və jínni ə/ state of the east-central United States on the Atlantic Ocean. Capital: Richmond. Population: 6,733,996 (1997). Area: 109,624 sq. km/42,326 sq. mi. —**Virginian** *n, adj*

Virginia Beach largest city in Virginia, in the southeast of the state, on the Atlantic Ocean. Population: 430,295 (1994).

Virginia creeper *n* a climbing plant with leaves made up of five leaflets and bluish-black berries. *Parthenocissus quinquefolia*.

Virginia reel *n* a US country dance in which a caller instructs couples facing each other in long rows

Virginia stock *n* a plant with sweet-scented, white and pink four-petalled flowers. Native to: Mediterranean. *Malcolmia maritima*.

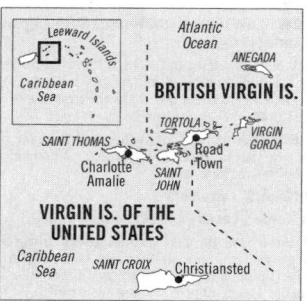

British Virgin Islands and Virgin Islands of the United States

Virgin Islands, British /vúrjin-/ dependent territory of the United Kingdom, consisting of 36 islands in the Caribbean. Capital: Road Town. Population: 13,195 (1996). Area: 153 sq. km/59 sq. mi.

Virgin Islands of the United States unincorporated external territory of the United States in the Caribbean, consisting of three main islands and over 60 smaller islands and islets. Capital: Charlotte Amalie. Population: 97,120 (1996). Area: 153 sq. km/59 sq. mi.

virginity /vər jínnəti/ *n* **1** the state of being a virgin **2** the state of being untouched, unexplored, or unspoilt

Virgin Mary *n* in Christian tradition, the mother of Jesus Christ

Virgin Queen *n* a name used for Elizabeth I, queen of England

virgin's bower *n* a clematis that has clusters of small white flowers. Native to: E North America. *Clematis virginiana*.

virgin soil *n* **1** soil that has not yet been used for cultivation **2** a thing that has not been used, developed, or exploited, or a person who does not have experience of something

virgin wool *n* wool that has not already been used to make something

Virgo /vúrgō/ (*plural* **-gos**) *n* **1 LARGE CONSTELLATION** a large constellation on the celestial equator containing the binary star Spica. See illustration at **constellation 2 SIXTH SIGN OF ZODIAC** the sixth sign of the zodiac, represented by a virgin and lasting from approximately 23 August to 22 September **3 Virgo** (*plural* **-gos** *or* **-goans**) SOMEBODY BORN UNDER VIRGO somebody whose birthday falls between 23 August and 22 September [Pre-12C. < Latin, 'maiden'.] —**Virgo** *adj* —**Virgoan** *n*

virgo intacta /vúrgō intáktə/ *n* a girl or woman whose hymen remains unbroken [< Latin, 'intact virgin']

virgulate /vúrgyoōlət/ *adj* shaped like a rod [Mid-19C. < Latin *virgula*, diminutive of *virga* 'rod, staff, twig'.]

virgule /vúr gyool/ *n* PRINTING = **solidus** *n*. **1** (*technical*) [Mid-19C. Via French, 'comma, little rod' < Latin *virgula* (see VIRGULATE).]

viricide /vírə sīd/, **virucide** *n* a drug or other agent that neutralizes or destroys a virus or viruses [Mid-20C. < VIRUS.] —**viricidal** /vírə sīd'l/ *adj*

viridescent /vírri déss'nt/ *adj* being or becoming green [Mid-19C. < late Latin *viridescent-*, present participle of *viridescere* 'become green' < *viridis* 'green'.] —**viridescence** *n*

viridian /vi ríddi ən/ *n* **1** a green pigment made from a hydrated chromic oxide **2** a bluish-green colour —**viridian** *adj*

viridity /vi ríddəti/ *n* (*literary*) **1** the state of being green **2** the state of being inexperienced

virile /vírrīl/ *adj* **1 MASCULINE** relating to or having the characteristics of an adult male **2 POTENT** able to carry out the male sexual function **3 STRONG** showing strength and forcefulness [15C. < Latin *virilis* < *vir* 'man, husband'.]

virilism /vírralizəm/ *n* the development of male secondary sex characteristics culturally considered to be unusual in a woman, e.g. body hair or a deep voice

virility /və rílləti/ *n* the state of being male, having male characteristics, or male sexual potency

virilocal /vírri lōk'l/ *adj* describes a form of marriage or the custom where, after the wedding, the bride moves to her new husband's family home [Mid-20C. < Latin *virilis* 'of a man' (see VIRILE).]

virion /vírri ən/ *n* the form taken by a virus when it is outside living cells and capable of causing infection, consisting of a core of DNA or RNA surrounded by a protein coat, sometimes covered by an outer envelope [Mid-20C. < French < *virien* 'viral' + -ON[1].]

viro- *prefix* virus, viral ○ *virology* [< VIRUS]

viroid /vír oyd/ *n* an infectious RNA particle that is like a virus but smaller [Mid-20C. < VIRUS.]

virology /vī rólləji/ *n* the scientific study of viruses and the diseases caused by them —**virologic** /vīrə lójjik/ *adj* —**virological** *adj* —**virologically** *adv* —**virologist** *n*

virtu /vur toó/, **vertu** *n* **1** a love of or taste for fine art objects or curios **2** fine art objects or curios [Early 18C. < Italian, 'virtue'.]

⚡**virtual** /vúrchoo əl/ *adj* **1 BEING SOMETHING IN PRACTICE** being something in effect even if not in reality or not conforming to the generally accepted definition of the term **2 HYPOTHETICAL** describes a particle whose existence is suggested to explain observed phenomena but is not proved or directly observable **3 GENERATED BY COMPUTER**

simulated by a computer for reasons of economic convenience, or performance [14C. < medieval Latin *vi tualis* < Latin *virtus* (see VIRTUE).] —**virtuality** /vúrchoo állət *n*

⚡**virtual assistant** *n* a user of computer and phor links to work from a distance as a personal assistant t somebody else ○ *'There are many reasons why home-base business owners are hiring virtual assistants'.* (Washington Post; December 1998)

⚡**virtual community** *n* a group of people con municating with each other via the Internet ○ *'… a interactive virtual community where local residents can d anything from look for local work to book seats at the loc cinema'.* (BBC website; April 1999)

⚡**virtual disk** *n* random-access memory used as a dis drive

virtual focus *n* the point from which divergent reflecte or refracted light rays seem to originate

virtual image *n* an image from which reflected o refracted light rays appear to diverge

virtually /vúrchoo əli/ *adv* **1** in effect even if not in fac **2** almost but not quite

⚡**virtual machine** *n* a program running on a compute that creates a self-contained operating environmen and presents the appearance to the user of a differen computer

⚡**virtual memory**, **virtual storage** *n* a technique fo creating the illusion that a computer has more memor than it really has by swapping blocks or pages of dat between memory and external storage

⚡**virtual reality** *n* **1** a technique by which a compute simulates a three-dimensional physical environmen using visual and auditory stimuli with and within which people can interact **2** a computer-generated en vironment that simulates three-dimensional reality

⚡**Virtual Reality Modelling Language** *n* full form o VRML

⚡**virtual space** *n* a computer-generated simulation of a environment that is experienced by a human operato ○ *You can enter virtual spaces to conduct real-time type conversations.*

⚡**virtual storage** *n* COMPUT = **virtual memory**

virtue /vúrchoo/ *n* **1 GOODNESS** the quality of being morall good or righteous ○ *a paragon of virtue* **2 GOOD QUALITY** particular quality that is morally good ○ *Patience is virtue.* **3 ADMIRABLE QUALITY** a particular quality that i good or admirable, but not necessarily in terms of mor ality **4 CHASTITY** the moral quality of being chaste, es pecially in a woman **5 WORTH** the worth, advantage, o beneficial quality of something ○ *knew the virtue of thrif* **6 EFFECTIVE FORCE** the power or efficacy that something contains to do something (*archaic*) ■ **virtues** *npl* ORDER OF ANGELS the fifth of the nine traditional orders in th hierarchy of angels [12C. Via Old French *vertu* < Latin 'manliness, excellence, worth' < *vir* 'man, husband'.] — **virtueless** *adj* ◇ **by** *or* **in virtue of** because of, through the power of, or by the authority of something ◇ **make a virtue of necessity** to do something with good grace when you are obliged to do it anyway

virtuosi plural of **virtuoso**

virtuosity /vúrchoo óssəti/ *n* **1** great skill or technique shown by somebody who excels at doing something especially performing music **2** interest in, or knowledge and appreciation of, fine art objects

virtuoso /vúrchoo óssō/ (*plural* **-sos** *or* **-si** /-óssi/) *n* **1** EX CEPTIONAL PERFORMER a musician who shows exceptiona ability, technique, or artistry **2 TALENTED PERSON** a persor who shows exceptional technique or ability in some thing **3 CONNOISSEUR** a person who is knowledgeable and cultivated in appreciating the fine arts [Early 17C. < Italian, 'skillful, versed' < late Latin *virtuosus* 'good' < Latin *virtus* (see VIRTUE).] —**virtuosic** /-óssik/ *adj* —**virtuosically** *adv*

virtuous /vúrchoo əss/ *adj* **1** having or showing moral goodness or righteousness **2** not having sexual intercourse with anyone except a partner in marriage, especially a husband —**virtuously** *adv* —**virtuousness** *n*

virucide *n* MED = **viricide**

virulent /vírrooliənt, vírryoō-/ *adj* **1** extremely poisonous, infectious, or damaging to organisms **2** showing great bitterness, malice, or hostility ○ *virulent criticism* [14C. < Latin *virulentus* 'poisonous' < *virus* 'poison, venom'.] — **virulence** *n* —**virulently** *adv*

viruliferous /vìrrō líffərəss, vírryŏō-/ *adj* describes an organism that contains or carries a virus [Mid-20C. < VIRULENT.]

virus /vírəss/ *n* 1 SUBMICROSCOPIC ENTITY a minute parasitic particle of a nucleic acid surrounded by protein that can only replicate within a host cell 2 VIRAL DISEASE a disease caused by a virus 3 DISRUPTIVE COMPUTER PROGRAM a short computer program, hidden within another, that makes copies of itself and spreads them, disrupting the operation of a computer that receives one. ◊ **Trojan Horse** *n.* 3, **worm** *n.* 8 4 SOMETHING THAT CORRUPTS anything that has a corrupting or poisonous effect, especially on people's minds [Late 16C. < Latin, 'poison, venom, medicinal liquid'.]

Vis. *abbr* 1 Viscount 2 Viscountess

visa /véezə/ *n* 1 PASSPORT INSERTION an official endorsement in a passport authorizing the bearer to enter or leave, and travel in or through, a particular country or region 2 AUTHORIZATION any mark of official authorization ■ *vt* 1 SUPPLY DOCUMENT WITH VISA to insert a visa in a passport or other document 2 GIVE SOMEBODY A VISA to provide somebody with a visa [Mid-19C. Via French < Latin *visa* 'things seen' < past participle of *videre* 'see'.]

visage /vízzij/ *n* 1 somebody's face or facial expression (*literary*) 2 the appearance or look of something [13C. < Old French, < *vis* 'face, appearance' < Latin *visus*, past participle of *videre* 'see'.]

visagiste /vée zaa zhéest/ *n* a specialist in applying facial makeup [Mid-20C. < French, < *visage* (see VISAGE).]

vis-à-vis /véezə vée/ *prep* 1 REGARDING in relation to 2 OPPOSITE opposite to or face to face with ■ *adv* FACE TO FACE face to face, or opposite each other ■ *n* (*plural* **vis-à-vis**) 1 SOMEBODY OR SOMETHING FACING somebody or something that is face to face with another 2 COUNTERPART a person who is the counterpart of somebody else 3 HORSE-DRAWN CARRIAGE a horse-drawn carriage in which people sit facing each other [Mid-18C. < French, 'face to face' < Old French *vis* (see VISAGE).]

Visayan /vi saá yən, bi-/, **Bisayan** /bi-/ *n* 1 a member of a people of the central and southern islands of the Philippines 2 the Austronesian language of the Visayan people [Early 20C. < a language of the central Philippines.] —**Visayan** *adj*

Visby /vízbi/ port on the west of the island of Gotland, SE Sweden. Population: 57,110 (1990).

visc *abbr* viscosity

Visc. *abbr* 1 Viscount 2 Viscountess

visc- *prefix* = **visco-** (*before vowels*)

viscacha /vi skaáchə/, **vizcacha** *n* a burrowing, gregarious rodent with black and white markings on its face, related to and resembling the chinchilla. Native to: South America. *Lagostomus maximus*. [Early 17C. Via Spanish < Quechua *(h)uiscacha*.]

viscera /víssərə/ *npl* the internal organs of the body, especially those of the abdomen such as the intestines [Early 18C. < Latin, 'internal organs, entrails'.]

visceral /víssərəl/ *adj* 1 INSTINCTUAL proceeding from instinct rather than from reasoned thinking 2 EMOTIONAL characterized by or showing basic emotions 3 OF INTERNAL ORGANS relating to or affecting one or more internal organs of the body —**viscerally** *adv*

visceromotor /víssərō mṓtər/ *adj* relating to the nervous control of gut movements, especially to disorders of bowel movement

viscid /víssid/ *adj* 1 thick and sticky in consistency 2 describes a leaf or other plant part that is covered with a sticky substance [Mid-17C. < late Latin *viscidus* < Latin *viscum* (see VISCOUS).] —**viscidity** /vi síddəti/ *n* —**viscidly** *adv* —**viscidness** *n*

visco- *prefix* viscosity ○ *viscoelastic* [< VISCOUS]

viscoelastic /vískō i lástik/ *adj* describes asphalt and many polymers that exhibit both viscous and elastic properties when deformed —**viscoelasticity** /vískō ée la stíssəti/ *n*

viscometer /vi skómmitər/, **viscosimeter** /vískō símmitər/ *n* an instrument used to measure the viscosity of a substance —**viscometric** /vískō méttrik/ *adj* —**viscometrical** *adj* —**viscometry** /vi skómmətri/ *n*

Visconti /vi skónti/, **Luchino** (1906–76) Italian film and theatre director

viscose /vískōss/ *n* 1 rayon with a soft silky feel made from a cellulose solution 2 a cellulose solution of thick consistency. Use: rayon manufacture. [Late 19C. < late Latin *viscosus* (see VISCOUS).]

viscosimeter *n* PHYS = **viscometer**

viscosity /vi skóssəti/ (*plural* **-ties**) *n* 1 THICKNESS AND STICKINESS a thick and sticky consistency or quality 2 PROPERTY OF FLUID THAT RESISTS FLOWING the property of a fluid or semifluid that causes it to resist flowing 3 MEASURE OF SUBSTANCE'S RESISTANCE TO MOTION a measure of the resistance of a substance to motion under an applied force

viscosity index *n* an arbitrary scale for lubricating oils that is used to indicate how much the viscosity of the oil varies according to its temperature

viscount /ví kownt/ *n* 1 BRITISH NOBLEMAN a British nobleman of a rank above baron 2 COUNT'S SON OR YOUNGER BROTHER in European countries other than the United Kingdom, especially France, somebody whose father or elder brother is a count 3 COUNT'S REPRESENTATIVE in medieval Europe, somebody acting for or representing a count [14C. Via Anglo-Norman *viscounte*, Old French *vi(s)conte* < medieval Latin *vicecomes* < Latin *vice* 'in place of' (see VICE³) + *comes* 'companion'.] —**viscountcy** *n* —**viscounty** *n*

viscountess /ví kowntəss/ *n* 1 a woman who holds a rank equivalent to viscount 2 a wife or widow of a viscount

viscous /vískəss/ *adj* 1 thick and sticky, reluctant to flow, and difficult to stir 2 describes a fluid that has a relatively high resistance to flow [14C. < late Latin *viscosus* 'sticky' < Latin *viscum* 'mistletoe, birdlime made from mistletoe berries'.] —**viscously** *adv* —**viscousness** *n*

Visct. *abbr* 1 Viscount 2 Viscountess

viscus /vískəss/ *n* singular of **viscera**

vise /vīss/ *n, vt* US = **vice**

Vishakhapatnam /vi shaákə pútnəm/ city in SE India, on the Bay of Bengal. Population: 750,024 (1991).

Vishnu /vish noo/ *n* a Hindu god called the Preserver, the second member of the triad that includes Brahma the Creator and Shiva the Destroyer [Mid-17C. < Sanskrit *Viṣṇu*.]

visibility /vízzə bílləti/ *n* 1 ABILITY TO BE SEEN the fact of being able to be seen 2 DISTANCE IT IS POSSIBLE TO SEE the distance it is possible to see under the prevailing atmospheric or weather conditions 3 CLEAR VIEW the ability to provide somebody, especially the driver of a vehicle, with a good view of what is around him or her, or the view obtained from a particular position 4 PUBLIC PROMINENCE the degree to which somebody or something is easily noticed by and catches the attention of the public or a particular group of people ○ *the comparatively low visibility of the board of directors*

visible /vízzəb'l/ *adj* 1 ABLE TO BE SEEN capable of being seen by, or perceptible to, the human eye ○ *the visible spectrum* 2 IN SIGHT in somebody's sight at a particular time ○ *The building became visible again as soon as she turned the corner.* 3 OBVIOUS easily noticeable ○ *the very visible results of the recent floods* 4 DETECTABLE capable of being discovered by means of the mental faculties ○ *no visible prospect of a solution to the problem* 5 OFTEN SEEN PUBLICLY frequently in the public eye ○ *the company's very visible head of public relations* 6 DESIGNED TO KEEP SOMETHING IN VIEW designed to keep information or an item in view or able to be readily brought to view ○ *a visible index* 7 CONSISTING OF ACTUAL GOODS in the form of, or relating to, actual goods imported or exported, as opposed to other types of transaction affecting a country's balance of trade ○ *visible exports* [14C. < Latin *visibilis* < *vis-*, past participle of *videre* 'see'.] —**visibleness** *n* —**visibly** *adv*

visible speech *n* 1 a set of phonetic symbols intended to represent the position of the lips, tongue, and other speech organs in creating sounds 2 a visual representation of speech using a spectrograph that disperses radiation into a spectrum and photographs it

Visigoth /vízzi goth/ *n* a member of an ancient Germanic people who conquered parts of the Roman Empire during the 5th century, taking over parts of Spain and S France, where they established a kingdom that lasted until the start of the 8th century. ◊ **Ostrogoth** [Mid-16C. < late Latin *Visigothi* 'Visigoths'.] —**Visigothic** /vízzi góthik/ *adj*

vision /vízh'n/ *n* 1 EYESIGHT the ability to see 2 MENTAL PICTURE an image or concept in the imagination ○ *visions of power and wealth* 3 SOMETHING SEEN IN DREAM an image or series of images seen in a dream or trance, often interpreted as having religious, revelatory, or prophetic significance 4 FAR-SIGHTEDNESS the ability to anticipate possible future events and developments 5 TELEVISION PICTURE the picture on a television screen 6 SOMEBODY OR SOMETHING BEAUTIFUL a beautiful or pleasing sight [13C. < Latin *vision-* < *vis-* (see VISIBLE).] —**visional** *adj* —**visionally** *adv* —**visionless** *adj*

visionary /vízh'nəri/ *adj* 1 FULL OF FORESIGHT characterized by unusually acute foresight and imagination 2 IMAGINARY produced by, resulting from, or originating in the imagination 3 INCAPABLE OF BEING REALIZED so idealistic or unrealistic as to be unrealizable in practice 4 GIVEN TO DREAMINESS tending by nature to be dreamy or to have impractical schemes and ideas 5 RELATING TO MYSTICAL VISIONS relating to or seen in a mystical vision 6 HAVING VISIONS given to seeing mystical visions ■ *n* (*plural* **-ies**) 1 SOMEBODY WITH MUCH FORESIGHT somebody of unusually acute foresight and imagination 2 SOMEBODY WHO HAS VISIONS a person who has mystical visions 3 DREAMER a person who daydreams or indulges in impractical schemes and ideas —**visionariness** *n*

vision mixer *n* 1 a technician who mixes and combines the different camera shots during the production of a television programme or film 2 a piece of equipment used by a vision mixer in television or film production

vision quest *n* a personal spiritual search undertaken by an adolescent Native North American boy in order to learn by means of a trance or vision the identity of his guardian spirit

visit /vízzit/ *v* 1 *vti* GO TO SEE to go to see and spend time with somebody, especially as an act of affection or friendship ○ *Nobody visited him in hospital.* 2 *vt* STAY WITH to go to stay with somebody for a time as a guest in his or her home ○ *I'm going to visit my family during the holidays.* 3 *vti* GO TO SEE PLACE to go to see or stay at a place for a time, e.g. as a tourist 4 *vt* GO TO INSPECT PLACE to go to a place as an official inspector 5 *vt* INFLICT SOMETHING ON to inflict something unpleasant such as punishment or vengeance on somebody (*archaic*) ○ *visited them with plagues* 6 *vi US* CHAT WITH to engage in amiable or casual conversation with somebody ■ *n* 1 SOCIAL CALL a trip to see somebody and a period of time spent in his or her company 2 STAY IN A PLACE an extended temporary stay in a place, e.g. as somebody's guest or as a tourist 3 OFFICIAL INSPECTION an official call paid for the purpose of inspection 4 BOARDING OF SHIP the boarding of a ship on the high seas to carry out a search for contraband 5 *US* CHAT an amiable or casual conversation [12C. Directly or via French < Latin *visitare* 'go to see', < *visare* 'to view' < *vis-* (see VISIBLE).] —**visitable** *adj*

visitant /vízzitənt/ *n* 1 BIRDS = **visitor** *n.* 2 2 VISITOR a visitor (*archaic*) 3 VISITING SPIRIT a being thought to visit from the spirit world ■ *adj* MAKING VISIT paying a visit to somebody or something

visitation /vízzi táysh'n/ *n* 1 OFFICIAL VISIT an official visit for inspection or examination 2 SOCIAL VISIT a social visit to somebody's home, especially if it is unwelcome or lasts too long (*humorous*) 3 PUNISHMENT FROM GOD a punishment or, sometimes, a benefit received, especially one believed to be sent by God 4 APPEARANCE FROM SPIRIT WORLD a supposed appearance made by a supernatural being 5 *US* VISIT WITH CHILD GRANTED TO PARENT the right of a divorced parent to have access to a child for a specified period of time, or a period of time with the child granted by this right —**visitational** *adj*

Visitation *n* 1 the visit made by the Virgin Mary after the Annunciation to her cousin Elizabeth 2 a Christian festival celebrating the Visitation of the Virgin Mary to Elizabeth. Date: 2 July.

visiting card *n* a small card bearing the name and sometimes the address of a person, presented, especially in former times, when visiting or left behind when calling and finding that somebody is out. US term **calling card**

visiting fireman *n US* an important visitor who is entertained lavishly and impressively

visiting hours *npl* the period of time during which patients in a hospital may have visitors

visiting professor *n* a professor from one university who teaches at another for a term or academic year

visiting teacher *n US* EDUC = **home teacher**

visitor /vízzitər/ *n* 1 a person who visits somebody or a place 2 a migratory bird that regularly spends a short time in a place

visitor centre *n* a building offering information and services to visitors in a city or at a historical or archaeological site, a park, or a nature reserve

visitors' book *n* a book in which visitors, e.g. to a house, guesthouse, hotel, or art gallery, write their names, their home addresses, and often their comments on the visit. ◊ **guest book**

visitorship /vízzitər ship/ *n* the total number of tourists visiting a particular place

visitor's passport *n* a one-year British passport, phased out in 1995, that permitted the holder to visit certain countries for periods of up to three months

visna /víssnə/ *n* a chronic progressive pneumonia of sheep and goats [Mid-20C. < Old Norse, 'wither'.]

visor /vízər/, **vizor** *n* **1 TRANSPARENT FRONT OF HELMET** a hinged front part of a helmet, made of transparent or tinted plastic and designed to protect the face or eyes, especially on helmets worn by motorcyclists or welders **2 FRONT OF MEDIEVAL HELMET** a hinged metal front part of a medieval helmet in a suit of armour designed to protect the face and having slits for the eyes to see through **3 EYESHADE** a shade for the eyes attached to a band worn around the head **4** *US* **CAP PEAK** the peak of a cap **5 FLAP OVER A WINDSCREEN FOR GLARE** a flap mounted above the windscreen inside a car used to shield the eyes from glare [13C. < Anglo-Norman *viser* < French *vis* (see VISAGE).] —**visored** *adj*

vista /vístə/ *n* **1 SCENIC VIEW** a scenic or panoramic view **2 VIEW THROUGH NARROW OPENING** a view seen through a long narrow opening, e.g. between rows of trees or buildings **3 MENTAL PICTURE** a mental picture covering a wide range of objects or a long succession of events in the past or future ○ *open up vistas of expansion into hitherto untapped markets* [Mid-17C. < Italian, 'view' < past participle of *vedere* 'see' < Latin *videre*.]

Vistula /vístulə/ longest river of Poland, emptying into the Baltic Sea at the Gulf of Gdansk. Length: 1,090 km/675 mi.

visual /vízhoo əl, vízzyoo-/ *adj* **1 OF VISION** relating to vision or sight **2 VISIBLE** able or intended to be seen by the eyes, especially as opposed to being registered by one of the other senses or by a machine ○ *visual humour* **3 PERCEPTIBLE BY THE MIND'S EYE** able to be perceived as a picture in the mind rather than as an abstract idea ○ *a visual memory* **4 DONE BY SIGHT ONLY** done by sight only and without the use of scientific instruments or equipment ○ *visual navigation* ■ *n* **PIECE OF ILLUSTRATIVE MATERIAL** a photograph, picture, chart, or graph that displays information or promotional material in a way that appeals to the eye [15C. < late Latin *visualis* < Latin *visus* 'sight' < past participle of *videre* 'see'.] —**visually** *adv* —**visualness** *n*

visual acuity *n* acuteness of vision as determined by a comparison with the normal ability to identify letters at a distance of 6 m/20 ft

visual aid *n* something such as a model, chart, or film that is looked at as a complement to a lesson or presentation

visual arts *npl* arts such as painting or sculpture that are perceived by sight

visual binary *n* a star that can be seen to be a double star either with the naked eye or when viewed through a telescope

visual field *n* OPTICS = **field of vision**

visualisation *n* = **visualization**

visualise *vti* = **visualize**

visualize /vízhoo ə līz, vízzyoo-/ (**-izes, -izing, -ized**), **visualise** (**-ises, -ising, -ised**) *v* **1** *vti* **IMAGINE** to form a visual image of something in the mind **2** *vti* **CREATE POSITIVE MENTAL PICTURE** to create a vivid positive mental picture of something such as a desired outcome to a problem, in order to promote a sense of well-being **3** *vt* **MAKE IMAGE OF INTERNAL ORGANS** to produce an image of an internal organ or other part of the body by using X-rays or other means such as magnetic resonance imaging —**visualization** /vízhoo ə lī záysh'n, vízzyoo-/ *n* —**visualizer** *n*

visually impaired *adj* having reduced vision, especially having eyesight so poor that it interferes with the ability to perform day-to-day activities effectively

visual-motor coordination *n* the coordination of the body's visual and motor systems, as shown, e.g., in reaching for something being looked at

visual purple *n* BIOL = **rhodopsin**

visuomotor /vízhoo ō mōtər, vízzyoo-/ *adj* relating to or involving motor processes that are linked to vision, e.g. the coordination of movements

vital /vīt'l/ *adj* **1 CRUCIAL** extremely important and necessary, or indispensable to the survival or continuing effectiveness of something **2 LIVELY** full of animation or vigour **3 OF LIFE** relating to life **4 NEEDED FOR LIFE** required for the continuation of life [14C. < Latin *vitalis* < *vita* 'life'.] —**vitalness** *n*

SYNONYMS See ***necessary.***

vital capacity *n* a measure of the air that can be exhaled from the lungs after maximum inhalation

vitalise *vt* = **vitalize**

vitalism /vītəlizəm/ *n* a doctrine that maintains that life and the functions of a living organism depend on a nonmaterial force or principle separate from physical and chemical processes. ◊ **dynamism, mechanism** —**vitalistic** /vītə lístik/ *adj* —**vitalistically** *adv*

vitality /vī tálləti/ *n* **1 LIVELINESS** abundant physical and mental energy usually combined with a wholehearted and joyous approach to situations and activities **2 DURABILITY** the ability of something to live and grow or to continue in existence **3 VITAL PRINCIPLE** the nonmaterial force that, according to vitalism, distinguishes the living from the nonliving

vitalize /vītə līz/ (**-izes, -izing, -ized**), **vitalise** (**-talises, -talising, -talised**) *vt* **1** to cause somebody or something to live **2** to make somebody or something lively —**vitalization** /vītə lī záysh'n/ *n* —**vitalizer** *n*

vitally /vītəli/ *adv* extremely or indispensably

vitals /vīt'lz/ *npl* **1 ORGANS ESSENTIAL TO LIFE** the internal organs of the body that are essential to life, especially the stomach and intestines **2 GENITALS** the genitals, especially those of a man (*humorous*) **3 ESSENTIALS** the essential parts of something [Early 17C. < Latin *vitalia* 'vital things' < form of *vitalis* (see VITAL).]

vital signs *npl* the signs that indicate life, namely pulse, body temperature, breathing, and blood pressure

vital staining *n* the process of using a substance that colours only live cells in order to study the fate of certain cells in embryonic development

vital statistics *npl* **1** statistics of human births, deaths, marriages, and health **2** the measurements of a woman's bust, waist, and hips (*dated informal; considered offensive by many people*)

vitamin /víttəmin, vītə-/ *n* **1** any organic substance essential in small quantities to normal metabolism in most animals **2** a vitamin in a pill or capsule form [Early 20C. < German *Vitamine* < Latin *vita* 'life' + AMINE.] —**vitaminic** /víttə mínnik, vītə-/ *adj*

vitamin A, vitamin A_1 *n* a fat-soluble vitamin found in some vegetables, fish, milk, and eggs, important for normal vision

vitamin A_2 *n* a form of vitamin A obtained from fish liver

vitamin B *n* BIOCHEM **1** = **vitamin B complex 2** = **thiamine**

vitamin B_1 *n* BIOCHEM = **thiamine**

vitamin B_{12} *n* a water-soluble vitamin obtained only from animal products and fish, important for normal blood formation

vitamin B_2 *n* BIOCHEM = **riboflavin**

vitamin B_6 *n* BIOCHEM = **pyridoxine**

vitamin B complex *n* a group of water-soluble coenzyme vitamins found in many foods

vitamin C *n* a water-soluble vitamin found in fruits and leafy vegetables

vitamin D *n* a fat-soluble vitamin that occurs in fish-liver oils and eggs, essential for the formation of bones and teeth

vitamin D_2 *n* a form of vitamin D made by plants

vitamin D_3 *n* BIOCHEM a form of vitamin D formed by the action of sunlight on the skin. = **cholecalciferol**

vitamin E *n* a mixture of fat-soluble vitamins found in seed oils, essential for normal reproduction

vitamin G *n* US = **riboflavin**

vitamin H *n* US BIOCHEM = **biotin**

vitamin K *n* a fat-soluble vitamin essential for blood clotting

vitamin K_1 *n* a form of vitamin K found in green vegetables

vitamin K_2 *n* a form of vitamin K found in fish

vitamin P *n* BIOCHEM = **bioflavonoid**

vitellin /vi téllin/ *n* a protein in egg yolk [Mid-19C. < *vitellus*.]

vitelline /vi téll īn, -téllin/ *adj* **1** relating to egg yolk **2** of the yellow colour of egg yolk [< medieval Latin *vitellinu* < Latin *vitellus* 'egg yolk']

vitelline membrane *n* the membrane that encloses a fertilized egg

vitellus /vi télləss/ (*plural* **-luses** *or* **-li** /-lī/) *n* the yolk of an egg [Early 18C. < Latin, 'egg yolk'.]

vitiate /víshi ayt/ (**-ates, -ating, -ated**) *vt* **1 MAKE SOMETHING INEFFECTIVE** to destroy or drastically reduce the effectiveness of something, or make it invalid **2 MAKE SOMETHING DEFECTIVE** to cause something to become defective **3 DEBASE** to degrade something morally [Mid-16C. < Latin *vitiare* < *vitium* 'fault, vice'.] —**vitiable** *adj* —**vitiation** /víshi áysh'n/ *n* —**vitiator** *n*

viticulture /vítti kulchər/ *n* the science or practice of growing grapevines, especially for wine making [Late 19C. < Latin *vitis* 'vine'.] —**viticultural** /vítti kúlchərəl/ *adj* —**viticulturally** *adv* —**viticulturist** *n*

vitiligo /vítti lígō/ *n* a skin disorder in which smooth whitish patches appear on the skin [Late 16C. < Latin, 'skin eruption'.]

Vitoria /vi táwri ə/ capital of the Basque Country in N Spain. Population: 204,961 (1991).

Vitória /vi táwri ə/ port in E Brazil, on an island in Espírito Santo Bay. Population: 258,245 (1991).

vitr- *prefix* = **vitri-**

vitrain /vítttrayn/ *n* a narrow glassy band found in bituminous coal [Early 20C. < VITREOUS + *-ain* after FUSAIN.]

vitrectomy /vi tréktəmi/ (*plural* **-mies**) *n* a surgical operation to remove some or all of the vitreous humour of the eye

vitreous /víttri əss/ *adj* **1 SIMILAR TO GLASS** having the characteristics or appearance of glass **2 OF GLASS** relating to, consisting of, or derived from glass **3 OF VITREOUS HUMOUR** relating to the vitreous humour of the eye [Mid-17C. < Latin *vitreus* < *vitrum* 'glass'.] —**vitreosity** /víttri óssəti/ *n* —**vitreousness** /víttri əsnəss/ *n*

vitreous body *n* the transparent gel that fills the main cavity of the eyeball, between the lens and the retina

vitreous enamel *n* an opaque glassy coating applied to steel or other metals through firing

vitreous humour *n* the fluid component of the gel (**vitreous body**) that fills the main cavity of the eye between the lens and retina

vitreous silica *n* glass made solely from silica

vitrescent /vi tréss'nt/ *adj* capable of being made into glass [Mid-18C. < Latin *vitrum* 'glass'.]

vitri- *prefix* glass ○ *vitrify* [< Latin *vitrum*]

vitric /víttrik/ *adj* having the characteristics or appearance of glass [Early 20C. < Latin *vitrum* 'glass'.]

vitrification /víttrifi káysh'n/ *n* **1** the process of converting materials to glass **2** the point at which a pot loses its porosity during a firing

vitriform /víttri fawrm/ *adj* having the form or appearance of glass [Late 18C. < Latin *vitrum* 'glass'.]

vitrify /víttri fī/ (**-fies, -fying, -fied**) *vti* to become changed into glass, or to change materials into glass [Late 16C. < French *vitrifier* or directly < Latin *vitrum*, 'glass'.] —**vitrifiability** /víttri fī ə bílləti/ *n* —**vitrifiable** *adj*

vitrine /víttreen/ *n* a cabinet or case with glass walls for displaying specimens or art objects [Late 19C. < French, < *vitre* 'glass' < Latin *vitrum* 'glass'.]

vitriol /víttri əl/ *n* **1 BITTER HATRED** extreme bitterness and hatred towards somebody or something, or an expression of this feeling in speech or writing **2 GLASSY METALLIC SULPHATE** a glassy metallic sulphate such as that of copper or iron **3 SULPHURIC ACID** sulphuric acid (*archaic*) [14C. < medieval Latin *vitriolum* < Latin *vitrum* 'glass'.]

vitriolic /víttri óllik/ *adj* **1** filled with or expressing violent and bitter hatred towards somebody or something **2** resembling a glassy metallic sulphate —**vitriolically** *adv*

Vitruvius /vi troóvi əss/ (*fl.* 1st century BC) Roman architect and engineer

vitta /víttə/ (*plural* **-tae** /-tee/) *n* **1** a tube or cavity containing oil in the carpels of the family of plants that includes carrot, parsley, and celery **2** a stripe or band of colour on the body of an animal [Late 17C. < Latin, 'headband'.] —**vittate** *adj*

ittles /vítt'lz/ *npl* food or other provisions (*archaic*) [Variant of VICTUAL]

ituline /víttyŏŏ līn, -lin/ *adj* relating to or resembling a calf or veal [Mid-17C. < Latin *vitulinus* < *vitulus* 'calf'.]

ituperate /vī tyóopə rayt, vi-/ (**-ates, -ating, -ated**) *vti* to attack somebody in harshly abusive or critical language [Mid-16C. < Latin *vituperare* < *vitium* 'fault, vice' + *parare* 'make ready'.] —**vituperative** /vī tyóopərativ, vi-/ *adj* —**vituperatively** *adv* —**vituperativeness** *n* —**vituperator** *n* —**vituperatory** /vī tyóopərətəri, vi-/ *adj*

ituperation /vī tyóopə ráysh'n, vi-/ *n* **1** an outburst of violently abusive or harshly critical language **2** the use of violent abuse or extremely harsh criticism

va[1] /véevə/ *interj* used to express enthusiastic support for somebody ○ *Viva the president!* [Mid-17C. < Italian, 'may he, she, or it live', form of *vivere* 'to live' < Latin.]

va[2] /vívə/ *n* an examination, especially one taken as part of a university degree, in which a student is asked and answers questions in a spoken interview rather than on paper ■ *vt* (**-vas, -vaing, -vaed**) to examine a student orally [Late 19C. Shortening of VIVA VOCE.]

vace /vi vàachi/ *adv* in a lively and spirited manner (*musical direction*) ■ *n* a piece of music, or a section of a piece, played vivace [Late 17C. < Italian, 'lively' < Latin *vivac-* (see VIVACIOUS).] —**vivace** *adj*

vacious /vi váyshəss/ *adj* exhibiting or characterized by liveliness and high-spiritedness [Mid-17C. < Latin *vivac-* 'lively, long-lived' < *vivus* (see VIVID).] —**vivaciously** *adv* —**vivaciousness** *n*

vacity /vi vássəti/ *n* liveliness and high-spiritedness

valdi /vi váldi/, **Antonio** (1678–1741) Italian composer

varium /vī váiri əm/ (*plural* **-a** /-ri ə/ *or* **-ums**) *n* a transparent enclosure in which small animals are kept so that their behaviour can be studied [Early 17C. < Latin, 'game preserve, fishpond' < form of *vivarius* 'of living things' < *vivus* (see VIVID).]

va voce /vívə vṓchi/ *n* EDUC = **viva**[2] *n.* ■ *adv* by word of mouth [Mid-16C. < medieval Latin, 'with the living voice'.]

vax malaria /vī vaks-/, **vivax** *n* a form of malaria marked by convulsions that occur every 48 hours and that is caused by the parasite *Plasmodium vivax*

verrid /vī vérrid/ *n* a civet, mongoose, or other similar small carnivorous mammal with a long slender body. Family: Viverridae. [Early 20C. < modern Latin *Viverridae* (plural) < *Viverra* (singular) < Latin, 'ferret'.] —**viverrid** *adj*

vid /vívvid/ *adj* **1 VERY BRIGHT** strikingly bright or intense in colour **2 EXTREMELY CLEAR AND FRESH** characterized by striking clarity, distinctness, or truth to life when perceived either by the eye or the mind ○ *a vivid image* **3 GRAPHIC** producing strong and distinct mental images **4 INVENTIVE** active and inventive ○ *a vivid imagination* **5 LIVELY** characterized by spirit and animation [Mid-17C. < Latin *vividus* < vivus 'alive' < *vivere* 'to live'.] —**vividly** *adv* —**vividness** *n*

vify /vívvi fī/ (**-fies, -fying, -fied**) *vt* **1** to cause somebody or something to come to life **2** to give liveliness or vividness to something [14C. Via French *vivifier* < late Latin *vivificare* 'make alive' < Latin *vivus* (see VIVID).] —**vivification** /vívvifi káysh'n/ *n* —**vivifier** *n*

viparous /vi vípparəss/ *adj* **1 BEARING LIVE YOUNG** bearing live young rather than eggs. ◊ **oviparous** *adj.* **1 2 PRODUCING PLANTLETS** describes a plant, e.g. the spider plant, that produces plantlets or bulbils from the flower stem **3 PRODUCING SEEDLINGS ON PLANT** describes a plant, e.g. a mangrove, with seeds that germinate and develop into seedlings before being shed from the parent plant [Mid-17C. < Latin *viviparus* 'bringing forth alive' < *vivus* (see VIVID).] —**viviparously** *adv* —**viviparousness** *n*

visect /vívvi sekt/ *vti* to perform operations on living animals that involve cutting into their bodies in order to gain knowledge of pathological or physiological processes [Mid-19C. Back-formation < VIVISECTION.] —**vivisective** /vívvi sektiv, -séktiv/ *adj* —**vivisector** *n*

visection /vívvi séksh'n/ *n* the practice of operating on living animals in order to gain knowledge of pathological or physiological processes [Early 18C. < Latin *vivus* (see VIVID) after DISSECTION.] —**vivisectional** *adj* —**vivisectionally** *adv* —**vivisectionist** *n*

visectorium /vívvi sek táwri əm/ (*plural* **-ums** *or* **-a** /-táwri ə/) *n* an establishment where vivisection is practised [Late 20C. < VIVISECTION after EMPORIUM.]

vivo /véevō/ *adv* in a lively and energetic manner (*musical direction*) [Mid-18C. Via Italian < Latin *vivus* (see VIVID).]

vixen /víks'n/ *n* **1** a female fox **2** an offensive term that deliberately insults a woman regarded as vindictive and bad-tempered [15C. Variant of *fixen* < Old English *fyxe*, feminine of *fox* (see FOX).] —**vixenish** *adj* —**vixenishly** *adv* —**vixenishness** *n* —**vixenly** *adj, adv*

viz /viz/ *adv* namely [< Latin *videlicet* (see VIDELICET)]

vizcacha *n* ZOOL = **viscacha**

vizier /vi zéer/ *n* a high-ranking government officer in various Islamic countries and especially in the former Ottoman empire [Mid-16C. Via French or Spanish *visir* < Turkish *vezir* < Arabic *wazīr* 'vizier', earlier 'helper, assistant'.] —**vizierate** *n* —**vizierial** *adj* —**viziership** *n*

vizor *n* = **visor**

vizsla /vízhlə/ *n* a medium-sized hunting dog of a Hungarian breed with a short, smooth, reddish coat [Mid-20C. < ?]

VJ *abbr* video jockey

V-J day *n* 15 August 1945, the day of the Japanese surrender in World War II

vl *abbr* a variant reading [Latin *varia lectio*]

Vlach /vlaak/ *n* **1** a member of a SE European people who in the 13th century founded the principalities of Wallachia and Moldavia, later merged to become Romania, and who now live mainly in N Greece, the Former Yugoslav Republic of Macedonia, or Albania **2** a language of the Romance family that is spoken in SE Europe, especially that of the Vlach people [Mid-19C. < Bulgarian and Serbo-Croat, < Germanic, 'foreign'.] —**Vlach** *adj*

Vladimir /vláddi meer, vlə dée meer/ city in W Russia. Population: 353,000 (1990).

Vladivostok /vláddi vóstok/ major port in SE Russia. Population: 648,000 (1991).

Vlaminck /vlá mink/, **Maurice de** (1876–1958) French painter

VLCC *abbr* very large crude carrier

vlei /flay, vlay/ (*plural* **vleis**) *n S Africa* a stretch of low-lying ground that is either permanently marshy or is flooded in the rainy season to form a shallow lake [Late 18C. Via Afrikaans < Dutch *wallei* 'valley'.]

VLF, vlf *abbr* very low frequency

⚡**VLSI** *adj* made using technology that allows hundreds of thousands of components to exist on a single microchip. Full form **very large-scale integration**

VMD *abbr* Doctor of Veterinary Medicine

⚡**vn** *abbr* Vietnam (*in Internet addresses*)

V neck *n* **1** a neckline shaped like a letter 'V' (*hyphenated when used before a noun*) **2** a garment, especially a sweater or T-shirt, with a v-shaped neckline —**V-necked** *adj*

VO *abbr* **1** verbal order **2** Royal Victorian Order **3** very old (*used on labels for bottles of brandy, whisky, or port*) **4** voiceover

vo. *abbr* verso

VOC *abbr* volatile organic compound

voc. *abbr* vocative

vocab /vṓ kab/ *n* vocabulary (*informal*) [Early 20C. Shortening.]

vocable /vṓkəb'l/ *n* a single word considered only as a grouping of sounds or letters, not in terms of its meaning (*dated formal*) ■ *adj* capable of being pronounced or spoken (*formal*) [Mid-16C. Directly or via French < Latin *vocabulum* 'name' < *vocare* 'call, name'.] —**vocably** *adv*

vocabular /vō kábbyŏŏlər/ *adj* relating to words [Early 17C. < Latin *vocabulum* (see VOCABLE).]

vocabulary /vō kábbyŏŏləri/ (*plural* **-ies**) *n* **1 WORDS KNOWN** the words used by or known to a person or group, or contained in a language as a whole **2 LIST OF WORDS** an alphabetical list of words and phrases supplied with definitions or translations **3 RANGE OF EXPRESSIVE TECHNIQUES** a repertoire of expressive forms or techniques used by an artist or in an art form [Mid-16C. < medieval Latin *vocabularium* 'of words' < Latin *vocabulum* (see VOCABLE).]

SYNONYMS See ***language***.

vocal /vṓk'l/ *adj* **1 UTTERED** uttered with the voice **2 OF THE VOICE** relating to the voice **3 HAVING VOICE** having a voice or using a voice to produce speech or sound **4 OUTSPOKEN** using frank, forthright, or insistent speech **5 OF OR FOR SINGING** composed or arranged for singing, or relating to the art or techniques of singing **6 NOISY WITH VOICES** full of the sound of voices **7** PHON = **vocalic** ■ *n* **1 SUNG PART** the sung part of a piece of pop music or jazz **2 POP OR JAZZ SONG** a song in the pop or jazz style [14C. < Latin *vocalis* < *voc-*, stem of *vox* 'voice'.] —**vocality** /vō kálləti/ *n* —**vocally** *adv* —**vocalness** *n*

vocal cords, vocal chords *npl* a pair of fibrous sheets of tissue that span the cavity of the voice box (**larynx**) and produce sounds by vibrating

vocal folds *npl* a pair of folds in the wall of the voice box (**larynx**) situated just above the vocal cords

vocalic /vō kállik/ *adj* **1** relating to or containing vowels **2** used or acting as a vowel —**vocalically** *adv*

vocalise[1] *vti* = **vocalize**

vocalise[2] /vṓkə lees/ *n* **1** a voice training exercise in which a singer sings using only vowel sounds, especially one single vowel sound **2** a passage or composition for performance in which a singer sings only vowel sounds, especially one single vowel sound [Late 19C. < French, < *vocaliser* 'vocalize'.]

vocalism /vṓkəlizəm/ *n* **1 USE OF VOICE** the use of the voice in producing speech, singing, or other sounds **2 ART OF SINGING** the art or technique of singing **3 VOWELS OF A LANGUAGE** the range of vowels used in a specific language **4 VOWEL** a vowel sound

vocalist /vṓkəlist/ *n* a singer, especially of pop music or jazz —**vocalistic** /vṓkə lístik/ *adj*

vocalize /vṓkə līz/ (**-izes, -izing, -ized**), **vocalise** (**-ises, -ising, -ised**) *v* **1** *vti* **EXPRESS** to use the voice to express something **2** *vti* **TRANSFORM INTO A VOWEL** to transform a consonant into a vowel sound in speaking, or to be transformed into a vowel **3** *vt* PHON = **voice** *v.* **3 4** *vt* LING = **vowelize 5** *vi* **SING WITHOUT WORDS** to sing without words, using only one or more vowel sounds, especially as a vocal exercise to warm up the voice —**vocalization** /vṓkə lī záysh'n/ *n* —**vocalizer** *n*

vocal score *n* the score of a vocal work, especially an opera, that gives the vocal parts in full with the orchestral parts transcribed for piano

vocal tic *n* a sudden noise or shout produced involuntarily, especially as a symptom of Tourette's syndrome or a similar neurological condition

vocat. *abbr* vocative

vocation /vō káysh'n/ *n* **1** somebody's work, job, or profession, especially a type of work demanding special commitment **2** a strong feeling of being destined or called to undertake a particular type of work, especially a sense of being chosen by God for religious work or a religious life [15C. < Latin *vocation-* < *vocat-*, past participle of *vocare* 'call, name'.]

vocational /vō káysh'nəl/ *adj* **1** relating to education designed to provide the necessary skills for a particular job or career **2** relating to somebody's vocation —**vocationally** *adv*

vocational guidance *n* guidance in the form of interviews and tests to see which job or career would best suit somebody's individual abilities and personality

vocative /vókətiv/ *adj* **INDICATING SOMEBODY OR SOMETHING ADDRESSED** describes a grammatical case or a form of a word that indicates that somebody or something is being directly addressed by the speaker ■ *n* **1 VOCATIVE CASE** the vocative case (*informal*) **2 WORD IN THE VOCATIVE** a word or form in the vocative case [15C. < Latin *vocativus* < *vocat-* (see VOCATION).] —**vocatively** *adv*

vociferate /vō síffə rayt/ (**-ates, -ating, -ated**) *vti* to shout something out loudly [Late 16C. < Latin *vociferari* 'carry voice' < *voc-* (see VOCAL) + *ferre* 'carry'.] —**vociferant** *adj* —**vociferation** /-síffə ráysh'n/ *n* —**vociferator** /-raytər/ *n*

vociferous /vō síffərəss/ *adj* **1** shouting in a noisy and determined way **2** characterized by noisy and determined shouting [Early 17C. < Latin *vociferari* (see VOCIFERATE).] —**vociferously** *adv* —**vociferousness** *n*

⚡**vocoder** /vō kṓdər/ *n* an electronic device or computer program that converts speech into digital form and resynthesizes it at a later time or after transmission as artificial speech [Mid-20C. < VOICE + CODE.]

vodka /vódkə/ *n* a colourless distilled spirit originally from Russia that is made from a grain such as rye or wheat or from potatoes [Early 19C. < Russian, 'small water' < *voda* 'water'.]

vodoun /vō do͞on/, **vodun** *n* RELIG = **voodoo** *n.* 1 [Late 19C. < Fon *vodū* 'fetish'.]

voe /vō/ *n* in Orkney or Shetland, a small bay [Late 17C. < Norwegian *våg*, Icelandic *vogur* 'bay, inlet'.]

voetstoots /fo͝ot sto͞ots, vo͞ot-/ *adv S Africa* with the seller having no responsibility for any defects in the item sold or for any other problems arising from the sale [Late 20C. < Afrikaans.] —**voetstoots** *adj*

Vogel /vṓg'l/, **Sir Julius** (1835–99) British-born New Zealand statesman and journalist

vogue[1] /vōg/ *n* **1 PREVAILING FASHION** the prevailing fashion at a particular time **2 POPULARITY** the state of being widely popular and fashionable at a particular time ○ *in vogue* ■ *adj* **FASHIONABLE** currently popular or fashionable [Late 16C. < French, literally 'rowing' < *voguer* 'to row'.]

vogue[2] /vōg/ (**voguing** *or* **vogueing**) *vi* to dance by imitating the poses struck by fashion models [Late 20C. After *Vogue*, fashion magazine.] —**voguing** *n*

voguish /vṓgish/ *adj* **1** elegantly fashionable and stylish in appearance **2** enjoying brief or sudden popularity —**voguishly** *adv* —**voguishness** *n*

voice /voyss/ *n* **1 SOUND MADE USING VOCAL ORGANS** the sound produced by using the vocal organs, especially the sound used in speech **2 SOUND OF SINGING** the musical sound produced in singing **3 ABILITY TO USE VOICE** the ability to produce vocal sounds for speaking or singing ○ *have a good voice* **4 SOUND LIKE HUMAN VOICE** a sound similar to a human voice ○ *listen to the voice of the wind* **5 RIGHT TO STATE OPINION** a right to express an opinion ○ *sections of society that feel they have no voice* **6 EXPRESSED OPINION** an expressed opinion or desire ○ *hear the voice of the people* **7 REPRESENTATIVE EXPRESSION** a medium of communication or expression for somebody or something ○ *the voice of reason* **8 SINGER** a singer taking a part in a musical composition **9 SINGING PART** a sung part in a musical composition **10 VIBRATION OF VOCAL CORDS IN SPEAKING** the passing of air across the vocal cords so as to create audible vibrations **11 FORM OF VERBS** the form of a verb that indicates the relation of the subject to the verb ■ *vt* (**voices, voicing, voiced**) **1 UTTER** to express a sentiment or opinion verbally ○ *voice an opinion* **2 REGULATE THE TONE OF AN ORGAN** to regulate the tone of an organ pipe in order to produce the desired sound **3 PRONOUNCE USING THE VOCAL CORDS** to pronounce a consonant or vowel by passing air across the vocal cords so as to create audible vibrations [13C. Via Old French *vois* < Latin *vox*.] —**voicer** *n* ◇ **be in (good) voice** to be singing well or speaking well ◇ **with one voice** simultaneously or unanimously

⚡**voice-activated** *adj* operated by the user's spoken commands rather than physical input

voice box *n* ANAT = **larynx**

voiced /voyst/ *adj* describes a consonant or vowel pronounced by passing air across the vocal cords to create audible vibrations, as for the 's' sound in the word 'his' —**voicedness** *n*

voiceful /vóysf'l/ *adj* having a loud or ringing voice (*literary*) —**voicefulness** *n*

voiceless /vóyssləss/ *adj* **1 SAYING NOTHING** maintaining a silence **2 HAVING NO SAY** having no vote or influence **3 HAVING NO VOICE** not endowed with a voice **4 PRONOUNCED WITHOUT VIBRATION OF VOCAL CORDS** describes a consonant or vowel pronounced without passing air across the vocal cords and creating audible vibrations, as in the 's' sound in the word 'hiss' —**voicelessly** *adv* —**voicelessness** *n*

voice mail *n* an electronic communications system that stores digitized recordings of telephone messages for later playback (*hyphenated before nouns*)

voiceover /vóyss ōvər/ *n* the voice of, or the words spoken by, an unseen narrator, commentator, or character in a film or television programme

⚡**voice over Internet protocol** *n* full form of **VoIP**

⚡**voice-over-the-Net** *adj* describes voice communication using VoIP technology

voiceprint /vóyss print/ *n* a representation in graph form of the frequencies that make up somebody's voice [Mid-20C. < VOICE + FINGERPRINT.]

voiceprint identification *n* the use of the sound frequencies of speech as a method of identifying a person

⚡**voice recognition** *n* **1** COMPUT = **speech recognition 2** a computer function that enables the machine to recognize a particular voice or voices speaking into a microphone attached to it

voice vote *n* a vote taken in a parliament or other legislative body in which voters cry out 'aye' or 'no', or 'yea' and 'nay', with the louder cry winning the vote

void /voyd/ *adj* **1 NOT LEGALLY VALID** having no legal force ○ *declared the will null and void* **2 POINTLESS** ineffective or useless **3 DEVOID** totally lacking in something (*formal*) ○ *a personality void of all compassion* **4 NOT CONTAINING ANYTHING** having no contents **5 VACANT** having no incumbent, occupant, or holder **6 HAVING NO CARDS IN A SUIT** lacking any cards in a particular suit ■ *n* **1 VACUUM** an empty space, especially a large empty space **2 PRIVATION** a state of loss or privation, or a feeling of loneliness and emptiness **3 GAP** a gap or opening **4 LACK OF CARDS IN A SUIT** a complete lack of cards in a particular suit ○ *a void in spades* ■ *v* **1** *vt* **MAKE LEGALLY INVALID** to deprive something of legal force **2** *vt* **EMPTY CONTENTS OF** to empty out the contents of something, or empty something of its contents **3** *vti* **EMPTY BOWELS OR BLADDER** to empty the bowels or bladder [13C. < Old French *voide* 'empty' < assumed Vulgar Latin *vocitus*, alteration of Latin *vocivus*.] —**voidable** *adj* —**voidableness** *n* —**voider** *n* —**voidness** *n*

SYNONYMS See ***vacant***.

voidance /vóyd'nss/ *n* **1 INVALIDATION OF CONTRACT** the act of depriving a contract of legal force **2 ACT OF EMPTYING** the act of voiding or emptying something **3 VACANCY** the situation of having no incumbent or occupant, e.g. no bishop in a diocese

void deck *n* in Malaysia and Singapore, the empty ground floor of a block of flats, used for social events by people living in the block

voided /vóydid/ *adj* in heraldry, having the centre and a narrow surrounding area removed or left empty

voilà /vwa laá/ *interj* used to bring somebody's attention to something, especially in order to elicit appreciation or approval [Mid-18C. < French, < *voi* 'see!' + *là* 'there'.]

voile /voyl/ *n* a crisp lightweight translucent fabric made from cotton, synthetic fibres, or wool [Late 19C. < French, 'veil' < Latin *vela* (see VEIL).]

⚡**VoIP** *n* a technology that enables voice messages to be sent via the Internet, often simultaneously with data in text or other forms. Full form **voice over Internet protocol**

voir dire /vwaa deér/ *n* the preliminary examination of a witness or juror to determine his or her competence to give or hear evidence [Late 17C. < Law French < Old French *voir* 'truth' + *dire* 'speak'.]

voix céleste /vwaá sə lést/ *n* an organ stop that gives a light wavering otherworldly quality to the notes played [Late 19C. < French, < *voix* 'voice' + *céleste* 'heavenly'.]

vol. *abbr* **1** volcano **2** volume **3** volunteer

Volans /vṓ lanz/ *n* a small constellation of the southern hemisphere. See illustration at **constellation**

volant /vṓlənt/ *adj* **1 HAVING WINGS SPREAD** in heraldry, having the wings outspread as in flight **2 ABLE TO FLY** flying or having the power of flight **3 NIMBLE** moving quickly, lightly, and easily (*literary*) [Early 16C. < French, present participle of *voler* 'fly' < Latin *volare*.]

Volapük /vóllə pook, vṓlə-/ *n* a synthetic language based on English and German, invented by Johann Martin Schleyer in 1880 [Late 19C. < *vol*, alteration of WORLD + *pük* 'speech', alteration of SPEAK.]

volar /vṓlər/ *adj* relating to the palm of the hand or the sole of the foot [Early 19C. < *vola* 'hollow of the hand or foot' < Latin, 'sole, palm'.]

⚡**volatile** /vóllə tīl/ *adj* **1 CHANGING SUDDENLY** characterized by or prone to sudden change **2 UNSTABLE AND POTENTIALLY DANGEROUS** apt to become suddenly violent or dangerous **3 UNPREDICTABLE OR FICKLE** changeable in mood, temper, or desire **4 PRONE TO EVAPORATION** evaporating at a relatively low temperature **5 SHORT-LIVED** continuing for only a short time **6 LOSING DATA WHEN POWER IS OFF** describes a computer memory that does not store data when the power is turned off ■ *n* **VOLATILE SUBSTANCE** a substance that evaporates at a relatively low temperature [Late 16C. < Latin *volatilis* < *volat-*, past participle of *volare* 'fly'.] —**volatilely** *adv* —**volatileness** *n* —**volatility** /vóllə tílləti/ *n*

volatile organic compound *n* an organic compound such as ethylene, propylene, benzene, or styrene that evaporates at a relatively low temperature and co tributes to air pollution

volatilize /və látti līz/ (**-izes, -izing, -ized**), **volatili** (**-ises, -ising, -ised**) *vti* to change into a vapour, cause a solid or liquid to be changed into a vapour **volatilizable** *adj* —**volatilization** /və látti lī záysh'n/ *n* **volatilizer** *n*

vol-au-vent /vólō voN/ *n* a small light pastry shell fill with meat, fish, game, or fowl in a sauce and baked French, 'flight in the wind']

volcanic /vol kánnik/ *adj* **1 OF VOLCANOES** relating to originating from a volcano **2 CONSISTING OF VOLCANO** made up of or coming from volcanoes **3 SUDDEN A VIOLENT** characterized by sudden violent outbursts **volcanically** *adv*

volcanic arc *n* GEOG = **island arc**

volcanic bomb *n* a lump of lava ejected from a volca that has acquired a characteristic form as a result of solidification while travelling through the air

volcanic cone *n* a cone-shaped mass of material th has built up around the crater of a volcano

volcanic dust *n* fine particles of ash that are suspend in the atmosphere after a volcanic eruption

volcanic glass *n* natural glass formed when molt lava from a volcano cools too quickly to crystallize

volcanicity /vólkə níssəti/, **vulcanicity** /vúlkə níssəti/ the tendency or likelihood of a volcano or group volcanoes to erupt [Mid-19C. < French *volcanicité* < *volc* 'volcano'.]

volcanic plug, volcanic neck *n* a massive cylindric formation of solidified lava that once blocked the ve of a volcano, now exposed after erosion of softer su rounding material

volcanise *vt* = **volcanize**

volcanism /vólkənizəm/, **vulcanism** /vúlkənizəm/ *n* th processes involved in the formation of volcanoes, a in the transfer of magma and volatile material from t interior of the earth to its surface

volcanize /vólkə nīz/ (**-nizes, -nizing, -nized**), **volcani** (**-nises, -nising, -nised**) *vt* to cause something to chan as a result of volcanic activity —**volcanization** /vólkə záysh'n/ *n*

volcano /vol káynō/ (*plural* **-noes** *or* **-nos**) *n* **1** a natura occurring opening in the surface of the Earth throu which molten, gaseous, and solid material is ejected **2** mountain created by the deposition and accumulati of materials ejected from a vent in a central crater [Ea 17C. Via Italian < Latin *Volcanus*, *Vulcanus* 'Vulcan'.] **volcanian** *adj*

LITERARY LINK ***Under the Volcano***, a novel (1947) Malcolm Lowry. Set in Mexico on the annual Day of the De it describes the last hours of British consul Geoffrey Firm who, depressed by the failure of his marriage and the onset war, slowly drinks himself to death. A harrowing psychologic study, it can also be read as an allegory of the disintegrati of Western values.

volcanology /vólkə nólləji/, **vulcanology** /vúlkə nólləji/ the scientific study of volcanoes, including their fo mation, signs of an eruption, and other aspects of v canic activity —**volcanologic** /vólkənə lójjik/ *adj* **volcanological** *adj* —**volcanologist** /vólkə nólləjist/ *n*

vole[1] /vōl/ (*plural* **voles** *or* **vole**) *n* a small rodent simil to mice and rats but with a shorter tail and legs and stocky body. Native to: North America, Europe, Asi Genus: *Microtus*. [Early 19C. < Norwegian *voll mus* 'fie mouse'.]

vole[2] /vōl/ *n* a taking of all the tricks in a single hand a card game such as bridge [Late 17C. < French, proba < *voler* 'to fly' < Latin *volare*.]

Volga /vólgə/ longest river of Europe, in W Russia. It ris northwest of Moscow and flows southeast and sou before emptying into the Caspian Sea. Length: 3,5 km/2,194 mi.

Volgograd /vólgə grad/ city in SW Russia, on the Riv Volga. Population: 1,006,100 (1992).

volitant /vóllitənt/ *adj* **1** flying or capable of flig **2** moving about rapidly or constantly [Early 17C. < La *volitare* 'keep on flying' < *volare* 'fly'.]

volition /vō lísh'n/ *n* **1 CHOOSING** the act of exercising t will **2 ABILITY TO CHOOSE** the ability to make conscio choices or decisions **3 CHOICE MADE** the result of exercisi the will **4 ACT OF WILL** an act of will distinguished fro

MAJOR VOLCANOES OF THE WORLD

Cotopaxi *Ecuador*
Elevation [**19,347 ft / 5,897 m**]
World's highest active volcano

Mauna Loa *Hawaii*
Elevation [**13,680 ft / 4,170 m**]
Major eruption 1984

Erebus *Antarctica*
Elevation [**12,448 ft / 3,794 m**]
Major eruptions 1970s

Cameroon *Cameroon*
Elevation [**13,435 ft / 4,095 m**]
Major eruption 1982

Etna *Italy*
Elevation [**10,902 ft / 3,323 m**]
Over 90 recorded eruptions

Ruapehu *New Zealand*
Elevation [**9,177 ft / 2,797 m**]
Major eruptions 1995, 1996

Saint Helens *United States*
Elevation [**8,365 ft / 2,550 m**]
Major eruption 1980

Vesuvius *Italy*
Elevation [**4,190 ft / 1,277 m**]
Major eruption 79 AD — destroying Roman Pompeii

Soufriere Hills *Montserrat*
Elevation [**3,002 ft / 915 m**]
Major eruption 1997 — much of island left uninhabitable

Krakatau *Indonesia*
Elevation [**2,667 ft / 813 m**]
Major eruption 1883 — tidal waves from eruption estimated to have caused over 30,000 deaths

the intended physical movement it causes [Early 17C. Directly or via French < Latin *volition-* < *vol-* (see VOLUNTARY).] —**volitional** *adj* —**volitionally** *adv* —**volitionary** *adj*

volitive /vóllətiv/ *adj* **1** relating to or beginning in the will **2** GRAM = **desiderative** *adj.* 2 [15C. < medieval Latin *volitivus* < Latin *volition-* (see VOLITION).]

volk /folk/ *n S Africa* a people or nation, especially the nation of Afrikaners [Late 19C. Via Afrikaans < Dutch, 'nation, people'.]

Völkerwanderung /fólkər vandəròong, fṓlkər vaandəròong/ *n* a movement of peoples, especially the migration of Germanic and Slavic peoples into southern and W Europe from the 2nd to 11th centuries [Mid-20C. < German, 'migration of nations'.]

Volkslied /fólks leed/ (*plural* **-lieder** /-leedər/) *n* a traditional German folk song [Mid-19C. < German, 'people's song'.]

volley /vólli/ *n* **1** FIRING OF WEAPONS a simultaneous discharge of several weapons, especially firearms **2** MISSILES FIRED a discharge of missiles or other projectiles fired simultaneously **3** SIMULTANEOUS EXPRESSION OF a simultaneous rapid expression of something, e.g. curses or protests **4** SWING AT A BALL a swing, kick, or hit at a ball, e.g. in tennis or football, before it touches the ground or court **5** BALL the flight of a ball or the ball itself **6** ROCK BLASTING a simultaneous explosion of several blastings of rock ■ *v* (**-leys, -leying, -leyed**) **1** *vti* STRIKE A BALL BEFORE IT LANDS to hit or kick a ball before it reaches the ground, e.g. in tennis or football **2** *vti* FIRE SIMULTANEOUSLY to fire weapons simultaneously **3** *vti* SAY RAPIDLY to say something forcefully or loudly and rapidly, or to be spoken forcefully and rapidly **4** *vi* MOVE RAPIDLY to move or rush rapidly or loudly [Late 16C. < French *volée* < Latin *volare* 'to fly'.] —**volleyer** *n*

volleyball /vólli bawl/ *n* **1** a sport played on a rectangular court, in which two teams can each use up to three hits to pass a large ball over a high net **2** a large, usually white inflated ball used to play volleyball —**volleyballer** *n*

volost /vṓ lost/ *n* **1** a rural elected council in the former Soviet Union **2** in tsarist Russia, a peasant community made up of several villages [Late 19C. < Russian.]

volplane /vól playn/ *vi* (**-planes, -planing, -planed**) **1** GLIDE TO THE GROUND to glide towards the ground in an aeroplane with the engine turned off **2** MOVE BY GLIDING to travel or move by gliding ■ *n* ACT OF GLIDING a glide towards the ground in an aircraft with the engine turned off [Early 20C. < French *vol plané* 'planed flight'.]

vols. *abbr* volumes

volt[1] /vōlt/ *n* (*symbol* **V**) the unit of electromotive force and electric potential difference equal to the difference between two points in a circuit carrying one ampere of current and dissipating one watt of power [Late 19C. After Alessandro VOLTA.]

volt[2] /volt/, **volte** *n* **1** a circular movement executed by a horse in dressage **2** a sudden leap made in fencing to elude an opponent's thrust [Late 16C. Via French *volte* < Italian *volta* (see VOLTA).]

volta /vóltə/ (*plural* **-te** /-tay/) *n* **1** ITALIAN DANCE an fast Italian dance of the 16th and 17th centuries **2** VOLTA MUSIC the music for a volta **3** ONE PLAYING OF A MUSICAL PASSAGE a single playing of a passage of music that may then be repeated [Late 16C. < Italian, 'a turn' < *volgere* 'to turn' < Latin *volvere* 'to roll'.]

Volta /vóltə/ river in SE Ghana, emptying into the Atlantic Ocean. Length: 1,500 km/930 mi.

Volta, Alessandro, Count (1745–1827) Italian physicist

voltage /vṓltij/ *n* electric potential expressed in volts

voltage divider *n* a series of resistors or a single resistor used to provide various voltages that are fractions of the source voltage

voltaic /vol táy ik/ *adj* relating to or denoting direct electric current produced by chemical action [Early19C. < After Alessandro VOLTA.]

Voltaic /vol táy ik/ *adj* relating to the Gur group of languages, spoken chiefly in Burkina-Faso and Ghana [Mid-20C. < the River VOLTA.]

voltaic battery *n* an electric battery made up of one or more primary cells

voltaic cell *n* ELEC = **primary cell**

voltaic couple *n* two different metals immersed in an electrolyte that produce a potential difference due to chemical action

voltaic pile *n* a stack of dissimilar metal discs separated by a porous material soaked in electrolyte that acts as a battery

Voltaire /vol táir/ (1694–1778) French writer and philosopher. Born **François Marie Arouet**

voltaism /vóltə izəm/ *n* PHYS = **galvanism** *n.* 1

volte *n* RIDING, FENCING = **volt**[2]

volte-face /vólt fáass/ *n* **1** a sudden reversal in opinion or policy **2** a change in position so as to be facing the opposite direction [Early 19C. Via French < Italian *voltafaccia* 'turn of the face'.]

voltmeter /vṓlt meetər/ *n* an instrument calibrated in volts that measures the electromotive force or potential difference between two points in a circuit

voluble /vóllyòob'l/ *adj* **1** talking or spoken easily and at length **2** twining or twisting [14C. Directly or via French < Latin *volubilis* < *volvere* 'to roll'.] —**volubility** /vóllyòo bílləti/ *n* —**volubleness** *n* —**volubly** *adv*

volume /vóllyoom/ *n* **1** SPACE INSIDE AN OBJECT (*symbol* **V**) the size of a three-dimensional space enclosed within or occupied by an object **2** AMOUNT the total amount of something **3** LOUDNESS the loudness of a sound **4** SOUND CONTROL the knob or button on a radio, television, or audio player that controls loudness **5** THICKNESS the thick quality or appearance of somebody's hair ○ *Apply to roots for added volume.* **6** BOOK a bound collection of printed or written pages **7** BOOK OF A SET a single book that belongs to a set of books **8** CONSECUTIVE MAGAZINE ISSUES a set of issues of a periodical spanning one calendar year **9** SCROLL a roll of parchment or papyrus ■ *adj* INVOLVING LARGE QUANTITIES using or involving large amounts or quantities ○ *The factory is offering volume discounts on carpet sales.* [14C. Via Old French < Latin *volumen* 'roll, scroll, book' < *volvere* 'to roll'.] ◇ **speak volumes** to be highly expressive or significant

volumed /vóllyoomd/ *adj* **1** published in a series or set of a specified number of books (*usually in combination*) ○ *three-volumed set* **2** forming or rolling in a rounded mass (*literary*)

volumetric /vóllyòo méttrik/ *adj* of, relating to, or using measurement by volume —**volumeter** /vo lyóomitər/ *n* —**volumetrically** *adv*

volumetric analysis *n* **1** an analysis of liquids using measured volumes of standard chemical reagents **2** an analysis of gas by volume

voluminous /və lóominəss/ *adj* **1** LARGE having great size, capacity, or fullness **2** EXTREMELY LONG very lengthy and taking up many pages or books ○ *a voluminous report* **3** PROLIFIC producing a large amount of creative work ○ *a voluminous novelist* **4** WINDING winding or coiling (*archaic*) [Early 17C. < late Latin *voluminosus* 'with many coils' < Latin *volumen* (see VOLUME).] —**voluminosity** /və lóomi nóssəti/ *n* —**voluminously** /və lóominəssli/ *adv* —**voluminousness** *n*

voluntarism /vóllәntərizəm/ *n* **1** PHILOSOPHICAL THEORY the theory that regards the will rather than the intellect as the essential principle of the individual or cosmos **2** RELIANCE ON VOLUNTARY CONTRIBUTIONS the use of or dependence on voluntary contributions rather than government funds to keep an institution such as a school or church in existence **3** NO INTERFERENCE the belief that no level of government or law should interfere in the process of collective bargaining or the organization of trade unions —**voluntarist** *n* —**voluntaristic** /vóllәntə rístik/ *adj*

voluntary /vóllәntəri/ *adj* **1** OF FREE WILL arising, acting, or resulting from somebody's own choice or decision rather than because of external pressure or force **2** WITHOUT PAY performing, working, or done without financial reward **3** USING VOLUNTEERS composed of, functioning, or requiring volunteers **4** NOT PART OF GOVERNMENT not part of statutory provision, e.g. of social services, and usually maintained at least in part by private charitable donations rather than by government or other official support ○ *Many organizations in the UK voluntary sector receive state funding* **5** HAVING WILL having the capacity required to make conscious choices or decisions **6** WITHOUT LEGAL OBLIGATION not involving legal obligation, coercion, or persuasion **7** DONE ON PURPOSE performed or carried out with intention rather than by accident **8** GIVEN WITHOUT PAYMENT IN RETURN done or given freely with no promise of money or other recompense ■ *n* (*plural* **-ies**) **1** SHORT COMPOSITION a short musical composition, often played on a solo instrument, that introduces a longer work **2** CHURCH MUSIC a piece of music or improvisation for the organ, played before, during, or at the end of a church service **3** VOLUNTEER a volunteer, particularly somebody who joins the army (*archaic*) [14C. < Latin *voluntarius* < *voluntas* 'will, choice' < *vol-*, stem of *velle* 'to wish'.] —**voluntarily** /vóllәntərəli, -térrəli/ *adv* —**voluntariness** *n*

voluntary arrangement *n* a procedure in which a failing business can make arrangements with its creditors to resolve its financial problems, often after a court order

voluntaryism /vóllәntəri izəm/ *n* PUBLIC ADMIN = **voluntarism** *n.* 2 —**voluntaryist** *n*

voluntary muscle *n* a muscle, usually made up of striated fibres, that is consciously controlled by the individual

volunteer /vóllən téer/ *n* **1** SOMEBODY WHO WORKS FOR NOTHING a person who works without being paid **2** SOMEBODY WHO DOES SOMETHING VOLUNTARILY a voluntary doer of something, especially something undesirable **3** VOLUNTARY RECRUIT TO ARMED FORCES a person who has freely offered to serve in the armed services **4** CULTIVATED PLANT GROWING NATURALLY a cultivated plant, especially a crop plant, that grows without having been intentionally sown or planted **5** SOMEBODY ACTING WITHOUT LEGAL OBLIGATION a performer of an act or participant in a transaction who is not legally bound to do so and does not expect to be paid **6** SOMEBODY GIVEN PROPERTY a recipient of property who does not have to pay for it or give anything in return ■ *v* **1** *vti* OFFER FREE HELP to do charitable or helpful work without receiving pay for it ○ *volunteers his time* **2** *vti* DO SOMETHING BY CHOICE to perform or offer to perform work of your own free will ○ *volunteered to work the night shift* **3** *vt* TELL SOMETHING WITHOUT BEING ASKED to tell somebody something or give information without being asked ○ *to volunteer information* **4** *vt* OFFER SOMEBODY

ELSE'S HELP to suggest somebody else as a helper ○ *volunteered her secretary for a few days* **5** *vi* OFFER TO DO MILITARY SERVICE to offer to serve in one of the armed services without being required to join by law [Late 16C. Via French *volontaire* < Latin *voluntarius* (see VOLUNTARY).]

volunteer army *n* an army that relies on recruiting people who enlist voluntarily rather than conscripting recruits by law

volunteerism /vóllən teérizəm/ *n US* the practice of using volunteer workers in community service organizations and programs

volunteer vacation *n US* a holiday during which somebody does volunteer work such as cleaning up the environment or housing construction and repair

~~voluptious~~ incorrect spelling of **voluptuous**

voluptuary /və lúpchoo əri/ (*plural* **-ies**) *n* somebody whose life is devoted to enjoying luxury and the pleasures of the senses [Early 17C. < Latin *voluptuarius* < *voluptas* 'pleasure'.]

voluptuous /və lúpchoo əss/ *adj* **1** sensual in appearance or providing sensual pleasure **2** inclined or devoted to a luxurious sensual life [14C. Directly or via French *voluptueux* < Latin *voluptuosus* < *voluptas* 'pleasure'.] —**voluptuously** *adv* —**voluptuousness** *n*

volute /və lóot, vóllyoot/ *n* **1** SPIRAL SHAPE a spiral form or structure such as the whorl in the shell of a snail **2** DECORATIVE SCROLL a carved spiral decoration, usually on an Ionic capital **3** TROPICAL MOLLUSC a gastropod mollusc with a colourful spiral shell. Native to: tropical waters. Family: Volutidae. ■ *adj* SPIRALLING moving in or following a spiral path [Mid-16C. Directly or via French < Latin *voluta*, feminine past participle of *volvere* 'roll'.]

volutin /vóllyòotin/ *n* an easily stained substance found in the cytoplasm of some bacterial and fungal cells that serves to store phosphates for the energy needs of the cell [Early 20C. < modern Latin *Spirillum volutans* 'rolling spirillum', bacterium in which first found < Latin *volutare*.]

volution /və lóosh'n/ *n* **1** a shape that coils, twists, or turns around a centre **2** a spiral segment of a gastropod's shell [15C. < late Latin *volution-* < Latin *volvere* 'to roll'.]

volvox /vól voks/ *n* freshwater green algae that form communities made up of hollow multicellular spheres. Genus: *Volvox*. [Late 18C. < modern Latin, < Latin *volvere* 'to roll'.]

volvulus /vólvyòoləss/ (*plural* **volvuli** /-lī, -lee/) *n* an abnormal twisting of the digestive tract that leads to partial or complete obstruction and a reduction in blood supply [Late 17C. < medieval Latin, < Latin *volvere* 'to roll'.]

vomer /vṓmər/ *n* a thin plate of bone that forms part of the septum dividing the nasal passages inside the nose [Early 18C. < Latin, 'ploughshare'; because of its shape.] —**vomerine** /vṓmə rīn/ *adj*

vomit /vómmit/ *vti* **1** THROW UP STOMACH CONTENTS to expel the contents of the stomach through the mouth as a result of a series of involuntary spasms of the stomach muscles **2** GUSH FORTH to send something out in a forceful stream, or to be ejected forcefully ○ *to vomit curses* ■ *n* **1** EXPELLED STOMACH CONTENTS the stomach contents expelled through the mouth. Technical name **vomitus** **2** ACT OF VOMITING the act of expelling the stomach contents through the mouth [15C. Directly or via Anglo-French < Latin *vomitus*, past participle of *vomere* 'eject, vomit'.] —**vomiter** *n*

vomitory /vómmitəri/ *adj* **vomitory, vomitive** CAUSING VOMITING causing the vomiting of stomach contents (*dated*) ■ *n* (*plural* **-ries**) **1** OPENING an opening through which matter is ejected **2** ANCIENT ROMAN PASSAGEWAY a passageway, usually in an amphitheatre or stadium, connecting a tier of seats with an outside entrance [Early 17C. < Latin *vomitorius* < *vomitus* (see VOMIT).]

vomitus /vómmitəss/ *n* vomited contents of the stomach (*technical*) [Early 20C. < Latin (see VOMIT).]

Von Braun /von brówn/, **Wernher** (1912–77) German engineer

Vo Nguyen Giap /vṓ əng gòo yen-/ (*b.* 1912) Vietnamese military leader

Vonnegut /vónni gut/, **Kurt** (*b.* 1922) US writer

von Neumann /von nóymən/, **John** (1903–57) Hungarian-born US mathematician. Born **Johann von Neumann**

Von Sternberg /von stúrn burg/, **Josef** (1894–1969) Austrian-born US film director. Born **Jonas Sternberg**

Von Stroheim /von strṓ hīm/, **Erich** (1885–1957) Austrian-born US actor and film director

voodoo /vóodoo/ *n* (*plural* **voodoos**) **1** CARIBBEAN RELIGION a religion practised throughout Caribbean countries, especially Haiti, that is a combination of Roman Catholic rituals and the animistic beliefs of enslaved labourers, involving magic and communication with ancestors **2** PRACTITIONER OF VOODOO a practitioner of voodoo **3** SOMETHING MAGIC a charm, spell, or fetish regarded by those who practise voodoo as having magical powers ■ *vt* (**voodoos, voodooing, voodooed**) CAST A SPELL ON to cast a voodoo spell on somebody [Early 19C. Via Louisiana French *voudou* < Fon *vodū* 'fetish'.]

voodooism /vóodoo izəm/ *n* **1** the practises and beliefs of voodoo **2** an attempt to control or affect the world by using magic or sorcery —**voodooist** *n* —**voodooistic** /-ístik/ *adj*

voop /voop/ *n Carib* in cricket, a wild uncontrolled swing at the ball by a batsman ■ *vi Carib* in cricket, to make a wild uncontrolled swing at the ball when batting

Voortrekker /fóor trekər/ *n S Africa* a member of a band of Afrikaner pioneers who, in the early 19th century, left the British-ruled Cape for the E Cape and the interior of South Africa [Late 19C. Via Afrikaans < Dutch, 'before-trekker'.]

VOR *abbr* very-high-frequency omnidirectional radio range

voracious /və ráyshəss/ *adj* **1** desiring or consuming food in great quantities ○ *a voracious appetite* **2** unusually eager or enthusiastic about an activity ○ *a voracious reader* [Mid-17C. < Latin *vorac-* < *vorare* 'devour'.] —**voraciously** *adv* —**voraciousness** *n* —**voracity** /və rássəti/ *n*

Vorlage, vorlage *n* a skiing position in which a skier leans forward from the ankle but keeps his or her heels on the skis [Mid-20C. < German, 'forward position'.]

Voronezh /və rónnezh/ city in W Russia. Population: 895,000 (1990).

-vorous *suffix* eating, having a particular kind of food ○ *herbivorous* [< Latin *-vorus* < *vorare* 'to swallow']

Vorster /fáwrstər/, **John** (1915–83) South African statesman. Born **Balthazar Johannes Vorster**

vortex /váwr teks/ (*plural* **vortexes** *or* **vortices** /váwrti seez/) *n* **1** a whirling mass of something, especially water or air, that draws everything near it towards its centre **2** a situation or feeling that seems to swamp or engulf everything else [Mid-17C. < Latin, variant of *vertex* (see VERTEX).]

vortical /váwrtik'l/ *adj* relating to or moving in a vortex [Mid-17C. < Latin *vortic-*, stem of *vortex* (see VORTEX).] —**vortically** *adv*

vorticella /váwrti séllə/ (*plural* **-lae** /-lee/) *n* an underwater protozoan with a bell-shaped body. It is usually attached to something such as a plant by a slender stalk. Genus: *Vorticella*. [Late 18C. < modern Latin, 'little vortex' < Latin *vortic-* (see VORTICAL).]

vorticism /váwrtissizəm/ *n* a short-lived early 20th-century British movement in art and literature that was both abstract and concerned about the future and the machine age [Early 20C. < Latin *vortic-* (see VORTICAL).] —**vorticist** *n*

vorticity /vawr tíssəti/ *n* the state of a fluid moving in a vortex [Late 19C. < Latin *vortic-* (see VORTICAL).]

vorticose /váwrti kōss/ *adj* = **vortical** *adj.*

Vosges /vōzh/ mountain range in NE France. Length: 190 km/120 mi. Highest peak: Grand Ballon1424 m/4,672 ft.

Vostok /vóstok/ *n* any of seven spacecraft launched by the former Soviet Union, beginning in April 1961 [Mid-20C. < Russian.]

votary /vṓtəri/ (*plural* **-ries**), **votarist** /-rist/ *n* **1** a person who has sworn to dedicate his or her life to religious worship or service **2** a dedicated follower of something, such as a religion or cause [Mid-16C. < Latin *vot-*, past participle of *vovere* 'vow'.]

vote /vōt/ *n* **1** FORMAL CHOICE FOR OR AGAINST a formal indication of somebody's choice or opinion, especially in an election or referendum **2** ACT OF CHOOSING the act of making a choice or stating a preference to determine the outcome of something **3** BALLOTS CAST the total number of ballots cast by eligible voters ○ *They got 83 per cent of the vote.* **4** SUFFRAGE the right to express opinions and preferences by casting a ballot ○ *Women struggled for many years to get the vote.* **5** MEANS OF EXPRESSING A VOTE the ticket, ballot, or other method by which somebody expresses a vote **6** RESULT OF BALLOTING the outcome of an election or referendum ○ *Yesterday's vote indicates that people are tired of being lied to.* **7** OPINION EXPRESSED th[e] preference of a group of people as indicated by a ballo[t] ○ *Politicians can no longer ignore the youth vote.* **8** PROPOSA[L] a proposal to be voted for or against, usually by [a] committee ■ *v* (**votes, voting, voted**) **1** *vti* INDICATE FORMA[L] PREFERENCE to express an opinion or preference in a[n] election or referendum ○ *How did you vote in the las[t] election?* **2** *vt* VOTE FOR OR AGAINST to decide the outcom[e] of an election by voting for or against somebody ○ *It'[s] difficult to vote an incumbent out of office.* **3** *vt* VOTE T[O] MAKE SOMETHING AVAILABLE to create something or mak[e] something available by casting a vote ○ *The city counc[il] refused to vote additional funds for the new building.* **4** [*vt*] VOTE FOR SOMEBODY TO WIN to vote for a candidate to win [a] competition or title ○ *He was voted 'Waiter of the Year'.* **5** [*vt*] SHOW OPINION ON to agree on how successful or enjoyabl[e] something is (*informal*) ○ *The meal was voted a grea[t] success.* **6** *vt* SUGGEST to make a suggestion ○ *I vote tha[t] we eat out.* [13C. < Latin *votum* 'vow' < *vovere* 'to vow', late 'desire'.] —**votable** *adj* —**voter** *n*

vote down *vt* to defeat a proposal or candidate in a vot[e]

Vote /vōt/, **Votic** /vṓtik, vóttik/ *n* a Uralic language of th[e] Finno-Ugric group spoken by a very small group o[f] people living around the Russia-Estonia border —**Vot[e]** *adj*

vote-catcher *n* POL = **vote-winner**

voteless /vṓtləss/ *adj* without the right to choose o[r] express a political opinion

vote of confidence *n* **1** a vote in which voters expres[s] their continuing approval of the leadership of a par[-] ticular party or policy **2** a formal or informal expressio[n] of continuing support for somebody or something

vote of no confidence *n* in a parliamentary system a vote originating with an opposition party that cen[-] sures an act or policy of the government in power and if passed, requires that the government resign

vote-winner, vote-catcher *n* a policy or strategy tha[t] will attract a high proportion of votes

Votic *n* LANG = **Vote** —**Votic** *adj*

voting booth *n US* POL = **polling booth**

votive /vṓtiv/ *adj* **1** showing or symbolizing a wish o[r] desire ○ *a votive prayer* **2** given, done, or offered i[n] fulfilment of an oath or vow ○ *a votive offering* [Late 16C < Latin *votivus* < *votum* (see VOTE).] —**votively** *adv* —**votiveness** *n*

Votyak /vót yak/ (*plural* **-yak** *or* **-yaks**) *n* LANG = **Udmur[t]** *n.* **2** [Mid-19C. < Russian.] —**Votyak** *adj*

vou. *abbr* voucher

vouch /vowch/ *vt* in English law, to summon somebod[y] to court to prove ownership of land (*archaic*) [14C. Vi[a] French *voucher* 'summon' < Latin *vocare* 'call'.]

vouch for *vt* **1** to give an assurance that somebod[y] will behave well or appropriately **2** to guarantee tha[t] something such as a document or statement is accurat[e] or genuine

vouchee /vów cheé/ *n* somebody for whom anothe[r] person vouches

voucher /vówchər/ *n* **1** SUBSTITUTE FOR MONEY WHEN BUYING a card, token, or other document that can be exchanged for goods and services in place of money **2** DOCUMENTARY EVIDENCE a document that provides supporting evidence for a claim, e.g. a receipt proving that a purchase was made **3** GUARANTOR somebody or something that guar[-] antees or provides proof of something **4** CREDENTIALS FOR UK RESIDENCE a document that entitles a British national born outside the United Kingdom to live in Britain

vouchsafe /vówch sáyf/ (**-safes, -safing, -safed**) *vt* **1** to undertake or deign to grant or give something, es[-] pecially a reply **2** to promise, agree, or allow something (*formal*)

voussoir /voo swaár/ *n* a wedge-shaped brick or stone used to form the curved parts of an arch or vault [14C < French, < Latin *volvere* 'to roll'.]

Vouvray /vóo vray/ *n* a dry white wine produced in the Loire Valley of France [Late 19C. After a village in Indre-de-Loire, France.]

vow /vow/ *n* SOLEMN PLEDGE a solemn promise to perform a certain act, carry out an activity, or behave in a given way ■ **VOWS** *npl* RELIGIOUS PROMISE a solemn promise to join a religious order and live in accordance with its rules ■ *v* **1** *vt* PLEDGE to promise something solemnly and seriously **2** *vti* DEDICATE to promise somebody to a pledge or task, or to somebody such as a deity **3** *vt*

ASSERT to assert or declare something [13C. Via Old French *vou* < Latin *votum* (see VOTE).] —**vower** *n*

owel /vówəl/ *n* a speech sound, or the corresponding letter of the alphabet, produced by the passage of air through the vocal tract, with relatively little obstruction [14C. Via Old French *vouel* < Latin *vocalis* (see VOCAL).]

owel gradation *n* LING = ablaut

owelize /vówə līz/ (**-izes, -izing, -ized**), **vowelise** (**-ises, -ising, -ised**) *vt* to mark the vowel points in a Hebrew or Arabic text —**vowelization** /vów ə lī záysh'n/ *n*

owel mutation *n* LING = umlaut *n*. 1

owel point *n* a diacritical mark placed above or below a consonant to show a preceding or following vowel, used especially in languages such as Arabic and Hebrew that lack symbols for vowel sounds

ox angelica /vóks ən jéllikə/ *n* a quiet organ stop, usually with vibrato, that enriches the tone of other quiet stops [< Latin, 'angelic voice']

oxel /vóksəl/ *n* the smallest unit of three-dimensional space in a computer image, equivalent to a three-dimensional pixel [Blend of VOLUME + PIXEL]

ox humana /vóks hyoo maánə/ *n* an organ reed stop that produces a tone resembling the human voice [< Latin, 'human voice']

ox pop /vóks póp/ *n* the impromptu opinions of ordinary members of the public as gathered by a radio or television interviewer (*hyphenated before nouns*) [Shortening of VOX POPULI]

ox populi /vóks póppyōō lī/ *n* popular public opinion ○ *Let's see if we can detect the vox populi.* [< Latin, 'voice of the people']

oyage /vóy ij/ *n* **1** LONG TRIP a journey by sea or air, especially one to a distant place **2** SPACE JOURNEY a journey into space **3** JOURNEY EVENTS the events of an exploratory trip regarded as a story (*literary*) **4** NARRATIVE a story of an exploratory trip ■ *vti* (**-ages, -aging, -aged**) TRAVEL to make a long journey to, through, or over a place [13C. Via Old French *voiage* < Latin *viaticus* 'of a road or journey' < *via* 'road'.] —**voyager** *n*

oyager /vóy ijər/ *n* the name of two US spacecraft, Voyager 1 and Voyager 2, designed for exploring the outer planets of the solar system without a crew and launched in 1977

oyageur /vóy ə júr/ *n* Can a boatman, woodsman, trapper, or explorer hired by fur companies to carry furs and supplies from one remote station to another, especially in Canada and the NW United States [Late 18C. < French, 'voyager'.]

oyeur /vwī yúr/ *n* **1** a person who gains pleasure from watching, especially secretly, other people's bodies or the sexual acts in which they participate **2** a fascinated observer of distressing, sordid, or scandalous topics or events [Early 20C. < French, 'somebody who sees' < *voir* 'see' < Latin *videre*.] —**voyeurism** *n* —**voyeuristic** /vwī yur rístik/ *adj* —**voyeuristically** *adv*

oysey /vóyzi/, **Charles** (1857–1941) British architect and designer

P *abbr* **1** verb phrase **2** Vice President

PL *abbr* visible panty line

R *abbr* **1** variant reading **2** virtual reality **3** Volunteer Reserve **4** Victoria Regina

raisemblance /vráy soN blóNss/ *n* the quality of seeming to be true or likely [Early 19C. < French, 'true appearance'.]

RI *abbr* Victoria, Queen and Empress [Latin *Victoria Regina et Imperatrix*]

RML *n* a computer-graphics programming language used to create images of three-dimensional scenes. Full form **Virtual Reality Modelling Language**

room /vroom/ *n* the loud noise of an engine when it is being revved up or is running at high speed (*informal*) ■ *vi* to move noisily at high speed [Mid-20C. An imitation of the sound.]

VS, v. *abbr* versus

v.s. *abbr* vide supra

V-shaped *adj* having the shape of a 'V'

V-sign *n* **1** a hand sign that indicates victory, approval, or solidarity, made by holding up the index and middle fingers so that they form a 'V' with the palm facing outwards **2** a hand sign that indicates contempt, anger, or abuse, made by holding up the index and middle fingers so that they form a V with the palm facing inwards

VSO *n* an organization that sends volunteers to work and teach in developing countries. Full form **Voluntary Service Overseas** ■ *adj* used to indicate that brandy or port is between 12 and 17 years old. Full form **very superior old**

VSOP *adj* used to indicate that brandy or port is between 20 and 25 years old. Abbr of **very special old pale, very superior old pale**

VSS. *abbr* **1** verses **2** versions

V/STOL /veé stol/ *abbr* vertical and short takeoff and landing

vt *abbr* verb transitive

Vt *abbr* Vermont

VT *abbr* **1** vacuum tube **2** variable time **3** Vermont

VTOL /veé tol/ (*plural* **VTOLs**) *n* **1** a system used by some aircraft that enables them to take off and land vertically. Full form **vertical takeoff and landing 2** an aircraft capable of vertical takeoff and landing

VTR *n* (*plural* **VTRs**) video-tape recorder

⚡**VU** *abbr* Vanuatu (*in Internet addresses*)

vug /vug/ *n* a small hole in a rock or vein that often contains a mineral lining that differs from that of the surrounding matrix [Early 19C. < Cornish *vooga*.] —**vuggy** *adj*

Vuillard /vweé aar/, **Édouard** (1868–1940) French painter

Vul. *abbr* Vulgate

Vulcan /vúlkən/ *n* in Roman mythology, the god of fire. Greek equivalent **Hephaestus** —**Vulcanian** /vul káyni ən/ *adj*

vulcanian /vul káyni ən/ *adj* **1** relating to or caused by a type of explosive volcanic eruption resulting when the pressure of gases trapped in viscous magma is sufficient to blow off overlying solidified material **2** relating to or consisting of metalworking or metal craft

vulcanicity *n* GEOL = volcanicity [Late 18C. < French *vulcanicité*, variant of *volcanicité* (see VOLCANICITY).]

vulcanise *vt* = vulcanize

vulcanism *n* GEOL = volcanism

vulcanite /vúlkə nīt/ *n* a hard rubber produced by vulcanizing natural rubber with large amounts of sulphur [Mid-19C. After VULCAN.]

vulcanize /vúlkə nīz/ (**-nizes, -nizing, -nized**), **vulcanise** (**-nises, -nising, -nised**) *vt* to strengthen a material such as rubber by combining it with sulphur and other additives and then applying heat and pressure —**vulcanizable** *adj* —**vulcanizer** *n*

vulcanology *n* GEOL = volcanology

vulg. *abbr* **1** vulgar **2** vulgarly

Vulg. *abbr* Vulgate

vulgar /vúlgər/ *adj* **1** CRUDE AND INDECENT crude or obscene, particularly about sex or bodily functions ○ *vulgar language* **2** TASTELESSLY OSTENTATIOUS showing a lack of taste or reasonable moderation **3** LACKING REFINEMENT lacking in courtesy and manners **4** OF ORDINARY PEOPLE'S LANGUAGE relating to a form of a language spoken by people generally **5** OF ORDINARY PEOPLE relating to the majority of people (*archaic*) ■ *npl* ORDINARY PEOPLE people regarded or spoken of as a majority group ○ *She believes that fine food and wine are beyond the taste of the vulgar.* [14C. < Latin *vulgaris* < *vulgus* 'the common people'.] —**vulgarly** *adv*

vulgar fraction *n* MATH = simple fraction

---

vulgarian /vul gáiri ən/ *n* a wealthy but tasteless or ostentatious person

vulgarise *vt* = vulgarize

vulgarism /vúlgərizəm/ *n* **1** a crude or indecent word or phrase **2** a word or phrase from the language spoken by people generally, as contrasted with a more formal or refined usage **3** = vulgarity

vulgarity /vul gárrəti/ (*plural* **-ties**) *n* **1** a vulgar state or way of behaving **2** a crude or tasteless joke, remark, or act

vulgarize /vúlgə rīz/ (**-izes, -izing, -ized**), **vulgarise** (**-ises, -ising, -ised**) *vt* **1** to make something less refined or reduce the quality of something **2** to present or treat something in a way that makes it accessible to ordinary people —**vulgarization** /-rī záysh'n/ *n* —**vulgarizer** *n*

Vulgar Latin *n* the form of Latin that was the common spoken language of the W Roman Empire

vulgate /vúl gayt/ *n* **1** the everyday informal use of a language **2** a text generally accepted among experts as being the best or most accurate version [Early 17C. < Latin *vulgatus*, past participle of *vulgare* 'make public or common' < *vulgus* 'the common people'.]

Vulgate *n* a Latin version of the Bible produced by Saint Jerome in the 4th century [Early 17C. < Latin *vulgata editio* 'edition made public, edition for ordinary people' < *vulgatus* (see VULGATE).]

vulnerable /vúlnərəb'l/ *adj* **1** WITHOUT ADEQUATE PROTECTION open to emotional or physical danger or harm **2** OPEN TO ATTACK exposed to an attack or possible damage **3** EXTREMELY SUSCEPTIBLE easily persuadable or liable to give in to temptation **4** PHYSICALLY OR PSYCHOLOGICALLY WEAK unable to resist illness, debility, or failure **5** LIABLE TO INCREASED STAKES in bridge, liable to higher penalties as well as bonuses, having won one game of a rubber [Early 17C. < late Latin *vulnerabilis* < Latin *vulnerare* 'to wound' < *vulnus* 'wound, injury'.] —**vulnerability** /vúlnərə bílləti/ *n* —**vulnerableness** *n* —**vulnerably** *adv*

vulnerary /vúlnərəri/ *adj* capable of or used for healing wounds (*archaic*) ■ *n* (*plural* **-ies**) a drug or other agent used in treating and healing wounds (*archaic*) [Late 16C. < Latin *vulnerarius* < *vulnus* 'wound, injury'.]

Vulpecula /vul pékyoolə/ *n* a constellation of the northern hemisphere [< Latin, diminutive of *vulpes* 'fox']

vulpine /vúl pīn/ *adj* **1** typical of or resembling a fox **2** having or displaying a trait such as cunning that is commonly associated with foxes [Early 17C. < Latin *vulpes* 'fox'.]

vulture /vúlchər/ *n* **1** a large bird of prey with dark plumage and broad wings that feeds on carrion. Native to: Europe, Asia, Africa, the Americas. Family: Accipitridae and Cathartidae. **2** a person who waits for the chance to exploit somebody who is vulnerable [14C. Via Anglo-Norman *vultur* or Old French *voltour* < Latin *vultur*.]

vulturine /vúlchə rīn/ *adj* **1** typical of or resembling a vulture **2 vulturine, vulturous** having a trait commonly associated with vultures, e.g. opportunism or greed

vulva /vúlvə/ (*plural* **-vae** /-vee/ *or* **-vas**) *n* the external female genitals. These include two pairs of fleshy folds, the labia majora and labia minora, that surround the opening of the vagina, and the clitoris. [14C. < Latin, variant of *volva* 'womb' < *volvere* 'to roll'.] —**vulval** *adj* —**vulvar** *adj* —**vulviform** *adj*

vulvectomy /vul véktəmi/ (*plural* **-mies**) *n* the surgical removal of all or part of a woman's external genitals

vulvitis /vul vītiss/ *n* painful swelling and redness of the vulva

vulvovaginitis /vúlvō vaji nítiss/ *n* painful swelling and redness of the vulva and vagina

VV *abbr* Victoria

vv. *abbr* **1** verses **2** (first and second) violins **3** volumes

VW[1] (*plural* **VWs**) *n* any car manufactured by Volkswagen

VW[2] *abbr* very worshipful

VX *n* an oily, liquid, highly lethal, nerve gas

Vyatka /vyátkə/ former name for **Kirov** (1780–1934)

vying present participle of **vie**

Ww

W[1] /dúbb'l yoo/ (*plural* **w's**), **W** (*plural* **W's** *or* **Ws**) *n* the 23rd letter of the English alphabet, representing a consonant or sometimes a vowel

W[2] *abbr* **1** week **2** wicket(s) **3** wide(s) **4** width **5** wife **6** with

W[1] /dúbb'l yoo/ (*plural* **W's** *or* **Ws**) *n* something shaped like a letter 'W'

W[2] *symbol* **1** tungsten **2** watt **3** weight **4** work

W[3] *abbr* **1** Wales **2** Warden **3** Wednesday **4** Welsh **5** West **6** Western **7** women's (*used of clothing sizes*)

W/ *abbr* with

W3 *abbr* World Wide Web

W8 *abbr* wait (*in e-mails*)

W8ING *abbr* waiting (*in e-mails*)

WA *abbr* **1** Washington (State) **2** Western Australia **3** with average

WAAC /wak/ *abbr* Women's Army Auxiliary Corps

WAAF[1] /waf/ (*plural* **WAAFs**), **Waaf** (*plural* **Waafs**) *n* a member of the Women's Auxiliary Air Force or the Women's Auxiliary Australian Air Force (*dated*) [Mid-20C. < WAAF².]

WAAF[2] /waf/ *abbr* Women's Auxiliary Air Force (*dated*)

Waal /waal/ southernmost branch of the River Rhine in the Netherlands. Length: 84 km/52 mi.

wabbit /wábbit/ *adj Scotland* weary or exhausted [Late 19C. < ?]

wack /wak/, **wacker** /wákər/ *n* used to address a friend (*regional*) [< ?]

wacko /wákō/ (*plural* **wackos** *or* **wackoes**), **whacko** (*plural* **-os** *or* **-oes**) *n* an offensive term that deliberately insults somebody regarded as unconventional, unpredictable, or unusual (*slang*) [Late 20C. < WACKY.]

wacky /wáki/ (**-ier, -iest**), **whacky** (**-ier, -iest**) *adj* **1** an offensive term meaning unconventional or unpredictable (*slang*) **2** entertainingly silly (*informal*) [Mid-19C. Probably from the phrase *out of whack* 'out of order' (see WHACK).] —**wackily** *adv* —**wackiness** *n*

Waco /wáykō/ city in central Texas. Population: 105,892 (1994).

wad /wod/ *n* **1** SOFT MATERIAL a small rounded mass of soft material, usually used to pack or stuff something ◇ *The vase was carefully packed in wads of cotton.* **2** BUNDLE a roll or small bundle of paper money ◇ *a wad of notes* **3** COMPRESSED MATERIAL a rounded compressed lump of something soft, especially tobacco or gum for chewing **4** POWDER PLUG a plug of material such as paper or cloth used to hold the powder charge in a muzzle-loading gun or cannon **5** DISC IN SHOTGUN CARTRIDGE a disc made of felt or paper, used to hold the powder or shot in a shotgun cartridge **6** *US, Can* **A LOT OF MONEY** a large amount of money (*informal*) **7** *US* **MANY** a large quantity of something (*informal*) ◇ *She has wads of friends.* **8** MINERAL MIXTURE IN BOGGY GROUND a fine-grained mixture of hydrated barium manganese oxide and other hydrated oxide minerals. Source: poorly drained boggy ground. **9** BIT OF HAY OR STRAW a segment of a bale of hay or straw **10** BUN a small bread roll (*slang*) ■ *v* (**wads, wadding, wadded**) **1** *vti* COMPRESS TIGHTLY to form or compress something into a small mass ◇ *He wadded up the speeding ticket and threw it away.* **2** *vt* PUT WADDING INTO to stuff or plug something with wadding ◇ *She wadded her ears so she wouldn't hear the noise.* **3** *vt* KEEP CHARGE IN PLACE to hold a charge of powder or shot in place **4** *vt* INSERT

WADDING INTO GUN to insert a piece of wadding into a gun [Mid-16C. < ?] —**wadder** *n*

wada /vúddə/, **vada** *n S Asia* a fried lentil ball eaten as a popular snack, particularly in South India [< Hindi *vadā*]

wadding /wódding/ *n* **1** SOFT PROTECTIVE MATERIAL soft material used to protect something, especially in packaging **2** GUN WADS material used to hold powder or shot in a gun or cartridge **3** PADDING MATERIAL USED IN SEWING a bonded fibre material produced in different thicknesses. Use: interlining, patchwork quilt padding.

Waddington /wóddingtən/, **Conrad Hal** (1905–75) British embryologist and geneticist

waddle /wódd'l/ *vi* (**-dles, -dling, -dled**) to walk with short steps, causing the body to tilt slightly from one side to the other ■ *n* a way of walking, taking short steps with the body tilting slightly from one side to the other with each step [Late 16C. < WADE.] —**waddler** *n* —**waddly** *adj*

wade /wayd/ *v* (**wades, wading, waded**) **1** *vti* WALK IN WATER to walk against the pressure of water or mud **2** *vi* GO THROUGH SOMETHING WITH DIFFICULTY to read through something with difficulty, especially because it is very long or boring ◇ *wading through a tome on Greek philosophy* ■ *n* WALK TAKEN IN SHALLOW WATER an act or instance of walking in shallow water [Old English *wadan* < Indo-European, 'go'] —**wadable** *adj*
wade in *vti* **1** **wade in, wade into** to interrupt somebody forcefully or with determination **2** to intervene in a situation in an attempt to help or restore order

Wade /wayd/, **Virginia** (*b.* 1945) British tennis player

wader /wáydər/ *n* **1** a person who or animal that wades through something **2** = wading bird **3** = shore bird ■ **waders** *npl* waterproof boots or combined boots and trousers that reach to the hips or chest, worn as protection while fishing

wadi /wóddi/ (*plural* **wadis** *or* **wadies**), **wady** (*plural* **-dies**) *n* **1** a steep-sided water course in dry regions of North Africa and S Asia through which water flows only after heavy rainfall **2** an oasis, especially in North Africa [Early 17C. < Arabic *wādī* 'valley, river bed'.]

wading bird *n* a long-legged bird such as a crane, heron, or stork that stands in water and hunts for its food that includes fish, frogs, invertebrates, carrion, and algae

wading pool *n* a shallow pool, sometimes near a larger pool, for small children to play in. ◊ **paddling pool**

Wad Medani /waåd mi daåni/ capital of El Gezira Province, central Sudan. Population: 218,714 (1993).

wady *n* GEOG = wadi

WAEF *abbr* when all else fails (*in e-mails*)

Wafd /woft/ *n* an Egyptian nationalist party that emerged after an Egyptian delegation was refused a hearing at the Versailles Treaty negotiations following World War I

wafer /wáyfər/ *n* **1** THIN CRISP BISCUIT a thin, crisp, and sometimes sweetened biscuit, usually in a rectangular, fan, or cone shape, often eaten with ice cream **2** BREAD IN CHRISTIAN COMMUNION SERVICE a very thin disc of unleavened bread used to represent the body of Jesus Christ in the Christian Communion **3** ELECTRONICS = chip *n*. **4** ADHESIVE MATERIAL a small thin disc of adhesive material, used to seal letters and formal documents **5** MEDICINE CASING a piece of rice paper or dried flour paste. Use: formerly, to encase a powdered medicine. (*archaic*) ■ *vt* **1** FASTEN WITH WAFER to fasten something such as a letter or formal document with a wafer

2 ENCASE MEDICINE to encase a powdered medicine in rice paper or dried flour paste (*archaic*) [14C. Via Angl Norman *wafre*, variant of French *gaufre*, < Middle Lc German *wāfel*, < Germanic.]

wafer-thin *adj* extremely thin or narrow

waffle[1] /wóff'l/ *vi* (**-fles, -fling, -fled**) to speak or write length without saying anything important or inte esting (*informal*) ■ *n* speech or writing that is length and irrelevant (*informal*) [Late 17C. < *waff* 'yelp or bar an imitation of the sound; literally 'keep on waffling'.] - **waffly** *adj*

waffle[2] /wóff'l/ *n* a thick light pancake, crisp on tl outside, that is baked in a waffle iron to give a patte of indentations on both sides [Mid-18C. < Dutch *wa*▮ (see WAFER).]

waft /woft, waaft/ *vti* FLOAT GENTLY to float gently throug the air, or move something gently through the air ■ **1** SOMETHING CARRIED THROUGH AIR something such as a sce▮ carried on the air or by a breeze **2** WAVING MOTION a gent waving or fluttering motion **3** LIGHT BREEZE a brief gent gust of air **4** SIGNALLING FLAG a hoisted flag formerly use for signalling at sea (*archaic*) **5** SIGNAL USING FLAGS a sign formerly sent at sea using flags (*archaic*) [Early 16▮ Back-formation < *wafter* 'an armed ship used to guard convoy' < Dutch *wachter* < *wachten* 'guard'.]

wag[1] /wag/ *v* (**wags, wagging, wagged**) **1** *vti* MOVE SOMETHIN RAPIDLY TO AND FRO to move part of the body to and fr or move to and fro ◇ *The dog wagged its tail.* **2** *vi* GOSS to gossip about somebody or other people, especial disapprovingly ◇ *Tongues are wagging.* ■ *n* MOTION GOI▮ TO AND FRO a motion that goes to and fro [Old Englis *wagian* 'move backwards and forwards' < Germanic]

wag[2] /wag/ *vti* (**wags, wagging, wagged**) to be absent fro▮ school without permission (*slang*) ■ *n* a humorou or witty individual (*dated*) [Mid-16C. < ? Originally a affectionate term for a mischievous boy.] —**waggery** - **waggish** *adj* —**waggishly** *adv* —**waggishness** *n*

wage /wayj/ *n* **1** PAYMENT FOR WORK a sum of money paid ▮ a worker in exchange for services, especially for wo▮ performed on an hourly, daily, weekly, or piece-ra▮ basis (*often plural*) **2** wages RESULT the deserved outcom of a wrong or unwise action (*literary*; + *singular ver* ◇ *the wages of sin* ■ *vt* (**wages, waging, waged**) ENGAGE FIGHT to engage in war or in a serious fight to achiev an end ◇ *wage war* [14C. < Anglo-Norman or Old N Frenc < Germanic, 'pledge'.] —**wageless** *adj* —**wagelessness** ▮

SYNONYMS *wage, salary, pay, fee, remuneratio▮ emolument, honorarium, stipend*

CORE MEANING: money given for work done

wage a fixed regular payment made on an hourly, weekly, daily basis, especially to manual workers; **salary** a fixe regular annual sum, usually paid on a monthly basis, e pecially to clerical or professional workers; **pay** a wage salary; **fee** a payment made to a professional person by client; **remuneration** payment for work, goods, or service **emolument** (*formal*) any payment for work; **honorariu▮** money given in exchange for services for which there normally no fixed charge; **stipend** a regular payment allowance for living expenses, especially one made to member of the clergy or a student.

wage differential *n* any difference in wages betwee workers with different skills working in the same in dustry or workers with similar skills working in di▮ ferent industries or regions

wage earner *n* **1** somebody in a family or household who is earning a wage or salary **2** a person who works by the hour, day, or week for wages and not a fixed salary

wage incentive *n* additional money paid to a worker in order to improve that person's productivity

wage packet *n* a wage or salary that is paid to somebody

wager /wáyjər/ *n* **1 BET ON OUTCOME** an agreement between two people that whoever loses a bet on an uncertain outcome will pay the other a particular amount or some other form of compensation **2 AMOUNT BET** a sum of money, property, or other compensation to be paid to the person who wins a bet **3 PLEDGE** formerly, a pledge to engage in combat, especially in order to establish guilt or innocence by single combat ■ *vt* **BET MONEY** to risk or bet money or property on the outcome of a game, event, or uncertain situation [14C. < Anglo-Norman *wageure* < *wagier* 'to pledge' < *wage* 'pledge'.] —**wagerer** *n*

wage scale *n* a scale of the different wages paid to employees who are performing different jobs within a single company or industry

wage slave *n* a person who totally depends on work in order to live (*informal*)

Wagga Wagga /wóggə wóggə/ city in S New South Wales, Australia. Population: 42,848 (1996).

waggle /wágg'l/ *vti* (**-gles, -gling, -gled**) to move rapidly back and forth, or make something move rapidly back and forth ■ *n* a quick shaking or wobbling motion [Late 16C. < WAG[1].] —**waggly** *adj*

waggon *n* TRANSP = **wagon**

waggonette *n* TRANSP = **wagonette**

waggonload *n* MEASURE = **wagonload**

Wagner /vaágnər/, **Richard** (1813–83) German composer —**Wagnerian** /vaag neéri ən/ *adj, n*

Wagner /wágnər/, **Robert F.** (1877–1953) German-born US politician

wagon /wággən/, **waggon** *n* **1 WHEELED VEHICLE** a rectangular vehicle that is used to carry heavy loads and is pulled by an animal or tractor or is motor-powered **2** *US* **DELIVERY VEHICLE** a van used to sell or deliver something **3** *US, Can* **POLICE PATROL WAGON** a van used by the police to transport suspects or criminals **4** *US, Can* **CHILD'S FOUR-WHEELED CART** a low four-wheeled cart with a long handle that a child can use to pull the cart or to control the direction of the front wheels **5** *US* **SERVING CART** a four-wheeled rectangular cart used to display or serve food or drink **6 FREIGHT TRUCK** a railway truck for goods, particularly an open one [15C. < Dutch *wagen* < Germanic.] —**wagoner** *n* ◇ **be off the wagon** to resume drinking alcohol after a period of abstinence ◇ **be on the wagon** to abstain from drinking alcohol

wagonette /wággə nét/, **waggonette** *n* a light four-wheeled horse-drawn vehicle with two lengthwise seats facing each other behind a crosswise driver's seat

wagon-lit /vággon leé/ (*plural* **wagon-lits** *or* **wagons-lits**) *n* **1** a sleeping car on a European railway **2** an individual compartment in a railway sleeping car [< French, < *wagon* 'railway coach' + *lit* 'bed']

wagonload /wággən lōd/, **waggonload** *n* the amount that a wagon does or can hold

wagon train *n* a line of two or more animal-drawn wagons travelling cross-country and carrying people, food supplies, or goods

wagon vault *n* ARCHIT = **barrel vault**

Wagram /vaág ram/ village in NE Austria, site of Napoleon's defeat of the Austrians in July 1809

wagtail /wág tayl/ *n* a songbird with a long tail that bobs up and down when it walks and especially when it lands. Native to: Europe, Asia, Africa. Family: Motacillidae.

Wag the Dog syndrome *n US* a situation in which a US president uses military attacks on other nations as a diversionary tactic to deflect intense public and media scrutiny from a personal scandal (*slang*) ○ *'Was the bombing of Iraq really a result of Wag the Dog syndrome?'* (*Vanity Fair*; March 1999) [Late 20C. *Wag the Dog* < a film title.]

Wahhabi /wə haábi/ (*plural* **-bis**), **Wahabi** (*plural* **-bis**) *n* a member of a very conservative Islamic group that rejects any innovation that occurred after the 3rd century of Islam [Early 19C. < Arabic *wahhābī*, after Muhammad ibn bd-al- *Wahhāb* (1703–92), its founder.] —**Wahhabism** *n*

wahine /waa heéni/ *n* **1** *Hawaii, NZ* a Hawaiian or Maori woman or wife **2** *Hawaii* a young woman surfer (*informal*) [Late 18C. < Hawaiian or Maori.]

wahoo /waá hoo, waa hoó/ (*plural* **-hoos**) *n* a large fast-swimming fish of the mackerel family that weighs up to 120 pounds. Native to: tropical seas. *Acanthocybium solanderi*. [Early 20C. < ?]

wah-wah /waá waa/, **wa-wa** *n* **1 WAVERING SOUND OF WIND INSTRUMENT** the wavering sound made by alternately covering and uncovering the bell of a brass instrument **2 ELECTRONIC SOUND** a sound resembling a wah-wah, created for electronic instruments **3 ELECTRONIC DEVICE** an electronic device attached to a musical instrument for producing a wah-wah sound [Early 20C. An imitation of the sound.]

wah-wah pedal *n* a foot pedal attached to an electronic musical instrument, used to create a wavering sound

waiata /wī aatə/ *n NZ* a Maori song [< Maori]

waif /wayf/ *n* **1 ABANDONED CHILD** a homeless or friendless person, especially an abandoned child **2 STRAY ANIMAL** a stray animal whose owner is unknown **3 THIN YOUNG PERSON** somebody, usually a young person, with a thin fragile appearance who looks in need of care **4 UNCLAIMED ITEM** any item found whose owner is unknown (*literary*) **5 UNCLAIMED PROPERTY** any property that, if found ownerless and unclaimed, becomes the property of the Crown or lord of the manor [14C. < Anglo-Norman *weyf*, earlier *gwayf* 'lost property', < N Germanic.] —**waif-like** *adj*

Waiheke Island /wī heéki-/ island off the northeastern coast of the North Island, New Zealand, in the Hauraki Gulf. Population: 6,286 (1996). Area: 93 sq. km/36 sq. mi.

Waikaremoana /wī kurrəmō unə/ lake in the eastern part of the North Island, New Zealand. Area: 54 sq. km/21 sq. mi.

Waikato /wīk aatō/ longest river in New Zealand, rising in Lake Taupo in the centre of the North Island and emptying into the Tasman Sea. Length: 434 km/270 mi.

Waikiki /wī kee kee/ beach resort on S Oahu Island, Hawaii

wail /wayl/ *v* **1** *vti* **MAKE MOURNFUL CRY** to express pain, grief, or misery in a long mournful high-pitched cry or in words uttered in a mournful way ○ *He could only wail when he heard the news.* **2** *vi* **MAKE LONG HIGH-PITCHED NOISE** to make a long loud high-pitched sound ○ *The sirens wailed.* **3** *vt* **LAMENT** to express grief over somebody or something (*archaic*) ■ *n* **1 LONG HIGH-PITCHED SOUND** a long loud high-pitched sound or cry **2 PROTEST** a loud plaintive expression of protest, resentment, or disappointment [13C. < an Old Norse word, < *vei* 'woe'.] —**wailer** *n* —**wailful** *adj* —**wailfully** *adv*

SPELLCHECK Do not confuse ***wail*** with ***wale*** or ***whale***, which sound similar. Beware: your spellchecker will not catch this error.

Wailing Wall *n* = **Western Wall**

wain /wayn/ *n* a farm wagon or cart (*archaic or literary*) [Old English *wæ(g)n* < Germanic]

wainscot /wáynskət, wáyn skot/ *n* **1 WOODEN PANELS LINING ROOM** a lining for the walls of a room, especially one made of wood panelling **2 LOWER PART OF WALL OF ROOM** the lower part of the wall of a room, especially when it is panelled in wood or finished differently from the upper part **3 OAK PANELLING** a fine grade of oak used as wall panelling ■ *vt* (**-scots, -scoting** *or* **-scotting, -scoted** *or* **-scotted**) **COVER WALL WITH PANELLING** to cover a wall, especially with wood panelling [14C. < Middle Dutch *waghenscote* or Middle Low German *wagenschot* 'wagon-boarding'.]

wainscoting /wáynskəting, wáyn skotting/, **wainscotting** *n* **1** BUILDING = **wainscot** *n.* 1 **2** the material, especially wood, used to cover a wall

wainwright /wáyn rīt/ *n* a maker and repairer of wagons

Wairarapa, Lake /wī raa raápə/ lake in the southern part of the North Island, New Zealand. Area: 80 sq. km/50 sq. mi.

Wairau /wīr ow/ river in the northern part of the South Island, New Zealand. Length: 169 km/105 mi.

waist /wayst/ *n* **1 BODY AREA BETWEEN RIBS AND HIPS** the part of the human trunk between the rib cage and the hips, usually narrower than the rest of the trunk **2 PART OF CLOTHING** the part of a garment that fits around the waist of the body **3 NARROW PART** the narrow middle part of something, such as the middle of a violin **4 MIDDLE OF DECK** the middle part of a ship or a ship's deck between the raised sections at the bow and stern **5 MIDDLE OF AEROPLANE** the middle section of an aircraft's fuselage **6 MIDDLE OF INSECT** the narrow part of an insect's body between the thorax and the abdomen [14C. < ?] —**waisted** *adj* —**waistless** *adj*

SPELLCHECK Do not confuse ***waist*** with ***waste***, which has a similar sound. Beware: your spellchecker will not catch this error.

waistband /wáyst band/ *n* a band of fabric that circles the waist at the top of a garment such as a skirt or pair of trousers

waistcloth /wáyst kloth/ *n* a loincloth (*archaic*)

waistcoat /wáyss kōt, wáyst-/ *n* **1** a man's or woman's sleeveless and collarless waist-length garment, usually with buttons down the front, worn over a shirt and traditionally worn by men under a suit jacket **2** a man's sleeveless garment reaching to the hips or knees, worn under a doublet in the 16th century —**waistcoated** *adj*

waistline /wáyst līn/ *n* **1** the measurement round the narrowest part of the waist **2** the level, usually near the waist, where the bodice and skirt of a dress meet ○ *a low waistline*

wait /wayt/ *v* **1** *vi* **DO NOTHING EXPECTING SOMETHING TO HAPPEN** to stay in one place or do nothing for a period of time until something happens or in the expectation or hope that something will happen ○ *I'll wait for you here until noon.* **2** *vi* **STOP SO SOMEBODY CAN CATCH UP** to stop or slow down in order to allow somebody else to catch up ○ *Wait for me!* **3** *vi* **BE HOPING** to be hoping for something or on the lookout for something ○ *He is waiting for a job opportunity.* **4** *vi* **BE DELAYED OR IGNORED FOR NOW** to be postponed or put off until later ○ *Fame would just have to wait.* **5** *vi* **BE READY OR AVAILABLE** to be ready or available for somebody to take or use ○ *Your mail is waiting for you.* **6** *vt* **DELAY** to delay something, especially a meal, because somebody is expected to arrive soon (*informal*) ○ *We waited dinner for you.* **7** *vti* **BE A WAITER** to work as a waiter ○ *She waits at the local restaurant.* ■ *n* **TIME SPENT WAITING** a period of time spent while expecting something to happen ○ *The wait seemed like forever.* ■ **waits** *npl* **BAND OF MUSICIANS** a band of musicians who play and sing Christmas carols in the streets (*archaic*) [12C. Via Old N French *waitier* 'spy, prepare to ambush' < Frankish.] ◇ **lie in wait for somebody** *or* **something** to be waiting to catch or attack somebody or something

LITERARY LINK ***Waiting for Godot***, a play (1954) by Samuel Beckett. A classic drama of the theatre of the absurd, it has two main characters, the tramps Estragon and Vladimir. They indulge in idle conversation and games while waiting for Godot, who they hope will give some meaning to their futile existence. Godot does not arrive and the tramps decide to go, but they do not leave the stage.

SPELLCHECK Do not confuse ***wait*** with ***weight***, which has a similar sound. Beware: your spellchecker will not catch this error.

USAGE See ***await***.

wait on *vt* **1 SERVE SOMEBODY BY BRINGING REQUESTED ITEMS** to go and get the things that somebody asks for, usually continuously for a period of time ○ *It's nice to be waited on for a change.* **2 SERVE SOMEBODY AT TABLE** to bring food and drink to people sitting at a table, usually in a restaurant **3 SERVE RETAIL CUSTOMER** to attend to a customer's purchasing needs **4 WAIT FOR** to wait for somebody or something (*informal*) **5 VISIT** to pay a formal visit to somebody (*archaic*) ■ *interj ANZ* **HOLD ON** used to tell somebody to wait a while

wait out *vt* to stay in one place or do nothing until something ends ○ *We decided to wait out the storm.*

wait up *vi* to delay going to bed to await an event or somebody's arrival ○ *I'll be home late; don't wait up.*

wait upon *vt* = **wait on** *v.* 1, **wait on** *v.* 2, **wait on** *v.* 3, **wait on** *v.* 5

Waitaki /wī táki/ river in the southeastern part of the South Island, New Zealand. Length: 209 km/130 mi.

Waitangi /wī túngi/ historic site in the northern part of the North Island, New Zealand. A treaty between the Maori people and the British government was signed there in February 1840.

Waitangi Day /wī tungi-/ *n* in New Zealand, a national day and public holiday marking the signing of the Treaty of Waitangi in 1840 by Maori chiefs and representatives of the British government. Date: 6 February. [After WAITANGI]

Waitemata Harbour /wítə mátə haárbər/ arm of the Pacific Ocean on the northeastern coast of the North Island, New Zealand

waiter /wáytər/ *n* **1 SOMEBODY WHO SERVES AT TABLES** somebody employed to bring food and drink to people, usually in a restaurant **2 TRAY** a tray for carrying dishes or serving food **3 MESSENGER** a messenger at the London Stock Exchange or Lloyd's [14C. Via Anglo-Norman, 'attendant, watchman' < Old N French, or directly < WAIT.]

waiting game *n* a tactic whereby somebody delays taking any action or making a move in a contest or negotiation, hoping that his or her position will improve with the passage of time

waiting list *n* a list of people waiting for something that is not immediately available, e.g. a hospital bed, a table in a restaurant, a place in a school, or an out-of-stock product

waiting room *n* a room in which people may wait, e.g. for a doctor's appointment or a train

Waitomo Caves /wī tṓmō-/ limestone cave system in the western part of the North Island, New Zealand

waitperson /wáyt purss'n/ (*plural* **waitpeople** *or* **waitpersons**) *n US* a man or woman employed to serve at tables, usually in a restaurant

waitress /wáytrəss/ *n* a woman who serves food or drink at tables, usually in a restaurant

waitron /wáytrən/ *n US* a person who serves at tables (*slang*) [Late 20C. Blend of WAITER or WAITRESS and AUTOMATON, suggesting mechanical, repetitive work.]

waitstaff /wáyt staaf/ *n US* the group of waiters and waitresses in a café or restaurant

ϟ**wait state** *n* a period of time during which a central processing unit in a computer sits idle while a slower component, such as a memory or bus, functions

waive /wayv/ (**waives, waiving, waived**) *vt* **1 SURRENDER CLAIM** to give something up voluntarily, especially a right or claim ○ *She waived her right to remain silent.* **2 NOT ENFORCE** to refrain from enforcing or applying something in a particular instance ○ *They decided to waive the restrictions.* **3 TEMPORARILY DELAY** to put off something for a time [13C. < Anglo-Norman *weyver* 'make a waif of, abandon' < *weyf* (see WAIF).]

SPELLCHECK Do not confuse ***waive*** with ***wave***, which has a similar sound. Beware: your spellchecker will not catch this error.

waiver /wáyvər/ *n* **1** a voluntary giving up of a right or claim **2** a document or formal statement relinquishing a right or claim, or an action indicating an intention to waive something

Wajda /vídə/, **Andrzej** (*b.* 1926) Polish film director

wakame /waa kaámi/ (*plural* **-mes** *or* **-me**) *n* an edible brown seaweed. Use: dried, in Japanese and Chinese cooking. Native to: coasts of Japan, China, and Korea. *Undaria pinnatifida*. [Mid-20C. < Japanese.]

Wakashan /waa káshən/ *n* a family of languages spoken by Native North American peoples in British Columbia and Washington State. Native speakers: 3,000. [Late 19C. < Nootka *waukash* 'good'.] —**Wakashan** *adj*

Wakatipu /waákə típpoo/ lake in the southwestern part of the South Island, New Zealand. Area: 293 sq. km/113 sq. mi.

Wakayama /wákə yaámə/ port of S Honshu Island, Japan. Population: 396,553 (1990).

wake[1] /wayk/ *v* (**wakes, waking, woke** /wōk/, **woken** /wṓkən/) **1** *vti* **END SOMEBODY'S OR YOUR OWN SLEEP** to come back, or bring somebody back, to a conscious state after sleeping ○ *I woke suddenly at dawn.* **2** *vti* **END INACTIVITY** to become alert and active, or make somebody alert and active, after being inactive, in a daydream, or preoccupied **3** *vti* **MAKE SOMEBODY REALIZE SOMETHING** to make somebody aware of something ○ *Their pleas woke us to the situation.* **4** *vi* **WATCH OVER CORPSE** to hold a vigil over the body of somebody who has died **5** *vi* **STAY AWAKE** to be or to remain awake ○ *'Fled is that music — Do I wake or sleep?'* (John Keats, *Ode to a Nightingale*; 1819) **6** *vti* **KEEP WATCH** to keep watch over somebody or something (*archaic*) ■ *n* **1 WATCH KEPT OVER CORPSE** a watch or vigil held over a corpse before burial or cremation **2 FESTIVE GATHERING ASSOCIATED WITH A DEATH** a social gathering held after a funeral or, in Ireland, often after the death but before the funeral **3 wakes ANNUAL HOLIDAY** an annual one- or two-week holiday, originally to celebrate a parish church festival in the industrial areas of N England, when the local factories shut down (*regional; + singular or plural verb*) [Old English *wacan* 'become awake' < Indo-European, 'be active or lively'] —**waker** *n*

LITERARY LINK *Finnegans Wake*, a novel (1939) by Irish writer James Joyce. Joyce's last novel recounts a single night in the life of a Dublin publican, Humphrey Chimpden Earwicker, and his family. An extraordinary multilayered work consisting chiefly of extended interior monologues, it is crammed with multilingual puns, poetry, and literary and historical allusions that emphasize the universal and cyclical nature of human experience.

USAGE See ***awake***.

wake up *v* **1** *vti* = **wake**[1] *v.* **1**, **wake**[1] *v.* **2**, **wake**[1] *v.* **3 2** *vt* to make something look more interesting or attractive

wake[2] /wayk/ *n* **1 TRACK IN WATER** the track left in water by a vessel or any other body moving through it **2 DISTURBED AIR BEHIND VEHICLE** the stream of turbulence in the air left by an aircraft or land vehicle passing through it **3 POSITION BEHIND** a position or the area behind somebody or something that is moving ahead fast ○ *left the rest of the field trailing in her wake* **4 AFTEREFFECTS** the aftermath or aftereffects of a dramatic event or powerful thing ○ *The bomb left destruction in its wake.* [15C. Via Middle Low German < Old Norse *vok* 'hole in ice (made by a boat)'.] ◇ **in the wake of something** immediately after and usually as a result of something

wakeboarding /wáyk bawrding/ *n* a water sport in which somebody riding a single board is pulled behind a motor boat and performs jumps while crisscrossing the wake of the boat [Late 20C. After SKATEBOARDING.] —**wakeboard** *vi* —**wakeboarder** *n*

Wakefield /wáyk feeld/ city in N England. Population: 73,675 (1991).

Wakefield, Edward Gibbon (1796–1862) British-born New Zealand social theorist

wakeful /wáykf'l/ *adj* **1 NOT SLEEPING** unable to sleep **2 SLEEPLESS** passed without sleep ○ *a wakeful night* **3 ALERT** awake, especially while watching or guarding something ○ *promised to remain wakeful* —**wakefully** *adv* —**wakefulness** *n*

wakeless /wáykləss/ *adj* uninterrupted by waking, or spent in uninterrupted sleep

waken /wáykən/ *vti* to become, or make somebody, conscious after sleeping, active after being inactive, or aware after being unaware —**wakener** *n*

USAGE See ***awake***.

wake-robin (*plural* **wake-robins** *or* **wake-robin**) *n* **1** = **cuckoopint 2** a member of a group of early-blooming North American arums, e.g. the arrow arum

wake-up call *n* **1** a telephone call or a personal visit made to awaken somebody, especially a telephone call from or arranged by hotel staff made at an agreed time to awaken a guest **2** a frightening experience that is interpreted as a sign that a major change is needed in the way somebody lives or conducts business

wakil LAW = **vakil**

Wal. *abbr* Walloon

Walachia /wolláyki ə/ former region in SE Europe, in present-day S Romania —**Walachian** *n, adj*

Walcott /wáwlkət/, **Derek** (*b.* 1930) St Lucian writer

Waldemar I /vaáldə maár/ (1131–82) king of Denmark (1157–82). Known as **Waldemar the Great**

Waldemar II (1170–1241) king of Denmark (1202–41). Known as **Waldemar the Conqueror**

Waldenses /wawl dénseez, wol-/ *npl* the members of a small Christian denomination, originating in S France, that broke with the Roman Catholic Church in the 12th century and experienced much persecution [Mid-16C. < medieval Latin, < *Waldensis*, variant of Peter *Valdes* (d. 1205), who founded the movement.] —**Waldensian** *adj*

Waldheim /wáwld hīm, vaált-/, **Kurt** (*b.* 1918) Austrian statesman

Waldorf salad /wáwld awrf-, wóld-/ *n* a salad made of diced raw apples, celery, and walnuts with a mayonnaise dressing [Early 20C. After the *Waldorf-Astori*… Hotel in New York, USA.]

waldsterben /vált shtàirbən/ *n* widespread disease an… death of trees, thought to be the result of atmospheri… pollution [Late 20C. < German, 'forest dying'.]

wale /wayl/ *n* **1 SKIN WELT** a raised mark on the skin mad… by a blow, particularly with a whip **2 RIDGE ON FABRIC** … ridge on the surface of a woven fabric such as corduro… **3 WEAVE OF FABRIC** the weave or texture of a fabric wit… ribs **4 VERTICAL ROW OF KNITTING** a vertical row of stitche… in knitting **5 WOOD FORMING SIDES OF SHIP** any strong hori… zontal plank forming the sides of a wooden ship ■ … (**wales, waling, waled**) **1 RAISE WELT ON SKIN** to raise a re… swollen mark on the skin by striking a blow, par… ticularly with a whip **2 WEAVE RIDGED FABRIC** to weav… fabric with ridges [Old English *walu* 'ridge' < Germanic]

SPELLCHECK See ***wail***.

Wales /waylz/ principality in Great Britain, part of th… United Kingdom of Great Britain and Northern Ireland… Capital: Cardiff. Population: 2,921,000 (1996). Are… 20,766 sq. km/8,018 sq. mi.

Walhalla, Walhall *n* MYTHOL = **Valhalla**

walk /wawk/ *v* **1** *vi* **MOVE ON FOOT** to move or travel on leg… and feet, alternately putting one foot a comfortabl… distance in front of, or sometimes behind, the other an… usually proceeding at a moderate pace ○ *a toddler jus… learning to walk* **2** *vt* **TRAVEL THROUGH PLACE ON FOOT** to trave… along or through something on foot ○ *walking the coasta… path* **3** *vt* **TAKE ANIMAL FOR EXERCISE BY WALKING** to lead o… exercise an animal, usually a dog on a leash ○ *walke… the dog* **4** *vt* **WALK WITH SOMEBODY TO A PLACE** to accompan… somebody on foot as far as a particular place such as … home or car ○ *I'll walk you home.* **5** *vt* **CAUSE SOMEBODY T… WALK** to help or force somebody to walk by holding an… pushing from behind ○ *We kept walking him till he wa… able to stand on his own.* **6** *vti* **MOVE LARGE OBJECT BY ROCKIN…** to move, or move something, in a way that suggest… walking, e.g. by pivoting a large heavy object al… ternately on its corners and swinging the other sid… forwards ○ *The wardrobe's too heavy to lift; we'll have t… walk it into the bedroom.* **7** *vt* **MEASURE SOMETHING BY WALKIN…** to measure or inspect something by walking over o… along it, especially the boundaries of an area or piec… of property ○ *walk the west property line* **8** *vi* **LIVE I… PARTICULAR WAY** to conduct your life in a particular wa… (*archaic*) ○ *walk with God* **9** *vti* **COME BACK AS A GHOST** t… return to earth after death as a ghost ○ *She walks th… tower.* **10** *vi* **BE STOLEN** to disappear or be stolen (*informa…* ○ *The petty cash seems to have walked.* **11** *vi US* **GO ON STRIK…** to go out on strike (*slang*) ○ *threatened to walk* **12** *vi U…* **LEAVE IN PROTEST** to leave a job, event, or meeting t… express disagreement (*slang*) ○ *I'd better get an apolog… or I'm walking!* **13** *vi US* **BE FREED FROM JAIL OR ACQUITTED** t… be released from prison or found innocent of a crim… (*slang*) ○ *I couldn't believe they walked after what they did* **14** *vi* **ACKNOWLEDGE BEING OUT BY LEAVING WICKET** in cricket, t… leave the wicket without waiting to be given out by th… umpire **15** *vi* **GO TO FIRST BASE** in baseball, to proceed or allow the batter to proceed, to first base after fou… deliveries from the pitcher, none of which was in th… strike zone or swung at **16** *vi* **TAKE STEPS ILLEGALLY** to tak… more than two steps in basketball without dribblin… while holding the ball ■ *n* **1 ROUTE** a regular route of … street vendor or delivery person **2 MARCH** a processio… **3 JOURNEY ON FOOT** a journey made on foot, especially fo… pleasure or exercise ○ *a walk in the woods* **4 DISTANCE O… TIME OF FOOT JOURNEY** the distance travelled or the time i… takes to go somewhere on foot ○ *a four-mile walk* ○ *a ten minute walk from home* **5 HORSE'S SLOWER GAIT** a relativel… slow-paced way of moving for a horse or other four… legged animal, in which two feet are always on th… ground ○ *The mare started at a walk, then broke into … trot.* **6 WAY OF WALKING** somebody's characteristic way o… walking ○ *She's got a graceful walk.* **7 PLACE FOR PEDESTRIAN…** a place designed or set aside for the use of people o… foot **8 ROUTE FOR PEOPLE WALKING** a route or path for trav… ellers on foot ○ *The miners' trail is an easy scenic walk* **9 RACE** a race in which the competitors walk a specified distance **10 AREA FOR ANIMALS** an enclosed area for exercising or pasturing domestic animals such as horses **11 ROWS OF TREES** a plantation of widely spaced trees o… shrubs **12 SPACE BETWEEN ROWS** the space between rows of widely spaced trees or shrubs **13 ILLEGAL HOLDIN… INSTEAD OF DRIBBLING** in basketball, illegally moving while holding the ball **14** *US* **SOMETHING VERY EASY** something that is very easy to do (*informal*) ○ *We'll certainly bea… them. It'll be a walk.* **15 FOREST** a section of a forest con-rolled by a single keeper (*archaic*) [Old English *wealcan* 'roll, toss' and *wealcian* 'roll up' < Germanic] —**walkable** *adj* ◇ **walk it** to gain victory or success easily (*informal*) ◇ **walk all over somebody** to ignore somebody's rights or feelings ◇ **walk tall** to feel and display self-confidence and pride in your achievements

walk away *vi* **1 ABANDON PROBLEM** to refrain from becoming, or refuse to become, involved in a situation or problem **2 HAVE MINOR INJURIES** to survive an accident uninjured or with few and minor injuries and be able to walk from the scene **3 DEFEAT SOMEBODY** to defeat or outdo another person or team easily **4 WIN** to win or achieve something ○ *She walked away with the first prize.*

walk in on *vt* to enter a place without warning, causing an interruption or intrusion ○ *She walked in on them in the middle of an argument.*

walk off v **1** *vi* to leave a place abruptly ○ *She walked off without a word.* **2** *vt* to get rid of something such as an injury or feeling of sickness by walking

walk off with *vt* **1** to steal something ○ *walked off with all the jewels* **2** to win something effortlessly

walk out *vi* **1 LEAVE WITHOUT EXPLANATION** to leave, especially in anger or protest, without explanation **2 GO ON STRIKE** to go on strike **3 LEAVE SOMEBODY PERMANENTLY** to leave a spouse, partner, or family permanently ○ *My wife walked out on me last summer.*

walk out on *vt* to leave or abandon somebody (*informal*)

walk over *vt* to win or defeat an opponent easily (*informal*) ○ *That horse will walk over the rest.*

walk through *vt* **1 REHEARSE OR PERFORM A PLAY SKETCHILY** to rehearse something in a simple, unelaborate way, mainly practising basic moves and positions, or perform something in a perfunctory, uncommitted way, as if still in rehearsal **2 REHEARSE WITHOUT CAMERAS** to rehearse a television programme without cameras **3 GIVE SOMEBODY STEP-BY-STEP EXPLANATION** to go through the various stages of something with somebody in advance in order to make it familiar and understandable ○ *They walked their client through the whole cross-examination procedure.*

walkabout /wáwkə bowt/ *n* **1** *Aus* **JOURNEY THROUGH BUSH** an extended journey through a remote area made by an Australian Aborigine wishing to experience or return to a traditional way of life and to traditional beliefs **2 PUBLIC WALK** an informal walk among the people by royalty or a celebrity **3 WALK** a walking trip (*informal*) ◇ **go walkabout 1** *Aus* to go for an extended journey on foot in remote country, traditionally alone and living off the land (*informal*) **2** *Aus* to leave your normal surroundings ○ *to be stolen* (*informal*)

walker /wáwkər/ *n* **1** a person who walks, especially for exercise or in competition **2** = **baby walker 3** a lightweight waist-high framework, usually with four legs and rubber feet, used to help somebody who cannot walk without support

Walker /wáwkər/, **Alice** (*b.* 1944) US writer

Walker, John George (*b.* 1952) New Zealand athlete

walkie-talkie /wáwki táwki/, **walky-talky** (*plural* **walky-talkies**) *n* a hand-held, battery-operated radio transmitter and receiver often used by emergency personnel to communicate with one another [Mid-20C. Playful variant of WALK + TALK.]

walk-in *adj* large and spacious enough to enter ○ *a walk-in cupboard*

walking /wáwking/ *adj* **1 ABLE TO WALK** capable of walking **2 FOR WALKING** used or designed for the purpose of walking ○ *walking shoes* **3 OF WALKING** that involves travelling on foot ○ *a walking tour* ◇ **a walking dictionary** *or* **encyclopaedia** somebody who is very knowledgeable

walking bass *n* a bass accompaniment, usually consisting of small steps or intervals up and down the scale in 4/4 time

walking boot *n* **1** a heavy stout boot worn to support the ankle when hiking or trekking over rough terrain **2** a lightweight rigid knee-length boot with a reinforced sole and straps that fasten around the leg. Use: support after a sprain or fracture.

walking catfish *n* a freshwater catfish with special organs that enable it to breathe on land for short periods while it moves to another body of water. Native to: tropical Asia. *Clarius batrachus.*

walking delegate *n* **1** *US* a labour union representative appointed to visit local unions and their employers to ensure compliance with contracts and sometimes to represent the local union in negotiations **2** *NZ* a trade union official in a dock area

walking fern, **walking leaf** *n* a fern whose long arching fronds take root at the tip, sprouting new plants. Native to: E North America. *Camptosorus rhizophyllus.*

walking papers *npl US* official notification that somebody has been fired from a job or dismissed from military service (*informal*)

walking stick *n* **1** a cane or stick used to assist in walking **2** *US* a long brown or green insect that resembles a twig, especially a North American species that feeds on leaves, *Diapheromera femorata.*

walking wounded *npl* **1** casualties of war, terrorism, or disaster who are able to walk despite their injuries **2** people who continue to be affected by great emotional pain experienced during their lives

Walkman /wáwkmən/ *tdmk* a trademark for a small portable cassette player with earphones

walk of life *n* somebody's occupation or social or economic class ○ *people from all walks of life*

walk-on *n* **1** a small part, usually a nonspeaking one, in a stage or film production **2** an actor who has a small part, usually a nonspeaking one, in a stage or film production

walkout /wáwk owt/ *n* **1** an organized strike by employees in which workers walk out of the building or off the premises **2** a departure in protest or anger about something

walkover /wáwkōvər/ *n* **1** an easy victory or one that is obtained without a contest, e.g. because the opposing side did not turn up (*informal*) **2** a horserace in which only one horse is entered

walk-through *n* an early play rehearsal without props or costumes, or a television rehearsal without cameras, usually to practise basic moves and positions

walk-up *n US* **1** a building of several stories without a lift (*informal*) **2** a flat in a building without a lift

walkway /wáwk way/ *n* **1** a specially constructed path for pedestrians **2** a passage above ground level designed for pedestrian use, e.g. one connecting buildings or passing over a roadway

Walkyrie *n* MYTHOL = **Valkyrie**

walky-talky *n* COMMUNICATION = **walkie-talkie**

wall /wawl/ *n* **1 FLAT SIDE OF BUILDING OR ROOM** a vertical structure forming an inside partition or an outside surface of a building **2 STANDING STRUCTURE THAT SURROUNDS OR BLOCKS** a narrow upright structure, usually built of stone, wood, plaster, or brick, that acts as a boundary or keeps something in or out ○ *a garden wall* **3 SOMETHING IMPENETRABLE** something similar to a wall in appearance or impenetrability ○ *met with a wall of reporters* **4 SOMETHING THAT PREVENTS COMMUNICATION** an obstacle to understanding or communication between people **5 LINE OF DEFENSIVE PLAYERS** in soccer, a line of defensive players who must stand at least ten yards from a free kick and who try to block a shot on goal **6 BODY MEMBRANE OR LINING** a membrane or lining enclosing or bounding an organ, blood vessel, or cavity of the body ○ *the uterine wall* **7 RIGID COVERING FOR CELLS** a rigid covering over the outer membranes of plant cells and of some prokaryotic animal cells **8 ROCK FACE** a vertical or nearly vertical rock face ○ *a sheer wall of granite* **9 DEFENSIVE STRUCTURE** a structure of earth or stone built for defensive purposes **10 BARRIER TO FLOODING** a structure built as a barrier to flooding ■ *vt* **1 SURROUND SOMETHING WITH WALLS** to fortify or surround something or somebody with a wall ○ *They walled in the back garden.* **2 SEPARATE SOMETHING WITH WALLS** to put up a wall to separate one area from another **3 CLOSE SOMETHING WITH WALL** to close an opening with a wall ○ *wall up the passage* **4 TRAP OR BURY BEHIND WALLS** to seal something or something in a space with a wall [Pre-12C. < Latin *vallum* 'rampart' < *vallus* 'stake'.] —**walled** *adj* ◇ **be climbing the wall** *or* **walls** to be extremely bored or frustrated (*informal*) ◇ **drive somebody up the wall** to annoy or irritate somebody to an extreme degree (*informal*) ◇ **go to the wall** to be destroyed or ruined, especially financially ◇ **hit a brick wall** to encounter an insurmountable difficulty

walla *n* = **wallah**

wallaby /wólləbi/ (*plural* **-bies**) *n* a marsupial that resembles a small kangaroo. Native to: Australia and New Guinea. Family: Macropodidae. ■ **Wallabies** *npl* the Australian Rugby Union team (*informal*) [Early 19C. < Dharuk *walabi* and *waliba*.]

Wallaby

Wallace /wólliss/, **Alfred Russel** (1823–1913) British naturalist

Wallace, Edgar (1875–1932) British writer

Sir William Wallace:
Commemorative statue near
Melrose, Scotland

Wallace, Sir William (1272?–1305) Scottish patriot

Wallace's line /wóllissiz-/ *n* a hypothetical boundary separating the SW Pacific into two biogeographical regions with distinctly different types of wildlife [Mid-19C. After Alfred Russel WALLACE.]

wallah /wóllə/, **walla** *n* somebody in charge of a particular thing or associated with a particular service or occupation (*dated informal*) ○ *a legal wallah* [Late 18C. Via Hindi *-vālā* '(somebody) responsible for something or some duty' < Sanskrit *pālaka* 'keeper'.]

wallaroo /wóllə roō/ (*plural* **-roos** *or* **-roo**) *n* a large and sturdy kangaroo. Native to: rocky upland areas of Australia. *Macropus robustus* and *Macropus bernardus.* [Early 19C. < Dharuk *walāru*.]

Wallasey /wóllassi/ town in NW England. Population: 60,895 (1991).

wall bars *npl* a series of horizontal bars attached to a wall and used for exercises

wallboard /wáwl bawrd/ *n* BUILDING = **plasterboard**

wallchart /wáwl chaart/ *n* a chart designed to be displayed on a wall to provide information or aid in instruction

wall creeper *n* a songbird with a long slender beak and black wings with scarlet markings. Native to: mountains of Europe and Asia. *Tichodroma muraria.*

Wallenberg /vaálən berg, waálən búrg/, **Raoul** (1912–47?) Swedish diplomat

Waller /wóllər/, **Fats** (1904–43) US singer, pianist, and composer. Born **Thomas Wright Waller**

⚡**wallet** /wóllit/ *n* **1 POCKET-SIZED FOLDED CASE FOR MONEY** a small flat folding case usually made of leather or plastic that holds paper money and credit cards and is usually carried in a pocket or handbag **2 SOFTWARE FOR ONLINE PURCHASES** a software program to carry out transactions for online purchases made on the Internet (*in e-commerce*) **3 FOLDER** a folder for holding items such as papers, photographs, or maps **4 KNAPSACK** a bag or knapsack for carrying articles on a trip (*archaic*) [14C. Probably via Anglo-Norman, 'travelling pack' < Germanic, 'roll'.]

walleye /wáwl ī/ (*plural* **walleye** *or* **walleyes**) *n* **1 EYE THAT APPEARS WHITE** an eye with a white or streaked iris, giving the appearance of a pale ring round the pupil **2 WHITE IN CORNEA** an eye with an opaque white cornea, or the condition that causes this opacity **3 OUTWARDS TURNING EYES** a form of squint (**strabismus**) in which one or both eyes turn outwards **4 FRESHWATER FISH** a large predatory freshwater fish with large eyes that is related to the perch. Native to: NE North America. *Stizostedion vitreum*. [Early 16C. Back-formation < WALLEYED.]

walleyed /wáwl īd/ *adj* **1** having any of the medical conditions known as walleye **2** having bulging or staring eyes [14C. < N Germanic , 'speckle-eyed'.]

walleyed pike *n* ZOOL = **walleye** *n*. 4

walleyed pollack *n* a fish of the cod family resembling a pollack. Native to: N Pacific. *Theragra chalcogramma*.

wallflower /wáwl flow ər/ *n* **1 SPRING-FLOWERING GARDEN PLANT** a common spring-blooming garden plant with rather woody erect stems. Flowers: fragrant, yellow, orange, or brownish, clustered at top of stem. Genera: *Cheiranthus* and *Erysimum*. **2 PLANT WITH FRAGRANT COLOURFUL FLOWERS** a wild plant often found growing on walls, rocks, and cliffs. Flowers: fragrant, colourful. Native to: S Europe. *Cheiranthus cheiri*. **3 SOMEBODY UNNOTICED AT SOCIAL EVENT** a shy or retiring person who remains unnoticed at social events, especially a woman without a dance partner (*informal*)

wall fruit *n* **1** a fruit of a tree or bush that has been trained to grow against a wall **2** a fruit-bearing tree or bush that has been trained to grow against a wall

wall game *n* a variant on association football unique to Eton College in which a ball is moved along a wall in a field by two teams using hands and feet

wall hanging *n* a tapestry or other large flat object hung on a wall as a decoration

wallies /wálliz/ *npl Scotland* a set of false teeth (*informal humorous*) [Plural of WALLY², 'made of china']

Wallis /wólliss/, **Sir Barnes Neville** (1887–1979) British aeronautical engineer

Wallis and Futuna Islands /wólliss ənd fə tyōōnə-/ island group in the SW Pacific Ocean. It is an overseas territory of France. Capital: Mata Utu. Population: 13,705 (1988). Area: 200 sq. km/77 sq. mi.

wall knot *n* a bulky knot made at the end of a rope by unwinding the strands and tying them together

wall lizard *n* a lizard that can be found on walls and rocks. Family: Lacertidae.

wall mustard *n* PLANTS = **wall rocket**

wall of death *n* an attraction at a fairground in which a motorcyclist rides round the inside wall of a large cylinder

wall of sound *n* recorded sound on pop records achieved by overdubbing or layering many different instruments around a pop tune

Walloon /wo lōōn/ *n* **1** a member of a French-speaking people living in S Belgium, mainly in the autonomous region of Wallonia, and in neighbouring parts of France. ◊ **Fleming** *n*. 2 **2** a dialect of French spoken in S Belgium and nearby areas of France [Mid-16C. Via French *Wallon* < medieval Latin *wallo(n)*- 'foreigner' < Germanic.] — **Walloon** *adj*

wallop /wólləp/ *vt* (*informal*) **1 BEAT** to give somebody a sound physical beating **2 HIT SOMEBODY VERY HARD** to strike something or somebody with great force ○ *She can really wallop the ball.* **3 DEFEAT SOMEBODY DECISIVELY** to defeat a person or team decisively ■ *n* **1 HARD HIT** a powerful blow (*informal*) **2 ABILITY TO HIT HARD** the ability to strike a powerful blow (*informal*) ○ *He's got a wallop that could make him heavyweight champion.* **3 ABILITY TO IMPRESS** the ability to create a powerful impression on others (*informal*) **4 BEER** beer (*dated slang*) [14C. < Old French *waloper*, variant of *galoper* 'gallop, run well' < Germanic.]

walloping /wólləping/ *n* (*informal*) **1 BEATING** a sound physical beating **2 DECISIVE DEFEAT** a decisive defeat or victory ■ *adj* **BIG** very large or impressive (*informal*) ○ *The angler came back with a walloping catch.* ■ *adv* **VERY** to an extreme degree (*informal*) ○ *a walloping big lie*

wallow /wóllō/ *vi* **1 ROLL** to lie down and roll around in something ○ *pigs wallowing in mud* **2 INDULGE HEAVILY** to immerse yourself in something, e.g. an emotion or material wealth, in a self-indulgent way ○ *wallowing in self-pity* **3 HAVE HUGE AMOUNT** to be amply or overly supplied with something ○ *We suddenly found ourselves wallowing in kittens.* **4 WALK WITH DIFFICULTY** to move clumsily, as if in mud ■ *n* **1 ACT OF WALLOWING** an instance of wallowing in something such as mud, emotion, or material luxury **2 PLACE WHERE ANIMALS ROLL** a muddy, wet, or dusty place which animals use to roll around in **3 DEPRESSION FORMED BY ANIMAL** a sunken area in the ground made by a rolling animal [Old English *wealwian* 'to roll' < Indo-European] —**wallower** *n*

⚡**wallpaper** /wáwl paypər/ *n* **1 PAPER TO DECORATE WALLS** paper, usually printed with a pattern, that is pasted on walls and sometimes ceilings **2 BACKGROUND PATTERN FOR SCREEN** the background pattern for a computer screen, composed of graphics **3 SOMETHING BLAND AND DULL** something that is so bland and unexciting that it serves as a hardly noticed background (*informal*) ■ *vti* **PUT UP WALLPAPER** to cover a surface with wallpaper

wall pass *n* a movement in football in which one player passes the ball to another and runs forward to receive the return

wall pepper *n* a stonecrop with creeping stems and leaves with a peppery taste. Flowers: yellow. Native to: Europe, Asia. *Sedum acre*.

wall plate *n* a horizontal structural member placed along the top of a wall to support the ends of beams, joists, or trusses

wall plug *n* a receptacle in the wall connected to an electric circuit, into which appliances can be plugged

wall rock *n* the rock that surrounds a vein, mineral deposit, or fault

wall rocket *n* a cruciferous plant that grows on walls and waste ground. Flowers: yellow. Native to: Europe. *Diplotaxis muralis* and *Diplotaxis tenuifolia*.

wall rue *n* a small delicate fern that grows in fan-shaped clusters on walls or in rocky crevices. *Asplenium ruta-muraria*.

Wallsend /wáwlz end/ town in NE England. Population: 45,280 (1991).

Wall Street /wáwl-/ *n* **1** the street in Manhattan, New York City, where the New York Stock Exchange and many major financial institutions of the United States are located **2** the US financial market, especially as represented by the publicly owned companies comprising the stock markets

wall-to-wall *adj* **1** completely covering a floor or floors ○ *wall-to-wall carpeting* **2** completely filling, covering, or pervading something, or occurring nonstop (*informal*) ○ *fed up with wall-to-wall pop music*

wally¹ /wólli/ (*plural* **-lies**) *n* an offensive term that deliberately insults somebody's intelligence or common sense (*slang*) [Mid-20C. < ?]

wally² /wálli/ *adj Scotland* **1 SPLENDID** splendid **2 CHINA** made of china **3 TILED** lined with ceramic tiles [15C. < ?]

walnut /wáwl nut/ *n* **1 EDIBLE NUT** a deeply wrinkled nut that is enclosed in a hard shell and a thick leathery husk **2 VALUABLE WOOD** a light ornamental wood. Use: cabinetwork, panelling, veneers. (*often before nouns*) **3 LIGHT-BROWN COLOUR** a light yellowish-brown colour like that of walnut wood **4 TREE VALUED FOR NUTS AND WOOD** a deciduous tree with fragrant compound leaves and drooping catkins, grown worldwide for its shade, wood, and walnuts. Genus: *Juglans*. [14C. < Old English *wealhnutu* 'foreign nut', < *wealh* 'foreign, Welsh, Celtic'.] —**walnut** *adj*

Walpole /wáwlpōl/, **Horace** (1717–97) British writer

Walpole, Sir Robert, 1st Earl of Orford (1676–1745) English statesman

Walpurgis Night /val pŏŏrgiss-/ *n* **1** in German folklore, the witches' feast night on the Brocken in the Harz mountains. Date: 30 April. **2** a wild celebration or a nightmarish situation [Early 19C. Translation of German *Walpurgisnacht*, after *Walpurga*, 8C Anglo-Saxon saint.]

walrus /wáwlrəss, wóll-/ (*plural* **-ruses** *or* **-rus**) *n* a large sea mammal related to seals and sea lions, with tough wrinkled skin, large tusks, and bristly whiskers. Native to: Arctic. *Odobenus rosmarus*. [Early 18C. < Dutch *walrus*, *walros* 'whale-horse' < *walvis(ch)* 'whale'.]

walrus moustache *n* a thick drooping moustache resembling a walrus's whiskers

Wałęsa /və wénssə/, **Lech** (*b*. 1943) Polish trade unionist and statesman

Walsall /wáwl sawl, wól-/ industrial town in central England, near Birmingham. Population: 174,739 (1991).

Walsingham /wáwlsingəm, wóls-/ village in Norfolk, hundreds of years a Christian pilgrimage centre

Walter /váltər/, **Bruno** (1876–1972) German-born US co[nductor]. Born **Bruno Walter Schlesinger**

Walter /wáwltər/, **John** (1739–1812) British newspap[er] publisher

Walter Mitty /wáwltər mítti, wóltər-/ (*plural* **Wal[ter] Mitties**) *n* an unremarkable person who daydrea[ms] about great personal adventure and success [Mid-20[C.] After the hero of 'The Secret Life of Walter Mitty', a 19[39] short story by James Thurber, about such a daydreamer.] **Walter Mittyish** *adj*

Walters /wáwltərz/, **Barbara** (*b*. 1931) US television jo[ur]nalist and presenter

Waltham Forest /wáwlthəm-, wólt-/ residential borou[gh] in NE London. Population: 221,100 (1995).

Walton /wáwlt'n/, **Ernest T. S.** (1903–95) Irish physicis[t]

Walton, Izaak (1593–1683) English writer

Walton, Sir William (1902–83) British composer

waltz /wawlss, wolss, wawlts/ *n* (*plural* **waltzes**) **1 DANCE** [FOR] **COUPLES IN TRIPLE TIME** a ballroom dance in triple time which a couple turn continuously while moving rou[nd] **2 MUSIC FOR WALTZ** the music for a waltz **3 SOMETH[ING] EASY** something that can be accomplished effortles[sly] (*informal*) ■ *v* (**waltzes, waltzing, waltzed**) **1** *vti* **DA[NCE] WALTZ** to dance or lead somebody in a waltz ○ *walt[zed] him round the room* **2** *vi* **MOVE IN RELAXED MANNER** to mo[ve] in a relaxed and confident manner (*informal*) ○ *She j[ust] waltzed right in and demanded more money.* **3** *vi* **GO THROU[GH] SOMETHING EASILY** to accomplish something [ef]fortlessly [Late 18C. < German *Walzer* < *walzen* 'waltz, r[oll,] revolve'.] ◇ **waltz Matilda** *vt Aus* to wander arou[nd] looking for work carrying your belongings in a pa[ck] (*dated slang*)

Waltzing Matilda /wáwlssing-/ *n* a traditional A[us]tralian song that tells the story of a vagrant work[er] (**swagman**) who commits suicide at a water hole [to] avoid being arrested for sheep-steali[ng] (*informal*) [Because of the dancing motion of a pack carr[ied] on somebody's shoulder; *Matilda* 'personal pack, bundle' the name]

Walvis Bay /wáwlviss-/ port in W Namibia, on the A[t]lantic coast. Population: 16,652 (1985).

wame /waym/ *n Scotland* the belly, abdomen, womb [15C. Variant of WOMB.]

Wampanoag /wómpə nō ag/ (*plural* **-ag** *or* **-ags**) *n* member of an Algonquian people who lived in Rho[de] Island and Massachusetts [Late 17C. < Narraganset, 'ea[st]erners'.] —**Wampanoag** *adj*

wampum /wómpəm/ *n* small polished beads made fr[om] shells, threaded on string, and used by some Nati[ve] North Americans as decoration, for ceremonial pu[r]poses, or formerly for money [Mid-17C. Shortening [of] *wampumpeag* < Algonquian, 'white strings' < *wap* 'white' *umpe* 'string'.]

wan /won/ *adj* (**wanner, wannest**) **1 PALE** unhealthily pa[le,] especially from illness or grief **2 INDICATIVE OF LOW SPIR[ITS]** suggesting ill health or unhappiness ○ *He gave me a w[an] look.* **3 FAINT** lacking brightness ○ *a wan star* ■ *vti* (**wa[ns,] wanning, wanned**) **MAKE OR BECOME PALE OR ILL** to ma[ke] something pale, or become pale or unhealt[hy] (*literary*) [Old English *wann* 'dark, dusky, grey' < ?] —**wa[nly]** *adv* —**wanness** *n*

⚡**WAN** /wan/ *abbr* wide area network

Wanaka /wə náakə/ town in the southern part of Sou[th] Island, New Zealand, on Lake Wanaka. Populati[on:] 1,335 (1991).

Wanaka, Lake lake in the southern part of Sou[th] Island, New Zealand. Area: 194 sq. km/75 sq. mi.

⚡**wand** /wond/ *n* **1 ROD WITH MAGICAL POWERS** a thin rod [be]lieved to possess magical powers, used by suppos[ed] magicians, wizards, and supernatural beings **2 ST[AFF] SHOWING AUTHORITY** a thin staff carried as a symbol [of] office **3 VACUUM CLEANER PART** an attachment betwe[en] the hose and cleaning tool of a vacuum cleaner t[hat] resembles a pipe **4 BAR-CODE SCANNER** a hand-held opti[cal] scanning device used to read and enter bar-code [in]formation into a computer **5 BATON** a conductor's ba[ton] **6 SLENDER PLANT SHOOT** a slender bendable shoot of a shr[ub] or tree (*archaic*) [12C. Via Old Norse *vondr* 'straight flexi[ble] stick' < Germanic, 'turn'.]

wander /wóndər/ *v* **1** *vti* **TRAVEL WITHOUT A DESTINATION** [to] move from place to place, either without a purpose [or] without a known destination ○ *They wander the co[...]*

tryside looking for work. **2** *vi* **TAKE A BENDY PATH** to follow a winding course ○ *The river wandered through the meadows.* **3** *vi* **STROLL SOMEWHERE** to go somewhere at a leisurely pace **4** *vi* **LEAVE A FIXED PATH** to stray from a particular course ○ *Don't wander far from the path.* **5** *vi* **DAYDREAM** to lose the ability to concentrate on or listen to a particular thing ○ *My mind was wandering.* **6** *vi* **FAIL TO THINK OR SPEAK CLEARLY** to lose the ability to think, speak, or write in an organized and coherent way ■ *n* **AIMLESS STROLL** an aimless or leisurely moving from place to place [Old English *wandrian* < Germanic, 'turn'] —**wanderer** *n* —**wandering** *adj* —**wanderingly** *adv*

wandering albatross *n* a large albatross that has a white body and black wings and tail and spends most of its life in flight at sea. Native to: southern seas. *Diomedea exulans.*

wandering Jew *n* any of three trailing plants widely grown as houseplants for their variegated foliage. Flowers: white, rose-red. Native to: tropical America. *Tradescantia fluminensis, Tradescantia albiflora,* and *Zebrina pendula.*

Wandering Jew *n* in medieval legend, a Jewish man, sometimes named as Ahasuerus, condemned to remain alive wandering the earth until Judgment Day for having mocked Jesus Christ on the day of the Crucifixion

wanderlust /wóndər lust/ *n* a strong desire to travel [Early 20C. < German, 'desire to travel'.]

wane /wayn/ *vi* (**wanes, waning, waned**) **1 SHOW LESS LIGHTED AREA** to show a decreasing illuminated surface between a full Moon and new Moon (*refers to the Moon or a planet*) **2 GET SMALLER OR LESS** to decrease gradually in intensity or power ○ *His interest was waning.* **3 FINISH** to draw to a close ○ *Winter is waning at last.* ■ *n* **1 DECREASE IN INTENSITY** a gradual lessening of power or intensity **2 TIME DURING MOON'S WANE** the period during which the Moon's visible illuminated surface is decreasing in size **3 PERIOD OF LESSENING** a period of gradual decrease **4 END OF PERIOD** the conclusion of a time or season ○ *the wane of summer* **5 IRREGULARITY ON PLANK'S EDGE** a defective edge left on a rough-sawn plank [Old English *wanian* 'lessen' < Germanic, 'lacking'] ◇ **be on the wane** to decrease or pass out of fashion

Wanganui /wóngə noō i/ **1** river in the southwest of the North Island, New Zealand. Length: 290 km/180 mi. **2** city in the southwestern part of the North Island, New Zealand, on the Wanganui River. Population: 41,097 (1996).

Wangaratta /wáng gə rátta/ city in N Victoria, Australia. Population: 15,984 (1991).

wangle /wáng g'l/ *vt* (**-gles, -gling, -gled**) **1 GET SOMETHING DEVIOUSLY** to get something using indirect and sometimes deceitful methods (*informal*) ○ *I'm trying to wangle some time off work.* **2 FALSIFY ACCOUNTS** to manipulate accounts or records, usually deceitfully ■ *n* **DISHONEST METHOD** a devious means of accomplishing something [Late 19C. < ?] —**wangler** *n*

wank /wangk/ *vi* a highly offensive term meaning to masturbate (*taboo*) ■ *n* (*taboo*) **1** a highly offensive term for an act of masturbation **2** a highly offensive term for self-indulgent, pretentious, or arrogant behaviour [Mid-20C. < ?]

Wankel engine /wángk'l-, váng-/ *n* an internal-combustion engine in which an approximately triangular rotor inside an elliptical combustion chamber replaces the pistons of a conventional engine, thus reducing the number of moving parts [Mid-20C. After Felix *Wankel* (1902–88), German engineer.]

wanker /wángkər/ *n* **1** a highly offensive term for somebody who masturbates (*taboo*) **2** a highly offensive term for an unpleasant, self-indulgent, pretentious, or arrogant person (*insult*)

wanna /wónnə/ *vt* want to (*nonstandard*) ○ *I wanna go!* [Late 19C. Alteration of *want to.*]

wannabe /wónnə bee/ *n* a person who tries to be like another person or to belong to a specific group (*informal disapproving*) [Late 20C. Alteration of *want to be.*]

want /wont/ *vt* **1 DESIRE** to feel a need or desire for something ○ *We want a new car.* **2 WISH SOMETHING DONE** to desire to do something or that something be done ○ *I don't want you being late.* ○ *He wants his steak well done.* **3 MISS** to feel the lack of something ○ *After a week on the road, I want my own bed.* **4 WISH SOMEBODY'S PRESENCE** to wish to see or speak to somebody ○ *He's wanted on the phone.* ○ *Someone wants you at the door.* **5 SEEK SOMEBODY AS CRIME SUSPECT** to seek somebody in connection with a crime (*usually passive*) ○ *wanted for two felonies* **6 SHOULD** used to indicate that something is desirable or advisable (*informal*) ○ *You want to see a doctor about that.* **7 NEED** to have a need for something (*informal*) ○ *What that kid wants is some discipline!* ○ *The cupboards want cleaning.* **8 DESIRE SOMEBODY SEXUALLY** to feel sexual desire for somebody (*informal*) ■ *n* **1 NEEDED THING** something that somebody desires or needs (*usually plural*) ○ *All your wants can be easily supplied.* **2 LACK** an absence or shortage of something ○ *no want of snow for the skiers this winter* **3 POVERTY** the state of being poor ○ *Freedom from want is a fundamental human right.* [12C. Via Old Norse *vanta* 'be lacking' < Germanic, 'lacking'.] —**wanter** *n* ◇ **for want of** through the lack of something ○ *No one should be left behind for want of opportunity.*

SYNONYMS *want, desire, wish, long, yearn, covet, crave*

CORE MEANING: to seek to have, do, or achieve something

want to feel a need or desire for something; **desire** to want something very strongly; **wish** to have a strong, sometimes unrealistic, desire to have or to do something; **long** to have a strong desire for somebody or something, especially something difficult to achieve; **yearn** to want something very much, especially with a feeling of sadness when it seems unlikely that it can ever be obtained; **covet** to have a strong desire to possess something that belongs to somebody else, or (*formal*) to want something very much; **crave** to want something very much, especially when this desire is physical.

want for *vt* to experience the lack of something ○ *The family wants for nothing.*

want in *vi* to wish to be included in something, especially to want to invest in a business deal (*informal*) ○ *Do you want in?*

want out *vi* to wish to be excluded from or to leave something, especially a business deal (*informal*) ○ *We want out before we get into trouble.*

want ad *n US* a classified advertisement in a newspaper or magazine (*informal*)

wanting /wónting/ *adj* not meeting expectations or requirements ○ *found wanting in the area of security* ■ *prep* missing something necessary ○ *a chair wanting one leg*

wanton /wóntən/ *adj* **1 SEXUALLY INDISCRIMINATE** without restraint or inhibition, especially in sexual behaviour **2 RANDOM** without reason or provocation ○ *wanton violence and destruction* **3 DESIRING TO DO HARM** done out of a desire to cause harm **4 EXCESSIVE** unrestrained, heedless of reasonable limits, or characterized by greed and extravagance ○ *wanton indulgence* **5 UNRULY** lacking discipline **6 LUSH** growing luxuriantly (*archaic*) **7 PLAYFUL** engaged in play that is carefree (*archaic*) ■ *n* **1 SOMEBODY WITHOUT SEXUAL RESTRAINT** a lascivious or sexually uninhibited person **2 SOMEBODY PLAYFUL** a playful person (*archaic*) **3 SOMEBODY GROWING UNRULY** an undisciplined person (*archaic*) ■ *vi* **BE WANTON** to behave in a wanton manner (*archaic*) [14C. < Old English *wan-* 'un-' + *togen,* 'disciplined', < *tēon* 'train, discipline, pull'.] —**wantonly** *adv* —**wantonness** *n*

ϟ**WAP** /wap/, **Wap** *n* a standard protocol for the transmission of electronic data between hand-held narrowband devices, e.g. mobile phones and pagers and other sources of digital information such as the Internet ○ *WAP technology.* Full form **wireless application protocol**

wapentake /wóppən tayk/ *n* a historical subdivision of some counties in northern and midland England, equivalent to the hundred in other counties [Pre-12C. < Old Norse *vápnatak* 'weapon-taking'.]

wapiti /wóppiti/ (*plural* **-tis** *or* **-ti**) *n* a large deer that has tall branched antlers and lives in herds. Native to: mountainous W North America. *Cervus elaphus.* [Early 19C. < Shawnee *wapiti* 'white rump'.]

war /wawr/ *n* **1 ARMED FIGHTING BETWEEN GROUPS** an armed conflict between countries or groups that involves killing and destruction ○ *The two countries are at war.* **2 PERIOD DURING WAR** a period of armed conflict ○ *during the Vietnam War* **3 METHODS OF WARFARE** the techniques or the study of the techniques of armed conflict **4 CONFLICT** any serious struggle, argument, or conflict between people ○ *The candidates are at war.* **5 SERIOUS EFFORT TO END SOMETHING** an effort to eradicate something harmful ○ *a war against drugs* ■ *vi* (**wars, warring, warred**) **1 MAKE WAR** to engage in an armed conflict with somebody **2 BE IN A STRUGGLE** to be involved in a serious disagreement with somebody or a struggle to combat or eradicate something [12C. Via Old N French *werre,* Old French *guerre* < Germanic, 'strife, confusion'.]

LITERARY LINK ***War and Peace,*** a novel (1865–69) by Russian writer Leo Tolstoy. This monumental work is set in Russia during and after the Napoleonic Wars (1805–14). Though it focuses on five fictional families, the story incorporates historical accounts and philosophical essays to create an extraordinarily comprehensive portrait of Russian society that touches on almost every aspect of human experience, from love and happiness to grief and war.

SYNONYMS See ***fight.***

war. *abbr* warrant

War. *abbr* Warwickshire

waragi /waárəgi/ (*plural* **-gis** *or* **-gi**) *n* a Ugandan alcoholic drink made from bananas [Early 20C. < Kiswahili *wargi.*]

~~**waranty**~~ incorrect spelling of **warranty**

waratah /wórrə taá, -taa/ (*plural* **-tahs** *or* **-tah**) *n* an Australian shrub that is the emblem of New South Wales. Flowers: large dark red, globular. Native to: New South Wales. *Telopea speciosissima.* [Late 18C. < Dharuk *warrada.*]

war baby *n* a baby born or conceived during a war

Warbeck /wáwr bek/, **Perkin** (1474?–99) Flemish royal pretender to the English throne

War Between the States *n* HIST = **Civil War** *n.* 1

warble[1] /wáwrb'l/ *vti* (**-bles, -bling, -bled**) **1 SING NOTES WITH TRILLS** to sing a song or note with trills or other vocal modulations ○ *a songbird warbling outside my window* **2 SING** to sing, or express something in song ○ *warble a tune* ■ *n* **1 MODULATED SINGING** singing with trills or other vocal modulations **2 MODULATED SOUND** a sound with trills or quavers [14C. < Old N French *werbler* 'sing with trills' < Frankish, 'whirl, trill'.]

warble[2] /wáwrb'l/ *n* **1 SWELLING IN HORSES AND CATTLE** a swelling under the skin that forms usually on the back in horses and cattle, caused by the warble fly maggot **2 WARBLE FLY OR ITS LARVA** the warble fly, or the maggot of the warble fly **3 LUMP ON HORSE'S BACK FROM SADDLE** a hard tumorous lump of tissue on the back of a riding horse caused by the rubbing of the saddle [Late 16C. < ?]

warble fly *n* a large hairy fly, the larvae of which form painful swellings under the skin of cattle and horses. Family: Oestridae.

warbler /wáwrblər/ *n* **1 THRUSH RELATIVE** a songbird that is related to the thrush. Native to: Europe, Asia. Family: Sylviidae. **2 SMALL SINGING BIRD** a small songbird that eats insects and is often brightly coloured. Native to: North and South America. Family: Parulidae. **3 SOMEBODY WHO WARBLES** a person who warbles or sings

war bride *n* a woman who meets and marries a serviceman during wartime, especially one from another country

war chest *n US* funds collected to pay for a war or a campaign of any sort

war clouds *npl* signs of impending war

war correspondent *n* a journalist reporting from a war

war crime *n* a crime committed during wartime that is in violation of international agreements concerning the conventions of war, e.g. the mistreatment of prisoners or genocide (*often plural*) —**war criminal** *n*

war cry *n* = **battle cry** *n.* 1

ward /wawrd/ *n* **1 CITY DIVISION** an administrative or electoral division of an area such as a city, town, or county **2 ROOM IN HOSPITAL** a room in a hospital, especially one for several patients being given similar treatment **3 PRISON DIVISION** a division in a prison **4 SOMEBODY UNDER OFFICIAL CARE** somebody, especially a child or young person, who is under the care of a guardian or a court **5 AREA IN CASTLE** an open area within the walls of a castle **6 CUSTODY** a state of official custody or protection **7 DEFENCE MOVEMENT** a movement or stance used as a means of protection, e.g. in fencing **8 LOCK OR KEY FEATURE** a ridge or groove in a key or a lock that makes one fit the other ■ *vt* **PROTECT** to guard or protect somebody or something (*archaic*) [Old English *weard* < Germanic, 'be on guard']

ward off *vt* **1** to parry or repel a blow or attack **2** to keep away or avert something bad

Ward /wawrd/, **Frederick** (1835–70) Australian bushranger. Known as **Captain Thunderbolt**

Ward, Sir Joseph George (1856–1930) Australian-born New Zealand statesman

-ward, -wards *suffix* **1** in a particular direction, or towards a particular place ○ *earthward* **2** lying or occurring in a particular direction ○ *rightward* ○ *windward* [Old English *-weard* < Indo-European, 'to turn']

war dance *n* a dance performed as a ceremony before a battle or to celebrate victory, e.g. by Native North Americans

warded /wáwrdid/ *adj* describes locks or keys that have grooves or ridges

warden /wáwrd'n/ *n* **1 SOMEBODY IN CHARGE OF BUILDING** a person who is in charge of a building **2 SOMEBODY IN CHARGE OF INSTITUTION** a person who is in charge of an institution such as a college or school **3** *US* CRIME = **governor** *n.* 3 **4 OFFICIAL CONCERNED WITH REGULATIONS** an official, e.g. a traffic warden or air-raid warden, who makes sure that regulations are enforced **5** CHR = **churchwarden** *n.* 1 [12C. < Anglo-Norman *wardein* < Germanic, 'be on guard'.] —**wardenry** *n* —**wardenship** *n*

warder /wáwrdər/ *n* **1** a prison officer **2** a guard [14C. Via Anglo-Norman < Old N French *warder* 'to guard', variant of French *garder*.]

ward heeler *n* *US* a person who does minor tasks for a local or city politician (*informal*)

ward manager *n* a nurse in charge of a ward

ward of court *n* somebody, especially a minor, who is under the protection of a court or a court-appointed guardian

wardrobe /wáwrdrōb/ *n* **1 PLACE FOR CLOTHES** a large cupboard with a rail or shelves for clothes and shoes **2 CLOTHES COLLECTION** all the clothes that belong to a particular person **3 CLOTHES FOR A PURPOSE** a collection of clothes for a particular season or purpose **4 THEATRE COSTUMES** the costumes used by a theatrical company **5 PLACE FOR COSTUMES** a place in a theatre where costumes are kept **6 ROYAL DEPARTMENT** the department in a royal or noble household in charge of robes and jewels [14C. < Old N French *warderobe*, variant of French *garderobe* < French *garder* 'guard' + *robe* 'robe'.]

wardrobe mistress *n* a woman in charge of the costumes in a theatre or on a film set

wardrobe trunk *n* a large upright trunk with a rail on which clothes can be hung

wardroom /wáwrd room, -rŏŏm/ *n* **1** a room on a warship used by all the officers except the captain **2** the officers on a ship who can use the wardroom

-wards *suffix* = **-ward**

wardship /wáwrdship/ *n* the state of being in the care of a guardian appointed by parents or a court

ward sister *n* MED = **sister** *n.* 4

ware[1] /wair/ *n* **1 SIMILAR THINGS** similar things, or things that are made of the same material (*usually in combination*) **2 CERAMICS** ceramic articles of a particular kind or made by a particular manufacturer ○ *delftware* ■ **wares** *npl* **1 THINGS FOR SALE** articles offered for sale **2 MARKETABLE SKILLS** skills or talents offered as a service or a commodity [Old English *waru* probably < the same word as WARD, with the underlying idea 'something taken care of']

SPELLCHECK Do not confuse ***ware*** with ***wear*** or ***where***, which sound similar. Beware: your spellchecker will not catch this error.

ware[2] /wair/ *vti* (**wares, wared, waring**) to beware (*archaic*) ■ *adj* wary or prudent (*archaic*) [Old English *warian* < Germanic, 'be on guard']

warehouse /wáir howss/ *n* (*plural* **-houses** /-howziz/) **1 STORAGE BUILDING** a large building in which goods, raw materials, or commodities are stored **2 BIG SHOP** a large store or shop, especially one where goods are sold wholesale ■ *vt* (**-houses** /-howziz/, **-housing** /-howzing/, **-housed**) **STORE IN A WAREHOUSE** to store materials, goods, or commodities in a warehouse

warehouseman /wáir howssmən/ (*plural* **-men** /-mən/) *n* a worker in or owner of a warehouse

warehousing /wáir howzing/ *n* the accumulation of a particular security in the hope that demand will push the price up as the result of the reduced supply on the open market

~~**warf**~~ incorrect spelling of **wharf**

warfare /wáwr fair/ *n* **1** the act or fact of engaging in a war **2** conflict or struggle ○ *economic warfare*

warfarin /wáwrfərin/ *n* $C_{19}H_{16}O_4$ a colourless crystalline compound. Use: rodenticide, anticoagulant in medicine. [Mid-20C. < initial letters of *Wisconsin Alumni Research Foundation* + the ending of COUMARIN.]

war game *n* **1** a military exercise that simulates battle conditions **2** a game in which models of soldiers, battlefields, and equipment are used to refight historical battles —**war gaming** *n*

war-game (**war-games, war-gaming, war-gamed**) *v* **1** *vi* to take part in a war game **2** *vt* *US* to try out a military operation or strategy using simulation —**war-gamer** *n*

warhead /wáwr hed/ *n* the part of a bomb, ballistic or guided missile, rocket, or torpedo that contains the biological, chemical, explosive, incendiary, or nuclear material intended to damage the enemy

Warhol /wáwrhōl/, **Andy** (1928–87) US artist. Born **Andrew Wahola**

warhorse /wáwr hawrss/ *n* **1 HORSE IN BATTLE** a horse ridden in battle **2 SURVIVOR OF A CONFLICT** a participant in and survivor of many conflicts (*informal*) **3 STANDARD WORK** a play or a piece of music that is familiar and hackneyed because of too frequent performance (*informal*)

Waring /wáiring/, **Marilyn Joy** (*b.* 1952) New Zealand politician and writer

warison /wárriss'n/ *n* a note played on a bugle as a sign for soldiers to attack [13C. < Old French, variant of *garison* 'provision' (see GARRISON).]

Warks *abbr* Warwickshire

warlike /wáwr līk/ *adj* **1 HOSTILE** hostile and inclined to fight **2 RELATING TO WAR** relating to war or warfare **3 MARTIAL** martial or military

warlock /wáwr lok/ *n* a male sorcerer or wizard [Old English *wærloga* 'oath-breaker' < *wær* 'oath, pledge' + *-loga* 'liar' < Indo-European, 'true']

Warlock /wáwr lok/, **Peter** (1894–1930) British composer and musicologist. Pseudonym of **Philip Arnold Heseltine**

warlord /wáwr lawrd/ *n* a military leader, especially a powerful one, operating outside the control of government —**warlordism** *n*

warm /wawrm/ *adj* **1 QUITE HOT** moderately or comfortably hot **2 PROVIDING WARMTH** providing warmth or protection against cold **3 WITH TOO MUCH HEAT** having or feeling an undesirable amount of heat, from exertion or ambient temperature **4 FRIENDLY** showing or feeling kindness and friendliness ○ *a warm person* **5 PASSIONATE** showing passion or liveliness **6 ENTHUSIASTIC OR ARDENT** showing or feeling great enthusiasm **7 QUICK TO ANGER** excitable or easily angered **8 SUGGESTING WARMTH** with a colour suggesting warmth, especially yellow or red **9 HEATED BY METABOLISM** giving off the heat that arises normally in warm-blooded creatures **10 FRESH** describes a scent in hunting that is fresh and strong **11 CLOSE** close to the hidden object in a game or to guessing a secret (*informal*) ○ *You're getting warm.* **12 UNCOMFORTABLE** uncomfortable because of danger (*informal*) ■ *v* **1** *vti* **MAKE WARM** to increase the temperature of something to a desirable or comfortable level, or become warm **2** *vt* **MAKE SOMEBODY HAPPY** to make somebody or something cheerful or happy ○ *warmed by the presence of all their children* **3** *vi* **BECOME ENTHUSIASTIC** to become enthusiastic about something ○ *warmed to the idea of buying a new car* **4** *vi* **BECOME FRIENDLY** to become fond of somebody ○ *She warmed to him.* ■ *n* (*informal*) **1 WARM PLACE** a warm environment **2 GETTING WARM** an act of making something warm or becoming warm ○ *Have a warm by the fire.* [Old English *wearm* < Indo-European] —**warmer** *n* —**warmish** *adj* —**warmness** *n*

warm down *vi* to get back to a normal level of activity after strenuous physical exertion in a way that avoids cramp, usually by gentle exercising (*informal*)

warm over *vt* *US, Can* **1** to reheat food **2** to suggest something again, without having greatly altered it

warm up *v* **1** *vi* **PREPARE FOR EXERCISE** to prepare for physical exercise by stretching or practising **2** *vi* **PREPARE FOR** to prepare for something that is going to happen **3** *vti* **GET WARM** to become, or make something become, warm or warmer **4** *vti* **GET TO OPERATING TEMPERATURE** to run something such as an engine to bring it to a temperature at which it works efficiently, or to reach this condition **5** *vti* **GET ANIMATED** to become, or make somebody, enthusiastic, animated, or eager

war machine *n* the combined military resources with which a country can fight a war

warm-blooded *adj* **1** passionate, impetuous, and en[thusiastic] **2** maintaining a nearly constant body tem[perature], usually higher than, and independent of, th[e] environment —**warm-bloodedness** *n*

⚡**warmboot** /wáwrm boot/ *vt* to restart a computer witho[ut] switching it off, e.g. by pressing the control, Alt, an[d] delete keys together. ◊ **coldboot**

warm front *n* the gently sloping advancing edge of warm air mass that displaces colder air, bringing temperature increase and heavy rain where the fro[nt] makes contact with the ground

warm-hearted *adj* having or showing a kind and sym[pathetic] nature —**warm-heartedly** *adv* —**warm-hear[t]edness** *n*

warming pan *n* formerly, a long-handled metal pa[n] that was filled with hot coals and placed in a bed t[o] warm it

warmly /wáwrmli/ *adv* **1** with enthusiasm, fondness, [or] passion **2** in a way that will keep somebody war[m] ○ *dressed warmly*

warmonger /wáwr mung gər/ *n* a person who is eager f[or] war or tries to start a war —**warmongering** *n*

warm sector *n* a wedge of warm air within the low pressure region between the cold front and warm fro[nt] of a storm

warmth /wawrmth/ *n* **1 WARM STATE** the feeling, quality, o[r] state of being warm **2 AFFECTION** affection and kindne[ss] **3 AMOUNT OF HEAT** a moderate amount of heat prese[nt] in something **4 EXCITEMENT** strong emotion, especiall[y] anger or zeal **5 EFFECT OF COLOUR** the effect gained fro[m] using colours such as red and yellow

warm-up, warmup *n* an exercise, or period spent ex[ercising], before a contest or event

warn /wawrn/ *v* **1** *vti* **TELL OF RISK** to tell somebody abou[t] something that might cause injury or harm **2** *vt* **TE[LL] SOMEBODY IN ADVANCE** to tell somebody about somethin[g] in advance **3** *vt* **SCOLD** to admonish somebody **4** *vt* **KE[EP] SOMEBODY FROM DOING** to tell somebody to desist fro[m] doing something or going somewhere ○ *warned us o[f] driving over the pass in the storm* [Old English *war(e)nian* Germanic, 'be cautious'] —**warner** *n*

SPELLCHECK Do not confuse ***warn*** with ***worn***, which has similar sound. Beware: your spellchecker will not catch th[is] error.

warn off *vt* **1** to tell somebody to leave or keep awa[y] from a place, usually in an authoritative or forcef[ul] manner ○ *Sightseers were warned off by security guard[s]* **2** to advise somebody to avoid something, usually i[n] an authoritative manner ○ *warned customers off buyin[g] cheap imitations*

warning /wáwrning/ *n* **1 SIGN OF SOMETHING BAD COMING** threat or a sign that something bad is going to happe[n] **2 ADVICE TO BE CAREFUL** advice to be careful or to sto[p] doing something ○ *If you're late again, you'll get a writte[n] warning.* **3 NOTICE** a notice (*archaic*) ■ *adj* **MEANT TO WAR[N]** intended to warn somebody —**warningly** *adv*

warning coloration *n* markings on an animal warnin[g] predators that it is poisonous or dangerous. Man[y] insects and amphibians have warning coloration.

warning shot *n* a shot fired deliberately off target as warning to somebody to stop doing something

war of nerves *n* a conflict in which psychological tacti[cs] are used against an opponent

warp /wawrp/ *v* **1** *vti* **GET TWISTED** to become or make some[thing] twisted or out of shape **2** *vti* **CHANGE FOR WORSE** t[o] change something so that it no longer follows its usu[al] course, or become distorted or strange **3** *vti* **MOVE SHIP B[Y] PULLING ON ROPES** to move a ship by pulling on rop[es] fastened to a dock or fixed buoy, or to move in this wa[y] **4** *vt* **ARRANGE THREADS** to arrange threads to form the war[p] in a loom ■ *n* **1 DISTORTION** a twist or distortion i[n] something, e.g. in wood that curls when dried **2 PE[R]VERSION** a deviation or perversion of mind or characte[r] **3 THREADS RUNNING LENGTHWISE** the threads that run length[wise] on a loom or in a piece of fabric. ◊ **weft** *n.* 1 **4 RO[PE] FOR TOWING** a rope used to warp a vessel [Old Englis[h] *weorpan* < Germanic, 'throw'] —**warpage** *n* —**warper** *n*

war paint *n* **1** paint used to decorate the body before battle, e.g. that formerly used by some Native Nort[h] American peoples **2** face make-up (*informal*)

warpath /wáwr paath/ *n* formerly, a route taken by Nativ[e] North Americans on the way to war ◇ **on the warpat[h]** angry and in the mood for a confrontation (*informal*)

warplane /wáwr playn/ *n* an aircraft used in war

warrant /wórrənt/ *n* **1 AUTHORIZATION** something that authorizes somebody to do something **2 WRITTEN AUTHORIZATION** a written authorization or certifying document **3 DOCUMENT AUTHORIZING POLICE** a document that gives police particular rights or powers, e.g. the right to search or arrest somebody **4 OPTION TO BUY STOCK** a document authorizing a stockholder to buy shares from a company at a later date and at a given price **5 WARRANT OFFICER'S CERTIFICATE** a warrant officer's certificate of appointment ■ *vt* **1 SERVE AS A REASON** to serve as a justifiable reason to do, believe, or think something **2 GUARANTEE** to guarantee something such as the truth or dependability of something or somebody **3 AUTHORIZE** to give authority to somebody **4 GUARANTEE TITLE** to guarantee the title to property **5 STATE CONFIDENTLY** to state something with the confidence that it is true or will happen (*archaic*) [12C. < Old N French *warant*, variant of Old French *guarant* < Germanic, 'be on guard'.] —**warranter** *n*

warrantable /wórrəntəb'l/ *adj* able to be justified or permitted —**warrantability** /wórrəntə bíllәti/ *n*—**warrantably** *adv*

warrantee /wórrən tée/ *n* somebody to whom a warrant is given or a warranty is made

warrant officer *n* an officer in the armed services of a rank between a commissioned and a noncommissioned officer

warrantor /wórrən tawr/ *n* a person who gives a warranty to somebody

warrant sale *n Scotland* the enforced sale of a debtor's belongings in order to raise money to pay off the debts

warranty /wórrənti/ (*plural* **-ties**) *n* **1 GUARANTEE** a guarantee on purchased goods that they are of the quality represented and will be replaced or repaired if found defective **2 INSURED PERSON'S UNDERTAKING** a condition in an insurance contract in which the insured person guarantees that something is the case **3 GUARANTEE OF TITLE** a covenant guaranteeing the security of the title to property being sold **4 JUSTIFICATION** a justification or authorization for an action

warren /wórrən/ *n* **1 RABBIT HABITAT** a group of connected burrows where rabbits live and breed **2 RABBIT COLONY** a colony of rabbits **3 CROWDED BUILDING OR AREA** an area or building that is crowded or has a complicated layout **4 AREA FOR GAME ANIMALS** a piece of ground where game animals are kept and bred [14C. < Anglo-Norman *warenne* 'enclosed area for breeding game'.]

warrener /wórrənər/ *n* a gamekeeper or keeper of a rabbit warren

~~warrent~~ incorrect spelling of **warrant**

Warrington /wórringtən/ town in NW England. Population: 154,900 (1994).

warrior /wórri ər/ *n* a person who fights or is experienced in warfare [13C. < Old N French *werreior*, < *werre* 'war' (see WAR).]

Warrnambool /wáwrnəm bool/ city in SW Victoria, Australia. Population: 23,946 (1991).

Warrumbungle Range /wórrəm búng g'l-/ range of volcanic peaks in N New South Wales, Australia. Highest peak: Mount Exmouth 1,228 m./4,028 ft.

Warsaw /wáwr saw/ capital of Poland, in the centre of the country. Population: 1,632,500 (1997 estimate).

warship /wáwr ship/ *n* an armoured ship that is equipped with weapons and is used in war

wart /wawrt/ *n* **1** a small benign rough lump that grows usually on the hands, feet, or genitals, caused by a virus **2** any abnormal growth that looks like a wart and is found on a plant [Old English *wearte* < Indo-European, 'raised spot'] —**warted** *adj* —**warty** *adj* ◇ **warts and all** including any flaws, faults, or disadvantages (*hyphenated before nouns*)

wart hog *n* a wild pig with tusks, a coarse mane, and warty growths on its face. Native to: Africa, south of the Sahara. *Phacochoerus aethiopicus.*

wartime /wáwr tīm/ *n* a period during which a war is being fought

war-torn *adj* disrupted by war, especially war between different groups from one country

Warwick 1 town in central England. Population: 22,476 (1991). **2** town in SE Queensland, Australia. Population: 10,371 (1991).

Warwickshire /wórrikshər/ county in central England. Area: 1,981 sq. km/765 sq. mi.

wary /wáiri/ (**-ier, -iest**) *adj* **1** cautious and watchful ○ *wary of hidden rocks in the water* **2** showing caution or watchfulness ○ *a wary approach* [15C. < WARE².] —**warily** *adv* —**wariness** *n*

SYNONYMS See ***cautious.***

was (*stressed*) /woz/; (*unstressed*) /wəz/ past tense of **be** (*with I, he, she, it, and singular nouns*) [Old English *wæs*, form of *wesan* 'be' < Indo-European, 'stay, dwell']

wasabi /wə saábi/ *n* **1** a strong-tasting green powder or paste from a plant root. Use: condiment in Japanese cooking. **2** (*plural* **-bis** *or* **-bi**) a plant whose root is ground to make wasabi powder or paste. Native to: Asia. *Eutrema wasabi.* [Early 20C. < Japanese.]

wash /wosh/ *v* **1** *vt* **CLEAN** to clean something with water, usually with added soap or detergent **2** *vti* **REMOVE SOMETHING BY WASHING** to remove something with water and usually with soap, or be removed in this way ○ *couldn't get the stain to wash out* **3** *vr* **CLEAN YOURSELF** to clean yourself, especially your hands or face, with soap and water **4** *vi* **BE WASHABLE** to be capable of being washed without fading or being damaged (*refers to garments or fabrics*) ○ *curtains that wash well* **5** *vti* **LICK TO CLEAN** to clean something by licking ○ *The cat washed her kittens.* **6** *vi* **WASH CLOTHES** to clean clothes in soap and water or in a washing machine ○ *spent the morning washing* **7** *vt* **MOISTEN** to wet or moisten something (*literary*) ○ *lashes washed with tears* **8** *vt* **FLOW OVER** to flow over the surface of something ○ *washed by the tides* **9** *vt* **ERODE SOMETHING WITH WATER** to erode something by the action of water **10** *vt* **MOVE SOMETHING ON WATER** to carry something along or away on water, or as if on water **11** *vt* **PURIFY** to remove something corrupting ○ *the power to wash away sins* **12** *vt* **SEPARATE SOMETHING BY WASHING** to separate something such as precious stones or valuable minerals by sifting earth or gravel through water **13** *vt* **APPLY THIN COATING TO** to brush a thin coating or layer over something **14** *vi* **BE CONVINCING** to be convincing or believable (*informal*) ○ *That story won't wash with her.* **15** *vt* **PUT GAS THROUGH LIQUID** to pass a gas or vapour through a liquid to remove contaminants ■ *n* **1 ACT OF WASHING** the act or process of washing something or somebody **2 QUANTITY OF CLOTHES** a quantity of clothes that have been or are to be washed **3 THIN LIQUID COATING** a thin or weak liquid, especially one used to rinse or coat something **4 SKIN TREATMENT** a lotion, antiseptic, or cosmetic that is applied to the skin **5 FLOW OF WATER** the flow of water against a surface, or the sound made by this **6** *Southwest US* **DRY STREAM BED** the dry bed of a stream that flows only after heavy rains, often found at the bottom of a canyon **7 LAYER OF COLOUR** a thin layer of colour applied with a brush **8 PAINTING TECHNIQUE** the technique of using washes in painting **9** ART = **wash drawing 10 SURGE OF DISTURBED WATER OR AIR** the surge of disturbed water, air, or other fluid caused by something such as an oar, propeller, or jet engine moving through the fluid **11 REMOVAL OF SOIL** removal of soil by the action of flowing water **12 SEDIMENT** alluvial material carried and left by the movement of water **13 LAND PERIODICALLY COVERED BY WATER** land that is periodically covered by a sea or river, e.g. by a tide **14 ORE** material such as gravel from which precious stones and valuable minerals can be extracted by washing **15** AGRIC = **swill** *n.* 1 **16 FERMENTED MALT** the liquor from fermented malt before it is distilled [Old English *wæscan* < Germanic]

wash down *vt* **1** to wash something thoroughly and completely ○ *had to wash down the kitchen walls afterwards* **2** to follow something drunk or eaten with another drink ○ *washed down the cake with a glass of milk*

wash out *v* **1** *vt* **CLEAN INSIDE OF** to clean something by washing the inside of it **2** *vti* **REMOVE BY WASHING** to come out or get something out by washing **3** *vt* **CANCEL** to cancel something because of rain **4** *vti* **MOVE AWAY ON WATER** to carry away something, or be carried away, on water ○ *washed out to sea* **5** *vti* **WEAR AWAY** to wear something away, or be worn away, by water

wash over *vt* **1** to cover something in a flowing or overflowing manner, as a liquid does **2** to well up in somebody (*refers to feelings*) ○ *A wave of homesickness washed over him.*

wash up *v* **1** *vti* **WASH DISHES** to wash the dishes after a meal **2** *vi US* **WASH FACE AND HANDS** to wash your face and hands **3** *vti* **ARRIVE BY WATER** to deposit something on the shore, or land on the shore from tidal or wave action ○ *Look what the tide washed up!*

Wash /wósh/ shallow inlet of the North Sea, on the coast of E England. Area: 855 sq. km/330 sq. mi.

Wash. *abbr* Washington

washable /wóshəb'l/ *adj* capable of being washed without being damaged —**washability** /wóshə bíllәti/ *n*

wash-and-wear *adj* easily washed and dried and needing little or no ironing

washbasin /wósh bayss'n/ *n* a bowl or basin for washing the face and hands or small articles

washboard /wósh bawrd/ *n* **1 RIDGED BOARD** a board with a corrugated surface on which clothes that are being washed can be rubbed to help get them clean **2 MUSICAL INSTRUMENT** a board resembling a washboard, used as a musical instrument to produce a scratching sound **3 PROTECTIVE FEATURE ON A BOAT** a thin plank on the gunwale of a boat to stop water from splashing over the side ■ *adj* **MUSCULAR** describes a man's stomach that has well-defined muscles

washbowl /wósh bowl/ *n* HOUSEHOLD = **washbasin**

washcloth /wósh kloth/ *n US, Can* = **facecloth**

washday /wósh day/ *n* a day when clothes are washed, usually the same day each week

wash drawing *n* a drawing made in ink to which a wash of colour is applied, or a painting made using washes

washed-out, washed out *adj* **1** faded or without colour **2** exhausted or lacking vitality and strength

washed-up, washed up *adj* no longer likely to continue or succeed (*informal*)

washer /wóshər/ *n* **1 SMALL RING** a small disc or ring used to keep a screw or bolt secure or prevent leakage at a joint **2 WASHING APPLIANCE** an appliance used for washing, especially a washing machine **3 SOMEBODY WHO WASHES SOMETHING** a person who washes something **4** *Aus* **FACECLOTH** a facecloth (*informal*)

washer-dryer *n* a machine that both washes and dries clothes

washer-up (*plural* **washers-up**) *n* a hired washer of dishes (*informal*)

washerwoman /wóshər wŏŏmən/ (*plural* **-en** /-wimin/), **washwoman** /wósh wŏŏmən/ (*plural* **-en** /-wimin/) *n* a woman who is employed to wash clothes

wash house *n* a building where laundry or other washing is done

washing /wóshing/ *n* **1 CLOTHES FOR WASHING** clothes to be washed, being washed, or just washed **2 DOING LAUNDRY** the act or process of washing clothes **3 THIN COAT** a thin coat of something ○ *a washing of silver* **4 LIQUID USED FOR WASHING** the liquid that has been used to wash something (*often plural*)

washing machine *n* a machine for washing clothes, usually an electric one

washing powder *n* detergent in powder form, used for washing clothes. US term **laundry detergent**

washing soda *n* a crystalline form of sodium carbonate. Use: washing and cleaning.

Washington /wóshingtən/ **1** state of the NW United States, on the Pacific coast. Capital: Olympia. Population: 5,610,362 (1997). Area: 182,949 sq. km/70,637 sq. mi. **2** town in NE England. Population: 61,500 (1996). —**Washingtonian** /wóshing tṓni ən/ *n, adj*

Washington, D.C. /-dee sée/ capital of the United States, in the east-central part of the country. The city of Washington has the same boundaries as the District of Columbia, a federal territory. Population: 543,000 (1996).

Washington /wóshingtən/, **Booker T.** (1856–1915) US educator. Full name **Booker Taliaferro Washington**

Washington, George (1732–99) US general, statesman, and 1st president of the United States (1789–97)

washing-up *n* **1** the cleaning of dishes, cutlery, and other items used for cooking and eating **2** the items that need to be washed after a meal

washing-up liquid *n* detergent in liquid form, used for washing dishes. US term **dishwashing liquid**

wash-off *adj* removable by washing or by the use of water with soap or a detergent

washout /wósh owt/ *n* **1 FAILURE** a complete failure or fiasco (*informal*) **2 INEFFECTUAL PERSON** somebody regarded as lacking in competence or effectiveness (*insult*) **3 EROSION CAUSED BY RUNNING WATER** erosion caused by running

Library of Congress

George Washington

water, e.g. during a flash flood **4 CHANNEL WASHED OUT** a hole or channel made by floodwater

washroom /wósh room, -ro͝om/ *n* **1** a room, especially in a public place, with toilet and washing facilities **2** *US* a euphemism for a public toilet

wash sale *n US* **1** the illegal practice of buying and selling almost simultaneously a particular stock to give the impression that the stock is being actively traded **2** the repurchase of stock sold within 30 days of the time it was sold

washstand /wósh stand/ *n* a stand on which a basin and jug can be placed for washing the face and hands

washtub /wósh tub/ *n* a large container in which clothes can be washed

wash-up *n* **1** *Aus* **FINAL PHASE** the final phase or summing up of a process (*informal*) ○ *In the wash-up on TV after the election, the senator admitted that government policy was out of step with the public.* **2** *Aus* **OUTCOME** the outcome of a process or series of events **3** *Wales* **KITCHEN SINK** a kitchen sink (*informal*)

washwoman *n* OCCUPATIONS = **washerwoman**

washy /wóshi/ (**-ier, -iest**) *adj* **1 WEAK** watery or weak **2 PALE** faint or faded **3 NOT FORCEFUL** without intensity or vitality —**washily** *adv* —**washiness** *n*

wasn't /wózz'nt/ *contr* was not

wasp /wosp/ *n* a slender black-and-yellow striped social stinging insect that typically has well-developed wings, biting mouthparts, and a narrow stalk connecting the abdomen and thorax. Families: Vespidae and Sphecidae. [Old English *wæsp* < Indo-European, 'weave']

Wasp /wosp/, **WASP** *n US* an offensive term for a white person who has a Protestant Anglo-Saxon background and is viewed as belonging to the dominant and most powerful level of US society (*informal insult*) [Mid-20C. Acronym < *White Anglo-Saxon Protestant*.]

waspish /wóspish/, **waspy** /wóspi/ (**-ier, -iest**) *adj* **1 OF WASPS** like a wasp, or relating to wasps **2 EASILY IRRITATED** easily irritated or annoyed **3 SPITEFUL** showing spite —**waspishly** *adv* —**waspishness** *n*

wasp waist *n* a very slender waist, or one that is corseted to make it appear slender —**wasp-waisted** *adj*

waspy *adj* = **waspish**

wassail /wóssayl/ *n* (*archaic*) **1 FESTIVE SALUTATION** a salutation or drinking toast made during festivities **2 FESTIVE OCCASION** a festive occasion at which people drink a great deal **3 ALCOHOLIC DRINK** an alcoholic drink, usually mulled wine or ale, drunk on a festive occasion **4 DRINKING OR CHRISTMAS SONG** a drinking song or a song sung at Christmas ■ *v* **1** *vi* **DRINK IN CELEBRATION** to celebrate by drinking (*archaic*) **2** *vi* **SING CHRISTMAS SONGS** to go from house to house at Christmas, singing carols and greeting people (*archaic regional*) **3** *vt* **TOAST** to drink to somebody's health (*archaic*) [12C. < Old Norse *ves heill* 'be healthy', *heill* < Germanic.] —**wassailer** *n*

Wassermann test /wássərmən-, vássər-/, **Wassermann reaction** *n* a test for syphilis infection, based on determining the presence in a blood sample of antibodies to the syphilis bacterium [After August Paul *Wassermann* (1866–1925), German bacteriologist]

wast /wost, wəst/ 2nd person past singular of **be** (*archaic*)

wastage /wáystij/ *n* **1 AMOUNT WASTED** an amount that is lost or wasted **2 LOSS** loss caused when something is used, is worn, decays, or leaks **3 REDUCTION IN NUMBERS** the reduction in numbers of people working in a place because of deaths and resignations, rather than from redundancies

waste /wayst/ *v* (**wastes, wasting, wasted**) **1** *vt* **USE SOMETHING CARELESSLY** to use something or use something up carelessly, extravagantly, or without effect **2** *vt* **FAIL TO USE** to fail to make use of something such as an opportunity **3** *vti* **GET WEAKER OR MORE ILL** to become gradually weaker or thinner, e.g. as a result of disease, or make somebody become gradually weaker or thinner ○ *children wasting away from malnutrition* ○ *a body wasted by illness* **4** *vt* **EXHAUST** to make somebody exhausted **5** *vt* **DESTROY** to ravage or devastate something **6** *vt* **KILL** to kill or murder somebody (*slang*) ■ *n* **1 ACT OF WASTING** a failure to use something wisely, properly, fully, or to good effect **2 UNWANTED MATERIAL** unwanted or unusable by-products ○ *chemical waste* **3 FOOD REMAINDER** the undigested remainder of food expelled from the body as excrement **4 WILD AREA** an uncultivated, desolate, or wild area (*often plural*) **5 DESTROYED AREA** a place or region that has been destroyed or ruined **6 RUBBISH** rubbish or refuse ○ *household waste* **7 PROPERTY DEPRECIATION** loss of value in a property or estate caused by damage done by the tenant **8 USED OR CONTAMINATED WATER** used or contaminated water from domestic, industrial, or mining applications **9 ROCK ASSOCIATED WITH A MINERAL** enclosing rock mined with a mineral, or ore with insufficient mineral content to justify further processing ■ *adj* **1 NOT NEEDED** superfluous, useless, or not needed **2 UNPRODUCTIVE** unproductive, uninhabited, or uncultivated ○ *waste ground* **3 REJECTED FROM BODY** expelled from the body as unwanted and indigestible ○ *waste matter* **4 FOR WASTE** used to carry off or store waste [12C. Via Old N French < Latin *vastus* 'empty'.] —**wastable** *adj* ◇ **lay something (to) waste** to destroy or devastate something

SPELLCHECK See ***waist***.

wastebasket /wáyst baaskit/ *n US* = **wastepaper basket**

wasted /wáystid/ *adj* **1 NOT USED** not used or exploited **2 USELESS** useless because it achieves nothing **3 WITHERED** shrunken or ravaged **4 EXHAUSTED** exhausted from exertion (*slang*) **5 INTOXICATED** under the influence of drink or drugs (*slang*)

waste disposal, waste disposal unit *n* an electrical device, fitted in a kitchen sink, that grinds up food so that it can go into the waste pipe. US term **garbage disposal**

wasteful /wáystf'l/ *adj* **1** using resources unwisely **2** causing waste or devastation —**wastefully** *adv* —**wastefulness** *n*

waste heat recovery *n* the reclaiming of heat that would otherwise be unused, from such sources as furnaces, kilns, or engines, for use in another process, e.g. preheating air or water

wasteland /wáyst land, wáystlənd/ *n* **1** an area of land that is desolate or barren and not used **2** an environment that is thought to be spiritually or intellectually barren ○ *the wasteland of daytime TV*

LITERARY LINK ***The Waste Land***, a poem by US-born British poet T. S. Eliot (1922). One of the 20th century's major poetic works, it portrays the disintegration of Western values, the soullessness of modern society, and humankind's desperate search for salvation. It consists of five seemingly disconnected sections made up of fragmented verses written in a variety of styles but linked by imagery, symbols, and diverse literary and historical references.

waste management *n* activities that deal with waste before and after it is produced, including its minimization, transfer, storing, separating, recovering, recycling, and final disposal

wastepaper /wáyst páypər/ *n* paper that is not needed and has been thrown away

wastepaper basket, wastepaper bin *n* a small container for rubbish, especially paper. US term **wastebasket**

waste pipe *n* a pipe that carries excess or used fluids from a container such as a sink or bathtub

waste product *n* a useless or unwanted byproduct of a process

waster /wáystər/ *n* **1 SOMEBODY WHO WASTES** a person who wastes something **2 SOMETHING THAT WASTES** something that destroys or wastes something **3 LAZY PERSON** a lazy or worthless person (*informal insult*) **4 RUINED ARTICLE** an article that has been spoiled during manufacture, especially a ceramic piece

wastewater /wáyst wawtər/ *n* water that has been use ○ *a wastewater treatment plant*

wasteweir /wáyst weer/ *n* GEOG = **spillway**

wasting /wáysting/ *adj* taking away strength an energy —**wastingly** *adv*

wasting asset *n* an asset, especially a natural resourc such as a mine, that cannot be renewed and that lose its value over time

wastrel /wáystrəl/ *n* somebody regarded as wastefu spendthrift, or lazy (*insult*) [Late 16C. < WASTE + *-rel*, a ending indicating 'little' or derogatory sense.]

Wastwater /wóst wawtər/ lake in the Lake District, NV England. Area: 4 sq. km/1.5 sq. mi. Depth: 79 m/25 ft.

wat /wot/ *n* a Buddhist monastery or temple in Thailan Cambodia, or Laos [Mid-19C. Via Thai < Sanskrit *vā* 'enclosure'.]

watch /woch/ *n* **1 PERSONAL CLOCK** a small clock worn on th wrist or carried in a pocket **2 TIME SPENT OBSERVING** period of time spent observing something closely **3 DUT ON SHIP** a fixed period of a day spent on duty on boar a ship **4 CREW ON DUTY** the members of a ship's crew wh are on duty at a particular time **5 DIVISION OF NIGHT** one the periods of time into which the night was former divided **6 GUARD'S DUTY** the period during which a guar is on duty **7 PEOPLE WATCHING** a person or group th guards or observes something, especially at nigh ○ *posted a watch around the house, day and night* ■ *v* **1** **LOOK CAREFULLY** to look at something carefully or close **2** *vi* **KEEP LOOKOUT** to keep a lookout for something th might appear or happen ○ *Your job is to watch for anyo coming.* **3** *vti* **MONITOR** to keep something or somebod under observation ○ *has to watch his weight and avo fatty foods* **4** *vi* **KEEP VIGIL** to stay awake and keep vigil [Assumed Old English *wæccan* 'keep watch, be awake < Germanic] —**watcher** *n* ◇ **be on the watch for some body** *or* **something** to look out for somebody or some thing ◇ **watch it** to be careful (*informal*)

watch out *vi* **1** to be careful, alert, or wary **2** to look an wait for something or somebody

watch over *vt* to look after, supervise, or guard some body or something

watchable /wóchəb'l/ *adj* **1** apparent or capable of bein observed **2** interesting and enjoyable to watch ○ *a ve watchable detective series* —**watchability** /wóchə bílləti/ *r*

watchband /wóch band/ *n US, Can, Aus* a strap for wristwatch

watch cap *n* a dark-blue, close-fitting knitted wooll cap worn in cold weather, especially by sailors

watchdog /wóch dog/ *n* **1 DOG FOR GUARDING** a dog used f guarding property or people **2 GUARD AGAINST UNDESIRAB PRACTICES** a person or organization guarding again illegal practices, unacceptable standards, or i efficiency ○ *a government watchdog* ■ *vti* (**-dogs, -dog ging, -dogged**) **BE A WATCHDOG** to act as a watchdog o something

watch fire *n* a fire kept burning at night either as signal or for the comfort of somebody keeping watch

watchful /wóchf'l/ *adj* **1** carefully observant or ale ○ *watchful for signs of recovery* **2** not asleep (*archaic*) – **watchfully** *adv* —**watchfulness** *n*

watch glass *n* **1** a piece of glass or plastic fitted to watch to cover and protect its face. US term **crystal** *n.* **2** a shallow round glass dish used to evaporate liqui or to cover something

watchmaker /wóch maykər/ *n* a maker or repairer watches

watchman /wóchmən/ (*plural* **-men** /-mən/) *n* somebod employed to patrol or guard buildings or an area

watch night *n* **1** the last night of the year, marked some churches by a service that spans the midnig transition from the old year to the new one. Date: th night of 31 December. **2** the night before Christma Day, marked in some churches by a service that spa midnight. Date: the night of 24 December.

watchphone /wóch fōn/ *n* a watch with a built-in mobi phone

watchstrap /wóch strap/ *n UK, NZ* a strap for a wris watch. ◊ **watchband**

watchtower /wóch tow ər/ *n* a high tower in which se tries keep watch for the approach of an enemy

watchword /wóch wurd/ *n* **1** a word or slogan that e capsulates a mode of action, a set of beliefs, or me bership of a group **2** a word or phrase that somebody has to say to prove a right to be in a particular place

water /wáwtər/ n **1** LIQUID OF RAIN AND RIVERS H_2O the clear colourless liquid, odourless and tasteless when pure, that occurs as rain, snow, and ice, forms rivers, lakes, and seas, and is essential for life **2** AREA OF WATER an area or body of water, such as a river, stream, lake, or sea **3** SURFACE OF WATER the surface of a body of water ○ *swim under water* **4** ELEMENT in ancient and medieval philosophy, one of the four elements **5** TRANSPORT OVER WATER a means of transport over or through water, especially a boat ○ *can only get there by water* **6** WATER SUPPLY a supply of water to a house, town, or region **7** A WATERING the action of giving water to a plant **8** SOLUTION OF SUBSTANCE IN WATER a solution of a particular chemical or substance in water ○ *lavender water* **9** BODY FLUID any watery fluid present in or secreted by the body, e.g. urine, sweat, saliva, or tears **10** WAVY PATTERN a lustrous wavy pattern on the surface of some fabrics such as silk **11** BRIGHTNESS the quality of brightness of a gem, e.g. **first water** ■ **waters** npl **1** FLUID SURROUNDING FOETUS the amniotic fluid that surrounds the foetus in the womb (*sometimes singular*) ○ *Her waters have broken.* **2** PARTICULAR AREA OF SEA a particular region of sea, e.g. that belonging to a specific nation ○ *territorial waters* **3** WATER CONTAINING MINERALS naturally occurring water containing minerals, e.g. that found at a spa and used for health reasons ■ v **1** vt SPRINKLE OR SOAK SOMETHING WITH WATER to sprinkle, wet, or soak something with water **2** vt IRRIGATE LAND to take water to crops or fields **3** vti GIVE OR GET WATER to give drinking water to an animal, or get or take water as an animal does **4** vi FILL WITH TEARS WHEN IRRITATED to fill with tears, especially because of irritation (*refers to eyes*) **5** vi PRODUCE SALIVA to produce saliva, particularly in pleasant anticipation of food (*refers to the mouth*) **6** vi TAKE ON WATER SUPPLY to take on a supply of water **7** vt GIVE WAVY SHEEN to give a lustrous wavy pattern to material, especially silk [Old English *wæter* < Indo-European, 'water'] —**waterer** n ◇ **be dead in the water** to have no chance of success or survival ◇ **be water under the bridge** to be something that is in the past and that cannot be altered ◇ **clear (blue) water** a marked difference or differentiation between two political parties ◇ **hold water** to be well-founded, or stand up under scrutiny ◇ **in deep water** in a difficult or complicated situation ◇ **in hot water** in trouble because of having done something wrong ◇ **muddy the waters** to cause confusion or trouble ◇ **pour** or **throw cold water on** or **onto** or **over something** to discourage a plan or idea by showing a lack of interest in it or rejecting it as impractical ◇ **throw water** W Africa to offer somebody a bribe ◇ **tread water 1** to keep afloat without moving forwards, by moving the legs and arms **2** to make no progress but manage to keep a situation the same for a period of time ◇ **water off a duck's back** something said that has absolutely no effect on the attitude or behaviour of the person to whom it is said

water down vt **1** to weaken or dilute something by adding water to it **2** to moderate or attenuate something in order to make it less difficult, offensive, or controversial ○ *The producers want to water down her original script.* —**watered-down** adj

waterage /wáwtərij/ n **1** the carrying of passengers or cargo by water **2** money paid for the carrying of passengers or cargo by water

water arum n an aquatic plant cultivated for its glossy heart-shaped leaves and large white funnel-shaped cone surrounding the flower spike. Native to: northern temperate regions. *Calla palustris.*

water bag n **1** a bag made of leather, canvas, or similar material used for carrying water **2** the thin protective sac (**amnion**) around the growing foetus, and the watery fluid (**amniotic fluid**) it contains that is expelled just before or during childbirth

water ballet n the performance of dance movements in water

water bear n ZOOL = **tardigrade** n.

Water Bearer n ZODIAC = **Aquarius** n. 2

water bed n a bed with a special mattress filled with water

water beetle n a member of a group of beetles that live mainly in water. Family: Hydrophilidae.

water bird n a bird that lives mainly near, and wades in or swims on, water, especially fresh water

water biscuit n a thin plain biscuit made from flour and water, often served with cheese

water blister n a blister that contains clear watery fluid without blood or pus

water bloom n a growth of algae on a body of water such as a lake

water boatman n any insect that lives mainly at the bottom of ponds and has oar-shaped flattened hind legs used for swimming. Family: Corixidae.

waterborne /wáwtər bawrn/ adj **1** travelling on or transported by water ○ *a waterborne vessel* **2** transmitted or transported by water, as certain infectious agents are

water brash n the sudden filling of the mouth with acidic juices from the stomach, usually accompanied by heartburn and often resulting from indigestion

waterbuck /wáwtər buk/ (*plural* **-bucks** or **-buck**) n a large antelope with a shaggy dark-grey or reddish coat, found in grassland and woodland near open water. Native to: South Africa. *Kobus ellipsiprymnus.*

water buffalo n a large widely-domesticated buffalo with a grey-black coat and long backward-curving horns. Kept for: haulage, milk. Native to: Southeast Asia. *Bubalus bubalis.*

water bug n an aquatic insect, e.g. the water boatman or pond skater

waterbus /wáwtər buss/ n a boat carrying passengers in a regular service across a river or lake

water butt n a large barrel for collecting rainwater, usually from a drainpipe

water caltrop n PLANTS = **water chestnut**

water cannon n an apparatus usually mounted on a lorry that produces a jet of high-pressure water and is used to disperse crowds

Water Carrier n ZODIAC = **Aquarius** n. 2

water chestnut n **1** CRUNCHY NUT-SHAPED CORM a round white crunchy stem (**corm**) of a Chinese aquatic plant, often used in Asian cooking **2** AQUATIC PLANT an annual aquatic plant that forms rosettes of diamond-shaped floating leaves, has feathery submerged leaves, and bears hard spiny dark-grey fruit containing edible seeds. Native to: Europe, Asia. *Trapa natans.* **3** CHINESE PLANT WITH AN EDIBLE STEM a Chinese sedge that produces edible stems (**corms**). *Eleocharis tuberosa.*

water clock n = **clepsydra**

water closet n a small room fitted with a toilet and, often, a washbasin **2** a flush toilet (*archaic*)

watercolor n US = **watercolour**

watercolour /wáwtər kullər/ n **1** PAINTING a painting created with pigments mixed with water rather than oil **2** PIGMENT MIXED WITH WATER painting pigments, or a pigment, mixed with water rather than oil (*often plural*) **3** METHOD OF PAINTING the method of painting with pigments mixed with water rather than oil —**water-colourist** n

water-cool vt to cool an engine or machine by means of water, typically by circulating water in a water jacket or by pipes —**water-cooled** adj

water cooler n a device that dispenses cooled drinking water ■ adj US popular enough to be the subject of everyday conversation, e.g. between colleagues around the water cooler in the workplace (*informal*) ○ *water cooler TV*

watercourse /wáwtər kawrss/ n **1** a river or stream channel, or an artificial channel, through which water flows **2** the water of a river or stream that flows along a watercourse

watercraft /wáwtər kraaft/ n **1** a vessel used for travelling on water (*formal*) **2** skill in swimming, handling boats, or other water-related activities

watercress /wáwtər kress/ n a perennial aquatic plant, widely cultivated for its peppery-flavoured leaves and stems, used in salads. Native to: Europe, Asia. *Nasturtium officinale.*

water cure n a session of treatment by hydrotherapy or hydropathy

water cycle n the constant circulation of water between atmosphere, land, and sea by evaporation, precipitation, and percolation through soils and rocks

water diviner n somebody who dowses for water, especially underground water, usually by using divining rods

water dog n **1** a dog that likes water, especially one trained to hunt or retrieve game in water **2** a person

who likes being in, on, or near water, e.g. a keen sailor or swimmer (*informal*)

water dropwort n **1** a perennial plant of the carrot family that grows alongside watercourses and has a hollow grooved stem and compound leaves. Flowers: small, white, in flat-topped clusters. *Oenanthe fistulosa.* **2** any plant related to water dropwort

WORLD'S HIGHEST WATERFALLS

1	**Angel Falls**	
Height	[3,212 ft / 979 m*] (also single largest leap, [2,647 ft / 807 m*])	
Location	*Venezuela*	
2	**Tugela Waterfall**	
Height	[3,110 ft / 948 m*]	
Location	*South Africa*	
3	**Mtarazi Waterfall**	
Height	[2,500 ft / 762 m*]	
Location	*Zimbabwe*	
4	**Yosemite Falls**	
Height	[2,425 ft / 739 m*]	
Location	*United States*	
5	**Cuquenán Waterfall**	
Height	[2,000 ft / 610 m*]	
Location	*Venezuela*	
6	**Sutherland Falls**	
Height	[1,904 ft / 580 m*]	
Location	*New Zealand*	
7	**Kile Waterfall**	
Height	[1,840 ft / 561 m*]	
Location	*Norway*	
8	**Kahiwa Waterfall**	
Height	[1,748 ft / 533 m*]	
Location	*United States*	
9	**Mardal Waterfall**	
Height	[1,696 ft / 517 m*]	
Location	*Norway*	
10	**Takakkaw Falls**	
Height	[1,650 ft / 503 m*]	
Location	*Canada*	

* Total height may include more than one leap

waterfall /wáwtər fawl/ n a vertical stream of water that occurs where a river or stream falls over the edge of a steep place

water fern n PLANTS = **mosquito fern**

water filter n an appliance or fitting for removing unwanted matter from water, especially bacteria or harmful chemicals from drinking water

water flea n a tiny crustacean that swims with rapid jerky movements, using its large forked antennae. Suborder: Cladocera.

Waterford /wáwtərfərd/ **1** county in Munster Province, in the south of the Republic of Ireland. Area: 1,838 sq. km/710 sq. mi. **2** city in the southeast of the Republic of Ireland. Population: 66,692 (1996 estimate).

waterfowl /wáwtər fowl/ n (*plural* **-fowl** or **-fowls**) any bird that swims on water ■ npl swimming game birds such as ducks, considered collectively

waterfront /wáwtər frunt/ n **1** the part of a town that lies alongside a body of water **2** land beside an area of water

water gap n a deep valley through a mountain ridge, in which water flows

water gas n a toxic mixture of carbon monoxide and methane generated by passing air and steam over hot, glowing coals. Use: fuel for heating, lighting, and power.

water gate n **1** CIV ENG = floodgate **2** a gate that gives access to an area of water

Watergate /wáwtǝr gayt/ n **1** a political scandal stemming from a break-in by Republican operatives at the 1972 US Democratic National Committee headquarters, which were in the Watergate complex in Washington, D.C. The scandal led to the resignation of President Nixon **2** a public scandal involving politicians or officials abusing power, especially if a cover-up is also attempted

water gauge n a device that indicates the quantity or level of water in a tank, boiler feed, reservoir, or stream

water glass n **1** DRINKING GLASS a drinking glass, especially for water **2** THICK CHEMICAL SOLUTION an extremely viscous solution of sodium silicate. Use: cement, waterproofing and fireproofing agent, egg preservative. **3** GLASS GAUGE a water gauge consisting of a glass tube **4** DEVICE FOR EXAMINING UNDERWATER OBJECTS an instrument such as an open box or tube with a glass bottom, used for looking at objects under the water's surface

water gum n any of various Australian trees that grow near water

water gun n US a toy gun that squirts water

water hammer n a hammering or stuttering sound in a pipeline that sometimes accompanies a sudden and significant change in the flow rate of the fluid through the pipeline

water hemlock n any of various poisonous highly scented plants found in marshy areas. Flowers: small, white, in dense flat-topped clusters. Native to: N hemisphere. Genus: *Cicuta*.

water hen n a bird that lives near water, e.g. a rail or a coot. Family: Rallidae.

water hole n a natural hollow in the ground containing water, especially one where animals drink

Waterhouse /wáwtǝr howss/, **Alfred** (1830–1905) British architect

Waterhouse, George Marsden (1824–1906) British-born New Zealand statesman

water hyacinth n a perennial aquatic plant that has glossy rounded leaves with bulbous stalks. Flowers: lilac-blue. Native to: subtropical America. *Eichhornia crassipes*.

water ice n a frozen dessert of sweet-flavoured ice

watering can n a container with a handle and a spout, often with a perforated nozzle, used for watering plants

watering hole n **1** GEOG = water hole **2** a place such as a pub where people meet socially to drink (*informal*)

watering place n **1** GEOG = water hole **2** LEISURE = watering hole n. **2 3** a place where people go to drink or bathe in the local water for health reasons **4** a place by the sea to which people go for swimming and other leisure activities (*dated*)

waterish /wáwtǝrish/ adj a bit watery

water jump n a place in a race where the runners or horses have to jump over an obstacle that includes a stream, ditch, or pool

waterless /wáwtǝrlǝss/ adj **1** lacking water **2** not needing water in the making or use of something —**waterlessness** n

water level n **1** the level of the surface of a body of water **2** SHIPPING = water line n. **1 3** GEOL = water table n. **1**

water lily n a perennial aquatic plant with rounded leaves that float on the water. Flowers: cup-shaped, often fragrant. Family: Nymphaeaceae.

water line n **1** a line on a ship's hull indicating the level to which the ship can sink into the water under various conditions **2** the line to which a body of water rises or reaches

waterlogged /wáwtǝr logd/ adj **1** saturated with water ○ *a waterlogged pitch* **2** filled with water and therefore hard to steer —**waterlog** vt

Waterloo[1] /wáwtǝr loó/ town in central Belgium, site of Napoleon's defeat by British and Prussian forces on 18 June 1815. Population: 27,860 (1991).

Waterloo[2] /wáwtǝr loó/, **waterloo** ◊ **meet your Waterloo** to be decisively defeated or overcome

water louse n any freshwater crustacean related to the woodlouse. Genus: *Asellu*.

water main n a large underground pipe supplying water

waterman /wáwtǝrmǝn/ n (*plural* **-men** /-mǝn/) a person who works on or hires out boats

⚡ **watermark** /wáwtǝr maark/ n **1** HIDDEN MARK IN PAPER a design or mark in paper that can be seen when the paper is held up to the light, or the metal tool used to make such a design **2** SHIPPING = water line n. **1 3** LINE LEFT BY WATER a line showing where the edge or surface of water has been ■ vt PUT WATERMARK OR PATTERN IN PAPER to put a watermark into paper while it is being made, or impress a particular pattern as a watermark ■ n EMBEDDED PATTERN IN DATA FILE a pattern of bits digitally embedded in a data file, used in detecting unauthorized copies ■ vt EMBED IDENTIFYING PATTERN IN DATA FILE to embed a pattern of bits in a data file for identification and detection of unauthorized copies

water meadow n a meadow that is often flooded by a stream or river

watermelon /wáwtǝr melǝn/ n **1** a large oval or round fruit with a hard green skin and sweet and juicy pink, red, or yellow flesh, usually with many black seeds **2** a climbing plant that produces watermelons. Native to: Africa. *Citrullus lanatus*.

water meter n a device that records the amount of water that passes through a pipe, usually for billing purposes

water milfoil n a perennial aquatic plant that has submerged leaves made up of many feathery segments and bears slender spikes of tiny flowers above the water surface. Genus: *Myriophyllum*.

water mill n a mill that has machinery powered by moving water

water mint n a perennial plant of swampy areas with toothed hairy leaves and a hairy stem, that emits a strong scent when crushed. Flowers: lilac-pink, in whorls. *Mentha aquatica*.

water moccasin n **1** a venomous semiaquatic snake belonging to the pit viper family that has an olive to brownish back and indistinct black bars. Native to: S United States. *Agkistrodon piscivorus*. **2** a snake that resembles the venomous water moccasin but is harmless. Genus: *Nerodia*.

water mould n any fungus that inhabits fresh or brackish water and feeds mainly on dead organic material but is sometimes parasitic on fish, plants, and other living organisms. Order: Saprolegniales.

water nymph n **1** in folklore and classical mythology, a nymph that lives in water **2** a water plant, such as a water lily

water of crystallization, water of crystallisation n water molecules incorporated in a crystalline substance that are typically necessary for its properties and structure

water of hydration n water molecules incorporated in a substance that can be removed without affecting its essential chemical composition

water on the brain n MED = hydrocephalus

water on the knee n the accumulation of watery fluid in or around the knee indicating disease or injury of the knee joint

water opossum n ZOOL = yapok

water ouzel n BIRDS = dipper n. **2**

water park n a leisure area or theme park with water-based facilities such as slides with flowing water

water penny n circular beetle larvae that cling like tiny suction cups to rocks in swift streams. Family: Psephenidae.

water pennywort n a creeping plant that grows in water or moist places. Genus: *Hydrocotyle*.

water pepper n an annual plant widely distributed in damp places that has lance-shaped leaves and a hot peppery taste. Flowers: inconspicuous, pink or greenish, in slender spikes. *Polygonum hydropiper*.

water pipe n **1** a pipe for transporting water from one place to another **2** a pipe for smoking something, especially marijuana, that is filled with water in order to cool the smoke by drawing it through the water

water pistol n a toy pistol that squirts out water. US term **squirt gun**

water plantain n a perennial plant found in water or wet places, with a rosette of pointed oval leaves.

Flowers: pinkish or white, in branching heads. Genus *Alisma*.

water polo n a game played in a swimming pool by two teams of seven players whose object is to score by sending a large ball into the opposing team's goal

water power n **1** power, usually generated from an elevated water supply, that is converted to electricity through the use of hydraulic turbines **2** the descent or a watercourse capable of providing water power

waterproof /wáwtǝr proof/ adj IMPERVIOUS TO WATER treated or constructed so as to be impenetrable or unaffected by water ■ n **1** ITEM OF WATERPROOF CLOTHING an item or waterproof clothing **2** TEXTILE IMPERVIOUS TO WATER a textile that has been made or treated so as to be impenetrable by water ■ vt MAKE SOMETHING WATERPROOF to make something such as a house or an item of clothing impenetrable by water —**waterproofness** n

water purslane n a creeping annual plant growing in moist places with fleshy rounded leaves. Flowers small, purplish, growing at leaf base. *Lythrum portula*.

water rail n a bird with a long red bill, grey underparts with black-striped flanks, and mottled brown back and wings. Native to: marshes of Europe and Asia. *Rallus aquaticus*.

water rat n **1** ZOOL = water vole **2** US ZOOL = muskrat n. **3** a large amphibious rat with broad paddle-shaped hind feet for swimming. Native to: Australia, New Guinea, Philippines. Subfamily: Hydromyinae. **4** US a criminal, loafer, or hooligan who often frequents water front areas (*slang*)

water-repellent, water-resistant adj treated or constructed so as to prevent water being absorbed or passing through

water right n **1** the right to use a water source, especially for irrigation (*often plural*) **2** the right to sail on particular rivers, lakes, or seas

Waters /wáwtarz/, **Muddy** (1915–83) US blues musician Born **McKinley Morganfield**

water sapphire n a precious stone that is a blue form of cordierite. Source: river gravel. Use: gems.

waterscape /wáwtǝr skayp/ n a view or picture of an expanse of water

water scorpion n an aquatic insect that lies submerged in water breathing through a long tubular siphon, and that catches prey by using the front pair of legs. Family: Nepidae.

water seal n water that lies in a waste pipe and forms a seal that prevents the escape of unpleasant smells

watershed /wáwtǝr shed/ n **1** LINE BETWEEN CATCHMENT AREAS the boundary separating the catchment basins of different rivers. US term **divide** n. **2 2** REGION DRAINING INTO RIVER OR OCEAN the land area that drains into a particular lake, river, or ocean **3** TURNING POINT an important period time, event, or factor that marks a change or division [Early 19C. Anglicization of German *Wasserscheid* 'water divide'.]

water shield n **1** a widely distributed perennial aquatic plant with floating leaves that are purple underneath and covered in a layer of clear jelly. Flowers: purple *Brasenia schreberi*. **2** any of various aquatic plants with roundish floating leaves or finely divided needle-shaped submerged leaves. Genus: *Cabomba*. [Because the leaves are shaped like shields]

water-sick adj describes land that has been made unproductive by excessive irrigation

waterside /wáwtǝr sīd/ n land alongside an area of water ■ adj living or working beside an area of water

water sign n any one of the three signs of the zodiac Pisces, Cancer, or Scorpio, that are associated with emotional sensitivity

waterski /wáwtǝr skee/ n **water ski** a ski designed for skiing over water ■ vi (**-skis, -skiing, -skied**) to ski over water while being towed by a boat —**waterskier** n —**waterskiing** n

water snake n **1** a snake that lives in or near water **2** a nonvenomous snake that lives in marshes and other wet places. Native to: North America, Europe, and Southeast Asia. Genus: *Natrix*.

water softener n **1** a device that removes or reduces hardness in water, usually by means of ion-exchange resins **2** a substance used to reduce water hardness, e.g. by precipitating out the minerals causing the hardness

ater-soluble *adj* capable of being dissolved completely by water

ater spaniel *n* a dog with a thick curly water-resistant coat, belonging to a breed developed for retrieving game from water

ater spider *n* a spider that lives underwater in a bell-shaped web that it spins amongst vegetation and fills with air bubbles transported from the surface in its body hairs. Native to: Europe, Asia. *Argyroneta aquatica*.

ater splash *n* a section of road where a stream flows across it

ater sports *npl* 1 sports carried out on or in water 2 an offensive term for sexual activity in which urine or the act of urination provides gratification (*slang*)

aterspout /wáwtər spowt/ *n* 1 a funnel-shaped tornado, sometimes hundreds of feet wide, extending from the surface of the sea or a lake to the cloud base and caused by violent circulation of air 2 a hole or spout through which water flows, e.g. from the gutter of a building

ater sprite *n* in folklore and classical mythology, a sprite that lives in water

ater strider *n* US INSECTS = **pond-skater**

ater supply *n* 1 the water distributed to a town, community, or region 2 the source or delivery system supplying water to an area, e.g. reservoirs, pipes, or purification plants

ater system *n* 1 a river with all its tributaries 2 a system for delivering water to a group of users or a town or region

ater table *n* 1 the upper surface of ground water, below which pores in the rocks are filled with water 2 a moulding or band that projects from a wall and is intended to divert rainwater

ater taxi *n* a motorboat used to ferry passengers between destinations separated by water for a fare

ater thrush *n* a small songbird of the wood warbler family with markings similar to the thrush, found near streams, ponds, and swampy ground. Native to: North America. Genus: *Seiurus*.

atertight /wáwtər tīt/ *adj* 1 not allowing water to pass in, out, or through 2 without loopholes or flaws ○ *a watertight argument* —**watertightness** *n*

ater torture *n* a form of torture in which water is used, especially one in which water is dripped steadily onto somebody's forehead

ater tower *n* 1 a tower for water storage where the prevailing water pressure is not sufficient for either firefighting or general distribution 2 a firefighting apparatus for lifting hoses to high levels

ater vapour *n* water in vapour form, but usually below boiling point

ater vole *n* an amphibious vole that lives near rivers and streams, often burrowing into the banks. Native to: Europe, Asia. Genus: *Arvicola*.

aterway /wáwtər way/ *n* 1 a navigable channel such as a river or canal used by boats or ships 2 a drain for water at the edge of the deck of a boat

aterweed /wáwtər weed/ *n* PLANTS = **pondweed** *n.* 2

ater wheel *n* 1 a simple wheel driven by water flowing or falling onto vanes or into buckets on the edges of the wheel, used to power machinery 2 a wheel with buckets fixed to its rim, used for lifting water

ater wings *npl* a pair of air-filled supports that fit closely around the upper arms of a swimmer, especially a child learning to swim

ater witch *n* PARANORMAL = **water diviner**

aterworks /wáwtər wurks/ *n* (*plural* **-works**) 1 SYSTEM FOR SUPPLYING WATER the entire system of treating, storing, supplying, and managing the distribution networks of pumps and pipes that provide water to a community or region (*+ singular or plural verb*) 2 COMPONENT OF WATER SYSTEM a single component of a waterworks system such as a pumping station 3 DISPLAY OF MOVING WATER a display of water that has been made to move artificially such as a fountain 4 URINARY SYSTEM the bodily system involved in excreting urine (*informal; + plural verb*) 5 TEARS a display of crying (*informal; + plural verb*)

aterworn /wáwtər wawrn/ *adj* smoothed or eroded by the action of water

atery /wáwtəri/ *adj* 1 RELATING TO OR CONTAINING WATER relating to, containing, soaked with, or like water 2 HAVING EXCESSIVE WATER containing too much water ○ *watery coffee* 3 FILLED WITH TEARS filled with tears, from either emotion or physical irritation ○ *watery eyes* 4 LACKING FORCE lacking the usual full force and appearing thin or weak ○ *A watery sun hung in the autumn sky.* 5 WEAK lacking strength or sincerity ○ *a watery smile* 6 FULL OF FLUID discharging, secreting, or filled with a watery fluid ○ *watery blister* —**wateriness** *n*

Watford /wótfərd/ town in south-central England. Population: 113,080 (1991).

Watson /wóts'n/, **Chris** (1867–1941) Chilean-born Australian statesman. Full name **John Christian Watson**

Watson, James D. (*b.* 1928) US biochemist. Full name **James Dewey Watson**

Watson-Crick model *n* the three-dimensional double-helix model of the DNA molecule proposed by James Watson and Francis Crick in 1953 [Mid-20C. After J. D. WATSON and F. H. C. CRICK.]

watt /wot/ *n* (*symbol* **W**) the international (**SI**) unit of power equal to the power produced by a current of one ampere acting across a potential difference of one volt [Late 19C. After James WATT.]

Watt /wot/, **James** (1736–1819) British inventor

wattage /wóttij/ *n* electrical power measured in watts

Watteau /wóttō/, **Antoine** (1684–1721) French painter

watt-hour *n* a unit of electrical energy equal to that of one watt operating for one hour

wattle /wótt'l/ *n* 1 STAKES INTERWOVEN WITH BRANCHES stakes or poles interwoven with branches and twigs, used for walls, fences, and roofs 2 MATERIAL FOR WATTLE material such as branches or stakes used to make wattle 3 SKIN HANGING FROM ANIMAL'S THROAT a loose, often highly coloured fold of bare skin hanging from the throat or cheek of birds and lizards 4 AUSTRALIAN ACACIA TREE a drought-resistant tree or shrub, often planted for shade or ornament, whose feathery-looking leaves are sometimes replaced by flattened green leaf stalks in maturity. Native to: Australia. Genus: *Acacia*. ■ *vt* (**-tles, -tling, -tled**) 1 MAKE FROM WATTLE to construct something from wattle 2 WEAVE BRANCHES INTO WATTLE to weave branches or twigs into wattle [Old English *watul*, < ?] —**wattled** *adj*

wattle and daub *n* building material consisting of wattle covered with mud or clay, often containing lime, dung, or straw (*hyphenated when used before a noun*)

wattlebird /wótt'l burd/ *n* a slender-bodied grey-brown or olive-brown bird with a long bill, a brush-tipped tongue for lapping nectar, and wattles on the cheeks. Native to: Australia. Genus: *Anthochaera*.

wattmeter /wót meetər/ *n* an instrument designed to measure the magnitude of the power in an electric circuit. It may be scaled in watts, kilowatts, or megawatts.

Watts /wots/, **George Frederick** (1817–1904) British painter and sculptor

Waugh /waw/, **Evelyn** (1903–66) British novelist

waul /wawl/, **wawl** *vi* to cry out shrilly like a cat or baby ■ *n* a shrill cry, like that of a cat or baby [Early 16C. An imitation of the sound.]

waulk /wawk/ *vt Scotland* to make cloth, such as tweed, thicker and more felted by soaking and beating it [15C. < Dutch or Low German *walken*.]

waulking song /wáwking-/ *n Scotland* a Gaelic work-song traditionally sung while fulling cloth

waur /wawr/ *adj, adv Scotland* worse [Late 18C. Scots dialect variant of WAR.]

wave[1] /wayv/ (**waves, waving, waved**) *v* 1 *vti* MOVE HAND REPEATEDLY AS SIGNAL to move the hand or arm from side to side or up and down as a greeting, farewell, or signal 2 *vti* MOVE SOMETHING REPEATEDLY IN AIR to move or cause something such as a flag to move from side to side or up and down ○ *The flag waved in the wind.* 3 *vt* DIRECT SOMEBODY OR SOMETHING BY WAVING to direct somebody or something by waving a hand, arm, or object ○ *The police waved the traffic around the procession.* 4 *vti* MAKE INTO OR BE IN UNDULATIONS to make something into or be in the form of swells, ridges, or swirls ○ *a field of grain waving in the wind* 5 *vti* BE OR MAKE SLIGHTLY CURLED to be slightly or gently curled, or make hair slightly curled 6 *vt* GIVE MATERIAL A RIPPLED PATTERN to create a rippled pattern in a fabric such as silk [Old English *wafian* < Germanic, 'move back and forth']

SPELLCHECK See ***waive***.

wave aside *vt* to dismiss something or somebody as trivial or inconsequential

wave down *vt* to stop a vehicle by waving to the driver to halt

wave off *vt* to watch and wave to somebody who is leaving

wave[2] /wayv/ *n* 1 MOVING RIPPLE ON LIQUID OR OCEAN any ripple moving across the surface of a liquid, especially a large raised ridge of water moving across the surface of the sea 2 ACT OF WAVING THE HAND an instance of moving the hand or arm as a signal or greeting 3 LINE CURVING IN ALTERNATING DIRECTIONS a line, shape, surface, or pattern that curves in one direction and then another, especially one with repeated curves 4 UNDULATING MOTION a movement on a surface or edge that is similar to a wave ○ *The wind made waves across the field of grain.* 5 SUDDEN REPETITION OF EVENTS a sudden occurrence of repeated activity ○ *a crime wave* 6 OVERWHELMING FEELING a sudden overwhelming feeling ○ *a wave of sorrow* 7 INCOMING GROUP an advancing or incoming group of people ○ *a wave of immigrants* 8 LOOSE CURVE IN HAIR a soft, usually large, curve or ripple in the hair where the lie of the hair changes direction, either naturally or after setting 9 OSCILLATION OF ENERGY an oscillation that travels through a medium by transferring energy from one particle or point to another without causing any permanent displacement of the medium ○ *sound waves* 10 RIPPLED PATTERN a rippled pattern in material such as silk 11 *US* SPORTS = **Mexican wave** ■ **waves** *npl* SEA the waves of the ocean, or the ocean itself [15C. Alteration of obsolete *waw* under the influence of the verb WAVE[1].] ◇ **make waves** to cause a disturbance or trouble, e.g. by suggesting or introducing changes or making criticisms

Wave *n US* a member of the WAVES

waveband /wáyv band/ *n* a range of radio frequencies within which transmissions occur

wave energy *n* energy produced for domestic or industrial use by harnessing and converting the energy of sea waves

wave equation *n* in physics, an equation, usually a partial differential equation, that defines the propagation of a wave through a medium

⚡**wave file** *n* a computer file containing a digitized representation of sound waves

waveform /wáyv fawrm/ *n* in physics, the profile or shape of a wave, especially the graphic representation of one of its characteristics, e.g. frequency or amplitude, relative to time

wavefront /wáyv frunt/ *n* in physics, a line or surface that joins points of the same phase in a wave travelling through a medium

wave function *n* in quantum physics, an equation that shows how a wave's amplitude varies in space and time

waveguide /wáyv gīd/ *n* in electronics, a transmission line consisting of a hollow metal conductor used as a path to convey microwave energy along its length

wavelength /wáyv length/ *n* 1 (*symbol* **λ**) in physics, the distance between two points on adjacent waves that have the same phase, e.g. the distance between two consecutive peaks or troughs 2 in broadcasting, the wavelength of the fundamental radio wave used by a broadcasting station ◇ **be on the same wavelength** to have the same opinions, attitudes, or tastes

wavelet /wáyvlət/ *n* a small wave, e.g. a ripple

wavellite /wáyvəlīt/ *n* a soft light grey, yellow, or brown hydrated aluminium phosphate mineral, forming clusters of radiating crystals. Source: slates and shales. [Early 19C. After William *Wavell* (d. 1829), British physician.]

wave mechanics *n* a form of quantum theory in which happenings on the atomic scale are explained in terms of interactions between systems of waves, represented by wave functions (*+ singular verb*)

wavemeter /wáyv meetər/ *n* an instrument for measuring wavelengths

wave number *n* (*symbol* **σ**) in physics, the number of waves in a given unit distance

waveoff /wáyv of/ *n* a signal or instruction to an aircraft that it is not to land

wave-particle duality *n* a fundamental concept of quantum theory holding that energy sometimes behaves like particles and sometimes behaves like waves, so that descriptions of energy as one or the other are inadequate

wave pool *n* a public swimming pool equipped with a device to produce waves

wave power *n* = wave energy

waver /wáyvər/ *vi* **1 FLUCTUATE BETWEEN POSSIBILITIES** to go back and forth between possibilities, or be indecisive in making a choice **2 BEGIN TO CHANGE OPINION** to become unsure or begin to change from a previous opinion **3 MOVE IN DIFFERENT DIRECTIONS** to move one way and then another in an irregular pattern **4 FLUCTUATE, ESPECIALLY IN TONE** to vary or fluctuate, e.g. as the voice does from emotion **5 FLICKER** to go on and off, especially due to burning unsteadily (*refers to a light or a flame*) ■ *n* **ACT OF WAVERING** an instance or act of wavering [14C. < Old Norse *vafra*.] —**waverer** *n* —**waveringly** *adv*

SYNONYMS See *hesitate*.

WAVES /wayvz/ *n* the women's branch of the US Naval Reserve that was organized in World War II. It no longer exists as a separate entity. Full form **Women Accepted for Volunteer Emergency Service**

wave theory *n* the theory that the behaviour of light or any other electromagnetic radiation can be explained by assuming that it travels in waves. ◊ **corpuscular theory**

wave train *n* in physics, a series of similar waves produced at equal intervals and travelling in the same direction

wavy /wáyvi/ (**-ier, -iest**) *adj* **1 REPEATEDLY CURVING** forming a series of smooth curves that go in one direction and then another **2 HAVING SOFT CURVES** having loose open waves ○ *wavy hair* **3 CONTAINING WAVES** full of waves or having a surface covered by waves **4 MOVING LIKE A WAVE** moving with an up-and-down or side-to-side motion **5 WAVERING** wavering or changeable —**wavily** *adv* —**waviness** *n*

waw *n* ALPHABET = vav

wa-wa *n* MUSIC = wah-wah

wa-wa pedal *n* MUSIC = wah-wah pedal

wawl *vi, n* = waul

wax[1] /waks/ *n* **1 NATURALLY-OCCURRING GREASY SUBSTANCE** a hard or soft and mouldable substance of animal, plant, or mineral origin that feels slightly greasy or oily to the touch **2 PREPARATION FOR POLISHING** a preparation containing wax used for polishing floors, cars, and other surfaces **3** INDUST = **beeswax** *n*. 2 **4** MED = **earwax 5 RESINOUS MIXTURE USED IN SHOEMAKING** a resinous mixture rubbed onto thread used in shoemaking **6 SOMETHING EASILY MOULDED** an easily moulded, shaped, or manipulated person or thing **7 RECORD** a gramophone record (*dated informal*) ■ *vt* (**waxes, waxing, waxed, waxed** *or* **waxen** *archaic* /wáks'n/) **1 POLISH SOMETHING WITH WAX** to coat or polish something such as a floor or car with wax **2 REMOVE HAIR WITH WAX** to remove unwanted hair from the skin using heated wax that is left to dry and then removed [Old English *wæx* < Germanic] —**waxer** *n*

wax[2] /waks/ *vi* **1 APPEAR LARGER EACH NIGHT** to show a gradually increasing illuminated surface, as does the Moon between its new and full phases (*refers to the Moon or a planet*) **2 INCREASE** to increase in size, power, or intensity (*literary*) **3 BECOME SOMETHING STATED** to get into a particular emotional or behavioural state (*literary*) ○ *waxed philosophical* [Old English *weaxan* < Indo-European, 'to increase']

wax[3] /waks/ *n* a fit of temper or anger (*dated informal*) [Mid-19C. < ?]

wax bean *n* US a variety of string bean that is yellow

waxbill /wáks bil/ *n* a small brightly-coloured finch with a red conical bill. Native to: Africa. Family: Estrildidae.

wax cap *n* a mushroom with a cap that has waxy gills. Family: Hygrophoraceae.

waxcloth /wáks kloth/ *n* TEXTILES = oilcloth

waxed jacket *n* a jacket for outdoor use made from fabric that has been coated with wax to repel moisture

waxed paper *n* DOMESTIC = greaseproof paper

waxen /wáks'n/ *adj* **1 LIKE WAX** resembling wax in texture and colour **2 MADE OF WAX** covered with, permeated with, or made of wax **3 PALE AND UNHEALTHY-LOOKING** lacking the rosy glow of life or health ○ *a waxen face* **4 EASY TO SHAPE** easily shaped, changed, or manipulated

wax flower *n* a plant that has waxy flowers, especially a hoya

wax insect *n* any scale insect that secretes wax. Superfamily: Coccoidea.

wax light *n* a candle or taper made of wax

wax moth *n* a small brownish moth whose larvae develop inside beehives, feeding on the wax of the honeycombs and often damaging the honey and the honey bee larvae. *Galleria mellonella*.

wax museum *n* = waxworks *npl*.

wax myrtle *n* TREES = bayberry *n*. 2

wax palm *n* TREES = carnauba *n*. 1

wax paper *n* US = greaseproof paper

waxwing /wáks wing/ *n* a bird marked by a crest, buff-brown plumage, and waxy-looking red tips on the upper flight feathers. Native to: northern regions. Genus: *Bombycilla*.

waxwork /wáks wurk/ *n* **1 WAX MODEL** a realistic model, usually of a famous person, made from wax **2 WAX OBJECT** an object made of wax, especially an ornament **3 ART OF USING WAX FOR MODELLING** the art of using wax as a modelling or expressive medium

waxworks /wáks wurks/ *n* (*plural* **waxworks**) **1** an exhibition, usually in a museum, of life-like wax models, usually of people who are famous **2** a museum containing a waxworks (+ *singular or plural verb*) US term **wax museum**

waxy /wáksi/ (**-ier, -iest**) *adj* **1 LIKE WAX** resembling wax in appearance, colour, texture, or pliability **2 COVERED WITH WAX** covered with, having a lot of, or made of wax **3 HAVING HARD DEPOSITS LIKE WAX** containing deposits of a hard substance resembling wax (**amyloid**) resulting from tissue degeneration —**waxiness** *n*

way /way/ *n* **1 MANNER OR METHOD** a means, manner, or method of doing or achieving something ○ *You do it your way, I'll do it mine.* **2 EXAMPLE** a feature, aspect, or example of something ○ *In some ways, my sisters are very similar.* **3 CONDITION** the state or condition of somebody or something, especially with regard to health or finances ○ *He was in a bad way after the accident.* **4 PREFERENCE** something somebody wants to happen or to do ○ *You can't always get your own way.* **5 CHARACTERISTIC ASPECT OF BEHAVIOUR** a usual, characteristic, or distinctive activity or style of behaviour ○ *How do you put up with those irritating ways of theirs?* **6 TRADITION OR CUSTOM** the customary style or practices of somebody's life ○ *the way of the Sufi* **7 TYPICAL HAPPENING** the usual occurrence or pattern of events ○ *Isn't it usually the way that all the cabs are taken when you're late?* **8 PATH** a path or physical means of getting from one place to another ○ *The way out is through here.* **9 DOOR OR OPENING** a door or opening leading or providing access to or from somewhere ○ *Come in the front way.* **10 JOURNEY OR ROUTE** a particular journey or the route followed or to be followed ○ *on my way to the office* **11 PROGRESS THROUGH LIFE** progress on or a path through life and its experiences or difficulties **12 DIRECTION** a direction such as left, right, up, or down **13 MANNER OF PLACING** the manner in which something is placed, arranged, or arranged, or the direction it faces **14 SPACE FOR ACTION** path, room, territory, or space allowing movement, progress, or action ○ *Get out of the way! I tried to take photographs but people kept getting in the way.* **15 AREA** an area or district, e.g. around somebody's home (*informal*) ○ *out our way* **16 DISTANCE** a distance away in space or time ○ *Graduation is still a long way off.* **17 AMOUNT** the extent or amount to which somebody does something ○ *He's fallen for her in a big way.* **18 way, Way STREET** a street, usually a small or narrow one (*often in placenames*) **19 SUBPART** each of a particular number of parts into which something divides or is split ○ *They're going to split the prize four ways.* **20 GUIDE OR SUPPORT** a surface used to guide or provide support to moving parts of a machine tool such as a lathe (*often plural*) **21 MOVEMENT THROUGH WATER** movement or speed of a ship through water ○ *The vessel now had some way on.* ■ *adv* **1 VERY MUCH** to a considerable degree or at a considerable distance (*informal*) ○ *That's way out of our price range.* **2** ⚠ **VERY** to a great extent (*slang*) [Old English *weg* < Indo-European, 'to go'] ◊ **by the way** used to introduce something that is not strictly part of the subject at hand ◊ **by way of something 1** as a means of or for the purpose of something **2** via ◊ **every which way 1** US in all directions **2** US in every way possible (*informal*) ◊ **get into the way of doing something** to get into the habit of doing something ◊ **give way 1** to give in or give precedence to somebody else **2** to collapse or break under pressure ◊ **give way to** to be overcome by an emotion that you have been trying to resist ◊ **go out of**

your way to do something to do more than is usual or necessary ◊ **have a way with somebody** *or* **somethin** to be good at dealing with somebody or something ◊ **have it both ways** to have the benefits of opposir situations or actions ◊ **in a way** from a certain point (view ◊ **(in) the worst way** US very much, very bad! or very intensely ◊ **make way (for somebody something)** to move aside to make room for someboc *or* something ◊ **make your way 1** to go somewher especially when getting there requires overcomir some obstacle, e.g. finding the route or some transpo **2** to become successful ◊ **no way** used as an emphat negative ◊ **there are no two ways about it** there no room for dispute ◊ **way to go** Can, US used congratulate somebody on something that he or sl has done (*informal*)

waybill /wáy bil/ *n* a document that gives informatic about goods being shipped or carried

wayfarer /wáy fairər/ *n* a traveller, especially someboc who makes a journey on foot (*literary*) —**wayfaring** *adj*

wayfaring tree *n* a bush with red berries that tur black. Flowers: white in flat-topped clusters. Native t Europe, W Asia. *Viburnum lantana*. [Probably because can provide the traveller with shade]

Wayland /wáyland/, **Wayland Smith, Wayland the Smi** *n* in N European folklore, a magical smith who was t king of the elves [< Old Norse *Völundr*. First mentioned the 13C *Poetic Edda*.]

waylay /way láy/ (**-lays, -laying, -laid** /-láyd/, **-laid**) *vt* **1** lie in wait for somebody, especially as part of an attac or ambush **2** to stop or accost somebody, e.g. in ord to talk —**waylayer** *n*

wayleave /wáy leev/ *n* the right of way over someboc else's property, for which payment is usually made

waymark /wáy maark/ *n* **waymark, waymarker** a signpo or other marker used to guide travellers, especial walkers ■ *vt* to mark out a path with waymarks

John Wayne

Wayne /wayn/, **John** (1907–79) US actor. Born **Mari Michael Morrison**. Known as the **Duke**

way of life *n* the particular habits and behaviour th characterize a person or group of people ○ *had an i creasingly sedentary way of life*

Way of the Cross *n* a series of pictures representir Jesus Christ's progress on the road to Calvary

way-out *adj* **1** unusual, peculiar, or unconvention (*informal*) **2** excellent or exciting (*dated informal*)

waypoint /wáy poynt/ *n* a point on a journey or rou where a traveller can stop or change course

ays /wayz/ *n* **1** *US* a distance travelled or to be travelled (*informal; + singular verb*) ○ *The next gas station is quite a ways from here.* **2** the tracks a ship slides down to be launched (*+ singular or plural verb*)

ways *suffix* in a particular direction or position ○ *edgeways* [Old English *weges*, form of *weg* 'way, of (such a) way']

ays and means *npl* **1** methods of accomplishing or achieving something, especially finding a way of paying for something **2** methods, e.g. legislation, used by a government to raise money

ays and Means *npl* in the United States, a legislative committee in charge of methods of raising money for government

ayside /wáy sīd/ *n* the side of a road or path ■ *adj* situated at the side of a road or path ◇ **fall by the wayside** to fail to continue or complete something ○ *Several students fell by the wayside after the first few weeks.*

ay station *n US* **1** a station between the major stations on a railway **2** a point or stopping place on a route

ayward /wáyward/ *adj* **1** characterized by wilfulness or disobedience **2** behaving in an erratic, apparently perverse, or unpredictable manner [14C. Alteration of *awayward*.] —**waywardly** *adv* —**waywardness** *n*

SYNONYMS See *unruly*.

ayworn /wáy wawrn/ *adj* worn out or weary from travelling

ayzgoose /wáyz gooss/ *n* formerly, an annual outing for people working at a printing house [Mid-18C. Alteration of *waygoose* < ?]

azzock /wázzək/ *n* an offensive term that deliberately insults somebody's intelligence or common sense (*slang insult*) [Late 20C. < ?]

b *abbr* **1** water ballast **2 wb, WB, W/B** waybill **3** westbound

Vb *symbol* weber

VB *abbr* welcome back (*in e-mails*)

VBA *abbr* World Boxing Association

VBC *abbr* **1** white blood cell **2** World Boxing Council

VbN *abbr* west by north

V boson *n* PHYS = **W particle**

VbS *abbr* west by south

VC[1] *abbr* **1** water closet **2** West Central (London)

VC[2] *abbr* who cares (*in e-mails*)

.c. *abbr* without charge

VCC *abbr* World Council of Churches

d *abbr* **1** ward **2** wood **3** word **4 wd, w/d** warranted

VD *abbr* War Department

VDA *abbr* **1** writing-down allowance **2** Welsh Development Agency

VDM, wdm *abbr* wavelength division multiplex

dth *abbr* width

VDV *abbr* written-down value

VDYT *abbr* what do you think (*in e-mails*)

e (*stressed*) /wee/; (*unstressed*) /wi/ *pron* **1 REFERS TO SPEAKER AND OTHERS** refers to the speaker or writer and at least one other person (*first person plural personal pronoun, used as the subject of a verb*) ○ *We are going on holiday.* ○ *We grown-ups should protect our children's rights.* ○ *We all want our children to have a better future.* **2 REFERS TO PEOPLE IN GENERAL** refers to all people or to people in general ○ *We are getting closer to the election.* **3 USED INSTEAD OF 'I'** used by a writer or speaker to include the listener or speaker in what is being said, especially to talk about how a book or talk is organized or by a monarch as the people's symbolic head ○ *We will now consider the causes of World War I.* **4 USED INSTEAD OF 'YOU'** used sarcastically or condescendingly by a speaker ○ *How are we today? Are we getting better?* [Old English *wē* < Indo-European]

USAGE ***we*** or ***us***? Personal pronouns often appear with nouns that are 'appositives' (i.e. the nouns immediately follow the pronouns, are synonymous with them, and serve to further identify the pronouns). Some writers have trouble identifying the appropriate grammatical form (e.g. the subjective ***we*** or the objective ***us***) for the pronouns. A good rule to follow is to identify the subject and/or object of the sentence right away. If the pronoun is the subject, it goes into the subjective case (***we***); if the pronoun is the object, it goes into the objective case (***us***). This usage is correct: *We pilots flew five missions last night.* This sentence is incorrect: *Us pilots few five missions last night.* Leave out the noun in apposition (i.e. *pilots*) and the subjective choice ***we*** is clear: *We flew...*, for you would never say *Us flew....* This usage is correct: *For us pilots, the mission schedule has been exhausting*, where *for* is a preposition and ***us*** is the object, and *pilots* is a noun in apposition to the pronoun. You would not say *For we pilots...*, just as you would not say *For we, the mission schedule was exhausting*.

WEA *abbr* Workers' Educational Association

weak /week/ *adj* **1 NOT STRONG OR FIT** not physically or mentally strong **2 EASILY DEFEATED** easily overcome or defeated **3 LACKING STRENGTH OF CHARACTER** not having strength of character **4 NOT INTENSE** not powerful or intense ○ *weak winter sunshine* **5 LACKING SKILLS OR ABILITIES** not having particular skills or abilities **6 WATERY OR TASTELESS** watery or lacking flavour ○ *weak tea* **7 NOT WORKING TO FULL CAPACITY** not working as well as normal **8 UNCONVINCING** not persuasive or convincing ○ *a weak argument* **9 NOT STRONG POLITICALLY** not politically strong or powerful **10 UNSTRESSED** describes a syllable or word that is not stressed or accented **11 HAVING ACCENT ON NORMALLY UNSTRESSED SYLLABLE** describes verse that has the accent on a syllable that is normally unstressed **12 CHARACTERIZED BY REGULAR INFLECTIONAL ENDINGS** describes a verb whose forms are characterized by regular inflectional endings, not by vowel changes **13 CHARACTERIZED BY FALLING PRICES** falling in price, or characterized by falling prices ○ *a weak market* **14 LACKING IN CONTRAST** not having much contrast between tones [13C. < Old Norse *veikr* 'pliant' < Germanic.]

SPELLCHECK Do not confuse ***weak*** with ***week***, which has a similar sound. Beware: your spellchecker will not catch this error.

SYNONYMS ***weak, feeble, frail, infirm, debilitated, decrepit, enervated***

CORE MEANING: lacking physical strength or energy

weak not physically fit or mentally strong; **feeble** lacking physical or mental strength or health; **frail** in a physically weak state as a result of illness or advanced years; **infirm** lacking strength as a result of long illness or advanced years; **debilitated** with strength and energy temporarily diminished as a result of illness or physical exertion; **decrepit** (*archaic or humorous*) made weak by advanced years; **enervated** made weak and tired by physical or mental exertion.

weaken /wéekən/ *vti* to make somebody or something weak or weaker, or become weak or weaker —**weakener** *n*

weaker sex *n* an offensive term for women considered as a group (*dated*)

weakfish /week fish/ (*plural* **-fish** *or* **-fishes**) *n* ZOOL = **sea trout** *n.* **2** [Late 18C. < obsolete Dutch *weekvisch* 'soft fish' < *week* 'soft' + *visch* 'fish'.]

weak force *n* PHYS = **weak interaction**

weak interaction *n* the fundamental interaction between elementary particles that is mediated by the W and Z particles. It is involved in radioactive decay, which occurs by electron production, and particle decay. One of the four fundamental interactions, it is only effective at distances of less than 10^{-15} metres and is a million million times weaker than the strong interaction.

weak-kneed /-neéd/ *adj* easily persuaded or intimidated (*informal*) —**weak-kneedly** *adv* —**weak-kneedness** *n*

weakling /wéekling/ *n* a person who lacks physical strength or a strong character

weakly /wéekli/ *adj* (**-lier, -liest**) sickly or delicate ■ *adv* with little strength or force ○ *She nodded weakly.* —**weakliness** *n*

weak-minded *adj* **1** easily persuaded or convinced (*disapproving*) **2** an offensive term meaning of low intelligence —**weak-mindedly** *adv* —**weak-mindedness** *n*

weakness /wéeknəss/ *n* **1 LACK OF STRENGTH OR DETERMINATION** lack of strength, power, or determination **2 WEAK POINT** a weak point or flaw in something ○ *Unfortunately, the escape plan had a serious weakness.* **3 CHARACTER FLAW** a failing or defect in somebody's character **4 FONDNESS** a strong liking for something ○ *a weakness for chocolate* **5 OBJECT OF DESIRE** an irresistible object of desire ○ *My weakness is adventure stories.*

weak sister *n US* **1** an offensive term for somebody regarded as a weak or unreliable member or component of a group (*insult*) **2** an offensive term for somebody regarded as timid or cowardly

weak-willed *adj* not having a strong will

weal[1] /weel/ *n* **1** a raised or reddened area on the skin, caused by being hit with something. US term **wheal** *n.* **1** **2** a short-lived raised area on the skin, often red and itchy, caused by something such as a nettle or insect sting or by exposure to an allergen. US term **wheal** *n.* **2** [Early 19C. Alteration of WALE under the influence of WHEAL.]

weal[2] /weel/ *n* **1 STATE OF WELLBEING** a general state of wellbeing, prosperity, and happiness (*literary*) **2 PROSPERITY** fortune or prosperity (*archaic*) **3 BODY POLITIC** the state or the body politic (*archaic*) [Old English *wela* < Indo-European, 'to wish']

Weald /weeld/ once-wooded region in SE England. Area: 1,300 sq. km/500 sq. mi.

wealth /welth/ *n* **1 LARGE AMOUNT OF MONEY** a large amount of money or possessions **2 STATE OF HAVING MUCH MONEY** the state of having plenty of money or possessions ○ *came from a background of great wealth* **3 ABUNDANCE** an abundance or great quantity of something ○ *quoted a wealth of statistics to prove the point* **4 VALUE OF ASSETS** the value of assets owned by an individual or a community ○ *need to determine the college's wealth* **5 WELLBEING** wellbeing or prosperity (*archaic*) [13C. < WEAL[2].]

wealth management *n* a service offered by banks and similar institutions to private customers to assist them in making the best use of their financial assets

wealth tax *n* a tax levied on financial assets above a fixed level. ◊ **capital gains tax**

wealthy /wélthi/ (**-ier, -iest**) *adj* **1** having a large amount of money or possessions **2** enjoying an abundance or great quantity of something —**wealthily** *adv* —**wealthiness** *n*

wean[1] /ween/ *v* **1** *vti* **GIVE FOOD OTHER THAN MOTHER'S MILK** to start feeding a baby or young animal food other than its mother's milk **2** *vt* **STOP SOMEBODY HAVING** to cause somebody to go without something that has become a habit or that is much liked ○ *She had weaned herself away from watching all the soaps on TV.* **3** *vt* **ACCUSTOM SOMEBODY TO SOMETHING FROM CHILDHOOD** to accustom somebody to something from an early age ○ *children weaned on computer games and videos* [Old English *wenian* 'accustom' < Germanic] —**weanedness** /wéenədnəss, weénd-/ *n*

wean[2] /wayn, ween/ *n* a child, especially a young one (*regional*) [Late 17C. Contraction of *wee ane*; *ane* a dialect form of ONE.]

weaner /wéenər/ *n* **1** a young animal that has recently been weaned, especially a pig **2** a person who weans animals, or something used in weaning animals

weanling /wéenling/ *n* a child or young animal that has just been weaned ■ *adj* newly weaned ○ *a weanling lamb*

weapon /wéppən/ *n* **1 DEVICE DESIGNED TO INJURE OR KILL** a device designed to inflict injury or death on an opponent **2 SOMETHING USED TO GAIN ADVANTAGE** something used as a way of getting an advantage in a situation ○ *A teacher's best weapon can be humour.* **3 ANIMAL'S PROTECTIVE PART** an animal part, e.g. claws, used for defence or attack ■ *vt* **GIVE ARMS** to provide somebody with weapons [Old English *wǣpen* < Germanic] —**weaponed** *adj* —**weaponless** *adj*

weaponeer /wéppə neér/ *n* **1** a preparer of a nuclear weapon for detonation **2** a designer of nuclear weapons

weaponry /wéppənri/ *n* **1** all the weapons possessed by an individual, group, or nation **2** techniques for producing weapons

weapons system, weapon system *n* a weapon consisting of two or more major components, e.g. a missile and its ground-based radar guidance

wear[1] /wair/ *v* (**wears, wearing, wore** /wawr/, **worn** /wawrn/) **1** *vt* **USE TO COVER OR ADORN BODY** to have something on all or part of the body as clothing, jewellery, protection, or for another purpose, e.g. to aid sight or hearing, either temporarily or habitually **2** *vt Malaysia, Singapore* **PUT ON** to put on a piece of clothing **3** *vt* **DISPLAY ON FACE** to display, show, or present an expression or physical manifestation of an emotion on the face ○ *wear a smile* **4** *vti* **DAMAGE BY USING OR RUBBING** to damage or alter something by using or rubbing it, or be damaged or altered in this way ○ *The lettering had been worn away by years of use.* **5** *vti* **PRODUCE BY USING OR RUBBING** to produce something, especially a hole, through continued use, pressure, or friction, or be produced in this way ○ *had worn a hole in his sweater* **6** *vti* **RUB OFF** to rub something off or away, or be rubbed off or away **7** *vti* **TIRE OUT** to tire somebody out, or become exhausted **8** *vi* **LAST IN SAME CONDITION** to last in the same, especially good, condition with much use ○ *That fabric doesn't look as if it would wear well.* **9** *vti* **PASS SLOWLY** to pass time slowly, or be passed slowly ○ *We wore the evening away worrying about him.* **10** *vt* **ACCEPT OR TOLERATE** to accept or put up with something (*informal*) ○ *She'll never wear that idea.* **11** *vt* **FLY FLAG** to fly a particular flag or colours as a ship's identification ■ *n* **1 ACT OF WEARING** the act of wearing something, or the condition of being worn **2 DAMAGE FROM BEING USED** damage or deterioration from something being used **3 ABILITY TO LAST** the ability to last without deteriorating **4 CLOTHING OF PARTICULAR KIND** clothing, especially clothing of a particular kind (*often in combination*) ○ *beachwear* [Old English *werian* < Germanic] —**wearer** *n* ◇ **the worse for wear 1** in a poor condition because of much use **2** looking unwell, especially because of being tired ◇ **wear thin 1** to weaken or fail ○ *My patience is wearing rather thin.* **2** to become unacceptable or implausible because of excessive use ○ *That excuse is beginning to wear a bit thin.*

SPELLCHECK See ***ware***.

wear down *vti* to overcome or weaken somebody or something by a gradual process, or be overcome or weakened in this way

wear off *vi* to lose effectiveness or strength gradually

wear out *v* **1** *vti* to use something heavily or for a long time until it is no longer useful, or to become useless through long use **2** *vt* to tire somebody out

wear[2] /wair/ (**wears, wearing, wore** /wawr/, **worn** /wawrn/) *vti* to bring a ship about by turning the stern to windward, or come about in this way [Early 17C. < ?]

Wear /weer/ river in N England, flowing past the city of Durham and emptying into the North Sea. Length: 107 km/67 mi.

wearable /wáirəb'l/ *adj* suitable and in a condition to be worn ■ *n* an item of clothing that can be worn —**wearability** /wáirə bílləti/ *n*

ϟ**wearable computer** *n* a computer small enough to be worn as a fashion accessory

wear and tear /-táir/ *n* damage caused by using something over a period of time

weariful /wéereef'l/ *adj* **1** tedious and causing annoyance or fatigue **2** tired and weary —**wearifully** *adv* —**wearifulness** *n*

weariless /wéereeləss/ *adj* not feeling or showing tiredness —**wearilessly** *adv*

wearing /wáiring/ *adj* **1** tiring or tedious ○ *found the long journey very wearing* **2** made or designed to be worn ○ *wearing apparel* —**wearingly** *adv*

wearing course *n* the upper layer of an asphalt or bitumen carriageway

wearisome /wéereessəm/ *adj* physically or mentally tiring and tedious ○ *a wearisome task* —**wearisomely** *adv* —**wearisomeness** *n*

wearproof /wáir proof/ *adj* able to withstand normal wear or use

weary /wéeri/ *adj* (**-rier, -riest**) **1 TIRED** tired, especially in having run out of strength, patience, or endurance **2 TIRING** tiring or exhausting **3 SHOWING TIREDNESS** showing or characterized by tiredness ■ *vti* (**-ries, -rying, -ried**) **BECOME OR MAKE TIRED OR IMPATIENT** to become or cause somebody to become tired or impatient [Old English *wērig* < Germanic] —**wearily** *adv* —**weariness** *n* —**wearying** *adj* —**wearyingly** *adv*

weasel /wéez'l/ *n* (*plural* **-sels** *or* **-sel**) **1 SMALL MAMMAL WITH LONG BODY** a small carnivorous mammal with a long body and tail, short legs, and brown fur that in northern species may turn white in winter. Genus: *Mustela.* **2 SOMEBODY SLY** a sly or underhand person (*informal insult*) ■ *vi* (**-sels, -selling, -selled**) *US, Can* **BE EVASIVE** to be evasive or try to mislead others [Old English *wesule* < Germanic] —**weaselly** *adj*

weasel out *vi* to try to get out of an obligation or commitment, especially in a cowardly way (*informal*)

weasel words *npl* deliberately misleading or ambiguous language (*informal*) —**weasel-worded** *adj*

weather /wé*th*ər/ *n* **1 STATE OF THE ATMOSPHERE** the state of the atmosphere with regard to temperature, cloudiness, rainfall, wind, and other meteorological conditions **2 BAD WEATHER** adverse weather such as a storm, or the effects of this ○ *protection from the weather* ■ *adj* **1 USED IN WEATHER FORECASTING** used in or relating to weather forecasting **2 WINDWARD** towards the wind ■ *v* **1** *vti* **EXPOSE SOMETHING TO THE WEATHER** to expose something to the weather, or be exposed to it **2** *vti* **CHANGE BECAUSE OF EXPOSURE TO WEATHER** to change colour or become worn because of prolonged exposure to the weather, or cause such a change **3** *vi* **ENDURE THE EFFECTS OF THE WEATHER** to endure the damaging effects of the weather **4** *vt* **COME SAFELY THROUGH A CRISIS** to come safely through a crisis or difficult time **5** *vt* **SAIL WINDWARD OF** to sail on the windward side of something **6** *vt* **SLANT SOMETHING TO KEEP OFF RAIN** to give a slope to something such as a roof to keep off rain [Old English *weder* < Indo-European, 'to blow'] —**weatherability** /wé*th*ərə bílləti/ *n* —**weatherer** *n* ◇ **make heavy weather of something** to make a task that is quite easy to do seem more difficult than it is ◇ **under the weather** slightly unwell

SPELLCHECK Do not confuse ***weather*** with ***wether*** or ***whether***, which sound similar. Beware: your spellchecker will not catch this error.

weather balloon *n* a balloon used to carry meteorological instruments

weather-beaten *adj* damaged, worn, or marked by exposure to the weather ○ *a weather-beaten face*

weatherboard /wé*th*ər bawrd/ *n* **1 BOARD ON BOTTOM OF DOOR** a sloping piece of wood fitted to the bottom of a door to allow rain to run off **2 GROOVED BOARD FOR CLADDING** a grooved piece of timber used as part of a series of overlapping horizontal pieces forming cladding for walls or roofs **3 WINDWARD SIDE** the windward side of a ship ■ *vt* **COVER WITH WEATHERBOARDS** to fit a building with weatherboards

weatherboarding /wé*th*ər bawrding/ *n* weatherboards collectively

weatherbound /wé*th*ər bownd/ *adj* delayed or kept from functioning by bad weather ○ *a weatherbound plane*

weather bureau (*plural* **weather bureaus** *or* **weather bureaux**) *n US* = **weather centre**

weathercast /wé*th*ər kaast/ *n US* METEOROL = **weather forecast** [Mid-19C. Contraction of WEATHER FORECAST.]

weather centre *n* an agency that collects meteorological information and provides weather forecasts. US term **weather bureau**

weather chart *n* = **weather map**

weathercock /wé*th*ər kòk/ *n* **1 WEATHER VANE** a weather vane shaped like a farmyard cock **2 SOMEBODY FICKLE** somebody who changes opinion or allegiance frequently ■ *vi* **TURN IN THE DIRECTION OF THE WIND** to tend to turn in the direction of the wind (*refers to aircraft*)

weather deck *n US* an open deck on a ship

weathered /wé*th*ərd/ *adj* **1 WORN BY EXPOSURE TO WEATHER** worn, damaged, or seasoned by exposure to the weather **2 GIVEN A WEATHERED APPEARANCE** given an artificial appearance of having been exposed to weather **3 ERODED BY WEATHER** describes rocks that have been eroded or changed by the action of the weather **4 WITH A SLOPING SURFACE** having a sloping surface so that rain can run off ○ *a weathered roof*

weather eye *n* **1** the eye of somebody trained to watch for changes in the weather **2** alertness or watchfulness, especially an alertness to change (*informal*) ◇ **keep a weather eye open, keep a weather eye on something** to be alert and watchful for any change or development in something

weather forecast *n* a radio or television broadcast announcing weather conditions —**weather forecaster** *n*

weatherglass /wé*th*ər glaass/ *n* **1** an instrument such as a barometer used to indicate changes in atmospheric conditions **2** = **storm glass**

weathering /wé*th*əring/ *n* **1** the effect of prolonged exposure to the weather on, e.g. a building **2** the disintegration and decomposition of rocks and minerals by natural processes such as the action of frost or percolating groundwater

weatherly /wé*th*ərli/ *adj* capable of sailing close to the wind

weatherman /wé*th*ər man/ (*plural* **-men** /-men/) *n* a man who works as a professional weather forecaster

weather map *n* a map or chart showing the m[eteorological] conditions over a large area

weatherperson /wé*th*ər purss'n/ *n* a profession[al] weather forecaster

weatherproof /wé*th*ər proof/ *adj* able to withstand ex[posure] to rain or bad weather ■ *vt* to make somethin[g] able to withstand exposure to rain or bad weather —**weatherproofness** *n*

weather satellite *n* a satellite that records cloud di[s]tribution and temperature to help in predicting weathe[r] patterns

weather ship *n* a ship that collects meteorological in[formation]

weather station *n* an observation post where me[teorological] conditions are observed and recorded

weather strip *n* a thin piece of material fitted around [a] door or window to stop wind, rain, and cold fro[m] coming through

weatherstrip /wé*th*ər strip/ (**-strips, -stripping, -strippe[d]**) *vt* to put a weather strip around a door or window

weather stripping *n US* = **weather strip**

weather tourist *n* somebody who visits places in orde[r] to be able to experience extreme weather conditio[ns] such as tornadoes and hurricanes —**weather tourism**

weather vane *n* a device, usually mounted on a roo[f] that turns to point in the direction the wind is blowin[g]

weather window *n* a period of time in which weathe[r] conditions are suitable for a particular activity

weather-wise *adj* **1** good at predicting what th[e] weather will be **2** good at predicting what publi[c] opinion will be

weatherworn /wé*th*ər wawrn/ *adj* worn or damaged b[y] exposure to the weather

weave[1] /weev/ *v* (**weaves, weaving, wove** /wōv/ *or* **weave[d]**, **woven** /wōv'n/ *or* **weaved**) **1** *vti* **MAKE CLOTH** to make clot[h] by interlacing threads vertically and horizontally, es[pecially] on a loom **2** *vt* **MAKE SOMETHING BY INTERLACIN[G] STRANDS** to make something by interlacing strands o[r] strips of any material **3** *vti* **SPIN A WEB** to spin somethin[g] such as a spider's web **4** *vt* **CONSTRUCT A STORY** to constru[ct] something such as a story by combining separate par[ts] **5** *vt* **INTRODUCE PARTS INTO SOMETHING LARGER** to introduc[e] separate parts into something larger ○ *weaving ne[w] elements into the plot* ■ *n* **WAY IN WHICH SOMETHING IS WOVE[N]** the way in which something is woven and the patter[n] formed by it ○ *a fabric with an open weave* [Old Englis[h] *wefan* < Germanic] ◇ **get weaving** to hurry and sta[rt] doing something (*dated informal; often a command*)

weave[2] /weev/ (**weaves, weaving, weaved**) *vi* to mov[e] forwards on a zigzag course [Late 16C. < ?]

weaver /wéevər/ *n* **1** a person who weaves, especiall[y] professionally **2** BIRDS = **weaver bird**

weaverbird /wéevər burd/, **weaver finch** *n* a gregariou[s] finch known for its communal woven nest. Native t[o] Africa, Asia. Family: Ploceidae.

web /web/ *n* **1 WOVEN FABRIC** a piece of fabric created b[y] weaving **2 SPIDER'S CONSTRUCTION** a delicate structure o[f] threads woven by a spider or other arachnid to catc[h] prey **3 MEMBRANE BETWEEN ANIMAL TOES** a membrane of ski[n] joining the digits of an animal's foot, especially the foo[t] of a bird or amphibian **4 COMPLEX NETWORK** a comple[x] structure, network, or design ○ *a web of interconnectin[g] wires* ○ *a web of deceit* **5 THIN METAL PLATE** a thin plate o[r] strip of metal such as the blade of a saw **6 BARBS ON TH[E] SHAFT OF A FEATHER** the barbs on either side of the shaft o[f] a feather **7 RIBBED SURFACE IN A VAULT** a ribbed surfac[e] within a vaulted structure **8 PRINTING PAPER** a roll of pape[r] that is used on a rotary printing press ■ *vi* (**web[s], webbing, webbed**) **FORM A WEB** to form or produce [a] web [Old English < Indo-European, 'weave'] —**webbed** *a[dj]*

ϟ**Web** /web/ *n* the World Wide Web (*informal*)

Webb /web/, **Sir Aston** (1849–1930) British architect

webbing /wébbing/ *n* **1 STRONG COARSE FABRIC** strong coars[e] fabric. Use: belts, harnesses, upholstery support. **2 SKI[N] OF THE FOOT** the membrane of skin joining the digit[s] of an animal's foot, especially the foot of a bird o[r] amphibian **3 SOMETHING FORMING A WEB** something tha[t] forms a web

ϟ**Web browser, web browser** *n* a program used fo[r] displaying and viewing pages on the World Wide We[b]

ϟ**Web bug** *n* a minute inclusion in a web page or e[-]mail message designed to record information about th[e] person reading it

Webcam /wéb kam/, **webcam** *n* a video camera recording pictures that are broadcast live on the Internet [Late 20C. Blend of WEB + CAMERA.]

Webcast /wéb kaast/, **webcast** *n* a broadcast made on the World Wide Web ○ *'...they spent $5 million promoting the live Webcast of their Spring Fashion Show ...'* (*The New York Times*; April 1999) [Late 20C. Blend of WEB + BROADCAST.]

Webcasting /wéb kaasting/, **webcasting** *n* the use of the World Wide Web as a medium to broadcast information [Late 20C. Blend of WEB + BROADCASTING.]

Web crawler, web crawler *n* a program used to search through pages on the World Wide Web for documents containing a particular set of words, a phrase, or a topic

Web-enable *vt* to make a device such as a mobile phone capable of accessing the Internet —**Web-enabled** *adj*

Weber /váybər/ *n* (*symbol* **Wb**) the SI unit of magnetic flux, equal to 1 joule per ampere or 1 volt-second [Late 19C. After Wilhelm Eduard *Weber* (1804–91), German physicist.]

Weber /váybər/, **Carl Maria von** (1786–1826) German composer

Weber, Max (1864–1920) German economist and sociologist

Webern /váybərn/, **Anton Friedrich Wilhelm von** (1883–1945) Austrian composer

Web folio *n* a collection of Web pages with an underlying defining theme, e.g. the pages of an electronic book or the electronic images of an artist's portfolio

Webfoot /wéb fòot/ (*plural* **webfeet** /-feet/) *n* **1** a foot that has the toes joined by a membrane of skin **2** an animal with webbed feet —**web-footed** /wéb fòotid/ *adj*

Webhead /wéb hed/, **webhead** *n* a frequent user of the World Wide Web (*slang*)

Webisode /wébbi sōd/, **webisode** *n* an episode, preview, or promotion of a film, television programme, or music video on a website (*slang*) [Late 20C. Blend of WEB + EPISODE.]

Webliography /wébbli óggrəfi/ (*plural* **-phies**), **webliography** (*plural* **-phies**) *n* **1** a list of particular documents available on the World Wide Web **2** a list or catalogue of all the Web-based material relating to a particular subject [Late 20C. Blend of WEB + BIBLIOGRAPHY.]

Weblish /wéb lish/ *n* the form of English used globally online, with characteristic features such as the omission of apostrophes and capital letters, the use of abbreviations, and the rapid absorption of new words [Late 20C. Blend of WEB + ENGLISH.]

Weblog /wéb log/ *n* a frequently updated personal journal chronicling links to a website, intended for public viewing —**Weblogger** *n*

Webmaster /wéb maastər/, **webmaster** *n* a creator, organizer, or updater of information on a website

Web member *n* a brace that links the top and bottom flanges of a lattice girder or truss

Web offset *n* offset printing carried out on a web press

Web page, web page *n* a computer file, encoded in hypertext markup language (**HTML**) and containing text, graphics files, and sound files, that is accessible through the World Wide Web

Webphone /wéb fōn/ *n* a phone that uses the Internet to make connections and carry voice messages

Web press *n* a printing press that is fed paper from a large roll

Web ring, web ring *n* a series of interlinked websites that are visited in sequential order, eventually returning to the original site

Web server, web server *n* a program such as a Web browser that serves up Web pages when requested by a client

Website /wéb sīt/, **Web site** *n* a computer program that runs a Web server that provides access to a group of related Web pages

Web spinner *n* an insect that spins a web, especially one with glands that produce a kind of silk used to construct a web. Order: Embioptera.

Webster /wébstər/, **John** (1580?–1623?) English playwright

Webster, Noah (1758–1843) US lexicographer

Web storefront *n US* a virtual store on the World Wide Web providing merchant information about the retailer, a product catalogue, and secure payment facilities (*in e-commerce*)

webwheel /wéb weel/ *n* a wheel with no spokes but a web or plate instead, or a wheel with the centre formed from one piece

webworm /wéb wurm/ (*plural* **-worms** *or* **-worm**) *n US* a caterpillar, especially a tiger moth caterpillar, that spins a web in which it feeds or rests

⚡**Webzine** /wéb zeen/ *n* ONLINE = **e-zine**

wed /wed/ (**weds, wedding, wedded** *or* **wed**) *v* **1** *vt* MARRY to marry somebody (*formal or literary*) **2** *vi* GET MARRIED to become married to somebody **3** *vt* JOIN A COUPLE IN MARRIAGE to join two people in marriage **4** *vt* UNITE THINGS to bring two things together or regard them as linked ○ *The two concepts had become wedded in his mind.* [Old English *weddian* < Indo-European, 'pledge']

we'd /weed/ *contr* **1** we had **2** we would

Wed. *abbr* Wednesday

wedded /wéddid/ *adj* **1** MARRIED united in marriage **2** OF MARRIAGE relating to marriage ○ *wedded bliss* **3** COMMITTED strongly attached or committed to something ○ *wedded to the idea of reform*

Weddell Sea /wédd'l-/ arm of the South Atlantic Ocean, south of Cape Horn and the Falkland Islands

wedding /wédding/ *n* **1** MARRIAGE CEREMONY a marriage ceremony, or the act of marrying (*often before nouns*) ○ *a wedding veil* **2** WEDDING ANNIVERSARY the anniversary of a marriage (*in combination*) ○ *a silver wedding* **3** UNITING OF TWO THINGS the bringing together of two things ○ *the wedding of form and function*

wedding band *n US* = **wedding ring**

wedding breakfast *n* a celebratory meal served after a wedding ceremony

wedding cake *n* a cake, often a fruit cake, decorated with icing, usually white, and arranged in tiers, served at a wedding reception

wedding-cake *adj* characterized by an extremely ornate style of architecture

wedding dress *n* a dress worn by a bride at her wedding

wedding march *n* a piece of music in march time played during a marriage ceremony, usually when the bride enters the church

wedding ring *n* a ring, usually a gold band, worn on the third finger of the left hand by somebody who is married

Wedekind /váydə kint/, **Frank** (1864–1918) German playwright. Full name **Benjamin Franklin Wedekind**

~~**Wedensday**~~ incorrect spelling of **Wednesday**

wedge /wej/ *n* **1** TAPERING BLOCK a solid block that is thick at one end and thin at the other, used to secure or separate two objects **2** WEDGE-SHAPED OBJECT an object that has a wedge shape ○ *a wedge of cake* **3** SOMETHING THAT ACTS AS A WEDGE something that acts as a wedge, e.g. by causing division ○ *drove a wedge between the two families* **4** CLOTHING = **wedge heel** **5** GOLF CLUB a golf club with a markedly slanted head, used to hit the ball along a high arcing trajectory **6** STROKE IN CUNEIFORM WRITING a wedge-shaped stroke used in cuneiform writing ■ *v* (**wedges, wedging, wedged**) **1** *vt* FORCE APART WITH A WEDGE to force something apart or open with a wedge **2** *vt* SECURE WITH A WEDGE to secure or tighten something with a wedge **3** *vti* SQUEEZE to squeeze or pack something into a small space, or to be squeezed or packed in this way ○ *Hundreds of people were wedged into the room.* [Old English *wecg* < Germanic, probably < Indo-European, 'ploughshare, wedge'] —**wedgy** *adj*

wedge heel *n* **1** a shoe heel shaped like a wedge, forming a solid extension of the sole so that there is no gap under the instep **2** a shoe with a wedge heel

wedge-tailed eagle *n* a large eagle with dark brown or black plumage and tail feathers in the form of a wedge. Native to: Australia. *Aquila audax.*

wedgie /wéjji/ *n* **1** a wedge heel (*informal*) **2** *Aus* a practical joke that involves grabbing the top of somebody's pants or panties and giving a sharp upward pull

Wedgwood /wéj wòod/, **Josiah** (1730–95) British potter

Wedgwood blue *adj* pale grey-blue in colour [Early 20C. After Josiah WEDGWOOD.] —**Wedgwood blue** *n*

wedlock /wéd lok/ *n* the state of being married [12C. By folk etymology from *wedlac* 'action of pledging' < *wed* 'pledge', by association with LOCK[1].] ◇ **born** *or* **conceived out of wedlock** born to *or* conceived by parents who are not married (*formal*)

Wednesday /wénz day, -di/ *n* the third day of the week, coming after Tuesday and before Thursday [Old English *wōdnesdæg* 'Odin's day' < *Woden* 'Odin' (chief deity of the Germanic peoples) + *dæg* 'day', a translation of Latin *Mercurii dies* 'Mercury's day']

Wednesdays /wénz dayz, -diz/ *adv* every Wednesday ○ *Wednesdays I leave a little early.*

~~**Wednsday**~~ incorrect spelling of **Wednesday**

wee[1] /wee/ *adj* very small ■ *n Scotland* a brief period of time ○ *bide a wee* [Old English *wǣg* 'weight']

wee[2] /wee/ *n* (*informal or babytalk*) **1** URINE urine **2** ACT OF URINATING an act or instance of urinating ■ *vi* (**wees, weeing, weed**) URINATE to urinate [Mid-20C. An imitation of the sound of urinating.]

weed[1] /weed/ *n* **1** UNWANTED PLANT a plant, especially a wild plant, growing where it is not wanted **2** UNWANTED PLANTS weeds in general (*often before nouns*) ○ *weed control* **3** PLANT GROWING IN WATER a plant that grows in water, especially seaweed **4** TOBACCO tobacco or cigarettes (*slang*) **5** MARIJUANA marijuana for smoking as a drug (*slang*) **6** WEAK PERSON a weak or strikingly thin person (*informal*) **7** INFERIOR ANIMAL an inferior animal, especially a horse that cannot be bred ■ *v* **1** *vt* REMOVE WEEDS FROM THE GROUND to clear an area of weeds ○ *to weed the garden* **2** *vi* PULL UP WEEDS to pull up and remove weeds ○ *spent several hours weeding* [Old English *wēod* < Germanic] —**weeder** *n*

weed out *vt* to separate out or remove somebody or something undesirable or unwanted ○ *a test to weed out unsuitable candidates*

weed[2] /weed/ *n* something worn as a sign of mourning, especially a black band around a sleeve or hat ■ **weeds** *npl* the black clothes once traditionally worn by widows (*archaic or literary*) [Old English *wǣd* < Germanic, 'garment']

weedkiller /wéed killər/ *n* a chemical that kills plants by attacking the root, leaf, or vascular system

weedy /wéedi/ (**-ier, -iest**) *adj* **1** FULL OF WEEDS filled with or containing many weeds ○ *a weedy patch of ground* **2** LIKE A WEED resembling or having the characteristics of a weed ○ *weedy plants* **3** THIN strikingly thin and weak-looking (*insult*) **4** WEAK physically or morally weak (*informal*) —**weedily** *adv* —**weediness** *n*

Wee Free /wée frée/ *n Scotland* a member of the Free Kirk, a body that broke away from the Free Church of Scotland in 1900 (*offensive in some contexts*) [Early 20C. Because it was a minority body of the Free Church of Scotland.]

wee hours *npl* = **wee small hours**

week /week/ *n* **1** 7-DAY PERIOD a period of seven consecutive days **2** CALENDAR WEEK a period of seven days beginning from a particular day, usually Sunday ○ *the middle of the week* **3** WORKING WEEK the days of the week on which somebody works, or the time that is spent working ○ *goes to bed early during the week* **4** SPECIAL WEEK a week containing a particular holiday, or dedicated to a particular cause ○ *Easter week* ■ *adv* ONE WEEK AFTER A PARTICULAR DAY one week after or before a particular day ○ *arranged to meet on Thursday week* [Old English *wice* < Germanic, 'series, succession']

SPELLCHECK See ***weak***.

weekday /wéek day/ *n* a day of the week other than Sunday, or, sometimes, other than Saturday or Sunday ○ *only open on weekdays*

weekend /wéek énd/ *n* the end of the week, from Friday evening until Sunday evening ■ *vi* to spend a weekend or weekends in a particular place

weekend bag *n* a bag or small suitcase used to carry clothes and other items needed for a short trip or holiday

weekender /wéek éndər/ *n* **1** somebody spending a weekend somewhere, especially on a regular basis **2** *Aus* a holiday house (*informal*)

weekends /wéek éndz/ *adv* at or during the weekend (*informal*)

weeklong /wéek lóng/ *adj* lasting for a whole week

weekly /wéekli/ *adj* **1** HAPPENING ONCE A WEEK happening, produced, or done once a week or every week **2** CALCULATED BY THE WEEK worked out by the week ○ *weekly pay* ■ *adv* **1** ONCE A WEEK once each week ○ *does the shopping weekly* **2** EVERY WEEK every single week **3** BY THE WEEK by the week ○ *gets paid weekly* ■ *n* (*plural* **-lies**) SOMETHING PUBLISHED ONCE A WEEK a newspaper or magazine published once a week

weeknight /weék nīt/ *n* the evening or night of a weekday ○ *I'm not letting you go out on a weeknight.*

weenie /weéni/ *n US* 1 an offensive term for somebody regarded as weak or insignificant (*slang insult*) 2 an offensive term for a penis (*slang*)

weensy /weénzi/ *adj* = **weeny** (*informal*)

weeny /weéni/ (**-nier, -niest**) *adj* very small (*informal*) [Late 18C. < WEE[1] after *tiny*.]

weeny-bopper *n* a child, especially a young girl, who is keen on pop music and the latest fashions (*informal*) ◊ **teenybopper**

weep /weep/ *v* (**weeps, weeping, wept** /wept/, **wept**) 1 *vi* CRY to shed tears ○ *They walked behind the coffin, weeping silently.* 2 *vt* EXPRESS SOMETHING WHILE CRYING OR BY CRYING TEARS to express something while crying or by crying tears 3 *vti* MOURN to lament or cry tears for somebody or something (*literary*) 4 *vti* LEAK FLUID to leak, drip, or ooze drops of liquid ○ *The eye was inflamed and weeping* ■ *n* SPELL OF CRYING a period of time spent crying [Old English *wēpan* < Germanic]

weeper /weépər/ *n* 1 SOMEBODY WHO WEEPS a person who weeps 2 SIGN OF MOURNING something that is worn as a sign of mourning such as a black armband or a veil 3 HOLE FOR WATER TO ESCAPE a hole in a wall or foundation that allows accumulated water to escape ■ **weepers** *npl* SIDEBURNS long sideburns (*informal*)

weepie /weépi/, **weepy** (*plural* **-ies**) *n* a film, play, or book that tends to move people to tears, especially one that is blatantly sentimental in tone (*informal*)

weeping /weéping/ *adj* 1 WITH DROOPING BRANCHES having slender drooping branches ○ *a weeping birch* 2 CRYING shedding tears 3 LEAKING FLUID leaking, dripping, or oozing drops of liquid —**weepingly** *adv*

weeping fig, weeping ivy *n* a small fig tree with glossy leaves, often grown as a houseplant. *Ficus benjamina.*

weeping willow *n* a popular ornamental willow tree with long drooping branches and narrow leaves. Native to: China. *Salix babylonica.*

weepy /weépi/ *adj* (**-ier, -iest**) 1 inclined to weep (*informal*) 2 tending to make people cry ■ *n* (*plural* **-ies**) CINEMA, THEATRE = **weepie** (*informal*) —**weepily** *adv* —**weepiness** *n*

wee small hours *npl* the early hours of the morning, especially those just after midnight

weever /weévər/, **weeverfish** /weévər fish/ (*plural* **-fishes** *or* **-fish**) *n* a small marine fish with a single long spine on each gill cover and several on its back. Family: Trachinidae. [Early 17C. Probably < Old N French *wivre* (see WYVERN).]

weevil /weév'l/ *n* 1 DESTRUCTIVE BEETLE WITH A SNOUT a beetle with a long head that forms a snout or rostrum. Family: Curculionidae. 2 PEA OR BEAN PEST a beetle whose larvae live in the seeds of peas and beans. Family: Bruchidae and Lariidae. 3 BEETLE LIKE A WEEVIL any beetle similar to a weevil including many that are pests. Family: Rhynchophora. [Old English *wifel* 'beetle' < Indo-European, 'move quickly'] —**weevily** *adj*

wee-wee *n* (*informal babytalk*) 1 ACT OF URINATING an act or instance of urinating 2 URINE urine (*offensive in some contexts*) ■ *vi* (**wee-wees, wee-weeing, wee-weed**) URINATE to urinate (*babytalk*) [Repetition of WEE[2]]

weft /weft/ *n* 1 HORIZONTAL THREADS the horizontal threads of a woven fabric or a tapestry. ◊ **warp** *n.* 3 2 YARN FOR THE WEFT yarn used for the weft 3 SOMETHING WOVEN an article or piece of woven fabric [Old English < Indo-European, 'weave']

Wegener /váygənər/, **Alfred** (1880–1930) German meteorologist

Wehrmacht /váir maakht, -maakt/ *n* the German armed forces, especially the army between 1935 and 1945 [Mid-20C. < German, 'defence force'.]

weigela /wī jeélə, wi geélə/ *n* a shrub with bell-shaped pink, white, or red flowers. Native to: Asia. Genus: *Weigela*. [Mid-19C. < modern Latin *Weigela*, after Christian E. *Weigel* (1748–1831), German physician.]

weigh[1] /way/ *v* 1 *vt* FIND THE WEIGHT OF to find out the weight of somebody or something ○ *He weighed himself regularly.* 2 *vi* BE A PARTICULAR WEIGHT to be of a particular weight 3 *vt* MEASURE BY WEIGHT to measure or distribute something by weight ○ *weighed out a kilo of onions* 4 *vt* EVALUATE to consider or evaluate something, especially so as to be able to come to a decision or choice ○ *had to weigh all possible options* 5 *vi* HAVE IMPORTANCE to have importance or be influential 6 *vt* GUESS THE WEIGHT OF to hold something in the hand in order to assess its weight 7 *vi* BE BURDENSOME to be burdensome, oppressive, or worrying to somebody ○ *The problem weighed heavily on my mind.* 8 *vti* RAISE ANCHOR to raise the anchor of a vessel [Old English *wegan* 'weigh, carry' < Indo-European, 'carry'] —**weighable** *adj* —**weigher** *n*

SPELLCHECK See ***way***

weigh against *vt* 1 to assess the relative importance of one thing in relation to another ○ *had to weigh the added costs against the gain in speed* 2 to have a negative part in influencing a decision with regard to somebody or something ○ *Her lack of experience weighed against her in the final selection.*

weigh down *vt* 1 to be oppressive or burdensome to somebody ○ *weighed down by grief* ○ *weighed down with extra paperwork* 2 to press somebody or something down by exerting weight ○ *trees weighed down with fruit*

weigh in *vi* 1 BE WEIGHED FOR A RACE OR CONTEST to be weighed before or after a race or contest such as a boxing match or horse race 2 HAVE BAGGAGE WEIGHED to have baggage weighed before a flight 3 CONTRIBUTE A COMMENT to contribute or produce something such as an argument or comment, especially in an assertive way (*informal*)

weigh up *vt* 1 to consider something carefully, especially so as to come to a decision or choice ○ *weighing up the pros and cons* 2 to judge the qualities or character of somebody or something (*informal*) ○ *The two boys weighed each other up.*

weigh[2] /way/ [Late 18C. By folk etymology < WAY by association with WEIGH[1] in *weigh anchor*.] ◇ **under weigh** while a ship is in motion, not in port or at anchor

weighbridge /wáy brij/ *n* a weighing machine for vehicles, consisting of a metal plate set into a road

weigh-in /wáy in/ *n* the weighing of a competitor before or after a race or contest

weight /wayt/ *n* 1 HEAVINESS the heaviness of somebody or something ○ *Just feel the weight of it!* 2 MEASURE OF SOMEBODY'S HEAVINESS the specific amount that a person or animal weighs ○ *I had lost 10 pounds in weight.* 3 SYSTEM FOR MEASURING HEAVINESS a system of standard measures of weight 4 FORCE CAUSED BY GRAVITY (*symbol* W) the vertical force experienced by a mass because of gravity 5 UNIT OF WEIGHT a unit used as a measure of weight 6 HEAVY OBJECT a heavy object used to hold something down 7 MENTAL BURDEN a mental or moral burden or load 8 HEAVY LOAD a heavy load to carry ○ *had to put him down since he was a heavy weight* 9 IMPORTANCE importance or significance ○ *a motion that did not carry much weight with the judge* 10 GREATER PART the preponderance or greater part of something 11 HEAVINESS OF TYPEFACE the heaviness or thickness of a typeface 12 OBJECT USED IN WEIGHTLIFTING a heavy object used in weightlifting or for exercise (*often plural*) 13 THICKNESS OF CLOTH the heaviness or thickness of cloth (*often in combination*) ■ *vt* 1 ADD WEIGHT TO to add weight or weights to something 2 BIAS to slant something in somebody's favour ○ *The choice of candidate was heavily weighted in her favour.* 3 INCREASE DENSITY OF FABRIC to treat fabric so as to increase its density 4 ASSIGN A HORSE A HANDICAP WEIGHT to assign a handicap weight to a horse [Old English *wiht* < Indo-European] —**weighter** *n* ◇ **be worth its** *or* **your weight in gold** to be extremely valuable ◇ **pull your weight** to do your fair share of work or take your fair share of responsibility ◇ **throw your weight around** *or* **about** to be domineering

SPELLCHECK See ***wait.***

weighted /wáytid/ *adj* adjusted by the addition of a statistical value

weighting /wáyting/ *n* additional pay given in particular cases, e.g. to somebody who has to live in a place where the cost of living is higher ○ *The job carries an inner London weighting.*

weightless /wáytləss/ *adj* having no weight, especially by virtue of being in an atmosphere in which there is no gravitational pull —**weightlessly** *adv* —**weightlessness** *n*

weightlifting /wáyt lifting/ *n* the sport of lifting heavy weights, either for exercise or in competition —**weightlifter** *n*

weight training *n* physical training using weights to strengthen the muscles

weighty /wáyti/ (**-ier, -iest**) *adj* 1 HEAVY weighing a great deal 2 IMPORTANT of an important or serious nature ○ *discussing weighty matters* 3 INFLUENTIAL able to exert influence 4 OPPRESSIVE oppressive or burdensome ○ *weighty responsibility* —**weightily** *adv* —**weightiness** *n*

Weil /vīl/, **Simone** (1909–43) French philosopher and mystic

Weill /vīl/, **Kurt** (1900–50) German-born US composer

Weil's disease /vílz-/ *n* a severe form of leptospirosis usually resulting from contact with the urine of infected animals such as rats [Late 19C. After H. Adolf *Weil* (1848–1916), German physician.]

Weimar /vím aar/ city in east-central Germany. Population: 61,583 (1990).

Weimaraner /vímə raanər, wímə-, -raánər/ *n* a large hunting dog of a breed with a short-haired silver-grey coat, originally bred in Germany [Mid-20C. After WEIMAR.]

Weimar Republic /vím aar-/ *n* the government of Germany between 1919 and 1933, so named because the National Assembly met in Weimar in 1919 to establish a new republic and draw up a constitution

Weiner /weénər/, **Lawrence** (*b.* 1942) US conceptual arti

weir /weer/ *n* 1 a dam built across a river to regulate the flow of water, divert it, or change its level 2 a fence placed in a stream to catch fish [Old English *wer* < Indo-European, 'cover']

Weir /weer/, **Peter** (*b.* 1944) Australian film director

weird /weerd/ *adj* 1 ODD strange or unusual 2 SUPERNATUR belonging to or suggesting the supernatural 3 OF FA relating to or influenced by fate (*archaic*) ■ *n Scotland* FATE fate or destiny (*archaic*) ○ *to dree your weird* [Old English *wyrd* 'fate' < Indo-European, 'turn'] —**weirdly** *adv* —**weirdness** *n*

weirdie /weérdi/, **weirdy** (*plural* **-ies**) *n* a strange or unconventional person (*informal*)

weirdo /weérdō/ *n* an offensive term for somebody who behaves in a way regarded as strange or unconventional, especially somebody whose sexual taste or habits are regarded as unusual

weird sisters, Weird Sisters *npl* 1 the Fates 2 the three witches in Shakespeare's play *Macbeth* [*Weird* in the meaning of 'having the power to control fates']

weirdy *n* = **weirdie** (*informal*)

Weismann /vísm'n/, **August** (1834–1914) German biologist

Weismannism /víssmənizəm/ *n* the principle that the inherited characteristics of any organism are determined solely by material (**germ plasm**) contained in the male and female sex cells from which the organism develops [Late 19C. After August WEISMANN.]

Weizmann /vítsmən/, **Chaim** (1874–1952) Russian-born Israeli chemist and statesman

weka /wáykə/ *n* a flightless fast-running bird with mainly brown and black plumage. Native to: scrubland of New Zealand. *Gallirallus australis*. [Mid-19C. < Maori, an imitation of bird's call.]

welch *vi* = **welsh**

welcome /wélkəm/ *adj* 1 RECEIVED GLADLY received or entertained glady and generously ○ *a welcome gift* 2 EAGERLY AND DELIGHTEDLY ACCEPTED accepted or anticipated with delight and eagerness, often because it answers a nee ○ *It was a welcome break after two solid weeks of writin* 3 FREELY INVITED OR PERMITTED freely and willingly invite or permitted ○ *You're welcome to stay for dinner.* 4 WI NOTHING EXPECTED IN RETURN with no obligation incurre by a courtesy, favour, gift, or something else give ○ *You're very welcome, it was no trouble.* ■ *n* 1 AC NOWLEDGMENT OF SOMEBODY'S ARRIVAL a greeting or receptio given to somebody upon arrival or being met ○ *a war welcome to their guests* 2 REACTION TO a particular respons or reaction to something ○ *Local authorities have extend a cautious welcome to the new proposals.* ■ *vt* (**-come -coming, -comed**) 1 RECEIVE IN A PARTICULAR WAY to gree receive, or entertain somebody in a particular wa 2 ACCEPT IN A PARTICULAR WAY to accept or receive some thing in a particular way ○ *We welcome any feedback fro our customers.* ■ *interj* USED AS GREETING used to expres a friendly or courteous greeting to somebody who ha just arrived or is a stranger [Old English *wilcuma* 'welcor guest' (influenced by WELL[2] and either Old Norse *velkominn* or Old French *bien venu*) < *willa*] —**welcomely** *adv* —**welcomeness** *n* —**welcomer** *n* ◇ **be welcome to something** used to indicate that the speaker is happy for somebody to have something (*often used ironically*) ◇ **wear out** *or* **outstay** *or* **overstay your welcome** to stay longer than is polite or accept somebody's hospitality for too long

welcome mat *n* a doormat, especially one with the word 'welcome' on it ◇ **put out** *or* **roll out the welcome mat for somebody** *US* to make somebody feel very welcome (*informal*)

welcome page *n* ONLINE = **home page** *n.* 1

welcome swallow *n* a swallow with a long forked tail, glossy dark-blue back and wings, grey underparts, and a reddish throat. Native to: S and E Australia. *Hirundo neoxena*.

weld[1] /weld/ *v* 1 *vti* FUSE MATERIAL BY HEATING to join together pieces or parts of some material by heating, hammering, or using other pressure, or to be joined in this way ○ *to weld two pieces of iron together* 2 *vt* REPAIR OR CONSTRUCT SOMETHING BY FUSING to repair or construct something by heating its pieces or parts so that they fuse together ○ *to weld a metal sculpture* 3 *vti* ASSOCIATE OR BECOME ASSOCIATED to join or become joined in a union or a close association ■ *n* 1 FUSION OF PARTS the union or fusion of parts or pieces 2 JOINT FORMED BY FUSION a joint where pieces or parts have been fused together [Late 16C. Alteration of WELL[1] (verb) in the obsolete meaning of 'liquefy by heating'; influenced by its past participle *welled*.] —**weldability** /wéldə bíllәti/ *n* —**weldable** *adj* —**welder** *n*

weld[2] /weld/ *n* a yellow dye extracted from the dyer's rocket plant. Use: colourant for wool and other fabrics. [14C. Ultimately < Germanic.]

Weld /weld/, **Frederick Aloysius** (1823–91) British-born New Zealand statesman

welfare /wél fair/ *n* 1 PHYSICAL, SOCIAL, AND FINANCIAL WELLBEING the physical, social, and financial conditions under which somebody may live satisfactorily 2 *US, Can* AID TO PEOPLE IN NEED financial aid and other benefits for people who are unemployed, below a specified income level, or otherwise requiring assistance, especially when provided by a government agency or programme ■ *adj* 1 AIDING PEOPLE IN NEED concerning or designed to aid people who are poor, unemployed, or in need of assistance in some other way ○ *a welfare agency* 2 *US, Can* RECEIVING GOVERNMENT AID OWING TO NEED receiving government financial aid or benefits because of income level, unemployment, or other conditions that create a need for assistance ○ *welfare clients* [14C. Contraction of *well fare*.]

welfare state *n* 1 a political system in which a government assumes the primary responsibility for assuring the basic health, education, and financial wellbeing of all its citizens through programmes and direct assistance 2 a nation whose government assumes primary responsibility for the social welfare of its citizens

welfare work *n US* the efforts of an organization, community, or agency to improve the living conditions and economic status of its socially disadvantaged members, residents, or citizens —**welfare worker** *n*

welfarism /wél fair izәm/ *n* the policies, practices, and beliefs that characterize the welfare state (*disapproving*) —**welfarist** *n*

welkin /wélkin/ *n* the sky, heaven, or the upper air (*archaic or literary*) [Old English *weolcen, wolc(e)n* 'cloud, firmament' < Germanic]

Welkom /wélkәm, vélk-/ town in central South Africa. Population: 185,500 (1985).

well[1] /wel/ *n* 1 HOLE MADE TO DRAW UP FLUIDS a hole or shaft that is dug or drilled into the ground in order to obtain water, brine, petroleum, or natural gas ○ *an oil well* 2 SPRING OF WATER a place where water comes out of the ground as a natural source ○ *get their water from a well* 3 SOURCE a source of a freely and abundantly available supply of something ○ *a well of information* 4 CONTAINER FOR LIQUID a container or sunken area for holding ink or another liquid ○ *a well on a cutting board* 5 VERTICAL PASSAGE IN A BUILDING a vertical space within or enclosed by a building, often used as a passageway for stairs or lifts or for air and light 6 SPACE IN CENTRE OF COURTROOM the open space in the centre of a courtroom 7 ENCLOSURE FOR A SHIP'S PUMPS an enclosed area in the hold of a ship in which the pumps are located 8 SHIPBOARD CONTAINER FOR FISH a compartment in a fishing boat in which freshly caught fish are held 9 ENCLOSING COMPARTMENT a compartment that encloses or is used to store something temporarily such as the retracted wheels of an aircraft in flight ■ *v* 1 *vti* RISE OR BRING TO THE SURFACE to rise or flow to the surface from inside the earth or the body, or to cause something to do this ○ *Tears welled up in his eyes.* ○ *The fountain welled a stream of clear water into the basin below.* 2 *vi* GROW STRONGER to surge from within or grow stronger so as to threaten to burst forth ○ *Fear welled up inside me.* 3 *vi* BECOME FILLED WITH LIQUID to become filled with a pool of water, tears, or another liquid ○ *My eyes welled with tears.* [Old English *wella* 'spring of water' and *wellan* 'boil' < Indo-European, 'turn']

well[2] /wel/ (**better** /béttәr/, **best** /best/) CORE MEANING: a grammatical word indicating that something is satisfactory or is performed in a satisfactory way ○ *She did very well in her test.*

1 *adv* PLEASINGLY OR DESIRABLY in an efficient, satisfying, or otherwise desirable way (*often in combination*) ○ *I thought the party went very well.* 2 *adv* ETHICALLY OR PROPERLY in an ethical, proper, or courteous way ○ *He always treated the children very well.* 3 *adv* SKILFULLY OR EXPERTLY with proficiency, skill, or expertise (*often in combination*) ○ *She plays tennis really well.* 4 *adv* JUSTLY AND APPROPRIATELY with justice and good reason ○ *I could not very well refuse her request.* 5 *adv* COMFORTABLY in ease and comfort (*often in combination*) ○ *I just want to be rich enough to live well.* 6 *adv* ADVANTAGEOUSLY in a way that promotes somebody's advantage and wellbeing (*often in combination*) ○ *She married well – her husband is wealthy.* 7 *adv* CONDUCIVE TO GOOD HEALTH in a way that promotes health and physical wellbeing (*often in combination*) ○ *Both mother and baby are doing well.* 8 *adv* CONSIDERABLY to a considerable extent, distance, or degree (*often in combination*) ○ *I was well prepared for the exams.* 9 *adv* FULLY AND THOROUGHLY in a complete and thorough way (*often in combination*) ○ *Stir the mixture well, then turn it out onto a baking sheet.* 10 *adv* WITH CERTAINTY with no doubt whatever about something ○ *As you well know, I will not tolerate any laziness* 11 *adv* FAMILIARLY AND INTIMATELY in a familiar and intimate way ○ *I knew them well when they were students.* 12 *adv* GOOD-NATUREDLY taking something in a tolerant or good-humoured way ○ *I teased him but he took it well.* 13 *adv* VERY very or completely (*slang*) ○ *He was well drunk last night.* 14 *adj* IN GOOD HEALTH mentally and physically healthy ○ *I don't feel very well.* ○ *There's a well baby clinic every Wednesday.* 15 *adj* PROPER OR APPROPRIATE suitable, proper, or appropriate in the circumstances ○ *It is as well that you apologized to her.* 16 *adj* HIGHLY SATISFACTORY in a good, pleasing, or satisfying condition ○ *Is everything well with you?* 17 *interj* EXPRESSING EMOTION expresses surprise, agreement, indignation, disapproval, or some other emotion ○ *Well! You've finally come back!* 18 *interj* INTRODUCING OR RESUMING introduces a comment or statement, or resumes a conversation ○ *Well, it looks as if we'll be waiting a while.* [Old English *wel(l)* < Indo-European, 'to wish'] ◇ **as well** in addition to something ○ *The members were mostly young couples, but there were several grandparents as well.* ◇ **as well as** to an equal degree or extent ○ *Banking, as well as other businesses, will take the demographics into consideration.* ◇ **be as well to do something** to be advisable or sensible to do something ○ *It would be as well to look at all the building societies before investing your savings.* ◇ **be well out of something** to be fortunate in having escaped from a difficult or unhappy situation ○ *You're well out of it – they weren't treating you very well in that job.* ◇ **that's** *or* **it's just as well** used to indicate that something is fortunate ○ *It's just as well that she's going to be a bit late, because we're not quite ready.* ◇ **well and good** indicating qualified approval ○ *If he wants to come with us, well and good, but he'll have to pay his share.*

USAGE as well or **aswell**? ***As well***, as in *You know as well as I do that the answer is wrong*, is spelt as two words.

USAGE *Well* works as an adjective and an adverb, as in *All's well that ends well*, where the first ***well*** is an adjective and the second ***well*** is an adverb. The adjective ***well*** is used chiefly after verbs, as in *She is not at all well this morning*, i.e. she is sick. It occasionally appears before the noun it modifies, as in *He is not a well man. They have established a well-woman clinic.* ***Well*** and *good* can appear with the sensory verb *feel*, as in *I don't feel well this morning. I don't feel good this morning*, i.e. I feel sick or unwell. In one instance, however, *good* is the only choice: if the meaning is 'uneasy', as in *I don't feel good* [not *well*] *about this development*, i.e. I'm worried about this development.

USAGE See ***good***.

---

we'll /weel, wil/ *contr* 1 we will 2 we shall

well-adjusted *adj* (*not hyphenated after verbs*) 1 successfully adapted to prevailing conditions 2 content with your own self and life and therefore emotionally and psychologically stable

well-advised *adj* acting with good sense (*not hyphenated after verbs*) ○ *You would be well advised to leave before the storm hits.*

Welland Canal /wéllәnd-/, **Welland Ship Canal** canal system in Ontario, Canada, linking Lake Ontario and Lake Erie. It is part of the St Lawrence Seaway. Length: 44 km/28 mi.

well-appointed *adj* equipped, furnished, or arranged with whatever is necessary or desired (*not hyphenated after verbs*)

well-balanced *adj* (*not hyphenated after verbs*) 1 psychologically or emotionally stable 2 organized, conducted, or constructed so that all the parts are appropriately and sensibly proportioned or coordinated

well-behaved *adj* behaving, operating, or occurring properly and as expected (*not hyphenated after verbs*)

wellbeing /wél bee ing/ *n* a good, healthy, or comfortable state

well-beloved *adj* (*not hyphenated after verbs*) 1 DEARLY LOVED truly and dearly loved 2 RESPECTED highly respected or honoured ■ *n* (*plural* **well-beloved**) DEARLY LOVED PERSON a dearly loved person

wellborn /wél báwrn/ *adj* born into an aristocratic, highly respected, or wealthy family ■ *npl* people who are born in aristocratic, highly respected, or wealthy families (+ *plural verb*)

well-bred *adj* (*not hyphenated after verbs*) 1 possessing or displaying good manners or other marks of a good upbringing 2 born as an animal from a good breed or of good stock

well-built *adj* (*not hyphenated after verbs*) 1 having a sturdy and strong physique 2 of strong or sound construction

well-chosen *adj* selected carefully so as to be suitable or appropriate (*not hyphenated after verbs*)

well-connected *adj* having relatives, friends, or acquaintances in important or influential positions who can provide help when necessary (*not hyphenated after verbs*)

well-defined *adj* (*not hyphenated after verbs*) 1 stated or described with clarity and without ambiguity 2 having a clearly observable outline or form

well-disposed *adj* feeling or inclined to be approving, friendly, kindly, or sympathetic and potentially helpful (*not hyphenated after verbs*) ○ *She seemed well disposed towards us.*

well-done *adj* (*not hyphenated after verbs*) 1 carried out or performed correctly, properly, or skilfully 2 cooked right through to the centre

well-dressed *adj* wearing stylish and fashionable clothes (*not hyphenated after verbs*)

well dressing *n* in the United Kingdom, the practice of decorating a well with flowers at Whitsuntide in a traditional ancient ceremony

well-earned *adj* fully deserved, especially as a result of hard work or effort (*not hyphenated after verbs*) ○ *sat down for a well-earned rest*

well-endowed *adj* 1 OFFENSIVE TERM an offensive term meaning having a large penis or large breasts (*slang*) 2 AFFLUENT provided with substantial property, a sizable income, or a good source of income (*not hyphenated after verbs*) 3 NATURALLY EXCELLENT talented or capable as a result of a natural gift (*not hyphenated after verbs*)

Orson Welles

Welles /welz/, **Orson** (1915–85) US actor and director

well-established having been in existence for a sufficiently long time to have won general respect or achieved widespread success (*not hyphenated after verbs*)

~~wellfare~~ incorrect spelling of **welfare**

well-fed *adj* (*not hyphenated after verbs*) **1** having a diet that provides proper nourishment **2** overweight, especially as a result of having eaten a great deal of good or rich food

well-formed *adj* fully conforming to the rules of grammar and syntax in a language (*not hyphenated after verbs*) —**well-formedness** *n*

well-found *adj* properly and fully fitted out or equipped (*not hyphenated after verbs*)

well-founded *adj* based on sound reasons, information, or evidence or on undisputable facts (*not hyphenated after verbs*)

well-groomed *adj* (*not hyphenated after verbs*) **1** clean, neat, and well-dressed **2** carefully cleaned, brushed, or tended

well-grounded *adj* (*not hyphenated after verbs*) **1** encompassing or thoroughly familiar with the essential details or knowledge of a subject **2** = **well-founded**

wellhead /wél hed/ *n* **1** SOURCE OF A SPRING OR STREAM the place where a spring emerges from the earth or a stream begins **2** SOURCE a principal or primary source of something **3** STRUCTURE ON TOP OF A WELL a structure or enclosure at the upper end of a water, oil, or natural-gas well, e.g. one containing pipes and pumping equipment

well-heeled *adj* having a large income or substantial property (*informal; not hyphenated after verbs*)

well-hung *adj* (*not hyphenated after verbs*) **1** OFFENSIVE TERM an offensive term meaning having a large penis or a large penis and testicles (*slang*) **2** HANGING AS DESIRED OR REQUIRED suspended or attached so as to hang in a way that is desired or required **3** HUNG FOR THE PROPER TIME hung up long enough to mature and be good to eat ◇ *He liked his venison well hung.*

wellie /wélli/, **wellie boot**, **welly** (*plural* -ies), **welly boot** *n* a Wellington boot (*informal*) [Mid-20C. Shortening and alteration.] ◇ **give it some wellie** to put some effort into doing something (*informal; usually a command*)

well-informed *adj* having a broad and detailed knowledge of something, especially of the world and current events or of a particular subject (*not hyphenated after verbs*)

Wellingborough /wéllingbərə/ town in central England. Population: 41,602 (1991).

wellington *n* CLOTHING = **wellington boot**

Wellington /wéllingtən/ **1** capital of New Zealand, built around a deep harbour at the southern end of the North Island. Population: 165,200 (1998 estimate). **2** administrative region of New Zealand, occupying the southern tip of the North Island and including the city of Wellington. Population: 416,019 (1996). Area: 15,821 sq. km/6,109 sq. mi.

Wellington, Mount mountain in S Tasmania, Australia. Height: 1,270 m/4,167 ft.

Wellington /wéllingtən/, **Arthur Wellesley, 1st Duke of** (1769–1852) British general and prime minister (1828–30)

wellington boot, **wellington** *n* **1** a loose waterproof rubber boot extending to the knee or just below it and worn in wet weather or muddy conditions **2** a leather boot that reaches to the top of or above the knee in the front but is cut lower in the back [Early 19C. After the 1st Duke of WELLINGTON.]

wellingtonia /wéllingtóni ə/ (*plural* -**as** *or* -**a**) *n* = giant sequoia [Mid-19C. < modern Latin, after the 1st Duke of WELLINGTON.]

well-intentioned *adj* intended to be helpful or useful in some way but producing a negative effect or result (*not hyphenated after verbs*)

well-kept *adj* (*not hyphenated after verbs*) **1** carefully maintained or looked after **2** not revealed to anyone or to only a few people

well-knit *adj* (*not hyphenated after verbs*) **1** BOUND BY CLOSE TIES bound or joined together by close relationships or ties **2** FIRMLY CONSTRUCTED constructed or produced in such a way that the parts are firmly joined together or are integrated well **3** COMPACT IN PHYSIQUE with a compact and strong physique

well-known *adj* (*not hyphenated after verbs*) **1** known to many people **2** fully known or understood

well-man *adj* monitoring men's health and advising men on ways to prevent illness. ◇ **well-woman**

well-mannered *adj* behaving with politeness and courtesy (*not hyphenated after verbs*)

well-meaning *adj* trying to be helpful or useful in some way, but often producing a negative effect or result (*not hyphenated after verbs*)

well-meant *adj* arising from a desire to be helpful or useful, but often producing a negative effect (*not hyphenated after verbs*)

wellness /wélnəss/ *n* US physical wellbeing, especially when maintained or achieved through good diet and regular exercise

well-nigh *adv* nearly or almost ◇ *well-nigh impossible*

well-off (**better-off, best-off**) *adj* **1** FAIRLY WEALTHY having a good income or enough money to live comfortably (*not hyphenated after verbs*) **2** FAVOURABLY PLACED in a good or favourable situation or circumstances ◇ *It's not a good idea to change jobs, you're better off where you are.* **3** WITH PLENTY having a good supply of something ◇ *well off for fuel right now*

well-oiled *adj* (*not hyphenated after verbs*) **1** functioning, operating, or carried out efficiently **2** having drunk too much alcohol (*informal*)

well-ordered *adj* (*not hyphenated after verbs*) **1** arranged or organized so that things are in the proper place or run smoothly **2** in mathematics, having the property that every subset with members has an element that precedes all other elements in that subset

well-padded *adj* having a greater body weight than is desirable or advisable (*informal; not hyphenated after verbs*)

well-preserved *adj* in good condition or maintaining a good appearance or good health in spite of advanced age (*not hyphenated after verbs*)

well-read /-réd/ *adj* knowing much about many things or a particular field from having read widely and thoroughly (*not hyphenated after verbs*)

well-rounded *adj* (*not hyphenated after verbs*) **1** WITH EXPERIENCE IN MANY AREAS having abilities, experience, or achievements in a wide and balanced variety of fields **2** COMPREHENSIVE AND VARIED encompassing or including a wide, desirable, and balanced variety of subjects or activities **3** SHAPELY having a rounded or otherwise pleasingly shaped body

Wells /welz/ city in SW England, known for its medieval cathedral. Population: 9,763 (1991).

Wells, H. G. (1866–1946) British writer. Full name **Herbert George Wells**

well-set *adj* (*not hyphenated after verbs*) **1** strong and solid in physique **2** solidly established or fixed

well-spoken *adj* (*not hyphenated after verbs*) **1** speaking clearly, articulately, and in a refined accent, and with an accent that is regarded as the product of a good education **2** selected or expressed appropriately

wellspring /wél spring/ *n* **1** a source of a spring or stream **2** a plentiful source or supply of something ◇ *a wellspring of artistic talent*

well-stacked *adj* an offensive term meaning having large breasts (*slang*)

well-taken *adj* (*not hyphenated after verbs*) **1** performed or executed skilfully or effectively **2** based on sound reasons, information, or evidence or on indisputable facts

well-tempered *adj* tuned so as to permit playing in any key (*not hyphenated after verbs*)

well-thought-of *adj* regarded with respect or esteem or enjoying a good reputation (*not hyphenated after verbs*)

well-thought-out *adj* carefully and skilfully planned (*not hyphenated after verbs*)

well-thumbed *adj* with pages that show signs of having been turned many times (*not hyphenated after verbs*)

well-timed *adj* done or occurring at an appropriate or opportune moment (*not hyphenated after verbs*)

well-to-do *adj* having a good income or enough money to live comfortably

well-tried *adj* thoroughly tested or used and so known from experience to be reliable (*not hyphenated after verbs*) ◇ *a well-tried publishing formula*

well-turned *adj* (*not hyphenated after verbs*) **1** GRACEFULLY OR ATTRACTIVELY SHAPED having a graceful or attractive shape ◇ *a well-turned ankle* **2** SKILFULLY STATED skilfully expressed or worded ◇ *a well-turned phrase* **3** MANUFACTURED WITH A GRACEFUL SHAPE turned on a lathe or formed so as to have a pleasing, graceful shape

well-wisher *n* a person who wishes success or good luck to another or good will towards somebody or something —**well-wishing** *adj, n*

well-woman *adj* monitoring women's health and advising women on ways to prevent illness. ◇ **well-man**

well-worn *adj* (*not hyphenated after verbs*) **1** showing signs of wear as a result of much use **2** trite or hackneyed as result of being used too often in speech or writing

welly, **welly boot** *n* CLOTHING = **wellie** (*informal*)

wels /velss/ (*plural* **wels**) *n* a large freshwater catfish. Native to: central and eastern Europe. *Silurus glanis*. [Late 19C. < German.]

welsh /welsh/, **welch** *vi* an offensive term meaning to fail to fulfil or honour an obligation entered into or incurred [Mid-19C. Probably < WELSH.] —**welsher** *n*

Welsh /welsh/ *npl* the people of Wales ■ *n* a Celtic language spoken in Wales. Native speakers: 50,000. [Old English *Wēlisc*, *Wǣlisc*. < *W(e)alh* 'Briton, Celt, Welshman' ('foreigner'), via Germanic 'foreign'. < Latin *Volcae* 'Celtic people of southern Gaul'.] —**Welsh** *adj* —**Welshman** *n* — **Welshwoman** *n*

Welsh cob *n* a horse with a strong neck, powerful shoulders, and compact body, used as a saddle and harness horse

Welsh corgi *n* ZOOL = **corgi**

Welsh dresser *n* a sideboard with cupboards and drawers in the lower part and open shelves in the top part

Welsh English *n* the variety of English spoken in Wales

Welsh harp *n* a harp with three rows of strings that allow the production of a chromatic scale

Welsh mountain pony *n* a pony of a breed that has tiny pointed ears and a compact body. Native to: Wales.

Welsh pony *n* a pony descended from crosses between Welsh cobs and Welsh mountain ponies, slightly larger than the latter

Welsh poppy *n* a poppy that forms branching tufts of deeply divided compound leaves. Flowers: yellow, borne singly on long slender stems. Native to: W Europe. *Meconopsis cambrica*.

Welsh rarebit /-ráir bit/, **Welsh rabbit** *n* a dish made of hard cheese melted with seasoning, then spread on toast and grilled until bubbling and golden [Late 18C. Alteration of *Welsh rabbit*.]

Welsh terrier *n* a wire-haired terrier of a breed originally developed for hunting, that resembles an Airedale and has a long thick, typically black-and-tan coat

welt /welt/ *n* **1** RIDGE ON THE SKIN a raised ridge or bump on the skin caused by a lash from a whip, a scratch, or a similar blow **2** LASH FROM A WHIP CAUSING A RIDGE a lash from a whip or a similar blow that causes a raised ridge or bump on the skin **3** STRIP SEWN INTO A SHOE a strip of leather or other material that is sewn into a shoe or boot between the upper and the sole in order to strengthen the seam **4** REINFORCEMENT FOR A SEAM a folded strip of cloth, sometimes wrapped around a cord, that is sewn into a seam in a garment or pillow as a reinforcement or decoration ■ *vt* **1 BEAT SOMEBODY SEVERELY** to beat or hit somebody severely, especially with a whip or switch **2 RAISE SMALL RIDGES ON THE SKIN** to cause raised ridges or bumps on the skin as a result of a lash from a whip or switch **3 STITCH SOMETHING REINFORCING OR DECORATIVE** to stitch or supply something with a strip of material as a reinforcement or decoration [15C. < ?]

Weltanschauung /vélt an show ŏong/ (*plural* **-ungen** /-ŏongən/) *n* a comprehensive and usually personal conception or view of humanity, the world, or life [Mid-19C. < German, 'world view' < *Welt* 'world' + *Anschauung* 'view'.]

Welter /wéltər/ *n* **1 CONFUSED MASS** a confused or jumbled mass of something **2 CONFUSED CONDITION** a state of confusion or chaos or a disorderly or chaotic situation **3 SURGING MOTION OF WATER** a surging, rolling, or heaving motion made by the sea or waves **4 WELTERWEIGHT** a welterweight (*informal*) ■ *vi* **1 WALLOW IN** to wallow or roll around in something **2 LIE DRENCHED WITH LIQUID** to lie soaked or bathed in water, blood, or some other liquid **3 BE COMPLETELY IMMERSED IN** to be completely or deeply involved, absorbed, or entangled in something **4 SURGE OR ROLL IN WATER** to surge, roll, or heave in the sea or waves [14C. < Middle Dutch or Middle Low German *welteren* 'roll'.]

welterweight /wéltər wayt/ *n* a sports contestant ranked by body weight between a lightweight and a middleweight, especially a professional boxer weighing between 61 kg/135 lb and 66.5 kg/147 lb [Early 19C. < *welter* 'heavyweight rider or boxer' < ?]

Weltschmerz /vélt shmairts/, **weltschmerz** *n* sadness felt at the imperfect state of the world, especially at the behaviour of human beings [Late 19C. < German, < *Welt* 'world' + *Schmerz* 'pain'.]

Eudora Welty

Welty /wéltee/, **Eudora** (*b.* 1909) US writer

welwitschia /wel wíchi ə/ (*plural* **-as** or **-a**) *n* a desert plant that produces two large strap-shaped leaves from the base of a short trunk and scarlet cones in which flowers develop. Native to: southern Africa. *Welwitschia mirabilis*. [Mid-19C. < modern Latin, after Friedrich *Welwitsch* (1806–72), Austrian botanist.]

Welwyn Garden City /wéllin-/ town in SE England. Population: 42,000 (1994).

Wemba-Wemba /wémbə wémbə/ *n* an Australian Aboriginal language of New South Wales, now almost extinct [< an Aboriginal language] —**Wemba-Wemba** *adj*

Wembley /wémbli/ *n* residential area in NW London

wen[1] /wen/ *n* **1** a cyst containing material secreted by a sebaceous gland of the skin, usually on the scalp or genitals **2** a very large overpopulated city [Old English *wen(n)* < ?]

wen[2] *n* ALPHABET = **wynn**

Wenceslas IV /wénsəss láwss, -laàss/ (1361–1419) king of Bohemia (1378–1419) and Holy Roman Emperor (1378–1400)

Wenceslaus /wénsəsləss/, **St, Duke of Bohemia** (907?–929) Known as **Good King Wenceslaus**

wench /wench/ *n* **1 SERVANT GIRL** a girl or young woman who works at a paid job, usually as a servant or on a farm (*archaic*) **2 COUNTRY GIRL** a girl or young woman who lives in a rural area (*archaic*) **3 OFFENSIVE TERM** an offensive term for a prostitute or a woman who is regarded as sexually promiscuous **4 OFFENSIVE TERM** an offensive term for a young woman ■ *vi* **OFFENSIVE TERM**

an offensive term meaning to engage in sex with prostitutes or with women considered to be promiscuous (*archaic*) [13C. Shortening of obsolete *wenchel* 'child, enslaved labourer, prostitute' < Old English *wencel* 'child' < Germanic, 'to falter'.] —**wencher** *n*

wend /wend/ *vti* to proceed along a course or route ○ *The boat wended its way through the reefs.* [Old English *wendan* 'turn, proceed' < Germanic, 'turn']

Wend /wend/ *n* a member of a Slavic people who lived in NE Germany in medieval times [Late 18C. < German *Wende*.]

Wendish /wéndish/ *n* a Slavic language spoken in E Germany. Native speakers: 100,000. —**Wendish** *adj*

Wendy house /wéndi-/ *n* a model house that is large enough for small children to go inside and play in. US term **playhouse** *n*. **2** [Mid-20C. After the house built around the character *Wendy* in the play *Peter Pan* (1904) by J. M. Barrie.]

wenge /wéng gay/ *n* the dark brown wood of an African tree, often used as a veneer for furniture. *Millettia laurentii*.

Wensleydale /wénzli dayl/ *n* **1** a white crumbly hard English cheese with a slightly tangy flavour **2** one of a breed of sheep that has a blue-grey head and ears and dark mottled legs. Kept for: fleece. Native to: N England. [Late 19C. After *Wensleydale*, valley in N Yorkshire.]

went past tense of **go**[1]

wentletrap /wént'l trap/ *n* a marine gastropod mollusc with a spiral prominently ribbed shell that is typically white but is sometimes tinged with brown. Family: Epitoniidae. [Mid-18C. < Dutch *wenteltrap* 'winding stair' from the appearance of the shells.]

Wentworth /wént wurth/, **W. C.** (1793–1872) Australian explorer and politician. Full name **William Charles Wentworth**

wept past tense, past participle of **weep**

were (*stressed*) /wur/; (*unstressed*) /wər/ past tense of **be** [Old English *wæron* (plural past indicative), *wæren* (plural past subjunctive), and *wære* (2nd person singular past indicative and singular past subjunctive), forms of *wesan* 'be' (see WAS)]

USAGE where or **were**? The word *where* is an adverb: *Where* [not *Were*] has she gone? *Were* is a past form of the verb to be: *We were there yesterday.*

we're /weer/ *contr* we are

weren't /wurnt/ *contr* were not

werewolf /wáir woolf, weér-/ (*plural* **-wolves** /-woolvz/), **werwolf** (*plural* **-wolves**) *n* a person believed to have been transformed into a wolf, or to be able to change into a wolf and then back into a human being [Old English *werewulf* < *were-* 'man' + *wulf* 'wolf' < Indo-European, 'man']

Wergaia /wur gî ə/ *n* an Aboriginal language of South Australia and W Victoria [Late 19C. < an Aboriginal language.] —**Wergaia** *adj*

wernerite /wúrnə rīt/ *n* MINERALS = **scapolite** [Early 19C. After Abraham Gottlob *Werner* (1750–1817), German mineralogist.]

Wernicke-Korsakoff syndrome /váirnikə káwrssə kof-/ *n* a form of brain damage occurring in long-term alcoholics that results from severe nutritional deficiencies [Mid-20C. After Karl *Wernicke* (1848–1905), German neurologist, and Sergei Sergeevich *Korsakov* (1854–1900), Russian psychiatrist.]

wersh /wursh/ *adj* Scotland **1** bitter or sour-tasting **2** having little or no taste or flavour [Probably contraction of obsolete *wearish* (except for dialect) *wearish*]

wert past tense of **be** (*archaic*)

werwolf *n* PARANORMAL = **werewolf**

Weser /váyzər/ river in NW Germany, emptying into the North Sea. Length: 483 km/300 mi.

weskit /wéskit/ *n* a waistcoat (*archaic*) [Mid-19C. Alteration of WAISTCOAT.]

Wesley /wézli/, **John** (1703–91) British religious leader

Wesleyan /wézzli ən/ *adj* based on, consisting of, or resembling the teachings, practices, and beliefs of the Christian preacher John Wesley and his brother Charles, or of Methodism. ◊ **Methodist** *adj*. ■ *n* a follower of the Christian preacher John Wesley and his brother Charles, or a believer in their teachings or those of Methodism —**Wesleyanism** *n*

Wessex /wéssiks/ former Anglo-Saxon kingdom in S England

west /west/ *n* **1 DIRECTION IN WHICH THE SUN SETS** the direction that lies directly ahead of somebody facing the setting Sun or that is located towards the left-hand side of a conventional map of the world **2 COMPASS POINT OPPOSITE EAST** the compass point that lies directly opposite east **3 west, West AREA IN THE WEST** the part of an area, region, or country that is situated in or towards the west **4 west, West POSITION EQUIVALENT TO WEST** the position equivalent to west in any diagram consisting of four points at 90-degree intervals ■ *adj* **1 IN THE WEST** situated in, facing, or coming from the west of a place, region, or country **2 BLOWING FROM WEST** blowing from the west ○ *a west wind* ■ *adv* **TOWARDS THE WEST** in or towards the west [Old English < Indo-European, 'evening, night'] ◊ **go west** to die, disappear, or be destroyed (*informal*)

West /west/, **west** *n* **1 EUROPE AND THE AMERICAS** the countries of Europe and North and South America. ◊ **western hemisphere 2 COUNTRIES WITH GRAECO-ROMAN AND CHRISTIAN TRADITIONS** those countries of the world, especially in Europe and North and South America, whose culture and society are most influenced by traditions rooted in Greek and Roman culture and in Christianity **3 NON-COMMUNIST COUNTRIES IN THE COLD WAR** the non-Communist countries of Europe and North and South America during the Cold War **4 W UNITED STATES** the part of the United States west of the Mississippi River or west of the Allegheny Mountains during early phases of the country's history

West /west/, **Benjamin** (1738–1820) US artist

West, Mae (1892–1980) US actor and comedian

West, Morris (1916–99) Australian novelist

West, Nathanael (1903–40) US writer. Born **Nathan Wallenstein Weinstein**

West, Dame Rebecca (1892–1983) British writer. Pseudonym of **Cicily Isabel Andrews**. Born **Cicily Isabel Fairfield**

West Bank

West Bank disputed territory in the Middle East, on the western bank of the River Jordan, bordered by Israel and Jordan. Population: 1,600,000 (1996). Area: 5,860 sq. km/2,263 sq. mi.

West Bengal state in NE India. Capital: Calcutta. Population: 73,600,000 (1994). Area: 87,853 sq. km/33,920 sq. mi. ◊ **East Bengal**

West Berlin western part of the city of Berlin, officially part of West Germany between 1945 and 1990 —**West Berliner** *n*

westbound /wést bownd/ *adj* leading, going, or travelling towards the west

West Bromwich /-brómmich, -brómmij/ town in west-central England. Population: 146,386 (1991).

west by north *n* the direction or compass point midway between west and west-northwest —**west by north** *adj*, *adv*

west by south *n* the direction or compass point midway between west and west-southwest —**west by south** *adj*, *adv*

West Coast 1 administrative region of New Zealand, occupying the western coast of the South Island. Population: 35,671 (1996). Area: 36,116 sq. km/13,944 sq. mi. **2** region of the W United States, including California, Oregon, and Washington

West Country area in SW England, comprising the counties of Cornwall, Devon, and Somerset

West Dunbartonshire /-dun baart'nshər/ council area in west-central Scotland. Area: 162 sq. km/63 sq. mi.

wester /wéstər/ *n* a wind blowing from the west, especially one blowing ahead of or with a storm ■ *vi* to move or appear to move across the sky to the west (*refers to the Sun, Moon, or other astronomical bodies*)

westerly /wéstərli/ *adj* **1 IN THE WEST** situated in or towards the west **2 COMING FROM THE WEST** blowing from the west ■ *n* (*plural* **-lies**) **WIND FROM THE WEST** a wind blowing from the west ■ *adv* **1 FROM THE WEST** coming from the west **2 TOWARDS THE WEST** moving towards the west —**westerliness** *n*

western /wéstərn/ *adj* **1 IN THE WEST** situated in the west of a region or country **2 FACING WEST** situated in or facing the west ○ *The house has a western aspect.* **3 western, Western OF THE WEST** typical of or native to the west of a region or country **4 COMING FROM THE WEST** blowing from the west ○ *a western wind* **5 WEST OF THE PRIME MERIDIAN** lying west of the prime meridian [Old English *westerne* < WEST + a suffix denoting direction] —**westernness** *n*

Western, western *adj* **1 INFLUENCED BY GRAECO-ROMAN AND CHRISTIAN TRADITIONS** found in or typical of countries, especially in Europe and North and South America, whose culture and society are greatly influenced by traditions rooted in Greek and Roman culture and in Christianity **2 OF NON-COMMUNIST COUNTRIES IN THE COLD WAR** found in or belonging to the non-Communist countries of Europe and North and South America during the Cold War **3 TYPICAL OF THE AMERICAN WEST** found in or relating to the part of the United States west of the Mississippi River or west of the Allegheny Mountains during early phases of the country's history **4 FOUND IN EUROPE AND AMERICAS** located in or relating to Europe and North and South America **5 CATHOLIC AND PROTESTANT** based on, consisting of, or resembling the teachings, practices, and beliefs of Roman Catholicism and Protestantism, as opposed to those of the Eastern Orthodox Church ■ *n* **FILM OR BOOK ON THE AMERICAN WEST** a film, radio or television programme, novel, or story set in the W United States, usually during the second half of the 19th century —**Westernness** *n*

Western Australia state occupying the western part of Australia. Capital: Perth. Population: 1,766,000 (1996). Area: 2,525,500 sq. km/975,100 sq. mi.

Western blotting, Western blot *n* a technique that analyses mixtures of proteins by separating them and then binding them to specific antibodies [After *Southern blot*]

Western Cape province in SW South Africa. Capital: Cape Town. Population: 4,055,000 (1996). Area: 129,386 sq. km/49,943 sq. mi.

Western Church *n* the Christian Church as found in or influenced by that of Europe, especially the Roman Catholic Church

westerner /wéstərnər/ *n* a person who comes from the western part of a country or region

Western European Time *n* the standard time in the time zone centred on 0° longitude (**the prime meridian**), which includes the United Kingdom

Western European Union *n* an association of European countries, inaugurated in 1955, whose main function is to coordinate defence, economic, and social policy

Western Front *n* the battle line between the French and British armies and the German armies in W Europe during World War I. It extended from Belgium to the Swiss border.

Western Ghats mountain range in S India. Highest peak: Doda Betta 2,637 m/8,652 ft.

western hemisphere *n* the half of the Earth that is to the west of the Greenwich meridian, including North and South America and portions of W Europe and Africa

western hemlock *n* a coniferous tree with drooping foliage, widely grown for ornament and timber. Native to: W North America. *Tsuga heterophylla.* ◊ **hemlock** *n.* 3

westernise *vti* = **westernize**

Western Isles[1] council area in the Outer Hebrides, W Scotland. Population: 29,600 (1991). Area: 2901 sq. km/1120 sq. mi.

westernism /wéstərnizəm/, **Westernism** *n* **1** a custom or practice typical of the countries of Europe and North and South America **2** a word or idiom chiefly used in the western part of a country or region, especially the W United States

westernize /wéstər nīz/ (**-izes, -izing, -ized**), **westernise** (**-ises, -ising, -ised**) *v* **1** *vti* to adopt or cause a person, country, or culture to adopt the customs, practices, or beliefs of the people of Europe or North and South America **2** *vt* to change a law, custom, practice, or belief so that it resembles or is replaced by its European or North American counterpart —**westernization** /wéstər nī záysh'n/ *n*

westernmost /wéstərn mōst/ *adj* situated farthest west

western red cedar *n* TREES = **red cedar** *n.* 2

western roll *n* a high jump in which the body is half-turned over the bar

Western saddle *n* a large and heavy saddle for a horse with a raised pommel. It was originally used on ranches in the western and SW United States. US term **stock saddle**

Western Sahara disputed region in NW Africa. Area: 267,000 sq. km/103,000 sq. mi.

Western Samoa former name for **Samoa**

western sandwich *n US, Can* a sandwich with a filling of an omelette made with diced ham, green pepper, and onion

Western Standard Time *n* a time zone lying west of the 120th meridian and including the whole of Western Australia

western swing *n* country and western music played on guitars, steel guitars, fiddles, and other instruments and incorporating elements of swing music

Western Wall *n* a wall in Jerusalem believed to be part of the Second Temple, destroyed in AD 70 by the Romans

West Germanic *n* a subgroup of Germanic languages that consists of English, German, Yiddish, Dutch, Flemish, Afrikaans, and Frisian

West Germany republic of W Europe from 1945 to 1990 —**West German** *n, adj*

West Highland terrier, West Highland white terrier *n* a small terrier of a hardy long-haired breed with a pure white coat, originally bred for hunting small mammals but now kept as a pet [< its having originated in the western Highlands of Scotland]

West Indies /-ín deez/ former name for the islands of the Caribbean, now used only in certain contexts, such as the West Indies cricket team —**West Indian** *adj, n*

westing /wésting/ *n* **1** the distance due west between two points on a course heading in a westwards direction **2** travel or progress in a westwards direction

West Irian /-írri ən/ former name for **Irian Jaya**

West Lothian council area and historic county in central Scotland. Area: 425 sq. km/164 sq. mi.

Westm. *abbr* Westminster

Westmeath /wést meéth/ county in Leinster Province, in the central part of the Republic of Ireland. Area: 1,764 sq. km/681 sq. mi.

Westminster /wéstminstər/ borough in central London. Population: 195,300 (1995).

Westminster Abbey *n* a large Gothic church in London, originally a Benedictine abbey, in which British monarchs are traditionally crowned

West New Guinea former name for **Irian Jaya**

West Nile fever, West Nile disease *n* a mosquito-borne viral infection affecting birds, horses, and humans that causes fever, rash, headache, muscle pain, enlarged lymph nodes, and, in some cases, inflammation of the brain [Because first identified in the W Nile district of Uganda]

West Nile virus *n* **1** a virus, carried by mosquitos, that causes West Nile fever **2** = **West Nile fever**

west-northwest *n* the direction or compass point midway between west and northwest ■ *adj, adv* in, from, facing, or towards the west-northwest —**west-northwesterly** *adj, adv*

Weston /wést'n/, **Edward** (1886–1958) US photographer

Weston standard cell *n* a portable, highly accurate, voltage source used as a standard for calibration purposes [Early 20C. After Edward *Weston* (1850–1936), English-born electrical engineer.]

Weston-super-Mare /wést'n sōōpər máir/ resort town in SW England. Population: 65,000 (1991).

Westphalia /west fáyli əl/ former province in N Germany —**Westphalian** *n, adj*

Westphalian ham *n* German ham that is cured an eaten raw, very thinly sliced

West Point *n* the site of the US Military Academy, o the Hudson River in New York State, or the Academ itself

Westport /wést pawrt/ town on the northwestern coa of the South Island, New Zealand. Population: 4,2 (1996).

West Riding /-rīding/ former county in Yorkshire, I England

West Saxon *n* **1** a dialect of Old English used in Wesse during Anglo-Saxon times as the main literary diale **2** a person who came from Wessex during Anglo-Saxo times —**West Saxon** *adj*

west-southwest *n* the direction or compass poir midway between west and southwest ■ *adj, adv* i from, facing, or towards the west-southwest —**wes southwesterly** *adj, adv*

West Sussex county in SE England. Area: 1,989 s km/768 sq. mi.

West Virginia state of the east-central United State Capital: Charleston. Population: 1,815,787 (1997). Are 62,761 sq. km/24,232 sq. mi. —**West Virginian** *n, adj*

westward /wéstwərd/ *adj* towards or in the west ■ a direction towards or a point in the west ■ *adv* **westwards** —**westwardly** *adv, adj*

USAGE westward or **westwards**? ***Westward*** is the on form available for the adjective: *In a westward directio* ***Westwards*** is commonly used as well as ***westward*** for th adverb: *The ship was moving slowly westward/westwards.*

westwards /wéstwərdz/ *adv* in a westerly direction

Westwood /wést wŏŏd/, **Vivienne** (*b.* 1941) British fashio designer

wet /wet/ *adj* **1 SOAKED WITH WATER** covered, soaked, c dampened with water or some other liquid **2 NOT YE DRY** not completely dry **3 NOT YET SET** not yet firm c solidified ○ *wet cement* **4 RAINY, SHOWERY, MISTY, OR FOGG** characterized by rain, showers, mist, or fog ○ *a we weekend* **5 WITH RAINY WEATHER** subject to frequent heav rain, showers, mist, or fog ○ *a wet climate* **6 USING OR DON WITH LIQUID** using or done in water or another liqui **7 UNASSERTIVE** regarded as weak and lacking resolutio or decisiveness (*informal insult*) **8** *US, Can* **ALLOWING SALE OF ALCOHOL** allowing the legal manufacture, storag transportation, and sale of alcoholic beverag (*informal*) ○ *a wet town* **9** *US* **FAVOURING SALES OF ALCOHO** favouring the legal manufacture, storage, trans portation, and sale of alcoholic beverages (*informal*) ○ *wet representative* ■ *n* **1 LIQUID OR MOISTURE** water o another liquid, or moisture from it **2 RAINY OR DAM WEATHER** rainy, showery, misty, or foggy weather ○ *Com in out of the wet.* **3** *Aus* **N AUSTRALIAN WET SEASON** the we season in N Australia that lasts from December t March **4 WET GROUND** a wet area or surface **5 UNASSERTIV PERSON** a weak, irresolute, or indecisive person (*informa insult*) **6 LIBERAL CONSERVATIVE** a Conservative politicia whose policies some other Conservatives consider nc to be sufficiently pure or doctrinaire (*informal*) **7** *U* **SUPPORTER OF LEGAL SALES OF ALCOHOL** a supporter of th legal manufacture, storage, transportation, and sale o alcoholic beverages (*informal*) ■ *v* (**wets, wetting, we** *or* **wetted**) **1** *vti* **MAKE OR BECOME WET** to become or caus something to become damp or soaked with water o some other liquid **2** *vt* **MAKE WET BY URINATING** to caus something to be damp or soaked with urine **3** *vt* **MAK TEA** to make tea with boiling water (*regional*) [Old Englis *wǣt*, *wǣta* (noun), *wǣt* (adjective), and *wǣtan* (verb) Indo-European, 'water, wet'] —**wetly** *adv* —**wetness** *n* — **wettability** *n* —**wettable** *adj* —**wetter** *n* —**wettish** *adj* < **all wet** *US, Can* completely mistaken or wrong

WET *abbr* Western European Time

weta /wéttə/ *n* a heavy-bodied wingless insect that re sembles a locust. Native to: New Zealand. Genus: *De inacrida*. [Mid-19C. < Maori.]

wetback /wét bak/ *n US* a highly offensive term for Mexican person recently arrived in the United States especially somebody who has entered the country il legally to work as a labourer (*taboo*) [Early 20C. < Mexica immigrants having waded or swum across the Rio Grand river to enter the United States.]

et bar *n US, Can* a small bar equipped with a sink in a house or hotel room, used for mixing alcoholic drinks

et blanket *n* a person who spoils or diminishes other people's enthusiasm or enjoyment (*informal*) [< the use of wet blankets to smother small fires]

et-bulb thermometer *n* a thermometer that records the temperature at which pure water must be evaporated to saturate a given volume of air

et cell *n* a primary cell that contains a free-flowing electrolyte. ◊ **dry cell**

et dream *n* a dream that has sexual content and leads to the ejaculation of semen (*offensive in some contexts*)

et fish *n* fresh fish for sale, as distinguished from frozen or cooked fish

et fly *n* a fishing lure resembling a fly that slips beneath the surface of the water after it is cast. ◊ **dry fly**

ether /wéthər/ *n* a male sheep or goat that has been castrated before becoming sexually mature [Old English *weþer* < Germanic]

SPELLCHECK See *weather*

etland /wétlənd/ *n* a marsh, swamp, or other area of land where the soil near the surface is saturated or covered with water, especially one that forms a habitat for wildlife (*often plural*)

et look *n* **1** a glossy finish on a material that gives an appearance of wetness **2** a glossy sheen given to the hair by the use of a special hair gel that gives an appearance of wetness —**wet-look** *adj*

et nurse *n* a woman who breast-feeds and takes care of another woman's baby

et-nurse (**wet-nurses, wet-nursing, wet-nursed**) *vt* **1** to breast-feed and take care of another woman's baby **2** to bestow excessive care or attention on somebody (*informal disapproving*)

et pack *n* a piece or pieces of material dampened with hot or cold water and wrapped around a patient's body for therapeutic purposes

et rot *n* rot that affects moist or wet timber, caused by fungi and characterized by brown discoloration of the wood. ◊ **dry rot** *n.* 1

et steam *n* steam that is under low pressure and contains water droplets

et suit *n* a tight-fitting garment worn by a diver, made of foam neoprene rubber or a similar material

etting agent *n* a chemical agent that allows a liquid to spread more easily across or into a surface by lowering the liquid's surface tension

NEU *abbr* Western European Union

Vexford /wéksfərd/ **1** county in Leinster Province, SE Republic of Ireland. Area: 2,353 sq. km/908 sq. mi. **2** port in the SE Republic of Ireland. Population: 9,544 (1991).

Veymouth /wáyməth/ **1** resort and ferry port in S England, on Weymouth Bay, an inlet of the English Channel. Population: 46,065 (1991). **2** town in E Massachusetts. Population: 46,065 (1991).

vf *abbr* **1** wf, w.f. wrong font **2** Wallis and Futuna Islands (*in Internet addresses*)

vff *abbr* well-formed formula

NFTU *abbr* World Federation of Trade Unions

vg, WG *abbr* **1** water gauge **2** wire gauge

Ng Cdr *abbr* Wing Commander

V. Glam. *abbr* West Glamorgan

Nh *abbr* watt-hour

vh. *abbr* white

NHA *abbr* World Hockey Association

vhack /wak/ *v* **1** *vti* **HIT WITH A LOUD SHARP BLOW** to hit somebody or something with a swift sharp blow that produces a loud noise **2** *vt* **PLACE CASUALLY AND QUICKLY** to put or place something somewhere casually and quickly (*informal*) **3** *vti* **CUT OR CHOP** to cut or chop something with a swift sharp blow ■ *n* **1 SHARP BLOW** a swift sharp blow **2 SOUND OF A SHARP BLOW** the sound made by a swift sharp blow **3** *vt* **ATTEMPT** an attempt at doing something (*informal*) ○ *That looks like fun – can I take a whack at it?* **4 SHARE** a share or portion of something, especially one deserved or due (*informal*) **5 COST** the amount that something costs (*informal*) ■ *vt US* to kill

somebody (*slang*) [Early 18C. Probably an imitation of the sound.] —**whacker** *n*

whack off *vti* a highly offensive term meaning to masturbate (*taboo*)

whacked /wakt/ *adj* **1** *UK, Can* very tired or exhausted (*informal*) **2** *US* relaxed, excited, or euphoric as a result of taking drugs, especially marijuana (*slang*)

whacked-out *adj* **1** very tired after physical or mental exertion (*informal*) **2** *US* relaxed, excited, or euphoric from taking illegal drugs, especially cannabis (*slang*)

whacking /wáking/ *adj* very large or impressive (*informal*) ■ *adv UK, Can* to an extreme degree (*informal*)

whacko /wakō/ *n* = **wacko** (*slang offensive*)

whacky /wáki/ *adj* = **wacky**

Whakatane /fúkə taʻa nay/ coastal town in the NE of the North Island, New Zealand. Population: 17,493 (1996).

whale[1] /wayl/ *n* **1 BIG MARINE MAMMAL** a large marine mammal that breathes through a blowhole on the top of its head and has front flippers, no hind limbs, and a flat horizontal tail. Order: Cetacea. **2 IMPRESSIVE EXAMPLE OF** an impressive, very large, or very enjoyable example of something (*informal*) ■ *vi* (**whales, whaling, whaled**) **HUNT WHALES** to hunt for and kill whales [Old English *hwæl* < Germanic]

SPELLCHECK See *wail*.

whale[2] /wayl/ (**whales, whaling, whaled**) *vt* **1** to beat somebody severely as a punishment **2** *US* to defeat somebody soundly or completely [Late 18C. < ?]

whaleback /wáyl bak/ *n* **1** something large and rounded like the back of a whale, e.g. an ocean wave or a small hill **2** a cargo vessel with a rounded bow and arched upper deck designed to allow the water from waves breaking on it to run off more easily

whaleboat /wáyl bōt/ *n* a long, narrow, easily manoeuvred boat with a pointed bow and stern, originally rowed in pursuit of whales but now often powered and used as a lifeboat

whalebone /wáyl bōn/ *n* **1** ZOOL = **baleen 2** a piece or strip of a hard elastic material found in some whales. Use: formerly, corset stays, whips. [13C. Originally in the sense 'ivory from an animal confused with a whale such as a walrus'.]

whalebone whale *n* ZOOL = **baleen whale**

whale catcher *n* a boat with a harpoon launcher mounted in its bow, used for pursuing and catching whales

Whale Island uninhabited volcanic island off the NE of the North Island, New Zealand, in the Bay of Plenty. Area: 4 sq. km/2 sq. mi.

whale oil *n* a yellowish oil manufactured by rendering the blubber of whales. Use: formerly, lamp fuel, soap, candles.

whaler /wáylər/ *n* **1** a hunter or harpooner of whales, or processer of killed whales **2** a ship used for hunting whales or processing killed whales **3** SHIPPING = **whaleboat**

whale shark *n* the largest of all sharks, found in warm oceanic waters worldwide, with a white-spotted dark body up to 15 m/50 ft in length. *Rhincodon typus*.

whaling /wáyling/ *n* the activity or industry of hunting and processing whales

wham /wam/ *n* (*informal*) **1 FORCEFUL BLOW** a solid forceful blow or impact **2 SOUND OF FORCEFUL BLOW** the loud noise produced by a solid forceful blow ■ *vti* (**whams, whamming, whammed**) **HIT SOMETHING WITH LOUD NOISE** to hit or crash into somebody or something with a loud noise (*informal*) ○ *The car whammed into the brick wall.* ■ *interj* **USED TO INDICATE THE SOUND OF BLOW** used to imitate the sound of a forceful blow or impact (*informal*) ■ *adv* **SUDDENLY AND FORCEFULLY** with a startling or jarring suddenness (*informal*) ○ *I ran wham right into my ex-husband.* [Early 20C. An imitation of the sound.]

whammy /wámmi/ *n* (*plural* **-mies**) *n* (*informal*) **1** a jinx or hex **2** something with unpleasant or damaging consequences [Mid-20C. < ?]

whang[1] /wang/ *n* **1 THONG** a thong, especially a thong made from leather **2 UNTANNED ANIMAL HIDE** untanned hide from cattle or other animals **3** *US* **OFFENSIVE TERM** an offensive term for a penis (*slang*) ■ *vt* **HIT SOMEBODY SEVERELY** to beat, whip, or thrash somebody [Early 16C. Alteration of *thwang*, a variant of THONG.]

whang[2] /wang/ *n* **1 RESOUNDING BLOW** a blow that resounds when it hits something **2 SOUND OF RESOUNDING BLOW** the sound produced by a heavy blow when it hits something ■ *vti* **HIT WITH RESOUNDING SOUND** to hit something and produce a loud resounding sound [Early 19C. An imitation of the sound.]

Whangarei /fáàngə ráy/ coastal town in the northern part of the North Island, New Zealand. Population: 45,892 (1996).

whangee /wang eè/ *n* **1** a walking stick or cane made from a piece of bamboo **2** a bamboo plant whose stems are used to make whangees. Native to: China. Genus: *Phyllostachys*. [Late 18C. < Chinese (Mandarin) *huang* 'bamboo sprouts too old for eating'.]

whap /wop/ *n, vti* = **whop**

wharf /wawrf/ *n* (*plural* **wharves** /wawrvz/ *or* **wharfs**) **1 LANDING PLACE FOR SHIPS** a structure built alongside or out into the water as a landing place for boats and ships, sometimes with a protective covering or enclosure **2 SHORE** a riverbank or seashore (*archaic*) ■ *v* **1** *vti* **MOOR A BOAT AT A WHARF** to moor a vessel at a wharf, or to be moored there **2** *vt* **UNLOAD OR STORE CARGO ON A WHARF** to unload cargo onto or store it on a wharf **3** *vt* **EQUIP A PLACE WITH A WHARF** to provide a place with a wharf or wharves [Old English *hwearf* 'embankment, wharf' < Germanic, 'turn']

wharfage /wáwrfij/ *n* **1 USE OF A WHARF** the use of a wharf or wharves **2 FEE TO USE A WHARF** a fee that is paid for the use of a wharf or wharves **3 WHARVES** wharves collectively, especially the wharves in a particular location

wharfie /wáwrfi/ *n Aus* a worker at a dock or wharf (*informal*)

wharfinger /wáwrfinjər/ *n* a wharf owner or supervisor of activity on a wharf or group of wharves [Mid-16C. Alteration of obsolete *wharfager*.]

Edith Wharton

Wharton /wáwrt'n/, **Edith** (1862–1937) US writer. Born Edith Newbold Jones

wharve /wawrv/ *n* a wheel or similar part on a spindle. Use: pulley on spinning machine, flywheel on spinning wheel. [Old English *hweorfa*, < *hweorfan* 'turn' < Germanic]

wharves plural of **wharf**

what /wot/ CORE MEANING: a grammatical word used in direct and indirect questions to request further information, e.g. about the identity or nature of somebody, or about the purpose of something ○ (det) *What time do you make it?* ○ (det) *I'm not sure what kind of sauce goes best with this dish.* ○ (pron) *What are they doing?* ○ (pron) *Do you know what she does for a living?*

1 *det, pron* **THAT WHICH** the person or persons that, or the thing or things that ○ (det) *We spent what money we did have.* ○ (pron) *picking their way through what remained of the house* **2** *det* **EMPHASIZING A REACTION** used in exclamations to emphasize a reaction or opinion ○ *What fantastic news!* ○ *What a miserable day it's been.* **3** *adv* **HOW** in what respect or to what degree ○ *What does it matter now that they've gone?* **4** *adv* **AT A GUESS** used to indicate a guess or approximation of an amount or value ○ *It must be, what, ten years since we first met.* **5** *interj* **EXCLAMATION** used as an exclamation when expressing an emotion such as surprise, anger, or disappointment ○ *The plane will be delayed by two hours. – What?* [Old English *hwæt* < Indo-European] ◊ **give somebody what for** to scold or punish somebody severely (*informal*) ◊ **what about ... 1** used to suggest that somebody or something be taken into consideration ○ *What about all* *the money we've already paid then?* **2** used to suggest that somebody might like to do something ○ *What about going on a fishing trip?* ◇ **what for** asking the reason for or the purpose of something ◇ **what have you** other things similar to those just mentioned ◇ **what if 1** used to make a suggestion about a possible course of action **2** used to ask what might or would happen in a given situation ◇ **what of it?** used to suggest that something is not important ◇ **what's what** the true facts or actual situation (*informal*) ◇ **what with** used to introduce the reason or reasons for something ○ *I didn't get there until ten, what with all the traffic and setting out late.*

USAGE If you use ***what*** as the subject of a clause, ***what*** takes a plural verb if its complement (i.e. the word or phrase completing the sentence) is plural: *She makes what seem* [not *seems*] *to be exaggerated claims.* If you use ***what*** as the subject of a clause, ***what*** takes a singular verb if its complement is singular: *I see what looks like a deer on the track.* The same rule applies to ***what*** clauses that occur at the beginning of sentences: *What we wanted was fairness. What we wanted were fairness and truth.* If both singular and plural complements are involved, the number of the verb in the ***what*** clause usually mimics the number of the complement closest to it: *What we expected was truthfulness and honest claims. What we got were fraudulent claims and mendacity.*

whatchamacallit /wóchəmə kawlit/ (*plural* **-its** *or* **-um** /wóchəmə kawləm/) *n* something whose name is forgotten or is not known [Early 20C. < a pronunciation of *what you may call it.*]

whatever /wot évvər/ CORE MEANING: a grammatical word used to refer to everything of a particular type, without limitation ○ (pron) *Feel free to say whatever you like.* ○ (det) *He lost whatever interest he may have had in it.*

1 *pron, adj* NO MATTER WHAT being the case in all circumstances ○ (pron) *She always seems to succeed, whatever she does.* ○ (adj) *Whatever problem you come up with they'll deal with.* **2** *pron* **what ever, whatever** EMPHATIC 'WHAT' an emphatic form of 'what' used to express an emotion such as surprise or perplexity ○ *Whatever is the matter now?* **3** *adv* OF ANY KIND used for emphasis ○ *I can see no reason whatever why you shouldn't go.* **4** *adv* EXPRESSING MILD DISAGREEMENT indicates that the speaker disagrees with what has just been said but is not prepared to argue (*informal*) ○ *OK, if that's what you think, whatever.* ◇ **or whatever** used to refer generally to something else of the same kind ○ *any tool such as a hoe, fork, or spade, or whatever*

USAGE whatever or **what ever**? ***Whatever***, written as one word, is a relative pronoun used in statements or commands: *I'll have whatever you're having. Take whatever things you need. I don't want it, whatever it is.* It is also spelt as one word as an adverb used to reinforce negative statements: *I've no idea whatever about that.* ***What ever*** is sometimes written as two words when each word retains its separate meaning and the expression is equivalent to *what on earth*, usually in questions: *What ever are they doing?*

what-if *n* a situation, difficulty, or obstacle that could arise in the future (*informal*)

whatnot /wót not/ *n* **1** SOMEBODY THE SAME OR SIMILAR something of the same or a similar kind **2** SET OF SHELVES a set of light shelves for displaying small ornamental items **3** SOMETHING UNIMPORTANT something nondescript, trivial, or unimportant [Late 16C. < *what not?*]

what's /wots/ *contr* **1** what does **2** what has **3** what is

whatshername /wótsər naym/ *pron* a woman or girl whose name you has been forgotten or is not known (*informal*)

whatshisname /wótsiz naym/ *pron* a man or boy whose name has been forgotten or is not known (*informal*)

whatsit /wótsit/ *n* something whose name you have forgotten or do not know (*informal*) [Contraction of *what-is-it*]

whatsitsname /wótsits naym/ *pron* something whose name you have forgotten or do not know (*informal*)

whatsoever /wót sō évvər/ *adv* used to emphasize a negative statement, after words such as 'none', 'no one', and 'anyone' ○ *Did you have any doubts? – None whatsoever.* ■ *pron, det* whatever (*archaic*)

whaup /wawp/ *n Scotland* a curlew [Mid-16C. An imitation of the sound of its cry.]

wheal /weel/ *n* **1** = **weal**[1] *n.* **1 2** = **weal**[1] *n.* **2** [Variant]

wheat /weet/ *n* **1** EDIBLE GRAIN grain harvested in temperate regions from a widely cultivated annual grass, which is ground into flour. Use: bread, pasta, and other foods. **2** GRASS WITH EDIBLE GRAIN an annual grass of a genus that includes types cultivated for wheat. Native to: SW Asia, the Mediterranean. Genus: *Triticum*. **3** PALE YELLOW COLOUR a pale yellow colour [Old English *hwǣte* 'that which is white' < Indo-European, 'white'] —**wheat** *adj*

wheatear /wéet eer/ *n* a small thrush typically having a white rump and black face. Native to: Europe, Asia, Africa, North America. Genus: *Oenanthe*. [Late 16C. Back-formation < *wheatears*, probably by folk etymology < WHEAT + EAR.]

wheaten /wéet'n/ *adj* **1** made from or with wheat or milled wheat flour **2** pale yellow in colour —**wheaten** *n*

wheaten terrier *n* a terrier of a medium-sized breed that has a soft, wavy, wheat-coloured coat and a docked tail

wheat germ *n* the embryonic centre of the wheat grain, rich in B vitamins, that is sold milled finely, and sometimes toasted, for sprinkling over cereals or used in cooking

wheatgrass /wéet graass/ *n* wheat grains sprouted to a height of around 17 cm/7 in, cut, and pulped to produce a highly nutritious juice that is drunk in very small quantities

wheatish /wéetish/ *adj S Asia* light creamy brown, or with a light brown complexion

wheatmeal /wéet meel/ *n* wheat flour that has had some of the bran and germ removed [Old English *hwǣtemelu*]

wheat rust *n* **1** a disease of wheat caused by various fungi and marked by blackish, brownish, or yellowish streaks on the leaves and stems **2** a fungus that causes rust in wheat

Wheatstone bridge /wéetstən-/ *n* a device consisting of an electrical circuit, three known resistances, and a galvanometer that is used for measuring an unknown resistance [Late 19C. After Sir Charles *Wheatstone* (1802–75), English physicist.]

wheatworm /wéet wurm/ (*plural* **-worms** *or* **-worm**) *n* a small nematode worm that lives as a parasite on and is destructive to wheat. *Anguina tritici.*

whee /wee/ *interj* used to express exhilarating or unrestrained joy, pleasure, or excitement [Early 20C. Natural exclamation.]

wheech /hweekh/ *vt Scotland* to take something or put something somewhere with a swift and energetic movement

wheedle /wéed'l/ (**-dles, -dling, -dled**) *v* **1** *vti* to coax or try to persuade somebody to do something using flattery, guile, or other indirect means **2** *vt* to obtain something from somebody by coaxing, flattery, guile, or other indirect means of persuasion [Mid-17C. < ?] —**wheedler** *n* —**wheedlingly** *adv*

wheel /weel/ *n* **1** ROTATING ROUND PART a ring or disc that revolves or is turned by a central shaft or pin, sometimes having a central hub with radiating spokes attached to a circular rim (*often in combination*) ○ *a wagon wheel* **2** ROUND MACHINE PART THAT TURNS ANOTHER a rotating circular part of a mechanism, often with projections on the outer edge, used to turn another part **3** STEERING WHEEL a steering wheel ○ *The instructor had to take the wheel.* ○ *He fell asleep at the wheel.* **4** SPINNING WHEEL a spinning wheel (*informal*) **5** CASTOR a small rotating or swivelling circular part fitted to the base of something such as a piece of furniture or luggage to make it easier to move **6** POTTER'S WHEEL a potter's wheel (*informal*) **7** MEDIEVAL TORTURE DEVICE a medieval instrument of torture in the form of a large wheel to which the victim was tied **8** ROTATING FIREWORK a flat round or coiled firework that spins as it burns (*often in combination*) **9** WHEEL OF FORTUNE an imaginary wheel said to be spun by fate **10** ROUND FRAME SPUN IN GAMBLING a circular device that is spun in games of chance such as roulette in order to determine who wins in a random way **11** SOMETHING RESEMBLING A WHEEL something that resembles a wheel in shape, form, or function **12** TURN a turn or revolution **13** MOVEMENT IN A CIRCLE a turning, spinning, pivoting, or circular movement **14** MILITARY FORMATION a military formation in which the inner unit remains in one place, as a pivot, while the outer units change direction and make an arc around it **15** SET OF RHYMING LINES a group of rhyming lines that end a stanza of verse ■ **wheels** *npl* **1** CAR a car, especially for personal use (*slang*) **2** DRIVI FORCE OR WORKINGS the system or influences controllir the way something functions or operates ○ *the wheels government* ■ *v* **1** *vti* MOVE ON WHEELS to push somethir that has wheels or to roll along ○ *wheeled her bicycle u the steep hill* **2** *vt* TRANSPORT SOMEBODY IN A WHEELED OBJECT move or carry somebody or something in a conveyan with wheels such as a trolley or wheelchair ○ *wheel the patient out of the room* **3** *vt* PROVIDE SOMETHING WI WHEELS to fit something with a wheel or wheels **4** *vi* TU QUICKLY to move quickly in a circle **5** *vi* MAKE A CIRCUL MOVEMENT to do something with a circular or curvir movement ○ *Her arms wheeled frantically in the air as s tried to signal for help.* **6** *vi* MOVE SMOOTHLY to mov smoothly and easily ○ *He wheeled through the gatherin making all his appointed stops.* **7** *vt* to transmit bu electric power generated by another utility or ge erating company along a grid system [Old English *hwē* < Indo-European, 'go round'] —**wheeled** *adj* —**wheelles** *adj* ◇ **reinvent the wheel 1** to waste time recreatir something that already exists in a perfectly usable an acceptable form (*disapproving*) **2** to produce a ne version of something very basic and familia (*disapproving*) ◇ **wheel and deal** to use complex an skilful, sometimes slightly dishonest, negotiating tec niques in order to secure something

wheel about *vi* **1** to turn round quickly or suddenl **2** to reverse or radically change an opinion, positio practice, or belief.

wheel around *vi* = **wheel about**

wheel in *vi* to approach or enter a place quickly an confidently (*informal*)

wheel out *v* **1** *vt* to present somebody or use somethin readily or repeatedly **2** *vi* to leave a place quickl (*informal*)

wheel round *vi* = **wheel about**

wheel and axle *n* a simple machine, often used t raise or lower loads, typically consisting of a cylindric drum and wheel mounted on the same axle with rope wound about each

wheel animalcule /-ani mál kyool/ *n* ZOOL = **rotifer**

wheelbarrow /wéel barō/ *n* a small cart used to transpo things, usually in the form of an open container with single wheel at the front and two handles at the bac ■ *vt* to move or transport something in a wheelbarro

wheelbase /wéel bayss/ *n* the distance between the fro axle and the rear axle of a motor vehicle, usually meas ured in inches

wheel bug *n* a large and powerful insect belonging t the assassin bug family that preys on other insects an has an outgrowth on its back resembling a gear. *Arilu cristatus.*

wheelchair /wéel chair/ *n* a chair with two small wheel at the front and two large wheels at the sides, used a a way of moving around by somebody who cann walk

wheelchair housing *n* houses and flats designed o adapted for people who use wheelchairs to enable the to move around easily

wheel clamp *n* a metal device fitted over the wheel c an illegally parked car to immobilize it until a fine i paid. US term **Denver boot** —**wheel-clamp** *vt*

wheeler /wéelər/ *n* **1** WHEELED VEHICLE a vehicle that has particular number of wheels (*in combination*) ○ *a three wheeler* **2** SOMEBODY WHO WHEELS somebody or somethin that wheels or pushes something with wheels **3** WHEE MAKER OR REPAIRER a maker or repairer of wheels, es pecially the wheels of carriages or wagons

Wheeler /wéelər/, **Sir Mortimer** (1890–1976) Britis archaeologist

wheeler-dealer *n* an adroit negotiator who use complex or sometimes dishonest techniques to obtai what he or she wants, especially in business or politic (*informal*) —**wheeler-dealing** *n*

wheel horse *n US, Can* a steady, diligent, and reliabl worker, especially in a political organization

wheelhouse /wéel howss/ (*plural* **-houses** /-howziz/) NAUT = **pilot house**

wheelie /wéeli/ *n* a manoeuvre performed on a movin or stationary bicycle or motorcycle in which the ride raises the front wheel off the ground and balances o the back wheel

wheelie bin *n* a large rubbish bin that has two wheel at either side of its base so that it can be manoeuvre easily

wheeling /wéeling/ *n* the transmission by an electricity company of electricity produced by another utility or generating company along its own distribution network

Wheeling /wéeling/ city in N West Virginia. Population: 32,541 (1998 estimate).

wheel lock *n* in some old firearms, a firing mechanism in which a steel spring-wound wheel strikes sparks from a piece of iron pyrites

wheelman /wéelmən/ (*plural* **-men** /-mən/) *n US* NAUT = **helmsman** *n*. 1

wheel of fortune, Wheel of Fortune *n* a revolving wheel said to determine random changes in the course of somebody's life, used as a symbol of the inconstancy of fortune

wheelsman /wéelzmən/ (*plural* **-men** /-mən/) *n US* = **helmsman**

wheel-thrown *adj* made by being turned on a potter's wheel

wheelwork /wéel wurk/ *n* an arrangement of interlocking wheels or gears within a machine or other device, e.g. the gear train in a mechanical timepiece

wheelwright /wéel rīt/ *n* a maker or repairer of wheels, especially the wheels of carriages and wagons

wheen /hween/ *n Scotland* a considerable amount or number [14C. Representing Old English *hwēne* 'somewhat', form of *hwōn* 'a few'.]

wheesht *interj, vti, n Scotland* = **whisht**

wheeze /weez/ *v* (**wheezes, wheezing, wheezed**) **1** *vi* BREATHE WITH A HOARSE WHISTLING SOUND to breathe with an audible whistling sound and with difficulty, usually because of a respiratory disorder such as asthma **2** *vt* SAY SOMETHING WITH A NOISY WHISTLING SOUND to say or express something while breathing noisily and with difficulty **3** *vi* MAKE A WHISTLING OR PUFFING SOUND to make a noisy whistling or puffing sound that resembles wheezing ○ *The old locomotive wheezed and puffed up the steep slope.* ■ *n* **1** NOISY BREATHING SOUND noisy and difficult breathing, or the hoarse whistling sound of this **2** CLEVER IDEA a good idea or clever plan (*dated informal*) **3** OFTEN REPEATED JOKE a hackneyed story, joke, or saying (*informal*) [15C. < ?] —**wheezer** *n* —**wheezily** *adv* —**wheeziness** *n* —**wheezy** *adj*

whelk[1] /welk/ (*plural* **whelk** *or* **whelks**) *n* a predatory marine gastropod mollusc with a conical spiralling shell. Family: Buccinidae. [Old English *weoloc*, altered perhaps by association with WHELK[2]]

whelk[2] /welk/ *n* a raised spot or mark on the skin such as a pimple, boil, or weal [Old English *hwylca* 'pustule, tumour'] —**whelky** *adj*

whelm /welm/ *vt* (*literary*) **1** to engulf or submerge something in water **2** to overpower or overburden somebody or something [14C. Probably alteration of Old English *āhwylfan* 'cover over, submerge', influenced by *helmian* 'cover'.]

whelp /welp/ *n* **1** YOUNG ANIMAL a young animal, especially the young of carnivorous mammals such as wolves, lions, bears, and dogs **2** RUDE YOUNG MAN a boy or young man regarded as showing inappropriate boldness or lack of deference (*insult*) **3** CHILD a child or young person (*dated humorous*) **4** RIDGE ON CAPSTAN OR WINDLASS a projection on the barrel of a capstan or windlass **5** TOOTH ON A WHEEL a tooth on a sprocket wheel ■ *vti* BEAR YOUNG to give birth to young (*refers to animals, especially carnivores*) [Old English *hwelp* < Germanic]

when /wen/ CORE MEANING: an adverb used to ask at what time or at what point things happen ○ *When can we expect you?* ○ *When should you use your rearview mirror?*
1 *conj* WHILE at or during the time that ○ *When I was a child, I lived in the country.* **2** *conj* AS SOON AS as soon as somebody does something or something happens ○ *Call me when you get home.* **3** *conj* AT SOME POINT at some point during an activity, event, or circumstance ○ *We got him when he was still a pup.* **4** *conj* EACH TIME each time something happens ○ *When it thunders the whole house shakes.* **5** *conj* IF considering the fact that ○ *Why walk when you can ride?* **6** *conj* ALTHOUGH in spite of the fact that ○ *They think I'm really easygoing, when in fact I'm not.* **7** *adv* AT OR DURING WHICH TIME indicates a time at or during which something happens ○ *When did it happen?* ○ *Since when has that been a problem?* ○ *He remembered a time when he could run a mile without any difficulty.* **8** *n* UNSPECIFIED TIME PERIOD used to refer to the time that something happened or will happen (*often plural*) ○ *We're having trouble determining the whens and hows of the thing.* [Old English *hwonne, hwænne* < Indo-European]

USAGE See *if*.

whenas /wen áz/ *conj* (*archaic*) **1** WHENEVER at such time as **2** WHILE at or during the time that **3** ALTHOUGH in spite of the fact that

whence /wenss/ *adv* **1** FROM WHERE from what place or source (*archaic or literary*) ○ *Can we know whence comes this good luck?* **2** FROM WHICH PLACE from the place or thing previously referred to (*archaic or literary*) ○ *that envy whence comes hate* **3** AS A RESULT from which cause or origin (*formal*) ○ *You have treated her badly, whence her anger.* [13C. < *whennes* 'of or from when'.]

USAGE whence or **from whence**? Both uses now sound old-fashioned or literary in tone, but ***from whence***, as an attempt to bring the form up to date, fits rather better in the structures of modern English. In everyday English, however, the word can normally be avoided altogether: *They did not know from whence they came* can easily be recast as *They did not know where they came from.*

whencesoever /wénssō évvər/ *adv, conj* from whatever cause, origin, or source (*archaic*) ○ *accept the gifts whencesoever they come*

whene'er /wen áir/ *adv, conj* whenever (*literary*)

whenever /wen évvər/ *conj* **1** AT ANY TIME at whatever time ○ *Whenever you need me I'll be there.* **2** EACH AND EVERY TIME at every time or occurrence ○ *Whenever you're around, the dog growls.* ■ *adv* (*informal*) **1 when ever, whenever** WHEN used as an intensive form of 'when' ○ *When ever will you learn?* **2** SOMETIME at another time

USAGE whenever or **when ever**? ***Whenever*** is written as one word when it is a conjunction (*Come whenever you can*), or an adverb used informally: *I'll do it at the weekend or whenever.* In questions in which *ever* is a reinforcing word, the two words are usually written separately: *When ever did I say that?*

whensoever /wenssō évvər/ *adv, conj* used as an intensive form of 'whenever'

whenua /fen óo ə/ *n NZ* land [< Maori]

where /wair/ CORE MEANING: an adverb used to ask a question about the place somebody or something is in, at, coming from, or going to ○ *Where are my keys?* ○ *Where are you going?* ○ *Guess where I've been. – Where?*
1 *adv, rel adv* IN OR TO A PLACE used to indicate the place in which something is located or happens ○ *I want to live where it's warm.* ○ *Nobody really knew where she had gone.* ○ *They went to the beach, where they spent the afternoon.* **2** *adv* WHAT PURPOSE used to ask questions about the purpose or goal of something ○ *Where will all your hard work get you?* **3** *rel adv* IN ANY SITUATION in any situation in which ○ *Where there's life, there's hope.* ○ *They're at a stage where they can now talk about their problems.* **4** *n* UNKNOWN PLACE used to refer to an unspecified place or event (*usually plural*) ○ *Let us know the wheres and whens of your itinerary.* [Old English *hwær, hwar* < Indo-European]

SPELLCHECK See ***ware***.

USAGE Avoid usages in which ***where*** follows nouns that are unrelated to the ideas of place and space: *This is a case where we must confer with a specialist. This is a situation where the accountants are wrong.* In formal writing, substitute *in which* for ***where*** in both these sentences. The preposition *from* is needed with ***where*** when the context involves a point of origin: *Where did that cat come from? From where we sit, we can see the stage clearly.* In formal writing, avoid the redundant, dangling use of *at* with ***where***. Thus: *He doesn't know where the car is* not *He doesn't know where the car is at.* Also avoid using the preposition *to* with ***where*** when ***where*** is used in contexts involving destination. Thus, *Where are you going?* not *Where are you going to?*

USAGE See ***were***.

whereabouts /wáir ə bowts/ *adv* in, at, or near what location ○ *Do you know whereabouts the hotel is?* ○ *I've forgotten whereabouts I parked the car.* ■ *n* the approximate place where somebody or something is ○ *Could you give us any information regarding the whereabouts of your brother?*

whereafter /wair áaftər/ *rel adv* after which time or event (*formal*) ○ *She left, whereafter he also departed.*

whereas /wair áz/ *conj* **1** WHILE IN CONTRAST while on the other hand ○ *She was saving money, whereas you were living in the fast lane.* **2** BECAUSE for the reason that (*formal*) ○ *Whereas you've proven your worth, you're welcome to join the team.* **3** CONNECTING SERIES used to introduce each clause in a series (*formal*)

whereat /wair át/ *rel adv* towards or at which place (*archaic*) ■ *conj* because or as a consequence of which (*archaic*)

whereby /wair bī/ *rel adv* by means of or through which ○ *the invention whereby he made his millions*

where'er /wair áir/ *adv, rel adv* wherever (*literary*)

~~whereever~~ incorrect spelling of **wherever**

wherefore /wáir fawr/ *n* REASON a reason or purpose for something ○ *I don't want to know the whys or the wherefores of your decision.* ■ *adv* (*archaic*) **1** THEREFORE for the foregoing reason **2** FOR WHAT REASON for what reason or purpose

wherefrom /wair fróm/ *adv* from what place or origin (*archaic*) ○ *Do we know wherefrom this stranger comes?*

wherein /wair ín/ *adv* HOW in what particular way or respect (*archaic*) ○ *Wherein did I misspeak myself?* ■ *rel adv* (*archaic*) **1** WHERE in which particular place ○ *the country wherein they dwelled* **2** DURING WHICH during the time that ○ *the years wherein we were ignorant and happy*

whereof /wair óv/ *rel adv* of or about what thing or person (*formal or archaic*) ○ *Do you know whereof you speak?*

whereon /wair ón/ *adv* on which thing or place (*archaic or formal*) ○ *the couch whereon she lay*

wheresoever /wáirssō évvər/ *adv, conj* used as an emphatic form of 'wherever' (*archaic*)

whereto /wair tóo/, **whereunto** /wair ún too/ *adv* where or to which (*archaic formal*) ○ *the place whereto you've brought me*

whereupon /wáirə pón/ *conj* at which time or as a result of (*formal*) ○ *The rain began to come down hard, whereupon we ran for the house.* ■ *adv* on or upon which (*archaic or formal*) ○ *the pillow whereupon she laid her head*

wherever /wair évvər/ *conj* **1** TO ANY PLACE in, at, or to any place ○ *I'll go wherever you go.* **2** EVERY TIME OR PLACE THAT on every occasion or in every place that ○ *Take exercise wherever possible.* ○ *I crossed the fields wherever there was a gate.* ■ *adv* **1** NO MATTER WHERE at or in an indefinite place ○ *I'll sleep on the couch, the floor, wherever.* **2** AT AN UNKNOWN PLACE to, in, or at an unknown or unidentified place or position **3 wherever, where ever** WHERE INDEED used as an emphatic form of 'where' ○ *Where ever have my glasses gone?*

USAGE wherever or **where ever**? ***Wherever*** is written as one word when it is a conjunction: *You can go wherever you like* or an adverb used informally: *I'll stop in Paris or wherever.* In questions in which *ever* is a reinforcing word, the two words are usually written separately: *Where ever did they go?*

wherewith /wair wíth/ *rel adv* with or by means of which (*archaic*) ○ *the tool wherewith the deed was done*

wherewithal /wáirwith awl/ *n* the money or resources required for a purpose

wherry /wérri/ (*plural* **-ries**) *n* **1** a small light rowing boat used in inland waters **2** a small barge, once used for commercial purposes in parts of England, now used largely for pleasure cruises [15C. < ?] —**wherryman** *n*

whet /wet/ *vt* (**whets, whetting, whetted**) **1** SHARPEN A TOOL OR WEAPON to sharpen the cutting edge or blade of a tool or weapon, usually by rubbing it on a stone **2** STIMULATE to make a feeling, sense, or desire more keen or intense ○ *The thought of easy money whetted my enthusiasm for the undertaking.* ■ *n* **1** SHARPENING OR INTENSIFYING an act of sharpening, intensifying, or stimulating something **2** SHARPENING BLOCK something that sharpens a cutting edge **3** SOMETHING THAT STIMULATES THE SENSES something that stimulates a feeling, sense, or desire, especially a small amount that makes somebody want more (*informal*) [Old English *hwettan* 'sharpen' < Germanic, 'sharp'] —**whetter** *n*

whether /wéthər/ *conj* **1** INTRODUCES ALTERNATIVES used to indicate alternatives in an indirect question or a clause following a verb that expresses or implies doubt or the possibility of choice ○ *We should try to meet them whether it's raining or not.* **2** INTRODUCES AN INDIRECT QUESTION used to introduce an indirect question ○ *I wonder whether it's worth the effort.* **3** EITHER used to introduce doubt regarding two equal possibilities ○ *She said she'd get here whether by car or by train.* [Old English *hwæþer, hweþer* <

Indo-European] ◇ **whether or no** whatever the circumstances might be

SPELLCHECK See ***weather***.

whetstone /wét stōn/ *n* **1** a stone used to sharpen the cutting edge or blade of a tool or weapon by rubbing **2** something that makes a feeling, sense, or desire more keen or intense

whew /fyoo, hyoo/ *interj* used to express great relief, surprise, or discomfort [15C. Natural exclamation.]

whey /way/ *n* the watery liquid that separates from the solid part of milk when it turns sour or when enzymes are added in cheese making [Old English *hwæg, hweg* < Germanic] —**wheyey** *adj*

SPELLCHECK See ***way***

wheyface /wáy fayss/ *n* **1** a very pale face (*informal*) **2** somebody whose face is regarded as too pale (*insult*) —**wheyfaced** *adj*

whf *abbr* wharf

which /wich/ CORE MEANING: used to ask for something to be identified from a known larger group or range of possibilities ○ (det) *Which part of it don't you understand?* ○ (pron) *Which would you like?* ○ (pron) *Which of the colours do you prefer?* ○ (adj) *At which stage do we start to cut our losses?*

1 *pron* **INTRODUCES A RELATIVE CLAUSE** used to introduce a clause that provides additional information about something previously mentioned ○ *The cabin, which we bought last spring, sits high on the dunes.* ○ *A success for which she is to be congratulated.* **2** *pron* **THAT** used to introduce a relative clause that provides necessary information about its antecedent ○ *Please return the money which I loaned to you.* **3** *pron* **REFERS BACK TO A PHRASE OR SENTENCE** used to refer back to an entire verb phrase or sentence ○ *Swimming after eating, which I've told you not to do, can be very dangerous.* **4** *det, pron* **ONE FROM KNOWN SET** one of a range of things or possibilities specified or implied by the immediate context ○ (det) *I can't decide which activity would be the most fun.* ○ (pron) *He decided which to buy and paid the money.* **5** *det, pron* **INDICATES CHOICE** used to indicate one or any number of things ○ (det) *Use which method best suits you.* ○ (pron) *Take which you prefer.* [Old English *hwilc* 'of what form, like what' < Germanic]

SPELLCHECK Do not confuse ***which*** with ***witch***, which has a similar sound. Beware: your spellchecker will not catch this error.

USAGE See ***that***.

whichever /wich évvər/ *det, pron* used to refer to any one or any number of items in a class ○ (det) *Whichever job you take, starting out will be hard.* ○ (pron) *I'll buy whichever you think best.*

whichsoever /wíchssō évvər/ *pron, det* whichever (*archaic*)

whicker /wíkər/ *vi* to neigh softly [Mid-17C. An imitiation of the sound.] —**whicker** *n*

whidah *n* BIRDS = **whydah**

whiff /wif/ *n* **1 SLIGHT OR BRIEF ODOUR** a faint smell of something, pleasant or unpleasant, often perceived briefly ○ *a whiff of disinfectant* **2 TRACE** a slight sign or trace of something ○ *a whiff of corruption* **3 GENTLE GUST OR PUFF** a short light gust, puff, or breath of wind **4 SNIFF** a sniff, smell, or brief inhalation of something ○ *took one whiff of the concoction and started coughing* **5 SMALL SKIFF** a narrow skiff for one rower **6 COMPLETE MISS** in golf, a swing that completely misses the ball ■ *v* **1** *vti* **WAFT OR PUFF** to come or send something in short light gusts or puffs ○ *The smoke whiffed and curled around the room.* **2** *vt* **SNIFF SOMETHING** to sniff, smell, or inhale something ○ *The hyena whiffed the night air for predators.* **3** *vi* **SMELL BAD** to have an unpleasant smell (*informal*) **4** *vi* **FAIL TO HIT A BALL** in golf, to swing at and miss a ball completely [Late 16C. Thought to suggest a light puff of wind that carries a smell.] —**whiffer** *n*

whiffle /wiff'l/ (**-fles, -fling, -fled**) *v* **1** *vi* **BEHAVE ERRATICALLY** to be indecisive or unpredictable in thought or action **2** *vti* **BLOW GENTLY** to blow or move in short light variable gusts or puffs, or to blow or move something in this way **3** *vi* **WHISTLE** to whistle softly [Late 17C. < WHIFF.] —**whiffler** *n*

whiffletree /wiff'l tree/ *n Northeast US* AGRIC = **swingletree** [Mid-19C. Variant of WHIPPLETREE.]

whiffy /wiffi/ (**-ier, -iest**) *adj* having an unpleasant smell (*informal*)

Whig /wig/ *n* **1 MEMBER OF A FORMER BRITISH POLITICAL PARTY** a member of a reforming British political party that supported the aristocracy and later the business community, finally becoming the core of the Liberal Party **2** *US* **SUPPORTER OF THE REVOLUTION AGAINST BRITISH** a supporter of the American side against the British in the War of American Independence **3** *US* **MEMBER OF 19C US POLITICAL PARTY** a member of a 19th-century US political party that favoured loose interpretation of the Constitution and opposed the Democratic Party **4 CONSERVATIVE IN THE BRITISH LIBERAL PARTY** a conservative member of the Liberal Party in the United Kingdom **5 SUPPORTER OF FREE ENTERPRISE** an opponent of government intervention in commerce and the economy **6** *Scotland* **SCOTTISH PRESBYTERIAN** a 17th-century Presbyterian in Scotland [Mid-17C. Shortening of obsolete Scots dialect *whiggamaire* 'horse driver'.] —**Whiggery** *n* —**Whiggish** *adj* —**Whiggishly** *adv* —**Whiggishness** *n* —**Whiggism** *n*

whigmaleerie /hwígmə léeri/ *n Scotland* a fanciful ornament or trinket [Mid-18C. < ?]

while /wīl/ *conj* **1 AT OR DURING SAME TIME** at or during the same time that ○ *We can talk while I fix supper.* **2** ⚠ **EVEN THOUGH** in spite of the fact that ○ *While I admire your tenacity, I cannot support your aims.* **3 BUT IN CONTRAST** but on the contrary ○ *An older car would be cheaper to buy while a newer one might be more reliable.* **4** *Scotland* **UNTIL** until ■ *n* **PERIOD OF TIME** a period of time or some interval ○ *It's been a while since I saw her.* [Old English *hwīl* 'period of time' < Indo-European, 'rest, period of rest'] ◇ **once in a while** very occasionally ◇ **worth (somebody's) while** **1** deserving somebody's time, money, or support **2** rewarding in terms of money or advantage

SPELLCHECK Do not confuse ***while*** with ***wile***, which has a similar sound. Beware: your spellchecker will not catch this error.

USAGE while or **whilst**? In all the main meanings ***while*** and ***whilst*** are interchangeable, but ***whilst*** is used more in the north of Britain than in the south. Some people dislike the use of ***while*** to mean 'even though', as in *While we agree with some of what you say, we do not accept your conclusions.*

while away *vt* to pass time in an idle, leisurely, and usually pleasant way

whiles /wīlz/ *adv* at some times (*archaic*) ■ *conj* while (*archaic*)

whilom /wīləm/ *adv* at or during some past time (*archaic*) ■ *adj* having been at an earlier time (*archaic*) [Old English *hwīlom*, form of *hwīl* (see WHILE)]

whilst /wīlst/ *conj* = **while** *conj.* 1, **while** *conj.* 2, **while** *conj.* 3 [15C. < WHILES.]

USAGE See Usage at ***while***.

whim /wim/ *n* **1** a sudden thought, idea, or desire, especially one based on impulse rather than reason or necessity **2** a winch used to lift ore or water from a mine, drawn by a horse [Mid-17C. < ?]

whimberry /wímbəri/ (*plural* **-ries**) *n Wales* a bilberry (*informal*) [Mid-19C. Alteration of *wineberry*]

whimbrel /wímbrəl/ (*plural* **-brel** *or* **-brels**) *n* a large shore bird with a long downward-curving bill, related to the curlew. *Numenius phaeopus.* [Mid-16C. < obsolete dialect *whimp* 'whimper' (with reference to the bird's cry), or < WHIMPER.]

whimper /wímpər/ *v* **1** *vi* **SOB SOFTLY** to make repeated weak plaintive crying or whining sounds of pain, distress, or fear **2** *vi* **COMPLAIN PEEVISHLY** to complain in a weak, whining, or irritated manner **3** *vt* **SAY SOMETHING PLAINTIVELY** to say something in a plaintive or whining voice ■ *n* **1 WHINE** a weak plaintive cry or whine **2 COMPLAINT** a feeble or peevish complaint [Early 16C. < *whimp* 'whimper', an imitation of the sound.] —**whimperingly** *adv*

whimsey *adj* = **whimsy**

whimsical /wímzik'l/ *adj* **1 FANCIFUL** imaginative and impulsive **2 AMUSING** slightly odd, old-fashioned, or playful, especially in an endearing way ○ *He gave me that whimsical smile of his.* **3 ERRATIC OR UNPREDICTABLE** behaving in such a way as to be impossible to predict ○ *She distrusted his whimsical nature.* [Mid-17C. < WHIMSY.] —**whimsicality** /wímzi kállәti/ *n* —**whimsically** *adv* —**whin**sicalness *n*

whimsy /wímzi/, **whimsey** *n* (*plural* **-sies**; *plural* **-sey**
1 ENDEARING QUAINTNESS OR ODDITY the quality of bein quaint, odd, or playfully humorous, especially in a endearing way ○ *There's a touch of whimsy about the o cottage.* **2 IMPULSIVE NOTION** an idea that has no im mediately obvious reason to exist ○ *We can't always catering to their whimsies.* ■ *adj* (**-sier, -siest**) **ENDEARING DIFFERENT** having the quality of quaintness or oddne (*archaic*) [Early 17C. Probably based on WHIM-WHAM, perha after words like *dropsy*.]

whim-wham *n* a quaint, odd, or fanciful object such a an ornament, toy, or device (*archaic*) ○ *some whim-wha he bought somewhere* [< ?]

whin[1] /win/ (*plural* **whin** *or* **whins**) *n* PLANTS = **gorse** [15 Probably < a N Germanic word related to Old Danish *hvin græs* 'rough grass'.]

whin[2] /win/ *n* = **whinstone** [13C. < ?]

whinchat /wín chat/ (*plural* **-chat** *or* **-chats**) *n* a sma songbird of the thrush family with mottled brown an white plumage and a streaky reddish-brown breas Native to: Asia, Europe. *Saxicola rubetra.* [Late 17C. WHIN[2] + CHAT 'warbler'.]

whine /wīn/ *v* (**whines, whining, whined**) **1** *vi* **MAKE A HIG SORROWFUL SOUND** to cry, moan, or plead with a lon plaintive, high-pitched sound **2** *vi* **GRUMBLE PEEVISHLY** complain or protest about something, often in an a noyingly plaintive voice **3** *vt* **UTTER SOMETHING IN A WHININ VOICE** to say something in a plaintive high-pitched voi **4** *vi* **MAKE A HIGH-PITCHED SOUND** to make a continuous hig pitched sound ○ *The wind whined and moaned throug the trees.* ■ *n* **1 HIGH-PITCHED CRY** a long, plaintive, hig pitched cry **2 PEEVISH COMPLAINT** a complaint or protes especially one made repeatedly in a whining voi **3 CONTINUOUS HIGH-PITCHED SOUND** a long or continuou high-pitched sound ○ *The whine of the jet engines wo me up.* [Old English *hwīnan* '(of an arrow) to whistle throug the air', of imitative origin] —**whiner** *n* —**whiningly** *adv* — **whiny** *adj*

SPELLCHECK Do not confuse ***whine*** with ***wine***, which ha a similar sound. Beware: your spellchecker will not catch th error.

SYNONYMS See ***complain***.

whinge /winj/ *vi* (**whinges, whingeing, whinged**) (*informa* **1 GRUMBLE PEEVISHLY** to complain annoyingly or con tinuously about something perceived as relatively un important **2 MAKE IRRITATING SORROWFUL SOUND** to cry c whimper annoyingly or continuously ■ *n* **PEEVISH COM PLAINT** an irritable, peevish complaint about somethin (*informal*) [Old English *hwinsian* 'whine', an imitation of th sound of a whining dog] —**whinger** *n* —**whingy** *adj*

whingeing Pom *n Aus* an English person, especiall one perceived as constantly complaining, particularl about life in Australia (*informal insult*)

whinny /wínni/ *v* (**-nies, -nying, -nied**) **1** *vi* **NEIGH** to neig softly **2** *vi* **MAKE A NEIGHING SOUND** to make a neighin sound, especially when laughing **3** *vt* **UTTER WITH A NEIGH ING SOUND** to say or express something with a neighin sound ■ *n* (*plural* **-nies**) **NEIGHING SOUND** a soft neigh o neighing sound [Mid-16C. An imitation of the sound.]

whinstone /wín stōn/ *n* a hard, dark, fine-grained roc such as basalt or chert [Early 16C. < WHIN[2] + STONE.]

whip /wip/ *v* (**whips, whipping, whipped**) **1** *vt* **LASH** to strik a person or animal repeatedly with a flexible rod, lengt of rope, thin strip of leather attached to a handle, o something similar, especially as a punishment **2** *v* **STRIKE AGAINST SOMETHING SHARPLY** to strike something o somebody very hard, sharply, or repeatedly ○ *The ic rain whipped our faces.* **3** *vt* **CRITICIZE SOMEBODY SEVERELY** t criticize or reproach somebody very strongly or se verely **4** *vti* **MOVE RAPIDLY** to move very quickly, forcefull or suddenly, or make something move in this way ○ *Sh whipped around guiltily as I came in.* **5** *vt* **MOVE SOMETHIN WITH RAPID ACTION** to move, remove, or produce some thing very quickly, suddenly, or forcefully **6** *vt* **DEFEAT** t defeat, overcome, or outdo somebody (*informal*) **7** *v* **BEAT LIQUID UNTIL STIFF** to make food such as batter o cream stiff and creamy by adding air to it with shor quick movements using a fork, whisk, or electric beate **8** *vt* **BIND THE END OF A ROPE** to wind thread, cord, or twin around the end of a rope or cable to keep it from frayin or ravelling **9** *vt* **LIFT BY A ROPE AND PULLEY** to lift somethin by means of a device consisting of a rope passe

through a single pulley **10** *vt* **SEW IN WHIPSTITCH** to sew the edge of a piece of fabric using whipstitch **11** *vt* **SPIN TOP** to make a top start to spin **12** *vt* **STEAL** to steal something or remove something (*informal*) ■ *n* **1 INSTRUMENT FOR INFLICTING PAIN** a flexible rod, a length of rope, or a thin strip of leather attached to a handle, used to strike people or animals **2 LASHING STROKE OR BLOW** a stroke or blow with a whip or something similar ○ *a whip across the face* **3 SOMETHING RESEMBLING A WHIP** something that resembles a whip in form, motion, or flexibility **4 SOMEBODY WHO USES A WHIP** an experienced or skilled user of a whip, e.g. the driver of a horse-drawn carriage **5 SOMEBODY IN CHARGE OF PARTY DISCIPLINE** an elected representative in a legislative body such as Parliament or the US Congress who has special responsibility for ensuring discipline and attendance among his or her party's representatives **6 CALL FOR PARTY SOLIDARITY** a call issued to a party's elected legislators to ensure they attend for an important vote and vote the party line **7 WEEKLY LEGISLATIVE AGENDA** in Parliament, a weekly agenda sent to a party's members that indicates which items are routine, important, or urgent **8 SWEET DISH** a light creamy dessert made from whipped cream with added sweetening and flavouring **9 HOISTING APPARATUS** a device that consists of a rope, a pulley, and a snatch block. Use: raising heavy cargo. **10 FLEXIBLE PERCUSSION INSTRUMENT** a percussion instrument with two flexible strips of wood attached in the shape of a V that make a loud clapping sound when they are waved in the air **11** FIELD SPORTS = **whipper-in** *n.* **12 WINDMILL VANE** a sail or arm of a windmill **13 FAIRGROUND AMUSEMENT** a ride at an amusement park with small cars that travel with sudden rapid jerking movements round a track **14 WRESTLING THROW** in wrestling, a throw in which an opponent is seized by an outstretched arm and thrown to the floor **15** *US* **LONG FLEXIBLE BRANCH** a long, slender, flexible branch of some trees such as willows ○ *furniture made of willow whips* [13C. Probably < Middle Low German or Middle Dutch *wippen* 'swing', < Germanic, 'move quickly'.]
◇ **crack the whip** a game in which children join hands in a line and pull each other around sharply

whip in *v* **1** *vi* to keep a pack of hounds under control **2** *vt* to keep the members of a political party in line with the party's aims

whip through *vt* to do something very quickly (*informal*)

whip up *vt* **1 EXCITE SOMETHING** to arouse or provoke a strong feeling or reaction in a group of people **2 MAKE SOMETHING RISE UP** to stir or disturb something with force so that it rises or flies up **3 PREPARE SOMETHING RAPIDLY** to make something quickly, especially an impromptu meal (*informal*)

whip bird *n* **1** a bird that has a long tail and prominent crest and emits a loud whistling sound that ends with a whip crack note. Native to: Australia. *Psophodes olivaceus* and *Psophodes nigrogularis.* **2** a bird with a call that that resembles that of a whip bird

whipcord /wíp kawrd/ *n* **1** a strong cotton or woollen fabric woven with diagonal ribs **2** a tough twisted cord. Use: whips.

whip graft *n* a way of grafting two plants by inserting the cut end of a scion into a similar cut in a rootstock and tying them securely together until they join

whip hand *n* **1** the most powerful or advantageous position in a particular situation ○ *She has the whip hand.* **2** a hand that holds a whip, especially one used to drive horses

whiplash /wíp lash/ *n* **1 FLEXIBLE PART OF WHIP** the flexible part of a whip **2 LASHING BLOW** a stroke or blow from a whip, or something that resembles this in motion, speed, or force **3 INJURY TO THE NECK** an injury to the muscles, ligaments, vertebrae, or nerves of the neck caused when the head is suddenly thrown forward and then sharply back

whipper-in /wíppər-/ (*plural* **whippers-in**) *n* an assistant to a fox hunter in controlling a pack of hounds

whippersnapper /wíppər snapər/ *n* an impudent and unimportant person, especially somebody who is young (*dated*) [Late 17C. < ?]

whippet /wíppit/ *n* a fast slender short-haired dog of a breed that resembles but is smaller than a greyhound [Mid-16C. < WHIP in the sense 'move quickly'.]

whipping /wípping/ *n* **1 PUNISHMENT** a beating, spanking, or flogging with a whip or something similar **2 BINDING CORD** thread, cord, or twine wound round the end of a rope or cable to keep it from fraying or ravelling **3 DEFEAT** a convincing defeat (*informal*) ○ *Didn't they give us a whipping in that last game?*

whipping boy *n* a person who assumes blame or punishment for the mistakes or wrongdoings of more important people [Originally, this referred to a boy raised and educated with a prince. If the prince misbehaved, the boy would be punished in his place.]

whipping cream *n* a heavy cream containing a high proportion of butterfat, which causes it to stiffen when whipped

whippletree /wípp'l tree/ *n* AGRIC = **swingletree** [Mid-18C. < WHIP.]

whippoorwill /wíppərwil/ *n* a nocturnal bird of the nightjar family, with spotted dark plumage and a distinctive song. Native to: North America. *Caprimulgus vociferus.* [An imitation of its call]

whip-round *n* an informal and often impromptu collection of money from a group of people for a particular purpose, often buying a present for somebody (*informal*)

whipsaw /wíp saw/ *n* any kind of saw that has a flexible blade, e.g. a band saw ■ *vt* (**-saws, -sawing, -sawed** *or* **-sawn**) to saw something with a whipsaw

whip scorpion *n* a terrestrial invertebrate related to the scorpion but with a whip-shaped appendage at the end of its abdomen. Native to: tropics, subtropics. Order: Uropygi.

whip snake *n* a fast-moving nonpoisonous snake that pursues its prey. Native to: North America, Asia, Europe, Africa. Genus: *Coluber.*

whipstall /wíp stawl/ *n* a manoeuvre in a small aircraft in which it goes into a vertical climb, pauses briefly, then drops towards the earth nose first

whipstitch /wíp stich/ *n* a small stitch that passes over the edge of a piece of fabric, used to finish the edge or baste two pieces of fabric together ■ *vt* to sew the edge of a piece of fabric using a whipstitch

whipstock /wíp stok/ *n* the handle of a whip

whiptail /wíp tayl/ *n* a lizard with a long thin tail. Native to: South America, Mexico. Genus: *Cnemidophorus.*

whipworm /wíp wurm/ *n* a nematode worm found in human intestines. *Trichuris trichiura.*

whir *vti, n* = **whirr**

whirl /wurl/ *v* **1** *vti* **TURN OR SPIN RAPIDLY** to turn or spin very quickly, or to make something revolve in this way **2** *vti* **MOVE WHILE TURNING QUICKLY** to move along while turning or spinning very quickly, or to make something move along in this way ○ *The dancers whirled round the floor.* **3** *vi* **FEEL DIZZY OR CONFUSED** to seem to spin with dizziness, confusion, or excitement ○ *So much information at one time made my head whirl.* **4** *vti* **MOVE VERY FAST** to move very quickly or make something move very quickly on a straight or curved course ○ *Cars whirled past on the highway.* ■ *n* **1 SPINNING MOTION** a rapid turning or spinning movement ○ *gave the prayer wheel a whirl* **2 SOMETHING THAT WHIRLS** something that moves or is moved with a rapid circular or spiral motion ○ *Whirls of dust filled the air.* **3 SENSATION OF SPINNING** a spinning sensation caused, e.g. by confusion, excitement, or dizziness ○ *So much good luck had my head in a whirl.* **4 THINGS HAPPENING IN QUICK SUCCESSION** the bustling activity of an endless series of events or engagements ○ *the whirl and bustle of a large city* **5 BRIEF TRIP OR RIDE** a short trip, ride, or dance (*informal*) ○ *Let's go for a whirl in my new car.* [13C. Probably < Old Norse *hvirfla* < Indo-European, 'turn around'.] —**whirler** *n* —**whirly** *adj* ◇ **give something a whirl** to have a try at something (*informal*)

whirlabout /wúrl ə bowt/ *n* a turn, spin, or revolution

whirligig /wúrligig/ *n* **1 SPINNING TOY** any toy that spins or turns very quickly **2 MERRY-GO-ROUND** a merry-go-round or carousel **3 SOMETHING THAT WHIRLS** something that revolves rapidly or changes continuously ○ *Her life's a whirligig since she took over the business.* **4** INSECTS = **whirligig beetle** [15C. < *whirling* or *whirly* + *gig* 'spinning top'.]

whirligig beetle *n* an aquatic insect with a smooth, oval, flattened body, usually seen spinning around on the surface of calm freshwater in groups. Family: Gyrinidae.

whirling dervish *n* **1** a dervish of a group known for whirling **2** a person who busily does many things in quick succession ○ *Once we sent out the invitations, he became a whirling dervish, cleaning, shopping, and cooking.*

whirlpool /wúrl pool/ *n* **1** a spiralling current of water in a stream or river **2** something that has or seems to have the action, motion, or power of a whirlpool ○ *a whirlpool of despair* **3** *US* = **whirlpool bath**

whirlpool bath *n* a bath or outdoor pool with powerful underwater jets that keep the water constantly moving or swirling around your body. US term **whirlpool** *n.* 3

whirlwind /wúrl wind/ *n* **1 SPINNING COLUMN OF AIR** a column of air rotating rapidly round a core of low pressure **2 SOMETHING HAPPENING OR CHANGING SWIFTLY** something that happens very quickly, or a rapid succession of events (*often before nouns*) ○ *a whirlwind romance* ○ *a whirlwind visit* **3 SOMETHING VERY DESTRUCTIVE** something that has a terrible destructive force ○ *swept up in the whirlwind of war* [14C. < Old Norse *hvirfilwindr.*]

whirlybird /wúrli burd/ *n* a helicopter (*informal*)

whirr /wur/, **whir** *vti* (**whirs, whirring, whirred**) to make a continuous soft buzzing or humming sound, usually by vibrating or turning very quickly, or to cause something to make such a sound ■ *n* a continuous soft buzzing or humming sound like that of something vibrating or turning very quickly [14C. Probably < N Germanic.]

whish /wish/ *v* **1** *vi* **MAKE OR MOVE WITH A RUSHING SOUND** to make the soft smooth rushing sound of something moving quickly through the air, or to move with such a sound ○ *Water whished along the boat as we rowed upstream.* **2** *vt* **MOVE SOMETHING QUICKLY WITH RUSHING SOUND** to cause something to make or move with a whishing sound ○ *The dog whished its tail.* ■ *n* **WHISHING SOUND OR MOVEMENT** a soft whistling or rushing sound, or a movement that makes such a sound ○ *the whish of the windscreen wipers* ■ *adv* **WITH A WHISHING SOUND** moving or falling with a whishing sound ○ *Whish, the branch came down.* [Early 16C. An imitation of the sound.]

whisht /hwisht/, **whist** /hwist/, **wheesht** /hweesht/ *interj Scotland* **CALL FOR SILENCE** used to command a person or a group to be silent ■ *vti Scotland* **BE SILENT** to silence somebody or something, or become or remain silent ■ *n Scotland* **SILENCE** the state or condition of making no noise [Mid-16C. An imitation of the sound made by someone calling for silence.]

whisk /wisk/ *n* **1 UTENSIL FOR WHIPPING** a kitchen tool, usually with curved or coiled wires attached to a handle, used with short quick movements to make a soft or liquid substance thick and frothy **2 BRUSHING MOVEMENT** a quick light brushing or sweeping movement ○ *He wiped the table with a whisk of his hand.* **3 SOMETHING USED TO SWEEP THINGS AWAY** a small brush or similar implement made of a bundle of twigs, straw, or grass, used to sweep or stir things ■ *v* **1** *vt* **MAKE THICK AND SMOOTH** to make a soft or liquid substance thick and smooth by beating it with a fork, whisk, or other device to create air bubbles in the mixture **2** *vt* **BRUSH AWAY LIGHTLY** to remove something with a quick light sweeping movement ○ *He whisked the crumbs from the table.* **3** *vt* **PLACE WITH A SWEEPING MOTION** to move or place something somewhere with a quick light sweeping motion **4** *vti* **MOVE QUICKLY** to move or take somebody or something somewhere very quickly or suddenly ○ *They whisked her off to hospital.* [14C. < N Germanic.]

whisker /wískər/ *n* **1 HAIR NEAR ANIMAL'S MOUTH** a long stiff hair growing near the mouth of some mammals, e.g. cats, mice, and rabbits **2 HAIR ON SOMEBODY'S FACE** a short stiff hair growing on somebody's face, especially on the cheeks, chin, or upper lip **3 SMALL MARGIN** a very small amount or margin ○ *We came within a whisker of losing everything.* **4 whisker, whisker boom LIGHT POLE** a light pole used for extending the corners of a sail **5 THIN CRYSTAL** a strong thin hair-shaped crystal of a metal or mineral ■ **whiskers** *npl* **SOMEBODY'S FACIAL HAIR** a short growth of hair growing on somebody's cheeks, chin, or upper lip [15C. < WHISK.] —**whiskered** *adj* —**whiskery** *adj*

whiskey /wíski/ (*plural* **-keys**) *n US, Ireland* whisky. ◊ **Irish whiskey**

whiskey sour *n* BEVERAGES = **whisky sour**

whisk fern *n* a simple plant with slender branching stems and tiny scale-shaped leaves, that reproduces by means of spores. Native to: tropical and subtropical regions. *Psilotum nudum.*

whisky /wíski/ (*plural* **-kies**) *n* **1** an alcoholic beverage made from a fermented grain, such as corn, rye, or barley, that is sometimes aged or blended **2** a drink or measure of whisky [Early 18C. < Scottish Gaelic *usquebea, usque beatha* 'water of life' < *usque* 'water' and *bethu* 'life'.]

Whisky /wíski/ *n* a code word for the letter 'W', used in international radio communications

whisky jack *n US, Can* = **grey jay** [< *whiskey john*, by folk etymology < Cree *wiskatjan*]

whisky mac *n* a drink made of whisky and ginger wine

whisky sour, whiskey sour *n* a mixed drink containing whisky, often an American whiskey such as bourbon, lemon juice, and sugar

whisper /wíspər/ *v* 1 *vti* **BREATHE WORDS VOICELESSLY** to speak or say something very softly, without using the vocal cords 2 *vti* **SPEAK OR SUGGEST SOMETHING SECRETLY** to speak or say something in a confidential or furtive manner, often to spread gossip, reveal a secret, or conspire with somebody ○ *Whisper so that no one else hears.* 3 *vi* **RUSTLE SOFTLY** to make a soft rustling sound ■ *n* 1 **VERY LOW VOICE** a soft speaking sound that uses the breath but not the vocal cords ○ *She spoke in a whisper.* 2 **SOMETHING SAID IN SOFT VOICE** something said in a whisper 3 **RUSTLING SOUND** a soft rustling sound 4 **FAINT HINT** a hint or trace of something ○ *a whisper of perfume* 5 **RUMOUR** a rumour expressed confidentially or furtively ○ *Ignore the whispers of the crowd.* [Old English *hwisprian* < Germanic] —**whisperer** *n*

whispering campaign /wíspəring-/ *n* the spreading of scandalous rumours in order to damage or destroy the reputation of a person or group

whispering gallery *n* a space or gallery beneath a dome or vault with acoustic properties such that a faint sound made at one point travels round the entire circumference and is audible at any point on it

whist[1] /wist/ *n* a card game in which two pairs of people try to take a majority of the tricks and the trump suit is determined by the last card dealt [Mid-17C. < ?]

whist[2] *interj, vti, n* = **whisht**

whist drive *n* a card party at which the winning players of each hand of whist move to different tables and play the losers of the preceding hand

whistle /wíss'l/ *v* (**-tles, -tling, -tled**) 1 *vi* **MAKE A SHRILL SOUND THROUGH PURSED LIPS** to make a shrill or musical sound by forcing the breath through a small gap between the lips or the teeth 2 *vi* **PRODUCE A SHRILL SOUND** to produce a shrill sound or signal by forcing steam or air through a narrow opening (*refers to trains, kettles, etc.*) ○ *heard the train whistle as it came round the bend* 3 *vi* **MOVE WITH A SHRILL SOUND** to move at great speed through the air, making a shrill sound ○ *bullets whistling by overhead* 4 *vt* **MAKE A MUSICAL SOUND BY WHISTLING** to produce music or give a signal by whistling ○ *whistling a tune* 5 *vti* **ISSUE A CALL OR ORDER BY WHISTLING** to express a summons or order to a person or animal by whistling 6 *vi* **EMIT A SHRILL CHARACTERISTIC CALL** to make a characteristically shrill sound, using the mouth or throat or by other means (*refers to birds or animals*) ■ *n* 1 **DEVICE PRODUCING A SHRILL SOUND** a device or instrument that produces a shrill or musical sound when air or breath is forced through it 2 **WHISTLING SOUND** a sound or signal made by a person, animal, or object whistling ○ *He let out a low whistle.* 3 **ACT OF WHISTLING** an act of whistling [Old English *hwistlian* < Germanic, 'whistle, hiss'] ◇ **blow the whistle (on somebody** *or* **something)** to report somebody for doing something wrong or illegal, especially within an organization ◇ **wet your whistle** to have a drink, especially of alcohol (*dated informal*)

whistle for *vt* to expect something that is not going to happen or be given (*informal*)

whistle up *vt* to summon a person or animal by making a whistling call

whistle-blower *n* an exposer of wrongdoing, especially within an organization [< the idea of a police officer sounding the alarm when witnessing a crime] —**whistle-blowing** *n*

whistler /wísslər/ *n* 1 **WHISTLING PERSON OR OBJECT** somebody or something that whistles 2 **RADIO DISTURBANCE** an interference signal in a radio receiver, resembling a whistling sound of decreasing pitch and caused by lightning or other electromagnetic disturbance 3 **WHISTLING AUSTRALIAN FLYCATCHER** an often brightly coloured flycatcher with a particularly melodious whistling call. Native to: Australia. Genus: *Pachycephala*. 4 **HORSE WITH A RESPIRATORY PROBLEM** a horse with a breathing defect that causes it to make a whistling noise when it breathes in

Whistler /wísslər/, **James Abbott McNeill** (1834–1903) US artist

whistle stop *n* 1 **SHORT STOP** a short stop to make a brief public appearance, especially one made by a political candidate during an election campaign 2 *US* **SMALL RAILWAY STATION** a town or railway station where trains stop only when signalled to do so 3 *US* **SMALL TOWN** a small town or community (*slang*)

whistle-stop *adj* **HAVING FREQUENT STOPS** conducted very rapidly with frequent brief stops or visits, especially in order to make public appearances or deliver election speeches ○ *a whistle-stop tour of the state* ■ *vi* (**whistle-stops, whistle-stopping, whistle-stopped**) 1 **TOUR SMALL TOWNS** to make a rapid tour that features many stops in small towns 2 **MAKE A BRIEF STOP** to make a short stop in a place as part of a rapid tour, especially as a political candidate

whistling duck *n* a long-legged duck with an upright stance and often a whistling call. Native to: tropical waters. Genus: *Dendrocygna*.

whit /wit/ *n* the smallest imaginable degree or amount (*dated*) ○ *I don't care a whit whether they succeed or fail.* [15C. Alteration of WIGHT.]

Whit /wit/ *n* = **Whitsuntide** ■ *adj* occurring at or relating to Whitsuntide [Mid-16C. Shortening of *Whitsun* or *Whit Sunday*.]

Whitaker /wíttəkər/, **Sir Frederick** (1812–91) British-born New Zealand statesman

Whitby /wítbi/ fishing port and resort in N England, on the North Sea. Population: 14,000 (1994).

white /wīt/ *adj* (**whiter, whitest**) 1 **SNOW-COLOURED** of the colour of fresh snow, resulting from the reflection of nearly all light from visible wavelengths 2 **LACKING COLOUR** without colour or hue 3 **white, White PALE-SKINNED** belonging or relating to a people with naturally pale skin, especially one of European ancestry 4 **COMPARATIVELY LIGHT** light in colour in comparison with others of the same kind ○ *white cabbage* 5 **MADE FROM WHITE GRAPES** describes wine made from pale-skinned grapes 6 **LACKING PIGMENT** describes hair that has lost most or all of its pigment, usually as a result of aging 7 **HAVING A VERY PALE COMPLEXION** unusually pale in the face, e.g. from fright or shock 8 **HAVING WHITE PARTS OR COLOURINGS** describes plants or animals with light or white parts or colourings ○ *white bass* 9 **WITHOUT BRAN OR GERM** describes flour that has had the bran and wheat germ removed 10 **MADE FROM WHITE FLOUR** made using white flour 11 **SERVED WITH MILK** served with milk added ○ *white coffee* 12 **UNMARKED BY WRITING** not written on or printed on 13 **PURE** unblemished, especially in character 14 **WEARING WHITE** dressed in white, or characterized by the wearing of white ○ *a white wedding* 15 **white, White POLITICALLY CONSERVATIVE** conservative or royalist in political outlook 16 **INCANDESCENT** heated to such a high degree that the substance turns white in colour 17 **HAVING SNOW** accompanied or characterized by the presence of snow ○ *a white Christmas* 18 **LACKING TONAL WARMTH** relating to a pure musical tone that lacks warmth, colour, and resonance ■ *n* 1 **COLOUR OF SNOW** the colour of fresh snow 2 **WHITE PAINT** a paint or dye that is or is near to the colour of fresh snow 3 **WHITE OBJECT** a white object, substance, or fabric, or the part of something that is white, e.g. an unprinted area on a page 4 **WHITE CLOTHING** clothing that is white (*usually plural*) 5 **white, White PALE-SKINNED PERSON** a member of a people with pale skin, especially one of European ancestry 6 **PART OF EGG** the transparent liquid that surrounds the yolk of an egg and turns white when the egg is cooked 7 **PART OF EYE** the part of the eyeball surrounding the iris 8 **PART OF TARGET** the white outermost ring of an archery target or a shot that lands in it 9 **GAME PIECE OR PLAYER** a white or light-coloured piece or set of pieces in a game such as chess or draughts, or the player using them 10 **BUTTERFLY** a butterfly that is predominantly white in colour. Family: Pieridae. ■ *v* (**whites, whiting, whited**) 1 *vt* **LEAVE BLANK SPACES IN** to make or leave blank spaces in something, especially something printed 2 *vti* **WHITEN** to become or cause something to become white (*archaic*) [Old English *hwīt* < Indo-European, 'shine'] —**whiteness** *n* —**whitish** *adj*

white out *v* 1 *vt* to cover a mistake in written, printed, or typed material using white correction fluid 2 *vi* to lose visibility in daylight because of snow or fog

White /wīt/, **Patrick** (1912–90) British-born Australian writer

white admiral *n* 1 a butterfly that has brown wings with white marks. Native to: Europe, Asia. *Limenitis camilla*. 2 a butterfly that has bluish-black wings with a large white band on them. Native to: North America. *Limenitis arthemis*.

white alkali *n* a whitish deposit of mineral salts that is sometimes seen on the surface of very alkaline soils

Patrick White

white ant *n* INSECTS = **termite**

white area *n* an area of land not yet subject to plannin proposals or limitations [< The idea of its not being code in any particular colour on planning maps]

white ash *n* 1 an ash tree that has leaves with a pal silvery underside. Native to: North America. *Fraxinu americana*. 2 the wood of the white ash tree. Use: oars. [the pale colour of the undersides of its leaves]

White Australia Policy *n* the policy of limiting th number of non-white people migrating to Australia embodied in the Immigration Restriction Act of 190 and officially abandoned in 1945

whitebait /wīt bayt/ (*plural* **-bait**) *n* 1 a small young fis fried and eaten whole, especially a young herring 2 small marine fish that swims into brackish and fres water to spawn. Native to: Australia, New Zealand *Galaxias attenuatus*. [Mid-18C. *White* < the silvery colour o most of the fish.]

white bass *n* an edible silvery freshwater fish of th bass family. Native to: Great Lakes, Mississippi valley *Morone chrysops*.

whitebeam /wīt beem/ *n* a deciduous tree whose leave have pale hairy undersides. Native to: Europe, Asia *Sorbus aria*. [Early 18C. < the white undersides of its leaves.]

white belt *n* 1 the belt worn by a beginner in a martia art such as karate or judo 2 a martial arts novice

white blood cell *n* an unpigmented large cell in blood that helps protect the body against infection and als plays a role in inflammation and allergic reactions

whiteboard /wīt bawrd/ *n* a board for writing on, similar to a blackboard but with a white plastic surface that is written on with erasable marker pens, used in teaching and in giving presentations [Mid-20C. < WHITE, after *blackboard*.]

white book *n* in some countries, an official government report published in a white binding

white bread *n* bread made from flour that has had the bran and wheat germ removed

white-bread *adj* (*informal*) 1 bland, conventional, and unimaginative 2 *US* relating to, belonging to, or considered typical of white, middle-class North America

white bryony *n* a climbing plant with lobed leaves and reddish-black berries. Native to: Europe, Asia, North Africa. Genus: *Bryonia*. [< its greenish-white flowers]

whitecap /wīt kap/ *n* the white crest of a breaking wave

white cedar *n* 1 light-coloured durable wood from either of two coniferous trees. Use: boatbuilding, telegraph poles. 2 either of two coniferous trees that have leaves resembling scales and yield white cedar. Native to: E North America. *Chamaecyparis thyoides* and *Thuja occidentalis*. [< the light colour of their wood]

white cell *n* PHYSIOL = **white blood cell**

white chip *n* 1 a betting chip with the lowest possible value 2 a thing of little value

white chocolate *n* a cream-coloured confection containing the same ingredients as chocolate but lacking cocoa powder

white Christmas *n* a Christmas when there is snow, especially on Christmas day

white cloud, white cloud mountain fish *n* a small brightly coloured freshwater fish of the minnow family, popular for aquariums. Native to: Asia. *Tanichthys albonubes*. [Mid-20C. After *White Cloud*, English name of a mountain northeast of Guangzhou (Canton), China, where the fish was discovered.]

white clover *n* a perennial plant grown with grass as pasture for livestock. Flowers: small, white, attractive to honey bees. Native to: Europe, Asia, naturalized in North America. *Trifolium repens.*

white coal *n* flowing water considered as a source of hydroelectric power

white-collar *adj* relating to jobs that are usually salaried and do not involve manual labour. ◊ **blue-collar, pink-collar** [< the white shirts traditionally worn by people in such jobs]

white-collar crime *n* crime committed in the workplace by white-collar workers, e.g. embezzlement and fraudulent accounting practices

white corpuscle *n* = **white blood cell**

white-crowned sparrow *n* a sparrow with black-and-white bands on its head. Native to: W and N North America. *Zonotrichia leucophrys.*

white currant *n* **1** a greenish white berry, usually eaten raw **2** a variety of redcurrant that produces white currants. *Ribes sativum.*

whitedamp /wīt damp/ *n* a mixture of poisonous gases that collects in coalmines [After BLACKDAMP]

whited sepulchre *n* a hypocrite, especially somebody who is falsely righteous or pious [< the Bible (Matthew 23:27), which compares such people to whitewashed tombs]

white dwarf *n* a small, dim, extremely dense star that has collapsed on itself and is in the final stages of its evolution [< its colour]

white elephant *n* **1 SOMETHING COSTLY TO MAINTAIN** an expensive and often rare or valuable possession whose upkeep is a considerable financial burden **2 POSSESSION OF QUESTIONABLE VALUE** something with a questionable or at least very limited value **3 CONSPICUOUS FAILED VENTURE** a much publicized or keenly anticipated venture that proves to be a spectacular flop **4 DISCARDED OBJECT** an unwanted object of possible use to somebody else (*dated; hyphenated before nouns*) **5 ALBINO ELEPHANT** a rare albino Indian elephant regarded as sacred in India and in neighbouring parts of Southeast Asia [Said to derive from the practice of the King of Siam of giving a white elephant to troublesome courtiers, who would be ruined by the cost of keeping it]

White Ensign *n* the flag of the British Royal Navy, showing a red cross on a white background with the Union Jack in the upper corner nearest the hoist

white-eye *n* a small green or greenish-brown songbird with a ring of white feathers round the eye. Native to: tropical and subtropical regions. Family: Zosteropidae.

whiteface /wīt fayss/ *n* white makeup for the face, particularly as used by clowns

white-faced *adj* **1** having a face that has turned pale through fear, anger, or some other strong emotion **2** having white markings on the face, especially when this distinguishes one species from other similar species

white-faced heron *n* a medium-sized heron that has grey plumage, yellow legs, and a white face. Native to: Australia. *Ardea novaehollandiae.*

white fish *n* any or all edible marine fish with whitish flesh, including cod, hake, and whiting, as distinct from flat fish such as plaice and oily fish such as mackerel

whitefish /wīt fish/ (*plural* **-fishes** /-fish/ *or* **-fish**) *n* **1** a freshwater fish with large scales and a small mouth. Native to: North America. Family: Coregonidae. **2** the pale flesh of a whitefish eaten as food

white flag *n* a white cloth or improvised flag waved as an international sign of truce or surrender

white flight *n* the movement of white people that sometimes occurs from neighbourhoods where members of other groups are settling, especially because of racism

white flour *n* flour from which most of the bran and wheat germ has been removed

whitefly /wīt flī/ (*plural* **-flies** *or* **-fly**) *n* a minute insect with a white waxy coating on the body. Many species suck the sap from garden and house plants. Family: Aleyrodidae.

white fox *n* the arctic fox in its white winter coat. Its coat is dark grey in summer.

white friar, White Friar *n* a member of the Carmelite order of monks [< the white habits of the monks]

white frost *n* METEOROL = **hoar frost**

white gold *n* a silvery-looking gold alloy that contains gold mixed with palladium, nickel, or sometimes zinc and is typically used in jewellery

white goods *npl* **1** large household appliances such as refrigerators, cookers, and dishwashers, typically finished with white enamel **2** household goods made of fabric, e.g. bed linens, towels, and tablecloths

white gum *n* any eucalyptus tree with a whitish bark. Native to: Australia. Genus: *Eucalyptus.*

white-haired *adj* having hair that has become white with advanced age

Whitehall /wīt hawl/ *n* **1 CENTRAL LONDON STREET** a street in central London, between Trafalgar Square and the Houses of Parliament, containing the main offices of the British civil service **2 BRITISH GOVERNMENT** a collective term for the administration and civil service departments of the British government, many of which are located in Whitehall **3 TRINIDADIAN PRIME MINISTER'S RESIDENCE** the official residence of the prime minister of Trinidad

ϟ **white hat hacker** a hacker hired by a firm to predict and counteract attacks on its computer systems. ◊ **black hat hacker**

Whitehaven /wīt hayv'n/ fishing port in NW England. Population: 26,542 (1991).

whitehead /wīt hed/ *n* a small pimple with a whitish top formed when a sebaceous gland becomes blocked. Technical name **milium** [Mid-20C. After *blackhead.*]

Whitehead /wīt hed/, **Alfred North** (1861–1947) British mathematician and philosopher

white-headed *adj* **1** having white markings on the feathers, hair, or fur of the head, especially when this distinguishes one species from other similar species **2** favoured over others and considered blessed by luck

white heat *n* **1** an extremely high degree of heat characterized by the emission of white light **2** a state of intense excitement or activity

white hole *n* a hypothetical region in space from which stars, light, and other forms of energy explosively emerge [After *black hole*]

white horse *n* **1** = **whitecap 2** the outline of a horse carved in prehistoric times in exposed chalk on a hillside [In the sense of 'whitecap', from its imagined resemblance to a horse's head and flowing mane]

Whitehorse /wīt hawrss/ capital of the Yukon Territory, Canada, on the Yukon River. Population: 19,157 (1996).

white-hot *adj* **1** so hot that white light is emitted **2** characterized by intense excitement or activity

White House *n* **1 OFFICIAL RESIDENCE OF US PRESIDENT** the large white mansion in Washington, D.C. that is the official residence of the president of the United States **2 EXECUTIVE BRANCH OF THE US GOVERNMENT** the executive branch of the US government **3 RUSSIAN PARLIAMENT BUILDING** the Russian parliament building in central Moscow

white hunter *n* a white man hunting big game professionally or working as a safari guide, especially in Africa in former times

White Island /wīt-/ uninhabited volcanic island off the northeastern coast of the North Island, New Zealand, in the Bay of Plenty. Area: 3.2 sq. km/1.2 sq. mi.

white knight *n* **1** a rescuer of a person or situation from disaster **2** a person or organization that rescues a business company, especially from an undesirable takeover

white-knuckle *adj* causing or characterized by fear, apprehension, nervousness, or uncertainty [< the appearance of nervously clenched fists]

white-knuckle ride *n* **1** a situation, experience, or encounter that causes fear, anxiety, or uncertainty **2** a frightening or exhilarating fairground ride, especially a roller coaster

white lady *n* a cocktail made with gin, Cointreau™, and lemon juice

white lead *n* **1** $2PbCO_3.Pb(OH)_2$ lead carbonate in the form of a poisonous heavy white powder, used as a pigment in paints and in putty **2** putty made from white lead suspended in boiled linseed oil

white leather *n* soft leather treated with salt and alum for a white finish

Whiteley /wītli/, **Brett** (1939–92) Australian artist

white lie *n* a lie perceived or intended not to harm, but told in order to avoid distress or embarrassment

SYNONYMS See *lie.*

white light *n* light such as sunlight that contains all the wavelengths from red to violet at approximately equal intensity

white lightning *n US* strong, illegally distilled alcohol, usually whisky (*regional*) [*White* because it is usually colourless]

white line *n* a white line along the middle or edge of a road, used to mark the edge of a road or to separate lanes of traffic, especially those moving in opposite directions

white list *n* a list of people, organizations, or items deemed acceptable. ◊ **blacklist** [After *blacklist*] —**white-listed** *adj*

whitely /wītli/ *adv* showing a face pale with anger, fear, or shock

white magic *n* supposed magic practised for good purposes or as an antidote to evil [After *black magic*]

white mahogany *n US* INDUST = **primavera**[1] *n.* **2**

white man's burden *n* the supposed responsibility of Europeans and their descendants to impose their allegedly advanced civilization on the non-white original inhabitants of the territories they colonized (*often considered offensive*)

white marlin *n* a large marine fish with a light-coloured belly, one of the smaller species of marlin. Native to: W Atlantic. *Tetrapturus albidus.*

white matter *n* the whitish nerve tissue of the brain and spinal cord, consisting mostly of myelinated nerve fibres. ◊ **grey matter**

white meat *n* light-coloured meat, especially chicken, turkey, or pork, that is usually lower in fat than red meat, more tender, more delicate in flavour, and requires a shorter cooking time

white metal *n* a light-coloured alloy, especially one with a high tin or lead content such as pewter or babbitt

white mica *n* MINERALS = **muscovite**

white mulberry *n* **1** the edible berry of a Chinese mulberry tree. **2** a mulberry tree that bears white mulberries. Native to: China. *Morus alba.*

whiten /wīt'n/ *vti* to become or cause something to become white or lighter in colour

whitener /wīt'nər/ *n* **1** any substance used to colour something white or enhance its whiteness, e.g. a dye for sports shoes or bleach **2** a substance added to tea or coffee as a substitute for milk, usually in powder form and lower in calories or with a longer shelf life than milk

White Nile section of the River Nile from near the Sudan-Uganda border to its junction with the Blue Nile at Khartoum. Length: 2,084 km/1,295 mi.

white noise *n* low-volume electrical or radio noise of equal intensity over a wide range of frequencies [By analogy with white light, which contains light from the whole range of visible frequencies]

white oak *n* **1** an oak tree with evenly lobed hairless leaves and pale wood. Native to: E North America. *Quercus alba.* **2** TREES = **roble** *n.*

whiteout /wīt owt/ *n* **1** an atmospheric condition in which low clouds merge with a snow-covered landscape, greatly restricting visibility, and only darker objects are discernible **2** a blizzard that is so severe it reduces visibility to virtually zero [Mid-20C. After BLACKOUT.]

white paper *n* **1** in many countries, an official report setting out government policy on a particular issue to be voted on by the country's parliament or congress. ◊ **green paper 2** an official, authoritative, or heavily researched report on a topic, e.g. a report produced by a group of journalists [Because such reports are customarily printed as white pamphlets]

white pepper *n* light-coloured pepper made from peppercorns that have had their dark husk removed

white perch *n* a silver-coloured edible fish that is a variety of sea bass. Native to: W Atlantic, freshwater streams of E North America. *Morone americana.*

white pine *n* **1 WOOD OF PINE TREE** the soft durable wood of a North American pine tree (*hyphenated before nouns*) **2 N AMERICAN PINE** a fast-growing pine tree that is planted for white pine. Native to: E North America. *Pinus* strobus. **3 SIMILAR PINE TREE** a pine that resembles the white pine, particularly in having five-needle clusters [< its light-coloured wood]

white poplar n 1 the straight-grained wood of a poplar tree (*hyphenated before nouns*) **2** a poplar tree that has white woolly leaves and yields white poplar. Native to: Europe, Asia. *Populus alba.*

white potato n the edible tuber of a potato with whitish flesh, or the plant that it grows on

white pudding n a sausage made from light-coloured offal, e.g. brain and sweetbreads, and bound with oatmeal or a similar starchy ingredient but not mixed with blood

white rice n rice that has had both the outer husk and the bran layer removed. ◊ **brown rice**

white room n SCI = **clean room**

White Russian n 1 PEOPLES = **Belarusian** n. 1 **2** an opponent of the Bolsheviks during the Civil War (1918–21) that followed the 1917 Russian Revolution **3** a cocktail made from vodka, coffee liqueur, and cream

whites /wīts/ npl **1 WHITE LAUNDRY** white or light-coloured laundry, usually washed separately from coloured laundry items **2 SPORTS CLOTHES** white or off-white clothing of a particular kind, especially as worn by sportspeople such as tennis players or cricketers **3** US **WHITE DRESS MILITARY UNIFORM** the white dress uniform of a military service such as that of the US Navy or Coast Guard **4 LEUCORRHOEA** leucorrhoea (*informal*)

white sale n a sale of household linen

white sapphire n a precious stone that is a colourless variety of corundum. Use: gems.

white sauce n a pale milk sauce, thickened with butter and flour or cornflour and variously seasoned or flavoured

White Sea arm of the Barents Sea on the coast of NW Russia. Area: 95,000 sq. km/36,700 sq. mi.

white shark n ZOOL = **great white shark**

white sheep n ZOOL = **Dall sheep**

white slave n a white girl or woman sold into prostitution against her will —**white slaver** n —**white slavery** n

whitesmith /wīt smith/ n **1** a maker or repairer of objects made from metal, especially tin and other white metals **2** somebody whose job is smoothing and polishing metal articles that have been forged [14C. After BLACKSMITH.]

white space n an area of a page or other printed surface where no text or pictures appear

white spirit n a colourless liquid derived from petroleum and used like turpentine, e.g. to clean paintbrushes and to thin paint

white spruce n **1** the soft wood of a North American spruce tree **2** a spruce tree that has short blue-grey needles and whitish shoots and that yields white spruce. Native to: N North America. *Picea glauca.* [< its silvery-brown bark]

white squall n a violent tropical or subtropical storm that stirs up the surface of the sea into whitecaps, but is limited to a very localized area, often with no storm clouds present

white stick n a white-coloured walking stick used by a visually-impaired person to detect obstacles in his or her path

white stork n a stork with black-and-white plumage, reddish feet, and a reddish bill. Native to: Europe, Asia. *Ciconia ciconia.*

white supremacy n the view that white people are supposedly genetically and culturally superior to all other people or races and should therefore rule over them —**white supremacist** n

white-tailed deer, **whitetail** /wīt tayl/ n a deer with a greyish or reddish-brown coat and a tail that is white on the underside. Native to: North America. *Odocoileus virginianus.*

whitethorn /wīt thawrn/ n TREES = **hawthorn** [13C. *White* < the fact that its bark is lighter in colour than the blackthorn's.]

whitethroat /wīt thrōt/ n **1** a small songbird with a white throat. Native to: Europe, Asia, North Africa. Genus: *Sylvia.* **2** BIRDS = **white-throated sparrow**

white-throated sparrow n a sparrow with a prominent white throat and black-and-white bands on its head. Native to: North America. *Zonotrichia albicollis.*

white tie n **1** a white bow tie worn as part of a man's formal evening dress. ◊ **black tie 2** a man's full formal evening clothes, consisting of a black suit with a tail coat and a white bow tie

white-tie adj requiring evening dress for women and full formal evening clothes for men, with tail coats and white bow ties

white trash n US an offensive term for a white person or group of white people considered as possessing the stereotypical characteristics of members of a lower-income group in society (*slang; takes a singular or plural verb*)

white van man, **White Van Man** n a stereotyped figure, typically the driver of a white delivery van, caricatured as young, aggressive, urban, and with bad driving habits (*informal*)

white vitriol n CHEM = **zinc sulphate**

whitewall /wīt wawl/, **whitewall tyre** n a vehicle tyre with a band of white on the outside sidewall

whitewash /wīt wosh/ n **1 WHITE PAINTING SOLUTION** lime suspended in water, often with glue or sizing, and used like paint for whitening walls **2 COVER-UP** a coordinated attempt to hide unpleasant facts, especially in a political context (*informal*) **3 THOROUGH DEFEAT** a resounding defeat, especially one in which the losing player or team does not score at all (*informal*) ■ v **1** vt **PAINT SOMETHING WITH WHITEWASH** to paint something, usually a wall, with whitewash **2** vti **HIDE TRUTH ABOUT** to conceal the unpleasant facts about something **3** vt **DEFEAT SOMEBODY DECISIVELY** to defeat an opposing player or team resoundingly, especially by preventing the player or team from scoring at all —**whitewasher** n

white water n **1** fast-flowing water with a foamy, choppy surface **2** lighter-coloured sea water visible in shallow areas

whitewater rafting n the outdoor leisure pursuit of floating on a raft down a fast-flowing river

white wedding n a wedding that takes place in a Christian church, with the bride wearing a traditional white dress

white whale n a small white fish-eating whale with a bulbous head. Native to: Arctic waters. *Delphinapterus leucas.*

white-winged dove n a dove with white patches on its wings. Native to: S United States, Mexico. *Zenaida asiatica.*

white-winged scoter n a sea duck that is mostly black with a white patch on each wing. Native to: North America. *Melanitta fusca.*

white witch n a witch whose supposed magic is designed to do good or to counter evil magic [*White* because such a witch practises white magic]

whitewood /wīt wood/ n **1** the pale wood of some deciduous trees **2** a deciduous tree such as the tulip tree, cottonwood, or basswood

whitey /wītī/ (*plural* **-eys**), **whity** (*plural* **-ies**) n an offensive term for a white person (*slang*)

whither /wīthər/ adv, rel adv to what place (*archaic or literary*) ■ adv to what state, condition, outcome, or degree (*literary or humorous*) ○ a debate entitled 'Whither capitalism?' [Old English hwider < Germanic]

whiting¹ /wīting/ (*plural* **-ing**) n **1 EUROPEAN FISH** a small sea fish related to the cod, with a silvery underside. Native to: Europe. *Merlangus merlangus.* **2 PACIFIC AND ATLANTIC FISH** a commercially important fish such as the American silver hake or corbina that is similar to the European whiting. Native to: Pacific and Atlantic oceans. Genera: *Merluccius* and *Menticirrhus.* **3 WHITING AS FOOD** the white flesh of the whiting as food, commercially important throughout Europe [15C. < Dutch *wijting*, < *wijt* 'white'.]

whiting² /wīting/ n pure powdered chalk used as an ingredient in various commercial preparations such as putty and whitewash [15C. < WHITE.]

Whitlam /wītləm/, **Gough** (b. 1916) Australian statesman

Whitley Council /wītli-/ n a consultative committee or organization consisting of representatives from the management and staff of a company or industry, set up to discuss industrial relations, working conditions, and other work-related issues [Early 20C. After J. H. *Whitley* (1866–1935), British politician.]

whitlow /wītlō/ n a pus-filled infection on the skin at the side of a fingernail or toenail [14C. Alteration of earlier *whitflawe* < WHITE + FLAW¹.]

Walt Whitman

Whitman /wīt mən/, **Walt** (1819–92) US poet and essayist. Born **Walter Whitman**

Whit Monday n the Monday after Pentecost, formerly a public holiday in England, Ireland, and Wales [After WHIT SUNDAY]

Whitney /wītnee/, **Eli** (1765–1825) US inventor

Whitstable /wītstəb'l/ fishing port in SE England. Population: 28,907 (1991).

Whitsun /wīts'n/ n = **Whitsuntide** ■ adj relating to or happening on Whitsuntide or Whit Sunday [13C. Back-formation < WHIT SUNDAY, understood as 'Whitsun day'.]

Whit Sunday n CHR = **Pentecost** n. 1 [Old English hwīta sunnandæg 'white Sunday', because of the white robes the priests wear on this day]

Whitsunday Islands group of approximately 70 islands off the coast of SE Queensland, Australia, in the Coral Sea. Area: 98 sq. km/38 sq. mi.

Whitsuntide /wīts'n tīd/ n the days around and including the Christian festival of Pentecost [13C. < WHITSUN + TIDE in obsolete sense of 'period of time'.]

whittle /wīt'l/ v (**-tles**, **-tling**, **-tled**) vti to carve something out of wood, usually something small enough to hold in the hand, by cutting away small pieces of wood [Mid-16C. < *whyttel* 'knife', variant of *thwitel*, 'tool for paring' < Old English *þwītan* 'pare, cut'.] —**whittler** n

whittle away vt to deplete something by using or spending a little of it at a time

whittle down vt to reduce or diminish something gradually by taking away a little of it at a time

Whittle /wīt'l/, **Sir Frank** (1907–96) British engineer

whittlings /wītlingz/ npl pieces of wood that have been whittled off a larger piece and discarded

Whitworth screw thread /wīt wurth-/ n the thread form used in the United Kingdom for all screws, produced in a series of standard sizes. It has a 55° flank angle and a rounded top and foot. [Late 19C. After Sir Joseph *Whitworth* (d. 1887), English inventor.]

whity n = **whitey** (*slang, offensive*)

whiz /wīz/, **whizz** v (**whizzes**, **whizzing**, **whizzed**) **1** vi HOW to make a humming, hissing, or buzzing noise **2** vti MOVE WITH A HUMMING NOISE to move swiftly with a humming, hissing, or buzzing noise, or to cause something to move in this way ○ bullets whizzing past **3** vi MOVE QUICKLY to move or travel somewhere rapidly ○ whiz down to the shops **4** vt PROCESS IN FOOD MIXER to blend or liquidize something using a food mixer or food processor (*informal*) **5** vi US OFFENSIVE TERM an offensive term meaning to urinate (*slang*) ■ n (*plural* **whizzes**) **1 HUMMING SOUND** a humming, hissing, or buzzing sound **2 FAST MOVEMENT** a fast movement, often accompanied by a humming, hissing, or buzzing sound **3 EXPERT** a person who is very skilled at something (*informal*) ○ a computer whiz **4 AMPHETAMINES** amphetamine drugs taken for nonmedical reasons (*slang*) **5** US OFFENSIVE TERM an offensive term for an act of urinating (*slang*) [Mid-16C. An imitation of the sound.]

whiz-bang, **whizz-bang** n (*informal*) **1 ARTILLERY SHELL** a lightweight artillery shell used in World War I **2 SOMEBODY OR SOMETHING EXCELLENT** somebody or something that is outstandingly successful or effective, loud, or fast ■ adj EXCELLENT, FAST, OR LOUD outstandingly successful or effective, loud, or fast (*informal*) ○ a whiz-bang presentation

whiz kid, whizz kid, wiz kid *n* a young and exceptionally talented and successful person in a given field (*informal*)

whizz *vti, n* = **whiz**

whizz-bang *n, adj* = **whiz-bang** (*informal*)

whizz kid *n* = **whiz kid** (*informal*)

who /hoo/ *pron* **1** used to introduce a question asking about the name or identity of a person or people ○ *Who's that at the door?* ○ *Who did you see there?* **2** used to introduce a relative clause giving information about a person or people ○ *meals for people who are too busy to cook* [Old English *hwā* < Indo-European, 'who, what']

USAGE who or **whom**? ***Whom*** as the form for the object of a verb or preposition has fallen into disuse in many contexts, and constructions with ***who*** take its place, especially in British English. In speech, *Do you remember whom you saw?* may be expressed as *Do you remember who you saw?*, and *The man to whom I was talking* as *The man who I was talking to* (often with ellipsis of the relative pronoun). In formal contexts, ***whom*** is still preferred by careful writers. Note that ***whom*** is incorrect in sentences where ***who*** refers to the subject of the verb: *The woman who* [not *whom*] *we thought was dead is still alive.* The relative pronoun ***who*** is the subject of *was* [not *is*] and is not the object of *thought*.

WHO *abbr* World Health Organization

whoa /wō/ *interj* used to order an animal, or humorously, a person, to stop [Mid-19C. Variant of HO².]

who'd /hood/ *contr* **1** who had **2** who would

whodunit /hoo dúnnit/, **whodunnit** *n* a novel, film, or play centring on the solving of a crime, usually a murder [Mid-20C. Alteration of 'who done it?'.]

whoever /hoo évvər/ *pron* **1 INTRODUCES AN EMPHATIC QUESTION** introduces an emphatic question indicating surprise or disbelief ○ *Whoever would do such a thing?* **2 ANY PERSON WHO** indicates a person or people whose identity is not known ○ *Whoever takes over from her will have difficult decisions to make.* **3 NO MATTER WHO** indicates a person or people whose identity is not important ○ *You can bring whoever you like to the party.*

USAGE whoever or **whomever**? ***Whoever*** is a relative pronoun used in statements or commands: *Whoever made this has done a good job. Ask whoever you like.* ***Whomever***, used for an object (*Ask whomever you like.*), is falling out of use just as *whom* is, and ***whoever*** is generally considered acceptable.

whole /hōl/ *adj* **1 ENTIRE** complete, including all parts or aspects, with nothing left out **2 UNDIVIDED** not divided into parts or not regarded as consisting of separate elements **3 RELATING TO DURATION OR EXTENT** relating to or representing the full duration or extent of something ○ *stayed up the whole night* **4 UNBROKEN** not damaged or broken ○ *not a single item of furniture left whole* **5 UNIMPAIRED** not wounded, impaired, or incapacitated ○ *no longer a whole man* **6 HEALED OR HEALTHY** healed or restored to health physically or psychologically ○ *made him whole again* **7 HAVING COMMON PARENTS** having both parents in common with your siblings ○ *a whole sister* **8 NOT FRACTIONAL** containing no vulgar or decimal fractions ■ *adv* **1 AS A SINGLE PIECE** in a single piece rather than in several pieces ○ *Many snakes swallow their food whole.* **2 COMPLETELY** completely and in every way (*informal*) ○ *a whole different approach* ■ *n* **1 SOMETHING COMPLETE** something that is complete and has no parts missing **2 SINGLE ENTITY OR UNIT** something regarded as a single and complete unit or entity, as opposed to a set of components [Old English *hāl* < Indo-European, 'sound, propitious'] ◇ **as a whole** as a single and complete entity ◇ **on the whole 1** as a rule or in general **2** taking all relevant factors into account

SPELLCHECK See ***hole***.

whole cloth *n US* complete fiction or fabrication ○ *an explanation made out of whole cloth* [< the underlying meaning 'cut from new material, in any shape you please']

whole enchilada *n US* the entirety of something (*slang*)

wholefood /hōl food/ *n* food that has undergone very little processing and has been grown or produced without the use of synthetic pesticides or fertilizers

whole gale *n* a wind of force 10 on the Beaufort scale, travelling at 87 to 102 km/55 to 63 mi. per hour and capable of causing considerable structural damage

wholegrain /hōl grayn/ *adj* describes food containing or made with whole unprocessed grains of a cereal ○ *wholegrain muffins* ○ *wholegrain mustard*

wholehearted /hōl háartid/ *adj* characterized by enthusiasm, passion, or commitment —**wholeheartedly** *adv* —**wholeheartedness** *n*

whole hog *adv* in every way or to the fullest extent (*informal*) [< ?]

~~**wholely**~~ incorrect spelling of **wholly**

wholemeal /hōl meel/ *adj* **1** not having had the bran and wheat germ taken out. US term **whole-wheat** *adj.* 1 **2** made using wholemeal flour. US term **whole-wheat** *adj.* 2

whole milk *n* cow's milk from which no fat has been removed

whole note *n US* MUSIC = **semibreve** [*Whole* < the fact that it lasts for one full bar in common time]

whole number *n* a positive or negative number, including zero, that does not contain a vulgar or decimal fraction

wholesale /hōl sayl/ *n* **TRADE IN QUANTITY** the business of buying and selling goods in quantity at discounted prices, usually direct from manufacturers or distributors, in order to sell them on to the consumer ■ *adj* **1 OF TRADE IN QUANTITY** relating to the buying and selling of goods in quantity at discounted prices **2 DONE ON LARGE SCALE** done on a large scale and indiscriminately ■ *adv* **1 IN BULK** on a large scale and at a discounted price **2 INDISCRIMINATELY** as a whole, without exercising any judgment or taking individual cases into account ■ *vti* (**-sales, -saling, -saled**) **BUY OR SELL GOODS WHOLESALE** to buy or sell goods in large quantities at a discounted price, especially selling to retailers, instead of direct to the consumer, or to be bought or sold in this way [15C. < the phrase 'by whole sale', that is, sold in a single lot for redistribution at retail.] —**wholesaler** *n*

wholesome /hōlssəm/ *adj* **1 HEALTH-GIVING** beneficial to physical health, usually by virtue of being fresh and naturally produced **2 MORALLY BENEFICIAL** leading to or promoting improved moral wellbeing **3 SENSIBLE** based on openness, honesty, and common sense **4 HEALTHY AND FIT** having a fit, healthy appearance that suggests clean living —**wholesomely** *adv* —**wholesomeness** *n*

whole step *n US* MUSIC = **whole tone**

whole tone *n* a musical interval consisting of two semitones, such as exists between the notes D and E or A and B. US term **whole step**

whole-tone scale *n* a musical scale that begins on any of two notes that are a semitone apart and goes up or down in whole notes for one octave

whole-wheat *adj US* **1** = **wholemeal** *adj.* 1 **2** = **wholemeal** *adj.* 2

who'll /hool/ *contr* **1** who shall **2** who will

wholly /hōl li/ *adv* **1** totally and in every way or to the fullest extent **2** solely and to the exclusion of all other things

whom /hoom/ *pron* (*formal*) **1** used to introduce a question asking about the name or identity of a person or people ○ *Whom did you expect to see?* **2** used to introduce a relative clause giving information about a person or people ○ *Birch and her colleagues studied 162 infants, none of whom were born prematurely.* [Old English *hwǣm* < Germanic]

USAGE See ***who***.

whomever /hoom évvər/ *pron* a formal word for 'whoever' when used as the object of a verb or preposition (*formal*)

USAGE See ***whoever***.

whomp /womp/ *v US* **1** *vti* **STRIKE** to hit somebody or something with great force, especially noisily **2** *vt* **DEFEAT** to subject somebody to a crushing defeat (*informal*) ■ *n US* **BLOW OR NOISE OF A BLOW** a heavy blow or the loud deep sound it makes [Early 20C. An imitation of the sound.]

whomp up *vt US* to arouse, incite, or stir up interest or enthusiasm (*dated*)

whomsoever /hoom sō évvər/ *pron* an emphatic form of 'whomever' (*formal*)

whoop /woop, hoop/ *v* **1** *vi* **CRY OUT** to make a loud howling cry of excitement or joy **2** *vt* **EXCLAIM** to exclaim something loudly and with great excitement **3** *vt* **URGE OR DRIVE SOMEBODY FORWARD** to urge somebody on, chase after somebody, or drive a person or animal forward with a whooping call **4** *vi* **WHEEZE** to breathe in with the sharp wheezing sound associated with whooping cough ■ *n* **1 LOUD CRY** a loud howling cry of excitement or joy **2 BATTLE CRY** a cry uttered before a battle or hunt, by a warrior, soldier, or hunter **3 CALL MADE BY BIRD OR ANIMAL** a loud call or hoot, e.g. from a bird or animal **4 WHEEZING SOUND** a sharply wheezing inhalation associated with whooping cough [14C. An imitation of the sound.] ◇ **whoop it up 1** to have fun or celebrate in an extravagant or noisy way (*informal*) **2** *US* to express and try to arouse enthusiasm for somebody or something (*informal*)

whoop-de-do /woop di doo/, **whoop-de-doo** *n US* (*informal*) **1 PARTY** a large-scale party or celebration that is lively or noisy **2 PUBLICITY** noisy activity meant to attract attention ○ *the whoop-de-do surrounding the film's release* **3 FUSS** a noisy public commotion or outcry ■ *interj US* **EXPRESSING EXCITEMENT** used to express excitement (*informal; often ironic*) [Mid-20C. Expressive alteration of WHOOP.]

whoopee /woo pée/ *interj* used to express great and sudden excitement (*informal; often used ironically*) [Mid-19C. Alteration of WHOOP.] ◇ **make whoopee** /wóoppi/ **1** to celebrate noisily and exuberantly (*dated informal*) **2** to engage in sexual activity (*dated informal*)

whoopee cushion /wóoppi-/ *n* a practical joker's toy in the form of an inflatable cushion with a small opening, designed to make a noise resembling flatulence when somebody sits on it

whooper /hóopər, wóo-/ *n* **1** = **whooping crane** **2** = **whooper swan**

whooper swan *n* a large white swan with a yellow-and-black bill, straight neck, and loud whooping cry in flight. Native to: Europe, Asia. *Cygnus cygnus*.

whooping cough /hóoping-/ *n* an infectious bacterial disease that causes violent coughing spasms followed by sharp, shrill inhalation. It affects children in particular. Technical name **pertussis**

whooping crane /hóoping-/ *n* a large white crane with black wing tips that makes a loud whooping cry in flight and is now an endangered species. Native to: North America. *Grus americana*.

whoops /woops/, **whoops-a-daisy** *interj* used to express surprise, concern, or embarrassment at making a mistake or having a slight accident [Mid-20C. < ?]

whoosh /woosh/, **woosh** *n* **1 NOISE OF RUSHING AIR OR WATER** the sound made by rushing air or water **2 SWIFT MOTION OR RUSH** a swift motion, spurt, or rush ■ *vi* **1 MAKE RUSHING SOUND** to make the sound of rushing air or rushing water **2 MOVE FAST** to move rapidly, with a whooshing sound ○ *whooshed into the room* [Mid-19C. An imitation of the sound.]

whop /wop/, **whap** /wap/ *vt* (**whops, whopping, whopped; whaps, whapping, whapped**) (*informal*) **1 HIT** to strike somebody or something forcefully **2 DEFEAT SOMEBODY DECISIVELY** to subject an opponent to a crushing defeat ■ *n* **BLOW OR NOISE OF BLOW** a heavy blow or the loud dull sound it makes [14C. Variant of *wap* 'strike, slap', also 'blow' < ?]

whopper /wóppər/ *n* (*informal*) **1** something that is much bigger than others of its kind **2** a blatant and outrageous lie [Late 18C. < WHOPPING.]

whopping /wópping/ *adj* very big or great (*informal*) ■ *adv* extremely (*informal*) [Early 18C. < WHOP.]

whore /hawr/ *n* **1** an offensive term for a prostitute **2** an offensive term for somebody regarded as being sexually indiscriminate **3** an offensive term for somebody who is regarded as willing to set aside principles or personal integrity in order to obtain something, usually for selfish motives (*insult*) ■ *vi* (**whores, whoring, whored**) **1** an offensive term meaning to work as a prostitute **2** an offensive term meaning to be a regular customer of prostitutes [Old English *hōre* < Indo-European, 'to desire'] —**whoredom** *n*

whore after *vt* an offensive term meaning to pursue something desperately, making whatever sacrifices of principles or personal integrity are necessary

whorehouse /háwr howss/ (*plural* **-houses** /-howziz/) *n* an offensive term for a brothel or other place of prostitution

whoremonger /háwr mung gər/ *n* an offensive term for a sexually indiscriminate man, especially one who frequents prostitutes (*archaic*) —**whoremongery** *n*

whoreson /háwrss'n/ *n* **1** an offensive term for a boy or man whose paternity is unknown or has not been established (*archaic*) **2** an offensive term for a man regarded as dishonest, treacherous, or otherwise disreputable (*archaic insult*) ■ *adj* an offensive term meaning contemptible or loathsome (*archaic*) [14C. Translation of Anglo-Norman *fiz a putain*.]

Whorf hypothesis /wáwrf-/ *n* PSYCHOL = **Sapir-Whorf hypothesis**

whorish /háwrish/ *adj* **1** an offensive term meaning characteristic of the behaviour stereotypically ascribed to prostitutes **2** an offensive term meaning relating to prostitutes or prostitution —**whorishly** *adv* —**whorishness** *n*

whorl /wurl/ *n* **1 SOMETHING SPIRAL-SHAPED** something in the shape of a spiral, coil, or curl **2 PATTERN ON FINGER** a series of concentric circular or elliptical ridges in the pattern of lines on the gripping surface of a finger or thumb, or this shape seen in a fingerprint **3 CIRCLE OF PLANT PARTS** a circular arrangement of three or more leaves, petals, or other plant parts arising at the same level on a stem or other axis, like spokes on a wheel **4 SPIRAL IN SHELL** a turn or coil in a mollusc's shell [15C. Alteration of WHIRL.] —**whorled** *adj*

whortleberry /wúrt'lbəri/ (*plural* **-ries**) *n* **1 EDIBLE BERRY** a small sweet edible blue-black fruit **2 PLANT WITH EDIBLE BERRIES** a low-growing plant found in heathland and mountainous areas that bears whortleberries. Flowers: greenish-pink. Native to: Europe. *Vaccinium myrtillus*. **3 PLANT RELATED TO THE WHORTLEBERRY** any of several plants related to the whortleberry that have edible berries, e.g. the blueberry [Late 16C. Dialect variant of *hurtleberry*.]

who's /hooz/ *contr* **1** who has **2** who is

SPELLCHECK Do not confuse ***who's*** with ***whose***, which has a similar sound. Beware: your spellchecker will not catch this error.

USAGE See ***whose***.

whose /hooz/ *pron, det* a grammatical word used to talk or ask about the person or thing something belongs to ○ *Whose are these boots?* ○ *'It wasn't my idea'. – 'Well, whose was it then?'* ○ *a theatre whose doors will always be open to such a talented performer* ○ *Whose car shall we use?* ○ *He wanted to know whose the scarf was.* [Old English *hwæs*, genitive of the pronouns *hwa* (masculine) 'who' and *hwæt* (neuter) 'what'. Influenced in Middle English by *who* and *whom*.]

SPELLCHECK See ***who's***.

USAGE whose or **who's**? ***Whose*** denotes possession or association: *These are the children whose father we saw yesterday. There was a church whose steeple had been struck by lightning.* (Some people dislike the use of ***whose*** to refer to things, but it is a well established use and the alternatives are usually awkward.) ***Who's*** is a contraction of *who is* or *who has*: *She's the one who's coming to dinner next week. Who's got my pen?*

whosoever /hoòssō évvər/ *pron* whoever (*formal*)

Who's Who *tdmk* a trademark for a reference work giving brief biographical sketches for notable people

WH question *n* a question that starts with *who, what, where, when, why,* or *how*. It cannot be answered by 'yes' or 'no'.

whs. *abbr* warehouse

whsle *abbr* wholesale

whump /wump/ *n* the sound of a dull thump or muffled explosion ■ *vti* to make the sound of a dull thump or muffled explosion, or to hit somebody or something with such a sound [Late 19C. An imitation of the sound.]

whup /wup, wòop/ (**whups, whupping, whupped**) *vt* **1** *US* to subject an opponent to a crushing defeat (*informal*) **2** *Southern US* to beat somebody with a whip [Late 19C. Dialect variant of WHIP.]

why /wī/ CORE MEANING: an adverb used to ask or talk about the reason, purpose, or cause of something ○ *Why didn't you call?* ○ *I wish you'd tell me why you're so unhappy.* ○ *He could not say why he'd done it.* ○ *It seems clear to me why.*

1 ⚠ *rel adv* for or on account of which ○ *There's no reason why you shouldn't go.* **2** *interj* an exclamation used to express surprise, shock, or indignation ○ *Why, John, how could you!* [Old English *hwȳ*, instrumental case form of *hwæt* 'what'] ◇ **why not** used to express agreement with a suggestion or proposed course of action ○ *'Would you like another coffee?' – 'Why not?'*

USAGE Since people disagree as to whether *reason why* is redundant, the safest course is to avoid using it in formal writing: *The reason the experiment failed is that our test procedures were flawed* rather than *The reason why the experiment failed is that our test procedures were flawed.*

Whyalla /wī állə/ port in SE South Australia, on the Spencer Gulf. Population: 23,382 (1996).

whydah /wíddə/ (*plural* **-ah** *or* **-ahs**), **whidah** (*plural* **-ah** *or* **-ahs**) *n* a weaverbird, the male of which has long black tail feathers during the breeding season. Native to: Africa. Genus: *Vidua*. [Late 18C. After *Ouidah*, West African town.]

whys and wherefores *n* all the reasons and explanations for something ○ *Without going into all the whys and wherefores, let's just say the wedding's off.*

WI *abbr* **1** West Indian **2** West Indies **3** Women's Institute **4** Wisconsin

Wicca /wíkə/ *n* a religious practice involving nature-worship and witchcraft [Mid-20C. A deliberate revival of Old English *wicca* 'wizard'.] —**Wiccan** *n, adj*

Wichita /wíchi taw/ city in south-central Kansas. Population: 320,395 (1996).

wick /wik/ *n* **1 MATERIAL HOLDING FUEL THAT BURNS** a string or piece of fabric that uses capillary action to draw the fuel to the flame in a candle, oil lamp, or cigarette lighter **2 MATERIAL THAT DRAWS UP LIQUID** any piece of material that draws liquid up by capillary action, e.g. a strip of gauze put into a wound to drain it ■ *vti* **MOVE LIQUID BY CAPILLARY ACTION** to take in or transfer liquid by capillary action, or to be taken in or transferred in this way ○ *synthetic materials that wick moisture away from the skin* [Old English *wēoc* < ?] ◇ **get on somebody's wick** to annoy or irritate somebody greatly (*slang*)

Wick /wik/ port near the NE tip of Scotland. Population: 7,681 (1991).

wicked /wíkid/ *adj* **1 VERY BAD** very wrong or very bad **2 DANGEROUS** capable of causing harm to somebody ○ *a knife with a wicked blade* **3 DISTRESSING** causing discomfort, distress, or disappointment (*informal*) ○ *I've got a wicked headache.* **4 DISGUSTING** tasting or smelling disgusting and repulsive **5 MISCHIEVOUS** liking to tease people playfully or cause them slight trouble, but without upsetting them seriously ○ *a wicked sense of humour* **6 MEAN** liking to say very unpleasant things to people ○ *She has a really wicked tongue sometimes!* **7 VERY GOOD** very impressive or very skilful (*slang*) ○ *What do you think of the car, then? Pretty wicked, eh?* ■ *adv US* **VERY** extremely (*slang*) ○ *It was wicked good!* ■ *npl* **BAD PEOPLE** people who do very bad things [13C. Related to Old English *wicca* 'sorcerer' (see WITCH).] —**wickedly** *adv* —**wickedness** *n*

wicker /wíkər/ *n* **1** CRAFT = **wickerwork** *n*. 1 **2** any one of the twigs, canes, or reeds woven together to make such things as baskets or chairs **3** something such as a basket made of twigs, canes, or reeds [14C. < N Germanic < Indo-European, 'bend'.]

wickerwork /wíkər wurk/ *n* **1** thin twigs, canes, or reeds woven together to make objects such as baskets and chairs **2** objects such as baskets and chairs made by weaving together thin twigs, canes, or reeds

wicket /wíkit/ *n* **1 SMALL DOOR OR GATE** a small door or gate, especially one close to or forming part of a larger one **2** *US* **SMALL OPENING FOR COMMUNICATION** a small opening or window in a wall or door through which people can communicate **3 GATE CONTROLLING WATER FLOW** a gate used to control the flow of water at a lock or water wheel **4 UPRIGHT STICKS DEFENDED BY CRICKET BATSMAN** in cricket, either of two sets of three upright sticks (**stumps**) on which are balanced two shorter sticks (**bails**) and in front of which the batsman or batswoman stands **5 PART OF CRICKET PITCH** the part of a cricket pitch between the two sets of stumps, which are placed 20 m/22 yd apart **6 TURN OF BATTING** in cricket, a batsman's or batswoman's turn of batting, or that of a pair of batsmen or batswomen ○ *a fifth-wicket partnership between Crawley and Hussein* **7 ENDING OF TURN OF BATTING** in cricket, the ending of somebody's turn of batting, by knocking down the stumps or catching the ball **8** *US* **CROQUET HOOP** a hoop through which the ball is hit in croquet [13C. < Old N French *wiket* < Germanic, < Indo-European, 'bend'.]

wicketkeeper /wíkit keepər/ *n* in cricket, the player positioned behind the wicket to catch the ball or knock the bails off the stumps

wicket maiden *n* in cricket, an over in which no rur are conceded and at least one wicket is taken by th bowler

wicking /wíking/ *n* material used to make wicks

wickiup /wíki up/, **wikiup** *n* a hut made by Nativ North Americans of the SW United States by coverin a framework of arched poles with mats of bark, gras or branches [Mid-19C. < Fox *wikiapi*.]

Wicklow /wíklō/ **1** county in Leinster Province, SE Re public of Ireland. Area: 2,025 sq. km/782 sq. mi. **2** tow in the E Republic of Ireland, on the Irish Sea. Popu lation: 6,215 (1991).

Wicklow Mountains mountain range in the Republic of Ireland. Highest peak: Lugnaquill 92 m/3,039 ft.

Wicliff = **Wycliffe**

widdershins /wíddərshinz/ *adv* = **withershins**

widdle /wídd'l/ *vi* (**-dles, -dling, -dled**) to urinate (*informa usually by or to children*) ■ *n* an act or instance of urinatin (*informal; usually by or to children*) [Mid-20C. Alteration c PIDDLE.]

wide /wīd/ *adj* (**wider, widest**) **1 WITH SIDES OR EDGES FAR APAR** having a relatively large distance or space between on side or edge and the other **2 BEING A SPECIFIED DISTANC APART** having a specified distance between one side c edge and the other ○ *three inches wide* **3 OPENED TO GREA EXTENT** opened to a great extent or as far as possibl ○ *staring at him with wide eyes* **4 WITH MANY TYPES OR CHOICE** including many varieties, offering many choices, o having a large range ○ *a wide selection of cheeses* **5 IN VOLVING MANY PEOPLE** from, involving, or given to man people ○ *wide support for the plan* **6 LARGE IN SCOPE** with large scope ○ *a very wide gap between living standards her and in developing countries* **7 NOT HITTING TARGET** goin some distance away from the intended, expected, o correct place **8 GOING BEYOND DETAILS** looking beyond th particular issue involved toward the more genera aspects of something rather than the details ○ *We nee to look at the wider implications of these proposals.* **9 FITTIN LOOSELY** not fitting tightly round the body **10 CLEVER AN UNSCRUPULOUS** shrewd and slightly dishonest or un scrupulous (*slang*) ○ *There's some pretty wide character in this game.* **11** PHON = **lax** *adj*. 4 ■ *adv* (**wider, widest**) **1 TO GREAT EXTENT** to a great extent or as much as possibl ○ *Stand with your legs wide apart.* **2 OVER LARGE AREA** ove an extensive area ○ *scattered far and wide* **3 TO SIDE O TARGET** to one side of the intended target ○ *A few shot were fired but they all went wide.* ■ *n* **BALL BOWLED BEYON BATSMAN'S REACH** in cricket, a ball bowled beyond th reach of the batsman or batswoman, for which one rur is awarded to the batting side [Old English *wīd* < Indo European, 'apart'] —**wideness** *n* —**widish** *adj*

-wide *suffix* effective throughout a particular plac ○ *statewide* ○ *storewide* [< WIDE]

wide-angle *adj* **1** describes a camera lens that gives ar unusually wide field of view by making things appea smaller or further away than they really are **2** relating to or using a camera lens with an unusually wide field of view ○ *a wide-angle shot*

ϟ**wide area network** *n* a network of computers and peripheral devices linked by cable and satellite over a broad geographic area

wide-awake *adj* **1 FULLY AWAKE** completely awake and alert (*not hyphenated after verbs*) **2 ALERT** very aware o surroundings and watching for advantageous possibilities (*informal*) ○ *a wide-awake young go-getter* ■ *n* **wide-awake, wide-awake hat FELT HAT** a soft felt hat with a wide brim and a low crown —**wide-awakeness** *n*

wide ball *n* CRICKET = **wide** *n*.

wide boy *n* a shrewd and rather unscrupulous man who makes his money in dishonest ways (*informal*) ○ *He's a bit of a wide boy, your mate.*

wide-eyed *adj* **1** with eyes that are wide open, e.g. in amazement or fear **2** lacking experience, wisdom, or common sense and therefore easily fooled by other people

widely /wídli/ *adv* **1 WITH SPACE BETWEEN** with a relatively large distance between ○ *Plant them fairly widely apart.* **2 MAKING SOMETHING SPREAD OR OPEN WIDE** in such a way as to make something open or spread as much as possible or to a great extent ○ *smiling a little too widely* **3 OVER LARGE AREA** over an extensive area ○ *She is very widely travelled.* **4 OVER LARGE RANGE** so as to cover an extensive range ○ *The conversation ranged widely, from politics to bee-keeping.* **5 BY MANY PEOPLE** by a large number of people

○ *It is not widely known that he was once an acrobat.* **6 GREATLY** to a great degree ○ *widely different examples of this phenomenon*

wide-mouthed *adj* **1** with a mouth that is notably wider than average **2** with the mouth open wide, e.g. in surprise

widen /wíd'n/ *vti* to become wider or to make something wider —**widener** *n*

wide-open *adj* (*not hyphenated after verbs*) **1 OPEN TO GREAT EXTENT** open to a great extent, or as much as possible ○ *The door was wide open.* **2 UNPREDICTABLE** not as yet decided or even predictable in outcome ○ *The match is still wide open.* **3 VULNERABLE TO ATTACK** unprotected and therefore able to be attacked easily **4** *US* **WITHOUT LAWS OR LAW-ENFORCEMENT** with few laws regulating such things as prostitution, gambling, or the sale of alcohol, or not stringently enforcing the laws that do exist (*informal*)

wide-ranging *adj* **1** dealing with a great variety of matters **2** affecting a large number of people or things ○ *a decision that has wide-ranging implications*

wide receiver *n* in American football, a player who positions himself to the side of the offensive formation, and whose role is to catch long passes from the quarterback

wide-screen *adj* **1** describes a type of film projection in which the image is substantially wider than it is tall **2** describes a television whose screen is noticeably larger than average —**wide screen** *n*

widespread /wíd spred/ *adj* **1** existing or happening in many places, or affecting many people **2** spread or extending far apart ○ *with arms widespread*

SYNONYMS ***widespread, prevalent, rife, epidemic, universal***

CORE MEANING: occurring over a wide area

widespread existing or happening in many places, or affecting many people; **prevalent** occurring commonly or widely as a dominant feature; **rife** full of or severely affected by something undesirable that occurs frequently or in great numbers over a wide area, especially when it appears to be uncontrollable; **epidemic** spreading more quickly and more extensively than expected; **universal** affecting the whole world or everyone in the world.

widgeon *n* BIRDS = **wigeon**

widget /wíjjit/ *n* **1** any little device or mechanism, especially one whose name is unknown or forgotten (*humorous*) **2** a hypothetical manufactured object, considered to represent the typical product of a manufacturer [Early 20C. < ?]

Widnes /wídniss/ town in NW England, on the River Mersey. Population: 57,162 (1991).

widow /wíddō/ *n* **1 WOMAN WHOSE HUSBAND HAS DIED** a woman whose husband has died, especially when she has not remarried **2 WOMAN LEFT BEHIND** a woman whose partner regularly goes away from her to take part in a particular activity (*only in combination*) ○ *a golf widow.* ◊ **grass widow** **3 SHORT FINAL LINE OF PARAGRAPH** a short line at the end of a paragraph, especially when occurring as the top line of a page or column of text. ◊ **orphan** *n.* 3 **4 EXTRA HAND OF CARDS** an extra hand of cards dealt out in some card games ■ *vt* **MAKE SOMEBODY WIDOW OR WIDOWER** to cause somebody to become a widow or widower (*usually passive*) ○ *She was widowed a year ago.* [Old English *widuwe* < Indo-European, 'to separate'] —**widowhood** *n*

widow bird (*plural* **widow birds** *or* **widow bird**) *n* BIRDS = **whydah**

widower /wíddō ər/ *n* a man whose wife has died, especially when he has not remarried —**widowerhood** *n*

widowmaker /wíddō maykər/ *n* something that is so dangerous that it might kill anyone who uses it or tries it

widow's benefit *n* a sum of money paid weekly to a widow under the National Insurance scheme in the United Kingdom

widow's cruse *n* a source that provides an unending supply of something [< the biblical story of the widow's cruse of oil that supplies Elijah during a famine (I Kings 17:8–16)]

widow's mite *n* a contribution that, although small, is generous because it comes from somebody who has very little to give [< the poor widow's contribution of two copper coins to the treasury in the Bible (Mark 12:42)]

widow's peak *n* a V-shaped line across the top of a person's forehead behind which the hair grows [< the superstition that this feature portends early widowhood]

widow's walk *n* a walkway with a rail around it on the rooftop of a house, especially one that was used to keep watch for incoming ships [Because, while pacing along it, wives commonly looked for signs of their husbands returning from sea]

widow's weeds *npl* the black clothes once traditionally worn by widows (*archaic or literary*)

width /width, witth/ *n* **1 DISTANCE ACROSS** the distance from one side or edge of something to the other **2 STATE OF BEING WIDE** the fact of being wide or how wide something is **3 SIDE TO SIDE DISTANCE OF POOL** the distance from one side of a swimming pool to the other ○ *Learners begin by swimming widths rather than lengths.* **4 MATERIAL OF FULL WIDTH** a piece of material of its full width

widthwise /width wīz, witth-/, **widthways** /width wayz/ *adv* from one side or edge to the other

~~**wiegh**~~ incorrect spelling of **weigh**

~~**wieght**~~ incorrect spelling of **weight**

Wieland /veé lant/, **Christoph Martin** (1733–1813) German writer

wield /weeld/ *vt* **1** to have and be able to use something, especially power or authority ○ *the immense economic power wielded by large companies* **2** to hold and use a weapon or tool [Old English *wielden* 'rule', variant of *wealden* < Indo-European, 'be strong'] —**wieldable** *adj* —**wielder** *n*

wieldy /weéldi/ (**-ier, -iest**) *adj* easily handled or used, or easy enough to manage

wiener /weénər/ *n* FOOD = **frankfurter** [Late 19C. Shortening of WIENERWURST.]

Wiener /weénər/, **Norbert** (1894–1964) US mathematician

Wiener schnitzel /veénər shnits'l/ *n* a thin slice of veal coated in egg and breadcrumbs and fried

wienerwurst /weénər wurst/ *n* FOOD = **frankfurter** [Late 19C. < German, < *Wiener* 'of Vienna' + *Wurst* 'sausage'.]

~~**wier**~~ incorrect spelling of **weir**

~~**wierd**~~ incorrect spelling of **weird**

Wiesbaden /veéss baad'n/ capital of Hesse State in west-central Germany. Population: 266,400 (1995).

Wiesel /veéz'l/, **Elie** (*b.* 1928) Romanian-born US writer. Full name **Eliezer Wiesel**

Wiesenthal /veéz'n taal/, **Simon** (*b.* 1908) Polish-born Austrian war-crimes investigator

wife /wīf/ (*plural* **wives** /wīvz/) *n* **1 SPOUSE** the woman to whom a particular man is married **2 MARRIED WOMAN** a woman, especially a married one (*archaic*) **3 MATURE WOMAN** a woman, especially a mature woman (*regional*) [Old English *wīf* 'woman, wife' < ?] —**wifehood** *n*

wifely /wífli/ (**-lier, -liest**) *adj* showing the attitudes or behaviour stereotypically expected of a wife —**wifeliness** *n*

wig[1] /wig/ *n* **1** a covering of hair or something resembling hair worn on the head for adornment, ceremony, or to cover baldness **2** a toupee (*informal*) [Late 17C. Shortening of PERIWIG.] —**wigged** *adj*

wig[2] /wig/ (**wigs, wigging, wigged**) *vt UK* to speak sternly to somebody who has done something wrong (*dated informal*) [Early 19C. < WIG[1].]

Wigan /wíggən/ town in NW England. Population: 77,000 (1994).

wigeon /wíjjən/ (*plural* **-geons** *or* **-geon**), **widgeon** (*plural* **-geons** *or* **-geon**) *n* **1** a freshwater duck with a white patch on each wing. Native to: Europe, Asia. *Anas penelope.* **2** a duck, the male of which has a white crown. Native to: North America. *Anas americana.*

wigged-out /wigd ówt/ *adj US* experiencing an extreme emotional or psychological state such as nervousness or anxiety (*slang*) ○ *wigged-out from staying up all night*

wigging /wígging/ *n* a severely critical scolding (*dated informal*)

wiggle /wígg'l/ *vti* (**-gles, -gling, -gled**) **MAKE SMALL BACK AND FORTH MOVEMENTS** to move from side to side in small quick movements, or to make something move in this way ■ *n* **1 INSTANCE OF WIGGLING** a small quick side-to-side movement **2 WAVY LINE** a line with irregular curves in it [13C. < Low German or Dutch *wiggelen* < Germanic.] —**wiggler** *n*

wiggly /wígg'li/ (**-glier, -gliest**) *adj* **1** moving from side to side with small quick movements, or able to be moved in this way (*informal*) **2** with many irregular curves ○ *a wiggly line*

wight /wīt/ *n* a living being, especially a human being (*archaic*) [Old English *wiht* < Germanic]

Wight, Isle of /wīt/ island off the coast of S England, in the English Channel. Population: 125,100 (1995). Area: 381 sq. km/147 sq. mi.

wiglet /wígglət/ *n* a small hairpiece for a woman, worn as an addition to a hairstyle rather than to cover the head

wigmaker /wíg maykər/ *n* a professional maker of wigs

wigwag /wíg wag/ *vti* (**-wags, -wagging, -wagged**) **1 MOVE FROM SIDE TO SIDE** to wave or swing from side to side in an arc about a fixed point, or to make something such as a flag move in this way **2 SIGNAL BY WAVING** to send a message by waving something such as an arm or a flag ■ *n* **1 PROCESS OF WIGWAGGING** the method of communicating by waving an arm or a flag **2 MESSAGE SENT BY WIGWAGGING** a message communicated by the moving of arms or flags [Late 16C. Reduplication of WAG[1].] —**wigwagger** *n*

wigwam /wíg wam/ *n* **1** a Native North American hut made by covering a conical or dome-shaped framework of poles with woven rush mats or sheets of bark **2** a light tent in the shape of a wigwam for a child to play in [Early 17C. < Abenaki *wikewam*.]

Wik /wik/ *n* a judgment passed by the High Court of Australia in 1996, ruling that the granting of a pastoral lease did not necessarily extinguish all native title rights to land

wikiup *n* = **wickiup**

wikiwiki /wíki wiki/ *adv Hawaii* quickly

Wilberforce /wílbər fáwrss/, **William** (1759–1833) British politician and political reformer

wilco /wílkō/ *interj* used to indicate that you understand what has just been said in a radio message and will do what is necessary [Mid-20C. Blend and shortening of *will comply*.]

Wilcoxon test /wil kóks'n-/ *n* a statistical test of the equality of similar or matched groups of data to determine whether they differ significantly from one another, without any assumptions about the underlying distribution patterns [Mid-20C. After Frank *Wilcoxon* (1892–1965), Irish statistician.]

wild /wīld/ *adj* **1 NOT TAME OR DOMESTICATED** not kept as a pet or used for display, work, or experimentation, but living freely in a natural habitat **2 NOT CULTIVATED** growing in a natural state rather than being cultivated in fields, parks, or gardens ○ *picking wild strawberries* **3 PRODUCED BY WILD ANIMALS** produced by animals living freely rather than by domesticated animals ○ *wild honey* **4 ROUGH, DESOLATE, AND BARREN** not inhabited or able to be inhabited by humans because of being barren, remote, or desolate **5 OFFENSIVE TERM** an offensive term meaning supposedly culturally inferior **6 STORMY** rough and stormy, with a strong wind **7 ENTHUSIASTIC OR EAGER** feeling enthusiastic or eager or showing enthusiasm or eagerness ○ *I'm not wild about the idea.* **8 UNRULY** lively and showing a disregard for rules ○ *The kids next door are really wild.* **9 OVERWHELMED BY EMOTION** overwhelmed by or showing a strong emotion such as anger, grief, or desire ○ *wild with grief* **10 UNRESTRAINED** marked by a lack of restraint or prudence, especially in things considered to be vices ○ *a really wild party* **11 UNTIDY** not neat or well-groomed ○ *His hair was wild.* **12 NOT CAREFULLY THOUGHT OUT** not based on rational thought, evidence, or probability ○ *I just made a wild guess.* **13 POORLY AIMED** not carefully aimed ○ *throwing wild punches* **14 UNCONVENTIONAL** unconventional, exciting, and slightly irrational (*informal*) ○ *a wild idea* **15 EXCELLENT** excellent (*dated slang*) ○ *Hey, man, that's really wild!* **16 WITH VALUE ASSIGNED BY PLAYER** describes a playing card that has any value that the player using it wishes to give it ○ *Jokers are wild.* ■ *adv* **1 IN UNCULTIVATED WAY** in a natural state rather than being cultivated in fields, parks, or gardens ○ *flowers that grow wild in the fields* **2 IN UNCONTROLLED WAY** in an uncontrolled, unpredictable, or unplanned way ○ *She just lets her kids run wild.* **3** *Ireland* **EXTREMELY** to an extreme degree (*informal*) ○ *That was wild stupid.* ■ *n* **UNDOMESTICATED STATE** the natural, free state of an undomesticated animal ○ *Most people have never actually seen a panda in the wild.* ■ **wilds** *npl* **UNINHABITED AREA** an area that is completely uninhabited or only very sparsely populated because it is remote or rugged (*sometimes singular*) ○ *They live somewhere out in the wilds.* [Old English *wilde* < Indo-European, 'wild, woods'] —**wildish** *adj* —**wildness** *n*

SYNONYMS See *unruly*.

Wild /wīld/, **Jonathan** (1682?–1725) English criminal

wild boar *n* a wild pig with a coat ranging from pale grey to black, dense bristles, a thin body, and small tusks. Native to: Europe, Asia. *Sus scrofa*.

wild brier *n* = **wild rose**

ϟ**wild card** *n* **1 SOMEBODY OR SOMETHING UNPREDICTABLE** somebody or something that is important to a plan or course of action, but whose behaviour cannot be predicted (*informal*) **2 EXTRA PLAYER OR TEAM IN COMPETITION** an extra player or team selected to take part in a competition although not technically qualified to do so **3 COMPUTER SYMBOL REPRESENTING ANY CHARACTER** a symbol, usually *, that can be used to represent any single character or multiple characters that may appear in the same position in a computer search argument **4 CARD OF NO FIXED VALUE** in card games, a card that can have whatever value its player assigns it

wild carrot *n* PLANTS = **Queen Anne's lace**

wildcat /wīld kat/ *n* (*plural* **-cats** *or* **-cat**) **1 WILD EUROPEAN OR ASIAN CAT** a cat that resembles the domestic tabby but is heavier and has a bushy tail. Native to: Europe, Asia, Africa. *Felis sylvestris*. **2** *US, Can* **MEDIUM-SIZED WILD FELINE** any medium-sized wild feline such as the bobcat, caracal, lynx, and ocelot **3 QUICK-TEMPERED PERSON** an easily angered person **4 SPECULATIVE OIL OR GAS WELL** an exploratory or speculative well drilled in an area not yet known to be productive of oil or gas **5** *Can, US* **FINANCIALLY UNSOUND BUSINESS** a financially unsound business ■ *adj US, Can* **NOT FINANCIALLY SAFE** practising unethical or financially risky business methods, or characteristic of such methods ○ *wildcat stocks* ■ *vti* (**-cats, -catting, -catted**) **DRILL EXPLORATORY WELL** to drill an exploratory well, or take samples in an area not yet known to have any reserves of what is being sought, especially oil or gas —**wildcatting** *n, adj*

wildcat strike *n* a sudden strike not authorized by the trade union that the strikers belong to

wildcatter /wīld katər/ *n US, Can* **1 PROSPECTOR** a prospector for oil in areas not yet known to be productive (*informal*) **2 UNETHICAL BUSINESSPERSON** a developer or promoter of risky or fraudulent business ventures **3 WILDCAT STRIKE PARTICIPANT** a participant in a sudden strike not authorized by the trade union he or she belongs to

wild cherry *n* a tree, ancestral to cultivated sweet cherries, that flowers in spring before the leaves emerge and bears clusters of red berries. Flowers: white. Native to: Europe, West Asia, North Africa. *Prunus avium*.

wild dog *n* any wild member of the dog family, especially the dingo, the African hunting dog, or the dhole

AKG London

Oscar Wilde

Wilde /wīld/, **Oscar** (1854–1900) Irish writer

wildebeest /vildə beest, wildə-/ (*plural* **-beests** *or* **-beest**) *n* ZOOL = **gnu** [Early 19C. < Afrikaans, 'wild beast'.]

wilder /wildər/ *vti* (*archaic*) **1** to go astray or lead somebody or something astray **2** to become confused by a number of complex options, or to confuse somebody in this way [Early 17C. < ?] —**wilderment** *n*

Wilder /wīldər/, **Billy** (*b.* 1906) Austrian-born US film director. Born **Samuel Wilder**

Wilder, Thornton (1897–1975) US writer

wilderness /wildərnəss/ *n* **1 NATURAL UNCULTIVATED LAND** a mostly uninhabited area of land such as a forest or mountainous region in its natural uncultivated state, sometimes deliberately preserved like this **2 BARREN AREA** an area that is empty or barren ○ *in the vast wilderness of outer space* **3 DELIBERATELY UNCULTIVATED LAND IN GARDEN** a piece of land, e.g. in a garden, that is deliberately not cultivated but is left to grow wild **4 LOSS OF INFLUENCE** the state of being without power or influence for a time after having been in a position of leadership or authority, especially in politics, **5 UNCOMFORTABLE SITUATION** a place, situation, or multitude of people or things that makes somebody feel confused, overwhelmed, or desolate ○ *the wilderness of the big city* [Old English *wilddēornes* < *wilddēor* 'wild beast' < *wilde* 'wild' + *dēor* 'animal'] ◇ **be (a voice) crying in the wilderness** to be giving advice or suggestions that are very unlikely to be followed

wilderness area *n US* a protected area set aside for preservation in as natural a state as possible, with restrictions on most human activity except for non-motorized forms of outdoor recreation ○ *backpacking in the wilderness areas*

wild-eyed *adj* **1** with eyes that are wide and glaring because of fear, anger, or a psychological disorder **2** marked by or advocating ideas that are so extreme and far-fetched as to be completely impracticable

wildfire /wīld fīr/ *n* **1 RAPIDLY SPREADING FIRE** a fierce fire that spreads rapidly, especially in an area of wilderness **2** SCI = **will-o'-the-wisp** *n.* **1** **3 LIGHTNING WITHOUT THUNDER** lightning that occurs without audible thunder **4 INFLAMMABLE MATERIAL AS WEAPON** any inflammable material formerly used in warfare ◇ **like wildfire** very rapidly

wild flower *n* a flowering plant growing in a natural, uncultivated state, or the flower of such a plant

wildfowl /wīld fowl/ (*plural* **-fowl**) *n* a bird that is hunted for food or sport, e.g. a duck or a goose —**wildfowler** *n* —**wildfowling** *n*

wild ginger *n* a herb with two heart-shaped leaves and an aromatic root. Flowers: single, reddish-brown. Native to: North America. *Asarum canadense*.

wild-goose chase *n* a futile search for something that there is no chance of finding, especially because it does not exist [Originally of an irregular course, like the patterned flight of wild geese]

wild hyacinth *n* PLANTS = **bluebell** *n.* **1**

wilding /wīlding/ *n* **1 WILD PLANT OR TREE** a plant that grows wild or one that has escaped from cultivation, especially a wild crab-apple tree **2 FRUIT** the fruit of a plant that grows wild or that has escaped from cultivation, especially a wild crab apple **3 WILD ANIMAL** a wild animal ■ *adj* **UNCULTIVATED** uncultivated or undomesticated

wildlife /wīld līf/ *n* wild animals, birds, and other living things, sometimes including vegetation, living in a natural undomesticated state

wildlife park *n* LEISURE = **safari park**

wildling /wīldling/ *n* BIOL = **wilding** *n.* **1**, **wilding** *n.* **2**, **wilding** *n.* **3**

wildly /wīldli/ *adv* **1 WITH ENTHUSIASM** in a very enthusiastic way ○ *cheering wildly* **2 WITHOUT CAREFUL THOUGHT** not considering something carefully **3 VERY** to a great extent (*informal*) ○ *not wildly enthusiastic about the idea* **4 IN WAY THAT SHOWS FEAR** in an uncontrolled way that betrays fear or anxiety, and often with eyes that are wide and staring ○ *looking wildly in all directions* **5 STRONGLY** in a fierce and rough way ○ *The wind blew wildly through the trees*.

wild man *n* **1** a man who has extreme or radical opinions, especially in politics **2** an offensive term for a man regarded as supposedly being culturally inferior (*archaic*)

wild mustard *n* PLANTS = **charlock**

wild oat *n* a weedy annual grass of temperate regions that resembles cultivated oats. *Avena fatua*. ◇ **sow your wild oats** to behave in an uncontrolled way, especially sexually, while young

wild pansy *n* a plant of the violet family. Flowers: blue, violet, and yellow. Native to: Europe, Asia. *Viola tricolor*.

wild pitch *n* a baseball pitch that a catcher could not have caught and that results in a runner advancing to the next base

wild rice *n* **1** the dark grain of an aquatic grass, used as food **2** a tall perennial aquatic grass that yields wild rice. Native to: North America. *Zizania aquatica*.

wild rose *n* any wild-growing rose such as the dog rose and sweetbrier

wild rubber *n* rubber obtained from uncultivate rubber trees

wild silk *n* **1** silk fibre obtained from wild silkworm **2** fabric woven from the silk of wild silkworms, or a imitation of this made with short silk fibres

wild type *n* the form of an organism, strain, or gene tha results from natural breeding, as opposed to mutan forms or those resulting from selective breeding

wild water *n* = **white water** *n.* **1**

Wild West *n* the W United States in the second half c the 19th century, regarded as a time of lawlessness

Wild West show *n* a North American form of en tertainment involving the demonstration of skills as sociated with the Wild West, e.g. shooting, riding, an roping cattle, especially performed by people dresse as cowboys

wildwood /wīld wŏŏd/ *n* natural uncultivated woodlan (*archaic or literary*)

wile /wīl/ *n* **TRICK** a trick or cunning ruse ■ **wiles** *n* **TRICKERY MEANT TO PERSUADE** trickery intended to persuad somebody to do something, especially in the form o insincere charm or flattery ■ *vt* (**wiles, wiling, wiled PERSUADE SOMEBODY BY WILES** to trick or entice somebod into doing or not doing something (*dated*) [12C. < ?]

SPELLCHECK See *while*.

Wilfrid /wilfrid/, **Wilfrith** /wilfrith/, **St** (634–709?) Englis prelate

wilful /wilf'l/ *adj* **1** done deliberately, especially with th intention of harming somebody or in spite of knowin that it will harm somebody **2** always determined to ac on a desire, regardless of the opinions or advice o others —**wilfully** *adv* —**wilfulness** *n*

SYNONYMS See *unruly*.

Wilhelmshaven /vil helmz haavən, vil helms haafən/ por in NW Germany. Population: 89,900 (1989).

Wilkes /wilks/, **John** (1725–97) British political leader an reformer

Wilkins /wilkinz/, **Maurice** (*b.* 1916) New Zealand-bor British biophysicist

will[1] /wil/ CORE MEANING: a modal verb used to indicat future time ○ *Delegates from all over Europe will attend th forum.* ○ *Will you ever be able to forgive him?* ○ *Your sui will be ready for collection tomorrow.*

v **1** *vi* **RESOLUTION** indicating intent, purpose, or de termination ○ *I will be staying with Jean when I come t England.* ○ *I will study harder for these exams.* **2** *vi* **POLIT QUESTIONS** used in questions to make polite invitation or offers ○ *Will you sit down, please?* ○ *Will you have mor coffee?* **3** *vi* **REQUESTS** used in questions to make request ○ *Will you take the washing out for me please?* ○ *Phone th garage, will you?* **4** *vi* **COMMANDS** used when ordering somebody to do something ○ *You will do exactly as I say.* ○ *Examination candidates will not start writing until tol to do so.* **5** *vi* **CUSTOMARY BEHAVIOUR** used to indicate th way that something usually happens or the way tha somebody usually does something ○ *The wetter the roa conditions, the harder it will be for a vehicle to stop.* ○ *When they're out together they will shop till they drop!* **6** *v* **WILLINGNESS** used to indicate that somebody is willing t do something ○ *I will mail your letters for you.* ○ *I will no tolerate this kind of behaviour.* **7** *vi* **ABILITY** used to indicat the ability or capacity of something ○ *That wardrobe wil not fit in your bedroom.* ○ *The truck will carry loads of up t 10 tons.* **8** *vi* **EXPECTATION** used to express surmise o likelihood ○ *That will be them at the door now.* ○ *He wil have left the country by now.* **9** *vi* **INCLINATION** used t indicate the inevitability of something happening o being true ○ *She will stay up till all hours in front of th TV.* **10** *Scotland* **POLITE WAY OF ASKING** used in statement to avoid the impoliteness of a question (*informal*) ○ *Thi will be your brother.* [Old English *wyllan* < Indo-European]

USAGE See *shall*.

will[2] /wil/ *n* **1 PART OF MIND THAT MAKES DECISIONS** the part o the mind with which somebody consciously decide things **2 POWER TO DECIDE** the power to make decision ○ *This lawn mower seems to have a will of its own!* **3 PROCES OF MAKING DECISIONS** the use of the mind to make decision about things **4 DETERMINATION** the determination to do something ○ *She has lots of ability but she lacks the will t succeed.* **5 DESIRE OR INCLINATION** a desire or inclination to d something **6 ATTITUDE TOWARD SOMEBODY ELSE** the attitude o feelings somebody has toward somebody or something **7 SOMETHING DESIRED BY SOMEBODY TO HAPPEN** what a person or group, especially one in authority, wants to happen (*formal*) ○ *It was her will that he should never be told the truth.* **8 STATEMENT DETERMINING DISTRIBUTION OF DECEASED'S PROPERTY** a statement of what somebody wants to happen to his or her property after he or she dies, or a legal document containing this statement. ◊ **living will**

■ *vt* **1 TRY TO CAUSE SOMETHING BY THOUGHTS** to make or try to make something happen or somebody do something by the power of the mind ○ *He willed himself to stay awake.* ○ *Her parents were watching her run, willing her on.* **2 LEAVE SOMEBODY SOMETHING IN WILL** to give something officially to somebody by declaring it in a will **3 WANT OR DECIDE** to want something to happen or to decide that something will happen (*archaic or formal*) ○ *It shall be as God wills.* [Old English *willa* (noun), *wyllan* (verb), and *willian* (verb < noun) < Indo-European, 'to will, wish'] —**willable** *adj* —**willer** *n* ◊ **at will** when somebody wishes (*formal*) ○ *They are free to come and go at will.* ◊ **with a will** with energy and enthusiasm (*formal*) ○ *He set about the task with a will.* ◊ **with the best will in the world** indicates that somebody cannot do something however much he or she wishes or tries to do it ○ *With the best will in the world we won't be able to supervise her all the time.*

Villadsen /villads'n/, **Steen** (b. 1944) Danish geneticist

villemite /villa mīt/ *n* a colourless fluorescent brown, green, or red zinc sulphate mineral [Mid-19C. After *Willem* I (1772–1843), king of the Netherlands.]

villet /villit/ *n* a large grey shore bird with a long, straight, moderately stout bill, long legs, and a distinctive black-and-white wing pattern. Native to: North America. *Catoptrophorus semipalmatus.* [Mid-19C. An imitation of its call.]

villful *adj* US = **wilful**

villfull incorrect spelling of **wilful**

William /willyam/, **Prince** (b. 1982) the first child of Prince Charles and Diana, Princess of Wales

William I (1028?–87) king of England (1066–87). Known as **William the Conqueror**

William II (1056?–1100) king of England (1087–1100). Known as **William Rufus**

William III (1650–1702) king of England, Scotland, and Ireland (1689–1702). Known as **William of Orange**

William IV (1765–1837) king of the United Kingdom (1830–37). Known as **the Sailor King**

William (of Malmesbury) (1090?–1143?) English monk and chronicler

Williams /willyamz/ (*plural* **-liams**), **Williams pear** *n* a variety of pear with juicy white flesh and yellow skin. US term **Bartlett** [Early 19C. After *William's* Nursery of Middlesex.]

Williams, Emlyn /willyamz/ (1905–87) British playwright, novelist, and actor

Williams, Fred (1927–82) Australian painter. Full name **Frederick Ronald Williams**

Williams, Hank (1923–53) US country musician. Born **Hiram Williams**

Williams, John (b. 1941) Australian-born British classical guitarist

Williams, J. P. R. (b. 1949) Welsh Rugby Union footballer. Full name **John Peter Rhys Williams**

Williams, Ted (b. 1918) US baseball player. Full name **Theodore Samuel Williams**

Williams, Tennessee (1911–83) US playwright. Born **Thomas Lanier Williams**

Williams, William Carlos (1883–1963) US writer

Williamsburg /willyamz burg/ city in SE Virginia, site of a restored colonial-era town. Population: 11,530 (1990).

Williamson /willyams'n/, **David Keith** (b. 1942) Australian playwright

Williamson, Henry (1895–1977) British novelist

willie *n* = **willy** (*informal, offensive*)

willies /williz/ *npl* an uncomfortable, anxious, or fearful feeling (*informal*) [Late 19C. < ?]

willing /willing/ *adj* **1 READY TO DO SOMETHING VOLUNTARILY** ready to do something without being forced to **2 HELPFUL** cooperative and enthusiastic **3 OFFERED VOLUNTARILY** offered or given by somebody readily and enthusiastically —**willingly** *adv* —**willingness** *n*

willing horse *n* a hard and willing worker

Willis /willis/, **Norman** (b. 1933) British trade union leader

williwaw /willi waw/ *n US, Can* a violent gust of cold wind blowing down from a mountainous region to the coast and out to sea, especially in the Straits of Magellan and in Alaska [Mid-19C. < ?]

will-o'-the-wisp /will ə thə wisp/ *n* **1** a phosphorescent light sometimes seen at night over marshy ground, caused by the spontaneous combustion of gases given off by rotting organic matter **2** somebody or something that is misleading or elusive, e.g. a false hope [< *Will*, shortening of the forename *William*, + OF + THE + WISP] —**will-o'-the-wispish** *adj*

willow /willō/ *n* **1 TREE WITH LONG FLEXIBLE BRANCHES** a tree or bush with long flexible branches, narrow leaves, and catkins containing small flowers without petals. Genus: *Salix*. **2 WILLOW WOOD** the wood of a willow tree **3 CRICKET BAT** a cricket bat (*informal*) **4 MACHINE WITH SPIKES** a machine with a revolving spiked cylinder inside a box that is also fitted with spikes. Use: cleaning or loosening fibrous materials such as cotton, wool, or rags. [Old English *welig* < Germanic] —**willowish** *adj*

LITERARY LINK *The Wind in the Willows*, a children's story (1908) by British writer Kenneth Grahame. Originally written as a bedtime story for Grahame's son, it recounts the mishaps that befall four animals – Mole, Ratty, Toad, and Badger – when they venture outside their natural habitats. Much-loved by children, the tales are also enjoyed by adults as entertaining allegories of human behaviour.

willowherb /willō hurb/ *n* PLANTS = **rosebay willowherb**

willow pattern *n* a pattern used to decorate china, usually blue on a white background, featuring a Chinese landscape with a willow tree, pagoda-style buildings, a bridge, and two swallows (*hyphenated when used before a noun*)

willow tit *n* a black-capped member of the tit family. Native to: forest and scrub in N Europe and Asia. *Parus montanus.*

willow warbler *n* a small woodland bird of the leaf warbler family, distinguishable from a chiffchaff by its song. Native to: Europe, Asia. *Phylloscopus trochilus.*

willowware /willō wair/ *n* china decorated with the willow pattern

willowy /willō i/ (**-ier, -iest**) *adj* **1 GRACEFUL** describes somebody who is slim, graceful, and elegant, partly because of being tall **2 FLEXIBLE** able to be bent easily, and springing back into place **3 COVERED BY WILLOWS** covered or shaded by willow trees

willpower /wil pow ər/ *n* a combination of determination and self-discipline that enables somebody to do something despite the difficulties involved

Wills /wilz/, **Helen Newington** (1906–98) US tennis player. Also known as **Helen Wills Moody**

Wills, William John (1834–61) British-born Australian surveyor and explorer

willy /willi/ (*plural* **-lies**), **willie** *n* an offensive term for a penis (*informal*) [Early 20C. < Shortening of the proper name *William*.]

willy-nilly /willi nilli/ *adv* **1 NOT CONTROLLABLY** whether or not somebody wants it to happen ○ *He won't be rushed willy-nilly into a quick decision.* **2 HAPHAZARDLY** in a disorganized or unplanned way ○ *Totally confused by now, I handed out the invitations willy-nilly.* ■ *adj* **1 HAPPENING WITHOUT CHOICE** happening or existing without plan or choice **2 HAPHAZARD** lacking direction or organization [Early 17C. < *will I, nill I* 'whether I wish it or do not wish it'.]

willy-willy *n Aus* a dust storm or whirlwind [Late 19C. < Aboriginal.]

Wilmut /wilmət/, **Ian** (b. 1944) Scottish embryologist

Wilson /wilss'n/, **Alexander** (1766–1813) British-born US ornithologist

Wilson, Sir Angus (1913–91) British writer

Wilson, Edmund (1895–1972) US literary critic

Wilson, Harold, Baron Wilson of Rievaulx (1916–95) British statesman

Wilson, Robert Woodrow (b. 1936) US astrophysicist

Library of Congress

Woodrow Wilson

Wilson, Woodrow (1856–1924) US statesman and 28th president of the United States (1913–21) —**Wilsonian** /wil sōni ən/ *adj*

Wilson's disease *n* a rare hereditary disease resulting from an inability to metabolize copper and marked by cirrhosis of the liver, damage to other organs, and psychiatric disorder [Early 20C. After S. A. Kinnier *Wilson* (1878–1937), English neurologist.]

Wilson's petrel *n* a small dark seabird of southern oceans that breeds in Antarctica but sometimes wanders to the N Atlantic. *Oceanites oceanicus.* [After Alexander WILSON.]

Wilson's Promontory /wilss'nz prómməntəri/ peninsula in SE Victoria, Australia, the most southerly point on the mainland

wilt[1] /wilt/ *v* **1 DROOP OR SHRIVEL** to droop or shrivel, or make a plant droop or shrivel through lack of water, too much heat, or disease **2** *vi* **BECOME WEAK** to become weak and tired, e.g. because of heat **3** *vti* **LOSE CONFIDENCE** to lose confidence, composure, or enthusiasm, or to make somebody do this ■ *n* **1 DROOPING OR SHRIVELLING** the drooping of plants or shrivelling of leaves because of a lack of water, too much heat, or disease **2 PLANT DISEASE** a plant disease caused by fungi, bacteria, or viruses that make plants droop and leaves shrivel **3 ACT OF WILTING** an instance of wilting or the condition of having wilted [Late 17C. < ?]

wilt[2] *vti* 2nd person present singular of **will**[1] (*archaic*)

Wilton /wiltən/ *n* carpet with a thick velvety pile [Late 18C. After *Wilton*, Wiltshire.]

Wilts *abbr* Wiltshire

Wiltshire /wiltshər/ county in SW England. Area: 3,486 sq. km/1,344 sq. mi.

wily /wīli/ (**-lier, -liest**) *adj* skilled at using clever tricks to deceive people —**wilily** *adv* —**wiliness** *n*

wimble /wimb'l/ *n* a hand-held tool used for boring holes ■ *vt* (**-bles, -bling, -bled**) to bore a hole with a wimble [13C. < Anglo-Norman, probably < Middle Dutch *wimmel* 'augur'.]

Wimbledon /wimb'ldən/ suburb of S London, site of annual international tennis championships

wimp /wimp/ *n* an offensive term that deliberately insults somebody as being weak, timid, unassertive, or ineffectual (*informal insult*) [Early 20C. < ?] —**wimpish** *adj* —**wimpy** *adj*

wimp out *vi* to fail to do or finish doing something because of fear or a weakness of character (*slang*)

⚡ WIMP[1] /wimp/ *n* a graphical user interface for computers designed to make them more user-friendly that includes windows, icons, mice, and pull-down menus. Full form **windows, icons, mice, and pull-down menus**

WIMP[2] /wimp/ *n* a hypothetical nonbaryonic subatomic particle that has been proposed as a possible form of dark matter. Full form **weakly interacting massive particle**

wimple /wimp'l/ *n* **1 WOMAN'S HEAD COVERING** a cloth covering for a woman's head and neck. The wimple was common in medieval Europe and it is still worn by some orders of nuns. **2 FOLD IN CLOTH** a fold or pleat in a piece of cloth ■ *v* (**-ples, -pling, -pled**) **1** *vi* **RIPPLE** to form small undulating waves **2** *vt* **DRESS SOMEBODY IN WIMPLE** to put a wimple on somebody (*archaic*) [Old English *wimpel*]

win /win/ *v* (**wins, winning, won** /wun/, **won**) **1** *vti* **ACHIEVE VICTORY** to beat any or every opponent or enemy in a competition or fight **2** *vt* GET SOMETHING FOR DEFEATING OTHERS to get something as a prize by beating other competitors using skill, effort, or luck ○ *proud of the cups he had won for swimming* **3** *vt* MAKE SOMEBODY SUCCEED IN GETTING to be the reason why somebody is first in something or receives something as a prize ○ *Their attacking play won them the game.* ○ *That photo is sure to win you a prize.* **4** *vt* GAIN to gain something such as respect or friendship, e.g. because of something done or said or an ability shown, or to make somebody do this ○ *His attitude won him few friends in the company.* **5** *vt* GET to obtain something by hard work (*literary*) ○ *winning his livelihood by the sweat of his brow* **6** *vt* REACH PLACE WITH EFFORT to arrive somewhere by great effort or with difficulty (*literary*) **7** *vt* CAPTURE SOMETHING USING FORCE to capture something such as a city using force (*formal*) **8** *vt* GAIN SUPPORT to persuade somebody to do something or agree to something, or to gain somebody's sympathy or support **9** *vt* EARN THE LOVE OF to persuade somebody to love or marry you **10** *vt* GET SOMETHING BY MINING to mine coal, oil, or ore from a source **11** *vt* PREPARE LODE FOR MINING to discover a source of coal, oil, or ore and prepare it for mining **12** *vt* EXTRACT SOMETHING FROM ORE to extract a metal or mineral from its ore ■ *n* **1** VICTORY success in a competition, game, or bet ○ *The team has had six wins in a row.* **2** AMOUNT OF MONEY WON the amount of money won, e.g. in a bet [Old English *winnan* < Indo-European, 'to desire'] —**winnable** *adj* ◇ **some you win, some you lose** used to indicate philosophically or humorously that in life everyone has some successes and some failures

win out, win through *vi* to be successful or dominant after a struggle

win over *vt* to persuade somebody to agree with you, support you, or give you permission

wince /winss/ *vi* (**winces, wincing, winced**) **1** MOVE BODY BACK SLIGHTLY to make an involuntary movement away from something because of pain or fear **2** MAKE PAINED EXPRESSION to make an expression of pain with the face because of seeing or thinking of something unpleasant or embarrassing ■ *n* **1** EXPRESSION OF PAIN a facial expression of pain or fear **2** SLIGHT MOVEMENT AWAY a slight movement away from something because of pain or fear **3** EXPRESSION OF DISPLEASURE OR EMBARRASSMENT a facial reaction to seeing or thinking of something unpleasant or embarrassing [13C. < Anglo-Norman, variant of Old French *guencir* 'turn aside' < Germanic.] —**wincer** *n*

SYNONYMS See ***recoil***.

wincey /wínssi/ *n* a cloth made of linen and wool [Early 19C. Probably variant of *woolsey* in LINSEY-WOOLSEY.]

winceyette /wínssi ét/ *n* cloth made of cotton that has a raised surface [Early 20C. < WINCEY.]

winch /winch/ *n* **1** LIFTING MACHINE a machine for lifting loads by means of a rope or chain that is wound round a cylinder turned by an engine or by hand **2** CRANK OR HANDLE the handle used to turn a machine ■ *vt* MOVE SOMETHING WITH WINCH to lift or pull something by means of a winch [Old English *wince* < Germanic] —**wincher** *n* —**winchman** *n*

winchester /wínchistər/ *n* a large bottle with a short narrow neck. Use: carrying or storing liquid chemicals. [Early 18C. After WINCHESTER, where standards for liquid and dry measures were once kept.]

Winchester /wínchistər/ city in S England. Population: 34,700 (1994).

Winckelmann /wínk'l man/, **Johann Joachim** (1717–68) German archaeologist and art historian

wind[1] /wind/ *n* **1** MOVING AIR air moving across the surface of the planet or through the atmosphere at a speed fast enough to be noticed **2** AIR MOVED ARTIFICIALLY air that is being made to move by a device such as a fan **3** FLOW OF PARTICLES INTO SPACE a flow of particles ejected into space from the surface of the Sun or a star **4** SOCIAL OR ECONOMIC FORCE a force or movement bringing something such as change or destruction (*formal*) ○ *'The wind of change is blowing through the continent'.* (Harold Macmillan, *Speech to South African parliament*; 3 Feb 1960) **5** BREATH the breath of normal breathing and talking **6** POWER TO BREATHE the power to breathe, especially when making an effort such as running **7** MUSICAL INSTRUMENTS a group of musical instruments that requires a flow of air to produce a sound, including both woodwind and brass instruments ○ *the wind section of the orchestra* **8** STOMACH GAS gas that builds up in the stomach and intestines while food is being digested **9** IDLE TALK talk that is empty and meaningless **10** HINTING INFORMATION news that brings information of something intended to be secret ○ *If wind of this gets out, we've had it.* **11** AIR CARRYING A SCENT the air on which a scent, e.g. that of a hunter, is carried **12** DIRECTION OF WIND the direction from which the wind blows (*literary*) ■ **winds** *npl* PLAYERS OF WIND INSTRUMENTS the musicians in an ensemble, especially an orchestra, who play wind instruments ■ *v* **1** *vt* MAKE SHORT OF BREATH to make somebody unable to breathe in enough air, e.g. because of too much exertion or by a blow to the abdomen **2** *vt* MAKE BABY RELEASE STOMACH GAS to help a baby bring up gas from its stomach, e.g. by patting and rubbing its back **3** *vt* LET HORSE REST to allow a horse to rest after exertion **4** *vti* SMELL to get a scent of somebody or something in the air **5** *vt* PURSUE ANIMAL BY SCENT to pursue an animal in a hunt by following its scent **6** *vt* EXPOSE TO WIND to expose something to the wind, e.g. in order to dry it [Old English < Indo-European, 'to blow'] —**winded** *adj* ◇ **be in the wind** to be about to happen or be likely to happen ◇ **break wind** to pass intestinal gas through the anus ◇ **get the wind up** to become nervous or fearful (*informal*) ◇ **get wind of something** to hear indirectly about something ◇ **piss in the wind** an offensive phrase meaning to do something that is likely to have little or no effect (*slang*) ◇ **put the wind up somebody** to make somebody nervous or fearful (*informal*) ◇ **sail close to the wind** to come very close to breaking the law or a rule ◇ **see which way** *or* **how the wind is blowing** to wait and find out the nature of a situation before making a decision ◇ **swing** *or* **twist in the wind** to be left in a difficult or unpleasant situation without any help or support from other people (*informal*) ◇ **take the wind out of somebody's sails** to make somebody feel deflated, silly, or embarrassed, or put somebody at a disadvantage

wind[2] /wīnd/ *v* (**winds, winding, wound** /wownd/, **wound**) **1** *vti* GO ALONG PATH WITH BENDS to move along a course with many bends and twists in it, or to make a route with many bends and twists in it ○ *The river winds lazily through the valley.* ○ *The procession wound its way slowly up the hill.* **2** *vi* FOLLOW SPIRAL PATH to go in a spiral path ○ *smoke winding slowly up into the air* **3** *vti* GO OR PUT ROUND to go round something in a coil or coils, or to wrap something round something else in a coil or coils ○ *winding the thread onto the bobbin* **4** *vt* WRAP SOMETHING WITH COILS to cover or decorate something by wrapping something else round it in coils ○ *She wound the injured arm with a scarf.* **5** *vt* MOVE SOMETHING UP OR DOWN to move or lift something by turning a handle or pressing a button ○ *I wound the car window down.* **6** *vti* MOVE SOMETHING BACKWARD OR FORWARD to move something such as a film forwards or backwards by turning a handle or pressing a button, or to be moved in this way ○ *Let's wind the tape back and see that part again.* **7** *vt* MAKE SOMETHING REVOLVE to turn something such as a crank with a circular motion **8** *vt* MAKE A CLOCKWORK MECHANISM WORK to turn a key or handle in a clock or clockwork device in order to make the mechanism operate, usually by means of a spring that tightens on being wound ■ *n* **1** CURVE OR BEND a bend or twist in something such as a river or a path **2** ACT OF WINDING the act of winding something such as a clock or motor, or a single turn in this process [Old English *windan* < Germanic]

wind down *v* **1** *vi* RELAX to relax after a period of feeling stressed or tense **2** *vti* STEADILY REDUCE WORK to gradually reduce the amount of work done before stopping completely **3** *vi* GO MORE SLOWLY to operate more and more slowly and then stop because the spring by which a mechanism works is losing or has lost its tension

wind up /wīnd-/ *v* **1** *vt* CLOSE BUSINESS DOWN to close down a business, bringing trading to an end **2** *vt* FINISH ACTIVITY to conclude something or to bring an activity to an end **3** *vi* END UP to come to be in a particular place or situation as a result of, or at the end of, a series of earlier events (*informal*) **4** *vt* LIE TO SOMEBODY AS A JOKE to tease or trick somebody by telling him or her things that are not true (*informal*) ○ *You're winding me up, aren't you?* **5** *vt* MAKE SOMEBODY TENSE to make somebody nervous or irritated, usually deliberately (*informal; often passive*)

wind[3] /wīnd/ (**winds, winding, winded** *or* **wound**) *v* **1** *vti* to blow a horn or bugle to create a sound **2** *vt* to make a signal by blowing a horn [14C. < WIND[1].]

windage /wíndij/ *n* **1** DEFLECTION CAUSED BY WIND the amount of deflection the wind will produce in a projectile **2** ALLOWANCE MADE FOR WIND DEFLECTION the amount needed to adjust the aim of a projectile to counter wind deflection **3** DIFFERENCE BETWEEN BORE AND PROJECTILE the amount by which the bore of a gun is larger than the bullet or shell it fires, so that gases can escape **4** PART OF SHIP ABOVE WATER the part of a ship's body that is above the water and consequently causes wind resistance **5** FRICTION BETWEE[N] AIR AND MOVING PARTS the friction between air and th[e] moving parts of a machine, which tends to slow th[e] machine

windbag /wínd bag/ *n* **1** a talkative person who is though[t] to have little of interest or value to say (*informal insul[t]*) **2** the bag in a set of bagpipes into which air is force[d] by the player's lungs or a set of bellows and from whic[h] it flows to produce sound

windball cricket /wínd bawl-/ *n* a form of cricket playe[d] with a wooden bat and a tennis ball

wind-bell /wínd-/ *n* a light bell that rings when the win[d] moves it

windblast /wínd blaast/ *n* the harmful effect of air frictio[n] on a pilot who has ejected from an aircraft travelling a[t] high speed

windblown /wínd blōn/ *adj* **1** BLOWN BY THE WIND blow[n] about by the wind ○ *They came back from their wal[k] looking a bit windblown.* **2** GROWING IN SHAPE CAUSED B[Y] WIND growing in a shape caused by the action of th[e] prevailing winds **3** *NZ* BLOWN DOWN blown down by th[e] wind

wind-borne /wínd-/ *adj* carried or dispersed by the win[d]

windbound /wínd bownd/ *adj* unable to sail because th[e] wind is blowing in the wrong direction

windbreak /wínd brayk/ *n* **1** something such as a wall o[r] hedge that breaks the force of the prevailing wind **2** a[n] object consisting of a wide piece of cloth with severa[l] sticks along it that can be pushed into the ground t[o] provide shelter from the wind

wind-broken /wínd-/ *adj* describes a horse that has impaired breathing, e.g. because of heaves

windburn /wínd burn/ *n* redness and inflammation of th[e] skin caused by exposure to harsh wind —**windburn[t]** /-burnt/ *adj*

windcheater /wínd cheetər/ *n* a warm windproof outer jacket with tight-fitting neck, cuffs, and waistband, an[d] sometimes with a hood

wind chest /wínd-/ *n* a compartment in an organ tha[t] stores wind from the bellows under pressure before i[t] goes to the pipes

wind-chill factor /wínd-/, **wind-chill** *n* a temperature in calm conditions that has the equivalent effect o[n] exposed skin as the combination of a given temperature and wind speed

wind chime /wínd-/ *n* a musical decoration consisting of objects such as beads or metal tubes suspended o[n] strings so that they will make a pleasant noise whe[n] moved by the wind

wind cone /wínd kōn/ *n* = **windsock**

winder /wíndər/ *n* **1** SOMETHING THAT WINDS UP a key, knob, or other device that is used to wind up a spring-powered mechanism such as a clock **2** HOISTING MECHANISM OR OPERATOR a mechanism for hoisting or lowering a cage in a mineshaft, or an operator of such a mechanism **3** SOMEBODY OR SOMETHING THAT WINDS a person or device that winds thread or textiles around a spool, cone, or tube **4** OBJECT FOR WINDING SOMETHING AROUND a spool or bobbin around which something such as thread is wound **5** STEP IN SPIRAL STAIRCASE a step in a spiral staircase or at the turn of a staircase that is narrower at the inside of the curve

Windermere, Lake /wíndər meer/ largest lake in England, in the Lake District in the north west of the country. Area: 16 sq. km/6 sq. mi.

windfall /wínd fawl/ *n* **1** something good that is received unexpectedly, especially a sum of money **2** something that the wind has blown down, especially a piece of ripe fruit blown off a tree

wind farm /wínd-/ *n* an area of land with a large number of electricity-generating windmills or wind turbines

windflaw /wínd flaw/ *n* METEOROL = **flaw**[2] *n.* 1

windflower /wínd flowər/ *n* an anemone plant such as the wood anemone

windgall /wínd gawl/ *n* a fluid-filled swelling around the fetlock joint of a horse, usually not associated with loss of function or lameness

wind gap /wínd-/ *n* a shallow pass or gap in a mountain ridge, often originally a water gap

wind gauge /wínd-/ *n* an attachment to the sight on a musket or rifle showing how much the aim should be adjusted to allow for the effect of the wind on the bullet

wind harp /wínd-/ *n* MUSIC = **aeolian harp**

Windhoek /wínd hòok, wínt-, vínt-/ capital of Namibia. Population: 169,000 (1997 estimate).

windhover /wínd hovər/ *n* a kestrel (*regional*) [Late 17C. < its habit of hovering in the air.]

winding /wínding/ *adj* **1** TWISTING AND CURVING made up of many consecutive curves or twists **2** SPIRALLING arranged or moving in a spiral ■ *n* **1** SOMETHING WOUND something wound or coiled round an object, or a single turn of it **2** ACT OF COILING the act or process of coiling something **3** CURVING COURSE the bending or curving course that something follows **4** WIRE COIL CARRYING ELECTRICITY a wire coil designed to have an electric current passing through it, forming part of numerous electrical devices such as electric motors and transformers —**windingly** *adv*

winding drum *n* a revolving drum with a wire rope coiled round it that acts as the lifting mechanism of a hoist or winch

winding sheet, winding-sheet *n* a sheet that a corpse is wrapped in before it is buried

wind instrument /wínd-/ *n* a musical instrument, such as a trumpet or flute, played by causing air to vibrate by blowing into or across a tube

windjammer /wínd jammər/ *n* **1** a large sailing ship, especially a large and fast merchant ship **2** = **windcheater** (*dated*) [Late 19C. Because of its huge sail area.]

windlass /wíndləss/ *n* a device that uses a rope or cable wound round a revolving drum to pull and lift things, especially the mechanism on a ship to raise and lower the anchor ■ *vt* to raise or pull something using a windlass [14C. Alteration of Old Norse *vindáss* < *vinda* 'wind' + *áss* 'pole'.]

wind machine /wínd-/ *n* **1** a device used backstage in a theatre to simulate the sound of wind blowing, or a large fan that simulates windy weather on a film set **2** a machine that creates a strong current of air, e.g. a device that produces warm air to protect crops from frost

windmill /wínd mil/ *n* **1** BUILDING WITH REVOLVING BLADES a building with a set of wind-driven revolving sails or blades fitted to the site of its roof that drive a grinding machine inside **2** REVOLVING BLADES OR GRINDING MECHANISM the set of revolving sails or blades on a windmill, or the grinding mechanism inside the building **3** DEVICE HARNESSING WIND POWER a building or device fitted with a set of revolving blades designed to harness the power of the wind, e.g. to pump water or generate electricity **4** CHILD'S TOY WITH SPINNING BLADES a child's toy consisting of a stick with a set of plastic or paper blades fitted to it, which spin round when the wind blows them. US term **pinwheel** *n.* 1 ■ *v* **1** *vti* SPIN LIKE WINDMILL to spin or turn like the sails of a windmill, or to be spun or turned in this way **2** *vi* ROTATE UNPOWERED to rotate solely by wind force and with no engine power ◇ **tilt at windmills** to struggle against imagined enemies or opponents

window /wíndō/ *n* **1** GLASS-COVERED OPENING IN BUILDING an opening in a wall of a building, usually with an inner frame of wood or metal with glass fitted to it, to let in light or, when opened, air **2** GLASS-COVERED OPENING LETTING LIGHT IN any glass-covered opening designed to let in light or, when opened, air, e.g. in a vehicle **3** = **windowpane 4** DISPLAY IN SHOP WINDOW the area immediately behind a large window in the wall of a shop, where goods are put on display **5** OPENING WHERE SOMETHING IS DISPENSED an opening above a counter where somebody provides information, goods, or services to customers **6** OPENING SIMILAR TO WINDOW an opening that makes it possible to see something behind or underneath, e.g. the opening on some envelopes **7** PERIOD OF AVAILABLE TIME a period of free time in a schedule available for use, or a limited time during which conditions are right for something to take place **8** OPPORTUNITY an opportunity to see or experience something **9** SECTION ON COMPUTER SCREEN a rectangular frame on a computer screen in which images output by application programs can be displayed, moved around, or resized **10** PART OF ELECTROMAGNETIC SPECTRUM the range of the electromagnetic spectrum that a given medium will allow to pass through it **11** AIR FORCE = **chaff**[1] *n.* 3 [Pre-12C. < Old Norse *vindauga* < *vindr* 'wind' + *auga* 'eye'.] ◇ **go out of the window** to be lost for good (*informal*)

window box *n* **1** a soil-filled box on a window ledge with plants growing in it, or a box made to be used in this way **2** either of the spaces in the sides of the frame of a sash window that conceal the weights, ropes, and pulleys that raise and lower the window's separate sections

window dressing *n* **1** a display of goods for sale in a shop window **2** a deceptively appealing presentation of something, intended to conceal flaws

window envelope *n* an envelope with a transparent panel at the front that makes it possible to see the address to which the letter is being sent on the letter inside

windowpane /wíndō payn/ *n* a sheet of glass that forms part of a window

window seat *n* **1** an indoor seat fixed to a wall under a window, especially a window that is set into a recess **2** a seat by a window in a plane, train, or bus

window-shop (**window-shops, window-shopping, window-shopped**) *vi* to look at goods displayed in shop windows without a serious intention of buying anything —**window-shopper** *n*

windowsill /wíndō sil/ *n* the shelf on the bottom edge of a window, either a projecting part of the window frame or the bottom of the wall recess that the window fits into

window tax *n* a tax on windows that was levied between 1691 and 1851, the evasion of which accounts for the blocked-up windows in some old houses

windpipe /wínd pīp/ *n* the tube in air-breathing vertebrates that conducts air from the throat to the bronchi, strengthened by incomplete rings of cartilage. Technical name **trachea**

wind-pollinated *adj* pollinated by pollen that is carried to the plant by the wind

wind power *n* the force of the wind harnessed by windmills and wind turbines that convert it into electricity, or the electricity produced in this way

windproof /wínd proof/ *adj* resisting the force of the wind

wind rose *n* a circular diagram indicating the range of wind speeds and directions for a particular place over a given time period

windrow /wíndrō/ *n* **1** ROW OF DRYING HAY a long thin pile of cut hay or grain designed to catch the wind and dry quickly **2** PILE BLOWN TOGETHER BY WIND a long thin pile of things, especially leaves or snow, heaped up by the wind ■ *vt* GATHER HAY INTO WINDROWS to gather cut grass, hay, or other crop material into windrows for drying —**windrower** *n*

windsail /wínd sayl/; *nautical* /wíndss'l, wínss'l/ *n* **1** a tube or funnel of sailcloth rigged over a companionway or hatch to catch breezes and provide ventilation for a ship **2** a sail on a windmill

wind scale *n* a scale for measuring the strength of a wind, e.g. the Beaufort Scale

windscreen /wínd skreen/ *n* **1** the piece of glass or plastic that forms the front window of a motor vehicle. US term **windshield** *n.* 1 **2** *US* = **windshield** *n.* 2

windscreen wiper *n* a motorized device consisting of a rubber blade attached to a metal arm that is fixed just below a vehicle's windscreen, used for wiping rain and snow off the windscreen. = **windscreen wiper**

wind shake /wínd-/ *n* a crack between the growth rings of a tree, thought to be caused when the tree bends violently in the wind

wind shear /wínd-/ *n* the amount by which the speed of the wind varies at different altitudes, often causing difficulties for aircraft

windshield /wínd sheeld/ *n* **1** *US* AUTOMOT = **windscreen** *n.* 1 **2** a screen used to protect somebody or something from the wind, e.g. sunbathers on a beach or plants in a garden. US term **windscreen** *n.* 2

windsock /wínd sok/ *n* a fabric tube or cone attached at one end to the top of a pole, so that it blows like a flag to show which way the wind is blowing

Windsor /wínzər/ **1** town in S England, on the River Thames, the site of Windsor Castle. Population: 27,400 (1991). **2** town in SE New South Wales, Australia. Population: 21,317 (1996).

Windsor, Duke of title granted to Edward VIII after his abdication from the British throne in 1936 and subsequent marriage to Wallis Simpson in June 1937. ◊ **Edward VIII**

Windsor chair *n* a wooden chair that traditionally has a back formed of spindles, a saddle-shaped seat, and splayed legs [Mid-18C. After WINDSOR in England.]

Windsor knot *n* a large triangular knot in a man's tie, made by putting an extra turn on each side of the loop that lies beneath the knot [Mid-20C. Probably after the Duke of WINDSOR.]

windstorm /wínd stawrm/ *n* a storm consisting of very strong winds and little or no rain or other precipitation

wind-sucking /wínd suking/ *n* the habit some horses have of biting the edge of a stall or fence while gulping air or sucking in air by making certain head and neck movements —**wind-sucker** *n*

windsurf /wínd surf/ *vi* to ride and steer a sailboard fitted with a movable sail —**windsurfer** *n*

Popperfoto

Windsurfing

windsurfing /wínd surfing/ *n* the sport of riding and steering a sailboard

windswept /wínd swept/ *adj* **1** EXPOSED TO WIND exposed to the wind and usually very windy **2** DISHEVELLED dishevelled in appearance as a result of exposure to the wind **3** FASHIONED TO LOOK WINDBLOWN fashioned so as to look blown by the wind ○ *a windswept hairstyle*

wind tee /wínd-/ *n* a T-shaped weather vane at an airfield that shows which way the wind is blowing

wind tunnel /wínd-/ *n* a tunnel-shaped chamber through which air can be passed at a known speed in order to test the aerodynamic properties of an object such as an aircraft or automobile placed inside it

wind-up /wínd up/ *n* **1** TEASE a tease, especially a lie told in order to get a reaction (*informal*) **2** ENDING the bringing to a close of something, such as the closing down of a business ■ *adj* OPERATED BY TURNING HANDLE made to work by turning a handle or key that winds an internal spring

windward /wíndwərd/ *adj* FACING THE WIND facing the wind, or on the side of something, especially a boat, that is facing the wind. ◊ **leeward** ■ *adv* INTO THE WIND towards where the wind is coming from. ◊ **leeward** ■ *n* SIDE FACING WIND the side facing the wind, or the direction that the wind is blowing from. ◊ **leeward**

Windward Islands /wíndwərd-/ group of islands in the E Caribbean Sea, including Martinique and the independent island states of Dominica, St Lucia, Grenada, and St Vincent and the Grenadines. Area: 3,657 sq. km/1,412 sq. mi.

windway /wínd way/ *n* an opening or passage allowing air through, e.g. a ventilation shaft in a mine

windy /wíndi/ (**-ier, -iest**) *adj* **1** WITH WIND BLOWING with strong winds blowing **2** WHERE WINDS BLOW where strong winds tend to blow ○ *a high and windy hill* **3** FULL OF EMPTY WORDS full of long and important-sounding though largely meaningless words designed to impress people (*informal*) **4** FLATULENT suffering from flatulence (*informal*) **5** NERVOUS nervous or frightened (*dated informal*) —**windily** *adv* —**windiness** *n*

wine /wīn/ *n* **1** ALCOHOL FERMENTED FROM GRAPES an alcoholic drink made by fermenting the juice of grapes **2** ALCOHOL FERMENTED FROM OTHER FRUIT an alcoholic drink made by fermenting the juice or an infusion of fruit other than grapes, or the juice or an infusion of other plants **3** SOMETHING STIMULATING OR INTOXICATING something that has a stimulating or intoxicating effect resembling that of wine (*literary*) **4** DARK PURPLISH-RED COLOUR a dark purplish-red colour, like that of red wine [Old English *wīn* < Latin *vinum* < Indo-European] —**wine** *adj* ◇ **wine and dine** to enjoy, be treated, or treat somebody to an expensive meal out

SPELLCHECK See *whine.*

wine bar *n* a bar that specializes in serving wine, although beer and spirits may also be served

wine cellar *n* **1** a cellar where wine is stored, or any dark cool room used for storing wine **2** a stock of wine

wine cooler *n* **1** a container filled with ice or a refrigerant and used to keep one or more bottles of wine cool **2** a mixture of wine and fruit juice, sometimes with carbonated water, sold in bottles

wine gallon *n* an obsolete British unit of capacity equal to 231 cubic inches or 3.79 litres, which is smaller than the imperial gallon but exactly equal to the standard US gallon

wineglass /wín glaass/ *n* **1** a glass suitable for drinking wine, with a bowl mounted on a stem and usually a rounded base **2** the amount of liquid that the average wineglass will hold, around four fluid ounces or 0.11 litres, for mixing cocktails or for cooking purposes

wine grower *n* a grower of grapes for making wine, especially the owner or manager of a vineyard who also oversees the winemaking

winemaking /wín mayking/ *n* the art or business of producing wine, from the growing of the grapes to the finished product —**winemaker** *n*

wine palm *n* a palm tree whose fermented sap is used to make palm wine

winepress /wín press/ *n* a piece of winemaking equipment that squeezes the juice from grapes

winery /wínəri/ (*plural* **-ies**) *n US, ANZ* a place where wine is made

wineskin /wín skin/ *n* a container for wine made from the skin of a sheep or goat sewn into a bag

wine tasting *n* **1** the sampling of a variety of wines, either as a preliminary to buying wine or as instruction in the appreciation of wine **2** a gathering to sample, learn about, and enjoy drinking a variety of wines

Winfrey /wínfri/, **Oprah** (*b.* 1954) US talk show host and actor

wing /wing/ *n* **1** BIRD'S LIMB FOR FLYING either of a bird's feather-covered limbs that are typically used for flying **2** INSECT'S OR BAT'S LIMB FOR FLYING any large membrane-covered limb on an insect or a bat that is used for flying **3** FLAT SURFACE PROJECTING FROM AIRCRAFT'S SIDE either of the large flat surfaces sticking out from the sides of an aircraft's body that provide the aircraft's main source of lift **4** FLAT PROJECTING PART either of a pair of flat parts that stick out from the main body of something, e.g. the outgrowths of a wind-dispersed seed case or the ends of an old-fashioned collar **5** FLIGHT a means or manner of flying **6** PART OF BUILDING PROJECTING FROM MIDDLE one of the parts of a building that project from the main part **7** LONGER SIDE OF SPORTS FIELD either of the longer sides of the field of play in some sports, at right angles to the sides where the goals are **8** ATTACKING PLAYER ON SIDE OF FIELD an attacking player who plays down one side of the field in some team sports such as football and hockey, or this position the person plays **9** FOOTBALL = **wingman** *n.* **2** **10** SUBDIVISION OF POLITICAL GROUP a faction within a political party or movement, especially either of two broad factions, one more conservative, the other more liberal **11** SUBSIDIARY GROUP a group attached and subordinate to a parent organization **12** CORNER OF CAR any of the corner parts of the body of a motor vehicle that surround each wheel. US term **fender** *n.* **4** **13** AIR FORCE UNIT an air force unit that is larger than a group but smaller than a division **14** PART OF MILITARY FORMATION the left or right part of a large military formation such as a field army or a fleet **15** SCENERY PIECE AT SIDE OF STAGE a piece of scenery at the side of the stage ■ **wings** *npl* **1** SIDE OF THEATRE STAGE the areas of a theatre to the sides of the stage, unseen by the audience **2** QUALIFIED PILOT'S BADGE a badge with a design in the shape of wings, worn by a trained and qualified pilot ■ *v* **1** *vti* MOVE SWIFTLY to move or travel somewhere swiftly, or send something with great speed **2** *vt* WOUND BIRD BY HITTING WING to wound a bird superficially by hitting it on its wing **3** *vt* WOUND OR DAMAGE SUPERFICIALLY to wound somebody superficially, especially in the arm or leg, or cause only superficial damage to something **4** *vt* PREPARE PERFORMANCE AT LAST MINUTE to prepare a performance as a last-minute replacement actor, learning the lines in the wings immediately before going on, or perform a part without having thoroughly learned or prepared it [12C. < N Germanic < Indo-European, 'to blow'.] ◇ **be (waiting) in the wings** to be ready and prepared to do something, or available for use when needed ◇ **take somebody under your wing** to look after or protect somebody ◇ **wing it** to improvise (*informal*) ◇ **with wings** to be taken away rather than consumed on the premises (*informal*) ○ *one cappuccino with wings*

wing and wing *adv* with sails extended on each side

wingback /wíng bak/ *n* **1** an offensive back in American football who lines up outside an end, or the position taken by this player **2** in football, an essentially defensive player who also makes attacking runs and who plays close to the touchlines on either side of the defence

wing-case *n* INSECTS = **elytron**

wing chair *n* an armchair with a high back and large side panels

wing collar *n* a high stiff collar on a man's shirt, worn with the points at the upper corner turned down over the tie as part of formal dress

wing commander *n* a commissioned officer in the Royal Air Force of a rank above squadron leader

wing covert *n* a small feather on a bird's wing, covering the base of the wing quills

wingding /wíng ding/ *n US* **1** a party or celebration, especially a noisy and boisterous one (*dated*) **2** a wild or violent outburst, e.g. a fit of anger (*slang*) [Early 20C. < ?]

winged /wingd, wíngid/ *adj* **1** able to fly because of having wings **2** moving swiftly in a manner resembling flying (*literary*)

winger /wíngər/ *n* SPORTS = **wing** *n.* **8**

wingman /wíng man/ (*plural* **-men** /-men/) *n* **1** a pilot who flies in a position behind, and to the side of, the leader of a flying formation **2** in Australian Rules football, either of two players playing in positions on either side of the centre circle

wing nut *n* a nut that has flat projections on its sides for the fingers to grip

wingover /wíng ōvər/ *n* a flying manoeuvre to turn an aircraft in which the pilot puts the aircraft into a steep banking climb to a near stall and then allows the nose to fall

wingspan /wíng span/, **wingspread** /wíng spred/ *n* the distance from tip to tip of an aircraft's wings, or of the outstretched wings of a bird or insect

wing tip *n* **1** the tip of the wing of a bird, insect, or aircraft that is the point furthest away from the centre of its body **2** *US* CLOTHING = **brogue**[2] *n.* **1**

wink /wingk/ *v* **1** *vti* GESTURE BY CLOSING ONE EYE BRIEFLY to close one eye briefly, usually either as a friendly greeting or to show that something just done or said is a joke or a secret **2** *vi* SHINE INTERMITTENTLY to shine intermittently or faintly ■ *n* **1** BRIEF CLOSING OF ONE EYE a brief closing of one eye as a greeting or signal **2** TWINKLING LIGHT a twinkling or faintly flashing light **3** SHORT TIME the briefest period of time **4** SHORT NAP a brief nap or very short period of being asleep (*informal*) [Old English *wincian* 'close your eyes' < Indo-European] ◇ **tip somebody the wink** to give somebody information privately or confidentially (*informal*)

wink at *vt* to pretend not to notice an offence or wrongdoing (*informal*)

winker /wíngkər/ *n* **1** SOMEBODY WHO WINKS somebody or something that winks **2** FLASHING LIGHT a light that winks or flashes, especially an indicator on a motor vehicle **3** *US* EYE OR PART OF EYE an eye, or a part of the eye such as an eyelid or eyelash (*informal*) ■ **winkers** *npl* BLINKERS a racehorse's blinkers

winkle /wingk'l/ *n* a small edible mollusc with a spiral shell. Native to: coastal waters. Genus: *Littorina.* [Late 16C. Shortening of PERIWINKLE[1].]

winkle out *vt* to extract something such as information with difficulty [< the practice of extracting molluscs from their shells]

winkle-pickers *npl* shoes with narrow pointed toes, popular in the 1950s (*informal*) [Because the shoe's pointed toe resembles a pin used for removing winkles from their shells]

Winnebago[1] /wínni báy gō/ (*plural* **-go** *or* **-gos** *or* **-goes**) *n* **1** a member of a Siouan people who lived in Wisconsin and Illinois, and now live mainly in Wisconsin and Nebraska **2** the Siouan language of the Winnebago people [Mid-18C. < Algonquian *wi:nepye:ko:ha* 'person of the dirty water'.]

Winnebago[2] *tdmk* a trademark for a large motor vehicle with cooking and sleeping facilities

Winnebago, Lake /wínni báy gō/ lake in E Wisconsin, forming part of the course of the Fox River. Area: 557 sq. km/215 sq. mi.

winner /wínnər/ *n* **1** somebody or something that wins a competition or contest **2** a very successful or popular person or thing, or one that seems likely to become successful or popular

winner's enclosure, winner's circle *n* an enclosure at a racecourse where the winning horses are unsaddled and prizes awarded to owners, trainers, and jockeys

winning /wínning/ *adj* **1** VICTORIOUS victorious or bringing victory **2** CHARMING very charming, to the extent that people are won over ■ **winnings** *npl* MONEY WON money or other valuables that are won, especially from gambling —**winningly** *adv* —**winningness** *n*

winningest /wínningist/ *adj US* winning the highest number of victories or prizes, or the most prize money (*informal*) ○ *a list of the all-time winningest baseball coaches*

winning gallery *n* an opening in a side wall of a real tennis court into which the ball is hit from the other side of the net in order to win a point

winning post *n* the post that marks the finish line on a racecourse

Winnipeg /wínni peg/ capital of Manitoba, Canada, in the southern part of the province. Population: 618,477 (1996).

Winnipeg, Lake freshwater lake in central Manitoba, Canada. Depth: 18m/60 ft. Area: 24,390 sq. km/9,417 sq. mi.

winnitude /wínni tyood/ *n* success or the fact of being successful [Late 20C. < WIN, after such words as *plenitude.*]

winnow /wínnō/ *v* **1** *vti* USE AIR TO REMOVE CHAFF to separate grain from its husks (**chaff**) by tossing it in the air or blowing air through it **2** *vt* EXAMINE SOMETHING TO REMOVE BAD PARTS to examine something in order to remove the bad, unusable, or undesirable parts ■ *n* PROCESS OF WINNOWING the process of separating grain from chaff, or a device used to do this [Old English *windwian* < *wind* 'wind'] —**winnower** *n*

wino /wínō/ (*plural* **-os**) *n* an offensive term for somebody who is addicted to alcohol, especially wine, and usually is also homeless (*informal insult*)

winsome /wínssəm/ *adj* charming, especially because of a naive, innocent quality [Old English *wynsum* 'pleasant' < *wynn* 'joy' < Indo-European, 'to desire'.] —**winsomely** *adv* —**winsomeness** *n*

winter /wíntər/ *n* **1** YEAR'S COLDEST SEASON the coldest season of the year, which runs in the northern hemisphere from around November or December to February or March and in the southern hemisphere from June to August **2** CLOSING PERIOD OR PERIOD OF INACTIVITY the closing part or period of something, or a period of decline or inactivity **3** YEAR one of a number of years, especially a great number (*literary*) ■ *v* **1** *vi* SPEND WINTER SOMEWHERE to spend the winter in a particular place, especially away from home **2** *vt* KEEP SOMETHING SOMEWHERE IN WINTER to keep something, especially farm animals, in a particular place during the winter [Old English, < Indo-European, 'wet']

winter aconite *n* a low-growing plant with a single yellow flower that blooms in winter or early spring. Native to: Europe, Asia. *Eranthis hyemalis.*

winterberry /wíntərbəri/ (*plural* **-ries** *or* **-ry**) *n* a deciduous holly with bright red berries and leaves that turn black in the autumn. Native to: E North America. *Ilex verticillata.*

winterbourne /wíntər bawrn/ *n* a stream that flows only or mostly in winter, after heavy rains

winter cherry *n* **1** PLANTS = **Chinese lantern** *n.* **2** **2** a small plant with round red fruit, often grown as a pot plant. *Solanum capsicastrum.* **3** the fruit of the winter cherry

wintercress /wíntər kress/ *n* a plant of the mustard family, formerly used as a winter salad. Flowers: yellow. Genus: *Barbarea.*

winterfeed /wíntər feed/ (**-feeds, -feeding, -fed** /-fed/ **-fed**) *vt* to feed livestock in winter, e.g. on hay or silage, when there is little or no grazing

winter flounder *n* **1** a reddish-brown flounder that is a popular food fish in winter. Native to: NW Atlantic. *Pseudopleuronectes americanus.* **2** a dark-brown flounder, fished commercially for food. Native to: South Atlantic coast, Gulf of Mexico. *Pseudopleuronectes americanus.*

winter garden *n* **1** a garden planted with evergreen plants, to give growth even in winter **2** a greenhouse or conservatory that contains winter plants

wintergreen /wíntər green/ (*plural* **-greens** *or* **-green**) *n* **1** a low-growing evergreen bush with red berries and fragrant leathery leaves from which an oil (**oil of wintergreen**) is distilled. Native to: E North America. *Gaultheria procumbens.* **2** = **oil of wintergreen** [Mid-16C. Translation of Dutch *wintergroen.*]

winter heliotrope *n* a creeping winter-flowering perennial plant. Flowers: lilac-coloured, vanilla-scented. *Petasites fragrans.*

winterize /wíntə rīz/ (**-izes, -izing, -ized**), **winterise** (**-ises, -ising, -ised**) *vt US, Can* to prepare something, especially a house or a car, to withstand cold winter conditions —**winterization** /wíntə rī záysh'n/ *n*

winter jasmine *n* a variety of jasmine that has yellow flowers in winter. Native to: China. *Jasminum nudiflorum.*

winter moth *n* a brown moth with no wings in the female whose larvae crawl with a series of looping movements. *Operophtera brumata.*

Winter Olympics, Winter Olympic Games *npl* an international gathering for athletes competing in a variety of winter sports, taking place every four years

winter sports *npl* sports such as skiing and ice skating performed on snow and ice

winter squash *n US* a slow-maturing squash that grows on long trailing vines, has a tough skin, and stores well. ◊ **summer squash**

wintertide /wíntər tīd/ *n* wintertime (*archaic or literary*)

wintertime /wíntər tīm/ *n* the season of winter

winterweight /wíntər wayt/ *adj* made of thick heavy fabric and designed to protect somebody or something from cold weather

winter wheat *n* a variety of wheat planted in autumn, left in the ground over winter, and harvested the following spring or early summer

wintery *adj* = **wintry**

Winthrop /wín throp/, **John** (1588–1649) English-born American colonial governor

wintry /wíntri/ (**-trier, -triest**), **wintery** (**-terier, -teriest**) *adj* **1** relating to or typical of winter, especially in being cold **2** cheerless or unfriendly ○ *She gave him a wintry smile.* —**wintrily** *adv* —**wintriness** *n*

win-win *adj* describes a situation in which all parties benefit in some way ○ *a win-win scenario*

winy /wīni/ (**-ier, -iest**) *adj* like wine in taste or appearance

winze /winz/ *n* a steeply inclined or vertical shaft between levels in a mine [Mid-18C. Alteration of obsolete *winds* < ?]

WIP *abbr* work in progress

wipe /wīp/ *v* (**wipes, wiping, wiped**) **1** *vt* RUB SOMETHING WITH LIGHT STROKES to rub something with long light strokes with a soft material, or rub something lightly on a soft material ○ *wiped their hands on the towel* **2** *vti* REMOVE OR BE REMOVED BY RUBBING to remove something such as dirt with long light rubbing strokes, usually with a soft material, or be removed in this way ○ *The mark wiped off easily.* **3** *vt* REMOVE RECORDING FROM TAPE to remove recorded material from an audiotape or video tape **4** *vt* REMOVE to remove something or get rid of it as if by wiping ○ *wiped from my memory* **5** *vt* APPLY SOMETHING WITH LIGHT RUBBING to apply something, especially a liquid or cream, by rubbing it on lightly, e.g. with a cloth or the hand ■ *n* **1** LIGHT RUBBING STROKE one or more long light rubbing strokes **2** DISPOSABLE CLEANING CLOTH a soft disposable cloth or tissue soaked with a cleansing liquid, used for cleaning something such as the skin ○ *'Remember trash bags, wipes, and napkins. It's no fun sitting next to banana peel for five hours'.* (*Washington Post*; July 1998) **3** ONE PICTURE PUSHING OTHER OFF SCREEN an effect in which one picture on the screen appears to be pushed off the side of the screen by another, often used to move from scene to scene [Old English *wīpian* < Indo-European, 'move back and forth']

wipe out *v* **1** *vt* DESTROY SOMETHING IN LARGE NUMBERS to destroy large numbers of things or kill large numbers of people, especially suddenly and violently (*informal*) **2** *vt* MURDER to murder or assassinate somebody (*slang*) **3** *vi* FALL FROM SURFBOARD to fall from a surfboard, either because of losing control or because of being knocked off by a wave, or fall or crash in some other sport (*informal*)

wiped out *adj* thoroughly exhausted (*slang*)

wipeout /wīp owt/ *n* (*informal*) **1** FALL IN SURFING a fall from a surfboard, or a fall or crash in other sports, e.g. skiing and cycling **2** FAILURE OR DEFEAT a total failure or a crushing defeat **3** RECEIVING OF RADIO SIGNAL MASKING OTHERS the receiving of a radio signal that is so strong it makes receiving other signals impossible

wiper /wīpər/ *n* **1** AUTOMOT = **windscreen wiper** **2** a cam that projects from a rotating shaft and is designed to move, dislodge, or lift another component **3** an electrical device in which a conducting arm may be rotated or moved over a row of contacts, e.g. a rheostat

WIPO /wīpō/, **Wipo** *abbr* World Intellectual Property Organization

Wiradhuri /wi rájjəri/, **Wiradjuri** *n* an Australian Aboriginal language of New South Wales and S Queensland, now extinct [Late 19C. < an Aboriginal language < Wiradhuri *wirai* 'no'.] —**Wiradhuri** *adj*

wire /wīr/ *n* **1** STRAND OF METAL metal in the form of thin flexible strands, or a single strand of it **2** METAL STRAND CARRYING ELECTRIC CURRENT a strand of metal, usually copper, that is encased in plastic or another insulating material and is used to carry an electric current **3** CABLE PROVIDING TELECOMMUNICATIONS LINK a cable that provides a telecommunications link **4** MESH STRUCTURE a mesh made of strands of metal, or a structure such as a fence made of the mesh **5** *US* ANY END OR FINISH the end of anything, or the time when something ends (*informal*) ○ *writing in their exam books right down to the wire* **6** *US* ELECTRONIC LISTENING DEVICE a slimline electronic listening device concealed in somebody's clothes (*slang*) **7** TELEGRAM OR TELEGRAPH a telegram or the telegraph system ■ *vt* (**wires, wiring, wired**) **1** FASTEN SOMETHING WITH WIRE to use wire to fasten or secure something **2** CONNECT ELECTRICAL EQUIPMENT to connect a piece of electrical equipment to a power source or to another piece of equipment **3** PROVIDE A PLACE WITH NECESSARY EQUIPMENT to provide a place with the equipment, especially electrical or electronic equipment, needed to give it a particular facility or capability (*informal*) **4** *US* FIT SOMEBODY WITH A LISTENING DEVICE to fit somebody or a place with a concealed electronic listening device (*slang*) **5** SEND A TELEGRAM to send a telegram to somebody, or send something to somebody by means of a telegram [Old English *wīr* 'metal thread' < Indo-European, 'twist'] ◇ **go to the wire** to risk your reputation, job, or life in order to help somebody (*informal*) ◇ **have** *or* **get your wires crossed** have a misunderstanding

wire brush *n* a brush with short stiff wires instead of bristles

wire cloth *n* a flexible mesh of soft fine wires woven closely together, used to make strainers and some types of screening

ϟ **wired** /wīrd/ *adj* **1** SUPPORTED BY WIRE supported or strengthened by wire **2** EQUIPPED FOR INTERNET having computer equipment that allows use of the Internet (*informal*) ○ *'Ireland has seen Dublin go wired'.* (*Newsweek*; November 1998) **3** *US* FITTED WITH LISTENING DEVICES fitted with one or more concealed electronic listening devices (*slang*) **4** NERVOUS full of nervous energy, especially because under the influence of drugs (*slang*)

wiredraw /wīr draw/ (**-draws, -drawing, -drew** /-droo/, **-drawn** /-drawn/) *vt* **1** to reduce the diameter of a wire by pulling it through successively smaller dies **2** to spin something out to great lengths, overrefining it and treating it with excessive subtlety [Late 16C. Back-formation < *wiredrawer* 'somebody skilled in drawing metal into threads'.]

wire entanglement *n* a barrier of barbed wire used to keep enemy troops back

wirefree /wīr free/ *adj* describes telephone systems that do not use electrical wires in order to operate ○ *'Today, more than 1.7 million people subscribe to our wirefree services'.* (*Marketing Week*; December 1998)

wire gauge *n* **1** a gauge used to measure the thickness of wire or sheet metal **2** a standard system of sizes for measuring wire

wire gauze *n* a fine mesh of thin wires woven closely together

wire glass *n* glass reinforced with a sheet of wire mesh embedded in it

wire grass *n* a coarse grass with tough wiry roots

wirehaired /wīr háird/ *adj* having a coat of coarse stiff hair

wireless /wīrləss/ *n* **1** RADIO a radio or a radio set (*dated*) **2** TELECOM = **wireless telegraphy** ■ *adj* **1** WITHOUT WIRES lacking wires **2** NOT USING WIRES using radio signals rather than wires —**wirelessly** *adv*

ϟ **wireless markup language** *n* a standardized system for tagging text files, based on XML, that specifies the interfaces of narrowband wireless devices

wireless telegraphy *n* a system that sends telegrams using radio signals rather than wires

wireline /wīr līn/ *adj* operating or transmitting by means of a connecting wire, as opposed to wirelessly

wireman /wīrmən/ (*plural* **-men** /wīrmən/) *n US* **1** an installer or repairer of electrical or telecommunications cables **2** an expert at installing and operating electronic listening devices (*slang*)

wire netting *n* mesh made of medium to thick wire that is stronger, less flexible, and has larger spaces than wire gauze

wirer /wīrər/ *n* a snarer of animals (*informal*)

wire recorder *n* an early type of magnetic recorder that used stainless steel wire instead of magnetic tape to record sound

wire rope *n* strong thick rope made of plaited strands of wire

wire service *n US* a news agency that sends out syndicated news items to various media by means of wire or satellite

wiretap /wīr tap/ *vti* (**-taps, -tapping, -tapped**) to make a wire connection to a telephone line in order to listen in secret to somebody's conversations ■ *n* a connection made to a telephone line in order to listen secretly to somebody's conversations —**wiretapper** *n*

wire wheel *n* **1** a motor vehicle wheel that has wire spokes connecting the hub to the rim **2** a disc of coarse wires designed to be attached to a power tool and used for rubbing down metal

wire wool *n* = **steel wool**

wirework /wīr wurk/ *n* **1** LAYOUT OF WIRES an arrangement or system of wires **2** SOMETHING MADE OF WIRE something made by shaping or weaving wire **3** TIGHTROPE ACROBATICS acrobatics performed on a tightrope

wireworks /wīr wurks/ (*plural* **-works**) *n* a factory where wire is made, or where wire articles are made

wireworm /wīr wurm/ *n* the long thin hard-bodied larva of various kinds of beetle that feeds on plant roots and is a serious agricultural pest

wiring /wīring/ *n* a network of electrical wires

wirra /wírrə/ *interj Ireland* used to express concern, sorrow, confusion, or annoyance [Early 19C. < Irish *a Mhuira* 'oh, Mary!'.]

Wirral /wírrəl/ peninsula in NW England, between the rivers Dee and Mersey. Area: 218 sq. km/84 sq. mi.

wiry /wīri/ (**-ier, -iest**) *adj* **1** SLIM BUT STRONG slim but muscular and strong **2** COARSE stiff and coarse like wire **3** PRODUCED BY VIBRATING WIRES produced by or sounding as though produced by vibrating wires —**wirily** *adv* —**wiriness** *n*

wis /wiss/ (**wisses, wissing, wissed** *or* **wist** /wist/, **wissed** *or* **wist**) *vti* to know, think, or suppose something (*archaic*) [Old English *wissian*]

Wis. *abbr* Wisconsin

Wisbech /wíz beech/ town in E England. Population: 24,981 (1991).

Wisc. *abbr* Wisconsin

Wisconsin /wi skónssin/ state of the north-central United States. Capital: Madison. Population: 4,891,769 (1990). Area: 169,642 sq. km/65,499 sq. mi. —**Wisconsinite** *n*

Wisd. *abbr* Wisdom of Solomon

Wisden /wízdən/, **John** (1826–84) British cricketer and founder of *Wisden's Cricketer's Almanack.*

wisdom /wízdəm/ *n* **1** GOOD SENSE the knowledge and experience needed to make sensible decisions and judgments, or the good sense shown by the decisions and judgments made **2** ACCUMULATED LEARNING accumulated knowledge of life or of a particular sphere of activity that has been gained through experience **3** OPINION WIDELY HELD an opinion that almost everyone seems to share or express **4 SAYINGS** ancient teachings or sayings [Old English *wīsdōm* < *wīs* (see WISE[1])]

Wisdom literature *n* a speculative or didactic form of religious writing, exemplified in the Bible by the books of Job, Proverbs, and Ecclesiastes, and the Apocryphal books, the Wisdom of Solomon and Ecclesiasticus

Wisdom of Jesus, the Son of Sirach *n* BIBLE = **Ecclesiasticus**

Wisdom of Solomon *n* a book of the Apocrypha expounding Jewish doctrines in the terminology of Greek philosophy. It was probably written in the 1st century BC.

wisdom tooth *n* one of the four teeth at the back of each side of the upper and lower jaw of human beings [Translation of Latin *dens sapientiae*]

Wisdom writings *n* BIBLE = **Wisdom literature**

wise[1] /wīz/ (**wiser, wisest**) *adj* **1 KNOWING MUCH FROM EXPERIENCE** able to make sensible decisions and judgments on the basis of knowledge and experience **2 SENSIBLE** showing good sense or good judgment **3 LEARNED** knowledgeable about many subjects **4 SHREWD** capable of achieving some purpose or goal by cunning **5 SKILLED IN OCCULT PRACTICES** skilled in magic or fortune telling (*archaic*) [Old English *wīs* < Indo-European, 'see, know'] —**wisely** *adv* ◇ **be** *or* **get wise (to something)** to be or become aware of something, usually something dishonest or secret (*informal*) ◇ **put somebody wise (to something)** to let somebody know about something, or give somebody information about something (*informal*) **wise up** *vti* to become, or make somebody, aware or informed (*informal*)

wise[2] /wīz/ *n* a way or manner (*archaic*) [Old English *wīse* < Germanic, 'shape, form, something seen']

-wise *suffix* in a particular manner or direction ○ *crabwise* ○ *coastwise* [Old English *-wīsan* < *wīse* 'manner' (see WISE[2])]

USAGE Many critics object to words ending in the suffix ***-wise*** when the meaning is 'with regard to, with respect to', as in these controversial examples: *moneywise, timewise,* and *politicswise*, e.g. *Politicswise, this has been an exciting year.* The use of words ending in ***-wise*** is acceptable when the meaning of the suffix is 'in a particular manner or direction', as in *clockwise, anticlockwise,* and *lengthwise.*

wiseacre /wīz aykər/ *n* a person who speaks with irritating authority or self-assurance, especially when not truly knowledgeable (*informal*) [Late 16C. Alteration of Middle Dutch *wijsseggher* 'soothsayer'.]

wisecrack /wīz krak/ *n* a flippant or sarcastic remark (*informal*) ■ *vi* to make flippant or sarcastic remarks (*informal*) —**wisecracker** *n*

wise guy *n US, Can* somebody inclined to make impudent or sarcastic remarks (*informal*)

wise man *n* **1 LEARNED MAN** a scholar or a very learned man **2 ANCIENT PRACTITIONER OF OCCULT ARTS** a man who, in ancient times, practised any of the occult arts such as magic or astrology (*archaic*) **3 SPECIAL ADVISER** a man chosen as a special senior adviser to a government or other authority (*informal*) **4 ONE OF MAGI** one of the three Magi who came to pay homage to the infant Jesus Christ

wisent /wee'z'nt/ *n* a bison with a head that is smaller and higher than that of the North American bison. Native to: Europe. *Bison bonasus.* [Mid-19C. Via German < Old High German *wisunt* < Indo-European.]

wisewoman /wīz wŏŏmən/ (*plural* **-en** /-wimin/) *n* a woman who is skilled in the art of using herbs to heal people and ease the pains of childbirth

wish /wish/ *v* **1** *vt* **DESIRE** to have a strong desire for something **2** *vt* **DEMAND** to want or demand something ○ *I wish you to leave him alone.* **3** *vti* **EXPRESS DESIRE** to express or feel a desire that something is true or will come to pass ○ *They wished me a safe journey.* ○ *We only wish for peace.* **4** *vt* **WANT SOMETHING TO BE OTHERWISE** to desire somebody or something to be in a particular state ○ *We all wish it were different.* **5** *vt* **GREET** to greet somebody in a particular way ○ *She wished me good afternoon as I left.* ■ *n* **1 YEARNING** a desire or strong yearning for something ○ *I certainly had no wish to speak to him.* **2 EXPRESSION OF DESIRE** an expression of a desire or longing for something **3 SOMETHING WISHED** something that is desired **4 HOPE** a hope for somebody's welfare or health (*usually plural*) ○ *Give him our best wishes.* **5 POLITE REQUEST** a polite request (*formal; often plural*) [Old English *wȳscan* < Indo-European, 'to desire'] —**wisher** *n*

SYNONYMS See ***want.***

wish on *vt* to wish that something, usually something unpleasant, would happen to somebody ○ *I wouldn't wish that on my worst enemy.*

wishbone /wish bōn/ *n* the V-shaped bone, actually two fused collarbones, found between the breasts of a chicken or other bird. Technical name **furcula**

wishbone boom *n* the boom on a sailboard that a windsurfer holds on to. It has two curving arms, one on either side of the sail, joined at the ends.

wishful /wishf'l/ *adj* wishing for something, or expressing a wish or longing —**wishfully** *adv* —**wishfulness** *n*

wish fulfilment *n* in psychoanalytic theory, the process by which unconscious desires are realized in the imagination, mainly through dreams and fantasies

wishful thinking *n* the unrealistic belief that something that is wished for is actually true or will be realized

wish list *n* an often informal list of things somebody would like to have or would like to happen

wish-wash *n* (*archaic*) **1** an unpleasantly weak or tasteless drink **2** uninteresting and uninspiring talk or writing [Late 18C. Doubling of WASH, in the sense 'thin, weak'.]

wishy-washy /wishi woshi, wishi wóshi/ *adj* (*informal*) **1** changeable or fluctuating in character, especially unable to make firm decisions or develop clear opinions **2** weak, lacking taste, or unattractively pale [Late 17C. Doubling of *washy* 'thin, watery' < WASH.] —**wishy-washily** *adv* —**wishy-washiness** *n*

wisp /wisp/ *n* **1 SOMETHING RESEMBLING THREAD** something that is thin and delicate like thread, especially a lock of hair, a piece of straw, or a streak of smoke **2 SOMEBODY SLENDER AND DELICATE** somebody or something that is slender and delicate ○ *a wisp of a child* **3 SOMETHING INSUBSTANTIAL** something that is vague and fleeting ○ *a wisp of a memory* **4 BUNDLE** a bundle of something, especially a bundle of hay or straw ■ *v* **1** *vt* **BUNDLE STRAW OR HAY** to make a handful of straw or hay into a bundle **2** *vi* **MOVE LIKE WISP** to float like something delicate or faint [14C. < ?] —**wispily** *adv* —**wispiness** *n* —**wispy** *adj*

wist (*archaic*) **1** past participle, past tense of **wis 2** past participle, past tense of **wit**[2]

wisteria /wi steéri ə/ (*plural* **-as** *or* **-a**) *n* a deciduous climbing shrub. Flowers: blue, pink, or white, hanging in clusters. Native to: North America, Asia. Genus: *Wisteria.* [Early 19C. < modern Latin, after Caspar *Wistar* (1761–1818), US anatomist.]

wistful /wistf'l/ *adj* deep in sad thoughts, especially thoughts of something yearned for or lost, or expressing this sad yearning [Early 17C. < obsolete *wistly* 'intently'.] —**wistfully** *adv* —**wistfulness** *n*

wit[1] /wit/ *n* **1 INGENIOUS HUMOUR** apt, clever, and often humorous association of words or ideas, or a capacity for it **2 SPEECH OR WRITING SHOWING WIT** speech or writing that shows an apt, clever, and often humorous association of words **3 WITTY PERSON** somebody known for using wit **4 INTELLIGENCE** mental acumen, intelligence, or reasoning power **5 COMMON SENSE** knowledge, information, or common sense (*regional*) ■ **wits** *npl* **SHREWDNESS** mental acumen, shrewdness, or reasoning power [Old English *wit* 'mind, understanding' < Indo-European, 'see, know'] ◇ **be at your wits' end** to be in despair as to how to cope with something ◇ **live by your wits** to use cunning and ingenuity in order to survive

wit[2] /wit/ (**wits** *or* **wot** /wot/, **witting, wist** /wist/, **wist**) *vti* to know or become aware of something (*archaic*) [Old English *witan* < Germanic] ◇ **to wit** that is to say

witan /witt'n/ *n* an assembly of the king's counsellors in Anglo-Saxon England [Early 19C. Revival of Old English, 'counsellors' < *wita* 'counsellor, one who knows'.]

Witbank /wit bank/ town in NE South Africa. Population: 83,400 (1998).

witblits /vítblits/ *n S Africa* illegally distilled alcoholic liquor, usually made from grapes [Mid-20C. < Afrikaans, 'white lightning'.]

witch /wich/ *n* **1 SOMEBODY WITH MAGIC POWERS** somebody, especially a woman, who is supposed to have magical or wonder-working powers that are most often used malevolently **2 FOLLOWER OF NATURE RELIGION** a follower of Wicca, a pre-Christian natural religion **3 OFFENSIVE TERM** an offensive term that deliberately insults a woman regarded as ugly, vicious, or malicious **4 SEDUCTIVE WOMAN** an alluring or seductive woman (*informal; offensive in some contexts*) ■ *vt* **EXERCISE WITCHCRAFT** to cause or change something by witchcraft [Old English *wicce* 'witch' and *wicca* 'wizard']

SPELLCHECK See ***which.***

witchcraft /wich kraaft/ *n* **1 EXERCISE OF MAGICAL POWERS** the art or exercise of magical powers **2 EFFECT OF MAGICAL POWERS** the effect or influence of magical powers **3 SEDUCTIVE CHARM** alluring or seductive charm or influence (*informal*)

witch doctor *n* **1** in tribal societies, somebody who practices healing, divining, or other magical powers **2** in some African cultures, somebody who detects or identifies supposed witches

witch elm *n* TREES = **wych elm**

witchery /wichəri/ *n* **1** the practice of witchcraft or magic (*dated or literary*) **2** charm or influence that has a bewitching quality or effect

witches' brew *n* **1** a malevolent or diabolical mixture of different things ○ *an article that was a witches' brew of spite and innuendo* **2** a potion concocted by a witch or witches

witches' broom *n* an abnormal tufted growth of shoots on a tree or woody plant, usually caused by parasitic fungi

witches' butter *n* FUNGI = **jelly fungus**

witches' Sabbath *n* an assembly to celebrate Wicca rites

witchetty grub /wichiti-/ *n* the wood-eating larva of a number of species of Australian moth, used as food by Aboriginal people and people who live in the bush [Mid-19C. Probably < Australian Aboriginal words meaning 'climb' or 'hooked stick' and 'grub'.]

witch grass *n* **1** a grass with creeping roots. Native to: North America. *Panicum capillare.* **2** PLANTS = **couch grass** [Probably alteration of QUITCH GRASS]

witch hazel, wych hazel *n* **1** a tree or bush that has toothed egg-shaped leaves and blooms in autumn or winter. Flowers: small, yellow with strap-shaped petals. Genus: *Hamamelis.* **2** a mixture of water, alcohol, and extract from the bark and dried leaves of the witch hazel. Use: astringent, embrocation. [< Old English *wice* (see WYCH ELM)]

witch-hunt, witch hunt *n* **1** an intensive systematic campaign directed against those who have done something wrong or who hold different views **2** a persecution of people believed to be witches —**witch-hunter** *n*

witching /wiching/ *adj* **1 SUITABLE FOR WITCHCRAFT** suitable for or resembling witchcraft (*archaic*) **2 BEWITCHING** bewitching (*literary*) ■ *n* **WITCHCRAFT** witchcraft or sorcery (*archaic*)

witching hour *n* midnight, said to be the time when witches appear

witchweed /wich weed/ *n* a parasitic plant native to South Africa and introduced into the S United States. Flowers: small, red. Genus: *Striga.*

Wite-Out /wīt owt/ *tdmk* a trademark for a white fluid used to cover up mistakes in writing, typing, or printing

with /with/ *prep* **1 IN THE COMPANY OF** used to indicate that somebody is accompanying or is in the company of another person or people, or that something is accompanying something else ○ *at the theme park with their children* ○ *Do you still want me to go with you?* **2 USED TOGETHER** used together or at the same time ○ *He made Yorkshire pudding to go with the roast beef.* **3 INVOLVING** involving that person or people ○ *He organized the meeting together with the head of his department.* **4 AGAINST** in opposition to ○ *students competing with each other for a limited number of spaces* **5 BY MEANS OF** by the means of or using a particular object, substance, or system ○ *After 18 months, all the rats treated with the altered virus were healthy.* **6 CARRYING** carrying or having in one's possession ○ *He came into the office with a box full of files.* **7 HAVING** having as a possession, attribute, or feature ○ *The film is in French with English subtitles.* **8 BECAUSE OF** in a particular condition as a result of something ○ *I felt heartsick and faint with anxiety.* **9 ON OR IN** used to indicate that something has a substance or things on or in it ○ *brightly painted walls covered with photographs of Italy* **10 CONCERNING** used to indicate the person or thing that a state, quality, or action relates to or affects ○ *not happy with the service provided* **11 IN THIS WAY** used to indicate the way something is done, or the degree to which it is done ○ *sitting with her head on his shoulder* **12 ACCOMPANIED BY** used to indicate the feeling, gesture, sound, or facial expression that accompanies or causes an action ○ *walks with a limp* **13 IN THE LIGHT OF** in the light of or given the situation mentioned ○ *With all the problems you have, the last thing you need is a lawsuit.* **14 IN SPITE OF** in spite of the situation mentioned ○ *With all his charm and good breeding, he's not a man to be trusted.* **15 AT TIME OF** at the same time as ○ *He woke with the alarm and hurriedly dressed.* **16 FOLLOWING THE DIRECTION OF** in the same direction as ○ *They were to sail with the tide the next day.* **17 ACCORDING TO** used to indicate that something happens or is true according to something else ○ *how much the risk of death increases with age* **18 AFTER** following on from ○ *With a final wave goodbye she turned the corner.* [Old English *wiþ* 'with, against' < Indo-European, 'apart'] ◇ **be with it 1** to be fashionable or up to date with fashion (*informal*) **2** to be able to understand what is going on in a situation (*informal*) ◇ **be with somebody 1** to understand somebody **2** to approve of or support somebody ○ *Are you with us or not?* ◇ **with that** immediately after saying or doing something specified ○ *With that, she turned to go.*

USAGE Use a singular verb when a singular subject of a sentence is followed by a noun or noun phrase introduced by ***with*** instead of *and*: *The report, together with the supporting documents, has been filed for reference.* It makes no difference that the number of the entities in the noun phrase is plural, because ***with*** is a preposition rather than a conjunction. Of course, if the situation is reversed, and the subject of the sentence is plural, use a plural verb: *The supporting documents, together with the report itself, have been filed for reference.*

withal /wi*th* áwl/ *adv* (*archaic*) **1 MOREOVER** along with the rest or in addition **2 NEVERTHELESS** in spite of that ■ *prep* **WITH** with (*archaic*) [12C. < WITH + ALL.]

withdraw /wi*th* dráw/ (**-draws, -drawing, -drew** /-dróo/, **-drawn** /-dráwn/) *v* **1** *vt* **REMOVE** to remove or take back something that was previously provided or in place **2** *vt* **RETRACT STATEMENT** to deny the truth or validity of something that was previously stated **3** *vi* **RETREAT FROM POSITION** to retreat or retire from a position **4** *vt* **TAKE MONEY FROM ACCOUNT** to take money out of an account —**withdrawable** *adj* —**withdrawer** *n*

withdrawal /wi*th* dráw əl/ *n* **1 TAKING MONEY FROM BANK** the act of taking money from a bank or building society account, or the amount of money taken out **2 PERIOD OF FIGHTING ADDICTION** a period during which somebody addicted to a drug or other addictive substance stops taking it, causing the person to experience painful or uncomfortable symptoms **3 TAKING SOMETHING AWAY** the act or condition of taking something away or no longer taking part in something **4 RETREAT OF ARMY** retreat or retirement of an army or other military force from an area in which it was fighting

withdrawing room *n* a drawing room (*archaic*)

withdrawn /wi*th* dráwn/ past participle of **withdraw** ■ *adj* **1** not friendly or sociable but quiet and thoughtful, especially to an unusual or worrying degree **2** removed from circulation, competition, or activity —**withdrawnness** *n*

withdrew past tense of **withdraw**

withe /with, wi*th*/ *n* **1 FLEXIBLE STEM** a strong flexible twig or stem used to bind something **2 FLEXIBLE TOOL HANDLE** a shock-absorbing flexible handle for a tool ■ *vt* (**withes, withing, withed**) **BIND SOMETHING WITH WITHES** to bind something with withes [Old English *wiþþe* < Indo-European, 'twist, bend']

wither /wi*th*ər/ *v* **1** *vti* **SHRIVEL** to shrivel or dry up as part of the process of dying, or make something, especially a plant or part of a plant, shrivel in this way **2** *vi* **FADE AWAY** to fade or lose freshness or vitality **3** *vti* **MAKE SOMEBODY LOSE CONFIDENCE** to make somebody feel embarrassed, foolish, or incapable of activity as the object of scorn or contempt, or lose confidence in the face of somebody's scorn [14C. Probably variant of WEATHER 'expose to the elements'.] —**withered** *adj* —**witherer** *n*

withering /wi*th*əring/ *adj* expressing scorn or contempt with the intention of causing somebody to feel embarrassed or foolish ○ *'When he assumed this attitude in the courtroom, ears were always pricked up, as it usually foretold a flood of withering sarcasm'.* (Willa Cather, *The Troll Garden*; 1905) —**witheringly** *adv*

witherite /wi*th*ə rīt/ *n* a rare greyish-white barium carbonate mineral. Source: lead ores. Use: source of barium. [Late 18C. After William *Withering* (1741–99), English scientist.]

withers /wi*th*ərz/ *npl* the ridge between the shoulder bones of a horse, sheep, ox, or similar four-legged animal, forming the highest part of its back [Early 16C. Probably < Old English *wiþer* 'against'.]

withershins /wi*th*ər shinz/, **widdershins** /wíddər-/ *adv Scotland* (*literary*) **1** in the direction that is contrary to the natural course **2** anticlockwise or in the direction that is contrary to the course of the sun [Early 16C. Alteration of Middle Low German *weddersinnes* < Middle High German *widersinnes* < *wider* 'against, opposite' + *sin* 'sense, direction'.]

withhold /wi*th* hṓld/ (**-holds, -holding, -held** /wi*th* héld/, **-held**) *v* **1** *vti* to refuse to do or give something until something else is done **2** *vt* to collect or deduct tax from a salary —**withholder** *n*

withholding tax *n* **1** tax deducted at source from dividends paid to nonresidents of a country **2** *US* part of an employee's wage or salary withheld and remitted to the government by an employer in payment of taxes

within /wi*th* ín/ *prep, adv* **1 INSIDE** used to indicate that somebody or something is inside or enclosed by a place, area, or object ○ (prep) *goods manufactured within a country* ○ (prep) *A natural pool lay within a copse of young trees.* ○ (adv) *The door was locked from within.* **2 HAPPENING INSIDE** happening inside an organization, system, or society ○ (prep) *keeping companies within a given industry technologically competitive* ○ (adv) *A lot of our Internet development activity is coming from within.* **3 INSIDE YOURSELF** inside the body or mind ○ (adv) *Her new-found happiness was from within.* ○ (prep) *He needed to find the strength within him to carry on.* ■ *prep* **INSIDE LIMITS OF** inside the limits or rules of ○ *Try to keep within your budget and avoid overspending.* ■ *adv* **INDOORS** indoors (*literary*) ■ *prep* **NOT BEYOND** not beyond the scope, experience, range, time, or distance of ○ *regulations requiring that all accidents be reported within 48 hours* [Old English *wiþinnan* 'on the inside' < WITH + *innan* 'from within']

USAGE See ***inside***.

with-it *adj* fashionable and modern in dress and behaviour (*dated informal*)

~~**withold**~~ incorrect spelling of **withhold**

without /wi*th* ówt/ *prep* **1 NOT HAVING** used to indicate that somebody or something does not have the thing mentioned ○ *left without proper tools to finish the job* **2 NOT ACCOMPANIED BY** not with somebody, or not having the involvement of somebody ○ *We can't really make any decisions without him.* **3 BEYOND** beyond (*archaic*) **4 NOT HAPPENING** used to indicate that something does not happen or occur ○ *The bill was passed without a dissenting voice.* ■ *prep, adv* **OUTSIDE** on, at, or to the outside of somewhere (*archaic or literary*) ○ (prep) *Without the town the air was fresher.* ○ (adv) *She knocked and waited without.* ■ *prep* **LACKING** lacking a feeling of ○ *The accused engaged in physical abuse without remorse or intent to change.* ■ *conj* **UNLESS** unless (*nonstandard*) [Old English *wiþūtan* 'on the outside of', < WITH + *ūtan* 'from the outside'] ◇ **be** *or* **do without** to manage in spite of not having something considered necessary or desirable ○ *a form of power he could not buy or do without*

withstand /wi*th* stánd/ (**-stands, -standing, -stood** /-stŏŏd/, **-stood**) *vti* to be strong enough to stand up to somebody or remain unchanged by something such as extremes of heat or pressure —**withstander** *n*

withy /wí*th*i/ *n* (*plural* **-ies**) **1** TREES, CONSTR = **withe** *n.* 1 **2** a willow tree, especially an osier ■ *adj* tough and pliable, like withes (*dated*) [Old English *wīþig* 'willow' < Indo-European, 'twist, bend']

witless /wíttləss/ *adj* lacking intelligence or common sense —**witlessly** *adv* —**witlessness** *n*

witling /wíttling/ *n* a person who wishes to be witty (*archaic*)

witness /wítnəss/ *n* **1 SOMEBODY WHO SEES AN OCCURRENCE** a person who gives evidence after seeing or hearing something **2 SIGNATORY OF A DOCUMENT** a person who signs a document to show that it, or another signature, is genuine **3** *US* **SOMEBODY WHO TESTIFIES TO CHRISTIAN BELIEFS** a person who publicly states his or her strong Christian beliefs **4** *US* **PUBLIC STATEMENT OF CHRISTIAN BELIEFS** a public statement of strong personal Christian beliefs ■ *v* **1** *vt* **SEE SOMETHING HAPPEN** to see something happen, especially a crime or an accident **2** *vt* **COUNTERSIGN A DOCUMENT** to affirm the authenticity of a document or a signature on a document by signing it **3** *vt* **EXPERIENCE IMPORTANT EVENTS** to experience important events or changes, or be the time in which they occur **4** *vt* **BE SIGN OF** to be a sign or proof of something that is happening **5** *vi US* **SPEAK PUBLICLY ABOUT RELIGIOUS BELIEFS** to talk in public about strong personal Christian beliefs [Old English *witnes*, < *wit* (see WIT[1])] —**witnessable** *adj* —**witnesser** *n* ◇ **bear witness (to something)** to prove or be evidence that something is true or that something happened

witness box *n* the enclosed place in a courtroom where witnesses give evidence. US term **witness stand**

witness stand *n US* LAW = **witness box**

Wittenberg /vít'n burg/ city in east-central Germany where Martin Luther began his campaign for the reform of the Roman Catholic Church in 1517. Population: 53,400 (1989).

witter /wíttər/ *vi* to chatter or babble at undue length (*informal*) [Early 19C. < ?]

wittering /wíttəring/ *n* continuous pointless chatter (*informal*)

Wittgenstein /vítgən stīn/, **Ludwig** (1889–1951) Austrian-born British philosopher

witticism /wíttissizəm/ *n* a witty or clever remark [Late 17C. Blend of WITTY + CRITICISM.]

witting /wítting/ *adj* **1** done deliberately or intentionally **2** responsible and fully aware —**wittingly** *adv*

witty /wítti/ (**-tier, -tiest**) *adj* **1** using words in an apt, clever, and amusing way **2** strikingly clever, stylish, or original in design or execution —**wittily** *adv* —**wittiness** *n*

Witwatersrand /wit wáwtərz rand/ rocky ridge in NE South Africa, the most productive gold-mining area in the world. Length: 100 km/60 mi.

wive /wīv/ (**wives, wiving, wived**) *v* (*archaic*) **1** *vti* to marry a woman **2** *vt* to supply somebody with a wife [Old English *wīfian* < *wīf* 'woman, wife']

wivern *n* HERALDRY = **wyvern**

wives plural of **wife**

wiz /wiz/ (*plural* **wizzes**) *n* = **whiz** *n.* 3 (*informal*) [Early 20C. Partly shortening of WIZARD; partly variant of WHIZ.]

wizard /wízzərd/ *n* **1 MALE WITCH** a man who is supposed to have magical or wonder-working powers **2 SOMEBODY EXCELLING** a person who is extremely skilled in or knowledgeable about something (*informal*) ■ *adj UK* **VERY GOOD AT SOMETHING** extremely proficient or adept at something (*dated*) [15C. Variant of *wisard*, < *wise*.] —**wizardly** *adj*

wizardry /wízzərdri/ *n* **1** the art, activities, or accomplishments of a wizard **2** extreme skill, ability, or accomplishment

wizened /wízz'nd/ *adj* looking wrinkled, shrivelled, or dried up [Early 16C. Past participle of *wizen*, < Old English *wisnian*, < Germanic.] —**wizen** *adj, vi*

wiz kid *n* = **whiz kid** (*informal*)

wk *abbr* **1** weak **2** week **3** work

wkly *abbr* weekly

wkt *abbr* wicket

WL *abbr* **1 WL, w.l.** water line **2** wavelength

Wm. *abbr* William

wmk. *abbr* watermark

ϟ **WML** *abbr* wireless markup language

WMO *abbr* World Meteorological Organization

WNF *abbr* West Nile fever

WNV *abbr* West Nile virus

WNW *abbr* west-northwest

WO, W.O. *abbr* **1** warrant officer **2** wireless operator **3** War Office

w/o *abbr* without

woad /wōd/ *n* **1** a blue dye obtained from the leaves of a European plant. Use: body paint in ancient times. **2** a plant formerly cultivated for woad. Native to: Europe. *Isatis tinctoria.* [Old English *wād* < Germanic]

ϟ **w.o.b.** *abbr* **1** washed overboard **2** without a boyfriend (*in e-mails*)

wobble /wóbb'l/ *v* (**-bles, -bling, -bled**) **1** *vti* **MOVE FROM SIDE TO SIDE** to move or cause something to move in a swaying, shaking, or trembling way **2** *vi* **QUAVER** to vary uncertainly in pitch or volume **3** *vi* **BE UNABLE TO DECIDE** to be unable or unwilling to reach a decision ■ *n* **WOBBLING**

EFFECT a wobbling movement or sound [Mid-17C. Probably < Low German *wabbeln* < Germanic.] —**wobbler** *n* — **wobblingly** *adv*

wobbler syndrome *n* a condition in horses and dogs characterized by an unsteady gait and sometimes falling, due to a misalignment of vertebrae in the neck, which impinges on the spinal cord

wobbly /wóbbli/ (**-blier, -bliest**) *adj* **1** moving unsteadily from side to side **2** feeling weak and unable to keep balanced (*informal*) —**wobbliness** *n* ◇ **throw or chuck a wobbly** to become very angry or frightened suddenly (*informal*)

Wobbly /wóbbli/ (*plural* **-blies**) *n* US a member of the Industrial Workers of the World (*informal*) [Early 20C. < ?]

Wodehouse /woód howss/, **P. G.** (1881–1975) British writer. Full name **Sir Pelham Grenville Wodehouse**

Woden /wṓd'n/ *n* an Anglo-Saxon god, the equivalent of the Norse god Odin

wodge /woj/ *n* a large lump or chunk of something (*informal*) ○ *They caught him stuffing wodges of banknotes into his pockets.* [Mid-19C. Blend of WAD + WEDGE.]

woe /wṓ/ *n* **1** UNFORTUNATE HAPPENING a serious affliction or misfortune **2** GRIEF grief or distress resulting from a serious affliction or misfortune ■ *interj* EXPRESSING GRIEF used to express grief or distress (*archaic or literary*) [Old English *wā* < Germanic < Indo-European] ◇ **woe betide somebody** used as a threat to indicate that somebody is going to regret something or be punished in some way ○ *Woe betide him if he turns up late for work again.* ◇ **woe is me** used to indicate that the speaker is in distress or feels unhappy or unfortunate (*literary or humorous*)

woebegone /wṓ bi gon/ *adj* feeling or looking distressed or sorrowful [13C. < WOE + *begon* 'beset' (< Old English *gān*).]

woeful /wṓf'l/ *adj* **1** UNHAPPY feeling or expressing great distress or sorrow **2** CAUSING GRIEF bringing or causing great distress or sorrow **3** PATHETICALLY BAD pitifully or regrettably bad —**woefully** *adv* —**woefulness** *n*

wog[1] /wog/ *n* a highly offensive term for a member of any people that has dark skin (*taboo*) [Early 20C. Probably shortening of GOLLIWOG.]

wog[2] /wog/ *n* Aus influenza or a similar illness (*informal*) [Mid-20C. < ?]

woggle /wógg'l/ *n* the thin ring of leather through which a Scout's neckerchief is drawn and secured [Mid-20C. < ?]

Wöhler /vṓlər, vṓlər/, **Friedrich** (1800–82) German chemist

wok /wok/ *n* a large thin metal pan with a curved base, used for stir-frying, steaming, and braising food, especially in Chinese and other East Asian styles of cooking [Mid-20C. < Chinese (Cantonese).]

woke past tense of **wake**[1]

woken past participle of **wake**[1]

Woking /wṓking/ town in SE England. Population: 92,667 (1991).

Wokingham /wṓkingəm/ town in S England. Population: 38,063 (1991).

wold /wōld/ *n* upland or rolling country, especially when treeless [Old English *wald, weald* 'forest' < Indo-European, 'wild']

Wolds /wōldz/ range of chalk hills in E England, divided into the Yorkshire Wolds and the Lincolnshire Wolds

wolf /woolf/ *n* (*plural* **wolves** /woolvz/) **1** CARNIVORE THAT HUNTS IN PACKS any one of several predatory animals that are related to the dog and hunt in packs, especially the grey wolf. Native to: North America, Europe, Asia. Genus: *Canis*. **2** ANIMAL RESEMBLING WOLF an animal that resembles a wolf but is not of the dog family, e.g. the Tasmanian wolf **3** FUR OF WOLF the fur of the wolf **4** GREEDY AND CRUEL PERSON a greedy and cruel person **5** MAN WHO PURSUES WOMEN a sexually aggressive or predatory man (*informal*) **6** DESTRUCTIVE LARVA the destructive larva of several moths and beetles that sometimes infests granaries **7** DISCORD an unpleasant discord produced on a string or keyboard instrument (*often before nouns*) ■ EAT QUICKLY AND GREEDILY to eat food quickly and greedily or in gulps [Old English *wulf* < Indo-European] ◇ **a wolf in sheep's clothing** a person who looks harmless or pleasant but is in fact dangerous or unpleasant ◇ **cry wolf** to give a false alarm or cry for help too many times, so that when help is really needed, no one will give it ◇ **keep the wolf from the door** to be enough to prevent

hunger or starvation ◇ **throw somebody to the wolves** to abandon somebody to be destroyed by enemies in order to save yourself

Wolf /woolf/ *n* ASTRON = **Lupus**

Wolf, **Hugo** (1860–1903) Austrian composer

Wolf Cub *n* a Cub Scout

wolf dog *n* **1** a dog used to hunt wolves **2** an offspring of a wolf and a dog

Wolfe, **James** (1727–59) British general

Wolfe, **Thomas** (1900–38) US writer

wolfer *n* = **wolver**

wolffish /woolf fish/ *n* (*plural* **-fish** *or* **-fishes**) *n* a large fish with sharp teeth and no pelvic fins. Native to: N Atlantic. Genus: *Anarhichas*. [< its voracious appetite]

wolfhound /woolf hownd/ *n* a large dog of a breed that was originally bred to hunt wolves

wolfish /woolfish/ *adj* resembling or characteristic of a wolf —**wolfishly** *adv*

Wolfit, **Sir Donald** (1902–68) British actor and theatre-company manager

wolf pack *n* **1** a group of wolves that hunt together **2** a group of submarines engaged in hunting and attacking enemy convoys during World War II

wolfram /woolfrəm/ *n* tungsten (*archaic*) [Mid-18C. < German, 'wolframite' < *Wolf* 'wolf' + German dialect *Rahm* 'soot, dirt'.]

wolframite /woolfrə mīt/ *n* a brownish-black crystalline mineral consisting of iron manganese tungstate. Use: source of tungsten. [Mid-19C. < German (see WOLFRAM).]

wolfsbane /woolfs bayn/ *n* (*plural* **-banes** *or* **-bane**) *n* any of several wild or cultivated poisonous plants. Flowers: yellow or purplish-blue. Use: medicines. Genus: *Aconitum*. [Mid-16C. Translation of Greek *lukoktonon* 'wolf-killer', from the poison found in the plants.]

Wolfsburg /woolfs burg, vólfs boȯrk/ city in north-central Germany. Population: 126,800 (1995).

wolf spider *n* a ground spider that hunts its prey instead of using a web. Family: Lycosidae.

wolf whistle *n* a whistle given to signal sexual interest in or admiration of somebody that may give offence

wolf-whistle *vti* to make a wolf whistle at somebody, especially a woman passer-by

wollastonite /wólləstə nīt/ *n* a fibrous grey-white calcium silicate mineral. Source: metamorphosed limestone. [Early 19C. After William Hyde *Wollaston* (1766–1828), English physicist.]

Wollongong /wólləng gong/ coastal city in E New South Wales, Australia. Population: 219,761 (1996).

Mary Wollstonecraft: Portrait (1790) by John Opie

Wollstonecraft /wóllstən kráft/, **Mary** (1759–97) British feminist

Wolof /wól of/ (*plural* **-lof** *or* **-lofs**) *n* **1** a member of a people who live in West Africa, mainly in Senegal but also in Gambia and Mauritania **2** a Niger-Congo language spoken in Senegal and the Gambia. Native speakers: 2 million. [Early 19C. < Wolof.] —**Wolof** *adj*

Wolsey /woolzi/, **Thomas** (1475–1530) English clergyman and statesman. Known as **Cardinal Wolsey**

wolver /wolvər/, **wolfer** *n* a hunter of wolves

Wolverhampton /woolvər hámptən/ city in west-central England. Population: 244,300 (1995).

wolverine /woólvə rín/ (*plural* **-ines** *or* **-ine**) *n* a strong dark-furred, usually solitary member of the weasel family. Native to: forests of N Europe, Asia, North America. *Gulo gulo*. [Late 16C. Probably < WOLF.]

wolves plural of **wolf**

⚡**WOM** *abbr* word of mouth (*in e-mails*)

woman /wʊ́mmən/ (*plural* **-en** /wímmin/) *n* **1** FEMALE ADULT an adult female human being **2** WOMEN AS GROUP women collectively or in general **3** FEMININITY feminine qualities or feelings **4** DOMESTIC EMPLOYEE a woman who is a domestic employee **5** WIFE OR GIRLFRIEND a wife, female lover or girlfriend (*informal; offensive to some people*) [Old English *wimman*, variant of *wīfman*, < *wīf* 'woman, wife' + *man* 'person'] —**woman-like** *adj* ◇ **to a woman** used to indicate that every one of a group of women does or thinks something, without any exceptions

LITERARY LINK *Little Women*, a novel (1868–69) by US writer Louisa May Alcott. An abidingly popular family saga set in 1860s New England, it recounts the emotional and intellectual development of four sisters – Meg, Jo, Beth, and Amy – as they progress through adolescence to adulthood. It was followed by two sequels, *Little Men* (1871) and *Jo's Boys* (1886).

USAGE See *girl* and *person*.

womanfully /wʊ́mmənfəli/ *adv* in a way that shows or is characteristic of womanly spirit or energy [Early 19C. After *manfully*.]

womanhood /wʊ́mmənhoȯd/ *n* **1** the state or condition of being a woman **2** women in general, or as a group

womanise *vti* = **womanize**

womanish /wʊ́mmənish/ *adj* an offensive term meaning having qualities stereotypically attributed to women e.g. weakness or fussiness —**womanishly** *adv* —**womanishness** *n*

womanist /wʊ́mmənist/ *adj* having a respect for and a belief in the abilities and talents of women [Late 20C. After *humanist*.]

womanize /wʊ́mmə nīz/ (**-izes, -izing, -ized**), **womanise** (**-ises, -ising, -ised**) *vi* to be constantly in search of casual sex with women (*disapproving; refers to men*) — **womanizer** *n*

womankind /wʊ́mmən kīnd/, **womenkind** /wímmən-/ *n* women collectively or in general

womanly /wʊ́mmənli/ *adj* having positive characteristics or qualities, especially warmth, calmness, and competence, attributed to mature women —**womanliness** *n*

woman of the house *n* a woman who is in charge of or who is the primary woman of a household

woman of the world *n* a socially experienced and sophisticated woman

womanpower /wʊ́mmən powər/ *n* **1** women as part of the workforce in society **2** the influence and impact of women in society [Early 20C. After MANPOWER.]

woman suffrage *n* POL = **women's suffrage**

woman-to-woman *adj* **1** marked by directness and candour between 2 women in sports such as women's football, hockey, or basketball, having each defender of one team mark a corresponding attacker of the other team —**woman-to-woman** *adv*

womb /woom/ *n* **1** UTERUS OF WOMAN the uterus, especially that of a woman (*not used technically*) **2** PLACE OF ORIGIN a place where something is conceived and nurtured **3** PLACE OF SECURITY a place that offers protection and shelter, or a state of mind that provides comfort [Old English *wamb* < Germanic]

wombat /wóm bat/ *n* a burrowing marsupial that is short, robust, covered in dense wiry hair, and has a stumpy tail and wide blunt snout. Native to: Australia. *Vombatus ursinus* and *Lasiorhinus latifrons*. [Late 18C. < Dharuk *wambaty*.]

womblike /woóm līk/ *adj* resembling a womb, especially in being reassuring, all-enclosing, and giving a feeling of security

women plural of **woman**

womenfolk /wímmin fōk/ *npl* women collectively, or a particular group of women, especially those belonging to the same family or society (*dated*)

womenkind /wímmin kīnd/ *n* = **womankind**

AKG London

Wombat

Women's Institute *n* a worldwide organization of affiliated groups of women, especially in rural areas, who hold regular meetings for social and cultural activities, or a group belonging to this

women's lib *n* women's liberation (*informal*) —**women's libber** *n*

women's liberation *n* a political movement intended to free women from oppression, or the act of a woman's freeing herself

women's movement *n* a movement seeking to promote and improve the position of women in society

women's refuge *n* a place where women and children can stay after leaving home to escape domestic violence. US term **women's shelter**

women's room *n US* a public toilet for women and girls to use

Women's Royal Voluntary Service *n* a British service run by women that provides support for people in need

women's shelter *n US* = **women's refuge**

women's studies *n* a course of study examining the historical, economic, and cultural roles and achievements of women (+ *singular or plural verb*)

women's suffrage *n* the right of women to vote in elections

womenswear /wímminzwair/ *n* clothing and accessories for women

womera *n* = **woomera**

won[1] /won/ (*plural* **won**) *n* see table at **currency** [Mid-20C. < Korean *wǎn*.]

won[2] past participle, past tense of **win**

wonder /wúndər/ *n* **1 AMAZED ADMIRATION** amazed admiration or awe, especially at something very beautiful or new **2 SOMETHING MARVELLOUS** a miracle or other cause of intense admiration or awe ▪ *adj* **EXTRAORDINARILY GOOD** exciting admiration or amazement by virtue of being extraordinarily good, effective, or unusual ▪ *v* **1** *vti* **SPECULATE ABOUT** to speculate or be curious to know about something **2** *vi* **BE AMAZED** to be in a state of amazed admiration or awe [Old English *wundor*, < Germanic] —**wonderer** *n* ◊ **for a wonder** as a matter of astonishment or surprise ◊ **no** *or* **small** *or* **little wonder** used to indicate that something is not surprising ◊ **work** *or* **perform** *or* **do wonders** to achieve remarkable results or be very effective in solving a problem

Wonder /wúndər/, **Stevie** (*b.* 1950) US singer and songwriter. Born **Steveland Judkins**

wonder drug MED = **miracle drug**

wonderful /wúndərf'l/ *adj* **1** of a quality that excites admiration or amazement **2** suiting somebody perfectly —**wonderfully** *adv* —**wonderfulness** *n*

wonderland /wúndər land/ *n* a land where wonderful things happen or exist

LITERARY LINK *Alice's Adventures in Wonderland*, a children's story (1865) by Lewis Carroll. This extraordinarily inventive and immensely popular tale was based on stories that the author made up to entertain his friends' children. A girl called Alice dreams that she falls down a rabbit hole into a surreal world inhabited by eccentric characters including the Mad Hatter, the March Hare, and the King and Queen of Hearts. The expressions 'Curiouser and curiouser!' and 'Oh my fur and whiskers!' are direct quotations from this book. The often-used expressions 'grin like a Cheshire cat','wild as

a March hare', and 'mad as a hatter' have associations with characters in the book.

wonderment /wúndərmənt/ *n* **1** amazed admiration or awe **2** puzzled surprise

wonderwork /wúndər wurk/ *n* something made or done that arouses amazed admiration or awe —**wonderworker** *n*

wondrous /wúndrəss/ *adj* so good or admirable as to inspire wonder or awe (*literary*) ▪ *adv* wondrously or extraordinarily (*literary*) [15C. Alteration (influenced by MARVELLOUS) of obsolete *wonders* < WONDER.] —**wondrously** *adv* —**wondrousness** *n*

wonk /wongk/ *n* **1** an expert in matters of policy, especially in government, the economy, or diplomacy ○ *The dinner conversation was dominated by deep discussions among the government's policy wonks.* **2** a student who works unduly hard or long (*disapproving informal*) [Early 20C. < ?]

wonky /wóngki/ *adj* (**-kier, -kiest**), *adv* (*informal*) **1** not to be relied on to be steady or secure or to function correctly **2** not straight or level [Early 20C. < ?] —**wonkily** *adv* —**wonkiness** *n*

wont /wónt/ *adj* ACCUSTOMED accustomed or likely to do something (*formal*) ○ *He is wont to be rather quick of temper when tired.* ▪ *n* **SOMEBODY'S CUSTOM** a habit or custom followed by a particular person or group of people (*formal*) ▪ *vti* (**wonts, wonting, wont** *or* **wonted**) BE ACCUSTOMED to have or give somebody the habit of doing something (*archaic*) [12C. < past participle of Old English *wunian* 'be accustomed'.]

SYNONYMS See *habit*.

won't /wónt/ *contr* will not

wonted /wóntid/ *adj* usual or typical (*literary*) —**wontedly** *adv* —**wontedness** *n*

SYNONYMS See *usual*.

won ton /wón tón/ *n* **1** in Chinese cookery, a small dumpling made from a square of noodle dough with a little filling in the middle, boiled in soup or deep-fried **2 won ton, won ton soup** Chinese soup with boiled small dumplings in it [Mid-20C. < Chinese (Cantonese) *wǎn t'ǎn*.]

WOO /woo/ (**woos, wooing, wooed**) *vti* **1** to seek the affection or love of a woman in order to marry her (*literary*) **2** to try to please in order to gain something, especially acceptance, fame, or approval [Old English *wōgian* < ?] —**wooingly** *adv*

wood /wood/ *n* **1 SUBSTANCE OF TREES** a hard fibrous substance that chiefly composes shrubs and trees and is found beneath their bark **2 FUEL OR BUILDING MATERIAL** wood from trees, cut and dried for use as a fuel or a building material or in other areas of craft and manufacture **3 AREA WITH TREES** an area of land covered by shrubs or trees **4 GOLF CLUB** a golf club with a head formerly made of wood, but now usually made of stainless steel or titanium **5** BOWLS = **bowl**[2] *n.* **1** ▪ *adj* **1 OF WOOD** made of or used for wood **2 AMONG TREES** located or living in a forested area ▪ *v* **1** *vt* **COVER AREA WITH TREES** to cover an area of land with trees **2** *vti* **FUEL SOMETHING WITH WOOD** to supply somebody or something or be supplied with wood as fuel [Old English *wudu* < Germanic] —**wooded** *adj* ◊ **cannot see the wood for the trees** used to indicate that somebody is too concerned with the details to appreciate the general nature of a situation or problem ◊ **out of the woods** out of danger or difficulty (*informal*) ◊ **touch wood** used, whether you are actually touching wood or not, to try to avoid the bad luck that is supposed to come from being too confident or hopeful

SPELLCHECK Do not confuse **wood** with **would**, which has a similar sound. Beware: your spellchecker will not catch this error.

Wood /wood/, **Sir Henry** (1869–1944) British conductor

Wood (the Elder), John (1704?–54) British architect and town planner

Wood (the Younger), John (1728–81) British architect and town planner

wood alcohol *n* CHEM = **methanol**

wood anemone *n* a spring-flowering anemone that grows in shady places. Flowers: single, white to crimson. Native to: North America, Europe. *Anemone quinquefolia* and *Anemone nemorosa*.

wood avens *n* PLANTS = **herb bennet**

woodbine /wood bīn/ *n* (*plural* **-bines** *or* **-bine**) *n* a honeysuckle with fragrant yellow flowers. Native to: Europe, Asia, North Africa. *Lonicera periclymenum*. [Old English *wudubinde*, < *wudu* 'wood' + *bindan* 'bind'; because the plant grows around trees]

woodblock /wood blok/ *n* **1** = **woodcut** *n.* **1 2** a hollow block of wood used as a percussion instrument in an orchestra or band **3** a small flat piece of wood laid in a pattern with others to make a floor surface

woodborer /wood bawrər/ *n* a medium sized moth with a stocky body that, as a large fleshy larva, bores into wood, causing considerable damage. Family: Cossidae.

Wood Buffalo National Park national park and nature reserve in central Canada, on the Alberta-Northwest Territories border. Area: 44,807 sq. km/17,300 sq. mi.

woodcarving /wood kaarving/ *n* **1** the art of carving wood **2** a decorative article carved from wood

woodchat /wood chat/ *n* (*plural* **-chats** *or* **-chat**), **woodchat shrike** *n* a songbird of the shrike family with black-and-white plumage and a reddish-brown crown. Native to: Europe, North Africa. *Lanius senator*.

woodchop /wood chop/ *n* a wood-chopping competition held at country fairs in Australia

woodchopper /wood chopər/ *n* a person who chops wood, especially somebody who chops down trees

woodchuck /wood chuk/ (*plural* **-chucks** *or* **-chuck**) *n* a heavy-set short-legged marmot with brownish fur streaked with grey. Native to: N North America. *Marmota monax*. [Late 17C. By folk etymology from an Algonquian word.]

wood coal *n* **1** = **brown coal 2** = **charcoal** *n.* **1**

woodcock /wood kok/ (*plural* **-cocks** *or* **-cock**) *n* either of two small stocky ground-dwelling birds related to the snipe, with short legs and rounded wings, and a long bill. Genus: *Scolopax*.

woodcraft /wood kraaft/ *n* **1** skill in travelling, living, or working in woods or forests **2** *US* skill in carving or making objects from wood —**woodcrafter** *n* —**woodcraftsman** *n*

woodcreeper /wood kreepər/ *n* (*plural* **-ers** *or* **-er**) *n* a forest bird that clings to tree trunks with its short strong legs and probes for insects with its bill. Native to: Central and South America. Family: Dendrocolaptidae.

woodcut /wood kut/ *n* **1** a block of wood carved with a picture or design from which prints are made **2** a print made by pressing a woodcut onto a colouring substance and then onto paper

woodcutter /wood kutər/ *n* **1** a person who cuts down trees **2** a maker of and printer from woodcuts

wood duck *n* a crested duck that nests in tree cavities near water, the male of which has black, chestnut, green, purple, and white plumage. Native to: North America. *Aix sponsa*.

wooden /wood'n/ *adj* **1 MADE OF WOOD** made or consisting of wood **2 UNGAINLY** lacking flexibility, relaxation, and grace **3 INEXPRESSIVE** lacking animation, emotion, or responsiveness ○ *a wooden prose style* **4 DULL IN SOUND** making a dull unresonant sound ○ *spoke in a toneless, wooden voice* —**woodenly** *adv* —**woodenness** *n*

wood engraving *n* **1** the art or process of engraving a picture or design with a burin on a block of wood **2** an engraving made with a burin on a block of wood, or a print from one —**wood engraver** *n*

woodenhead /wood'n hed/ *n* an offensive term for a person considered to be unintelligent (*informal insult*) —**woodenheaded** /wood'n héddid/ *adj* —**woodenheadedly** *adv* —**woodenheadedness** *n*

Wooden Horse *n* = **Trojan Horse** *n.* **1**

wooden spoon *n* a prize awarded for being last in a race or competition

woodenware /wood'n wair/ *n* dishes or utensils made from wood

woodfree /wood free/ *adj* describes paper made from wood pulp that has been chemically treated to remove impurities

wood frog *n* a frog that lives in woodland and is light brown with darker markings on the head. Native to: E North America. *Rana sylvatica*.

woodgrain /wood grayn/ *n* a material or finish that imitates the natural grain of wood

woodgrouse /wŏŏd growss/ (*plural* **woodgrouse** *or* **woodgrouses**) *n* BIRDS = **capercaillie**

wood hedgehog *n* a pale buff fungus that has a spiny underside to the cap and is found in broad-leaved woodland. *Hydnum repandum.*

wood hyacinth *n* PLANTS = **bluebell** *n*. 1

wood ibis *n* 1 a stork with white plumage, a bare red face, and a yellow bill. Native to: Africa. *Mycteria ibis.* 2 BIRDS = **wood stork**

woodie *n* US = **woody** *n*. (*slang offensive*)

woodland /wŏŏddlənd/ *n* land that is covered with trees, shrubs, or bushes —**woodlander** *n*

woodlark /wŏŏd laark/ (*plural* **-larks** *or* **-lark**) *n* a small lark noted for its song in flight. Native to: Europe, Asia. *Lullula arborea.*

woodlouse /wŏŏd lowss/ (*plural* **-lice** /-līss/) *n* a small land-dwelling crustacean that lives in damp woody places and is capable of rolling into a ball. Genera: *Oniscus* and *Porcellio.*

woodman *n* = **woodsman**

wood mouse *n* a small mouse that lives in woodlands in western and central Europe and North Africa. *Apodemus sylvaticus.*

woodnote /wŏŏd nōt/ *n* a natural musical note, call, or song, e.g. that made by a wild bird (*literary*)

wood nymph *n* 1 WOODLAND NYMPH a nymph that lives in woodland, e.g. a dryad 2 BUTTERFLY any one of several brown butterflies, especially one with a broad yellow band and black-and-white eyespots on each front wing. Family: Satyridae. 3 HUMMINGBIRD a tropical hummingbird. Native to: Central and South America. Genus: *Thalurania.*

wood opal *n* wood impregnated and fossilized by silica preserving the grain

wood owl *n* BIRDS = **tawny owl**

woodpecker /wŏŏd pekər/ *n* a tree-climbing bird with boldly-patterned plumage, a stiff tail, and a hard bill for hammering against wood and extracting insects. Family: Picidae.

wood pigeon *n* a pigeon that has a white patch on each side of the neck and lives in woodland. *Columba palumbus.*

woodpile /wŏŏd pīl/ *n* a heap or stack of firewood

wood pitch *n* the sticky residue left after wood tar has been distilled

woodprint /wŏŏd print/ *n* CRAFT = **woodcut** *n*. 1

wood pulp *n* wood that has been mechanically and chemically broken down for use in making paper and paper products

wood rat *n* ZOOL = **pack rat**

Woodridge /wŏŏdrij/ village in NE Illinois. Population: 29,382 (1998 estimate).

Woodroffe, Mount /wŏŏd rof/ highest peak in South Australia, in the NW of the state. Height: 1,439 m / 4,721 ft.

woodruff /wŏŏd ruf/ (*plural* **-ruffs** *or* **-ruff**) *n* any of several plants with sweet-scented flowers. Use: perfumery, flavouring for wines and liqueurs. Genera: *Asperula* and *Galium.* [Old English *wudurofe*, < *wudu* 'wood' + *rofe* ?]

Woodruff key *n* a self-aligning key that is semicircular in cross-section, designed to fit into the recess of a shaft [Late 19C. After the *Woodruff* Manufacturing Co. in Hartford, Connecticut.]

woodrush /wŏŏd rush/ *n* a plant with flat leaves fringed with hairs. Native to: cold and temperate areas of the N hemisphere. Genus: *Luzula.*

woods /wŏŏdz/ *npl* 1 a forested or wooded area or region 2 the woodwind instruments of an orchestra

LITERARY LINK *Stopping by Woods on a Snowy Evening*, a poem (1923) by US poet Robert Frost. In this much-anthologized poem the narrator pauses on horseback, drawn into the dark beauty of the woods in snow. He lingers, attracted by the quiet, solitude, and, according to many critics, the prospect of death, while yet considering the practical obligations of society. It ends with the famous lines, 'But I have promises to keep,/ And miles to go before I sleep,/ And miles to go before I sleep'.

Woods /wŏŏdz/, **Tiger** (b. 1975) US golfer. Born **Eldrick Woods**

wood sage *n* a downy aromatic plant found in woods and heaths. Native to: Europe. *Teucrium scordonia.*

woodscrew /wŏŏd skroo/ *n* a tapered metal screw that can be driven into wood by a screwdriver

woodshed /wŏŏd shed/ *n* an outbuilding or connected room in which firewood and tools are stored

woodsia /wŏŏdzi ə/ (*plural* **-as** *or* **-a**) *n* a small fern that has wiry fronds and is found in northern often mountainous regions. Genus: *Woodsia.* [Mid-19C. < modern Latin after Joseph *Woods* (1776–1864), English botanist.]

woodsman /wŏŏdzmən/ (*plural* **-men** /-mən/), **woodman** /wŏŏdmən/ (*plural* **-men** /-mən/) *n* a person who is skilled at living, working, or travelling in the woods

wood sorrel *n* a herb with a creeping stem and heart-shaped leaves. Flowers: white, with coloured veins. Genus: *Oxalis.*

wood spirit *n* CHEM = **methanol**

Woodstock /wŏŏd stok/ 1 town in central England. Population: 2,898 (1991). 2 city in S Ontario, Canada. Population: 30,075 (1991). 3 town in SE New York State, best known for a rock music festival in 1969. Population: 6,241 (1998 estimate).

wood stork *n* a large stork with a long heavy bill, bare head, white plumage, and black wing tips. Native to: wooded marshes in North, Central, and South America. Genus: *Mycteria americana.*

wood sugar *n* CHEM = **xylose**

woodsy /wŏŏdzi/ (**-ier, -iest**) *adj US, Can* relating to or reminiscent of the woods (*informal*)

wood tar *n* a black viscous tar produced as a by-product in the destructive distillation of wood, used as a protective coating for rope and timber

wood thrush *n* a large woodland thrush with a reddish-brown head and a pale spotted breast. Native to: E North America. *Hylocichla mustelina.*

wood tick *n* a tick that transmits the pathogenic micro-organism that causes Rocky Mountain spotted fever. Native to: W North America. Genus: *Dermacentor.*

wood vinegar *n* CHEM = **pyroligneous acid**

wood warbler *n* 1 a small yellowish-green songbird that lives in woods. Native to: Europe. *Phylloscopus sibilatrix.* 2 a small, insect-eating, often brightly coloured songbird. Native to: North and South America. Family: Parulidae.

Woodward /wŏŏdwərd/, **Robert B.** (1917–79) US chemist. Full name **Robert Burns Woodward**

Woodward, Roger Robert (b. 1944) Australian pianist

wood wasp *n* = **horntail**

woodwind /wŏŏd wind/ *n* 1 MUSICAL INSTRUMENTS the family of wind instruments, originally made of wood, that includes the flute, clarinet, oboe, and bassoon (+ *singular or plural verb*) 2 MUSICAL INSTRUMENT an instrument belonging to the woodwind family 3 PLAYERS IN ORCHESTRA the players of woodwind instruments in an orchestra, considered collectively (+ *singular verb*) —**woodwind** *adj*

woodwork /wŏŏd wurk/ *n* 1 MANUFACTURE OF WOODEN ITEMS the skill or craft of making items out of wood. US term **woodworking** *n*. 2 ITEMS MADE FROM WOOD items or components made from wood, especially the interior parts of a building, e.g. the frames of windows, staircases, and doors 3 FRAME OF FOOTBALL GOAL the goalposts and crossbar of a football goal (*informal*) ◇ **crawl** *or* **come out of the woodwork** to appear suddenly and unexpectedly in large numbers (*slang*)

woodworking /wŏŏd wurking/ *n US* = **woodwork** *n*. 1 ■ *adj* relating to woodwork or used in making things from wood

woodworm /wŏŏd wurm/ *n* 1 a worm or insect larva that bores into and weakens wood, e.g. in joists or stairs inside a building 2 the damaged condition of wood from its infestation by wood-boring insects, especially larvae

woody /wŏŏdi/ *adj* (**-ier, -iest**) 1 HAVING MANY TREES containing or covered with many trees 2 RELATING TO WOOD relating to, typical of, or situated in wood 3 MADE OF WOOD made of or containing wood or a material resembling wood 4 RESEMBLING WOOD resembling wood in some way, e.g. in appearance, texture, or smell ■ *n*

(*plural* **-ies**) **woody** (*plural* **-ies**), **woodie** *US* OFFENSIVE TERM an offensive term for an erect penis (*slang*)

woodyard /wŏŏd yaard/ *n* a place where wood is cut and stored

woody nightshade *n* a woody plant with poisonous red fruits resembling berries. Flowers: purple. Native to: Europe, Asia. Genus: *Solanum dulcamara.* US term **bittersweet** *n*. 2

woof[1] /wŏŏf/ *n* SOUND OF BARKING DOG the sound made by a dog when it barks ■ *interj* REPRESENTATION OR IMITATION OF BARKING a representation or imitation of the sound made by a barking dog ■ *vi* MAKE BARKING SOUND to produce woof [Early 19C. An imitation of the sound.]

woof[2] /wŏŏf/ *n* 1 CRAFT = **weft** *n*. 1 2 a woven fabric or its texture [Old English *owef* 'weave on' < *wefan* 'weave' < Indo-European]

woofer /wŏŏfər/ *n* a loudspeaker used to reproduce low-frequency sounds. ◇ **tweeter** [Mid-20C. As a metaphor < WOOF[1].]

wool /wŏŏl/ *n* 1 SHEEP'S HAIR the short curly overlapping hair of sheep and some other mammals, e.g. the llama and the alpaca 2 YARN USED TO MAKE CLOTHES yarn spun from the wool of sheep or other mammals. Use: knitting, weaving. 3 WOOLLEN MATERIAL material knitted or woven using wool 4 HAIR OF INSECT LARVA the furry hair of some insect larvae, e.g. caterpillars (*informal*) 5 HAIR GROWING ON PLANT a mass of soft hairs that grows on some plants [Old English *wull* < Indo-European] —**woolled** *adj* ◇ **pull the wool over somebody's eyes** to deceive or trick somebody

wool clip *n* the annual wool yield of a farm, district, or country

woolen *adj, n US* = **woollen**

wooly *adj, n US* = **woolly**

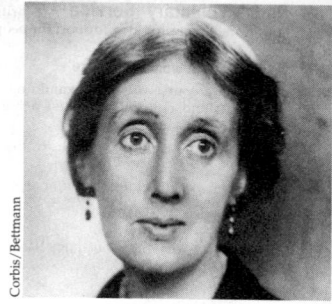

Virginia Woolf

Corbis/Bettmann

Woolf /wŏŏlf/, **Virginia** (1882–1941) British novelist and critic. Born **Virginia Adeline Stephen**

wool fat *n* PHARM = **lanolin**

woolgathering /wŏŏl gathəring/ *n* daydreaming or absent-mindedness [Mid-16C. Originally 'gathering the bits of wool torn from sheep by bushes'.] —**woolgather** *vi* —**woolgatherer** *n*

wool grease *n* a fatty wax that coats the fibres of sheep's wool and yields lanolin

woolgrower /wŏŏl grō ər/ *n* a person who keeps sheep in order to sell their wool —**woolgrowing** *n*

woollen /wŏŏllən/ *adj* 1 MADE FROM WOOL knitted or woven using wool 2 PRODUCING WOOL OR WOOLLEN ITEMS relating to the production of wool or items made from wool ■ *n* WOOLLEN GARMENT a garment made from wool, especially a sweater or cardigan

Woolley /wŏŏlli/, **Sir Leonard** (1880–1960) British archaeologist

woolly /wŏŏlli/ *adj* (**-lier, -liest**) 1 MADE OF WOOL knitted or woven using wool 2 COVERED WITH INSECT HAIR describes an insect larva, e.g. a caterpillar, that is covered with furry hair resembling wool 3 CONFUSED confused, vague, and lacking focus ◇ *woolly thinking* 4 COVERED WITH PLANT HAIRS describes a stem, leaf, or other plant part that is covered with long, soft, white hairs 5 US UNCIVILIZED AND UNRULY rough and boisterous in a way that is reminiscent of the frontier days of the American West (*informal*) ■ *n* (*plural* **-lies**) WOOLLEN GARMENT a garment made from wool (*informal*) ■ **woollies** *npl US* LONG WOOLLEN UNDERWEAR long underwear made of wool —**woollily** *adv* —**woolliness** *n*

woolly aphid *n* a tiny insect that secretes a waxy substance in long filaments that gives it a woolly appearance. Family: Aphididae.

woolly bear *n* the caterpillar of various moths, especially the tiger moth, that has a coat of dense woolly hairs

woolly-headed *adj* **1** confused, vague, and lacking focus **2** having thick curly hair that looks or feels like wool

woolly mammoth *n* an extinct mammoth with a shaggy coat that lived in cold regions across North America and Eurasia during the Ice Age. Genus: *Mammuthus primigenius*.

Woolner /wóolnər/, **Thomas** (1825–92) British sculptor and poet

woolpack /wóol pak/ *n* **1** the coarse material, usually jute or canvas, used to wrap a bale of wool **2** a package in which a bale of raw wool is transported

woolsack /wóol sak/ *n* a sack for holding wool

Woolsack *n* the seat traditionally stuffed with wool from which the Lord Chancellor presides over the House of Lords

woolshed /wóol shed/ *n ANZ* a building or group of buildings in which sheep are sheared and their wool is prepared and packed for market

wool-sorter *n* a person who sorts wool into different grades

wool-sorter's disease *n* pulmonary anthrax resulting from the inhalation of spores of an anthrax bacterium that contaminates wool

wool stapler *n* **1** = **wool-sorter 2** a dealer in wool

Woolwich /wóollij, -ich/ district of London, located on the S bank of the River Thames

Woolworth /wóolwərth/, **Frank W.** (1852–1919) US retailer. Full name **Frank Winfield Woolworth**

woomera /wóommərə, wóom-/ (*plural* **-as**), **woomerah** (*plural* **-ahs**), **womera** *n* a wooden stick with a notch at one end, used by Australian Aboriginals to launch a spear [Early 19C. < Dharuk.]

Woop Woop /wóop woop/ *n Aus* a remote town or area that is regarded as lacking the facilities and sophistication of the city (*informal humorous*) [Early 20C. Mock Australian Aboriginal.]

woosh *n, vi* = **whoosh**

Wootton /wútt'n/, **Barbara Frances, Baroness Wootton of Abinger** (1897–1988) British social scientist. Born **Barbara Frances Adam**

woozy /wóozi/ (**-ier, -iest**) *adj* **1** weak and unsteady or dizzy **2** confused or unable to think clearly [Late 19C. < ?] —**woozily** *adv* —**wooziness** *n*

wop /wop/ *n* a highly offensive term for an Italian person (*taboo*) [Early 20C. < Italian dialect *guappo* 'tough, bold' < Spanish *guapo* 'dandy'.]

Worcester /wóostər/ **1** city in west-central England. Population: 91,100 (1995). **2** city in central Massachusetts. Population: 169,759 (1990).

Worcester china, Worcester porcelain, Worcester *n* fine china made in Worcester since 1751, or the articles made from this china

Worcester sauce *n* a thin pungent table sauce flavoured with soy, tamarind, and spices, originally made in Worcestershire. US term **Worcestershire sauce**

Worcestershire /wóostərshər/ county of west-central England. Area: 1735 sq. km/670 sq. mi.

Worcestershire sauce *n* FOOD = **Worcester sauce**

Worcs. *abbr* Worcestershire

word /wurd/ *n* **1 MEANINGFUL UNIT OF LANGUAGE SOUNDS** a meaningful sound or combination of sounds that is a unit of language or its representation in a text **2 BRIEF UTTERANCE** a brief comment, announcement, discussion, or conversation ○ *Could I have a word with you in my office, please?* **3 INFORMATION** information or news about somebody or something ○ *Is there any word on your daughter?* **4 RUMOUR** rumour or gossip ○ *The word is that she's leaving the company.* **5 PROMISE** a promise, assurance, or guarantee ○ *I give you my word.* **6 COMMAND** a command, order, or authorization ○ *He gave the word to attack.* **7 PASSWORD** a password or verbal signal ○ *Don't let anyone in unless they give the word.* **8 FIXED NUMBER OF PROCESSED BITS** a number of bits, e.g. 32, 48, or 64, processed as a single unit by a computer ■ **words** *npl* **1 ANGRY TALK** angry or quarrelsome speech ○ *had words with him over the shoddy merchandise he sold us* **2 TEXT OF SONG** the text or lyrics of a song, musical, or opera ■ *vt* **PHRASE** to express something in words [Old English < Indo-European] —**worded** *adj* ◇ **a man of his word, a woman of her word** somebody who keeps his *or* her promise ◇ **be as good as your word** to do as promised ◇ **eat your words** to admit humbly that you were wrong or mistaken (*informal*) ◇ **get a word in edgeways** to succeed in speaking when other people are talking nonstop (*usually in negative statements*) ◇ **in a word** briefly or very concisely expressed ◇ **my word** used to express surprise or astonishment (*dated*) ◇ **put in** *or* **say a good word for somebody** to speak well of or recommend somebody ◇ **put something into words** to express something such as a feeling or emotion clearly ◇ **put words in somebody's mouth** to say that somebody has said something when in fact he or she did not say it

Word *n* **1** in Christian theology, the divine rational principle as epitomized by Jesus Christ **2 Word, Word of God** in Christianity, the Bible or Scriptures, considered as revealing divine truth

wordage /wúrdij/ *n* **1 NUMBER OF WORDS** the number of words in a text **2 WORDS COLLECTIVELY** words considered as a group **3 WORDINESS** the use of too many words to express something **4 WORDING** the choice of words made by a writer or speaker

word association *n* a method of assessing somebody's mental state or personality by asking the person to respond with the first word that comes to mind when a given word is heard

word blindness *n* MED = **alexia** —**word-blind** *adj*

wordbook /wúrd bòok/ *n* a dictionary, vocabulary, or lexicon

wordbreak /wúrd brayk/ *n* the point in a word where it can be divided if there is insufficient room at the end of a line for the entire word

word class *n* a category of words that have the same form or function, e.g. parts of speech

word count *n* the calculation of the number of words in a piece of text, or the result of such a calculation

word deafness *n* the loss of the capacity to understand spoken words, especially when caused by a cerebral lesion —**word-deaf** *adj*

word finder *n* a book that lists words according to meaning or subject, designed to help users find the word that best expresses the meaning they want to convey

word for word *adv* **1 IN SAME WORDS** in exactly the same words as originally used **2 LITERALLY** by translating each word used in a spoken or written piece of foreign language individually ■ *adj* **word-for-word 1 USING SAME WORDS** using exactly the same words as the original spoken or written text **2 LITERAL** translating each word used in a spoken or written piece of foreign language individually

word game *n* **1** a game in which players have to construct, find, or change the form of words **2** disingenuous language intended to mislead, misrepresent, conceal, or put a spin onto a usually awkward situation or issue (*slang; often plural*) ○ *Please stop the word games and give me a truthful answer.*

word-hoard *n* the total number of words that somebody is able to use or understand

wording /wúrding/ *n* the choice of words made by a writer or speaker

wordless /wúrdləss/ *adj* **1** communicating without the use of speech **2** incapable of speech, especially temporarily —**wordlessly** *adv* —**wordlessness** *n*

Word of God *n* CHR = **Word** *n.* **2**

word of honour *n* a solemn promise or undertaking to do something

word of mouth *n* communication using the spoken word, as distinct from written communication

word-of-mouth *adj* made by using oral communication, not written ○ *A small business thrives on word-of-mouth recommendation.*

word-perfect *adj* **1 KNOWING OR PERFORMING SOMETHING PERFECTLY** having memorized, spoken, or sung with total accuracy. US term **letter-perfect** *adj.* **1 2 KNOWN OR PERFORMED PERFECTLY** memorized, spoken, or sung with total accuracy. US term **letter-perfect** *adj.* **2 3 ABSOLUTELY CORRECT** accurate in every detail

word picture *n* a vivid description of something in words

wordplay /wúrd play/ *n* the witty, subtle, or ingenious use of words, e.g. in taking advantage of their multiple meanings

ϟ **word processing** *n* the creation, retrieval, storage, and printing of text using a computer or other electronic equipment (*hyphenated before nouns*)

ϟ **word processor** *n* **1 MACHINE FOR MANIPULATING TEXT** a piece of electronic equipment that has a keyboard and video display unit and is used to create, retrieve, modify, store, and print text **2 COMPUTER PROGRAM FOR MANIPULATING TEXT** a computer program that is used to create, retrieve, modify, store, and print text **3 SOMEBODY PROCESSING WORDS** a person who does word processing

wordsmith /wúrd smith/ *n* somebody such as a professional writer or journalist who uses words skilfully

word square *n* a puzzle consisting of a square grid to be constructed of words that read the same vertically and horizontally

word stress *n* the placing of stress on the syllables of a word, or an instance of this

Wordsworth /wúrdz wurth/, **Dorothy** (1771–1855) British writer

Wordsworth /wúrdzwərth/, **William** (1770–1850) British poet —**Wordsworthian** /wúrdz wúrthi ən/ *adj*

ϟ **word wrap, word wrapping** *n* a feature of word-processing programs in which a word that exceeds a preset line length is moved automatically to the next line

wordy /wúrdi/ (**-ier, -iest**) *adj* **1** using an excessive number of words in writing or speech **2** relating to or consisting of words —**wordily** *adv* —**wordiness** *n*

SYNONYMS ***wordy, verbose, long-winded, rambling, prolix, diffuse***

CORE MEANING: too long or not concisely expressed

wordy using an excessive number of words in writing or speech; **verbose** expressed in language that is wordy and not precise; **long-winded** tediously wordy in speech or writing; **rambling** excessively long with many changes of subject, making it difficult to follow; **prolix** tiresomely wordy; **diffuse** lacking organization and conciseness.

wore past tense of **wear**[1]

work /wurk/ *n* **1 PAID JOB** paid employment at a job ○ *people looking for work* **2 DUTIES OF JOB** the duties or activities that are part of a job or occupation ○ *Much of my work involves talking on the phone.* **3 SOMEBODY'S PLACE OF EMPLOYMENT** the place where somebody is employed ○ *spends all her time at work* **4 TIME SPENT AT PLACE OF EMPLOYMENT** the time that a person spends carrying out his or her job ○ *meet you after work* **5 PURPOSEFUL EFFORT** the physical or mental effort directed at doing or making something ○ *It was a lot of work, but it was worth it.* **6 SOMETHING MADE OR DONE** that which has been made or done as part of a job or as a result of effort or activity requiring skill (*often in combination*) ○ *Your work is not satisfactory.* **7 ARTISTIC OR INTELLECTUAL CREATION** an artistic or intellectual composition, e.g. a book, treatise, painting, sculpture, film, or piece of music (*often plural*) **8 MEANS FOR ENERGY TRANSFER** (*symbol* **W**) the transfer of energy, measured as the product of the force applied to a body and the distance moved by that body in the direction of the force **9 SOMETHING MANUFACTURED** that which has been or is in the process of being worked on or manufactured ■ *v* (**works, working, worked** *or* **wrought** *archaic* /rawt/, **worked** *or* **wrought** *archaic*) **1** *vi* **HAVE JOB** to have a paid job **2** *vti* **EXERT OR CAUSE EFFORT** to exert or make somebody exert physical or mental effort in order to do, make, or accomplish something **3** *vti* **FUNCTION** to function or operate or cause something to function or operate ○ *The television doesn't work.* ○ *It's stopped working altogether now.* **4** *vi* **BE SUCCESSFUL** to be effective or achieve a desired result ○ *Our relationship just isn't working.* **5** *vti* **WORK IN SPECIFIC PLACE** to carry on an operation or activity in a particular place or area ○ *You'll be working the southern region.* **6** *vi* **EXERT INFLUENCE** to produce results or exert an influence ○ *Everything seemed to be working against them.* **7** *vti* **SHAPE** to shape, bend, form, or forge a material, or to be shaped, bent, formed, or forged in a specified way **8** *vt* **CULTIVATE LAND**

to cultivate land in order to grow crops on it **9** *vt* **ACHIEVE** to effect something or bring something about **10** *vti* **ATTAIN SPECIFIED CONDITION** to attain or cause something to attain a specified condition slowly or gradually **11** *vti* **MOVE SLOWLY AND WITH EFFORT** to move or progress slowly and with effort, or to cause something to move or progress in this way ○ *He worked his way through the crowd.* **12** *vt US, Can* **SOLVE MATHEMATICAL PROBLEM** to solve a mathematical problem or puzzle **13** *vti* **EXERCISE** to move or exercise a muscle or part of the body **14** *vt* **PROVOKE EMOTIONAL RESPONSE IN** to arouse or stir up emotions in somebody **15** *vt* **MAKE SOMETHING IN NEEDLEWORK** to make or decorate something by hand in needlework or embroidery **16** *vi* **MOVE LOOSELY** to move in a loose way that results in friction and wear (*refers to machinery*) **17** *vt* **ARRANGE** to arrange or exploit something in order to gain an advantage (*informal*) ○ *He managed to work it so that he got every other Friday off.* **18** *vt* **CHARM** to use charm and personal influence on somebody in order to attain popularity or acclaim **19** *vti* **FERMENT** to ferment or cause something to ferment **20** *vi* **STRAIN SLIGHTLY IN ROUGH WATER** to give slightly in rough water so that the joints move slightly and the fastenings become loose (*refers to ships*) **21** *vi* **SAIL INTO WIND** to sail against the wind [Old English *weorc* < Indo-European] ◇ **at work 1** engaged in employment **2** in operation ◇ **have your work cut out (for you)** to be faced with a difficult task ◇ **make short work of somebody** *or* **something** to dispose of or deal with somebody or something very quickly ◇ **work to rule** *UK, Can* to take part in a labour protest in which workers make a point of adhering strictly to the rules of the workplace so that work will slow down

USAGE See ***wrought***.

work in *vt* **1** to add something gradually while blending it with another substance **2** to arrange a time or place for something in a given situation ○ *I'll see if I can work you in on Friday.*
work off *vt* **1 work off, work at** to pay back a debt by doing work rather than by paying the money owed **2** to use up or get rid of something by the effort of working
work on, work upon *vt* **1 AFFECT** to influence or attempt to influence somebody or something **2 MAKE OR FIX** to spend time making, improving, or fixing something **3 USE SOMETHING AS BASIS** to use something as a starting point for further investigation or enquiry
work out *v* **1** *vt* **SOLVE OR CALCULATE** to solve a problem or find an answer to a question by reasoning or calculation **2** *vt* **RESOLVE DIFFICULTY** to resolve differences or find a way of dealing with a difficulty **3** *vt* **THINK SOMETHING UP** to devise something, especially a course of action **4** *vt* **COMPREHEND** to understand somebody or something fully **5** *vt* **ACHIEVE SOMETHING BY EFFORT** to succeed in doing something after working long and hard at it **6** *vt* = **work off** *v.* 1 **7** *vt* **EXHAUST MINE BY EXTRACTION** to extract all the valuable material from a mine or deposit **8** *vi* **END SATISFACTORILY** to have a satisfactory or successful result **9** *vi* **END IN PARTICULAR WAY** to have a particular result **10** *vi* **EXERCISE** to train or take part in strenuous physical exercise as a way of keeping fit ○ *How do you find the time for working out?* **11** *vi* **MAKE TOTAL** to come to a particular amount

SYNONYMS See ***deduce***.

work over *vt* **1 REDO** to do something again **2 EXAMINE SOMETHING THOROUGHLY** to work at or examine something thoroughly and in detail **3 GIVE SOMEBODY A BEATING** to give somebody a severe beating or subject somebody to severe physical punishment (*informal*)
work through *vt* to deal with an emotional problem by thinking about it often until it is understood or its impact is lessened
work up *v* **1** *vt* **EXCITE EMOTIONS IN** to arouse or stir up emotions in somebody **2** *vt* **CREATE** to create something or cause it to grow ○ *working up a sweat* **3** *vt* **IMPROVE** to develop, refine, or improve something **4** *vi* **BECOME MORE INTENSE** to grow or develop in intensity **5** *vt* **EXAMINE A PATIENT THOROUGHLY** to subject a patient to a thorough diagnostic examination
work up to *vt* to gradually reach a particular level by effort

workable /wúrkəb'l/ *adj* **1** able to be accomplished or carried out ○ *The plan is not workable.* **2** capable of being operated or handled ○ *workable steel* —**workability** /wúrkə bílləti/ *n* —**workableness** *n* —**workably** *adv*

workaday /wúrkə day/, **workday** /wúrk day/ *adj* **1** ordinary or part of the experience of most people **2** suitable for work or for a working day [Mid-16C. < ?]

workaholic /wúrkə hóllik/ *n* a compulsively hard worker [Mid-20C. < WORK + -AHOLIC.]

⚡**workaround** /wúrkə rownd/ *n* a technique that enables somebody to overcome a fault or defect in a computer program or system without actually putting the fault or defect right

workbag /wúrk bag/, **workbasket** /wúrk baaskit/ *n* a bag for holding materials and tools for work, especially sewing or knitting

workbench /wúrk bench/ *n* a table or surface on which work is done, e.g. by a carpenter or mechanic

workboat /wúrk bōt/ *n* a boat used solely for work, e.g. for fishing or transporting cargo

workbook /wúrk bŏŏk/ *n* **1 STUDENT'S EXERCISE BOOK** a book of exercises and questions for students, usually with spaces for answers to be written in **2 INSTRUCTION BOOK** a book of instructions on how to do or operate something **3 RECORD OF WORK** a book in which a record is kept of work done or to be done

work camp *n* **1** a camp where volunteers, especially young people or members of a religious organization, work on a project of benefit to the community **2** a camp in which prisoners are forced to work

workday /wúrk day/ *n* **1** *US* = **working day** *n.* 1 **2** = **working day** *n.* 2 ■ *adj* US = **workaday**

worked /wurkt/ *adj* produced, decorated, or treated with craft and skill [Late 16C. Originally 'that has been worked on'.]

worked up *adj* full of anger or other strong emotion (*informal*)

worker /wúrkər/ *n* **1 PERSON OR THING THAT WORKS** a person, animal, or device that is engaged in or used for a task of some kind **2 EMPLOYEE** an employee of somebody or something **3 MEMBER OF WORKING CLASS** a member of the working class, especially a factory employee or manual labourer **4 INSECT THAT WORKS** a member of a colony of social insects, especially sterile females, that carry out all the work, e.g. gathering food or feeding larvae

worker participation *n* the involvement of ordinary employees in making decisions at all levels in a business

worker-priest *n* a Roman Catholic priest who also has a secular job

workers' compensation *n* **1** in the United States, a form of insurance required from employers that provides money as compensation for workers who are injured at work or who contract an occupational disease **2** in the United States, money paid as compensation to a worker who is injured at work or who contracts an occupational disease

workers' cooperative *n* a business that is owned jointly by those who work in it

work ethic *n* a dedication to work, or belief in the moral value of hard work ○ *hasn't got much of a work ethic*

workfare /wúrk fair/ *n* a government scheme that obliges unemployed people to do community work or attend training schemes in return for benefit payments [Mid-20C. Blend of WORK + WELFARE.]

workflow /wúrkflō/ *n* the progress or rate of progress of work done by a business, department, or individual

workforce /wúrk fawrss/ *n* **1** all of the workers employed in a company or industry **2** all of the people who are employed or able to work, e.g. in a country

work function *n* (*symbol* Φ) the minimum energy needed to remove an electron from within a solid to a point outside its surface in a vacuum

work-harden *vt* to increase the hardness or strength of a metal by subjecting it to compression, tension, or another mechanical process

workhorse /wúrk hawrss/ *n* **1 HORSE USED FOR HEAVY WORK** a horse used for heavy work such as hauling, rather than for riding **2 HARD-WORKING PERSON** a hard and diligent worker, often assuming extra duties (*informal*) **3 RELIABLE TOOL OR MACHINE** something such as a machine that performs well over long periods

workhouse /wúrk howss/ (*plural* **-houses** /-howziz/) *n* formerly, a publicly run institution in Britain in which people living in poverty were given food and accommodation in return for unpaid work

work-in *n* a form of industrial action in which the workers of a business that is threatened with closure occupy the premises but continue to work

working /wúrking/ *adj* **1 FUNCTIONING** capable of being used or operated **2 WORN AT WORK** suitable for use while at work **3 HAVING PAID JOB** engaged in doing paid work **4 SPENT AT WORK** taken up with work ○ *all his working life* **5 GIVEN OVER TO WORK** spent doing work at a time when work is not normally done ○ *a working lunch* **6 ADEQUATE** good enough for a purpose, though not perfect or complete ○ *a working knowledge of Italian* **7 PROVIDING BASIS** usable as a basis for further work ○ *a working theory* ■ *n* **1 PROCESS OF SHAPING** the shaping, bending, forming, or forging of a material **2 JERKING MOTION** the convulsive, involuntary motion of a part of the body, caused by excitement or tension (*formal*) ■ **workings** *npl* **1 FUNCTIONING** the operation of something or the way in which it operates **2 USED PARTS OF MINE** the parts of a mine or quarry in which work is carried on

working capital *n* **1** the money that a business has available for use **2** the amount of current assets that remains after current liabilities are deducted

working class *n* **1** the part of society made up of people who work for hourly wages, not salaries, especially manual or industrial labourers (*often used in the plural*) **2** in Marxist theory, the proletariat or revolutionary class

working-class *adj* relating to or belonging to the part of society made up of people who work for hourly wages, not salaries, especially manual or industrial labourers ○ *a working-class neighbourhood*

working day *n* **1** a day on which people work, usually but not always a weekday. US term **workday** *n.* 1 **2** the part of a day during which somebody works. US term **workday** *n.* 2

working dog *n* a dog that is kept in order to do work, e.g. herding, guarding, or guiding

working drawing *n* a detailed scale drawing of something, for use as a guide in building or manufacturing

working girl *n* **1** a young woman who works for a living (*informal*) **2** a woman who is a prostitute (*slang*)

working group *n* US = **working party**

working hours *npl* the part of the day during which most people normally work and shops and offices are open

working man *n* a man who works for wages, especially at manual labour

working memory *n* the contents of a person's consciousness at the present moment

working paper *n* a document created as a basis for discussion rather than as an authoritative text

working party *n* a group of people appointed to study and report back on a particular subject. US term **working group**

⚡**working storage** *n* the amount of storage in a computer's memory that is assigned for data stored only while a program is running

working substance *n* a substance, especially a fluid, that undergoes changes in form or degree that are used to operate something such as an engine

working title *n* the provisional title by which a project, especially a film or novel, is known while it is still being worked on

Workington /wúrkingtən/ port in NW England. Population: 25,579 (1991).

working week *n* the amount of hours or days worked in a week. US term **workweek**

working woman (*plural* **working women** /-wimmin/) *n* a woman who works for wages, especially in a manual job

work-in-progress (*plural* **works-in-progress**) *n* a piece of artistic work, e.g. a novel or musical composition, that has not yet been finished but may be printed, exhibited, or performed

workless /wúrkləss/ *adj* having no work or employment —**worklessness** *n*

workload /wúrk lōd/ *n* **1** the amount of work assigned to a person or a group, and that is to be done in a particular period **2** the amount of work that a machine does or can do in a particular period

workman /wúrkmən/ (*plural* **-men** /-mən/) *n* **1** a man who works for hourly wages, not a salary, especially at a manual job **2** a man described or judged according to his skill or diligence as a worker ○ *a tidy workman*

workmanlike /wúrkmən līk/, **workmanly** /wúrkmənli/ *adj* done in a way that is thorough and satisfactory, without being imaginative or exciting

workmanship /wúrkmənship/ *n* 1 ART OR SKILL OF WORKER the skill or craft of a worker or artisan 2 QUALITY OF SKILL the level of skill used in making or doing something 3 PRODUCT OR RESULT OF WORKER'S SKILL the product or result of the skill of a worker or artisan

workmate /wúrk mayt/ *n* a person who works with or in the same place as another

work of art *n* 1 a piece of fine art, e.g. a painting or sculpture 2 something made or done exceptionally well ○ *The second goal was an absolute work of art.*

workout /wúrk owt/ *n* 1 a session of strenuous physical exercise or the practising of physical skills intended as a way of keeping fit or as practice for a game or athletics competition 2 a tough practical test of the capability or performance of a person, animal, or device

workpeople /wúrk peep'l/ *npl* hourly workers, especially those with manual jobs

workpiece /wúrk peess/ *n* something that has been, or is in the process of being, worked on or manufactured

workplace /wúrk playss/ *n* the place where somebody works, e.g. a factory or office

work print *n* a print of a film used in various stages of editing and as a guide in cutting the original negative from which the final commercial prints are made

work-release *n US* a system of allowing prisoners to take on paid work outside prison while serving their sentences

workroom /wúrk room, -rŏom/ *n* a room in which work is done, especially one equipped for manual work

works /wurks/ *n* (*plural* **works**) PLACE FOR INDUSTRIAL PRODUCTION a place where industrial work, especially manufacturing, is done ○ *an engineering works* ■ *npl* 1 SYRINGE FOR INJECTING NARCOTICS a syringe used to inject narcotics (*slang*) 2 EVERYTHING all things that are available (*informal*) ○ *A hot dog with the works, please.* 3 *US* BAD BEATING a severe beating or punishment (*slang*) 4 INNER MECHANISMS the interior moving parts of a mechanism ○ *The works of the clock are rusty.* 5 ACTS deeds or actions ◇ **in the works** being prepared or worked on

works council, works committee *n* a group of representatives of employers and employees in a company that meet to discuss matters of common interest relating to the running of the business

worksheet /wúrk sheet/ *n* 1 SHEET OF QUESTIONS FOR STUDENTS a sheet of questions or tasks for students on a recent lesson 2 SHEET RECORDING WORK a sheet of paper used for keeping a record of work done or scheduled 3 SHEET FOR DRAFT a sheet of paper used for making a rough draft or preliminary notes

workshop /wúrk shop/ *n* 1 a place where manual work is done, especially manufacturing or repairing 2 a group of people working on a creative project, discussing a topic, or studying a subject ○ *a song writing workshop*

workshy /wúrk shī/ *adj* lazy and unwilling to work [Early 20C. Translation of German *arbeitsscheu*.]

work song *n* a song sung by people working, usually with a repetitive rhythm that guides the rhythm of the work being done

Worksop /wúrk sop/ town in east-central England. Population: 37,247 (1991).

workspace /wúrk spayss/ *n* an area set aside for an individual worker or a business

workstation /wúrk staysh'n/ *n* 1 WORKING AREA a small area in a workplace assigned to one worker, especially a desk with a computer 2 TERMINAL OF NETWORK OR MAINFRAME a computer terminal, usually connected to a network in a business environment, that runs application programs and serves as an access point to the network 3 POWERFUL SPECIALIZED COMPUTER a powerful stand-alone computer, often with a high-resolution display, used for computer-aided design and other complex and specialized applications

work stoppage *n* an occasion when a group of employees stop work, often as a protest or as a bargaining tool

work-study *n* an investigation into the most efficient way of doing a job

work surface *n* a rigid flat area on which work is done, e.g. a tabletop or the top of a kitchen unit

worktable /wúrk tayb'l/ *n* a table at which work is done, e.g. writing or drawing

worktop /wúrk top/ *n* a rigid flat surface on which work is done, especially the flat top fitted onto kitchen units, used when preparing food

work-to-rule *n UK, Can* a labour protest in which workers make a point of adhering strictly to the rules of the workplace so that work will slow down

workup /wúrk up/ *n* a complete diagnostic medical examination

workwear /wúrk wair/ *n* clothes worn at work, especially at manual work

workweek /wúrk week/, **work week** *n US* = **working week**

world /wurld/ *n* 1 PLANET EARTH the planet Earth 2 EARTH AND EVERYTHING ON IT the Earth, including all of its inhabitants and the things upon it 3 HUMAN RACE all of the human inhabitants of the Earth ○ *Soon, the world would know the truth.* 4 SOCIETY human society ○ *in the eyes of the world* 5 PART OF EARTH a particular part of the Earth, considered in terms of time or space ○ *the western world* 6 AREA OF ACTIVITY a specified area of human activity and the people involved in it ○ *the world of fashion* 7 UNIVERSE all the galaxies that are known or thought to exist in space 8 DOMAIN a sphere, realm, or domain ○ *the world of reptiles* 9 INHABITED BODY an astronomical body considered to be inhabited, e.g. a planet 10 EVERYTHING IN SOMEBODY'S LIFE all that relates to or makes up the life of an individual ○ *Her entire world collapsed.* 11 CONDITION OF EXISTENCE a condition or state of existence ○ *the world of tomorrow* 12 GREAT DEAL OR AMOUNT a very large amount, degree, or distance ○ *They're still worlds apart.* 13 SECULAR EXISTENCE secular life and its ways ○ *a man of the world* ■ *adj* 1 OF THE ENTIRE WORLD relating to the entire world ○ *the world champions* 2 EXERTING INFLUENCE GLOBALLY exerting influence over the whole of the world ○ *a world figure* 3 AFFECTING WHOLE WORLD involving or affecting the whole of the Earth ○ *a world crisis* [Old English *woruld* 'human existence, age, Earth' < Germanic, 'age of man'] ◇ **come down in the world** to have less money or power than previously ◇ **for all the world** exactly and in every detail ◇ **have the best of both worlds** to have the advantage of the best features of two different situations ◇ **in the world** expresses puzzlement, surprise, or dismay, or gives emphasis to a statement ○ *What in the world have you done?* ◇ **not for the world** no matter what happens ○ *Not for the world would I think of doing such a thing.* ◇ **out of this world** extraordinarily good in some way (*informal*) ◇ **the world is your oyster** there are limitless opportunities available for you to be successful ◇ **think the world of somebody** to be extremely fond of somebody

World Bank *n* a specialized agency of the United Nations established in 1944 that guarantees loans to member nations for the purpose of reconstruction and development. Full form **International Bank for Reconstruction and Development**

world-beating *adj* surpassing all others in a particular field —**world-beater** *n*

world-class *adj* ranked among the best or most prominent in the world ○ *a world-class downhill racer*

World Council of Churches *n* an international ecumenical organization founded in 1948 that links Protestant and Eastern churches from around the world for the purpose of coordinated and cooperative action in religious and secular areas

World Court *n* LAW = **International Court of Justice**

World Cup *n* a sports tournament, especially in football, contested by the national teams of qualifying countries, held every four years on a different continent and in a different country

world economy *n* the economy of the world, considered as an international exchange of goods and services

World English *n* the English language in all its varieties as it is spoken and written over the world

world-famous *adj* renowned throughout the world

World Health Organization *n* a specialized agency of the United Nations that helps countries to improve their health services and coordinates international action against diseases

World Heritage Site *n* an area or structure designated by UNESCO as being of global significance and conserved by a country that has signed a United Nations convention pledging its protection

world language *n* 1 a language that is used in many countries, e.g. English, Spanish, or Arabic 2 a language created for international use, e.g. Esperanto or Interlingua

world leader *n* 1 a leader of a politically and economically powerful country 2 a company, organization, or country that is the biggest or best in a particular field

world-line *n* the path of a particle in time and space, which is straight if the particle moves in a uniform way

worldling /wúrldling/ *n* somebody more interested in everyday material things than in spiritual matters

worldly /wúrldli/ *adj* 1 BELONGING TO PHYSICAL WORLD relating to everyday material existence ○ *all my worldly goods* 2 MATERIALISTIC much more interested in everyday materialistic concerns than in the spiritual side of life 3 EXPERIENCED IN LIFE experienced in and knowledgeable about human society and its ways

worldly-minded *adj* = **worldly** *adj.* 2, **worldly** *adj.* 3

worldly-wise *adj* = **worldly** *adj.* 3

world music *n* popular music from or influenced by countries outside the western world and its traditions

world power *n* a country or alliance of countries powerful enough to influence events on a global scale

World Series *tdmk* a trademark for a series of baseball games played in the United States, between the winners of the American League and the National League to decide the major leagues championship

world's fair *n* an exhibition of commercial and cultural products from many different countries

world-shaking, world-shattering *adj* = **earthshattering**

world soul *n* a spirit believed to animate the world in the same way that the human soul animates the body

World Trade Organization *n* an international organization founded in 1995 to promote and regulate trade between countries

world-view, worldview *n* a comprehensive interpretation or image of the universe and humanity

world war *n* a war involving a number of countries on each side, with fighting spread over much of the world

World War I *n* a war fought in Europe from 1914 to 1918, in which an alliance including Great Britain, France, Russia, Italy, and the United States defeated the alliance of Germany, Austria-Hungary, Turkey, and Bulgaria

World War II *n* a war fought in Europe, Africa, and Asia from 1939 to 1945, in which an alliance including Great Britain, France, the Soviet Union, and the United States defeated the alliance of Germany, Italy, and Japan

world-weary *adj* tired of or bored with life —**world-weariness** *n*

worldwide /wúrld wīd/ *adj* affecting or found throughout the entire world ■ *adv* all over the world

ϟ**World Wide Web** *n* a set of rules to access, manipulate, and download a very large set of hypertext linked documents and other files located on computers connected through the Internet

ϟ**worm** /wurm/ *n* 1 LONG CYLINDRICAL INVERTEBRATE an invertebrate that has a slender, soft, cylindrical or flat body and no apparent appendages, especially an annelid, nematode, or flatworm (*often in combination*) 2 INSECT LARVA the larva of an insect, e.g. a caterpillar, grub, or maggot 3 ANIMAL LOOKING OR MOVING LIKE WORM an animal that looks or moves like a worm, e.g. the shipworm or the slowworm 4 OFFENSIVE TERM an offensive term that deliberately insults somebody regarded as contemptible, especially somebody who behaves in a grovelling way (*insult*) 5 SOMETHING THAT TORMENTS something that torments, undermines, or corrupts a person from within ○ *a worm of discontent* 6 THREADED SHAFT a shaft with a helical thread that is the part of a gear that meshes with a toothed wheel 7 SPIRAL CONDENSER IN STILL a spiral pipe in a still in which alcohol condenses 8 INVASIVE COMPUTER PROGRAM a computer program that invades computers on a network, replicates itself to prevent deletion, interferes with the host computer's operation, and often carries a virus. ◊ **virus** *n.* 3, **Trojan Horse** *n.* 3 ■ *v* 1 *vt* PROCEED DEVIOUSLY to make progress deviously or obsequiously 2 *vt* OBTAIN SOMETHING DEVIOUSLY to obtain something from somebody by devious or underhanded means ○ *They wormed his secret out of him.* 3 *vt* TREAT SOMEBODY FOR PARASITIC WORMS to treat a person or animal in order to prevent or remove an infestation of parasitic worms **4** *vt* **WIND YARN ROUND ROPE** to wind yarn round a rope so as to give it a smooth surface **5** *vi* **MOVE LIKE WORM** to move in a slow, slithering way **6** *vi* **SEARCH FOR WORMS** to search for worms, especially for use as fishing bait [Old English *wurm* < Indo-European] —**wormer** *n* —**wormish** *adj*

ϟ**WORM** /wurm/ *n* a computer storage medium, usually optical, in which data cannot be changed after it is stored but can be read. Full form **write once read many (times)**

wormcast /wúrm kaast/ *n* a small spiral mound of earth or sand that has been excreted by a burrowing earthworm or lugworm

worm-eaten *adj* **1 EATEN INTO BY WORMS** weakened by worms burrowing into it **2 DECAYED** affected by decay or rot **3 DILAPIDATED** old or worn-out

worm fence *n* a fence consisting of crossed poles that support interlocking rails in a zigzag pattern

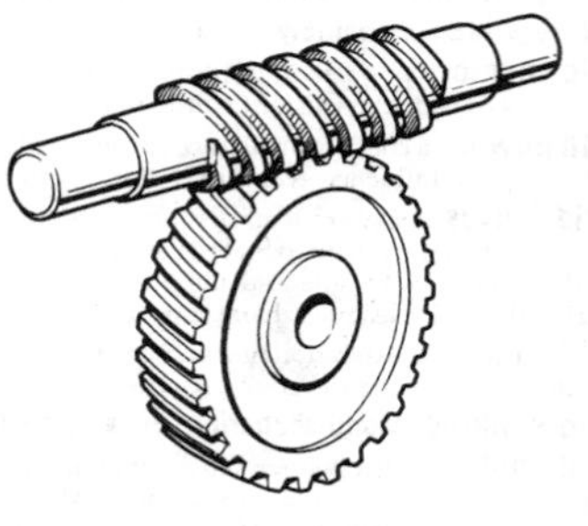

Worm gear

worm gear *n* **1** a gear consisting of a shaft with a helical thread that meshes a toothed wheel to transfer rotary motion between two shafts at right angles to one another **2** ENG = **worm wheel**

worm grass *n* PLANTS = **pinkroot** *n.* 1

wormhole /wúrm hōl/ *n* **1** a hole made by a burrowing worm, e.g. in wood **2** a hypothetical passage in space-time connecting widely separated parts of the universe —**wormholed** *adj*

worm lizard *n* ZOOL = **amphisbaena** *n.* 1

worms /wurmz/ *n* an infestation of parasites, especially pinworms or tapeworms, affecting the intestines or other parts of a person's or animal's body (+ *singular verb*)

Worms /wurmz, vawrmz/ city in SW Germany. Population: 78,415 (1993).

worm's-eye view *n* a view of somebody or something from a lower or inferior position

worm snake *n* a small nonvenomous snake with vestigial eyes. Native to: central and E United States. Genus: *Carphophis*.

worm wheel *n* the toothed wheel that meshes with the threaded shaft in a worm gear

wormwood /wúrm wŏŏd/ *n* **1** a plant that yields a bitter extract. Use: flavouring for absinthe, formerly, medicine for intestinal worms. Genus: *Artemisia*. **2** something that causes somebody to feel bitter (*literary*) ○ *Her ingratitude was wormwood to him.* [14C. By folk etymology < Old English *wermod*, by association with WORM, because the plant was used as medicine for intestinal worms.]

wormy /wúrmi/ *adj* **1** full of or eaten into by worms **2** resembling or characteristic of a worm —**worminess** *n*

worn /wawrn/ past participle of **wear**[1] ■ *adj* **1 SHOWING EFFECTS OF WEAR** weakened or frayed by use **2 SHOWING EFFECTS OF FATIGUE** showing the effects of fatigue, worry, illness, or age **3 HACKNEYED** used so much as to have lost meaning —**wornness** *n*

SPELLCHECK See ***warn***.

worn-out *adj* (*not hyphenated after verbs*) **1 DAMAGED OR WEAKENED BY LONG USE** so damaged or affected by prolonged use as to be no longer usable **2 EXHAUSTED** very tired **3 OUTDATED** no longer relevant, useful, or fashionable

worrisome /wúrrissəm/ *adj* **1** causing anxiety or distress **2** having a tendency to worry —**worrisomely** *adv*

worry /wúrri/ *v* (**-ries, -rying, -ried**) **1** *vti* **BE OR MAKE ANXIOUS** to feel anxious or to cause another person to feel anxious about something unpleasant that may have happened or may happen **2** *vt* **ANNOY ANOTHER** to annoy another person by making insistent demands or complaints **3** *vt* **TRY TO BITE ANIMAL** to try to wound or kill an animal by biting it ○ *a dog suspected of worrying sheep* **4** *vt* = **worry at** *v.* 1 **5** *vi* **PROCEED DESPITE PROBLEMS** to proceed persistently despite problems or obstacles ○ *worried the project along despite continued delays* **6** *vt* **TOUCH SOMETHING REPEATEDLY** to touch, move, or interfere with something repeatedly ○ *Stop worrying that button or it'll come off.* ■ *n* (*plural* **-ries**) **1 ANXIOUSNESS** a feeling of anxiety or concern **2 CAUSE OF ANXIETY** something that causes anxiety or concern **3 PERIOD OF ANXIETY** a period spent feeling anxious or concerned [Old English *wyrgan*. Originally in the sense 'strangle'.] —**worried** *adj* —**worriedly** *adv* —**worriedness** *n* —**worrier** *n* —**worrying** *adj* —**worryingly** *adv* ◇ **not to worry** used to tell somebody that something is not important and need not be a cause of concern ○ *Not to worry. We'll do better next time.*

SYNONYMS ***worry, unease, care, anxiety, angst, stress***

CORE MEANING: a troubled mind

worry a troubled state of mind resulting from concern about current or potential difficulties; **unease** a feeling of anxiousness or lack of satisfaction with a situation; **care** a state of troubled anxiety; **anxiety** nervous apprehension about a future event or a general fear of possible misfortune; **angst** nonspecific chronic anxiety about the human condition or the state of the world; **stress** the worry and nervous apprehension related to a particular situation or event, for example a job or the process of moving house.

worry at *vt* **1** to shake or tear at something with the teeth **2** to think about a problem repeatedly in an effort to find a solution

worry beads *npl* a string of beads for fingering or playing with when feeling tense

worryguts /wúrri guts/ (*plural* **-guts**) *n* somebody who tends to worry needlessly (*informal*) US term **worrywart**

worrywart /wúrri wawrt/ *n US* = **worryguts** (*informal*)

worse /wurss/ comparative of **bad, badly, ill** ■ *adj* **1 LESS GOOD THAN SOMETHING ELSE** less good in quality or effect than before or than somebody or something else ○ *did a worse job on the decorating than the previous workers* **2 MORE SEVERE** more severe than before or than something else of the same kind ○ *The patient's fever is worse this morning.* **3 SICKER** more ill than before ○ *The patient is worse today.* ■ *adv* **TO A WORSE DEGREE** to a degree worse than before ■ *n* **SOMETHING WORSE** somebody or something that is worse than another ○ *Of the two of them, this one's the worse.* [Old English *wyrsa* < Germanic] ◇ **be none the worse for something** to experience no harm or ill effects from something ◇ **if worse comes to worst** if the situation reaches an intolerable state

worsen /wúrss'n/ *vti* to become or cause something to become worse

worser /wúrssər/ comparative of **bad** (*nonstandard*)

worship /wúrship/ *v* (**-ships, -shipping, -shipped**) **1** *vti* **TREAT SOMEBODY OR SOMETHING AS DEITY** to treat somebody or something as divine and show respect by engaging in acts of prayer and devotion **2** *vt* **LOVE SOMEBODY DEEPLY** to love, admire, or respect somebody or something greatly and perhaps excessively or unquestioningly **3** *vi* **TAKE PART IN RELIGIOUS SERVICE** to take part in a religious service ■ *n* **1 RELIGIOUS ADORATION** the adoration, devotion, and respect given to a deity **2 RELIGIOUS RITES** the rites or services through which people show their adoration, devotion, and respect for a deity **3 GREAT DEVOTION** great or excessive love, admiration, and respect felt for somebody or something [Old English *weorþscipe* 'condition of worth' < *weorþ* 'worth'] —**worshippable** *adj* —**worshipper** *n* —**worshippingly** *adv*

Worship *n UK, Can* a title of respect for a mayor, magistrate, or other similar dignitary ○ *His Worship, the Mayor*

worshipful /wúrshipf'l/ *adj* **1** showing or expressing deep reverence and devotion **2** **worshipful, Worshipful** used as the honouring adjective in the titles of some dignitaries, e.g. mayors, and of the ancient guild companies of the City of London —**worshipfully** *adv* —**worshipfulness** *n*

worst /wurst/ superlative of **bad, badly, ill** ■ *adj* **LEAST GOOD** least good, most unpleasant, or most unfavourable ○ *your worst enemy* ○ *My worst forebodings were soon realized.* ■ *adv* **LEAST WELL** in the least good, most unpleasant, or most unfavourable way ■ *n* **LEAST GOOD THING** the least good, least pleasant, or least favourable aspect or part of something, or the worst thing that could happen or be done ○ *fear the worst* ○ *The worst was over* ■ *vt* **DEFEAT** to get the better of or defeat an opponent [Old English *wyrsta* < Indo-European, 'confuse'] ◇ **get the worst of it** to be defeated, or get the least benefit from something

worst case *n* the least desirable, most disastrous situation or result that can be envisaged (*hyphenated before nouns*) ○ *the worst-case scenario*

worsted /wŏŏstid/ *n* **1** smooth closely-woven woollen cloth without a nap, made from tightly twisted yarn **2** the tightly twisted yarn, made from long-fibred wool, from which worsted cloth is made [13C. After the village of *Worstead* in Norfolk,.]

wort[1] /wurt/ *n* a medicinal plant (*usually in combination*) [Old English *wyrt* < Indo-European, 'branch, root']

wort[2] /wurt/ *n* a sugary liquid produced from crushed malted grain and water, to which yeast and hops are added in the brewing of beer [Old English *wyrt* < Germanic]

worth /wurth/ *n* **1 VALUE IN MONEY** the value of something, especially in terms of money ○ *The necklace has little real worth, but it means a lot to me.* **2 AMOUNT EQUALLING GIVEN VALUE** the amount of something that can be bought for a particular sum of money or that will last for a particular length of time ○ *twenty pounds' worth of petrol* **3 MORAL OR SOCIAL VALUE** the goodness, usefulness, or importance of something or somebody, irrespective of financial value or wealth ○ *A diploma from that place has little worth.* **4 WEALTH** the wealth of a person, group, organization, or other entity ■ *adj* **1 EQUAL IN VALUE TO STATED AMOUNT** equivalent in value to the amount stated ○ *How much is it worth?* ○ *a painting worth thousands* **2 IMPORTANT ENOUGH TO JUSTIFY** important, large, or good enough to justify something ○ *His friendship is not worth having.* [Old English *weorþ* < Indo-European, 'turn'] ◇ **for all you are worth** as fast, energetically, or enthusiastically as possible ◇ **for what it's worth** used to suggest that what you say may not be true or of much value ○ *Here's my opinion on the issue, for what it's worth.*

Worthing /wúrthing/ seaside resort in SE England. Population: 95,732 (1991).

worthless /wúrthləss/ *adj* **1** having no financial or other value or usefulness **2** bad, incompetent, or totally lacking good, attractive, or admirable qualities —**worthlessly** *adv* —**worthlessness** *n*

worthwhile /wúrth wíl/ *adj* rewarding or beneficial enough to justify the time taken or the effort made [Mid-17C. Shortening of *worth the while*.] —**worthwhileness** *n*

USAGE One word or two? ***Worthwhile*** is now usually written as one word, and the traditional rule that it should be written as two words after a verb (*It seemed worth while* but *It was a worthwhile thing to do*) is largely disappearing.

worthy /wúrthi/ *adj* (**-thier, -thiest**) **1 DESERVING** fully deserving something, usually as a suitable reward for merit or importance ○ *That remark is not worthy of a reply.* **2 RESPECTABLE** morally upright, good, and deserving respect **3 GOOD BUT DULL** having good qualities, good intentions, or the best of motives, but being boring and pedestrian ■ *n* (*plural* **-thies**) **SOMEBODY GOOD OR MORAL** a good, morally upright, or reputable person (*often ironic*) ○ *colonial governors and other 18th-century worthies* —**worthily** *adv* —**worthiness** *n*

wot[1] /wot/ *pron, det, adv* a spelling of 'what' (*informal or humorous*) ○ *Wot they done then?*

wot[2] 1st person present singular, 3rd person present singular of **wit**[2] (*archaic*)

Wotan /vṓ taan, -tan/ *n* in Germanic mythology, the supreme god and the god of war

wotcher /wóchər/, **wotcha** /wóchə/ *interj* hello (*slang*) [Late 19C. Contraction of 'what cheer'.]

would /wŏŏd/ CORE MEANING: used to express the sense of 'will' in reported speech or when referring to an event that has not happened yet ○ *Susan didn't think she would pass.* ○ *It would be wrong to suggest otherwise.*

vi **1 USED WITH 'IF' CLAUSES** used in stating what will, or suggesting what might, happen under the circumstances described in the conditional clause ○ *You would know him if you saw him.* ○ *My mother would be annoyed if I were late.* **2 POLITE REQUEST** used in making polite requests or offers ○ *Would you mind closing the window?* ○ *Would you like more coffee?* **3 HABITUAL ACTION** used to indicate that a past action was habitual ○ *Every Sunday we would drive out to Henley.* ◇ **would that** used to introduce a strong desire or wish, usually one that is not expected to be fulfilled (*formal*) ○ *Would that we had never met.*

SPELLCHECK See ***wood***.

USAGE See ***should***.

USAGE would have or **would of?** Substituting ***would have*** for *had* in an *if* clause (one stating a condition contrary to fact) is a grammatical error. Do not write: *If they would have done it right to begin with, these problems would not exist.* Write instead: *If they had done it right...* or, more formally, *Had they done it right to begin with, these problems would not exist.* Avoid the incorrect form *they'd + have*, as in *If they'd have done it right...*; here *they'd* is a contraction for *they had*. Write instead *If they'd done it right...* or *If they had done it right...* Although the nonstandard form *would of* sounds similar to the contracted form *would've*, it is incorrect to use it for *would have*: *It would have/would've* [not *would of*] *been nice if you'd told me this before.*

would-be *adj* who hopes, or is trying, to do or be something ○ *a would-be poet* ■ *n* a person who is hoping or trying to become something or achieve the status of something (*informal*) ○ *The reception was attended by all the major candidates for office and other would-bes.*

wouldn't /wo͝odd'nt/ *contr* would not

would've /wo͝oddəv/ *contr* would have

Woulfe bottle /wo͝olf-/ *n* a vessel with more than one neck. Use: bubbling gases through liquids. [After Peter Woulfe (1727?–1803), English chemist]

wound[1] /woond/ *n* **1 INJURY TO BODY** an injury in which the skin, tissue, or an organ is broken by some external force, e.g. a blow or surgical incision, with damage to the underlying tissue **2 EMOTIONAL INJURY** a lasting emotional or psychological injury ○ *still recovering from the wounds of a bitter divorce* ■ *vti* **1 INJURE** to cause a wound in the body of somebody or something, especially using a knife, gun, or other weapon ○ *He was wounded in the leg.* **2 CAUSE EMOTIONAL WOUND** to cause somebody emotional or psychological distress by saying or doing something ○ *cutting remarks intended to wound* [Old English *wund* < Indo-European, 'beat'] —**woundable** *adj* —**wounded** *adj* —**wounder** *n* —**wounding** *adj* —**woundingly** *adv* —**woundless** *adj*

wound[2] /wownd/ past participle, past tense of **wind**[2]

Wounded Knee /wo͝ondid née/ village in SW South Dakota, site of a massacre of mostly unarmed Native North Americans in 1890

woundwort /wo͝ond wurt/ (*plural* **-worts** *or* **-wort**) *n* **1** betony or a related plant of the mint family. Use: formerly, to treat wounds. Genus: *Stachys*. **2** any plant formerly used to treat wounds

wove past tense of **weave**[1]

woven /wōvən/ past participle of **weave**[1] ■ *adj* made or manufactured by the process of weaving ○ *woven synthetic textiles*

wove paper *n* paper made using a roller with a fine mesh that leaves a faint mesh imprint

wow[1] /wow/ *interj* **EXPRESSING SURPRISE** used to express surprise, admiration, wonder, or pleasure (*informal*) ■ *vt* **IMPRESS SOMEBODY GREATLY** to impress or delight somebody greatly (*informal*) ○ *The acrobats wowed the audience with their daring moves.* ■ *n* **GREAT SUCCESS** a great success or an object of great admiration (*informal*) [Early 16C. A natural interjection.]

wow[2] /wow/ *n* a distortion in recorded sound in the form of slow fluctuations in the pitch of long notes, caused by variations in the speed of the reproducing or recording equipment [Mid-20C. An imitation of the acoustic effect.]

WOW *abbr* waiting on weather

wowser /wówzər/ *n* ANZ (*informal*) **1** somebody with a puritanical disposition who disapproves of activities such as drinking and dancing **2** a person who disrupts or ruins the fun of others [Late 19C. < ?]

⚡**WP** *abbr* **1** weather permitting **2** without prejudice **3** word processing **4** word processor

W particle *n* an elementary particle with a relatively large mass and either positively or negatively charged, believed to mediate weak interactions between other particles in which the charges on the particles change

WPB, w.p.b. *abbr* waste paper basket

WPC *abbr* woman police constable

WPGA *abbr* Women's Professional Golfers' Association

WPI *abbr* wholesale price index

wpm *abbr* words per minute

wpn *abbr* weapon

Wraac /rak/ *n* Aus a member of the Women's Royal Australian Army Corps

WRAC /rak/ *abbr* Women's Royal Army Corps

wrack[1] /rak/ *n* **1 MARINE VEGETATION** seaweed floating in the sea or growing on the shoreline **2 BROWN SEAWEED** any brown seaweed, e.g. bladderwrack. Family: Fucaceae. **3 WRECKED SHIP** a wrecked ship, especially one driven onto the shore (*archaic*) **4 WRECKAGE** wreckage or a piece of wreckage (*archaic*) ■ *vti* **WRECK OR BE WRECKED** to wreck something or be wrecked (*archaic*) [14C. < Dutch *wrak* 'wreck'.]

wrack[2] *n* = **rack**[6]

WRAF /raf/ *abbr* Women's Royal Air Force

wraith /rayth/ (*plural* **wraiths**) *n* **1** the ghost of a dead person, or any ghostly and insubstantial apparition **2** a vision of a person still alive, said to appear as a premonition of that person's death [Early 16C. < ?] —**wraith-like** *adj*

Wrangel Island /ráng g'l-/ island of NE Russia, in the Arctic Ocean. Area: 4,660 sq. km/1,800 sq. mi.

Wrangell Mountains /ráng g'l-/ mountain range in SE Alaska. Highest peak: Mount Blackburn 4,996 m/16,390 ft.

wrangle /ráng g'l/ *v* (**-gles, -gling, -gled**) **1** *vi* **ARGUE NOISILY** to argue noisily and persistently ○ *wrangled for hours over the wording of the agreement* **2** *vt* **GET SOMETHING BY PERSISTENT ARGUMENT** to obtain something or persuade somebody by arguing persistently (*informal*) ○ *managed to wrangle a commitment to peace out of the opposing side* **3** *vt* US, Can **HERD ANIMALS** to herd horses or cattle ■ *n* **LONG ARGUMENT** a lengthy or noisy and bad-tempered argument or dispute [14C. < Germanic.]

wrangler /ráng glər/ *n* **1** Can, US **SOMEBODY WHO LOOKS AFTER HORSES** a worker who takes care of horses kept for riding on a ranch **2 SOMEBODY INVOLVED IN LENGTHY ARGUMENT** a noisy and persistent arguer, or a participant in a lengthy argument **3 MATHS STUDENT WITH FIRST CLASS HONOURS** at Cambridge University, somebody who achieves first class honours in the final undergraduate examinations in mathematics

wrap /rap/ *v* (**wraps, wrapping, wrapped**) **1** *vt* **COVER SOMETHING UP** to cover something up by winding or folding a pliable material such as cloth or paper around it ○ *The package was wrapped in plain brown paper.* **2** *vti* **COIL AROUND** to wind, fold, or clasp something, oneself, or itself around somebody or something else ○ *He wrapped his arms around the pole and wouldn't let go.* **3** *vt* **FOLD SOMETHING UP** to fold or roll something up into a compact bundle ○ *linen napkins neatly wrapped* **4** *vt* **ENVELOP** to envelop and obscure or conceal something ○ *Fog wrapped the harbour.* **5** *vt* **GIVE SOMETHING AURA** to surround something with a particular type of atmosphere or quality such as secrecy or scandal ○ *The whole affair was wrapped in secrecy.* **6** *vt* **ENGROSS** to occupy the mind and attention of somebody fully ○ *wrapped in thought* **7** *vi* **FINISH FILMING** to finish filming or video-taping something ○ *We're scheduled to wrap at the end of the month.* **8** *vi* US **FINISH** to come to an end ○ *'The government's antitrust case ... was supposed to wrap by the end of the year'.* (*Newsweek*; November 1998) **9** *vti* **TAKE SOMETHING OVER TO NEXT LINE** to take a word or piece of text over to the next line automatically on reaching the margin, or to be taken over in this way **10 wrap, rap** *vt* Aus **PRAISE** to sing somebody's praises ■ *n* **1 OUTER GARMENT** an outer garment such as a shawl, cloak, or coat to be wrapped or folded around the wearer **2 MATERIAL FOR WRAPPING** material, or a piece of material, used to wrap something **3 COMPLETION OF FILMING** the completion of filming or video-taping something ○ *All right, everybody, that's a wrap!* **4 FILLED TORTILLA SANDWICH** a sandwich consisting of fillings enclosed in a tortilla **5** Aus **PIECE OF PRAISE** a praising comment or assessment of something (*informal*) [14C. < ?] ◇ **keep something under wraps** to keep something secret ○ *Our new product is being kept under wraps for the moment.*

wrap up *v* **1** *vt* **COVER SOMETHING WITH MATERIAL** to cover something completely with material such as paper, plastic, or foil **2** *vi* **DON WARM CLOTHES** to put on warm clothes for protection from the cold, wind, or rain ○ *Wrap up well, it's freezing outside.* **3** *vt* **COMPLETE** to complete something or bring it to an end (*informal*) ○ *We'll wrap up the editing phase of the project next week.* **4** *vt* US **SUMMARIZE** to give a short final summary of something such as the news **5** *vi* **BE SILENT** to stop talking and be silent (*informal; usually a command*) **6** *vt* Aus **PRAISE** to sing somebody's praises (*informal*) ◇ **wrapped up in somebody** *or* **something** completely absorbed by or preoccupied with somebody or something ○ *She is completely wrapped up in her career.*

⚡**wraparound** /ráppə rownd/, **wrapround** /ráp rownd/ *adj* **1 DESIGNED FOR WRAPPING AROUND BODY** designed to be worn wrapped around the body and tied in position with one edge overlapping the other rather than fastened with buttons or a zip **2 CURVING AROUND SIDES** curving around the sides of whatever it is fitted to ■ *n* **1 WRAPAROUND GARMENT** a wraparound skirt or other piece of clothing **2 WRAPAROUND FITMENT** a fitment that is shaped to curve around the sides of something **3 COMPUTER FUNCTION AUTOMATICALLY STARTING NEW LINE** a function of a computer program or visual display unit that makes text automatically begin a new line as soon as the last character space in the previous line is filled **4 PAPER STRIP AROUND BOOK'S DUST COVER** a strip of paper fastened around the dust cover of a book, e.g. to announce a price reduction **5 PLATE FOR ATTACHING TO PRESS CYLINDER** a plate of flexible material that can be attached to the cylinder of a rotary press

wrapover /ráppōvər/ *adj* CLOTHING = **wraparound** *adj.* 1 ■ *n* CLOTHING = **wraparound** *n.* 1

wrapped /rapt/ *adj* Aus extremely pleased (*informal*) [Mid-20C. Blend of *wrapped (up in)* + RAPT.]

wrapper /ráppər/ *n* **1 MATERIAL WRAPPED AROUND** the paper, plastic, or other material wrapped around something that is sold **2** PUBL = **dust jacket 3 PAPER AROUND MAGAZINE OR NEWSPAPER** a piece of paper wrapped around a magazine or newspaper sent by post **4 TOBACCO LEAF FORMING OUTSIDE OF CIGAR** a tobacco leaf wrapped around a cigar to form its outer skin **5 LOOSE LOUNGING GARMENT** a garment such as a dressing gown that wraps loosely around the body (*dated*)

wrapping /rápping/ *n* the paper, plastic, or other material used to wrap something

wrapround *n, adj* = **wraparound**

wrap-up *n* **1** US a short summary at the end of something such as a news bulletin **2** Aus a praising comment or assessment of something (*informal*)

wrasse /rass/ (*plural* **wrasses** *or* **wrasse**) *n* a fish with protruding lips and well-developed canine teeth. Native to: temperate and tropical seas. Family: Labridae. [Late 17C. < Cornish *wrah* 'old woman'.]

wrath /roth/ *n* **1 GREAT ANGER** fury often marked by a desire for vengeance **2 DIVINE RETRIBUTION** God's punishment for sin **3 VENGEANCE** the vengeance, punishment, or destruction wreaked by somebody in anger (*literary*) ■ *adj* **FURIOUS** full of anger (*archaic or literary*) [Old English *wrǣþþu* < *wrāþ* 'angry'] —**wrathful** *adj* —**wrathfully** *adv* —**wrathfulness** *n* —**wrathless** *adj*

SYNONYMS See ***anger***.

Wrath, Cape /roth/ the northernmost point of the west of mainland Scotland

Wray /ray/, **Fay** (*b.* 1907) Canadian-born US actor

wreak /reek/ *vt* **1 CAUSE HAVOC OR DESTRUCTION** to cause something violent and destructive ○ *a storm that wreaked vast destruction* **2 INFLICT REVENGE** to inflict something violent, especially revenge or punishment, on somebody **3 EXPRESS ANGER OR HATRED** to express anger, hatred, or another violent emotion in action against somebody (*literary*) [Old English *wrecan* 'drive out' < Indo-European] —**wreaker** *n*

SPELLCHECK See ***reek***.

USAGE See ***wrought***.

wreath /reeth/ (*plural* **wreaths** /reethz, reeths/) *n* **1 CIRCULAR ARRANGEMENT OF FLOWERS** a circular arrangement of flowers and greenery placed as a memorial on a grave, hung up as a decoration, or put on somebody's head as a sign of honour **2 REPRESENTATION OF WREATH** a representation of a circular arrangement of flowers, vines, or other things, e.g. in a carving or on a coat of arms

3 CIRCULAR SHAPE a hollow circular shape formed by something such as smoke [Old English *wriþa* < *wrīþan* (see WRITHE)] —**wreathless** *adj*

wreathe /reeth/ (**wreathes, wreathing, wreathed**) *v* 1 *vt* PUT WREATH ON OR AROUND to encircle, surround, or cover something with a wreath or wreaths or a similar type of decoration 2 *vt* MAKE SOMETHING INTO WREATH BY INTERTWINING to make things into a wreath by twisting and intertwining them 3 *vti* WRITHE OR COIL to move, or to cause something to move, in coils, curves, or spirals [Mid-16C. Partly < WREATH, partly back-formation < *wrethen* 'twisted', obsolete past participle of WRITHE.]

wreck /rek/ *vt* 1 DESTROY OR DAMAGE to destroy something completely or damage it beyond repair 2 DESTROY SHIP to cause a ship to sink or run aground and be destroyed ■ *n* 1 DESTRUCTION OF SHIP the sinking or destruction at sea of a ship from accidental causes 2 BADLY DAMAGED SHIP a very badly damaged or sunken ship 3 CARGO FROM WRECKED SHIP cargo or other goods that are washed ashore after a shipwreck 4 REMAINS OF SOMETHING DESTROYED something that has been totally destroyed, or its shattered remains 5 SOMETHING BADLY DAMAGED something that is in very poor condition, damaged, or dilapidated 6 SOMEBODY LOOKING OR FEELING TERRIBLE a person who is physically or emotionally exhausted or broken down 7 DESTRUCTION the ruin or destruction of something 8 *US* = **crash**[1] *n.* 1 [13C. < Anglo-Norman *wrec* < N Germanic.]

wreckage /rékij/ *n* 1 the broken pieces left after something has been extremely badly damaged or destroyed 2 the wrecking, ruining, or destruction of something (*formal*)

wrecked /rekt/ *adj* 1 very tired or exhausted (*informal*) 2 in an intoxicated or drugged state (*slang*)

wrecker /rékər/ *n* 1 DESTROYER OR SPOILER a person who destroys or spoils something, especially deliberately, maliciously, or with pleasure ○ *He's a wrecker of others' dreams.* 2 *US, Can* SOMEBODY DEMOLISHING BUILDINGS OR DISMANTLING CARS somebody whose job is to demolish buildings or dismantle old cars for salvage 3 *US* AUTOMOT = **breakdown lorry** 4 SOMEBODY LURING SHIPS TO DESTRUCTION formerly, somebody who lured ships onto rocks in order to steal the cargo or other goods on board

wrecker's ball *n US* BUILDING = **wrecking ball**

wreckfish /rék fish/ (*plural* **-fish** *or* **-fishes**) *n* ZOOL = **stone bass** [Late 19C. < its habit of following wreckage.]

wrecking ball *n* a heavy ball attached by a cable to a crane and swung to knock down parts of buildings that are being demolished

wrecking bar *n* a short crowbar forked at one end and bent at the other to provide leverage

Wrekin /réekin/ hill in west-central England, near the River Severn. Height: 407 m/1,335 ft.

wren /ren/ *n* 1 a small songbird with a long slender downturned bill, usually brown feathers, and a short upright tail. Native to: Europe, Asia, North and South America. Family: Troglodytidae. 2 = **fairy wren** [Old English *wrenna*]

Wren /ren/ *n* a member of the former Women's Royal Naval Service [Early 20C. < WRNS.]

Wren /ren/, **Sir Christopher** (1632–1723) English architect, scientist, and mathematician

wrench /rench/ *v* 1 *vti* PULL AND TWIST SOMETHING AWAY to pull something away forcefully, often using a twisting movement ○ *He angrily wrenched the bag away from the cashier and left the shop.* 2 *vt* INJURE SOMETHING BY TWISTING to injure part of the body by twisting it suddenly and forcibly 3 *vt* DISTRESS to make somebody feel very sad or distressed 4 *vt* SKEW MEANING OR FUNCTION to distort something in order to make it mean or appear to be something different ■ *n* 1 FORCEFUL TWISTING PULL a forceful twisting pull at something, especially to free it 2 ADJUSTABLE SPANNER a spanner, especially a large one, with adjustable jaws 3 *US* = **spanner** *n.* 4 SADNESS AND LOSS ON PARTING a difficult parting from a person or place, or the feelings of sadness and loss that accompany such a parting ○ *Leaving New York was a terrible wrench after having lived there for 30 years.* 5 SURGE OF EMOTION a sudden surge of emotion, e.g. pity or empathy ○ *the wrench we felt when viewing film footage of the flood's devastation* 6 SPRAIN CAUSED BY TWISTING a sprain caused by a sudden forceful twisting movement of a part of the body [Old English *wrencan* < Indo-European, 'turn']

wrest /rest/ *vt* 1 GAIN CONTROL OR POWER to take something such as control or power from somebody in the face of opposition or resistance 2 PULL SOMETHING AWAY FORCIBLY to seize something with the hands and take it away from somebody by using physical force 3 GET SOMETHING WITH EFFORT to get or extract something with an effort or struggle 4 ALTER SOMETHING'S MEANING to change or twist the meaning of something ■ *n* FORCEFUL PULL a sharp wrench or pull at something [Old English *wrǣstan* < Germanic] —**wrester** *n*

wrestle /réss'l/ *v* (**-tles, -tling, -tled**) 1 *vti* FIGHT BY GRIPPING AND PUSHING to fight somebody using special holds and moves in an attempt to force his or her shoulders onto a mat 2 *vti* HAVE A STRUGGLING FIGHT to fight with somebody by gripping and pushing rather than hitting him or her 3 *vi* HAVE DIFFICULTY to struggle to deal with something difficult or intractable ○ *I spent the evening wrestling with my accounts.* 4 *vti* MANOEUVRE SOMETHING AWKWARD to struggle to lift or move something ○ *We wrestled the trunk down the hall.* ■ *n* 1 FIGHT BETWEEN WRESTLERS a wrestling match or a fight in which people wrestle rather than hit each other 2 A STRUGGLE WITH SOMETHING DIFFICULT a struggle to deal with something difficult or intractable [Old English. < *wrǣstan* (see WREST).] —**wrestler** *n*

wrestling /réssling/ *n* 1 a sport in which two contestants fight by gripping each other using special holds, each trying to force the other's shoulders onto a mat 2 the action of having a struggling fight with somebody

wretch /rech/ *n* 1 SOMEBODY MISERABLE a troubled or distressed person who evokes pity in others 2 ANNOYING PERSON a person who causes mild irritation or annoyance (*humorous*) 3 DESPICABLE PERSON a person viewed with contempt or disapproval (*formal*) [Old English *wrecca* < W Germanic]

SPELLCHECK See *retch*.

wretched /réchid/ *adj* 1 UNHAPPY OR ILL feeling very unhappy or ill 2 APPEARING MISERABLE OR DEPRIVED in a state of great hardship, deprivation, and hopelessness and arousing sympathy in others ○ *living in wretched conditions* 3 INADEQUATE OR OF LOW QUALITY seriously inadequate or of very low quality 4 IRRITATING provoking irritation or anger ○ *The wretched car won't start!* —**wretchedly** *adv* —**wretchedness** *n*

Wrexham /réksəm/ town in NE Wales, near the border with England. Population: 41,300 (1995).

wrick *vt, n* MED = **rick**[2]

wrier comparative of **wry**

wriest superlative of **wry**

wriggle /rigg'l/ *v* (**-gles, -gling, -gled**) 1 *vti* TWIST AND TURN to make quick small twisting and turning movements with the body, or to cause the body to make these movements 2 *vi* MOVE WHILE TWISTING AND TURNING to move by making quick twisting and turning movements ○ *managed to wriggle out of the sleeping bag* ■ *n* 1 TWISTING OR TURNING MOVEMENT a short twisting or turning movement 2 TWISTING PASSAGE OR COURSE a twisting passage or line [14C. Probably < Middle Low German *wriggelen* < *wriggen* 'turn'.] —**wriggler** *n* —**wriggly** *adj*

wriggle out of *vt* to avoid doing something or suffering the consequences of something by making excuses or using deception

Wright /rīt/, **Billy** (1924–94) British footballer. Born **William Ambrose Wright**

Wright, Frank Lloyd (1869–1959) US architect

Wright, Joseph (1734–97) British painter. Known as **Joseph Wright of Derby**

Wright, Joseph (1855–1930) British philologist

Wright, Judith Arundell (*b.* 1915) Australian poet.

Wright, Orville (1871–1958) US inventor and aviation pioneer.

Wright, Peter (*b.* 1916) British intelligence officer

Wright, Wilbur (1867–1912) US inventor and aviation pioneer

wring /ring/ *vt* (**wrings, wringing, wrung** /rung/, **wrung**) 1 TWIST AND COMPRESS to twist and compress something in order to force liquid out of it ○ *Wring the towel out and hang it up to dry.* 2 FORCE OUT LIQUID BY TWISTING to force liquid out of something by twisting and compressing it 3 EXTRACT SOMETHING WITH DIFFICULTY to extract something from somebody with great difficulty ○ *finally managed to wring an answer out of him* 4 TWIST SOMETHING FORCIBLY AND PAINFULLY to twist something forcefully, e.g. an animal's

Library of Congress

Wilbur (right) and Orville Wright

neck, usually causing pain or death 5 CAUSE DISTRESS to cause somebody emotional pain and distress ■ *n* TWIST GIVEN TO WET MATERIAL a twist or squeeze given to wet material in order to force out water or other liquid [Old English *wringen* < Germanic]

SPELLCHECK See *ring*.

wringer /ríngər/ *n* HOUSEHOLD = **mangle**[2] *n.* ◇ **put somebody through the wringer** *US* to subject somebody to a very difficult or stressful experience (*informal*)

wringing wet *adj* extremely wet

wrinkle /ríngk'l/ *n* 1 FACIAL LINE FROM AGEING a line or crease between small folds of skin that forms on the face as a result of ageing or exposure to the sun 2 SMALL FOLD IN MATERIAL a small untidy or unintentional fold in cloth or paper 3 PROBLEM something that causes trouble or inconvenience ○ *We need to iron out the wrinkles in the plan before implementing it.* 4 NEW FEATURE an ingenious trick, method of doing something, or feature of something (*informal*) ○ *We've added a couple of new wrinkles to the policy.* ■ *vti* (**-kles, -kling, -kled**) 1 MAKE OR GET SMALL UNTIDY FOLDS to make small untidy or unintentional folds in something, or to come to have untidy folds ○ *This fabric wrinkles easily.* 2 MAKE OR GET LINES ON SKIN to develop lines or to cause lines to develop in the skin as a result of ageing or exposure to the sun 3 CONTRACT PART OF FACE to tighten the muscles in part of the face so that it contracts or creases [14C. < ?] —**wrinkled** *adj* —**wrinkleless** *adj*

wrinkly /ríngkli/ *adj* (**-klier, -kliest**) covered with wrinkles ■ *n* an offensive and condescending term for somebody of advanced age (*slang offensive*)

wrist /rist/ *n* 1 the lower end of the forearm or the joint between the forearm and the hand together with the tissue surrounding it 2 the part of a sleeve or glove that covers the wrist [Old English < Germanic]

wristband /ríst band/ *n* 1 ABSORBENT BAND WORN ROUND WRIST an absorbent band of material worn round the wrist to keep sweat from running onto the hand 2 WATCH STRAP the strap of a wristwatch 3 IDENTIFICATION BAND WORN ROUND WRIST an identification band worn round the wrist, e.g. when in hospital 4 PART OF SOMETHING COVERING WRIST a band of material that fits over the wrist, e.g. at the end of a long sleeve or on a glove

wrist-drop *n* inability to move the muscles that raise the wrist and move the fingers, caused by damage to or compression of the radial nerve

wristlet /rístlət/ *n* a close-fitting band of material worn round the wrist, especially a decorative one that is attached to the top of a glove or the end of a sleeve

wristlock /ríst lok/ *n* a hold in wrestling in which the wrist is held and twisted, rendering an opponent helpless

wrist pin *n US, Can* MECH ENG = **gudgeon pin**

ϟ**wrist support, wrist rest** *n* a long rectangular pad in front of a keyboard on which a keyboarder's wrists can rest, designed to help prevent repetitive strain injury

wristwatch /ríst woch/ *n* a watch on a band that is worn round the wrist

wristy /rísti/ (**-ier, -iest**) *adj* using a lot of wrist movement when hitting a ball

writ[1] /rit/ *n* 1 a written court order demanding that the addressee do or stop doing whatever is specified in the order 2 a piece of written text (*archaic*) [Old English, 'something written' < *wrītan* (see WRITE)]

writ[2] past tense, past participle of **write** (*archaic*)

write /rīt/ (**writes, writing, wrote** /rōt/ *or* **writ** *archaic* /rit/, **written** /rítt'n/ *or* **writ** *archaic* /rit/) *v* **1** *vti* PUT WORDS ON PAPER to put words, letters, numbers, or musical notation on a surface using a pen, pencil, or similar instrument **2** *vti* CREATE BOOK, POEM, OR MUSIC to create or compose something for others to read or listen to, e.g. a letter or note, an article, a poem, or a piece of music **3** *vti* COMPOSE AND SEND LETTER to compose and send a letter to somebody ○ *I wrote her a long letter.* **4** *vi* COMPOSE MATERIAL FOR PUBLICATION to create books, poems, or newspaper articles for publication, often as part of a job **5** *vt* FILL IN FORM to fill in the details on a form such as a cheque, prescription, or other document and, usually, sign it ○ *I'll write you a cheque.* **6** *vt* TELL SOMETHING IN WORDS to say something in a letter, book, or article ○ *He wrote that he would be home on Tuesday.* **7** *vt* SPELL to spell a word or words ○ *two words that are written the same but mean different things* **8** *vi* WORK AS WRITING TOOL to function as a writing instrument ○ *There's something wrong with this pen: it won't write.* **9** *vti* USE CURSIVE SCRIPT to employ a cursive script when setting down words **10** *vt* DISPLAY to reveal or exhibit something clearly ○ *She had glee written all over her face.* **11** *vt* INSUR = **underwrite** *v.* 1 **12** *vt* PREDETERMINE to ordain or prophesy what will happen in the future (*usually passive*) ○ *It is written: your future is preordained.* **13** *vt* STORE COMPUTER DATA to transfer data to a storage medium such as a magnetic or optical disc or tape **14** *vt* DISPLAY SOMETHING ON SCREEN to display text or images on a computer monitor [Old English *wrītan* 'score, draw, write' < Germanic, 'to tear']

write away *vt* to send off an order for goods of some kind to a distant supplier ○ *wrote away for new upholstery materials*

write down *vt* **1** RECORD SOMETHING IN WORDS to record something in writing, usually so that the information is not lost or forgotten ○ *I wrote down her address.* **2** OVERSIMPLIFY SOMETHING FOR UNSOPHISTICATED AUDIENCE to write in excessively simplified language for the benefit of an audience considered to be unsophisticated, inexperienced, or unintelligent **3** WRITE DISPARAGINGLY ABOUT to write slightingly or disparagingly about somebody **4** REDUCE THE ENTERED VALUE OF to reduce the price or value of something, especially the value of an asset as entered in the accounts of a business

write in *v* **1** *vt* WRITE DETAILS IN FORM to write additional words into a text or document ○ *wrote in all the personal health data required* **2** *vi* WRITE TO AN ORGANIZATION to send a letter to an organization **3** *vt US* ADD NAME TO BALLOT to add somebody's name to a ballot paper in an election in order to vote for that person

write off *v* **1** *vi* WRITE TO AN ORGANIZATION to send a letter to an organization, usually in order to obtain something from it ○ *I wrote off for a brochure.* **2** *vt* DECIDE SOMEBODY OR SOMETHING IS WORTHLESS to dismiss somebody or something as worthless or unsuccessful and not worth continued attention or performance (*informal*) **3** *vt* DAMAGE VEHICLE TOO BADLY TO REPAIR to damage a vehicle so badly that it is not economic to repair it **4** *vt* REDUCE VALUE OF to reduce the estimated value of an asset for accounting purposes **5** *vt* REMOVE BAD DEBT OR VALUELESS ASSET to remove a debt considered irrecoverable or an asset with no value from the accounts of a business

write out *v* **1** *vt* WRITE IN COMPLETE FORM to write something in its complete form ○ *write out your name* **2** *vt* SAY IN WRITING to express something in written form **3** *vt* REMOVE FROM A SERIES to remove a regular character from a radio or television series ○ *He's been written out of the show.* **4** *vr* WRITE TO POINT OF EXHAUSTION to write so much that your ideas or stamina are exhausted ○ *By midnight I was written out after 12 hours at the keyboard.*

write up *vt* **1** WRITE SOMETHING FROM EARLIER NOTES to write a report or account of something from notes made earlier **2** WRITE REVIEW OF to write a review of something such as a new play or book **3** UPDATE JOURNAL OR DIARY to bring something such as a journal or log up to date by writing additional entries **4** *US* REPORT SOMEBODY FOR UNLAWFUL ACT to report somebody in writing for violating a law or rule ○ *wrote the motorist up for illegal parking* **5** *US* OVERVALUE ASSETS to overvalue corporate assets

write-down *n* a reduction in the value of an asset as entered in the books of a business

write-in *n US* **1** a vote cast in an election by adding somebody's name to the ballot paper **2** a candidate added to a ballot paper by a voter

~~**writeing**~~ incorrect spelling of **writing**

~~**writen**~~ incorrect spelling of **written**

write-off *n* **1** VEHICLE DAMAGED BEYOND REPAIR something, especially a vehicle, that is so badly damaged that it is not economic to repair it ○ *Nobody was injured but the car was a write-off.* **2** REDUCTION IN VALUE a reduction in the estimated value of an asset **3** SOMETHING REDUCED IN VALUE an asset that has had its estimated value reduced **4** AMOUNT OF REDUCTION IN VALUE the monetary amount by which something such as a corporate asset has been reduced in value

⚡**write-protected** *adj* describes computer storage space that cannot be altered or erased

writer /rítər/ *n* **1** SOMEBODY WHO WRITES AS PROFESSION a person who writes books or articles professionally **2** PERSON WHO WROTE DOCUMENT the person who wrote a particular text or document **3** SOMEBODY WHO CAN WRITE a person who can write, who writes well, or who enjoys writing **4** SCRIBE a scribe (*archaic*)

writer's block *n* an inability on the part of a writer to start a new piece of writing or continue an existing one

writer's cramp *n* a muscular spasm that results from a prolonged period of writing and affects the muscles of the forearm, hand, and fingers, causing temporary cramping and pain

Writer to the Signet (*plural* **Writers to the Signet**) *n* in Scotland, a member of an ancient society of solicitors who have the exclusive power to prepare crown writs [Originally a clerk who prepared writs for the royal signet]

write-up *n* **1** a written account of material, especially a published review of a new play, book, or film **2** *US* a deliberate overvaluation of company assets

writhe /rīth/ *v* (**writhes, writhing, writhed**) **1** *vi* TWIST OR SQUIRM to make violent twisting and rolling movements with the body, especially as a result of severe pain ○ *writhing in agony* **2** *vti* MOVE IN TWISTING WAY to move in a twisting, squirming way, or to cause the body to move in this way **3** *vi* EXPERIENCE STRONG EMOTION to feel a particular emotion, especially embarrassment or shame, very strongly, and experience internal stress as a result of it ■ *n* WRITHING MOVEMENT a twisting or squirming movement [Old English *wrīþan* < Germanic] —**writher** *n*

writing /rīting/ *n* **1** WORDS WRITTEN DOWN words or other symbols, e.g. hieroglyphics, written down as a means of communication **2** WRITTEN MATERIAL written material, especially considered as the product of a writer's skill **3** ACTIVITY OF CREATING BOOKS the activity of creating written works, especially as a job **4** = **handwriting** *n.* 2 ■ **writings** *npl* ALL AUTHOR'S WRITTEN OUTPUT all the publications and written work of a writer ○ *Churchill's writings on the war.* ◇ **the writing on the wall** something that suggests that a disaster of some kind is about to happen ○ *She should have seen the writing on the wall when her boss asked her if she had ever thought of a change of career.*

writing case *n* a portable case with compartments for holding paper, pens, and other materials for writing

writing desk *n* **1** a desk with a surface for writing on and compartments for holding paper, envelopes, and other writing materials **2** a portable case used for carrying writing materials, often with a hard surface for writing

writing paper *n* paper of a quality good enough to write on with ink

Writings *npl* JUDAISM = **Hagiographa**

written past participle of **write**

Written Law *n* JUDAISM = **Torah** *n.* 2

~~**writting**~~ incorrect spelling of **writing**

WRNS *abbr* HIST Women's Royal Naval Service

wrnt *abbr* warrant

Wroclaw /vrót swaaf/ city in SW Poland, on the River Oder. Population: 644,000 (1992).

wrong /rong/ *adj* **1** INCORRECT not correct or accurate ○ *That's the wrong answer.* **2** MISTAKEN holding an incorrect opinion about a person, thing, or matter ○ *I thought it would be fun, but I was wrong.* **3** NOT MEANT not the intended or desired one ○ *It was sent to the wrong address.* **4** NOT IN NORMAL STATE not in the normal satisfactory state ○ *What's wrong with you today?* **5** NOT CONFORMING TO ACCEPTED STANDARDS not in accordance with law, morality, or with people's sense of fairness, justice, and what is acceptable behaviour ○ *It's wrong to steal.* **6** UNSUITABLE unsuitable, or showing poor judgment on the part of the person who chooses, does, or says it ○ *It's the wrong time of year to be planting seeds.* **7** NOT WORKING not functioning properly ○ *Something's gone wrong with the television.* **8** NOT VISIBLE describes the side of a fabric or garment that is not intended to be seen ○ *I always iron knitted garments on the wrong side.* **9** REVERSED OR INVERTED opposite to the normal, proper, or intended side, way, or direction ○ *This picture is the wrong way up.* ■ *adv* **1** INCORRECTLY incorrectly or in a way that leads to failure or a different result from the one intended ○ *You've spelt that wrong.* **2** IN WRONG DIRECTION in a direction that is different from or opposite to the right or intended direction ■ *n* **1** ACTION NOT CONSIDERED MORAL an action or situation that does not conform to ideas of morality or justice **2** UNACCEPTABLE BEHAVIOUR behaviour that is morally or socially unacceptable ○ *Children have to be taught the difference between right and wrong.* **3** LAW = **tort** **4** INFRINGEMENT OF SOMEBODY'S LEGAL RIGHTS an infringement, abridgment, or violation of another party's rights under the law ■ *vt* **1** TREAT UNJUSTLY to judge or treat somebody unjustly ○ *He felt he had been wronged.* **2** DISCREDIT to discredit somebody by saying malicious but untrue things about him or her **3** BRING DISHONOUR ON to seduce a woman and thereby bring about her dishonour (*archaic*) [Old English *wrange* 'wrongful act'. The adjective *wrang* probably existed in Old English, but is not found before the 12C.] —**wronger** *n* —**wrongly** *adv* —**wrongness** *n* ◇ **get somebody wrong** to misunderstand somebody ○ *Don't get me wrong: I'm very grateful for your help.* ◇ **get something wrong 1** to make a mistake in an answer or calculation **2** to misunderstand something ◇ **go wrong 1** to go badly or not according to plan **2** to make a mistake **3** to fail to conform to ideas of morality or justice ◇ **in the wrong 1** at fault for something **2** mistaken

wrongdoing /róng doo ing/ *n* behaviour or an action that fails to conform to standards of law or morality —**wrongdoer** *n*

wrong-foot *vt* **1** to put somebody at a disadvantage or in an embarrassing position by doing or saying something unexpected **2** to cause an opponent to anticipate wrongly the direction in which a move is going to be made or a ball hit or kicked

wrongful /róngf'l/ *adj* **1** not done according to the law ○ *wrongful dismissal* **2** not just or fair —**wrongfully** *adv* —**wrongfulness** *n*

SYNONYMS See ***unlawful***.

wrong-headed *adj* **1** completely contrary to reason or good sense **2** obstinately sticking to a false belief, opinion, or course of action —**wrong-headedly** *adv* —**wrong-headedness** *n*

wrong number *n* an incorrectly dialled telephone number that connects the caller with the wrong person

wrong'un /róngən/ *n* (*informal*) **1** somebody regarded as having a bad character or criminal tendencies **2** a googly [Late 19C. Contraction of 'wrong one'.]

wrote past tense of **write**

wroth /rōth, roth/ *adj* extremely angry (*archaic or literary*) [Old English *wrāþ* < Germanic]

wrought past tense, past participle of **work** (*archaic*) ■ *adj* **1** made in a skilful or decorative way (*often in combination*) ○ *a delicately wrought ebony screen* **2** describes decorative metalwork shaped by hammering and welding

USAGE As the term *wrought iron* suggests, ***wrought*** is a rare past tense not of *wreak* (for which the past tense is *wreaked*) but of *work*, though *worked* is the common, modern past tense of this verb. ***Wrought*** is seen in only a few, rather specialized situations such as ones relating to metalwork, and in the set phrase *What hath God wrought* (used by Samuel Morse in the first successful test of the telegraph). *Wrought havoc* is not correct; it should be *wreaked havoc.*

wrought iron *n* a highly refined form of iron that is easy to shape but is strong and fairly resistant to rust. Use: decorative metalwork. —**wrought-iron** *adj*

wrought-up, wrought up *adj* tensely nervous, agitated, or excited

WRP *abbr* Worker's Revolutionary Party

⚡**WRT** *abbr* (*in e-mails*) **1** with regard to **2** with respect to

wrung past tense, past participle of **wring**

WRVS *abbr* Women's Royal Voluntary Service

wry /rī/ (**wrier** *or* **wryer, wriest** *or* **wryest**) *adj* **1** AMUSING AND IRONIC combining, or expressing a mixture of, mild amusement and irony ○ *a wry remark* **2** CHARACTERIZED BY IRONIC ACCEPTANCE characterized by or showing a slightly ironic acceptance of something not particularly pleasant or desirable ○ *a wry grin* **3** TWISTED out of shape or twisted to one side [Old English *wrīgian* 'to turn' < Indo-European] —**wryly** *adv* —**wryness** *n*

wrybill /rī bil/ *n* a shore bird of the plover family whose bill is bent to one side so that it can search for food beneath pebbles. Native to: New Zealand. *Anarhynchus fontalis.*

wryneck /rī nek/ *n* **1** a bird of the woodpecker family that has mottled brown plumage and a short sharp bill, eats insects and lives in holes, but does not drill into trees. Native to: Europe, Asia. *Jynx torquilla* and *Jynx ruficollis.* **2** MED = **torticollis**

⚡**WS** *abbr* Samoa (*in Internet addresses*)

⚡**WS** *abbr* **1** Western Samoa **2** Samoa

WSW *abbr* west-southwest

wt *abbr* weight

WTA *abbr* **1** Women's Tennis Association **2** World Tennis Association

WTO *abbr* World Trade Organization

Wu /woo/ *n* a group of Chinese dialects spoken mainly in the Jiangsu and Zhejiang provinces of China, the colloquial language of Shanghai. Native speakers: 90 million. [Early 20C. < Chinese *wú*.]

Wuhan /woo hán/ capital of Hubei Province, in central China. Population: 3,860,000 (1993 estimate).

wulfenite /woolfə nīt/ *n* an orange, yellow, or brown mineral consisting of lead molybdate. Use: source of molybdenum. [Mid-19C. After F. X. von *Wulfen* (1728–1805), Austrian scientist.]

wunderkind /wúndər kind, voóndər-/ (*plural* **-kinds** *or* **-kinder** /-kindər/) *n* **1** a person who is extremely successful at a young age **2** a child who is unusually talented at something [Late 19C. < German, 'wonder child'.]

Wundt /voont/, **Wilhelm** (1832–1920) German psychologist

Wuppertal /voopər taal/ city in NW Germany. Population: 382,400 (1995).

Wurlitzer /wúrlitsər/ *tdmk* **1** a trademark for a type of electric organ **2** a trademark for a jukebox

wurst /wurst, woorst, voorst/ *n* **1** a sausage made in Germany and Austria, especially a large sausage intended to be sliced and eaten cold **2** *US* sausage of any kind [Mid-19C. < German *Wurst* 'sausage' < Indo-European, 'confuse'.]

Würzburg /vúrts burg, vúrts berk/ city in south-central Germany. Population: 127,700 (1995).

wushu /woo shoo/, **wu shu** *n* Chinese martial arts considered collectively [Late 20C. < Chinese *wŭ shù* 'military technique'.]

wuss /woos/ *n* an offensive term that deliberately insults somebody regarded as weak or ineffectual (*slang insult*) [Late 20C. < ?] —**wussy** *adj*

wuthering /wúthəring/ *adj* *N England* **1** describes a wind that blows strongly and makes a loud roaring sound **2** subject to persistent blustery or noisy winds [Late 18C. < obsolete *wuther* 'rush'.]

WV *abbr* **1** West Virginia **2** (Windward Islands) St Vincent

W.Va. *abbr* West Virginia

WWF *abbr* **1** World Wide Fund for Nature **2** World Wrestling Federation

WWI *abbr* World War One

WWII *abbr* World War Two

⚡**WWW** *abbr* **1** World Wide Wait (*in e-mails*) **2** World Wide Web

WY, Wy *abbr* Wyoming

Wyandot /wī ən dot/ (*plural* **-dot** *or* **-dots**), **Wyandotte** (*plural* **-dotte** *or* **-dottes**) *n* a member of an Iroquois people who lived west of Lake Huron, and now live mainly in Oklahoma [Mid-18C. Via French *Ouendat* < Huron *Wendat*.]

Wyandotte *n* a medium-sized North American domestic chicken. [Late 19C. Variant of WYANDOT.]

Wyatt /wī ət/, **James** (1746–1813) British architect

Wyatt, Sir Thomas (1503–42) English courtier and poet

wych elm /wich-/, **witch elm** *n* an elm with prominently tipped leaves and clusters of winged green fruit. *Ulmus glabra.* [Old English *wice* < Indo-European 'bend, be pliant']

Wycherley /wíchər li/, **William** (1640?–1716) English playwright

wych hazel *n* TREES = **witch hazel**

Wycliffe /wíklif/, **Wyclif, Wycliff, John** (1330?–84) English philosopher and religious reformer —**Wycliffite** *n, adj*

wye /wī/ *n* **1** the letter 'y' **2** something shaped like the letter 'Y' [Mid-19C. Probably representing the letter's pronunciation.]

Wye /wī/ river of SW Wales and W England, emptying into the estuary of the River Severn. Length: 20 km/130 mi.

Wyeth /wī əth/, **Andrew** (*b.* 1917) US artist

Wykeham /wíkəm/, **William of** (1324–1404) English statesman

Wykehamist /wíkəmist/ *n* a pupil or former pupil of Winchester College [Mid-18C. After William of WYKEHAM.]

wyn *n* = **wynn**

wynd /wīnd/ *n* *Scotland* a narrow lane in a town [15C. Probably < WIND[2].]

wynn /win/, **wyn, wen** /wen/ *n* a runic letter used in Old English [Old English *wyn* 'joy'. Runes were named using words beginning with their sound.]

Wyo. *abbr* Wyoming

Wyoming /wī ṓming/ state of the NW United States. Capital: Cheyenne. Population: 528,964 (1997). Area 253,347 sq. km/97,818 sq. mi. —**Wyomingite** *n*

⚡**WYSIWYG** *abbr* what you see is what you get (*describes relation of a word processor's output on a display to its printed output*)

Wyvern

wyvern /wívərn, -urn/, **wivern** *n* in heraldry, a mythical creature depicted as having two legs, a dragon's head, wings, and a long tail [Late 16th C. Via Old French *wivre* < Latin *vipera* 'snake'.]

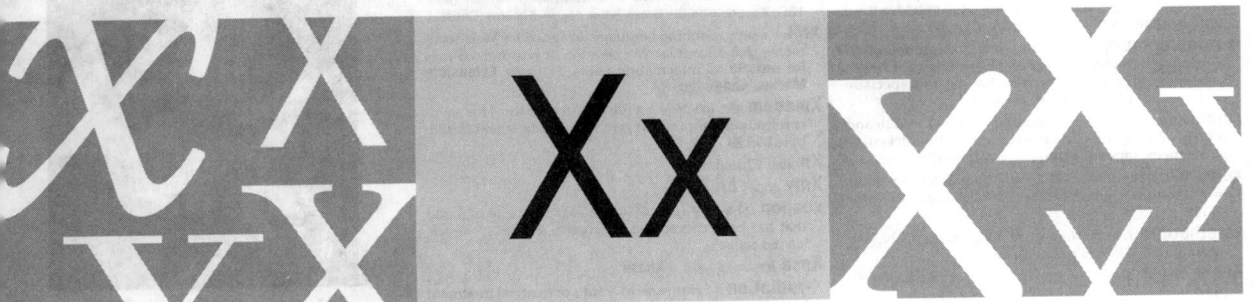

x^1 /eks/, **X** *n* (*plural* **x's**; *plural* **X's** *or* **Xs**) **1** 24TH LETTER OF ENGLISH ALPHABET the 24th letter of the English alphabet, representing a consonant sound **2** 'X'-SHAPED SYMBOLIC MARK an 'x'-shaped mark used to indicate a vote, to show that something is incorrect, to represent a kiss, or in place of a signature by somebody who cannot write **3** SYMBOL USED TO REPRESENT AN UNKNOWN a letter 'x' or an 'x'-shaped mark used to represent something or somebody unknown or unspecified **4** ROMAN NUMERAL FOR 10 the Roman numeral for 10 ■ *vt* (**x-es** *or* **x'es, x-ing** *or* **x'ing, x-ed** *or* **x'ed; X-es** *or* **X'es, X-ing** *or* **X'ing, X-ed** *or* **X'ed**) MARK OR SIGN WITH 'X' to mark or sign something with an 'x'

x out, X out *vt US* to cross something out

x^2 *symbol* **1** an algebraic variable **2** any card that is not an honour **3** by (*used when giving dimensions*) **4** a Cartesian coordinate along the x-axis **5** ex **6** extension **7** multiplied by

X^1 /eks/ (*plural* **X's** *or* **Xs**) *n* **1** something shaped like a letter 'X' **2** a censorship classification used in the United Kingdom until 1982 for films that could not be shown publicly to anyone under 18 and until 1990 in the United States for films considered unsuitable for under-17s. Now called **18**

X^2 *symbol* reactance

Xanadu /zánnə doo, zánnə dóo/ (*plural* **-dus**) *n* an idyllically beautiful place [Mid-20C. After the residence of KUBLAI KHAN in Samuel Taylor Coleridge's poem *Kubla Khan* (1816).]

xanth- *prefix* = **xantho-**

xanthan gum /zánthən-/ *n* a natural gum with a high molecular weight. Source: bacterial fermentation of glucose. Use: food stabilizer. [Mid-20C. < modern Latin *Xanthomonas*, a bacterium < Greek *xanthos* 'yellow' + late Latin *monas* (stem *monad-*: see MONAD).]

xanthate /zán thayt/ *n* any salt or ester of xanthic acid. Use: extraction of metals, manufacture of rayon. [Mid-19C. < XANTHIC ACID.]

xanthene /zán theen/ *n* CH$_2$(C$_6$H$_4$)$_2$O a yellow crystalline compound. Use: fungicide, basis of some organic dyes.

xanthic acid /zánthik-/ *n* ROC(S)SH where R is an organic group any unstable organic sulphur-containing acid

xanthine /zán theen, -thīn/ *n* **1** C$_5$H$_4$N$_4$O$_2$ a yellow-white crystalline compound, the precursor of uric acid, found in blood, urine, and some plants **2** a derivative of xanthine such as caffeine, theophylline, or theobromine

xantho- *prefix* **1** yellow ◦ *xanthopterin* **2** xanthic acid ◦ *xanthate*

xanthoma /zan thốmə/ (*plural* **-mas** *or* **-mata** /-mətə/) *n* a yellow lipid-filled lesion on the skin, especially on the eyelids, that indicates a disorder of fat metabolism —**xanthomatous** *adj*

xanthomatosis /zànthōmə tốssiss/ *n* the presence of multiple xanthomas on the skin

xanthone /zán thōn/ *n* C$_{13}$H$_8$O$_2$ a colourless crystalline compound. Use: basis of some yellow dyes.

xanthophyll /zánthōfill/ *n* a yellow or brown oxygenated carotenoid pigment that colours autumn leaves —**xanthophyllic** /zànthō fíllik/ *adj*

Xavier /závvi ər, závyi ər/, **St Francis** (1506–52) Spanish missionary

x-axis *n* **1** the horizontal axis in a two-dimensional co-ordinate system **2** an axis in the three-dimensional Cartesian coordinate system, conventionally the horizontal one

X-certificate *adj* containing explicitly sexual or violent material or unsuitable for children, as in the former UK classification for cinema films. US term **X-rated** *adj.* **2**

X chromosome, X-chromosome *n* a chromosome present in both sexes that plays a role in determining the sex of an individual. ◊ **Y chromosome**

x-coordinate *n* the position of a point in space with reference to the x-axis in the Cartesian coordinate system, defined in conjunction with the y- and z-

XD, xdiv *abbr* ex dividend

Xe *symbol* xenon

xebec /zeébek, záy-/, **zebec** *n* a small Mediterranean ship with three masts rigged with both square and triangular sails [Mid-18C. Via French *chebec* < Arabic *šabbāk*.]

xen- *prefix* = **xeno-** (before vowels)

Xenakis /ze naákis/, **Yannis** (1922–2001) Romanian-born Greek composer

xeno- *prefix* foreign, strange, different ◦ *xenophile* ◦ *xenolith* [Via modern Latin < Greek *xenos* 'stranger, foreigner']

xenobiotic /zénnō bī óttik, zeéna-/ *adj* describes a chemical compound, e.g. a drug or pesticide, that is foreign to the body of a living organism ■ *n* a xenobiotic chemical compound

Xenocrates /ze nókrə teez/ (396–314 BC) Greek philosopher

xenocryst /zénnōkrist/ *n* a crystal in an igneous rock introduced from an external source and not crystallized from the magma [Late 19C. < XENO- + CRYSTAL.]

xenodiagnosis /zénnō dī əg nốssiss/ (*plural* **-noses** /-nố seez/) *n* the diagnosis of a parasitic infection by allowing a noninfected disease-carrying organism, e.g. a mosquito, to feed on an infected person's blood and then examining the organism for infection —**xenodiagnostic** /-nóstik/ *adj*

xenogeneic /zénnōjə náy ik/ *adj* coming from or derived from a different species [Mid-20C. After SYNGENEIC.]

xenogenesis /zénnō jénnəssiss/ *n* **1** the supposed production of offspring completely different from either parent **2** the existence in the life cycle of an organism of two or more alternating forms or reproductive modes, e.g. sexual and asexual cycles —**xenogenetic** /zénnōjə néttik/ *adj*

xenograft /zénnō graaft/ *n* MED = **heterograft**

xenolith /zénnōlith/ *n* a fragment of rock that is different in origin from the igneous rock in which it occurs —**xenolithic** /zénnō líthik/ *adj*

xenon /zeén on, zén-/ *n* (*symbol* **Xe**) a heavy colourless odourless gaseous element that is relatively inert. Source: in minute quantities in air. Use: electronic tubes, specialized lamps. [Late 19C. < Greek *xenon*, neuter of *xenos* 'stranger, foreigner'.]

Xenophanes /ze nóffə neez/ (*fl.* late 6th-early 5th centuries BC) Greek philosopher and poet

xenophile /zénnō fīl/ *n* a person who likes the people, customs, and culture of other countries, or things from abroad —**xenophilia** /-fílli ə/ *n* —**xenophilous** /ze nóffiləss/ *adj*

xenophobe /zénnōfōb/ *n* a person who hates the people, customs, and culture of other countries, or things from abroad

xenophobia /zénnə fốbi ə/ *n* an intense fear or dislike of foreign people, their customs and culture, or foreign things —**xenophobic** *adj*

Xenophon /zénnəf'n/ (430?–355? BC) Greek historian and soldier

xenopus /zénnəpəss/ *n* an aquatic frog. Native to: southern Africa. Genus: *Xenopus*. [Late 19C. < modern Latin, < Greek *xeno-* 'stranger, foreigner' + *pous* 'foot'.]

xenotime /zénnə tīm/ *n* a yellowish-brown mineral consisting of yttrium phosphate, usually with small amounts of other rare-earth elements [Mid-19C. < XENO- (probably by confusion with Greek *kenos* 'empty, vain') + Greek *timē* 'honour'; because the yttrium in xenotime was wongly thought to be a new element.]

xenotransplant *vt* /zénnō transs plaänt/ TRANSPLANT SOMETHING TO DIFFERENT SPECIES to transfer a tissue or organ between members of different species ■ *n* /zénnō tránss plaänt/ **1** OPERATION TRANSPLANTING TISSUE TO DIFFERENT SPECIES a surgical operation in which a tissue or organ is transferred between members of different species **2** SOMETHING TRANSPLANTED TO DIFFERENT SPECIES a tissue or organ that is transferred between members of different species —**xenotransplantable** /zénnō transs plaäntəb'l/ *adj*

xenotransplantation /zénnō tránss plaan táysh'n/ *n* the process of transplanting organs from one species to another, especially from animals to humans

xer- *prefix* = **xero-** (before vowels)

xeric /zeérik/ *adj* relating to or living in a dry habitat —**xerically** *adv*

Xeriscape /zeéri skayp, zérri-/ *tdmk US* a trademark for a method of landscaping gardens that emphasizes water conservation, used especially in areas with an arid climate

xero- *prefix* dry, dryness ◦ *xerothermic* [< Greek *xēros* 'dry']

xeroderma /zeèrō dúrmə/, **xerodermia** /-dúrmi ə/ *n* a mild form of the hereditary disorder ichthyosis, marked by discoloured dry hard scaly skin —**xerodermatic** /-dur máttik/ *adj* —**xerodermatous** *adj*

xeroderma pigmentosum /-píg mən tốssəm/ *n* a rare and often fatal hereditary condition beginning in infancy in which the skin and eyes are damaged by sunlight. It results in freckles, discoloured patches, and skin cancers.

xerodermia *n* = **xeroderma**

xerography /zeer róggrəfi/ *n* a method of photocopying in which the image is formed by attracting a resinous powder to an electrostatically charged plate, then transferred to paper and fixed by heating —**xerographer** *n* —**xerographic** /zeèrō gráffik/ *adj* —**xerographically** *adv*

xerophilous /zeer róffiləss/ *adj* thriving in or adapted for a hot dry habitat —**xerophile** /zeèrō fīl/ *n* —**xerophily** /zeer róffili/ *n*

xerophthalmia /zeèr ō thálmi ə/ *n* an eye disease caused by vitamin A deficiency, marked by dryness and ulceration of the conjunctiva and cornea —**xerophthalmic** *adj*

xerophyte /zeèrə fīt/ n a plant that is adapted for a dry habitat, e.g. a cactus —**xerophytic** /-fíttik/ adj —**xerophytically** adv —**xerophytism** /-fītizəm/ n

xeroradiography /zeèrō ráydi óggrəfi/ n high-definition X-ray photography, often used in screening for breast cancer, in which the image is first made on a specially coated metal plate then transferred to paper

xerosis /zeer róssiss/ n abnormal dryness of the skin and mucous membranes of the eye, caused by thickening of the membranes —**xerotic** /zeer róttik/ adj

xerostomia /zeèrō stṓmi ə/ n an abnormal lack of saliva in the mouth, caused by disease, poisoning, or some drugs

xerothermic /zeèrō thúrmik/ adj very hot and having little rainfall ○ a xerothermic climate

Xerox /zeèr roks/ tdmk a trademark for a photocopying process

Xerxes I /zúrk seez/ (519?–465 BC) king of Persia (486–465 BC)

x-height n the height of the lower-case letter x in a particular typeface, used as a measure of the height of the main body of all lower-case letters in that typeface

Xhosa /kṓssə, káwssə/ (plural -**sa** or -**sas**), **Xosa** (plural -**sa** or -**sas**) n 1 a member of a Bantu-speaking people of South Africa 2 the Bantu language of the Xhosa people. Native speakers: 7 million. [Early 19C. < Nguni.] —**Xhosan** adj

xi /zī, sī, ksī, ksee/ (plural **xis**) n the 14th letter of the Greek alphabet

Xiamen /shyaà mén/ seaport in SE China, on Xiamen Island in the Taiwan Strait. Population: 579,500 (1998 estimate).

Xi'an /shyaan/ capital of Shaanxi Province, N China. Population: 2,790,000 (1992 estimate).

Xiangtan /shyang tán, syang tán/ city in S China. Population: 525,448 (1991).

xi hyperon, xi-particle n a neutral or negatively charged elementary particle present in cosmic rays and in high-energy collisions in particle accelerators

Xi Jiang /sheè jyáng/ river in S China, rising in Yunnan Province and flowing east to the South China Sea. Length: 2,100 km/1,300 mi.

Xining /sheè níng/ capital of Qinghai Province, central China. Population: 777,983 (1991).

Xinjiang Uygur /shín jyáng weègər/ autonomous region in NW China. Capital: Urumqi. Population: 15,550,000 (1991). Area: 1,646,800 sq. km/635,833 sq. mi.

xi-particle n PHYS = **xi hyperon**

xiphisternum /ziffi stúrnəm/ (plural -**na** /-nə/) n the third and lowest segment of the breastbone (**sternum**) in humans

xiphoid /zíffoyd/ adj 1 shaped like a sword 2 relating to the xiphisternum ■ n **xiphoid, xiphoid process** ANAT = **xiphisternum**

XL abbr extra large (used of clothing sizes)

Xmas /kríssməss, éksməss/ n Christmas (informal) [Mid-16C. X represents the Greek letter chi, in Khristos 'Christ'.]

⚡XML n a programming language designed for Web documents that allows for the creation of customized tags for individual information fields. Full form **Extensible Markup Language**

⚡Xmodem /éks mō dem/ n a file transfer protocol for asynchronous communications in which data is sent in 128-byte blocks

Xn abbr Christian

Xnty abbr Christianity

xoanon /zṓ ə non/ (plural -**na** /-nə/) n an image of a god that has been carved out of wood [Early 18C. < Greek, 'carved statue'.]

Xosa n PEOPLES, LANG = **Xhosa**

X-radiation n 1 exposure to X-rays or medical treatment by means of X-rays 2 radiation in the form of X-rays

X-rated adj 1 containing explicit sex scenes or descriptions of sex (informal) 2 US CINEMA = **X-certificate**

X-ray, X ray, x-ray, x ray n 1 ELECTROMAGNETIC RADIATION a high-energy electromagnetic radiation 2 PHOTOGRAPHIC IMAGE USING X-RAYS an image produced on photographic film by X-rays passing through objects or parts of the body, often used in medicine and science as a diagnostic tool 3 CODE WORD FOR THE LETTER 'X' a code word for the letter 'X', used in international radio communications ■ vt 1 PHOTOGRAPH SOMETHING USING X-RAYS to expose something, e.g. a part of the body, to X-rays in order to obtain a photographic image of it 2 EXAMINE PATIENT USING X-RAYS to examine or treat somebody using X-rays [Late 19C. Translation of German X-Strahl, X signifying 'unknown'.]

X-ray astronomy n the branch of astronomy in which the properties of astronomical objects are determined using the X-rays they emit

X-ray crystallography n the study of crystal structures using the diffraction patterns produced by scattered X-rays

X-ray diffraction n the diffraction of X-rays produced by the atoms within a crystal, used to determine information about the crystal's structure

X-ray star, X-ray source n a celestial object that emits X-rays in addition to other types of radiation

X-ray therapy n the medical application of X-rays in treating illnesses such as cancer

X-ray tube n an evacuated tube in which a stream of high-energy electrons is made to strike a metal target to produce X-rays

XS abbr extra small (used of clothing sizes)

Xt. abbr Christ

Xtian abbr Christian

xtn abbr extension

Xty abbr Christianity

xu /soo/ (plural **xu**) n see table at **currency** [Mid-20C. Via Vietnamese < French sou (see SOU).]

xyl- prefix = **xylo-** (before vowels)

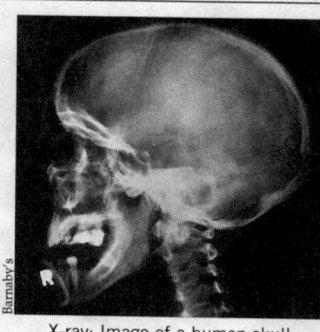

X-ray: Image of a human skull

xylan /zī lan/ n a polysaccharide (**pentosan**) found in plant cell walls and woody tissue

xylem /zīləm, zī lem/ n plant tissue that carries water and dissolved minerals from the roots through the stem and leaves [Late 19C. Via German < Greek xulon 'wood'.]

xylene /zī leen/ n C_8H_{10} any of three flammable volatile colourless liquid hydrocarbon isomers. Source: petroleum, natural gas, coal tar. Use: solvents, manufacture of aviation fuel, resins, and dyes.

xylidine /zíli deen, zīli dīn, zílli-/ n $C_8H_{11}N$ any of six toxic amines derived from xylene. Use: manufacture of dyes, organic synthesis.

xylo- prefix 1 wood ○ xylograph 2 xylene ○ xylidine [< Greek xulon 'wood']

xylogenous /zī lójjənəss/ adj adapted to or living in or on wood

xylograph /zílə graaf, -graf/ n 1 WOOD ENGRAVING an engraving made on wood 2 PRINT FROM XYLOGRAPH a print made from an engraving made on wood ■ vt MAKE A XYLOGRAPH to take a print from an engraving made on wood —**xylographer** /zī lóggrəfər/ n —**xylographic** /zílə gráffik/ adj —**xylographical** adj —**xylographically** adv —**xylography** /zī lóggrəfi/ n

xylol /zī lol/ n CHEM = **xylene**

xylophagous /zī lóffəgəss/ adj feeding on or living in wood —**xylophage** /zīlō fayj/ n

xylophone /zīləfōn/ n a musical instrument with a row of wooden bars of different lengths that are laid out like a keyboard and produce a tone when struck with a mallet —**xylophonist** /zī lóffənist/ n

xylose /zī lōz, -lōss/ n a five-carbon sugar that forms the units in xylan. Use: in diabetic foods.

xystus /zístəss/ (plural -**tuses**), **xyst** /zist/ n 1 in ancient Greece, a long walkway with a roof supported by pillars, used for athletics 2 in ancient Rome, a covered or open path in a garden, lined with trees or pillars [Mid-17C. Via Latin < Greek xustos 'covered colonnade', literally 'smooth' (from its polished floor) < xuein 'to scrape'.]

Y¹ /wi/ (*plural* **y's**), **Y** (*plural* **Y's** *or* **Ys**) *n* the 25th letter of the English alphabet, representing a consonant sound or sometimes a vowel

Y² *symbol* **1** an algebraic variable **2** a Cartesian coordinate along the y-axis **3** y-axis **4** yocto-

Y³ *abbr* year

Y¹ /wi/ (*plural* **Y's** *or* **Ys**) *n* **1** something shaped like a letter 'Y' **2** US a YMCA or YWCA hostel (*informal*)

Y² *symbol* **1** admittance **2** an unknown factor **3** yotta- **4** yttrium

Y³ *abbr* **1** yen **2** yuan

-y¹, -ey *suffix* **1** consisting of or characterized by ○ *muddy* **2** somewhat, like ○ *chilly* ○ *wintry* **3** tending towards ○ *sleepy* [Old English *-ig* < Germanic]

-y² *suffix* **1** a condition, state, or quality ○ *infamy* **2** an activity ○ *chandlery* **3** the place where an activity is carried on, or the result or product of an activity ○ *colliery* ○ *laundry* **4** a body or group ○ *soldiery* [Via Old French *-ie* < Latin *-ia*]

-y³ *suffix* = **-ie**

Y2K *n* used to refer to the year 2000, especially with regard to the millennium bug [Abbreviation]

YA *abbr* yet another (*in e-mails*)

yabber /yábbər/ *vti Australian* to talk a lot or say something rapidly, often so that it is incomprehensible ■ *n Australian* rapid speech that is often incomprehensible (*informal*)

yabby /yábbi/ (*plural* **-bies** *or* **-by**), **yabbie** (*plural* **-bies** *or* **-bie**) *n Aus* a small freshwater crayfish. Native to: Australia. Genus: *Cherax*. [Late 19C. < Wembawemba *yabij*.]

YAC /yak/ *abbr* yeast artificial chromosome

yacht /yot/ *n* **1 SAILING BOAT** a sailing boat, often one that has living quarters and is used for cruising or racing **2 MOTORBOAT FOR CRUISING** a large motorboat used for cruising ■ *vi* **SAIL IN YACHT** to sail in a yacht for leisure or sport [Mid-16C. < obsolete Dutch *jaghte*, shortening of *jaghtschip* 'chasing ship'.]

yachtie /yótti/ *n* a person who owns a yacht or enjoys sailing, cruising, or racing in yachts (*informal*)

yachting /yótting/ *n* the sport or pastime of sailing or sailing a yacht

yachtsman /yótsmən/ (*plural* **-men** /-mən/) *n* an owner or sailor of a yacht —**yachtsmanship** *n*

yachtswoman /yóts wŏŏmən/ (*plural* **-en** /-wimmin/) *n* a woman who owns or sails a yacht

yack *vi*, *n* = **yak²** (*informal*)

yacker *n ANZ* = **yakka** (*informal*)

yackety-yak /yákəti yák/ *vi* (**yackety-yaks, yackety-yakking, yackety-yakked**), *n* = **yak²** (*informal*) [Mid-20C. An imitation of the sound.]

yadda yadda yadda /yáddə yaddə yáddə/ *n US* boring, trite, superficial, unending talk (*slang*) ○ *just a lot of yadda yadda yadda on the talk shows tonight* [Late 20C. < ?]

YAG /yag/ *n* a synthetic mineral containing yttrium, aluminium, and garnet. Use: infrared lasers, gems. [Mid-20C. Acronym < *yttrium, aluminium, garnet*.]

Yagara /yaágərə/ *n* an Australian Aboriginal language of Queensland, now extinct —**Yagara** *adj*

Yagi aerial /yaági-/ *n* a directional radio or television aerial consisting of several elements arranged in line [Mid-20C. After Hidetsugu Yagi (1886–1976), Japanese electrical engineer.]

yah¹ /yaa/ *interj* used to express derision or defiance [Early 17C. Natural exclamation.]

yah² /yaa/ *adv* yes (*informal; especially parodying affected upper-class accents*) ○ *Okay, yah, super.* [Mid-19C. Representing a pronunciation.]

yahoo¹ /yaa hoó, yə-, yaá hoo/ (*plural* **-hoos**) *n* a person regarded as unruly, crude or brutish (*informal insult*) [Early 18C. After the *Yahoos* in Jonathan Swift's *Gulliver's Travels* (1726).] —**yahooism** *n*

yahoo² /yə hoó/ *interj* used to express enthusiasm, approval, or celebration (*informal*) ○ *Yahoo! Let's go!* ■ *n* (*plural* **-hoos**) a cry of yahoo (*informal*)

Yahrzeit /yaáwrt sīt/ *n* in Judaism, the anniversary of somebody's death, celebrated by near relatives with the lighting of a memorial candle and the saying of the Kaddish [Mid-19C. < Yiddish *yortsayt* 'year's time'.]

Yahveh *n* JUD-CHR = **Yahweh**

Yahvism *n* JUD-CHR = **Yahwism**

Yahvist *n* JUD-CHR = **Yahwist**

Yahvistic *adj* JUD-CHR = **Yahwistic**

Yahweh /yaá way/, **Yahveh** /-vay/, **Jahveh, Jahweh** *n* a name of God, expanded from the four letters, YHWH (**Tetragrammaton**), that form the name of God in Hebrew [Late 19C. < Hebrew.]

Yahwism /yaáwizəm/, **Yahvism** /yaáv-/ *n* the use of 'Yahweh' to represent the name of God or to worship God

Yahwist /yaáwist/, **Yahvist** /yaáv-/ *n* the unknown writer of the parts of the Old Testament of the Bible in which a set of four letters (**Tetragrammaton**) is used to refer to God

Yahwistic /yaa wístik/, **Yahvistic** /-vístik/ *adj* relating to Yahweh, Yahwism, or the Yahwist

yak¹ /yak/ (*plural* **yaks** *or* **yak**) *n* a large long-haired ox that has long curved horns and is found both wild and domesticated. Native to: Tibetan highlands. *Bos grunniens.* [Late 18C. < Tibetan *gyag*.]

yak² /yak/, **yack** *vi* (**yaks, yakking, yakked**) to talk continuously, usually about unimportant matters (*informal*) ■ *n* continuous talking, usually about unimportant matters, or an instance of this (*informal*) [Mid-20C. An imitation of the sound.]

Yakama /yákəmə/ (*plural* **-ma** *or* **-mas**) *n* the Penutian language of the Yakama people. Native speakers: 3,000. [Mid-19C. < Sahaptin.]

yakitori /yáki táwri/ *n* a dish of Japanese origin consisting of small pieces of grilled chicken that are basted on skewers with a sauce of soy, stock, sugar, and mirin [Mid-20C. < Japanese, 'grilling fowl'.]

yakka /yákə/, **yakker** /yákər/, **yacker** *n ANZ* work (*informal*) [Late 19C. < ?]

Yakut /ya kŏŏt/ (*plural* **-kut** *or* **-kuts**) *n* **1** a member of a people who live in NE Siberia, mainly in the Russian republic of Sakha **2** the Turkic language of the Yakut people. Native speakers: 300,000. [Mid-18C. Via Russian < Yakut.] —**Yakut** *adj*

Yakutsk /yə kŏŏtsk/ capital of the republic of Sakha, NE Russia. Population: 197,600 (1992).

yakuza /yə kŏŏzə/ (*plural* **-za**) *n* **1** a Japanese criminal organization involved in illegal activities such as drug-dealing, extortion, and prostitution **2** a member the yakuza [Mid-20C. < Japanese, 'gambler' < *ya* 'eight' + *ku* 'nine' + *-za* 'three', the worst hand in a card game.]

y'all *contr Southern US* = **you-all** (*informal*)

Yallourn /yál awrn/ town in S Victoria, Australia. Population: 15,512 (1996).

Yalta /yáltə, yóltə/ resort in S Ukraine, on the Black Sea that was the site of an Allied conference in 1945 between Joseph Stalin, Franklin Roosevelt, and Winston Churchill. Population: 89,000 (1991).

Yalu /yaá loo/ river in East Asia, forming most of the boundary between North Korea and China. Length: 790 km/490 mi.

yam /yam/ *n* **1** a vine root that resembles a large white floury potato and is eaten cooked as a vegetable **2** a tropical vine that produces yams. Genus: *Dioscorea*. [Late 16C. Via Portuguese *inhame* or Spanish *iñame*, < a W African language.]

Yamim Nora'im /yaa mím nawr aa ím/ *npl* in Judaism, the period of repentance lasting from Rosh Hashanah to Yom Kippur [< Hebrew, 'Days of Awe']

yammer /yámmər/ *vi* (*informal*) **1 TALK LOUDLY AND AT LENGTH** to talk, chat, or chatter noisily and continuously **2 WHINE** to whine or complain persistently about something **3 HOWL OR WAIL** to make repeated howling sounds of pain or distress ■ *n* (*informal*) **1 NOISY CHATTERING** noisy continuous talk, chat, or chattering **2 COMPLAINT** a whining sound or persistent complaint [15C. Probably < Middle Dutch *jammeren* 'mourn'.] —**yammerer** *n*

Yamoussoukro /yámmŏŏ sŏŏkrō/ capital of Côte d'Ivoire, in the central part of the country. Population: 100,000 (1988).

Yana /yaánə/ (*plural* **-na** *or* **-nas**) *n* **1** a member of a Native North American people of N California **2** the Hokan language of the Yana people, now extinct [Late 19C. < Yana, 'person, people'.] —**Yana** *adj*

Yan'an /yán án/ town in NE China. Population: 113,277 (1991).

yang /yang/, **Yang** *n* the principle of light, heat, motivation, and masculinity in Chinese philosophy that is the counterpart to yin. ◊ **yin** [Late 17C. < Chinese *yáng* 'sun, positive'.]

Yangon /yang gón/ capital of Myanmar, in the south of the country. Population: 2,513,023 (1983).

Yangtze /yáng see, yáng tsee/, **Yangzi** longest river in China, rising in the Kunlun Mountains and flowing southwards and then eastwards to the East China Sea. Length: 5,470 km/3,400 mi.

yank /yangk/ *v* **1** *vti* **PULL SHARPLY** to pull or jerk somebody or something suddenly and sharply **2** *vt* **REMOVE SOMEBODY OR SOMETHING SWIFTLY** to remove somebody or something suddenly and quickly ■ *n* **SHARP PULL** a sudden sharp pull or jerk [Early 19C. < ?]

SYNONYMS See **pull**.

Yank /yangk/ *n* an offensive term for somebody from the United States (*informal*) [Late 18C. Shortening of YANKEE.]

Yankee /yángki/ *n* **1** PEOPLES = **Yank** (*informal*) **2** *US* **SOMEBODY FROM A NORTHERN US STATE** somebody who comes from a Northern state of the United States, especially a soldier fighting on the side of the Union during the American Civil War (*offensive in some contexts*) **3** *US* **SOMEBODY FROM NEW ENGLAND** a person who comes from one of the states of New England (*offensive in some contexts*) **4** **CODE WORD FOR LETTER 'Y'** a code word for the letter 'Y', used in international radio communications [Mid-18C. < ?] —**Yankeedom** *n*

Yankee Doodle /-doód'l/ *n* a song first popular during the American War of Independence ■ PEOPLES = **Yank**

Yankeeism /yángki izəm/ *n* an expression or other characteristic considered typical of Yankees

Yankton /yángktən/ city in SE South Dakota. Population: 13,884 (1996).

yanqui /yángki/ (*plural* **-quis**) *n* an offensive term used by some Latin Americans to refer disparagingly to an English-speaking US citizen [Early 20C. Spanish-style spelling of YANKEE.]

Yao /yow/ (*plural* **Yao**) *n* **1** a member of a people who live in the mountains of S People's Republic of China **2** the language of the Yao people, belonging to the Miao-Yao group of languages. Native speakers: 1 million. [Mid-19C. < Chinese, literally, 'precious jade'.] —**Yao** *adj*

Yaoundé /yaa oónd ay/ capital of Cameroon, in the southwest of the country. Population: 1 million (1997 estimate).

yap /yap/ *vi* (**yaps, yapping, yapped**) **1** **MAKE HIGH BARKING SOUND** to make a short loud high-pitched barking noise **2** **CHATTER ANNOYINGLY** to talk continuously about trivial things, often in a loud or high-pitched voice (*informal*) ■ *n* **1** **SHORT HIGH-PITCHED BARK** a short, loud, high-pitched bark **2** **TRIVIAL CONVERSATION** a trivial or meaningless conversation (*informal*) **3** **MOUTH** somebody's mouth (*slang*) [Early 19C. An imitation of a dog's bark.] —**yapper** *n* —**yappy** *adj*

Yap /yap/ state of Micronesia, comprising a group of islands, islets, and atolls in the Caroline Islands of the W Pacific Ocean. Population: 10,886 (1991). Area: 119 sq. km/46 sq. mi.

yapok /yáppok/ (*plural* **-poks** *or* **-pok**) *n* an amphibious nocturnal opossum that has dense fur, webbed hind feet, a long tail, and feeds on aquatic organisms such as shrimp. Native to: Central and South America. *Chironectes minimus*. [Early 19C. After the river *Oyapok*, border between N Brazil and French Guiana.]

Yaqui /yáki/ (*plural* **-qui** *or* **-quis**) *n* **1** a member of a Native North American people of Arizona and Sonora, Mexico **2** the Uto-Aztecan language of the Yaqui people. Native speakers: 20,000. [Early 19C. Via Spanish < Yaqui *Hiaki*.] —**Yaqui** *adj*

yarborough /yaárbərə/ *n* a hand in bridge or whist consisting of 13 cards, each of which has a value lower than nine [Late 19C. After Charles Anderson Worsley (1809–97), 2nd Earl of *Yarborough*.]

yard[1] /yaard/ *n* **1** a unit of length equal to 0.9144 m/3 ft **2** MEASURE = **yardstick** *n.* 1 **3** a long spar that supports the head of a square sail, lugsail, or lateen [Old English *gerd* 'rod' < W Germanic] ◇ **the whole nine yards** *US* the totality or full extent of something (*informal*)

yard[2] /yaard/ *n* **1** **ENCLOSED PAVED PIECE OF LAND** an area of ground that is usually paved and enclosed, and is next to or surrounded by a building or buildings **2** *US, Can* = **garden** *n.* 1 **3** **AREA USED FOR BUSINESS OR ACTIVITY** an area of ground, sometimes with associated buildings, used for a particular purpose (*often in combination*) ○ *a builder's yard* **4** **RAILWAY STORAGE AREA** an area of railway tracks used for storing rolling stock or locomotives and for making up trains **5** **LIVESTOCK ENCLOSURE** an enclosed area of land for livestock **6** *US, Can* **WINTER GRAZING AREA** an area of land where deer, moose, or other animals graze in winter ■ *vt* **KEEP LIVESTOCK IN A YARD** to put or keep livestock in a yard [Old English *geard* 'enclosure, garden' < Germanic]

Yard ◇ **the Yard** Scotland Yard (*informal*)

yardage[1] /yaárdij/ *n* measurement in yards, or an amount measured in yards

yardage[2] /yaárdij/ *n* **1** the use of a livestock yard for storing animals before transporting them **2** a fee charged for storing livestock in a yard

yardarm /yaárd aarm/ *n* an end of the yard used to support a sail

yardbird /yaárd burd/ *n US* **1** **SOLDIER ASSIGNED MENIAL DUTIES** a soldier who is assigned menial tasks or is confined to a limited area, usually as a punishment (*informal*) **2** **INEPT RECRUIT** an untrained and inept military recruit (*dated informal*) **3** **CONVICT** a convict or prisoner (*dated informal*) [Mid-19C. After JAILBIRD.]

yard goods *npl* COMM = **piece goods**

yard grass *n* a coarse annual grass with ground-hugging leaves and grouped spikes that grows widely as a weed. *Eleusine indica*.

Yardie /yaárdi/ *n* a member of a criminal syndicate that originated in Jamaica

yardman /yaárdmən/ (*plural* **-men** /-mən/) *n* **1** a worker in a yard, especially a railway yard or a timberyard **2** *US* somebody employed to look after a lawn or garden

yard of ale *n* **1** a long narrow drinking glass, sometimes shaped like a horn, approximately one yard long and holding two to three pints of beer **2** the contents of a yard of ale

yard sale *n US* a sale at which personal possessions and household items are sold, usually held in the garden of somebody's house

yardstick /yaárd stik/ *n* **1** a measuring stick one yard long, usually marked in feet and inches **2** a standard used to judge the quality, value, or success of something

yare /yair/ *adj* **1** **EASY TO HANDLE** describes a ship that is easy to handle and responsive **2** **READY** ready or prepared (*archaic*) **3** **QUICK** quick or lively (*archaic*) ■ *adv* **QUICKLY** quickly or nimbly (*archaic*) [Old English *gearo* 'ready' < Germanic] —**yarely** *adv*

yarmulke /yaármoolkə/, **yarmulka, yarmulkah** *n* a small round cap worn by Jewish men and boys [Mid-20C. Via Yiddish < Polish *jarmułka*.]

yarn /yaarn/ *n* **1** **THREAD** a continuous twisted strand of wool, cotton, or synthetic fibre. Use: knitting, weaving. **2** **STRAND OF GLASS OR METAL** a continuous strand of a material such as glass or metal **3** **LONG STORY** a long or involved tale, especially one that relates exciting or incredible events (*informal*) ■ *vi* **TELL A YARN** to relate a long tale full of incredible events (*informal*) [Old English *gearn* < Indo-European, 'entrail']

yarn-dyed *adj* dyed in the form of yarn before being woven or knitted

Yaroslavl /yaáro slaávəl/ city in central European Russia, on the Volga River. Population: 636,000 (1990).

Yarra /yárrə/ river in S Victoria, Australia. Length: 250 km/155 mi.

yarrow /yárrō/ (*plural* **-rows** *or* **-row**) *n* a plant of the daisy family with leaves like ferns. Flowers: usually white, in broad flat clusters. Native to: Europe, Asia. *Achillea millefolium*. [Old English *gearwe* < W Germanic]

yashmak /yásh mak/, **yashmac** *n* a veil worn by some Muslim women in public [Mid-19C. < Turkish *yaşmak*.]

yataghan /yáttəgən/, **yatagan, ataghan** /áttəgən/ *n* a Turkish sword with no handle guard and a single-edged blade that curves inwards then outwards [Early 19C. < Turkish *yatağan*.]

yatra /yáttrə/ *n* a holy pilgrimage for Hindus [Early 19C. < Sanskrit *yātrā* < *yā* 'undertake a trip'.]

yatter /yáttər/ *vi* to talk continuously, especially about trivial things (*informal*) ■ *n* continuous talk, especially about trivial things, or an instance of this (*informal*) [Mid-19C. An imitation of the sound.]

yaup *vi, n US* = **yawp**

yautia /yáwti ə/ (*plural* **-as** *or* **-a**) *n* **1** a brown starchy tuber, cooked and eaten as a vegetable **2** a plant of the arum family that produces yautias. Native to: Caribbean. Genus: *Xanthosoma*. [Early 20C. Via Spanish < Taino.]

yaw /yaw/ *vti* **1** **GO OR PUT OFF COURSE** to deviate from a straight course, or to make a boat or ship do this **2** **TURN AROUND A VERTICAL AXIS** to turn around the vertical axis, or to make an aircraft turn in this way **3** **ZIGZAG** to move unsteadily on a zigzag course, or to make somebody or something advance in this way ■ *n* **1** **DEVIATION FROM COURSE** the deviation of a ship from a straight course **2** **MOVEMENT ABOUT VERTICAL AXIS** the movement of an aircraft about its vertical axis [Mid-16C. < ?]

Yawelmani /yaá wel maáni/ (*plural* **-ni**) *n* **1** a member of a Native North American people living in California **2** the Yokuts language of the Yawelmani people [Early 20C. < Yawelmani.] —**Yawelmani** *adj*

yawl /yawl/ *n* **1** a sailing vessel rigged fore-and-aft with a large mainmast and a smaller mizzenmast towards the stern **2** a small boat kept on a ship, rowed by four or six people [Mid-17C. < Dutch *jol*.]

yawn /yawn/ *v* **1** *vi* **OPEN MOUTH WIDE** to open the mouth wide and take a long deep breath, usually involuntarily, because of tiredness or boredom **2** *vt* **SAY SOMETHING WHILE YAWNING** to say something while yawning, or in a tired or bored voice **3** *vi* **BE WIDE OPEN** to open wide or be wide open, especially in a threatening or alarming manner ■ *n* **1** **ACT OF YAWNING** an involuntary response to tiredness or boredom in which the mouth is opened wide and a long deep breath is taken **2** **SOMEBODY OR SOMETHING BORING** a boring person, thing, or event (*informal*) [Old English *ginian*] —**yawning** *adj* —**yawningly** *adv*

yawner /yáwnər/ *n* **1** a person who yawns **2** = **yawn** *n.* 2 (*informal*)

yawp /yawp/, **yaup** *vi US* (*informal*) **1** **TALK COARSELY** to talk or complain loudly, coarsely, and sometimes meaninglessly **2** **UTTER A YELP** to utter a sharp loud yelp ■ *n US* (*informal*) **1** **YELP** a sharp loud yelp **2** **COARSE TALK** loud, coarse, and sometimes meaningless talk [14C. < ?] —**yawper** *n*

yaws /yawz/ *n* an infectious tropical disease marked initially by red skin eruptions and later by joint pains. It mainly affects children and is caused by the bacterium *Treponema pertenue*. (+ *singular or plural verb*) [Late 17C. < Carib *yaya*.]

y-axis *n* **1** the vertical axis in a two-dimensional coordinate system such as a graph **2** one of the axes in the three-dimensional Cartesian coordinate system, conventionally the vertical one

Yb *symbol* ytterbium

⚡**YBS** *abbr* you'll be sorry (*in e-mails*)

YC *abbr* Young Conservative

Y chromosome, Y-chromosome *n* the sex chromosome that determines the male sex in humans and other mammals. ◊ **X chromosome**

yclept /i klépt/ *adj* called by the name of (*archaic or humorous*) [Old English *geclipod*, past participle of *geclipian* 'to call']

yd *abbr* yard

YDT *abbr* Yukon Daylight Time

ye[1] /yee/; *unstressed* /yi/ *pron* plural of **thou** (*archaic or regional*) [Old English *gē* < Germanic]

⚡**ye**[2] *abbr* Yemen (*in Internet addresses*)

yea /yay/ *adv, n* yes (*archaic*) ■ *adv* indeed (*archaic*) ○ *'Yea, though I walk through the valley of the shadow of death, I will fear no evil'* (*Psalm 23, Authorized Version*) [Old English *gēa* 'yes' < Germanic]

Yeager /yáygər/, **Chuck** (*b.* 1923) US aviator. Full name **Charles Elwood Yeager**

yeah /yaa, yair/ *interj* yes (*informal*) [Early 20C. Variant of YEA.]

year /yeer, yur/ *n* **1** **TWELVE-MONTH PERIOD FROM JANUARY 1** a period of 365 days (or 366 in a leap year), measured from 1 January to 31 December **2** **TWELVE-MONTH PERIOD FROM ANY DATE** a period of 365 or 366 days, measured exactly or approximately from any date ○ *The company's financial year ends on 31 July.* **3** **SOLAR YEAR** the time it takes the Earth to orbit the Sun, approximately 365.25 days **4** **TIME OF PLANET'S ORBIT AROUND SUN** the time taken for a planet to orbit once round the Sun **5** **PERIOD OF PARTICULAR ACTIVITY** the time occupied by a particular activity within a twelve-month period ○ *academic year* **6** **AGE BAND IN SCHOOL OR COLLEGE** a group of students, usually of approximately the same age, who start school or college at the same time and study together in one or more classes ■ **years** *npl* **1** **LONG TIME** a very long time (*informal*) ○ *It's years since I last saw him.* ○ *We haven't been back for years.* **2** **AGE** age, especially advanced age ○ *a man of his years* **3** **TIME IN GENERAL** time in the past, present, or future ○ *in years to come* **4** **PARTICULAR PERIOD OF TIME** a particular period of time, usually in the past ○ *her early years* [Old English *gēar* < Indo-European] ◇ **since the year dot** for an extremely long time (*informal*) ◇ **year in, year out** in a regular or repeated way over a long period of time, especially when this is seen as monotonous (*informal*)

yearbook /yeér boŏk, yúr-/ *n* **1** a book published annually containing details of events in the previous year, usually within a particular organization or field of interest **2** in the United States, a book compiled by members of a graduating class of a high school or college, commemorating their school year and usually including photographs of the students

year-end *n* the end of a financial year or calendar year ■ *adj* occurring or done at the end of a financial or calendar year

yearling /yéerling, yúr-/ *n* **1 YOUNG ANIMAL** an animal, e.g. a calf or deer, between one and two years of age **2 YEAR-OLD RACEHORSE** a racehorse that is one year old, as reckoned from 1 January in the year after it was born **3 BOND MATURING IN ONE YEAR** a bond that comes to term after one year

yearlong /yéer lóng, yúr-/ *adj* lasting for a year or continuing throughout a year

yearly /yéerli/ *adj* **1 ANNUAL** happening, done, appearing, or published once a year, or every year **2 RELATING TO ONE YEAR** relating to or lasting for a period of twelve months ■ *adv* **1 ONCE A YEAR** once every year **2 PER YEAR** during each year ■ *n* (*plural* **yearlies** /yéerliz/) **ANNUAL EVENT OR ISSUE** something that happens or appears once a year, especially an annual publication

yearn /yurn/ *vi* **1** to want somebody or something very much, often with a feeling of sadness because of the difficulty or impossibility of fulfilling the desire **2** to feel affection, tenderness, or compassion [Old English *giernan* < Indo-European, 'to want'] —**yearner** *n* —**yearningly** *adv*

SYNONYMS See **want**.

yearning /yúrning/ *n* a very strong desire, often tinged with sadness

year of grace, **year of our Lord** *n* a particular year of the Christian era

year out *n EDUC* = **gap year**

year-round *adj* existing, continuing, or operating throughout the year ■ *adv* throughout the year

yea-sayer *n US* **1** a confident and optimistic person **2** a person who always agrees submissively with a superior

yeast /yeest/ *n* **1 SMALL SINGLE-CELLED FUNGUS** a small single-celled fungus that ferments sugars and other carbohydrates, and reproduces by budding. Genus: *Saccharomyces*. **2 PREPARATION OF YEAST CELLS** a commercial preparation of yeast cells. Use: brewing, baking, food supplement. **3 FROTH** the yellowish froth that forms on the surface of a fermenting liquid such as beer, contains yeast cells and carbon dioxide, and promotes fermentation **4 FOAM** any foam or froth, e.g. on sea waves **5 CAUSE OF FERMENT OR ACTIVITY** something or somebody that causes ferment, activity, or unrest ■ *vi* **FERMENT** to ferment, froth, or foam [Old English *gist* < Germanic]

yeast artificial chromosome *n* a sequence of DNA taken from another organism and inserted in a yeast to reveal its function

yeast extract *n* a thick sticky brown food obtained from yeast and eaten as a spread or used in cooking

yeast infection *n* an overgrowth of a fungus in the vagina, intestines, skin, or mouth, causing irritation and swelling. Technical name **candidiasis**

yeasty /yéesti/ (**-ier**, **-iest**) *adj* **1 RELATING TO YEAST** relating to, containing, tasting, or smelling of yeast **2 CAUSING FERMENTATION** fermenting, or causing fermentation **3 FROTHY** full of foam **4 RESTLESS** marked by or causing agitation or restlessness **5 ENERGETIC** full of vitality, productivity, or creativity **6 FRIVOLOUS** light and frivolous — **yeastily** *adv* —**yeastiness** *n*

Yeats /yayts/, **William Butler** (1865–1939) Irish poet and dramatist

yech /yekh, yek/ *interj US* used to express disgust (*informal*) [Mid-20C. Natural exclamation.]

yegg /yeg/ *n US* a burglar, especially a safecracker (*slang*) [Early 20C. < ?]

yeild incorrect spelling of **yield**

Yekaterinburg /ye kátta rèen burg/ city in central Russia, on the eastern slopes of the Ural Mountains. Population: 1,280,000 (1995).

Yekaterinodar /ye kátta rèena daar/ former name for **Krasnodar**

yell /yel/ *vti* **SHOUT LOUDLY** to shout or speak something, or to speak in a very loud voice ◊ *Stop yelling at me!* ■ *n* **1 LOUD CRY** a loud shout, scream, or cry **2** *US, Can* **CHEER OF SUPPORT** a rhythmic word or phrase chanted together by people to give support or encouragement [Old English *giellan* < Indo-European, 'to call'] —**yeller** *n*

William Butler Yeats

Yell /yel/ one of the Shetland Islands, N Scotland. Population: 1,075 (1991). Area: 210 sq. km/81 sq. mi.

yellow /yélló/ *adj* **1 OF THE COLOUR OF BUTTER** having or being near the colour of butter or ripe lemons **2 COWARDLY** cowardly or afraid (*insult*) **3 OFFENSIVE TERM** an offensive term meaning from or born in Asia **4 SENSATIONALIST** using scandalous or sensational material, often greatly exaggerating or distorting the truth. ◊ **yellow journalism, yellow press** ■ *n* **1 YELLOW COLOUR** a colour such as that of butter or ripe lemons that lies between orange and green on the visible spectrum. It is one of the three primary colours of pigment and one of the three subtractive colours. **2 YELLOW PIGMENT** a yellow pigment or dye ◊ *using a bright yellow to complement the green* **3 YELLOW FABRIC** yellow clothing or fabric ◊ *dressed in yellow* **4 YELLOW OBJECT** something yellow **5 YELLOW SNOOKER BALL** a yellow ball in a cue game such as snooker ◊ *pot the yellow* **6 EGG YOLK** the yolk of an egg ■ **yellows** *npl* **PLANT DISEASE** a plant disease marked by a yellowing of foliage that may be caused by a mineral deficiency, virus, or some other infectious agent ■ *vti* **BECOME YELLOW** to become or make something yellow [Old English *geolu* < Indo-European, 'to shine'] —**yellowish** *adj* —**yellowishness** *n* —**yellowly** *adv* —**yellowness** *n* —**yellowy** *adj*

SYNONYMS See **cowardly**.

yellow-bellied *adj* **1** cowardly or afraid (*informal insult*) **2** with a yellow underside

yellow-belly *n* somebody regarded as cowardly (*insult*)

yellow bile *n* MED, HIST = **choler** *n.* 2

yellow brain fungus *n* FUNGI = **jelly fungus**

yellow cake *n* the concentrated semirefined oxide of uranium ore

yellow card *n* in football, a card shown by the referee to a player guilty of serious or persistent foul play as an indication that the player has been cautioned. ◊ **red card**

yellow cress *n* a cress that is related to watercress, but is not limited to growing at water margins. Flowers: yellow.

yellow-dog contract *n US* an illegal employment contract in which the employee agrees not to join a trade union

yellow fever *n* an infectious, often fatal viral disease of warm climates, transmitted by mosquitoes and marked by high fever, haemorrhaging, vomiting of blood, liver damage, and jaundice

yellow flag *n* **1** SHIPPING = **quarantine flag** **2** a signal in motor racing advising caution on the racetrack and prohibiting the passing of another vehicle

yellow-green alga *n* an alga that lives in soil and other moist environments and contains brown and bright yellow pigments that mask the chlorophyll. Division: *Chrysophyta*.

yellowhammer /yélló hamər/ *n* a stout-billed songbird of the bunting family, the male of which has a bright yellow head, neck, and breast. Native to: Europe. *Emberiza citrinella*. [Mid-16C. < YELLOW + ?]

yellow jack (*plural* **yellow jacks** *or* **yellow jack**) *n* **1** yellow fever (*archaic*) **2** SHIPPING = **quarantine flag** **3** a large yellowish food fish. Native to: Atlantic coast of North, South, and Central America. *Caranx bartholomaei*.

yellow jacket *n US* a social wasp with black-and-yellow bands on its body that nests in the ground or in the hollows of trees, and can sting repeatedly. Family: Vespidae.

yellow jasmine *n* TREES = **Carolina jasmine**

yellow jersey *n* in the Tour de France, the jersey awarded to the cyclist with the fastest elapsed time at a completed stage of the race

yellow journalism *n* a style of journalism that makes unscrupulous use of scandalous, lurid, or sensationalized stories to attract readers. ◊ **yellow press** [Late 19C. After the *Yellow Kid* cartoons, in yellow ink, in the sensationalistic *New York World*.]

Yellowknife /yélló nìf/ capital of the Northwest Territories, Canada, on the northern shore of the Great Slave Lake. Population: 17,275 (1996).

yellowlegs /yélló legz/ (*plural* **-legs**) *n* a large shore bird of the sandpiper family with bright yellow legs, mottled brown plumage, and white underparts. Native to: Americas. Genus: *Tringa*.

yellow line *n* in the United Kingdom, a line painted in yellow at the edge of a road, indicating that parking is allowed only for limited periods or at specified times

yellow ochre *n* a yellow-brown pigment containing iron. Use: artists' colours.

Yellow Pages *tdmk* a trademark for a telephone directory printed on yellow paper and containing names, addresses, and telephone numbers of businesses and other organizations listed according to the products or services offered

yellow peril, **Yellow Peril** *n* a highly offensive term referring to the perceived threat to Western nations posed by the nations of East Asia, especially China (*dated taboo*)

yellow pine *n* a strong yellowish pine wood

yellow poplar *n* **1** TREES = **tulip tree** **2** INDUST = **tulipwood**

yellow press *n* collectively, the newspapers that make unscrupulous use of scandalous, lurid, or sensationalized stories to attract readers. ◊ **yellow journalism**

yellow rain *n* a fungal toxin that occurs as a form of precipitation in Southeast Asia

yellow rattle *n* a plant with yellow flowers whose seeds rattle in their pouches when they are shaken. Native to: Europe, North America. *Rhinanthus minor*.

Yellow River = **Huang He**

Yellow Sea arm of the Pacific Ocean between NE China and the Korean Peninsula. It merges with the East China Sea to the south. Chinese **Hwang Hai**

yellow spot *n* OPHTHALMOL = **macula** *n.* 2

Yellowstone /yélló stōn/ river in the W United States, rising in NW Wyoming and flowing into the Missouri River in North Dakota. Length: 1,110 km/692 mi.

Yellowstone National Park the world's first national park, established in 1872 in parts of Wyoming, Montana, and Idaho. Area: 8,983 sq. km/3,468 sq. mi.

yellowtail /yélló tayl/ (*plural* **-tails** *or* **-tail**) *n* **1** a marine game fish with a yellowish tail. Native to: coastal waters of California and Mexico. *Seriola lalandei*. **2** a small greenish fish with silver underparts and a yellow tail and fins that is commonly used as bait. Native to: S Australian and New Zealand waters. *Trachurus novaezelandiae*.

yellowthroat /yélló thrōt/ *n* a small warbler that nests in dense undergrowth and has a yellow breast and throat, a black mask, and a brownish back. Native to: North America. *Geothlypis trichas*.

yellowwood /yélló wòod/ (*plural* **-woods** *or* **-wood**) *n* **1 YELLOWISH WOOD OF NORTH AMERICAN TREE** the yellowish wood of a leguminous North American tree. Use: source of yellow dye. **2 YELLOWISH WOOD OF SOUTHERN AFRICAN TREE** the yellowish wood of a southern African coniferous tree **3 US TREE WITH YELLOW WOOD** a leguminous tree that yields yellowwood. Native to: S United States. *Cladastris lutea*. **4 SOUTHERN AFRICAN TREE** a coniferous tree that yields yellowwood. Native to: southern Africa. *Podocarpus falcatus*.

yellowwort /yélló wurt/ (*plural* **-worts** *or* **-wort**) *n* a perennial plant that has grey waxy foliage and is usually found on chalky turf. Flowers: yellow. *Blackstonia perfoliata*.

yellow-yite /yéllō yīt/ (*plural* **yellow-yites** *or* **yellow-yite**) *n Scotland* a yellowhammer [Early 19C. < ?]

yelp /yelp/ *v* 1 *vi* **BARK OR CRY SHARPLY** to utter a short sharp high-pitched bark or cry, usually of pain 2 *vt* **UTTER SOMETHING WITH YELPING SOUND** to say something in a sharp high-pitched bark or cry ■ *n* **SHORT BARK OR CRY** a short high-pitched bark or cry [Old English *gielpan* 'to boast' < Indo-European, 'to call'] —**yelper** *n*

Yeltsin /yéltsin/, **Boris** (*b.* 1931) Russian statesman

Yemen

Yemen /yémmən/ country on the S Arabian Peninsula, bordering the Red Sea and the Gulf of Aden. Capital: Sana'a. Population: 16,600,000 (1996). Area: 536,869 sq. km/207,285 sq. mi. —**Yemeni** *n, adj*

yen[1] /yen/ (*plural* **yen**) *n* see table at **currency** [Late 19C. Via Japanese *en* < Chinese *yuán* 'round'.]

yen[2] /yen/ *n* a strong yearning for something ■ *vi* (**yens, yenning, yenned**) to have a strong yearning for something [Early 20C. Probably < Chinese (Cantonese) *yăn*.]

Yenisey /yénni say/ river in central Siberian Russia, rising in S Siberia and flowing northwards into the Kara Sea. Length: 4.090 km/2,540 mi.

yenta /yéntə/, **yente** *n US* a person, often a woman, known as a meddler or a gossip (*disapproving slang; offensive in some contexts*) [Mid-20C. Via Yiddish *yente* < woman's name *Yente* < Latin *gentilis* 'of the same family'.]

yeoman /yṓmən/ *n* (*plural* **-men** /-mən/) 1 **NAVY SIGNALS OFFICER** a noncommissioned or petty officer in the Royal Navy or the Marines who is in charge of signals 2 **FARMER WITH SMALL FREEHOLD** a member of a former class of English commoners who owned and cultivated their own land 3 **SHERIFF'S ASSISTANT** formerly, an assistant to a sheriff or other official in the past 4 **ATTENDANT TO NOBILITY OR ROYALTY** formerly, a servant or minor official employed in a royal or noble household 5 **YEOMAN OF THE GUARD** a yeoman of the guard ■ *adj* **PERFORMED DILIGENTLY** characterized by loyalty, diligence, and reliability ○ *performed yeoman service in completing the task on time* [13C. < ?]

yeomanly /yṓmənli/ *adj* 1 **RELATING TO YEOMAN** relating to or characteristic of a yeoman or yeomen 2 **STAUNCH AND DEPENDABLE** dependable, loyal, and brave (*archaic or literary*) ■ *adv* **BRAVELY** in a brave and loyal way

yeoman of the guard *n* a member of a British royal guard who perform ceremonial duties, especially as guards of the Tower of London

yeomanry /yṓmənri/ *n* 1 a former class of English commoners who owned and cultivated their own land 2 a British cavalry force organized as a home guard in 1761 that became part of the Territorial Army in 1907

Yeovil /yṓvil/ town in SW England. Population: 35,000 (1993 estimate).

yep /yep/ *adv* yes (*informal*) [Late 19C. Alteration of YES.]

YER *abbr* yearly effective rate

yerba /yáirbə, yúr-/, **yerba maté** *n TREES* = **maté** [Early 19C. < Spanish.]

Yerevan /yérrə vaán/ capital of Armenia, in the west of the country. Population: 1,305,000 (1995 estimate).

yersinia /yur sínni ə/ *n* any gram-negative bacterium that may cause disease in humans and animals. Genus: *Yersinia*. [Mid-20C. < After A. E. J. Yersin (1863–1943), Swiss-born French bacteriologist.]

yersiniosis /yur sínni ōssis/ *n* a condition, mainly found in children and young adults, caused by a bacterium and characterized by intestinal pain and symptoms that resemble appendicitis [Late 20C. < YERSINIA, which causes it.]

yes /yess/ *adv* 1 **ASSENT INDICATOR** used especially in speech to indicate assent, agreement, or affirmation ○ *'Do you mean it's all over?' 'Yes, I suppose I do'.* ○ *97 per cent of respondents answered yes* 2 **INDICATES CONTRADICTION** used to indicate contradiction in response to a negative proposition ○ *'He won't believe you'. 'Oh yes he will'.* 3 **MARK OF ATTENTION** used to indicate that somebody is ready to give his or her attention to somebody who has asked for it ○ *'Doctor?' 'Yes?'* 4 **ACCEPTANCE** used to accept an offer or a request ○ *'Would you like some tea?' 'Yes, please'.* ■ *n* 1 **yes** (*plural* **yeses** *or* **yesses**) **AFFIRMATIVE RESPONSE** an affirmative response to a question ○ *Was that a yes or a no?* 2 **AFFIRMATIVE VOTER** a person who votes in the affirmative ○ *The yeses have 65 per cent and the noes 35 per cent, so the motion is carried.* [Old English *gēse < gēa* (see YEA) + *sīe* 'may it be (so)', form of the verb *to be*] ◊ **say yes** to express agreement or consent

yeshiva /yə shēvə/ (*plural* **-vas** *or* **-vot** /-vot/ *or* **-voth**), **yeshivah** (*plural* **-vahs** *or* **-vot** /-vot/ *or* **-voth**) *n* a seminary for orthodox Jewish, usually unmarried, men where they study the primary source of Jewish law, the Talmud [Mid-19C. < Hebrew *yĕšīḇāh < yāšab* 'sit'.]

yes man, **yes-man** *n* a person who enthusiastically and uncritically agrees with the ideas and views of a superior

yes/no question *n* a question that can be answered with 'yes' or 'no' and that in English begins with an actual or implied verb

yessir /yéssər/, **yessiree** /yés surée/ *interj* used, often ironically or humorously, to express submissive assent or obedience (*informal*) [Early 20C. Representing a casual pronunciation of *yes, sir.*]

yester- *prefix* used to refer to a time in the past denoted by the suffix ○ *yestermorning* [Old English *geostran* < Germanic]

yesterday /yéstərday, -di/ *n* 1 **DAY BEFORE TODAY** the day before this one 2 **PAST** a time in the past ■ *adv* 1 **ON THE PREVIOUS DAY** on the day before today 2 **IN THE PAST** at a time in the past

yesterevening /yéstər eevning/ *adv* yesterday in the evening (*archaic or literary*) ■ *n* the evening of yesterday (*archaic or literary*)

yestermorning /yéstər mawrning/ *adv* yesterday in the morning (*archaic or literary*) ■ *n* the morning of yesterday (*archaic or literary*)

yesternight /yéstər nīt/ *adv* yesterday in the night (*archaic or literary*) ■ *n* the night of yesterday (*archaic or literary*)

yesteryear /yéstər yeer, -yur/ *n* 1 the not very recent past 2 the year before this one

yet /yet/ *adv* 1 **SO FAR** so far, or up to now (*often used with a negative or interrogative*) ○ *The information has not yet been analysed.* 2 **NOW** now, as opposed to later (*often used with a negative*) ○ *I can't come over just yet.* 3 **EVEN** even or still (*often used with a comparative*) ○ *This spurred her on to yet greater efforts.* ○ *Yet again, we find the same reluctance to act.* 4 **IN SPITE OF EVERYTHING** used to indicate that it is still possible that something will happen despite everything ○ *We'll solve this problem yet.* 5 **UP TO NOW** used with superlatives to indicate that something is, e.g., the best, worst, or most impressive up to now ○ *This study is the largest yet – a 14-year study of 87,000 nurses.* 6 **FOR LONGER** used to indicate that something will go on happening for a specified time ○ *It would take hours yet for the space telescope photos to arrive on Earth and be processed.* 7 **NEVER UP TO NOW** used to indicate that somebody has not done something up to now ○ *The largest hotel in the town, the Queen's Head, has yet to welcome a member of the royal family.* ■ *conj* **NEVERTHELESS** however or nevertheless ○ *They can't find the cause, yet the researchers agree that one must be found.* [Old English *gīet* < ?]

USAGE *Did she go yet?* In the simple past tense **yet** is not used in this way in British English; the perfect tense (*Has she gone yet?*) is used. The simple past is usual, however, in American English. In some meanings, **yet** and *still* are largely interchangeable: *This has still to be decided* or *This has yet to be decided.*

yeti /yétti/ (*plural* **-tis**) *n* a mysterious hairy humanoid animal said to live in the Himalayas [Mid-20C. < ?]

⚡ **yettie** /yétti/ *n* a young, technologically knowledgeable entrepreneur who is involved in e-commerce and who typically buys and trades technology shares (*slang*) [Late 20C. Acronym < *y*oung, *e*ntrepreneurial, *tech*(nology)-based after YUPPIE and similar words.]

Yevtushenko /yévtə shéngkō/, **Yevgeny Aleksandrovich** (*b.* 1933) Russian poet

yew /yoo/ *n* 1 **WOOD** the fine-grained wood of a poisonous evergreen tree 2 **EVERGREEN TREE** a poisonous evergreen tree or shrub that yields yew and has flat dark-green needles and scarlet fruits (**arils**) that resemble berries. Genus: *Taxus*. 3 **YEW BOW** an archer's bow made from yew [Old English *īw* < Germanic]

Yezidi /yézzidi/ *n* a member of a Kurdish religious group, founded by an Muslim mystic in the 12th century but incorporating many elements of Iranian myth and tradition [Early 19C. < ?] —**Yezidism** *n*

Y-fronts *tdmk* a trademark for men's or boys' underpants that have an opening at the front with seams in the shape of an inverted Y

Yggdrasil /ígdrə sil/, **Ygdrasil** *n* in Norse mythology, the great ash tree that overshadows the world, binding together earth, heaven, and hell [< Old Norse]

YHA *abbr* Youth Hostels Association

YHWH, **YHVH, JHVH, JHWH** *n* the transliteration of the four letters (**Tetragrammaton**) representing the name of God in the Bible. ◊ **Adonai, Yahweh**

Yi /yee/ *n* a Korean dynasty that ruled Korea from 1392, following a period of Mongol invasions, until 1910, and that restored aristocratic dominance and Chinese influence

yid /yid/ *n* a highly offensive term for a Jewish person (*taboo*) [Late 19C. Via Yiddish *yidish < Middle High German *jüde* 'Jew' (see YIDDISH).]

Yiddish /yíddish/ *n* a language derived from a medieval German dialect and written in Hebrew script, spoken by some Jews in Europe, Israel, and North and South America [Late 19C. Via Yiddish *yidish* (*daytsh*) 'Jewish (German)' < Middle High German *jüdisch diutsch < jüde* 'Jewish person' < Latin *Judaeus* (see JEW).] —**Yiddish** *adj*

yield /yeeld/ *v* 1 *vt* **PRODUCE** to produce something naturally or as a result of cultivation ○ *The field yields a good crop.* 2 *vt* **GIVE SOMETHING AS RESULT** to produce something as the result of work, activity, or calculation ○ *The research has yielded some interesting results.* 3 *vt* **GIVE PROFIT** to gain an amount as a return on an investment ○ *bonds that yield 9 per cent* 4 *vi* **GIVE WAY** to give way or give up further resistance ○ *She refused to yield despite our pleas.* 5 *vt* **GIVE SOMETHING UP TO** to give something up to somebody else or concede it ○ *He eventually yielded control of the company to his daughter.* 6 *vi* **GIVE WAY TO PRESSURE** to move or bend under pressure or with the application of force ○ *The window was painted shut and wouldn't yield.* 7 *vi* **SURRENDER** to admit defeat and surrender 8 *vi* **BE REPLACED BY** to be replaced by something else ○ *Older houses and gardens were gradually yielding to modern purpose-built flats.* 9 *vi US* **LET ANOTHER PASS** to slow down or stop in order to let another vehicle pass ○ *yield to traffic on the right* ■ *n* 1 **AMOUNT PRODUCED** the amount of something, especially a crop, produced by cultivation or labour ○ *Yields per acre were slightly lower than last year.* 2 **RETURN ON INVESTMENT** a part of a return on investment coming from the receipt of interest or dividends ○ *The yield on the account was disappointing.* 3 **PRODUCT FROM A CHEMICAL REACTION** the quantity of product resulting from a chemical reaction or process, often expressed as a percentage of the amount that is theoretically obtainable 4 **EXPLOSIVE FORCE** the amount of energy released in a nuclear explosion expressed as the amount of TNT that would have the same explosive force [Old English *geldan* 'pay' < Germanic] —**yieldability** /yéeldə billəti/ *n* —**yieldable** *adj* —**yielder** *n*

SYNONYMS yield, capitulate, submit, succumb, surrender

CORE MEANING: to give way

yield to give way to something such as force, pressure, entreaty, or persuasion; **capitulate** to cease to resist a superior force, especially one that seems invincible, sometimes without having offered strong opposition; **submit** to accept somebody else's authority or will, especially reluctantly or under pressure; **succumb** to give in to something due to weakness or the failure to offer effective opposition; **surrender** to give way to the power of another person and stop offering resistance, usually after active opposition.

yield up *vt* to reveal something formerly hidden or secret

yielding /yeélding/ *adj* 1 SOFT AND BENDING inclined to give or bend under pressure 2 COMPLIANT tending to obey others 3 PRODUCING productive of a good or bad yield or crop —**yieldingly** *adv* —**yieldingness** *n*

yikes /yīks/ *interj* used when suddenly startled (*informal*) [Late 20C. < ?]

yin /yin/ *n* the principle of darkness, negativity, and femininity in Chinese philosophy that is the counterpart to yang. ◊ **yang** [Late 17C. < Chinese *yīn* 'shade, feminine, moon'.]

Yinglish /yíng glish/ *n* a type of English influenced by Yiddish words and syntax, spoken by early Jewish immigrants to the United States [Mid-20C. Blend of YIDDISH + ENGLISH.] —**Yinglish** *adj*

yip /yip/ *vi* (**yips, yipping, yipped**) to give a high-pitched bark ■ *n* a high-pitched bark [An imitation of the sound]

yipe /yīp/ *interj US* used to express fear or alarm (*informal*) [Mid-20C. < ?]

yippee *interj* used to express joy and excitement (*usually by or to children*) [Early 20C. A natural exclamation.]

yips /yips/ *npl* nervousness that impairs the performance of a sportsman or sportswoman, especially a golfer [Mid-20C. < ?]

YIU *abbr* yes, I understand (*in e-mails*)

yizkor /yíz kawr/ *n* a memorial prayer for deceased relatives recited in synagogue on Festivals and Yom Kippur [Mid-20C. < Hebrew *yizkōr* 'may He remember'.]

-yl *suffix* a group of atoms forming a radical ○ *carbonyl* [Via French *-yle* < Greek *hulē* 'wood, organic matter']

ylang-ylang /eé lang eé lang/, **ilang-ilang** *n* a tree with flowers that yield a fragrant oil used in perfumery. Native to: tropical Asia, N Australia. *Cananga odorata.* [Late 19C. < Tagalog *ilang-ilang.*]

ylem /íləm/ *n* hypothetical matter that, according to the big bang theory of the origin of the universe, was the substance from which the chemical elements were formed. ◊ **big bang** [Mid-20C. < medieval Latin *hylem* 'universal matter' < Greek *hulē* 'wood, matter'.]

Y-level *n* a rotatable level mounted on a Y-shaped frame, used in surveying

YM *abbr* you mean (*in e-mails*)

YMCA *abbr* Young Men's Christian Association ■ *n* (*plural* **YMCAs**) a building or other centre where social, sports, or educational facilities are provided by the YMCA for its members

YMHA *abbr* Young Men's Hebrew Association

Ymir /eé meer/ *n* the forefather of all the giants of Norse mythology

Ymodem /wī mōdem/ *n* a variation of the Xmodem file transfer protocol in which data is sent in 1-kilobyte blocks

YNK *abbr* you never know (*in e-mails*)

yo /yō/ *interj* used as a greeting or to get somebody's attention [15C. Natural exclamation.]

yob /yob/ *n* a young hooligan (*informal*) [Mid-19C. Backward spelling of BOY.] —**yobbery** *n* —**yobbish** *adj*

YOB *abbr* year of birth

yobbo /yóbbō/ (*plural* **-bos**) *n* = **yob** (*informal*)

yocto- indicates 10^{-24} in measurements ○ *yoctojoule* [Late 20C. Modelled on OCTO-.]

yod /yod/, **yodh** *n* the 10th letter of the Hebrew alphabet [Mid-18C. < Hebrew *yōḏ*.]

yodel /yṓd'l/, **yodle** *vi* (**-dels, -delling, -delled; -dles, -dling, -dled**) to sing, changing rapidly between a normal and falsetto voice ■ *n* a song or passage that features yodelling [Early 19C. < German *jodeln* an imitation of the sound.] —**yodeller** *n*

yodh *n* ALPH = **yod**

yodle *vi, n* MUSIC = **yodel**

yoga /yṓgə/ *n* 1 a Hindu discipline that promotes the unity of the individual with a supreme being through a system of postures and rituals 2 a system or set of breathing exercises and postures derived from or based on Hindu yoga [Late 18C. < Sanskrit *yogaḥ* 'union'.]

yogh /yog/ *n* a letter ʒ used in Middle English [13C. < ?]

yoghurt /yóggərt, yṓgərt/, **yogurt, yoghourt** *n* milk fermented by bacteria to give a tangy or slightly sour flavour and a lightly set or thick and creamy consistency [Early 17C. < Turkish *yoğurt.*]

yogi /yṓgi/ (*plural* **-gis**), **yogin** /yṓgin/ *n* 1 a practitioner of yoga 2 a student of a guru or other spiritual teacher [Early 17C. < Sanskrit *yogī* < *yogaḥ* 'yoga'.]

yogic /yṓgik/ *adj* relating to the practice of yoga

yogurt *n* FOOD = **yoghurt**

Yogyakarta /yóggyə kaártə/ city in SW Indonesia, on Java. Population: 412,059 (1990).

yo-heave-ho *interj* formerly used by sailors as a rhythmic accompaniment to hauling work

yoicks /yoyks/ *interj* used to encourage hounds in a foxhunt [Mid-18C. < ?]

yoke /yōk/ *n* 1 ANIMAL HARNESS a wooden frame for harnessing two draught animals 2 FRAME FOR CARRYING LOADS a frame designed to fit across somebody's shoulders with balanced loads suspended at each end 3 RESTRICTIVE BURDEN something that is oppressive and restrictive 4 FITTED PART OF A GARMENT the fitted part of a garment, usually around the shoulders or waist, from which an unfitted part is suspended 5 BOND a bond or tie that keeps people together ○ *the yoke of marriage* 6 *Ireland, N Ireland* WHATSIT OR THINGUMABOB any gadget or implement whose proper name is not known ○ *I need a yoke to fix this screw in.* 7 CROSSED SPEARS an archway made of crossed spears under which defeated enemies of the ancient Romans were forced to march 8 JOINED ANIMALS two animals joined by a yoke 9 RUDDER CROSSBAR a crossbar fitted to the top of a rudder and connected to the front of a boat by ropes or cables for steering 10 CATHODE RAY DEVICE a device fitted to the neck of a cathode ray tube to control the scanning motion of the electron beam 11 EQUIPMENT FOR MULTI-TRACK RECORDING equipment for recording or reproducing sounds or music on more than one track simultaneously, by joining together two or more magnetic recording heads 12 AIRCRAFT PART the handle of the steering mechanism for an aeroplane's ailerons ■ *vt* (**yokes, yoking, yoked**) 1 FIT ANIMALS WITH A YOKE to put a yoke on two draught animals 2 CONNECT AN ANIMAL TO A VEHICLE to connect a draught animal to a plough or vehicle 3 LINK THINGS TOGETHER to join or link two things forcibly or surprisingly ○ *Foxhunters were yoked together with farmers on the issue.* [Old English *geoc* < Indo-European, 'join']

SPELLCHECK Do not confuse ***yoke*** with ***yolk***, which has a similar sound. Beware: your spellchecker will not catch this error.

yokel /yṓk'l/ *n* an offensive term that deliberately insults a country dweller, regarded as lacking sophistication, education, or other qualities thought typical of city dwellers (*insult*) [Early 19C. < ?] —**yokelish** *adj*

Yokohama /yṓkō haámə/ port of SE Honshu Island, Japan. Population: 3,265,000 (1994).

Yokuts /yṓ kuts/ (*plural* **-kuts**) *n* 1 a member of a closely related group of Native North American peoples of central California 2 the group of languages spoken by the Yokuts people, now virtually extinct [Late 19C. < Yawelmani *yokhoc'* 'a Native American'.] —**Yokuts** *adj*

yolk /yōk/ *n* 1 the round yellow portion of a bird's or reptile's egg, containing protein and fats that provide nourishment for the developing young 2 a greasy substance from the skin of sheep that collects in wool [Old English *geol(o)ca* < *geolu* (see YELLOW)] —**yolky** *adj*

SPELLCHECK See ***yoke***.

yolk sac *n* a thin membrane surrounding the embryo in birds, fish, reptiles, and mammals. In birds, fish, and reptiles, it encloses the yolk.

Yom Arafat /yom árrə fat/ *n* an Islamic festival during which people on the hajj gather at the plain of Arafat near Mecca and Muslims elsewhere remember them in prayer. Date: 9th day of Dhu al-Hijjah.

Yom Hashoah /yòm hə shṓ ə/, **Yom Ha-Shoah** *n* = **Holocaust Day** [Late 20C. < Hebrew.]

Yom Kippur /yom kíppər, -ki poór/ *n* the holiest day of the Jewish year, on which Jewish people fast and say prayers of penitence. Date: 10th day of Tishri [< Hebrew *Yōm Kippūr* 'day of atonement']

yomp /yomp/ *vi* to walk while heavily laden or over difficult terrain (*informal*) [Late 20C. < ?]

yom tov /yóm tóv, yómtəv/ (*plural* **yamim tovim** /yaa meém to veém/) *n* a Jewish religious festival [Directly and via Yiddish *yontef* < Hebrew *yōm ṭōḇ* 'good day']

yon /yon/ *adv* yonder, over there (*regional*) ■ *det Scotland, N England* that or those over there [Partly shortening of YONDER, partly < Old English *geon* 'that one']

yonder /yóndər/ *adv* over there (*regional*) ■ *det* that over there (*regional*)

yoni /yṓni/ (*plural* **-nis**) *n* in Hinduism, a representation of the female genitals regarded as a manifestation of the feminine principle [Late 18C. < Sanskrit *yoniḥ* 'womb'.]

Yonkers /yóngkərz/ city in SE New York State. Population: 190,153 (1998 estimate).

yonks /yongks/ *n* a very long time (*informal*) [Mid-20C. < ?]

yoo-hoo /yoó hoo/ *interj* used to get somebody's attention, especially when the speaker is at a distance ■ *vti* (**yoo-hoos, yoo-hooing, yoo-hooed**) to say or shout 'yoo-hoo' to attract somebody's attention [Early 20C. Natural exclamation.]

yore /yawr/ *n* time long past (*literary*) [Old English *geāra* < ?]

york /yawrk/ *vt* in cricket, to get a batsman out or to attempt to get a batsman out by bowling a ball so that it pitches immediately under the bat [Late 19C. Back-formation < YORKER.]

York[1] /yawrk/ *n* the branch of the Plantagenet dynasty that ruled England from 1461 to 1485. It was named after its founder, Edward, Duke of York (**Edward IV**).

York[2] /yawrk/ historic city in N England. Population: 105,500 (1991).

Yorke Peninsula /yáwrk-/ peninsula in SE South Australia, between the Gulf of St Vincent and the Spencer Gulf

yorker /yáwrkər/ *n* a ball bowled in cricket so that it pitches on the ground immediately under the bat [Probably after the city of YORK[2]]

yorkie /yáwrki/, **Yorkie** *n* a Yorkshire terrier (*informal*) [Early 19C. Shortening.]

Yorkist /yáwrkist/ *n* a supporter or member of the House of York that ruled England from 1461 to 1485

York rite *n* a masonic ceremony that confers different degrees at different levels of the membership [Late 19C. After YORK[2].]

Yorks. *abbr* Yorkshire

Yorkshire /yáwrkshər/ former county in N England, traditionally divided into the East, West, and North Ridings

Yorkshire Dales area of wild moorlands divided by fertile valleys in N England

Yorkshire fog *n* a common grass of the British Isles that has downy leaves and white or pink flower heads. *Holcus lanatus.*

Yorkshire pudding *n* a flour-based batter that is traditionally cooked in the drippings of roast meat and served with gravy

Yorkshire terrier *n* a very small long-haired terrier with a long silky brown-and-grey coat

Yorkton /yáwrktən/ town in SE Saskatchewan, Canada. Population: 15,154 (1996).

Yoruba /yórrŏŏbə/ (*plural* **-ba** *or* **-bas**) *n* 1 MEMBER OF W AFRICAN PEOPLE a member of a West African people living mostly in Nigeria 2 W AFRICAN LANGUAGE a Niger-Congo language spoken in SW Nigeria, Benin, and Togo. Native speakers: 20 million. 3 REGION OF CITY-STATES IN NIGERIA a region of city-states that developed in N Nigeria around AD 1200, notable for the population's animistic religion and their artistic work, in particular wood and bronze pieces [Mid-19C. < Yoruba.] —**Yoruba** *adj* —**Yoruban** *adj*

Yosemite Falls /yə sémməti-, yō-/ waterfall in the Yosemite National Park. Height: 739 m/2,245 ft.

Yosemite National Park national park in central California. Area: 3,079 sq. km/1,189 sq. mi.

yotta- *prefix* indicates 10^{24} in measurements ○ *yottabyte* [Late 20c. Probably < Italian *otto* 'eight'.]

ϟ **yottabyte** /yóttə bīt/ *n* a unit of computer memory or disk storage equal to 1,024 zettabytes

you (*stressed*) /yoo/; (*unstressed*) /yŏŏ/; /yə/ *pron* 1 PERSON BEING ADDRESSED refers to the person or people being addressed or written to ○ *I'm fine – how about you?* 2 PERSON OR PEOPLE UNSPECIFIED refers to an unspecified person or people in general ○ *You have to see it to believe it.* ○ *You mix all the dry ingredients together in a bowl.*

3 THOSE BEING REFERRED TO used to refer to the person you are talking to, as well as other people of the same type or class (*before a plural*) ○ *Isn't it time you kids were in bed?* **4 PERSONALITY OF PERSON ADDRESSED** refers to the personality of the person addressed or something's suitability to express it (*informal*) ○ *Don't buy that suit – it's not really you!* **5** US **YOURSELF** yourself (*informal*) ○ *You'll have to get you a job.* [Old English *īow* < *gē* (see YE)]

USAGE See *yourself.*

you-all /yawl/ *pron Southern US* used to address more than one person (*informal*)

you'd /yood/ *contr* **1** you had **2** you would

you'll /yool/ *contr* **1** you will **2** you shall

young /yung/ *adj* **1 NOT VERY OLD** having lived or been in existence a relatively short time ○ *a young person* **2 OF YOUTH** relating to somebody's youth **3 YOUTHFUL** looking or behaving like a young or younger person **4 FOR YOUNG PEOPLE** designed for or appropriate to young people **5 RECENTLY BEGUN** recently begun or in an early stage **6 NOT SIGNIFICANTLY ERODED** in a relatively early stage of landscape formation and therefore steep and largely uneroded ■ *npl* **1 OFFSPRING** offspring, especially when still completely dependent on parents **2 YOUNG PEOPLE** young people in general [Old English *geong* < Indo-European, 'youth, vigour'] —**youngish** *adj* —**youngness** *n*

Young /yung/, **Arthur** (1721–1820) British agriculturist and writer

Young, Brigham (1801–77) US religious leader

Young, Cy (1867–1955) US baseball player. Born **Denton True Young**

Young, Nat (*b.* 1947) Australian surfer

Young, Thomas (1773–1829) British physicist and Egyptologist

youngberry /yúngbəri/ (*plural* **-ries**) *n* **1** a large, sweet, dark-purple fruit, a hybrid of the blackberry and dewberry **2** the trailing bramble that bears youngberries. Native to: SW United States. [Early 20C. After B. M. *Young,* US horticulturist.]

young blood *n* fresh, new, and vigorous ideas or people

young fogy *n* a young person whose ideas and outlook are old-fashioned and conservative (*disapproving*)

young lady *n* **1** used to refer to or address a girl or young woman, often in annoyance or exasperation **2** a man's or boy's girlfriend (*dated*)

youngling /yúngling/ *n* a young person or a young animal

young man *n* **1** used to refer to or address a boy or young man, often in annoyance or exasperation **2** a girl's or woman's boyfriend (*dated*)

young offender *n* **1** in the UK, somebody under 18 who has committed a criminal act. US term **youthful offender 2** *Can* in Canada, somebody between the ages of 12 and 18 who has committed a crime and must be treated according to the terms of the Young Offenders Act, 1984

Young Pretender ♦ **Stuart, Charles Edward**

youngster /yúngstər/ *n* **1** a child or young person **2** a young horse

SYNONYMS See *youth.*

Young Turk *n* **1** a member of a liberal pro-democratic Turkish nationalist movement in the early 20th century that brought about a short-lived revolution in 1908 **2** a young person, especially one of a group, who attempts to wrest control of an organization from an older, established, more conservative group

young'un /yúngən/ *n* an infant or child (*informal*)

younker /yúngkər/ *n* (*archaic*) **1 YOUNG MALE** a young man **2 CHILD** a child **3 YOUNG NOBLE** a young nobleman [Early 16C. < Middle Dutch *jonckher* < *jonc* 'young' + *hēre* 'lord'.]

your (*stressed*) /yawr, yoor/; (*unstressed*) /yər/ *det* **1 BELONGING TO PERSON SPOKEN TO** refers to something that belongs to or relates to an addressee ○ *What's your phone number?* **2 BELONGING OR RELATING TO SOMEBODY** refers to something that belongs or relates to an unspecified person or people in general ○ *The house is on your left as you come down the road.* **3 INDICATES TOPIC** refers to somebody or something as an example or topic (*informal*) ○ *Take your Queen, for example.* [Old English *ēower* < *gē* (see YE)]

USAGE your/you're The word *your* is a possessive determiner (*Your* [not *You're*] *e-mail password must be*

protected), and *you're* is a contraction of 'you are' (*You're* [not *Your*] *protecting your e-mail password, aren't you?*). Beware: your spellchecker will not catch this error.

Yourcenar /yoòrsə naar/, **Marguerite** (1903–87) Belgian-born French US writer. Pseudonym of **Marguerite de Crayencour**

you're (*stressed*) /yoor, yawr/; (*unstressed*) /yər/ *contr* you are

USAGE See *your.*

yours /yawrz, yoorz/ *pron* **1** refers to something that belongs or relates to the person or people being addressed ○ *I'm taking my tea through to the sitting-room – shall I take yours as well?* **2 yours, Yours** used at the end of letters before somebody signs his or her name ○ *Sincerely yours, Marcia Klein*

yourself /yawr sélf, yoor-, yər-/ *pron* **1 SOMEBODY BEING ADDRESSED** refers to the person or people being addressed or written to ○ *Be careful not to hurt yourself.* **2 MAKING REFERENCE TO SOMEBODY SPOKEN TO** refers emphatically or politely to the person or people being addressed or written to ○ *'Consider', he replied, 'how you yourself really feel about such things'.* **3 YOUR NORMAL SELF** your normal or usual self ○ *You are not yourself tonight.*

USAGE The primary uses of *yourself* are as a reflexive pronoun (*Don't hurt yourself*) and as a reinforcing pronoun (*Can you do it yourself?*). In formal writing it should not be used as an alternative for *you* in sentences of the type: *That's up to you* [not *up to yourself*].

yours truly *pron* me, myself, or I (*informal*) ○ *Of course, everyone's going to be there except yours truly.*

yous /yooz/, **youse** *pron* used to address more than one person (*nonstandard regional*) [Late 19C. < YOU.]

youth /yooth/ *n* **1 TIME WHEN SOMEBODY IS YOUNG** the period of human life between childhood and maturity **2 BEING YOUNG** the state of being young **3 YOUNG PERSON** a young person, especially a boy or young man **4 EARLY STAGE** an early stage of something **5 EROSION STAGE** the first stage in landscape formation in which fast-flowing streams travel down steep mountain valleys ■ *npl* **YOUNG PEOPLE** young people in general [Old English *geoguþ* < Germanic]

SYNONYMS *youth, child, kid, teenager, youngster*
CORE MEANING: somebody who is young
youth a man or boy who is in his teens or early twenties; **child** a young person between birth and the onset of puberty; **kid** (*informal*) a child or young person; **teenager** somebody between the ages of thirteen and nineteen; **youngster** somebody who is young, or (*humorous*) somebody younger than others mentioned or present.

youth club *n* a centre that provides organized activities for young people during their leisure time

Youth Court *n* a provincial court in Canada with jurisdiction over all cases involving offenders under the age of 18

youth custody *n* in the United Kingdom, a custodial sentence of four to eighteen months for an offender aged 15 to 21

youth custody centre *n* in the United Kingdom, a penal institution for young offenders

youthful /yóothf'l/ *adj* **1 LIKE YOUTH** typical of or possessing youth **2 VIGOROUS** vigorous and energetic **3 NOT FULLY DEVELOPED** in early development and not yet mature **4 MILDLY ERODED** steep, rugged, and relatively uneroded **5 NEAR SOURCE** describes a fast-flowing stream close to its source —**youthfully** *adv* —**youthfulness** *n*

youthful offender *n US LAW* = **young offender** *n.* 1

youth hostel *n* an establishment offering cheap accommodation for travellers, especially young travellers

Youth Training Scheme *n* in the United Kingdom, a former government scheme providing work-related training courses and work experience for jobless school-leavers

you've /yoov/ *contr* you have

yow /yow/ *interj* used to express pain, surprise, or alarm (*informal*) [Mid-19C. Natural exclamation.]

yowl /yowl/ *vi* to cry out mournfully or as an expression of pain ■ *n* a long mournful wail [12C. Probably an imitation of the sound.] —**yowler** *n*

⚡**YOYO** *abbr* you're on your own (*in e-mails*)

yo-yo /yó yō/ *n* (*plural* **yo-yos**) **1 TOY WITH STRING WOUND ON SPOOL** a toy consisting of a long string wound onto a spool that is dropped and raised repeatedly using the force of gravity and momentum to unwind and rewind the string **2 FLUCTUATING THING** something that repeatedly goes up and down or fluctuates between one extreme and another **3** *US, Can* **OFFENSIVE TERM** an offensive term that deliberately insults a person's intelligence or judgment (*slang insult*) ■ *vi* (**yo-yos, yo-yoing, yo-yoed** **FLUCTUATE** to fluctuate between two extremes or directions [Early 20C. < ?]

yo-yo dieting *n* a situation in which somebody repeatedly loses weight through dieting and then regains the weight that he or she has lost

Ypres /éeprə/ town in SW Belgium, site of several major battles during World War I. Population: 35,100 (1989).

Ypsilanti /ípsə lánti/, **Alexander, Prince** (1792–1828) Greek soldier

yr *abbr* **1** year **2** younger **3** your

Yrs *abbr* Yours (*used at end of letter*)

YST *abbr* Yukon Standard Time

⚡**yt** *abbr* Mayotte (*in Internet addresses*)

⚡**YT** *abbr* **1** yours truly (*in e-mails*) **2** Yukon Territory

YTD *abbr* year to date

YTS *abbr* Youth Training Scheme

ytterbia /i túrbi ə/ *n CHEM* = **ytterbium oxide** [Late 19C. After *Ytterby* (see YTTERBIUM).]

ytterbium /i túrbi əm/ *n* (*symbol* **Yb**) a soft silvery metal of the lanthanide group of rare-earth elements. Source: monazite, bastnaesite. Use: strengthening steel, in laser devices and portable X-ray units. [Late 19C. After *Ytterby* a Swedish quarry.] —**ytterbic** *adj*

ytterbium oxide *n* Yb_2O_3 a colourless oxide of ytterbium. Use: alloys, ceramics.

yttria /íttri ə/ *n CHEM* = **yttrium oxide** [Early 19C. After *Ytterby* a swedish quarry.]

yttriferous /i tríffərəss/ *adj* yielding or containing yttrium

yttrium /íttri əm/ *n* (*symbol* **Y**) a silvery-grey metallic element. Source: uranium, rare-earth ores. Use: superconducting alloys, permanent magnets. [Early 19C. < YTTRIA.] —**yttric** *adj*

yttrium metal *n* a metal in the group that includes yttrium and related rare-earth elements such as holmium, erbium, thulium, ytterbium, and lutetium

yttrium oxide *n* Y_2O_3 a yellowish powder. Use: optical glass, ceramics, lasers, microwave components.

⚡**yu** *abbr* Yugoslavia (*in Internet addresses*)

yuan /yoo án/ (*plural* **-an**) *n* see table at **currency** [Early 20C. < Chinese *yuán* 'round'.]

Yucatán /yoˇokə taàn/ peninsula in E Central America, comprising three Mexican states, Belize, and part of N Guatemala. Area: 181,300 sq. km/70,000 sq. mi.

yucca /yúkə/ *n* an evergreen plant widely grown for its sharp lance-shaped leaves and clusters of white flowers that grow in vertical spikes. Native to: SW United States, Mexico. Genus: *Yucca.* [Mid-16C. Via Spanish *yuca* < Taino.]

yucca moth *n* a small white moth that pollinates the yucca plant, laying its eggs in the ovaries of the yucca's flowers. Native to: North America. *Tegeticula alba.*

yuck /yuk/, **yuk** *interj* used to express disgust or revulsion (*informal*) [Mid-20C. An imitation of the sound of vomiting.]

yucky /yúki/ (**-ier, -iest**), **yukky** (**-kier, -kiest**) *adj* disgusting or unpleasant (*informal*) —**yuckiness** *n*

Yug. *abbr* Yugoslavia

yuga /yoˇogə/ *n* in Hinduism, any one of the four stages in each cycle of history, each worse than the one before [Late 18C. < Sanskrit *yugam* 'yoke, era'.]

Yugo. *abbr* Yugoslavia

Yugoslavia

ugoslavia /yoŏgō slaåvi a/ republic in SE Europe, consisting of Serbia and Montenegro. Capital: Belgrade. Population: 10,574,000 (1996). Area: 102,173 sq. km/39,449 sq. mi. —**Yugoslav** /yoŏgō slaav/ n, adj — **Yugoslavian** adj, n

■k interj = **yuck**

■kky adj = **yucky**

■kon /yoŏk on/ river in NW North America, rising in S Yukon Territory, Canada, and flowing through Alaska to the Bering Sea. Length: 3,190 km/1,980 mi.

■kon Territory territory in NW Canada. Capital:

Whitehorse. Population: 30,766 (1996). Area: 483,450 sq. km/186,660 sq. mi.

Yukon Time n the time observed in the Yukon Territory and in a section of more or less equivalent longitude extending southwards from there, being nine hours behind Universal Coordinated Time

yulan /yoŏ lan/ n a deciduous tree or shrub of the magnolia family that flowers profusely in spring before the leaves emerge. Flowers: white, fragrant, cup-shaped. Native to: China. *Magnolia denudata*. [Early 19C. < Chinese *yùlán* 'jade orchid'.]

Yule /yool/, **yule** n Christmas day or the Christmas season (*archaic literary*) [Old English *gēol* 'mid-winter festival, Christmas' < Germanic]

yule log n a large log traditionally placed on the hearth fire on Christmas Eve

Yuletide /yoŏl tīd/ n the Christmas season

Yuma /yoŏma/ n a member of a Native North American people of SW Arizona and neighbouring areas [Early 19C. < Pima *yumī*.] —**Yuma** adj

Yuman /yoŏman/ n a family of languages spoken in the SW United States and in N Mexico. Native speakers: 4,000. —**Yuman** adj

yummy /yúmmi/ (-**mier**, -**miest**) adj very appealing to taste or smell [Late 19C. < *yum*, an imitation of the sound of smacking the lips.] —**yumminess** n

Yunnan /yoŏ nán/ province in S China. Capital: Kunming. Population: 39,390,000 (1994). Area: 390,000 sq. km/150,600 sq. mi.

Yün Shoup'ing /yůn shō píng/ (1633–90) Chinese artist

yup /yup/ adv yes (*informal*) [Early 20C. Representing a casual pronunciation of YES.]

Yupik /yoŏpik/ (*plural* -**pik** *or* -**piks**) n 1 a member of an aboriginal people of W Alaska and parts of coastal Siberia, related to the Inuit of the Canadian Arctic and Greenland 2 the group of Eskimo-Aleut languages spoken by the Yupik people. Native speakers: 3,000. [Mid-20C. < Alaskan Yupik *Yup'ik* 'real person'.] — **Yupik** adj

yuppie /yúppi/ n a young educated city-dwelling professional, especially when regarded as materialistic [Late 20C. < *y(oung) u(rban) p(rofessional)*, after HIPPIE.]

yuppie flu, **yuppie disease** n chronic fatigue syndrome (*informal*)

yuppify /yúppi fī/ (-**fies**, -**fying**, -**fied**) vt to cause an area to be increasingly populated by young educated city-dwelling professionals or to modify something with the values ascribed to yuppies —**yuppification** /yúppifi káysh'n/ n

yurt /yurt/ n a collapsible circular tent of skins stretched over a pole frame, used by Central Asian nomadic peoples [Late 18C. Via Russian *yurta* < Turkic *jurt*.]

Yuwaalaraay /yoo waàla rī/ n an extinct Australian Aboriginal language of New South Wales, now being revived —**Yuwaalaraay** adj

YWCA abbr Young Women's Christian Association ■ n a building or other centre where social, sports, or educational facilities are provided by the YWCA for its members

YWHA abbr Young Women's Hebrew Association

Zz

z[1] /zed/, **Z** *n* (*plural* **z's**; *plural* **Z's** *or* **Zs**) the 26th and final letter of the English alphabet, representing a consonant sound ■ **z's** *npl* sleep, from the traditional transcription of the sound of snoring (*informal*)

z[2] *symbol* **1** an algebraic variable **2** atomic number **3** a Cartesian coordinate along the z-axis

z[3] *abbr* **1** zaïre **2** z-axis **3** zepto- **4** zetta- **5** zone

Z[1] /zed/ (*plural* **Z's** *or* **Zs**) *n* something shaped like a letter 'Z'.

Z[2] *symbol* **1** atomic number **2** impedance **3** zetta-

Z[3] *abbr* zone

⚡**Z39.50** *n* a standard communication protocol used in accessing bibliographic data in databases

⚡**za** *abbr* South Africa (*in Internet addresses*)

Zaanstad /zaan shtát/ city in the W Netherlands. Population: 133,817 (1996).

zabaglione /zább'l yóni, zábba lyóni/ *n* a dessert made of egg yolks, sugar, and Marsala wine beaten over hot water until pale and foamy [Late 19C. < Italian.]

zaddik *n* JUDAISM **= tzaddik**

zaffer /záffər/, **zaffre** *n* an impure form of cobalt oxide. Use: blue colouring agent in enamels and glass. [Mid-17C. Via Italian *zaffera* < French *safre*.]

zaftig /záftig/ *adj* with a full-figured body [Mid-20C. Via Yiddish < Middle High German *saftec* 'juicy' < *saft* 'juice'.]

zag /zag/ *n* a direction or segment of a course running opposite to a zig ■ *vi* (**zags, zagging, zagged**) to change direction quickly [Late 18C. < ZIGZAG.]

Zagreb /záa greb/ capital of Croatia, in the north of the country. Population: 706,770 (1991).

Zagros Mountains /zág ross-/ mountain range in SW Iran. Highest peak: Zard Kuh 4,548 m/14,921 ft. Length: 1,600 km/1,000 mi.

Zaharias /zə háiriee ass, -hárriee-/, **Babe Didrikson** (1913–56) US athlete. Born **Mildred Didrikson**

Zaharoff /zə khaárəf/, **Sir Basil** (1849–1936) Turkish-born French arms dealer. Born **Zacharias Basileor Zaharoff**

zaibatsu /zí bat soó/ (*plural* **-su**) *n* a large industrial combine created in Japan in the 1890s, usually by a single family, as part of the process of industrialization [Mid-20C. < Japanese, < *zai* 'wealth' + *batsu* 'clique'.]

zaikai /zí kí/ *n* the business and financial community of Japan [Mid-20C. < Japanese, < *zai* 'wealth' + *kai* 'world'.]

zaïre /zaa eer/ (*plural* **-ïre** *or* **-ïres**) *n* a former unit of currency in the Democratic Republic of Congo [Mid-20C. After *Zaire*, local name for the Congo River.]

Zaire /zí eer, zaa-/ **1** former name for **Congo, Democratic Republic of the 2** former name for **Congo** —**Zairean** /zí eerən/ *adj*

zakat /zə kaát/ *n* a tax that goes to charity, obligatory for all Muslims, set traditionally at 2.5 per cent of somebody's annual income and capital [Early 19C. Via Persian and Urdu *zaka(t)* or Turkish *zekat* < Arabic *zaka(t)* 'alms-giving'.]

Zakinthos /zákin thoss, zə kínthoss/, **Zakynthos** one of the Ionian Islands, SW Greece, in the Ionian Sea. Population: 30,014. Area: 401 sq. km/155 sq. mi.

zakuski /zə koóski/, **zakuska** /zə koóskə/ *npl* a variety of blinis and breads with savoury toppings, especially caviar and other accompanying titbits, served in Russia with vodka [Late 19C. < Russian, plural of *zakuska* 'hors d'oeuvre'.]

Zambezi /zam beézi/ river in southern Africa, flowing through Zambia, Angola, Botswana, Zimbabwe, and Mozambique to the Indian Ocean. Length: 3,540 km/2,200 mi.

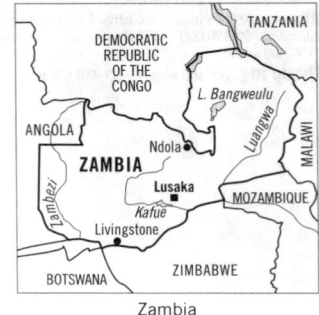
Zambia

Zambia /zámbi ə/ republic in south-central Africa. Capital: Lusaka. Population: 9,715,000 (1996). Area: 752,614 sq. km/290,586 sq. mi. —**Zambian** *n*, *adj*

zamia /záymi ə/ *n* a small tropical tree (**cycad**) that resembles a palm tree, with a short thick trunk, spiky leaves, and upright woody cones that contain seeds. Genus: *Zamia*. [Early 19C. < modern Latin, misreading of Latin *azaniae* 'pine cones'.]

zamindar /zə meen daár/, **zemindar** *n* **1** TAX COLLECTOR IN MUGHAL INDIA a collector of property taxes in Mughal India **2** TAXPAYER IN BRITISH COLONIAL INDIA a landlord in British colonial India liable for tax on his holdings **3** LANDOWNER IN INDIA OR PAKISTAN a traditional owner of land in South Asia [Late 17C. Via Urdu < Persian *zamīndār* < *zamīn* 'land' + *dār* 'holder'.]

zamindari /zə meen daári/ (*plural* **-is**), **zemindary** (*plural* **-ies**), **jamindari** (*plural* **-is**) *n* the system of traditional land ownership in South Asia, or the area of land owned [Mid-18C. Via Urdu < Persian *zamīndārī* < *zamīndār* (SEE ZAMINDAR.)]

zanana /zə naánə/ *n* **1** in South Asia, an area reserved for women in some trains and waiting rooms in railway stations **2 = zenana** [Mid-18C. < Persian, Urdu *zanānah* < *zan* 'woman'.]

zander /zándər/ (*plural* **-der** *or* **-ders**) *n* a freshwater fish of the perch family, harvested for food. Native to: central Europe. *Stizostedion lucioperca*. [Mid-19C. Via German < Low German *sandat*.]

ZANU /záa noo/, **Zanu** *abbr* Zimbabwe African National Union

zany /záyni/ *adj* (**-nier, -niest**) AMUSINGLY UNCONVENTIONAL entertainingly strange or amusingly unusual ■ *n* (*plural* **-nies**) **1** CLOWN a fool, buffoon, or clown **2** STOCK CHARACTER a stock character in Renaissance comedies who mimicked other characters [Late 16C. Via French *zani* < Italian dialect *Zanni*, variant of *Gianni*, pet form of *Giovanni*, character in the commedia dell'arte who tried to mimic the clown.] —**zanily** *adv* —**zaniness** *n* —**zanism** *n*

Zanzibar /zánzi baar/ island of Tanzania, in the India Ocean. Population: 375,539 (1988). Area: 1,650 s km/637 sq. mi.

zap /zap/ *v* (**zaps, zapping, zapped**) (*informal*) **1** *vt* DESTR to kill or finish somebody or something off with sudde force **2** *vti* CHANGE TV CHANNELS USING REMOTE CONTROL change channels on a television set using a remo control device, especially to change channels rapid **3** *vi* MOVE QUICKLY to move about or accomplish somethi very rapidly **4** *vt* COOK SOMETHING IN MICROWAVE to co something in a microwave oven ○ *I'll just zap this fo minute and then we can eat.* **5** *vt* Malaysia, Singapore PHO COPY to photocopy something ■ *n* (*informal*) **1** ENER energy and excitement **2** TIME IN MICROWAVE a short peri of time in a microwave oven ■ *interj* EXPRESSION FORCEFUL ACTION used especially in comic books to i dicate sudden and violent force (*informal*) [Early 20C. imitation of the sound of a lightning strike or electric spark

Zapata /saa paátaa, zə paáta/, **Emiliano** (1879–191 Mexican revolutionary

Zapata moustache *n* a thick moustache that curv down around the edges of the mouth [Mid-20C. Af Emiliano ZAPATA.]

zapateado /záppə tay aádó/ (*plural* **-dos**), **zapateo** /záp táy ó/ (*plural* **-os**) *n* a Spanish or Latin American danc involving rhythmic tapping of the feet [Mid-19C. Spanish < *zapatear* 'tap with the shoe' < *zapato* 'shoe'.]

Zapopan /zaápō pan/ city in SW Mexico. Populatic 668,323 (1990).

Zaporizhzhya /záppə rózhyə/ city in SE Ukraine. Pop lation: 897,000 (1993).

Zapotec /zápə tek/ (*plural* **-tec** *or* **-tecs**) *n* **1** a memb of a Native Central American people who found a Mesoamerican civilization in the region of Oaxac Mexico, between the 7th century BC and the 11th centur AD, and now live in the highlands of the same regi **2** the Oto-Manguean language of the Zapotec peop Native speakers: 500,000. [Late 18C. Via Spanish *zapote* < Nahuatl *tzapotecatl* 'person from the place of the sap tilla'.] —**Zapotecan** *adj*

zapper /záppər/ *n* US (*informal*) **1** a remote control fo television or video recorder **2** a device that attracts a electrocutes insects

zappy /záppi/ (**-pier, -piest**) *adj* lively and forcefully i pressive (*informal*)

ZAPU /záppoo/, **Zapu** *abbr* Zimbabwe African Peopl Union

Zaragoza /zárrə gózə/ capital of Zaragoza Province in autonomous region of Aragon, NE Spain. Populatic 607,900 (1995).

Zarathustra /zárrə thoóstrə/ **= Zoroaster**

zaratite /zárrə tīt/ *n* an amorphous green mineral c sisting of hydrated nickel carbonate [Mid-19C. < Span *zaratita* < the surname *Zarate*.]

zareba /zə reébə/ *n* an outdoor enclosure, especially c made of thorn bushes and used as protection aroun a campsite or village in various parts of No Africa [Mid-19C. < Arabic *zarība* 'cattle pen'.]

zarf /zaarf/ *n* a metal frame for holding a cup, used in Middle East [Mid-19C. < Arabic *zarf* 'vessel'.]

zari /zaàri/, **jari** *n S Asia* gold brocade used to decorate clothes [Mid-20C. Via Urdu < Persian *zarī* < *zar* 'gold'.]

Zaria /zaàri ə/ city in north-central Nigeria. Population: 369,800 (1995 estimate).

zart /zaart/ *interj S W England* a mild expression of surprise or annoyance [Alteration of *God's heart*]

zarzuela /zaar zwáylə/ *n* Spanish musical theatre, usually comic, combining dialogue, music, and dance [Late 19C. < Spanish.]

Zátopek /záttəpek/, **Emile** (*b.* 1922) Czech athlete

zawster /záwstər/ *n S W England* a seamstress [Variant of obsolete *sewster*]

zax /zaks/ *n* a tool similar to a hatchet used for cutting and shaping slate [Mid-17C. Representing Old English *seax* 'knife' < Indo-European.]

z-axis *n* one of the axes of the Cartesian coordinate system that provides a reference in three-dimensional space

zayin /zaàyin/ *n* the seventh letter of the Hebrew alphabet [Early 19C. < Hebrew, 'weapon'.]

zazen /zaà zen/ *n* a form of meditation in Zen, practised sitting in a prescribed position [Early 18C. < Japanese, 'sitting zen'.]

Z boson *n* PHYS = **Z particle**

Z chart *n* a chart used in business and industry to illustrate production data

z-coordinate *n* one of three numbers that provide a reference to a position in three-dimensional space, conventionally the vertical one

zeal /zeel/ *n* energetic and unflagging enthusiasm, especially for a cause or idea [14C. Via late Latin *zelus* < Greek *zēlos* 'eager rivalry'.]

Zealand /zeèlənd/ = **Sjaelland**

zealot /zéllət/ *n* a zealous supporter of a cause, especially a religious cause [Mid-16C. Via late Latin < Greek *zēlōtēs* < *zēloun* 'be jealous' < *zēlos* 'eager rivalry'.] —**zealotry** *n*

Zealot /zéllət/ *n* a member of a group of Jewish rebels who attempted the military overthrow of Roman rule in Palestine in the 1st and 2nd centuries AD

zealous /zélləss/ *adj* actively and unreservedly enthusiastic [Early 16C. < medieval Latin *zelosus* < *zelus* (see ZEAL).] —**zealously** *adv* —**zealousness** *n*

zeatin /zeè ətin/ *n* a naturally occurring growth promoter found in many plants [Mid-20C. < modern Latin *Zea* (see ZEIN) + -IN.]

zebec *n* = **xebec**

Zebedee /zébbəddi/ *n* in the Bible, a fisherman, and the father of the apostles, James and John (Matthew 4:21)

zebra /zébbrə, zeèbrə/ *n* an animal resembling a horse that has a black-and-white or brown-and-white striped hide. Native to: Africa. Genus: *Equus*. [Early 17C. < Italian, Spanish, or Portuguese, originally 'wild ass'.] —**zebraic** /zi bráy ik/ *adj* —**zebrine** /zéb rīn, zeèb-/ *adj* —**zebroid** *adj*

zebra crossing *n* a pedestrian crossing marked by white stripes in the road, at which drivers of vehicles must stop if a pedestrian is waiting to cross

zebra finch *n* a finch that has a reddish-orange bill, grey head and back, and a black-and-white striped tail and is a popular cage bird. Native to: inland Australia. *Poephila guttata*.

zebra fish *n* a small freshwater fish with a blue body and longitudinal silvery or gold stripes, popular for aquariums. Native to: South Asia. *Brachydanio rerio*.

zebra mussel *n* a freshwater mussel regarded as a nuisance in the Great Lakes in the United States and surrounding waterways where it was accidentally introduced. Native to: Europe, Asia. *Dreissena polymorpha*.

zebra plant *n* a tropical evergreen plant with green-and-purple striped leaves. Native to: South America. *Calathea zebrina*.

zebrawood /zébbrə wòod, zeèbrə-/ *n* **1 STRIPED WOOD** wood in two distinct colour bands, from any of various tropical trees. Use: furniture. **2 HARDWOOD TREE WITH STRIPED WOOD** a tropical hardwood tree producing zebrawood. *Connarus guianensis*. **3 TREE WITH STRIPED WOOD** any other tropical tree producing zebrawood

zebu /zeè boo/ (*plural* **-bu** *or* **-bus**) *n* a domesticated ox of Asia with a humped back, curving horns, floppy ears, and a large dewlap. *Bos indicus*. [Late 18C. < French *zébu*.]

zecchino /ze keènō/ (*plural* **-ni** /-nee/ *or* **-nos**) *n* MONEY = **sequin** *n*. 2 [Early 17C. < Italian (see SEQUIN).]

Zechariah /zékə rī ə/ *n* **1** in the Bible, a Hebrew priest and prophet of the 6th century BC **2** a book in the Bible containing the prophecies of Zechariah, including his visions of the rebuilding of the Temple in a restored Jerusalem

zechin /zékin/ *n* MONEY = **sequin** *n*. 2 [Late 16C. < Italian *zecchino* (see SEQUIN).]

zed /zed/ *n* a written representation of the sound of the letter 'Z'. US term **zee** [15C. Via French *zède* < Greek *zēta* (see ZETA).]

Zedekiah /zéddi kī ə/ *n* in the Bible, the last king of Judah (597–586 BC). After rebelling against Nebuchadnezzar, he was imprisoned in Babylon, where he died in captivity (2 Kings 24–25) (2 Chronicles 36).

zedoary /zéddō əri/ (*plural* **-ies**) *n* **1** an aromatic powder obtained from crushing the dried roots of a South Asian tree. Use: a condiment, in cosmetics, perfume, medicinally as a stimulant. **2** a plant with starchy aromatic rhizomes that yield zedoary. Flowers: yellow. Native to: South Asia. *Curcuma zedoaria*. [15C. < medieval Latin *zedoarium* < Persian *zadwār*.]

zedonk /zeè dónk, zé-/ *n* the offspring of a male zebra and a female donkey [Late 20C. < ZEBRA + DONKEY.]

zee /zee/ *n US* = **zed** [Late 17C. Alteration of Latin *zeta* (< Greek *zēta*: see ZETA) after *b*, *p*, etc.]

Zeebrugge /zeè brŏogə/ port in NW Belgium

Zeeland /zeèlənd/ province in the SW Netherlands. Population: 367,400 (1996). Area: 1,800 sq. km/695 sq. mi.

Zeeman /zeèmən/, **Pieter** (1865–1943) Dutch physicist

Zeeman effect *n* the splitting of single lines in a spectrum into two, three, or more polarized lines when the source of the spectrum is placed in a magnetic field [Late 19C. After Pieter ZEEMAN.]

Zeffirelli /zéffə rélli/, **Franco** (*b.* 1923) Italian film, stage, and opera director

Zeil /zīl/ highest mountain in the Northern Territory, Australia, in the south of the state. Height: 1,510 m/4,954 ft.

zein /zeè in/ *n* a powder of proteins obtained from corn, with various applications in industry and manufacturing [Early 19C. < modern Latin *Zea* via Latin *zea* 'emmer' < Greek *zeia*, kind of wheat.]

Zeiss /tsīss, zīss/, **Carl** (1816–88) German manufacturer of optical instruments

Zeitgeist /zít gīst, tsít-/, **zeitgeist** *n* the ideas prevalent in a period and place, particularly as expressed in literature, philosophy, and religion [Mid-19C. < German, 'spirit of the time'.]

zelkova /zélkəvə/ *n* a tree of the elm family cultivated for its resistance to Dutch elm disease. Native to: Asia. Genus: *Zelkova*. [Late 19C. Via modern Latin < a Caucasian language.]

zemindary *n* HIST = **zamindari**

Zen /zen/, **Zen Buddhism** *n* a major school of Buddhism originating in 12th century China that emphasizes enlightenment through meditation and insight [Early 18C. Via Japanese *zen*, Chinese *chán* < Sanskrit *dhyānam* 'meditation'.]

zenana /zə naànə/, **zanana** *n* in South Asia, the part of the house reserved for women and girls in a Muslim household [Mid-18C. < Persian, Urdu *zanānah* < *zan* 'woman'.]

Zen Buddhism *n* BUDDHISM = **Zen**

Zend /zend/ *n* **1** RELIG = **Zend-Avesta** **2** LANG = **Avesta**

Zend-Avesta *n* the canonical writings of Zoroastrianism, preserved in the Pahlavi language [Mid-17C. Via French < Persian *zand-awastā* 'Avesta with interpretation'.]

zener diode /zénnər-/ *n* a semiconductor used as a voltage regulator because of its ability to maintain a constant voltage during fluctuating current conditions [Mid-20C. After Clarence M. *Zener* (1905–93), US physicist.]

zenith /zénnith/ *n* **1** the point of the celestial sphere that is directly over the observer and 90 degrees from all points on that person's horizon **2** the high point or climax of something [14C. Via Old French and medieval Latin < Arabic *samt (ar-ra's)* 'path (over the head)'.] —**zenithal** *adj*

zenithal projection *n* a map projection of the Earth onto a plane tangential to a point on the surface of the Earth such as the North Pole or the equator

Zeno of Citium /zeènō əv síshee əm/ (*fl.* late 4th–early 3rd centuries BC) Greek philosopher

Zeno of Elea /-eèli ə/ (*fl.* 5th century BC) Greek mathematician and philosopher

zeolite /zeè ə līt/ *n* one of a large group of amorphous hydrated aluminium silicate minerals containing various other elements. Source: weathered igneous rocks, hydrothermal veins. Use: water purification. [Late 18C. < Greek *zein* 'to boil'.] —**zeolitic** /zeè ə líttik/ *adj*

Zephaniah /zeffə nī ə/ *n* **1** in the Bible, a minor Hebrew prophet of the 7th century BC **2** a book in the Bible, traditionally attributed to Zephaniah. It urges repentance by the people of Judah, and predicts a day of judgment.

zephyr /zéffər/ *n* **1** a light warming breeze **2** a delicate usually woollen fabric or garment [Pre-12C. Via Latin < Greek *zephuros* 'west wind'.]

Zephyrus /zéffərəss/ *n* in Greek mythology, the god who personified the west wind and was always mild and gentle in character. ◊ **Boreas** *n*. 1

zeppelin /zéppəlin/ *n* a rigid cylindrical airship consisting of a covered frame and a suspended compartment for engines and passengers [Early 20C. After Count Ferdinand von *Zeppelin* (1838–1917), German inventor.]

zepto- *prefix* indicates 10^{-21} in measurements ○ *zeptosecond* [Late 20C. Modelled on SEPTI-.]

Zermatt /tsur mát/ ski resort in SW Switzerland. Population: 4,225 (1996).

zero /zeèrō/ *n* (*plural* **-ros** *or* **-roes**) **1 SYMBOL 0** the numerical symbol 0, representing the absence of any quantity or magnitude **2 NUMBER WITH THE VALUE OF 0** the number that, when added to another number, results in that number, e.g. 0 + 4 = 4 **3 STARTING POINT FOR VALUES ON GAUGE** the starting or centre point for values on a counter, scale, or gauge ○ *Set the counter to zero.* **4 LOW TEMPERATURE** the temperature indicated by 0 on a thermometer scale, especially that corresponding to the freezing point of water on the Celsius scale ○ *It got down to zero last night.* **5 LOW POINT** the lowest possible point or degree ○ *Her spirits are at zero.* **6 NOTHING** nothing or nil ○ *They beat us five zero.* **7** *US* **FAILURE** a person who is regarded as a complete failure (*informal insult*) **8 ABSTRACT REALIZATION OF A MORPHEME** a variant form of a morpheme (**allomorph**) that is purely abstract and does not exist in any physical phonetic form **9 SETTING ON A GUN SIGHT** a setting on a gun sight indicating the centre of a target ■ *vt* (**-roes, -roing, -roed**) **SET TO ZERO** to set an instrument, gauge, counter, or similar measuring device to zero ■ *adj* **1 NONE** not any (*informal*) ○ *zero growth* ○ *our chances of getting away with it are zero* **2 WITH LIMITED VISIBILITY** describes a level of visibility limited to 15 m/50 ft vertically or 50 m/165 ft horizontally [Early 17C. Via French and Italian < Arabic *ṣifr* 'emptiness'.]

zero in *vi* **1** to find the precise position of a target and move towards it or aim a weapon at it, threateningly or inexorably **2** to identify something precisely and concentrate all efforts on dealing with it ○ *The report zeroed in on the weaknesses inherent in the management structure.* [< the technique of setting a gun sight exactly on a target by cancelling out the effects of elevation and wind deflection]

zero-base, zero-based *adj* relating to a budget or budgeting that considers each item on its merits without reference to previous practice or expenditure

zero-coupon *adj* not paying interest but sold at a discount and redeemable at maturity ○ *a zero-coupon bond*

zero-defect *adj* with no defects or flaws

ϟ **zerofill** /zeèrō fil/, **zeroize** /zeèrō īz/ *vti* in computing, to fill empty storage space with zeros

zero gravity *n* a condition of apparent weightlessness resulting from the centrifugal force on an object counterbalancing the gravitational force attracting it

zero grazing *n* a system of feeding cattle or other livestock in which freshly cut forage is brought daily to animals that are permanently housed instead of being allowed to graze

zero growth *n* no increase in the growth or development of something, especially when an increase might have been expected and where any increase is measured as a percentage ○ *predictions of zero growth in the economy*

zero hour *n* **1** the time set for the start of a military operation **2** the time or date when something important is due to happen

zero option *n* an offer to limit the number of short-range nuclear missiles or remove them altogether if an opposing side agrees to do the same

zero population growth *n* a situation in which the number of new births is no greater than the number of people dying, so that the overall population size remains the same

zero-rate (**-rates, -rating, -rated**) *vt UK, Can* to make goods or services exempt from a value-added tax —**zero-rated** *adj* —**zero rating** *n*

zero-sum *adj* relating to a situation in which a gain by one side or person requires any other side or person involved in it to sustain a corresponding loss

zeroth /zeer ōth/ *adj* preceding number one in a series

zero tolerance *n* the absence of any leniency or exception in the enforcement of a law, rule, or regulation, especially a law against antisocial behaviour

ϟ **zero wait state** *n* in computing, a condition in which instructions are immediately executed or data is immediately transferred

zero-zero *adj* describes flying conditions in which cloud is so thick and low that the pilot can see nothing ahead and nothing above or below the aircraft [Shortening of *zero ceiling, zero visibility*]

zero-zero option *n* MIL = **double-zero option**

zest /zest/ *n* **1** HEARTY ENJOYMENT lively enjoyment and enthusiasm ○ *zest for life* **2** EXCITING ELEMENT ADDING TO ENJOYMENT an exciting or interesting quality that makes something particularly enjoyable **3** CITRUS PEEL USED AS FLAVOURING the thin outer rind of the peel of a citrus fruit that is cut, scraped, or grated to yield a sharp fruity flavouring for foods and drinks **4** PIQUANT FLAVOUR a pleasantly sharp flavour ■ *vt* **1** GRATE THE SKIN OF CITRUS FRUIT to cut, grate, or scrape the rind of a citrus fruit in order to flavour foods and drinks **2** MAKE SOMETHING MORE STIMULATING AND ENJOYABLE to make an experience more enjoyable by adding excitement or interest to it [15C. < French.] —**zestful** *adj* —**zestfully** *adv* —**zestfulness** *n* —**zesty** *adj*

zester /zéstər/ *n* a small utensil with a row of tiny sharpened holes or edges at its tip for cutting strips of zest from oranges, lemons, or other citrus fruits

zeta /zeétə/ *n* the sixth letter of the Greek alphabet [Early 18C. < Greek *zēta*, of Phoenician origin.]

Zethus /zeéthəss/ *n* in Greek mythology, a son of Zeus and Antiope and the twin of Amphion

zetta- *prefix* indicates 10^{21} in measurements ○ *zettahertz* [Late 20C. Probably < Italian *sette* 'seven'.]

ϟ **zettabyte** /zéttə bīt/ *n* a unit of computer memory or disk storage space equal to one sextillion bytes or 1,024 exabytes

zeugma /zyoógmə, zoóg-/ *n* a figure of speech in which an adjective or verb is used with two nouns but is appropriate to only one of them or has a different sense with each, as in 'During the race he broke the record and his leg' [Late 16C. Via Latin < Greek, 'joining'.] —**zeugmatic** /zyoog máttik, zoog-/ *adj* —**zeugmatically** *adv*

Zeus /zyooss/ *n* in Greek mythology, the god of the sky, ruler of the Olympian gods, and spiritual father of gods and mortals. Roman equivalent **Jupiter** *n.* 1

Zhangjiakou /jáng jyaá kō/ city in NE China. Population: 673,901 (1991).

Zhang Zhidong /jáng jee túng/ (1837–1909) Chinese reformer and statesman

Zhao Mengfu /jów məng foó/ (1254–1322) Chinese artist

Zhejiang /jé jáng/ province in E China, on the East China Sea. Capital: Hangzhou. Population: 42,940,000 (1994). Area: 100,000 sq. km/38,600 sq. mi.

Zhengzhou /júng jō/ capital of Henan Province, E China, on the Huang He. Population: 2,001,109 (1991).

zho *n* ZOOL = **dzo**

Zhou /jō/ *n* a Chinese dynasty that ruled from the 12th to the 3rd centuries BC, during which China was divided into feudal states and the religions of Confucianism and Taoism arose [Late 18C. < Chinese *zhōu*.]

Zia ul-Haq /zeé ə oŏl haák/, **Muhammad** (1924–88) Pakistani general and national leader

zibeline /zíbbə līn/, **zibelline** *n* a thick soft fabric with a long nap, made of wool, especially mohair or alpaca, or of the hair of another animal such as a camel [Late 16C. Via French < Italian *zibellino* 'sable' < Slavic.]

zibet /zíbbit/ *n* a species of civet native to Southeast Asia. *Viverra zibetha*. [Late 16C. Via medieval Latin *zibethum* or Italian *zibetto* < Arabic *zabād* 'musky perfume obtained from civets'.]

zichel /zíchəl/ *pron S W England* suchlike [Alteration]

zidovudine /zī dṓvvyoō deen/ *n* PHARM = **AZT** [Late 20C. Probably alteration of AZIDOTHYMIDINE.]

Ziegfeld /zíg feld/, **Florenz** (1869–1932) US theatre producer

zig /zig/ *n* a sharp line, direction, movement, or course that forms part of a zigzag ■ *vi* (**zigs, zigging, zigged**) to move in a sharp line, direction, movement, or course that forms part of a zigzag [Mid-20C. < ZIGZAG.]

ziggurat /zíggoō rat/ *n* an ancient Mesopotamian pyramid-shaped tower with a square base, rising in storeys of ever-decreasing size, with a terrace at each storey and a temple at the very top [Late 19C. < Assyrian *ziqquratu* 'pinnacle'.]

zigzag /zíg zag/ *n* **1** LINE TAKING ALTERNATING TURNS a line going at an angle first one way, then sharply the opposite way, then back the first way, and so on, like the outline of a saw's teeth **2** SOMETHING REPEATEDLY SWITCHING DIRECTIONS SHARPLY something that follows a sharply alternating line or course, e.g. a road with sharp bends alternating right and left ■ *adv* IN SHARPLY ALTERNATING DIRECTIONS along a sharply alternating line or course ■ *v* (**-zags, -zagging, -zagged**) **1** *vti* PROCEED IN A SHARPLY ALTERNATING PATH to follow a sharply alternating line or course, moving rapidly ○ *They zigzagged across the field, dodging enemy bullets.* **2** *vt* MAKE A SHARPLY ALTERNATING PATTERN to make a pattern of sharply alternating lines or directions, e.g. by sewing something with herringbone stitches [Early 18C. Via French < German *Zickzack*.] —**zigzaggedness** /zíg zagidnəss/ *n*

zigzag fence *n Northeast US* a fence made of split rails each resting on and set at angles to the next, forming a zigzag

zila *n* HIST = **zillah**

zila parishad /zíllə púrrishəd/, **zilla parishad, zillah parishad** *n* a local council that governs an administrative district in India

zilch /zilch/ *pron* zero or nothing at all (*informal*) ○ *They take all the profits and we're left with zilch.* [Mid-20C. < ?]

zill /zil/ *n* either one of a pair of tiny cymbals that belly dancers hold in their fingers and play in time to their dancing [< Turkish *zil* 'cymbals']

zillah /zíllə, zíllaa/, **zilla, zila** *n* an administrative district in India when the country was under British rule [Early 19C. Via Persian and Urdu < Arabic *ḍila'* 'division'.]

zilla parishad, zillah parishad *n* PUBLIC ADMIN = **zila parishad**

zillion /zíllyən/ *n* a number of people or quantity of things so huge it cannot be counted or determined (*informal*) ○ *Zillions preferred the new model to the old one.* [Mid-20C. After MILLION and BILLION, with *z* representing the last in a series.] —**zillion** *det*

zillionaire /zílyə náir/ *n* an extremely wealthy person (*informal*) [Mid-20C. After MILLIONAIRE.]

Zimbabwe /zim baábwi, -baáb way/ republic in southern Africa. Capital: Harare. Population: 11,515,000 (1996). Area: 390,759 sq. km/150,873 sq. mi. —**Zimbabwean** *n, adj*

Zimmer /zímmər/ *tdmk* a trademark for a lightweight metal tubular frame with four rubber-tipped legs, designed to support somebody who needs help in walking

zinc /zingk/ *n* **1** BLUISH METALLIC ELEMENT (*symbol* **Zn**) a bluish-white metallic element. Source: calamine, sphalerite, franklinite. Use: in alloys such as brass and nickel-silver, as a protective corrosion-resistant coating for other metals, especially steel and iron. **2** GALVANIZED IRON corrugated iron with a protective zinc coating (*informal*) ■ *vt* (**zincs, zincing** *or* **zincking, zinced** *or* **zincked**) COAT WITH ZINC to cover a metal, especially iron or steel, with a protective corrosion-resistant coating of zinc [Mid-17C. < German *Zink*.] —**zincic** *adj* —**zincky** *adj* —**zincoid** /zíngk oyd/ *adj*

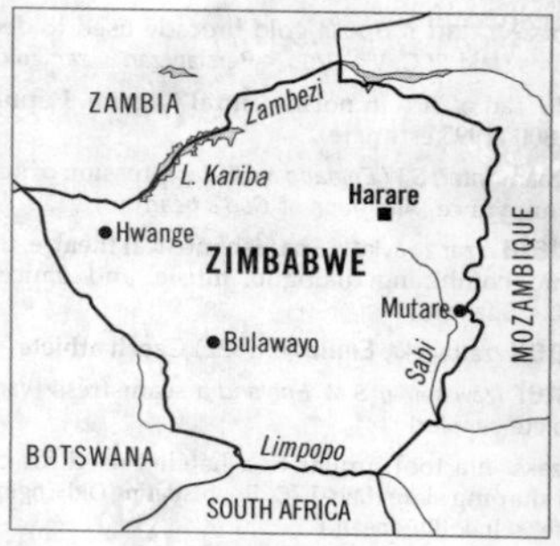

Zimbabwe

zincate /zíng kayt/ *n* a salt derived from zinc hydroxide

zinc blende *n* MINERALS = **sphalerite**

zinc chloride *n* $ZnCl_2$ a poisonous soluble salt. Use: wood preservative, antiseptic, catalyst.

zinc hydroxide *n* a colourless crystalline compound. Use: in chemical synthesis, as an absorbent.

zinciferous /zing kíffərəss/ *adj* containing or yielding zinc, especially as an ore

zincite /zíngk īt/ *n* a reddish-orange zinc oxide mineral

zinckenite *n* MINERALS = **zinkenite**

zinco /zíngkō/ (*plural* **-cos**) *n* a zincograph (*informal*) [Late 19C. Shortening.]

zincograph /zíngkə graaf, -graf/ *n* **1** a printing plate made of zinc that has the design to be printed etched into its surface **2** a print taken from a zincograph —**zincographer** /zing kóggrəfər/ *n* —**zincographic** /zíngkə gráffik/ *adj* —**zincographical** *adj* —**zincography** /zing kóggrəfi/ *n*

zinc ointment *n* an antiseptic ointment containing zinc oxide in a base of petroleum jelly or lanolin. Use: treatment of skin disorders.

zinc oxide *n* ZnO an odourless water-insoluble white powder. Use: pigment, astringent, antiseptic.

zinc sulphate *n* $ZnSO_4$ a colourless crystalline powder. Use: pigment, emetic, wood preservative, crop spray.

zinc sulphide *n* ZnS a crystalline white or yellowish powder. Use: pigment, phosphor on X-ray and television screens.

zinc white *n* zinc oxide used as a white pigment in paint

zindabad /zíndə bad/ *interj S Asia* expresses loud approval, acclaim, or enthusiasm ■ *n S Asia* a loud shout of approval, acclaim, or enthusiasm [Mid-20C. < Urdu, 'may. . . live'.]

Zinder /zíndər/ city in south-central Niger. Population: 120,900 (1988).

ϟ **zine** /zeen/ *n* a self-published paper, Internet magazine, or other periodical, issued at irregular intervals with and usually appealing to a specialist readership (*informal*) [Mid-20C. Shortening of MAGAZINE.]

Zinfandel /zínfən del/ *n* **1** a variety of black grape used, especially in California, to make a light fruity red or rosé wine **2** a light-bodied fruity red or rosé wine, or less commonly a hearty red wine, made from the Zinfandel grape, especially in California [Mid-19C. < ?]

zing /zing/ *n* **1** SHARP SINGING SOUND a short high-pitched humming or buzzing sound, e.g. the sound of a bullet whizzing through the air **2** LIVELY AND EXCITING QUALITY a lively exciting aspect of something that makes it particularly enjoyable (*informal*) ○ *The rhythm guitar gives the tune extra zing.* ■ *v* (*informal*) **1** *vi* MAKE A HUMMING NOISE to make or move with a short high-pitched humming or buzzing noise **2** *vt US* ATTACK WITH WORDS to criticize somebody sharply, especially in a swift and clever way [Early 20C. An imitation of the sound.] —**zingy** *adj*

zinger /zíngər/ *n US* (*informal*) **1** SOMEBODY OR SOMETHING ENERGETIC AND SURPRISING an energetic person or thing that produces startling results **2** CLEVER REMARK SKILFULLY DELIVERED a remark delivered with great skill and speed, especially a sharp and perfectly timed witticism or criticism **3** SHOCKING AND UNEXPECTED HAPPENING a shocking and unexpected turn of events such as an abrupt shift in the plot of a film, play, or book

injanthropus /zin jánthrəpəss/ (*plural* **-pi** /-pī/ *or* **-puses**) *n* a hominid fossil found in 1959 at Olduvai Gorge in East Africa. Originally classified as a distinct genus and species, it is now recognized as an australopithecine. [Mid-20C. < modern Latin, < medieval Arabic *Zinj* 'East Africa' + Greek *anthrōpos* 'person'.] —**zinjanthropine** *adj, n*

~~**ink**~~ incorrect spelling of **zinc**

inkenite /zíngkən īt/, **zinckenite** *n* a dark-grey lead antimony sulphide mineral [Mid-19C. After J. K. L. *Zincken* (1790–1862), German mineralogist.]

innia /zínni ə/ (*plural* **-as** *or* **-a**) *n* a plant of the daisy family with large colourful flowers that is widely grown as a garden plant. Native to: Mexico. Genus: *Zinnia*. [Mid-18C. < modern Latin, after J. G. *Zinn* (1727–59), German botanist.]

inzendorf /tsín tsən dáwrf/, **Nikolaus Ludwig, Graf von** (1700–60) German religious reformer

ion /zí ən/ *n* **1** one of the hills of Jerusalem, in Biblical times emblematic of the house or household of God and later by extension the Jewish people and their religion **2** in Christian belief, the place where God lives and is worshipped on earth or in the kingdom of heaven [Pre-12C. Via late Latin and Greek < Hebrew *ṣīyôn*.]

ionism /zí ənizəm/ *n* a worldwide movement, originating in the 19th century, that sought to establish and develop a Jewish nation in Palestine

ionist /zí ənist/ *n* **1** a supporter of 19th-century Zionism, or a modern supporter of the state of Israel **2** *S Africa* a member of an independent Christian church in South Africa that incorporates traditional African beliefs and forms of worship —**Zionist** *adj* —**Zionistic** /zí ə nístik/ *adj*

ip /zip/ *n* **1 FASTENER WITH INTERLOCKING TEETH** a fastener for clothes, bags, or other items, consisting of two rows of interlocking metal or plastic teeth with an attached sliding tab pulled to open or close the fastener. US term **zipper 2 LIVELY AND EXCITING QUALITY** a lively exciting aspect of something that makes it particularly enjoyable (*informal*) **3 BRIEF HISSING SOUND** a brief sibilant sound such as the sound of a bullet whizzing through the air ■ *v* (**zips, zipping, zipped**) **1** *vti* **FASTEN WITH ZIP** to fasten something, or to be fastened, with a zip **2** *vi* **MAKE OR MOVE WITH HISSING SOUND** to make or move with a rapid sibilant sound (*informal*) **3** *vti* **GO OR MOVE VERY FAST** to go somewhere or move something somewhere very fast (*informal*) **4** *vt* **COMPRESS A FILE** to compress a computer file for storage or transmission [Late 19C. An imitation of the sound.]

IP code, zip code *n US* MAIL = **postcode** [Acronym < *Zone Improvement Program*]

ip fastener *n* CLOTHING = **zip** *n.* 1

ip file *n* a computer file with the extension .zip containing data that has been compressed for storage or transmission.

ip gun *n US, Can* a homemade pistol, especially one that uses a spring or a rubber band as the firing mechanism (*slang*)

ipless /zíppləss/ *adj* **1** not fitted with, or fastened using, a zip **2** passionate and lasting only a short time [Late 20C. In the sense 'passionate' from the idea of clothes coming off without the awkward undoing of zips.]

ipper /zíppər/ *n* CLOTHING = **zip** *n.* 1

ippered /zíppərd/ *adj US* = **zip-up**

ippy /zíppi/ (**-pier, -piest**) *adj* (*informal*) **1** showing or having spirit or energy **2** with good acceleration

ip-up *adj* fitted with, or fastened using, a zip. US term **zippered**

ircalloy /zúrk álloy, zúrkə loy/, **zircaloy** *n* an alloy of zirconium with tin, chromium, and nickel that is resistant to heat and corrosion, making it a useful material in the nuclear power industry

ircon /zúr kon/ *n* a very hard zirconium silicate mineral. Use: source of zirconium, gems. [Late 18C. < German *Zirkon*.]

irconia /zur kṓni ə/ *n* CHEM = **zirconium oxide**

irconium /zur kṓni əm/ *n* (*symbol* Zr) a greyish-white, corrosion-resistant, metallic element. Source: zircon, zirconia. Use: coating fuel rods in nuclear reactors. —**zirconic** /-kónnik/ *adj*

zirconium oxide *n* ZrO_2 a heavy water-insoluble white powder. Use: pigment, abrasive, manufacture of heat-resistant materials and ceramics.

zit /zit/ *n* a pimple on the skin (*slang*) [Mid-20C. < ?] —**zitty** *adj*

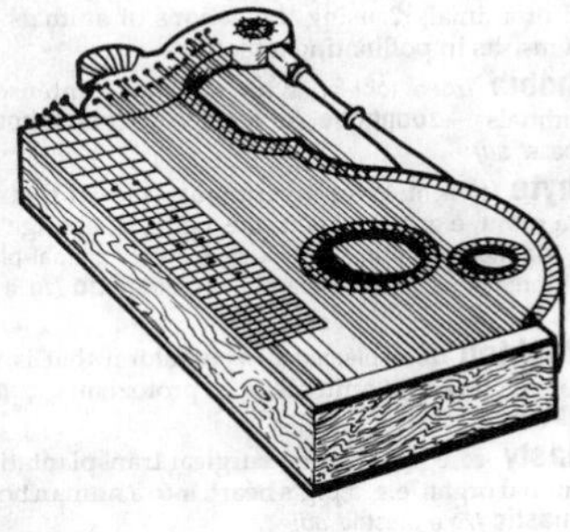

Zither

zither /zíthər/ *n* a musical instrument consisting of a flat shallow sound box with metal strings stretched across it that are plucked [Mid-19C. Via German < Latin *cithara* (see CITHARA).] —**zitherist** *n*

ziti /zee tee/ *n* pasta in the form of medium-sized tubes, longer and thicker than macaroni [Mid-19C. < Italian, plural of *zito* 'boy'.]

zizz /ziz/ *n* a brief sleep (*informal*) ■ *vi* to have a brief sleep (*informal*) [Mid-20C. < zzz.]

Zl *abbr* zloty

Z line *n* a narrow dark line across striated muscle fibres that marks the boundaries between adjacent segments [< abbreviation of German *Zwischenscheibe* 'intervening disc']

zloty /zlótti/ (*plural* **-ties** *or* **-ty**) *n* see table at **currency** [Early 20C. < Polish *złoty* 'golden' < *złoto* 'gold'.]

ϟ**zm** *abbr* Zambia (*in Internet addresses*)

ϟ**Zmodem** /zéd mōdem/ *n* a variation of the Xmodem file transfer protocol in which data is sent in 512-byte blocks without waiting for acknowledgment from the recipient between blocks

Zn *symbol* zinc

zo /zō/ *n* ZOOL = **dzo**

zo- *prefix* = **zoo-** (*before vowels*)

zoarium /zō áiri əm/ (*plural* **-ums** *or* **-a** /zō áiri ə/) *n* a collection of distinct organisms that together form a compound organism [Late 19C. < Greek *zōion* 'animal' (see -ZOON).]

zod. *abbr* zodiac

zodiac /zṓdi ak/ *n* **1 PART OF THE SKY CONTAINING THE MAJOR CONSTELLATIONS** a narrow band in the sky in which the movements of the major planets, Sun, and Moon take place, astrologically divided into twelve sections named after the major constellations **2 ASTROLOGER'S CHART** a chart linking twelve constellations to twelve divisions of the year, used as the astrologer's main tool for analysing character and predicting the future **3 RECURRING SET** a set of things or sequence of events that repeats itself cyclically (*literary*) [14C. Via French and Latin < Greek *zōidiakos kuklos* 'circle of animal figures' < *zōidion* 'small animal' < *zōion* (see -ZOON).] —**zodiacal** /zō dī́ ək'l/ *adj*

zodiacal constellation *n* a constellation that a sign of the zodiac is named after

zodiacal light *n* a faint glow in the sky, seen before sunrise to the east and after sunset to the west, and caused by small particles reflected in sunlight

Zog I /zōg/ (1895–1961) king of Albania (1922–24)

Zohar /zṓ haar/ *n* a 13th-century Jewish mystical text that is the primary text of Cabbalistic writings [Late 17C. < Hebrew *zōhar* 'light, splendour'.]

-zoic *suffix* **1** relating to a particular geological era ○ *Mesozoic* **2** having a particular kind of animal existence [< Greek *zōē* 'life' < Indo-European, 'to live']

zoisite /zóy sīt/ *n* a grey or green hydrated calcium aluminosilicate mineral. Source: metamorphic rocks. [Early 19C. After Baron Sigismund *Zois* von Edelstein (1747–1819), Slovenian scholar.]

zol /zol/ *n S Africa* (*slang*) **1** cannabis for smoking as a drug **2** a hand-rolled cannabis cigarette

Zola /zṓlə/, **Émile** (1840–1902) French novelist

Zollverein /zólfə rīn, tsól-/ *n* **1** a customs union formed in the 19th century by a number of German states to establish uniform import tariffs from other countries and free trade among themselves **2** any customs union formed to establish uniform import tariffs [Mid-19C. < German, 'tariff union'.]

zombie /zómbi/, **zombi** *n* **1 OFFENSIVE TERM** an offensive term for a person considered to lack energy, enthusiasm, or the ability to think independently (*informal*) **2 DEAD BODY GIVEN LIFE BY VOODOO** in voodoo, a dead body brought back to life again without a soul **3 VOODOO SPIRIT REVIVING A DEAD BODY** in voodoo, a spirit that brings a dead body back to life again **4 SNAKE GOD OF VOODOO** a snake god of Caribbean, Brazilian, and West African voodoo religions **5 VERY STRONG RUM COCKTAIL** a very strong alcoholic cocktail made with various kinds of rum **6 ARMY CONSCRIPT ASSIGNED FOR HOME DEFENCE** in Canada, a conscripted soldier assigned to home defence during World War II (*slang*) [Early 19C. Via Caribbean Creole < Kimbundu *n-zumbi* 'ghost, snake god'.] —**zombiism** *n*

zombify /zómbi fī/ (**-fies, -fying, -fied**) *vt* to convert somebody into a zombie

zonal /zṓn'l/, **zonary** /zṓnəri/ *adj* **1** relating to a zone or zones **2** divided up into zones —**zonally** *adv*

zonal soil *n* soil whose nature is established by the action of the climate and vegetation of the area in which it is found

zona pellucida /zṓnə pə lóossidə/ *n* a thick transparent envelope that surrounds a developing ovum, allowing only one sperm cell through to fertilize the ovum [< modern Latin, 'transparent band']

zonary *adj* = **zonal**

zonate /zṓ nayt/, **zonated** /zō náytid/ *adj* **1** divided up into zones **2** distinguished by zones, e.g. of colour or texture —**zonation** /zō náysh'n/ *n*

zone /zōn/ *n* **1 SEPARATE AREA WITH A PARTICULAR FUNCTION** an area regarded as separate or kept separate, especially one with a particular use or function ○ *a loading zone* **2 SUBSECTION OF A PARTICULAR AREA** one of the smaller, usually named or numbered sections that a particular area is divided into, e.g. those of a transport network or a sports field **3 HORIZONTAL CLIMATIC BAND AROUND THE EARTH** any of five horizontal bands across the Earth's surface, separated by the Arctic Circle, the Tropic of Cancer, the Tropic of Capricorn, and the Antarctic Circle, that marks climates **4 TIME ZONE** a time zone **5 AREA WITH DISTINCT PLANTS AND ANIMALS** an area with characteristic types of organisms determined largely by its environment, e.g. any of the belts of vegetation on a mountain **6 UNIT OF ROCK FORMATION WITH FOSSILS** a unit of a rock formation characterized by its fossil content **7 PART OF A SPHERE** the portion of a sphere included between two parallel planes meeting the sphere, one of which may be tangent to the sphere or both of which may intersect it ■ *vti* (**zones, zoning, zoned**) **1 SPLIT INTO ZONES** to divide up an area into zones **2 DESIGNATE AREA** to declare officially that an area is to be used for a particular purpose or to be developed in a particular way (*often passive*) ○ *The canal areas have been zoned for leisure and recreation.* [15C. Via French and Latin < Greek *zōnē* 'belt, girdle'.] —**zoning** *n*

zone melting *n* METALL = **zone refining**

zone of saturation *n* an area of soil or rock below the level of the water table where all the voids are filled with water

zone refining *n* a technique for greatly purifying metals in which a molten area is made to pass along an otherwise solid bar so that impurities become concentrated at one end

zonetime /zṓn tīm/ *n* the standard time that exists throughout a particular time zone

zonk /zongk/ *vti* to lose consciousness or become stupefied from exhaustion or an intake of alcohol or narcotic drugs, or to make somebody do this (*slang*) [Early 20C. An imitation of the sound of a heavy blow.]

zonked /zongkt/, **zonked out** *adj* **1** unconscious, stupefied, or sleeping, especially as a result of the effects of alcohol or a drug (*slang*) **2** exhausted (*informal*)

zoo /zoo/ (*plural* **zoos**) *n* **1** a park where live wild animals from different parts of the world are kept in cages or enclosures for people to come and see, and where they are bred and studied by scientists **2** a place characterized as being full of noisy obstreperous people creating confusion and disorder (*informal*) [Mid-19C. Shortening of ZOOLOGICAL GARDEN.]

zoo- *prefix* **1** animal, animal kingdom ○ *zootoxin* **2** motile organism ○ *zoospore* [< Greek *zōion* (see -ZOON)]

zooflagellate /zṓ ə flájələt/ *n* a colourless protozoan that ingests organic matter, is often parasitic, and has one or more flagella

zoogeography /zṓ ə ji óggrəfi/ *n* the scientific study of the areas where different animals live and the causes and effects of such distribution, especially distributions on a large or global scale —**zoogeographer** *n* —**zoogeographic** /zṓ ə jeé ə gráffik/ *adj*

zoogloea /zṓ ə gleé ə/ (*plural* **-as** *or* **-ae** /-ee/), **zooglea** (*plural* **-as** *or* **-ae** /-ee/) *n* a colony of microbes embedded in a gelatinous matrix [Late 19C. < modern Latin, < Greek *zōion* 'animal' + *gloios* 'glutinous substance'.] —**zoögloeal** *adj*

zoography /zō óggrəfi/ *n* a branch of zoology that deals with describing animals and their habitats —**zoographer** *n* —**zoographic** /zṓ ə gráffik/ *adj*

zooid /zṓ oyd/ *n* an individual invertebrate animal that reproduces nonsexually by budding or splitting, especially one that lives in a colony in which each member is joined to others by living material, e.g. a coral [Mid-19C. < ZOO- + -OID.] —**zooidal** *adj*

zookeeper /zoó keepər/ *n* somebody whose job is looking after the animals in a zoo

zool. *abbr* **1** zoological **2** zoology

zoolatry /zō óllətri/ *n* **1** in some ancient cultures, the worshipping of animals **2** an excessive devotion to animals, especially domestic pets (*humorous*) —**zoolater** *n* —**zoolatrous** *adj*

zoological /zṓ ə lójjik'l, zoó-/ *adj* **1** relating to the scientific study of animals **2** relating to or about animals

zoological garden *n* a zoo (*dated*)

zoology /zō ólləji, zoo-/ (*plural* **-gies**) *n* **1 SCIENTIFIC STUDY OF ANIMALS** the branch of biology that involves the scientific study of animals and all aspects of animal life **2 ANIMALS LIVING IN REGION** the animal life of a particular region **3 ANIMAL'S OR ANIMAL GROUP'S CHARACTERISTICS** the physical and biological characteristics of a particular animal or group of animals [Mid-17C. Via modern Latin < Greek *zōologia* 'the study of life' < *zōion* (see -ZOON).] —**zoologist** *n*

zoom /zoom/ *v* **1** *vi* **MOVE SPEEDILY** to move very fast, especially while emitting a loud low-pitched buzzing noise **2** *vi* **MAKE LOUD BUZZING NOISE** to emit a loud low-pitched buzzing or humming noise **3** *vi* **INCREASE SUDDENLY** to rise or increase suddenly and significantly **4** *vti* **CARRY OUT STEEP CLIMB IN AIRCRAFT** to make an aircraft climb rapidly at a very steep angle, or to be piloted in this way ■ *n* **1 LOUD BUZZING NOISE** a loud low-pitched buzzing noise, especially one caused by rapid movement **2** PHOTOGRAPHY = **zoom lens 3 SHOT WITH ZOOM LENS** a shot in which a zoom lens is used to make the object in focus appear to move closer or farther away while the camera itself stays still [Late 19C. An imitation of a buzzing sound.]
zoom in *vi* to make an object appear bigger or closer, or to decrease the area in view, by use of a zoom lens or a graphic imaging device
zoom out *vi* to make an object appear smaller or farther away, or to increase the area in view, by use of a zoom lens or a graphic imaging device

zoom lens /zoóm lenz/ *n* a camera lens assembly with adjustable focal lengths that make an object being photographed or filmed appear closer or farther away than it really is

zoomorphism /zṓ ə máwrfizəm/ *n* **1** the representation of gods as animals, or the attributing of animal characteristics to gods **2** the use of animal figures in art and design, or of animal symbols in literature —**zoomorphic** *adj*

-zoon *suffix* animal, zooid ○ *epizoon* [Via modern Latin < Greek *zōion* 'living being, animal' < Indo-European, 'to live']

zoonosis /zṓ ə nṓssiss, zō ónnəssiss/ (*plural* **-ses** /zoó ə nṓ seez/) *n* a disease, e.g. rabies, anthrax, or ringworm that can be transmitted from vertebrate animals to humans [Late 19C. < ZOO- + Greek *nosos* 'disease'.] —**zoonotic** /zṓ ə nóttik/ *adj*

zoophilia /zṓ ə filli ə/ *n* a sexual attraction to animals

zoophilic *adj* ZOOL = **zoophilous**

zoophilism /zō óffilizəm/ *n* a strong affinity for animals and a devotion to protecting or rescuing them from human activities, e.g. vivisection, that exploit or endanger them

zoophilous /zō óffiləss/, **zoophilic** /zṓ ə fillik/ *adj* **1** very fond of animals **2** using the actions of animals other than insects in pollinating a plant

zoophobia /zṓ ə fṓbi ə/ *n* an unusually intense fear of animals —**zoophobe** /zṓ əfōb/ *n* —**zoophobous** /zō óffəbəss/ *adj*

zoophyte /zṓ ə fīt/ *n* an invertebrate animal that looks like a plant, e.g. a sea anemone, coral, or sponge [Early 17C. Via modern Latin < Greek *zōiophuton* 'animal-plant' < *zōion* 'animal' + *phuton* 'plant'.] —**zoophytic** /zṓ ə fíttik/ *adj*

zooplankton /zṓ ə plángktən/ *n* plankton that is made up of microscopic animals, e.g. protozoans. ◊ **phytoplankton**

zooplasty /zṓ ə plasti/ *n* the surgical transplantation of an animal organ, e.g. a pig's heart, into a human body —**zooplastic** /zṓ ə plástik/ *adj*

zoosperm /zṓ ə spurm/ *n* BIOL = **spermatozoon** —**zoospermatic** /zṓ ə spur máttik/ *adj*

zoospore /zṓ ə spawr/ *n* a spore of some algae and fungi that is capable of independent movement —**zoosporal** /zṓ ə spáwrəl/ *adj* —**zoosporic** /-spórrik/ *adj*

zoosterol /zō óstə rol/ *n* a sterol produced by an animal

zootomy /zō óttəmi/ *n* **1** the study of the anatomy of animals, especially comparative anatomy **2** the dissection of animals [Mid-17C. < ZOO-, after ANATOMY.] —**zootomic** /zṓ ə tómmik/ *adj* —**zootomically** *adv* —**zootomist** *n*

zootoxin /zṓ ə tóksin/ *n* a poisonous substance produced by an animal, e.g. snake venom —**zootoxic** /zṓ ə tóksik/ *adj*

zoot suit /zoót-/ *n* a man's suit, popular in the 1940s, that had a long jacket heavily padded at the shoulders and baggy high-waisted trousers tapering to narrow bottoms —**zoot suiter** *n*

zoo TV *n* a genre of television programme that encourages emotional and often uncontrolled reactions from the participants such as those featuring debates or personal disclosures in front of live audiences (*slang*)

zooxanthella /zṓ əzan théllə/ (*plural* **-lae** /-thélli/) *n* a microscopic yellow-green alga that lives symbiotically within the cells of some marine invertebrates, especially corals [Late 19C. < modern Latin, 'small yellow animal' < Greek *zōion* 'animal' + *xanthos* 'yellow'.]

zori /záwri, zórri/ (*plural* **-ri** *or* **-ris**) *n* a simple Japanese sandal with a flat sole and a single thong, originally made of straw but now also made of rubber or felt [Early 19C. < Japanese, 'straw sole'.]

zorilla /zo rillə/, **zorille** /zórril/, **zoril** *n* a carnivorous mammal of the weasel family that looks like a skunk and has long black-and-white fur. Native to: Africa. *Ictonyx striatus*. [Late 18C. Via French and modern Latin < Spanish *zorilla* 'little fox' < *zorro* 'fox'.]

Zoroaster /zórrō ástər/, **Zarathustra** (630?–550? BC) Persian prophet

Zoroastrianism /zórrō ástri ənizəm/ *n* an ancient religion founded by the Persian prophet Zoroaster, the principal belief of which is in a supreme deity and in a cosmic contest between two spirits, one good and one evil —**Zoroastrian** *n, adj*

zoster /zóstər/ *n* **1** shingles (*technical*) **2** a belt worn by men, especially soldiers, in ancient Greece [Early 18C. Via Latin < Greek *zōstēr* 'girdle'.]

Zouave /zoo aáv/ *n* **1** a member of a former French infantry unit composed of Algerian soldiers, noted for their colourful uniforms and precision drill **2** a member of an army unit imitating the uniform of the French Zouaves, especially those on the Union side during the US Civil War [Mid-19C. Via French < Kabyle *Zouaoua*, tribe in Algeria.]

zouk /zook/ *n* a style of dance music originating in Guadeloupe and Martinique played with guitars and synthesizers that combines a strong fast disco beat and Caribbean rhythms [Late 20C. Via French < Antillean Creole.]

zounds /zowndz/ *interj* a mild expression of surprise or annoyance (*archaic*) [Late 16C. Contraction of *by God's wounds!*]

zoysia /zóyssi ə/ *n* a low-growing grass plant often used for lawns. Native to: Asia. Genus: *Zoysia*. [Mid-20C. < modern Latin, after Carl von *Zoys* zu Laubach (1756–1800?), Austrian botanist.]

Z particle *n* a short-lived electrically neutral elementary particle considered to mediate the weak interaction between other elementary particles

ZPG *abbr* zero population growth

ϟ **zr** *abbr* Zaire (*in Internet addresses*)

Zr *symbol* zirconium

zucchetto /zoo kéttō/ (*plural* **-tos**) *n* a small round skull cap worn by members of the Roman Catholic clergy that varies in colour depending on the rank of the person wearing it [Mid-19C. Alteration of Italian *zucchett* 'headlet' < *zucca* 'gourd, head' (see ZUCCHINI).]

zucchini /zoo keéni/ (*plural* **-ni** *or* **-nis**) *n Aus, Can, US* **courgette 1** a small summer squash that is shaped like a cucumber with a smooth thin dark-green or yellow skin and is eaten cooked as a vegetable **2** the plant that produces zucchini [Early 20C. < Italian, plural of *zucchin* 'courgette' < *zucca* 'gourd' < late Latin *cucutia*, variant of Latin *cucurbita*.]

~~**zuchini**~~ incorrect spelling of **zucchini**

zugzwang /zoóg zwang/ *n* a chess situation in which a player is forced into making a disadvantageous move, especially one that involves the loss of a piece ■ *vt* to force a chess opponent into a disadvantageous situation, especially one that involves the loss of one of the opponent's pieces [Early 20C. < German, 'being forced to move'.]

Zuider Zee /zídər zeé/ former inlet of the North Sea in the N Netherlands. After completion of the Ijsselmeer Dam in 1932, parts of it were drained, and the remainder now forms the Ijsselmeer.

Zukerman /zoókər man/, **Pinchas** (*b.* 1948) Israeli-born US violinist

Zulu /zoó loo/ (*plural* **-lu** *or* **-lus**) *n* **1 MEMBER OF SOUTH AFRICAN PEOPLE** a member of a people of South Africa who live mainly in N Natal province **2 SOUTH AFRICAN LANGUAGE** a Bantu language spoken in E South Africa closely related to Xhosa. Native speakers: 8 million **3 CODE WORD FOR LETTER 'Z'** a code word for the letter 'Z' used in international radio communications [Early 19C. < Zulu *umzulu*.] —**Zulu** *adj*

Zululand /zoóloo land/ historic region in South Africa, now incorporated into KwaZulu-Natal Province

Zuni /zoóni/ (*plural* **-ni** *or* **-nis**), **Zuñi** /zoónyi/ (*plural* **-ñi** *or* **-ñis**) *n* **1** a member of a Pueblo people of W New Mexico **2** the language of the Zuni people, unrelated to other languages. Native speakers: 5,000. [Mid-19C. < American Spanish, < Keresan.] —**Zuni** *adj*

Zurich /zoórik/, **Zürich** largest city in Switzerland, in the north of the country. Population: 336,821 (1998).

Zurich, Lake of lake in N Switzerland. Area: 88 sq km/34 sq. mi.

ϟ **zw** *abbr* Zimbabwe (*in Internet addresses*)

Zwickau /zwík ow, tsvík ow/ city in E Germany. Population: 103,900 (1995).

zwieback /zweé bak/ *n* a piece of bread, sliced and baked again until crisp and dry [Late 19C. < German, 'twice bake'.]

Zwingli /zwínglee/, **Huldreich** (1484–1531) Swiss religious reformer

Zwinglian /zwín gli ən, zwíngli ən/ *adj* relating to the life, works, or beliefs of the Swiss Protestant theologian Huldreich Zwingli, who believed that the Communion wafer and wine were only symbolic of Christ's body and blood ■ *n* a follower of the Swiss Protestant theologian Huldreich Zwingli or a believer in his doctrines —**Zwinglianism** *n*

zwitterion /zwíttər ī ən, tsvíttər-/ *n* an ion that has both a negative and a positive pole [Early 20C. < German, 'hybrid ion'.]

Zwolle /zwóllə/ capital of Overijssel Province, in the north-central Netherlands. Population: 105,819 (2000).

Zworykin /zwáwrikin/, **Vladimir** (1889–1982) Russian-born US inventor

zydeco /zídikō/ *n* a style of dance music originating in Louisiana that is usually played on accordion, guitar, and violin and combines traditional French melodies with Caribbean and blues influences [Mid-20C. Probably

< Louisiana creole *Les haricots (sont pas salés)* 'the beans (are not salted)', a well-known dance tune.]

yg- *prefix* = **zygo-** (*before vowels*)

ygo- *prefix* **1** yoke, pair ○ *zygomorphic* **2** union, reproduction ○ *zygogenesis* [< Greek *zugon* 'yoke, pair' < Indo-European, 'join']

ygodactyl /zígō dáktil/ *adj* **zygodactyl, zygodactylous** with toes arranged in pairs, two facing forwards and two backwards, like those found on woodpeckers ■ *n* a bird that has two pairs of toes, e.g. the woodpecker — **zygodactylism** *n*

ygogenesis /zígō jénnəssiss/ *n* reproduction involving the fusion of male and female nuclei — **zygogenetic** /zígōjə néttik/ *adj*

ygoma /zī gốmə/ (*plural* **-mata** /-mətə/) *n* **1** a cheekbone (*technical*) **2** ANAT = **zygomatic arch 3** ANAT = **zygomatic process** [Late 17C. < Greek *zugōma* 'joining' < *zugoun* 'to join'.] — **zygomatic** /zígə máttik/ *adj*

ygomatic arch *n* a slender bar of bone connecting the cheekbone with the temporal bone on the side of the skull

ygomatic bone *n* a cheekbone (*technical*)

ygomatic process *n* a bony projection that forms part of the zygomatic arch and is joined to the cheekbone

ygomorphic /zígō máwrfik/ *adj* producing identical halves only when divided along a vertical axis — **zygomorphism** *n* — **zygomorphy** /zígō mawrfi/ *n*

zygosis /zī gốssiss/ *n* BIOL = **conjugation** *n*. **6** [Late 19C. < Greek *zugōsis* < *zugoun* 'to join'.] — **zygose** /zígōss/ *adj*

zygosity /zī gốssəti/ *n* a particular characterization of a genetic trait, zygote, or embryo, e.g. whether twins have resulted from the division of one zygote or from two different zygotes (*often in combination*) [Mid-20C. < ZYGOSIS.]

zygospore /zígō spawr/ *n* a thick-walled sexual spore formed from the union of two gametes in some fungi and green algae — **zygosporic** /zígō spórrik/ *adj*

zygote /zígōt/ *n* an ovum that has been fertilized by a spermatozoon [Late 19C. < Greek *zugōtos* 'joined' < *zugoun* 'to join'.] — **zygotic** /zī góttik/ *adj* — **zygotically** *adv*

zygotene /zígə teen/ *n* a stage of the first meiotic cell division in which homologous chromosomes are paired [Early 20C. < French *zygotène* < *zygo-* 'zygo-' + *-tène* 'ribbon' (< Latin *taenia*).]

-zygous *suffix* having a particular kind of zygotic constitution ○ *hemizygous* [< Greek *zugos* 'yoked, paired', < *zugon* (see ZYGO-)]

zym- *prefix* = **zymo-** (*before vowels*)

zymase /zím ayss, -ayz/ *n* an enzyme or enzyme complex obtained from yeast that ferments sugars [Late 19C. < Greek *zumē* 'leaven' (see ZYMO-).]

zymo- *prefix* **1** fermentation ○ *zymology* **2** enzyme ○ *zymogen* [Via modern Latin < Greek *zumē* 'leaven' < Indo-European, 'to mix']

zymogen /zíməjən/ *n* BIOCHEM = **proenzyme**

zymogenesis /zímō jénnəssiss/ *n* the transformation of a zymogen into an enzyme

zymogenic /zímō jénnik/, **zymogenetic** /zíməjə néttik/, **zymogenous** /zī mójjənəss/ *adj* **1** relating to a zymogen **2** causing or producing fermentation

zymology /zī mólləji/ *n* the study of fermentation and the action of enzymes during it — **zymologic** /zímə lójjik/ *adj* — **zymologist** *n*

zymolysis /zī mólləssiss/ *n* the action of enzymes in the process of fermentation (*technical*) — **zymolytic** /zímə líttik/ *adj*

zymometer /zī mómmitər/ *n* an instrument that measures degrees of fermentation

zymosis /zī mốssiss/ *n* BIOCHEM = **zymolysis** [Early 18C. < Greek *zumōsis* 'fermentation' < *zumoun* 'to leaven' < *zumē* (see ZYMO-).]

zymotic /zī móttik/ *adj* relating to, producing, or produced by fermentation [Mid-19C. < Greek *zumōtikos* 'causing fermentation' < *zumōsis* (see ZYMOSIS).] — **zymotically** *adv*

zymurgy /zímərji/ *n* the scientific study of fermentation processes involved in the production of alcoholic drinks [Mid-19C. < ZYMO-, after METALLURGY.] — **zymurgic** /zī múrjik/ *adj*

zzz /zz/ (*plural* **zzz's**) *n* a representation of the sound made by somebody sleeping or snoring, often used in cartoons (*humorous*)